W9-AOY-803

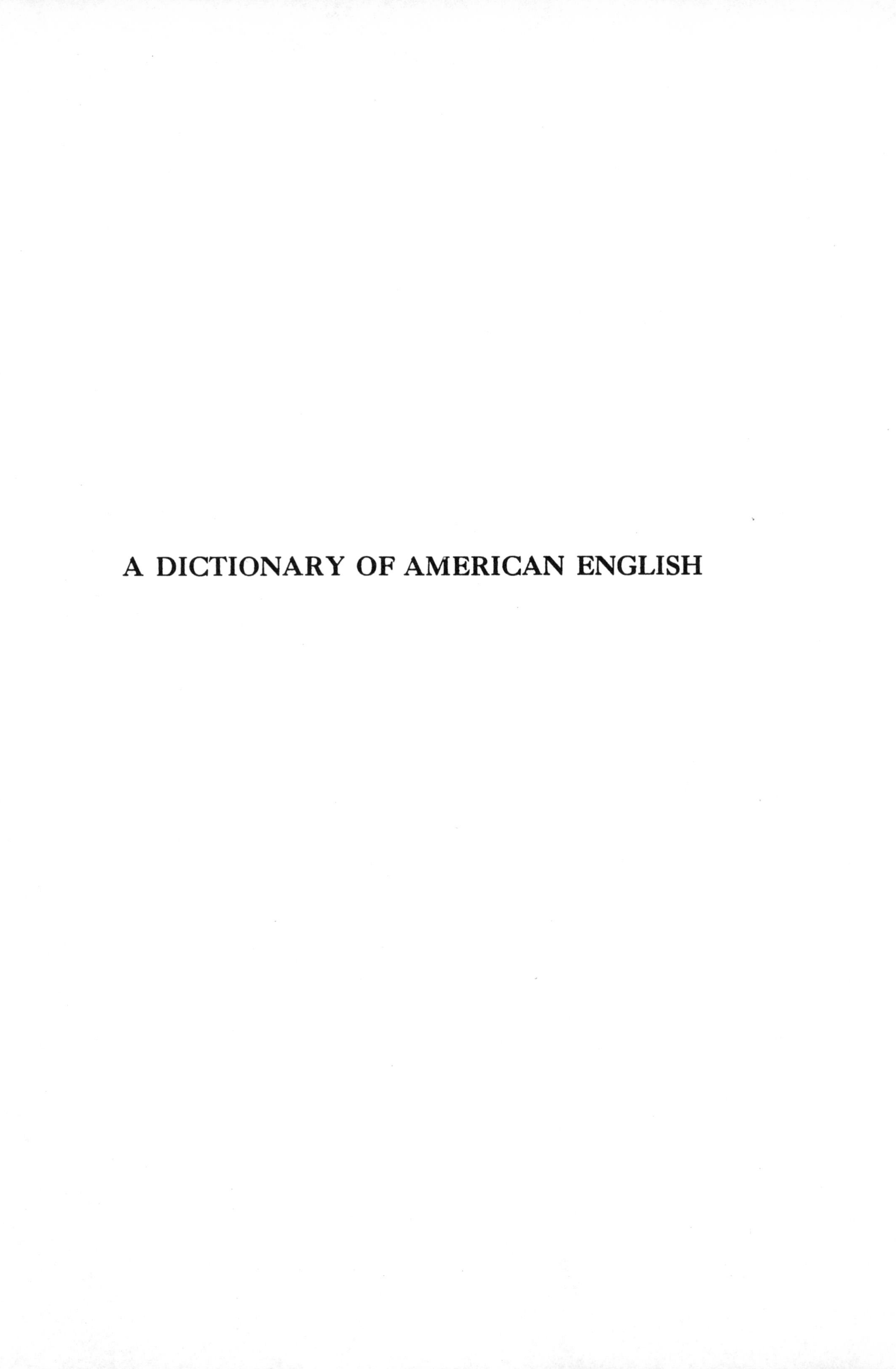

A DICTIONARY OF AMERICAN ENGLISH

A DICTIONARY OF AMERICAN ENGLISH

ON HISTORICAL PRINCIPLES

Compiled at

THE UNIVERSITY OF CHICAGO

under the editorship of

SIR WILLIAM A. CRAIGIE

Co-editor of the Oxford English Dictionary

and

JAMES R. HULBERT

Professor of English, the University of Chicago

VOLUME III, HONK—RECORD

THE UNIVERSITY OF CHICAGO PRESS · CHICAGO · ILLINOIS

THE UNIVERSITY OF CHICAGO PRESS, CHICAGO 37
Oxford University Press, London, England
The University of Toronto Press, Toronto 5, Canada

 Published 1942. Fourth Impression 1960. Printed in the U.S.A.

PREFATORY NOTE TO VOLUME III

THIS third volume of the dictionary covers a larger number of the letters of the alphabet than its predecessors, viz., the concluding portion of H, the whole of I and the letters following this up to Q, and the earlier pages of R. The number of pages respectively occupied by these are H 27 (additional to 66 in Volume II), I 33, J 31, K 24, L 79, M 114, N 42, O 46, P 202, Q 11, R 31. The unusual number of letters is due partly to a natural disproportion, as may be seen in ordinary dictionaries, and partly to the fact that the limited scope of this work permits the omission of a large number of abstract or scientific terms having no special American interest.

As in the prefatory notes to the previous volumes, the following survey of the contents of these pages is not intended to be exhaustive, but only to indicate some of the main features of a vocabulary which is both extensive and of varied interest. Even with such limitation, it is difficult to summarize in a few pages the wealth of material which is here for the first time collected for the information either of the casual reader or of the serious student of the language in its various aspects. For ease of comparison, the order of the sections in this survey is the same as in the previous prefatory notes.

The terms relating to the country fall into two main classes, those denoting natural or topographical features and those designating parts or places to which distinctive names have been given. To the former class belong such words as *interval(e)*, *key*[3], *kill* n.[1], *lagoon*, *lake*, *lick*, *marsh*, *meadow*, *mountain*, *neck*, *old field*, *panhandle*, *park*, *pass*, *pine barren*, *pineland*, *pitch* n.[2], *plain*, *pocoson*, *point*, *pond*, *prairie*, and *rapid*. The second class consists of a large number of proper names, many of which are of native origin, as *Illinois*, *Iowa*, *Kansas*, *Kentucky* (with its variants *Kentuck* and *Kaintuck*), *Mackinaw*, *Manhattan*, *Massachusetts*, *Michigan*, *Nantucket*, *Nebraska*, *Ohio*, *Oklahoma*, and *Oregon*, or have been devised and imposed at various times by the colonists, as *Louisiana*, *Maryland*, *New England*, *(New) Jersey*, *New Orleans*, *New York*, *North Carolina*, *Pennsylvania*, *Philadelphia*. These are included in the dictionary because it is necessary to illustrate the attributive collocations into which they frequently enter, as *Jersey pine*, *New Orleans moss*, etc. A number of them have also given rise to derivative nouns and adjectives, as *Illinoi(s)an*, *Iowan*, *Kansan*, *Michigander*, etc. To these may be added such descriptive terms as the *Middle West*, *Out West*, *Middle states*, *Northern state*, *Keystone State*, *Lone-Star State*, *Prairie state*, *Quaker City*, and *Queen City*, and the use of *Indian* with *country*, *land*, *reservation*, *territory*, etc., together with the native river names *Mississippi* and *Missouri*. Different types of names for localities are represented by a few terms, as *municipality*, *national park*, *parish*, *patent* n. 1, 2, *precinct*, *province*, *purchase*, and *quarter (section)*.

Means of communication and transport range from the *plank walk* and *plank road* to the *pike* n.[3], *mail road*, *post road*, *national road*, *railroad* and *railway;* connected with the latest of these are *interurban* and *L* (=elevated). Vehicles are represented by *horse car*, *Jersey wagon*, *mail coach*, *mail wagon*, *overland coach*, *prairie schooner*, and on the railway by *palace car*, *parlor car*, and *Pullman*. Other means of transport by land include *pack horse*, *pack mule*, *pony express*, and *portage*. Transport and carriage by water are illustrated by *log canoe, horse boat, keel* and *keel boat, Kentucky boat* and *flat, mail boat, Moses* (*boat*), *packet, packet boat,* and *packet ship*. The *hurricane deck* as part of a steamer is a specifically American term.

The vocabulary connected with building is not extensive, but includes *house* and some of its parts or appendages, as *parlor, keeping room, kitchen, L* (=ell), *lean-to* or *linter, piazza, porch,* and *lightning-rod;* also *mansion* (*house*), *meetinghouse, hotel, inn, ordinary, hospital, log cabin, log house,* and the Indian *long house*.

Under the heads of administration and public service the number of historically interesting terms is well up to the average, and includes both adjectives, as *municipal* and *national*, and nouns or composite expressions, as *legislature; House of Assembly, of Burgesses, of Delegates, of Representatives; lower house; joint committee, joint convention, junto, kitchen cabinet; Interior Department, Indian affairs, Indian bureau, land office, loan office, patent office; income tax; Maine law, prohibition*. The names of officials or persons in authority include *Indian agent, inspector, magistrate, marshal, mayor, messenger, minister, office-holder, officer, overseer, postmaster* (*general*), and *president*. The enforcement of *law and order* contributes *judge, judiciary, jury, justice, penitentiary, police, posse,* and *prison*.

Terms of politics are similarly in evidence to an extent which shows the prominent place held by these in American life. Among the more noteworthy are *Jacobin, Jacobinism, Know-nothing, Know-Nothingism, lobby* n. and v., *lobbying, lobbyist, logrolling, machine, nativism, nativist, office-seeker, party, pipelaying, plank, platform, plurality, political, politician, politics, popular sovereignty, populist party, public, radical,* and the colloquial or slang personal designations *hunker, old hunker, kicker, lame duck, locofoco, mossback,* and *mugwump*. Other terms more or less closely associated with politics are *impeachment, inaugural* (*address*), *inaugurate, mass meeting, Missouri Compromise, Monroe Doctrine, naturalize, naturalization, ratification; poll, primary, primary election* and *meeting, prox, proxy; ironclad oath*.

Various incidents, institutions, persons, etc., of historical interest are commemorated in *Independence Day, Ku-Klux Klan, Liberty Boys, Liberty pole* or *tree, lost cause, loyalist, Lynch* (or *Lynch's*) *law* (now definitely assigned to its real originator), *manor, Mayflower, Memorial Day, minute-man, mountain boy, night rider, non-importation, non-intervention, nullification, nullifier, Palatine, partisan, Paxton boys, Pinkerton, Pilgrim father, Pope Day* and *Night, Raines Law,* and *rebel*.

Military and naval terms are not specially prominent but include (1) *military* n. and a., *muster* n. and v., *National Guard, picket, picket guard, platoon, post* n.[3]; *inspector general, provost, provost marshal, quartermaster, ranger; palisade, parade ground; musket, Minié rifle, Parrott gun;* (2) *marine, marine corps, naval academy, officer,* and *school; navy, navy department,* etc.; *privateer* and *monitor*.

Varieties of religious belief and practice or their adherents supply *Hopkinsian, -ianism, Independent, Jack Mormon, jerker, Josephite, Latter-Day Saint, Lutheran, Mennonite, Methodism, Methodist, Millerism, Millerite, Moravian, Mormon, Mormonism, -ite, New Light, New school, Old school, Presbyterian, Protestant, Puritan, Quaker,* and *Ranter*. Other terms connected with religion or with the various churches are *lecture, lecture day, mission, monthly* and *quarterly meeting, platform, presbytery; missionary, parson, pastor*[1], *preacher, priest, prophet, mourner,* and *mourner's bench*.

Various grades of education are well represented by the defining terms applied to 'school,' as *Latin, law, manual labor, medical, normal, old field, parochial, preparatory, primary, private* and *pub-*

lic school. Other types of educational institutions are the *junior* and *medical college*, *lyceum*, *polytechnic* and *kindergarten*, with the curious hybrid *kitchengarten*. Other educational terms of interest are *president*, *prex(y)*, *proctor*, *professor*, *provost; junior*, *minor*, *parietal*, *postgraduate*, and *Phi Beta Kappa*.

A few terms relate to games of chance, as *jack pot*, *joker*, *keno*, *lay-out*, *monte*, *pedro*, *penny ante*, *poker*[2], and *policy*. Of outdoor sports only the *Kentucky Derby*, *lacrosse*, and the *infield* and *outfield* in baseball call for special mention.

Designations of persons from the names of states, as *Iowan*, *Kansan*, have been mentioned above. To these may be added *North American*, *Native American* (also *native-born*), *Hoosier*, *mountaineer*, *mountain man*, *pike* n.[4], and *poor white*, along with the immigrant *Irish* and *Pennsylvania Dutch*, and the Canadian *Kanuck*. Naturally prominent in themselves and in attributive use are *Negro* and *nigger;* less so are *mestizo*, *mulatto*, *mustee*, *octoroon*, and *quadroon* (with the variants *quatroon* and *quartero(o)n*). The *Indian*, who in various connections occupies no less than nineteen columns of the letter I, is represented by a large number of tribal names, as *Huron*, *Iroquois*, *Kickapoo*, *Mandan*, *Mingo*, *Navajo*, *Pawnee*, etc., as well as by the epithets *Praying* and *Pueblo Indian*. Other words having Indian associations are *nation*, *native*, and *Mound-Builder*. Indian names for the white man are *Long knife* and *Paleface*. Jocular names for members of different groups or races are *Jonathan*, *Jim Crow*, *John Chinaman*, and *Lo*.

Different phases in the occupation and development of the country are indicated by *immigration*, *locate*, *location*, *lot*, *plantation*, *pre-empt*, *pre-emption*, *ranch* and *rancho*, and the personal designations *hunter*, *immigrant*, *mover*, *old settler*, *pathfinder*, *Pike's Peaker*, *pioneer*, *planter*, *proprietary*, and *proprietor*. To the cultivation of the soil belong *irrigate*, *irrigation*, *list* n.[1] and v.[2], *mowing ground*, *mowing machine*, *new ground*, *patch*, *plough*, while cattle raising is scantily represented by *maverick*, *pasture*, *ranch*, and *range*.

Business and commerce, industry and its products, are naturally the sources of a large number of entries. Some of the leading activities are indicated by *King Cotton*, *logging*, *lumber* (with *lumberer*, *lumbering*, etc.), *mill*, *mining*, *prospecting*, *prospector*, *quartz*, *oil*, *petroleum*, *kerosene*, *naphtha*. Among manufactured articles are *jean* (also *Kentucky jean*), *osnaburg(s); kerosene lamp*, *Kodak*, *linotype*, *megaphone*, *phonograph*, *notions*, *oleomargarine*, the tobaccos *kitefoot* and *Oronoco*, and *long-nine* cigars. Abstract terms connected with business include *insurance*, *interstate commerce*, *market*, *merger*, *patent*, *pool*, *protection*, and *protective*. Dealings in property or stocks are represented by *land company*, *land jobber*, *real estate*, *manipulate*, *manipulation*, *margin*, and the adjective *long* as used on the stock exchange. Banking and currency provide *land bank*, *national bank; currency*, *dollar*, *money*, *paper bill*, and *postal currency; note-shaver*, *-shaving*, *post note; joe*, *johannes*, *nickel*, *ninepence*, *penny*, *picayune*, *pistareen*, *pistole*, and *quarter*.

The names of plants and trees form a numerous class. Many of these, as *hop*, *hornbeam*, *juniper*, *maple*, etc., are common both in British and American use, but have frequently been transferred to different species or even different genera in the new country. Among those which are more distinctively American, either in currency or in importance, are *huckleberry*, *Indian corn*, *ironwood*, *Jamestown* or *Jimson weed*, *Jersey pine*, *Judas tree*, *kalmia*, *killi-* or *kinnikinnick*, *lambkill*, *live oak*, *loblolly bay* and *pine*, *loco(weed)*, *locust*, *loganberry*, *magnolia*, *mesquit(e)*, *moosewood*, *ninebark*, *Osage orange*, *overcup oak*, *palmetto*, *papaw* or *pawpaw*, *partridge berry*, *peanut*, *pecan*, *pepperidge*, *persimmon*, *pig-*

nut, poison ivy, poke, pokeberry, post oak, and *pumpkin.* Of popular or fanciful names some of the most interesting are *Johnny-jump-up, Kentucky coffee, life everlasting, life-of-man, morning-glory, pieplant, pretty-by-night,* and *pride of India* or *China.*

Animal life presents a varied collection of names of quadrupeds, birds, fishes, etc. To the first of these belong *horse* (the importance of which is indicated by the nine columns occupied by it and its compounds), *mule, mustang, paint horse, pinto; ibex, moose, mountain sheep, prongbuck, prong-horn(ed) antelope; mountain cat, painter*[2] or *panther, polecat, prairie wolf; jack rabbit, rabbit; marten, mink, muskrat, musquash, opossum* or *possum, prairie dog* or *squirrel, raccoon; kangaroo mouse* and *rat.* Among the birds are the *killdee* or *-deer, kingbird, logcock, martin, mocking bird, oxeye, oyster-catcher, partridge, passenger pigeon, pewee* or *pewit, pheasant, phoebe, pigeon, pigeon hawk, pinnated grouse, prairie chicken* or *hen,* and *quail.* Names of fishes are less numerous, but include *killifish, kingfish, Lafayette, lake bass,* etc., *pigfish, pogy* or *porgy,* and *quinnat.* Of reptiles the chief are the *horn* or *horned snake, moccasin* 2 (or *m. snake*), *racer,* and *rattlesnake,* and of insects the *hopper* or *hoppergrass, katydid,* and *locust.* A number of specific names of animals, birds, etc., may also be found under the adjectives or nouns which form the distinguishing epithet, as *hooded, horned, mountain, prairie,* and the entries following upon these words.

Articles of food and drink are varied if not abundant, as *Indian bread, johnnycake* or *journey cake, pone, mush, pandowdy, pie, pumpkin pie, parched corn, popcorn,* and *Indian meal;* also *jerked beef, porterhouse steak, ice cream* (the attributive uses of which become more frequent after 1870), *maple sugar,* and *muscovado.* Of drinks there are *julep* and *mint julep, moonshine, peach brandy,* and the Mexican *mescal* and *pulque.*

The familiar, colloquial, and slang element in the more modern portion of the vocabulary, for the most part of American origin and of exclusively or distinctively American currency, is very large. Any classification of this would be difficult, and those terms included in the following selective list are given in alphabetic order, viz., *honk* v., *hoodlum, hooter, hub* 3, *hunky, hunky-dory, jag, jam* n. and adv., *jamboree, jayhawk, -hawker, -hawking, Jesse, jibe* v., *jig-saw, jimberjawed, joint* n. 3, *joker, josh* n. and v., *Juba, kalsomine* n. and v., *ker-* (in *kerchunk,* etc.), *ki-yi* n. and v., *knickerbocker, 'lasses, level-headed, lickety* (*-cut, -split,* etc.), *lick-log, linguister, loaf* v., *loafer, loco* a. and v., *lope* n. and v., *mammy, marm, mosey* v., *mucker*[1], *muss, nary, nation* n.[2], a., and adv., *nifty, norther, O.K.* (for which much new material has been found), *oodles, pard, pardner, peeler*[1], *pesky, peter* v.[1], *pickaninny, pigeonwing, piker*[2], *plank* v., *plug-ugly, podunk, puke, punch* v., *punky,* and *ragtime.* In addition to these a number of phrases consisting of two or more words may be noted, as (*great*) *horn spoon, hot air, hurrah's nest,* (*poor as*) *Job's turkey, jumping-off place, to be* (or *get*) *left, to face the music,* (*like*) *all nature, all outdoors,* and many more, which are entered under the significant word.

Less colloquial or trivial in character, and deserving of mention for one reason or another, are *improve* v. (=use), *Indian summer, kinepox* (substituted for *cow-pox*), *lengthy, level* (with *head, best*), *mammoth, medicine* (in its Indian sense), *mitten* n. 2, *overalls, overcoat, picture, pile* n.[2], and *puncheon.*

In the great majority of the words in this volume the senses requiring notice do not amount to more than one or two. Those in which a greater number appear, many of them originating in, and confined to, American use, are the nouns *jack, king, outfit, paper, point, pole,* and the verbs *jump, knock, lay, let, make, play,* and *put.* Both noun and verb figure in this respect in *line, pan, raft, raise,* and *range.*

Attributive collocations, as usual, account for a large number of separate entries. The nouns which form the first element in these are especially *horse, house, hunting, ice, iron, land, line, liquor, log, mail, market, marsh, meadow, meat, medicine, mill, mining, mission, money, moose, mountain, mud, mule, Negro, ox, oyster, pack, paper, party, pine, pipe, pork, potato, powder, prairie, pumpkin, rag, rail,* and *railroad.* Many of these collocations are purely American; in others the evidence for American use antedates, sometimes by many years, the examples so far noted from British sources. A few adjectives also yield a number of special entries, as *Indian, Mexican, old, open, patent, public, purple.*

The list of words adopted from other languages is much longer than in the previous volumes. Conspicuous in this respect is the number of adoptions from Spanish and the various Indian dialects, which are not completely covered by the following examples. Spanish has contributed *jacal, javalina, jornada* and *journada, laguna, lariat, lasso, llano, macheer, madroño, malpais, mañana, manta, mantilla, manzanita, mayordomo, mesa, mescal, mesquit(e), mestizo, mochila, mustang, ocotillo, olla, padre, paisano, paloverde, panoche, patio, penitente, peon, periagua, peyote, piñon, pinto, pitahaya, placer, placeta, plaza, pompano, poncho, presidio, pueblo, pulque, quirt, ranch(o), rancheria,* and *ranchero.* Of the Indian words a fair number have come into general use as the ordinary or only name for the thing, animal, etc., denoted by them. They include *huskanaw, kenticoy* (=canticoy), *killhag* (=culheag), *killi-* or *kinnikinnick, kiskatoma, Mackinaw, macock, mananosay, manito, massasauga, matchcoat, menhaden, mico, moccasin, moonack, mugwump, mummichog, muskellunge* (with the variants *mascalonge,* etc.), *musquash, namaycush, netop, nocake* or *nokehick, opossum* or *possum, papoose, peag* or *peak, pecan, pekan, pembina, pemmican, persimmon, pipsissewa, pocoson, poke, pone, potlatch, powwow, puccoon, punk, quahog, quinnat,* and *raccoon.* Next in number come the borrowings from French, of which the principal are *lagniappe, levee, loup-cervier* or *lucivee, Mardi gras, Mauvaise(s) terre(s), motte, parfleche, padgo* or *patgo, patroon*[1], *pelage, picayune, pirogue,* and *prairie.* From Dutch are derived *kill* n.[1], *lute, marshbanker* or *mossbunker, olykoek, overslaugh* n. and v., *patroon*[2], and *pinkster.*

From this survey it will be evident that the present volume of the dictionary is fully equal to either of its predecessors in the linguistic and historic interest of its contents.

The funds necessary for the editing of Volume III have been provided by Mrs. R. S. Maguire and the Rockefeller Foundation. The University is very appreciative of these generous contributions.

EXPLANATION OF SPECIAL LETTERING AND SYMBOLS

The size of the (boldface) type used for the heading of each entry indicates the relative importance of words with respect to their history or present currency.

The date of the quotation is usually followed by the author's name in capitals, or in small letters when he is quoting a source or when the name is that of the editor of the work.

* indicates that the word or sense is found in English before 1600.

+ indicates that the word or sense clearly or to all appearance originated within the present limits of the United States.

|| indicates that the term or sense is known only from the passage cited and may be an individualism.

{ } encloses the earliest, latest, or inclusive dates (so far as known) for the occurrence of the word or sense in England (or in other than American English), or a statement relative to this. When a definition is not preceded by a + mark but is followed by a date in braces later than that of the earliest quotation, it has been assumed that the sense is not (or is not with certainty) of American origin.

When none of these symbols is used, the inference is that the word or sense is to all appearance part of the common stock of English, although lexicographical evidence for deciding its precise origin is lacking.

† before a form in boldface type denotes that that spelling is obsolete.

[ ] frequently contains the etymology.

Editorial additions briefly elucidating some matter in a quotation are also given within brackets.

When enclosing quotations, brackets denote that such illustrations are inserted with a qualification, being sometimes anticipative of more definite American usage or illustrative of historical use and being sometimes the work of a non-American writer or of an American in a foreign environment.

' ' in the reference encloses the pseudonym under which the author produced the work quoted.

In references, large capitals indicate volumes, small capitals parts or sections, and lower-case letters chapters or prefatory pages, e.g. III., ɪɪ., xxi.

When a subordinate sense marked **b** follows a sense which is not marked **a,** this signifies that the subordinate sense is derived from (i.e. is not collateral with) this antecedent sense.

Numbered paragraphs, (1), (2), etc., are used to illustrate different contexts in which the word occurs.

Paragraphs preceded by (*a*), (*b*), etc., exhibit different forms or spellings of the word.

The printing of a word in small capitals signifies that further information will be found under that word.

LIST OF ABBREVIATIONS

(In addition to many others that are obvious)

a (before a date)	= *ante*, before
a., *adj.*, adj.	= adjective
abbrev.	= abbreviation
absol., absol.	= absolute, -ly
ad. (in etymologies)	= adaptation of
adv., adv.	= adverb
app.	= apparently
attrib.	= attributive, -ly
B. '48 (etc.)	= Bartlett, 1848 (1859, 1877)
B. and L.	= Barrère and Leland (1889)
c (before a date)	= *circa*, about
Cent.	= Century Dictionary (1889–91)
Cf., cf.	= compare
Cl.	= Clapin (1902)
colloq.	= colloquial, -ly
colloq.[2]	= a lower grade of colloquialism
comb.	= combination
dial., dial.	= dialect
Dict.	= Dictionary
E.	= East
E.	= English
ellipt., ellipt.	= elliptical, -l
Eng.	= England
esp.	= especially
F.	= Farmer (1889)
F., Fr.	= French
f. (in etymologies)	= formed on
F. and H.	= Farmer and Henley (1890–1904)
fem.	= feminine
fig., fig.	= figurative, -ly
freq.	= frequent, -ly
intr.	= intransitive
It.	= Italian
L.	= Latin
masc.	= masculine
mod.	= modern
Mex.	= Mexican
n., n.	= noun
Obs., obs.	= obsolete
occas.	= occasional, -ly
O.E.D.	= Oxford English Dictionary
Pg.	= Portuguese
Pick.	= Pickering (1816)
p.p.	= past participle
ppl. a., ppl. a.	= participial adjective
pple.	= participle
prep., prep.	= preposition
pron.	= pronoun
pronunc.	= pronunciation
Prov.	= Provençal
pr. pple.	= present participle
p.t.	= past tense
q.v.	= *quod vide*, which see
refl., refl.	= reflexive
S.	= South
Sc., Sc.	= Scotch
sc.	= *scilicet*, namely
S.E.	= South-East
Sp.	= Spanish
spec., spec.	= specifically
Stand.	= Standard Dictionary (1893–95)
s.v.	= *sub voce*, under the word
S.W.	= South-West
Th.	= Thornton *Glossary*
Th. S.	= Thornton *Supplement*
tr.	= transitive
transf., transf.	= transferred sense
v., vb.	= verb
var.	= variant of
vbl. n.	= verbal noun
W.	= West
W. '06 (etc.)	= Webster, 1806 (1828, etc.)
Worc.	= Worcester (1846, 1860)

+**Honk**, *v.*

1. *intr.* and *quasi-tr.* Of wild geese: To utter their cry. See HONKING for earlier quotations.

1868 HOLMES *Old Vol. of Life* 169 As the air grows colder, the long wedges of geese flying south, with their 'commodore' in advance, and *honking* as they fly, are seen high up in the heavens. **1874** J. LONG *Wild-Fowl* 234 They always commence cackling and honking loudly. **1904** *Automobile* 15 Oct. 429 The touring cars poured in over the road like flocks of honking geese to their feeding ground. **1911** J. F. WILSON *Land Claimers* 22 Wild geese honked their way overhead.

2. To sound the horn on a car. *To honk by,* to go by while sounding the horn. Also quasi-tr. with *way.*

1895 REMINGTON *Pony Tracks* 256 The irrepressible Dan begins to 'honk' on his horn. **1911** HARRISON *Queed* 6 Now and then a chauffeur honked by, grim eyes roving for the unwary pedestrian. **1915** *Lit. Digest* 4 Sept. 467/1 To-day nearly a dozen autos may be always seen 'honking' their way through Nome's busy thoroughfares.

+**Honker.** A wild goose. — *a***1841** W. HAWES *Sporting Scenes* I. 178 We have killed wild geese . . . and we know what it is to bring down a glorious gaggle of honkers to our stool. **1879** *Scribner's Mo.* Oct. 836/2 Two of the 'old honkers' tumble headlong into the lake. **1884** *Forest & Stream* 22 May 324 'My First Honker.'—Well do I remember the morning on which he measured his length on the grass. **1907** LILLIBRIDGE *Trail* 126 The swelling, diminishing note . . . of the grey Canada honker. **1917** *Birds of Amer.* I. 158 Canada Goose. *Branta canadensis canadensis.* . . . [Also called] Canada Brant; Honker; Long-necked Goose.

+**Honking.** The action of the verb HONK. — **1846** ABERT *Rep. N. Mexico* 28 Oct., The wild geese are flying about us in great numbers, and keep up an incessant 'honking.' **1854** THOREAU *Walden* 292, I was startled by the loud honking of a goose.

Honor. *Educ.* **1.** *attrib.* Designating a person or group that has done excellent academic work. +**2.** *Honor system,* the administration of examinations without the usual supervision, so that examinees are placed on their honor not to cheat. — (1) **1871** BAGG *At Yale* 42 *Appointment,* position upon the faculty's honor-roll of scholarship. **1877** *Harper's Mag.* Dec. 109/2 You, an honor man at college, marking bulletin-boards! (2) **1904** *Pittsburgh Gazette* 3 Dec. 4 The most successful plan of combating the tendency of college students to cheat in examinations has been some form of an 'honor system' by which the pupil is implicitly trusted and his statement accepted that he used no dishonest aids.

***Honorable, Honourable,** *a.* Applied as a prefix to the names of various persons of distinction or to a body of public officials. Often abbreviated. (See HON.)

There is no official rule for the application of this adjective. In general, it is applied to legislators and the more important public officials. It is, moreover, applied to any person whenever it is desired to show him special courtesy.

1640 BRADFORD *Hist.* 445 Freedomes granted in ye said letters patents by ye said right Honble. Counsell for New-England. **1704** S. KNIGHT *Journal* 66, I stayed a day here Longer than I intended by the Commands of the Honble Governor Winthrop to stay and take supper with him. **1721** *Mass. H. Rep. Jrnl.* III. 155 If any ill consequence . . . should insue from the Honourable House refusing to Supply the Treasury, . . . the Council must, and do clear themselves from the Blame of it. **1776** *N.J. Archives* 2 Ser. I. 39 Whereas by a resolution of the Honorable Continental Congress, a third battalion is recommended immediately to be raised for this colony. **1789** MACLAY *Deb. Senate* 71 But now a discourse was raised again, whether the members should be styled honorable on the minutes. **1833** T. HAMILTON *Men & Manners* I. 241 The members of the Federal Senate are addressed generally in the northern states, with the prefixture of Honourable, but the New Englanders go further, and extend the same distinction to the whole body of representatives, a practice followed in no other part of the Union. **1892** *Harper's Weekly* 9 Jan. 42/4 It is only permissible in the United States to place before the name of one man the prefix 'Honorable,' and that man is the Lieutenant-Governor of Massachusetts, upon whom the title is conferred by law. **1912** NICHOLSON *Hoosier Chron.* 195 There's one of the bright lights now—the Honorable Ike Pettit, of Fraser.

+**Hoochinoo.** (See quotation.) — **1899** *Boston Jrnl.* 11 Jan. 4/5 The name of fire-water in Alaska is 'hoochinoo,' and recently the House gave its official sanction to the word by enacting that no whisky, beer or 'hoochinoo' shall be sold in Alaska. . . . When the United States laws established prohibition for Alaska the natives of that land began furnishing a mixture of rum and molasses, which has gradually taken the name of 'hoochinoo.'

***Hood.** Also †**hud.**

***1.** A covering for the head and neck made of flexible material.

1644 *Essex Probate Rec.* I. 35 One sad collored Carsy gowen and hud sutable. **1711** *Boston News-Letter* 19 Feb. 2/2 (*advt.*), Stolen or carried privately away out of the House of Capt. John Bonner . . . , two white Muslin Hoods. **1768** in *Copley-Pelham Lett.* 41, I also send a Gown, Hood, and Band, by which to finish the Drapery. **1835** HOFFMAN *Winter in West* I. 240 He sallied out to cut wood, with his two sons, axe in hand, all clad in their belted capotes and white woollen hoods. **1896** WILKINS *Madelon* 49, I am going to get my hood and cloak, and then I am going to Lot Gordon's.

+**2.** The covering over the motor of an automobile.

1909 *Index of Patents 1908* 422 Robinson, E. T., assignor to St. Louis Car Company, St. Louis, Mo. [has invented a] Hood for automobiles. **1922** *Automotive Industries* XLVII. 158 On all of the six-cylinder models, nickel beading has been put on the cowl at the rear end of the hood.

Hooded,** *a.* In the specific names of birds: Having feathers suggestive of a hood. — *c1730** CATESBY *Carolina* I. 60 *Parus cucullo nigro.* The Hooded Titmouse. This is about the size of a Goldfinch. . . . They frequent thickets and shady places in the uninhabited parts of Carolina. **1828** BONAPARTE *Synopsis* 79 The Hooded Flycatcher, *Muscicapa cucullata,* . . . inhabits the United States during summer only; rare north of Maryland; common to the south. **1874** COUES *Birds N.W.* 78 Hooded Fly-catching Warbler. . . . This is essentially a southern bird. **1881** *Amer. Naturalist* XV. 216 The hooded troupial (*Icterus cucullatus*) and the Bullock's troupial (*Icterus bullockii*) are the most common around Tucson. **1917** *Birds of Amer.* II. 4 Masked Bob-white. . . . Other Names.—Arizona Bob-white; Hooded Quail.

+**Hooded merganser.** A small merganser (*Lophodytes cucullatus*), having a hoodlike crest on the head of the adult male. — **1823** in James *Exped.* I. 267 *Mergus cucullatus*—Hooded merganser. **1835** AUDUBON *Ornith. Biog.* III. 246 The Hooded Merganser is a most expert diver, and so vigilant that at times it escapes even from the best percussion gun. **1897** *Outing* XXX. 58/1 The hooded merganser, generally termed 'fan-head' owing to its beautiful crest, is a fish duck and worthless for the table.

+**Hooded oriole.** *S.W.* Any of various subspecies of the oriole *Icterus cucullatus,* having, in the male, a hood-shaped colored area about the head and neck. — **1869** *Amer. Naturalist* III. 186 The most peculiar birds [in Calif.] not yet mentioned are . . . the Little Vireo (*Vireo pusillus*) and Hooded Oriole (*Icterus cucullatus*), also migratory [etc.]. **1878** *Nat. Museum Proc.* I. 135 The Hooded Oriole . . . [breeds] with individuals of its own species only. **1886** *Ib.* VIII. 19 This new form may be appropriately named *Icterus cucullatus nelsoni,* Arizona Hooded Oriole. **1917** *Birds of Amer.* II. 255 Sennett's Oriole. *Icterus cucullatus sennetti,* . . . [Also called] Sennett's Hooded Oriole. *Ib.* 256 The Arizona Hooded Oriole, or Nelson's Oriole (*Icterus cucullatus nelsoni*) is similar to Sennett's Oriole, but paler and with its forehead entirely yellow.

+**Hooded sheldrake.** =HOODED MERGANSER. — **1844** *Nat. Hist. N. Y., Zoology* II. 320 The Hooded Sheldrake, *Mergus Cucullatus,* . . . it breeds from Carolina, . . . to high northern latitudes. **1883** *Nat. Museum Bul.* No. 27, 163 *Lophodytes cucullatus.* Hooded Sheldrake. . . . Whole of North America. **1917** *Birds of Amer.* I. 112.

+**Hooded warbler.** A warbler (*Wilsonia citrina*), having in the male a hood-shaped coloring about the head and neck. — **1844** *Nat. Hist. N.Y., Zoology* II. 107 The Hooded Warbler, . . . *Wilsonia mitrata,* . . . builds in low bushes. . . . A bold, courageous bird, feeding on insects which it takes on the wing. **1865** BURROUGHS in *Atlantic Mo.* May 521/2 In only one locality, full of Azalea and Swamp-Huckleberry, I am always sure of finding the hooded warbler. **1899** VAN DYKE *Fisherman's Luck* 22 He looks up carefully through the needles and discovers a hooded warbler, a tiny, restless creature, dressed in green and yellow. **1917** *Birds of Amer.* III. 164/1 The black domino of the Maryland Yellow-throat is replaced in the male Hooded Warbler by a broad yellow mask.

+**Hoodlum.**

This word originated in San Francisco about 1870, but its derivation is unknown. Many theories were concocted about 1877 to account for it, but none of them is supported by evidence: see 1883 *Manchester* (N.H.) *Notes & Queries* Sept.

1. A street rowdy; a loafer; a gangster or criminal. *colloq.*

1872 *Sacramento Wkly. Union* 24 Feb. (Th.), All the boys to be trained as . . . polite loafers, street hounds, hoodlums and bummers. **1877** 'E. MARTIN' *Hist. Great Riots* 420 The bitterest enemies of the Mongolians are the 'Hoodlums,' or the idle loafers, street loungers, and 'bummers,' of the city. **1877** *Congregationalist* 26 Sept. 310/6 A newspaper man in San Francisco, in attempting to coin a word to designate a gang of street Arabs under the beck of one Muldoon, hit upon the idea of dubbing them the *noodlums;* that is simply the reversing the leader's name. In writing the word the strokes of the *n* did not correspond in hight [*sic*], and the compositor took it for hoodlum. **1885** *Santa Fé Wkly. New Mexican* 23 July 1/1 What do we care about the grumblings of a few lately imported hoodlums and their prejudiced organs? **1897** CRANE *Third Violet* 136 We are a kind of a band of hoodlums, you know. **1913** LONDON *Valley of Moon* 25 'Watch me go across an' win her from them cheap skates.' 'Butchertown hoodlums,' Mary sniffed.

attrib. **1877** *Congregationalist* 26 Sept. 308/5 In San Francisco the citizens who believe in law and order have been driven to exert themselves to prevent deplorable and deadly 'hoodlum' riots against the Chinese element of their population. **1893** *Amer. Missionary* XLVII. 396 Indignities and outrages thrown upon them [the Chinese] by not only the hoodlum elements of the sandlots, but by the not less disgraceful hoodlum exhibit in the National Congress.

b. *Hoodlum wagon,* (see quotation).

1913 W. C. BARNES *Western Grazing Grounds* 382 Hoodlum Wagon.—The extra wagon taken with the chuck wagon on the roundup to haul grain, extra bedding, and at times wood and water. **1920** HUNTER *Trail Drivers Texas* I. 299.

2. *fig.* The English sparrow.

1917 *Birds of Amer.* III. 17 English Sparrow. *Passer domesticus.* . . . Other Names.—European House Sparrow; Gamin; Tramp; Hoodlum.

+**Hoodlumism.** The acts and practices of hoodlums. — **1872** *Newton Kansan* 14 Nov. 4/1 The Rev. Dr. Cunningham in a recent sermon traced the history of 'Hoodlumism.' **1875** *Scribner's Mo.* July 276/2 The selfish 'Trades Unions,' which virtually exclude apprentices from the mechanical pursuits, have been, I think, the principal cause of Hoodlumism. **1884** *Boston Journal* 10 Oct. 1 (*caption*), Fatal Result of Hoodlumism at Castine, Me. **1904** *Brooklyn Eagle* 7 June 4 This outbreak of lawlessness and hoodlumism which the magistrates and police have set out to break up.

+**Hoodoo,** *n.* [Probably a variant of VOODOO.]

1. One who practices voodooism; a Negro sorcerer or voodoo.

1881 *Harper's Mag.* April 736/1 Who seed yo' las' moon-risin' w'en Hoodoos met? *Ib.* 738/2 Suddenly she . . . rushed forward with an African yell and joined in the dance as wild as any Hoodoo among them.

b. *transf.* Anything that has a strange or malignant character or a fantastic shape. Also fig. (Cf. sense 3, quot. 1879.)

1882 *Harper's Mag.* April 691/1 So substantial are most of these 'hoodoos,' . . . that all along the line of the mountain railways the ruined construction camps are easily recognized by those who understand what purpose the odd little abandoned huts once served. **1884** H. BUTTERWORTH *Zigzag Journeys West. States* 54 A region . . . full of lofty stone monuments, the remnants of erosion, called hoodoos. **1909** WEBSTER 1032/3 *Hoodoo*, . . . a natural rock pile or pinnacle of fantastic shape. *Western U.S.*

2. A thing that supposedly causes bad luck; a person whose presence is supposed to bring on bad luck; a Jonah.

1883 BEADLE *Western Wilds* 558 If you can find an Indian tradition to match it, your 'hoodoo' is complete. **1890** RYAN *Told in Hills* 211 A sure 'hoodoo' it must be, to warp a man's judgment like that! **1900** GARLAND *Eagle's Heart* 226, I'm a hoodoo, Cory; nobody is ever in luck when I'm around. **1904** *Omaha Bee* 1 Aug. 4 What is the reason of the hoodoo which the railways are trying to put on Omaha in the matter of freight rates on coal? **1907** 'O. HENRY' *Roads of Destiny* vii. 110 Each one throwing the hoodoo on his own particular district.

3. *attrib.* **a.** In sense 1 with *enticement, land, meeting.*

1879 WHITMAN *Spec. Days* 148, I had wanted to go to the Yellowstone river region—wanted specially to see . . . the 'hoodoo' or goblin land of that country. **1881** *Harper's Mag.* April 737/2 Maum Dulcie had made strong resolutions of abstinence as to Hoodoo enticements. *Ib.*, How I should like to see a Hoodoo meeting!

b. In sense 2 with *planet, ship, town.*

1904 *N.Y. Globe* 2 April 1 It is hard to find a crew for a 'hoodoo' ship. Men desert from a vessel with an uncanny reputation. **1907** 'O. HENRY' *Roads of Destiny* vii. 110 [Saturn is] the hoodoo planet of the heavens. **1914** GERRY *Masks of Love* 168 Kansas City had always been a 'hoodoo town' for Newbold's productions.

+**Hoodoo,** *v.* **1.** *tr.* To bring bad luck to; to bewitch. **2.** To drive *away* by persecution. **3.** *intr.* To get greatly excited; to make a great outcry *about.* — (1) **1888** *Judge* July 239 A Washington paper . . . drops into . . . poetry, which is sufficient to hoodoo the organization for the balance of the season. **1890** RYAN *Told in Hills* 16, I've never got rid of the sight of her face. It—it hoodooed me. **1894** *Outing* XXIV. 374/1 The thing was as simple as that! And yet, see how we were hoodooed! **1902** BELL *Hope Loring* 254 Those girls reminded me that it was Friday, and the thirteenth of the month, and they told me I would hoodoo the whole school if I didn't wait until the next day. **1913** MULFORD *Coming of Cassidy* 108 Perhaps the case-keeper [at faro] had hoodooed him. (2) **1895** *Chicago Strike of 1894* 107 As soon as you are found out to be a member of the American Railway Union you were . . . hoodooed away from the property as quick as possible. (3) **1900** *Congress. Rec.* 27 Feb. 2336/2, I will tell you what they [the Democrats] . . . are hoodooing about.

+**Hoodooism.** (See quotation.) — **1881** *Harper's Mag.* April 737/1 'What *is* Hoodooism anyhow?' 'It's de ole African r'ligion, honey. It's jes' like white folk's r'ligion on'y it's heathenism, an' dey worships de debbil.'

+**Hoodwort.** The mad-dog skullcap. — **1784** CUTLER in *Mem. Academy* I. 463 *Scutellaria*. . . . Hoodwort. Blossoms blue. By fences in Sandwich. August. **1832** WILLIAMSON *Maine* I. 131.

***Hoof,** *n.*

1. a. *collect.* Cows, horses, etc. ***b.** A hoofed animal as the smallest unit of a herd. {-*a*1592, 1859}

(a) 1683 *Plymouth Rec.* 174 Which bridge shalbe for hoof and foot. **(b) 1820** WEBSTER *Works* (1851) III. 16 Small freeholders parted with their last hoof, and the last measure of corn from their granaries, to supply provisions for the troops. **1891** O'BEIRNE *Leaders Ind. Territory* 116/2 Mr. Muncrief has had much experience with the wild Indians . . . and lost many a hoof through the agency of these midnight marauders. **1898** CANFIELD *Maid of Frontier* 181 Every hoof and horn missed in this country was charged to me. **1901** WHITE *Westerners* 30 If you try to shoot us up any, we'll kill every hoof you have. **1903** A. ADAMS *Log of Cowboy* viii. 110 Not a hoof would bed down.

+**2.** *On (the) hoof.* Used in phrases dealing with the sale or transportation of beef cattle: Alive; under the cattle's own motive power.

1817 *Niles' Reg.* XII. 287/1 An ox, bred at Springfield, Mass. weighs on the hoof, 3,100 lbs. **1830** N. AMES *Mariner's Sk.* 163 We generally bought our beef 'on the hoof,' and swam them off alongside. **1845** FRÉMONT *Exped.* 197, I had purchased at the mission some California cattle, which were to be driven on the hoof. **1866** *Wkly. New Mexican* 17 Nov. 2/4 Sealed proposals in duplicate will be received . . . for the delivery of five thousand head of Beef Cattle, on the hoof, for the use of captive Indians. **1874** COUES *Birds N.W.* 382 Early in the fall it was deemed advisable to 'jerk' all the beef that remained on the hoof. **1890** *Stock Grower & Farmer* 4 Jan. 4/2 [Monroe] shipped on the hoof, and did all of his killing near the large cities which he supplied.

b. *To sell corn on the hoof,* to convert into money a crop of corn, not by direct sale to a consumer, but by feeding it to cattle later to be sold alive.

1902 LORIMER *Lett. Merchant* 78 It seems to take a farmer a long time to learn that the best way to sell his corn is on the hoof.

Hoof, *v.* {1641-} *S.* +*tr.* 'To kill (game) by shooting it on the ground' (*Cent.*).

+**Hoof ail.** =FOOT ROT. — **1838** in *Rep. Comm. Agric. 1884* 246 A number of the 'Farmer and Gardener' . . . contains an article on the 'Hoof-ail' of cattle. **1867** *Ib. 1866* 77 In New York, either grub, foot-rot, 'hoof-ail,' black tongue, scab or other diseases are found. **1871** *Ill. Agric. Soc. Trans.* VIII. 182 The most damaging disease, because the most difficult of eradication, is that known as Foot-Rot—sometimes called Hoof-Ail.

+**Hoof-and-mouth disease.** A disease affecting the feet and mouth of live stock. {foot and mouth d., 1862-} — **1884** LOWELL *On Democracy* 5 Would it account for the phylloxera, and hoof-and-mouth disease, and bad harvests . . . and the German bands? **1914** *Hoard's Dairyman* 11 Dec. 577/2 Guernsey cattle with the hoof and mouth disease . . . entirely recovered and did not disseminate the disease to other cattle.

+**Hoofed locust.** *W.* An opprobrious name given sheep by cattlemen. — **1897** *Science* V. 894 The feet of these 'hoofed locusts,' crossing and recrossing the faces of steep slope [*sic*], tread out the plants sheep do not relish.

+**Hoofrot.** =FOOT ROT. — **1863** RANDALL *Pract. Shepherd* 25 These miserable animals brought along with them scab and hoof-rot, those dire scourges of the ovine race. **1869** *Ill. Agric. Soc. Trans.* VII. 458 A large number of sheep suffering either from scab or hoof-rot.

Hooick. A cry uttered to call pigs or other stock to the feeding trough. — **1895** REMINGTON *Pony Tracks* 250 Dan sat on his pony and blew his old cow's horn, and yelled: 'Hooick! hooick!'

***Hook,** *n.*

1. [Perhaps influenced by Du. *hoek*, 'corner,' 'nook.'] A sharp bend in the course of a river or channel. {1670-}

1670 *Docs. Col. Hist. N.Y.* XII. 474 A Plantation wth proporcon of meadow ground for Hay for their cattle on Verdrietiges or Trinity Hook at Delaware. **1677** *Jamaica* (L.I.) *Rec.* I. 260 A sartain hook or nook of water . . . puts up westwerd from ye River. **1781** *Deane Papers* 161, I am just informed that the British Fleet have again sailed from the hook. **1848** BARTLETT 179 *Hook.* (Dutch, *hoek*, a corner.) This name is given in New York to several angular points in the North and East rivers; as, *Corlear's Hook, Sandy Hook, Powles's Hook.* **1895** *Educational Rev.* Nov. 357 This . . . forming an array of mud-flats . . . hooks and deltas.

+**2.** *pl.* A person's hands or feet. *slang.*

1846 *Spirit of Times* 18 April 85/3 He heard the rough voice of the husband grumble out—'*Take away your hooks!*' **1903** LEWIS *Boss* 96 A pickpocket has to have plenty of sleep to keep his hooks from shakin'.

+**3.** A district in New York City.

1851 GREELEY in *Whig Almanac 1852* 12/2 The 'Five Points' is the most 'Democratic' district of our city [New York]; 'The Hook' follows not very far behind it. **1859** [see HOOKER 1].

4. *Boxing.* A blow delivered with the elbow bent and rigid.

1898 *Kansas City Star* 21 Dec. 3/1 Round 1—After some slow work Hawkins got in a left hand hook on Mac's stomach. **1903** LEWIS *Boss* 14 The blow was of the sort that boxers style a 'hook.' **1908** LORIMER *J. Spurlock* i. 18 She . . . then fetched him a left hook under the jaw that made him take the count.

5. *On* (or *upon*) *one's own hook,* on one's own responsibility; on one's own account. (Cf. GO *v.* 11.) {1849-}

1812 *Boston Gazette* 23 Nov. (Th.), [Commodore] Rodgers himself says that he went upon his own hook. **1832** HONE *Diary* I. 58 Some troops are marching about the street, 'upon their own hook,' I suppose. **1846** SOL. SMITH *Theatr. Apprent.* 7 We were traversing together the fertile plains and piny woods of Georgia—you as candidate for Congress on your own hook. **1866** 'MARK TWAIN' in *Harper's Mag.* Dec. 107 This morning Captain called up the two quarter-boats, and said one would have to go off on its own hook. **1896** HARRIS *Sister Jane* 339, I allowed I'd git my head took off over here, an' I come primed to do some taking on my own hook.

6. Special combinations and phrases.

Hook-and-Eye Dutch, =HOOKER 2; *h. jump,* (see quot. 1912); *h. slide,* a slide in baseball in which the runner hooks the bag with his foot.

1903 *N.Y. Times* 9 Sept., A young farmer . . . [who] was a member of the Amish sect, commonly known as the Hook and Eye Dutch. **1912** MATHEWSON *Pitching* 222 Pitchers . . . are always trying for new curves in the spring practice, and out of the South . . . drift tales each spring of the 'fish' ball and the new 'hook' jump and the 'stop' ball and many more eccentric curves. **1917** — *Sec. Base Sloan* xi. 145 A dexterous hook-slide that kept him far out of reach of the baseman's sweep.

***Hook,** *v.* +*tr.* To make (a rug) by looping strips of cloth, yarn, etc., through burlap with a hook; to crochet. — **1882** *Harper's Mag.* Dec. 126/1 Cynthy Ann . . . hooked rugs from early in the morning until late into the night. **1898** *Boston Transcript* 16 April 14/5 A Detroit lady joyfully boasted: 'I have just hooked my husband a lovely pair of mittens.'

+**Hook-and-ladder company.** A fire company provided with a carriage containing ladders and large hooked instruments for tearing down walls.

1821 *Boston Selectmen* 187 Mr. George G. Channing . . . declines taking command of the Fire Hook & Ladder company. **1833** *N.Y. City Ordinance* 10 Dec., All firemen attached to any fire engine, hose, or hook and ladder company. **1856** *Porter's Spirit of Times* 8 Nov. 164/2 Two rival Hook and Ladder Companies of our Fire Department here, have for a long time been disputing as to the relative superiority of each other's valued horses. **1883** 'Mark Twain' *Life on Miss.* lviii. 566 Davenport has . . . an admirable paid fire department, consisting of six hook and ladder companies, four steam fire engines. **1898** *Engineering Mag.* Feb. 789 The fire department of the city of New York has . . . 22 hook and ladder companies. **1923** Watts *L. Nichols* 68 The only clean place in the vicinity was the Bald Eagle Engine-House and Hook-and-Ladder Company 17.

+**Hook-and-ladder man.** A member of a hook-and-ladder company. — **1825** Brayley *Boston Fire Dept.* 156 The engineers, the firemen and hosemen, and hook and laddermen are competent to manage all the machines. **1830** *Mass. Statutes* 5 March 338 Enginemen, hosemen, hook and laddermen, and clothmen.

+**Hook-and-ladder truck.** A fire truck carrying hooks and ladders. — **1882** McCabe *New York* 603 There are employed in the service of the department 42 steam fire-engines, . . . and 18 hook and ladder trucks. **1891** *Harper's Mag.* June 118/2 The fire department . . . consisted of four steam-engines, . . . one hook-and-ladder truck, and five hose carriages. **1904** *McClure's Mag.* Jan. 290/1 The crew of a hook and ladder truck were opening the forward hatch.

***Hook and line. 1.** A fishing apparatus consisting of a line with a hook or hooks attached to it. +**2.** Used as an adverb: Completely. (Cf. Hook, line, and sinker.) +**3.** Used as an adjective: Fully equipped. — (1) **1709** Lawson *Carolina* 155 The Dog-Fish are a small sort of the Shark kind; and are caught with Hook and Line. **1818** *Amer. Monthly Mag.* II. 294 Fresh cod . . . are taken off Sandy-Hook and the Jersey shore by the hook and line. **1854** *Harper's Mag.* Oct. 675/1 The fish [mackerel] are caught with hook and line, each fisherman using two lines. **1911** *Rep. Fisheries 1908* 316 Black Bass . . . are caught with hook and line and furnish a considerable quantity of excellent food. (2) **1834** C. A. Davis *Lett. J. Downing* 44 Its all over with you and the Bank—you'll all go 'hook and line.' (3) **1900** Bacheller *E. Holden* 215 When we came back, 'hook an' line' for another vacation, the fields were aglow with color.

+**Hooked rug.** A rug consisting of strips of cloth, yarn, etc., hooked back and forth through burlap. — **1880** Howells *Undiscovered Country* 415 Hooked rugs and embroidered tidies, were as worthy a place in Mrs. Ford's simple house as most of the old-fashioned things. **1882** *Harper's Mag.* Dec. 126/1 Her hooked rugs were in demand now, for several summer boarders had admired and purchased them. **1894** Howells *Traveler from Altruria* 163 Home-made hooked rugs, in rounds and ovals, [were] scattered about the clean floor.

***Hooker.** +**1.** (See quotation.) +**2.** A popular name for an Amish Mennonite. +**3.** (See quot. 1881.) +**4.** A cow that tries to catch people, etc., on its horns. — (1) **1859** Bartlett 201 *Hooker.* A resident of the Hook, i.e. a strumpet, a sailor's trull. So called from the number of houses of ill-fame frequented by sailors at the Hook (i.e., Corlear's Hook) in the city of New York. (2) **1880** *Lib. Universal Knowl.* IX. 700 The Amish Mennonites . . . are sometimes called Hookers, because they substitute hooks for buttons on their clothes. (3) **1881** Ingersoll *Oyster Industry* 245 *Hooker*, . . . in sponging, the man who hooks up the sponges from the bottom. (Florida reefs.) **1883** *Nat. Museum Bull.* No. 27, 125 As soon as a Sponge is sighted, the boat is quickly stopped, and the 'hooker' thrusts down his spear and fastens into it. (4) **1885** 'Craddock' *Prophet* 48 The red cow jes' hooked down the bars, bein' a turrible hooker. **1902** Lorimer *Lett. Merchant* 84 Of course, you want to . . . learn to distinguish between a cow that's a kicker, but whose intentions are good if she's approached with proper respect, and a hooker, who is vicious on general principles.

+**Hook Jack,** *v.* 'To play truant. New England' (B. '77).

+**Hook, line, and sinker.** Used adverbially in sense: Completely; without reservation. — **1865** *Weekly New Mexican* 25 August 1/3 Without him Chavez [a candidate for Congress] is gone hook, line, and sinker. **1906** *N.Y. Ev. Post* 8 May 1 A plan . . . was shown to Senator Aldrich, and one description has it, 'he took it, hook, line, and sinker.'

+**Hooks.** [Northern Eng. dial. *howks*, Old Sc. **holkis*.] *pl.* A disease affecting the eyes of horses. — **1846** *Congress. Globe* 1 June 894/2 The operation [of cutting for the 'simples'] . . . is only understood in the West. It comes from horse surgery—cutting a horse's eye for the hooks. The horse is subject to a disease of the eye, something like cataract, which blinds him; and, when emolient [*sic*] remedies fail, the knife is applied, the diseased part cut away, and then the animal sees clear. **1880** *Harper's Mag.* Nov. 930/2 He could . . . take the hooks out of a horse's eyes.

+**Hook-tender.** *Logging.* (See quot. 1905.) — **1893** *Atlantic Mo.* Feb. 196/1 Each man, being hired for a definite purpose, as chopper, hook-tender, barker [etc.], . . . keeps closely to his own job. **1900** *Monthly Summary of Commerce* (Bureau of Statistics) Nov. 1116 A logging crew consists of 1 foremen, . . . 2 swampers, 2 buckers, 3 hook tenders [etc.]. **1905** *Forestry Bureau Bul.* No. 61, 40 *Hook tender*, the foreman of a yarding crew; specifically one who directs the attaching of the cable to a turn of logs. (P[acific] C[oast] F[orest].)

Hooky.[1] Also **hookey.** *By hooky*, an interjection. {by the hooky, 1839–, Sc. and Eng. dial. variant of 'by the hokey'} — *c***1845** Paulding *American Comedies* 114 (1847) Look ye here, by the living Hookey, this is a free country, Count Stromboli. **1846** *Spirit of Times* 4 July 223/3 When we returned to my stand, and there saw my gun, and the ground unmercifully dug up, and no game—they both roared out, '*Buck ager, by hookey!*' **1890** Ryan *Told in Hills* 323 'A regular cave, by hooky!' said the moral guide from Idaho.

+**Hooky.**[2] Also **hookey.** *To play hooky*, to play truant; to stay away from school without permission.

1848 Bartlett 180. **1870** 'Mark Twain' *Sk., New & Old* 56 He would not play hookey, even when his sober judgment told him it was the most profitable thing he could do. **1883** Eggleston *Hoosier School-Boy* ix. 63 They remembered that the geography lesson was a hard one, and so they played 'hooky.' **1898** Westcott *D. Harum* xix, That's old Harum's boy Dave, playin' hookey. **1903** Hapgood *Autobiog. of Thief* 26, I was overflowing with spirits and arrogance, and began to play hooky. **1907** G. M. White *Boniface to Burglar* 169 Have you been playing hookey from school and got caught at it?

+**Hoolikan.** Variant of Eulachon.

***Hoop,** *n.*

***1.** A circular band of wood or metal, used esp. for binding together the staves of barrels, casks, etc.

1642 *New Eng. First Fruits* ii. v, The good hand of God . . . affording us many materials, as, . . . Clapboard, Hoops, Pipestaves, Masts. **1782** Crèvecœur *Letters* 180 [At Nantucket] some parts of it [the timber] are converted into useful articles for exportation, such as staves, scantlings, boards, hoops, poles, &c. **1891** Nichols *Business Guide* (ed. 28) 237 *Cooperage.*—Charges for putting hoops on casks or bales.

***2.** A circle or combination of circles made of flexible material, such as thin whalebone, for expanding a woman's skirts; a hoop petticoat. Usually pl.

1722 Franklin *Writings* II. 20 He saw four Gentlewomen with their Hoops half mounted in a Balcony. **1792** *Lady's Mag. & Repos.* (Phila.) Nov. 254 The hoop . . . is now so universally worn, that it is impossible for a person to walk the streets, without being turned off the pavement. **1856** *Porter's Spirit of Times* 25 Oct. 127/1 Hoops . . . increase in favor every day. They are not confined to the extreme fashionables—not even to the city—but they enter the village church, and make their way through the farm-house door. **1881** Rittenhouse *Maud* 39 We were all laughing and talking when we started across a crossing (Clara and I both had on hoops).

+**3.** A device used to simplify the carrying of two pails of water by keeping them away from the body.

1851 Cist *Cincinnati* 102 There are many still living who associate 'toting' water by hoop and buckets with their reminiscences of a washing day. **1857** E. Stone *Life J. Howland* 25 It fell to the lot of the boys, some of whom were negroes . . . to go with two pails and a hoop, across the bridge for a supply.

4. Attrib. in sense 1.

1638 *Md. Archives* IV. 89 One seale-ring. 2. hoope-rings. **1775** Adair *Indians* 144 Indians . . . thrashing their captive, with their long-knobbed hoop-flails. **1857** *Rep. Comm. Patents 1856* II. 179 Improved Hoop Machine. . . . [With it] I am . . . enabled to saw bent sticks. **1865** *Atlantic Mo.* XV. 331 A plump girl grown enough to be almost mistaken for a woman, bowling a hoop round the walks, with a hoop-stick in one hand. **1873** Roe *Army Lett.* 145 The nicest of all having been a pair of very large old-fashioned 'hoop' earrings.

***Hoop,** *v.* **1.** *intr.* To utter a whoop. +**2.** With *up:* To praise or ballyhoo (something). — (1) **1742** in *Travels Amer. Col.* 219 Before they came to us they hooped which our Indians Answered. **1816** U. Brown *Journal* ii. 222 [We] Holloos & Hoops untill Isaiah Wells hears us. (2) **1908** 'Yeslah' *Tenderfoot S. Calif.* iv. 42 These Californians who are eternally hooping up the glorious climate.

+**Hoop and poles.** Also **hoop and stick.** The equipment used in an Indian game or the game itself: (see quot. 1858). — **1823** James *Exped.* I. 186 The men in the mean time amuse themselves with hunting, playing with the hoop and stick, cards, dancing, &c. **1858** *Harper's Mag.* Sept. 463/1 Some of the young men selected a level spot, forty paces in length . . . and amused themselves with their favorite game of hoop-and-poles. . . . Rolling the hoop from one end of the course towards the other, two of the players chase it half-way, and at the same time throw their poles. He who succeeds in piercing the hoop wins the game.

+**Hoop ash. 1.** =Black ash 1. **2.** =Hackberry 1. — (1) **1763** in Durrett *Louisville* (1893) 132 [Boundaries] Beginning at a hoop-ash and buckeye, the lower corner of Major Edward Ward's land. **1897** Sudworth *Arborescent Flora* 325 *Fraxinus nigra.* Black Ash. . . . Common Names: . . . Hoop Ash (Vt., N.Y., Del., Ohio, Ill., Ind.) [etc.]. (2) **1787** Sargent in *Mem. Academy* II. i. 157 Black Ash, three feet diameter.

White Ash, to five feet diameter. Hoop Ash, of three, and three and a half feet diameter. **1810** MICHAUX *Arbres* I. 38 *Hackberry tree*, . . . *Hoop ash*, sur les bords de l'Ohio. **1832** BROWNE *Sylva Amer.* 133 On the Ohio it is called Hoop Ash, and in Kentucky, Hack Berry. **1897** SUDWORTH *Arborescent Flora* 185 *Celtis occidentalis.* Hackberry. . . . [In Vermont called] Hoop Ash.

Hooped petticoat. =HOOP PETTICOAT. — **1701** Felt *Customs New Eng.* 168 [The Rev. Solomon Stoddard, in a letter written to Judge Sewall, mentions] hooped petticoats.

+**Hoopee,** *interj.* An exclamation of delight. (See also WHOOPEE.) — **1845** HOOPER *Simon Suggs' Adv.* iii, Hoop-ee! won't they roll over the floor, and have chicken fits, a dozen at a time! **1857** *Knickerb.* XLIX. 426 A small boy . . . jumped up and down like a whip-saw, and halloa'd 'Hoop-ee' with all his might.

*__Hooper.__ The whooping or whistling swan. — **1709** LAWSON *Carolina* 146 The sort of Swans call'd Hoopers, are the least. They abide more in the Salt-Water, and are equally valuable, for Food.

Hoopid salmon. (See quotation.) — **1883** *Nat. Museum Bul.* No. 27, 474 *Oncorhynchus kisutch.* . . . Hoopid Salmon. . . . Pacific coast of North America from San Francisco northward to Bering Strait.

+**Hooping crane.** =WHOOPING CRANE. — *c*__1730__ CATESBY *Carolina* I. 75 *Grus Americana Alba*, The hooping Crane, is about the Size of the common Crane. . . . A white man . . . [told me] that he hath seen them at the Mouths of the Savanna, Aratamaha, and other Rivers nearer St. Augustine, but never saw any so far North as the Settlements of Carolina. **1744** F. MOORE *Voy. Georgia* 118 There is a hooping crane, a fowl with grey feathers, five or six feet high. **1828** BONAPARTE *Synopsis* 302 The Hooping Crane, *Ardea americana*, . . . inhabits throughout North America and the West Indies.

+**Hoop-la.** A stage-driver's cry adopted by others as an exclamation of joy or excitement; more generally, a furor or hullabaloo. — **1877** *N.Y. Tribune* 1 March (B.), The Stock Exchange to-day commenced its business of speculation with a grand 'hoop la,' regardless of the closing prices of yesterday. *c*__1877__ *Harper's Bazar* (B.), Hoop-la,—Melican man he heap much nice,—fetchee me home all light, top side up on slippery walk. **1902** CLAPIN 232 *Hoop-la.* An exclamation indicating jollification.

+**Hoople.** (See quot. 1848.) — **1848** BARTLETT 180 *Hoople.* (Dutch, *hoepel.*) The boys in the city of New York still retain the Dutch name *hoople* for a hoop. **1907** *St. Nicholas* June 676 Master Aldrich in his 'hoople' days.

Hoop petticoat. =HOOP SKIRT. {1711-} Also fig. — **1722** FRANKLIN *Writings* II. 20 A particular Fashion now reigning . . . namely, that of Hoop-Petticoats. **1724** *New-Eng. Courant* 10-17 Aug. 2/1, I discovered a Fleet of Hoop Petticoats bearing down upon me. **1742** *Md. Hist. Mag.* XX. 178 Two good Hoop Petticoats one a sise smaller and good Bone. **1787** TYLER *Contrast* (1790) II. i, When large hoops are in fashion, we often see many a plump girl lost in the immensity of a hoop-petticoat. **1842** HAWTHORNE *Twice-told Tales* 1879 II. 68 They were well content that the old gentlewoman, in her hoop petticoat and faded embroidery, should still haunt the palace.

Hoop-petticoated, *a.* Clad in a hoop skirt or petticoat. — **1842** HAWTHORNE *Twice-told Tales* (1879) II. 76 Neither of us would have wondered, had a hoop-petticoated phantom of Esther Dudley tottered into the chamber.

Hoop pole. A smooth, straight pole out of which hoops are made. {1807}

1645 *Dedham Rec.* III. 112 Samll Milles hath libtie to cut 400 lengthes of hoope poles on the common. **1703** *Suffield Doc. Hist.* 145 It was agreed . . . to impose a fine . . . upon any person, that shall presume hereafter, to cut . . . and carry away hoop-polls, from off any of our commons. **1775** ADAIR *Indians* 144 [The avengers] meet commonly in the dusk of the evening, near the town of the adulterer, where each of them provides a small hoop-pole with which they correct the sinners. **1797** *Wilmington* (N.C.) *Gazette* 26 Oct., A practice has existed for several years, of cutting and carrying away, without permission, from the lands of my Hillton plantation, fire-wood, hoop-poles, and timber of every kind. **1835** BIRD *Hawks of Hawk-H.* I. vi. 76 There was a bundle of green hoop-poles, at a cooper's shop. **1884** *Rep. Comm. Agric.* 140 In some counties the mania for hoop-poles has played havoc with young hickory and white oak.

b. Attrib. with *county, country, industry.*

1859 *Harper's Mag.* Oct. 712/1 Uncle Jim . . . saw a huge fellow . . . who hailed from the hoop-pole county of Marshall, Virginia, coming up Main Street. **1880** *Ib.* May 907/2 One day I accompanied the doctor on a long drive through the 'hoop-pole country' as a certain timbered district was called. **1884** SARGENT *Rep. Forests* 501 Partial returns of the hoop-pole industry give a production during the census year.

+**Hoop skirt.**

1. A skirt or petticoat expanded and held out by hoops.

1857 UNDERHILL & THOMPSON *Elephant Club* 193 Lady with hoop-skirt hails the driver. **1865** *Nation* I. 159 There is no article of dress which has heretofore caused so much trouble and annoyance as hoop skirts. **1880** *Harper's Mag.* June 30/2 The manufacture of hoop-skirts is said to engage ten thousand women. **1906** BELL *C. Lee* 11 As pitiable as a beautiful woman would be who paraded herself on Fifth Avenue in hoop-skirts and a cashmere shawl.

‖**b.** One of the hoops of a hoop skirt.

1882 McCABE *New York* 240 Horses have often been lamed by sewing-machine needles and hoop-skirts, which were left on the track.

2. Attrib. with *article, conflagration, factory.*

1865 STOWE *House & Home P.* 159 Look at the hoop-skirt factories. **1871** 'MARK TWAIN' *Screamers* 140 Ten or twelve thousand meet a similarly violent death . . . such as perishing by kerosene lamp and hoop-skirt conflagrations.

fig. **1906** *Springfield W. Repub.* 19 July 1 Populism was a 'hoopskirt' article of statesmanship, perhaps, but it produced no thieves.

+**Hoop snake.** 'A snake fabled to take its tail in its mouth and roll along like a hoop; specifically, *Abastor erythrogrammus*, a harmless species of the family *Colubridæ*, abundant in the southern United States' (*Cent.* 2879/3). — **1840** *S. Lit. Messenger* VI. 380/2, I never believed in the existence of hoop-snakes neither, until I went out into the western country.

Hoopwood. {1756} +=HOOP ASH. Also attrib. with *tree.* — **1770** WASHINGTON *Diaries* I. 428, I also marked . . . an Ash and hoopwood for the Beginning of another [corner] of the Soldiers Survey. **1787** V. W. Howard *Bryan Sta. Heroes* (1932) 145 A hoopwood, Buckeye and two Ashes. **1821** J. FOWLER *Journal* 21 We Set out at our ushal time at ten miles pased a point of Rocks and a Hoop wood tree on them. **1854** BANCROFT *Hist. U.S.* VI. 379 He would . . . set his mark on a maple, or elm, a hoop-wood, or ash, as the corner of a soldier's survey.

+**Hoorah place.** A disorderly or lawless place. (Cf. HURRAH'S NEST.) — **1883** SWEET & KNOX *Through Texas* xix. 257 [A railroad terminus in w. Texas] is what is called, in the classic vernacular of the country, 'a hoorah place.'

+**Hoosier.** Also **Hoosher, Hosier,** etc.

The origin of the word is uncertain. J. P. Dunn, in *Ind. Hist. Soc. Publ.* IV. No. 2 (1907), thinks it related to the Cumberland dialect word *hoozer*, said of anything unusually large. For other discussions of the word, see *Ind. Mag. Hist.* VII. (1911) 61-63, XXV. (1929) 101-03 and Shields McIlwaine *Southern Poor-White* (1939) p. xxiv.

1. A nickname for a resident or native of Indiana.

1832 *Ind. Democrat*, Ask for our 'hoosiers' good plantations. **1833** *Ind. Hist. Soc. Publ.* IV. 7 He hailed the house and then alighted. The 'Hoosher' met him at the door. **1842** *Life in West* 247 Walking by the lake side this evening, I found a regular encampment of Hoosiers. **1849** *Knickerb. Mag.* XXXIV. 407/2 Well, I allow our friend must hev got his skoolin along with that Hosier. **1870** O. LOGAN *Before Footlights* 310 At this moment, a genuine Hoosier, indigenous to the soil, rose up in the auditorium. **1885** *Outing* Nov. 152/2 Did you notice that young Hoosier and his bride who sat opposite me at breakfast? **1900** M. NICHOLSON *Hoosiers* 12 William M. Chase, the artist, [was] also a native Hoosier.

b. A local expression used by Hoosiers; a hoosierism.

1871 EGGLESTON *Hoosier Schoolm.* iv. 41 The 'big road' (Hoosier for *highway*) ran along the north-west side.

2. General sense: A rustic or frontiersman.

1857 GODKIN in R. Ogden *Life E. L. Godkin* I. 157 The mere 'cracker' or 'hoosier,' as the poor [southern] whites are termed. **1874** LONG *Wild-Fowl* viii. 144 'Greenhorns' and hoosiers, as the regular hunters call such fellows, . . . always commence to cry, 'Down! down! Here comes a duck!' **1900** 'FLYNT' *Tramping* 394 *Hoosier*, a 'farmer.' **1902** HARBEN *A. Daniel* 164 Pole Baker, yo're nothin' but a rag-tag, bob-tail mountain Hoosier, an' he's a slick duck from up North.

3. Attrib. with *boy, cake, candidate,* etc.

1871 EGGLESTON *Hoosier Schoolm.* 5 It has been in my mind since I was a Hoosier boy. **1859** BARTLETT 202 *Hoosier Cake*, a Western name for a sort of coarse gingerbread, which, say the Kentuckians, is the best bait to catch a hoosier with, the biped being fond of it. **1847** ROBB *Squatter Life* p. vii, I feel somewhat like the hoosier candidate described his sensations, when he first essayed to deliver a stump speech. *Ib.* 27 'Old fellar,' said a hoosier citizen, 'you'd better pick up your chicken fixens afore you go.' **1912** NICHOLSON *Hoosier Chron.* 145 Cussing the mules . . . almost spoiled my Hoosier dialect! **1899** *Mo. So. Dakotan* I. 183 Arthur Calvin Mellette was born and reared a hoosier farmer. **1840** *Crockett Almanac* 11/1 Luke had got married to one of them cornfed Conneticut Hooshur gals, that you'll see sot a-straddle on every fence in Ohio. **1878** BEADLE *Western Wilds* i. 18 No grammar of the 'Hoosier' language has ever been published. **1870** NOWLAND *Indianapolis* 66 A strolling player by the name of Crampton visited this place for the purpose of giving the denizens of the Hoosier metropolis the benefit of his entertainment. **1845** *Knickerb.* XXV. 374 You wouldn't think them soles had walked over three hundred miles of Hoosier mud. **1849** *Rep. Comm. Patents: Agric.* 434 A man . . . had a peach orchard . . . from the pits of 'Hoosier peaches,' to wit: small, worthless, late varieties, principally cling-stones. **1887** *Courier-Journal* 4 Jan. 1/5 (*caption*), Hoosier Politics. **1922** FOULKE *Hoosier Autobiog.* 39 The average Hoosier rural community is very democratic. *Ib.* 41 As the years went by I absorbed the Hoosier spirit more and more.

+**Hoosierdom. 1.** The West. **2.** A nickname for Indiana. — (1) **1848** *Congress. Globe* App. 7 Aug. 1119/3 In the West, every political thingumderry . . . does his little best to produce confusion in Hoosierdom. (2) **1850** *Knickerbocker* XXXVI. 71 The inhabitants of the Far West, . . . be they 'Buck-eyes,' 'Wolverines,' or citizens of 'Hoosier-dom' [etc.]. **1873** BEADLE *Undevel. West* xxxvi. 778 Seven days' riding from San Francisco brought me again to my native Hoosierdom. **1904** *N.Y. Tribune* 31 July, A flitting visit, after years of absence, to his boyhood home in Hoosierdom.

+**Hoosier frog.** (See quotation.) — **1883** *Amer. Naturalist* XVII. 945 The Mink or Hoosier Frog. . . . This frog (*Rana septentrionalis*) seems comparatively unknown, and is found in localities far apart.

+**Hoosierina.** A woman or girl who resides in Indiana. — **1843** 'CARLTON' *New Purchase* II. 5 And what could have deceived our Hoosierina? **1844** *Yale Lit. Mag.* IX. 264 Advancing to the door, I was met by a dame of goodly proportions, surrounded by some ten or twelve young Hoosiers and Hoosierina's.

+**Hoosierism.** A word, phrase, or idiom peculiar to the speech of Indianians. — **1843** 'CARLTON' *New Purchase* I. 63 Thus the cabin lady kept on doing up her small stock of English into Hoosierisms and other figures. **1878** BEADLE *Western Wilds* i. 18 The native of Indiana finds . . . that he must drop some of his 'Hoosierisms.'

+**Hoosierize,** *v. tr.* To render (a person) like the people of Indiana. — **1852** *S. Lit. Messenger* XVIII. 435/1 He was built after the model and structure of Bolingbroke in his youth, *American-ized* and *Hoosier-ized* a little by a 'raising in,' and an adaptation to, the Backwoods.

+**Hoosierland.** The state of Indiana. — **1848** *Congress. Globe* 25 April 668/3, I have spoken the result of our political lucubrations in Hoosierland. **1861** *Ladies' Repository* Nov. 698/2 Do not misunderstand me to have simply intended . . . to peep in at the railroad capital of Hoosier-land, and then possibly to straggle on. **1895** *N.Y. Dramatic News* 6 July 12/1 Well, we have left Hoosierland.

+**Hoosieroon.** Also **Hoosheroon.** An Indianian. — **1834** *Knickerb.* IV. 390 A few remote Kentuckians, or Indiana Hoosheroons. **1853** *Daily Morning Herald* (St. Louis) 27 April (Th.), He looks like a Hoosieroon; all he lacks is a chunk of gingerbread in his fist.

+**Hoosier State.** The state of Indiana. — **1834** *Indiana Democrat* 4 Jan., The Hoosier State like true democrats have taken the lead in appointing delegates to a National Convention. **1845** SOL. SMITH *Theatr. Apprent.* ii. 29, [I] trumped up a story . . . which induced the good folks of the 'Hoosier' state to give me corn-bread, bacon [etc.]. **1859** *Harper's Mag.* Sept. 574/1 My niece, Ella, . . . whose parents are domiciled in the interior of the 'Hoosier State,' is not much familiarized with the sable sons and daughters of 'Afric's golden sands.' **1912** NICHOLSON *Hoosier Chron.* 329, I beg to call your attention, sir, to the presence of many of the fair daughters of the old Hoosier State.

+**Hoot.** =HOOTER.[1] — **1883** BEADLE *Western Wilds* xxxviii. 615, I got onto my reaper and banged down every hoot of it [wheat] before Monday night. **1921** PAINE *Comr. Rolling Ocean* xii. 214, I am glad of that, even if he did tell me that as a supercargo I wasn't worth a hoot in hades. **1925** N. VENNER *Imperfect Impostor* iv, I can't see this place gives a hoot whether I'm here or not.

+**Hooter.**[1] A very small bit; a whit. Now shortened to HOOT. *colloq.*

1839 *Havana* (N.Y.) *Republican* 21 Aug. (Th.), Now the Grampus (a vessel) stopt, and didn't buge (budge) one hooter. *c***1849** PAIGE *Dow's Sermons* I. 178 What cares he about the 'honor of the nation'? . . . — Not a hooter. **1859** BARTLETT 202 *Hooter.* Probably a corruption of *iota.* Common in New York in such phrases as 'I don't care a *hooter* for him,' 'this note ain't worth a *hooter.*' **1889** *Cincinnati Commercial Gazette* 17 Oct. 4/1 It has not harmed the Republican cause in Ohio a hooter. **1900** DIX *Deacon Bradbury* 202 'Do you mean that you don't know anything about the matter at all?' . . . 'Not a hooter.'

Hooter.[2] +A kind of dance. — **1845** *Lowell Offering* V. 270 We could dance . . . an eight-handed reel, and an eight-handed 'hooter.'

Hoot owl. {1885-} +The barred owl: (see quot. 1917). — **1881** *Harper's Mag.* Oct. 693/1 A hoot-owl, sitting unseen above our heads, startles us. **1917** *Birds of Amer.* II. 103 Barred Owl. . . . Other Names.— Hoot Owl; Rain Owl; Wood Owl [etc.].

***Hop.**[1]

***1. a.** A twining Eurasian vine, *Humulus lupulus*, widely cultivated in America; +the native species, *H. americanus.* **b.** The ripened pistillate cones of these plants used in malt liquors, medicines, etc. Usu. in pl.

1647 *Springfield Rec.* I. 193 It is ordered yt no person shal gather any hops that grow in ye Swamps or in the comon grounds. **1677** WINTHROP in *Phil. Trans.* XII. 1068 The way of making Beer of Bread, is by breaking or cutting it into great lumps . . . to be mash'd, and so proceeded with as Malt, and the impregnated Liquor, as Woort, either adding or omitting Hopps, as is desired. **1685** BUDD *Penna. & N.J.* 33 *Hops* in some places grow naturally. **1781-2** JEFFERSON *Notes Va.* (1788) 36 Wild hop. *Humulus lupulus.* **1819** SCHOOLCRAFT *Mo. Lead Mines* 43 That useful vine, the Hop, grows spontaneously on the bottom lands, and is to be seen in great abundance, in the proper season, on the banks of the Platten, Apple Creek, and other places. **1883** *Rep. Indian Affairs* 17 The yield of hops last year was 28,431 pounds, as against 18,592 pounds the year before on the same ground.

2. Attrib. and comb. with *beer, dryer, house,* etc.

1629 *Mass. Bay Rec.* 25 To prouide to send for Newe England:— . . . wheate, rye, barly, oates, a hhed of each in the eare; . . . Potatoes; Hoprootes; Hempseede [etc.]. **1654** *Essex Probate Rec.* I. 182 A bed tick of Canvas & a hopp sack boulster. **1828** *Yankee* July 227/1 Oh what a luxury! everyone eats his fill, and washes it down with good old orchard, or hop beer, and all then go home, rain or shine. **1842** *Niles' Nat. Reg.* 9 July 304/1 The hop plantations in the neighborhood of East Retford are, it is said, seriously afflicted with fly and lice. **1875** KNIGHT 1118/1 *Hop-dryer.* A chamber in which hops are artificially dried. . . . Also called an *oast,* or *hop-kiln.* **1877** *Rep. Indian Affairs* 40 We have built one hop-house. **1884** 'CRADDOCK' *Tenn. Mts.* 279 It 'peared like 't would take a bar'l o' hop tea to get me quiet.

***Hop.**[2] A dance, formerly informal, now usually formal. *colloq.* {1731-} — **1757** Singleton *Social N.Y.* 172 She had no notion at her age of sacrificing all the dear pleasures of routs, hops, quadrille for a philosophical husband. **1849** A. MACKAY *Western World* I. 122 It is very common for the families of such members as live in the hotels to give weekly 'hops,' as they are called, which are neither more nor less than dancing parties, divested of some of the usual ceremonies of such assemblages. **1886** POORE *Reminisc.* I. 375 There were the customary receptions at the White House, and 'hops' at the hotels, but few large parties were given. **1899** C. KING *Trooper Galahad* 28 In June she led with Cadet Lieutenant Winn the german at the graduation hop at West Point. **1908** ADE *In Babel* 173 They move the chairs out of the dining-room every two weeks and have a 'grand hop.'

+**Hop butterfly.** A butterfly (*Thecla humuli*) that feeds upon the heads of the hop plant. — **1854** EMMONS *Agric. N.Y.* V. 262.

Hop clover. Any of several yellow-flowered herbs of the genus *Trifolium,* esp. *T. agrarium* and *T. procumbens.* {1679-} — **1787** WASHINGTON *Diaries* III. 261 Sowed . . . on the most Westerly square . . . 20 lbs. of Hop clover. **1817-8** EATON *Botany* (1822) 491 *Trifolium procumbens,* hop clover. **1843** TORREY *Flora N.Y.* I. 170 *Trifolium agrarium.* . . . Yellow Clover. Hop Clover. . . . Sandy soils and dry woods, . . . along the Hudson. **1850** S. F. COOPER *Rural Hours* 125 The downy 'rabbit-foot,' or 'stone-clover,' . . . the 'zig-zag,' and the 'hop clovers,' are all introduced.

Hop hornbeam. One of various trees of the genus *Ostrya,* +esp. *O. virginiana.* {1756- (*Compl. Body Husb.* 178)} — **1785** MARSHALL *Amer. Grove* 25 The Hop-Hornbeam. . . . The female flowers are produced in inflated chaffy katkins, much resembling a hop, from whence it acquired its name. **1814** BIGELOW *Florula Bostoniensis* 232 *Ostrya Virginica.* Hop Hornbeam. Iron wood. . . . This tree is generally of small size. **1861** *Ill. Agric. Soc. Trans.* IV. 407 Of the Carpineæ three are very common throughout the State, the hazelnut, the hornbeam, and the hop-hornbeam or ironwood. **1894** COULTER *Bot. W. Texas* III. 414 *Ostrya Virginica* (American Hop Hornbeam. Lever wood). **1901** MOHR *Plant Life Ala.* 83 These hillocks [w. of the spurs of the Cumberland highlands] . . . support . . . a stunted growth of . . . hop hornbeam (*Ostrya virginiana*).

+**Hopine.** *local.* (See quotation.) — **1888** *Texas Siftings* (F.), We don't get beer precisely but they sell a drink out there called hopine . . . the sale of which is not a violation of the liquor law.

+**Hopkinsian,** *n.* A believer in the doctrines of Hopkinsianism (q.v.). — **1795** BENTLEY *Diary* II. 139 The minister is what is called an Hopkinsian. It is the unsocial character of the professors of this sect which makes them odious. **1869** STOWE *Oldtown Folks* 72 Polly is a great Hopkinsian. **1882** Schaff *Religious Encycl.* I. 82/1 Some of the Hopkinsians would have preferred a larger modification of the catechism [than that of the 'Andover Theology'].

+**Hopkinsian,** *a.* Of or pertaining to the theological system of Hopkinsianism (q.v.). — **1797** BENTLEY *Diary* II. 213 The Hopkinsian opinions are distinguished, not so much by their intrinsic character as by the opposition of the Clergy, & the divisions in all the societies consequent upon that opposition, encouraged or patronised. **1835** T. FLINT in *Athenæum* 19 Sept. 716/2 This system, denominated Hopkinsian, has some other peculiar features and tenets. **1840** *Knickerb.* XVI. 89 Rev. Dr. B— was at his '17thly,' in the second of six divisions of a very comprehensive body of Hopkinsian divinity. **1853** M. BLAKE *Mendon Association* 33 The religious history of this town might be made to testify the practical workings of Hopkinsian theory. **1886** *Encycl. Brit.* (ed. 9) *Amer. Suppl.* III. 339/2 [Samuel Hopkins] was also noted as the founder of 'Hopkinsian divinity,' a modification of Calvinism.

+**Hopkinsianism.** The Calvinistic theological system of Samuel Hopkins (1721–1803), which, opposing the orthodox Calvinistic doctrines of original sin and the atonement, stressed the virtue of unselfish submission to the will of God, even to the point of willingly accepting damnation, as the means of bringing about the highest good for the universe as a whole.

1811 E. S. ELY (*title*), Contrast between Calvinism and Hopkinsianism. **1850** WHITTIER *Writings* VI. 131 Hopkinsianism, as a distinct and living school of philosophy, theology, and metaphysics, no longer exists. **1853** M. BLAKE *Mendon Association* 23 Without deciding whether President Edwards is to be considered the father of Hopkinsianism, it is certain that he believed . . . some of its leading peculiarities. **1876** C. G. FINNEY *Memoirs* xviii. 241 In preaching, I . . . took occasion to denounce Hopkinsianism; and said that they appeared to have too much of it in Philadelphia. **1882** Schaff *Religious Encycl.* I. 82/1 [The 'Andover Theology'] on the whole, adopts the substance of Calvinism as well as the substance of Hopkinsianism.

+**Hopkintonian,** *n.* and *a.* **1.** *n.*=HOPKINSIAN *n.* **2.** *adj.*=HOPKINSIAN *a.* Also absol. — **(1) 1788** BENTLEY *Diary* I. 104 Such are the exertions of a certain class of Preachers, called Hopkintonians that weekly, & almost daily, lectures are established in many towns of Essex. **(2) 1796** S. HOPKINS *Sk. Life* (1805) 97 In the latter end of the year 1769, or beginning of 1770, Mr. William Hart of Saybrook published a dialogue. . . . And soon after there was a small pamphlet published, which was doubtless by the same Mr. Hart. . . . To disgrace me before the public, he called them [my doctrines] *Hopkintonian* doctrines. This is the original of this epithet. **1853** M. BLAKE *Mendon Association* 30 *n.*, The term Hopkintonian, or Hopkinsian, was applied to this system of theology in 1777. ... It was previously styled Edwardean, and more generally 'New Divinity.' **1883** Schaff *Religious Encycl.* II. 1634/2 [New England divines] announced a few principles, which were called 'New-Light Divinity,' or 'New Divinity.' When a few more principles were added to their system, it was called 'Hopkintonian,' or 'Hopkinsian.'

+**Hop louse.** A plant louse, *Phorodon humuli*, esp. destructive to hops. Also *hop plant louse.* — **1868** *Rep. Comm. Agric. 1867* 238 The wheat midge, fruit blight, potato rot, black knot and hop louse were unknown. **1884** Nye *Baled Hay* 198 The brief but wonderful career of the hop-louse. **1888** *Amer. Naturalist* XXII. 68 The Hop Plant-louse, *Phorodon humuli*, ... passes the winter on plum trees.

* **Hopper.**

* **1.** A box or receptacle forming part of a machine or apparatus and designed to contain seed or material for grinding, sowing, etc.

1659 *Hempstead Rec.* I. 106 Halfe of the water-mill, (excepting) the hopper. **1754** Eliot *Field-Husb.* v. 118 The Hopper of the Wheat-Drill, holds about a Peck, and the Dung-Hopper two Bushels and an half. **1806** in *Amer. Philos. Soc.* VI. 239 The earth is dug and carried to hoppers of a very simple construction, which contain about fifty bushels. **1886** *Century Mag.* May 43/2 The wheat is first received in a hopper ... for weighing; then it goes into a bin.

+**b.** *Railroad.* A type of freight car shaped somewhat like a hopper and unloaded through an opening at its bottom. Also attrib.

1862 *N.Y. Tribune* 10 June 8/2 There were 183 iron hopper cars recovered and in a condition to be restored. Of the 57 hoppers thrown over Opequan Bridge, one half can be put into serviceable order again. **1891** C. Roberts *Adrift in America* 224 When the next train came I jumped, ... and held on by the top of the hopper which was higher than my head. **1900** *Engineering Mag.* XIX. 794/1 Development of the Structural Steel Hopper Car.

‖**2.** A hobble.

1847 in Howe *Hist. Coll. Ohio* 366 The first object of a new comer after selecting a location, and putting the 'hoppers' on the horse, ... was to cut some poles or logs, and build a cabin.

3. Short for Grasshopper.

Of recent origin in present-day use, though occurring once in early M.E.

***a*1870** Chipman *Notes on Bartlett* 202 *Hopper*, ... a grasshopper, especially the ravaging locust called grasshopper at the West. **1875** *Field & Forest* I. 31 Old residents of this State [Minn.] say that before the 'hoppers visited us one week ago we had ... the appearance of the best grain crop ever known in the State. **1885** *Century Mag.* XXXI. 29, I should think he had enough of 'em ... to last him till the 'hoppers come again. ***a*1918** G. Stuart *On Frontier* I. 65 The women also gathered many grasshoppers. On frosty mornings the hoppers would be stiff with cold and easily caught.

+**Hopper boy.** A mechanical device for spreading meal out to cool. — **1787** in *Rep. Comm. Patents 1849* 574 The other [device], denominated an hopper-boy, so constituted as to spread the meal over the floor of a mill to cool. **1813** *Niles' Reg.* V. Add. A. 6/2 Our Hopper-boy was an upright shaft revolving round with an arm.

+**Hopperdozer.** *Agric.* A contrivance for use in destroying grasshoppers and other insects: (see quot. 1892). — **1880** *Lib. Universal Knowl.* IX. 123 One of the most efficient pieces of apparatus [for destroying locusts] is the coal-tar pan, known as 'Robbins's hopperdozer.' **1889** *Rep. Secy. Agric.* 358 'Hopper dozers' ... should be worked during the warm days in the fall or spring in order to catch the hibernating species before they deposit their eggs. **1892** Kellogg *Kansas Insects* 48 A 'hopperdozer' is a machine for catching grasshoppers, usually in the nature of a broad tray containing coal-tar or kerosene, to be pushed or pulled over the infested field. **1903** *Div. of Entomology* (Dept. Agric.) *Circular* No. 53, 2 As hopperdozers are drawn over the ground ... the young locusts jump into the air, fall into the pan, and are wetted and killed by the kerosene.

+**Hoppergrass. 1.** A humorous perversion of 'grasshopper.' *colloq.* ‖**2.** (See quotation.) — **(1) 1829** *Virginia Lit. Museum* I. 458 *Hoppergrass.* This word is often used in the south for grasshopper. **1887** *Harper's Mag.* April 733/1, I see him hop over a ditch ... same's a hoppergrass. **1899** Chesnutt *Conjure Woman* 101 My mammy tol' me dat tale w'en I wa'n't mo' d'n knee-high ter a hopper-grass. **(2) 1875** *Chicago Tribune* 16 Aug. 2/6 This grass [in w. Mo.] is without a name. Since the hoppers brought a little good into the country [by bringing grass seeds from plains] ... why not call it 'hopper-grass'?

‖**Hoppine.** (See quotation.) — **1825** Wm. Biggs *Narr. Captivity* 34 [The Indians] had nothing to eat the last week I was with them, but Indian potatoes—some people call them hoppines, that grew in the woods, and they were very scarce.

+**Hopping John.** *S.* A highly seasoned stew of bacon, peas, and sometimes rice. — **1838** Gilman *Recollections* xviii. 124 Before me, though at the head of many delicacies provided by papa, was an immense field of *hopping John.* **1856** Olmsted *Slave States* 506 The greatest luxury with which they are acquainted is a stew of bacon and peas, with red pepper, which they call 'Hopping John.' **1886** *Amer. Philol. Ass. Trans.* XVII. 46 *Hopping-john* (stew of rice and peas).

+**Hoppy,** *a.* Of bread: Tasting of hops. — **1893** *Harper's Mag.* Feb. 458 'Jest so it don't tas'e hoppy, I ain't pertic'lar; but from hoppy bread deliver me!'

+**Hop-toad.** A toad. *colloq.* Also *hop-toady.* — **1827** *Mass. Spy* 28 Nov. (Th.), An inhabitant of the Middle States talks of 'hop-toads,'—as if all toads were not hoppers. **1847** *Knickerb.* XXIX. 183, I have so often ... a tender leaning towards little pigs and hop toads. **1899** *Animal & Plant Lore* 62 Hop-toad, and hop-toady, *Bufo lentiginosus.* [Name] somewhat general [in the United States]. **1906** Lynde *Quickening* 201 Why, I riccolect him when he wasn't no more'n knee-high to a hop-toad!

+**Hop tree.** A small tree, *Ptelea trifoliata*, bearing a fruit sometimes used in place of hops. — **1857** Gray *Botany* 75 *Ptelea.* Shrubby Trefoil. Hop-tree. **1877** Bartlett 296 *Hop-Tree.* (*Ptelia trifoliata.*) A tall shrub found in the Eastern States. The fruit, a wafer-like seed, grows in clusters, is a bitter tonic, and has been used as a substitute for hops. **1885** Havard *Flora W. & S. Texas* 458 Of the Rutaceae, two shrubs are common: the Hop-tree (*Ptelea trifoliata*) along the river [San Antonio] and the Prickly Ash. **1897** Sudworth *Arborescent Flora* 266.

Hopvine. The hop plant or its trailing stem. {1707-} Also attrib. — **1750** T. Walker *Explor. Kentucky* 50 Clover and Hop Vines are plenty here. **1850** S. F. Cooper *Rural Hours* 129 When hop-vines are used for screening the windows, which is often the case, the plant is not so easily restrained. **1868** *Amer. Naturalist* II. 333 We figure the Hop-vine Moth and the larva (Fig. 1) and pupa, which abound on hops the last of summer. **1896** E. Higginson *Land of Snow Pearls* 749 An' that hop-vine that you've got trained over your parlor window—set that out, too.

***Hopyard.** A field in which hops are grown. — **1702** Sewall *Diary* II. 62 Visit Mr. Fox, view the Hop-yards, come home. **1833** *Niles' Reg.* XLIV. 313/2 We passed a few fields of barley, of a scanty and meagre growth, and here and there a hop yard bristling up like quills upon the fretful porcupine. **1911** Jenks & Lauck *Immigration Problem* 217 The employment of Chinese in the orchards, fields, hop-yards and vineyards of California.

* **Horehound.**

1. A plant of the mint family (*Marrubium vulgare*) having an aromatic odor and widely used in medicine. (Cf. Black horehound.)

1737 Brickell *N. Carolina* 20 In these Parts ... several sorts of Horehound, Melilot, Bastard-Lovage. **1792** Imlay *Western Territory* 208 Of herbs, &c. we have of the wild sort ... winter-green, hore-hound, ladies mantle. **1819** *Niles' Reg.* XVI. *Suppl.* 101/1 After this each family is allowed to cook and eat their roasting-ears, but not before they drink a tea of wild horehound. **1858** Thoreau *Maine Woods* 108 Horehound, horsemint, and the sensitive fern grew close to the edge. **1901** Mohr *Plant Life Ala.* 705 Hoarhound. ... Introduced from Europe and naturalized from Ontario to the Gulf.

2. Attrib. in the names of confections or medicinal preparations made from this.

1840 *Picayune* 19 Sept. 2/1 Southern and Western agent in the sale of the celebrated Pease Horehound Candy. **1852** *Florida Plant. Rec.* 67, I have gave him Some Light Medicine and have him now drinking hoar hound water. **1899** *Caddo* (Okla.) *Herald* 24 Feb. 3/3 (*advt.*), Ballard's Horehound Syrup is the best known remedy. **1903** Burnham *Jewel* 105 I take horehound drops sometimes. **1910** 'O. Henry' *Strictly Business* 92, I take the horehound tea ... for old times' sake.

***Horizontal,** *a.* +Of tariff rates: Applied equally or uniformly to all articles. (Cf. Horizontal tariff.) — **1842** *Congress. Globe* 17 March 331/1 If they [members of the Ways and Means Committee] undertook ... to depart from the plain horizontal line of a tariff, ... they should be able to justify themselves before this House. **1845** *Ib.* 9 Dec. 35/2 What was the effect of their [1841-2] twenty per cent. horizontal duty? **1872** *Ib.* 28 March 2016/2 The horizontal reduction of duties ... would do incalculable injury. **1890** *Congress. Rec.* 9 May 4392/2 The Democratic bill made a horizontal cut of 20 per cent, thereby reducing the revenue $12,000,000 annually.

+**Horizontal,** *v.tr.* To terrace (land). — **1862** *Ill. Agric. Soc. Trans* V. 518 Side-hills were generally 'horizontaled;' that is, laid out in ridges.

+**Horizontalizing.** The process of making land level; terracing. — **1862** *Ill. Agric. Soc. Trans.* V. 518 This 'horizontalizing' is only required when the soil is loose. **1883** Smith *Geol. Survey Ala.* 386 This damage [done to the hillsides by heavy rains] has been checked to some extent by horizontalizing.

+**Horizontal tariff.** A tariff establishing a uniform ad valorem rate of duty on all imported goods or merchandise. — **1842** *Congress. Globe* 17 March 331/1 Was it expected that this committee would send in a horizontal tariff? **1844** *Ib.* App. 27 April 387 If you will not give us free trade, let us have the nearest approach to it—and that is a horizontal tariff. **1847** *Ib.* App. 22 Feb. 409/2, I am not for eking out the insufficiencies of a horizontal tariff by taxes upon tea and coffee.

* **Horn,** *n.*

* **1.** The hard bonelike appendage found on the heads of various mammals, esp. those of the ox kind, often prepared as a receptacle for gunpowder or as a bugle. Also fig.

1646 *Mass. H. S. Coll.* 4 Ser. VI. 334 Wequash Cooks brother tooke from him ... powder & bulletts, and a horne. **1704** S. Knight *Journal* 21, I on a suden was Rous'd from these pleasing Imaginations, by the Post's sounding his horn. **1791** in Jillson *Dark & Bl. Ground* 111 Above it hangs the rifle, horn and bullet pouch. **1810** Miner in Richardson & Miner

C. Miner (1916) 56 When I see a man . . . 'sounding the horn on the borders,' to call the people to support the man, on whom he depends for his office [etc.]. **1896** JEWETT *Pointed Firs* 67 Land sakes alive! Le' 's blow the horn for William. **1903** FOX *Little Shepherd* i, The rifle, he knew, was always loaded; there was not much powder in the horn.

+**2.** The high pommel of a saddle.

1847 PARKMAN in *Knickerb.* XXIX. 394 My long heavy rifle encumbered me, and the low sound it made striking the horn of my saddle startled him. **a1861** WINTHROP *Canoe & Saddle* 212, I threw Klale's bridle over his neck, and, grasping the horn, swung myself into the saddle. **1882** BAILLIE-GROHMAN *Camps in Rockies* 5 The frontiersman when on horseback usually carries his rifle in front of him across the Mexican saddle, attached by a simple leather arrangement to the 'horn.'

+**3.** *Mining.* (See quot. 1875.)

1869 J. R. BROWNE *Adv. Apache Country* 412 There was as nice a little deposit of pure gold in the bottom of the horn as ever I saw taken at random from any mine. **1875** KNIGHT 1121/1 *Horn*, . . . a spoon or scoop of horn, in which washings are tested in prospecting. **1896** SHINN *Story of Mine* 78 The quartz prospector prefers the horn, because he only pans out a few ounces of powdered rock, and the flakes are so much finer that a more manageable tool is required than in the case of the placer prospector.

+**4.** *In a horn*, (see quot. 1859). *slang. Obs.*

1840 *Picayune* 10 Sept. 2/5 A Horn Story.—The Baltimore Clipper tells the following story 'in a horn.' **1859** BARTLETT 203 *In a Horn.* A low phrase, now common, used to qualify a falsehood, equivalent to the English 'over the left.' A boy will say, 'I saw a man jump over the house,' and add *sotto voce*, 'In a horn;' meaning thereby directly the reverse. **1897** *Voice* 15 July 3/1 To give alms with 'a trumpet' and to pray to 'the house' are equally worship 'in a horn.'

5. *To lock horns* {1865}, +fig. and trans., to engage in combat; to compete. *colloq.*

a1846 *Quarter Race Ky.* 89, I knowed what it meant, so we locked horns without a word, thar all alone, and I do think we fit an hour. **1893** *Chicago Tribune* 28 April 16/1 Horns Still Locked. The Santa Fe and Rio Grande Keep Up Rate War. **1904** *N.Y. Times* 28 March 5 It was largely the advice of Cockran that induced Murphy to lock horns with David B. Hill for the control of the State Committee.

+**6.** *To haul in one's horns*, to recede from a position one has taken; to modify one's pretensions. *colloq.*

With reference to a snail's retracting its 'horns.' So Eng. with *pull* (1589), *pluck* (1678), and commonly *draw* (1824–).

1843 W. T. THOMPSON *Major Jones's Courtship* 79 The high-fliers that's been tryin to be stockrasy fokes has halled in ther horns sense Crotchett cut out. **1871** GOSS *Soldier's Story* iii. 67 But we told him we had 'hauled in our horns' considerably since our capture, which accounted for their not being visible.

***Horn,** *v.* +*fig. To horn off* (or *out*), to ward off or drive away. — **1851** HOOPER *Widow Rugby* 69 You horned me off to get a chance to get gaming witnesses out of the way. **1881** *Phila. Times* 5 June (Th.), There are others who believe that Mac Veagh is trying his best to horn Blaine out of the Cabinet herd, just as young buffalo bulls horn out the old ones from the herd when they get superannuated.

+**Horn ail.** Any one of various diseases of horned cattle, esp. hollow horn (q.v.), the seat or root of which is supposedly in their horns. — **1845** JUDD *Margaret* II. 284 Glad you got through with the pock so well . . . —it's worse than horn-ail, hoven or core. **1858** C. FLINT *Milch Cows* 271 Idiopathic or common fever, commonly called 'horn ail,' and often 'tail ail.' **1877** *Vt. Dairymen's Ass. Rep.* VIII. 49 Horn-ail, a disease formerly supposed to be very prevalent, is seldom heard of now. **1902** L. RICHARDS *Mrs. Tree* 165 Wasn't he the man that tried to cure Peckham's cow of the horn ail, bored a hole in her horn and put in salt and pepper,—or was it oil and vinegar?

***Hornbeam.** +An American tree, *Carpinus caroliniana*, having a hard white wood. Also attrib.

Cf. HOP HORNBEAM.

1671 *Providence Rec.* III. 107 Boundeth on . . . the norwesterne Corner with a horne beame or peckled tree marked on too sides. **1709** LAWSON *Carolina* 94 Horn-Beam grows, in some Places, very plentifully. **1774** in J. L. Peyton *Adv. Grandfather* (1867) 127 The forest of Kentucky consists of . . . sycamore, maple, horn-beam, dog wood [etc.]. **1819** E. DANA *Geogr. Sk.* 171 The soil is . . . thickly covered with timber; such as various species of . . . iron wood, hornbeam, chincapin [etc.]. **1886** *Outing* June 347/1 One spends his winters in tying flies, another in making horn beam-rods. **1905** *Forestry Bureau Bul.* No. 66, 36 The hornbeam, or ironwood (*Ostrya virginiana*), is reported to occur in Rock, Brown, Cherry, and Sioux counties, Nebr.

+**Hornbine.** =BLACK GUM. — **1793** *Mass. H. S. Coll.* 1 Ser. III. 167 The timber here growing is . . . spruce, beech, buttonwood, hornbine, and sassafras. **1894** *Amer. Folk-Lore* VII. 90 *Nyssa sylvatica*, . . . horn-bine, horn-pipe. Southern States.

+**Horn blow.** The blowing of a horn as a rising signal in the morning. — **1880** 'MARK TWAIN' *Tramp Abr.* xxviii, We had missed the morning horn-blow, and slept all day. **1902** WHITE *Blazed Trail* 68 Dyer should have been out of bed at first horn-blow.

***Hornblower.** +=HORNWORM. — **1850** *Rep. Comm. Agric. 1849* 320 The greater portion of the first *glut* reappear the same year as *Hornblowers* and breed myriads.

+**Horn-bound tree.** =BLACK GUM. *Obs.* (Cf. HORNBINE.) — **1634** WOOD *New Eng. Prospect* (1865) 19 The Horne-bound tree . . . requires so much paines in riving as is almost incredible. **1684** *Duxbury Rec.* 60 Beginning at a white oak tree, . . . and so to another horn bound tree. **1714** *Ib.* 93 Thence upward to a hornbound tree marked, viz a hornbound sapling standing in said swamp.

+**Horn-bowed,** *a.* Of spectacles: Having bows of horn. (Cf. BOW 2.) — **1845** JUDD *Margaret* I. 103 She provided him with a pair of broad horn-bowed bridge spectacles. **1893** *Columbus Dispatch* Sept. 28, The old man . . . slapped his horn-bowed spectacles upon his nose.

+**Horn-breeze.** (See quot. 1891.) *Obs.* — **1878** *Buffalo Hist. Soc. Publ.* IX. 405 [Since] there was no harbor at Buffalo of sufficient depth . . . , [the steamboat] was obliged to wait for a 'horn breeze,' as the sailors term it; by hitching on eight or ten pair of oxen [etc.]. **1891** WELCH *Recoll. 1830–40* 18 It was not necessary for vessels or steamboats to be launched and towed up against the current of the river by twenty Yoke of Ox-(s)team power (then called a 'Horn Breeze').

+**Horn bug.** Any one of various beetles, esp. the *Passalus cornutus*, having long jaws or hornlike processes on their heads. Also *horned bug*. — **1778** CARVER *Travels* 493 The Horned Bug, or as it is sometimes termed the Stag Beetle, is of a dusky brown colour. **1789** MORSE *Amer. Geog.* 62 Of the astonishing variety of Insects found in America, we will mention, . . . Horn Bug, Flea, Gnat [etc.]. **1878** STOWE *Poganuc People* 110 That Bill is saassy enough to physic a horn-bug. **1899** *Animal & Plant Lore* 63 Horn-bugs, May-bees, May-flies, June-bugs, *Lachnosterna*. Bernardston, Mass.

Horn comb. A comb made of horn. — **1790** *Penna. Packet* 19 April 4/2 John Murdock . . . has likewise for Sale, . . . Dressing, rake, and tail combs, Childrens crooked horn do. **1815** *Mass. H. S. Coll.* 2 Ser. IV. 124 The manufacture of horn combs and leather gloves is also carried on extensively. **1849** WILLIS *Rural Lett.* 61 There stood a pedlar chaffering for a horn-comb with a girl at a well.

***Horned,** *a.* In the names of insects, fishes, plants, etc.

See also HORNED DACE, FROG, etc.

1737 BRICKELL *N. Carolina* 162 There are several other different Species of Beetles here, but none so remarkable as these . . . except the Horned Beetle, Bull-Fly, or Flying-stag. **1839** STORER *Mass. Fishes* 85 *Catostomus tuberculatus.* The horned Sucker. **1874** COUES *Birds N.W.* 553 *Anser Rosii.* Horned Wavy; Ross' Goose. **1884** *Boston Jrnl.* 11 Oct. 2/4 Billions of insects have been killed by the electric lights in the Capitol at Washington. . . . They comprise . . . whirligigs, skippers, horned midgets [etc.]. **1901** MOHR *Plant Life Ala.* 562 American Horned Clover. . . . Widely distributed west of the Mississippi.

Horned cattle. Domestic animals having horns. {1756–} — **1776** *Jrnls. Cont. Congress* IV. 108 Resolved, That Mr. Aspden, be permitted to export . . . the produce or manufactures of these colonies, (horned cattle, sheep, hogs, and poultry . . . excepted) to Port-au-Prince. **1831** PECK *Guide* 169 A farmer [in Ill.] calls himself poor, with a hundred horned cattle around him. **1890** *Stock Grower & Farmer* 15 Feb. 5/4 These people shipped their household goods from Alamosa, . . . following later with their teams and a good lot of horned cattle.

transf. **1885** HOWELLS *S. Lapham* ix, I used to believe in what old Horace Greeley said about college graduates being the poorest kind of horned-cattle.

+**Horned dace.** Any one of various American fish resembling the carp, esp. *Semotilus astromaculatus.* (Cf. DACE.) — **1842** *Nat. Hist. N.Y., Zoology* IV. 199 The Horned Sucker is common in most of the fresh-water streams of this State. . . . It is known under the various popular names of *Barbel, Dace*, and *Horned Dace.* **1883** *Nat. Museum Bul.* No. 27, 486 *Semotilus corporalis.* . . . Horned Dace. . . . United States from Massachusetts southward to Georgia and west to Missouri. **1884** GOODE, etc. *Fisheries* I. 617 The Horned Dace—*Semotilus corporalis.* This species abounds in all small streams and ponds from Western Massachusetts to Nebraska and southward.

+**Horned frog.** =HORNED TOAD. — **1806** *Balance* V. 235/2 It may have been brought from Louisiana, where are salt mountains, horned frogs and prairie dogs. **1844** GREGG *Commerce of Prairies* I. 195 Another indigenous reptile is the horned-frog of the Prairies. **1885** ROOSEVELT *Hunting Trips* (1886) 205 The horned frog is not a frog at all, but a lizard.

+**Horned grebe.** A variety of small American grebe, *Colymbus auritus*. — **1823** JAMES *Exped. Rocky Mts.* I. 266 *Colymbus* (*Podiceps*, Lath.) *cornutus.* Horned grebe. **1849** AUDUBON *Western Jrnl.* (1906) 173 Here I saw . . . great numbers of the horned grebe. **1917** *Birds of Amer.* I. 5 Horned Grebes are commonly known as 'Hell-divers' or 'Water-Witches.'

Horned lark. A lark (*Otocoris alpestris*) having a tufted crest of feathers on the head. {1894–} — **1844** *Nat. Hist. N.Y., Zoology* II. 179 The Horned Lark is a northern species, which appears in this State in October. **1893** ROOSEVELT *Wilderness Hunter* 93 Little horned larks continually ran along the ruts of the faint wagon track, just ahead of the team.

+**Horned lizard.** =HORNED TOAD. — **1806** CLARK in *Lewis & C. Exped.* IV. (1905) 325 The Horned Lizzard is also common. **1844** GREGG *Commerce of Prairies* II. 231 The horned frog . . . or horned lizard, as those of earlier times more rationally called it, is the most famed and curious reptile of the plains. **1869** *Amer. Naturalist* III. 475 On March 10th . . . I obtained the first Horned Lizard (*Doliosaurus platyrhinos*).

***Horned owl.** One of several species of owls having conspicuous ear tufts, esp. the little horned owl and +the great horned owl. Also with specific modifiers. — **1837** WILLIAMS *Florida* 73 There are many birds in Florida, . . . Marsh Hawk, . . . Horned Owl, . . . Whooping Owl [etc.]. **1850** LEWIS *La. Swamp Doctor* 151 Suddenly one of those small screech, or horned owls, so common in the South and West, gave forth his discordant cry. **1858** THOREAU *Maine Woods* 105 Several times we heard the hooting of a great horned-owl. **1917** *Birds of Amer.* II. 109 Screech Owl. *Otus asio asio*. . . . Other Names.—Little Horned Owl; Gray Owl.

+**Horned pout.** =BULLPOUT. — **1839** STORER *Mass. Fishes* 102 The Horned Pout . . . is highly esteemed as an article of food. **1854** THOREAU *Walden* 190 At length you slowly raise, pulling hand over hand, some horned pout squeaking and squirming to the upper air. **1890** WIGGIN *Timothy's Quest* 126 The baby horned-pouts rustled their whiskers drowsily.

+**Horned snake.** =HORN SNAKE. — **1775** ADAMS *Works* (1850) II. 426 Every dip of his pen stung like a horned snake. **1784** FILSON *Kentucke* 27 Serpents . . . are such as are to be found in other parts of the continent, except the bull, the horned and the mockason snakes.

+**Horned toad.** *W.* and *S.W.* Any one of various small lizards having hornlike protuberances on their bodies. — **1806** *Massachusetts Spy* 16 July (Th.), A venerable Philosopher . . . surrounded by piles of . . . stuffed squirrel skins, and horned toads. **1885** *Weekly New Mexican Rev.* 18 June 4/6 In the hills about Santa Fe, and even in its streets, may be found . . . [the] little lizard called the horned toad. **1897** NORRIS *Third Circle* (1909) 105 The tarantulas and horned toads that you buy alive in glass jars.

***Hornet.**

***1.** Any one of various short, heavy-bodied wasps, +esp. *Vespa maculata*, the white-faced hornet. (Cf. BALD-FACED *a.* b.)

1737 BRICKELL *N. Carolina* 164 The Hornets are in great plenty in this province. **1789** MORSE *Amer. Geog.* 62 Of the astonishing variety of Insects found in America, we will mention, . . . Hornet, Fly, Sand Fly [etc.]. **1820** FLINT *Lett. from Amer.* 275 Wasps and hornets are extremely numerous. **1884** *Boston Jrnl.* 11 Oct. 2/4 Billions of insects have been killed by the electric lights in the Capitol. . . . They comprise . . . hornets, butterflies, moths [etc.].

+**2.** *Mad as a hornet*, very angry. Also in other contexts allusive to the ill-humor of the hornet.

1833 *Md. Hist. Mag.* XIII. 347, [I] broke his bridle—mad as a hornet—rode out to Mitchells mine. **1855** LONGFELLOW *Hiawatha* 224 Words of anger and resentment, Hot and humming, like a hornet. **1893** *Harper's Mag.* Feb. 378/1 They slap about and climb and snap with their jaws with the activity and malice of so many hornets.

Hornet's nest. 1. The nest or den of hornets. {1857–} Also transf. +**2.** =GUAYAVE 1. Also attrib. — **(1) 1783** in *Travels Amer. Col.* 673, I observed several petrifactions of the Shells formerly mentioned of Roots and of a hornets nest. **1872** *Newton Kansan* 26 Sept. 2/4 A young man threw a rock at a hornet's nest. **(2) 1848** ROBINSON *Jrnl. Santa Fe Exped.* (1932) 60 [We] found the inhabitants still friendly, giving us to eat of their pepper dishes and hornet's nest bread. **1849** *31st Congress 1 Sess.* Sen. Doc. 64, 62 When folded and rolled together, it [a guayave] does not look unlike (particularly that made from the blue corn) a 'hornet's nest' —a name by which it is sometimes called.

***Hornfish.** The garfish or a fish resembling this. — **1821** *Mass. H. S. Coll.* 2 Ser. X. 35 In the southerly part of this pond are . . . roaches, chubs, horn fish. **1843** MARRYAT *M. Violet* xliv, The horn fish is four feet long, with a bony substance on his upper jaw, strong, curved, and one foot long, which he employs to attack horses, oxen, and even alligators, when pressed by hunger.

Horn fly. {1706– (Phillips)} An American insect, esp. a small fly (*Lyperosia irritans*) that annoys cattle. — **1889** *Rep. Secy. Agric.* 17 The horn fly, a pest to horned cattle newly imported from Europe. **1892** KELLOGG *Kansas Insects* 113 The Horn Fly of Cattle (*Haematobia serrata*). . . . This cattle pest has not yet made its way into Kansas. **1897** BAILEY *Princ. Fruit-Growing* 25 A comparatively harmless insect in France becomes the dreaded horn-fly in America.

+**Horn frog.** =HORNED TOAD. — **1810** PIKE *Sources Miss.* 156 *n.*, I have seen . . . the horn frog, of which the prairie abounds.

***Horning.** +=CHARIVARI. — **1889** *Amer. Notes & Q.* IV. 81 The neighbor was engaged in giving him what is called in the despatches a 'charivari,' but is more idiomatically known in some of the rural parts of our country as a 'horning.'

+**Horn pout.** A catfish or horned pout. Also used of a stickleback of a variety found in New England. — **1798** *Gazette of U.S.* 3 Aug. (Th.), The company concluded to go, for the sake of seeing a horn pout—when at last I drew one up—and behold! what was it, but a cat fish! **1832** *N.H. Hist. Soc. Coll.* III. 87 On each side of their body and close to the head is a formidable weapon, called a *horn*, and hence the name of *Horn*-pout. **1877** HOWELLS *Out of Question* VI. i, I suppose you plank horn-pout, here. **1910** *Outlook* 9 July 529 On the other side of the pond we met Sam Noyes, who was catching hornpouts.

Horn shavings. *pl.* Thin slices of horn valued as fertilizer. {1744– (Ellis)} — **1749** ELIOT *Field-Husb.* 23 Sometimes they dress their Land . . . with Rags, Hogs and Cattles Hair, Horn-shavings and Ashes. **1825** LORAIN *Pract. Husbandry* 113 Horn shavings and turnings are still more powerful than bones. **1846** EMMONS *Agric. N.Y.* I. 360 All manufacturing establishments have various kinds of wastes, such as hair, wool, bones and animal matter, wood and horn shavings [etc.].

+**Horn snake.** Any one of various snakes reputed to have a particularly poisonous horn or sting in their tails.

1688 CLAYTON *Acct. Va.* in *Phil. Trans.* XVIII. 134 The Horn-Snake is, as they [=Virginians] say, another sort of deadly Snake. **1709** LAWSON *Carolina* 130 Of the Horn-Snakes I never saw but two, that I remember. **1791** W. BARTRAM *Travels* 276 These serpents are also called horn snakes, from their tail terminating with a hard, horny spur, which they vibrate very quick when disturbed. **1833** FLINT *D. Boone* 81 They had pleasant tales of horn-snakes, of such deadly malignity, that the thorn in their tails, struck into the largest tree in full verdure, instantly blasted it. **1896** P. A. BRUCE *Econ. Hist. Va.* I. 129 Other varieties of snakes were common, such as the puff adder, the moccasin, the corn, the black, the water, and the horn.

***Horn spoon.**

***1.** A spoon made from a horn.

1831 BUTTRICK *Travels* 66 A large horn spoon, perhaps three times the size of a common table spoon, was placed on the corn. **1899** CUSHMAN *Hist. Indians* 371 With a wooden or horn spoon, [they] helped themselves one after the other. **1907** ANDREWS *Recoll.* (1928) 214 Some took it with a little hornspoon so as not to soil their fingers.

+**2.** *By the (great) horn spoon(s)*, a euphemistic form of oath, used humorously. Also *by the sacred horn spoons*.

1842 *Amer. Nat. Song Bk.* II. 222 He vow'd by the great horn spoon, . . . He'd give them a licking, and that pretty soon. **1853** *Knickerb.* Feb. 115 'By the horn spoons!' repeated the skipper suddenly. **1857** UNDERHILL & THOMPSON *Elephant Club* 72 You do solemnly swear, by the sacred horn spoons. **1878** BEADLE *Western Wilds* 186 Swearin' by the great horn spoon of the Ancient Scottish Rites that he could whip any Morgan man. **1897** ROBINSON *Uncle Lisha* 231 'By the gre't horn spoon!' he whispered to himself.

+**3.** *Mining.* A small, dishlike receptacle made from a cow horn and used in washing tests for gold. (Cf. HORN *n.* 3.)

1875 BOURKE *Journal* 15 June, The quartz ledges, they have not thoroughly examined, not having any mercury, but have crushed the rock with mortar and pestle and found 'color' in horn-spoon. **1896** SHINN *Story of Mine* 78 The prospector then took it in his horn spoon, a flat vessel made from half of an ox horn.

+**Horn spree.** At Princeton, a procession of students creating discord and confusion by blowing upon fish horns. — **1879** HAGEMAN *Hist. Princeton* I. 281 A college horn-spree, in the year 1855, . . . was so disorderly that constable David Hullfish . . . attempted . . . to quell it. **1888** J. MCCOSH *20 Yrs. Princeton College* 36 We had horn-sprees and foolish bonfires kindled in the campus.

+**Hornswoggle, Hornswaggle.** *v. tr.* To hoax, deceive, bamboozle. *slang.* — **1829** *Va. Lit. Museum* 30 Dec. 458 *Hornswoggle.* 'To embarrass irretrievably.' *Kentucky.* **1866** C. H. SMITH *Bill Arp* 133, I'll be hornswaggled if the talkin and the writin and the slanderin has got to be done on one side any longer. **1904** *Boston Herald* 27 June 6 One practical working theory in advertising circles is that the ad's chief function is to hornswoggle the consumer. **1911** QUICK *Yellowstone Nights* 82 If you'll stand by . . . and see your old father hornswoggled out of his eye-teeth, you'll never see a cent of my money.

+**Hornworm.** Either one of two common larvae of hawk moths that feed upon the tobacco plant. — **1676** GLOVER *Acct. Va.* in *Phil. Trans.* XI. 635 When the [tobacco] plant is well grown they suffer damage by a Worm that devours the leaf, called a *Hornworm* (an *Eruca* or Caterpillar). **1784** SMYTH *Tour* II. 132 The other [species] is the horn-worm, . . . of a vivid green colour, with a number of pointed excressences [*sic*], or feelers, from his head like horns. **1850** *Rep. Comm. Patents 1849: Agric.* 459 The horn-worm is deposited on the smooth or upper surface of the leaf in an egg by the tobacco-fly. **1863** *Rep. Comm. Agric. 1862* 125 The larva [of the sphinx Carolina moth] . . . is sometimes called the horn worm.

+**Horny head.** Any one of various American fish of the family Cyprinidae the heads of which at certain seasons are covered with hornlike processes. — **1838** *So. Lit. Messenger* IV. 405, I dont 'spect to cetch any thing vut a few horny-heads no how, vut I'll fish on a while longer. **1879** [see FISH HOOK]. **1883** *Nat. Museum Bul.* No. 27, 485 *Ceratichthys biguttatus*. . . . Horny Head. . . . From Pennsylvania westward to the Great Basin of Utah.

***Horse.** Also (*colloq.*) **hoss.**

***1.** A well-known domestic animal of the genus *Equus*.

1631 *Mass. Bay Rec.* I. 86 If the cowes, horses, or goats, of any mans . . . shall trespass [etc.]. **1671** *Plymouth Laws* 290 None shall give, lend, or hire any Horse or Horse Colt to any Indian or Indians. *c***1790** T. COXE *View U.S.* 63 The produce, manufactures, and exports of Pennsylvania are very many and various, viz. . . . horses, horned cattle. **1849** *31st Congress 1 Sess.* Sen. Doc. 64, 106 As regards their [Navajos'] stock, . . . I should say that it consisted mainly of sheep and horses. **1890** *Stock Grower & Farmer* 8 March 6/2 Twenty thousand horses were required to round up the cattle on the ranges of the state [of Colo.] five or six years ago. **1925** TILGHMAN *Dugout* 70 'A ten-thousand acre ranch in Texas, with cattle and horses,' said Nate.

+**2.** A fellow or chap. Usually *hoss* or *old* (*ole*) *hoss. colloq.* {*c*1520– in derisive use}

In early use with connotation of strength, courage, etc. (Cf. HALF HORSE (AND) HALF ALLIGATOR.)

1844 *S. Lit. Messenger* X. 489/2 'Huzzah! Huzzah!' went round the crowd, while Jeptha's particular friends swore he was 'a horse.' **1846** CORCORAN *Pickings* 10 'You're right, hoss—I has,' said Jim. **a1846** *Quarter Race Ky.* 39 Good mornin', old hoss, ses I. **1850** LEWIS *La. Swamp Dr.* 41, 'I'm the hoss for you!' screamed I, doubling him up with a lick in the stomach. **1867** GOSS *Soldier's Story* 30, 'I guess you'd better not go down there, old hoss.' **1904** HARBEN *Georgians* 148 'Went back on us, ole hoss,' Jim said, cordially.

+**3.** *Policy.* (See quotation.)

1882 MCCABE *New York* 551 Three numbers make a 'gig,' and win from $150 to $225; four numbers make a 'horse,' and win $640.

+**4.** *To hold one's horse(s)*, to be patient or cool; to take one's time or go easy. *colloq.*

a1846 *Quarter Race Ky.* 120 Hold yer hosses, b'hoys! **1847** ROBB *Squatter Life* 24 Jest hold your hosses, boys—he'll come out directly. **1917** FREEMAN in *Woman's Home Comp.* Nov. 58 Now Phebe . . . you just hold your hosses and speak a little slower.

+**5.** *Horse and horse*, neck and neck; equally matched.

a1859 *Bunkum's Recoll.* (B.), I sot down to old sledge along with Jake Stebbins. It was horse and horse, and his deal. **1908** LORIMER *J. Spurlock* 3 It was horse and horse between the professors.

6. +*To play horse.* **a.** Of children: To ride (something) in play, as if upon a horse. **b.** To act in a violent manner; to play the fool; to bamboozle or ridicule. *slang.*

(a) **1885** *Santa Fé Wkly. New Mexican* 9 July 4/3 His bright little son 'playing horse' on the arm of the chair. **(b)** **1892** CRANE *Maggie* (1896) 24 Curious faces appeared in doorways, and whispered comments passed to and fro. 'Ol' Johnson's playin' horse agin'. **1896** ADE *Artie* 163 Do you think I'm goin' out ridin' with her and have a lot o' cheap skates stoppin' to play horse with her everywhere we go? **1901** WHITE *Westerners* 290 'I'm jest as willin' to play "horse" as anybody,' he said. **1904** W. H. SMITH *Promoters* 169 You've got to have some well-matured plan . . . if they try to play horse with you again. **1907** 'O. HENRY' *Heart of West* 311 I'll drop the tanglefoot and the gun play, and won't play hoss no more.

+**7.** *The man on the horse*, the person in authority. (Cf. HORSEBACK 2.)

1887 *Pall Mall Gaz.* 21 July 1/1 The man on the horse, . . . to use the picturesque American phrase, is not now Lord Salisbury.

8. *attrib.* and *comb.* **a.** Of or pertaining to a horse or to horses.

1872 HOLMES *Poet* iii. 75 Something like horse-ail, very likely—horses get it, you know, when they are brought to city stables. **1873** *Newton Kansan* 6 March 2/2 Parties desiring horse bills for the coming season can have the same neatly printed at this office. **1643** *Essex Prob. Rec.* I. 30, I give to him my horse booke alsoe a pitchforke. **1890** *Stock Grower & Farmer* 12 April 3/2 A horse exchange [at Albuquerque] will be a feature of the enterprise. **1883** *Harper's Mag.* Oct. 717/2 [He] has made the best [fortune] of all . . . by his high-grade horse farm. **1894** *Vt. Agric. Rep.* XIV. 99 There is a movement . . . to see about a Vermont Morgan Horse Register. **1892** *Ib.* XII. 153 Buyers come here, are continually through the horse sections of the State, picking up every promising colt as soon as old enough. **1858** D. PETERS *Kit Carson* 213 The Indians . . . were enjoying a breakfast on horse steaks, having already killed five of the stolen animals.

b. For a horse or for use on or in connection with a horse.

1854 M. J. HOLMES *Tempest & Sunshine* xix. 266, I'd as soon be married in the horse barn as there. **1650** *Boston Rec.* 414 Horse bells cost 10 li. **1832** *Louisville Public Advt.* 3 March, Whittemore's cotton and horse cards. **1831** PECK *Guide* II. 147 Rye for horse feed and distilleries. **1803** *Steele Papers* I. 395 A new Horse flatt not yet launched sufficiently large to take in a loaded Waggon & Team. **c1728** *MS. Inv. Toxhall's Estate, Bertie Co.* (N.C.H.C.), A pair of horse fleams. **a1861** T. WINTHROP *Canoe & Saddle* 282 Whatever can be found of asphodel or horse-fodder shall be your meed. **1781** *Steele Papers* I. 10, I was plundered of all my horses, dry cattle, horse forage, liquors, and family provisions. **1784** J. SMYTH *Tour U.S.* I. 115 A remarkable place in the Roanoak, named the Horse-ford; the only one where horses may cross the river, in that manner. **1755** L. EVANS *Analysis of Map Colonies* 23 A Horse Path may be conducted . . . without much Expence from the great Crossing to the Head of navigable Water. **1658** *Warwick* (R.I.) *Rec.* 158 A parcell of land adjoyning to Massapage pond westward be for a horse pasture. **1839** *Knickerb.* XIII. 449 Some relative or friend . . . may chance to encounter one, ready made, among the rubbish of his rat-traps, . . . horse-persuaders, . . . and other inventions. **1808** PIKE *Sources Miss.* 256 [We] came on eight miles further to a horse range of the marquis's. **1713** HEMPSTEAD *Diary* 27 In ye Lattr Part in ye woods cutting timber for Huttons horse Rooms. **1803** CUTLER in *Life & Corr.* II. 125 Keep your horse-stable free from dung. **1896** WILKINS *Madelon* 99 Madelon stepped forward impatiently towards the horse-stalls. **a1817** DWIGHT *Travels* IV. 26 About five miles of our way, we had no other than a horse track.

c. Drawn by a horse or operated by horse-power.

1881–5 MCCLELLAN *Own Story* 339 Stoneman moved with the advanced guard, consisting of the cavalry, horse-batteries, and two regiments of infantry. **1840** *Picayune* 22 Aug. 2/5 A new thing has appeared in the streets of New York in the shape of a horse broom for street sweeping. **1847** *Rep. Comm. Patents 1846* 83 One patent has been granted for a one-wheeled horse carriage. **1756** *N.E. Hist. & Gen. Register* XXIII. 159, I also give her . . . my part of the Horse Chair, and Tackling. **1821** COOPER *Spy* xii, At length, a single horse-chaise was seen. **1858** WARDER *Hedges & Evergreens* I. 62 This [the destruction of weeds] may be done by horse-cultivators and by hand-hoeing. **1867** J. MELINE *Santa Fé & Back* 298 Huge horse-mowers . . . are seen in the fields. **1736** HEMPSTEAD *Diary* 304 In the morn I rid out . . . to get Nathel Holts Horseplow. **1856** *Porter's Spirit of Times* 268/1 If she could have gone through it [the Louvre] in a horse rail-car, she would have liked it very well. **1889** *Cent.* 2893/2 *Horse-shovel*, . . . a road-scraper. **1782** *Broadside Verse* (1930) 107/3 The corpse of the murderer . . . was placed on a horse sled, dragged to an obscure place and buried. **1863** *Rep. Comm. Agric. 1862* 90 Since horse-thrashers are so universally employed, but few farmers keep a cleaning mill.

d. Large, coarse, loud.

1920 C. R. COOPER *Under Big Top* 202 The calliope player takes him along on parade and tells him the story of steam, to the accompaniment of the screaming notes of the howling, screeching 'horse piano.' **1858** *Harper's Mag.* June 133/1 A 'horse-rattle' which he was whirling round and round to the disturbance of the town. **1850** H. C. WATSON *Camp-Fires Revol.* 254 Bill Hurley had also brought with him an old horse-trumpet.

e. Designating persons dealing with horses or actions involving horses.

1849 *Cincinnati Commercial* 4 Dec. 2/2 A man with a light coat, black whiskers and stogy boots, a real specimen of a 'horse auctioneer.' **1807** IRVING, etc. *Salmagundi* xv. 345 He is always resorted to as an oracle to resolve any question about . . . farming, and horse-doctoring. **1883** *Century Mag.* June 223 Here met the capitalist . . . the steam-boat captain, the horse-fancier. **1876** HALE *P. Nolan's Friends* xi, Poor Nolan and his twelve horse-hunters in buckskin. **1894** WISTER in *Harper's Mag.* Sept. 508/2 The blizzard on Meacham's Hill, the horse-killing in the John Day Valley, Saw-Tooth stampede, and all the recent evils of the past. **1766** W. SMITH tr. *Bouquet's Exped.* (1868) 43 Four divisions, or brigades of pack-horses, each conducted by a horse master. **1876** HABBERTON *Jericho Road* 94 Some of the most determined horse-owners in each county formed secret societies. **1862** *Rep. Comm. Patents 1861: Agric.*, I hope . . . that every farmer as well as professional horse-raiser, and those who cultivate the animal for sporting purposes and for profit merely, will give more attention to the stock they propose to propagate. **1708** *Md. Hist. Mag.* XVII. 222 An Act . . . restraining Horse Rangers within this Province. **1772** in *Travels Amer. Col.* 526 As to Horse Stealing I do not find that ever he has brought any into this part. **1898** WESTCOTT *D. Harum* xxiv, I may 's well tell ye right now 't I've left all my prop'ty to the Institution fer Disappinted Hoss Swappers.

f. In the names of plants, trees, etc., usually denoting a large, strong, or coarse kind or variety.

1870 *Dept. Agric. Rep. 1869* 185 Horse Apple. Origin, Nash County, North Carolina; fruit, large; form, roundish oval. **1839** in *Mich. Agric. Soc. Trans.* VII. 419 *Smilax rotundifolia.* Horse brier. Green brier. **1843** TORREY *Flora N.Y.* I. 301 Horse Gentian. . . . It has long been a popular medicine. **1817–8** EATON *Botany* (1822) 493 *Triosteum perfoliatum*, fever root, horse-ginseng. **1894** *Amer. Folk-Lore* VII. 93 *Rhododendron maximum*, horse-laurel, White Haven, Pa. **1674** JOSSELYN *Two Voyages* 75 Horse Tobacco [has] . . . a broad long leaf piked at the end. **1840** Horse-weed [see HORSE BALM].

g. In the names of fish or insects of an unusually large size.

1884 GOODE, etc. *Fisheries* I. 323 The Cavally of the Gulf of Mexico and Eastern Florida—the 'Horse Crevallé' of South Carolina—occurs abundantly on our Southern coast. **1820** RAFINESQUE in *Western Rev.* II. 303 Red-tail Sucker. *Catostomus erythrurus.* . . . Vulgar names Red-horse, Red-tail, Horse-fish, Horse Sucker, &c. **1850** S. WARNER *Wide, Wide World* ix, The great wooden clock struck half-past five, with a whirling rickety voice, for all the world like a horse grasshopper.

*Horseback.

+**1.** A long, sharp ridge with somewhat precipitous sides. Cf. HOGBACK 2.

1851 SPRINGER *Forest Life* 41 The pumpkin Pine is . . . also [found] on abrupt ridges, called horsebacks, where the forest is dense. **1867** *Atlantic Mo.* Feb. 213/1 A friend . . . proposed to me to pass the intervening day or two in a drive with him northward along the 'horsebacks.' **1884** in D. Hurd *Hist. Norfolk Co., Mass.* 561/2 In various parts of [Weymouth, Mass.] . . . are unusually fine examples of the sharp, linear hills, called horse-backs or kames.

+**2.** *The man on horseback*, General U. S. Grant. Also transf. (Cf. HORSE 7.)

1879 *Congress. Rec.* 25 June 2324/2 An Army under President Hayes, or 'the man on horseback' if he should come back into power. **1880** *Ib.* 10 May 3200/1 The 'man on horseback' is the battle-cry . . . of the most dangerous element of the republican party. **1904** *Courier-Journal* 21 July 4 This is the lay-out. It is Parker, the Jurist and Patriot, against Roosevelt, the would-be Man-on-Horseback.

+**3.** *Horseback opinion*, an opinion given offhand without time for full consideration.

1879 *Congress. Rec.* 23 April 728/1, I am not here as a judicial authority or oracle. I can only give a horseback opinion. **1903** ADAMS *Log Cowboy*

72 My sister gives it as a horseback opinion that she'd been engaged to this fellow nearly eight months.

4. *Horseback ride, riding,* a ride or the action of riding on horseback. {1821–}

'*Horseback ride, riding,* are expressions used chiefly in U.S.; in England, *ride, riding* are understood to be on horseback, unless otherwise expressed or implied, as "a ride in a wagon," "a bicycle ride"' (*O.E.D.*).

1860 HOLMES *Professor* vii. 215 Hossback-ridin' a'n't for them,—except once a year,—on Fastday. **1875** *Fur, Fin, & Feather* 106 If they only knew how much of health and pleasure lay in a horseback-ride. **1880** 'MARK TWAIN' *Tramp Abroad* xxvi, [He] said horseback-riding was what the doctor had always recommended him to take. **1882** *Wheelman* I. 90 Walking, rowing, and horseback riding. Each of these have their objections. **1907** ANDREWS *Recoll.* (1928) 87 Captain Hunt invited me to take a horseback ride with him.

5. Attrib. in the sense: Of or pertaining to riding on horseback.

1877 H. C. HODGE *Arizona* 204 Two great stage lines have been in operation in Arizona for many years, and several minor ones, and horseback post routes. **1891** *Harper's Mag.* Aug. 364/1 This breeds the universal habit of horseback work. **1894** ROBLEY *Bourbon Co., Kansas* 64 Three times a week they had a horseback mail from Westpoint, Montevallo and Sarcoxie, Mo. **1895** REMINGTON *Pony Tracks* 1 Before accepting an invitation to accompany an Indian commission into the Northwest I had asked the general quietly if this was a 'horseback' or a 'wagon outfit.'

+**Horse balm.** An American plant of the genus *Collinsonia* having an exceptionally strong odor. — **1817–8** EATON *Botany* (1822) 244 *Collinsonia canadensis,* horse-balm, rich-weed.... Strong-scented, not unpleasant. **1840** DEWEY *Mass. Flowering Plants* 176 Horse Balm ... is sometimes called Horseweed. **1894** *Harper's Mag.* March 562/2, I passed a luxuriant clump of the plant known as 'horse-balm.'

Horse bean. Any one of several varieties of coarse beans grown usually for stock; also, the fruit of this. {1707–} — **1684** I. MATHER *Remark. Prov.* (1890) 216 The stone weighed about seven grains, being much in shape of our ordinary horse-beans. **1720** *Amer. Weekly Mercury* 26 May 2/1 Thunder and Lightning ... was followed by Hail as bigg as horse Beans. **1784** SMYTH *Tour* I. 293 Indian corn, which is in some places called Maize, is nearly as large as horse beans. **1913** LONDON *Valley of Moon* III. i, You see outside the fence there, clear to the wheel-tracks in the road—horse-beans.

Horse beef. Horse meat used as food. — **1716** CHURCH *Philip's War* I. 170 Taubut ... asked him, Whether he would eat Cow-beaf or Horse-beaf. **1758** C. REA *Journal* 14 A small portion of horse beef is their best allowance. **1859** *Ladies' Repository* May 294/1 'Ah,' said the gentleman, 'it is horse-beef.'

Horse billiards. Shuffleboard, a game played aboard ships. — **1869** 'MARK TWAIN' *Innocents Abr.* iv, Horse-billiards is a fine game. **1897** — *Following Equator* iv. 69 The short-voyage passenger gets his chief physical exercise out of 'horse-billiards'—shovel board.

Horse blanket. A coarse, heavy blanket suitable for use on a horse {1851–} — *c***1820** in *Knickerb.* XXIX. 470 But wiser Bill Van Snort, the jockey, ... Spread his horse-blanket in the manger. **1849** *31st Congress 1 Sess.* Sen. Doc. 64, 85 The doctor spreading out his horse-blanket and overcoat as a pallet for the night. **1890** *Stock Grower & Farmer* 15 March 3/4 The horse-blanket saves feed and flesh—less substance is used to make animal heat. **1917** MATHEWSON *Sec. Base Sloan* 90 The old horse blanket, now discarded as an article of bedding.

Horse block. A block, stump, or platform provided with steps and serving as a convenience in mounting a horse. {1753–} — **1713** *Charlestown Rec.* 207 Heatons Seller door & hors block [is] in the high way. **1825** JOHN NEAL *Bro. Jonathan* II. 12 The others [were] lolling about over the horse-blocks. **1877** BAGBY *Old Va. Gentleman* 8 The boy of the family was sure to be on the horse-block, begging permission to 'ride behind.' **1905** VALENTINE *H. Sandwith* 105 Jane stood on the horse-block, preparing to mount her steed.

* **Horse boat.**

* **1.** A ferryboat for horses. *Obs.*

1639 *Essex Inst. Coll.* V. 168/2 The ferry ... is now granted to Willm Dixye ... & he is to keepe an horse boate. **1645** *Plymouth Col. Rec.* XII. 126 Hee is to leaue the horse boate and skiff sufficiently fitt and serviceable for ... carrying ouer men and cattell. **1714** HEMPSTEAD *Diary* 34, I worked at Huttons al day about ye horse Boat or Scow. **1785** *Md. Hist. Mag.* XX. 49 The only time he went up in a larger boat, was in a horse boat, or one built for a ferry boat, and for carrying horses.

+**2.** A ferryboat propelled by horses.

1828 WEBSTER s.v., *Horseboat,* ... a boat moved by horses; a new species of ferry-boat. **1832** R. C. SANDS *Writings* II. 278 We embarked in an aquatic conveyance, called by the people of these parts a *horse-boat.* **1855** *Knickerb.* XLVI. 271 The horse-boat, which had superseded the tub-like scow. **1897** ROBINSON *Uncle Lisha* 257 They wended their way to the ferry just in time to see the horse boat come splashing into port, the four horses plodding their unprogressive journey on the revolving wheel.

Horse cake. (See quotation.) — **1859** BARTLETT 204 *Horse-Cake,* gingerbread rudely fashioned into the shape of a horse.

+**Horse car.**

1. A street car or railroad car drawn by a horse or by horses. Now hist.

1833 COKE *Subaltern's Furlough* v, We entered the several horse-cars, according to the numbered tickets we had received. **1869** *Boyd's Bus. Directory* 62 Passengers conveyed between Depots by Horse Cars upon the arrival of all trains. **1886** *Century Mag.* May 237/1 Horse-cars ... leave Bowdoin Square, Boston, every half-hour for Mt. Auburn. **1920** HOWELLS *Vacation of Kelwyns* 35 As the horsecar of those days tinkled toward his university suburb [etc.].

2. Attrib. with *bell, company, conductor,* etc. (See also HORSE-CAR LINE.)

1871 HOWELLS *Wedding Journey* 45 They seemed to have dreamed of a long horse-car pilgrimage. **1876** *Scribner's Mo.* April 912/1 There are round-eyed, wondering infants ... in the cradles of to-day who are to be the horse-car conductors and passinjares of the next generation. **1882** MCCABE *New York* 539 The entire structure ... includes a promenade of 13 feet, two railroad tracks, and four wagon or horse-car tracks. **1883** HOWELLS *Woman's Reason* xi, She gave Mrs. Sullivan everything she had in her porte-monnaie except some horse-car tickets. **1885** CRAWFORD *Amer. Politician* 55 The horse-car drivers on Tremont Street rang their bells furiously. **1888** BRYCE *Amer. Commw.* II. II. xliv. 163 *n.,* The president of a horse-car company. **1900** *Scribner's Mag.* Sept. 369/1 From the tracks on Brattle Street, came the drowsy tinkle of horse-car bells.

+**Horse-car line.** A transportation line or route upon which horse cars are used. — **1880** RANOUS *Diary of Daly Débutante* 207 Their horse-car lines [*i.e.,* in Boston] are simply maddening. **1894** *Vt. Agric. Rep.* XIV. 93 Electricity has displaced the horse-car lines. **1905** *McClure's Mag.* XXIV. 347 A scheme to buy up, equip with electricity, and not only run, but finance, the old horse-car lines of Providence.

* **Horse-chestnut.** +Any one of various American trees of the genus *Aesculus,* esp. *A. flava.* (Cf. BUCKEYE 1.)

1743 CATESBY *Carolina* App. p. xxiii, There are in Carolina these following: ... *Pavia.* Sweet flowering Horse Chesnut. *Siliquastrum.* The Judas-tree [etc.]. **1792** IMLAY *Western Territory* 128 By the middle of the month [of March], the buck-eye or horse chesnut is clad in its summer's livery. **1812** STODDARD *Sk. Louisiana* 123 Intermixed with the pines on the more elevated grounds, are the horse chesnut, and several kinds of oak. **1886** H. D. BROWN *Two College Girls* 156 Here stood by the roadside the old dying horse-chestnut.

attrib. **1785** WASHINGTON *Diaries* II. 360 Received from Colo. Henry Lee of Westmoreland, 12 Horse Chestnut Trees. **1899** GOING *Flowers* 55 The horse-chestnut buds, in later March, are no bigger than thimbles. **1912** T. R. SULLIVAN *Heart of Us* 260 Dorothy found joy ... in the more limited view ... through the horse-chestnut branches.

+**Horse conch.** A large marine shell found along the Florida coast. — **1869** *Amer. Naturalist* III. 464 At low tide can be collected ... the Horse Conch (*Fasciolaria gigantea*). **1871** *Harper's Mag.* XLIII. 191/2 The horse conch ... has a very rich face and lip, bearing the daintiest tint of rose and pink. **1881** INGERSOLL *Oyster-Industry* 245 *Horse Conch,* the largest species of Triton. (Florida reefs.)

Horse dealer. One who buys and sells horses. {1744– (Ellis *Mod. Husb.*)} — **1755** *Essex Inst. Coll.* LII. 81 Horse dealers here are great *Bites.* **1856** *Porter's Spirit of Times* 15 Nov. 178/2 A horse-dealer in Chicago has contrived an ingenious method of preventing the intrusion of constables on his premises. **1923** HERRICK *Lilla* 21 She was bought in by a stout horse dealer in Rome.

+**Horse devil.** A species of wild indigo, *Baptisia lanceolata.* — **1869** FULLER *Flower Gatherers* 261 The whole plant forms a globular mass, which, when dry, breaks away from the soil and rolls about in the wind, ... greatly to the discomfiture of horses; for which reason it has acquired the bad name of Horse-devil.

+**Horse disease.** =EPIZOOTIC. — **1872** *Newton Kansan* 21 Nov. 2/1 The notorious epizootic, or horse disease, continues to work its way westward. **1874** R. H. COLLINS *Kentucky* I. 235 The Canadian horse disease, the epizooty—recently epidemic all over the East, cities and country—reaches Cincinnati. **1875** [see EPIZOOTIC].

Horse doctor. One who doctors horses; a veterinarian. {1672–}— **1806** WEBSTER 113/2 *Farrier,* a man who shoes horses, a horsedoctor. **1839** HOFFMAN *Wild Scenes* 108 My father was a Connecticut horse-doctor. **1899** NORRIS *McTeague* 392 He's a horse doctor, this chap is.

+**Horse drama.** A form of drama in which trained horses were featured. — **1868** *Boston Evening Transcript* 7 May 2/2 The horse drama at the Howard is attracting very large audiences. **1880** N. M. LUDLOW *Dramatic Life* 337 The horse-drama did very well for both Mr. Brown and myself.

+**Horse drover.** One in charge of a drove of horses. — **1835** *So. Lit. Messenger* I. 645 Of the most conspicuous '*minora sidera,*' the Kentuckian horsedrover, the horsejockey, the ganderpuller, might be mentioned.

+**Horse fiddle,** *n.* A noise-producing contrivance consisting usually of a strong box well covered with rosin across which a scantling is drawn as a bow across a fiddle string. — **1843** *Knickerb.* XXI. 46 The clattering of pans, the grinding of horse-fiddles, the rolling of drums ... are sustained without intermission. **1870** NOWLAND *Indianapolis* 117 The principal musical instrument was a horse-fiddle. **1911** QUICK *Yellowstone Nights* 212 In addition to the horse-fiddles and bells and horns Absalom had arranged some private theatricals.

‖**Horse fiddle,** *v. tr.* To serenade (a person) with a horse-fiddle. — **1863** *Young Parson* 98 The last time [I went on a spree] was when Strapiron got married; then a parcel of us fellers did horse-fiddle him.

Horsefish. {1723–} +Any one of various American fish, esp. *Stizostedion canadensis,* the head of which suggests that of a horse. — **1672**

JOSSELYN *New Eng. Rarities* 96 Blew fish, or Horse . . . are as big usually as the Salmon, and better Meat by far. **1820** RAFINESQUE in *Western Rev.* II. 303 Red-tail Sucker. *Catostomus erythrurus*. . . . Vulgar names Red-horse, Red-tail, Horse-fish, Horse Sucker, &c. **1884** GOODE, etc. I. 322 This fish [*Selene setipinnis,* is] known on some parts of the coast as the 'Horse-fish.' *Ib.* 424 The 'Sauger' [is] known also as the . . . 'Horse-fish.'

***Horsefly.** Any species of two-winged flies of the family Tabanidae; also, any other species of flies that annoys horses.

1790 *Penna. Packet* 11 Oct. 3/4 A ganninipper is a kind of large horse-fly, frequent in pine woods, the sting of which is extremely poisonous as well as painful. **1832** CHILD *Frugal Housewife* 115 Horse-Flies.—Indigo-weed stuck plentifully about the harness tends to keep flies from horses. **1846** in Emory *Military Reconn.* 390 During the day, our animals suffered greatly from the horse-fly. **1879** *Diseases of Swine* 208 Ticks, screw-worm, and the large horse or cow fly have destroyed many animals. *a***1918** G. STUART *On Frontier* I. 173, [I] was bitten by several mosquitoes and saw the first horse fly of the season.

+**Horsefoot.** =next. — **1672** JOSSELYN *New Eng. Rarities* 13 They feed . . . upon a shell-fish called a Horse-foot. **1802** *Mass. H. S. Coll.* 1 Ser. VIII. 189 The horse-foot, or king crab, was formerly much used for manuring land. **1843** *Nat. Hist. N.Y., Zoology* VI. 56 This common species on our shores is known here under the popular name of Horse-foot. **1855** [see FIDDLER 2]. **1911** *Rep. Fisheries 1908* 311.

+**Horsefoot crab.** Any one of various large sea crabs, a king crab. — **1870** *Amer. Naturalist* IV. 257 This crustacean . . . bears also the popular names Horse Foot Crab, Horseshoe, and King Crab. **1918** LINCOLN *Shavings* 159 They walked along the beach, picked up shells, inspected 'horse-foot' crabs, jelly fish and 'sand collars.'

+**Horsefoot snipe. 1.** =CALICOBACK. **2.** The American knot, *Calidris canutus rufus.* — (1) **1813** WILSON *Ornithology* VII. 32 On the coast of Cape May and Egg Harbour this bird [the turnstone] is well known by the name of the Horse-foot Snipe. **1844** *Nat. Hist. N.Y., Zoology* II. 216 [The] Horsefoot Snipe . . . is very fond of the eggs of the *Limulus polyphemus*, or Horsefoot. **1917** *Birds of Amer.* I. 268 Ruddy turnstone. . . . Other Names. . . . Stone-pecker; Horsefoot Snipe; Brant-bird [etc.]. (2) **1888** G. TRUMBULL *Names of Birds* 179 Knot: Red-breasted Sandpiper: Red Sandpiper [etc.]. . . . At Pleasantville [N.J. it is called] . . . Horse-Foot Snipe. **1917** *Birds of Amer.* I. 231 Knot. . . . Other Names. Red Sandpiper; . . . Horsefoot Snipe [etc.].

Horse guard. {1647–}

+**1.** A fly that preys upon horseflies. (Cf. GUARD *n.* 4.)

1796 HAWKINS *Letters* 46 A large flie called the horse guard come at the same season. **1837** WILLIAMS *Florida* 71 Horse Guard, a species of large Hornet that burrows in the sand; destroys the flies. **1838** FLAGG *Far West* II. 108 A yellow insect . . . has made its appearance . . . and, from its sweeping destruction of the annoying fly, has been called the 'horse-guard.'

+**2.** One or more men detailed to keep watch over horses.

1843 FRÉMONT *Exped.* 10 Guard was mounted at eight o'clock, . . . the morning watch being horse guard for the day. **1856** *Harper's Mag.* XIII. 460/2 [He] was unexpectedly taken prisoner by a party of 'horse guards' belonging to that people [*sc.* the Crows]. **1865** PIKE *Scout & Ranger* (1932) 91 He sent his horses down into the bed of the stream, at the same time motioning me to go with the horse guard.

***Horsehead.** +The moonfish, *Argyreiosus vomer.* — **1883** *Nat. Museum Bul.* No. 27, 438 *Selene argentea*. . . . Horsehead. . . . Atlantic coast of the United States. **1884** GOODE, etc. *Fisheries* I. 323 In the Chesapeake this fish is often called by the names 'Horsehead' and 'Look-down.'

***Horseherd.** +A herd of horses. — **1884** *Century Mag.* May 141/1 Joseph and his elder daughter were . . . among the horse-herd, when the first charge was made. **1897** HOUGH *Story of Cowboy* 26 The cowboy will speak of the 'cavireyah' or 'cavireyard' (*caballado*) instead of the 'horse herd.'

+**Horse high,** *a.* **1.** Used in expressions descriptive of a fence too high for a horse to jump over. **2.** As high as a horse. — (1) **1880** TOURGEE *Fool's Errand* 194 The split-board paling . . . was 'horse-high, hog-tight, and bull-strong.' **1905** PRINGLE *Rice Planter* 176 The fence . . . is neither 'horse high, bull strong, nor pig tight,' and my cattle do not regard it at all. (2) **1896** WHITE *Real Issue* 147 In the summer the field stood horse-high with corn.

Horse-holder. *Milit.* In a cavalry unit, a soldier detailed to hold the horses of his comrades. — **1873** CUSTER in *Boots and Saddles* App. 282 The entire squadron (except the horse-holders) was dismounted and ordered to fight on foot. **1903** FOX *Little Shepherd* xxii, A horse-holder ran up from the rear, breathless, and announced that the Yankees were flanking.

+**Horse Indian.** A plains Indian accustomed to horseback riding. — **1839** MARRYAT *Diary in A.* II. 85 They are *Horse* Indians, as those who live on the prairies are termed. **1887** *Century Mag.* Jan. 448/2 There are no better horsemen in the world than our horse-Indians. **1888** *Ib.* May 39/1 The long, tedious, and bloody campaigns that finally broke the strength of the northern Horse Indians.

Horsejockey. {1782–} +A trafficker in horses; a sharper or knave. {jockey, 1638–1841; now *dial.*}

1789 MORSE *Amer. Geog.* 148 The gamester, the horse-jockey, and the knave, are equally despised. **1817** [see BLACKLEG *n.* 1]. **1865** *Atlantic Mo.* XV. 667/1 His father's tavern [was] a great resort for horse-jockeys, cattle-dealers [etc.]. **1905** LINCOLN *Partners* 145 His brother Sol . . . would skin the eye-teeth out of a Down-East horse jockey.

attrib. **1784** *Deane P.* 204 Ship Building is carried on with Vigor in this State, & the Horse Jockey business flourishes. **1851** *Harper's Mag.* June 37/1 'He's a down-Easter—a horse jockey chap, I'll be bound.'

+**Horse-jockeying,** *n.* Trafficking in horses. — **1783** in S. E. Baldwin *Simeon Baldwin* 129 The conversation was upon News—horsejockeying—& other indifferent subjects.

+**Horse-jockeying,** *a.* That sells or trades horses. — **1809** IRVING *Knickerb.* IV. iii, He swore that he would have nothing more to do with such a . . . cider-watering, horse-jockeying, notion-peddling crew.

Horse-keeping. The keeping or boarding of horses. — **1733** HEMPSTEAD *Diary* 259, I set out for home in the morn horsekeeping. **1746** *Ib.* 457, I p[ai]d Samll Post for horse keeping 4 nights 10s. **1799** in *Harper's Mag.* XLIV. 489/1 The estimates of horse-keeping are in neither instance greater than actually does arise. **1872** *Ib.*, For executive officers, from 1792 to 1798: . . . Horse-keeping, 2 horses $266.66.

***Horse litter.** A litter on poles suspended from two horses, one behind the other. *Obs.* — **1660** WILLIAMS *Letters* (1874) 309 Last week [he] was carried to Boston in a horse litter. **1715** SEWALL *Diary* III. 47 Capt. Warren . . . [was] Carried in a Horselitter to his Son-in-Law at Jones's River. **1735** HEMPSTEAD *Diary* 293 Old Ms Turnner was brot from Naraganset . . . in a Horse Litter.

+**Horse lot.** An enclosure in which horses are kept. — **1850** *Rep. Comm. Patents 1849: Agric.* 144 The man . . . has . . . no time to make manure, or to haul out and spread the little that is dropped in his horse-lot. **1884** HARRIS *Mingo* 57 As he passed out through his horse-lot, a cap and worm of a whisky-still . . . attracted his attention. **1890** *Century Mag.* May 125/2 A negro boy . . . was coming from the horse-lot across the road.

Horse mackerel. {1705–} +Any one of various sea fish of the family Thunnidae, esp. *T. secundodorsalis,* found along the Atlantic coast of America: (see also quots. 1884). — **1802** *Mass. H. S. Coll.* 1 Ser. VIII. 199 The other fishes in the harbour, and on the coast, are the sturgeon, . . . horse-mackerel, dog-fish, and several more. **1856** *Porter's Spirit of Times* 29 Nov. 205/1 The tail of the one [bluefish shark] caught by us was shaped precisely like that of a horse-mackerel. **1884** GOODE, etc. *Fisheries* I. 243 The name of Horse-mackerel . . . is used on our coasts with the greatest carelessness, being applied to *Elops saurus, Anoplopoma fimbria,* and *Merlucius productus,* as well as to various scombroids and carangoid fishes. *Ib.* 320 The most important of the Tunnies is the so-called Horse Mackerel, or Albicore, *Orcynus thynnus. Ib.* 324 The Jurel—*Caranx pisquetus* . . . [is known] at Fort Macon as the 'Horse-Mackerel.' *Ib.* 433 The Bluefish—*Pomatomus Saltatrix*. . . . This fish . . . is also known in Rhode Island as the 'Horse Mackerel.'

+**Horse mail.** A mail delivery by horse post. *Obs.* — **1825** *Catawba Jrnl.* 21 June, A horse mail will answer every purpose on the route between Salisbury and Raleigh. **1835** MARTIN *Description Va.* 134 A horse mail arrives thrice a week. **1837** W. JENKINS *Ohio Gaz.* 54 *The post office* . . . is supplied by a horse mail twice a week.

***Horseman.** Used in the possessive to designate articles belonging to or designed for a rider or a mounted soldier. Now hist. — **1622** 'MOURT' *Relation* 99 The Governour . . . provided a Horse-mans coat, of red Cotton, and laced with a slight lace. **1672** *Plymouth Laws* 166 Every trooper shall provide himselfe with a fix Carbine or horsmans peece. **1781** *Va. State P.* I. 431 These [stores] consist of . . . flints, lead, screws, brushes, & horse-mans' Sword. **1812** *Niles' Reg.* II. 131/1, 300 hospital, horsemen's and common tents . . . have been bought or made. **1829** COOPER *Wish-ton-Wish* iii, Turning to the double leathern sack, . . . he drew a pair of horseman's pistols from two well-contrived pockets in its sides.

+**Horse-mane oat.** (See quot. 1838.) — **1838** *Mass. Agric. Survey 1st Rep.* 33 The Tartarian, or as some call it, the Horse-Mane Oat, from the grain hanging together on one side of the panicle, is sometimes cultivated. **1862** *Ill. Agric. Soc. Trans.* V. 196 Four bushels of seed to the acre, of black Tartarian, or, as sometimes called, horse mane or side oats.

Horse market. A place where horses are bought and sold; the general financial or economic conditions affecting the sale of horses. {1894–} — **1790** *Penna. Packet* 3 March 3/3 At the Horse-Market on Dock-street, Will be Sold An Elegant English Phaeton. **1817** *Md. Hist. Mag.* XI. 372 This day spent in the Horse Market trying to sell the two Horses. **1894** *Vt. Agric. Rep.* XIV. 121 Never in the history of the United States and perhaps the world was the horse market in such a condition.

***Horse mill.** A mill operated by horsepower. Now hist.

1649 *Desc. Virginia* 5 They have . . . many Horse-mills of several kinds, and Hand-mills for several uses. **1685** *Southampton Rec.* II. 103 It is . . . granted to Mathew Howell Thomas Cooper and their copartners to set up a horse mill. **1795** *Ann. 3rd Congress* 1404 The works consist of . . . a milling machine, which is intended to be worked by the horse mill. **1812** *Emporium Arts & Sci.* (Phila.) May 75 The number of water and horse-mills employed in spinning cotton, on this exhibition, amounted to 330. **1889** CABLE in *Century Mag.* Feb. 520/2 You must have seen on plantations what they call a horse-mill—a long pole on which a man sits, and to which a horse or mule is hitched.

***Horsemint.** +Any one of various American plants of the genus *Monarda.* — **1784** CUTLER in *Mem. Academy* I. 460 Horse mint. Blossoms blue. By brooks, and in wet meadows. **1806** LEWIS in *L. & Clark Exped.* V. (1905) 61 During the time of his being in the sweat hole, he drank copious draughts of a strong tea of horse mint. **1858** THOREAU *Maine Woods* 108 Horehound, horsemint, and the sensitive fern grew close to the edge. **1891** WHITMAN *Good-bye My Fancy* 36 Ending our list . . . [there is] the horse-mint.

Horse mussel. Any one of various large sea mussels, esp. *Modiolus modiolus.* {1626-} — **1654** JOHNSON *Wonder-w. Prov.* 49 The Women once a day . . . resorted to the Mussells, and Clambankes, which are a Fish as big as Horse-Mussells. **1881** INGERSOLL *Oyster Industry* 245 *Horse Mussel.*—A large species of mussels. **1883** *Nat. Museum Bul.* No. 27, 237 *Modiola modiolus,* . . . the great 'horse-mussel,' is found from Greenland southward to New Jersey.

+**Horse nettle.** A weed, *Solanum carolinense;* also known as Carolina nightshade. — **1817-8** EATON *Botany* (1822) 463 *Solanum carolinense,* horse-nettle. **1864** *Ill. Agric. Soc. Trans.* X. 874 Horse-nettle or Wild Potato, a miserable weed. **1868** *Mich. Agric. Rep.* VII. 181, I discovered along the side of the railroad track . . . a plant . . . known in Virginia and Carolina as horse nettle. **1892** COULTER *Bot. W. Texas* II. 298.

+**Horse pen.** An enclosure for horses. Also *horse-penning.* — **1738** in Chalkley *Scotch-Irish Settlement Va.* II. 376 One of ye corners of Col. Carter's Horsepen. **1773** in Summers *Ann. S.W. Virginia* 592 Ordered that John Crockett and John Adams . . . view the nighest and best way from the horse pen to Captain Crockett in the Cove. **1839** TOWNSEND *Narrative* 210 Most of the men were immediately put to work . . . making horse-pens. **1884** *Harper's Mag.* Dec. 107/2 The logs for the horse-pen had been provided days before. — *Ib.* 106/1 It was the day fixed for the 'horse-penning' on Assateague Island.

***Horse plum.** +A common wild American plum or a variety of this. — **1797** S. DEANE *Newengland Farmer* (ed. 2) 266/1 The better sorts which are cultivated, are the horse plum, a very pleasant tasted juicy fruit, of a large size: The peach plum [etc.]. **1827** *Western Mo. Rev.* I. 322 The fruit is of the size of a common horse plum. **1884** SARGENT *Rep. Forests* 65 *Prunus Americana.* . . . Wild Plum. Canada Plum. Horse Plum.

Horse post.

1. A system established for transmitting postal material by carriers on horseback. {1668-}

1691 *Mass. H. S. Coll.* 3 Ser. VII. 53 No person . . . shall presume to . . . set up or employ any foot-post, horse-post, or pacquet boat whatsoever. **1792** *Ann. 2nd Congress* 61 If any person . . . shall be concerned in setting up any foot or horse post [etc.]. **1833** *Niles' Reg.* XLIV. 364/2 No person, other than the postmaster general, . . . *shall set up any foot or horse post* for the conveyance of letters and packets, upon any post road.

2. A post to which a horse or horses may be hitched; a hitching post.

1852 STOWE *Uncle Tom* vi, Sam and Andy . . . flew to the horse-posts, to be ready to 'help mas'r.' **1883** *Century Mag.* Nov. 28/1 A wide street with bright, clean, low houses; . . . here and there a horse-post, here and there lounging towns-folk. **1903** *Smart Set* IX. 96 Go out and argue with a wood pile, or a horse-post, or anything else that can't get away from you!

Horse power. {1806-} +A machine operated by one or more horses and supplying power to operate various contrivances. *Obs.* — **1841** CIST *Cincinnati* (*advt.*), Agricultural Machinery . . . including Horse Powers. **1851** — *Cincinnati* 169 These consist of . . . grain thrashing machines, and horse powers, for one, two, four and six horses. **1854** *Penna. Agric. Rep.* 80 Martin H. Cryell, Bucks county, 1 horse power and threshing machine. **1875** KNIGHT 1125.

***Horse race.** A race run by horses carrying riders. — **1721** *Amer. Weekly Mercury* 2 March 3/1 This Day was a famous Horse Race, run for the Sum of Sixty Pounds, between the Inhabitants of Queens County on the Island of Nassau, and Samuel Byard of the City of New York. **1741** *Ga. Col. Rec.* III. 397 Constant Clubs have been held, and Horse-races kept up by them. **1812** *Amer. Rev. Hist.* Oct. 370 Let there be a horse race, or a cock fight, . . . and notice the multitudes of able bodied individuals who attend them. **1883** WILDER *Sister Ridnour* 114 He is always found at the horse-races, at the theater and opera.

Horse-racer. {*c*1618-} +(See quotation.) — **1833** BROOKS *Zóphiël* note, The ring necked serpent is still sometimes seen in North America. . . . From the extreme swiftness of its movement, it received from the English settlers the name of horse-racer.

+**Horse rack.** A pole or heavy beam placed upon posts in such a way as to serve as a convenience for the hitching of horses. — *c***1845** THOMPSON *Chron. Pineville* 40 It was not uncommon to see a score of sore-backed, wind-broken rosinantes . . . 'hanging,' as we say in Georgia, to the horse-rack. **1860** S. MORDECAI *Virginia* 71 On either side of the capitol was a long horse-rack, for the convenience of the public and to diversify the odor. **1910** C. HARRIS *Eve's Husband* 17 There was a long line of horse-racks on the north side of the square.

***Horse-radish.** A tall, coarse herb (*Armorasia rusticana*) cultivated for its pungent root; also, the condiment made from the root. Also attrib. — **1651** *Mass. H. S. Coll.* 4 Ser. VI. 362, I send you by this vessell those horse radish roots you mention. **1709** LAWSON *Carolina* 77 The Garden-Roots that thrive well in Carolina, are . . . Radishes, Horse-Radish, Beet [etc.]. **1863** WHITMAN *Specimen Days* 38 After consulting the doctor, I gave him a small bottle of horse-radish.

+**Horse railroad.** A railroad upon which the cars are drawn by horses. Also attrib.

1857 *Mich. Gen. Statutes* (1882) I. 856 The said companies shall have the right to charge . . . fair compensation for the use of its said road and tunnel by the railroad companies or horse-railroad companies. **1861** NORTON *Army Lett.* 10, I then jumped on one of the cars of the horse railroad. **1872** MCCLELLAN *Golden State* 455 [In San Francisco] water and gas [have been] conducted everywhere, horse railroads running in every direction. **1874** *Dept. Agric. Rep. 1873* 411, I spent considerable time in the city of New York visiting the horse-railroad stables in that city. **1881** *Maine Laws* 137 Edward P. Chase [and his associates] . . . are hereby constituted a corporation . . . with authority to construct, maintain and use a horse-railroad. **1889** Salmons *Burlington Strike* 465 A horse railroad was finished at Quincy, Mass., about the same time that the Erie canal was completed.

+**Horse railway.** =prec. Also attrib. — **1863** WHITMAN *Specimen Days* 31 Campbell hospital, out on the flats, at the end of the then horse railway route, on Seventh street. **1878** *Harper's Mag.* Jan. 192 [He] thought some hunting grounds might be found near the terminus of the horse-railway. **1883** *Ib.* Sept. 648/1 The president of one of Boston's horse railways is trying to apply the civil service reform rules to his employés.

+**Horserake.** A rake drawn by a horse or by horses. {1843- (Ransome *Implem. Agric.*)} — **1817** *Ill. Hist. Soc. Trans. 1910* 147 The ground has to be clea(red of) the Cornstock by . . . cutting them down and drawing them togethe(r) with a horse Rake. **1857** *Lawrence* (Kansas) *Republican* 6 Aug. 4 Mowing machines and horse-rakes should be brought into requisition now if ever. **1906** *Indian Laws & Tr.* III. 204 The net proceeds . . . shall be expended . . . in the purchase of stock cattle, horse teams, . . . horserakes [etc.].

+**Horse ranch.** *W.* A ranch or farm suitably equipped for the raising of horses. (Cf. CATTLE RANCH.) — **1887** I. R. *Lady's Ranche Life Mont.* 13 One afternoon we drove up to the horse-ranche. **1890** *Stock Grower & Farmer* 8 March 4/4 Horse ranches in the Rocky mountains are improving the stock in that region.

Horse road. 1. A road or way suitable only for horseback travel. {1824-} +**2.** A street railroad operated by horse power. — (1) **1802** in R. Putnam *Memoirs* 431, I wish also to know what the expense will be . . . of a horse road twelve feet wide. **1854** BANCROFT *Hist. U.S.* III. 431 Trees had been blazed all the way for a 'horse-road.' (2) **1882** MCCABE *New York* 240 Some of the horse roads . . . are beginning to experience a return of their old prosperity.

+**Horse sense.** Practical common sense. *colloq.* — **1832** PAULDING *Banks of Ohio* II. 215 (Th.), He's a man of good strong horse sense. **1882** *Century Mag.* Oct. 834, I don't think myself . . . that ministers always show what we call horse sense. **1913** LA FOLLETTE *Autobiog.* 55 He had no humor, but much of what had been called 'horse-sense.'

+**Horse-shedding.** (See quots. 1856, 1888.) Also attrib. — **1846** COOPER *Redskins* xiv, The private discussions that were held between pairs under what is called the 'horse-shedding' process. **1856** HALL *College Words* (ed. 2) 258 *Horse-shedding.* At the University of Vermont, among the secret and literary societies, this term is used to express the idea conveyed by the word *electioneering.* **1888** BITTINGER *Hist. Haverhill* 361 Sometimes a little business was initiated [between services on Sunday], incipient steps taken toward purchases or trades. . . . The hour was a sort of exchange time, when seller and buyer . . . would talk, saying, 'If it was to-morrow, what and so.' This was generally . . . known as 'horse-shedding.'

***Horseshoe.** +=HORSEFOOT CRAB. In full *horseshoe crab.* — **1775** ROMANS *Nat. Hist. Florida* 302 It was no other than a crab of the kind called . . . to the northward a horse-shoe. **1797** BENTLEY *Diary* II. 234 A smaller number than usual of the Horse Shoe or Molucca Crab, tho' abundance of the small crab. **1838** HAWTHORNE in *U.S. Mag.* I. 192 Here we seized a live horse-shoe by the tail, and counted the many claws of that queer monster. **1883** *Nat. Museum Bul.* No. 27, 121 The curious Horseshoe Crab or King Crab (*Limulus Polyphemus*) . . . is occasionally eaten by man. **1885** HOLMES *Mortal Antipathy* viii, This horse shoe crab I fling at your feet is of older lineage than your Adam.

***Horse-shoer.** One who shoes horses. — **1789** *Boston Directory* 189 Kelly Andrew, horse-shoer. **1856** OLMSTED *Slave States* 567 So-and-so advertises 'a valuable drayman, and a good blacksmith and horse-shoer.' **1892** *York County Hist. Rev.* 71 Reider & Watson, General Blacksmiths and Horseshoers.

Horse show. A public competitive exhibition of horses and horsemanship. — **1856** *Porter's Spirit of Times* 181/2 The performances at the horse show . . . were very interesting. **1895** *N.Y. Dramatic News* 14 Dec. 6/1 The horse show . . . has had no detrimental effect on his business. **1903** C. L. BURNHAM *Jewel* 97 Father took me to the horse show.

+**Horse smoke.** (See quotation.) *Obs.* — **1807** in Pike *Sources Miss.* II. App. 22 The chief . . . filled a calumet, which several different Indians took from him, and handed the Osages to smoke. This was called the *horse-smoke,* as each person who took the pipe from the chief intended presenting the Osages a horse.

***Horse sorrel.** +=FIELD SORREL. Also attrib. — **1843** 'CARLTON' *New Purchase* II. 143 The excellent Servetus would have been . . . feasted in the tents on fried ham . . . and horse sorrel pies! **1892** *Amer. Folk-Lore* V. 102 *Rumex acetosella,* horse-sorrel. Mansfield, O. **1894** *Ib.* VII. 97 *Rumex acetosella,* . . . horse-sorrel, Minn.

+**Horse stamp.** A place where horses usually stand; an enclosure for horses. *Obs.* — **1791** BARTRAM *Travels* 355 A horse-stamp, where was a large squadron of those useful creatures. **1797** B. HAWKINS *Letters* 226 They have made free with the horses of the traders and some of the Indians who have horse stands or stamps. **1837** BIRD *Nick of Woods* II.

122, [I know] all the parts injacent and outjacent circumsurrounding the hoss-stamp.

+**Horse sugar.** A small tree (*Symplocos tinctoria*) found in the southern states; sweetleaf. — **1847** DARLINGTON *Weeds & Plants* 218 The *Symplocos* (Hopea) *tinctoria*, the 'Horse Sugar' of the South, . . . [is] a favorite food of cattle. **1892** APGAR *Trees Northern U.S.* 122 *Symplocos tinctoria*. . . . Horse Sugar. . . . A shrub or small tree, 10 to 20 ft. high. Delaware and south. **1913** MORLEY *Carolina Mts.* 47 Horse sugar, the only North American member of its family, which otherwise lives in South America, Asia, and Australia, is another early blossoming shrub.

+**Horse swap.** An exchange of horses. Also *horse-swapping*. — **1800** TATHAM *Agric. & Commerce* 80 The trade of *horse-swapping* is nearly as unlimited as the circle of society whose occasions this noble animal accommodates. **1813** *Wheeley's Baptist Ch. Min.* Dec. (N.C. Univ. MSS.), Brother Wills Lay in another Charge against Brother Whalock Concerning a horse Swap took place between him & James Millenner. **c1845** *Big Bear Ark.* 33 He was a general referee and umpire, whether it was a horse swap, a race, a rifle match, or a cock fight. **1865** PIKE *Scout & Ranger* (1932) 40 They had bantered me for a horse race and a horse 'swap.'

Horsetail.* Any one of various plants of the genus *Equisetum* somewhat resembling the tail of a horse. — **1672 JOSSELYN *New Eng. Rarities* 72 The hood shoots forth immediately from the Root, . . . having a Green sprig growing fast by it, like the smaller Horse Tayl. **1814** BIGELOW *Florula Bostoniensis* 259 *Equisetum hyemale*. Rough Horsetail. Scouring Rush. . . . The whole surface of the stem is rough, like a file, and is used in scouring and polishing metallic vessels. **1883** *Century Mag.* Sept. 718 A marsh overgrown with a semi-aquatic vegetation of water-cress and horse-tails. **1899** GOING *Flowers* 252 Those of the ferns and horsetails are green and leaf-like.

+**Horse thief.** One who steals a horse or horses. — **1768** *Boston Chronicle* 10 Oct. 388/3 People . . . who have assembled . . . with the view of driving all horse thieves . . . from amongst them. **1816** *Niles' Reg.* X. 334/1 A horse-thief, refusing to stop, was shot dead. **1867** *Wkly. New Mexican* 30 March 1/4 Col. Lane, of Fort Union, had a rencontre with a band of horse thieves and desperadoes last week. **1894** ROBLEY *Bourbon Co., Kansas* 109 Crawford sent this verbal answer: 'I don't exchange messages with horse-thieves,' and the crisis was on. **1916** THOBURN *Stand. Hist. Okla.* I. 347 Horse thieves and cattle rustlers were all too common.

+**Horse-thieving.** The stealing of horses. Also *ppl. a.* — **1835** BIRD *Hawks of Hawk-H.* II. xiii. 137 Down you rogue, or I'll indict you for horse-thieving. **a1861** WINTHROP *J. Brent* 71 Supposin' its more perarer wolves, or more rattlesnakes, or more horse-thieving, scalpin' Utes! **1874** GLISAN *Jrnl. Army Life* 463 These men are never so happy as when . . . in pursuit of a band of fleeing, horse-thieving, prairie Indians.

+**Horsetooth corn.** =DENT CORN. — **1872** *Vermont Bd. Agric. Rep.* I. 53 We cannot grow the Baldwin . . . with more success than we could grow the dent, or the horse-tooth corn of the south and west. **1887** J. KIRKLAND *Zury* 45 The 'dent' which occurs in the top of each kernel [of Indian corn] produces a withered appearance and gives it the name of 'horse-tooth' corn. **1892** *Amer. Folk-Lore* V. 105 *Zea mays*, horse-tooth corn. Central Ill.

+**Horse trade.** =HORSE SWAP. — **1846** *Knickerb.* XXVIII. 361 He was employed in . . . an action brought by a man against another for cheating him in a 'horse-trade.' **1867** 'LACKLAND' *Homespun* II. 181 At the Tavern were consummated cattle swaps and horse trades uncounted. **1912** NICHOLSON *Hoosier Chron.* 211 She has beat me on many a horse trade, that woman.

+**Horse-trader.** One who engages in trading or swapping horses. — **1850** GARRARD *Wah-To-Yah* vii. 9 The unfair horsetrader might have taken my scalp. **1876** HALE *P. Nolan's Friends* i, Sometimes a concealed horse-trader . . . passed the frontier eastward. **1912** COBB *Back Home* 3 The swapping ring below the wagonyard was . . . clamorous with the chaffer of the horse-traders.

+**Horse-trading.** The swapping or exchanging of horses. Also attrib. — **1826** FLINT *Recoll.* 64 Horse-trading . . . seems to be a favorite and universal amusement. **1863** 'E. KIRKE' *Southern Friends* vi. 84 All were . . . listening to a horse-trading narrative. **1913** LONDON *Valley of Moon* III. xiii, As extra man at the biggest livery stable, Billy's spare time was so great that he drifted into horse-trading.

+**Horse trail. a.** A trail made by the passage of horses. **b.** A path which can be taken by horses. — **1824** MARSHALL *Kentucky* I. 348 Captain Herndon . . . gave pursuit—and coming on the horse trail, took that. **1878** TAYLOR *Between Gates* 228 From this rock the horse-trail climbs to the right. **1913** LONDON *Valley of Moon* III. vii, The road was badly washed and gullied. . . . 'It peters out altogether farther down,' Billy said. 'From there on it's only horse trails.'

+**Horse trot.** A trotting match. — **1864** *Maine Agric. Soc. Returns 1863* 40 On the second day of the Fair, had the inevitable horse trot. **1884** *N.Y. Puck* Aug., He goeth to the horse-trot and betteth his money on the brown mare. **1918** RIDEOUT *Key of Fields* 262 [The tin peddler] used to . . . win money on horse trots at the fairs.

+**Horse trotting.** The trotting of horses in competitions or matches. — **1858** HOLMES *Autocrat of Breakfast Table* 38 Horse-*racing* is not a republican institution; horse-*trotting* is. **1874** *Vermont Bd. Agric. Rep.* II. 395 Mr. Kent, in naming some men to write essays on different branches of farming to be read at this meeting, named me to write one on horse trotting.

Horse trough. A trough at which horses are watered. {1837-} — **1833** COKE *Subaltern's Furl.* I. 120 A wash in the morning without glass, soap, or towel, at the pump or horse-trough. **1867** 'LACKLAND' *Homespun* I. 140 There were times . . . when the horse-trough was tight frozen. **1898** PAGE *Red Rock* 9 [He] dipped his handkerchief in the horse-trough.

Horseway.* A way or road by which a horse may pass. — **1637 *Dedham Rec.* III. 34 It may be lawful . . . to take & laye out in or through any mans lott: a sufficient Carteweye, horseway, or Footewaye. **1646** *New-Hampshire Doc. & Rec.* I. 186 It is ordered that Hampton should be allowed £5 out of the next Countery rate, so as they make a sufficient carte & horse way over the great marsh suddainly. **1681** *Huntington Rec.* I. 296 Thos. higbe and Joseph wood coper should make and mentain a good and sufficient foot and hors way over the water.

+**Horseweed.** =HORSE BALM. Also any one of various plants of the ragweed family. — **1791** *Amer. Philos. Soc.* III. 114 *Collinsonia canadensis* (Horse-weed, Knot-root), *Hydrophyllum canadensis* (Scaly-root). **1874** J. W. LONG *Wild-Fowl* 239 The hunter usually selects a position . . . amongst the high 'horse-weeds' bordering the field. **1924** CROY *R.F.D. No. 3* 28 A rotting heap with horse-weeds running up.

+**Horse wrangler.** *W.* Among cowboys, a herdsman having charge of the horses of a ranch, 'outfit,' or other unit. — **1888** ROOSEVELT in *Century Mag.* April 851 There are two herders, always known as 'horse wranglers'—one for the day and one for the night. **1902** WISTER *Virginian* x. 109 Then [came] the foreman of the 76 outfit, and the horse-wrangler from the Bar Circle-L. **1920** HUNTER *Trail Drivers Texas* I. 115 I was selected as horse-wrangler for the outfit.

Horticultural society. A society or group composed of those interested in horticulture. {1807-} — **1839** *S. Lit. Messenger* V. 758/2 The Maryland Horticultural Society was formed in 1832. **1879** *Mich. Gen. Statutes* I. (1882) 95 The secretary of the state horticultural society shall make a report annually.

* **Hose.**

* **1.** *collect.* Covering for the leg and foot; stockings.

c1638 R. WILLIAMS *Seven Lett.* (1825) 172 They got on hose and shoes, and departed in the night. **1774** J. ANDREWS *Letters* 27 A sixth [person presented him] with a pair of the best silk hose. **1865** *Yale Lit. Mag.* XXX. 295 (Th.), No stocking curbed her cunning toes, Nor hid her heel 'neath silken hose. **1917** *Sears, Roebuck & Co. Cat.* No. 135, 640 Mercerized Darning Cotton . . . for darning the better grades of cotton and silk hose.

* **2.** Flexible tubing for conducting and conveying water.

1780 *Heath P.* 28 The leather hose . . . might be directed to any part of the work on fire. **1840** *Picayune* 22 Oct. 2/5 The Treasurer [must] pay . . . for hose for washing the streets, ninety-nine dollars and twelve cents. **1889** BRAYLEY *Boston Fire Dept.* 45 The first mention of hose for the department is made on April 7 [1736], when Captain Sutton asked for a piece of new hose for his engine, which probably referred to a short piece for the pipe, as the regular hose was not used until after Boston became a city. **1904** *McClure's Mag.* Jan. 290 Line after line of hose had been stretched along the pier.

3. *attrib.* In sense 1 with *tax, yarn;* in sense 2 with *house, line*, etc.

1640 *Conn. Rec.* I. 453, 2 pre of stockings, a shirt & band and hose yarne. **1825** *Mass. Laws* X. 91 The Fire Department of the City of Boston shall hereafter consist of . . . Firemen, Hosemen, and Hook and Ladder men. **1832** WILLIAMSON *Maine* II. 499 Shoe and hose tax on Maine in 1780, was 1,016 pairs. **1851** CIST *Cincinnati* 168 Each of these companies is provided with Fire and Suction Engines and Hose Reel. **1867** S. W. MITCHELL in *Atlantic Mo.* XX. 469/2 The bulk of my patients were soap-fat-men, rag-pickers, oystermen, hose-house bummers, and worse. **1881** *Harper's Mag.* Jan. 197/1 The engines were ordered to form 'a hose line' in order to save the barn. **1889** BRAYLEY *Boston Fire Dept.* 251 A new hose-tower was also put in the house of Hose No. 5. **1898** *McClure's Mag.* X. 429 A dense knot of firemen was steadying a hose-nozzle on the sidewalk opposite. **1914** *Boston City Council Doc. 1913* I. No. 14, 59. Hose Wagons.—45 in service, 5 in reserve.

Hose carriage. A carriage upon which fire hose is carried. {1893-} — **1829** *Mass. Laws* XI. 237 If any person shall . . . damage or render useless any public Pump or Cistern, or any Engine, Hose Carriage or Sail Carriage, . . . [he] shall be convicted thereof. **1840** *Picayune* 22 Oct. 2/5 Resolved, That Fire Company No. 14 be authorized to procure a hose carriage. **1889** BRAYLEY *Boston Fire Dept.* 218 A new hose-carriage was ordered built for East Boston on September 6 [1851].

Hose cart. =prec. {1887-} — **1883** PECK *Bad Boy* 17 Feed your father a hose cart next, won't ye. **1904** 'O. HENRY' *Cabbages & Kings* xvii. 298 Tree frogs rattling like a hose cart going to a ten blow. **1909** — *Options* 111 Two years ago . . . I was a hose-cart driver for No. 98.

+**Hose company.** A group of men who manipulate a hose in fire-fighting. — **1806** *Mass. Spy* 21 May (Th.), The efforts of several hose and fire companies at length prevailed. **1833** *N.Y. City Ordinance* 10 Dec., All firemen attached to any fire engine, hose, or hook and ladder company. **1851** ROSS *In New York* 31 The department contains thirty-four engine companies, forty-seven hose companies, nine hook and ladder companies, three hydrant companies. **1889** BRAYLEY *Boston Fire Dept.* 200 No other company, or hose or hook-and-ladder company, was to leave. **1914** *Boston City Council Doc. 1913* I. No. 14, 13 A horse-drawn steam fire engine was installed in the station of Hose Company 48.

Hosier.* A dealer in hose and knitted goods. Also attrib. — **1649 *Charlestown Land Rec.* 101, I, Gardy James, bought [a lot] of John Power, hosier. **1780** *N.J. Archives* 2 Ser. IV. 409 The Subscriber . . . carries on the hosier business, where persons who choose to favour him with their custom, may depend on having their mitts, stockings and breeches-patterns wove with care. **1790** *Penna. Packet* 31 May 4/1 John Biggs, Hosier and Glover, Next door to the city Vendue-Store.

***Hospital.**

***1.** An institution for the care of the sick and wounded.

The word has a more general significance in the U.S. than in England where the terms private hospital and nursing home are employed to designate private institutions of this nature.

[**1613** PURCHAS *Pilgrimage* 634 Beyond James Towne . . . they were building an Hospitall with fourescore lodgings, and beds alreadie sent.] **1718** *Boston Rec.* 127 The Select men [shall] be impowered to Lease out a peice of Land . . . for the Erecting an Hospitall or Pest House there for the reception & entertainmt of Sick persons comeing from beyond Sea, and in Order to prevent the Spreading of Infection. **1835** HOFFMAN *Winter in West* II. 13 The hospital stands by itself on a slight knoll about a hundred yards from the barracks. **1879** *Scribner's Mo.* Dec. 200/2 By the will of Johns Hopkins . . . the sum of $7,000,000 was devoted to the endowment of a university and a hospital. **1914** 'BOWER' *Flying U Ranch* 163 They maligned the hospitals and Chicago doctors most unjustly.

***2.** A school, supported by charity, for giving shelter and education to needy children and young people. *Obs.* {*Obs.* exc. *Sc.*}

1713 C. MATHER *Diary* II. 180 That important affayr of setting up a Christian hospital, for the good education of poor children in this town. **1714** *Mass. Bay Currency Tracts* 80 Four Hundred Pounds per Annum to the Use of an Hospital or Charity School, for the Support and Education of the poor Children in the Town of Boston. **1774** *N.J. Gen. Assembly Acts* (1776) 404 No Servant or Servants bought, hired or otherwise procured from the Gaols, Hospitals and Workhouses of the neighbouring Colonies, shall gain any Settlement in this Colony.

3. An institution for the shelter of persons unfit to live in normal society; an insane asylum.

1766 *Va. House of Burgesses* 33 Resolved, That an Hospital be erected for the Reception of Persons who are so unhappy as to be deprived of their reason. **1775** BURNABY *Travels* 77 [In Phila.] there is also a noble hospital for lunatics, and other sick persons. **1796** A. BARTON *Disappointment* II. ii, I will build at my own expence, a comfitable hospital, for de reception of de poor penitent female prostitutes. **1835** J. TODD *Student's Manual* 148 The very intelligent and respectable Superintendents of the Insane Hospitals at Worcester and at Hartford. **1881** M. J. HOLMES *Madeline* 114 We put him in the hospital, usin' his little property to pay the bill. **1915** *Nation* 27 May 597/1 The madmen in the State Hospital.

4. *attrib.* and *comb.* **a.** Used in or at a hospital.

1865 C. A. DANA in *Recoll. Civil War* 286 The furniture of each prisoner is a hospital bed, with iron bedstead. **1850** A. LAWRENCE *Diary & Corr.* 281 Governor Briggs . . . was quite horrified to see me trundled about on a hospital chair. **1864** CUMMING *Hospital Life* (1866) 120/1 We lost nothing except a quantity of hospital clothing. **1863** *Ib.* 73/1 We are having hospital flags put up, but . . . it is said the enemy pay no respect to them. **1862** KETTELL *Hist. Rebellion* I. 168 The enemy's flight was so precipitate that he left in our hands a quantity of flour, fresh beef, intrenching tools, hospital furniture, and baggage. **1869** TOURGEE *Toinette* (1881) xxxii. 339 [She] donned again the soft grey hospital habit. **1865** *Atlantic Mo.* April 436/2 The very slaves . . . [now] had . . . [mutton] as hospital rations. **1907** 'O. HENRY' *Trimmed Lamp* 112 His objections came to be spread finally upon some police station blotter or a hospital register. **1823** THACHER *Military Jrnl.* 99 It was enjoined on me immediately to collect the sick and wounded, and as much of the hospital stores as possible.

b. Of or pertaining to a hospital or to hospitalization in general.

1893 PHILIPS *Making of a Newspaper* 174 The hospital bill was quite large. **1865** KELLOGG *Rebel Prisons* 302 An order was issued from headquarters, for the hospital camp to be moved. **1901** *Harper's Mag.* Dec. 215/1 The factory hospital corps was one of Standish's 'new notions.' **1794** *Ann. 3d Congress* 1424 For the Hospital Department, twenty thousand dollars. **1861** *Army Regulations* 285 The senior medical officer of each hospital . . . [will] transmit to him [the medical director] monthly . . . a copy of the 'statement of the hospital fund.' **1914** GERRY *Masks of Love* 114 The room was the usual bare, white, painfully orderly hospital room. **1880** LAMPHERE *U.S. Govt.* 47/2 A report showing the amount of money collected from seamen on account of hospital tax. **1865** *Atlantic Mo.* XV. 237 There is here, too, a hospital ward, with the requisite nurses and medical attendance. **1817** PAULDING *Lett. from South* II. 249 The statue of old William Penn . . . stands in the hospital-yard in Philadelphia.

c. Denoting one who works in or performs some service at a hospital.

1902 WHITE *Blazed Trail* 85 A hospital agent is always welcome. **1856** Hospital attendant [see HOSPITAL STEWARD]. **1866** MOORE *Women of War* 249 Early in 1864, the United States Sanitary Commission had determined to employ 'hospital visitors,' in order to secure a more thorough and faithful distribution of articles intended for soldiers.

d. Designating vehicles, boats, etc., used for conveying patients to a hospital.

1864 'PENNIMAN' *Tanner-Boy* 296 Being carried in a hospital-ambulance from the field in company with one of his staff to a place of quiet, he soon expired. **1862** MOORE *Rebellion Rec.* V. II. 223 Twenty-five are severely wounded, and are now on board the hospital-boat. **1866** — *Women of War* 26 In the removal to Richmond Mrs. Ricketts was able to secure for him a hospital car, instead of the rude box cars. **1862** MCCLELLAN in *Own Story* 452 Went on the hospital-steamer to see Clitz yesterday. **1874** B. F. TAYLOR *World on Wheels* I. xxiv. 162 The saddest train upon which the writer ever took passage was the Hospital Train, with its maimed and mangled burden, that ran from the still, white tents of Stevenson, Ala., to Nashville, Tenn., just after the battle of Chickamauga. **1866** MOORE *Women of War* 84 A letter published in the Princeton Standard, . . . describing a trip on a hospital transport from St. Louis to Young's Point.

+**Hospital steward.** A noncommissioned officer in the Hospital Corps of the United States Army: (see quot. 1865.) — **1856** GLISAN *Jrnl. Army Life* 350 Besides the sick, hospital steward, hospital attendants, and some three others, there will be no troops. **1865** KELLOGG *Rebel Prisons* 247 Hiram Buckingham . . . was detailed as hospital steward, or Doctor's clerk. **1895** *Outing* Dec. 255/2 The non-commissioned staff comprises a sergeant-major, a quartermaster-sergeant, a commissary-sergeant, and a hospital steward.

Hospital tent. *Mil.* A tent serving as a hospital. Also transf. — **1812** *Niles' Reg.* II. 131/1, 300 hospital, horsemen's and common tents . . . have been bought or made. **1862** in Billings *Hardtack* (1888) 357 One hospital tent will be allowed for office purposes at Corps Headquarters. **1879** *Scribner's Mo.* July 345/2, 'I have a family of orphans to take care of!' . . . she said, stooping over a basket. . . . It was the 'hospital tent,' and as she uncovered it, a brood of belated chickens stretched out their thin necks with plaintive peeps. **1890** CUSTER *Following Guidon* 71 The sitting-room was a hospital tent which is perhaps fourteen by sixteen.

Hoss. Colloq. variant of HORSE.

***Hostage.** +An Indian given and held in pledge. — **1654** JOHNSON *Wonder-w. Prov.* 198 The Indians being slow in their performance, had their hostages returned home before the Wapom was paid. **1693** SEWALL *Diary* I. 382 [The Indians] have sent 3 Hostages. **1721** *Mass. H. Rep. Jrnl.* III. 29 We observe an Article . . . paid Joseph Bean, Interpreter to the Indian Hostages, for his time in bringing them to Boston. **1877** *Rep. Indian Affairs* 15 The Indians . . . delivered up five of their number as hostages.

+**Hostile,** *n.* An Indian unfriendly to the whites. Usu. pl. — **1855** BARNUM *Life* 193 There was a good number of 'hostiles' who would not come in. *a*1872 LARPENTEUR *Forty Years* (1898) 366 They were fired upon by a party of concealed hostiles, about 40 in number. **1877** *Rep. Indian Affairs* 14 An all-day fight with the hostiles near the head of the Rosebud. **1894** WISTER in *Harper's Mag.* June 132/1 A lieutenant with two men was wading across after some hostiles that had been skirmishing with his troop.

***Hostile,** *a.* +Of Indians: Unfriendly towards or at war with the whites. — **1850** GARRARD *Wah-To-Yah* i. 14 At a party in a Missouri frontier settlement, a lady asked a mountaineer, fresh from the Platte if 'hostile Indians are as savage as those who serve on foot!' **1884** MATTHEWS & BUNNER *In Partnership* 32 They are hostile Comanshies. **1890** LANGFORD *Vigilante Days* (1912) 499 Hope of a safe and speedy passage through the two thousand miles of hostile Indian country. **1916** EASTMAN *From Deep Woods* 53 Custer's gallant command was annihilated by the hostile Sioux.

***Hot,** *a.*

+**1.** *Hot biscuit*, a biscuit fresh from the oven.

1867 G. W. HARRIS *Sut Lovingood* 82 The suckit-rider, a-travelin to'ards sumbody's hot biskit an' fried chicken. **1893** *Harper's Mag.* Feb. 454 Small hot biscuits were offered instead of bread, and eaten with the golden mountain butter. **1920** HOWELLS *Vacation of Kelwyns* 29 And could you . . . give us some of your hot biscuit?

+**2.** *Baseball.* Of a ball: Thrown or batted very hard or with great speed. Often *hot ball.*

1868 CHADWICK *Base Ball* 41 Hot Balls.—This term is applied to balls sent very swiftly to the hands from the bat, or thrown in swiftly. **1878** *De Witt's Base-Ball Guide* 19 He should have the pluck to face hot balls direct from the bat. **1884** NYE *Baled Hay* 28 [At a baseball game] he gets a 'hot ball' in the pit of his stomach. **1887** *Courier-Journal* 2 Feb. 8/3 Hot drives to the infield should be held or handled if they go directly to the player. **1912** E. V. COOKE *Baseballogy* 19 And could they play The game today And bat, or stop hot liners? **1917** MATHEWSON *Sec. Base Sloan* 125 The players . . . had not handled a ball since the summer before and the 'hot ones' made them wince and yell.

+**3.** In constant use, as if heated by friction.

1888 *Harper's Mag.* Oct. 679/2 The New York and Washington wire is kept 'hot' for eight hours every night. **1900** *Congress. Rec.* 31 Jan. 1343/2 The Government had kept the cable wires hot in its efforts to secure bidders for those bonds in Europe.

Hot air.

1. *attrib.* Designating furnaces or modes of heating by hot air. {1854–}

1841 CIST *Cincinnati* (*advt.*), Manufacturers of Hot Air Furnaces, Stoves, &c. **1879** *Scribner's Mo.* Nov. 147/2 The hot-air engine is less troublesome. **1892** *York County Hist. Rev.* 7 A specialty is made of hot air, hot water, steam heating and ventilating.

+**2.** Empty boasting talk; humbug; bombast. *slang.* Also attrib.

1873 'MARK TWAIN' & WARNER *Gilded Age* xliv. 399 The most airy scheme inflated in the hot air of the Capital only reached in magnitude some of his lesser fancies, the by-play of his constructive imagination. **1899** ADE *Fables in Slang* (1902) 126 They strolled under the Maples, and he talked what is technically known as Hot Air. **1904** E. ROBINS *Magn. North* II. 67 He has more hot air to offer than muscle. **1913** LONDON *Valley of Moon* I. xv, I'm no hot-air artist.... What'll I say, Saxon?

Hotbed. *Agric.* A bed of rich earth glassed in and heated by fermenting manure to stimulate or force the growth of plants. {1626-} Also attrib. — **1753** *Holyoke Diaries* 13 Planted Gourds, Cucumb[ers] & Lettuce in ye Hot Bed. **1848** *Rep. Comm. Patents 1847* 145 A garden frame was placed over two plants in a hot-bed and preserved there free. **1859** *Ill. Agric. Soc. Trans.* III. 501 For a hot bed, choose a warm, dry spot. **1890** *Stock Grower & Farmer* 26 April 5/2, [I] find on my return ... hot beds and cold frames and vegetables growing. **1897** *Outing* May 176/2 Now I should surely have got that trout, but just as I was ready to try, the accursed guide came clambering over the logs with all the silent grace of a horse galloping over hot-bed sashes.

+**Hot box.** A journal box or bearing overheated by friction, as on a railroad coach. — **1855** *Knickerb.* XLV. 199 They shout orders about 'couplings' and 'switches' and 'hot-boxes,' until the waiting passengers almost swear with disappointment and cold. **1873** 'MARK TWAIN' & WARNER *Gilded Age* xlvi. 419 It seemed as if the train would never reach Baltimore.... A hot box had to be cooled at Wilmington. **1898** *McClure's Mag.* X. 400 He came up and said he had a hot box on the last car. **1910** J. HART *Vigilante Girl* x. 140 If that near hind box was to begin to talk different, I'd pull up and examine it right away. Mebbe I'd save a hot box by doin' it.

Hot cake.

1. A fresh-baked cake or small pone of bread; a pancake. **1683** PENN *Select Works* (1782) IV. 309 Their entertainment was ... twenty bucks, with hot cakes of new corn, both wheat and beans, which they make up in a square form, in the leaves of the stem, and bake them in the ashes. **1791** W. BARTRAM *Travels* 241 Fine Corn flour ... being fried in the fresh bear's oil makes very good hot cakes or fritters. **1835** HOFFMAN *Winter in West* I. 191 The usual settlers' dinner of fried bacon, venison cutlets, hot cakes, and wild honey, with some tolerable tea and Indian sugar, ... was soon placed before us. **1914** 'BOWER' *Flying U Ranch* 89 Patsy was lumbering about the stove frying hot-cakes.

+**2.** *To sell* (or *go*) *like hot cakes*, to sell or be disposed of readily. **1860** in O. J. Victor *Hist. Southern Rebellion* I. 46 Revolvers and patent fire-arms are selling like hot cakes. **1876** *Wide Awake* 343/1 The paper-dolls 'went,' as Nora Blake said they would, 'like hot cakes.' **1896** FREDERIC *Damnation of T. Ware* 94 The model performance ... went swimmingly along through scented summer seas of pretty rhetoric, teaching nothing, it is true, but pleasing a good deal and selling like hot cakes.

+**Hotchkiss.** *attrib.* Designating one of various small arms or cannons of a type designed by Benjamin B. Hotchkiss (1826–85), an American inventor. — **1886** *Harper's Mag.* Oct. 793/2 The types adopted by the United States navy are the Hotchkiss revolving cannon and rapid-firing single-shot guns. **1893** *Ib.* Jan. 233/2 There's twelve thousand dollars' worth of stuff on her altogether, counting the Hotchkiss guns and the ammunition. **1916** EASTMAN *From Deep Woods* 107 We distinctly heard the reports of the Hotchkiss guns.

+**Hot corn.** *collect.* Freshly boiled ears of Indian corn. Also comb. — **1842** 'UNCLE SAM' *Peculiarities* I. 40 Some other niggers are crying from their wheelbarrows—'hominy' and 'hot corn.' **1852** J. W. BOND *Minnesota* 276 Mr. Kittson ... celebrated our arrival by a sumptuous dinner, in which hot corn and potatoes, onions, &c., ... formed the principal item in the vegetable line. **1870** *Scribner's Mo.* I. 115 There are many negro women among the mysterious 'hot corn' sellers. **1875** *Chicago Tribune* 10 Nov. 3/2 If Chicago men want to hear the cry of 'Hot corn,' let them pile up this year's crop.

Hotel.

1. A public house for the accommodation of travelers and strangers. {1765-} **1776** R. KING in *Life & Corr.* I. 20 By a Gentleman who lately came out of Boston I was informed that they have two bake houses constantly employed in baking for their hotels. **1839** BRIGGS *H. Franco* II. xxi. 203 It was just at dark when I landed on the levee, in New Orleans, and after seeing my baggage deposited at Bishop's hotel, I took a stroll through the town. **1894** ROBLEY *Bourbon Co., Kansas* 68 But they found [in 1857] that even at the best hotel the bed consisted of a straw tick and a buffalo robe. **1907** ANDREWS *Recoll.* (1928) 164 We were at Knoxville one afternoon and night, at the best hotel.

+**b.** A dining hall. **1829** *Va. Lit. Museum* 336/1 The Proctor is required to make a monthly report to the Chairman of the Faculty [of the Univ. of Va.], of the state of the dormitories, hotels, and public buildings.

2. *attrib.* and *comb.* **a.** Accustomed to work in or for a hotel. **1852** STOWE *Uncle Tom* xii, She sprung to the side of the boat, in hopes that, among the various hotel-waiters who thronged the wharf, she might see her husband. **1869** W. MURRAY *Adventures* 35 The 'hotel guides' are paid so much per month by the hotel-keepers, and by them furnished to their boarders and such as come unprovided. **1885** *Century Mag.* Aug. 584/1 Good hotel-caterers provide for the extra demand when salmon, spring lamb, or strawberries first appear. **1902** WISTER *Virginian* xxxv, I couldn't change my room, and the hotel man, he apologised to me next mawnin'. **1902** HARBEN *A. Daniel* 53, I only get to go with hotel girls. **1906** 'O. HENRY' *Heart of West* 75 Behind him closely followed ... a hotel detective, if ever white Alpine hat, hawk's nose, implacable watch chain, and loud refinement of manner spoke the truth.

b. Designating parts of a hotel building. **1866** A. D. WHITNEY *L. Goldthwaite* vii, A little girl presently appeared, running from the hotel portico at the front. **1897** BRODHEAD *Bound in Shallows* 1 A dull sound of hammering ... reduced to mere intonations the voices of the two elderly men on the hotel porch. **1898** CANFIELD *Maid of Frontier* 126 Standing upon his hotel piazza, ... Hornung thought of the tremens, and the small houses in the ardent sun danced fantastically before his eyes. **1912** NICHOLSON *Hoosier Chron.* 182 A number of idlers in the hotel lobby regarded him with a new interest.

c. Designating a vehicle operated in the interest of a hotel. **1878** *Harper's Mag.* Jan. 194 The traveller reaches his stopping-place by hotel 'bus, carriage, or ... street cars. **1881** HOWELLS *Modern Instance* xxvii. 328 Marcia watched him drive off toward the station in the hotel barge. **1882** LATHROP *Echo of Passion* ix, He was careful to ride in the hotel coach, while she went to the station in a carriage.

+**Hotel car.** A railroad coach in which passengers may sleep and have their meals. — **1870** RAE *Westward by Rail* 29 No Royal personage can be more comfortably housed than the occupant of a Pullman car, provided the car be an hotel one. **1875** *Chicago Tribune* 11 Sept. 1/7 Pullman hotel cars are also run on the western part of the road. **1895** *N.Y. Dramatic News* 30 Nov. 8/2 One of the clowns ... has slept in a chair for five nights, the hotel car being overcrowded.

+**Hotel clerk.** =CLERK *n.* 7. — **1856** OLMSTED *Slave States* 333 An easy and gentleman-like employment as that of hotel-clerk and bar-keeper. **1882** SWEET & KNOX *Texas Siftings* 23 The hotel clerk is a young man who was originally created to fill an Emperor's throne. **1923** FOSTER *Beachcomber in Orient* 264 A hotel clerk reached out the 'glad-hand,' and introduced me to a young man.

Hotel-keeper. +**1.** One who runs or supervises a dining hall. (Cf. HOTEL 1 b.) **2.** One who keeps or runs a hotel. — **(1) 1829** *Va. Lit. Museum* 336/1 The Proctor is required to make a monthly report ... of any matters relating to the students or hotel-keepers which may be worthy of being noticed. *Ib.*, The hotel keepers are required to furnish a list of such of their boarders as are absent from breakfast. **(2) 1851** *Polly Peablossom* 29 The extortions of hotel-keepers ... formed the year's staple of conversation. **1879** *Scribner's Mo.* June 242/1 Her husband had left town suddenly on a horse belonging to the hotel-keeper.

+**Hotel office.** The place where the business of a hotel is transacted; the lobby. — *a*1861 WINTHROP *C. Dreeme* 77, I heard here at the hotel-office [etc.]. **1897** HOWELLS *Open-eyed Conspiracy* xv, They dawdled through the thronged hotel office. **1912** NICHOLSON *Hoosier Chron.* 243 Harwood waylaid Allen in the hotel office a moment after Marian had gone to her room.

Hotel parlor. A room in a hotel suitably arranged and equipped for conversation, rest, reception of visitors, etc. — **1853** *Harper's Mag.* Jan. 193/1 There were several of the sedate groups that Nature always permits in hotel-parlors, to preserve the balance—so much lead to so much elixir. **1885** *Century Mag.* Aug. 581/2 Time was when gaudiness reigned in hotel-parlors. **1913** LA FOLLETTE *Autobiog.* 144 Sawyer said that he had been unable to secure a room and requested me to go with him to the hotel parlors on the second floor.

+**Hotel privilege.** The privilege or right to erect and operate a hotel. — **1884** *Congress. Rec.* 27 May 4550/2 'Do I understand the Senator from Missouri that there are seven hotel locations in the [Yellowstone] park?' ... 'Yes, sir; seven hotel privileges.' **1886** *Ib.* 2 Aug. 8354/2 There was a lease drawn up ... that did give a monopoly both of transportation and hotel privileges [in Yellowstone Park].

+**Hotel runner.** An employee of a hotel who solicits patronage. — **1848** JUDSON *Mysteries N.Y.* II. 57 Many of our readers may have noticed the almost professional look ... of an outside hotel-runner. **1867** DIXON *New America* I. 6 It was sweet to hear the cry of the hotel-runner (a tout is here called a runner). **1878** *Harper's Mag.* Jan. 194 The perspiring, shouting, excited crowds of hotel, boarding-house, and doctors' runners, hackmen, and porters. **1903** LEWIS *Boss* 11 A special trade had grown up among the piers; the men to follow it were called hotel runners.

+**Hot-foot,** *v. intr.* To go in haste. Often with *it. colloq.* — **1896** ADE *Artie* 22 When the night come ... I hot-foots up to the dance. **1900** — *More Fables* 159 He brushed away the Crumbs and Hot-Footed up to see the Boss. **1912** WASON *Friar Tuck* xl. 272, I slid down the path and hot-footed it into the ravine.

***Hothouse.** +Among American Indians, a cave or hut used for winter residence or for taking sweat baths. — **1643** R. WILLIAMS *Key* (1766) 211 This Hot-house is a kind of little Cell or Cave, ... [and] into this frequently the men enter after they have exceedingly heated it.... Here doe they sit ... sweating together. **1702** C. MATHER *Magnalia* (1853) I. 558 Their hot-house is a little cave, about eight foot over, where, after they have terribly heated it, a crew of them go sit and sweat and smoke for an hour together, and then immediately run into some very cold adjacent brook, without the least mischief to them; it is this way they recover themselves from some diseases, particularly from the French. **1792** POPE *Tour S. & W.* 55 This Rum-Drinking or Spewing-Match was held in the public Square, contiguous to their Hot-House. **1805** CLARK in *Lewis & C. Exped.* III. (1905) 63 Passed a Hot hous covd with Earth on the 1st fork. **1833** FLINT *D. Boone* 147 The waiter . . . placed a couple of blocks of wood . . . opposite the door of a circular cabin, called the hot-house, in the centre of which was the council fire.

+**Hot Scotch.** A drink of Scotch whisky and hot water. — **1882** HOWELLS *Modern Instance* xxiv, The bar-keeper said there was nothing like a hot-scotch to make you sleep. **1891** WELCH *Recoll. 1830–40* 368 The thirsty could slake their thirst, or lunch, by visiting the saloon within the theater, taking their 'mug of ale,' 'hot Scotch,' or 'julep.'

+**Hot sling.** A drink of warmed spirituous liquor. *Obs.* — **1827** J. HOWE *Journal* 17 Here I had some hot sling and a warm breakfast. **1856** GOODRICH *Recoll.* I. 63 Under the influence of this advent of new notions, some took . . . to hot slings.

Hot spring. A spring the water from which is hot. Usu. pl. {1669– (Simpson *Hydrologia Chymica* II. 148)} — **1806** *Ann. 9th Congress* 2 Sess. 1133 They returned to the camp at the hot springs. **1845** FRÉMONT *Exped.* 174 My attention was attracted by a smoke on the right side of the river, . . . where I found on the low bank, near the water, a considerable number of hot springs, in which the temperature of the water was 193°. **1890** *Stock Grower & Farmer* 29 March 6/4 Major Barrow with his wife and daughter have been for some time past stopping at Las Vegas hot springs.

+**Hotspur State.** (See quotation.) — **1883** J. FISKE in *Harper's Mag.* Feb. 425/1 After the union of the States under the Constitution the political conduct of South Carolina was so imperious and so unreasonable that she was not uncommonly known as the 'Hotspur State,' or as the 'vixen sister.'

Hot stuff. +A kind of spiced rum; fig., anything violent or full of action. *colloq.* — [**1841** HONE *Diary* II. 103 We were treated with coffee, spiced rum (known in the Dutch nomenclature as hot stuff), nice bread and butter, Dutch cheese, herrings, doughnuts, New Year's cookies, crullers, mince pies, and waffles.] **1853** BALDWIN *Flush Times Ala.* 162 Cave, . . . refreshing himself with about a pint of hot-stuff, rose, turned his back to the fire, and . . . began. **1895** REMINGTON *Pony Tracks* 208 'That's that outpost of the Twenty-seventh guarding the building.' . . . It fairly crackled now—'giving 'em hot stuff.' **1904** 'O. HENRY' *Roads of Destiny* xviii. 305 We want to introduce a little hot stuff in the way of campaigning.

+**Hot tamale.** A Mexican food consisting of highly seasoned ground meat coated with corn meal and steamed in corn husks. Also attrib. — [**1894** J. C. FOX (*title*), Hot Tomales, an original comedy in 3 acts.] **1896** *Cincinnati Enquirer* 21 Aug. 6/7 Thomas Gates [was arrested] . . . on the charge of passing a counterfeit silver dollar on . . . an old colored hot tamale man. **1900** *Boston Transcript* 22 Aug. 11/4 A valiant Bostonian . . . promptly established a champion record as a tamale-eater, consuming three hot tamales in swift succession. **1906** HOWELLS *Certain Delightful English Towns* 160 Our national fickleness has relegated to a hopeless backnumbership the hot-tamale-man, in his suit of shining white with his oven of shining brass, and impoverished our streets of their joint picturesqueness.

+**Hot wave.** =HEAT WAVE. — **1888** J. D. WHITNEY in *Encycl. Brit.* XXIII. 805/1 The occasional occurrence of 'hot waves' which sweep over large areas of country, raising the temperature much above its normal height, is one of the most . . . disagreeable features of the [U.S.] climate.

Hot wind. *W.* A natural current of air heated by passing over hot plains or prairies. {*c*1790– in Egypt} — **1869** *Repub. D. Jrnl.* 4 March, The sun and hot winds heating the sap on the south side of the tree. **1898** *Mo. So. Dakotan* I. 127 Occasionally these breezes continue during the day, and when the days are unusually warm the air becomes heated and they are then known everywhere on the Plains-country as 'Hot Winds.' **1918** CATHER *My Antonia* 383 At some distance behind the house . . . [was] an apple orchard, sheltered by a high hedge from the hot winds.

Houdan. A breed of chickens originated in France; a chicken of this breed. {1885–} — **1871** LEWIS *Poultry Bk.* 23 The Brahma, Cochin, Leghorn, Poland, and Houdan stand relatively in the position here named [as egg-layers]. **1876** INGRAM *Centennial Expos.* 679 The Houdans were chickens which have black bodies, and the crests on the head is [*sic*] of white and black.

*Hound.

***1.** A dog of a breed valued mainly for the chase.

1697 *Boston Rec.* 227 Noe Hounds or Hunting Dogs shall be suffered to Goe at Large in the Town. **1742** HEMPSTEAD *Diary* 388 Joshua . . . bro[ugh]t home 2 stout Rackoons th[a]t he killed in my Swamp with the help of a Hound. **1834** PECK *Gaz. Illinois* 35 Many of the settlers keep hounds to guard against the depredations of this animal [the prairie wolf]. **1895** *Outing* XXVIII. 74/2 A good bear dog . . . must be a mongrel; a cross of the hound with the mastiff or bull-dog is the best.

+2. A member of a gang of rowdies and desperadoes formerly found in San Francisco. *Obs.*

1850 W. RYAN *Adv. Calif.* II. 257 Amongst the most prominent and notorious disturbers of the public peace figured an association . . . known by the cognomen of the 'Hounds.' . . . They were a desperate set of brawlers, gamblers, and drunkards. **1855** SOULÉ, etc. *Ann. San Francisco* 554 The 'hounds' had perpetrated many outrages before public indignation was fully aroused. *Ib.* 559 Witnesses were . . . called . . . who proved the existence of the association called the 'hounds.' **1872** MCCLELLAN *Golden State* 133 The 'Sydney Ducks' and 'Hounds'—classes of desperadoes—were ever on the alert for booty.

3. Attrib. and comb. in sense 1 with *appetite, bitch, keeper, puppy.*

1768 WASHINGTON *Diaries* I. 255 A Hound Bitch . . . [was] shut up. **1769** *Ib.* 332 Two hound puppies . . . came from Musick and Rockwood. **1897** *Outing* XXIX. 440/2 Fresh doe venison largely contributed to their lack of the usual voracious hound-appetite. *Ib.*, The old hound-keeper declared that Tambelle would never come back.

+**Hound dog.** A hound. *colloq.* — **1649** *Dedham Rec.* 162 That care be taken that the young hound doges be in time taught to hunt. **1768** WASHINGTON *Diaries* I. 293 She was shut up with a hound dog, old Harry. **1835** LONGSTREET *Ga. Scenes* 213 Well, I've had bad luck too. Billy's hound-dogs broke up most all my nests. **1898** HARRIS *Tales of Home Folks* 10, I do hope you haven't asked your friends to bring their hound-dogs with them. **1911** SAUNDERS *Col. Todhunter* xix. 289 He made me feel like a cowardly hound-dog.

***Houndfish.** ‖=BLUEFISH 1. — **1672** JOSSELYN *New Eng. Rarities* 24 Blew-fish, or hound-fish, two kinds,—speckled hound-fish and blew hound-fish (called horse-fish).

Hounding. The pursuing, hunting, or driving of deer, moose, etc., with hounds. {1887 fig.} — **1854** THOREAU *Walden* 299 The old hound burst into view with muzzle to the ground . . . ; but spying the dead fox she suddenly ceased her hounding. **1901** *Munsey's Mag.* June 385/1 With the prohibition of hounding, and of killing does by any means, the native deer have more than doubled in number.

***Hound's-tongue.** Any one of various coarse weeds of the genus *Cynoglossum.* — **1784** CUTLER in *Mem. Academy* I. 414 *Cynoglossum.* . . . Houndstongue. Blossoms pale blue. Roadsides in Dedham. July. It has a very disagreeable smell. **1814** BIGELOW *Florula Bostoniensis* 47 *Cynoglossum officinale.* Common Hounds tongue. . . . An erect, downy plant, exhaling an unpleasant odour. **1872** *Vermont Bd. Agric. Rep.* I. 285 *Cynoglossum officinale*, Hound's Tongue, and *C. Morisoni*, Beggar's Lice, are common in open woods. Vile weeds.

*** Hour.** +Used in phrases to indicate the position of the sun above the horizon in the morning or the afternoon.

1637 *Essex Inst. Coll.* IX. 66 The keeper . . . [is] to take the Cattle at the pen at Sun halfe an hour highe. **1700** SEWALL *Diary* II. 14 Set out for Salem about an hour by sun. **1762** *Narrag. Hist. Reg.* II. 219 [We] got to the Ferry the sun about two hours high at night. **1822** J. FOWLER *Journal* 101 [We] set out the Sun about one Hour High. **1873** ALDRICH *Marj. Daw* 156 When I awoke the sun was several hours high. **1907** M. H. NORRIS *Veil* 3 The sun was an hour high when he entered a narrow road overgrown with grass.

***Hourglass.** A sandglass that measures an hour. — **1646** *Conn. Rec.* I. 482 An hower glasse, . . . 1 pewter quarte, 1 halfe pinte, 1 beker. **1707** *Boston News-Letter* 25 Aug. 2/2 (*advt.*), Grindstones & Ragstones, Hour Glasses [etc.]. **1835** HAWTHORNE *Note-books* I. 8 In the pulpit there was an hour-glass on a large and elaborate brass stand. **1887** ALDEN *Little Fishers* vi, [They] tie a sash around it, and it looks like an hour-glass.

* House.

***1.** A building in which people live.

1622 MOURT *Relation* 72 Wee agreed that every man should build his owne house. **1750** T. WALKER *Journal* 24 March, We went to Stalnakers, helped him to raise his house and camped about a quarter of a mile below him. **1804** *Md. Hist. Mag.* IV. 3 We rode to the house of . . . a neighboring farmer, where we found good accommodations. **1909** WHITE *Rules of Game* III. i, He could make out several other scattered houses, each with its dooryard.

***b.** A church or meetinghouse.

1644 *Springfield Rec.* I. 176 Thomas Cooper is to build ye house in length 40 foote. **1749** *Springfield Church Rec.* 4 April, Voted that the house be 26 feet in height between joynts. **1798** *Phila. Ordinances* (1812) 93 Sundry religious societies . . . have erected . . . houses of religious worship. **1856** GOODRICH *Recoll.* I. 309 The house seemed small, the galleries low, the pulpit mean.

***c.** The den or habitation of a beaver.

1748 H. ELLIS *Hudson's-Bay* 160 The Construction of these Creatures [beavers] Dens, Burroughs, or, as they are commonly called, Houses, are [*sic*] very curious and strong.

***2.** The name of various legislative bodies. **+a.** The representative assembly of an American colony.

1619 *Va. House of Burgesses* I. 5 All the Burgesses had taken the oath of supremacy, & were admitted into the House. **1638** *Md. Archives* I. 4 The freemen assembled at any time to any number above ten persons, . . . shalbe a house to all purposes. **1703** *N.J. Gen. Assembly Jrnl. Hse. of Rep.* (1872) 3 The House then proceeded to the choice of a Speaker. **1719** *Mass. H. Rep. Jrnl.* II. 126 A Petition . . . [was] presented to the House and Read. **1775** *Extracts from N.J. Provincial Congress Proc.* (1835) 14 A copy . . . will be transmitted to the speaker of your honorable house.

+b. The Continental Congress; also, a quorum of this body.

1775 J. ADAMS *Familiar Lett.* (1876) 99 There had not been members enough to make a House, several colonies being absent. **1776** JEFFERSON *Writings* IV. 34, I enclose you a copy of the Declaration of Independence, as agreed to by the House, and also as originally framed. **1778** *Jrnls. Cont. Congress* XI. 752 The Minister shall then bow to the President and the House, and they to him.

+**c.** Either of the two branches of the national Congress.
1787 *Constitution* ii. § 3 [The President] may, on extraordinary Occasions, convene both Houses, or either of them. **1801** CUTLER in *Life & Corr.* II. 47 By accounts this evening, both Houses will be unusually full. **1803** *Ann. 8th Congress* 1 Sess. 119 The small States having a majority in this House [=the Senate] and a majority of the [state] Legislatures, may defeat it if they choose. **1857** BENTON *Exam. Dred Scott Case* 108 Mr. Benton, fearing the loss of the Oregon bill in the disagreement between the two Houses, moved that the Senate recede from its amendment. **1894** [see HOUSE OF REPRESENTATIVES 2].

+**d.** =HOUSE OF REPRESENTATIVES 2.
1789 *Ann. 1st Congress* I. 17 The Senate have appointed one of their members to sit at the Clerk's table to make a list of the votes as they shall be declared; submitting it to the wisdom of the House to appoint one or more of their members for the like purpose. **1797** *Ann. 5th Congress* I. 333 The House went into a Committee of the Whole. **1849** J. DIXON *Tour through U.S.* 27 On leaving the Senate, we entered the House, as it is called, meaning the House of Representatives. **1885** CRAWFORD *Amer. Politician* 227 We should have as many Democrats in Congress as possible, in the Senate as well as in the House. **1913** LA FOLLETTE *Autobiog.* 429 He was taken by the leaders here in the House and afterward in the Senate.

+**e.** Either of the two branches of a state legislature.
1793 *Penna. Gen. Assembly Jrnl. of Senate 1793–5* 45 All bills, orders, resolutions, votes, and amendments of either House . . . shall be presented to the other. **1839** *Indiana H. Rep. Jrnl.* 208 Resolved, That, whereas a communication has been made to the Legislature of Indiana by Dr. I. Coe, one of the canal fund commissioners relative to the property received by said commissioners from the Cohens, . . . that the Senate be respectfully requested to transmit to this House, a copy. **1888** BRYCE *Amer. Commonw.* III. VI. c. 404 The [railway] companies might succeed in 'capturing' individual legislators or committees of either or both Houses.

*__3.__ A college; the fellows and students composing this. (Cf. HOUSE OF STUDENTS.)
1646 *Harvard Rec.* I. 27 If any Scholar shall transgresse any of the Lawes of God or the House out of perversnesse or apparant negligence, after twice admonition hee shall be liable . . . to correction. **1708** *Boston News-Letter* 12–19 Jan. 2/2 The Reverend Mr. John Leveret was this Day declared President of Harvard Colledge in this Place, . . . agreeable to the Choice of the Fellows of the House, and Votes of the Council & Assembly in their Last Session. **1748** in J. Maclean *Hist. Coll. New Jersey* (1877) I. 147 If, finally, money cannot be raised for the House and to support the necessary officers, the thing must be given up. **1848** ELIOT *Hist. Harvard Coll.* 9 The laws for the government of the house have not continued thus unchanged.

*__4.__ A theater or an audience.
1751 *New York Post-Bay* 21 Jan., Several Reports have been unkindly spread, that Mr. Kean . . . had caused a greater Number of Tickets to be printed than the House would hold. **1815** IRVING in P. M. Irving *Life W. Irving* I. (1862) 344 Cooper . . . is apt to fall into [a monotonous manner], in consequence of acting so often before indifferent houses. **1880** RANOUS *Diary of a Daly Débutante* 192 We had a splendid house at night—that is, the place was as full as it could be—and the audience was delighted. **1895** *N.Y. Dramatic News* 23 Nov. 4/4 Just now the craze among the managers is advertising their houses as 'absolutely fireproof.'

*__5.__ An inn, tavern, or hotel for the accommodation of the traveling public.
1771 FRANKLIN *Autobiog.* 255 Here . . . is one place that entertains strangers, but it is not a reputable house. **1857** *Lawrence* (Kan.) *Republican* 11 June 3 This House is new, and is well supplied throughout with good new furniture, making it a desirable stopping-place for strangers visiting Lawrence. **1882** MCCABE *New York* 170 On the east side of the avenue . . . is the massive red-brick front of the Windsor Hotel, one of the most elegant and costly houses in the city.

6. *attrib.* and *comb.* **a.** Designating a portion of ground at or near a house or upon which a house is built.
1893 *Harper's Mag.* April 654/2 A row of house gardens has been built on the roofs of the river-side storehouses. **1637** *Essex Inst. Coll.* IX. 58 Richard Addams . . . desires some house ground. **1677** *Conn. Probate Rec.* 201, 5 acres of house Lands & all other parcels of Land. **1913** LONDON *Valley of Moon* III. i, Father's house-patch of tomatoes was eaten by the black beetles. **1639** *Dedham Rec.* III. 68 Uplands or house places. **1924** RAINE *Land of Saddle-Bags* 10 Where hills are somewhat rounded, a 'house-seat' is often chosen upon one of the knobs. **1638** *Dedham Rec.* III. 39 He may confer ye same upon one or 2: freinds afterward for house scituacions we aloweing unto such his sayd freinds.

b. Used in the names of birds and other creatures that frequent houses, and of animals kept as pets.
1778 CARVER *Travels* 478 The Wall or House Adder, the Striped or Garter Snake. *c***1785** SARAH PEARS *Narrative* (MS.) 8 He had not killed anything save a [bear] cub not biger than a house cat. **1827** WILLIAMS *West Florida* 29 The house-frog always becomes very musical before a rain; and may be termed the poor man's barometer. **1853** *Knickerb.* Aug. 172 The house-martins, in their glossy, blue-black livery, flew back and forth into their miniature dwelling beneath the eaves. **1709** LAWSON *Carolina* 125 Of Rats we have two sorts; the House-Rat, as in Europe; and the Marsh-Rat, which differs very much from the other. **1781–2** JEFFERSON *Notes Va.* (1788) 77 House swallow. *Hirundo rustica.* **1708** *N.C. Col. Rec.* I. 682 After the numerous hazards of unseasonable weather, lack of Plants, the Fly, the ground worme the house wormes, . . . the freightes have not had near the vallue of their labour.

c. Pertaining to those who work near a dwelling house or perform housework.
Esp. used in the South to distinguish slaves employed about the house from those who worked in the fields. (See also HOUSE GIRL and cf. FIELD 5 d, FIELD HAND, etc.)
1788 WASHINGTON *Diaries* III. 301 Set the home house gang to cording the Wood which had been cut for Brick. **1732** *S.C. Gazette* 32/1 The personal Estate of the said Croft, consisting of several sorts of Household stuff, choice House-slaves [etc.]. **1857** *Harper's Mag.* May 848/2 The house-waiter . . . in a land where the pure flunky is unknown, stands at great disadvantage. **1769** *Md. Hist. Mag.* XII. 285 If you remove Henny from the Island, a good house wench must be sent there in her stead.

d. Articles used in a house or home or forming part of its equipment or construction.
1759 *Newport Mercury* 26 June 4/3 To be sold . . . House, and all other Sorts of Brushes. **1796** A. BARTON *Disappointment* II. i, He'll not be able to buy a house-cloth to wipe the flure. **1790** *Penna. Packet* 4 Jan. 1/3 Now Landing from the Brigantine Eleanor . . . House-coal of a good quality. **1902** HOWELLS in *Harper's Mag.* March 623 St. John, in his bare bald head and the négligé of a flannel house-coat. **1638** in Lechford *Note-Book* (1885) 57 The saide Captine Sedgwicke shall . . . cause to be clapboarded round the house frame of the said Samuel Cole. **1925** *Sears, Roebuck & Co. Cat.* No. 150, 28 A neat, trim gingham house or porch frock is an asset to every woman's wardrobe. **1836** *Knickerb.* VIII. 681 These showers afford some relief for a time from the heat which comes down in regular streams, like blasts of caloric from a house-furnace. **1765** HABERSHAM *Letters* 40 He had even sold all his House Furniture. **1880** CABLE *Grandissimes* xli. 320 [Honoré] saw his kinsmen handing house-keys to strangers. **1920** LEWIS *Main Street* 226 She realized that Kennicott had forgotten to turn off the houselights. **1863** A. D. WHITNEY *F. Gartney* xxxiii, My box of best house linen . . . stands besides the press in the northwest chamber. **1887** ALDEN *Little Fishers* xxii, All this joy was over an old, somewhat wheezy little house-organ which stood in the second story unused room. **1856** *Mich. Agric. Soc. Trans.* VII. 52 Cowing & Co. . . . [exhibited] brass house-pump.

+**e.** Pertaining or belonging to the lower house of Congress or a state legislature.
1888 BRYCE *Amer. Commonw.* II. III. lxxiii. 596 What the Americans call 'House caucuses,' *i.e.* meetings of a party in the larger House of the legislature, are not uncommon in England. **1894** *Harper's Mag.* Feb. 480/1 A new tariff bill . . . was made public by the House Committee of Ways and Means. **1898** *Kansas City Star* 21 Dec. 2/5 Populists Propose Changes That Will Give Them Perfect House Control. **1881** *Harper's Mag.* March 552/2 House members are the busiest people in the country, with their caucuses, their incessant committee meetings [etc.]. **1886** ALTON *Among Law-Makers* 20 The House-pages are double in number those of the Senate. **1860** *36th Congress 1 Sess.* H. R. Rep. No. 249, 133 If you have any connexion with the House printing, under or with the House printer, please state what that connexion is.

f. Special combinations.
House line, the line formed by the fronts of a row of houses; *h. mason*, a bricklayer who builds houses; *h. sack*, a dressing sack worn within a house; +*h. share*, =HOUSE LOT.
*c***1850** BAGBY *Old Va. Gentleman* 250 The front of this building . . . stands a little back from the house-line of the street. **1837** W. JENKINS *Ohio Gaz.* 421, 1 cabinet maker, 3 house masons, 2 wagon and carriage makers. **1903** WALTZ *Pa Gladden* 65 She was quite dressy, and had on a pink house-sack trimmed with white lace. **1643** *Providence Rec.* II. 7 All the land that he hath lying in the Bounds of prouidence excepting his house share and housing.

+**House bill.** A bill that originates in the house or lower branch of Congress or of a state legislature. — **1868** *N.Y. Herald* 2 July 3 Mr. Loughbridge . . . reported the House bill for the relief of the grantees of Ann D. Durelling. **1873** *Harper's Mag.* XLVI. 628 The aid proposed by the House bill . . . would be adequate to revive education. **1912** NICHOLSON *Hoosier Chron.* 435 Haven't got House Bill Ninety-five in your pocket, have you?

+**House-burn,** *v. tr.* and *intr.* To undergo injury, or to injure (tobacco), by disease, etc., during the curing process in a tobacco house. — **1640** *Md. Archives* 98 Bad Tobacco shall be judged ground leafes Second Crops leafs notably brused or worm eaten or leaves house burnt sun burnt. **1772** *Md. Hist. Mag.* XIV. 363 For 3 weeks past the Weather has been very unfavourable for the tob[acc]o Cured by fier very much & I suppose has House burnt all tob[acc]o not fierd. **1820** *Amer. Farmer* I. 395 If hung too close it will 'house burn' and the leaves drop off from the stalk. **1850** *Rep. Comm. Patents 1849: Agric.* 321 Splitting tobacco is admired by many who contend that it cures brighter . . . and [is] less likely to house-burn.

+**House-burning.** Of tobacco: Suffering injury during the curing process in a house. — **1772** *Md. Hist. Mag.* XIV. 291 Every day we have had very damp foggy mornings, fiers Have been kept to prevent House burning. *Ib.* 359 We are obliged to keep fiers in all Houses at no small risque . . . to prevent House burning & Mold. **1850** *Rep. Comm. Patents 1849: Agric.* 324 In this crop every leaf was saved, none lost by worms, nor by 'house-burning,' (that is, suffering, or even rotting from being hung too thick).

+**House car.** =BOXCAR. *Obs.* — **1858** W. P. SMITH *Railway Celebrations* 92 Equipment of the Marietta and Cincinnati Railway. . . . Cars. . . . Box Freight (or 'House'), 221; Live Stock, 212. **1862** *N.Y. Tribune* 10 June (Chipman), [The] house-cars were all burned to the trucks, and are a total loss. **1877** 'E. MARTIN' *Hist. Great Riots* 33 Engine No. 423 started off westward with a train of house cars at the same time that the coal train left.

House carpenter. A carpenter who builds frame houses. {1688-} — **1643** *Md. Archives* IV. 212 John Thatcher house-carpenter. **1711** *Boston News-Letter* 12 March 2/2 A Likely Negro Man about 18 years of age Speaks good English and served some time to a House Carpenter, To be Sold. **1792** WEBSTER in E. E. Ford *Notes on Life of N. Webster* I. 315 The bearer of this, Mr. John Leffingwell, is a Joiner (or in Pensylvania dialect) a house Carpenter. **1869** *Causes Reduct. Tonnage* (1870) 18 House-carpenters in Fall River received thirty-five cents an hour.

House-cleaning. The cleaning of a house, esp. the elaborate annual or semi-annual cleaning. Also fig. — **1863** 'HARLAND' *Husks* 140, I offered to have the house-cleaning done. **1870** TOMES *Decorum* 100 The necessary evil of house-cleaning, or pickling, . . . is [not] to be endured more patiently by twelve months of daily anticipatory fussing. **1894** ALLEN *Ky. Cardinal* iii, Most I love to see Nature do her spring house-cleaning in Kentucky. **1909** PARKER *G. Cleveland* 13 When I assisted Mr. Cleveland in the work of house-cleaning, after his first return from the White House, we found many publications dealing with his family history.

House detective. A detective employed by a hotel, business house, etc., to safeguard its interests. — **1898** *McClure's Mag.* X. 525/2 A house detective [had] observed the whole transaction. **1916** DU PUY *Uncle Sam* 50 The house detective telephoned to the special agents of the Department of Justice.

House dress. A dress worn in the house or suitable for wear by a woman doing housework. — **1897** *McClure's Mag.* X. 66 She looked charming in her long, soft house-dress. **1900** MUNN *Uncle Terry* 83 When she came in later, wearing her new house-dress, she drew her chair close to her brother's. **1915** CAMPBELL *Proving Virginia* 53 Put on my lavender silk house-dress. **1923** *Sears, Roebuck & Co. Cat.* No. 146, 57 One-Piece House or Porch Dress of washable solid color gingham.

+**House finch.** Any one of several varieties of small red-headed finches found principally in the southwestern part of the United States. — **1869** *Amer. Naturalist* III. 183 About the gardens [in California] are the House Finch . . . , the Black Pewee (*Sayornis nigricans*) [etc.]. **1874** COUES *Birds N.W.* 107 *Carpodacus Frontalis*, . . . Crimson-fronted Finch; House Finch; Burion. **1917** *Birds of Amer.* III. 7.

House girl. A girl, esp. a Negro, who works in a house. — **1851** *Knickerb.* XXXVIII. 394 The baker stops a moment to chatter with the house-girl. **1884** HARRIS *Mingo* 191 Jenny, the house-girl, refused to sleep at the quarters. **1898** — *Tales of Home Folks* 20 The house-girl came into Mary's room with a lighted candle and quickly kindled a fire.

Household goods. The furniture, utensils, etc., of a household. {1726-} — **1665** Pelletreau *Early L.I. Wills* 277, I give unto . . . Henry . . . all my household goods, cattle and chatels what soever. **1710** *N.H. Probate Rec.* I. 650 All my household goods and four Cows. **1887** *Courier-Journal* 1 May 4/2 He was engaged in moving the household goods of a lady. **1892** *York County Hist. Rev.* 29 George Hoyer, Household and Fancy Goods.

+**House joiner.** A carpenter. *Obs.* — **1785** WASHINGTON *Diaries* II. 378 One Richd. Boulton, a House joiner and undertaker, recommended to me. **1803** LEWIS in *L. & Clark Exped.* VII. (1905) 288 Among the party from Tennissee is a blacksmith and House-joiner—these may be of service in our present situation. **1852** REYNOLDS *Hist. Illinois* 316 He learned the trade of a house-joiner, or carpenter.

+**House log.** A log for use in building a log house. — **1825** *Austin P.* (1924) II. 1026, I wish yoo to furnish Him with tools to git me a set of House Logs. **1871** FLAGG in *Harper's Mag.* Dec. 46 Though barely sixteen years of age, according to the tenth row of notches cut upon one of the house-logs [etc.]. *a***1918** G. STUART *On Frontier* I. 263 The nearby mountains furnished an abundance of house logs . . . and soon log houses made their appearance on all sides.

+**House lot.** A lot or parcel of land of a size regarded as sufficient or suitable for a dwelling house or home.

1636 *Springfield Rec.* I. 158 It is agreed that no man except Mr. William Pynchon shall have above 10 acres for his house lott. **1682** *Conn. Rec.* III. 102 The land they have granted . . . one acre, or two at the most, as house lott. **1703** *Manchester Rec.* 105 One half of a common rite which hous lot is now in the posession of Ezekiell knowlton purcheser. **1800** *Mass. H. S. Coll.* VI. 218 A new road has been opened from North bridge, around the shore, as far as the mills, and it will afford some excellent house lots. **1837** W. JENKINS *Ohio Gaz.* 281 The town plat contains 1,000 house lots, each being 90 feet wide, and 180 feet long, with spacious airy streets, and extensive commons. **1885** HOLMES *Mortal Antipathy* Introd., He can add as many acres as he will to the narrow house-lot.

attrib. **1882** Godfrey *Nantucket* 87 In the olden time all the land, except such pieces as were set aside for homesteads, and designated as 'house-lot land,' was held in common by the twenty-seven original proprietors.

+**House-mover.** One who moves houses. — **1840** *Picayune* 15 Oct. 2/2 Mr. Banker, a Yankee house mover, has undertaken to remove a bridge. **1867** *Atlantic Mo.* Jan. 106/2 Jedwort had over a house-mover from the North Village.

+**House Negro.** Before the Civil War, a Negro slave who worked in the master's house. Now hist. Also attrib. — **1711** *Boston News-Letter* 21 May 2/2 (*advt.*), A Young House-Negro Wench of 19 Years of Age that speaks English to be Sold. **1771** *Md. Hist. Mag.* XIV. 135 You will have it that my People are not well fed, it is true they do not live so well as our House negroes, But full as well as any Plantation negroes. **1781** *Va. State P.* I. 613 List of fourteen 'Field negroes' and two 'House negroes,' entered and recorded by Nicholas Eveleigh. **1884** HARRIS *Mingo* 191 The house negroes stood in mortal dread of Blue Dave.

+**House of Assembly.** The legislative body of certain of the colonies and states; one, usually the lower, of the two houses of a state legislature.

1653 *Va. House of Burgesses* 88 By the Unanimous Opinion of the House of Assembly. It is ordered that John Baldwin shall . . . keep his place. **1775** *Extracts from N.J. Provincial Congress Proc.* (1835) 14 The Congress . . . are sorry . . . that they can[not] comply with your request, in giving you extracts . . . to take with you to the honorable house of assembly of the colony of Connecticut. **1790** in *History of Congress* (1834) 178 Signed by order of the House of Assembly [of Delaware]. **1790** *Ky. Petitions* 154 [He] Continued in publick Business . . . either as a Deligate in the House of Assembly or as a melitia officer in the Jersey State. **1809** KENDALL *Travels* I. 20 The governor [of Connecticut] is by statute president of the upper house of assembly. *a***1817** DWIGHT *Travels* II. 277 The Legislature [of New York State] is formed of a Senate and House of Assembly. **1914** *N.J. Legisl. Minutes of 138th Gen. Assembly* 245, I am directed by the Senate to inform the House of Assembly that the Senate has passed the following bills.

+**House of Burgesses.** In colonial times, the representative assembly of Virginia. Now hist.

1658 *Va. House of Burgesses* 111 The Burgesses . . . are not dissolvable by any power now extant in Virginia, but the House of Burgesses. **1695** *Ib.* 4 Mr. Speaker & Gentlemen of the house of Burgesses. **1724** H. JONES *Virginia* 29 The House of Burgesses . . . is not unlike the House of Commons. **1766** in *S. Lit. Messenger* XXVII. 117/2 [The chair] shall have no influence, whether I am in or out of the House of Burgesses. [**1854** J. E. COOKE *Va. Comedians* I. 22 He is a justice, and has sat often in the House of Burgesses.]

House of Commons. {1621-} +The name given to the lower branch of the North Carolina legislative body from 1776 to 1868. — **1776** *North Carolina Colonial Rec.* X. 1007 The legislative Authority shall be vested in two distinct Branches, . . . to wit, a Senate and House of Commons. **1837** *U.S. Mag.* I. 18 The people . . . entrusted him with the civil duties of a legislator, by an election to the House of Commons of North Carolina. **1867** *N.C. Senate Journal* 23 Jan. 187 A message was received from the House of Commons, informing the Senate . . . that the House was ready for the transaction of business.

***House of correction.** A penal institution to which those guilty of misdemeanors are sent for possible reformation. — **1632** *Mass. Bay Rec.* I. 100 It is ordered, that there shalbe a howse of correccion & a house for the beadle built att Boston. **1712** *Boston Rec.* 93 'Tis now made a Bridewell & House of Correction, wch Obstructs many Honest Poor Peoples going there. **1833** SNELLING *Exposé of Gaming* 25 A promising young lawyer was standing between two late graduates from the house of correction. **1881** *Mich. Gen. Statutes* I. (1882) 538 Any person committed . . . to the state house of correction and reformatory at Ionia . . . may be discharged by any two justices of the peace.

+**House of Delegates.** **1.** The lower house of the state legislature in certain states, as Maryland and Virginia. **2.** 'The lower house of the General Convention of the Protestant Episcopal Church (in full, *House of Clerical and Lay Delegates*)' (*Cent.*). — **(1) 1792** IMLAY *Western Territory* 161 The representatives of the State [of Ky.] . . . consist of two houses, *i.e.* the house of delegates and the senate. **1814** *Ann. 13th Congress* 1 Sess. I. 620 The Legislature of Maryland is composed of two branches. . . . The House of Delegates are annually elected. **1833** J. STUART *Three Years N.A.* II. 107 The legislature was in session; and I went to the House of Delegates, (for so the House of Representatives is here [in Richmond, Va.] called.) **1875** *Scribner's Mo.* Nov. 12/1 This chair and stove were removed to the Capitol of Richmond—the chair continuing to be that of the Speaker of the House of Delegates. **1918** *Va. Acts of Assembly* 788 Resolved, by the senate, the house of delegates concurring [etc.].

***House of easement.** =HOUSE OF OFFICE. *Obs.* — **1658** *Boston Rec.* 148 Itt is ordered that there bee two houses of easement sett upp about the dock for the accomdation of strangers and others. **1701** *Ib.* 12 [No person shall erect] any House of office or Easement within this Town . . . within forty foot of any Street lane or high way.

House of entertainment. An inn, tavern, or other house providing accommodations for travelers. Also *house of public* (or *private*) *entertainment.* {1848-}

1638 *R.I. Col. Rec.* I. 55 Will. Balston shall erect and sett up a howese of entertainment. **1671** *Boston Rec.* 58 A house of publique Entertainment for the sellinge of Coffee & Chuchaletto. **1801** HAWKINS *Letters* 379 Your father is desirous that his red children would consent to establish houses of entertainment and ferries on these roads. **1830** *Va. Lit. Museum* 597/1 My friend proposed we should stay all night at a small house of private entertainment in the neighborhood. **1857** *Ill. Agric. Soc. Trans.* II. 314

Even the rough 'grater' was the instrument to provide the weary and hungry traveler a supper and a breakfast at the 'houses of private entertainment.' **1865** *Nation* I. 557, I came to a large white house with several outbuildings. . . . Knowing it to be professedly a house of entertainment, I preferred a request for lodging.

***House of office.** A privy. *Obs.* — **1652** *Boston Rec.* 109 It is ordered that noe house of Office . . . shall stand within twentie foot of any hie way. **1701** [see HOUSE OF EASEMENT]. **1711** SEWALL *Diary* II. 308 Mr. Evans's Jury Acquit . . . Maria . . . of Murdering her Child, by letting it fall into the House of Office.

House of refuge. An institution or home for the destitute, the fallen, etc. {1866-} — *c***1835** in Martineau *Society* III. 324 Pennsylvania. 1832 and 1833. . . . Expenditures. . . . House of Refuge, [$]5,000. **1845** *Lowell Offering* V. 21 We have houses of Refuge and Magdalen Asylums for those who would return to the path of right. **1872** BRACE *Dangerous Classes N.Y.* 44 Those who instruct or govern 'Houses of Refuge,' or 'Reform Schools.' **1874** *Statutes at Large* XVIII. III. 125 The Secretary of the Treasury is hereby authorized to establish life-saving stations, life-boat stations, and houses of refuge, for the better preservation of life and property from shipwreck.

+**House of Representatives.**

1. a. The lower house of certain colonial legislatures.

1692 *Mass. Acts & Resolves* I. 65 [No] member of the house of representatives . . . shall be chosen to the office of constable. **1703** *N.J. Gen. Assembly Jrnl. Hse. of Rep.* (1872) 12 The Question being put, That Mr. Hartshorn should sit in ye Hs. of Representatives as a Member thereof, . . . It past in the negative. **1704** *Boston News-Letter* 21 Aug. 2/2 The House of Representatives have Voted Thanks to be given to Col. Church. **1775** CUTLER in *Life & Corr.* I. 52 Was in the galleries to hear the debates in the House of Representatives [in Mass.].

b. The lower house of certain state and territorial legislatures.

1791 *Phila. Ordinances* (1812) 82 Be it enacted by the senate and house of representatives of the commonwealth of Pennsylvania. **1802** *Penna. Gen. Assembly Jrnl. Hse. of Rep. 1802-3* 3 A number of gentlemen, elected members of the House of Representatives, sufficient to constitute a quorum met. **1850** *31st Congress 1 Sess.* Sen. Doc. No. 74 iii. § 2 The members of the House of Representatives shall be chosen by the qualified electors, and their term of office shall be two years from the day of their general election. **1874** J. S. PIKE *Prostrate State* 12 [In] the House of Representatives [of S.C.] sit one hundred and twenty-four members.

2. The lower house of the United States Congress.

1787 *Constitution* i. § 1 All legislative Powers herein granted shall be vested in a Congress of the United States, which shall consist of a Senate and House of Representatives. **1828** COOPER *Notions* II. 195 Cadwallader and myself had descended from the hall of the house of representatives to the caucus. **1846** POLK *Diary* (1929) 133 Mr. Woodworth of New York . . . called and informed me that the New York Democratic members of the House of Representatives had held a caucus tonight at which he was present. **1857** *N.Y. Tribune* 2 March (B.), The House of Representatives broke down upon the corruption committee's bill to protect the integrity of members of Congress, having first passed it for buncombe. **1894** *Harper's Mag.* Oct. 802/1 The House of Representatives adopted, after a six month's debate on the floors of both Houses and in Conference Committee, a Senate substitute for the Wilson tariff bill.

+**House of students.** (See quotations.) — **1860** *Ann. Amherst College* 29 A legislative body, called the 'House of Students' was organized in this memorable Summer term of 1828. **1871** CUTTING *Student Life at Amherst* 93 In the summer term of 1828, a legislative body was formed in college, known as the 'House of Students.' Its object was to enact such laws . . . as the good of a college community would seem to require.

House-painter. One whose occupation is painting houses. {1689-} — **1809** CUMING *Western Tour* 223 Pittsburgh [has] . . . two book binders; four house and sign painters; two portrait painters [etc.]. **1852** *Harper's Mag.* Nov. 854/2 To be taken for both an oyster-peddler and a house painter, in one day! **1902** ALDRICH *Sea Turn* 231, I propose to be a painter on a larger scale—a house-painter.

+**House-raising.** A community gathering for assisting a neighbor in the erection of a house. — **1704** *Essex Inst. Coll.* VIII. 223, I was at my L. Lords house raising. **1783** *Maryland Jrnl.* Aug. 29 (Th.), A dispute having arisen between Mr. C. S. and myself, at a house-raising last year, in which we both got warm and angry. **1843** *Amer. Pioneer* II. 451 The frequent necessity for united effort at house-raisings, log-rollings, corn-huskings, &c., produced in him habitual charity. **1901** *Scribner's Mag.* April 392/2 There are still log-rollings, house-raisings, house-warmings, [etc., in the southern mountains].

+**House snake.** The milk snake or spotted adder, *Lampropeltis triangulum.* — **1807** *Mass. H. S. Coll.* 2 Ser. III. 54 The milk or house snake, speckled like a rattlesnake. **1842** *Nat. Hist. N.Y., Zoology* III. 39 The Milk Snake, *Coluber eximius,* . . . is called Chicken Snake, Thunder and Lightning Snake, House Snake, and Chequered Adder. **1884** 'MARK TWAIN' *H. Finn* xxxix. 396 [We] grabbed a couple of dozen garters and house-snakes.

House sparrow. {1674-} +The chipping sparrow. In full usually *little house sparrow.* (Cf. EUROPEAN HOUSE SPARROW.) — **1791** W. BARTRAM *Travels* (1792) 289 *Passer domesticus;* the little house sparrow or chipping bird. **1885** *Knickerb.* XLVI. 22 The small house-sparrow, or, as he is generally known, the 'chippin-bird' comes to our very doors. **1877** *Harper's Mag.* April 658 Even the little house sparrow (*Spizella socialis*) cunningly wove it [moss] into the foundation of its dwelling. **1917** *Birds of Amer.* III. 41.

+**House wren.** The common American brown wren, *Troglodytes aedon.* — **1808** WILSON *Ornithology* I. 129 House Wren. *Sylvia Domestica. Ib.* 133 The House wren inhabits the whole of the United States, in all of which it is migratory. **1850** S. F. COOPER *Rural Hours* 90 Among all the varieties of birds flitting about our path during the pleasant months, there is not one which is a more desirable neighbor than the house-wren. **1904** GLASGOW *Deliverance* 442 A half-finished nest which a house-wren had begun.

***Housewright.** One who builds houses. *Obs.* — **1705** *Charlestown Land Rec.* 169 This Indenture [is] made . . . [between] Robert Wyer, Inholder, and Eleizer Bateman, house Wright. **1789** *Boston Directory* 175 Bell, John, house-wright and cistern-maker.

+**Houseyard.** A yard adjoining a dwelling. — **1863** MITCHELL *My Farm* 26 An ample stream . . . came with a gushing fulness upon the very margin of the quiet little houseyard that compassed the dwelling. **1893** *Harper's Mag.* Feb. 350/1 Apples as they fell to the ground could be heard on every side in the quiet house-yards.

Houstonia. [Wm. *Houston,* Eng. botanist (?1695-1733).] A genus of American plants of the madder family; a plant of this genus. — **1762** CLAYTON *Flora Virginica* 18 Houstonia primo vere ubique florens. **1814** BIGELOW *Florula Bostoniensis* 35 *Houstonia longifolia.* Long leaved Houstonia. . . . Flowers purplish. . . . June, July. **1842** THOREAU *Journal* 311 The popped corn is a perfect winter flower, hinting of anemones and houstonias. **1887** BURROUGHS in *Century Mag.* July 333 We have one flower which grows in vast multitudes, yet which is exquisitely delicate and beautiful in and of itself; I mean the houstonia, or bluets.

+**Houstonize,** *v. tr.* To beat up (a Congressman). In allusion to a beating administered by Sam Houston to Representative William Stanberry, April 13, 1832. — **1837** *Congress. Globe* App. 13 Oct. 326/1 The president pronounced us liars all the way from Washington to the Hermitage, and said here we ought to be Houstonized.

***Hovel.**

***1.** A shed, barn, outhouse, etc., used as a shelter for cattle or for grain, tools, etc. *Obs.*

1654 *New Haven Col. Rec.* 224 He went into the woods, intending to cut some crutches for a hovell. **1684** I. MATHER *Providences* (1856) x. 227 [The wind blew] a large hovel of peas from its supporters, and . . . [settled] it cleaverly upon the ground, without any considerable damage to the thatch. **1716** CHURCH *Philip's War* 15 About a dozen of them ran right over the Log into the Fort, and took into a sort of a Hovel that was build with Poles, after the manner of a corn crib. **1750** HEMPSTEAD *Diary* 560 Adm fetched a Ld of Seaweed & put on the hovel. *a***1862** THOREAU *Maine Woods* 254 There was a deserted log camp here, . . . with its 'hovel' or barn for cattle.

+**2.** (See quotations.)

1813 WILSON *Ornithology* VIII. 54 It is vain to pursue them [*sc.* Canada geese]; they [the hunters] therefore form a row of huts, made of boughs, at musquet-shot distance from each other, and place them in a line across the vast marshes of the country. Each stand, or *hovel,* as they are called, is occupied by only a single person. **1905** *Forestry Bureau Bul.* No. 61, 40 *Hovel,* a stable for logging teams. N[orth] W[oods], [Lake] S[tates Forest].

***How,** *adv.*

+**1.** An interrogative used in asking for the repetition of something not quite understood. *colloq.*

1839 MARRYAT *Diary* II. 34 The English *what?* implying that you did not hear what was said to you, is changed in America to the word *how?* **1858** HOLMES *Autocrat* 88, I was thinking,—he said indistinctly.—How? What is 't?—said our landlady. **1870** 'MARK TWAIN' *Sk., New & Old* 25 'What is that multitude of people gathered in the street for? How?—'looking at the lightning-rods!'

2. *How are you off for* (something)? how well supplied are you with (something)?

1776 C. LEE in Sparks *Corr. Rev.* II. 485 How are you off in the article of intrenching tools? **1848** *R.I. Words* (Bartlett MS.), 'How are you off for money or anything else' simply meant how much have you.

+**How,** *interj.* A word of greeting, assent, willingness, etc.; attributed to Indians or in imitation of their speech: (see also quot. 1911).

1817 BRADBURY *Travels* 95 We were interrupted by one of the chiefs crying 'How,' signifying amongst the Indians 'Come on,' or 'let us begin.' *c***1837** CATLIN *Indians* II. 172 'How! how!' vociferated all of them, thereby approving what was said, giving assent by the word *how,* which is their word for yes. **1867** TROBRIAND *Vie Militaire Dakota* 100 Nous n'échangeons avec la poignée de main que le mot 'Hoe' qui est une expression générale de bienvenue, de salutation et d'approbation. **1884** W. SHEPHERD *Prairie Exper.* 61 Seated round the camp-fire at night, you hear a gruff 'How!' like a bark just behind your back. . . . A red man has walked silently up. **1895** REMINGTON *Pony Tracks* 241 After gaining erectness, they brush the snow from their clothes, borrow a tin cup, and say, 'How! how!' **1911** *N.Y. Ev. Post* 28 Jan. Suppl. 3 The expression 'How,' used by army men in giving a toast, is equivalent to the expression, 'Here's to your health.' Some think it is merely the Indian corruption of 'How d'ye do?' abbreviated by the Indian to 'How.' Others believe the expression is derived from the Indian language direct.

+**Howdy,** *interj.* and *n. S.* A word of greeting, short for 'How do you do?' *colloq.* — **1863** Hopley *Life in South* I. 43 As we passed these people, they greeted my companion thus, 'Oh Mi' Cinta, *how'*dy?' The last word rhymes with rowdy pronounced quickly, and is intended for 'how do you do?' Howdy, being the common salutation of both white and black throughout the South. **1876** *Wide Awake* 150/2 When you come to live up here, I'll send a '*How-dy?*' by her, sometimes. **1905** *N.Y. Ev. Post* 14 Oct., The road was deserted. In 20 miles I met one man who gave me a 'Howdy' as he passed. **1913** Morley *Carolina Mts.* 181 'How-dy' is the usual form of salutation, and the people have the friendly habit, in common with the rustic communities of all civilized countries, of courteously greeting the stranger they may meet.

+**Howdy,** *v. tr.* and *intr.* To address (a person) with *howdy;* to greet. *colloq.* — **1864** Nichols *Amer. Life* I. 387 When people salute each other at meeting, he [the southerner] says they are howdyin' and civilizin' each other. **1884** Harris *Mingo* 138, I'm a-huntin' airter you, an' the business I come on hain't got much howdyin' in it. **1887** *Harper's Mag.* March 545/1, [I] howdyed to him as he sot in his peazzer [=piazza].

Howel. (See quot. 1875.) — **1805** Lewis in *L. & Clark Exped.* II. (1904) 140 To be deposited in this cash: . . . some chissels, a cooper's Howel, some tin cups [etc.]. **1870** *Rep. Comm. Patents 1868* II. 447/1 The howel and croze are so combined that the work of both may be done with one tool. **1875** Knight 1138 *Howel.* (Coopering.) A plane with a convex sole, used for smoothing the insides of barrels and casks.

Howeling. The action of smoothing with a howel. {1883-} Also attrib. — **1847** *Rep. Comm. Patents 1846* 339 What I claim therein as new . . . is the attaching the howeling, crozing, and chamfering cutters. **1850** *Ib. 1849* 386, I also claim the apparatus for chamfering and howelling and crozing. **1870** *Ib. 1868* II. 447/1 The howeling tool . . . may be used without the croze.

Howitz. =next. *Obs.* {1687-1709} — **1777** *Md. Hist. Mag.* V. 225 Their Howitz are now up to the Hubs in Water. **1781** in Sparks *Corr. Revol.* III. 458 Two field-pieces, some howitz, and perhaps a mortar.

Howitzer. Also †**hobitzer.**

1. A kind of light cannon. {1695-} Also transf. (Cf. Mountain howitzer.)

1760 R. Rogers *Journals* 195 Next morning the Light Infantry, . . . with a company of the royal artillery, with two pieces of cannon, and some hobitzers, entered the town. **1761** Niles *Indian Wars* II. 502 Our men . . . opened two batteries, and mounted two 18-pounders, two brass twelves, four sixes, and four royal howitzers of eight inches. **1778** Hamilton *Works* VII. 543 'Tis said he saved . . . four brass howitzers. **1823** James *Exped.* I. 145 The council was opened by a few rounds from the howitzers. **1858** Glisan *Jrnl. Army Life* (1874) 404 The two howitzers were abandoned with the other things. **1895** G. King *New Orleans* 302 The detachment of sailors and marines in United States uniform, . . . preceded by two howitzers, crossed Lafayette square. **1903** 'O. Henry' *Heart of West* 70 If I held her to it she would slide out and round up Uncle Emsley with his . . . hip-pocket howitzer.

2. Attrib. with *ball, drill, mortar.*

1761 Niles *Indian Wars* II. 499 The engineer had but just finished the first batteries of cannon the last night, which were to be mounted, . . . with six 24-pounders and two howitzer mortars. **1839** *S. Lit. Messenger* V. 325/2 Having already in their possession a quantity of howitzer balls, . . . they lost no time. **1886** Dorsey *Midshipman Bob* II. i. 101 A division of the corps were going through howitzer-drill.

Howling wilderness. A bleak, dreary, inhospitable region. {1611}

1680 *Mass. H. S. Coll.* 4 Ser. V. 50 The first-comers hither in the year 1620 . . . [are] willingly conflicting with many grievous difficulties and sufferings in this waste, howling wilderness, amongst wild men and wild beasts. **1761** Niles *Indian Wars* I. 215 They were marching through the vast howling wilderness. **1813** *Niles' Reg.* IV. 33/2 Many hundred miles from our families, in the howling wilderness, we did not continue in a state of indolence. **1893** *Harper's Mag.* May 936/1 If those Dutchmen and Puritans and things who settled the East could have landed out here on the plains, the thirteen original colonies would have been a howling wilderness filled with savages to-day. **1902** White *Conjuror's House* 65 Suppose your eyes—like mine—have rested on nothing but a howling wilderness.

***Hub.**

1. The central part of a wheel; the nave. {1649-}

'Although used by Blithe in 1649, and (from him) by several 17th c. writers, and in Bradley's *Fam. Dict.* 1725 (s.v. *Elm*), this word appears to have been merely dialectal, being unrecognized by the Dictionaries till the 19th c., when it appears first in the American Webster (1828) and Worcester (1846). It has received literary currency mainly from O. W. Holmes, and has recently become generally known in connexion with bicycles. Forby gives under *hob, hub,* "the hilt or guard of a weapon," with which he connects *up to the hub,* "as far as possible"; this phrase is in American use associated with the hub of a wheel, as implying "deeply, to a great extent, inextricably involved"' (*O.E.D.*).

1806 Webster 146/2 *Hub* or *Hob,* the nave of a wheel. **1837** *Harvardiana* III. 237 My squashes are frozen as hard as the hubs of my wagon wheels. **1858** Holmes *Poetical Works* (1895) 159/1 There is always somewhere a weakest spot,—In hub, tire, felloe, in spring or thill. **1897** *Outing* June 279/2 Here are the workmen lacing the spokes into the hubs and putting on the wooden rims. **1907** Andrews *Recoll.* 194 A few wagons had sunk down to their hubs in the sand in some places, and were not up until after dark. **1922** *Automotive Industries* XLVII. 73 A very good example of work on a forged hub . . . is the boring and reaming operation on a hub for the Yellow Cab. Mfg. Co. of Chicago.

2. *To* (or *up to*) *the hub,* to the middle part or nave of a wheel. Usually with reference to miring.

1815 Ticknor in *Life, Lett., & Jrnls.* I. 31 One horse fell, and the carriage, as the phrase is, 'mired up to the hubs.' **1877** Talmage *Sermons* 337 Wild flowers up to the hub of the carriage wheel. **1904** Stratton-Porter *Freckles* 122 We drove away in, and it was dreadful—over stumps and logs, and in to the hubs.

b. *fig.* (See note under 1 above.) *colloq.*

1800 *Aurora* (Phila.) 23 May (Th.), This is not a half measure—I like to do things by the lump—and this bill you will allow is up to the hub. **1827** *Hallowell* (Me.) *Gaz.* 20 June 2/2 Mr. M. H. Wickliffe said, he was a Jackson man up to the hub. **1838** Hone *Diary* I. 323 The Van Buren men have agreed upon a ticket for Congress. Loco-foco to the hub. **1884** 'Mark Twain' *H. Finn* xx. 194, I'm in, up to the hub, for anything that will pay.

+**3.** The State House at Boston, Massachusetts, or the city itself, thought of as being the center of culture and progress. Often in phrases *Hub of the Solar System* (or *Universe*), etc.

1858 Holmes *Autocrat* vi. 143 Boston State-House is the hub of the solar system. **1862** F. Moore *Rebellion Rec.* V. II. 600 One might imagine as he left the metropolis and journeyed eastward toward the 'Hub of the Universe,' he were going away from the action of the centrifugal forces to where the people never went off in tangents, or got excited. **1864** *N.Y. Herald* 5 April 4/5 Codfish aristocracy of 'the Hub.' **1880** *Harper's Mag.* Jan. 317/1 A town within twenty-five miles of the 'Hub.' **1887** George *40 Years on Rail* iv. 62, I soon found the country too far from the 'Hub of the Universe' to suit my tastes.

b. *transf.* Applied to places other than Boston.

1883 *Harper's Mag.* July 263/1 Cincinnati is 'the hub of the universe.' **1887** *Courier-Journal* 8 May 5/3 Take Massachusetts, the 'hub' of free schools, free labor, and boasted intelligence, as a fair representative.

4. *attrib.* **a.** In sense 1 with *auger, band.*

1810 *Austin P.* (1924) I. 168, 10 hub Bands. **1854** *Penna. Agric. Rep.* 363 Hub auger and box setter, H. Sidle, a good article.

b. In sense 3 with *city.*

1861 *Vanity Fair* 13 April 180/2 The appointment of One Palfrey to the postmastership of Boston may be looked upon as a very judicious measure, considering that a single hub city naturally classes as a One-Horse Town.

+**Hubbard squash.** An American squash of the winter variety. Also fig. — **1868** *Mich. Agric. Rep.* VII. 349 Thos. Smith, Hamtramck, [exhibited] 8 Hubbard squashes. **1898** Westcott *D. Harum* xxiii, Turnips, Hubbard squash, succotash. **1918** Lincoln *Shavings* 259 They probably wouldn't [bother] anybody with a head instead of a Hubbard squash on his shoulders.

+**Hubbardston.** Also **Hubbard stone, Hubbardston nonesuch.** [*Hubbardston,* Mass.] A well-known winter apple of superior quality. — **1846** B. Alcott *Journals* 176, I set out six apple trees. . . . They were Hubbard Stone, Nonesuch, Bell Flower, and Hood's Early Sweeting. **1849** *New Eng. Farmer* I. 25 The Hubbardston Nonsuch is one of our best late fall apples. . . . Origin, Hubbardston, Mass. **1868** *Mich. Agric. Rep.* VII. 430 Apples [recommended include] . . . Cooper's Market, Hubbardston Nonsuch, Dominie [etc.]. **1895** A. Brown *Meadow-Grass* 211 The Hubbardston, a portly creature—quite unspoiled by the prosperity of growth, and holding its lovely scent and flavor like an individual charm.

+**Hub(b)ite.** A citizen of Boston, Mass. (Cf. Hub 3.) — **1876** *Wide Awake* 111/1 She has filled the house with a 'picked' party of her friends, nearly all Boston people—Hubites, all of whom, in their own manner of speech, I 'admire' to know. **1877** *Congregationalist* 28 April (*Cent.*), As wide awake as a veritable New Englander, and as a native-born Hubbite.

+**Hubbly,** *a.* Rough, uneven. *colloq.* {hobbly, *dial.*, *a*1825} — *a***1870** Chipman *Notes on Bartlett* 206 *Hubbly.* Said of the surface of ice on roads and streams. . . . N[ew] E[ngland]. **1896** *N.Y. Wkly. Witness* 23 Dec. 4/1 Where the snow had been swept off the ice by the wind, some places were hubbly. **1903** *Springfield Repub.* 9 Oct. 8 Stumbling as over a hubbly field.

+**Hubbub.** (See quot. 1887.) — **1634** Wood *New Eng. Prospect* II. xiv. 85 The Indians . . . have two sorts of games, one called *Puim,* the other *Hubbub,* not much unlike Cards and Dice, being no other than Lotterie. **1764** Hutchinson *Hist. Mass.* I. 470 Another game they call hubbub, the same the French called jeu de plat, the game of the dish among the Hurons. **1887** *Notes & Queries* 11 June 472/2 Hubbub was a game played by the Indians . . . which was accompanied by a continual shouting of 'Hub-hub!' or 'Hubbub!'

+**Hubby,** *a.* (See quot. 1848.) Cf. Hubbly. — **1848** Bartlett 183 *Hubby.* Applied to rough roads, particularly when frozen; as, the road is hubby. **1858** T. Weed in *Autobiography* 18 The dozen journeys I made barefooted over the frozen and 'hubby' road in December.

+**Hub-deep,** *a.* Of mud: Deep enough to cover a wheel up to its hub. — **1833** S. Smith *Major Downing* 192 The longer horses and waggons stand knee and hub deep in mud, the less able they'll be to git out on 't. **1865** *Atlantic Mo.* June 751/1 Wagons went hub-deep in the mud. **1897**

H. PORTER *Campaigning with Grant* xxvi. 415 The mud was nearly hub-deep.

+Huckleberry. (Cf. HURTLEBERRY.)

1. The fruit or berry of any one of various species of *Gaylussacia*, esp. *G. baccata;* also, the bush or shrub which produces this.

See sense 4 for earlier attrib. uses.

1685 BUDD *Penna. & N.J.* 31 Fruits that grow natural in the Countries are Strawberries . . . Huckleberries [etc.]. **1705** BEVERLEY *Virginia* II. 15 There are Three Sorts of Hurts, or Huckleberies, upon Bushes, Two to Ten Foot high. **1791** J. LONG *Voyages* 45 A feast is prepared of dog's flesh boiled in bear's grease, with huckle berries. **1854** THOREAU *Walden* 188 If you would know the flavour of huckleberries, ask the cow-boy or the partridge. **1891** RYAN *Pagan of Alleghanies* 175 A few bushes grew—just a straggle of huckleberries. **1916** THOBURN *Stand. Hist. Okla.* I. 5 Of wild fruits there are a number of species, including plums, . . . huckleberries, currants [etc.].

2. *fig.* and *transf.* A small amount, degree, or extent; something worthless or negligible.

1832 PAULDING *Westward Ho!* I. 182, [I once got] within a huckleberry of being smothered to death. **1889** 'MARK TWAIN' *Conn. Yankee* xxvi, The Saracen . . . is no huckleberry himself. **1920** BOK *Americanization* 165 He always kept 'a huckleberry or two' ahead of his readers.

3. Phrases. **a.** *As thick as huckleberries*, very thick or plentiful.

1833 S. SMITH *Major Downing* 167 Congressmen . . . we shall have them here as thick as huckleberries. **1845** KIRKLAND *Western Clearings* 211 They were as thick as huckleberries.

b. *A huckleberry above* (one's) *persimmon*, (see PERSIMMON).

c. *To be one's huckleberry*, to be particularly suited or adapted to one.

1881 HAYES *New Colorado* v. 68 The first words that we heard him speak settled his nationality, for . . . he sententiously remarked, 'Hi'm 'is 'uckleberry.' **1883** HAY *Bread-Winners* x. 77 Then I'm your huckleberry. **1908** LORIMER *J. Spurlock* 72 If she were looking for a kind, considerate, thoughtful husband . . . you were her huckleberry.

d. *To get the huckleberry*, to be laughed at, to incur ridicule. *slang.*

1883 *Century Mag.* June 280/2 He got the huckleberry, as we used to say in college, on that particular text.

4. Attrib. and comb. with *county, district, field*, etc.

1892 Walsh *Literary Curiosities* 497 A number of persons happened to meet at the store in a village in one of the 'huckleberry counties.' **1867** HOLMES *Guardian Angel* xviii, He became what they call a 'clerk' in what they call a 'store' up in the huckleberry districts. **1878** STOWE *Poganuc People* xix. 211 The pair were well on their way to the huckleberry-field. **1682** *Topsfield Rec.* 40 An Iland Caled hocellbarey Iland. **1864** *Ohio Agric. Rep.* XVIII. 144 We think this is quite an item for the 'huckle berry knobs' of little Jackson. **1751** J. BARTRAM *Observations* 13 The land hereabouts is middling white oak and huckleberry land. **1869** STOWE *Oldtown Folks* 560 Every stick and stone, every sweetbrier-bush and huckleberry patch in Oldtown, will always be dear to me. **1868** *N.Y. Herald* 20 July 4/2 [Mr. Hill gave] an exposition of the principles and purposes of the republican party, as understood among the 'huckleberry' plantations. **1663** *Oyster Bay Rec.* I. 7 Ffrances Weeks have a teen eaker lot at huckelberie poynt. **1845** HOOPER *Simon Suggs' Adv.* vii. 89 He's . . . got the mark of the huckle-berry ponds on his legs yit. **1859** *Harper's Mag.* Nov. 859/1 Last year the Conference sent him [*sc.* a preacher] to the 'Fish Crook' Circuit, a barren, lonely, uncultivated, huckleberry region. **1833** COKE *Subaltern's Furlough* I. 150 My steed . . . carried me safely through the Huckleberry swamps and forest for six miles.

5. Special combinations.

Huckleberry apple, a gallnut found on huckleberry bushes; *h. grunt*, (see quotation); *h. heaven*, an imaginary place of perfect bliss; *h. road*, a railroad facetiously referred to as passing through a region where huckleberries abound; *h. train*, a train supposed to make slow time because of frequent stops to permit passengers to pick huckleberries. *humorous.*

*a***1862** THOREAU *Cape Cod* vii, That kind of gall called Huckleberry-apple. **1918** *Dialect Notes* V. 25 *Huckleberry grunt*, huckleberry dumpling. General in northern Oregon. **1856** W. G. SIMMS *Eaton* 403 He'll make as good a husband for the gal as she'll find 'twixt here and huckleberry heaven. **1871** *Harper's Mag.* Oct. 799/2 A gentleman . . . took the train a few days since on what is termed 'the huckleberry road,' running between Avon and Mount Morris. **1901** MERWIN-WEBSTER *Calumet 'K'* xv. 296 You'd have thought he was running a huckleberry train from the time he took.

+Huckleberry bush. Any one of various American shrubs or bushes of the genus *Gaylussacia.* — **1846** THORPE *Myst. Backwoods* 182 [A 'cat'] instantly leaped to the ground from a height of over forty feet, . . . throwing a sort of rough somerset, and then starting off as sound in limb and wind as if he had leaped off a 'huckleberry' bush. **1867** 'LACKLAND' *Homespun* I. 67, I remember . . . how we used to . . . secure them [the leaves] with little twigs of the huckleberry bush. **1894** *Harper's Mag.* March 524/2 He would move round the campfire like a cub bear around a huckleberry bush.

+Huckleberry hill. A hill upon which huckleberries abound. — **1749** *N.H. Probate Rec.* III. 751 The Remender . . . is to be Made up from the Marked pine tree on the fare Huckellberry hill streght to the head of Allon Andorsons uper Meadow. **1854** THOREAU *Walden* 126 All the Indian huckleberry hills are stripped, all the cranberry meadows are raked into the city. **1865** WHITTIER *Poetical Works* (1895) 404/1 Dread Olympus at his will Became a huckleberry hill.

+Huckleberrying. The seeking or gathering of huckleberries; an outing devoted to this purpose. — **1779** *Narragansett Hist. Reg.* I. 92 Went huckleberring [*sic*]. **1834** C. A. DAVIS *Lett. J. Downing* 324, I went out huckleberryin, and not bein very particular, I suppose I eat a leetle too many on 'em. **1884** ROE *Nature's Story* 336 A party of children who were out huckleberrying on the mountain were separated from home by the swollen brook.

+Huckleberry pasture. A tract of comparatively poor land overgrown with huckleberry bushes. Also *huckleberry pasture lot.* — **1854** LOWELL *Writings* I. 70 The greater part of what is now Cambridgeport was then (in the native dialect) a 'huckleberry pastur.' **1860** HOLMES *E. Venner* iv, There were huckleberry-pastures on the lower flanks of The Mountain. **1871** STOWE *Sam Lawson* 179 It all comes back to me again,—the image of that huckleberry-pasture. **1878** — *Poganuc People* xiv. 157 Widder Brown . . . lives up by the huckleberry pastur'-lot.

+Huckleberry pie. A pie made of huckleberries. — **1775** FITHIAN *Journal* II. 68 We have . . . boil'd potatoes, & huckleberry-pie. **1867** G. W. HARRIS *Sut Lovingood* 120 Yu cud onkiver a huckleberry pie wif a case-knife. **1888** GRIGSBY *Smoked Yank* xiii, Right this way for your ham and eggs with johnny-cake, and huckleberry pie for dessert.

+Huckleberry pudding. A pudding made of huckleberries. — **1828** NEAL *R. Dyer* 210 You'll never eat another huckleberry-puddin' in this world. **1845** *Knickerb.* XXVI. 367 After making a hurried dinner on roast mutton, boiled ham, huckleberry pudding, and a few apple tarts, I departed. **1857** UNDERHILL & THOMPSON *Elephant Club* 235 His complexion bore a close resemblance to the outside of a huckleberry-pudding.

***Huckster. 1.** A hawker or peddler, usually of provisions. **2.** Attrib. with *shop, wagon, woman.* — **(1) 1682** *Boston Rec.* 154 A complaint was exhibited to the inhabitants against Lindall & others did as Hucksters forestale ye market by goeinge out into ye necke . . . to buy vp the provisions . . . & the[n] sell the same againe at extraordinary deare rates. **1798** *Phila. Ordinances* (1812) 157 No person who follows the business of a huckster, or of selling provisions . . . at second hand, shall . . . sell . . . within the limits of the market, any provisions. **1843** 'CARLTON' *New Purchase* II. 291 Will not he who feasts like Homer's heroes despise the meannesses of a huckster's life? **1923** WATTS *L. Nichols* 19 The hucksters they got to have a license because they drive round an' wear out th' roads, I guess? **(2) 1827** J. L. WILLIAMS *West Florida* 10 A cargo of spoiled codfish arrived from Havana, and was distributed among the little huckster-shops along the bay. **1845** *Indiana Mag. Hist.* XXIII. 180, I have myself seen as many as fourteen huckster wagons at one camp meeting. **1846** MAGOFFIN *Down Santa Fé Trail* (1926) 90 [The rancheros] are like the huxter-women after a steamboat.

+Huddup! *interj.* Get up! A word of command to a horse. — **1858** HOLMES *Poetical Works* (1895) 160/1 'Huddup!' said the parson.—Off went they. **1891** COOKE *Huckleberries* (1896) 329 Huddup, Whitey!

Hudsonian, *a.* In the specific names of North American birds: (see quotations and see also HUDSONIAN GODWIT). — **1858** BAIRD *Birds Pacific R.R.* 744 *Numenius Hudsonicus.* Short-billed or Hudsonian Curlew. . . . Atlantic and Pacific coasts of North America. **1887** RIDGWAY *Manual N.A. Birds* 564 *P[arus] hudsonicus.* Hudsonian Chickadee. **1917** *Birds of Amer.* II. 116 American Hawk Owl *Surnia ulula caparoch.* . . . Other Names.— . . . Canadian Owl, Hudsonian Owl. *Ib.* 169 Pipit *Anthus rubescens.* . . . Other Names.—American Pipit; . . . Hudsonian Wagtail; Brown Lark.

+Hudsonian godwit. The American black-tailed godwit, *Limosa haemastica.* — **1835** AUDUBON *Ornith. Biog.* III. 426 The Hudsonian Godwit, *Limosa Hudsonica*, . . . is scarcely ever found farther south along the coast than the State of Maryland. **1874** COUES *Birds N.W.* 494 *Limosa Hudsonica*, Hudsonian or Black-tailed Godwit. **1917** *Birds of Amer.* I. 240 Hudsonian Godwit. *Limosa hæmastica.* . . . North and South America.

+Hudson River red antwerp. A variety of raspberry: (see quot.). — **1862** *Rep. Comm. Patents 1861: Agric.* 167 On the Hudson river fields are planted with a variety of the Red Antwerp, which has received its American cognomen from that stream, the Hudson River Red Antwerp.

+Hudson River sea horse. (See quotation.) — **1842** *Nat. Hist. N.Y., Zoology* IV. 322 The Hudson-river Sea-horse. *Hippocampus hudsonius.* . . . We believe that the animals of this genus stand alone among the fishes, in having a prehensile tail.

Hudson's Bay. *attrib.* **1.** In the names of birds and animals associated with the region about Hudson Bay. **2.** In the names of articles sold by the Hudson's Bay Co. or similar articles. — **(1) 1826** GODMAN *Nat. Hist.* II. 138 The Hudson's Bay Squirrel . . . is very common in the northern and western parts of this Country. **1839** PEABODY *Mass. Birds* 402 The Hudson Bay Titmouse, *Parus Hudsonicus*, . . . has been found . . . in Brookline. **(2) 1888** SHERIDAN *Memoirs* I. 61 The fugitive was armed with only an old Hudson's Bay flint-lock horse-pistol which could not be discharged. *a***1918** G. STUART *On Frontier* I. 241 We bought four fine Hudson's Bay shirts from him @ $3.00 each.

Hugag. Variant of HEWGAG.

+**Huge Paw.** (See quot. 1848.) *Obs.* — **1839** *Eastern Argus* (Portland, Me.) 24 Sept. 2/3 (Th.), How do you account for this, Mr. Huge Paw? **1846** *N.Y. Herald* 7 Oct. (B.), The huge paws ought to have another meeting at Tammany Hall before they make their nominations. **1848** *Bartlett* 183 *Huge Paws*, a nickname given to the working-men of the Loco Foco party in New York.

+**Hug-me-tight. 1.** A close-fitting vest. **2.** A buggy having a narrow seat barely sufficient for two passengers. Also attrib. — **(1) 1860** *Godey's Lady's Bk.* Dec. 544 Hug me tight. A garment to be worn under a cloak. **1869** ALCOTT *Little Women* II. 68 She . . . used to . . . demand . . . the meaning of a hug-me-tight, or wonder how a little thing composed of three rosebuds, a bit of velvet and a pair of strings, could possibly be a bonnet. **1910** *N.Y. Ev. Post* 24 Dec. Suppl. 3 Hug-me-tights and mittens, all knit at home by grandmother. **(2) 1901** HARBEN *Westerfelt* 6, I seed 'em takin' a ride in his new hug-me-tight buggy yesterday. **1902** — *A. Daniel* 42 He's got a new buggy—a regular hug-me-tight.

+**Huisache.** [Sp. from Nahuatl *huixachin.*] A thorny shrub (*Vachellia farnesiana*) found in the southern states. — **1892** *Dialect Notes* I. 190 *Huisache* (also *huaji, guaje*): a small tree or shrub with very sweet smelling yellow flowers (*Acacia Farnesiana*). From Mexican *huaxin.* [Texas.] **1898** CANFIELD *Maid of Frontier* 204 The huisache bore yellow blossoms faintly sweet.

+**Hulled corn.** (See quot. 1877.) — **1805** *Pocumtuc Housewife* (1906) 36. **1877** BARTLETT 302 *Hulled Corn.* Indian corn scalded or boiled in lye, until the hulls come off. It is then rinsed and boiled, making a most palatable dish. **1881** MCLEAN *Cape Cod Folks* vii. 137 After the season of hulled corn, came the reign of baked beans. **1904** WALLER *Wood-Carver* 136 Twiddie rushed in with . . . a bowl of fresh hulled-corn.

Humane society. An organization attempting to alleviate suffering. {1776–}

The earliest American humane societies, founded in Philadelphia (1780) and Boston (1786), were modeled on the Royal Humane Society of London (1774), and concerned themselves with matters of health and especially the prevention of drowning. More recently the name has been applied to organizations encouraging the kind treatment of animals.

*c***1786** (*title*) The Institution of the Humane Society of the Commonwealth of Massachusetts. **1787** in W. P. Young *Palladium of Knowledge*, Directions for recovering persons supposed to be dead. Published by the Humane Society of Philadelphia. **1795** in Kittredge *Old Farmer* (1904) 162 Directions for recovering persons apparently dead from drowning; as recommended by the Humane Society. **1824** *New Eng. Farmer* II. 311 The Trustees of the Humane Society have awarded twenty dollars to James S. Cade. **1883** PECK *Bad Boy* 183 A man who will take a poor kitty by the neck . . . ought to be looked after by the humane society. **1904** KITTREDGE *Old Farmer* 163 The Massachusetts Humane Society . . . was one of the earliest charitable associations founded in this part of the world. It was instituted in 1785, definitely organized in the next year, . . . and incorporated in 1791.

+**Humbird.** =HUMMING BIRD: (see also quot. 1871). — **1634** WOOD *New Eng. Prospect* I. viii. 28 The Humbird is one of the wonders of the Countrey, being no bigger than a Hornet. **1687** BLOME *Isles & Terr. in Amer.* 235 Here are great variety of Fowls, as Pheasants, . . . the Humbird. **1806** *Mass. Spy* 1 Jan. (Th.), Rattlesnakes are frequent and humbirds common in New England. **1871** DE VERE 377 The tiny *Mango* Humming-bird (*Trochilus colubris*) . . . is known familiarly . . . as *Humbird* or *Hummer* simply. **1891** COOKE *Huckleberries* (1896) 167, I never see a humbird fuller o' buzz.

***Humblebee.** =BUMBLEBEE. — **1743** CATESBY *Carolina* II. p. xxxvii, The particular genus's [of insects] I observed in Carolina [include] . . . The Humble-bee. **1781** PETERS *Hist. Connecticut* 260 The Humble-bee is almost as large as the humming-bird. **1876** WHITMAN *Specimen Days* (1892) 85 All have done much for me, and still do. But for the last two days it has been the great wild bee, the humble-bee, or 'bumble,' as the children call him.

Humhum. A coarse cotton cloth imported from India. *Obs.* {hammome, 1620; hummum, 1687–96} — **1745** in J. F. Watson *Philadelphia* 179 Quilted humhums, turkettees, grassetts, single allopeens [etc.]. **1790** *Penna. Packet* 19 Oct. 3/2 Richard and James Potter are rapidly disposing of their . . . Humhums. **1801** in Cist *Cincinnati* (1841) 179 Among other goods . . . humhums. **1820** *Massachusetts Spy* 5 Jan. (Th.), Our fine twilled linen shall be as much superior to the bleach rotted linen . . . imported, or the sleazy humhum, as they are to a cobweb.

***Humility.** +Any one of several snipe found on the New England coast. — **1634** W. WOOD *New Eng. Prospect* (1635) 26 The Humilities or Simplicities (as I may rather call them) bee of two sorts, the biggest being as big as a greene Plover, the other as big as birds we call Knots in England. **1832** WILLIAMSON *Hist. Maine* I. 149 The *Humility* [*Tringa interpres*] has long yellow legs, long neck, is gray spotted, . . . and is nearly as large as a pigeon. **1870** *Amer. Naturalist* III. 638 Black-necked Stilt . . . is well known to the gunners of Ipswich, who occasionally meet with it, and by whom it is ironically named 'Humility.'

Hummel. {hommels, *dial.*, 1876} (See quot. 1856.) *colloq.*² *Obs.* — **1856** HALL *College Words* (ed. 2) 261 *Hummel.* At the University of Vermont, a foot, especially a large one. **1894** R. E. ROBINSON *Danvis Folks* 42, I'd ruther be shakin' my hummels tu this sort of a jig.

Hummer. {1605–} +=HUMMING BIRD: (see also quot. 1871). — **1871** DE VERE 377 The tiny *Mango* Humming-bird (*Trochilus colubris*) . . . [is] known familiarly . . . as *Hum-bird* or *Hummer* simply. **1874** COUES *Birds N.W.* 269 The Hummers constitute a very large family of very small birds. **1881** *Harper's Mag.* June 27/2 Both male and female hummers come with their strange, eccentric manners under my daily notice. **1917** *Birds of Amer.* II. 181/1 The distinctive fact about this Hummer [Rivoli's humming bird] is that it doesn't hum.

+**Humming bird.** Any one of various American birds of the family Trochilidae, noted for their small size and brilliant plumage. {1657–}

1637 MORTON *New Canaan* 73 There is a curious bird to see to, called a hunning [*sic*] bird, no bigger then a great Beetle. **1672** JOSSELYN *N.E. Rarities* 6 The Humming Bird, the least of all Birds, little bigger than a Dor. **1709** LAWSON *Carolina* 145 The Humming-Bird is the Miracle of all our wing'd Animals. **1789** MORSE *Amer. Geog.* 61 The Humming-bird is the smallest of all the feathered inhabitants of the air. **1858** BAIRD *Birds Pacific R.R.* 129 There is no group of birds so interesting to the ornithologist or to the casual observer as the humming birds . . . almost the most abundant in species of any single family of birds. **1874** COUES *Birds N.W.* 270 Wilson knew but one North America Humming-bird. . . . In 1872 I was able to recognize eleven species. **1917** *Birds of Amer.* II. 181/2 Many years ago it was established beyond a doubt that the diet of Humming-birds consists largely of insects.

+**Humming-bird moth.** (See quot. 1899.) — **1850** S. F. COOPER *Rural Hours* 202 The whole tribe of hawk-moths are now sometimes called humming-bird moths, from these same insects. **1854** EMMONS *Agric. N.Y.* V. 217 The hummingbird moths, or sphinges, fly in the early morning, or in the dusk of evening, when they visit the gardens. **1899** *Animal & Plant Lore* 63 Humming-bird moth, any large sphinx moth, family *Sphingidæ.* General in the United States.

***Hummock.** Also **hom(m)ock, homok.**

+**1.** A tract of land somewhat higher than an adjacent marsh, swamp, creek, etc., and usually well wooded. Often with special reference to Florida. (Cf. HAMMOCK².)

1635 *Boston Rec.* 9 There stands 3 homocks, with pyne trees upon the south side of the marsh neare the water. **1684** *Southold Rec.* II. 60 His meadow and broken homoks of land lying against the mill pond. **1716** *Narragansett Hist. Reg.* IV. 168 For the hummock by the watering place, to John Briggs, . . . £5. **1766** in Darlington *Memorials Bartram & Marshall* 438, I thrice visited the River St. John, often landed upon each shore, exploring the swamps and hummocks, pine barrens, and sand barrens. **1840** IRVING in *Knickerb.* Oct. 339 When Florida was ceded by the Spaniards to the English, the Indians generally retired . . . [into the] intricate swamps and hommocks, and vast savannahs of the interior. **1883** C. F. ADAMS in *Prince Soc. Publ.* XIV. 11 Tradition still points out a small savin-covered hummock . . . as his [an Indian's] subsequent dwelling-place.

+**2.** *W.* A portion of land, usually inferior in fertility, higher than the surrounding prairie.

1869 *Overland Mo.* III. 130 There is the 'chocolate' prairie, . . . the 'hummock,' (yielding principally small honey-locusts) and the 'wire-grass.' **1870** KEIM *Sheridan's Troopers* 133 The plain . . . [was] covered with a number of hummocks of red earth and gravel. **1919** L. F. CODY *Buffalo Bill* 325 Below can be seen . . . the hills of Colorado and hummocks of Wyoming.

+**Hummock land.** =HAMMOCK LAND. — **1812** STODDARD *Sk. Louisiana* 123 Hummock land . . . rises in tufts or small mounts among the pines. **1883** SMITH *Geol. Survey Ala.* 21 These Second Bottom deposits, or hummock lands, are always above overflow, and vary in thickness from sixty feet and upwards in the central parts of the State, to less than ten near the gulf.

Hump, *n.* **1.** The protuberance on the back of a buffalo. {1774–} Used for food. {1807–} (Cf. BUFFALO HUMP.) +**2.** *To get a hump on*, to move fast. *colloq.* — **(1) 1779** *Travels Amer. Col.* 627 The hump or that remarkable rising on the shoulders of a Buffalo is formed by the Spiral Processes of the nine first Vertebrae of the back gradually rising in hight from the ninth to the third. **1806** LEWIS in *L. & Clark Exped.* V. (1905) 206 We killed a buffaloe cow as we passed throug[h] the plains and took the hump and tonge which furnish ample rations for four men one day. **1862** *Harper's Mag.* Sept. 461/2 Certain moving objects in the distance revived my buffalo fever, and awoke . . . a longing for 'hump steaks.' **1865** PIKE *Scout & Ranger* (1932) 56 We took nothing but the humps and a few tongues, leaving the remainder as a feast for wolves. **(2) 1892** *Harper's Mag.* Feb. 487/2 'We went fast enough then.' 'We do seem to be gittin' a leetle less hump on oursel's than we did then.'

Hump, *v.* {1840–} +*tr.* and *intr.* To hurry or hasten; to put forth one's best efforts. Usually with *it*, or reflexively. *colloq.*

*c***1845** *Big Bear Ark.* 126 He was breathin' sorter hard, his eye set on the Governor, humpin' himself on politics. **1848** RUXTON *Life Far West* ix, Now, you all go right ahead—Every one of you hump it. **1870** 'MARK TWAIN' *Sk., New & Old* 24 This iron being . . . said 'he would now proceed to hump himself.' **1884** — *H. Finn* xxix. 307, I never hunted for no back streets, but humped it straight through the main one. **1897** *Advance* 25 Feb. 263/1 Young man, take hold, hang on and hump. **1908** LORIMER *J. Spurlock* v. 92 Back to Broadway for yours, Ferdinand, and hump yourself.

transf. **1882** BAILLIE-GROHMAN *Camp in Rockies* 57 'That yar white powder as makes bread git up and hump itself,' as an old trapper called it. **1896** *N.Y. Wkly. Witness* 2 Dec., Would make the liver hump and get, This sulphur and molasses.

Humpback. {1697–}

+**1.** Any one of various whales of the genus *Megaptera.* See also HUMPBACKED *a.*

1725 DUDLEY in *Phil. Trans.* XXXIII. 258 Both the Finbacks and Humpbacks are shaped in Reeves longitudinal from Head to Tail on their Bellies and their Sides. **1782** CRÈVECŒUR *Letters* 169 The following are the names . . . of the various species of whales known to these people: . . . The hump-backs, on the coast of Newfoundland [etc.]. **1832** WILLIAMSON *Maine* I. 164 Such [whales] as we now see, are the *Humpback,* which are the most common, . . . severally yielding from 15 to 25 barrels of oil. **1867** *Amer. Naturalist* I. 224 Among the Humpbacks, the females exceed the males in size.

+**2.** A species of salmon, *Oncorhynchus gorbuscha.*

1881 *Amer. Naturalist* XV. 182 The hump-back, taken in salt water about Seattle, shows the same peculiarities. **1891** *Fur, Fin, & Feather* 151 The salmon most plentiful in the Alaska waters is known as the hump-back or garbusche.

3. *attrib.* In the names of fishes and whales. (Cf. HUMPBACKED *a.*)

1844 LEE & FROST *Oregon* 92 In the month of January following, two large hump-back whales were driven ashore in the same vicinity. **1881** *Amer. Naturalist* XV. 177 The fact that the hump-back salmon runs only on alternate years in Puget sound . . . is well attested. **1911** *Rep. Fisheries 1908* 318 The common whitefish . . . is found in the Great Lakes region and is known as 'humpback,' 'bowback,' and 'highback' whitefish.

Humpbacked, *a.* {1681–} In the names of fishes and whales: (see quotations and cf. HUMPBACK 3). — **1816** *Niles' Reg.* X. 199/1 On the 26th of March, two hump-backed whales were killed and caught by the crew of two boats. **1884** GOODE, etc. *Fisheries* I. 323 The Blunt-nosed Shiner . . . is a frequent summer visitor all along the coast as far north as Wood's Holl, Massachusetts, where it has a peculiar name . . . the 'Hump-backed Butterfish.' **1896** JORDAN & EVERMANN *Check-List Fishes* 241 *Xyrauchen cypho.* Razor-back Sucker; Hump-backed Sucker.

+**Hump rib.** One of the ribs to which the hump of a buffalo grows. Also transf. — **1846** W. G. STEWART *Altowan* II. ii. 92 The cry for 'hump ribs' succeeded a horn of brandy. **1848** BRYANT *California* vii. 96 The choice pieces of a fat cow, are . . . the hump-ribs; and . . . the 'marrow-gut.' **1850** GARRARD *Wah-To-Yah* ix. 123 Perchance astonishing with the recital of the number of 'Yutes' whose 'humpribs' have been savagely tickled.

Hunch. {1630–} A hint; an intuitive premonition. *colloq.*[2] {1901–} — **1899** ADE *Fables in Slang* (1902) 123 She didn't know how to make a Showing, and there was nobody in Town qualified to give her a quiet Hunch. **1907** LONDON *Road* 74, I had a 'hunch' that Niagara Falls was a 'bad' town for hoboes. **1924** CROY *R. F. D. No.* 3 154 The idea just struck me all of a sudden. It's queer how a fellow gets such hunches, isn't it?

* **Hundred.** +In some colonies and states, a small political division of a county: (see quot. 1914).

1621 in Stith *Hist. Virginia* App. iv. 33 The other council . . . shall consist for the present, of the said council of state, and of two burgesses out of every town, hundred, or other particular plantation. **1695** *Md. Hist. Mag.* I. 8 Ordered that the Justices of each hundred enquire into their respective hundreds who will be purchasers of the late Court house and land adjoining. **1723** *Amer. Wkly. Mercury* 7–14 Nov. 4/2 Run away the 5th of this Instant November, from William Hugh of White-Clay Creek Hundred, in the County of New-Castle, a Servant Man. **1815** *Niles' Reg.* IX. 92/1 The upper or most northern county, is divided into nine hundreds. **1896** P. A. BRUCE *Econ. Hist. Va.* I. 210 At certain intervals . . . houses were put up, the occupants of which formed a guard . . . for the population of the Hundreds. **1914** *Cycl. Amer. Govt.* II. 136/2 Hundreds were established in the colonies of Maryland and Delaware; and the name appears in the early records of Virginia and Maine. In Delaware the principal subdivisions of the counties are still called hundreds.

attrib. **1723** *Huntington Rec.* II. 351 It was voated and agreed to Rais 6 shillings on Each hundred Right in or belonging to this town.

***Hungarian,** *a.* Of a kind or sort found in or resembling that of Hungary. — **1850** MITCHELL *Lorgnette* I. 53 The Hungarian balsam is in new demand. **1855** BROWNE in *Trans. Amer. Inst. N.Y.* 590 White Hungarian wheat, (*blé blanc de Hongrie,* of the French,) [introduced] from the south of France, . . . well deserves a trial in this country. **1891** WELCH *Recoll. 1830–40* 183 Slouch hats, of wool, did not come into use here until the would-be liberator of Hungary, Kossuth's, visit to the country early in the fifties. The Kossuth, or Hungarian hats, were worn here [in Buffalo, N.Y.] with ostrich feather. **1895** *Dept. Agric. Yrbk.* 1894 425 This method is applicable to turf formers, also used to hold embankments, such as couch grass, Hungarian brome, Johnson grass, and Bermuda grass.

Hungarian grass. 1. =BENGAL GRASS. **2.** Attrib. with *crop, seed.* — **(1) 1861** *Ill. Agric. Soc. Trans.* IV. 319 Hungarian grass is a sure preventive. **1881** *Rep. Indian Affairs* 88 Millet and Hungarian grass, as it is called, seemed, from the short period of maturing, to afford the best promise of success. **1883** *Ib.* 23 About 12 acres were planted with Hungarian grass, from which 24 tons of hay was cut. **(2) 1863** *Mich. Statute* I. (1882) 447 Fifty pounds for a bushel of millet or Hungarian grass seed. **1864** *Ohio Agric. Rep.* XVIII. p. xxvi, Every farmer, almost, undertakes to grow . . . potatoes, turnips, sorgho, and some add to these tobacco, broom-corn, and Hungarian grass crops.

+**Hunk,** *n.*[1] [Du. *honk,* 'goal.'] In games, a goal or place of safety. *Obs.* — **1848** BARTLETT 185 *Hunk.* (Dutch, *honk.*) A goal, or place of refuge. A word much used by New York boys in their play.

+**Hunk,** *n.*[2] (See quotation.) *slang.* — **1896** *N.Y. Herald* 13 Jan. 3/4 The average Pennsylvanian contemptuously refers to these immigrants as 'Hikes' and 'Hunks.' The 'Hikes' are Italians and Sicilians. 'Hunks' is a corruption for Huns, but under this title the Pennsylvanian includes Hungarians, Lithuanians, Slavs, Poles, Magyars and Tyroleans.

+**Hunk,** *a.* =HUNKY. *colloq.* (Cf. HUNK *n.*[1]) — **1847** FIELD *Drama in Pok.* 50 'I've doated on roast pig ever since I read that chawming paper [by Lamb].' 'Well, I allow you're just *hunk,* this time, then,' interposed Mrs. Wilson, 'for we've got the sweetest roaster for dinner you ever did see!' **1856** *N.Y. Tribune* 30 Dec. (B.), Now he felt himself all hunk, and wanted to get this enormous sum out of the city. **1903** LEWIS *Boss* 181 'Do you approve my proposition?' . . . 'The proposition's all hunk.'

+**Hunker.**

1. A member of the conservative element of the Democratic party in New York State *c*1840–1850. Now hist. (Cf. OLD HUNKER.)

1843 in Weed *Autobiog.* 553 Let the 'Hunkers' and 'Barn-burners' contend. **1853** *Knickerb.* XLII. 653 What and who entered into the contest? . . . 'Hunkers' and 'Barnburners' in 'flocks,' carefully tended by their various shepherds. **1884** BLAINE *20 Years of Congress* I. 84 The result of the two contests left the Van Buren wing . . . in majority over the Hunkers. **1909** *N.Y. Ev. Post* 1 Nov., In 1847 Tammany, weakened by the factional fight between Hunkers and Barnburners, was defeated by the Whig candidate.

b. *transf.* A member of a similar party in another state; a conservative.

1849 *N.Y. Ev. Post* 11 July (B.), He is now the leader of the hunkers of Missouri. **1864** *Boston Commonw.* 3 June, The judge, a white-haired old man, well preserved, and a stickler for law and precedent and a 'hunker.'

2. Attrib. with *Democrat, majority.*

1848 *Whig Almanac 1849* 9/1 At the Syracuse Convention . . . one of the last acts was the laying on the table by the Hunker majority a resolution proposed by the Barnburners which affirmed the principle of the Wilmot Proviso. **1884** R. GRANT *Average Man* 225, I'm a Hunker Democrat, and Stoughton's a Dyed-in-the-wool Republican.

+**Hunkerish,** *a.* [f. prec.] Old-fashioned; conservative; old-fogyish. *colloq.* — **1857** *Lawrence* (Kan.) *Repub.* 2 July 3 This has in times past, been considered rather a hunkerish neighborhood. **1888** W. LAWRENCE *A. A. Lawrence* 139 His Kansas experience did not move Mr. Lawrence from his hunkerish sympathies in politics. **1905** *Springfield W. Repub.* 8 Sept. 1 Intelligent forward movements in legislation are met and hampered by the hunkerish conservatism which Mr. Cannon and the Senate stand for.

+**Hunkerism.** The political philosophy of the Hunkers; extreme conservatism. — **1859** HOLLAND *Gold Foil* xviii. 219 The 'fogyism' and 'hunkerism' of politics. **1865** S. ANDREWS *South since War* (1866) 186 The cold hunkerism of this people, however, stands immovably in his way, and gives him [*sc.* the Negro] little chance. **1906** *Springfield W. Repub.* 6 Dec. 8 Thus does the president compromise in his advanced position with the old republican hunkerism.

+**Hunky,** *a.* Also **hunkey.** [Cf. HUNK *a.*] Safe; all right; fine; first-rate. Often *all hunky. colloq.*

1861 'ARTEMUS WARD' in *Vanity Fair* 15 June 273/1 He (Moses) folded her to his hart, with the remark that he was 'a hunkey boy.' **1868** CHADWICK *Base Ball* 36 The moment he sets foot on third base he is what the boys call 'hunky,' that is, 'he's at home.' **1878** HARTE *Drift from Two Shores* 38 North . . . ventured to ask how the child was doing. . . . 'She's all hunky, and has an appetite.' **1894** 'MARK TWAIN' *Those Twins* vii, We're all hunky, after all. **1902** MCFAUL *Ike Glidden* iii. 21 If yer hit right you're all right an hunky, but if yer hit wrong why there yer be.

+**Hunky-dory,** *a.* Also **hunkidori.** Fine; first-rate; quite to one's liking. Also in phrases. *colloq.* — **1868** in Odell *Annals N.Y. Stage* VIII. 390 [Even Samuel Slater admitted that Tostee, when and if she sang, was] hunky-dory. **1875** BURNHAM *Three Years* 66 He was all 'hunky-dory,' in certain quarters. **1894** CLARK *On Cloud Mt.* 137 'Oh, *we're* hunkidori in a box!' declared the bridegroom. **1894** WISTER in *Harper's Mag.* April 784/2 You're all right, and the spot is hunky-dory, and it's the durned old boat hez made the mistake. **1913** LONDON *Valley of Moon* III. iv, 'It's all hunkydory,' he called as he approached.

* **Hunt,** *v.*

+**1.** *tr.* To seek (land) suitable for settling upon.

1818 E. P. FORDHAM *Narrative of Travels* 221 The next day I shall cross the Little Wabash to 'hunt land.' **1834** *Visit to Texas* i. 10 An old Tennessean and his wife with their sons . . . were going 'to hunt land' as the familiar term is for exploring new regions, for a place to form a settlement.

2. *To hunt up,* to seek for, to go in quest of. {1844–}

1741 *S.C. Hist. Soc. Coll.* IV. 33 The general . . . sent out the Indians to hunt up the Spanish Horses and Cattell. **1792** *Ann. 2d Congress* 1146 Colonel Trotter marched on the morning of the 18th October . . . in order to hunt up Indian camps. **1847** DRAKE *Pioneer Life Ky.* iii. 43, I was sent out to hunt up the cow. **1900** *Congress. Rec.* 22 Jan. 1036/2 He is usually hunting up a point on somebody.

+**3.** *To hunt one's bed* (or *blanket*), to retire, go to bed. *colloq.*

1891 RYAN *Told in Hills* 309 All were sleepy enough to hunt beds early. **1903** A. ADAMS *Log Cowboy* iii. 38 Flood . . . suggested that all hands hunt their blankets and turn in for the night.

Hunt club. A club made up of those interested in hunting. Also attrib. — **1886** LODGE in *Century Mag.* July 342/1 In Livingston county, New York, in the valley of the Genesee, from which it takes its name, there is a hunt-club. **1894** *Harper's Mag.* June 157/1 He is working on the Hunt Club ball committee. **1895** *Century Mag.* Aug. 625/1 Hitherto the hunting has been done individually. Now hunt clubs are being formed.

* **Hunter.** One who hunts; a huntsman. Also attrib.

1692 *Lancaster Rec.* 130, I am advised yt Lancaster hunters have lately seen a company of Indians near Wachusett. **1704** *Boston News-Letter* 3 July 1/2 Peace is made with the Maqua's in the Pardon which the King has a second time given the Hunters. **1807** GASS *Journal* 23 The hunters killed five deer and caught two beaver. **1818** SCHOOLCRAFT *Journal* 43 We are now at the last hunter-settlement on the river. . . . It consists of two families, Holt and Fisher by name. **1821** BRYANT *Poetical Works* (1903) 38 Then came the hunter tribes, and thou didst look, For ages, on their deeds in the hard chase. **1841** THOREAU *Journal* 25 April, When the flicker's cackle is heard in the clearings, the musing hunter is reminded that civilization has imported nothing into them. **1897** ALLEN *Choir Invis.* ii, A grave, proud Chickasaw hunter . . . strode by with inward grief and shame, wounded by the robbery of his people.

b. =BEE-HUNTER.

1830 RAY *Letter*, Our hunter brings us plenty of honey, which he gets from the *'honey-trees.'* **1887** *Century Mag.* Jan. 443/1 The hunters set out shortly after breakfast, Mr. Wimpy, besides his professional tackle, carrying the biggest bucket for the spoil.

Hunter spider. The tarantula. — **1867** *Amer. Naturalist* I. 409 This very large hunter-spider makes its appearance in Texas some years as early as the twenty-fifth of May.

* **Hunting.**

* **1.** The action of taking or pursuing game.

For eighteenth-century examples see A-HUNTING.

1627 *Plymouth Laws* 30 That fowling fishing and hunting be free. **1787** S. S. SMITH *Ess. Complexion* 16 The Anglo-Americans on the frontiers of the states, who acquire their sustenance principally by hunting. **1818** SCHOOLCRAFT *Journal* 40 Schools, learning, and religion are alike unknown. Hunting is the principal, most honourable, and the most profitable employment. **1895** *Century Mag.* Aug. 625/1 Hunting in Southern fashion requires a genius for leisure. **1921** *Outing* Feb. 212/3 We discovered during the course of our hunting that a portage . . . would bring us to the shores of another lake.

2. *attrib.* and *comb.* **a.** Undertaken or set out upon for the purpose of hunting.

1837 IRVING *Bonneville* I. 238 It was not in the plan of the present hunting campaign to go near the *caches* on Green River. **1856** M. J. HOLMES *L. Rivers* xxvi. 282 He had gone off on a hunting excursion. **1846** SAGE *Scenes Rocky Mts.* xii, A hunting expedition that included my self with six others. **1674** *Mass. H. S. Coll.* 1 Ser. I. 156 Sundry of our Indians, in their hunting journeys, converse and traffick with those Indians. **1866** *Rep. Indian Affairs* 293 Nearly all the Indians who were able made their usual hunting tours. **1805** *Ann. 9th Congress* 2 Sess. 1102, I set off . . . in company with a party of young Indian men, . . . on a hunting voyage, and to procure horses.

b. Of or pertaining to hunting.

1846 FARNHAM *Prairie Land* 345 Their hunting-dances are no more seen at evening! **1837** IRVING *Bonneville* I. 113 The two hunters cooked, and ate again and again, until, perfectly gorged, they sank to sleep before their hunting fire. **1745** BRAINERD *Journal* (1902) 104 It was supposed a great part of their [*sc.* Indians'] hunting lands was much endangered, and might speedily be taken from them. **1821** NUTTALL *Trav. Arkansa* 167 The cane brake . . . we here crossed by a hunting path. **1775** ADAIR *Indians* 346 They scouted off . . . to the hunting place, both for their own security, and to give the alarm. **1886** E. F. SMITH *Kentucky* 7 This region was known as the common park, or hunting range. **1762** *Huntington Rec.* II. 450 [We] do fully & absolutely give . . . unto them the said trustees . . . all the Soyl Right Planting and Hunting right and all the remainder. **1824** DODDRIDGE *Notes* 61 Hunting snows usually commenced about the middle of October. **1843** N. BOONE *Journal* (1917) 192 Followed until 2 O'clock the great Osage hunting trail until it left the waters of the creek.

c. Designating articles or tools worn or used by hunters.

1835 BIRD *Hawks of Hawk-H.* II. xx. 249 He sat down . . . his knife loosened in the sheath, and his little hunting-axe lying at his feet. **1836** CROCKETT *Exploits* 131 She placed it in his hunting bag. **1828** *Western Mo. Rev.* I. 577 In autumn the passengers of the hunting boats . . . saw him. **1857** STROTHER *Virginia* 61 Hunting-jackets have a rowdy look, so Miss Minnie thinks. **1825** NEAL *Bro. Jonathan* II. 109 A wet bandanna handkerchief, about which a sort of hunting-net was carelessly bound. **1840** HOFFMAN *Greyslaer* I. 122 He took a cup from his hunting-pouch, and . . . dipped up the water and let it fall again. **1886** ROOSEVELT in *Outing* March 615 No hunting-rifles in the world possess greater accuracy, range, and penetration. **1888** CABLE *Bonaventure* 146 Some sportsman's cast-off hunting-shoes minus the shoe-strings. **1874** LONG *Wild-Fowl* xix. 215 For this reason they are not as useful as the regular hunting-skiff. **1897** *Outing* May 121/2 We wore only our hunting togs. **1839** HOFFMAN *Wild Scenes* 171 The lad doesn't love to have his hunting-tools discomboborated. **1854** *Penna. Agric. Rep.* 98 Quinn & Palmer . . . for neat hunting wagon.

d. Taking part in hunting.

1847 RUXTON *Adv. Rocky Mts.* (1848) 77 One of the mules, which from its docility and good temper, I promoted to be my hunting-mule, was a short, stumpy animal. **1886** *Outing* April 7/1, I was riding a well-trained hunting pony.

+**Hunting cabin.** A temporary shelter used by Indians on a hunt. *Obs.* — **1753** WASHINGTON *Diaries* I. 45 The Half-king was out at his hunting-Cabbin on little *Beaver*-Creek. **1760** CROGHAN *Journal* 109, I met three Indians who informed me that the Deputys I sent from Fort Pitt had passed by their hunting Cabin Eight days agoe. **1791** W. BARTRAM *Travels* 344, I saw an Indian hunting cabin on the side of a hill.

+**Hunting camp.** The temporary headquarters of a party of huntsmen. Often used of Indian hunters. — **1751** GIST *Journals* 71 We lodged at a hunting Camp of an Indian Captain named Oppaymolleah. **1789** *Steele P.* I. 34 The South Carolina Commr. informed us at our last meeting that two Cherokees have lately been killed, and their hunting camp plundered. **1808** PIKE *Sources Miss.* 44, [I] dispatched Miller and Huddleston to the lower hunting-camp. **1847** L. COLLINS *Kentucky* 490 Owen . . . participated in the action which routed the Indians in their hunting camps. **1897** *Outing* July 374/2 What will be necessary for the smaller hunting camp . . . will find its place later on.

Hunting dress. The garb or dress worn by a hunter. {1859} — **1837** IRVING *Bonneville* I. 88 The mountaineers in their rude hunting dresses . . . looked like banditti. **1840** *Knickerb.* Aug. 159 Turning round, I saw a man at a short distance from me, in a hunting-dress. **1883** 'MARK TWAIN' *Life on Miss.* App. D., He then laid aside his hunting-dress and accoutrements.

+**Hunting frock.** =HUNTING SHIRT. — **1794** in *Amer. Pioneer* II. 222 Dressed in a hunting frock, breechcloth and leggins. **1835** HOFFMAN *Winter in West* I. 257 A tall backwoodsman, in a fringed hunting-frock, was stretched on several chairs. **1870** 'O. OPTIC' *Field & Forest* 287, I had dressed myself in my best clothes, discarding forever my hunting frock and skin cap.

+**Hunting ground.** A district or region of considerable extent frequented esp. by Indians in search of game. Usually pl. {1777-} (Cf. HAPPY HUNTING GROUND.)

1721 *Mass. H. Rep. Jrnl.* III. 20 Constantly Scouting, hunting and discovering the Rivers, Ponds, Carrying-places and Hunting Grounds. **1788** *Steele P.* I. 23 He shall endeavour to obtain from the said Indians an Extension of the Boundary between the citizens of this State and the hunting grounds of the Indians. **1812** MARSHALL *Kentucky* 23 The Indians . . . saw their perpetual enemy, taking possession of their hunting ground. **1892** *S.Dak. Hist. Coll.* I. 49 Many Indian tribes . . . used its 220,000,000 acres for shifting lodging camps and hunting grounds, unwilling to make farms and stock ranches upon them. **1923** J. H. COOK *On Old Frontier* 229 It was then or never that the white man could be stayed from doing as he pleased in the valuable hunting grounds which the chief had so long contested with the Crows.

+**Hunting house.** =HUNTING CABIN. — **1608** SMITH *Works* (1884) I. 22 In certaine olde hunting houses of Paspahegh we lodged all night. **1643** R. WILLIAMS *Key* (1866) 74 [The Indians] remove to a hunting house in the end of the yeere. **1765** ROGERS *Acct. N. America* 247 The Indian hunting houses are generally but the work of half an hour at the most. *a***1817** DWIGHT *Travels* II. 21 It was called his hunting-house because he spent the summer here in hunting.

Hunting knife. A sharp, heavy knife used by a hunter. {1842-} — **1829** COOPER *Wish-ton-Wish* iii, All turned their attention to the long sharp hunting-knife that he deposited by the side of the pistols. **1836** CROCKETT *Exploits* 139 They were both armed with rifles and hunting knives. **1884** *Century Mag.* Oct. 803/2 Northern and Southern soldiers were alike in their fondness for hunting-knives and revolvers. *a***1918** G. STUART *On Frontier* II. 173 A wolfer's outfit [included] . . . a hunting knife and a supply of strychnine.

Hunting party. A company of men engaged in hunting; a hunting expedition. {1788-} — **1770** WASHINGTON *Diaries* I. 367, I [went] to Mr. Rt. Alexander's on a hunting Party. **1805** *Ann. 9th Congress* 2 Sess. 1087 Besides these, there are rambling hunting parties of them [*sc.* Choctaws] to be met with all over Lower Louisiana. **1890** HARTE *Waif of Plains* 96 Shortly after the departure of the hunting party Clarence should ask permission to mount and exercise one of the team horses. **1924** CUMMINS *Sky-high Corral* 71 His great plans for making a clean-up taking hunting and tourist parties into the game and fish paradise of the Kolac Forest had not panned out.

Hunting quarter. The encampment of Indians engaged in hunting; the area over which Indians hunt. Usu. pl. — **1697** *Md. Hist. Mag.* XV. 116 Their time of moving to their hunting Quarters was in June. **1709** LAWSON *Carolina* 59 We met with about 500 Tuskeruros in one Hunting-Quarter. **1714** *N.C. Col. Rec.* II. 140 Ye same [land] is reserved for hunting Quarters for some of ye Tuskurora Indyans.

Hunting season. The season when hunting is engaged in. — **1743** *Ga. Col. Rec.* VI. 61 A proper Person [shall] be . . . employ'd to spend at least one week in every Month at the said Cowpen during the Hunting Season. **1800** HAWKINS *Sk. Creek Country* 46 The Indians . . . put their corn there for their support, during the hunting season. **1891** RYAN *Pagan of Alleghanies* 279 Here is the hunting-season almost upon us. **1902** W.

HULBERT *Forest Neighbors* (1903) 208 The hunting season had come, and half-a-dozen farmers from lower Michigan had camped beside the Glimmerglass.

+Hunting shirt. A long, loose, coatlike frock often made of deerskin ornamented with fringe and worn by hunters.

1774 in Peyton *Adv. Grandfather* (1867) 132 Providing myself, Charles and Annetta with good rifles, . . . ammunition and Indian dresses, consisting of hunting shirts, buckskin leggins and moccasins. **1824** DODDRIDGE *Notes* x. 113 The hunting shirt was universally worn [by frontiersmen]. **1857** *Lawrence* (Kan.) *Republican* 11 June 4 The trapper entered . . . dressed in his deer skin hunting shirt and trousers. **1886** Z. F. SMITH *Kentucky* 8 The hunting-shirt was a loose frock with cape, made of deer skins dressed. **1898** N. E. JONES *Squirrel Hunters of Ohio* 9 A coon-skin cap and gloves—deer-skin breeches and leggins, and a wolf-skin 'hunting shirt' made the weather right at all times with the hunter. **1916** THOBURN *Stand. Hist. Okla.* I. 263 The hunting shirts which were commonly worn by the men were also home spun.

transf. **1824** *Free Press* (Halifax, N.C.) 17 Sept., Bobtails and hunting shirts! you are a set of d—d ignorant fellows.

b. Attrib. with *comrade, gentry, uniform.*

1775 FITHIAN *Journal* II. 31 This town in arms. All in a hunting-shirt uniform & bucks tale in their hats. **1835** HOFFMAN *Winter in West* II. 183 There is a group of the white beaver and hunting shirt gentry collected at this moment around a blood-horse, whose points a groom is showing off. **1838** J. MCDONALD *Biographical Sketches* 187 This short pathetic speech, found its way to the sympathetic hearts of his leather-hunting-shirt comrades.

Hunting suit. A suit designed for a huntsman. — **1845** *Knickerb.* XXV. 242 Holabee received a full hunting-suit. **1891** RYAN *Told in Hills* 42 [The] brand-new hunting suit bespoke the 'got-up-regardless' tourist. **1916** EASTMAN *From Deep Woods* 31, I wore my hunting suit.

+Huntington root. A coarse variety of beet, mangel-wurzel. Also *Huntingdon root. Obs.* — **1788** *Amer. Museum* IV. 100/2 Mr. Laurens has now growing at Mepkin plantation upwards of 1600 plants of the Huntington (or scarcity) root, all in flourishing condition. *Ib.* 436/2 The Huntingdon (or scarcity) root.

+Hunting town. An encampment of Indians engaged in hunting. — **1608** SMITH *Works* (1884) I. 18 The next night I lodged at a hunting town of Powhatams. **1751** GIST *Journals* 69, [I] encamped on the SW Side about 1 M from a small Hunting Town of the Delawares from whom I bought some Corn.

Hurdy-gurdy. {1749-} *+W.* A water wheel driven by a jet of water under pressure. In full *hurdy-gurdy wheel.* — **1871** RAYMOND *3d Rep. Mines* 86 An eight-stamp mill, run by a 'hurdy-gurdy' wheel 8 feet in diameter, using 75 inches of water under a pressure of 75 feet. **1881** — *Mining Glossary, Hurdy-gurdy wheel,* a water-wheel operated by the direct impact of a stream upon its radially-placed paddles. **1882** *47th Congress 1 Sess.* H. R. Ex. Doc. No. 216, 628 The actuating power of the derrick is, generally, a hurdy-gurdy. This is a peculiar kind of impact wheel made to utilize water under high pressure.

+Huron. Also **†Hiroon.** [OFr. 'unkempt person,' 'ruffian.']

1. An Indian belonging to one or other of four confederated tribes formerly occupying a region adjacent to Lake Huron; in pl., this confederation of tribes.

[**1632** *Relat. Jésuites* (1858) I. 14 Ie vy arriuer les Hurons.] **1658** GORGES in *Maine H. S. Coll.* II. 67 The Hiroons, who being neuters are friends both to the one [the Iroquois] and the other [the French]. **1721** *Mass. H. Rep. Jrnl.* III. 111 The Algonquins, The Hurons, The Mikemaks, The Mountaniers on the North-side. **1789** *Ann. 1st Congress* I. 40 Resolved, That the Superintendent of Indian Affairs for the Northern Department inform the Five Nations, the Hurons, and other Indian nations, . . . that Congress . . . received their said representation. **1826** COOPER *Mohicans* iv, He is one of those you call a Huron. **1841** — *Deerslayer* x, The Iroquois, or Hurons, as it would be better to call them, were entirely ignorant of the proximity of her lover.

2. Attrib. with *husband, Indian, language, village.*

1786 *Mem. Academy* II. I. 125 The Huron, or Wyandot language having no affinity to the Shawanese, Delawares, and other nations. **1811** *Ann. 12th Congress* 1 Sess. II. 2123/4 The Prophet . . . is at a small Huron village, about twelve miles from his former residence. **1841** COOPER *Deerslayer* xxiii, Will you desart your duty . . . and take a Huron husband. **1888** *Amer. Naturalist* XXII. 803 Jerusalem Artichoke, *Helianthus tuberosus,* . . . was cultivated by the Huron Indians.

+Hurrah boy. 1. A blindly enthusiastic partisan: (see quotation). **2.** *pl.* construed as *sing.* (Usually hyphened.) A demonstration of excitement; a furor. — (1) **1836** *Congress. Globe* App. 17 Feb. 115/1 [Some have declared] that his election had been brought about by the '*hurrah boys,*' and those who knew just enough to shout 'hurrah for Jackson.' (2) **1841** COOPER *Deerslayer* xi, [A squall] came down upon us night afore last, in the shape of an Indian hurrah-boys! **1885** HOWELLS *S. Lapham* xiv, When there's such a hurrah-boys as there was then, you can't tell which is which.

||**Hurrah-bush.** (See quotations.) — **1853** SIMMS *Sword & Distaff* 81 We're in a pretty close thick, you see of gall and 'hurrah-bushes.' *Ib.*, The wild, matted, tangled, tough, and altogether indescribable shrub, which the woodman described as the 'hurrah-bush,' and for which we have no better name, constitutes, in poor soil . . . one of the most formidable . . . of forest-walls.

+Hurrah's nest. A place that is in confusion and disorder. *colloq.*

1829 LONGFELLOW in S. Longfellow *H. W. Longfellow* I. 164 A queer looking Dutchman, with a head like a 'hurra's nest' and a great wooden pipe. **1840** DANA *Two Years* ii. 10 Everything was pitched about in grand confusion. There was a complete 'hurrah's nest,' as the sailors say, 'everything on top and nothing at hand.' **1885** 'CRADDOCK' *Prophet* xiii. 246 That thar spun-truck . . . looks like a hurrah's nest. **1895** A. BROWN *Meadow-Grass* 134, I'll clear up this kitchen; it's a real hurrah's nest, if ever there was one. **1910** WALCOTT *Open Door* xxvi. 337 Here's this room looking like a hurrah's nest.

***Hurricane.** Also **†hiracano, hurrycane.**

***1.** A cyclone or violent storm, usually accompanied by rain and lightning, in which the wind blows with extraordinary violence.

1639 *Maine Hist. Soc. Coll.* III. 88 Monday about 4 o'clock in the afternoon, a fearful storm of wind began to rage, called a *hurricane.* **1670** I. MATHER *Life R. Mather* 68 There arose a fearful Storm (which the Americans are wont to call an Hiracano) by means whereof they were in no small danger. **1713** HEMPSTEAD *Diary* 27 A Storm or Hurrycane. **1797** B. HAWKINS *Letters* 108 There had been recently a hurrycane which had twisted and broken the little trees. **1863** O. W. NORTON *Army Lett.* 146 The wind blows almost a hurricane. **1896** *N.Y. Wkly. Witness* 30 Dec. 13/2 Our candidate swept the hundred logging-camps like a hurricane.

+2. An area devastated by a hurricane.

1735 HEMPSTEAD *Diary* 291, The Stack . . . was made in the Hurrycane this Side the Swamp. **1833** *Sketches of Crockett* 196 We were soon on foot, moving merrily forward to a small hurricane which had been agreed upon for a drive. **1891** SWASEY *Early Days Calif.* 15 In Missouri, cause and effect had been blended in the common designation of 'hurricane.'

b. Attrib. with *ground, hill, thick, tree.*

1775 ROMANS *Nat. Hist. Florida* 307 Travelled chiefly through pine land, and some hurricane ground. **1775** ADAIR *Indians* 337 They had passed over a boggy place of the creek, upon an old hurricane-tree. **1837** WETMORE *Gaz. Missouri* 80 That part of the county of Howard commonly termed the hurricane-hills is rich and picturesque; and the track of the tempest and the whirlwind, marked by the bare and branchless trunks of scathed oaks, lends a thrilling interest to the scenery. **1855** SIMMS *Forayers* 255, I was in a 'harricane thick,' on the butt-eend of an almighty big tree.

+Hurricane deck. The upper deck of a river steamer; the weather deck.

1833 *Niles' Reg.* XLIV. 261/1 The hull of the boat sunk, leaving a part of the hurricane deck . . . floating on the surface. **1841** STEELE *Summer Journey* 170 We hastened up to the hurricane deck. **1864** NICHOLS *Amer. Life* I. 166 The *Louis Philippe* gave rise to the more jokes because her hurricane deck was entirely covered with cabbages. **1889** *Boston Jrnl.* 6 Jan. 2/3 The steamboat Paris C. Brown . . . sank to the hurricane deck. **1901** CHURCHILL *Crisis* 182 Stephen stood apart on the hurricane deck, gazing at the dark line of sooty warehouses.

b. *transf.*

1857 *Lawrence* (Kan.) *Republican* 11 June 3 The New York Second Avenue Railroad Company have placed on the route some cars with an upper or 'hurricane deck.' **1887** *Outing* June 253/2, I have even known it [*sc.* the river] to be fished from the hurricane-deck of a cayuse, so that all lovers of the gentle art may be accommodated. **1923** J. H. COOK *On Old Frontier* 38 After he quit bucking I was still on his hurricane deck.

+Hurricane roof. =prec. — **1849** *Commercial* (Wilmington, N.C.) 27 Nov. 1/6 (Th. S.), The after part [of the boiler] shot through the main cabin floor, . . . passing obliquely through the hurricane roof immediately over the ladies' cabin. **1867** RICHARDSON *Beyond Mississippi* i. 21 [The snag] penetrated her hull . . . and came out at the hurricane roof. **1883** *Century Mag.* June 222/1 The tall, broad, frail-looking steamers . . . hidden to their hurricane roofs in cargoes of cotton bales.

+Hurrygraph. A hurriedly written note or communication. — **1851** WILLIS (*title*), Hurry-Graphs; or, Sketches of Scenery, Celebrities and Society. **1862** *Independent* 31 July 1/5 But I must close this hurrygraph, which I have no time to review. **1879** WHITMAN *Prose Wks.* (1892) 502, I set out on the following hurrygraphs of a breezy early-summer visit to New-York City.

***Hurtleberry.** Also **hirtleberry.** **+1.** =HUCKLEBERRY. **+2.** Attrib. in place names. — (1) **1629** *Mass. H. S. Coll.* 1 Ser. I. 119 Walnuts, smalnuts, hurtleberies, and hawes of whitethorne . . . grow in plentie here. **1682** M. RAWLINSON *Narr. Captivity* 69 [She had] nothing to eat or drink but water, and green Hirtle-berries. **1716** CHURCH *Philip's War* 34 He perceived they were gathering of Hurtle-Berries. **1774** FITHIAN *Journal* I. 195 Every Day [we have] good Fruit for Dinner, caudled Apples, Hurtle-Berries with milk. (2) **1654** *Boston Rec.* 27 More or lesse lately the land of William Curtiss called hurtlebury hill. **1677** *Plymouth Rec.* I. 153 The Towne have Graunted unto Thomas hewes a Certaine swamp Called hurtleberry swamp.

Hush,** *v.* **+intr.* Used imperatively to denote enthusiastic approval or appreciation. — *a***1846** *Quarter Race Ky.* 88 Oh hush! It makes my mouth water now to think what a beautiful row we had. **1898** DUNBAR *Folks from Dixie* 62 'Then you can sell chickens and eggs, and we'll go halves on the profits.' 'Hush, man!' cried 'Lias in delight.

***Husk**, *n.*

+**1.** The bracts or outside covering of an ear of Indian corn.

1677 WINTHROP in *Phil. Trans.* XII. 1067 The Husks about the Ear are good Fodder, given for change sometimes after Hay. **1823** JAMES *Exped.* I. 194 [Among the Omaha Indians] the poor who have no kettles, place the ear, sufficiently guarded by its husk, in the hot embers until properly cooked. **1884** ROE *Nature's Story* 412 He had planned and composed it while at work stripping the husks from the yellow corn. **1899** *Mo. So. Dakotan* I. 175 In the corn field the dry blades beating, the crackling husks and creaking stalks made deafening confusion.

b. (See quotation.)

1894 EGGLESTON in *Century Mag.* April 851/1 Husk is applied in the middle belt and in the South to the bran of corn-meal. . . . In this sense the word has largely lost its final letter. . . . In a particular life of Crockett which I saw in childhood, but of which I can find not a single copy existing today, 'huss' occurs for the bran of corn-meal. . . . 'She sifted the meal, she gimme the huss; She baked the bread, she gimme the crus'.'

+**2.** (See quotation.)

1881 INGERSOLL *Oyster-Industry* 245 *Husks.*—Oyster shells.

3. Attrib. in sense 1 with *bed, collar, mattress,* etc.

1857 *Ill. Agric. Soc. Trans.* II. 361 In these aboriginal times [c1800] husk collars were mostly used [in southern Ill.]. **1862** S. HALE *Letters* 13 One thing I shall rejoice at,—my own bed,—for this husk thing we sleep on is a beast. **1872** *Newton Kansan* 29 Aug. 4/3 E. W. asks how to make husk mattresses. **1881** *Harper's Mag.* Sept. 579/1 You may hanker after more black-flies, and mosquitoes, . . . and baked beans, and husk beds, and so forth. **1902** G. C. EGGLESTON *D. South* 82 When Arthur came down stairs the next morning he found the maids busily polishing the snow-white floors with pine needles and great log and husk rubbers.

***Husk**, *v.*

+**1.** *tr.* To strip (Indian corn) of its husk. Also with *out.*

1642 *Md. Archives* 195 An attachment or execution shalbe judged sufficiently served upon corne afore it be husked. **1724** *Mass. H.S. Coll.* 2 Ser. VIII. 247, I have gathered in the most part of my field and husked the same. **1737** E. PARKMAN *Diary* 36 About 18 or 20 hands husked out all my Corn. N.B. In my absence Winter Apples gathered in. **1786** WASHINGTON *Diaries* III. 139 Rid to the Ferry, Dogue run, and Muddy hole Plantn., gathering and husking Corn at all of them. **1836** GILMAN *Recoll.* (1838) iv. 35 Joseph, when a boy, was employed in tying fagots, driving cows, husking corn, hoeing potatoes, etc. **1898** *Mo. So. Dakotan* I. 44 See that load of corn? That's what I can husk in half a day.

+**2.** (See quotation.)

1881 INGERSOLL *Oyster-Industry* 245 *Husk.*—To remove the shells from an oyster or 'open' it. (Georgia.)

+**Huskanaw**, *n.* [Amer. Indian.] (See quot. 1907.) Now hist. — **1705** BEVERLEY *Virginia* III. 41 The *Appamattucks*, formerly a great Nation, tho' now an inconsiderable People, made an *Huskanaw* in the year 1690, and brought home the same number they carried out. **1907** HODGE *Handbook Amer. Indians* I. 592 *Huskanaw*, an Algonquian word applied to certain initiation ceremonies of the Virginia Indians, performed on boys at puberty, which were accompanied by fasting and the use of narcotics.

+**Huskanaw**, *v.* Also **husquenaugh, huskanoy.** *tr.* To subject (an Indian youth) to a huskanaw. *Obs.* Also transf. — **1705** BEVERLEY *Virginia* III. 39 The choicest and briskest young men of the Town, and such only as have acquired some Treasure by their Travels and Hunting, are chosen out by the Rulers to be *Huskanawed;* and whoever refuses to undergo this Process, dares not remain among them. **1709** LAWSON *Carolina* 233 It is always at Christmas that they *husquenaugh* their Youth, which is by bringing them into this House, and keeping them dark all the time, where they more than half-starve them. **1733** BYRD *Journey to Eden* (1901) 326 And the Joy of meeting my Family in Health made me in a Moment forget all the Fatigues of the Journey, as much as if I had been husquenawed. **1788** JEFFERSON *Writings* VII. 94 Luzerne . . . is a good man, too, but so much out of his element, that he has the air of one huskanoyed.

+**Husker.** One who husks Indian corn. (Cf. CORN-HUSKER 2.) — **1780** E. PARKMAN *Diary* 279 Breck was very generous in treating ye Huskers with Liquor. **1845** KIRKLAND *Western Clearings* 95 Parties of 'huskers' [are not wanting] to give a human interest to the picture. **1888** BITTINGER *Hist. Haverhill* 360 The unhusked corn was piled in a heap, . . . and the huskers . . . sat around the fire on the floor.

+**Husking.**

1. =HUSKING BEE.

1693 C. MATHER *Wond. Invis. World* 142 At another time this Deponent was desired by the Prisoners to come unto an Husking of Corn. **1764** *N.H. Hist. Soc. Coll.* IX. 166 At night had a husking. **1805** in Kittredge *Old Farmer* (1904) 168 If you make a husking, keep an old man between every two boys, else your *husking* will turn out a *losing.* **1855** THOREAU *Cape Cod* (1894) iii. 44 He had been to a husking . . . where five hundred bushels were husked in one evening. **1890** *Boston Jrnl.* 20 Oct. 2 Old-fashioned huskings have by no means fallen into disuse. **1903** W. E. CURTIS *True Abraham Lincoln* 66 The guest of honour at dinners, receptions, quiltings, huskings, weddings, and other entertainments.

2. Attrib. with *ballad, feast, night, supper.*

1828 *Yankee* May 147/1 A husking supper was composed of Indian pudding, and pork-and-beans baked, and a dessert of apple-pie and cheese. **1829** COOPER *Wish-ton-Wish* iv, Mutton will not be wanting for the husking-feast. **1841** *Lowell Offering* I. 292 Farewell, the merry husking-night, Its pleasant after scenes. **1850** WHITTIER *Poetical Works* (1895) 364/1 The master of the village school . . . a husking-ballad sung.

+**Husking bee.** A community gathering of friends and neighbors at the home of a farmer for assisting him to husk his Indian corn. (Cf. CORN-HUSKING, CORN-SHUCKING.) — **1848** *Knickerb.* XVIII. 217 The long round of husking-bees . . . furnish sources of enjoyment. **1887** GEORGE *40 Yrs. on Rail* i. 18 Fourth of July was a great day to us, of course, and we had, in the autumn and winter, husking-bees, dancing parties, and sleigh rides to our heart's content. **1900** MUNN *Uncle Terry* 19 He did not escort some other young lady to the husking-bees, barn dances, or church sociables.

+**Husking frolic.** =HUSKING BEE. — **1771** in *New England Mag.* ns. XII. 349/1, [I] was interrupted in my slumbers by son Johnny coming in from a husking frolic. **1807** JANSON *Stranger in America* 406 In some provinces of the United States, the farmers, on getting in the corn harvest, give a rural fete, in imitation of the ancient English custom of harvest home. This they call a *husking frolic.* **1827** COOPER *Prairie* xviii, Ellen herself getting her shining hair ready for a dance or a husking frolic! **1855** MITCHELL *Fudge Doings* I. iii. 45 His Cousin Phoebe . . . played barefooted at the old husking-frolics of Newton. **1887** TOURGEE *Button's Inn* 50 She went with him and his mother to a husking-frolic.

+**Husking match.** A competition in husking Indian corn. — **1853** THOMAS *J. Randolph* 97 After this, we got to the husking-match safe. **1873** *Harper's Mag.* March 513 Plenty to eat and drink—meat, cabbage, turnips! Same thing at de huskin' matches. **1885** HOLMES *Mortal Antipathy* ix, Carpet of her room looked like a barn floor after a husking-match.

+**Husking party.** =HUSKING BEE. — **a1892** WHITMAN *Prose Wks.* (1892) 491 [I recall] . . . the Western husking party. **1905** *Springfield W. Repub.* 27 Oct. 14 Mr. and Mrs. Whitham's house was the scene of a merry husking party Monday evening.

+**Husky**, *n.* [In sense 1 possibly from *Eskimo.*]

1. An Eskimo dog.

[**1886** *Colonial & Indian Exhibition* (London) (*Cent.*) 75 The original Husky has always been an animal requiring firm treatment.] **1903** *N.Y. Ev. Post* 31 Oct., The Alaska 'husky dogs' or 'huskies,' as they are called, resemble wolves strikingly in their appearance, manner, and carriage, and do not suggest dogs, save secondarily. **1904** WHITE *Silent Places* xiv. 148 Picked up a pretty good dog. Part 'husky.'

2. A strong, powerful person. (Cf. HUSKY *a.*)

1884 'MARK TWAIN' *H. Finn* xxix. 281 That big husky had me by the wrist. **1902** WHITE *Conjuror's House* iii. 35 Suppose some old Husky up on Whale River should send you word that you weren't to trap in the Whale River district next winter. **1919** H. L. WILSON *Ma Pettingill* iv. 113, I saw a kind of a slight young man . . . lick three big huskies that set on him.

***Husky**, *a.* +Strong, robust, vigorous. — **1869** STOWE *Oldtown Folks* xvii. 191 Them wild Injuns, . . . they're so kind o' wild, and birchy, and husky as a body may say. **1908** MULFORD *Orphan* ii. 24 Seven husky Apaches are too much for one man to go out of his way to fight. **1925** FOSTER *Trop. Tramp Tourists* 84 Several husky longshoremen caught our ropes and tied us fast.

Huss. +Variant of HUSK *n.* 1 b.

Hustle, *n.* {1715-} +Energetic effort; briskness, animation. *colloq.* — **1892** *Home Missionary* (N.Y.) July 120 The hustle and stir of our day. **1898** *Daily Chronicle* (London) 3 Dec. 5/1 With characteristic 'hustle,' excursions in the United States have already been organised to Hawaii. **1906** *N.Y. Ev. Post* 7 Sept. 6 What the Kaiser hopes from Herr Dernburg is what is popularly known as American 'hustle'—the ability to go right to the point, to decide quickly, to act aggressively by means of simple and direct methods.

Hustle, *v.* {1684-} +**a.** *tr.* To pick *up* smartly. +**b.** *intr.* To exert oneself, work busily *for* something. — **1840** *S. Lit. Messenger* VI. 414/2 Can't you go out to the woodpile and hustle me up a few chips to start this fire? **1890** *Stock Grower & Farmer* 28 June 3/1 Feeders will be hustling for steers and they should go up another point. **1898** *McClure's Mag.* X. 214 The boys were hustling for dear life. **1906** 'O. HENRY' *Four Million* 62 Do you think I'm going to let you hustle for wages while I philander in the regions of high art?

Hustler. {1882-} +(See quot. 1899.) — **1886** *Publishers' Weekly* 18 Dec. 965/1 Young man, a 'hustler' in every respect, wants a strictly first-class position with a 'live' book house. **1894** SHUMAN *Steps into Journalism* 64 [The staff man] is an excellent 'hustler.' **1899** ADE *Doc' Horne* 238 In the United States of America a hustler is one who is busy, persistent, resourceful and combative, usually that he may accumulate money. **1920** LEWIS *Main Street* 413 Mr. Blausser was known as a Hustler.

+**Hutchins's goose.** A variety of the Canada goose that migrates through the United States. — **1835** AUDUBON *Ornith. Biog.* III. 526 Hutchins's Goose. *Anser Hutchinsii.* . . . I have no doubt that it is the very species which has been named in honour of Mr. Hutchins, and that its periodical appearance along our eastern coast will ere long be fully established. **1856** *Porter's Spirit of Times* 13 Dec. 242/1 Hutchins' goose, or, as it is sometimes called, Hutchins' Brant, greatly resembles the Brent goose, both in size and appearance. **1917** *Birds of Amer.* I. 160/2 Hutchins's Goose (*Branta canadensis hutchinsi*) is precisely like the Canada Goose in everything except size.

+**Huttonweed.** *local.* The wild teasel. — **1894** *Amer. Folk-Lore* VII. 90 *Dipsacus sylvestris*, . . . Huttonweed, English thistle, water-thistle. West Va.

***Hyacinth.** Any one of various well-known plants of the genus *Hyacinthus*. — **1792** IMLAY *Western Territory* 207 Every part of the country abounds in a variety of natural flowers . . . daffodil, jonquil, hyacinth. **1829** SHERWOOD *Gaz. Georgia* (ed. 2) 18 The jessamine, woodbine, althea, hyacinth, and jonquil were in all the verdure of spring. **1910** C. HARRIS *Eve's Husband* 32, I began to take a sad, weeping-willow joy in the heartiness of the white hyacinths, narcissuses and pale trumpet lilies.

***Hydra.** +An officer in the first Ku Klux Klan organization. — **1867** in Lester & Wilson *Ku Klux Klan* 136 The officers . . . shall consist of a Grand Wizard of the Empire and his ten Genii; a Grand Dragon of the Realm and his eight Hydras [etc.].

Hydrangea. Also **hydrangia.** Any one of various common plants of the genus *Hydrangea*. {1753-} Also attrib. — **1785** MARSHALL *Amer. Grove* 61 *Hydrangea frutescens*. Virginian Shrubby Hydrangea. This hath a spreading woody root, from which are produced, generally several soft, pithy, ligneous stalks. **1827** WILLIAMS *West Florida* 8 Broken fragments [of limestone] lie in large piles, interspersed with dogwood, chicasa plumb, hydrangia shrubs, and vines. **1865** *Atlantic Mo.* Feb. 148 There are red houses, with white, and on the door-step of one a green tub that flames with a great pink hydrangea. **1915** CAMPBELL *Proving Virginia* 138 Mrs. Kirkland . . . superintended the decorations: ferns and pink carnations in the big room, daffodils and clematis in the dining-room, hydrangeas in the lower adjoining rooms.

+**Hydrant.** [f. Gr. ὕδωρ water.]

1. An upright cylinder or street fixture from which water may be drawn from a city main.

1806 *Phila. Ordinances* (1812) 197 If any person . . . shall wilfully injure . . . the hydrants . . . [he] shall forfeit . . . five dollars. **1851** *Knickerb.* XXXVIII. 604 Fire-men were attaching their hose to the hydrants. **1876** KNIGHT 2425/1 [Street-sprinklers] are usually filled from the public hydrant or fire-plug. **1889** BRAYLEY *Boston Fire Dept.* 214 The hydrant from which the supply of water was received was at the corner of Hanover and Cross streets.

2. A smaller outlet for water for domestic use; a faucet.

1849 G. G. FOSTER *N.Y. in Slices* 69 He can regale himself on pumpkin pie at four cents the quarter-section, with a cup of Croton, fresh from the hydrant, gratis. **1861** *Ladies' Repository* March 181/1 The flowers in the garden plot in front were hung with glittering water-drops from the neighboring hydrant.

3. Attrib. and comb. with *head*, *maker*, *man*, etc.

1834 *N.Y. City Ordinance* 8 March, It shall be the duty of the hydrant-men, on an alarm of fire, to proceed to the hydrants and attend to the proper letting out of the water. **1841** Cist *Cincinnati* (*advt.*), Pump and Hydrant Maker. **1841** CIST *Ib.* 69 The 'hydrant water' of our city . . . is reputed to be healthy. **1878** PINKERTON *Strikers* 270 There stood a ruffian on a hydrant-head with his arm about a lamp-post. **1904** *Daily Pub. Opinion* (Watertown, S.D.) 28 Dec. 1/3 A bunch of bills was allowed, covering hydrant rental from July to January, six months, at $2,504.

Hydraulic, *n.* {1626-} +A contrivance for using water in mining. — **1856** *San Francisco Call* 5 Dec. (Th.), I've used them things enough in the mines to know that that 'ere all-fired machine is not hydrollicks. **1872** McCLELLAN *Golden State* 259 The pan gave way to the rocker, the rocker to the sluice and shovel, and finally to the use of powder and the hydraulic. **1880** *Cimarron News & Press* 17 June 3/2 The New York *Sun* party have been at work at the head of Red river, preparing to work those placers with hydraulics.

Hydraulic, *a.* {1656-} +Pertaining to hydraulic mining. — **1869** BROWNE *Adv. Apache Country* 310 Put you through the hydraulic process after your arrival at Placerville, and your washings are worth $14 per ounce. **1871** RAYMOND *3d Rep. Mines* 55 The most important [improvements in mining] . . . are the improved hydraulic nozzles and the new drilling and boring machines. *Ib.* 59 Important improvements have been made in the manner of using water in the hydraulic diggings. **1876** — *8th Rep. Mines* 97 The company has nine hydraulic chiefs or giants, the streams from which are forced out under a pressure of 250 feet of water. **1883** RITCH *Illus. N. Mex.* 129 A hydraulic company . . . is expected to have twelve miles of pipe down and arrangements completed for extensive placer washing.

Hydraulic cement. Cement that hardens in water. {1851-} — **1843** *Nat. Hist. N.Y., Geology* IV. 455 At West-Vienna, this rock is burned for hydraulic cement, and is said to produce a very good quality. **1851** Ross *In New York* 16 It consists of broken stone, sand, gravel, and hydraulic cement. **1898** *Mo. So. Dakotan* I. 7 It is sufficient to burn Hydraulic or Natural cement only until the most of the carbonic acid is expelled.

+**Hydraulicing.** Hydraulic mining. — **1880** INGHAM *Digging Gold* ix. 243 Two steam pumps have been in operation near the city, forcing water from French Creek up to these dry diggings for hydraulicing, and with most satisfactory results. **1882** *47th Congress 1 Sess.* H. R. Ex. Doc. No. 216 Reed's Hydraulic mine . . . is being refitted for hydraulicing the coming spring.

+**Hydraulic mine.** A mine in which hydraulic mining is practiced. — **1881** RAYMOND *Mining Glossary, Clean-up*, the operation of collecting all the valuable product of a given period or operation in a stamp mill, or in a hydraulic or placer mine. **1894** *Youth's Companion* 22 Nov. 562/1 A hydraulic mine is one where the gold lies imbedded in the soil and has to be washed out.

+**Hydraulic mining.** A method of mining which employs a powerful jet of water for disintegrating auriferous earth; the mines using this method. Also attrib. — **1856** *Porter's Spirit of Times* 22 Nov. 194/2 Near San Juan North . . . hydraulic mining is very successful. **1876** RAYMOND *8th Rep. Mines* 125 During late years hydraulic mining has been carried on in the outer edges of the old drift-diggings. **1880** *Cimarron News & Press* 28 Oct. 2/1 The next morning a part of the party visited the placers and hydraulic mining of the Moreno valley. **1882** *47th Congress 1 Sess.* H. R. Ex. Doc. No. 216, 13 During the coming year . . . hydraulic and drift mining will probably be pursued with renewed energy. **1889** *Century Mag.* April 879/2 But the little washerwoman told . . . how they had sent a man to dig a little channel from the main hydraulic mining ditch to her cabin.

Hydraulic ram. A self-acting pump which utilizes the energy of moving water to raise a portion of it to a point higher than its source. {1808-} — **1850** *New Eng. Farmer* II. 225 Improved Hydraulic Ram. . . . This is a perfectly simple and effective machine for forcing a portion of a brook or spring to any required distance or elevation. **1857** WILLIS *Convalescent* 322 [The stream's] elevation, forty or fifty feet above the brook, suits it for the action of the hydraulic ram. **1892** *York County Hist. Rev.* 83/2 The stock carried embraces . . . wind mills, the 'Gawdrop' hydraulic rams, paints, oils, glass, etc.

+**Hydraulion.** A form of hydraulic engine used by fire-fighters. *Obs.* Also attrib. — **1830** *Mass. Statutes* 9 March, The number of enginemen shall not exceed fifty to every hydraulion or suction engine. **1845** *Transcript & Chronicle* (Providence) 8 Jan. 2 The Annual Meeting of 'The Providence Association of Firemen for Mutual Assistance' will be held at Hydraulion house, No. 1.

+**Hydrographic Bureau.** =next. — **1873** *Republic* I. 23 The Hydrographic Bureau . . . takes cognizance of the geography of the sea.

+**Hydrographic Office.** A bureau under the direction of the Navy Department having charge of charts and studies of the geography of the sea. — **1866** *Statutes at Large* XIV. 69 There shall be a hydrographic office attached to the bureau of navigation in the Navy Department. **1889** *Century Mag.* March 705/1 The attention of mariners has been called to the value of oil for stilling waves . . . by the published reports . . . issued by Commander J. R. Bartlett, United States Navy, Chief of the United States Hydrographic Office, Navy Department. **1892** *Boston Jrnl.* 17 Dec. 3/4 Word was received today by the Hydrographic Office that the old wreck of the schooner Wyer G. Sargent had been sighted again.

Hydrometer. An instrument for determining the specific gravity of liquids. {1675-} — **1781** *Salem Gazette* 3 July, Isaac Greenwood . . . makes . . . Lemon Squeezers, Serenges, Hydrometers, Shaving Boxes and Brushes. **1833** SILLIMAN *Man. Sugar Cane* 36 An instrument called the Saccharometer, or Hydrometer of Baumé, is frequently used, in order to learn the saccharine richness of cane liquor. **1880** LAMPHERE *U.S. Govt.* 105/1 He may prescribe, for use in the prevention and detection of frauds by distillers of spirits, such hydrometers, saccharometers, weighing and gauging instruments as may be necessary.

Hyla. A tree frog or tree toad. — **1839** STORER *Mass. Reptiles* 242 *Hyla squirella*. . . . The little peeping Hyla. **1894** GARLAND in *Harper's Mag.* June 144/1 As evening drew on, the hylas began to peep from the pools, and their chorus deepened. **1922** A. BROWN *Old Crow* xlii. 468 When the dusk came down and the hylas peeped . . . she would lose courage.

+**Hylodes.** A large genus of New World frogs; a frog of this genus. — **1839** STORER *Mass. Reptiles* 240 *H[ylodes] Pickeringii*. Pickering's Hylodes. **1852** THOREAU *Autumn* 57, I hear a hylodes (?) from time to time. **1858** — *Maine Woods* 139 We also heard the hylodes and tree-toads.

Hyperion. +(See quot. 1895.) *Obs.* — **1759** BROOKS *Days of Spinning-Wheel* (1886) 11 The use of Hyperion or Labradore Tea, is every day coming into more general vogue among people of all ranks. **1895** COFFIN *Daughters of Revolution* 116 Strawberry and other domestic teas were called by the high sounding name Hyperion [in 1769].

Hyson. =HYSON TEA. {1740-} — **1770** *Md. Hist. Mag.* XIII. 75 Cash Expended . . . for 6 lb of Hyson & 2 lb of Common Tea. **1816** *Ann. 14th Congress* 1 Sess. 1873 Duty on tea from China . . . hyson and young hyson, fifty-six cents per pound. **1832** L. M. CHILD *Frugal Housewife* 84 Young Hyson is supposed to be a more profitable tea than Hyson. **1846** *Spirit of Times* 6 June 171/1 Recollecting that I had a pound paper of the real Hyson, I begged him to prepare some for me.

Hyson skin. An inferior grade of hyson tea. — **1810** *Columbian Centinel* 6 Jan. 1/2 John Parker & Sons . . . have for sale . . . hyson, hysonskin, . . . clayed Sugars. **1839** *Knickerb.* XIII. 231 How nicely is it [tea] adapted, by its delicately varying shades, to every especial palate! There is your . . . Hyson, and Young Hyson, Hyson-skin [etc.]. **1867** COZZENS *Sayings* i. 5 The refuse goes by the name of 'Hyson Skin.'

Hyson tea. A kind of tea imported from China. {1756-} — **1744** *Md. Hist. Mag.* XXI. 247, 2 lb. Hyson Tea. **1790** *Columbian Centinel* 15 Sept. 3/3 [For sale:] 1 pipe Madeira Wine of an excellent quality, Souchong and Hyson Tea;—Also, two Copper Stills. **1891** WELCH *Recoll. 1830-40* 183 The elderly ladies used it [snuff], sometimes to excess as they did Bohea or Hyson teas.

+**Hystericky,** *a.* Given to having hysterics; hysterical. *colloq.* — **1823** COOPER *Pilot* II. xiv. 239 In order that the women need not be 'stericky in squalls. **1867** HOLMES *Guardian Angel* xi. 127 That queer woman, the Deacon's mother,—there's where she gets that hystericky look. **1894** WILKINS in *Harper's Mag.* Sept. 605/2 You'd better go to bed, Sophy Anne; you're gittin' highstericky.

I

Ibex. {1607–} The name of various wild goats of the Old World, +applied to the Rocky Mountain sheep and similar American animals. Also attrib. — **1805** CLARK in *Lewis & C. Exped.* II. (1904) 297, I killed a Ibix. *Ib.* III. (1905) 105 The women dress in a Shirt of Ibex or Goat (Argalia) Skins. **1807** GASS *Journal* xxi. 222 They saw a number . . . of the ibex or big-horn. **1812** STODDARD *Sk. Louisiana* 358 Among other animals incident to the country may be noticed the Ibex, or Antelope of California, called by the Spaniards mountain sheep. **1831** R. COX *Adv. Columbia R.* xxiv. 255 The animals found in the various passes of the mountains are the buffaloes, ibex, big-horns, or mountain sheep, bears, and sometimes a few wolves. **1847** COYNER *Lost Trappers* 152 [The mountain mutton] is the flesh of the mountain sheep, which is variously called the big-horn by the trappers, the asahto by the Mandans, and the argali and ibex by others.

***Ibis.** A wading bird with downward-curving bill, found in warm climates. (See also GLOSSY, SCARLET, etc., IBIS.) — **1839** AUDUBON *Ornith. Biog.* V. 334 Brown Ibis. *Tantalus Fuscus*. . . . Two specimens . . . of this large Ibis were shot by me on the Bayou leading from the Silver Springs to the St. John's River in Florida. **1858** BAIRD *Birds Pacific R.R.* 683 *Ibis Rubra*. . . . Red or Scarlet Ibis. . . . The occurrence of this *Ibis* as a North American bird is very problematical. **1895** GRAHAM *Stories of Foot-Hills* 171 A bronze ibis arose from the tules at the water's edge, and flapped slowly westward.

Icarian, *n.* and *adj.* {1865–} [f. Fr. *Icarie,* the name of the imaginary republic described in the *Voyage en Icarie* (1840) of Etienne Cabet (1788–1856).]

1. *n.* A follower of the French communist Etienne Cabet. Now hist.

The Icarians came from France to the United States in 1848–9. Settling at first in Texas, they removed (1849) to Nauvoo, Ill. Subsequently they settled in Iowa.

[**1851** in Cabet *Colonie icarienne aux Etats-unis d'Amérique* (1856) 51 Les Icariens forment entre eux une véritable Société.] **1867** DIXON *New America* II. 217 The Socialists had to quit New Lanark; the Rappists had to sell Harmony; the Icarians have been swept from Nauvoo. **1873** BEADLE *Undevel. West* xxxii. 694 After the Mormons came a people even more curious than they, but quite harmless: the Icarians, or French 'Fraternal Society' of Communists. **1883** Ely *French & German Socialism* 43 The Icarians . . . are highly courteous and intelligent.

2. *adj.* Of or pertaining to the Icarians. Now hist.

1851 *Ill. Private Laws* 114 Etienne Cabet, J. Pendant, P. J. Tavard, Andre Thebant, Alfred Pignnard and Jean J. Witzig . . . are hereby constituted a body politic and corporate, by the name and style of the 'Icarian Community.' **1875** NORDHOFF *Communistic Soc. U.S.* 393 The Icarian system is as nearly as possible a pure democracy. **1883** Ely *French & German Socialism* 44 At present the 'New Icarian Community' . . . have about one thousand and eighty-five acres. *Ib.*, The official inventory of the 'New Icarian Society' [was] made on Jan. 1, 1883. **1895** in Hinds *Amer. Communities* (1902) 351 The Icarian Community is dissolved.

Icarianism. Communism as taught by Etienne Cabet. Now hist. — **1883** ELY *Fr. & German Socialism* iii. 50 The apostles of Icarianism should . . . convert the world by teaching, preaching . . . and by setting good examples.

***Ice.**

1. A frozen dessert; now usually sweetened and flavored water or fruit juice artificially frozen. {1716–}

In the United States at the present time a distinction is made between an *ice* and *ice cream*.

1821 QUITMAN in Claiborne *Life Quitman* I. 59 Your stewed terrapins, your chicken salad, your confectionery and ices. **1864** NICHOLS *Amer. Life* I. 267 For four months in a year Americans eat ices and drink iced drinks. **a1882** in McCabe *New York* 218 A chocolate ice had not agreed with her. **1893** *Harper's Mag.* May 883/1 If she wished for an ice, it appeared by magic.

+b. An iced drink.

1888 RITTENHOUSE *Maud* 413 All the time I was making saucy comments on his compliments, dancing, laughing, sipping ices.

2. In colloq. phrases.

To chop one's own ice, to do one's own work; *to cut ice,* (see CUT *v.* 25 g); *on ice,* 'in the bag'; unapproachable, beyond reach.

1890 GUNTER *Miss Nobody* xx. 231 For Election. Gussie de P. Van Beekman. . . . On ice! **1894** FORD *P. Stirling* 328 They say she's never been able to find a man good enough for her, and so she's keeping herself on ice. **1904** *Daily Ev. Telegraph* 20 June 6 Do not think that Teddy Roosevelt is making any mistake in chopping his own Presidential ice.

3. Attrib. and comb. in general sense with *apple, baron, bill,* etc.

1891 WELCH *Recoll. 1830–40* 411 The trees of which seemed loaded with the sparkling winter fruit of the place called 'ice apples,' (frozen balls of snow). **1906** *N.Y. Ev. Post* 29 June 7 The ice 'barons' of this city have again raised the price of ice to the dealers. **1888** *Vt. Agric. Rep.* X. 14 In cream gathering the ice bill is large. **1874** LONG *Wild-Fowl* 75 We were shooting together from an ice blind at the edge of an air-hole. **1884** *Lisbon Star* 30 May, A crib has been built around the piles in the centre of the river and filled with stone, thereby forming a good and substantial ice-break. **1874** R. H. COLLINS *Kentucky* I. 76 Breaking up of the ice-bridge in the Ohio river. **1852** *Knickerb.* March 290 We heard one [cobbler singing] . . . while [we were] waiting for 'Young Knick.'s ice-brogans, 'on tap' at that period. **1853** KANE *Grinnell Exped.* 468 While three men were out on a low berg . . . one of them . . . struck his ice-chisel against the mass. **1823** *New Eng. Farmer* II. 125, I herewith hand you a sketch of my ice closet attached to my ice house. **1892** *Harper's Mag.* Feb. 441/2 What's the matter with the ice-cooler? **1853** BUNN *Old Eng. & New Eng.* 28 The 'ice-crop' (as it is drolly called) proved to be a fair average one. **1888** *Boston Jrnl.* 2, Jan. 5/8 Blizzards may be more correctly termed cloud-bursts of what has been aptly called ice-dust, of great extent, violence, and long duration. **1883** 'MARK TWAIN' *Life on Miss.* xxxix. 410 Like Vicksburg and New Orleans, she [Natchez] has her ice factory. **1905** *Forestry Bureau Bul.* No. 61, 40 *Ice guards.* Heavy timbers fastened fan shaped about a cluster of boom piles at an angle of approximately 30 degrees to the surface of the water. They prevent the destruction of the boom by ice, through forcing it to mount the guards and be broken up. (N[orthern] F[orest].) **1880** *Scribner's Mo.* Aug. 490/1 The ice had moved up thirty feet, the width of the ice-harvester's canal above, and had stopped. **1852** E. F. ELLET *Pioneer Women* 268 Along the ice on the lake shore, [he] fell into an 'ice hole' some distance from the land. **1884** *Nat. Museum Bul.* No. 27, 1053 Ice-hooks. . . . Used for lifting ice by hand or for hoisting it. **1838** *N.Y. Advertiser & Exp.* 24 Feb. 4/5 The ice-mongers need not have felt alarm on account of the warm weather the early part of the Winter. **1860** HOLMES *Professor* (1902) 212 It is rather the east wind, as it . . . clasps a clear-eyed wintry noon on the chill bridal couch of a New England ice-quarry. **1912** DREISER *Financier* 36 He was an adept at turning all sorts of practical tricks, such as . . . taking the agency for the sale of a new kind of ice-skate from an ice-skate company. **1876** 'MARK TWAIN' *Punch, Brothers, Punch!* (1878) 17 We have to credit the weather with . . . the ice-storm.

4. Special combinations.

+*Ice apron,* a pointed structure for preventing ice from injuring the supports of a bridge; +*ice chair,* a chair supplied with runners so that it can be moved over ice; +*ice gull,* the glaucous gull or burgomaster; +*ice gush,* in a glacier, ice and water at the bottom of a crevasse; +*ice palace,* an edifice built of ice and made the occasion of a public celebration or winter carnival; +*ice station,* a place at which ice is collected for shipment; *ice yacht,* =ICE BOAT 2. {1882}

1866 LOSSING *Hudson* 304 Rockland Lake village . . . , opposite Sing Sing, [is] the most extensive ice-station on the [Hudson] river. **1871** *Scribner's Mo.* II. 170 It [has been] necessary to construct enormous breakwaters, having ice-aprons of strong oak timber. **1888** *St. Paul Globe* 22 Jan., If every man in St. Paul would only do a little booming for the coming ice palace the amount of good it would do is almost incalculable. **1889** *Boston Jrnl.* 26 Dec. 16/5 There are great numbers of ice-yachts all ready for racing on the Upper Hudson. **1904** *Franklin Inst. Jrnl.* Oct. 304 Never once did one [horse] . . . refuse to climb out of an ice gush when called upon to do so. **1913** A. B. EMERSON *R. Fielding at Snow Camp* 88 The boys took turns in pushing her about in an ice-chair. **1917** *Birds of Amer.* I. 41 Glaucous Gull. *Larus hyperboreus*. . . . [Also called] Ice Gull; Harbor Gull.

Ice boat. **1.** A stout steamboat used for breaking ice in a river or harbor. {1842–} **2.** A frame or boat, equipped with sails and runners, used for sport on the ice. {1819–} — **(1)** **1839** *Hazard's Register* 13 Feb. 14/2 The city Ice Boat has this winter more than repaid all her cost, by the service of a few days in keeping open the navigation during the late inclement weather. [Phila.] **1841** *Knickerb.* XVII. 301 Let this paper be considered as the ice-boat, which goes before, and clears the way for, the magnificent squadron which is to follow. **1857** *Ib.* XLIX. 419 The Company's powerful Ice-boat . . . was to leave in the morning. **(2)** **1866** LOSSING *Hudson* 277 The river had offered good sport for skaters, and the navigators of ice-boats. **1896** *N.Y. Wkly. Witness* 23 Dec. 4/1 He had never sailed on an ice-boat before. **1902** CLAPIN 237 *Ice-boat,* a kind of yacht on skates, which furnishes an exhilirating [*sic*] winter pastime on the frozen rivers and lakes of the Northern regions.

+Ice box. A box containing ice and used for keeping food cool; a refrigerator car. {1884-} — **1855** *Amer. Inst. N.Y. Trans.* 397 Ice boxes for domestic purposes may be constructed on the same principle. **1898** CAHAN *Imported Bridegroom* 243 A little later a cheap alarm-clock and an ice-box were brought in. **1907** LONDON *Road* 137, I pulled out of Evanston in the ice-boxes of an 'orange special,' a fast freight laden with fruit from sunny California. **1920** COOPER *Under Big Top* 127 Residents of the neighborhood began to complain that their houses were being burglarized, ice boxes robbed.

+Ice-breaker. 1. (See quot. 1889.) **2.** (See quot. 1875.) — **(1) 1833** *Niles' Reg.* XLIV. 179/1 The ice breaker had been enlarged during the season to an extent of 575 feet in length by 60 in breadth. **1889** *Cent.* 2966/2 *Ice-breaker*, ... a structure of masonry or timber (as a pier or row of piles) for the protection of bridge-piers or of vessels in dock from moving ice. **(2) 1875** KNIGHT 1161/2 An ice-breaker for harbors is a steam-vessel provided with means for opening or keeping open a channel for ships. **1880** *Congress. Rec.* App. 20 May 178/2 Such ice as forms in the Choptank is not strong enough at any time to resist the power of an ordinary ice-breaker. **1902** LORIMER *Lett. Merchant* 114 You'll find that you can't push within a mile of her even on a Soo ice-breaker.

+Ice cart. A cart used for delivering ice. — **1842** *Knickerb.* XX. 205 Before an omnibus or hotel or restaurant or ice-cart had assumed its popular cognomen. **1864** NICHOLS *Amer. Life* I. 247 Every morning the ice-cart comes round.

Ice cellar. A storage cellar for beer, meat, etc., that is kept cool with ice. — [**1771** J. R. FORSTER tr. Kalm *Travels into N. Amer.* III. 232 Some of the people of quality [in Quebec] make use of ice-cellars, to keep beer cool in, during summer, and to keep fresh flesh.... These ice-cellars are commonly built of stone, under the house.] **1810** *Columbian Centinel* 20 Jan. 4 A new green-house and ice-cellar. **1883** *Harper's Mag.* July 261 [In Cincinnati] I visited one of the largest whiskey distilleries, and also one of the largest beer factories, and took copious—notes about ... the ice cellars colder than Siberia ever dared to be.

+Ice chest. An ice box or refrigerating chamber. {1897-} — **1841** CIST *Cincinnati* (*advt.*), Manufacturer of Packing-boxes, Ice-chests, Trunk and Segar Boxes, &c. **a1846** *Quarter Race Ky.* 166, I shall put it [fresh salmon] in my ice-chest. **1869** E. PUTNAM *Receipt Bk.* 319 It is quite ... necessary to have ... a large ice chest for the cellar. **1912** *N.Y. Ev. Post* 26 Aug. 6 (Th. S.), Agents Baffle Government Officials and Bring 'Chinks' Across Border in Coffins, Ice Chests and Box Cars.

+Ice company. A company which deals in ice. — **1834** *Congress. Deb.* 14 Feb. 544 He then read the prices of various stocks of banks, ice companies, ... at the South. **1873** BAILEY *Life in Danbury* 141 The Still-River ice-company have been engaged in the past week securing their crop of ice. **1882** MCCABE *New York* 364 Above Canal street the ice companies ... have their depots.

Ice cream.

1. A smooth, creamy, frozen confection, variously made with cream, milk, eggs, sugar, etc., and flavored with vanilla, chocolate, etc. {iced cream 1688; ice cream 1769-}

1744 *Penna. Mag. Hist.* I. 126 Among the Rarities of which it [the dessert] was Compos'd, was some fine Ice Cream which, with the Strawberries and Milk, eat most Deliciously. **1830** [see ICE HOUSE]. **1853** *Harper's Mag.* Sept. 567/2 Sitting in the little stalls ..., eating ice-creams, and indulging ... [in] 'Roman ice punch.' **1858** C. FLINT *Milch Cows* 214 The richest quality of ice-cream is made from cream. **1915** CAMPBELL *Proving Virginia* 102 Let us all drive down to Anderson's for ice-cream.

2. Attrib. and comb. with *cake, candy, day*, etc.

1905 *N.Y. Ev. Post* 4 Aug. 7 Angel cake, sponge cake, and ice-cream cake have conspired to relegate the seed cake to practical oblivion. **1873** BAILEY *Life in Danbury* 273 And a package of ice-cream candy. **1886** H. D. BROWN *Two College Girls* 90 It was Wednesday, ice-cream day. **1893** *Harper's Mag.* March 593 The groups gathered here and there enjoy themselves about as they do at church sociables and ice-cream and strawberry festivals in their home villages. **1853** *Ib.* Sept. 567/2, I was sitting in an ice-cream garden, pretending to lick an ice-spoon. **1904** M. KELLY *Little Citizens* 203 They expected some word of farewell—perhaps even an ice-cream party. **1873** BEADLE *Undevel. West* xxviii. 623 Two months vigorous courting will cost more than that—particularly in the ice cream-season. **1841** STEELE *Summer Journey* 43 The restless mankind part, repaired to the shops, to inspect the manufactures of the town, or to refresh themselves at the soda-water, and ice-cream shops. **1873** *Winfield* (Kan.) *Courier* 15 May 3/2 The Ladies of the Congregational church will hold an Ice Cream Sociable at the residence of Capt. John Lowrey. **1887** *Courier-Journal* 11 Jan. 3/4 Annie Heinrich ... clerked for ... the proprietress of an ice-cream and confectionery store. **1915** CAMPBELL *Proving Virginia* 106 Viviette insisted on stopping at Anderson's for ice-cream sundaes. **1898** *Kansas City Star* 18 Dec. 3/6 (*advt.*), We will show (occupying the space formerly used by our ice cream tables) the handsomest lot of Christmas Candy Novelties ever brought to the West. **1867** *Atlantic Mo.* Jan. 83/2, I won't send for her—till ice-cream time. **1877** PHELPS *Story of Avis* 137 The college-boys fitted for biennial under the tutelage of the ice-cream vender.

+Ice-cream freezer. A device used for freezing ice cream. Also fig. — **1854** *Penna. Agric. Rep.* 363 Three ice cream freezers. **1873** BAILEY *Life in Danbury* 101 As calm and cool as the lid of an ice-cream freezer. **1873** *Winfield* (Kan.) *Courier* 14 Aug. 1/7 Flirts are always pretty, have big hearts, and when once caught you'll find them worth a dozen iceberg girls, who are only useful as icecream freezers. **1901** HEGAN *Mrs. Wiggs* 146 The grocery boy, staggering under the weight of an ice-cream freezer and carrying something wrapped in white paper, came up the path.

+Ice-cream parlor. A shop which specializes in serving ice cream. — **1897** *Ore. State Jrnl.* 17 April 5/2 Engine Co. No. 1 met Thursday night at the Firemen's Hall ... [after which] they adjourned to the ice cream parlors of the Bonbonierre. **1903** ADE *People You Know* 42 The only Chance that Florine had to mingle with the Popular Boys was to go down Town in the Afternoon and just happen to meet one of them at the Ice-Cream Parlor. **1923** WATTS *L. Nichols* 11 [You] must hold your own against the hectic distractions of the city—saloons, ice-cream parlors, Shriners' parades, and fire-engines on the run.

+Ice-cream saloon. =ICE-CREAM PARLOR. — **1849** G. G. FOSTER *N.Y. in Slices* 31 The following scene had taken place at a fashionable ice-cream saloon in Broadway. **1864** TAYLOR *H. Thurston* xvi. 217 Transparencies gleamed before ice-cream saloons. **1906** BELL *C. Lee* 276 We took every child on the scene ... to an ice-cream saloon and treated them.

+Ice-cream soda. Soda water to which ice cream has been added. — **1887** HAYES *Jesuit's Ring* 56 The days of bright summer, and lawn tennis, ... and ice-cream soda. **1893** *Critic* 8 April 226/1 Our national beverage 'ice-cream soda.' **1904** *N.Y. Ev. Post* 9 July 5 There were four clerks in the drug store. One was serving ice-cream soda. **1909** STRATTON-PORTER *Girl of Limberlost* ix. 166 It was their custom to ... take turns in treating to expensive candies, ice-cream sodas, hot chocolate [etc.].

+Ice-cutter. 1. A device used in cutting or chopping ice. **2.** A man engaged in cutting ice. — **(1) 1851** WORTLEY *Travels in U.S.* 143 The clear polished ice is cut into blocks, about two-and-twenty inches square, for which operation a machine expressly constructed and invented, is used (called the ice-cutter). **1884** *Nat. Museum Bul.* No. 27, 1053 *Ice-cutter.* A flat chisel-shaped piece of steel, with saw-like teeth on the lower edge.... Used for chopping up ice for the purpose of packing fresh fish. **(2) 1854** THOREAU *Walden* 315 These ice-cutters are a merry race, full of jest and sport. **1899** *Scribner's Mag.* XXV. 124/1 An ice-cutter should make the best of ice-handlers in summer. **1917** MCCUTCHEON *Green Fancy* 45 Jim Roudebush,—one of our leadin' ice-cutters.

+Ice dealer. One whose business is dealing in ice. — **1851** CIST *Cincinnati* 50 [In Cincinnati there are three] ice dealers. **1871** GROSVENOR *Protection* 115 The ice dealer will scarcely need protection until there is an increased supply of pauper labor about the North Pole. **1895** *Chicago Tribune* 6 April 1 Patrick Fleming, a well-to-do ice dealer, ... died at midnight.

+Iced tea. Tea chilled with ice. Also attrib. — **1886** ALTON *Among Law-Makers* 275 The Senators [had] ... their large coolers of iced-tea, to mitigate the force of the weather. **1897** 'THANET' *Missionary Sheriff* 62 'Iced tea?' said Pauline. **1918** *Sears, Roebuck & Co. Cat.* No. 136, 624 Iced tea spoons ... set of six $1.68.

Iced water. Variant of ICE WATER. — **1855** *Harvard Mag.* I. 4 The man of color ... on hot days, serves to you the glass of refreshing iced-water and the mug of invigorating root-beer. **1870** O. LOGAN *Before Footlights* 263 A character quite peculiar to America is the boy or man who brings around iced water to thirsty travellers. **1881** *Harper's Mag.* Dec. 148/2 Iced-water ... [is] the American national drink.

+Ice gorge. An obstruction in a river caused by an accumulation of ice. Also fig. — **1862** *Congress Globe* 24 June 2896/1 [League] Island is below the bend of the Delaware, and hence mainly out of danger from ice gorges. **1873** *Newton Kansan* 2 Jan. 2/1 An ice gorge ... destroyed a large number of steamboats. **1887** *Courier-Journal* 21 Jan. 8/7 The monster ice-gorge which has been forming for the past ten days at the head of Six-Mile Island broke loose. **1896** *Congress. Rec.* 5 Feb. 1329/2 The closing days of the session, when there is a perfect ice gorge of measures contending for precedence.

+Ice harbor. A harbor for ships available for use when other harbors are closed by ice. — **1876** *Congress. Rec.* 17 July 4655/1 When the ice forms in the river, it is necessary that the shipping coming in from the ocean should have some place of refuge. Hence that ice-harbor at that point was established. *Ib.*, With reference to the ice-harbor at New Castle, we have but comparatively very little commerce at that point. **1884** *Ib.* 10 June 4967/1 The establishment of an ice-harbor at Bellaire [Ohio] is a matter of interest to all.

Ice house. A building used for the storage of ice: (see also quot. 1830). {1687-}

1785 WASHINGTON *Diaries* II. 434 Having put in the heavy frame into my Ice House, I began this day to seal it with Boards. **1804** CUTLER in *Life & Corr.* II. 153 The President filling his ice-house. **1830** WATSON *Philadelphia* 202 Ice Houses ... have all come into use among us since the war of Independence. After them came the use of ice creams.... Public ice houses for the sale of ice, is a more modern enterprise than either. **1850** *New Eng. Farmer* II. 48 The same principle applies to the construction of out-buildings, such as corn-cribs, ice-houses, smoke-houses, or hog-pens. **1904** WALLER *Wood-Carver* 211, I heard the tinkle of ice—she had been to the ice-house!

b. Such a building used for preserving provisions.

[**1853** FOWLER *Home for All* 116 My ice-house consists of *two stories*—the upper one for ice, the lower, a room kept cool by the ice and its drippings, a preservatory for keeping fruit, butter, eggs, fresh meat, fish, bacon, pies, etc.] **1855** *Amer. Inst. N.Y. Trans. 1854* 395 The grand purpose of an ice house he contended should not be to store ice, but to store and preserve perishable commodities. **1880** *Harper's Mag.* July 216/2 Two of the members [of the club] took a couple of ducks from the ice-house. **1891** CHASE & CLOW *Industry* II. 110 In many places the meat is placed, as soon as killed, in ice-houses, and cooled down to freezing point.

+**Ice machine.** A machine for making ice. — **1872** *Newton Kansan* 12 Sept. 4/4 From what we can learn of the operations of the various newly-invented ice-machines it is not improbable that this welcome commodity will soon be supplied to each family. **1883** BEADLE *Western Wilds* xxxvi. 591 On the river at Charleston [Ariz.] . . . is an ice machine, and every morning the ice wagon goes its rounds. **1897** 'MARK TWAIN' *Following Equator* iii. 62 The ice-machine has traveled all over the world, now, and brought ice within everybody's reach.

Iceman. {1855-} +**1.** A man employed in harvesting ice for sale. +**2.** A man whose business is delivering ice. — **(1) 1854** THOREAU *Walden* 209 Though . . . the ice-men have skimmed it once, it is itself unchanged, the same water which my youthful eyes fell on. **(2) 1870** 'F. FERN' *Ginger-Snaps* 179 Let no grocer boy or ice-man fondly hope to retain the celestial spark, while he briefly deposits his wares in my kitchen. **1890** *Harper's Mag.* April 746/1 [Lucilla saw] a burly ice-man, his iron pincers dangling from his hand. **1902** LORIMER *Lett. Merchant* 11 He couldn't write up a satisfactory account of the Ice-Men's Ball.

+**Ice merchant.** An ice dealer. — **1855** *Amer. Inst. N.Y. Trans.* 374 In building ice houses . . . the best thing, as has been fully proved by Mr. Tudor, the great ice merchant of Boston, is hollow walls, containing a statum [*sic*] of air. **1905** THWAITES *Early West. Trav.* XXI. 12 Wyeth finally . . . settled down to the humdrum role of ice-merchant in Cambridge.

+**Ice party.** A party at which people amuse themselves by skating on ice ponds, rivers, etc. — **1884** JAMES in *Century Mag.* July 339/2 The wonderful, brilliant New York winter, . . . the sunsets on the snow, the ice-parties in the frosty clearness, the bright, hot, velvety houses. **1905** WIGGIN *Rose* 91 Claude Merrill . . . was very much in evidence at the Saturday evening ice parties.

+**Ice pick.** An implement, somewhat like a stiletto, used in chipping ice, or dividing a block of ice into smaller blocks. — **1879** STOCKTON *Rudder Grange* i, It is not probable that I can sell that ice-pick after you have used it for ten years. **1885** CUSTER *Boots & Saddles* xxii. 210 It looks more like a large ice-pick. **1898** WESTCOTT *D. Harum* 210 David . . . began a struggle to unwire the same [bottle] with an ice-pick.

+**Ice pitcher.** A pitcher used for holding ice or ice water. — **1865** *Nation* I. 159 At this season of the year nothing adds more to one's comfort than to drink freely of the contents of our new pattern richly double-plated ice pitchers. **1876** SCUDDER *Dwellers* iii. 55 The big Britannia ice-pitcher and the half-dozen silver spoons . . . had been brought up-stairs. **1893** *Harper's Mag.* Feb. 458, I'm dyin' for a swingin' silver-plated ice-pitcher, an' have it I will. **1912** COBB *Back Home* 321 On opposite side-walks they [2 negroes] stood, sweating like brown stone china ice pitchers.

Ice plant. A plant (*Mesembryanthemum crystallinum*) having foliage covered with glistening dots or vesicles. {1753-} — **1817-8** EATON *Botany* (1822) 353. **1859** *U.S. & Mex. Bound. Survey Rep.* II. I. 16 Growing with the *Albronias* a species of ice-plant . . . is frequently found. *c***1887** STURTEVANT *Notes Edible Plants* 363 The ice plant . . . is advertised in American seed lists of 1881 as a desirable vegetable for boiling like spinach, or for garnishing.

+**Ice pond.** A pond from which ice is cut to fill ice houses. — **1851** *S. Lit. Messenger* XVII. 687/1 The waters which flow past Norfolk into the sea, divide . . . the ice ponds of the North from the cotton fields at the South. **1892** TORREY *Foot-Path Way* 156 [A piece of wood] is bounded on the further side by a wet meadow, and at the eastern end by a little ice-pond. **1917** MCCUTCHEON *Green Fancy* 153 The crick . . . was dammed a little ways up to make the ice-pond 'tween here an' Spanish Falls.

+**Ice wagon.** A wagon used for delivering ice to residences, stores, etc. — **1873** *Winfield* (Kan.) *Courier* 17 July 3/1 Our ice wagon has changed hands. . . . Mr. Stewart now holds the reins, and is prepared to deliver ice to any part of the city. **1901** HEGAN *Mrs. Wiggs* 64 All of a suddint a ice-wagon come rattlin' up behin' him.

Ice water. {1722}

1. Water chilled by the addition of ice. {1773-1797, in Italy}

1832 KENNEDY *Swallow Barn* II. xvii. 220 The injured part should be bathed frequently with ice-water. **1867** L. BAKER *U.S. Secret Service* 58 I stepped forward to a table on which stood a pitcher of ice-water. **1880** 'MARK TWAIN' *Tramp Abroad* xlvi. 536 America is healthier than Europe, notwithstanding her 'deadly' indulgence in ice-water. **1897** FLANDRAU *Harvard Episodes* 182 The orator calms himself with ice-water from the bedroom pitcher that is always prominent on those occasions. **1916** DU PUY *Uncle Sam* 232 We are alone with the pitcher of ice water.

2. Attrib. with *boy, jug, pitcher.*

1863 A. D. WHITNEY *F. Gartney* xxi, With quick, professional instinct, Miss Sampson sprang forward, seizing, as she did so, an ice-water pitcher from the table. **1893** *Harper's Mag.* March 498 The $2 or $3 a week to the waiter at table, the fees to the bell-boys and the ice-water boy and bootblack. **1897** 'THANET' *Missionary Sheriff* 62 A glass jug of tea stood by a plated ice-water jug of a pattern highly esteemed before the war.

+**I dad,** *interj.* Euphemism for 'by God.' *colloq.* {edad, 1710} — **1843** 'CARLTON' *New Purchase* I. 173 And, I dad, if she didn't read clean through all our church histories. *Ib.* 174 Nancy, I dad, says I, I do believe I'll jist take old Bet. **1848** BARTLETT 187, I Dad! An exclamation used in the Western States.

***Idea.** +A small drink. *colloq.* — **1830** *Ky. Gazette* 20 Aug., [I] ventured a tiff of Bramin and an idea of water. **1836** CROCKETT *Exploits* 129 'Let us take an ideer.' So we walked up to the bar, [and] took a nip.

***Ilex.** A plant of the genus *Ilex* of the holly family, Ilicaceae. Also attrib. — **1734** *Ga. Col. Rec.* III. 97 [Received] By Capt Wood Twenty one pieces of Timber, the Growth of Georgia, whereof Two Mahogany, One Ash, One Sycamore, Three Ilex and Fourteen Red Bay. **1836** HOLLEY *Texas* v. 88 Among the underwood are found the bay laurel . . . [and] the ilex.

+**Illinoian.** Also **Illinoisan, Illinoisian.** A native or inhabitant of the state of Illinois.

(*a*) **1835** HOFFMAN *Winter in West* II. 204 Why now, squire, the Yankees are becoming great people here north of us, in Michigan and so on, and they call us old Illinoians 'Suckers.' **1846** FARNHAM *Prairie Land* 63*n.*, ['Sucker' is] the cognomen of the Illinoians, answering to the Buckeye of Ohio, the Wolverine of Michigan, the Corn-cracker of Kentucky, &c. **1867** RICHARDSON *Beyond Mississippi* xi. 132 Most readers have heard Ohioans spoken of as 'Buckeyes,' . . . Illinoians as 'Suckers.'

(*b*) **1836** *Public Ledger* 14 Oct. (Th.), The Illinoisans are called Suckers. **1855** *Ill. Agric. Soc. Trans.* II. 63 Illinoisans—men—men who know their rights and dare maintain them. **1865** TROWBRIDGE *Three Scouts* xxx. 313 Grim and pleased looked the tall Illinoisan as he drew near. **1877** HABBERTON *Jericho Road* x. 97 Small parties of discharged Illinoisans and Indianians had frequently passed through.

(*c*) **1862** *Rep. Comm. Patents 1861: Agric.* 549 Jack Rossiter was a native Illinoisian, and his exploits may be found in the racing calendar. **1890** WHITMAN *Prose Wks.* (1892) 504 Abraham Lincoln, familiar, our own, an Illinoisian.

+**Illinois.** [Amer. Indian.]

1. An Indian of a confederation of Algonquian tribes formerly living in Illinois and adjacent states.

[**1670** *Relations des Jésuites* (1858) 86 Les Ilinois peuples tirans au Sud, ont cinq grands Bourgs. **1722** COXE *Carolana* 17 Besides the Illicoueck, are the Nations Prouaria, the great Nation Cascasquia and Caracontauon.] **1766** ROGERS *Ponteach* II. ii, This same Chekitan a Captive led The fair Donanta from the Illinois. **1775** ADAIR *Indians* 142 The Illinois . . . remember when adultery was punished among them with death. **1834** PECK *Gaz. Illinois* 102 [Marquette and Joliet] were hospitally [*sic*] received by the Illinois, a numerous nation of Indians who were destitute of the cruelty of savages.

2. *attrib.* **a.** In the names of plants and animals.

1785 MARSHALL *Amer. Grove* 69 *Juglans pecan.* The Pecan, or Illinois Hickery. This tree is said to grow plenty in the neighborhood of the Illinois river. **1836** in Hall *Statistics of West* x. 149 The Illinois grazier, a most useful race of sheep, . . . is a short-legged, stout sheep, with a long-stapled soft wool. **1849** EMMONS *Agric. N.Y.* II. 265 Illinois, or Lady-finger corn, . . . is an unproductive kind, bearing sometimes four ears upon a stalk. **1862** *Rep. Comm. Patents 1861: Agric.* 190 *Fragaria Illinoiensis*—Illinois strawberry. **1863** *Ill. Agric. Soc. Trans.* V. 869 *Cicer Arietunum* . . . has again been heralded as a valuable acquisition upon the prairies under the name of *Illinois coffee*, or 'Australian coffee.'

b. With reference to the Indians of the Illinois tribes.

1835 HOFFMAN *Winter in West* I. 279 This natural battlement was the scene of a desperate conflict between the fierce and haughty Pottawattamies and one band of the Illinois Indians.

c. With reference to the state of Illinois.

1835 HOFFMAN *Winter in West* I. 226 An Illinois man . . . was on the spot shortly afterwards. **1837** PECK *New Guide* 288 Nothing is more common than for an Illinois farmer to go among his stock, select, shoot down, and dress a fine beef. **1840** *N.Y. American* 24 Nov. 3/2 The overshadowing sycamore . . . was a scraggy affair whose butt-cut would hardly make a back-log for an Illinois cabin.

d. In nicknames applied to Abraham Lincoln.

1865 RICHARDSON *Secret Service* xxiv. 355 [*The Appeal*] was noticeably free from vituperation, calling the President 'Mr. Lincoln,' instead of the 'Illinois Baboon.' **1866** CARPENTER *At White House* 120 In various sections of the Eastern and Middle States, the antecedents and even the name of Mr. Lincoln were entirely unknown. The newspapers announced the nominee as the 'Illinois Rail-splitter'; and however popular this title may have been with the masses . . . it seemed to many people a very extraordinary qualification for the Presidency. **1866** W. REID *After the War* 30 The Rebel owner has the satisfaction of . . . calculating the profits which might have gone into his own pockets, but for the frantic determination . . . never to submit to the tyrannical rule of the Illinois gorilla.

Illinois(i)an. Variant of ILLINOIAN.

+**Illinois nut.** The pecan, *Carya illinoensis.* — **1781-2** JEFFERSON *Notes Va.* (1788) 37 Paccan, or Illinois nut. . . . It grows on the Illinois, Wabash, Ohio, and Missisipi [*sic*]. **1786** WASHINGTON *Diaries* III. 54 Also 21 of the Illinois Nuts. **1804** C. B. BROWN tr. Volney *View* 123 It is the same with the . . . pakan or Illinois nut. **1884** SARGENT *Rep. Forests* 132 *Carya olivæformis.* . . . Pecan. Illinois Nut.

***Illuminate,** *v.* +*tr.* (See quotations.) *slang. Obs.* — **1851** HALL *College Words* 167 *Illuminate*, to interline with a translation. *Ib.*, Illuminated books are preferred by good judges to ponies or hobbies, as the text and translation in them are brought nearer to one another.

***Illuminating,** *a.* Of gas or oil: Used for lighting. — **1859** *Rep. Comm. Patents 1858* I. 678 Improvement in Apparatus for Generating Illuminating Gas. **1875** *Amer. Cycl.* XIII. 371/2 Mineral sperm is the name given by Joshua Merrill, of the Downer kerosene oil company, to a petroleum product discovered by him. This is an illuminating oil. **1886**

WINCHELL *Walks & Talks* 152 Cannel Coals . . . were used in the earliest manufacture of illuminating gas and kerosene, or 'coal oil.'

***Illuminator.** +A highly polished convex reflector placed behind a light to intensify it. — **1851** GLISAN *Jrnl. Army Life* 77 The slow procession . . . moves onward with burnished muskets flashing their reflected light . . . like so many calcium illuminators. **1897** BRODHEAD *Bound in Shallows* 90 Buck Sherrer's house, with an illuminator behind the oil lamp on its porch, flashed in sight.

***Illusion. 1.** A delicate, semitransparent lace; a form of tulle. {1887} **2.** A stage device used for spectacular effect. **3.** Attrib. in sense 1 with *dress, waist.* — **(1) 1871** *Harper's Mag.* Aug. 385 She put down the bow of pretty ribbon she was pinning together on a heap of bonnet wire and illusion, and went out into the yard. **1881** *Reinbeck* (Iowa) *Times* 6 Jan. 1/5 [The dress] will be square cut with inside illusion and white kid boots. **1887** *Courier-Journal* 21 Jan. 4/6 There were draperies of silver illusion, and the gown was one of Worth's creations. **(2) 1895** *N.Y. Dramatic News* 14 Dec. 8/3 The new department . . . will introduce a series of illusions hitherto entirely unknown in this country. **(3) 1857** *Lawrence* (Kan.) *Repub.* 28 May 3 The most fashionable Millinery Goods . . . Lace, Gimp, Straw, Silk, Blend, Hair and Illusion Bonnets. **1873** ALDRICH *Marj. Daw* 14 An emerald-colored illusion dress looped up after the fashion of a Dresden china shepherdess. **1878** *Decorum* 279 Puffed illusion waists . . . should be used to cover the neck and arms.

***Illy,** *adv.* Badly, ill. {now *dial.*}

The use of this word in the United States has been often condemned. See second group of quotations below.

(1) **1787** JEFFERSON *Writings* VI. 223 Distresses brought on themselves by a feebleness of mind which calculates very illy its own happiness. **1794** WASHINGTON *Writings* XII. 431, I can very illy spare the money. **1812** in J. Cutler *Top. Descr. Ohio* 167 The weather was now very severe, and the lodges illy calculated to shelter us from it. *c***1834** CATLIN *Indians* II. 30 An independent-feeling . . . illy harmonized with rules and regulations. **1865** S. A. DRAKE ed. Hubbard *Narrative* II. 10*n.*, [This] illy agrees with the Catholicity with which he is usually credited. **1886** DORSEY *Midshipman Bob* II. xiv. 261 There are very few young men that could be so illy spared from the service. **1925** BRYAN *Memoirs* 357 Mr. Bryan was not illy prepared for this work.

(2) **1816** PICKERING 107 The adverb has been much used in America, both in conversation and in writing. It is not to be found in the English Dictionaries, nor is it now used by English authors; the word *ill* (like *well*) being always employed by them both as an *adverb* and *adjective.* *Illy* has been thought by some persons to be of American origin; but this is not the fact. **1829** *Va. Lit. Museum* 30 Dec. 458 *Illy.* This adverb cannot, perhaps, be said to be of American origin; it has, however, been employed by so few of the older English writers; and is now never used in England, that we mention it here. *Ill* is equally an adverb and adjective; and hence, *illy,* to say the least of it, is unnecessary. **1829** T. R. BECK in *Trans. Albany Institute* I. 30 *Illy.* The use of this adverb cannot be too frequently condemned, and it is to be regretted that a man of the eloquence and general accuracy in writing, of Mr. Clay, should have given it the sanction of his example, which he did on taking his seat as Speaker, in December, 1817. I have subsequently seen the word used, in some communication to the Legislature of New-York, but did not the time note, and I cannot now recall it. **1866** LOWELL *Biglow P.* 2 Ser. p. xxxiii, The objection to *illy* is not an etymological one, but simply that it is contrary to good usage; a very sufficient reason.

Immediatism. {*a*1825–} +*Hist.* The policy of abolishing slavery at once. — **1835** H. G. OTIS in *Liberator* V. 144 [Abolitionists] have enriched the nomenclature with a new word, *immediatism.* This . . . is the opposite of *gradualism,* another new coinage. **1880** O. JOHNSON *W. L. Garrison* 45 Mr. Garrison had learned the doctrine of immediatism from Dr. Beecher.

+Immediatist. 1. *Hist.* One who favored the immediate abolishment of slavery. **2.** One who favors immediate action. — **(1) 1835** H. G. OTIS in W. P. & F. J. Garrison *W. L. Garrison* I. 500 [Christ] was not an immediatist. **1852** W. GOODELL *Slavery & Anti-Slavery* 424 [Some] professed to be opposed to slavery, and in favor of its gradual removal, while they only deprecated the imprudent measures of the *immediatists.* **(2) 1888** *Andover Rev.* Oct. 361 The gospel of the Immediatist,—work while the day lasts.

+Immigrant. (Cf. EMIGRANT.)

Pickering discusses *immigrant, immigrate,* and *immigration* at some length. See also A. Matthews in *Nation* LXX. 10.

1. One who has come from a foreign country to settle in the United States.

1789 MORSE *Amer. Geog.* 253 There are in this state [N.Y.] many immigrants from Scotland, Ireland, Germany, and some few from France. **1796** *Boston Rec.* X. 219 Society for the aid of Immigrants. **1815** DRAKE *Cincinnati* v. 181 The diseases to which immigrants are most liable, are bilious and typhous fevers. **1849** *Whig Almanac 1850* 38/2 Mr. Walker estimated the coin brought into the U.S. by immigrants from abroad at $8,000,000 yearly. **1880** *Harper's Mag.* Dec. 70 The strong local prejudice against our Asiatic immigrants . . . [keeps] 'Chinatown' practically a sealed book. **1911** PERSONS, etc. *Mass. Labor Laws* 56 Places [in the factories] were filled with Irish immigrants.

2. One who has migrated from one part of the United States to another, as from the East to newly opened territory in the West.

The quotation dated *c*1787 by the *O.E.D.* is dubious, as an 1836 printing of the speech has *emigrant.*

1798 *Doc. Hist. N.Y. State* I. 675 New England had not been settled so long as to produce Native Immigrants when E. Hampton [L.I.] was first settled. *a***1817** DWIGHT *Travels* II. 232 Immigrants are crowding to it [Maine] from New-Hampshire, Massachusetts, and Rhode Island. **1857** *Lawrence* (Kan.) *Republican* 18 June 2 Among the immigrants of the present season, there are some Free-State men who doubt the propriety of the course hitherto adopted. **1872** MCCLELLAN *Golden State* 137 Immigrants and gold-seekers were still coming. **1874** GLISAN *Jrnl. Army Life* 481 The more sensible immigrants took up claims in the beautiful Willamette Valley.

3. Attrib. with *fund, interest, train,* etc.

1835 COOPER *Monikins* xxiv, The 'immigrunt interest,' as Noah termed it, had actually carried a candidate on each of the two great opposing tickets. **1867** RICHARDSON *Beyond Miss.* 26 A confused picture of immense piles of freight, horse, ox, and mule teams receiving merchandise from the steamers, scores of immigrant wagons, and a busy crowd of whites, Indians [etc.]. **1900** *Congress. Rec.* 31 Jan. 1354/1 In 1849 . . . many immigrant trains crossed the great plains through Arizona Territory. **1903** *Statutes at Large* XXXII. I. 1213 Money thus collected [by a head-tax on entry of aliens] . . . shall constitute a permanent appropriation to be called the 'immigrant fund.' **1911** PERSONS, etc. *Mass. Labor Laws* 175 In the investigation of immigrant women, evidence was obtained [etc.].

Immigration. {1658–}

+1. The action of moving into the United States from another country, or into one part of the United States from another, for the purpose of settlement.

1790 MACLAY *Deb. Senate* 178 Immigration is a source of population to us, and they wish to deprive us of it. **1804** C. B. BROWN tr. Volney *View* 262*n.*, There is a large party in the state who abhor and discourage immigration. **1837** *Diplom. Corr. Texas* I. (1908) 196 Immigration is partially suspended. **1857** *Lawrence* (Kan.) *Republican* 4 June 3 We are having an unprecedented rush of immigration this season, which will add tens of thousands to the number of mouths to be fed next winter. **1884** *N. Mex. Terr. Rep.* 15 The present 'Bureau of Immigration' . . . reduced the secretary's salary from $100 to $75 monthly. **1893** PAGE in *Harper's Mag.* Dec. 4/1 Of later years the tendency of immigration has been towards those more fertile sections, the rich lands of the Valley and of the Southwest.

+2. A (or the) body of immigrants.

1852 STANSBURY *Gt. Salt Lake* 126 In the autumn, another large immigration arrived under the president, Brigham Young, which materially added to the strength of the colony. **1857** *Lawrence* (Kan.) *Republican* 2 July 2 The whole immigration of this season . . . was excluded from the ballot-box. **1857** *Ill. Agric. Soc. Trans.* II. 365 The immigration [into Ill.] was generally a moral, correct people. . . . They emigrated from the various old states.

3. Attrib. with *boom, department, officer,* etc.

1872 *Atlantic Mo.* April 456/1 Natives of Europe and the British Provinces who came from and through Canada and New Brunswick . . . not included in the immigration reports were [etc.]. **1890** *Stock Grower & Farmer* 25 Jan. 7/2 Col. Edward Haren, of the immigration department of the Santa Fe, is in the city on his return from Albuquerque. **1890** *Ib.* 22 Feb. 3/2 This territory has never had an immigration 'boom'. **1903** *Statutes at Large* XXXII. I. 1217 The United States Public Health and Marine-Hospital Service shall be reimbursed by the Immigration Service for all expenditures incurred in carrying out the medical inspection of aliens. *Ib.* 1218 To prevent the landing of any such alien from such vessel at any time or place other than that designated by the immigration officers.

Impatience. [Bot. L. *impatiens* (Linnaeus).] The balsam or jewelweed. — **1885** *Harper's Mag.* Nov. 820/1 There was plenty of loosestrife along this bank, and some impatience and wild parsley.

***Impeachment.**

+1. In Congress or a state legislature, the presentation of formal charges against a public official by the lower house, trial to be before the upper house.

1779 *Mass. Const. Convention Jrnl.* (1832) 203 The House of Representatives shall be the Grand Inquest of this Commonwealth; and all impeachments made by them shall be heard, and tried by the Senate. **1787** *Constitution* i. § 2 The House of Representatives shall . . . have the sole Power of Impeachment. **1798** *Ann. 5th Congress* I. 809 Mr. McDowell wished to call the attention of the House to . . . the subject of William Blount's impeachment. **1830** *Congress. Deb.* 13 Dec. 3 The Court of Impeachment for the trial of Judge Peck, of Missouri, was opened in due form by proclamation from the Marshal of the District of Columbia. **1868** *N.Y. Tribune* 16 May 1/1 Speculation and rumor fill the Capital to-night, relative to the result of the expected vote on impeachment [of Pres. Johnson] to-morrow. **1893** *Harper's Mag.* April 707/1 Edmund G. Ross . . . forfeited the confidence of his constituents by voting against the impeachment of President Johnson. **1900** *Congress. Rec.* 20 Feb. 1988/1 The chief justice and the two associate justices . . . are subject to impeachment before the senate.

+2. Attrib. and comb. with *manager, trial.*

1868 *N.Y. Herald* 4 July 6/1 Mr. Butler, of the Committee of Impeachment Managers, made a report. **1870** *Nation* 13 Jan. 21/2 You must have valuable information in your possession, now, about the impeachment trial.

Imperial, *n.* [Fr. *impériale.*] A form of goatee. — **1841** *Knickerb.* XVII. 460 Two wigs, moustaches, an imperial, a gay vest. **1856** I. BIRD *Englishwoman Amer.* 366 [Americans] also indulge in eccentricities of appearance in the shape of beards and imperials, not to speak of the goatee. **1893** HOWELLS *Coast of Bohemia* 36 His little dot of an imperial had become lost in the beard which he wore. **1911** SAUNDERS *Col. Todhunter* i. 2 Colonel Todhunter carried his spare but stalwart frame with an ease that somewhat belied the grizzled gray of his hair and the white of his soldierly mustache and old-fashioned 'imperial.'

***Imperial,** *a.* In names of plants, trees, fruits, birds. — **1815** *Lit. & Phil. Soc. N.Y. Trans.* I. 172 Our Dutch forefathers . . . introduced . . . wall flowers, tulips, imperial flowers, the white lily. **1839** AUDUBON *Ornith. Biog.* V. 313 Imperial Woodpecker. *Picus Imperialis.* **1862** *Rep. Comm. Patents 1861: Agric.* 197 Imperial Crimson [strawberry] . . . Imperial Scarlet [strawberry]. *Ib.* 541 Of plums, Jefferson, imperial gage and purple gage [succeeded best]. **1892** APGAR *Trees Northern U.S.* 127 *Paulownia imperialis.* (Imperial Paulownia.)

Imperialism. {1858–} *Polit.* +(See quot. 1914.) — **1899** CARNEGIE in *N. Amer. Rev.* Jan. 5 Imperialism implies naval and military force behind; moral force, education, civilization, are not the backbone of Imperialism. **1900** 'FLYNT' *Notes Itinerant Policeman* 194 They are very scantily informed in regard to his notions about expansion and imperialism. **1914** *Cycl. Amer. Govt.* II. 152/1 As used in American politics, imperialism is employed to designate the policy upon which the United States has embarked of acquiring territory not a part of the United States proper, nor contiguous to it. **1925** BRYAN *Memoirs* 125, I did agree to the plank making imperialism the paramount issue.

Imperialist. {1603–} *Polit.* +One favoring a policy of imperialism for the United States. Also attrib. or adj. — **1900** *Congress. Rec.* 11 Jan. 766/2 The trouble with these imperialists is that they confound the Government of the United States with their puny President. *Ib.* 29 Jan. 1260/1 [A] brilliant speech has been heralded by the imperialist press as the slogan of twentieth-century Republicanism.

Imperial tea. A superior grade of Chinese tea. Also shortened to *imperial.* {1747–} — **1741** *Penna. Gazette* 29 Dec. 4/1. **1816** *Ann. 14th Congress* 1 Sess. 1873 Imperial, gunpowder, and gomee [tea shall bear a duty of] fifty cents per pound. **1839** *Knickerb.* XIII. 231 How nicely is it adapted . . . to every especial palate! There is . . . Gunpowder, and Imperial [etc.]. **1856** P. CARTWRIGHT *Autobiog.* 243 Often he . . . drank . . . sage tea for imperial. **1892** WALSH *Tea* 74 Imperial—Derives its trade name from being the make or style of tea used in the Imperial household and [among] the wealthier Chinese. . . . The true Imperial tea . . . [is] considered the 'perfection of tea.'

Imphee. Any of several African varieties of sorghum. {1880–} Also attrib. — **1859** *Ill. Agric. Soc. Trans.* IV. 108 A meeting was convened . . . for the purpose of discussing all matters of interest connected with the culture and manufacture of the Chinese Sugar Cane and Imphee. **1863** *Rep. Comm. Agric. 1862* 131 The Imphee canes are from the southeastern coast of Africa. **1867** *Iowa Agric. Soc. Rep.* 177 The African Imphee is raised to some extent. **1880** *Vt. Agric. Rep.* VI. 222 Sixteen varieties of sorghum [introduced] from Africa . . . received the general name of Imphees.

+**Implete,** *v. tr.* To fill. — **1862** *N.Y. Independent* 31 July 4 It was the purpose of Mr. Calhoun . . . to implete the Government silently with Southern principles. **1886** BEECHER in *Homiletic Rev.* May 421 [God] impletes all lands, all breadths, above, below, everywhere.

Implied power. Power not specifically granted by the Constitution of the United States but implied from enumerated powers. Freq. pl. — **1791** *Ann. 1st Congress* 1909 He did not pretend that it [*i.e.*, the last paragraph of Section 8 of the Constitution] gives any new powers; but it establishes the doctrine of implied powers. **1819** MARSHALL in *Supreme Ct. Rep.* XVII. 357 The implied powers of the constitution may be assumed and exercised, for purposes not really connected with the powers specifically granted, under color of some imaginary relation between them. **1883** WAITE in *Supreme Ct. Rep.* CX. 432 Otherwise the assertion and exercise by Congress of any implied power, irrespective of facts or circumstances, would destroy all limitations, and give to the implied powers a greater force than the express powers themselves.

***Import,** *n.*

+**1.** A system of taxation on imported articles.

1789 in *S. Lit. Messenger* Jan. 36/1, I am sorry that the opinion of those who wished to adopt the plan of Import, of [17]83, had not been followed; . . . the Legislature would have had leisure to digest a proper law of Import. **1802** *Steele P.* I. 259, I do not believe that the Import will produce the sum which he estimates.

2. A commodity imported from abroad. {1690–}

1789 *Ann. 1st Congress* I. 120 A bill to regulate the mode of collecting duties on imports and tonnage. **1865** *Atlantic Mo.* Jan. 80/2 Something like a quarter of all New York imports go in the first instance to the bonded warehouse. **1874** WELLS *Practical Economics* (1885) 5 The first feasible and ready way of collecting a revenue through taxation, that suggested itself, was by duties on imports, and the Texan legislators accordingly took to the tariff after the most approved American fashion. **1914** *Cycl. Amer. Govt.* III. 482/1 Duties which are levied upon imports may be either specific . . . or ad valorem.

3. Attrib. in sense 2 with *duty, law, trade.*

1789 in *S. Lit. Messenger* XXVIII. 35/2, I am well pleased that the Import Law has at last passed. **1865** *Atlantic Mo.* Feb. 166 [Servant girls] spend their earnings in costly goods of foreign manufacture, all now paying an excessive import duty. **1880** CABLE *Grandissimes* xxxix. 310 [Louisiana] wanted an unwatched import trade!

***Import,** *v. tr.* To bring in (foreign goods).

1704 *Boston News-Letter* 29 May 1/2 Have lately Imported a considerable Quantity of Gold dust. **1737** FRANKLIN *Poor Richard's Almanac 1738* 21 Just imported And to be sold by B. Franklin, . . . Large Bibles. **1776** *Jrnls. Cont. Congress* IV. 62, 462 quarter casks of powder were imported. **1851** MELVILLE *Moby-Dick* 120 Every year importing into our harbors a well reaped harvest of $7,000,000. **1880** CABLE *Grandissimes* vii. 46 They import cargoes of Africans.

Importation. {1601–} *local.* +The action of moving into a place to occupy land. *Obs.* — **1694** *N.C. Col. Rec.* I. 394 John Barrow proves three rights by importation. *Ib.* 432 Henry Brooks proves his right to fifty acres of land by the Importacion of himselfe. **1704** *Ib.* 612 Wm. Williams proves his Right to 50 acres of Land by the Importacion of himselfe.

Importer. One who imports goods or slaves from abroad. {1845–} — **1700** SEWALL *Diary* II. 16 There is a motion . . . to get a Law that all Importers of Negros shall pay 40 *s* per head. **1789** *Boston Directory* 193 Minot, Samuel, goldsmith and importer of plated and jewelry-ware. **1837** *U.S. Mag.* I. 112 The largest importer . . . bought and sold . . . on credit. **1875** WELLS *Practical Economics* (1885) 30 The importers . . . pointed to the clear and explicit provision of the tariff.

***Impost,** *n.* A tax or duty. Also attrib. Now chiefly hist. — **1643** *Mass. Bay Rec.* II. 34 Collectors of customs, subsedies, & imposts. **1695** SEWALL *Diary* I. 399 Voted . . . an additional Impost for a fund of 4000. Bills of Credit. **1707** *Boston Rec.* 60 Ordered that a competent number of Blank Certificates be Printed & Lodged at the Impost office. **1735** *Ib.* 122 There is no Argument for Retaining the Impost upon such Goods as are re-exported. **1789** JEFFERSON *Writings* VII. 329 *Impost* is a duty paid on any imported article, in the moment of its importation, and of course it is collected in the seaports only. *Excise* is a duty on any article, whether imported or raised at home, and paid in the hands of the consumer or retailer; consequently, it is collected through the whole country.

+**Impost,** *v. tr.* (See first quotation.) Hence *imposter.* — **1884** *Harper's Mag.* June 57/2 The entry papers . . . [are] sent to an official who imposts them, or, in other words, classifies the articles therein described in separate columns according to the rate of duty that each is liable to pay. *Ib.*, From the imposter the entries pass to other hands. *Ib.*, Again they pass into the hands of the imposting and statistical clerks.

Impost officer. An official who collects imposts. *Obs.* — **1705** *Boston News-Letter* 5 Nov. 2/1 All Officers of Customs [and] Naval and Impost Officers . . . are hereby Commanded to take notice. **1727** *Mass. H. S. Coll.* 4 Ser. II. 177 The governor has also the negativing of treasurers, . . . impost officers, and collectors of excise.

***Impound,** *v. tr.* To place (stray domestic animals) in a pound: (see also quot. 1876). Also absol.

1633 *Plymouth Laws* 34 Every Cunstablericke [shall] have a sufficient pound to impound cattle. **1675** *Ib.* 175 It shalbe lawfull . . . to impound the beast that hath treaspased in a pound house. **1701** *Boston Rec.* 15 It shall . . . be lawfull for such persons . . . to impound such horse, neet cattle or sheep so found. **1790** *Dallas' Rep.* II. 69 The usage . . . has been, both before and since our act of assembly, to impound on the premises. **1858** WARDER *Hedges & Evergreens* 148 The owner of land is obliged to fence it against cattle, and if his land is not fenced he can neither recover damages, nor impound for trespass. **1876** J. A. ALLEN *Amer. Bison* 275 The Indians . . . [are] in the habit of hunting the buffalo by impounding them, or by driving them into an artificial enclosure.

Impounder. One who impounds cattle. *Obs.* — **1646** *Cambridge Rec.* 53 Rescuing two Hogs from ye Impounder. **1658** *Boston Rec.* 145 One halfe of the fines shall bee allowed to the enformer or impounder. **1664** *Springfield Rec.* II. 71 The said impounder shall have the like allowance.

Impress, *n.* Impressment; the action of impressing men, horses, etc., for public service. *Obs.* {1602–1832} — **1689** *Maine Doc. Hist.* V. 1 Wee haue many Impresses for men, butt can get butt few. **1764** HUTCHINSON *Hist. Mass.* I. 146 They prayed that . . . they might be freed . . . from the impresses made of them or their children or servants into the war. **1780** in Sparks *Corr. Revol.* III. 22 We have been using every exertion to procure a number of teams, as well voluntarily as by impress. **1781** *Virginia Mag. Hist. & Biog.* V. 378 Impresses I beg leave to consider as a civil matter, and will receive such a number of horses from the executive as have been collected by their authority.

***Impress,** *v.*

***1.** *tr.* To enlist (men) by force into military service. Now hist.

1690 *Plymouth Laws* 231 The persons which shall be appointed press masters to Impress Souldiers for . . . service shall have full power to Impress any men. **1705** *Boston News-Letter* 12 Nov. 2/1 The Souldiers Impressed and sent down to the Service of this Province . . have several of them lately deserted the Service there. **1822** *Ann. 17th Congress* 1 Sess. I. 68 A negro man, . . . having been impressed into the service of the United States, was killed during the invasion.

transf. **1821** JEFFERSON *Writings* I. 160, I then meant . . . to withdraw from political life, into which I had been impressed by the circumstances of the times.

2. To seize (men, money, horses, wagons, etc.) for public service. {1749–}

1698 *Mass. Charters & Laws* (1814) 320 It shall . . . be lawful . . . for any fence viewer . . . to impress workmen and teams. **1713** *N.C. Col. Rec.* II. 3 Benjamin Tull under pretence of authority hath Impress'd and Kill'd severall Beefs of which he hath rendred noe account. **1755** WASHINGTON *Writings* I. 194, I impressed his wagons, and compelled him by force to assist in this work. **1885** *Century Mag.* June 296/1 General Jackson . . . started for Richmond with impressed horses.

+**Impressional,** *a.* Related to impressions; impressionable. — **1860** EMERSON *Conduct of Life* 111 He must be musical, Tremulous, impressional, Alive to gentle influence Of landscape and of sky. *a***1882** QUINCY *Figures of Past* (1883) 279 The resemblance . . . could scarcely be called physical, and I am loath to borrow the word impressional from the vocabulary of spirit mediums.

Impressment. The impressing of men or materials needed for public service. {1829–} Also attrib.

1787 T. Speed *Danville Polit. Club, Ky.* (1894) 126 Ought the inhabitants . . . submit to the impressment of their arms and accouterments? **1796** MORSE *Univ. Geog.* I. 689 The loss to the citizens directly by the . . . British army, and indirectly by American impressments. **1809** WEEMS *Washington* (1867) xvi. 236 Our persons have been free from the violence of impressments and conscriptions. **1892** HARRIS *On Plantation* 124 After this came the impressment law, which gave the Confederate officials the right to seize private property, horses, mules, and provisions.

+**b.** *spec.* The practice of impressing American sailors for service on British ships.

1807 J. Q. ADAMS *Diary* 45 The impressment of men from our ships. **1813** CLAY *Speeches* (1860) I. 46 Who is prepared to say, that American seamen shall be surrendered as victims to the British principle of impressment? **1835** HOFFMAN *Winter in West* I. 98 We should regard and treat impressment like piracy or kidnapping on the highway. **1842** TYLER in *Pres. Mess. & P.* IV. 169 The impressment of seamen from merchant vessels of this country by British cruisers.

* **Improve,** *v.*

American uses of this verb have been discussed by Franklin (*Writings* X. 76–7) and Pickering.

* **1.** *tr.* To make use of (something). *Obs.* {–*c*1710; now *dial.*}

1650 in Quincy *Hist. Harvard Univ.* (1840) I. 518 Such young scholars who . . . become utterly unfit to improve . . . the liberty of students in the College. **1700** *Springfield Rec.* II. 357 No Stranger . . . shal box any trees or Improve the sam for Turpintine. **1781** WITHERSPOON *Druid P.* No. 7, He improved the horse for ten days. This is used in some parts of New England for riding the horse.

2. To bring (land) under cultivation; to fence, provide with buildings, etc. {1684–}

1632 *Mass. Bay Rec.* I. 94 If the . . . said John Winthrop shall . . . suffer the said ileland to lye wast, and not improue the same, then this present demise to be voide. **1653** *Lancaster Rec.* 27 How Longe every man shall hold and Improue the said lands. **1686** *Maine Doc. Hist.* VI. 241 Francis Small built a house & Improued ye sd. land considerably aboue thirty years last past. **1713** *Charlestown Land Rec.* 179 That part of the land . . . that he shall Improve by ffenceing. **1777** *Va. State P.* I. 279 He settled and Improved a Plantation on the Monongahela River. **1826** J. BRADFORD *Kentucky Notes* 19 In the same year James Harrod from Monongehely, headed a party whose object it was to improve land (as they termed it) in Kentucky, under an expectation of obtaining 400 acres for every cabbin they should build. **1877** JOHNSON *Anderson Co., Kansas* 154 He resided there until the fall of 1862, and had in the meantime improved a good farm. **1906** BELL *C. Lee* 293, I could refuse an offer to improve my land, denuded and mortgaged as it is.

b. *absol.*

1642 *Mass. Charters & Laws* (1814) 65 If one man shall improve his land, . . . he who shall so improve, shall secure his lands against other men's cattle. **1667** *Plymouth Rec.* I. 95 The Towne of Plymouth . . . [has] bound unto Richard Wright fifty acrees of upland . . . where the said Richard hath begun to settle or Improve. **1702** *Groton Rec.* 123 Three acers of madow whare thay ust to Improue.

+**3.** *New Eng.* To occupy, inhabit, make use of (a place or piece of property).

1647 *Conn. Probate Rec.* I. 17 It being my will that . . . my sayd Howsing & Lande . . . bee improved by the overseers of this my will for the maintenence and education of my children. **1677** HUBBARD *Narrative* II. 2 Other Places . . . [were] improved for Trading and Fishing. **1684** *Essex Inst. Coll.* XXII. 2 The end of the house next the street [shall] be at her dispose to live in and Improve for her own. **1751** *Boston Rec.* 259 Forty six years ago Mr. Thomas Hunt occupied & improved a Blacksmith's Shop. **1782** *R.I. Col. Rec.* IX. 512 Josiah Flagg . . . [shall] have the liberty of improving the cellars under the state house in Providence, as repositories for the public stores. **1803** CUTLER in *Life & Corr.* II. 114 The octagon hall . . . seemed to be improved as a levee room. **1828** WEBSTER s.v., *Improve*. . . . To use; to occupy; to cultivate. The house or farm is now improved by an industrious tenant. This application is perhaps peculiar to some parts of the U. States. **1862** HAWTHORNE in *Atlantic Mo.* Dec. 712/2 The hall . . . has come to base uses in these latter days,—being improved, in Yankee phrase, as a brewery and wash-room.

+**4.** *New Eng.* To employ (a person). *Obs.*

1640 *Conn. Hist. Soc. Coll.* VI. 11 The Townsmen [shall] haue liberty to Improue men for the killing of woolfs. **1679** *Conn. Rec.* III. 30 It is by this Court recommended to the townesmen . . . to improve their inhabitants in cleareing the comon roades. **1703** in Sheldon *Hist. Deerfield, Mass.* I. 289 Our children of 12 or 13 years and under we have been afraid to improve in the field for fear of the enemy. **1722** in B. Peirce *Hist. Harvard Univ.* (1833) 232 Voted . . . that Mr. Judal Monis be *improved* as an instructor of the Hebrew language in the College. **1789** FRANKLIN *Writings* X. 76 A deceased Country Gentleman . . . had been for more than 30 years *improved* as a Justice-of-Peace. This Use of the Word *improved* is peculiar to New England. **1829** *Va. Lit. Museum* 30 Dec. 458 To improve. 'To occupy, make use of, employ'—as to 'improve as a tavern'—'to improve a schoolmaster.' 'to improve their children in labour &c.' New England.

Improved *a.* {1617–} +Of land: In use; under cultivation; fenced and provided with farm buildings. Often *improved land.* — **1643** *Plymouth Laws* 74 By ymproved lands are understood meddow land plowed land and howed lands. **1703** *N.J. Archives* III. 20 A hundred or Fifty Acres of improved Land (as it's call'd). **1787** in *Mag. Amer. Hist.* I. 435 Stopped at a very beautiful improved farm . . . where one Craig lives in an excellent stone house. **1832** WILLIAMSON *Maine* II. 159 The school tax was from a half-penny to a penny per acre on improved lands. **1870** *Dept. Agric. Rep. 1869* 8 The vague and meaningless distinctions of 'improved' and 'unimproved' land should be replaced by more . . . useful divisions.

* **Improvement.** (See also INTERNAL IMPROVEMENT.)

* **1. a.** The bringing (of land) under cultivation; cultivation, agricultural use.

1634 WOOD *New Eng. Prospect* (1865) 59 A well skilled and industrious husbandman, for tillage and improvements of grounds. **1675** *Conn. Rec.* II. 339 Haueing recd good inteligence of the comodiousnes of land for improuement . . . [they] came and built and planted. **1693** *Brookhaven Rec.* 79 The sd Coll. Willm Smith . . . hath been at much more considerable charge and expence in the purchaseing and improvement of a certain neck or peninsula. **1720** *Boston Rec.* 143 It [shall] be left wth the Selectmen to put that peice of the Townes Land . . . under Some Improvemt as they Shall think Advantagious.

+**b.** The use or occupation of land, buildings, etc.

1670 *Plymouth Col. Rec.* V. 45 The said Cowin, during the time of his improuement of the said land, shall not make hauocke or destroy the timber thereon. **1699** *Braintree Rec.* 41 Benjamin Webb should have ye improvement of ye old School House untill the next Town Meeting. **1707** *Ib.* 66 Then voted that ye salt meadow yt has been in Mr. Fisks improvement be now let out by a Committee . . . for one year Mr. Fiske haveing the refusal thereof cheaper than an other man. *a***1736** in *New Eng. Hist. & Gen. Reg.* IV. 112 As to the rest and residue of my Estate both Real and Personal I give the Improvement benefit and Income thereof to my Dear Wife. **1763** *Cambridge Prop. Rec.* 357 A pi[e]ce of common m[a]rshland . . . Shall Remain in his Improvement untell the propriators Shall order otherwise. **1838** *Mass. Agric. Survey 1st Rep.* 38 He has never been the owner of more than 10½ acres of land, but has often hired land for improvement.

2. a. *pl.* Buildings, fences, etc.

1640 in *New Haven Col. Rec.* 43 If they remove, to sell nothing butt improvements. **1748** *Virginia Mag. Hist. & Biog.* V. 279 The County Court . . . ordered John Savage . . . to make a new Survey, . . . having Regard to the Buildings and Improvements then standing. **1792** IMLAY *Western Territory* 148 Plantations with orchards and other improvements, may be purchased from 1 l. to 1 l. 5 s. per acre. **1818** FEARON *Sketches of A.* 219 The price of land varies very much, according to situation and the proximity of townships. Farms which are called *improved* can be bought at from 8 to 30 dollars per acre; the *improvements* often consist of the erection of rough log buildings, and about from 12 to 20 acres under middling cultivation. **1856** DERBY *Phoenixiana* xxxiii. 202 Three other small buildings, unoccupied, a fence, and a grave-yard, constitute all the 'improvements' that have been made at the 'Playa.' **1891** O'BEIRNE *Leaders Ind. Territory* 37/2 He gave his farm to the children of his first wife, and is at present employed erecting new improvements. **1908** *Indian Laws & Tr.* III. 382 Any person who . . . shall be an actual resident upon any one such lot and the owner of substantial and actual improvements thereon.

b. The paving of roads and sidewalks, the laying of water pipes, sewers, etc., in a town or town site.

1884 *Century Mag.* March 648/1 The rights of property-owners were disregarded, and they were assessed for 'improvements' when their property was ruined.

3. A piece of land under cultivation and provided with fences, buildings, etc.; a cultivated farm. *Obsolescent.* {1773–; now *obs.*}

1691 *Maine Doc. Hist.* V. 294 Ye heathen . . . haue been a sore scourge to us, & still distress us, by holding us off from our improuements. **1751** in Sheldon *Hist. of Deerfield, Mass.* I. 576 We have been great sufferers in the last War, in being Drove from our improvements so that we have been obliged to go into the lower Towns. **1779** in Hardenbergh *Journal* (1879) 62 The Infantry . . . marched on 16 miles within 5 miles of Yorkham's where we encamped on a small improvement called Burrows' farm.

1812 MARSHALL *Kentucky* 59 In 1776, the M'Afee's . . . raised corn on Salt River, principally at James M'Afee's improvement. **1853** *Mich. Agric. Soc. Trans.* 631 The fields . . . look more like what is commonly called brush land than they do like a white man's improvements.

+**4.** Employment.

1703 SEWALL *Letter-Book* I. 282 Very few gray hairs are to be found in the Colony, in civil or sacred improvement.

5. *New Eng.* 'The profitable spiritual application of a text' (*O.E.D.*).

1677 I. MATHER *Preval. Prayer* (1864) 268 That is the special Improvement which should be made of what hath been discoursed. **1816** PICKERING 112 *Improvement*, of a sermon; the conclusion. Ex. 'To make some improvement of the whole.' This expression, though probably much more common here than in Great Britain, is by no means peculiar to us. **1829** *Va. Lit. Museum* 30 Dec. 458. **1850** MITCHELL *Lorgnette* I. ix. 212, I leave it all, Fritz, the text, the woman, and the 'improvement' to the preacher.

6. *pl.* The latest household conveniences in plumbing, heating, lighting, etc.

1875 *N.Y. Tribune* 10 Aug. 9/2 Will be rented very low to a good tenant, a desirable house, with all the modern improvements, near depot. **1884** *N.Y. Herald* 27 Oct. 2/1 Furnished, handsome four-story residence, 20 East 73d; all improvements; perfect order; immediate possession. **1918** *N.Y. Times* 15 Jan. 21/5 Delightful home built to order; owner moved to California; a sacrifice for a fine semi-bungalow; 7 rooms and bath; all up-to-date improvements.

7. Attrib. with *cabin, district, lease,* etc.

1794 *Ann. 4th Congress* 2 Sess. 2803 The people in the western counties . . . complained of the decisions of the State courts, which discountenanced improvement titles, and gave the preference to paper titles. **1839** *Indiana H. Rep. Jrnl.* 368 An amount may be realized sufficient . . . to discharge the entire amount of interest on the improvement loans down to the year 1850. **1849** CHAMBERLAIN *Indiana Gazetteer* 34 They rented land on improvement leases. **1850** GARRARD *Wah-To-Yah* i. 3 [He] was to receive ten thousand dollars improvement money for his farm in Ohio. **1851** *Whig Almanac 1852* 9/1 'The party' is essentially hostile to the Improvement policy. **1876** *Ill. Dept. Agric. Trans.* XIII. 330 Succeeding the systems of commons and common fields came the grants of 'head rights' of 400 acres each, 'improvement rights' of 250 acres, and 'militia rights' of 100 acres, under acts of congress. **1883** *Ill. Rev. Statutes* 265 Any city or village . . . may lay off such city or village . . . into what shall be known or called improvement districts. **1886** Z. F. SMITH *Kentucky* 29 The men dispersed . . . to build on such locations improvement cabins.

+**Improvement company.** A company engaged in building or in developing real estate, transportation, etc. — **1880** 'E. KIRKE' *Garfield* 57 The Credit Mobilier Company is . . . authorized by its charter . . . to make advances of money and credit to railroad and other improvement companies. **1884** MATTHEWS & BUNNER *In Partnership* 150 There was already an Avoca Improvement Company, building a big hotel, advertising right and left, and prophesying that the day of Saratoga and Sharon and Richfield was ended.

+**Improvement society.** A group of persons working together for the betterment of local conditions. — **1880** *Harper's Mag.* Dec. 147 The village improvement societies are signs of the wish to remedy congenital defects of rural communities. **1894** *Ib.* June 156/1 The president of our improvement society.

Improver. One who makes use of land, fishing rights, etc.; one who 'improves' land; in later use, a settler in a hitherto unoccupied territory. {1649-} — **1656** *Conn. Hist. Soc. Coll.* VI. 110 The order made by the Improvers and possessors of the Swamp on the other side the great Riuer shall stand in force. **1687** *Doc. Hist. N.Y. State* I. 160 The Dutch are great improvers of land. **1738** W. STEPHENS *Proc. Georgia* 73 Mr. Hird a Constable, and one of the principal Improvers. **1812** MARSHALL *Kentucky* 27 The Indians . . . surprised a small company of improvers, at a new settlement about four miles from Harrodsburgh. **1886** Z. F. SMITH *Kentucky* 60 Other improvers appeared in Mason County this year.

Inaugural, *n.* = INAUGURAL ADDRESS.

1832 *Congress. Deb.* 5 May 2778 The President, in his inaugural, . . . [hoped for] 'instruction and aid from the co-ordinate branches.' **1846** *Whig Almanac 1847* 6/1 Mr. Polk in his Inaugural avowed his firm faith in our claim to Oregon and his resolution to maintain it. **1857** *Lawrence* (Kan.) *Republican* 4 June 2 On our fourth page will be found the inaugural of our new Governor. **1886** LOGAN *Great Conspiracy* 187 Bitter indeed must have been President Lincoln's disappointment and sorrow at the reception of his Inaugural. **1925** BRYAN *Memoirs* 328 In his second inaugural President Wilson said [etc.].

transf. *a*1861 WINTHROP *Open Air* 134, I must give them a little sharp talk by way of Inaugural.

Inaugural *a.* Pertaining to or used at the inauguration of an official. {1689-} — **1798** A. HOLMES *E. Stiles* 253 This Inaugural Oration [of President Stiles at Yale] was printed. **1801** HAMILTON *Works* VII. 223 What, then, are we to think of the ostentatious assurance in the Inaugural Speech as to the preservation of Public Faith? **1899** CHESNUTT *Wife of His Youth* 103 On the evening following the White House inaugural ball, the colored people of Washington gave an 'inaugural' ball at a large public hall.

Inaugural address. +The speech made by a president of the United States, or a governor of a state or territory, at his inauguration.

1805 JEFFERSON *Writings* XI. 69, I observe . . . with great pleasure . . . the satisfaction you express with the last inaugural address. **1821** J. Q. ADAMS *Memoirs* V. 302 The question yet remains undetermined whether any inaugural address is to be delivered or not. **1828** COOPER *Notions* II. 287 After a momentary delay, the new president commenced what is called his 'inaugural address.' **1850** *31st Congress 1 Sess.* Sen. Ex. Doc. No. 76, 5 Inaugural Address of Governor Manuel Alvarez, of New Mexico, of July 4, 1850. **1861** *Ladies' Repository* April 256/1 With the Inaugural address of President Lincoln there are three classes of men who are dissatisfied. **1893** HARRISON *Public Papers and Addresses* 26 Inaugural Address: March 4, 1889.

transf. **1884** BLAINE *20 Years of Congress* I. 256 In his message to the Confederate Congress, Mr. Davis apparently attempted to cure the defects of his Inaugural address.

Inaugurate, *v.* {1604-}

+**1.** *tr.* To induct (a president of the United States) into office.

1789 *Ann. 1st Congress* 232 The President of the United States was inaugurated [on April 30]. **1838** *U.S. Mag.* I. 154 When Jefferson was elected, but not yet inaugurated, he [John Marshall] was promoted to the high . . . office of Chief Justice of the Supreme Court of the United States. **1884** *N.Y. Tribune* 14 Nov. 2/3 The manufacturers . . . are still confident . . . that Blaine has not only been honestly elected but that he will be inaugurated. **1904** *Atlantic Mo.* Oct. 551 When Mr. Cleveland was inaugurated he found the gold reserve in the treasury at the lowest point.

+**2.** To induct (a governor or administration of a state or territory) into office.

1865 PIKE *Scout & Ranger* (1932) 50 The official term of Governor Runnells expired, and Gen. Sam. Houston was inaugurated in his place. **1872** MCCLELLAN *Golden State* 415 Frederick F. Low was inaugurated on the first Monday in December. **1902** E. FIELD *State of Rhode Island* I. 327 The vote [in 1835] was very close and there were many questions regarding fraudulent votes to be decided by the grand committee on 'Election Day' at Newport, before the new administration could be inaugurated.

* **Inauguration.**

+**1.** The induction of a president of the United States, or a similar public official, into office.

1789 HAMILTON *Works* VII. 44 The day . . . of the inauguration of the President, which completed the organization of the Constitution. **1822** *Boston Selectmen* 252 Make suitable arrangements for . . . the Inauguration of the Mayor in Faneuil Hall. **1846** POLK *Diary* (1929) 105 A greater number of persons (strangers) are said to be in Washington than have been at any time for many years, unless at the inauguration of a President. **1867** *Wkly. New Mexican* 11 May 2/2 Soon after his inauguration, Governor Mitchell began his adventures in politics. **1886** POORE *Reminisc.* I. 105 A parade, an inauguration, or the funeral of a distinguished person would receive brief mention. **1905** PHILLIPS *Plum Tree* 314 It was now less than a month before inauguration.

2. Attrib. with *cake, speech, suit, week.*

1805 *Steele P.* I. 445 This last, they say, not less than the first is a departure from the broad and generous principle avowed in the President's inauguration speech. **1841** *Niles' Nat. Reg.* 6 Feb. 368/1 We were yesterday shown . . . a splendid piece of black broad cloth . . . designed for the inauguration suit of general Harrison. **1841** *Picayune* 21 Feb. 2/2 An Inauguration Cake has been prepared at Georgetown, D.C., which is a model of the Capitol at Washington. **1849** *Knickerb.* XXXIII. 368 A friend who was present gives us an amusing description of matters and things in Washington during 'inauguration-week.'

+**Inauguration ball.** A ball given on the occasion of the inauguration of an official. Also transf. — **1817** in Morison *Life H. G. Otis* (1913) II. 206 A grand inauguration Ball in the even'g [for Monroe's inauguration]. **1841** *Picayune* 8 Dec. 2/1 The Inauguration Ball in honor of the opening of the St. Louis Hotel, will take place to-night, in the Ball-room. **1852** *Knickerb.* XL. 52 Ten years after, I was present at an inauguration-ball at Milledgeville. **1885** *Wkly. New Mexican Rev.* 11 June 2/6 The inauguration ball to be given in Santa Fe when our new governor is inaugurated will be the grandest ever witnessed in the territory.

Inauguration Day. {1686-} +The day of the induction into office of a public official; spec., the day of the inauguration of the president of the United States. (Cf. ELECTION DAY 2.) — **1886** TRUMBULL *Memorial Hist. Hartford Co., Conn.* 189 It was the duty of a selected company . . . to escort the governor on 'Election Day' as inauguration day was always styled [in Conn.]. **1887** *Narragansett Hist. Reg.* V. 343 The day upon which state officers are engaged—the day called in other states [than Rhode Island] Inauguration day. **1893** WIGGIN *Polly Oliver* (1894) xvii. 185 As it chances to be a presidential year, we will celebrate Inauguration Day.

+**Inca dove.** A dove (*Scardafella inca*) found in the southern states. — **1887** RIDGWAY *Manual N.A. Birds* 216 *S[cardafella] inca*. . . . Inca Dove. **1917** *Birds of Amer.* II. 52 The little Inca Dove . . . often seems very tame or very stupid. . . . One cannot live in Tucson for a day without making the acquaintance of the little Inca Dove.

+**Incense cedar.** Any one of various trees belonging to the genus *Libocedrus*, esp., on the west coast, *L. decurrens*. — **1884** SARGENT *Rep. Forests* 176 *Libocedrus decurrens*. . . . White Cedar. Bastard Cedar. Post Cedar. Incense Cedar. **1897** SUDWORTH *Arborescent Flora* 64.

Inch board. A board or plank one inch thick. {1646–} — **a1649** WINTHROP *Hist.* I. 184 They made divers shot through her [a pinnace], (being but inch board,) and so raked her fore and aft, as they must needs kill or hurt some of the Indians. **1704** *N.C. Col. Rec.* I. 605 Anthony Alexander . . . Complaines for twelve Hundred foot of good Inch board. **1869** *Rep. Comm. Agric. 1868* 253 A narrow strip of inch board or three or four inch batten.

Inch of candle. (See CANDLE b.)

Inch plank. =INCH BOARD. — **1725** *Bristol* (Va.) *Vestry Bk.* 23 The floors lay'd with inch-plank & Each Chapple ceal'd with halfe inch-plank. **1810** *Steele P.* II. 630, I was told that you had some seasoned Inch plank suitable for hogshead heading.

+**Inch plant.** (See quotation.) — **1892** *Amer. Folk-Lore* V. 104 *Tradescantia crassifolia*, . . . inch-plant.

Inchworm. A measuring worm. — **a1861** WINTHROP *Open Air* 123 All the green inch-worms vanish on the tenth of every June. **1881** *Harper's Mag.* Oct. 656/1 A wriggling inch-worm, . . . awaiting . . . an opportunity to measure the length of your nose. **1899** *Animal & Plant Lore* 63 Inch-worm, larvae of geometrid moths. Cambridge, Mass.

Incline. {1600–} **1.** *Mining.* A shaft that is not vertical; the inclined part of a shaft. +**2.** =INCLINED RAILWAY. — **(1) 1872** 'MARK TWAIN' *Sk., New & Old* 284 Say you go down on it with a shaft, straight down, you know, or with what you call 'incline.' **1876** RAYMOND *8th Rep. Mines* 85 The incline-shaft is down 800 feet. **1877** W. WRIGHT *Big Bonanza* 172 When this incline car has been hauled up as far as the bottom of the vertical shaft, that is, to within 1,300 feet of the surface. **1896** SHINN *Story of Mine* 224 Vertical winzes are in reality shafts; sloping winzes are inclines. **(2) 1880** *Harper's Mag.* Dec. 52 The nerve-trying 'inclines' . . . scale the bold cliffs of Coal Hill. **1883** *Ib.* Aug. 328/2 The Portage Railroad . . . received travelers by the canal route . . . and conveyed them over the mountain by inclines and stationary engines.

+**Inclined railway.** A cable-car line used on a steep incline. Also attrib. — **1833** COKE in *Select Circulating Library* II. 398/2 A melancholy accident occurred to a party of four gentlemen . . . upon the inclined railway connected with the quarries, by the chain to which the car was attached suddenly breaking. **1883** *Harper's Mag.* July 264/2 The adoption of the inclined railway system . . . has changed these once unpeopled heights into resorts and suburban residence sites unique of their kind in all the world. **1906** LYNDE *Quickening* 311 He took an electric car . . . on the line connecting with the inclined railway running up the mountain to Crestcliffe Inn.

Inclosed ground, etc. (See ENCLOSED GROUND, etc.)

***Incomer.** One who comes into a community from outside it; an immigrant. — **1649** *Southampton Rec.* I. 58 The land lying in the great playne, which is apoynted by this towne for incomers is at length laid out. **1676** *Conn. Rec.* II. 290 The Court granted to Robbin Cassacinamon six of the Incomers or captiues, to keep them as servants. **1721** *N.H. Prov Papers* III. 817*n.*, All Pedlers and Incomers yt shall trade in this Province of New Hampshire shall pay 2½ per cent. for all their trade. **1894** EGGLESTON in *Century Mag.* April 849 The incomer is puzzled by a compound familiarly called in the hill-country 'rine-injun.'

Income tax. A tax on income. {1799–}

Before the Civil War some of the states had levied taxes upon income. In 1861 Congress enacted a federal income tax which, with revisions, was continued until 1871. A second federal income tax, levied in 1894, was declared unconstitutional. An amendment to the Constitution in 1913 gave Congress power to levy an income tax 'without regard to any census or enumeration.'

1813 *Ann. 13th Congress* 1 Sess. 366, I am myself attached to a system of income taxes. **1861** *Statutes at Large* XII. 309 One principal assessor and one principal collector in each of the States . . . [shall] assess and collect the internal duties or income tax imposed by this act. **1863** *Rio Abajo Press* 1 Dec. 3/1 Persons liable to pay income tax . . . are directed to report without delay. **1865** *Nation* 16 Nov. 615/1 My income tax paid to the United States collector last summer . . . was over $100. **1894** *Supreme Ct. Rep.* CLVIII. 629 The stress of the argument is thrown . . . on the assertion that an income tax is not a property tax at all. **1900** MATTHEWS *Confident To-Morrow* 178 Mr. Dircks wishes to shift the burdens of the worthy poor upon the shoulders of the idle rich [with] special remedies like the single-tax or the income tax. **1913** *Statutes at Large* XXXVIII. I. 166 In addition to the income tax provided under this section (herein referred to as the normal income tax) there shall be levied . . . an additional income tax (herein referred to as the additional tax).

attrib. **1880** *Harper's Mag.* Nov. 920/1 In 1866 our income-tax returns showed 771,000 incomes of $500 per week and over. **1894** *Ib.* April 804/1 The House of Representatives, on February 1st, passed the Wilson tariff bill with the income-tax clause by a vote of 204 to 140.

Incomunicado. *a.* [Sp.] Without opportunity for communicating with others; in solitary confinement. — **1844** KENDALL *Santa Fé Exped.* II. 255 Now that I was incomunicado—now that all intercourse with my friends was cut off, . . . my situation became irksome in the extreme.

Incorporator. {1829–} +One who participates in the formation of a town corporation or of a business corporation. — **1877** *Mich. Gen. Statutes* I. (1882) 1013 An affidavit made by three or more of the incorporators, that the signatures to such articles and consent and agreement are genuine. **1898** PAGE *Red Rock* 209 Among the incorporators were himself, Hiram Still, Still's son, and Mr. Bolter.

Incubator. An apparatus or machine for hatching chickens. {1857–} Also attrib. — **1872** *Rep. Comm. Patents 1870* II. 988/1 Incubator [patented by] Jacob Graves, Reading, and Henry Graves, Boston, Mass. **1894** *Vt. Agric. Rep.* XIV. 173, I hire my eggs hatched in an incubator, and raise the chickens under hens. **1923** HERRICK *Lilla* 131 She bought a dozen incubator chicks in February.

Incurve. *Baseball.* +A pitched ball which curves toward the batter. — **1886** CHADWICK *Art of Pitching* 14 It is essential to change the direction of the curve from an 'out curve' to an 'in-curve,' and from an 'up-shoot' to a 'down-shoot.' **1887** *Outing* May 99/1 The 'in curve' [is] the one most easily attained by a left-hand pitcher. **1906** *Spalding's Base Ball Guide* 112 An In-curve . . . is a ball which curves in towards the batsman as he stands in his position.

+**Indeedy,** *adv.* A jocose or dial. variant of *indeed.* — **1856** *Knickerb.* Dec. 620 'Is thy eye not opened?' 'Yes, indeedy,' says I. **1873** 'MARK TWAIN' & WARNER *Gilded Age* iii. 39 An' d' you spec' he gwyne to let 'em off 'dout somebody ast him to do it? No indeedy! **1890–2** *Dial. Notes* I. 22, 78, 216.

***Indent,** *n.* +**1.** A certificate of indebtedness issued by the federal government soon after its organization. *Obs.* **2.** A certificate of indebtedness issued by a state. *Obs.* (Cf. INDENT OF INTEREST.) — **(1) 1790** MACLAY *Deb. Senate* 225, [I] proposed . . . that indents should be given to all persons entitled to them. **1801** *Hist. Review & Directory* I. 188 It may be discharged in certificates (called *indents*) granted for interest due on continental governmental securities. **(2) 1786** *Jrnls. Cont. Congress* XXX. 431 The board . . . are of opinion, that the continuation of the issue of indents in that state [Penna.] would not be improper. **1790** *Penna. Packet* 22 Dec. 1/2 Wanted, South Carolina State Indents, for which the highest Cash Price will be given. **1791** *S.C. Rep.* (Bay) I. (1809) 121 An indented certificate, commonly called a general indent of the said state of South-Carolina. **1809** MARSHALL *Writings Fed. Const.* (1839) 124 The indents issued upon them [state bonds] for interest, were drawn by David Rittenhouse.

***Indent,** *v. tr.* To engage (a servant) by indenture or contract. {1787–} *Obs.* — **1727** *Md. Hist. Mag.* XVIII. 228, I desire you will order to be procured and sent me . . . a Shoemaker Indented for as long a time as they can be had. **1732** *Ib.* XIX. 300 Have him indented to serve me here for 4 years.

***Indented,** *a.* Engaged by an indenture or contract. {1758–} — [**1758** *Acc. Micmakis & Maracheets* 105 He had been an indented servant in New England.] **1771** *Md. Hist. Mag.* XIII. 174 If an Indented servant get Him on the best terms you Can. **1794** *N.C. Gen. Ass. Public Acts* II. 53 And every person who shall knowingly sell, buy or hire such slave or indented servant of colour, shall in like manner forfeit and pay the sum of one hundred pounds for each and every slave or servant of colour so sold, bought or hired. **1817** H. M. Brooks *Gleanings* 137 Ran away from the subscriber, an indented apprentice, of the name of James Bails. **1835** C. P. BRADLEY *I. Hill* 13 He was never an indented apprentice.

+**Indent of interest.** =INDENT *n. Obs.* — **1786** *Jrnls. Cont. Congress* XXX. 432 The commissioners . . . [shall] give orders for the continuation of the issue of indents of interest in the state of Pennsylvania. **1790** *Statutes at Large* I. 140 The said certificates issued in payment of interest, commonly called indents of interest. **1790** *Statutes at Large* I. 140 The sums which shall be subscribed . . . [shall] be payable in . . . [certificates] issued for the payment of interest, commonly called indents of interest. **1822** *Ib.* III. 697 [All] indents of interest which . . . shall be outstanding, may be presented at the treasury.

* **Indenture.** Also †**endenture.** The contract by which an apprentice or servant is bound to his master for a specified term of years. *Obs.*

1664 *Boston Rec.* 21 Josiah Clarke shall not haue liberty to kepp open shop . . . vntell he hath fully compleated his endenture. **1694** *N.C. Col. Rec.* I. 401 His former Indenture of ffive years. **1705** BEVERLEY *Virginia* IV. 35 Servants . . . serve only for a few Years, according to the time of their Indenture, or the Custom of the Country. **1845** SOL. SMITH *Theatr. Apprent.* 30 She had one negro . . . who had been brought from Kentucky under indentures.

b. A printed form on which such a contract is made.

1733 FRANKLIN *Poor Richard's Almanac 1734* 23 Sold by the Printer . . . Servants Indentures. **1794** *Ann. 3d Congress* 1309 Apprentices' indentures, 15 cents.

Indentured servant. A servant bound to his employer by an indenture. {indentured, 1757–} — **1723** *Amer. Wkly. Mercury* 11–18 April 4/1 A Certain Number of Palatines (being all Indentured Servants) were Imported into this Province [Penna.]. **1759** FRANKLIN *Works* III. (1840) 466 The enlisting of apprentices and indentured servants would greatly disserve her Majesty's interest. **1847** T. FORD *Hist. Illinois* (1854) 32 Such slaves were then called indentured and registered servants.

Independence. {1640–}

+**1.** Freedom from the political control of England; political separation from England.

1768 *N.H. Prov. Papers* VII. 250 The House of Burgesses [of Va.] . . . have therefore thought proper to represent . . . That they do not affect independence of their parent Kingdom. **1776** JEFFERSON *Writings* IV. 255, I suppose they will tell us what to say on the subject of independence. **1786** in *Mag. Amer. Hist.* I. 179 Being the anniversary of Independence the troops fired three rounds as well as the cannon. **1842** *Whig Almanac 1843* 23/2 Mr. Clay renewed his efforts in favor of Protection to American Industry,—that great cause, the success of which he regarded as essential to the completion of our Independence. **1920** HOWELLS *Vacation of Kelwyns* 176 It's a good deal for the hundredth anniversary of our Independence to decide!

b. Used in official dating of documents.

1796 *State P.* III. 21 In the year one thousand seven hundred and ninety-five, and the twentieth year of American independence. **1816** Pickering 2 On the twenty ninth day of May, A.D. 1816, and in the fortieth year of the independence of the United States of America. **1847** POLK in *Pres. Mess. & P.* IV. 522 The 20th day of April, A.D. 1847, and of the Independence of the United States the seventy-first. **1856** PIERCE *Ib.* V. 393 The 28th day of May, A.D. 1856, and of the Independence of the United States of America the eightieth. **1913** WILSON in *N.Y. Times* 24 Oct. 10/7 Done at the City of Washington this 23d day of October, in the year . . . of the independence of the United States of America the one hundred and thirty-eighth.

+2. =INDEPENDENCE DAY. *Obs.* Also attrib.

1799 J. COWLES *Diary* 28 Thursday. Independence, which they celebrate. **1804** *Lewis & Clark Exped.* VII. (1905) 110 The party all in good Spirits keeping up the 4th. of July &c as Independence. **1834** in *Atlantic Mo.* XXVI. 743/2 Met sundry laughing lads and lasses, in curricles; returning, probably, from some place of pleasure, where they had spent 'Independence,' as the 4th. is called here [Northampton, Mass.]. **1845** KIRKLAND *Western Clearings* 27 It is an object of no small solicitude to the soberer classes in the new country to devise some mode of celebrating 'Independence' that shall not end in bloodshed and mortal quarrels. **1865** B. ALCOTT *Journals* 372 Emerson comes and spends Independence evening.

+3. The separation of Texas and California from Mexico.

1836 *Diplom. Corr. Texas* I. (1908) 93 Public Meetings are getting up in all directions petitioning Congress to recognise our Independence. **1848** *Calif. Claims* (Senate Rep. 23 Feb.) 12 The movement for independence was one of self defence on the part of the American settlers in that part of California.

4. (See quotation.)

1864 DICK *American Hoyle* (1866) 185 *Independence.*—When a player [in the game of Boston] agrees to name a trump and take more than five tricks; thus, when a player bids six tricks, it is termed an *Independence of six;* when he bids seven tricks, it is called an Independence of seven; and so on up to an Independence of thirteen, which is also called Grand Slam.

+Independence Day. The anniversary of the adoption of the Declaration of Independence, July 4, 1776. Also attrib.

1841 *Knickerb.* XVII. 276 The enthusiasm which is annually rekindled . . . by the return of 'Independence day.' **1855** *Harper's Mag.* XI. 419/2 On 'Independence Day' we took steamer for the county of Rockland, determined to pass the Fourth in peace. **1894** *Ib.* LXXXIX. 318/1 On the occasion of this Independence-day celebration the first untoward event was the explosion of the cannon. **1904** *Courier-Journal* 2 July 6 It is too much to hope that Independence Day this year will be celebrated in a way to avoid frightful killings and woundings.

Independency. {1611–} +=INDEPENDENCE 1. *Obs.* — **1775** in Johnston *N. Hale* 173 Congress had declared independency. **1776** A. ADAMS *Familiar Letters* 149, I hear that you have declared an independency. **1790** WASHINGTON *Diaries* IV. 135 This day being the Anniversary of the declaration of Independency the celebration of it was put of[f] until tomorrow. **1865** PHILLIPS *Amer. Paper Curr.* II. 48 The idea of independency grew more in favor among the people.

Independent, *n.* Also †**independant.**

1. A member of an Independent church; a Congregationalist. {1644–} Now hist. (Cf. CONGREGATIONAL *a.*, note.)

*c***1679** R. WILLIAMS *Ans. to Coddington* 8 Alas what doth the Pope, . . . Doctors, Presbyters, Independants, Baptists, Foxians prate of the Christian name? **1711** *N.C. Col. Rec.* I. 771 There are many of them Presbyterians or Independants unfit for such an office. **1750** J. BIRKET *Cursory Remarks* 22 There is Nineteen different places of Worship in the Town [of Boston] (to wit) thirteen of the Independents Presbyterians & newlights. **1756** BOWNAS *Acct. Life* 78 Churchmen, Presbyterians, Independents, and others, all preach themselves, and for their own Advantage in this World. **1789** ANBUREY *Travels* II. 285 [In Penna.] there are . . . Moravians, Independants, [and] Anabaptists. **1834** BANCROFT *Hist. U.S.* I. 290 The Independents had, it is true, been nearly exterminated.

+2. One who has separated from the Mormon church.

1862 *N. Amer. Rev.* July 221 In the catalogue of Mormon members, M. Remy reckons two thousand 'schismatics' and 'independents' in Texas, Pennsylvania, and Michigan.

+3. *Polit.* One who is not a member or regular adherent of either of the two major political parties, the Republican or the Democratic.

1886 ALTON *Among Law-Makers* 20 [The Senate occasionally includes] a few Independents—men who talk and vote sometimes with the Democrats and sometimes with the Republicans. **1888** LOWELL *Independent in Politics* 6, I shall . . . indicate why there is a necessity that the Independent should have a place in politics.

b. =INDEPENDENT REPUBLICAN 2.

1888 BRYCE *Amer. Commonw.* II. III. lvi. 379 The case of these Independents, or Mugwumps, is an illustrative one. **1888** *Amer. Almanac* 204 The [Dakota] Legislature of 1887–88 stands: . . . House, . . . 7 Democrats, 3 Farmers' Alliance, 1 Independent.

4. A business enterprise which is outside the combine or trust which dominates its field.

1904 TARBELL *Hist. Standard Oil Co.* I. 93 The independents [in oil-selling] . . . demanded open rates, with no rebates to anyone.

Independent, *a.* {1611–} **1.** Pertaining to the sect of Independents or Congregationalists. **2.** *Polit.* Not attached to a political party or machine.

(1) 1642 LECHFORD *Plain Dealing* 79 The Congregationall independent government, whereof I have had some experience. **1704** S. KNIGHT *Journal* 36 A little too much Independant in their principalls. *c***1792** T. COXE *View U.S.* 373 There are and have been in the legislative, executive, and judicial branches of the general government, persons of the following denominations—Episcopalian, Presbyterian, Independent or Congregational, Quaker [etc.]. *a***1817** DWIGHT *Travels* II. 40 It contains three Presbyterian, one Independent, and one Baptist, Congregations. **(2) 1885** *Century Mag.* Jan. 462/2 The 'independent voter' . . . has contributed to the placing of the executive power in the hands of a party which has hitherto been regarded by Republicans as unlikely to do its duty by the negro. **1902** E. C. MEYER *Nominating Systems* 46 At the primary election, also, the increasing strength of the independent candidate, who has been defeated in a regular 'machine-controlled' convention, testifies to a growing freedom and independence of thought on part of the voter.

+Independent Day. =INDEPENDENCE DAY. *Obs.* — **1803** E. S. BOWNE *Life* 161 We are in expectation of great entertainment on fourth of July—Independent day! as they laugh at us Yankees for calling it. **1840** DANA *Two Years* xxxi. 383 Monday, July 4th. This was 'independent day' in Boston.

+Independent Republican. *Polit.* **1.** One belonging to the moderate Democratic-Republican party in Pennsylvania, after the division of *c*1805. Now hist. **2.** A member of the group in the Republican party that refused in 1884 to support the candidacy of James G. Blaine for the presidency; a Mugwump. Now hist. — **(1) 1818** FEARON *Sketches* 139 The moderate democrats [are] called by the several names of 'Independent Republicans,' 'Democrats of the Revolution,' and 'Old Schoolmen.' **(2) 1888** BRYCE *Amer. Commonw.* II. III. lvi. 379 The Independent Republicans of 1884 did not venture to start a programme or candidate of their own.

Indess. An American Indian woman. *Obs.* — **1672** JOSSELYN *New Eng. Rarities* 49 Of the Moss that grows at the roots of the white Oak the Indesses make a strong decoction. **1674** — *Two Voyages* 124 The *Indesses* that are young, are some of them very comely.

+Index board. A signboard put up on streets and roads to give information to wayfarers. — **1830** WATSON *Philadelphia* 725, I remember very well that when a boy, about the year 1800, we first saw index boards on the walls, to show the streets. **1850** W. MILES *Journal* (1916) 23 Follow a broad frequented wagon road, directed by index boards. **1858** *Texas Almanac 1859* 23 It is made the duty of overseers . . . to put up index-boards at the forks of public roads, pointing to the most noted places to which the roads lead.

***India.** *attrib.* Imported from India; pertaining to India.

1725 *Boston News-Letter* 29 Oct., Chintz, muzlin, & sundry other India goods. **1755** FRANKLIN *Writings* III. 294 When you incline to buy china ware, chinces, India silks, or any other of their flimsey, slight manufactures. **1768** FRENEAU *Poems* (1809) I. 31 Pullcats, India teas; Improv'd by age, and now grown very old. **1788** H. M. Brooks *Gleanings* 59 A few pieces best India bandannoes. **1789** *Ann. 1st Congress* I. 173 If drawbacks were not allowed, it would be a very considerable restraint on commerce, particularly on the India trade. **1853** B. F. TAYLOR *Jan. & June* 192 Their pencils glide so freely . . . over the polished surface of the India card. **1860** M. J. HOLMES *Maude* xv. 164 It's my India shawl. **1877** *Harper's Mag.* March 565 In Easter-week Dolly was married, and in trailing robes of India muslin, and a cloud of tulle about her beautiful head, looked more child-like than ever.

***Indian,** *n.* Also (*dial.*) **Ingen, Injun,** etc.

+1. A member of one of the native tribes found by explorers and settlers in America. {1553, of the West Indies} Cf. BLANKET INDIAN.

(a) 1602 BRERETON *Virginia* 6 We saw manie Indians, which are tall big boned men. *a***1649** [see INCH BOARD]. **1682** *Plymouth Laws* 195 If any Indian who is a servant to the English shall run away amongst any Indians such Indians whither such a runaway Indian is come shall forthwith give notice of the said Runaway. **1707** SEWALL *Diary* II. 197 Mr. Coffin of Nantucket is appointed by the Govr. and Council to have an oversight of the Indians there. **1751** FRANKLIN *Representative Selections* (1936) 217 America is chiefly occupied by Indians, who subsist mostly by Hunting. **1812** MARSHALL *Kentucky* 38 White men in their wars against the Indians, became themselves Indians in practice. *a***1862** THOREAU *Maine Woods* 206 The Indian said that the Umbazookskus . . . was a good place for moose. **1890** CUSTER *Following Guidon* 287 Many Indians might hide or desperadoes lie in wait. *a***1918** G. STUART *On Frontier* I. 149 Marjeau . . . struck a village of Ute Indians and had a good trade.

(b) 1670 *East-Hampton Rec.* I. 330 Obadia the engiane was hiered to keepe the cattell. **1680** *N.H. Hist. Soc. Coll.* VIII. 55 The ingens have showed themselves. **1758** *Essex Inst. Coll.* XLVI. 211 A hous wass Burnt down a littell while afore by the Indjons. **1825** NEAL *Bro. Jonathan* I. 104 Where's the injunn? what's become o' him? **1870** 'MARK TWAIN' *Sk., New & Old* 199 Fine old family—great-grandmother was an Injun. **1889**

MUNROE *Golden Days* 118 No more attention was paid to the shooting of an 'Injun' than if he were a coyote.

fig. and *transf.* a**1861** WINTHROP *J. Brent* xxii. 242 But these yer fall storms is reg'lar Injuns. **1905** N. DAVIS *Northerner* 173 Watson . . . sat erect, staring at Falls silently. . . . 'You—you old Indian!'

+**2.** One or other of the languages spoken by the Indians.

1637 *Mass. H. S. Coll.* 4 Ser. VI. 215 He came from a trading howse . . . & can speake much Indian. **1675** *Ib.* 311 There is an English youth amongst them, . . . one that speaks good Indjan. **1700** SEWALL *Letter-Book* I. 233 The Savoy-Confession of Faith, Engl. on one side and Indian on the other, has been lately printed here. **1791** W. BARTRAM *Travels* 440 The chief . . . speaks in Indian, commanding them to proceed. **1830** WATSON *Philadelphia* 73 Both her and her husband, spoke Indian readily. **1865** PIKE *Scout & Ranger* (1932) 39 He went on delivering a lengthy discourse, still speaking in Indian.

+**3.** =INDIAN CORN, INDIAN MEAL. (See also INDIAN HARVEST.)

1641 *Dorchester Rec.* 286, I Re[ceive]d in wheate and Indein 3l. 8s. **1652** *Springfield Rec.* I. 224 This pay to bee payd halfe merchandable indian and halfe merchandable wheat. c**1680** HULL *Diaries* 221 A very dry summer; most of the grain in the Bay and southward almost scorched up; much Indian eaten up with worms. **1780** E. PARKMAN *Diary* 200 Elias went today with a Bushel of Indian. **1828** W. DUNLAP *Trip to Niagara* (1830) 49 As soon as I have put the Indian in the pot. **1849** COOPER *Sea Lions* xxiii, There were . . . a few barrels of cornmeal, or 'injin,' as it is usually termed in American parlance. **1894** EGGLESTON in *Century Mag.* April 849 The newcomer from another part of the country, when first he crosses the Connecticut River, is startled at being asked by an innocent-looking girl waiter in a village tavern if he will have some 'fried Indian.'

+**4.** A white man disguised as an Indian, for the purpose of committing violence. Applied to the Anti-renters of New York.

1845 *N.Y. Wkly. Tribune* 16 Aug. 5/2 Several 'Indians' from Delaware county are now in the State Prison. **1882** *Amer. Univ. Cycl.* I. 534 During . . . 1845 some alarming outrages were committed by 'Indians' of the anti-rent associations.

+**5.** Phrases: *To sing Indian,* to act in a proud or defiant manner; *to do (play) the sober Indian,* (see quot. 1832); *to play Indian,* to preserve a stolid countenance; of children playing, to pretend to be Indians; *to see Indians,* to suffer from an excess of strong drink; *to turn Indian,* to revert to a wild state. (See also HONEST INJUN.)

1829 *Western Mo. Rev.* II. 467 A native young Kentuckian, . . . warmed with the idea of getting rid of death and the doctor, began to sing Indian, after reading this. **1832** FERRALL *Ramble* 221 During these drinking fits, there is always one at least of the party who remains sober, in order to secure the knives, &c. Hence the Americans derive the cant phrase of 'doing the sober Indian' which they apply to any one of a company who will not *drink fairly*. **1840** *Knickerb.* XVI. 265, I tried to keep my countenance, and to play Indian, but it would not do. **1850** LEWIS *La. Swamp Doctor* 118 In one of the upper apartments was a private patient, labouring under the disease indifferently known as the blue-devils, red-monkeys, seeing injuns, or man-with-the-poker. **1862** *Rep. Comm. Patents 1861: Agric.* 356 The oft-quoted proverb of reclaimed swamps turning Indian was rehearsed for my especial benefit. **1876** MILLER *First Families* xxi. 184, He had had his carouse, and was now playing sober Indian. **1907** *St. Nicholas* XXXIV. 641/1 Both boys and girls delight in 'dressing up' and playing Indian.

Indian. *attrib.* and *adj.*

I. +**1. a.** Designating persons of a certain rank or class in an Indian tribe.

See also INDIAN DOCTOR, GUIDE, etc.

1638 *New Haven Col. Rec.* 1 Momaugin ye Indian Sachem of Quinopiocke. **1665** WINTHROP *Letters* (1882) 98 Some English maids at Hadly were with some Indian Squars or maids gathering berries in the woods. **1773** *Hist. of Brit. Domin. N. Amer.* I. 68 The scouts or Indian hunters, in time of war, used to carry packs. **1832** WILLIAMSON *Maine* II. 270 The Indian file-leader, hooded with a large hawk-skin, . . . raised a hideous yell, and quickened his pace. **1835** HOFFMAN *Winter in West* I. 61 The speech of an Indian chief before the council of Pennsylvania [etc.]. **1851** GLISAN *Jrnl. Army Life* 59, I marched into garrison as proudly as an Indian warrior with his dozen scalps dangling to the breeze. **1899** CUSHMAN *Hist. Indians* 38 There was but little difference between the 'Indian Magician' and the Indian 'Medicine Man.'

+**b.** Designating Indians who were servants or slaves to members of the white race. Now hist.

1682 *Plymouth Laws* 195 The Indian Constable . . . shall Imediatly apprehend such Indian servant. **1686** *Relat. Invasion of Fla.* 70 The Cacique of Cutifachiqui stole away from the Indian slaves who carried her. **1705** *Boston News-Letter* 8 Oct. 2/2 Ran away from his Master, Samuel Niles, of Kingston, . . . an Indian Man Servant, aged about 26 Years. **1708** *Boston News-Letter* 15–22 Nov. 4/2 A Lusty Carolina Indian Woman fit for any Dairy Service, to be Sold on Reasonable Terms. **1744** *S.C. Gazette* 9 Jan. 4/1 Run away some Time since from the Subscriber . . . an Indian Wench about 40 Years of Age.

+**2.** Of or pertaining to the speech or writing of the Indians.

1647 ELIOT *Day-Breaking* 1 [We were] not so farre acquainted with the Indian language as to expresse our hearts herein before God. **1718** SEWALL *Diary* III. 180, I gave her 10s to give her sister Weld for her Indian Bible. **1819** E. DANA *Geogr. Sks.* 276 Indian hieroglyphics are engraved on the walls. **1916** EASTMAN *From Deep Woods* 32 He took out his Bible and hymn-book printed in the Indian tongue.

+**3.** Designating articles or objects made by or in the manner of the Indians: **a.** Pottery, household articles, etc.

See also INDIAN BASKET, BEADS, etc., and cf. sense 5 b.

1624 SMITH *Gen. Hist. Va.* IV. 108 The houses . . . [are] couered aboue with strong boards, and some matted round with Indian mats. **1645** *Conn. Probate Rec.* I. 21, 2 hamers, a gymlett, 2 Indean baggs. **1648** *Conn. Rec.* I. 486 Earthen ware, . . . 2 Indian trayes. **1806** in *Ann. 9th Congress* 2 Sess. 1121 They threw up several broken pieces of Indian pottery. **1819** W. AMPHLETT *Emigrant's Directory* 155 Great quantities of broken ancient earthern-ware are found in the country above Natchez, but none of it has ever been glazed: it is generally called Indian ware. **1851** *Knickerb.* XXXVII. 498 The child had an Indian rattle, formed of the bone of some wild animal, and ornamented with curlew-feathers.

+**b.** Articles of clothing.

See also INDIAN SHOE, STOCKING.

1701 WOLLEY *Journal N.Y.* (1902) 35 Their ordinary habit is a pair of Indian Breeches. **1744** MOORE *Voy. Georgia* I. 120 Those who walk the woods much, wear what they call Indian boots, which are made of coarse woolen cloths, much too large for the legs, tied upon their thighs and hang loose to their shoes. **1753** WASHINGTON *Diaries* I. 63, I put myself in an Indian walking Dress, and continued with them three Days. **1784** J. SMYTH *Tour U.S.* I. 181 On their feet they . . . generally [wear] Indian moccossons, . . . which are made of strong elk's, or buck's skin. **1819** E. EVANS *Pedestrious Tour* 103 An Indian apron . . . was about eighteen inches square, covered with fine bear skin, trimmed with fur, and having over the lower part of it a net for game. **1834** BRACKENRIDGE *Recoll.* 23 The Indian sandal, or moccasin, . . . [is] worn here [in La.] by both sexes. **1835** HOFFMAN *Winter in West* I. 208 A fleet rider, whose tall figure and Indian head-dress had hitherto guided me, had been just unhorsed.

+**c.** Water craft and other vehicles.

1690 SEWALL *Diary* I. 317 An account of the danger they were in at Casco of an Assault from the Enemy, 30 Indian Canoes being seen. **1791** A. BRADMAN *Narr. Sufferings R. Forbes* (1792) 4 They undertook to hall [*sic*] on Indian sleighs, or handsleds [their provisions and four children]. **1836** IRVING *Astoria* II. 55 They followed down [the Snake R.] for a short distance, in search of some Indian rafts made of reeds, on which they might cross. **1880** *Harper's Mag.* Aug. 396 The Indian birch and dug-out . . . belong to the canoe group. **1885** *Rep. Indian Affairs* 129 The Flat-head Lake must be crossed by an Indian ferry-boat.

+**4. a.** Designating various dwellings of the Indians.

See also INDIAN LODGE.

1634 *Relation of Beginnings of Md.* 17 The Indian houses are all built heere in a long halfe Ouall. **1737** *Md. Hist. Mag.* III. 49 This Deponent Saw but a few Indian Cabbins and a little Hutt made of logs. **1837** *S. Lit. Messenger* III. 689 We saw on either side of the river several Indian tents made of straw mats. **1858** D. PETERS *Kit Carson* 239 Near the mountains, to the east of Fernandez de Taos, is located an Indian Pueblo which is very interesting to the traveler. **1893** in *S. Dak. Hist. Coll.* I. 301 Still further on in the timber are the Indian wigwams. **1907** *St. Nicholas* XXXIV. 651/1 The young folks who were playing in it explained that they had read of Indian tepees.

+**b.** Designating areas occupied by Indians. Sometimes in place names.

See also INDIAN COUNTRY, LAND, RESERVATION, etc.

1647 *Md. Hist. Mag.* VI. 372 The Easte side of St. Clements Bay, about 2 miles from Little Brittaine commonly knowen by the name of the Indian Quarters. **1658** *Hartford Land Distrib.* 216 One parcell of Indian Meadow lying in the South Meadow. **1788** M. DEWEES *Journal* (MS.), 19 We passed by Norris Towne on the Indian shore a Clever little situation with ten Cabbins. **1805** CLARK in *Lewis & C. Exped.* III. (1905) 62 I saw near an old Indian encampment a Swet (Sweat) house Covered with earth. **1854** BENTON *30 Years' View* I. 27/1 The victories of General Jackson over the Creeks . . . made the first great breach in this vast Indian domain. **1865** PIKE *Scout & Ranger* (1932) 75 We were in a country celebrated as an Indian hunting-ground, and therefore it would be folly for us to proceed further.

+**c.** Designating trails, passages, etc., made or used by the Indians.

See also INDIAN ROAD, TRAIL.

1668 *Plymouth Rec.* I. 103 A bush which standeth on the southwest syde of an old Indian path. **1673** *Plymouth Rec.* 132 Over Jones River by the Indian bridge by the herring weire. **1810** CUMING *Western Tour* 238 An old Indian trace, now the post road from Louisville to Vincennes. **1831** WITHERS *Chron. Border Warfare* 206 Proceeding by forced marches to the Indian crossing at the mouth of the Sandy fork of Little Kenhawa, he remained there nearly three days.

+**d.** Designating lines of demarcation between the whites and the Indians.

1666 *Duxbury Rec.* 15 Beginning the measurement on the north side the Indian fence, from a red oak tree marked on four sides. **1706** *Ib.* 80 From thence we ran about fifty five rods by John Boneys line, to the Indian line, then we ran by the Indian line near South. **1791** W. BARTRAM *Travels* 46 Excursions, through uninhabited wildernesses, and an Indian frontier. **1835** HOFFMAN *Winter in West* I. 186, I am now within eight or ten miles of the Indian boundary. **1873** BEADLE *Undevel. West* 804 It was then [1839] 'far up country,' on the Indian border.

+5. a. Designating various incidents, practices, etc., associated with the conflict between the whites and the Indians.

See also INDIAN SCARE

1668 WINTHROP *Letters* (1882) 127 The impossibility almost that full discoveries [of minerals] should be made, whiles these Indian warrs continue. **1746** *N.H. Hist. Soc. Coll.* IX. 130, [I] went to Boston to carry news of ye Indian mischief. **1767** HUTCHINSON *Hist. Mass.* II. 107 The terror of the Indian gantlet seems to have inspired Dunstan with resolution. **1829** COOPER *Wish-ton-Wish* i, Indian alarms, as they were termed, were not unfrequent. **1838** *U.S. Mag.* I. 300 There is a Lebanon cedar tree . . . which is immortalized by some wild tale of Indian massacre and miraculous escape. **1866** *Wkly. New Mexican* 24 Nov. 2/1 The deplorable condition of our Territory for want of protection from Indian raids demands some means for the protection of our people. **1877** W. WRIGHT *Big Bonanza* 118, I shall but briefly sketch this first and last Indian trouble in Nevada. **1884** MATTHEWS & BUNNER *In Partnership* 71 In New Mexico . . . there was an abundance of the pleasant sport of Indian fighting. **1916** EASTMAN *From Deep Woods* 117, I tried to make it clear that there was no 'Indian outbreak' in 1890–91.

+b. Designating implements or weapons used by the Indians in warfare or hunting.

See also INDIAN ARROW 1, GUN.

*c***1750** HUTCHINSON *Diary & Lett.* I. 52 He had supplied the Frenchman wth Indian hatchets. **1808** BARKER *Indian Princess* II. ii, Or shoot thy bird-bolt from an Indian bow. **1835** HOFFMAN *Winter in West* I. 34 Loose bones and Indian weapons . . . are at this day continually found amid piles of stone in the adjacent woods. **1860** HOLMES *Professor* 308 At Cantabridge, near the sea, I have once or twice picked up an Indian arrowhead in a fresh furrow. **1877** HODGE *Arizona* 108 Many other traditions exist . . . of golden Indian bullets found after straggling Indian fights. **1890** CUSTER *Following Guidon* 7 An Indian shield . . . is made of the thickest part of the buffalo-hide.

+c. Designating white men who fought, killed, or were hostile to the Indians. Now hist.

See also INDIAN-FIGHTER.

1835 HOFFMAN *Winter in West* I. 227 It is therefore useless to argue with an Illinois 'Indian-hater.' **1843** *Amer. Pioneer* II. 312 His reputation as an Indian hunter was . . . great. **1845** KIRKLAND *Western Clearings* 206 I have supposed it [the story] to descend to her through the old Indian-killer, from the more genial and impulsive South. **1847** *Santa Fe Republican* 25 Dec. 2/2 This distinguished mountaineer and Indian slayer, has opened a Hotel in the lower part of town. **1885** *Wkly. New Mexican Rev.* 11 June 3/3 Gonzales has been noted as the best guide and Indian trailer in this country [near Laredo, Tex.]. **1886** *Century Mag.* Nov. 14/1 Either a spirit of revenge . . . or a sportsmanlike pleasure . . . made him a determined Indian-stalker.

+6. a. Designating governmental actions, legislation, etc., intended to aid, compensate, or govern the Indians.

See also INDIAN TREATY.

1682 *Plymouth Laws* 195 Overseers and Constables shalbe accomptable to the Treasurer for all Indian rates and fines. **1835** HOFFMAN *Winter in West* II. 75 The sight of such a miserable remnant . . . would suggest doubts of the humanity of our Indian policy. **1840** *Niles' Nat. Reg.* 11 April 95/1 The officers of the army employed in paying Indian annuities. **1847** LANMAN *Summer in Wilderness* 141 He was on his annual visit to the North, to attend the Indian payments. **1857** *Lawrence* (Kansas) *Republican* 28 May 2 The President . . . has issued his proclamation for the sale of the Indian Trust Lands in Kansas Territory. **1862** KETTELL *Hist. Rebellion* I. 68 Mr. Russell induced Godard Bailey . . . to abstract from the department, $871,000 of stocks belonging to the Indian fund, and loan them to him. **1868** *N.Y. Herald* 17 July 8/3 So the Indian Appropriation bill was taken up. **1873** *Harper's Mag.* XLVI. 469 Indian scrip locations, 5,760.00 [acres]. **1881** *Rep. Indian Affairs* 13 It were better to encourage Indians . . . to take up the land under the 'Indian homestead act.'

+b. Designating various official persons or agencies that deal with the Indians.

See also INDIAN AGENCY, AGENT, BUREAU, etc.

1682 *Plymouth Laws* 195 Such Indians . . . shall forthwith give notice of the said Runaway to the Indian Constable. **1775** ADAIR *Indians* 252, I had the pleasure to see, at Augusta in Georgia, the honourable gentleman who was our first Indian super-intendant. **1866** *Rep. Indian Affairs* 260 The Indian committee refused to act upon the treaty until said decision was had. **1880** LAMPHERE *U.S. Govt.* 274/1 Indian inspectors [are appointed by the president]. **1885** *Wkly. New Mexican Rev.* 29 Jan. 3/1 An amendment was adopted [in Congress] appropriating $25,000 for the erection of an Indian industrial school at Santa Fe. **1904** in *Indian Laws & Treaties* III. 37 For compensation of judges of Indian courts, twelve thousand dollars.

+c. Designating private persons, agencies, actions, etc., concerned with educating and otherwise helping the Indians.

1699 *Mass. H. S. Coll.* 4 Ser. I. 27, I was put in to be an Indian preacher by the Gentlemen who have the oversight of yt work. **1829** in M'Kenney *Memoirs* (1846) I. 226 This Association shall be known by the style of 'The Indian Board, for the Emigration, Preservation and Improvement of the Aborigines of North America.' **1864** *Weekly New Mexican* 25 Nov. 3/2 Preposterous as it may seem in these days of Indian philanthropy, for an 'outsider' to speak of the depredations committed by the 'noble savage' [etc.]. **1872** *Rep. Indian Affairs 1871* 182 Indian aid societies have been formed. *Ib.*, An Indian peace association has been formed in Philadelphia, that furnish [*sic*] clothing, books, &c. **1885** *Weekly New Mexican Rev.* 25 June 2/2 The Indian sympathizers of the east are everlastingly parading Penn's treatment of the Indians. **1916** EASTMAN *From Deep Woods* 87 An ambition implanted by my earlier Indian teachers.

+7. Designating legal actions, political bodies, etc., connected with the Indians' efforts to live peaceably with the whites.

See also INDIAN CLAIM, DEED, etc.

1683 *Mass. H. S. Coll.* 4 Ser. V. 106 The deed . . . was given and received only as a confirmation of the English title, long before truly made by purchase, but not so amply confirmed by writing, which was not thought so necessary unto Indian conveyances until of later times. **1763** *N.C. Col. Rec.* VI. 991, I before acknowledged the receipt of Your Lordship's letter about the Indian Congress which is appointed at Augusta on the 15th of October. **1771** HABERSHAM *Letters* 160 If the Indian Cession of the Lands should take place, . . . Mr. Graham has desired me to mention Mr. John Jamieson to you. **1847** LOWELL *Biglow P.* 1 Ser. iv. 60 Town Meetings, . . . Parliaments, Diets, Indian Councils, Palavers, and the like.

+8. Designating objects, persons, etc., connected with commerce with the Indians.

See also INDIAN GOODS, STORE, TRADE, etc.

1709 LAWSON *Carolina* 215 The Indian stole . . . Blankets, Powder, Shot and Rum, (this being the Indian Store-House, where the Trading Goods were kept.) **1725** in *Travels Amer. Coll.* 103 It Amounted to 1341 wt of leather at Indian Price. **1766** ROGERS *Ponteach* I. 1, I'm unacquainted with your Indian Commerce, And gladly would I learn the Arts from you. **1772** in *Travels Amer. Col.* 549 In ClayCatskee are Sixty Gun Men and three Indian factors. **1835** HOFFMAN *Winter in West* I. 67 Fort Pitt began to assume commercial importance from the Indian fur trade then [*c*1790] carried on with vigour from this point. **1854** BENTON *30 Years' View* I. 20/2 The experience of the Indian factory system is an illustration of the unfitness of the federal government to carry on any system of trade.

+9. Designating celebrations, war cries, dances, etc., of the Indians.

See also INDIAN DANCE, POWWOW, etc.

1764 HUTCHINSON *Hist. Mass.* I. 78 No sound that was ever made can be more horrid than the Indian yell. **1805** LEWIS in *Ann. 9th Congress* 2 Sess. 1057 This Indian fair is frequently attended by the Yanktons of the north and Ahnah. **1837** IRVING *Bonneville* II. 184 The attention of the quarrellers was arrested by a strange kind of Indian chant or chorus, that seemed to operate upon them as a charm. **1844** *Knickerb.* XXIV. 240 It was the grove wherein stood the council-house, and wherein . . . they had celebrated their Indian festivals. **1883** 'MARK TWAIN' *Life on Miss.* 44 When he was done they all fetched a kind of Injun war-whoop. **1891** O'BEIRNE *Leaders Ind. Territory* 73/2 Mr. Sawyers will travel in the states next winter, giving stereoptican exhibitions of the Indian war dances. **1913** LONDON *Valley of Moon* III. viii, Mark Hall's sister . . . three times tumbled him ignominiously heels over head in a bout of Indian wrestling.

10. Designating natural objects associated with Indian arts or work.

1794 *N.Y. State Soc. Arts* I. 134 The remaining two acres I manured with shells called Indian shells, that is, the shells of clams, oysters, wilks and scollops, collected by Indians, and by length of time settled under the surface of the ground, and so dissolved as to be broken in pieces and mixed with the earth. **1798** *Amer. Philos. Soc.* IV. 439 The immense oysterbeds, which have been quitted by the ocean, are vulgarly called *Indian* oysterbanks. **1847** in *31st Congress 1 Sess.* H. R. Ex. Doc. No. 5, II. 731 The banks [of a stream] rise on either side . . . worn in some places into 'hog backs' or more like our 'Indian ridges,' being only two or three feet wide on the top and extending along the river for a considerable distance. **1902** CLAPIN 318 *Pot-holes*, naturally formed depressions in rock, due to the action of water, and which, from being circular in shape, were at one time thought to have been made by the early aborigines, for grinding and pounding corn in. Also called *Indian Mortars*. **1904** *N.Y. Ev. Post* 18 June, On the grounds are a number of 'Indian Kettles,' or potholes in the rocks.

+11. Special combinations.

Indian bed, (see quotation); *I. coffee*, a poor coffee made by using the grounds a second time; *I. liquor*, alcoholic liquor adulterated with water, spices, etc.; *I. ranch*, the headquarters of an Indian tribe; a rancheria; *I. ward*, an Indian whose affairs are taken care of by the government; *I. windmill*, (see quotation).

1848 BARTLETT 188 An *Indian bed* of clams is made by setting a number of clams together on the ground with the hinge uppermost, and then kindling over them a fire of brushwood, which is kept burning till they are thoroughly roasted. **1884** SHEPHERD *Prairie Exper.* 61 Water is poured on [the grounds], and the liquid set to boil; this second decoction . . . goes by the name of Indian coffee. **1859** *Nat. Intelligencer* 10 July A barrel of the 'pure Cincinnati' . . . is a sufficient basis upon which to manufacture one hundred barrels of 'good Indian liquor!' **1856** GLISAN *Jrnl. Army Life* 344 The agent . . . got the commanding officer of this post to send out three or four men to examine the Indian ranches for arms, etc. **1900** *Congress. Rec.* 31 Jan. 1350/2 It contains no change of the general policy of the Government in regard to its Indian wards. **1889** MUNROE *Golden Days* 120 [Acorns] were ground to a coarse meal, in the holes of the flat rock, which was called by the miners an 'Indian wind-mill.'

II. +12. Of or pertaining to Indian corn.

See also INDIAN HARVEST, MEAL.

1646 *Conn. Probate Rec.* I. 16 Two bush[els] of Indean molt. **1648** SHEPARD *Clear Sunshine* 15 A homely dinner, perhaps parcht Corne or *Indian* stalks. **1747** in Chalkley *Scotch-Irish Settlement Va.* I. 26 Daniel Kidney acquitted of stealing Indian fodder from Henry Christwell. **1805** PARKINSON *Tour* 223 A farmer's waggon in America, when she comes into market, is something like a pedlar's pack: it consists of butter, eggs, . . . geese, turkeys, wheat-flour, Indian-flour. **1817** *Niles' Reg.* XII. 212/1 The cut worm, or grub, . . . is if possible more destructive to the Indian crop this season than that of the last year.

+b. Designating foods prepared from Indian corn meal.

See also INDIAN BREAD, CAKE, DUMPLING, etc.

1789 MORSE *Amer. Geog.* 131 He breakfasts . . . on three small indian hoe-cakes. **1806** LEWIS in *L. & Clark Exped.* IV. (1905) 10 The root of the thistle . . . is . . . at other times pounded fine and mixed with could water untill reduced to the consistency of sagamity or indian mush. **1828** LESLIE *Receipts* 61 Indian Pound Cake. **1849** *New Eng. Farmer* I. 380 [Recipe] Indian Flap Jacks. **1867** *Common Sense Cook Book* 8 [Recipe] Indian Batter Cakes. **1877** BARTLETT 312 *Indian Dab*, a kind of batter-cake. Pennsylvania. **1881** TOURGEE *'Zouri's Christmas* v, The fish with its red-clay case and Indian-pone cover lay exposed upon her lap.

III. 13. Derived from India.

1813 *Austin P.* (1924) I. 231 Indian Calico. **1838** INGRAHAM *Burton* II. 138 A large Indian shawl which Caroline had thrown aside caught her eye at the instant. **1850** BROWNE *Poultry Yard* 24 Those writers, by a pleasant legerdemain, . . . transform one of the wild Indian cocks into a barn-door fowl. **1894** *Harper's Mag.* May 946/2 The sidewalks were covered with the remains of Indian crackers, and the whole air was redolent of gunpowder.

IV. +14. In names of plants, trees, fish, birds, and animals. **a.** Of plants.

As used in plant names, *Indian* freq. means *wild*.

1737 BRICKELL *N. Carolina* 23 The herb Mastick, Indian-all-heal, Cinquefoil. **1815** DRAKE *Cincinnati* ii. 77 [Plants growing in Miami country include] Indian arrow-wood. **1892** TORREY *Foot-Path Way* 80 The common greenbrier (cat-brier, horse-brier, Indian-brier) of my boyhood. **1847** DARLINGTON *Weeds & Plants* (1860) 59 *Mollugo verticillata.* . . . Carpet-weed. Indian Chickweed. **1743** CLAYTON *Flora Virginica* 205 Agaricus orbiculatus circulatim cristatus, intus viridi-flavescens. Indian Cork. **1722** BEVERLEY *Virginia* (ed. 2) 253 [The Indians] dish up [roots, herbs, etc.] various ways, and find them very delicious Sauce to their Meats . . . ; such are the Indian Cresses [etc.]. **1792** IMLAY *Western Territory* 207 Of herbs, &c. we have of the wild sort . . . thyme, Indian leaf, rosemary. **1791** BARTRAM *Travels* 42 A very singular and elegant plant, of an unknown family, called Indian Lettuce, made its first appearance in these rich vales. **1894** *Amer. Folk-Lore* VII. 101 *Agave*, sp., Indian maguey. New Mex. **1893** *Ib.* VI. 141 *Pyrus Americana*, Indian mozemize. . . . Ferrisburgh, Vt. **1785** MARSHALL *Amer. Grove* 147 This is called Indian Pipe Shank, from the pithy stems being used by the natives for that purpose. **1869** *Amer. Naturalist* III. 6 The Indian Pipestem (*Monotropa uniflora*) will be found rarely in low woods [in central Ill.]. **1687** CLAYTON *Va.* in *Phil. Trans.* XLI. 150 There is another Herb, which they [*i.e.*, Virginians] call the Indian Purge. This Plant . . . bears yellow Berries round about the Joints. **1737** BRICKELL *N. Carolina* 21 Oak of Jerusalem, Indian-purger, Swallow-wort. **1817–8** EATON *Botany* (1822) 238 *Cinna arundinacea*, indian reed. **1737** BRICKELL *N. Carolina* 17 The Indian Rouncival, or Miraculous Pea, so called from their long Pods and great Increase. **1847** DARLINGTON *Weeds & Plants* 170 *E[upatorium] perfoliatum.* . . . Perfoliate Eupatorium. Thorough-stem. Boneset. Indian Sage. **1881** *Harper's Mag.* March 526/1 He saw moving with the wind a quantity of Indian salt commonly known as sumac, which when ripe presents a red appearance. **1800** TATHAM *Agric. & Commerce* 136 There is a species of wild plant, which, among the people of the country, is vulgarly called *wild hemp*, sometimes *wild silk, Indian hemp, Indian silk, silk grass*, &c. **1832** WILLIAMSON *Maine* I. 132 Grasses.—Barn; . . . Herds; Indian-sweet; Knot [etc.]. **1894** *Amer. Folk-Lore* VII. 90 *Dipsacus sylvestris*, . . . Indian thistle, Huttonweed. . . . West Va.

b. Of trees.

1847 PARKMAN in *Knickerb.* XXIX. 310 The rich flowers of the Indian-apple were there in profusion. **1705** BEVERLEY *Virginia* II. 13 The Third sort is call'd the Indian Cherry, and grows higher up in the Country, than the Others do. **1838** FLAGG *Far West* II. 177n., Indian date, by the French called Placiminier, *Diosporus Virginiana.* **1737** BRICKELL *N. Carolina* 82 The Indian-Nut Tree grows to be very tall, large, and smooth. **1791** BARTRAM *Travels* 41, I observed . . . some very curious new shrubs and plants, particularly the Physic-nut, or Indian Olive. . . . The fruit is yellow when ripe, and about the size of an olive. The Indians, when they go in pursuit of deer, carry this fruit with them, supposing that it has the power of charming or drawing that creature to them. **1832** WILLIAMSON *Maine* I. 112 *Leatherwood* or *Indian Wickape* is a small tree which grows on the best hardwood land and none other: . . . even when dry, it is sufficiently limber and flexible to be used in lieu of twine or cords.

c. Of fish.

1820 RAFINESQUE in *Western Rev.* II. 238 Kentuckian Shiner, *Luxilus Kentuckiensis.* . . . Vulgar names, Indian Chub, Red tail, Shiner, &c. **1839** STORER *Mass. Fishes* 153 *Echeneis naucrates.* The Indian Remora. **1814** MITCHILL *Fishes N.Y.* 438 Indian Trumpet Fish. *Fistularia chinensis.* . . . Colour of a yellowish brown, with a ruddy tinge.

d. Of birds.

1835 AUDUBON *Ornith. Biog.* III. 275 [In S.C. the night heron] is named 'the Indian Pullet,' in Lower Louisiana the Creoles call it '*Gros-bec*,' the inhabitants of East Florida know it under the name of 'Indian Hen.'

e. Of animals.

1851 SPRINGER *Forest Life* 66 A dangerous specimen of the feline species, known by woodsmen as the 'Indian devil,' had prowled from time immemorial. **1857** *Harper's Mag.* July 150/2 The Doctor and I shot a deer and several Indian rabbits, which are much larger than our common rabbits at home.

‖**Indian,** *v. intr.* To move about like an Indian. — **1869** STOWE *Old-town Folks* 189 Jack Marshall and me has been Indianing round these 'ere woods more times 'n you could count. **1871** — *Sam Lawson* 55 Lordy massy! when a feller is Indianin' round, these 'ere pleasant summer days, a feller's thoughts gits like a flock o' young partridges.

Indian affairs.

+1. Matters affecting the relationship of the American Indians with the colonies and the United States as calling for adjustment by commissioners, superintendents, etc.

1703 SEWALL *Letter-Book* I. 287 The Commissioners for the Indian Affairs, are to have a Meeting at the Council-Chamber. **1754** *Mass. H. S. Coll.* 3 Ser. V. 19 He would direct the Secretary or Agent for Indian affairs to attend them with the records of that office. **1788** *Mass. Spy* 3 April 2/2 The superintendent of Indian affairs has sent messengers to invite the chiefs of Indian nations in the northern district [of Penna.] to a general treaty. **1822** *Ann. 17th Congress* 1 Sess. I. 137 The petition was read and referred to the Committee on Indian Affairs. **1873** *Newton Kansan* 2 Jan. 2/1 Dr. James Wright . . . has been appointed Superintendent of Indian Affairs for Montana Territory. **1913** LA FOLLETTE *Autobiog.* 377 Upon one of the committees, indeed, that of Indian affairs, I found immediately most congenial service.

2. In general sense.

1714 SEWALL *Diary* II. 433 Discours'd Mr. Mayhew largely of the Indian affairs. **1792** *State P.* I. 35, I cannot dismiss the subject of Indian affairs, without recommending to your consideration [etc.]. **1854** BENTON *30 Years' View* I. 21/1 The difficulty of detecting and redressing abuses in the management of our Indian affairs. **1873** *Newton Kansan* 6 Feb. 1/5 In the present state of Indian affairs we cannot afford to allow the bad Indians to score a victory against the government.

+Indian agency. The headquarters of an Indian agent. — **1822** MORSE *Rep. Indian Affairs* I. 39 Should the Government establish a military post here it will be very important . . . that . . . an Indian agency should be planted, at the same time, near it. **1866** *Rep. Indian Affairs* 73 [The Grande Ronde] reservation [in Ore.] consists of two townships and two fractional townships . . . , and upon it is located the oldest Indian agency in the superintendency. **1892** in *S.Dak. Hist. Coll.* I. 47 A rude frame covered with tarpaulin was the beginning of Dakota's first Indian agency of the government type. **1904** HANDSAKER in *Pioneer Life* 16 Near the bank of the river was a large building, an Indian agency.

+Indian agent. One serving as an agent among the Indians; in later use, an official representing the United States in dealings with an Indian tribe or tribes.

1766 in Rogers *Journals* (1883) 216 As Commandant and Indian Agent, it will be extremely difficult to check him, or detect him. **1807** *Ann. 10th Congress 1 Sess.* I. 670 James Seagroves was Indian agent for the Southern nations. **1831** PECK *Guide* 277 The intrigue and perfidy of the British Indian agents and Traders. **1883** *Rep. Indian Affairs* p. x, In addition to this, many of the Indian agents have to live in houses which are in wretched condition. **1916** EASTMAN *From Deep Woods* 76 After reporting to the Indian agent, I was shown to my quarters.

+Indian arrow. 1. An arrow made by the Indians to shoot from their bows. (Cf. ARROW 1.) **2.** =BURNING BUSH 1. — (1) **1654** JOHNSON *Wonder-w. Prov.* 50 He felt something brush hard upon his shoulder, which was an *Indian* arrow shot through his Coat, and the wing of his buffe-Jacket. **1654** *Md. Council Proc.* 303 The Indian Arrowes Mencioned to be allowed me. (2) **1843** TORREY *Flora N.Y.* I. 141 Burning-bush, Indian arrow, . . . [grows in] moist woods and along rivers, in the western part of the State. **1892** *Amer. Folk-Lore* V. 94 *Euonymus atropurpureus*, Indian arrow. Salem, Ind.

+Indian barn. (See quotation 1736.) Now hist. — **1634** *Mass. Bay Rec.* I. 121 What hurt the swyne of Charlton hath done amongst the Indean barnes of corne. **1668** *East-Hampton Rec.* I. 287 Nathaniell steers hide waighed forty five pound which steer fell into an Indian barne. **1736** GYLES *Mem. Captivity* 11 We put some into Indian Barns, i.e. in Holes in the Ground lin'd and cover'd with Bark, and then with Dirt. [**1898** J. R. TRUMBULL *Hist. Northampton Mass.* I. 173 Evidence . . . exists that they had receptacles for storing corn and other articles, 'Indian barns,' the settlers called them.]

+**Indian basket.** A basket made by Indians. — **1647** ELIOT *Day-Breaking* 4 Wee bid them looke upon that *Indian* Basket that was before them, there was black and white straws. **1713** SEWALL *Letter-Book* II. 22 I offer to your view a small Indian basket of summer fruit. **1848** B. B. MASON *Official Rep.* 17 Aug., About 200 men were at work in the full glare of the sun, washing for gold,—some with tin pans, some with close woven Indian baskets. **1880** *Harper's Mag.* Sept. 534/2 The ceilings [were] hung with . . . Indian baskets filled with the family clothing.

+**Indian('s) beads.** *pl.* =WAMPUM. *Obs.* — **1640** *Mass. H. S. Coll.* 4 Ser. VII. 339 He carried one hundred twenty od yeards of Indians beades with him. **1704** S. KNIGHT *Journal* 42 Also Wampom, vizt Indian beads wch serves for change.

+**Indian bean.**

1. Any one of various edible beans found in colonial times in use among the Indians. *Obs.*

1637 *Conn. Rec.* I. 9 Weathersfeild [is to provide] 1 bushell of Indian Beanes; Windsor 50 peeces of Porke. **1654** JOHNSON *Wonder-w. Prov.* 173 Indian Beans at 16 s. per bushel. **1793** *Mass. H.S. Coll.* 3 Ser. V. 129 His Indian beans [were] ready to be eaten as stringed beans.

2. A tree of the genus *Catalpa;* usually *C. bignonioides.*

1843 TORREY *Flora N.Y.* II. 25 *Catalpa syringæfolia.* Catalpa. Indian Bean. . . . About habitations. . . . The Catalpa is more esteemed for ornament than for use. **1857** GRAY *Botany* 279 Catalpa. Indian Bean. **1884** SARGENT *Rep. Forests* 115 *Catalpa bignonioides.* . . . Catalpa. . . . Cigar Tree. Indian Bean. **1892** APGAR *Trees Northern U.S.* 128 *Catalpa bignonioides.* (Indian Bean. Southern Catalpa.) *Ib., Catalpa speciosa.* . . . (Indian Bean. Western Catalpa.)

+**Indian blanket.** A blanket made by or for Indians. — **1765** in Chalkley *Scotch-Irish Settlement Va.* I. 450 One rifel gun . . . , one snafel bridle, and one Indian blanket. **1807** IRVING, etc. *Salmagundi* iii. 58 The shawl scarlet, . . . thrown over one shoulder, like an Indian blanket, with one end dragging on the ground. **1835** HOFFMAN *Winter in West* I. 243 A couple of rifles, with a powderhorn and a pair of Indian blankets, lay without. **1845** *Whig Almanac 1846* 6/2 Our Government . . . [obtained] the needed supplies under the pretence of purchasing 'Indian blankets.'

Indian bread. {1633–}

+**1.** Bread made with corn meal; corn bread. Also *Indian mixed bread.* (Cf. RYE AND INDIAN BREAD.)

1654 JOHNSON *Wonder-w. Prov.* 84 The want of English graine . . . proved a sore affliction to some stomacks, who could not live upon Indian Bread. **1704** S. KNIGHT *Journal* 47 But the Pumpkin and Indian mixt Bred had such an Aspect, and the Bare-legg'd Punch so awkerd or rather Awfull a sound, that we left both. **1765** TIMBERLAKE *Memoirs* 30 Fried meats of several kinds, and very good Indian bread, baked in a very curious way. **1805** D. MCCLURE *Diary* (1899) 91 The young man presents . . . some cakes of indian bread. **1863** *Rio Abajo Press* 26 May 4/1 Indian Bread.—Take two quarts of Indian meal, pour on boiling water enough to make the meal quite wet [etc.].

+**2.** (See quotations.)

1848 BARTLETT 366 *Tuckahoe.* . . . The Virginia truffle. A curious Vegetable, sometimes called by the name of Indian bread, or Indian Loaf, found in the Southern States, bordering on the Atlantic. **1903** *Dialect Notes* II. 318 *Indian bread* or *Indian pone,* a hard, perhaps fungous, growth found in the woods. It is black outside and white within and nearly globular. Is said to have been used for food by Indians.

+**Indian bureau.** A bureau of the federal government concerned with the welfare of the Indians. — **1846** M'KENNEY *Memoirs* I. ix. 212 When the Indian Bureau was organized, it was made the repository of all transactions relating to this branch of the public service. **1866** *Rep. Indian Affairs* 207, I respectfully submit the following report of an occurence of interest to the Indian bureau. **1888** WHITMAN *November Boughs* 409 Let me give a running account of what I see and hear through one of these conference collections at the Indian Bureau. **1908** *Indian Laws & Tr.* III. 380 One of said commissioners shall be a person holding tribal relations with said Indians, one a representative of the Indian Bureau, and one a resident citizen of the State of Montana.

+**Indian cake.** Cake made with Indian meal; INDIAN BREAD. — **1777** A. PANTHER *Narr. of Young Woman* 5 She refreshed us with . . . a kind of apples, some indian cake, and excellent water. **1805** *Pocumtuc Housewife* (1906) 21 Indian Cake or Bannock is sweet and cheap food. **1844** *Knickerb.* XXIV. 229 If the bread was whiter than usual or the Indian-cakes lighter and sweeter, they were so because Lucy had made them. **1896** WILKINS *Madelon* 45 Madelon . . . put pieces of Indian cake into her untasting mouth.

+**Indian camp.** Temporary quarters occupied by Indians; an Indian encampment. — **1775** FITHIAN *Journal* II. 81 We saw many 'Indian Camps,' small crotched Sticks covered with thick Bark. . . . On the Bank of a Brook . . . we came to a Fire, some Indians or others had encamped there last Night. **1807** GASS *Journal* 42 [We passed] an old Indian camp, where we found some of their dog-poles, which answer for setting poles. **1883** *Rep. Indian Affairs* 62 Stenches arising from the offal of an Indian camp. *c***1908** CANTON *Frontier Trails* 59 Every thing was quiet as a graveyard, not even a dog barking, which seemed singular in an Indian camp.

+**Indian cattle.** Cattle of a longhorn breed formerly common in the southwestern United States. Also attrib. — **1872** *Newton Kansan* 3 Oct. 2/2 No person shall be allowed to drive . . . any cattle from the country south of Kansas, commonly known as Indian cattle, or Texas cattle. **1882** *Nation* 9 Nov. 392/3 Any one who has grown rich as an Indian-cattle and Star-route contractor.

+**Indian claim. a.** The claim of ownership made by Indians to a piece of land, or the land so claimed. **b.** A right to a piece of land acquired or alleged to have been acquired from Indian owners.

1674 *Plymouth Laws* 172 Concerning Indian claimes that are . . . made to any lands within this Government; which are now orderly possesed by the English those which doe lay claime to them shall orderly comence and prosecute their claime as farre as hee or they are able. **1683** *Mass. H.S. Coll.* 4 Ser. V. 107 Major Savage might defend his right and possession against his imaginary, pretended Indian claim, rightfully, we believe. **1749** *N.J. Archives* 1 Ser. VII. 344 The other 5th [of the rioters] possess lands under the Indian Claim and not more than ⅓ of that ⅕ first settled the lands they possess on an Indian Title. **1789** *Ann. 1st Congress* I. 40 The practice of the late English colonies and Government, in purchasing the Indian claims, has firmly established the habit in this respect, so that it cannot be violated but with difficulty, and an expense greatly exceeding the value of the object. **1806** in *Ann. 9th Congress* 2 Sess. 969 Grants [were] obtained . . . probably by men who cared little whether the land was within the Indian claim or the limits of South Carolina. **1818** Morse *Rep. Indian Affairs* (1822) II. 113 No Commissioners should be appointed to buy out the Indian claim to this country.

+**Indian college.** A college or building erected or proposed for the education of Indians. — **1698** SEWALL *Diary* I. 480 The old Brick Colledge, commonly called the Indian Colledge, is pull'd down to the ground. **1822** MORSE *Rep. Indian Affairs* II. 315, I should think this the place [=Fox River] for the ultimate establishment of the Indian College.

+**Indian commissioner.** A federal official dealing with Indian affairs. — **1849** *31st Congress 1 Sess.* Sen. Ex. Doc. No. 64, 107 Particular care was taken, both by the colonel commanding and the Indian Commissioner, to make the chiefs [of the Navahos] comprehend the full import of the treaty. **1868** *N.Y. Herald* 4 July 10/1 He was referred by the Indian Commissioner, Taylor, to consult about the best method of procuring acquittal. **1888** WHITMAN *November Boughs* 409 A wise man . . . makes a short speech, apparently asking something. Indian Commissioner Dole answers him. **1913** *Indian Laws & Tr.* III. 563 For the expenses of the Board of Indian Commissioners, $4,000.

+**Indian corn.** Maize (*Zea mays*), a native American cereal first cultivated by the Indians; the ripe ears of this plant; a growing crop of it.

*c***1621** in J. Smith *Works* (1884) 261 Better graine cannot be then the Indian corne, if we will plant it vpon as good ground as a man need desire. **1699** E. WARD *Trip New-Eng.* 55 Husking of Indian-Corn, is as good sport for the Amorous Wag-tailes in New-England, as Maying amongst us is for our forward Youths and Wenches. **1704** *Boston News-Letter* 26 June 1/2 While our People were Tearing up the Indian Corn, they fired on them. **1778** CARVER *Travels* 521 Maize or Indian Corn grows to the height of about five or six feet, on a stalk full of joints, which is stiff and solid, and when green, abounding with a sweet juice. **1814** J. TAYLOR *Arator* 89 To the stalks are to be added the blades, tops, shucks and cobs of the Indian corn, all in some degree a food, and a plentiful litter. **1892** in *S. Dak. Hist. Coll.* I. 70 Indian corn is a fair test of climate. It has been grown by the Indians in the country as far back as tradition leads.

b. Attrib. with *crop, flour, harvest,* etc.

1642 *Essex Inst. Coll.* V. 219/2 Other poore people shalbe repayed . . . at the next Indian corne harvest. **1701** WOLLEY *Journal N.Y.* (1902) 40 Indian Corn Flower fifteen shillings a hundred. **1806** *Balance* V. 268/1 Principles in Agriculture, Leading to the improvement of land by the mode of culture . . . and the application of it to the Indian Corn crop. **1856** in *Amer. Legion Mag.* XXIII. 58/2, 2 families gave out, being frightened at getting nothing for 3 days but Indian corn stirabout. *a***1870** CHIPMAN *Notes on Bartlett* 213 *Indian Corn-Hills.* . . . In Essex Co., M[as]s., plat of ground where hummocks look like the hillocks in which maize has grown. **1888** WHITMAN *November Boughs* 412 On the floor of the big kitchen, toward sundown, would be squatting a circle of twelve or fourteen 'pickaninnies,' eating their supper of pudding (Indian corn mush) and milk.

+**Indian corn bread.** Bread made of Indian corn meal. — **1799** WELD *Travels* (1800) I. 183 Indian corn bread . . . is a coarse, strong kind of bread, which has something of the taste of that made from oats. **1822** J. WOODS *English Prairie* 258 Mr. Hamilton had only Indian corn bread. **1864** NICHOLS *Amer. Life* I. 117 The long narrow table through the centre of the cabin is covered with Yankee luxuries—hot Indian-corn bread, milk-toast, hot rolls [etc.].

+**Indian country.** Unsettled territory occupied only, or chiefly, by Indians; an extensive district dominated by Indians; (see also quot. 1885).

1715 *Boston News-Letter* 15 Aug. 2/2 By Letters from South Carolina . . . We are informed, That they are still daily Battling with the Indian Enemy, . . . and unless some speedy help comes not to their relief, they're afraid it will soon become an Indian Country. **1796** *Ann. 4th Congress* 2 Sess. 2889 It shall be lawful for the President of the United States to establish trading-houses at such posts and places on the western and southern frontiers, or in the Indian country, as he shall judge most convenient. **1823** KEATING *Narrative* 166 Chicago is, perhaps, one of the oldest settlements in the Indian country. **1885** *Century Mag.* Aug. 599/1 The modern idea of an Indian Country—a scope of territory set apart for the occupancy of the aboriginal tribes—was first suggested by President Jefferson. **1893** *Harper's Mag.* April 798/1 As long as the buffalo roamed through the Indian country, the settlement of the land and the extinction of the Indian title was practically an impossibility. **1902** ALDRICH *Sea Turn* 286 If them tenderfoots was in the Indian country their scalps wouldn't be on their empty heads a quarter of an hour.

+**Indian cucumber (root).** =CUCUMBER ROOT. — **1784** CUTLER in *Mem. Academy* I. 437 *Medeola*. . . . Indian Cucumber. The roots . . . are esculant and of an agreeable taste. The Indians made them a part of their food. **1814** PURSH *Flora Amer.* I. 244 *Medeola virginica* . . . is known by the name Indian Cucumber. **1839** in *Mich. Agric. Soc. Trans.* VII. 408 *Gyromia virginica*. Indian cucumber. **a1862** THOREAU *Maine Woods* 309 The prevailing flowers and conspicuous small plants . . . were . . . *Medeola Virginica* (Indian cucumber-root), etc. **1887** BURROUGHS in *Century Mag.* July 323 Indian cucumber root, one of Thoreau's favorite flowers, is named after the sorceress Medea, and is called 'medeola.'

+**Indian dance.** A dance performed by Indians. — **1705** BEVERLEY *Virginia* III. 22 Antique Indian Dances, perform'd both by Men and Women, and accompany'd with great variety of Wild Musick. **1839** PLUMBE *Sk. Iowa* 84 The savage can be here seen in his wildest state, and an Indian dance will be no rare occurrence. **1893** *Harper's Mag.* April 761/1 Dolly had announced her intention of going with them to see the Indian dance.

+**Indian deed.** A deed attesting transfer of land from Indians to white settlers or a town. *Obs.* (Cf. DEED *n.* 2.) — **1664** *Brookhaven Rec.* 12 The Copey of the Indian Deydes vpon recorde. **1698** *Braintree Rec.* 39 Peter Webb delivered the indian deed into the hands of Mr. C Hubbard Moderate. **1747** *N.J. Archives* VII. 31 Another Indian Deed of Sale and Confirmation, to the Town of Newark, from the Owners of the Great Mountain, . . . bearing Date the 13th of March, 1677-8. **1832** WILLIAMSON *Maine* I. 365 Jeremisquam, Sebascodegan, and other islands . . . were purchased of the natives; when the practice of obtaining 'Indian Deeds' became fashionable, till nearly the whole patent was covered by them.

+**Indian department.** A federal department or subdivision of a department charged with the management of Indian tribes and of the transactions of the government with them. — **1794** *Ann. 3d Congress* 1424 For the Indian Department, fifty thousand dollars. **1806** PIKE *Sources Miss.* 90, I spent the day in . . . settling the affairs of the Indian department with Mr. Dickson. **1887** *Amer. Missionary* Oct. 283 Nor do we question the motives of the heads of the Indian Department.

+**Indian doctor.** An Indian herb doctor, or a white practitioner employing his methods. — **1724** JONES *Virginia* 131 Drugs for the Apothecaries Service . . . abound there; such as Sassafras, Saxafras, Snakeroot. . . . Many of them be understood by the Indian Doctors. **1847** DARLINGTON *Weeds & Plants* 207 The crimson Cardinal-flower . . . is sometimes used by the 'Indian doctors' under the name of '*High-belia*.' **1881** *Rep. Indian Affairs* 9 The Indian doctor still holds his sway.

+**Indian dog.** A dog bred and owned by Indians. — **1672** JOSSELYN *New Eng. Rarities* 15 The Indian Dog is a Creature begotten 'twixt a Wolf and a Fox, which the Indians lighting upon, bring up to hunt the Deer with. **1823** JAMES *Exped.* II. 150 An Indian dog . . . had followed us thus far. **1870** KEIM *Sheridan's Troopers* 114 So close were some of the troopers that the Indian dogs could be heard barking.

+**Indian dumpling.** (See quot. 1782.) — **1751** J. BARTRAM *Observations* 60 Last of all was served a great bowl, full of Indian dumplings, of new soft corn, cut or scraped off the ear. **1782** CRÈVECŒUR *Letters* 210 Indian Dumplings, are a peculiar preparation of Indian meal, boiled in large lumps. **1818** in Kittredge *Old Farmer* 191 Planting time is close by and we begin to think of Indian dumplings and puddings. **1851** *Knickerb.* XXXVIII. 392 He scattered far and wide corn-meal, with recipes for making pone and Indian dumplings.

‖**Indianesque,** *a.* Somewhat Indian; resembling the Indians. — **a1861** WINTHROP *J. Brent* iv. 45 This was the Indianesque Saxon who greeted me. **a1861** — *Canoe & Saddle* ii. 14 Indianesque, not fully Indian, was her countenance.

+**Indian farm.** A farm owned by an Indian. — **1843** FRÉMONT *Exploration Rocky Mts.* 10 We had passed several good-looking Indian farms. **1866** *Rep. Indian Affairs* 75 As the number and extent of the Indian farms increase, the demand for both teams and tools increases also. **1885** *Ib.* 122 When I say 'we' I mean the Indian as well as the agency farm.

+**Indian fashion,** *n.* and *adv.* **1.** *n.* The fashion or manner followed by Indians. **2.** *adv.* In the manner of Indians. — (1) **1751** GIST *Journals* 60, I stayed here, and sweated after the Indian Fashion, which helped me. **1831** WITHERS *Chron. Border Warfare* 80 He became satisfied from observation, that to combat Indians successfully, they must be encountered in their own way; and he accordingly instructed his men in the Indian mode of warfare, dressed them after the Indian fashion, and fought after the Indian manner. **1873** *Newton Kansan* 5 June 4/3 The advice . . . 'to fight Indians in Indian fashion' is in order now. (2) **1855** SIMMS *Forayers* 275 Dugout—a canoe hollowed, Indian fashion, from a cypress. **1912** NICHOLSON *Hoosier Chron.* 117 Sylvia turned round and knelt, paddling Indian fashion. **1923** J. H. COOK *On Old Frontier* 46 He had thrown his bed blanket over his head and shoulders, Indian fashion, in place of an overcoat.

+**Indian field.** A field cleared and tilled, or formerly tilled, by Indians. Freq. with *old*.

'The Aborigines cleared considerable spaces on the Sea Islands along the Georgia Coast, planting them with maize, pumpkins, gourds, beans, melons, &c. These indications of early agriculture were not infrequent in various portions of the State. The richest localities were selected by the Aborigines for cultivation' (1878 C. C. Jones *Dead Towns of Ga.* 55*n.*).

1634 *Relation of Beginnings of Md.* 22 All is high wood, but in the Indian fields, which are some parcells of ground cleared for Corne. **1699** J. DICKENSON *God's Protecting Prov.* 62 The place was an old Indian-Field on a high bleak hill. **1735** in *Ga. Hist. Soc. Coll.* II. 57 There is an old Indian field to be seen, which shows it was formerly inhabited by them. **1837** WILLIAMS *Florida* 143 It appears like an old Indian field. **1877** JOHNSON *Anderson Co., Kansas* 19 [They] planted a crop of corn, on an old Indian field, and raised a fair crop therefrom.

Indian fig. {1712–} Any of various American kinds of prickly pear; also, their fruit. — **1737** BRICKELL *N. Car.* 23 The Sun-Flower, the Indian-Figg, or Prickly-Pear, the Fruit of this Vegetable is frequently eaten, and is very sweet and luscious. **1802** DRAYTON *S. Carolina* 70 Common Indian fig, or prickly pear. (*Cactus opuntia.*) Grows plentifully on the sea islands. **1854** BARTLETT *Personal Narrative* 193*n.*, The name [*organos del tunal*] is probably derived, first from the flutings of the stem, which resemble the pipes of an organ; and second, from the resemblance which the fruit [pitahaya] has in taste to the *tunal* or Indian fig. **1877** CAMPION *On Frontier* 304 Tunas are the fruit of the prickly pear or Indian fig.

+**Indian-fighter.** A frontiersman accustomed to fighting against Indians. Now hist. — **1832** *Louisville Directory* 97 Our fellow townsmen . . . were no doubt animated by the hardy gallantry so universally characteristic of the backwoods hunters and Indian fighters, as they were termed in those days. **1853** RAMSEY *Tennessee* 505 The emigrants being well armed, would, with the guard of fifty practiced woodsmen and Indian-fighters, constitute a formidable corps. **1884** MATTHEWS & BUNNER *In Partnership* 28 Experienced Indian fighters say the signs of a speedy going on the war-path are not to be mistaken. **1903** *McClure's Mag.* Nov. 22 He's an old Indian fighter.

+**Indian file.** A single file, the characteristic way in which groups of Indians traveled through the woods. {1814–} — **1758** *Essex Inst. Coll.* XVIII. 179 They march'd in Indian file. **1799** in *Ann. 7th Congress* 2 Sess. 1399 And then followed the foot, marching up in Indian (single) file. **1823** LONG *Exped.* I. 149 In a short time they [the Pawnees] appeared leisurely in a narrow pathway, in *Indian file*, led by the grand chief. **1890–3** TABER *Stowe Notes* 41 On these gray cloud-tattered skies, an Indian file of crows, clamoring as they go, gives a wild kind of charm.

+**Indian fort.** A stronghold constructed by Indians or as a defense against them. — **1672** *Hempstead Rec.* I. 290 A point of Indian land . . . lying norwest from the ould Indian fort the medow containing four or five akers. **1775** *Mass. H. S. Coll.* 2 Ser. II. 231 At Norridgewalk are to be seen the vestiges of an Indian fort and chapel. **1821** J. FOWLER *Journal* 28 Found an Indean fort which might Contain about 60 men. **1871** DE VERE 25 Indian Forts are inclosures, found in large numbers in New York and Pennsylvania, . . . occupying high bluff points or headlands, scarped on two or more sides and naturally easy of defence.

+**Indian gift.** A gift for which the giver expects a return; a revoked gift. — **1764** HUTCHINSON *Hist. Mass.* I. 469*n.*, An Indian gift is a proverbial expression, signifying a present for which an equivalent return is expected. **1853** *Harper's Mag.* VII. 841/2 Among children . . . a present made, and then revoked, is called an 'Indian gift.' **1879** B. F. TAYLOR *Summer-Savory* xxvi. 207 She is glad it [the check] is an 'Indian gift,' that the conductor did not present it to her outright, that he will relieve her of it in due time.

+**Indian giver.** (See quot. 1848.) — **1848** BARTLETT 189 *Indian Giver.* When an Indian gives anything, he expects an equivalent in return, or that the same thing may be given back to him. This term is applied by children in New York and the vicinity to a child who, after having given away a thing, wishes to have it back again. **1892** *Amer. Folk-Lore* V. 68 If an American child, who has made a small gift to a playmate is indiscreet enough to ask that the gift be returned, he (or she) is immediately accused of being an Indian-giver, or, as it is commonly pronounced Injun-giver. **1909** *Dialect Notes* III. 399 *Injun-giver.* One who takes what he has given. 'I don't want to be an Injun-giver, but let me have the sporting section of that paper.' [n.w. Ark.]

+**Indian giving.** The practice of making a present with the expectation of its being returned or reciprocated. — **1837** IRVING *Bonneville* II. 71 Captain Bonneville was suitably affected by this mark of friendship; but his experience in what is proverbially called 'Indian giving,' made him aware that a parting pledge was necessary on his own part, to prove that this friendship was reciprocated. **1911** SAUNDERS *Col. Todhunter* vii. 104 You're sure about it, too, ain't you? She ain't doin' no Injun-givin' in your case?

+**Indian goods.** Goods used in trade with the Indians. — **1685** *N.J. Archives* 1 Ser. I. 504 Which money [*i.e.*, four pounds in beaver pay] wee disbursed ffor indean trade which sayd indean goods went to the purchase of the . . . land. **1723** *Doc. Hist. N.Y. State* I. 716 This Government . . . did by a severe law prohibit the selling of any Indian Goods to the French. **1786** E. DENNY *Journal* 78 Captain O'Hara . . . arrived with a large cargo of Indian goods and stores for the commissioners. **1840** COOPER *Pathfinder* I. 184 Two batteaux loaded with Indian goods have been taken. **1871** *Rep. Indian Affairs* (1872) 458 All goods of the character denominated 'Indian goods' have been excluded [from the agency trading house].

+**Indian grass.** Any one of several grasses growing wild in the U.S. Also attrib. — **1764** HUTCHINSON *Hist. Mass.* I. 480n., The natural upland grass of the country commonly called Indian grass, is poor fodder. **1810** CUMING *Western Tour* 137 In an Indian grass hammock, lay Mr. Hunt. **1843** TORREY *Flora N.Y.* II. 477 *Andropogon nutans.* Wood-grass. Indian-grass. . . . Sandy and sterile fields: frequent. **1894** COULTER *Bot. W. Texas* III. 494 *Chrysopogon nutans.* (Indian grass.) . . . Common in rather dry soil throughout the United States, but more abundant in the South.

+**Indian grave.** An Indian burial mound; a grave in which bones and relics of Indians are found. — **1809** CUMING *Western Tour* 97 Mrs. Tomlinson obligingly permitted one of her sons to guide us to what is called the Indian grave. . . . It is a circular mound . . . about one hundred and eighty yards in circumference round the base. **1818** J. FLINT *Lett. from Amer.* 101 By the road side are many conical mounds of earth, called Indian graves. **1823** JAMES *Exped.* I. 55 Indian graves are extremely numerous about St. Louis.

+**Indian guide.** An Indian acting as a guide to individuals or parties of white settlers. — **1654** JOHNSON *Wonder-w. Prov.* 113* Certaine Indian guides . . . with the close of the day brought them to a small river. **1826** COOPER *Mohicans* iv, We trusted to an Indian guide to take us by a nearer though blinder path. **1866** *Rep. Indian Affairs* 125, I have made several trips to different parts of the Territory, accompanied by Indian guides, in the endeavor to have an interview with Black Hawk.

+**Indian gun.** A gun of a type designed for the Indian trade. *Obs.* (Cf. INDIAN TRADER 2.) — **1740** W. STEPHENS *Proc. Georgia* 574, I should give a light Indian Gun out of the Stores. **1755** *Lett. to Washington* I. 89, 4 Indian Guns. **1756** *Ib.* II. 4 Majr. Lewis will send You some Indn. Guns for the Catawbas.

+**Indian harvest.** The harvest of Indian corn. *Obs.* — **1642** *Dorchester Rec.* 46 The order of yoakinge [is] to continue vntil Indian Harvest and ringinge. **1690** *Plymouth Col. Rec.* VII. 308 Capt. John Williams . . . [was summoned] to answer his presentment for selling severall pots of cyder to the Indians, in Indian harvest last past. **1707** *N.H. Prov. Papers* II. 566 Dover and Portsmouth should each send out the same number [of men] . . . till the Indian Harvest is over. **1726** PENHALLOW *Indian Wars* 57 It being now the height of Indian harvest, they dispersed themselves into all parts, and did considerable mischief. **1780** *N.H. Hist. Soc. Coll.* IX. 188, [I] went on with Indian Harvest.

Indian hemp. +An American plant (*Apocynum cannabinum*) whose root is used medicinally and from whose bark fibers used in rope-making were derived.

1619 *Va. House of Burgesses* 10 For hempe also both English & Indian . . . wee doe require . . . all householders . . . to make tryal thereof. **1637** MORTON *New Canaan* 25 Threeds, made of their Indian hempe, which their groueth naturally. **1701** WOLLEY *Journal N.Y.* 74 The Indians, make . . . another sort of brownish thread of a small weed almost like a Willow, which grows in the Wood about three foot high, which is called Indian Hemp, of which they likewise make Ropes and bring them to sell, which wears as strong as our Hemp, only it wont endure wet so well. **1808** ASHE *Travels* vii. 63, I must mention one plant, a native of this place [near Pittsburgh], and which grows in many places, known commonly by the name of Indian hemp. **1830** WATSON *Philadelphia* 444 The Indians made their ropes, bridles, and twine for nets, out of a wild weed, growing abundantly in old corn fields, commonly called Indian hemp—(i.e. *Linum Virginianum.*) **1899** GOING *Flowers* 309 There is another variety of dogbane, the Indian-hemp or *Apocynum cannabinum.*

+**Indian hen.** =AMERICAN BITTERN. — **1781-2** JEFFERSON *Notes Va.* (1788) 73 *Ardea stellaris Americana* . . . [is known as] Brown bittern [and] Indian hen. **1813** WILSON *Ornithology* VIII. 35 American bittern. . . . This is another nocturnal species. . . . In some places it is called the Indian Hen. **1835** AUDUBON *Ornith. Biog.* III. 275 The inhabitants of East Florida know it [the night heron] under the name of 'Indian Hen.' **1844** *Nat. Hist. N.Y., Zoology* II. 226 The American Bittern [is] also familiarly known under the names of Poke, Indian Hen [and] Indian Pullet. **1917** *Birds of Amer.* I. 181 Bittern. *Botaurus lentiginosus.* . . . [Also called] Bog Bull; Indian Hen; Marsh Hen.

+**Indian horse.** A small hardy horse of a type formerly domesticated by Indians in the West and Southwest. (Cf. AMERICAN HORSE.) — **1805** CLARK in *Lewis & C. Exped.* III. (1904) 16 The Indian horses pass over those clifts hills beds & rocks as fast as a man. **1868** W. E. WATERS *Life among Mormons* 51 The California horse, or the Indian horse, . . . is a native of the plains or mountains. **1887** *Century Mag.* Jan. 448/2 [The Indians' horses] were undersized, as compared with our thoroughbreds, though larger than the average Indian horse.

+**Indian hug.** A hold used in wrestling. Also attrib. — **1825** NEAL *Bro. Jonathan* I. 257 Giving out his challenge . . . in a loud voice, for 'Indian hug'; half hug [etc.]. **1853** *S. Lit. Messenger* XIX. 471/2 To wrestle with the subject Indian-hug fashion. **1916** DU PUY *Uncle Sam* 46 Like a flash his head was in the tall man's chest, all his strength was in his arms, and he was administering that treatment known in his youth as the 'Indian hug.'

+**Indian-hunting.** **a.** The practice of hunting Indians. **b.** (See quot. 1818.) — **1818** FORDHAM *Narr. Travels* 179 He has killed more men than Boon has, and most of them in single fights, or Indian hunting, as it is called. **1847** ROBB *Squatter Life* 125 Massa Dick's soon goin' Ingin huntin'—sure! **1869** W. MURRAY *Adventures* 225 Jack Murdock . . . learned his horsemanship from buffalo and Indian hunting on the Plains.

+**Indianian.** A resident of Indiana. — **1833** HOFFMAN *Winter in West* I. 190 The term 'Hooshier' . . . bears nothing invidious with it to the ear of an Indianian. **1860** *36th Congress 1 Sess.* H. R. Rep. No. 648, 573 A club composed of Indianians temporarily resident in Washington. **1900** *Congress. Rec.* 5 Feb. 1508/2 The nation . . . mourns the death of this distinguished soldier, and Indianians feel it as a personal loss.

+**Indian interpreter.** One who serves as interpreter in dealings with Indians. — **1805** in *Ann. 9th Congress* 2 Sess. 1088 Mr. Francis Grappe . . . [has] been Indian interpreter for the Spanish Government for many years past. **1856** GLISAN *Jrnl. Army Life* 272 He is the best Indian interpreter on the coast. **1894** EGGLESTON in *Harper's Mag.* Feb. 467/1 This young man . . . was evidently . . . Indian interpreter, ambassador, topographer, and guide.

+**Indianism.** **1.** The customs and culture of the American Indians. ||**2.** An Indian word or expression. — (1) **1710** SEWALL *Letter-Book* I. 401 Though some of their aged men are tenacious enough of Indianisme . . . Others of them as earnestly wish that their people may be made English as fast as they can. **1871** *Rep. Indian Affairs* (1872) 181 We were in our original Indianism. (2) **1855** BRISTED in *Cambridge Essays* 68 The term ['Yankee'] is therefore additionally remarkable, as being the only *Indianism* that has found a place among Americanisms.

Indianize, *v.* {1829-} **1.** *intr.* To adopt the ways of the Indians. *Obs.* **2.** *tr.* To make Indian in manners or appearance. — (1) **1689** C. MATHER *Way to Prosperity* 27 How much do our people Indianize? **1702** — *Magnalia* (1853) II. 400 We have shamefully Indianized in all those abominable things. (2) **1837** BIRD *Nick of Woods* I. 49 A bad thing for her, to have an Injunized father. **1844** GREGG *Commerce of Prairies* II. 44 But, though quite 'Indianized,' he was exceedingly polite. **1879** *Mass. H. S. Coll.* 5th Ser. VI. 375n., More than one hundred of the whites have been 'Indianized' to each Indian who has been civilized.

+**Indian kale.** Any one of several large-leaved arums having edible roots. — **1810** CUMING *Western Tour* 297 He made me observe some ginger in a thriving state, and the cullaloo or Indian kail. **1817** S. BROWN *Western Gaz.* 236 Most kinds of tropical fruits flourish here, such as the sweet orange, guinea corn, [and] Indian kail.

+**Indian ladder.** (See quot. 1859.) *Obs.* — **1791** W. BARTRAM *Travels* 247 Having provided ourselves with a long snagged sapling, called an Indian ladder, . . . we both descended. **a1855** J. F. KELLY *Humors* 68 An Indian ladder, that is, a scrubby saplin', trimmed with footholds left on it, was laying against the old tree. **1859** BARTLETT 214 *Indian Ladder*, a ladder made of a small tree by trimming it so as to leave only a few inches of each branch as a support for the foot. Southern.

+**Indian land.** A piece of land or a district occupied, or formerly occupied, by Indians.

1658 *Conn. Hist. Soc. Coll.* VI. 121 One acker of ye Indian land which Belonges to ye Towne. **1744** MOORE *Voy. Georgia* I. 98 Above the Town is a parcel of land called Indian lands. **1802** DRAYTON *S. Carolina* 93 The Yamassee resided in that part of Beaufort district, which is still known by the name of *Indian land.* **1885** *Century Mag.* Jan. 447 The Indian lands are scattered through the valley among the farms of the whites. **1905** *Forestry Bureau Bul.* No. 62, 9 Permits [are given] to stockmen for the use of Indian lands suitable for grazing.

+**Indian lodge.** A cabin or tepee built by Indians for use as a residence. — **1827** MCKENNEY *Tour to Lakes* 212 Our Voyageurs found, where an Indian lodge had been, several articles of value to these poor creatures. **1898** *Mo. So. Dakotan* I. 16 A few Indian lodges were scattered about, but the large body of Indians were out on a hunt. **a1918** G. STUART *On Frontier* I. 125 We all lived in elk skin Indian lodges and were very comfortable.

+**Indian maize.** Indian corn. — **1637** MORTON *New Canaan* 72 The black bird . . . is a small sized Choffe that eateth the Indian maisze. **1676** B. TOMPSON *Poet. W.* 49 The dainty Indian Maize Was eat with Clampshells out of wooden Trayes. **1849** *S. Lit. Messenger* XV. 414/1 A delicious food which has since been known among the Choctaws as the sweet *ton-cha* or Indian maize.

+**Indian meal.** =CORN MEAL.

1635 *Mass. Bay Rec.* I. 140 Noe person whatsoeuer shall from henceforth transport any Indean corne or meale out of this jurisdiccon, till the nexte harvest. **1697** *East-Hampton Rec.* II. 386 That he . . . pay unto her yearly . . . ten bushels of good Indian Meale. **1743** BRAINERD *Diary* (1902) 112 Through divine goodness I had some Indian meal, of which I made little cakes and fried them. **1796** F. BAILY *Tour* 103 Hoe-cake . . . is simply a mixture of Indian meal and water. **1818** SCHOOLCRAFT *Journal* 27 We have not enough Indian meal to last more than one day more. **1891** WILKINS *New Eng. Nun* 220 The lounging men watched him furtively as he bought some Indian meal and matches at the counter.

b. (See quotations.)

1865 *Atlantic Mo.* XV. 288 His rations were eight ounces of Indian meal, cob and kernel ground together. **1867** GOSS *Soldier's Story* 94 The heating nature of Indian meal—the cob ground with the corn, also had its effects in producing an unhealthy condition of things.

c. Attrib. with *gruel, moth, shorts.*

1797 ASBURY *Journal* II. 344 My diet is chiefly tea, potatoes, Indian-meal gruel, and chicken broth. **1876** 'MARK TWAIN' *Tom Sawyer* vi. 65 Barley-corn, Barley-corn, injun meal shorts. **1895** *Yearbook Dept. Agric. 1894* 285 A phycitid moth allied to the preceding and known as the Indian-meal moth is widely distributed and injurious to a great variety of edibles.

Indian millet. 1. Durra; also, a species of *Pennisetum*, esp. *P. glaucum*. {1640–} +**2.** (See quotation.) — **(1) 1792** IMLAY *Western Territory* 208–9 Indian millet, *Holcus laxus*. **1847** DARLINGTON *Weeds & Plants* 412 *S[orghum] vulgare*. . . . Indian millet. **1855** BROWNE in *Amer. Inst. N.Y. Trans. 1854* 593 Indian Millet, or Dourah Corn, (*Holcus sorghum*,) . . . has also been introduced into . . . the southern and middle portions of the United States. **1896** BEAL *Grasses of N.A.* I. 187 *P[ennisetum] typhoideum*. Pearl, Indian, African, Cat-tails, or Horse Millet. **(2) 1888** *Dept. Agric. Bot. Div. Bul.* No. 6, 53 *Oryzopsis cuspidata* (Indian millet) . . . has a wide distribution through all the interior region of Utah, Nevada, New Mexico, Texas, Colorado, and Nebraska to the Missouri River. It is a perennial, growing in dense tufts, whence its common name of bunch-grass.

+**Indian mound.** A mound or barrow constructed by prehistoric peoples, perhaps of Indian stock, for burial or other purposes; also, a hill similar in appearance to such a mound. — **1791** *Mass. H. S. Coll.* 1 Ser. III. 24 There is an Indian mound, the base of which is about three hundred paces round, and rises in a conic form about one hundred feet. **1821** NUTTALL *Travels Arkansa* 39 At Mountplace [Ind.] . . . there are two or three Indian mounds, upon one of which our visitor had built his house, and in digging had discovered abundance of human bones, as well as several stone pipes, and fragments of earthen ware. **1883** 'MARK TWAIN' *Life on Miss.* 600 Troy . . . is situated on three large Indian mounds, circular in shape.

+**Indian nation. a.** A tribe of Indians. **b.** =INDIAN TERRITORY 2. — **1763** in Gist *Journal* (1893) 196, I wold attempt to undertake ye Negocieatory Maters with a Number of Indian Nations. **1819** E. DANA *Geog. Sketches* 54 The *Indian Nations* occupying the west plains and forests within the region of the Mississippi, Missouri, and their respective tributary streams, above St. Louis, consist of about seventy distinct tribes. **1835** SIMMS *Yemassee* II. 27 Did it include the Indian nations generally—twenty-eight of which, at that time, occupied the Carolinas? **1865** PIKE *Scout & Ranger* (1932) 11 At Fort Smith we entered the Indian Nation—the first we met being Choctaws. **1897** HOUGH *Story of Cowboy* 5 In 1867 a venturous drover took a herd across the Indian Nations, bound for California.

+**Indian office.** A federal office through which transactions with the Indians are carried on. — **1871** *Rep. Indian Affairs* (1872) 174 We then nominated Mr. Smith, who had been in the Indian office in Detroit. **1875** *Chicago Tribune* 15 Nov. 4/2 It would not be surprising that in the Land Office, the Indian Office, the Pension Office, and the Patent Office . . . there should be corruption or dishonesty to some extent. **1905** *Forestry Bureau Bul.* No. 62, 9 Action must be taken . . . upon the results of careful examinations made for the . . . Indian Office. **1915** in J. S. CALHOUN *Correspondence* ix, Maps and books and papers that were not needed for the current business of the Indian Office . . . were deposited in the basement, exposed to furnace heat and dirt.

||**Indianologist.** An expert in Indian anthropology. — **1894** *Nation* 31 May 417/3 His ears, in the view of Indianologists, were a sure mark of aboriginal origin.

+**Indian orchard.** (See quot. 1859.) *Obs.* — **1798** C. WILLIAMSON *Descr. Genesee* ii, The old Indian orchards had been dressed up, and the fruit secured from depredation. **1859** BARTLETT 215 *Indian Orchard*, an old orchard of ungrafted apple-trees, the time of planting being unknown. New York.

+**Indian paint. a.** =BLOODROOT 1. **b.** The hoary puccoon, *Lithospermum canescens*. — **1826** DARLINGTON *Flora Cestrica* 57 *S[anguinaria] canadensis*. . . . *Vulgo*—Red-root. Blood-root. . . . Indian Paint. **1894** *Amer. Folk-Lore* VII. 95 *Lithospermum canescens*, . . . Indian paint. Minn. **1899** *Animal & Plant Lore* 119 *Lithospermum canescens* is called 'Indian paint,' because the Indians are said to have used it in painting themselves. Southwestern Missouri.

+**Indian paintbrush.** Also **Indian's paintbrush.** The painted cup. — **1892** *Amer. Folk-Lore* V. 101 *Castilleia coccinea*, Indian paint-brush. Mass. **1898** *Atlantic Mo.* Oct. 497/2 The scarlet painted cup, otherwise known as the Indian's paint-brush and prairie fire, splendid for color. **1923** 'BOWER' *Parowan Bonanza* ii. 21 He plucked a bright red 'Indian paintbrush' from beside a rock.

+**Indian peach.** A wild peach. Also attrib. — **1709** LAWSON *Carolina* 110 Of this sort, we make Vinegar; wherefore we call them Vinegar-Peaches, and sometimes Indian-Peaches. **1737** BRICKELL *N. Carolina* 101 The Indian-Peach Tree, is a kind of Peach common amongst the Indians, which they claim as their own, and affirm that they had it growing amongst them before any Europeans came to America. . . . Of this sort there is made Vinegar, therefore some call them Vinegar Peaches. **1801** *Hist. Review & Directory* I. 261 This is frequently called the *Indian Peach*, and is the first for flavor, size and beauty. **1881** *Harper's Mag.* April 745/2 A robe of gauze the color of an Indian peach garlanded with pale clear blooms.

+**Indian peas.** *pl.* Peas, or beans, similar to kidney beans, supposed to have been cultivated by the Indians. *Obs.* — **1649** *Description of Virginia* 4 They have store of Indian Pease, better then ours, Beans, Lupines, and the like. **1709** LAWSON *Carolina* 17 We found great Store of Indian Peas, (a very good Pulse) Beans [etc.]. **1786** WASHINGTON *Diaries* III. 57 The early Corn, and Indian Pease at this place were coming up. **1822** J. WOODS *English Prairie* 221 Here are a few Indian peas in growth, leaf and blossom, much like a kidney-bean; the pods are very long, and contain from nine to sixteen peas in each.

+**Indian physic.**

1. =BOWMAN'S ROOT.

1743 CLAYTON *Flora Virginica* 55 Ipecacuanha, or Indian Physick. **1788** CUTLER in *Life & Corr.* II. 285 A plant called *Indian Physic*, or *Indian Root*; . . . [it] blossoms, I believe, early in the year, for the seed was ripe in August. **1809** KENDALL *Travels* III. 36 *Spiræa trifoliata*, otherwise called Indian Physic, with its pink blossoms and pale green leaves, is frequent, but is less conspicuous. **1824** DODDRIDGE *Notes* 148 Indian physick, or bowman root, a species of epicacuanha was frequently used for a vomit.

2. The long-leaved cucumber tree.

1810 MICHAUX *Arbres* I. 33 The ear-leaved Magnolia, . . . Indian Phisic, dénomination plus usitée par les habitans des montagnes, . . . [ou] long leaved cucumber tree. **1814** PURSH *Flora Amer.* II. 382 *Magnolia auriculata*. . . . The bark of this and some of the foregoing species is esteemed a valuable medicine, particularly in intermitting fevers; from which circumstance it is known in some places by the name of Indian Physic. **1832** BROWNE *Sylva* 207 [*Magnolia auriculata*] is designated by the names of *Long-Leaved Cucumber Tree*, and of *Indian Physic*. **1860** CURTIS *Woody Plants N.C.* 68 Long-Leaved Cucumber Tree. (*M[agnolia] Fraseri*.)—Found only in ravines of the mountains, where it is known by this name, and also as *Wahoo* and *Indian Physic*.

+**Indian pine.** A pine (*Pinus taeda*) of the southern states; also, any one of several varieties of red pine found in the western states. — **1806** SHECUT *Flora Carolinæensis* I. 122 Almiggim wood, supposed to be the Indian Pine. **1860** GREELEY *Overland Journey* 268 In Ruby Valley, they have one [mail-station cabin] of red or Indian-pine. **1897** SUDWORTH *Arborescent Flora* 26 Loblolly Pine. . . . Common names [include] . . . Indian Pine (Va., N.C.).

+**Indian pink.** Any of several wild plants, esp. the pinkroot, *Spigelia marilandica*. — **1738** CATESBY *Carolina* II. 78 The Indian Pink. . . . This Plant rises usually with four or five stalks, of about twelve or fourteen inches in height; every one of which has three or four pair of sharp-pointed leaves, set opposite to each other. . . . A decoction made of this Plant is good against worms. **1802** DRAYTON *S. Carolina* 63 Pink root, or Indian Pink, (*Spigelia Marilandica*,) . . . has become a profitable article of trade with the Cherokee Indians, . . . and is used in worm cases, with much success. **1877** BURDETTE *Rise of Mustache* 18 Your boy . . . knows where the last Indian pink lingers, a flame in the brown and rustling woods, in the autumn days. **1905** N. DAVIS *Northerner* 286 She was standing, poised lightly upon a stone, pursuing a clump of Indian pink.

+**Indian pipe.** The wax plant, *Monotropa uniflora*. — **1817–8** EATON *Botany* 357 *Monotropa uniflora*, birds nest, indian-pipe. . . . Whole plant ivorywhite at first. **1832** WILLIAMSON *Maine* I. 131. **1850** S. F. COOPER *Rural Hours* 182 That ghost-like plant, the Indian-pipe, is in flower, and quite common here. **1877** *Field & Forest* III. 39 Above 5000 feet we met . . . plants of decidedly northern aspect, *Monotropa uniflora*, (Indian Pipe). **1903** WIGGIN *Rebecca* xvii. 187 There was the spot where the Indian pipes grew.

+**Indian poke.** The American hellebore, *Veratrum viride*. — **1784** CUTLER in *Mem. Academy* I. *Veratrum*. . . . White Helebore. Poke-root. Indian Poke. Common in wet meadows and swamps. June. **1817–8** EATON *Botany* 506 *Veratrum viride*, itch-weed, indian poke, white hellebore. . . . Useful in rheumatisms and many cutaneous eruptions. **1874** GARROD & BAXTER *Materia Med.* (1880) 382 American or Green Hellebore; called also Swamp Hellebore and Indian Poke.

+**Indian police.** A police force consisting of Indians, under the supervision of white officials, for maintaining order among Indians; also as pl., members of this. — **1877** *Rep. Indian Affairs* 1 Provision for the preservation of order and the enforcement of laws by means of Indian police, composed of Indians under white officers. **1883** *Ib.* 146 The three Indian police of this agency do not display the zeal I could wish. **1891** O'BEIRNE *Leaders Ind. Territory* 41/1 The severity of his wounds obliged him to adopt the business of book agent and fur trader until 1889, when he was appointed a member of the U.S. Indian Police. **1916** EASTMAN *From Deep Woods* 85 My Indian police seem to be powerless.

+**Indian pony.** A small horse used by the Indians. — **1752** in *Travels Amer. Col.* 314 He is given us for an Indian poney in his place. **1831** PECK *Guide* 165 Wild horses . . . are the offspring of the horses brought there by the first settlers. . . . The Indians of the west have many such horses, which are commonly called Indian ponies. **1923** J. H. COOK *On Old Frontier* 52 [We] drove the entire bunch, Indian ponies and all, to the spot where our own animals were tied.

+**Indian posy. a.** One of several American everlastings. **b.** The butterfly weed. — **1846** *Knickerb.* XXVII. 287 [On one end of the island] were scattered dwarf cedars, interspersed with golden-rods, lobelias, Indian posies. **1894** *Amer. Folk-Lore* VII. 92 *Gnaphalium polycephalum*, Indian posy. Stonington, Ct. moonshine, Dorset, Vt. balsam, N.Y. rabbit-tobacco, N.C.

+**Indian potato.** Any of several plants whose roots were used by the Indians for food. — **1737** WESLEY *Journal* I. (1909) 402 In Fresh pineland [in Ga.], Indian potatoes grow well—which are more luscious and larger than the Irish. **1788** BIGGS *Captivity* 34 They had nothing to eat . . . but indian potatoes—some people call them hoppines. **1837** IRVING *Rocky Mts.* I. 40 Game was scanty, and they had to eke out their scanty fare with wild roots and vegetables, such as the Indian potato, the wild onion, and the prairie tomato. *a*1912 J. B. DUNBAR in Blackmar *Kansas* (1912) I. 41 The rich soil [of Kansas] spontaneously afforded a variegated growth of grass, flowering plants, and native fruits, nuts, Indian potatoes, etc.

+**Indian powwow.** An Indian priest or medicine man; a noisy assembly or frolic. — **1649** ELIOT *Glorious Progress* 3 The Indian Pawwawes gave him over for a dead man. **1693** C. MATHER *Wonders Invis. World* 74 The Indian *Powawes*, used all their Sorceries to molest the first Planters here. **1826** FLINT *Recoll.* 366 If I could describe its Indian powwows, its Spanish fandangos, its French balls, and its American frolics.

+**Indian pudding.** A pudding boiled or baked with Indian meal as one of the principal ingredients: (see also quot. 1792). — **1722** *New-Eng. Courant* 19–26 March 2 A Plain Indian Pudding, being put into the Pot and boil'd the usual Time, it came out of a Blood-red Colour, to the great Surprise of the whole Family. **1771** J. ADAMS *Diary* Works II. 276 Reached Bissell's . . . just as they had got their Indian pudding and their pork and greens upon the table. **1792** *Affecting Hist.F. Manheim* 18 [The Indians] for want of other food, ate his [a man's] whole body, and of his head made, what they called, an Indian pudding. **1825** NEAL *Bro. Jonathan* II. 174 There were among the native preparations . . . baked beans . . . ; Indian pudding; custards [etc.]. **1885** EGGLESTON in *Century Mag.* April 882/2 One of the commonest dinner dishes in New England, especially in winter, was the Indian pudding.

+**Indian purchase.** The sum or amount involved in a purchase made from Indians; the transaction itself. *Obs.* — **1642** *Springfield Rec.* I. 170 If ye Indian purchase be payd. **1682** *Huntington Rec.* I. Twenty shillings . . . is the Indian purchas for the whole forme. **1777** *Va. State P.* I 289 He was further fixed in his Determination not to be concern'd in any Indian Purchase whatever.

+**Indian reservation.** An area set apart by the government for the occupancy of Indians. — **1821** NUTTALL *Travels Arkansa* 103 On the opposite side, or Indian reservation, the hills approach within six or eight miles of the river. **1841** BUCKINGHAM *America* II. 128 In general, when treaties were made between the government of the United States and any of the Indian tribes, certain portions of land were set apart for their use, either as hunting-grounds or for cultivation. These were called 'Indian Reservations.' **1892** *S. Dak. Hist. Coll.* I. 63 General George A. Custer's march to the Black Hills began to please all white Dakotans who had been eager, but forbidden, to search for rumored gold on that well guarded Indian reservation.

+**Indian reserve.** =INDIAN RESERVATION. — **1838** *Indiana House Rep. Jrnl.* 27 These lands . . . embrace, all the Indian Reserves, so called, that have yet been surveyed. **1849** CHAMBERLAIN *Indiana Gazetteer* 431 The taxable land amounts to 199,637 acres, and there are about 4,000 acres of Indian Reserves and United States land in the county. **1901** DUNCAN & SCOTT *Allen & Woodson Co., Kansas* 582 All of Woodson County and a small strip off the south side of Coffey County was included in the New York Indian Reserve.

+**Indian rice.** A perennial wild rice (*Zizania aquatica*) which grows in the United States and is used for food. — **1843** TORREY *Flora N.Y.* II. 416 *Zizania aquatica.* . . . Tuscarora Rice. Water Oats. Indian Rice. . . . The grain of this plant is a favorite article of food among the Indians, and cattle are very fond of the herbage. **1889** VASEY *Agric. Grasses* 33 *Zizania aquatica* (Wild Rice; Indian Rice). . . . The grass abounds in the small lakes of Minnesota and the Northwest, and is there gathered by the Indians for food. The husk is removed by scorching with fire. It is a very palatable and nutritious grain. **1901** MOHR *Plant Life Ala.* 362 *Zizania aquatica.* . . . Wild Rice. Indian Rice. . . . Copious in water . . . in the estuaries of the rivers emptying into Mobile Bay.

+**Indian road.** A road made, or supposed to have been made, by Indians. — **1730** *Md. Hist. Mag.* XVIII. 13 Ordered, that the Road formerly cleared from the long Calm to Mr. Gist's be continued into the road . . . called the old Indian Road. **1752** C. GIST *Journals* 77 We found an old Indian Road up this Creek. **1846** W. G. STEWART *Altowan* I. 221 A few hundred yards through the thick wood brought him back on the Indian road.

+**Indian runner.** An Indian messenger or courier who travels on foot. — [**1725** *Travels Amer. Col.* 158 This morning I recd the following Letter . . . by one of the Indians runners.] *a***1772** WOOLMAN *Journal* 195 An Indian runner had been at that place a day or two before us. **1822** MORSE *Rep. Indian Affairs* I. 70 Indian runners are prodigies in respect to their long continued rapidity in conveying messages to distant tribes. **1866** *Rep. Indian Affairs* 125, I have also sent several Indian runners to find and endeavor to induce him to meet me. **1885** *Wkly. New Mexican Rev.* 5 Feb. 3/1 The Indian runners informed Lieutenant McDonald that more mutineers were coming to water at Pilot Knob.

+**Indian saddle.** ? A roughly fashioned saddle made and used by Indians; a saddle suited to carrying goods used about the camp. *Obs.* — **1850** GARRARD *Wah-To-Yah* iii. 44 Smith's squaw, a woman of thirty years or thereabout, with prominent cheek bones and other Indian peculiarities, rode astride of a high-pommelled Indian saddle. *c***1908** CANTON *Frontier Trails* 53 The hunters again appeared in Buffalo . . . leading a pinto pony, on which was an Indian saddle packed with a beef hide. **1923** J. H. COOK *On Old Frontier* 52 We took some of the Indian saddles and blankets . . . , for we knew that squaw-saddles were better than none.

+**Indian scalp.** A scalp taken from the head of an Indian. — **1690** SEWALL *Letter-Book* I. 113 Writt to Cousin Hull per Mr. Sergeants Ketch sent 4 Ind. Scalps in Barrals mark'd with Ink. **1711** *Boston News-Letter* 12 Nov. 2/1 On Monday last Lieut. Hilton Brought here three Indian Scalps for which the Government paid him the premium. **1726** PENHALLOW *Indian Wars* 27 The general assembly . . . enacted, that forty pounds should be given for every Indian scalp. **1871** *Scribner's Mo.* II. 386 British troops [in 1775] . . . expected to send home Indian scalps as trophies gathered in the wilds of Cape Cod.

+**Indian scare.** An alarm caused by an imminent or threatened attack by Indians. *Obs.* — **1882** *N. Mex. Terr. Rep.* (1884) 101 By this time the Indian scare was over with, and I can assure you . . . if they had come along they would have had a warm reception. **1883** RITCH *Illus. N. Mex.* 106 They have seen a great mine stand idle in their midst, and for years unsalable on account of Indian scares and raids. **1912** DAWSON *Pioneer Tales of Oregon Trail* 162 The Indian Scare of 1869. *Ib.* 163 Nothing of serious consequence occurred during this Indian scare.

+**Indian school.** A school maintained for Indians. — **1766** *N.H. Hist. Soc. Coll.* IX. 69, I am inform'd of a Donation of £100 Sterling in Goods, made by you to this Indian School. **1775** BURNABY *Travels* 30 The professor of the Indian school has 60 l. sterling. **1819** in Morse *Rep. Indian Affairs* (1822) II. 166 An Indian School has been originated in Kentucky, near the Great Crossings. **1866** *Rep. Indian Affairs* 84, I have the honor to submit the following report of the Indian school under my charge. **1898** *Mo. So. Dakotan* I. 66 The government Indian school at Flandreau is rapidly developing into an institution of magnitude and great educational worth.

+**Indian scout. 1.** An Indian employed as a scout. **2.** A white man who scouts Indians. **3.** A scouting expedition against Indians. — **(1)** **1837** IRVING *Bonneville* II. 18 Rising ground . . . might betray his little party to the watchful eye of any Indian scout. **1873** *Newton Kansan* 20 Feb. 3/4 An Indian scout dressed in soldier uniform came riding up to them and representing himself as being a chief. **1899** CUSHMAN *Hist. Indians* 444 The Indian scouts . . . learned the place of their rendezvous. **1923** J. H. COOK *On Old Frontier* 169, I am Lieutenant Gatewood, and these men are Indian scouts. **(2)** **1838** *S. Lit. Messenger* IV. 294 He became an Indian scout or ranger, and passed his days upon the frontier. **(3)** **1852** WATSON *Nights in Block-House* 147 John Whetzel and Veach Dickerson associated to go on an Indian scout. **1866** *Wkly. New Mexican* 25 May 1/3 Captain Krause's men have returned from their Indian scout.

Indian service. +**1.** Missionary service among the Indians. +**2.** =INDIAN DEPARTMENT. +**3.** Military service against the Indians. — **(1)** **1725** *Harvard Rec.* II. 525 Voted, That Campbel be allowed out of Mr Boyle's Donation for the Indian service fourty pounds for this year of his sophimoreship, to be paid Quarterly. *c***1749** in Brainerd *Journal* (1902) 237 The Correspondents . . . prevailed with Mr. Azariah Horton to relinquish a call to an encouraging parish, and to devote himself to the Indian service. **(2)** **1846** POLK *Diary* I. 323 During my walk this evening I met Senator Turney, who resumed the conversation about an appointment in the Indian Service which he desired to obtain for his nephew, Gideon C. Matlock. **1900** *Congress. Rec.* 3 Feb. 1472/1 Congress for the two years appropriated over $19,000,000 for the Indian schools and Indian service. **1916** C. A. EASTMAN *From Deep Woods* 135, I resigned my position in the Indian service, and removed with my family to the city of St. Paul. **(3)** **1866** MOORE *Women of War* 112 She is now with the detachment that has crossed the great plains and the Rocky Mountains for Indian service on the distant western frontier.

+**Indian shoe. 1.** A moccasin. **2.** The lady's-slipper or moccasin flower. — **(1)** **1704** *N.H. Prov. Papers* II. 422 Mr. Thomas Packer's Debenter . . . for entertaining an Express, and some friend Indians about making Indian shoes &c. was allowed. **1709** *Conn. Rec.* XV. 556 Such persons as receive snow-shoes, mogginsons or Indian shoes . . . [shall] be allowed for keeping them in good condition . . . two shillings *per annum.* **1778** CARVER *Travels* 155 An Indian woman . . . had been employed . . . to make him a pair of Indian shoes, out of curious elk-skin. **(2)** [**1764** REUTER *Wachau* 569 *Lady Shoes*, some call it *Indian Shoes.* It is a Snakeroot, and the Indians know how to use it for many things. Has a yellow or white blossom which is exactly the shape of a wooden shoe. Grows in rich Uplands.] **1909**– in dicts.

+**Indian sign.** A track, trace, or other indication of the presence of Indians. Usually collective or pl. — **1812** MARSHALL *Kentucky* 131 A report of Indian sign . . . gave occasional, and momentary recollections of danger—produced a little bustle—perhaps forced out a scouting party. **1860** CLAIBORNE *Sam. Dale* i. 17 A foraging party from an adjoining settlement . . . had discerned Indian 'signs.' **1900** DRANNAN *Plains & Mts.* 372 After we struck North Platte we saw considerable Indian sign every day. *a***1918** G. STUART *On Frontier* I. 115 Plenty of Indian signs, saw signal fires on the mountains to westward.

+**Indian stocking.** A stocking worn by the Indians; ? a stocking not knitted but made of material sewed together. *Obs.* — **1647** *Conn. Rec.* I. 478 A pair of Indean stockins. **1755** *Lett. to Washington* I. 89 Indian Goods at Fort Cumberland . . . [include] 33p blue Indian Stockgs. **1793** *Mass. H.S. Coll.* 3 Ser. V. 152 Besides, they all have Indian stockings, made of woollen cloth.

+**Indian store.** A store maintained for trade with Indians. — **1798** C. WILLIAMSON *Descr. Genesee* i, At the Genesee River I found a small Indian store and tavern. **1878** I. L. BIRD *Rocky Mts.* 162 The Indian stores and fur stores and fur depôts [in Denver] interested me most.

Indian strawberry. An herb (*Duchesnea indica*) from the East Indies naturalized in the United States. — **1841** STEELE *Summer Journey* 108 Our friends kindly gathered for me a variety of these, among which was a fine scarlet lilium superbum, blue bells, and kinni kanic, or Indian tobacco, and a pretty plant called Indian strawberry. **1869** FULLER *Flower Gatherers* 78 One species, known as the Indian Strawberry, has yellow blossoms and a round, red berry, without taste.

+**Indian sugar.** Maple sugar. — **1835** HOFFMAN *Winter in West* I. 191 The usual settlers' dinner of fried bacon, venison cutlets, hot cakes, and wild honey, with some tolerable tea and Indian sugar,—as that made from the maple-tree is called at the West,—was soon placed before us.

1880 *Harper's Mag.* Dec. 43/1 Chippewas . . . came to her door offering potatoes and Indian sugar.

+Indian summer.

Some of the attempts to explain the origin of the term are given in the following quotations. **1803** C. F. VOLNEY *Œuvres* (1825) IV. 251 Vers novembre, reparaît une série de beaux jours, appelés l'été *sauvage* (*Indian-summer*): c'est ce que nous appelons en France l'été de la Saint-Martin. **1804** C. B. BROWN tr. C. F. Volney *View U.S.* 210 A series of fine days are expected near November, which is called the Indian summer. In France, an interval like this is termed St. Martin's summer, and in England All-hallown summer. *Ib. n.*, Its American name it probably owes to its being predicted by the natives to the first emigrants, who took the early frosts as the signal of winter. **1812** J. FREEMAN *Sermons on Partic. Occasions* viii. 278 *n.*, This charming season is called the Indian Summer, a name which is derived from the natives, who believe that it is caused by a wind, which comes immediately from the court of their great and benevolent God Cautantowwit, or the southwestern God. **1823** W. FAUX *Memorable Days* 232 The Indian Summer . . . is caused by millions of acres . . . being in a . . . flaming, blazing, smoking fire. . . . Why called Indian? Because these fires seem to have originated with the native tribes . . . who by these means start, disturb, and pen up the game. **1824** DODDRIDGE *Notes* 266 After the apparent onset of winter, the weather became warm; the smokey time commenced and lasted for aconsiderable number of days. This was the indian summer, because it afforded the indians another opportunity of visiting the settlements with their destructive warfare.

1. A period of mild, warm weather in late October or early November, after the first frosts of autumn.

1778 CRÈVECŒUR *Sk. 18th-Cent. Amer.* (1925) 41 A severe frost succeeds [the autumn rains] which prepares it [the earth] to receive the voluminous coat of snow which is soon to follow; though it is often preceded by a short interval of smoke and mildness, called the Indian Summer. **1794** in E. DENNY *Journal* 13 Oct., Pleasant weather. The Indian summer here [near Erie, Pa.]. Frosty nights. **1818** FORDHAM *Narr. Travels* 199 November. 40° to 70°. A few days of hazy weather, succeeded by the Indian Summer, during which the sky was always obscured as if by smoke. The weather warm and pleasant. **1836** NICKLIN *Peregrination* 31 The autumn, or as the Philadelphians call it, the Fall, is the most delightful part of the year, and is sometimes eked out by the Indian Summer as far as Christmas. **1852** BRISTED *Upper Ten Th.* ii. 40 One fine day in Indian summer (a delightful appendix to the warm weather which the northern states enjoy in November) the two were seen walking arm in arm. **1891** WELCH *Recoll. 1830–40* 38 The true period of 'Indian Summer' is or should be looked for between the middle of October to the middle of November; lasting about a fortnight or half a moon, between its first and fourth quarters. **1902** GORDON *Recoll. Lynchburg* 10 It was in the month of November. . . . The haze of Indian Summer added its attractive features to the season.

b. *transf.* A return of the happiness associated with youth; a period of serenity and tranquillity near the end of life.

1843 WHITTIER *Poetical Works* 387/1 The warm light of our morning skies,—The Indian Summer of the heart! **1867** HOLMES *Guardian Angel* 340 By and by an Indian summer of serene widowhood. **1877** PHELPS *Story of Avis* 429 Her heart went to meet that Indian summer of married life, which after the rain, settles down upon the purple air. **1881** *Harper's Mag.* Jan. 273/2 Perhaps in the Indian Summer of his life he may put his heart into a poem . . . even more worthy of his genius.

2. Attrib. with *atmosphere, day, honeymoon,* etc.

1832 KENNEDY *Swallow Barn* II. 92 [The] foggy tint which is said . . . to spread such a charm over an Indian-summer landscape. **1833** *Knickerb.* I. 2 It was in the afternoon, . . . during one of those delicious 'Indian-summer' days, the peculiar boast of our climate. **1865** STOWE *House & Home P.* 91 The red maples and sumachs, the purple and crimson oaks, all stood swathed and harmonized together in the hazy Indian-summer atmosphere. **1898** FORD *Tattle-Tales* 89 The young couple had enjoyed . . . a recurring Indian-summer honeymoon of two months in front of their own fireside. **1899** *Mo. So. Dakotan* I. 175 The Indian summer smoke, banked back by the wind, hangs on the horizon.

+Indian-summerish, *a.* Like Indian summer. — **1852** THOREAU *Autumn* 79 It is a warm, Indian-summerish afternoon. **1898** *Advance* 12 May 627/2 The cradle-like rock of the Hebrew parallelisms [of the Psalms] . . . tend[s] to so calm body, mind, and soul, that your thoughts become Indian summerish.

‖**Indian-summery,** *a.* =prec. — **1881** WHITMAN *Spec. Days* 189 Out here on a visit—elastic, mellow, Indian-summery weather.

+Indian sweat. A sweat bath of the kind taken by Indians. *Obs.* Also fig. — **1797** WEEMS *Letters* II. 83 This moment I have got out of an Indian sweat of fright. **1807** GASS *Journal* 219 We gave him an Indian sweat and he is some better.

+Indian tea. One or other plant used for making a drink similar to tea, esp. a species of holly (*Ilex vomitoria*) common in the southern states. In full, *Indian tea tree.* — **1709** LAWSON *Carolina* 91 This Plant is the Indian Tea, us'd and approv'd by all the Savages on the coast of Carolina, and from them sent to the Westward Indians, and sold at a considerable Price. **1737** BRICKELL *N. Carolina* 87 The Indian-Tea Tree, which in their Language is called Yaupan, and Cassena, grows in great plenty in this Province. **1809** KENDALL *Travels* II. 143 Where the pine only is found, the ground beneath is nearly bare, sustaining but dwarfish plants, such as the *partridge-berry,* sometimes called the *tea plant* and *Indian tea.*

+Indian territory.

1. Any one of several areas set aside for or recognized to be the residence of Indian tribes; Indian country.

1792 *Ann. 2nd Congress* 1037 A great part of this is within the Indian territory. **1803** in *Ann. 8th Congress* 2 Sess. 1503 When compared with the Indian Territory, the face of the country in Upper Louisiana is rather more broken. **1834** J. HALL *Sk. of West* (1835) I. 103 The United States claims the right of navigation on all navigable rivers which pass through an Indian territory.

2. (Both words capitalized.) The territory (orig. approximately that of the present state of Okla.) provided for the residence of the 'five civilized tribes' of Indians. Also attrib.

1835 (*title*), The Annual Register of Indian Affairs within the Indian (or Western) Territory. **1863** *Chicago Tribune* 6 Sept., The Indian Territory is now clear of rebels. **1884** 'MARK TWAIN' *H. Finn* (1933) 455 There is a desprate gang of cutthroats from over in the Ingean Territory. **1887** *Courier-Journal* 14 Feb. 6/2 An Indian Territory special says: 'Reports from the Territory show that stock have wintered well and is in a fair condition.' **1916** EASTMAN *From Deep Woods* 146, I also visited for the first time the 'Five Civilized Tribes' of the Indian Territory, now in the state of Oklahoma.

+Indian title.

1. A legal right to the possession of land, derived from the original Indian owners. (Cf. INDIAN DEED.)

1683 *Mass. H.S. Coll.* 4 Ser. V. 107 He purchased no propriety unto himself or unto any other, but only procured the confirmation of the common right, from the Indian title, to his own and to every other particular inhabitant's lands and possessions. **1717** *Conn. Rec.* VI. 13 No conveyance of native right or Indian title, without the allowance or approbation of this Assembly as aforesaid, shall be given in evidence of any man's title. **1765** ROGERS *Acct. N. America* 33 Being not satisfied with their Indian title, they this year obtained a grant from the aforesaid company. **1873** BEADLE *Undevel. West* xxi. 417 Bear in mind, this is not an 'Indian title,' so called, . . . but a patent of the United States. **1883** *Century Mag.* Sept. 657/2 One of the most interesting things with regard to the relations between the whites and the Indians is the occasional appearance, to this day, in the Massachusetts law reports . . . of suits relating to Indian titles.

2. The legal right or claim which the Indians had to the land which they occupied.

[**1660** *Dedham Rec.* IV. 26 Lieft Fisher & Sergent Ellice are deputed to treat . . . with the Indians . . . and cleere the place from all Indians title.] **1802** *Amer. State P.: Public Lands* I. 126 The United States shall, at their own expense, extinguish, for the use of Georgia, . . . the Indian title to the country of Talassee. **1812** *Niles' Reg.* II. 19/1 That part of the state of Tennessee to which the Indian title is not extinguished. **1822** MORSE *Rep. Indian Affairs* I. 68 The Indian title . . . is certainly to be respected, until it be legitimately extinguished. **1899** CUSHMAN *Hist. Indians* 433 It was now falsely claimed that the Indian title was extinguished east and south of the Ohio River.

+Indian tobacco. Any of several N.A. plants, esp. *Lobelia inflata, Nicotiana rustica,* and any variety of *Antennaria.* — [**1764** REUTER *Wachau, Indian Tobacco* has leaves much like Brown Betonia, though rougher.] **1792** BELKNAP *Hist. New-Hampshire* III. 126 [Poke] is known to the hunters by the name of Indian tobacco. **1804** LEWIS in *L. & Clark Exped.* VI. (1905) 157 The corolla of the Indian Tobacco as prepared for the purpose of smoking . . . is mixed with a small quantity of Buffaloes Tallow, previous to charging the pipe. **1841** [see INDIAN STRAWBERRY]. **1889** *Cent.* 2429/2 *Gagroot,* . . . the *Lobelia inflata,* so called from its emetic properties: more usually known as *Indian tobacco.* **1892** *Amer. Folk-Lore* V. 98 *Antennaria plantaginifolia,* Indian tobacco. N.E.; Nebraska. **1894** *Amer. Folk-Lore* VII. 95 *Nicotiana rustica,* Indian tobacco, real tobacco. N.Y.

+Indian town. A town established and occupied by Indians.

1657 *Suffolk Deeds* III. 144 Wee Peter, Josias Hoddin and Solomon Inhabitants of the Indian Towne of wip sufferage. haue . . . freely & fully Graunted [etc.]. **1676** GLOVER *Acct. Va.* in *Phil. Trans.* XI. 626 While he was in an Indian town adjacent to the Mountains, there came four Indians on an Embassie to the King of that town, from a King that lived on the other side of the Mountains. **1732** HEMPSTEAD *Diary* 251, I went . . . to the Indian Town to get a squaw to botom chairs [for] Brother Talmage. **1792** *Mass. H.S. Coll.* 1 Ser. I. 113 Tatnuck and Boggochoag hills are remarkable for having formerly had Indian towns on them. **1823** in *S. Dak. Hist. Coll.* I. 184 From the situation of the Indian towns, it will be difficult for a small force to oust them without a six-pounder. **1872** HOLLAND *Marble Prophecy* 107 Straight up the river an Indian town Filled the soft air with its musical hum.

+Indian trade. Trade with the Indians.

1644 *Conn. Rec.* I. 113 The propositions of the Commissioners concerneing a generall Indean trade (except corne, fishe and venison) is also approued. **1692** *Md. Hist. Mag.* XIII. 208 They found him in his store, . . .

having great store of Indian trade therein. **1790** R. PUTNAM in *Memoirs* 235 All the beef, pork, & mutton . . . will come to the seaports of Verginia, Maryland & Pennsylvania to market, as will also most of the furs skins, etc. obtained by the Indian Trade to those places & New York. **1822** MORSE *Rep. Indian Affairs* I. 12 You will report such facts, as . . . will suggest such improvements in the present system of Indian trade, as in your opinion will render it better calculated to secure peace between them and us. **1853** R. GLISAN *Jrnl. Army Life* 104 His prospects are flattering as the command is large and the Indian trade increasing. *a*1918 G. STUART *On Frontier* I. 149 Dempsy and Jackson also came over here and camped near by, and later another French Canadian moved in with a stock of goods for the Indian trade.

+Indian trader.

1. One whose chief occupation is trading with Indians. Now hist.

1696 Scottow *Massachusetts* 42 The first English Blood-shed was of an Indian trader. **1709** LAWSON *Carolina* 184 The Indian Traders are those which travel and abide amongst the Indians for a long space of time; sometimes for a Year, two, or three. **1775** FITHIAN *Journal* II. 70 On passing over this Creek, I met, an Indian Trader, with his Retinue. **1852** MARCY *Explor. Red River* (1854) 2 The only information we had upon the subject was derived from the Indians and semi-civilized Indian traders. **1923** J. H. COOK *On Old Frontier* 214 Indian traders and agency employees . . . might tell conflicting stories.

2. (See quotation.)

1835 LONGSTREET *Georgia Scenes* 222 *Indian-traders* (a long, cheap, but sometimes excellent kind of gun, that Mother Britain used to send hither for traffic with the Indians).

+Indian-trading, *a.* Of or pertaining to trade with the Indians. — **1676** I. MATHER *King Philip's War* (1862) 99 [Resolved] that the Indian Trading-houses, whereby the Heathen have been debauched and scandalized against Religion, be suppressed. **1716** *N.C. Col. Rec.* II. 257 A resolution of the General Assembly, impowering a Committee of this House to buy a certain quantity of Indian trading goods, arms and ammunition. **1733** *S.C. Gazette* 4 Aug., Just Imported . . . indian trading strouds, . . . coarse shalloons, . . . coverlids. **1775** ADAIR *Indians* 289 So widely different is our Indian-trading conduct from that of the French. **1822** MORSE *Rep. Indian Affairs* I. 62 The Indian Trading Fund of $300,000, now yielding no income to the Government, and no substantial benefit to the Indians, . . . would be withdrawn.

+Indian trail. A trail made by Indians. Also attrib. — **1817** *Niles' Reg.* XII. 335/2 On the morning of the 23d we fell in with an Indian trail, which we followed a circuitous route. **1846** SAGE *Scenes Rocky Mts.* iv, Indian trails . . . consist of a number of well-beaten, parrallel [*sic*] footpaths. **1888** M. A. GREEN *Springfield* (Mass.) 3 It was, in fact, an Indian trail centre. **1890** CUSTER *Following Guidon* 36 Finally the Indian trail, so long looked for, was struck.

+Indian treaty. A meeting or conference with Indians for the purpose of making a treaty; a treaty made with a tribe of Indians. — **1787** *Ann. 1st Congress* I. 41 On the 12th of October, 1787, Congress resolved: 'That twenty thousand dollars be, and hereby are, appropriated for the purpose of Indian treaties, whenever the same shall hereafter be judged necessary by a majority of the United States in Congress assembled.' **1817** *Ann. 14th Congress* 2 Sess. 201 An act . . . for carrying into effect certain Indian treaties. **1836** in *Knickerb.* XX. 1 It is unusual for 'Indian treaties' to pass off with so little disturbance.

+Indian turnip. 1. A plant of the genus *Arisaema*, esp. *A. triphyllum*, the jack-in-the-pulpit; also, the root of such a plant. **2.** =BREADROOT. — (1) **1806** in *Ann. 9th Congress* 2 Sess. 1142 Persicaria, Indian turnip, wild carrot, wild onion, . . . and bastard indigo [grow near the Ouachita R.]. **1850** *New Eng. Farmer* II. 12 The Indian Turnip, or *Arum*, with its singular flower, variegated inside with stripes of pale green or brown. **1897** ROBINSON *Uncle Lisha* 32 A crowded cluster of scarlet berries . . . marked the place where the fiery bulb of the Indian turnip was hidden. (2) **1857** GRAY *Botany* 94 *P[soralea] esculenta*, . . . the *Indian turnip*, *Pomme Blanche*, or *Pomme de Prairie*, [is] used as food by the aborigines.

+Indian village. 1. A village of Indians. **2.** A group of Indians customarily dwelling together in a village. — (1) *c*1805 R. PUTNAM *Memoirs* 42 Passed an Indian Village of about 40 Hutts, belonging to the Tonicas. **1847** PARKMAN in *Knickerb.* XXX. 290 We spent most of our evenings in the Indian village. **1872** MCCLELLAN *Golden State* 84 We came unexpectedly into a large Indian village. (2) **1843** FRÉMONT *Explor. Rocky Mts.* 55 We reached a place where the Indian village had crossed the river. **1846** SAGE *Scenes Rocky Mts.* xxxii, The Indian village . . . on its way in quest of buffalo, visited the fort.

+Indian weed.

1. (See quotation.)

1687 CLAYTON *Va.* in *Phil. Trans.* XLI. 145 The Indians . . . have indeed various very good Wound-herbs, as an Herb commonly called Indian-weed, which perhaps may be referred to the Valerians, and be said to be *Plantani foliis*.

2. Tobacco.

1730 E. COOK *Sotweed Redivivus* 10 Leaving behind, to raise up Seed, And tend a stinking Indian Weed, Scotch, English, and Hybernians wild. **1790** FRENEAU *Poems* (1795) 125 Tobacco. This Indian weed, that once did grow On fair Virginia's fertile plain. **1844** *Knickerb.* XXIV. 394 The '*Experiences of a Tobacco Smoker*' will suggest to the lover of the Indian weed . . . some important truths. **1867** DIXON *New America* I. 71 The red men have taught the whole world how to smoke the Indian weed. **1900** WINCHESTER *W. Castle* vi. 124 You know that smoking and chewing the vile Indian weed are great evils.

Indian wheat. +1. Indian corn, maize. Now chiefly hist. {1720} **2.** Tartarian buckwheat. — (1) **1622** 'MOURT' *Relation* 30 Wee went to another place, which we had seene before, and digged, and found more corne, viz. two or three Baskets full of Indian Wheat, and a bag of Beanes. **1674** JOSSELYN *Two Voyages* 56 Their Summer is hot and dry proper for their *Indian* Wheat; which thrives best in a hot and dry season. **1746** E. KIMBER *Itinerant Observ.* 43, I have known them [*sc.* horses] to go six Days Journey without a Feed of Corn; having nothing but the Stalks of Indian Wheat, and such other Litter as they could pick up. (2) **1838** *Mass. Agric. Survey 1st Rep.* 33 [Tartarian buckwheat] is known under the name of Indian wheat. **1868** GRAY *Field Botany* 289 *F[agopyrum] tartaricum*, Tartary or Indian Wheat. Cult[ivated] for flour on our N.E. frontiers and N.

+Indian whoop. A whoop or yell of the kind given by Indians. — **1761** NILES *Indian Wars* II. 578 The Indian whoop went directly after from front to rear of the line of both flanks. **1798** I. ALLEN *Hist. Vermont* 34 The expert marksmen were to fire, one by one at him, until he fell from his horse, then to give an Indian *whoop* and raise their ambuscade. **1845** *Knickerb.* XXVI. 521 He turned round and laughed; and shaking his gun toward the enemy, gave an Indian whoop of defiance!

India rubber.

1. Caoutchouc, an elastic material derived from the juice of various tropical plants. {1799–}

The first quotation may belong to sense 2.

1790 [see GUM ELASTIC 1]. **1830** *Va. Lit. Museum* 537 The successful experiments of Dr. Mitchell of Philadelphia in making bladders of the caoutchouc, or India rubber, so light that when inflated with hydrogen, they became real balloons. **1851** *S. Lit. Messenger* XVII. 690/2 We all recollect when the only uses to which India-rubber was applied, were to rub out pencil marks and make trapballs for boys. **1884** ROE *Nature's Story* 50 My foot bounded up and back as if I had been india-rubber.

+2. *pl.* Overshoes, made of rubber.

1840 *Knickerb.* XVI. 207 He gave such answers as suited him to the gentleman in the India-rubbers, taking especial care not to invite him to alight. **1848** *Ib.* XXXI. 56 The mud is pituitous, and sucks off your India-rubbers. **1877** HALE *G. T. T.* 143 She took also her cloak, her india-rubbers which she had not time to put on, and her carpet-bag.

3. An eraser made of rubber.

1857 M. J. HOLMES *Meadow-Brook* v, Taking my India-rubber, I erased it [the writing] while my scholars were settling the matter of seats.

4. Attrib. with *blanket, cloak, poncho, umbrella.*

1835 *Boston Directory* 14 (*advt.*) India Rubber, Silk, Gingham and Oil Cloth Umbrellas of every variety. **1847** PARKMAN in *Knickerb.* XXIX. 504 My india-rubber cloak conducted twenty little rapid streamlets to the ground. **1860** GREELEY *Overland Journey* 79 Our trust, under Providence, is in buoyant hearts and an India-rubber blanket. **1888** SHERIDAN *Memoirs* I. 325 My command received only a few overcoats and a small supply of India-rubber ponchos.

India-rubber boat. A boat made of India-rubber cloth. *Obs.* — **1843** FRÉMONT *Explor. Rocky Mts.* 11 The carts had been unloaded and dismantled, and an India-rubber boat, which I had brought with me for the survey of the Platte river, placed in the water. **1858** D. PETERS *Kit Carson* 181 Among the rest of the forethought supplies, there was an India-rubber boat.

India-rubber cloth. Cloth one side of which is covered with India rubber. — **1833** *Niles' Reg.* XLIV. 420/2 The India rubber cloth may be obtained on application to George Spring. **1847** *Rep. Comm. Patents 1846* 212 The outsides of boats have been made of India-rubber cloth. **1847** PARKMAN in *Knickerb.* XXIX. 504 We lay upon india-rubber cloth, placed between our blankets and the soil.

India-rubber shoe. A shoe or overshoe made of India rubber. Usually pl. — **1833** *Niles' Reg.* XLIV. 4/2 A pair of India rubber shoes passed through that post office. **1855** J. E. COOKE *Ellie* 73 The comfortable merchant, with his great coat and India-rubber shoes, . . . smiled. **1870** 'F. FERN' *Ginger-Snaps* 182 Yesterday I went out with only one India-rubber shoe on.

India-rubber tree. Any one of various trees which yield rubber. — **1838** C. NEWELL *Revol. Texas* 176 The India Rubber tree has been lately discovered, and is abundant upon the timber lands on the River Colorado, a few miles from Bastrop. **1884** SARGENT *Rep. Forests* 127 *Ficus pedunculata*. . . . Wild Fig. India-rubber Tree. **1897** SUDWORTH *Arborescent Flora* 191 *Ficus aurea*. . . . Golden Fig. . . . India Rubber Tree (Fla.). *Ib.*, *Ficus populnea*. . . . Poplarleaf Fig. . . . India-Rubber Tree (Fla.).

India wheat. =INDIAN WHEAT 2. — **1857** *Lawrence Republican* 18 June 4 If you cannot get buckwheat, take India wheat if you can. **1874** *Vermont Bd. Agric. Rep.* II. 222 Our shiftless neighbor, if we had one, was sure to send us his kind regards in the shape of cockle, India wheat, or something more lasting. **1877** *Ib.* IV. 76 In the opinion of some good farmers, India wheat is the only paying [grain] . . . in the State.

***Indication.** *Mining.* Evidence of the presence of profitable ore. Usu. pl. — **1861** *Harper's Mag.* Jan. 157/1 That's a speculator from San Francisco. See how wildly he grasps at every 'indication,' as if he had a lease of life for a thousand years. **1872** 'MARK TWAIN' *Roughing It* lxi. 443 '*Prospecting*' is hunting for a '*placer*'; '*indications*' are signs of its presence. **1878** Beadle *Western Wilds* 468 The indefatigable prospectors had dotted all the slopes with holes in search of 'indications.' **1884** Harte *Story of Mine* 394 Luckily the fertile alluvium of these valleys . . . offered no 'indications' to attract the gold-seekers.

***Indictment.** Also †**indictement.** *Law.* The formal statement charging a crime, brought in by a grand jury. Often in phrase *bill of indictment.* — **1647** *Conn. Rec.* I. 159 The Jury find the bill of indictement. **1747** *N.J. Archives* 1 Ser. VII. 87 The prisoner . . . was committed at the Suit of the King by Vertue of a writt on an Indictment for high treason. **1802** *Ann. 7th Congress* 1341 Such bills of indictment as shall be found in the circuit court . . . shall . . . be transmitted by the clerk of the said court. **1911** *Okla. Session Laws* 3 Legisl. 166 Any person violating any provision of the laws of this state enacted for the suppression of the liquor traffic . . . shall be guilty of being an habitual violator of the prohibition laws of this state, and shall be so charged in the presentment or indictment.

+**Indignation meeting.** A meeting held to express public indignation at some abuse. — **1846** Cooper *Redskins* xii, Is 't possible! What, have you no 'indignation meetin's' in Jarmany? We count a great deal on our indignation meetin's and both sides have 'em in abundance. **1883** Howells *Woman's Reason* xi, The passengers in the saloon were divided between two minds, and inclined in about equal numbers to hold a service of song and thanksgiving for their delivery from danger, and to organize an indignation meeting for the adoption of resolutions condemning the captain. **1905** N. Davis *Northerner* 53 Indignation meetings were held daily at the different houses of the officials of the societies and guilds.

***Indigo.** Also †**indico.**

***1.** A powder used for a blue dye, obtained esp. from plants of the genus *Indigofera.*

1646 *Essex Prob. Rec.* I. 51, 20 li. of Indico at 3s. 6d. **1682** Ash *Carolina* 16 Indigo they have made, and that good: The reason why they have desisted I cannot learn. **1773** in Peyton *Adv. Grandfather* (1867) 60 The principal crop is indigo, which is the staple production of the territory [Louisiana]. **1802** Ellicott *Journal* 133 The making of indigo, and raising tobacco, were carried on with spirit some years ago. **1837** Williams *Florida* 109 Indigo was the principal staple of the Florida planters, while the British possessed the country. **1872** *Atlantic Mo.* April 398 A Carolinian could not sell a pound of his indigo to France where so much of it was used.

2. A plant from which indigo is obtained. {1600-} Also collective. (See also Wild indigo.)

1649 *Desc. Virginia* 4 Indico begins to be planted, and thrives wonderfully. **1709** Lawson *Carolina* 95 The Indico grows plentifully in our Quarters. **1781-2** Jefferson *Notes Va.* (1788) 40 Indico yields two cuttings. **1819** E. Dana *Geog. Sketches* 25 Indigo and rice have been found to flourish well here, but they have latterly been neglected for the more profitable crops of cotton and sugar. **1888** Cable in *Century Mag.* Dec. 254/2 [He] bought a very fine plantation, where he cultivated indigo. **1920** Hunter *Trail Drivers Texas* I. 381 The cloth was dyed with a weed called '*Indigo*' that grew in the creek nearby.

3. *slang.* A serious or strait-laced student: (see quot. 1851). Cf. Blue *n.* 3.

1842 *Dartmouth* IV. 117 Success to every student, That rooms in Dartmouth Hall, Unless he be an Indigo, Then, no success at all. **1851** Hall *College Words* 169 *Indigo.* At Dartmouth College, a member of the party called the Blues.

4. Attrib. with *bag, bush, cotton,* etc.

1825 Neal *Bro. Jonathan* I. 188 A hanging shelf . . . loaded with cheeses; . . . rennet bags; indigo dittos; and heaps of blue woollen yarn. **1860** Curtis *Woody Plants N.C.* 104 *Indigo bush* (*Amorpha fruticosa.*) A very pretty shrub. . . . It is said to have been used for the manufacture of Indigo, but, I imagine, with not much profit. **1896** Wilkins *Madelon* 11 Not a girl . . . could wear a gown of brocade with the grace . . . with which Madelon Hautville wore indigo cotton. **1874** *Rep. Comm. Agric. 1873* 260 In the county of Orangeburgh, S.C., there are six indigo-farms, carried on by some of the older men of the county. **1645** *Mass. H. S. Coll.* 4 Ser. VI. 150a Your man hath some Indico seeds for yourselfe & Mr. Peter. **1796** *Boston Directory* 287 Tileston Lemuel, indigo store, No. 5, Ann street. **1737** Brickell *N. Carolina* 82 The Indico Tree (which is a kind of Woad, such as Dyers use to dye Cloth) grows plentifully in this Province, but I have never known any uses made of it. **1850** Judd *R. Edney* xii. 173 You are the dregs of an indigo-tub! **1754** *S.C. Gazette* 1 Jan. 4/1 On the said plantation there are two good barns, and one set of cypress indico vats, the sleeper 15 feet square, and was built this year. **1843** *Knickerb.* XXI. 114 He said nothing, but sat down again, threatening to fall backward with the indigo-water.

+**Indigo bird.** =next. — **1785** Pennant *Artic Zool.* II. 365 The Americans call it [the indigo bunting] the Indigo bird. **1808** Wilson *Ornithology* I. 100 [The] Indigo Bird, *Fringilla Cyanea,* . . . is numerous in all the settled parts of the middle and eastern states; in the Carolinas and Georgia it is also abundant. **1865** Burroughs in *Atlantic Mo.* May 520/1 [The white-eyed flycatcher's] song . . . is a little hard and shrill, like that of the Indigo-Bird or Oriole. **1898** Torrey *Ib.* April 462/1 In imagination I was already beholding them [the woods] populous with chats, indigo-birds, wood pewees, wood thrushes, and warblers.

+**Indigo bunting.** A small finch (*Passerina cyanea*), the male of which is notable for its deep blue color. — **1783** Latham *Gen. Synopsis Birds* II. 205 Indigo B[unting]. . . . It is common at New York. **1844** *Nat. Hist. N.Y., Zoology* II. 173 The Indigo-Bird. *Spiza Cyanea.* . . . Indigo Bunting. **1887** Ridgway *Manual N.A. Birds* 448 Eastern United States and more southern British Provinces, west to edge of Great Plains. . . . *P[asserina] cyanea.* Indigo Bunting. **1917** *Birds of Amer.* III. 71 Indigo Bunting. *Passerina cyanea.*

+**Indigo finch.** =prec. — **1828** Bonaparte *Ornithology* II. 91 Female Indigo Finch. *Fringilla Cyanea.* **1917** *Birds of Amer.* III. 71.

Indigo plant. Any plant from which indigo is obtained, esp. a plant of the genus *Indigofera:* (see also quot. 1898). {1757-} — **1791** Bartram *Travels* 76 Here were large plantations of the Indigo plant. **1841** W. Kennedy *Texas* I. 95 The indigo plant is indigenous, and only demands careful management to render it a valuable article of export. **1848** Bryant *California* ii. 28 Among the flowers and plants which I have noticed today, are the verbena and the indigo-plant. **1874** *Dept. Agric. Rep. 1873* 260 A correspondent of Clinch County, Georgia, recently sent to the Department a specimen of the indigo-plant which grows wild in that section and in great abundance. On examination it proves to be *Indigofera anil.* **1898** Creevey *Flowers of Field, Hill, & Swamp* 418 False or Wild Indigo. *Baptisia tinctoria.* . . . This common, well-known 'indigo' plant is found everywhere.

Indigo plantation. A plantation on which indigo is grown. *Obs.* {1888-} — **1757** *Lett. to Washington* II. 174 What adds to make this Place at present disagreeable is that most of the Gent of Note are out at their Indigo Plantations, so that We have nothing left but a Set of trading Ones. **1774** Finlay *Journal* 64 We came to an indigo plantation. **1797** Imlay *Western Territory* (ed. 3) 253 It is also scarce possible to keep any animal on an indigo plantation in any tolerable case, the fly being so troublesome, that even poultry thrive but little where indigo is made.

Indigo planter. A planter who grows indigo. *Obs.* {1849-} — **1772** Habersham *Letters* 202 We have had a great Quantity of Rain fall, which must hurt the Indigoe Planters. **1789** Morse *Amer. Geog.* 49 The indigo planters carry them [*sc.* oyster shells] away in large boat loads. **1880** Cable *Grandissimes* vi. 37 Old De Grapion . . . married her . . . to young Nancanou, an indigo-planter on the Fausse Rivière.

+**Indigo snake.** = Gopher snake. — **1885** Kingsley, etc. *Riverside Nat. Hist.* III. 367 *Spilotes couperi* . . . is known by the negroes as the indigo or gopher-snake.

Indigo weed. Any wild plant popularly regarded as a kind of indigo, esp. the wild indigo, *Baptisia tinctoria.* {1884-} — **1784** Cutler in *Mem. Academy* I. 473 *Indigofera.* . . . Indigoweed. . . . A durable pale blue may be obtained from the leaves and small branches. Fomentations of the plant, it is said, will abate the swelling, and counteract the poison in the bite of rattle-snakes. **1789** Morse *Amer. Geog.* 429 The soil [in South Carolina] . . . produces moderately good indigo weed. **1832** Child *Frugal Housewife* 115 Indigo-weed stuck plentifully about the harness tends to keep flies from horses. **1852** *Mich. Agric. Soc. Trans.* III. 197 My timber is generally oak, with some hickory, indigo weed, tea weed.

Indigo work. A building in which indigo dye is extracted from plants. — **1687** Blome *Isles & Terr. in Amer.* 14 There [are] already above eighty Indico-Works. **1748** *Georgia Col. Rec.* VI. 225 [He] intends to carry on a large Indigo Work. **1797** Imlay *Western Territory* (ed. 3) 252 An indigo work should always be remote from the dwelling-house.

***Indirect,** *a.* Of taxes: Not collected directly from those who ultimately bear the burden. {1845-} — **1787** *Const. Convention Rec.* (1911) II. 277 Indirect taxes . . . it seemed to be understood were to form the principal revenue of the new Govt. **1797** *Ann. 4th Congress* 2 Sess. 2168 The House then resolved itself into a Committee of the Whole on the subject of indirect taxes. **1833** Story *Commentaries on Constitution* 340 It is not necessary to determine, whether a tax on the produce of land be a direct or an indirect tax. **1882** Wells *Practical Economics* (1885) 71 Federal taxes, both direct and indirect, with very few exceptions, are levied on commodities. **1886** Alton *Among Law-Makers* 59 The Government depends for its hundreds of millions upon indirect taxation.

Industrial education. Education that fits one for industrial employment. — **1868** *Rep. Comm. Educ.* 305 A combined and persistent effort for the appropriation of National lands to encourage industrial education. **1881** *Harper's Mag.* Feb. 476/2 An amendment . . . provides for the instruction of women . . . in such branches of . . . industrial education as are suited to their sex. **1891** *Atlantic Mo.* June 812/1 One district school . . . well illustrated the advantage of industrial education.

Industrial school. A school in which trades and practical skills are taught. {1853-} — **1853** Brace *Dangerous Classes N.Y.* (1872) 92 'Boys' Sunday Meetings' have already been formed. . . . With these we plan to connect 'Industrial Schools,' . . . where they can learn an honest trade. **1881** *Rep. Indian Affairs* p. lxv, The principal agency by which these Indians can be elevated is believed to be the 'industrial school.' **1912** Monroe, etc. *Cycl. Educ.* III. 431/2 It will undoubtedly be a considerable time before any general agreement among manufacturers will be reached to allow learners in their establishments to attend industrial schools during the working hours. **1912** *Indian Laws & Tr.* III. 548 For support and maintenance of day and industrial schools among the Sioux Indians, . . . two hundred thousand dollars.

+**Infant industry.** An undeveloped industry, regarded as in need of governmental aid or protection in its competition with foreign rivals. — **1870** *Congress. Globe* App. 29 March 240/3 But, argue our defenders of monopoly, let us protect our infant industries, and when they have grown to manhood, . . . they will need no further protection. **1884** *Congress. Rec.* 1 May 3660/2 The [protective] system was first commended to the people on the ground that it was needed for the encouragement of infant industries. **1897** *Ib.* 26 March 382/1 The people have been taxed to furnish princely estates . . . for infant industries.

+**Infant manufacture.** =prec. — **1789** *Ann. 1st Congress* I. 106 Some [duties are] calculated to . . . protect our infant manufactures. **1831** PECK *Guide* 81 Were protection to the sugar making business to be wholly abandoned, . . . the result would be more disastrous to the south and west, than the influx of foreign goods was to the infant manufactures of the north, and to the whole country.

*****Infantry.** Also **infantery. 1.** A body of foot soldiers; collectively, soldiers who serve afoot. **2.** Attrib. with *cap, flag, tactics.* — **(1) 1759** *Essex Inst. Coll.* XIX. 145 We went on and Landed ye Rangers Light infantery and granaders. **1781** HAMILTON *Works* VIII. 39 A handsome command . . . in the light infantry. **1812** *Ann. 12th Congress* 1 Sess. II. 1449 An engrossed bill for the more perfect organization of the infantry of the United States was read the third time, and passed. **1892** M. A. JACKSON *Gen. Jackson* xvii. 345 The river here is only about half a mile wide, and having a level and pebbly bottom, from two to three feet deep, the infantry were able to ford the stream. **(2) 1861** *Army Regulations* 138 The recruits . . . to be well drilled in the Infantry Tactics. **1866** 'F. KIRKLAND' *Bk. Anecdotes* 235 A large infantry flag, almost new. **1894** ALDRICH *Two Bites* 161 The dustmen went about in cast-off infantry caps.

Infant school. A school for very young children. {1833–} Now hist. — **1829** ROYALL *Pennsylvania* II. 63 Of a piece are their infant schools, now getting up. **1835** ABDY *Journal* III. 154 The system of infant schools is not so popular in the United States as it was at its introduction. **1884** ROOSEVELT *Amer. Backlogs* (1928) 23 When Helen was about a year and a half old she was sent to what was then [c1830] called an 'infant-school.'

*****Infare.** Also **infair.** The celebration, on the day following a wedding, of the couple's entrance into their new home. {*Sc.* and *dial.*} — **1744** J. MACSPARRAN *Diary* (1899) 18 Dr. Hazard and Betty Gardiner went to . . . Billy Hazard's weding. . . . They are both gone again to Mr. Robinson's to the Infair. **1839** *S. Lit. Messenger* V. 473/1 You must have an infair for the bride and bridegroom. **1873** BEADLE *Undevel. West* xxi. 408 Mrs. Thomson's youngest daughter was married yesterday to a white young man, . . . and we arrived in the middle of the 'infair.' **1924** RAINE *Land of Saddle-Bags* 83 When we war married, there was a heap o' doin's. We had an infare and waiters.

Inferior court. {1754–} A court from which an appeal can be made. Freq. *inferior court of (common) pleas.*

1636 *Plymouth Laws* 41 Inferior Courts . . . shall be allowed by this Court in other places of this Government. **1687** *Mass. H. S. Coll.* 4 Ser. V. 157 The witnesses may be sworn before the Judge of the Inferior Court of Pleas. **1721** *Mass. H. Repr. Jrnls.* III. 13 An Act for Removing the Court of General Sessions of the Peace, and Inferiour Court of Common Pleas. **1771** in *New Eng. Mag.* ns. XII. 352/2 Inferior court sits twice a year here. **1829** SHERWOOD *Gaz. Georgia* (ed. 2) 22 The power of administering the laws is vested in a superior and inferior courts, and in a magistrates' court. **1853** STOWE *Key* 77 The judge in the inferior court charged the jury that . . . in law the defendant was guilty.

Infield. {1606–}

+**1.** *Baseball.* (See quot. 1867.)

1867 CHADWICK *Base Ball Reference* 138 The In-Field.—That portion of the field within the base lines. **1896** — *Base Ball Guide* 167. **1910** *Spalding's Base Ball Guide* 338 The infield is bounded by the base-running paths, which extend from base to base. **1912** MATHEWSON *Pitching* 290 The soil of the infield was mixed with a form of clay which, when wet and then rolled, was almost as hard as concrete.

+**2.** *collect.* The players who perform in the infield.

1889 CAMP *College Sports* (1893) 170 The first sensation of a college infield on meeting a professional nine is one of hurry. **1917** MATHEWSON *Sec. Base Sloan* xiv. 194 Our infield's pretty good as it is.

+**3.** Attrib. in sense 1 with *fly, hit, position, work.*

1885 CHADWICK *Art of Pitching* 118 Backing each other up is one great feature of the play of first-class basemen. Indeed, infield work can never be effectually attended to without it. **1886** — *Art of Batting* 60 To cover infield positions properly, a degree of intelligence in the players is required which the majority do not as a general rule possess. **1910** *Spalding's Base Ball Guide* 381 In cases of the base runner being declared 'out' . . . on an infield fly, the 'out' should be credited [etc.]. **1912** MATHEWSON *Pitching* ii. 23 Devore beat out an infield hit.

+**Infielder.** *Baseball.* A player stationed in the infield. — **1867** CHADWICK *Base Ball Reference* 138 The infielders include the first six players of a nine. **1868** — *Base Ball* 41 There are six in-fielders in a nine of a match, viz., catcher, pitcher, first, second, and third base men, and shortstop. **1910** *Spalding's Base Ball Guide* 368 The batsman is out . . . if . . . he hit a fly ball . . . that can be handled by an infielder.

+**Infit,** *v. local. tr.* To supply (a seaman) with necessaries for shore life, usu. on credit. — **1887** GOODE, etc. *Fisheries U.S.* V. II. 226 The merchant is as anxious to 'infit' as he was to 'outfit' him, but the man must now bring an order from the agent or owner of the vessel.

+**Infitter.** *local.* (See quotation.) — **1887** GOODE, etc. *Fisheries U.S.* V. II. 226 The outfitters are also 'infitters,' that is, they furnish the men with such supplies and articles of clothing as they may need when the vessel returns.

*****Inflation.**

+**1.** Of money and prices: Overexpansion. {1887–}

1841 in MacLeod *F. Wood* 75 We have been periodically visited by panics, revulsions, and distresses, inflations and reäctions. **1870** [see INFLATIONIST]. **1885** WELLS *Practical Economics* 58 The maintenance, further inflation, or redemption of the then 'legal-tender' (irredeemable paper) currency. **1924** *Lit. Digest* 13 Sept. 82/1 Another period of inflation . . . is looked for by many financial experts.

+**2.** Attrib. with *organ, party,* etc.

1874 *N.Y. Tribune* 26 Nov. 5 An Inflation Party [has been organized] . . . reaffirming, in effect, the financial plank of the Indiana Independents. **1875** *Chicago Tribune* 2 July 4/2 With the states of New York, Connecticut, and New Jersey against any Democratic candidate on a repudiation or inflation platform, it will puzzle the *Enquirer* to tell how he is to be elected. *Ib.* 27 Nov. 8/7 The wild-cat inflation organ, which believes only in irredeemable, fluctuating, depreciated scrip for money. **1887** *Century Mag.* Jan. 432/1 Wages . . . are now as high or higher in gold coin than they were in paper money at the highest point . . . in the paper-money inflation period of 1864 to 1867.

+**Inflationist.** One who favors inflation of the currency. {1889–} Also attrib. — **1870** *Nation* 3 March 129 The work of inflation by adding fifty million dollars to the currency . . . [is] part of an arrangement between the Western inflationists, who want more greenbacks, and the Eastern tariff men, who are opposed to a reduction of duties. **1876** *N. Amer. Rev.* Oct. 451 The election of Tilden would spike the whole inflationist battery. **1890** *Voice* 17 July, If the government accedes to the demand of the inflationist it is just as likely to do so the second and third time. **1905** *Springfield W. Repub.* 8 Sept. 1 The inflationists, although defeated at the polls, appear after all to be the real winners in contemporary politics. **1918** *Nation* 7 Feb. 129/1 There is a pretty obvious inflationist trend to the proposal.

*****Influence.** *Polit.* +The ability to secure political offices for others; the person exercising such power; 'pull.' *colloq.* — [**1792** in Bowers *Jefferson & Hamilton* 161 Favoritism, influence and monopoly.] **1882** *Nation* 31 Aug. 265 There is no good reason now, under the spoils theory, why individual members of Congress should not . . . sell their 'influence' openly for a fixed sum to be used in procuring their reëlection. **1888** BRYCE *Amer. Commonw.* III. IV. lxxxviii. 177 This position gave him a vast amount of 'influence,' which he continued to use for his own advantage until the board was abolished in 1870. **1903** *N.Y. Ev. Post* 8 Dec. 7 It is an axiom of the Departments that the more incompetent the employee the greater his 'influence,' for by a natural law the employee knows that he must have something to stand on, and so what he lacks in ability he hastens to make up by cultivating political backers. **1904** DERVILLE *Other Side of Story* 49 Asked me how I liked Washington, how I liked my work, how old I was and who was my influence.

*****Information.** *Law.* A charge brought against a person by some public officer; in some states, a formal accusation brought by the public prosecutor, in place of an indictment found by a grand jury. — **1688** SEWALL *Letter-Book* I. 87 Mr. Sherlock . . . serv'd a seal'd parchment Writt of Intrusion on Jeremiah Balchor, and left an Information with him. . . . Balchor came and brought the Information. **1734** *Penna. Col. Rec.* III. 562 Now it is required they should plead to the Several Informations exhibited against them. **1877** JOHNSON *Anderson Co., Kansas* 227 An information was filed against him for the murder of Ruth. **1911** *Okla. Session Laws* 3 Legisl. 160 When it is shown upon the taking of such testimony that there is probable cause to believe that any person has violated any provision of this act, the county attorney shall immediately prepare an information.

Infract, *v.* [Back formation from *infraction.*] *tr.* To infringe, violate. {1819–} 'Chiefly *U.S.*' (*O.E.D.*). — **1798** WASHINGTON *Writings* XIV. 127, I think every nation has a right to establish that form of government, under which it conceives it shall live most happy; provided it infracts no right, or is not dangerous to others. **1801** HAMILTON *Works* VII. 226 The treaties of the United States had been infracted by State laws. **1816** PICKERING 115 To *infract.* This is used by some American authors instead of the verb *to infringe,* which is commonly employed by English writers. **1897** *Columbus Dispatch* 5 March 1/6 The galleries infracted the senate rules by applauding vigorously as Mr. Hanna took the oath of office.

+**Ingersollian,** *a.* Favoring the agnostic views of Robert Green Ingersoll (1833–99). — [**1892** STEVENSON & OSBOURNE *Wrecker* xi, I don't know if you quite believe in prayer, I'm a bit Ingersollian myself.] **1898** *Mo. So. Dakotan* I. 117 Then follows an analysis of the several petitions of the Lord's prayer, which, were the author not redeemed from the charge by his earnestness and by his final deductions would lead the reader to set him down as a scoffer of the Ingersollian school.

+**Ingersollistic,** *a.* =prec. — **1896** *Advance* 2 April 477/3 We could wish that the expressions had been less ambiguous and seemingly Ingersollistic.

+**Ingersollite.** A believer in agnosticism as taught by Robert Green Ingersoll (1833–99). — **1883** *Home Missionary* Nov. 281 Nowhere is skepticism more prevalent. . . . Many of our ablest men . . . are Ingersollites.

Ingrain. {1858–} +=next. — **1863** 'M. HARLAND' *Husks* 20 Sarah's carpet was common ingrain, neither pretty nor new. **1893** *Stand.* 925/3.

+**Ingrain carpet.** A carpet dyed in the grain, *i.e.,* in the yarn before it is woven. — **1836** *Penny Cycl.* VI. 314/1 Kidderminster or Scotch carpets, or, as the Americans more descriptively term them, in-grain carpets, are wholly of worsted or woollen, or, as is most common, the chain is of worsted and the shoot of wool. **1879** WHITMAN *Diary* (1904) 57 The same error [*i.e.,* spoiling the effect] in Capitol Hill at Washington,—exploiting the designs of ingrain carpets, with sprawling and meaningless lines. **1905** Lincoln *Partners* 29 There were two or three straight-backed chairs set squarely in their places on the ingrain carpet.

+**Ingrain carpeting.** The fabric from which ingrain carpets are made. — **1847** *Rep. Comm. Patents 1846* 75 Letters patent have been granted for improvements in looms for weaving ingrain carpeting. **1860** *Ladies' Repository* May 141/2 A breadth of Ingrain carpeting rolled upon the floor. **1861** *Vanity Fair* 1 June (*advt.*), Three Ply and Ingrain Carpeting, Rugs, Mats, ... at a great Reduction in Prices.

*__Inhabitant.__ +**1.** *pl.* In colonial times, a region or district settled or inhabited by colonists. *Obs.* +**2.** *Law.* One who technically resides in a particular area or jurisdiction. — **(1) 1753** Washington *Diaries* I. 43 In company with those persons [I] left the Inhabitants the Day following. **1784** Ellicott in Mathews *Life A. Ellicott* 23 Tomorrow we shall set off for the Inhabitants. **(2) 1787** *Constitution* i. § 2 No person shall be a representative who shall not ... be an inhabitant of that state in which he shall be chosen. **1834** *Cases Contested Elections 1789–1834* (H.R. Com. on Elections) 411 An inhabitant of a State, within the meaning of the ... constitution, is one who is *bona fide* a member of the State, subject to all the requisitions of its laws, and entitled to all the privileges ... which they confer. **1883** E. Channing *Town & County Govt. Eng. Col. N. Amer.* (1884) 12 To this [parish] meeting all those who had benefit of the things there transacted might come; that is to say, all householders, and all who manured land within the parish. Such were technically termed inhabitants, even though they dwelt in another town.

*__Inheritance.__ Land possessed as an inheritance. Formerly used in the descriptions of property in county records. — **c1700** *Md. Hist. Mag.* XIX. 345 Spryes Inheritance. *Ib.* 348 Aquilas Inheritance. *Ib.* XXI. 338 Johns Inheritance.

+**Initiation fee.** The fee paid when one is initiated into a society. — **1871** Baggs *At Yale* 121 The initiation fee of fifteen to twenty-five dollars is collected. **1875** 'Mark Twain' *Old Times on Miss.* i. 121 The initiation fee had been raised to fifty dollars. **1897** Flandrau *Harvard Episodes* 140 You'll have to make him an honorary member, won't you? Can he pay his initiation fee?

Initiative. {1793–} *Initiative and referendum,* the right or power of citizens to initiate legislation, constitutional amendments, etc., and to vote on proposed legislation. {referendum and initiative 1889–, in Switzerland} — **1893** *Arena* VII. 697 In the Massachusetts town meetings, ... the Initiative and Referendum have been in force from the beginning of our national history, although unnamed and unnoticed. **1902** *Independent* 20 Nov. 2789/1 The extent to which the popular movement for the Initiative and Referendum has advanced within the past three or four years is not generally recognized. **1925** Bryan *Memoirs* 186 His views on the initiative and referendum and prohibition have not altered.

+**Injun.** (See Indian *n.*)

Injunct, *v.* [Back formation from Injunction.] *tr.* To enjoin, forbid. *colloq.* {1890–} — **1871** De Vere 653 A whole class of violent contractions [arose], derived from well-known and well-formed words, like *burgled, injuncted,* and *excurted.* **1880** *Christian Advocate* (N.Y.) 11 March (Th.) Stoddards have successfully injuncted Scribner's from taking and using subscription lists procured by [them]. **1887** *Ohio State Jrnl.* 1 Sept., Foraker proposed to 'injunct' the return of the rebel flags.

*__Injunction.__ *Law.* A writ granted by a court of equity, requiring a party to do or, more often, to refrain from doing certain acts. — **1694** *N.C. Col. Rec.* I. 402 The defen[dan]t craves an Injunction. **1715** *Ib.* II. 207 No injunction or wager of Court ... shall be allowed or admitted of. **1835** Clay in *Congress. Deb.* 4 Feb. 297 The judges of the courts of Georgia are restrained from granting injunctions, so that the only form in which the Indian can come before them is in the form of an appeal. **1911** *Okla. Session Laws* 3 Legisl. 164 The injunction shall be granted at the commencement of the action, and no bond shall be required.

Ink ball. {1884–} An oak gall used in the making of ink. Also attrib. with *oak.* — **1817–8** Eaton *Botany* (1822) 419 *Quercus coccinea,* scarlet oak, ink-ball oak: ... the leaves of this species become reddish, and even scarlet in autumn. Produces brownish-purple nut-galls. **1888** *Century Mag.* Sept. 765/2 The juice of poke-berries, compounded with vinegar, or the distillation of a vegetable product known as 'ink balls' usurped the place of ink.

+**Inkberry.** The gall berry (*Ilex glabra*), a shrub of the holly family; also, the berry of this shrub. — **1817–8** Eaton *Botany* (1822) 410 *Prinos glaber,* ink-berry. ... A low shrub. **1850** *New Eng. Farmer* II. 109 The Ink Berry is another low, evergreen shrub, of a handsome appearance. **1858** Warder *Hedges & Evergreens* 275 The *Prinos glaber,* or Winter-Berry, is a handsome shrub, growing three or four feet high, and bearing black berries, called ink-berries. **1901** Mohr *Plant Life Ala.* 116 Excepting the ink berry (*Ilex glabra*), scarcely any tree or shrub shades the ground [of the pine-barren flats].

*__Inkhorn.__ A small portable container for ink. — **1638** *Md. Archives* IV. 75, 13 pamphletts an ink horne, & pewter spoone. **1747** *N.H. Probate Rec.* III. 483, I also give him my Wigg & brass inkorn. **1852** Stowe *Uncle Tom* xiv, Pulling out an old inkhorn, he proceeded to fill out a bill of sale.

+**Ink-slinger.** (See quot. 1877.) Also *ink-slinging. colloq.*[2] — **1877** Bartlett 786 *Ink-Slinger,* one who habitually writes for publication; particularly an editor or reporter of a newspaper. **1888** *Texas Siftings* 13 Oct. (F.), You don't consider that insignificant ink-slinger ... a big gun, do you? **1894** *Daily News* (Lond.) 2 May 6/3 High-bred women who were not given to what modern Americans call 'ink-slinging.'

Inkstand. A device to hold ink bottles, pens, etc.; an ink-container. {1773–} — **1781** *Salem Gazette* 3 July, Isaac Greenwood ... makes ... Buckle-Brushes, Ink-Stands, Paper-Folders, Sand-Boxes, Bannisters for Stair-cases, &c. &c. **1790** *Penna. Packet* 10 May 4/3 John Sparhawk ... Has For Sale ... blank books, tambour ink stands, backgammon and chess boards. **1864** Taylor *H. Thurston* xxiii. 295 The rude country children ... drew pictures on their slates and upset the inkstands over their copy-books. **1893** *Harper's Mag.* March 643/1 He reached over and took a sheet of paper and a pen, dipped his pen in his silver inkstand, and with a look of determination on his face, squared himself to write.

Inkwell. A container, freq. in a desk, for holding ink ready for use. {1876–} — **1875** Knight 1188/2 *Ink-well,* an ink-cup adapted to occupy a hole in a desk. **1876** Ingram *Centennial Exp.* x. 333 The swinging ink-well adapts the desk to marine purposes. **1891** *Boston Jrnl.* 9 April 43 The expectant young man opened his certificate blank book and dipped his pen in the inkwell before him.

Inkwood. A small tree (*Exothea paniculata*) with purple fruit which grows in Florida and the West Indies. — **1889** *Cent.* 3103/2. **1897** Sudworth *Arborescent Flora* 296.

+**Inland alewife.** A river fish of the Mississippi Valley, *Pomolobus chrysochloris.* — **1884** Goode, etc. *Fisheries* I. 594 The Inland Alewife or Skipjack ... is abundant throughout the Mississippi Valley in all the larger streams.

+**Inland swamp.** (See quotations.) — **1802** Drayton *S. Carolina* 116 The plantations which produce this grain [rice], are of two kinds, *river swamp,* and *inland swamp.* The first are immediately connected with fresh water rivers; the latter are situated on low inland swamp, unconnected with tides or navigation. **1842** Buckingham *Slave States* I. 38 There are no less than six classes or kinds of soil in this territory: the first of these is the tide swamp, near the sea; the second is the inland swamp, above the reach of the tide-water range.

In-lot. {a1661} +A lot within a town, village, or new settlement. — **1779** *Ky. Petitions* 51 [We] pray that every Actual settler ... may be entituled to Draw a free lott; ... the lotts to consist of half acre in lott and five acre out lott. **1815** Drake *Cincinnati* iii. 139 Bonfires, and all other conflagrations on the streets or in-lots, are ... forbidden. **1838** J. McDonald *Biog. Sketches* 31 [Massie] offered each of the first twenty-five families, as a donation, one in-lot, one out-lot, and one hundred acres of land, provided they would settle in a town he intended to lay off at his settlement. **1841** Cist *Cincinnati* 16 As an inducement to settlers the new proprietors agreed to give an 'in lot six rods by twelve ... and an out lot.

*__Inn.__ A public house for the lodging and boarding of travelers, visitors to a town, etc.; a hotel.

1633 *Plymouth Laws* 35 None [shall] be suffered to retale wine or strong water or suffer the same to be drunke ... except it be at some inne or victualling house. **1715** *Boston News-Letter* 7 Feb. 2/2 (*advt.*), The Globe Tavern or Inn at Salem, ... situated in the Main Street of said Town. **1794** *Ann. 3d Congress* 1455 Persons, who, as keepers of taverns, inns, or houses of entertainment, ... shall vend or sell really and truly for consumption ... wines or distilled spirituous liquors. **1817** Webster *Letter to Pickering* 25 *Tavern* and *inn* are used indifferently in this country, because we unite the uses of both, in the same house. **1877** *Harper's Mag.* April 677/1 Old Wiley was an object of perennial interest to that estimable class of people who hang around village inns and stores with a painful amount of leisure on their hands.

*__Innholder.__ =Innkeeper. *Obs.* exc. in legal use. — **1650** *Suffolk Deeds* I. 134 Wm. Hudson of Boston Inhoulder ... granted unto Tho[mas] Dudley Governr: all his Brewhouse in Boston neere to his dwelling house. **1693** *Boston Rec.* VII. 215 There are under consideration by the quarter Sessions for Inholders or Retailers in the town of Boston the persons hereafter named. **1721** *Mass. H. Rep. Jrnl.* III. 30 That which most of all surprizes us is the Sum ... paid to Mary Smith, Innholder for Sundries, supplied the Press Gangs Impressing Sailors. **1832** Williamson *Maine* I. 349 The innholders, or 'ordinaries' licensed [in 1653], were John Davis of York, and Hugh Gunison of Kittery.

*__Inning.__ *Baseball.*

+**1.** The period of play in which both sides have a turn at bat; a turn at bat. Formerly sometimes plural in singular sense. {1746– in cricket}

1868 Chadwick *Base Ball* 41 An innings, in base ball, is played when three men on the batting side have been put out. **1886** *Outing* May 239/1 The game was fairly played and exciting up to the fourth inning. **1897** *N.Y. Journal* 5 Sept. 41/6 After the fifth inning is played and the game is called whichever team is ahead wins. **1917** Mathewson *Sec. Base Sloan* 238 Two runs obtained in the first inning.

b. *transf.* An opportunity; a period of action or influence. *colloq.* {1855–, in pl.}

1884 'Mark Twain' *H. Finn* xxvi. 264 Then Mary Jane she took another inning, and went in sweet and lovely again—which was her way. **1885** *N.Y. Mirror* 23 May 7/3 (*caption*), An Inning for the Lyceum Pupils. **1889** 'Mark Twain' *Conn. Yankee* vii. 88 Step to the bat, it's your innings. **1905** N. Davis *Northerner* 146 Mr. Caldwell is quite welcome to his innings.

+**2.** Often used as the second element in combinations with numbers to form adjectives.

1918 Sandburg *Cornhuskers* 19 A sixteen-inning game ended by darkness.

***Innkeeper.** One who keeps an inn. Now legal or hist. — **1636** *Boston Rec.* 10 None shall keepe any victualling houses . . . but onely such as are allowed thereunto as Inkeepers. **1787** CUTLER in *Life & Corr.* I. 207 If he made as good a judge, when on the bench, as he does an innkeeper, he must have excelled many of his brethen in office. **1807** IRVING, etc. *Salmagundi* iv, Travel-mongers . . . write whole volumes about themselves, . . . interspersed with anecdotes of innkeepers, droll sayings of stage-drivers [etc.]. **1898** HARPER *S. B. Anthony* I. 3 He settled in Portsmouth R.I. and became a land-owner, an innkeeper, and an office holder.

***Innocence.** +=BLUET 1. — **1821** BARTON *Flora* I. 119 Fairy-flax-Bluett. Innocence. Venus' Pride. **1863** *Rep. Comm. Agric. 1862* 159 The 'Bluets,' 'Innocence,' 'Dwarf Pink,' with, perhaps, some other common name, is one of the prettiest ornaments of our spring meadows. **1892** *Amer. Folk-Lore* V. 97 *Houstonia cærulea*, innocence. Boston, Mass.

*** Inoculate,** *v. tr.*

1. To impregnate (a person or animal) with the virus or germs of a disease, esp. smallpox. {1722-}

1721 *New-Eng. Courant* 7 Aug. 1/2 The bold undertaker of the Practice of the Greek old Women, notwithstanding the Terror and Confusion from his Son's Inoculation-Fever, proceeds to inoculate Persons from Seventy Years of Age and downwards. **1763** *Huntington Rec.* II. 455 We the subscribers the Trustees of the said town for the time Being do ennact that no Docter shall Presume to Innoculate any person or persons within the Limmits afore sd. **1823** THACHER *Military Jrnl.* 54 Orders are given to inoculate for the smallpox, all the soldiers and inhabitants in town. **1913** *Amer. Phil. Soc. Proc.* LII. 226 When a chicken was inoculated with a weakened culture of the chicken cholera bacillus it became sick but soon recovered.

2. *intr.* To receive an inoculation.

1776 *Warren-Adams Lett.* I. 260 In Boston they have given up all thoughts of stopping it, and everybody is inoculating. **1779** *Essex Inst. Coll.* XXI. 278 None shall EnockoLate till they Go in the Pest Houses and there to Stay till Clensed.

Inoculist. One who inoculates. {1886} *Obs.* — **1776** *Narrag. Hist. Reg.* V. 352 Practitioners and Inoculists may be served with them [*sc.* medicines], if applied for soon.

***Inquest.** A legal inquiry, esp. into the cause of death, made by, or before, a coroner and jury; the jury which makes such an inquest. — **1661** *Portsmouth Rec.* 107 The Crounars inquest beinge paneled thay made inquirey hou he came by his death. **1709** *N.J. Archives* 1 Ser. III. 454 The Free-holders summon'd to serve upon the grand inquest . . . did all answer to their names. **1845** *Ill. Rev. Statutes* 518 The coroner . . . shall take immediate measures to bury the body which may have been the subject of the inquest. **1879** STOCKTON *Rudder Grange* vii, The constable, who was also coroner of our township, had gone . . . to hold an inquest.

+Inquiry meeting. (See quot. 1835.) *Obs.* — **1835** REED & MATHESON *Visit* II. 15 *Conference or Inquiry Meetings.*—These are instituted for those persons who have become anxiously concerned for their salvation; and who need the more exact guidance and encouragement, which discreet conversation can best supply. **1850** GALLAHER *Western Sketch-Book* 242 A church was organized. . . . I appointed an inquiry meeting, to be held early in the morning.

+Inquiry room. A room, usually in a church, in which persons troubled about their prospects of salvation may ask for information and guidance. — **1850** GALLAHER *Western Sketch-Book* 243 He came into the inquiry room, and told me, very frankly, that he had been living in sin, and that unmerited grace alone had held him up from a deserved hell. **1877** *Boston Bulletin* Feb. (B.), They had a tough subject in the inquiry-room this week. Moody wrestled with him, and Sankey sang with him, but the man seemed to despair of forgiveness.

+Insane asylum. A public asylum for insane patients. Usually supported by the state. — **1860** HOLMES *E. Venner* vi, Penitentiaries and insane asylums take care of most of the right-angle cases. **1883** 'MARK TWAIN' *Life on Miss.* 528 Died in the insane asylum three or four years ago. **1895** *Dept. Agric. Yrbk. 1894* 90 The land and buildings reverted to the State and are now used for an insane asylum. **1907** ANDREWS *Recoll.* 223 He took me in September to visit the insane asylum.

Insect. *Zoöl.*

1. Any of a large number of species of small invertebrate creatures with bodies divided into sections or segments. {1601-}

1684 I. MATHER *Providences* (1856) vi. 125 The devil may by his art produce insects and vermin. **1789** MORSE *Amer. Geog.* 62 Of the astonishing variety of insects found in America, we will mention, The Glow Worm [etc.]. **1877** *Rep. Indian Affairs* 49 If insects and drought destroy the gardens, they are no worse off than the whites. **1917** *Dept. Agric. Yrbk. 1916* 273 This insect . . . came to be known as the white scale, or fluted scale.

2. Attrib. and comb. with *blight, destroyer, enemy,* etc.

1855 *Amer. Inst. N.Y. Trans.* 332 Prof. Mapes . . . described the insect lamp and the preventive principles of the melon box. **a1862** THOREAU *Maine Woods* 220 My companion . . . defended his face and hands with the insect-wash. **1867** *Amer. Naturalist* I. 328 Another insect-hunter is the singular *Ranatra fusca.* **1867** *Ill. Agric. Soc. Trans.* VII. 503 The *insect blight* is caused by the *Scolytus Pyri.* **1875** KNIGHT 1189/2 *Insect-destroyer,* a device for killing noxious insects. **1883** *Harper's Mag.* Oct. 706/2, I generally had . . . my insect forceps in my pocket. **1883** *Century Mag.* Oct. 811/1 No port . . . has more rigid laws of quarantine than are now enforced in California against these insect enemies. **1892** KELLOGG *Kansas Insects* 101 Several insect parasites attack the Maple-worm, much to the advantage of the maple tree. **1899** GOING *Flowers* 300 Insect-eating leaves are probably a device to supply the plant with nitrogen by means of the foliage.

Insect powder. A powder used for killing insects. {1893-} — **a1872** in Brace *Dangerous Classes N.Y.* 355 There were some hundred children; their occupations were as follows: They put up insect-powder, drive wagons, tend oyster-saloons [etc.]. **1882** PECK *Sunshine* 43 One lady said that she had tried all the aesthetic insect powder that was advertised. **1885** *Harper's Mag.* Jan. 228/1 Make no trip to the Gulf in a yacht without a goodly store of insect powder, for there be many things that crawl on shipboard. **1924** *Sears, Roebuck & Co. Cat.* No. 148, 482 Insect Powder for Killing All Kinds Insects.

+Inshore cod. (See quot. 1884.) — **1884** GOODE, etc. *Fisheries* I. 201 [Cod] fish which live near the shores, but which are less closely limited to the reefs . . . are called 'Shoal-water Cod,' 'Shore Cod,' 'Inshore Cod' [etc.]. **1889** *Cent.* 1082/2 *Clam-cod,* inshore cod which feed on clams.

***Inside,** *a.* and *n. attrib.* +In the confidence of those who control something; confidential; not commonly known. *colloq.* — **1870** *Congress. Globe* 3 Feb. 1022/1, 'I ask the gentleman from Ohio to name the ships which he says have been sold for a song. The gentleman is inside on all these matters.' . . . 'I am no more inside than [Mr. Eldridge].' **1894** LEAVITT *Our Money Wars* 11 *n.*, A few lines of inside history are worth whole books of that usually printed. **1912** MATHEWSON *Pitching* ix. 184 Behind this game is some 'inside' history that has never been written.

Inside, *adv. Inside of* (with reference to time), within the space of. {1889-, in Australia} — **1877** *Boston Jrnl.* 27 April (B.), They would pollute the society of Heaven inside of twenty-four hours. **1888** *Missouri Republican* 22 Feb. (F.), He is very desperate, and inside of thirty days shot at four men. **1904** *Springfield W. Repub.* 29 July 6 The textbook would be ready for distribution inside of a week.

Inside man. A servant whose duties are within a house {1894-}; +a burglar who enters houses to rob them. *colloq.* — **1886** HOWELLS *Minister's Charge* 368 Look at the Blue-book, where our nobility is enrolled; it's the apotheosis of farm-boys, mechanics, insidemen, and I don't know what! **1892** — *Mercy* 116 James, the inside-man, opened the door. **1924** HENDERSON *Keys to Crookdom* 79 If there are two, one is an 'inside man,' and the other an 'outside man.'

Insider. {1875-} **1.** (See quotation.) **2.** One who is 'on the inside'; one who possesses private information concerning the financial status of a company, plans for managing a stock, etc. — **(1) 1848** W. ARMSTRONG *Stocks* 7 A certain classification of operators in Stocks [exists] by which they are divided into Insiders and Outsiders. Insiders are those by whom and through whom all transactions are made in and about the Exchange. . . . This class comprehends all the regular brokers who are members of either Board, and also all . . . curb-stone brokers. **(2) 1880** INGHAM *Digging Gold* xxi. 452 As a mine the North Ophir was not worth three cents a mile, but as a speculation it was a success—to the insiders. **1892** *Courier-Journal* 1 Oct. 11/2 The only other important change for the day was in Distillers, which is taken care of by the insiders. **1900** NELSON *A B C Wall St.* 148 *Insiders,* the men who own the controlling interest of stock in railroad and industrial companies and shape the course of prices.

Inside track. +*fig.* A favored position; the greatest advantage. — **1867** MELINE *Santa Fé & Back* 24 The railroad from Omaha appears to have, in point of time, what is called the inside track. **1885** HOWELLS *S. Lapham* xx, I guess I've got the inside track. **1892** *Harper's Mag.* Feb. 440/2 My gentleman friend in our office has the inside track, and got me the pass. **1914** ATHERTON *Perch of Devil* ii. 361 When a woman knows where she stands, and has the inside track, . . . the man has no show whatever.

Insinuendo. (See quot. 1913.) — **1885** MATTHEWS in *Longman's Mag.* Dec. 151 Could I not damn with faint praise and stab with sharp insinuendo?—to use the labour-saving and much-needed word thoughtlessly invented by the sable legislator of South Carolina. **1902** L. MEAD *Word-Coinage* 102. **1913** *Boston Transcript* 9 July 16/6 'Portemanteau' Words. . . . Insinuendo—a compound from innuendo and insinuation.

Inspect, *v.* {1623-} *intr.* To prove or turn out to be upon inspection. — **1865-6** *Ill. Agric. Soc. Trans.* VI. 638 All Flour that inspects 'Sound' and full weight shall be branded.

+Inspection house. A house in which tobacco is examined. — **1773** *Md. Hist. Mag.* II. 358 To compel all the Owners or Makers of Tobacco to send it to certain Inspection Houses whence it cannot be again removed till it is put on Board a Ship. **1818** *Niles' Reg.* XV. 139/2 Adjoining the inspection house, on Queen street [in Baltimore], two frame dwellings . . . were burnt to the ground.

+Inspection law. A law providing for the inspection of various articles of commerce to determine their fitness for transportation or sale. — **1753** *Md. Hist. Mag.* III. 366 Which made me apprehend they intended some Opposition to the Inspection Law. **1773** *Ib.* XV. 286 Prohibiting their Delegates from Proceeding to Business unless the inspection Law was Previously obtained. **1790** MACLAY *Deb. Senate* 188 Read the law for giving effect to the inspection laws of the States.

Inspector. {1602-}

+1. An official who examines various articles as brick, tobacco, etc., to determine their suitableness for sale or conformity to regulations.

1685 *Boston Rec.* 173 Inspectors of Bricke. **1693** *Ib.* 213 Officers for the year . . . were chosen as followeth . . . Inspectors of Brickemacors,—

John Gooding, Rich Scates. **1763** *Md. Hist. Mag.* 171 Mr. John Johnson, Inspector at St. Leonard's Creek warehouse . . . was seized with an apoplectic fit. **1796** *Boston Directory* 288 Townsend, David, inspector of nails and pot-ash, Middle street. **1822** *Ann. 17th Congress* 1 Sess. I. 168 Regulations of the pay of Weighers, Gaugers, inspectors. **1840** *Niles' Nat. Reg.* 26 Sept. 64/2 Inspectors attention! We have complaints from England that the tare of barrels are fraudulently marked.

2. A police, military, or governmental officer charged with particular supervisory duties: (see quot. 1815). {1840–}

1711 *Boston Rec.* 78 Those Gentlem[en] whom they shall chuse as Inspectors of the Schools, Together with ye ministers of the Town [etc.]. **1788** *Mass. Centinel* 30 April, The Inspectors of the Police . . . have caused the law respecting the same to be published. **1802** *Ann. 7th Congress.* 1 Sess. 1306 There shall be . . . one adjutant and inspector of the army, to be taken from the line of field officers. **1815** *View N.Y. State Prison* 16 The government of this institution [the state prison] has been committed by the Legislature to a body of men appointed for that purpose, who are denominated *Inspectors.* **1867** Richardson *Beyond Miss.* vi. 88 A military board, consisting of . . . inspector, quartermaster [etc.]. **1891** 'Thanet' *Otto the Knight* 239 'You were a—an inspector, a warden,' he said huskily. **1912** F. J. Haskin *Amer. Government* 86 An Indian inspector suggested the thumbprint in addition to the mark, and all new Indian deeds bear this imprint.

+3. An official appointed to see that an election is conducted in a lawful manner.

1800 *Phila. Ordinances* 100 An act to . . . choose two inspectors of the general election for each . . . of the said wards. **1818** Fearon *Sketches of A.* 140, I was astonished to witness the anxiety felt by leading men, that *their* party should be elected *inspectors.* **1875** *Mich. Gen. Statutes* I. (1882) 708 The inspectors of such election, after the close of the polls, shall canvass the ballots.

+4. (See quotations.)

1814 *Harvard Coll. Laws* 58 One of the members of the Immediate Government shall have the office of Inspector of the College. His duty shall be from time to time to examine the exterior and interior State of the College public buildings . . . and to cause such repairs of them to be made as may to him appear necessary or proper. **1837** *Yale Coll. Laws* 22 And all estimates of damages, particularly stated, the Inspectors shall deliver to the President in writing with their names subscribed. **1851** Hall *College Words* 171 *Inspector of the college.* At Yale College, a person appointed to ascertain, inspect, and estimate all damages done to the College buildings and appurtenances, whenever required by the President.

Inspector general. An officer in charge of the system of inspection in an army or body of militia. {1702–}

1777 *Jrnls. Cont. Congress* IX. 1024 It is essential . . . that an appointment be made of inspectors general. . . . The duty of these officers [shall] be as follows: To review . . . the troops, and to see that every officer and soldier be instructed in the exercise and manœuvres which may be established by the Board of War: that the rules of discipline are strictly observed, and that the officers command their soldiers properly, and do them justice. **1798** *Ann. 5th Congress* I. 623, I nominate Alexander Hamilton, of New York, to be Inspector General of the Army, with the rank of Major General. **1844** Featherstonhaugh *Slave States* 29 In New York a young lawyer, for political services, is named *Inspector-General* of the Militia—an office without duties and without emolument, as the militia never assembles in a body. **1881–5** McClellan *Own Story* 124 The duties of the Inspector-General's Department, during the whole period of my command of the Army of the Potomac, were performed by Col. D. B. Sackett. **1897** *Outing* April 77/2 General George L. Beal was also appointed Inspector-General [of the National Guard of Maine].

Install,** *v.* **+tr.* (See quot. 1828.) — **1788** *Presb. Church Constitution* 405 The presbytery shall . . . ordain and install him pastor. **1828** Webster s.v., To install a clergyman or minister of the gospel, is to place one who has been previously ordained, over a particular church and congregation, or to invest an ordained minister with a particular pastoral charge. **1874** Aldrich *P. Palfrey* xi, The Rev. James Dillingham was formally installed pastor of the Old Brick Church.

***Instal(l)ment.** +The action of installing an ordained minister in a new charge. — **1759** *Essex Inst. Coll.* XLIX. 2, I went to an Instalment at Stoneham where Mr. John Serls took upon him the pastoral Charge of the Church. **1788** *Presb. Church Constitution* 405 When a call shall be presented to any minister or candidate, it shall always be viewed as a sufficient petition from the people for his instalment.

+Instal(l)ment man. A man who collects payments from purchasers of goods on the installment plan. — **1887** *Courier-Journal* 18 Jan. 3/7 Installment men and agents generally will find just what they need by addressing Installment Dealers' Supply Co. **1909** 'O. Henry' *Roads of Destiny* 47 The poor . . . when they get money . . . exhibit a strong tendency to spend it for stuffed olives . . . instead of giving it to the instalment man.

+Instal(l)ment plan. The plan or method of paying for goods in installments. Also fig. (Cf. the British *hire-purchase system.*) — **1886** Howells *Minister's Charge* 206 Lemuel . . . was told, when he said he could not afford the suit he fancied, that he might pay for it on the instalment plan. **1897** Flandrau *Harvard Episodes* 91 Pay on the instalment plan for thirty or forty years . . . the way people do when they buy a piano or a set of Kipling—or any old thing. **1909** Fort *Outcast Manufacturers* 317 You can get anything on the instalment plan nowadays. **1921** Paine *Comr. Rolling Ocean* 187 This is still a valuable ship, . . . even if she is floating around the high seas on the installment plan.

***Institute.**

+1. A school or college, often of a specified type; also, the building used by such an institution.

1830 Watson *Philadelphia* 248 The simple, unassuming apellation [*sic*] of 'school' was the universal name till about the year 1795; after that time 'academies,' 'seminaries,' 'lyceums,' 'institutes,' &c. were perpetually springing up in every quarter among us. **1868** *Rep. Comm. Agric. 1867* 326 The Institute of Technology is a purely scientific school. **1882** Lathrop *Echo of Passion* i, The Institute was a large, nondescript wooden building with an immense colonnade, where they were boarding; so called because in winter it served the purpose of a country academy for young women. **1883** *Century Mag.* Sept. 793/1 An elaborate plan for Girard College, that it might be organized . . . as a technical institute. **1898** Canfield *Maid of Frontier* 146 Abla . . . had received the best of training from Mons. Guillaume, especially imported by the Smithville Ladies' Institute at tremendous salary. **1908** *Mass. Inst. Technology Cat.* Dec. 33 In these Courses . . . the Institute aims to afford . . . the additional instruction . . . essential to a liberal education.

2. A somewhat loose association organized for the purpose of affording adults a means of increasing their knowledge of various subjects. {1829–}

1841 *Lowell Offering* I. 142 Martha . . . mentioned the evening schools for . . . factory girls. She also spoke of the Lyceum, and Institute, and other lectures. **1877** *Harper's Mag.* April 724/2 Social libraries embrace the athenæums, young men's associations, institutes, and subscription libraries in general.

+3. A short series of meetings planned to improve the professional knowledge and methods of teachers, farmers, etc.

1890 J. G. Fitch *Notes Amer. Sch. & Training Coll.* 90 By an 'Institute' is meant a sort of normal class, held periodically for the teachers of a district, and furnishing instruction in the art and practice of education, and an opportunity for the discussion of methods. Institutes are, in fact, migratory and occasional academies. **1902** Clapin 240 Farmer's institutes, lasting two or three days, with lectures and discussions, are especially very common at the West. **1906** *Springfield W. Repub.* 3 May 12 A well-attended teachers' institute under the direction of the board of education was held in the high school Friday.

***Institution.** +Used particularly with reference to the practice in the southern states of keeping slaves. *Obs.* (Cf. Peculiar institution.)

Illustrated extensively by Thornton.

1835 Channing *Slavery* iii, There are masters who . . . see slavery as it is. . . . They deplore and abhor the institution. **1844** Featherstonhaugh *Slave States* 38 Revolting as all these atrocious practices are, still this 'Institution'—a term with which some of the American statesmen dignify slavery and the circumstances inherent to it . . . does not appear to me to have been fairly placed before the judgment of mankind. **1854** Lincoln in Victor *Hist. Southern Rebellion* I. 142/2 When it is said that the institution exists, . . . I can understand and appreciate the saying. **1881** *Congress. Rec.* 28 April 418/2 Down with it [the defeated South] . . . went the institution, and there ended that 'irrepressible conflict.'

***Institutor.** +A bishop or one who acts for him in instituting a minister into a church or parish. — **1808** *P.E. Ch. Bk. Com. Prayer* (1823) 674/2 Then shall the Priest who acts as the Institutor receive the Incumbent within the rails of the Altar.

***Instruct,** *v.* **+1.** *tr.* To direct (an elected representative or delegation) how to vote regarding a particular candidate or matter. Often as *ppl. a.* in the phrase *instructed delegation.* **+2.** *To instruct out,* of a state legislature, to direct a United States senator to vote in a way that is so repugnant to his own views as to result in his resignation. *Obs.* — (1) **1817** [see Instruction]. **1828** *Niles' Reg.* 2 Feb. 879/2 Mr. Barnard presented a resolution of the legislature of Pennsylvania, instructing the senators, and requesting the representatives from that state in congress to procure the establishment of such a tariff [etc.]. **1841** *Congress. Globe* App. 9 June 74/2 The twenty-four towns of the Congressional district of the honorable gentleman from Massachusetts have a right to instruct him. **1904** *New York Times* 31 March 8 A delegation instructed for Judge Parker will go to St. Louis from this State. **1916** Thoburn *Stand. Hist. Okla.* II. 702 Barnes [used his influence] . . . to secure an instructed delegation from Oklahoma. (2) **1862** *N.Y. Tribune* 22 Jan. 4/6 Mr. Tyler . . . opposed the removal of the U.S. deposits from the U.S. Bank by General Jackson's order, and was in 1836 instructed out of the Senate on that issue, having previously been very strongly sustained by the Legislature [of Virginia].

***Instruction.** +The giving, by state legislatures, conventions, etc., of specific voting directions to senators, representatives, delegates, etc.; *pl.*, the directions themselves.

1817 Calhoun *Works* II. 177 The ear of this House [the House of Representatives] . . . is closed to truth and reason. What has produced this magic spell? Instructions! . . . Have the people of this country snatched the power of deliberation from this body? *Ib.* 177–8 This doctrine of implied instruction . . . is very different . . . from the old doctrine, that the constituents have a right to assemble and formally to instruct the representative; and though I would not hold myself bound to obey any such instructions, yet I conceive that the doctrine is not of a very dangerous character. **1827** CLAY *Speeches* (1860) I. 300 An instruction . . . [is addressed] only to the Senators of the United States. **1841** *Congress. Globe* App. 9 June 74/2 Minorities may petition, majorities enjoy the higher right of instruction. **1904** *N.Y. Globe* 30 March 2 The state convention will send 78 delegates to St. Louis with ironclad instructions for Judge Parker.

+**Instructive ballot.** (See quotation.) — **1897** *Congress. Rec.* 18 Feb. 1970/1 [The law of Illinois] provided, also, that accompanying these ballots should be eight 'instructive ballots'—ballots prepared for the instruction of the voters, sample ballots.

***Instructor.** Also **instructer.** +A college teacher. Applied usually to one whose rank is below that of professor.

1722 in Peirce *Hist. Harvard University* 232 Voted . . . that Mr. Judal Monis be *improved* as an instructor of the Hebrew language in the College. **1763** *Ib.* 234 That Sir Sewall, B.A., be the Instructer in the Hebrew and other learned languages for three years. **1817** *N. Amer. Rev.* Nov. 147 The officers of the University are, at present, twenty Professors, . . . Private Instructer in Mathematics, and Instructer in the French and Spanish Languages. **1834** PECK *Gaz. Illinois* 86 Erastus Colton, A.B. Instructor in the Preparatory Department. **1891** *Univ. of Chi. Official Bul.* No. 1, 11 Lecturers and Teachers . . . shall be Classified as follows: . . . The Instructor [etc.]. **1921** PAINE *Comr. Rolling Ocean* i. 10 A better income than the salaries of some of the instructors at Follansbee College.

Instrument-maker. One who makes instruments, esp. mathematical or scientific instruments. {*a*1691–} — **1695** SEWALL *Diary* I. 397 Jacob Mason, the Instrument-maker, died last night very suddenly. **1789** *Boston Directory* 187 Hagar William G. mathematical instrument-maker. **1799** in H. M. Brooks *Gleanings* 43 Samuel Thaxter, Mathematical Instrument Maker.

***Insurance.**

1. The act of insuring property or life against loss or damage; the amount for which property or life is insured; the contract by which provisions for such protection are made. {1651–}

'*Assurance* . . . is retained in Great Britain in the nomenclature and use of the majority of life insurance companies. But in general popular use, insurance is the prevalent term' (*O.E.D.*).

1649 *Boston Rec.* 256 Pray you pay Mr. Farrell for his paines & for the insurance. **1738** W. STEPHENS *Proc. Georgia* 130 He had fixed up an Office of Insurance, where he would insure any of their Safeties after the Rate of from 5 to 15 per Cent. **1839** *S. Lit. Messenger* V. 7/1 By these policies, insurance in New York is effected by the mere act of shipment, upon all goods shipped by the packets. **1840** *Niles' Nat. Reg.* 16 May 165/1 In case of death of the wife, . . . the amount of the insurance may be made payable . . . to her children. **1885** HOWELLS *S. Lapham* xxvii, If he . . . had looked after the insurance of his property [etc.]. **1912** NICHOLSON *Hoosier Chron.* 389 Stories as old as the hills about Jews burning down their clothing-stores to get the insurance.

2. Attrib. with *affair, business, commissioner,* etc.

1774 J. ROWE *Diary* 266, I had a Long Conversation with Tristram Dalton on the Insurance affairs. **1808** *Ann. 10th Congress* 2 Sess. 24 It would be found that no property was more sought after than insurance stock. **1869** Insurance business [see INSURANCE COMPANY]. **1894** WARNER *Golden House* xv, If the Street knew this it would say it was insurance-money. **1911** *Okla. Session Laws* 3 Legisl. 119 A tax . . . is hereby levied . . . to be collected . . . by the insurance commissioner.

Insurance agent. An agent for an insurance company. — **1866** *Internal Revenue Guide* 73 Insurance agents shall pay ten dollars. **1887** *Courier-Journal* 2 Feb. 8/4 He has been a practising lawyer and insurance agent for some years. **1898** *Kansas City Star* 19 Dec. 1/4 James S. Bailey, insurance agent, was a great shock to the lawyers. **1916** DU PUY *Uncle Sam* 98 The next day the insurance agent deposited for discount a sixty-day note for $300.

Insurance company. A company, or corporation, organized for the purpose of undertaking insurance of one or more kinds (life, fire, accident, etc.).

1784 in Brooks *Days of Spinning-Wheel* (1886) 62 The Gentlemen forming this Insurance Company, whose names are inserted in each Policy. **1820** *Plough Boy* I. 302 One Insurance Company, incorporated last year, in New York, has to pay about 50,000 dollars to the sufferers by the fire at Savannah. **1869** *Mich. Gen. Statutes* I. (1882) 1104 The term agent . . . shall include . . . any other person . . . who shall in any manner aid in transacting the insurance business of any insurance company not incorporated by the laws of this state. **1884** 'CRADDOCK' *Where Battle Was Fought* 178, Other people have some rights under the law—even an insurance company. **1911** PERSONS, etc. *Mass. Labor Laws* 320 No insurance company to issue policy for over three years.

Insurance man. =INSURANCE AGENT. — **1879** *Harper's Mag.* July 215 The insurance men . . . would . . . insure the lives of the hands who were at work there. **1916** DU PUY *Uncle Sam* 103 In Royerton it was easy to find many intimates of the insurance man.

Insurance office. An office kept for carrying on insurance business. {1651–} — **1759** in Brooks *Days of Spinning-Wheel* (1886) 63 The Insurance Office . . . kept in . . . King-Street: where the Business of Insurance is carried on as usual. **1807** *Mass. H.S. Coll.* 2 Ser. III. 30 There are at Nantucket two banks and two insurance offices. **1874** ALDRICH *P. Palfrey* iv, He would cover his maladroit move by getting his nephew into a New York banking-house or an insurance office at once.

Insurgent. A rebellious member of a group {1765–}, as +one who opposed the excise laws in the Whisky Rebellion, a supporter of the Confederacy in the Civil War, or a rebellious member of a political party. Also attrib. — **1794** *Ann. 3d Congress* 954 Resolved, That provision be made by law, for compensating the sufferers by the depredations of the insurgents in the Western counties of Pennsylvania. **1823** THACHER *Military Jrnl.* 512 Lincoln however, conducted with such address and energy, that the insurgents were routed from one town to another. **1866** CARPENTER *At White House* 214 Mr. Lincoln . . . suggested that there was a question as to the right of the insurgent States to return at once. **1904** CRISSEY *Tattlings* 390 'Sugarlips' Sunridge . . . can tell almost as good a story as the Insurgent candidate.

***Insurrection.** A revolt against established authority. — **1689** *Doc. Hist. N.Y. State* II. 37 The Obligations lying upon me . . . [are] neither . . . (notwithstanding the Sd. Invasion insurrection, or other troubles) . . . any ways vacated or Superceded. **1747** *N.J. Archives* 1 Ser. VI. 472 This insurrection has happen'd in the County where the next term is to be held. **1794** *Ann. 3d Congress* 907 We might [inquire] into the causes of the [Whisky] insurrection. **1840** *Niles' Nat. Reg.* 14 Nov. 176/2 We learn . . . that a plot has been discovered among the slaves of the parish of St. Mary, for insurrection. **1857** in Johnson *Anderson Co., Kansas* 38 In consequence of insurrection throughout Kansas Territory . . . the probate and commissioners' court were unable to hold their regular or adjourned court.

+**Inswamp,** *v. tr.* and *intr.* To take refuge in a swamp; to conceal in a swamp. *Obs.* (Cf. ENSWAMPED *a.*) — **1676** *Conn. Rec.* II. 458 Who presently inswamped themselves in a great spruce swamp. **1775** ADAIR *Amer. Indians* 315 The violent exercise of running a great distance under the violent rays of the sun . . . would not allow him to inswamp. *Ib.* 386 [They] take an oblique course, till they inswamp themselves again, in order to conceal their tracks.

Intangible, *a.* and *n.* {1845} +Of property: (see quot. 1888). — **1888** BRYCE *Amer. Commonw.* II. II. xliii. 129 The largest part of a rich man's wealth, consists in what the Americans call 'intangible property,' notes, bonds, book debts, and Western mortgages. At this it is practically impossible to get, except through the declaration of the owner. **1914** *Cycl. Amer. Govt.* III. 496/1 The term 'personal property' . . . includes . . . visible property and intangibles.

Intelligence office. {1692–} +An employment bureau for household servants and domestic help.

1768 *Boston Gazette* 25 July. **1830** WATSON *Philadelphia* 220 Intelligence Offices. These offices for finding places for servants, began within a very few years and upon a very small scale. **1852** M. L. DUNCAN *America* 227 The same method of hearing where servants are to be found, is used in the United States as with us. What is here called a Register, is there called an Intelligence Office. **1876** SCUDDER *Dwellers* i. 19, I keep an intelligence-office. You will see . . . that I have unrivaled means for securing the most valuable help from all parts of the world. **1904** *N.Y. Ev. Post* 2 March 5 The intelligence offices in New York city supply fully one-half of the families having household help.

comb. **1866** *Internal Revenue Guide* 73 Intelligence-office keepers shall pay ten dollars.

+**b.** (See quot. 1828.) Also attrib.

1828 WEBSTER s.v., *Intelligence-office*, an office or place where information may be obtained. **1849** COOPER *Sea Lions* i, Nantucket itself had not more of this intelligence office propensity, or more of the true whaling *espirit [sic] de corps.* **1857** *Lawrence* (Kansas) *Republican* 28 May 1 General Land Agency, and Emigrant's Intelligence Office.

Intendant. {1652– in France; 1696–7– in England} An officer having various functions in certain colonies and in French and Spanish parts of North America. *Obs.* Also *intendant general.*

[**1744** A. DOBBS *Hudson's Bay* 21 The Intendant of Canada wanted to discover these Countries from thence.] **1776** *R.I. Col. Rec.* VII. 572 There shall be two persons annually appointed by this General Assembly, as intendants of trade. **1789** MORSE *Amer. Geog.* 428 Charleston was . . . divided into 13 wards, who choose as many wardens, who, from among themselves, elect an intendant of the city. **1814** BRACKENRIDGE *Views La.* 89 The mode of carrying on the Indian traffic [in La. under Sp. rule] . . . was by monopolies, in which the interest of the governor or intendant was alone consulted. **1829** SHERWOOD *Gaz. Georgia* (ed. 2) 135 Milledgeville is governed by an Intendant and four Commissioners. **1857** BENTON *Exam. Dred Scott Case* 55 The American Governor . . . was to replace the Spanish Intendant General in that important province.

transf. **1855** MARETZEK *Crotchets* 18 Some of the male members of the chorus . . . were occupied in a game of cards with the 'General Intendant' of Mr. Fry's Opera.

Intercollegiate, *a.* Pertaining to contests between teams representing two or more colleges. {1884–} Also absol. — **1873–4** *Harvard Univ. Cat.* 248 Write not less than four, or more than eight, pages upon one of the following subjects: — . . . Intercollegiate regattas [etc.]. **1897** *Outing* May 179/2 Mr. Davies of Harvard defeat[ed] Mr. Taylor of the same college . . . in the two-mile bicycle race at the inter-collegiate games in New York city. **1899** QUINN *Penna. Stories* 196 He's doing the distance in fifty seconds now, and will be down to my time by the Inter-collegiate. **1914** J. H. GARDINER *Harvard* 137 The coach . . . is a member of the Intercollegiate Rules Committee. *Ib.* 144 Harvard also sends a [track] team to take part in the Intercollegiate games.

***Interest.** +A plantation or landed estate. Often in proper names. — **1663** *Charlestown Land Rec.* 84 Fencing Stuffe from of our wood interest on Maulden Common. **1700** in *Md. Hist. Mag.* XX. 185 Johns Interest. **1836** GILMAN *Recoll.* (1838) xiii. 90 Papa was visiting his planting interest on Edisto.

+**Interest lands.** *pl.* Lands set aside to secure the payment of interest on bonds. — **1859** *Ill. Central Railroad Lands* 16 The Company's lands are respectively designated as Construction, Free-lands, and Interest Lands.

Interference. {1783–} +**1.** *Patent law. attrib.* Pertaining to conflicting claims to prior right in a patent. +**2.** *Football.* The action of interfering with a tackler, or tacklers, so as to make the way clear for the runner. — **(1) 1888** *Scribner's Mag.* Aug. 190/2 An application for a patent which, after an interference litigation with Edison, was finally issued to Maxim. **1903** *Congress. Directory* (58th Congress Extraord. Sess.) 251 The Commissioner of Patents, . . . has appellate jurisdiction in the trial of interference cases. **(2) 1894** *Outing* XXIV. 112/2 The special feature of American Rugby arises from the principle of interference to aid the man running with the ball. **1903** *N.Y. Ev. Post* 23 Nov. 6 Much that seemed intentional rough play was the 'interference' which, forbidden by the English rules, is the most characteristic feature of our game. **1923** D. C. FISHER *Rough-Hewn* xxv, Neale [was] uselessly buried under the interference.

+**Interior Department.** A division or branch of the federal government that deals with matters, as pensions, Indians, education, etc., not included within the scope of other departments.

1859 BUCHANAN in *Pres. Mess. & P.* V. 543 According to a report from the Interior Department . . . the lands given to the States amount to 6,060,000 acres. **1883** *Century Mag.* Aug. 512/2 In 1852, a report in regard to these Indians was made to the Interior Department by the Hon. B. D. Wilson, of Los Angeles. **1898** *Kansas City Star* 18 Dec. 4/1 [The bill] did not contain a single item which had not been approved by the . . . Interior department. **1900** *Independent* LII. 412/2 The transfer of these and various other related bureaus to the Department of Commerce would greatly relieve . . . the Treasury and Interior Departments. **1917** S. MATHER in *Nat. Park Service Rep.* 16 The Interior Department . . . will control the destinies of the Sand Dunes National Park.

+**Interline,** *a. Railroad.* Of or pertaining to two or more lines or roads. — **1897** *Columbus Dispatch* 26 Feb. 9/3 Among the subjects [for discussion] will be . . . uniform contract for interline ticket. **1903** E. JOHNSON *Railway Transportation* 124 If the shipment made is to be through freight, a 'joint' or 'interline' way-bill of merchandise is used.

***Interlinear.** +*College.* A book containing text in a foreign language with a translation between the lines. — **1850** THAXTER *Poem before Iadma* 20 Then [he] devotes himself to study, with a steady, earnest zeal, And scorns an 'Interlinear,' or a 'Pony's' meek appeal. **1851** HALL *College Words* 171 *Interlinear*, a printed book, with a written translation between the lines.

Interliner. {1652} + =prec. — **1832** *Tour through College* 25 Ponies, Interliners, Ticks, Screws, and Deads (these are all college verbalities) were all put under contribution. **1852** FELTON *Mem. J. S. Popkin* p. lxxvii, He was a mortal enemy to translations, 'interliners,' and all such subsidiary helps in learning lessons.

Interlock, *v.* {1632–} +*intr.* Of the heads or sources of rivers that flow in different directions: To lie or be situated between or adjacent to each other. Also transitive.

[**1693** T. CLAYTON in *Phil. Trans.* XVII. 791 The Heads of the Branches of the Rivers interfere and lock one within another . . . after the manner that an Indian explained . . . to me, when . . . he clapt the Fingers of one hand 'twixt those of the other, crying, they meet thus.] **1749** in J. Winsor *Miss. Basin* (1895) 241 This Branch [of the Susquehanna] interlocks with the Branches of Allegeny and the North Branch of Potomack. **1756** *Ib.* 217 [The] head-springs [of one of the branches of the Mississippi] interlocked on a neighboring mountain with the head-springs of another large river. **1770** WASHINGTON *Diaries* I. 418 [It] interlocks with the Branches of Split Island Creek. **1796** MORSE *Univ. Geog.* I. 718 A branch of the Hiwassee, called Amoia, almost interlocks a branch of the Mobille. **1808** PIKE *Sources Miss.* II. 135 The dry branches of [the Osage and Arkansas] . . . interlock within 20 yards of each other. **1840** BANCROFT *Hist. U.S.* III. 122 The journey, by way of the Ottawa and the rivers that interlock it, was one of more than three hundred leagues.

***Interlocutor.** +In a group of Negro minstrels, the performer who occupies the middle seat in the row, converses with the end men, and acts as chairman. — **1880** E. JAMES *Negro Minstrel's Guide* 2 An Amateur Negro Minstrel band . . . arranged on the stage as follows: Interlocutor or Middle Man, in the Center [etc.]. **1915** MATTHEWS in *Scribner's Mag.* June 756/1 The dignified interlocutor took his place in the middle of the semicircle.

Intermediate school. +(See quot. 1911.) — **1866** *Rep. Indian Affairs* 252 The branches usually taught in primary and intermediate schools receive attention here. **1893** *Harper's Mag.* April 806 Oh, she was a rose half-budded, in the intermediate school, And her face and form I studied twice as much as task or rule. **1911** MONROE, etc. *Cycl. Educ.* II. 430/2 In the North Atlantic group of states, the term 'intermediate school' is frequently still retained to designate the upper primary and the lower grammar grades of the elementary school.

+**Intermontane, Intermountain,** *a.* Between or amid mountains. — **1807** MEASE *Geol. Acct. U.S.* 59 Whatever of saline . . . the soil of the upland contains, is thus floated or rolled along to the low lands, and constitutes with proportional diversity and mixture, the intermontane soil. **1893** *Harper's Mag.* April 700/2 The irresistible tendency of emigration to the intermontane regions of the West, and the Northwest, already dedicated to freedom. **1900** *Congress. Rec.* 24 Jan. 1147/2 Polygamy . . . was taught by the Mormon Church throughout the whole of the intermountain country as a religious duty. **1907** *Springfield W. Repub.* 13 June 2 The opposition in the intermountain states will not find anything comforting in the president's remarks.

+**Intern(e).** [F.] A medical student who, having completed the courses of instruction in a medical school, is serving for a prescribed time as an assistant in a hospital in preparation for private practice. Also *internship.* — **1879** WEBSTER *Suppl.* 1563/1. **1914** GERRY *Masks of Love* 123 The young interne, standing before them, very trim in his white uniform, had alarmed them. **1923** WYATT *Invis. Gods* II. v. 85 The older man . . . became . . . attached to the young surgical interne. **1924** *Scribner's Mag.* Feb. 183/1, I was at that time just finishing my internship.

***Internal,** *a.* +Of taxes: Levied upon or derived from commerce and industry, etc., within the United States.

1792 HAMILTON *Works* III. (1850) 298 There can surely be nothing in the nature of an *internal duty* on a *consumable* commodity, more incompatible with liberty, than in that of an external duty, on a like commodity. **1802** CUTLER in *Life & Corr.* II. 60 Question to inquire into the expenditures in collecting each duty of the internal tax—Salt, loaf Sugar, Tea, and Coffee. **1838** *U.S. Mag.* I. 145 That ascendency, which launched our American Government on a sea of troubles, in the midst of such rocks of the *British channel* as a funding system, national bank, internal taxation, soon stranding Washington's administration on the quicksands of civil war. **1884** WELLS *Practical Economics* (1885) 163 Previous to the imposition of internal taxes by the Federal Government in 1862, raw or common whiskey was retailed freely throughout the country at from seven to fifteen cents per quart. **1914** H. E. SMITH *U.S. Federal Internal Tax Hist.* 291 The people of the United States, as a whole, did not oppose the internal taxes.

+**Internal improvement.**

1. Improvement of conditions within the country, esp. by the construction of means of transportation, as roads and canals, at national expense.

1819 *Amer. Farmer* I. 30 Virginia, . . . following the example of New-York, has begun the work of internal improvement. **1850** *Western Jrnl.* IV. 86 You are aware that a Board of Internal Improvement was established by authority of the Legislature of Missouri in 1839, and that during its existence examinations and surveys were made of the Osage, the Meramac, the North Grand, and the Salt rivers, of this State, and a route for a railroad was located from this city to the Iron mountain. **1851** *Whig Almanac 1852* 9/1 Opposed to the instinct of boundless acquisition stands that of Internal Improvement.

b. *concrete.* A public improvement in transportation, communication, etc.

1827 *Mass. Resolves 1824–8* 479 The Governor of the Commonwealth . . . is authorized to appoint . . . a Board of Internal Improvements, whose duty it shall be to attend to the examination of such routes for Canals and Railways, as the Legislature may . . . direct. **1874** GLISAN *Jrnl. Army Life* 484 The effect of these internal improvements has been to stimulate all branches of industry. **1891** WELCH *Recoll. 1830–40* 352 The policy of the general government was opposed to 'internal improvements.'

2. Attrib. with *branch, county, party.*

1832 BENTON *30 Years' View* I. 219/1 The Bank of the United States . . . wields at its pleasure, the whole high tariff and federal internal improvement party. **1839** *Indiana H. Rep. Jrnl.* 269 The county of Fayette, an internal improvement county, has decreased $719. **1848** POLK in *Pres. Mess. & P.* IV. 662 Involving the principle of the internal-improvement branch of the 'American system.'

Internal revenue.

1. Revenue derived from excise taxes, income taxes, etc., in distinction to customs duties.

1796 *Ann. 4th Congress* 1 Sess. 379 Mr. W. Smith moved the order of the day on the report of the Committee of Ways and Means on the Internal Revenue. **1865** in Fleming *Hist. Reconstruction* I. 173 That the Secretary of the Treasury proceed to nominate for appointment assessors of taxes and collectors of customs and internal revenue and such other officers as are authorized by law. **1886** ALTON *Among Law-Makers* 59 One species of indirect taxation is what is styled the 'Internal Revenue,' which taxes domestic evils, like the liquor traffic. **1914** *Cycl. Amer. Govt.* III. 214/1 The collection of internal revenue is made by a bureau of the Treasury Department.

2. Attrib. and comb. with *collection, collector,* etc.

1873 *Newton Kansan* 2 Jan. 2/1 The most important bills . . . are those reducing the internal revenue force. **1883** *Harper's Mag.* July 260/2 Covington and Newport . . . figure quite as largely as Hamilton County upon the tax list of the internal revenue collector. **1887** *Courier-Journal* 8 Jan. 4/2 The repeal of the internal revenue system was one of those things the people had no right to expect from the Democratic party. **1903**

A. B. HART *Actual Govt.* 7 The interior and the coast together are divided into 63 internal-revenue collection districts.

***Interpreter.** +One who interprets the statements of Indians to white men and vice versa: (see also quot. 1721). Cf. INDIAN INTERPRETER.

1619 *Va. House of Burgesses* 15 Captaine Henry Spelman . . . was examined by a relation upon oath of one Robert Poole Interpreter what conference had passed between the said Spelman & Opochancano. **1721** *New-Eng. Courant* 14–21 Aug. 4/2 The Treaty was managed by Interpreters from the Mingoe Language to the Delaware, and from that into English by different Persons. **a1772** WOOLMAN *Journal* 184 In conversation with them [the natives of Wehaloosing] by an interpreter, . . . I believed some of them were measurably acquainted with that Divine Power which subjects the rough and froward will of the creature. **1805** LEWIS in *L. & Clark Exped.* II. (1904) 361 Capt. Clark arrived with the Interpreter Charbono. **1836** IRVING *Astoria* I. 234 He was engaged to serve . . . as guide and interpreter when they should reach the country of the Crows. **1891** O'BEIRNE *Leaders Ind. Territory* 129/1 His mother was a Miss Ellis, daughter of Ellis, the great white interpreter, who transacted business between the United States government and the Choctaw people.

***Intersection.** The place where streets, railroads, etc. meet or cross. — **1858** HAWTHORNE *Fr. & It. Jrnls.* 22 We came to an intersection with another street. **1868** *N.Y. Herald* 28 July 4/1 Verdict, nobody to blame, with a recommendation that a flagman be stationed at the intersection.

+Interstate, *a.* Carried on between the states of the United States; pertaining to the interrelation of the states.

*a***1845** J. STORY cited by Worc. '60. **1855** in Hambleton *H. A. Wise* 242 He would . . . abolish the inter-State slave trade. **1865** *Nation* I. 63 The unsealing of the ports followed by the removal of all restraints on interstate traffic. To these is now added the farewell address of the managers of the Sanitary Commission. **1895** CHAMBLISS *Diary* 305 Those terms were invented by fanatics and foreigners to aggravate our interstate quarrel. **1903** *Chicago Chronicle* 11 April 2/1 Whenever the control of competing interstate carriers is secured . . . the antitrust law is violated.

+Interstate commerce. Commerce among the states of the United States. Also attrib.

1872 *Sup. Ct. Rep.* LXXXII. 272 The question . . . calls upon us to trace the line . . . between the limits of State sovereignty in imposing taxation, and the power and duty of the Federal government to protect and regulate interstate commerce. **1883** *Century Mag.* Sept. 783/2 On the question of inter-state commerce . . . our public men have nothing to say. **1887** GEORGE *40 Years on Rail* xi. 228 Before the Inter-State Commerce Bill became a law everybody . . . wanted a pass. **1913** LA FOLLETTE *Autobiog.* 461 My valuation measure . . . had been bottled up in the Committee on Interstate Commerce.

+b. *Interstate Commerce Commission,* an administrative board, with quasi-judicial powers, established in 1887 for the regulation of transportation and communication.

1887 *Statutes at Large* XXIV. 383 A Commission is hereby created and established to be known as the Inter-State Commerce Commission. **1903** E. JOHNSON *Railway Transportation* 92 The Interstate Commerce Commission, however, and the United States Supreme Court have not adopted this rule. **1913** LA FOLLETTE *Autobiog.* 461 After the Interstate Commerce Commission had ascertained the value of the physical properties of the railroads.

+Interstate commerce law. A federal law regulating commerce among the states. — **1887** *Courier-Journal* 5 May 4/3 He is greatly disappointed in the criticisms being made by the press and the public on the interstate commerce law. **1890** *Stock Grower & Farmer* 8 Feb. 3/4 The trunk lines will be compelled to accept the cars of the Ohio Railroad company under the provisions of the Inter State commerce law. **1903** *McClure's Mag.* Nov. 110/1 Congress . . . in 1887 passed an interstate commerce law forbidding railroad discrimination.

+Interterritorial, *a.* Pertaining to relations among territories of the United States. — **1888** *Philadelphia Ledger* 4 Dec. (*Cent.*), A call for an inter-territorial convention of the four north-western Territories—the two Dakotahs, Montana, and Washington. **1903** in Thoburn *Stand. Hist. Oklahoma* II. 755 At a nonpartisan interterritorial statehood convention held in this city today, . . . the following resolutions were unanimously adopted.

Interurban, *a.* and *n.* **1.** *adj.* and *n. attrib.* Connecting cities or towns. +Applied usually to electric railroads. +**2.** *n.* An interurban electric railroad. — (1) **1883** *Harper's Mag.* May 927/1 [The] increasing volume of inter-urban commerce. **1897** *Columbus Dispatch* 2 April, The families that lived to the left of the interurban bridge at Minneapolis have been driven out. **1903** *Sci. Amer. Suppl.* 16 May 22822/1 In a majority of cases the interurban lines have been specially constructed for operation by electricity. **1912** NICHOLSON *Hoosier Chron.* 405 An interurban car landed him in town at eleven o'clock. (2) **1914** *Electric Ry. Jrnl.* 3 Jan. 8 (*caption*), The Central Electric Railway Association and the Interurbans. **1925** *Ib.* 13 June 930/1 The suggestion . . . that the interurbans in the central territory should be consolidated is certainly a good one.

***Interval.**

'The following are the early forms: Enteruail, Enterual, Entervail, Entervaile, Enterval, Entervale, Entervall, Intervail, Intervaile, Interval, Intervale, Intervall, Intervayle, Intrevall. By about 1750 these had been reduced to the two forms [*i.e.*, interval, intervale] now common' (A. Matthews in *Mass. Col. Soc. Pub.* VI. 142).

+1. =INTERVAL LAND.

1647 *Suffolk Deeds* I. 85 Fifty Acres of Interval. **1754** in G. Powers *Hist. Sketches Coos* (1860) 21 And on this river there is a great quantity of excellent interval. **1805** T. BIGELOW *Journal* (1876) 5 The famous tract of interval in this town called the Great Rainbow is not within sight of the great road. **1837** PECK *Gaz. Illinois* I. 3 The term 'bottom' is used throughout the west to denote the alluvial soil on the margin of rivers, usually called 'intervals' in New England. **1888** J. D. WHITNEY *Names & Places* 231 An interval . . . is the space between a river and hills or mountains by which the lower, level portion of the river-valley is bounded.

2. Attrib. with *cornfield, farm, hay,* etc.

1736 GYLES *Captivity* 14 We cross'd a large Interval-Corn-Field. **1780** E. PARKMAN *Diary* 255 Elias carrys one Load of ye Interval Hay to Capt. Fisher. **1863** *Rep. Comm. Agric. 1862* 98, I have grown it on interval or alluvial soil. **1892** *Vt. Agric. Rep.* XII. 132 From Hardwick to Fairfax nearly all of our interval farms are under a high state of cultivation.

***Intervale.** +=INTERVAL LAND.

'From 17th c. in New England, associated with *vale*' (*O.E.D.*).

1653 *Lancaster Rec.* 29 We Covenant . . . to proportion to every ten pounds three acors of Land two of vpland and one of Entervale. **1673** *Groton Rec.* 46 The countrey hye way . . . was for the most part lyeing in the Intervailes wheirin their are seuerall soft places and litle brookes. **1736** *Lunenburg Rec.* 93–4 A Town way or Rode Laid out . . . Down to Mullipus Entervail . . . , and then Runing across a narrow peice of Entervail of Aberaham Sanderson. **1790** in Belknap *Hist. New-Hampshire* III. 397 They . . . desired to know what reason I had to think New-Hampshire would consent, inasmuch as it would take off a large tract of Pigwacket Intervales. **1816** *N. Amer. Rev.* III. 428 There are no boats or canoes in the river, and no place where they could be used, except in the intervales and millponds. **1856** WHITTIER *Poetical Works* 49/1 From the lake that never fails, Falls the Saco in the green lap of Conway's intervales. **1889** — in Pickard *Life Whittier* 740 This rainy season has left the mid-summer greener if possible than June, and I never saw the Saco intervales more lovely.

attrib. **1663** *Lancaster Rec.* 75 He is willing to take the 12 acres of medow for medow . . . and the swamp for soe much medow as it is worth, according as the intervaile swamp is ordered. **1892** *Vt. Agric. Rep.* XII. 126 Generally, away from the rivers with their fine intervale meadows, the farms are less stony, but composed of good land.

+Intervale land. =next.

1653 *Lancaster Rec.* 27 For the maintainanc of the minestree of Gods holy word . . . there shall be laid out . . . thirty acors of vppland and forty acors of Entervale Land and twelue acors of meddowe. **1694** *Mass. H. S. Coll.* 4 Ser. I. 103 Through this place runs a very curious river . . . ; and it has, on each side, several parcels of pleasant, fertile, intervale land. **1749** ELIOT *Field-Husb.* ii. 23 Planters . . . who settled by the large Rivers and Intervale Lands. **1794** S. WILLIAMS *Hist. Vermont* 35 In this descent and passage to the ocean, all the large rivers in this part of America, have also formed large tracts of intervale lands. **1815** *Mass. H. S. Coll.* 2 Ser. IV. 55 On this stream there is much meadow or intervale land. [**1884** S. E. DAWSON *Hand-Bk. Domin. Canada* 108 The spring freshets flood these wide valleys, and produce what is called 'intervale land' of great fertility.]

+Interval land. Flat alluvial land by the side of a river or other stream. (Cf. BOTTOM LAND.)

1683 in Temple & Sheldon *Hist. Northfield, Mass.* (1875) 95 Every person that has 60 acres granted of interval land, shall settle two inhabitants upon it. **1694** *Mass. H. S. Coll.* 4 Ser. I. 104 A curious river runs through the town, on ye banks of which yr is some interval land. **1736** *Concord* (N.H.) *Rec.* 28 A Committee to let out the Interval Land belonging to the School Right for the Year ensuing. **1788** in Imlay *Western Territory* (ed. 3) 597 The house-lots, in their nearest approach to the Ohio, are . . . separated from it by the last mentioned creek, and low interval lands of the first quality. **1809** KENDALL *Travels* III. 193 The *interval,* intended in New England geography, is the *interval* or *space between a river and the mountains*. . . . Hence, *interval-lands,* include meadow and uplands, and in general the whole of the narrow valley. . . . Among the interval-lands are to be reckoned the *swales,* or rich hollows, lying behind the uplands. **1832** BROWNE *Sylva* 309 [The white elm] delights in low, humid, substantial soils, such as in the Northern States are called *interval lands.* **1867** *Congress. Globe* 13 Feb. 1230/2 League Island is a common low interval land.

+Interval lot. A lot in a tract of interval land. *Obs.* — **1653** *Lancaster Rec.* 29 He which hath now more then his estate Deserveth in home Lotts and entervale Lotts shall haue so much more. **1717** *Ib.* 176 The entervale . . . was formerly granted to Danill Gaines to make up his entervale Lott. **1736** *Concord* (N.H.) *Rec.* 26 The Selectmen shall be a Committee to let out the Intervall Lots belonging to the School Rights.

Interventor. {1727–41} (See quotations.) — **1803** in *Ann. 8th Congress* 2 Sess. 1521 The interventor superintends all public purchases and bargains. **1889** *Cent.* 3157/2 *Interventor,* . . . an inspector in a mine, whose duty it is to report upon the works carried on, and upon the use made of supplies. Gregory Yale. (Western U.S.)

***Interview,** *n.* +A colloquy between a reporter and another person, in which an effort is made to obtain information for publication; the article in which the information is embodied; a statement made to the press. {1884–} — **1869** *Nation* 28 Jan. 67 The 'interview,' as at present managed, is generally the joint product of some humbug of a hack politician and another humbug of a newspaper reporter. **1871** *Harper's Mag.* Nov. 934/1 Unquestionably all reports of 'interviews' are seriously distrusted, so that if a writer or an orator should make statements and arguments, founded upon the tales of 'interviewing' reporters, he would fall into great discredit. **1894** SHUMAN *Steps into Journalism* 68 The newspaper interview is peculiarly an American product. **1925** BRYAN *Memoirs* 20 My correspondent had given out an interview denying that there had been any change in my name.

***Interview,** *v.* +*tr.* To have an interview with (a person); to obtain information from (a person) in conversation for purposes of publication in the press. {1869-} Also *interviewing* vbl. n. — **1869** *Nation* 28 Jan. 66 'Interviewing' is confined to American journalism. **1870** LONGFELLOW in S. Longfellow *H. W. Longfellow* III. 144 A northwest newspaper, in which I have been 'interviewed,' and private conversation reported to the public. **1879** RANOUS *Diary of Daly Débutante* 66 We were warned never to allow a reporter to 'interview' us on any pretext whatever. **1889** *Voice* 14 March, Congressman F. W. Rockwell . . . said he did not care to be interviewed. **1922** LORD *Young Man & Journalism* 32 Interview everybody [on] effect of his death on the election, get White House comment.

+**Interviewer.** A reporter who seeks to obtain information by interviewing. {1880-} — **1869** *Nation* 28 Jan. 67/2 'Interviewing' helps to establish the curious device of looking on the correspondent, whether interviewer or not, as . . . not at all under editorial control. **1875** STOWE *We & Neighbors* 291 Your press interviewers beset them on every hand. **1886** JAMES *Bostonians* 123 He was the most brilliant young interviewer on the Boston press. **1894** FORD *P. Stirling* 104 The interviewer's next remark is best represented by several 'blank its.' **1919** W. G. BLEYER *Feature Articles* 57 In studying an interview article, one can generally infer what questions the interviewer used.

Intolerant, *a.* {*a*1735-} +Unable to endure heavy shade. — **1898** PINCHOT *Adirondack Spruce* 22 If the intolerant species can get the start, . . . they may hold their position by growing above the other trees about them, as do Tamarack and Pine. **1905** *Forestry Bureau Bul.* No. 61, 14.

***Introduce,** *v.* *Commerce.* +*tr.* To offer for sale (a new product). — **1899** ADE *Doc' Horne* 203 He found employment as a house-to-house salesman and 'introduced' a new kind of soap.

Invalid chair. A reclining chair, usually on wheels, designed for the use of invalids. — **1865** WHITNEY *Gayworthys* 336 Jane Gair [was] sitting in her invalid chair, with her invalid gown and cap on. **1908** STEVENS *Liberators* 7 The only modern thing in the room was the invalid chair. **1924** HASKIN *Amer. Govt.* 379 Several employees . . . had to be brought to their jobs in invalid chairs.

+**Invalid pension.** A pension paid to a former soldier on account of invalidism. — **1793** *Ann. 2d Congress* 804 An engrossed bill to regulate the claims to Invalid Pensions was read. **1865** *Atlantic Mo.* Feb. 240/1 [During] July and August the relief agents brought to a successful issue . . . 203 cases of invalid pensions. **1887** *Courier-Journal* 2 Feb. 1/2 Representative Taulbee, for the Committee on Invalid Pensions, today reported adversely the Senate bill to pension the widows of Gen. Logan and Gen. Blair.

+**Invalid pensioner.** A former soldier to whom the federal government has granted a pension because of ill health. *Obs.* — **1782** *N.H. Comm. Safety Rec.* 307 Ordered that Lt. Joseph Huntoon & Capt. Chase Taylor continue on Quarter instead of Half pay, as Invalid Pensioners. **1789** *Ann. 1st Congress* I. 914 The House then went into a Committee on the bill making provision for the invalid pensioners. **1809** *Steele P.* II. 604 Sherwood Haywood Agent for Invalid pensioners.

Investigating committee. A committee appointed by legislative action to inquire into some matter of public importance. — **1838** *N.Y. Advertiser & Exp.* 14 March 1/2 Some of the New Jersey witnesses in the case of Ruggles are now here, and have been before the Investigating Committee of the Senate. **1894** *N.Y. Tribune* 10 June 1/3 E. R. Chapman . . . was the first witness before the Sugar Trust Investigating Committee to-day. **1924** *N.Y. Times* 13 March 1/7 [It would] be the first act of the investigating committee to call upon the Attorney General.

+**Invisible Empire.** One or other of the two Ku-Klux Klans. — **1870** W. H. HOLDEN *Proclamations Govr. N.C.* 31 There is a widespread and secret organization in this State, partly political and partly social in its objects; . . . known . . . as 'The Invisible Empire.' **1880** TOURGEE *Invisible Empire* iv, During 1866 the 'Invisible Empire' was organized in Tennessee. **1898** PAGE *Red Rock* 407 Go home . . . and leave the Invisible Empire to execute its dread decrees. **1924** MECKLIN *Ku Klux Klan* 108 Here is a large and powerful organization offering to solace his sense of defeat by dubbing him a knight of the Invisible Empire for the small sum of ten dollars.

Invisible green, *n.* and *a.* (See quot. 1864.) — **1864** WEBSTER 714 *Invisible green*, a very dark shade of green, approaching to black, and not easily distinguished from it. **1877** JEWETT *Deephaven* 61 Miss Martha Lorimer's invisible-green watered silk. **1887** *Harper's Mag.* July 306/2 His little tight jacket with the glass buttons I made for him outer my old invisible green dress.

+**Involuntary servitude.** Forced employment, esp. Negro slavery. — **1845** *Whig Almanac 1846* 44/1 North of said Missouri compromise line, slavery, or involuntary servitude (except for crime,) shall be prohibited. **1853** PIERCE *Ib. 1854* 14/2, I believe that involuntary servitude, as it exists in different states of this confederacy, is recognized by the constitution. **1864** in Fleming *Hist. Reconstruction* I. 121 Involuntary servitude is forever prohibited, and the freedom of all persons is guaranteed in said State.

+**Iowa, Ioway.** [Amer. Ind.]

1. An Indian of a Siouan tribe formerly resident in the Middle West; in pl., this tribe.

1836 IRVING *Astoria* I. 161 The Osage warriors . . . returned from a successful foray against the Ioways, in which they had taken seven scalps. **1840** *Niles' Nat. Reg.* 2 May 136/3 A band of Iowas, exceeding one hundred in number, have assumed a hostile attitude. **1841** BUCKINGHAM *Amer., N. States* I. 109 The Sioux and Ioways . . . were not so fine a race of men as the Sauks and Foxes.

2. *attrib.* **a.** In sense 1 with *Indian, tribe.*

1810 *Ann. 12th Congress* 1 Sess. II. 1858 An Iowa Indian informs me, that two years ago this Summer, an agent from the British arrived at the Prophet's town. **1839** VAN BUREN in *Pres. Mess. & P.* III. 512, I lay before you . . . a treaty concluded with the Omaha, Ioway, and Otoe tribes of Indians.

b. In the names of plants and trees associated with the state of Iowa.

1853 *Knickerb.* XLII. 202 Then hoe the corn, (Iowa-white, an esteemed present, that hung all winter long from the buck-horns in our town-sanctum,) which is now higher than our head by four inches. **1862** *Rep. Comm. Patents 1861: Agric.* 190 *Fragaria Iowensis*—Iowa strawberry. **1897** SUDWORTH *Arborescent Flora* 209 *Pyrus ioensis*. . . . Iowa Crab.

+**Iowan.** Also †**Iowaian.** A native or citizen of Iowa. — **1856** N. H. PARKER *Iowa as It Is* 56 Our ferry is busy all hours in passing over the large canvas-backed wagons, densely populated with becoming Iowaians. **1889** *Amer. Notes & Q.* IV. 81 An Iowan has just been acquitted, upon a second trial. **1893** 'THANET' *Stories* 43 The wayfarer may catch bird's-eye glimpses of the city, the vast river that the Iowans love, and the three bridges. **1909** PARKER *G. Cleveland* 134 Delegations of Iowans . . . had come to town in great force.

+**Ipecac. 1.** Any one of various North American plants, esp. *Tithymalopsis ipecacuanhae*, the roots of which have emetic properties. **2.** A medicine prepared from the root of this or of the South American ipecacuana. — (1) **1788** CUTLER in *Life & Corr.* I. 409 Examined several vegetables, the Pawpaw, Ipecac, Redbud, Spanish Oak, Honey-locust. **1857** GRAY *Botany* 114 *G[illenia] stipulacea*. . . . American Ipecac. . . . [Grows] from W. Pennsylvania and New York to Illinois and Kentucky. (2) **1852** *Florida Plant. Rec.* 80 It seames Like Nothing will brake the Fever hear Except Calomel, Ippecac and Qinine. **1876** HABBERTON *Jericho Road* 12 One day he was half mad with whisky, and went to the drug-store and ordered two ounces of arsenic, but the clerk gave him ipecac.

Ipecacuanha. {1682-} +=prec. 1.

*c*1729 CATESBY *Carolina* I. 24 *Anapodophyllon Canadense Morini*. . . . The May Apple. This Plant grows about a Foot and half high. . . . The root is said to be an excellent Emetic, and is used as such in Carolina; which has given it there the Name of Ipecacuana, the stringy Roots of which it resembles. **1788** CUTLER in *Life & Corr.* I. 427 Found vast quantities of Ipecacuanha on a hill. **1843** TORREY *Flora N.Y.* I. 201 *Gillenia stipulacea*. . . . American Ipecacuanha. . . . In the western part of the State. **1896** *Garden & Forest* IX. 282 Ipecacuanha. . . . A name for several North American plants, of which the roots, like those of the officinal *Cephaëlis*, possess emetic qualities (*Podophyllum, Euphorbia, Gillenia*, etc.).

attrib. **1832** WILLIAMSON *Maine* I. 125 *Ipecacuanha-spurge* has a large pulpous root. . . . It is a powerful emetic.

+**Ipswich sparrow.** (See quot. 1917.) — **1892** TORREY *Foot-Path Way* 54 The Ipswich sparrow . . . I have now seen at Nahant . . . from October to April. **1917** *Birds of Amer.* III. 24 Ipswich Sparrow, *Passerculus princeps*, . . . is a songless Sparrow which . . . seems to have been first discovered near Ipswich, Mass., in 1868.

***Iris.** A genus of plants of the family Iridaceae having large, bright flowers; also, one or other of the many species, esp. the blue flag. — **1818** *Mass. H. S. Coll.* 2 Ser. VIII. 170 In July the lover of plants is gratified with . . . the white spirea, agrimony, the common iris. **1844** *Lowell Offering* IV. 217 The lilac and the iris . . . by their fading hues foretold a speedy farewell. **1880** CABLE *Grandissimes* 237 Yonder . . . [were] constellations of water-lilies, the many-hued iris [etc.]. **1916** L. H. BAILEY *Manual Gardening* 378 Irises thrive best in a rather moist soil.

***Irish,** *n.*

+**1.** *pl.* Irish immigrants in America. Also attrib. and transf.

1655 *Plymouth Laws* 100 That all such Scotes and Irish as are in any Township in this Government shall beare armes and traine. **1744** BRAINERD *Diary* (1902) 162, [I] went and preached, first to the Irish, and then to the Indians [in N.J.]; and in the evening was a little comforted. **1838** DRAKE *Tales & Sketches* 75 The Kentuckians have been called the Irish of America. **1872** 'MARK TWAIN' *Roughing It* xlvii. 334 His word was, 'No Irish need apply!' **1884** *Lisbon* (Dak.) *Star* 22 Aug., The Irish bolt continues. The Telegraph, a paper whose proprietors are Irish and Catholic, . . . entered the canvass for Cleveland.

2. Anger, passion. *colloq.* {Yorks. dial.}

1834 CROCKETT *Narr. Life* 30 Her Irish was up too high to do any thing with her. **1856** 'MARK TWAIN' *Adv. Snodgrass* 21 She'd got her Irish up now, and din't keer a scratch for bars and nothin else. **1859** BARTLETT 217 Col. Dick Johnson . . . used this Western substantive in one of his Eastern speeches: 'My friends say that my *Irish* is getting up.'

***Irish**, *a.*

1. Of textiles, etc.: Made or resembling those made in Ireland. (See also IRISH LINEN.)

1637 *Md. Council Proc.* 67 Shipped upon the good vessel . . . sixteene paire of irish stockings. **1684** I. MATHER *Providences* 27 [They] covered them with some Irish-Cloth of their own Garments. **1754** *S.C. Gazette* 1 Jan. 4/2 The goods on hand consist in . . . check mantuas and Irish stuffs, everlastings [etc.]. **1871** ROE *Army Lett.* 29, [I] shall wear my pearl-colored Irish poplin. **1913** LONDON *Valley of Moon* II. vi, She made ruffled chemises of sheer linen, . . . and nightgowns . . . trimmed with Irish lace.

2. Of places: Settled by Irish immigrants.

1800 TATHAM *Agric. & Commerce* 150 That powerful extent of rich and fertile vales, called the Irish Tract, that populous country which is situated between the Blue and Allegany ridges. **1809** CUMING *Western Tour* 177 Passing Millersburgh, and one of the first settlements, called the Irish station, . . . I spurred my horse past Nicholasville Court house. **1836** T. POWER *Impressions Amer.* 185 Enter an Irish village [in Penna.] . . . and a dozen [youngsters] will be under your horses feet in a moment.

3. Of persons: From Ireland; of Irish descent.

1708 *Boston News-Letter* 6 Dec. 4/2 Ran-away from his Master Ambrose Vincent, . . . an Irish lad call'd Darby Ragan, aged about 17 years. **1841** *N. Amer. Rev.* Jan. 209 The Irish laborer in America . . . undergo[es] privations, that in many cases, make his condition little better than it was at home. **1858** *Atlantic Mo.* Aug. 341/1 The Irish girls have found their way into the farmer's kitchen. **1868** *N.Y. Herald* 1 July 5/6 Some dispute arose between a party of Irish laborers . . . and some darkies. **1891** HOWELLS *Imperative Duty* i, Olney was uncomfortably aware of the Irish waiter standing . . . behind his chair.

4. Of plants and trees: Associated in some way with Ireland.

1856 OLMSTED *Slave States* 24, I noticed these, as well as the Irish and palmated ivy, growing . . . in the private gardens. **1868** GRAY *Field Botany* 100 Irish Broom, so called, but is from Portugal, is another species [of *Cytisus*], not hardy here. **1879** *Scribner's Mo.* Nov. 38/1 Close by are arranged . . . Irish yews. **1892** APGAR *Trees Northern U.S.* 199 Var. *Hibernica* (Irish Juniper) grows erect like a column.

5. Special combinations.

Irish dividend, an assessment on stock or shares in ownership; *Irish hint*, a broad or obvious hint; *Irish pendant* (*Naut.*), a piece of rope, etc., hanging loose; *Irish spoon*, a spade. *humorous* or *slang.*

1834 NOTT *Novellettes* I. 8 Various young men . . . intimated, in what might be called Irish hints that they had espied the worthy Mr. Hunt. **1840** DANA *Two Years* xxii. 221 There was no rust, no dirt, no rigging hanging slack, no fag ends of ropes and 'Irish pendants' aloft. **1862** NORTON *Army Lett.* 73 One company just passed armed with 'Irish spoons,' going out to work in the trenches. **1881** *Harper's Mag.* May 805/2 Members [of the N.Y. Philharmonic Society] found themselves in debt and obliged to declare an 'Irish dividend' to make the accounts balance.

+**Irish American**, *n.* An Irish immigrant in America; a son of Irish immigrants. — **1836** T. POWER *Impressions Amer.* I. 185 The accent of the Irish American . . . differ[s little] from that of the settler of a year. **1878** *N. Amer. Rev.* CXXVII. 9 It may be doubted whether . . . the young Irish-American is a better or safer citizen than his parent from Cork. **1900** *Congress. Rec.* 14 Feb. 1799/1 Out on the prairies of that great State [Missouri], . . . we do not hear any such terms as German-American, Irish-American . . . or French American.

+**Irish American**, *a.* Pertaining to Irish immigrants in the United States. — **1832** *New-Eng. Mag.* June 490 Irish-American Literature. **1900** *Congress. Rec.* 15 Jan. 805/1 The great body of our German and Irish American citizens are in favor of it.

Irisher. {1830– *dial.*} An Irish settler in the U.S. *colloq.* — **1807** C. SCHULTZ *Travels* I. 8 The inhabitants are mostly of German descent, and still, in a great measure, retain their national prejudices, and consider all who do not speak their own language either as *Yankees* or *Irishers*. **1827** *Western Mo. Rev.* I. 385 He could flog, in a fair fist fight, any Dutchman, Irisher, or Yankee in the place. *Ib.* 386 Jacob Barndollar . . . [asked] the fair Irisher, if she would marry him? **1836** T. POWER *Impressions Amer.* I. 185 All strangers [in a Penna. Dutch village] are suspected of being Irishers.

Irish linen. Linen produced in Ireland. Also attrib. — **1754** *S.C. Gazette* 1 Jan. 2/2 Samuel Peronneau hath just imported . . . a large assortment of Irish linnens, sheeting [etc.]. **1796** *Boston Directory* 270 Neil Getty, Irish linen store, Hanover street. **1837** SHERWOOD *Gaz. Georgia* (ed. 3) 20 A piece of broad-cloth, a piece of Irish linen, a cask of Tobacco-pipes. **1910** W. H. DOOLEY *Textiles* 179 French and Belgian linens while fine in thread are not as serviceable as Irish linen.

***Irishman.** **1.** An Irish immigrant in America; an American of Irish descent. **2.** (See quotation.) — **(1)** **1704** *Boston News-Letter* 8 May 2/2 Stollen the 4 instant . . . by an Irish man, speaks bad English. **1867** EDWARDS *Shelby* 66 We had two heavy guns in battery— . . . well served bv as reckless a lot of devil-may-care Irishmen as ever lit a port-fire. **1885** CRAWFORD *Amer. Politician* 40 Everything else is so thick with steam-engines and Irishmen that one could not possibly go across country. **1913** LONDON *Valley of Moon* I. iv, His elbow powerfully crushed on the ribs of a big Irishman who gave room. **(2)** **1709** LAWSON *Carolina* 159 The flat or mottled Pearch are shaped almost like a Bream. They are called Irish-men, being freckled or mottled with black, and blue Spots.

Irish potato. The common white potato. {1664} — **1685** in Blome *Isles & Terr. in Amer.* (1687) 123, I have planted the Irish Potatoes, and hope to have a brave encrease to transplant next year. **1750** J. BIRKET *Cursory Remarks* 9 They have . . . abundance of Garden Culture as Beans, . . . Asparagus, English or whats commonly called Irish Potatoes also the Sweet Potatoe. **1883** SWEET & KNOX *Through Texas* 64 In January he planted Irish potatoes. **1904** *N.Y. Globe* 28 March 3 His hide was as pink as a freshly scrubbed Irish potato.

***Iron.**

***1.** A silver-white metallic element of great malleability and ductility.

1607 Smith *Works* I. p. xlvi, The head [of the river] . . . where they gat . . . their Iron. **1643** *N.E. First Fruits* 11 Mineralls [have been] discovered and proved, as of Iron in sundry places. **1748** ELIOT *Field-Husb.* i. 2 In the early Times of the Country, the most of the Iron made and in use, was Taunton Iron, made of Bog Oar, and so coarse and brittle as to break in the working. **1794** *Mass. H. S. Coll.* 1 Ser. III. 175 Vast quantities of iron, both cast and wrought, have been made in this part of the country, for more than an hundred years past; but it was chiefly out of bog ore. **1821** *Amer. Jrnl. Science* III. 45 On the head of the river Trinity . . . were several blocks of native iron, from one thousand to seven or eight thousand pounds weight. **1883** RITCH *Illus. N.Mex.* 34 The resources of the Territory consists . . . likewise of copper, lead, manganese and iron. **1910** T. D. WEST *Amer. Foundry Practice* 314 The small cupolas are only practicable for melting small quantities of iron.

***2.** *pl.* Fetters or shackles.

1635 *Md. Council Proc.* 34 A new Sheriff . . . to whom he committed the keeping of the Prisoners in Irons. **1685** SEWALL *Diary* I. 111 James Morgan ordered to have Irons put on him. **1705** *Boston News-Letter* 4 June 2/1 Thomas Odell the Forger of the Bills of Credit of the Colony of the Massachusetts-Bay, being in Irons on Board Derick Adolph, . . . made his escape. **1775** *Jrnls. Cont. Congress* III. 378 He who is guilty of drunkenness . . . shall be put in irons until he is sober. **1837** *Diplom. Corr. Texas* I. (1908) 270 The passengers . . . were all stripped and searched . . . and four of them . . . were immediately put in double irons. **1867** RICHARDSON *Beyond Miss.* 150 They bore them triumphantly to a blacksmith's shop and cut off their irons.

+**3.** The rails of a railroad.

1871 *Republican Rev.* 16 Sept. 1/4 The ties for seventy miles were all bedded and the iron was on the way which it was expected to lay in ten days. **1880** *Cimarron News & Press* 19 Aug. 1/6 Thirty-five miles of iron are now in the Albuquerque yards. **1885** *Santa Fé Wkly. New Mex.* 30 July 4/3 Nearly a mile of iron has been laid on this end of the Los Angeles and San Gabriel valley railroad.

4. *attrib.* and *comb.* **a.** Designating places yielding iron.

1661 *Md. Council Proc.* 415 On Marettico or the iron hill mett them two Indians comeing from the Minquas Country. **1844** *Whig Almanac 1845* 5/1 Mr. Polk received large majorities in nearly every Iron County of New-York, New-Jersey and Pennsylvania. **1854** WHIPPLE *Prelim. Report Explor. Ry. Route* 13 The iron mountains [of Ark.] near the Missouri line are alone worthy a railroad. **1887** *Courier-Journal* 19 Feb. 5/3 Organized last week for the development of 17,000 acres of iron and manganese lands. **1902** HARBEN *A. Daniel* 137 She said she knew one [branch railroad] in the iron belt in Alabama that didn't own a car or an engine.

b. Designating the trade, industry, factories, etc., associated with iron.

1812 *Ann. 12th Congress* 1 Sess. II. 2073 The Directors of the New Hampshire Iron Factory . . . have expended a large sum of money in erecting furnaces . . . for the purpose of manufacturing bar iron and various sorts of cast iron ware. **1840** *Niles' Nat. Reg.* 20 June 242/3 The iron manufacture. . . . It appears that the manufacture of iron has increased in a remarkable degree. **1865** *Atlantic Mo.* June 694/1 Another branch of the Lake trade, . . . which promises to reach vast proportions in a few years, is the iron and copper trade of Lake Superior. **1880** *Harper's Mag.* Dec. 65 The oil industry has lent a powerful hand to the iron industry of Pittsburgh.

c. Designating persons engaged in the iron industry.

1846 *Whig Almanac 1847* 14/1 Whether this shall go farther or not will depend directly on the ability of our Iron-Makers to continue their operations under the new act. **1871** GROSVENOR *Protection* 238 As long as the iron-producers maintain their association, . . . the experience of 1832 and 1846 is likely to be repeated. **1898** *McClure's Mag.* X. 526/1 He was an iron molder and a good workman. **1906** LYNDE *Quickening* 343 Has the old iron-melter been taken in on it, do you think?

+**Iron City.** Pittsburgh, Pennsylvania: (see also quot. 1887). — **1853** BUNN *Old Eng. & New Eng.* 100 We told you . . . that New York was one of the dirtiest places we ever happened to have been in, but the Iron City (as Pittsburg is called), . . . throws it completely into shade. **1859** *Ladies' Repository* Jan. 51/1 Pittsburg, Pennsylvania, is the 'Iron City,' from its iron trade and manufactures. **1880** *Harper's Mag.* Dec. 57 Your true Pittsburgher glories in his city's name. . . . The great Iron City's mills and her wonderful furnaces are inspiring. **1887** *Courier-Journal* 8 May 16 (*advt.*), The Iron City! . . . South Pittsburg, Tenn., . . . is the manufacturing center of the world-famed Sequachee Valley.

Ironclad, *n.*

1. An armored naval vessel. {1863–}

1862 in F. Moore *Rebellion Rec.* V. II. 177 Next came . . . four of the 'iron-clads,' followed by the two ordnance and one supply steamer. **1865**

Nation I. 36 This extraordinary torpedo was not only adequate to blowing up a fleet of iron-clads, but to destroying whole regiments when employed in the army. **1875** *Chicago Tribune* 24 Nov. 1/7 Orders were issued to-day at the Navy Department . . . for the fitting up of five more iron clads. **1898** *Boston Herald* 1 June 12/4 In her day she was a battleship, but she . . . would be little more than sport for a modern ironclad. **1901** CHURCHILL *Crisis* III. 419 Those clumsy ironclads of his can't move backward or forward.

+**2.** *transf.* (See quotations.)

1867 EDWARDS *Shelby* 483 The West Pointers were the iron-clads in our wooden navy. **1889** 'MARK TWAIN' *Conn. Yankee* xxxix. 503 Things began to look serious to the ironclads [*i.e.*, knights in armor]. **1892** O. F. WHITNEY *Hist. Utah* I. 547 The ravages of the 'iron-clads' [grasshoppers] were wide-spread and far-reaching.

Ironclad, *a.*

1. Of a naval vessel: Protected by or cased with iron or steel plates. {1859–}

1861 *N.Y. Herald* 23 Sept. 5/2 Our government have at length made up their mind to build . . . iron clad ships. **1862** in McClellan *Own Story* 269 An iron-clad boat must attack Yorktown. **1868** NORTON & VALENTINE *Rep. Munitions War* 140 The armor plates of this vessel . . . (as will be seen when we come to speak of iron-clad ships) are, mainly six inches thick. **1897** C. A. DANA *Recoll. Civil War* 37 First came seven ironclad turtles and one heavy armed ram.

b. Of plants or trees: Able to resist cold.

1872 *Vermont Bd. Agric. Rep.* I. 54 Currants and gooseberries are iron clad as regards climate. **1882** *Maine Bd. Agric. Rep.* XXVI. 336 It is an early winter fruit, the tree not perfectly 'iron clad,' notwithstanding its origin, yet hardy enough for most places.

2. *fig.* Extremely strict or rigorous; unyielding; absolutely fixed. {1887–} (Cf. next.)

'Chiefly *U.S.*' (*O.E.D.*).

1884 *Boston Jrnl.*, 25 April, The law [relating to oleomargarine] . . . was drawn with care and is presumably ironclad. **1888** SHERIDAN *Memoirs* I. 198, I had then endeavored to persuade him to modify his iron-clad interpretation of the order. **1892** *Courier-Journal* 3 Oct. 6/4 There would be an iron-clad agreement. **1911** HARRISON *Queed* 114 He insisted on doing it after an ironclad schedule.

+**Ironclad oath.** *Hist.* (See quot. 1914.)

1866 *Congress. Globe* 14 Feb. 835/1 Traitors never would be troubled with the 'iron-clad oath,' for they never would have a chance to take it. **1880** TOURGEE *Bricks* 42 Every member of such board of registration should be able to take . . . the 'iron-clad oath,' that is, an oath that he had never engaged in, aided, or abetted any rebellion against the Government of the United States. **1886** POORE *Reminisc.* II. 251 Some of those applying, however, had served in the Confederate army, and were not able to take what was known as the 'iron-clad oath.' **1914** *Cycl. Amer. Govt.* II. 239 *Iron-Clad Oath*, a name given the stringent oath of office prescribed by Congress in 1862 and applied at the close of the Civil War for office holders in the reconstructed states. It aimed at the exclusion of all who had participated in the 'rebellion.'

b. In transferred and figurative use.

1873 MILLER *Amongst Modocs* xxvi. 304 Some hard, iron-clad oaths and then shot after shot. **1900** *Congress. Rec.* 25 Jan. 1207/1 Members-elect . . . could be kept out by the exaction of an iron-clad oath.

Ironer. {1880–} One who irons laundry. {1883}

1782 *Royal Gazette* (Charleston, S.C.) 13 July 4/1 To be sold, a bargain, twelve negroes, among whom are two young wenches, who are good cooks, washers, and ironers. **1835** INGRAHAM *South-West* II. 197 The planter . . . inquired of the girl her capabilities as seamstress, nurse, and ironer. **1852** in Stowe *Key* 139/1 We have now on hand . . . a large and well-selected stock of Negroes, consisting of field-hands, house-servants, mechanics, cooks, seamstresses, washers, ironers, etc. **1895** 'CRADDOCK' *Myst. Witch-Face Mt.* 241 She was what is known as a 'beautiful washer and ironer.' **1913** LONDON *Valley of Moon* I. i, Occasionally an ironer lost the stride for an instant, gasped or sighed, then caught it up again.

Iron fence. A fence made of iron rods, bars, etc. — **1847** *Santa Fe Republican* 24 Sept. 1/4 Iron Fences are becoming common in the U. States, and will soon be made cheap. **1850** *New Eng. Farmer* II. 171 This cut represents an iron fence. . . . It is well adapted to cemeteries, front yards, and other purposes. **1907** *St. Nicholas* Oct. 1117 The crowd proceeded slowly to the iron fence.

Iron founder. One who is engaged in the founding or casting of iron. {1817–} — **1777** *N.J. Archives* 2 Ser. I. 290 Deserted, . . . a certain John Williams, . . . an iron-founder by trade. **1818** FLINT *Lett. from Amer.* 61 Enumeration of the manufacturing people of Pittsburg: . . . 4 Iron Founders. **1865** *Atlantic Mo.* XV. 466, I had Fred immediately apprenticed to an iron-founder in the neighborhood.

Iron foundry. An establishment in which iron products are cast or made. {1784–} — **1815** DRAKE *Cincinnati* 143 Cincinnati has no iron foundery; but is well supplied with blacksmiths. **1831** PECK *Guide* 199 At Mount Carmel in Wabash county is an iron foundry. **1878** in Summers *Ann. S.W. Va.* 1557 We have three large and well-kept hotels, nine variety stores, . . . a billiard saloon, an iron foundry. **1890** HOWELLS *Boy's Town* 57 Sometimes the schoolboys ventured inside of the flour-mill and the iron-foundry.

Iron furnace. A furnace used for reducing iron ore. — **1775** BURNABY *Travels* 47 There is an iron furnace, a forge, two saw-mills, and a bolting-mill [in Va.]. **1801** W. STRICKLAND *Agric. U.S.* 30 At Elizabeth iron furnace, some of the head men have £90. per annum. **1880** *Harper's Mag.* Sept. 587 He at last persuaded Bezy to let him go to work in the iron furnace at Hampton Falls. **1906** LYNDE *Quickening* 26 On the banks of the river, there was the antiquated iron-furnace.

Ironhead. 1. *local.* =GOLDEN-EYE 1. **2.** The wood ibis, *Mycteria americana.* — (1) **1888** G. TRUMBULL *Names of Birds* 79 At Morehead, N.C., [the American golden-eye, *Glaucionetta clangula americana*, is called Iron-head. **1917** *Birds of Amer.* I. 138. (2) **1917** *Ib.* I. 179 'Goard Head,' 'Iron Head,' and 'Gannet' are the appellations given to these birds by many swamp-dwellers to whom the name Wood Ibis is unknown.

+**Iron horse.** A locomotive. Also transf. — **1846** *Congress. Globe* 6 Feb. 323 The iron horse (the steam-car) with the wings of the wind, his nostrils distended with flame, salamander-like vomiting fire and smoke. **1854** THOREAU *Walden* 127 The stabler of the iron horse was up early this winter morning by the light of the stars amid the mountains, to fodder and harness his steed. **1891** WELCH *Recoll. 1830–40* 422 The Iron Horse has acquired a speed as of 'a rushing mighty wind.' **1913** BARNES *Western Grazing Grounds* 23 In 1867 began the movement to relieve the Texas ranges of their surplus cattle by establishing those great trails . . . into Kansas. There they met the iron horse and found an opening to the eastern markets.

Ironing board. A large board upon which clothes are ironed. — **1854** CUMMINS *Lamplighter* xxxiii. 307 She carried over one arm a dress . . . , together with other articles evidently fresh from the ironing-board. **1889** *Century Mag.* April 912/1 [She] faced her visitor across the ironing-board. **1905** VALENTINE *H. Sandwith* 97 The light fleecy blankets her grandmother . . . had woven and bequeathed with strict injunction they should never be used 'for the ironing board.'

Ironing table. A table upon which clothes are ironed. {1840–} — **1856** STOWE *Dred* I. 62 She stands there at her ironing table. **1875** — *We & Neighbors* 164, 'I don't really know whether I shall go,' . . . said Mrs. Betsey confidentially to Dinah over her ironing-table. **1887** ALDEN *Little Fishers* vi, 'For curtains?' said Mrs. Smith, coming back with a start from her ironing-table.

Iron man. {1617–} A workman in an iron factory; a manufacturer of iron. {1875} — [**1649** *Descr. Virginia* 5 Skilfull Iron-men for the Works sent out of England.] **1654** *Mass. H. S. Coll.* 4 Ser. VI. 290 Mr. Foote . . . tould me that you had speech with him about his getting of jron men to Pequt. **1783** in Chalkley *Scotch-Irish Settlement Va.* II. 410 Henry Miller, Iron Man. *Ib.* 411 Isaac Zane, Iron Man. **1870** MEDBERY *Men Wall St.* 186 He was brought much in contact with iron men, and kept the books for two large houses concerned in this trade. **1906** LYNDE *Quickening* 85 It'd be a thousand pities to spoil a good iron man and engineer to make a poor preacher, Martha.

Iron master. The master or owner of an ironworks. {1674–} — **1819** SCHOOLCRAFT *Mo. Lead Mines* 55 Mr. Miller, an iron-master of Augusta county, Virginia, . . . thought the ore of an excellent quality. **1850** *Rep. Comm. Patents 1849* 442 Letters patent have been granted for a machine, the invention of a well known iron master. **1905** VALENTINE *H. Sandwith* 4 The retirement from active business life of the Quaker iron-master, Joshua Sandwith.

***Iron mill.** A mill which processes iron. {*Obs.*} — **1654** JOHNSON *Wonder-w. Prov.* 45 Here is also an Iron Mill in constant use. **1680** *N.J. Hist. Soc. Coll.* IV. 3 His Iron Mills, his manours, and divers other buildings. **1873** BAILEY *Life in Danbury* 170 Iron mills roar day and night without cessation. **1881** *Harper's Mag.* May 859/2, I am interested in iron; that is I have iron mills and—other things.

Iron mine. A mine from which iron ore is obtained. Also attrib. {1601–} — **1657** *Suffolk Deeds* III. 160 The said Iron workes, Iron mines lands woods, howses Edifices, and buildings. **1784** CUTLER in *Life & Corr.* I. 101 On one side appeared to be a fine iron mine, the stream that ran from it of a deep rusty color. **1847** in Stowe *Key* 187/1 The forests and iron mines of the South supply . . . the materials out of which these things are made. **1889** *Century Mag.* March 780/1 The camp was forming into crowds. There were the iron-mine crowd, the famous Chrysolite crowd, the Evening Star crowd.

***Ironmonger.** A dealer in iron ware. (Now supplanted by *hardware dealer*). Also attrib. — **1645** *Harvard Rec.* I. 8 For Nayles & other appurtenances from the Iron Monger, 4[s]-8[d]. **1681** *Boston Rec.* 150 [Sold] unto Richard Hutchinson . . . Ironmonger three full and cleare quarter parts of the Docke. **1714** *Ib.* 208 William Adkinson Iron monger wth his wife . . . Signified their desires. **1811** SUTCLIFF *Travels* (1815) 56 There was but one ironmonger's shop in the place.

Ironmongery. Ironware, hardware. {1711–} Also attrib. — **1746** in *Mag. Amer. Hist.* I. 611 Peter Cloppen . . . is a sadler and keeps iron mongery ware. **1800** *Columbian Centinel* 24 Dec. 3/2 Ironmongery & Hardware, Imported in the ship Harriot. **1818** DARBY *Emigrant's Guide* 258 Of ironmongery, are now made sheet iron, nails and nail rods. **1892** *Century Mag.* Dec. 218/2 The broad veranda . . . had the customary array of . . . hanging lamps set with bosses of colored glass, and much ironmongery in spirals and curlicues.

Iron oak. {1884–} +One of several American oaks, esp. the post oak, *Quercus stellata.* — **1775** *Amer. Husbandry* I. 377 White iron oak, very durable, is reckoned the best of all for ship-building. **1814** PURSH *Flora Amer.* II. 632 The Upland White Oak, or Iron Oak is a spreading tree about fifty or sixty feet high; its timber is of great value in ship-building. **1884** SARGENT *Rep. Forests* 139 *Quercus obtusiloba*. . . . Post

Oak. Iron Oak. **1897** SUDWORTH *Arborescent Flora* 154 *Quercus minor.* ... [Called] Iron Oak (Del., Miss., Nebr.).

Iron ore. Any ore complex containing iron in sufficient quantity to be extracted with profit. {1601–}

1631 *Va. House of Burgesses* 125 Of Iron Oare Capt. Tucker hath taken in some quantitie from a place adioyninge neere unto us. **1721** *Mass. H. Rep. Jrnl.* III. 23 To take care of the Iron Oar belonging to the Town. **1847** L. COLLINS *Kentucky* 159 There are several varieties of iron ore found in Kentucky. **1880** *Cimarron News & Press* 1 July 3/2 Within a radius of a very few miles from a point in the Cimarron cañon there are found large deposits of brown and red hematite and magnetic iron ore.

b. Attrib. and comb. with *baron, bed, dust, mining.*

1821 *Amer. Jrnl. Science* III. 57, I visited a few months since, the iron ore bed, and the iron works, in Bennington, Vermont. **1883** WELLS *Practical Economics* (1885) 93 The representatives of the iron-ore-mining interests in the United States have recently agreed to ask of Congress an increase in the duties imposed on the importation of foreign ores. *c***1888** *Chicago Inter-Ocean* (F.), I have observed in all the 'steam rail baron's' reply to 'fair trade' that he calls upon the 'iron ore barons,' ... and the 'labor barons' to aid him in meeting European competition in steel rails. **1897** *McClure's Mag.* X. 75 Iron-ore dust must be put into such form that it could be shipped and smelted.

Iron sand. Sand containing iron ore. {1876–} Also attrib. — **1805** D. MCCLURE *Diary* 29 The soil abounds in iron sand Ore. **1843** *Nat. Hist. N.Y., Geology* IV. 426 Magnetic iron sand and garnet sand are also found in considerable quantities, and collected for writing sand. **1894** *Harper's Mag.* Jan. 409 'Iron-sand' is a form of magnetite ... consisting of silicious particles mixed with grains of iron ore.

***Ironstone.** Any of several hard iron ores containing other elements.

1630 HIGGINSON *New-England* 7 For Stone, here is plentie of Slates at the Ile of Slate in Masathulets Bay, and ... Iron-Stone, and Marble-stone also. **1740** W. STEPHENS *Proc. Georgia* 603 [He] found in it a plentiful Quarry of Iron Stone. **1877** H. C. HODGE *Arizona* 126 A formation of limestone, ironstone and manganese. **1881** *Harper's Mag.* May 837/2 The dusty quarters of the manufacture of iron-stone and Rockingham.

+**Iron store.** A store dealing in wrought and cast iron products; a hardware store. — **1837** W. JENKINS *Ohio Gaz.* 138 There are ... 3 wholesale and many retail grocery stores, 1 iron store [etc.]. **1849** CHAMBERLAIN *Ind. Gazetteer* 199 There are now in Covington fourteen dry goods stores, two drug stores, four groceries, two iron stores.

***Ironware.** Tools, utensils, etc., made of iron. — **1652** *Suffolk Deeds* I. 217 William Awbrey shall ... Receiue and take into his care and Custodie ... all such Iron and Ireron [*sic*] wares and other Commodities as shalbe made in Newe England and deliuered to him. **1727** *Md. Hist. Mag.* XVIII. 226 Iron ware. Six good Strong frying pans. **1789** MORSE *Amer. Geog.* 260 Upwards of twelve hundred sleighs entered the city daily ... loaded with ... iron ware. **1837** PECK *New Guide* 174 Pittsburgh, ... from its manufacturing enterprise, especially in iron wares, has been denominated the 'Birmingham of the West.' **1892** *Hist. Rev. York Co.* 54/2 The stock carried embraces a finely selected line of ... house furnishing goods, iron and copper ware.

Iron wedge. A V-shaped iron implement used for splitting wood, timber, etc. {1613–} — **1634** WOOD *N.E. Prospect* I. 52 [Each settler should bring] all manner of Augers, ... Beetles heads, and Iron-wedges. **1648** *Conn. Rec.* I. 491 Axes, handsaw, beetle rings, iron wedges. **1851** *Florida Plant. Rec.* 442 Received 7 Sacks of Salt and 2 iron wedges from El Desteno.

Ironweed. {1827} +**a.** Any species or plant of the genus *Vernonia.* +**b.** Blue vervain. — **1823** FAUX *Memorable Days* 185 Found iron-weed all day, and fine extensive peach orchards. **1835** AUDUBON *Ornith. Biog.* III. 56 Locusts ... were gathered by boys from the trunks of trees and the 'iron weeds,' a species of wild hemp very abundant in that portion of the country. **1872** EGGLESTON *End of World* i. 15 [She] nervously broke off the top of a last year's iron-weed. **1894** *Amer. Folk-Lore* VII. 96 *Verbena hastata*, ... iron-weed, Jones Co., Iowa. **1900** H. ROBERTSON *Red Blood & Blue* 191 There was a worm-fence of rails, in the corners of which iron-weed and mullein crowded shoulder-high.

Ironwood. {1657–} Any of a large variety of trees and shrubs noted for the extreme hardness of their wood, +esp. the hop hornbeam (*Ostrya virginiana*).

1762 CLAYTON *Flora Virginica* 151 Nostratibus Iron-wood, Belgis Noveboracensibus Yzerhout. **1814** BIGELOW *Florula Bostoniensis* 232 *Ostrya Virginica.* Hop Hornbeam. Iron wood.... The wood is hard, close grained, and heavy. **1831** AUDUBON *Ornith. Biog.* I. 204 The Virginian Hornbeam, or Iron-Wood Tree.... The common name in America is *Iron-wood*, which it receives on account of the great hardness of the wood. **1871** *Dept. Agric. Rep. 1870–71* 411 Iron-wood, (*Olneya tesota,*) ... grows in the most desolate and rocky places of Arizona and Sonora. **1884** SARGENT *Rep. Forests* 158 *Ostrya Virginica.*... Hop Hornbeam. Iron Wood. Lever Wood. **1905** *Bureau of Forestry Bul.* No. 66, 36 The hornbeam, or ironwood (*Ostrya virginiana*), is reported to occur.

attrib. **1785** MARSHALL *Amer. Grove* 9 *Andromeda plumata.* Plumed Andromeda, or Carolinian Iron-wood Tree. **1851** MELVILLE *Moby-Dick* cxiii. 540 Perth was standing between his forge and anvil, the latter placed upon an iron-wood log.

***Ironwork.** A factory in which iron is smelted, or where heavy iron articles are manufactured. Now in pl. — **1623** *Va. House of Burgesses* 24 Otherwise he could not but hear of our Proclamations for the Advancement of Staple Commodities ... ; the Iron-Works in great Forwardness. **1734** *Doc. Hist. N.Y. State* I. 734 We have a great many Iron mines ... but as yet no Iron Work is set up in this province. **1818** DARBY *Emigrant's Guide* 197 Several iron works are, and have been many years in operation, both in east and west Tennessee. **1884** *Century Mag.* Feb. 594/1 On railroad construction the average annual rate of mortality, for 1879 and 1880, was 47 to the thousand, ... at the iron-works it was 54.

***Ironworker.** One working in iron or employed in ironworks. — **1832** WATSON *Hist. Tales N.Y.* 27 His ship having accidentally burned, he built another on the East River; a first demonstration to the simple natives of the superior skill of the Charistooni—iron workers. **1882** *Nation* 20 July 44/3 The great iron-workers' strike is now over in the St. Louis district. **1905** VALENTINE *H. Sandwith* 182 A number of the iron-workers had been locked up in the jail.

+**Iroquois.** [Amer. Indian.]

1. =FIVE NATIONS; an Indian belonging to one of the tribes included in this. Also attrib.

[**1603** CHAMPLAIN *Œuvres* (1870) II. 9 Lesdicts Irocois ... sont en plus grand nombre que lesdicts Montagnés.] **1666** *Doc. N.Y. Col. Hist.* III. 134 The Irocquois Indians should not cômit any Act of hostilety. **1764** H. GRACE *Hist. Life & Sufferings* 31 We crossed the River to the Iroquois Nation. **1826** COOPER *Mohicans* v, Every Indian who speaks a foreign tongue is an Iroquois, whether the castle of his tribe be in Canada, or be in York. **1854** *S. Lit. Messenger* XX. 396 The Iroquois never made themselves felt, south of the northern border of Virginia. **1872** W. H. VENABLE *School Hist. U.S.* 19 To say 'as savage as an Iroquois warrior' is to exhaust the power of simile. **1896** WILKINS *Madelon* 11 The first Hautville ... had espoused an Iroquois Indian girl.

2. The Iroquoian language. Also attrib.

1713 in Swift *Works* XVI. (1883) 27 Lest you should not have your Iroquoise Dictionary at hand, 'Brother, I honour you and all your tribe.' **1851** *Harper's Mag.* Aug. 390/2 He fancied he heard her mutter in Iroquois one word—'revenged!'

Irredeemable, *a.* {1609–} +Of paper money: Not convertible into cash. {1879–} — **1790** HAMILTON *Wks.* II. 78 The subscriber ... [is entitled] to have the whole sum funded at an annuity or yearly interest of four per cent., irredeemable by any payment exceeding five dollars per annum. **1837** D. WEBSTER *Works* (1851) I. 374, I abhor paper; that is to say, irredeemable paper, paper that may not be converted into gold or silver at the will of the holder. **1884** BLAINE *20 Years of Congress* I. 429 A government cannot ... maintain a state of solvency by the continuous issuing of irredeemable paper.

Irrepressible conflict. +*Hist.* The conflict between freedom and Negro slavery; the Civil War (1861–5). Also transf. — **1858** SEWARD *Works* IV. 292 This collision ... is an irrepressible conflict between opposing and enduring forces, and it means that the United States must ... become either entirely a slaveholding nation, or entirely a free-labor nation. **1862** NORTON *Army Lett.* 126 Seward was right—the 'irrepressible conflict' will continue till freedom or slavery rules the nation. **1881** *Congress. Rec.* 28 April 418/2 Another 'irrepressible conflict' has arisen in this country ... between the people for their liberties, and arrogant, bloated corporate power and monopoly. [**1892** WALSH *Lit. Curiosities* 566 *Irrepressible Conflict*, a locution current during the anti-slavery agitation, supposed to have been originated by William H. Seward in an address to a public meeting at Rochester, New York, October 25, 1858.... If not invented, the phrase at least was brought into prominence by him through this utterance.]

Irrigate, *v.* {1615–}

1. *tr.* To supply (land or fields) with water. {1623–}

1821 in *Mass. Agric. Repository & Jrnl.* VII. 79 From this pond ... I have opened a small ditch, by which I irrigate the principal part of the land. **1848** ROBINSON *Santa Fe Exped.* (1932) 25 [At Santa Fe] they also irrigate their cornfields. **1873** COZZENS *Marvellous Country* 34 They irrigated their ground. **1880** *Stock Grower & Farmer* 11 Jan. 4/1 Enough water to irrigate two or three states is just now going to waste in Arizona. **1900** *Congress. Rec.* 26 Jan. 1222/2 The higher lands, upon the prairie, that can not be irrigated, are practically worthless for agricultural purposes in their present condition. **1921** *Dept. Agric. Yrbk. 1920* 204 Only 5 acres out of every 100 acres [in the western states] can be ultimately irrigated.

+**b.** *absol.* To provide water by a system of ditches.

1849 *31st Congress 1 Sess.* Sen. Doc. 64, 197 They are obliged here [Dona Ana], as in all places in New Mexico, to irrigate, as without this the soil would produce nothing. **1864** *Weekly New Mexican* 24 June 2/3 This is favorable to those who farm and irrigate along the river.

+**2.** *W. intr.* To take a drink of liquor. *slang.* Also *irrigating* vbl. n.

1856 DERBY *Phoenixiana* 104 [He] was invited by the urbane proprietor to irrigate. **1881** HAYES *New Colorado* 120 This person taking out a large flask, asked, 'Stranger, do you irrigate?' **1905** A. ADAMS *Outlet* 298 Sponsilier called every one to the bar to irrigate. **1909** *Denver Republican* Feb. (Th. S.), We've cut out the type of rancher ... Who thinks that irrigatin' means a-quenchin' of his thirst.

Irrigating canal. A canal that supplies water for irrigation purposes. — **1866** *Rep. Indian Affairs* 120 The first thing necessary to insure success is an irrigating canal. **1876** W. M. FISHER *Californians* 11 Irrigating canals intersect the district in many directions. **1890** *Stock*

Grower & Farmer 11 Jan. 7/1 [The canal company's] object is to construct an irrigating canal between the towns of Aztec and Farmington in New Mexico.

+**Irrigating ditch.** A ditch used for irrigating a field. — **1854** *Harper's Mag.* April 582/2 The numerous irrigating ditches . . . are the inseparable assistants of New Mexican agriculture. **1883** *Century Mag.* Aug. 527/2 The women were at work in the fields, some hoeing, some clearing out the irrigating ditches. **1912** RAINE *Brand Blotters* 78 She got into the rig and drove round the corral to the irrigating ditch.

Irrigation. {1612–}

1. The conveying of water to farm land by canals or ditches. Esp. common in the West. {1626–}

1821 in *Mass. Agric. Repository & Jrnl.* VII. 78, [I adopted] a system of irrigation . . . on my farm in Newton [Mass.]. **1850** GARRARD *Wah-To-Yah* xx. 250 [The] strongest argument against farming in New Mexico was that the soil required irrigation. **1884** W. SHEPHERD *Prairie Exper.* 216 Where there are rivers, the water is taken out for irrigation. **1900** *Congress. Rec.* 31 Jan. 1352/2 The country demanding irrigation—one-half of the territory of our own country—can be developed and expanded by irrigation.

+**2.** *W.* Refreshment by means of alcoholic liquor. *slang.*

1856 DERBY *Phoenixiana* 162 Being of a naturally arid disposition, and perhaps requiring irrigation at that particular moment, you unguardedly invite Brown, and your new friend Jones of course, to step over to Parry and Battens, and imbibe.

3. Attrib. in sense 1 with *bill, pump, rancher,* etc.

1883 *Century Mag.* Oct. 805/1 The appliances . . . belonging to these irrigation systems add much to the picturesqueness of South California landscapes. **1890** *Stock Grower & Farmer* 22 March 6/2, 75,000 gallons of water raised 20 feet at an expense of 100 lbs. of soft coal seems wonderful. The Greely Irrigation Pump does it, just the same. **1909** 'O. HENRY' *Roads of Destiny* 91 Senator Kinney had an irrigation bill that he wanted passed for the benefit of his own section. **1910** PINCHOT *Fight for Conservation* 31, I have been impressed with the peculiar advantages which surround the irrigation rancher. **1913** LONDON *Valley of Moon* III. xvi, Let them hunt their white sparrows in the Sacramento islands and the irrigation valleys.

+**Irrigation ditch.** =IRRIGATING DITCH. — **1870** HUNT *Own Story* (MS.) 1 Irrigation ditches were dug for as much of the land as could be covered with water. **1897** *Outing* XXIX. 457/2 Irrigation ditches are crossed at a bound. **1912** *Indian Laws & Tr.* III. 544 The sum of fifteen thousand dollars [is] to be expended in the payment of taxes, . . . maintenance and repair of irrigation ditches [etc.].

+**Irrigationist.** One who favors extension of irrigation. — **1887** *Detroit Free Press* 21 May 2/4 Of interest to irrigationists. **1894** *Voice* 18 Oct. 3/4 The Denver congress of irrigationists was a body of importance.

Isabella. +=next. — **1846** *Knickerb.* XXVII. 419 A snaky-looking vine . . . from which glorious bunches of Catawbas and Isabellas may be gathered. **1850** *Western Journal* IV. 127 The Isabella is not preferable for wine, and is only used for table use. **1890** HOWELLS *Shadow of Dream* 49 Over staggering trellises the grape-vines clung, and dangled imperfect bunches of Isabellas and Concords.

+**Isabella grape.** A cultivated variety of the northern fox grape, *Vitis labrusca.* Also attrib. (Cf. FOX GRAPE note.) — **1833** VIGNE *Six Months in Amer.* I. 150 At Boston I tasted a grape called the Isabella grape. **1854** *Penna. Agric. Rep.* 93 The wines manufactured from Catawba and Isabella grape . . . are rich, firm and luscious. **1856** *Rep. Comm. Patents 1855: Agric.* 305 In the region of Lake Erie, but more particularly of Cleveland, the 'Isabella' grape had been found in the greatest perfection.

***Isinglass.** Mica. {1747–} Also attrib. — **1737** WASHINGTON *Diaries* III. 222 The soil of these appeared loamy, slightly mixed with Isinglass and originally had been good. **1792** BELKNAP *Hist. New-Hampshire* III. 193 In various parts of the country is found that transparent substance, which is commonly called Ising-glass, (*Lapis specularis.*) **1832** WILLIAMSON *Maine* I. 178 *Mica* (commonly called Isinglass,) . . . is seen in different parts of Maine. Anciently it was much used for window glass, particularly in war-ships, as being proof in the discharge of cannon. **1880** INGHAM *Digging Gold* 246 There is also in the vicinity [of Hayward] a mica deposit, sheets of which have been procured five by eight inches of pure isinglass.

***Island.**

+**1.** A piece of ground rising from a level tract; a hill.

1638 *Dedham Rec.* III. 51 Abraham Shawe selleth vnto Ferdinando Adam one portion of Grownd called an hill or Iland as it lyeth to his home lott. **1703** *Providence Rec.* V. 61 A litle Island of upland in sd meaddow. **1794** S. WILLIAMS *Nat. Hist. Vt.* 35 The small islands in these intervales, are of a different soil, and . . . are evidently the tops of small hills, which have not been covered by the inundations of the rivers. **1802** *Mass. H. S. Coll.* 1 Ser. VIII. 112 There are on it [a ridge] one or two hills, which the neighbouring inhabitants call islands.

+**2.** A grove or clump of trees in a plain or prairie.

1656 *Southold Rec.* I. 42 Ten acres of meadow . . . buting against a little creeke at the east end, and to an Island of trees on the West. **1770** WASHINGTON *Diaries* I. 443 Large Planes 30 Miles in length without a Tree except little Islands of Wood. **1828** *Western Mo. Rev.* I. 514 Above it [the Missouri Valley] is the vast and beautiful Mamelle prairie, dotted with green islands of woods. **1853** F. W. THOMAS *J. Randolph* 61 Here and there, arising from the immense body of the prairie, were what are called islands—that is, great clumps of trees, covering sometimes many acres.

+**3.** *Island City,* New York City; *Island State,* Rhode Island.

1855 M. THOMPSON *Doesticks' Letters* 57, I left . . . the sweet retiracy of the swamps of Michigan, to become a denizen of the Island City. **1870** WHITTIER *Poetical Works* 229/1 Once more the Island State repeats The lesson that he taught her.

+**Island cotton.** =SEA-ISLAND COTTON. — **1802** DRAYTON *S. Carolina* 134 That raised on lands adjacent to the sea and salt water, called *island* or *sea shore cotton,* being black seed, is preferred to the *green seed* cotton.

+**Island money.** An interest-bearing paper money authorized in March, 1780, by the Pennsylvania assembly: (see quot. 1874). — **1874** SCHUCKERS *Finances & Paper Money of Rev. War* 89 The assembly set apart as a further security a number of city lots in Philadelphia and the Province Island. . . . Hence the emission was called 'the Island money.' **1892** W. G. SUMNER *Financier & Finances of Amer. Rev.* I. 97 The so-called 'island money' of Pennsylvania became as good as specie or better, because it bore interest, and the amount of it which was issued was not equal to the value of the tract of land which was pledged as security for it.

+**Islay.** A western plum tree, *Prunus ilicifolia;* its cherrylike fruit or its juice. — **1867** COZZENS *Sayings* v. 33 A little more of the Islay; thank you. **1884** SARGENT *Rep. Forests* 70 *Prunus ilicifolia.* . . . Islay. **1893** *Amer. Folk-Lore* VI. 140 *Prunus ilicifolia,* islay. S. Cal. and W. Arizona. **1897** SUDWORTH *Arborescent Flora* 247.

***Islet.** +=ISLAND 2. — **1791** W. BARTRAM *Travels* 117 Interspersed with hommocks or islets of evergreen trees. **1814** BRACKENRIDGE *Views La.* 110 To the left, we behold the ocean of prairie, with islets at intervals.

+**Issuance.** The sending out or emission of proclamations, notes, documents, etc. — **1863** *National Almanac* 545/2 A proclamation of neutrality . . . was issued [May 13, 1861] by Victoria, Queen of England. . . . A brigade of British Volunteers [which] had been enlisted in the North, . . . disbanded after its issuance. **1875** *Chicago Tribune* 23 Aug. 7/2 The issuance of blank summons by a Justice of the Peace. **1886** *Lit. World* 11 Dec. 469/1 There appeared to be sufficient reason for the issuance of just such a 'royal order' through the proper channel. **1925** BRYAN *Memoirs* 218 In the New England States . . . the Grange . . . [demanded] the issuance of greenbacks by the Federal Government.

***Issue.**

+**1.** The act of issuing government supplies to soldiers or Indians; supplies so issued.

1861 *Army Regulations* 283 His descriptive list, . . . on which the surgeon shall enter all payments, stoppages, and issues of clothing to him in hospital. **1881** *Rep. Indian Affairs* p. x, They agreed to go as soon as the issue of beef (which was in progress) had been made. **1911** QUICK *Yellowstone Nights* 309, I had fixed up a deal to go with Miss Ainsley an' her friends on a campin' trip, lastin' up to the day of the issue. **1916** EASTMAN *From Deep Woods* 79 It so happened that this was the day of the 'Big Issue.'

b. Attrib. with *cattle, room, tobacco.*

1877 *Rep. Indian Affairs* 60 A new issue room, 22 by 120 feet. **1916** EASTMAN *From Deep Woods* 117 Moreover, the Government herd of 'issue cattle' was found to be greatly depleted. **1924** *Scribner's Mag.* Dec. 651/2 He traded issue tobacco for three gallons of wine.

2. *Polit.* A crucial point in controversy between opposing parties or candidates. {in legal sense, 1511–}

1834 *Congress. Deb.* 2 Jan. 112 A great issue . . . is made up, and between great parties. . . . The issue itself is a great one; the parties to it are eminent. **1884** *Boston Jrnl.* 20 Sept. (Th. S.), The attempt of the Republicans to introduce the tariff as one of the issues of the campaign. **1903** *Evanston (Ill.) Press* 11 April, Public meetings of various kinds found in him an interested participant, and he was frequently called upon to act as chairman or to present the issues.

+**Issue day.** The day on which government supplies are issued to Indians. — **1874** GLISAN *Jrnl. Army Life* 447 They gave the white physicians much annoyance by coming for medicine only on issue or ration day. **1877** *Rep. Indian Affairs* 43 The Utes are in the habit of going out on brief hunting expeditions . . . between 'issue days.' **1895** WISTER *Red Men & White* 24 It was issue day, but no families remained after drawing their rations.

+**Issue house.** A house from which supplies are issued to Indians. — **1878** *Rep. Indian Affairs* 39 Other mechanics are putting up new store and issue-houses. **1881** *Ib.* 1, I found commodious buildings, ample for all agency purposes, (except a corral, slaughter and issue house), in a fair state of preservation. **1911** QUICK *Yellowstone Nights* 316 The way we . . . hit the trail f'r the Issue House was a high-class piece o' teamin'.

***It,** *pron.* or *quasi-n.* +In group games, the person singled out for a special duty, e.g., in the game of tag, the one who chases and tags someone else. {Sc. and n. dial. in form *hit*} — **1888** H. C. BOLTON *Counting-out Rhymes* 2 The child not set free by the magic word is declared to be 'it.' **1891** *Amer. Folk-Lore* IV. 230 The boy who is 'it' places the wicket . . . against the tree. **1899** CHAMPLIN & BOSTWICK *Cycl. Games & Sports* (ed. 2) 206/2 In this country the one who takes such a part is called 'It.' In England he is sometimes called 'He,' in France *Le* (It), and in Germany he is said to be *daran* (in). Sometimes to be It is a desirable thing, and sometimes not.

Italian, *n.* +A native of Italy settled in America or a descendant of such a settler. — **1768** *Boston Chronicle* 26 Sept., On August 17, about two hundred of the Spaniards and Italians [in Charleston, S.C.] . . . rose and seized a schooner. **1842** *Picayune* 4 January 1/6 The Italian gave exaggerated accounts of the force and intentions of the Texans. **1902** WISTER *Virginian* xvi, 'Was Delmonico one of them I-talians?' inquired a fascinated mutineer. **1922** P. M. ROSE *Italians in Amer.* 80 The Italian is an individualist by nature and by circumstance.

Italian,* *a.* In specific names of plants supposed to have been derived from Italy. — **1838 ELLSWORTH *Valley of Wabash* 47 The Italian wheat I put in also late, and it succeeded admirably. **1840** DEWEY *Mass. Flowering Plants* 66 *Trifolium incarnatum.* Italian Clover. **1849** EMMONS *Agric. N.Y.* II. 142 Italian Spring Wheat. . . . Kernels clustered, irregularly arranged upon the spike. **1894** COULTER *Bot. W. Texas* III. 510 *S[etaria] Italica.* . . . (Italian millet.) . . . Introduced from Europe and cultivated in all parts of the United States.

Italian chair, chaise. (See quotations.) — **1754** *S.C. Gazette* 15–22 Jan. 2/3 Two new genteel Italian chairs, with iron axle-trees, red wings, and lined with worsted coffoy [will be sold]. **1775** BURNABY *Travels* 114 Return home in Italian chaises, (the fashionable carriage in this [N.Y.] and most parts of America, Virginia excepted, where they make use only of coaches; and these commonly drawn by six horses).

+**Italian mulberry.** Also **Italian white-fruited mulberry.** A species of mulberry imported from Italy in connection with silk culture. Also attrib. — **1743** CATESBY *Carolina* App. p. xxi, The Italian or silk-worm mulberry . . . [was] introduced into Virginia by Sir William Berkley. *c***1790** T. COXE *View U.S.* 45 We have a large nursery of the white Italian mulberry established here this summer. **1796** WANSEY *Excursion U.S.* 193 Near Princetown are large plantations of the Italian mulberry tree, for the culture of the silk worm. **1831** PECK *Guide* 139 [Silkworms] thrive . . . on the Italian mulberry. **1846** BROWNE *Trees Amer.* 444 *Italian White-fruited Mulberry; Mûrier d'Italie,* of the French; with lobed leaves.

Italian poplar. (See quotations.) {1766–} — **1817–8** EATON *Botany* 405 *Populus dilatata,* lombardy poplar, italian poplar. . . . It is said no pistillate plant of this species has been brought to America. **1847** DARLINGTON *Weeds & Plants* 332 Dilated Populus. Lombardy Poplar. Italian Poplar. . . . Introduced to [Philadelphia] . . . , from England, in the year 1784.

Italian rye grass. A European grass, *Lolium multiflorum.* (Cf. RYE GRASS.) {1834–} — **1858** FLINT *Milch Cows* 170 Italian Rye Grass (*Lolium italicum*). **1878** KILLEBREW *Tenn. Grasses* 99 Italian Rye Grass, *Lolium Italicum,* . . . can be forced by manures and irrigation to a greater extent than any other known species of hay. **1889** VASEY *Agric. Grasses* 74 *Lolium perenne* (Italian Rye Grass). A perennial grass, introduced from Europe.

***Item.**

***1.** (See quot. 1816.) *Obs.* {–1786}

'Now *U.S. local*' (*O.E.D.*).

1816 PICKERING 118 *Item.* An intimation, a hint. *Ex.* I had an *item* of his designs. This is a low word, and is used here only by the illiterate. **1818** FEARON *Sketches* 124 *Q.* What is her sickness? *A.* Consumption. *Q.* I had an item (a supposition) of that. **1853** 'P. PAXTON' *Yankee in Texas* 129 The minute you get item that I'm back, catch up your horses, meet me at the cross-roads.

+b. *To give item,* (see quot. 1889).

1829 *Va. Lit. Museum* 266, I had horrid luck [at cards] that night. . . . At length I detected one of the fellows 'giving item' to my adversary. **1889** FARMER 319/1 Among gamblers, confederates give *items* or hints by looking at the players' hands, and signalling their value. A complete code of secret signs is employed for the purpose.

+2. A brief article in a newspaper.

1848 *Santa Fe Repub.* 15 May 2/1 Our Devil has laid before us a hatful of 'items' which will have their proper place in our next. **1864** 'MARK TWAIN' *Sk., New & Old* 163 Getting at least twelve hours ahead of the morning paper boys with this most magnificent 'item' that ever fell to the lot of the craft. **1889** — *Conn. Yankee* ix. 109, I wanted to sample . . . reporter-material. . . . The priest did very well. . . . He got in all the details, and that is a good thing in a local item.

+**Itemize,** *v.* (See quot. 1864.) {1890–} Also *itemized* ppl. a. — **1857** PAYNE *Rep. Railroads Tenn.* 13 Itemized Cost of Road. . . . Bridges and trestles, [$]340,367.23. **1864** WEBSTER 721/2 *Itemize,* to state in items, or by particulars; as, to *itemize* the cost of a railroad. (*Local, U.S.*) **1891** *Harper's Mag.* June 119/2 It contains a minutely itemized account of the expenditures of the past year. **1919** *Detective Story Mag.* 25 Nov. 14 'Was the list itemized?' 'Not entirely. In some instances several articles were grouped under a single item.'

+**Itemizer.** **1.** One who itemizes; one who writes 'items' for a newspaper. **2.** One who interprets or applies single passages from the Bible without consideration of their contexts. — **(1) 1860** *Congregationalist* 21 Sept. (Chipman), An itemizer of the *Adams Transcript.* **(2) 1887** *Bible Society Rec.* Feb. 27/2 The itemizers have often been huge misinterpreters of the gospel.

Ithuriel's-spear. [f. *Ithuriel,* an angel in Milton's *Paradise Lost.*] +A plant (*Brodiaea laxa*) found in California and Oregon. — **1889** *Cent.* 3203/3 Ithuriel's-spear. . . . The Californian liliaceous plant *Brodiæa* (*Triteleia*) *laxa.* **1915** M. ARMSTRONG *Field Bk. West. Wild Flowers* 24 Ithuriel's Spear. Very much like Harvest Brodiaea but rather taller. . . . Common on hillsides and in adobe fields.

Itinerant, *n.* A traveling preacher. {1641–} — **1714** *N.C. Col. Rec.* II. 122 The fatigue of being an itinerant I am not able longer to undergo. **1765** *Mass. Col. Soc. Publ.* VI. 110 He has not held forth since in Public, . . . the Usage this Itinerant met with in so refined a Place . . . having given him little Encouragement. **1865** RICHARDSON *Secret Service* 23 Methodist itinerants and other clergymen still preach at long intervals.

***Itinerant,** *a.* Of preachers: Traveling; moving from place to place. — **1745** *Duxbury Rec.* 274 The town voted to choose some persons to take care of their meeting house, to keep out of it itinerant preachers. **1846** *Ind. Mag. Hist.* XXIII. 264 He had been a kind of an itinerant local preacher, who had given himself much to the work, particularly at popular meetings. **1891** WILKINS *New Eng. Nun* 119 The minister, an itinerant one—this poor parish had no settled preacher—in a solemn voice requested the congregation to be seated.

+**Ivorybill.** =IVORY-BILLED WOODPECKER. {1893–} — **1872** COUES *N. Amer. Birds* 191 The ivory-bill and the flicker stand nearly at extremes of the family, the little diversity of which is thereby evident. **1885** M. THOMPSON *By Ways & Bird Notes* 37 The question arises . . . whether the ivory-bill is an example of the highest development, from the downy woodpecker, say. **1917** *Birds of Amer.* II. 138 Ivory-billed Woodpecker. *Campephilus principalis.* . . . Other Names. . . . Logcock; Woodchuck; Ivory-bill.

+**Ivory-billed coot.** The common American coot, *Fulica americana.* — **1889** *Cent.* 3205/2 *Ivory-billed coot,* the common American coot or whitebill, *Fulica americana.* **1917** *Birds of Amer.* I. 214 Coot. *Fulica americana.* . . . Other Names. . . . Pond Hen; Mud Coot; Ivory-billed Coot.

+**Ivory-billed woodpecker.** The largest of the North American woodpeckers (*Campephilus principalis*), found chiefly in the South. {1893–} — **1811** WILSON *Ornith.* IV. 20 Ivory-billed Woodpecker: *Picus principalis* . . . [has] a distinguished characteristic in the superb carmine crest and bill of polished ivory. **1828** BONAPARTE *Synopsis* 44 The Ivory-billed Woodpecker . . . inhabits the southern states and Mexico: common, resident. **1831** AUDUBON *Ornith. Biog.* I. 341 The Ivory-billed Woodpecker confines its rambles to a comparatively very small portion of the United States, it never having been observed in the Middle States. **1858** BAIRD *Birds Pacific R.R.* 81 Ivory-billed Woodpecker. . . . Southern Atlantic and Gulf States. **1917** *Birds of Amer.* II. 138 The Ivory-billed Woodpecker is a bird of astonishing strength and vigor.

+**Ivory-bill woodcock.** =prec. — **1784** FILSON *Kentucke* 26 The ivory-bill wood-cock, of a whitish colour with a white plume, flies screaming exceeding sharp. It is asserted, that the bill of this bird is pure ivory.

Ivory gull. A small white arctic gull, *Pagophila alba.* — **1858** BAIRD *Birds Pacific R.R.* 856. **1917** *Birds of Amer.* I. 39 The Ivory Gull is a glutton whenever it can obtain the flesh of seals or the blubber of whales.

+**Ivory plum.** **a.** The wintergreen (*Gaultheria procumbens*), or its fruit. **b.** The creeping snowberry (*Chiogenes hispidula*), or its fruit. — **1828** NEAL *R. Dyer* 55 The more brilliant ivory-plumbs or clustered bunch-berries rattled among the withered herbage. **1847** DARLINGTON *Weeds & Plants* 213 *Procumbens Gaultheria.* . . . Ivory Plum. Partridge-berry. **1891** *Amer. Folk-Lore* IV. 149 *Gaultheria procumbens* seems to have an almost endless variety of epithets. . . . In South Berwick, Me., . . . the berries are called *Ivory Plums.* **1892** *Ib.* V. 99 *Chiogenes serpyllifolia,* ivory plums. Washington Co., Me.

+**Ivorytype.** (See quot. 1875.) — **1861** *Chicago Tribune* 26 May 1/9 (*advt.*), Ivorytypes, the original style, and only safe method, taken by Fassett & Cook. **1873** ALDRICH *Marjorie Daw* vii, There is an exquisite ivorytype of Marjorie, in passe-partout, on the drawing-room mantelpiece. **1875** KNIGHT 1207/2 *Ivorytype,* . . . a kind of picture in which two finished photographs are taken, one light in color, made translucent by varnish, tinted on the back, and placed over a stronger picture, so as to give the effect of a photograph in natural colors.

***Ivy.** (Cf. ENGLISH IVY.)

1. The Virginia creeper, *Parthenocissus quinquefolia.*

Cf. AMERICAN IVY.

[**1620** PARKINSON *Paradisus* 612 *Vitis, seu potius Hedera Virginensis.* The Virginia Vine, or rather Ivie.] **1784** CUTLER in *Mem. Academy* I. 423 *Hedera.* . . . Woodbine. Ivy. It is planted by walls and buildings, upon which it will ascend.

+2. The mountain laurel.

1743 CLAYTON *Flora Virginica* 160 *Andromeda.* . . . The common Laurel, vulgarly called Ivy. **1750** T. WALKER *Journal* 45 There is much Holly in the Low grounds & some Laurel and Ivy. **1832** WILLIAMSON *Maine* I. 116 [The lambkill] has been called *mountain Laurel, Spoonwood, Ivy* and *Calico Bush.* **1888** WARNER *On Horseback* 29 In this region the rhododendron is called laurel, and the laurel (the sheep-laurel of New England) is called ivy.

+3. Poison ivy.

1788 MAY *Jrnl. & Lett.* 65, I have been clearing land for eight days, and now begin to feel the effects of poison—from ivy, doubtless. **1848** PARKMAN in *Knickerb.* XXXI. 4 In the morning Shaw found himself poisoned by ivy.

***Ivyberry.** +Wintergreen. — **1840** *S. Lit. Messenger* VI. 518/2 There were the fringed polygula, the butter-cup, wild geranium, bunch-plum, ivy-berry. [**1892** *Amer. Folk-Lore* V. 100 *Gaultheria procumbens,* ivy-berry. N.B.]

J

Jabiru. The American wood ibis or gourdhead, *Mycteria americana.* {1774–} — **1815** *Lit. & Phil. Soc. N.Y. Trans.* I. 137 The jabiru, or crane of Surinam, is larger than a stork . . . ; it lives entirely on fish, and is domesticated [in the U.S.] in poultry yards. **1883** *Nat. Museum Bul.* No. 27, 144 *Mycteria americana.* . . . Jabiru. Tropical America, north to Southern Texas. **1887** RIDGWAY *Manual N.A. Birds* 126.

+**Jacal, Jackal.** *S.W.* [Mex. Sp. fr. Nahuatl *xacalli*, 'wigwam'.]

1. A Mexican or Indian hut, usually built of upright poles or sticks and plastered with mud; an adobe house; a hogan. (Cf. HACKAL.)

1838 'TEXIAN' *Mexico v. Texas* 249 It was a little *Jacal*, or cabin, built with large unburnt bricks, called *adobes*, in the language of the country. **1865** NORTON *Army Lett.* 273 A pretty senorita . . . called at a jacal where I stopped a while. **1872** POWERS *Afoot & Alone* 164 The common jacal of the peon is built of stakes set in the ground. **1888** SHERIDAN *Memoirs* I. 30 The Mexicans quickly closed in around the Indians and forced them out of the house—or rude jackal—where the 'ball' was being held. **1898** CANFIELD *Maid of Frontier* 203 A jacal is a hut built of crooked mesquite poles, driven upright into the ground, and roofed with 'tules.' **1909** 'O. HENRY' *Roads of Destiny* 150 A stone's cast away stood . . . a jacal such as the Mexicans erect—a one-room house of upright poles daubed with clay and roofed with grass or tule reeds.

b. A temporary shelter, similarly constructed, used by sheep herders.

1849 AUDUBON *Western Journal* (1906) 54 The ranchos are forlorn 'Jacals' (a sort of open-work shed covered with skins and rushes and plastered with mud, here so full of lime and marl that it makes a hard and lasting mortar.) **1888** J. J. WEBB *Adventures* 105 The *jacal* was full—packed so thick it was impossible to count [the sleepers]. **1894** *Congress. Rec.* 18 Jan. 1011/1 Sheep-herders, many of whom doubtless exist in jacals, men whose employment compels them to be out on the hills among the cacti.

2. The material or method used in building such a hut or shelter. Also comb.

1850 AUDUBON *Western Journal* (1906) 230 We . . . saw a comfortable (for this country), log and jacal built house. **1885** *Santa Fé Weekly New Mexican* 10 Dec. 2/6 Found on the land a very miserable shanty of jack-all, unfit to be a hog pen for a fourth-class clerk. **1894–5** *Amer. Bureau Ethnol. Rep.* 108 This method is known to the Mexicans as 'jacal,' and much used by them. It consists of a row of sticks or thin poles set vertically in the ground and heavily plastered with mud.

Jacana. [Pg.] {1753–} +=MEXICAN JAÇANA. — **1894** *Dialect Notes* I. 324 *Jacána:* A tropical bird of the rail family found along the north banks of the Rio Grande, its northern limit.

***Jack,** *n.*[1]

***1.** A mechanical device for turning a roasting spit. *Obs.*

1633 *N.H. Doc. & Rec.* I. 80, 1 jack to roast meate. **1674** *Harvard Rec.* I. 61 Kitchins Utensils. . . . 1 small Jack to turn spitts. **1775** *Essex Inst. Coll.* XIII. 186, 1 Jack, 2 Spits. [**1853** FELT *Customs New Eng.* 39 Jacks and Spits . . . were in general use, till they began to be superseded, sixty years ago, by tin kitchens.]

***2.** Any one of various other labor-saving devices operating as a roller, winch, lever, etc.

1666 *Essex Inst. Coll.* XXV. 146 It[em] in the garret . . . boulster and Hangings an old Jacke & Hammocke. **1775** *Ib.* XIII. 186, 1 Jack for Boots. 1 Barn Lanthorn. **1850** *Annual of Sci. Discovery* 51 'Jacks' . . . take the wool or roping that has previously been prepared by the cards, and spin it into thread for warp or filling. **1901** MERWIN & WEBSTER *Calumet 'K'* 296, I was chief wrecker, and I had an old Scotch engineer that you couldn't move with a jack.

3. Used as the name of various fishes, animals, and birds. +**a.** One of various American fishes; =JACKFISH.

1709 LAWSON *Carolina* 159 The Jack, Pike, or Pickerel, . . . are very plentiful with us in Carolina, all our creeks and Ponds being full of them. **1797** PRIEST *Travels* 70 [The Delaware River] also abounds in cat-fish, perch, jack, eels, and a great variety of others. **1883** *Nat. Museum Bul.* No. 27, 438 *Caranx chrysus.* . . . Jack, Buffalo Jack. . . . Atlantic coast of the United States north to Cape Ann. . . . The fish is abundant, but has little commercial importance. **1897** *Outing* XXIX. 231/2 Other game fishes of Florida are the 'jack,' or crevallé, also called carvalho. **1911** *Rep. Fisheries 1908* 311 *Jack.*—A name applied to the common pickerel (*Esox reticulatus*) in the South, to the bocaccio (*Sebastodes paucispinis*) on the Pacific Coast, and to the wall-eyed pike (*Stizostedion vitreum*) in the South.

+**b.** =JACKASS.

1785 WASHINGTON *Diaries* II. 458 Dispatched at his own reqt. the Spaniard who had the charge of my Jack from Spain. **1799** — *Writings* XIV. 197, I have two or three young Jacks . . . and several she asses, that I would dispose of. **1836** EDWARD *Hist. Texas* 50 Mingled with the herds of mustangs, are often seen jacks, jennies, and mules. **1868** *Iowa Agric. Soc. Rep. 1867* 133 G. H. Bacon . . . writes that there is one blooded jack, owned by G. H. Fitzgerald. **1888** ROOSEVELT in *Century Mag.* March 661/2 A wild stallion fears no beast except the grizzly . . . ; yet it is a curious fact that a jack will almost always kill one in a fair fight.

+**c.** =JACK RABBIT.

1887 *Outing* May 111/1 Besides, there hain't nothing to do, and the 'jacks' is thicker'n tumble-weeds on the prairie. **1890** *Buckskin Mose* viii. 123 You may find a Jack or two . . . down the valley. **1899** *Mo. So. Dakotan* I. 181 Some straddling 'Jack' now come upon unwary, With backward ears is bounding o'er the prairie. **1911** *N.Y. Ev. Post* 21 Dec. 7/2 (Th. S.), In western Kansas . . . the 'jacks' have been causing much trouble for farmers.

+**d.** =JACK CURLEW.

1917 *Birds of Amer.* I. 252 Hudsonian Curlew. . . . [Also called] Jack Curlew; Jack.

+**4.** =FLAPJACK[1] or APPLEJACK.

1832 KENNEDY *Swallow Barn* I. 57 She was usually occupied in paring apples to be baked up into tough jacks for our provender. **1850** W. RYAN *Adv. Calif.* I. 238 Though some over fastidious stomachs may turn at the bare notion of eating such an unpromising preparation, . . . [I soon] set to work upon the 'jacks.' **1894** *Dialect Notes* I. 331 In Salem, Sussex, and Burlington counties [N.J.], where apple whiskey is made, it is commonly called 'jack.'

5. The lowest face card in each of the four suits making up a pack of playing cards; the knave. {1674–80–}

1845 HOOPER *Simon Suggs' Adv.* 58 He staked his winnings and the original stake on the Jack. **1876** INGRAM *Centennial Exp.* 731 Three queens and a jack . . . he shoved under the seat when he sat outside of the church playing draw-poker. **1922** T. A. MCNEAL *When Kansas Was Young* 188 Major Drumm had three aces and the Texas gentleman had three jacks.

+**6.** A lantern used by hunters and fishermen for attracting game and fish at night; a jack lamp. (Cf. FIRE-HUNTING 2, FLOATING *n.*, JACK *v.* 1.)

1859 *Harper's Mag.* July 175/1 'A jack' composed of a bit of tin, acting as a reflector on one side and as a shade on the other, is bent round a piece of wood holding a candle. **1885** *Outing* Oct. 75/1 If you can shoot behind the jack, . . . Bullock will be glad to paddle you within range of an old buck. **1895** *Ib.* April 61/1 Standing with my eyes below the level of the flaming jack, I could scan every foot of the shallow waters, and readily detect the skulking fish. **1902** WHITE *Blazed Trail* 61 On soft moccasined feet they stole about in the evening with a bull's eye lantern fastened on the head of one of them for a 'jack.'

7. In various slang phrases. +**a.** *To tear up* (or *raise*) *jack*, to make (or create) a commotion or disturbance; *to be full of jack*, to be full of mischief. (Cf. CAIN 1.)

1845 *Lowell Offering* V. 104 The mill has been started on sometime now, and the girls always tear up Jack, in my absence. **1867** S. HALE *Letters* 23 The street is narrow, so it looks quite deep,—and full of Arabs raising Jack all the time. **1872** *Ib.* 96 Mr. Holmes . . . and James Lowell were full of Jack, chaffing each other and going on.

+**b.** *To make one's jack*, to achieve one's object, to secure a great deal of money.

1867 CRAWFORD *Mosby* 282 Frankland having given up the office of Quartermaster . . . to take command of Company F, . . . thought it an excellent opportunity to make his 'Jack.' . . . He determined to attack the enemy at all hazards. **1877** BARTLETT 378 *Made his Jack.* Carried his point; was fortunate in his undertaking. **1901** H. ROBERTSON *Inlander* 25 You've come here to make your jack, and I've always heard that a good way to do that is to dress as if you'd already made it.

+**8.** *attrib.* and *comb.* **a.** With *colt, lamp, light,* etc.

1788 WASHINGTON *Diaries* III. 400 Brought the Jenny with the Jack Colt from Muddy hole, and turned them, . . . into the Clover Paddock.

a1841 W. HAWES *Sporting Scenes* I. 228 A stranger . . . presented in the glare of the jack-light an object of fear and admiration. **1888** *Harper's Mag.* Sept. 510/1 Occasionally a caribou is killed at night by the light of a jack-lamp. **1895** REMINGTON *Pony Tracks* 247 Guess I'll go to jack-punchin', 'nen I kin use a dry club.

+**b.** In names of certain American plants, animals, etc. (See also JACK BEAN, JACK-IN-THE-PULPIT, etc.)

1812 J. CUTLER *Topographic Descr. Ohio* 96 The land in this distance is mostly clothed with jack bushes and tall woods. **1848** *Rep. Comm. Patents 1847* 465 The Ohio, I believe to be a native, and may be the same as the jack grape of the Mississippi. **1871** *Penna. Laws* 276 The species commonly known as Susquehanna salmon, pike, perch, jack salmon, and by the scientific name of *stigostedium americanum,* shall henceforth not be taken . . . during their spawning time. **1882** G. C. EGGLESTON *Wreck of Red Bird* 18 They call them blue fish up North, I believe, but we call them skip-jacks or jack-mackerel. **1892** *Amer. Folk-Lore* V. 102 *Nepeta Glechoma,* creeping Charlie; Jack-over-the-ground. . . . E. Mass. **1899** *Animal & Plant Lore* 62 Jack-come-up-the-world, ant-lion. Eastern Ohio.

***Jack,** *n.*[2] A drinking vessel, usually of leather. *Obs.* — **1633** *N.H. Doc. & Rec.* I. 80, 1 jack of leather to drink in. **1640** *Conn. Rec.* I. 449 An Inventory: . . . 2 Jacks . . . two drinkeing horns. **1790** *Penna. Packet* 1 March 1/1 This Day. . . . Will commence the Sale of . . . pewter mugs and jacks.

Jack, *n.*[3] {1633–} +(See quot. 1889.) Also attrib. — **1839** *Knickerb.* XIII. 43 The body was brought on deck, laid on the lee-gangway-board, and covered with a jack. **1889** *Cent.* 3208/3 In the United States naval service the jack is a blue flag with a white five-pointed star for each State in the Union. It is hoisted on a jack-staff at the bowsprit-cap when in port, and is also used as a signal for a pilot when shown at the fore.

Jack, *n.*[4] (See JACK ROSE.)

Jack, *v.*

+**1.** *intr.* To hunt or fish at night with the aid of a jack. Also *jacking* vbl. n. (Cf. JACK *n.*[1] 6.)

a1841 HAWES *Sporting Scenes* I. 219 Not a man on Long Island can clam, crab, jack, shoot, or draw a net for bony fish with the skill and success of those who have inherited the honorable name of 'Smith.' **1885** *Outing* Oct. 80/1 'Sportsmen' . . . had 'still-hunted,' 'jacked,' and 'drove.' **1895** *Ib.* April 61/1 Some may characterize jacking as unsportsmanlike and cruel. **1902** *N.Y. American* 21 Dec. 64/1 'Jacking' for deer . . . is hunting it by the aid of a strong lantern which has a brilliant reflector . . . attracting the game up to it, so that it may be easily shot.

+**2.** *local. tr.* (See quotation.)

1871 DE VERE 211 Any owner of a large herd considers himself authorized to brand a maverick which he finds on or near his ranche, and this operation is called *to jack a maverick.*

3. *To jack up.* {1873–} +In slang uses. **a.** To call to account; to bring (a person) to a sense of his duty. **b.** To suspend in disgrace. **c.** To raise or increase; to force up.

(a) 1896 ADE *Artie* xii. 107 He was goin' to clean the streets and jack up the coppers. **1914** S. H. ADAMS *Clarion* 100, I think I'll jack up our boys in the city room by hinting that there may be a shake-up coming under the new owner. **(b) 1898** HAMBLEN *Gen'l Manager's Story* 298 The engineer was, of course, discharged; and the head brakeman . . . was jacked up for thirty days. **(c) 1904** *N.Y. Tribune* 8 May 10 The management thought it saw a chance to jack up rents, and made a sudden announcement of a raise. **1917** FREEMAN & KINGSLEY *Alabaster Box* 57 We could have sold it on easy terms the next year for six thousand; but in process of trying to jack up our customer to seven, we lost out on the deal.

Jackal.[1] Variant of JACAL.

Jackal.[2] {1603–} +The smaller American prairie wolf or a creature resembling this. — **1699** E. WARD *Trip New-Eng.* 15 Jackall. These are very numerous in New-England. They are the color of a Grey Rabbit; something less than a Fox. **1858** PETERS *Kit Carson* 22 There are two species of these animals [wolves] found on the western prairie. One is small, called the Jackal.

Jackass. A male ass. {1727–}

1786 WASHINGTON *Diaries* III. 15 Began the yards back of the Green house designed for the Jack Ass. **1796** *Ann. 4th Congress* 2 Sess. 2685 The other revenues of the State arise from specific taxes . . . on stud horses and jack asses, at various rates. **1852** A. T. JACKSON *Forty-Niner* (1920) 221 Pard rolls out at daybreak to fire rocks at the jackass, who insists on giving us an early concert every morning.

+**b.** A symbol of the Democratic party. (Cf. DONKEY 3.)

[**1870** *Harper's Wkly.* 15 Jan. 48/1 [A cartoon by Thomas Nast showing a donkey, labelled 'Copperhead papers,' kicking a lion, E. M. Stanton, with the caption] A Live Jackass kicking a Dead Lion.]

+**Jackass rabbit.** =JACK RABBIT. *Obsolescent.* — **1847** HENRY *Campaign Sk.* 61 [We] started a number of hares (called jackass rabbits), and had no little amusement in witnessing some animated runs; their speed is wonderful. **1862** *N. Amer. Rev.* July 202 The jaws of the *callotis,* or 'jackass rabbit,' may make . . . havoc with the crops. **1873** COZZENS *Marvellous Country* 376 He fell headlong to the ground, again seemingly on 'all fours,' to again straighten up with a bound that would have done credit to a 'jack-ass rabbit.' **1898** HARTE *Stories in Light & Shadow* 46 We had to grub on pine nuts and jackass-rabbits.

+**Jack bean.** Any one of various tropical American plants of the genus *Canavalia* having purple and white blossoms and white seeds in long pods. Also attrib. — **1885** 'CRADDOCK' *Prophet* 280 He sat upon the cabin porch beneath the yellow gourds and the purple blooms of the Jack-bean. **1887** *Harper's Mag.* Dec. 66/1 A brave jack-bean—a friend of the sheltering eaves—made shift to bloom purple and white. **1888** 'CRADDOCK' *Despot* 69 The jack-bean vines that hung above her head blossomed lilac and white.

Jack boot. A stout boot reaching above the knee. {1686–} — **1711** *Springfield Rec.* II. 42 A pair of Jackeboots. **1766** *Essex Inst. Coll.* LI. 292 [The papers stamped according to the Stamp Act] together with a Jack-boot, . . . should be affixed to a long Pole. **1836** *Harvardiana* II. 218 Black Tom . . . came forward arrayed in a pair of . . . revolutionary jack-boots. **1902** LORIMER *Lett. Merchant* 173 Her old man wore jack-boots and she wore congress shoes.

+**Jack coat.** A jacket. — **1682** *Providence Rec.* VI. 96 A sarge jack coat, & a sarge paire of breeches. **1711** *Springfield Rec.* II. 41 A coate, 18 shillings, a Jackcoate, 12 shillings. **1818** E. PETTIGREW *Let. to Ann Pettigrew* 12 Feb. (Pettigrew P.), Airy . . . stole one the negroe men's Jack coats.

Jack curlew. {1866–} +The Hudsonian curlew. (Cf. CURLEW 2 a.) — **1805** LEWIS in *L. & Clark Exped.* VI. (1905) 133 [*Symphemia semipalmata*] is about the size of the yellow leged plover common to the U'States, and called the jack curloo by some. **1844** *Nat. Hist. N.Y., Zoology* II. 233 The Jack Curlew, or Short-billed Curlew, appears on the seacoast of this State. **1884** COUES *Key to Birds* (ed. 2) 645 *Numenius hudsonicus* (of Hudson's Bay), Hudsonian Curlew, Jack Curlew. **1917** *Birds of Amer.* I. 253 The Hudsonian Curlew, or Jack Curlew, as it is commonly called by gunners, is an illustration of the Darwinian theory.

***Jackdaw.** +One of several varieties of American grackle, esp. the boat-tailed grackle. Also *purple jackdaw.* — **c1728** CATESBY *Carolina* I. 12 *Monedula purpurea.* The Purple Jack-Daw. . . . At a distance they seem all black, but at a nearer view, they appear purple. **1808** ASHE *Travels* 159 American birds . . . described by Catesby . . . [include] purple jackdaw, blackbird [etc.]. **1884** COUES *Key to Birds* (ed. 2) 412 Boat-tailed Grackle, Jackdaw. Of large size, with long, much keeled and graduated tail. **1917** *Birds of Amer.* II. 270 Boat-Tailed Grackle. . . . This is the 'Jackdaw' of the South. . . . It got its popular name from the early settlers of the country on account of its superficial resemblance to the European Jackdaw.

Jacker. + =JACK POT. — **1887** *Courier-Journal* 24 Jan. 2/4 Fortune varied one way and then another and finally they played a jacker in which the opener was promptly raised $500. [**1895** *Thompson Street Poker Club* 6, *Jacker*—Jack-pot—The combined contributions of all who play, each one contributing the same amount.]

***Jacket,** *n.*

***1.** A long-sleeved coat reaching to or just below the waistline. (Cf. FATIGUE JACKET.)

1647 *Conn. Rec.* I. 477 A Jackette, . . . 1 Racoone skine coate. **1707** *Boston News-Letter* 15 Sept. 2/2 (*advt.*), Ran-away from her Master. . . . [She] had on a striped red blue and white Homespun Jacket, & a red one. **1841** EMERSON *Nature, Addresses, & Lect.* 275 Before the young American is put into jacket and trowsers, he says, 'I want something which I never saw before.' **1903** WIGGIN *Rebecca* 103 We'll hang your soppy hat on the nail, put your jacket over the chair-rail.

2. A vest or waistcoat. *Obs.* {1843– *dial.*}

1705 *Boston News-Letter* 10 Dec. 4/2 (*advt.*), Ran-away from his Master . . . , a Negro Man-Slave named Peter, . . . has on a mixt gray homespun Coat, white home spun Jacket and Breeches. **1738** *N.H. Probate Rec.* II. 622 Five Strait bodied Coats five Jackets. **1800** BOUCHER *Glossary* p. xlix, A *Jacket;* a waistcoat.

+**3.** A folder or envelope for filing official papers.

1888 *Congress. Rec.* 12 June 5174/1 You can not get that information by taking one case or several cases, and taking the jacket down and getting an abstract. **1889** *Cent.* 3210/2 *Jacket,* . . . a folded paper or open envelop containing an official document, on which is indorsed an order or other direction respecting the disposition to be made of the document, memoranda respecting its contents, dates of reception and transmission, etc.

Jacket, *v.* ‖To file with related material in a folder or envelope. (Cf. JACKET *n.* 3.) — **1888** *American* 16 May (F.), Another record was made in the book of the office of letters received and jacketed.

Jackfish. {1847–} +Any one of various kinds of American fish, particularly a small pike or pickerel. (Cf. JACK *n.*[1] 3 a.) — **1855** SIMMS *Forayers* 277, I've caught . . . three fine cat, seven perch and two jackfish, in an hour. **1884** GOODE, etc. *Fisheries* I. 331 The Amber-fish—*Seriola carolinensis* . . . is . . . rather common on the Carolina coast, where it is known as the 'Jack-fish.' **1904** *N.Y. Sun* 23 Aug. 9 Mr. and Mrs. Eure were crossing a brook when a jack fish jumped into the buggy.

+**Jack hunter.** A sportsman who hunts with a jack. (Cf. JACK *n.*[1] 6.) — **1888** *Harper's Mag.* Sept. 510/1 The jack-hunter hears them [*sc.* caribou] prowling among the bushes.

+**Jack hunting.** The act or process of hunting with a jack. Also *Jack hunt.* (Cf. JACK *v.* 1.) — **1881** *Harper's Mag.* Oct. 690/2 It is the only way to get venison in that season of the year which intervenes between Jack-hunting and still-hunting. **1901** STILLMAN *Autobiog. Journalist* I. 254 One night we went out 'jack-hunting' to enable him to realize that ambition. *Ib.* 255 We had no other opportunity for the 'jack-hunt,' and so Emerson went home unsatisfied in this ambition.

+Jack-in-the-pulpit. Any one of various American lily-like plants, esp. the dragon-root, *Arisaema triphyllum.*

1847 WOOD *Botany* 519 Jack-in-the-Pulpit.... A curious and well-known inhabitant of wet woodlands. **1869** FULLER *Flower Gatherers* 36 Little bluets, great broadleaf trilliums and waterarum (Jack-in-the-pulpit we called it then). **1880** *Harper's Mag.* June 75/1 That grotesque Jack-in-the-pulpit, rising above that crumbling log, is named more to my mind. **1906** *N.Y. Ev. Post* 16 June 2 (Suppl.) In these woods I made acquaintance with Jack-in-the-pulpits, or, as the English call them, 'Lords and Ladies.'

+Jackknife, *n.*

1. A large pocket clasp knife: (see also quot. 1828).

1711 *Springfield Rec.* II. 39 One Dozen of Jack Knives, at six pence the Knife. **1770** *Boston Gaz.* 12 March 4/3 (Ernst), Penknives, Jack knives. **1828** *Yankee* April 135/3 What is called a jack-knife here (a large knife used by sailors). **1873** COZZENS *Marvellous Country* 81 He has been known to start from home with an old blind horse, a jack-knife, and a smooth quarter. **1914** 'BOWER' *Flying U Ranch* 225 He had his jack-knife out, and was already slashing carefully the shirt of Happy Jack, that he might inspect the wound.

attrib. **1879** B. F. TAYLOR *Summer-Savory* 138 Here is the wooden bench beside the stone, covered with jack-knife sculpture.

b. Such a knife given as a prize for homeliness. *Obs.*

1804 FESSENDEN *Orig. Poems* 31 Peter Grievous, and his black wife, Though they both have had the jack-knife. **1846** *Knickerb.* XXVII. 470 They have a practice at the west of giving to the ugliest man in all the 'diggin's' round about, a jack-knife.

2. (See quotations.)

1883 KNIGHT *Suppl.* 510/1 *Jack-knife,* ... a form of commutator used in telephone central stations. It is a square piece of brass fixed to an upright board by means of two bolts. **1889** *Cent.* 3211/1 *Jack-knife,* ... a form of terminal used for making connections in central telephone-stations.

+Jackknife, *v.* **1.** *tr.* To cut (someone or something) with a jack-knife. **2.** *intr.* To double up, like the folding blade of a jackknife. — **(1) 1806** *Balance* V. 228/2 A sailor ... Jacknifed (as he termed it) the poor creature in several places about the head. **1889** *Amer. Annals Deaf* Oct. 277 Some of the class-rooms had desks ink-stained and jack-knifed like those of a country school. **(2) 1888** *Century Mag.* June 251/2 The practice, for instance, of dodging shots, 'jackknifing' under fire, proceeds from a nervousness which is often purely physical. **1897** H. PORTER *Campaigning with Grant* 140 One of their amusements in camp ... was to throw stones and chips past one another's heads, and raise a laugh at the active dodging and bending the body low, or 'jack-knifing' as the men called it.

+Jackleg. An impostor, incompetent workman, or shyster. *colloq.*[2] Often used of lawyers. Also attrib. — **1853** 'PAXTON' *Yankee in Texas* 284 These men were 'jack-leg' carpenters. **1891** *Harper's Mag.* June 160/1 Why, once I was called a jack-leg and shyster—epithets calculated to goad any self-respecting lawyer almost to madness. **1894** 'MARK TWAIN' *Those Twins* Introd., He has been told many a time how the born-and-trained novelist works. Won't he let me round and complete his knowledge by telling him how the jack-leg does it? **1904** HARBEN *Georgians* 69 [These gillies] swallow every dose that's give to 'em from any jack-leg preacher that comes along.

+Jack-legged, *a.* Professionally incompetent. Used esp. of a lawyer. — **1839** *Congress. Globe* App. 19 Jan. 127/3 That party contains no *jack-legged pettifogging lawyers.* They are all distinguished gentlemen. **1870** NOWLAND *Indianapolis* 37 About that time there was a kind of 'Jack-legged lawyer' (as they were then called) here. **1892** *Congress. Rec.* 27 May 4777/1 He goes away, and a jack-legged [army] officer could do nothing except to mark him as a deserter.

+Jack-leg lawyer. A poorly trained, incompetent, or unprincipled lawyer. *colloq.* — **1853** 'P. PAXTON' *Yankee in Texas* 137 They had with them a long-legged chap, a sorter jack-leg lawyer. **1888** *Florida Times Union* 11 Feb. (F.), It seems that the State Bar Association is disposed to draw the line between attorneys and Jack-leg Lawyers. **1901** HARBEN *Westerfelt* 259, I'm jest a plain Cohutta Mountain, jack-leg lawyer. **1911** QUICK *Yellowstone Nights* 130 Out comes what Elkins called our Nemmysis in the form of a jack-leg lawyer.

+Jack Mormon. A non-Mormon who is friendly toward Mormons; a half Mormon. Also attrib. Usu. *contemptuous.*

1847 T. FORD *Hist. Illinois* (1854) 330 The county contained a goodly number of inhabitants in favor of peace.... These were stigmatized by the name of *'Jack Mormons.'* **1850** *Congress. Globe* App. 27 June 822/2 [Pickett] was a non-resident, a Jack Mormon in religion and a renegade Democrat in politics. **1878** BEADLE *Western Wilds* 505 The jury, as finally settled upon, consisted of nine Mormons, three Gentiles, and one 'Jack-Mormon.' **1890** *Stock Grower & Farmer* 26 July 6/3 A Jack Mormon from up about Greeley ... hadn't an idea above an irrigation ditch. **1900** *Congress. Rec.* 24 Jan. 1129/2 Here we have the inspiring spectacle of a 'Jack-Mormon' county attorney overruling the supreme court of Utah.

+Jack oak. a. =BLACK JACK OAK. **b.** The shingle oak, *Quercus imbricaria.* Also attrib. — **1816** U. BROWN *Journal* I. 266 Ugly Hills ... abounded with pines of a scruby kind, Jack Oaks and other Scrub Wood. **1836** EDWARD *Hist. Texas* 68 The post-oak and jack-oak are considered in Texas as every man's property. **1889** RILEY *Pipes o' Pan* 37 Clean out o' sight o' home, and skulkin' under kivver Of the sycamores, jack-oaks, and swamp-ash and ellum. **1897** SUDWORTH *Arborescent Flora* 173 *Quercus marilandica....* Jack Oak. *Ib.* 176 *Quercus imbricaria....* Shingle Oak.... Jack Oak (Ill.). **1901** DUNCAN & SCOTT *Allen & Woodson Co. Kansas* 581 The 'jack oak hills' have been fenced.

Jack(o')lantern. {man with lantern, 1663–} +A Hallowe'en lantern made of a scooped-out pumpkin in which openings have been carved to resemble the features of a human face; a synthetic imitation of this. Also attrib. (Turnip lanterns are so called in North England and Scotland. Cf. *O.E.D.*) — **1831** HAWTHORNE *Twice-told Tales* (1879) 169 Hide it [the great carbuncle] under thy cloak, sayest thou? Why, it will gleam through the holes and make thee look like a jack-o'lantern! **1889** *Cent.* 3211/1 *Jack-o'-lantern,* ... a lantern used in children's play, made of the rind of a pumpkin or of a similar vegetable, in which incisions are made to represent eyes, nose, and mouth; a pumpkin-lantern. **1890** WIGGIN *Timothy's Quest* 99 They never hearn tell o' cat-o'-nine tails, nor jack-lanterns, nor see-saws. **1923** *Ladies' Home Jrnl.* Oct. 130 An orange Jack-o'-lantern card with quaint inked features reveals the name of the guest.

Jackonet. (See JACONET.)

+Jack pine. Any one of several North American varieties of pine; a tree belonging to one of these. — **1894** *Amer. Folk-Lore* VII. 100 *Pinus Banksiana,* ... jack-pine. Mich. and Minn. **1900** BRUNCKEN *N. Amer. Forests* 9 As you go south, the first additional trees you meet with will be the little jack pine. **1916** WILSON *Somewhere* 42 The hammock between the two jack pines at the back of the Arrowhead ranch house had lured me to mid-afternoon slumber.

Jack plane. A long smoothing plane for coarse work. {1812–16–} Also attrib. — **1835** HOFFMAN *Winter in West* I. 167 The house [of two settlers in Mich.] ... is of their own manufacture; a saw, an axe, a wood-knife, and a jack-plane, being their only tools. **1876** INGRAM *Centennial Exp.* 191 The old-time laborious process of shoving and drawing, jack-plane fashion, an immense block of marble over the surface of the block to be polished. **1890** FREDERIC *Lawton Girl* 165, I saw Ben Lawton fooling around inside with a jack-plane, fixing up a table.

+Jack pot.

1. a. A round or game at draw poker in which a pot cannot be opened until a player has a pair of jacks or better. Also *progressive jack pot:* (see quot. 1887). **b.** The pot or stakes in such a game. {1897–}

1887 KELLER *Draw Poker* 38 The result is the progressive jack pot, viz: If a pot is not opened on the first deal the opening hand for the next deal increases from jacks, or better, to queens or better; ... on the second deal ... from queens, or better, to kings, or better. **1888** *St. Louis Globe-Democrat* 27 Feb. (F.), I never saw such a big game as that was.... They played tremendous Jack-Pots. **1909** WASON *Happy Hawkins* 117 He came in an' blurted out, right while we was boostin' up a jack-pot. **1922** T. A. MCNEAL *When Kansas Was Young* 187 On the third round it was proposed to make it a jack pot.

b. *fig.* and *transf.*

1887 *Courier-Journal* 21 Jan. 3/3 There are thirty-eight applicants in the 'jack-pot,' and the man naming the winner is a prophet, who will get honor in every country. **1903** MARCHMONT *When I Was Czar* 6 'It was a fine bluff.' 'Too dangerous for me to see him,' returned the Prince with a smile, falling readily into the language of the pool room. 'And the worst of it was he knew it and claimed the jack pot.'

2. (See quotation.)

1905 *Forestry Bureau Bul.* No. 61, 40 *Jackpot.* 1. A contemptuous expression applied to an unskillful piece of work in logging. (N[orthern] F[orest].) 2. An irregular pile of logs. (App[alachian Forest].)

+Jack rabbit. Any one of several varieties of long-legged, long-eared hares found in the West and Southwest. (Cf. JACKASS RABBIT.) — **1870** BEADLE *Utah* 222 The jack-rabbit is about four times as large as the common 'cotton-tail.' **1885** *Wkly. New Mexican Rev.* 14 May 2/3 Thinking he had merely fired at a jack-rabbit, the general warned him to be careful. **1911** *N.Y. Ev. Post* 21 Dec. 7/2 (Th. S.), Garden City, Kan., Dec. 20.—Twelve hundred jack rabbits were shipped from this city to Topeka last night. **1914** 'BOWER' *Flying U Ranch* 116 'Mh-hm-I thought maybe you'd run up against a hostile jackrabbit, or something,' Pink purred.

+Jack rose. =JACQUEMINOT. Also *Jack.*—**1883** *Harper's Mag.* Jan. 241/1 The box contained a ... nosegay, with a 'Jack' rose in the centre. **1888** *Scribner's Mag.* Dec. 757/2 'What roses?' said Mrs. Van Corlear. 'Why, I ordered some Jacks this morning. Didn't they come?' **1902** BANKS *Newspaper Girl* 252 The village florist he says the roses is what you call 'Jack roses.'

Jackscrew. 1. A mechanical device for raising heavy weights or exerting great pressure. {1769–} Also attrib. **2.** (See quotation.) — **(1) 1776** *Essex Inst. Coll.* XLIX. 100 Sold ... hand screws and jack screws. **1810** *Austin P.* (1924) I. 168 Invoice.... 1 Jack Screw [etc.]. **1851** CIST *Cincinnati* 50 Occupations [include] ... Jackscrew maker, 1. **1883** *Harper's Mag.* Jan. 206/2 Chinese laborers easily roll them [*sc.* logs] down upon the cars, aiding themselves with cant-hooks [and] jack-screws. **1893** *Chicago Tribune* 23 April 1/5 Six jack-screws twenty feet long were braced against the south face of the wall at a point fifteen feet from its base. **(2) 1889** *Cent.* 3211/2 *Jack-screw,* ... the screw-mechanism forming part of a dental instrument called a *screw-jack* ..., for regulating the teeth.

Jacksnipe. {1663–} +Any one of several American species of snipe or sandpiper. — **1844** *Nat. Hist. N.Y., Zoology* II. 242 It passes under the various names of Meadow Snipe, Jack Snipe, Short-neck, and ... Fat-

Bird. **1846** *Spirit of Times* 25 April 97/1 The jack snipe in the low grounds [of the Rio Grande country] were found in flocks. **1858** BAIRD *Birds Pacific R.R.* 720 *Tringa maculata*, . . . Jack snipe. . . . Of rather frequent occurrence on the coast of the Atlantic, and rearing its young in the northern States of the Union. **1897** *Outing* Aug. 449/2 The alouettes came in flocks, . . . and the jack-snipe and the golden plover also.

+**Jackson.** [Andrew *Jackson* (1767–1845), president of the United States (1829–1837).] In attrib. uses.

1. Designating various persons, measures, organizations, etc., dominated by or related to Jackson as the president of the United States or as the leader of the Democratic party. (Cf. ANTI-JACKSON; see also JACKSON MAN, PARTY.)

1828 *Niles' Reg.* XXXV. 209/2 The Jackson ticket has prevailed in Louisiana. **1830** HAYNE in W. MacDonald *Jacksonian Democracy* (1906) 150–1 The Adams and Clay men, a few seceders from the Jackson ranks and the dissatisfied of all parties. **1832** *Niles' Reg.* XLII. 125/1 At a meeting of the Jackson members of the legislature of the state of New Jersey, the following resolutions were adopted. **1842** 'UNCLE SAM' *Peculiarities* I. 289, I always pay cash, in hard Jackson money, at auctions. **1844** *Niles' Reg.* LXVI. 196/2 'An old Jackson democrat' . . . charges . . . a conspiracy between some whigs, money-brokers, and a few democrats. **1851** GREELEY in *Whig Almanac 1852* 12/1 The Tariff of 1828 . . . was framed by a Jackson Committee, passed by a Jackson Congress, and boasted of as a Jackson measure. **1855** ANDREWS *Recoll.* 96 Those men are not principally Massachusetts abolitionists, but to my own personal knowledge are mostly democrats of the Jackson stamp. **1860** *Harper's Mag.* Jan. 280/1 During the summer of that year the Democrats got up 'a Jackson funeral'; and as the members of that party were death on the General in his lifetime, they were, of course, enthusiastic in their funeral ovations.

b. Designating articles of clothing named for Jackson, or fashioned after the clothes worn by him.

1834 *Albany Ev. Jrnl.* 8 Aug. 2/1 Our very habiliments may bear some evidence of the impress of his bloated reputation. We have Jackson hats, and Jackson coats, and Jackson jackets, and Jackson trousers, and Jackson boots, and Jackson shoes, and Jackson slippers.

2. Designating things named after or in honor of Jackson as a military man.

1877 BARTLETT 319 *Jackson crackers.* Fire crackers. South-western. **1884** *N.Y. Herald* 9 Jan. 3/4 The annual 'Jackson' Banquet . . . took place at the Parker House this afternoon.

b. *Jackson Day*, January 8, celebrated, esp. by the Democratic party, in honor of Jackson's defeat of the British at New Orleans in 1815. (Cf. GLORIOUS EIGHTH.) Also *Jackson's Day.*

1885 *N.Y. Herald* 9 Jan. 2/3 The Iowa democrats observed Jackson's Day in old fashioned style. **1891** *Ib.* 9 Jan. 4/5 'Jackson Day' was celebrated in grand style to-night by the Young Men's Democratic Association [in Phila.]. **1909** *Springfield W. Repub.* 14 Jan. 1 'Jackson day' has always been January 8—a day seldom celebrated in this part of the country.

+**Jacksonian,** *n.* A political supporter of Andrew Jackson. *Obs.* — **1831** *Troy* (N.Y.) *Watchman* 12 Nov. (Th.), 'The anti-Kemble Jacksonians of the Fourth Ward' issued a manifesto signed 'Several Old Hickories.' **1833** *Niles' Reg.* XLV. 161/2 In the legislature of Rhode Island, the Jacksonians, aided by the anti-masons, have succeeded in electing Mr. Potter.

+**Jacksonian,** *a.* Pertaining to or characteristic of Andrew Jackson or his political supporters. (Cf. JACKSON.)

1828 *Niles' Reg.* XXXV. 147/1 In some instances, counties decidedly Jacksonian, gave me majorities. **1872** POWERS *Afoot & Alone* 33 The typical piney-woods man is tall and gaunt . . . ; hair coarse and Jacksonian; fingers bony and long. **1886** LOGAN *Great Conspiracy* 23 The 'Jacksonian Congress' passed the [Tariff] Act [of 1828]. **1889** H. C. POTTER *Scholar & State* (1897) 41 The Jeffersonian simplicity . . . in due time came to be only another name for the Jacksonian vulgarity.

+**Jacksoniana.** The name of a state proposed in 1841. — **1841** *Tenn. Senate Jrnl.* 15 Dec. 345 The expediency . . . of ceding that portion of this State lying west of the Tennessee River . . . for the purpose of being formed into a separate . . . State to be called Jacksoniana. *Ib.*, The disposition of said States [Ky. and Miss.] to cede . . . a portion of their territory, to be embraced in and form a part of the contemplated State of Jacksoniana when formed.

+**Jacksonian democracy.** The democratic political ideals reflected in the administrative policies of President Andrew Jackson; also, collect., the supporters and followers of these policies. — **1838** MAYO *Polit. Sk. Washington* (1839) 49 The reader is enabled to appreciate the sacrifice I have made . . . in pursuing the phantom of 'Jacksonian-democracy.' **1879** *N.Y. Herald* 9 Jan. 4/4 The Jacksonian democracy were the determined foes of monopoly. **1913** A. C. COLE *Whig Party in So.* 31 [The Whig party's] object stood out clearly from the beginning—to check Jackson and Jacksonian democracy, to 'cure the sea of Jacksonism.'

+**Jacksonism.** The political principles and policies advocated or established by Andrew Jackson and his followers. — **1827** in T. Weed *Life T. Weed* II. 32 If anything can be done to save this State [N.Y.] from the devouring gulf of Jacksonism, it is time we were about it. **1842** *Whig Almanac 1843* 3/2 The popularity of Jacksonism and the power of official patronage and party discipline had secured his [Harrison's] defeat. **1913** [see JACKSONIAN DEMOCRACY.] **1922** MCCORMAC *Biog. Polk* 130 Admiration for the man had obscured the vision of many who would otherwise have been quick to detect the inherent evils of Jacksonism.

+**Jacksonite.** = JACKSON MAN. Now hist. Also attrib. — **1830** J. Q. ADAMS *Memoirs* VIII. 247 Although counteracted by a double opposition, federalist and Jacksonite, I have received nearly three votes in four, throughout the district. **1831** S. SMITH *Major Downing* 60 It was a plaguy shame there should be any such wicked parties as Federalists . . . or Jacksonites. **1902** CLAPIN 242 *Jacksonites.* Said of the followers of general Andrew Jackson (1821–32). Their opponents were called Adamites.

+**Jacksonize,** *v. local. tr.* In allusion to Andrew Jackson's fame as an Indian-fighter: To defeat or overwhelm in battle. — **1815** *Niles' Reg.* IX. 64/2 But the Sacs and Foxes, west of the Mississippi, it is thought, must be brought to a sense of justice through feeling—they must be *Jacksonized*, as the saying is in the west.

+**Jackson man.** A friend and supporter of Andrew Jackson, or of the political beliefs attributed to him; a member of the Jackson party. Now hist.

1830 J. Q. ADAMS *Memoirs* VIII. 240 What with Anti-Masonic and Jackson men, parties were all broken up. **1833** *Niles' Reg.* XLV. 292/1 At the late election for mayor [of Boston], gen. Lyman . . . , though called a 'Jackson man,' was elected. **1834** *Congress. Deb.* 19 March 1007 That meeting [in New Orleans] was composed of . . . Jackson men and anti-Jackson men [etc.]. **1847** T. FORD *Hist. Illinois* (1854) 75 At this time Gov. Duncan was a thorough Jackson man, as the friends of Gen. Jackson were then called. *a***1882** WEED *Autobiog.* 203 S. G. Andrews . . . was then [in 1825] a Jackson man, although two years afterwards, he, together with Mr. Whittlesey, became first anti-Masons and then Whigs. **1906** W. MACDONALD *Jacksonian Democracy* 34 It was not until some years later [than 1826] that the name 'Jackson men' was generally relinquished in favor of 'Democrats.'

+**Jackson party.** The political following which elected Andrew Jackson to the presidency of the United States; later an unofficial title for the Democratic party. Also *Jackson–Van Buren party.* Now hist. — **1833** *Niles' Reg.* XLV. 161/2 The great body of the national republican and Jackson parties acted together and supported a combined ticket. **1836** TICKNOR in *Life, Lett., & Jrnls.* I. 488 [Mr. Legaré] seems to belong to the Jackson party, only from the circumstance that he was of the Union party in South Carolina; for his views are quite too broad and high for any faction, and he is as far from being a Democrat as any man in the United States. **1839** MAYO *Polit. Sk. Washington* p. v, The Jackson–Van Buren party, is . . . made up of odds and ends of all parties. **1843** in Hambleton *H. A. Wise* (1856) 40 This same republican portion of the Whig party was that fragment of the old Jackson party that had gone off under the white flag of '36.

Jackstone.

1. *pl.* A children's game played with a few small pebbles or five or six specially shaped bits of metal, glass, etc., and often a ball. {1837– *dial.*} Also fig.

1814 BRACKENRIDGE *Views La.* 251 The women . . . amuse themselves with a game something like jack-stones; five pebbles are tossed up in a small basket, with which they endeavor to catch them again as they fall. **1878** B. F. TAYLOR *Between Gates* 37 Beyond . . . the scraggy ridges where giants played 'jack-stones.' **1923** WIGGIN *My Garden of Memory* 10 We played paper dolls, jackstraws and jackstones.

2. A pebble, bit of metal, etc., designed for or suitable for such a game. Usually pl. {1879–}

1854 SHILLABER *Mrs. Partington* 61 Ike, unwatched, was weighing his knife and five Jackstones in the bright brass scale on the other counter. **1873** BAILEY *Life in Danbury* 277 A West-Street boy secreted a set of jack stones in his father's boot for safe keeping. **1877** BARTLETT 787 *Jack-stone.* A metal toy, consisting of several arms with globular termini. It is so tossed and caught that the player may keep as many of the toys as possible in motion at the same time.

Jackstraw.

1. *pl.* A game in which the players in turn attempt to remove single strips of wood from a heap of such strips without disturbing the remainder. {1801–}

1833 NEAL *Down-Easters* I. 1 Pushpin, tetotum, and jackstraws (cards being prohibited) . . . had all been tried . . . to relieve the insipidity of a pleasant voyage. **1873** PHELPS *Trotty's Wedding* v, Lill played jack-straws with him. **1881** *Rep. Indian Affairs* 73 Various games, such as jackstraws and nine pins, and other amusements, were provided for them, in which they take great pleasure. **1923** [see JACKSTONE 1].

2. One of the small pieces of wood used in this game.

1840 COOPER *Pathfinder* i, The vast trunks which had been broken and driven by the force of the gust lay blended like jack-straws. **1870** *Scribner's Mo.* I. 53 The rest crowd around the Doctor, . . . their mallets thrust at him like a medley of jack-straws. **1914** GERRY *Masks of Love* 70 You *good* women play with the huge forces that make and murder like a child tossing jackstraws.

Jacobea lily. A Mexican bulb cultivated in gardens in the United States for its single bright red flower. Also *Jacobæan lily.* {1760–} — **1840** DEWEY *Mass. Flowering Plants* 193 *Amaryllis formosissima.* Jacobea

Lily. A splendid plant from tropical North America, sometimes found in gardens. **1861** WOOD *Botany* 694 Jacobea Lily. . . . *S[prekelia] formosissima.* **1868** GRAY *Field Botany* 331 *Amaryllis formosissima*, Jacobæan or St. James's Lily, . . . cultivated from South America.

***Jacobin,** *n.* +*Polit.* One opposed to the political beliefs and practices of the Federalists; an Antifederalist. Now hist.

So called in allusion to the Jacobin or extreme revolutionary group in France. {1790–}

1798 CUTLER in *Life & Corr.* II. 8 Mr. Gerry . . . was at first little noticed by the first Federal characters, but attended by almost all the Jacobins. **1800** J. ADAMS *Works* IX. 83 The jacobins infer from this disapprobation designs in such Federalists [etc.]. **1804** A. BURR in C. Biddle *Autobiog.* 405 Our intemperate and unprincipled Jacobins who have been for years reviling H[amilton] as a disgrace to the country . . . are now the most vehement in his praise. **1809** KENDALL *Travels* III. 2 Among the more modern compellations . . . of the anti-federalists, are *jacobins, French tories, republicans* and *democrats.* **1833** NEAL *Down-Easters* I. 47 Blue-lights, jacobins, tories, democrats and enemies to the country.

Jacobin, *a.* {1795–} +Of or pertaining to Jacobins or Antifederalists; radical. Now hist.

*c***1798** FESSENDEN *Orig. Poems* (1806) 28 She weeps lest her sons should by . . . jacobin phrensy be driven To fraternize with . . . France. **1800** J. ADAMS *Works* IX. 83 Porcupine's gazette, and Fenno's gazette . . . have done more to shuffle the cards into the hands of the jacobin leaders, than all the acts of administration. **1803** J. Q. ADAMS *Diary* 17 Coalition of the Jacobin party so called with the Junto. **1868** *N.Y. Herald* 10 July 6/2 The delegates . . . were called together by pure patriotism and by a resolve to stand by the constitution, now threatened by Jacobin revolutionists.

Jacobinic, Jacobinical, *a.* {1793–} +Characteristic of or pertaining to the American Jacobins; radical. Now hist. — **1802** HAMILTON *Works* VII. 325 If his [Jefferson's] plan has been to rise to power on the ladder of Jacobinic principles [etc.]. **1822** J. Q. ADAMS *Diary* 282 Archer was a Radical and inclined to be Jacobinical. **1878** STOWE *Poganuc People* 105 The Rev. Mr. Coan rejoiced in the result of the election. Not that he was by any means friendly to the ideas of the Jacobinical party by whose help it had been carried.

Jacobinism. {1793–} +The principles and policies of American Jacobins, or those attributed to them. Now hist.

1792 JEFFERSON *Writings* VIII. 444 They endeavored . . . to conjecture up the ghost of antifederalism, and to have it believed that this and republicanism were the same, and that both were Jacobinism. **1800** *Steele P.* I. 190 The General Assembly have commenced their annual Session, with a higher tone of Jacobinism than has ever heretofore appeared. **1801** J. ADAMS *Works* IX. 98 The imputation of jacobinism . . . will have no weight with me. **1804** CUTLER in *Life & Corr.* II. 158 Never before have I seen the demon of Jacobinism display the cloven hoof with equal audacity. **1869** STOWE *Oldtown Folks* 222 We are both stanch Federalists, and make the walls ring with our denunciations of Jacobinism and Democracy.

Jacobinize, *v.* {1793–} +*tr.* To win to the cause or support of the Antifederalists. — **1801** F. AMES *Works* (1854) I. 291 Great efforts will be made to jacobinize Massachusetts, and to elect Gerry [governor].

Jacob's ladder. {1733–} +An American wild flower, *Polemonium reptans.*

1791 MUHLENBERG *Index Florae* 163 *Polemonium reptans.* Jacobs-Ladder. **1843** TORREY *Flora N.Y.* II. 94 Jacob's Ladder . . . [is found in] moist woods and meadows. Cattaraugus county. **1857** GRAY *Botany* 330 Jacob's Ladder. . . . Shady river banks, W. New York to Wisconsin and southward.

+b. A flowering weed, *Smilax peduncularis.*

1817–8 EATON *Botany* (1822) 462 *Smilax peduncularis*, jacob's ladder. **1845** LINCOLN *Botany* App. 168/2.

+c. A popular name for any one of many other United States plants.

1784 CUTLER in *Mem. Academy* I. 434 *Uvularia*, . . . Bellwort, Sweet-smelling Solomon's Seal, Jacob's Ladder. **1892** *Amer. Folk-Lore* V. 94 *Celastrus scandens*, Roxbury wax-work. E. Mass. Jacob's ladder. Stratham, N.H. *Ib.* 101 *Linaria vulgaris*, Jacob's ladder. Parts of N.E. **1900** BACHELLER *E. Holden* 58 The straight road, . . . glorious in a double fringe of golden rod and purple aster and yellow John's-wort and the deep blue of the Jacob's ladder.

***Jacob('s) staff. 1.** A strong, iron-pointed rod used by surveyors as a compass support. +**2.** (See quotation.) — (1) **1838** W. T. SHERMAN in *Sherman Lett.* 5 You have become quite an expert engineer,—much better acquainted with 'Jacob staffs,' chains, compasses, etc., than you used to be with Euclid and Virgil. **1843** *Amer. Pioneer* II. 379 A council of war was held forthwith to devise a plan for attacking Bruin. One, proposed by John Stinson, was with the marker's tomahawk and my steel-pointed jacob staff. (2) **1891** COULTER *Bot. W. Texas* I. 33 *Fouquiera splendens* . . . [is] common on rocky mesas from the Colorado to the Pecos and westward. Known as 'Jacob's staff' or 'Ocotillo.'

Jaconet. A fine, lightweight cotton cloth, frequently printed, originally made in India. Also *jaconet muslin.* {1769–} — **1790** *Columbian Centinel* 9 Oct. 31/2 Will be sold at Publick Vendue . . . Black Modes, . . . Jackonet Muslins, . . . Castor Hats. **1800** *Ib.* 8 Feb. 4/2 Now selling off . . . a Handsome assortment of 6–4 plain, striped, checked, sprigged, and spotted Jaconet Muslins. **1861** *Chicago Tribune* 26 May 1/8 Choice styles of French Muslins, Figured Jaconets, French Prints [for sale]. **1875** *Ib.* 26 July 1/1 We are offering splendid Bargains in . . . Lawns, Swisses, Books, Nainsooks, Jacinets, etc.

Jacqueminot. A hybrid variety of rose of a deep red color. {1863–} Also attrib. — **1882** *Harper's Mag.* Dec. 51/2 A lovely Jacqueminot rose on its tall stem . . . makes its vivid crimson felt by the eye from a long distance. **1883** *Century Mag.* Aug. 583/1 They went into the rose-house, and he gave her . . . a Jacqueminot so big, so rich and lustrous in its dark beauty that she could not help crying out with delight. **1884** ROE *Nature's Story* 230 The heat of the day had so far developed half a dozen Jacqueminot rosebuds that they were ready for gathering. **1893** POST *Harvard Stories* 19 Other faces, not so conspicuous, are apparently equally interesting over the top of glowing bunches of Jacqueminots, or of violets, as the case may be.

Jaeger. (See JÄGER.)

Jag. Also **jagg.**

***1.** A small load *of* hay, wood, etc. Now dial. {Now *dial.*}

1633 *Plymouth Col. Rec.* I. 41 One small jag of hay. **1683** *Cambridge Prop. Rec.* 158 He brought a Jagg of wood with his two cattle for Andrew Boedman. **1748** HEMPSTEAD *Diary* 507 Ben . . . bro[ugh]t home a Jagg of Pumkins. **1892** [see sense 2].

b. *transf.* An indefinite amount or quantity.

1818 FEARON *Sketches* 93 What a jag (a load) there is of them 'ere salt-water fish lately come into the States. **1833** S. SMITH *Major Downing* 190 As there was a very little rale money in the country, the Bank, went and bo't a good jag on't in Europe. **1881** INGERSOLL *Oyster-Industry* 245 *Jag.*—A lot, parcel, or quantity of oysters of indefinite size; *e.g.* 'I sold a *jag* of 75 bushels to A, B, & Co.' **1898** NICHOLAS *Idyl of Wabash* 198 Old Mis Green . . . up an' died, . . . an' left him her little jag o' proputty. **1902** LORIMER *Lett. Merchant* 34, I had delivered quite a jag of that wheat to his father myself.

2. One's fill of alcoholic drink, or the intoxicated condition resulting from this. *slang.* {1678–, *dial.*} Also transf.

1887 *Courier-Journal* 27 Jan. 2/6 The main question . . . [was] whether the three respectable ladies had 'jags' on last night and attempted to 'do up' the police. **1892** *Amer. Notes & Q.* VIII. 150 When I was a boy in the country, any fraction of a load of hay was called a 'jag'; that is, a small load. By an easy transition, one heated with wine was said to have a load or be loaded, but nowadays it is common to hear him described as 'having a frightful old jag on,' meaning the biggest kind of a load. **1895** *N.Y. Dramatic News* 26 Oct. 7/2 The Duke of Malmsbury, a gentleman with a passion for drink, and an ability to acquire a 'jag' in a wonderfully short space of time and with a single drink. **1913** LONDON *Valley of Moon* I. xv, 'Aw, it's only one of his cryin' jags,' Mary said. **1920** ALSAKER *Eating for Health* 479 Those who overeat of starches and sweets often manufacture much alcohol in the digestive tract. They go on a jag without knowing what makes them feel gay.

3. Attrib. in sense 2 with *artist, cure, factory, mill.*

1894 MATTHEWS in *Harper's Mag.* Jan. 226/1 Say! ain't they a jag-factory somewheres round here? Come in and have one with me. **1895** *N.Y. Dramatic News* 26 Oct. 7/3 W. S. Hart, as the lightning 'jag' artist, was unable to save the part. **1896** *Congress. Rec.* 15 April 4024/1 [Is it] the policy of the Board to run a saloon at one of the institutions and a 'jag cure' at the other? **1904** *Topeka Capital* 9 June 4 The mayor and marshal allow gambling dens to run on High street and a notorious jag mill to run on Main street.

Jäger. Also †**jager.** [G., 'hunter.']

+**1.** A German mercenary rifleman employed by Great Britain during the American Revolution. Now hist. {1783–}

1776 in F. Moore *Songs Amer. Revol.* (1856) 125 *n.*, [The British government] has . . . succeeded in raising a legion of Jagers, people brought up to the use of the rifle-barrel guns, in boar hunting. **1778** *Penna. Mag.* VI. 197, 40 Jagers made an Excursion mounted and surprised a party of Rebels.

2. A large, predatory sea bird belonging to one of several varieties, and resembling a sea gull. {1826– (Stephens *Shaw's Zool.* XIII. I. 210)}

1853 KANE *Grinnell Exped.* 99 The Fulmar petrel, a solitary jager (*Larus parasitica*), the Stunt jager of Marten [etc.] . . . complete the list. **1858** BAIRD *Birds Pacific R.R.* 837 The Skua Gulls; the Jagers. . . . There are four Arctic species found both in Europe and North America. **1869** *Amer. Naturalist* III. 235 Skua Gulls, or Jagers, are placed among the *Laridae.* **1880** *Lib. Universal Knowl.* VIII. 829 The jägers or gull hunters, so called because they pursue the smaller gulls, and rob them of . . . food. **1894** *Outing* XXIII. 366/2 We also killed some jaegers and small bladder-nosed seals.

b. With differentiating adjectives. { 1826– Arctic jäger (*Ib.* 211)}

1835 AUDUBON *Ornith. Biog.* III. 396 The Pomarine Jager, *Lestris Pomarinus*, . . . alighted on the water like a gull. *Ib.* 470 The Arctic Jager, *Lestris Parasiticus*, . . . generally passes through the air at a height of fifty or sixty yards, . . . ranging over the broad bays, on which gulls of various kinds are engaged in procuring their food. **1839** PEABODY *Mass. Birds* 382 Richardson's Jager, *Lestris Richardsonii.* . . . Its flight is firm and long continued. **1874** COUES *Birds N.W.* 611 Parasitic Jaeger. . . . North Atlantic Ocean, and sea-coasts of Europe and America. *Ib.* 615 Buffon's or the Long-tailed Jaeger. . . . Coasts of North America and Europe, chiefly in higher latitudes. **1883** *Nat. Museum Bul.* No. 27, 173 Richardson's Jaeger. . . . South in winter to New York, Illinois, Colorado (!), and even to coast of Brazil.

+**Jagged,** *a.* Intoxicated, drunk, 'on a jag.' *slang.* — **1737** *Penna. Gazette* 13 Jan. 1/3 He's Jagg'd. **1907** 'O. HENRY' *Trimmed Lamp* 162 What I want is a masterful man that slugs you when he's jagged and hugs you when he ain't jagged.

Jaguar. [Sp. and Pg., of Tupian origin.] One of the largest of the great spotted cats (*Felis onca*), ranging as far north as Texas and Arizona. {1604–} — [**1774** GOLDSMITH *Hist. Earth* (1822) II. 430 The Jaguar or Panther of America . . . is also said to be lower upon its legs, and less than the leopard of Senegal.] **1817** BENTLEY *Diary* IV. 444, I visited the Jaguar from Brazil brought into this town [Salem, Mass.]. **1872** POWERS *Afoot & Alone* 224 That terrible yell! Is it a lion, or a jaguar? There is another. They fight. **1899** *Boston Transcript* 8 July 24/1 There are plenty of deer and turkeys, as well as the 'yow-yow' and many other kinds of cats. The 'yow-yow,' so pronounced, is spelled jaguar in Spanish, but few Americans know how to call properly its name, which is a phonetic rendering of the animal's cry. **1917** *Mammals of Amer.* 150 The jaguar ranged as far north as latitude 37°, but like many others of our large-game animals, has gradually receded before the trend of civilization.

***Jail.** A place of confinement, usually maintained by a county, for one awaiting trial or receiving punishment for a crime; a prison or lockup. (Cf. GAOL, GOAL.[1])

1776 LEACOCK *Fall Brit. Tyranny* III. ii, Other houses of our God converted into . . . barracks, and common jails, where you will perish with want. **1873** *Newton Kansan* 6 March 3/5 Jester . . . broke jail. **1899** CHESNUTT *Conjure Woman* 3 There were two or three hotels, a courthouse, a jail, stores, offices, and all the appurtenances of a county seat. **1923** DUTTON *Shadow On Glass* 205, I had the idea he was still held in the jail at Westerly.

+**b.** *transf.* (See quotation.)

1900 *Dialect Notes* II. 43 College Words and Phrases [include] . . . *jail*, Dormitory for women students. Ta[lladega Coll., Ala.].

2. Attrib. with *bleach, bond, door,* etc.

1851 CIST *Cincinnati* 215 Dorr, Thompson & Magness . . . manufacture . . . gratings and balconies, iron stairs, jail doors and vaults. **1873** *Winfield* (Kansas) *Courier* 11 Jan. 3/1 The elections for jail and railroad bonds were declared void on account of an informality in the call. **1888** 'CRADDOCK' *Despot* 29 A man with that singular pallor acquired by years of indoor life, and known as 'jail bleach.' **1894** *Harper's Mag.* Feb. 484/2 Lindman had spent the night in the jail parlor. **1898** CANFIELD *Maid of Frontier* 90 He had long been made acquainted with . . . court attendance and jail duty. **1911** *Okla. Session Laws* 3 Legisl. 27 The board of county commissioners may allow such jail guards as are necessary. **1917** SINCLAIR *King Coal* 195 They say he has a jail-record.

***Jailer.** Also †**jaylor,** †**goaler.** The warden of a jail or prison. — **1636** *Plymouth Laws* 48 As Jaylor to keepe such as shall be comitted. **1754** *S.C. Gazette* 8 Jan., It is said that the goaler of the chatelet is put in prison. **1800** in Rothert *Muhlenberg Co.* 46 Sheriff Samuel Russell was appointed Jailor of this county. **1896** WILKINS *Madelon* 60 He was writing a letter when the bolt shot and the jailer entered with Madelon.

+**Jail house.** A building used for the retention or confinement of prisoners; a jail. *colloq.* — **1812** ASBURY *Journal* III. 399 We left our lodging in the jail-house, and came away to Green Hill's. **1904** *Dialect Notes* II. 419, I can find my way when I get past the jail-house.

+**Jake.** Short for COUNTRY JAKE. *colloq.* — **1895** *Dialect Notes* I. 389 *Jake:* a rough, uncouth country fellow. N.C., Tenn., Mo., Kan. **1915** *Ib.* IV. 199 He's no jake even though he did come from a Nebraska farm.

Jalap. Also **jallop,** etc. [F. from Sp. *jalapa*, fr. *Jalapa* (fr. Nahuatl *Xalapan*), a Mexican place name.]

1. Any one of several American tuberous plants, particularly *Exogonium jalapa*, yielding medicinal jalap.

[**1668** J. WINTHROP *Letters* (1882) 136 Some vegetables of this country, & one especially wch might be accounted a kind of jalap, but that it causeth to vomit as well as purge.] **1772** in P. L. Phillips *Notes on B. Romans* (1924) 47 A specimen of the Jalap of this Country . . . has been lately discovered within the Province by Mr. Romans—But I cannot take upon me to Say whether it may prove to be the real Jalap or not.

2. The purgative root of such a plant, or a drug made from it. {1675–} Also *jalap root.*

1682 *S.C. Hist. Coll.* II. 34 Drugs—Jallop, Sassaparilla, Turmerick, Sassafras, Snake-root and divers others. **1724** *New-Eng. Courant* 10–17 Feb. 2/2 To be sold at his Shop, . . . good Jallop Root at 23s. per Pound. **1782** in S. E. Baldwin *Simeon Baldwin* 115 The natural consequences of a potion of powdered Jallap . . . keeps me very busy. **1856** GOODRICH *Recoll.* I. 376 A family that held to brandy, would hardly hold intercourse with another which held to jalap. **1888** *Century Mag.* Aug. 551/2 He done his lev'lest best; not only bleedin', but calomel and jalap.

Jam, *n.*[1] A kind of preserves made by boiling mashed fruit with sugar. {1730–6–} Also attrib. — **1791** *Phil. Trans.* III. 75 Whether he had found . . . relief from the pain of the stone, from the Blackberry Jam, of which he took large quantities. **1878** *Amer. Home Cook Book* 170 You may make a charlotte with any sort of jam. **1912** N. WOODROW *Sally Salt* 92 Sally straightened herself up from the jam-pots.

Jam, *n.*[2]

+**1.** An accumulation of timber, driftwood, ice, etc., blocking a stream; a log jam. Also attrib.

1805 SIBLEY in *Ann. 9th Congress* 2 Sess. 1076 Its overflowing [is] occasioned by a jam of timber choking the river. **1850** JUDD *R. Edney* xvi. 199 At the head of the pond was probably also a jam of ice. **1902** WHITE *Blazed Trail* 358 Down at the booms the jam crew received the drive as fast as it came down. **1905** *Forestry Bureau Bul.* No. 61, 39 An expert river driver who, during the drive, is stationed at a point where a jam is feared . . . [is called a] jam cracker. (P[acific] C[oast] F[orest].) **1905** WIGGIN *Rose* 95 By the time the jam neared the falls . . . it was made up of tier after tier of huge ice cakes. **1909** WHITE *Rules of Game* I. xii, 'Where's the drive, doctor?' asked the lumberman. 'This is the jam camp,' replied the cook.

+**2.** A crowded social gathering; a party. *Obs.* {a crowd 1806–}

1827 LONGFELLOW in S. Longfellow *H. W. Longfellow* I. 123, I have been several times to her evening jams; but, as it was Lent, there was no dancing. **1853** KANE *Grinnell Exped.* 260 At those funny little jams, that we call in Philadelphia 'parties.' **1889** S. HALE *Letters* 213 We left at ten-thirty, and might have gone on to Mrs. Secretary Whitney's jam.

+**Jam,** *n.*[3] *pl.* =JIMJAM. *slang.* — **1888** *Boston Globe* 4 March (F.), My fader's de best doctor in Boston, an' . . . keeps de medicine to stave off de jams already mixed. **1894** WISTER in *Harper's Mag.* July 208/1 That's the kind of clock gives a man the jams. Sends him crazy.

+**Jam,** *a.* Excellent, ideal, topnotch. Freq. with *up. colloq.*

1838 *Lexington Observer* 2 June, There was something jam about Nance, that they couldn't hold a candle to. **1839** F. TROLLOPE *Domestic Manners* xxix. 272 There they go, that's jam! and now we must set to slick. *Ib.* 273 Say no more, that's a jam gal. **1841** *S. Lit. Messenger* VII. 54/2 Reaching him a hand, Received him, introduced him to 'the jam-Up little company' in his command. **1855** HALIBURTON *Nature & Human Nature* (1859) 277 The temperature must have been perfect [in Paradise], and connubial bliss, I allot, was rael jam up. **1899** GREEN *Va. Word-Book* 202 *Jam-up*, a degree of high perfection.

Jam, *v.* {1719–}

+**1.** *intr.* Of logs, floating ice, etc.: To collect in an immovable mass, blockading a stream.

1706 SEWALL *Diary* II. 156 The Ice jam'd and made a great Damm. **1848** THOREAU *Maine Woods* 33 Just above McCauslin's, there is a rocky rapid, where logs jam in the spring. **1875** *Mich. Rep.* XXXI. 339 There are three miles of rapids, upon which logs coming down in the spring of 1872 had jammed. **1901** WHITE *Claim Jumpers* (1916) 132 Down near our way the timber began to jam, and it is all choked up. **1905** *Forestry Bureau Bul.* No. 61, 40 *Jam, to break a*, to start in motion logs which have jammed.

+**2.** *tr.* (See quotations.)

1860 *Harper's Mag.* April 607/1 No amount of judgment can select with any certainty a favorable location for 'jamming' or turning a river. **1909** *Cent. Suppl.* 665/3 *Jam*, . . . to push (a bill or measure) through the regular routine of a legislative body by the brute force of a majority controlled by 'the machine,' without proper consideration or discussion. (Political slang.) *N.Y. Com. Advertiser*, April 11, 1901.

+**Jam,** *adv.* Also **jamb.** *colloq.*

1. *Jam up.* **a.** Closely pressed, crowded. **b.** Completely, without reservation. **c.** Excellently, perfectly. **d.** Close to, pressing close upon.

(a) 1825 NEAL *Bro. Jonathan* II. 52 He had been sitting, for two or three hours, without opening his mouth, 'jam up' in a back seat. **1837** *Baltimore Transcript* 24 June 2/4 (Th.), I was standing by the Doctor jam up to him. **(b) 1835** CROCKETT *Tour* 192 [Andrew Jackson] went jam up for war; but the cabinet got him down to half heat. **1846** *Congress. Globe* 22 May 852 Their notion is that we go jam up to 54°40', and the Russians come jam down to the same. **(c) 1866** C. H. SMITH *Bill Arp* 61 Linton played his part of the program jam up. **(d) 1874** EGGLESTON *Circuit Rider* xvi. 142 Jam up fifty miles, and over tough roads.

2. *Jam (up) against,* smack against or into, as close to as possible.

1842 *Amer. Pioneer* I. 184 The next moment the sloop ran jamb against it. **1850** LEWIS *La. Swamp Doctor* 66 The snake-box was placed . . . jam up, as luck would have it, against one of the chimneys. **1852** STOWE *Uncle Tom* I. 49 It'll stand, if it only keeps jam up agin de wall!

3. *Jam full,* closely filled, packed.

1882 S. HALE *Letters* 139 A car came along, and I climbed up on it with difficulty, to find it jam full and people sticking out of the doors and windows. **1884** 'MARK TWAIN' *H. Finn* xxiii. 226 The house was jam full of men. **1894** — *P. Wilson* vi, De house is plum' jam full o' people.

Jamaica. [An island in the West Indies.]

1. Jamaica rum or spirits. {1848–}

1775 ADAIR *Indians* 339 A large dose of old Jamaica and qualified mercury. **1823** COOPER *Pioneers* xix, It's not the stuff to raise the heat in my body, neither; the raal Jamaiky being the only thing to do that. **1855** SIMMS *Forayers* 237 Here comes Little Peter . . . bringing out a jug of Jamaica which I ordered for the use of your troop.

2. *attrib.* **a.** In names of various things imported from Jamaica.

1707 *Boston News-Letter* 27 Jan. 2/2 To be Sold . . . in Boston near the Swing-Bridge, . . . Jamaica & Leeward-Islands fine Sugar. **1715** *Ib.* 16 May 2/2 To be Sold Mens and Womens Shoes from England, . . . Jamaica Sole Leather very Good, cheaper than New-England Leather. **1807** J. R. SHAW *Life* (1930) 96 [We] got a good breakfast in the morning with a bumper of Jamaica spirits to wash it down. **1832** *Louisville Pub. Advertiser* 3 March, 8 puncheons Jamaica rum; 2 ceroons indigo. **1876** *Wide Awake* 147/2 'He'll get his death a-cold.' . . . 'If we only had some Jamaica ginger.'

b. Designating various species of fish and plants: (see quotations).

*c*1830 *Waldie's Select Library* II. 88/3 The land crab, which is common to many of the West India islands, is more generally known as the Jamaica crab, because it has been most frequently described from observation in that island. **1897** SUDWORTH *Arborescent Flora* 264 *Ichthyomethia piscipula*. . . . Jamaica Dogwood (Fla.).

+**Jamaica fish.** Codfish of an inferior grade which is exported from New England to Jamaica. — **1792** BELKNAP *New-Hampshire* III. 214 The fish of the summer and fall fares is divided into two sorts, the one called merchantable, and the other Jamaica fish. **1800** *Mass. H. S. Coll.* VII. 249 The summer codfish, called Jamaica fish, which goes to the West-Indies, is about three dollars a quintal.

+**Jambone.** (See quotation.) — **1864** DICK *Amer. Hoyle* (1866) 83 Jambone is a word unknown to Webster, but, as applied to Euchre, means that a party who plays Jambone plays a lone hand with his cards exposed upon the table.

+**Jamboree.** **1.** (See quotation.) **2.** An unrestrained celebration or merrymaking; a big party or spree. — **(1) 1864** DICK *Amer. Hoyle* (1866) 85 Jamboree signifies the combination of the five highest cards, as, for example, the two Bowers, Ace, King, and Queen of trumps in one hand, which entitles the holder to count sixteen points. **(2) 1868** *N.Y. Herald* 10 July 8/3 The Seventh regiment has gone on a jamboree to Norwich, Connecticut. **1884** *Boston Jrnl.* 10 Dec. 2/3 It is very creditable to Mr. O'Brien that he did not open a jamboree at the Parker House on the night of his election. **1895** *N.Y. Dramatic News* 7 Dec. 10/3 After the coons were paid off on Saturday, some of them started on a jamboree. **1920** COOPER *Under Big Top* 224 That jamboree was something which made you gasp in horror when you read about it.

+**James River.** **1.** Tobacco grown in the James River region of Virginia. **2.** *James River fever,* (see quotation). — **(1) 1785** in *S. Lit. Messenger* XXVIII. 37/2 Some very low sales of tobacco from Britain has much reduced the price here; James River to about 4 d. and Rappahannock to a Guinea. **(2) 1866** MOORE *Women of War* 39 Here were hundreds and hundreds languishing with that low, dull fever that overcame so many who shared in that [Peninsular] campaign, and which was called in the army the 'James River fever.'

+**Jamestown lily.** *local.* [Cf. JAMESTOWN WEED.] =JIMSON WEED. — **1894** *Amer. Folk-Lore* VII. 95 *Datura Stramonium* . . . stinkweed, West Va.; Jamestown lily, Lincolnton, N.C.

+**Jamestown weed.** [fr. *Jamestown,* Va.] Orig. form of JIMSON WEED.

1687 J. CLAYTON *Acct. Va.* in *Phil. Trans.* XLI. 160 The Soldiers . . . lighting in great Quantities on an Herb called James-town-weed, they gathered it; and by eating thereof in plenty, were rendered apish and foolish, as if they had been drunk, or were become Idiots. **1709** LAWSON *Carolina* 78 Mint, James-Town Weed, so called from Virginia, the Seed it bears is very like that of an Onion; it is excellent for curing Burns, and asswaging Inflammations, but taken inwardly brings on a sort of drunken Madness. **1781–2** JEFFERSON *Notes Va.* (1788) 36 James-town weed. *Datura Stramonium.* **1832** KENNEDY *Swallow Barn* I. 180 A rank crop of Jamestown weed grew up within. **1877** *Harper's Mag.* Dec. 79/1 [The house] stood in a field overgrown with thistles and Jamestown weed. **1904** GLASGOW *Deliverance* 273 Well, you must persuade her to use a liniment of Jamestown weed steeped in whisky.

+**Jam-up,** *a.* (See JAM *a.*)

***Janitor.** {doorkeeper, *c*1630–} The caretaker of a building. Also attrib.

'Sc. and *U.S.' O.E.D. Suppl.*

1868 *Mich. Agric. Rep.* VII. 22 The above amount embraces all expenditures in this department, and includes expenses for wood, furniture, janitor work, &c. **1882** GODFREY *Nantucket* 23 Mr. Swain is also the janitor of the building, and applications for renting the hall should be made to him. **1902** MCFAUL *Ike Glidden* 32 During the hours in which Ike was alone at the office Rastus, the colored janitor of the building, became an habitual caller. **1910** *N.Y. Ev. Post* 27 Oct. 2 Most of the school janitors are paid according to the floor space they must attend to. **1923** HERRICK *Lilla* 132 He could play god . . . [to] the teachers and janitors of the county schools.

+**Janitorship.** The office or position of janitor. Also attrib. — **1878** HARTE *Drift from 2 Shores* 144 A desire for rural repose led him to seek the janitorship of Doemville Academy. **1893** *Columbus Dispatch* 12 July, The janitorship fight is expected to rear its 'hideous form' in the meeting of the Board of Education tomorrow night.

Janitress. {1806–} +A scrubwoman; a female janitor. — **1890** *Advance* 20 Nov. 864/2 She's janitress in one of those industrial schools. **1903** *N.Y. Sun* 29 Nov. 8 The janitors object to allowing the janitresses to be so styled. 'Scrubwomen' is the term which they insist upon applying to their female rivals. **1908** 'O. HENRY' *Options* 29, I'd ask the janitress for one, but I don't want 'em hep just yet to the fact that I'm pounding the asphalt for another job.

+**January thaw.** A thaw or spell of mild weather occurring in the month of January: (see also quot. 1832). — **1832** WILLIAMSON *Maine* I. 100 'The January thaw,' when the rain sometimes freezes as it falls [and] covers the face of the earth with a glare ice. **1847** *Knickerb.* XXX. 239, I do not know precisely what makes a January thaw so pleasant. **1857** DANA *Great West* 144 There is generally an unbroken winter from the middle of November till January, when there is almost invariably a 'January thaw'; after which the weather is generally mild. **1873** BEADLE *Undevel. West* 711 No 'January thaw' need be apprehended.

Japan. {1613–} +In attrib. uses designating various plants, trees, etc., introduced into the United States from Japan.

1854 *Penna. Agric. Rep.* 73 For pair Japan fowls, $2.00. **1855** BROWNE in *Amer. Inst. N.Y. Trans.* 597 Japan pea . . . has been since cultivated with remarkable success. **1865** RICHARDSON *Secret Service* 39 Japan plums hung ripe. **1868** GRAY *Field Botany* 131 Japan Allspice, . . . *Chimonanthus fragrans.* Shrub with long branches, . . . hardy S. of Penn. **1879** *Scribner's Mo.* May 55/1 One of the very best on our lawn is the Japan Judas-tree. **1889** *Rep. Secy. Agric.* 29 Tests have been made . . . with olives, Japan persimmons, pine-apples, etc. **1892** APGAR *Trees Northern U.S.* There are a great number of Japan Maples, many of them probably varieties of this species [*Acer palmatum*].

Japan cedar. A valuable timber tree (*Cryptomeria japonica*), introduced into the United States from Japan. {1852–} — **1889** *Rep. Secy. Agric.* 115 An avenue of the Japan cedar . . . had each alternate tree root-pruned in August. **1892** APGAR *Trees Northern U.S.* 198 *Japan Cedar.* . . . A beautiful tree from Japan, 50 to 100 ft. high.

+**Japan clover.** A cloverlike plant introduced into the United States before 1846 from Japan. (Cf. *Japanese clover* s.v. JAPANESE *a.*) — **1868** *Rep. Comm. Agric. 1867* 253 The Japan clover (*Lespedeza striata,*) . . . has already extended over large districts in the more southern States, proving itself to possess extraordinary merit, both for fodder and grazing. **1878** in Killebrew *Tenn. Grasses* 209 Japan Clover, or Sing Grass, *Lespedeza striata,* . . . seems especially adapted to the Southern states, not flourishing above 36°, [and] growing with great luxuriance on the poorest soils. **1889** VASEY *Agric. Grasses* 95 *Lespedeza striata* (Japan Clover) . . . was introduced in some unknown way, over forty years ago, from China into the South Atlantic States.

Japanese, *a.* {1719–} In the names of various American plants: (see quotations). {1866– (*Treas. Bot.* s.v. *Yam*)} (Cf. JAPAN.) — **1879** WHITMAN *Diary* (1904) 57, I stop long before a tall clump of the Japanese sunflowers. **1890** *Cent.* 4738/3 California privet, the Japanese privet, sometimes misnamed *Ligustrum Californicum.* **1891** *Ib.* 7007/2 The Chinese or Japanese yam . . . excited considerable interest in Europe and America, at the time of the potato rot, as a possible substitute for that crop. **1892** APGAR *Trees Northern U.S.* 196 Japanese Arbor-Vitae. . . . Beautiful small trees or generally shrubs (in this country), of a score of named varieties of many colors and forms of plant and foliage. **1901** MOHR *Plant Life Ala.* 54 The Japanese clover (*Lespedeza striata*) . . . has now spread over thousands of square miles, west to Louisiana, and southern Arkansas, and as far north as Maryland.

+**Japan lily.** Any one of several large-flowered lilies introduced into the United States from Japan. — **1836** LINCOLN *Botany* App. 111 [*Lilium*] *japonicum,* (Japan lily,) corolla elongated into a tube; flowers very large, pure white, with a streak of blue. **1850** *New Eng. Farmer* II. 126/2 The *L[ilium] superbum* is the most magnificent of our wild herbaceous plants,—far more showy than the much-lauded new Japan lily, (*L. lancifolium*). **1899** GOING *Flowers* 204 The white day or Japan lily opens about sundown, giving forth an alluring sweetness.

Japanner. A craftsman who lacquers various articles for sale. {1695–} — **1712** SEWALL *Diary* II. 333 Pendleton, the Japanner, making more haste than good, . . . jumping from a Sloop broke his Legg. **1715** *Boston Rec.* 238 She is entertained at ye House of Mr. William Randoll Jappanner in Queen Street. **1809** CUMING *Western Tour* 222 Pittsburgh [has] . . . seven coppersmiths, tinplate workers, and japanners.

Japonica. Any one of various ornamental plants originating in Japan; also, a blossom of one of these plants. {1819–} — **1851** MELVILLE *Moby-Dick* xlii. 207 Whiteness refiningly enhances beauty, . . . as in marbles, japonicas, and pearls. **1854** M. J. HOLMES *Tempest & Sunshine* xviii. 252 A single japonica rested among the curls of her bright hair. **1859** A. VAN BUREN *Sojourn in South* 134 That richest and sweetest blossomed of tropical shrubs—the japonica—that never blossoms only in winter. **1865** *Atlantic Mo.* XV. 424 The deserted house was embowered in . . . japonicas, bananas, oranges. **1905** 'O. HENRY' *Heart of West* 33, I have a movement on foot that . . . leaves you writing to the society column to inquire whether the best man wears a japonica or seamless socks at the wedding.

+**Japonicadom.** (See quot. 1859.) — **1851** A. O. HALL *Manhattaner* 123 The general society of New Orleans is still in a chaotic state, and she has no located, acknowledged empire of Japonicadom. **1859** BARTLETT 219 *Japonicadom* [is] a word invented by N. P. Willis to denote the upper classes of society. *a*1870 CHIPMAN *Notes on Bartlett* 219 *Japonicadom.* . . . Allusive to the flower known as the Japonica lily.

+**Jaquima.** *S.W.* [Sp. *jáquima.*] (See quotations and cf. HACKAMORE.) — **1877** BARTLETT 321 *Jaquima,* . . . the head-stall of a halter, used in

Texas and California for breaking wild horses. **1894** *Dialect Notes* I. 324 *Jáquima:* the headstall of a halter; often pronounced somewhat like *hackamore*.

+**Jar.** (See quot. 1863.) — **1863** Randall *Pract. Shepherd* 73 Those usually short, detached, not very coarse, glistening particles of hair found in the fleece, termed 'jar,' are very objectionable. **1878** *Ill. Dept. Agric. Trans.* XIV. 239 The jar in coarse hair invariably found in the wrinkled fleeces.

+**Jarabe.** [Sp. *jarabe*, 'syrup.'] A Mexican dance. — **1834** A. Pike *Sketches* 103 In the jarabes, or singular dances of the fandango, her first partner was always Rafael. **1844** Kendall *Santa Fé Exped.* II. 347 A party of dancers . . . were executing one of the rude jarabes of the country. **1910** J. Hart *Vigilante Girl* 157 The fandango was danced by the lower orders, generally combined with the jarabe, a Mexican dance.

+**Jarfly.** Any one of various cicadas or harvest flies which make jarring noises. — **1880** M. Allan-Olney *New Virginians* I. 110 There is the thing they call the 'jar-fly,' for instance. . . . It makes a noise like a watchman's rattle. **1897** Glasgow *Descendant* 10 The low chirping of insects began in the hedges, the treble of the cricket piercing shrilly above the base of the jar-fly. **1902** Gordon *Recoll. Lynchburg* 44 The jar-flies, as if in sympathy, sang out their prophecies of a sultry day.

+**Jasm.** *local.* Energy, enthusiasm, 'drive.' — **1860** Holland *Miss Gilbert* xix. 350 If you'll take thunder and lightning and a steamboat and a buzz-saw and mix 'em up and put 'em into a woman, that's jasm. **1871** — in *Scribner's Mo.* II. 433/2 When a man has genuine 'jasm' and irrepressibility, a way of carrying out big enterprises to brilliant and successful issues, . . . we are apt to wink at his processes and praise his pluck. **1886** *Harper's Mag.* Sept. 579/2 Willin', but hain't no more jas'm than a dead corn-stalk.

***Jasmine.** Any of various plants, +esp. the Carolina jessamine. — **1802** Drayton *S. Carolina* 6 Their undergrowth is covered with a profusion of shrubbery; and jassmines. **1846** Thorpe *Myst. Backwoods* 166 The roe eat up the dahlias, jasmines, or other choice flowers of the neighbouring gardens. **1872** *Atlantic Mo.* May 548 They got among tangled jasmine-vines and green brier. **1899** Going *Flowers* 239 The bean, jasmine, wistaria, and convolvulus turn always in the contrary direction to the hands of a watch, or against the sun. **1912** N. Woodrow *Sally Salt* 113 He lifted his head, sniffing the odor shaken from the insignificant green bells of a night-blooming jasmine by a wandering breeze.

***Jasper.** An opaque varicolored variety of quartz. — **1789** Morse *Amer. Geog.* 487 Here also are mines of gold . . . and a great quantity of excellent crystal and jasper. **1818** Schoolcraft *Journal* 5 Our path this day has lain across an elevated ridge of land . . . strewed with fragments of sandstone, quartz, and a species of coarse, flinty jasper. **1873** *Harper's Mag.* March 620/2 The material of these splintered stones consists of jaspers, quartzites, . . . and less frequently of black flint.

Java. [An island in the Dutch East Indies.]

+**1.** Coffee grown in Java, or a drink prepared from this. In modern slang, any coffee.

1850 Garrard *Wah-To-Yah* xiii. 169 Partaking of the nectar-like Java, . . . we smoked. **1853** *Harper's Mag.* VII. 276/1 Sh'd be glad to sell you a lot of damag'd Java . . . very cheap. **1902** Lorimer *Lett. Merchant* xiv, He had changed his face for the one which he wore when he sold an easy customer ground peas and chicory for O. G. Java. **1907** London *Road* 124, I shared my Java and grub with him.

+**2.** A breed of chickens; also, a fowl of this breed. Also attrib. with *fowl.*

1849 *New Eng. Farmer* I. 386 *Java* fowls were shown by John Giles. **1871** Lewis *Poultry Book* 70 The Black Javas. This species of birds are said to be among the most valuable breeds of this country.

3. *attrib.* Designating birds brought from or native to Java. {Java sparrow, 1861–}

1859 Stowe *Minister's Wooing* ii, A Java dove comes whirring down and settles on her finger. **1884** *Amer. Naturalist* XVIII. 949 [The principal occupation of] a male white Java sparrow . . . [was] the pecking and pulling out of feathers of the cutthroat finch.

+**Javalina.** Also **javelina, havalena,** etc. *S.W.* [Sp. *jabalina*, 'wild sow.'] 'Peccary; a hog-like mammal formerly common to parts of Texas and Mexico' (Bentley). — **1822** Dewees *Lett. from Texas* 25 We are obliged to use great care when hunting for them [*sc.* bears], lest the *havalenas* (meaning the peccary) kill our dogs. **1877** Cozzens *Young Trail Hunters* 46 (Bentley), Soon afterwards they discovered the tracks of the havilinas. **1894** *Scribner's Mag.* May 603/1 Lucky indeed will be the guest who shall be invited to partake of . . . stewed 'jabalin.' **1900** Smithwick *Evolution of State* 309 Occasionally we . . . ran into a drove of javalinas—Mexican hogs. **1900** Webster *Suppl.* Javelina. **1923** J. H. Cook *On Old Frontier* 27 A javalina (musk hog) when in battle resembled more than anything else, a 'ball of hair with a butcher knife run through it.'

***Jawbone.** +**1.** A castanet. *slang.* **2.** ?=Jew's-harp. Also *jawbone lute.* — (1) **1844** *Cincinnati Misc.* 14 Fowler . . . found the truant as he expected at a dance house on Columbia st, with his slippers off, dancing and playing the *jaw bones* or Castanets. (2) **1845** *Knickerb.* XXVI. 336 The frequent sound of the violin, banjo, or jaw-bone lute is . . . an indication. **1869** Dumont *Benedict's Congress Songster* 50, I can play the old jawbone, and can use the fiddlebow.

Jawbreaker. {1839–} +**1.** A kind of hard candy. *colloq.* +**2.** (Hyphened.) A machine for crushing ore. — (1) **1875** *Chicago Tribune* 21 Nov. 2/6 Each one had grown tired of jaw-breakers and popcorn balls. **1905** Lincoln *Partners* 4 Jars of striped stick candy with boxes of 'jaw-breakers' and similar sweetmeats. **1909** *Dialect Notes* III. 399 *Jawbreakers* are the same as all-day suckers. (2) **1877** Raymond *8th Rep. Mines* 421, I speak of the rolls as more applicable for completing the crushing of the ore as it comes in small pieces from the jaw-breaker.

+**Jaw-cracker.** (See quot. 1840.) *colloq.* {jawbreaker, 1839–} — **1840** *Congress. Globe* 5 May 367/1 The gentleman had brought up many hard words, which he said he could scarcely spell, nor pronounce them after he had spelt them. They were in fact what in Virginia they termed 'jaw-crackers.' **1842** *Amer. Pioneer* I. 375, I found in his office a dictionary of jaw-crackers, of new coined words, Greek, Latin, and phrases not used by English readers. **1861** *Ladies' Repository* XXI. 180/1 We have what we call *jaw-crackers, muscle-stretchers, tongue-twisters,* etc.

+**Jaw-crusher.** =Jawbreaker 2. — **1877** Raymond *8th Rep. Mines* 420 The jaw-crusher, and also the rolls, . . . simply break up the ore.

***Jay,** *n.* +Any of various American birds of the subfamily Garrulinae of the crow family.

1688 Clayton *Va.* in *Phil. Trans.* XVII. 991 The *Pica Glandarea*, or Jay, is much less than our English Jay. **1709** Lawson *Carolina* 140 Jays are here common, and very mischievous, in devouring our Fruit, and spoiling more than they eat. **1784** Smyth *Tour U.S.* I. 149 There are . . . also wood-peckers and jays of several different kinds. **1839** Hoffman *Wild Scenes* 62 The incessant call of the jay, with the ever-changing cry of the loon. **1893** Roosevelt *Wilderness Hunter* 132 Jays and chickadees came round camp, and woodpeckers hammered lustily in the dead timber.

+**Jay,** *a.* Rustic, countrified, naïve. *colloq.* — **1890** Bunner *Short Sixes* 91 'T ain't neuralogy, you jay pill-box, she's cooked! **1894** Hoyt *Texas Steer* (1925) II. 28 When I fixed myself all up to please him, he thought I looked jay,—and . . . wouldn't let me go down to dinner. **1912** Nicholson *Hoosier Chron.* 268 He's only a state senator from the jayest county in Indiana. **1916** Wilson *Somewhere* viii. 348 He puts it up with the press agent of this big hotel to have the poor things [Indians] sleep up on the roof, . . . so them jay New York newspapers would fall for it, and print articles about these hardy sons of the forest.

Jay bird. {1851–} +=Blue jay.

1661 *Dedham Rec.* IV. 41 En Dani Fisher is creditor to the Towne for his sonne catching of Jaybirds: the sume of one shiling twoopenc. **1805** Lewis in *L. & Clark Exped.* II. (1904) 295, I saw also . . . a blue bird about the size of the common robin. It's action and form is somewhat that of the jay bird. **1872** Powers *Afoot & Alone* 248 Then there was the bluejay. 'Jaybird, jaybird, what'll you take for your tail?' **1896** Harris *Sister Jane* 84, I hear a flutter in the chaney-berry tree and look up and see a jaybird.

b. Attrib. with derogatory implication.

1887 *Courier-Journal* 2 May 6/5 The man who has one or more good mares to breed can . . . make a very ridiculous ass of himself . . . in using some jay-bird stallion to breed them to.

+**Jayhawk,** *v. tr.* and *intr.* To harass (someone); to steal (something); to raid or act as a jayhawker. *slang.* (Cf. Jayhawking.)

1884 'Craddock' *Where Battle Was Fought* 48 There's no use in jayhawking me. **1893** *Scribner's Mag.* XIII. 381/2 Every man suddenly discovering that somebody has jayhawked his boots or his blanket. **1901** Duncan & Scott *Allen & Woodson Co., Kansas* 595 About this time lumber was obtained for a new school house, but I am told the greater portion of it was 'jayhawked' by a wagon maker who had a shop near by. **1912** Cobb *Back Home* 94 He was jayhawkin' back and forth along the State line here, burnin' folks' houses down over their heads.

b. (See quotation.)

1905 *Forestry Bureau Bul.* No. 61, 40 *Jay hawk, to,* to strip one 4-foot length of bark from a tanbark oak, leaving the tree standing. (P[acific] C[oast] F[orest].)

+**Jayhawker.** [Origin unknown.]

1. Originally, one who took part in the irregular war (1854–60) waged in Kansas over slavery; during the Civil War, a free-lance soldier, freebooter, or guerilla operating in Kansas; latterly, any lawless marauder or robber.

1860 *Ashtabula Sentinel* (Jefferson, Ohio) 26 Dec. 5/3 By the term 'Jayhawkers' is here [in Mound City, Kan.] understood the active, fighting abolitionists. **1867** Edwards *Shelby* 418 Shelby . . . gained the glorious opportunity . . . of meeting these jayhawkers—these robbers, who for four years had desolated Missouri with fire and sword. **1881** Buel *Border Outlaws* 12 The border counties of Missouri and Kansas suffered terribly from the incursions of 'Jayhawkers' and 'Border Ruffians.' **1888** M. Lane in *America* 11 Oct. 15/3 *Jayhawker.*—A term in use in the Western States to describe the lawless unenlisted guerillas. They were in the late war, much such a class, in the Western border states, as were the Cowboys in the Revolutionary War—lawless plunderers and freebooters. **1900** Goodlander *Fort Scott* 8 We may be attacked by the Jayhawkers before morning, and you must use it [a gun]. **1910** Villard *J. Brown* 350 A leader of 'jayhawkers,' he had but little respect for man-made laws. **1920** Hunter *Trail Drivers Texas* I. 148 A Kansas jay-hawker had been . . . exacting toll from the herds.

2. a. *Jayhawker State*, Kansas.

1885 *Santa Fé Wkly. New Mexican* 3 Sept. 4/3 Mr. Hutchinson . . . has seen the Jayhawker state rise from an arid waste. **1907** *Boston Transcript*

9 Nov., A list of the popular names of the States: . . . Jayhawker—Kansas.

b. A native or citizen of Kansas.

1875 *Chambers's Jrnl.* 13 March 171 Kansas . . . is occupied by Jayhawkers. **1890** *Opelousas* (La.) *Democrat* 14 June 3/2 Some did not understand what was meant by 'Jay-hawker.' . . . This is the name that is applied to all citizens of Kansas.

3. Attrib. in sense 1 with *party, war.*

1862 *Knickerb.* LIX. 392 Guess she must a-had Secesh beaux And gone to Jayhawker parties from her youth up. **1888** *St. Louis Globe Democrat* 20 Jan. (F.), He was connected with what is known as the Jayhawker war that raged on the borders of Kansas about twenty-five years since.

+**Jayhawking.** Stealing, raiding, oppressing, etc. *slang.* Also attrib. — **1861** *N.Y. Times* 27 Dec. (Chipman), Charges of jayhawking, oppression, and so forth. **1873** BEADLE *Undevel. West* 210 'Jayhawking' was adopted into the language as a delicate euphemism for 'taking what you really needed when you couldn't pay for it.' **1886** EBBUTT *Emigrant Life* 16 We might have some wood to burn or for fences, and not be entirely dependent upon 'jay-hawking,' which is the term for stealing wood off Government land. **1888** CODY *Wild West* 471 Consequently I abandoned the jay-hawking enterprise, for such it really was. **1897** BARTON *Hero in Homespun* 218 The warning conveyed by the horseman had been of the supposed approach of the rebels, and . . . the 'jay-hawking' might now be looked for at every foot of the way.

***Jean.** Also **jeen.**

'The form *Jeans* is used in U.S.' (*O.E.D.*).

***1.** A twilled cotton cloth; a cloth of coarse material. (Cf. KENTUCKY JEAN.)

In quots. 1743–1809, as a real plural, the meaning is 'kinds of this cloth.'

1743 *Boston Weekly Messenger* 22 Aug. (Th.), Fustian Dimothys, Jeans. **1789** MORSE *Amer. Geog.* 91 A cotton manufactory has lately been established at Philadelphia, at which are made jeans, fustians, velvets, velverets and corduroys. **1809** KENDALL *Travels* II. 26 Jeans, fustians, thicksetts, velvets and other fabrics are manufactured in Providence. **1854** M. J. HOLMES *Tempest & Sunshine* v. 67 He took off his beard and put on 'a bran new suit of jeens.' **1898** B. H. YOUNG *Jessamine Co., Ky.* 240 He . . . manufactured cotton cloth and jeans.

2. *pl.* A garment of this material, esp. a pair of trousers. {1879}

1846 SOL. SMITH *Theatr. Apprent.* 48 My friend in the jeans and white hat informed me that my failure to meet my appointment had caused great consternation. **1879** BURDETTE *Hawkeyes* 198 He wears butternut jeans, and a fur cap. **1901** WHITE *Claim Jumpers* (1916) 44 The stranger was a tall, scraggly individual, dressed in the usual flannel shirt and blue jeans. **1910** RAINE *B. O'Connor* 21 Dig up, Mr. Pullman. Go way down into your jeans.

3. Attrib. in sense 1 with *britches, coat, overalls,* etc.

1787 *Md. Gazette* 1 June 4/1 A deep claret-coloured coat, much faded, with white fustian or jean waist coat and breeches. **c1845** *Big Bear Ark.* 41 His woollen jean britches did not taste well. **1846** FARNHAM *Prairie Land* 99 He was clad in a blue jeans coat, and pantaloons of the same. **1884** HARRIS *Mingo* 43 He wore a wool hat, a homespun shirt, jeans pantaloons, and cotton suspenders. **1904** GLASGOW *Deliverance* 5 He carefully wiped the blade of his knife on the leg of his blue jean overalls.

+**Jebacco boat.** = CHEBACCO BOAT. — **1799** BENTLEY *Diary* II. 304 We had an opportunity of seeing the fashion of mooring Boats commonly called Jebacco Boats. **1817** *Ib.* IV. 478 The sight of Jebacco boats building for the bay fishery . . . was very impressive.

***Jeer,** *v. tr.* To deride or treat with open mockery. {-1852; 'the earlier Eng. usage, now obs.' (Horwill)} — **1880** 'MARK TWAIN' *Tramp Abroad* xvii. 151 Everybody turned up their noses at him, and some openly jeered him. **1904** PRINGLE *Rice Planter* 90 She said some one had jeered her on the road. **1906** *N.Y. Herald* 1 Oct. 7 The motorman and conductor remained in the car and the mob jeered them.

+**Jeff,** *v. Printers' slang. intr.* To gamble by throwing quadrats as dice. — **1837** *Baltimore Commercial Transcript* 7 Nov. 2/1 (Th.), We move that the printers of the U.S. divide off in halves, and 'jeff' to see which shall go to digging ditches or picking stone coal for a living. **1888** *Amer. Humorist* (F. and H.), He never set any type except in the rush of the last day, and then he would smouch all the poetry, and leave the rest to jeff for the solid takes.

+**Jeff Davis.** [Short for *Jefferson Davis* (1808–1889), president of the Confederate States of America (1861–1865).] **1.** *Jeff Davis Grays,* a nickname for one of the regiments of the Confederate army. **2.** Used in various quips and phrases: (see quotations). *Obs.* — **(1) 1865** *Atlantic Mo.* June 746/1 Jeff-Davis Grays . . . fired with patriotism and whiskey, proud to be in Richmond. **(2) 1870** O. LOGAN *Before Footlights* 202, I thought perhaps they imagined I was a female Jeff Davis, and were going to make a *'charge a la bayonette'* instanter. **1871** DE VERE 283 The *Musical-Box* of the Confederates was also known as *Jeff Davis' Box:* it was the humorous name given by the men to the lumbering, ill-built army-wagons, which were apt to creak horribly for want of greasing.

+**Jeffdom.** [Cf. prec.] The Confederate States of America. — **1861** *N.Y. Tribune* 11 July 4/4 To attempt to issue a Union journal . . . in any city of Jeffdom, would be . . . stark mad.

+**Jefferson.** [Thomas *Jefferson* (1743–1826), third president of the United States (1801–9).] **1.** *Jefferson's giant sloth,* (see quotation). **2.** A name given a certain style of high top shoe formerly worn: (see quot. 1847). Also attrib. with *boot, shoe.* **3.** A variety of plum. — **(1) 1826** GODMAN *Nat. Hist.* II. 197 Jefferson's Giant Sloth. *Megatherium Jeffersonii.* . . . The only fragments yet obtained of the skeleton of this extinct species were discovered in a salt-petre-cave, . . . in Green Briar county, Va. **(2) 1838** *S. Lit. Messenger* IV. 639/1 Slippers, pumps, bootees, Jefferson shoes. **1843** 'CARLTON' *New Purchase* I. xi. 72 Shoes he wore, it is true—but one a coarse cow-hide laced boot, the other a calfskin Jefferson, or some other presidential name. **1847** J. S. HALL *Book of Feet* 144 The Jefferson boot, which was introduced at about the time when Mr. Jefferson came into the presidency, . . . and which that gentleman was himself fond of wearing, was laced up in front, as high as the ankles, in some instances perhaps higher. **1861** *Army Regulations* 482 Boots: . . . For all Officers—ankle or Jefferson. **(3) 1862** *Rep. Comm. Patents 1861: Agric.* 163 Plums are very productive, and those that are most prominent are the Green Gage, the Damson, and the Jefferson.

+**Jeffersonia.** (See quot. 1879.) — **1869** FULLER *Flower Gatherers* 63 [The rheumatism root] was named *Jeffersonia Diphylla,* in honor of Thomas Jefferson. **1879** WEBSTER *Suppl.* 1563/3 *Jeffersonia,* . . . A genus of American plants of the barberry family, bearing a handsome white flower, an inch in diameter; found in woods from Western New York to Wisconsin, and southwards.

+**Jeffersonian,** *n.* [See JEFFERSON.] A political follower or supporter of Thomas Jefferson (1743–1826); an advocate of political principles attributed to Jefferson; a Democrat. Also transf.

1809 *Ann. 10th Congress* 2 Sess. 1065 The fact was . . . that no Administration, even if composed of Adamites, Pickeronians, Jeffersonians, and Madisonians, . . . could uphold this navy system in time of peace. **1817** *Ann. 14th Congress* 2 Sess. 795 Persons who at that time were staunch Federalists, and since that time have been staunch Jeffersonians, Madisonians, and Monroites. **1844** 'UNCLE SAM' *Peculiarities* II. 79, [I] experienced the misery of being placed in a large room, with no other company than Inquirers, Couriers, Jeffersonians, Suns, and Polar Stars. **1880** *Lib. Universal Knowl.* I. 91 The Jeffersonians were eager for discriminations against England. **1888** BRYCE *Amer. Commonw.* II. III. liii. 326 The Jeffersonians had more faith in the masses and in leaving things alone, together with less respect for authority.

+**Jeffersonian,** *a.* [See JEFFERSON.] Of or pertaining to Thomas Jefferson, or to the political doctrines held by or attributed to him.

1799 *Spectator* (N.Y.) 3 April (Ernst). **1806** *Balance* V. 35/3 It is presumed, that he means occlusion, which is a Jeffersonian word. **1813** *Niles' Reg.* IV. *Suppl.* 65/1 This is true Jeffersonian, Madisonian, democratic economy, which has . . . beggared the people. **1837** *U.S. Mag.* I. 8 We have endeavored to state the theory of the Jeffersonian democracy, to which we profess allegiance, in its abstract essence. **1844** *Lexington Observer* 2 Oct. 3/4 The Democratic party . . . receive them as the genuine offspring of the Jeffersonian creed. **1854** BENTON *30 Years' View* I. 224/2 It was a message of the Jeffersonian school. **1900** *Congress. Rec.* 16 Feb. 1868/2 It is the plain duty of Jeffersonian expansionists to maintain our established policy in our treatment of the people inhabiting the new acquisitions. **1909** PARKER *G. Cleveland* 50 If we had stood faithfully by Jeffersonian principles [etc.].

b. *Jeffersonian simplicity,* the absence of pomp or ceremony in political and social matters.

1886 *Congress. Rec.* 29 June 6302/2 (Th. S.), What would a man wedded to 'Jeffersonian simplicity' do with $16,000 worth of new furniture? **1904** *N.Y. Sun* 21 Aug. 4 A coat of arms is an article easily cut to order in these days, when the Democrats are returning to Jeffersonian simplicity. **1914** *Cycl. Amer. Govt.* II. 251 *Jeffersonian Simplicity.* An expression denoting the dislike and disregard for display, . . . [which] has been used to denote principles of democratic equality and simplicity.

+**Jeffersonian Democrat.** A member of the Democratic party who believes in the principles of government advocated by Thomas Jefferson. — **1865** *Atlantic Mo.* Feb. 150/1 The Squire was a thorough-going Jeffersonian Democrat. **1884** H. S. CUMMINGS *Dartmouth Class 1862* 118 He is a 'Jeffersonian Democrat' in politics.

+**Jeffersonianism.** The political principles and doctrines advocated by or attributed to Thomas Jefferson. — **1876** H. C. LODGE in *N. Amer. Rev.* July 137 Ultimately, Jeffersonianism must have prevailed, but at the time of its actual triumph it came too soon.

+**Jeffersonian Republican.** A Democratic Republican who followed the leadership of Thomas Jefferson. — **1888** BRYCE *Amer. Commonw.* II. III. liii. 333 One of these two parties carried on, under the name of Democrats, the dogmas and traditions of the Jeffersonian Republicans. **1900** *Congress. Rec.* 6 Feb. 1587/2 Randolph, Jeffersonian Republican, said that the power to settle disputes as to boundaries involved the power of extending boundaries.

+**Jeffersonite.** [Named in 1822 after Thomas *Jefferson.*] A variety of pyroxene containing some zinc and manganese. — **1822** *Amer. Jrnl. Science* V. 402 Jeffersonite . . . has a great resemblance to pyroxene. **1857** DANA *Mineralogy* (1872) 151 *Polyite, Hudsonite,* and *Jeffersonite* fall here [in the category of dark-colored pyroxene]. **1889** *Cent.* 3224/2 *Jeffersonite* . . . is peculiar in containing some zinc and manganese. It occurs, with franklinite, zincite, etc., at Franklin Furnace, Sussex county, New Jersey.

+**Jefferson's Manual.** A popular name for a manual of parliamentary practice drawn up by Thomas Jefferson and published in 1800, orig.

for the use of the Senate of the United States. — **1837** *Congress. Deb.* 15 Sept. 626 The rules of parliamentary practice comprise Jefferson's Manual, and shall govern the proceedings of the House in all cases in which they are not inconsistent with the rules of the House. **1900** *Congress. Rec.* 1 Feb. 1375/2 The Secretary will read what Jefferson's Manual says in relation to it.

+**Jeffite.** *attrib.* 'A follower of Jefferson Davis; a rebel' (Chipman). — **1861** *N.Y. Tribune* 11 July 5/4 Whispers . . . come up from Washington that his [Henry May's] mission has for its object a disgraceful and humiliating peace with the Jeffite traitors, upon their own terms.

+**Jeffrey pine.** [John *Jeffrey*, Scottish botanical explorer.] A long-needled pine (*Pinus jeffreyi*), of the Northwest. — **1897** Sudworth *Arborescent Flora* 22 Black Pine. . . . Jeffrey Pine.

+**Jell,** *n.* [Shortened form of Jelly.] =Jelly 1. *colloq.* — **1870** 'F. Fern' *Ginger-Snaps* 262 Meantime my excellent country friends put up pounds and quarts of 'jell' every fall. **1894** Garland in *Harper's Mag.* June 148/1, I jest brought a chicken up, an' some jell an' things the women sent.

+**Jell,** *v. intr.* To congeal into a jelly. — **1869** Alcott *Little Women* II. 60 The jelly won't jell—and I don't know what to do! **1880** *Scribner's Mo.* April 823/1 Mrs. Foote's charming drawing suggests one of the gravest questions in the domestic economy,—whether the jelly will 'jell.'

* **Jelly.**

*1. A preparation of fruit juices boiled down with sugar having a characteristic soft, elastic, and semitransparent consistency: (see also quot. 1882).

1761 in Singleton *Social N.Y.* 364 To be sold, wholesale and retail, by William Keen, grocer and confectioner on Rotten Row: . . . Preserves of all Sorts, such as Currants, Jellys, Quinces [etc.]. **1784** in *Mem. Academy*, I. 439 The fruit of these species [of *Vaccinium*] are agreeable to children, either eaten by themselves, or in milk, or in tarts and jellies. **1863** Norton *Army Lett.* 170 The sutler makes no bones of charging seventy-five cents for a tumblerful of jelly. **1877** *Harper's Mag.* Feb. 429/1 Many a country housewife . . . will make cakes, whip-custards, and all manner of fancy creams and jellies fit for a royal table. **1882** Rittenhouse *Maud* 79 Jellies (gelatine) with ripe, sweet strawberries and bananas in them. **1902** *Harper's Mag.* Jan. 284/1 She put up preserves and jellies and cordials, and did the most beautiful embroidery. **1923** Watts *L. Nichols* 223 He had carted tons of jellies, fruits [etc.] . . . to every hospital and Home in the city.

+2. A jellyfish.

1882 *Harper's Mag.* Jan. 181/1 One of these large jellies was observed . . . moving lazily along.

3. Attrib. in sense 1 with *bread, cake, closet,* etc.

1678 *New Castle Court Rec.* 267, 7 gelly Pots & 2 small boxes with medsons. **1842** *Knickerb.* XIX. 447 All the affairs of the household . . . were managed with singular energy . . . as Saturday's good pie and pudding . . . and also my wife's jelly closet, abundantly testified. **1870** W. Baker *New Timothy* 49, I'm dying for a little more of that delicious jelly-cake. **1876** *Wide Awake* 21/2 Yours, Effie, is the jelly-custard pie. **1923** Watts *L. Nichols* 33, I bet she eats her meals that same way—cup of coffee once, an' mebbe another time a slice of jelly-bread, standin' up somewhere.

Jemima. Also **Jemimy.** [f. the feminine name, prob. affected by Jeminy, Jiminy.] A mild oath. — **1887** J. C. Harris in *Century Mag.* Sept. 713/2 Well, the great Jemimy! What's her name, maw? **1888** *Outing* May 108 After which I advanced to 'Great Caesar!' '*Jemima!*' '*Jerusalem!*' (prolonging the *je* in both cases).

Jeminy. Also **Jeeminy.** =Jiminy. — *a***1846** *Quarter Race Kentucky* 121 But, oh! Jeminy! see Dick run! **1851** *Polly Peablossom* 53 Jeemeny, criminy! if you'd only bin what I was! **1869** Browne *Adv. Apache Country* 45 'Oh, Gosh!' groaned George. . . . 'Oh, Jeeminy Gosh!'

Jenneting. A variety of early apple. {1601–} Also attrib. with *apple.* — **1790** Deane *New-Eng. Farmer* 11 One sort [of apple] is ripe in June; therefore called a jenneting apple. **1818** *Amer. Jrnl. Science* I. 372 August 7. Early jenneting apples ripe. **1856** *Rep. Comm. Patents 1855: Agric.* 292 Winter apples [include] . . . Rawles' Jennetting, Roman Stem, Small Romanite.

Jenny. {1600–} A spinning jenny. {1797– (*Encycl. Brit.* V. 488)} — **1796** Morse *Univ. Geog.* I. 440 The filling of the cotton goods is spun with jennies. **1857** *Lawrence* (Kan.) *Republican* 25 June 3 Every cotton-spinner knows that jennies are always on the go.

+**Jenny Lind.** [A Swedish operatic soprano (1820–87).] The name of various fashions and things. Usually attrib.

1850 Mitchell *Lorgnette* I. 123 The nurses will take good care to pinch the noses of the young bawlers into the Jenny Lind shape. **1854** *Penna. Agric. Rep.* 128 To S. P. Hamilton, . . . for a Jenny Lind Carriage. **1855** [see Jibe *v.*]. **1857** *Lawrence* (Kan.) *Republican* 28 May 3 Ladies' Fine Kid Jenny Lind Boots . . . for sale. **1862** *Rep. Comm. Patents 1861: Agric.* 186 Jenny Lind, and Burr's New Pine are good early strawberries. **1874** *Gold Hill* (Nev.) *News* 21 April, A splendid Jenny Lind table in the saloon for players. **1885** *Harper's Mag.* March 559/1 Some blocks [of granite] are polished by a great machine called a Jenny Lind. **1894** *Ib.* May 847/2 The fair hair [was] arranged 'Jenny Lind fashion.' **1901** Churchill *Crisis* 267 A 'Jenny Lind' passed them. Miss Belle recognized the carriage immediately.

Jeopardize, *v. tr.* To put into jeopardy. {1646, 1834–} — **1816** Pickering 119 *To Jeopardize.* This verb is often seen in the Debates of Congress, as they are reported in the newspapers. . . . It is hardly necessary to remark, that *to jeopardize* is not in any of the dictionaries. **1836** L. Matthews *Lectures* 130 We sometimes see . . . *jeopardize*, . . . *grade*, and *lengthy* in books, and hear *missionate, variate*, . . . in conversation or prayer. . . . But none of these I presume can be said to have the stamp of good use among us? **1843** *Diplom. Corr. Texas* III. (1911) 873 It is hoped and believed that . . . your eventual success [will not be] jeopardized by adhereing [*sic*] to the first plan. **1848** Bartlett 190 *To jeopardize.* . . . This word is much used in the United States, and less frequently in England. **1855** I. C. Pray *Mem. J. G. Bennett* 410 Hence the absurd propositions which merchants themselves are most forward in making, to jeopardize the interests of their own class.

+**Jerk,** *n.*[1] Jerked meat; a piece of such meat. (Cf. the earlier Jirk.) — **1831** Buttrick *Travels* 64 The venison for want of salt to preserve it, is cut in slices, dried and smoked, which makes what they call jerk. **1841** *S. Lit. Messenger* VII. 53/2 For ten long months I've pass'd and tasted no cake, Nor aught but buffalo jerks. **1851** W. De Hass *Hist. Early Settlement W. Va.* VII. iii. 389 As soon as daylight appeared, the captain started to where they left some jerk hanging on the evening before.

* **Jerk,** *n.*[2]

+1. *pl.* An involuntary spasmodic movement of the body or face experienced during certain religious excitement.

1807 McNemar *Ky. Revival* 62 Such as were seized with the jerks, were wrested at once . . . from under their own government. **1834** *Biblical Repertory* VI. 350 The dread of the jerks was great in many, both religious and careless. *c***1843** B. W. Stone *Biography* (1847) 39 The bodily agitations or exercises attending the excitement in the beginning of this century, were various, and called by various names;—as, the falling exercise—the *jerks*—the dancing exercise—the barking exercise—the laughing and singing exercise, &c. **1846** *Indiana Mag. Hist.* XXIII. 424 Brother Whitten . . . who had felt some of the symptoms in the former part of the sermon was well nigh thrown into the 'jerks' of a former day, by resisting his emotions. **1856** Goodrich *Recoll.* I. 202 Others still were agitated by violent and revolting convulsions and twitchings, which obtained the popular name of the *jerks.* All classes of persons who came within the atmosphere of the mania—Methodists, Presbyterians, and Quakers—men and women—became subjects of these extraordinary agitations. **1898** N. E. Jones *Squirrel Hunters of Ohio* 132 In the period from 1800 to 1810 . . . there existed a singular manifestation, called the '*jerks.*'

+2. *Baseball.* A manner of delivery by the pitcher.

1885 Chadwick *Art of Pitching* 8 The pitcher having the choice of the simple toss of the ball, the jerk, the regular pitch, or the underhand or overhand throw.

+3. A branch line of a railroad. *slang.*

1907 London *Road* 26 By mistake I had missed the main line and come over a small 'jerk' with only two locals a day on it.

Jerk, *v.*[1] Also **jirk, jurk.** [Corrupted f. Amer. Sp. *charquear*, f. *charque, charqui*, Peruv. *echarqui*, 'dried beef.'] *tr.* To cure (meat or fish) by cutting it into long strips and drying it in the sun or at a fire. {in Jamaica, 1707 (jirk); 1748– (jerk)}

In some of the early examples, the meaning may simply be 'to cure.'

1775 Cresswell *Journal* 76 The meat is laid on this [gridiron] and a slow fire put under it, and turned until it is done. This is called jerking the meat. **1804** Clark in *Lewis & C. Exped.* I. (1904) 40 After Jurking the meet killed yesterday and Crossing the hunting party we Set out at 6 oClock. **1807** Gass *Jrnl.* 19 At 12 we stopped to jirk our meat, and again proceeded at two. **1852** *Mich. Agric. Soc.* III. 232 The young fish [sturgeons] are good for cooking or packing. The Indians . . . jerk them as they do venison. **1872** Powers *Afoot & Alone* 152 They had been employing the time in jerking beef. Everybody had a rope stretched from his wagon to everybody else's wagon, and three whole beeves slit and hung thereon. **1881** C. M. Chase *Editor's Run in N.Mex.* 204 Fresh meat is cured by hanging it out doors, 'jerked,' as they say, into strips. **1923** J. H. Cook *On Old Frontier* 157 The following morning I instructed our new-found friends in the art of jerking meat.

***Jerk,** *v.*[2] +1. *intr.* To move convulsively while under the influence of religious excitement. +2. *tr.* To yank (an ear of corn) off its stalk. +3. To draw (beer) at a bar. *slang.* +4. With *up:* To arrest. *slang.* — (1) **1807** McNemar *Ky. Revival* 69 About the latter end of the year 1804, there were regular societies of these people in the state of Ohio; . . . praying, shouting, jerking, barking, or rolling. **1874** Eggleston *Circuit Rider* 130 He jerked violently—his jerking only added to his excitement. **1898** Dunbar *Folks from Dixie* 12 Every now and then some mourner would spring half up, with a shriek, and then sink down again trembling and jerking spasmodically. (2) **1859** T. D. Price *Diary* (MS.) 4 Oct., Put up some corn. Jerked about one load for hogs. **1907** *Farmers' Bul.* No. 313, 17 The total amount of work required to jerk the corn and afterwards husk it is considerably greater than that required to husk it from the standing stalk. (3) **1884** Miller *Memorie & Rime* 20 They stared at me, but went on jerking beer behind the counter. (4) **1901** Merwin & Webster *Calumet 'K'* 222 He'll probably try to make out a case of criminal carelessness against me, and get me jerked up. **1910** McCutcheon *Rose in Ring* 122 The cops . . . jerk up a circus man on the slightest excuse.

Jerked, *a.* [f. Jerk *v.*[1]] Of meat: Cured by the process of jerking. (See also Jerked beef.)

1784 Smyth *Tour U.S.* I. 302 [We] eat heartily of our jerked (or dried) venison. **1817** Bradbury *Travels* 53 We had also . . . a little jerked buffaloe meat. **1852** J. Reynolds *Hist. Illinois* 80 Our hardy backwoodsmen, . . . their knapsacks on their backs, filled with parched corn and jerked meat, waded thro' mud and water. **1870** Keim *Sheridan's Troopers* 56 At last the chance of jerked horse-flesh was exhausted. **1894** Robley *Bourbon Co., Kansas* 38 They had nothing to eat but jerked buffalo and Pawnee macarroni [*sic*].

Jerked beef. Beef that has been cured by the process of jerking.

[**1712** W. Rogers *Cruising Voyage* 199 [The people of Guyaquil] export . . . some dry'd Jerkt Beef.] **1775** in J. Hall *Sk. of West* (1835) II. 263 We struck whilst the iron was hot, fixed Mr. Cocke off with a good Queen Anne musket, plenty of ammunition, . . . and no small quantity of jerked beef. **1834** Baird *Valley Mississippi* 240 Our shipping will here receive its salted and jerked beef. **1885** *Outing* VII. 24/2 The old and young squaws had cut and dried large packages of 'jerked' beef. **1916** Thoburn *Stand. Hist. Okla.* I. 262 Every well-appointed plantation and farm had its smoke-house, which hung full of cured pork and 'jerked' beef.

***Jerker.** +**1.** One who in religious excitement has the jerks. +**2.** (See quotations.) — (1) **1807** McNemar *Kentucky Revival* 62 Head dresses were of little account among the female jerkers. **1851** Judd *Margaret* viii. 48 The jumpers of Wales were outdone by the jerkers of Kentucky. **1871** De Vere 235 At a large revival . . . flew about in seemingly uncontrollable madness, countless *jerkers*. **1889** [see Jumper 6]. (2) **1884** Goode, etc. *Fisheries* I. 617 The 'Horny-head,' 'River Chub,' or 'Jerker' is one of the most widely-diffused of fresh-water fishes. **1889** *Cent.* 3226/3 *Jerker*, . . . a cyprinoid fish, *Hybopsis kentuckiensis*: same as *hornyhead*.

+**Jerking.** Attrib. with *line, rack:* Designating devices for drying jerked meat. — **1851** M. Reid *Scalp Hunters* xxvii. 201 Yonder goes the jerking-line! **1885** *Outing* VII. 79/2 In front of the shanty was a 'jerking rack'; two parallel poles, fifteen feet in length and three feet apart.

+**Jerking exercise.** =Jerk *n.*[2] 1. — **1847** Howe *Hist. Coll. Ohio* 46 The phenomena of '*bodily exercises*,' then common in the west . . . have been classified by a clerical writer as 1st, the *Falling* exercise; 2d, the *Jerking* exercise.

Jerkings. *pl.* +=Jerk *n.*[2] 1. — **1842** Buckingham *E. & W. States* II. 427 At a great Camp-Meeting in Kentucky . . . the women were seized with convulsions, called at that time 'jerkings.'

+**Jerk line.** A line used in place of reins to guide the lead horse of a team. Also fig. — **1888** Grigsby *Smoked Yank* xix. (1891) 164 The driver rode on the near wheel mule and drove the leader with a jerk-line. **1904** Steedman *Bucking the Sagebrush* 22 They were driven with a 'jerk line' manipulated by the 'mule skinner' who rode the nigh wheeler. **1907** White *Arizona Nights* 287 Sang would get a wiggle on him . . . if he had a woman ahold of his jerk line. **1910** J. Hart *Vigilante Girl* 140 An iron 'jockey-stick' ran from the near leader's hames to the off leader's bit—this pushed or pulled his head as his mate moved in answer to the 'jerk-line.'

+**Jerk rein.** =prec. — **1895** *Forum* June 475 The big freight wagon, with its six or eight mules guided by a single jerk-rein.

+**Jerkwater.** [Orig. a railroad word, probably for a water tank from which water was 'jerked' for the engines. (Cf. Jerk *n.*[2] 3.)] *colloq.* **1.** *attrib.* Designating things regarded as small townish or of no significance. **2.** (See quotation and cf. Jerk *n.*[2] 3.) — (1) **1897** *Chicago Tribune* 25 July 15/2 *Jerkwater*, insignificant. 'John J. Ingalls regards the Swiss Mission as a jerkwater job, and would not take it if it were offered to him.' **1904** Crissey *Tattlings* 48 More distinguished statesmen got off at that little jerkwater station . . . than had ever been in the country before. **1908** Lorimer *J. Spurlock* xii. 326 You'd simply have swapped railroads, and have a bang up dividend-paying system, instead of a bum jerkwater one. **1911** Harrison *Queed* 225 The spring found West stronger and more contented with his lot as president of a jerkwater college. (2) **1905** *Dialect Notes* III. 84 *Jerkwater* (*train*), n. Train on a branch railway. 'Has the *jerkwater* come in yet?

+**Jerky.**[1] [Sp. *charqui.*] Jerked meat. — **1850** Colton *3 Years Calif.* 298 A tin cup of coffee, a junk of bread, and a piece of the stewed jerky. **1877** Campion *On Frontier* 63 He would certainly sleep six hours, then arise, eat a few yards of jerky, take a drink from the river, and start. **1893** Coues *Lewis & Clark Exped.* I. 31*n.*, Jerked meat is known as *jerky*. **1904** White *Silent Places* 98 We can stock her up with jerky, and there's no reasons she shouldn't make it.

+**Jerky.**[2] Also **jirky.** *W.* A wagon or carriage without springs: (see quot. 1882). — **1871** Roe *Army Lett.* 2 We came all that distance in a funny looking stage coach called a 'jerkey,' and a good name for it, too. **1882** *Century Mag.* Oct. 864/1 The 'jerky' is a sort of cross between a coach proper and a common wagon. **1894** Robley *Bourbon Co., Kansas* 63 Between Fort Scott and Jefferson City, Mo., . . . the stage, an old bob-tailed 'jerky,' such as is now to be seen only in 'Wild West shows,' made the trip once a week. **1904** Steedman *Bucking the Sagebrush* 15 We left early in the morning and upon arriving at York, took a 'jerky' or one-horse stage to Nephi. *a***1918** G. Stuart *On Frontier* II. 103 Here we changed for a covered jirky.

Jerry-builder. One who builds inferior or insubstantial houses merely for the purpose of selling them on their appearance. {1881–} Also fig. — **1882** *Century Mag.* March 791/2 The absence of this simple precaution, especially in the so-called 'jerry-builder's' work, . . . ultimately results . . . in repairs and doctor's bills. **1889** *Ib.* Feb. 633/2 The exploits of the 'jerry-builder,' of the 'real-estate fraud,' . . . possess rather a curious than a personal interest for most readers. **1898** *N.Y. Journal* 26 Aug. 9/4 The frightened jerry builder kept out of the way of the District Attorney's men. **1924** Mumford *Sticks & Stones* 100 Richardson was in a biological sense a 'sport' surrounded by jerry-builders.

***Jersey.** Also (*dial.*) **Jarsey.**

+**1. a.** *pl.* The colonies of East New Jersey and West New Jersey; later, the single colony or state of New Jersey.

East New Jersey and West New Jersey, formed by a division in 1676, were united in a royal colony in 1702.

1683 *N.J. Archives* 1 Ser. I. 429 We desired it may be examined . . . whether he had Power to sell . . . Land in Jersey's. **1687** *Doc. Hist. N.Y. State* I. 159 Our neighbors . . . desire nothing more than to be a part of this Government . . . the Jerseys wishing the like as having once been a part of us [New York]. **1707** *Boston News-Letter* 3 Nov. 2/2 The Assembly of the Jerseys are now sitting. **1745** *N.Y. Ev. Post* 2 Sept. 4/1 [Mr. Witfield] designs to take his Departure this Day for the Jersies. **1809** Cuming *Western Tour* 186 Marshon is from the Jerseys. **1835** Kennedy *Horse Shoe Robinson* I. 28 The colonel then told me to watch my chance and make off to you in the Jarseys. **1854** H. H. Riley *Puddleford* 33, I know'd your mother when she made cakes and pies down in the Jarseys. **1863** 'M. Harland' *Husks* 37 She was a native of New Jersey, 'the Jarseys' she had heard it called in her father's house.

+**b.** *sing.* The colony or state of New Jersey.

1795 Freneau *Poems* I. 36 Perhaps in Jersey is this creature known, Perhaps New-England claims him for her own. **1790** *Mass. Spy* 7 Oct. (Th.), Instead of half-joes or guineas, I have brought some quadrangular stones back with me to Jersey, as matters of curiosity.

+**c.** American English as spoken in New Jersey.

1886 S. W. Mitchell *R. Blake* 236 Uncle John and I will arrange all that on the 'mashes.' Isn't that good Jersey, Uncle John?

+**2.** =Jersey wagon.

1834 Simms *Guy Rivers* 491 A small Jersey—a light wagon in free use in that section—contained all his wardrobe, books, papers, etc.

3. A breed of dairy cattle originally from the island of Jersey in the English channel. Usu. pl. {1862– (*Jrnl. R. Agric. Soc.* 2 Ser. XVII. 229)}

1856 *Porter's Spirit of Times* 20 Dec. 262/2 We do not wish to be understood that Ayrshires and Jerseys may not be good for beef or for work. **1862** *Rep. Comm. Patents 1861: Agric.* 464 The Jerseys are so totally unlike any other of the improved breeds that they are recognized at a glance. **1868** *Ib. 1867* 345 Later fairs have called out a better show of Jerseys than in 1851. **1878** *Ill. Dept. Agric. Trans.* XIV. 283 Again, not only is the quantity of the product of the little Jerseys remarkable, but in quality it is superior to the butter product of the 'beef breeds.' **1894** *Vt. Agric. Rep.* XIV. 70 The Jersey is a superior butter cow.

4. A knitted, close-fitting jacket. {1836–}

1883 *Harper's Mag.* Nov. 900/1 Scarcely one girl in three ventures to wear a jersey, mainly because she knows too well that this tell-tale jacket only becomes a good figure. **1891** Howells *Imperative Duty* i, They seemed fond of wearing red jerseys, which accented every fact of their anatomy. **1895** *N.Y. Dramatic News* 12 Oct. 8/3 Jennie Yeamans . . . wears a black Jersey decorated with Defenders and Yachting emblems.

5. *attrib.* and *comb.* +**a.** In sense 1 with *boy, brigade*, etc.

1724 *New-Eng. Courant* 6 April 2/2 To be sold, a very likely Jersey Boy's Time for Eight Years (from Christmass last). **1844** Barber & Howe *Hist. Coll. U.S.* 413 After the successful mutiny of the Pennsylvania line at Morristown, a part of the Jersey brigade . . . revolted. **1850** Burke *Reminisc. Georgia* 240 Chairs, tables, beds and bedsteads, cradles for babies, and coops for chickens, all heaped upon cotton Jersey carts. **1856** Thompson *Plu-ri-bus-tah* 71 Put him in a Jersey clam boat. **1884** Matthews & Bunner *In Partnership* 151 Winter was still on the Jersey flats on the last day of March. **1770** *Boston Gazette* 7 May (Th.), To be sold, five years Time of a likely active Jersey girl. **1903** *N.Y. Tribune* 18 Oct. 8 Even with a faithful judge . . . 'Jersey justice' did not shine as brilliantly as usual. **1778** *Boston Gazette* 25 Aug. 373 (Ernst), Handy, light, Jersey made wagon. **1713** *Boston News-Letter* 5 Oct. 2/2 A Jersey Maids times for four years and an half very good Servant to be disposed of. **1778** *Md. Journal* 20 Jan. (Th.), Last week, the Jersey militia took a Prize, and began to unload her. **1800** Weems *Letters* II. 154, O that I had but a Jersey Stage and a couple of good strong horses! **1857** Vaux *Villas* 104 The window-dressings, angles, etc., may be of hard Jersey stone. **1844** Barber & Howe *Hist. Coll. N.J.* 413 In the winter of 1780–'81, some of the Jersey troops were stationed . . . at Pompton. **1910** J. Hart *Vigilante Girl* 207 It's made of whiskey and hard cider—Jersey whiskey at that.

+**b.** In the names of fruits and plants cultivated or originating in New Jersey.

1817 W. Coxe *Fruit Trees* 129 Jersey, or Rhode-Island Greening. Sometimes called the Burlington Greening. **1827** Drake & Mansfield *Cincinnati* 73 The durability of the boats built upon the Ohio has in some instances even surpassed that of boats constructed in the east, from the Jersey oak. **1838** C. Newell *Revol. Texas* 169 The so-much celebrated Jersey peach, found in Philadelphia and New York markets, will not compare with [the Texas peach]. **1830** *Illinois Mo. Mag.* 13 Every negro in New Orleans might afford to eat Jersey pippins. **1875** Burroughs *Winter Sunshine* 163 With a tree of the Jersey sweet . . . in bearing, no man's table need be devoid of luxuries. **1836** *Knickerb.* VIII. 58 He held forth his bony, knuckle-knobbed hand, in which was clasped . . . a green 'Jersey-sweetin.'

+**c.** In sense 3 with *breed, cattle,* etc.

1853 *Whig Almanac 1854* 39/2 The Jersey Breed of Cows is one of the best we have in this country for milk. **1868** *Rep. Comm. Agric. 1867* 292 A committee of New York gentlemen recently visited several of the dairies of Chester county as representatives of an incipient organization, the 'American Jersey Cattle Club.' **1862** *Rep. Comm. Patents 1861: Agric.* 465 The milk of the Jersey cow is particularly rich in butyraceous particles, and is of a deep yellow. **1898** E. C. HALL *Aunt Jane* 195 A plate of golden butter, a pitcher of Jersey milk, and a bowl of honey in the comb.

Jerseyan. +A resident of New Jersey. — **1854** SIMMS *Southward Ho* 21 The courage and enterprise of the Jerseyans had plucked the rugged oyster from his native abodes.

+**Jersey blue.**

1. A name at first applied to the colonial New Jersey soldier because of his blue uniform; later extended to any native or resident of New Jersey.

1758 *Essex Inst. Coll.* XVIII. 110 Excepting ye Yorkers and Jersy Blews all ye Provincials didn't loose more than 100 men. **1761** NILES *Indian Wars* II. 509 July 2d, 16 of the Jersey Blues were sent without the camp to gather some brush for the general's baker. **1775** J. MELVIN *Journal* (1857) 26 Hear that they have brought three hundred Jersey blues, prisoners, to town. **1849** COOPER *Sea Lions* i, Distinctions . . . do certainly exist between the Eastern and the Western man, . . . the Buckeye or Wolverine, and the Jersey Blue. **1854** SIMMS *Southward Ho* 24 The Jersey Blues had enjoyed a very honorable reputation for valor from the Revolutionary period. **1864** *Congress. Globe* 15 June 2968/2 The early history of the 'Blue Hen's Chickens' . . . is as proud as that of the early 'Jersey Blues.'

b. In allusive use.

1866 LOWELL *Biglow P.* II. xi. 242 A Nothun Dem'crat o' th' ole Jarsey blue Born copper-sheathed an' copper-fastened tu.

2. A breed of chicken.

1871 LEWIS *Poultry Book* 60 The color of the Jersey Blue is a light blue, sometimes approaching a dun. **1897** *Farmers' Bul.* No. 51, 10 The Jersey Blues . . . are one of the largest breeds of poultry.

3. (See quotation.)

1902 CLAPIN 243 *Jersey blue,* the color of uniform worn by Jersey troops before the War of the Revolution.

4. *attrib.* **a.** In sense 1 b. **b.** In sense 2.

(a) 1798 *Aurora* (Phila.) 13 Dec. (Th.), They said I was a Jarzy Blue Dog, and they would cut my head off. **1859** *Harper's Mag.* June 133/2 A Jersey Blue correspondent says that a . . . gentleman in Newark has been deeply interested in the promotion of Sunday-schools among the blacks. **(b) 1850** BROWNE *Poultry Yard* 77 The Jersey-Blue Fowl . . . is another large mongrel of a bluish cast. **1854** *Penna. Agric. Rep.* 205 [To] D. O. Gher, for best pair Jersey blues chicken, [a prize].

+**Jerseyite.** A New Jerseyan. — **1854** SIMMS *Southward Ho* 21 Perhaps, the most exciting of recent events is the oyster war between the Gothamites and Jerseyites. **1896** *Home Missionary* July 133 There are but few real Jerseyites in the Congregational Churches of New Jersey. Their wealth and culture came to them from across the Hudson.

+**Jersey lightning.** =APPLEJACK 2. *slang.* — **1860** *Harper's Mag.* April 581/2 Every particle of sap in his system had been dried up by the combined effect of the weather and 'Jersey lightning.' **1866** GREGG *Life in Army* 96 When his brains become addled by too much 'Jersey lightning,' he is not fit to drive a decent mule team. **1875** BURNHAM *Three Years* 131 He had plainly been indulging in more than one draught of 'Jersey Lightning.' **1892** *Boston Jrnl.* 14 April 8/1 Jersey lightning will still be distilled and sold to the honest, unsuspecting public as fine old French brandy.

Jerseyman. {1825} +A native or resident of New Jersey. (Cf. JERSEY 1, note.)

1679 *Boston Rec.* 58 Thomas Begretia [entertained] at James Wardens, Jersiman. **1689** SEWALL *Diary* I. 281 But in the morning, by putting out our Ancients, find them to be Jersey-Men, our Friends. **1705** *Boston News-Letter* 17 Sept. 2/1, 2 Seamen, one Abraham Parker of York near Piscataqua, the other a Jersey man and his own Negro, . . . are drown'd. **1798** *Aurora* (Phila.) 13 Dec. (Th.), [He] only said so to make fun of me, cause I was a Jarzyman. **1858** *Harper's Mag.* Oct. 709/1, I am not a Yankee, I am a *Jerseyman.* I come from the State of New Jersey. **1886** S. W. MITCHELL *R. Blake* 258 Did you hear Uncle John say . . . that whenever a mosquito bites a Jerseyman it dies 'pizened'? **1905** *N.Y. Ev. Post* 9 Dec. (Horwill MS.), They were evidently Jerseymen, for a bottle of applejack was moved about the table to show whose deal came next, and it grew lighter after each shove.

+**Jersey pine.** The scrub pine, *Pinus virginiana.* — **1743** CLAYTON *Flora Virginica* 191 The common Jersay-Pine. **1785** MARSHALL *Amer. Grove* 102 *Pinus virginiana.* Two-leaved Virginian or Jersey Pine. **1832** BROWNE *Sylva* 234 The Jersey Pine has probably been so named from its abounding in the lower part of New Jersey. **1860** CURTIS *Woody Plants N.C.* 20 Jersey Pine. (*P. inops*). . . . This tree is too small, often crooked, and generally with too much sap-wood, to be of any value. **1884** SARGENT *Rep. Forests* 546 The manufacture of pumps and water-pipes from logs of the Jersey pine (*Pinus inops*) at one time an important industry in Louisville, has . . . become unremunerative.

+**Jersey red.** One of a breed of hogs closely allied to, but larger than, the Duroc-Jersey. Also attrib. (Cf. DUROC.) — **1879** *Diseases of Swine* 120 Claims [of immunity to swine plague] were made in behalf of Chester Whites and Jersey Reds. **1883** [see DUROC]. **1893** G. W. CURTIS *Horses, Cattle* 301 At the first meeting of the National Swine Breeders' Association at Indianapolis, Indiana, 1872, a committee was appointed on 'Jersey Red Swine.' *Ib.* 302 The old Jersey Red or Duroc was a coarse, heavy, raw-boned, lop-eared and 'lank-sided' animal.

+**Jersey tea.** The New Jersey tea, *Ceanothus americanus.* (Cf. NEW JERSEY TEA.) — **1814** BIGELOW *Florula Bostoniensis* 57 *Ceanothus Americanus.* Jersey tea. . . . The leaves were used, among other substitutes, for tea, during the American revolution. **1846** in Emory *Military Reconn.* 387 The wild rose was still in bloom, and mingled its pink flowers with the beautiful white clusters of the Jersey tea. **1850** *New Eng. Farmer* II. 60 The Jersey Tea is a small shrub, found in dry soils. **1870** *Amer. Naturalist* IV. 583 The *Ceanothus,* or Jersey tea, is a frequent inhabitant of the prairies.

+**Jersey wagon.** A light, four-wheeled carriage once popular in New Jersey; a dearborn or similar carriage.

1811 Sutcliff *Travels* p. viii, Jersey waggons . . . are made very light, hung on springs with leather braces, and travel very pleasantly. **1814** ASBURY *Journal* III. 439, I sat in the end of my little Jersey wagon, screened by the drawn curtain behind me. **1818** F. HALL *Travels* 126 At Queenston I commenced a new, and infinitely more convenient mode of traveling, viz. in my own carriage; this being a light Jersey waggon, (a machine I have already described, by the name of a Dearborn). **1833** *Knickerb.* II. 351 Every body has seen a Jersey waggon, and knows what it was of old, and is now. **1844** KENDALL *Narr. Santa Fé Exped.* I. 67 General Lamar provided a neat Jersey wagon, drawn by two mules, and covered so as to protect us from the sun and rain during the long marches. **1870** W. BAKER *New Timothy* 69 In a few moments they are off, Charles in his buggy with John, the General following in his Jersey wagon. **1904** *N.Y. Tribune* 29 May, The low basket Jersey wagon of ante-bellum days.

attrib. **1813** *Salem Gazette* 5 Nov. 3/2 Last evening arrived the remarkably fast-sailing, new, tandem-rigged, Baltimore-pilot-boat-built, coppered and copper-fastened Jersey-wagon Dash, from Vermont bay.

Jerusalem.

1. *attrib.* Used in the specific or popular names of plants and fruits.

1787 *Amer. Academy Mem.* II. I. 157 Honey locust or Jerusalem Thorn . . . armed in the trunk & limbs with sharp thorns. **1847** DARLINGTON *Weeds & Plants* 140 *Cucumis Anguria.* . . . Prickly cucumber. Jerusalem Cucumber. **1850** *New Eng. Farmer* II. 288 The Tomato. This plant or vegetable, sometimes called *Love Apple,* or *Jerusalem Apple,* . . . was first found in South America. **1857** GRAY *Botany* 318 *Phlomis.* Jerusalem Sage. . . . An old Greek name of a woolly species, of obscure derivation. **1894** COULTER *Bot. W. Texas* III. 494 *Sorghum vulgare.* . . . This species includes the many varieties cultivated as sugar sorghum, Kaffir corn, Jerusalem corn, and broom corn.

+**2.** Used alone or in phrases as a mild oath.

1861 NEWELL *Orpheus C. Kerr* I. 234 Jerewsalem crickets! I'm like a fellow jist out of a feather bed. **1888** *Outing* May 108/1, I tried . . . the very mildest [words] first. . . . After which I advanced to 'Great Cæsar!' '*Je*mima!' '*Je*rusalem!' (prolonging the *je* in both cases). **1891** COOKE *Huckleberries* (1896) 44 Oh, Jeerus'lem! **1914** *N.Y. Herald* 21 May 3/7 All he said to Mr. Morgan over the phone was 'Jerusalem.'

Jerusalem artichoke. A perennial American sunflower, *Helianthus tuberosus;* the tuber of this plant used as a vegetable. {1620–} — **1705** BEVERLEY *Virginia* IV. 57 The poorer Sort brew their Beer with . . . *Jerusalem Artichoke,* which some People plant for that use. **1792** POPE *Tour S. & W.* 8, I observed about an Acre of Ground well beset with Jerusalem Artichokes. . . . To this Vegetable, Swine and horned Cattle of every Description, particularly Sheep, are surprisingly attached. **1819** *Amer. Farmer* I. 109 The Jerusalem artichoke, or *helianthus tuberosus,* grows spontaneously over the country. **1879** GRAY *Structural Botany* 59 The eyes of . . . Jerusalem artichoke are axillary buds. **1901** MOHR *Plant Life Ala.* 828.

+**Jerusalem cherry.** One of two species of *Solanum,* esp. *S. pseudocapsicum;* also, the fruit. — **1788** CUTLER in *Life & Corr.* I. 428 Landlady gave me Jerusalem cherries, and Vandaver's Apple. **1840** DEWEY *Mass. Flowering Plants* 167 *Solanum pseudo-capsicum.* Jerusalem Cherry. Winter Cherry. A small ornamental shrub. **1868** GRAY *Field Botany* 268 *Solanum Pseudo-Capsicum,* Jerusalem Cherry. Shrubby house-plant from Madeira, cultivated for the ornamental bright red berries, resembling cherries. **1901** MOHR *Plant Life Ala.* 713.

Jerusalem oak. {1771– (Hanbury *Compl. Body Planting* Index); *oak of Jerusalem} An aromatic oak-leaved goosefoot (*Chenopodium botrys*), or an allied species. Also attrib.

1759 in Commons, etc. *Documentary Hist.* I. 109 The Breeding wenches [*i.e.,* slaves] more particularly you must instruct the Overseers to be Kind and Indulgent to. . . . Give them every Spring & Fall the Jerusalem Oak seed for a week together. **1775** ROMANS *Nat. Hist. Florida* 254 The stincking weed which is known by the name of Jerusalem Oak, and in those provinces is the most efficacious vermifuge, and the safest medicine especially for children. **1802** DRAYTON *S. Carolina* 65 Jerusalem oak. (*Chenopodium Anthelminticum.*) A noxious weed, growing in dry grounds; which having a long tap root, is with difficulty destroyed. **1894** COULTER *Bot. W. Texas* III. 368 Jerusalem oak. Feather geranium. . . . Across the continent, but not common in the West. **1901** MOHR *Plant Life Ala.* 488 Jerusalem Oak. . . . Introduced from southern Europe, all over temperate and warmer North America.

Jessamine. {17th c.–} [Var. of JASMINE.] +**1.** The yellow jessamine or related species. +**2.** The matrimony vine, *Lycium halimifolium.* +**3.** *S.W.* A low shrub: (see quotation). — **(1) 1709** LAWSON *Carolina* 63 Myrtles, Jessamines, Wood-bines, . . . interweave themselves with the loftiest Timbers. **1792** IMLAY *Western Territory* 207 Every part of the country abounds in a variety of natural flowers, . . . may-flowers, jessamine, columbine. **1839** 'M. PENCIL' *White Sulphur P.* 47 We gathered a bouquet of jessamines and went on to the Sweet. **1889** DELAND *Florida Days* 68 The grass is thick in the wet darkness along the walls under the tangle of jessamine. **(2) 1892** *Amer. Folk-Lore* V. 101 *Lycium vulgare,* jessamine. Stratham, N.H. **(3) 1894** *Ib.* VII. 94 *Macrosiphonia brachysiphon,* . . . jessamine. Arizona.

+**Jesse, Jessie, Jessy.** [Of obscure origin.] *colloq.*

1. *To give* (a person) *Jesse*, or *particular Jesse*, to scold or handle severely; to beat soundly: (see also quot. 1888).

1844 *Nauvoo Neighbor* 17 April (Th.), Lo, the Saints, the Mormons, bless ye! Felt thy glory most severely, When Missouri gave them jesse. **1846** *Spirit of Times* 6 June 176/2 Our boys did give them '*most particular Jesse*,' and that is all I have time to tell you about the battle. *a***1855** J. F. KELLY *Humors* 212, I told Van to go it, give the rascal jessy, and Van did. **1865** A. H. STEPHENS *Diary* (1910) 518 While I thought I was giving you Jesse on hearts, you were giving me fits on spades. **1885** COOKE *Deacon's Week* 19, I'd opened my mouth to give him Jesse. **1888** M. LANE in *America* 11 Oct. 15 *Give Them Jessie.*—Jessie was the name of the wife of General John C. Fremont, and the old saying was adopted as a campaign cry when he became a candidate for the Presidency.

2. Used in other phrases.

1846 *Spirit of Times* 4 July 223/3 One of the combatants 'caught Jessie.' **1847** ROBB *Squatter Life* 59 The afarr [affair] raised jessy in Nettle Bottom. **1858** VIELÉ *Following Drum* 172 General Harney . . . had come down . . . to administer 'jesse' generally to all delinquents. **1863** *Rocky Mountain News* 2 April (Th.), Wherever we go [after vaccination] we are sure to catch jesse on our sore arm.

***Jesuit.**

***1.** A member of the Roman Catholic Society of Jesus.

1643 WILLIAMS *Key* 27 To this question some put an edge from the boast of the Jesuits in . . . Maryland. **1649** *Md. Archives* 245 Whatsoever person . . . shall . . . in a reproachful manner . . . call or denominate any person . . . Prespiterian popish prest, Jesuite, Jesuited papist . . . or any other name or terme in a reproachfull manner relating to matter of Religion shall . . . loose the some of tenne shillings. **1721** *Mass. H. Rep. Jrnl.* III. 89 The Indians . . . have marched in hostile manner, under French Colours, accompanied by two Jesuits. **1834** PECK *Gaz. Illinois* 102 To investigate this question [whether the Mississippi communicated with the western ocean], P. Marquette, a jesuit, and Joliet, were appointed by M. Talon, the intendant of New France. **1837** IRVING *Bonneville* II. 134 The peninsula of California was settled in 1698, by the Jesuits, who . . . have generally proved the most beneficent of colonists. **1872** POWERS *Afoot & Alone* 250 The Indians had very wicked and profane 'sweat-houses' for keeping themselves healthy. The Jesuits immured them in religious dungeons, or huts so outrageous that they burned them periodically to suppress the vermin.

2. *transf.* A political manipulator; an intriguer. {1640–} +Applied esp., as an opprobrious term, to the Tories during the Revolutionary period.

1774 J. ADAMS *Works* IX. 337, I admire the Jesuits! . . . Bowing . . . to persons whom . . . they would gladly butcher. **1777** — *Familiar Lett.* 306 Some Jesuits, who call themselves Quakers, . . . love money and land better than liberty and religion. **1779** HAMILTON *Works* VII. 576 He has given up Dr. Gordon, of Jamaica Plains. You will remember the old Jesuit. **1878** *N. Amer. Rev.* May–June 504 One-fourth of all power is in these ignorant masses, and they are in the hands of the political Jesuits of the South.

3. Attrib. with *father, mission, missionary, priest.*

1822 MORSE *Rep. Indian Affairs* II. 144 The two last Jesuit Missionaries at Mackinaw and L'Abre Croche, were Fathers Le Franc and Du Jaunay, who were sixty years in this country. **1870** *Republican Rev.* 3 Dec. 3/3 The Jesuit Fathers have opened two schools this winter in Albuquerque, one for boys and one for girls, gratis. **1885** *Wkly. New Mexican Rev.* 16 April 4/1 The famous medical springs, . . . eulogized so highly for its hygenienic [*sic*] and curative properties by the Jesuit priests and Franciscan friars, after being lost for more than two centuries has been recently discovered. **1890** *Century Mag.* Dec. 183 The Jesuit Missions [were] established in Lower California.

Jesuit's bark. Also **Jesuit bark. 1.** Peruvian bark, a medicinal bark of a species of *Chinchona.* {1694–} +**2.** *local.* The marsh elder. — **(1) 1723** *Amer. Wkly. Mercury* 1–8 Jan. 2/2 Lately imported from Peru, a Choice Parcel of Jesuits Bark, To be sold by Joseph Haynes. **1748** FRANKLIN *Poor Richard's Almanac 1749* That famous specific for the cure of intermitting fevers, agues, &c. called the Jesuits Bark, . . . fell into general disrepute. **1775** ROMANS *Nat. Hist. Florida* 239 Continue taking a bitter infusion, composed of the bark of the root of the *magnolia major* (which the French on the Mississippi substitute in lieu of Jesuit's bark) . . . in good Madeira or Lisbon wine. **1829** WEEMS *B. Franklin* xxxv. 175 As if it were not just as pleasing to him . . . as warding off the ague and fever by jesuit's bark. **1843** 'CARLTON' *New Purchase* I. 294, [I] set right to work, assisting the partly renovated son and daughter in getting wood, in boiling water, and in handling along jesuit bark, and sulphate of quinine. **(2) 1894** *Amer. Folk-Lore* VII. 92 *Iva frutescens,* . . . Jesuit's bark. N.Y.

***Jetty.** A part of a structure, esp. an upper story, that projects out over the wall. {–1664} *Obs.* — **1624** WINSLOW *Good Newes* 4 Wee thought it most needfull to impale our towne, . . . making foure bulwarkes or ietties without the ordinarie circuit of the pale. **1677** *Boston Rec.* 109 The widdow Walker hath set vp 4 posts vpon the towne land to support the Gettie of her house. **1688** *Ib.* 194 Nicholas Paige Esq was incloseinge the Towne ground on yt pte of the streete vnder the Jettie of his dwelling house. **1701** *Ib.* 11 Ordered, That no person shall Erect or set up any Pentice, jetty or Pendal over any of the Streets, lanes or highwayes of this town.

***Jew,** *n.* Any person of the Hebrew people or whose religion is Judaism. Also attrib.

1678 *Doc. Hist. N.Y. State* I. 92 There are Religions of all sorts, one church of England, . . . some Jews but presbiterians & Independents most numerous & Substantiall. **1737** W. STEPHENS *Proc. Georgia* 43 After Dinner walked out to see what Improvements of Vines were made by one Mr. Lyon, a Portuguese Jew. **1765** ROGERS *Acct. N. America* 72 The religious persuasions here [N.Y.] are very numerous; there being . . . Moravians, Quakers, and Jews. **1819** SHECUT *Top. Sk. Charleston* 30 There can be no argument that goes more fully to illustrate the correct principles of our government than that of a reference to the Jews who have settled among us. **1860** *Harper's Mag.* April 607/1 A small town was built, . . . goods came pouring in, Jew clothiers, rum-dealers, and gamblers followed the crowds of working men. **1868** M. H. SMITH *Sunshine & Shadow* 452 Persons in search of a house [in N.Y.] invariably ask 'Are there any Jews in the block?' **1900** *Outlook* 22 Sept. 213/1 Most of the children [in the Henry Booth House Kindergarten, Chicago] came from the homes of orthodox Jews. **1922** *Nation* 14 June 708/1 Harvard is not the first American university to limit the proportion of Jews in its midst. It is merely the frankest.

Jew, *v.*

1. *tr.* To overreach or cheat by sharp practice or trickery. {*a*1845–} *Obsolescent.*

*a***1834** L. DOW *Dealings of God* (1849) 189 If they [the Jews] will *Jew* people, they cannot flourish among Yankees, who are said to '*out-jew*' them in trading. **1859** BARTLETT 220 To *Jew* a person, is considered, in Western parlance, a shade worse than to 'Yankee' him. **1863** 'M. HARLAND' *Husks* 130 She shopped largely and judiciously . . . ; 'Jewed' her butcher; watched her pantry, and served up poorer dinners than ever. *a***1870** CHIPMAN *Notes on Bartlett* 220 *To Jew.* . . . This word is used all over the U.S. In N[ew] E[ng.] Jews themselves use it in the same way. **1888** BILLINGS *Hardtack* 204 It's just like that fraud of a quartermaster to jew a recruit out of a part of his outfit.

+**2. a.** *intr.* To haggle and bargain by way of lowering a price. **b.** *tr.* =next.

(a) 1872 *Chicago Tribune* 14 Oct. 8/2 The prices [for lodging] asked vary —the lodger being generally asked as much as it is thought he will give. If he jews, he will get it for comparatively little. **1887** W. R. HOUSTON, etc. *Rules of Etiquette* (ed. 11) 100 Avoid 'jewing,' and never give insult by offensively suggesting that you can do better elsewhere. **(b) 1890** *Stock Grower & Farmer* 19 April 7/1 Don't 'jew' the owner of a stallion in the price he asks for the service of his horse.

+**3.** *To jew down,* to bring (a payment or price) lower by bargaining or forcing down; to argue (a person) into lowering the price of something.

1870 *Congress. Globe* 7 July 5340/1 This bill supposes that Congress . . . is ready to commence jewing down the pay of its General. **1880** *Congress. Rec.* 16 March 1605/1 They might be able, living in New York, to jew the compositors down to a lower figure. **1883** 'MARK TWAIN' *Life on Miss.* xliii, There's one thing in this world which a person don't ever try to jew you down on. That's a coffin. *c***1895** NORRIS *Vandover* (1914) 259, I jewed him down . . . from twenty-five thousand I brought him right down to, say eight thousand.

***Jeweler.** One who works in precious stones; a dealer in jewels, watches, etc. — **1723** *New-Eng. Courant* 7 Jan. 2/2 Mr. James Boyer, Jeweller, from London, living at Mr. Enstone's, . . . setts all manner of Stones in Rings, &c. **1754** *S.C. Gazette* 1 Jan. 2/2 John Paul Grimke, Jeweller, has just imported . . . a fine fashionable assortment of jewellers work. **1819** MCMURTRIE *Sk. Louisville* 138 There are at this moment, in Louisville . . . three watch makers and jewellers. **1869** *Boyd's Business Directory* 14 Skiff M. M. jeweler, 358. **1921** *Ladies' Home Jrnl.* Jan. 165/4 For over 45 years the house of Jason Weiler & Sons, of Boston, has been . . . selling [diamonds] to jewelers.

+**Jewelhead.** (See quotation.) — **1884** GOODE, etc. *Fisheries* I. 370 Another name [for the fresh-water drum] used in the southwest is 'Jewelhead.'

***Jewelry.** The products of a jeweler's labor: gems, rings, watches, etc. Also transf. — **1805** tr. F. A. Michaux *Travels* 127 Fine jewellery, cutlery, ironmongery, and tin ware [are imported from England]. **1842** *Niles' Nat. Reg.* 9 April 93 In favor of low duties on jewelry in order to prevent their business being thrown into the hands of smugglers. **1845** *Knickerb.* XXVI. 466 Frequently, when the officers entered the cells, they would find the prisoners without chains, when suddenly every fellow would jump to his 'jewelry,' and clamp it on with magic celerity. **1849** *New Mexican* 28 Nov. 2/1 These young men have just received from the States, a very large lot of exceedingly well selected stock of Jewelry, etc. **1911** Vance *Cynthia* 327 'But why back?' she insisted in a gasp. 'Why don't we wait here?' 'To get Madame Savaran's jewelry,' he replied.

+Jewelry store. A shop where jewelry is sold. — **1847** Collins *Kentucky* 304 Frankfort contains . . . two hardware stores, two jewelry stores, four commission houses. **1877** Johnson *Anderson Co., Kansas* 181 W. Huff, . . . in 1869, . . . opened a jewelry store. **1894** *Harper's Mag.* Oct. 806 A man whom we may call Billson had for some time carried on a jewelry store in this town. **1904** H. R. Martin *Tillie* 113 He'll make his livin' in Lancaster city by keepin' a jew'lry-store.

+Jewelweed. Any plant of the genus *Impatiens*, esp. *I. biflora*, with an orange-yellow, brown-spotted flower, and *I. pallida*, with a pale yellow flower. — **1817–8** Eaton *Botany* (1822) 317 *Impatiens nolitangere*, jewelweed, touch-me-not. **1821** *Mass. H. S. Coll.* 2 Ser. IX. 151 Plants, which are indigenous in the township of Middlebury, [Vermont, include] . . . *Impatiens biflora*, Jewel-weed. **1843** Torrey *Flora N.Y.* I. 25 Balsam-weed, Jewelweed. . . . *Impatiens fulva*. **1869** Fuller *Flower Gatherers* 223, I have seen . . . the wild jewel-weed in our meadow. **1907** *St. Nicholas* July 842/2 A sudden thrust of the lantern into this clump of jewel weed near our path, produces a shower of miniature drops.

+Jewett red. A variety of apple. Also *Jewett's fine red.* — **1847** Ives *New Eng. Fruit* 49 *Jewett's Fine Red.*—This apple originated in Hollis, N.H. . . . It is among the best native apples of our country. **1909** Webster 1162 *Jewett red*, an American variety of apple, of round-oblate form, yellow color, and subacid flavor.

Jewfish. Any of several large marine fish, esp. of the family Epinephelidae. {1697–} — **1775** Romans *Nat. Hist. Florida* App. 19 A little to the north hereof is a small reef . . . where vast quantities of groopers, . . . yellow-tails, Jew-fish, &c. may be taken. **1837** Williams *Florida* 42 Highly prized . . . are the Jew-fish, porgy, hog-fish, and bass. **1880** *Lib. Universal Knowl.* VIII. 299 *Jew-fish*, a common name of several species of the serranidæ. . . . The jew-fish of California is the *stereolepis gigas*. **1886** *Nat. Museum Proc.* VIII. 208 In the fish-market at Indianapolis, I examined recently a large black 'jew-fish.' (*Epinephelus nigritus*). **1890** *Boston Jrnl.* 13 April 2/3 The largest jewfish ever caught on the Gulf coast . . . weighed 348 pounds, was 6 feet in length and 8 feet in circumference just back of the gills. **1911** *Rep. Fisheries 1908* 311 Jewfish. . . . The name is also applied to the . . . tarpon (*Tarpon atlanticus*) in Georgia and Florida.

+Jewhilliken(s), *interj.* Also **jewhilikins.** (See quot. 1859.) Also used as an adjective. (Cf. Gee whillikins.) — **1851** *Polly Peablossom* 52 Jewhilliken, how he could whip er nigger! **1859** Bartlett 220 *Jewhilikens!* A Western exclamation of surprise. **1877** Johnson *Anderson Co., Kansas* 115 Anderson, somewhat intoxicated, . . . in a loud voice, said: 'Great Jewhilikins! who ever heard of such a warrant—to bring a man dead or alive!' **1885** Baylor *On Both Sides* 372, 'Why aren't you gambolling like the playful antelope, Heathcote?' . . . 'I leave that to Ramsay, who is an all-fired jewhillikens scratch at it, as you say over here.'

+Jewlark, *v.* [? F. *jeu*, 'play' and *lark*, 'to frolic.'] *intr.* To sport *round;* to play. *colloq.* — **1851** Hooper *Widow Rugby* 59 Wonder if I'll ketch that rascal Jim Sparks jewlarkin' round Betsy, down at old Bob's!

***Jew's-ear.** An edible fungus (*Auricularia auricula-judae*) that grows on tree trunks. — **1624** *Va. House of Burgesses* 29 Famine compelled us wholly to devoure those Hogges . . . as alsoe Toadstooles, Jewes eares, or what els we founde growing upon the grounde. **1743** Clayton *Flora Virginica* 205 *Agaricus substantiæ tenellæ gelatinæ, auriculæ forma.* Jews Ear. **1791** W. Bartram *Travels* 270, I saw at the root of a small shrub, . . . a large kind of Fungus which we call Jews ears.

***Jew's-harp.** A small musical instrument played by holding it in the teeth and striking a bent metal tongue attached to the frame of the instrument. Also attrib. — **1637** *Md. Council Proc.* 67 Shipped vpon the good vessell . . . knives, combes, fish hooks iewes-harpes. **1756** *Lett. to Washington* I. 364 Brass Jews-harps @ 21/—but few left. **1815** in H. M. Brooks *Gleanings* 138 Jews-Harp Club. The first meeting of this Society will be holden . . . for the purpose of electing Officers and organizing the Society. **1912** Cobb *Back Home* 17 Did you notice a tall sort of a saddle-colored darky playing a juice harp in front of that there sideshow?

Jib. {1661–} **1.** *The cut of one's jib*, one's personal appearance. {1823–} **2.** *To up jib*, (see quot. 1859). — (1) **1787** Freneau *Misc. Works* 420 But I know what you are by the cutt of your jibb. **1886** Dorsey *Midshipman Bob* 176 He's not quite such a good-looking chap; but he isn't bad. Look at the cut of his jib—his nose, I mean. (2) **1848** J. Mitchell *Nantucketisms* 40 *Up jib.* Be off. **1859** Bartlett 494 *To Up Jib*, to be off. A sailor's phrase, much used in familiar language in Nantucket.

+Jibe, *n.* A sharp blow or push. *colloq.* — **1843** A. E. Silliman *Gallop* 5 [The river] stretched tranquilly onwards, undisturbed save by the occasional jibe of the boom, or lazy creak of the rudder of some craft. **1851** Springer *Forest Life* 66 After an untold number of stumbles over old windfalls, and jibes from the limbs, knots, and protruding boughs of trees, we reached [the log cabin]. **1870** *Scribner's Mo.* I. 58 Richard gave the boat an impatient jibe.

+Jibe, *v. intr.* To fit *in;* to agree *with;* to be in accord. (Cf. Gibe.)

1843 Stephens *High Life N.Y.* II. 40 The streaked mittens marm knit for me when my yaller gloves wore out, they didn't exactly jibe with my other fix up. **1855** Thompson *Doesticks* xiv. 113, [I] placed before her the 'Jenny Lind Polka,' which she at once began to play—I attempting to sing the words of 'Old Hundred,' which didn't seem to jibe. **1880** *Harper's Mag.* Dec. 91/2, 'I don't see how you make them idees jibe with 'lection and fore-ordination,' rejoined Aunt Polly. **1892** Harte *Col. Starbottle* 116 You'd better find out first how all the schoolin' and trainin' of Jack's is goin' to jibe with the Ranch. **1924** Croy *R.F.D. No. 3* 347 As I told you before, him and me didn't jibe, but I don't see as why I should hold that ag'in the kid.

Jiffy. Also **jiffin(g).** A very short space of time; a moment. {1785–} — **1776** Leacock *Fall Brit. Tyranny* IV. iii, He'll hoist his sheet-anchor presently; he'll be up in a jiffin. **1815** Humphreys *Yankey* 53 *C't.* Deliver it, and bring an answer—quick—quick. *Doo.* In a jiffing: and I'll be back, to rights. **1837** Neal *Charcoal Sk.* (1838) 65 Just hold my horse a minute. I'll be back in a jiffey, Salix; in less than half an hour. **1881** *Harper's Mag.* Jan. 195/2 Whenever there was a fire any where, all the engines were out in a jiffy. **1904** Crissey *Tattlings* 393 Our whole strength will go to you in a jiffy.

***Jig.**

1. *The jig is up* (or *over*), the game is up; the scheme or plan has failed.

1777 *Md. Journal* 17 June (Th.), Mr. John Miller came in and said, 'The jig is over with us.' **1800** *Aurora* (Phila.) 27 Dec., As the Baltimore paper says 'The jig's up, Paddy.' **1832** S. Smith *Major Downing* 93, [I] told 'em how the jig was up with us, that the British were going to have the land, without any fighting about it. **1875** in Summers *Hist. S.W. Va.* (1903) 655 Some of the doctors may take a dose of his own medicine one of these days, and if so, the jig is certainly up with him. **1898** Westcott *D. Harum* xlii, Did you think 'the jig was up an' the monkey was in the box?' **1909** Wason *Happy Hawkins* 291, I could tell by their talk that Barbie had told him about Dick, an' then I knew the jig was about up.

+2. One of various contrivances for catching fish, as a spinner, spoon, etc.

1846 *Knickerb.* XXVII. 513 See that your jigs are in prime order, for if we do get hold of 'em, our lines and hooks will have to take it. **1857** *Harper's Mag.* Sept. 540/2 A dog-fish . . . swallowing all the bait, and . . . taking in also every jig which crosses his path. **1858** *N.Y. Tribune* 22 July 3/3 [He] seized . . . a long, stout line, at the end of which was a shining spoon-shaped piece of pewter terminated by a large hook. This apparatus he called a jig. **1881** *Amer. Naturalist* XV. 368 The only gear is a peculiar hook called a 'jig,' and a couple of fathoms of 'mackerl' line. **1883** *Nat. Museum Bul.* No. 27, 190 The *Ommastrephes* . . . are also captured by using 'jigs' or groups of hooks which are moved up and down in the water. **1897** *Outing* XXX. 258/1 [He] seized one of the jigs, and after giving its brass wire a swift, sure turn, threw it overboard once more.

+3. *Mining.* A machine for shaking up ore in a fluid medium.

1849 *31st Congress 1 Sess.* H. R. Ex. Doc. No. 5, II. 479 Assay and analysis of the washed metals from the jigs at the Boston and Pittsburg Company's mine. **1873** Raymond *Silver & Gold* 493, [I] recommend a continuous jig, designed by Dr. F. M. Stapff, M.E.

Jigamaree. {1847} Also **gigamaree,** etc. +A 'thingumajig.' *colloq.* — **1824** *Old Colony Memorial* (Plymouth) 6 March (Th.), O the wonderation, what a nation sight of jiggermarees! **1843** W. T. Thompson *Major Jones's Courtship* 116 Mary was sowin something mighty fine and white with ruffles and jigmarees all round it. **1848**—*Major Jones's Sk. Travel* 156 (Th.), I axed the captain what sort of a gigamaree he had got up thar for a flag. **1851** *Polly Peablossom* 71 One uv them ar all-fired yankee pedlars come er long with er outlandish kind uv er jigamaree to make the wimmin's coat sorter stick out in the t'other eend.

Jigger.[1]

1. =Chigoe 1. {1756–}

1827 Williams *West Florida* 29 Of these [insects] the jigger is the most troublesome; it enters the skin, most usually of the feet, and produces an excessive itching and inflammation. **1854** Emmons *Agric. N.Y.* V. 148 *Aphaniptera.* . . . The chigre, or jigger, *Pulex penetrans*, of the West Indies, belongs to this family. **1869** *Amer. Naturalist* III. 386 As I was not in the habit of going entirely barefooted, I cannot say whether I would have been more troubled by the nigua (Spanish)—or jigger (Florida), or chigoe or chique (French) . . . —than with shoes. **1899** *Animal & Plant Lore* 63 Jigger, chigger, *Sarcopsylla penetrans.* Illinois and Missouri.

+2. Applied to various harvest ticks, esp. *Trombicula irritans:* (see quots. 1873, 1889).

1851 D. B. Woods *At Gold Diggings* 22 [We were] ourselves likewise the sport of innumerable swarms of musquitoes, ticks, fleas, and jiggers. This latter insect, though very small, is the occasion, at times, of great inconvenience and suffering. **1873** *Amer. Naturalist* VII. 17 We have, however, in the southwestern States, two other mites which cause great annoyance from harvest time till into October. . . . Both of them are six-legged, reddish, microscopic specks, and both are popularly termed jiggers. **1889**

Cent. 3232/3 *Jigger*, . . . in the United States, a name of sundry harvest-mites or harvest-ticks which, though normally plant-feeders, fasten to the skin of human beings and cause great irritation.

Jigger.[2] {1675-}

+**1.** A small glass or metal cup holding about one fluid ounce, used to measure out alcoholic liquor for a drink; such a glassful of liquor. Also attrib.

1836 W. O'BRYAN *Travels* 107 These canal labourers have a boy to supply them with Whiskey, called a *Jiggar boss*, who goes on the canal and carries a half gill (half noggin) of Whiskey to every man sixteen times a day! **1857** *Harper's Mag.* March 443/1 Betsy . . . would drink numerous consecutive jiggers of raw whisky without winking. **1870** NOWLAND *Indianapolis* 361 By jiggers was meant a small cup of whisky, say about a gill; they had cups made on purpose for this use. **1889** *Lisbon* (Dak.) *Star* 15 Feb. 3/1 After giving him [an Indian] two small 'jiggers' the civilities were brought to an end. **1925** *Scribner's Mag.* Oct. 21 (*advt.*), A silver 'jigger set' has a bottle opener, a corkscrew, and a flattened funnel, which all fit together in a pigskin case.

+**2.** (See quotation.)

1841 *S. Lit. Messenger* VII. 646/2 He then dressed himself, with more than ordinary care; . . . discarding his 'stitch downs' for his 'jiggers' (his pumps).

3. +**a.** A fishing smack used on the northeast coast. **b.** A small vessel furnished with a jigger sail. {1891}

1842 BUCKINGHAM *E. & W. States* I. 107 Vessels collectively he [the Bay of Fundy fisherman] calls *craft*, and subdivides them into *Pinkies*, *Pogies*, *Jiggers*, &c. **1852** *32d Congress 2 Sess.* H. R. Ex. Doc. No. 23, 260 Chebacco-boats and small schooners are known to him [*sc.* the boat-fisherman of the Bay of Fundy] as *pinkies*, *pogies*, and *jiggers*. **1859** BARTLETT 221 *Jigger*, . . . a small fishing vessel. New England. **1875** KNIGHT 1214/1 *Jigger*, . . . a fishing-vessel whose rig corresponds to that of a cutter, excepting a small mizzen in the stern. **1880** *Harper's Mag.* Aug. 350/2 The jigger, a small schooner of perhaps forty feet long by ten feet beam, with a considerable hold, and a cabin of four bunks. **1888** *St. Louis Globe-Democrat* 10 March, The owner of the jigger said that his name was Catlin. . . . He was bound for Jupiter Inlet.

+**4.** *Mining.* An apparatus for separating ore into various grades of fineness.

1853 *Harper's Mag.* April 580/1 The *jigger* is a kind of low tub, with a bottom of sheet brass finely perforated. **1874** RAYMOND *6th Rep. Mines* 499 The mining laboratory now contains . . . a little hand-jigger, a rotary pulverizer, and a fan-blower. **1890** *Congress Rec.* 12 Aug. 8454/1 After it [the tin ore] is ground fine it is sent into what is termed a 'jigger.'

+**5.** (See quotation.)

1889 *Cent.* 3232/3 *Jigger*, . . . a small street-railway car, drawn by one horse, and usually without a conductor, the driver giving change and the fare being deposited in a box.

+**6.** (See quotation.)

1889 *Cent.* 3232/3 *Jigger*, . . . a machine now generally used in the produce exchanges of American cities, which exhibits on a conspicuous dial the prices at which sales are made as the transactions occur. The hand or pointer is controlled by electric mechanism connected with a keyboard.

+**7.** Among tramps: (see quotation). *cant.*

1900 'FLYNT' *Tramping* 394 *Jigger*, a sore, artificially made, to excite sympathy.

+**Jiggling board.** (See quotation and cf. JOGGLING BOARD.) — **1859** BARTLETT 221 *Jiggling-Board*, a board the ends of which are placed upon frames or stools, upon which a person stands and springs up—also called a jolly-board.

+**Jig saw,** *n.* Also **gig saw.** (See quot. 1875.)

1873 J. RICHARDS *Wood-working Factories* 128 With respect to jig saws, the band saw and duplicating machines have driven the most of them out of use. **1874** *Vermont Bd. Agric. Rep.* II. 745 Then, if the stock is designed for mantles, it goes to a 'jig saw,' from thence to the rubbing bed. **1875** KNIGHT 965/2 *Gig-saw*, a thin saw to which a rapid vertical reciprocation is imparted, and which is adapted for sawing scrolls, frets, etc. **1886** *Harper's Mag.* July 174/1 The world's people made a city . . . still more fantastic, by the aid of paint and the jig-saw.

b. Attrib. with *carving*, *porch*, *puzzle.*

1884 *Century Mag.* May 49/2 A bastard structure with . . . much riottous ornamentation in sanded zinc and jig-saw carving. **1887** *Harper's Mag.* Nov. 950/1 Several wooden houses across the street . . . were adorned with jig-saw porches. **1916** PORTER *David* 289 It's a jig-saw puzzle, David. All these little pieces fitted together make a picture, you see.

+**Jig-saw,** *v. tr.* To cut or shape with a jig saw; to design in the manner of jig-saw work. Hence *jig-sawed* ppl. a. and *jig-sawing* vbl. n. — **1873** J. RICHARDS *Wood-working Factories* 128 What may be said of jig-sawing need not consume much space here. **1881** HOWELLS *Modern Instance* i. 5 Some houses of more modern taste, . . . looked, with their mansard roofs and jig-sawed piazzas and balconies, intrusive and alien. **1883** — *Woman's Reason* 185 [She saw] comic designs *jig-sawed* out of white-wood. **1897** BRODHEAD *Bound in Shallows* One of them [*sc.* roads], sheering abruptly, crossed the railway at the jig-sawed station near the knoll.

Jim. +Used alone or in combination in mild oaths. — **1866** 'F. KIRKLAND' *Book Anecdotes* 444 By Jim! Major, you got out of that snarl completely—slick! **1897** STUART *Simpkinsville* 56, I'd give every dog gone cent . . . ef I'd been raised to swear—jim-blasted ef I wouldn't. **1911** SAUNDERS *Col. Todhunter* 7, I'll be jim-swizzled if I don't believe [etc.].

+**Jimberjawed,** *a.* Having a projecting lower jaw. *colloq.*

1834 CARRUTHERS *Kentuckian* I. 195 Some . . . pushed out the under jaw, like a person who (to use a Southern term) is jimberjawed. **1857** *Harper's Mag.* March 443/2 In physiognomy and manner he reminds one of a 'jimber-jawed' bull-dog—one of those fellows who never let go. **1871** EGGLESTON *Duffels* 158 She was 'jimber-jawed'—that is, her lower teeth shut a little outside her upper. **1885** 'CRADDOCK' *Prophet* 74 His long chin, of the style familiarly denominated jimber-jawed, was still smooth and boyish. **1923** WATTS *L. Nichols* 290 [They] moved away, all but th' oldest girl, that there jimber-jawed one, remember her?

+**Jim Crow.**

1. The name of an old Negro song; a Negro character in this song. (Cf. CROW 4.)

1838 *Harvardiana* IV. 299 'Zip Coon' and 'Jim Crow' . . . are hymns of great antiquity. **1841** *Picayune* 7 May 2/2 Rice was fond of riding, and frequently visited . . . a very droll negro hostler, who used to dance grotesquely and sing odd fragments of a song about one *Jim Crow*.

2. A song and dance based on the Negro song, written and first performed by Thomas D. Rice in 1832; the Negro character in this song, and, by extension, the actor performing his part.

1835 CROCKETT *Tour* 32 The landlord, Dorrance, and others were to go with me to see Jim Crow. **1837** HONE *Diary* I. 266 The Bowery, with Jim Crow, who is made to repeat nightly, almost *ad infinitum*, his balderdash song, which has now acquired the stamp of London approbation to increase in *éclat*. **1841** *Picayune* 7 May 2/2 In half an hour Rice was master of symphony, melody, and all the steps, words and drollery of the far-famed and irresistible Jim Crow! **1867** *Atlantic Mo.* Nov. 608/2 As a national or 'race' illustration, behind the footlights, might not 'Jim Crow' and a black face tickle the fancy of pit and circle?

b. *To jump Jim Crow*, to jump or dance according to the routine of this or a similar song and dance.

The phrase is taken from the song: (see quot. 1836).

1833 *Sketches D. Crockett* 41 You nebber get to Heben till you jump Jim Crow. **1836** WESTON *Visit* 69 Turn about, jump about, turn about so; Ebery time I turn about, jump Jem Crow. **1844** 'UNCLE SAM' *Peculiarities* II. 174 That black devil has been jumping Jim Crow ever since we have been on board. **1893** M. A. OWEN *Voodoo Tales* 3 She could, as actively as a girl, . . . 'jump Jim Crow.'

3. A Negro. Also fig.

1838 'UNCLE SAM' in *Bentley's Misc.* IV. 582 Don't be standing there like the wooden Jim Crow at the blacking maker's store. **1841** H. PLAYFAIR *Playfair Papers* I. 3 A portmanteau and carpet-bag . . . were snatched up by one of the hundreds of nigger-porters, or Jim Crows, who swarm at the many landing-places to *help* passengers.

4. A small card resembling a currycomb used by Negroes in rural districts instead of a comb.

1899 CHESNUTT *Conjure Woman* 22 He wuk at it ha'f de night wid er Jim Crow.

5. *attrib.* **a.** In sense 2.

Quot. 1835 may be used in sense 3.

1835 *Knickerb.* V. 47 Some jolly slaves . . . were waiting to take us into a ferry-boat, which they rowed, singing some Jim Crow song. **1847** *Chicago Jrnl.* 7 Oct., We do not mean *Jim Crow* dances and poor songs worse sung. **1847** J. SPENCE *Ship & Shore* 88 Here . . . are two boys of the Jim Crow school, singing charcoal songs to a checkered crowd. **1891** WELCH *Recoll. 1830–40* 371 In August, '35, at the old Eagle Street Theatre, Mr. Rice, known as the original 'Jim Crow Rice,' sang and jumped 'Jim Crow,' in negro character.

b. Passing into adj.: Dexterous or tricky; double-dealing; deceptive. *Obsolescent.*

1838 *N.Y. Advertiser & Exp.* 18 April 2/1 Gov. Marcy's message, Mr. Secretary Woodbury's Letter [etc.] . . . are Jim Crow performances. **1890** *Stock Grower & Farmer* 11 Jan. 3/4 The *stock grower* has refused to puff a fraudulent jim crow ditch scheme whose projectors have handled a big profit before the 'preliminary survey' was made. *Ib.* 3 May 7/4 Many people have become slaves to the vile opium habit from the use of that drug by these jim-crow physicians. **1897** A. H. LEWIS *Wolfville* 193 He hangs about Wolfville an' Red Dog alternate turnin' little jim-crow tricks for the express company.

c. In sense 3 with *Bible*, *line.*

1852 STOWE *Uncle Tom* xx, I thought she was rather a funny specimen in the Jim Crow line. **1908** LORIMER *J. Spurlock* 132 Our pasture has done promised us niggers dat we'll all be white in heben, and we jest natchelly won't buy no Jim-Crow Bibles.

d. Designating things set aside for the exclusive use of the Negroes, and laws intended to segregate the Negroes from the whites. (Cf. JIM CROW CAR.)

1903 *N.Y. Sun* 29 Nov. 7 The members of the committee have arranged with the parents of negro children to send them all to the Jim Crow school, thus entirely separating the white and negro pupils. **1904** *Nation*

17 March 202 Writing of the 'Jim Crow' bills now before the Maryland Legislature, the Cardinal expressed his strong opposition. **1904** *Richmond Times-Dispatch* 25 May 10 The Norfolk and Southern Railroad was fined $300 to-day for violating the 'Jim Crow' law by allowing negroes to ride in the same car with whites. **1904** *Churchman* 11 June 728 Many opposed it [a proposal at the Presbyterian Assembly for the organization of presbyteries for a special race] as constituting 'Jim Crow presbyteries.' **1910** *N.Y. Ev. Post* 2 June (Th.), An attempt to get the Supreme Court of the United States to pass on the authority of common carriers engaged in interstate commerce to make 'Jim Crow' regulations, met with failure today when the court dismissed the so-called Chiles appeal.

e. *Jim-crow planing machine,* (see quotation).

1875 KNIGHT 1216/1 The jim-crow planing-machine is furnished with a reversing tool, to plane both ways, and named from its peculiar motion, as the tool is able to 'wheel about and turn about.'

+**Jim Crow car.** A car, as on a railway train, designated for the use of Negroes. Also attrib. (Cf. JIM CROW 5 d.) — **1861** H. JACOBS *Life Slave Girl* 265, I was now put into a 'Jim Crow car,' on our way to Rockaway. **1887** GEORGE *40 Years on Rail* 160 An educated colored man . . . found, on going from Boston to Salem, his home, that he must ride in the 'Jim Crow' car. **1898** *Boston Morning Herald* 19 April 12/1 South Carolina's 'Jim Crow car law' provides that the act shall not apply to nurses on trains, to narrow gauge roads, to relief trains in case of accident, to through vestibule trains, nor to officers or guards transporting prisoners. **1909** 'O. HENRY' *Options* 89 Lee surrendered; . . . cotton went to nine cents; Old Crow whiskey and Jim Crow cars were invented.

+**Jim-dandy,** *n.* A person or thing that is unusually fine or admirable. *colloq.* — **1887** *Courier-Journal* 12 Jan. 2/1 Dear Sir: Though a stranger to you (yet a Democrat), let me say you are a 'Jim Dandy.' **1894** H. GARDENER *Unofficial Patriot* 255 A battery is a jim-dandy of a place. I get to ride all the time. **1902** WISTER *Virginian* xxvii, He killed a big fighter on the other side who was another jim-dandy. **1914** ATHERTON *Perch of Devil* 242, I've got a . . . jim dandy of a limousine.

+**Jim-dandy,** *a.* Unusually good; excellent. *colloq.* — **1888** *Chicago Inter-Ocean* 14 Feb. (F.), George C. Ball came upon the floor yesterday arrayed in a jim-dandy suit of clothes. **1902** WISTER *Virginian* xxvii, He cert'nly must have been a jim-dandy boy if that is all true. **1909** 'O. HENRY' *Roads of Destiny* 160 What a jim-dandy place for a hold-up! **1923** *Dialect Notes* V. 212 That was a jim dandy meal [McDonald Co., Mo.]

Jiminy. Also **gimini.** [Cf. JEMINY.] **1.** A mild oath. {gemony, 1664–; gemini, 1666–} +**2.** In various phrases in same sense. — **(1) 1836** SIMMS *Mellichampe* 47 'Gimini!' exclaimed Thumbscrew. 'Gimini! if the major was only here now.' **1848** BARTLETT 191 By *Jiminy!* An exclamation. **1883** BEADLE *Western Wilds* 615 [We] thought, by jiminy, the whole ground was moving. **1905** N. DAVIS *Northerner* 227 Jiminy! . . . This beats out all creation! **(2) 1848** J. MITCHELL *Nantucketisms* 40 *By Jiminy Cricket,* an exclamation of surprise. **1893** *Harper's Mag.* Dec 67/2 Jiminy crackers! but I wush 't I'd 've knew it. **1898** F. H. SMITH *C. West* 288 Jiminy-whiz, but it's soapy out there! See 'er take that roller! Gosh! **1910** J. HART *Vigilante Girl* 305 She's going to try and separate Salem's heirs from some of Salem's money, and by jimminy crick, Yarrow, I think she'll make it go.

***Jimjam.** *pl.* Delirium tremens; the fidgets; a fit of nervousness. {1885–} — **1852** JACKSON *Forty-Niner* 157 He had a bad attack of the jim-jams, and his nearest neighbor, O'Neil, heard him yelling and shrieking like all possessed. **1883** DE VERE in *Encycl. Brit.* (ed. 9) *Amer. Suppl.* I. 196/2 The sad effects of 'indulging in it' [drinking] are often called the '*jim-jams.*' **1888** *St. Louis Globe-Democrat* 16 Feb. (F.), Burbridge . . . began to drink very excessively. . . . He had the Jim-Jams yesterday evening, and last night he raved like a madman. **1892** HARTE *First Family of Tasajara* 5 He'll either go off his head with jim-jams or jump into the creek. **1911** FERBER *Dawn O'Hara* 29 You'll give yourselves nervous jim-jams and then you'll have to go home to be patched up.

Jimmy.[1] [Var. of *jemmy* {1753–}] An iron bar used by burglars to force a lock, window, etc. {jemmy, 1811–} — **1854** *Alta Californian* 23 Feb., Officer Powers, . . . upon examining the lock, found it had been broken open with a 'jimmy.' **1872** MCCLELLAN *Golden State* 409 He nimbly plies his 'jimmey,' skeleton-keys, and chloroform. **1882** MCCABE *New York* 511 When small safes are to be forced open, they use only a jimmy and a hammer. **1898** *Kansas City Star* 21 Dec. 4/1 And when the judge had seen the delicate pick locks and jimmies he fined Powell $15. **1904** LORIMER *Old Gorgon Graham* 159 You can't break a big merchant with a jimmy and a stick of dynamite.

+**Jimmy.**[2] 'A freight-car used for carrying coal; a coal-car' (*Cent.*). — **1887** *N.Y. Semi-Weekly Tribune* 18 March (*Cent.*), The express train . . . ran into a freight. . . . The second car on the freight was lifted from the rails and carried on top of two jimmies loaded with coal.

+**Jimmy-john.** *S.* =DEMIJOHN. — **1884** HARRIS *Mingo* 28 Ole Marster he ain't say nothin', but he tuck a fresh grip on de jimmy-john. **1888** 'CRADDOCK' *Despot* 200 Jes' ketch a-holt o' the handle o' that thar jimmy-john in the corner, an' haul it hyar. **1898** HARRIS *Tales of Home Folks* 107 There he'd get his jimmy-john filled, and then he'd go back home.

+**Jimpsecute.** Also **jimpsycute.** *S.* (See quotations.) *colloq.* — **1869** *Overland Mo.* III. 131 When a Texan goes forth on a sparking errand, he does not go to pay his devoirs to his Amaryllis, . . . but . . . his 'jimpsecute.' **1891** *Amer. Notes & Q.* VIII. 60 In the State of Mississippi, I several times heard the word jimpsycute used in the sense of 'sweetheart,' it being always, so far as I remember, applied to the young lady in the case.

+**Jimpson weed.** Also **gympson weed.** =JIMSON WEED. — **1832** BENTON *30 Years' View* I. 256/2 An eagle . . . [was] by a pig under a jimpson weed . . . caught and whipt. **1855** *Knickerb.* XLVI. 600 The schooners . . . are manned by a primitive race of people who live principally upon . . . crabs, shrimps, and a species of gympson (Jamestown) weed. **1876** 'MARK TWAIN' *Tom Sawyer* i, [She] looked out among the tomato vines and 'jimpson' weeds that constituted the garden. **1884** — *H. Finn* 209 Hardly anything in them [*sc.* gardens] but jimpson-weeds, and sunflowers, and ash-piles. **1924** CROY *R.F.D. No. 3* The jimpson weed was about to go to seed—it had to be cut.

+**Jimson.** Also **gimson.** *ellipt.* =JIMSON WEED. Also attrib. — **1842** *Amer. Pioneer* I. 314 She said her principal dressings were made of . . . the leaves of stramonium, or 'jimson.' **1867** G. W. HARRIS *Sut Lovingood* 177 They makes soup outen dirty towils, an' jimson burrs. **1873** *Kansas Bd. Agric. Trans. 1872* 423 Bur-grass, cockle-bur, jimson, and smartweed were contending for the mastery, in this field, when we first took hold of it. **1910** C. HARRIS *Eve's Husband* 299, [I] passed up the path between clumps of sweet jimson and borders of balsam and pinks.

+**Jimson weed.** Also **gimson weed.** [From *Jamestown,* Va.] A name applied to a poisonous Asiatic weed (*Datura stramonium*), naturalized in the United States. (Cf. JAMESTOWN, JIMPSON WEED, JIMSON.)

1850 S. F. COOPER *Rural Hours* 107 The gimson weed, or Datura, is an Abyssinian plant. **1872** EGGLESTON *End of World* xi. 77 Long may you wave, like . . . a jimson-weed on the sunny side of a board-fence. **1885** — in *Century Mag.* April 883/2 Some of the soldiers in Bacon's rebellion, . . . after eating its leaves, . . . suffered a delirium of several days, whence the plant got its name of Jamestown weed, long since corrupted to its present form of 'jimson weed.' **1899** GOING *Flowers* 214 All along the Ohio valley and in the alluvial country westward . . . the commonest night flower is the Jamestown or jimson-weed. **1903** *Atlantic Mo.* July 82 The smell of jimson-weed was heavy on the evening air.

+**Jim-swinger.** (See quot. 1895.) *colloq.* — **1895** *Dialect Notes* I. 389 *Jim-swinger:* long-tailed coat, especially a 'Prince Albert.' **1898** DUNBAR *Folks from Dixie* 52 He walked to church, flanked on one side by Aunt Caroline . . . and on the other by her husband stately in the magnificence of an antiquated 'Jim-swinger.'

***Jingle.** +=GOLD SHELL 2. — **1881** E. INGERSOLL *Oyster-Industry* 245 *Jingle.*—Any species of *Anomia.* (Long Island sound.) **1887** GOODE, etc. *Fisheries* v. 543 A more fragile shell, such as a scallop, mussel, or jingle (*Anomia*) is certainly better.

+**Jingle bob. 1.** *W.* An earmark used on cattle: (see quot. 1913). **2.** A cow bearing this earmark. — **(1) 1890** *Stock Grower & Farmer* 11 Jan. 11/2 Ear marks, double jinglebob left ear. **1913** BARNES *Western Grazing Grounds* 382 *Jingle Bob.*—An ear-mark made by cutting the ear on the upper side, so as to break the back of the ear. This allows it to hang down along the side of the face much as do the long ears of the Angora goat. **1920** HUNTER *Trail Drivers Texas* I. 298 A *jingle bob* is to split the ear to the head and let the pieces flap. **(2)** *Ib.* I. 15 Mr. Charles Goodnight went the western route . . . , afterwards trailing the 'Jingle Bobs' or the John Chissum cattle north.

***Jingler.** {1829–} *local.* +=GOLDEN-EYE 1. — **1888** G. TRUMBULL *Names of Birds* 79 At Pleasantville [N.J., the American golden-eye is called] . . . Jingler. **1917** *Birds of Amer.* I. 138.

+**Jinglet. 1.** The loose metal ball serving as a clapper in a sleigh bell. **2.** (See quotation.) — **(1) 1881** *Scientific Amer.* XLIV. 323 This sand core, with the jinglet inside, is placed in the mould of the outside [etc.]. **1885** *American* IX. 350 The little iron ball [of the sleigh bell] is called 'the jinglet.' **(2) 1893** *Stand.* 964/3 *Jinglet,* . . . any small jingling appendage, especially one shaped like a sleigh-bell.

‖ **Jingo,** *v. tr.* To force into action by an aggressively chauvinistic policy. — **1898** *Westminster Gaz.* 28 Feb. 7/1 President McKinley is reported to have declared that he 'will not be jingoed into war.'

Jinks.[1] *pl.* (See quot. 1870.) — *a***1870** CHIPMAN *Notes on Bartlett* 221 *Jinks;* Jinkins. By Jinks! An expletive in N[ew] E[ngland]. Perhaps traceable to Wales or its borders. Jenkin, [illegible]kins, Jenks. (Jan-kin, John). **1890** C. KING *Sunset Pass* 67 By Jinks! [illegible] swear to it as long as it can possibly hold good. **1902** WISTER *Virginian* xxiv. 276 'My jinks!' said Scipio, quietly, and he shut the door.

+**Jinks.**[2] The checkerberry: (see quotation). — **1892** *Amer. Folk-Lore* V. 100 *Gaultheria procumbens,* . . . jinks or chinks. N.H.; Mass.

+**Jirk.** =JERK *n.*[1] — **1799** J. SMITH *Acct. Captivity* 65 [This] we kept to stew with our jirk as we needed it. **1807** GASS *Journal* 19 *n.*, Jirk is meat cut into small pieces and dried in the sun or by a fire. The Indians cure and preserve their meat in this way without salt. **1825** W. BIGGS *Narr. Captivity* 13 They sat down to eat their jirk. **1842** *Amer. Pioneer* I. 52 They took the whole of our two months' work, breakfast, *jirk,* skins and all.

+**Jirks.** =JERK *n.*[2] 1. — **1824** R. H. BISHOP *Hist. Church Ky.* 353 The first bodily exercise, which appeared in our worshipping assemblies, was *falling.* This was succeeded by . . . the *jirks.*

***Joan.** ?=next. — **1793** *Mass. Spy* 16 May 3/3 New goods imported this Spring include: . . . wildbore, joans, black russel, black lasting. **1812** *Niles' Reg.* II. 9/1 Much of it [*i.e.,* wool] . . . may be wrought into . . . joans.

Joan's spinning. A kind of cloth. — **1790** *Penna. Packet* 2 Jan. 1/4 A compleat assortment of Stuff Goods; such as, durants, tammies, Joan's spinning, calimancoes.

Job.[1] +*Job's cat*, a symbol of patient poverty (cf. JOB'S TURKEY); +*Job's Coffin*, Delphinus, or the Dolphin, a northern constellation nearly west of Pegasus; *Job's ox*, a symbol of great patience. — **1830** S. SMITH *Major Downing* 24 It broke the Sinnet wheel right in tu, and left it so flat, that all Job's oxen never could start it. **1854** — *'Way Down East* 184, I should rather be as poor as Job's cat all the days of my life. **1883** WILDER *Sister Ridnour* 133, I chanced to get a glimpse of the stars in 'Job's coffin.'

Job.[2] {*a*1627–}

+**1.** A more or less permanent position of employment for which wages or a salary is paid; a situation. *colloq.*

***a*1861** WINTHROP *E. Brothertoft* 38, I will find you a fat job and plenty of pickings! **1872** POWERS *Afoot & Alone* 38 Ragged land-workers strolled in legions in the road, 'looking for a job.' **1893** *Harper's Mag.* Jan. 323/1 Yes, I've got a job. Two dollars a day and board, and it's yours. **1896** ADE *Artie* xiv. 129 That guy up in your place don't know nothin' on earth except how to hold down his measly job. **1905** PHILLIPS *Social Secretary* 79 Ever since the second week in my 'job' I've realized that nothing could be easier than to put the Burkes well to the front.

2. Short for *job lot*.

1887 *Courier-Journal* 13 Jan. 8/5 (*advt.*), Three special jobs in Children's Underwear.

3. *attrib.* and *comb.*

Job gardener, a gardener who hires himself out to do odd jobs of gardening; *j.-holder*, one who holds a political job.

1870 *Nation* 20 Jan. 45/1 The navvy and job-gardener have had the work all their own way, and have compelled the landscape gardener to languish for want of work. **1904** CRISSEY *Tattlings* 275 There'll be a brass band and a lot of job holders waiting with glad hands at the station to meet me.

Jobber.

1. a. One who does work by the job. {1706–}

1770 *Md. Hist. Mag.* XII. 368 My Jobbers are not my strongest Hands. **1785** WASHINGTON *Diaries* II. 348, I set the jobbers to pounding the plaister of Paris by hand. **1823** COOPER *Pioneers* vi, An unfortunate jobber suffered a fracture of his leg by the tree that he had been felling.

+**b.** A contractor who undertakes to drive a season's logs.

1902 WHITE *Blazed Trail* 7 Customarily a jobber is paid a certain proportion of the agreed price, . . . so much when the 'drive' down the waters of the river is finished. **1905** *Forestry Bureau Bul.* No. 61, 40 *Jobber's sun*, a term applied to the moon in a jobber's or contractor's logging camp, on account of the early and late hours of commencing and ending work. (N[orth] W[oods], L[ake] S[tates Forest].)

2. One who buys from the producer or importer and sells to the retailer or other small dealer. {1670–}

1819–27 J. BERNARD *Retrosp.* 37 This curious class of mammalia, the 'Down-Easter' as it is often called, is divisible into three species—the swapper, the jobber, and the pedler. **1839** BRIGGS *H. Franco* I. 76 Mr. Smith Davis . . . told me he was not a retailer, but a jobber, and advised me if I wanted to negotiate for a vest pattern to go into Chatham street. **1864** *Wkly. New Mexican* 3 June 1/1 Stettaeur & Bro., Jobbers in Fancy and Staple Dry Goods. **1892** *Courier-Journal* 1 Oct. 6/4 The jobber read with profound delight An order by mail from Jeweler Dwight. **1908** LORIMER *J. Spurlock* 241 You can wire your jobbers to double their orders.

Jobbing. {1735–} The action of using opportunities in public office or service for private gain or graft. {1784–} Cf. LAND JOBBING. — **1841** BUCKINGHAM *Amer. N. States* I. 314 The department for the sale of the public lands is reputed to be a fertile source of jobbing and corrupt patronage. **1854** BENTON *30 Years' View* I. 207/2 Randolph—friend of the people, . . . of economy and hard money—scourge and foe to all corruption, plunder and jobbing. **1866** 'F. KIRKLAND' *Book Anecdotes* 647/1 No sort of approach at official 'jobbing' ever had any encouragement from him.

+**Jobbing house. 1.** A firm that deals in stock-jobbing. **2.** A firm that buys from the manufacturer or importer and sells to the retailer. — **(1) 1870** MEDBERY *Men Wall St.* 166 Mr. Fisk's maturity dates with his entrance as partner in a well-known Boston jobbing-house. **(2) 1878** *Harper's Mag.* April 760/2 We were all employed in the old jobbing-house down town.

Jobbing trade. Trade that results from the bulk buying of goods by a middleman for resale in smaller quantities to retailers. — **1875** *Chicago Tribune* 15 Oct. 6/1 The Jobbing Trade of the City Still Increasing. **1879** *Harper's Mag.* Dec. 38/2 The jobbing trade in dry-goods alone amounts to some millions of dollars annually. **1898** *Kansas City Star* 18 Dec. 5/2 This, of course, shows heavy jobbing trade in furniture and furniture supplies.

+**Job office.** A printing office that does job printing. — **1840** *Picayune* 17 Oct. 2/1 We are pouring out bills of all kinds from our Job Office now. **1855** *Chicago W. Times* 6 Sept. 1/1 The Times Job Office contains as well selected an assortment of Job Materials as any office in the country. **1873** *Winfield* (Kan.) *Courier* 11 Jan. 1/7 The Courier Job Office [is] prepared to do all kinds of job work . . . at reduced rates. **1884** MATTHEWS & BUNNER *In Partnership* 54 Mr. Kilburn, recognising the acknowledged merits of our job-office, had given us the contract. **1898** *Internat. Typogr. Union Proc.* 63 The union has made several attempts to unionize this office and also the job offices.

+**Job printer.** A printer who does job work. — **1838** MAYO *Polit. Sk. Washington* (1839) 15, I would also add, the establishment of a servile monopoly, and that too, under the pretence of selecting a job printer. **1869** *Boyd's Business Directory* 521 B. Hermon Smith, Job Printer. **1901** DE VINNE *Correct Composition* 283 The exclamation-point is sometimes used by job printers at the end of displayed lines, for no other reason than its convenience in filling up an otherwise short line.

+**Job printing.** Commercial printing of various kinds done by the job; also, the printing of special notices in a newspaper: (see quot. 1846). — **1832** *Congress. Deb.* 5 May 2767 The job printing, binding, and stationery, for each department, shall be furnished by contract. **1846** MCKENNEY *Memoirs* I. 196 Among the first to profit by this state of things, was General Duff Green, whose 'reward' was conferred in the job-printing of the government in his paper. **1872** *Newton Kansan* 12 Dec. 3/2 All kinds of job printing executed. **1892** *York County Hist. Rev.* 52 The office is thoroughly stocked with a line of new type for display and job printing.

***Job's-tears.** *pl.* **1.** An Asiatic grass, *Coix lacryma-jobi;* the hard pearl-like seeds of this plant. +**2.** (See quotation.) — **(1) 1791** MUHLENBERG *Index Florae* 179 *Coix Lacryma*, Jobs-tears. **1832** WATSON *Hist. Tales N.Y.* 153 It was very common for children and working women to wear beads made of Job's-tears, a berry of a shrub. **1899** *Animal & Plant Lore* 100 Seeds of Job's tears . . . worn as a necklace, are thought to be good for children teething. **(2) 1894** *Amer. Folk-Lore* VII. 102 *Smilacina racemosa*, . . . Job's tears, N.Y.

Jobster. {1892–} One who uses a public trust for the promotion of private gain; one who gives or takes jobs in public service in return for political favors. — **1897** *N.Y. Times* 15 Nov., The Hawaiian jobsters are astir again, and they talk with buoyant confidence. They seem to feel sure of the administration. **1913** LA FOLLETTE *Autobiog.* 167 He was not in favor of the spoilsman or the jobster.

+**Job's turkey.** An imaginary turkey having the qualities of patience and poverty, in allusion to the qualities of Job. Used as a type of comparison.

1824 *Troy Sentinel* 22 May (Th.), We have seen fit to say 'the patience of Job's turkey,' instead of the common phrase, 'as patient as Job.' **1830** *Va. Lit. Museum* 496/2, I am left by my new house, Poor as Job's turkey, or a starv'd church mouse. **1845** *S. Lit. Messenger* XI. 668/1 He don't own nothing: he's poor as Job's turkey, and he ain't got chick nor child. **1853** SIMMS *Sword & Distaff* 130 He's dead now as Job's turkey, with a loss of all the profits of his trade. **1903** WIGGIN *Rebecca* 193 'They're poor as Job's turkey,' whispered Mrs. Robinson. **1913** LONDON *Valley of Moon* III. v, The Dalmatians . . . were miserable immigrants—poorer than Job's turkey.

Job work. {1803–} +Printing that deals only with special jobs, as handbills, cards, etc. — **1832** *Congress. Deb.* 5 May 2766 [In] the publication of the laws, and the occasional advertising and job-work for the Government, . . . there were employed about one hundred printers. **1849** CHAMBERLAIN *Ind. Gazetteer* 168 There are three printing offices in the town, one of which publishes the Herald, another the Christian Record, the other principally job work. **1871** *Republican Rev.* 17 Oct. 2/2 When we have to do job work or other interruptions occur we are consequently heavily taxed for time. **1892** *York County Hist. Rev.* 74 He is prepared for all kinds of job work, circulars, cards, bill heads . . . and general printing.

***Jockey.**[1]

+**1.** Short for JOCKEY CAP.

1759 *Boston Gazette* 13 Aug., Sattin Jockeys with Feathers for Boys, brocaded silk, black sattin and Russel Shoes. **1775** DEANE *Correspondence* 254 The Light Infantry are green faced with buff; vests &c. as the others, except the cap, which is a hunter's cap, or jockey. **1853** FELT *Customs New Eng.* 162 Previously and subsequently to 1765, the black satin jockey, as well as hats of the same material, appeared in considerable numbers. **1865** STOWE *House & Home P.* 165 That's my jockey, papa, with a plume *en militaire*.

2. a. One who trades in horses; a horse dealer. {1638–1841, now *obs.* or *dial.*} (Cf. HORSEJOCKEY.) **b.** The rider of a horse in a horse race. {1670–}

1774 FITHIAN *Journal* I. 138 My horse seems (as jockeys say) in good Flesh. [**1787** GRIEVE tr. Chastellux *Travels N.A.* I. 415 *Jockey.* [Note:] The name given in America to horse-dealers, as well as those who take care of horses.] **1792** BRACKENRIDGE *Modern Chivalry* (1937) 6 The jockeys were of opinion . . . that the horse was what they call a bite, and that under the appearance of leanness and stiffness, there was concealed some hidden quality of swiftness. ***c*1845** *Big Bear Ark.*, etc. 14 Here may be seen jostling together the wealthy Southern planter, . . . the Northern merchant, and the Southern jockey. **1855** SIMMS *Forayers* 71 His horse . . . was unfavorably marked, in the estimation of the jockeys, by four white feet. **1897** HOWELLS *Open-eyed Conspiracy* xiv, The horses for the first race had already appeared, with their jockeys in vivid silk jackets of various dyes.

+**3.** A type of jacket.

1879 *Harper's Mag.* Dec. 67/1 The scissors . . . changed the relic of stately awkwardness [a waistcoat] into a jaunty 'jockey' or jacket.

4. A fraudulent bargainer; a swindler. {1683–1790}

1884 *Century Mag.* Feb. 520/1 There was no registry of flocks, and jockeys sold grade sheep, numbered, lamp-blacked, and oiled up to the desired blackness and greasiness, for full bloods at prices ten-fold beyond their real worth.

5. Attrib. in sense 2 with *purse, yard.*

1837 *Knickerb.* X. 410 Captain Joplin's colt . . . had been entered for the jockey purse. **1874** *Vermont Bd. Agric. Rep.* II. 604 For the want of success in farm enterprise they sell and buy, hoping to better themselves, like men in a jockey-yard, until they trade themselves nearly homeless.

+**Jockey.**[2] [f. the verb.] A horse deal. — **1867** LACKLAND *Homespun* II. 181 [The Tavern] served for their Exchange; and never did a dicker or a jockey occur, but the profit and the loss were each congratulated and consoled with sundry social drinks.

Jockey cap. A cap with a peak or visor on its front. {1748-} — **1746** *Boston News-Letter* 20 Feb. 2 Run away . . . a young Negro Fellow, . . . took with him an old Hatt, and a Leather Jocky-Cap. **1750** *Boston Ev. Post* 22 Oct 3/2 [A Negro wearing] a Frock and Trouzers, and a Leather Jocky Cap. **1764** *Boston Selectmen* 121 [A fireman] shall . . . at every Fire wear a black Leather Jocky Cap with a Pewter Blaze in the front of it. **1804** *Steele P.* II. 792 Each rider shall be dressed in a colored Jacket with sleeves, with a Jockey cap or colored hank[erchie]f on his head.

Jockey club.

1. A club or association formed to promote or direct the affairs of horse racing. {1775-}

1772 WASHINGTON *Diaries* II. 82 Dined at the Coffee House with the Jocky Club. **1856** *Porter's Spirit of Times* 15 Nov. 179/1 The fourth annual meeting of the St. Mary's County Jockey Club was held on the course near Leonardtown, on Tuesday. **1863** *Rio Abajo Press* 19 May 2/3 The Spring meeting of the Albuquerque Jockey Club was held at the Valverde Course. **1872** *Atlantic Mo.* Feb. 189 It was not very uncommon for the clergyman of a parish to be president of its jockey-club, and personally assist in the details of the race-course. **1883** *Harper's Mag.* Oct. 716/2 At one side of the town [of Lexington, Ky.] is the track of the Lexington Jockey Club, the oldest active association of its kind in the United States, founded in 1795.

b. The clubhouse of such an association.

1856 *Porter's Spirit of Times* 25 Oct. 128/2 Instead of sitting on the soft sofas of their jockey-clubs . . . gentlemen at the head of the turf should enter into practical reforms.

2. A kind of perfume. Also comb. {1855}

1859 *Great Republic Mo.* Jan. 70 (B.), I became wildly extravagant, . . . used cologne, hair oil, and scented my handkerchief with 'jockey-club.' **1866** 'F. KIRKLAND' *Book Anecdotes* 492 One morning the subscriber received a gilt-edged jocky-club scented note.

Jockey hat. A riding hat. — **1871** *Harper's Mag.* July 268 Here he tipped her jockey hat over her eyes, and she retorted by pulling his hair.

Jockeying. {a1770-} Adroit manipulation for the purpose of gaining an advantage; tricky management. {1810-} — **1779** *Essex Inst. Coll.* XLIII. 202 The Makers of Money sent it to their servants to purchas goods and thay knew it was to be out of circulation in a few months. It would be called by some Jockeing. **1789** MACLAY *Deb. Senate* 138 This week has been one of hard jockeying between the Senate and House of Representatives. **1809** KENDALL *Travels* I. 87 The farmers impeached their honesty, accusing them of unfair dealing; or, as their phrase is, of *jockeying.*

+**Jockey stick.** (See quotations.) — **1887** CUSTER *Tenting on Plains* 352 [In driving a prairie schooner] a small hickory stick, about five feet long, called the jockey-stick, not unlike a rake-handle, is stretched between a pilot [mule] and his mate. **1910** [see JERK LINE].

+**Jo-darter.** An excellent specimen of anything. *slang.* — **1851** *Polly Peablossom* 151, I could hit him a jo-darter.

Joe.[1] Also jo.

+**1.** A Portuguese gold coin current in the American colonies and states at a value of about $17; a double Johannes. *Obs.* (Cf. HALF JOE, JOHANNES.)

1765 *Boston Ev. Post* 14 Oct. (Th.), Into the L . . . rs hands (full) many a Jo We've slily put. **1782** *Warren-Adams Lett.* II. 185, I received the two Joes you was so good as to send for interest. c**1790** HOPKINS in *Amer. Poems* (1793) 138 For twenty joes the cure is done. **1825** NEAL *Bro. Jonathan* I. 160, I shows him a handful of the royal goold. . . . I do lay one of 'em out—jest a joe.

2. =JOHANNES: (see quotations and cf. HALF JOE.) {1783-}

Apparently a misunderstanding by later writers.

1870 G. T. CURTIS *Life D. Webster* I. 586 *n.*, Jo is a Portuguese coin of eight dollars, common in this country at one period. **1891** WELCH *Recoll. 1830-40* 168 The gold coins most popular in circulation [in upper New York] were the 'Carolus Doubloons,' standard value $16, there were half pieces called 'Joes,' eight dollars.

Joe.[2] +(See quotation.) Also comb. — **1851** HALL *College Words* 271 *Joe,* a name given at Yale and Hamilton colleges to a privy. . . . The following account of *Joe-burning* is by a correspondent from Hamilton College.

+**Joe boat.** *Ky.* A small rowboat, used on a river. — **1874** R. H. COLLINS *Kentucky* I. 238, 5 persons, while crossing the Big Sandy river in Floyd co. in a joe boat, caught in the ice and drowned. **1887** *Courier-Journal* 15 Feb. 6/4 The Noise of the Midnight Hammer is Heard in the Land, Building 'Joe Boats' to Be Used in the Second-story of High Houses.

+**Joe Brown's Pets.** In allusion to the governor of Georgia during the Civil War, Joseph E. Brown (1821-1894): (see quotation).—**1863** CUMMING *Hospital Life* (1866) 104/1 A young man came in and told Mrs. B. that the soldier was pretending that he was one of 'Joe Brown's Pets,' as the Georgia militia are called.

+**Joe-flogger.** (See quotations.) *colloq.* — **1852** *32d Congress 2 Sess.* H. R. Ex. Doc. No. 23, 260 [The boat-fisherman of the Bay of Fundy] is kind and hospitable in his way; and the visitor . . . is treated to *fresh smother, duff,* and *jo-floggers.* [Note:] Potpie of sea-birds, pudding and pancakes. **1889** MUNROE *Dorymates* 47 The cook made them [the crew] a great dish of Joe-floggers (peculiar pancakes stuffed with plums) for breakfast.

+**Joe-pye.** =next. — **1817-8** EATON *Botany* (1822) 278 *Eupatorium purpureum,* purple thoroughwort, joe-pye. **1895** WIGGIN *Village Watch-Tower* 42 Purple asters and gay Joe Pye waved their colors by the roadside.

+**Joe-pye('s) weed.** Either of two tall perennial weeds (*Eupatorium maculatum* and *E. purpureum*) having tubular flower heads. — **1817-8** EATON *Botany* (1822) 278 *Eupatorium verticillatum,* joe-pye's weed. **1857** GRAY *Botany* 186 *E[upatorium] purpureum.* (Joe-Pye Weed. Trumpet-Weed.) **1903** WALTZ *Pa Gladden* 144 In other Septembers the slope was lovely with joepye-weed.

+**Joe rocker.** (See quotation.) — **1884** GOODE, etc. *Fisheries* I. 774 In Vineyard Sound and Buzzard's Bay it [the green crab] is known to the fishermen as the 'Joe Rocker.'

+**Jo-fired,** *a.* Goldarned; terrible. *slang.* (Cf. ALL-FIRED *a.*) — **1824** *Woodstock* (Vt.) *Observer* 24 Feb. (Th.), Whate'er joe fir'd racket they keep up. **1835** D. P. THOMPSON *Adv. T. Peacock* 168, I have lately found out a most Jo-fired discovery. **1861** NEWELL *Orpheus C. Kerr* I. 234 A Jofired Wagon-trade.

+**Jo-fired,** *adv.* Exceedingly, darned. *slang.* — **1833** 'ELMWOOD' *Yankee among Nullifiers* 29 He's a jo-fired smart horse for all that. **1853** 'P. PAXTON' *Yankee in Texas* 219 The jo-fired mean whelp wouldn't stake me.

Jog. {1715-} +Any receding or projecting break in a surface or line. — **1845** JUDD *Margaret* I. xiv. 118 Directly on the right of the sunsetting was an apparent jog or break in the line of the woods and hills. **1876** SCUDDER *Dwellers* iii. 56 The house . . . was set back from the others in a jog of the court. **1884** *Boston Jrnl.* 10 Oct., The houses or rooms are one above the other to three or more stories high, but between each story there is a jog or recess the full width of the room below. **1892** MAHAN *Sea Power & Fr. Rev.* I. 80 [Spain's] maritime advantages were indeed diminished by the jog which Portugal takes out of her territory.

+**Joggling board.** A long, springy board, mounted on standards, upon which children play. (Cf. JIGGLING BOARD.) — **1882** G. C. EGGLESTON *Wreck of Red Bird* 14 The best way to get acquainted with a joggling board . . . is to get on it. . . . Don't be afraid. **1883** *Amer. Philol. Ass. Trans.* XIV. 50 Joggling is a favorite amusement of children in South Carolina, and the joggling-board . . . is a common sight. **1904** *Kansas City Star* 18 Aug. (Th. S.), A 'Joggling-board' is the latest contrivance for exercise that has made its appearance in these parts and it is liable to become the poor man's horse.

+**Johannes, Joannes.** [*Joannes* V of Portugal (1703-1750).] A Portuguese gold coin valued at about $8.81, once current in America. *Obs.* (Cf. HALF JOE, HALF JOHANNES.)

1758 *Essex Inst. Coll.* XII. 151 Exchanged my horse . . . for a young mare, gave a Johannas to boot. **1768** *N.H. Prov. Papers* VII. 175 Counterfeit coin, mostly Dollars, Bistareens & Joannes. **1788** *Mass. Spy* 3 July (Th.), A considerable number of base Johannes have lately been brought [to Philadelphia] from the state of Massachusetts. **1831** W. SLOCOMB *Amer. Calculator* 92 Coins which pass current in the United States [include] . . . a Johannes, . . . a Doubloon [etc.].

+**b.** *Double johannes,* =JOE.[1] *Obs.*

1765 *N.H. Prov. Papers* VII. 77 A Double Johannes or gold coin of Portygal of the value of Three pounds twelve shillings sterling at four pounds sixteen shillings. **1789** FRANKLIN *Writings* X. 74 In this way he got of me sometimes a double Joannes.

***John.** A masculine first name.

+**1.** =JOHN CHINAMAN.

1855 HELPER *Land of Gold* 91 The Americans salute them [*sc.* Chinese] all indiscriminately by the easy and euphonious appellation of 'John.' **1860** GREELEY *Overland Journey* 288 'John' does not seem to be a very bad fellow, but he is treated worse than though he were. **1869** BROWNE *Adv. Apache Country* 388 Poor John is taxed by the State, by the Government, by every white pilgrim who jogs along with pick and shovel, by his own people, and finally by the Digger Indians. **1873** BEADLE *Undevel. West* 771 The melancholy 'Johns,' with glazed caps and black pig-tails, looking like a lot of half-drowned crows.

2. In the names of birds and fishes.

1883 *Nat. Museum Bul.* No. 27, 503 *Epinephelus drummond-hayi* . . . John Paw; Spotted Hind. **1917** *Birds of Amer.* I. 80 Fulmar. *Fulmarus glacialis glacialis.* . . . [Also called] Molly Hawk; John Down; Sea Horse. *Ib.* 141 Old-Squaw. *Harelda hyemalis.* . . . [Also called] Old Billy; John Connolly; Uncle Huldy.

3. Special combinations.

John Yankee, a familiar name for a New Englander; *John the Baptist,* a colloquial name for a copper cent.

1778 J. ADAMS in *Warren-Adams Lett.* II. 40, I never was however much of John Bull. I was John Yankee and such I shall live and die. **1888** *Arkansaw Traveler* Oct. (F.), Mebbe he gwine ter gimme a John de Baptist' [*sic*]—dat's one cent.

+**John Brown.** Used attrib. in honor of or in allusion to John Brown (1800–1859), the abolitionist. — **1865** *Atlantic Mo.* XV. 512, I see in the 'Mercury,' . . . that some of your Northern scum are making preparations for another John Brown raid into Virginia. **1867** LOCKE *Swingin' Round* 78 In Kentucky we are hangin men uv the John Brown style. *c***1870** BAGBY *Old Va. Gentleman* 295 A suffusion of the eyes . . . ill became veteran soldiers who had taken part in the John Brown war. **1874** PINKERTON *Expressman & Detective* 18, I had always been a man somewhat after the John Brown stamp, aiding slaves to escape, or keeping them employed, and running them into Canada when in danger.

+**John Chinaman.** An appellation for any Chinaman. *colloq.* (Cf. JOHN 1.) — **1868** W. E. WATERS *Life among Mormons* 47 The primitive mode of mining has ceased to be profitable to all save 'John Chinaman.' **1869** BROWNE *Adv. Apache Country* 308 John Chinamen, with long tails rolled up on the backs of their heads, running distractedly through the crowd in search of their lost bundles. **1873** BEADLE *Undevel. West* 313, I feel no anxiety about 'John Chinaman,' either as a political problem, a disturbing social power, or a source of injury to the laboring classes. **1913** LONDON *Valley of Moon* III. v, There are . . . apple canneries and cider and vinegar factories. And Mr. John Chinaman owns them.

+**Johnkannaus.** (See quotation.) — **1861** H. JACOBS *Life Slave Girl* 179 Every child rises early on Christmas morning to see the Johnkannaus. . . . These companies, of a hundred each, turn out early in the morning, and are allowed to go around till twelve o'clock, begging for contributions.

+**John Mariggle.** The ten-pounder, *Elops saurus.* — **1896** JORDAN *Check-List N.A. Fishes* 279 *Elops saurus* . . . [is called] Tenpounder; John-Mariggle; Bony-fish; Bone-fish; Big-eyed Herring; [etc.]. . . . Common north to the Gulf of California and to Long Island on the Atlantic Coast. **1911** *Rep. Fisheries 1908* 317.

Johnny, Johnnie. The familiar diminutive of the name *John*, applied to various men {1673–} and things.

‖**1.** ? = JOHANNES.

1766 in Duane *Lett. to Franklin* (1859) 190, I shall be obliged to you for a Johney and the New England song.

+**2.** A Chinaman. *colloq.*

1857 GUNN *N.Y. Boarding Houses* 275 *He* knows. He's seed the *Johnnies* goin' into that there doorway next block. *a***1870** CHIPMAN *Notes on Bartlett* 221 *Johnny.* . . . A Chinaman.—Recent use in Cal., &c. **1884** W. SHEPHERD *Prairie Exper.* 140 The American atmosphere of independence . . . has breathed into Johnny the spirit of equality.

+**3.** A Confederate soldier. So called esp. by the Federal soldiers. *colloq. Obs.*

1865 KELLOGG *Rebel Prisons* 194 The 'cheekiest' thing that had been done by the 'Johnnies' . . . was an attempt to secure the services of our men as artillerists. **1865** BOUDRYE *Fifth N.Y. Cavalry* 171 The Johnnies were scarcely prepared for the onset that was made upon them. **1867** GOSS *Soldier's Story* i. 25 A detachment of dilapidated rebels [was] coming around a corner with the shuffling, unmilitary gait, which is peculiar to the Johnnies. **1888** *Century Mag.* Nov. 159/2 We did not complain for a sutler's wagon If the 'Johnnies' got it. [**1898** *Boston Transcript* 25 July 6/6 The name 'Johnny' was bestowed in the first year of the war by the soldiers of the Army of the Potomac on the Confederates opposed to them in Virginia.]

+**4.** A name locally applied to one of two species of fish: (see quotation).

1884 GOODE, etc. *Fisheries* I. 259 'Johnny' is applied only to very little Sculpins along the shore [of the Pacific], notably *Oligocottus maculosus.* The same name is given in the Ohio Valley to fishes of precisely similar habits, the *Etheostomatinae.*

+**5.** (See quotation.) *colloq.*

1888 *Boston Record* 24 Sept. 1/4 A very large number of 'Johnnies' as small English schooners are called, were entered at the custom house this morning.

+**6.** (See quotation.)

1892 *Dialect Notes* I. 236 *Johnnies*, a popular name for violets [in Jackson Co., Mo.]. Also used in Michigan.

+**7.** In various colloq. names and expressions.

Johnny bread, = JOHNNYCAKE; *J.-come-lately*, a newcomer; *J. Congress*, a familiar name for Congress; *J. Newcome*, a newcomer.

1827 *Western Mo. Rev.* I. 445 In the rural, but significant speech of the swains, this body is called Johnny congress. **1855** *Harper's Mag.* XII. 37/1 [Yellow fever] don't take the acclimated nor the 'old uns;' . . . but let it catch hold of a crowd of 'Johnny come latelys,' and it plants them at once. **1885** *Congress. Rec.* 7 Jan. 512/2 His Hawaiian Majesty,—a king with more alien Johnny Newcomes and coolies than subjects. **1915** *Dialect Notes* IV. 239 *Journey bread*, Johnny bread:—originally so called because Indian corn bread was often carried by travelers.

+**Johnnycake.**

Origin uncertain: (see JOURNEY CAKE, note, and JONAKIN).

1. A flat cake made of a mixture of corn meal and other ingredients, cooked in various ways—on a board before an open fire, on a griddle, or in a pan in an oven; corn bread.

1739 *S.C. Gazette* 22 Dec. 4/2 (Th. S.), New Iron Plates to cook Johnny Cakes or gridel bread on. **1765** DEANE *Diary* 310 So we breakfasted on tea and johnny cake, without butter, and fled for our lives. **1805** PARKINSON *Tour* 332 The lower class of people mix the flour . . . with water, make a sort of paste, and lay it before the fire, on a board or shingle, to bake, and generally eat it hot, as it is but very indifferent when cold. This is called a Johnny cake. **1859** BARTLETT 221 A New England Johnny-cake is invariably spread upon the stave of a barrel-top, and baked before the fire. **1903** K. M. ABBOTT *Old Paths & Legends New Eng.* 463 The 'real Johnie-cake' or 'journey' cake, made of Rhode Island meal ground by the mills on Aquidneck Isle, is a unique breakfast delicacy. **1917** *Nation* 21 June 724/1 Johnny-cake, of the deep, seductive shade of a mandarin's yellow-jacket, . . . has always been considered one of America's rare delicacies.

b. *Land of johnnycake*, New England.

1844 *Lowell Offering* IV. 26 This was the mystery connected with his visit to the land of johnnycake and wooden nutmegs.

2. A New Englander. *colloq.*

[**1840** DANA *Two Years* viii. 65, I've been through the mill, ground, and bolted, and come out a regular-built down-east johnny-cake.] **1842** DICKENS *Amer. Notes* 58 Down Easters and Johnny Cakes can follow if they please. I an't a Johnny Cake, I an't. I am from the brown forests of the Mississippi, I am.

‖**3.** *quasi-adj.* Pleasant; good-natured. *colloq.*

1889 S. HALE *Letters* 227 Emily, of herself, 'got good' and was yesterday all smiles and johnny cake.

+**Jo(h)nnycake board.** A flat board on which johnnycake is cooked before an open fire. — **1852** REYNOLDS *Hist. Illinois* 265 The bread used at these frolics, was baked generally on jonny, or *journey*-cake boards. **1886** Z. F. SMITH *Kentucky* 63 The hackberry tree, out of the side of which Samuel Williams cut a Johnny-cake board, . . . was standing in 1803.

+**Johnny Crapeau.** Also **Johnny Crapaud.** [f. Fr. *crapaud*, 'toad.'] A Frenchman or the French people. *colloq.* — **1840** COOPER *Pathfinder* xvi, We are no Johnny Crapauds to hide ourselves behind a . . . fort on account of a puff of wind. **1847** BRIGGS *Tom Pepper* I. 173, I have tried Johnny Bull and Johnny Crapeau, but give me Uncle Sam, after all. **1886** *Harper's Mag.* Aug. 330/1 The Indian maiden soon learned to prefer Johnny Crapeau for a husband.

+**Johnny Grindle.** The bowfin, *Amia calva.* — **1884** GOODE, etc. *Fisheries* I. 659 The Bowfin . . . is also abundant . . . in all parts of the Mississippi Valley, where it is variously called the 'Johnny Grindle,' 'Bowfin,' and 'Dogfish.'

+**Johnny jump.** The shooting star: (see quotation). — **1894** *Amer. Folk-Lore* VII. 94 *Dodecatheon Meadia*, Johnny jump. So. Cal.

+**Johnny Jumper.** = JOHNNY-JUMP-UP AND KISS ME. — **1859** BARTLETT 221. **1884** ROE *Nature's Story* 402 In the hot weather they were almost as small as johnny-jumpers.

+**Johnny-jump-up. a.** One of various American species of violet, as the early blue violet or the bird's-foot violet. **b.** A popular name given the wild pansy. **c.** The daffodil.

1842 *Knickerb.* XIX. 115 Mr. Ketchup had now kissed little Chip and stuck a johnny-jump-up in his cap. **1858** *Congress. Globe* 19 May 2244/2 You stand here, and with smiling faces spend $60,000 a year for morning-glories and johnny jump-ups! **1863** *Rio Abajo Press* 28 April 3/1 Gold is fluctuating like a johnny-jump-up. **1892** *Amer. Folk-Lore* V. 92 *Viola tricolor*, Johnny-jump-up. O. and Ill. **1898** E. C. HALL *Aunt Jane* 274, I used to call 'em Johnny-jump-ups, till Henrietta told me that their right name was daffydil. **1904** NESBIT *Trail to Boyland* 57 The johnny-jump-ups, noddin' soft when I go by.

+**Johnny-jump-up and kiss me.** (See quotation.) — **1859** BARTLETT 221 *Johnny Jump up and Kiss me. Johnny Jump up. Johnny Jumper.* Names given to the Heart's Ease, or Violet. This name is also given to the breastbone of a goose, with its two ends brought together by a twisted string held by a stick passing through it and stuck fast at the end by a piece of wax.

+**Johnny Navajo.** *S.W.* A familiar name for the Navahos. *colloq.* — **1863** *Rio Abajo Press* 17 Nov. 2/3, I must 'pitch in' and portray some of the characters now engaged in stirring up Johnny Navajo. **1864** *Wkly. New Mexican* 23 Dec. 1/3 Johnny Navajoe is rampant, and no mistake. **1865** *Ib.* 14 July 1/4 We'll first chastise then civilize bold Johnny Nav-a-jo.

+**Johnny on the spot,** *n.* and *a. colloq.* **1.** *n.* A person who makes a point of being on hand when anything happens. **2.** *adj.* On hand, present. — (1) **1896** ADE *Artie* iii. 24, I could see that a Johnny-on-the-spot with a big badge marked 'Committee' was tryin' to keep cases on her. [**1899** *Boston Transcript* 18 Feb. 21/5 At the Grand Opera House . . . 'Johnny on the Spot,' a new farce comedy which is said to rank among the best of its kind.] (2) **1913** LONDON *Valley of Moon* II. x, He's Johnny-on-the-Spot whenever street car men are licked into shape. **1914** 'BOWER' *Flying U Ranch* 106 Well, when it arrives I'm sure Johnny-on-the-spot.

+**Johnny Reb.** = JOHNNY 3. — **1865** *Nation* I. 584 They begun to talk to the old man, an' he talked too. They said he was a Johnny Reb. **1866** GREGG *Life in Army* 249 A man of sense and patriotic impulses . . . must bear a vast amount of insult . . . from these swaggering 'Johnny Rebs.' **1875** *Chambers's Jrnl.* 13 March 172/1 Confederate soldiers were Johnny Rebs. **1908** 'O. HENRY' *Options* 192 The Yankees commenced to holler for help, and the Johnny Rebs answered the call.

+**Johnny smokers.** (See quotation.) — **1893** *Amer. Folk-Lore* VI. 141 *Geum triflorum*, Johnny smokers. Rockford, Ill.

+**Johnny verde.** [Sp. *Juan verde.*] (See quotations.) — **1884** GOODE, etc., *Fisheries* I. 413 The Johnny Verde—*Serranus nebulifer* . . . is common only from San Pedro southward to Magdalena Bay. **1911** *Rep. Fisheries 1908* 308 *Cabrilla.*—A name applied indiscriminately to several serranoid fishes of the southern coast of California. They are also called 'rock bass,' 'kelp salmon,' 'Johnny Verde,' [etc.].

+**Johnson.** [Andrew *Johnson* (1808–1875), seventeenth president of the United States (1865–1869).] Used attrib. with *man, party, Unionist.* — **1866** *Wkly. New Mexican* 27 Oct. 2/2 In Pennsylvania the Johnson party has lost two members of Congress. **1867** LOCKE *Swingin' Round* 253 Vote ez a Johnson Unionist, or ez a Democratic Johnsonian—but vote. **1914** *Cycl. Amer. Govt.* I. 402/1 The Conservatives or Johnson men were the adherents of President Johnson in his contest with Congress over the question of reconstruction.

+**Johnson grass.** [Wm. *Johnson*, of Alabama.] A tall perennial grass (*Sorghum halepense*), first planted for pasture and hay, but now often regarded as a pest. Also fig. — **1884** VASEY *Agric. Grasses* 51 *Sorghum halapense.* (Cuba grass, Johnson grass, Means grass, false Guinea grass, Evergreen millet, Arabian millet.) **1890** *Stock Grower & Farmer* 18 Jan. 7/1 Several of our subscribers have asked for some method of exterminating Johnson grass, which has proven a rank failure for any purpose whatever. **1894** *Congress. Rec.* 17 July 7587/2 When you destroy cocoa grass, [or] Johnson grass, . . . you are improving his [a man's] private property. **1903** 'O. HENRY' in *McClure's Mag.* Dec. 147 Have I been sodded down with Johnson grass by a pink-eyed snoozer, or what?

+**Johnsonian,** *n.* A follower of Andrew Johnson. (See JOHNSON). — **1867** LOCKE *Swingin' Round* 212 There were twenty Johnsonians in this hamlet.

+**Johnsonian,** *a.* According to the policies of Andrew Johnson. — **1880** TOURGEE *Bricks* 209 The Black Codes, which were adopted by the legislatures first convened under what has gone into history as the 'Johnsonian' plan of reconstruction, were models of ingenious subterfuge.

+**Johnsonize,** *v. tr.* To indoctrinate with the principles of Andrew Johnson. Also *ppl. a.* — **1867** *Congress. Globe* 16 March 144/1 There are few Democratic negroes, and they cannot be Johnsonized. **1869** *Ib.* 20 March 181/3 A portion of the Republican party are struggling . . . [to] prevent President Grant from removing from office the Johnsonized political bands who were floated upon the surface after his treachery.

John's-wort. The St. John's-wort. — **1753** HEMPSTEAD *Diary* 611 Wee pulld up the yellow Blossoms (alias Johnsworth) in the upper end & back Side the Lot. **1818** *Mass. H. S. Coll.* 2 Ser. VIII. 170 In July the lover of plants is gratified with . . . two species of pyrala, the small geranium, several species of hypericum or John's wort.

***Join,** *v. To join* (*a* or *the*) *church,* to become a member of a church. — **1829** *Va. Lit. Museum* 30 Dec. 458 Join the church—'to become a member of the church.' **1846** *Indiana Mag. Hist.* XXIII. 428 The whole town, or nearly so, joined church, and became religious. **1871** DE VERE 231 The *church* is not only the building, but, contrary to English usage, the congregation. . . . To *join* it, application is made to the pastor or the deacon. **1881** *Harper's Mag.* Feb. 437/2 That child jined the church when she were eleven year old. **1925** BRYAN *Memoirs* 23 Just when he joined the church I do not know.

***Joiner.** Also (*colloq.*) **jiner.**

***1.** A craftsman who makes furniture, etc., by joining pieces of wood. Distinguished from a carpenter by the lighter nature of his work. *Obsolescent.* (Cf. HOUSE JOINER.)

1626 *Plymouth Laws* 28 No handy craftsman . . . as taylors, shoemakers carpenters joyners . . . shall use their science or trades . . . for any strangers or foreigners. **1641** *Conn. Rec.* I. 65 Sufficient able Carpenters, . . . Masons, Joyners, Smithes and Coopers, shall not take aboue 20d. for a dayes worke. **1720** *Amer. Wkly. Mercury* 14 July 3/2 Run away on the 26th of June last . . . Alexander Taylor, by Trade a Joiner. **1785** MARSHALL *Amer. Grove* 113 The timber [of the cherry tree] . . . is frequently sawed into boards and used by joiners, cabinet-makers, etc. for many purposes. **1840** *Picayune* 17 Sept. 2/6 Wanted, A Ship Joiner, to finish the cabin of a small vessel. **1857** VAUX *Villas* 26 Lumber-merchants . . . [and] joiners . . . live by the constant demand for the exercise of this art of building. **1880** [see GLASS *n.* 6 c].

+**2.** A person who makes a practice of joining clubs, lodges, etc.

1894 RITTENHOUSE *Maud* 570 Miss Rittenhouse called me a 'jiner' last winter. Now that Christmas is past I seem doomed to be a jiner again. **1900** ADE *More Fables* 144 The real Joiner loves to sit up on an elevated Throne, wearing a Bib and holding a dinky Gavel. **1920** *3d Nat. Country Life Conf. Proc.* 83 More simply stated the farmer is not, and never can be, a club man or 'joiner.'

***Joint,** *n.*

+**1.** *New Eng. building.* The place where a stud joins either with the sill of the frame or with the plate. *Obs.*

1644 *Springfield Rec.* I. 176 Cooper is to build ye house . . . 9 foote betwixt Joynts. **1647** *Watertown Rec.* 18 Schoole house . . . 9 foot betwene Joynts. **1697** *Braintree Rec.* 36 The dimensions of the house to bee twenty foot long the width sixteen foot: and seven foot between joynts. **1705** *Charlestown Land Rec.* 172 [To be built] a Dwelling house which shall be Twenty foot Long, and Eighteen foot wide, nine foot stud Between Joynts. **1723** *Manchester Rec.* I. 155 It was voted that a scool hous should be buelt forthwith of 24 foot Long 17 foot wide & 7 foot betwen Joynts.

+**2.** (See quotation.)

1863 RANDALL *Pract. Shepherd* 74 When the change of condition [in a sheep] . . . takes place from a low and unhealthy state to a healthy and fleshy one—it generally occasions 'a joint' in the wool,—i.e., the place in the fibers where the change began, is so weak that a slight pull will detach the two parts.

+**3. a.** An illegally kept place for opium-smoking, drinking, or gambling. Later often applied to such places that are legally open. *slang.* (Cf. OPIUM JOINT.) Also fig.

1883 *Harper's Mag.* Nov. 944/2, I have . . . smoked opium in every *joint* in America. **1890** *Stock Grower & Farmer* 22 Feb. 3/2 The *Stock Grower and Farmer* . . . will see that the frauds do not use this territory as a bunko joint, through which to rob eastern capitalists. **1893** *Harper's Mag.* April 708/2 Club drinking and 'joints' are not unknown, but the saloon has vanished [from Kansas]. **1897** *Boston Jrnl.* 4 Jan. 2/8 Many think this the only method by which they can ever hope to crush out the drug-store system of saloons and 'joints.' **1901** 'FLYNT' *World of Graft* 72 There's joints what ain't on the level, an' that means graft. **1909** WASON *Happy Hawkins* 344 Jim got cleaned out by the cattle crowd, an' opened his joint in Laramie.

+**b.** A term, usually disparaging, for any place or establishment. *slang.*

1887 *Lippincott's Mag.* Aug. 290 The student, upon reaching his 'joint,' as the club is called, hurriedly bolts a few mouthfuls of breakfast. **1896** ADE *Artie* xviii. 169 You go along Prairie avenue and see all o' them swell joints where the fat boys with side whiskers hang out. **1896** *Chicago Record* 15 Jan. 4/6 This is the last time I bring me wash to this joint. **1901** WHITE *Westerners* 116 He owns this joint here, he says. **1908** SINCLAIR *Metropolis* 40 He added that they were to meet at the 'Hawks' Nest,' which he said was an automobile joint. **1913** LONDON *Valley of Moon* II. xvii, That's the swell joint where fellows like Roy Blanchard hangs out, blowin' the money we sweat for them.

***Joint,** *v.* +**1.** *Carpentry. tr.* (See quot. 1864.) +**2.** *intr.* Of grain; To form nodes in growth. — (**1**) **1815** *Niles' Reg.* IX. 36/1 Two horses . . . with a man and a boy can dress and joint, in a superior manner, the staves necessary for one hundred barrels, hogsheads or pipes in twelve hours. **1864** WEBSTER 728/2 *Joint,* . . . to prepare so as to fit closely; to fit together; . . . as, to *joint* boards. (**2**) **1772** *Md. Hist. Mag.* XIV. 289 I am apprehensive it [the wheat and rye] will be too thick and Joint if the weather proves warme. **1904** *Topeka Capital* 1 June 8 Wheat has not done well, though it is jointing now.

+**Joint ballot.** *Parl. law.* A ballot taken at a joint session. — **1815** *Niles' Reg.* IX. 110/2 Alleghany county has 4 federalists—and in joint ballot, for governor, United States' senator, &c. that party has an apparent majority in the legislature of one vote. **1831** PECK *Guide* 281 The judges are chosen by joint ballot of the legislature. **1844** *Lexington Observer* 11 May 3/6 The Whig majority in the House of Delegates will be sufficient to control the Locofoco majority of the Sen[ate] on [a] Joint Ballot! **1885** *Wkly. New Mexican Rev.* 5 Feb. 3/1 The election of Governor Stanford [to the U.S. Senate] was confirmed today on a joint ballot [of the California legislature].

+**Joint committee.** A committee made up of members of both houses of a legislative body.

Appointed by concurrent resolutions of the two houses.

1778 *N.Y. Laws* 27 March, The joint Committee . . . [shall] canvas and estimate the votes. **1790** *Ann. 1st Congress* II. 1792 A Joint Committee of the House and Senate should be appointed for the purpose. **1854** BENTON *30 Years' View* I. 9/2 The joint committee acted, and soon reported a resolution in favor of the admission of the State.

+**Joint convention. 1.** A joint session of a legislative body, specifically convened to elect a public officer or to consider matters arising out of an election. **2.** A political convention composed of delegates of two or more parties. — (**1**) **1844** *Ind. Senate Jrnl.* 166 Resolved, That the Senate be invited . . . in the Hall of the House of Representatives, to go into joint convention for the purpose of electing president judges in the 1st, 2d, and 3d judicial circuits. **1873** *Republic* I. 54/1 That scrutiny . . . had not enabled Congress to reach any ultimate conclusion . . . for counting the vote [of La. voters for presidential electors] in joint convention. **1887** *Courier-Journal* 11 Jan. 1/2 The law does not require or contemplate a joint convention in counting the vote. (**2**) **1900** *Congress. Rec.* 14 Feb. 1801/2 In 1884, . . . our Republican gold-standard, gold-bond friends . . . made a bargain with our Greenback friends in the State, had a joint convention and gave to our Greenback folks half the electoral ticket, and voted a solid vote against the Democratic party.

***Jointed,** *a.* Used in the specific names of plants: (see quotations). **1761** ROGERS *Journals* 231 We found . . . some rich savannahs of several miles extent, without a tree, but clothed with jointed grass near six feet high. **1817–8** EATON *Botany* (1822) 328 *Lathyrus articulatus*, jointed pea. **1868** GRAY *Field Botany* 56 *Raphanus Raphanistrum*, Wild Radish or Jointed Charlock. Troublesome weed in cultivated fields.

Jointer. 1. A tool for jointing boards, staves, etc. {1678–} **2.** A workman who makes junctures between parts of an electric wire. {1876–} — (**1**) **1654** *Essex Probate Rec.* I. 198, 2 Joynters . . . Trussing hoopes, 2 Cresses. (**2**) **1858** in Prescott *Telegraph* 192 Two cable-splicers and a gutta-percha jointer here waiting to make a splice in shore-end.

Joint grass. {1790} +A creeping grass (*Paspalum distichum*), which roots at the joints. — **1835** SIMMS *Partisan* 55 Rebellion grows like joint-grass when it once takes root. **1878** in Killebrew *Tenn. Grasses*

223 Joint Grass [makes] . . . excellent forage; cattle very fond of it. **1894** COULTER *Bot. W. Texas* III. 499 Joint grass. . . . Moist places throughout Texas and across the continent.

+**Joint resolution.** A resolution adopted jointly by the two houses of a legislative body.

A distinction is sometimes made between a *joint* and *concurrent resolution*, the former, like a bill, requiring the approval of the executive (see, for instance, *Constitution* i. 7), the latter requiring no such approval, since it affects only the business of the legislative body.

1838 *Indiana H. Rep. Jrnl.* 85 Mr. Judah asked leave to introduce a joint resolution relative to postponing the election of United States' Senator. **1840** *Niles' Nat. Reg.* 18 July 315/1 The joint resolutions for the exchange of books and public documents for foreign publications. **1848** in Benton *Exam. Dred Scott Case* (1857) 109 The Joint Resolution for annexing Texas to the United States, approved March 1st, 1845. **1886** LOGAN *Great Conspiracy* 169 The House Joint Resolution was then adopted by 24 yeas to 12 nays. **1900** *Congress. Rec.* 9 Jan. 702/2 Mr. Butler introduced a joint resolution . . . proposing an amendment [etc.]. **1924** E. W. HUGHES *Amer. Parliamentary Guide* 613 In recent years Congress has endeavored to restrict the use of joint resolutions in law-making to matters of minor importance or merely temporary laws.

+**Joint session.** A session of a legislative body in which the two houses sit together. — **1863** *Rio Abajo Press* 15 Dec. 2/2 Last Wednesday, about noon the Governor read his annual message to both Houses of the Legislature, in joint session, in the hall of the House of Representatives. **1887** *Courier-Journal* 11 Jan. 1/2 (*caption*), An Alleged Joint Session of the Indiana Legislature Counts Robertson In. **1917** *N.Y. Times* 3 April 1/6 President Wilson appeared before a joint session of the Senate and House and invited it to consider the fact that Germany had been making war upon us.

+**Joint shingle.** A shingle with its edges planed so as to fit into the shingles next to it. Also attrib. — **1799** in Rothert *Muhlenberg* Co. 45 A joint shingle roof put on with pegs, except the outside rows with nails. **1806** *Austin P.* (1924) I. 105 Some Keggs Cut Nails for Joint Shingles and others for lathing of the smallest kind.

+**Joint snake.** =GLASS SNAKE. — **1789** MORSE *Amer. Geog.* 61 The Joint Snake is a great curiosity. Its skin is as hard as parchment and as smooth as glass. It is beautifully streaked with black and white. It . . . has so few joints, and those so unyielding, that it can hardly bend itself into the form of a hoop. **1873** *Winfield* (Kansas) *Courier* 24 July 1/5 The maple worm . . . is constructed like a joint snake, a concertina, . . . or something of the kind. **1899** *Animal & Plant Lore* 87 A snake known as the 'joint snake' can be broken into many pieces, which will then reunite into a living snake.

Joint-stock company. A company organized for profit, consisting of a number of individuals who own shares in a common capital stock. {1808–} — **1834** *N.Y. Rep.* (11 Wendell) 87 The defendants were members of a joint stock company for the building of the Bowery Theatre. **1842** *Knickerb.* XIX. 113 Alas! Thou hast fallen under the cui-bono clutches of a joint-stock company. **1865** *Atlantic Mo.* XV. 86 On the 31st day of December, 1863, there were 101 joint-stock companies for the underwriting of fire-risks. **1911** A. M. SIMONS *Soc. Forces Amer. Hist.* 161 Joint stock companies, as corporations were still called [in 1819], had been organized in great numbers.

***Joint stool.** A stool fitted together by a joiner. *Obs.* — **1649** *Conn. Rec.* I. 496 An Inventory of the Estate of Mr. William Whiting: . . . a courte cubberd, 6 joint stooles. **1678** *N.H. Probate Rec.* I. 220, I give to . . . Richd Joce ye best bed in ye House . . . with ye Table-Board & Joyn-stooles. **1698** CHAMBERLAIN *Lithobolia* (1914) 73 A Form that stood in the Entry (or Porch) was set along by the Fire side, and a joint Stool upon that, with a Napking spread thereon.

+**Jointweed.** A jointed, spikelike herb, *Polygonella articulata*. — **1817–8** EATON *Botany* (1822) 401 *Polygonum articulatum*, joint-weed. . . . Very abundant on the sandy plains west of Albany. **1892** TORREY *Foot-Path Way* 60 [Plants in Mass. in Dec. include] two kinds of groundsel, fall dandelion, and jointweed. **1899** MACMILLAN *Minn. Plant Life* 258 Those with the small leaves are called knotweeds, jointweeds [etc.].

Jointworm. {1706} +The larva of any of several small chalcid flies of the genus *Harmolita*, such as that which attacks wheat, *H. tritici*. Hence *jointworm fly*. — **1855** *Amer. Inst. N.Y. Trans.* 328 The Joint-worm or, as naturalists generally call it, *Euritoma*, . . . has done much mischief [to wheat] this year, especially to the South. **1858** *Mich. Agric Soc. Trans.* IX. 232 The Joint-worm (*Eurytoma hordei*) . . . has committed great depredations in the wheat crops of Virginia, and other parts of the United States. **1862** *Ill. Agric. Soc. Trans.* V. 488 The larvae of these *chalcis flies*, called by Dr. Fitch the *joint worm fly*. **1882** *Ill. Entom. Reports* XI. 81, I have obtained another specimen of this species from a gall in a stalk, produced evidently by the regular joint-worm (*Isosoma hordii*). **1918** *Farmer's Bul.* No. 1006, 2 This jointworm can be controlled in Virginia, Tennessee, and Kentucky by plowing down wheat stubble deeply after harvest wherever this is practicable.

‖**Jo. Johnson cap.** (See quotation.) — **1857** B. YOUNG in *Jrnl. Discourses* V. 97 (Th.), [When I was a boy] my sisters would make me what was called a Jo. Johnson cap for winter.

Joke. {1670–} +*To throw at the joke*, (see quotation). — **1833** WATSON *Hist. Tales Phila.* 152 They used to have a play at the time of the fairs, called 'throwing at the joke.' A leather cylinder, not unlike a high candlestick, was placed on the ground over a hole. The adventurers placed their coppers on the top of the joke, then retired to a distance and tossed a stick at it.

Jokee. A person made the object of a joke. {1869–} — **1851** HALL *College Words* 302 The jokee is said to be 'hard up.' **1851** *Polly Peablossom* 92 Our unlucky jokee . . . concluded to 'hitch up.'

Joker. {1729–}

+**1.** Anything with which a trick is played; spec., the pea used in the game of thimblerig or the game itself. Usually *little joker*.

1856 THOMPSON *Plu-ri-bus-tah* 176 Yunga-Merrakah . . . Knew the game of triple thimbles, Thimbles three and 'little joker.' **1858** HOLMES *Autocrat* 39 The racer is . . . essentially something to bet on, as much as the thimble-rigger's 'little joker.' The trotter is essentially . . . useful. **1888** in Fleming *Hist. Reconstruction* II. 86 Several hundred of these 'little jokers' bounced out and were counted just as though they had been honestly voted. **1895** *Rev. of Reviews* (London) Jan. 70/2 These little jokers were attached to the left thumbs of certain judges of election as the ballots were being counted. These jokers are made of rubber and have a cross on them. They are really rubber stamps. As these judges picked up the ballots they took hold of them in such a way that their left thumbs, with jokers attached thereto, pressed upon the squares opposite the name of the candidate they wished to aid. By thus pressing upon said squares crosses were left in them. [Chicago.]

+**2.** An extra card in a deck of cards that counts in certain games as a trump. Also in allusive context.

1885 GREENOUGH *Queen of Hearts* iii, The White Knight, called the Joker, otherwise the Best Bower. **1887** KELLER *Draw Poker* 84 Some fun may be extracted from the use of the joker in Poker, but the game is complete without it. **1894** *Sat. Review* 26 July (F. and H.), It is true that American manufacturers of playing cards are wont to include a blank card at the top of the pack; and it is, alas! true that some thrifty person suggested that the card should not be wasted. This was the origin of the Joker. **1910** MULFORD *Hopalong Cassidy* 52 [They] began to back away, glancing around in an endeavour to locate the joker in the deck.

+**3.** *Legislation.* An unobtrusive clause inserted in a bill to affect its operation in a way not consistent with its apparent purpose. Also transf.

1904 *N.Y. Ev. Post* 11 May 1 They are all nervous over the possibility that there may be a hitherto unperceived joker in the present bill. **1906** *Ib.* 30 April 6 The Malby 'joker' to the Adirondack Reserve bill applies to a bill drawn to prevent deforestation an amendment permitting the damming of Adirondack streams for purposes of 'water storage.' Ostensibly an effort to give to the adjoining towns reasonable facilities for water supply, this amendment will permit the wholesale flooding and destruction of forest lands for manufacturing purposes. **1908** *Nation* 30 Jan. 96/1 The various 'jokers' which have got into important statutes were not put there by accident. **1914** S. H. ADAMS *Clarion* 241 Even her simple mind grasped the joker in the contract.

+**Jollier.** One who jokes and kids a lot. — **1896** ADE *Artie* 78 He's one o'f [*sic*] the biggest jolliers that ever come over the hills. **1901** MERWIN & WEBSTER *Calumet 'K'* 12 Oh, he's a good-looking young chap. . . . He's a great jollier. **1904** 'O. HENRY' *Roads of Destiny* xviii. 309 Old Denver has got to make good as a jollier and a silver-tongued sorcerer, or else give up all the medals he's earned.

Jolly, *v.* {1610–} +*tr.* To talk to or kid (a person) in a good-natured way so as to put him in a good humor. Often with *along* and *up*. *colloq.*[2] — **1890** H. PALMER *Stories of Base Ball Field* 81, I jollied him along as strong as I could. **1892** GUNTER *Miss Dividends* 232 You've left her alone all to-day—you ain't been near to jolly her up. **1901** ADE *40 Modern Fables* 178 He advised every one to give up the mad Race for Wealth and be a Philanthropist, . . . jollying up the Orphans and planting sweet Flowers along Life's Rugged Pathway. **1907** 'O. HENRY' *Trimmed Lamp* 78, I'm supposed to go to dinner with you and help jolly you along so you'll trade with old Lizzy. **1918** LINCOLN *Shavings* 129 My wife is pretty good at that, she jollies him along.

Jolly board. (See JIGGLING BOARD.)

Jolly-boat. [Perhaps from Du. *jol*, 'yawl,' influenced by E. *jolly*.] A ship's boat used for small work and usually carried across the stern. {1727–} (Cf. the earlier JOLLY SHIP.) — **1800** *Essex Inst. Coll.* X. III. 76 Sent the jolly boat with the Surgeon's mate on board the Juno. **1838** COOPER *Homeward B.* xix, Mr. Dodge began incontinently to scull the jolly-boat, in the best manner he could, off to the launch. **1847** ROBB *Squatter Life* 104 The other [hand] grasped the painter of the jolly-boat towing astern.

‖**Jolly ship.** =prec. — **1678** SEWALL in *Mass. H. S. Coll.* 5 Ser. VI. 14* Mr. Josiah Allen . . . was slain on board of Benj. Gillam's ship by the accidental firing of a fowling piece, out of a Boat of Joss. Gillam, as they were going from the jolly Ship.

+**Jonah crab.** A large crab (*Cancer borealis*) of the eastern seaboard. — **1883** *Nat. Museum Bul.* No. 27, 110 The Rock and Jonah Crabs (*Cancer irroratus* and *borealis*) are eaten only to a slight extent. **1911** *Rep. Fisheries 1908* 308.

+**Jonakin, Jonikin.** [Of obscure origin.] Possibly the original form of JOHNNYCAKE. (Quot. 1850, if a genuine example of survival rather than a literary usage based on knowledge of Tompson's work, indicates the meaning of the word.) — **1675** B. TOMPSON *New England's Crisis*, Then times were good, merchants car'd not a rush For other fare than Jonakin and mush. **1850** S. F. COOPER *Rural Hours* 388 We have . . . Jonikin, thin, wafer-like sheets, toasted on a board; these are all eaten at breakfast, with butter.

Jonathan.

+**1.** A generic nickname for the American people or, more particularly, the New Englanders. (Cf. BROTHER JONATHAN 1.)

[**1724** JONES *Virginia* 54 Except the last Sort [*i.e.*, the deported convicts], for the most Part who are loose Villains, made tame by *Wild*, and then enslaved by his *Forward Namesake*. . . . These if they forsake their Roguery together with the other Kids [indentured servants] of the later Jonathan, when they are free, may work Day-Labour, or else rent a small Plantation for a Trifle almost.] **1778** *Royal Gazette* (N.Y.) 3 Oct. 3/2 As Jonathan so much desir'd To shine in martial story, D'Estaing with politesse retir'd To leave him all the glory. **1779** *Ib.* 14 July 3/1 The troops faced about, drove Jonathan from his fancied fortress and then set fire to these few alone which had emboldened and afforded cover to their enemies. **1812** *Niles' Reg.* II. 351/2 '*Jonathan*' was ready for *John Bull* in any way. **1827** *Hallowell* (Me.) *Gaz.* 20 June 2/2 Let any man from any part of Jonathan's dominions visit the Kingdom of John Bull, and he will forthwith receive the appellation of Yankee. **1856** *Harper's Mag.* Dec. 125/2 Jonathan has not been as anxious as John to build monuments. **1884** W. SHEPHERD *Prairie Exper.* 17 The Americans tell you that all Englishmen inherit money from their parents. . . . The great purpose of Nature is to relieve this plethora by transferring the cash into the pockets of Jonathan.

+**b.** *St. Jonathan*, the patron saint of the United States. *humorous.*

1855 *U.S. Rev.* XXXV. 106 But we sons of Columbia . . . will invoke no saint but St. Jonathan, . . . resolving that henceforth and for ever St. Jonathan shall be the patron-saint of the universal Yankee nation—and the Fourth of July, St. Jonathan's Day.

+**2.** An individual American or a New Englander. (Cf. BROTHER JONATHAN 2.)

1780 *Royal Gazette* (N.Y.) 27 May 2/4 [The loyalists] also took and destroyed a piece of cannon, which the Jonathans in vain endeavoured to defend. **1782** in F. Moore *Songs & Ballads Amer. Revol.* (1856) 375 *n.*, [A letter] from a dejected Jonathan, a prisoner taken in the South Carolina, to his brother Ned at Philadelphia. **1824** WHEATON *Journal* 193 One may see a *posse* of long-legged Jonathans gathering about a stage at a tavern in America. **1830** N. AMES *Mariner's Sk.* 240 The English, I must confess, seemed to be more liberal than the Jonathans, whose calculating, money making disposition always shews itself on any emergency. **1844** 'UNCLE SAM' *Peculiarities* II. 290 A jew broker . . . made the . . . assertion that his 'peoples' could not make a good living among the keen Jonathans. **1849** WILLIS *Rural Letters* 157 The itching to be doing something, . . . in one shape or another, belongs to every genuine Jonathan.

+**3.** A typically rustic but shrewd American.

[**1787** TYLER *Contrast* II. ii, How sweet will the contrast be between the blundering Jonathan and the courtly and accomplished Jessamy!] **1828** ROYALL *Black Book* II. 63 Jonathans are awkward young fellows from the country, who come to market, and afford great amusement for the *cits.* **1843** *Yale Lit. Mag.* IX. 44 Occasionally . . . you will see some honest country Jonathan, with his wagon full of 'Yankee notions.' **1848** THOREAU *Maine Woods* 18 The Province man was now the only real Jonathan, or raw country bumpkin, left so far behind by his enterprising neighbors that he didn't know enough to put a question to them. **1857** *Lawrence* (Kan.) *Republican* 2 July 4 Among the arrivals was . . . a regular no-mistake Jonathan—with his eyes wide open at the novelties he met.

+**4.** A variety of apple.

[**1842** *Catalogue of Fruits Cultivated in Garden of Hortic. Soc.* (ed. 3) 21 Apples . . . Jonathan.] **1845** A. J. DOWNING *Fruits America* 113 The Jonathan is a very beautiful dessert apple. **1847** J. M. IVES *New England Bk. of Fruit* 47 *Jonathan.*—This winter fruit was considered by the late Judge Buel, who first described and brought it into notice, as one of the very best apples he had ever seen. **1849** *New Eng. Farmer* I. 90 *Jonathan.*—This is a beautiful and excellent apple, of medial size, very popular in some parts of New York, and some other sections of the country. **1867** *Ill. Agric. Soc. Trans.* VII. 520 If a man knows the delicious apple he purchases is a Jonathan or Fameuse . . . when he asks for apples again he will name the variety he wants.

+**Jonathanism.** ? A tall story. — **1841** *Picayune* 4 Dec. 4/1 The original version, which is greatly superior in humor to those monstrosities called Jonathanisms, is, we believe, as follows.

+**Jonathanization.** Americanization. *colloq.* — **1854** EMERSON *Corr. Carlyle & Emerson* (1883) II. 235 John Bull interests you at home. . . . Come and see the Jonathanization of John. [**1894** *Sat. Review* 15 Dec. 652/1 The Jonathanization of John is going on so rapidly that we already notice many of the symptoms of American corruption and misrule.]

Jonquil. A bulbous plant (*Narcissus jonquilla*), with yellow or white flowers similar to those of the daffodil; the flower of this plant. {1629–} — **1792** IMLAY *Western Territory* 207 Every part of the country abounds in a variety of natural flowers . . . daffodil, jonquil, hyacinth. **1817–8** EATON *Botany* (1822) 360 *Narcissus jonquilla*, jonquil. E[xotic]. **1835** HOFFMAN *Far West* I. 144, I thought of the various vines and flowers . . . jonquils and amaranth, the purple foxglove and saffron-coloured silkweed. **1898** PAGE *Red Rock* 60 Just then a young girl came around the corner of the house, . . . her hands full of jonquils and other early flowers.

+**Joree.** =CHEWINK. *colloq.* — **1884** HARRIS *Mingo* 179 We seem to agree, Brother Brannum, like the jay-bird and the joree,—one in the tree and t'other on the ground. **1917** *Birds of Amer.* III. 58 Towhee. *Pipilo erythrophthalmus erythrophthalmus*. . . . [Also called] Jo-ree; Marsh Robin.

Jornada, Jornado. {1656, 1667} *S.W.* [Sp.] +**a.** A journey; a day's travel over an arid stretch. *Obs.* +**b.** An expanse of more or less desert country; spec., one or other of two such areas in New Mexico. *Obsolescent.* (Cf. JOURNADA.)

The American use of this word represents an independent borrowing from the Spanish in the Southwest.

1845 FRÉMONT *Exped.* 260 The caravans sometimes continue below to the end of the river, from which there is a very long *jornada* of perhaps sixty miles. **1846** SAGE *Scenes Rocky Mts.* xxi, A reach of little more than one *jornada* (day's travel) leads over the mountain range. **1847** *Santa Fe Republican* 27 Nov. 2/1 Capt. Skillman then left and returned to the *Jornada*, where he met the troops, and again returned to El Paso. **1867** *Wkly. New Mexican* 6 July 2/1 Agents Henderson and Ward . . . have visited every pueblo from Taos to the Jornada. **1872** POWERS *Afoot & Alone* 137 We reached the uppermost spring of the Concho, and encamped to prepare for the dreadful jornada across the Staked Plain. **1880** *Cimarron News & Press* 15 April 2/3 The buckboard carrying the U.S. mail was taken by our braves last week near Aleman on the Jornado. **1890** *Stock Grower & Farmer* 10 May 5/1 A garden is growing on the Jornado, three miles from the river, which is irrigated by this system.

***Joseph.** An outer garment or kind of riding habit worn usually by women. {1659–} — **1825** NEAL *Bro. Jonathan* III. 7 With every swing of her body, [she betrayed] the rich dress underneath her 'Joseff.' **1848** BARTLETT 192 A garment made of Scotch plaid, for an outside coat or habit, was worn in New England about the year 1830, called a *Joseph*, by some a *Josey*. **1852** E. F. ELLET *Pioneer Women* 433–4 She wore a dark calico dress; . . . over this a 'joseph,' or short riding dress of brown cassimere.

+**Josephite.** [f. *Joseph* Smith, the younger (1860–1914).] A member of the Reorganized Church of Jesus Christ of Latter Day Saints, which was established by Mormons who chose to follow the son of the prophet rather than Brigham Young. *colloq.* Also attrib. or adj. — **1867** DIXON *New America* I. 322 Under the name of Josephites, a band of Mormons are now gathering round these sons of the Prophet. **1870** BEADLE *Utah* 275 Some three years ago a 'Josephite,' or recusant Mormon, . . . conceived that he was Adam sent back to the flesh. **1883** Schaff *Religious Encycl.* II. 1579/2 The Josephites . . . have headquarters at Plano, Ill. **1890** H. H. BANCROFT *Hist. Utah* 643 In Utah . . . four distinct and organized attempts were made to throw off the yoke of Brigham. . . . [Among] these were the Gladdenite secession in 1852, the Josephite schism in 1860. **1890** *Congress. Rec.* 2 April 2933/1 The Josephites to a man repudiate polygamy and bigamy.

Joseph's-coat. +Either of two ornamental plants: (see quotations). — **1866** LINDLEY & MOORE *Treas. Bot.* I. 48/1 In the gardens of the Southern United States, these hues are so richly developed as to have procured for it [*Amaranthus tricolor*] the appellation of Joseph's coat. **1894** *Amer. Folk-Lore* VII. 96 *Coleus Blumei*, Joseph's coat. general.

Josey. Variant of JOSIE.

+**Josh,** *n.*[1] *slang* or *colloq.*

1. (See quot. 1869.) *Obs.*

1869 *Overland Mo.* III. 129 The cant designation in the Rebel army for a man of Arkansas was 'Josh.' . . . Just before the battle of Murfreesboro, the Tennesseeans, seeing a regiment from Arkansas approaching, cried out, . . . 'Thar come the tribes of Joshua!'

2. (See quotation.)

1870 MEDBERY *Men Wall St.* 136 *Josh*, a word shouted at the Exchange in order to wake up a sleepy member.

3. a. Bantering talk; joking. **b.** A joke; a speech intended to take someone in.

1896 ADE *Artie* iii. 30 That ain't no josh, neither. **1897** *Chicago Tribune* 22 July 1/3, I did say something of the kind. But it was all 'josh.' **1902** WISTER *Virginian* ii, That's straight. That's no bar-room josh. **1906** QUICK *Double Trouble* 231 Here, damn you, this is all a josh! **1914** 'BOWER' *Flying U Ranch* 188, I d'no, by cripes, why it is a feller can always think uh lies and joshes by the dozens, and put 'em over O. K. when there ain't nothing to be made out of it except hard feelin's.

Josh, *n.*[2] =JOSS 1. — **1873** BEADLE *Undevel. West* 180 Within were two enormous 'Joshes' ten feet high, one in each corner, . . . while behind the altar the Boodhist priests and attendant boys were going through a ceremony.

+**Josh,** *v. tr.* To tease or take in (someone) by telling elaborate lies or tall stories; to 'kid' (someone); to banter and joke (a person) in a good-humored manner. *colloq.*— **1887** FRANCIS *Saddle & Moccasin* 185 [He] liked nothing better than to get into a circle of young cow-punchers, and chin and josh with them. **1891** *Century Mag.* Nov. 63 Oh go away . . . ; I fear that you are joshing me. **1895** *San Fran. W. Exam.* 19 Sept. 4 The boys joshed Mr. Durrant some about it—about the disappearance of the young lady. **1899** NORRIS *McTeague* 399 Everyone of them knew Cribbens, and almost invariably joshed him on his venture. **1903** *N.Y. Sun* 22 Nov. 1 Senator Hanna said that he had nothing whatever to say about politics, and he joshed and jollied everybody who tried to get him to talk on the subject. **1912** MATHEWSON *Pitching* viii. 176 It used to be quite the fad in the League to 'josh' 'Bob' about his wig.

+**Josher.** One who joshes. *colloq.* — **1899** NORRIS *McTeague* 57 What a josher was this Marcus! Sure, you never could tell what he would do next. **1904** *N.Y. Sun* 21 Aug. 10 Others said that Mr. Taggart had turned out to be a josher and a jollier. **1913** LONDON *Valley of Moon* II. vii, 'He's just teasing you,' Saxon soothed. 'He always was a josher.'

Joshua. +(See quotations.) Also *Joshua tree, yucca.* — **1875** *Amer. Naturalist* IX. 141 We recognized one of the principal objects of our journey in the singular forms of that remarkable desert production, *Yucca brevifolia* Engel. This is universally known among the Mormon settlers under the name of '*The Joshua.*' **1884** SARGENT *Rep. Forests* 219 *Yucca brevifolia*. . . . The Joshua. Joshua Tree. **1897** SUDWORTH *Arborescent Flora* 106 *Yucca arborescens*. . . . Joshua Yucca. . . . Common Names. . . . The Joshua (Utah). Joshua Tree (Utah, Ariz., N.Mex.).

+**Josie.** [A contraction of JOSEPH with a derived meaning.] A close-fitting outer waist worn by women; a bodice. — **1848** [see JOSEPH]. **1885** BAYLOR *On Both Sides* 168 She wore that very frock . . . and the countess asked to be allowed to take off the pattern of her josie, saying that she had not seen anything like it before. **1886** *Harper's Mag.* July 297/2 And I hope to gracious you 'ain't made the josie too tight! I busts my josies awful. **1894** CHOPIN *Bayou Folk* 170 She wore a coarse white cotton 'josie,' and a blue calico skirt.

Joss. 1. A Chinese image of a deity. {1711–} Also transf. **2.** *Joss stick*, an incense stick covered by a paste made of the dust of fragrant woods, or a cylinder filled entirely with such paste. {1883} **3.** *Joss paper*, gold and silver paper, cut in the shape of coins or ingots, burned by the Chinese in religious ceremonies. {1884} — **(1) 1873** BEADLE *Undevel. West* 182 The word 'Josh,' or 'Joss,' is not Chinese, but 'Pigeon-English,' a language used in the ports of China. **1883** DE VERE in *Encycl. Brit.* (ed. 9) *Amer. Suppl.* I. 198/1 *Joss*, though only a slang word, has most strangely as such recovered the meaning of its original form, which was not Chinese at all, but the pure Castilian word Dios. **1901** RIIS *Making of an American* 374 The Mulberry Street idea of friendship includes the loaves and fishes first and last, and pull is the Joss it worships. **(2) 1871** [see JOSS HOUSE]. **(3) 1883** HOWELLS *Woman's Reason* xi, They stood huddled together in the bow . . . as they tried to free the wet joss-papers that clung to their fingers.

Joss house. A Chinese house of worship. {1771–} *colloq.* — **1871** DE VERE 155 *Joss-houses* with ample supplies of *joss-sticks* are now quite common in San Francisco and other parts of California. **1876** CROFUTT *Trans-continental Tourist* 141 Placerville contains a goodly number of schools, and churches of almost every denomination, including a 'Joss' House. **1880** *Harper's Mag.* Dec. 72 The walls of the hall and stair-case of the principal Joss-house were covered with colored slips of paper . . . containing the names of the donors to the idols. **1918** RIDEOUT *Key of Fields* 297 Nearing home, Mr. Weechurch paused . . . above the southern façade of the joss house.

+**Jour.** Short for JOURNEYMAN. *colloq.* — **1845** *Knickerb.* XXVI. 415 [You] discover the 'boss' and two or three 'jours,' each seated on a low form. **1847** ROBB *Squatter Life* 11 John Earl, the subject of our story, was a true and veritable specimen of the genus *Jour Printer*,—intelligent, reckless, witty, . . . and unsteady. **1857** *Harper's Mag.* May 749/1, I traveled round when I was a jour'; then I served in the army a while. **1863** HALE *If, Yes, & Perhaps* (1868) 35, I stopped at one or two cabinet-makers, and talked with the 'jours' about work. **1898** *Milwaukee Sentinel* 16 Jan. II. 2/7 Where the hundreds of old time-honored 'jours,' that drifted about the country in the palmy days of typesetting, have gone to, no one seems able to determine.

+**Journada, journado.** =JORNADA. — **1849** *31st Congress 1 Sess.* Sen. Doc. 64, 197 After marching 23 1/8 miles, we reached the river again at the southern extremity of the Journado, making the entire distance across the desert 77½ miles. **1862** *Harper's Mag.* Sept. 455/2 Between the Cimarron and the crossing of the Arkansas lies a long arid stretch or *journada*. **1869** BROWNE *Adv. Apache Country* 278 Whenever it became necessary to make a long stretch we started in the afternoon, travelled till midnight, camped till day-light, and then made the rest of the *journada* by noon.

***Journal.**

1. The daily record of the proceedings of a deliberative body such as Congress. {1647–}

1680 (*title*), Journal of the House of Burgesses att a Genrll Assembly Begunne at James City at the house of Mrs. Susanne ffisher . . . June 1680. **1693** *Penna. Col. Rec.* I. 399, I desire you to provide a Clark to keep the Journalls of your votes and other proceedings **1775** J. ADAMS *Familiar Letters* 127, I hope the Journal of the Session will be published soon. **1787** *Constitution* i. § 5 Each House shall keep a journal of its proceedings. **1834** JACKSON in *Pres. Mess. & P.* III. 87 It appears by the Journal of the Senate that . . . twenty-six Senators . . . voted for the resolution on its final passage. **1900** *Congress. Rec.* 17 Feb. 1901/2 Next Monday, immediately after the reading of the Journal, I will stand by the gentleman from New York in a demand for an hour.

2. A personal record of daily events; a military daily record. {1610–}

1698 *Witchcraft Cases* 58 Being an Exact and True Account (by way of Journal). **1699** SEWALL *Diary* I. 497 See my Journal of meeting the Govr. June, 7th. **1704** S. KNIGHT *Journal* 27 But poor weary I slipt out to enter my mind in my Jornal. **1764** HUTCHINSON *Hist. Mass.* I. 213 Goffe kept a journal or diary. **1861** *Army Regulations* 99 Commanding officers of troops marching through a country little known, will keep journals of their marches according to the form and directions hereto annexed. **1892** M. A. JACKSON *Gen. Jackson* 87 His journal subsides into merely jotting of places and objects.

3. Any periodical publication that deals with affairs of current interest. {1692– (*The Gentleman's Journal*)}

1727 (*title*), The New England Weekly Journal [Boston]. **1787** (*title*), The New-York Journal, and Daily Patriotic Register. **1790** (*title*), Farmer's Journal [Danbury, Conn.; weekly]. **1827** *Hallowell* (Me.) *Gaz.* 20 June 3/1 The establishment of well-conducted literary journals is not a greater evidence of the prevalence of good taste. **1842** *Diplom. Corr. Texas* III. (1911) 951 The subject of annexation voted in your Congress, has been noticed and discussed by our leading journals. **1873** *Newton Kansan* 6 March 2/2 We will go as far as any journal . . . in advocating any and all measures which have for their object the real benefit of the ex soldier. **1900** ADE *More Fables* 161 He discovered that Alcohol was a Food long before the Medical Journals got onto it. **1920** *3d Nat. Country Life Conf. Proc.* 222 The agricultural journals will naturally be of very great service.

Journalism. The business of writing or publishing journals or newspapers {1833–}, +esp. as taught in a school or college. — **(1) 1869** R. E. LEE in S. L. Williams *20 Yrs. Educ. for Journalism* 4 The proposition recommending the institution of 50 scholarships [at Washington College, Lexington, Va.] for young men proposing to make printing and journalism their life work and profession. **1873** 'MARK TWAIN' & WARNER *Gilded Age* xliii. 391 He himself and all that he did still emitted an odor of sanctity now that he had diverged into journalism and politics. **1883** in S. L. Williams *20 Yrs. Educ. for Journalism* 14, I do not agree with you about the possibility of a professorship of journalism at the University. **1908** *Harper's Wkly.* 27 June 22/1 The State University of Missouri . . . has just put a widely mooted proposal into practice by the establishment of a School of Journalism, co-ordinate with its schools of law, medicine, [etc.]. **1921** HUFF *Laboratory Journalism* 6 The students in the first term of journalism should spend one day a week in special laboratory work on the paper. **1923** [see JOURNALIST].

Journalist. One who writes for newspapers or other publications; a newspaper man. {1693–} — **1724** *New-Eng. Courant* 8–15 June 1/2 These are to give Notice to . . . all Journalists, Gazetteers and Couranteers, . . . That they may be supply'd at Boston in New England with a Perfect Pattern for News Writers. **a1817** DWIGHT *Travels* I. 19 Other writers, particularly literary journalists, have united with them in the pursuit. **1885** *Century Mag.* Oct. 838, I am a journalist, and I am on the staff of the 'Gotham Gazette.' **1923** WYATT *Invisible Gods* 176 The authors appeared barefacedly as persons . . . who had gone out with the crass directness of journalism to learn all they could on the subject they were writing about. In fact, 'journalists' was the epithet of reproach most frequently hurled at them.

‖**Journal letter.** A letter written in the form of a journal. — **1869** ALCOTT *Little Women* II. x. 141, I shall keep a journal-letter, and send it once a week.

+**Journey cake.** =JOHNNYCAKE 1.

The evidence here, which is later than that for *johnnycake*, fails to support the suggestion that *journey cake* is the original form of that word. For neither form, however, can the evidence be regarded as complete. Both words may be rationalized forms of *jonakin* (q.v.).

1754 in Fries *Moravians in N.C.* II. 530 Today I bak'd Journey Cakes, it went well. **1775** ROMANS *Nat. Hist. Florida* 125 Rice . . . is (for our use) only fit for puddings, and to put in soops, or to make the wafer-like bread called journey cakes in Carolina. **1800** BOUCHER *Glossary* p. xlix, A *Johnny-Cake*; (sometimes supposed to have originally been a *Journey Cake*;) a kind of thin cake, made of Indian meal, baked before the fire, and made crisp, and extremely palatable. **1809** WEEMS *Marion* (1833) 124 But the most comfortable sight of all, was the fine supper which the tories had cooked! three fat roasted pigs, and six turkeys, with piles of nice journey-cakes. **1845** SIMMS *Wigwam & Cabin* 2 Ser. 99 [At] the breakfast table . . . we had enjoyed all the warm comforts of hot rice-waffles, journey-cake [etc.]. **1868** G. G. CHANNING *Recoll. Newport* 25 The 'journey-cake,' vulgarly called *Johnny-cake*,—how can I sufficiently extol it?

+**Journey cake board.** (See JOHNNYCAKE BOARD quot. 1852.)

***Journeyman.** Also †**jo(u)rnyman.** A tradesman or craftsman who, having served his apprenticeship, works for an employer at day wages.

1663 *Boston Rec.* 17 Robert Orchard fined 20s. for entertaineing John White as a Journyman. **1668** *Mass. Col. Laws* (1889) 260 You are also required to take a list of the names of those young persons . . . [who] do not serve their Parents or Masters, as Children, Apprentices, hired Servants, or Journey men ought to do. **1716** *Boston Selectmen* 12 George Weeks a Butcher now a Jorny-man . . . [was] warned to depart out of this Town. **1771** FRANKLIN *Autobiog.* 239, I was to serve as an apprentice till I was twenty-one years of age, only I was to be allowed journeyman's wages during the last year. **1831** PECK *Guide* 297 There were at that time one steam saw mill, . . . one cooper with six journeymen, and three apprentices, . . . and one retail store. **1889** *Century Mag.* Jan. 403/1 When old enough, and able to do a full day's work, [the lad] . . . is to apply for a second examination, which, if passed, entitles him to be considered a journeyman.

transf. **1835** HOFFMAN *Winter in West* I. 65 Every mechanic here [in Pittsburgh], of any pretension, has one of these tremendous journeymen [steam engines] at work in his establishment.

b. Attrib. with *baker, bootmaker, coppersmith*, etc.

1714 *Boston News-Letter* 23–30 Aug. 2/2 This is to give notice, that a Journyman Pewterer . . . may have constant Work. **1722** *New-Eng. Cou-*

rant 12–19 Feb. 1/2, I am pester'd . . . with a young Fellow who calls himself a Merchant, but I am afraid he is a Journeyman Gentleman. **1790** *Penna. Packet* 4 Jan. 1/2 Wanted Immediately, A good Journeyman Coppersmith. . . . Also, a good Journeyman Tinman. **1811** in H. M. Brooks *Gleanings* 141 Six Journeyman Bakers of other Towns. **1818** Fearon *Sketches* 30 A journeyman gilder would not succeed. **1840** *Picayune* 4 Oct. 2/6 Five or six good journeymen Bootmakers wanted.

+**Jovite.** (See quot. 1898.) — **1897** *Current History* VII. 646 Recent tests of the explosive known as 'jovite' indicate its great promise as to its effectiveness for navy shells. **1898** *Boston Transcript* 25 June 24/6 The explosive employed in her projectiles is wet guncotton. Before long . . . she will use 'jovite' instead. . . . Jovite is the invention of a Swede named Blomen. It is a mixture of certain coal-tar products with a metallic nitrate.

Jower, *v.* Also **jour.** *intr.* (See quot. 1923.) {1628–} *'Dial.* and *local U.S.'* (*O.E.D.*). — **1883** *Amer. Philol. Ass. Trans.* XIV. 50 *Jower* or *jour*, quite common in the South in the sense of persistent quarrelling or scolding. **1884** Monteith *Parson Brooks* vii. 45 We won't hev no jowerin' 'bout it. **1923** *Dialect Notes* V. 212 *Jar*, to wrangle, to quarrel, to argue: Also *Jower.* [McDonald Co., Mo.]

+**Juba.** Also **jubah.** A noisy, rollicking dance formerly popular among Negroes. Usually in the phrase *to dance juba.* Also transf.

1834 Carruthers *Kentuckian* I. 113 A man looks so unromantic with his teeth, and his hands, and his feet all in motion like a negro dancing 'Juba.' **1837** *Raleigh* (N.C.) *Standard* 25 Oct. 3/4 (Th. S.), Your last potato is 'dancing Juba' to the melancholy music of a tea-kettle. **1869** *Atlantic Mo.* July 75/1, [I saw] a water-color representation of myself, with one arm and one leg elevated, in the act of performing 'Juba' over the heads and carts and carriages of the passers-by. **1873** 'Mark Twain' & Warner *Gilded Age* xvi, The twang of a banjo became audible as they drew nearer, and they saw a couple of negroes, from some neighboring plantation, 'breaking down' a juba. **1880** *Harper's Mag.* Aug. 368/1 There lounged a dozen men watching black Sam pick the banjo and dance Juba. **1888** Billings *Hardtack* 70 Sometimes a real negro was brought in to enliven the occasion by patting and dancing 'Juba.'

attrib. **1848** Judson *Mysteries N.Y.* I. 91 A 'juba dancer' was on the floor. **1885** *Library Mag.* July 1 On the rude floor of the forecastle, they [the Negroes] danced their vigorous hoe-downs, jigs and jubah-shuffles.

+**b.** *To pat juba,* to keep time to this dance by patting with the hands or feet.

1847 Field *Drama in Pokerville* 14 The niggers were patting Juba on every corner, but the pleasurable excitement among the 'first families' was scarcely less remarkable. **1855** *Harper's Mag.* Oct. 597/2 [The bears] the while keep time with their paws, and give no mean imitations of 'patting Juba.' **1887** Custer *Tenting on Plains* 234 The fattest darkey of all waddled down next and did a break-down, at which all the assembly patted juba. **1900** Smithwick *Evolution of State* 20 Let's go round there and see those fellows [Negroes] pat Juba.

+**Juba dance.** =Juba. — **1857** *Harper's Mag.* July 149/2 H—— gave them the Juba dance, which . . . they appreciated to its fullest extent. **1888** *Century Mag.* Sept. 770/1 The juba-dance and the corn-shucking were equally invested with elements of the unreal and the grotesque. **1900** Smithwick *Evolution of State* 20 A regular series of hand-claps going on . . . naturally reminded us of the 'Juba' dance among the negroes.

Jubilee.** +Used attrib. to designate Negro folk songs or singers. (Cf. Jubilee singer.) — *c1872** T. F. Seward (*title*), Jubilee Songs as Sung by the Jubilee Singers, of Fisk University. **1873** G. D. Pike *Jubilee Singers* 163 The excellent rendering of the Jubilee Band is made more effective . . . by the comparison of their former state of slavery . . . with the present prospects and hopes of their race. **1884** *Boston Transcript* 13 Dec. 2/6 Colored Jubilee Concert Company and Sam Lucas, Reserved Seats, 25 and 50 cents. **1922** *Amer. Folk-Lore* XXXV. 248 Every Time I Feel the Spirit. This is one of the most thrilling of the later jubilee songs.

+**Jubilee singer.** One of a group of Negro singers who gave concerts of Negro songs, orig. in celebration of emancipation. *Obsolescent.* — **1872** *N.Y. Tribune* 17 Feb. 3/6 Unique Vocal Concert by the Jubilee Singers. **1876** *Ib.* 12 February 11/5 Sacred Concert at Steinway Hall . . . by the famous and original Wilmington Colored Jubilee Singers. The largest, best, and most popular slave band of jubilee singers ever before the public. **1881** *Harper's Mag.* May 804/1 Thomas's Symphony concerts and the . . . Jubilee Singers all find an appreciative audience.

Judas tree. {1668–} +Any one of various American trees of the genus *Cercis*, esp. *C. canadensis*, the redbud. Also *American Judas tree.*

1785 Marshall *Amer. Grove* 32 Red-bud, or Judas Tree. This grows naturally in several parts of North-America. **1808** Ashe *Travels* 225 Besides these there were . . . the judas tree, the dog wood and many others. **1843** Torrey *Flora N.Y.* I. 188 American Judas-tree. . . . Niagara county. . . . The flowers are acid, and are said to be used by the French Canadians for salads and pickles. **1850** *New Eng. Farmer* II. 411 The American Judas-tree, sometimes called the Red Bud, is an early flowering, small tree. . . . It received the appellation of Judas-tree from the supposition that it was the one on which the traitor hung himself; but Gerard, an old English botanist, says that it was the Elder on which Judas committed suicide! **1870** *Amer. Naturalist* IV. 215 The Red-bud, or Judas Tree, . . . with its branches all aflame in early spring, is a small, graceful tree. **1894** Torrey *Fla. Sketch-Book* 27 Spring blossoms were beginning to make their appearance . . . —violets in abundance (*Viola cucullata*), . . . the Judas-tree, or redbud [etc.].

***Judge.**

***1.** The official who presides over a court of justice, hearing and trying cases.

1638 *R.I. Col. Rec.* I. 52 We that are freemen Incorporate of this Bodie Politick do Elect and Constitute William Coddington, Esquire, a Judge amongst us. **1682** *Plymouth Laws* 198 Where there shalbe soe neare relation between any Judge and either of the p[ar]tyes as father and son . . . such Judge . . . shall . . . not have power to centance therin as a Judge. **1703** Sewall *Diary* II. 83 Governour's note to me to instruct a Meeting of the Judges next Monday is in my Court Book. **1776** *Decl. Independence*, He has made judges dependent on his will alone, for the tenure of their offices, and the amount and payment of their salaries. **1807** Janson *Stranger in Amer.* 323 Judges throughout the United States are addressed —*your honors.* **1835** Clay in *Congress. Deb.* 4 Feb. 297 The judges of the courts of Georgia are restrained from granting injunctions, so that the only form in which the Indian can come before them is in the form of an appeal. **1905** Steffens in *McClure's Mag.* Feb. 345/2 The General Assembly [of R.I.] 'elects' judges, sheriffs, and fills most of the offices in between.

+**b.** *Judge-Marshall,* a local official in the province of Maine: (see quotation). Now hist.

*a***1647** Gorges *Descr. New-Eng.* iv. 46, I added a Marshall for the managing of the Militia, who have for his Lievetenant a Judge-Marshall, and other Officers to the Marshall Court, where is to be determined all Criminall and Capitall matters.

2. Such an official *of* a specified jurisdiction or type.

1647 *R.I. Col. Rec.* I. 163 It is allso Rebellion to threat, assault or strike a Judge of Record. **1719** *Mass. Bay Currency Tracts* 193 Ministers, School-Masters, Judges of the Circuit, President & Tutors at Colledge, Widows and Orphans, &c. are pincht and hurt more than any. **1779** *Penna. Col. Rec.* XI. 713 Resolved, That the Hon'ble George Ross, Esq'r, be commissioned Judge of the Admiralty of this State. **1809** Kendall *Travels* I. 178 The courts of the United States are a district-court, with a resident judge, and a circuit-court, held by the judges of the federate republic. **1841** *Diplom. Corr. Texas* III. (1911) 1333 The undersigned Judge of the fourth Judicial District and Associate Justice of the Supreme Court. **1851** *California Laws* 515 Whenever any dispute arises respecting the ownership, mark, or brand of any horse, mule, jack, jenny, or horned cattle, it shall be the duty of the Judges of the Plains to decide on such dispute.

+**b.** *Judge of probate,* the official who presides over a probate court.

1707 Sewall *Diary* II. 205 Some desire that it may be put in the Bill that Mr. Leverett Lay down all his Civil offices; as Judge of Probat, and judge of the Superior Court. **1788** *Mass. Spy* 20 Nov. 1/1 Four months further are allowed by the Hon. Joseph Dorr, Esq.; Judge of Probate for the County of Worcester, to the several creditors of the estate of Thomas Bascom. **1865** in Fleming *Hist. Reconstruction* I. 175 The appointment of Judge of Probate and Sheriff in each county will be made specially. **1877** *Mich. Gen. Statutes* I. (1882) 233 The judge of probate of such county may, on application of the officer so elected, approve of the bond and sureties thereto.

+**c.** *Judge of election,* one appointed to see that the laws relating to an election are complied with.

1871 De Vere 272 When the whole [vote] is examined by official judges of election, the majority is securely established. **1875** *Chicago Tribune* 5 Oct. 2/2 The Republican County Committee . . . appointed a sub-committee to prepare a list of trustworthy citizens to be recommended to the County Commissioners for judges of election. **1877** Johnson *Anderson Co., Kansas* 69 The county commissioners . . . appointed judges of election for each precinct. **1901** Duncan & Scott *Allen & Woodson Co., Kansas* 12 On the 19th of August, 1856, the Board met and appointed judges of election for the first Monday in October for members of the Territorial legislature.

+**3.** Used as a mere title of respect or courtesy.

1800 J. Maude *Visit Niagara* 74 Captain Williamson was himself here best known as 'the Judge.' **1845** *Knickerb.* XXVI. 221 One 'Squire Rawson, now *Judge* Rawson, ('judge' by courtesy) had gleaned the legal field. **1869** Browne *Adv. Apache Country* 394 My friend was called the Judge, though I believe he claimed to be of no higher rank than an attorney at law. All popular lawyers, however, are judges in Nevada, whether they practice at the bar or sit upon the bench. **1872** Powers *Afoot & Alone* 103 [The Mississippi planter] comes in his broad-brimmed hat, and his honest Kentucky jeans. . . . The 'Count' or the 'Duke' may be a born churl, but your 'Judge' or your 'Colonel' seldom. **1873** 'Mark Twain' & Warner *Gilded Age* v. 61 His title of 'Squire' came into vogue again, but only for a season; for, as his wealth and popularity augmented, that title, by imperceptible stages, grew up into 'Judge.' **1905** *N.Y. Ev. Post* 18 March The title of 'Judge' stuck to him from the time he was a justice of the peace.

Judge advocate. *Mil. & Nav.* An officer appointed to serve as prosecutor at a court-martial. {1689– (*Act 1 William & Mary* 170)} Also transf. — **1757** *General Orders* 42 A Genll Cort Mareschal . . . Lieut. Col: Young President—Capt. Woodall Judge Advocate. **1797** *Ann. 4th Con-*

gress 2 Sess. 2330 One Judge Advocate . . . shall be taken from the commissioned officers of the line. **1862** STRONG *Cadet Life W. Point* 80 The earnest and eloquent appeals of the judge-advocate doing his utmost to defend me, dispelled finally all the suspicions I had at first entertained of its illegality. **1897** C. A. DANA *Recoll. Civil War* 278, [I] then delivered them [*sc.* letters] to Judge John A. Bingham, special judge advocate in the conspiracy trial.

Judge-Advocate-General. {1802– (James *Mil. Dict.* s.v. *Court*)} **1.** In the U.S. army, an officer of the rank of brigadier general, who serves as the chief of the legal bureau. **2.** In the U.S. Navy, an officer serving a similar function. — **(1) 1862** *Statutes at L.* XII. 598 The President shall appoint, . . . a judge advocate general, with the rank, pay, and emoluments of a colonel of cavalry. **1881–5** MCCLELLAN *Own Story* 123 Col. Gantt performed the duty of judge-advocate-general. **(2) 1865** *Statutes at Large* XIII. 468 The President . . . is hereby, authorized to appoint, . . . an officer in the Navy Department to be called the Solicitor and Naval Judge-Advocate-General.

+**Judge Lynch.** The personification of lynch law. — **1837** WETMORE *Gaz. Missouri* 61 This banditti . . . are now lodged in jail, with the hope that punishment may overtake them by due course of law, without the expense of an extra term of Judge Lynch's court. **1844** GREGG *Commerce of Prairies* II. 12 The importunate creditor . . . committed him at once to the care of 'Judge Lynch' for trial. **1887** *Courier-Journal* 31 Jan. 27 The people of Washington are sorry that the state of affairs in their county calls for the service of Judge Lynch. **1900** *Congress. Rec.* 25 Jan. 1205/1 When Judge Lynch decides that a man ought to be hanged, he decides, too, that the method of procedure is immaterial.

***Judger.** +*Judger of fence*, =FENCE-VIEWER. *Obs.* — **1689** *Tisbury Rec.* 22 John Manter and Thomas Look shall stand in the place of savairs [=surveyors] and judgers of fence for this following year.

***Judgment.** The decision of a court of justice, esp. one whereby a debt is established. Also attrib. — **1656** *Suffolk Deeds* II. 303 Ye aboue bargained premisses . . . is free and Cleere . . . [of all] Entajles Judgements executions [etc.]. **1733** *Md. Hist. Mag.* XIX. 303, I have had a Land Warrant . . . to be renewed & . . . have applyed to y[ou]r Clerk who refuses to do it unless I sign a judgement Bond. **1796** *Ann. 4th Congress* 2 Sess. 2696 Taxes . . . must be paid out of the assets in the hands of executors, prior to any judgments, mortgages, or debts whatsoever. **1846** POLK *Diary* (1929) 124 Judgments had been recovered against him in the courts of [Illinois]. **1887** *Courier-Journal* 13 Jan. 8/2 (*headline*), Tarleton Awarded a Judgment For Money Lost In a Brace Poker Game.

***Judicial,** *a.* Of or pertaining to the administration of justice or to courts of justice. — **1644** WINTHROP *Hist.* II. 212 There is a threefold power of magistratical authority, viz., legislative, judicial, and consultative or directive. **1789** *Ann. 1st Congress* I. 46 Mr. Lee . . . reported a bill to establish the judicial courts of the United States. **1821** COOPER *Spy* ii, Laying aside the sword, to assume the ermine on the benches of the highest judicial authority. **1900** *Congress. Rec.* 6 Feb. 1576/1 The question as to whether or not certain territory has been or should be acquired is a political and not a judicial one. **1913** LA FOLLETTE *Autobiog.* 152 It might prove an important factor in his judicial career.

+**Judicial circuit.** =CIRCUIT 1. — **1848** *Indiana Mag. Hist.* XXII. 86 Jas. W. Borden was on yesterday elected President Judge of the 12th Judicial Circuit. **1870** *Nation* 10 March 147/1 The chief topics in the Senate have been the Funding Bill, the bill to compensate Southern loyalists, and the bill to alter the judicial circuits. **1888** J. KIRKLAND *McVeys* 119 [There] were sitting in amicable, anecdotal confab, the judge and the attorneys of the —th Judicial Circuit, comprising eight counties.

+**Judicial district.** =prec. — **1841** *Diplom. Corr. Texas* III. (1911) 1333 Henry J. Jewett Attorney of the republic for the third Judicial District. **1854** BENTON *30 Years' View* I. 84/1 Mr. Smythe . . . had voted for the establishment of a judicial district in Western Virginia. **1872** *Newton Kansan* 12 Dec. 2/1 Senator Pomeroy has introduced a bill into the senate to create a new judicial district. **1897** *R.I. Secy. State Manual* 225 First Judicial District. (County of Newport.) **1914** *Cycl. Amer. Govt.* I. 503 In the United States, courts of common pleas are now to be found in New Jersey, Pennsylvania, Delaware and Ohio, one or more counties forming a judicial district for such courts.

***Judiciary.** +=FEDERAL JUDICIARY.

1787 JEFFERSON *Writings* VI. 131 The idea of separating the executive business of the confederacy from Congress, as the judiciary is already, in some degree, is just and necessary. **1814** *Ann. 13th Congress* 1 Sess. I. 852 That the Committee on the Judiciary be instructed to inquire into the expediency of making it the duty of the Attorney General . . . to keep his office at the seat of Government during the session of Congress. **1829** CHANNING *Works* (1886) 637/1 We pass to another method by which the government is to strengthen the Union. We know not a more important one. It is, to give dignity and independence to the national judiciary. **1902** *Harper's Mag.* April 698/1 The evening receptions to . . . the Judiciary, Congress, and the Army and Navy, are things long to be remembered.

+**b.** Used of a state system of courts and judges.

1797 IMLAY *Western Territory* (ed. 3) 335 The judiciary [consists in Kentucky] in the supreme court of appeals, and such inferior courts as the legislature may establish. **1872** *Congress. Globe* 6 April 2244/1 The gentleman in his remarks has chosen to make an attack upon the judiciary of my State [Virginia].

c. Attrib. with *circuit, department, system.*

1789 JEFFERSON *Writings* VII. 423 Were I called upon to decide, whether the people had best be omitted in the legislative or judiciary department, I would say it is better to leave them out of the legislative. **1792** in *History of Congress* (1834) 136, I cannot forbear to bring again into the view of the legislature the subject of a revision of the judiciary system. **1829** SHERWOOD *Gaz. Georgia* (ed. 2) 22 There are eight Judiciary Circuits.

+**Judiciary committee.** In a legislative body, a committee having supervision of matters affecting the judiciary. — **1789** *Ann. 1st Congress* I. 19 Mr. Carroll and Mr. Izard were added to the Judiciary Committee. **1842** *Whig Almanac 1843* 28/2 A bill was reported by the Judiciary Committee to enforce the collection of the revenue. **1877** *Harper's Mag.* March 627/1 The House Judiciary Committee, January 3, presented a majority and a minority report on the admission of the Representative from Colorado. **1911** PERSONS, etc. *Mass. Labor Laws* 25 These petitions were referred as received, in January and February, to the judiciary committee.

Judy. {1812–} +(See quotation.) *Obs.* — **a1870** CHIPMAN *Notes on Bartlett* 222 *Judy*, . . . a lamp formerly used in N[ew] E[ngland] for burning blubber.—Eastern Mass.

***Jug,** *n.*

***1.** A cylindrical vessel, usually of earthenware, equipped with a handle on one side; +now one tapering rapidly at the top to a small orifice with a stopper; also, ellipt., a jugful.

1651 *Essex Probate Rec.* I. Gally potts & drinking pots, and holand juggs. **1704** *Boston News-Letter* 8 May 2/1 Four Indians Seized a Servant Maid . . . who went about 150 Yards from the Garrison to a Spring, for a Jugg of Water. **1837** IRVING *Bonneville* II. 52 The Shoshokoes . . . construct bowls and jugs out of a kind of basket-work formed from small strips of wood plaited. **1905** PRINGLE *Rice Planter* 199, I really do not miss ice now that my little brown jug is swung in the well.

b. A vessel of this kind used as a container for whisky.

1853 'P. PAXTON' *Yankee in Texas* 197 Whether Colonel Rhoads ever paid three dollars for his jug of whiskey and deck (pack) of cards, I could not find out. **1862** LOCKE *Struggles Nasby* 74 Send me a eucher deck, a two-gallon jug uv corn joose. **1898** *McClure's Mag.* X. 348 He brought out a jug of whiskey.

2. A prison or jail. *slang.* {stone-jug, 1796–; jug, 1834–}

1815 *Niles' Reg.* IX. Suppl. 190/1 A full grown villain, who, with an accomplice, were shortly after safely lodged in the *jug*. **1842** 'UNCLE SAM' *Peculiarities* I. 104 You should have followed, and helped to put the prisoner in the jug. **1885** *Lisbon* (Dak.) *Star* 18 Sept., I didn't care for the jug, and, so as the officer was willing, I climbed into the wagon and away we went. **1924** CROY *R. F. D. No. 3* 229 'Where's the marshal?' they called. 'Get him. Throw him in the jug.'

Jug, *v.* {1681–} **1.** *tr.* To put (a person) in prison. *slang.* {1890–} (Cf JUG. *n.* 2.) **2.** To preserve (cherries) in a jug.—**(1) c1834** CATLIN *Indians* II. 30 The poor fellow was soon 'jugged up.' **1865** TROWBRIDGE *Three Scouts* xiii. 240 We'll go with you . . . and see your prisoner jugged. **1887** EGGLESTON *Graysons* xviii, The watchman had jugged him. **1918** RIDEOUT *Key of Fields* 224 You don't jug me for that! **(2) 1862** T. D. PRICE *Diary* (MS.) 13 Aug., Picked 1/2 bushel of cherries to jug and dry; stored them, put up two jugs and dried balance.

+**Jug-fishing.** =JUGGING. — **1889** *Cent.* 3249/2 Jug-fishing . . . [is a] method of fishing with empty jugs or bottles, which are corked and thrown overboard to serve as buoys, carrying a line, at the end of which is the hook.

Jugful. {1893–} +*By a jugful*, by a great deal, usu. in expressions of negation. *slang.* — **1833** NEAL *Down-Easters* I. 126, I have a right . . . to indemnify thee according to law. Not by a jug-full; cant obleege me at law, frind. **1853** BALDWIN *Flush Times Ala.* 149 Blass, did you ever hear of my telling a lie? No, not by a jug-full. **1893** *Congress. Rec.* 2 Oct. 2048/1 Take the Republicans one at a time and they are very clever sort of gentlemen . . . , but take them en masse and they will not do to tie to, by a jugful. **1911** SAUNDERS *Col. Todhunter* 33 'You hear the flutter of their wings!' 'No, I don't, not by a jugful.'

+**Jugging.** (See quot. 1884.) — **1872** *Kansas Mag.* Feb. 178 Jugging for catfish in the chutes of the Missouri and the Kaw. **1884** GOODE, etc. *Fisheries* I. 628 The 'Mud Cat' . . . and other of the larger Catfishes, are often caught by 'jugging,' the bait being attached to a jug filled with air, which will in time tire out the fish and bring it to the surface. **1911** *Rep. Fisheries 1908* 308 [Catfish] are caught by means of nets, traps, hand lines, and jugging.

Jug handle. 1. *attrib.* =JUG-HANDLED *a.* +**2.** (See quot. 1913.)— **(1) 1846** SOL. SMITH *Theatr. Apprent.* 118 Not perceiving the entire justice of this arrangement, it being somewhat on the jug-handle principle, all on one side. **a1882** in McCabe *New York* 85 This jug-handle style of architecture has become so universal that we have grown accustomed to it. **(2) 1913** BARNES *Western Grazing Grounds* 382 *Jug Handle.*—A mark made in cattle by slitting the dew lap about 4 inches so that the outside strip hangs free from the animal.

+**Jug-handled,** *a.* One-sided, not evenly proportioned, unfair. *colloq.* — **1881** *Congress. Rec.* 8 Dec. 60/2 English reciprocity in pleasure travel, however, like their often proposed commercial reciprocity, is comparatively jug-handled. **1886** *Ib.* 2 April 3053/2 Gentlemen of the South, this is no 'jug-handled' question; you are receiving a reasonably fair share of our revenue and customs. **1896** *Ib.* 1 May 4693/2 [This amendment] is infinitely better than the one-sided, jug-handled proposition of the gentleman from Pennsylvania. **1904** *Boston Herald* 28 Sept. 6 At the present time the trade between Canada and the United States is distinctly jug-handled, with the handle altogether on the side of our people.

+**Jug swallow.** =CLIFF SWALLOW. — **1868** *Amer. Naturalist* II. 217 I had nailed a board . . . under the eaves of a barn to form a resting-place for the nests of the Cliff or Jug-swallow. **1917** *Birds of Amer.* III. 84 Cliff Swallow. . . . Other Names.—Eave Swallow; Jug Swallow.

+Jug trade. Traffic in whisky contained in jugs. *colloq.* — **1887** *Courier-Journal* 1 Jan. 2/4 (*caption*), The Prohibitory Law at the Health Resort Results in a Boom in the Jug Trade. **1908** *Amer. Rev. of Reviews* April 468/2 The jug trade from the 'wet' into the 'dry' counties [in Ga.] became so great and annoying [etc.].

***Juice.**

***1.** The fluid found in certain trees or plants. Also attrib. and comb.

1792 IMLAY *Western Territory* 113 It has been long known that sugar could be made from the juice of this tree [the maple]. **1834** in Commons, etc. *Doc. Hist.* I. 281 Women are appointed one to put them [*sc.* sugar canes] into the machines for grinding them, and another to draw them out after the juice has been extracted. **1869** *Rep. Comm. Agric. 1868* 163 A press, or other juice-rendering machine, can work as many beets of rich quality as of inferior. *Ib.* 171 Wages were paid at the following rates: . . . For juice gutter: 2 boys, at 23 cents, 46 cents; same for night. **1880** *Vt. Agric. Rep.* VI. 222 The juice of maize contains as much if not a larger proportion of sugar than that of sugar cane. **1887** *Century Mag.* Nov. 113/2 Next the juice is pumped into an iron cylinder called the 'juice-heater.'

+b. *Juice of corn,* = CORN JUICE.

1857 *Lawrence* (Kan.) *Republican* 13 Aug. 1 Walker, a little higher than usual, in consequence of the inspiring qualities of the juice of corn.

+2. Electric current. *colloq.*

1896 *Boston Herald* 25 Dec. 4/5 Now we know what a blessing the trolley is—when the juice isn't turned off. **1911** VANCE *Cynthia* 218 Engine-room flooding rapidly, ship sinking by head. Will stick by post as long as possible or until juice gives out.

***Julep.** +A sweetened spirituous drink, often artificially cooled and flavored with mint. (Cf. MINT JULEP.)

1787 *Amer. Museum* I. 215 [A middle-class Virginian] rises in the morning about six o'clock. He then drinks a julap, made of rum, water, and sugar, but very strong. **1789** ANBUREY *Travels* II. 329 [A Virginian] drinks what he calls a julep, which is a large glass of rum sweetened with sugar. **1834** *Knickerb.* III. 350, I had never fancied their amusements of riding to the Lamb tavern for a julep, . . . or playing at faro. **1891** F. H. SMITH in *Century Mag.* March 733 Last I yeard from 'em dey was hollerin' for juleps. **1900** ROBERTSON *Red Blood & Blue* 134 [At] Syracuse, . . . the most elegant ladies not only drank juleps with him, but they drank julep for julep.

+b. Attrib. and comb. with *fountain, tippling, wise.*

1848 IRVING *Knickerb.* (rev. ed.) IV. ix, He denounced them as a pack of lazy, . . . julep-tippling . . . upstarts. **1849** G. G. FOSTER *N.Y. in Slices* 4 Let us hurry . . . past this palatial refectory cooled by a julep-fountain in the basement. **1851** A. O. HALL *Manhattaner* 58 Old jokers will tell you of mosquitoes who contemptuously spurn bars and netting; and . . . suck you (julep wise) from without.

+Julep pitcher. A pitcher for julep or mint julep. — **1842** *S. Lit. Messenger* VIII. 407/1 This mantel-piece had notoriously a remarkable capacity for holding sugar dishes, whole battalions of mint phials, not to omit a great julep pitcher. **1881** *Harper's Mag.* May 888/1 Mrs. Brinkly brought the julep pitcher.

Jumble. A soft cookie, esp. a drop cookie or one baked in the form of a ring; also, a fried cake. {jumbal 1615–1769; jumble, 1851–, chiefly *dial.*} — **1828** LESLIE *Receipts* 57 [Recipe for] Jumbles. **1845** NOAH *Gleanings* 74 She feels a little faint with walking, and intends eating a tart or a jumble, or drinking a glass of lemonade. **1898** DELAND *Old Chester Tales* 164 There was always a dish of apples on a side-table (or jumbles, if it was summer). . . . When collect class was over, the apples or jumbles were handed around, and each child took one. **1908** GALE *Friendship Village* 73 Abigail Arnold [was there], with a huge basket of gingerbread and jumbles from her home bakery.

Jump, *n.*[1] An under bodice formerly worn by women. {1706–} Usually pl. — **1666** *New Eng. Hist. & Gen. Register* XVIII. 329, I give to my sonn Williams wife, ye jump which was my sister Sarah Caps. **1764** in Singleton *Social N.Y.* 226 English, French turn'd and Mecklenburg Stays and Jumps [for sale]. **1790** *Penna. Packet* 23 Sept. 4/4 S. Finlass, Stay-Maker, . . . [sells] Riding Stays, turned stays, jumps, &c.

***Jump,** *n.*[2] In various colloq. phrases. **+a.** *From the* (*first* or *very*) *jump,* from the very beginning. Also *from the very first jump.*

1831 *Maysville* (Ky.) *Eagle* 12 July, I'll give you a history of Henry Clay, from the *first jump* of him. **1836** SIMMS *Mellichampe* i, I seed the whole business, from the very first jump. **1856** — *Charlemont* 224 The great desire which he felt . . . to make him display the qualities of both from the very jump. **1897** LEWIS *Wolfville* 192 It's cl'ar from the jump he ain't meant by Providence for the cattle business. **1911** FERBER *Dawn O'Hara* 32 Asked for you, right from the jump.

+b. (*At a*) *full jump,* at full speed.

1854 M. J. HOLMES *Tempest & Sunshine* i. 12 What you ridin' Prince full jump down the pike for? **1870** KEIM *Sheridan's Troopers* 39 The irate quadruped made for our party, coming at a 'full jump.'

+c. *On the* (*keen*) *jump,* (see first quot. 1889); also, at once, abruptly. {on the jump, 1900–}

1859 *S. Lit. Messenger* XXVIII. 143, I run down stream, an I meets Bill on the jump. **1861** *Atlantic Mo.* Sept. 293/1 De tar-kittle's a-bilin' on de keen jump. **1865** *Ib.* April 421/1, I went upstairs 'on the jump.' **1889** *Cent.* 3251/3 *On the jump, on the keen jump,* on the go; on the rush; busily engaged; hard at work. (Colloq., U.S.) **1889** 'MARK TWAIN' *Conn. Yankee* xxxiv. 442 We heard it [the hunt] coming—and coming on the jump, too. **1913** LONDON *Valley of Moon* II. xii, The receivin' hospital went outa commission on the jump.

***Jump,** *v.*

I. +1. *tr.* In hunting: To cause (game) to start from cover. Also with *up.*

1836 GILMAN *Recoll.* (1838) 211 The boys were ordered to stick close to the dogs, and if they jumped the buck, to catch him. **1874** LONG *Wild-Fowl* 205 The most successful method of hunting ducks is identical with . . . 'jumping them up' along the creeks and rivers which they frequent. **1890** CUSTER *Following Guidon* 9 Yesterday while looking for camp, . . . we jumped a prairie-wolf. **1900** DRANNAN *Plains & Mts.* 58 We jumped up a band of fifty elk, which was considered a small herd then.

+2. To skip over, omit, neglect.

1844 EMERSON *New Eng. Reformers* Ess. 2 Ser., They jumped the Greek and Latin and read law, medicine, or sermons, without it. **1873** BEADLE *Undevel. West* 186 New sects always preach the New Testament till they get into power, then jump it and go back to the Old Testament.

+b. To evade (an obligation or responsibility). Freq. *to jump bail.*

1859 MATSELL *Vocabulum* 47 *Jumped his bail,* run away from his bail. **1884** *Boston Jrnl.* 23 July, Agents have been working for them on the quiet to jump their contracts. **1888** *Chicago Herald* (F.), Slumbering lightly, he arose at early dawn, and jumped his bill like a true American. **1911** VANCE *Cynthia* 177 He's jumped bail on a bigamy indictment.

+c. To quit (something), to leave (a place). Also *absol.*

1876 MILLER *First Families* 94 Even the head man of the company . . . jumped a first-class poker game . . . to come in and weigh out dust. **1885** *Santa Fé Wkly. New Mexican* 17 Sept. 4/3 Jumped the Springs. Some trouble Brewing at the Valles Hot Springs. **1897** LEWIS *Wolfville* 313 The Deef Woman ain't seemin' to regard the Major's jumpin' the outfit as no loss, however. *a***1904** WHITE *Blazed Trail Stories* ii. 30 The men, discouraged, . . . would begin to 'jump,' would ask for their 'time,' and quit. **1921** PAINE *Comr. Rolling Ocean* 260, I told you about jumping the town because I had stove up a limousine for an old boy I was chauffeur for.

+d. Of sailors: To leave (a ship) with no intention of returning to one's duties aboard it.

1897 CLOVER *Paul Travers' Adv.* 146 The lad, . . . having signed articles for Sydney, was amenable to discipline if detected in an attempt to 'jump the ship.'

+3. To take possession of or occupy (a cabin, etc.) without the ordinary legal procedure. (Cf. 12.)

1860 GREELEY *Overland Journey* 163 'How do you live in Denver?' . . . 'O, I've jumped a cabin.' As jumping a cabin was rather beyond my experience, I . . . learned that, finding an uninhabited cabin that suited him, he had quietly entered and spread his blankets. **1872** 'MARK TWAIN' *Roughing It* xlvii. 334 When some roughs jumped the catholic bone-yard and started in to stake out town-lots in it. **1892** *Harper's Mag.* March 650/1 Bilfinger cast his eye on the public square in the middle of the town, and at once 'jumped it' as a homestead claim. **1901** NORRIS *Octopus* 450 They may jump the ranch, Pres, . . . if they try hard enough, but they will never do it while I am alive.

+4. *Checkers.* To pass over in moving; to take (an opponent's man).

1887 *Lippincott's Mag.* Sept. 350 If your checkers are jumped off the board so fast, you won't get any in the king-row.

+5. To attack, apprehend, come to grips with.

1891 *Harper's Mag.* Nov. 883/1 He kept ever on the trail . . . going from camp to camp to 'jump' whiskey peddlers and gamblers. **1893** ROOSEVELT *Wilderness Hunter* 244 A war party of Comanches . . . 'jumped' a neighboring camp, killing one man and wounding two more. **1903** FOX *Little Shepherd* xiii, Then Tad thar jumped me, and I whooped him.

+6. To get aboard (a train) surreptitiously as a tramp or hobo. *slang.*

1891 C. ROBERTS *Adrift America* 123, I jumped a freight here, and not being able to get into a car I rode the drawheads. **1903** KILDARE *My Mamie Rose* 173 To save our small capital, we were to walk or 'jump' freight trains. *a***1910** 'O. HENRY' *Rolling Stones* 118, I've grabbed my hat and jumped a freight and rode 200 miles to identify him.

+7. To elevate (an officer) in rank; to place (someone) in a particular position; to pass over (another) on being promoted.

1897 C. A. DANA *Recoll. Civil War* 96 He was jumped almost at a stroke, without much previous service, to be a lieutenant general. **1899** *Boston Transcript* 24 Feb. 6/1 The appointee has received a promotion . . . by influence, and in doing it has jumped many of his fellow-officers quite as good or better than he. **1902** WISTER *Virginian* xvii, I'd happened to come along, and he jumped me into the vacancy. **1903** *N.Y. Sun* 20 Nov. 12 Four hundred and 94 officers are jumped by Gen. Wood.

II. With adverbs.

+8. *To jump off*, (see quotation).

1847 PARKMAN in *Knickerb.* XXIX. 316 It was resolved to remain one day at Fort Leavenworth, and on the next to bid a final adieu to the frontier; or in the phraseology of the region, to 'jump off.'

+9. *To jump up*, of a town or village, to arise or spring up. *Obs.*

1818 *Niles' Reg.* XIV. 310/2 The improvements in the navigation of this important river [the Roanoke] has [*sic*] caused new towns and thriving villages to 'jump up' as suddenly as in any part of the western country. **1833** *Ib.* XLIV. 198/1 A new and flourishing town of fifty houses, called Amsterdam, has jumped up on the Big Black river.

III. In phrases.

See also CUT *n.* 9 c and TRACK *n.*

+10. *To jump the blind*, (see quotation). *slang.*

1902 CLAPIN 246 *Jump the blind.* In the West, to steal a ride on the platform of a baggage-car.

+11. *To jump a bounty*, to obtain a military bounty by enlisting and then deserting the service. (Cf. BOUNTY JUMPER, BOUNTY JUMPING *vbl. n.*)

1884 *Congress. Rec.* 28 March 2388/1, I shall not vote for this bill until I am ready to put the man upon the pension-roll 'who broke his leg attempting to jump a bounty.'

12. *To jump a claim*, to secure another person's mining claim by taking possession in the absence of the owner or by resorting to legal technicalities: (see also quot. 1899). {1854–, Australia} Also transf.

1848 E. H. SMITH *Black Hawk* 276 If, through mistake, I jumped a man's claim, as soon as I knew it I jumped off again. **1877** JOHNSON *Anderson Co., Kansas* 59 He jumped the claim made by one Card. **1889** *Cent.* 3251/3 *To jump a claim*, . . . to take possession of public land to which another has previously acquired a claim, the first occupant, by squatter law and custom, and under the preëmption laws of the United States, having the first right to the land. **1899** *Harper's Weekly* 8 April 341/3 Halstead promptly jumped the so-called 'Discovery' claim that Whipple was trying to reserve for himself. **1904** *N.Y. Sun* 3 Sept. 7 The villains failed to jump Jim's claim when that miner was busy attending to his sick baby. **1925** TILGHMAN *Dugout* 98 Why they had not already jumped the claim did not appear from the Mexican's story.

***Jumper.**[1]

+1. A crude or rough kind of sled or sleigh.

1823 COOPER *Pioneers* xxix, He was seen drawing one of those jumpers that they [*sc.* pioneers] carry their grain to mill in. **1835** HOFFMAN *Winter in West* I. 166 Have you ever seen a *jumper?* . . . It is a primitive kind of sledge, or *traineau.* **1871** EGGLESTON *Hoosier Schoolm.* xxxiv. 224 Driving Martha to a wedding in a 'jumper' was the one opportunity Bud needed. **1898** *New Eng. Mag.* June 455/1 My pulse quickens as I recall the glorious times with our 'jumper,' and the hair-breadth escapes from posts and barberry bushes, in our swift descent upon the ice. **1904** ATHERTON *Rulers of Kings* 23 Her remains were placed on the 'jumper'—a low sledge—and driven through the snowdrifts. The jumper was on runners.

+2. (See quotation.)

1850 BROWNE *Poultry Yard* 71 *Jumpers*, from their halting gait, are rather to be considered as accidental deformities collected from unhealthy families of Bantams, than as constituting any distinct variety.

+3. One who jumps a claim.

1851 A. T. JACKSON *Forty-Niner* (1920) 67 They are good friends of ours and will keep the jumpers off [our claim]. **1880** INGHAM *Digging Gold* iv. 127 There were no courts convenient to settle [gold-claim] disputes, and a class of miners called 'Jumpers,' taking advantage of this fact, became very numerous. **1893** HARTE *Susy* 105 Only then did Jim Hooker condescend to explain the reason of his warlike occupation, with dark hints of the outlying 'squatters' and 'jumpers.' **1925** TILGHMAN *Dugout* 102 She stopped there, rather than at the house, because the road ran by it, and there the jumpers would first reach the claim.

+4. (See quotations.)

1884 GOODE, etc. *Fisheries* I. 401 In Kentucky it [the large-mouth black bass, *Micropterus salmoides*] is called 'Jumper.' *Ib.*, The Small-mouth [black bass, *Micropterus dolomiei*] shares with the Large mouth in the Southern States the names 'Jumper,' 'Perch,' and 'Trout.'

+5. A contrivance upon which fire hose is wound. Also attrib.

1889 BRAYLEY *Boston Fire Dept.* 326 The new-style hose-carriage, or wagon, was fast taking the place of the old-fashioned 'jumper,' or reel. **1903** *N.Y. Ev. Post* 17 Oct., Next came firemen's day—a long eight hours of flashing uniforms, . . . of sudden dashes by swift hose 'jumper' men.

+6. =JERKER 1.

1889 *Pop. Science Mo.* June 148 Examples of this [religious excitement] in America are seen in the 'Jumpers,' 'Jerkers,' and various revival extravagances.

+7. One who has quit his job. *colloq.* (Cf. JUMP *v.* 2 c.)

1903 WHITE *Blazed Trail Stories* ii. 33 Silver Jack . . . took one of the 'jumpers' in the cutter with him.

+8. A boy who delivers packages from a delivery wagon. *colloq.*

1905 *Washington Star* 24 Nov. 20 (*advt.*), Wanted—boys for jumpers on delivery wagons.

Jumper.[2] One or other of a number of variously styled garments, esp. a jacket or blouse worn over a shirt, guimpe, etc. — **1853** KANE *Grinnell Exped.* 45 The most popular article of attire [on the island of Disko in Davis Strait] was the *karah*, a 'jumper' or close jacket, slipping on like a shirt, and hooded like the cowl of a Franciscan monk. **1870** HARTE *Luck Roaring Camp* 61 Clad in a loose duck 'jumper' and trousers streaked and splashed with red soil, his aspect . . . [was] quaint. **1879** PHELPS *Old Maid's Paradise* (1885) 156 A green-check cotton waist or blouse sewed into a belt—the masculine uniform of Fairharbor; he calls it a jumper. **1917** SINCLAIR *King Coal* 112 He wore a pair of common miner's 'jumpers,' but even so, he was not to be taken for a workingman. **1904** M. KELLY *Little Citizens* 111 Her jumper was red, with golden buttons. *Ib.* 324 'Teacher's jumper!' shouted the children. . . . 'Missis Bailey's got a green waist.'

***Jumping,** *n.* **1.** The action of leaping, as an athletic exercise or sport. Also attrib. **+2.** (See quot. 1879.) Also transf. (Cf. JUMP *v.* 3.) — **(1) 1789** MORSE *Amer. Geog.* 148 Jumping . . . and prison-bass [*sic*] are universally practised in the country. **1841** COOPER *Deerslayer* xx, Accustomed to the rude sports of wrestling and jumping, then so common in America, more especially on the frontiers, Hurry possessed an advantage. **1896** A. LEE *Track Athletics* 51 The jumping costume should consist of a jersey suit. **1906** D. A. SARGENT *Physical Education* 47 Nearly all of the city athletic clubs have grounds where their athletes practice running, jumping, and like sports. **(2) 1850** HINES *Voyage* 198 Here was no jumping of claims, . . . all were satisfied to select from that part of the vast surface of the whale around which lines had not been run. **1879** *Scribner's Mo.* Oct. 806/1 Next came a period of 'jumping,' that is, getting forcible or fraudulent possession of property. **1885** *Wkly. New Mexican Rev.* 21 May 4/6 Doc Stenley was arrested at Lake Valley on the complaint of Mr. Speed, charged with ranch jumping and unlawful entry.

***Jumping,** *a.* **+1.** In the names of various American fish and animals characterized by jumping: (see quotations). **+2.** In expletives: (see quotations). — **(1) 1766** J. BARTRAM *Journal* 35 Saw a mullet jump three times in a minute or two, which they generally do before they rest, so are called jumping-mullets. **1831** R. COX *Adv. Columbia R.* 319 The jumping-deer, or chevreuil, . . . frequent the vicinity of the mountains in considerable numbers. **1872** *Harper's Mag.* April 663/2 An infernal beast with long legs, a bristling back, and immense proboscis . . . frightened Miss Lilly dreadfully. She told me it was a 'ridge-back'—a 'jumping alligator,' a 'sub-soiler.' **(2) 1815** HUMPHREYS *Yankey* 106 *Jumping jings, jingoes*, expletives indicative of confirmation. **1923** *Dialect Notes* V. 212 *Jumpin' Jesus*, an exclamation of great surprise. [McDonald Co., Mo.]

+Jumping bean. =JUMPING SEED. {1896–} — **1889** *Cent.* 3252/2 *Jumping seed.* . . . Also called *jumping-bean, devil-bean.*

Jumping exercise. +=JERK *n.*[2] 1 — **1834** *Biblical Repertory* VI. 349 We saw another who had, what was termed, 'the jumping exercise;' which resembled that of the jumpers in Wales.

Jumping jack. +1. *local.* (See quotation.) **2.** A small toy figure of a man the limbs of which are made to jump by means of strings. {1793–} — **(1) 1861** *Ill. Agric. Soc. Trans.* V. 416 There is scarcely an individual . . . to be found who is unacquainted with the 'Spring-beetles,' or as they are often termed, 'Jumping-Jacks.' **(2) 1883** *Harper's Mag.* Jan. 277/1 Barley-candy statuettes, jumping-jacks, and other . . . toys. **1888** *Century Mag.* Sept. 771/1 Jumping-jacks, or 'supple sawneys,' were made of pasteboard. **1896** HARRIS *Sister Jane* 351 You're setting there acting for all the world like a jumping-jack!

Jumping mouse. {1839–} +=KANGAROO MOUSE.

1826 GODMAN *Nat. Hist.* II. 95 The jumping-mouse is found in this country from Canada to Pennsylvania, and no doubt still farther south. **1842** *Nat. Hist. N.Y., Zoology* I. 72 It proved to be one of these *wood-mice*, or *jumping mice.* **1857** *Rep. Comm. Patents 1856: Agric.* 96 This animal is known as the . . . 'Kangaroo Mouse,' 'Jumping Mouse,' 'Buck Mouse,' 'Wood Mouse,' and other names. **1867** [see JUMPING RAT]. **1889** *Cent.* 1498/1 The American jumping-mouse, *Zapus hudsonius*, . . . [has] enlarged hind quarters and hind feet, by means of which it clears several feet at a bound. **1917** *Mammals of Amer.* 264 Jumping Mice . . . are slender and graceful Mice with exceptionally long tails.

+Jumping-off place.

1. A derogatory designation for an out-of-the-way place, the farthest limit of anything settled or civilized.

1826 FLINT *Recoll.* 366 Being, as they phrase it, the 'jumping off place,' it is necessarily the resort of desperate, wicked, and strange creatures who wish to fly away from poverty, infamy, and the laws. **1828** SHERBURNE *Memoirs* xi. 234 Olean point was denominated the *'jumping-off place.'* **1844** *Knickerb.* XXIV. 303 We have . . . a rhyming correspondent who sends us from 'the Jumping-off Place in Maine' what he calls 'an effusion.' **1906** LITTLE *Lady of Decoration* 116, I had often heard of the Jumping Off Place, but I never expected to actually see it. **1907** STEWART *Partners* 15, I couldn't see what a high-toned man like him was going up to that jumping-off place for.

2. A place at the end of a given portion of a journey as a point of departure for further travel. {1884–} Also transf.

1834 BRACKENRIDGE *Recollections* x. 111, I had no jumping off or jumping up place, like those who prepare their exordium and perorations, and leave the body of the speech to take care of itself. **1841** *Picayune* 28 May 2/2 To-morrow I set out for Austin, which may be considered the 'jumping off place,' as from there we leave the settlements altogether [in the journey to Santa Fe]. **1869** BROWNE *Adv. Apache Country* 46 We reached Cariso, the last inhabited station on the road. . . . Here was the jumping-off place. Beyond this, . . . we were at the mercy of the sands and storms and burning suns of Colorado. **1882** *Uncle Rufus & Ma* 51, I have . . . arrived at the 'jumping-off-place,' on the Northern Pacific Railroad. . . . The train could go no farther. **1883** *Harper's Mag.* May 820/1 There is a definite fascination in having arrived at the 'jumping-off place.' **1887** S. HALE *Letters* 189 From the plateau the town is on, you look off of this jumping-off place, over the fertile plain to snowy mountains.

b. The extreme limit of the earth; the end or edge of the earth. Also fig.

*c***1845** PAULDING *Amer. Comedies* (1847) 197, I have hunted all over them parts, almost clean out to the jumping off place of creation. *c***1862** THOREAU *Maine Woods* 178 He . . . only reached the jumping-off place of his wonder at white men's institutions. **1870** KEIM *Sheridan's Troopers* 224 Religious superstition also teaches that the earth is a great plain, and that there is a jumping off place. **1884** 'CRADDOCK' *Where Battle Was Fought* 54, I think we have come to the financial jumping-off place. **1898** *Outing* April 24/1, I stood upon the edge of the earth, it seemed, the 'jumping-off place' of the fairy tales. **1899** TARKINGTON *Gentleman from Ind.* xv, He had come to a jumping-off place in his life—why had they not let him jump?

+**Jumping rat.** =KANGAROO RAT. — **1867** *Amer. Naturalist* I. 394 The *Saccomyinæ* . . . are known in the vernacular as 'Kangaroo' or 'Jumping' Rats and Mice, and are entirely confined to Transmississippian regions.

Jumping rope. =JUMP ROPE. {1870–, *Sc.*} — **1859** *Ladies' Repository* XIX. 668/2 A merry party they made with their satchels, jumping-ropes, tops, and other things.

+**Jumping seed.** The seed of various Mexican shrubs animated by the contained larva of a small moth. — **1876** *Field & Forest* II. 53 We have recently had the pleasure of examining . . . these so-called jumping seeds received from California. **1889** [see JUMPING BEAN].

+**Jump-off.** A precipitous descent. *colloq.* — **1873** BEADLE *Undevel. West* 490 In this [bayou] we encountered dangerous whirls and jump-offs. **1884** PHILLIPPS-WOLLEY *Trottings of Tenderfoot* v. 129 The broad stem of a fallen giant gives you 150 feet of splendid wooden road; but . . . you find you have been gradually ascending, and now stand on what the Americans would call a 'jump off.' **1909** WASON *Happy Hawkins* 26 The lantern shed a splash o' light on the shelf, but the jump-off looked like the mouth o' the pit.

Jump rope. Skipping the rope; the rope used for this purpose. — [**1887** *Nation* 14 April 317/1 Various small side-shows in the way of 'jump-rope,' 'grace-sticks,' and 'class-ball.'] **1894** FORD *P. Stirling* 49 The old clothes-line . . . served for a jump-rope.

Junco. +**1.** A shrub or small tree (*Koeberlinia spinosa*), usu. leafless, found in the southwestern part of the U.S. +**2.** Any one of various small American finches; a snowbird. — (1) **1872** POWERS *Afoot & Alone* 146 The junco has no foliage, except immense, green thorns. **1894** *Scribner's Mag.* May 597/1 There is an almost unvarying succession of the . . . 'junco.' (2) **1887** RIDGWAY *Manual N.A. Birds* 422–4 [Gives eight U.S. species.] **1898** *Atlantic Mo.* Oct. 492/2 Birds which had been isolated . . . might be presumed to have acquired . . . some slight but real idiosyncrasy of voice and language. But if this is true of the Carolina junco, I failed to satisfy myself of the fact. **1904** *N.Y. Ev. Post* 2 Jan., There was a flickering of white tail-feathers as the juncos flew away. **1917** *Birds of Amer.* III. 45 Slate-colored Junco. *Junco hyemalis hyemalis.* . . . [Also called] Eastern Junco.

Junction. {1711–}

1. The place at which two or more streams join.

1792 *Ann. 2d Congress* 1037 A grant of 200,000 acres to Richard Henderson . . . on Powel's and Clinch's rivers, extending . . . down Clinch's from their junction in a breadth not less than twelve miles. **1807** GASS *Journal* 146 We stopped a short distance above the junction of this with another large river. **1843** N. BOONE *Journal* 226 The river flows a little south of East after the junction in a sandy bed a mile wide. **1867** 'E. KIRKE' *On Border* 105 [It was] a small town at the junction of the Big Sandy with the Ohio.

2. The joining or intersection of a railroad track with another track or with a thoroughfare. {1846–}

1856 *Porter's Spirit of Times* 22 Nov. 192/3 He was driving the horse near the junction when the train appeared. **1884** MATTHEWS & BUNNER *In Partnership* 152 She's gotter get along mighty lively to keep ahead of the express from Philadelphia till she gets to the junction and goes on a siding till the express goes past. **1885** *Santa Fé Wkly. New Mex.* 1 Oct. 2/7 A Las Vegas schemer . . . made written contracts with the flock owners to deliver their fall clip at Lamy junction. **1905** RICE *Sandy* 254, I could swear I saw him hiding in the bushes between here and the Junction.

***June,** *n. attrib.* In the names of various fruits and flowers that ripen or come to perfection in June..

[**1760** WASHINGTON *Diaries* I. 146 Grafted 10 of a pretty little early (June) Pear from Collo. Mason's.] **1821** NUTTALL *Travels Arkansa* 98 A species of *Vitis*, called the June grape, from its ripening at that early period, was also nearly in blossom. **1832** in Williamson *Maine* I. 109 [The wild plum tree, *Prunus sylvestris*, is] called also pomegranate, wild pear, and June-plum. **1853** *S. Lit. Messenger* XIX. 221/1 She was painted up like a doll; her withered old face streaked like a June apple. **1856** *Rep. Comm. Patents 1855; Agric.* 291 The 'Red' and 'Yellow June Harvest,' and other kinds of summer apples, are drugs in the market.

+**June,** *v. W. colloq.* **1.** *intr.* To go rapidly. **2.** *tr.* To drive briskly. — (1) **1869** *Overland Mo.* III. 127 A trig, smirk little horse is a 'lace-horse,' and he often has to 'june,' or 'quill.' **1889** FARMER 328/1 *June, To* (Texas).—To go. (2) **1903** A. ADAMS *Log of Cowboy* 228 To june a herd of cattle across in this manner would have been shameful.

+**June berry.** Any one of various American shadbushes or the fruit of one of these. — **1810** MICHAUX *Arbres* I. 32 *June berry*, nom donné a cet arbre [*Mespilus arborea*] dans tous les Etats du milieu. **1832** BROWNE *Sylva* 217 The wood of the June berry is of a pure white. **1850** S. F. COOPER *Rural Hours* 72 Just now, the leaves of the June-berry are dark reddish brown. **1892** *Amer. Folk-Lore* V. 95 *Amelanchier Canadensis*, June berry. Various parts of N.E. and Central States.

June bug. {*a*1800–, *dial.*} +Any one of various large beetles of the genus *Phyllophaga;* also, =FIG-EATER.

Cf. MAY BEETLE.

1835 LONGSTREET *Ga. Scenes* 78 You'll see me down upon him like a duck upon a June-bug. *a***1846** *Quarter Race Ky.* 90 They make a man swaller tobacker jist to look at 'em, and feel sorter like a June bug was crawlin up his trowses and the waistband too tite for it to git out. **1872** *Harper's Mag.* Nov. 803/2 Phemie Bonner whirled him round like a June-bug tied to a string. **1884** 'CRADDOCK' *Tenn. Mts.* 14 The critter war ez peart and lively as a June-bug. **1894** 'MARK TWAIN' *P. Wilson* viii, It is better to be a young June-bug than an old bird of paradise.

fig. **1873** *Winfield* (Kan.) *Courier* 17 July 1/4 Sometimes I can hear the June bugs of despondency buzzing in my ears.

+**b.** Attrib. with *breastpin, order.*

1857 STROTHER *Virginia* 110 [A Negro], dressed in his holiday suit, with a ruffled shirt of red calico, a June-bug breast-pin, a brass-headed cane [etc.]. **1909** 'O. HENRY' *Options* 129 He spent his life seining the air for flying fish of the June-bug order, and then sticking pins through 'em and calling 'em names.

+**June butter.** Butter made in June. (Cf. FALL BUTTER 2.) — **1839** *Mass. Agric. Survey 2d Rep.* 71 June butter . . . and September butter . . . are generally of a superior quality to that made at other seasons. **1873** *Vermont Bd. Agric. Rep.* II. 186 This butter is not what is usually called 'winter butter,' but is equal in flavor and color to 'June butter.' **1902** *Boston Ev. Globe* 18 Feb. 4/5 Gathered cream butter in June 20 to 21 cents; renovated and best June butter, after being in cold storage, 23 cents.

+**June grass.** =BLUE GRASS; also, a tufted grass (*Koeleria cristata*) found in prairie regions. — **1855** *Mich. Agric. Soc. Trans.* VI. 160 One tree of the damson variety, standing in a stiff June grass sod plat. **1870** *Rep. Comm. Agric. 1869* 169 The best grasses for permanent lawns are red top (*Agrostis vulgaris,*) and June grass (*Poa pratensis*). **1919** *Maine My State* 336 How fair her fields when June-grass waves!

+**June rise.** (See quot. 1871.) — **1847** ROBB *Squatter Life* 134 The varmint's [a rival's] countenance looked as riled as the old Missouri in a June rise. **1857** CHANDLESS *Visit Salt Lake* 2 Except during the 'June rise' side-wheel boats rarely go up [the Missouri]. **1871** DE VERE 181 This leads to a peculiar phenomenon, called the *June Rise* of the Missouri, when suddenly all the headwaters come roaring and rushing down from the high table-lands, from which the great river springs, and swell it to its full height. The rise begins generally in June, though it is sometimes delayed till July, and of course affects the Mississippi also.

+**Juney bug.** = JUNE BUG. — *c***1866** BAGBY *Old Va. Gentleman* 45 The humming-birds and the bumble-bees and Juney-bugs, which knew them [*sc.* butterflies] once shall know them no more. *c***1870** *Ala. Hist. Soc. Trans.* IV. 484 Why a hog has no more chance to live among these thieving negro farmers than a juney bug in a gang of puddle ducks.

***Junior.**

+**1.** In American colleges and secondary schools, a student in the third year of the regular four-year academic course: (see also quot. 1847).

*c***1764** in Woolsey *Hist. Disc. Yale* (1850) 55 A Senior may take a Freshman from a Sophimore, a Bachelor from a Junior, and a Master from a Senior. **1819** A. PEIRCE *Rebelliad* 19 He look'd so queer The Juniors shouted in the rear. **1842** *Yale Lit. Mag.* VIII. 46 The aspiring Junior is already anticipating the high enjoyments, and, perchance, the *ease* of Senior year. **1847** WEBSTER 635/2 *Junior*, . . . one in the first year of his course at a theological seminary. **1850** *Yale Lit. Mag.* XV. 208 He sprees, is caught, rusticates, returns next year, mingles with feminines, and is consequently degraded into a spooney Junior. **1888** BRYCE *Amer. Commonwealth* III. VI. cii. 453 In an American college the students . . . of the third year [are called] juniors. **1906** *University* (Chicago) *High School Wkly.* 10 Oct. 1 To the Juniors we [Seniors] give our commanding dignity, which we hope they will in time learn to use. **1915** CAMPBELL *Proving Virginia* 10 Alan is a Junior and he studies.

+**b.** (See quotation.)

1889 *Century Mag.* Jan. 403/1 When the trade-school course is finished and he has proved by an examination held by a committee of master mechanics that he has profited by it, he is to enter a workshop as a 'junior.'

2. Attrib. with *exhibition, prom, society, year.*

1851 HALL *College Words* 45 At Hamilton College, it is customary for the Sophomores to appear in a class cap on the Junior Exhibition day. **1884** R. GRANT *Average Man* 10 It was the end of my Junior year, and I was feeling terribly blue . . . over a condition in chemistry. **1897** FLANDRAU *Harvard Episodes* 159 The junior society seemed made to his hand. **1914** GERRY *Masks of Love* 79 [Her tears] were a tribute not only to the lover but to all the years of sheltered sweetness with which he was associated, . . . her 'junior prom' at college [etc.].

+**Junior bachelor.** (See quot. 1851.) *Obs.* — **1790** *Harvard Laws* 19 No Junior-bachelor shall continue in the College, after the Commencement in the summer vacation. **1851** HALL *College Words* 176 *Junior Bachelor,* one who is in his first year after taking the degree of Bachelor of Arts.

Junior class. +A class in college made up of those who are in the third year of the academic course: (see also quot. 1720).

1720 D. NEAL *Hist. New-Eng.* I. 185 [At Harvard] the Junior Class are called fresh Men the first Year . . . : The second Year they bear the Title of Sophimores: the third of Junior Sophisters, and the fourth of Senior Sophisters. **1770** FITHIAN *Journal* I. 7 Mr. Hunter and myself, were admitted into the junior-Class [at Princeton] . . . after a previous Examination by the president. **1839** CASWALL *America* 200 These classes are known as the Senior, Junior, Sophomore, and Freshman. **1856** HALL *College Words* (ed. 2) 67 At Union College, as a mark of distinction, a class cane was for a time carried by the members of the Junior Class. **1882** THAYER *From Log-Cabin* xxi. 313 James passed the examination without any difficulty, and was admitted to the Junior class [at Williams College].

+**b.** (See quotation.) *Obs.*

1816 *Ann. 14th Congress 2* Sess. 270 Those [in the militia] between the age of twenty-one and thirty-one years of age, shall be called the junior class.

+**Junior college.** A college, operating as a separate institution or as part of a standard college, which does not offer courses more advanced than those of the sophomore year. Also attrib. — **1899** *Univ. of Chicago Reg. 1898–99* 37/1 The Faculties of the Schools of Arts, Literature, and Science have been organized as follows: (1) The Faculty of the Junior Colleges; (2) The Faculty of the Senior Colleges [etc.]. **1919** F. M. MCDOWELL *Junior College* 6 The junior college is in the experimental stage. **1925** L. V. KOOS *Junior-College Movement* 10 Many less well-established institutions have taken recourse to the junior-college status as a means of finding a recognized place in the school system.

Junior Ex. [Abbrev. of *Junior exhibition;* cf. EXHIBITION 1.] A program designed to display the literary and, sometimes, the musical and dramatic talents of members of the junior class. — **1887** RITTENHOUSE *Maud* 379 Last night went to the 'Junior Ex' from Emily's. Some of the orations were dreadful, and the poor young orators awkward, nervous, and stiff. **1901** *Albion* (Mich.) *Recorder* 25 April, The Junior Ex. was a financial success, the total receipts being $55. **1920** *Ib.* 15 April (*advt.*), Junior Ex. Big Program and 3 act Comedy 'Tommy's Wife.'

Junior preacher. In the Methodist church, a minister subordinate in rank to another. — **1846** *Indiana Mag. Hist.* XXIII. 242 Elliott being only a probationer in the conference and Brown being an elder of some years' standing, he thought his dignity invaded by being a junior preacher under a probationer, so that the elder deemed it expedient to change him with the junior preacher on Lawrenceburg circuit. **1874** EGGLESTON *Circuit Rider* 194 He had, therefore, sent him as 'second man' or 'junior preacher' on a circuit.

+**Junior senator.** A senator who has been in Congress a shorter time than the other senator from his state. — **1885** CRAWFORD *Amer. Politician* 142 The junior senator for Massachusetts died this morning, and there may be an election at any moment. **1900** *Congress. Rec.* 11 Jan. 766/2 The details of the amendment offered by the junior Senator from Massachusetts . . . might be considerably extended.

+**Junior sophister.** (See quot. 1847.) *Obs.*

[**1654** H. DUNSTER (Harvard Univ. MS.), Ad 3m deinde pervenientes Annum termino Paschali Juniores Sophistae appellantur.] **1708** *Broadside Verse* (1930) 23 A Solemn Lacrymatory for the Grave of Jonathan Marsh, Junior-sophister: Who Deceas'd at Harvard College. **1734** *Harvard Rec.* I. 139 If any Resident Bacheour, Senior or Junior Sophister shall neglect to analyse, in his course according to the direction of the President, . . . he shall be punished by the President. **1766** in B. Peirce *Hist. Harvard* (1833) 246 The Junior Sophisters shall attend *B* on Mondays. **1818** *N. Amer. Rev.* March 423 The following are . . . the several classes [at Harvard]: . . . Freshmen . . . Sophomores . . . Junior sophisters . . . Senior sophisters. **1847** WEBSTER 635/2 *Junior,* . . . one in the third year of his collegiate course in an American college, formerly called *Junior Sophister.*

***Juniper.**

The following examples indicate the loose way in which the term has been used in the United States.

1832 BROWNE *Sylva* 146 At New York, New Jersey and Pennsylvania, it is known by the name of White Cedar, and in Maryland, Virginia and North Carolina, by that of *Juniper.* **1834** in *Atlantic Mo.* XXVI. 491/2 Hemlock trees, exactly what we in Louisa [Co., Va.] have called juniper, on river hills. **1856** OLMSTED *Slave States* 151 A great many long rough poles of the juniper, under the name of 'cedar-rails,' are sent to New York. **a1862** THOREAU *Maine Woods* 213 The Indian called these [larch trees] juniper. **1894** *Amer. Folk-Lore* VII. 99 *Larix Americana,* . . . juniper, Penobscot Co., Me., Grand Lake region of Penobscot River, Me.

+**1.** Any one of various American coniferous trees resembling those of Europe belonging to the genus *Juniperus.*

1622 'MOURT' *Relation* 10 They found it to be a small neck of Land [near Cape Cod Bay]; . . . all wooded with Okes, Pines, Sassafras, Iuniper, Birch, Holly, Vines, some Ash, Walnut. **1720** D. NEAL *Hist. New-Eng.* I. 16 The Entrance [to Cape Cod Bay is] . . . encompass'd all round, even to the very Sea with Oaks, Pines, Juniper, Sassafras, and other sweet Woods. **1799** WELD *Travels* 102 [The Dismal Swamp] is entirely covered with trees; juniper and cypress trees grow where there is most moisture. **1825** NEAL *Bro. Jonathan* I. 127 [The graveyard] was now overgrown with patches of juniper—ground hemlock—mullein—thistle—and sweet briar. **1883** SMITH *Geol. Survey Ala.* 289 The usual growth in the bottom lands consists of magnolia, bay, ti-ti, sweet-leaf, juniper. **1916** THOBURN *Stand. Hist. Okla.* I. 5 The most common species of trees in Oklahoma include . . . walnut, juniper (two species), pine [etc.].

2. Attrib. with *bucket, bush, kind,* etc.

1785 MARSHALL *Amer. Grove* 70 *Juniperus.* The Juniper Tree. . . . The flowers are Male and Female on different plants. **1832** WILLIAMSON *Maine* I. 107 The red Cedar is the largest of the juniper kind. **1838** *S. Lit. Messenger* IV. 25 The juniper soil, which is vegetable, might perhaps be used as peat. **1866** A. D. WHITNEY *L. Goldthwaite* vi, An enormous valley, . . . over whose tall pines and cedars one looked, as if they were but juniper and blueberry bushes. **1882** *Nation* Dec. 503/2 Roper . . . is doing a prosperous business in cutting up shingles and staves for juniper buckets. **1899** GOING *Flowers* 298 When the cedar- and juniper-seed are ripe the succulent globes which enclose them become purple.

Juniper berry. The berry of the juniper tree.

1724 *New-Eng. Courant* 10–17 Feb. 2/2 To be sold at his Shop, . . . good Jallop Root at 23s. per Pound, . . . and Juniper Berrys at 2s. per Pound. **1797** TRUMBULL *Hist. Conn.* I. 25 Juniperberries, barberries and bayberries, which are of the medicinal kind grow spontaneously in Connecticut. **1852** STOWE *Uncle Tom* xv, I'll have the first juniper-berries that get ripe in our garden by the lake brought in. **1878** *Rep. Indian Affairs* 115 The choke cherry and the juniper berry, are not palatable or nutritious.

attrib. **1852** STOWE *Uncle Tom* xv, Juniper-berry tea is good for sick-headache.

***Junk.**

+**1.** A tobacco pipe. *Obs.*

1704 S. KNIGHT *Journal* 29 Having 'litt, [he] makes an Awkerd Scratch wth his Indian shoo, and a Nodd, sitts on ye block, fumbles out his black Junk, dipps it in ye Ashes, and presents it piping hott to his muscheeto's, and fell to sucking like a calf, without speaking. **1723** *New-Eng. Courant* 15–22 July 1/1 The Engine whence ascends this fragrant Funk [tobacco smoke], Modern Interpretations render *Junk.*

+**2.** Miscellaneous secondhand or discarded articles of little or no value. Also attrib.

1842 *Congress. Globe* 23 Feb. 261 Champagne was charged for under the head of 'old junk.' **1851** *Yale Tomahawk* Feb., The all receiving shop of some dealer in old junk. **1879** *Scribner's Mo.* May 34/1 These piers . . . are too narrow even for the circulation of a junk-cart. **1920** ALSAKER *Eating for Health* 195 You and I have to conform to the laws of nature, or else we are thrown into the junk heap.

+**Junk bottle.** A heavy bottle of thick, dark glass.

1805 *Naval Chron.* XIV. 65 The following article was found in a junk-bottle, taken up at the southward of the Vineyard. **1819** SCHOOLCRAFT *Mo. Lead Mines* 81 The principal kinds are the black junk bottle, and the common green bottle. **1881** *Maine Hist. Soc. Coll.* IX. 217 Sawyer drank the last drop of rum from his junk bottle. **1898** HARPER *S. B. Anthony* I. 36 It was said that great numbers of junk bottles had been laid under the floor to give especially nice tone to the fiddles.

+**Junk dealer.** A dealer in marine stores; one who buys and sells secondhand or cast-off articles. — **1869** *Boyd's Business Directory* 39 Junk Dealers, McCarthy C. & P. **1882** SALA *Amer. Revisited* (1885) v. 70 The marine store or 'junk' dealer, as he is styled in New-York. **1912** NICHOLSON *Hoosier Chron.* 499 It was my car that got smashed! It looked like a junk dealer's back yard when they pulled us out.

Junker. +(See quotation.) — **1889** *Boston Herald* 3 Feb. 3/4 What was termed the junkers, parties who buy up old vessels and anything they think there is a little money in.

***Junket.** +(See quotation 1886.) Also transf. — **1886** *Detroit Free Press* 4 Sept. 4/2 The term 'junket' in America is generally applied to a trip taken by an American official at the expense of the government he serves so nobly and unselfishly. **1888** *Boston Journal* 10 Dec., An increasing city debt and extravagant expenditures for jobs and junkets are bad for the poor man as well as for the rich. **1894** *Columbus Dispatch* 6 Dec. 4/1 Delegates . . . regard a convention, not as a junket, but as serious business and are content if they are provided with facilities for doing their work. **1912** C. MATHEWSON *Pitching* 229 At last, after the long junket through the South . . . is ended, comes a welcome day, when the new uniforms are donned.

Junketer. {1825–} +An official who takes part in a political junket. (Cf. JUNKET.) — **1862** *N.Y. Tribune* 14 June (*Cent.*), On what principle . . . are these junketers . . . allowed the use of steamboats at an expense of from $300 to $500 per day? **1892** *Columbus Dispatch* 20 Oct., It would have been a matter of selfish precaution for the State and Legislative junketers to invite Dr. Probst to accompany them to Chicago.

***Junketing.**

+1. A political feast or banquet; a trip, refreshments, etc., enjoyed at public expense; indulging or participating in such outings. (Cf. JUNKET.) Also attrib. and ppl. a.

1809 IRVING *Knickerb.* VI. viii, The dinner went off much the same as do our great corporation junkettings and fourth of July banquets. **1843** *Pathfinder* 22 April, After all the parades, junkettings and speeches, . . . is there a single man who can honestly say that his lot has been improved by the result [of the election]? **1883** E. M. BACON *Dict. Boston* 359 Money spent in junketing by the city-fathers and their favourites. **1884** *Boston Jrnl.* 19 Sept., The Final Spasm of Junketing. A statement of the expenditures for refreshments charged to the city by members of the Common Council . . . shows a total of $546.10. **1891** *Boston Journal* 11 March 4/3 This was not to be a junketing trip, but a trip undertaken for a very serious purpose. **1899** *Chicago Record* 27 Jan. 2/2 The commission takes the place of the junketing committees that have hitherto visited the institutions.

2. Going on an excursion or pleasure trip; picnicking. Also attrib.

1820 *Amer. Farmer* I. 369 The frequent custom of husband and wife going a junketing on the same horse or 'beast,' as in those days it was more commonly called. **1884** 'MARK TWAIN' *H. Finn* xviii. 162 Sometimes a stack of people would come there . . . and have such junketings round about and on the river. **1888** *Century Mag.* May 112/2 Stories were current of reckless Virginia clergymen making junketing trips through the neighboring province [N.C.], and defraying their expenses by baptizing the people at so much a head.

+Junkman. A dealer in secondhand or discarded articles. — **1880** *Scribner's Mo.* Oct. 862/1 He is a day laborer, a truckman, a junkman or a rag-picker. **1895** *Outlook* 24 Aug. 304/2 What the Sheriff could get for the goods sold in a lump for cash . . . with possibly only a junkman for a bidder. **1901** *Scribner's Mag.* April 421/2 He had become the horse of a wandering junkman.

Junk shop. {1800–} +A shop in which miscellaneous secondhand or discarded articles are kept for sale. Also fig. — **c1849** PAIGE *Dow's Sermons* I. 256 Trash that wouldn't fetch two cents in the market of heaven, and but a trifle more in the junk-shops of hell. **1861** NEWELL *Orpheus C. Kerr* I. 86 If you find any old cannon around the junk-shops, just send them along. **1875** *Scribner's Mo.* Nov. 129/1 Tom has a mass of old rubbish collected at junk-shops. **1907** M. C. HARRIS *Tents of Wickedness* 398 Those trunks full of papers . . . worth just so much per pound as waste papers in the junk-shops.

+Junk store. =prec. — **1882** MCCABE *New York* 583 They gather up whatever they can find, and sell it to the junk and rag stores. **1888** *St. Louis Globe Dem.* 10 March (F.), A Junk Store Rifled. The second-hand store of Joseph Laschkowtz . . . was rifled of a large lot of goods early yesterday morning.

+Junk yard. An area or enclosure where secondhand or wornout articles are collected. — **1880** CABLE *Grandissimes* 192 You may still here and there see one [villa] standing . . . among founderies, cotton and tobacco-sheds, junk-yards, and longshoremen's hovels. **1891** WELCH *Recoll. 1830–40* 141 Those boats which were hurriedly built and early relegated to the junk yard.

Junta. {1623–} *S.W.* [Sp.] A deliberative council or meeting. — **1836** HOLLEY *Texas* xiii. 311 A junta and regency were established, at the head of which was placed Iturbide. **1847** *Santa Fe Republican* 9 Oct. 2/1 A *junta* of the principal generals of the army took place yesterday. **1885** *Wkly. New Mexican Rev.* 30 April 2/5 Had your minds not been inflamed in secret 'juntas' and by-places by lies most damnable, this disgrace . . . could not have occurred.

Junto. {1641–} A meeting of a deliberative body; a political clique, faction, or cabal. (Cf. ESSEX JUNTO.)

1666 ALSOP *Maryland* (1869) II. 47 Burgesses . . . commonly sit in Junto about six weeks. **1702** C. MATHER *Magnalia* (1853) I. 176 This Junto made a law, which prohibited the inhabitants of any town to meet about their town affairs above once in a year. **1789** S. LOW *Politician Outwitted* IV. i, You and your vile junto of perfidious politicians want to *Latin* us out of our liberties. **1803** J. Q. ADAMS *Diary* 17 Coalition of the Jacobin party so called with the Junto. **1806** in *Life & Corr. Cutler* II. 326 J. Randolph and some of his fast friends lead the Southern Junto. **1813** CLAY *Speeches* (1860) I. 38 He . . . shall live only in the treasonable annals of a certain junto. **1893** *Advance* 26 Oct., By administration [of N.Y. City] I mean that junto of cut-throats, whiskey-guzzlers, harlot-keepers and dive-manipulators, beneath whose heel our city is groveling.

+b. (See quotation.)

1771 FRANKLIN *Representative Selections* (1936) 58, I had formed most of my ingenious Acquaintance into a Club of mutual Improvement, which we called the Junto.

Jurel. One or other species of carangoid fishes, esp. *Paratractus crysos*, found along the southern coast of the U.S. {1772, near S. Amer.} — **1884** GOODE, etc. *Fisheries* I. 324 The Jurel . . . is occasionally brought to the New York market, but is of no special importance as an article of food north of the Gulf of Mexico. **1896** JORDAN & EVERMANN *Check-List Fishes* 346 *Caranx crysos.* Hard-tail; Runner; Jurel; Yellow Mackerel. . . . Cape Cod to Brazil. *Ib.*, *Caranx caballus.* Cocinero; Jurel; Cocinero Dorado. Pacific Coast of tropical America, San Diego to Panama. *Ib.*, *Caranx latus.* Jurel; Xurel; Horse-eye Jack. All warm seas, north to Virginia.

***Juror.** Also †**jurer.** A member of a jury. Also attrib. — **1636** *Conn. Rec.* I. 4 A Jurer shalbe wthdrawen. **1721** *Boston Rec.* 164 Voted that there be new Books procured for Entring Jurors Names. **1833** *Trial E. K. Avery* 4 The regularly drawn jurors, fourteen in number, were called. **1911** *Okla. Session Laws* 3 Legisl. 151 [The money is] to be paid out of the court fund in favor of the legal holders of juror vouchers issued by the district clerk of Greer county.

***Jury.** A body of men legally impaneled and empowered to render a verdict upon the basis of evidence presented before them.

1623 *Plymouth Laws* 28 It was ordained . . . that all criminall facts . . . should be tried by the verdict of twelve honest men to be impanelled by authority in forme of a jury upon their oath. **1692** *Witchcraft Cases* 172 What can the Jury or Judges desire more, to convict any man of witchcraft? **1724** SEWALL *Diary* III. 329 The Jury returned that he was *Non Compos.* **1776** *Decl. Independence*, For depriving us, in many cases, of the benefits of trial by jury. **1828** NEAL *R. Dyer* 96 You cannot address the jury. **1893** *Harper's Mag.* May 976/2 The counsel glanced up at the judge . . . and then at the jury. 'I would like to poll the jury,' he said. **1900** *Penna. Rep.* CXCVII. 550 The language of the district attorney . . . was a statement to the jury of the position taken by the commonwealth.

b. *Jury of trial(s)*, a trial jury. *Obs.*

1675 *Topsfield Rec.* I. 18 Jacob towne Is Chosen to sarue one the Juri of trialls at Ipswich Corte next insuing. **1695** *Manchester Rec.* 68 John Elathorpe & Samuell Lee . . . serve in ye Jury of tryalls att ye superior court of judicature cort of Assize. **1698** SEWALL *Diary* I. 483 Inpanel'd a Jury of Trial.

+c. *Jury of view*, (see quotation). *Obs.*

1895 'CRADDOCK' *Myst. Witch-Face Mt.* 96 This engine of the law . . . consist[ed] of one road commissioner and two freeholders, the trio still . . . denominated a 'jury of view.'

d. Attrib. with *bench, lawyer, list, trial.*

1799 in Rothert *Muhlenberg Co.* 45 The cracks of the house to have shaved boards . . . and a sufficient number of jury benches. **1835** *S. Lit. Messenger* I. 423 Our statesmen have been governed by a fixed design to bring jury-trial itself into disrepute. **1902** WHITLOCK *13th District* 53 General Bancroft . . . was the best jury lawyer we ever had there. **1917** SINCLAIR *King Coal* 152 There are some three hundred men on our jury-list, and we know them all.

Jury box.

+1. A box in which the names of prospective jurors are deposited.

1738 *Boston Selectmen* 159 [The names of] Persons . . . Qualified and lyable to Serve on the Petit Jury, . . . may be put into the Jury Box, as the Law directs. **1832** WILLIAMSON *Maine* II. 349 Others [legislative acts], in 1760, made it the duty of towns to keep two jury-boxes,—from one of which all jurors were to be drawn, except the petit jurors to the Common Pleas and Sessions, who were to be taken from the other box. **1843** *Knickerb.* XXI. 190 He had read . . . the names which had been put into the jury-box.

2. The enclosed space occupied by a jury. {1826–}

1823 COOPER *Pioneers* xxxiii, At either of its [the room's] ends were rows of seats, rising one over the other, for jury-boxes. **1847** in Stowe *Key* 94/2 If any of them were disturbed with doubts or scruples on this point, he scarcely supposed they would have gone into the jury-box. **1887** *Courier-Journal* 12 Jan. 4/3 A great lawyer . . . used always to keep his eye on the most idiotic-looking face in the jury-box, as a test of the progress he was making. **1899** in *Congress. Rec.* 15 Jan. (1900) 824/2 Your life may be placed in the hands of your neighbor who is summoned to sit in the jury box.

Jury duty. a. The obligation of a citizen to serve on a jury. **b.** Jury service. — **1837** *S. Lit. Messenger* III. 644 The same free person of color enjoys an exemption from militia, from patrol, from fire and jury duty. **1857** OLMSTED *Journey through Texas* 127 Though everyone was glad to be rid of jury-duty . . . no one liked to be classed . . . as unfit for it. **1893** *Harper's Mag.* April 708/1 Women are exempt from jury duty, from military service and from work upon the highways.

+Jury-fixer. One who bribes or attempts to bribe or otherwise illegally influence a juror. Also *jury-fixing. colloq.* — **1882** *Washington Post* 18 March (Th.), There was an idea abroad that there might be some scope in the proceedings before the Grand Jury for a 'jury fixer.' **1887** *Library Mag.* April 531/2 Bribery and jury-fixing would speedily disappear [if the requirement of unanimous verdicts were abolished]. **1890** *N.Y. Tribune* 8 Aug. (Th. S.), The juries were at the mercy of the jury-fixers, then as now. **1895** *Nation* 9 May 357/3 Clearly, nobody but the criminals and the 'jury fixers' are interested in the continuance of the present state of things. **1901** FLYNT *World of Graft* 159 The Powers that Rule . . . to whom he [the thief] pays the greater part of his corruption fund, are the policeman, the district attorney, the 'court,' and the 'jury fixer.'

***Juryman.** A member of a jury; a juror. — **1637** *Conn. Rec.* I. 9 It is ordered yt every Juryman shall haue six pence for every accion that is given to them vppon evidence. **1708** *Boston News-Letter* 22–29 March 2/2 Just out of the Press, . . . A Guide to Jury men, Constables, Surveyors of Highways, . . . &c. As also their Oaths, Power and Duty. **1819** *Western Rev.* I. 101 Jurymen, taken from the community indiscriminately, have a mutual interest with those whose causes they determine. **1890** LANGFORD *Vigilante Days* (1912) 145 One of the jurymen said that the prisoners ought never to have been tried by a jury, but in a miners' court.

Jury-packing. The placing, on a jury, of persons who are expected to favor a particular verdict. {1887–} *colloq.* — **1870** *Nation* 31 March 202/1 Jury-packing is a device very soon exhausted, and which, like all prostitution of judicial forms, rouses popular indignation. **1887** *Courier-Journal* 18 Feb. 5/2 Sexton had already placed a motion referring to jury-packing.

Jury room. A room for the use of a jury during its deliberations. {a1832–} — **1770** in Summers *Ann. S.W. Va.* 77 A log cabbin . . . for a Court House, with a clapboard roof with two small sheads, one at each end for jury rooms. **1806** in Commons, etc. *Doc. Hist.* III. 133 If you take this book into the jury room with you, when you retire [etc.]. **1853** BALDWIN *Flush Times Ala.* 322, [I] took him into the vacant jury-room on the same floor. **1902** HARBEN *A. Daniel* 295 Abner Daniel leaned in the doorway opening into one of the jury-rooms.

+**Jury wheel.** A revolving device used in an effort to insure the operation of chance in the drawing of names of prospective jurors. — **1882** S. D. THOMPSON & E. G. MERRIAM *Juries* 624 The jury wheel shall be secured against tampering [by being sealed]. **1904** *Phila. Public Ledger* 8 Dec. 1 Some 7,000 names from which will be drawn those men who will sit as jurors next year were placed in the jury wheel yesterday. **1912** COBB *Back Home* 11 The clerk spun the jury wheel, which was a painted wooden drum on a creaking wooden axle, and drew forth a slip of paper with the name of a talesman written upon it.

***Just,** *adv.* +Used before a demonstrative or an interrogative introducing a subject clause. — **1884** GOODE, etc. *Fisheries* II. 543 Just what makes the best lodgement for oyster spawn . . . has been greatly discussed. *Ib.* 544 Just how many bushels a man will place on an acre depends upon both his means and his judgment. **1900** *School Rev.* June 322 Just this happened in Latin.

***Justice.** A public official authorized to hold court and try cases; a judicial officer.

1. A judge presiding over a criminal or civil court, as a justice of the peace, a judge of quarter sessions, etc.

a1649 GORGES *Descr. New-Eng.* iv. 47 There is assigned one Lieveten-ant, and eight Justices, to administer Justice for maintenance of the Publique Peace. **1690** *N.H. Hist. Soc. Coll.* I. 135 We had only the Justices and Inferior officers left. **1692** *Mass. Acts & Resolves* I. (1869) 356 The justices of the said courts . . . are hereby impowred and authorized . . . to chancer the forfeiture. **1707** *N.J. Archives* 1 Ser. III. 200 Raising this money was to desolve the then Assembly and get new Justices. **1794** *Ann. 4th Congress* 2 Sess. 2829 To every judge, justice, sheriff, brigade inspector . . . residing in the western counties, a letter was addressed. **1873** *Newton Kansan* 27 Feb. 4/3 About two thirds of the suits decided by the female justices of Wyoming are appealed and the verdicts set aside. **1887** *Courier-Journal* 11 Jan. 6/3 Although formerly a 'fat' place, several of the Justices [city magistrates] are scarcely able to make a living out of the perquisites and fees of the office now. **1907** *St. Nicholas* May 632/1 The justice decided as he had also in the morning, that Jim need not be imprisoned.

+**2.** One of the judges of a state or federal court. *Justice of the Supreme Court,* a judge in the supreme court of a state or of the United States.

1789 MORSE *Amer. Geog.* 180 The salaries of governor and justices of the supreme court, cannot be diminished. **1809** *Ann. 10th Congress* 2 Sess. 1832 Justice of the supreme court shall thereupon issue his order, in the nature of a certiorari. **1839** *Knickerb.* XIII. 2 In this city [New York] alone, are three law courts; a superior court with three justices; a court of common pleas, with five, and a circuit judge of the first circuit. **1857** BENTON *Exam. Dred Scott Case* 125 Two of the Justices dissent entirely from the opinion of the Court, and give well reasoned arguments against that opinion, and in favor of a different one. **1894** *Harper's Mag.* April 797/1 His father is justice of the Supreme Court. **1907** ANDREWS *Recoll.* 39 His brother, . . . then a justice of the Supreme Court of the United States, had been Secretary of the Treasury. **1910** J. HART *Vigilante Girl* 307 He could not continue to appear in the case before the circuit court with his uncle as presiding justice.

***Justice court.** Also **justice's** or **justices' court.** A court presided over by a justice of the peace. Also attrib. — **1828** COOPER *Notions* II. 205 The lowest tribunal known to the laws, is what is called a justices, court, or the suits before a justice of the peace. **1867** 'LACKLAND' *Homespun* 240 Justice Courts furnish one of the staple entertainments of a country town, or village. **1881** *Harper's Mag.* May 879/2 He lived at the cross-roads, the justice's court ground, three miles further south from Dukesborough. **1893** 'THANET' *Stories* 106 Tommy . . . was graduated with honors, and came back to a large, ready-made justice court's practice.

***Justice of the peace.** A local officer whose duties consist chiefly of administering justice in minor cases, and committing those accused of graver offenses to a superior court for trial.

1630 *Mass. Bay Rec.* I. 74 Any justice of the peace may imprison an offender, but not inflict any corporall punishmt. **1665** in Hutchinson *Collection Orig. Papers Mass. Bay* (1769) 424 The commissioners, for necessity sake, have appoynted the best whom they could find, in each place, to be a justice of peace. **1693** *Boston Rec.* 215 At a meeting of the Selectmen with 2 of the Justices of the Peace . . . to consider and assigne places for Still houses. **1708** E. COOK *Sot-Weed Factor* 15 In the County-Court of Mary-Land, very few of the Justices of the Peace can write or read. **1788** FRANKLIN *Autobiog.* 375 The office of justice of the peace I try'd a little, by attending a few courts, and sitting on the bench to hear causes. **1809** KENDALL *Travels* I. 18 Justices of the peace . . . are considered as the civil authority of the town in which they dwell. **1893** *Harper's Mag.* Feb. 484 It was 'long about June, somewhere back in the seventies, when I was runnin' for justice o' the peace. **1913** LONDON *Valley of Moon* I. xiv, The next afternoon, at five, she and Billy were to go before a justice of the peace and be married.

Jute.

1. The fiber of either of two plants native to the East Indies and imported into the United States for making sacking, twine, etc.; the plant itself. {1746–}

1862 *Rep. Comm. Patents 1861: Agric.* 106 A cheap, thin article, . . . sold in this country as 'hemp carpeting,' is not hemp at all, but made of *jute.* **1867** HOLMES *Guardian Angel* 5 Several announcements of 'Feed,' whatever that may be . . . —also of 'Shorts,'—terms mysterious to city ears as *jute* and *cudbear* and *gunnybags* to such as drive oxen in the remote interior districts. **1870** *Rep. Comm. Agric. 1869* 58 The wholesale importation of jute and jute-butts has injured the market for this fiber [flax]. **1875** *Ib. 1874* 295 He was also led to believe that jute might attain its full growth in from three to four months. **1876** CROFUTT *Trans-continental Tourist* 148 Their principal business, at present, is the manufacture of burlaps for bags and wool-packs, from 'jute' imported from the West Indies.

2. Attrib. with *butt, canvas,* etc.

1870 Jute butt [see JUTE 1]. **1874** *Rep. Comm. Agric. 1873* 268 The first trial of a regular jute-culture has just been made in Louisiana. **1887** *Postal Laws* 333 Jute-Canvas Mail Sacks [are] . . . designed for printed and third and fourth class matter not registered. **1913** LONDON *Valley of Moon* I. xi, You worked in the jute mills, the cannery, the paper-box factory, the laundry.

+**Juvenile asylum.** A refuge for vagabond or homeless children. — **1856** *Porter's Spirit of Times* 18 Oct. 108/2 'The New York Juvenile Asylum' . . . [is designed] to provide a refuge for all the little vagabond children of both sexes, found prowling about the streets. **1856** MACLEOD *F. Wood* 289 Thus sat the Hon. Fernando Wood, Mayor of the City of New-York, . . . Director of the New-York Juvenile Asylum, Member of the Board of Trustees of the Astor Library, in his chair of state.

+**Juvenile court.** *Law.* A court, or a special part of a court, in which children's cases are tried. {1908– (*Act 8 Edw. VII* § 111)} Also attrib. — **1899** *Ill. Laws* 132 A special court room, to be designated as the juvenile court room, shall be provided . . . , and the court may, for convenience, be called the 'Juvenile Court.' **1914** *Cycl. Amer. Govt.* I. 500/1 In most of the states of the Union having juvenile courts, the law covers dependent, neglected and delinquent children. **1923** WATTS *L. Nichols* 39 Social workers, juvenile-court officials, humanitarians of every brand, would long since have reported the case.

K

+**Ka-.** =CA-. (Cf. KER-.) — **1848** *S. Lit. Messenger* XIV. 686/2 Jim Collins . . . commonly fishes in a boat, and the dexterity with which he 'Kawallups' the fish upon his lap is truly astonishing. **1855** 'P. PAXTON' *Capt. Priest.* 93 There he goes kalumpus right by the big apple tree. *a***1859** *N.Y. Spirit of Times* (B.), I kasoused the old cock into a bucket of boilin' water. **1914** ATHERTON *Perch of Devil* i. 45 She had been 'brought up' rich, . . . and then come down kaplunk.

+**Kadoodle,** *v. intr.* To sport, play. *colloq.* — **1875** HOLLAND *Sevenoaks* 232, I have a little game with a rovin' angel that comes kadoodlin' round me.

+**Kaeding('s) petrel.** [f. Henry B. *Kaeding.*] A species of petrel (*Oceanodroma leucorhoa kaedingi*) found on the Pacific coast. — **1898** *Auk* XV. 37 Kaeding's Petrel [is found] . . . from Socorro and Clarion Islands to Southern California. **1917** *Birds of Amer.* I. 86 On Three Arch Rocks off the Oregon coast, we found both the Forked-tailed and the Kaeding Petrels nesting.

Kaf(f)ir corn. Any of several grain sorghums derived from *Sorghum vulgare*, used for forage esp. in the Southwest. {1836–} +Hence *Kafir corner*, (see quot. 1913).

1889 VASEY *Agric. Grasses* 37 *Sorghum vulgare.* This name as at present applied includes . . . millo maize, Kaffir corn, dourra, and broom corn. **1896** W. A. WHITE *Real Issue* 79 The kaffir corn, the grass, . . . curled up under their fiery breath from the southwestern desert. **1897** *Okla. Governor Rep.* 26 The farmers planted largely of Kafir corn up to as late as July 10. **1901** MOHR *Plant Life Ala.* 135 Various kinds of sorghum, known as durrha or kafir corn, millo maize, and pearl millet. **1913** BARNES *Western Grazing Grounds* 89 During the past few years a new type of settler, the dry farmer or 'kafer corn-er,' as he is often called, has worked great changes in the western ranges, especially in the Great Plains region lying east of the Rocky Mountains.

+**Kaintuck.** Also **Caintuck.** =KENTUCK. Often in the phrase *Old Kaintuck. colloq.*

1795 J. & E. PETTIGREW *Let.* 25 May (Univ. N.C. MS.), They expect to set off for Caintuck about the first of september. **1819** QUITMAN in Claiborne *Life Quitman* I. 42 Made fast at night to the Kentucky shore. Nine cheers went up for 'Old Kaintuck.' **1835** HOFFMAN *Winter in West* II. 119 No, stranger, there's no place on the universal 'arth like old Kaintuck: she whips all 'Out-west' in prettiness. **1864** NICHOLS *Amer. Life* I. 387 The south-western man was born in old Kaintuck, raised in Mississippi. **1894** CHOPIN *Bayou Folk* 132 Ole Kaintuck. . . . Dat ain't no sech kentry as dis heah.

b. Attrib. with *bill, fashion, rifle.*

1850 LEWIS *La. Swamp Doctor* 85 Here's a five-dollar Kaintuck bill, take your pay and gin us the change. **1855** *Amer. Inst. N.Y. Trans.* 583 Seventy years ago, some American made rifles in the Western country, . . . which soon bore the name of *Kain Tuck rifle.* **1872** *Harper's Mag.* XLIV. 544/1 If you and I should ever have the pleasure of meeting again, you must expect me to defend myself *Kaintuck* fashion.

*****Kale.** Also **kail. 1.** A variety of cabbage with curled leaves that do not form a dense head. +**2.** Money. Originally *kale seed. slang.* — **(1) 1804** LEWIS in *L. & Clark Exped.* VI. (1905) 143 It is a species of rope or kail, it grows on the beach of the river, when young my men used it [as] a boiled green and found [it] healthy and pleasant. **1817–8** EATON *Botany* (1822) 211 *Brassica napus*, kale or cole. **1895** *Dept. Agric. Yrbk. 1894* 391 In the following cases a large portion, though perhaps not one-half, of the seeds are foreign grown: Cabbage, celery, chervil, kale, and lettuce. **(2) 1902** MUNN *Rockhaven* 4 'Wal,' he says, pullin' out a roll o' bills. . . . 'Here's the kale seed.' **1922** PARRISH *Case & Girl* 313, I've got just as much right to all that kale as she has.

*****Kali.** Also †**kaly.** The glasswort, *Salsola kali.* — **1766** STORK *Acct. E. Florida* 49 This herb resembles entirely our samphire in England, and is called Barilla or kaly. **1792** *Ann. 2d Congress* 1030 The salts of various plants, particularly of the seaweed [*sic*] kali or kelp, constitute the essential ingredients.

Kalmia. [After Peter *Kalm*, Swedish botanist (1715–79).] A genus of North American evergreen shrubs of the family Ericaceae, the principal species being the American laurel, *K. latifolia;* a plant or flower of this genus. Also attrib. {calmia, 1784–}

1785 MARSHALL *Amer. Grove* 71 Kalmia, or American Laurel. **1805** BENTLEY *Diary* III. 166 The young ladies furnished themselves with the Kalmia, swamp apples, etc. **1878** COOKE *Happy Dodd* 347 With . . . glittering clusters of Kalmia leaves . . . she adorned all the rooms. **1887** PERRY *Flock of Girls* 16 Judy had a knot of scarlet kalmias on her shoulder.

b. With distinguishing adjectives.

1785 MARSHALL *Amer. Grove* 72 Narrow leaved Kalmia . . . delights in moist or swampy places. *Ib.* 72 Broad leaved Kalmia. **1821** *Amer. Jrnl. Science* III. 276 June 4. Visited the bog in Goshen, [Mass.] where I found . . . the glaucous kalmia.

Kalsomine, *n.* Also **calcimine.** (See quotations 1864 and 1875.) {1840–} — **1864** WEBSTER 184/3 *Calcimine*, . . . a superior kind of white or colored wash for walls. *Hart.* **1875** KNIGHT 1222/1 *Kalsomine*, a mixture of clear glue, Paris white, and water, laid on a wall as whitewash. **1883** *Harper's Mag.* March 503/2 Violent storms occur, and paint and kalsomine can not be counted upon for long duration. **1906** PRINGLE *Rice Planter* 415, I have bought some kalsomine, and every minute which can be spared from getting in the hay Jim is kalsomining.

Kalsomine, *v.* Also **calcimine.** *tr.* (See quot. 1864.) Also *vbl. n.* and *adj.* {1888–} — **1864** WEBSTER 184 *Calcimine*, to wash or cover with calcimine; as, to *calcimine* walls. **1873** [see KALSOMINER]. **1891** BUNNER *Zadoc Pine* 166 Inside of it there were white kalsomined bedrooms. **1916** WILSON *Somewhere* 135 [He] began to paper and paint and grain and kalsomine.

+**Kalsominer.** Also **calciminer.** A workman whose business is kalsomining. — **1873** *Winfield* (Kan.) *Courier* 11 Jan. 1/2 Painting, Sign-writing, Kalsomining, Paper hanging and all kinds of work in the painting line. Paper-hangers, Kalsominers and Gilders. **1885** *Advance* 4 June 361 Yesterday the calciminers invaded our dwelling. **1916** WILSON *Somewhere* 128 He was a painter and grainer and kalsominer and paperhanger.

+**Kamas.** =CAMAS. Also attrib., esp. with *root.* — **1832** WYETH *Journal* 172 [The] Indians . . . dig the Kamas root. *Ib.* 202 Kamas in bloom. The Indians are taking large quantities of it. **1851** M. REID *Scalp Hunters* 305 There were also dried fruits and vegetables, chilé, roots of the kamas, etc. *a***1861** WINTHROP *Canoe & Saddle* iii. 33 [The Whulgeamish Indians] dig sweet kamas bulbs in the swamps. **1873** BEADLE *Undevel. West* 751 The staple food of the Diggers is of acorns, grass-seeds, pine nuts and kamas roots.

Kanaka. Also **Kanacka.** +A native of a Pacific island, settled or working in California.

[**1840** DANA *Two Years* xx. 198 The Catalina had several Kanakas on board.] **1848** BRYANT *Calif.* 303 The natives of the Sandwich Islands (*Kanackas*, as they are called) are, without doubt, the most expert watermen in the world. **1849** T. T. JOHNSON *Sights in Gold Region* 141 Pitching our tent on the borders of the American River, we found ourselves surrounded by Peruvians, Chilians, Mexicans, Kanakas and our own countrymen. **1859** J. W. PALMER *New & Old* 89 (*Cent.*), In the rough winter of Forty-nine and Fifty the poor *Kanakas* of San Francisco, quite childlike in their helplessness, . . . died under filthy sheds of hide, and in the bush. **1890** HARTE *Heritage of Dedlow Marsh* 33 You'll go out among the hounds ez allowed your mother was a Spanish nigger or a kanaka.

+**Kangaroo court.** An unauthorized or irregular court conducted with either a disregard for or a perversion of legal procedure, as a mock court held by prisoners in a jail, or an irregularly conducted court in a frontier district. *colloq.*

1853 'P. PAXTON' *Yankee in Texas* 205 By a unanimous vote, Judge G. . . . was elected to the bench, and the 'Mestang' or 'Kangaroo Court' regularly organized. **1890** *Stock Grower & Farmer* 17 May 5/3 Organizing 'kangaroo courts' for the slightest offense, were some of their every day amusements. **1895** *Harper's Mag.* April 718/2 The most interesting of these impromptu clubs is the one called in the vernacular the 'Kangaroo Court.' It is found almost entirely in county jails. **1912** THORNTON 507 *Kangaroo court*, a sham trial court, especially one conducted by prisoners.

+**Kangaroo mouse.** {1888 Australia}

1. a. =DEER MOUSE. Loosely applied. **b.** Any of various jumping mice of the genus *Zapus.*

1857 *Rep. Comm. Patents 1856: Agric.* 96 This animal is known as the 'Long-tailed Deer Mouse,' 'Fob-tailed Mouse,' 'Kangaroo Mouse.' **1876** MILLER *First Families* 243 Wood-rats, kangaroo-mice, . . . had gone into winter-quarters under the great logs. **1909** WEBSTER 1171/3 They [jumping mice] undergo true hibernation in winter. Called also, erroneously, *kangaroo mouse.*

2. a. =KANGAROO RAT. Loosely applied. **b.** Any of various pocket mice of the genus *Perognathus.*

1874 COUES *Birds N.W.* 366 In the stomachs of those [buzzards] examined I found the remains of burrowing pouched-rats, . . . kangaroo-mice (*Dipodomys ordii*) and some *Arvicolae.* **1889** *Cent.* 3265/1 The kangaroo-mice are closely related to the species of *Dipodomys* . . . but are smaller. They inhabit the same parts of the United States.

Kangaroo rat. {1788– in Australia} +Any of several pouched rodents of the genera *Dipodomys, Perodipus,* and *Microdipodops*, found in the West. — **1867** *Amer. Naturalist* I. 394 They are known in the vernacular as 'Kangaroo' or 'Jumping' Rats and Mice, and are entirely confined to Transmississippian regions. *Ib.* 395 The Pouched Kangaroo Rat . . . is one of the most abundant of the Rodents about Fort Whipple [in Ariz.], where it more nearly takes the place of the house rat. **1890** *Stock Grower & Farmer* 4 Jan. 7/2, I also found a queer sort of kangaroo rat, a mouse with jackass ears, and another kind of a mouse with pockets in its cheeks . . . in the Grand Canon. **1917** *Mammals of Amer.* 260 It is unfortunate that the name 'Kangaroo Rat' has become attached to this group of beautiful rodents; for . . . 'they are as unratlike as they are widely removed from the Marsupials.'

+**Kani(c)kani(c)k.** =KINNIKINNICK. — **1839** TOWNSEND *Narrative* ii. 146 He smokes the article called kanikanik,—a mixture of tobacco and the dried leaves of the poke plant. **1847** LANMAN *Summer in Wilderness* 87 A bag of ka-nick-a-nick and tobacco was circulated, and a cloud of fragrant smoke ascended to the sky.

+**Kansa, Kansas.** Also **Kans, Konsas,** etc.

1. One of a tribe of Siouan Indians formerly in Kansas, but now in Oklahoma; also, usu. in pl., this tribe.

For variants of the name and for earlier non-English references, see Hodge *Amer. Indians* I. 655 f.

1741 D. COXE *Carolana* 11 Upon the river Ousoutiwy . . . dwell . . . the Kansæ, Mintou Erabacha and others. **1804** CLARK in *Lewis & C. Exped.* I. (1904) 64 We camped after dark . . . opposit the 1st old village of the Kanzes which was Situated in a Valley. **1808** PIKE *Sources Miss.* 140 The Kans had stolen some horses. **1824** *18th Congress 1 Sess.* Sen. Doc. No. 56, 9 The tribes personally known to me . . . [include] the Kansas, whose permanent residence is on the Kansas river. **1843** MARRYAT *M. Violet* ix, The same original tribe having given birth to the Konsas, the Mandans, the Tetons, the Yangtongs, [etc.]. **1847** PARKMAN in *Knickerb.* XXIX. 313 The Shawanoes . . . both in appearance and in character form a marked contrast to our late acquaintance, the Kanzas. **1867** RICHARDSON *Beyond Miss.* 29 'Kansas,' signifying 'smoky,' is the name of a degraded and nearly extinct Indian tribe. **1907** HODGE *Handbook* I. 654/1 The Kansa figured but slightly in the history of the country until after the beginning of the 19th century.

2. Attrib. with *Indian, nation, tribe.*

1806 in Pike *Sources Miss.* 107 You are to turn your attention to the accomplishment of a permanent peace between the Kanses and Osage nations. **1844** LEE & FROST *Oregon* x. 115 We reached the Kanzas Indians, who are located seven days' journey from Independence. **1847** COYNER *Lost Trappers* 27 Big White said they were the Kansas tribe, a fierce and warlike nation.

+**Kansan.** A person who resides in Kansas. — **1868** J. N. HOLLOWAY *Hist. Kansas* 574 At a favorable opportunity the Kansans seized the Ruffians, . . . and held them for trial. They gave them a drum-head trial. **1882** *N.Y. Tribune* 12 July, Time will establish a local character by which the West Kansan may be ticketed and characterized. The East Kansan is already a well-marked species. **1888** D. D. FIELD *Speeches, Arguments* (1890) III. 369 Nebraskan, Kansan, Arkansan, Minnesotan, are the true designations of the citizens of those flourishing States, from whose names they are derived.

+**Kansas.** [From KANSA.] A territory and state of the United States. Used attrib.

1. Designating things associated in some way with Kansas.

1848 BRYANT *California* iv. 47 We counted, . . . on our arrival, to be received and entertained by the female *élite* of the Kansas aristocracy. **1857** DANA *Great West* 201 This Kanzas marble exists in abundance, and makes very beautiful and substantial buildings. **1888** *Harper's Mag.* June 39/2 People speak of its strongest gales as 'Kansas zephyrs.' **1898** *Kansas City Star* 18 Dec. 2/3 After the Kansas boom collapsed the property of Mr. Collins shrank. **1907** *St. Nicholas* June 692/1 He could talk interestingly on a hundred subjects, and could be as breezy as a Kansas cyclone.

2. Designating things associated with the struggle over the admission of Kansas as a state.

1856 *Porter's Spirit of Times* 25 Oct. 126/1 In our happy and beautiful Territory [Minnesota], where we have no bloody Kansas scenes to deplore, there yet roam the buffalo and the elk. **1857** *Lawrence* (Kan.) *Republican* 28 May 1 Twenty-one were sentenced by the Kansas Jeffries to five years hard labor with ball and chain. **1859** WILMER *Press Gang* 123 Is the Kansas issue . . . a matter which concerns the people of the United States more than that tremendous system of corruption?

+**Kansas-Nebraska Bill.** Also **Kansas and Nebraska Bill, Kansas-Nebraska Act.** An act passed by Congress in 1854, organizing the territories of Kansas and Nebraska, and leaving the question of slavery to local option.

Cf. NEBRASKA.

1855 in Hambleton *H. A. Wise* 192, I know very little about the Kansas and Nebraska Bill. **1857** BENTON *Exam. Dred Scott Case* 37 This fundamental Territorial law . . . became the basis of all Territorial governments down to the passage of the Kansaz-Nebraska Act in 1854. **1857** *Lawrence* (Kan.) *Republican* 28 May 1 The Kansas-Nebraska bill was violently opposed . . . by a decided majority of the northern representatives. **1872** TICE *Over Plains* 27 The abrogation of the Missouri Compromise . . . and the passage of the Kansas-Nebraska bill by Congress, actually initiated the conflict which culminated in the rebellion and abolition of slavery. **1907** ANDREWS *Recoll.* 73 The year 1854 was memorable for the reopening of the slavery agitation by the passage of the Kansas-Nebraska bill, repealing the Missouri Compromise.

+**Kansas stable.** (See quot. 1886.) — **1885** *Harper's Mag.* June 5/1 Near by [was] the 'Kansas stable,' with its one horse only sheltered as to its head. **1886** EBBUTT *Emigrant Life in Kansas* 199 The stables were of the kind known as '*Kansas stables*,' that is built with a few forked posts stuck into the ground, with poles laid across, and the roof and sides built up with sods, brush, manure, and rubbish of all sorts.

+**Kansian.** =KANSAN. *Obsolescent.* — **1855** WHITMAN *Leaves of Grass* 58 Not only the free Utahan, Kansian, or Arkansian. **1873** BEADLE *Undevel. West* 214 It was laid out by a town company of ambitious Kansians. **1879** WHITMAN *Spec. Days* 141 We found a train ready and a crowd of hospitable Kansians to take us on to Lawrence.

+**Kanuck.** Also **Kanuk.**

1. =CANUCK 1.

1835 TODD *Notes* 92 Jonathan distinguishes a Dutch or French Canadian, by the term *Kanuk.* **1855** WHITMAN *Leaves of Grass* 16 Growing among black folks as among white, Kanuck, Tuckahoe, Congressman, Cuff, I give them the same. **1870** 'O. OPTIC' *Field & Forest* 280, I hedn't no 'fection for them pesky half breeds, nor them French Kanucks nuther. They are thick enough all along the [Arkansas] river. **1882** HOWELLS *Modern Instance* ix, Fridays I make up a sort of chowder for the Kanucks; they're Catholics, you know. **1888** ROOSEVELT in *Century Mag.* Oct. 832/2 One was a short, square-built, good-humored Kanuck . . . who interlarded his conversation with a . . . mixture of . . . French and English profanity.

2. A Canadian horse.

1860 HOLLAND *Miss Gilbert* 29, I'll hang on the tail of it and try legs with that little Kanuck of his.

+**Kanyon.** =CAÑON. (Cf. CANYON, KENYAN.) — **1843** FRÉMONT *Explor. Rocky Mts.* 58 In about three miles, we reached the entrance of a *kanyon*, where the Sweet Water issues upon the more open valley we had passed over. **1849** STANSBURY *Salt Lake* 275 Road leaves the river, and passes over hills to avoid kanyons. **1870** RAE *Westward by Rail* 94 The word 'Canyon' . . . is always used to denote those sudden depressions . . . which are common in Colorado, Utah, Nevada, and California. Some persons write the word in its Spanish form; others spell it 'Kanyon.'

Kaolin. A fine white clay used in the making of chinaware. {1727–41–} Also attrib. — **1807** JANSON *Stranger in Amer.* 229 Different kinds of clay are found here, among which it is believed, is the real kaolin, to which the porcelain of China owes its reputation. **1831** PECK *Guide* 45 In this cove [of Washita] are all kinds of earth . . . used in glass manufactories and iron foundries, amongst which is kaolin, for making porcelain, and abundance of materials for glass. **1868** *Rep. Comm. Agric. 1867* 113 Immense beds of kaolin and superior buhrstone and marl in Barnwell and other districts [of S.C.]. **1881** *Harper's Mag.* Feb. 361/1 Analyses have proved American kaolins to be both richer and finer than foreign clays. **1888** *Outing* May 108 The logging does not, of course, affect the quicksands nor the kaolin beds that one comes across.

+**Karimption.** *W.* 'A squad' (B. '59). **1859** *Cairo* (Ill.) *Times* (B. '59), A whole karimption of Dutch emigrants were landed here yesterday.

Katherine. =CATHERINE PEAR. — **1709** LAWSON *Carolina* 109 The Warden-Pear here proves a good eating Pear; . . . Katharine excellent. **1749** *Holyoke Diaries* (1911) 11 Katherine Pears ripe.

+**Katowse.** (See quotation.) — **1859** BARTLETT 224 *Katowse,* (Germ. *Getöse,*) a din, tumult, rumpus; as, 'What a *katowse* you are making!' New England.

+**Katydid.** Also **Kittydid.** [Echoic.] Any of several large, green, arboreal, orthopterous insects of the family Locustidae, which produce a noise suggested by the name. (Cf. CATADED, CATYDID.)

1784 J. F. D. SMITH *Tour U.S.* II. 387 There is a very singular insect in this island [L.I.], which I do not remember to have observed in any other part of America. They are named by the inhabitants here *Katy did's.* **1811** SUTCLIFF *Travels* (1815) 268, I was entertained with the harmony . . . of the bull frogs, tree frogs, kittydids . . . , and a variety of other animals. **1835** *Knickerb.* VI. 184 Bull-frogs, screech-owls, and katydids performed the musical part of the drama. **1850** S. WARNER *Wide, Wide World* xxxix, The cricket and grasshopper and tree toad and katy-did, and nameless other songsters, kept up a concert. **1875** 'MARK TWAIN' *Sk., New & Old* 127 At the head of the column a great band of Bumble-Bees, Mosquitoes, Katy-Dids and Crickets discoursed martial music. **1900** MUNN *Uncle Terry* 269 She sat on the porch and heard the katydids in the fast thinning foliage of the elms.

+**Kaw.** =KANSA. — **1844** GREGG *Commerce of Prairies* I. 41 The Kaws (or Kansas Indians) . . . prowl about those prairies, and steal from the caravans. **1868** *N.Y. Herald* 4 Aug. 8/1 The Kiowas have . . . made war upon the Kaws. **1872** *Newton Kansan* 26 Sept. 2/1 [The Quaker Indians] are something like the Kaws. **1873** *Ib.* 10 April 2/1 The Kaw Indians are to be removed south to the new reservation.

Kay. =KEY.[3] {kaay, 1726} — **1761** J. GLEN *Descr. S. Carolina* 63 A pretty many Indians among the Kays, about the Cape of Florida, . . . might be easily secured to the British Interest. **1859** BARTLETT 224 *Kay, Cay, Key,* (Span. *cayo,*) a small island or rock in the sea. The term is generally applied to those on the Florida coast.

+**Kayuse.** Also **Cayuse.** In pl., a tribe of Indians formerly occupying territory in Washington and Oregon. (Cf. CAYUSE.) — **1838** PARKER *Jrnl.* 126 We called at an encampment of Cayuse Indians of about a dozen lodges. **1843** DE SMET *Lett. & Sk.* 220 Several of the nation, have been baptized; . . . also the Shuyelpi . . . Kayuses, Attayes [etc.]. **1850** HINES *Voyage* 12 The merits of the different portions of the country were considered, the Flat Heads, the Nez Perces, the Kayuses, and other tribes.

+**Kazoo.** A musical instrument used by children, consisting of a tube, inside which is stretched a piece of cat gut which vibrates and makes a sound when one hums into it. — **1884** *Lisbon* (Dak.) *Star* 31 Oct., A kazoo is an instrument invented to give pleasure and satisfaction to the small boy. **1885** *Century Mag.* August 511/1 Banjos, and musical tools of even greater deadliness, are now brought out. The 'kazoo' is admired. **1904** *N.Y. Sun* 2 Sept. 5 Dear Edna sang as usual out of tune and with a quality of voice that resembled a solo on the gentle kazoo.

+**Kearneyism.** [Denis *Kearney*, Irish-American labor agitator (1847–1907).] (See quot. 1914.) — **1879** *Congress. Rec.* 13 Feb. 1266, I believe in the rights of property; I believe in peace and order; I have no sympathy with Kearneyism. *Ib.* App. 28 Jan. 51/1 Kearneyism, with all that the term implies, is not the cause of the discontent and clamor coming from the Pacific coast. **1914** *Cycl. Amer. Govt.* II. 277/1 *Kearneyism*, a term signifying the policy of driving out Chinese laborers by violent measures if necessary [etc.]

+**Kearnyite.** (See quotation.) — **1885** *Mag. Amer. Hist.* Feb. 201/2 *Kearnyites.*—Followers of one Dennis Kearny, a Communist, who a few years since commanded quite a strong faction among discontented working men. For a time he made his headquarters in what were known as the 'Sand Lots,' near San Francisco.

+**Keboodle.** =CABOODLE. — **1884** L. W. BALDWIN *Yankee School Teacher in Va.* 27, I wish the hull keboodle on ye a Merry Christmas. **1898** *Mo. So. Dakotan* I. 135 Good boy, come, clk, clk, confound the brute, he'll wake up the whole keboodle! Nice doggie.

* **Keel,** *n.*[1] [Du. *kiel*, 'ship,' 'boat.'] A cargo boat, narrow, not so large as a barge, and used chiefly on rather narrow, shallow rivers. Now hist. (Cf. KEEL BOAT.)

1785 DENNY *Journal* 57 Our fleet now consists of twelve small keels and batteaux. **1803** LEWIS in *Journals of L. & Ordway* 55 Overtook two keels from Louisville bound to Kaskaskias loaded with dry goods and whiskey. **1810** CUMING *Western Tour* 75 The navigation of the Allegheny is easy for boats called *keels* from fifty to seventy feet long, sharp at both ends, drawing little water, carrying a good burden, and calculated to be set against the stream, so as to surmount it from eight to twenty miles a day in proportion to the strength of the current operating against them. **1836** J. HALL *Statistics of West* 218 [Pirogues] were succeeded by the barge [and] the keel. . . . Of the two . . . the keel was longer, had less depth, and was better fitted to run in narrow and shallow channels. **1883** 'MARK TWAIN' *Life on Miss.* i, Some hundreds [of rivers subordinate to the Mississippi] . . . are navigable by flats and keels.

***Keel,** *n.*[2] [ON *kjölr*, 'keel.'] +A yacht constructed with a keel instead of a centerboard. Also attrib. — **1883** *Harper's Mag.* Aug. 443/2 Two keels are being laid down to every centre-board designed.

+**Keel,** *v.* [f. KEEL *n.*[1]]

+**1.** *intr.* To turn over, faint, collapse. Freq. with *up*, *over*. {1895–}

1832 S. SMITH *Major Downing* 98 [The horse] keeled up and couldn't go another step. **1850** LEWIS *La. Swamp Doctor* 174 Vim! I tuck him over the head, and, cochunk, he keeled over. **1851** MELVILLE *Moby-Dick* cxxix. 588 If thou speakest thus to me much more, Ahab's purpose keels up in him. **1861** NEWELL *Orpheus C. Kerr* I. 20, I only keeled for the shake of a tail. **1896** ADE *Artie* xiv. 125 This afternoon I thought I'd keel over. **1918** FREEMAN *Edgewater People* 161, I believe I'd never keeled over in the first place if I'd had anything decent to eat.

+**2.** *tr.* To upset or capsize (a person or thing); to kill. Also with *over*, *up*.

1843 STEPHENS *High Life N.Y.* II. 208, I wish to gracious the old shote had got up and keeled me over with both fists tu once. **1848** WEBBER *Old Hicks Guide* 92 He keeled one of them [*sc.* wolves] over with his air-gun. **1852** STOWE *Uncle Tom* xi, I've got free papers for 'em all recorded, in case I gets keeled up any o' these times, and they knows it. **1856** CARTWRIGHT *Autobiog.* 204 As I was not in the habit of using spirits at all, I knew that a very little would keel me up. **1872** EGGLESTON *End of World* 239 S'posin' they was a woodpecker on that air stump, wouldn't I a keeled him over?

Keel boat. {1695–} + =KEEL *n.*[1] Also attrib.

1786 in *Mag. Amer. Hist.* I. 176 Great numbers of Kentucke and keel boats passing every day; some to the Falls, others to Post Vincent — Illinois Country &c. **1797** F. BAILY *Tour* 256 Dr. Watrous . . . left us in order to proceed down the river in a keel boat. **1812** MELISH *Travels* II. 85 Keel-boats, so called from being built upon a small keel, are constructed to draw but little water. **1837** PECK *New Guide* 133 Before the introduction of steam-boats on the western waters, its immense commerce was carried on by means of keel-boats and barges. The former is much in the shape of a canal boat, long, slim-built, sharp at each end, and propelled by setting-poles and the cordelle, or long rope. **1880** 'MARK TWAIN' *Tramp Abroad* xv. 130 She had nine keel-boats hitched on behind and following after her in a long, slender rank. **1891** 'THANET' *Otto the Knight* 217 It is an ancient town for Arkansas: in keelboat times it was bustling and prosperous. **1904** *Kansas State Hist. Soc. Trans.* IX. 272 The keelboat . . . had . . . a draft of thirty inches light, and cost, usually, from $2000 to $3000.

+**Keel boating.** The action of carrying on commerce in keel boats. Also attrib. — **1883** 'MARK TWAIN' *Life on Miss.* iii, Then keelboating died a permanent death. *Ib.* xxxix, [Natchez, Miss.] had a desperate reputation, morally, in the old keelboating and early steamboating times.

+**Keel boatman.** A man who works on or owns a keel boat. *Obs.* — **1839** HOFFMAN *Wild Scenes* 109 Keel-boatmen from the Mohawk . . . for customers. **1843** *Amer. Pioneer* II. 162 The packers, who had been the lions of the day, were succeeded by still greater lions, the keel boatmen, who will be noticed hereafter. **1883** 'MARK TWAIN' *Life on Miss.* iii. 41 The steamers did all of the up-stream business, the keelboatmen selling their boats in New Orleans, and returning as deck-passengers in the steamers. **1898** CUSHMAN *Hist. Indians* 479 Under the disguise of keeping a store for the accommodation of keel and flat-boatmen, he enticed them into his power.

* **Keeler.** A small tub. *Obs.* or *local.*

1646 *Essex Probate Rec.* I. 55 One barrell & keeler. **1662** *Essex Inst. Coll.* XLII. 133 One tub, two keelirs, . . . 2 beere vessels & pails. **1758** FRANKLIN *Writings* III. 464 A shallow tray, or keeler, should be under the frame, to receive any water that might drip from the wetted cloths. **1844** *Lexington Observer* 25 Sept. 4/3 Wooden Ware, &c. 75 Doz. Painted Buckets, 20 Nests do Tubs and Keelers, . . . for sale. **1859** MATSELL *Vocabulum* 47.

Keeler tub. =prec. — **1866** LOWELL *Biglow P.* 2 Ser. p. lviii, A few phrases not in Mr. Bartlett's book which I have heard [include] . . . *Keeler-tub:* one in which dishes are washed.

+**Keeley cure.** [Dr. Leslie E. Keeley, Amer. physician (1832–1900).] The methods of cure for alcoholism in use at the Keeley institutes. (Cf. GOLD TREATMENT.) — **1895** *N.Y. Dramatic News* 6 July 8 Keeley Cure Not Certain. The treatment for dipsomania invented by Dr. Leslie A. Keeley does not appear to be universally efficacious.

+**Keener.** *W.* 'A very shrewd person, one sharp at a bargain, what in England would be called "a keen hand"' (B. '59).

* **Keep,** *n.*

+**1.** *New Eng.* One who takes care of animals; a herdsman. *Obs.*

The examples are doubtful, as the manuscripts may have an abbreviation for *er.* Cf., however, BARKEEP.

[**1638** *Dorchester Rec.* 32 The rest [are] to bring their Cowes be yound Mr. Stoughtons dore or elce the keep' [is] to driue away the heard not to stay for the rest.] **1641** *Boston Rec.* 60 If any goates shall be found without a keep after the 14th day of the next moneth, . . . the owners of them shall forfett for every goate soe found halfe a bushell of Corne. **1643** *Ipswich Rec.* 25 March, The keeps are to have iijs iid by the head, for soe long as the keeps attend the herd.

+**2.** *For keeps*, for permanent ownership; for good; finally. *colloq.*

1861 *Ladies' Repository* Oct. 627/1 Pay him! Nothing. He and I played for 'keeps,' and I was the best player and won all his. **1871** *Wright County Monitor* (Clarion, Iowa) 29 Nov., Winter has at last come 'for keeps' in this section of the country. **1886** *Advance* 9 Dec. 794/1 We, the undersigned, promise not to play marbles for keeps, nor bet, or gamble in any way. **1893** *Columbus Dispatch* 30 Dec., Montgomery's exaltation was short-lived and he was hustled back to the inside there to remain for keeps. **1901** RYAN *Montana* 78 When they learn 'for keeps,' that I'm not a marrying man, they'll let up. **1907** LONDON *Road* 177 The private car and engine went east, and the tracks died for keeps. **1920** LEWIS *Main Street* 451 That darn collar certainly is gone for keeps.

+**3.** Any game of marbles in which the play is 'for keeps.'

1876 'MARK TWAIN' *Tom Sawyer* xvi. 135 Next they got their marbles and played 'knucks' and 'ring-taw' and 'keeps.' **1894** — *P. Wilson* iv, Tom staked him with marbles to play 'keeps' with.

* **Keep,** *v.*

* **1.** *intr.* To dwell, reside, live. *colloq.* and *obsolescent.*

'Now only *colloq.*, esp. at Cambridge University and in U.S.' (*O.E.D.*). **1669** *N.Y. State Col. Hist.* XII. 463 Coleman being well verst in the Indian language amongst whome both he & t'other keep, may . . . do mischiefe. **1710** *Boston Rec.* 123 At present She keeps at ye House of Solo-man Townsend. **1818** FEARON *Sketches* 123 Do you keep at Boston? . . . No. . . . Where do you keep? . . . Fairfield. **1851** HALL *College Words* 176 *Keep*, to lodge, live, dwell, or inhabit. This word, though formerly used extensively, is now confined to colleges and universities. **1889** *Boston Jrnl.* 8 July 3/3 Just where Mrs. Stevens kept in Boston is unknown to history.

+**2.** Of a school: To be in session.

1845 *Knickerb.* XXVI. 277 One afternoon, when 'school didn't keep,' some one got into the house. **1867** 'LACKLAND' *Homespun* I. 123 The District School has not 'kept' since the week began. **1882** THAYER *From Log-Cabin* iii. 53 School will keep through the winter. **1903** G. C. EGGLESTON *First of Hoosiers* 31 The bound girl or bound boy always went to school . . . whenever 'school kept,' as the phrase went—that is to say, whenever there was a school open in the neighborhood. **1908** FREEMAN *Shoulders of Atlas* 68 School ain't going to keep to-day.

+**b.** *Not to care whether school keeps or not*, not to care what happens.

1896 W. A. WHITE *Real Issue* 174 The Colonel was wedded to his idols and didn't care whether school kept or not. **1913** LONDON *Valley of Moon* III. i, We're not in a hurry, and we don't care whether school keeps or not.

+3. *absol.* To keep school. (Cf. SCHOOL *n.*)

1797 J. COWLES *Diary* 1 Miss Sally did not keep. I went to St. John's.

***Keeper.**

*1. One who takes care of domestic animals. +a. *New Eng.* A town officer who looked after the live stock of townsmen who paid for the service. *Obs.*

1635 *Cambridge Rec.* 20 Itt is ordered Every man shall put his Goats to the keeper before the 20th of March. **1636** *Dorchester Rec.* 22 All that have Cowes shall put them to the Keepers to be kept in the ordinary Cow pasture. **1657** *Boston Rec.* 137 Every person that putt any sheep upon the Common shall pay to the keeper 8*d.* for every sheep and 3*d.* for every Lamb. **1658** *Dedham Rec.* IV. 2 In case the Town . . . cannot attayne a keeper . . . ther is common land . . . [where] our drye Cattell might be put thether.

*b. The guardian of a private herd. *Obs.*

1639 *Plymouth Rec.* 5 None shall suffer any goates to goe without a keeper. **1658** *Dedham Rec.* IV. 2 Drye Cattell goeing at libertie without a keeper.

*2. One who has charge or oversight of any of several things, as a prison, lighthouse, records, etc.

1642 *Mass. Bay Court Assistants Rec.* II. 125 George Roberts was committed to the keeper for his ill carriage. **1674** *Conn. Rec.* II. 245 The markes of the creatures . . . shall be entered with the keeper of the brand booke. **1734** *Mass. H. Rep. Jrnl.* XII. 19 A Memorial of Robert Ball, Keeper of the Light-House at the Entrance of the Harbour of Boston. **1789** *Ann. 1st Congress* I. 45 Every member of the present Congress, who is not yet furnished with a copy of the journals of the late Congress, shall, on application to the Keeper of the Records of the late Congress, be entitled to receive a complete set of such journals. **1815** *View N.Y. State Prison* 12 The apartments in the center of the building [in the prison] are appropriated to the use of the Inspectors and Agent, the Keeper, his family, and Assistants. **1874** R. H. COLLINS *Kentucky* I. 162 Gen. Palmer orders the arrest—tonight—of all dealers in or keepers of faro or faro banks. **1877** BARTLETT 330 *Keeper*, a custodian of attached property, appointed by a constable or sheriff. **1900** MUNN *Uncle Terry* 112, I'm keeper o' the light at the end o' Southport Island.

Keeping room. *New Eng.* The sitting room of a house: (see quot. 1849). {1787–,} Also attrib.

1771 *Copley-Pelham Lett.* 141, I forget weither or not there was to be a Clossit in the Keeping Room. **1791** WEBSTER in E. E. F. Ford *Notes on N. Webster* I. 351 Altered my keeping-room Chimney. **1809** KENDALL *Travels* III. 264 The latter spent his evening in the parlour, or, as it is called, the *keeping-room*. **1836** DUNLAP *Mem. Water Drinker* (1837) I. 92 Woodward re-entered, literally dragging the yellow-faced crow—the preaching tailor—into the 'keeping room,' by the collar of his coat. **1849** COOPER *Sea Lions* xx, The deacon and his niece were alone together in the 'keeping-room'—as it was, if it be not still, the custom among persons of New England origin to call the ordinary sitting apartment. **1856** GOODRICH *Recoll.* I. 74 [In Conn.] carpets were then [early in 19th c.] only known in a few families, and were confined to the keeping-room and parlor. **1898** HARPER *S. B. Anthony* I. 7 Then there were the spacious 'keeping' or sitting room, with the mother's bedroom opening out of it, the great-weaving-room [etc.].

+**Keet.** The guinea fowl. *local.* — **1859** [see GUINEA 5 c]. **1899** *Animal & Plant Lore* 61 *Keets*, young Guinea fowls. Chestertown, Md.

Keg, *n.* (Cf. CAG.)

1. A small barrel or cask. {1632–}

1707 *Boston News-Letter* 25 Aug. 2/2 (*advt.*), Fine Pistol Powder in small Keggs of about 12 pound weight each, . . . to be Sold. **1797** HAWKINS *Letters* 253 The goods he wants are . . . 7 bags salt, 1 keg of brandy [etc.]. **1840** *Picayune* 2 Aug. 2/6, 75 Kegs fresh Goshen Butter, received per ship St. Mary, for sale by the keg or retail. **1861** *Chicago Tribune* 19 July 1/1 One rebel was killed and two kegs of powder captured. **1897** *Outing* April 61/2 There's a keg of water, a cook-stove and a skillet in that fish-house. **1914** STEELE *Storm* 96 A dozen bales of tobacco and thirty kegs of rum were swung over the rails.

+b. *Battle of the kegs*, (see quotations).

In January, 1778, some Americans above Philadelphia floated kegs of gunpowder down the Delaware River, which were arranged to explode when touched. The object was to injure the British shipping at Philadelphia. The British, however, were warned, and to avoid any calamity they spent the day firing at everything that looked like a keg floating on the river.

1778 in *Amer. Museum* I. 56/1 Not a chip, stick, or drift log, passed by, without experiencing the vigour of the British arms. . . . In short, Monday the 5th . . . day of January, 1778, will be ever memorable in history, for the renowned *battle of the kegs*. **1833** WATSON *Hist. Tales Phila.* 297 Among the amusing and facetious incidents of the war . . . was that of the celebrated occurrence of 'the Battle of the Kegs' at Philadelphia.

+2. Of one's drinking capacity: The stomach. *slang.*

1877 W. WRIGHT *Big Bonanza* 366 His 'keg' was evidently 'full' to overflowing, yet he was still athirst. **1877** F. FRANCIS *Saddle & Moccasin* 270 (F. and H.), We'd been having a time and my keg was pretty full too.

3. Attrib. with *hat, raisin.*

1855 MITCHELL *Fudge Doings* I. 128 There is the head clerk . . . with fingers sticky with keg-raisins. **1895** *Century Mag.* Aug. 570/1 Sam he had on a keg hat, all shiny silk.

Keg, *v.* {1630} +*reflex.* and *absol.* To abstain from alcohol for a set time. Also vbl. n. *slang.* — **1789** ANBUREY *Travels* I. 193, 'I'll *keg* myself for six months, directly I get home.' The word *keg* . . . is a cant word that the soldiers have among them, when they wish to refrain from liquors. [**1832** J. MACGREGOR *British America* I. 221 From the cheapness of rum, the labouring people [in Newfoundland], . . . acquire habits of excessive drinking, which they have only resolution to resist by swearing, . . . that they will not taste rum, or spirits of any kind. This act is called Kegging, extending to one or more years, and often for life.] **1855** BARNUM *Life* 36 Once in a while he would 'keg,' as he called it; that is, he would abjure strong drink for a certain length of time.

Keg-maker. One who makes kegs. — **1765** *Boston Gazette* 29 April 3/2 We have . . . tub, kegg and can makers. **1789** *Boston Directory* 180 Cary Jonathan, keg-maker. **1796** *Ib.* 233 Carey, Jonathan, keg maker, Fish street.

+**Keister.** [perhaps f. Ger. *kasten* 'a chest.'] A suitcase or handbag. *local* or *cant.* — **1882** PECK *Sunshine* 227 The boy took the Knight's keister and went to the elevator. *Ib.* 229 He looked around at them, picked up his boots and keister and started for the door.

+**Keithian.** [Geo. *Keith*, Eng. Quaker (?1639–1716).] (See quotations.) Also attrib. — *a*1854 in Bowden *Hist. Soc. Friends in Amer.* II. 102 The Keithian Quakers ended in a kind of transformation into Keithian Baptists. **1882** Schaff *Religious Encycl.* II. 1230/1 Keith was condemned by the Annual Meeting, but formed a body of his own, known as the 'Christian Quakers,' or 'Keithians.' **1888** *Century Mag.* May 115/1 He managed . . . to rend the little newly planted Pennsylvania world into two parties, leading out in 1691 a sect of those who modestly distinguished themselves as the *Christian* Quakers, but who were popularly known as Keithian Quakers.

+**Kellogg's oak.** [Albert *Kellogg*, Amer. botanist (1813–87).] (See quotation.) — **1897** SUDWORTH *Arborescent Flora* 169 *Quercus californica.* . . . California Black Oak. . . . [Commonly called] Kellogg's Oak ([in] Cal.).

+**Kellupweed.** The oxeye daisy. — **1894** *Amer. Folk-Lore* VII. 91 *Chrysanthemum leucanthemum*, Kellup weed, Rhode Island clover, Montpelier, Vt.

***Kelp.**

*1. Any of several large brown seaweeds of the families Laminariaceae and Fucaceae, +esp. the seaweed (*Macrocystis pyrifera*) of the Pacific coast. (Cf. DEVIL'S-APRON.)

1722 *New-Eng. Courant* 2–9 April 2/2 Rock-Weed or Kelp is good Manure for Hemp Lands. **1800** CUTLER in *Life & Corr.* II. 40 Sent two teams to West Beach for kelp and seaweed. **1846** EMORY *Military Reconn.* 115 The kelp (*fucus gigantens*) occupies a space in front of the harbor. **1857** DANA *Great West* 300 Immense quantities of kelp are thrown up by the waves—an article that now forms the most available material for the manufacture of iodine, and is also excellent as a compost for arid soils, like those of this state. **1890** *Cent.* 3273/1 *Bullhead kelp, Nereocystis Luetkeana* of northwestern America, the long filaments of which are used by the Indians for fishing-lines. *Ib., Great kelp*, of California, the *Macrocystis pyrifera*.

2. The ash of seaweeds when burned, the source of carbonate of soda, iodine, etc. {1678–}

1814 *N.Y. State Soc. Arts* III. 79 Kelp is employed in the manufacture of glass, alum and hard soap.

3. Attrib. and comb. in the names of plants and fishes.

1784 CUTLER in *Mem. Academy* I. 425 *Salsola.* . . . Kelpwort. Blossoms greenish. On the sea shore. September. **1883** *Nat. Museum Bul.* No. 27, 112 Crabs . . . regarded as edible on the Pacific coast [include] . . . Kelp Crab (*Epialtus productus*), Yellow Shore Crab [etc.]. **1884** GOODE, etc. *Fisheries* I. 275 The Kelp-fish, of California, . . . is found in the kelp about Santa Catalina Island. *Ib.* 413 The Cabrilla—*Serranus clathratus.* This species is called at Monterey, where it is not common, the 'Kelp Salmon.'

Kelter. (See KILTER.)

+**Kench.** [Origin unknown.] A box or bin in which fish or skins are salted. — **1852** SABINE *Fisheries* 207 The fish taken are split, salted, and put in 'Kenches' or piles. **1874** SCAMMONS *Marine Mammals* 161 The [seal] skins are all taken to the salt-houses, and are salted in kenches, or square bins. **1884** *Nat. Museum Bul.* No. 27, 1059 Kench of Bank cod at Trefethen's sheds waiting to be dried. **1887** GOODE, etc. *Fisheries U.S.* v. 370 Sliding planks, which are taken down and put up in the form of deep bins, or boxes—kenches, the sealers call them.

Kendal cotton. [*Kendal*, Westmorland.] A woolen fabric having a nap, made in Westmorland, England. *Obs.* {Kendal, 1606– (*Stat. at L.* VII. (1763) 201)}

1732 *S.C. Gazette* 136/2 Lately imported, and to be sold, . . . welsh plains and kendal cottons. **1746** *Md. Hist. Mag.* XXI. 379 Invoice of goods . . . 4 ps. Kendal Cotton. **1813** *Niles' Reg.* III. 295/1 [List of military supplies:] Kendall cotton, 392 yards. **1832** *Congress Deb.* 22 June 3715 The fifth amendment . . . [was amended] so as to read plains, kerseys, or Kendal cottons. **1854** BENTON *30 Years' View* I. 347/1 The passage of the bill, being a political, not a legislative action, . . . [was] openly carried in the Senate by a *douceur* to some men, not in 'Kendal Green,' but Kendal cotton.

+**Kenion.** =CANYON. — **1846** W. G. STEWART *Altowan* I. 222 Three or four spruce trees ... seemed to have grown there to form a natural shade and shelter in the rough bosom of the kenion.

+**Kennebunker.** [f. *Kennebunk*, Me.] (See quotations.) — **1895** *Dialect Notes* I. 390 *Kennebunker:* valise in which clothes are put by lumbermen when they go into camp for a 'winter operation.' Me. woods. **1902** *Amer. Folk-Lore* XV. 245 *Kennebunker,* a word of comparatively recent origin used to denote 'the valise (for clothes) which Maine lumbermen take with them to the woods.'

***Kennel.**[1] A gutter that drains a street. *Obs.* Also attrib. — **1769** *Philadelphia Ordinances* (1812) 29 Great complaint is made ... that distillers, soap-boilers and others ... discharge ... stinking liquors, ... into the kennels of the public streets. **1788** FRANKLIN *Autobiog.* 383 The next rain wash'd it quite away, so that the pavement and even the kennel were perfectly clean. **1833** *N.Y. City Ordinance* 13 Aug., The side walks or foot walks between the lines of the streets and kennels.

***Kennel.**[2] =DOG-HOUSE 1. — **1823** COOPER *Pioneers* xxvii, He has got on the rock back of the kennel, and let the dogs loose by fastening his knife to a stick. **1872** ROE *Army Lett.* 69 The little dog is chained to a kennel all the time. **1893** M. HOWE *Honor* 286 He still ... had a general supervision of his patron's town and country places, as well as of his stables, his kennels and his steam-yacht. **1920** *3d Nat. Country Life Conf. Proc.* 12 They put me in a dog kennel.

+**Keno.** Also **kino.** [Cf. F. *quine*, 'five winning numbers.']

1. A gambling game in which the players cover numbers on their cards as those numbers happen to come out of the keno goose or from a wheel of chance, the first five numbers in a row on a card winning the purse. {1884}

1845 NOAH *Gleanings* 133 They were employed at a game called *lotto* or *kino*—the master drew the numbers from a wheel, while the company covered such as appeared on small placards before them, and when they obtained a certain number, they claimed and took the purse. **1869** BREWER *Rocky Mt. Lett.* 14 He monotonously calls out in a loud tone the numbers of Keno, in progress in a neighboring gambling saloon. **1881** C. M. CHASE *Editor's Run in N.Mex.* 134 Mexican monte, keno, faro, high ball, etc., are the prevailing games, and everybody [in Socorro, N.M.] indulges. **1905** F. A. MATHEWS *B. Duane* 244 It's keno and roulette and the bridge that carries us all over or under. **1910** 'O. HENRY' *Strictly Business* 70, I've heard of places in this here town where a fellow could have a good game of old sledge or peg a card at keno.

2. The exclamation given when a player has winning numbers; also, transf., an exclamation of approval or satisfaction.

1907 MULFORD *Bar-20* 193 He wants to know where th' cards are stacked an' why he can't holler 'Keno.' **1920** in Hunter *Trail Drivers Texas* I. 205, Shake yer spurs an' make 'em rattle! Keno! Promenade to seats.

3. Attrib. with *dive, establishment,* etc.

1871 *Figaro* 15 April, The police pulled every Keno establishment in the city. **1873** *Scribner's Mo.* July 271/1 The keno and monte players had any quantity of tents all about this section. **1876** HARTE in *Scribner's Mo.* XII. 45 Your suggestion ... is worthy of a short-card sharp and a keno flopper, which I have ... long suspected you to be. **1878** S. C. UPHAM *Notes on Voyage to Calif.* 225 The *roulette, keno, rattle-and-snap* and other small-fry gamblers pay less [saloon rental] amounts. **1887** *Courier-Journal* 20 Jan. 6/2 The case against Frederick Therwanger, the proprietor of the largest keno dive in the city, was called. **1889** MUNROE *Golden Days* 40 We'll have the drawin' over in Slim Jim's keno-ranch.

b. *Keno goose,* a receptacle from whose spout the numbered balls of keno are taken.

1887 *Courier-Journal* 20 Jan. 6/2 (*headline*), Fred Therwanger Manipulates a Keno Goose for Edification of the Court.

+**Kensington stitch.** Crewel stitch, or crewelwork. — **1883** *Century Mag.* Sept. 787/1 They know little of Kensington stitch or of Eastern-woven portières. **1884** *Ib.* Jan. 473/2 In the 'woman's department' it is half smothered by the Kensington stitch.

***Kental.** Also †**kintall, kentle,** etc. Variant of QUINTAL. — **1645** *Suffolk Deeds* I. 65 One thousand Kintall of dry Cod fish. **1689** in Sewall *Letter-Book* I. 92, I have Shipt on board the ship ... one Hundred kentals of Marchandable Cod fish. **1724** *Essex Inst. Coll.* XLV. 92 Having about fifteen hundred Kentalls on board ... we Halld off into ye Harbour. **1816** PICKERING 121 Mr. Webster's orthography, which is *Kentle,* ... is conformable to the common pronunciation of the word. **1890** JEWETT *Strangers* 168, I wouldn't give a kentle o' sp'iled fish for the whole on 'em.

+**Kenticoy,** *n.* Also **kinticoy,** etc. [Apparently an Algonquian word.] Among the Indians of the Northeast, a ceremonial dance or festival; a ritualistic meeting. (Cf. CANTICOY.)

1671 *N.Y. State Col. Hist.* XII. 485 The Proposall to have the Murderers destroyed was to cause a Kinticoy to bee held, & in the midst of their Mirth, That then one should be hired to knock him i' the head. **1675** in Easton *Indian War* 126 Several Indyans ... are in a few Dayes to have a great Kintecoy at Seaquetalke. **1701** WOLLEY *Journal N.Y.* (1860) 37 Their Kin-tau-Kauns, or time of sacrificing is at the beginning of winter. **1757** W. SMITH *Hist. N.Y.* 41 These Conventions are called Kenticoys; ... such Accounts of their Conduct, naturally lead one to imagine, that they pay a joint Homage and Supplication to some invisible Being. **1840** HOFFMAN *Greyslaer* II. 18 This was the seat of the mysterious Kenticoys, or solemn meetings of the Mohawks. **1866** WHITTIER *Writings* V. 144 [An Indian girl] told us that they did still hold their Kentikaw, or Dance for the Dead.

+**Kenticoy,** *v. intr.* To dance in the ceremony of the kenticoy. *Obs.* — **1675** *N.J. Archives* I. 183 They return thanks and fall a kintacoying with expressions of thanks, singing *kenon, kenon.* **1675** in Easton *Indian War* 126 A Speciall Warrant sent to Huntington to Demand the Indyans Armes of Rockaway and Seaquatalke, who are to Kintecoy there.

Kenting. A kind of fine linen. *Obs.* {1657-} Also attrib. (Cf. BOOK-KENTING.) — **1711** *Springfield Rec.* II. 39 One peice of Kenting, being eight yards. **1714** *Boston News-Letter* 8-15 March 2/2 To be Sold by Publick Vendue or Outcry ... Knives and Forks, very Good, Scotch Kentings. **1763** *Essex Inst. Coll.* XLIX. 84 [List of stolen goods:] Kenting, Linen and Silk Handkerchiefs in Pieces. **1784** *Mass. Centinel* 4 Sept. 3/3 To be sold ... a general assortment of European goods, consisting of ... kerseymeres, ... scarf twist, ... kenting handkerchiefs.

***Kentish,** *a. Kentish cherry,* a variety of cherry; *K. tern,* (see quot. 1917). — **1815** *Mass. H. S. Coll.* 2 Ser. III. 216 The various kinds of plums that used to prosper, and the kentish cherry, which used to abound, have almost wholly disappeared. **1917** *Birds of Amer.* I. 59 Cabot's Tern, *Sterna sandvicensis acuflavida.* ... [Also called] Kentish Tern.

Kentle. Variant of KENTAL.

+**Kentuck.** Also **Kentucke.** (Cf. KAINTUCK.)

The final -e spelling may be intended to indicate the pronunciation as shown in 'Kentucky.'

1. The territory or state of Kentucky. Often *Old Kentuck.*

1784 FILSON *Kentucke* 8 About the year 1767, ... [John Finley] travelled over the fertile region, now called Kentucke. **1786** *New Haven Gazette* 16 Feb. 15/3 (Th. S.), You have certainly heard of the fertility of Kentucke. **1798** *Filson Club* (Ky.) *Publ.* No. 31, 153 If Kentuck cannot pay a continental tax of thirty-six thousand pounds ... her opinion ... cannot weigh very heavily in the scale. **1819** FAUX *Memorable Days* 190 At five this evening I entered the city, the far-famed metropolis of old Kentuck. **1835** HOFFMAN *Winter in West* II. 194 It would take half of old Kentuck to pile up the stuff the way it lies there. **1842** *Lowell Offering* II. 357 Hurra for Yankee Land and old Kentuck! **1854** M. J. HOLMES *Tempest & Sunshine* iv. 52 Kentuck hain't many like her, nor never will have.

b. In figurative and allusive contexts: An ideal place. (Cf. 4 b.)

1826 FLINT *Recoll.* 64 Heaven is a Kentuck of a place. **1834** CARRUTHERS *Kentuckian* I. 190 [New York is] a real Kentuck of a place.

2. An inhabitant of Kentucky.

1826 FLINT *Recoll.* 15 You learn the received opinion, that a 'Kentuck' is the best man at a pole. **1830** *Western Mo. Review* III. 357 His captain had deported, like a real Kentuck. **1835** INGRAHAM *South-West* I. 105 Here are congregated the primitive navies of Indiana, Ohio, and the adjoining states, manned ... by 'real Kentucks.' **1842** 'UNCLE SAM' *Peculiarities* II. 23 You put me in mind of a Kentuck I saw yesterday. **1856** M. J. HOLMES *L. Rivers* viii. 93 How do you git along down amongst them heathenish Kentucks & niggers?

3. In phrase *Old Kentuck,* Kentucky whiskey.

1869 L. SIMONIN *Grand-Quest* x. 120 Quel bouquet, mon ami, et quelle liqueur traîtresse que cet *old Kentuck!*

4. *attrib.* **a.** In sense 1.

1834 CARRUTHERS *Kentuckian* I. 25 When we Kentuck boys gits at it, it won't all end like a log rollin'. *Ib.* I. 98 He asked me if I had ever seen an auction of a ship cargo; I said no, I had never seen more nor a Kentuck vendue. **1841** *S. Lit. Messenger* VII. 53/2 A segment of an old Virginia hoe-cake, ... In Kentuck phrase, 'would not be bad *toe* take.' **1852** STOWE *Uncle Tom* x, Them plantations down thar, stranger, an't jest the place a Kentuck nigger wants to go to. **1852** WATSON *Nights in Block-House* 27, I say, you Kentuck screamer, ... what kind o' livin' had you while you were up the stream?

b. In sense 1 b.

1850 *Knickerb.* XXXV. 370 Heaven is a real Kentuck sort of a place.

c. *Kentucke clover,* a variety of clover.

1785 WASHINGTON *Diaries* II. 426 Also sowed about a tablespoonful of the Buffalo or Kentucke Clover.

+**Kentuck boat.** Also **Kentucke boat.** =KENTUCKY BOAT. — **1786** [see KEEL BOAT]. **1788** MAY *Jrnl. & Lett.* 42 Three Kentuck boats were captured by the savages. **1789** *Mass. Spy* 11 June (Th.), A Kentuck boat of 40 feet long will cost about one dollar per foot. **1842** *Amer. Pioneer* I. 63 They all came, with their teams, wagons and furniture, in *one* Kentuck boat to the point of destination.

+**Kentuckian,** *n.* Also **Kentuckyan.**

1. An inhabitant or native of Kentucky.

1779 G. R. CLARK *Campaign in Ill.* (1869) 85 If not deceived by the Kentuckyans, I should still be able to compleat my design. **1797** F. BAILY *Tour* 273 They were mostly Kentuckians with us, who are all men of a fiery temper. **1816** *Niles' Reg.* X. 233/2 A colonel ... described to him, in the most terrible terms, the ferocity of the *Kentuckians.* **1826** AUDUBON *Journal* I. 141 We breakfasted as quickly as if we had been Kentuckians.

1833 T. HAMILTON *Men & Manners* II. 179 The Kentuckians are the only Americans who can understand a joke. There is a kind of native humour about them which is very pleasant. **1857** STROTHER *Virginia* 119 He brags like a Kentuckian. **1873** *Newton Kansan* 13 Feb. 2/3 The Kentuckians of Kansas held a preliminary meeting in Topeka. **1901** *Munsey's Mag.* XXIV. 508/1 The murder of the girl . . . roused the chivalrous Kentuckians to a fever heat.

2. Any person inhabiting the Ohio Valley.

1807 C. SCHULTZ *Travels* II. 21 A Kentuckian would scorn to shoot a squirrel, or even a swallow, unless with a rifle. **1810** *Ib., note,* All the inhabitants on the Ohio are here called Kentuckians.

3. A Kentucky-bred horse.

1835 HOFFMAN *Winter in West* I. 111 There was . . . the sleek spongy-looking Ohio horse, and the clean-limbed quickly-gathering Kentuckian.

+**Kentuckian,** *a.* In, from, belonging to, or pertaining to, Kentucky.

1804 C. B. BROWN tr. Volney *View* 71, I have observed the Kentuckian bank of the river to be formed of similar ridges. **1819** FLINT *Lett. from Amer.* 168 Henry Clay, a Kentuckian lawyer, . . . has for eight years made a distinguished figure in . . . the House of Representatives. **1822** WOODS *English Prairie* 110 The best boat channel to pass the Falls is on the Indiana side, it is called the Indian shoot; . . . the other the Kentuckian shoot. **1880** CABLE *Grandissimes* 75 One of those Kentuckian dealers in corn and tobacco whose flat-boat fleets were always drifting down the Mississippi. **1885** BAYLOR *On Both Sides* 145 A handsome carriage . . . drawn by a beautiful pair of Kentuckian thoroughbreds.

+**Kentucky.** Also *dial.* **Kaintucky.** [Amer. Indian: the original meaning is uncertain.] The name, used attributively, of a southern territory or state. (Cf. KENTUCK, KAINTUCK.)

1. Designating various things or actions characteristic of, found in, or coming from, Kentucky.

1854 *Harper's Mag.* March 456/2 By previous arrangement, strong Kentucky bagging has been so placed as to cover the upper and lower side of the pressed cotton. **1830** N. AMES *Mariner's Sk.* 147 It was not difficult to perceive that in the Indian hug or Kentucky bite, I should stand no chance at all. **1889** *Harper's Mag.* Sept. 566/2 The Kentucky fair, which began as a cattle-show, seems likely to end with being a horse-show. **1837** PECK *New Guide* 318 Fencing it [the Ill. farm] into four fields, with a Kentucky fence of eight rails high, with cross stakes. **1903** FOX *Little Shepherd* xvii, A great turkey supplanted the venison, and last to come . . . was a Kentucky ham. **1858** *Texas Almanac 1859* 67 The Kentucky Harvester is most used, and is generally preferred. **1817** FORDHAM *Narr. Travels* 158, I had on . . . a pair of Kentucky leggings. **1847** L. COLLINS *Kentucky* 156 It is in these cliffs of the Kentucky river, and in the adjacent country that we find what is called Kentucky marble. **1807** *Ann. 10th Congress* 1 Sess. I. 429 Blannerhasset paid me off in Kentucky notes. **1904** TARBELL *Hist. Standard Oil Co.* I. 5 'Seneca Oil' . . . was followed by a large output of Kentucky petroleum sold under the name 'American Medicinal Oil.' **1832** F. A. BUTLER *Journal* I. 290 Danced sundry quadrilles; and, finally, what they called a Kentucky reel,—which is nothing more than Sir Roger de Coverly turned Backwoodsman. **1841** BUCKINGHAM *America* II. 68 In that year [1805] a very remarkable excitement or agitation of the public mind on the subject of religion took place in Kentucky, and is known by the name of the 'Kentucky Revival.' . . . The excitement was occasioned by the preaching of some Presbyterian missionaries who had been sent into the Western States from New-England. **1892** *Outing* March 477/2 The Woodburn Stud . . . is another of the celebrated Kentucky stud farms. **1852** STOWE *Uncle Tom* xi, You have an idea of the jollities of a Kentucky tavern. **1845** SOL. SMITH *Theatr. Apprent.* xviii. 119 A still louder laugh . . . presently increased into a real *Kentucky yell.*

2. Designating various produce and live stock of Kentucky. (Cf. KENTUCKY HORSE.)

1858 D. K. BENNETT *Chron. N.C.* 86 On our way down we met 373 head of Kentucky cattle in one drove. **1849** EMMONS *Agric. N.Y.* II. 265 Kentucky corn. . . . Kernel white, somewhat shrivelled, elongated and pointed. **1834** H. TUDOR *Tour* II. 9 About two thousand large Kentucky hogs, which we unluckily encountered in one of the very narrowest defiles of the mountains. **1882** *Congress. Rec.* 22 June 5229/2 The fatted calf—the Kentucky ox—was killed for the returning prodigals. They were feasted on Bourbon and burgoo. **c1845** PAULDING *Amer. Comedies* (1847) 190 Like a real Kaintucky porker a-rootin' in the woods. **1881** *Harper's Mag.* April 728/2 Such horses as awaited them! Kentucky stock full-blooded and fit for warriors. **1900** *Outing* Sept. 645 The Master of Woodburn did more to improve the Kentucky thoroughbred . . . than all of his contemporaries combined. **1868** *N.Y. Herald* 22 July 7/3 The demand for Kentucky tobacco is mainly confined to the low grades.

3. Designating persons living in, or native to, Kentucky.

1868 *N.Y. Herald* 3 July 3/2 Our Kentucky correspondent says, 'I . . . never . . . saw a greater outcome in wheat.' *Ib.* 6 July 3/3 Kentucky 'corn-crackers' and Illinois 'suckers' might have joined labors yesterday. **1847** PARKMAN in *Knickerb.* XXIX. 162 The parties of emigrants . . . professed great disinclination to have any connexion with the 'Kentucky fellows.' **1887** *Southern Bivouac* V. 576/2 An accomplished Kentucky horseman like James B. Clay. **1907** ANDREWS *Recoll.* 145 At Traverse des Sioux we dined with Judge Flandrau and his first wife, a lovely Kentucky lady. **1895** G. KING *New Orleans* 246 'Bear up, my dear fellow, you are too brave to die,' bade a kind-hearted Kentucky major.

4. a. In the specific names of plants.

1871 DE VERE 416 The Coffee-tree (*Gymnocladus canadensis*), often called Kentucky Coffee-tree, or Kentucky Locust, derives its name from the fact that in the days of early settlements the seeds were frequently used as a substitute for coffee, a practice renewed during the late Civil War. **1847** DARLINGTON *Weeds & Plants* 111 Canadian Gymnocladus. Kentucky Coffee-tree. Kentucky Mahogany. . . . This fine tree has been introduced into the Eastern States, from the West. **1846** *Knickerb.* XXVIII. 38 The Kentucky rose is not excelled by any plant in America for the plenitude of its blossoms. **1849** EMMONS *Agric. N.Y.* II. 139 Kentucky White-bearded, Canada Flint, Hutchinson Wheat. In Western New-York, it has become a favorite variety.

b. In the specific names of apples.

1856 *Rep. Comm. Patents 1855: Agric.* 290 The 'Tennessee Milam,' and 'Kentucky Red,' are our best early winter apples. **1870** *Rep. Comm. Agric. 1869* 186 Buckingham. Synonyms: . . . Kentucky Queen, Lexington Queen [etc.].

c. In the specific names of birds.

1894 *Harper's Mag.* May 926 (*title*) A Kentucky Cardinal. **1917** *Birds of Amer.* III. 155 Kentucky Warbler. . . . Other Name.—Kentucky Wagtail.

5. With *broadhorn, man, ship,* =KENTUCKY BOAT.

1884 Kentucky broadhorn [see BROADHORN 1]. **1788** MAY *Jrnl. & Lett.* 33, I was obliged to put my stores and baggage on board a small ferry-boat in order to put them on board the Kentucky-man. *Ib.* 66 The house . . . I am in hopes to raise in eight or ten days; for I am not very comfortable on board my Kentucky ship.

6. *Kentucky Resolutions,* a set of resolutions, passed by the Kentucky Legislature (1798–9), defining the strict-constructionist view of the relative powers of the state and federal governments. Sometimes associated with the Virginia Resolutions in the phrase *Kentucky and Virginia Resolutions.*

1798 JEFFERSON *Writings* X. 62, I enclose you a copy of the draught of the Kentucky Resolutions. **1821** *Nation* XLIV. 382/3 The doctrine we held . . . was the doctrine of the old Republican party, of Mr. Madison's report of '98, and of the Kentucky resolutions penned by Mr. J[efferson] himself. **1856** *Democratic Conv. Proc.* 25 *Resolved,* . . . That the Democratic party will faithfully abide by and uphold, the principles laid down in the Kentucky and Virginia resolutions of 1798. **1886** *Southern Bivouac* March 581/1 The first seven of the Breckinridge or Kentucky resolutions are the same as these numbers of the Jefferson draft, . . . but the 8th and 9th of the Breckinridge or Kentucky set are radically different from these numbers in the Jefferson series. **1894** JAMESON *Dict. U.S. Hist.* 349 The close union of political feeling with Virginia was shown by the passage of the 'Kentucky and Virginia Resolutions' of 1798 and 1799, which protested against the passage of the Alien and Sedition Acts.

+**Kentucky ark.** An arklike Kentucky boat, freq. used to accommodate families migrating to the West. (Cf. ARK 1.) — **1824** BLANE *Excursion U.S.* 102 [Boats] of about 150 tons' burthen . . . are called Kentucky Arks, and indeed they contain almost as great a medley of eatables, furniture, animals, &c. &c. as ever Noah could have stored in his miraculous vessel. **1852** E. F. ELLET *Pioneer Women* 180 [They] arrived at Marietta, coming down the Ohio in 'Kentucky arks,' or flatboats.

+**Kentucky blue grass.** =BLUE GRASS 1. — **1849** EMMONS *Agric. N.Y.* II. 68 An earlier kind of grass than timothy, is the Spear grass, Meadow grass, or Kentucky blue grass. **1869** *Rep. Comm. Agric. 1868* 177 The well known Kentucky blue-grass (*Poa pratensis*) which grows luxuriantly as far north as Kotzebue Sound. **1879** (New Orleans newspaper), The Bermuda, the Gramma and Guinea grasses, are to tropical and semi-tropical climates what Kentucky blue grass and other species are to more Northern climates.

+**Kentucky boat.** Any of several slightly varying kinds of large flat-bottomed river boats of a rectangular shape, propelled by man power, and made for carrying agricultural produce, household furniture, and other freight. Often used by families migrating into the West. Now hist.

So called from the importance of Kentucky in the river traffic of the West during the first decades of the republic. (Cf. ARK, BROADHORN 1, DURHAM BOAT, FAMILY BOAT, FLATBOAT, KENTUCK BOAT, KENTUCKY ARK, KENTUCKY SHIP, ORLEANS BOAT.)

1785 DENNY *Journal* 57 Our fleet now consists of . . . batteaux, besides two large flats called Kentucky boats. **1796** F. BAILY *Tour* 152 Accordingly, as soon as the [Ohio] river was reported to be navigable, all the *Kentucky boats* (as this flat-bottomed craft is termed) were in motion. **1802** ELLICOTT *Journal* 122 If Kentucky boats (as they are called,) fall within the draught of this upper current, it will be extremely difficult to relieve them. **1807** C. SCHULTZ *Travels* I. 129 Kentucky boats are strong frames of an oblong form, varying in size from twenty to fifty feet in length. **1818** J. PALMER *Travels U.S.* 56 Our conveyance was one of the long Kentucky boats, in common use here for transporting produce and manufactures *down* the Ohio. **1847** in H. Howe *Hist. Coll. Ohio* 207 Boats similarly constructed on the northern waters, were then called *arks,* but on the western rivers, they were denominated *Kentucky boats.*

+**Kentucky coffee.**

1. (See quotation.)

1859 BARTLETT 227 *Kentucky Coffee.* The fruit of *Gynonoclades* [*sic*] *canadensis.* A large tree, resembling the locust tree, bearing a pod with berries which are used for coffee.

2. *Kentucky coffee tree,* a tall caesalpiniaceous tree of North America, *Gymnocladus dioica* (var., *G. canadensis*), having pods with brown seeds.

1785 WASHINGTON *Diaries* II. 360 Eight Nuts from a tree called the Kentucke Coffee tree. **1814** PURSH *Flora Amer.* I. 304 *Gymnocladus canadensis.* . . . A large tree, known by the name of Kentucky Coffee Tree, and among the Canadians Chicot. **1850** S. F. COOPER *Rural Hours* 477 The Kentucky Coffee-tree, with its peculiar blunt branches, is also found in rich woods, on the banks of the rivers. **1860** CURTIS *Woody Plants N.C.* 50 Kentucky Coffee tree, . . . occasionally cultivated about houses as a handsome shade tree. **1900** H. L. KEELER *Native Trees* (1902) 109 Kentucky coffee tree, stump tree.

+**Kentucky Derby.** The classic of American horse races, run since 1875 at Churchill Downs, Louisville, Kentucky. — **1875** *Courier-Journal* 18 May 4/3 The second race was the event of the day—the Kentucky Derby, a dash of 1½ miles for three-year olds, fifty dollars entrance, p.p., the Association adding $1,000. **1881** *Ib.* 1 May 4/7 The Kentucky Derby is one of the grandest and most important races in the country, and has always been won by a first-class colt. **1903** *Amer. Almanac 1904* 638 Principal Stake Events of 1903: . . . Kentucky Derby. 1¼ miles. Judge Himes [winner]. **1920** *N.Y. Times* 9 May VIII. 1/1 Nearly 60,000 persons . . . saw Paul Jones . . . win the fortysixth renewal of the historic Kentucky Derby, at a mile and a quarter, with $30,000 added.

+**Kentucky flat.** =KENTUCKY BOAT. — **1812** STODDARD *Sk. Louisiana* 374 Most of the produce of the upper country is floated to market in what are called Kentucky flats, or arks. These are of various sizes, generally from forty to sixty feet long, and from twelve to fifteen broad, with roofs of thin boards to secure their cargoes from the water. **1829** CUMINGS *Western Pilot* 7 The Barge, the Keel boat, the Kentucky Flat, or Family boat, . . . and many others, formerly floated in great numbers down the current of the Ohio and Mississippi. **1849** E. DAVIES *Amer. Scenes* 95 In the vernacular phrase, these boats are called 'Kentucky flats,' or 'broad-horns.'

+**Kentucky horse.** A horse bred in Kentucky. — **1881** *Harper's Mag.* April 730/2 The two Kentucky horses were trotting along the beach. **1885** BAYLOR *On Both Sides* 279 A handsome landau and a dog-cart drawn by two pairs of beautiful Kentucky horses. **1887** *Southern Bivouac* V. 498/2 In the very fullest sense Nutwood is a representative Kentucky horse. He was bred in this State, and here, too, were bred his sire, his dam, and the sire of his dam. **1925** BRYAN *Memoirs* 273 We watched as he rode out on Governor, his shiny black Kentucky horse.

+**Kentucky jean.**

1. Homemade twilled cotton cloth made in Kentucky. *colloq.* (Cf. JEAN.)

1835 INGRAHAM *South-West* II. 175 The young Mississippian . . . dresses plainly, . . . often in pantaloons of Kentucky jean, a broad brimmed white hat, brogans, and a blanket coat. **1847** ROBB *Squatter Life* 119 The first was a man about middle stature, . . . clad in a dilapidated suit of Kentucky jean. **1862** *Prelim. Rep. 8th Census* 67 Satinets, Kentucky jeans, and other fabrics of which the warp is cotton. **1884** *Harper's Mag.* Aug. 345/1 Kentucky jean or denim has been known to take upon itself the semblance of Oriental drapery.

2. *pl.* Trousers or other garments made of this material.

*c***1845** W. T. THOMPSON *Chron. Pineville* 18 He no longer tolerated Kentucky-jeans and thick-soled shoes. **1855** 'P. PAXTON' *Capt. Priest* 60 Youths . . . so very green, that they had not yet shed their 'Kentucky jeans.' **1876** *Ill. Dept. Agric. Trans.* XIII. 337 The Kentucky jeans and the copperas-colored clothing of home manufacture, so familiar to our boyish eyes, have given place to the cassimeres of Harris or of local factories. **1880** *Harper's Mag.* Jan. 227/1 They play in solemn fashion, occasionally giving way to bursts of boyish spirits, which . . . are speedily checked, in due deference to order—and the Kentucky jeans. **1889** P. BUTLER *Recollections* 54 Some were dressed in Kentucky-jeans.

3. Attrib. with *coat, vest.*

1843 'CARLTON' *New Purchase* I. 73 He had on a Kentucky-jean vest. **1845** SOL. SMITH *Theatr. Apprent.* v. 47 A gentleman in a Kentucky jeans coat and white hat.

+**Kentucky oyster.** (See quotation.) — **1898** DUNBAR *Folks from Dixie* 103 There was hog jole and cold cabbage, ham and Kentucky oysters, more widely known as chittlings.

+**Kentucky rifle.** An extremely accurate, double-sighted, long-barreled, small-caliber, flintlock rifle of a type used by the first white settlers of Kentucky. — **1839** HOFFMAN *Wild Scenes* 132 The British bayonet was no match then for the Kentucky rifle. **1853** MCCONNEL *Western Char.* 208 At his belt hung a long knife, and in his hand he carried a heavy 'Kentucky rifle.' **1896** SHINN *Story of Mine* It might be a fellow with buckskins and Kentucky rifle. **1913** LONDON *Valley of Moon* 322 What does old Susan do, but get out an old, long-barreled Kentucky rifle?

+**Kentucky warbler.** A warbler (*Oporornis formosus*) common in the eastern part of the United States. — **1811** WILSON *Ornithology* III. 85 [The] Kentucky Warbler, *Sylvia Formosa,* . . . inhabits the country whose name it bears. It is also found generally in all the intermediate tracts between Nashville and New Orleans. **1844** *Nat. Hist. N.Y., Zoology* II. 105. **1868** *Amer. Naturalist* II. 181 The Kentucky Warbler (*Oporornis formosus*) . . . has been discovered on Long Island several times. **1917** *Birds of Amer.* III. 156/1 The Kentucky Warbler is a lover of heavily timbered country.

+**Kenyan, Kenyon.** =CAÑON. (Cf. KANYON.) — **1838** S. PARKER *Journal* 83 The place of our encampment was such as would naturally fill the mind with solemnity—just above a very deep and narrow defile which we had to pass, called by the hunters Kenyan. **1843** FARNHAM *Travels Prairies* I. 267 About midway from the Great Gap and the Kenyon of the south Fork of the Platte.

+**Ker-.** The first element in various echoic formations heightening the idea of impact or sound. *colloq.*

Some of these formations are occasionalisms as *kerbim, kerblip, kerplumpus,* but others as *kerchunk, kerplunk,* and *kerflummux* have considerable frequency. (Cf. CA-, KA-.)

1843 'CARLTON' *New Purchase* I. 268 In he splasht'd kerslush, like a hurt buffalo bull. *c***1849** PAIGE *Dow's Sermons* I. 179 Genius . . . comes down ker-whop, bruises itself not a little. **1851** *Polly Peablossom* 52 He cussed 'nuff to send twenty preachers like old Hoe Slater . . . right kerplumpus into h—. *Ib.* 70 She turned 'round an' took me kerbim right 'tween the eyes! *a***1859** *N.Y. Spirit of Times* (B.), And then Kerswollop went one rider clear over the horse's head. **1859** *Harper's Mag.* Aug. 318/2 In his eagerness to grasp a magnificent lily, [he] was plunged 'ker swop!' . . . to the muddy bottom of the lake. **1884** 'MARK TWAIN' *H. Finn* xxiii. 234 'Long come de wind en slam it to, behine de chile, ker-*blam!* **1903** 'O. HENRY' *Cabbages & Kings* vi. 95 Now and then a ripe cocoanut would drop kerblip in the sand. **1906** FREEMAN *'Doc' Gordon* 8 It is only because I'm a poor devil that I don't go kerflop the minute I set eyes on you. **1916** PORTER *David* 227 Along comes the news that somethin's broke kersmash in that bank.

b. *Kerchunk, kerplunk, kerflummux.*

*c***1849** PAIGE *Dow's Sermons* I. 166 Ere the middle round [of the ladder] be reached, the bottom slips, and down you come ker-flummux. **1850** NORTHALL *Yankee Hill* 39 'Jump in' says he, and he took me by the coat-collar and pulled me in kerchunk. **1871** STOWE *Sam Lawson* 213 He sot out full tilt and come down on him ker chunk, and knocked him head over heels. **1884** NYE *Baled Hay* 79 We hear the low, sad kerplunk of the wheel, the loud burst of earnest, logical profanity. **1897** ROBINSON *Uncle Lisha* 18, I went a kerflummuxin' daown yunder through the bushes right slap ontu a snag o' ducks. **1908** MCGAFFEY *Show-Girl* 228 The outfit fell into the water kerplunk.

+**Kerboodle.** =CABOODLE. — **1877** BARTLETT 331 *Kerboodle,* all; the whole. **1880** HARTE *Story of Mine* (1896) 253 Down we go, the whole kerboodle of us, plump into the Stanislaus!

***Kerchief.** A square of cloth used as a covering for the head and shoulders; a handkerchief. — **1807** IRVING, etc. *Salmagundi* i, Mrs. Oldmixon pins her kerchief a hair's breadth awry. **1838** *S. Lit. Messenger* IV. 58/1 His white 'kerchief was barely perceptible in his pocket corner. **1860** HOLMES *E. Venner* vii, Mrs. Crane bedewed her own kerchief with some of the *eau de Cologne* of native manufacture,—said on its label to be much superior to the German article. **1890** HOWELLS *Boy's Town* 13 [She] always wore a dress of Quakerish plainness, with a white kerchief crossed upon her breast. **1898** PAGE *Red Rock* 283 An old negro woman in a white kerchief stood in the door dropping courtesies as though she were in a play.

+**Kerchunk.** (See Ker- b.)

+**Kerosene.** Also **kerocene.** [Gr. κηρός, 'wax.'] Named by Abraham Gesner, Canadian geologist (1797–1864).

1. A mixture of liquid hydrocarbons, distilled from mineral wax, bituminous shale, etc., or from petroleum; coal oil. {=paraffin}

1855 *Rep. Comm. Patents 1854* 462 This [fluid] the inventor calls *A. Kerocene.* **1865** *Atlantic Mo.* XV. 394 She would put kerosene on her fire to make it burn. **1871** *Scribner's Mo.* I. 537 For many months this was the only street lamp in town; but afterwards the streets were lighted with kerosene, and still later with gas. **1882** LATHROP *Echo of Passion* xi, The smell of kerosene from the lamps became painfully noticeable. **1883** *Century Mag.* July 338/2 The new illuminating fluid obtained from the earth, . . . is still widely known by that name [coal oil] or by the Greek appelation [*sic*] kerosene, originally taken as a trade-mark by one of the early distillers of cannel coal. **1909** 'O. HENRY' *Options* 149 On them stood his stores of flour, bacon, lard, talcum-powder, kerosene, baking-powder, soda-mint tablets [etc.].

2. Attrib. with *can, factory,* etc.

1855 *Rep. Comm. Patents 1854* 462 Abraham Gesner, assignor to the Asphalt Mining and Kerocene Gas Company. **1870** *Mass. Bureau Statistics of Labor Rep.* I. 371 [A list of occupations:] Kerseymeres, Knitting machines, Kerosene works, Lime [etc.]. **1873** *Pat. Off. Gazette* IV. 89/2 Kerosene Heater. . . . The heating-vessel, adapted to be used in connection with a lamp and its chimney, consists of two concentric compartments. **1873** BAILEY *Life Danbury* 298 The kerosene kindlers have adopted this plan. **1875** CARLETON *Farm Legends* 54 Let's sit here a while, by this kerosene light. **1882** PECK *Sunshine* 40 [He] calls for the kerosene can, and pours a little oil into the crevice. **1883** *Century Mag.* July 338/2 The great petroleum refineries of Hunter's Point . . . are the successors of one of the earliest kerosene factories in the United States.

+Kerosene lamp. A lamp in which the wick is fed from a reservoir of kerosene.

1859 *Texas Almanac 1860* 265 All descriptions of . . . Kerosen, Solar and Coal Oil Lamps. **1868** *N.Y. Herald* 29 July 6 A girl . . . was terribly burned a day or two since by the explosion of a kerosene lamp. **1875** B. W. HOWARD *One Summer* i, The prim, cheerless room, lighted by one kerosene-lamp, which stared down at her from the high wooden mantel. **1882** SWEET & KNOX *Texas Siftings* 107 Even the stage robbers are not as dangerous as a kerosene lamp to handle. **1907** LILLIBRIDGE *Trail* 67 That tiny frontier room with the smoke-blackened ceiling and the single kerosene lamp sputtering on the wall. **1917** MCCUTCHEON *Green Fancy* 69 A single kerosene lamp gave out a feeble, rather ghastly light.

attrib. **1869** *Boyd's Business Directory* 601 Scovill Manufacturing Co., Manufacturers of . . . Kerosene Lamp Burners and Hand Lamps.

+Kerosene oil. =KEROSENE 1. Also attrib.

1858 *Boston Directory* 114/2 Downer, Samuel, kerosene oil, 76 Water. **1862** *Prelim. Rep. 8th Census* 73 In 1854 the Kerosene Oil Company, on Long Island, commenced the first manufacture of carbo-hydrogen oil under patents secured by Dr. Gesner. **1867** *Atlantic Mo.* Feb. 156/1 Sharpley trimmed the kerosene-oil lamps freshly. **1885** CUSTER *Boots & Saddles* viii. 101 She held out the can of kerosene oil to him. **1897** F. C. MOORE *How To Build* 40 Kerosene-oil alone . . . [is] free from the danger of spontaneous ignition.

+Kerrite. [W. C. *Kerr*, Amer. geologist (1827–85).] A kind of vermiculite found in North Carolina: (see quotations). — **1873** *Amer. Philos. Soc.* XIII. 396 Kerrite . . . consists of innumerable fine scales, which under the microscope do not present a definite shape. **1890** *Cent.* 3277/1 *Kerrite*, named after W. C. Kerr, a State geologist of North Carolina.

+Kerry pippin. A variety of apple. — **1847** IVES *New Eng. Fruit* 38 *Kerry Pippin.*—Fruit of medium size; the form oblong, flattened at the eye and stalk.

***Kersey.** Also **cars(e)y, keirsy,** etc.

***1.** A kind of woolen cloth, usually coarse and ribbed; freq. in pl., a make or variety of this cloth.

1640 *Md. Archives* 97 A Servant at the end of his Service shall have . . . one good Cloth suite of Keirsy or broadcloth. **a1656** BRADFORD *Hist.* 311 They were forced to buy of the fisher men . . . cottens & carseys & other such like cloath. **1732** *S.C. Gazette* 136/2 Lately imported, . . . yorkshire kerseys. **1759** *Newport Mercury* 10 April 4/2 To be Sold by Simon Pease, Jun. . . . German Serges, Devonshire Kerseys. **1775** *Jrnls. Cont. Congress* III. 318 That as much duffiels or Kersey, as will make up three hundred watch coats, be purchased. **1833** *Niles' Reg.* XLIV. 380/2 [We] dealt freely during that year [1828] in flushings or fearnaughts, drab kerseys, broadcloths [etc.]. **1903** WHITE *Forest* 12 A pair of oilskin trousers turns the wet better than does kersey.

2. Attrib. with *cloth, coat, doublet*, etc.

1644 *Essex Probate Rec.* I. 35 One sad collored Carsy gowen and hud sutable. **1699** J. DICKENSON *God's Protecting Prov.* 67 The chiefest man of the Sentinall took a Kersey-Coat and gave my Wife to cover her. **1771** *Essex Gazette* 14 May, A Negro Man named Cato . . . had on a kersey Jacket and leather Breeches. **1835** HOFFMAN *Winter in West* I. 259 Shaking the flaps of his rough kersey doublet like a pair of wings, he crowed and swore that he could throw any man of his weight in the mines. **1856** *Mich. Agric. Soc. Trans.* VII. 65 Mrs. C. Hadsell . . . 1 piece linen wove kearsey cloth.

Kerseymere. [A corruption of CASSIMERE by erron. association with KERSEY.] Cassimere, or a garment made of it. {1798–}

1784 *Mass. Centinel* 4 Sept. 3/3 To be sold . . . a general assortment of European goods, consisting of . . . kerseymeres, . . . scarf twist, . . . kenting handkerchiefs. **1797** *Ann. 4th Congress.* 2 Sess. 2271 It was not fitting to put them [*sc.* cotton goods] upon the same footing with respect to duty as kerseymeres, fine linen, &c. **1833** NEAL *Down-Easters* I. 94 The midshipman . . . was just pouring down a tumbler of porter, . . . showering his white kerseymeres with a new color. **1846** in J. Hawthorne *N. Hawthorne & Wife* I. 309 The pantaloons [to be] of kerseymere or broadcloth. **1872** *Newton Kansan* 7 Nov. 2/2 They should soil their silks or kerseymeres by the contact. **1909** WEBSTER 341/1 Kerseymere . . . is woven with one third of the warp always above and two thirds below each shoot of the weft.

+Ke-souse. (See KER-.) — **1841** *Knickerb.* XVII. 154, I swear, I had a twelve-pounder out of the water, when my cussed line broke, and *kesouse* he went.

Ketch. Also **catch, cetch.** *Naut.* A strongly rigged two-masted vessel, usually with several jibs, up to 250 tons burden. {1655– later form of **catch*}

1636 *Mass. H. S. Coll.* 4 Ser. VII. 55 At the closing of this letter came the cetch from the Naragansets with corne, and I have tacken one hondard buchils of it. **1671** in Neill *Va. Carolorum* 336 What number of ships do trade yearly to and from your plantation, and of what burthen are they? . . . Few New England ketches; but of our own we never yet had more than two, at one time, and those not more than twenty ton burthen. **1687** SEWALL *Diary* I. 184 Brother . . . brings word that two Salem Catches are taken by the French, of which his Newbury Ketch is one, and the whole Fare due to him, so that his Livelihood is in a manner taken away. **1704** *Boston News Letter* 24 April 2/2 They found the aforesaid Shallop . . . and a Ketch at Tarpolian Cove, who were all Fishing Vessels belonging to Marblehead of Salem. **1705** *Ib.* 30 July 2/1 We daily expect more Men of War with Fire-Ships and a Bomb Ketch to joyn them. **1884** *Nat. Museum Bul.* No. 27, 652 The so-called ketches . . . were [illegible]ll and heavy built, with a peculiar rig that was at first invented for a bomb vessel (the mainmast standing about amidships to give room for ordnance forward), but afterwards came into great favor for yachts and fishing crafts.

***Kettle.** Also *dial.* **cattel, kittle.**

The form *cattell* occurs in older Scottish (1506–1640). *Kittle* is widely current in Eng. dialects.

***1.** A metal vessel for boiling something over a fire.

1622 'MOURT' *Relation* 21 We found a great Ketle, which had beene . . . brought out of Europe. **1633** *N.H. Doc. & Rec.* I. 75, 4 kittles, [£]3. **1677** *Hempstead Town Rec.* I. 312 He saw severall fathums of wampom and two greate cattells. **1786** in *Mag. Amer. Hist.* I. 309 At present there are about 100 kettles boiling [salt]. **1833** SILLIMAN *Man. Sugar Cane* 56 The syrup is conveyed from the kettles, by a trough, into the receiving cisterns. **1891** WILKINS *New Eng. Nun* 164 'Now fill up the kittle, an' fry the sassages,' she said to Mrs. Carey. **1925** TILGHMAN *Dugout* 33 'Now,' said Kiowa, as he rinsed the kettle, 'you git out them packages of red pepper and I'll fetch some more water.'

b. Often preceded by name of metal of which it is made.

1624 SMITH *Gen. Hist. Va.* III. 75 We wrangled out of the King ten quarters of Corne for a copper Kettell. **1633** *N.H. Doc. & Rec.* I. 77, 1 brasse kettle. **1650** *Essex Inst. Coll.* XLIII. 71 A gird ieren & a iern Kettell & a ould posnett. **1760** *Ib.* 198 [We] took our Blankets and Tin Kittles and other things. **1817** *Indian Laws & Tr.* II. 143 The United States do also bind themselves to give to all the poor warriors . . . one blanket and one brass kettle. **1871** *Rep. Indian Affairs* (1872) 418 The amount expended for beaver-traps, if used for the purchase of sheet-iron kettles, would be of much more service to the Indian.

c. Often preceded by name of the substance boiled in it. (Cf. TEAKETTLE.)

1664 *Brookhaven Rec.* 12, 3 pekle kettels. **1704** S. KNIGHT *Journal* 15 The sause was of a deep Purple, wch. I tho't was boil'd in her dye Kettle. **1790** *Penna. Packet* 2 Jan. 3/3 He can furnish pot-ash kettles. **1859** BARTLETT 19 *Bagasse* . . . is used as fuel under the sugar-kettle.

+2. ? A kettle-shaped container.

1674 JOSSELYN *Two Voyages* 70 Many of these Trees [Birches] are stript of their bark by the *Indians*, who make of it their Canows, Kettles, and Birchen-dishes.

+3. 'A pail, as of tin-plate; a dinner-pail. N. England' (B. '77).

4. Attrib. and comb. with *maker, man*, etc.

1833 SILLIMAN *Man. Sugar Cane* 15 During the cutting season . . . forty hands with knives . . . [and] six kettle men [are employed]. **1856** A. CARY *Married* 293 If she knew where to find a good kettle-maker she would have enough brass taken out of her husband's face to make a forty or fifty gallon one. **1857** *Ill. Agric. Soc. Trans.* II. 461 You will not send your old 'bull's eye,' for repairs, to a kettle tinker. **1872** *Vermont Bd. Agric. Rep.* I. 220 We do not hesitate to pronounce this [the siphon system of sugar-making] as great an improvement upon Mr. Northrop's four pan system, as that is upon our original kettle system.

+Kettle bail. (See quotation.) — **1881** INGERSOLL *Oyster-Industry* 245 *Kettle Bail.*—A dredge used in catching scallops, which has the blade adjusted to swing in the eyes of the arms, in order to prevent its sinking into the mud of the soft bottom on which it is used. (Rhode Island.)

+Kettled, *a.* **1.** Rendered in kettles. **2.** *Geol.* Worn into kettle-shaped hollows. — **(1) 1869** *Ill. Agric. Soc. Trans.* VII. 432 Kettled lard . . . sold at 16 c. **(2) 1898** *Amer. Geologist* Nov. 298 Crevasses and moulins would be formed . . . producing such a profusely kettled surface as in the Glacier Garden.

***Kettledrum.** An informal tea party held in the afternoon. {1861–} (Cf. DRUM *n.* 4.) — **1867** DIXON *New America* II. 51 In the face of our surplus million of spinsters, the saying is a pleasantry, as you may see at any crush-room, kettle-drum, and croquet party. **1879** WEBSTER *Suppl.* 1564. **1882** 'HARLAND' *Eve's Daughters* 298 The late dinners *à la Russe*, ladies' lunches, kettle-drums and high teas are a surprise and a strain to her faculties. **1887** *Courier-Journal* 8 May 20/2 She and several of her friends were at a fancy dress kettledrum. **1898** ATHERTON *Californians* 297 She also gave many dinners and breakfasts, kettle-drums and theatre parties.

Kettlings. =CHITLINGS 1. — **1869** *Overland Mo.* III. 130 Then there are the delusive 'kettlings,' among the 'low-down' people. . . . I will simply say that it is fried sausages, minus all the unhealthy and absurd meat which most people insist on stuffing into the intestinal integuments.

***Key.**[1] Variant of 'quay,' a wharf. *Obs.* — **1638** *Dedham Rec.* 42 For a parcell of grownd layd downe by him at the Keye. **1686** *Conn. Rec.* III. 408 Customs are duly paid . . . [and] no goods . . . landed upon any key. **1715** *Va. State P.* I. 183 The Ground or Beach for which a Patent is desired, is part of the Common Key or Landing place formerly laid out for this Port and Town.

***Key.**[2]

***1.** An instrument, usually of metal, for moving back and forth the bolt of a lock.

1644 *Harvard Rec.* I. 6 Expenses: . . . for nayles, locke & key, . . . 5 [s] 10 [d]. **1799** BROWN *A. Mervyn* iv, The door was fastened by several bolts and a lock. The bolts were easily withdrawn, but the key was removed. **1869** TOURGEE *Toinette* vii. 86 He put his hand in his pocket and felt the key of the wardrobe. **1911** VANCE *Cynthia* 69 [He] snatched the key from her unresisting grasp.

+2. A key-shaped emblem of a fraternity, as the Phi Beta Kappa key.

1912 *Independent* 19 Dec. 1436/2 [Members of Phi Beta Kappa] carry a gold key, and that badge is all the distinction they get.

3. *attrib.* and *comb.* **a.** In sense 1.

1871 *Rep. Comm. Patents 1869* I. 557/1 A key-ring, . . . as a new article of manufacture. **1871** BAGG *At Yale* 21 The steward's office is now used as a dormitory by an indigent student who has charge of the key-box. **1882** PECK *Sunshine* 30 He will be apt to look up at the key rack and tell them everything is full. **1902** BELL *Hope Loring* 233 Hope searched for her father's key-chain, and took the key to the wine-cellar.

+b. *Keyman*, a telegrapher.

1907 *Washington Star* 30 Sept. 9 Some of the leading keymen are sounding as their shibboleth the cry of 'government ownership of the telegraph systems.'

Key.[3] [Sp. *cayo*, 'shoal, reef.'] A low island or reef. Chiefly off the Florida coast. {1697-, in Central America} (Cf. KAY.)

1772 D. TAITT in *Travels American Colonies* 549 He says that there is always vessels fishing and cutting Lumber amongst the Keys about Cape Florida. **1799** ELLICOTT in Mathews *Life A. Ellicott* 186 Along the Florida Reef, and among the Keys, a great abundance and variety of fish may be taken: such as . . . red, and gray snappers. **1802** — *Journal* 243 [We] sailed to the anchor ground between the main land and southern Key. **1837** WILLIAMS *Florida* 98 The Black Mangrove covers most of the low islands and shores of the keys. **1886** *Boston Jrnl.* 11 Aug. 2/3 The keys from Biscayne Bay to Key West contain many thousand new trees. **1907** *Harper's Mag.* Jan. 214 On one of the keys of Alligator Bay is the principal plume-bird rookery left in Florida.

+Key basket. A small basket used to carry or keep keys in. — **1836** GILMAN *Recoll.* (1838) 172 Mama had carefully placed hers in her key-basket. *c*1866 BAGBY *Old Va. Gentleman* 54 The good wife of the native Virginian, with her check apron, key-basket, and knitting sheath. **1880** *Harper's Mag.* July 263/2, I heard keys jingling in her key basket as she moved across the floor. **1889** *Century Mag.* April 841/1 A mob-cap covering her grey hair, and key-basket in hand, the wife of Washington must have offered a pleasant picture.

Keyboard. {1819-} **1.** A board on which telegraphic keys are placed. **2.** The set of keys on a typewriter. {1851-} — **(1) 1848** *Sci. Amer.* 2 Dec. 83/1 The letters on it [House's Printing Telegraph] are detained to print by a key board like that of a piano, . . . [hence] the letters can be printed just as quick as the key board can be operated. **1860** PRESCOTT *Telegraph* 147 The key-board is similar in appearance to the House. **1870** MEDBERY *Men Wall St.* 31 A grave-faced man has his fingers on the key-board, and is spreading the news of this fierce 'bear' raid. **(2) 1871** C. L. SHOLES in Weller *Early Hist. Typewriter* 46, I have now a machine . . . which is an entirely different thing. . . . The key board is not the same. **1918** OWEN *Typewriting Speed* 34 This third finger should be made as strong . . . because the keys which it operates might be termed more 'popular' than any of the other letters on the keyboard.

+Key City. A nickname for Dubuque, Iowa. — **1859** *Ladies' Repository* XIX. 51/2 Dubuque, Iowa, is the 'Key City,' as it is said to open the doors of trade to the north-west and the Pacific.

Keyhole saw. A narrow saw suitable for cutting keyholes. {1816} — **1777** *Essex Inst. Coll.* XLIX. 106 Sold, . . . key hole saws, at 2 s. **1832** *Louisville Pub. Advertiser* 3 March 4/1 (*advt.*), John D. Thorpe . . . is now opening a general assortment of Hardware . . . [including] mill, cross cut, . . . key hole and wood saws.

+Key log. In river driving, a log or one of several logs so caught or wedged that a jam is formed and held.

1851 SPRINGER *Forest Life* 166 It may be thought best to cut off the key-log, or that which appears to be the principal barrier. **1860** *Harper's Mag.* March 452/1 The most vulnerable point—the 'key-log' of the jam—is sought. **1873** BEADLE *Undevel. West* 719 There is generally what is called a 'key-log,' and by attaching a rope thereto the whole mass is loosened. Climbing over the 'jam,' hunting for this 'key-log,' and loosening it, is a most perilous business. **1893** *Scribner's Mag.* June 714/2 Teams hitched to lines, at the end of which is a hook similar to a cant-hook are used to loosen the 'key-log.' **1900** BRUNCKEN *N. Amer. Forests* 86 Many lives have been lost by the impetuous rush of the logs when those key-logs had begun to move. **1908** WHITE *Riverman* 40 A good riverman . . . knows how to look for the key-log in breaking jams.

+Key State. =KEYSTONE STATE. — **1851** J. F. W. JOHNSTON *Notes on Amer.* II. 326 With more dignity, those of New Hampshire speak of their home as the Granite State, . . . of New York as the Empire State; of Pennsylvania as the Key State; and of Virginia, proudly as the Old Dominion!

Keystone. {1637-}

1. In fig. context: +A state or city occupying a position similar to that of a keystone in an arch.

1818 *Niles' Reg.* XIV. 23/1 The powerful population and ample resources of Pennsylvania, together with her local position, standing as the key-stone of the federal arch. **1834** *Congress. Globe* 31 May 408/1 The State of Pennsylvania . . . was still the key-stone of the Union. **1870** *Ib.* 19 April 2801/3 Pennsylvania . . . is the keystone of this Union much more than in name. **1903** FOX *Little Shepherd* xxvii, Atlanta, the keystone of the Confederate arch.

+2. =KEYSTONE STATE. Also attrib.

1844 *Congress. Globe* App. 4 June 662/3 The old Keystone has never furnished the Union with either President or Vice President, and it causes her to feel badly. **1873** W. CARLETON *Farm Ballads* 89 Mid old Key-stone's rugged riches, which the miner's hand await. **1892** *Review of York County* 70/1 The Keystone Felting Mills can quote satisfactory prices to the trade anywhere.

+Keystone City. The city of Philadelphia. — **1846** WYSE *America* II. 114 General Fritz, was . . . a working stone-cutter, in this 'keystone city,' as Philadelphia is often called.

+Keystone Commonwealth. =next. — **1899** *Success* 6 May 391 They emigrated to the Keystone commonwealth when the northern portion of the state was a howling wilderness.

+Keystone State. A sobriquet for the state of Pennsylvania, in allusion to its being in the center of the thirteen original states.

1836 *S. Lit. Messenger* II. 277 The little German farmer . . . in the Key Stone State . . . would not wish the property of the country to be thrown in jeopardy. **1842** *Knickerb.* XIX. 160 A worthy immigrant from either the Granite or the Key-stone state. **1856** *Democratic Conv. Proc.* 50 [James Buchanan] will receive a large and overwhelming majority in the Keystone State. **1875** BURNHAM *Three Years* 338 An Academy . . . is still flourishing there, and is now considered one of the finest educational institutions of its class in the great Key-stone State. **1904** *N.Y. American* 4 April 4 The Pennsylvania men agreed with the Tammany leader that the Keystone State should send an uninstructed delegation.

b. In allusion to its position among the states holding their elections before November in the years of presidential elections.

1885 *Century Mag.* Feb. 635/2 The only Northern States now holding elections before November are Vermont, Maine, and Ohio. Pennsylvania was once the 'Keystone State' of the political arch, but its citizens . . . transferred their State contest to November.

+Key West. [The name of a city of Florida, situated on an island in the Gulf of Mexico.] In the specific names of birds. — **1858** BAIRD *Birds Pacific R.R.* 607 Key West Pigeon. . . . Key West, Florida, and West Indies. **1917** *Birds of Amer.* III. 110/2 The Small White-eyed Vireo . . . is similar in color to the Key West Vireo.

+K. G. C. Abbreviation for KNIGHTS OF THE GOLDEN CIRCLE. *Obs.* — **1860** *Richmond Enquirer* 20 April 4/7 (Th.), Every day strengthens my conviction that the whole K. G. C. enterprise will end in smoke. **1861** *Congress. Globe* 23 Jan. 532/1 *n.*, The K. G. C.—A secret and oath-bound association the members of which call themselves the Knights of the Golden Circle, has existed for many months throughout the cotton States. **1865** *Nation* I. 66 Wendell Phillips and Barnwell Rhett are relieved from the suspicion of being K. G. C.'s.

Khaki. A stout twilled cotton or wool fabric of a dull brownish color {1857-}; soldiers dressed in this. {1899-} Also attrib. — **1898** *N.Y. Journal* 16 Sept. 4/2 Evening dress and khaki talked much sport and a little war over 'high balls' or chicken livers. **1900** *Boston Ev. Globe* 26 Jan., The men looked very businesslike in khaki and putties. **1908** BEACH *Barrier* 90 [He] fashioned her a pillow out of a bundle of smaller ones, around which he wrapped his khaki coat. **1918** SANDBURG *Cornhuskers* 141 The boys and men in winding lines of khaki.

Kiaka elm. (See quotation.) — **1892** APGAR *Trees Northern U.S.* 136 *Planera acuminata.* (Kiaka elm or Japan Planer-tree.) . . . This is a larger, more hardy, and finer tree than the American Planer-tree, and should be more extensively cultivated.

+Kib(b)lings. 'Parts of small fish used by fishermen for bait on the banks of Newfoundland' (B. '48). — **1843** in Goode, etc. *Fisheries* v. (1887) 160 Metal hooks baited with parts of small fish (by us called kiblings).

***Kick,** *n.*

1. The recoil of a gun when discharged. {1846}

1826 COOPER *Mohicans* vii, The kick of the rifle disconcerts your aim.

+2. A complaint or vigorous objection. *slang.*

1887 *Courier-Journal* 13 Jan. 5/6 (*caption*), Kicks Sent to Congress. **1893** *Daily Press Gazette* (Oklahoma City) 18 Sept. (Th. S.), The kick came from those who paid . . . for a certificate in the deluded idea that it was exchangeable for a claim or a town lot. **1904** W. H. SMITH *Promoters* 219 The whole thing is strictly business, and as a business man of the modern type, you ought to have no kick coming. **1920** LEWIS *Main Street* 115 But then I've got no kick. I do what I please.

***Kick,** *v.*

1. *tr.* Of a gun: To strike in the recoil when fired. {*intr.* 1832-}

1776 TRUMBULL *M'Fingal* I. 19 But as some musquets so contrive it, . . . Bear wide and kick their owners over. **1872** ROE *Army Lett.* 43 The big thing rudely 'kicked' me over on my back, and the bullet . . . is still on its way to Mars.

+2. To reject (a suitor). *colloq.*[2]

1848 BARTLETT 194 Miss A has *kicked* the Hon. Mr. B, and sent him off with a flea in his ear. **1881** PIERSON *In the Brush* 8 They did not say the lady rejected or 'mittened' her suitor, but, 'She kicked him.' **1895** *Outing* XXVII. 74/2 Some years ago . . . a Suffolk gal kicked me.

+3. a. *intr.* (with advs.) To walk or go. *slang.*

1839 KIRKLAND *New Home* xxv. 195 We heard that he was better, and would be able to 'kick around' pretty soon. **1908** MCGAFFEY *Show-Girl* 47 The other evening I kicked down to a show I once worked in.

+b. *tr.* To put (something, as a railroad car) into motion by a quick, sudden impact.

1898 *McClure's Mag.* X. 211/1, I was about to step directly in front of a rapidly approaching car which an engine had kicked in on that track. *Ib.* 212/1 A conductor . . . pulled the coupling pin on the crippled car, and gave his engineer a signal to kick it in. . . . The kicked car fetched up.

4. With adverbs. *To kick about,* to be neglected or disregarded; to be here and there according to shifts of fortune. {1877–, *dial.*}

1867 'LACKLAND' *Homespun* I. 80 [The] doctor, whose instruments . . . lie kicking about like ordinary household trumpery. **1884** R. GRANT *Average Man* 251 Its stock had been kicking about on the market for about fourteen dollars a share. **1896** SHINN *Story of Mine* 157 The stock has been 'kicking about the street,' to use the broker's phrase, which means that it was like so much waste paper.

+5. *To kick one's self,* (see quot. 1892). *colloq.*

1891 *Voice* 29 Jan., In the absence of any of the committee to kick I went home kicking myself, and it wears on the constitution to be both kicker and kickee at the same time. **1892** WALSH *Lit. Curiosities* 584 To kick one's self, often used with an infinite variety of adjuncts,—*i.e.,* to kick one's self 'all over the house,' 'all over the place,' etc.,—means to feel or express violent dissatisfaction with one's self, to be mortified or chagrined.

+Kickapoo. Also **Kickepoo,** etc. A member of an Algonquian tribe of Indians once inhabiting northern Illinois, but now on reservations in Kansas, Oklahoma, and Mexico; also, pl., a tribe of these Indians.

[**1670** *Relations des Jesuites* (1858) 100/1 A quatre lieues d'icy sont les Kikabou, et les Kitchigamich.] **1776** *Kentucky Petitions* 40 They were apprehensive the Kiccapoos would strike their Brothers the Long Knives. **1779** G. R. CLARK *Campaign Illinois* (1869) 79 Calling together the neighbouring Nations, Peankeshaws, Kickepoes, & others, . . . [I] made a very long Speach to them. **1805** PIKE *Sources Miss.* I. App. 2 [They] seem to ascribe the murder to the Kickapoos. **1831** HOLLEY *Texas* (1833) 98 The Kickapoos and Shawnees, driven by the people of the United States to the west of the Mississippi, sometimes extend their hunting parties to the settlements on the Brazoo. **1835** HOFFMAN *Winter in West* I. 276 The Indians that frequent the neighbourhood of Chicago, . . . are chiefly Pottawattamies and Ottawas, with a few Chippewas . . . , and a straggling Kickapoo or Miami. **1865** PIKE *Scout & Ranger* (1932) 72 We soon found the . . . Indians, who proved to be a band of Kickapoos. **1898** *Kansas City Star* 18 Dec. 4/1 The bill contains . . . items . . . for the Mexican Kickapoo Indians, known as the 'kicking Kickapoos.'

b. Attrib. with *community, Indian, land.*

1776 in J. Hall *Sk. of West* (1835) II. 245 It will most certainly be the terror of our savage enemies, the Kickeboos Indians. **1897** in *Congress. Rec.* 4 Jan. (1900) 647/2 Such a provision, however, was embodied . . . in the act of March 3, 1893, providing for the disposal of the Kickapoo lands in Oklahoma. **1912** *Indian Laws & Tr.* III. 544 Said sum to be paid to the treasurer of a corporation to be known as the Kickapoo community of Mexico.

***Kicker.**

+1. *Polit.* One who bolts his party; a bolter. *colloq.*

1885 *Mag. Amer. Hist.* Feb. 202/1 *Kicker.*—One who revolts against party discipline—kicks over the traces, as it were. **1893** *Chicago Tribune* 26 April 10/6 He says the rank and file of the 'kickers' who made up the Populist vote are not for a third party but relief from oppression. **1900** *Congress. Rec.* 5 Feb. 1522/2 You Republicans came in under a good deal of pressure. You had a 'kickers' caucus around here that had eighty-five members in it. **1902** WHITLOCK *13th District* 129 We had to deal with the Sprague kickers.

+2. Anyone who objects or rebels; one who makes kicks. *colloq.*

1889 MUNROE *Golden Days* 40 There were some kickers, of course, but the crowd agreed. **1893** *Harper's Mag.* April 709/2 The pioneer is radical, impatient of dogmas, and a 'kicker' by instinct. **1900** WINCHESTER *W. Castle* 203 Every one of the kickers has left. **1924** R. CUMMINS *Sky-High Corral* 71 His people had been kickers—they had kicked over the grub, and the cooking and the camp sites.

+Kicking colt. The spotted jewelweed. — **1892** *Amer. Folk-Lore* V. 93 *Impatiens fulva,* kicking colt. N. Mass.

Kick-up. {*a*1793–} +A dance. *colloq.* — (1) **1778** *Md. Hist. Mag.* III. 116 We Collected the Girls in the neighbourhood and had a kick up in the Evening. **1804** FESSENDEN *Orig. Poems* (1806) 30 See what lasses we can pick up For our famous village kick up.

***Kid.**[1]

I. +1. a. (See quotations and cf. FREE-WILLER 1 and KIDNAP *v.*)

1724 JONES *Virginia* 53 The Ships . . . often call at Ireland to victual, and bring over frequently [to Va.] white Servants which are . . . bound by Indenture, commonly call'd *Kids,* who are usually to serve four or five Years. [**1893** EGGLESTON *Duffels* 31 The ship [in 1751] was already taking aboard a lot of kids and freewillers out of the cook houses, where some of them had been shut up for weeks. **1895** BALLAGH *White Servitude Va.* 34 The great body of servants [consisted of] . . . free persons . . . who wished to go to the colony as settlers to better their condition, but were too poor to bear the charges of their transportation. . . . This class of so-called 'Kids' was supplemented by a smaller class of persons who went on agreements for fixed wages for a definite time.]

+b. 'A kidnapper' (Chipman).

1862 *N.Y. Tribune* 9 April 6/4 Attempted Kidnapping in Washington. The kidnappers Caught and Locked up. . . . The 'Kids' were . . . sent into town to the Provost Marshal's office.

2. A young person. {a child, 1690–} **a.** Often applied as a nickname to men having a certain youthful appearance or size. {1812– 'in low sporting or criminal circles'}

1880 *Cimarron News & Press* 30 Dec. 2/2 The 'Kid' Captured. At last the leaders of the Pecos and White Oaks desperadoes have been hunted down and forced to surrender. **1898** *Kansas City Star* 18 Dec. 3/1 'Kid' McCoy, the rising young Hoosier pugilist . . . made a chopping block of game Dan Creedon, the Australian pugilist. **1905** 'O. HENRY' *Roads of Destiny* 138 'It sounds to me!' said the Kid, nodding his head. **1925** W. N. BURNS *Saga of Billy the Kid* 115 The Kid's a wise hombre. . . . He'll listen to reason.

+b. Applied as a familiar or intimate term to any young person. *colloq.*

1890 *Stock Grower & Farmer* 17 May 5/3 It was a wild and reckless set of kids that started out with the T. V. wagon. **1896** *Emporia Gazette* 15 Aug., Then we have discovered a kid without a law practice and have decided to run him for attorney general. **1908** HORNBLOW *Profligate* 44 One drunken kid . . . had lost $200,000, settled in promissory notes. **1915** CAMPBELL *Proving Virginia* 126 They're nice kids, aren't they? **1920** SANDBURG *Smoke & Steel* 89 Do you love me, kid?

II. 3. *attrib.* **a.** Of gloves or footwear: Made of kid leather or a substitute. (See also KID GLOVE.)

1759 WASHINGTON *Writings* II. 138, 1 light duffel Cloak with silver frogs. 8 pr kid Mitts. **1850** LEWIS *La. Swamp Doctor* 157 Pride, that sticks a pretty foot in a kid slipper in the dead of winter. **1875** HOWARD *One Summer* i, [She] eyed the tips of her delicate French kid boots. **1891** WELCH *Recoll. 1830–40* 175 Lane's French kid slippers, black or bronzed, cut very low, the soles quite thin, without heels. **1893** *Harper's Mag.* March 489 There she strode, in white kid shoes, with a white sailor hat on her head. **1893** *Chicago Tribune* 28 April 8 Ladies' Fine Imperial Kid Blucher Oxfords, with patent leather tips—sold at $3.00.

+b. (Passing into adj.) Younger. *slang.*

1898 *Mo. So. Dakotan* I. 103 Yer kid brothers kin run the place all right.

Kid.[2] {1769–} +'A large box in fishing vessels into which fish are thrown as they are caught. In New England' (B. '48). — **1846** *Knickerb.* XXVII. 511 The scaly denizens tumbling into the kids.

***Kiddle.** Also **†kedle.** A contrivance with nets set in a stream for catching fish. — **1724** *Penna. Col. Rec.* III. 233 An act for demolishing . . . Fishing Dams, Wears & Kedles set across the River Schuylkill. **1871** *Penna. Laws* 278 Such contrivances for the catching of fish as are commonly known as fish baskets, eel weirs, kiddles, brush or fascine nets . . . are declared common nuisances.

Kid glove.

1. A glove made of the skin of a kid or of an imitation of this leather. {1832–}

1711 *Boston News-Letter* 20 Aug. 2/2 A Parcel of fine Kidd and Lamb Gloves of the best sort for Men and Women, . . . To be Sold. **1734** *Ib.* 27 Nov. 2/2 Men's and women's kid gloves. **1762** in H. M. Brooks *Gleanings* 37 Mens and Womens Kid and Lamb Gloves. **1865** WHITMAN *Spec. Days* 64, I saw Mr. Lincoln, drest all in black, with white kid gloves and a claw-hammer coat. **1890** *Stock Grower & Farmer* 5 July 7/1 Those who wear kid gloves are probably not aware that many of the skins . . . came from New Mexico.

+b. *With kid gloves,* in a gentle way; without roughness.

1864 in *Wkly. New Mexican* 3 June 2/3 We have handled the Yankees with kid gloves far too long for our good. **1888** BRYCE *Amer. Commonw.* II. III. lviii. 410 The Americans who think that European politics are worked, to use the common phrase, 'with kid gloves.'

2. Attrib. with *excursion, officer, opening, pilot.*

1846 MELVILLE *Typee* xxiv. 217 [The man] remained there but two weeks, sleeping every night on board his ship, and taking little kid-glove excursions ashore in the daytime. **1866** GREGG *Life in Army* 106 The many starched-up, kid glove, and band-box officers of our army, have proven to be a great nuisance. **1873** 'MARK TWAIN' & WARNER *Gilded Age* iv. 48 What he don't know about the river ain't worth knowing—a regular gold-leaf, kid-glove, diamond-breastpin pilot Wash Hastings is. **1875** *Chicago Tribune* 7 Sept. 1/2 Immense Kid Glove Opening Today. Paris Glove Store.

Kidnap, *v.* [f. *kid* a child and *nap* v.] *tr.* Originally, to abduct and carry off (a child or other person) for use as a servant in the American colonies; hence, to carry off (any person) by illegal force. {1682–}

1693 I. MATHER *Further Acct. Tryals* (1862) 241 A Servant, who was Spirited or Kidnapt . . . into America. **1779** *N.J. Archives* 2 Ser. III. 291 The infamous Weart Banta . . . was shot through the knee, and it is supposed will . . . be disabled from kidnapping and plundering the loyal subjects of this state in the future. **1809** WEEMS *Marion* (1833) 29 [He prattled] a great deal to him about the 'cursed hardship' . . . of kidnapping poor clodhoppers at this rate. **1819** *Niles' Reg.* XVI. 322/2 Nancy Gamble . . . was indicted and tried for kidnapping, stealing, and conveying away an infant female child. **1865** *Atlantic Mo.* XV. 154 Edward Prigg and others were indicted in Pennsylvania for kidnapping a negro woman on the 1st of April, 1837. **1894** *Ib.* LXXIV. 326/1 Celeste Barbeau was kidnapped on her wedding day. **1925** *N.Y. Times* 11 Nov. 2/4 [A woman] was kidnapped last night on Henry Street, . . . by two men who . . . threw a blanket over her head, lifted her into an automobile and drove away.

Kidnapper. **a.** A person whose business was to kidnap others to make them servants or slaves in America. *Obs.* {1678–} **b.** Anyone who kidnaps another.

[**1678** E. PHILLIPS *New World Eng. Words* (ed. 4), *Kidnappers*, . . . those that make a trade of decoying and spiriting away young children to Ship them for foreign Plantations.] **1778** HAMILTON *Works* VII. 541 Punishing kidnappers or persons who aid the enemy in carrying off the peaceable inhabitants. **1827** COOPER *Prairie* viii, Who is a kidnapper? . . . Am I to be called to account for every lie they put in print throughout the States? **1837** CHANNING *Works* (1886) 766/2 In incorporating this region with the Union to make it a slave-country, we send the kid-napper to prowl through the jungles, and to dart, like a beast of prey, on the defenceless villages of Africa. **1857** *Lawrence* (Kan.) *Republican* 25 June 2 In the case of the kidnappers of Solomon Northrup, we learn that a *nol. pros.* has been entered and they are now at large. **1869** STOWE *Oldtown Folks* 355 These kidnappers always make for the New York State line. **1925** *N.Y. Times* 20 July 3/5 The General Electric Company offered a reward of $2,500 for the kidnapper.

* **Kidney.**

1. Applied to kidney-shaped things: **a.** =KIDNEY POTATO. {1796–} **b.** A vein of ore.

1854 *Mich. Agric. Soc. Trans.* V. 208 Some of the more approved kinds [of potato] are the Ash Leaved Kidney, the Cumberland Kidney [etc.]. **1887** TOURGEE *Button's Inn* 178 He picked up the potatoes, . . . delicate white 'Kidneys.' — **1883** RITCH *Illust. New Mexico* 82 The Rappahannock . . . shows a vein of like character, . . . with kidneys of peacock copper. **1886** *Outing* IX. 226/2 The ore of the Blue Nose [mine] occurs principally in pockets or kidneys.

2. *attrib.* and *comb.* +**a.** In the specific names of plants. (Cf. KIDNEY BEAN.)

1817–8 EATON *Botany* (1822) 517 *Woodwardia angustifolia*, kidney-fern. . . . About a foot high. **1819** *Western Rev.* I. 92 As a striking instance . . . I shall select . . . *Cacalia reniformis*, Kidney weed. **1821** *Mass. H. S. Coll.* 2 Ser. IX. 158 Plants, which are indigenous in the township of Middlebury [Vermont, include] . . . *Viola asarifolia*, Kidney-leaf violet. **1829** EATON *Botany* (ed. 5) 241 *Hepatica americana*, kidney-liverleaf. . . . Grows chiefly in woods, prefering [*sic*] the south side of hills and mountains. **1843** TORREY *Flora N.Y.* I. 13 *Ranunculus abortivus*. . . . Kidney-leaved Crowfoot. . . . A common species in rocky woods, meadows, etc.; beginning to flower towards the end of April, and continuing through May. **1898** BRITTON & BROWN *Illus. Flora Northern U.S.* III. 307 *Eupatorium purpureum*. Joe-Pye or Trumpet-weed. . . . Called also Kidney-root, Queen of the Meadow.

+**b.** *Kidney punch*, a fighter's blow to the kidney; *k. shot*, a shot that wounds an animal in the abdomen, but does not kill it.

1896 ADE *Artie* 3 Miller gave him a friendly blow known to ringside patrons as a 'kidney-punch.' **1923** J. H. COOK *On Old Frontier* 85, I kept on and was soon close enough to the big bull to give him what was called a 'kidney shot.'

* **Kidney bean.** Any bean of the genus *Phaseolus*, esp. the common bean, *P. vulgaris;* the seed of such a plant. Also attrib.

1699 E. WARD *New-England* 16 With hard Eggs Pulveriz'd they thicken their Broth; Indian-Corn and Kidney-Beans boil'd. **1709** LAWSON *Carolina* 77 The Kidney-Beans were here before the English came, being very plentiful in the Indian Corn-Fields. **1743** CATESBY *Carolina* II. p. xviii, *Phaseoli*. Kidney-Beans. Of the Kidney-bean kind there are in Carolina and Virginia, eight or ten different sorts, which are natives of America. **1805** PARKINGTON *Tour* 341 Kidney-beans are very productive, and are much in use. **1825** LORAIN *Pract. Husbandry* 123 The kidney bean, when it comes up through the soil, brings the seed with it. **1843** TORREY *Flora N.Y.* I. 160 *Phaseolus diversifolius*. . . . Various-leaved Kidney-bean. . . . Common on sandy shores, particularly in the neighborhood of New-York. August–September. **1871** *Rep. Comm. Agric. 1870* 422 *Kidney bean*, (*Phaseolus*.)—A large bean growing wild among the mountains around Fort Whipple, Arizona.

Kidney potato. A kidney-shaped variety of potato. {1744– (Ellis *Mod. Husb.* I. II. 108)} (Cf. KIDNEY 1.)

1790 S. DEANE *New-England Farmer* 224/2 Soon after this [*c*1740], the white kidney potatoe appeared. **1830** WATSON *Philadelphia* 718 The earliest potatoes . . . were small bright yellow ones, called kidney potatoes. **1856** *Rep. Comm. Patents 1855: Agric.* 225 The flavor was like that of a fine Kidney potato, and the yam was very white.

+**Kidney seed cotton.** Seed cotton produced by the cotton shrub, *Gossypium brasiliense*. — **1829** SHERWOOD *Gaz. Georgia* (ed. 2) 266 The kidney seed cotton . . . was tried.

+**Kidney worm.** One of various species of parasitic nematode worms that live in the kidneys. — **1845** *Cultivator* ns. II. 125/1 He keeps 100 head of cattle, and a 'right smart chance' of hogs, but they are dying with the kidney worm.

***Kilderkin.** A cask for liquids, butter, etc., of definite but varying capacity. Now hist. — **1636** WINTHROP *Letters* (1869) 157 Two kilderkins of butter [*i.e.*, 112 lbs. each]. **1651** *Plymouth Laws* 94 It is ordered, That all Coopers shall make full sized cask barrells and hoggsheads for meat and fish; and that Cask for Tarr bee either barrells or kilderkins. **1687** *Conn. Rec.* III. 426 Every barrel . . . shall contain thirty-two gallons, every kilderkin sixteen gallons, and every firkin eight gallons. **1783** *S.C. Gazette* 3 June 2/2 They will dispose of . . . porter in half hogsheads and kilderkins. **1896** EARLE *Colonial Days N.Y.* 118 Great hogsheads of corned beef, barrels of salt pork . . . kilderkins of home-made lard.

+**Kilham Hill.** A variety of apple. — **1847** IVES *New Eng. Fruit* 38 *Kilham Hill.*—Originated on the farm of Doctor Kilham, in Wenham, Essex county, Mass. The size is sometimes large, the form round, a little oblong.

Kilkenny rug. A rug made in Kilkenny, Ireland. — **1634** *N.H. Doc. & Rec.* I. 93 It[em], 3 Irish blanketts and 2 Kilkany ruges.

+**Kill,** *n.*[1] [Du. *kil.*] A channel, stream, or creek. Frequent in place names. Local in New York, New England, etc.

1669 *Doc. Col. Hist. New York* XII. 464 Some Familyes from Maryland may haue liberty to come and settle upon ye Kill below Apoquenimi, lying and being within their Government [etc.]. **1677** *New Castle Court Rec.* 113 Owners of a Certain mill standing on a Creeke in Christina Kill in delowar River [are] debarred from Cutting wood. **1703** in Munsell *Annals Albany* IV. 178 A certain Piece of Pasture ground . . . on the third kill or creek, commonly called or known by the name of the Fossen kill. **1794** S. WILLIAMS *Hist. Vermont* 31 The head of this river in Bromley, is not more than thirty feet from the head of Batton Kill. **1840** HOFFMAN *Greyslaer* II. 61 There was an old hunter camped down by the kill, Who fished in this water and shot on that hill. **1879** BURROUGHS *Locusts & Wild Honey* 169 We can take another slice or two of the Catskills . . . without being sated with kills and dividing ridges.

b. Locally used as the name of a strait, esp. for the straits separating Staten Island, New York, from New Jersey. Often pl. in singular sense. Also attrib.

1771 FRANKLIN *Autobiog.* 250 A squall . . . tore our rotten sails to pieces, prevented our getting into the Kill and drove us upon Long Island. **1828** *Englishman's Sketch-Book* 25 We took the right hand passage round Staten Island, called the Kills. **1838** INGRAHAM *Burton* II. 78 Isabel, indeed, had commenced her system of spying even upon the officer commanding the boats that came to convey her from 'the Kills' to the city. **1886** *Congress. Rec.* 19 May 4665/1 The number of vessels plying through the Kills is annually increasing. . . . There are ten thousand vessels employed in the Arthur Kill traffic. **1888** *Newark Advertiser* (F.), The new Baltimore and Ohio bridge across the Kills, below Elizabethport, commences to assume imposing proportions.

***Kill,** *n.*[2] One or more animals killed by a hunter. {1878–} — **1858** JACKSON *Diary* 520 All off for the elk grounds. . . . Tom and Black Hawk to butcher the kill of yesterday and I to follow the elk trail. **1894** *Columbus Dispatch* 10 Nov. 4/2 Those who go out to shoot quail can only use their kill for themselves.

***Kill,** *n.*[3] Var. of **Kiln.**

* **Kill,** *v.*

+**1.** Used in the infinitive form after another verb with adverbial force: To a great or impressive degree. *colloq.* (Cf. FIT *a.* b.)

1845 *N.Y. Ev. Express* 5 March 2/4 Mrs. Polk . . . dresses 'to kill.' **1848** BARTLETT 194 *To kill.* To do anything *to kill*, is a common vulgarism, and means to do it to the uttermost; to carry it to the fullest extent; as, 'He drives *to kill*;' 'She dances *to kill*.' **1862** LOWELL *Biglow P.* 2 Ser. ii. 54 'T was Concord Bridge a-talkin' off to kill With the Stone Spike thet's druv thru Bunker Hill. **1884** RITTENHOUSE *Maud* 270, I ran out and ushered Mr. Lyons in, gotten up to kill in his Prince Albert coat.

+**2.** **a.** *tr.* To damage the machinery of (a boat); to put (an engine) out of working order. *colloq.*

1884 'MARK TWAIN' *H. Finn* 92 It was a steamboat that had killed herself on a rock. **1886** *Phila. Ev. Telegraph* 20 March (*Cent.*), The hose was cut, fire dumped out, . . . pins removed, and engines *killed* so that it will take days to bring them to life again. **1888** *Denver Republican* 29 Feb. (F.), They had run the engine away from the train to which it was attached and had killed it.

+**b.** To make (a gasoline engine) go dead, as by putting too heavy a load on it.

1907 FIELD *Six-Cylinder Courtship* 9, I lost no time in starting. What a blessing that I hadn't killed my engine!

+**3.** *Journalism.* To cancel or scrap (a story or article, or a part thereof) before publication: (see also quot. 1924).

1887 *Courier-Journal* 29 Jan. 5/4 Please kill the deer story sent by Associated Press this morning. **1894** SHUMAN *Steps into Journalism* 23 Get the pith and point of your whole article into . . . the first paragraph, so that the rest of the story might be 'killed' and the news would still be 'covered.' **1897** *Scribner's Mag.* XXII. 460/2, I saw an article that told how to crack a safe. I kicked to the proprietor about it, and he killed it. **1903** SHUMAN *Pract. Journalism* 62 The editor can make room by killing the last paragraphs of the other stories. **1924** *Publisher's Weekly* CVI. 188 *Dead matter*—type which has been 'killed,' i.e., not to be included in the printing.

4. In comb. forming nouns: +*Kill-me-quick, kill preacher,* names of intoxicating drinks.

1861 NEWELL *Orpheus C. Kerr* I. 236, I druv down to the tavern . . . and the fust feller I see was hisself, a standin' in the door, and sippin' kill-me-quick. **1890** D'OYLE *Notches* 24 He spread through all that section yet another name for whisky—'Kill Preacher.'

***Kill-cow.** +(See quotation.) — **1894** *Amer. Folk-Lore* VII. 103 *Eleocharis tenuis*, poverty-grass, kill-cow, West Va.

+**Killcu.** *local.* [Echoic.] =YELLOWLEGS. — **1888** TRUMBULL *Names Birds* 168 [The greater yellowlegs, *Totanus melanoleucus*] in New Jersey at Dennisville, Cape May C. H., and Cape May City, [is called] *Kill-cu;* this name being used by many of the gunners for [the yellowlegs, *T. flavipes*] . . . as well.

+**Killdee.** Variant of KILLDEER.

1781-2 JEFFERSON *Notes Va.* (1788) 74. **1789** MORSE *Amer. Geog.* 59 The following catalogue [of Amer. birds] is inserted: . . . The Chattering Plover or Kildee [etc.]. **1840** *S. Lit. Messenger* VI. 416/1 The kildees are so poor, that they have to let down the draw-bars to enable them to go into a field. **1897** *Outing* XXX. 25/1 The kildee oscillates its body, with its hip-joints as points of support. **1908** 'O. HENRY' *Options* 204 They was going to give us the biggest blowout, complimentary, alimentary, and elementary, that ever disturbed the kildees on the sand-flats. **1917** *Birds of Amer.* I. 259 Kill deer. . . . [Also called] Kildee.

b. In allusive or figurative contexts.

1835 LONGSTREET *Ga. Scenes* 167 Ladies . . . entered the room in the same style, which seemed to have been strictly copied from the movement of the Killdee. **1868** BAGBY *Old Va. Gentleman* 205 He called the cadets of the Virginia Military Institute. . . . 'Kildees,' a title which, as it seemed to belittle them, made the cadets very angry. **1884** 'CRADDOCK' *Where Battle Was Fought* 259 He walked, sir, same as a kildee!

+**Killdeer.** Also **kildeer.** [Echoic.] A plover, *Oxyechus* (syn. *Aegialitis*) *vociferus.*

1731 *Phil. Trans.* XXXVII. 176 The Chattering Plover. In Virginia they are called Kildeers, from some resemblance of their Noise to the Sound of that Word. **1737** BRICKELL *N. Carolina* 192 The Kill-Deer, is a Bird in these parts, so called, from it's frequent repeating those Words. **1832** WILLIAMSON *Maine* I. 147 The Kildeer is a long-legged drooping bird, not seen often in this quarter. **1867** *Ohio Laws 1866-7* 101 It shall be unlawful . . . to catch, kill, injure or destroy . . . any meadow lark or kill-deer. **1874** GLISAN *Jrnl. Army Life* 493 There is abundance of game along the coast, such as . . . kildeer, plover, snipe [etc.]. **1884** 'CRADDOCK' *Tenn. Mts.* 2 Then she saw only a stream . . . with the laurel and pawpaw close in to its banks, and the kildeer's nest in the sand.

+**Killdee(r) plover.** =prec. — **1813** WILSON *Ornithology* VII. 73 Kildeer Plover. . . . This restless and noisy bird is known to almost every inhabitant of the United States. . . . Their cries of Kildeer, Kildeer, as they winnow the air over head, . . . are shrill and incessant. **1885** M. THOMPSON *Byways & Bird Notes* 125 There was an island a mile up the river whither we often went . . . to sketch kildee-plover and sand-pipers. **1892** TORREY *Foot-Path Way* 39 The winter of 1888-89 will long be familiar in the ornithological annals of New England as the winter of killdeer plovers.

***Kill-devil.**

1. West Indian rum. *colloq.* Now hist. {*c*1651-1796, in West Indies}

1639 in Josselyn *Two Voyages* 26 Captain Thomas Wannerton . . . drank to me in a pint of Kill-devil *alias* Rhum at a draught. **1654** *Conn. Rec.* I. 255 Berbados Liquors, commonly called Rum, Kill Devill, or the like. **1699** E. WARD *Trip New-Eng.* 10 Rum, alias Kill Devil, is as much ador'd by the American English, as a dram of Brandy is by an old Billingsgate. **1736** in *Amer. Hist. Review* I. 88 They will give some other Name to their Rum, which they may safely do, because it gos by that of Kill-Devil in this country from its banefull qualitys. **1885** EGGLESTON in *Century Mag.* April 884/2 Rum, or 'kill-devil,' as it was everywhere called, was rendered plentiful by the trade with the West Indies and by the New England stills.

+**2.** A kind of lamp: (see quotation).

1882 *Narragansett Hist. Reg.* I. 215 They furnished a lamp, which consisted of a wick drawn through an iron ring and elevated to burn, the other end drawing from an open vessel of grease or oil in an open pot, which contrivance was called a 'Kill Devil.'

+**Killegenico.** =KILLIKINICK. — **1799** J. SMITH *Acct. Captivity* 11 [They] gave me a . . . polecat skin pouch which . . . contained tobacco, killegenico, or dry sumach leaves, which they mix with their tobacco.

***Killer.**

1. An insect that kills other insects, +as the locust-killing wasp. *colloq.*

1868 *Amer. Naturalist* II. 217 The 'killer' had seized one of our August locusts, and was endeavoring to rise from the ground with it. **1872** HOLMES *Poet* 288 [The spider] is a killer and a cannibal among other insects.

+**2.** One who slaughters animals for food.

1883 SWEET & KNOX *Through Texas* 584 The killer, as he is called, rides as near to the herd as he can without alarming the buffalo. **1895** *Dept. Agric. Yrbk. 1894* 34 If the inspection is worth anything at all to killers, packers, and dealers in fresh or cured meats, they should pay for it. **1898** *Kansas City Star* 20 Dec. 8/3 A bunch of . . . lambs which were covered with mud sold to the killers at $4.65.

+**3.** One who readily or wantonly kills others. *colloq.*

1885 *Wkly. New Mexican Rev.* 5 Feb. 2/6 Aragon is an old time killer and numbers fully a dozen men on his dead list. **1922** MULFORD *Tex* 118 A natural-born killer. They say he's chain lightnin' on th' draw.

+**Killhag.** (See quot. 1848 and cf. CULHEAG.) — **1848** BARTLETT 194 *Killhag*, (Indian,) a wooden trap, used by the hunters in Maine. **1864** *Bradford Times* (De Vere), The first furs were brought into town yesterday, and already a number of killhags have been put up everywhere.

+**Killie.** =next. Also transf. — **1848** BARTLETT 403 *Killifish*, . . . a small fish found in the salt water creeks and bays. . . . They are often called *killies.* **1897** *Congress. Rec.* 6 Jan. 518/1 While you are feeding country 'killies' to great newspaper sharks, you ought . . . to have some regard for the great publishing interests. **1898** HAMBLEN *Gen'l Manager's Story* 243 Frank had remained for a bit seated on a stone behind me, watching the 'killies' swimming in the shallow water.

+**Killifish.** Also **killiefish.** Any of several minnowlike cyprinodont fishes of the genus *Fundulus* or allied genera, esp. *F. heteroclitus*, found on the eastern and southern coasts of the United States. — **1814** MITCHILL *Fishes N.Y.* 441 Sheep's-Head Killifish. *Esox ovinus.* . . . Length about an inch and a half; and remarkably large in the girth. **1842** *Nat. Hist. N.Y., Zoology* IV. 217 The Big Killifish, *Fundulus viridescens*, . . . abounds in the salt water creeks and brackish streams in the neighborhood of New-York. **1860** *Harper's Mag.* March 489/1 Our minnow—or, as it is called around New York, killie-fish—is not the same as the English fish which goes by that name. **1897** *N.Y. Forest, Fish, & Game Comm. 2d Rep.* 232 *Fundulus majalis.* . . . Killifish.—This large killifish is found all the year in Gravesend Bay.

+**Killikin(n)ick.** Also **killicanic, killekinic.** =KINNIKINNICK. Also attrib. — **1792** POPE *Tour S. & W.* 63 Killicanic or Sumac Leaves, which when mixed with Tobacco, emit a most delightful Odour from the Pipe. *a***1811** HENRY *Camp. Quebec* 223 A half part of Red-willow bark, added to as much of the dryed sumach forms the killekinic. **1865** *Nation* I. 209 The windows of half the shops make a display of earthen pipes, bundles of tobacco [etc.]. . . . One is everywhere attracted by such titles as 'the Celebrated Killikinnick.' **1878** JACKSON *Travel at Home* 289 The ground was gay with yellow lupines, daisies, and great mats of killikinnick vines (the bear-berry). **1889** MUNROE *Golden Days* 284 Put that in your pipe and smoke it, along with your killikinick.

***Killing,** *n.* +**1.** The action of shooting or knifing a man dead. *slang.* Also attrib. +**2.** A financial coup; a clean-up. *slang.* — (1) **1875** *Chicago Tribune* 28 July 2/2 A killing scrape occurred at Johnson City. **1890** *Stock Grower & Farmer* 12 July 6/1 No, son, there ain't no murderin much on the range. There's a heap of killin', which is different, killin' being moral an' decent. **1911** ROLT-WHEELER *Boy with Census* 9, I thought the Kentucky 'killings' had stopped ten or fifteen years ago. (2) **1902** WILSON *Spenders* 435 There's always goin' to be a big killing made in Wall Street to-morrow. **1908** MCGAFFEY *Show-Girl* 196, I was out with a party who is interested in the bet placing business at all of the big tracks, and he said he was hep to a few killings. **1920** SANDBURG *Smoke & Steel* 214 [They] make a killing in steel.

***Killing,** *a.* Excruciatingly funny. {1901} — **1887** I. R. *Lady's Ranche Life Mont.* 67 Frank's rendering, to a tune of his own, and playing his accompaniment with one finger, was killing. **1889** 'MARK TWAIN' *Conn. Yankee* viii. 112 A lecturer . . . flooded an ignorant audience with the killingest jokes for an hour.

Killing time. {1687-} On farms, the season or time of year when animals are usually slaughtered. {1818-} — **1666** *East-Hampton Rec.* I. 244 A barrell of beef Merchantable to be paid unto the aforesaid Mr. Stanbrough att killinge time. **1841** LYELL *Trav. N.A.* (1845) I. 157, I was told it was 'killing time,' this being the coldest season of the year. **1891** *Harper's Mag.* Oct. 824/1 Sausages (after 'killing-time') were hung to dry.

+**Kill lamb.** =LAMBKILL. — **1832** CHILD *Frugal Housewife* 28 [Winter evergreen] resembles the poisonous kill-lamb, both in the shape and the glossiness of the leaves. **1869** FULLER *Flower Gatherers* 65 One of the Andromedas, with *deciduous* or falling leaves has acquired the bad name of 'Kill-Lamb,' because it is thought to poison sheep if they eat it. *a***1870** CHIPMAN *Notes on Bartlett* 228 *Kill-Lamb*, C[onnecticu]t Usage. See Lamb-Kill.

Killock. Also **kelleck,** etc. A heavy stone used by small boats as an anchor; an anchor. *To come to a killock,* to come to anchor. {1670-} — *a***1649** WINTHROP *Hist.* I. 55 The wind overblew so much at N.W. as they were forced to come to a killock at twenty fathom. **1663** *Boston Rec.*

16 If any belonging to any vessell or vessells doe drop any ancor, Grapnell or Kelleck upon the flatts or within the Coue and haue noe Boy theareunto theay ar to pay tenn shillings. **1722** *New-Eng. Courant* 3–10 Sept. 2/2 They told him they were us'd to weighing Anchors, but did not understand pulling up Killicks. **1846** *Spirit of Times* 11 July 229/3 They would straighten all their Cod hooks and 'up killock and mainsail.' *a***1870** CHIPMAN *Notes on Bartlett* 226 *Kellock.* A boat's anchor. In use at Salem, Mass. An anchor. . . . Kellock is properly a stone—sometimes in, sometimes not in—a frame.

+**Killy fish.** =KILLIFISH. — **1859** BARTLETT 228 *Killy-fish*, or *Killy*, . . . a small fish found in the salt water creeks and bays. . . . They are so called from the 'Kills' in which they abound.

Kilmarnock willow. (See quotation.) — **1869** *Rep. Comm. Agric. 1868* 202 Kilmarnock willow (*Salix caprea*, var. *pendula*) . . . becomes one of the most distinct of the hardy weeping plants which we possess. **1892** APGAR *Trees Northern U.S.* 166 The Goat-willow is the one generally used for the stock of the artificial umbrella-formed 'Kilmarnock Willow.'

* **Kiln.** Also **kill. a.** A furnace or oven for hardening, drying, or burning anything. **b.** A pile of green bricks arched to receive heat underneath them. (Cf. BRICKKILN, LIMEKILN.)

1644 *New Haven Rec.* 151 A Kill of bricks w[hi]ch was to be devided betwixt Steven Medcalfe, John Medcalfe and himselfe. **1677** *Phil. Trans.* XII. 1069 [The malt] may be washed, and then presently dry'd on a Kiln, or in the Sun. **1709** *Boston Rec.* 93 The Select men do judg the burning a Kiln in that place to be a Nusance. **1741** W. STEPHENS *Proc. Georgia* II. 169 [My visit] happened not to be at a right Season, for his Kiln was now burning. **1807** *Ann. 10th Congress* 1 Sess. I. 429, I was hired on the island to help to build a kiln for drying corn. **1857** *Lawrence* (Kan.) *Republican* 4 June 3 Messrs. Totten & Green are just burning a fine kiln of 168,000 bricks, already contracted for the Free State hotel. **1895** *Dept. Agric. Yrbk. 1894* 45 Inquiries have been made, and are in progress, as to the principles and effectiveness of dry kilns for lumber.

+**Kiln-dryer.** A kiln specially devised for drying grain. — **1808** in *Niles' Reg.* V. Add. A. 16/1 The Kiln-Dryer.—To kiln-dry the meal after it is ground. **1813** *Ib.* III. Add. 7/2 The machinery invented . . . consisted of . . . an improved *kiln dryer*.

Kilter, *n.* Also **kelter.** Good condition or order. Used esp. in the phrases *in good kelter* and *out of kilter.* {1674–}

'Widely diffused in Eng. dial. from Northumb. and Cumb. to Cornwall, and occasional in literature. More frequent in U.S. (in form *kilter*)' (*O.E.D.*).

1638 *Conn. Rec.* I. 17 When they are certified to bee in good kelter there must be a speedy course taken by ye Courte. **1643** WILLIAMS *Key* (1866) 201 Their Gunnes they have from the French, and often sell many a score to the English, when they are a little out of frame or Kelter. **1722** *Conn. Rec.* VI. 335 Mending, cleansing and keeping in good kelter the firelocks. **1833** A. GREENE *Yankee among Nullifiers* 30 My hoss looks so kind of shabby and out of kilter. **1887** WILKINS *Humble Romance* 404 It's more 'n half that's got your nerves out of kilter—sweepin' an' scrubbin' from mornin' till night. **1910** BOSTWICK *Amer. Pub. Library* 242 Two or three badly fixed points of this kind may throw a whole branch system 'out of kilter.'

Kilter, *v. tr.* To put in good condition. {kelter, 1868–, Yorks. *dial.*} — **1712** HEMPSTEAD *Diary* 8, I was kiltering my Saw att Lieut Richards. **1718** *Ib.* 75, I was at home al day plowing & killtering a whipsaw for Mr Coit.

***Kimnel.** A tub used for various household purposes. *Obs.* — **1650** *Mayflower Desc.* X. 23 One kimnell [1*s.* 6*d.*]. **1652** *Ib.* XI. 90, 4 trayes one kimnell one bowle, [7*s.*]. **1682** *Providence Rec.* VI. 79, 1 New Kenmill [*sic*].

Kind.

1. In phrase *kind of* (sometimes corrupted to *kinda, kind o', kinder*), used adverbially: To some extent, somewhat. *colloq.* {1849–}

1775 *Broadside Verse* (1930) 141 Captain Davis had a gun, He kind of clapt his head on 't. **1804** FESSENDEN *Orig. Poems* (1806) 81, I kind of love you, Sal—I vow. **1839** *Knickerb.* XIV. 72 Hanson kind o' hesitated a little, and looked as if he didn't want to go. **1843** 'CARLTON' *New Purchase* I. 139 A three year old black geldin, come next spring, with a switch tail, but a kind a eat off by his other colt. **1863** MITCHELL *My Farm* 243 Waal—no; kinder back-achin' work to weed carrits. **1870** 'MARK TWAIN' *Sk., New & Old* 23 All that was needed now . . . was to kind of touch up the other chimneys a little. **1911** VANCE *Cynthia* 344 You're kinda all in about Miss Cynthia, ain't you? **1920** LINCOLN *Mr. Pratt* 269 He's kind of knocked off swearing lately.

2. *Of a kind*, of the same rank. Said of playing cards.

1887 KELLER *Draw Poker* 13 Triplets are sometimes known as Three of a Kind.

+**3.** *The worst kind*, (see WORST *a.*).

Kindergarten. A school for young children wherein instruction is given by making use of the normal aptitude of children for play, building things, etc. {1855–}; the instruction given in this kind of school.

1862 *Atlantic Mo.* Nov. 586/1 Neither is the primary public school a Kindergarten. *Ib.* 593/1 In New England, parents would not consent to be so much separated from their children, and a few hours of Kindergarten in the early part of the day will serve an excellent purpose. **1878** *Harper's Mag.* March 604/2 The first . . . Kindergarten for these Arabs of the street was . . . kept . . . by a young lady voluntarily. **1887** *Courier-Journal* 25 Jan. 8/1 The Kindergarten was opened yesterday morning at the Holcombe Mission, on East Jefferson street. **1919** *Rep. Comm. Educ.* 85 In many places there are no public-school kindergartens.

b. Attrib. with *education, law, movement*, etc.

1866 *Rep. Indian Affairs* 311 Having recently . . . made some investigation into the educational operations in the State of New York, modelled after the German Kindergarten schools, I beg leave to submit my report. **1870** *Rep. Comm. Educ.* 359 As yet there is but one Kindergarten normal school in America. **1887** in *Harper's Mag.* LXXXVI. 668/1 [Pratt Institute was founded in 1887] to establish for other schools a type of what kindergarten and primary education should be. **1919** *Rep. Comm. Educ.* 83 The influence of the kindergarten movement in California and Texas has made itself felt in Arizona, and a kindergarten law was enacted by the legislature of 1919.

Kindergartening. Kindergarten instruction; the action of giving such instruction. Also fig. — **1871** *Boston School Com. Ann. Rep.* 353 Miss Peabody says, 'she has always known it is quite impossible to have Kindergartening in the public education without a normal department in the city Normal School.' **1891** *Harper's Mag.* July 210/2 One more ride will be the final polish of his primary schooling. The Kindergartening has been omitted. **1899** STOCKTON *Associate Hermits* 92, I offered to teach her a much better system of kindergartening than she was using.

Kindergartner. Also **kindergartener.** One who is prepared to teach in a kindergarten. — **1871** *Boston School Com. Ann. Rep.* 354 In five months she can train a reasonably-sized class of Kindergarteners. **1889** *Advance* 11 July, Already a thoroughly trained kindergartner has offered her services. **1899** STOCKTON *Associate Hermits* 92 There were young women in the place who were not kindergartners, but who would like to become so. **1919** *Rep. Comm. Educ.* 86 Before the war . . . the kindergartner was going to the homes of the foreign mothers and giving them friendly help and advice.

***Kindler.** Something used for starting a fire; kindling wood. {1854} — **1845** JUDD *Margaret* I. ii. 6 Put some kindlers under the pot. **1887** *Harper's Mag.* July 272/1 The children . . . fed the fire, . . . squabbling for the possession of the one cane-knife to split kindlers.

* **Kindling.** Material that kindles readily for lighting a fire; kindling wood. {–*a*1568, 1824–} +Sometimes in pl.

1839 KIRKLAND *New Home* xii. 82, I guess they'll do better for kindlin's than any thing else, here. **1848** DRAKE *Pioneer Life Ky.* v. 92 To chop . . . [and to] pick up chips in the corn basket for kindling in the morning, were regular labors. **1865** *Atlantic Mo.* XV. 396 So I put some kindling in the stove. **1876** HABBERTON *Jericho Road* vii. 69 [He] industriously devoted himself to the preparation of kindlings for the morning's fire. **1890** HOWELLS *Boy's Town* 93 Others made them split kindling and carry in wood, and even saw wood. **1907** *Harper's Mag.* Feb. 450 Ezra and Abner cut kindling and frantically thrust it into the stove.

Kindling wood. Dry wood cut up into fine pieces so as to kindle easily; splinters used for starting a fire. {1850} Often fig. — **1833** S. SMITH *Major Downing* 177 We'll git a stumper from Philadelphy one of these days, that will nock us all into kindlin wood. *a***1846** *Quarter Race Ky.* 88 A perfect mule from Stock Creek hit *me* a wipe with a pair of windin blades: he made kindlin-wood of them, an I lit on him. **1854** CUMMINS *Lamplighter* x. 80 After stirring up the coals, and making free with all True's kindling-wood, [she] waited long enough to hear the roaring. **1882** 'M. HARLAND' *Eve's Daughters* 72 Willy splits kindling-wood for the kitchen-fire. **1904** *N.Y. Ev. Post* 30 Sept. 6 His calm verdict upon the struggle for the gold standard makes kindling wood of the Republican platform.

+**Kinepox.** Also **kinepock.** A pustular eruptive disease of a cow's udder, which when used as a vaccine will protect the human body against smallpox; the vaccine of this disease. — **1800** BENTLEY *Diary* II. 357 The use of the Kine Pox has not been unequivocally successful, & we hear that Waterhouse has written to some patients. **1802** C. PETTIGREW *Let. to E. Pettigrew* (Univ. N.C. MS.), I found Dr. Norcom had inoculated her children with the *kine pox*, & that it had taken very well. **1810** *Columbian Centinel* 31 Jan. 4/1 A lottery has been granted by the Legislature of Maryland, for the benevolent purpose of furthering the distribution of Kine Pock among the citizens. **1813** *Ann. 12th Congress* 2 Sess. 947 Benjamin Waterhouse, medical doctor, of Boston, . . . wishes to undertake the inoculation of the Army of the United States with the 'kine-pock inoculation.' **1816** *Ann. 14th Congress* 2 Sess. 254 The use of the kine pock has been thus greatly promoted in almost every section of the United States.

+**Kinetograph.** [Named by Thomas Alva Edison (1847–1931).] A camera for taking pictures of objects in motion. *Obs.*—[**1891** *Times* (London) 29 May 5/1 [Mr. Edison said] the kinetograph is a machine combining electricity with photography.] **1894** *Voice* 5 April, Edison has recently invented what he calls a kinetograph and a kinetoscope.

+**Kinetoscope. 1.** (See quotation.) **2.** A motion-picture camera, or a machine for projecting motion pictures; also, a series of motion pictures. — **(1) 1864** WEBSTER 739/2 *Kinetoscope*, . . . a sort of movable panorama. **(2)** [**1894** *Daily Telegraph* (London) 18 Oct. 5/3 With his [Edison's] kinetoscope . . . he reproduces most realistically the movements of a Spanish ballet-girl.] **1896** *N. Amer. Rev.* Sept. 377 When Mr. Edison first made his kinetoscope, . . . he foretold that he would enlarge the effects produced by it, and give life-sized pictures of people, all sorts of animals and mechanisms or other objects in action. **1896** *N.Y. Dramatic News* 29 Aug. 11/1 We have a profusion of 'scopes this week—the Vitascope at Elitch's, Phantascope at Manhattan, and Kinetoscope in the entrance of the Tabor. **1897** *McClure's Mag.* X. 78 The public . . . thought Mr. Edison to be resting upon the laurels won by the electric light, the kinetoscope, or the phonograph. **1908** LORIMER *J. Spurlock* i. 9 That was where the bear came into the kinetoscope.

***King.**

+1. The head of an Indian nation; the chief of an Indian tribe. Now hist.

1587 HAKLUYT tr. Laudonnière *Notable Hist.Fla.* in *Voyages* III. (1600) 339 The widow of king Hiocaia . . . sent me backe . . . certaine baskets full of the leaues of Cassine, wherwith they make their drinke. **1634** WOOD *New Eng. Prospect* II. x. 79 The Kings have no Lawes to command by, nor have they any annuall revenewes. **1676** GLOVER in *Phil. Trans.* XI. 631 The Indians . . . live together in Towns, and every town is under a several King. **1707** *N.C. Col. Rec.* I. 660 When the Poackyacks killed their King they were by the English brought from thence and placed on the Blackwater aforementioned as Tributarys. **1725** in *Travels Amer. Col.* 101 The Ceremony being over, the King made the following speech to me. **1784** FILSON *Kentucke* 102 A long Council-house extends the whole length of the town, where the King and Chiefs of the nation frequently meet, and consult. **1831** WITHERS *Chron. Border Warfare* 40 The spot which had been selected by the Ohio company, as the site for a fort, was occupied by Shingess, king of the Delawares. **1841** COOPER *Deerslayer* xxviii, The first colonists, bringing with them to this hemisphere the notions and opinions of their own countries, often dignified the chief men of those primitive nations with the titles of kings and princes.

***2.** Any of the male rulers of England who had sovereign power in the American colonies before the Revolution. Now hist.

[**1606** *1st Va. Charter* i, James, by the grace of God, King of England, Scotland . . . etc. [do] . . . vouchsafe unto them our Licence to make Habitation, Plantation, and to deduce a Colony of sundry of our People into that Part of *America*, commonly called Virginia.] **1638** in Hutchinson *Hist. Mass.* I. (1764) 507 Wee are ready to yield all due obedience to our soueraigne Lord the King's Majesty. **1676** *Mass. H. S. Coll.* 4 Ser. IX. 187 Seize ye p'sons above mencioned as Trayters to ye King & Country. **1774** GAGE in *Jrnls.Cont.Congress* I. 114, I have . . . strongly urged it to people here [Boston] to pay for the tea, and send a proper memorial to the king. **1776** *Decl. Independence,* The history of the present King of Great Britain is a history of repeated injuries and usurpations. **1900** *Congress. Rec.* 6 Feb. 1589/2 The proposition that 'the just powers of government are derived from the consent of the governed' is as correct to-day as it was when American patriots hurled it in the teeth of King George.

b. As a possessive in the names of various things, legal instruments, etc.

1606 in West *Source Book Amer. Hist.* 29 [They [various persons residing in England] shal be called the King's Council of Virginia.] **1670** *R.I. Col. Rec.* II. 321 Two of our men . . . were inoffensiuely rideing on the King's highway. **1688** SEWALL *Letter-Book* I. 91 Probably ere long you may be Press'd, and then you will only have the King's Pay. **1692** *Huntington Rec.* II. 112 These are to give you notes by the Kings writ . . . to summons you to be at the next court of comon pleas. **1693** *Penna. Col. Rec.* I. 389 Lay outt the king's road, where it may fall into the king's old road. **1726** FRANKLIN *Writings* II. 55 The King's yards and docks employ abundance of men, who, even in peace time, are constantly building . . . men-of-war for the King's Service. **1767** *Cambridge Prop. Rec.* 325 One [horse-block] Standing on the Kings way leading from Menotomy Meeting house to Watertown.

+c. *King George man,* (see quotation).

1885 *Century Mag.* April 834 'Boston man' was the Chinook term for all Americans,—Englishmen and Canadians being called 'King George men.'

3. +a. Anything of great economic importance. (Cf. COTTON 3 b, KING CAUCUS, KING COTTON.)

1861 NEWELL *Orpheus C. Kerr* I. 202 When economy can be thus artistically blended with plentitude . . . money ceases to be king and butcher-bills dwindle. **1872** *Vermont Bd. Agric. Rep.* I. 348 In the South cotton is called king, in the West wheat and corn are king, but in Vermont grass, if it is not king, is the foundation of all good farming. **1884** W. SHEPHERD *Prairie Exper.* 121 The dollar is king here as elsewhere.

+b. The leading business man or manufacturer in any designated field; a captain of industry. (Cf. CATTLE, RAILROAD, etc., KING.)

1846 J. G. SAXE *Progress* (1847) 28 How would she [the Muse] strive, in fitting verse, to sing The wondrous Progress of the Printing King! **1862** *Rep. Comm. Patents 1861: Agric.* 185 He has been called the 'Strawberry King' . . . [because of] unquestionable pre-eminence in this branch of fruit culture. **1870** MEDBERY *Men Wall St.* 119 The kings of the stock market are not prone to let the street understand their tactics. **1885** HOWELLS *S. Lapham* viii, He left me yesterday afternoon to go and offer his allegiance to the Mineral Paint King. **1890** *Stock Grower & Farmer* 8 Feb. 5/4 Mr. W. E. Anderson, of . . . Rocky Ford, Colorado, is rapidly winning his title of the alfalfa king of the southwest. **1893** M. HOWE *Honor* 155 Gwendolin O'Shaunessey, the daughter of old O'Shaunessey the Western pork-king. **1908** HORNBLOW *Profligate* 13 There were multi-millionaires, social leaders, actresses, kings of finance, captains of industry [etc.].

+c. A favored man at a king's ball (q.v.).

1852 REYNOLDS *Hist. Illinois* 52 These four kings are to give the next ball. These are called 'King balls.'

+d. *King of Rivers,* the Mississippi River.

1855 *S. Lit. Messenger* XXI. 669/1 The current of the King of Rivers and its affluents was strong and rapid.

+4. a. One or other of several varieties of apples so named. **b.** A variety of cotton.

1861 DOWNING *Fruits N.A.* 116 King. A native of western North Carolina. **1875** BURROUGHS *Winter Sunshine* 155 Now a Vandevere [apple] or a King rolls down from the apex above. **1910** TYLER *Varieties Amer. Upland Cotton* 20 This group is composed of King and its derivatives and some other cottons developed in North Carolina and Tennessee.

+5. *attrib.* **a.** With names of animals in sense: Male.

1748 CATESBY *Carolina* App. 11 *Scarabæus pilaris Americanus.* The Tumble-Turds. . . . [The males] are commonly called King Tumble-Turds, tho' by what appears, they assume no pre-eminence. **1862** in F. Moore *Rebellion Rec.* V. II. 245 The old man, game as a king-eagle, begged to be permitted to drive the rebels home. **1901** RYAN *Montana* 93 You're strong as a mountain lion, or an old king buffalo. **1904** STRATTON-PORTER *Freckles* 293 She's just about where the old king rattler crosses to go into the swamp.

b. In the names of plants.

1846 EMORY *Military Reconn.* 77 In one view could be seen . . . the cactus, (king) cactus, (chandelier) green wood acacia, &c. **1878** in Killebrew *Tenn. Grasses* 209 Japan Clover, or King Grass, *Lespedeza striata,* . . . seems especially adapted to the Southern states. **1890** *Cent.* 4167/3 *O[smunda] regalis* being the royal fern or osmund royal, also called *bog-onion, buckhorn-brake, ditch-fern,* and *king-fern.* **1898** BRITTON & BROWN *Illus. Flora Northern U.S.* III. 284 King-devil . . . in north-central New York . . . a troublesome weed. Naturalized from Europe.

c. In the names of fish.

1884 GOODE, etc. *Fisheries* I. 234 The King Hake, *P. regius,* . . . has also been found near the shore in the vicinity of Cape Hatteras, in Chesapeake Bay, and at the eastern end of Long Island. *Ib.* 316 The King Cero of the Florida Keys grows to be five or six feet long and to twenty or thirty pounds in weight.

6. Special combinations.

King's apple, a variety of red apple; *king's base,* a children's game similar to baseball; *king beat,* (see quot. 1902); *king's cure-all,* (see quot. 1893); *king's ex(cuse),* (see quot. 1890); *king's gift,* (see quot. 1800); *King Kleagle,* an officer of the second Ku-Klux Klan; *King's Mountain Day,* (see quot. 1909).

1676 GLOVER in *Phil. Trans.* XI. 628 The Countrey . . . affords . . . all sorts of English Apples, as Pear-mains, . . . Marigolds, Kings-apples, Magitens, Batchelours, and many others. **1800** HAWKINS *Sk. Creek Country* 66 These negroes were, many of them, given by the agents of Great Britain to the Indians, in payment for their services, and they generally call themselves 'King's gifts.' **1883** EGGLESTON *Hoosier School-Boy* xxv. 165 They agree to play that favorite game of Greenbank. . . . It is called 'king's base.' **1890** *Dialect Notes* I. 65 *King's excuse.* . . . Abbreviated to *king's ex.* In playing base, when a boy falls down, to keep from being caught he says, 'King's ex.' [Ky.] **1893** *Amer.Folk-Lore* VI. 142 *Oenothera biennis,* king's cure-all, Southern States. **1902** CLAPIN 249 *King-beat,* in newspaper parlance, exceedingly important news which have been obtained in advance of other papers. **1909** *N.Y. Ev. Post* (s.-w. ed.) 7 Oct. 8 'King's Mountain Day,' the anniversary of the battle of King's Mountain, S.C., in which 900 'mountain men' won a victory over a British force numbering 1,200, on October 7, 1780. **1923** *Imperial Night-Hawk* 29 Aug. 6/1 When trouble seemed unavoidable the King Kleagle of Pennsylvania is said to have ordered the marchers to return to the hill.

Kingbird. {1779–} +Any of various tyrant flycatchers, esp. the common kingbird, *Tyrannus tyrannus;* the bee-martin.

See also ARKANSAS 5, BEE-MARTIN, CASSIN, FIELD MARTIN, etc.

1778 CARVER *Travels* 475 The King Bird is like a swallow, and seems to be of the same species as the black martin or swift. **1796** WANSEY *Excursion U.S.* 194 Of some kinds of birds they have great plenty [in N.J.], such as robins, swallows, cat birds, and king birds, or men of war, as some call them. **1810** WILSON *Ornithology* II. 69 The death of every King-bird is . . . an actual loss to the farmer, by multiplying the numbers of destructive insects. **1844** *Nat. Hist. N.Y., Zoology* II. 119 The Great-Crested King-Bird, *Tyrannus crinitus,* . . . enters Louisiana in March. **1858** *Rep. Comm. Patents 1857: Agric.* 123 The king-bird, or 'Field Martin,' as it is sometimes called in the Southern States, remains at the North during the spring and summer. **1892** HARRIS *On the Plantation* 73 One of the hawks . . . was pounced on by a kingbird, which Jim-Polk called a bee martin. **1917** *Birds of Amer.* II. 192.

Kingbolt. {1825–} +A large bolt connecting the forward axle and wheels of a wagon or buggy with the other parts of the vehicle. — **1856** WHIPPLE *Explor. Ry. Route* I. 17 Wagons needed repairing. There were king-bolts to be made at Little River, and a guide to be sought. **1900** WINCHESTER *W. Castle* iv. 89 Suddenly the king-bolt of the buggy broke.

1904 WALLER *Wood-Carver* 23 The last time I used it [a wagon], the king-bolt chinked just as I heard it a minute ago.

+**King caucus.** A name applied to the Congressional caucus in allusion to the great political power it once wielded: (see CONGRESSIONAL CAUCUS note). *colloq.* — **1826** *Spirit of '76* I. 322 Your adversaries, the friends and agents of king and kitchen caucus, have assumed many names. **1854** BENTON *30 Years' View* I. 49/2 King Caucus is as potent as any other king. **1902** E. C. MEYER *Nominating Systems* 15 The congressional caucus was doomed. The people had won a decisive battle. King Caucus was dethroned.

+**King Cotton.** A popular personification of cotton in allusion to its economic supremacy in the South. (Cf. COTTON 3 b.)

1860 LOWELL *Writings* V. 22 Mr. Hammond has proclaimed the accession of King Cotton. **1863** HOPLEY *Life in South* I. 257 He dilated on the importance of 'King Cotton,' and how impossible it was for the world to exist without it. **1865** *Atlantic Mo.* XV. 627 King Cotton turns out to be a thorough citizen-king and adapts himself very readily to changed events. **1885** *Century Mag.* May 4/2 The people of the lower Mississippi Valley . . . thought that the proper place to glorify King Cotton was in the chief city of the cotton-belt. **1887** *Ib.* March 771/1 King Cotton's days of prosperity, it was gravely predicted, would end forever with the emancipation of the slaves.

King crab. Any of several large marine arthropods of the genus *Limulus*, esp. *L. polyphemus* (syn. *Xiphosurus sowerbyi*). {1698-} — **1796** MORSE *Univ. Geog.* I. 227 King Crab, or Horse Shoe *Monoculus polyphemus.* **1802** *Mass. H. S. Coll.* 1 Ser. VIII. 149 Besides sea weed and the king crab on their shores, there are also spots which contain clay, a well known fertilizer of a sandy soil. **1863** *Ladies' Repository* Nov. 679/1 The king crab, which is to-day a denizen of our New England shores, is only a lost prince of a royal house. **1884** GOODE, etc. *Fisheries* I. 829 The curious form of marine animal called 'Horseshoe Crab' [and] 'King Crab' . . . is not, however, a true Crab. . . . Some naturalists regard it as a low type of crustacean, while others place it among the *Arachnida*, or scorpions and spiders. Its nearest allies all occur as fossils.

+**King duck.** =next. — *c*1785 PENNANT *Arctic Zoology* II. 554. **1839** PEABODY *Mass. Birds* 390 The King Duck, *Fuligula spectabilis*, . . . sometimes, in the depths of winter, wanders into our borders. **1876** DAVIS *Polaris Exped.* xvi. 378 The Esquimaux shot three king-ducks.

King eider. A species of eider duck (*Somateria spectabilis*), which lives in the far North; a duck of this species. {1824- (Shaw *Gen. Zool.*)} — **1858** BAIRD *Birds Pacific R.R.* 810 King Eider. . . . King Duck. **1865** *Atlantic Mo.* XV. 203 Isn't it a king eider? **1883** *Nat. Museum Bul.* No. 27, 162 King Eider. . . . Circumpolar regions; in North America, south in winter to the Great Lakes and coast of California. **1911** in *Birds of Amer.* (1917) I. 148/1 The King Eider is an arctic species and its habits resemble those of the common Eider.

Kingfish. {1750-}

+**1.** The cero, *Sierra cavalla;* also, the spotted cero or pintado, *Scomberomorus regalis.*

It is not clear whether the first two quotations belong under 1 or 2.

1775 ROMANS *Nat. Hist. Florida* App. 7 Groopers are in great plenty, king-fish, Spanish mackrel and Barrows are often caught towing. **1799** ELLICOTT in Mathews *Life A. Ellicott* 186 A great abundance and variety of fish may be taken: such as . . . king-fish. **1884** GOODE, etc. *Fisheries* I. 316 It is more than likely that this [*Scomberomorus regalis*] and the preceding species [*S. caballa*] are both included by the Key West fishermen under the name 'King-fish.'

+**2.** One of various marine sciaenoid fish of the genus *Menticirrhus*, esp. *M. saxatilis*, prevalent on the Atlantic coast. (Cf. BARB.)

1814 MITCHILL *Fishes N.Y.* 408 King-fish, *Sciaena nebulosa*. . . . Length sixteen or eighteen inches. **1842** *Nat. Hist. N.Y., Zoology* IV. 78 The King-fish . . . is exceedingly abundant on the coast of Carolina and Florida where it is known as the Whiting. **1897** *N.Y. Forest, Fish, & Game Comm. 2d Rep.* 243 Kingfish . . . was formerly abundant in Gravesend Bay, but it seldom makes its appearance there now.

+**3.** One or other of two California fishes, *Seriphus politus* and *Genyonemus lineatus.*

1884 GOODE, etc. *Fisheries* I. 380 The Queen-fish—*Seriphus politus*. This species is known as 'King-fish' or 'Queen fish.' **1890** *Cent.* 3290/3 *King-fish*, . . . a sciænoid fish, the little roncador, . . . common on the coast of California: so called in the San Francisco markets.

***Kingfisher.** Any of several nonpasserine birds of the family Alcedinidae, +esp. the belted kingfisher. (Cf. BELTED *a.*)

*c*1730 CATESBY *Carolina* I. 69 *Ispida.* The King-Fisher. This kind of King's-fisher is somewhat larger than a Black-bird. **1796** LATROBE *Journal* 17 Had we been furnished with firearms we might have had plenty of wild ducks, Indian hens, and kingfishers [in Va.]. **1805** [see FISHER 5]. **1846** THORPE *Myst. Backwoods* 42 The kingfisher may be seen the live-long day. **1872** *Atlantic Mo.* Feb. 163 What created thing can seem more patient than yonder kingfisher on the sea-wall? **1917** *Birds of Amer.* II. 132 The American Kingfishers are a well-marked group of birds.

Kinglet. {1603-} Any of several small birds of the genus *Regulus* {1839-}, the two chief American species being: +**a.** The golden-crested kinglet, *R. satrapa.* (Cf. GOLDEN-CRESTED a.) +**b.** The ruby-crowned kinglet, *R. calendula.*

1865 *Atlantic Mo.* XV. 528 Autumn arrives, bringing Finches, . . . Kinglets from the North. **1875** BURROUGHS *Winter Sunshine* 28 The regular winter residents go in little bands, . . . the jays . . . in advance . . . and the creepers and kinglets . . . last of all. **1882** *Vt. Agric. Rep.* VII. 72 Kinglets should also be encouraged. **1890-3** TABER *Stowe Notes* 41, I have before seen kinglets in the company of nuthatches. **1917** *Birds of Amer.* III. 219 The Kinglets and Gnatcatchers are closely related to the Thrushes.

+**King nut.** A name applied to different species of hickory. Properly applied to *Carya laciniosa.* — **1884** SARGENT *Rep. Forests* 134 *Carya tomentosa*. . . . Whiteheart Hickory. King Nut. **1894** COULTER *Bot. W. Texas* III. 411 *Hicoria sulcata.* (Big shell-bark-king nut.) . . . Rich soils, extending into eastern Texas. **1894** *Amer. Folk-Lore* VII. 98 *Carya alba*, king-nut, West Va. **1897** SUDWORTH *Arborescent Flora* 114 *Hicoria laciniosa*. . . . Common Names [include] . . . Thick Shellbark Hickory (N.C., Ark.). King Nut (Tenn.).

+**King Philip corn.** =BROWN CORN. — **1856** *Rep. Comm. Patents 1855: Agric.* p. xi, The Improved King Philip or Brown Corn . . . was extensively disseminated in all the States north of New Jersey, and throughout the mountainous districts of Pennsylvania, Maryland, and Virginia.

King-pin. {1801-} +*fig.* A person or thing holding together a complex system. — **1882** *Century Mag.* Aug. 541 It's meet that the market should stiffen when the king-pin is rolling in rocks. **1884** R. GRANT *Average Man* 251 A controlling interest in the property had been acquired by a syndicate, of which Peter Idlewild was the king-pin. **1895** *Library Jrnl.* June 202 Mr. Vinton . . . believed cataloging to be the king-pin of the library system. **1914** S. H. ADAMS *Clarion* 23 To-day we come pretty near to being king-pins in this town, you and I, Hal.

+**King plover.** =next. — **1858** BAIRD *Birds Pacific R.R.* 694 King Plover. . . . Common on the Atlantic.

+**King rail.** A long-billed large rail, *Rallus elegans.* — **1835** AUDUBON *Ornith. Biog.* III. 28 Hunters . . . now and then obtained a few of these birds, which they considered as very rare, and knew only by the name of 'King Rails.' **1858** BAIRD *Birds Pacific R.R.* 746 King Rail; Marsh Hen. . . . Middle and southern States on the Atlantic ocean. **1874** COUES *Birds N.W.* 535 The King Rail is more limited in dispersion than any other one of our species of the family. **1911** in *Birds of Amer.* (1917) I. 203/1 The King Rail closely resembles the Virginia Rail except in size.

King row. *Checkers.* The row at either end of the board. Also fig. — **1847** LONGFELLOW *Evangeline* II. 45 The old men . . . Laughed when a man was crowned, or a breach was made in the king-row. **1887** *Lippincott's Mag.* Sept. 350 If your checkers are jumped off the board so fast, you won't get any in the king-row. **1901** *McClure's Mag.* Dec. 146 In 1877 it was that he [Platt] pushed himself into the king-row, and was elected chairman of the Republican State convention.

+**King salmon.** The quinnat salmon, *Oncorhynchus tschawytscha.* — **1881** *Amer. Naturalist* XV. 177 These species may be called the quinnat or King salmon . . . or *Oncorhynchus chouicha.* **1899** *Fish. Comm. Bul.* XVIII. 6 In the opinions of the canners . . . coho should rank next after the king salmon in food value. **1900** NORRIS *Blix* 129 There were . . . sheaves of fishing-rods, from the four-ounce wisp of the brook-trout up to the rigid eighteen-ounce lance of the king-salmon and sea-bass. **1908** BEACH *Barrier* 16 His cache was filled with fish of which the bulk were dried king salmon.

+**King('s) ball.** (See quot. 1851.) — **1832** HALL *Leg. of West* 153 He continued to make a voyage of three or four months annually, and spent the remainder of his time in cultivating his crop, smoking his pipe, attending the king-balls, and playing the fiddle. **1851** A. O. HALL *Manhattaner* 122 We have [in New Orleans] . . . a 'king's' ball, at which you must make one of the guests. . . . Certain of the youngsters among us, at every yearly winter's ball of the neighborhood, are presented with bouquets by the ladies, who have been the chosen queens of the festivities then concluding; and each bouquet present*ee* is crowned the king of the next year's ball. . . . Each king accordingly selects a queen, and under their united auspices the ball is given. **1852** [see KING 3 c].

King's man. {*a*1639-} +One who supported the English cause at the time of the American Revolution; a Tory. *Obs.* — **1797** FRENEAU *Poems* (1809) II. 11 Whate'er some angry king's-men say, You play a game that must be won. **1838** *S. Lit. Messenger* IV. 114/2 Her master, I expect was a kingsman. **1857** *Ladies' Repository* XVII. 83/1, I never feed kingsmen if I can help it.

+**King snake.** A large, colubrid, harmless snake (*Lampropelti getulus*) of the southern United States, or any related species. — **1709** LAWSON *Carolina* 132 The King-Snake is the longest of all others, and not common. **1827** WILLIAMS *West Florida* 28 The king snake kills them [*sc.* poisonous snakes] whenever they cross his path. **1848** *Santa Fe Republican* 29 Jan. 4/1 There is a species of snake commonly called in the southern states the king snake, perhaps because he is the most formidable enemy of the rattlesnake. **1881** *Amer. Naturalist* XV. 562 The length of the king snake was forty-two inches. **1909** *Dialect Notes* III. 399 *King-snake*, a kind of snake found in N.W. Arkansas.

Kink, *n.* {1678-}

+**1.** *fig.* An odd notion or quirk; a whimsical mental twist. *colloq.*

1803 JEFFERSON *Writings* VIII. (1897) 280 Should the judges take a kink in their heads. **1812** *Ib.* (1905) XIII. 157 Adair too had his kink. He believed all the Indians of America to be descended from Jews.

1833 S. SMITH *Major Downing* 181 Little things sometimes give us a kink, and a notion of bigger ones. 1857 HAMMOND *Northern Scenes* 71 The strange 'kinks,' as you call them, . . . got into my head between the fever and the Doctor's opiates. 1887 J. HAWTHORNE *Great Bank Robbery* iv, She had got a kink in her head that diamonds she must have.

+b. An individual or clever way of doing something; a twist or angle; a device or fad.

1825 NEAL *Bro. Jonathan* III. 291 There he goes, now!—there! there!—that's a new kink! 1830 S. SMITH *Major Downing* 38 You always want to find out all the kinks about politiks. 1879 BURROUGHS *Locusts & Wild Honey* 239 They have kinks and ways of their own. 1887 *Courier-Journal* 1 May 1/3 See the latest kink in Full Dress Shirts.

+c. *To take the kinks out of* (someone or something), to strip of any illusions; to restore to a sensible attitude.

1886 in W. F. Crafts *Sabbath for Man* (1894) 267 It did more in one week to . . . take the kinks out of our thinking . . . than the rattling of all our pulpits could avail in a score of years. 1904 CRISSEY *Tattlings* 223 There's nothing like the whirligig of time to take the kinks out of a crooked politician.

+2. a. A temporary stiffness in one's legs, back, etc. {1868–, *dial.*}

1848 *Yale Lit. Mag.* XIV. 82 (Th.), Come! wake up, and shake the kinks out of your land legs. 1873 ALDRICH *Marjorie Daw* 235, I resolved to get the kinks out of me by walking from the station. 1901 NORRIS *Octopus* 23 A little turn through the country, to get the kinks out of the muscles.

+b. An obstacle or difficulty.

1868 *Congress. Globe* 16 May 2492/2 There would have been kinks in it [the Arkansas bill], and somebody would have wanted to send it back. 1888 *Missouri Repub.* 11 Feb. A kink arose in the non-payment of rent by Samuels, and Strauss wished to compel him to pay it.

3. A tight curl. +Freq. in reference to the hair of Negroes.

1861 LOWELL *Writings* I. 56 A Declaration of Independence that hangs the franchise of human nature on the kink of a hair. 1868 *Congress. Globe* 11 Jan. 466/1 Shall we measure a man's rights in this free country by the kinks in his hair and the length of his heel?

Kink, *v.* {1697–} +*tr.* To confuse with odd notions. — 1801 JEFFERSON *Writings* X. 189 A head, entangled and kinked as his is.

Kinkle. {1855–} +=KINK 2 a. — 1862 LOWELL *Biglow P.* 2 Ser. ii. 7 To shake the kinkles out o' back an' legs.

+**Kinky,** *a.*

1. Of hair, esp. of the Negroes: Full of kinks or short tight curls. Often in combination with *haired, headed.*

1844 *Congress. Globe* App. 6 Jan. 42/3 [The Negro's] skull is as thick, his hair is as kinkey, . . . and his skin as black, as they were the day he was first introduced. 1861 in F. Moore *Rebellion Rec.* I. III. 137 A marked distinction is laid Between the rights of the mistress, And those of the kinky-haired maid. 1865 *Public Opinion* 31 Dec. 726 Sambo the blubber-lipped . . . the kinky-haired. 1876 MILLER *First Families* 24 Before midnight the little kinky-headed Israelite had not a shirt . . . in the shop. 1921 PAINE *Comr. Rolling Ocean* 252 This kinky-headed, limber-tongued, son-of-a-sea-cook of a Mendosa is aboard this ship as a fireman.

2. 'Queer, eccentric, crotchety' (B. '59).

+**Kinnikinnick.** Also **kinnikineck,** etc. [Algonquian, 'a mixture.'] (Cf. KILLIKINICK.)

1. a. A mixture of the dried leaves and bark of certain plants, such as sumac, and tobacco, used for smoking. b. The bark and leaves of certain plants used for smoking without tobacco.

1817 BRADBURY *Travels* 91 They did not make use of tobacco, but the bark of *Cornus sanguinea*, or red dog wood, mixed with the leaves of *Rhus glabra*, or smooth sumach. This mixture they call kinnikineck. 1839 C. A. MURRAY *Travels* I. 310 *Kinnekinnick* . . . , which is smoked by all the Indians of the western regions, is usually composed of the dried leaves of the shumack and the inner bark of the red willow. 1863 J. L. FISK *Exped. Rocky Mts.* 18 Our . . . guests passed round their long pipe filled with Kinnikinnick. The mixture that the mountain Indians smoke is one-half tobacco and one-half *uve ursa*, a small-leaved evergreen, of a pleasant smell and taste. 1890 CUSTER *Following Guidon* 101 The oldest of the chiefs . . . took a whiff, then the others followed with a prolonged inhaling of the fragrant kinni-kinnic. 1905 *N.Y. Ev. Post* 6 May, Nahgonahgahnabe, as he filled his pipe with kinnikinnick, looked the approval that he would not speak.

2. Any of various plants supplying the leaves or bark for such mixtures.

1817–8 EATON *Botany* (1822) 178 *Arbutus uva-ursi*, bear berry, kinnikinnick. . . . Dry, barren sand plains. 1841 STEELE *Summer Journey* 108 Our friends kindly gathered for me a variety of these, among which was a fine scarlet lilium superbum, blue bells, and kinni kanic, or Indian tobacco. 1857 CHANDLESS *Visit Salt Lake* I. 143 Small shoots of the kinnik-kinnik that grows like willow along the stream sides. 1876 *Atlantic Mo.* XXXVIII. 679 You will have a picture of the shape, the set of the leaf, the thick matting of the branches, and the utter unrestrainedness of a root of kinnikinnick.

3. Attrib. with *bag, bark,* etc.

1805 ORDWAY in *Jrnls. Lewis & O.* 199 Some Indians had hung up . . . a Scraper a paint bag with 1/2 an ounce in it, kinikaneck bags, flints [etc.]. 1853 J. W. BOND *Minnesota* 303 Some dry Kinne-kin-nick bark is generally carried along, cut very fine for the purpose of smoking. 1876 *Atlantic Mo.* Dec. 683/2 The little mound is kept green with the faithful kinnikinnick vines. 1898 WISTER *Lin McLean* 137 That's a kinni-kinnic seed.

+**Kino.** Variant of KENO.

+**Kinspeople.** *pl.* Persons of the same kin; relatives. {=kinsfolk} — 1866 HOWELLS *Venetian Life* xviii, Kinspeople of herself or her husband. 1881 *Harper's Mag.* July 266/1 Pike was . . . free-handed, especially to his kinspeople. 1888 *Nation* 12 Jan. 35/3 The facts got from friends and kinspeople and from letters, are material in abundance [for this book]. 1891 WINSOR *Columbus* v. 86 Here his kinspeople ruled.

Kinticoy. Variant of KENTICOY.

+**Kioting.** =COYOTING. — 1888 FERGUSON *Exp. Forty-niner* 170 The miners did not understand how to contend with the water . . . , nor did they know anything about driving, or kioting.

+**Kiowa.** Also **Kioway, Kiawa, Kyaway.**

For variants of the name and for earlier non-English references, see Hodge *Amer. Indians* I. 700 f.

1. A member of a warlike tribe of plains Indians apparently of a distinct linguistic stock; *pl.*, the tribe of this Indian.

1808 PIKE *Sources Miss.* II. App. 16 The only nations with whom the Pawnees are now at war, are the Tetaus, Utahs, and Kyaways. 1821 J. FOWLER *Journal* 54 Kiawas and Padducas the Continu to Increes. 1848 RUXTON *Life Far West* vii, The Kioway loves the pale-face, and gives him warning. 1849 *31st Congress* 1 *Sess.* Sen. Doc. No. 64, 211 Beaver pronounces the saddle and moccasins the same kind as those of the Kioways. 1868 *N.Y. Herald* 31 July 5/4 The Senate . . . ratified treaties with the Potawatamies, Sacs . . . the Wyomings and Navajoes . . . the Kiowas and Comanches.

b. Attrib. with *chief, country, feather cap,* etc.

1821 J. FOWLER *Journal* 64 The Kiawa cheef with his nation had stoped and intended we shold stop with them. 1865 PIKE *Scout & Ranger* (1932) 50 Houston's design was to carry the war into the Comanche and Kiowa country. *Ib.* 113 Most of the stampede party sported Kiowa feather caps. 1870 KEIM *Sheridan's Troopers* 30 They met many of the chiefs and headmen of the Kiowa and Comanche tribes at the Council Camp. *Ib.* 197 The Kiowa women wear an ornamented flap, attached to the top and rear part of the leggins, which trails at the heels.

2. *Geol.* A formation of the Lower Cretaceous in Kansas. Also attrib.

1895 *Amer. Geol.* XVI. 162 The Kiowa shales. *Ib.* The upper part of the Kiowa. 1924 PIRSSON & SCHUCHERT *Text-Book of Geol.* II. 541 The change from the Kiowa or Denison fauna to the Woodbine of the Upper Cretaceous shows little if any greater contrast [etc.].

***Kip.** The hide of a young animal used as leather. Also attrib. — 1843 'CARLTON' *New Purchase* I. 212 We did give credit for kip and neatsleather, even where it was doubtful whether our political friends would pay. 1852 in Stowe *Key* 179/1 Had on, when taken up, . . . pants, . . . a new cotton shirt, a pair of kip boots, an old cloth cap and wool hat. 1864 'PENNIMAN' *Tanner-Boy* 29 Tanned leather, my son, is of three kinds,—hides, kips, and skins. 1872 *Congress. Globe* 7 May 3917/1 Then, except the matter of gloves and mittens, it is foot-gear only that is made of kipskins? 1891 CHASE & CLOW *Industry* II. 81 The skins of small or yearling cattle are called *kips*.

Kippered, *a.* Of fish: Cured by cleaning, rubbing with salt, and drying. {1773–} — a1861 WINTHROP *Canoe & Saddle* 37 After our lunch on kippered cod and biscuits, we had not tarried. *Ib.* 137 He packed a good supply of kippered salmon, and filled his pouch with kinni kinnick. 1884 *Nat. Museum Bul.* No. 27, 1087 Kippered Herring. One dozen 1-pound oval cans.

+**Kirmess.** [Du. *kermis.*] An indoor entertainment and carnival. (An independent borrowing from the Dutch; the usual English form is *kermis.*) — 1885 *Boston Journal* 16 April 2/3 The kirmess which opened yesterday in New York is a festival which originated in the Netherlands many years ago. 1888 *Ib.* 12 Dec. 1/8 Salem Mechanic Light Infantry Kirmess . . . is destined to prove a brilliant success.

+**Kirtland money.** Currency issued by a Mormon bank in Kirtland, Ohio, about 1830. — 1845 *S. Lit. Messenger* XI. 477/2 'Kirtland money' was as plenty in the West at that time as have been the issues of similar equally well-founded institutions since that period.

+**Kirtland's owl.** [J. P. *Kirtland*, Amer. naturalist (1793–1877).] The Acadian owl. — 1871 *Amer. Naturalist* V. 119 Occurrence of Kirtland's Owl in Maine.—A characteristic specimen of the *Nyctale albifrons* Cassin, was shot at Norway, Me. 1917 *Birds of Amer.* II. 107 Saw-Whet Owl. . . . [Also called] Kirtland's Owl.

+**Kirtland's warbler.** [See prec.] A rare warbler (*Dendroica Kirtlandi*) that breeds in Michigan. — 1858 BAIRD *Birds Pacific R.R.* 286 Kirtland's Warbler. . . . Of this species but a single specimen is known to be extant. It was killed by Dr. Kirtland . . . in May of 1851. 1917 *Birds of Amer.* III. 146 Kirtland's Warbler, *Dendroica kirtlandi*. . . . Jack-pine Warbler.

+**Kiskatom(a).** Also **kiskythomas, kiskitoma,** etc. [Amer. Ind.] The hickory nut, or the tree on which it grows. Also attrib. with *nut.* — 1810 MICHAUX *Arbres* I. 20 *Shell bark hickery,* [*sic*] . . . nom le plus en usage dans tous les Etats-Unis.... *Kiskythomas*, par les Hollandois du New-Jersey. **a1817** DWIGHT *Travels* IV. 58 On these grounds, grow the chesnut, the shag-bark or Kiskatoma, and several other trees. **1832** BROWNE *Sylva* 184 The Dutch settlers ... near the city of New York, call it [Shellbark Hickory] Kisky Thomas Nut. **1850** *Lit. World* 2 Nov. 353/2 Hickory, shell-bark, kiskitomas nut! Or whatsoever thou art called. **1894** *Amer. Folk-Lore* VII. 98 *Carya alba*, kiskytom, Otsego Co., N.Y.

***Kiss.** A term applied to different kinds of candy, as a small ball of taffy or a confection made of sugar and egg whites. {1825-} — **1828** LESLIE *Receipts* 58 [Recipe for] Kisses. **1842** *Civilian & Galveston City Gazette* 1 Oct 1/3 Candies and Confectionaries, ... Hoarhound, Kisses. **1876** *Wide Awake* 38/2 A factory-weaver's family ... had the most lovely of patties, and kisses, and sugar-plums sent them for their Christmas dinner last year. **1892** *Harper's Mag.* Jan. 266/2 Three jars of candy ... held red kisses and white, little hard gum drops, and fat black sticks of licorice.

+**Kissing bee.** A term used facetiously for a party. *colloq.* — **1853** *Turnover* 6 (Th.), [He was about] to shave and dress for a 'party' or 'kissing-bee.' **1900** DRANNAN *Plains & Mts.* 188, I sat in a corner like a homely girl at a kissing-bee, and had nothing to say.

+**Kissing bug.** Any of several hemipteran insects that sometimes bite the lip, causing a painful sore. — **1899** *Pop. Sci. Mo.* Nov. 33 Several persons suffering from swollen faces visited the Emergency Hospital in Washington and complained that they had been bitten by some insect while asleep.... Thus began the 'kissing bug' scare. *Ib.* 35 The kissing bug, in its own way and in the short space of two months, produced almost as much of a scare as did the San José scale in its five years of Eastern excitement. **1904** *N.Y. Ev. Post* 4 Aug. 1 The doctors were unable to decide whether he had been bitten by a mosquito or a kissing bug.

Kiss-in-the-ring. A variety of DROP THE HANDKERCHIEF. {1825-} — **1817** J. GALLATIN *Diary* 26 Dec. 117 We were allowed to play kiss-in-the-ring, suppressing the kiss; it was like 'Hamlet' minus the Prince of Denmark.

+**Kiss-joke.** =KISS-JOKE TICKET. Hence *kiss-joking*, the action of casting kiss-jokes. *slang. Obs.* — **1879** *Congress. Rec.* 24 April 843/1 In many States ... ballot-stuffing, kiss-joking, bulldozing, and murder have been ... unrestrained. **1880** *Ib.* 26 May 3809/1 Only upon rare occasions was one of these 'kiss-jokes' destroyed. It was a neat and safe way to establish a democratic majority—to put in a few hundred extra fraudulent democratic votes and then take out and destroy the same number of republican votes.

+**Kiss-joker.** =next. *slang. Obs.* — **1879** *Congress. Rec.* 24 April 844 In 1878 it [Charleston, S.C.] cast for a democrat ... 22,707 votes, kiss-joker and all, and for a republican 14,096.

+**Kiss-joke ticket.** *Polit.* A party ticket printed on very thin paper to permit a dishonest voter to cast several of them folded within a large ballot. *slang. Obs.* (Cf. SUGAR TICKET.) — **1880** *Congress. Rec.* 26 May 3809/1 Then [in 1878, in Charleston] came in those kiss-joke tickets, printed on very thin tissue paper.

Kiss-me. {1877-} +(See quotation.) — **a1870** CHIPMAN *Notes on Bartlett* 230 *Kiss-me.* Used, as is 'Thank-you-Ma'am,' for a ridge or hollow place across a roadway; a jolting obstruction to vehicles.—N[ew] E[ngland].

Kiss-me-quick. (See quot. 1848.) {1852-} Also attrib. — **1845** *Knickerb.* XXV. 375 Seen from the Bowery, it [a church] looks like a barn with a 'kiss-me-quick' hood on. **1848** BARTLETT 403 *Kiss-me-quick*, a homemade quilted bonnet which does not extend beyond the face. **1855** HALIBURTON *Nature & Hum. Nature* I. 287 She has a new bonnet on.... It has a horrid name, it is called a kiss-me-quick.

***Kit.**

1. A collection of various articles packed up for use on a journey; the knapsack or container in which these articles are carried. {1785-}

1819 QUITMAN in Claiborne *Life Quitman* 41 We furnish our own kit, and do our own cooking. **1847** RUXTON *Adv. Rocky Mts.* (1848) 273 All our very primitive 'kit' [was] overhauled to render it serviceable for the journey across the grand prairies. **1878** BEADLE *Western Wilds* 265 We here overhauled our kit, brushed up a little, and put on our best gear for a visit. **1890** HARTE *Waif of Plains* 145 He purchased some herrings, smoked beef, and biscuits, as future provisions for his 'pack' or kit. **1899** *Boston Ev. Globe* 20 July 9/6 Owing to the failure to supply the brigade with individual kits, haversacks, canteens and other articles, no considerable march outs will be attempted.

+**2.** *fig.* A personal or political following.

1901 *McClure's Mag.* Dec. 148 At the next session of the legislature Platt came up with a some-what large kit.... At the end of that session he was a power.

3. Colloq. phrases in sense: A number of persons or things viewed as a whole. Used contemptuously. {the whole kit, 1785-} +**a.** *The whole kit and biling.*

1859 BARTLETT 32 The phrase *the whole* (or more commonly *hull*) *kit and bilin*, means the whole lot, applied to persons or things. **1869** in De Vere 583 At one time there was good reason to fear that the whole kit and biling, as our men invariably called our traps, would be swept away. **1884** 'MARK TWAIN' *H. Finn* xxxvii. 378 Go 'long now, the whole kit and biling of ye. **1920** LEWIS *Main Street* 50 The whole kit and bilin' of 'em are nothing in God's world but socialism in disguise.

+**b.** *The whole kit and boodle.*

a1861 WINTHROP *J. Brent* xxviii. 296, I motioned we shove the hul kit an boodle of the gamblers ashore on logs. **1875** HOLLAND *Sevenoaks* xii. 160 The whole kit an' boodle of 'em is gone. **1899** A. THOMAS *Arizona* 21 Wasn't he the best of 'em—the whole kit and boodle? **1904** E. ROBINS *Magn. North* I. 93 The whole kit and boodle of us can drink.

+**c.** (*The whole*) *kit and caboodle.*

1888 *Boston Globe* 5 Feb. 1/3 If any 'railroad lobbyist' cast reflections on his character he would wipe out the whole kit and caboodle of them. **1900** GARLAND *Eagle's Heart* 103 They 'low me settlin' h'yer will bring others, which is shore about right, fer h'yer you be, kit an' caboodle. **1913** LONDON *Valley of Moon* II. vi, They look more like a real kid than the whole kit an' caboodle.

+**d.** *The whole kit and tuck.*

1871 EGGLESTON *Hoosier Schoolm.* iv. 50 He'll beat the whole kit and tuck of 'em afore he's through.

+**Kitcaboodle.** Contraction of *kit and caboodle.* — **1891** *Amer. Folk-Lore* IV. 70 *Kitcaboodle*, used in New England, in the same sense as the preceding [*kerhoot*]. 'The whole kitcaboodle.'

+**Kit Carson hitch.** [Christopher or *Kit Carson*, a frontiersman of the Far West (1809-68).] =DIAMOND HITCH. — **1882** BAILLIE-GROHMAN *Camps in Rockies* 45 You have at last managed the famous 'diamond' or 'Kit Carson' hitch to the lash rope.

***Kitchen.**

***1.** The room or part of a house, restaurant, etc., in which food is cooked or prepared.

c1640 *Harvard Rec.* I. 15 The highest Chamber over the Kitchen. **1798** BROWN *Wieland* vi, On the eastern side, were wings, divided in like manner into an upper and lower room; one of them comprised a kitchen, and chamber above it for the servant. **1826** G. POWERS *New York Prison at Auburn* 73 The basement story contains a kitchen, store-rooms, and pantries. **1845** JUDD *Margaret* I. 11 The house was divided by the chimney into two principal apartments, one being the kitchen or commons, the other a work-shop. **1867** *Atlantic Mo.* March 344/2 They are rather religious club-houses, and some of them are provided with a complete kitchen and restaurant apparatus. **1920** HOWELLS *Vacation of Kelwyns* 49 Somebody ought to go into the farm kitchens and teach the women ... that cookery is a science.

b. A separate building in which food is cooked. Chiefly on the plantations of the South. (Cf. next.)

1675 *New Castle Court Rec.* 63 The houses and Land knowne by the name of the greate house with the blokhouse and kitching with the erves thereto belonging. **1704** *Boston News-Letter* 8 May 2/2 To be Let or Sold, ... a Plantation, having on it a large new Brick house, and another good house by it for a Kitchin, & work house. **1788** *Edenton* (N.C.) *Intelligencer* 9 April, Upon which [plantation] there is ... a well built Barn 20 feet by 40, Cribs, Kitchens, Quarters &c. **1825** in Commons, etc. *Doc. Hist.* I. 252 Upon the premises there is a good dwelling house of six rooms, a good kitchen, Overseer's house [etc.]. **1833** J. HALL *Harpe's Head* 17 The kitchen, the ice-house, the smoke-house, being each a separate building. **1881** *Rep. Indian Affairs* 9 The dormitories, wash-rooms, kitchen, and store-room are all built of adobes. **1904** GLASGOW *Deliverance* 533 And now go —through the back door and past the kitchen to the piece of woods beyond the pasture.

+**c.** (See quotation.)

1824 DODDRIDGE *Notes* 174, I saw that the slaves and convicts [in Md.] lived in filthy hovels called kitchens.

+**2.** *fig.* (See quotation.)

1903 FOX *Little Shepherd* xv, He was told that in everything but mathematics he must go to the preparatory department until the second session of the term—the 'kitchen' as it was called by the students.

+**3.** 'A kind of oven for roasting meat, as before an open fire' (W. '09). Cf. TIN KITCHEN.

4. *attrib.* **a.** Designating various utensils, furnishings, etc., used in or located near a kitchen.

1824 *N.H. Hist. Soc. Coll.* I. 244 The only furniture found near the house was a kitchen chair. **1856** EMERSON *Eng. Traits* 59 The kitchen-clock is more convenient than sidereal time. **1889** JEWETT *Betty Leicester* xv. 222, I heard a clacketing in the kitchen closet. **1859** ELWYN *Glossary* 32 Other meanings [of clout] we have kept as we had them from our ancestors, *i.e.* a kitchen-cloth, etc. **1862** *Ill. Agric. Soc. Trans.* V. 161 It is brought up and set in the warm kitchen cupboard. **1887** ALDEN *Little Fishers* xviii, Jerry sitting on the doorstep fashioning a bracket for the kitchen lamp. **1875** STOWE *We & Neighbors* 55 Thence to the kitchen and kitchen pantry, where she looked into the flour barrel, the sugar barrel, the safe. **1853** FOWLER *Home for All* 132 One of these cisterns also connects with the copper boiler attached to the kitchen range. **1903** WIGGIN *Rebecca* 218 Miranda removed the shawl from her head and sank into the kitchen-rocker. **1898** *Kansas City Star* 18 Dec. 10/4 Kitchen Safe, 5 shelves, ... worth $6. **1876** *Wide Awake* 68/1 Mr. Brewer ... was washing his hands and face at the tin wash-basin in the kitchen sink. **1887** ALDEN *Little Fishers* ix, He was fashioning [a stick] into a proper shape to do duty as a towel-rack for Mrs. Job Smith's kitchen towel. **1674** *Harvard Rec.* I. 61 Kitchins Utensils ... 1 clever.

b. Designating various tools or equipment used with, or about, the kitchen fire.

1759 *Newport Mercury* 26 June 4/3 Imported . . . and to be sold by Jacob Richardson, . . . Parlor and Kitchen Bellows. **1835** *24th Congress 1 Sess. H. R. Doc.* No. 64, 20 Boiler, kitchen, J. and W. C. Bailey, Farmington, Maine, May 22. **1693** SEWALL *Diary* I. 376 Our kitchin chimney fell on fire about noon. **1898** WESTCOTT *D. Harum* xxvii, He . . . made out to assist Nature, as the sayin' is, by stirrin' on't with the kitchen poker. **1859** STOWE *Minister's Wooing* xvii, Candace . . . stood frowning and gloomy over the top of her long kitchen-shovel. **1871** — *Sam Lawson* 4 He only took up the great kitchen-tongs, and smote on the hickory forestick.

c. Designating persons who work in a kitchen.

1835 INGRAHAM *South-West* II. 253 There are some Yankee 'kitchen girls,' . . . who can do more house work . . . than three or four negro servants. **1873** *Newton Kansan* 8 May 4/3 The frenzied proprietor promoted laundresses, kitchen scrubs, bell boys. **1903** FOX *Little Shepherd* ix, General Dean was walking swiftly down the hill, with Snowball's mammy, . . . rushing after him, and the kitchen servants following. **1722** *New-Eng. Courant* 13–20 Aug. 1/2 The scandalous and Monstrous Fashion of Hoop-Petticoats, which are worn by all our Females (from the best Lady to the poorest Kitchen-Wench).

d. Special combinations.

+*Kitchen back*, the back of a two-story house in which the kitchen is only of one story; +*k. dance*, a dance held in a kitchen; *k. loft*, a loft over a kitchen; +*k. oyster*, (see quotation); +*k. shower*, a shower of various kitchen utensils given to engaged couples just before they get married; *k. tent*, a tent where cooking is done.

1787 in *Mag. Amer. Hist.* I. 382 These houses add much to the beauty of [Fort Harmar, near Pittsburgh]. . . . The Colonel's is two story high, with a kitchen back. **1880** *Harper's Mag.* Dec. 89/2 The younger people had their berrying frolics, sleigh-rides, kitchen dances, nuttings, and the like. **1648** *Conn. Rec.* I. 508 In the Kitchin Lofts and Garritts . . . 1 saddle, 1 cloakbag, 1 pillion, 1 sidesaddle and pillion cloath. **1881** INGERSOLL *Oyster-Industry* 245 *Kitchen Oyster.*—Small oyster for cooking. (New Orleans.) **1924** CROY *R. F. D. No.* 3 89 It was a 'kitchen shower.' The glittering array was piled high, like a special sale in a racket store—dish-pans, saucepans, pie pans, an egg beater, . . . and so on. **1885** CUSTER *Boots & Saddles* v. 52 The little sheet-iron cooking-stove . . . was placed in the kitchen-tent on stormy nights.

Kitchen cabinet. +A coterie of personal, unofficial advisers to President Andrew Jackson (1829–1837), chief among whom were: Frank P. Blair, Isaac Hill, Amos Kendall, and William B. Lewis; any group of unofficial advisers to a president or a state governor. At first a derisive term. *colloq.*

1832 in A. C. Cole *Whig Party in So.* (1913) 13 *n.*, If there be no other mode of preventing its [a mission's] being given to the most despicable of all the Protegees of the Kitchen Cabinet [*i.e.*, Van Buren]. **1834** *Ib.* 31 The Nullifiers of the South have always professed to cherish the Union. . . . It is now more in danger from the triumph of the Kitchen Cabinet than any other circumstance. **1838** *N.Y. Advertiser & Exp.* 21 Feb. 1/1 The Kitchen Cabinet in Washington understands how the strings are pulled in New York. **1844** 'UNCLE SAM' *Peculiarities* I. 233 The whole of the kitchen cabinet, knows nothing of it. **1886** *Congress. Rec.* 9 June 5721/2 Don't you think Mr. Adams, of New York, is one of the members of that kitchen cabinet? **1904** *N.Y. Herald* 14 Sept. 5 The kitchen cabinet is a development of the ascendency of Governor Odell in republican affairs. It consists of the body guard of his closest friends and advisers. *attrib.* **1842** 'UNCLE SAM' *Peculiarities* I. 212 We will hurl the Kitchen cabinet tyrants from their stools. *a***1855** J. F. KELLY *Humors* 76, I'd like to inquire if those Kitchen cabinet disclosures of the Pennsylvania Senator, were true. **1867** *Wkly. New Mexican* 30 March 2/2 [Gov.] Mitchell [of N.M.] having failed in his 'kitchen cabinet' diplomacy, Perea turned his eyes upon the Senate.

+**Kitchen caucus.** ? A private caucus held by persons without official status in the government. — **1826** [see KING CAUCUS].

+**Kitchen chamber.** A chamber over, or adjacent to, a kitchen. — **1649** *Conn. Rec.* I. 497 An Inventory of the Estate of Mr. William Whiting: . . . In the kitching chamber . . . a bed, . . . In the Kittching . . . 2 brass pots. **1692** SEWALL *Diary* I. 366 Din'd in his Kitchin Chamber. **1715** *Boston Rec.* 224 Agreed that the Kitchin Chamber of ye House . . . be ceiled over head. **1780** E. PARKMAN *Diary* 227 Ye Fire, . . . kindled in ye Kitchen Chamber. **1865** A. D. WHITNEY *Gayworthys* xxxvii. 346 The kitchen-chamber at the head of the 'end staircase,' was what had been Joanna's room.

* **Kitchen garden.**

***1.** A garden to supply vegetables and fruits for the table.

1634 WOOD *New Eng. Prospect* I. x. 37 Dorchester . . . is the greatest Towne in New England; well woodded and watered; . . . faire Cornefields, and pleasant Gardens, with Kitchin-gardens. **1776** *N.J. Archives* 2 Ser. I. 32 To Be Sold. A plantation in the township of Amwell, Hunterdon County, West New-Jersey, containing . . . a good kitchen garden. **1842** KIRKLAND *Forest Life* I. vi. 54 She has not only provided for the kitchen-garden, but ventured upon a little stand of exotics for the parlor. **1881** WHITMAN *Spec. Days* 10 There [was] the well, the sloping kitchen-garden, and . . . the dwelling of my great-grandfather. **1912** WOODROW *Sally Salt* 179 She sauntered down through her kitchen garden to observe her drooping tomato vines.

Kitchen gardening. +(See quot. and cf. next.) — **1893** *Daily News* (London) 26 Jan. 5/5 'Kitchen-gardening' is the curious name bestowed upon their labours by the ladies of an American city, who teach a class of poor children to sew, cook, dust, sweep, make beds, and wash clothes.

+**Kitchengarten.** [Wrongly formed after KINDERGARTEN.] A class for children in which cooking, sewing, etc., is taught. *local.* — **1893** Barrows *World's Parl. of Religions* II. 1483 Kindergartens, kitchengarten, and nightschools [etc.] . . . are among the methods employed [by the Woman's Home Missionary Society].

Kitchen hatch. {1750} *College.* +(See quot. 1851.) — **1734** *Harvard Rec.* I. 146 The waiters . . . shall receive the Plates and Victualls at the Kitchen Hatch, & carry the same to the severall tables. **1851** HALL *College Words* 177 *Kitchen-Hatch*, a half-door between the kitchen and the hall in colleges and old mansions.

+**Kitchen mule.** A pack mule that carries kitchen ware. — **1873** in Abbott *C. Carson* 296 As Loring fled with the speed of an antelope, he met the first animal, which happened to be the kitchen mule. He was so called, because he had very large open bags or panniers, into which we put all our cooking utensils. **1880** *Scribner's Mo.* May 128/1 When a bread-pan is taken, it is lashed bottom up on the top of the kitchen-mule's pack.

Kitchen stove. A cookstove or cooking range. — **1845** *Knickerb.* XXV. 106 He wished her in the south of France, or the kitchen-stove, rather than there. **1863** A. D. WHITNEY *F. Gartney* xxiii, The fire was down,—the kitchen stove immaculate in blackness from fresh polish. **1883** RITTENHOUSE *Maud* 244 There isn't even a fire in the kitchen stove or a 'girl' in the kitchen-door-way. **1907** ANDREWS *Recoll.* 259 None of the houses had any stoves, fireplaces or even chimneys, except the kitchen-stoves. **1913** LONDON *Valley of Moon* II. i, The first morning he had insisted upon getting up with her and building the fire in the kitchen stove.

* **Kite,** *n.*

***1.** Any of several hawklike birds of the family Falconidae.

The chief American species are the EVERGLADE KITE, the MISSISSIPPI KITE, the white-tailed kite, *Elanus leucurus*, and the swallow-tailed kite, *Elanoides forficatus*.

1637 MORTON *New Canaan* 71 There are Crowes, kights and rooks that doe differ in some respects from those of England. **1737** BRICKELL *N. Carolina* 175 The Kites . . . are mortal Enemies to the Snakes, for which reason the Planters seldom kill them, or destroy their Eggs. **1767** J. ROWE *Diary* 140 Coming home we saw a Kite attack a full grown Duck, he struck his Tallons into her side. **1858** BAIRD *Birds Pacific R.R.* 36 Sub-Family [in Falconidae] Milvinae.—The Kites. **1874** COUES *Birds N.W.* 332 *Nauclerus forficatus.* . . . Swallow-tailed Kite. . . . Marked among its kind by no ordinary beauty of form and brilliancy of color, the Kite courses through the air [etc.]. **1917** *Birds of Amer.* II. 58 The Eagles, Hawks, and Kites comprise the family *Buteonidæ*.

2. A contrivance consisting of a frame over which paper or cloth is stretched, which can be flown by means of a long string attached. {1664–} Also attrib.

1752 FRANKLIN *Writings* III. 99 This kite is to be raised when a thunder-gust appears to be coming on. **1809** J. ADAMS *Works* IX. 613, I spent my time in shooting, skating, swimming, flying kites. **1876** 'MARK TWAIN' *Tom Sawyer* xxxi. 244 He took a Kite-line from his pocket. **1890** HOWELLS *Boy's Town* 89 The Kites were of various shapes: bow Kites, two-stick Kites, and house Kites.

+**3.** *Higher than a kite*, very high, with unusual force. Also *higher than Gilderoy's kite.*

E. C. Brewer, in *Notes and Queries* (7 Ser. V. 357/1), suggests a Scottish ballad as the possible source of *Gilderoy's kite*.

1867 *Wkly. New Mexican* 24 Aug. 2/2 The Cleverites have thrown him higher than a kite. **1869** 'MARK TWAIN' *Innocents* xxv. 256 She squandered millions of francs on a navy . . . , and the first time she took her new toy into action she got it knocked higher than Gilderoy's Kite—to use the language of the Pilgrims. **1885** HOWELLS *S. Lapham* i, The war broke out; and it knocked my paint higher than a kite. **1887** STOCKTON *Hundredth Man* xii, That would 'a' knocked the eatin' house proprietor higher 'n a kite.

Kite, *v. colloq.*

1. *intr.* or *quasi-tr.* (See quot. 1864.)

1839 BRIGGS *H. Franco* II. 35 He stuffed half a dozen blank checks into his hat, and said he must go out and kite it to save his credit. **1864** WEBSTER 740/3 *Kite*, . . . to raise money, or sustain one's credit, by the use of mercantile paper which is fictitious. **1891** NICHOLS *Business Guide* (ed. 28) 241 Kiting or Kite flying.—Exchanging checks on different banks, for the purpose of obtaining the use of money for a single day.

2. *intr.* To move *along* quickly or smoothly; to fly away; to soar *around* as a kite. {1863–}

1854 'O. OPTIC' *In Doors & Out* (1876) 92 You did not use to be fond of 'kiting' round in this manner. **1857** *Lawrence* (Kan.) *Republican* 18 June 4 The team is hitched to the plow, and on it goes, kiting along the surface. **1863** *Rio Abajo Press* 2 June 1/3 Fortunately for us, petroleum is non-explosive; otherwise we . . . might go 'kiting' into the regions of illimitable space. **1877** HARTE *Story of Mine* (1896) 253 The other way is to whip up and yell, and send the whole six kiting by like h—ll! **1883** PECK *Bad Boy* 176 When they struck the step they went kiting. **1898** WESTCOTT *D. Harum* ii, I seen the deakin putterin' 'round, an' I waved my hand to him an' went by a-kitin'.

+3. To go up in price.

1874 *Congress. Rec.* 31 Jan. 1085/1 Gold went up as soon as that law passed, kiting, kiting, almost out of sight. **1902** WILSON *Spenders* 355 The stock is bound to kite.

* **Kitefoot, Kite's foot.** +A kind of tobacco processed to a color resembling the kite's foot. *Obs.* Also attrib. with *tobacco.*

[**1688** CLAYTON *Va.* in *Phil. Trans.* XVII. 943 Aranoko Tobacco, whose Scent is not much minded, their . . . aim being . . . to procure it a bright Kite's-foot colour.] **1790** *Penna. Packet* 13 July 1/4 Fine Cut Tobacco, for chewing; Kitefoot and common ditto, for smoaking. **1795** WINTERBOTHAM *Hist. View* III. 36 Two articles are said to be peculiar to Maryland, viz. the genuine white wheat, . . . and the bright kite's foot tobacco. **1805** PARKINSON *Tour* 56 The other [situation offered me was] upon Elk-Ridge (where the fine kite-foot tobacco was formerly grown), in the road between Alexandria and Baltimore. **1835** TODD *Notes* 50 The adjacent state of Maryland produces . . . the Bright Kite's Foot Tobacco.

+**Kit fox. a.** (See quot. 1890.) **b.** 'A related species (*V. macrotis*), with larger ears, [which] inhabits the southwestern United States' (W. '09). — **1805** LEWIS in *L. & Clark Exped.* II. (1904) 216 The party who were down with Capt. Clark also killed a small fox. . . . It is so much like the comm[on] small fox of this country commonly called the kit fox that I should have taken it for a young one of that species. **1890** *Cent.* 3296/1 *Kit-fox,* . . . the American corsak, or swift-fox, *Vulpes velox,* a small fox peculiar to western North America, where it lives in holes in the prairies. **1917** *Mammals of Amer.* 77 The Kit Foxes might be considered as Red Foxes that had left the timbered regions to dwell in open, semi-arid areas and had become bleached out by exposure to the hot sun, as well as suffering a reduction in size.

Kiting. *attrib.* Designating acts or things associated with improper manipulation of bonds, stocks, etc. — **1866** *Congress. Globe* 29 June 3482/1 Every kiting charter like this one—I speak of the National Telegraph Company. **1872** *Ib.* 3 April 2128/2 (Th.), They may . . . hold the bonds, as has often been done in kiting corporations, and then take the property they have thus swindled the public . . . out of. **1878** *Ib.* 5 June 4124/2 This is to make the Government party to a kiting operation. **1916** DU PUY *Uncle Sam* 34 He believed that the story of the bookkeeper of the kiting bank was to be enacted before his eyes.

+**Kittatinny.** [*Kittatinny* Mountains of New Jersey and Pennsylvania.] A garden variety of blackberry. Also attrib. — **1874** *Rep. Comm. Agric. 1873* 187 Six years ago he planted ten rows of Kittatinny and ten of Wilson. . . . None of the Kittatinny canes bore fruit.

Kittereen. Also **kittern, kettering, kittareen.** {1831–} A kind of top carriage drawn by a single horse: (see quot. 1754). *Obs.* — **1745** *N.Y. Wkly. Post-Boy* 18 March, Several very good Riding Chairs and Kittereens to be sold. **1754** *Boston News-Letter* 29 Aug. 4/2 A two-wheel chair, commonly call'd a Kittern. **1758** *Boston W. Advertiser* 9 Jan. 2/3 To be sold, a good handsome Kettering. **1792** *Descr. Kentucky* 42 In 1787 were exported Chaises 40, Kittareens 10, Sulkeys 7. **1794** *Gazette of U.S.* (Phila.) 6 Jan. (Th.), He undertakes to make and repair . . . coaches, chaises, kittereens, &c.

+**Kittereen box.** =prec. — **1750** *New-York Gazette* 22 Jan., Chaise-Boxes, chair and Kittereen Boxes, with all Sorts of Wheels and Carriages for the Same, are made by James Hallett.

Kittiwake. Any of several gulls of the genus *Rissa*, having the hind toe rudimentary, esp. *R. tridactyla.* {1661–} Also attrib. with *gull.* — **1828** BONAPARTE *Synopsis* 359 The Kittiwake Gull . . . inhabits the north of both continents. **1835** AUDUBON *Ornith. Biog.* III. 186 High above the mast-head of our tallest man-of-war, the Kittiwakes float gracefully in wide circles. **1874** COUES *Birds N.W.* 644 The Common Kittiwake. . . . Arctic regions of both hemispheres. South in winter on the Atlantic coast to the Middle States. **1917** *Birds of Amer.* I. 39.

+**Kittly-benders.** Also **kiddly-benders, kettle-de-benders.** 'Thin bending ice; act of running over such ice' (W. '09). *colloq.* Also fig. — **1854** THOREAU *Walden* 353 Let us not play at kittlybenders. **1858** G. M. DALLAS *Series of Lett. from London* (1869) II. 7 This will enable our ministers here to walk, on this treacherous element of dress, as on thick ice, not as heretofore on what boys call 'kiddly benders.' **1872** E. E. HALE *How to Do It* iii. 46 You will, with unfaltering step, move quickly over the kettle-de-benders of this broken essay.

Kitty. {1825–} 'A pool into which each player in a card-game puts a certain amount of his winnings, to be used in meeting expenses, as for room-rent, refreshments, etc.' (*Cent.*). {1892} Also fig. — **1887** KELLER *Draw Poker* 12 *Widow,* or *Kitty*—A percentage taken out of the pool to defray the expenses of the game or the cost of refreshments. **1909** 'O. HENRY' *Roads of Destiny* xiii. 213 Your thousand dollars is gone into the kitty of this corrupt country on that last bluff you made.

Kitty-cornered, *a.* and *adv.* Variant of CATER-CORNERED. Also *kitty-corner* v. — **1890** *Dialect Notes* I. 8 *Kittycornered* . . . would be an easy development from *cattycornered. Ib.* 78 [In the Seguachee Valley, Tenn.] catty-*cornered* . . . is sometimes called *kitty-catty-cornered.* **1892** *Ib.* 236 *Kitty-corner,* . . . to cut off a corner by going across lots.

+**Kiva.** [Hopi, 'sacred chamber.'] *S.W.* An assembly chamber for the observance of religious rites among the Pueblo Indians. (Cf. ESTUFA 1.) — **1875** *Scribner's Mo.* Dec. 205/2 This kiva, as it is called in their own tongue, is called '*Estufa*' by the Spaniards, and is spoken of by writers in English as the 'Sweat House.' **1904** *N.Y. Tribune* 29 May, The secret ceremonies [of the Indians] are for the most part held in underground kivas, or secluded chambers.

+**Kiverlid.** (See COVERLID.)

+**Ki-yi,** *n. slang.* [Echoic.] **1.** A howl or yelp, as of a dog. **2.** A dog. — (**1**) **1883** HAY *Bread-Winners* 29 You ought to have heard the Ki-yi's that followed. **1888** *Detroit Free Press* 4 Aug. (F.), Now and then you will hear a joyous Ki-yi come from the direction of some woolley-headed worker. **1895** REMINGTON *Pony Tracks* 27 The men from Tongue River greeted the men from Pine Ridge . . . with *ki-yis* of delight. (**2**) **1904** *Buffalo Express* 20 June 4 A butcher in Brussels made sausage of the carcass of a zoo elephant which had been killed. Doubtless the Brussels kiyis yelped for joy. **1913** LONDON *Valley of Moon* I. x, But them sickenin', sap-headed stiffs, with the grit of rabbits and the silk of mangy ki-yi's, a-cheerin' me—*me!*

+**Ki-yi,** *v. intr.* To yelp. *slang.* Also fig. — **1850** GARRARD *Wah-To-Yah* vii. 95 The poor victim to savage appetite . . . ki-yi-ed until his little canine spirit departed for elysium. **1869** STOWE *Oldtown Folks* 332 Hang him [a dog] we did, and he ki-hied with a vigor that strikingly increased the moral effect. **1894** *Harper's Mag.* Sept. 642/2 One of those little Skye-terrier tugs . . . began to ki-yi right under our stern.

+**K. K.** Abbreviation for KU-KLUCKER. — **1870** B. YOCUM in *Report on Public Frauds, S.C.* (1878) 26 If the governor is going to arm the white K. K.'s to operate against them, he, the Gov., can take back the guns and commissions that has been already sent to this county. **1898** PAGE *Red Rock* 322 You better watch out for de K. K.'s.

+**K. K. K.** [Abbreviation for KU-KLUX KLAN.] The original Ku-Klux Klan or one of its members; the reorganized Klan. Also attrib. — **1872** in Fleming *Hist. Reconstruction* II. 132 We advanced upon the supposed K. K. K.'s with an intrepidity that reflected credit upon the troops. **1877** J. M. BEARD *K. K. K. Sketches* 35 The horses of the raid were . . . furnished with all those *cap-a-pie* appointments of K. K. K. regalia. **1879** TOURGEE *Fool's Errand* xxviii. 180 Three colored men were whipped by the K. K. K. **1921** in Fry *Modern Ku Klux Klan* (1922) 55 You gentlemen at headquarters will probably be pleased to know what rapid strides the K. K. K. is making in this State [Miss.]. **1923** *Imperial Night-Hawk* 29 Aug. 5/3 The electric K. K. K. sign (a cross) was torn from the leading automobile.

+**Klan.** =KU-KLUX KLAN. — **1868** in *Century Mag.* XXVIII. 409/1 The Klan now, as in the past, is prohibited from doing such things. **1870** *N.C. Governor Proclamations* 31 The County governments have . . . omitted to ferret out and bring to justice those of this Klan who have thus violated the law. **1884** *Century Mag.* July 402 The way was prepared for the rapid growth and spread of the Klan.

+**Klondike.** Used attrib. in reference to a region in Alaska to which a gold rush was made in 1897–9. — **1898** *Century Mag.* March 695 During the rush of 1897 only two routes into the Klondike country were followed. *Ib.* 697/2 These men made their way home, as best they could, out of the wreckage of the first Klondike rush. **1898** *Kansas City Star* 21 Dec. 7/3 For the first time, though, there are a number of military dolls and quite a number of Klondike dolls. **1901** (*play title*), A Klondike Diamond.

+**Klucker.** A member of the Ku-Klux Klan. (Cf. KU-KLUCKER.) — **1879** TOURGEE *Fool's Errand* xxvii. 141 Ef dere's any mo' Kluckers raidin' roun' Burke's Corners, dar'll be some funerals tu.

+**Klu Klux.** Erron. variant of KU KLUX. — **1872** *Congress. Globe* 21 May 3707/3 Since 1868, when we handled this organization without gloves, we have had no Klu Klux in Arkansas. **1924** *Imperial Night-Hawk* 14 Feb. 8 We understand that a member of your firm ran for Mayor on the Klu Klux ticket.

+**K.N.** =KNOW-NOTHING 2. Used attrib. — **1855** *Chicago W. Times* 2 Sept. 1/2 The Philadelphia *Sun,* an original K.N. organ, draws a picture of the greedy office seekers among the Hindoos.

+**Knackaway.** [See quot. 1896.] The anaqua, a tree or shrub found in the southwestern part of the United States. — **1884** SARGENT *Rep. Forests* 114 *Ehretia elliptica.* . . . Knackaway. Anaqua. **1896** *Garden & Forest* IX. 282 *Knackaway* (*Ehretia elliptica*), a corruption of the Mex.-Span. anaqua, shortened from anacahuite, which is from Aztec *nanahuaquahuitl,* 'lues venera tree,' so called from the medicinal use of its roots. **1902** CLAPIN 18 *Anaqua* . . . (Sp.), a tree or shrub of the borage family (*Ehretia elliptica*), found in South-Western Texas. Also called *knackaway.*

Knapsack. A sack or bag worn by soldiers as a receptacle for their necessities. {1603–} — **1608** SMITH *Works* I. 20 One [man] . . . vsually carried my Gowne and Knapsacke. **1775** *Jrnls. Cont. Congress* II. 188 Each soldier [shall] be furnished with . . . twelve flints and a knapsack. **1820** *Amer. Antiq. Soc. Trans.* I. 283 The knapsack is an old blanket, and contains some parched corn flour, jerked meat, and leather to patch their [warriors'] mocasons with. **1862** F. MOORE *Rebellion Rec.* V. II. 268 Nothing was to be found on this portion of the field but killed and wounded Yankees and their guns and knapsacks. **1897** *Outing* XXIX. 488/2 The flour, salt, sugar and coffee were carried in rubber-cloth bags . . . and stored away . . . in the knapsacks.

* **Knapweed.** A plant of the genus *Centaurea* introduced into the United States from Europe. — **1829** EATON *Botany* (ed. 5) 167 *Centaurea jacea,* knapweed. . . . Naturalized. **1898** CREEVEY *Flowers of Field* 202 Centaurea, or Knapweed. Star-thistle.

* **Knawel.** A low weed (*Scleranthus annuus*), found in the eastern part of the United States. — **1762** CLAYTON *Flora Virginica* 16 Knawel sive Polygono affinis erecta ramosa [etc.]. **1814** BIGELOW *Florula Bostoniensis*

107 *Scleranthus annuus*. Common Knawel. . . . A small, obscure plant in gravelly soils, road sides, &c. **1850** S. F. COOPER *Rural Hours* 106 It will be easy to name a number of these: . . . the prinpernel [*sic*], celandine, and knawel. **1892** TORREY *Foot-Path Way* 38 Found chickweed and knawel in bloom.

***Kneading trough.** A wooden trough in which dough is kneaded. — **1647** *Essex Probate Rec.* I. 64 A kneeding trough & other lumber. **1674** *Harvard Rec.* I. 61 Kitchins Utensils: . . . 1 kneading or sifting trough. **1859** STOWE *Minister's Wooing* vii, Candace lifted her great floury fist from the kneading-trough.

***Knee.**

***1.** A piece of timber having a natural crook or bend which makes it useful in shipbuilding.

1640 *Mass. H. S. Coll.* 4 Ser. VI. 143 And the towne agreed not to cutt any great tymber which is fitt for shipping planckes or knees &c. **1795** *Ann. 4th Congress* 2 Sess. 2575 He will have all the timber in the six yards in the month of May next, excepting the knees, all of which he thinks cannot be got of live oak. **1839** BRIGGS *H. Franco* II. 240 Green and white paint are very indifferent substitutes for strong oak ribs and stout hanging knees. **1893** *Harper's Mag.* Jan. 168 There has been no apparent effort to imitate the massive beams, the peculiar 'knees,' . . . of our coast boat-builders.

attrib. **1741** *Ga. Hist. Soc. Coll.* I. 165 Near the sea, where the ground is more upon a level, there is a great quantity of excellent knee timber.

b. Such a piece of timber used in erecting houses, making canoes, etc.

1717 *N.J. Archives* 1 Ser. IV. 318 The carpenters represented, that they could not go on for want of Knees, . . . which are little crooked sticks not so big as my arm. **1764** HUTCHINSON *Hist. Mass* I. 467 The other sort [of canoes] were made of the bark or rind of the birch tree, with knees or ribs. **1807** GASS *Journal* 108 This evening the canoes were finished except the putting in some knees. **1872** *Ill. Dept. Agric. Trans.* 174 It makes excellent wagon timbers, plow beams, threshing machine knees.

+2. (See quotation and cf. BUTTING POLE.)

1791 in Jillson *Dark & Bl. Ground* 109 The knees are pieces of heart timber laid above the butting poles to prevent the poles rolling off.

+3. =CYPRESS KNEE: (see also quot. 1858).

1823 JAMES *Exped.* III. 178 The innumerable conic excrescences called knees . . . give a gloomy . . . aspect to the scenery of those cypress swamps. **1830** ROYALL *Southern Tour* I. 164 [The cypress trees] stand as thick as a cane-brake, and the few crevices that are left, are filled with *knees*—knee is the name of young cypress, and is like nothing else in the world. **1854** SIMMS *Southward Ho* 277 [She] passed into the low flat land, strewed with gray cypresses, with their thousand *knees*, or abutments. **1856** *Harper's Mag.* Sept. 444/1 Pools of black, slimy water, from which rose the broad-based cypress, and grouped around those strange contorted roots, called knees, gnarled and knotted like stalagmites in a cave. **1858** WARDER *Hedges & Evergreens* 244 One of the physiological peculiarities of these plants [of Abietineae] is that the roots do not develop buds; hence they never sucker, although they run near the surface, and often rise above it, forming knees. **1891** 'THANET' *Otto the Knight* 13 Even the hideous 'knees' that spike the ground are transformed.

Knee action. In a horse: Action or muscular articulation or co-ordination at the knee joint. — **1868** WOODRUFF *Trotting Horse* iv. 62 [The colt] continually hit himself in the elbows, by reason of excessive knee-action as it appeared. **1884** *N.Y. Herald* 27 Oct. 1/2 (*advt.*), A Very Handsome Dapple Gray Horse, 15¾ hands high, 6 years old; cannot be surpassed for style and knee action. **1898** WESTCOTT *D. Harum* 21 Deakin Perkins has got a hoss that don't jest suit him—hain't got knee-action enough at times. **1903** A. ADAMS *Log Cowboy* xv. 100 They will discuss how to shoe that filly so as to give her certain knee action which she seems to need.

Knee band. A band that encircles the leg at the knee; a garter. — **1787** FRENEAU *Misc. Works* 411 A tailor by trade (and a dabster was he To make a silk knee-band set snug to the knee). **1835** IRVING *Tour of Prairies* 30 [The Creeks] have leggins of dressed deer skins, or of green or scarlet cloth, with embroidered knee bands and tassels. **1855** S. WILLARD *Mem. Youth & Manhood* I. 319 Boots with yellow tops inverted, and coming up to the knee-band, were commonly worn by men somewhat advanced in years.

Knee buckle. A buckle, usually of ornamental design, worn at the knee. {1772–} — **1754** *S.C. Gazette* 1–8 Jan. 4/3 To Be Sold . . . shoe and knee buckles, snuffers, gun hammers. **1791** *Ann. 1st Congress* II. 2130 Duties . . . shall be laid on . . . shoe and knee buckles, on gold and silver lace [etc.]. **1845** *Knickerb.* XXV. 445 His silver knee-buckles wore the same brightness. **1884** ROOSEVELT *Amer. Backlogs* 8 Those were the days when gentlemen wore . . . long black silk stockings with knee-buckles.

Knee-high, *a.*

1. Of a height sufficient to reach to the knee. **a.** Of persons. (Often in contexts having reference to extreme youthfulness). Also fig.

1799 BROWN *A. Mervyn* xv, I never cried in my life, since I was knee-high. **1808** J. N. BARKER *Indian Princess* I. ii, You followed him as I have, from a knee-high urchin. **1853** SIMMS *Sword & Distaff* 78, I've seen and talked with him years ago, when he wasn't knee-high. **1884** *Century Mag.* Nov. 108, I doubt if my patriotism, during my first three-weeks' drill, was quite knee high. **1902** HARBEN *A. Daniel* 121 He's known me since I was knee-high.

b. Of plants. {1745– (Ellis *Mod. Husb.* III. II. 83)}

1855 *Fla. Plantation Rec.* 132 The Cotton in the lower most cut of prelow will avrige knee high. **1878** B. F. TAYLOR *Between Gates* 281 Nearly everything will grow in California. It seldom gets knee-high. **1887** I. R. *Lady's Ranche Life Mont.* 108 Another time we would picket our horses and go afoot, through bunch-grass knee-high. **1902** WISTER *Virginian* xiv, There was rutted sand and lumpy, knee-high grease wood in our short cut.

+c. *Baseball.* (See quotation.) *Obs.*

1868 CHADWICK *Base Ball* 42 *Knee-High.*—This is one of the terms used by the batsman, when he is requested to show the pitcher where he wants a ball delivered.

+2. *Knee-high to a duck*, etc., used in comparisons as a means of emphasizing the extreme youthfulness of the person described.

1824 *Microscope* (Albany, N.Y.) 12 June 55/1 (Th.), He has lived with me ever since he was 'knee high to a musquitoe.' **1833** NEAL *Down Easters* I. 78 A bit of a rogue he was too, when he want more'n knee high to a bumbly-bee. **1841** SIMMS *Kinsmen* ii. 63 (Th.), He has been known in the Congaree ever since I was knee high to a splinter. **1856** *Porter's Spirit of Times* 15 Nov. 172/1 Not since I have been old enough to discriminate between a good and a bad animal, and that has been since I was knee-high to a grasshopper. **1904** HARBEN *Georgians* 89, I know'd 'im when he wasn't kneehigh to a duck.

b. Esp. with *frog, toad*, etc.

1833 *Louisville Herald* 20 March, It is really the best version of an old story we have heard 'ever since we were knee-high to a frog.' **1840** THOMPSON *Green Mt. Boys* II. 221 Why man, I have known him ever since he was knee high to a toad. **1845** JUDD *Margaret* I. xvi. 141 They an't knee high to a toad to 't. **1880** *Harper's Mag.* March 570/2 She was knee-high to a hop-toad, as you may say. **1893** *Ib.* Dec. 59/2 He warn't no mo'n knee-high to a toad-frog.

Kneeling desk. A desk at which one kneels; a prie-dieu. *Obs.* {1853–} — **1647** *Md. Archives* IV. 321 A kneeling desk, & a picture of Paules.

Knee pants. Pants or trousers extending to the knees. — **1869** *Atlantic Mo.* July 74/2, I made my initial bow before the foot-lights, in my small Canton flannel knee-pants. **1896** ADE *Artie* xvii. 154, I'll come hot-footin' in here with my knee-pants and a dinky coat. **1917** MCCUTCHEON *Green Fancy* 1 She was afraid of the big, strange man . . . who wore 'knee pants' and stockings like a boy on Sunday.

Knee-sprung, *a.* Of animals: Having overstrained or bent knees; bow-legged. Also transf. — **1875** HARTE in *Scribner's Mo.* XII. 208 Particularly when that animal's foundered and knee-sprung. **1907** STEWART *Partners* 204 Old John, which was the second cook, was so kneesprung you could see through his apron.

+Knickerbocker. [Diedrich *Knickerbocker*, pretended author of Irving's *A History of New York* (1809).]

1. A New Yorker, esp. one descended from the original Dutch settlers.

[**1809** IRVING *Knickerb.* 83 Lastly, came the Knickerbockers, of the great town of Schahtitoke, where the folk lay stones upon the houses in windy weather, lest they should be blown away.] **1841** *Corr. R. W. Griswold* (1898) 74 We Knickerbockers, I fear, do not sufficiently appreciate the leaven of Eastern scholarship. **1852** BRISTED *Upper Ten Th.* ii. 47 A genuine Knickerbocker from the start, . . . he learned a little of everything. **1886** *Harper's Mag.* Nov. 941/2 She is not a bad match even for a Knickerbocker.

transf. **1880** CABLE *Grandissimes* 101 The Creoles—the Knickerbockers of Louisiana.

b. (See quot. 1881.)

1857 *Harper's Mag.* March 451/1, I am an Albany Knickerbocker—a Dutchman of purest Belgic blood—and I justly claim to be heard. **1881** *Ib.* March 533/1 It has become common to speak of the *élite* of Albany as Knickerbockers—a name derived from Knik-ker-bak-ker (pronounced as spelled), a baker of knickers [marbles].

2. *pl.* Short, loosely fitting trousers gathered at the knee. {1859–}

1864 G. A. SALA in *Daily Telegraph* 19 Oct., Imagine a South-Western Robin Hood, with a tawny beard, homespun knickerbockers, and a Rip-Rap hat. **1883** *Wheelman* April 6/1 We donned our knickerbockers, . . . and bicycled to the wharf. **1893** M. HOWE *Honor* 129 [She] darned the great holes which the boys' knees wore in stockings and knickerbockers. **1913** LA FOLLETTE *Autobiog.* 488 He soon made his appearance, wearing linen knickerbockers.

3. Attrib. in sense 1 with *literature, name, parlor*, etc.

1830 WATSON *Philadelphia* App. 39 It was one of the grand links of union in the Knickerbocker social compact. **1844** *Lexington Observer* 16 Oct. 1/1 The fine old Knickerbocker parlor was in its primmest order. **1878** *Harper's Mag.* Jan. 307/1 That 'Knickerbocker literature' which the Nation pungently described some years ago. **1884** *Congress. Rec.* App. 25 June 343/1 Upon mattresses laid on the bare ground within this tent twenty-five of us were 'bundled' in true Knickerbocker style, without regard to sex, side by side. **1903** *N.Y. Times Sat. Rev.* 7 Nov. 790 A young woman who bears a Knickerbocker name beginning with Van.

Knicker. [Du. *knikker.*] +(See quot. 1859.) — **1859** Bartlett 231 Knicker or Nicker, . . . a boy's clay marble; a common term in New York. **1881** [see Knickerbocker 1 b].

*** Knife,** ***n.***

1. *a. A well-known instrument for cutting or thrusting consisting of a blade with a sharpened edge fixed securely in a handle.

1607 in Smith *Works* I. p. xliii, [We] presented . . . gyftes of dyvers sortes, as penny knyves, sheeres. **1681** *New Castle Court Rec.* 462 Fower Kniues and fower alls. **a1772** Woolman *Journal* 120 We . . . let them [the horses] feed on the wild grass, which was plentiful, in the mean time cutting with our knives a store against night. **1820** *Amer. Antiq. Soc. Coll.* 64 Then we delivered our presents, consisting of axes, knives [etc.]. **1896** Wilkins *Madelon* 37 She kept on swiftly, holding her knife under her cloak. **1916** Eastman *From Deep Woods* 175, I took with me little that belonged to the white man, except his guns, fishing tackle, knives and tobacco.

***b.** An instrument of this type designed for use at table.

1644 *Conn. Rec.* I. 457 An Inuentory [includes] . . . kniues & a spoone [etc.]. **1719** Sewall *Letter-Book* II. 106 A duzzen of good ivory-hafted knives and forks. **1850** Colton *3 Years Calif.* i. 22 Plain knives and forks cost ten dollars the dozen. **1870** Tomes *Decorum* 215 A silver knife and fork and spoon are served upon the small plate, with the finger-bowl and doily. **1876** *Wide Awake* 11/2 [She made] haste to fetch plates and knives from the corner-cupboard.

2. Attrib. and comb. with *basket, belt, blade, board,* etc.

1873 *Harper's Mag.* Jan. 194 A man . . . [was] busily engaged in finishing the centre piece of a knife-basket. **1861** *Vanity Fair* 18 May 233/1 We have just . . . taken up our knife belt two holes. **1828** Neal *R. Dyer* 222 His critical reproduction of the knife-blade. **1863** A. D. Whitney *F. Gartney* v, Over the knife-board she . . . sharpened at length the keen edge of desperate resolution. **1869** Alcott *Little Women* II. i. 12 A knife-cleaner that spoilt all the knives. **1923** J. H. Cook *On Old Frontier* 13 Almost every dispute [in Texas] had to be settled with a gun- or knife-fight or else assassination. **1807** Irving *Salmagundi* iii. 56–7, I would sooner hold sweet converse with the wheel of a knife-grinder than endure his monotonous chattering. **1898** Westcott *D. Harum* 212 David, shoveling a knife-load of good things into his mouth. **1923** Wyatt *Invisible Gods* 25 Mrs. Marshfield in a pale blue cashmere morning dress with knife pleats and lace cascading down the front. **1870** E. B. Foote *Plain Talk* 421 We have knife-sharpeners, scissors-sharpeners, and pencil-sharpeners. **a1841** Hawes *Sporting Scenes* II. 164, I consider myself entering a butcher's knife-shop. **1851** Cist *Cincinnati* 215 Among the principal articles, are tea-caddies and chests, knife trays, trunks, lard and lard-oil lamps. **1898** *Kansas City Star* 20 Dec. 10/3 Dr. Monahan, assistant police surgeon, sewed up a knife wound in his side.

Knife, *v.* {1865–} *fig.* +*tr.* To strike at or try to defeat (a candidate, ticket, etc.) in an underhand manner. — **1888** *Nation* 5 July 3/1 He speaks favourably of them in a leading article, and 'Knifes' them slyly in paragraphs or extracts. **1892** *Boston Jrnl.* 5 Nov. 12 The idea is to knife Moise for Congress. **1904** *N.Y. World* 9 Nov. 2 Thousands of voters who declare allegiance to Tammany Hall in the open went to the polls yesterday and knifed the ticket. **1912** Nicholson *Hoosier Chron.* 403 If Thatcher had knifed Bassett men or if Thatcher men had been knifed at Bassett's behest, evidence of such perfidy was difficult to adduce from the returns.

Knife box. A box in which table knives are kept. {1848–} — **1779** *York Co., Va., Rec.: Wills* XXII. 28 April, [Alex. Purdie.] 2 walnut knife boxes 40/. **1855** Simms *Forayers* 404, I gone up-stairs with the knife-box, to put 'em on the table. **1865** A. D. Whitney *Gayworthys* v. 50 [In city churches] people . . . [are] stuck in rows, like knives in a knife-box.

Knife case. =prec. — **1790** *Pennsylvania Packet* 6 Jan. 1/4 Steel and gilt hat buckles, and A few inlaid mahogany knife cases. **1853** Simms *Sword & Distaff* 341 A variety of other articles, including knife-case, with knives and forks, decanters, glasses, and sundry small things.

Knife-handle. +Any one of various marine clams having a long thin shell; a razor clam. *colloq.* — **1881** Ingersoll *Oyster-Industry* 245 *Knife-Handle.*—See *Razor-fish.* (Massachusetts bay.) **1883** *Nat. Museum Bul.* No. 27, 232 *Ensatella americana* . . . is the 'razor-clam' or 'razor-fish' of commerce; and is also called the 'razor' and 'knife-handle.' **1884** Goode, etc. *Fisheries* I. 707 Our Razor-shell . . . passes under the various names of 'Razor-fish,' 'Razor-clam,' 'Knife-handle,' etc. **1890** *Cent.* 3302/1 *Knife-handle,* . . . a mollusk, the razor-shell, *Solen ensis.*

+Knife man. (See quotations.) *Obs.* — **1643** R. Williams *Key* (1866) 66 Whence they call English-men Chàuquaquock, that is, *Knivemen.* **1764** Hutchinson *Hist. Mass.* I. 478 The French [writers] speak of others [Indians], viz. that, at certain repasts, they never make use of knives; it is not probable they ever had any to use, on any occasion, until they were brought to them from Europe, they called the first English, Knifemen.

Knife sheath. A sheath or case for a knife. — **1652** *Essex Probate Rec.* I. 149 Duzen kniffe sheaths, . . . fyles, . . . 1 sawe. **1861** *Chicago Tribune* 26 May 1/8 We are now extensively engaged in manufacturing Dragoon Equipments, . . . [including] Cartridge Boxes, Belts, Knife-Sheaths, &c. **1873** Beadle *Undevel. West* 619, I find my Navajo whip and knife sheath . . . missing. **1894** 'Mark Twain' *P. Wilson* xix, [He] reached for his prize and seized it, dropping his knife-sheath.

Knife work. Stabbing, cutting, etc., with a knife in a fight. — **1845** Simms *Wigwam & Cabin* 2 Ser. 143 But none of your knife-work, le' me tell you. **1916** Wilson *Somewhere* 322, I bet his brother-in-law did most of the knifework.

***Knight.** +**1.** A member of any one of various secret orders, *Knights of Labor, Knights of the Golden Circle,* etc. **2.** Often used in slang or jocular phrases denoting one who follows a particular occupation, as *Knight of the yard stick,* (see quotation); *Knight of the grip,* a drummer or traveler; *Knight of the green cloth,* a gambler. — (1) **1876** Ingram *Centennial Exp.* 650 There were not less than 7,500 Knights in line. **1886** Logan *Great Conspiracy* 559 Whether . . . many other prominent Congressmen of that sort,—were merely in close communion with these banded 'Knights,' or were actual members of their secret organizations, may be an open question. **1891** 'Thanet' *Otto the Knight* 21 Now the Knights are down on me. (2) **1859** Matsell *Vocabulum* 49 *Knight of Alsatia,* a person that treats the whole company. *Ib., Knight of the Post,* a fellow that will swear anything for money. **1877** Bartlett 787 *Knight of the Yard-Stick,* a retail dry-goods clerk; a 'counter-jumper.' **a1889** *N.Y. Slang Dict.* (B. and L.), Gamblers are called knights of the green cloth. **1891** O'Beirne *Leaders Ind. Territory* 72/2 He built a fine hotel which is being fitted up in a stylish manner to suit the tastes of the most fastidious knights of the grip.

+Knights of Labor. A secret organization founded in 1869 to safeguard the rights of workingmen, or the members composing this. Now hist. Also attrib. — **1885** *Century Mag.* Sept. 802 The Knights of Labor have a scheme on foot in some of the Western States by which tracts of land are to be purchased by the State. **1887** *Courier-Journal* 4 Jan. 3/1 A secret circular has been issued by District Assemblies Nos. 57 and 136, Knights of Labor, of Chicago, as a boycott against Armour & Co. **1891** 'Thanet' *Otto the Knight* 21, I didn't want no more Knights of Labor in [my boarding house]. **1894** Warner *Golden House* xvii, One of these was joining a Knights of Labor lodge. **1903** Ely *Evolution of Industrial Soc.* 348 The Knights of Labor endeavored to secure a unity like that of the republic indivisible which was the ideal of the leaders of the French Revolution.

+Knights of Pythias. A secret society founded in Washington, D.C., in 1864 for social and benevolent purposes; the members composing this order. — **1864** in Shackleford *Knight's Armor* (1869) 41 It was resolved, that this Order be styled the Knights of Pythias. **1876** Ingram *Centennial Exp.* 660 The Knights of Pythias cannot boast of any antiquity as to their order, it having been established in Washington only ten years ago. **1904** (*title*), Reports of Grand Officers, Thirty-fifth Annual Convention of the Grand Lodge, Knights of Pythias, Domain of Illinois.

+Knights of the Golden Circle. A secret organization founded in Cincinnati in 1854 which during the Civil War became an avowed advocate of the Southern cause; the members of this organization. Now hist. (Cf. Golden Circle.) — **1861** in Logan *Great Conspiracy* 250 A Conspiracy for the overthrow of the Government through the military organizations, the dangerous secret order, the 'Knights of the Golden Circle,' 'Committees of Safety,' Southern leagues, [etc.]. **1865** Pike *Scout & Ranger* (1932) 124 He was a member of the Knights of the Golden Circle. **1886** Logan *Great Conspiracy* 559 The 'Knights of the Golden Circle' (otherwise known as the 'Order of the Sons of Liberty,' and 'O. A. K.' or 'Order of American Knights'). **1891** *Century Mag.* Jan. 413/1 It was predicted that hundreds, perhaps thousands, of 'Knights of the Golden Circle' and 'Sons of Liberty' would flock to his [General Morgan's] standard.

+Knights of the White Camelia. A name applied to one of various local secret organizations that sprang up in the South soon after the Civil War; the members of this organization. *Obs.* — **1870** *Congress. Globe* 19 April 2794/3 The society called the Knights of the White Camelia . . . [wanted] to maintain the integrity and superiority of the white race. *Ib.,* Its individual members . . . coöperated with the Democratic party . . . as Democrats, and not as 'K. W. C.'s,' or Knights of the White Camelia. **1877** Dibble *Why Reconstr. Failed* 21 Thousands of men . . . sought relief . . . through the agency of . . . the Knights of the White Camelia, Regulators, . . . and such kindred secret organizations.

Knights Templar. {1610–} An order of Freemasons or the members of this order. Also sing. — **1769** in Gould *Hist. Freemasonry* IV. (1889) 553 Davis . . . was accordingly made [a Royal Arch Mason] by receiving the four steps, that of Excellent, Superexcellent, Royal Arch and Knight Templar. **1876** Ingram *Centennial Exp.* 650 On May 30th and 31st the Knights Templar held their Twenty-third Annual Conclave in Philadelphia. **1898** *Kansas City Star* 19 Dec. 1/3 Del Harbaugh, the detective who was hired by the Knights Templar.

***Knitter.** A machine for knitting. — **1890** Tourgee in *Advance* 12 June 456/2 The man had come from the West just before the war, bringing with him some sort of an invention. . . . It was . . . a knitter.

*** Knitting.** *attrib.* and *comb.* Of or pertaining to knitting by hand.

1818 Fearon *Sketches* 223 [The women who have sent gifts] are invited to the preacher's house, to partake of a supper. . . . This is termed a knitting frolic. **1843** *Lowell Offering* III. 27, I hunted up my knitting work, which Aunt Letty had kindly begun for me. **1850** *Rep. Comm. Patents 1849* 491 The needle itself, and thimble will be exhibited in museums with distaffs, spinning-wheels, knitting-wires [etc.]. **1852** Eastman *Aunt Phillis's Cabin* 104 Her youngest child, Lydia, . . . followed the old lady everywhere, carrying her key and knitting-basket. **1882** J. Hawthorne in *Macmillan's Mag.* XLVI. 310 He could discourse upon the subject most vital to his happiness as composedly as if it were a question of matching knitting-yarns.

b. With reference to knitting by machinery.

1843 *Niles' Nat. Reg.* 24 June 262/3 A *rotary knitting loom,* invented . . . by Mr. Erasmus French, of Springfield, Conn., . . . knits stockings and hosiery of all kinds of perfect shape without seam or blemish. **1880** *Harper's Mag.* Sept. 629/2 Go into the knitting-room to see the busy machines and the growing piles of mittens. **1907** in Persons, etc. *Mass. Labor Laws* (1911) 283 Describe what you would consider an ideal knitting mill in which 150 persons are employed.

+**Knitting bee.** A social gathering of girls and women who knit for some helpful or charitable purpose. *Obs.* — **1855** *Chicago Times* 19 March 2/6 This girl had been at a knitting bee, at the house of a friend. **1880** *Harper's Mag.* Sept. 508/1 In winter they sometimes had knitting bees.

Knitting machine. A machine for knitting. {1858–} — **1838** *25th Congress 2 Sess.* Senate Doc. No. 105, 9 Knitting machine, John McMullen and Joseph Hollen, jr. **1859** *Rep. Comm. Patents 1858* I. 605 It is not new to use a belt-shipping apparatus in a knitting-machine. **1867** *Atlantic Mo.* May 527/1 Two men in Boston—one a mechanic, and the other a capitalist—were striving to produce a knitting-machine. **1875** KNIGHT 1236/2 The Bickford knitting-machine . . . is a specimen of the circular system.

* **Knitting needle.** A small, straight, slender rod, usually of steel, used in knitting. — **1678** *New Castle Court Rec.* 362, 4 parcells of knitting needles. **1711** *Springfield Rec.* II. 41 Knetting needles, one Pound & a Half. **1837** HAWTHORNE *Twice-told Tales* (1879) I. 234 Nothing broke the stillness but the regular click of the matron's knitting-needles. **1920** *Sears, Roebuck & Co. Cat.* No. 140, 536 A. C. E. Steel Knitting Needles. . . . American Red Cross Size.

Knitting pin. (See quot. 1890.) {1870–} — **1776** *N.J. Archives* 2 Ser. I. 196 An assortment of dry goods, . . . among which are . . . thimbles, knitting pins, penknives [etc.]. **1805** CLARK in *Lewis & C. Exped.* III. (1905) 130 We purchased forty dogs for which we gave articles of little value, such as bells, thimbles, knitting pins, brass wire and a few beeds. **1890** *Cent.* 3304/1 *Knitting-pin,* . . . a small bar or rod used for knitting, having a button at one end. It is made of ivory, bone, guttapercha, wood, etc., and is used in pairs for knitting large work, such as shawls. **1920** *Sears, Roebuck & Co. Cat.* No. 140, 536 Celluloid Knitting Pins. . . . For heavy knitting.

* **Knob.** A prominent rounded hill or knoll. {1650–}
Cf. CEDAR KNOB.

1796 IMLAY *Western Territory* (ed. 3) 522 The rich lands near Cumberland river are considerably broken by knobs or short hills. **1814** BRACKENRIDGE *Views La.* 106 Flint knobs present themselves, strewed with rude masses of horn stone and affording a scanty nourishment to a few straggling black jacks. **1862** in F. Moore *Rebellion Rec.* V. II. 514 We came upon an open knob, where we found Gen. McCook and all his staff watching some beautiful artillery practice. **1898** *McClure's Mag.* X. 431 The first thing Grant tried to do was . . . to get hold of two knobs, or low hills, where the Confederates had their advance guard. **1924** RAINE *Land of Saddle-Bags* 10 Where hills are somewhat rounded, a 'house-seat' is often chosen upon one of the knobs.

b. *pl.* As the name of a particular region.

1823 JAMES *Exped.* I. 27 On the Kentucky side they [the Silver Creek hills] constitute the commencement of a rugged and barren district, called the *Knobs.* **1835** HOFFMAN *Winter in West* II. 145 We were now entering what is called the knobs of Kentucky. **1849** CHAMBERLAIN *Ind. Gazetteer* 12 About five miles below the Falls of the Ohio, commences a range of hills called the Knobs.

+**Knobcone pine.** A pine (*Pinus attenuata*) found on the Pacific coast. — **1884** SARGENT *Rep. Forests* 196 *Pinus tuberculata.* . . . Knobcone Pine. **1897** SUDWORTH *Arborescent Flora* 25 *Pinus attenuata.* . . . Knobcone Pine.

* **Knock,** *v.*

+**1.** *tr.* To break down (cotton stalks) by striking with a stout stick preparatory to planting a new crop. *colloq.*

1847 *Florida Plant. Rec.* 216, 15 hand knocking cotton stalks.

+**2.** Ellipt. for 'knock down,' 'knock out,' etc., in the sense: to surpass, beat, overcome, cure. *colloq.*

1853 *Knickerb.* XLII. 55 He 'knocked' all the adjacent male population, native and imported, in the matter of looks. **1877** BURDETTE *Rise of Mustache* 19 Your boy . . . has a formula . . . [which] will cause warts to disappear from the hand, or, to use his own expression, will 'knock warts.' **1887** J. KIRKLAND *Zury* 112 Them [*i.e.*, the physicians] 's kin tell what'll knock all complaints, they station in the big cities.

3. In colloquial and slang phrases.

For other phrases see BOTTOM, COCKED HAT, HINDSIGHT, etc.

a. *To knock along,* to wander about or proceed in a leisurely fashion. {*dial.*}

a1846 *Quarter Race Ky.* 148, I knocks along up and down and about, until at last I finds out where Colonel Lamar lived. **1890** *Stock Grower & Farmer* 29 March 7/2 If you ever met Dandy going anywhere, . . . you would see 'Old Smoky' a knocking along directly as if he owned the world.

+**b.** *To knock (a)round,* to wander around or about somewhat aimlessly. {knock about, 1851–; 1884}

1877 HARTE *Story of Mine* (1896) 163 I'm not 'company' today and didn't put on my best harness to knock round in. **1892** HARRIS *On the Plantation* 81, I'm a-gwine dis night fer ter knock aroun' wid you! **1900** *Congress. Rec.* 11 Jan. 784/1, I quit school at 17, about the time the Senator did, and I have been knocking around for a living ever since.

* **c.** *To knock down.* +(1) To bring down (game) with a shot. +(2) Of a conductor, ticket-taker, etc.: To steal or appropriate (fares, money, etc.). +(3) *To knock down and drag out,* to vanquish completely. (Cf. KNOCKDOWN *n.* 1.) Also fig.

(1) **1733** BYRD *Journey to Eden* (1901) 311 We pursued our Journey thro' uneven and perplexed Woods, and in the thickest of them had the Fortune to knock down a young Buffalo, 2 Years old. **1809** WEEMS *Marion* (1833) 100 Many a family goes without dinner, unless the father can knock down a squirrel in the woods.

(2) **1860** HOLLAND *Miss Gilbert* xii. 220 Now tell a feller: is there any chance to knock down? **1889** 'MARK TWAIN' *Conn. Yankee* xl. 513 They would 'knock down' fares—I mean rob the company. **1904** *N.Y. Ev. Post* 5 April 9 Two conductors on surface cars were convicted of petit larceny to-day. The men were accused of 'knocking down' fares on their cars.

(3) **1842** *Knickerb.* XX. 491 If the wife ran in debt, or . . . knocked down and dragged out a fellow-citizen, the man and wife were one. **1882** C. B. LEWIS *Lime-Kiln Club* 291 To say that the prominent members were pleased, gratified, knocked down and dragged out, would not cover the case.

d. *To knock off* {1611–}, +to auction off, to 'knock down.'

1747 *Boston Selectmen* 15 April, He being the highest bidder, the same was knocked off to him. **1843** STEPHENS *High Life N.Y.* II. 35, I'll jest go down to the bar-room and see when the critter is going to be sold, and what madam it is that's going to knock her off. **1883** HOWELLS *Woman's Reason* v. 98 The auctioneer intoned his chant . . . varied with a quick 'Sold!' as . . . he knocked off this lot or that.

* **e.** *To knock out.* +(1) Of a hound: To lose the trail or scent in a chase. +(2) *fig.* To eliminate, get rid of (something).

(1) **1835** LONGSTREET *Ga. Scenes* 195 At about two o'clock, P.M., right in the big road, near Richland Creek, the dogs 'knocked out,' and could never be *knocked in* again. (2) **1900** *Congress. Rec.* 23 Jan. 1066/1 Will the court knock that out . . . leaving the remainder of the amendment stand? **1904** *N.Y. Sun* 5 Aug. 4 In power, the Democrats wouldn't knock out protection if they could.

* **f.** *To knock up,* to prepare or get (food) ready quickly.

1869 ALCOTT *Little Women* II. v. 61 Don't cry, dear, but just exert yourself a bit, and knock us up something to eat. **1890** *Harper's Mag.* May 894/2, I jest killed a chicken, and knocked up a few biscuit.

Knockabout. {1887–} +**1.** A small pleasure boat or yacht. +**2.** A rough-and-tumble fight. *colloq.* — (1) **1897** *Outing* XXX. 497/1 The cat-boat, knock-about, and special classes of small yachts are well filled. **1904** *N.Y. Ev. Post* 21 May 6 There are numerous knockabouts and other small yachts in the Pawcatuck River. (2) **1903** LEWIS *Boss* 316 He was all for th' strong-arm, an' th' knock-about! It's a bad system. Nothin's lost by bein' smooth, Gov'nor.

Knockdown, *n.* {1698–}

‖**1.** A 'knocker-down'; a pugilist or boxer.

1843 *Knickerb.* XXI. 484 'Tom and Jerry' ushered before a Park audience the scientific Mr. T. Belcher Kay, one of the great knockdowns of foreign celebrity.

‖**2.** The careening of a ship under the impact of heavy seas.

1888 *Scribner's Mag.* May 526/1 Every bit of that water came in through the hatch at the time of the knock-down.

3. *Knockdown and drag-out,* a free for all, rough and tumble fight. *colloq.* Also attrib. and transf.

1827 COOPER *Prairie* iv, It was thinking of what you call consequences . . . that prevented me from . . . making it a real knock-down and drag-out. **1834** CARRUTHERS *Kentuckian* I. 61 It's what I would call a regular row; I never saw a prettier knock down and drag out in all the days of my life. **1851** *Polly Peablossom* 146 Mike . . . in a regular knock-down-and-drag-out row, was hard to beat. **1884** 'CRADDOCK' *Tenn. Mts.* 255 [He] makes a right smart show in a reg'lar knock-down and drag-out fight. **1906** *Springfield W. Repub.* 22 Nov. 3 It is well to give Potter a knockdown and dragout, but it is a pity that this involves the defeat of Mr. Gilmore.

Knockdown, *a.* {1690–}

+**1.** Constructed so as to be easily taken apart for packing or shipment.

1795 WINTERBOTHAM *Hist. View* III. 305 Articles of exportation [were] . . . 231,776 Barrels of dried and pickled fish . . . 48,860 Shook or knock-down casks. **1875** KNIGHT 1239/2 The shook may be said to be a knock-down barrel. **1877** ROE *Army Lett.* 162 In the front half will be packed . . . the knock-down bed, mess-chest [etc.]. **1888** *Scientific Amer.* LIX. 187 To make a knockdown wigwam, the framing should be lashed together with ropes or twine, and the bark tied to the rafters with twine.

+**2.** Of or pertaining to fees paid for 'knocking down' or selling property at auction. *colloq.*

1888 *Harper's Mag.* Nov. 934/2 Bills for knock-down fees are presented for payment to auctioneers every month. *Ib.* 937/2 The knock-down book records the price, buyer, and all particulars of every sale in the Auction-room.

***Knocker.** A metal fixture placed on a door for use in attracting the attention of those inside.

1759 *Newport Mercury* 26 June 4/3 To be sold by Jacob Richardson, ... Latches, Brass Knockers, Steel and Iron-plate-saws. 1809 IRVING *Knickerb.* III. iii, [The front door] was ornamented with a gorgeous brass knocker, curiously wrought, sometimes in the device of a dog, and sometimes of a lion's head. 1863 A. D. WHITNEY *F. Gartney* xvi, Nobody rang the bell or lifted the old-fashioned knocker, here at Cross Corners. 1896 WILKINS *Madelon* 7 He raised the knocker, and knew when it fell that a girl's heart within responded to it with a wild beat.

Knock out. {1854-} In polo, the privilege of knocking a ball out of a given position. — 1894 in M. H. Hayes *Mod. Polo* (1896) 314 When the ball goes out ends, the side defending that goal is entitled to a knock out from the point at which it crossed the line. When the player having the knock out causes unnecessary delay, the Referee may throw a ball on the field and call play. 1897 *Outing* XXX. 486/2 The ball ... is the property of the side defending that goal, the captain of which team is entitled to a knockout from the point at which the ball crossed the line.

+Knock-out drops. Drops of some drug producing unconsciousness or stupor in one who takes them or to whom they are administered. *colloq.* — 1896 ADE *Artie* xviii. 173 They get out the bottle o' knock-out drops and get ready to do business. 1901 — *40 Modern Fables* 301 While he was under the influence of Knock-Out-Drops or something else equally Potent, she spirited him away in a Hack. 1903 — *In Babel* 111 Doc must have slipped me a few knock-out drops. 1909 WASON *Happy Hawkins* 47 He said that if he hadn't 'a' had that chance he would 'a' put knock-out drops in the coffee that night.

***Knoll.** Also †**knole, knowl(e).** A small hill, a hillock.

1656 *Boston Rec.* 130 Itt is ordered that the gallowes shall bee removed to the next knole of land. 1691 *Plymouth Rec.* 203 Where as a knowle of land was ... granted to William Harlow. 1787 WASHINGTON *Diaries* III. 259 Yield as follow: From 56 sqr. yds. laid on a poor Washed Knowl, gulld., 3 Pecks. 1850 JUDD *R. Edney* xx. 259 Richard stood with Melicent on a knoll overlooking the very pretty sheet of water. 1922 A. BROWN *Old Crow* 469 The knoll was across the road overlooking the house.

b. (See quot. 1772.) *Obs.*

1772 DE BRAHM *Hist. Georgia* (1849) 45 The second Species of Pine ... is only met with on the Knowls (small Islands in Swamps). 1802 DRAYTON *S. Carolina* 8 In these swamps, knolls or small rising grounds sometimes present themselves; on which grow the laurel.

***Knot.** +A billet of firewood or lightwood, esp. a piece of pine composed largely or wholly of a knotty excrescence found where limbs once grew from the pine trunk.

[1674 JOSSELYN *Two Voyages* 66 The knots of this Tree [Fir] and fat-pine are used by the *English* instead of Candles.] 1705 BEVERLEY *Virginia* III. 12 [The Indians] generally burn Pine, or Lightwood, (that is, the fat Knots of dead Pine). 1724 H. JONES *Virginia* 57 In some of the poorer Parts of the Country abounding in Pine, do they gather up the *Light-wood,* or Knots of the old Trees, which will not decay. 1851 SPRINGER *Forest Life* 131 The lovers of this recreation are careful to select a store of pitchy knots, whose brilliant combustion relieves them from all the inconvenience of darkness. 1884 'CRADDOCK' *Tenn. Mts.* 106 Tom, ... put on some more of them knots.

***Knotgrass.** A common weed (*Polygonum aviculare*) having small greenish flowers. — 1784 CUTLER in *Mem. Academy* I. 440 *Polygonum.* ... Knotgrass. Blossoms reddish white. Common by the roadsides. June–September. 1814 BIGELOW *Florula Bostoniensis* 93 Knot grass.... A hardy weed growing every where. 1843 TORREY *Flora N.Y.* II. 152. 1874 *Vermont Bd. Agric. Rep.* II. 779 *Gastrophysa caeruleipennis.* Feeds upon the leaves of knotgrass.

+Knotroot grass. An American grass (*Muhlenbergia mexicana*), valued as hay and as a soil preserver. — 1895 *Dept. Agric. Yrbk. 1894* 434 *Knot-root grass* is very common along river banks, usually where the soil is somewhat sandy.

Knotting. A disease to which pears are subject. — 1867 *Ill. Agric. Soc. Trans.* VII. 505 *Knotting,* or hardening of the fruit, is a disease not very prevalent [in the pear].

***Know,** *v.* In various colloq. and dial. expressions.

(*Not*) *to know beans,* see BEAN 2.

+1. *As I know on,* as I know of, so far as I know.

1835 *Jrnl. Excursion U.S. 1834* 159 A few of the Yankeeisms [are] ... a tarnal lie—not as I know on [etc.]. 1877 JEWETT *Deephaven* x. 199 You need n't be so forth-putting, as I knows on! 1887 WILKINS *Humble Romance* 72, I don' know what you mean as I knows on.

+2. (*I*) *want to know,* well, well! do tell! is it possible?

1840 *Knickerb.* XVI. 20, 'I want to know!' said the lady; 'precious soul!' 1869 STOWE *Oldtown Folks* 196 'Want to know?' said Sam. 'Wal, that 'ere does beat all.' 1921 PAINE *Comr. Rolling Ocean* 169 And you come from North Dakoty! I want to know.

Know-nothing.

1. One who is extremely ignorant. {1839-}

1828 COOPER *Red Rover* ii, The fellow is a know-nothing! *c*1845 *Big Bear Ark.* 16 They were real know-nothings, green as a pumpkin-vine—couldn't, in farming, I'll bet, raise a crop of turnips. 1883 *Harper's Mag.* July 260/2 Not to know Cincinnati's soap and candles is to argue one's self a know-nothing. 1887 *Courier-Journal* 21 June 4/2 The chief spokesman of these modern know-nothings is the editor of the New York Independent, a nondescript religio-political journal.

+2. A member of the Know-Nothing party (q.v.); sometimes in pl., the party itself. Now hist.

1854 *Harper's Mag.* Aug. 400/1 A secret combination designated as 'Know-Nothings,' ... have operated with much success in local elections in many of the larger places. 1859 WILMER *Press Gang* 141, I have nothing to do with the 'Know-Nothings,' and never was a member of their mysterious association. 1872 *Newton Kansan* 3 Oct. 4/3 Mr. Wilson was a Know-Nothing. 1884 BLAINE *20 Years of Congress* I. 117 The American party ... had a fitful and feverish success and in 1854–5 under the name of *Know-Nothings,* enrolled tens of thousands in secret lodges.

3. Attrib. in sense 2 with *excitement, hat,* etc.

1854 *S. Lit. Messenger* XX. 540/1 This Know Nothing movement will prove to be ... a giant evil. 1855 in Hambleton *H. A. Wise* 232 Catholic Louisiana fought full as bravely ... as Know Nothing Massachusetts against Catholic Mexico in the war of 1846–'47. *Ib.* 334 The Know Nothing Legislature of Abolition Massachusetts ... has disbanded that Irish regiment. 1857 T. H. GLADSTONE *Englishman in Kansas* 119 Judge O'Trigger ... wore a 'Know-Nothing' hat, and had a black coat on his back. 1888 *N.Y. World* May (F.), During the days of Know Nothing excitement [he] was an active sympathizer with that party.

Know-Nothingism. {1866-} +The principles of the Know-Nothing party. Now hist.

1854 SIMMS *Southward Ho* 252 Know-Nothingism had not then become a fixed fact in the political atmosphere. 1856 *Democratic Conv. Proc.* 27 The reading of the resolutions on Know-Nothingism and the Kansas-Nebraska question was followed by long continued and enthusiastic applause. 1859 WILMER *Press Gang* 141 It is the common trick of the Anti-American newspaper press ... to check all inquiry ... by raising the hue and cry of 'Know-Nothingism.' 1864 NICHOLS *Amer. Life* II. 90 The conspiracy of nativism or know-nothingism, with its machinery of oath-bound secret societies, failed. 1886 Z. F. SMITH *Kentucky* 596 Nor had the latter party recovered the full confidence of the public, after the demoralizing experience with Know Nothingism. 1903 *N.Y. Ev. Post* 28 Oct. 4 Irishmen who were fixed for life in the Democratic party by the bitter Knownothingism of years ago.

+Know-Nothing party. =AMERICAN PARTY. Now hist. — 1854 *S. Lit. Messenger* XX. 542/2 The great Know Nothing party desire a presidential candidate. 1855 M. THOMPSON *Doesticks* ii. 19, I had as much difficulty ... as the Know-Nothing party ... had, in determining the nativity of their candidate for Governor. 1874 SCHARF *Chron. Baltimore* 576 The Constitutional Union Convention [was] composed almost wholly of the old Whig party and the warring organization known as the 'American' or 'Know-Nothing' party. 1886 POORE *Reminisc.* I. 406 The main effect of Kossuth's visit to the United States was an extraordinary impetus given to 'The Order of United Americans,' from which was evolved that political phenomenon, the American, or Know-Nothing, party. 1911 OVINGTON *Half a Man* 196 Since the death of the Know-nothing Party, New York has ceased any organized attempt to lessen the power of the foreigner.

+Know-Something. A member of a projected political order or party in opposition to the Know-Nothings. *Obs.* — 1855 *Mich. Agric. Soc. Trans.* VII. 495 There are among us so many who are either Whigs or Democrats, or Republicans, or Know-Somethings, or Know-Nothings, that [etc.]. 1856 (*title of broadside*), Platform of principles of New York know somethings.

Knuck. [Eng. dial.]

1. *pl.* +(See quot. 1902.)

1840 *S. Lit. Messenger* VI. 385/1 [In] the game of marbles he ... is counted a proficient particularly in knucks and five in the ring. 1876 'MARK TWAIN' *Tom Sawyer* xvi. 135 They got their marbles and played 'knucks' and 'ring-taw.' 1886 *Harper's Mag.* Dec. 41/2 They were playing 'knucks' together. 1902 CLAPIN 252 *Knucks,* a game of marbles in which the winner shoots at his adversary's knuckles.

+2. A thief. *slang.*

1848 JUDSON *Mysteries N.Y.* I. 33 There is a house in Cherry street ... [that] has been known to the 'crossmen' and 'knucks' of the town as 'Jack Circle's Watering place' and 'fence.' 1859 MATSELL *Vocabulum* 49 *Knuck,* a pickpocket. 1893 *Congress. Rec.* 6 Oct. 2242/2 [The Republicans] employed knucks, bounty-jumpers ... and all other criminal vermin and riff-raff. 1903 LEWIS *Boss* 168 But knucks, dips, sneaks, ... an' strong-arm men have got to quit.

+3. *pl.* =BRASS KNUCKLES, KNUCKLE-DUSTER.

1913 *Sat. Ev. Post* 17 May 50 The fat fist armed with a set of murderously heavy knucks. 1918 SANDBURG *Cornhuskers* 88, I slipped my fingers into a set of knucks.

Knuckle, *v.* {1740-} +*To knuckle down,* and variants of this: To apply oneself earnestly and seriously. — 1864 WEBSTER 743/3 *To knuckle to,* ... to apply one's self vigorously. 1892 HARRIS *On the Plantation* 38 He spoke to the dog again.... 'Come, knuckle down! Try 'em, old fellow!' 1907 ANDREWS *Recoll.* 130, I would ... have knuckled down to law practise and ignored everything else.

***Knuckled,** *a.* +Of a horse: Having cocked ankles. — 1846 *Spirit of Times* 11 July 229/1 If you will take one [a horse] that is knuckled, or a little shaky on his pins . . . , we can buy you one for half the money. **1868** WOODRUFF *Trotting Horse* 131 Some of the poor decrepit animals we sometimes see staggering about, . . . twisted up and knuckled behind.

+**Knuckle-dabster.** (See quotation.) — **1890** HOWELLS *Boy's Town* 82 You could use a knuckle-dabster of fur or cloth to rest your hand on [in playing marbles], but it was considered effeminate.

+**Knuckle-duster.** (See quot. 1858 and cf. BRASS KNUCKLES, KNUCK 3, KNUCKLES.) — **1858** *Times* (London) 15 Feb. (F. and H.), Knuckle-duster, . . . a formidable American instrument, made of brass, which slips easily on to the four fingers of the hand, and having a projecting surface, across the knuckles, is calculated, in a pugilistic encounter to inflict serious injury on the person against whom it is directed. **1861** *All Year Round* 13 July 372 What the crew most feared, was the free use of the 'brass knuckles' or 'knuckle dusters.' **1903** LEWIS *Boss* 14 Take him to the station! . . . he struck me with a knuckle duster.

+**Kodak,** *n.* [A proprietary name: see quot. 1899.]

1. A small photographic camera made by the Eastman company. Also applied to cameras of other makes.

1888 *Patent Off. Gazette* XLIV. 1072/1 Photographic Cameras and Sensitized Plates and Film Therefor.—The Eastman Dry Plate and Film Company. . . . 'The word "Kodak." ' **1889** M. M. BALLOU *New Eldorado* 348 At that moment a lady passenger in our car aimed her 'kodak' at them, and, presto! they were photographed in the twinkling of an eye. **1896** *Typographical Jrnl.* IX. 361 C. F. Whitmarsh . . . gathered in a number of interesting pictures with his little kodak. **1899** *Scribner's Mag.* XXV. Advt. 65 'There *is* no Kodak but the Eastman Kodak.' 'Kodak' is a Trade Name applied by us to cameras and other goods of our manufacture. We originated and registered the word 'Kodak.' The trade-mark is our exclusive property. **1908** 'YESLAH' *Tenderfoot S. Calif.* 39 You dump your overcoat, and your kodak . . . into the nearest rig.

2. Attrib. with *camera, girl, shot.*

1890 *Amer. Notes & Q.* 12 April (*advt.*), New Kodak Cameras. 'You press the button, we do the rest.' **1912** NICHOLSON *Hoosier Chron.* 323 This item was among the 'Kodak Shots' subjoined to the 'Advertiser's' account of the convention. *Ib.* 450, I reckon you can hardly call Marian a kodak girl.

+**Kodak,** *v. intr.* and *tr.* To photograph with a kodak. — **1891** *Internat. Ann.: Anthony's Photogr. Bul.* IV. 59 A next door neighbor, who is just beginning to 'kodak.' **1894** HAY in W. R. Thayer *Life J. Hay* II. 113 M. swore that he would have me kodaked in my clothes, so that I would never dare to run for President. **1904** 'O. HENRY' *Cabbages & Kings* 8 The tintype man, the enlarged photograph brigand, the kodaking tourist . . . carry on the work.

+**Konkus.** Also **konchus.** (See quot. 1851 and cf. CONK.[2]) Also attrib. — **1851** SPRINGER *Forest Life* 99 There is a cancerous disease peculiar to the Pine-tree, to which lumbermen give the original name of 'Conk' or 'Konkus.' **1858** THOREAU *Me. Woods* 111 Here and there . . . was a full-grown, tall, and slender, but defective one [white pine], what lumbermen call a *konchus* tree. **1860** *Harper's Mag.* March 444/2 Many [trees] . . . which to the uninitiated appear to be perfect . . . exhibit to the lumberman the mark of the insidious 'konkus,' which is infallible.

+**Kooyah.** ['From one of the Shahaptian or Shoshonean dialects' (Hodge).] The root of *Valerian edulis*, used as food by Indians of the Northwest. Also attrib. — **1843** T. TALBOT *Journals* 45 We traded some Kooyah or Black root, . . . a black, sticky, suspicious looking compound, of very disagreeable odor. **1843** FRÉMONT *Exped.* 135, I ate here, for the first time, the *kooyah*, or tobacco root, (*valeriana edulis,*) the principal edible root among the Indians who inhabit the upper waters of the streams on the western side of the mountains. **1845** *Ib.* 273 The kooyah plant . . . is the best remedial plant known among those Indians.

+**Korl.** (See first quot.) Also comb. — **1861** *Atlantic Mo.* April 435/1 In the neighboring furnace-buildings lay great heaps of the refuse from the ore after the pig-metal is run. *Korl* we call it here [in the iron mills]: a light, porous substance, of a delicate, waxen, flesh-colored tinge. *Ib.* 450/2 A wan, woful face, through which the spirit of the dead korl-cutter looks out.

+**Kossuth hat.** [Louis *Kossuth*, Hungarian patriot (1802–94), who visited the United States in 1851.] A hat having an oval, flat-topped crown and a roll brim. — **1853** BUNN *Old Eng. & New Eng.* 282 He goes out to parties in a Kossuth hat. **1866** 'F. KIRKLAND' *Bk. Anecdotes* 342 Having on a light colored and broad brimmed Kossuth hat, and a rubber overcoat, was unquestionably his bodily salvation. **1905** VALENTINE *H. Sandwith* 8 David Sandwith, entering the shed, shaking the sparks from his Kossuth hat.

+**Kouse.** =COWISH. Also attrib. with *root.* — **1896** *Garden & Forest* IX. 282 *Kouse, or Kouse-root.*—From *kowish*, the Nez-Perce (Shahaptian) name of the root, which is used by these and other Indians for bread making. **1900** *Dept. Agric. Yrbk. 1899* 308 In Oregon and Washington an immense amount of food was gathered from the camass root, and also from the kouse root. **1907** HODGE *Handbook* I. 728 *Kouse.* A plant (*Peucedanum ambiguum*) used by the Indians of the Columbia-Oregon region for making bread.

+**Krieker.** [See quot. 1888.] The pectoral sandpiper, *Pisobia maculata.* — **1888** G. TRUMBULL *Names of Birds* 176 At Newport, R.I., on Long Island . . . , and at Barnegat, N.J., [the pectoral sandpiper is called] Krieker. . . . It was not applied . . . because of the bird's creaking note, but because of its crouching or squatting habit—German *Kriecher*, a cringing person. **1917** *Birds of Amer.* I. 233.

+**Kriss Kringle.** Also **Christ-kinkle.** [Cf. Ger. *Christkindl*, 'Christ child.'] Santa Claus, St. Nicholas. Also attrib. — **1830** WATSON *Philadelphia* 242 Every father in his turn remembers the excitements of his youth in Belsh-nichel and Christ-kinkle nights. **1874** B. F. TAYLOR *World on Wheels* 188 A cur of a fact, that should have been born with its nose in a muzzle, [should not be set] upon Santa Claus or Kriss Kringle.

+**Krout.** Sauerkraut, a food prepared from cabbage. — **1828** H. FINN, etc. *Whimwhams* 65 She had not wanted many *sparks*, But was as sour as krout; And look'd so black on them, that all Who came, full soon went out. **1842** *S. Lit. Messenger* VIII. 202/2 The captain's stentor voice sung out Fire away boys, and save the krout. **1861** *Army Regulations* 245 Fresh vegetables (potatoes, onions, &c.), pickles, krout, and dried fruits, can only be purchased and paid for out of the hospital fund and issued to the sick.

+**Kruller.** (See CRULLER.)

+**Ku-Klucker.** A member of the Ku-Klux Klan. (Cf. KLUCKER.) — **1880** TOURGEE *Bricks* 274 Jes let 'em come. . . . Ku Kluckers or sheriffs, it don't make no difference which.

+**Ku-Klux,** *n.*

1. =KU-KLUX KLAN; also, a member of this. *Obs.*

1868 in Fleming *Hist. Reconstruction* II. 365 The negroes have entirely deserted one prairie in Attakapas since the election, having been run out by the Ku-Kluxes. **1874** *Chicago Times* 24 Feb. 7/4 Communism in Kentucky. Ku-Klux Attempts to Drive Labor Out of Franklin County. **1877** BEARD *K.K.K. Sketches* 40 The Ku-Klux themselves were about as intangible examples of ghostliness as were ever wrapped in loose-fitting bombazine. **1888** *Boston Jrnl.* 4 Aug. 2/1 The Ku-Klux in Florida. **1898** PAGE *Red Rock* 519 It was a body of Ku Klux making their way back home. **1908** 'O. HENRY' *Options* 192 The old party lines drawn by Sherman's march and the Kuklux and nine-cent cotton and the Jim Crow street-car ordinances faded away. **1920** *N.Y. Times* 11 Oct. 1/2 Ginnery Owners, Farmers and Merchants Are Warned to Hold Cotton. Negroes Think It Ku Klux.

2. Attrib. with *bill, outrage, prosecution, robe.*

1870 *Proclamations by Gov. of N.C.* 19 Proclamations [were] issued from the Executive office . . . in reference to various Ku Klux outrages and disorders in the counties of Jones, Lenoir, Alamance, etc. **1871** *Harper's Mag.* Aug. 471/1 The [Democratic] resolutions recognize the new Constitutional amendments, denounce the Ku-Klux bill, and favor universal amnesty. **1872** *Atlantic Mo.* March 387 The Ku-Klux prosecutions vanished into thin air. **1884** *Century Mag.* July 407/1 He held it there till every drop of the water was poured into a gum or oiled sack concealed beneath the Ku Klux robe.

+**Ku-Klux,** *v. tr.* To treat (one) in the way employed by the Ku-Klux Klan; to beat, kill, etc. *Obs.* — **1871** *Ku Klux Klan Rep.* VI. 107 [The Negro] supposed . . . that he was going to ku-klux the Ku-Klux. *Ib.* 364, I considered that I had done nothing to be Ku-Kluxed for. **1874** R. H. COLLINS *Kentucky* I. 217/2, 7 Radical negroes, at 2 A.M., called out of his house one who voted the Democratic ticket, and kukluxed him by shooting him with bird-shot. **1879** *Phila. Inquirer* 28 Nov. 1/5 Ten men . . . were to-day taken . . . on a charge of kukluxing a man named McAlpine.

+**Ku-Kluxism.** The principles and practices of the Ku-Klux Klan. *Obs.* — **1868** *N.Y. Herald* 30 July 5/2 A Bill to Punish Ku-Kluxism—Selection of Electors. **1880** TOURGEE *Invisible Empire* vii. 437 Two lists of names . . . which perhaps gives a more vivid idea of the horrors of Ku-Kluxism. **1884** *American* VIII. 72 [He] was not only a Confederate but was sent to the Albany Penitentiary for Ku-Kluxism. **1893** *Amer. Missionary* June 189 Despite the bitterness of the days of reconstruction and Ku Kluxism, he enjoyed the esteem of the whites and the confidence of the colored people.

+**Ku-Klux Klan.** *Hist.* A secret organization that arose in the South immediately after the Civil War, designed chiefly to preserve native white supremacy in the South.

1868 *N.Y. Herald* 1 July 6/4 If the Democratic Convention can only be induced . . . at the dictation of the Knights of the Golden Circle and the Ku Klux Klan, to place upon their ticket some copperhead opponent of the war, the radicals will have a clear track next November. **1868** in *Century Mag.* XXVIII. 408/2 The blacks in the counties of Marshall, Maury, Giles, and Lawrence are organized into military companies, with the avowed determination to make war upon and exterminate the Ku Klux Klan. **1877** DIBBLE *Why Reconstr. Failed* 21 Thousands of men . . . sought relief . . . through the agency of the Kuklux Klan, . . . Bulldozers, and such kindred secret organizations. **1886** POORE *Reminisc.* II. 273 It soon became evident, too, that the whites were determined, by a well-disciplined legion, known as the Ku-Klux Klan, . . . to intimidate the colored voters. **1890** *Century Mag.* Dec. 306, I was warned against the Ku Klux Klan, that's all.

b. A secret organization, based on the earlier Klan, which advocated native white Protestant supremacy.

1920 *N.Y. Times* 11 Oct. 1/2 The old Ku Klux Klan has been reorganized and is regularly chartered under the laws of Georgia. **1923** *What is Ku Kluxism?* 2 Although the Ku Klux Klan was reorganized in 1915, the writer . . . was not aware of its serious activities until early in the year 1921. **1924** *Imperial Night-Hawk* 10 Sept. 6 The district meeting of the Ku Klux Klan held recently at Twin Lakes, Realm of Iowa, was a huge success.

L

∗**L.** The twelfth letter of the alphabet.

+**1.** A wing to a building, often built at right angles with the main building, the whole forming the shape of a capital L. Also attrib. (Cf. ELL[2] 2.)

[**1708** *Boston Rec. Comm. Rep.* XXIX. 188 To Thomas Hobart to Erect a Timber building . . . with a Return in form of an L.] **1843** 'CARLTON' *New Purchase* I. 80 [There] were two rooms, . . . connected with a Lilliputian half-story kitchen forming an L as near as possible. **1874** *Vermont Bd. Agric. Rep.* II. 510 To save expense, it is apt to be the case that no cellar is put under the L part of the house. **1900** DIX *Deacon Bradbury* 236 Steps came up the path leading from the gate to Mr. Clark's office in the 'L' of his home. **1905** *N.Y. Ev. Post* 20 March 1 In the rear of the building was an L section.

+**2.** Abbreviation for *elevated* (railroad). *colloq.* Also attrib.

1879 *N.Y. Herald* 19 Sept. 8/4 The crowds at the Park place station of the Metropolitan 'L' road, . . . have apparently been unprecedently large. **1881** MARSHALL *Through Amer.* 24 The effect of the 'elevated'—the 'L,' as New Yorkers generally call it—is, to my mind, anything but beautiful. **1899** J. L. WILLIAMS *Stolen Story* 189 He took the L train for Cortlandt Street. **1904** A. DALE *Wanted, a Cook* 85 Woman Drops Dead in L Station—Sitting bolt upright in an elevated railroad station in Brooklyn. **1919** *Chicago Daily News* 26 April 3/5 Seek 5 Cent 'L' Fare.

Labadist. Also **Labady.** [Jean de *Labadie* (1610–74).] A member of a primitivistic sect transplanted from the Netherlands to America. {1753–} Also attrib. — **1756** S. BOWNAS *Acct. Life* 58 After we had dined, we took our Leave, and a Friend, my Guide, went with me, and brought me to a People call'd *Labadies*, where we were civilly entertained in their Way. **1881** *Century Mag.* Dec. 217/1 Bohemia Manor, in Cecil County, Maryland, where the Labadists under Peter Schluter had formed a settlement. **1884** *Ib.* Jan. 441/2 The Labadist travelers complained in 1680 that the garden vegetables in one part of Maryland were 'few and coarse.'

∗**Labor.**[1] Also **labour.**

'The spelling with *-our* is preferred in the British Isles, while in the U.S. *-or* is more common' (*O.E.D.*).

+**1.** A plot of land to which the owner has acquired title by labor done on it. (Cf. sense 6 c, quot. 1816.)

1694 *N.C. Col. Rec.* I. 410 The dividing line . . . shall begin about the length of a chaine up the swamp from a little house built upon Alexander Speeds labour and shall run paralel wth Cornelius Lerrys side line.

2. a. In the production of wealth, the service rendered by laborers as opposed to the service rendered by capitalists. {1690– (Locke *Government* II. v. § 40)} **b.** The body of laborers, operatives, and artisans who help produce wealth. {1880–}

1792 *Ann. 2d Congress* 972 Nothing can afford so advantageous an employment for capital and labor, as the conversion of this extensive wilderness into cultivated farms. **1824** *Ann. 18th Congress* 1 Sess. 2035 Agriculture, commerce, and navigation . . . all furnish employment for American capital and American labor. **1885** *Wkly. New Mexican Review* 9 April 3/3 We sometime think that labor ought to fight like a son-of-a-gun. **1898** *Kansas City Star* 18 Dec. 2/2 The leaders of labor, the members of labor unions, are engaged in a great and noble cause. **1925** BRYAN *Memoirs* 217 The age-long question between capital and labor.

+**3.** Among the Shakers, the dancing used in their ceremonies of worship.

1832 WILLIAMSON *Maine* II. 699 The Shakers live in families, having . . . a house of public worship, which they call their *Temple*. Here both sexes join in acts and exercises of devotion, which they denominate 'labor.' **1838** *Knickerb.* XI. 535 And now, at a signal, the 'music' strikes up, to a wild, irregular chant, and the 'labor' begins. **1841** BUCKINGHAM *America* II. 359 The assembly then formed itself into another order for the dancing, which is called by them 'labour.'

+**4.** In the names of various agencies, officials, and organizations, in sense 2.

Cf. GREENBACK-LABOR PARTY, KNIGHTS OF LABOR, etc.

1884 *Statutes at Large* XXIII. 60 There shall be established in the Department of the Interior a Bureau of Labor, which shall be under the charge of a Commissioner of Labor. **1886** *N.Y. Tribune* 12 Dec. 1/4 The association shall be known as the American Federation of Labor. **1888** *Statutes at Large* XXV. 183 The Bureau of Labor, as now organized and existing, shall continue its work as the Department of Labor until the Department of Labor shall be organized in accordance with this act. **1903** *Ib.* XXXII. I. 825 There shall be at the seat of government an executive department to be known as the Department of Commerce and Labor. **1911** PERSONS, etc. *Mass. Labor Laws* 260 The former commissioner of labor in New York, P. Tecumseh Sherman. **1913** *Statutes at Large* XXXVII. I. 736 There is hereby created an executive department in the Government to be called the Department of Labor, with a Secretary of Labor.

+**5.** (See quotation.)

1890 *Cent.* 3317/1 *Labor*, . . . in the quicksilver-mines of California, any place where work has been or is going on; especially, in the plural, those parts of the mine from which ore is being extracted in some quantity; workings.

6. *attrib.* and *comb.* **a.** In sense 2 b with *agitator, association, boss*, etc.

1894 FORD *P. Stirling* 160 The labor agitator proved quite a good man. **1911** PERSONS, etc. *Mass. Labor Laws* 63 There were present 32 delegates representing 22 organized labor associations located in different parts of the state. **1903** *McClure's Mag.* Nov. 40/1 The arrogance of the Labor Boss . . . is largely traceable to this courting of the labor monopoly by both parties. **1872** *Bureau Stat. Labor 4th Rep.* 13 Industrial partnerships and co-operation are the most important subjects for inquiry by . . . the Massachusetts Labor Bureau. **1851** CIST *Cincinnati* 313 The next great effect will be, the general up-rising of the labor class in agriculture—the tenant farmers at the east. **1873** *Harper's Mag.* April 792/1 The bill for the establishment of a Labor Commission . . . was passed by the House over a year ago. **1866** *39th Congress 1 Sess.* Sen. Ex. Doc. No. 27, 60 In returning the labor contract bill, he [the governor of Alabama] states [etc.]. **1889** *Cent.* 1232/3 *Contractor*, . . . one who contracts or covenants . . . to perform any work or service, at a certain price or rate: as, a paving-*contractor;* a labor-*contractor.* **1883** WELLS *Practical Economics* (1885) 117 Our existing national fiscal or economic policy was . . . entailing so much of labor discontent and disturbance, that [etc.]. **1845** *Lowell Offering* V. 96 The petitioners to the Legislature for a reduction of labor hours are but a very small proportion of the whole number of laborers. **1904** *McClure's Mag.* Feb. 366/1 The employers of San Francisco are flat on their backs . . . ; when a labor leader makes a demand we give in without a word. **1911** PERSONS, etc. *Mass. Labor Laws* p. xvi, Legislative Reviews and summaries, published annually by the American Association for Labor Legislation. **1870** *Scribner's Mo.* I. 71 The preacher . . . beats about . . . in a dissertation on . . . the 'labor movement.' **1895** ROBINSON *Men Born Equal* 284 Threats . . . were being made . . . that the members of other labor organizations would be 'called out.' **1866** *39th Congress 1 Sess.* Sen. Ex. Doc. No. 27, 60 Idleness was extremely prevalent, and contracts might answer to restrain their disposition. 'Labor regulations' were therefore issued from [the Freedmen's Bureau]. **1868** *Rep. Comm. Agric. 1867* p. ix, The change in the labor system of these [southern] States . . . has been [radical].

+**b.** Designating persons or actions of various labor groups, such as the Knights of Labor, the Labor party, etc.

1872 *N.Y. Herald* 23 Feb. 10/1 The National Labor Convention reassembled at ten o'clock this morning. **1888** *Amer. Almanac* 222 Of the scattering votes, . . . 4,434 [were] for the Labor candidate for Governor.

c. Special combinations.

Labor baron, a man of influence and power among laborers; *l. lot*, = sense 1; *l. pass*, a railroad pass to a place where labor is needed, as at harvest time; *l. school*, an Indian school in which the students do the cooking, housework, farming, etc.

1816 U. BROWN *Journal* I. 269 Finds ½ a ½ & ¾ Labor Lots taxed in the name of George Dyke. **1871** *Rep. Indian Affairs* (1872) 404, [I] respectfully recommend that a labor-school be established as soon as practicable. *a***1889** *Chicago Inter-Ocean* (F.), I have observed in all the 'steam rail baron's' reply to 'fair trade' that he calls upon the 'iron ore barons' . . . and the 'labor barons' to aid him in meeting European competition. **1891** ROBERTS *Adrift America* 194 Knowing that there was a chance of getting sent out on a 'labour pass' to almost any part of the States from Kansas City in Missouri, I determined to go there.

+**Labor.**[2] Also **labour** by assimilation to LABOR.[1] *S.W.* [Sp.] A measure of land, usually of about 177 acres. *Obs.* except in legal cases.

1824 DEWEES *Lett. from Texas* 50 Every single man, who receives land under the Mexican government, on marrying, is entitled to an augmentation of his claim, to a league and labor of land. **1825** *Austin P.* (1924) II. 1022, I have made choice of the seventh Labour, on the west side of the river. **1835** A. PARKER *Trip to Texas* 151 This land is laid off into what is called *labors* of one hundred and seventy-seven acres. **1845** T. J. GREEN *Texian Exped.* xiii. 212 The valley—a basin of about thirty by sixty English miles, [is] laid off in labours. **1883** SWEET & KNOX *Through Texas* 213 To the man who brought a colony of a hundred families to Texas was granted five leagues and five labors of land. **1905** *Forestry Bureau Bul.* No. 62, 33 Under the law to which reference was made the unit of measurement was a vara (about 331-3 inches); a square of land measuring 1,000 varas on a side was a labor (about 177 acres).

Laboratory. 1. A factory engaged in manufacturing ammunition. {1716-} **2.** A building, rooms, or room in which experiments and studies in natural science are conducted. {1605-} — **(1) 1776** *Jrnls. Cont. Congress* VI. 860 *Resolved,* That ye Board of War be directed to prepare a plan for establishing a continental Laboratory, and a military Academy. **1777** *Essex Inst. Coll.* XIII. 115 Those men who Inlisted out of last Regiment had furlows and where [*sic*] Indulged to work In the Laboratory. **1867** EDWARDS *Shelby* 108 There came up a great cry for arms and ammunition and General Hirdman built manufactories; opened laboratories [etc.]. **1890** *Cent.* 3317/3 In Great Britain laboratories are in charge of officers of the Royal Artillery; in the United States they are under the officers of the Ordnance Department. **(2) 1797** MORSE *Amer. Gaz.* 1 Philadelphia . . . [has] a medical theatre, a laboratory, an amphitheatre. **1803** *Lit. Mag.* (Phila.) Oct. 64 A fire broke out in the chemical laboratory of Mr. Hunter. **1902** G. M. MARTIN *Emmy Lou* 228 Classes went to the laboratory for this subject, filing into an amphitheatre of benches.

+Labor Day. The first Monday in September, a legal holiday in honor of labor: (see also first quotation). Also attrib.

1887 *Oregon Laws* 86 The first Saturday of June of each and every year [shall] be . . . set apart and declared to be a public holiday under the name and title of Labor day. **1887** *Colo. Laws* 327 The first Monday in September . . . is hereby declared a public holiday, to be known as 'Labor Day.' **1894** *Statutes at Large* XXVIII. 96 An Act Making Labor Day a legal holiday. . . . The first Monday of September . . . , being the day celebrated and known as Labor's Holiday, is hereby made a legal public holiday. **1897** *N.Y. Journal* 5 Sept. 41/6 Three great sprinters . . . will be seen at the Labor Day games. **1904** *N.Y. Sun* 5 Sept. 10 Labor Day is a misnomer. It might now more properly be called sports day, or excursion day, or salt water day, for aside from the annual parade in which a small fraction of the trades unionists will march, labor, as such, will in nowise be conspicuous in the general celebration. **1922** *N.Y. Times* 5 Sept. 2/3 A steady downpour drenched the marchers in the annual Labor Day parade [in Boston].

***Laborer.** One who does physical labor, esp. work requiring little or no skill. (Cf. DAY LABORER.)

1756 *Penna. Col. Rec.* VII. 37 We are drained of our hired Labourers. **1775** FITHIAN *Journal* II. 147 The whole expense here per Annum of a labourer for diet, washing, & lodging was only five pounds. **1811** in H. M. Brooks *Gleanings* 141 Wanted, two Laborers about the yard, two months or more. **1835** CHANNING *Works* (1886) 719/2 Our slave-holding brethren, who tell us that the condition of the slave is better than that of the free labourer at the North, talk ignorantly and rashly. **1882** WELLS *Practical Economics* (1885) 68 What chance has the laborer for successful resistance, with . . . an annual import of 700,000 foreign laborers, ready to compete for . . . domestic employment? **1923** *Lit. Digest* 31 March 36/1 The wife of a 'boss roller' finds satisfaction in the knowledge that she stands head and shoulders above the wife of a common laborer.

Labor exchange. {1832-} An employment agency for laborers. {1893-} — **1869** BRACE *New West* 53 The intelligence and humanity of this new community was [shown in] the establishment, in 1868, of the 'Labor Exchange.' **1872** — *Dangerous Classes N.Y.* 60 The success of . . . the Commissioners of Emigration in their 'Labor Exchange,' indicate what might be accomplished. **1882** MCCABE *New York* 662 A labor exchange is established in the building, where those who wish to procure work can secure situations.

***Laboring,** *a.*

***1.** *Laboring man,* =LABORER. Also collect.

1651 *Rowley Rec.* 72 Labering men to have 18 d. a day in Summer. **1674** *Huntington Rec.* I. 207 All sufficient laboring men that shall labor at the mill work, shall have per day 2 shillings and six pence. **1729** FRANKLIN *Writings* II. 137 What can be more disheartening to an industrious labouring man than this? **1872** BRACE *Dangerous Classes N.Y.* 64 A laboring-man . . . returns to his tenement-house after a hard day's work, 'dragged out' and craving excitement. **1880** *Harper's Mag.* Oct. 726/2 These . . . labor-saving inventions are apparently much more hostile to the interests of the 'laboring-man' than all the Chinamen that ever came in through the Golden Gate. **1900** *Congress. Rec.* 16 Jan. 875/1 They have built trust upon top of trust, until they are now impoverishing the laboring man whom they claim they are benefiting. **1917** SINCLAIR *King Coal* 205 The old Swede was staying, in the home of a labouring-man nearby.

2. *Laboring class,* +that class of American society made up of day laborers, mill workers, servants, etc.

1807 *Ann. 9th Congress* 2 Sess. 303 The laboring classes of the community receive but a very small portion of relief from a total abolition of the salt tax. **1851** CIST *Cincinnati* 327 The heavy disbursements have proved a seasonable and sensible benefit to the laboring class. **1865** STOWE *House & Home P.* 209 The girls of New England . . . left the whole business of domestic service to a foreign population . . . because they would not take positions in families as an inferior laboring-class. **1883** *Century Mag.* July 471/1 A vast deal more remains to be done to raise the amusements and recreations of the laboring class. **1900** *Congress. Rec.* 31 Jan. 1339/1, I defy any man to point to any provision in the bill which will benefit the laboring classes from one end of the country to the other.

Labor party. {1886-} +Any of various U.S. political parties claiming to represent the interests of labor. — **1886** *Public Opinion* 13 Nov. 1/1 These voters wish to be considered the Labor party, as if there were no other. **1887** *Courier-Journal* 8 May 16/2 Will the Labor party cut any figure in the next contest? **1911** PERSONS, etc. *Mass. Labor Laws* p. xx, The part played by the labor party and labor organizations outlined by Mr. Persons in his study of the origins of labor legislation, found a counterpart in their efforts during the following decade. **1913** LA FOLLETTE *Autobiog.* 17 A Labor party was organized to agitate the problems of capital and labor.

+Labor reform. a. Reform in the working conditions of the laboring classes. **b.** *attrib.* Designating various organizations seeking such reform. — **1847** (*title*), Conditions of Labor. An address to the Members of the Labor Reform League of New England by one of their number. **1872** *Atlantic Mo.* June 771 The size of the vote caused a good deal of wonder, as no one supposed that Labor Reform, as an independent political movement, could muster so many supporters. **1911** PERSONS, etc. *Mass. Labor Laws* 107 This later convention seems to have assembled under the auspices of the Labor Reform party. *Ib.* 109 The Labor Reform Association was reorganized in 1867, as a result of a mass meeting in which Wendell Phillips was the leading spirit.

+Labor reformer. One associated with a labor-reform organization. — **1872** *Atlantic Mo.* June 771 It was in great measure to the discontent of the Crispins . . . that the heavy vote thrown at the Labor-Reformers was at that time attributed. **1883** *Century Mag.* Oct. 901/1 'We are Labor Reformers,' said the spokesman.

Labor-saving, *a.* Designating a device or machine that saves labor in the performance of a given task. {c1775-} — **1792** *Ann. 2d Congress* 1026 Expectations . . . are derived from some late experiments of being able to extend the use of labor-saving machines in the coarser fabrics of linen. **1812** *Niles' Reg.* II. 336/1 Numerous works, by labor-saving machinery . . . have been commenced since the British orders in council, blockades, and impressments from 1803 to 1807. **1862** *Ill. Agric. Soc. Trans.* V. 691 We flaunt our labor-saving farm machinery in the faces of slow and fogy Germany. **1900** *Congress. Rec.* 31 Jan. 1352/2 Various labor-saving devices and combinations are constantly lessening the opportunities for the wage-workers to get employment. **1919** J. COBB *Canning Fishery Products* 1 In fish canning labor saving devices have been brought to a high state of efficiency.

+Labor union. A union of laborers, esp. of those engaged in a particular craft. {=trade-union}

1866 in Commons, etc. *Doc. Hist.* IX. 133 The Executive Board shall have power to levy a tax of twenty-five cents a year upon each member belonging to the National Labor Union. **1883** HAY *Bread-Winners* 183 The labor unions have ordered a general strike. **1885** *N. Amer. Rev.* Jan. 60 The most important of these is the Central Labor Union of New York City, in which nearly one hundred thousand wage-workers are represented. **1898** DUNBAR *Folks from Dixie* 208 [The only remedy] was to pay him [the labor agitator] two dollars and immediately organise a local branch of the Miners' Labour Union. **1908** LORIMER *J. Spurlock* iii. 43 The Governor remembered Teddy Roosevelt and labour unions in the same prayer. **1923** WATTS *L. Nichols* 162 Events variously explained as resulting from the War, . . . the disagreement between labor-unions and employers, and so on.

Labrador.

+1. =LABRADOR TEA 1 and 2. *Obs.*

1767 *Boston Gazette* 2 Nov. 2/2 There is a certain Herb, lately found in this Province, which begins already to take Place in the Room of Green and Bohea Tea. . . . It is called Labrador. **1767** *Newport Mercury* 28 Dec. 3/3 Where . . . noxious Bohea sheds a pois'nous Stream, There let balsamick Labrador regale.

2. *attrib.* **+a.** *Labrador pine,* the jack pine, *Pinus banksiana.*

1803 LAMBERT *Descr. Genus Pinus* 7 Labrador Pine. . . . Habitat in Americâ septentrionali. **1858** WARDER *Hedges & Evergreens* 246 Labrador Pine is also a low, scrubby, or straggling tree, rising only five or eight feet. *a***1862** THOREAU *Maine Woods* 275.

+b. In names of birds.

1869 *Amer. Naturalist* III. 383 The Pied or Labrador duck . . . is a very interesting bird to the naturalist. **1877** MINOT *Land-Birds & Game-Birds New Eng.* 405 Those very small wiry, compactly feathered, weather-tanned birds [woodcocks] . . . are called, perhaps locally, Labrador twisters. **1917** *Birds of Amer.* I. 18 Puffin. . . . [Also called] Labrador Auk. *Ib.* III. 213/2 Another subspecies [of the Acadian Chickadee] is the so-called Labrador Brown-capped Chickadee.

+Labrador tea.

1. Tea made with the leaves of an evergreen: (see sense 2).

1767 [see HIPERION TEA]. **1768** *Boston Gazette* 9 May, They took Labradore Tea and Coffee for their Support, and finished their work. **1828** SHERBURNE *Memoirs* iii. 69 We were driven into store houses, and furnished with a kind of tea, which they called Labrador tea.

2. The evergreen shrub (*Ledum groenlandicum*), from which the tea is made.

1784 CUTLER in *Life & Corr.* I. 103 There were large beds of what is called the Labrador tea, of a very aromatic taste and smell. **1814** PURSH *Flora Amer.* I. 301 *Ledum latifolium.* . . . Commonly called Labrador Tea. **1832** WILLIAMSON *Maine* I. 131 Labrador-tea, (*Laedum Latifolium,*) is a shrub. . . . Its leaves make a palatable tea;—used to check the dysentery. **1850** S. F. COOPER *Rural Hours* 122 Several native plants were prepared at that time to take the place of the prohibited souchong and bohea . . . [as] the 'Labrador tea,' a low evergreen with handsome white flowers. **1870** *Amer. Naturalist* IV. 217 Labrador Tea . . . with its delicate white clusters and leaves rusty-woolly beneath, is likewise full of beauty.

+**Labrick.** *Missouri.* A fool. *slang.* — **1889** 'MARK TWAIN' *Conn. Yankee* xxx. 382 As a rule, a knight is a lummux, and sometimes even a labrick. **1893** — *P. Wilson* i, He's a labrick—just a Simon-pure labrick, if ever there was one.

***Laburnum.** A genus of small shrubs or trees of the family Fabaceae much cultivated for their bright flowers; any species or tree of this genus. Also attrib. with *tree.*

1832 S. J. HALE *Flora* 84 Laburnum. *Cytisus.* . . . A genus of about 12 species; 6 of which belong to America. **1842** KIRKLAND *Forest Life* II. 142 The flowering currant . . . [is] already strung with golden, clove-scented wreaths looking at a little distance like miniature laburnum. **1877** *Harper's Mag.* Jan. 269/2 Her keen grey eyes looked out beyond her father to the dusky laburnums at the garden gate. **1888** M. DELAND *J. Ward* 14 He stooped down to pull some matted grass from about the roots of a laburnum-tree, whose dark leaves were lighted by golden loops of blossoms. **1892** APGAR *Trees Northern U.S.* 92 *Laburnum vulgare.* (Laburnum. Golden-chain. Bean-trefoil Tree.) . . . A low, very ornamental tree, 10 to 20 ft. high, often cultivated.

***Lace.**

***1. a.** An ornamental braid used as a trimming on men's coats, hats, etc. *Obs.* except in *gold* or *silver lace.* **b.** An openwork fabric, usually arranged with an inwrought pattern.

1634 *Mass. Bay Rec.* I. 126 The ordinary weareing of silver, golde, & silke laces, girdles, hatbands, &c., [is forbidden]. **1651** *Mass. Col. Laws* (1887) 5 No person within this Jurisdiction, nor any of their relations depending upon them, . . . shall wear any Gold or Silver lace. **1695** *N.C. Col. Rec.* I. 457 Some of ye Perticulars [were] taken out [of the box] as a parcel of Harrow lace. **1725** *New-Eng. Courant* 7–14 June 2/2 To be sold . . . a Parcel of Fine Lace and Edgings. **1768** FRENEAU *Poems* (1795) 9 Laces and lawns would draw each rural maid. **1875** STOWE *We & Neighbors* 162, I'll take your laces to the mender's. **1925** N. KNEELAND *Negligees* 31 Hand-made, or real lace, is softer and more irregular than the machine-made.

2. *attrib.* and *comb.* **a.** Designating articles made of, or trimmed with, lace.

1711 *Boston News-Letter* 13 Aug. 2/2 A Carolina Indian Maid-Servant . . . has carried away . . . several pair of Stockings, & several Lace Caps. **1875** STOWE *We & Neighbors* 471 She's just going in that satin gown . . . with a great lace collar as big as a platter. **1879** HOWELLS *Lady of Aroostook* 6 Little winders at the top, and white lace curtains to the bed. **1876** *Wide Awake* 352/1, I can give you each a reg'lar bang-up lace hankercher to cry on. **1771** A. G. WINSLOW *Diary* 5, I intend to send Nancy Mackky a pair of lace mittens. **1800** E. S. BOWNE *Life* 42 Why can't you go and see McLellan's lace shades? **1865** STOWE *House & Home P.* 186 Here is a man that will buy his wife a diamond bracelet and a lace shawl. **1853** *Harper's Mag.* VI. 195 Her light lace skirt, lifted by the whirl, flew against me. **1904** GLASGOW *Deliverance* 149 The thought of Maria's lace stockings came to him all at once. **1896** WILKINS *Madelon* 13 Madelon, her brown throat swelling above her lace tucker, . . . stood in the midst of the men.

b. Designating persons who make lace.

1796 *Boston Directory* 226 Bensey Peter, lace weaver. *Ib.* 230 Bright, John and William, upholsterers and lace-manufacturers. **1853** B. F. TAYLOR *Jan. & June* 103 [She] kept the weary lace-maker . . . full two hours longer at her task.

c. *Lace boot,* a boot fastening with laces. *Obs.*

1790 *Penna. Packet* 5 Feb. 3/3 Nathaniel Prentiss . . . has now the following assortment, viz. . . . Womens Lace Boots, Plain and lined and bound Shoes [etc.].

***Laced,** *a.* Ornamented or trimmed with lace or braid. *Obs.* {1665–}

1683 *Portsmouth Rec.* 299 The Body of a man . . . hanging by the head by a linin lact neckcloth. **1711** *Boston News-Letter* 19 Feb. 2/2 Stolen or carried privately away out of the House of Capt. John Bonner . . . , three pair of laced Sleves. **1733** *S.C. Gazette* 203/2 Delivered, by Mistake, . . . a Box . . . in which was two Dozen of laced Hats, and some Wigg Cauls. **1755** *Lett. to Washington* I. 89, 1 fine Laced Coat. **1757** *Ib.* II. 179 Youl scarce believe that the Colonel never appears here but in full dressed laced Suits—so great a change has Carolina produced.

Laced jacket. +(See quotation.) — **1824** DODDRIDGE *Notes* 100 When annoyed by the claimants under those [tomahawk] rights, . . . [settlers] deliberately cut a few good hiccories, and gave them what was called in those days 'a laced jacket,' that is a sound whipping.

+**Lace flower.** The wild carrot. — **1894** *Amer. Folk-Lore* VII. 89 *Daucus Carota,* lace-flower, Philadelphia, Pa. **1899** GOING *Flowers* 349 There are places west of the Mississippi where wild-carrots, despised intruder on Eastern lawns, is cosseted and extolled under the appropriate alias of 'lace flower.'

+**Lacer.** A dash of liquor used to flavor a beverage. — **1854** SIMMS *Southward Ho!* iv. 32 A bowl of coffee and a cracker is the initial appetizer, with possibly a tass of brandy in the purple beverage, as a lacer.

Lacewing. Any of various insects having lacelike wings. {1863–} — **1854** EMMONS *Agric. N.Y.* V. 159 Another insect . . . the lacewing, unceremoniously thrusts its curved beak into the sides of the aphis, and sucks the insect dry. **1862** *Ill. Agric. Soc. Trans.* V. 734 The Lace Wing clears off plant lice.

+**Lacrosse.** [Fr. *la crosse* a hooked stick.] A field game similar to hockey, the ball being caught, carried, and thrown with long-handled rackets carried by the players. Also attrib. (Cf. BALL-PLAY 1, CROSS *n.* 2.) — **1718** in Beckwith *Ill. & Indiana Indians* 168 They play a good deal in La Crosse in summer, twenty or more on a side. [**1808** PIKE *Sources Miss.* 18 Passed the Racine river, also a prairie called Le Cross, from a game of ball played frequently on it by the Sioux Indians.] **1886** *Outing* March 665/2 Lacrosse . . . is the offspring of the American savage. It was born and bred upon the plains of the South and West. **1898** *Outing* April 10/1 This Union is composed of . . . the Hockey Club, the Lacrosse Association, the Golf Club and the Fencing Club.

***Ladder.**

***1.** An appliance consisting, in its simplest form, of two supports connected by cross pieces, by means of which one may climb up or down.

1636 *Plymouth Laws* 56 Every householder within this Colony & Government shall have one sufficient ladder or ladders at least about his house which will reach ye top. **1663** *Jamaica Rec.* I. 177 Every Dwelling howse shall have a sufficient ladder to reach within two foot of the Ridge of the howse. **1723** HEMPSTEAD *Diary* 132, I fell off ye Ladder Climbing to get black Cherrys in ye orchard. **1788** FRANKLIN *Autobiog.* 354 The small fines . . . have been apply'd to the purchase of fire-engines, ladders, . . . and other useful implements. **1806** *Mass. Laws 1805–6* 98 The enginemen . . . [shall] attend fires . . . , with axes, firehooks, fire-sails and ladders. **1884** ROE *Nature's Story* 380 Webb, from the top of a tall ladder in the orchard, happened to glance that way.

+**2.** *To see through a ladder,* to see something that is obvious.

1837 MARTINEAU *Society* I. 337 One asked if such an one was not a 'smart fellow.' 'He! he can't see through a ladder.' **1852** STOWE *Uncle Tom* vi, Can't ye see through a ladder, ye black nigger? Missis don't want dis yer Mas'r Haley to get Lizy's boy; dat's de go! **1897** BRODHEAD *Bound in Shallows* 86, I can see through a ladder when the rungs ain't too close together.

3. *attrib.* and *comb.* +**a.** With special reference to the ladders of a fire company. (Cf. HOOK-AND-LADDER COMPANY, MAN, etc.)

1889 BRAYLEY *Boston Fire Dept.* 139 Almost the first act of this board was . . . the enlargement of the ladder-house. *Ib.* 173 On September 21 the members of the ladder company were provided with caps like those worn by the enginemen. *Ib.* 297 Ladder companies [included]: foreman, assistant foreman, and twelve ladder-men. *Ib.* 466 They had a narrow excape [*sic*] from a collision with Ladder Truck No. 8.

+**b.** In the names of several American woodpeckers.

1869 *Amer. Naturalist* III. 474 The resident species not found westward of this valley [the Colorado Valley in Calif.] were the Ladder Woodpecker (*Picus scalaris*) [etc.]. **1884** COUES *Key N.A. Birds* (ed. 2) 485 *Picoïdes americanus.* . . . Ladder-backed Three-toed Woodpecker. **1917** *Birds of Amer.* II. 149/1 The Ladder-back Woodpeckers are divisible into three regional varieties, the American, the Alaska (*Picoides americanus fasciatus*), and the Alpine (*Picoides americanus dorsalis*).

+**Ladder pole.** A long pole for use in making a ladder. — **1678** *Springfield Rec.* II. 160 To Goodm[an] Mirricke for ladder Poles, . . . 2 [shillings]. **1737** HEMPSTEAD *Diary* 316, I cut a black ash ladder pole. **1744** *Ib.* 424 Wee found 51 Pine Logs besides 1 Ladder pole & 7 Sparrs fitt for yards.

Ladies'. The possessive pl. of lady in special combinations. (See also LADIES' AID (SOCIETY), etc., and, for plant names, LADY'S-DELIGHT, LADY'S-EARDROP(S), etc.)

1818 FESSENDEN *Ladies Monitor* 94 Ladies-Academies are well, perhaps, As theatres in which to set our caps. **1841** BUCKINGHAM *America* II. 441 At the Tremont House in Boston . . . about the same number of persons dined at what is called the ladies' table, and where gentlemen (but only those who are accompanied by ladies) sit. **1846** SAXE *Progress* (1847) 13 Nor less, O Progress, are thy newest rules Enforced and honored in the 'Ladies' Schools.' **1863** WHITMAN *Diary* (1904) 50 The ladies' gallery in the House [in Congress] is about half of the whole room devoted to the public. **1875** *Chicago Tribune* 8 July 7/6 Adelphi Theatre Thursday Evening, July 8—Ladies Night. **1876** INGRAM *Centennial Exp.* 639 There were also committee-rooms, a ladies' parlor, invalids' room, . . . and gentlemen's parlor [in the Ind. state building]. **1885** *Harper's Mag.* March 552/2 They took possession of the ladies' room, which Anastasia, who had seen many, pronounced a very good one. **1893** *Voice* 20 July, Patrons of the 'cocktail' route know that the ladies' entrance is more disastrous to morals . . . than any other vice. **1914** 'BOWER' *Flying U Ranch* 202 He had been invited to dance 'Ladies' choice' with the prettiest girl in the crowd.

+**Ladies' Aid (Society).** **1.** During the Civil War, a women's organization devoted to sending garments, bandages, etc., to the soldiers.

2. One of various societies of church women devoted to raising money for the church. — (1) **1866** Moore *Women of War* 214 Mrs. Wittenmeyer, as president of the Ladies' Aid Society of Iowa. (2) **1893** 'Thanet' *Stories* 185 The furnishing of the church . . . is in charge of the Ladies' Aid Society. **1898** *Kansas City Star* 18 Dec. 2/4 Contributions to the shoe fund of the Catholic Ladies' Aid Society. **1908** Gale *Friendship Village* 81 The Ladies' Aid had got the floor [of the church] broom-clean.

Ladies' cabin. On a ship, a cabin reserved for the use of women passengers. Also attrib. — **1834** *S. Lit. Messenger* I. 74 We went to the ladies' cabin, where I was introduced with all due form, to Mrs. M. **1849** *Wilmington* (N.C.) *Commercial* 27 Nov. 1/6 (Th. S.), Passing obliquely through the hurricane roof immediately over the ladies' cabin. **1870** O. Logan *Before Footlights* 198 The dinners are wastefully luxurious, the ladies' cabin never without the inevitable grand piano. **1875** 'Mark Twain' *Old Times* v. 84 It's been up on the lady's-cabin guards two days drying.

+**Ladies' car.** On a train, a car reserved for the use of women passengers and their escorts. — **1864** Daly in J. F. Daly *A. Daly* 62 Brutes and blackguards in the so-called ladies' car! **1873** 'Mark Twain' & Warner *Gilded Age* xxiv. 218 You were about to enter the 'ladies' car' without knowing it. **1884** 'Craddock' *Where Battle Was Fought* 25 'Glad to see you back,' said a young man who was entering from the 'ladies car.' **1887** Custer *Tenting on Plains* i. 35 There was a ladies' car, to which no men unaccompanied by women were admitted.

Ladies' day. A day on which special privileges are given to women: (see also quot. 1882). — **1787** Washington *Diaries* III. 225 Dined with a Club. . . . The Gentlemen . . . met every Saturday . . . accompanied by the females every other Saturday. This was the ladies' day. **1882** McCabe *New York* 329 January 2d . . . is 'Ladies' Day,' and is devoted by the fair sex to calling upon each other. **1906** *American Mag.* Oct. 595 Ladies' Day in Carbury Mine.

+**Ladies' fair.** A bazaar held by women for some charitable purpose. — **1843** Fuller in *Dial* July 13 Governor's of Ladies' Fairs are no less engrossed by such a charge, than the Governor of the State by his. **1855** Thompson *Doesticks* 132 There was soon to be a ladies' fair, in aid of the poor, given by the benevolent ladies of the Church.

+**Ladies' twist (tobacco).** Pigtail tobacco. — **1824** *Shipping & Commercial List* (Pettigrew P.) 31 July, Tobacco . . . Ladies' Twist, Cavendish, Sweet scent. **1832** *Louisville Pub. Advertiser* 7 March, T. K. Byrne has received . . . 15 boxes ladies' twist and Cavendish tobacco. **1843** Lumsden *Amer. Memoranda* 14 My next communication will probably contain full details of the methods adopted by the Virginian planters in the manufacturing of the nigger-head, ladies'-twist [etc.]. **1864** E. Burritt *Walk from London to John O'Groat's* 290 An American tobacco-chewer, of fifty years' standing, would not have asked a cut from a neighbor's 'lady's twist,' or 'pig-tail' in more perfect good faith.

+**Ladino.** (See quotation.) — **1891** *Dialect Notes* I. 191 *Ladino.* In Spanish, learned, knowing Latin; then crafty, cunning. In Texas as a noun, a vicious, unmanageable horse, full of cunning and tricks.

*Ladle.

*1. A large spoon-shaped utensil used for lading liquids.

1634 Wood *New Eng. Prospect* (1865) 109 If her husband come to seeke for his Squaw and beginne to bluster the English woman betakes her to her armes which are the warlike Ladle, and the scalding liquors. **1757** *Lett. to Washington* II. 158 Had we Copper & tinn, the Ladles & Measures might be made, as also the Lanthorn. **1804** Fessenden *Orig. Poems* (1806) 142 And snatch'd up a ladle for broth. **1890** *Century Mag.* Nov. 54/2 Mynheer leaned across the table and took the ladle out of her hand.

+2. (See quot. 1833.)

1833 Burritt *Geog. of Heavens* (1839) 85 Ursa Major. The Great Bear. —This constellation is readily distinguished from all others by means of a remarkable cluster of seven bright stars, forming what is familiarly termed the *Dipper* or *Ladle.* **1841** *Lowell Offering* I. 26, I was just endeavoring to point out to my cousins the constellation vulgarly called 'The Ladle.'

+Ladron(e). *S.W.* [Sp. *ladrón*, pl. *ladrones.*] A thief.

Used occas. by British and American writers with reference to Spain, but as current in the United States a new borrowing from Mexican Spanish.

1844 Kendall *Santa Fé Exped.* II. 70 The ladrones, or common thieves, could now reap a rich harvest of plunder. **1867** *Wkly. New Mexican* 6 April 1/4 The soldiers would not be able to discriminate the good Indian from the ladrone. **1879** *Cimarron News & Press* 27 Nov. 3/2 These Mora county *ladrones* never seem to get enough of Colfax county cattle.

Lad's-love. =Boy's-love. {a1825–, *dial.*} — **1891** A. M. Earle *Sabbath* 40 A large bunch of aromatic southernwood, or 'lad's-love' . . . had been brought to meeting by the matron in the next pew. **1899** *Animal & Plant Lore* 115 *Artemisia abrotanum*, the southernwood, is called 'boy's love,' 'lad's love,' etc., in the Northeastern and Central States, probably from a general belief in its aphrodisiac qualities. New England to Illinois.

*Lady.

See also Ladies' and Ladies' aid (society), etc.

*1. A woman of high social standing. Also as title.

a1649 Winthrop *Hist.* II. 126 The lady Moodye, a wise and anciently religious woman, . . . [was] taken with the error of denying baptism to infants. **1747** Franklin *Exper. on Electricity* 16 The same if another gentleman and lady . . . salute. **1807** Irving, etc. *Salmagundi* x, At a tea-party the ladies in general are disposed close together, like a setting of jewels. **1886** James *Bostonians* 43 Of course she knew principally ladies; the time hadn't come when a lady-doctor was sent for by a gentleman. **1914** A. Lowell *Sword Blades* 242 A Lady. You are beautiful and faded Like an old opera tune Played upon a harpsichord.

b. In loose and excessively polite usage, a woman.

Many writers have commented upon this weakening of the word. See especially Farmer. The corresponding sense of gentleman (q.v., sense 1 b) is much less widely used.

1815 *Massachusetts Spy* 23 Aug. (Th.), If our friends knock at the door, our lady and gentleman 'hired helps' do not understand who is meant. **1816** 'Scene Painter' *Emigrant's Guide* 27 For every white female is a lady by Columbian courtesy; an equality of rank, therefore, entitles a pot-wrestler to a place on the same seat with her employers. **1833** in *Century Mag.* Sept. (1885) 782/1 A High School for young colored Ladies and Misses. **1835** *Jrnl. Excursion U.S. 1834* 136 The title lady is applied in America to all females; even a white servant would be affronted if she were not styled a young lady. **1837** Martineau *Society* III. 83 This noble word [woman], spirit-stirring as it passes over English ears, is in America banished, and 'ladies' and 'females' substituted: the one to English taste mawkish and vulgar; the other indistinctive and gross. **1891** O'Beirne *Leaders Ind. Territory* 194/1 Mr. Watkins married a Choctaw lady in 1870. **1894** *Harper's Mag.* May 970/2 Every unmarried woman is a 'young lady' by courtesy south of Mason and Dixon's line. **1904** Tarbell *Hist. Standard Oil Co.* I. 41, I paid my washerwoman and the lady I boarded with.

+2. Used as a title for the wife of a president of the United States.

1832 F. Trollope *Domestic Manners* I. 256, I was often amused by the evident fondness which the Americans shew for titles. The wives of their eminent men constantly receive that of 'Lady.' We heard of Lady Washington, Lady Jackson, and many other 'ladies.' **1861** McClellan in *Own Story* 91, I had another bouquet this morning, one from the 'Lady President.'

3. *Lady of the house*, the mistress of the house. Also transf.

1832 Bryant *Letter to F. Bryant* (MS.) 3 June, The lady of the house . . . had been sitting with the guests in the parlour. **a1882** in McCabe *New York* 220, [I] told the lady of the house what had occurred. **1886** Stockton *Mrs. Lecks* 53 As for me, I'm goin' to ask the lady of the house, and if she don't like me she can lump me. **1903** Wiggin *Rebecca* 140 She asked, 'Is the lady of the house at home?' [He said] 'I am the lady of the house at present.'

+b. *Lady of the White House*, the presiding lady in the household of the president of the United States. (Cf. sense 2.)

1841 *Picayune* 20 April 2/3 The Lady of the White House.—A daughter of the venerable Thomas Cooper, Esq., . . . will now, it is said, be presiding lady at the President's Mansion in Washington. **1857** *N.Y. Chronicle* 14 March 43/4 Lady of the White House. . . . Miss Lane, a niece of the President, will dispense the hospitalities of the Executive mansion. **1881** L. C. Holloway *Ladies of the White House* 3 The Ladies of the White House have had no biographers.

4. In names of fruits, plants, and insects. Used attributively and in possessive. (See also Lady's-delight, etc.)

1904 Stuart *River's Children* 57 Cloth-of-gold, musk-cluster, Lady-bank . . . mingled in harmonious relations with honeysuckle. **1868** *Mich. Agric. Rep.* VII. 175 Quite a number of lady-beetles have been noticed on the vines. **1868** *Rep. Comm. Agric. 1867* 132 Lady's Blush, Trumbull Sweet, Fenton Sweet [are names for the apple called Higby Sweet]. **1854** Emmons *Agric. N.Y.* V. 210 The caterpillar [*Cynthia Huntera*] is said by Drury to be green, with black rings around the body, and feeds on balsam or lady's-jewels. **1784** Cutler in *Mem. Academy* I. 486 *Orchis.* . . . Lady's Plume. Female-Handed Orchis. Blossoms in large spikes; white, or purplish, or flesh colour'd. In wet meadows. **1892** *Amer. Folk-Lore* V. 94 *Impatiens fulva*, lady's pocket, Mansfield, O. **1868** *Rep. Comm. Agric. 1867* 133 Lady's Sweet. . . . [Also called] Ladies' Sweeting. . . . [The color of the apple is] pale yellowish green. **1833** Eaton *Botany* (ed. 6) 244 *Oxalis corniculata*, lady's wood-sorrel.

Lady apple. A small apple of attractive appearance. {1876} — **1817** W. Coxe *Fruit Trees* 117 *Pomme D'Apis.* This apple is called in New-York the Lady apple from the beauty of its appearance. **1847** Ives *New Eng. Fruit* 41 *Lady Apple.*—This size is small, the form flat, the skin at maturity is a bright yellow. **1860** Holmes *Professor* iii. 64 How some of us fellows remember . . . Joe, with his cheeks like lady-apples, and his eyes like black-heart cherries. **1870** *Rep. Comm. Agric. 1869* 446 When living in New York City, in 1868, a friend had sent him some 'lady apples' to sell. The apples brought $25 per barrel.

***Ladybird.** 1. Any one of various species of small beetles, useful in destroying plant lice. {1704–} +2. The pintail duck. — (1) **1737** Brickell *N. Carolina* 158 The Lady Bird is a beautiful small Insect (with red Wings and black spots thereon) which . . . is to be met with in Carolina in the Summer time, and is a wonderful Cordial, curing all Fevers. **1854** Emmons *Agric. N.Y.* V. 161 Plant lice have numerous foes. . . . Among these foes we rank the numerous species of *Coccinella*, or ladybirds. **1856** *Rep. Comm. Patents 1855: Agric.* 113 The lady-bird . . . is a most valuable auxiliary to the cotton-planter, as it destroys the cotton-louse. **1892** Kellogg *Kansas Insects* 74 Several predaceous beetles, conspicuous among them certain 'lady-birds' . . . , consider the soft-bodied lice to be dainty tid-bits. (2) **1890** *Cent.* 3328/2 *Ladybird,* . . . the pintail duck, *Dafila acuta:* so called from its graceful form. **1917** *Birds of Amer.* I. 128 Pintail. *Dafila acuta.* . . . [Also called] Winter Duck; Ladybird; Long-necked Cracker.

Ladybug. =LADYBIRD 1. {1787– *dial.*}

'*Dial.* and *U.S.*' (*O.E.D.*).

1844 *Knickerb.* XXIII. 549 He 'sticks a pin' . . . [into] any thing from a lady-bug . . . to an offensive black beetle. **1867** *Amer. Naturalist* I. 223 The natural-insect enemies of the Plant-lice now abound; such are the Lady-bugs (*Coccinella*) [etc.]. **1883** *Century Mag.* Oct. 816/1 [The bee's] time of danger is when apricots are ripe and lady-bugs fly. **1904** *Wilmington Every Evening* 1 Dec. 8 As an enemy of the dreaded San Jose scale, which dotes on peach trees, the lady-bug is a rank failure.

+**Lady cake.** A kind of butter cake variously flavored. — **1849** G. G. FOSTER *N.Y. in Slices* 72 It would be sacrilege to eat any thing heartier than ice-cream and lady-cake till the crisis comes off. **1855** COOKE *Ellie* 247 What would fifty lady-cakes, two for a cent, come to in money? **1883** HOWELLS *Woman's Reason* viii, In a plated basket in the center of the table was a generous stack of freshly-sliced lady-cake.

Lady crab. {1882–} +An edible crab (*Ovalipes ocellatus*), noted for its pleasing color and markings. — **1843** *Nat. Hist. N.Y., Zoology* VI. 10 It is not much esteemed as an article of food. By the shore-dwellers, it is often designated as the Lady Crab, from the beauty of its colors. **1883** *Nat. Museum Bul.* No. 27, 111 The Lady Crab (*Platyonichus ocellatus*) is occasionally taken for food on the Atlantic coast, . . . but is rarely seen in the markets. **1884** GOODE, etc. *Fisheries* I. 774 The 'Lady Crab,' or 'Sand Crab,' is abundant on nearly all our sandy shores from Cape Cod to Florida. **1911** *Rep. Fisheries U.S.* 308.

Lady finger. {ladies finger, 1670–; lady-finger-grass, 1743–}

+**1.** A variety of apple.

1709 LAWSON *Carolina* 109 Lady-Finger, the long Apple. **1875** BURROUGHS *Winter Sunshine* 154 Others are indeed lady apples . . . like the egg-drop and lady-finger.

2. 'A finger-shaped variety of the potato formerly common' (*Cent.*).

+**Lady finger corn.** (See ILLINOIS 2 a. quot. 1849.)

Ladyfish. {1712–} +One or other of several species of fish found along the southeastern coast of the United States. — **1878** *Nat. Museum Proc.* I. 384 *Albula vulpes.*—Lady Fish. **1884** GOODE, etc. *Fisheries* I. 612 With us it [*Albula vulpes*] is usually called the 'Lady-fish.' **1897** *Outing* May 148 The 'bony fish,' or 'lady fish,' . . . abounds in all Florida rivers, and has been malignantly christened by some bilious scientist a *Lagodon rhomboides.*

+**Lady pea. a.** The everlasting pea, *Lathyrus latifolius.* **b.** A species of field pea. — **1788** WASHINGTON *Diaries* III. 324 Below, were sowed, or rather planted, the everlasting (or Lady Pease) sent me by the Honble. James Mercer. **1825** LORAIN *Pract. Husbandry* 513 The Albany and lady pea are lenient plants. **1837** WILLIAMS *Florida* 112 The cow pea, lady pea, and chickasaw pea, produce excellent crops during the heat of summer. **1912** COBB *Back Home* 78 He overturned a little wooden measure that held a nickel's worth of dried lady-peas.

+**Lady's-delight.** One or other species of wild pansy. — **1841** CHILD *Lett. New York* i. 14, I am like the Lady's Delight, ever prone to take root. **1865** A. D. WHITNEY *Gayworthys* ix. 86 A Sunday nosegay for his mother, of late pinks and . . . ladies' delights, and bits of coriander. **1895** A. BROWN *Meadow-Grass* 254 Dorcas . . . remembered he loved ladies'-delights.

Lady's-eardrop(s). 1. Any of various species of fuchsia, esp. the small-flowered fuchsia, *Fuchsia coccinea.* +**2.** One or other of certain American plants such as the spotted jewelweed, balsamweed, etc. — **(1) 1836** LINCOLN *Botany* 159 The ladies' ear-drop, *Fuschsia,* . . . is a beautiful exotic. **1868** GRAY *Field Botany* 147 Short-flowered Fuchsias, or Ladies' Eardrops. **(2) 1887** WILKINS *Humble Romance* 195 He cut lavishly sprays of dioletra, or lady's ear-drop, snowballs, daffodils. **1892** *Amer. Folk-Lore* V. 94 *Impatiens fulva,* balsam-weed, slipper-weed, lady's ear-drop, Mansfield, O. **1893** *Ib.* VI. 137 *Dicentra spectabilis,* lady's ear-drops, Concord, Mass. **1901** MOHR *Plant Life Ala.* 487 *Brunnichia cirrhosa.* . . . Ladies' Ear Drops.

Lady slipper. =next. {1894–} — **1863** *Horticulturist* XVIII. 127 Lady Slippers . . . are very beautiful. **1872** *Rep. Comm. Agric. 1871* 413 Mr. Rand treats . . . a number of favorite herbaceous flowers, as the lung wort, . . . lily of the valley, the lady-slipper, moccasin.

***Lady's-slipper.**

***1.** Any of several varieties of wild orchid having an inflated lip shaped somewhat like a woman's slipper. (Cf. MOCCASIN FLOWER.)

1738 CATESBY *Carolina* II. 72 *Helleborine.* The Lady's Slipper of Pensylvania. . . . The slipper is of a greenish yellow, with a tincture of red. **1784** CUTLER in *Mem. Academy* I. 486 *Cyrripedium* [*sic*]. Lady's Slipper. . . . Catesby says, the flowers of this plant . . . were in great esteem with the Indians for decking their hair. **1806** LEWIS in *L. & Clark Exped.* V. (1905) 173, I also met with the plant in blume which is sometimes called the lady's slipper or mockerson flower. **1845** JUDD *Margaret* II. i. 193 Chilion brought out a neatly made box in which he wished her to set a venus shoe or ladies slipper. **1893** S. HALE *Letters* 281, I had been to look after the lady's slippers; they are still in bud.

b. With distinguishing adjectives. (See also SHOWY LADY'S-SLIPPER, etc.)

1843 TORREY *Flora N.Y.* II. 287, *Cypripedium acaule.* . . . Noah's Ark. Purple Lady's-slipper. . . . Woods, in both dry and moist situations: not rare. **1893** DANA *Wild Flowers* 180 Pink Lady's Slipper. Moccason-Flower. **1901** MOHR *Plant Life Ala.* 452–3 [Lists three species].

+**2.** The garden balsam, *Impatiens balsamina.*

1836 LINCOLN *Botany* 101 *n.*, The Impatiens of the garden is sometimes called *Ladies'-slipper,* sometimes *Balsamine.* **1857** GRAY *Botany* 74 *I[mpatiens] Balsamina* is the Balsam or Ladies' slipper of the garden. **1892** *Amer. Folk-Lore* V. 94 *Impatiens fulva,* Lady's slipper. Plattsburg, N.Y.; Mansfield, O.

***Lady's-smock.** Also **ladiesmock, ladysmock.** The cuckoo-flower. — **1784** CUTLER in *Mem. Academy* I. 467 *Cardamine.* . . . Ladysmock. Blossoms white. Near small brooks. Not common. May–June. **1791** MUHLENBERG *Index Florae* 174 *Cardamine,* Ladiesmock. **1868** GRAY *Field Botany* 55 *Cardamine pratensis,* Cuckoo-Flower or Ladies' Smock.

+**Lady's-thumb.** The common persicary, having a spike shaped somewhat like a thumb. — **1843** TORREY *Flora N.Y.* II. 149 *Polygonum Persicaria.* . . . Lady's-thumb. . . . Waste places, gardens, and often in low grounds. **1850** S. F. COOPER *Rural Hours* 106 It will be easy to name a number of these, . . . the lady's thumb and May-weed [etc.]. *a*1862 THOREAU *Maine Woods* 319. **1890** *Cent.* 3329/2 *Lady's-thumb,* . . . the common persicaria, . . . so called from its dense oblong reddish spike.

***Lady's-tress, -trace.** Any orchid of the genus *Spiranthes.* Usually pl.

1814 BIGELOW *Florula Bostoniensis* 207 *Neottia cernua.* Drooping Neottia. Ladies traces. . . . In moist ground. **1840** DEWEY *Mass. Flowering Plants* 200 *Neottia tortilis.* Ladies Tresses. . . . [In] cold, wet meadows and pastures. June. **1869** FULLER *Flower Gatherers* 240, I see you have Ladies' Tresses there, Mary. **1887** JACKSON *Between Whiles* 158 A curious little white flower called 'Ladies'-Tress' grew there in great abundance. **1892** TORREY *Foot-Path Way* 208 School-girls and botanists . . . pull up the gerardias and ladies-tresses.

b. With distinguishing adjectives.

1821 *Mass. H. S. Coll.* 2 Ser. IX. 152 *Neottia pubescens,* Blood-vein ladies' tresses. **1843** TORREY *Flora N.Y.* II. 282 *Spiranthes gracilis.* . . . Slender Lady's-tresses. . . . Meadows and dry open woods: common. *Ib.* 283 *Spiranthes cernua.* . . . Nodding Lady's-tresses. . . . Wet meadows and moist thickets: common. **1901** MOHR *Plant Life Ala.* 456–7 [Lists five species].

Lafayette. [f. the Marquis de *Lafayette,* French general (1757–1834).]

+**1.** The spot, *Leiostomus xanthurus.*

1842 *Nat. Hist. N.Y., Zoology* III. 69 The Lafayette . . . visits us in almost incredible numbers at irregular . . . intervals. One of these visits happened to coincide with the arrival of . . . La Fayette at New York, in the summer of 1824. **1855** BAIRD in *Smithsonian Rep.* 329 The Lafayette. . . . When perfectly fresh they are most delicious—excelled in flavor by no species on the coast. **1884** GOODE, etc. *Fisheries* I. 370 The Lafayette, or 'Spot,' . . . is found along our coast from New York to the Gulf of Mexico. **1898** JORDAN & EVERMANN *Fishes No. & Mid. Amer.* II. 1458. **1903** *N.Y. Sun* 15 Nov., The fish are small—something like Lafayettes.

+**2.** The butterfish or dollarfish.

1890 *Cent.* 3329/3 *Lafayette,* . . . a stromateoid fish, *Stromateus triacanthus.* **1896** JORDAN & EVERMANN *Fishes No. & Mid. Amer.* I. 967 *Rhombus Triacanthus.* . . . Dollar-fish; Harvest-fish; Butter-fish; La Fayette. . . . Maine to Florida; very abundant northward.

+**3.** Attrib. with names of articles of food and dress.

1824 *Free Press* (Halifax, N.C.) 3 Dec., Mrs. S. expects to receive . . . an elegant assortment of *La Fayette Bonnets. Ib.,* La Fayette gloves, belts, buckles, &c.—all of which will be sold at the lowest *Petersburg prices.* **1828** LESLIE *Receipts* 67 [Recipe for] Lafayette Gingerbread.

Lafitte. +A follower of Jean Lafitte (died *c*1825), a French pirate operating in the Gulf of Mexico. (Cf. BARATARIAN.) — **1817** *Niles' Reg.* XIII. 289/1 The Barratarians, among whom the Lafittes may be classed foremost, and most actively engaged in the Galvezton trade.

+**Lager.** *ellipt.* =LAGER BEER. — **1855** COOKE *Ellie* 13 He was rotund, red and solemn—'lager' was written in his eyes. **1860** MORDECAI *Virginia* 244 Lager has gone ahead of all other beverages. **1870** WARNER *Summer in Garden* viii, The chair in which the president sat, while declining to take a glass of lager, I have had destroyed. **1883** 'MARK TWAIN' *Life on Miss.* 260 Give an Irishman lager for a month and he's a dead man.

Lager beer. Also **lager bier.**

1. A beer which is slowly fermented at a low temperature and stored for some time in lager casks. {1853 in Germany}

In the United States the term *beer* is now generally equivalent to *lager beer.*

1855 COOKE *Ellie* 212 My frents, . . . h'ist me up one glass of lager bier. **1863** E. DICEY *6 Mo. Federal States* II. 80 Neither for love nor money could a stranger obtain a drink more intoxicating than lager beer. **1872** POWERS *Afoot & Alone* 82, I thought to cheer my thirsty soul with lager beer. It was a very small glass of very mean beer, but the price was twenty-five cents. **1881** *Harper's Mag.* April 716/2 The other great fact in Milwaukee is lager-beer. **1894** ALDRICH *Two Bites* 174 Bleeker and I passed the evening with 'Lager-beer and Meyerbeer,' as my lively kinsman put it. **1901** CHURCHILL *Crisis* 117 [In] South St. Louis . . . lager beer took the place of Bourbon, and black bread and sausages of hot rolls and fried chicken.

2. Attrib. and comb. with *cask, cellar, restaurant,* etc.

1855 THOMPSON *Doesticks* xxxi. 272 Within the American shield, two lager-bier casks supporting a rum-bottle rampant. **1861** *Atlantic Mo.* April 433/1 The long rows of houses, except an occasional lager-bier shop, were closed. **1869** *Overland Mo.* III. 53 Who has not met graduates of the German Gymnasia, all through this country, in the capacity of wood-sawyers, organ-grinders, . . . [and] drivers of lager-beer wagons. **1870** MEDBERY *Men Wall St.* 244 On Williams Street . . . is a basement floor, now radiant with the brass-mounted counters of a flourishing lager-beer restaurant. **1877** W. WRIGHT *Big Bonanza* 80 Mrs. Comstock finally ceased to roam; she came to anchor in a lager-beer cellar in Sacramento.

+**Lager-beer saloon.** A saloon which dispenses chiefly lager beer. — **1855** THOMPSON *Doesticks* 259 Benedict Arnold has opened a Lager-bier saloon, and left a vacancy for S. A. Douglas (white man). **1862** *Ill. Agric. Soc. Trans.* V. 542 Even the sweepings of the whisky and lager beer saloons, will give the market gardener the very element for his business. **1872** *Newton Kansan* 29 Aug. 1/7 A wag, . . . while in Skelian's lager-bier saloon, met an enterprising painter. **1882** *Wheelman* I. 173 [The] enlivening interchanges of sentiment which take place in . . . city lager-beer saloons may also be freely overheard.

+**Lagniappe.** Also **lanyappe,** etc. A small present given when a purchase is made; a gratuity. Also transf.

'*Lagniappe* is composed of the French *la,* "the," and a French adaptation of Spanish *ñapa,* which is taken in turn from Kechuan *yapa,* "a present made to a customer"' (W. A. Read *Louisiana-French* 142).

1849 *Knickerb.* XXXIV. 407/1 Ime sum pumpkins in that line; but he's a huckleberry above my persimmon, and right smart lanyope too, as them creole darkies say. **1853** 'P. PAXTON' *Yankee in Texas* 47 He would usually put off the winner with . . . a dubious note that he had received as 'lanyappe.' **1883** 'MARK TWAIN' *Life on Miss.* i, The English were trading beads and blankets to them [*sc.* Indians] for a consideration, and throwing in civilization and whiskey, 'for lagniappe.' **1893** *Harper's Mag.* Feb. 380/2 'Take that for a lagniappe' (pronounced lan-yap), says a storekeeper [in New Orleans] as he folds a pretty calendar into the bundle of stationery you have purchased. **1897** LEWIS *Wolfville* 267 She'd swap the whole Mexican outfit for a word from Mace, an' throw herse'f in for laniyap. **1910** 'O. HENRY' *Strictly Business* 125 When I got to the hotel I hurriedly paid it the fifty cents it demanded (with approximate lagniappe, I assure you).

Lagoon. Also **lagune.**

1. a. An area of shallow salt or brackish water separated from the sea by sand dunes. {lagoon, 1789–; lagune, 1697–, in Mexico} +**b.** A bay, inlet, or sound, as between the mainland and adjacent islands.

It is not always possible to assign quotations definitely to 1 or 2.

1750 *Georgia Col. Rec.* VI. 349 George Glaner . . . begs to take for his Property that uncultivated Plantation near him at the Lagoon of our long Bridge. **1763** W. ROBERTS *Nat. Hist. Florida* 8 This river running a course of 70 miles nearly South-west, and sometimes almost due South, forms a lagune at the mouth, and enters the gulf of Mexico about four leagues . . . from Pensacola. **1807** *Mass. H. S. Coll.* 2 Ser. III. 56 The common eel is very abundant in all the harbours, lagunes, and ponds. **1827** WILLIAMS *West Florida* 6 The seacoast is indented with bays, bayous, and lagoons, abounding with fish of all kinds. **1836** HOLLEY *Texas* iv. 70 Salt lagunes are scattered in every section of this wide territory. **1865** *Atlantic Mo.* Jan. 77/2 The main-land is . . . separated from it by tortuous and difficult lagoons. **1911** VANCE *Cynthia* 325 That's a siren whistle. . . . Sounded as though it came from the lagoon.

+**2.** A shallow, fresh-water pond or lake, sometimes artificially formed and usually located near or connected with a lake, river, etc. (Cf. next.)

'In regions where Spanish is or formerly was the current language, the word *lagoon* is likely to be used with more latitude of meaning, since in the Spanish language *laguna* is applied to ordinary lakes [etc.].' *Cent.* Use of the word in its broader meanings is not now confined to areas of Spanish influence.

1766 J. BARTRAM *Journal* 31 We rowed to the east-side of the lake, near which is the mouth of a fine lagoon, a mile long and half as wide. **1784** SMYTH *Tour* I. 359 As we descended the stream of the Mississippi we observed several lakes, or as they are termed here *Lagunes,* sometimes on one side, sometimes on the other side of the river. **1802** ELLICOTT *Journal* 136 A continued, and correct survey of this river will scarcely ever be obtained on account of the swamps, lagoons, thickets, etc. **1847** LONGFELLOW *Evangeline* II. 92 Now through rushing chutes, . . . They emerged into broad lagoons. **1872** *Amer. Naturalist* VI. 725 This pond is a fine representative of a peculiar feature of the bottom-lands of the western and southern rivers, locally termed bayous, lagoons or ponds. **1890** HARTE *Waif of Plains* 98 Before them opened a vast expanse of bottom land, slightly sloping on the right to a distant half-filled lagoon. **1893** *Outing* Dec. 210/2 Sydow hurried on . . . across the wide, free spaces of the Exposition grounds. . . . Smooth as a mirror lay the waters of the lagoon. **1897** HOUGH *Story of Cowboy* 15 Sometimes this artificial water supply of the ranch is supplemented by a few natural lagoons of fresh water.

+**Laguna.** [Sp.] **1.** =LAGOON 1 b. **2.** =LAGOON 2. — **(1) 1811** J. BLACK tr. Humboldt *Polit. Essay New Spain* II. 185 Interior basins [along the shores of Santander and Texas] . . . go by the name of *lagunas,* or salt-water lakes. **1854** BARTLETT *Personal Narr.,* II. 532 The navigation here is carried on with boats of light burden through the shallow bays or lagunas, which line the west and north-west shores of the Gulf of Mexico. **(2) 1838** 'TEXIAN' *Mexico v. Texas* 163 The whole company spread themselves about, following the banks of the laguna, and looking for the track. **1856** WHIPPLE *Explor. Ry. Route* I. 61 The stream, as we ascended, bore a greater volume of water; forming lagunas, and fertilizing some very broad bottoms. **1865** NORTON *Army Lett.* 274 Every few miles on the road we came to 'lagunas' or lakes of fresh water, that had no apparent outlet or inlet. **1895** GRAHAM *Stories of Foot-Hills* 162 Every crease and wrinkle in the velvet of the encircling hills was reflected in the blue stillness of the laguna.

Laid work. Couched work; embroidery made by couching. — **1884** *Harper's Mag.* Aug. 346/1 [A silk-canvas foundation for tapestry] resembles, in effect, 'laid-work,' or 'couching,' as seen in the grounds of so many old embroideries. **1891** WILKINS *New Eng. Nun* 95 When Liddy was married she had a whole chistful of clothes, real fine cotton cloth, all tucks an' laid-work.

***Lake.**

***1.** An inland body of water.

1658 *Suffolk Deeds* III. 108 The Lord Protector . . . did giue graunt and Confirme Vnto . . . Thomas Temple and William Crowne, . . . all those Lands, Islands, fforts, Seas rivers Lakes woods vnderwoods, [etc.]. **1692** *Conn. Rec.* IV. 68 Comeing over the lake to doe spoyle upon the plantations in these partes. **1760** *New Eng. Hist. & Gen. Register* XXXVI. 32 On arriving on the Lake, I took the bearing of a Notch or Break in the Mountains. **1798** I. ALLEN *Hist. Vermont* 159 A neck of land, two miles and a half in length, . . . connected the two lakes. **1840** COOPER *Pathfinder* xxix, The Lord who governs the lake and the forest alike . . . keep you happy and worthy to be so! **1882** *Harper's Mag.* March 554/1 The surface of the lake is flecked with the . . . overgrown, and stanch double-enders known as Mackinac boats. **1910** J. W. TOMPKINS *Mothers & Fathers* 204 Their climb terminated on a rocky shelf that hung over a lavish prospect of lakes and glowing hillsides.

+**2.** *pl.* The Great Lakes. (Cf. GREAT LAKE 2.)

1759 P. COLLINSON in Darlington *Memorials J. Bartram & H. Marshall* 217, I don't remember ever reading of any [goats] in the country about the lakes, nor with you. **1798** C. WILLIAMSON *Descr. Genesee* iii, While the Lakes and Alleghany Mountains are in existance so long will the inhabitants of the Genesee Country be blessed with their present temperate climate. **1803** *Steele P.* I. 367 The Ocean, the Mexican Gulf, the Mississippi, & the Lakes must be our boundaries. **1813** *Niles' Reg.* IV. 47/1 This river opposite to Detroit . . . [has] sufficient depth to carry any vessels which navigate the lakes. **1835** HOFFMAN *Winter in West* I. 199 Although one of the most ancient French trading-posts on the Lakes, [Chicago] can only date its growth as a village since the Indian war. **1888** *Forum* June 421 The story of the lakes is not completely told by explaining the origin of their basins.

3. *attrib.* **a.** With reference to navigation on lakes, esp. the Great Lakes.

1814 *Ann. 13th Congress* 1 Sess. I. 1142 They are . . . taking seamen from all their stations to man the Lake fleets. **1835** HOFFMAN *Winter in West* I. 276 A line of four steam-boats, of the largest class of lake-boats, and regular lines of brigs and schooners, are now established. **1842** *Amer. Pioneer* I. 283 He was a lake boatman until some time after the commencement of the war. **1847** ROBB *Squatter Life* 83 The good steamer Constitution, . . . under the care of Doty, one of the best lake engineers. **1891** WELCH *Recoll. 1830–40* 154 Captain Allen, if I be not mistaken, is the oldest Lake captain now living. **1902** WHITE *Blazed Trail* 245 Lake schooners lay in a long row during the summer months.

b. Designating a place or area situated on or near a lake.

1837 W. JENKINS *Ohio Gaz.* 60 Ashtabula, a lake county, situated on the southern shore of lake Erie. **1887** *Courier-Journal* 3 Feb. 2/1 It is nonsense to talk about defending our lake cities by batteries and other works. **1896** *N.Y. Dramatic News* 29 Aug. 12/4 There are now eight lake resorts during [*sic*] a good business here. **1902** WHITE *Blazed Trail* 393 Thorpe descended at Twelfth Street in Chicago. . . . For a moment he faced the long park-like expanse of the lake front.

c. In names of plants.

1817–8 EATON *Botany* (1822) 471 *Sparganium americanum,* lake burreed. . . . Grows plentifully in a small lake in Troy, about a mile east of . . . the Old Bank place. **1839** in *Mich. Agric. Soc. Trans.* VII. 417 *Ranunculus lacustris.* Lake crowfoot. **1847** WOOD *Botany* 455 *L[imnanthemum] lacunosa.* . . . Lake-flower. **1817–8** EATON *Botany* (1822) 400 *Polygonum coccineum,* lake knotweed. **1843** TORREY *Flora N.Y.* II. 412 *Carex lacustris.* . . . Lake Sedge. . . . Deep swamps and borders of lakes.

d. In names of fish. (See also LAKE BASS, HERRING, etc.)

Only a selection of examples is given.

1884 GOODE, etc. *Fisheries* I. 236 The Burbot is known as . . . 'Lake-cusk' in Lake Winnipiseogee. **1842** *Nat. Hist. N.Y., Zoology* IV. 210 The Black-Headed Dace, *Leuciscus atromaculatus.* . . . They are popularly termed Lake Chub and Lake Dace. **1823** COOPER *Pioneers* viii, A great favorite of the epicures . . . bore the title of 'lake-fish.' **1883** *Nat. Muse-*

um Bul. No. 27, 479 Lake Mullet. Great Lakes. Eastern United States from Vermont to South Carolina. **1856** *Porter's Spirit of Times* 20 Dec. 253/2 The same kind of fish [as the pike-perch of the Ohio River], is brought from the lakes and sold in our markets [in Cincinnati], and the fishermen tell me that on the lake shore they are called lake pickerel, but here salmon. **1897** *Outing* Aug. 435/2 Most abundant . . . was the 'sheepshead' (freshwater drum), a good-looking silvery fish, somewhat like the lake shad. **1842** *Nat. Hist. N.Y., Zoology* IV. 73 The Lake Sheepshead, *Corvina oscula*, . . . is a very common fish in Lake Erie. **1863** *Rep. Comm. Agric. 1862* 55 The fishes of Maine . . . which are known to spawn in fresh water [are] . . . lake trout, *Salmo confinis;* lake white fish, *Ceregonus albus* [etc.]. **1883** *Nat. Museum Bul.* No. 27, 422 Lake Whiting. Great Lake Region; lakes of the Adirondacks.

+**Lake bass.** Any of several basses found in lakes. — **1795** J. Scott *U.S. Gazetteer* s.v. *Vermont*, The rivers are stored with a great variety of fish, as . . . a species of fish called lake bass. **1858** *Harper's Mag.* Oct. 621/1, I should not forget to mention a fine brace of lake bass, which Eliphalet . . . had hauled in. **1883** *Century Mag.* July 376/2 The black bass . . . have received names somewhat descriptive of their habitat, as, lake, river, marsh, pond, . . . and Oswego bass.

Lake country. Any of several districts abounding in lakes; the Great Lakes region. — **1826** in Peck *Guide* 205 The lake country is . . . much of it swampy. **1842** *Amer. Pioneer* I. 211 No where was the pressure or want of money more sensibly felt than in the lake country [near Buffalo]. **1848** Thoreau *Maine Woods* 36 The country is an archipelago of lakes,—the lake country of New England. **1873** *Harper's Mag.* Jan. 275/1 Chester is a town in the lake country of New York, quiet, old-fashioned, sleepy, and pleasant.

+**Lake fever.** Malaria. — **1807** C. Schultz *Travels* I. 24 [A town near Lake Ontario] is said to contain about thirty houses, but mostly deserted, on account of what they call the lake fever. **1819** F. Wright *Soc. & Manners in Amer.* (1821) 199 We found the intermitting or *lake* fever, as it is styled in the country, prevailing very generally. **1832** Ferrall *Ramble through U.S.* 82 Whilst on the banks of Lake Erie, having heard a great deal of conversation about the 'lake fever,' I made several inquiries.

+**Lake fly.** 'An ephemerid, *Ephemera simulans*, which swarms on the Great Lakes late in July' (*Cent.*).

+**Lake herring.** One or other of several species of cisco found in the Great Lakes, esp. *Leucichthys artedi:* (see also first quot.). — **1842** *Nat. Hist. N.Y., Zoology* IV. 267 The Lake Moon-eye, *Hyodon clodalis*, . . . is common in Lake Erie. At Buffalo and Barcelona, it is called . . . Lake Herring. **1875** *Amer. Naturalist* IX. 135, I received . . . a collection of deep-water 'Siscoes.' . . . Compared with Coregonus most of the species have a more slender form; hence their popular name of 'lake herrings,' although their resemblance to the sea herring is quite superficial. **1884** Goode, etc. *Fisheries* I. 541 The Lake Herring is one of the most abundant fishes of the Great Lake region. **1902** *Amer. Folk-Lore* XV. 243 [The name *cisco* is] applied to certain species of fish found in the Great Lakes and adjoining waters, . . . [including] the lake herring (*Coregonus artedi*).

+**Lake lawyer. a.** =Dogfish 2. **b.** =Dogfish 3. — **1838** in *Nat. Hist. N.Y., Zoology* IV. 270 The *Dog-fish* is found in Lake Erie, where it is frequently called *'The Lake Lawyer.'* **1848** Bartlett 198 Lake Lawyer . . . [or] the Western Mud-fish . . . is found in Lakes Erie and Ontario, where it is known by the name of Dog-fish. **1896** Jordan *Check-List N.A. Fishes* 495 *Lota maculosa* [is called] . . . Burbot; Lake Lawyer; Ling; Alekey Trout.

+**Lake port.** A port, harbor, or town on the shore of a lake, esp. one of the Great Lakes. Also attrib. — **1872** *Atlantic Mo.* April 455 There is no difficulty in determining the number who landed at our sea-ports and the lake-ports since October 1, 1819. *Ib.* 456 These, with the 31,987 presumed to have come across the border, added to the sea-port and lake-port arrivals, make 200,000. **1881** *Harper's Mag.* April 707/2 All lake-port and sea-port citizens are very familiar with [grain elevators] . . . and their use. **1893** *Advance* 10 Aug. 606/3 [Work like that of the Boston Seaman's Friend Society] ought to be inaugurated in every seaport and lakeport of considerable size.

Laker. {1798–}

+**1.** One accustomed to boating on a lake or lakes; one who works on a lake steamer.

1838 Cooper *Home as Found* xix, After fishing a few hours, the old laker [Captain Truck] pulled the skiff up to the Point. **1840** — *Pathfinder* xxv, Jasper, as a laker, . . . knows all that is necessary to be done on the water. **1900** 'Flynt' *Notes Itinerant Policeman* 157 [The] rough element . . . is composed largely of 'lakers,' men who work on the lakes during the open season.

+**2.** One or other species of lake trout, esp. *Cristivomer namaycush.*

1823 Cooper *Pioneers* xxiv, I see a laker there, that has run out of the school. **1853** Lowell *Writings* I. 41 Telemachus caught a laker of thirteen pounds and a half. **1876** *Wide Awake* 145/1 You must state that this is no laker nor togue, but a genuine spotted trout. **1884** Goode, etc. *Fisheries* I. 488 The Lake Trout has other appellatives, such as . . . 'Tyrant of the Lake,' 'Laker,' 'Red Trout.'

+**3.** A lake steamer; *spec.*, one operating on the Great Lakes.

1882 *Tenth Census* VIII. IV. 221 A representative laker is the Boston, a fine steamer, carrying 83,000 bushels of wheat. **1887** *Century Mag.* Aug. 484/2 A twenty-foot laker can slip through any lock without scratching her paint.

+**4.** (See quotation.)

1905 *Forestry Bureau Bul.* No. 61, 41 *Laker*, a log driver expert at handling logs on lakes. (N[orthern] F[orest].)

+**Lake sailor.** One employed as a sailor on a boat operating on the Great Lakes. — **1881** *Harper's Mag.* Jan. 219/2 The poor parson's cooking was passed from one incompetent hand to another—lake-sailors' wives, wandering emigrants, moneyless forlorn females [etc.]. **1898** *N. Amer. Rev.* June 723 Whalebacks, or 'pigs,' as the lake sailors call [Great Lakes steamers of a certain type]. **1922** Parrish *Case & Girl* 244 Neither Hogan, nor the man Mark, bore any resemblance to a lake sailor.

+**Lake salmon.** A species of large trout (*Cristivomer namaycush*) found in the Great Lakes. — **1842** *Nat. Hist. N.Y., Zoology* IV. 239 The well known Lake Salmon . . . appears to possess all the coarseness of the halibut, without its flavor. **1856** *Porter's Spirit of Times* 20 Dec. 253/1 Dr. Unzicker . . . was confident . . . that the Ohio fish called salmon is identical with the lake salmon. **1884** *Century Mag.* Dec. 202 The Indians were sent down to our old camp on the lake for a couple of loads of lake salmon. **1911** *Rep. Fisheries 1908* 311.

+**Lake state. 1.** A state bordering on one of the Great Lakes. **2.** (Both words usually capitalized.) Michigan. — **(1) 1845** *S. Lit. Messenger* XI. 578/1 The Lake States will be there, with their plans for the common defence and their own safety in war. **(2) 1871** De Vere 660 Michigan, surrounded by the four magnificent lakes, . . . derives from this position also the name of *Lake State.* **1875** *Chambers's Jrnl.* 13 March 171/2 Michigan is Lake State or Wolverine State; Wolverines, not Lakers, have there a habitation.

+**Lake steamer.** A steamer operating on a lake, esp. on one of the Great Lakes. — **1847** *Knickerb.* XXX. 456 He has been inspired by looking down through the iron foot-grating of a great lake-steamer. **1850** *Ib.* XXXVI. 295 It is to be regretted that the cars reach the lake-steamer by a route so circuitous. **1882** *Harper's Mag.* March 554/1 The lake steamers pass by [the shores of the islands in L. Mich.] . . . unless in need of wood. **1888** Ferguson *Exp. Forty-Niner* 11 [At Cleveland] I embarked on the lake steamer *A. D. Patchen* for Chicago. *c***1900** R. L. Hale *Log of Forty-Niner* 101 He had been away from home for a number of years, acting as captain of a lake steamer.

Lake trout. {1668–} Any one of several varieties of trout or salmon found in lakes, +esp. the salmon trout of the Great Lakes. — **1830** *Cabinet of Nat. Hist.* I. 147 In the outlet, or stream from the lake [Silver Lake, Penna.], none of the lake trout were ever found. **1839** Hoffman *Wild Scenes* 31 Storing our canoe with a good supply of brook and lake trout. *a***1862** Thoreau *Maine Woods* 271 In the midst of our dreams of giant lake-trout, . . . our fisherman drew up a diminutive red perch. **1888** *Outing* July 307 Lake trout, white fish, and black bass from the State hatchery were put in plentifully fifteen years ago. **1897** *N.Y. Forest, Fish, & Game Comm. 2d Rep.* 225 *Cristivomer namaycush*, . . . Lake Trout; Salmon Trout.

+**Lallygag,** *v. intr.* To fool around, or carry on. Also *vbl. n. colloq.*[2] — **1890** *Amer. Folk-Lore* III. 311 Lallygag.—To 'spoon,' make love. Maine. **1893** M. A. Owen *Voodoo Tales* 160 He bin kip 'wake o' nights a-lissenin' at de gigglin' an' lallygaggin' (humbugging, chaff). **1902** Lorimer *Lett. Merchant* 224 The old fellows were playing poker in the smoking-room and all the young ones were lallygagging under the boats.

+**Lamanite.** According to the Book of Mormon, a follower of Laman, cursed with a dark skin. Applied by Mormons to the American Indians. — **1830** *Book of Mormon* (1920) Jac. 3: 5 The Lamanites your brethren . . . ye hate because of their filthiness and the cursing which hath come upon their skins. **1862** *N. Amer. Rev.* July 199 Besides the white Gentiles . . . there are 'Lamanites,' which is the Saints' name for Indians.

***Lamb.**

***1.** A young sheep.

1643 *Suffolk Deeds* I. 42 [They] granted unto Richard Russell of Charlstowne thirty Sheepe & Lambs. **1760** Washington *Diaries* I. 127 Sent 4 Yews and Lambs to the mill to be fatted. **1851** T. D. Price *Diary* (MS.) 19 June, Dipped the lambs in tobacco [juice] today [to kill sheep ticks]. **1906** Pringle *Rice Planter* 326 There is one splendid ram and the lambs are beauties.

2. The meat of the lamb, used for food. {1620–} Also attrib. and fig.

1784 Cutler in *Life & Corr.* I. 99 A fine house, and grand provisions—cucumbers, peas, lamb, etc. **1840** *Picayune* 15 Oct. 2/2 She would have given the Recorder his 'lamb and sallad,' a figurative expression, the literal meaning of which we could not precisely comprehend. **1865** Stowe *House & Home P.* 248 All the edible matters . . . would form those delicate dishes of lamb-chop, which . . . are so ornamental. **1898** Page *Red Rock* 301 One came in an old wagon and brought two or three chairs . . . ; another sent over a mahogany table; a third came with a quarter of lamb.

+**3.** An inexperienced speculator who loses money in the stock market. {one who is cheated, esp. at cards, 1668–}

1880 *Cimarron News & Press* 18 March 2/3 Messrs. Chaffee and Elkins have been unloading lately to the detriment of eastern lambs. **1886** Gladden *Applied Christianity* 204 A recent estimate . . . puts the amount of which the 'lambs' are shorn in the New York stock market alone at eight hundred million dollars a year. **1894** Leavitt *Our Money Wars* 252 Two thousand millions were added to the nominal values of stocks, which were afterward unloaded upon the 'lambs.' **1900** NELSON *A B C Wall St.* 150 *Lamb*, a novice in Wall Street.

Lambaste, *v.* {1637-} +*tr.* To scold severely. Also *vbl. n. slang.* — **1886** *Harper's Mag.* July 321/2 A more complete lambasting and more vigorous and thorough roasting than Wise gave Boutelle was never known. **1893** *Ib.* Feb. 483 You never heard such a lambasting as he gave me in your life, all the time keeping a running fire at me, asking what I was 'in for,' etc. **1908** *Springfield W. Repub.* 26 March 5 They may be exhorted in sermons, lambasted in presidential messages, ridiculed in newspaper paragraphs. **1923** NUTTING *Massachusetts* 61 [We] have in our generation lambasted our ancestors for their lack of artistic appreciation.

Lambkill. {1888} +The sheep laurel, *Kalmia angustifolia.* — **1814** BIGELOW *Florula Bostoniensis* 103 *Kalmia angustifolia*, . . . a low shrub with rose coloured flowers, very common in low grounds, and known by the names *sheep poison, lambkill, low laurel,* &c. **1832** WILLIAMSON *Maine* I. 116 Lamb-kill . . . has been called mountain Laurel, Spoonwood, Ivy and Calico Bush. Its wood is dense and hard. *a***1862** THOREAU *Maine Woods* 314 *Kalmia angustifolia* (lamb-kill). **1898** CREEVEY *Flowers of Field* 515 Lambkill . . . is a low shrub . . . with narrow, evergreen leaves in whorls of three.

Lambrequin. {1725-} +A narrow valance hanging from a shelf or from a casing at the top of a window. — **1872** *Rep. Comm. Patents 1870* 40/2 Claim.—The construction of lambrequins in sections, which can be adjusted to windows of different sizes. **1875** STOWE *We & Neighbors* 23 Visions of certain brackets and lambrequins that are to adorn my spare chamber visit my pillow nightly. **1887** ALDEN *Little Fishers* x, Their pinkish lambrequins of the same gay-flowered goods as the sofas, had been cut and scalloped. **1920** LEWIS *Main Street* 233 She pictured . . . a suite in Paris, immense high grave rooms, with lambrequins and a balcony.

***Lamb('s-)lettuce.** Corn salad, *Valerianella locusta.* — **1817-8** EATON *Botany* (1822) 280 *Fedia olitoria*, lamb lettuce. E[xotic]. **1848** BARTLETT 136 *Fetticus*, . . . corn salad, or lamb's-lettuce. **1889** *Amer. Notes & Q.* IV. 22 The plant called corn-salad, or lamb-lettuce, is called *fetticus*, or *vettekost*, by gardeners.

Lamb's-quarter(s). The goosefoot. Commonly used for greens. {1773-} — **1804** CLARK in *Lewis & C. Exped.* I. 1(904) 79 In those small Praries or Glades I saw wild Timothy, lambs-quarter, Cuckle burs, & rich weed. *a***1862** THOREAU *Maine Woods* 311 Plants commonly regarded as introduced from Europe: . . . *Plantago major* (common plantain), *Chenopodium album* (lamb's-quarters) [etc.]. **1875** BOURKE *Journal* 1 June, A couple of principle [*sic*] dishes were furnished by the country. Roast Elk meat and lambs-quarter boiled as greens with bacon. **1886** EBBUTT *Emigrant Life* 75 Lamb's quarter . . . in the spring, when young, was cooked and eaten like spinach.

***Lamb('s-)tongue.** +One of several American plants as the yellow adder's-tongue. — **1873** MILLER *Amongst Modocs* x. 128 [Winter] cut down the banners of the spring that night, lamb-tongue, Indian turnip and catella. **1894** *Amer. Folk-Lore* VII. 102 *Erythronium Americanum*, lambs' tongues, Banner Elk, N.C.

+**Lame distemper.** (See quotations.) *Obs.* — **1733** *S.C. Gazette* 221/2 A Receipe, being an effectual Cure for all Distempers arising from an inveterate Scurvy, such as the Yawes, Lame Distemper [etc.]. **1775** ROMANS *Nat. Hist. Florida* 249 The chronic diseases are . . . among blacks the leprosy, elephantiasis, and body yaws; which last in Carolina is called the lame distemper.

Lame duck. {1761-} +An officeholder who has not been re-elected, esp. a defeated member of the short session of Congress after a November election. Also attrib. (Cf. DEAD DUCK.)

By the 20th amendment to the Constitution the lame duck session of Congress was abolished in 1933.

1863 *Congress. Globe* 14 Jan. 307/1 In no event . . . could it [the Court of Claims] be justly obnoxious to the charge of being a receptacle of 'lame ducks' or broken down politicians. **1910** *Springfield W. Repub.* 8 Dec. 1 The Congress which assembled Monday for its last session is full of what they call 'lame ducks,' or representatives who failed of re-election in November and senators who will fail when the Legislatures meet. **1910** *N.Y. Ev. Post* 8 Dec. 8 'Lame Duck Alley' . . . is the name they [*sc.* reporters] have given to a screened-off corridor in the White House offices, where statesmen who went down in the recent electoral combat may meet. **1924** *Outlook* 17 Dec. 627/1 A 'lame duck' Congress is not likely to be very competent, because it is not really representative. **1925** G. W. NORRIS in *Independent* 21 Feb. 213/1 The proposed Constitutional amendment . . . has been usually designated as the 'lame-duck' amendment.

***Lamp.** A device for utilizing oil, electricity, or other means for the purpose of illumination. (Cf. ELECTRIC LAMP, etc.)

1622 'MOURT' *Relation* 142 Bring . . . cotton yarne for your Lamps. **1684** I. MATHER *Providences* (1856) v. 101 The man, at his going to bed, put out his lamp. **1730** J. SECCOMB *Father Abbey's Will* xii, A rusty Lamp, Two Quarts of Samp, And half a Tallow Candle. **1771** *Phila. Ordinances* (1812) 36 At such other times and places as they, the said wardens, shall appoint, to maintain, preserve and take care of the lamps already erected. **1846** *29th Congress 1 Sess.* H. R. Doc. No. 140, 1321 My improvement in the lamp for burning lard and other fatty substances. **1879** *N.Y. Tribune* 22 Dec. 4/4 The new Sawyer-Man-Edison lamp . . . will probably prove a useful addition to other forms of electric lighting. **1909** *Sears, Roebuck & Co.* Cat. No. 118, 712 This is a very large and effective lamp for very little money. **1923** *Ladies Home Jrnl.* Dec. 34/1 A carefully chosen lamp is one of the nicest of Christmas gifts.

Lamper eel. a. =LAMPREY. {1824-} (Cf. LAMPREY EEL.) +**b.** *New Eng.* The eelpout or mutton fish, *Zoarces anguillaris.* — [**1709** *N.H. Hist. Soc. Coll.* III. 53 Edward Taylor was slain by the Indians at Lamper-eel river.] **1834** C. A. DAVIS *Lett. J. Downing* 23 Mr. Van Buren hung on like a lamper-eel, till he was kinder jerked up like a trounced toad. **1884** GOODE, etc. *Fisheries* I. 247 The Mutton-fish, . . . called Congo Eel . . . and also Lamper Eel, especially by Maine fishermen, is often seen near the shore north of Cape Cod. **1897** *Outing* Aug. 440/1 The lamprey, or lamper-eel, may once have been considered a delicacy.

Lampist. One engaged in the manufacture or repair of lamps. {1839-} — **1876** *U.S. Official Register 1875* 224 S. V. Poor, lampist. **1889** *Ib. 1889* I. 247 George King, Lampist [Chicago Post Office].

Lamplighter.

1. A man employed to light street lamps. {1750-}

1774 *Boston Selectmen* 1 March, Edward Smyth [is] to have £.40- Ster[lin]g . . . for overseeing the Lamps & Lamplighters. **1850** S. WARNER *Wide, Wide World* i, The lamp-lighter . . . hooked his ladder on the lamp-irons, ran up and lit the lamp. **1885** *Wkly. New Mexican Rev.* 15 Jan. 4/5 A well known colored citizen, for three years employed as lamp-lighter for the City Gas Company, was . . . severely beaten. **1907** *Outlook* 4 May 5/1 A strike of street lamplighters . . . was declared in New York City last week.

+**2.** A slim roll of paper or similar device used to light lamps.

1833 NEAL *Down-Easters* II. 115 One side is clean, said she—and it will do for lamplighters! **1849** J. D. WHITNEY *Life & Lett.* 103, I very deliberately rolled the letter up into lamplighters. **1859** *Harper's Mag.* Feb. 342/1 Mr. Beebe tore off the margin of the newspaper and commenced rolling a lamp-lighter after the most approved pattern. **1893** *Ib.* April 760/1 Mrs. Franklin . . . knocked off a chair accidentally the lamplighters which she had just completed.

+**3.** (See quot. 1876.)

*a***1876** *Ohio Fish Comm. 1st Rep.* 77 *P*[*omoxys*] *hexacanthus.* . . . Strawberry Bass; . . . Lamp-lighter, of Portsmouth; Grass Bass, of Kirtland. **1911** *Rep. Fisheries 1908* 308.

+**Lamp mat.** An ornamental mat on which to set a lamp. — **1854** *Penna. Agric. Rep.* 139 [A prize was given] To Mary Jane Schofield, for a Lamp Mat. **1887** WILKINS *Humble Romance* 99 With Mrs. Hemans' poems and the best lamp in a bead lamp-mat on it. **1893** 'MARK TWAIN' in *Harper's Mag.* CIV. 602/1 Wall-paper and framed lithographs, and bright-colored tidies and lamp-mats, and Windsor chairs.

Lamp-post. 1. A post, usually of iron, supporting a street lamp. {1790-} +**2.** A shell used by the Northern forces during the Civil War. *colloq.* — **(1) 1797** *Phila. Ordinances* (1812) 146 If any person . . . shall . . . destroy . . . any of the public lamps, lamp-posts, watch-houses, . . . [he] shall forfeit and pay . . . one hundred dollars. **1871** *Chicago Tribune* 6 Oct. 1 A lamp-post . . . still marks . . . the names of two beautiful streets. **1885** *Wkly. New Mexican Rev.* 5 Feb. 4/5 It is unlawful to throw stones at, climb upon or hitch horses or other animals to street lamp posts. **1910** TOMPKINS *Mothers & Fathers* 107 Under the next lamppost he paused and . . . noted down a name and address. **(2) 1885** *Century Mag.* XXX. 449/2 The gun-boats . . . opened fire, . . . throwing those awe-inspiring shells familiarly called by our men 'lamp-posts,' on account of their size and appearance. *Ib.*, The Yankees throwed them lamp-posts about too careless like.

***Lamprey.** Any one of various eel-like, scaleless fishes having a jawless, suctorial mouth. (Cf. LAMPER EEL a.)

1612 SMITH *Virginia* 15 Of fish we [have] . . . Rockfish, Eeles, Lampreyes. **1705** BEVERLEY *Virginia* II. 31 There come up likewise into the Freshes from the Sea, . . . some few Lampreys, which fasten themselves to the Shad. **1832** WILLIAMSON *Maine* I. 153 The Lamprey is . . . darker coloured and less slimy than a silver eel. **1909** *St. Nicholas* May 651/2 In the spring lampreys in large numbers ascend the streams and even waterfalls to their spawning places.

b. With distinguishing adjectives.

1839 STORER *Mass. Fishes* 195 *P*[*etromyzon*] *Americanus.* . . . The American Lamprey. . . . This species . . . is taken in large quantities in the Merrimack River, at Lowell. *Ib.* 197 *P. nigricans.* . . . The bluish Lamprey. . . . This species . . . is frequently affixed to mackerel. **1842** *Nat. Hist. N.Y. Zoology* IV. The Small Lamprey, *Petromyzon appendix*, . . . from the Hudson river. *Ib.* 383 The Plain Mud Lamprey. *Ammocoetes unicolor.* . . . Its popular name in this state is Lamper Eel. **1877** *Ohio Fish Comm. 1st Rep.* 50 *Petromyzon nigrum*, . . . Black Lamprey. *Petromyzon argenteus*, . . . Silvery Lamprey. *Ammocetes bicolor*, . . . Blind Lamprey. **1885** [see LAMPREY EEL].

Lamprey eel. The sea lamprey (*Petromyzon marinus*), found in inland waters during spawning season, or a related fish.

[**1726** PENHALLOW *Indian Wars* 31 Next day, they kill'd Edward Taylor near Lamprey-Eel River.] **1789** MORSE *Amer. Geog.* 208 About four miles northeast of Providence lies a small village . . . famous for lamprey eels. **1831** R. COX *Adv. Columbia River* 85 We got . . . some lamprey eels, . . . which were oily and very strong. **1844** LEE & FROST *Oregon* xv. 156 A fire was struck, some dried salmon and lamprey-eels roasted; and we sat down and made a good hearty Indian supper. **1883** *Harper's Mag.* Dec. 102/1 Very similar in its habit of erecting a nest is the lamprey-eel (*Petromyzon marinus*). **1885** *Amer. Naturalist* Sept. 922 The lamprey eel of Kansas . . . proves to be usually the *chestnut* lamprey.

Lancasterian, Lancastrian, *a.* [Joseph *Lancaster*, Eng. educator (1778–1838).] *Educ.* Pertaining to the monitorial method of instruction in schools. {1807–} — **1815** *Niles' Reg.* IX. 152/1 A 'Lancastrian' seminary at Cincinnati, received more than four hundred scholars in the course of the first week. **1822** *Missionary Herald* XVIII. 107 A school house, 24 feet by 36, is nearly completed, constructed on the Lancasterian plan, and designed to accommodate 100 children. **1836** EDWARD *Hist. Texas* 120 All ought to be taught to read and write by the priests and Lancasterian schools which have been established in many places. **1861** *Amer. Jrnl. Education* X. 362 Lancasterian or Monitorial Schools were established in New York, Albany, . . . Washington, and other principal cities, which . . . finally have lost all the distinctive features of the original model.

***Lance. a.** A military weapon consisting of a long wooden staff with a sharp-pointed metal head; a similar instrument used for killing large game. Freq. used by Indians. Also attrib. **b.** An early form of bayonet. *Obs.* — **1687** SEWALL *Diary* I. 193 His Excellency with . . . 15 or 20 Red-coats with small Guns and short Lances in the Tops of them, set forth for Woodcocks. **1808** PIKE *Sources Miss.* III. App. 10 Their other weapon of offence is a lance of 15 feet in length. **1854** BARTLETT *Personal Narr.* I. 329 Their bows, arrows, and lances were the same. **1907** J. R. COOK *Border & Buffalo* (1938) 80 There would be from ten to fifteen lance horses, and each lancer would be armed with a lance-blade about fourteen inches long, fastened by sinews to a staff seven to eight feet long.

Lance-leaved, *a.* Also **lance-leaf.** +In the names of American plants: (see quotations). {1811–} — **1785** MARSHALL *Amer. Grove* 108 Lance-leaved Balsam Tree (*Populus balsamifera lanceolata.*). **1843** TORREY *Flora N.Y.* I. 72 *Viola lanceolata*. . . . Lance-leaved Violet. . . . Wet meadows; common in the valley of the Hudson. **1897** SUDWORTH *Arborescent Flora* 143 Lanceleaf alder. *Ib.* 275 Lanceleaf Dwarf Sumach. **1901** MOHR *Plant Life Ala.* 632 Lance-leaf Loosestrife. . . . Central Prairie region to Coast plain. Low damp places. Montgomery and Mobile counties. *Ib.* 633 Lance-Leaf Meadow Beauty.

***Lancer.** +**1.** A hunter who kills buffalo, etc., by means of a lance. **2.** *pl.* A form of quadrille. {1862–} — **(1)** **1854** BARTLETT *Personal Narrative* I. 360, I also had with me a Mexican lancer, . . . to direct us to . . . the watering places. **(2)** **1860** in Christy *Ethiopian Joke Book No. 3* 70, I always knew you could dance *quadrilles* and excelled in de *lancers*, but now I find you can't be beat at a *break-down*. **1884** RITTENHOUSE *Maud* 274, I had promenaded a double length in one figure of the lancers with Mr. Carnes. **1891** WELCH *Recoll. 1830–40* 378 The attractive military formal dance, 'The Lancers,' the outcome of the Crimean War, did not become a fashionable dance here until somewhere about 1855. **1902** LORIMER *Lett. Merchant* 148 Doc . . . wasn't one of those elders who would let a fellow dance the lancers if he'd swear off on waltzing.

***Land,** *n.*

I. ***1.** Ground or territory viewed as a property, either private or public. (Cf. PUBLIC LAND.)

1627 *Plymouth Laws* 29 It was agreed in a full court about division of lands as followeth. **1645** *New Haven Col. Rec.* 199 A certayne quantity of land, fit for a small plantation, hath bin purchased of the Indians. **1717** *Mass. H. Rep. Jrnl.* I. 196 A Petition . . . praying that 600 Acres of Land . . . may be laid out in some Unappropriated Land of this Province. **1778** *Jrnls. Cont. Congress* X. 406 Every soldier who shall accompany his captain shall receive fifty acres of land, one ox, one cow, and two hogs. **1803** *Statutes at Large* II. 225 The following several tracts of land in the state of Ohio . . . are hereby appropriated for the use of schools in that state. **1873** *Republic* I. 33 The law . . . gives to every soldier who desires it for a homestead, one hundred and sixty acres of land, free of cost. **1913** *Indian Laws & Tr.* III. 556 The price of said lands entered as homesteads under provisions of this act shall be as follows.

2. In grandiloquent or high-flown phrases meaning +**a.** America or the United States.

1770 *Boston Chronicle* 1 March, The said horse . . . was not imported from England, but manufactured in this land of liberty. **1817** PAULDING *Lett. from South* II. 209 He heard of America, the Sweet Land of the Exile, where the industrious stranger is ever welcome. **1825** NEAL *Bro. Jonathan* II. 67 America—as everybody knows, *there*—is the land of liberty and equality. **1861** NEWELL *Orpheus C. Kerr* I. 196 Our Union, my boy—our Land of the Eagle—is stricken sorely. **1885** BAYLOR *On Both Sides* 10 Even in the 'land of the free,' . . . there was something about her that made Bridget stammer when asking if she was the woman that wanted a 'gurl.'

+**b.** A particular state or region of America. (Cf. LAND OF STEADY HABITS.)

1817 PAULDING *Lett. from South* I. 83 The prospect . . . will allure many of the young ones of the East, to the Land of Promise in the West. **1830** ROYALL *Southern Tour* I. 168 He was another great, over-fed glutton, and from the land of snags [Vermont]. **1856** P. CARTWRIGHT *Autobiog.* 22 Many hard and bloody battles were fought, and thousands killed on both sides; and rightly was it [Kentucky] named the 'land of blood.' **1861** Moore *Rebellion Record* I. III. 92/2, I wish I was in de land o' cotton, . . . In Dixie land. **1868** *N.Y. Herald* 2 July 4/2 From Maine, the land of lumber, there is a respectable share of a delegation. *c***1873** DE VERE *MS. Notes* 661 *Oregon*=Land of Red Apples. **1883** WILDER *Sister Ridnour* 110 Adeline had the pleasure . . . of seeing Evangeline and her mother start for the land of perpetual youth [Florida]. **1887** *Three* (San Francisco) Aug. 3/2 Let the California Amateurs all join hands and cry, 'Hurrah for our land of gold!'

+**3.** In exclamations and exclamatory phrases. (See also GOOD LAND, LAND ALIVE, LAND'S SAKE.)

1825 NEAL *Bro. Jonathan* I. 108, I know *you;* don't care for *you;* land o' liberty; walk *into* you, any time, for half a sheet o' gingerbread. **1880** *Harper's Mag.* Dec. 91 Land! ef I was to set sail on them seas o' divinity I should be . . . drownded right off. **1882** *Century Mag.* July 341 Land knows I've had to drown every blessed batch [of kittens]. **1885** HOWELLS *S. Lapham* xvii, Why, what in the land *did* he want? **1885** JACKSON *Zeph* 17 Land o' the livin'! What a hole! **1887** *Little Fishers* iv, I wish to the land you could have such a comfortable room all the time. *Ib.* xiv, 'For the land of pity!' said Mrs. Decker. **1901** CHURCHILL *Crisis* 364 My land! . . . there's no doubt about your sentiments, anyhow. **1918** LINCOLN *Shavings* 224 'Miss her! My land of Goshen!'

II. *attrib.* and *comb.*

+**4. a.** Designating various agencies, instruments, actions, etc., that pertain to the disposal and settlement of unoccupied or public land.

1831 PECK *Guide* 316 Hillsboro' [contains] . . . a post office, a land agency office by John Tillson, Esq., and a Presbyterian meeting-house. **1868** in *S. Dak. Hist. Coll.* I. 456 [The] tract, when so selected, certified, and recorded in the 'land book,' . . . shall cease to be held in common. **1854** BENTON *30 Years' View* I. 116/2 He voted against . . . all the modern revolutionary pensions and land bounty acts. **1873** EGGLESTON *Myst. Metrop.* 320 The collapse of the land-bubble and the opening of railroads destroyed it. **1833** S. SMITH *Major Downing* 119 So you see, I am pretty well to live in the world, without any of your land speculations. I cant seem to see how 'tis they all make money so fast in that land business. **1841** *Diplom. Corr. Texas* III. (1911) 247 The preliminary arrangements Mr. Burnley and myself have made with certain land emigrating companies. **1814** *Steele P.* II. 728, I have sealed and placed it [the certificate] to the credit of your Accot. in payment for the Land-Entry above mentioned. **1845** KIRKLAND *Western Clearings* 2 A friend . . . became quite a proficient in the mysteries of land-finding. **1868** *N.Y. Tribune* 11 July 5/3 Kansas Land-Frauds. **1871** *Rep. Indian Affairs* (1872) 269, I should think money might be obtained from the 'land fund.' **1873** *Newton Kansan* 9 Jan. 2/2 It beats all the land gobbles and swindles that the country has ever yet seen. **1876** W. M. FISHER *Californians* 114 'Land grabs,' 'mining grabs,' [etc.] . . . are enabling a few persons 'to fill themselves with gold as a sponge fills itself with water.' **1839** Land-hunting [see LAND-LOCATOR]. **1872** *Chicago Tribune* 27 Dec. 4/7 Crafty politicians lifted up by railroad and land jobs and all sorts of rings have been able to control Legislatures in other States. **1910** J. HART *Vigilante Girl* 46 His opinion was asked by a street tribunal over a 'land-jumping.' **1911** *Okla. Session Laws* 3 Legisl. 332 The assessor shall keep a book to be known as the 'land list.' **1884** HARRIS *Mingo* 65 The Hog Mountain land-lot covered a vein of gold. **1882** THAYER *From Log-Cabin* 100 It is certain that the opportunity to labor in that State came to him through the 'Western land mania.' **1845** KIRKLAND *Western Clearings* 5 Watching the land-market for bargains. **1916** *Statutes at Large* XXXIX. I. 361 Farm loan registrars . . . [shall] have no connection with . . . the business of making land mortgage loans or selling land mortgages. **1854** BENTON *30 Years' View* I. 106/2 The new States of the West were the sufferers by this federal land policy. **1842** *Whig Almanac 1843* 17/2 The Whigs contend that the Land Proceeds should be fairly and equally distributed to the several States. *a***1844** *Indiana Mag. Hist.* XXII. 376, I then set out into the land purchase in search of such a quarter of land as I have never seen. **1830** *Congress. Deb.* 26 Feb. 210/1 The task will be comparatively easy of striking out a plan for the final adjustment of the land question. **1814** *Steele P.* II. 730, [I] am hurried by those who wish land Receipts &c. and therefore do not recollect any other business done by the Assembly which would be new to you. **1854** BENTON *30 Years' View* I. 12/2 The passage of this land relief bill was attended by incidents which showed the delicacy of members at that time. **1801** *Spirit Farmers' Mus.* 205 He bought lands in Boston at the time all their great men got caught in the Georgia land trap.

+**b.** Designating persons involved in the business of disposing of and settling on unoccupied or public land.

1898 *Scribner's Mag.* XXIV. 425/1, I should have suspected a land-boomer in the doctor had there been anything aggressive or boastful in his manner. **1798** I. ALLEN *Hist. Vermont* 27 These severities were used . . . to prevent aid being given to the land claimants of New York. **1846** MACKENZIE *Van Buren* 260 He was a land contractor. **1873** 'MARK TWAIN' & WARNER *Gilded Age* 279 He's made the riffle on the Injun; great Injun pacificator and land-dealer. **1896** *Congress. Rec.* 16 March 2840/2 [Many men have had] to spend all they have . . . to purchase the claims of professional land jumpers. **1894** *Congress. Rec.* 11 July 7339/2 This bill is in the interest of land lawyers, and no other class of citizens. No . . . honest man can afford to support it. **1848** IRVING *Knickerb.* (rev. ed.) II. ix, He was accompanied by Mynheer Ten Breeches, as land-measurer, in case of any dispute with the Indians. **1798** I. ALLEN *Hist. Vermont* 21 In the mean time the persecutions of the settlers were carried on by the Governor and his land-monopolists. *Ib.* 43 The plan of the land monopolizers of New York was . . . to occupy the lands contiguous to Champlain. **1887** *Courier-Journal* 2 Feb. 5/4 The country is full of land prospectors. **1853** J. W. BOND *Minnesota* 364 Land-Receiver at Stillwater—William H. Holcombe, of Minnesota . . . Land-Register at Stillwater—T. M. Fullerton, of Minnesota. **1845** GREEN *Texian Exped.* xvii. 319 The old governor . . . [demanded] what that land robber meant by insulting him. **1860** GREELEY *Overland Journey* 84 We are far beyond the stakes of the land-surveyor. **1776** *Vt. Hist. Soc. Coll.* 17 The Monopolising Land Traders of New York . . . did present a petition.

5. Designating birds and animals that live on land.

*c***1830** in *Waldie's Select Library* II. 88/2 A vast number of the small land crabs . . . occupy burrows or caves dug in the marshy soil. **1866** HOLMES in Morse *Life O. W. Holmes* I. 8 Story about his talking of 'land-eels,' meaning *snakes* thereby. **1836** HOLLEY *Texas* 104 Land and water moccasin, coach whip, and copper heads are the only venomous snakes, besides the rattlers. **1844** LEE & FROST *Oregon* 71 Beaver was valued at two dollars per skin, though worth five dollars; land otter at fifty cents, though worth five dollars. **1836** HOLLEY *Texas* 107 Of the testaceous animals or shell fish, the most prominent are the oyster . . . and land-snail. **1676** GLOVER *Va.* in *Phil. Trans.* XI. 631 There are also some other sorts of Land-Snakes, all of which are more or less venemous; besides there are very many Water-Snakes, that keep the Springs and Rivers. **1709** LAWSON *Carolina* 133 The Land-Terebin is of several Sizes, but generally Round-Mouth'd, and not Hawks-Bill'd.

6. Designating vehicles, routes, etc., that pertain to travel or transportation on land.

*a***1861** WINTHROP *J. Brent* 98 The great blue land-arks, each roofed with its hood of white canvas stretched on hoops. **1829** *Amer. Traveller* 14 Sept. (Ernst), The engraving above exhibits what may emphatically be called a Land Barge . . . with a Cabin, Births, etc. below, . . . a promenade deck, awning, seats, etc. above. **1855** BARNUM *Life* viii. 205 At Vicksburg we sold all our land-conveyances, excepting four horses and the 'band waggon.' **1862** MOORE *Rebellion Rec.* V. II. 246 Our tremendous land-fleet was sailing down two roads. **1850** *Rep. Comm. Patents 1849* 600 Snow . . . causes the wheels of land locomotives to slip upon . . . the rail. **1835** *Diplom. Corr. Texas* I. (1908) 53 You will write in duplicate and order one to be forwarded by the Land Mail by way of Fort Jessup. *a***1846** *Quarter Race Ky.* 115 [Uncle Billy] was well known as the captain of a 'land-packet'—in plain terms, the driver of an ox-team. **1775** ADAIR *Indians* 318 From that place, the land-path was mostly level. **1862** MCCLELLAN in *Own Story* 234 The second base of operations . . . affords the shortest possible land route to Richmond.

+7. Special combinations.

Land association, an association that invests money in land and land mortgages; *l. day*, a day formerly set aside for the sale of land warrants; *l. fence*, a fence on land as distinguished from one on the water's edge; *l. hog*, one who destroys the fertility of land by improper farming; *l. scout*, (see quot. 1741); *l. security*, land used as security for the issuance of currency; *l. state*, a state in which public lands are open to homestead; *l. waiter*, a customs-control officer formerly at the harbor in New York.

1644 *Southampton Rec.* I. 34 The little common shall be sufficiently fenced . . . both for land fence and for water fence. **1714** *Mass. Bay Currency Tracts* 134 Our Fathers about Twenty eight years ago, entred into a Partnership to Circulate their Notes founded on Land Security, stamped on Paper, as our Province Bills. **1741** *Georgia Hist. Soc. Coll.* II. 114 That the indented servants . . . when their time of servitude was expired, were under the necessity of listing in the service of a bad paymaster, or starving, because there was a land scout and water scout to keep them from leaving the place by land or water. **1763** HABERSHAM *Letters* 10 The Governor [of S.C.] . . . has issued Warrants the last Land Day to the amount of four hundred thousand acres. **1774** *Doc. Hist. N.Y. State* I. 760 The Custom House officers are Eight in Number; viz. The Collector, . . . Land Waiter, Tide Surveyor and Three Tide Waiters [etc.]. **1874** *Penna. Laws* 99 All land and building associations are hereby authorized to make sale of . . . the ground-rents created as aforesaid. **1900** *Congress. Rec.* 4 Jan. 648/1 [The bill] will give to the land States . . . 5 per cent . . . upon all lands that were disposed of by bounty land laws. **1913** LONDON *Valley of Moon* 432 'Land-hogs,' he snapped. 'That's our record in this country.'

***Land,** *v.* **+1.** *tr.* To drive (a sheep) out of a dipping basin. **+2.** *intr.* Of a plow: To furrow into the ground. **+3.** To run *out* on a person; to leave. *slang.* — **(1) 1856** *Mich. Agric. Soc. Trans.* VIII. 166 The sheep may be 'landed.' **(2) 1857** *Lawrence* (Kan.) *Republican* 18 June 4 If it [the plow] lands too little, regulate it the other way. **(3) 1882** MCCABE *New York* 393 When he was tired of me he landed out, an' I've never seen him since.

Land agent. {1846-}

+1. An official of Massachusetts or Maine who administered public lands in the state of Maine. Now hist.

By the terms governing the separation of Maine from Massachusetts in 1820 the latter state retained for some years title to a large portion of the public lands in Maine.

1828 *Maine Laws* III. (1831) 243 The Land Agent . . . is hereby authorized to execute deeds [etc.]. **1829** *Mass. Resolves* 116 The Report of the Land Agents of the sales they have made of the Public Lands. [**1833** in *Pres. Mess. & P.* III. 423 A letter . . . complaining of the 'conduct of certain land agents of the States of Maine and Massachusetts in the territory in dispute between the United States and Great Britain.']

+2. An agent of a land company or of a land-owning railroad; a broker or agent who helps settlers acquire title to public or private land.

1847 ROBB *Squatter Life* 124 The Land Agent . . . informed the unsuspecting squatter, that the stranger had . . . entered the claim. **1870** 'O. OPTIC' *Field & Forest* 282 Matt owns the quarter section, as an actual settler. I found the paper signed by a land agent. **1883** *Harper's Mag.* Nov. 943/2 To read the 'land agents' literature' of the railroads which have land to sell in it [Missouri] one would think it a veritable land of Goshen. **1890** *Stock Grower & Farmer* 22 Feb. 8 Upson and Garrett, Land Agents and Conveyancers, Roswell, New Mexico.

+Land alive. A mild expletive. (Cf. LAND *n.* 3.) — **1865** A. D. WHITNEY *Gayworthys* 324 Land alive! Why, Grace, child, what's happened you?

Landau. A four-wheeled closed carriage, the top of which, divided into halves, can be closed or thrown open. {1743-} — **1759** *Penna. Gazette* 19 Nov. 1/3 Coaches, chariots, landaus, phaetons, two and four wheeled chaises, open or close, to take off and fix on, as occasion may require. **1851** LONGFELLOW in S. Longfellow *H. W. Longfellow* II. 210 Drove down to Nahant in a landau. **1912** IRWIN *Red Button* 38, I hired a landau from a livery-stable, an' every day I drove up Fifth Avenue.

Land bank.

1. A bank that issues currency notes secured by landed property {1696-}; +esp., the land bank organized in 1740 in Massachusetts. Now hist. Also attrib.

The early quotations relate only to proposed land banks as a means of obtaining more currency. (Cf. MANUFACTURE BANK.)

1714 *Let. from One in Boston to Friend in Country* 2, I apprehend they had left the foundation too fluctuating and changeable for a Land Bank [for Mass.], . . . tho' the Possessor of the Bills Emitted, had good Security. **1720** J. COLMAN in *Mass. Bay Currency Tracts* 367 That a suitable Sum be agreed on, and that a Land Bank be Erected, for we have no other Foundation to build upon. **1731** *Money the Sinews of Trade* 6 Had we [in Mass.] Gold & Silver, there would not be occasion for a Land Bank, or any other at present. **1740** DOUGLASS *Discourse Currencies* 42 Land . . . rises in Denominative Value . . . . Hence it is, that a Land Bank is so much desired, by those who are in Debt or Mortgage. **1766** ROWE *Diary* 99, [I] heard the tryal between the Commissioners of the Land Bank & the Heirs. **1832** WILLIAMSON *Maine* II. 203 Such was the 'Land Bank.' . . . As soon as the establishment of the Bank was known in England, the Parliament dissolved the Company. **1898** *Quart. Jrnl. Econ.* XIII. 70 A Connecticut Land Bank of the Eighteenth Century.

+2. a. One of twelve federal banks authorized in 1916 to facilitate loans on farm lands. Usually *federal land bank.* Also attrib.

1916 *Statutes at Large* XXXIX. I. 362 The Federal Farm Loan Board shall establish in each Federal land bank district a Federal land bank. **1916** MYRICK *Fed. Farm Loan System* 67 All directors of the land bank must have been residents of the district for at least two years.

+b. (See quot. 1917.)

1917 *Fed. Land Bank of Baltimore Circular No. 1*, 1 National Farm Loan Associations are in reality cooperative land banks, . . . organized to obtain through Federal Land Banks mortgage loans on lands:—they are chartered corporations under a law of Congress. **1923** *Joint Stock Land Bank Bonds* 22 The mortgages made by the San Antonio Joint Stock Land Bank have averaged only 40.1% of such valuations.

+3. Attrib. and comb. with *apartment, appraiser, bill*, etc.

1741 *Boston News-Letter* 1-8 Jan. 2/2 To be Sold for Land Bank Money. **1741** *Ib.* 5 Feb. 2/1 There is good . . . Wheat to be sold . . . for Bills of Credit of any Currency except those Bills call'd Manufactory or Land Bank Bills. **1741** in Williamson *Maine* II. 208 It was moulded to the liking of the land bank party and others. **1813** BENTLEY *Diary* IV. 152, I visited the Land Bank apartment in the State House. **1916** *Statutes at Large* XXXIX. I. 361 The Federal Farm Loan Board shall appoint . . . one or more land bank appraisers for each land bank district and as many land bank examiners as it shall deem necessary.

+Land banker. One who advocated or supported the Massachusetts land bank. — **1741** B. LYNDE *Diary* 162 Election, where most of the number were Land Bankers, Capt. Watts for Speaker and negatived.

+Land bill. A legislative bill relating to the sale or the granting of public lands. — **1806** *Balance* V. 326/3 The refusal . . . to deliver up the documents relative to the land bills of this state. **1833** *Niles' Reg.* XLIV. 1/1 If the land-bill fails in the house, some also believe that the tariff bill will hardly pass the senate. **1842** *Whig Almanac 1843* 32/1 His Land Bill was again brought up by Mr. Clay. **1857** *Harper's Mag.* March 550/1 The New York *Times* . . . affirmed that proofs of the truth of the accusation could be produced, . . . specifying in particular the case of the Minnesota Land Bill. **1873** *Newton Kansan* 27 Feb. 2/1 The soldiers' bounty land bill has been adversely reported.

‖**Landboard.** [On the analogy of *seaboard.*] The land bordering on the western frontier. — **1790** JEFFERSON *Writings* XVII. 306 If Great Britain establishes herself on our whole land-board our lot will be bloody and eternal war. **1793** *Ib.* III. 277 The position and circumstances of the United States leave them nothing to fear on their land-board. . . . But on their sea-board they are open to injury.

Land carriage.

1. Conveyance or transport by land. {1613–}

1734 *Boston Rec.* 81 Grain, Meal, Apples, . . . brought into the Town by Land carriage, may be sold. **1775** *Jrnls. Cont. Congress.* III. 269 Your Committee think Provision should be made to facilitate Land Carriage. **1792** IMLAY *Western Territory* 35 There is scarce any place in all the back parts of America, where art may not reduce the land carriage to a very small distance. **1847** COYNER *Lost Trappers* 157, 'I am confident,' says he, 'in asserting there can be established the best communication on this side of the Isthmus of Darien, between the Atlantic and Pacific oceans; as, admitting the utmost, the land carriage would not be more than two hundred miles.'

+**2.** In contrast to a boat, a vehicle for use on land.

1800 HAWKINS *Sk. Creek Country* 30 Wood for fuel is at a great and inconvenient distance, unless boats or land carriages were in use. **1816** *Ann. 14th Congress* 1 Sess. 30 Mr. Ruggles presented the memorial . . . praying the renewal of his patent right to certain improvements in propelling vessels and land carriages. **1859** *36th Congress 1 Sess.* H. R. Rep. No. 648, 740 A temporary contract has recently been awarded . . . for the conveyance of the United States mail . . . in steamships, steamboats, and land carriages.

+**Land certificate.** A negotiable certificate guaranteeing to the grantee the ownership of a given amount of public land; a certificate of ownership of a certain tract of public land. Also in ellipt. contexts. — **1837** in Gouge *Fiscal Hist. Texas* (1852) 70 The acting paymaster-general had issued upwards of thirty thousand acres of land-certificates for discharged soldiers. **1838** *Indiana Mag. Hist.* XXII. 451 He was to pay in land and made an assignment on a land certificate on which Goldsby lived. **1883** *Rep. Indian Affairs* p. xxv, Payne issues 'land certificates' to persons who do not desire to go down themselves by which he guarantees them 160 acres of land in the 'Oklahoma Colony.'

+**Land claim.**

1. A claim to a given portion of public land, based upon the claimant's conforming to the requirements of the land law; the land involved in such a claim. (Cf. CLAIM *n.* 2.)

1812 *Steele P.* II. 695 In the prosecution of several very valuable land claims in Tennessee, I have to encounter a set of men well practiced in the art of forging. **1851** *Harper's Mag.* III. 276/1 The Governor of Maine . . . complains of the illiberal conduct of Massachusetts, in regard to the land-claims within the State of Maine. **1877** JOHNSON *Anderson Co., Kansas* 110 In November, 1858, a Free State squatters' court was organized . . . for the trial of contested land claims, etc. **1907** C. C. ANDREWS *Recoll.* (1928) 84 There is a store there, and a registry of land claims has been established there by the squatters.

b. The document certifying this claim.

1847 ROBB *Squatter Life* 117 Dick Kelsey's Signature to his Land Claim.

2. In formerly Spanish areas, a claim on land based upon a Spanish or Mexican grant.

1860 *Statutes at Large* XII. 71 The private land claims in the Territory of New Mexico . . . are hereby confirmed. **1825** *Austin P.* (1924) II. 1061 He advises his sone to not sell his land claims in Texas.

Land company. {1630} A company which deals in land, +esp. in the promotion of settling the West.

1805 *Ann. 8th Congress* 2 Sess. 1044 Having never thought of purchasing any land from the Georgia land companies, I made no inquiry about the acts of the Legislature. **1833** *Knickerb.* I. 283 'Look,' said an old man . . . to the agent of the land company. **1854** LOWELL *Writings* I. 72 Nothing else but an American land-company ever managed to induce settlers upon territory of such uninhabitable quality. **1865** *Atlantic Mo.* XV. 193 The Scioto Company turned out to be a swindling land-company, the precursor of many that have resembled it. **1887** *Courier-Journal* 11 Jan. 4/7 A full car-load of Montgomery investors left for booming Decatur tonight for Gordon's organization, the Decatur Land Company. **1909** RICE *Mr. Opp* 107 Mr. Opp . . . set to work to call a meeting of the Turtle Creek Land Company.

Land crab. 1. A crab that lives mostly on land. {1638–} +**2.** A landsman. *slang.* — (1) **1624** SMITH *Virginia* v. 200 Land Crabs . . . as thicke in their Borowes as Conies in a Warren. **1839** KEMBLE *Journal* 136, I encountered a curious creature walking all sideways, a small cross between a lobster and a crab. One of the negroes to whom I applied for its denomination informed me that it was a landcrab. (2) **1861** *New Haven Palladium* 27 Dec. (Chipman), We 'Old Whales' . . . are not supposed by some 'land-crabs' to have much of a taste for the feathery tribe done up brown.

+**Land district.** One of the districts into which a territory or state is divided for convenience in the disposition of public land. Also attrib.

1812 *Ann. 12th Congress* 2 Sess. 28 The Board of Land Commissioners, for the western land district in the State of Louisiana. **1817** *Ann. 14th Congress* 2 Sess. 873 A bill, to define and enlarge the boundaries of the land district of Edwardsville, in the Illinois Territory. **1831** PECK *Guide* 257 The State is divided into land districts, which are designated by Congress. **1849** CHAMBERLAIN *Ind. Gazetteer* 24 In every land district is a land office where all the public lands belonging to that district are sold. **1857** in *36th Congress 1 Sess.* H. R. Rep. No. 648, 172 After concluding your investigations in the Delaware district, you will then immediately proceed to the *Pawnee land district* land office at Lecompton. **1883** *Rep. Indian Affairs* 187 An Act to create three additional land districts in the territory of Dakota.

+**Landeritt chaise.** A kind of chaise: (see LANDRIGHT). — **1761** *Boston Post Boy* 1 June 4/2 A new Landeritt Chaise . . . to be sold.

+**Land fever.** A powerful urge to acquire title to public land. With special reference to the speculations of 1835. — **1840** *Knickerb.* XVI. 205 'Seeing is believing,' certainly, in most cases; but in the days of the land-fever we who were in the midst of the infected district scarcely found it so. **1849** *Ib.* XXXIII. 174 A young man . . . was at that time (in 1835, the season of the 'land fever,') stopping in 'our village.'

Land-grabber. One who seizes land unfairly or selfishly. {1880–} — **1860** *Richmond Enquirer* 7 Aug. 1/7 (Th.), Is not John Bell an outrageous land-grabber? **1871** *Rep. Indian Affairs* (1872) 576 But for the agitation constantly kept up by land-grabbers and sharks generally, . . . they would soon be a prosperous and happy people. **1885** *Wkly. New Mexican Rev.* 5 March 3/4 After the close of this [Mexican] war there poured in from 'the states' a hungry hord[e] of land-grabbers and official schemers. **1900** *Congress. Rec.* 30 Jan. 1311/2 We had also become a world power among the land grabbers, and had become one of the family of nations to oppress and subject the weak and feeble.

+**Land grant.**

1. A grant of public land made to a railroad, a school, etc.

The first federal land grant to a railroad was to the Illinois Central R.R. in 1850. (Cf. CANAL LAND, LAND *n.* 1, quot. 1803, SCHOOL LAND.)

1862 *N.Y. Tribune* 21 March (Chipman), Some years since, the movement for a Pacific Railroad, attended by an enormous land-grant, assumed proportions that indicated the probable success of the movement. **1871** *Republican Review* 18 Feb. 1/3 The company that own the above Railroad and its munificent land grant made by Congress in 1866 have their road completed 315 miles southwest from St. Louis. **1883** *Harper's Mag.* Nov. 938/2 Congress . . . gave a land grant of 12,800 acres per mile in the States . . . to aid in the construction of the [Northern Pacific] road. **1895** *Dept. Agric. Yrbk. 1894* 91 After the passage of the Morrill act of 1862 the legislature of New York voted to give the whole of New York's share of the land grant to the 'People's College.' **1903** E. JOHNSON *Railway Transportation* 315 This agitation for the repeal of the land grants was due in part to the popular feeling against railroads that developed in connection with the effort to subject railroad corporations to public control.

2. In areas formerly Spanish, a grant of land made by the Spanish or the Mexican government.

1865 *Wkly. New Mexican* 16 June 2/2 Any man who can't see it, is an enemy to wholesale swindles in land grants, to speculation upon 'lo! the poor Indian.' **1877** H. C. HODGE *Arizona* 47 Near the upper part of the San Pedro Valley is one old Spanish-Mexican land-grant, said to be the only one in the Territory which is legal and valid. **1890** *Stock Grower & Farmer* 22 Feb. 4/4 Land grants in New Mexico do not cover but a small proportion of its immense area. **1900** *Congress. Rec.* 3 Jan. 637/2 Also, a bill . . . to confirm to the city of Albuquerque, in the county of Bernalillo and Territory of New Mexico, the Villa de Albuquerque land grant.

3. Attrib. in sense 1 with *act, bill, company,* etc.

1869 *Kansas Pacific Ry. Gold Loan* 5 Dabney, Morgan & Co. [etc.] . . . have accepted the Agency of the Kansas Pacific Railway Company for the sale of its new Seven Per Cent. Gold-bearing Railroad and Land-Grant Sinking Fund Bonds. **1873** *Newton* (Kan.) *Kansan* 13 March 2/1 The trunk lines are mainly land-grant roads. **1873** *Republic* I. 47 There are sixty-seven land-grant railroads in the United States. **1884** *Congress. Rec.* 27 June 5695/2 The vote by which the Backbone Railroad land-grant bill had failed to pass. **1895** *Dept. Agric. Yrbk. 1894* 96 The shares of the several States under the land-grant act of 1862 ranged from 24,000 acres for Alabama to 990,000 acres for New York. **1900** *Congress. Rec.* 4 Jan. 648/2 Patents subsequently issue from the Government to the land-grant company.

+**Land grant college.** Any state college created by the Morrill Land Grant Act of 1862, 'donating public lands to the several States and Territories which may provide colleges for the benefit of agriculture and mechanic arts [etc.].' — **1889** *Century Mag.* Jan. 404/2 The land-grant colleges graduate men fitted to superintend farms and workshops. **1917** *Bureau Ed. Bul.* No. 38, 37 The work of teacher training in the land-grant colleges. **1918** *Ib.*, No. 13, 5 The land-grant colleges have . . . led to the establishment of several new professions, to the stimulation of new achievement in both the great industrial fields to which they minister.

***Landgrave.** {A German title} +In the Carolina colonies, a county nobleman. Now hist.

1669 *Fundamental Constitutions of Carolina* ix, There shall be just as many landgraves as there are counties, and twice as many cassiques, and no more. **1679** *Warrants for Lands in S.C.* II. (1911) 3 You are forthwith to admeasure and lay out unto James Colleton one of the Landgraves of this province six hundred acres of land in some convenient place. **1702** *S.C. Statutes* I. (1836) 42 The upper house, consisting of the Landgraves and Casiques, . . . are . . . a middle state between Lords and Commons. **1706** *N.C. Col. Rec.* I. 638 The said Colony was divided into four Estates (viz) The Lords Proprietors or their Deputies, Landgraves Cassiques and Freeholders. **1738** BYRD *Dividing Line* (1901) 77 Neither land-graves nor Cassicks can procure one drop for their wives. **1884** *Century Mag.* Jan. 437/1 Smith was raised to the rank of landgrave, and made governor of the colony three years after the success of his rice-patch [in 1696].

+**Land-hunter.** One who searches for land for speculative purposes or with intention of settling on it.

1816 U. BROWN *Journal* I. 367 This John Hall was a Land Speculator & a Land Hunter & Informed him of the Vacancy. **1834** *Visit to Texas* xxiii. 214 These persons, commonly called land-hunters, were almost all from the United States, and generally from the South Western States. **1845** HOOPER *Simon Suggs' Adv.* 36 Rival land-hunters [were] intent upon the acquisition of the same 'first-rate eighty.' **1885** *Graceville* (Minn.) *Manuscript* 11 April 2/3 An O'Neill land-hunter, just returned from the Santee-Sioux reservation, says that between the Indians and local land-sharks the white folks will stand little or no show of securing locations. **1894** *Outing* June 172 Four or five rough-looking men—evidently land-hunters.

* **Landing.**

1. A place for discharging passengers or goods from a boat. {1609–1793} Often in place names.

1658 *Md. Council Proc.* 356, I doe charge him with ... Lewd behaviour Comitted on board of Covills ship Rideing in St. Georges River ... to Mr. Edward Packers Landing & from that Landing ... up the River to Mr. Thomas Mathews. **1729** *Md. Gazette* 3 June, [He] keeps carts and Horses, for carrying Goods by Land between ... Apoquinomy and Bohemia Landings. **1736** *Md. Hist. Mag.* III. 34, I made Directly to my Landing, where I kept my Flat. **1831** PECK *Guide* 17 Boats ply regularly from St. Louis to the towns and landings on its banks. **1857** *Lawrence* (Kan.) *Republican* 4 June 3 [It] possesses, without doubt, one of the best levees and the most unchanging landings, of any town in Kansas on the Missouri river. **1884** 'MARK TWAIN' *H. Finn* xiii, She was a visiting there at Booth's Landing.

+**2. a.** *S.* (See quotation.)

1844 *Zoologist* II. 706 Every extensive planter, whose estate borders on the [Alabama] river, has what is called a landing; that is a large building to contain bales of cotton.

+**b.** *Lumbering.* (See quot. 1902.)

1868 *Harper's Mag.* March 420/1 We emerged from the thick timber into an opening through which ran Tibbet's Brook. Here was what is called the 'landing.' ... We could see thousands of logs which had been cut and hauled from the surrounding forests. **1902** W. F. FOX *Hist. Lumber Industry N.Y.* 25 Logs ... were hauled ... to the shore of some stream, where they were piled in huge tiers on the 'banking grounds' as they were called on the Susquehanna, or 'landings' or 'rolling-banks,' in northern New York.

***3.** The action of coming to land, +with special reference to the landing of the Pilgrims in 1620.

1802 *Columbian Centinel* 22 Dec. 2/3 The 'Sons of the Pilgrims' will this day celebrate the 181st anniversary of the landing of The Fathers at Plymouth. **1826** [see FOREFATHER('s) DAY]. **1882** *Nation* 20 July 50/2 [You attempt to prove] that the design of the celebration of the 22d December has always been to commemorate the landing of the colonists from the *Mayflower*, and not from the shallop.

+**Landing day.** Any of various days commemorated in honor of the first landing in America of certain explorers or colonizers. — **1832** WATSON *Hist. Tales N.Y.* 19 The memorable *landing day* of the discoverer [Henry Hudson] and his crew was on the 3d September, 1609. **1845** — *Philadelphia* I. 15 The arrival, or *landing day* of Penn [Oct. 27, 1682], as a commemorative occasion, is but a modern institution, originally got up in 1824.

* **Landing place.** =LANDING 1.

1636 *Essex Inst. Coll.* VII. 19 All the Canooes ... shall be brought ... vnto the Cove of the common landing-place of the North River. **1679** *Manchester Rec.* 16 The current standing price of Coard wood at the landing place at Ketle Cove is ... four shillings 6d acoard. **1724** *New-Eng. Courant* 17–24 Aug. 2/2 To be sold, a very good Farm, situate at Woburn, ... within a mile of Mistick-Pond landing Place. **1752** in *Travels Amer. Col.* 315 Arrived at the landing place at the west end of the great bay. **1818** FLINT *Lett. from Amer.* 79 There is no wharf or artificial landing place [at Wellsburgh]. **1856** J. REYNOLDS *Peter Gott* (B.), The owners of vessels [in fishing districts] have a flake-yard in the vicinity of the landing-places, to which the fish are carried on being landed. **1893** *Harper's Mag.* May 818/1 This was the business centre of the town, because here were the landing places.

+**b.** A town at which river boats regularly call.

1818 FLINT *Lett. from Amer.* 103 Limestone ... is a considerable landing place on the Kentucky side of the river Ohio. **1831** PECK *Guide* 287 Chester is a landing place, and a river port on the Mississippi.

Land-jobber. Also **land-gobber.** +One who acquires title to, or speculates in, large tracts of public land with the purpose of later selling them in smaller lots. Now hist. {of private land *a*1745}

*c***1753** in Gist *Journals* (1893) 229 The late Governor and Council having made out large Grants to private persons Land-gobbers, to the amount of near 1,400,000 Acres. **1789** MORSE *Amer. Geog.* 261 The governors were many of them land-jobbers. **1812** MARSHALL *Kentucky* 105 The Indiana Company, was also a combination of land-jobbers, ... whose object was to engross western lands. **1842** in *Amer. Pioneer* I. 7 These land-jobbers were alarmed at this hostile carriage of the Indians.

Land-jobbing. Speculation in land. Used attrib. — **1781** *Mass. H. S. Coll.* 2 Ser. I. 186 Toryism, British interest, and Land-jobbing views, combine numbers without and within doors. **1825** DOUGHERTY *Light to People of Ky.* 1 It was the case of ... the first settlers of Kentucky ... against ... the famous John Kercheval, of land jobbing memory. **1885** *Century Mag.* April 826 When the bill to establish a State park at Niagara was on its passage, ... the great majority of the country members were opposed to it, fearing that it might conceal some land-jobbing scheme.

***Landlady.** A woman who rents a room, house, etc., to a person; also, a woman who keeps an inn or tavern. {1654–} — **1681** *Boston Rec.* 149 The Church [to pay] 31d. to his Landladie mony due to her. **1704** S. KNIGHT *Journal* 27, [I] left my Great Landl[ad]y with her Talkative Guests to themselves. **1810** M. DWIGHT *Journey to Ohio* 34 We stopt ... at a dismal looking log hut tavern. The landlady (I hate the word but I must use it,) talk'd about bigotry. **1898** HARPER *S. B. Anthony* I. 139 We stopped at a little tavern where the landlady was not yet twenty.

* **Land law.** +A law relating to ownership of land, esp. to the proving up of a land claim.

1812 MARSHALL *Kentucky* 122 By the land-law, commissioners were to be appointed ... to hear, determine and settle, all disputes relative to land-claims. **1837** *Diplom. Corr. Texas* I. (1908) 274 My interest in regard to the Land Law remains unabated. **1850** FILLMORE in *Pres. Mess. & P.* V. 87, [I] call your attention to the propriety of extending at an early day our system of land laws, ... over the State of California and the Territories of Utah and New Mexico. **1886** *Century Mag.* Nov. 12/1 The land laws of Kentucky had reduced to something like order the chaos of conflicting claims arising from the various grants ... under which settlers occupied their property. **1900** HANDSAKER in *Pioneer Life* 26 John and George bought the right to a choice tract of land [in Oregon] ... on the division line so that each could occupy the same house and still comply with the donation land laws then in force.

+**Land-layer.** *New Eng.* A town official whose duty was to lay out land for occupancy. Now hist. — **1673** *Essex Inst. Coll.* XXXVII. 221 Any two of those aforesayd land layers may act according to order from the town. *Ib.*, The town did chuse William Gager ... & John Coffin to be land layers and apoynted them to lay out John Gamedge's land & meadow.

+**Land-leaguer.** A member of an association of Kansas settlers on the Osage ceded lands, organized to fight the railroads' claims to their land. Now hist. — **1878** BEADLE *Western Wilds* 432 In August, 1873, I took a flying tour through the new counties in Southern Kansas. It was the year of Grangers, *land leaguers* and war on the railroads.

+**Land loafer.** [Cf. Ger. *landläufer.*] **a.** A landlubber. **b.** One who is unsettled in life; an idler. — **1836** *Knickerb.* VII. 21 'T would be too bad ... to be ... laughed at int' the bargain by every yaw-hawing land-loafer, about the borough. **1840** HOFFMAN *Greyslaer* II. 50 Kit, you land-lougher, stand up and measure heights with the capting. **1856** *Porter's Spirit of Times* 18 Oct. 113/1 Squirrels ... may still be ... ignobly plundered with shot-guns by land-loafers.

+**Land-locator.** One who seeks out or locates land. — **1816** BROWN *Journal* I. 364 Those present Land Locaters Surveys will hold good. **1839** *Congress. Globe* App. 23 Jan. 265/1 Land hunting soon became a distinct and profitable profession. Hence, sir, in the legal vocabulary of the day, the land 'locator' was as familiarly known by his name as the attorney and clerk of the court by their respective titles.

+**Land-locked salmon.** One or other variety of salmon which does not leave inland waters; spec., *Salmo sebago*, of northern New England. — **1869** *Rep. Comm. Agric. 1868* 324 The taking of trout and land-locked salmon by any other means than by hook and hand-line is prohibited. **1871** *Harper's Mag.* Aug. 466/1 Of great interest to American sportsmen ... are the so-called 'landlocked salmon,' found in Maine and elsewhere. **1884** Goode, etc. *Fisheries* I. 470 The 'Land-locked' or 'Freshwater' Salmon ... probably never visit salt water. **1892** *Vt. Agric. Rep.* XII. 157 Our waters abound in ... land-locked salmon, ... pike perch, and pickerel.

+**Landlooker.**

1. A person claiming to have looked at and appraised all the land in a given area: (see quotation). Now hist.

1840 *Knickerb.* XVI. 206 Another class of operators ... became popularly known as 'land-lookers.' These met you at every turn, ready to furnish 'water power,' 'pine-lots,' 'choice farming tracts,' or any thing else, at a moment's notice.

2. *Lumbering.* One employed to look for valuable timberland; a cruiser.

1887 *Courier-Journal* 2 Feb. 5/4 Most of these land-lookers come from the great Northwest. **1891** *Voice* 15 Oct., I took what woodsmen call a 'land-looker,' i.e. a timber expert whose business it is to locate pine timber land in Michigan. **1900** BRUNCKEN *N. Amer. Forests* 81 This has given rise to a peculiar class of people variously known as woodsmen, cruisers, landlookers, whose business it is to give information as to the existence of pine timber, its location, amount, value. **1902** WHITE *Blazed Trail* 116 This is the usual method of procedure adopted by landlookers everywhere.

+**Land-looking.** Used attrib. in senses: **1.** Looking for land on which to settle. **2.** Looking for and appraising tracts of timber. — (1) **1840** THOMPSON *Green Mt. Boys* II. x. 260 Remington seemed ... convinced that it would not be prudent to proceed any further in the land-looking excursion. (2) **1902** W. HULBERT *Forest Neighbors* (1903) p. xiii, Some thirty years ago, while out on one of his landlooking trips in the woods of Northern Michigan, my father came upon a little lake.

***Landlord.**

***1.** An owner of land; a person who leases land or houses to a tenant.

1662 *R.I. Col. Rec.* I. 477 Such as are in possestion of any such possestions as lands, howses, . . . may not . . . keepe out ther landlords out of ther sayd possestiones. **1728** *N.J. Archives* I Ser. V. 226 Land is so plenty and so very cheap in America, that there is no such thing as tenants . . . for every man is a landlord in fee of what he possesses. **1882** McCabe *New York* 331 Landlords reap a rich harvest here. **1911** *Okla. Session Laws* 3 Legisl. 146 The tenant, with the assent of the landlord, continues to occupy the premises after the expiration of the term [etc.].

2. The keeper of an inn, hotel, etc. {1654–}

1733 Byrd *Journey to Eden* (1901) 283 The Entertainment we met with was the less sumptuous by Reason of our Landlord's Indisposition. **1789** Low *Politician Outwitted* I. ii, Landlord Tipple, that keeps the ale-house at the sign of the Turk's Head. **1865** S. Andrews *South since War* 288 The landlord . . . reckoned he would have to get a stove into the office of the hotel pretty soon. **1900** Stockton *Afield & Afloat* 405 The landlord of the inn . . . was called upon to preside.

+Land lottery. **1.** A business in which land is disposed of by a lottery. **2.** A lottery in which the prizes are land. — **(1) 1808** Ashe *Travels* iv. 34 He could purchase a share in a capital house; or he might buy a land-lottery. **(2) 1832** Williamson *Maine* II. 530 Another expedient, which met with some success, was a *land-lottery*.

***Landmark.**

***1.** An object placed to mark a boundary of a piece of land.

1637 *R.I. Col. Rec.* I. 28 The oake tree having four marks [to serve] . . . till some other land marke be set for a certaine bound. **1645** *New Haven Col. Rec.* 174 Thomas Robinson was chardged for remoueing some land marks in Mr. Hooks & setting new stacks in Wm. Fowlers meddowe. **1674** *Jamaica* (L.I.) *Rec.* I. 79 A sertaine white oake tree marked for a Land Mark. **1782** Trumbull *M'Fingal* III. 106 Then stopp'd and seiz'd the stone that lay, An antient land-mark near the way. **1836** *Diplom. Corr. Texas* I. (1908) 90 All bona fide grants of land . . . shall not be adjudged defective for any failure to comply with . . . erecting land marks, paying annual fees . . . and the like.

2. An object or event of historic significance. {1859–}

1838 *S. Lit. Messenger* IV. 114/1, I felt inclined to . . . inquire for the ancient landmarks of the southern campaign. **1888** Roosevelt in *Century Mag.* May 39/1 The trail made by Custer's baggage train is to this day one of the well-known landmarks. **1908** 'O. Henry' *Roads of Destiny* 57 Citizens will gather at the nearest corners and weep over the destruction of a dear old landmark.

+3. *Landmark Baptist*, (see quotation).

1905 *Dialect Notes* III. 85 *Landmark Baptist.* Name used by and of that Baptist sect which stresses what it regards as the ancient landmarks, or, original principles of Baptist Christianity. [N.W. Ark.]

Land-monger. =Land-jobber. {1647} — **1776** in Rauck *Boonesborough* 234 People could make entries without money and without price; the country abounded with land-mongers. **1781** *Mass. H. S. Coll.* 2 Ser. I. 187 Any thing that can operate the delay and defeat of a measure, calculated . . . to preclude the avaritious views of certain Land mongers, will be industriously pressed. **1806** *Balance* V. 77/2 Much said he of land mongers. **1853** 'Ramsey' *Tennessee* 92 Land mongers penetrated fearlessly into the wilderness.

+Land office.

1. An office established by a colony, a state, or the federal government, in which business concerning public land is transacted.

Cf. General land office.

1681 *Md. Archives* VII. 242 An Act relating to the Land Office also passed in these words. **1759** Franklin *Hist. Rev. Penna.* 48 A Bill . . . to correct the Exorbitancies of the proprietary Land-Office, rendered them yet farther obnoxious. **1784** Filson *Kentucke* 37 After the entry is made in the land-office, there being one in each county, the person making the entry takes out a copy of the location. **1790** Maclay *Deb. Senate* 172 *Resolved*, that a land office be opened for the sale of the western territory. **1806** *Balance* V. 69/1 Now the old soldier may go to the land office and demand 100 acres of land. **1817** *Ann. 14th Congress* 2 Sess. 873 The bill to provide for the establishment of additional land offices in the Territory of Missouri. **1834** Peck *Gaz. Illinois* 97 There are eight land offices in Illinois, in as many districts, open for the sale or entry of public lands. **1858** *Texas Almanac 1859* 24 This act extends to preemption settlers or their assigns the time to return their field-notes to the Land Office for patent. **1883** *Century Mag.* Aug. 518/2 The Los Angeles land office has informed the Indians that, not being citizens, they cannot retain any claim. **1911** *Okla. Session Laws* 3 Legisl. 87 Such assignment . . . shall be duly recorded in a land office.

2. A privately owned office where the business of a land company is transacted.

1811 Sutcliff *Travels* (1815) 177 My hospitable friends showed me into the land-office of the Holland purchase. **1815** *Niles' Reg.* IX. 37/2 [The government does not] recognize any pretended *land office* for [the purpose of issuing military land warrants]. **1884** W. Shepherd *Prairie Exper.* 6 Sometimes railways or land offices pretend to supply information.

3. A building which houses either a private or public land office.

1838 Flagg *Far West* I. 38 The buildings . . . are a very conspicuous bank, courthouse, and a land-office for the southern district of Illinois. **1867** Richardson *Beyond Miss.* 81 The Border Ruffian capital . . . was composed of few dwelling-houses, many land-offices, and . . . saloons.

4. *attrib.* **a.** Designating a warrant or certificate entitling the grantee to ownership of certain land when given conditions are fulfilled.

1824 *Ky. Petitions* 180 There issued from the Land office of this commonwealth, a Land office Treasury Warrant . . . for 1462 acres. **1824** Doddridge *Notes* 99 Building a cabin and raising a crop of grain . . . entitled the occupant to four hundred acres of land, and a preemption right to one thousand acres more adjoining, to be secured by a land office warrant. **1839** *Indiana H. Rep. Jrnl.* 263 The fee simple of any tract of land is vested in the holder of a land office certificate to the land.

b. Designating various persons connected with a land office.

1853 J. W. Bond *Minnesota* 119 Whitney, at the time land-office receiver at St. Croix Falls. *Ib.* 120 Samuel Leech, land-office register at St. Croix Falls. **1873** Eggleston *Myst. Metrop.* 92 He is a land-office lawyer.

+Land-office business. A rushing business like that of a land office in boom times.

1865 'Mark Twain' *Sketches* (1926) 167 You can do such a land-office business on such a small capital. **1875** *Chicago Tribune* 3 Nov. 1/5 The tap-rooms adjoining the polls were all open and doing a 'land-office' business. **1880** *Cimarron News & Press* 24 June 3/2 The commission house of Brown of Manzanares . . . appears to be doing a 'land office business.' **1887** *Courier-Journal* 29 Jan. 2/1 The doughty burglar . . . has been doing a land-office business the past few days. **1895** *N.Y. Dramatic News* 7 Dec. 2/4 [The theater] appears to be doing a land-office business.

+Land-office money. (See quotation.) — **1822** Woods *English Prairie* 256 [In the Ohio-Illinois country] the paper money is of two kinds, called land-office and current money; land-office money is bank paper that will pass at the land-office, but this money frequently changes.

+Land officer. An officer in a land office. — **1814** *Niles' Reg.* V. 322/1 The land officers in these districts are progressing to a close in ascertaining the character and extent of the private claims. **1844** Tyler in *Pres. Mess. & P.* IV. 277 A letter . . . requesting certain information respecting the receipt by local land officers of fees not authorized by law. **1905** *Indian Laws & Tr.* III. 606 A homestead entry duly allowed by the local land officers.

+Land of steady habits. **1.** A nickname for the state of Connecticut (Cf. Blue law 2.) **2.** *transf.* New England. — **(1) 1825** Neal *Bro. Jonathan* I. 138 All the women, as usual, in this 'land of steady habits' getting as close to the wall as they could. **1834** in *Atlantic Mo.* XXVI. 490 Now I am in Connecticut! not only in Yankee land, but in the very land of steady habits, itself! **1845** *Knickerb.* XXVI. 180 The following communication . . . we derive from a welcome contributor in the 'land of steady habits.' **1904** *Congregationalist* 26 Nov. 786 Every 14th person in the Land of Steady Habits is a Congregationalist. **(2)** *c***1873** De Vere *MS. Notes* 661 New England—The 'Land of Steady Habits.'

+Land patent. A patent conferring ownership of a tract of public land. — **1841** *Niles' Nat. Reg.* 27 Feb. 412/3 On leave, Mr. Lincoln reported a bill to confirm land patents. **1873** *Winfield* (Kan.) *Courier* 27 May 2/3 Webb has filed . . . a petition for a mandamus on the secretary of the interior to compel him to issue land patents for certain lands in Kansas. **1884** Blaine *20 Years of Congress* I. 459 They had their land patents, which were certificates of patriotic service in the Revolutionary war.

+Land pike.

1. =Hellbender 1. *Obs.*

1687 Blome *Isles & Terr. in Amer.* 50 A Land-Pike is another strange Reptile, so called from its likeness to that Fish; but instead of Fins it hath four Feet.

2. A poor breed of pigs. Also attrib.

1841 *Cultivator* VIII. 152, I am anxious that he should soon get rid of his land-pikes and alligators at such prices as will enable him to buy a better breed. **1842** *Ib.* X. 37 Hogs, Landpike variety, are so cheap that stealing them is no longer petit larceny. **1855** *Mich. Agric. Soc. Trans.* VII. 716 The Suffolk swine . . . are of the same descent as the long-nosed, slab sided land pike, so often seen in the highways. **1879** *Diseases of Swine* 189, I have not learned of a single person [in St. John's Co., Fla.] having an improved breed of pigs. All depend on the 'razor-back' or 'land pike.' **1890** *Amer. Notes & Q.* V. 21, I think the term *land-pike* more frequently designates a thin, lank, half-wild swine.

Land pirate. **1.** A robber. {1609–} **+2.** (See quot. 1847.) — **(1) 1717** *Mass. H. S. Coll.* 6 Ser. V. 343 Thay that haue been land-pyrates by swaring men out of their rights will not stick at swaring any one out of their liues. **1853** 'P. Paxton' *Yankee in Texas* 370 Even two persons in whose hands he had intrusted his property . . . proved afterwards to have been of the number of the Land Pirates. **(2) 1847** Coyner *Lost Trappers* 70 The greater part of the country . . . was infested with a variety of tribes of Sioux, whose predatory habits had justly secured to them the title of 'land pirates.' **1899** Cushman *Hist. Indians* 479 Many efforts were made to break up this nest of land pirates.

+**Land plaster.** 'Rock-gypsum ground to a powder for use as a fertilizer' (*Cent.*). — **1887** *Courier-Journal* 24 Jan. 6/2 It is important that land plaster be sown early enough in the season to have it thoroughly dissolved by rains. **1894** *Vt. Agric. Rep.* XIV. 177 In order that the manure be all saved . . . sprinkle a little land plaster on the platform to absorb all moisture.

+**Land-poor,** *a.* Possessed of ample land but lacking in cash because of large tax payments, interest, etc.

1873 BEADLE *Undevel. West* 781 In the country, the old settlers are 'land-poor'—so rich that they can not pay their taxes. **1877** H. C. HODGE *Arizona* 82 Thousands of landholders complain of being 'land poor,' and the same may be said of hundreds of miners. **1884** ROE *Nature's Story* 101 Notwithstanding his many acres, he felt himself growing 'land-poor,' as country people phrase it. **1893** SANBORN *S. California* 134 The steam thresher would amaze some of our overworked, land-poor farmers. **1901** NORRIS *Octopus* 296 Buying! At twenty and thirty an acre! Why there's not one in ten that can. They are land-poor.

Land reform. +*ellipt.* A party or movement that advocated a policy of homesteading public lands free to actual settlers. Now hist. Also attrib. — **1846** *Whig Almanac 1847* 45/1 [Election return in N.Y.] *Land Reform.*—Governor, (Masquerier) 550. **1848** *Ib. 1849* 59/1 In New York and Ohio, 2,656 votes were given to the Land Reform Electors.

+**Landright.** =LANDERITT CHAISE. — **1760** *Boston Gazette* 14 April 3/3 Isaac Hawes . . . has to sell 2 second-hand chaises, one a fall-back, the other a landright.

Land sale. {1708-} +A sale of public land. Now hist. — **1834** PECK *Gaz. Illinois* 337 At the land sales of November, 1823, the tract on which the older portion of the town [of Springfield] is located, was purchased. **1845** *Indiana Mag. Hist.* XXIII. 8 The wonder is, that the country improved as fast as it did, under the grinding process of the land sales. **1849** CHAMBERLAIN *Ind. Gazetteer* 281 Digby had bought the town site at the United States land sale, at a little more than Congress price. **1850** *Indiana Mag. Hist.* XII. 229 After the land sales in May, 1808, and the sale of lots in Madison in 1811, the town and country commenced filling.

+**Land scrip.**

1. A land certificate issued to a person or land company.

1834 JACKSON in *Pres. Mess. & P.* III. 52 Mr. St. Clair . . . had permitted the clerk in his office to be the agent of speculations in land scrip. **1840** *Picayune* 31 July 3/1 The thief . . . rifled his pocket-book of . . . seven Certificates of Land Scrip to the amount of 35,000 acres. **1846** POLK *Diary* II. 67 Nothing occurred . . . except the presentation to me by a committee of Congress of a Bill appropriating $5,000,000 to be paid in land scrip for the payment of claims for French spoliations prior to 1800. **1871** *Rep. Indian Affairs* (1871) 251 He did then and there . . . sell and deliver to said defendant 28 pieces of Chippewa half-breed land-scrip. **1900** *Congress. Rec.* 4 Jan. 648/2 All of said lands . . . which hereafter may be sold, located, or disposed of by the United States for cash or bounty land warrants, or land scrip.

2. Scrip entitling states having insufficient or no public land to certain amounts of land in the public-land states.

Issued by the federal government for the support of colleges under the Morrill Act of 1862. (Cf. COLLEGE SCRIP.)

1862 *Statutes at Large* XII. 504 The Secretary of Interior is hereby directed to issue to each of the States in which there is not the quantity of public lands . . . land scrip to the amount in acres for the deficiency of its distributive share. **1863** *Mass. Acts & Resolves* 480 [The commissioner's] duty . . . shall be to locate . . . all the land scrip which may come into the possession of the Commonwealth. **1870** *Rep. Comm. Agric. 1869* 471 The proceeds of the sales of land scrip up to this time, deposited in the treasury of the State for the benefit of the university [*i.e.*, Cornell Univ.], amount in all to $328,300. **1872** *Congress. Globe* 2 March 1356/2 The land scrip given to the States for agricultural colleges has been generally sold for cash by the States. **1874** *Dept. Agric. Rep. 1873* 321 The amount already received by the colleges of the several States from the sales of the congressional land-scrip is $10,560,264.

+**Land-seeker.** One who seeks land on which to settle. — **1845** HOOPER *Simon Suggs' Adv.* iii, He overtook the land-seeker. **1848** WHITTIER *Crisis* 11 The pale land-seekers come, with eager eyes of gain. **1889** *Columbus Ev. Dispatch* 2 March, The ghost is suspected to be a land-seeker, who wished to scare the owners and buy the adjoining land cheap. **1892** *Aberdeen* (S.D.) *Sun* 6 Oct. 5/1 The land-seekers who are now going into the state are of a desirable character.

Land shark. {1769-}

+**1.** One who gets control of large tracts of public or other land for speculative purposes; a land-grabber.

1840 *Knickerb.* XVI. 211 You're a land-shark, then—swallowin' up poor men's farms. **1848** W. ARMSTRONG *Stocks* 37 He had settled a hundred thousand dollars upon his accomplished lady, which he very naturally refused to deprive her of for the sake of satisfying certain land sharks. **1870** *Rep. Comm. Agric. 1869* 427 Mr. Danielson . . . wrote to inquire if there is not some way by which the 'poor but honest farmer, who wishes land and a home, may escape the grasp of the middle-men, the land-sharks, those who come between the Creator and the tiller of the soil.' **1878** *Rep. Indian Affairs* p. viii, The reservations in such cases are at once infested by a class of land-sharks who do not hesitate to resort to any measure to defraud the Indians of their land. **1894** 'O. HENRY' *Rolling Stones* 218 A class of land speculators commonly called land sharks, unscrupulous and greedy. **1899** [see CLAIM *n.* 4].

+**2.** A gaunt breed of hog. Also attrib. (Cf. LAND PIKE 2.)

1840 *Cultivator* VII. 81 That vile race of animals which infest the country, and which, before the discovery of the name of 'land sharks,' used to be known by the name of hogs. **1849** *New Eng. Farmer* I. 338 They looked too well to be even distant relations of the *Land Sharks*, as the gaunt races [of swine] were called. **1850** *Rep. Comm. Patents 1849: Agric.* 107 In the county of Yates . . . there is . . . the full blood land-shark hog. **1860** *Indiana Bd. Agric. Rep. 1858-9* 303 Hogs.—All kinds of mixtures, consisting in part of Grazier, Berkshire, Russian and China, together with the original 'elm pealers,' or land sharks.

+**Landslide.**

1. The slipping of an embankment or of a mass of earth and rocks off a hill or mountain side; the place where such slipping has happened. {=landslip}

1838 *Niles' Nat. Reg.* 6 Oct. 96/1 *Land slide in Vicksburg.* . . . An avalanche or sinking of the earth on the margin of the landing at Vicksburg . . . threatens serious damage to the front street of that city. **1843** *Ib.* 2 Sept. 16/2 Land Slide at New Orleans. . . . The cause of this disaster . . . is said to have been an unusual rise in the Mississippi river. **1876** 'MARK TWAIN' *Tom Sawyer* xxxiii. 257 Do you see that white place up yonder where there's been a landslide? **1891** *Boston Jrnl.* 26 Oct. 1/6 A Big Land-Slide at New Orleans. **1903** *N.Y. Ev. Post* 17 Sept. 12 The trains are now running as usual, all washouts and landslides having been repaired.

2. *Polit.* An overwhelming majority of votes in an election. Also attrib.

1895 *Century Mag.* March 734 There was then a great landslide of votes for McClellan. **1903** *N.Y. Herald* 21 Oct. 8 The landslide under which Mr. Bryan was buried at the polls. **1912** *Commoner* 8 Nov. 1 It was a democratic landslide. Of 531 electoral votes Wilson and Marshall will have at least 400. **1913** LA FOLLETTE *Autobiog.* 169, I was a material help in saving him from defeat in that landslide year.

+**Land speculation.** Speculation in land; legitimate or illegitimate activities in the purchase and sale of unsettled land for profit; a single deal of this sort.

1807 *Ann. 10th Congress* 1 Sess. I. 605 We made a purchase of a single tract of land together. Perhaps you call that land speculations. **1821** NUTTALL *Travels Arkansa* 103 General Calamees and his brother, two elderly men out on a land speculation. **1831** PECK *Guide* 8 Having no connection with the business of land speculation, or town sites, . . . he has aimed to give a plain and unvarnished statement of things. **1860** GREELEY *Overland Journey* 36 The twin curses of Kansas . . . are land-speculation (whereof the manufacture of paper-cities and bogus corner-lots . . . is not half so mischievous as the grasping of whole townships by means of fraudulent pre-emptions and other devices . . .) and one-horse politicians. **1885** HOWELLS *S. Lapham* xx, He's been dabbling in . . . patent-rights, land speculations.

+**Land speculator.** A person engaged in land speculation.

1798 I. ALLEN *Hist. Vermont* 24 Lawyers and land speculators called on Mr. Allen. **1805** *Ann. 8th Congress* 2 Sess. 1046 Money is the bane of morals, when put in the hands of land speculators. **1848** BURTON *Waggeries* 171 The land speculator, hastening to the various sales expected to take place in the north-western states. **1875** STOWE *We & Neighbors* 12 Innumerable schemes of land speculators had attacked the old place. **1898** *McClure's Mag.* X. 523/1 The land speculators were in the habit of giving free excursions occasionally to prospective purchasers.

+**Land's sake.** Also **land('s) sake(s).** In expletive expressions, euphemistic for *Lord's sake.* (See LAND 3.)

1834 C. A. DAVIS *Lett. J. Downing* 232 'For the land's sake,' says I, 'jist look at it.' **1846** *Knickerb.* Jan. 18 Jedediah, for the land's sake, does my mouth blaze? **1863** A. D. WHITNEY *F. Gartney* ii, Land sakes, Miss Faith! I don't know what you mean. **1880** *Harper's Mag.* Dec. 80/2 Land's sakes! I can't see. **1896** JEWETT *Pointed Firs* 46 'Land sakes alive!' says she, . . . 'How you do lurch about steppin' into a bo't!' **1906** FREEMAN *By Light of Soul* 118 For the land's sake, there she is now! **1918** LINCOLN *Shavings* 320 Land sakes, I presume likely 'tis.

‖**Landstead,** *a.* Provided in respect of land. *Obs.* — **1688** *N.J. Archives* 1 Ser. II. 31 A gushet of about 2000 acres . . . I design to take vp for you, being good land; so I think by farr you will be the best land-stead of any concerned in the province.

+**Land tacks.** *pl.* In phrase (orig. nautical), *to take* (*our*, etc.) *land tacks on board,* to travel by land. *Obs.* — **1776** *Mass. H. S. Coll.* 2 Ser. II. 304 Maj'r Meigs & I agree'd to take our Land-Tacks on board and quit the boat. **1813** *Salem Gazette* 1 Oct. 3/3 The farms of Nantucket men were formerly upon the ocean, but Madison's war has obliged them to take land tacks on board, and pass the mountains. **1814** *Boston Spectator* 16 April 63/3 Are you lately arrived from a voyage? Yes, sir, and the longest voyage [*i.e.*, a trip on land] I ever made with my land tacks aboard.

***Land tax.** A tax on landed property. +Later, sometimes in the specific sense: The single tax.

1715 *N.C. Col. Rec.* II. 167 The heavy charge of a land tax, will make your debt 1000 pounds sterling money of England. **1785** in Ramsey *Tennessee* 297 It shall . . . be lawful for the aforesaid land tax . . . to be paid in the following manner. **1804** *Steele P.* I. 440 A few public bills have been introduced amongst which is a bill for equalising the land tax. **1817** BRADBURY *Travels* 292 No land tax is expected until five years after the purchase, when land becomes liable. **1835** J. HALL *Sk. of West* II. 208 The land tax is payable into the state treasury, on the first day of August, in each year. **1914** FILLEBROWN *Taxation* 147 Land taxes have as yet had little opportunity to show their worth in the United States.

+Land title. A title of ownership to land.

1812 *McDonogh P.* 11 The people . . . of Florida are . . . in a dissatisfied state, arising from this uncertainty in which their land titles are placed. **1814** BRACKENRIDGE *Views La.* 116 The uncertainty in a great number of land titles . . . presents an obstacle to the torrent of emigration. **1854** BENTON *30 Years' View* I. 280/1 The country had been afflicted for a generation with the curse of unsettled land titles. **1872** *Atlantic Mo.* Feb. 256 The money-order system is out of the question, and the registration of land-titles a dream. **1893** *Harper's Mag.* April 788/1 Vallejo visited Washington on business connected with his land titles.

Land tortoise. Any of various tortoises which live on land. {1666– in the Caribbean} — **1688** *Phil. Trans.* XVIII. 125 They have [in Va.] great store both of Land and Water Tortoises. **1791** W. BARTRAM *Travels* 18 The dens, or caverns, dug . . . in the sand hills by the great land-tortoise, called here Gopher, present a very singular appearance. **1805** PARKINSON *Tour* 313 There is the terrapin (or land-tortoise), weighing about one pound and a half which is eaten generally at suppers. **1822** WOODS *English Prairie* 258, I found a small land tortoise of about five inches over. **1894** *Scribner's Mag.* May 598/2 Racoons, 'possums, land-tortoises . . . fill out the list of animated life to be ordinarily looked for in these thorny recesses.

Land turtle. =LAND TORTOISE. {1697–} — **1607** in Smith *Works* I. p. xlix, He made ready a land turtle which we eate. **1672** JOSSELYN *N. E. Rarities* 34 The Land Turtle; they are found in dry sandy Banks, under old Houses, and never go into the water. **1778** CARVER *Travels* 488 The Tortoise or Land Turtle. The shape of this creature is so well known that it is unnecessary to describe it. **1842** *Nat. Hist. N.Y., Zoology* III. 24 The Common Box Tortoise, *Cistuda carolina*, . . . is designated in this State under the names of Box Tortoise and Land Turtle.

+Land warrant.

1. A negotiable warrant authorizing a surveyor or a land officer to grant to the holder a given amount of unlocated public land; a warrant wherein the land is described. Also attrib.

Cf. LAND OFFICE 4 a, MILITARY LAND WARRANT, WARRANT.

1742 *Md. Hist. Mag.* XX. 261, I will give him Eighty pounds sterling . . . Conditional he allso Assigns the fifty Acres Land want [*sic*]. **1769** *Ib.* XII. 285, I think you told me there was some land warrant due to you. **1826** BRADFORD *Kentucky Notes* 66 Virginia having passed a law opening a land office for the sale of land warrants. **1847** in Howe *Hist. Coll. Ohio* 441 The locations of land Warrants in the Virginia military district between the Scioto and the Little Miami, prior to 1790, were made by stealth. **1857** DUNLAP *Book Forms* 161 Application for land warrants. Application for taking out a warrant, by a Settler, for Lands settled on [by himself]. **1866** *Internal Revenue Guide* 69 Any person shall be regarded as a land-warrant broker who makes a business of buying and selling land-warrants, or of furnishing them to settlers. **1873** EGGLESTON *Myst. Metrop.* 165 To persuade Plausaby to raise money enough for him to buy a land-warrant with, . . . was the only course open. **1901** Duncan & Scott *Allen & Woodson Co., Kan.* 34 At that time land warrants being under par, I procured my land from the government for a little less than one dollar per acre.

2. a. *To locate a land warrant*, to locate or enter a particular claim on public land as described, or to the amount granted, in a land warrant. (Cf. LOCATE *v.* 2 b.)

1754 *Md. Archives* VI. 58 The method always followed here of Locating Land Warrants . . . has left the Land . . . [in] irregular small & incommodious Parcells. **1793** *History of Congress* (1834) 579 Resolved—That the petitioner be permitted to locate the land warrant, issued in his name, for his services in the late army. **1812** MARSHALL *Kentucky* 130 The great object which now absorbed public attention, was the entering and locating land warrants, of which great numbers had been obtained. **1867** RICHARDSON *Beyond Miss.* 138 The preëmptor 'locates' a land-warrant upon the claim.

b. *To survey a land warrant*, to survey land as described in, or to the amount of, a land warrant.

1834 M. BUTLER *Hist. Kentucky* 20 Land warrants were actually surveyed on the Kenhawa as early as 1772.

3. Special phrases.

Unlocated land warrant, a land warrant granting an amount of land, but not specifying its location; *executed land warrant*, a land warrant the instructions of which have been executed by a surveyor.

1787 JEFFERSON *Writings* VI. 394 Sharpers had duped so many with their unlocated land-warrants. **1788** WASHINGTON *Diaries* III. 398 A Mr. Oconnor, D. Surveyor in the Western Country, came here with some executed Land Warrants.

***Land way.** +'A road giving access to land' (*O.E.D.*). Now hist. — **1638** *Charlestown Land Rec.* 4 Ten acres of woodland . . . butting west upon the drift way towards the north river to the east upon the land way bounded on the south by Ed Convers. **1649** *Ib.* 94 Five acres of woodland . . . butting . . . east upon the land way. **1899** D. P. COREY *Hist. Malden* 90 The land-way and drift-way along the five acre lots ended at the head of the North River.

+Landy. A euphemism for *Lordy. colloq.* — **1877** JEWETT *Deephaven* x. 194 'Landy!' said she, 'if it ain't old Parson Lorimer!' **1909** STRATTON-PORTER *Girl of Limberlost* iv. 70 'Landy, ain't I a queen?' she murmured.

***Lane.**

***1.** A narrow road or street.

1689 *Plymouth Rec.* 196 The Lane . . . that leadeth downe to the seaside. *Ib.*, To the head of the above s(ai)d laine. **1721** *Providence Rec.* XIII. 42 Provided there be sufficiant Gates sett up and maintained in sd. Lane and highway. **1782** *Phila. Ordinances* (1812) 48 The streets, lanes and alleys . . . dedicated to public use by private persons. **1818** *Niles' Reg.* XIV. 310/2 New streets, lanes and alleys are opened, paved and built upon. **1877** *Harper's Mag.* Jan. 284/1 Every day they took their morning walk, up one side and down the other of our lane.

b. In place names.

1638 *Charlestown Land Rec.* 8 One homesteede . . . bounded on the southeast by garden Lane allias mault lane, . . . with one dwelling house. **1698** *Boston Rec.* 230 The High way Leading from the Black horse Lane to the mill.

2. *S.* A road which has a fence on each side.

1835 INGRAHAM *South-West* II. 107 The road, (always degraded, in the parlance of the country, when running between two fences, to a 'lane.') **1859** BARTLETT 236 In the Carolinas, all roads with fences on each side are called *lanes*. **1881** PIERSON *In the Brush* 21 Whenever, for a short distance, there was a fence on both sides of a road, *that* was called a 'lane.'

+Lane snapper. (See first quot.) — **1896** JORDAN & EVERMANN *Check-List Fishes N.A.* 382 *Neomænis synagris*. . . . Lane Snapper. . . . Florida Keys to Colon and Brazil. **1911** *Rep. Fisheries 1908* 316 The silk snapper . . . [and] the lane snapper . . . [are] fishes of food value common in the West Indies and southern Florida.

Langshan. A breed of fowl introduced from China. {1871–} — **1894** *Vt. Agric. Rep.* XIV. 173 For roasters . . . select the Brahma, Cochin, Langshan, or Plymouth Rocks.

Languister. Variant of LINGUISTER.

***Lanner(et).** Also **lanier.** +The prairie falcon. (Prob. erroneously identified in first quot.) — **1612** SMITH *Virginia* 14 Hawkes there be of diuerse sorts as . . . Lanarets, Goshawkes [etc.]. **1874** COUES *Birds N.W.* 339 *Falco Mexicanus* var. *Polyagrus*. . . . American Lanier, or Prairie Falcon. **1917** *Birds of Amer.* II. 87 Prairie Falcon. *Falco mexicanus*. . . . [Also called] American Lanner (female) or American Lanneret (male). . . . The Prairie Falcon is the American representative of the Lanners and Lannerets of the eastern hemisphere.

Lant. The sand launce. {Newfoundland 1620–; 1880–4} — **1883** *Nat. Museum Bul.* No. 27, 415 *Ammodytes personatus*. . . . Sand Launce; Lant. Monterey Bay and Puget Sound . . . ; entire coast of Alaska north to Point Belcher. . . . This little fish plays a very important part in the cod fishery, because of its great abundance and the greediness with which cod feed upon it. **1884** GOODE, etc. *Fisheries* I. 244. **1897** *N.Y. Forest, Fish, & Game Comm. 2d Rep.* 235 *Ammodytes americanus*, . . . Sand Launce, Sand Eel; Lant.—The species appears in Gravesend Bay in July, but is more plentiful in winter.

***Lantern.** Also †**lanthorne.**

***1.** A light inclosed in an easily portable case.

1651 *Essex Probate Rec.* I. 128 2 sives, 4 boot hauches & 1 lanthorne. **1702** *Essex Inst. Coll.* XLII. 160 Inventory of ship . . . three Lanthorns. **1796** *Ann. 4th Congress* 2 Sess. 2785 Water-casks, boats, lanterns, and all the tin work, are provided [for a frigate]. **1840** COOPER *Pathfinder* viii, I was right glad to see the lanterns come down to the water-side. **1884** 'MARK TWAIN' *H. Finn* xiii, It was a lantern hanging on the jackstaff of a double-hull ferry-boat. **1912** NICHOLSON *Hoosier Chron.* 29 Billy Sanderson . . . invested his first month's salary in a silver-mounted lantern.

2. In a lighthouse, the chamber containing the light. {1759– (Smeaton *Edystone Lighthouse* § 282)}

1789 MORSE *Amer. Geog.* 203 The heighth from the ground to the top of the cornice is 58 feet, round which is a gallery, and within that stands the lanthorn, which is about 11 feet high, and 8 feet diameter. **1809** KENDALL *Travels* II. 9 The height of the building [the lighthouse at the harbor of Newport, R.I.], measured from its base to the top of the lanthorn, is sixty-nine feet. **1832** WILLIAMSON *Maine* I. 30 On this head is Portland Lighthouse . . . an edifice of stone 72 feet in height, exclusive of the lantern. **1844** *Knickerb.* XXIV. 287 [At Sandy-Hook Light] huge polished steel reflectors . . . [are] surrounded by a lanthorn, no mean apartment in itself, with its plate glass sides, twelve or fifteen feet high.

3. A projector or magic lantern. {1884–} Also attrib.

1866 *Rep. Comm. Patents 1864* I. 434 The lantern is so constructed as to exhibit pictures upon a screen by reflected light. **1890** *Internat. Ann., Anthony's Photogr. Bul.* III. 144, I was expected to furnish some slides for the first lantern exhibition of the club. **1897** *Outing* XXX. 194/2 The exposure of bromide and velox paper, lantern slides by contact [etc.]. **1899** CHAMPLIN & BOSTWICK *Cycl. Games & Sports* (ed. 2) 472/2 The farther the lantern is from the wall or screen . . . , the larger the pictures will be.

+Lanyappe. (See LAGNIAPPE.)

Lap, *n.*[1] {1800–}

+1. ? A bundle, or a certain number, of hides.

1673 *N.J. Archives* I. 132 They presented about 20 deer skins, 2 @ 3 laps of Beaver, and 1 string of Wampum.

2. ? The space of ground inclosed in an angle of a rail fence.

1787 WASHINGTON *Diaries* III. 213 In the laps of the fence Inclosg. it 139 pumpkin hills were Planted.

+3. *Euchre.* Points scored in excess of the number necessary for winning a game. So called when the excess is applied to the player's score in a subsequent game. {1886} Also attrib. with *game.*

1864 DICK *Amer. Hoyle* (1880) 70 The *lap* . . . is simply counting upon the score of the ensuing game [etc.]. *Ib.*, When the Lap game is played, it is usual to count four points [etc.].

+4. =LAPSTREAK 2.

1876 TRIPP *Student-Life* 130 A few choice spirits . . . [would] buy an old 'lap.' from one of the upper classes. *Ib.* 151 A boat, the club 'lap.,' was slung into the 'gaskets.'

5. 'Any portion of railroad-track used in common by the trains of more than one system' (*Stand.*).

***Lap,** *n.*[2] *attrib.* **a.** Designating a covering worn over the lap. **+b.** Designating meals eaten with dishes held on the lap. — **1675** *Doc. Col. Hist. N.Y.* XII. 524 The Gov. presents them [*sc.* Indians] with 4 Coates & 4 lappcloathes. **1866** LOWELL *Biglow P.* 2 Ser. p. lviii, A few phrases not in Mr. Bartlett's book which I have heard [include] . . . *Laptea:* where the guests are too many to sit at table. **1889** *Century Mag.* April 853/2*n.*, [As the] last act of this woful tragedy [of over-eating], which, till now, had been what is innocently called in the Colorado vernacular a 'lap-party'—the guests were summoned to 'a *full* supper.' **1920** LEWIS *Main Street* 12 They made a specialty of sandwich-salad-coffee lap suppers.

+Lap, *n.*[3] [Var. of *lop.*] A twig or branch trimmed from a tree; a fallen piece of timber. — **1851** *S. Lit. Messenger* XVII. 45/2 The glancing of a squirrel in a fallen lap, attracts your attention. **1881** *Harper's Mag.* July 316/2 One pleasant Sunday . . . he started up a fox, which ran under a tree that had blown down, or, as it is called, the 'lap of a tree.'

Lap,** *v.*[1] *Racing. tr.* To pass or overlap (a rival). {1890–} — **1841** *Picayune* 11 Dec. 2/2–3. *a1846** *Quarter Race Ky.* 50, I told you the brown horse was a mighty fast one for a little ways. But soon I lapped him. **1857** *Lawrence* (Kan.) *Republican* 11 June 3 This certainly was a killing pace, but Mahen lapped him inside the first quarter. **1890** WEBSTER 829/2 The hinder boat lapped the foremost one.

***Lap,** *v.*[2] [Cf. LAP *n.*[3]] *+intr.* Of a bear: To pull or tear off branches or limbs of trees or vines in order to get fruit, nuts, etc. Also *lapping season.* — **1853** 'P. PAXTON' *Yankee in Texas* 18 Just you sight that muscadine vine, whar one of the varmint's [a bear] been a lappin'. **1868** *Amer. Naturalist* May 122 [Bears] climb in order to 'lap,' as the hunter says, described by Mr. Clapp as drawing in branches to get the fruit. **1881** *Scribner's Mo.* Oct. 858/2 The fall . . . is called the lapping season, as he [the bear] ensconces himself in a tree-lap and breaks the limbs to pieces, in gathering fruits and nuts.

Lapboard. A board placed across the lap and used as a table, esp. by seamstresses, tailors, etc. — **1840** *Picayune* 18 Sept. 2/3 Ashamed! why, I feel as flat as my own lapboard, and as dull as a blunt shears. **1866** A. D. WHITNEY *L. Goldthwaite* vi, Miss Craydocke slipped her lapboard—work and all—under her bureau. **1891** *Harper's Mag.* Jan. 222/1 He sat with the 'lap-board'—usually used in cutting out men's clothes—across his knee. **1902** G. M. MARTIN *Emmy Lou* 195 But it was not a school—it was only a Parlour; and there being a pupil more than there were accommodations, and Emmy Lou being the newcomer, her portion was a rocking-chair and a lap-board.

Lap dog. A small dog accustomed to lying in a person's lap. {1645–} — **1790** *Penna. Packet* 19 May 1/1 Strayed away . . . from the house of Mr. John Leamy, . . . a small White Lap-Dog. **1854** COOKE *Va. Comedians* I. 20 He unfortunately treads with his whole weight upon the long silky ear of his sister's favorite lapdog Orange.

***Lapidary.** A stonecutter, esp., a skilled worker in precious stones. — **1810** *Columbian Centinel* 20 Jan. 3/3 Andrew Faracy, Regular bred Optician and Lapidary. **1913** *Boston Directory* 2937 H. E. Alsterlund & Co. Special Jewelers and Lapidaries, Seal Engravers and Incrusters.

***Lapland.** **+1.** =LAPLANDER. **+2.** *attrib.* **a.** In names of birds: (see quotations and cf. LAPLAND LONGSPUR). **b.** With *azalea, rhododendron, rosebay:* a dwarf plant, *Rhododendron lapponicum.* — **(1) 1887** *Century Mag.* Nov. 16/2 A procession of little darkies [at Mount Vernon, Va.] . . . supporting plates of hot . . . griddle-cakes, love-puffs, beaten biscuit, laplands. **(2) 1844** *Nat. Hist. N.Y., Zoology* II. 177 The Lapland Snow-Bird. *Plectrophanes Lapponicus.* . . . This rare arctic bird is not an unfrequent visitor to this State, during the extreme cold of winter. **1917** *Birds of Amer.* III. 95 Bohemian Waxwing. . . . [Also called] Lapland Waxwing. — **1847** WOOD *Botany* 377 *R[hododendron] Lapponicum.* . . . Lapland Rhododendron. **1857** GRAY *Botany* 257 *R[hododendron] Lapponicum.* (Lapland Rose-bay.) . . . Alpine summits of the high mountains of Maine, New Hampshire, and New York. **1892** TORREY *Foot-Path Way* 31 The splendid Lapland azalea . . . is to be seen in all its glory upon the Mount Washington range, in middle or late June.

Laplander. {1637–} +A kind of muffin or gem. — **1882** F. E. OWENS *Cook Book* 133 Laplanders. One egg, one cup of milk, one cup of flour, pinch of salt; beat well.

+Lapland longspur. A long-clawed Arctic bird, *Calcarius lapponicus.* — **1828** BONAPARTE *Ornithology* II. 53 [The] Lapland Longspur, *Emberiza Lapponica,* . . . long since known to inhabit the desolate Arctic regions of both continents, is now for the first time introduced into the Fauna of the United States. **1858** BAIRD *Birds Pacific R.R.* 433 Lapland Longspur. . . . Eastern Northern America into the United States in winter. **1870** *Amer. Naturalist* III. 585 Lapland Longspur, *Centrophanes Lapponicus,* . . . is a very rare winter visitor in the interior of [Mass.]. **1917** *Birds of Amer.* III. 22/1 The Lapland Longspur and its varieties . . . inhabit a broad subarctic belt around the world during the breeding season.

+La Plata potato. (See quotations.) — **1838** *Mass. Agric. Survey 1st Rep.* 33 The kinds [of potato] raised [in Essex Co.] are . . . the Biscuit potato . . . ; the La Plata, or long red, well known; and the Chenango. **1839** *Ib. 2d Rep.* 90 In the starch manufactory at Williamstown, they have found the long red or La Plata potato unfit for their purposes until the spring.

+La Platte. (See quotation.) — **1808** PIKE *Sources of Miss.* II. App. 16 The third game [played by the Pawnees] alluded to, is that of La Platte, described by various travellers, and is played at by the women, children, and old men, who like grasshoppers, crawl out to the circus to bask in the sun, probably covered only with an old buffalo robe.

Lap(ped) shingle. A shingle so laid as to overlap another shingle. Also attrib. — **1765** in Chalkley *Scotch-Irish Settlement Va.*I. 494 The house to be covered with lap shingles, clear of the sap, and fourteen inches to the weather. **1784** in Summers *Ann. S.W. Virginia* 387 A house . . . covered with lapped shingles 18 inches to the weather clear of sap. **1844** *Cincinnati Misc.* I. 51 A new jail of hewed logs and lapt-shingle roof . . . was erected within less than two years.

Lapper. A machine for lapping cotton. — **1850** *Rep. Comm. Patents 1849* 195 [The] cotton batting . . . has been merely . . . spread in a lapper. **1883** [see LAP SCALE].

Lapping machine. A machine for forming cotton into layers or sheets. {1851} — **1850** *Rep. Comm. Patents 1849* 436 A very interesting lapping machine has been patented this year. **1875** [see LAP ROLLER].

Lapping title. (See quotation.) — **1843** HAWKS *D. Boone* 129 Entries of these certificates were made in a way so loose, that different men frequently located the same lands; one title would often lap over upon another; and almost all the titles conferred in this way became known as 'the lapping, or shingle titles.'

Lapp owl. (See quot. 1917.) — **1887** RIDGWAY *Manual N.A. Birds* 260 *S[cotiaptex] cinereum lapponicum* Lapp Owl. **1917** *Birds of Amer.* II. 106/2 The Lapp Owl (*Scotiaptex nebulosa lapponica*) is an Old World variant of the Great Gray Owl which occasionally strays into Alaska.

+Lap robe. A blanket or covering for the lap, legs, and feet. Freq. used in carriages, sleighs, etc. — **1866** [Ernst annotation]. **1875** STOWE *We & Neighbors* 373 He took her to ride in such a stylish carriage, white lynx lap-robe, and all! **1903** WIGGIN *Rebecca* xiv. 154 He tucked the old lap-robe cosily over their feet. **1914** ATHERTON *Perch of Devil* 121 He smiled directly into her resentful eyes . . . and tucked the lap-robe about her.

Lap roller. A cylinder or bobbin upon which layers of cotton, wool, etc., are rolled in the course of manufacture. — **1850** *Rep. Comm. Patents 1849* 160, I also claim the combination of burring apparatus . . . with the calendar and lap rollers. **1875** KNIGHT 1254/2 *Lap-roller,* . . . one in a lapping-machine, upon which the fleece or wadding is wound.

+Lap rug. =LAP ROBE. — **1876** A. D. WHITNEY *Sights & Insights* I. 27 On a sea voyage . . . she has a brown leather belt and reticule, and a brown veil and a sealskin-jacket, and a beautiful brown-shaded lap-rug.

Lap scale. (See quot. 1883.) — **1869** *Boyd's Business Directory* 73 Frederick Miller, . . . Agent for and Dealer in . . . Lap-Scales, Nuts, Oils [etc.]. **1883** KNIGHT *Suppl.* 526/2 *Lap Scale,* a scale with a pan in which a given quantity of wool or cotton is weighed to be spread upon a given length of the traveling feeding apron of the lapper or carding machine, as the case may be.

Lapse, *v.* {1611–} *+intr.* Of public land: To revert to the government because of nonimprovement by the grantee. Also *lapsed* ppl. a. {generic sense 1726–} — **1705** BEVERLEY *Virginia* IV. 43 Lapsed Land, is when any one having obtain'd a Patent as before, doth not Seat or Plant thereon within three Years, as the Condition of the Patent requires; but leaves it still all or part uninhabited, and uncultivated: In such Case it is said to be Lapsed. **1712** *N.C. Col. Rec.* I. 852 A Tract of Land on Nuse River Called Wilkison's point is Lapsed for want of Seateing. **1791** *Ann. 2d Congress* 1037 Of the remaining entries, many are certified void, and others understood to be lapsed, or otherwise voidable under the laws of the State [of N.C.].

+Lapstreak.

1. In a boat, a board so laid that its edge overlaps that of another board in the manner of clapboards. Also attrib. and comb., passing into adj.

1771 *Boston-Gazette* 11 March (Th.), Whale-boats and all sorts of Lapstreak Boats. **1815** *Essex Inst. Coll.* II. 60/2 [The boat] was lap-streak built and carried 3 lateen sails. **1874** LONG *Wild-Fowl* 89 The siding is put on commencing at the bottom in lap-streaks. **1895** *Outing* XXVI. 488/2 Their boat is of lap-streak construction. **1897** *Ib.* XXX. 113/1

The *Wanderer* was a sixteen-foot yawl, lap-streak, copper-riveted and built for salt water.

2. A boat built with lapstreaks.

1871 *Harper's Mag.* July 186 The boat races take place . . . between the third and fourth [class] in lap streaks. **1887** *Century Mag.* May 178/2 The Freshmen formed a practice-crew of their own, making use of the old lapstreak which had conquered in 1860.

+**Larb.** (See quot. 1871.) Also attrib. — **1846** SAGE *Scenes Rocky Mts.* xxvii, Frequent clusters of larb, richly laden with its deep red berry. *Ib.*, The larb-berry is of a deep red color, and somewhat larger than the common currant. **1871** *Rep. Comm. Agric. 1870* 413 *Bearberry, (arctostaphylos uva-ursi.)*—This plant is the killikinick of the Indians and larb of hunters.

***Larceny.** *Law.* The theft of personal property. — **1647** *R.I. Col. Rec.* I. 159 Under the Law for Menstealers—are comprehended those Lawes that concern Theft of men, Larcenie, Trespasses by Men or beasts [etc.]. **1796** *Mass. Rev. Statutes* (1836) 193 In any such case of fire, if any person shall purloin, . . . effects of the inhabitants, . . . [he] shall be deemed guilty of larceny. **1894** *Boston Jrnl.* 17 Nov. 9/7 John Long . . . appeared in the Municipal Criminal Court . . . on two charges of larceny. **1909** *Indian Laws & Tr.* III. 423 All Indians committing . . . any of the following crimes, namely—murder, manslaughter, . . . and larceny [etc.].

Larch.** Any coniferous tree of the genus *Larix* or related genera, +esp. the common tamarack, *L. laricina.* (See also AMERICAN, EUROPEAN LARCH.) — **1792** BELKNAP *Hist. New-Hampshire* III. 109 The Larch . . . is the only tree of the terebinthine quality which sheds its leaves in the autumn. **1814** BIGELOW *Florula Bostoniensis* 236 The Larch is a fine tree. . . . Its wood is strong and durable, and is used in ship building. *a1862** THOREAU *Maine Woods* 214 We continued along through the most extensive larch wood which I had seen. **1899** GOING *Flowers* 270 The larch and the 'bald'-cypress of the Southern States . . . are not evergreen.

Larch pine. (See quotation.) — **1858** WARDER *Hedges & Evergreens* 247 *Pinus laricio,* Corsican or Larch Pine, . . . is a useful timber-tree of rapid growth. Hardy as far north as Pennsylvania.

***Lard.**

***1.** Rendered pork fat.

1778 *Jrnls. Cont. Congress* XI. 594 There were 2,015 barrels of flour, . . . besides pease, Indian Meal, . . . rum, salt, candles and hogs lard. **1825** NEAL *Bro. Jonathan* I. 76 Here, were dough nuts, a kind of sweet cake fried in lard. **1840** *Niles' Nat. Reg.* 26 Dec. 272/3 We hear of a considerable sale of No. 1. lard. **1911** FERBER *Dawn O'Hara* 34 A motherly hug . . . enveloped me in an atmosphere of liquid face-wash, strong perfumery and fried lard.

2. *attrib.* and *comb.* Of or pertaining to lard or lard substitutes.

1881 *Chicago Times* 16 April, Very little lard-butter is now sold in Chicago. *Ib.*, Large amounts of butterine and lard-cheese were sold here as the genuine article. **1904** LAMBORN *Cottonseed Products* 162 Lard-compound . . . consists of summer white cottonseed-oil and oleo-stearin mixed in various proportions, and sometimes with a small percentage of genuine lard. **1887** *Courier-Journal* 2 May 4/3 Lard consumers have long since got accustomed to all kinds of deviled groceries. **1848** *Rep. Comm. Patents 1847* 529 Lard grease is computed to form eighty per cent. of all the fat used in making soap. **1883** WILDER *Sister Ridnour* 38 The lard jar was empty. **1851** CIST *Cincinnati* 345 The pork merchants paid me cash for my due bills, payable in barrels and lard kegs. **1891** *Fur, Fin, & Feather* March 195 Two empty lard pails with their covers . . . will complete the culinary outfit. **1896** *Alden's Living Topics Cycl.* II. 308 A trust corporation . . . owned: . . . cotton compressors, 3; lard and cottolene plants, 4 [etc.]. **1885** JEWETT *Marsh Island* xi. 143 The lard pots that's empt'ed. **1867** *Rep. Comm. Patents 1865* 810 Lard Press. . . . This invention consists in forming the bottom plate of the press of a convex shape [etc.]. **1857** *Quinland* I. 19 His solicitude in regard to the flour-barrel, lard-tub, and tea-canister. **1838** *N.Y. Advertiser & Exp.* 7 Feb. 3/3 In the [meat-]packing houses, 'Cutters,' 'Lard Venders,' 'Weighers,' and 'Packers,' have been paid two dollars per day.

Larder.** A room in which food supplies are stored; a pantry. — *c1640** *Harvard Rec.* I. 15 The study [is] in the chamber East off this over the Larder. **1842** *Knickerb.* XX. 545 The stores for the Sabbath were sent from the larder to the kitchen. **1904** T. E. WATSON *Bethany* 10 My mother afterward . . . used [it] as smoke-house, butler's pantry and larder.

+**Larder beetle.** A dark-colored insect (*Dermestes lardarius*), the larva of which feeds on dried meat, etc. — **1868** *Amer. Naturalist* II. 165 *Ptinus fur* . . . is destructive to cloth, furs, etc., resembling the Larder-beetle (*Dermestes*) in its habits. **1895** COMSTOCK *Manual Insects* 539 The Larder Beetle, *Dermestes lardarius*. . . . This pest of the larder is the most common of all the larger members of this family [Dermestidae]. **1905** KELLOGG *Amer. Insects* 264 The larder- or bacon-beetle . . . is about ⅓ inch long.

Lardine. A commercial name for a substitute for lard. {1888-} — **1884** *Vt. Agric. Rep.* VIII. 10 Oleomargarine, butterine, lardine, or any other villainous counterfeit, will not be preferred.

+**Lard lamp.** An illuminating device consisting of a dish, cup, etc., containing lard and provided with a wick. *colloq.* — **1844** *Lexington Observer* 25 Sept. 1/6 Patent solar lard lamps . . . $8.00. **1852** EASTMAN *Aunt Phillis's Cabin* 53 The lard-lamp . . . lit up everything astonishingly. **1898** N. E. JONES *Squirrel Hunters of Ohio* 292 The man . . . did his reading at night by the light of the furnace or a 'log-cabin luminary,' a lard lamp.

Lard oil. Oil made from lard. Used for illumination and lubrication. {1882} Also comb. with *manufacturer.* — **1845** *Cincinnati Misc.* I. 181/2, I know one lard oil manufacturer alone, whose capacity of producing lard oil . . . would require for his year's business 2,000,000 lbs. lard. **1860** *Texas Almanac* 248 Lard Oil, Sperm, Star, and Adamantine Candles [etc.]. **1913** *Boston Directory* 2207/3 Lard Oil Mfrs. Squire John P. & Co. 39 N. Market.

***Large,** *n. At large.* +**a.** Of an elector or representative: Chosen to represent the whole of a political unit such as a state or county, rather than one of its subdivisions. (Cf. CONGRESSMAN 2, ELECTOR-AT-LARGE.) **b.** Of the political unit: The whole.

1696 SEWALL *Diary* I. 427 At Large. . . . Saffin 39. **1741** B. LYNDE *Diary* (1880) 161, I was again chose a Counsellor in ye 1st 18, and my Coz. Wm. Browne chose a Counsellor at Large. **1872** *Statutes at Large* XVII. 28 In any State which by this law is given an increased number of Representatives, the additional Representative or Representatives . . . may be elected by the State at large. **1888** BRYCE *Amer. Commonw.* I. xiii. 166 The additional member or members are elected by the voters of the whole State on a general ticket, and are called 'representatives at large.' **1903** A. B. HART *Actual Govt.* 222 Whenever a State legislature has neglected to redistrict in order to provide for new members, the additional members may be chosen from the State 'at large,'—that is, by vote of the whole State.

***Large,** *a.*

+**1.** In specific names of trees and plants.

Only a selection of these names is given.

1810 MICHAUX *Arbres* I. 39 *American large aspen,* . . . nom donné par moi. **1814** BIGELOW *Florula Bostoniensis* 50 *Convolvolus sepium.* Large bindweed. . . . Perennial. **1843** TORREY *Flora N.Y.* II. 387 *Carex angustata*. . . . Large Bog Sedge. . . . Wet meadows; very common. **1832** BROWNE *Sylva* 226 The large buckeye attains the height of 60 or 70 feet. **1785** MARSHALL *Amer. Grove* 105 *Platanus occidentalis.* American Plane Tree or Large Button Wood **1868** GRAY *Field Botany* 354 *Arundinaria macrosperma,* Large Cane, forming the cane brakes. S[outh]. **1778** CARVER *Travels* 504 Shrubs. Spoon Wood, Large Elder, Dwarf Elder [etc.]. **1787** SARGENT in *Mem. Academy* II. I. 159 Trees, Northwest of the River Ohio . . . [include] Hazel, Alder, Elder, Large Laurel, Nine Bark [etc.]. **1810** MICHAUX *Arbres* I. 32 *Magnolia grandiflora*. . . . *The Large magnolia* . . . , dénomination la plus en usage parmi les habitans des villes des Etats méridionaux. **1833** EATON *Botany* (ed. 6) 362 *Thalictrum revolutum,* large meadow rue. **1814** BIGELOW *Florula Bostoniensis* 29 *Lechea major.* Large Pin weed. . . . An upright hairy plant . . . [which has] roundish capsules. *Ib.* 33 *Plantago major,* Large plantain, . . . grows at every one's door, and not the less for being trampled under foot. *Ib.* 241 *Populus grandidentata.* Large Aspen or Poplar. **1847** DARLINGTON *Weeds & Plants* 288 *E[uphorbia] hypericifolia*. . . . Hypericum-leaved Euphorbia. . . . Large Spotted Spurge. **1840** DEWEY *Mass. Flowering Plants* 70 *Urtica Canadensis.* Large Stinging Neetle. So strong are the fibres of the bark, that Mr. Whitlow proposed its culture as a substitute for hemp. **1843** TORREY *Flora N.Y.* I. 59 *Dentaria maxima,* Large Tooth-wort. . . . Western part of the State of New York. . . . Extremely rare. **1863** *Horticulturist* XVIII. 262/1 Of Apples, we may mention . . . Pearmain, Red Astrachan, Early Harvest, Large Yellow Bough [etc.]. **1785** MARSHALL *Amer. Grove* 111 *Prunus americana.* Large Yellow Sweet Plumb. . . . We have a great variety of these. **1840** DEWEY *Mass. Flowering Plants* 79 *V[iola] pubescens.* Large Yellow Woods Violet. . . . Middle-sized yellow flowers; woods; May.

+**2.** In specific names of birds, animals, and fishes.

1844 *Nat. Hist. N.Y., Zoology* II. 218 The Large Brown or Whooping Crane has not been observed by me in this State. **1805** *Lewis & Clark Exped.* VI. (1905) 187 The Prarie lark, bald Eagle, & the large plover have returned. [Between Sandy River and the Dalles.] **1844** *Nat. Hist. N.Y., Zoology* II. 287 The Large Shearwater. *Puffinus cinereus.* **1814** MITCHILL *Fishes N.Y.* 446 Large Silverside. *Atherina mordax.*

3. Combined with participles in specific names of birds, fishes, and plants. (See also LARGE-FLOWERED, etc.)

1835 AUDUBON *Ornith. Biog.* III. 599 The birds observed were Large-billed Puffins. **1843** TORREY *Flora N.Y.* I. 178 *Desmodium cuspidatum.* . . . Large-bracted Desmodium. . . . Banks of rivers, and rocky open woods. August. **1814** MITCHILL *Fishes N.Y.* 375 Large-lipped Blenny, *Blennius labrosus,* . . . was taken at sea among the cod fishes. **1843** TORREY *Flora N.Y.* II. 379 *Carex decomposita*. . . . Large-panicled Sedge. . . . Swamps. Yates county. **1897** SUDWORTH *Arborescent Flora* 286 Large-tooth Maple. . . . Common names. Western Sugar Maple, Hard Maple, . . . Large-toothed Maple.

***Large,** *adv.* In a boastful, exaggerated, or threatening manner. {-*c*1500} (See also BY AND LARGE.) — **1833** S. SMITH *Major Downing* 149 Other folks may talk larger and bluster more. **1872** *Ku Klux Klan Rep.* VI. 107 He had talked large about the Ku-Klux?

Large bread. ? Bread in loaves, in contrast to rolls, muffins, etc. Also attrib. — **1837** *S. Lit. Messenger* III. 660/1 [In New York] there are for sale hats, boots and shoes, . . . large bread, jewelry . . . : every thing on earth. **1876** SCUDDER *Dwellers* 7 There was a large-bread bakery at Skotos.

Large-flowered, *a.* +In specific names of plants and trees: Distinguished by having large flowers. — **1813** MUHLENBERG *Cat. Plants* 38 *Asculus macrostachya*, white, large-flow'r'd horse chestnut. **1843** TORREY *Flora N.Y.* I. 325 *Liatris scariosa*. Large-flowered Button-Snakeroot. . . . Sandy, moist bushy places; Long Island, particularly in Suffolk County. *Fl.* August–September. *Ib.* II. 296 *Trillium grandiflorum*. . . . Large-flowered Trillium. . . . Woods: western and southwestern counties: rare. **1846** BROWNE *Trees Amer.* 2 Of all the trees . . . the Large-flowered Magnolia is most remarkable for the . . . beauty of its flowers. **1868** GRAY *Field Botany* 77 Large-flowered Red Flax . . . has showy crimson-red flowers.

Large-fruited, *a.* +In the specific names of plants: Bearing large fruit. — **1813** MUHLENBERG *Cat. Plants* 48 *Cratægus punctata*, large-fruited hawthorn. *Ib.* 88 *Juglans compressa* [or] *squamosa macrocarpa*, large-fruited shell-bark [or] shag-bark walnut. **1843** TORREY *Flora N.Y.* II. 331 *Juncus stygius*. . . . Large-fruited Rush. . . . In an extensive sphagnous swamp.

Large-leaved, *a.* +In specific names of trees and plants: Having large leaves.

1785 MARSHALL *Amer. Grove* 93 *Morus rubra*. Large-leaved Virginian Mulberry Tree. **1810** MICHAUX *Arbres* I. 34 Large leaved magnolia, . . . nom donné par moi. **1832** BROWNE *Sylva* 212 The large-leaved umbrella tree arrives at the height of 30 or 35 feet. **1846** — *Trees Amer.* 78 *Acer macrophyllum*. . . . The Large-leaved Maple is one of the most graceful of trees. **1884** SARGENT *Rep. Forests* 21 *Magnolia macrophylla*. . . . Large-leaved Cucumber tree. **1892** APGAR *Trees Northern U.S.* 86 Large-leaved or California Maple. . . . Cultivated; from the Pacific coast. **1901** MOHR *Plant Life Ala.* 480 Birthwort Family . . . [includes] Virginia Snakeroot, . . . Large-leaved Pipe Vine [etc.].

+**Largemouth (black bass).** =next. — **1884** GOODE, etc. *Fisheries* I. 401 The Large-mouth is known in the Great Lake region . . . as the 'Oswego Bass.' **1893** *Outing* XXII. 94/1 In the fresh pond above Nag's Head . . . are found the large-mouth black-bass. **1897** *Ib.* XXX. 219/2 Doctor James A. Henshall, has killed Florida large-mouths weighing well up in the 'teens.' **1911** *Rep. Fisheries 1908* 313 The name 'perch' is also given to the large-mouth black bass (*Micropterus salmoides*) . . . in the Southern states.

+**Large-mouthed (black) bass.** A species of black bass, *Huro floridana* or *Micropterus salmoides*. — **1883** *Century Mag.* July 376/2 There are but two well-defined species, the large-mouthed bass and the small-mouthed bass. **1883** *Nat. Museum Bul.* No. 27, 446 Large-mouthed Black Bass. . . . Rivers and lakes of the United States.

***Larger,** *a.* +In specific names of plants and birds. — *c*1728 CATESBY *Carolina* I. 17/1 The larger red-crested Wood-pecker weighs nine ounces. **1843** TORREY *Flora N.Y.* I. 78 *Lechea major*. Larger Lechea. . . . Dry woods and on hill-sides. July–September. **1857** GRAY *Botany* 71 *L*[*inum*] *Boottii*, Planchon. (Larger Yellow Flax.) **1869** *Amer. Naturalist* III. 231 The larger White Egret . . . [is] occasionally tempted to visit our coast. **1883** *Nat. Museum Bul.* No. 27, 158 Larger White-cheeked Goose. . . . South to California in winter. **1901** MOHR *Plant Life Ala.* 502 Larger Whitlow-wort. . . . Coast of western Florida to Mississippi.

+**Largest red oak.** (See quotation.) — **1785** MARSHALL *Amer. Grove* 122 *Q*[*uercus*] *rubra maxima*. Largest Red Oak.

+**Large-toothed aspen.** (See quot. 1892.) — **1858** THOREAU *Maine Woods* 98 Its banks were . . . densely covered with . . . mountain ash, the large-toothed aspen [etc.]. **1860** CURTIS *Woody Plants N.C.* 73 Large toothed aspen (*P. grandidentata*). . . . This tree is occasionally seen adorning the streets of our villages. **1892** APGAR *Trees Northern U.S.* 168 *Populus grandidentata* (Large-toothed Aspen.) Leaves large, . . . with large, irregular, sinuate teeth.

+**Large tupelo.** A southeastern variety of the tupelo, *Nyssa aquatica*. — **1810** MICHAUX *Arbres* I. 29 *Large tupelo*, . . . nom le plus général dans les Etats du sud. **1832** BROWNE *Sylva* 222 The large tupelo . . . attains the elevation of 70 or 80 feet. **1892** APGAR *Trees Northern U.S.* 113 Large Tupelo. . . . In water or wet swamps; Virginia, Kentucky, and southward.

+**Lariat,** *n.* Also **lariatt, larriat.** [Sp. *la reata*, 'the rope.'] (See also LARIETTE.)

1. a. A long rope, made of rawhide, horse hair, or hemp, used for lassoing cattle, horses, etc.; a lasso. **b.** A similar rope used for tethering animals; a long halter.

1835 IRVING *Tour on Prairies* 36 He came . . . [with] coils of cordage at his saddle bow, which we were told were lariats, or noosed cords, used in catching the wild horse. **1841** FOOTE *Texas & Texans* II. 384 The ranchero . . . dashes among the herd . . . swinging about his head his coiled *lariat* —a platted raw-hide rope, with a running noose at the end. **1844** KENDALL *Narr. Santa Fé Exped.* I. 93 It is said that they [*sc.* rattlesnakes] will never cross a hair lariat. **1849** *31st Congress 1 Sess.* Sen. Ex. Doc. No. 64, 85 The sergeant, however, soon ascertained that the horse was an American one, and had a *lariat* (a long halter) upon him. **1853** 'P. PAXTON' *Yankee in Texas* 123 He got all his fixins ready for camping—his little wallet, and tin cup, and larriat to stake out his mule. **1873** *Winfield* (Kan.) *Courier* 5 June 3/1 A buffalo cow . . . will be offered as the prize to the first man who can catch her with horse and lariatt. **1919** CODY & COOPER *Buffalo Bill* 227 Will had cut one buffalo out from the great mass, and was pursuing it . . . , his lariat beginning to circle over his head.

2. Attrib. and comb. with *end, noose, pin*, etc.

1850 GARRARD *Wah-To-Yah* i. 9 The lariat noose is sure to fall on their [the mules'] unwilling necks. *Ib.* xi. 144 The riding animals . . . stood while their owners, with lariat ends in their hands . . . , raked out coals. **1875** *Chicago Tribune* 14 Oct. 7/1 The old camp-sites are marked by . . . lariat-stakes . . . to which the ponies have been attached. **1880** INGHAM *Digging Gold* 223 Young laid out the town, using a lariat rope instead of a surveyor's chain for a measure. **1881** *Rep. Indian Affairs* 93 [Manufactured] by the blacksmith: twenty-three beetle-rings, . . . one hundred and fifty lariat pins [etc.].

+**Lariat,** *v.*

1. *tr.* To catch with a lariat; to lasso.

1846 *Spirit of Times* 4 July 222/2 [The horse] has never been backed or before *lariated*. **1847** HENRY *Campaign Sk.* 85 One of the men was evidently lariated, and was probably choked to death before he was pulled off his horse. **1886** *Outing* IX. 104/2 A mustang was lariated, saddled, and . . . we were *en route* for the mountains.

2. To stake out (an animal) on a tether. Frequently with *out*. Also fig.

1850 TAYLOR *Eldorado* (1862) 104 My mules had already been caught and lariated. **1867** RICHARDSON *Beyond Miss.* 55 He lariated his mule upon the prairie to graze. **1869** *Overland Mo.* Aug. 127, I have even heard a Texan speak of land which he 'lariated out,' meaning thereby that he had just bought it from Government, but not occupied it yet. **1887** *Outing* April 11/1 In a troop of cavalry there are ordinarily two sentinels over the horses if they are herded or *lariated* out. **1888** *Red Man* (Carlisle, Pa.) Sept., Two [Indian] women took our mules and lariated them out.

+**Lariet(te).** =LARIAT *n.* 1. — **1843** N. BOONE *Journal* 199 This morning several horses were missing and evidence of foul play shown by the lariettes being cut. **1847** PARKMAN in *Knickerb.* XXIX. 508 They galloped around her [*sc.* a cow], trying in vain to noose her with their trail-ropes, which they had converted into *lariettes* for the occasion. **1864** *Wkly. New Mexican* 21 Oct. 2/3 Indians . . . cut the lariet that held two horses to the picket rope. **1876** BESANT & RICE *Golden Butterfly* 3 The horsehair lariette . . . serves the western Nimrod for lassoing by day and for keeping off snakes at night.

***Lark.**

1. a. =HORNED LARK. **b.** Any of several similar birds, +as the American titlark, *Anthus spinoletta rubescens*, or the meadow lark, *Sturnella magna magna*.

1637 MORTON *New Canaan* 70 The Larkes there are like our Larkes of England in all respects: sauing that they do not use to sing at all. **1709** LAWSON *Carolina* 144 The Lark with us resorts to the Savannas, or natural Meads, and green Marshes. **1851** GLISAN *Jrnl. Army Life* 88 The birds . . . most common to this country [Indian Territory], that are good for food, are teal, . . . plover, lark, robin [etc.]. *a*1918 G. STUART *On Frontier* II. 118 'Tis very pleasant to hear the larks, flickers, blackbirds, and curlews . . . singing.

+**2.** A person. *colloq.*[2]

1835 LONGSTREET *Ga. Scenes* 22 Fetch up your nag, my old cock; you're jist the lark I wanted to get hold of. **1840** SIMMS *Border Beagles* 133 The other lark told Betsy a different story. **1859** A. CARY *Country Life* i. 12 Old Wolverton's . . . was a moughty hard place for the gal, whatever kind of a lark she mought be.

+**Lark bunting. 1.** A bird of the genus *Calcarius*. With modifiers. **2.** The prairie bobolink, *Calamospiza melanocarys*. — **(1) 1839** AUDUBON *Ornith. Biog.* V. 44 Chestnut-Collared Lark-Bunting, *Emberiza Ornata*, . . . is by no means a common bird; keeps in pairs, and appears to live exclusively upon the ground. **1874** COUES *Birds N.W.* 121 *Plectrophanes pictus*. Painted Lark Bunting. **(2) 1869** *Amer. Naturalist* III. 296 That pretty and musical bird of the high plains, the Lark Bunting (*Calamospiza bicolor*), also occurred [along the upper Missouri R.]. **1874** COUES *Birds N.W.* 163 The Lark Bunting is one of the most singularly specialized of all our fringilline forms. **1917** *Birds of Amer.* III. 76/1 The Lark Bunting is a bird of the prairies.

+**Lark finch.** =next. — **1825** BONAPARTE *Ornithology* I. 47 [The] Lark Finch, *Fringilla Grammaca*, . . . frequent[s] the prairies, and very seldom, if ever, alight[s] on trees. **1877** *Field & Forest* III. 51 A pair of lark finches were seen and identified by Mr. Ridgway. **1917** [see next].

+**Lark sparrow.** A handsome American sparrow (*Chondestes grammacus*), widely distributed west of the Alleghenies. — **1887** RIDGWAY *Manual N.A. Birds* 414 *C*[*hondestes*] *grammacus*. . . . Lark Sparrow. **1917** *Birds of Amer.* III. 31 Lark Sparrow. . . . Other Names.—Quail-head; Road-bird; Lark Finch; Little Meadowlark.

***Larkspur.** Any one of various plants of the genus *Delphinium*. — **1737** BRICKELL *N. Carolina* 22 Prickly Bind-Weed, Larks-Spur, Hops, Flax and Hemp, the best and finest in the known World groweth in North Carolina. **1821** NUTTALL *Travels Arkansa* 148 These vast plains . . . were now enamelled with innumerable flowers, among the most splendid of which were the azure Larkspur, gilded Coreopsides [etc.]. **1852** STANSBURY *Gt. Salt Lake* 26 In the bottom of the creek a species of larkspur and wild-onion abound. *a*1918 G. STUART *On Frontier* II. 227 There were . . . several varieties of larkspurs and lobelia.

+**Lash rope.** A rope used for lashing or securing a pack on a horse.

1806 LEWIS in *L. & Clark Exped.* V. (1905) 114 Sergt. Gass, McNeal, Whitehouse and Goodrich accompanyed them [*sc.* Indians] with a view to procure some pack or lash ropes. **1843** *Amer. Pioneer* II. 162 Each horse was provided with . . . a lash rope to secure the load. **1882** BAILLIE-GROHMAN *Camps in Rockies* 45 The 'cinche' . . . and the lash-rope that is thrown over the load and round the animal are as taut as a strong man's arms can make them. **1893** ROOSEVELT *Wilderness Hunter* 178 A skilful professional packer . . . adjusts the doubles and twins of the lash-rope so accurately, that everything stays in place. *a***1918** G. STUART *On Frontier* I. 149 A pocket dictionary . . . [is] in a somewhat damaged condition from frequent pressures of the lash rope on our pack horses.

+**'Lasses.** Short for MOLASSES. *humorous* or *colloq.* Also attrib.

1775 *Broadside Verse* (1930) 141/1 The 'lasses they eat every day, Would keep an house a winter. **1792** C. PRENTISS *Fugitive Ess.* 155 Ye muses, who, round mount Parnassus, Lick *Helicon*, as sweet as 'lasses. **1842** *Spirit of Times* (Phila.) 3 Jan. (Th.), Every puppy that would be keeled over with a smaller of rum and 'lasses turns up his nose at him. **1854** M. J. HOLMES *Tempest & Sunshine* 317 Get along Jack, pokin' your fingers into the 'lasses cup. **1879** *Harper's Mag.* June 70/1 The appetite may be satisfied with . . . bread and 'lasses.' **1890** HARTE *Waif of Plains* 50 They is chickens and hamanaigs and hot biksquits, and lasses. **1909** CALHOUN *Miss Minerva* 174 Aunt Minerva's in the kitchen right now makin' me a 'lasses custard.

+**'Lasses candy.** Candy made of molasses. *colloq.* — **1807** IRVING, etc. *Salmagundi* x, This manufacture is called by the Bostonians *lasses candy.* **1834** CARRUTHERS *Kentuckian* I. 99 Some of them had their mouths daubed, like children suckin 'lasses candy. **1856** *Porter's Spirit of Times* 18 Oct. 109/1 The one who could object to so harmless an amusement [as trotting for purses at a horse fair], would deprive his baby of 'lasses' candy on a Sunday, for conscience' sake.

+**Lasset.** [F. *lacet.*] A rope used to stake out a horse to graze. *Obs.* — **1848** ROBINSON *Santa Fé Exped.* (1932) 19 Five hundred frightened horses (with their lassetts and pickets flying about them) ran wildly down the Arkansas. *Ib.* 44 A novel scene was presented—the [Nebajo] Indians catching their horses with the lasso, and catching the lassett from the ground when at full speed.

Lasso, *n.* Also †**laso, lazo.** *S.W.* A long rope, usually of rawhide or hair, having a noose at the end and used chiefly for catching cattle and horses. {laço, of Patagonia, etc., 1768–} Also attrib.

(*a*) **1833** CATLIN *Indians* I. 253 The laso is a long thong, of rawhide. *c***1836** *Ib.* II. 152 A line, with a sort of 'laso throw,' came from an awkward hand. **1837** IRVING *Bonneville* II. 142 The vaqueros, or Indian cattle-drivers, have also learnt the use of the laso from the Spaniards. **1880** *Cimarron News & Press* 9 Sept. 1/6 Ambrose threw the laso over the beast [a mountain lion] holding him secure and fast.

(*b*) **1834** A. PIKE *Sketches* 102 He was the best rider, the best thrower of the *lasso*, and the best hunter in the valley. **1847** J. PALMER *Rocky Mts.* 233 He accordingly prepared himself with a lasso rope. **1853** BREWERTON *With Kit Carson* (1930) 56 Juan galloped up with the truant mule which he had captured with his lasso. *a***1861** WINTHROP *J. Brent* ii. 13 They cantered off . . . and then, halting just out of lasso reach, stopped to reconnoitre me. **1887** *Outing* X. 15/2 The man rose in his stirrup and flung his lasso. **1923** J. H. COOK *On Old Frontier* 9 Longworth now threw his lasso on the pony he had first selected for me.

(*c*) **1836** CROCKETT *Exploits* 129 The mustangs . . . are taken by means of a lazo, a long rope with a noose, which is thrown around their neck. **1841** W. KENNEDY *Texas* I. 125 There are two modes of catching [mustangs]. . . . [One is] by noosing them with a cord made of twisted strips of raw hide, attached to a long pole, and called the *lazo. Ib.*, As soon as the lazo is thrown over the head of a horse, it is drawn tight, almost to suffocation. **1856** DAVIS *El Gringo* (1857) 209 The muleteers and cowherds are remarkably skillful in throwing the *lazo.*

Lasso, *v. S.W. tr.* To catch with, or as with, a lasso. {1807–} — **1834** *Visit to Texas* 60 A horse which has been lazoed is blindfolded, mounted by a rider [etc.]. **1880** *Cimarron News & Press* 9 Sept. 1/6 Mr. Ambrose and Mr. Goodman saddled their horses and prepared their riatas with a view of lasoing the animal. **1888** J. J. WEBB *Adventures* 212 There was a man in the corral lassoing a mule. **1907** *St. Nicholas* May 589/2 'You will, will you?' jeered Jo, who had just come in stealthily from behind, and now by a dexterous twist had Peace safely lassoed with a bath towel. **1924** R. CUMMINS *Sky-High Corral* 93 He sneaked up—an' lass'ed me—an' ground my elbows together behind.

Lassoer. One who lassoes. {1896–} — **1883** SWEET & KNOX *Through Texas* xli. 584 Juan Gonzales . . . is said to be the champion lassoer of the world. **1884** W. SHEPHERD *Prairie Exper.* 52 There are few good lassoers in this part of the country.

Lassoing. Catching with a lasso. {1864–} — **1838** 'TEXIAN' *Mexico v. Texas* 48 The men were collecting the mules, and when these were driven together, the lassoing began. **1850** GARRARD *Wah-To-Yah* xx. 238 Considerable chasing and final lassoing were necessary to capture the young brutes.

***Last.** A model of the foot. Used by shoemakers in making or repairing shoes.

1648 *Conn. Rec.* I. 491 In the working shopp . . . lasts, axes, handsaw [etc.]. **1742** *Md. Hist. Mag.* XX. 267 Send me one Dozen of Mens shoe Lasts Large and different sizes. **1835** *Stimpson's Boston Directory* Advt. 14 William Mitchell & Co. . . . have constantly on hand a choice selection of Shoe Stock, . . . and Lasts, Findings and Trimmings, &c. **1915** *Bur. Labor Statistics Bul.* No. 180, 37 The assembler . . . tacks the insole to a wooden last.

attrib. and *comb.* **1820** FLINT *Lett. from Amer.* 214 There are . . . one bellows-maker; two last-makers; one whip-maker. **1837** W. JENKINS *Ohio Gaz.* 158 A last factory, producing 14,000 lasts, 200 boot trees, and 200 crimping boards per annum.

Lasting. =EVERLASTING *n.* 1. {1782–} Also attrib.

1733 *Md. Hist. Mag.* XX. 61 A pair of Childs stays to be covered with some Lasting Silk and a Skirt of the same Silk. **1759** in H. M. Brooks *Gleanings* 33 Lastings of all colours, bombazine, . . . English oznabrigs. **1790** *Penna. Packet* 1 Jan. 3/4 At the city Auction Store, Will be sold by Public Vendue, . . . Lastings, Durants, Camblets [etc.]. **1827** *Hallowell* (Me.) *Gaz.* 20 June 3/5 (*advt.*), A large assortment of . . . Piece Goods, among which are Broadcloth; cassimeres; Lastings; Denmark Satins [etc.]. **1885** *Harper's Mag.* Jan. 280/1 Serges, lastings, ducks, drills, flannels, beavers, and all kinds of cloths are sold by the yard.

Lasting boot. A boot made in part of lasting. *Obs.* — **1832** *Louisville Pub. Advertiser* 17 March, An extensive assortment of . . . black and colored lasting boots . . . for sale. **1891** WELCH *Recoll. 1830–40* 173 Lasting or prunella boots with an Indian embroidered moccasin for the outside.

Latania. [Sp. and mod. L.] +=CABBAGE PALMETTO. — **1799** Cuming *Western Tour* 336 Some . . . cabins [were] covered over with a shrub like a large fan, called latania. **1819** E. DANA *Geogr. Sk.* 238 On the . . . outer margin of the cane, the palmetto, or latania, fill the slope between the cane and the inundated lands.

Latanier. [F.] +=prec. Also attrib. — **1827** *Western Mo. Rev.* I. 315 Palmetto, or latanier, peet, and long moss, add an aspect of novelty to the view in the eye of strangers. **1868** *Putnam's Mag.* I. 594/1 Here and there . . . is a 'latanier-hut,' with adobe walls and a roof thatched with . . . palmetto. **1897** SUDWORTH *Arborescent Flora* 104.

***Latch.** A fastening for a door or gate.

1678 *New Castle Court Rec.* 299, 7 prs of hinges & some other small Laches. **1712** HEMPSTEAD *Diary* 16, I came home & hanged ye Door made a Latch &c. **1847** FIELD *Drama in Pokerville* 158 [The mansion's] numerous unaffected cracks and spaces clearly showing that dropping the latch was a useless formality. **1916** DU PUY *Uncle Sam* 107 The latch was so set that the door locked.

b. As the name for a particular kind of earmark. *Obs.* Also attrib.

1665 *Hempstead Rec.* I. 188 One brindled two yeere old heifer marcked on the neer ear with a latch marke. **1689** *Ib.* 433 Jeams Jackson his eare marcke is a slot in ye neere eare and a lach on ye uppor side ye of eare. **1745** *Smithtown Rec.* 85 Samuel Smith his ear mark is a latch under the left ear.

Latchstring. A string that passes through a hole in a door and enables one outside to lift the latch and open the door. {1861–}

1791 in Jillson *Dark & Bl. Ground* 109 The doors and the window shutters are of oaken puncheons, secured by stout bars on the inside with a latch-string of leather hanging out. **1863** A. D. WHITNEY *F. Gartney* i, The latch-string was put forth. **1884** 'MARK TWAIN' *H. Finn* 352 You only have to pull a buckskin latch-string, they don't fasten the doors. **1903** FOX *Little Shepherd* i, He closed the door softly and caught the short, deer-skin latch-string to the wooden pin outside.

attrib. **1883** ZEIGLER & GROSSCUP *Alleghanies* 322, [I] approached a door through whose latch-string hole and gaping slits rays of light were sifting.

+**b.** *fig.* In various contexts having reference to leaving the latchstring hanging out as a sign of hospitality and welcome.

1858 *Ill. Agric. Soc. Trans.* III. 342 The people of the west . . . are always to be found with 'their latch strings out.' **1865** RICHARDSON *Secret Service* xii. 157 The two leading characteristics of Chicago residents . . . are, holding the ribbons and leaving out the latch-string. **1876** MILLER *First Families* 16 'The latch string,' to use the expression of the Sierras, hung on the outside to strangers. **1893** *Advance* 16 March 209 'Our latch string is out,' has become a classic expression of cordial hospitality. **1904** *Chicago Tribune* 30 Nov. 1 City's Latch-String Out. Commercial Association Plans to Make Visitors Welcome.

Lateral. {1635–} +In a system of irrigation a ditch leading directly out of the main canal or water supply. — **1890** *Stock Grower & Farmer* 26 April 4/3 The waters of Red river are to be divided and carried by ditches and laterals. **1901** *Congress. Rec.* 26 Feb. 3078/2 If you had lived at the tail end of a lateral as long as I have you would know something about this subject [irrigation]. **1912** *Indian Laws & Tr.* III. 534 For continuing the construction of necessary channels and laterals [etc.] . . . , thirty-five thousand dollars. **1913** LONDON *Valley of Moon* III. xiv, A five-inch stream of sparkling water splashed into the shallow main ditch of his irrigation system and flowed away across the orchard through many laterals.

Late unpleasantness. (See UNPLEASANTNESS.)

***Lath.**

1. A thin narrow strip of wood used by builders in forming a basis for plastering or roofing.

1634 WOOD *New Eng. Prospect* 52 [Each settler should bring] Froes . . . for the riving of Pailes and Laths. *c***1642** *Harvard Rec.* I. 12 Laths, . . . 3 [shillings]. **1758** *Lett. to Washington* II. 321, I shall take ye Roof off ye

House, as soon as ye Carpenters gets ye Laths for to shingle on. **1853** COZZENS *Prismatics* 47 Here and there large pieces of plaster had fallen, exposing the laths. **1899** *Boston Transcript* 14 Jan. 12/2 The word cat is still applied to the first rough coat in plastering which fills the space between the laths.

2. Attrib. and comb. with *cutting, saw, sword, wood.*

1771 *N.H. Gazette* 30 Aug., Such persons as are desirous of contracting for . . . hogshead and barrel staves, with heading, lathwood, ash oak rafters, etc. **1827** *Western Mo. Rev.* I. 80 A lath-cutting machine is also in operation which cuts them with great rapidity. **1853** J. W. BOND *Minnesota* 124 This mill . . . runs two upright saws, one circular, one cross-cut circular, and three lath saws. **1902** LORIMER *Lett. Merchant* 99 He was dangling head foremost in the air while Clarence was threatening his jugular with a lath sword.

Lather. One who puts on laths. — **1885** *Boston Directory* 1289 Lathers. Brown Robert T. **1889** *Home Missionary* May 3 Frank became an expert lather.

***Lathing.**

1. Material used for laths, lathwork. {1756–}

1636 *Springfield Rec.* I. 160 He [is] to undertak the getting of ye thatch and all other things belonging to it with lathing and nayls. **1897** F. C. MOORE *How to Build a Home* 7 The ceiling should be plastered on metallic lathing.

***2.** Putting on laths.

1641 *New Haven Col. Rec.* 55 Lathing and laying shingle. **1741** *Md. Hist Mag.* VIII. 359 For Lathing and plaistering Including the pulling down the old plaistering two shillings per yard.

3. Attrib. with *hammer, hatchet.*

1638 *Md. Archives* IV. 30, 1. hatchett & lathing hammer. **1812** *Niles Reg.* II. 376/2 Lathing hatchets would be a good substitute for tomahawks, if they cannot be had.

+Latin school. A preparatory school in which Latin is taught. Also *Latin schoolhouse, schoolmaster.*

Cf. GRAMMAR SCHOOL 1, and Du. *latijnsche school*, G. *lateinische schule.*
1651 *Mass. Bay Rec.* III. 242 Whosoeuer shall . . . cause Schollers belonginge to the Colledge or any other Latine Schoole . . . to spend any of theire time [etc.]. **1699** *Boston Rec.* 234 Voted, that an Assistant be Provided to be with Mr. Cheever in the Latine School. **1715** *Ib.* 113 Real Estate for the use of the Publick Lattin School. **1781** S. PETERS *Hist. Conn.* (1829) 148 Elms . . . surround the centre square, wherein are . . . the jail, and Latin school. **1838** *S. Lit. Messenger* IV. 361/2 The neighborhood viewed this novelty, a Latin school, as it was called, as an important acquisition to the country. **1865** *Atlantic Mo.* XV. 737 He is doomed to go into the Latin School, and spend three or four years in trying to learn what he never can learn well. **1915** *Handbook Best Private Schools* 152 Chicago Latin School for Girls . . . is an exclusive day school. — **1687** *Mass. Prov. Acts* VII. 640 Your Petitioners . . . Crave . . . Leave . . . to meet on the Sabbath daye to exercise our duties in the Lattin Schoolhouse. **1701** *Boston Rec.* 8 The building a House for the Lattin Schoolmaster.

***Latten.** Also **latin, letten,** *etc. attrib.* Designating various articles made of latten, a metallic alloy similar to brass. *Obs.* — **1638** *Md. Archives* IV. 30, 1. latin pott. 1. bagg. **1643** *Conn. Rec.* I. 456, 1 laten candlesticke, & tunell. **1652** *Mayflower Descendant* XI. 90 One letten pan and an earthen Dish, 00–01–04. **1674** *Essex Inst. Coll.* XXXVII. 98 Wearing apparell 8 sh; in pewter; & 2 latten peeces; 35 sh. **1684** *Ib.* XXV. 155 3 payles. 1 Lattin dripping pan. 1 sacke.

+Latter-Day Saint. A member of the Church of Jesus Christ of Latter-Day Saints; a Mormon.

1838 S. WOOD *Lett. from U.S.* 10 The Church of the Latter-day Saints originated in 1830, with a man of the name of Joseph Smith. **1847** PARKMAN in *Knickerb.* XXIX. 499 The people of Illinois and Missouri . . . have never been on the best terms with the 'Latter Day Saints.' **1884** *Century Mag.* May 114 It was a Mormon elder, come to preach . . . the strange doctrines of the Latter-Day Saints. **1890** in *Congress. Rec.* 23 Jan. (1900) 1102/2 My advice to the Latter-Day Saints is to refrain from contracting any marriage forbidden by the law of the land. *a***1918** G. STUART *On Frontier* I. 50 We stayed with the 'Latter Day Saints,' as the Mormons called themselves.

Laughing,** *n.* +An hysterical fit of laughter or involuntary facial distortion which afflicted persons attending religious revivals. *Obs.* Also attrib. (Cf. HOLY LAUGH and JERK *n.*[2] 1.) — **1824** R. H. BISHOP *Hist. Church Ky.* 353 *Falling* . . . was succeeded by involuntary convulsive *laughing*, by the *jirks* [etc.]. *c1843** B. W. STONE *Biography* (1847) 41 The laughing exercise was frequent, confined solely with the religious.

***Laughing,** *a.* +In the names of American birds whose notes resemble laughter. (Cf. LAUGHING GOOSE, etc.) — **1848** *S. Lit. Messenger* XIV. 531/1 The free open shout of the large laughing owl, so abundant in South Florida. **1888** *Century Mag.* XXXVI. 699/1 The collared turtle or laughing dove is usually catalogued as the ring-dove.

Laughing goose. The white-fronted goose, *Anser albifrons;* also, the tule goose, *Anser albifrons gambelli.* {1750– (Edwards *Nat. Hist. Birds*)} — **1828** BONAPARTE *Synopsis* 376 The White-fronted Goose. The Laughing Goose, *Anas albifrons*. . . . Rare and accidental in the middle states. **1850** BROWNE *Poultry Yard* 211 The domesticated goose is a combination of the 'grey-legged,' (*Anser palustris*,) 'white-fronted,' or 'laughing goose,' (*A. albifrons*,) and 'bean goose.' **1917** *Birds of Amer.* I. 158 White-fronted Goose. *Anser albifrons gambeli*. . . . [Also called] Laughing Goose; Harlequin Brant [etc.].

Laughing gull. {1839–} +The black-headed gull, *Larus atricilla.* — **1789** MORSE *Amer. Geog.* 59 American Birds [include] . . . Laughing Gull, Goose, Canada Goose [etc.]. **1823** James *Exped.* I. 266 *Larus ridibundus?*—Laughing gull. **1883** *Nat. Museum Bul.* No. 27, 169 Laughing Gull. . . . Atlantic coast, from Maine (casually) to mouth of the Amazon. **1917** *Birds of Amer.* I. 50/1 The Laughing Gull is well named, for seemingly it laughs.

***Laundress.** A woman whose occupation is laundering. — **1679** *Harvard Rec.* I. 67 The Colledge Laundress is allowed forty shillings per annum for washing the Colledge linnen. **1720** *Ib.* II. 453 The laundress [is] to be allowed twenty shillings per Quarter for Washing the College Linen. **1865** *Atlantic Mo.* April 510/2 Nancy [was] the laundress, of a gentleman residing at the capital. **1918** C. WELLS *Vicky Van* iii. 38, I believe the laundress and chore boy come by the day.

***Laundry.**

***1.** A place where linens, clothes, etc., are laundered.

1840 *Picayune* 8 Oct. 2/3 The laundry . . . is situated somewhat apart from the place where the other prisoners are. **1881** *Rep. Indian Affairs* 73 It is very difficult to drain the slops from the laundry and kitchen. **1913** LONDON *Valley of Moon* II. ii, I've worked in the laundry for years.

2. Attrib. with *cottage, girl, soap,* etc.

1838 F. A. KEMBLE *Journal* 24 The eldest son of our laundry-woman . . . is uncommonly bright. **1872** ROE *Army Lett.* 78 Everything had been carried off except a few candles on Mrs. Hunt's side, and a few cakes of laundry soap on mine. **1885** *Century Mag.* Jan. 266 Laundry Trays . . . are hardly to be regarded as a conspicuous element of the sanitary works of a house. *Ib.* 260 This trap (Putman) or something like it may probably come into universal use for wash-stands, baths, and laundry-tubs. **1885** *Santa Fé Wkly. New Mexican* 10 Sept. 4/7 George Handley, a laundryman at Albuquerque, has skipped the town. **1899** *Mo. So. Dakotan* I. 186 The laundry cottage at the State Insane Asylum . . . was burned. **1913** LONDON *Valley of Moon* II. v, You belonged to the laundry workers' union. *Ib.* III. x, Saxon felt that she was something more than a laundry girl and the wife of a union teamster.

***Laurel.**

1. a. Any tree or shrub of the genus *Laurus* or related genera. **+b.** The evergreen magnolia (*Magnolia grandiflora*), or related species. **+c.** Any one of various shrubs belonging to either of the genera *Kalmia* and *Rhododendron.* (Cf. AMERICAN, GREAT LAUREL.) **+d.** The madroña, *Arbutus menziesii.* Also attrib. with *tree.*

1637 MORTON *New Canaan* 92 There are divers aromaticall herbes . . . , Balme, Lawrell, Hunnisuckles, and the like. **1682** ASH *Carolina* 6 There are many other Fragrant smelling trees, the Myrtle, Bay and Lawrel, several Others to us wholly unknown. **1709** LAWSON *Carolina* 94 Bay and Laurel generally delight in a low, swampy ground. I know no Use they make of them, but for Fire-wood. **1815** *Mass. H. S. Coll.* 2 Ser. IV. 273 The first growth, after a pine lot has been felled, we have remarked to be . . . laurel, cross-wort, whortleberry [etc.]. **1852** E. F. ELLET *Pioneer Women* 206 [It] is so named from the profusion of . . . Kalmia latifolia, or laurel, which cluster along its rocky sides. **1886** Z. F. SMITH *Kentucky* 22 The forest, undergrown with brush and thick laurel, seemed to forbid a passage onward. *a***1918** G. STUART *On Frontier* I. 59 There were also . . . some beautiful madrona or laurel trees. **1924** RAINE *Land of Saddle-Bags* 133 Away up under a 'clift' a spring must be selected that flows under an impenetrable thicket of laurel (rhododendron).

+2. Attrib. in the specific names of American trees.

1744 MOORE *Voy. Georgia* 98 The trees in the grove are mostly bay . . . American ash, and the laurel tulip. **1827** *Western Mo. Rev.* I. 252 The handsomest of the family, is the laurel Almond, *laurus Caroliniensis.*

+Laurel brake. A thicket of laurel. (Cf. CANEBRAKE.) — **1853** P. KENNEDY *Blackwater Chron.* 73 A man could walk about for a week, . . . if he got into a big laurel-brake. **1853** *Harper's Mag.* Dec. 18/1 The settlers on its borders . . . regard it [a tract of land in Randolph Co., Va.] as an ill-omened region, filled with bears, panthers, impassable laurel-brakes, and dangerous precipices. **1872** *Ib.* Aug. 347/1 Dick . . . by a cruel ruse surprised a covey [of children] in a laurel break [*sic*].

Laurel cherry. {1787–} +An evergreen shrub (*Laurocerasus caroliniana*) found in the South. — **1850** *New Eng. Farmer* II. 221 Of the various kinds of cherry, the laurel or bird cherry is the most dangerous. **1897** SUDWORTH *Arborescent Flora* 246 Laurel Cherry . . . [is also called] Wild Peach, . . . Wild Orange, . . . Mock Orange [etc.]. **1901** MOHR *Plant Life Ala.* 552 Mock Orange. Laurel Cherry. Wild Peach. . . . North Carolina, valley Cape Fear River to Florida, west to eastern Texas.

Laurel-leaved, *a.* Designating various trees having leaves resembling those of laurel. {1787–} — **1785** MARSHALL *Amer. Grove* 82 *Magnolia.* The Laurel-Leaved Tulip-Tree. **1813** MUHLENBERG *Cat. Plants* 44 *Arbutus laurifolia*, laurel-leaved strawberry tree. **1874** *Dept. Agric. Rep. 1873* 255, I regard the laurel-leaved willow as one of the most beautiful which can be planted.

+Laurel magnolia. The evergreen magnolia (*Magnolia grandiflora*); the sweet bay (*M. virginiana*). — **1817** BROWN *Western Gaz.* 145 The laurel magnolia is the beauty of the forest. **1826** FLINT *Recoll.* 294 [Along the Miss. R. in La.] also you begin to discover the ever-verdant laurel magnolia, with its beautiful foliage of the thickness and the feeling of leather. **1850** S. F. Cooper *Rural Hours* 476 The small Laurel Magnolia, or Sweet Bay, is found as far north as New York, in swampy grounds.

+**Laurel oak.** Either of two American oaks (*Quercus laurifolia* and *Q. imbricaria*) having glossy, laurel-like leaves. — **1810** Michaux *Arbres* I. 23 *Laurel oak*, . . . dénomination secondaire dans les Etats a l'ouest des Monts Alléghanys. **1832** Browne *Sylva* 271 West of the [Allegheny] Mountains . . . it is called Jack Oak, . . . and sometimes from the form of the leaves, Laurel Oak. **1884** Sargent *Rep. Forests* 154 *Quercus imbricaria*. . . . Shingle Oak. Laurel Oak. **1901** Mohr *Plant Life Ala.* 131 Between Bon Secour and Perdido Bay low, sandy hills . . . support a high forest . . . of laurel oak and Cuban and long-leaf pine.

Laurel thicket. =Laurel brake. {1840} — **1750** T. Walker *Journal* 49 Just at the foot of the Hill is a Laurel Thicket. **1834** *S. Lit. Messenger* I. 97 The tangled laurel thickets affording them secure refuge from foes. **1853** Ramsey *Tennessee* 501 The dark laurel thickets . . . had hitherto, excluded even the hunter and Indian from an easy access to it [the mountain] in pursuit of game. **1883** Zeigler & Grosscup *Alleghanies* 264 In one of the dense woods I passed men engaged in clearing a laurel thicket.

+**Laurier almond.** =Laurel cherry. — **1818** Darby *Emigrant's Guide* 80 The most important vegetable productions [include]: . . . *Celtis crassifolia*, Hackberry, *Cerasus caroliniana*, Laurier almond [etc.]. **1819** E. Dana *Geogr. Sk.* 237 We subjoin a list of the vast variety of forest trees, growing in the Attacapas and Opelousas region—viz. . . . Laurier almond, dogwood, swamp dogwood [etc.]. **1829** *Western Mo. Rev.* III. 57 Laurier almond, and Bois d'arcs, the most beautiful trees of the American forest.

***Lavender.** Any one of various plants of the genus *Lavandula*, valued chiefly for their aroma. — **1737** Brickell *N. Carolina* 20 The Pot-Herbs . . . are . . . Lavender, Hyssop, which grows very large, Sweet Bazil, Groundsel. **1817–8** Eaton *Botany* (1822) 328 *Lavandula spica*, lavender. **1858** Holmes *Autocrat* iv. 87, I open a certain closet. . . . On its shelves used to lie bundles of sweet-marjoram and pennyroyal and lavender and mint and catnip. **1912** Nicholson *Hoosier Chron.* 591 She found in the linen chest the leaves of lavender that Mary had strewn among them.

***Law.**

***1.** A rule, proceeding from custom or from enactment by a legislative body, recognized as binding upon members of a given community.

1620 *Plymouth Laws* 19 [We] do enact, constitute and frame such just and equal laws, ordinances, . . . as shall be thought most meet. **1776** *Decl. Independence*, The present King of Great Britain . . . has refused his assent to laws the most wholesome and necessary for the public good. **1857** in Benton *Exam. Dred Scott Case* 10 And this Court held that their status or condition, as free or slave, depended upon the laws of Kentucky, when they were brought back into that State, and not of Ohio. **1920** *3d Nat. Country Life Conf. Proc.* 115 Ten or twelve states have co-operative credit-union laws.

2. *attrib.* Pertaining to the practice, interpretation, enforcement, or study of law.

1835 in Mackenzie *Life Van Buren* (1846) 259, I believe I some time since appointed you my law agent in Albany. **1912** Nicholson *Hoosier Chron.* 460 He opened the door of Dan Harwood's new office in the Law Building. **1789** Franklin *Autobiog.* 436 Ferdinand John Paris . . . managed for them all their law business in their great suit with the neighbouring proprietary of Maryland. **1898** Westcott *D. Harum* viii, This history will not concern itself to any extent with our friend's career as a law clerk. **1859** Bartlett 237 *Law Day*, the day on which a magistrate holds court at a country tavern. Common in thinly settled districts in the West. **1849** Chamberlain *Ind. Gazetteer* 45 In the winter of 1838, the institution was chartered as an University, and in 1842, a law department was established. **1817** *Yankee Traveller* 68, I gave the law-driver [a deputy sheriff] ten dollars, as a reward for his honesty and fidelity. **1776** J. Adams *Works* IX. 433 You must make yourself sufficiently acquainted with law-french and with the abbreviated law-hand, to read [etc.]. **1847** *Knickerbocker* XXIX. 349, [I] had heard law-lectures at Yale. **1853** *S. Lit. Messenger* XIX. 71/1 Simon gratified him, taking his law license in pawn for two dollars and a half. *a***1882** Weed *Autobiog.* 609 The landlord . . . recommended him to 'Squire Barton, the law partner of the famous Colonel Thomas H. Benton. **1819** in Mackenzie *Life Van Buren* (1846) 162, I have had some leisure for law reading and law labor. **1788** Freneau *Misc. Works* 223 A short cut to my law shop in another street. **1839** *S. Lit. Messenger* V. 97/2 John Mason died a year before my law-studies began. **1652** R. Williams *Letters* (1874) 236 When my public business is over, I am resolved to begin my old law-suit.

Law-abiding, *a.* Abiding by the law, peaceable. {1867–} — **1834** *Congress. Deb.* 25 Feb. 685 North Carolina was emphatically a law-loving and law-abiding state. **1855** *Congress. Globe* 26 Jan. 416/2 The people of Oregon are a law-abiding, honest, and gallant people. **1887** *Courier-Journal* 7 May 4/2 Louisville is a law-abiding city, and it must so remain. **1922** *Federal Reporter* Jan.-March 821 He has been a moral and law-abiding citizen.

Law and order. Law and its enforcement; a condition produced by proper respect for and observance of law and social orderliness. {1881–} Also attrib.

1796 *Ann. 4th Congress* 2 Sess. 1689 A military diploma, expressive of his patriotism and attachment to law and order. **1831** Peck *Guide* 71 They had better . . . compel it [=vice] to act under the trammels of law and order. **1883** *Century Mag.* Oct. 949/1 For this purpose, Law-and-Order Leagues have sprung into existence. **1903** Wiggin *Rebecca* 81 Minnie had spasms of bravery, when well surrounded by the machinery of law and order.

+**b.** Used particularly with reference to Dorr's Rebellion (q.v.), or to the days of vigilance committees in the West.

1858 *Harper's Mag.* Jan. 279/1 During the 'Dorr war' in Rhode Island every one that could shoulder a musket became suddenly valiant . . . in defense of 'Dorr and Free Suffrage,' or else for 'Law and Order.' **1897** Lewis *Wolfville* 118, I ain't none shore about the merits of what you-all calls law an' order. **1910** J. Hart *Vigilante Girl* 95 Nearly all the Northern men favor the Vigilantes. Nearly all the Southerners are Law and Order men.

+**Law and order party. 1.** (See quot. 1914.) Now hist. **2.** A name assumed by political groups wishing to appeal especially to law-abiding citizens. — **(1) 1857** *Lawrence* (Kan.) *Republican* 28 May 1 We arraign the self styled 'law and order party' of Kansas as guilty of high crimes and misdemeanors. *Ib.* 6 Aug. 2 In order to get this class of northern men to act with them, the pro-slavery party agreed . . . to change the name of the party from pro-slavery to the law and order party. **1914** *Cycl. Amer. Govt.* II. 312 *Law and Order Party*, a name taken by the pro-slavery party in Kansas during the struggle for the control of that territory following the Kansas-Nebraska Act . . . of 1854. **(2) 1879** *N.Y. Herald* 17 Sept. 5/2 The law and order party of Newark, led by a number of Presbyterian, Methodist, and Baptist clergymen, have resolved to nominate an independent ticket for Mayor and Aldermen.

***Law book.** A book containing laws or a code of laws; a textbook for the study of law. — **1672** *Conn. Rec.* II. 190 It is allso ordered that euery famely in the seuerall plantations in this Colony shall purchase one of our Law bookes. **1722** *Mass. H. Rep. Jrnl.* III. 175 Resolved, That a New Index be composed for the Law Book. **1847** *Santa Fe Republican* 27 Nov. 1/2 Law Books, Chittey's Pleading, Starkie on Evidence, & Archbold's Practice, for sale by W. S. McKnight. **1900** Stockton *Afield & Afloat* 147 This case . . . was . . . a mere matter of a will probably forged or altered, such as I have often read of in law books.

***Lawful money. a.** Money that is sanctioned by law. +**b.** Money having a standard weight of gold or silver, as distinguished from subsidiary coins.

1742 *Boston Rec.* 309 Pay the Sum of Twenty Shillings Lawful Money. **1776** M'Robert *Tour* 23 [In N.Y.] they have two denominations of currency, *viz.* Old tenor, and lawful money. Old tenor is of very small value. **1809** Kendall *Travels* I. 193 In those parts of the United States to which the present pages are confined, the dollar is estimated at six shillings currency, or as it is now called in the country, *lawful money*. For this, the ancient phrase is, *country pay*. **1864** *Statutes at Large* XIII. 109 Clearing-house certificates, representing specie or lawful money specially deposited for the purpose of any clearing-house association, shall be deemed to be lawful money. **1879** *Congress. Rec.* 23 May 1537/1, I believe the committee as a body will agree that 'lawful money' is money of value, gold and silver coin of the United States.

Law judge. A judge who decides questions of law as distinguished from questions of equity. — **1818** Fordham *Narr. Travels* 155 He is an associate Judge and sits on the bench with the circuit or law judge; but gives his opinion only on the equity of a case. **1856** *Knickerb.* XLVIII. 287 Mr. Stowder was a Pennsylvania Judge, of that description known in Vermont and other places as Flower-Pot Judges, as associate judges are there called to distinguish them from *law* judges.

Law library. A library composed of books of laws and books pertaining to law. {1799–} — **1818** *N. Amer. Rev.* March 429 The law students [of Harvard] are to have access to the University library, . . . as well as to the Law library, which shall be established. **1841** Catlin *Indians* I. 2, I very deliberately sold my law library. **1900** *Congress. Rec.* 8 Jan. 688/1 Some gentlemen have favored . . . a transfer of the Law Library to that space.

***Lawn.**[1] A finely woven cotton or linen fabric used for dresses, etc. Also attrib. — **1651** *Essex Probate Rec.* I. 139 A laune Cubbord Cloth & an croscloths. **1754** *S.C. Gazette* 1 Jan. 2/2 Samuel Peronneau hath just imported . . . a large assortment of Irish linnens . . . and long lawns. **1833** *Niles' Reg.* XLIV. 269/1 List of Linens to be admitted at an ad valorem duty of 15 per cent. under the act of 14th July, 1832 [includes] . . . Irish linen lawns. **1889** *Boston Journal* 12 Jan. 2/5 Let the goods be ginghams, batistes, dainty cambrics, chambreys and lawns.

***Lawn.**[2]

***1.** A grassy opening or glade in a forest.

1801 Asbury *Journal* III. 9 Jessamine flinging its odours far and wide; lawns and savannahs. *c***1835** Catlin *Indians* II. 91 This little lawn was surrounded by bunches and copses of the most luxuriant and picturesque foliage, consisting of the lofty bois d'arcs and elms. **1848** Cooper *Oak Openings* II. 54 There were the glades, vistas, irregular lawns and woods, shaped with the pleasing outlines of the free hand of nature. **1907** *St. Nicholas* July 791/1 Will looked around at the beautiful natural lawn.

2. A portion of smooth, grassy ground, usually closely mowed, in front of or about a dwelling. {1733–} Also transf.

1761 Glen *Descr. S. Carolina* 6 In many Places [are] fine Savannahs, . . . a Kind of natural Lawns, and some of them as beautiful as those made by Art. **1830** Cooper *Water Witch* II. x, Neither had an opportunity of making his observations on the condition of things in and about the villa, until they had . . . entered the narrow but fragrant lawn in its front. **1851** *Harper's Mag.* April 710/1 In the rear of the house was a lawn covered with appletrees. **1905** N. DAVIS *Northerner* 300 The terraced lawns yawned below them, leading to the road to town.

3. Attrib. and comb. with *rake, seat,* etc.

1863 *Horticulturist* March 15 New York Agricultural Warehouse ... Lawn Scythes and Scythe Stones, and Lawn Rakes. **1872** *Rep. Comm. Patents 1871* II. 969/2 Lawn-Sprinkler. ... A portable water-fountain and sprinkler. **1873** *Pat. Off. Gazette* IV. 515/1 Lawn-Seat. ... The back is solid and made wider than the seat. **1883** KNIGHT *Suppl.* 533/1 *Lawn Sprinkler,* a garden and lawn irrigator. **1908** CALHOUN *Miss Minerva* 31 The two little boys were soon comfortably settled facing each other in the big lawn-swing.

Lawn grass. +(See quotation.) — **1889** *Rep. Secy. Agric.* 389 *Paspalum platycaule,* called lawn grass or Louisiana grass, usually grows on low rich land, but is perfectly at home in poor pine land. As a pasture grass it can not be excelled, and is also an excellent lawn grass.

Lawn-mower. A machine for mowing lawns. {1872– (*Belgravia* Oct. 66)} — **1869** *Rep. Comm. Patents 1868* I. 547/1 Lawn Mower. ... The straight cutter bar acts in connection with the spiral rotating cutter. **1876** *Scribner's Mo.* March 745/1 The lawn-mowers, now within the reach of every one, make grass cutting on the lawn anything but hard work. **1882** PECK *Sunshine* 15 A lawn mower ... was in the barn. **1916** EASTMAN *From Deep Woods* 52 The green grass was evenly cut with lawn mowers.

Lawn sieve. A sieve the bottom of which is made of a lawn fabric. *Obs.* {1806, 1807} Also attrib. — **1674** *Harvard Rec.* I. 61 Kitchins Utensils, ... 1 Lawne sieve. 1 scummer. **1686** SEWALL *Letter-Book* I. 33 Six Duz. of Lawn sive Bottoms, not of the Largest size, all to be bordered with reed Leather. **1785** WASHINGTON *Diaries* II. 421 It was pulverized ... and sifted for use through a fine lawn sieve, and kept from wet.

Lawn tennis. A variety of tennis usually played in the open air; spec., tennis played on a grass court. {1874–} Also attrib. (Cf. TENNIS.) — **1878** *Harper's Mag.* Jan. 258/1 'Duck on the rock' ... is far ahead of ... pallone, lawn tenis [*sic*], or Aunt Sally. **1883** *Harper's Weekly* 8 Sept. 566/2 For three successive years Mr. Richard D. Sears has held the lawn tennis championship of the United States. **1886** *Harper's Mag.* July 169/1 Promenading ... [were] lawn-tennis young ladies conscious of being in the mode. **1898** *Outing* April 50 The Building of Lawn-Tennis Courts.

+**Law office.** The office of a lawyer. — **1819** in Mackenzie *Van Buren* 155, I considered it absolutely impossible for him to confine himself to so irksome an employment as a clerkship in a law office. *c***1845** W. T. THOMPSON *Chron. Pineville* 104 Our hero ... informed the inquirers ... that his was a law-office. **1893** PAGE in *Harper's Mag.* Dec. 22/2 [Men of Va.] began as ... clerks in law-offices ... and have worked themselves up to the highest positions of trust. **1911** VANCE *Cynthia* 63 First job, clerk in law-office—Higginbotham & Hunt, Wall Street.

+**Lawrence.** [George Newbold *Lawrence,* Amer. ornithologist (1806–1895).] Used in the possessive in bird names: (see quotations). — **1858** BAIRD *Birds Pacific R.R.* 181 *Myiarchus lawrencii.* Lawrence's Flycatcher. **1869** *Amer. Naturalist* III. 185 Other birds observed [near Cajon Pass, Calif.] were a flock of Pigeons ..., Lawrence's Goldfinch (*Chrysomitris Lawrencii*), and the Western Bluebird. **1887** RIDGWAY *Manual N.A. Birds* 486 Northeastern United States (New Jersey, etc.). *H[elminthophila] lawrencei.* Lawrence's Warbler.

+**Law sakes,** *interj.* An exclamation of surprise or astonishment. Also *law sakes alive. colloq.* — **1846** KIRKLAND *Western Clearings* 78 'Law sakes alive' was the reply, 'I ain't no how.' **1853** STOWE *Key* 22/2 Law sakes! she's just a-readin' on 't 'cause she could; don't s'pose it did her no good no way. **1855** HALIBURTON *Nature & Hum. Nature* (1859) 12 Law sakes alive man! Make a question between our nation and England about fifty deserters! **1898** NICHOLAS *Idyl of Wabash* 20 But law sakes, what could you expect of a man!

+**Law school.** A school, operating independently or forming a department in a university, in which instruction in law is given.

1818 *N. Amer. Rev.* March 428 A Law School is established at the University, under the superintendence of the University Professor of Law. **1848** ELIOT *Sk. Hist. Harvard* 122 The Law School dates, strictly, from the year 1817. **1870** EMERSON *Soc. & Solitude* i. 11 When he heard the best-bred young men at the law-school talk together, he reckoned himself a boor. **1909** 'O. HENRY' *Options* 316 He was a recent graduate of a southwestern law school.

+**b.** Attrib. with *allowance, classmate, man.*

1893 POST *Harvard Stories* 128 'You couldn't do that if you were a biographee,' reasoned Dane Austin, the law-school man. **1901** CHURCHILL *Crisis* 32 We've come out here with only a few thousand dollars, and the nine hundred I saved out of this year's Law School allowance. **1925** BRYAN *Memoirs* 65 Henry Trumbull ... the law-school classmate I have referred to.

+**Lawson's cypress.** [John *Lawson,* d. 1712.] The Port Orford cedar (*Chamaecyparis lawsoniana*), found in the West. — **1884** SARGENT *Rep. Forests* 179 *Chamaecyparis Lawsoniana.* ... Port Orford Cedar. ... Lawson's Cypress. Ginger Pine. **1892** APGAR *Trees Northern U.S.* 196 Lawson's Cypress. ... A magnificent tree in California, ... one of our best cultivated evergreens. **1897** SUDWORTH *Arborescent Flora* 82 Port Orford Cedar. ... [Commonly called] Lawson's Cypress (Cal., Oreg.).

+**Law sorts,** *interj.* An exclamation of surprise. *colloq.* — **1840** HOFFMAN *Greyslaer* II. 49 Law sorts, Capting Max, how your shoulders have spread.

+**Law souls,** *interj.* =prec. — **1789** DUNLAP *Father* II. i, Law souls! I protest I can't think, nor guess n'ither. *a***1848** in Northall *Yankee Hill* 192 Well, law Souls, I heard it; go on.

Law student. One who studies law. — **1843** *Knickerb.* Nov. 497 We have neither 'abused the law' nor yet 'the lawyers,' though ... at least some score of law-students would [seem to say so]. **1872** *Atlantic Mo.* Feb. 185 When he was a law-student, he kept a clock in his bedroom. **1909** PARKER *G. Cleveland* 31 His life at this time was not much out of the common run of the average law student.

+**Lawton blackberry.** [From personal name.] A variety of blackberry developed at New Rochelle, N.Y. — **1847** DARLINGTON *Weeds & Plants* 128 The kind known as the 'Lawton' or 'New Rochelle Blackberry,' is a splendid fruit, and is now becoming abundant in the markets of our cities. **1855** *Amer. Inst. N.Y. Trans.* 314 He has abundance of ... the Lawton blackberry. **1860** *Ill. Agric. Soc. Trans.* IV. 446 There is more danger the Lawton Blackberry will become a pest.

***Lawyer.** Also †**lawer.**

***1.** One whose profession is to give legal advice to clients or to conduct lawsuits.

1707 *N.J. Archives* 1 Ser. III. 199 This deponent further saith that this money was not raised to pay the Lawers. **1781** PETERS *Hist. Conn.* 284 In quarrels between the merchants and lawyers of a particular parish, the minister is allowed to stand neuter. **1842** *Knickerb.* XX. 491 There's a mighty chance of lawyers' lies in the papers. **1887** *Courier-Journal* 8 May 14/3 The first thing we do, let's kill all the lawyers. **1925** BRYAN *Memoirs* 112 Senator Vilas [was] a man of ... great ability as a lawyer.

attrib. **1891** 'THANET' *Otto the Knight* 218 He allus wears them lawyer clothes.

b. As a title.

1894 *Harper's Mag.* Nov. 955/1 Now Lawyer Sharp, conscious that his bill would be a shock to Miss Mehetable, had delayed sending it. **1905** *Hartford Courant* 10 Feb. 8 Young Lawyer Comerford ... bit off more than he could chew.

+**2. a.** The American avocet. **b.** The black-necked stilt, *Himantopus mexicanus.*

1813 WILSON *Ornithology* VII. 126 American Avoset: *Recurvirostra Americana;* ... from its perpetual clamour and flippancy of tongue, is called by the inhabitants of Cape May, the Lawyer. **1844** *Nat. Hist. N.Y., Zoology* II. 265 The Lawyer, *Himantopus nigricollis,* ... is known under the various popular names of Tilt, Stilt, Longshanks and Lawyer. **1917** *Birds of Amer.* I. 223 Black-necked Stilt. *Himantopus mexicanus.* ... [Also called] Longshanks; Lawyer.

+**3. a.** The American burbot, *Lota maculosa.* **b.** The bowfin or mudfish. **c.** The gray snapper (*Lutianus griseus*).

1857 HAMMOND *Northern Scenes* 45 That ... is a species of ling; we call it in these parts a *lawyer.* **1885** J. S. KINGSLEY, etc. *Stand. Nat. Hist.* III. 97 *Amia calva,* the bowfin ... or lawyer. **1896** JORDAN & EVERMANN *Check-List Fishes* 381 Lawyer. West Indies; ranging from New Jersey to Brazil. **1897** *N.Y. Forest, Fish, & Game Comm. 2d Rep.* 246 *Lota maculosa.* ... Ling; Lawyer. ... One of the most difficult of the fresh-water fishes to transport. **1903** T. H. BEAN *Fishes N.Y.* 75 The bowfin has various common names, among them mudfish, dogfish, lawyer, grindle, and John-a-grindle. **1911** *Rep. Fisheries 1908* 308, 316.

***Lay,** *n.*

+**1.** Price or rate; the terms or conditions of a sale, contract, employment, etc.: (see also quot. 1902). *colloq.*

1710 T. BUCKINGHAM *Naval Exped.* (1825) 98 At Whitney's, our breakfast and horse-meat, 19d a very reasonable lay. **1772** WASHINGTON *Diaries* II. 81 Agreed with my Overseer ... to continue another year on the same lay as the last. **1816** PICKERING 121 *Lay,* terms or conditions of a bargain; price. ... *A low word. New England.* **1890** TOURGEE *Pactolus Prime* 63, I've a fair enough lay, thanks to your endorsement. **1902** *Dialect Notes* II. 238 *Lay,* advantage afforded by a contract, situation or employment, as 'A good lay'—'A poor lay.' [Southern Ill.]

2. A share in the profits of a fishing or whaling voyage.

1849 COOPER *Sea Lions* iv, Yes, ship a goodly number of green hands. ... They work at cheap 'lays,' and leave the owners the greater profits. **1855** 'P. PAXTON' *Capt. Priest* 49 A few months saw him handling the ropes upon a whaler, at a good 'lay.' **1872** *Harper's Mag.* Jan. 256/2 The whale and cod fishermen make their voyages on a 'lay,' or share of the profits. **1906** *Ib.* April 677 In lieu of wages, a whaler's crew, from captain down to cabin-boy, receive each a 'lay'; that is to say, a certain proportion of the gross earnings of the voyage.

b. (See quots. 1871 and 1901.) Also transf.

1871 DE VERE 303 A kind of limited partnership is, in the West, not unfrequently called *to go on lays.* **1901** GRINNELL *Gold Hunting in Alaska* 90 A 'lay' is a lease given by a claim owner to a party to work a claim for a certain percentage of the outcome. **1909** 'O. HENRY' *Roads of Destiny* 322 We five are on a lay. I've guaranteed you to be square, and you're to come in on the profits equal with the boys.

+**3.** The plowshare of a moldboard plow.

1868 *Iowa Agric. Soc. Rep. 1867* 266 There is no clogging and the mould and lay are so hardened that they scour readily.

***Lay,** *v.*

I. +**1.** *tr.* To set aside or lay off (land) *for* a specified purpose or *to* a particular jurisdiction or use. *Obs.*

1640 *New Haven Col. Rec.* 48 Itt is ordered thatt after 2 years next ensueing be expired, the neck shall be layd for pasture. **1641** *Mass. Bay Rec.* I. 333 Squantums Neck & Mennens Moone are layd to Dorchester. **1645** *New Haven Col. Rec.* 188 It was ordered that 3 acres of land in the Oystershell feild, out of Mr. Brownings part shalbe layd to the ferry without rent.

II. Phrases.

In several of the phrases enumerated below, as 3 c and 5 d, the verb is the equivalent of *lie.*

***2.** *To lay by,* +to work (a crop) for the last time during the growing season.

1784 SMYTH *Tour* II. 123 Just before the last ploughing of the Indian corn (called *laying-it-by*). **1820** *Western Carolinian* 4 Aug., Attention ought always to be paid in laying by corn the last ploughing, never to plough every row, but every other one. **1858** *Texas Almanac 1859* 73 This last ploughing may be done with the solid sweep, if the ground is dry, but if wet, then with the turning-plough, while your hands, with trim hoes, make a finish, or lay the crop by. **1894** CHOPIN *Bayou Folk* 199 Baptiste's fine crop of cotton and corn was 'laid by' just now, waiting for rain.

***3.** *To lay down.* +**a.** To deliver (a commodity) at a given point or destination.

1865 *Atlantic Mo.* June 695/1 Grain can be laid down in New York ten cents a bushel cheaper than it now is done. **1885** *Santa Fé Wkly. New Mexican* 17 Sept. 2/7 The animal [a stallion] is 4 years old, and 'laid down' there [in Albuquerque] cost the carpet king $1,500.

‖**b.** To put away or store (butter) for future use.

1868 BRACKETT *Farm Talk* 37 'How do you "lay down" your butter?' . . . 'I pack [it] into stone jars, cover it with a layer of salt, and keep in the cellar until wanted for use or the market.'

c. To submit *to,* to give up, cease trying, fail to function. *colloq.*

1898 *Scribner's Mag.* XXIII. 453/2, I swear I hate to lay down to such a nincompoop. **1901** MERWIN & WEBSTER *Calumet 'K'* 64 You've never had to lay down yet, and you don't now. **1911** HARRISON *Queed* 87 Your body's got to carry your mind around, and if it lays down on you [etc.]. **1923** WATTS *L. Nichols* 157 The engine had laid down, he didn't know what was the matter.

***4.** *To lay in,* +to connive or arrange *with. colloq.*

1771 in Johnston *N. Hale* 148, [I] have Laid in with Mr. Strong for his Horse. **1833** A. GREENE *Dod. Duckworth* I. 28 They took no little pains to procure fresh supplies . . . partly by laying in with their female acquaintance to send them a specimen of the all-important cake. **1883** 'MARK TWAIN' *Life on Miss.* xliii, As I lay-in with the livery stables, of course I don't forget [etc.]. **1897** ROBINSON *Uncle Lisha* 63, I've laid in with a feller tu take ye tu Caverdy on his boat.

5. *To lay off.* **a.** To survey or plot out (land or grounds) in some way or for some purpose. {1765–}

1748 WASHINGTON *Writings* I. 4 This Morning began our Intended business of Laying of[f] Lots. **1787** in Summers *Ann. S.W. Va.* 820 David McGavock ordered to lay off 10 acres of land around the prison. **1815** DRAKE *Cincinnati* 43 Dayton, the chief town, is laid off on a fine tract of bottom land. **1852** REYNOLDS *Hist. Illinois* 116 The ordinance required townships of six miles square to be laid off. **1904** *N.Y. Times* 10 May 3 Col. Symons has given orders that grounds for the game be laid off in the northwest corner of the Monument Field.

fig. **1904** STRATTON-PORTER *Freckles* 14 Kindnesses that people are paid to lay off in job lots.

b. *Agric.* To mark off (a field) with rows or furrows preparatory to planting.

1787 WASHINGTON *Diaries* III. 187 Brought another of the Muddy hole plows home from French's, and set it to laying off the 20 acre cut designed . . . for Carrots. **1797** HAWKINS *Letters* 103 Lay off his cornfield in a proper manner. **1847** *Florida Plant. Rec.* 223, 2 [slaves] laying off cotton land in Redoak field.

+**c.** To plan or intend to do some specified thing. *colloq.*

1849 *S. Lit. Messenger* XV. 72/1 As soon as I heard that Northern gentleman was staying here, I laid off to tell you all about Mr. Jarvis. **1888** 'CRADDOCK' *Despot* 126 You'd better lay off to milk the cow-critters sooner'n common. **1896** HARRIS *Sister Jane* 148, I laid off to overtake 'im at the Baptizin' Creek.

d. To take a rest from work. {1868–, *dial.*}

1863 WHITMAN *Spec. Days* 41 Some of the men are cleaning their sabres (pleasant to-day,) some brushing boots, some laying off, reading, writing. **1886** JAMES *Bostonians* 18 She would expect him to be strenuous in return; but he couldn't—in private life, he couldn't; privacy for Basil Ransom consisted entirely in what he called 'laying off.' **1897** HOWELLS *Landlord at Lion's Head* (1908) 60 The husbands . . . want to lay off and rest.

e. To dismiss (a workman) from employment, usually for a short time.

1888 in Salmons *Burlington Strike* (1889) 363 General Manager Miller, of the St. Paul road, issued orders . . . to lay off every employe whose services were not absolutely necessary. **1894** CARWARDINE *Pullman Strike* 36 Three men who were members of the committee were 'laid off.' **1901** MERWIN & WEBSTER *Calumet 'K'* 82 That clerk that we laid off to-day . . . 'lowed that he was going to make trouble.

***6.** *To lay out.* **a.** To allot (land) for a particular purpose, to survey or plot out (grounds, roads, etc.). {1608–}

1627 *Plymouth Laws* 30 Every man of the surveighers [shall] have a peck of corne for every share of land layed out by them. **1663** *Dedham Rec.* IV. 71 Them that haue made improument at Woolomonupack cominge to the Select men & desireinge the highway might be confirmd as it was layd out by the comity. **1717** *Mass. H. Rep. Jrnl.* I. 198 A Tract of Land . . . was accordingly laid out. **1792** IMLAY *Western Territory* t.-p., By G. Imlay, . . . a Commissioner for laying out Land in the Back Settlements. **1857** *Lawrence* (Kan.) *Republican* 2 July 3 This town, recently laid out, is located in one of the most beautiful . . . portions of Kansas. **1883** 'MARK TWAIN' *Life on Miss.* 384 They are tastefully laid out in broad terraces.

b. To be on the lookout *for* something. *colloq.*

1825 NEAL *Bro. Jonathan* I. 54 Whenever a young she-yankee is 'laying out' for a husband, she gives what is there called a 'quilting frolick.'

+**c.** *fig.* To 'lay low,' or 'use up' completely. *colloq.* {1892} Freq. with *cold.*

1829 *Mass. Spy* 22 July (Th.), I want to lay out [this candidate] as cold as a wedge. **1836** *Quarter Race Ky.* (1846) 18 You'll lay him out cold as a wagon-tire. **1847** FIELD *Drama in Pokerville* 93 It is 'bound' to lay every thing in the way of architecture west of the Alleghanies 'out cold,' and no mistake! **1894** *Nation* 22 Nov. 373/2 Never . . . were so many demagogues laid out in one day as in the elections of a fortnight ago.

***7.** *To lay over.* +**a.** To interrupt or break a journey by stopping for a time.

1841 *Cultivator* VIII. 152 The stage lays over here this day. **1873** *Newton Kansan* 10 July 3/3 Passengers going west . . . have to lay over here until the next morning. **1900** DRANNAN *Plains & Mts.* 224 Here we laid over three days to let our horses rest up a little.

+**b.** To excel or surpass. *colloq.*

1865 'MARK TWAIN' *Sk., New & Old* 33 All said he laid over any frog that ever *they* see. **1880** — *Tramp Abroad* ii. 37 A bluejay can lay over anything, human or divine. **1903** *N.Y. Sun* 25 Nov. 10, I have heard a good many queer things here, but this lays over anything yet. **1923** WATTS *L. Nichols* 210 In Luther's own language, she laid over the whole bunch.

‖**c.** To turn (hay) over for curing.

1873 *Vermont Bd. Agric. Rep.* II. 188 Unless so rainy as to be impracticable, he lays it [the hay] all over.

***8.** *To lay up.* +**a.** To erect or put up (a log building). *Obs.*

1788 MAY *Jrnl. & Lett.* (1873) 86 To-day finished laying up the house, and put on the roof. **1844** LEE & FROST *Oregon* xxii. 289 [We] were so successful as to finish laying up the cabin . . . at the end of two weeks. **1847** in H. Howe *Hist. Coll. Ohio* 377 A block-house . . . was laid up of large beech logs, and rather open.

+**b.** Of a train: To lie by, to remain at a standstill.

1864 *Wkly. New Mexican* 25 Nov. 3/2 Large trains have been compelled to 'lay up' on the road.

c. To replenish (a fire) by placing fuel upon it.

1865 *Atlantic Mo.* XV. 354, I had just laid up the fire.

+**9.** *To lay* (something) *up against* (one), to hold something against a person. *colloq.*

1856 M. J. HOLMES *L. Rivers* vi. 63 The poor critter is sick, and I shan't lay it up agin her. **1887** WILKINS *Humble Romance* 35 You don't lay up anything agin me, Maria? **1903** — *Six Trees* 61, I hope you won't lay it up against her.

Lay-by. *attrib.* {1804–} +Designating the final flooding of a growing rice field. — **1854** in Commons, etc. *Doc. Hist.* I. 262 This is called the lay-by flow. Up to the time of this flow, is about ninety days for Rice sown the first week in April. **1859** *Harper's Mag.* Nov. 728/2 The 'lay-by water' . . . is kept on until the rice is fully headed and the blossoms have dropped.

***Lay elder.** +In the Congregational churches of New England, a lay official having authority over his congregation in matters of discipline and government. — **1722** *New-Eng. Courant* 5–12 Nov. 1/2 Having thus burlesq'd the Rev. Lay-Elder, he presents us with an ample Muster-Roll of shining Heroes his Predecessors. **1765** ROGERS *Acct. N. America* 37 There was a synod or convention of Ministers, with their lay elders, or delegates of the churches, called.

***Layer-out.** +In colonial times, one appointed to lay out or measure off land, roads, etc. *Obs.*

1635 *Essex Inst. Coll.* IV. 90/1 Overseers & layers out of lotts of ground for this presinct of Salem. **1647** *Portsmouth Rec.* 36 It is . . . ordered that the layers out shall lay out the hundered acres granted to mr. Thomas Cornell. **1678** *Southampton Rec.* II. 72 Iohn Iessup being one of the layers out of land for the town. **1708** *N.J. Archives* III. 280 The layers out of the High way were appointed. **1740** *East-Hampton Rec.* IV. 114 The passing highways above mentioned were allowed for . . . by us the layers out, as witness our hands.

Laying box. A box in which hens lay eggs. — **1871** LEWIS *Poultry Book* 8 Have the laying boxes cleaned and renewed frequently with straw, hay, or shavings. **1883** ALLEN *New Farm Book* 491 Crude kerosene oil . . . swabbed along the roosts and laying boxes . . . has proved destructive to [lice]. **1894** *Vt. Agric. Rep.* XIV. 169 Inside place a roost and the laying boxes.

+**Laying by.** (See quot. 1800 and cf. LAY *v.* 2.) — **1800** TATHAM *Agric. & Commerce* 56 What is termed the laying by of the crop in autumn . . . is, the last ploughing and hoeing which it requires before it is suffered to remain at rest and ripen like other fruits of the earth. **1850** *Rep. Comm. Patents 1849: Agric.* 169 Between the 'laying by' of the crop of cane and the rolling season, it grows luxuriantly.

+**Layman.** One who engages with others in mining operations for a share of the entire gains. (Cf. LAY *n.* 2 b.) — **1899** *Harper's Weekly* 8 April 344/1 The lay-men struck it the first hole, and out of thirty burnings took out $40,000. **1908** BEACH *Barrier* 190 Some of his laymen are quitting work. They've cross-cut in half a dozen places and can't find a color.

+**Lay-off.** The period during which an employee is absent from work or is 'laid off.' (Cf. LAY *v.* 5 d, e.) — **1897** LEWIS *Wolfville* 47 A gent as would begretch two pore, hard-workin' girls a lay-off of a week . . . ain't clean strain. **1904** *Minneapolis Times* 8 June 8 Those who have been working less than a year have to get along with only a five-day layoff. **1909** WASON *Happy Hawkins* 148 Now take a lay-off if you want to, . . . then come back here.

+**Layout.**

1. In various gambling games: **a.** The numbers or cards laid out for the players to bet on. Also transf. **b.** The equipment needed for one of these games.

1851 *Polly Peablossom* 112 As the fellers say at monte, he was a lay out I didn't want to bet on. **1864** DICK *Amer. Hoyle* (1866) 456 He deals out two [cards], one at a time, and places them side by side upon the table, with their faces up. This is called the 'lay-out' and upon these cards the players place their bets. **1890** *Cent.* 3382/2 *Faro lay-out*, the thirteen cards of a suit, which are fastened to the faro-table, and on or near which the stakes are placed. **1899** *Boston Transcript* 21 Aug. 10/6 A complete fantan layout and dominoes, cards, chips and dice-cup were seized by the liquor squad in a raid made yesterday afternoon at 4 Oxford place. **1908** WHITE *Riverman* 64 The professional gamblers sitting quietly behind their various lay-outs.

2. An 'outfit,' plan, situation, state of affairs, etc. *colloq.*

1869 MCCLURE *Rocky Mts.* 219 They get up a most expensive 'layout' for him. **1873** BEADLE *Undevel. West* 103 Apostle Sammy Richards truly had, as our companion expressed it, 'the softest layout in the business.' **1890** *Stock Grower & Farmer* 15 March 5/3 When he [*sc.* a cowpuncher] locates the layout [the calf tied up in process of being weaned], it is interesting to watch his antics. *Ib.* 26 April 3/1 Mr. Armour's daughters must have struck their pa for a new layout of spring clothes and somebody had to be squeezed. **1898** 'MARK TWAIN' in *Cosmopolitan* Aug. 426, I glanced at the list and my stomach threw a handspring. Of all the barbarous layouts that were ever contrived, this was the most atrocious.

b. A number of articles laid out for use, display, etc.

1890 *Saginaw Courier-Herald* 4 July, A fine layout of fruits and vegetables at C. Rimmele's, 122 North Hamilton. **1890** RYAN *Told in Hills* 100 'What did you find to cook?' he asked, glancing at the 'lay-out,' as Jim called it. 'I haven't been here since yesterday.'

3. A group, party, or company. *colloq.*

1869 *Overland Mo.* Aug. 128 Several persons in our 'lay-out' (*i.e.*, our company) in New Mexico 'swapped' good American horses for mustangs. **1878** BEADLE *Western Wilds* 538 It would be astonishin' for that lootenint and his layout to git into the fort without a skrimmage. **1884** 'CRADDOCK' *Tenn. Mts.* 222, I hearn ez how the whole lay-out footed it all the way ter New Helveshey. **1903** A. ADAMS *Log Cowboy* 100 Surround this layout, lads.

b. A group of relatives; a family.

1904 HARBEN *Georgians* 20, I hain't never seed nothin' good in him nur his layout.

3. A laying out; the order, arrangement, or disposition of a city, land, etc.

1888 *Harper's Mag.* July 285/1 Although the conception of its lay-out dates back nearly half a century, the tree planting that has added so much to Washington was begun only in 1872. **1890** *Conn. Rec.* XV. 448 *n.*, The lay-out [of the grant of land] is recorded in *Col. Record of Deeds.* **1898** TRUMBULL *Hist. Northampton, Mass.* I. 379 This was the second lay out of what is now known as Green Street. **1908** *Scientific Amer.* 22 Aug. 119 The construction of the new layout of the tracks called for some heavy and costly work.

Lay-over. {1777-} +**1.** A stop or interval for rest in a journey. (Cf. LAY *v.* 7 a.) +**2.** A transplanted oyster. — (1) **1873** BEADLE *Undevel. West* 758 Four exhausted passengers took a 'lay-over,' making room for the recuperated four to go on. **1903** A. ADAMS *Log Cowboy* xxi. 336 Flood . . . seemed rather convivial and quite willing to enjoy the enforced lay-over with us. (2) **1891** *Scribner's Mag.* Oct. 472/1 Young oysters so treated are termed 'lay-overs.'

Lay reader. In the Church of England and the Protestant Episcopal church, a layman given the right to read the prayers. {1873- (s.v. *reader*)} Also *lay reading* vbl. n. — **1751** MACSPARRAN *Diary* 47 God guard my chh against ye Inroad of Lay Readers. *Ib.*, I think it my Duty to bear Testimony against Lay-reading, especially in ye Eldest chh in ye Colony. **1822** MORSE *Rep. Indian Affairs* II. 80 *n.*, Mr. Eleazer Williams, at the earnest request of the Oneida Chiefs, was licensed by me about two years since, as their Lay-Reader, Catechist, and Schoolmaster. **1898** *Kansas City Star* 18 Dec. 2/3 He was commissioned as a lay reader in the Episcopal church.

***Lazaretto.** A building, ship, or quarantine station for isolating contagious diseases. — **1804** C. B. BROWN tr. Volney *View Soil U.S.* 252, I am . . . by no means an enemy to the establishment of lazarettoes and health-offices. **1840** *Niles' Nat. Reg.* 23 May 192/3 The ship Shenandoah at Philadelphia from Liverpool, has the small pox on board. She has been ordered to the lazaretto and no one permitted to board her for the present. **1844** *Lexington Observer* 13 July 1/4 A medical commission . . . has made a report recommending the establishment of a Lazaretto, and the removal of the sick to it. **1887** HARTE *Crusade of Excelsior* 111, I've an idea that we're in a sort of lazaretto, and the people outside won't trouble us often.

+**Lazuli bunting.** =next. Also *lazuli painted bunting.* — **1887** RIDGWAY *Man. N.A. Birds* 447 Western United States, east to Great Plains, south, in winter, to western Mexico. *P[asserina] amœna.* . . . Lazuli Bunting. **1917** *Birds of Amer.* III. 72 Lazuli Bunting. *Passerina amœna.* . . . [Also called] Lazuli Painted Bunting.

+**Lazuli finch.** An American finch or bunting (*Passerina amoena*), found in the western part of the United States. — **1825** BONAPARTE *Ornithology* I. 61 Lazuli Finch. *Fringilla Amœna.* **1839** AUDUBON *Ornith. Biog.* V. 64 The Lazuli Finch, one of the handsomest of its tribe, and allied to the Indigo Bird, . . . was added to our Fauna by Thomas Say. **1874** COUES *Birds N.W.* 170 The prettily-colored and delicate little Lazuli Finch is found to be common.

***Lazy,** *a.* Of a type of brand or of letters and figures in a brand: Lying on its side. — **1887** *Scribner's Mag.* II. 508/2 Words used in connection with . . . life on the plains: . . . *flying-brand; lazy-brand* [etc.]. **1907** WHITE *Arizona Nights* 76, I didn't see them any more after that until I'd hit the Lazy Y. **1921** F. S. HASTINGS *Ranchman's Recoll.* 232 Strange stories drifted in about a certain outlaw speckled yearling on the Lazy 7 Ranch—he had thrown every boy with rodeo aspirations who had tried to ride him.

Lazy-back. {1611-} +(See quotations.) Also attrib. — **1875** KNIGHT 1268/1 *Lazy-back*, . . . a high back-bar to a carriage-seat. It is sometimes made shifting, so as to be removed at will. **1887** *Pop. Science Mo.* XXX. 748 A lazy-back chair makes a capital observing-seat.

Leach, *n.* A quantity of wood ashes for use in soap-making; a receptacle for such ashes. {1673-; now *dial.*} — **1828** WEBSTER, *Leach*, . . . a quantity of wood ashes, through which water passes, and thus imbibes the alkali. **1875** T. D. PRICE *Diary* (MS.) 28 April, I made a leach and put up ashes. **1894** *Harper's Mag.* April 810/2 Her elbow struck the leach and knocked it into the soap-kettle.

***Leach,** *v. tr.* To cause a liquid to percolate through (some material) for the purpose, or with the result, of removing certain elements from that material. Also *leaching*, purifying (a liquid) by percolating it through a suitable material.

1796 MORSE *Amer. Geog.* I. 439 Cider . . . is first separated from the filth and dregs, either by leaching through sand, or straining it through flannel clothes. **1828** WEBSTER, *Leach*, . . . to wash, as ashes, by percolation, or causing water to pass through them, and thus to separate from them the alkali. **1840** J. BUEL *Farmer's Companion* 74 The wind and the sun dissipate its virtues, and rains leach it and waste its fertilizing powers. **1877** RAYMOND *Mines* 389 The tubs are kept constantly full and discharged into a series of tanks below. It takes eight or nine hours to leach the charge. **1877** N. S. SHALER in J. A. Allen *Amer. Bison* 458 Whenever the rocks lie above the line of the drainage, these salts have been leached away.

+**Leached ashes.** Ashes that have been leached. Used as a fertilizing agent. — **1839** BUEL *Farmer's Companion* 74 *Leached ashes* are in many cases beneficial, particularly within the influence of the marine atmosphere. **1850** *Rep. Comm. Patents 1849: Agric.* 122 Leached ashes, hen-house and hog-pen refuse are very valuable fertilizers. **1868** *Mich. Agric. Rep.* VII. 130, I propose, also, to test leached ashes in the same way, to ascertain from whence comes the beneficial action of wood ashes.

‖**Leach hole.** (See quotation.) — **1854** THOREAU *Walden* 313 The [ice-] cutters . . . showed me in another place what they thought was a 'leach hole,' through which the pond leaked out under a hill into a neighboring meadow.

+**Leach's petrel.** [W. E. *Leach*, Eng. natural scientist (1790–1836).] The white-rumped petrel (*Oceanodroma leucorhoa*). Also *Leach's fork-tailed petrel.* (Cf. FORK-TAILED PETREL.) — **1858** BAIRD *Birds Pacific R.R.* 830 Leach's Petrel. . . . Atlantic coast from Massachusetts to Baffin's Bay. **1883** *Nat. Museum Bul.* No. 27, 175. **1917** *Birds of Amer.* I. 85 Leach's Petrel. . . . [Also called] Leach's Fork-tailed Petrel.

+**Leachy,** *a.* Of soils: Of a loose or sandy formation; porous. — **1846** EMMONS *Agric. N.Y.* I. 247 [The soil] is rarely sufficiently tight to retain manures well, and yet they are not excessively leachy. **1879** *Scribner's Mo.* Dec. 247/1, I had my choice between a farm of cold stiff clay or light leachy sand. **1886** *Harper's Mag.* Sept. 533/2 The subsoil is too loose and leachy.

***Lead,** *n.*[1] A well-known, soft, lusterless metal.

In early examples as a material for making bullets. (Cf. b.)

1639 *Plymouth Laws* 63 If any man shall sell . . . leade or powder to any Indian [etc.]. **1675** in Easton *Indian War* 91 The Constables of the severall Townes [shall] take Care no Powder or Lead bee sold to the Indyans.

1794 *Ann. 3d Congress* 1448 It shall not be lawful to export from the United States any cannon, muskets, . . . musket balls, lead, bombs, grenades, . . . or saltpetre. 1814 BRACKENRIDGE *Views La.* 156 The immense quantity and cheapness of lead, naturally point out this country as the proper one for the . . . manufactures of . . . sheet lead, shot, red and white lead, &c. 1872 MCCLELLAN *Golden State* 279 Lead is abundant on the Pacific Coast.

*b. *collect.* Bullets made of lead. (Cf. COLD LEAD.)

1837 *Diplom. Corr. Texas* I. (1908) 190 We would give Mexico nothing but lead. 1893 WISTER in *Harper's Mag.* Dec. 57/1 All you want to do is stay covered and pump lead into 'em. 1920 MULFORD *J. Nelson* 47 Oh, if you'll only . . . give me half an excuse to throw lead!

2. Attrib. (passing into adj.) and comb. with *digging, district*, etc.

1651 *Essex Probate Rec.* I. 128, 2 pitchfork . . . lead wayte. 1833 *Niles' Reg.* XLIV. 183/1 There are some who wish to keep up an excitement on this subject, for the purpose of preventing the *lead region* from being overrun with miners. 1843 *Nat. Hist. N.Y., Geology* III. 60 The ore, being profusely distributed, and often in decomposed or altered rocks or cavities, calls for the use of the spade oftener than the blast; hence the term *lead diggings*, so frequently applied to these deposits. 1867 *Atlantic Mo.* June 665/2 The lead districts of Missouri include more than 6,000 square miles. 1877 PHELPS *Story of Avis* 148 The poisoned face of a lead-worker suddenly uplifted.

***Lead,** *n.*[2]

+**1.** *Mining.* A lode or vein.

1814 BRACKENRIDGE *Views La.* 148 Leads, (or loads) are the smaller fissures that connect with the larger, which are called by the miners, *caves.* 1852 W. KELLY *Diggings of Calif.* 133 When miners found their 'lead giving out' they devised some feasible pretext for selling out. 1891 *Century Mag.* Jan. 426/2 The vein in the copper mine was always going to widen out into a six-foot lead. 1923 'BOWER' *Parowan Bonanza* 37, I've got to go in on a lead, and I want the work to count as location work.

transf. 1875 *Scribner's Mo.* July 277/1 The genuine Californian never says he has made a fortunate investment; but he has 'struck a lead.'

+**2.** *Baseball.* The distance from base taken by a runner preparatory to running to the next base.

1893 CAMP *College Sports* 216 The runner should be coached to take as great a lead as he can with security.

+**3.** (See quotation.)

1905 *Forestry Bureau Bul.* No. 61, 41 *Lead*, a snatch block with a hook or loop for fastening it to convenient stationary objects, used for guiding the cable by which logs are dragged. (P[acific] C[oast] F[orest].)

Lead, *a.* Of an animal: That leads a team or herd, esp. the near front animal of a team. {1828} (Cf. LEAD MULE.)

1843 *Amer. Pioneer* II. 63 Two men could manage ten or fifteen horses . . . by tying one to the other in single file; one of the men taking charge of the lead horse to pioneer. 1846 SAGE *Scenes Rocky Mts.* xxxiii, Bidding them adieu, with my lead pack-animal returned to the mountains. 1869 *Overland Mo.* III. 127 With the Texan driver all oxen are 'steers,' and he has his 'wheel-steers,' his 'swing-steers,' and his 'lead-steers.' 1903 A. ADAMS *Log Cowboy* 89 The lead cattle were nearly up to the river. 1910 RAINE *B. O'Connor* 189 The man in charge circled round to head the lead cows in.

***Lead,** *v.* +**1.** *Boxing. intr.* To launch or direct a blow at one's opponent. **2.** *To lead out* {1776–}, +to set out. — (1) 1887 *Courier-Journal* 20 Jan. 5/3 Both sparred cautiously, looking for an opening. Danforth led for Harding's head with his left, but was short. *Ib.*, Fourth Round—Harding led, but it was short. (2) 1894 *Harper's Mag.* Feb. 354/2, I 'led out' for the casa at a rate of speed which the boys afterwards never grew weary of commending. 1903 A. ADAMS *Log Cowboy* xx. 312 The cattle led out as if walking on a wager.

Lead bar. The bar to which the traces of a draft animal working in the lead are attached; a whiffletree. {1890–} — 1840 *Congress. Globe* App. 5 March 227/2 The horse . . . broke loose from the coach, taking with him a part of what are now called 'lead bars.' 1897 *Outing* XXX. 253/1 When going steadily and easily your lead-bars should chatter.

+**Lead-colored gnat-catcher.** The plumbeous gnat-catcher (*Polioptila melanura*) of the Southwest. — 1869 *Amer. Naturalist* III. 474 Resident species not found westward of this valley [of the Colorado R.] were . . . the lead-colored Gnatcatcher (*Polioptila plumbea*), Malherbe's Flicker [etc.]. 1881 *Ib.* XV. 214 Later, in Arizona, I noticed the remaining species of gnat-catcher peculiar to our fauna, the Arizona or lead-colored gnat-catcher.

***Leader.**

1. *Mining.* **a.** A stream of water indicating, by its color, the presence of minerals. **b.** A small vein or branch leading to a larger vein. {1846–}

1809 A. HENRY *Travels* 231 A green-coloured water . . . issued from the hill; and this the miners called a *leader.* 1842 *Nat. Hist. N.Y., Geology* II. 345 A thin vein in the form of a *leader*, as they are sometimes called.

2. A leading article or editorial in a newspaper. {1844–}

1841 GREELEY in T. Weed *Memoir* (1884) 95 Give us a good, rousing leader, calling on the Whigs . . . to rally. 1873 'MARK TWAIN' & WARNER *Gilded Age* 118 He could write leaders with perfect ease, he was sure.

+**3.** *Angling.* A short line of strong, preferably transparent, material, used to attach a hook or bob to the casting line.

1848 *Knickerb.* XXXII. 80 The bending-on of leaders and hooks, and the adjustment of sinkers and floats, was soon completed. 1879 *Scribner's Mo.* Nov. 23/1 My customary tackle . . . is a twelve-foot rod of about eight and a half ounces; leaders eight feet long. 1893 *Outing* XXII. 123/1 Smoke-colored leaders of gut are . . . good things. 1919 HOUGH *Sagebrusher* 86 His fish . . . broke the gear and ran off with joy, a yard of leader attached to his mouth.

+**4.** *Comm.* **a.** An article of major importance in trade. **b.** An article especially featured or displayed and usually lowered in price to attract trade.

1851 CIST *Cincinnati* 319 These articles are the leaders, as they are called, in commercial transactions, with the west. 1888 *Chicago Tribune* 29 April 4/7 Goods advertised and sold below cost are technically known as 'leaders.' 1890 H. O. WELLS *Twice Born* 93 It is his big card, his 'leader,' and he knows how to play it for all it is worth. 1895 *Critic* 6 April 263/1 In several Sixth Avenue houses, new books by popular writers have long been used as 'leaders.'

Lead furnace. A furnace for smelting lead ore. — 1819 SCHOOLCRAFT *Mo. Lead Mines* 48 This village . . . has 3 stores, 2 distilleries . . ., 2 flour mills, 9 lead furnaces, 1 saw mill. 1831 PECK *Guide* 199 In Jo Davies county [Ill.] are ten lead furnaces.

+**Lead harness.** Harness for a draught animal that works in the lead or on the left side in a team. — 1871 *Atlantic Mo.* Nov. 574 Conversation sprung up on 'lead harness,' [and] the 'Stockton wagon that had went off the grade.' 1880 *Cimarron News & Press* 23 Dec. 3/1 Wheel and Lead harness, Collars, Lines, . . . and Stirrups at Porter's.

***Leading.** +An inner spiritual prompting toward proper action. — 1879 HOWELLS *Lady of Aroostook* 3 It's an opportunity; you might call it a leadin', almost, that it would be flyin' in the face of Providence to refuse. 1889 COOKE *Steadfast* 230, I had a leadin'; yes, a powerful leadin' to come over to Trumbull for to hear Priest Hall. 1889 M. C. LEE *Quaker Girl Nantucket* 8 Ann Millet . . . began to have 'leadings' at the age of four years.

+**Leading way.** (See quot. 1665.) *Obs.* — 1641 *Dedham Rec.* III. 79 Lay out a Cart way to our Water Mill for a common leading way. 1665 *Ib.* IV. 108 Whether the said space of grounde be onely a leading waye. that is for Cartes and teames. or Cattell kept in hand. or a Common drift waye for loose Cattell to goe at liberty in.

Lead mine. A mine from which lead ore is obtained. {1653–}

1658 *Mass. H. S. Coll.* 4 Ser. VII. 404, I shal . . . abide by what agrement you mack with him conserning the Led mine or the Iron worke. 1721 *Mass. H. Rep. Jrnl.* III. 24 The Lead Mines . . . are not yet laid out. 1812 *Ann. 12th Congress* 1 Sess. II. 1563 A bill concerning the lead mines in the Territory of Missouri. 1922 *Mineral Resources 1919* (Bur. of Mines) I. 245 The lead and zinc mines of northern Illinois are all in Jo Daviess County.

attrib. 1826 FLINT *Recoll.* 106 Boats are also constantly ascending to the lead-mine districts, on the upper Mississippi.

+**Lead mule. 1.** A mule that serves as a leader of a mule pack train. **2.** A mule that works at the head of a team or on the left side of it. — (1) 1860 GREELEY *Overland Journey* 169 The Frenchman . . . took one of our lead-mules by the halter. 1873 BEADLE *Undevel. West* 491 Two or three times the little lead mules were obliged to swim a rod or so. 1887 CUSTER *Tenting on Plains* 352 A broad piece of leather . . . divides over the shoulders of the lead or pilot mule. (2) 1895 REMINGTON *Pony Tracks* 149 A 'swing mule' tripped up a 'lead mule.' 1913 LONDON *Valley of Moon* III. viii, The lead-mule kicked e-o-wt the swing-mule's eye.

Lead ore. Ore that contains lead. {1653–} — 1637 MORTON *New Canaan* 85 Lead ore is there likewise, and hath bin found by the breaking of the earth. 1778 CARVER *Travels* 47 Mountains that lie about fifteen miles to the southward [in Wis.] . . . abound in lead ore. 1854 BENTON *30 Years' View* I. 104/2 Making money by boiling salt water, and digging lead ore. 1874 RAYMOND *6th Rep. Mines* 304 No adequate supply of lead-ores could be obtained.

Lead pencil. A pencil of graphite usually enclosed in wood. {1688–} Also attrib. — 1790 *Penna. Packet* 8 May 4/4 For Sale. . . . Middleton's black lead pencils per groce or dozen. 1832 WILLIAMSON *Maine* I. 181 The purest kind [of graphite] is manufactured into lead pencils. 1880 CABLE *Grandissimes* 161 The note was a lead-pencil scrawl, without date. 1887 PERRY *Flock of Girls* 124 Down went that blackest of black lead-pencils in a mark against the name of Gold. 1919 *Sears, Roebuck & Co. Cat.* No. 138, 541 Ladies Sterling Silver Lead Pencil.

+**Lead plant.** An American shrub of the genus *Amorpha*, esp. *A. canescens*, found in the West and reputedly indicating the presence of lead ore in the soil. — 1833 EATON *Botany* (ed. 6) 15 *Amorpha canescens*, lead plant. . . . Somewhat woody. . . . Galena. 1846 in Emory *Military Reconn.* 399 The lead plant, or tea plant, (*amorpha canescens*,) . . . is in some places so abundant as to displace almost every other herb. 1867 *Amer. Naturalist* I. 405 On the long spikes of flowers of the False Indigo and Lead-plant . . . bees and wasps were seen.

***Leaf.** *attrib.* passing into *adj.* Designating various insects that feed on or otherwise damage leaves of plants.

1868 *Iowa Agric. Soc. Rep. 1867* 189 The vines have been injured to some extent by the leaf-louse. 1875 *Rep. Comm. Agric. 1874* 127 An experiment has been instituted in order to prove the identity of the *Pemphygus vitifoliæ*, or leaf-gall-louse . . . with the *Phylloxera vastratix* [*sic*], or root-gall-louse. **1882** *Amer. Naturalist* XVI. 913 The Buckeye Leaf Stem Borer. **1889** *Rep. Secy. Agric.* 17 The orange-growers of Florida [complain] of a new pest in the shape of a leaf-mite which causes an injurious shedding of the foliage in the winter. **1891** WILKINS *New Eng. Nun* 162 His progress was hardly more perceptible than a scaly leaf-slug's. **1894** *Columbus Dispatch* 3 Aug., The cotton crop, . . . in years of bad infestation by the leaf worm, was estimated to be injured to the extent of $30,000,000.

Leaf beetle. Any of various beetles that feed on leaves. — **1852** T. W. HARRIS *Insects Injur. Veget.* (1862) 117 Beetles . . . which, as they derive their nourishment . . . from leaves alone, may be called leaf-beetles. **1856** *Rep. Comm. Patents 1855: Agric.* 90 A small leaf-beetle . . . is often found in the young flowers of the cotton, where it gnaws holes in the petals. **1876** *Vermont Bd. Agric. Rep.* III. 573 It is commonly called the three-lined leaf beetle, *Lema trilineata*. **1924** *Dept. Agric. Yrbk. 1923* 192 The beet leaf beetle . . . does its principal injury in alkali regions.

Leaf blight. A disease which attacks plants and causes their leaves to wither and die. — **1850** *Rep. Comm. Patents 1849: Agric.* 440 Our seedling pears were for the first time badly affected with 'leaf-blight.' **1867** *Ill. Agric. Soc. Trans.* VII. 505 The leaves [of the apples] died just in the same manner as the leaf blight in the pear. **1889** *Rep. Secy. Agric.* 416 The quince trees at Vineland, N.J., are annually affected with a number of diseases, chief among which are twig blight . . . and leaf blight (*Entomosporium maculatum*, Lév.). **1899** *Dept. Agric. Yrbk. 1898* 652 The leaf blights of potato and the potato rot have been widely distributed.

Leaf-cutter. {1815-} +(See quot. 1890.) — **1850** WARNER *Wide, Wide World* iii, Mrs. Montgomery . . . went on further to furnish the desk with an ivory leaf-cutter, a paper-folder [etc.]. **1890** *Cent.* 3387/1 *Leaf-cutter*, . . . a knife used to cut the leaves of a book: same as *paper-cutter*. (U.S., rare.)

+**Leaf hopper.** Any one of various small leaf-sucking insects. — **1852** T. W. HARRIS *Insects Injur. Veget.* (1862) 220 Leaf-hoppers . . . live mostly on the leaves of plants. **1867** *Amer. Naturalist* I. 327 The various leaf-hoppers, *Tettigonia* and *Ceresa*, abound on the leaves of plants, sadly blighting them. **1877** *Vermont Bd. Agric. Rep.* IV. 98 The little leaf hopper (*Tittigonia Rosæ*) . . . will be found nestled closely to the under side of the new leaves. **1924** *Dept. Agric. Yrbk. 1923* 192 The sugar-beet leaf hopper . . . exists in all fields through the growing season.

Leaf lard. Lard of a superior quality made from the leaf fat of hogs. — **1848** *Rep. Comm. Patents 1847* 528 The articles thus referred to are put up in these establishments, from the hams, . . . leaf lard [etc.]. **1870** *Ill. Agric. Soc. Trans.* VII. 478 The result in the aggregate . . . shows the comparative yield of leaf lard. **1878** BEADLE *Western Wilds* 485 On the edge of rich ore-seams little accretions of almost pure silver have run together, like 'leaf lard,' as it were.

Leaf-nosed bat. A bat that has a leaflike membrane on its nose. {1843- (Gray *Spec. Mammals* 21)} — **1867** *Amer. Naturalist* I. 283 The *Istiophora*, or Leaf-nosed Bats, are so called from having a curious membranous expansion of the snout, of a fancied foliaceous appearance, in which the nostrils are open. **1869** *Ib.* III. 472 A second species, at present known no farther west, is the Leaf-nosed Bat (*Macrotus Californicus*) from Fort Yuma.

Leaf-roller. The larva of various insects that roll up the leaves of plants they infest. {1830-} — **1851** BARRY *Fruit Garden* 374 *Leaf Rollers*.—In May and June these insects may be found on the leaves of fruit trees. **1861** *Ill. Agric. Soc. Trans.* V. 470 The larva of a small moth, belonging probably to the group known as 'leaf-rollers' (*tortrices*) has occurred by millions in McHenry county. **1881** *Amer. Naturalist* XV. 484 The book is indispensable to any one engaged in studying the parents of our 'leaf-rollers.' **1899** *Dept. Agric. Yrbk. 1898* 259 A caterpillar known as the bean leaf-roller or 'roller-worm' is injurious in the Gulf States to leguminous plants.

+**Leaf tobacco.** Tobacco in an unprocessed, whole-leaf condition.

1637 *Md. Archives* IV. 12 [They] owe . . . twelve hundred fiftie and two pound of good merchantable leafe-tobacco. **1706** *Boston News-Letter* 14 Jan. 2/2 [There] will be exposed to Sale . . . near the Dock in Boston, twenty nine half Barrels of Leaf, and 40 Rolls of Spun Tobacco. **1822** in McKenney *Memoirs* I. App. 288 It must be for the leaf tobacco, and that is not suited to the trade. **1917** (*title*), Stocks of Leaf Tobacco and the American Production . . . of Tobacco [Bureau of Census].

attrib. **1887** *Courier-Journal* 8 Jan. 4/3 The public prints in the various leaf-tobacco States are taking both sides of the question.

***Leafy,** *a.* +In the names of American plants. — **1785** MARSHALL *Amer. Grove* 158 Leafy Vaccinium or Indian gooseberry. **1833** EATON *Botany* (ed. 6) 310 *Rubus frondosus*, leafy raspberry. **1878** in Killebrew *Tenn. Grasses* 229 *Poa alsodes*, . . . Leafy Meadow Grass, . . . is a scattered growing grass.

***League.**[1] *S.W.* +**1.** In areas formerly a part of Mexico: A measure of land approximately 4,400 acres. Also attrib. +**2.** A linear measure of about 2.63 miles; the Spanish league. — (1) **1824** DEWEES *Lett. from Texas* 50 Every single man, who receives land under the Mexican government, on marrying, is entitled to an augmentation of his claim, to a league and labor of land. **1836** *Diplom. Corr. Texas* I. (1908) 56 We are of the opinion that in the next convention a stop should be put to granting league and quarter league tracts to all who come after that date. **1857** BRAMAN *Texas* 152 All persons who had . . . received their leagues of land . . . were entitled to additional quantity. (2) **1885** *Santa Fé Wkly. New Mexican* 24 Sept. 1/2 The legal league contains 100 cordels, or 5,000 varas.

***League.**[2]

+**1. a.** = UNION LEAGUE. **b.** = LOYAL LEAGUE. Also attrib.

1865 in Fleming *Hist. Reconstruction* I. 135 Some of the most prominent men of the League ask of you an interview. **1871** *Ku Klux Klan Rep.* VIII. 227 The negroes . . . had half a dozen league rooms, I suppose. *Ib.* 357 Agents of this [Freedmen's] Bureau . . . would send regular orders to the League members on the plantations. **1880** TOURGEE *Bricks* 145 The colored men should be encouraged to consider and discuss political affairs. . . . The League gives them this opportunity.

+**2.** A term used in the names of various religious and temperance organizations. Also attrib. (Cf. *Anti-saloon League*, s.v. ANTI-SALOON.)

1883 *Century Mag.* May 65 The Christian League of Connecticut. . . . This is the third annual convention of the League. **1883** RITTENHOUSE *Maud* 192 He had been invited to the [temperance] League meeting tonight and wanted to escort me. **1890** J. B. ROBINSON (*title*), The Epworth League. Its Place in Methodism.

+**3. a.** An association of baseball clubs. Also attrib. (Cf. CIRCUIT 4.)

1885 CHADWICK *Art of Pitching* 132 The following are the best fielding averages of the Eastern League players in championship games for 1885. **1891** *Scribner's Mag.* Oct. 459/1 In a base-ball game a few years ago, a League pitcher broke his humerus in this manner. **1896** *Cincinnati Enquirer* 5 July 2/2 Miller is no longer at the head of the columns of league batters. **1910** *Spalding's Base Ball Guide* 356 The Spalding National League Ball or the Reach American League Ball must be used in all games played under these rules. **1912** C. MATHEWSON *Pitching* 57 Many men, who shine in the minor leagues, fail to make good in the majors.

+**b.** A similar association of bowling clubs.

1898 *Kansas City Star* 18 Dec. 3/2 The Missouri Bowling club's team is now in the lead in the Kansas City bowling league's tournament.

***Leak,** *v.* ‖**1.** To shed tears. *humorous.* **2.** *To leak out*, fig., to become known despite efforts at concealment. {1884-} — (1) **1884** 'MARK TWAIN' *H. Finn* xxv, They bust out a-crying. . . . I never see two men leak the way they done. (2) **1831** S. SMITH *Major Downing* 58 If it should leak out that I was going, . . . somebody else might get the start of me. **1855** GLISAN *Jrnl. Army Life* 187 The news is beginning to leak out, and excites much alarm.

***Lean,** *v.* +*intr.* To run away, 'make tracks.' *colloq.* — **1833** CATLIN *Indians* I. 98 He darts forth . . . , wraps his robe around him and 'leans' as fast as possible for home. **1840** *Knickerb.* XV. 424 Mr. Bruce . . . plunged out of the window, . . . 'leaning' for home. **1851** *Polly Peablossom* 109 Lean, Sam, . . . she's goin' to rip, sartin.

***Lean-to.** Also †**leantoo, lento,** etc. (Cf. LINTER.[1])

***1.** A building or structure the rafters or supports of which butt against or lean upon another building.

1639 in Lechford *Note-Book* (1885) 54 The old house and leantoos, yard & garden thereto belonging. **1704** *N.H. Probate Rec.* I. 401 The said Benedictus Carr . . . [shall] build the same [cellar] under one of the Leanetoos. **1847** BRYANT *Let. to J. Olds* (MS.) Jan., [I prefer] a small cheap building, . . . one room, a bed room and a pantry, with perhaps a lean to. **1920** LEWIS *Main Street* 350 Attached to the rear was a lean-to of storm-streaked pine lumber.

2. Attrib. with *addition, bedroom, chamber*, etc. Also †*lean-to rail*, a handrail.

1666 *Dedham Rec.* IV. 122 The said bridge or foot plankes and leaneto rayles. **1704** S. KNIGHT *Journal* 48 Arriving at my apartment found it to be a little Lento Chamber furnisht . . . with a High Bedd [etc.]. **1879** *Harper's Mag.* Dec. 112/1 Joel . . . had just expired in the lean-to bedroom. **1896** SHINN *Story of Mine* 248 A small lean-to addition was the kitchen and dining room. **1916** PORTER *David* 3 From the little lean-to kitchen the sound of the sputtering suddenly ceased.

+**Leap-year party.** An entertainment to which women invite men. — **1880** *Cimarron News & Press* 26 Feb. 3/2 As the Leap Year party was given up some of the enterprising gentlemen of town, . . . got up an impromptu affair on Tuesday night. **1880** *Boston Ev. Transcript* 6 March 1/4 The ladies of the Hollis-street Society gave a leap-year party . . . last evening, and about fifty couples were present. **1883** RITTENHOUSE *Maud* 266 Early in the evening had given note to Elmer asking to take him to the leap year party next Thursday.

***Least,** *a.* +Used in the names of various American birds regarded as the smallest of their kind. (Cf. LEAST BITTERN, etc.) — **1796** MORSE *Univ. Geog.* I. 209 Least Golden Crown Thrush. **1858** BAIRD *Birds Pacific R.R.* 397 Least Tit. . . . Pacific coast of United States. **1881** *Amer. Naturalist* XV. 213 At Colton, Cal., I first found the nest of that diminutive little bird, the least bush titmouse [*Psaltriparus minimus*]. **1917** *Birds of Amer.* I. 87 The Least Petrel, a Pacific Ocean form, [is] seen occasionally off the coast of California. *Ib.* 182 Least Bittern. . . . [Also called] Least Heron.

+**Least bittern.** The dwarf bittern (*Ixobrychus exilis*), found in the temperate parts of North America. — **1813** WILSON *Ornithology* VIII. 37 Least Bittern: *Ardea exilis*; . . . is commonly found in fresh water meadows. **1839** PEABODY *Mass. Birds* 365 The Least Bittern . . . is so slender that it can pass between two books set an inch apart from each other. **1874** COUES *Birds N.W.* 528, I found the nests of the Least Bittern about three feet above the ground in a thick cluster of smilax and other briary plants. **1917** *Birds of Amer.* I. 182/2 Reed-grown ponds, grassy margins of lakes, and expanses of fresh-water marshes form the abiding places of the Least Bittern.

+**Least flycatcher.** The chebec, the smallest of the flycatchers (*Empidonax minimus*), found chiefly in the eastern part of the United States. — **1874** COUES *Birds N.W.* 254 The Least Flycatcher is . . . numerous during the breeding season along the Red River of the North. **1892** TORREY *Foot-Path Way* 9 All our common eastern Massachusetts species were present; the kingbird . . . and the least fly-catcher. *Ib.* 10 In his notes, the yellow-belly may be said to take after both the least flycatcher and the wood pewee. **1917** *Birds of Amer.* II. 210/1 The Least Flycatcher . . . makes up in energy of manner and emphasis of utterance what it lacks in size.

+**Least sandpiper.** A sandpeep (*Pisobia minutilla*), a common marsh and shore bird throughout America. — **1858** BAIRD *Birds Pacific R.R.* 721 Least Sandpiper. . . . Entire temperate North America. . . . Specimens from western localities seem to be slightly larger. **1874** COUES *Birds N.W.* 482 Least Sandpiper. . . . Abundant . . . in suitable places, throughout the United States. **1917** *Birds of Amer.* I. 236/1 The tiniest atom of its tribe, the Least Sandpiper, . . . is still with us, . . . thanks to the outlawry of shooting them.

+**Least tern.** The little striker or minute tern, *Sterna antillarum.* — **1858** BAIRD *Birds Pacific R.R.* 864 The Least Tern. . . . Texas to Labrador; western rivers. **1869** *Amer. Naturalist* III. 234 The Least Tern . . . and the Roseate Tern, still breed on our coast. **1917** *Birds of Amer.* I. 65/1 The most dainty of all the American sea-birds is the Least Tern.

***Leather.**

***1.** The tanned hide of an animal; a piece of this or something made from it. Also collect.

1622 'MOURT' *Relation* 87 They had . . . aboue their groynes to their wast another leather. **1666** *Md. Archives* II. 77 That Act Concerning Hides & other Skins with an Addition as to prohibite the export of Leather. **1767** *N.Y. State Doc. Hist.* I. 736 No mention is made of the great quantities of Leather being tanned in this country, as this branch of business has been carried on for many years. **1838** *S. Lit. Messenger* IV. 28/1, I caught the leathers on each side of the coach. **1885** HOWELLS *S. Lapham* vi, Jerry, suppose you let me have hold of the leathers [*i.e* reins] a minute. **1891** *Harper's Mag.* June 6/1 For long marches the saddle is comfortable, and the leathers are of about the proper length for the work. **1914** 'BOWER' *Flying U Ranch* 12 [He revealed] a wonderful saddle of stamped leather inlaid on skirt and cantle with more beaten silver.

+**2.** *To pull leather*, to hold on to the saddle with the hands in an effort to retain one's place on a bucking horse. *colloq.* Also transf.

1918 MULFORD *Man from Bar-20* 22, I manages to stick on th' job by pullin' leather. **1923** J. H. COOK *On Old Frontier* 16 He certainly made me 'pull leather,' and I clung to his mane as well in order to keep in close touch with him. **1924** RAINE *Troubled Waters* 190 Stick to the saddle, Mac. Don't you pull leather, old scout.

3. *attrib.* **a.** Made of leather; connected with leather as an article of use or commerce.

1643 *Conn. Rec.* I. 455, 1 lether bottell, . . . 4 hows, 4 axes [etc.]. **1721** *New-Eng. Courant* 7–14 Aug. 2/2 Mr. Nathanael Parkman . . . was accidentally kill'd at a Leather-Mill in Milton. **1772** in *Travels Amer. Col.* 561 The water . . . often rises twenty feet above its present Surface, which Obliges the Traders to Carry leather Canoes along with them. **1809** CUMING *Western Tour* 191 At some distance on the bank of the creek, he has a large tanyard and leather shop. **1864** 'PENNIMAN' *Tanner-Boy* 245 The unassuming leather-merchant of Illinois, was now the great conquering general of the West.

b. In the specific names of plants that in appearance or character resemble or suggest leather.

1789 MORSE *Amer. Geog.* 143 Among the flowering trees and shrubs in the forests, are the . . . leather tree, laurel [etc.]. **1817–8** EATON *Botany* (1822) 241 *Clematis viorna*, leather flower; . . . flowers solitary, bell-form.

c. In the specific names of birds and animals.

1811 *Niles' Reg.* I. 119/1 It is a Testudo Cariaria or Leather tortoise. **1842** *Nat. Hist. N.Y., Zoology* III. 4 The Leather Turtle, although a native of tropical American seas, is a great wanderer. **1917** *Birds of Amer.* I. 152 Ruddy Duck. . . . [Also called] Leather-back.

+**Leather bark.** Any one of various tough-barked trees of the genus *Thymelaea.* — **1751** J. BARTRAM *Observations* 28 Leather-bark or *thymelea* . . . is plentiful in all this part of the country. **1762** CLAYTON *Flora Virginica* 60 Leather bark or Thymelæa. **1855** *Mich. Agric. Soc. Trans.* VI. 149 The shrubs are crab-apple, . . . leather bark, elder [etc.].

Leather breeches. Breeches made of leather. Also attrib. and transf. {18th cent.} — **1684** MATHER *Providences* 104 When the man was a bed, he was beaten with a heavy pair of leather breeches. **1796** *Boston Directory* 259 Ives, James, leather breeches maker, No. 31, Marlborough street. **1837** BIRD *Nick of Woods* I. 168, The feel of wet leather breeches is quite uncomfortable. **1923** J. H. COOK *On Old Frontier* 57 Many were the poor old 'leather breeches' who came dragging themselves into camp.

Leather bucket. A bucket made of leather. {leathern bucket, 1719} — **1658** *Boston Rec.* 149 The Treasurer shall forthwith . . . gett the leather bucketts repayred for the townes use. **1721** *Ib.* 152 Voted that the Proposal for Leather Buckets be Refered unto the meeting in May. **1888** BILLINGS *Hardtack* 304 Each ambulance was required to carry . . . the following articles:—Three bed-sacks, . . . one leather bucket [etc.].

Leather-dresser. One whose profession is to dress leather. {1611–}

1631 *Va. House of Burgesses* 125 Tradesmen are wantinge, especially Shipwrites, . . . Tanners, Leatherdressers, Hempdressers. **1670** *Portsmouth Rec.* 154 His Trade beinge a Lether dresser. **1722** *New-Eng Courant* 19–26 Nov. 2/2 Mr. Benjamin Harris, late of Boston, Leather-Dresser. **1789** *Boston Directory* 173 Adams, Abraham, leather-dresser and breeches-maker. **1818** BENTLEY *Diary* IV. 561 He served in Salem with Woodbridge as a Leather dresser. **1891** HOLMES *Over Teacups* 231 He served an apprenticeship as a leather-dresser.

+**Leather-face(d),** *adj.* and *attrib.* Having a hard-featured, emotionless face. — **1834** SIMMS *G. Rivers* I. 77 What's to hinder us now, you leather-faced Jew? **1884** 'MARK TWAIN' *H. Finn* 287 You ain't one of these leather-face people.

Leatherhead. {1700–} +**1.** A nickname for an inhabitant of Pennsylvania. +**2.** A watchman or policeman in New York City. *slang. Obs.* — **(1) 1845** *Cincinnati Misc.* I. 240 The inhabitants of . . . Pennsylvania [are called] Leatherheads. **1872** *Harper's Mag.* Jan. 318/1 Nicknames given to the States and people of this republic . . . [include] Pennsylvania, Pennites, and Leatherheads. **(2) 1868** M. H. SMITH *Sunshine & Shadow* 148 The guardians of the city were watchmen . . . and were known as leather-heads, from the leather cap they wore. **1882** MCCABE *New York* 369 A patrol of civilians . . . wore a leather hat with a wide brim, something like a fireman's hat, and this won for them the name of 'Leatherheads.' **1888** *N.Y. Mercury* 21 July (F.), The old police or leatherheads tried to restrain them.

Leather jacket. {1770–} +**a.** A species of filefish or triggerfish. +**b.** A species of fish (*Oligoplites saurus*) having small scales embedded in the skin. — **(a) 1884** GOODE, etc. *Fisheries* I. 172 The Leather-jacket of Pensacola . . . occasionally finds its way as far north as Massachusetts. **1903** T. H. BEAN *Fishes N.Y.* 608 Balistes carolinensis. Leather Jacket; Turbot; Triggerfish. **(b) 1884** GOODE, etc. *Fisheries* I. 332 The Leather-jacket—*Oligoplites saurus.* This fish . . . [has] been several times observed between Florida and Newport, Rhode Island. **1911** *Rep. Fisheries 1908* 316.

+**Leatherleaf.** A shrub (*Chamaedaphne calyculata*) with tough coriaceous leaves. — **1817–8** EATON *Botany* (1822) 173 *Andromeda calyculata*, leather leaf. **1839** *Mich. Agric. Soc. Trans.* VII. 399 *Andromeda calyculata.* Leather-leaf. **1870** *Amer. Naturalist* IV. 217 The Leather Leaf (*Cassandra calyculata*), and *Andromeda polifolia*, are both worthy of attention.

Leather medal. 'An imaginary reward for stupidity' (Th.). *colloq.* — **1837** *Harvardiana* III. 147 (Th.), A leather medal his reward should be, A leather medal and an LL.D. **1851** HALL *College Words* 183 At Harvard College, the Leather Medal was formerly bestowed upon the laziest fellow in College. **1860** *Richmond Enquirer* 20 April 2/5 (Th.), The individual who conceived the leather medal idea [for identifying dogs] deserves a leather medal himself. **1865** *Nation* I. 103 If that mythical 'institution' of our boyhood, the leather medal, be not altogether a myth, . . . we would order a large supply.

Leather-sealer. In colonial times, an official who inspected leather and stamped it or affixed to it a seal indicative of quality. *Obs.* — **1662** *Conn. Rec.* I. 377 The leathr sealers . . . shal have allowed unto them for each Dicker of Leather they seale, 18 *d.* **1683** *Huntington Rec.* I. 359 At a towne meeting . . . Joseph Whitman was chossen leather sealler. **1798** I. ALLEN *Hist. Vermont* 272 Weights and measures, leather sealers &c. are regulated according to law.

+**Leatherside.** 'A small cyprinoid fish, the leather-sided minnow, *Tigoma tænia*, used in Utah as a bait for catching white-fish, or mountain herring, *Coregonus williamsoni*' (*Cent.*).

Leather stocking.

1. A stocking or legging of leather.

1701 PENN in *Penn-Logan Corr.* I. 56 My leather stockings are Christopher's.

+**2.** (Written as one word.) A wearer of stockings made of leather; a frontiersman. Often with particular reference to Natty Bumppo, or Leatherstocking, the central character in J. F. Cooper's *Leatherstocking Tales.*

1823 COOPER *Pioneers* xxxiii, The Leather-stocking made his appearance, . . . under the custody of two constables. **1831** HOLLEY *Texas* (1833) 43 The dress of these hunters is usually of deer-skin. Hence the appropriate name *Leather Stocking.* Their generic name . . . is *Frontiers-men.* **1843** 'CARLTON' *New Purchase* I. 100 One [house was occupied] by a very special sort of a squatter—the Leatherstocking of our tribe. **1853** *Knickerb.* XLII. 225 He was in truth a very good representative of the leather-stocking. **1897** *Outing* XXX. 435/1 The old Leatherstockings understood the habit of the fish. **1913** M. E. PHILLIPS *J. F. Cooper* 120 [They] paid a brief visit to West Point, thence to Catskill, where, like Leatherstocking, they saw 'Creation!'—as Natty said,—'all creation, lad.'

***Leather-wing(ed) bat.** Any one of various flying mammals belonging to the order of true bats. — **1805** LEWIS in *L. & Clark Exped.* II. (1904) 200, I have not seen the leather winged bat for some time. **1867** HARRIS *Sut Lovingood* 79 More room in a turnip-seed tu fly roun in than a leather-wing bat hes in a meetin-hous. **1899** *Animal & Plant Lore* 61 Leather-winged bat, for any of the family *Vespertilionidæ.* Chestertown, Md.

+Leatherwood.

1. The genus *Dirca;* also, a small shrub or tree of this genus (*D. palustris*) with tough, pliant bark and branches.

1743 CLAYTON *Flora Virginica* 155 Unde Leather-wood appellatur. **1785** MARSHALL *Amer. Grove* 41 *Dirca.* Leather Wood. **1843** TORREY *Flora N.Y.* II. 163 Leather-wood.... The branches of this shrub are so tough that the Indians use them for making cords. **1860** CURTIS *Woody Plants N.C.* 92 Leather-wood.... Widely diffused over the country.

2. *Cyrilla racemiflora,* the ironwood.

1901 MOHR *Plant Life Ala.* 122 Swamp dogwood ... interspersed with titi ..., leatherwood ..., holly ... and blue palmetto.

3. Attrib. with *bark, creek.*

1784 SMYTH *Tour U.S.* I. 275 My journey ... brought me to a large water-course, named Leatherwood Creek. **1787** Leatherwood bark [see next].

+Leatherwood bush. =LEATHERWOOD 1. — **1787** *Amer. Acad. Mem.* II. I. 159 Leather Wood Bushes. Leather Wood bark is an excellent substitute for cord ... : it grows only in low and very rich lands. **1789** MORSE *Amer. Geog.* 461 The prevailing growth ... and the more useful trees are, maple ... and leather wood bushes. **1887** EGGLESTON *Graysons* xiii, Bob now went to the brookside and cut up and stripped three or four leatherwood bushes.

Lebanon cedar. Cedar of Lebanon. In attrib. use. (Cf. CEDAR 1 c.) — **1838** *U.S. Mag.* I. 300 There is a Lebanon cedar tree ... which is immortalized by some wild tale of Indian massacre.

+Lecompton. [*Lecompton,* Kan.] *Hist.*

1. *Lecompton Constitution,* a constitution for the state of Kansas drawn up by proslavery leaders at Lecompton in 1857.

1858 LINCOLN in Logan *Great Conspiracy* 56 The Lecompton Constitution connects itself with this question [of popular sovereignty], for it is in this matter ... that ... Judge Douglas, claims such vast credit. **1860** *36th Congress 1 Sess.* H. R. Rep. No. 648, 56 Mr. Buchanan's belief that the existence of the Union would be endangered unless Kansas was admitted *under the Lecompton constitution.* **1870** *Congress. Globe* 18 March 2055/3 The 'Lecompton constitution' ... was somewhat national in its character. **1884** BLAINE *20 Years of Congress* I. 150 Until his break from the regular ranks in his opposition to the Lecompton Constitution, Douglas had enjoyed boundless popularity.

2. *attrib.* passing into *adj.* Pertaining to the political situation growing out of the struggle over the adoption or rejection of the Lecompton Constitution.

1858 in W. Lawrence *A. A. Lawrence* 112 The Lecompton state government is secured. **1861** in Logan *Great Conspiracy* 178 The Pro-Slavery Party in Kansas perpetrated, and the President and the South accepted, the Lecompton fraud. **1886** LOGAN *Ib.* 86 The split in the Democratic Party, between the Lecompton and Anti-Lecompton Democracy, was widened.

+Lecomptonist, Lecomptonite. One who favored the Lecompton Constitution. Now hist. — **1858** *N.Y. Tribune* 1 April 3/3 (Th.), Lecomptonists and the 'anti-Lecompton' Democracy of Lecompton went off on this bolt, doing it secretly. **1859** BARTLETT 239 *Lecomptonite,* an upholder of the pro-slavery constitution for Kansas promulgated at the city of Lecompton.

+Leconte. [John Lawrence *LeConte* (1825–1883), Amer. entomologist.] In possessive. **1.** With *mock thrush, thrasher:* A thrasher of the desert regions of the Southwest. **2.** With *bunting, sparrow:* A small sparrow (*Passerherbulus caudacutus*) of the west-central states. — **(1) 1869** *Amer. Naturalist* III. 188 The only peculiar bird known is Leconte's Mock-thrush (*Harporhynchus Lecontei*), which is also of a pale grayish brown. **1917** *Birds of Amer.* III. 184 Leconte's Thrasher. *Toxostoma lecontei lecontei....* It is a pity that this fine bird does not select a habitat more habitable for man. **(2) 1873** COUES in *Amer. Naturalist* VII. 748 LeConte's bunting (*Coturniculus LeContei*) long remained among our special desiderata. **1874** — *Birds N.W.* 134 *Coturniculus Lecontei.* Leconte's Sparrow. **1917** *Birds of Amer.* III. 29 On the prairie marshes of the Mississippi valley ... is another ... species, known as Leconte's Sparrow (*Passerherbulus lecontei*).

***Lecture.**

1. In colonial New England, a sermon, discourse, or other morally edifying exercise, often one of a series held at regular times. *Obs.* (Cf. LECTURE DAY.)

1633 *Mass. Bay Rec.* I. 110 It is therefore ordered, that hereafter noe lecture shall begin before one a clocke in the afternoone. **1680** *Conn. Rec.* III. 65 The ministers ... keep a lecture weekly ... in each county. **1722** *New-Eng. Courant* 12–19 March 1/2 Persons that idle away the Time (to say no worse) in and about the 'Change, on the Thursday Weekly Lectures. **1741** B. LYNDE *Diary* 125 Mr. Balch of Bradford preached his lecture on Grace thro' J. **1772** A. G. WINSLOW *Diary* (1894) 14 On thursday I attended my aunt to Lecture & heard Dr Chauncey preach a third sermon from Acts.

2. A public informative discourse on a subject of popular interest.

1767 *N.Y. Mercury* 20 July 3/2 Mr. Douglass proposes to deliver the Lecture on Tuesdays and Fridays, for the short Time he has to stay in Town. **1861** *Chicago Tribune* 26 May 1/9 Both Halls, or either, can be rented for Concerts, Lectures, Exhibitions, Balls, and the like. **1865** *Atlantic Mo.* XV. 362 The popular lecture, in the Northern States of America, has become 'an institution.' **1900** DIX *Deacon Bradbury* 71 They had been discussing ... the illustrated lecture of the fortnight before.

+3. A political speech.

1885 CRAWFORD *Amer. Politician* 55 The affair was called a 'lecture' in accordance with the time-honored custom of Boston.

4. Attrib. in sense 2 with *agent, bureau,* etc.

1864 NICHOLS *Amer. Life* I. 67 There are towns where a lecture-committee would not dare to invite Beecher or Phillips to lecture. **1865** *Atlantic Mo.* XV. 369 The platform of the lecture-hall has been common ground for ... all our social, political, and religious organizations. **1870** Lecture season [see LECTURE SYSTEM]. **1873** 'MARK TWAIN' & WARNER *Gilded Age* lviii. 527, I am a lecture-agent. **1880** ALDRICH *Stillwater Tragedy* xvi. 180 The Grecian lecture-bureau never sent him twice to the same town. **1890** FREDERIC *Lawton Girl* 150 It may take the form of ... a lecture course with elevating popular exhibitions. **1897** 'MARK TWAIN' *Following Equator* xv. 160, I had a curiosity to know about that man's lecture-tour and last moments. **1912** NICHOLSON *Hoosier Chron.* 381 You ought to consider going on the lecture platform.

Lecture day. {1616} In colonial New England, the day, as a Sunday or market day, appointed for a discourse by a lecturer: (see quotations). Now hist.

1637 *Dorchester Rec.* 21 They shall upon the next Lecture Day after Lecture read them [*sc.* acts] to the Company of free men. **1671** SEWALL *Letter-Book* I. 18 Mr. Wheelwright read the printed paper on a Lecture-day, and preached a sermon. **1704** S. KNIGHT *Journal* 39 Their Diversions in this part of the Country are on Lecture days and Training days mostly. **1779** PARKMAN *Diary* 94 Mr. Badcock has been with me to speak about ye Singing ... on proposed Lecture day. **1816** PICKERING 202 *Lecture-Day.* Used in New England for *holiday;* from the custom of excusing boys from going to school on those *week-days,* when there was a public *Lecture.* **1857** HOLLAND *Bay-Path* 118 The term 'lecture day' early became the synonym for holiday, and Wednesday was called by its real name hardly once in a twelvemonth. **1890** *Cent.* 3395/3 *Lecture-day....* In the New England colonies it seems to have been usually Thursday.

Lecture room. In a college building, a room in which students hear lectures. {1829–} — **1788** *Columbian Mag.* II. 673/1 On the lower floor, in the middle, was a hall, which served as ... a lecture-room for the professors. **1817** *N. Amer. Rev.* Jan. 284 There are three separate lecture-rooms, besides a laboratory. [Harvard.] **1893** POST *Harvard Stories* 233 Even if you never go near the library, you can learn much in the lecture-room.

Lecture sermon. A sermon given as a lecture (sense 1) or on a lecture day. *Obs.* {1751–} — **1703** SEWALL *Diary* II. 83 Mr. Thomas Bridge preaches his first Lecture-Sermon. **1711** *Ib.* 296 It seems the Governour's Lady was very much affected with Mr. Wadsworth's Lecture Sermon. **1736** J. ELIOT (*title*), The Two Witnesses.... Being the Substance of a Lecture-Sermon Preached at the North-Society in Lyme.

+Lecture system. The system of providing lectures, usually in 'courses,' for popular audiences. — **1854** *Harper's Mag.* Feb. 415/1 We can not ... look abroad over the varied panorama of life and society in our country, and not mark so striking a fact as the Lecture-system. **1870** O. LOGAN *Before Footlights* 489 As the lecture season draws nigh, there comes up a cry ... that the lecture system is dying out. **1875** *Scribner's Mo.* Dec. 281/2 The 'lecture system' ... is declining in its usefulness.

+Lecture time. In colonial New England, the time when a periodical lecture was given. *Obs.* — **1674** SEWALL *Diary* I. 3 News of Peace in Lecture time. **1702** *Ib.* II. 63 Got home in Lecture-time. After Lecture Council sets. **1779** STILES *Lit. Diary* II. 328, I had no Lecture to day, as just at Lecture time this Aft. a Brigade of 500 Contin. Troops came into Town to be stationed here.

***Ledge.** *Mining.* Metal-bearing rock; a lode or vein. {1863–} — **1847** EMERSON *Poems* 196 She ransacks mines and ledges, And quarries every rock. **1852** WHITMORE *Diary* 26 July, Worked for the Ill. and Wis. Quartz Mining Company drawing dirt from ledge. **1869** BROWNE *Adv. Apache Country* 231 Twenty distinct mines, ... forming what might be termed a perfect net-work of silver-bearing ledges. **1883** E. LORD *Control Mining* 98 The first locators were entitled to the exclusive possession of the section of the ledge included in their claim. **1896** SHINN *Story of Mine* 126 The Comstock ledge ... was very fine.

+Ledgy, *a.* Abounding in ledges or rocky ridges. — **1779** *N.H. Hist. Soc. Coll.* VI. 315 This swamp is not level, but has some considerable hills and ledgy mountains in it. **1810** *Mass. H. S. Coll.* 2 Ser. I. 181 There are no heaths, few ledgy hills, and scarcely any sunken lands. **1865** *Maine Bd. Agric. Rep.* X. 136 In the eastern part of the town the land is broken and ledgy. **1895** 'CRADDOCK' *Myst. Witch-Face Mt.* 124 The shadowy woods stood dense about the little open ledgy space on three sides.

***Leek.** A pungent bulbous plant of the genus *Allium* related to the onion. — **1622** 'MOURT' *Relation* 62 We found ... great store of Leekes, and Onyons. **1709** LAWSON *Carolina* 77 The Garden-Roots that thrive well in Carolina, are Carrots, Leeks, Parsnips. **1858** T. WEED *Autobiog.* 19 Leeks ... tainted everything, but especially the milk and butter. **1891** WELCH *Recoll. 1830–40* 119 The old squaws would bring the various green herbs, ... leeks, horseradish [etc.].

***Left.** *ellipt. Baseball.* + =LEFT FIELD. — **1875** *Chicago Tribune* 17 Aug. 5/6 Hall captured eight flys at left. **1899** QUINN *Penna. Stories* 49 The next batter sent a long fly out to left.

*Left, *p.p.* +*To get* (or *be*) *left*, to be left behind; fig., to be disappointed in something. *colloq.*

1882 *Chicago Tribune*, Destiny won't get left any in the mean time. **1882** *Century Mag.* Aug. 540, I may be 'left' if I prescribe a limit. **1889** MUNROE *Golden Days* 113 Perceiving that he was about to 'get left,' he followed the example of those about him. **1899** QUINN *Penna. Stories* 69 We determined not to be left entirely, and so we laid a plan to steal theirs in return. **1914** ATHERTON *Perch of Devil* 174 They tried to corral your mine . . . but got left.

+**Left center.** *Baseball.* That portion of the outfield slightly to the left of center field. — **1875** *Chicago Tribune* 3 Aug. 7/3 Pike's difficult fly to left-centre was muffed by Eggler after a desperate effort. **1880** N. BROOKS *Fairport Nine* ii. 25 Jo Murch . . . made a muff of a high fly ball, far out in the left centre in the eighth inning.

+**Left field.** *Baseball.* **1.** That portion of the outfield to the left of the batter as he faces the pitcher; the position of left fielder. **2.** The left fielder. — (1) **1867** CHADWICK *Base Ball Reference* 51 Suppose, also, that a ball similarly hit to the right or left fields [etc.]. **1874** WRIGHT *Boston Base Ball Club* 12 He will probably play left field. **1880** N. BROOKS *Fairport Nine* xiv. 183 Sam Booden at the bat . . . led off with a fly to the left field. **1897** *Outing* June 299/2 Greenway or Tearey can fill left field well. (2) **1870** in Wright *Boston Base Ball Club* (1874) 50 'He's caught him out!' shouted the boy, . . . as the left field took in a fly. **1878** *De Witt's Base-ball Guide* 20 The left field . . . should watch the play of the pitcher, and attend to his signals.

+**Left fielder.** *Baseball.* The player who covers left field. — **1867** CHADWICK *Base Ball Reference* 70 Suppose the left-fielder should be the third striker on the list, and the pitcher the eighth [etc.]. **1874** WRIGHT *Boston Base Ball Club* 13 [He is] one of the best left fielders of the country. **1885** CHADWICK *Art of Pitching* 109 The idea that a left fielder has only to attend to left field balls . . . is an exploded rule.

Left-hander. {1861–} +*Baseball.* A left-handed pitcher. — **1887** *Courier-Journal* 27 May 2/4 The big fellows . . . made twenty hits off the famous left-hander. **1897** *Outing* XXX. 204/2 Besides Hayden for the box, Bandeline, a left-hander, is about the best of the new men. **1912** MATHEWSON *Pitching* 30 He became the greatest lefthander in the country.

*Leg, *n.* +**1.** In slang phrases: *To show leg*, to run away; *to have by the leg*, to have at a great disadvantage. +**2.** The case or housing in which the vertical conveyor belt of a grain elevator operates. — (1) **1837** BIRD *Nick of Woods* I. 120, I'll fight for you, or run for you, take scalp or cut stick, shake fist or show leg. **1894** *Congress. Rec.* 9 April 3556/1 To use the language imputed to the President [Cleveland], 'the banks have got the country by the leg.' (2) **1881** *Harper's Mag.* April 708/2 Iron buckets [of grain] . . . travel up a sort of chimney, called a 'leg,' to this roof chamber. **1901** MERWIN & WEBSTER *Calumet 'K'* 212 Harahan Company are building the Leg.

Leg, *v.* {1601–} +*intr.* To bestir oneself *for* someone or something. *colloq.* — **1844** *Lexington Observer* 30 Nov. 3/5 There are a number of men here 'legging' for the Colonel. **1867** *Wkly. New Mexican* 20 July 1/4 Bob Mitchell and Jim Carleton have not helped Clever *much* in the 'diggings,' by legging for him. **1890** *Stock Grower & Farmer* 22 March 3/2 The way things start off it looks as though the Colorado Sanitary board intended to 'leg' for the Denver yards again this year. **1902** HARBEN *A. Daniel* 74 Durin' election . . . he was leggin' fer a friend o' his'n.

+**Legal cap.** Ruled writing paper made in long sheets folded at the top and often used for legal documents. Also attrib. — **1874** KNIGHT 455/2 *Cap-paper* . . . [Ruled] with red lines to form a margin on the left hand, and made to fold on the top, it is *legal cap*. **1884** 'CRADDOCK' *Tenn. Mts.* 115 He replaced the sheet of scrawled legal-cap in his pocket. **1902** C. MORRIS *Stage Confidences* 172 [The letter] was on legal cap. **1904** HARBEN *Georgians* 104 Abner . . . drew out several sheets of legal-cap paper pinned together at the top.

+**Legal holiday.** A holiday established by statute or proclamation, during which government and other business is usually suspended. — **1867** *Wkly. New Mexican* 30 March 1/4 New Jersey makes a legal holiday of President Lincoln's birthday. **1888** *Nation* 5 April 275/3 A legal holiday, called 'Labor Day,' has been created in Massachusetts, New York, New Jersey, Colorado, and Oregon. **1895** *Statutes at Large* XXVIII. 96 The first Monday of September . . . , being the day celebrated and known as Labor's Holiday, is hereby made a legal public holiday. **1918** *Bank & Public Holidays* 5 Governments . . . have sought to establish and define certain dates as legal holidays. This has been done . . . in the United States . . . by each State independently of all others.

Legal tender. Currency recognized by law as legal in the payment of monetary obligations {1816–}; hence used humorously for money, esp. paper money.

[**1739** W. DOUGLASS *Discourse Currency* 6 The Court of France were obliged to ordain, that there should be no other legal Tender but Silver-Coin.] **1797** *Ann. 5th Congress* I. 730 Bank notes were not a legal tender in any part of the United States. **1822** *Ann. 17th Congress* 1 Sess. I. 83 No State . . . [shall] . . . make anything but gold and silver a legal tender. **1875** *Chicago Tribune* 16 Aug. 8/2 [The] question was whether they [*sc.* greenbacks] should be a legal tender between individuals in the payment of debt. **1896** *Congress. Rec.* May 4935/2 A Bland dollar authorized in 1878 . . . itself is not a legal tender. **1911** VANCE *Cynthia* 60 The driver inspected the legal tender narrowly . . . and stuffed it in his pocket.

b. Attrib. with *act, currency, gold money*, etc.

1865 *Atlantic Mo.* XV. 190/1 The calamity of a worthless paper legal-tender currency added to the general discontent [in 1783 in Conn.]. **1882** *Nation* 30 Nov. 462/3 Add one plank—the repeal of the Legal-Tender Act and the retirement of the greenbacks. **1893** *Arena* March 471 All money . . . is given its legal-tender value . . . by an edict or law. **1894** LEAVITT *Our Money Wars* 109 Mr. Spaulding had, on January 7, 1862, reported a bill for $100,000,000 full legal-tender Greenbacks. **1900** *Congress. Rec.* 11 Jan. 771/1 Five hundred millions of legal-tender gold money created a gold standard.

+**Legal-tender note.** A currency note, as a non-interest-bearing treasury note, made legal tender by government fiat. — **1865** *U.S. Laws Concerning Money* (1910) 189 This act shall not be so construed as to give any authority for the issue of any legal-tender notes . . . beyond the balance unissued. **1884** BLAINE *20 Years of Congress* I. 481 The legal-tender notes . . . supplied an ample currency for the business of the country. **1894** LEAVITT *Our Money Wars* 109 Additional temporary loan certificates . . . would be redeemed in legal-tender notes. **1900** *Congress. Rec.* 7 Feb. 1620/2 The agents and friends of the national banks . . . sought to destroy silver, the greenbacks, and the legal-tender notes.

+**Leg drama.** *Theat.* A ballet or musical burlesque giving actresses opportunity for displaying their legs. *slang. Obs.* — **1872** *Chicago Tribune* 8 Dec., The history of the leg-drama, so well known under the title of *The Black Crook*.

Legging. Also **leg(g)in.** A covering for the leg frequently made of dressed deerskin. {1821–} Usually pl.

(*a*) **1751** *New Jersey Archives* XIX. 84 [He] had on when he went away . . . brown yarn leggins [etc.]. **1800** BOUCHER *Glossary* p. xlix, *Leggins;* a kind of loose, light gambadoes for the legs. **1836** IRVING *Astoria* II. 63 Each had a good buffalo or deer skin robe; and a deer skin hunting shirt and leggins. **1881** PIERSON *In the Brush* 32 For leggins I bought a yard and a half of butternut jean, which was cut into two equal parts.

(*b*) **1775** CRESSWELL *Journal* 61 Leggings . . . are pieces of coarse woollen cloth wrapped round the leg and tied below the knee with a string to prevent the snakes biting you. **1784** SMYTH *Tour U.S.* I. 180 On their legs they [backwoods riflemen] have Indian boots or leggings, made of coarse woolen cloth. **1823** JAMES *Exped.* I. 145 The Black Bird presented . . . a pair of handsome leggings. **1862** in *Harper's Mag.* LXXXIV. 496/1 The men appeared in gaudy array, with . . . blue or scarlet leggings. **1905** N. DAVIS *Northerner* 272 He ran to Falls and, grasping a strap of his legging, sought to draw him to Joan.

Leghorn.

1. A straw plaiting for hats made from a variety of wheat grown in Italy and exported from Leghorn; also, a hat made of this. {1804–}

See also LEGHORN BONNET and LEGHORN HAT.

1819 *Niles' Reg.* XVII. 143/2 [The hats] were closely compared . . . with the finest Leghorns worn by the ladies in the city of Hartford. **1845** NOAH *Gleanings* 10 Expensive leghorns [etc.] . . . convert our ladies into walking mines of wealth. **1903** WIGGIN *Rebecca* 10 She wore an odd little visored cap of white Leg-horn.

+**2.** A breed of small domestic fowl said to have been imported from Leghorn, Italy; also, a fowl of this breed. Also attrib. {1873– (Tegetmeier *Poultry Bk.* 173)}

1869 *Rep. Comm. Agric. 1868* 485, 15 hens, mostly Leghorns and Black Hamburgs. *Ib.*, Mixture of Leghorn and native breed. **1879** HOWELLS *Lady of Aroostook* 80 'He looks as if he were Leghorn. Leghorn breed,' she added. **1894** *Vt. Agric. Rep.* XIV. 173 If eggs is the object sought, then select the Minorca or Leghorn. **1912** WOODROW *Sally Salt* 40 A great flock of industriously pecking chickens, snow-white Leghorns, gray speckled Plymouth Rocks [etc.].

Leghorn bonnet. A bonnet made of leghorn. {1826– (*Stanford Dict.*)} — **1850** JUDD *R. Edney* 88 On the sofa lay . . . a leghorn bonnet. **1870** NOWLAND *Indianapolis* 155 Old 'oman wanted to know if they were gwine to have any more Leghorn bonnets with two crowns. **1905** VALENTINE *H. Sandwith* 19 She had on . . . a white plumed Leghorn bonnet.

+**Leghorn flat.** A broad-brimmed, low-crowned hat made of leghorn straw. Worn by women. — **1830** WATSON *Philadelphia* 176 Other articles of female wear . . . [include] a 'skimmer hat,' . . . of a very small flat crown and big brim, not unlike the present Leghorn flats. **1851** [see FLAT *n.*[1] 6]. **1891** WELCH *Recoll. 1830–40* 174 The ladies shopping, visiting or driving in summer . . . wore leghorn flats, shaped into bonnets according as the fashion dictated.

Leghorn hat. A hat made of leghorn straw. — **1740** *Penna. Gazette* 22 May 7/2. **1819** *Niles' Reg.* XVII. 143/2 Among the articles of wearing apparel were two elegant imitations of ladies Leghorn hats. **1873** 'MARK TWAIN' & WARNER *Gilded Age* vi. 63 She tripped down the street on a summer's day . . . with her wide Leghorn hat flapping down and hiding her face. **1904** GLASGOW *Deliverance* 128 A single tobacco blossom [was] waving over her leghorn hat.

Legislation. The enactment of laws {*a*1655–}, +esp. by Congress or a state legislature.

1788 *Federalist* II. 131 Does the period of two years bear no greater proportion to the knowledge requisite for federal legislation, than one year does to the knowledge requisite for state legislation? **1835** in Benton *30 Years' View* (1854) I. 610/2 We would say that the abolitionists can only be put down by legislation in the States in which they exist. **1861** in Logan *Great Conspiracy* 155, I believe, Mr. President, that . . . it must be by *Legislation;* which is more ready, more certain, and more likely to be satisfactory, than *Constitutional Amendment.* **1882** *Nation* 21 Dec. 524/3 The only practical and effective check, on speculation in anything, is the great losses sustained by the vast majority of those who speculate. No legislation can provide a substitute for this. **1912** *Rep. Indian Affairs* 5 For the recent development of the Government's policy, legislation in the early . . . eighties, . . . prepared the way.

Legislative, *a.* Of or pertaining to a legislature. {*c*1641–} — **1776** *Decl. Independence,* He has called together legislative bodies at places unusual, uncomfortable, and distant from the depository of their public records. **1816** *Ann. 14th Congress* 2 Sess. 354 Mr. Chairman, the source of all these evils is the practice of legislative caucussing. **1870** *Ill. Rev. Statutes 1874* 60 Legislative Department. . . . The legislative power shall be vested in a general assembly. **1900** *Congress. Rec.* 16 Jan. 853/2, I therefore move that the doors be closed as for legislative session. **1900** *Nation* 22 Nov. 400 'Ask Platt,' said Croker before the Legislative Committee.

+**Legislative assembly.** [F. *assemblée legislative* (1791).] The title of one or other of various territorial and state legislatures. — [**1836** *Southern Literary Messenger* II. 408 His [Madison's] second reason for having a Senate, or second branch of the Legislative Assembly, is thus stated.] **1855** *Santa Fe Gazette* 8 Dec., The legislative Assembly of the Territory of New Mexico convened in the Palace, in Santa Fe, on Monday. **1889** *N.D. Constitution* ii. § 29 The Legislative Assembly shall fix the number of Senators. **1917** *Oregon Blue Book* 55 Senators—Twenty-ninth Legislative Assembly.

+**Legislative caucus.** A party caucus in a state legislature. — **1816** *Ann. 14th Congress* 2 Sess. 351, I come now to the last and great complaint. . . . The deformity of a legislative caucus—State intrigues [etc.]. **1846** MACKENZIE *Van Buren* 190 Martin Van Buren having procured himself to be made Senator of the United States by the legislative caucus . . . then directed the following appointments to be made.

+**Legislative council. 1.** The title of a few territorial legislatures. Now hist. **2.** The upper house of the New Mexico territorial legislature. — (1) **1836** *Niles' Nat. Reg.* 24 Sept. 62/2 [Appropriations.] For arrearages of the expenses of the legislative council of the territory of Michigan, 3,553 40. **1837** WILLIAMS *Florida* 208 The Legislative Council this year [1824] established the counties of Watton, Leon [etc.]. (2) **1867** *Wkly. New Mexican* 9 March 1/4 The Legislative Assembly convened . . . and with the unanimous consent of the Legislative Council, I was appointed and commissioned as Attorney General.

Legislator. One who makes laws {1605–}, +esp. a member of a territorial or state legislature. Also used as a title. — **1788** *Federalist* liii, No man can be a competent legislator who does not [have] . . . a certain degree of knowledge of the subjects on which he is to legislate. **1820** FLINT *Lett. from Amer.* 189 The laying out of new counties . . . seems to be a gratifying duty to back-wood legislators. **1848** *S. Lit. Messenger* XIV. 494/2 This letter was post-marked *Richmond!* A striking circumstance, because Legislator Blarney . . . was there. **1863** *Rio Abajo Press* 24 Feb. 2 Our legislators have two sessions to consult in. **1885** *Century Mag.* April 821 It is almost impossible to actually convict a legislator of bribe-taking. **1916** EASTMAN *From Deep Woods* 157, I would soon find the legislator in question drumming up some objection to the bill.

Legislature. {1676–}

+**1.** The body or assembly of constituted representatives of a colony, state, or territory, vested with the authority to make laws for the governance of the body politic.

1729 FRANKLIN *Writings* II. 147 It would behove the Legislature most carefully to contrive how to prevent the Bills issued upon Land from falling with it. **1776** *Decl. Independence,* For suspending our own legislatures, and declaring themselves invested with power to legislate for us in all cases whatsoever. **1779** *N.J. Archives* 2 Ser. III. 598 David Smalley . . . intends to petition the legislature of this state. **1836** *Niles' Reg.* L. 371 All the states choose [electors] by general ticket except South Carolina, which chooses by the legislature. **1847** *Santa Fe Republican* 18 Dec. 2/2 The results of the deliberations of the Legislature, now in session in New Mexico. **1885** CRAWFORD *Amer. Politician* 136 The legislature should elect the new senator in place of the one deceased. **1891** O'BEIRNE *Leaders Ind. Territory* vi/1 The legislature convenes annually at Tishomingo, the capital. **1912** NICHOLSON *Hoosier Chron.* 159 At every session of the legislature I am charged with the grossest corruption.

+**2.** The federal Congress. Also *Legislature of the United States. Obs.*

1787 RANDOLPH in Elliot *Deb. Constitution* (1836) I. 144 Resolved, That a national executive be instituted, to be chosen by the national legislature. **1788** *Federalist* II. 150 All the local information and interests of the state [*i.e.,* each state] . . . may easily be conveyed by a very few hands into the legislature of the United States. **1798** *Ann. 5th Congress* I. 599 Any person . . . [who shall] traduce or defame the Legislature of the United States . . . shall be punished by a fine. **1809** FRENEAU *Poems* II. 268 *n.,* Occasioned by the intended removal of the Supreme Legislature of the United States from New York to Philadelphia. **1866** *Nation* II. 423/2 The present conflict between the legislature and the Executive possesses much political importance.

Legitimate, *a. Theat.*

1. Of or pertaining to stage plays having recognized theatrical and literary merit {1841– (*Monthly Mag.* Oct. 313)}; in later use, designating plays, theaters, etc., belonging to that part of the show business concerned with drama rather than with the circus, vaudeville, moving pictures, etc.

1839 *Chicago American* 3 Sept., [The] motto at the head of this article . . . conveys an idea of the useful tendencies of the legitimate drama. **1846** *Knickerb.* XXVIII. 108 The management confines itself solely to legitimate business. **1890** J. JEFFERSON *Autobiog.* 81 Anything like a legitimate production was a great treat. **1925** *Theatre Mag.* Jan. 39/2 Mrs. Carter, with no legitimate vehicle in sight, is playing a two-a-day sketch, while Robert Warwick is doing the same thing.

2. *absol.* The legitimate drama, stage, or theater.

1843 *Knickerb.* XXI. 485 Such honors as the grateful hearts of all admirers of the 'true legitimate' can bestow, have been showered upon this son of genius. **1849** FOSTER *N.Y. in Slices* 90 Sublime emanations of some police reporter enamored of the 'legitimate' and panting for the honors of a free admission. **1887** *Courier-Journal* 2 Feb. 5/5 They have gone to the top faster than any other stars who have attempted 'the legitimate.' **1911** J. F. WILSON *Land Claimers* 35, I was in legitimate at the old Alcazar.

+**Leg knife.** A heavy knife carried in one's legging or boot. *Obs.* — **1835** HOFFMAN *Winter in West* II. 69, I had struck my leg knife into the chine of the other [man]. **1840** — *Greyslaer* I. 14 The terrible leg-knife [was] worn beneath the beaded garters of his companion.

Leicester. A breed of long-wooled sheep developed in Leicestershire; also, a sheep of this breed. {1834–} In full *Leicester sheep.* — **1856** *Rep. Comm. Patents 1855: Agric.* 50 There are a few of the Leicester sheep in this section, and they are highly esteemed for mutton. **1863** RANDALL *Pract. Shepherd* 44 During the war of 1812 with England, some choice Leicesters . . . were captured by one of our privateers, and sold at auction in New York. **1870** *Rep. Comm. Agric. 1869* 386 Mr. Winne has long been a breeder of Leicester sheep from the finest imported stock.

***Lemon.** Also †**limon, lemmon.**

***1.** The well-known fruit of the lemon tree; also, the tree itself, *Citrus limonia.* Also attrib. with *tree.*

1634 *Relation of Beginnings of Md.* 21 We haue also . . . Limons, Melocotunes, Apples, Peares, Potatos. **1682** ASH *Carolina* 6 Fruit Trees there are in abundance of various and excellent kinds, the Orange, Lemon, Pomegranate, Fig and Almond. **1743** CATESBY *Carolina* II. p. xxi, *Mali Aurantia & Limonia.* The Orange and Lemon-Tree. . . . When they are planted near the Sea, or Salt-Water, they are less liable to be injured by frosts. **1784** *Mass. Centinel* 1 Sept. 4/3 To be Sold, by Daniel & Robert M'Neill . . . Lisbon Lemmons per Box. **1812** STODDARD *Sk. Louisiana* 168 The Delta produces various kinds of excellent fruit; . . . figs in great plenty, some lemons. **1872** MCCLELLAN *Golden State* 327 Nearly all the oranges, lemons, limes, and citron produced in the State are raised in Los Angeles county. **1917** *Dept. Agric. Yrbk. 1916* 271 The grapefruit, the orange, the lime, and the lemon are . . . readily infected with citrus canker.

2. *attrib.* **a.** In the names of confections and drinks prepared from lemons. (See also LEMON BUTTER, LEMON PIE.)

1742 *Holyoke Diaries* 32 [Sept.] 4. Stilld 11 pts of Lemmon Water. **1833** *Ib.* 181 [Sept.] 30 Made Lemon syrup for the wedding. **1845** J. W. NORRIS *Chicago Directory* 98 (*advt.*), The bar will be furnished with the best of Liquors, such as . . . Milk, Lemon and Roman Punches. **1870** EGGLESTON *Blake's Walking-Stick* 41 He had inquired if they had any lemon-drops in their pockets. **1882** 'M. HARLAND' *Eve's Daughters* 112 We had lollypops and barley-sticks, and clear lemon-bars. **1882** RITTENHOUSE *Maud* 49 Such a dinner—the turkeys, . . . fruit, lemon-cakes, white and fruit cake [etc.]. **1887** *Ib.* 393 Light rolls, lemon-sherbet and white mountain cake. **1890** HARTE *Waif of Plains* 127 The Commodore . . . [will] content himself with lemon soda.

b. In the specific names of plants and trees.

1817–8 EATON *Botany* (1822) 382 Lemon, or maple-leaf, geranium. **1848** *Rep. Comm. Patents 1847* 196 Fifteen specimens of Vandermark seedling (from the seed) of the lemon cling . . . measured over a foot in circumference! **1869** BRACE *New West* 37 Lemon-verbenas . . . are small trees. **1894** *Amer. Folk-Lore* VII. 96 *Melissa officinalis,* . . . lemon-balm, common balm. . . . N.E.

c. (See quotation.)

1890 *Cent.* 3406/2 *Lemon-fish,* . . . a sort of amber-fish, *Seriola stearnsi,* of the Gulf of Mexico. (Louisiana.)

Lemonade. A drink made of lemon juice, water, and sugar. {1663–; now less common than 'lemon squash'}

1804 FESSENDEN *Orig. Poems* (1906) 34 Give each buxom, rosy maid, Brimming glass of lemonade. **1836** *Harvardiana* III. 110, I received them . . . with a little treat of fruit and lemonade. **1886** POORE *Reminisc.* I. 74 The refreshments were iced lemonade, ice-cream, port wine. **1920** COOPER *Under Big Top* 213 Any guy who's tried to make a living selling ice-cold lemonade.

attrib. **1877** PHELPS *Story of Avis* 137 They became the abject preys of the soda-fountain and the lemonade-boy. **1883** PECK *Bad Boy* 54 They never prayed in circus, 'cept the lemonade butchers.

+**Lemon butter.** A spread made with lemon and other ingredients cooked to a butterlike consistency. — **1882** F. OWENS *Cook Book* 265 *Lemon Butter.* Use as sauce, filling for tarts, or as jelly for layer cake. **1917** [see BUTTER[1] 2].

Lemon dealer. One who deals in lemons. *Obs.* — **1789** *Boston Directory* 177 Booth Francis, lemon-dealer. **1800** *Columbian Centinel* 11 Jan.

2/3 The procession [for George Washington included] lemon-dealers, lightermen, limners [etc.].

+**Lemon pie.** A pie with a filling flavored with lemon. — **1876** M. F. HENDERSON *Practical Cooking* 237. **1893** *Harper's Mag.* Feb. 457 What you askin' fo' yo' lemon pies, Miss Simpkins? **1914** 'BOWER' *Flying U Ranch* 62 There's two lemon pies in the brown cupboard.

Lemon squeezer. An apparatus for expressing the juice from lemons. {1884–} Also attrib. — **1781** *Salem Gazette* 3 July, Isaac Greenwood . . . makes Flutes, . . . Billiard-Balls, Maces, Lemon Squeezers. **1857** UNDERHILL & THOMPSON *Elephant Club* 118 One . . . had been hit over the head with a lemon-squeezer. **1887** *Century Mag.* Aug. 489/1 The 'chunkers' were frequently of the 'lemon-squeezer' pattern.

***Length.** +A piece of something cut off and used as a unit of quantity or measure. *Obs.* — **1645** *Dedham Rec.* III. 112 Samll Milles hath lib[er]tie to cut 400 lengthes of hoopes poles on the common. **1650** *Rowley Rec.* 64 From Leu Joh Rementons to widow broklbank all thos lots nine lenths [of rail] is the streett Cald bradforth street. **1666** *Ib.* 169 In polipod lots 2 lenths John Stickney for one lenth.

+**Lengthily,** *adv.* At length, fully. {1827–} — **1787** JEFFERSON *Writings* VI. 394, I have written somewhat lengthily to Mr. Madison. **1894** *Columbus Dispatch* 23 March, Justh . . . lengthily extolled Kossuth's services.

+**Lengthy,** *a.* Of compositions or speeches: Long, often with implications of prolixity and tediousness. {1816–}

See Albert Matthews 'The Word "Lengthy"' in *Boston Evening Transcript* Nov. 2, 1895, p. 7/2. At the time he wrote this article his earliest example of the use of 'lengthy' was one of 1759, but he later placed at the editor's disposal the one of 1689 given below.

1689 *Mass. H. S. Coll.* 4 Ser. VIII. 370, I very much fear a dreadfull, lengthy, wasting Indian war. **1759** J. ADAMS *Diary* Works II. 59 But I grow too minute and lengthy. **1776** A. ADAMS *Familiar Letters* 161 The whole sheets I have wrote to you . . . were so lengthy as to be troublesome. **1816** PICKERING 123 This word . . . is applied by us, as Mr. Webster justly observes, chiefly to writings or discourses. Thus we say, a *lengthy* pamphlet, a *lengthy* sermon, &c. *a***1862** THOREAU *Maine Woods* 284 The Indian . . . once made an indirect, but lengthy apology. **1895** WISTER in *Harper's Mag.* March 541/2 Never before had Gilet's oratory seemed to him more welcome or less lengthy.

b. Used with reference to physical length. {1795–}

'*Rare* exc. U.S. and *techn.* of animals' (*O.E.D.*).

1760 *New Eng. Hist. & Gen. Register* IX. 341 There is an Hill . . . the most steep and lengthy to ascend which I have ever seen. **1808** PIKE *Sources Miss.* II. App. 4 [The estimate] would still leave the Arkansaw near 800 miles more lengthy than the White river. **1849** THOREAU *Week on Concord* (1894) 248 Many a lengthy reach we've rowed.

‖**Lengthy,** *adv.* At length, fully. — **1775** J. HANCOCK *J. Hancock His Book* (1898) 199 Do acquaint me every Circumstance Relative to that Dear Aunt of Mine; write Lengthy and often.

Lento. Variant of LEAN-TO.

***Leopard.** +**1.** The jaguar (*Felis onca*), found in the Southwest. +**2.** Jocose variant of TIGER *n.* — (1) **1858** *Texas Almanac 1859* 186 The game of the country [Webb Co., Tex.] consists of leopards, (here called tigers,) cougars, or South American lions, wild cats [etc.]. (2) **1890** LANGFORD *Vigilante Days* (1912) 93 Pinkham, with his faro boards and monte cards, 'giving the boys a chance for a tussle with the tiger and the leopard.'

Leopard cat. {1773–} +The American ocelot, *Felis pardalis.* — **1845** GREEN *Texian Exped.* 50 He took [the skin] from a leopard-cat in a Brasos canebrake. **1898** CANFIELD *Maid of Frontier* 205 He knew the track of the leopard cat. **1911** *Springfield W. Repub.* 19 Jan. 16 Quick work . . . saved the collection of more than 100 birds, a dozen monkeys, two young leopard cats [etc.].

+**Leopard frog.** An American frog (*Rana pipiens*), having green and black markings on the back suggesting the spots of a leopard. — **1839** STORER *Mass. Reptiles* 237 *Rana halecina* . . . [is] better known in this state as the leopard frog from its ocellated appearance. **1842** *Nat. Hist. N.Y., Zoology* III. 62 The Marsh Frog, *Rana palustris*, . . . is called, in various districts, Pickerel Frog, and also Tiger and Leopard Frog. **1860** HOLMES *E. Venner* iv, The shy and agile leopard-frog had taken the six-foot spring that plumped him into the middle of the pool. **1890** *Cent.* 3411/2.

+**Lepero.** *S.W.* [Sp.] (See quot. 1836.) — **1836** EDWARD *Hist. Texas* 122 The lower and poor sort of Creoles, however, [are] called *Leperos.* **1845** GREEN *Texian Exped.* 225 Our officer here discharged the lepero and his mule, and allowed us to hire some burros.

Lesser, *a.* Designating various birds of a smaller variety or species than common. {1678–} (Cf. LESSER REDPOLL.) — **1813** WILSON *Ornithology* VII. 81 The Lesser Tern . . . sometimes sits for hours together on the sands. **1874** COUES *Birds N.W.* 497 Lesser Yellowshanks. . . . More numerous and generally distributed east of the Rocky Mountains. **1883** *Nat. Museum Bul.* No. 27, 165 Lesser White-crested Cormorant. Coast of California. **1887** RIDGWAY *Manual N.A. Birds* 103 *A[ythya] affinis.* Lesser Scaup Duck. **1917** *Birds of Amer.* II. 100 Long-eared Owl. . . . Other Names. . . . Cat Owl; Lesser Horned Owl.

Lesser redpoll. The common redpoll (*Acanthis linaria*), found as a winter visitor in the northern and eastern portions of the U.S. {1776–(Pennant)} — **1811** WILSON *Ornith.* IX. 127 The Lesser Red-poll become[s] very fat, and . . . [is] then accounted delicious eating. **1844** *Nat. Hist. N.Y., Zoology* II. 168 The Lesser Red-Poll, *Linaria Minor*, . . . migrates from the north . . . , as far south as Pennsylvania, and in the interior to Ohio and Kentucky. **1869** *Amer. Naturalist* III. 384 Lesser Redpoll (*Linaria minor*), abundant during autumn and winter. **1917** *Birds of Amer.* III. 11 Redpoll. . . . [Also called] Lesser Redpoll.

***Lesson.** *Christian Science.* +=next. — **1899** EDDY *Church Manual* (ed. 10) 24 The readers must devote a suitable portion of their time to preparation for reading the Sunday lesson,—a lesson on which the prosperity of Christian Science largely depends.

+**Lesson-sermon.** Passages from the Bible and the Christian Science textbook, *Science and Health with Key to the Scriptures*, by Mary Baker Eddy, read in Christian Science church services. — **1899** EDDY *Church Manual* (ed. 10) 25 [The readers] shall make no remarks explanatory of the Lesson-Sermon at any time during the service. **1906** *Boston Herald* 11 June, The Lesson-Sermon consisted of the following citations from the Bible and Science and Health with Key to the Scriptures.

***Let,** *v. tr.* and *intr.* In colloq. phrases and expressions.

For phrases including a second verb, as *to let her rip*, see the second verb.

+**1.** *To let down the bars*, to cast off all restraints; to remove restrictions or obstructions.

1869 *Congress. Globe* 22 March 199/1 Why should we thus 'let down the bars' the first time a vacancy occurs? **1889** [see BAR *n.*[1] 2 *fig.*]. **1890** *Congress. Rec.* 8 May 4322/2 We have tried the experiment of 'letting down the bars.'

***2.** *To let in*, +to begin. *colloq.* and *slang.*

1904 HARBEN *Georgians* 143 When I tol' 'im I was [with Marse Eric] he let in to cussin' wuss 'n I ever heard anybody in my life. **1904** *Dialect Notes* II. 398 'The party will let in about nine o'clock.' Slang. N.Y. c.

3. *To let on.* **a.** To mention, disclose, betray. {1725–}

'*Dial.* and *U.S.*' (*O.E.D.*).

1823 *Nat'l. Intelligencer* 1 May 1/4 *Let-on*, v.a. To acknowledge: 'I never let on that I know'd him.' **1875** 'MARK TWAIN' *Sk., New & Old* 127 If he had discovered the sources meantime, he did not let on. **1917** FREEMAN & KINGSLEY *Alabaster Box* 128 And you didn't let on to me.

b. To pretend {1822 *dial.*}; also, to insinuate.

1828 *Yankee* (Portland, Me.) 23 April 132/3 [In the South] to let on signifies to make believe. **1884** 'MARK TWAIN' *H. Finn* 90, [I] let on to be interested—and I was, too. **1892** — *Amer. Claimant* xi. 108 He being, as he says to me, a *gentleman*, which is pretty plain letting-on that the boys ain't. **1901** ADE 40 *Modern Fables* 44 She would let on to be Annoyed.

***4.** *To let out.* +**a.** To give unrestrained vent to one's feelings or emotions; to 'speak out.' Also reflexive.

1847 FIELD *Drama in Pokerville* 23 Her vengeance foiled, and feelings outraged, she 'jest let out' as Mrs. Store-Shed Wilson graphically expressed it. **1847** ROBB *Squatter Life* 80 He 'let himself out,' on some of the measures he advocated. *Ib.* 142 Tom squared himself for a yarn, . . . took a small strip of Missouri weed, and 'let out.' **1866** KIRKLAND *Bk. Anecdotes* 269 The funniest animal in the world is a little negro when he 'lets himself out.' **1892** *Harper's Mag.* Feb. 440/2 There wasn't anything serious; only Melie and Tom letting themselves out.

+**b.** Of school or meeting: To dismiss or break up. Also *letting out.*

1867 'LACKLAND' *Homespun* 325 No impatient chap in school looks forward more wistfully to the 'letting out.' **1888** EGGLESTON *Graysons* x, [He] would meet her at the door of the Mount Zion tent when the meeting should 'let out.' **1898** N. BROOKS *Boys of Fairport* 173, I'll lick you when school lets out.

+**c.** To release or excuse (someone) from further responsibility. *colloq.*

1871 'MARK TWAIN' *Sk., New & Old* 299 That lets you out, you know, you chowder-headed old clam. **1883** PECK *Bad Boy* 67 He says that lets him out. He don't go into any more schemes with me. **1891** GARLAND *Main-travelled Roads* (1922) 142 That simply lets me out. **1904** *Montgomery W. Advertiser* 29 July 4 They are going the limit by making one word out of parts of a Russian and a Chinese one. That lets us out.

+**d.** To discharge or dismiss from employment.

1896 *Internat. Typogr. Union Proc.* 37/1 His scheme was to 'let out' the union men one at a time.

+**5.** *To let up*, to stop, slacken, or lessen.

1787 WASHINGTON *Diaries* III. 185 The Plows, after the rain let up, proceeded to finish this part of field No. 5. **1841** COOPER *Deerslayer* vi, Let up, you painted riptyles—let up! **1894** WARNER *Golden House* xxiii, I think you'd better let up a little, and run down and see Edith. **1905** *N.Y. Ev. Post* 16 Sept., Passenger traffic, of course, lets up considerably during the very cold months.

+**b.** *To let up on* (someone or something), to grant respite to, to desist from further activity against or concerning.

1875 'MARK TWAIN' *Old Times* iii. 52 [When the wheel on the steamboat] fights strong . . . let up on her a trifle. **1884** — *H. Finn* 311 Oh let *up* on this cussed nonsense. **1890** HARTE *Waif of Plains* 61 Let up on him, will you, . . . the boy knows what he's about. **1911** QUICK *Yellowstone Nights* 302 A man under them succumstances is supposed to let up on cussin'.

Letheon. (See quot. 1880.) *Obs.* {1847–} — **1848** *Santa Fe Republican* 12 Feb. 1/3 The Letheon is used successfully in Mexico in surgical operations. Dr. Barton has introduced it. **1880** *Lib. Universal Knowl.* X. 241 Dr. [W. T. G.] Morton [of Boston] obtained a patent for the use of ether [as an anaesthetic], under the name of 'letheon,' in 1846. **1891** HODGES *Introd. of Sulphuric Ether* 56 The term 'letheon,' commonly adopted immediately after the American patent was secured, had its origin in a meeting at the house of Dr. Gould. . . . Returning to his [Dr. Morton's] office, he said, 'I have found a name for the discovery, and am going to call it Letheon.'

Let-off. {1827-} Release, escape. — **1836** CROCKETT *Exploits* 52, I was for backing out and fighting shy; but there was no let-off, for the cock of the village . . . determined not to stay whipped.

***Letter.** Attrib. with *express, money*, etc. (Cf. LETTER BAG, etc.)

1691 *Mass. H. S. Coll.* 3 Ser. VII. 51 Be it therefore enacted . . . that there be from henceforth A General Letter Office erected and established in . . . Boston. **1839** *S. Lit. Messenger* V. 5/2 The business . . . between England and America [may be estimated] . . . by the single item 'letter money.' **1872** 'MARK TWAIN' *Roughing It* 37 We stirred up the hard leather letter-sacks. **1880** LAMPHERE *U.S. Govt.* 240/1 [To] the Blank Agency . . . is assigned the duty of supplying the post-offices entitled thereto with blanks, . . . twine, letter-balances, and cancelling-stamps. **1890** LANGFORD *Vigilante Days* (1912) 255 Dr. A. J. Oliver had been running a letter express between Bannack and Salt Lake City. **1897** FLANDRAU *Harvard Episodes* 206 Somebody-or-other's pamphlet . . . [was] slipped through his letter-slide one morning. **1903** *Chicago Chronicle* 11 April 1/4 Two more letter pouches had been stolen.

Letter bag. A bag in which letters are placed for conveyance to a destination. {1809-} — **1773** FINLAY *Journal* 17 Mr. Child . . . took the letter-bag of one of those vessels to the office. **1790** *Penna. Packet* 23 April 3/2 The letter bag of the ship Manchester, . . . will be taken from the Post-Office this day. **1831** HOLLEY *Texas Lett.* (1833) 37 The letter bag was the first object of curiosity, and its interesting contents were soon searched.

Letter book. A book for keeping letters or copies of letters. {1685- (*New Mills Cloth Manuf.* 86)} — **1696** SEWALL *Letter Book* I. 166, I find it Copied out in my Letter Book. **1776** J. ADAMS *Familiar Letters* 224 It would fill this letter-book to give you all the arguments for and against this measure. **1803** *Steele P.* I. 412, [I] suppose he has caused it to be entered in his Letter-Book. **1861** *Army Regulations* 20 The following books will be kept at each post: a Morning Report Book, . . . a Letter Book, each two quires foolscap. **1883** J. HAY *Bread-Winners* 181 His den . . . was a litter of letter-books, stock-lists, and the advertising pamphlets of wine-merchants.

Letter box.

1. A receptacle located at some convenient place into which letters may be dropped for forwarding by private carriers or by postal authorities. {1849-} Also attrib.

1772 *Virginia Gaz.* 26 Nov., A Letter Box, placed . . . at the Raleigh Tavern, . . . was stole. **1825** *Postal Laws* (1843) I. 20 Letter-box letters, one cent. **1872** POWERS *Afoot & Alone* 67 A wag in Montgomery, among other tricks, induced over a score of them [Negroes] to vote in the letter-box in the post-office. **1887** FREDERIC *Seth's Brother's Wife* 69 A youngster who . . . doesn't know the difference between a Custom House and a letter-box on a lamp-post! **1912** NICHOLSON *Hoosier Chron.* 87 The lawyer wrote a brief note which he . . . dropped later into a letter-box with his own hand.

2. A box in which letters are kept as souvenirs or for future reference.

1863 A. D. WHITNEY *F. Gartney* xiii, Faith, being in her own room, took out from her letter-box the last missive from abroad.

3. =BOX *n.*[2] 3.

1870 W. BAKER *New Timothy* 218 Any body hesitates a little in reference to going behind the letter-boxes and assisting in sorting the mails. **1882** LATHROP *Echo of Passion* vi, The dignity of the government was represented by a cage of letter-boxes.

***Letter-carrier.** One who carries and delivers letters; a postman.

1825 *Postal Laws* (1843) I. 20 Letter carriers sha *ll be* employed . . . for the delivery of letters. **1855** HOLBROOK *Among Mail Bags* 206 A boy twelve or thirteen years of age was employed as assistant to one of the letter carriers. **1882** *Nation* 20 July 44/1 The bill providing for a third grade of letter-carriers and for promotions was passed by the House. **1900** *Congress. Rec.* 3 Jan. 628/1 The petition . . . praying that he be granted compensation for overtime as a letter carrier. **1916** DU PUY *Uncle Sam* 110 The special agents . . . , through the postmaster and letter carriers, had been steadily watching this means of communication.

Letter case. A case for letters. {1672-}

1653 *Boston Rec.* 39 My Leather Letter case . . . comonly lyes upon my table. **1714** *Boston News-Letter* 11-18 Oct. 2/2 A Plain red Letter-Case, dropt at the lower end of Corn-Hill-Street Boston. **1790** *Penna. Packet* 8 May 4/4 Thomas Seddon, . . . has for Sale . . . Pocket books and letter cases of various sizes. **1865** A. D. WHITNEY *Gayworthys* xxxix, The old, worn, yellow letters . . . had been found in the faded, shapeless letter-case. **1868** *Mich. Agric. Rep.* VII. 357 Mrs. P. Hude, Detroit, [exhibited an] embroidered letter case. **1887** WILKINS *Humble Romance* 220 There were . . . a splint letter-case, a motto worked in worsteds [etc.].

+Letter drop. (See quot. 1890); also, a slit or opening through which letters are dropped in mailing. — **1890** *Cent.* 3421/3 *Letter-drop*, . . . on a postal or mail railroad-car, a plate with an opening closed by a hinged flap, for receiving letters for the post along the route of the train. **1904** WALLER *Wood-Carver* 52 The letter-drop is a simulated squirrel-hole.

Letter-founder. One who casts metal into type. {1683-} — **1771** FRANKLIN *Autobiog.* 291 Our printing-house often wanted sorts, and there was no letter-founder in America. **1786** — in W. Pepper *Medical Side B. Franklin* (1911) 104 Mr. James, a Letter-founder in the same Close. **1803** *Ann. 7th Congress* 2 Sess. 1288 Papermakers, letter founders, makers of umbrellas . . . [were] praying for protecting duties. **1819** SCHOOLCRAFT *Mo. Lead Mines* 141 The composition of the common type metal of the letter founders is stated to be 4 parts of lead to 1 of antimony.

Letterhead. {*a*1887} A sheet of letter paper having a heading printed or engraved upon it, or the heading itself. — **1888** *Harper's Mag.* March 649/2 He drew up a note upon the 'tavern' letter-head. **1894** *Ib.* May 972/1, [I] got three thousand letter-heads printed. **1902** LORIMER *Lett. Merchant* 53 The fellow . . . can't find any place to put it [*sc.* his coat of arms], except on his carriage door and his letter-head. **1918** OWEN *Typewriting Speed* 101 As you take up a letter head you may leave on it an indelible ink blur.

+Letter mail. Postal matter consisting of letters. — **1817** *Niles' Reg.* XII. 177/1 Three entire letter mails . . . did not even arrive. **1838** *N.Y. Advertiser & Exp.* 10 Jan. 3/1 The Express Mail . . . is no sort of benefit as a Letter Mail. **1860** BUCHANAN in *Pres. Mess. & P.* V. 597 In consequence of the diversion of a large part of the letter mail to the overland route, the postages derived from the California service have been greatly reduced.

Letter paper. Paper for use in writing letters. {1837-} — **1841** EMERSON in *Dial* April 528, [I] get indefinite quantities of sugar, hominy, . . . and letter paper, by simply signing my name . . . to a cheque. **1857** *Lawrence Republican* 11 June 3, 50 Reams Fine Letter Papers, 'Congress' and other brands, just received. **1904** WALLER *Wood-Carver* 90 If there's any left, . . . put it into stamps and good letter paper.

Letter postage. The amount or rate of postage charged on letters sent by mail. — **1839** *Diplom. Corr. Texas* I. (1908) 392 He will then credit himself . . . with a commission of 30 pr cent on the first hundred dollars . . . letter postage actually collected at each post office in Texas within the Quarter. **1844** TYLER in *Pres. Mess. & P.* IV. 349 There is a strong desire manifested . . . so to alter the tariff of letter postage as to reduce the amount of tax. **1876** RAYMOND *8th Rep. Mines* 354 The letter-postage per pound is only 96 cents.

+Letter sheet. A sheet of paper such as letters are usually written on. Also attrib. and comb. — **1851** CIST *Cincinnati* 188 Both these firms execute fine circulars, checks, . . . and indeed, every species of letter sheet printing. **1877** PHELPS *Story of Avis* 136 It was enclosed in a letter-sheet on which was written [etc.]. **1887** *Postal Laws* 84 The Postmaster-General is hereby authorized to . . . furnish for public use a letter-sheet envelope.

***Lettuce.** Also †**lettice.** Any plant of the genus *Lactuca*, esp. *L. sativa*, the leaves of which are used as a salad.

The term is also applied to other succulent plants.

1682 ASH *Carolina* 13 Their [planters'] Gardens begin to be supplied with such . . . Herbs as are necessary for the Kitchen, viz. Potatoes, Lettice, . . . Carrot and Reddish. **1709** LAWSON *Carolina* 77 The Sallads are the Lettice, Curl'd, Red, Cabbage, and Savoy. **1831** AUDUBON *Ornith. Biog.* I. 172 The food of the American Goldfinch consists chiefly of seeds of the Hemp, the Sun-flower, the Lettuce [etc.]. **1885** *Rep. Indian Affairs* 17 The estimated productions . . . by the boys'-boarding-school, . . . [are] peas, radishes, lettuce, horseradish, &c. **1903** *Dept. Agric. Yrbk. 1902* 569 Experiments dealing with fertilizers for lettuce have yielded some apparently very conflicting results.

attrib. **1790** DEANE *New-Eng. Farmer* 10 Mr. Ray sowed some lettuce-seed. **1912** NICHOLSON *Hoosier Chron.* 13 The Greek professor's cow . . . immured herself in Professor Kelton's lettuce frames. **1913** LONDON *Valley of Moon* III. iv, [She] surveyed . . . the sliced corned beef, the lettuce salad and sliced tomatoes.

+Lettuce bird. =AMERICAN GOLDFINCH. — **1781-2** JEFFERSON *Notes Va.* (1788) 75 American goldfinch. Lettuce bird. **1808** WILSON *Ornithology* I. 21 [Goldfinches] pass by various names expressive of their food, color, &c. such as Thistle-bird, Lettuce-bird, Sallad-bird [etc.]. **1917** *Birds of Amer.* III. 13 Goldfinch. . . . [Also called] Lettuce-bird.

+Let-up. Cessation; slackening; release from further strain or effort. (Cf. LET *v.* 5.)

1841 COOPER *Deerslayer* viii, There's no let-up in an Ingin's watchfulness when he's on a war-path. **1873** BEADLE *Undevel. West* 711 There will be no let-up from the middle of November to the middle of April. **1900** MUNN *Uncle Terry* 121, I shall keep you grinding eight full hours, six days a week, and no let-up until July first. **1925** *Scribner's Mag.* Oct. 39 (*advt.*), There is no let-up in all of the 317 pages [of the detective story].

b. *Stock exchange.* (See quotations.)

1870 MEDBERY *Men Wall St.* 136 A 'let up.' Employed when an artificial pressure upon money or any other cause leading to a stringency in the loan market suddenly disappears. **1885** *Harper's Mag.* Nov. 842/2 Some relief is afforded by a 'let up,' or the withdrawal from the market of the 'clique,' or 'pool,' or combination of operators that cornered him.

+Levee, *n.*[1] *S.* and *W.* [F. *levée* fr. *lever*, 'to raise.']

1. An embankment to afford protection for lowlands during high water, esp. from the overflowing of a river.

[**1719** in Winsor *Narr. & Crit. Hist.* V. 39 Devant la ville [New Orleans] il y a une levée et par derrière un fossé.] **1766** H. GORDON in *Travels Amer. Col.* 481 [They] are obliged to have Levée's of Earth to keep off the Floods. **1770** PITTMAN *Present State* 10 [New Orleans] is secured from the inundations of the river by a raised bank, generally called the Levée. **1805** in *Amer. Pioneer* II. 231 The ladies . . . set at their doors or walk on the levee. **1840** *Picayune* 9 Aug. 3/3 Proposals will be received . . . for the making a Levee in front of the Nun's faubourg in the city of Lafayette. **1888** CABLE *Bonaventure* 55 Under his trudging feet was the wagon-road along the farther levee of the Teche. **1918** RIDEOUT *Key of Fields* 270 The rails and ties of a disused freight line crossed the levee in this depression.

attrib. **1851** A. O. HALL *Manhattaner* 4 New Orleans . . . [is] walled by flat boats, . . . wrinkled with levee crevasses, and dotted with shipyards. **1877** BURROUGHS *Taxation* 4 A levee tax was laid on certain lands, and . . . they had been sold and purchased by the levee commissioners. **1881** *Nation* 19 Oct. 331/1 [Arkansas] repudiated the entire payment of her State Levee bonds. **1901** CHURCHILL *Crisis* 420 A trestle bridge . . . spanned the distance from the levee bank over the flood to a house.

2. A landing place or quay.

1842 H. CASWALL *City of Mormons* 3 The landing-place [at St. Louis] (or levée, as it is denominated) was literally swarming with life. **1851** *Polly Peablossom* 119 The 'Gen. Jackson' had hauled up to the miniature levee, and lay puffing, and paddling, and jerking cotton bales and negroes over her bow. **1872** EGGLESTON *End of World* 197 The boat ran on safely enough to Louisville, and tied up at the levee. **1907** *St. Nicholas* Aug. 948/1 Their moldering warehouses, levees, and wharves stand as monuments of former prosperity.

3. A district to which commercialized vice in a city is restricted.

1903 *N.Y. Sun* 8 Nov. 3 Three levees, one for each of the three leading parts of the city, are to be sanctioned by the city of Chicago. **1909** E. A. BELL *War on White Slave Trade* 257 The 'levee,' blazing with electric lights and floating in liquor, is regarded by thousands of visitors as one of the chief sights of Chicago.

Levee, *n.*[2] {1672–} A reception or formal gathering at any time of day. {1831} — **1766** M. CUTLER in *Life & Corr.* I. 12 A second grand levee at Ellis' Inn. **1842** DICKENS *Amer. Notes* viii, It was on the occasion of one of those general assemblies which are held on certain nights, between the hours of nine and twelve o'clock, and are called . . . Levees. **1870** M. H. SMITH *20 Years Wall St.* 33 Mrs. Adams wished to introduce at these levees of state the French custom of announcing visitors.

+**Levee,** *v.* [f. LEVEE *n.*[1]] *tr.* To provide (a river, land, etc.) with a levee. Also *to levee off.* — **1837** WILLIAMS *Florida* 45 Where there is clay enough in the soil, to form good embankments, the waters might be leveed off. **1845** *Indiana Senate Jrnl.* 364 An act to authorize the leveeing of Blue river, in Shelby county. **1847** PALMER *Rocky Mts.* 225 Several islands in the river might be leveed and successfully cultivated. **1877** W. H. BURROUGHS *Taxation* 75 An act incorporated certain persons for the purpose of leveeing and draining a district.

* **Level,** *n.*

1. An area or tract of land having a level surface. {1623–} Sometimes used in place names.

1700 *Md. Hist. Mag.* XIX. 348 New Parke . . . near a place called the Levil in the woods. **1738** BYRD *Dividing Line* (1901) 90 It was hardly possible to find a level large enough on the banks of the river whereupon to pitch our tent. **1829** WEEMS *B. Franklin* 184 The majestic grove . . . shaded the extended level on the western bank. **1841** J. C. BOOTH *Mem. Geol. Survey Md.* 89 The beautiful tract of land . . . appropriately called the *Levels*, is the dividing line of the waters. **1904** T. E. WATSON *Bethany* 4 They cleared off the forest, put the levels into cultivation . . . and raised cattle.

+**b.** *pl.* A name sometimes given to the prairies of Illinois and Texas.

1834 *Visit to Texas* ii. 24 The Prairies or levels of Texas may be generally described [etc.]. **1865** *Atlantic Mo.* XV. 8 Nowhere else—not even on the levels of Illinois—are the same features so constantly reproduced.

2. *Mining.* (See quot. 1881.) {1805–}

1721 *Conn. Rec.* VI. 253 Clearing and cleaning the said levels or shafts. **1815** *N. Amer. Rev.* I. 335 The proprietors . . . commenced running a level to [the vein]. **1872** *Harper's Mag.* Dec. 27/1 Numbers of miners were here engaged, some 'pushing the level.' **1881** RAYMOND *Glossary*, *Level*, a horizontal passage or drift into or in a mine. It is customary to work mines by levels at regular intervals in depth, numbered in their order below the adit or drainage level, if there be one.

3. *To take* (or *make*) *a level*, to ascertain the differences in elevation of a piece of land. {1693–}

1770 WASHINGTON *Diaries* I. 369 Went to the Mill with Jno. Ball to take the Level of the Run. **1798** I. ALLEN *Hist. Vermont* 4 In 1785 Captain Twist made a survey and level to ascertain the expence of a canal from the River St. Lawrence to Lake Champlain. **1816** *Ann. 14th Congress* 2 Sess. 264 It shall be the duty of the said commissioners . . . to cause all necessary surveys and levels to be taken, and accurate maps, field-books, and draughts thereof to be made.

4. *On the level* {1790–}, + in a fair, straightforward manner, honestly. *colloq.*[2]

1875 BURNHAM *Three Years* p. vii, On The Level, meeting a man with honorable intentions. **1896** ADE *Artie* 42 On the level, I'm surprised you ain't on to that. **1909** 'O. HENRY' *Roads of Destiny* ix. 157 Bud acted 'on the level.' **1923** VANCE *Baroque* 40 No, on the level: if it hadn't been for luck we'd still be guessin'.

* **Level,** *a.*

+**1.** Well-balanced or poised; possessing common sense. Said usually of the *head*, regarded as the seat of the understanding or judgment.

[**1870** *Orchestra* 12 Aug. 331/1 To tell a woman her head is level is apparently a compliment in America.] **1872** 'MARK TWAIN' *Sketches, New & Old* 180 With a great brain and a level head [the Englishman reminded] . . . the bar-keeper not to forget the strawberries. **1891** *Harper's Mag.* Aug. 447/1 If we don't keep our heads level, we'll go up the flume like a spring salmon. **1907** M. C. HARRIS *Tents of Wickedness* 136 Commend me to common sense . . . and a level head.

+**b.** *Level head*, a person possessed of common sense and poise.

1906 'O. HENRY' *Four Million* 204 James Williams belonged among the level heads.

+**2.** (One's) *level best*, (one's) utmost or very best. Often, *to do one's level best.*

1851 BYRN *Arkansaw Doctor* 87 (Th.), We put our horses out at their level best. **1867** 'MARK TWAIN' *Sk., New & Old* 74 Was he a leading of the choir—He done his level best. **1872** TICE *Over Plains* 53 A prairie wolf . . . was seen trying his 'level best' to get out of the way of the 'fire horse.' **1883** 'MARK TWAIN' *Life on Miss.* ii, An Indian chief who has taken off his last rag in order to appear at his level best. **1894** *Nation* 22 March 209/3 The Government is doing its level best to excogitate methods of economy.

+**b.** Similarly used with other superlatives; also, *levelest*, level best.

1884 'MARK TWAIN' *H. Finn* xxviii, He was on hand and looking his level pisonest. **1891** *Harper's Mag.* July 208/2 The pony will not do his level worst again. **1898** CANFIELD *Maid of Frontier* 97 She told me . . . that she was goin' to do her levelest to make our little home comfortable.

+**Level-headed,** *a.* **1.** Having good common sense and judgment. {1898–} (Cf. LEVEL *a.* 1.) **2.** Of a horse: Steady; not skittish. — **(1) 1879** TOURGEE *Fool's Errand* 8 Clear-headed, or, as they would now be called, level-headed, were these children of the Berkshire hills. **1886** *Harper's Mag.* Nov. 882/2 Sometimes a level-headed cow-boy was placed upon the judicial bench. **1893** *Boston Jrnl.* 6 Jan. 6/1 Hon. William C. Whitney is a level-headed man, and . . . doesn't want to imperil his political future. **(2) 1884** *N.Y. Herald* 27 Oct. 1/3 Wanted—Sound, Level Headed Horse.

+**Level-headedness.** **1.** In a horse: Steadiness. **2.** The quality of good judgment and sound reasoning. — **(1) 1876** *Vermont Bd. Agric. Rep.* III. 156 That same steadiness, or, in horse parlance, level-headedness, . . . is quite as essential on the race track . . . as any where else. **(2) 1886** *New Englander* (New Haven, Conn.) Feb. 179 This unexampled success is due . . . to the levelheadedness of its clerical guardians.

+**Lever bit.** A severe curb bit. — **1834** *Visit to Texas* vi. 60 [A rider puts] the terrible lever bits into his mouth. **1836** CROCKETT *Exploits* 183 Lever bits of the harshest description, able to break the jaws of their animals under a very gentle pressure.

Lever watch. A watch having a lever escapement. {1848–} — **1840** *Picayune* 14 Aug. 3/1 $20 Reward will be paid for the recovery of a gold patent lever Watch, with a golden dial. **1846** *Ind. Mag. Hist.* XXIII. 452 The preachers . . . purchased a valuable lever watch. **1854** MARCY *Explor. Red River* p. iii, [We] were under the necessity of making our observations with a pocket lever watch.

+**Leverwood.** The American hop hornbeam. (Cf. HOP HORNBEAM.) — **1755** *N.H. Hist. Soc. Coll.* II. 102 In this meadow, they left a bow, made of lever wood, and several arrows. **1814** PURSH *Flora Amer.* II. 624 *Ostrya virginica*, . . . a small tree, of exceeding hard and heavy wood, . . . generally known under the name of Iron-wood; in some parts they call it Lever-wood. **a1870** CHIPMAN *Notes on Bartlett* 242 *Lever-wood*. Ironwood; hop-hornbeam.—Ct. [=Conn.]; the use of it being in part for levers, 'prys,' and the like. **1897** SUDWORTH *Arborescent Flora* 147 *Ostrya virginiana*. . . . Hop Hornbeam. . . . [Also called] Leverwood (Vt., Mass., R.I., N.Y., Pa., Kans.).

+**Levy.** [*Ele*venpence.] The Spanish real or an equivalent amount of money (twelve and one-half cents). *Obs.* — **1829** SEALSFIELD in *Amer. Speech* XVI. 27. **1834** *Knickerb.* III. 349, I was soon eased on this point by an affirmation . . . that a *levy* was a coin; corresponding . . . to a New-York shilling. **1837** NEAL *Charcoal Sk.* (1838) 98 They want a fip's worth of dinner, or a levy's worth of sleep. **1857** *Oregon W. Times* 15 Aug. (Th.), A hungry boy . . . bought a fip custard for a levy.

+**Levy court.** In Delaware and formerly in other places, a body of county officials who administer the affairs of the county. — **1788** *Maryland Laws* II. Nov. ch. iv. - 3 Every person . . . who shall produce a certificate as aforesaid . . . at the levy court, shall, for every old wolf's head be allowed five pounds current money. **1794** *Ib.* II. ch. liii, An Act for the establishment and regulation of the levy courts in the several counties of this state. **1864** *Supreme Ct. Rep.* LXIX. 504 The Levy Court [is not] a corporation . . . with the capacity of suing and being sued. **1891** *Del. Rev. Statutes 1893* 78 The Levy Court of each county shall meet at the court house . . . three times in every year.

+**Lewis.** [Capt. Meriwether *Lewis*, Amer. explorer (1774–1809).] *attrib.* and *possessive.* In the names of various plants and fish found in the western part of the United States. (Cf. LEWIS'S WOODPECKER.) — **1813** MUHLENBERG *Cat. Plants* 36 *Berberis pinnata*, Lewis's Barberry. **1859**

BARTLETT 268 Mesquit Grass (*Stipa spata*), a fine, short grass, called also Lewis Grass, which grows with great vigor and beauty on the western prairies. **1869** *Amer. Naturalist* III. 125 Lewis' Trout (*Salmo Lewisii Girard*) . . . abounds in the headwaters of the Missouri.

+**Lewisite.** (See quot. 1888.) *Obs.* — **1804** *Mass. Spy* 2 May (Th.), Both Burrites and Lewisites are very polite to the Federalists. **1817** PAULDING *Lett. from South* I. 50 We find [the people of N.Y.] . . . submitting to be called Burrites, Lewisites, or Clintonians. **1824** in Mackenzie *Van Buren* 169 It is not very serviceable to talk much of Burrites, Lewisites, or the High minded. **1888** M. LANE in *America* 11 Oct. 16 Lewisites.—Followers of Morgan Lewis, Governor of New York, in 1804. It was too exclusive and aristocratic a faction to gain much popularity or to live long.

+**Lewis('s) woodpecker.** *W.* [See quot. 1917.] The black or crow woodpecker, *Asyndesmus lewisi.* — **1811** WILSON *Ornithology* III. 31 Lewis's Woodpecker, *Picus Torquatus*, . . . was eleven inches and a half [long]. **1852** in Stansbury *Gt. Salt Lake* 319 Lewis's Woodpecker . . . occurs abundantly along the western coast. **1880** *Cimarron News & Press* 23 Dec. 1/4 Another remarkable inhabitant of the mountains and cañons is the Lewis woodpecker, its head, back and wings black, with a bronzy-green iridescence. **1917** *Birds of Amer.* II. 159 Lewis's Woodpecker was one of the birds discovered on the Lewis and Clark expedition and was named in honor of [Captain Meriwether] Lewis.

***Ley.** Variant of LYE. *Obs.*

Leyden. *attrib.* [*Leyden*, Holland.] Designating a bottle or jar suitably prepared to serve as an electrical condenser. {1774– (*Phil. Trans.* LXIV. I. 389)} — **1749** FRANKLIN *Exper. Elect.* 77 It will represent the Leyden bottle. **1762** — *Writings* IV. 133, I formerly had an opinion, that a *Leyden* bottle . . . might retain its electricity for ever. **1825** NEAL *Bro. Jonathan* I. 29 She was . . . like a Leyden jar always ready to be let off. **1899** CHAMPLIN & BOSTWICK *Cycl. Games & Sports* (ed. 2) 464/2 Make a Leyden jar whose coatings can be removed while it is charged.

+**Leyed corn.** Variant of LYED CORN. *Obs.* — **1823** JAMES *Exped.* I. 114 Another very acceptable dish was called *leyed* corn. **1825** W. BIGGS *Narr. Captivity* 35 Sandy hill cranes [were] boiled in leyed corn.

Liberal, *n.* {1820–}

+**1.** One holding liberal rather than orthodox views on theological matters. (Cf. LIBERAL *a.*)

1821 *Mass. Const. Convention Jrnl.* (1853) 589 What the ultra liberals and the ultra royalists in religion had acquiesced in, seemed to be a point at which we ought to stop. **1887** *Boston Beacon* 8 Jan., In Boston a minister is called a liberal when he rejects the Andover creed, and, perhaps, the Apostles' Creed. **1925** W. P. MERRILL *Liberal Christianity* 11 [Machen] has even gone so far as to deny to liberals the right to be considered Christians at all.

+**2.** A member of the Liberal Republican party. Now hist. (Cf. LIBERAL REPUBLICAN.)

1872 *Newton Kansan* 17 Oct. 4/2 What pleases the Liberals, displeases the Rebels and Copperheads. **1885** *Mag. Amer. Hist.* Feb. 202/2 *Liberal.*—This term acquired its recent significance from a movement headed by Carl Schurz in Missouri, in 1870, and resulting in a division of the local Republicans into 'Liberals' and 'Radicals.'

+**b.** Attrib. with *party, ticket.*

1872 *Chicago Tribune* 9 Oct. 1/4 Cincinnati elects the Liberal ticket by 4,000. **1872** *Newton Kansan* 21 Nov. 2/4 It seems . . . that the 'Liberal' party would sweep over the country like an avalanche.

***Liberal,** *a.* Free from prejudice or orthodox zeal {1781–}; +in the United States often used in religious contexts to characterize Unitarians and Universalists. — **1823** (*title*), The Liberal Christian. **1846** HOLMES *Poetical Works* (1899) 56/2 Thine eyes behold A cheerful Christian from the liberal fold. **1876** FROTHINGHAM *Transcendentalism* 128 Liberal Christianity or Unitarianism.

+**Liberal construction.** (See CONSTRUCTION 1.)

+**Liberal Republican.** A member of a party formed 1870–2 by Carl Schurz, B. Gratz Brown, and other Republicans desirous of securing various reforms. — **1873** *Newton Kansan* 13 Feb. 4/2 The Democrats were willing to use Liberal Republicans as cat's paws. **1900** *Congress. Rec.* 14 Feb. 1800/1 The Liberal Republican element got control of the State of Missouri in 1870.

Liberated slave. A slave who has been freed; a freedman. {liberated galley-slave, 1794} — **1853** STOWE *Key* 19/2 The writer has conversed . . with a very considerable number of liberated slaves. **1885** *Century Mag.* June 275/1 This decree affirms the negro, the liberated slave, a citizen.

Liberator. {1650–} +Abraham Lincoln, the issuer of the Emancipation Proclamation. (Cf. EMANCIPATOR b.) — **1869** TOURGEE *Toinette* (1881) xlii, The Liberator had signed that proclamation [etc.].

***Liberty.**

***1.** The area or bounds within the jurisdiction of a town or township. *Obs.*

1636 *Essex Inst. Coll.* IV. 94/2 Every person that shall fell any tymber . . . within the libertyes of Salem. **1652** *Plymouth Laws* 96 Within the Liberties and precincts of theire seuerall towneships. **1701** *Phila. Ordinances* (1812) 2 Lands, tenements, rents, liberties, jurisdictions, franchises and hereditaments, to them and their successors, in fee-simple. **1711** *Providence Rec.* XI. 154 All swine within ye libertye of this our Towneshipp of Providence that shall . . . be found upon ye Common land.

b. *pl. Penna.* A suburb of a city. {1659–}

1769 *Phila. Ordinances* (1812) 26 No waggon, wain or cart whatsoever, belonging to any person or persons . . . inhabiting within the said city of Philadelphia, or within the Northern Liberties thereof [etc.]. **1816** 'SCENE PAINTER' *Emigrant's Guide* 41 The city [of Phila.] is bounded by two suburbs, Camptown and Southwark; or, as they are sometimes styled, the northern and southern liberties. **1818** DARBY *Emigrant's Guide* 257 A suburb [of Pittsburgh] has been laid out upon the Aleghany called the northern liberties. **1819** *Plough Boy* I. 148 During the week . . . 104 deaths occurred in Philadelphia and the liberties. **1832** DUNLAP *Hist. Amer. Theatre* 21 The manager had cautiously taken his stand without the precincts of the city authorities, in what is called the Southern Liberties.

+**2.** A watch cry of Americans, esp. during the Revolutionary period.

1775 P. HENRY in W. Wirth (1831) *Life Patrick Henry* 141 Give me liberty, or give me death! **1777** in Jenkins *B. Gwinnett* 227 It Contains the pillars of Liberty, [on] wh[ic]h a people . . . might Erect an Administration of Govt. **1779** *Boston Gazette* 8 March 2/2 A friend to Liberty presents his cplmts to the Gen. Court. **1830** WEBSTER in Benton *30 Years' View* I. 142/1 That other sentiment, dear to every true American heart—Liberty and Union. **1884** BLAINE *20 Years of Congress* I. 536 In their evangelization of Liberty the Democrats had halted at the color-line, but, as they alleged, only because the solemn obligations of the Constitution forbade a step beyond.

+**3.** Ease or facility of expression in preaching or praying.

1835 LONGSTREET *Ga. Scenes* 212 He's a mighty good man, and I think he prays with greater libity, than most any one of his age. **1872** BRACE *Dangerous Classes N.Y.* 277 He had held forth with peculiar 'liberty' on the sin of thieving.

+**4.** Attrib. in sense 2 with *bell, cause, color,* etc. (Cf. LIBERTY BOYS, LIBERTY CAP, etc.)

1769 *Boston Chronicle* 22 May, All persons . . . are . . . to call and receive their respective dues of T. Chase, at the venerable Liberty-Elm. **1775** HUTCHINSON *Diary & Lett.* I. 586 His wife's family . . . are high Liberty people. **1777** in Jenkins *B. Gwinnett* 233 Mr. Hornby a true Friend to the liberty side from this place. **1777** *Ib.* 238 He is the best Friend to the Liberty Cause it now has left. **1837** *N.H. Hist. Soc. Coll.* V. 84 [During the Revolution] many adopted the use of what was called *Liberty tea*, as a substitute for the Chinese herb. It was made of four-leaved loosestrife. **1866** A. D. WHITNEY *L. Goldthwaite* xvi, The liberty-colors flashed full in Rebel faces. **1896** (*title*), The Liberty Bell.

Liberty Boys. *pl.* {1760–} +Early active supporters of the American Revolution. (Cf. SONS OF LIBERTY.)

1781 PETERS *Hist. Conn.* 393 The liberty boys were instantly honoured with the presence of ministers, deacons [etc.]. **1819** *Plough Boy* I. 2 The patriots, who commenced that revolution, or rather those who first shed their blood in it, at Lexington, were called Liberty Boys. **1857** *Ladies' Repository* XVII. 82/2 She was among the first and most ardent in the support of liberty. She encouraged the 'liberty boys' as she called them. **1872** *Harper's Mag.* April 692/2 The close of the revolutionary war found New York politically in the hands of the Whigs of that day, who were controlled by the Liberty Boys, the most radical of their number.

+**b.** A similar organization interested in freeing Texas from Mexican rule. *Obs.*

1858 *Texas Almanac 1859* 33 The Liberty boys, always on hand on an emergency, joined Austin's Company.

+**Liberty bush.** The purple azalea. — **1839** AUDUBON *Ornith. Biog.* V. 70 The Liberty bush. *Azalea nudiflora.* . . . Occurs in dry situations in most parts of the United States, from their northern limits to Florida.

Liberty cap. A cap serving as a symbol of liberty. {cap of liberty, 1709–} — **1803** [see LIBERTY POLE]. **1843** L. M. CHILD *Lett. New York* (1846) 287 This age and country, in which liberty-caps abound, but no one is allowed to wear them. **1851** *N. Amer. Misc.* I. 139/2 Thirty little boys, dressed in 'white shirts, black pants, and liberty caps.' **1872** *Harper's Mag.* April 689/2 A pole, crowned with a liberty-cap, and bearing aloft a tomahawk, wampum, and other Indian paraphernalia, was planted in the earth.

Liberty Hall. {1773–} +The area under the Liberty Tree in Boston. *Obs.* — **1768** *Boston Rec.* 312 The Sons of liberty request all those who . . . would promote the peace . . . to assemble at Liberty Hall under Liberty tree on Tuesday. **1768** [see LIBERTY TREE].

Liberty man. {1758–} +**1.** During the American Revolution, one who was loyal to the cause of the colonists. Now hist. +**2.** (See quotation.) — **(1) 1774** HUTCHINSON *Diary & Lett.* I. 111 Some of the highest Liberty men begin to see they have carried the matter too far. **1855** SIMMS *Forayers* 139 But what's it to you, ef I'm king's or liberty man! **(2) 1867** DIXON *New America* II. 243 One party [of Perfectionists] putting freedom before holiness, were known as the 'Liberty men'; another putting sanctity before freedom were known as the 'Holiness men.'

+**Liberty party.** *Hist.* A political party organized about 1840 having as its main object the abolition of slavery. Now hist. (Cf. FREE-SOIL PARTY.) — **1843** WHITTIER *Writings* VII. 105 It is against this system . . . that the Liberty Party is . . . directing all its efforts. **1885** G. S. MERRIAM *Life S. Bowles* I. 52 The Liberty party was merged in the Free-soil, whose creed was the exclusion of slavery from the territories. **1922** McCORMAC *Biog. Polk* 263 In August, 1843, the Liberty party had nominated James G. Birney, of Michigan, on an anti-slavery ticket.

+**Liberty pole.** A tall pole or mast, usually having a cap or flag on it, and serving originally as a rallying place for the Sons of Liberty. Now hist.

1774 HUTCHINSON *Diary & Lett.* I. 264 The week before last our Sons of Lyberty here, put up a Lyberty Pole on the Green. **1797** *Mass. H. S. Coll.* V. 55 [The common] during the late war with our mother country, was decorated with a *towering liberty pole.* **1803** *Lit. Mag.* (Phila.) Dec. 172 Every few miles present us with a liberty pole towering near some dismal hovel, and decorated with party coloured flags and liberty caps. **1835** *S. Lit. Messenger* I. 217 One of the objects that have struck me most pleasingly, is the *Liberty Pole* in almost every village. **1857** *Lawrence* (Kan.) *Republican* 9 July 3 On a beautiful eminence near by, . . . a liberty pole had been raised. **1883** *Century Mag.* Aug. 513/2 They set up a tall liberty-pole, and bringing forth a United States flag . . . they flung it out to the winds.

attrib. **1774** in *Copley-Pelham Lett.* 281 The demolition of Liberty-Pole-Committee,—we could not come to, on that Day.

+**Liberty song.** During the Revolutionary period a song popular with American patriots. *Obs.* — **1769** J. ADAMS *Diary* Works II. 218 We had also the Liberty Song—that by the farmer, and that by Dr. Church, and the whole company joined in the chorus. **1774** FITHIAN *Journal* I. 96 There were parties in Rooms made up, some at Cards; . . . some singing 'Liberty Songs' as they call'd them.

+**Liberty tree.**

1. An elm in Boston upon which, during the excitement over the Stamp Act (1765), unpopular persons were hanged in effigy.

1766 *Boston Selectmen* 26 March 212 Complaint being made by a number of Inhabitants that the Chimnies of a House . . . Situate in Newbury Street near *Liberty Tree* . . . are Insufficient and dangerous. **1768** BERNARD in Tudor *Life J. Otis* (1823) 221 *n.*, Your lordship must know that Liberty tree is a large old Elm in the High Street, upon which the effigies were hung in the time of the Stamp Act, and from whence the mobs at that time made their parades. It has since been adorned with an inscription, and has obtained the name of Liberty Tree, as the ground under it has that of Liberty Hall. **1776** A. ADAMS in *Familiar Letters* 180, [I] ventured just as far as the stump of Liberty Tree. **1889** BRAYLEY *Boston Fire Dept.* 68 Engine 8 . . . [was] ordered to be removed to a piece of ground near . . . the 'Liberty Tree.'

2. A tree dedicated to liberty. Also fig.

1823 TUDOR *Otis* 223 In Providence, an inhabitant gave a deed to the Town of a small piece of ground containing a large tree, to be used as a 'Liberty Tree' forever. **1840** MATHEWS *Politicians* IV. iii, I had better have . . . lined my belly, than have spent my substance in planting liberty-trees that are as barren as crabs. **1868** G. G. CHANNING *Recoll. Newport* 269 The Liberty Tree, at the head of Thames Street, was surmounted with the star-spangled banner.

Librarian. {1670–} One in charge of a library. {1713–} — **1774** *Jrnls. Cont. Congress* I. 27 Ordered, That the Librarian furnish the gentlemen, who are to meet in Congress, with the use of such Books as they may have occasion for. **1808** *Ann. 10th Congress* 1 Sess. II. 2827 For all contingent expenses of the Library of Congress, and the Librarian's allowance . . . eight hundred dollars. **1870** *Republican Rev.* 7 May 1/4 The Librarian was there removing and assorting the books and papers. **1920** *3d Nat. Country Life Conf. Proc.* 145 The most progressive state commissions now employ a traveling librarian.

***Library.**

***1.** A room or place provided with books for reading and study; a collection of books.

*c***1640** *Harvard Rec.* I. 15 [The income for] the Great Chamber next the library . . . [is £]2 10[s]. **1702** *Boston Rec.* 26 Ordered that Mr. John Barnerd junr be desired to make a Cattalogue of all the bookes belonging to the Towns Liberary. **1771** FRANKLIN *Autobiog.* 311 By thus clubbing our books to a common library, we should . . . have each of us the advantage of using the books of all the other members. **1833** J. S. JONES *Green Mt. Boy* I. i, Go to the library, and bring me the last new novel. **1883** *Harper's Mag.* June 142/2 [Cooper] provided technical schools and lectures and reading rooms and libraries. **1910** 'O. HENRY' *Strictly Business* 17 [He] had $647,000 in cash in his (ranch) library just received for the sale of a drove of beeves.

+**b.** *Library of Congress*, the national library at Washington, D.C. (Cf. *Congressional Library*, s.v. CONGRESSIONAL *a.* 6.)

1803 CUTLER in *Life & Corr.* II. 128, I have taken out of the Library of Congress a work [etc.]. **1821** *Ann. 17th Congress* 1 Sess. I. 20 The Senate . . . [considered] the resolution for the appointment of a joint Committee on the arrangements for the Library of Congress. **1840** *Niles' Nat. Reg.* 1 Aug. 349/2 Resolution for the disposition of certain documents now deposited in the library of congress. **1872** *Harper's Mag.* Dec. 42 The first catalogue of the Library of Congress . . . embraced the titles of 212 folios [etc.]. **1910** BOSTWICK *Amer. Pub. Library* 29 The chief bond, however, between the Government at Washington and libraries throughout the country is the Library of Congress.

2. Attrib. with *board, committee, council*, etc. (Cf. LIBRARY ASSOCIATION, etc.)

1831 *Congress. Deb.* 7 Feb. 618 After a few words from Mr. Wickliffe . . . it was referred to the Library Committee. **1891** *Univ. of Chicago Official Bul.* No. 1, 13 There shall also be . . . a library-fee. **1903** *Evanston* (Ill.) *Press* 11 April, His long and efficient connection with the library board . . . make[s] his name a most excellent choice. **1910** BOSTWICK *Amer. Pub. Library* 203 [In some libraries such a meeting of heads of departments and assistants] is dignified by some such name as that of 'Library Council.' *Ib.* 354 Library institutes . . . occupy a position midway between the summer or other occasional class and the meeting of neighborhood librarians for discussion. **1911** *Okla. Session Laws* 3 Legisl. 201 Such a tax is to be levied and collected . . . and to be known as a 'Library Fund.'

+**Library association.** An organization composed of those who make contributions for founding and maintaining a library. — **1848** *Santa Fe Repub.* 29 Jan. 2/1 The citizens of Santa Fe have taken an interest in the establishment of a Library Association. **1853** *S. Lit. Messenger* XIX. 645/1 A Library Association has been formed in Petersburg [Va.]. **1876** *Amer. Library Jrnl.* I. 140/1 For the purpose of promoting the library interests of the country, . . . the undersigned form themselves into a body to be known as the American Library Association. **1881** RITTENHOUSE *Maud* 1 We were first introduced to the Social Science and Cairo Auxiliary, and the Woman's Club and Library Association.

+**Library company.** =prec. — **1745** FRANKLIN *Writings* II. 296 Our Library Company sends for about twenty pounds sterling worth of books yearly. **1788** — *Autobiog.* 417 Soon after my return to Philadelphia, our library company receiv'd . . . a glass tube, with some account of the use of it in making such experiments. **1837** W. JENKINS *Ohio Gaz.* 99 The public institutions [of Canton, Ohio] are a bank, a library company, and a mechanics society. **1877** *Harper's Mag.* April 723/1 This [subscription] library . . . exists today in the Philadelphia Library Company.

Library room. A room containing, or used in connection with, a library. {1785–} — **1805** *Ann. 8th Congress* 2 Sess. 1668 For defraying the expenses incidental to dismantling the late library room of congress. **1841** *Lowell Offering* I. 213 A query arose, why it was necessary to have a library room. **1893** in M. Philips *Making of a Newspaper* 56 After a few turns in the *Herald's* big library-room, the editor decided

Library table. A table suitable for use in a library. — **1741** *Harvard Rec.* II. 712 [The cross table was] compos'd of three Library Tables. **1873** HOLLAND *A. Bonnicastle* xxvii, I draw the chair to my library-table, to write these closing paragraphs. **1908** 'O. HENRY' *Options* 74 Barbara sat by the quartered-oak library table.

***License.**

***1.** Permission from the proper authority to do some specific thing or to engage in some particular activity; also, the document granting this permission.

1626 *Plymouth Laws* 29 That no corne beans or pease . . . be conveyed out of the colony without the leave and licence of the governour and counsell. **1721** *Mass. H. Rep. Jrnl.* III. 59 The Inn-holders, Taverners and Retailers . . . shall obtain Licence to Sell or Retail Strong Drink. **1790** *Harvard Laws* 35 No class-meetings shall be held, but with the special licence of the President. **1815** DWIGHT *Remarks Rev. Inchiquin's Lett.* 56 In order to obtain a license, and afterwards to be admitted to ordination, they [*sc.* divinity students] must in each case pass through the Associational or Presbyterial examination. **1898** *Kansas City Star* 18 Dec. 3/2 [Those] who are really entitled to licenses to hold boxing shows, have not received licenses as yet. **1920** COOPER *Under Big Top* 5 There is the general contracting agent . . . who arranges contracts for the exhibitions and parade licenses.

2. Attrib. with *bond, commissioner, court*, etc.

1692 in Munsell *Annals Albany* 121 Ordered that the sheriffe have a warrant to levy the lycence money from the 14th Oct. 1691, to 14th Oct. 1692. **1871** *Harper's Mag.* Aug. 368 The license bond for his marriage is still extant, written by his own hand. **1885** WELLS *Pract. Economics* 231 License taxes on rectifiers, wholesale and retail dealers, capacity taxes, etc. **1886** *Pop. Science Mo.* Feb. 464 The license-tax, as it is called there [in Wisconsin], applies to railroads, insurance, telegraph, and telephone companies. **1893** in M. Philips *Making of a Newspaper* 69 No press censorship could be more arbitrary than the License Courts of Philadelphia and Pittsburgh. **1911** PERSONS, etc. *Mass. Labor Laws* 353 A special license commissioner, or inspector, is appointed whose sole duty is the enforcement of the laws regulating employment agencies.

***Licensed,** *a.* Operating by virtue of a license; possessing a license. — **1669** *Plymouth Laws* 155 That all such lycenced ordinaries shall not suffer prophane singing daunceing or revelling in their houses. **1682** *Mass. H. S. Coll.* 4 Ser. V. 60 In the heart of the town, there may be but one licensed tavern. **1806** *Balance* 28 Jan. 31 (Th.), There are 174 licensed groceries in the city of Albany. **1866** *Rep. Indian Affairs* 112 Mr. A. M. White, licensed trader for these Indians, sent notices to the various pueblos. **1896** FREDERIC *Damnation of T. Ware* 10 There existed a dim feeling that these Licensed Exhorters . . . had taken rather too much for granted. **1900** NELSON *A B C Wall St.* 136 About 100 bales of cotton . . . to be delivered from a licensed warehouse in the port of New York.

License law. A law regulating the granting of licenses. — **1838** *Amer. Almanac 1839* 76 The old license law, as well as the new one, was a law of prohibition. **1848** *Knickerb.* XXXI. 37 She has reared the sugar-cane, . . . without the faintest shadowing-forth of distilleries or alcohol or license-laws. **1883** *Century Mag.* Oct. 957/1 A Pennsylvania judge has recently put a stop to the curious method of evading the license law, extensively practiced in the petroleum regions of that State.

Licensure. Act of licensing, esp. the granting of a license to preach. — **1846** WORCESTER 418/2 *Licensure*, act of licensing, license. *Godwin.* **1872** R. ANDERSON *Hist. Missions to Oriental Ch.* II. 411 Seven young men ... were carefully examined for licensure. **1898** YOUNG *Jessamine Co., Ky.* 259 There he sought licensure in the Methodist ministry.

Licentiate.* One licensed to exhort but not yet regularly ordained. {1854–} — **1824 R. H. BISHOP *Hist. Church Ky.* 119 'Each licentiate to exhort' was ordered 'to exercise himself in composition on any subject he might choose.' **1849** CHAMBERLAIN *Indiana Gazetteer* 71 This denomination [of Baptists] has in this State, ... 95 Licentiates. **1867** 'LACKLAND' *Homespun* 219 It would be hard to say that the condition of the minister settled in the country *is* just the pleasantest which might be imagined by a young licentiate.

Lichen. Any one of various small creeping plants often found growing like moss on rocks, trees, etc. {1601–} — **1838** *Mass. Agric. Survey 1st Rep.* 118 Where water stands for a length of time about the roots, it [the larch] becomes fogged or covered with lichens. **1847** WEBSTER 731/2 The term *moss* is also popularly applied to ... *lichens*, species of which are called *tree-moss, rock-moss, coral-moss*, &c. **1865** *Atlantic Mo.* XV. 46 A purple lichen ... clothes much of the rock. **1883** THAXTER *Poems for Children* 3 Mrs. Sandpiper had only drawn together ... a little pale green lichen, and a twig or two. **1899** *Boston Transcript* 7 Aug. 9/2 Tauric acid ... is obtained from tauric moss, a peculiar lichen, or fungus, which grows upon rocks and the roots of trees.

Lichnidia. The paniculate phlox, *Phlox paniculata*, or a similar plant. {lychnidea, 1731– (Miller *Gard. Dict.* s.v. *Lychnis*)} — **1835** HOFFMAN *Winter in West* I. 144, I thought of ... the deep-hued lichnidia and gorgeous golden rod, which, with jonquils and amaranth, the purple foxglove and saffron-coloured silk-weed, paint the surface of the soil. **1836** LINCOLN *Botany* App. 124 *Phlox ... paniculata*, (smooth-stem lichnidia).

Licitation. {1623–} +In parts of the United States formerly under Spanish rule, an auction at which property jointly owned is released for sale. — **1820** in Martin *La. Term Rep.* VII. 89 The sale made by the parish judge ... was a cant or licitation between the parties for the purpose of dividing the property, which had been held in common by their ancestors. **1887** MERRILL *Amer. & Eng. Encycl.* II. 721 Cant, or Licitation.—A mode of dividing property held in common by two or more persons.

***Lick,** *n.*

+1. A salt lick. (See also BUFFALO, DEER LICK.)

1750 T. WALKER *Journal* 51 At the mouth of a Creek ... is a Lick, and I believe there was a hundred Buffaloes at it. **1792** IMLAY *Western Territory* 43 A salt spring is called a Lick. **1814** *Niles' Reg.* VI. Suppl. 177/2 This lick was the great point of concentration of the buffaloe, the elk, the deer [etc.]. **1852** WATSON *Nights in Block-House* 232 Upon this run was a lick apparently much frequented by deer. **1888** *Century Mag.* Sept. 764/1 The salt springs and 'licks' of Virginia, east Tennessee, and the Indian Territory were furnishing constantly large quantities of [salt].

+b. In place names.

1774 D. JONES *Journal* (1865) 86 As I passed a certain place called the *Great Lick*, saw the last flock of parrots. **1777** *Va. State P.* I. 276 [They] had left their women and children ... at the Blue Licks on Kentucke River. **1781–2** JEFFERSON *Notes Va.* 32 The area of Bullet's lick is of many acres. **1791** W. BARTRAM *Travels* 35 We sat [*sic*] off from Augusta, early in the morning, for the Great Buffalo Lick, on the Great Ridge. **1838** ELLSWORTH *Valley of Wabash* 6 Near the French lick ... freestone ... may be readily obtained.

2. A brief race, esp. a quarter mile, or a spurt in racing; rate of speed; a burst of energy. Freq. pl. {to come with a lick, etc., 1809–, *dial.*} Cf. FAIR LICK.

1837 HALIBURTON *Clockmaker* 1 Ser. xv. 127 That are colt can beat him for a lick of a quarter of a mile. **a1846** *Quarter Race Ky.* 104 He gave his horse the spurs ... and crossed the river at a 'quarter lick' speed. ... He went up the opposite bank at the same lick, and disappeared! **1857** *Knickerb.* XLIX. 184 Old Van and Hiram were smoking great licks over a box of Operas. **1869** 'MARK TWAIN' *Innocents* v. 48 Somehow she don't keep up her lick here on the water—gets seasick, maybe. **1891** ROBERTS *Adrift America* 148, I went in big licks, and ... I chopped it all up. **1900** DRANNAN *Plains & Mts.* 550 When he struck the ground he lit running, and at his best licks, too.

+b. *To put in big* (or *best* or *solid*) *licks*, to put forth maximum or continued and substantial effort.

1847 ROBB *Squatter Life* 106 He was puttin' in the biggest kind a licks in the way of courtin'. **1851** *Polly Peablossom* 111, I saw comin' my gray mule, puttin' in her best licks, and a few yards behind her was a grizzly. **1883** PECK *Bad Boy* 71 Pa put in his best licks, and run up the track. **1902** WHITE *Blazed Trail* 294 So put in your best licks, old man. **1907** *Springfield W. Repub.* 22 Aug. 3 It is a time for those interested in the city's welfare to wake up and put in some solid licks for good government.

***Lick,** *v.*

1. *tr.* and *intr.* Of an animal: To pass the tongue over the soil at a lick.

1806 CLARK in *Lewis & C. Exped.* V. (1905) 174 A deer came in to lick at the Springs and one of our hunters killed it. **1847** DRAKE *Pioneer Life Ky.* 13 The deer and buffalo were in the habit, as at other salt springs, of 'licking' the surrounding earth.

2. To go rapidly. *colloq.* {1889– Austral.} +With *it.*

1850 GARRARD *Wah-To-Yah* i, 16 The mad animal ... charged. How they did 'lick it' over the ground! **1886** *Outing* IX. 198/1 He'd nothin' ter do but ter lick it like blazes, with the little dog a-follerin' along.

+3. *intr.* To plunge *into* or begin.

1889 RILEY *Pipes o' Pan* 104 He was ready to lick into it then and there.

+Lick block. A block of hard salt put out for stock to lick. — **1878** in Summers *Ann. S.W. Va.* 1602 A gang of horses had come in from the range to the lick-blocks, about one hundred yards from the house.

Licker, *n.* and *v.* Variant of LIQUOR.

+Lickety. Also **lickoty.** Used in various adverbial expressions, as *lickety-brindle, lickety-click*, etc., to denote rapidity of movement, quickness or impulsiveness of going, etc. *slang.* (Cf. next and LICKETY-SPLIT.)

1847 ROBB *Squatter Life* 116 Away they started, 'lickety-click,' and arrived at the winning-post within touching distance of each other. **1848** J. MITCHELL *Nantucketisms* 40 *Lickoty liner.* Going very fast. **1858** *Harper's Mag.* May 766/2 There they had it, lickety-switch, rough-and-tumble, till Cephe give in. **1876** *Wide Awake* 236/2 You can't describe a boy running down hill without saying he went 'lickety split,' or 'lickety brindle.'

+Lickety-cut, *adv.* =next. — **1859** BARTLETT 243 *Lickety Split.* Very fast, headlong. ... *Lickety cut* and *lickety liner* are also used. **1879** PHELPS *Old Maid's Paradise* (1885) 157 They went and pitched into the old chap, lickety-cut. **1898** WESTCOTT *D. Harum* 175, I up an' put fer the village lickety-cut. **1920** LINCOLN *Mr. Pratt* 248 [They] had races right through the main street; going it licketty-cut and scandalizing the neighbors.

+Lickety-split, *adv.* At full tilt, with a rush. *slang.*

1859 ELWYN *Glossary* 49 There he goes, lickity split. **1869** STOWE *Oldtown Folks* 358, I tell you if they didn't whip up an' go lickety-split down that 'ere hill. **1879** BURDETTE *Hawkeyes* 240, [I] saw old Flanigan comin' down the main line lickety split. **1904** *N.Y. Sun* 10 Aug. 2 The Coroner drove lickety-split to the Tenderloin. **1923** WATTS *L. Nichols* 354 [He] heard this machine coming towards him lickety-split.

+Licking place. A place to which animals resort to lick the ground for salt; a lick. Also *licking pond.* — **1751** J. BARTRAM *Observations* 68 [We travelled] down to a Licking-place ..., where our intruder ... shot at an Elk. *Ib.* 27 We found a *Liching* [*sic*] *Pond*, where we dined, the backs [*sic*] parts of our country are full of these liching ponds. **1762** in W. Darlington *Memorials* (1849) 238 Their bones or skeletons are now standing in a licking-place, not far from the Ohio. **1824** MARSHALL *Kentucky* II. 45 He traversed the vales, ... ruminating on the various modes of detecting their feeding, licking, or hiding places.

+Lick log. (See quot. 1889.) Also fig. *To stand* (*up*) *to one's lick log*, to meet something fairly and fully, as an unpleasant duty. (Cf. RACK *n.*)

1834 CROCKETT *Narr. Life* 170, I was determined to stand up to my lick-log, salt or no salt. **1840** HALIBURTON *Clockmaker* 3 Ser. xii, I like a man to be up to the notch, and stand to his lick-log. **1867** HARRIS *Sut Lovingood* 79, I 'tended the lick-log es reg'lar es the old bell cow. **1887** *Congress. Rec.* 17 Feb. 1880/1 It is not necessary to bait him [*sc.* a recusant witness] or to take him to a lick-log. **1889** ROOSEVELT *Winning West* II. 212 To provide for the latter [farm stock] a tree was chopped down and the salt placed in notches or small troughs cut in the bark, making it what was called a lick-log.

***Licorice.** Also **liquorice. a.** The root of the plant *Glycyrrhiza glabra;* an extract of this or a confection flavored with it. **+b.** The North American species, *G. lepidota;* also, a similar plant, esp. one or other of two species of cleavers. Freq. *wild licorice.*

1683 *Mass. H. S. Coll.* 4 Ser. V. 112 We drink barley-water; in which boil anise-seed, liquorice, figs sliced, ... and pimpernel. **1729** *Md. Hist. Mag.* XVIII. 332 To be had of Eyre & Beecher Druggists ... 16 lb. Juice Licorice. **1737** BRICKELL *N. Carolina* 22 White Hellebor, ... Fern, Male and Female, Liquorice. **1806** *Ann. 9th Congress* 2 Sess. 1142 Clover, sheep's clover, life everlasting, wild liquorice, ... wild hemp, bulrush. **1828** in *Albany Inst. Trans.* I. 19 (Wild liquorice,) found at St. Louis, on the Platte river and Rocky Mountains. **1876** 'MARK TWAIN' *Tom Sawyer* iv. 45 'What'll you give?' 'Piece of lickrish and a fish-hook.' **1904** *Dept. Agric. Yrbk. 1903* 344 Much valuable work on the subject of licorice in America has been done by Mr. Henry W. Rittenhouse of Philadelphia.

attrib. **1820** *Columbian Centinel* 5 Jan. 3/1 John A. Bacon. ... Has for sale ... 5 cases Liquorice Paste. **1879** B. F. TAYLOR *Summer-Savory* 138 The variety store of a hundred years ago, where needles and crowbars, goose-yokes and finger-rings, liquorice-stick and leather are to be had for cash or 'dicker.'

***Licorice root. +a.** (See quot. 1870.) **b.** The root of licorice, *G. glabra* or *lepidota.* — **1870** DALL *Alaska* 438 [The Indians pick] the roots of *Hedysarum Mackenzii*, the 'liquorice root' of the trappers. **1883** 'MARK TWAIN' *Life on Miss.* xliv, The shopman ... gives the child a bit of licorice-root. **1893** *Harper's Mag.* Feb. 459/1 She slipped a piece of licorice-root from her pocket to her mouth as she began a circuit of the room, chewing vigorously the while.

*Lie, *v.*

+1. *To lie around loose,* to be in an unattached, scattered, or neglected condition. *colloq.*

1856 *Knickerb.* XLVII. 617 One of the effects of their refreshment was to make things lie around loose in a promiscuous manner. **1865** *Atlantic Mo.* XV. 288 The means are tolerably sure to be lying around loose somewhere. **1879** *Congress. Rec.* 21 Jan. 609/2 The cipher dispatches were suffered to 'lie around loose.'

2. *To lie out* {1601–}, +of land, to remain in an uncultivated condition.

1850 *Rep. Comm. Patents 1849: Agric.* 402 After the corn crop, do not suffer the land to 'lie out.'

3. *To lie over* {1856–}, +to interrupt a journey by stopping for a time. (Cf. LAY *v.* 7 a.)

1849 *31st Congress 1 Sess.* Sen. Ex. Doc. No. 64, 186 But I shall make an early drive and 'lie over' to-morrow at the first water. **1854** BARTLETT *Personal Narr.* II. 538 We arrived there too late for the morning cars. We had, therefore, to lie over a day. **1903** A. ADAMS *Log Cowboy* 181 We overtook a number of wagons loaded with wool, lying over, as it was Sunday.

+**Lienor.** One who holds a lien. — **1890** *Law Times* LXXXIX. 165/1 If the lienors may insure, so may the owners of the injured ship and cargo. **1907** *N.Y. Rep. Suppl.* CIII. 679 Where a mechanic's lien has been discharged by the giving of a bond, the lienor may do either one of two things.

+**Lieutenant commander.** *Nav.* An officer ranking below a commander and above a lieutenant. — **1878** *N. Amer. Rev.* CXXVII. 224 Lieutenant-Commander J. G. Walker had been sent in the iron-clad Baron de Kalb. **1883** *Harper's Mag.* Nov. 950/1, I was a young lieutenant-commander.

***Lieutenant general.**

+1. (See quot. 1890.) Now hist.

1639 *Md. Council Proc.* 89 A high Constable . . . [is] to arrest all Offenders against the peace and them to send or bring to Our Lieutenant General. **1642** *Md. Archives* I. 178 The Lieut. General adjourn'd the house till the third Beating of drum afternoon. **1890** *Cent.* 3441/2 *Lieutenant-general,* . . . in the proprietary government of Maryland, the deputy of the proprietor, who acted as governor of the province for him.

2. *Mil.* An officer ranking next below a general and next above a major general. Also as a title. {1618–}

1798 J. ADAMS *Works* IX. 159, [I] congratulate them [the Senate] and the public on . . . [Washington's] acceptance of his appointment as Lieutenant-General and Commander-in-chief of the army. **1864** *Wkly. New Mexican* 27 May 1/4 Caterers . . . are in spasms at the report that the Lieutenant General [Grant] is about to banish their wares from the lines. **1865** *Atlantic Mo.* XV. 413 A peculiar kind of grit . . . is illustrated in Lieutenant-General Grant. **1903** W. E. CURTIS *True Lincoln* 255 As a reward for the victories of Donelson, Vicksburg, and Chattanooga, the President recommended the revival of the rank of lieutenant-general, which had been conferred only upon Washington and Scott. **1917** *Statutes at Large* XL. 411 The pay of the grades of general and lieutenant general shall be $10,000 and $9,000 a year, respectively.

***Lieutenant governor.**

1. The governor of one of the American colonies exercising authority under a governor-general. Now hist. {1693– (*Laws of Bermuda* 23)}

1690 *Me. Doc. Hist.* V. 94 Yt ye Major be Apointed by the Lt. governor of New Yorke. **1705** *Boston News-Letter* 25 June 2/2 No Governour, Lieut. Governour or Commander in Chief of this Province shall receive any Gift or Present from the Country. **1727** *Mass. H. S. Coll.* 4 Ser. II. 177, I should be glad . . . to know who is to be our Lieutenant Governor. **1752** J. MACSPARRAN *Amer. Dissected* 12 The present Lieutenant-Governor [of Virginia] is one Mr. Dinwoody, my Class-Mate at the College of Glasgow. **1772** A. G. WINSLOW *Diary* (1894) 73, I should have said the daughter of the Hon. Lieut. Governor of Connecticutt.

+2. A state official ranking next below the governor and succeeding that official in case a vacancy occurs in the governorship.

1788 in *Mem. T. Parsons* (1859) 462 For two things we need you in extremity,—the Lieutenant-Governor, and a very extraordinary message from the Governor. **1809** KENDALL *Travels* I. 6 The lieutenant-governor administered the oath to the governor-elect. **1850** *Mich. Gen. Statutes* I. (1882) 49 A lieutenant governor shall be chosen for [two years]. **1898** *Kansas City Star* 18 Dec. 4/4 A. M. Harvey, now lieutenant governor, . . . will be a candidate for the Populist nomination for governor in 1900. **1924** CROY *R.F.D. No. 3* 3 The Lieutenant Governor was to officiate [at a dedication ceremony].

***Life.**

1. *To save one's life,* for the life of one. Used as an intensive.

1863 HOPLEY *Life in South* II. 151, I could not help laughing, 'to save my life,' in Virginia phraseology.

+2. *Bet your life,* positively, most assuredly. *colloq.*

1872 POWERS *Afoot & Alone* 244 'You bet your life they do,' said he.

+3. *Not on your life,* by no means. *colloq.*[2] {1927}

1905 *N.Y. Ev. Post* 19 Aug. 2 The congressman was asked if there had been any gambling during the trip. 'Not on your life,' he said. **1913** LONDON *Valley of Moon* II. vii, 'You'd . . . vote the socialist ticket next election.' 'Not on your life,' Billy declined.

+**Life car.** A water-tight vessel moved by rope, by means of which persons can be brought ashore from wrecked ships through heavy seas. — **1851** *Harper's Mag.* July 162/1 The Life-Car is a sort of boat. **1858** *Statutes at Large* XI. 320 A metallic life-car, and necessary harness. **1878** *Harper's Mag.* Feb. 330/2 [They] were safely brought ashore in the life-car through a surf in which no boat could have lived. **1882** GODFREY *Nantucket* 344 The best and finest apparatus for saving life . . . , consisting of . . . floats, life-cars and lines, has been placed on this [island].

+**Life everlasting. a.** =CUDWEED. **b.** The pearly everlasting, *Anaphalis margaritacea.*

1629 PARKINSON *Paradisus* 374 *Argyrocome siue Gnaphalium Americanum.* Liue long or Life euerlasting. This siluer tuft or Indian Cotton weede, hath many white heads of leafes. **1784** CUTLER in *Mem. Academy* I. 480 Life-Everlasting. Blossoms white. In pastures and fields. September. **1806** *Ann. 9th Congress* 2 Sess. 1142 Common names of some of the . . . plants, growing in the vicinity of the Washita . . . [include] sheeps' clover, life everlasting, wild liquorice. **1877** WHITMAN *Spec. Days* 106, I pull a handful of the balsamic life-everlasting and stuff it down in my trowsers-pocket for scent. **1892** *Amer. Folk-Lore* V. 98 *Gnaphalium polycephalum,* life everlasting. N.E.; No. Ohio.

Life guard. {1648–} +One employed at a beach, swimming pool, etc., to prevent bathers' drowning. {1921 (*Daily Telegraph* 29 Aug. 9/3)} — **1896** HOWELLS *Impressions & Exper.* (1909) 159, I came out almost before the life-guard could get ready to throw me a life-preserver. **1904** *N.Y. Tribune* 13 March 21 The life guards . . . do not go on duty until June. **1923** DUTTON *Shadow on Glass* 111 The life guard did not see any.

Life insurance. Insurance on the life of a person. {1809–}

1841 *Picayune* 22 Aug. 1/5 (*caption*), Life Insurance. **1865** *Nation* I. 157 This plan of paying for a policy by a definite number of annual instalments . . . obviates one of the greatest objections to life insurance. **1894** *Harper's Mag.* July 297/2 My lungs were examined for life-insurance six months ago. **1895** E. CARROLL *Principles Finance* 298 Insurance is divided into . . . Fire Insurance, Life Insurance, Marine Insurance, etc. **1920** HOWELLS *Vacation of Kelwyns* 1 Kelwyn paid for his life insurance.

b. Attrib. with *agent, man, office, policy.*

1836 *Niles' Nat. Reg.* 17 Sept. 48/3 The late col. Heileman insured his life to the amount of six thousand dollars in the Life Insurance office in Baltimore. **1861** NEWELL *Orpheus C. Kerr* I. 360 He's not an economical man if he don't destroy his life-insurance policy. **1871** *Harper's Mag.* Oct. 799/1 That fearful creature, the Life Insurance Man, . . . came around to my office fourteen times in one morning. **1883** *Ib.* Sept. 624/1 The doctor had always supposed Northern women to be as little afflicted with timidity as life-insurance agents.

Life insurance company. A company that insures the lives of its policy-holders. — **1847** WEBSTER 16/1 *Actuary* . . . in America . . . is chiefly applied to the manager of a life insurance company. **1865** *Atlantic Mo.* XV. 86 The life insurance companies number thirteen. **1884** 'CRADDOCK' *Where Battle Was Fought* 175, I am a witness . . . in that Jartree suit against the life insurance company—shabby, shabby affair! **1912** NICHOLSON *Hoosier Chron.* 80 A ruthless life insurance company . . . seemed most unreasonably insistent in its collections.

Life line. {1794–} +At a beach or pool, a rope or chain running through the water, to be grasped as a support or guide by bathers. — **1896** HOWELLS *Impressions & Exper.* (1909) 163 The life-guard of the bathing-beach . . . pulls in the life-lines and the buoys.

+**Life-of-man.** Any one of various American plants as bush honeysuckle, mountain ash, etc.

1784 CUTLER in *Mem. Academy* I. 431 *Aralia.* . . . Pettymorrel. Life of Man. . . . It is aromatic. The berries give spirits an agreeable flavour. **1795** WINTERBOTHAM *Hist. View* III. 397 Among the native and uncultivated plants of New-England . . . employed for medical purposes . . . [is] Pettimorrel, or life of man. **1832** WILLIAMSON *Maine* I. 126 Life-of-man . . . bears clusters of purple berries, large as shot and wholesome; its root is excellent in a poultice. **1891** *Amer. Folk-Lore* IV. 148 A family visiting us from Maine called it *Life of Man,* and I have met the same name [for *Aralia racemosa*] elsewhere since then. **1893** *Ib.* VI. 142 *Sedum Telephium,* life of man. Concord, Mass. **1894** *Ib.* VII. 90 *Aralia racemosa,* life-o'-man, Fryeburg, Me.

Life policy. A contract providing for insurance upon life. — **1881** *Harper's Mag.* Jan. 274/2 Most of their bargains with the public are made in the shape of life policies. **1919** W. ALEXANDER *Life Insurance Co.* 46 In Chapter vii the net level premium on an ordinary life policy was computed.

Life-preserver. {1638–} A contrivance, usually made chiefly of cork, for buoying up a person in the water. {1804–} — **1838** COOPER *Homeward B.* xiv, I have . . . that life-preserver that you admire so much. **1865** *Atlantic Mo.* XV. 544 There was an old tin life-preserver hanging on a hook by the door. **1900** STOCKTON *Afield & Afloat* 225 On she came, with the men in the bow ready to throw over their life-preservers. **1913**

Seamen's Bill: Hearings 415 Was not a good bit of this trouble in the *Slocum* disaster due to a lack of life preservers?

Life-saver. {1883–} =LIFE GUARD. — **1887** *Courier-Journal* 10 Feb. 8/3 The Police and the Life-Savers Still Prying Into the Mystery of Smyser's Pond. **1898** *Century Mag.* April 932/1 One winter night the Barnegat life-savers launched their boat. **1903** *Boston Ev. Transcript* 20 Aug., According to a decision of the Election Commissioners a City Point life saver cannot vote. **1920** COOPER *Under Big Top* 222 The gangly roughneck was slated for the position of a life saver.

Life-saving, *a.* Of or pertaining to the saving of life from drowning or shipwreck. — **1858** *Statutes at Large* XI. 320 For contingencies of life-saving apparatus on the coast of the United States, twelve thousand dollars. **1874** *Ib.* XVIII. 127 The Secretary of the Treasury is hereby authorized to make all necessary regulations for the government of the life-saving service not inconsistent with law. **1877** *Harper's Mag.* Dec. 50/2 The life-saving car is passing from the vessel to the shore with living freight. **1882** MCCABE *New York* 367 They resolved to start a life saving corps, and quietly went to work. **1882** *Harper's Mag.* Feb. 360/2 Upon the wall hangs the India-rubber life-saving dress invented by Clark S. Merriman in 1852. **1883** WILDER *Sister Ridnour* 157 We have often been to Cape Cod, to Chatham, to the beach, and the 'life-saving hut.' **1898** *Century Mag.* April 925/1 In the United States these men [whose duty it is to patrol the coast] belong to what is known as the Life-saving Service. *Ib.* 926/2 To no life-saving crew does the term 'heroes of peace' more exactly apply than to that of the station at Evanston, Illinois, on Lake Michigan.

+**Life-saving station.** A building or establishment on a shore or coast, with apparatus and a crew of men for preventing loss of life by drowning. Also attrib. — **1858** *Statutes at Large* XI. 320 Twenty-eight life-saving stations on the coast of New Jersey. **1862** *Huntington Rec.* III. 469 So much of the land . . . as the United States may want for the purpose of placing a Life Saving Station house thereon. **1875** *Chicago Tribune* 2 July 5/4 Bids were opened in the Treasury Department yesterday for the construction of nine complete life-saving stations. **1886** DORSEY *Midshipman Bob* 172 Then Young dragged himself on those banged up legs ever so far . . . to the Life-Saving Station. **1903** *N.Y. Times* 25 Sept. 14 The plight of the sloop had been signalled at the life-saving station at Sandy Hook.

+**Life station.** =prec. — **1856** *Statutes at Large* XI. 97 For compensation of two superintendents for the life-stations on the coasts of Long Island and New Jersey, three thousand dollars.

Life tree. {1649–} +(See quotation.) — **1832** WILLIAMSON *Maine* I. 107 The white Cedar is believed to be the western life-tree.

***Lift,** *n.* +**1.** The difference between the minimum and the maximum depths of water in a lock. +**2.** *S. On the lift,* in the act of moving or changing residence. *colloq.* — (**1**) **1829** J. MACAULEY *Hist. New York* I. 170 This [canal] lock has an extent within the gates of one hundred and fourteen feet, with a breadth of thirty—the lift is nine feet. **1837** PECK *Gaz. Illinois* 55 Here are to be two locks [in a canal], ten feet lift each. **1840** TANNER *Canals & Railr. U.S.* 252 The difference between the levels is termed the *lift of the lock,* which ranges from 3 to 30 feet. (**2**) **1852** *S. Lit. Messenger* XVIII. 436/2 Bolus was on the lift for Texas.

* **Lift,** *v.*

‖**1.** *tr.* To please or satisfy.

1825 *Austin P.* (1924) II. 1120, I was very much lifted with your country.

+**2.** (See quotations.) Also *vbl. n.*

1829 *Va. Lit. Museum* 98/1 The stone is not to be laid on in shovel-fulls, but to be scattered over the surface, one shovel-full following another and being spread over a considerable space. This preparation of the road for the receipt of small stones is called *lifting.* *Ib.* 98/2 In some cases it would be unprofitable to *lift* and relay a road, even if the materials should have been originally too large.

+**3.** To pay off or redeem (a note, mortgage, etc.).

1834 CROCKETT *Narr. Life* 45, I would set in and work out the note so as to lift it for him. **1858** *Knickerb.* LII. 216, I bent my back in lifting notes, and I don't know that it will ever come straight again. **1868** BEECHER *Sermons* (1869) I. 190, I want to lift a mortgage, and two hundred dollars would lift it. **1908** *N.Y. Ev. Post* (s.-w.) 2 April 5 It is naturally the desire of the club to lift this debt as soon as possible.

‖**b.** To take back (a claim made for public land).

1825 *Austin P.* (1924) II. 1184 If anything has taken place that may in any wise effect my land Claims in Texas I would like to lift one or both and locate them anew.

+**4.** To obtain (a letter) by paying the postage due on it. *Obs.*

1863 *Congress. Globe* 20 Feb. 1154/3 The soldier, being disappointed in receiving his pay, is unable to provide his family with the pittance necessary to lift a letter from the office.

5. Of a conductor: To take up (a passenger's ticket).

1898 *Boston Herald* 3 July 14/8 The Pullman method for affixing the war tax stamps to parlor car seats is to have the conductors put them on when the ticket is lifted.

+**6.** *To lift the hair,* (see HAIR 2).

Lifting handle. a. A handle for use in lifting various articles. **b.** A handle that moves upon a hinge. — **1778** *Mass. Spy* 29 Oct. 4/3 To be sold . . . Lifting handles, desk and book-case locks. **1859** *Rep. Comm. Patents 1858* I. 522 A 'lifting handle' with the plate cast in any metal that can be bent, having the socket formed in the manner described. **1890** *Cent.* 3444/2 In another form [of lifting gear in a steam boiler] the lever is actuated by a rod passing out through a stuffing-box, and provided with a lifting-handle.

+**Lifting plow.** (See quotation.) — **1879** *Scribner's Mo.* Dec. 239/2 Let the first team be followed by a subsoil or lifting plow, which stirs and loosens in substratum without bringing it to the surface.

Lifting pump. A lift or displacement pump for raising and discharging a fluid. {1797–} — **1851** CIST *Cincinnati* 103 A lifting-pump . . . lifted the water from the river into a tank. **1856** *Mich. Agric. Soc. Trans.* VII. 53 A. O. & W. L. Peuf . . . [exhibited] three lifting pumps.

+**Lift lock.** A lock in a canal or stream for raising or lowering boats. — **1832** *Louisville Directory* 111 There is one guard and three lift locks combined. **1848** *Indiana Gen. Ass. Doc.* II. 145 Upon this portion of the line [of the canal] there will be five lift locks. **1881–5** MCCLELLAN *Own Story* 193 The lift-locks, above and below, are all large enough for the ordinary boats.

***Light,** *n.* **1.** *To see* (or *get*) *the light,* +to become convinced about a matter. +**2.** *To disappear between two lights,* to depart surreptitiously between sundown and sunup. — (**1**) **1812** *Niles' Reg.* III. 195/2 It is indispensably necessary that every man should 'see the light.' **1903** *N.Y. Ev. Post* 10 Sept., It is altogether likely that they, too, will see the light before another week has passed. (**2**) **1859** A. CARY *Country Life* 188 The feller what brought her, had shortly afterwards disappeared between two lights, leaving her with a limited amount of chink.

* **Light,** *v.*

+**1.** *To light out,* to run away, to depart in haste. *colloq.*

1873 *Newton Kansan* 14 Aug. 2/3 The young man thereupon could not wait but lit out. **1881** HAYES *New Colorado* 85 When he lit out, it took a four-mule team to freight his trunks. **1909** WASON *Happy Hawkins* 219 They settled with James, an' he lit out.

+**2.** *To light in,* to engage in a fight.

1878 BEADLE *Western Wilds* 187 The Irish . . . got wind of a free fight, and they double-quicked into town and lit in generally.

+**3.** *To light into,* to punish, to give a beating to. *colloq.*

1884 'MARK TWAIN' *Huck. Finn* xxii. 224 He lit into that horse with his whip and made him fairly hum.

+**4.** *To light down on* (someone), to take (someone) to task, to censure severely. *colloq.*

1884 R. GRANT *Average Man* 3 She was in love with Willis Blake, but her stern parent lit down on her.

+**Lightboat.** =LIGHTSHIP. — **1831** *Statutes at Large* IV. 491 Ten thousand dollars for building a light-boat to be stationed in the strait connecting Lakes Huron and Michigan. **1848** *Statutes at Large* IX. 298 For a light-boat to be stationed on Bartlett's Reef, Long Island Sound, twelve thousand dollars. **1863** in Moore *Rebellion Rec.* V. I. 10 The Commodore Perry found the lantern from the light-boat at the mouth of Roanoke River.

+**Light bread.** *S.* Wheaten bread leavened with yeast.

1821 *Western Carolinian* 27 March, Crackers and light Bread will always be found in his shop. **1847** MAGOFFIN *Down Santa Fé Trail* 240 She gave a cup of coffee with some nice light-bread and butter. **1868** REDFORD *Hist. Methodism Ky.* I. 395, I would . . . bake fifteen or twenty loaves of light-bread. **1887** HARRIS in *Century Mag.* Aug. 549/2 That everlastin' nigger went and made too much fire in the stove and tee-totally ruint my light-bread. **1897** BRODHEAD *Bound in Shallows* 84 She makes the meanest light bread I ever put to my mouth. **1920** HOWELLS *Vacation of Kelwyns* 17 You can give us light bread, I suppose?

+**Light-complected,** *a.* Having a light or fair skin; blonde. *colloq.*[2] (Cf. COMPLECTED *ppl. a.* and DARK-COMPLECTED *a.*) — **1806** LEWIS in *L. & Clark Exped.* III. (1905) 315 They are generally low in stature, proportionably small, reather lighter complected and much more illy formed than the Indians of the Missouri. **1872** M. HOLLEY *My Opinions* 245 A good lookin' light complected woman. **1902** L. RICHARDS *Mrs. Tree* 12 They made a handsome couple, if they be both light-complected. **1922** A. BROWN *Old Crow* 99 He's light-complected, blue eyes an' all.

Light dragoon. A lightly equipped dragoon. *Obs.* {1808–} — **1792** *Ann. 2d Congress* 80 That there shall be raised a squadron of light dragoons. **1797** *Ann. 5th Congress* I. 20 The bill for raising an additional corps of light dragoons was read the second time. **1867** EDWARDS *Shelby* 477 A general . . . who never . . . had his rear attacked by some swift, superb body of light dragoons.

* **Lighter.** A boat or barge for unloading or loading ships and for other harbor uses.

1623 in Bradford *Hist.* 192 Let him build you 2. catches, a lighter, and some 6. or 7. shalops. **1756** ROGERS *Jrnls.* 21 We immediately lightened our boats, and prepared to board her; but were prevented by two lighters coming up the lake. **1849** CHAMBERLAIN *Indiana Gazetteer* 317 Vessels can now be loaded and unloaded only from Lighters. **1894** *Harper's Mag.* April 805/1 He had repaired one of the lighters used in carrying materials for the foundation of the light-house.

***Lighterage.** The unloading or loading of cargo with a lighter; the hire of a lighter. — **1632** *Mass. H. S. Coll.* 2 Ser. VIII. 233 Paid Edward Bendall for lighterage of ordnance, . . . 15 [shillings]. **1792** *R.I. Commerce* II. 449 Lighterage is very high and hard to be commanded. **1895** E. CARROLL *Principles Finance* 294 *Lighterage,* the hire of a lighter or barge.

*__Lighterman.__ One who owns or is employed on a lighter. — **1647** *R.I. Col. Rec.* I. 153 Herdsmen, lighter-men and such as be left of necessity at Farmes, shall pay two shillings. **1796** *Boston Directory* 266 Martes Anthony, lighterman. **1872** *Harper's Mag.* Oct. 681/1 All cases of theft from closed piers, or from lighters, . . . are accomplished by collusion with the private watchmen, the lightermen, or the crews.

***Light horse.**

***1.** *Mil.* A body or unit of light-armed cavalry soldiers. Now hist.

1776 FITHIAN *Journal* II. 226 The militia . . . have taken already a number of their Light-Horse. **1790** D. FANNING *Narrative* 45 The light Horse under the command of Capt. Ramsay kept back, until our return. **1838** INGRAHAM *Burton* II. 179 Had we been in possession of a few hundred lighthorse to act as videttes . . . your approach would have been communicated to us.

+2. A mounted police guard among the Indians. Also *light-horseman.*

1820 in Morse *Rep. Indian Affairs* (1822) II. 172 The Cherokee Nation shall be laid off into Eight Districts . . . , and one company of light horse [is] to accompany each Circuit Judge on his official duties in his respective districts. **1844** GREGG *Commerce of Prairies* II. 266 [Among the Choctaws and Creeks] the executioners are called the 'light-horse,' a kind of police guard, also formerly in use by the Cherokees. **1864** *Ladies' Repository* April 200/2 The 'Light Horse,' a mounted police, were our only dependence in an emergency [in Indian Terr.]. **1883** *Rep. Indian Affairs* p. xii, The murderer was arrested by the Seminole Light Horse and brought into the Cheyenne and Arapaho Agency. **1899** CUSHMAN *Indians* 217 A company of armed and mounted police, called '*Light Horse Men*,' were organized from each district.

Lighthouse.

1. A tall, towerlike structure, usu. on a shore or coast, having a powerful beacon or light at the top to guide navigators. {1622–}

[**1689** SEWALL *Diary* I. 244 Saw the Light-House. **1715** *Boston News-Letter* 8 Aug. 2/2 An Act for Building and Maintaining a Light-House upon the Great Brewster.] **1789** *Ann. 1st Congress* I. 51 The House . . . had passed a bill for the establishment and support of light-houses, beacons, and buoys. **1812** *Ann. 12th Congress* 1 Sess. II. 2250 The plan of lighting light-houses, by reflecting and magnifying lanterns. **1893** *Harper's Mag.* April 768/1 Take me as far as the old light-house.

b. Attrib. and comb. with *board, inspector,* etc.

See also LIGHTHOUSE DISTRICT, -KEEPER.

1852 *Statutes at Large* X. 119 An officer of the army or navy [shall] be assigned to each district as a light-house inspector. *Ib.* 120 It shall be the duty of the Light-house Board to furnish . . . all the estimates of expense which the several branches of the light-house service may require. **1867** WHITTIER *Tent on Beach* 10 They saw . . . The lamp-fire glimmer down from the tall light-house tower.

+2. *transf.* (See quotations.) *slang.*

1859 MATSELL *Vocabulum* 51 *Light-house*, a man with a very red nose. **1900** FLYNT *Tramping* 386 'Lighthouse' . . . means a man who knows every detective of a town by sight.

+**Lighthouse district.** An area of coastal or interior waters directed by a superintendent in the U.S. Lighthouse Service. — **1852** *Statutes at Large* X. 119 The Light-house Board . . . [shall arrange] light-house districts. **1880** LAMPHERE *U.S. Govt.* 80/2 The following will give the limits and bounds of the 14 Light-House Districts.

Lighthouse-keeper. One who manages a lighthouse and tends the light. {1866} — **1738** *Mass. Prov. Acts* XII. (1904) 513 *Ordered* that the sum of Fifty one Pounds . . . be paid . . . for his services as Light House Keeper. **1900** *Congress. Rec.* 11 Jan. 762/1 The bill (S. 1800) providing for the retirement of John Briercliff Brown, light-house keeper at Point Bonito.

Light infantry. *Mil.* Infantry men trained for rapid operations. Also attrib. — **1759** *Essex Inst. Coll.* XIX. 184 One Capt. Canada belonging to gages Lite Infentery set off from Crown Point. **1823** THACHER *Military Jrnl.* 247 Two brigades have been selected . . . to form a corps of light infantry. **1841** COOPER *Deerslayer* xxxi, A sentinel, who wore the light infantry uniform of a royal regiment, paced the platform.

Light money. A tax levied upon ships to defray the expenses of maintaining lighthouses, lightships, etc. {1672–} — **1789** *Ann. 1st Congress* I. 289 There is not . . . a vessel of ours that goes to Europe, that does not pay, in light money and other charges, more than fifty cents per ton. **1816** *Ann. 14th Congress* 2 Sess. 1077 The citizens . . . [shall be required to pay] only the dues of . . . quayage, or light money. **1900** *Congress. Rec.* 2 Feb. 1446/2 One section imposes . . . a tax, called light money, of 50 cents per ton.

Lightning.

+1. *fig.* **a.** *To catch particular lightning*, to catch hell. **b.** A person with sudden and overwhelming power of action. *colloq.*

1871 *Harper's Mag.* Oct. 690/1 Ef *Pat* Role, or any other consarned Irishman, kicks up a muss 'bout these yer diggins, he'll kotch *par*tic'lar lightnin'. **1875** *Scribner's Mo.* Nov. 142/2 They said that I was 'lightning' when I 'got up on my ear!'

+2. Whisky of an inferior quality. *slang.* {gin, 1781–} Also attrib. (Cf. CHAIN LIGHTNING 2 and JERSEY LIGHTNING.)

1873 MILLER *Amongst Modocs* 94 Men were wont to meet at night, have stag-dances, and drink lightning. *Ib.* 141 All ranged themselves . . . before the bar, calling out 'Cocktail,' . . . 'Lightning straight,' . . . and so on. **1877** BARTLETT 27 This latter sort is also called 'Lightning Whiskey,' because 'warranted to kill at forty rods.' **1882** *Century Mag.* Sept. 767/1 Taking heart again from his full tumbler of Colorado lightning.

3. A decisive political upset; sudden political success or failure. *colloq.*

1879 *Congress. Rec.* 25 April 920/2 No danger of that kind of lightning in my district. **1891** *Ib.* 5 Jan. 925/1 When the doctrine of practical reciprocity is applied the lightning will strike next time somewhere about Arkansas.

+4. *Polit.* The policy of the Democratic party in Alabama (*c*1880–90), adopted in an effort to wrest political control of the state from the Republicans and Negroes. *Obs.* Also attrib.

For other material see Th. S.

1887 in *Congress. Rec.* 3 June (1890) 5547/2 [In 1886] the issue in the Democratic party between aspirants for the office of probate judge was understood to be 'honesty or the lightning process at elections.' **1890** *Congress. Rec.* 3 June 5548/1 The Progress was founded in May, 1887, . . . as an advocate of the lightning Democratic creed of 1880. *Ib.*, Before we went into lightning session Colonel Gaillard withdrew. *Ib.*, It was lightning in 1880; it was lightning in 1886.

+5. Attrib., passing into adj., in sense: Especially fast, quickly made, dexterous, etc. *colloq.* (Cf. LIGHTNING CALCULATOR, etc.)

1873 W. MATHEWS *Getting On in World* 242 Now . . . people travel by 'lightning lines,' going from New York to Chicago in twenty-nine hours. **1875** 'MARK TWAIN' *Old Times* vii. 130 If one of the boats has a 'lightning' pilot, whose 'partner' is a trifle his inferior, you can tell which one is on watch by noting whether that boat has gained or lost some. **1890** *Harper's Mag.* June 51/2 No more 'lightning change' from the sock to the cothurn was ever made in life's drama. **1899** ADE *Doc' Horne* 9 The lightning dentist turned up his coat collar and shivered with sympathy.

b. First-class, excellent.

1874 'MARK TWAIN' *Letters* I. 239, The 'Cloth of Gold' . . . is just *lightning* poetry.

Lightning-arrester. A device for protecting electrical apparatus from the occasional high voltages caused by lightning, etc. {1870–} — **1860** PRESCOTT *Electric Telegraph* 300 There have been several kinds of lightning-arresters. **1868** *Rep. Comm. Patents 1867* 1121/1 A lightning arrester in which one or more permanent or electro-magnets are combined with the telegraph wire or cable. **1879** PRESCOTT *Speaking Telephone* 28 A lightning arrester is provided in each box for the protection of the apparatus.

+Lightning bug. =FIREFLY.

1778 CARVER *Travels* 491 The Lightning Bug or Fire Fly is about the size of a bee. **1804** FESSENDEN *Orig. Poems* (1806) 133 Their love-lighted lustre outvies The lightning-bug's twinkle by night. *c***1849** PAIGE *Dow's Sermons* I. 90 The feeble, phosphorescent glow emanating from the tail-end of a lightning-bug. **1871** *Billings' Farmer's Allminax* 7 Thare iz about as mutch difference [between vivacity and wit] az thare iz between lightning and a lightning bug. **1899** *Animal & Plant Lore* 42 If a lightning bug comes into the house you will have a strange visitor. Alabama.

transf. **1842** *S. Lit. Messenger* VIII. 199/2 It will never do to tell *us* that there is any humbug in this business, or even that it is a mere *lightning-*bug. **1847** *Knickerb.* XXIX. 434, I am the star of the universe and the lightning-bug of the world!

+**Lightning calculator.** An adept at rapid calculation. — **1883** *Century Mag.* July 397 One of the board, commonly known as the 'lightning calculator' from his expertness in this sort of rascality, deliberately changed 2000 to the wrong column. **1887** *Courier-Journal* 18 Feb. 4/4 A lightning calculator gave an exhibition in Lansing, Mich. **1900** *Congress. Rec.* 17 Jan. 915/1 It will take a lightning calculator to estimate the amount of boodle which that bank will contribute.

+Lightning conductor. =LIGHTNING ROD. {1832–}

1792 in Roosevelt *Amer. Backlogs* (1928) 61 The lightning conductor was at the mast-head. **1814** W. BENTLEY *Diary* IV. 262 The post remained, retained on the side of the steeple by the Lightning conductors. **1853** B. F. TAYLOR *Jan. & June* 28 A bolder branch [of the everlasting pea] . . . discovered the Lightning Conductor. **1868** *Mich. Agric. Rep.* VII. 362 N. Brittan & Co., Coldwater, [exhibited] 1 continuous copper stick lightning conductor.

+Lightning express. A fast train.

1853 BUNN *Old Eng. & New Eng.* 160 You have direct communication from [Buffalo] . . . with New York . . . by what they term 'lightning expresses.' **1871** *Harper's Mag.* Oct. 690/2 The dépôt of the Great Western line was in its usual state of excitement . . . as the hour drew near for the departure of the Lightning Express. **1877** HALE *G. T. T.* 145 There is but one 'lightning express.' **1902** G. C. EGGLESTON *D. South* 308 It was the fashion to call trains that reached a maximum speed of twenty miles an hour, 'lightning expresses.'

attrib. and *transf.* **1880** 'MARK TWAIN' *Tramp Abroad* 456 The passenger-part of this glacier,—the central part,—the lightning-express part, so to speak,—was not due in Zeematt till the summer of 2378. **1889** MUNROE *Golden Days* 114 All the lightning express eating-houses in the States would get left so quick as would make 'em dizzy.

+**Lightning express train.** =prec. — **1860** HOLMES *Professor* vi. 163 The scenery of a long tragic drama flashed through his mind as the lightning-express-train *whishes* by a station. **1873** *Harper's Mag.* Jan. 173/1 We are sometimes inclined to be impatient even of our 'lightning express' trains. **1887** GEORGE *40 Years on Rail* 47 In these days of lightning express trains it is hard to realize that fifty years ago the locomotive was in its infancy.

+**Lightning rod.** Also **lightening rod.** A pointed, properly grounded, metallic rod, usually of copper, placed on a building or other structure as a protection against lightning.

1789 *Mass. Spy* 23 July 1/3 The house in Philadelphia . . . had two lightening rods. **1789** *Ann. 1st Congress* I. 688 John McPherson . . . [petitioned for] an exclusive privilege . . . to make and vend lightning rods upon an improved construction. **1823** *New Eng. Farmer* II. 77 People will never be persuaded to erect Lightning Rods, till they are in some measure convinced of their utility. **1851** CIST *Cincinnati* 216 Lightning Rods . . . are made here . . . of superior quality, and on an extensive scale. **1880** *Harper's Mag.* July 273/2 When Franklin proposed the protection of buildings by lightning-rods, it was looked upon as an impious thing. **1900** STOCKTON *Afield & Afloat* 391 It ran like a streak of gray electricity along the lightning-rod. **1924** CROY *R.F.D. No. 3* 61 On top of the horse barn were the lightning rods of twisted copper cable.

fig. **1800** WEEMS *Letters* II. 154 If the dark cloud shd. gather on the brow of Mrs. Campbell, you wd. play the Lightening rod for me. **1876** SCUDDER *Dwellers* 9 He had acted as a sort of lightning-rod to conduct the old scholar's bolts.

b. Attrib. and comb. with *agent, business, dispenser,* etc.

1873 BAILEY *Life in Danbury* 253 There were letters from nine different lightning-rod men. **1881** CARLETON *Farm Festivals* 89 This railroad smash reminds me . . . Of a lightning-rod dispenser that came down on me one day. **1883** *Century Mag.* Oct. 889/2 The young woman told who *he* was—in the lightning-rod business in Kalamazoo. **1891** GARLAND *Main-travelled Roads* (1922) 73 Guessed Bill had got hooked onto by a lightnin'-rod peddler, or somethin' o' that kind. **1900** R. GRANT *Unleavened Bread* 48, I set you down at first as one of those lightning-rod agents.

+**Lightning train.** =LIGHTNING EXPRESS TRAIN. — **1862** LOWELL *Biglow P.* 2 Ser. iii. 109 An' ary man thet's pop'lar's fit to drive a lightnin'-train. **1874** B. F. TAYLOR *World on Wheels* 66 In lightning trains he [the brakeman] is not given to much humor. **1893** *Harper's Mag.* April 788/2 This first experience in a lightning train was by no means unalloyed bliss.

Lightship. A ship equipped with a bright light or lights and often signals or other warning devices and anchored where it can serve the purposes of a lighthouse. — [**1837** MARTINEAU *Society* II. 11 The office of the light-ship is to tow vessels in the dark through the strait [between Lakes Michigan and Huron].] **1861** E. COWELL *Diary* 358 The Smith's Point lightship . . . had been carried off from Chesapeake Bay by the rebels. **1883** *Century Mag.* Sept. 656/2 Looking off to the light-ship on the Shoals. **1897** *Outing* XXX. 500/2 *Syce* . . . sailed a race from Sarah's Ledge to and round Bartlett's Reef lightship, thence to Cornfield lightship and return.

+**Light stand.** A small table or similar article of furniture upon which a light is placed. — **1863** A. D. WHITNEY *F. Gartney* xii, On the little 'lightstand' in the corner by the fireplace stood the self-same basket. **1896** WILKINS *Madelon* 233 A little light-stand, with his medicines and a candle, stood on his left. **1903** WIGGIN *Rebecca* 32 She folded Aurelia's letter and laid it in the light-stand drawer.

Lightwood. {1685–} *S.* +The dead, thoroughly dried heart of one or other species of pine; also, the dead root, knot, or limb of this. Used for fuel or kindling.

1705 BEVERLEY *Virginia* III. iii. 12 [The Indians] generally burn Pine, or Lightwood, (that is, the fat Knots of dead Pine). **1724** H. JONES *Virginia* 57 In some of the poorer Parts of the Country abounding in Pine, do they gather up the Light-wood, or Knots of the old Trees, which will not decay. **1784** SMYTH *Tour* I. 104 The light-wood (the roots and knots of pine, so named here [in N.C.]), . . . is their whole fuel. **1800** TATHAM *Agric. & Commerce* 115 Lightwood is the heart of the pine-tree, which, when fallen, retains the turpentine or resinous properties of the tree. **1822** SIMMONS *Notices E. Fla.* 35 (Th. S.), The lightwood . . . [burns] inextinguishably in the heaviest showers. **1843** *Amer. Pioneer* II. 453 In Carolina we had the real fat light-wood, not merely pine knots, but the fat straight pine. **1889** *Harper's Mag.* Jan. 243/2 A negro woman on her knees was hastily lighting a fire on the broad hearth with fat lightwood. **1905** PRINGLE *Rice Planter* 258 As I rowed up to the mills I came upon a flat heavily loaded with lightwood.

b. Attrib. with *brand, fire, soot,* etc. (Cf. LIGHTWOOD KNOT, etc.)

1709 LAWSON *Carolina* 183 Their Faces dawb'd over with Light-wood Soot, (which is the same as Lamp-black). **1725** in *Travels Amer. Col.* 150 [The Ditch] is Stuck full of light wood Spikes. *c***1845** THOMPSON *Chron. Pineville* 165 He had gone to the kitchen and lit a few light-wood splinters. **1847** *Knickerb.* XXIX. 534 A 'quantity' of children were gathered round the fire of a light-wood stump. **1853** SIMMS *Sword & Distaff* 458 M'Kewn . . . [was] satisfied with the sufficient blaze of the lightwood brands cast upon the fire. **1863** 'E. KIRKE' *Southern Friends* 290 An iron kettle filled with tar was already simmering over a light-wood fire.

+**Lightwood knot.** *S.* A dead, dried-out knot of any species of pine, used for kindling.

1800 HAWKINS *Sk. Creek Country* 80 They covered him with lightwood knots, burnt him [etc.]. **1836** GILMAN *Recoll.* (1838) 11, I see him now, in winter, throwing the oak logs or lightwood knots on the wide hearth. **1853** BALDWIN *Flush Times Ala.* 308 You can't put an inch or two of knife in a fellow, or lam him over the head a few times with a light-wood knot. **1895** *Outing* XXVII. 73 The guide piled some lightwood knots in the frying pan.

attrib. **1900** HARRIS *On the Wing* 149 He studied his books by a lightwood knot fire.

+**Lightwood torch.** *S.* A torch made of split pieces of lightwood. — **1709** LAWSON *Carolina* 210 [The] Indian Boys go in the Night, and one holding a Lightwood Torch, the other has a Bow and Arrows. **1834** *Knickerb.* III. 35 The girls . . . [were] holding aloft large lightwood torches. **1856** OLMSTED *Slave States* 450 All the negroes . . . marching in procession from the cabin of the deceased person to the grave, carrying lightwood torches, and singing hymns. **1884** HARRIS *Mingo* 192 When Aunt Tabby . . . started for her cabin after dark, she was accompanied by a number of little negroes bearing lightwood torches.

Lignite. A variety of coal at a stage between peat and bituminous coal; brown coal. {1808–} (Cf. BOVEY COAL.)

1821 NUTTALL *Travels Arkansa* 54 We came to for the night on a sand-bar, opposite the centre of the island, . . . scattered in every direction with lignite. **1853** Marcy *Explor. Red River* (1854) 155 Among the specimens in my hands is one of lignite. **1881** *Rep. Indian Affairs* p. xxx, After this year 'lignite' can be substituted for fuel. *a***1918** G. STUART *On Frontier* II. 111 Firey [*sic*] red cliffs, bluffs, and buttes evidently caused by the burning out of great beds of lignite and oily shales which once underlaid all this region.

attrib. **1874** RAYMOND *6th Rep. Mines* 322 They belong . . . to the great lignite formation extending along the eastern flank of the Rocky Mountains. **1880** *Scribner's Mo.* July 460/1 The fuel of the city is wholly lignite coal which comes from the foot-hills.

***Lignum-vitae.** Any one of various tropical American trees of the genus *Guaiacum,* esp. *G. officinale;* also, the wood of such a tree.

1686 SEWALL *Diary* I. 116, [I] discoursed with Ralf Carter, about *Lignum Vitae.* He saith thinks 'tis found no where but in America. **1776** *Jrnls. Cont. Congress* V. 424 Mr. Charles Walker . . . ought to be paid . . . four tons of lignum vitae. **1897** SUDWORTH *Arborescent Flora* 264 *Guajacum sanctum.* . . . Common Names. Lignum Vitæ (Fla.). Ironwood (Fla.).

+**b.** Attrib. with *club, mortar, sheaf.*

1742 *Md. Hist. Mag.* XX. 176, I would have them [*sc.* blocks for small boats] Lignum Vitae sheaves and pins. **1855** M. THOMPSON *Doesticks* xxxii. 283, I, too, felt a desire to serve the city by . . . carrying a lignum-vitae club. **1869** PUTNAM *Receipt Bk.* 318 It is quite . . . necessary to have . . . a lignum-vitae mortar.

Like, *a.* +*To feel like,* (see FEEL *v.* 2).

Likely-looking, *a.* Handsome, capable, strong, promising, etc. *colloq.* {1864–, *dial.*} — **1805** MCCLURE *Diary* 10 He had several likely looking children. **1898** WESTCOTT *D. Harum* 10 That's a putty likely-lookin' hoss. **1902** LORIMER *Lett. Merchant* 181, I noticed one of the boys on the mailing-desk, a mighty likely-looking youngster.

Lilac. {*attrib.* 1625–}

1. A shrub belonging to any one of numerous varieties of *Syringa,* esp. *S. vulgaris,* prized for its showy and fragrant blossoms. {1658–}

1786 WASHINGTON *Diaries* III. 12 The buds of the lylack were much swelled and seemed ready to unfold. **1842** KIRKLAND *Forest Life* I. 52 Lilacs and lilies, and even cauliflower and celery are mere superfluities. **1863** A. D. WHITNEY *F. Gartney* xxii, Up among the lilacs and evergreens, and barberries. **1868** — *P. Strong* 35 Wide turf spaces . . . under lilacs, snowballs, and seringas, and horse-chestnuts and maples. **1912** NICHOLSON *Hoosier Chron.* 114 Lilacs and snowballs bloomed, and Professor Kelton went serenely about among his roses.

+**2.** A shrub of the genus *Ceanothus,* esp. the blue myrtle, *C. thyrsiflorus.* Chiefly Pacific Coast.

1872 MCCLELLAN *Golden State* 163 In the State [of Calif.] are the wild nutmeg, . . . lilac, cherry, plum, grape-vine, vine-maple, and sequoia. **1889** *Garden & Forest* II. 279/1 The Ceanothus in these mountains [of the Santa Cruz range] are commonly called 'Lilacs.' **1896** *Amer. Folk-Lore* IX. 184 Rhamnaceæ. . . . *Ceanothus divaricatus,* Nutt., lilac, Santa Barbara County, Cal.

Lilac bush. =LILAC 1. — **1854** CUMMINS *Lamplighter* 150 A Persian lilac-bush in full bloom sent up a delicious fragrance. **1875** STOWE *We & Neighbors* 462 Doesn't it seem as if our bright, cosy, happy, free-and-easy home was throwing out as many side-shoots as a lilac bush. **1879** HOWELLS *Lady of Aroostook* 2 The hens were burrowing for coolness in the soft earth under the lilac bushes. **1902** *Harper's Mag.* May 943 Under a lilac-bush Lizbeth made mud pies, and the pies of the enchanted garden were the brownest and richest in all Our Yard.

***Lily.**

1. a. A plant or flower belonging to any one of numerous species of the genus *Lilium* or of the family Liliaceae. **b.** Any of numerous other plants or flowers having a real or fancied resemblance to the true lily.

1682 ASH *Carolina* 13 [Planters'] Gardens also begin to be beautified and adorned with . . . The Rose, Tulip, Carnation and Lilly, &c. **1778** CARVER *Travels* 520 Heart's Ease, Lilies red and yellow [are seen]. **1850** *New Eng. Farmer* II. 126/2 Lilies . . . are all fine. **1894** *Amer. Folk-Lore* VII. 102 *Erythronium albidum*, lily, Peoria, Ill. **1904** STRATTON-PORTER *Freckles* 365 Thistles grow from thistles, and lilies grow other lilies.

2. With defining or modifying term.

1672 JOSSELYN *New Eng. Rarities* 42 Red Lillies grow all over the Country innumerably amongst the small Bushes. **1806** LEWIS in *L. & Clark Exped.* (1905) V. 165 Neare our encampment we saw a great number of the yellow lilly with reflected petals in blume. **1843** TORREY *Flora N.Y.* II. 305 *Lilium superbum*. . . . Turk's-cap, or Superb Lily. . . . Moist meadows. **1885** F. M. CRAWFORD *Amer. Politician* 301 [She looked] down at the wild white lilies which she had been gathering.

3. Attrib. with *bed, pond, soup.* (Cf. LILY PAD, etc.)

1847 MAGOFFIN *Down Santa Fé Trail* 206 Here and there a rose bush, a lilly bed, or something of the kind. *a***1862** THOREAU *Maine Woods* 284 After the regular supper we attempted to make a lily soup of the bulbs which I had brought along. **1880** *Harper's Mag.* June 80 The blue flowers of the flag . . . deck the borders of the lily pond.

Lily iron. (See quotation 1839.) — **1839** STORER *Mass. Fishes* 51 The fishermen capture it [the swordfish] by means of an instrument called a 'lily iron,' from the form of its shafts or wings, which resemble the leaves of a lily. **1879** *Nat. Museum Bul.* No. 14, 83 Spears with detachable heads. Lily-irons. **1885** HOLDER *Marvels of Animal Life* 61 The harpooner found support and security when wielding his lily-iron. **1897** *Outing* XXIX. 470/1 The lily-iron is a short powerful harpoon . . . capable of killing at a single blow.

***Lily of the valley. a.** A perennial stemless herb (*Convallaria majalis*) having a creeping rootstock and producing fragrant, white, bell-shaped flowers; also, the flower itself. **+b.** One or other of various wild flowers resembling this. — **1815** *Lit. & Phil. Soc. N.Y.* I. 172 Our Dutch forefathers . . . introduced . . . lily of the valley, ladies' rose, violet, and gold flower. **1835** HOFFMAN *Winter in West* I. 145, I could fancy . . . the snow-white lily of the valley, the lilac-tinted adder's-tongue [etc.]. **1850** S. F. COOPER *Rural Hours* 104 The pretty little lily of the valley . . . grows wild in the Southern Alleghanies. **1892** *Amer. Folk-Lore* V. 104 *Maianthemum Canadense*, lily-of-the-valley; two-leaved Solomon's seal. N.H. **1892** M. A. JACKSON *Gen. Jackson* 473 His dear face was wreathed with the lovely lily of the valley. **1894** *Amer. Folk-Lore* VII. 93 *Pyrola elliptica*, . . . wild lily-of-the-valley, Concord, Mass.

+Lily pad. The broad flat leaf of the water lily. — **1814** BIGELOW *Florula Bostoniensis* 132 *Nymphœa advena*. Yellow water lily. . . . The floating leaves of this . . . are well known to anglers under the name of lily pads. **1847** PARKMAN in *Knickerb.* XXIX. 500 Three turtles . . . tumbled themselves off a broad 'lily pod' [*sic*]. **1883** *Century Mag.* XXVI. 383 Among the lily-pads, deer-tongue, and other aquatic plants. **1903** W. J. LONG *Beasts of Field* 100 A big pickerel, coming back to his den under the bank after his frog-hunting among the lily pads.

+Lily-padded, *a.* [f. prec.] Strewn with lily pads. — **1859** *Harper's Mag.* April 610/1 The lake . . . was not one of ordinary lily-padded lagoons, overrun with tall rank rushes.

***Lily root.** The root of a lily, esp. as used by the Indians for food. — **1682** M. RAWLINSON *Narr. Captivity* 61 They eat also . . . Lilly roots. **1699** E. WARD *Trip New-Eng.* 16 With hard Eggs Pulveriz'd, they [*sc.* the Indians] thicken their Broth; . . . Lilly-Roots, Pumpkins, Milions, and divers sorts of Berries; Cook'd after various manners. **1726** PENHALLOW *Indian Wars* 28 But that which heightened her affliction was being . . . many days together without subsistence, excepting . . . lilly roots. **1902** HULBERT *Forest Neighbors* (1903) 33 The Beaver and his wife left their lodge to look for lily-roots.

Lily-white. {*a*1700-} **+1.** A cosmetic made chiefly of chalk. **+2.** (See quotation.) — **(1) 1858** *Harper's Mag.* Sept. 566/2 Notable ladies . . . used lily white (prepared chalk), and made faces for themselves such as Nature had denied them. **1861** *Vanity Fair* 23 Feb. 85/2 There was the fresh pot of lily-white and the bottle of liquid rouge, just to touch up her cheeks. **(2) 1909** WEBSTER 1251/2 *Lily-white*. . . . One of a faction of Republicans in the South which desires to exclude negroes from the party and from political life generally.

+Lima. =next. — **1856** COZZENS *Sparrowgrass P.* 85 Put the Limas to the right . . . and as for the rest of the seeds, sweep them into the refuse basket. **1862** *Ill. Agric. Soc. Trans.* V. 785 Pole Beans.—Amongst these the Limas deservedly rank the highest. **1870** WARNER *Summer in Garden* ix, I put up the most attractive sort of poles for my limas.

Lima bean. [*Lima*, Peru.] **a.** A dwarf plant (*Phaseolus limensis*), cultivated for its edible fruit. {1834-} **b.** The Sieva bean (*P. lunatus*) or another related species.

1822 *Amer. Jrnl. Science* IV. 173 October 19, the Lima beans and peppers, of the second crop, have come almost to perfection. **1829** EATON *Botany* (ed. 5) 326 *Phaseolus lunatus*, carolina bean, lima bean. **1833** J. BOARDMAN *America* 89 A large species, and of good flavour, lately imported from Peru, called the Lima bean, is already much in vogue. **1859** *Ill. Agric. Soc. Trans.* III. 503 When the Lima beans reach the top of the pole the tops should be pinched off. **1887** *Harper's Mag.* Jan. 307/2 The delicious pale lima bean requires and deserves more attention. **1901** MOHR *Plant Life Ala.* 830 *Phaseolus lunatus*. Lima Bean.

attrib. **1841** *Knickerb.* XVII. 295 Did you look among the cabbages, and among the Lima bean-poles?

***Limb.**

***1.** A leg.

'Now only (esp. *U.S.*) in mock-modest or prudish use' (*O.E.D.*). Cf. quot. 1839 below.

1839 MARRYAT *Diary in Amer.* 1 Ser. II. 245, I am not so particular as some people are, for I know those who always say limb of a table, or limb of a piano-forte. **1888** *Congress. Rec.* 16 March 2178/1 This claimant is laboring under a disability equivalent to the loss of a limb above the knee. **1898** DELAND *Old Chester Tales* 237 She . . . informed him that he might stay until his 'limb' permitted him to walk. **1904** *Courier-Journal* 5 Sept. 1 Her limbs were void of shoes and stockings. **1916** WILSON *Somewhere* 184 'How bad was she hurt?' I asks. The poor thing looks down greatly embarrassed and mumbles: 'She has broken a limb.' 'Leg or arm?' I blurts out, forgetting all delicacy. . . . 'A lower limb,' says he.

attrib. **1895** *N.Y. Dramatic News* 14 Dec. 3/3 May Adams, of burlesque and darkey ditty note, is with Aaron's limb exhibit.

+2. *To get* (someone) *out on a limb*, to get (someone) at a great disadvantage. *colloq.*[2]

1897 LEWIS *Wolfville* 59 Seven of us . . . seein' whatever can we tie down an' brand, when some Mexicans gets us out on a limb.

Limber, *v.* {1748-} *To limber up*, to render limber or supple. — **1870** BEADLE *Utah* 219 [We] took a little hot coffee, . . . limbered up our joints, and traveled on. **1892** HARTE *Col. Starbottle* 182 It'd limber you fellows up to hear it. **1895** *Century Mag.* Sept. 675/2 Most of the boys . . . stops in here for a spell, to limber up their shins by our fire.

Limburger cheese. A moderately firm cheese, made originally in the province of Limburg in Belgium, having a characteristic odor and flavor. — **1871** HOWELLS *Wedding Journey* v. 113 On their plates were odorous crumbs of Limburger cheese. **1880** RANOUS *Diary of Daly Débutante* 224 Someone . . . asked me whether I would have some Limburger cheese! **1883** SWEET & KNOX *Through Texas* 291 Do you see . . . where those old cabbages and those boxes of Limburger cheese are piled?

***Lime,** *n.*[1]

***1.** The product obtained by calcining limestone, sea shells, etc.; quicklime, burnt lime.

*c*1638 *Harvard Rec.* I. 172 In part of payment for lime to be burnt for the Colledge, [£]1. **1662** *Providence Rec.* III. 8 Liberty to burne Lime upon the comon. **1770** WASHINGTON *Diaries* I. 380 Began . . . to carry wood round for burning Lyme. **1805** SIBLEY in *Ann. 9th Congress* 2 Sess. 1095 The lakes likewise afford plenty of shells for lime. **1863** MITCHELL *My Farm* 232 [The young farmer] has hardly seen his lime dumped upon his clover-field. **1912** *Dept. Agric. Yrbk. 1911* 185 The poultryman materially defends himself and his flock when he cleans up with powdered air-slaked lime.

2. Attrib. and comb. with *cask, contractor, hill*, etc.

1654 JOHNSON *Wonder-w. Prov.* 209 Masons, Lime, Brick, and Tilemakers. **1771** *Md. Hist. Mag.* XIV. 129 Give my Service to Mr. Deards & desier Him to send 1 Coarse lime sifter. **1801** *Phila. Ordinances* (1812) 174, I will faithfully . . . perform the duties of a hay, straw, and lime inspector for the city of Philadelphia. **1810** *Columbian Centinel* 17 Jan. 3/1 Wanted, from 50 to 300 Lime Casks. **1857** VAUX *Villas* 65 The outside surfaces of brick walls may . . . [be] covered with a coat of boiled oil, or with a limewash. **1883** SMITH *Geol. Survey Ala.* 255 Where the lignitic clays are so largely developed, the reaction . . . produces . . . a calcareous clayey, prairie, or 'lime-hills' soil. **1889** BRAYLEY *Boston Fire Dept.* 111 It was occupied by Elijah Loring as a lime-store. **1893** *Harper's Mag.* Jan. 287/1 [One student was] the son of a lime-contractor.

***Lime,** *n.*[2] Any one of various trees of the genus *Citrus*, or the fruit of such a tree. Also attrib.

1709 LAWSON *Carolina* 5 These more Southerly Parts will afford Oranges, Limons, Limes, and many other Fruits. **1774** FITHIAN *Journal* I. 206 We had after Dinner, Lime Punch & Madaira. **1812** STODDARD *Sk. Louisiana* 168 The Delta produces various kinds of excellent fruit; such as . . . limes, citrons, and shaddock. **1850** COLTON *3 Years Calif.* 447 He planted the cotton-tree, the lime, and a grove of olives. **1888** *Treasury Dept. Decisions* 125 The [imported] merchandise . . . consists of confectionery made in part of sugar and in part of gum-paste, and commercially known as 'lime-fruit jujubes.' **1917** COIT *Citrus Fruits* 81 Three kinds of limes are grown for home use . . . in California.

***Lime,** *v. tr.* To treat with lime; to dress (land) with lime. {1649-} Also absol. — **1796** J. ADAMS *Diary* Works III. 421 B. and S. making and liming a heap of manure. **1846** *Cultivator* ns. III. 211/2 One portion of his wheat he stirred and sunned *without* liming it. **1854** SIMMS *Southward Ho* 125 Lands which . . . were no longer profitable for tobacco the New-Yorkers have limed for wheat. **1885** *Harper's Mag.* Jan. 279/1 There are diverse opinions as to the relative value of liming or sweating.

***Lime-burner.** One whose occupation is to make lime by burning limestone, sea shells, etc. — **1657** *Charlestown Land Rec.* 144 A sale of a Hous and ground by Richard Arrington, lime burner. **1684** *Boston Rec.* 74 Eliatha Blake, Lyme burner, became surety . . . for William Bolderson. **1834** WEBSTER in Benton *30 Years' View* I. 419/1 This meeting . . . was composed of carpenters, . . . lime burners, plasterers [etc.]. **1898** WESTCOTT *D. Harum* 331 'Let me see it,' she says, in a voice dryer 'n a lime-burner's hat.

Lime-burning. Producing lime by burning limestone, sea shells, etc. — **1794** *Mass. H. S. Coll.* IV. 23 Too great attention [is paid] to lumbering and lime-burning. **1860** ABBOTT *South & North* 196 [Slaves are] employed . . . in lime-burning or fishing. **1881** *Rep. Indian Affairs* p. lviii, The already acquired industries of many of the Indians . . . [include] freighting, brick-making, lime and charcoal burning [etc.].

Lime grass. Variant of LYME GRASS.

Lime house. A temporary structure in which lime is stored. — **1733** *Harvard Rec.* II. 621 Lime-house. [Marginal entry.] Voted, that a small building be set up somewhere about the College, for Lime & mortar. **1807** C. SCHULTZ *Travels* I. 130 In the streets of New-York, where new houses are building, . . . [one finds] a lime-house.

***Limekiln.** A kiln or furnace in which lime is produced. — **1665** [see LIMEROCK]. **1701** *Boston Rec.* 12 No person shall hence forth make and fire any lime Kiln . . . but in such place . . . as the select men . . . shall approve. **1760** WASHINGTON *Diaries* I. 154 Cook Jack's plow was stoped he being employed in setting the Lime Kiln. **1823** COOPER *Pioneers* xx. Bake your cake in yonder lime-kiln. **1880** *Harper's Mag.* Aug. 344/1 Rude stone and timber lime kilns [were] faintly smoking like a row of barbaric fortresses.

Lime mortar. Mortar made of lime. {1839–} — **1701** *Boston Selectmen* 11 John Goodwin agrees to . . . Purge the Chimnyes with good Lime morter. **1764** *N.H. Hist. Soc. Coll.* IX. 168 Capt. Walker's son came and made my lime mortar. **1788** MAY *Jrnl. & Lett.* 27 The buildings are made of hewn logs, the chinks filled in with stones, and plastered over with lime-mortar. **1881** *Rep. Indian Affairs* 121 Boarding school partially complete, . . . walls of hewn logs, finished with lime mortar. **1897** MOORE *How to Build a Home* 19 Take . . . the simple precaution of throwing shovelfuls of ordinary lime-mortar into the hollow spaces.

***Lime pit.** A pit in which lime is utilized in tanning hides. — **1642** *Md. Archives* IV. 283 Thomas Todd . . . bindeth himselfe & his assignes to dresse completely & wth his best art the 46. skins now in the limepitt. **1792** BENTLEY *Diary* I. 365 On the line of Mrs. Webb's garden between his lime pits & Bark House.

Limerick. 1. Attrib. denoting gloves made in, or resembling those made in, Limerick, Ireland. {1804– (Edgeworth *Pop. Tales* 241)} **2.** A fishhook of a shape or design developed in Limerick, Ireland. In full *Limerick hook.* — **(1) 1795** *Columbian Centinel* 10 Jan. 4 Best superfine Limeric, habit and long Gloves. **1836** GILMAN *Recoll.* (1838) 208 Next came Mr. Prentiss, . . . his white shirt-cuffs in full sight over his Limerick gloves. **(2) 1846** *Spirit of Times* 25 April 97/1 He has lately received from 'Piscator,' a dozen of the genuine Limericks. **1856** *Porter's Spirit of Times* 11 Oct. 97/2 [The silver perch] affords good sport to the angler with shrimp bait and a No. 6 or 7 Limerick hook. **1859** *Harper's Mag.* July 165/1 The angler . . . attaches a single strand of gut with a sound Limerick to the end of his line. **1889** *Cent.* 2877/3 *Limerick hook,* a fish-hook . . . better adapted for artificial flies than for use with bait.

Limerock. a. A rock composed of limestone. **b.** =LIMESTONE. {1799} — **1665** *Providence Rec.* III. 66 Those Lime Rockes about Hackletons lime Killne shal be perpetually Common. **1783** *Mem. Academy* II. I. 44 The bank adjoining some of the principal springs is very steep, and bound with a broken ledge of lime rocks. **1813** *Niles' Reg.* V. Suppl. 189/2 Most of them were found enclosed in the softer kind of lime-rock. **1846** FARNHAM *Prairie Land* 300 A bold bluff of lime-rock rises abruptly. **1876** RAYMOND *8th Rep. Mines* 177 To the west of the lode a lime-rock comes in.

+**Lime sink.** *Geol.* A depression or sink hole in a limestone region. Also attrib. — **1837** WILLIAMS *Florida* 148 Nearly allied to these springs, are the sink holes, or lime sinks that are scattered all over the Territory. **1842** LYELL *Trav. N.A.* (1845) I. 176 Lime-sinks or funnel-shaped cavities, are frequent in this country arising from natural tunnels and cavities in the subjacent limestone. **1883** SMITH *Geol. Survey Ala.* 286 [The] Lime Sink Region . . . embraces an area of 6,570 square miles.

***Limestone.**

***1.** A species of rock composed chiefly of carbonate of lime.

1630 HIGGINSON *New-England* 7 Lime-stone, Free-stone, and Smooth-stone, . . . are in such store, that we haue great Rockes of it. **1709** LAWSON *Carolina* 82 We make our Lime of Oyster-Shells, tho' we have great Store of Lime-stone, towards the Heads of our Rivers. **1781–2** JEFFERSON *Notes Va.* (1788) 30 We see calcareous dropstones generating every day by the percolation of water through limestone. **1818** SCHOOLCRAFT *Journal* 47 The west bank of the river, at this place, consists of a rugged wall of lime-stone. **1882** *Econ. Geol. Illinois* II. 112 The limestone also forms the bank of the creek, from the low-water mark upward. **1916** THOBURN *Stand. Hist. Okla.* I. 4 The rock formations . . . include those commonly known as limestone, sandstone, granite, gypsum, and shale.

2. Attrib. with *belt, fence, prairie,* etc.

See also LIMESTONE COUNTRY, etc.

1775 FITHIAN *Journal* II. 104 From the top of the arch, upwards, . . . it is 45 feet; all which is solid Lime-stone rock. **1818** *Amer. Jrnl. Science* I. 219 Every where . . . [one] hears of 'limestone water.' **1821** FOWLER *Journal* 14 At 6 miles over High Rich lime stone pirarie We Camped. **1831** PECK *Guide* 14 The remainder [of the Mississippi Valley] is made up of abrupt hills, flint and limestone ridges, bluffs, and ravines. **1849** CHAMBERLAIN *Indiana Gazetteer* 191 The strip along the river . . . has a limestone soil. **1873** RAYMOND *Silver & Gold* 56 The limestone belt, on which are found the early placers noted for their immense yield from 1850–1855. **1892** J. L. ALLEN *Blue-Grass Region* 28 One hears of fewer lime-stone fences of late years.

Limestone country. A region on or near the surface of which limestone abounds. — **1781–2** JEFFERSON *Notes Va.* (1788) 31 In the limestone country are many caves, the earthy floors of which are impregnated with nitre. **a1817** DWIGHT *Travels* II. 374 From this line . . . the limestone country commences; and continues as far West at least as Lake Erie. **1847** PALMER *Rocky Mts.* 44 We found a limestone country, quite hilly, indeed almost mountainous. **1884** 'CRADDOCK' *Where Battle Was Fought* 1 The railway train thundering through the cavernous limestone country.

Limestone land. Land which abounds in limestone. {1685–} — **1805** PARKINSON *Tour* 71 The General's [Washington's] land is of great note, being what is termed limestone land, and more productive than any other in that country. **1816** U. BROWN *Journal* I. 270 Thence 12 Miles through a Beautiful Level country & rich Lime stone Land. **1836** EDWARD *Hist. Texas* 90 According to the quantity of lime-stone, and limestone land abounding, so did moss abound also. **1843** N. BOONE *Journal* 193 After getting on the limestone land a great change was observed in the vegetation.

Limestone spring. A spring the water of which is impregnated with carbonate of lime. — **1802** ELLICOTT *Journal* 240 The principal source of the Apalachy, is from a single lime stone spring. **1834** A. PIKE *Sketches* 62 About ten we arrived at a large clear limestone spring. **1843** *Nat. Hist. N.Y., Geology* I. 81 In Greene county, tufa was seen near a limestone spring three miles west of Athens. **1878** in Summers *Ann. S.W. Va.* (1929) 1615 On one farm . . . there are six springs, viz.: a chalybeate, alum, magnesia, sulphur, limestone and freestone.

Lime tree.[1] A tree of the genus *Citrus.* {1748} — **1666** *S.C. Hist. Coll.* II. 13 They have . . . Lime-trees; Orange, Lemon, and other Fruit-trees. **1765** J. BARTRAM *Journal* 11 This was the fatal night that destroyed the lime, citron and banana-trees in Augustine. **1847** WOOD *Botany* 205 *C[itrus] Limeta.* Lime Tree. . . . This like most other species, is native of Asia. **1883** *Century Mag.* Oct. 818/2 [On a ranch in s. Calif. are] a few orange, lemon, and lime trees.

Lime tree.[2] The European or American linden, *Tilia europaea* or *glabra,* or a related species. {1625–}

Cf. AMERICAN LIME(-TREE).

1785 WASHINGTON *Diaries* II. 343 Also four Lime or Linden Trees, sent by Govr. Clinton. **1814** PURSH *Flora Amer.* II. 362 This tree is known by the name of Lime- or Line-tree; Basswood; Spoonwood. **1832** BROWNE *Sylva* 307 In the maritime parts of the Carolinas and of Georgia, it has received no specific denomination and is simply called Lime Tree, to which we have added the epithet Downy. **1846** — *Trees Amer.* 39 *Tilia europaea.* European Lime-tree. **1847** DARLINGTON *Weeds & Plants* 68 European Tilia. Linden, or Lime tree. European Linden. **1897** SUDWORTH *Arborescent Flora* 301 *Tilia americana* Linn. Basswood. . . . Common Names [include] . . . Limetree (R.I., N.C., S.C., Ala., Miss., La., Ill.).

Limewater. a. A solution of lime in water. Used in medicine and commerce. {1677–} **b.** Limestone water. — **1666** *Maryland Archives* II. 124 For Lyme water 1/2 a pint . . . 4 lb. Tob[acco]. **1789** MORSE *Amer. Geog.* 265 Some lime-water, made of abalactiles brought from the subterranean cave at Rhinebec. **1811** *Niles' Reg.* I. 31/1 Soak the wheat in weak ley or lime water, brine or chamberlye. **1846** FARNHAM *Prairie Land* 146 The tender of a barrel of rain-water, . . . those only can appreciate who have undertaken to clean such a house with lime-water, and that to be brought a distance of some dozen rods.

+**Limited,** *n.* A limited train. Often the name of a particular train. (Cf. LIMITED *a.* 1.) — **1887** *Pop. Science Mo.* March 577 Let . . . the limited crash through a trestle. **1898** HAMBLEN *Gen'l Manager's Story* 179 There was no earthly hope of getting to the next siding ahead of the limited. **1904** *N.Y. Ev. Post* 6 May 2 The Sunset Limited of the Southern Pacific encountered a severe hailstorm. **1912** NICHOLSON *Hoosier Chron.* 600 You said you meant to get back to the city in time to catch that limited for New York.

***Limited,** *a.*

1. Of a railroad train: Making few stops; restricted as to the number of passengers carried or the type of accommodations provided. {1883–}

1879 STOCKTON *Rudder Grange* ix, Time flew like a 'limited express' train. **1887** *Courier-Journal* 20 Jan. 5/4 The New York limited express . . . arrived in the city at 10:30. **1890** *Harper's Mag.* Aug. 409/1 Coming up by the limited train, Miss Lee was not favorably impressed. **1904** *Dial* 16 Oct. 238 It is not a book for the limited express. **1918** *Gt. Lakes Recruit* Jan. 85 Special limited trains will leave Great Lakes for Chicago at 4:15 P.M. and every 10 minutes thereafter until 5:30 P.M.

+**2.** Of a railroad ticket: (See quot. 1891).

1891 *Cent.* 6328/2 *Limited ticket,* in railroad usage, a ticket not giving the holder all the privileges given by an ordinary ticket, as, for instance, one limited to a trip commenced on a specified day, or by a particular train, or excluding the right to break the journey by stopping on the way and taking a later train. **1899** MUIRHEAD *Baedeker's U.S.* p. xxi, A distinction is frequently made between 'Limited' and 'Unlimited' tickets.

***Limner.** A painter, esp. one who paints portraits. — **1701** *Boston Rec.* 8 Lawrence Brown, a Limner, asks admittance. **1796** *Boston Direc-*

tory 251 Gulagher, Christian, limner, Tremont street. **1854** BENTON *30 Years' View* I. 358/2 The graphic limner was in the eighty-sixth and last year of his life. **1885** EGGLESTON in *Century Mag.* April 879/1 The paintings . . . were portraits . . . made by some struggling provincial 'limner'—that was the genteel word [in the 18th century].

+**Limpkin.** =CARAU. — **1883** *Nat. Museum Bul.* No. 27, 156 Limpkin. . . . Greater Antilles, Florida, and coasts of Central America. **1917** *Birds of Amer.* I. 202 Limpkins at times are very noisy creatures.

Limpsy, *a.* Limp, lazy, flaccid. *colloq.* {1825 *dial.*} — **1833** S. SMITH *Major Downing* 147 Let a feller be all worn out and wilted down as limpsy as a rag. **1869** STOWE *Oldtown Folks* 343 There comes Sam Lawson down the hill, limpsy as ever. **1880** DEMING *Adirondack Stories* 168 [There was a] gradual weakening of the young man in the paws of the panther, until he became 'limpsy.' **1911** QUICK *Yellowstone Nights* 231 Hen fell back into his chair limpsy, like dropping a wet string.

***Lincoln.** A sheep of a breed developed in Lincolnshire, England; in pl., this breed of sheep or (quot. 1851) its breeders. {1837-} — **1851** L. A. MORRELL *Amer. Shepherd* 124 There was a long . . . contest between the Leicesters and the Lincolns for the point of supremacy. **1863** RANDALL *Pract. Shepherd* 50 The Lincolns are a less improved and larger variety of long-wools. **1869** *Ill. Agric. Soc. Trans.* VII. 454 Others, like the Lincolns and Leicesters, prefer moist, rich, alluvial valleys. **1914** *Farmers' Bul.* No. 576, 11 The Lincoln is shorter . . . than the Cotswold.

+**Lincoln Brotherhood.** [See LINCOLNITE.] (See quot. 1892.) *Obs.*— **1885** in Fleming *Hist. Reconstruction* II. 20 In order to work the negro with greater facility in the interest of Osborn and his gang, this secret league was named the Lincoln Brotherhood. **1892** WALSH *Lit. Curiosities* 637 *Lincoln Brotherhood*, political associations of negroes in the South after the close of the civil war, to protect their rights of suffrage.

+**Lincolndom.** [See LINCOLNITE.] During the Civil War a nickname used in the South for the northern section of the United States. — **1862** *N.Y. Tribune* 14 June 2/3 We hope our [Confederate] Government will soon find some means of marching an army into that State [Ky.]. . . . A more serious blow could not be struck at Lincolndom. **1862** in Moore *Rebellion Rec.* V. II. 11 To the B'hoys from Lincolndom—from Dixie.

+**Lincolnism.** [See next.] The political principles and policies of Abraham Lincoln. *Obs.* — **1861** in Richardson *Secret Service* 184 The whole power of Lincolnism is broken in the West. **1862** in Moore *Rebellion Rec.* V. II. 183 The city [of Memphis] is conquered, but her people are not crushed, or converted to Lincolnism.

+**Lincolnite.** [Abraham *Lincoln* (1809–65).] A believer in the political principles and policies of Abraham Lincoln; a Northern soldier or sympathizer in the Civil War. Now hist.

1861 in Kettell *Hist. Rebellion* I. 233 A squad of twelve men were sent . . . to arrest some Lincolnites. **1863** HOPLEY *Life in South* I. 361 The Lincolnites will see that it is useless to attempt to conquer us by force of arms. **1864** PITTENGER *Daring & Suffering* 49 Among other things we instanced to show the tyranny of the Lincolnites in Kentucky, was the expatriation law. **1888** BILLINGS *Hardtack* 20 Someone who was not a 'Lincolnite' would exclaim, in an angry tone. **1901** CHURCHILL *Crisis* 152 There lacked not detractors who swore that John Dibble and other Lincolnites had applied for torches for the mere pleasure of carrying them.

attrib. **1862** in Moore *Rebellion Rec.* V. II. 181, I leave this office to any Lincolnite successor.

+**Lincoln's finch.** [See first quot.] =next. — **1834** AUDUBON *Ornith. Biog.* II. 539 Lincoln's Finch. *Fringilla Lincolnii.* . . . I named it *Tom's Finch*, in honour of our friend [Thomas] Lincoln, who was a great favourite among us. **1872** in Coues *Birds N.W.* 136 Lincoln's Finch is abundant, and migratory [in Colorado]. **1917** *Birds of Amer.* III. 53.

+**Lincoln('s) sparrow.** [See prec., quot. 1834.] A small sparrow (*Melospiza lincolni*), found in the United States. — **1870** *Amer. Naturalist* III. 581 In avoiding the North-eastern states it resembles . . . *Melospiza Lincolnii* (Lincoln's Sparrow). **1874** COUES *Birds N.W.* 135 Lincoln's Sparrow. . . . In the Atlantic States it is apparently rare. **1917** *Birds of Amer.* III. 54/2 The food of the Lincoln Sparrow resembles that of the Song Sparrow.

***Linden.** +An American species of the genus *Tilia*, as *T. glabra;* the wood of such a tree. (Cf. AMERICAN LINDEN.)

1781-2 JEFFERSON *Notes Va.* (1788) 38 Linden, or lime. *Tilia Americana.* **a1797** Imlay *Western Territory* (ed. 3) 149 The sap . . . is carried and poured into store troughs . . . made of white ash, linden, bass wood, or white pine. **1819** E. DANA *Geogr. Sk.* 225 On the waters of Mermentau are several species of oak, . . . pine, linden, laurel, magnolia. **1848** BRYANT *California* iii. 44 The trees are chiefly oak, linden, and hickory. **1892** APGAR *Trees Northern U.S.* 72 Basswood. Whitewood. Linden. . . . Wild in rich woods and often cultivated. **1901** MOHR *Plant Life Ala.* 613 Maple, white ash, chestnut, and linden, indicate calcareous, fertile, and somewhat heavy strong soils.

+**b.** Attrib. with *tree.*

1823 JAMES *Exped.* I. 63 The linden tree attains great magnitude in the low grounds of the Missouri. **1860** MORDECAI *Virginia* viii. 122 Mr. Ellis's garden, embellished by a row of fine Linden trees. **1884** ROE *Nature's Story* 219 The linden-tree . . . furnishes the richest harvest for the honey-bees.

+**Lindentree borer.** (See quotation.) — **1854** EMMONS *Agric. N.Y.* V. 262 (*index*), [121. The *Saperda (Oberea) tripunctata* . . . attacks the linden, and, by burrowing beneath the bark, destroys the vitality of the tree].

***Line,** *n.*

I. ***1.** =FISHING LINE.

1634 WOOD *New Eng. Prospect* (1865) 38 These Macrills are taken with drails which is a long small line, with a lead and hooke at the end of it. **1765** TIMBERLAKE *Memoirs* 43 The Indians catch the fish with lines, spears, or dams. **1855** SIMMS *Forayers* 277 She was to make my lines for me—yet see what I have to fish with now—old cotton strings. **1899** VAN DYKE *Fisherman's Luck* 199 The only possible method of angling was to let the line . . . drift down the current. **1918** MULFORD *Man from Bar-20* 45 Ought to have some line, too; an' a reel somewheres.

2. *pl.* Reins used in driving. {1895 *dial.*} Also fig.

1833 S. SMITH *Major Downing* 190 Ever since they told the Squire to take the lines, they haint lost a linchpin. **1845** HOOPER *Taking Census* 120 Uncle Kit reassuming the lines, said—'Well, *now* I'm off sure.' **1905** RICE *Sandy* 250 She tried to take the lines, but he held her hands.

3. An electric wire, as for telegraphic or telephonic communication. {1851-}

1878 PINKERTON *Strikers* 199 The strikers certainly had some experienced telegraphers . . . capable of tapping the line. **1885** CUSTER *Boots & Saddles* 70 The Indians had such a superstition about molesting the wires, that the lines ran through even the most dangerous country. **1914** *Lit. Digest* 14 March 576/3 He had fixt the broken line and kept business going.

II. 4. +**a.** The boundary of a colonial town or colony. Sometimes preceded by a proper name.

1638 *Charlestown Land Rec.* 21 Foure acres of earable land by estimation . . . butting southwest upon Cambridge line, northeast upon the bridge way. **1640** *R.I. Col. Rec.* I. 109 Which line . . . is the Bounds between the Two Townes and to be sett out by marked Trees. **1648** *Providence Rec.* XIV. 37 On ye Southerne Side of Boston Line. **1702** *Conn. H. S. Coll.* VI. 206 The boundaries or Line between the Said towns on the East side the great River. **1746** E. KIMBER *Itinerant Observ.* 43 The next Night we got to the Line that divides Maryland from Virginia.

+**b.** The boundary between the United States and Canada or between the United States and Spanish possessions or Mexico.

1809 KENDALL *Travels* III. 259 The earlier counterfeiters . . . had commenced their business in Canada, or as it is here called, on the other side of *the line.* **1818** *Niles' Reg.* XIV. 64/2 They shield themselves under the protection of the Spanish line—but that line will not be respected if hostilities are carried on within it. **1827** PICKERING *Inquiries Emigrant* (1831) 92 The inhabitants are . . . 'blue bellies' of all sorts and condition, equal to any of the frontier towns on both sides of the 'lines.' **1854** PIERCE in *Pres. Mess. & P.* V. 280 The commission to establish the new line between the United States and Mexico . . . has been organized. **1910** RAINE *B. O'Connor* 53 He lit out across the line for Mexico.

+**c.** The boundary between the northern and the southern states. (Cf. MASON AND DIXON'S LINE.)

1845 F. DOUGLASS *Narrative* 101 We owe something to the slaves south of the line as well as to those north of it. **1881-5** MCCLELLAN *Own Story* 30 Events were precipitated . . . by the violent course of a comparatively small number of men, on both sides of the line. **1904** 'O. HENRY' *Roads of Destiny* 358 If you had come from below the line, I reckon I would have liked you right smart.

+**d.** The boundary of a state.

1869 TOURGEE *Toinette* xxviii. 296 Buck Lloyd . . . had a plantation over the line in Virginia. **1880** *Harper's Mag.* Sept. 535/1 Near the Tennessee line their huts are often merely sheds. **1890** *Stock Grower & Farmer* 22 Feb. 8/2 The southern canal . . . will irrigate more than 100,000 acres on the west side of the river, north of the Texas line. **1913** LONDON *Valley of Moon* III. xv, Wait till you get across the Oregon line into the Rogue River Valley.

+**5.** *pl.* The frontier.

1840 COOPER *Pathfinder* III. v, I do not think a truer-hearted lad lives on the lines than Jasper Western.

III. 6. +**a.** A system of communication or transportation operated over a particular route or way. (Cf. 7 a.)

1781 JEFFERSON *Writings* IV. 390 A Quartermaster is employed in establishing a similar line from hence to the army before Portsmouth. **1816** *Ann. 14th Congress* 1 Sess. 113 So great was the carriage . . . of goods . . . that it became necessary to use four distinct lines of transportation. **1837** in E. E. Sparks *Expansion* (1901) 277 Pioneer Fast Line, by Rail Road Cars and Canal Packets, From Philadelphia to Pittsburgh. **1847** ROBB *Squatter Life* 112 [Newspaper proprietors] have been . . . prating all along . . . about expresses to Washington, railroads to Oregon, regular lines to California [etc.].

+**b.** A number of public conveyances operated in succession over a regular route by one management. Used esp. of stagecoaches and boats. {1848-}

1786 *Boston Centinel* 11 Jan. 3/1 (Ernst), A line of stages. **1815** *Niles' Reg.* IX. 215/1 Completing a line of steam-boats . . . from New London to Baltimore. **1818** *Ib.* XIV. 14/2 A regular line of waggons and packets are established between the city of New-York and Detroit. **1835** *S. Lit. Messenger* IV. 92/2 The 'Kentucky' . . . belongs to the established line between Baltimore and Richmond. **1852** *Harper's Mag.* V. 545/1 A series of resolutions was adopted in favor of . . . liberal appropriations by Congress for a line of steamers between San Francisco and China and Japan. **1886** Poore *Reminisc.* I. 37 Stage books for the Providence line were kept in Boston. **1925** Bryan *Memoirs* 322 The ship belonged to the Ward line.

+**c.** A series *of* traps.

1857 Hammond *Northern Scenes* 331 We talk about a *line* of traps, because we blaze a line of trees, sometimes for miles, and set a trap every twenty or thirty rods. **1917** *Birds of Amer.* II. 216/2 The Magpie beat him in running the line of traps.

7. a. A railroad or a continuous part of a railroad. {1825–} (Cf. 6 a.)

1842 *Western R.R. Corp. Proc.* 16 In the spring of 1840 the Department requested us to put a mail-car on the line. **1872** Tice *Over Plains* 77 The land grant of Congress extends the whole length of the line. **1882** McCabe *New York* 187 During the five-cent hours the trains on all the [elevated] lines are crowded. **1890** *Stock Grower & Farmer* 22 Feb. 8/2 The important line of the Santa Fe system . . . will pass through the lands. **1897** *Boston Morning Herald* 11 Aug. 8/3 The Illinois Central has placed on all its western lines cafe cars, in which meals are served a la carte. **1903** E. Johnson *Railway Transportation* 242 The three California lines established a Transcontinental Freight Rate Committee.

+**b.** =Pipe line.

[**1881** *Mich. Gen. Statutes* I. (1882) 954 Any number of persons, not less than five, may form a company for the purpose of constructing and operating . . . a line or lines of pipes (pipe), for the conveying and transporting therein of brine.] **1904** Tarbell *Hist. Standard Oil Co.* I. 18 From the start the line was a success, carrying eighty barrels of oil an hour.

+**8.** *Baseball.* =Base line 2.

1868 Chadwick *Base Ball* 40 A fair ball is one sent from the bat and striking the ground *forward* of the lines of the bases.

IV. +**9. a.** A local division of a militia or fighting force. *Obs.* **b.** The fighting or combat force of the army or navy. {1802–, in narrower sense}

1781 *New Hampshire Hist. Soc. Coll.* IX. 242 A Devision Court Martial [was] hild in the Connecticut Line by order of Majr. Genl. Parson. **1844** *Whig Almanac 1845* 34/1 Pursers of Ships of the Line. **1866** H. Phillips *Hist. Sk. Paper Currency* 2 Ser. 148 The Connecticut line [in 1779–80] . . . assembled to return to their homes. **1870** *Nation* 17 March 169/2 The staff people . . . suffer many . . . slights at the hands of the line, because they possess no rank. **1881–5** McClellan *Own Story* 108 The organized armies . . . consist of two well-defined parts: the fighting force, or 'line,' and 'the staff.'

+**10.** *Football.* The players lined up even with the ball before the action of a down begins.

1887 *Century Mag.* Oct. 891/2 The two players on the ends of the line, the 'end-rushes,' stand slightly back of the main line. **1909** *Cap & Gown* 199 The line [of the Minnesota team] was said to weigh a Ton. **1920** *Ib.* 353 The line stiffened and held Illinois in four line drives.

+**11.** *fig.* A stock or supply of goods or commodities kept or offered for sale; a class, kind, or variety of goods. {an order for goods, 1882–}

1875 *Chicago Tribune* 7 Dec. 5/7 A full line of Fur Beaver and Chinchilla Cloaks, very cheap. **1886** *Harper's Mag.* June 93/1 Different lines of sugar have different names. **1902** Norris *Pit* ix, How are we going to unload our big line of wheat without breaking the price on us? **1906** 'O. Henry' *Four Million* 121 'Ikey,' said he, . . . 'get busy with your ear It's drugs for me if you've got the line I need.'

V. In phrases.

12. *To read the line,* =Deacon *v.* 1. {to give out the line, 1827–, *Sc.;* 1867 *Sc.*}

1779 E. Parkman *Diary* 96 Ps. 149 . . . was sung without reading the lines by the Deacon.

+**13.** *W. To ride the line,* to go on horseback along the boundary of an area in order to recover straying cattle or to mend fences. (Cf. Line-rider, -riding.)

1888 Roosevelt in *Century Mag.* March 669/1 Even for those who do not have to look up stray horses, and who are not forced to ride the line . . . there is apt to be some hardship. [**1923** J. H. Cook *On Old Frontier* 49 Indians had crawled up within about fifteen feet of the line where he was riding.]

+**14.** *To run a line,* to survey or mark out a boundary. Also fig.

1641 *R.I. Col. Rec.* I. 114 Mr. Porter . . . and Mr. Jeoffreys shall run the line between the Touns. **1679** *Dedham Rec.* V. 82 A order from Roxbury select men to rune the line betwixt thier Towne and ours. **1700** *Braintree Rec.* 46 A committe [was chosen] to Run the line with Weymouth men between ye Towns land & Mr. Torreys neck. **1721** *Mass. H. Rep. Jrnl.* III. 196 The Committee Appointed to Run the Line, between Dighton and Taunton. **1797** *Ann. 5th Congress* I. 42 The Commissioners may not run the line as the Indians expect. **1850** Hines *Voyage* 198 Here was no jumping of claims, but . . . all were satisfied to select from that part of the vast surface of the whale around which lines had not been run. **1892** Gunter *Miss Dividends* 63 He ran the lines in Nebraska when that State was a howling wilderness.

VI. In attributive use.

+**15. a.** In sense 4 a. **b.** In sense 6 b. **c.** In sense 9. **d.** In sense 1. **e.** In sense 3. **f.** In sense 10.

(**a**) **1638** *Charlestown Land Rec.* 1 Eight acres of earable land by estimation, more or lesse, scituate in the line feilde. **1680** *Derby Rec.* 118 The Towne . . . impower[s] ye sd men to Conclude ye line place & places. (**b**) **1842** Emerson *Transcendentalist* 347 The storm-tossed vessel at sea speaks the frigate or 'line-packet' to learn its longitude. (**c**) *a***1861** Winthrop *Open Air* 273 Our handsome Colonel . . . manoeuvres his thousand men of the line-companies on the parade for two or three hours. **1866** Moore *Women of War* 102 Convalescents, not able to return to line duty, were successively detailed for this purpose. (**d**) **1884** *Nat. Museum Bul.* No. 27, 963 *Line-floats.* Series of egg-shaped wooden floats with wood and quill tops. **1895** *Outing* XXX. 432/1 The local angler . . . still fishes with worms, minnows, . . . or any favorite line bait from his boat. (**e**) **1904** Stratton-Porter *Freckles* 45 A handful of crumbs on the top of a locust line-post. **1911** Quick *Yellowstone Nights* 32, I'm just through with a summer's line-work in the West. (**f**) **1907** *St. Nicholas* Sept. 1013/2 There was some discussion last year as to whether a line man could run from his position in the line and take the ball from the quarter. **1920** Line drive [see sense 10].

+**16.** Special combinations.

Line-ball, (see quotation); *Line road,* a road along the boundary line of a township or municipality.

1868 Chadwick *Base Ball* 42 A line ball is one sent from the bat, or thrown by a fielder on a line with the fielder to whom the ball is hit or thrown. **1881** *Mich. Gen. Statutes* I. (1882) 389 Whenever a line road shall have been laid out.

∗**Line,** *v.*

+**1.** *tr.* =Deacon *v.* 1. Freq. with *out.*

1822 *Mass. Spy* 13 Feb. (Th.), I was very sorry to observe that our custom of lining out the hymn as sung scarcely exists [on the Atlantic Coast]. **1859** *Harper's Mag.* Aug. 420/2 The old style [in Methodist churches] was [for] a 'brother' to 'lead the singing,' while the hymn was *lined* by the minister. **1875** Temple & Sheldon *Hist. Northfield, Mass.* 318 As few, except the pastor and deacons had books, it was customary to 'deacon' or 'line' the psalm. **1890** *Harper's Mag.* May 895/1 He does line out hymns beautiful.

+**2.** To trace (wild bees) to their hive by observing their line of flight.

1827 Cooper *Prairie* v, May I never hear the hum of another bee, or . . . fail in sight to line him to his hive! **1852** Thoreau *Autumn* 44 As none [of the bees] flew in the right direction for us, we did not attempt to line them. **1879** Burroughs *Locusts & Wild Honey* 20 Lining them [the bees] as well as I could, I soon reached the hilltop.

transf. **1827** Cooper *Prairie* xiv, We have lined the squatter into his most secret misdoings.

+**3.** (See quotation.)

1871 De Vere 131 Mules . . . are *lined* [rather than hobbled], that is, the forefoot is tied to the hindfoot on the same side.

+**4.** To straighten (railroad track).

1872 Huntington *Road-Master's Assistant* 66 Many suppose that after track is once well lined it needs no further attention.

‖**5.** To assign or accustom (a person) *to* a particular type of work.

1886 *Phila. Times* 21 March (*Cent.*), No actor of American birth and training can be lined to this class of work.

+**6.** (See quotation.)

1891 *Fur, Fin, & Feather* March 190 The lost camper . . . [should] look straight ahead and fix his eyes on some object on a line with him. Having walked to that object, he should line himself to another, and so on.

+**7.** *intr.* To fish with a line. *rare.*

1833 J. V. C. Smith *Mass. Fishes* 262 [The squeteague] is taken both by lining and seining.

+**8.** To border or form a line *with* something.

1881 *Harper's Mag.* Feb. 433/2 Three hundred acres of good fresh land, lining, on the east side, . . . with the Booker estate.

9. *To line out.* {1618–} (See also sense 1.) +**a.** *Baseball.* To hit (a ball) so that it follows a more or less low, straight line for a considerable distance.

1887 *Courier-Journal* 26 May 2/6 He smashed the first ball that came over the plate, and lined out a beautiful hit past second base. *Ib.* 27 May 2/4 Both Wolf and Cross lined out splendid two-baggers when the bases were crowded.

b. Of football players: To get in position for playing.

1893 Camp *College Sports* 105 As the players 'line out' they assume as nearly as possible the regular formation.

+**c.** To leave or depart *for* a place. *colloq.*

1897 Lewis *Wolfville* 90 Them towerists . . . lines out for Tucson.

10. *To line up* {1891–}, +to take a position or place as a competitor or rival *against* or *alongside* something or someone.

1897 *N.Y. Journal* 5 Sept. 41/4 The two elevens, 'varsity and scrub, will not line up against each other. **1907** LONDON *Road* 159, I 'lined' myself up alongside those road-kids.

+**Line boat.** A boat operated in a line of such vessels. (Cf. LINE *n.* 6 b.) — **1819** *Niles' Reg.* XVII. 112/1 A late Nashville paper notices the *arrival* there of . . . 'Line boat, No. 11.' **1835** A. PARKER *Trip to Texas* 10 The Line boats are owned by companies; and the captain told me that forty-five boats belonged to his line. **1849** NASON *Journal* 78 At nine o'clock, on board a line boat for Toledo. **1898** HARPER *S. B. Anthony* I. 47 The journey from here to Rochester was made . . . on a 'line boat' instead of a 'packet.'

+**Line breeding.** (See quot.) — **1879** WEBSTER *Suppl.* 1565 *Line-breeding*, . . . the breeding of animals with reference to securing descent from a particular family, especially in the female line.

+**Line camp.** A camp occupied by line-riders. — **1888** *Century Mag.* March 667/2 The men in the line camps lead a hard life. **1893** ROOSEVELT *Wilderness Hunter* 21 We generally carry rifles . . . while visiting the line camps. **1897** HOUGH *Story of Cowboy* 211 He takes a straight course across the country, on his way out to one of the 'line camps' of the ranch.

+**Line fence.** A fence on the boundary line between two properties. — **1854** HAMMOND *Hills, Lakes* 250 Later still, the old line fence was pulled away. **1874** B. F. TAYLOR *World on Wheels* 198 We purchased a sober horse and a modest carriage, and propped up the line fence and shingled the kitchen. **1906** LYNDE *Quickening* 279 The orchardist . . . makes the leisurely round of his line fence. **1914** 'BOWER' *Flying U Ranch* 93 Andy . . . loped along outside the line fence to a point opposite the sheep.

+**Line gale.** =LINE STORM. — **1836** *Knickerb.* VII. 17 That blamed line gale has kept me in bilboes such a dog's age.

Lineman. An electrician who works on a telegraph, telephone, or power line. {1876–} — **1887** *Courier-Journal* 21 Jan. 2/7 Lineman Frederick Simons . . . climbed a pole to cut the electric wires. **1891** E. S. ELLIS *Check 2134* 38 They'll have linemen out at break of day [to repair the wires]. **1913** LONDON *Valley of Moon* III. i, Beside the road they came upon a lineman eating his lunch.

***Linen.**

***1. a.** Cloth made from flax. **b.** A garment, tablecloth, sheet, etc., made of linen. In collective sense applied to garments, etc., formerly usually made of linen.

See also IRISH LINEN.

1641 *Mass. Bay Rec.* I. 320 In October last there was an order made for the incuragement of the makeing of linnen. **1674** *Harvard Rec.* I. 60 [It is ordered] that mr Gookin & Thacher be desired to ask an account of the Colledg linnen . . . in mr Danforths hands. **1688** SEWALL *Diary* I. 240 Shifted my Linen this day, Shirt, Drawers, N. Wastcoat, Binder. **1720** *Boston Rec.* 148 [Voted] That a Premium be allowed by the Town of five pounds for the first peice of Linnen Spun and Wove here. **1782** *Essex Inst. Coll.* XXXVIII. 54 For Linnen a nough for Six Shirts. **1833** *Niles' Reg.* XLIV. 269/1 *List of Linens* to be admitted at an ad valorem duty of 15 per cent. under the act of 14th July, 1832. **1867** EDWARDS *Shelby* 375 The kind lady of the house tore up her household linen for surgical purposes. **1875** STOWE *We & Neighbors* 74 Aunt Maria is a capital judge of linens and cottons. **1910** TOMPKINS *Mothers & Fathers* 213 She chose a pale pink linen, suited to a garden party.

2. Attrib. and comb. with *chest, cloth, handkerchief*, etc.

1643 *New Eng. First Fruits* 22 God favoured our beginnings . . . in prospering Hempe and Flaxe so well that its frequently sowen, spun, and woven into linnen Cloath. **1648** *Conn. Public Rec.* I. 488 Linnen yearne and Cotton wool yearne. **1761** in H. M. Brooks *Gleanings* IV. 29 Lawns of all Sorts, strip'd and flower'd kenting Handkerchiefs; cotton and linnen ditto; silk and gause ditto. **1818** FLINT *Lett. Amer.* 61 The manufacturing people of Pittsburg [include]: . . . 1 Linen Manufactory. **1833** *Niles' Reg.* XLIV. 269/1 To be admitted at an ad valorem duty of 15 per cent. . . . German, French and Flanders linen sheetings. **1859** STOWE *Minister's Wooing* iv, It's easy to see that *your* linen-chest will be pretty full by the time *he* comes along. **1900** STOCKTON *Afield & Afloat* 325 You're a linen merchant; that's what you are.

Linen cambric. Cambric made of linen as distinguished from cotton cambric; also, a handkerchief made of this. Also attrib. — **1833** NEAL *Down-Easters* I. 174 Wiping the inside of his palms with a linen cambric handkerchief. **1856** M. J. HOLMES *L. Rivers* x. 122 Her linen cambric went up to her forehead as if trying to smooth out the scowl. **1876** *Wide Awake* 11/1 [She] . . . purchased linen cambric, fine as gossamer.

***Linen draper.** A dealer in linen articles and related goods. *Obs.* — **1675** *Penna. Mag.* VI. 89 Here you need not . . . run to a Linnen-Draper for a supply, every one making their own Linnen. **1811** SUTCLIFF *Travels* (1815) 110 Her husband and family had been settled . . . as linen drapers and milliners.

+**Linen duster.** (See DUSTER 2.)

Linen press. An upright case or receptacle in which linens are kept. — **1852** STOWE *Uncle Tom* xviii, The store-room, the linen-presses, the china-closet, . . . all went under an awful review. **1854** CUMMINS *Lamplighter* 129 'Where shall I keep the linen press?' 'Can't it stand in the back entry?' **1857** VAUX *Villas* 195 The chamber plan supplies four bedrooms, . . . a bath-room and water-closet, a linen-press.

Linen wheel. =FLAX WHEEL. *Obs.* {1638–} — **1648** *Conn. Rec.* I. 490 1 kneading trough, . . . two linnen wheeles [etc.]. **1682** *Conn. Probate Rec.* I. 357 She shall have . . . a linen wheele, & the Nobed And Iron. **1723** *Narragansett Hist. Reg.* V. 156, 1 Linen Wheel.

+**Line officer.** In the army or navy, an officer in the combat or fighting force as distinguished from a staff officer. (Cf. LINE *n.* 9.) — **1868** in Custer *Following Guidon* 14, I found all the line-officers to-day in the classes. **1870** *Nation* 17 March 170/1 Every line-officer who executes an order is an executive officer, and entitled to precedence of all staff-officers. **1880** LAMPHERE *U.S. Govt.* 183/1 The Line-Officers of the navy are classed as follows. **1884** BLAINE *20 Years of Congress* I. 76 The line-officers appointed from civil life behaved gallantly.

***Liner.**

1. A vessel plying regularly between certain ports, esp. one belonging to a regular line. {1848–} (Cf. LINE *n.* 6 b.)

1838 *Knickerb.* XII. 174 He swept slowly past, on the deck of a 'liner,' with an old blue umbrella over his head. **1851** *S. Lit. Messenger* XVII. 689/1 The 'Liners' as the packet ships of New York came to be called, went on increasing in numbers and size. **1882** *Harper's Mag.* Aug. 364 Those faithful colored men . . . had learned their business before steamships had driven liners to the wall. **1905** N. DAVIS *Northerner* 321 In the dream . . . [was] a big liner ploughing her way on and on.

+b. A canal boat.

1874 B. F. TAYLOR *World on Wheels* 25 The mighty fleet of white-decked 'liners,' looking like . . . ant's eggs with windows in them, has had more to do with the march of civilization than all the aquatic armaments that ever thundered.

+2. *S.* One who lives on a dividing line or boundary.

1848 *Ala. Acts* 401 William Ogletree and Joseph Buck are declared liners between the counties of Perry and Marengo. **1901** *Ala. H. Rep. Jrnl.* 1200 Hugh W. Hardy . . . is a liner between Dallas and Lowndes counties.

+3. *Baseball.* A batted ball that travels in a straight line: (see also last part of first quot.).

1867 CHADWICK *Base Ball Reference* 137 A Liner.—A ball sent swift and straight from the bat without rising in the air; or one thrown similarly to a base. **1880** N. BROOKS *Fairport Nine* ii. 30 Peletiah Snelgro sent a hot liner to Pat Adams at third base. **1894** *Chicago Record* 12 May 2/1 Wilmot drove a hot liner straight at Pfeffer, on which Griffith and Ryan scored. **1917** MATHEWSON *Sec. Base Sloan* 166 It was a hot liner.

+**Line-rider.** *W.* One engaged in line-riding. (Cf. LINE *n.* 13.)

1888 ROOSEVELT in *Century Mag.* April 835/2 If the line-riders are caught in a blizzard [etc.]. **1898** CANFIELD *Maid of Frontier* 141 The line-riders, vaqueros and cooks crowded round in wonderment. **1909** *Indian Laws & Tr.* III. 404 For the employment of 'Line Riders' along the southern and eastern boundary of the Northern Cheyenne Indian Reservation . . . , one thousand five hundred dollars. **1920** HUNTER *Trail Drivers Texas* I. 298 The 'fence rider,' also called the 'line rider,' is employed to ride fences and repair them.

+**Line-riding.** *W.* Patrolling on horseback the boundaries of a ranch, cattle drift, etc. — **1888** ROOSEVELT in *Century Mag.* March 668/2 Line riding is very cold work, and dangerous too, when the men have to be out in a blinding snowstorm. **1890** *Harper's Mag.* July 240/1 Line riding . . . means a close inspection of the fences and the repair of all breaks and damages.

+**Line shooting.** (See quot. 1843.) — **1836** *Knickerb.* VIII. 575 We went out to practise, and the major soon put me in the way of line-shooting. **1843** 'CARLETON' *New Purchase* I. 129 Each man had three shots. And provided the three were within the circle, each was to be measured by a line from the centre of the diamond to the near edge of the bullet hole—except a ball grazed the centre, and then the line went to the centre of the hole—and then, the three separate lengths added were estimated as one string or line, the shortest securing the prize. This is called line shooting.

+**Line shot.** A shot in which the bullet or projectile strikes in line with the target. — **1883** SHIELDS *S. S. Prentiss* 72 General Foote fired first, his ball striking the ground immediately in front of Prentiss,—a line shot. **1910** J. HART *Vigilante Girl* 301 His bullet entered the ground some nine feet from where he stood, making a line shot.

+**Line storm.** *local.* A storm when the sun crosses the line. — **1850** KINGSLEY *Diary* 115 A fine day with a strong West wind; rather think the line storm is over. **1867** WHITTIER *Poetical Works* (1894) 259/1 Along their foam-white curves of shore They heard the line-storm rave and roar. **1874** *Vermont Bd. Agric. Rep.* II. 730 It is well enough to look for a line storm, study the almanac, and watch the thermometer. **1892** S. HALE *Letters* 274 It poured guns and blew blazes, the regular 'Line Storm.'

+**Line tree.** A tree located on the line or boundary of a survey. — **1743** *N.J. Archives* 1 Ser. VI. 161 Lett the line trees be markt with your notches on two sides where the line cutts them. **1817** *Niles' Reg.* XII. 99/1 The deputy surveyors are . . . to enter in their field books, . . . all those trees which fall in the lines, called station, or line trees. **1832** *Louisville Directory* 107 The practice of blocking out the chops on the corner and line trees of surveys, has been universally adopted. **1899** JEWETT *Queen's Twin* 176 The light axe . . . Isaac had carried to blaze new marks on some of the line-trees on the farther edge of their possessions.

+**Line tub.** (See quot. 1883.) — **1839** *Knickerb.* XIII. 382 Line-tubs, water-kegs, and wafe-poles, were thrown hurriedly into the boats. **1851** MELVILLE *Moby-Dick* 617 The two crews were . . . reaching out after the revolving line-tubs, oars, and other floating furniture. **1883** *Nat. Museum Bul.* No. 27, 302 Line tubs. Receptacles for the whale-line.

***Ling.** +The American burbot, *Lota maculosa;* also, applied locally to various other fishes.

1616 SMITH *New England* 29 [There were] whales, Grampus, . . . Cole, Cusk, or small Ling [etc.]. **1839** STORER *Mass. Fishes* 67 *Zoarcus anguillaris*, . . . the eel-shaped Blenny, . . . is incorrectly called by our fishermen 'ling.' **1883** *Nat. Museum Bul.* No. 27, 448 *Elacate canadus* . . . Sergeant-fish; Snooks; Ling. **1884** GOODE, etc. *Fisheries* I. 267 Cultus Cod (*Ophiodon elongatus* Girard). . . . About Puget Sound the English call it 'Ling.' **1897** *N.Y. Forest, Fish, & Game Comm. 2d Rep.* 246 *Lota maculosa*. . . . Burbot; Ling; Lawyer.—Perhaps one of the most difficult of the fresh-water fishes to transport. **1911** *Rep. Fisheries 1908* 312 *Ling*, a local name given to the hake (*Urophycis*) . . . ; to the mutton-fish . . . ; to the cobia . . . and to the cultus cod.

***Linguist.** +An interpreter between white people and Indians. *Obs.* — **1670** *S.C. Hist. Soc. Coll.* V. 167 Leauing that place which is called Sowee, carrying ye Caseeka of Kayawah wth us a uery Ingenious Indian & a great Linguist in this Maine. **1741** *Ib.* IV. 40 Thomas Jones, . . . being of Indian Extract, was Employed . . . as a Linguist to the Creeks and Euchees. **1749** *Georgia Col. Rec.* VI. 264 A White Servant of Mr. Bosomworths . . . was the Linguist.

+Linguister. Also †**languister.** An interpreter, esp. one between white people and Indians. *Obs.*

1670 *S.C. Hist. Soc. Coll.* V. 228 Thay left Captain Bayly in the Fryers hands and went away he being a person of verie good worth and a good linguister. **1713** in Sheldon *Hist. Deerfield, Mass.* I. 350, J Jmployed my Indian Languister to talk to her. **1725** in *Travels Amer. Col.* 108, I went to the Town House and carryed along with me King Crow and the Two Linguisters. **1777** *Va. State P.* I. 303 From the Linguister he employed . . . he was informed the Indians was in want of Goods. **1789** *Steele P.* I. 52 Bennet Belew applyed to sd. Forman for to assign him as linguister to bring about a liese or purchase of land from the Cherokee Indians. **1849** LANMAN *Alleghany Mts.* 97 [The preacher] wished to know if he should preach with the '*linguister*,' or interpreter, for the benefit of the young stranger. [**1889** F. R. GOULDING *Marooner's Isl.* (1890) 65 Linkster . . . is a word in common use in many parts [of Ga. and Fla.], being a corruption of linguister.]

||**b.** One skilled in languages.

1871 LOWELL *My Study Windows* 265 He who writes to be read does not write for linguisters.

Link.[1] =LYNX. *colloq.* — [**1804–6** *Lewis & Clark Exped.* VI. 107 Carkajous wolverine or Beaver eaters Loucirva Picpou or Links.] **1874** HOWELLS *Chance Acquaintance* 52, 'I deal in deer, . . . moose, cariboo, wild-cat, link'—'What?' 'Link—link! You say deer for deers, and link for lynx, don't you?' **1897** *Outing* XXIX. 380/1 A link is mighty curious an' is forever a-smellin', an' a-pryin' about.

***Link.**[2] +*To let out links*, to make increased exertion or effort. *colloq.* — **1868** WOODRUFF *Trotting Horse* 282 Lancet . . . in the third heat, let out the links in such a manner that he trotted it in 2m. 25½ s. **1880** BURNETT *Old Pioneer* 110 [The buffaloes] let out a few more links, and ran much faster.

***Linn.** Also †**lynn.** +The American linden, *Tilia glabra*, or a related species; also, the wood of such a tree. Also attrib.

1787 in *Amer. Acad. Mem.* II. I. 158 Lynn, of 3½ feet diameter, a light white wood very proper for finishing the inside of dwelling houses. **1797** MORSE *Gazetteer* s.v. *Territory*, The more useful trees, are . . . elm, cucumber tree, lynn tree, gum tree, iron-wood. **1814** BRACKENRIDGE *Views La.* 104 The timber is not as is usually found in swamps, but fine oak, ash, olive, linn, beech, and poplar of enormous growth. **1860** CURTIS *Woody Plants N.C.* 79 Southern Linn. (*T. pubescens*, Ait.)—This is confined to the Lower Districts of the Southern States. **1883** ZEIGLER & GROSSCUP *Alleghanies* 49 We noticed . . . thousands of sound lofty linns, ashes, buckeyes, oaks and sugar maples.

Linnaea. {1789– (Aiton *Hortus Kewensis*)} +The American twin-flower, *Linnaea americana.* — **1818** *Mass. H. S. Coll.* 2 Ser. VIII. 169 The linnaea is a small, creeping, woody plant. **1863** S. HALE *Letters* 15 The ground [was] carpeted with Linnaea. **1896** JEWETT *Pointed Firs* 70 He picked a few sprigs of late-blooming linnæa.

Linn bark. The bark of the linn tree. — **1799** J. SMITH *Acct. Captivity* 16 Poles [were] . . . tied together with lynn or elm bark. **1843** *Amer. Pioneer* II. 450 The manner of making ropes of linn bark, was to cut the bark in strips . . . and water-rot it. **1853** RAMSEY *Tennessee* 467 With a piece of linn bark, the hole in the canoe was at length covered.

***Linnet.** A small songbird of the family Fringillidae, +esp., in the West, the house finch, *Carpodacus mexicanus.* — **1805** LEWIS in *L. & Clark Exped.* II. (1904) 130, I observed among them the brown thrush, Robbin, turtle dove linnit goaldfinch [etc.]. **1862** *N.H. Laws* 2609 If any person shall . . . take, kill or destroy any of the birds called . . . linnets, fly-catchers or warblers; . . . he shall forfeit . . . the sum of one dollar. **1883** *Harper's Mag.* Oct. 707/1 The sage-brush abounded in the nests of . . . the linnet, pipit, and blackbird kinds. **1902** *Harper's Mag.* Feb. 490 Linnets and goldfinches . . . came to . . . [the water] regularly every day.

+Linotype. a. (See quot. 1924.) In full *linotype machine.* **b.** A bar of type that has been cast by this machine.

1888 *Pat. Off. Gazette* XLV. 1103/2 The linotype . . . [has] on its side face two or more ribs extending from top to bottom. **1890** *Detroit Free Press* 5 July, The Linotype. . . . The Linotype Machine made by this company under its patents, is now for lease or sale; is capable of an average speed of 8,000 ems per hour. *Ib.*, The use of any machine which casts, as a substitute for movable type, linotypes or type bars, each bearing the characters to print an entire line, . . . will render the user liable to a suit for infringement. **1896** *Typographical Jrnl.* 16 Nov. 407 When the contract expires, this newspaper will throw out its linotype machines. **1900** *Ann. Cycl. 1899* 623/2 In 1880 [Mergenthaler] . . . adopted the plan that he brought to perfection in the linotype. **1924** *Publisher's Weekly* CVI. 189/1 *Linotype.*—A typesetting machine which sets matter in slugs or solid lines.

+Linotyper. One who operates a linotype machine. — **1896** *Typographical Jrnl.* IX. 31 Mr. H. H. Murphy, an Express linotyper and treasurer of No. 172, . . . will spend the summer in Missouri. **1911** HARRISON *Queed* 83 The little knot of linotypers and helpers . . . now listened. **1913** BIGGERS *Seven Keys to Baldpate* 150 One of 'em . . . flies back to New York with a ten-page story of my vicious career all ready for the linotypers.

***Linseed.** Flax or the seed of flax. Also attrib. — **1666** in F. L. Hawks *Hist. N. Carolina* II. 39 The meadows are very proper for rice, rape-seed, linseed, &c. **1801** [see LINSEED CAKE]. **1868** WOODRUFF *Trotting Horse* 96 Some people give boiled flax-seed or linseed meal and the like to make their horses shed early.

Linseed cake. A cake made of pressed linseed: (see quot. 1801). Used as food for cattle. {1813} — **1801** W. STRICKLAND *Agric. U.S.* 66 What is called linseed cake, or oil-cake, being the remainder of the linseed after the oil is pressed out, might be purchased there. **1805** PARKINSON *Tour* 393 With purchased linseed-cakes . . . I fed each cow one week. **1825** LORAIN *Pract. Husbandry* 120 Linseed cake is said to be an excellent manure.

***Linseed oil.** Oil expressed from flaxseed.

1674 *Md. Archives* II. 406 The frames and Casements to be well laid in Lynseede Oyle . . . and glased. **1726** *Md. Hist. Mag.* XVIII. 216 Send . . . 20 Galls. Lineseed oile. **1801** W. STRICKLAND *Agric. U.S.* 66 Much linseed oil is used in the United States, where the houses, mostly built of wood, are painted on the outside. **1827** DRAKE & MANSFIELD *Cincinnati* 21 The principal exports are flour, pork, lard, . . . linseed oil [etc.]. **1885** HOWELLS *S. Lapham* i, It'll mix easily with linseed oil, whether you want to use it boiled or raw. **1902** ALDRICH *Sea Turn* 255 Self-respect . . . [is] about the only thing that's worth what it costs—that and first-class linseed oil.

attrib. and *comb.* **1862** *Rep. Comm. Patents 1861: Agric.* 111 A linseed oil manufacturer . . . is beginning to doubt whether even flax-seed will be much longer produced in this country. **1882** *Century Mag.* Feb. 595/1 He cares as much for the doings of society . . . as I do for the linseed-oil market—if there is a linseed-oil market. **1883** KNIGHT *Suppl.* 152/1 *Cake Grinder*, a machine for breaking linseed oil cake for food for stock.

Linseed-oil mill. A mill in which linseed oil is made. — **1788** CUTLER in *Life & Corr.* I. 397 One of the Brethren came and conducted us . . . [to the] water-works, spring, linseed oil mills, and other water-works [at Bethlehem, Pa.]. **1847** HOWE *Hist. Coll. Ohio* 110 This flourishing town has . . . 1 linseed oil and 1 saw mill. **1850** *Rep. Comm. Patents 1849: Agric.* 94 [In Bristol, Mass.] are about fifty cotton factories . . . [and] one linseed oil mill.

***Linsey.**

1. =LINSEY-WOOLSEY. {1771–}

1754 in Chalkley *Scotch-Irish Settlement Va.* I. 445 [The servant] had on when he went away an old felt hat, an old brown coat lined with brown linsey. **1800** TATHAM *Agric. & Commerce* 87 Linsey is spun and wove as in Europe. **1844** *Lexington Observer* 25 Sept. 1/3 Just received: . . . Jeans, Linseys, Flannels [etc.]. **1851** *S. Lit. Messenger* XVII. 545/1 Coarse linsey . . . was almost universally the dress of women on the frontier. **1892** J. L. ALLEN *Blue-Grass Region* 107 At the dry-goods stores: . . . gay cottonades . . . and linseys of prismatic dyes.

b. *pl.* Linsey trousers.

*c*1845 THOMPSON *Chron. Pineville* 43 [He] was in the habit of thrusting his legs somewhat farther through his copperas-coloured linseys than fashion required.

2. Attrib. in the names of garments.

1754 in Chalkley *Scotch-Irish Settlement Va.* I. 445 [The servant] had on . . . a linsey jaccoat wanting sleeves. **1803** *Lit. Mag.* (Phila.) Dec. 172 The dress of the women consisted of . . . the usual garment of coarse linen, and a linsey petticoat. **1824** DODDRIDGE *Notes* 129 The gentlemen dressed in shoepacks, . . . leggins, and linsey hunting-shirts, all home-made. **1869** STOWE *Oldtown Folks* 100, I'll have to make her a regular linsey working dress this fall. **1884** Z. F. SMITH *Kentucky* (1886) 125 The ladies [appeared] in linsey gowns.

***Linsey-woolsey.** A strong coarse fabric having a linen warp and a woolen woof.

1634 WOOD *New Eng. Prospect* 57 Callico stuffes, Linsey-woolsies, and blue Callicoe . . . for Housewives aprons. **1732** *Doc. Hist. N.Y. State* I. 722 Manufacture [by the people of N.Y.] extends no farther than . . . a few coarse Lindsey Woolseys for clothing, and linen for their own wear. **1854** RILEY *Puddleford* 243 The girls, dressed in linsey-woolsey, were boisterous. **1904** GLASGOW *Deliverance* 58 An aged negress, in a dress of linsey-woolsey which resembled a patch-work quilt, was pouring . . . coffee.

b. Attrib. (passing into adj.) in the names of garments.

1707 *Boston News-Letter* 15 Sept. 2/2 Ran-away from her Master. . . . Had on . . . a mixed blue and white Linsey Woolsey Apron. **1818** FORDHAM *Narr. Travels* 208 He wore a linsey woolsey coat. **1843** *Knickerb.*

XXI. 523 His legs [were] encased in a pair of massive boots, which were surmounted by a pair of linsey-woolsey breeches. **1880** *Harper's Mag.* Oct. 688/2 She made him a linsey-woolsey dress. **1889** *Century Mag.* April 933/1 Her severe linsey-woolsey gown defining her figure.

* **Lint.** +The fiber surrounding the seed of unginned cotton. {fiber of flax, 1375–, chiefly *Sc.*}

1835 INGRAHAM *South-West* II. 289 The teeth of the saws catch and carry through the lint from the seed. **1883** 'MARK TWAIN' *Life on Miss.* xxxiii, In sixteen hundred pounds crude cotton, four hundred are lint. **1896** HARRIS *Sister Jane* 80 The negroes . . . picked the lint from the cotton seed. **1911** *Dept. Agric. Yrbk.* 57 Some of the new types produce larger bolls and longer lint than any of the varieties now generally cultivated in Texas.

attrib. **1901** CABLE *Cavalier* xxi, The lint-box of the old cotton-press was covered with wet morning-glories.

+**Linter.**[1] Also **lintan, lintow.** Variant of LEAN-TO. *colloq.* {1893–} Also attrib.

1736 *N.H. Prov. Papers* IV. 714 The cause [of a fire] was from a spark falling out of the lintan chimney (which was lower than the house). **1779** *N.J. Archives* 2 Ser. III. 382 To be sold, A very good house . . . two stories high . . . with a linter to the house for a shop fit for any business. **1801** *Spirit Farmers' Mus.* 35 She conducted him into a back lintow, where a negro . . . usually slept. **1845** *Knickerb.* XXV. 444 A venerable pussy ran out of the cat-hole in the linter door. **1881** JEWETT *Country By-Ways* 109 Up-stairs there was a long, unfinished room . . . under the sloping roof, and . . . I remembered that I had once heard an old man say . . . that he had slept in just such a 'linter' chamber as this.

b. (See quotations.)

1819 in Kittredge *Old Farmer* (1904) 90 The barn-floor,—the linter—the flail, & the curry-comb are not to be neglected. *a***1870** CHIPMAN *Notes on Bartlett* 246 *Linter.* Essex Co., Mass. Place or thing for feeding cattle. Cow-or-ox-manger.

+**Linter.**[2] **1.** (See quotation.) **2.** The short-staple fiber stripped from cotton seed after ginning: (see quotation). — **(1) 1890** *Cent.* 3469/3 *Linter,* . . . a machine for stripping off the short-staple cotton-fiber which adheres to cotton-seed after ginning, preparatory to extraction of oil from the seed. . . . Also *linter-machine.* **(2) 1904** LAMBORN *Cottonseed Products* 50 The purpose of delinting is to remove more completely the short fibres which form the 'linters.'

+**Lint room.** A room for storing cotton from which the seed has been removed. — **1852** *Florida Plant. Rec.* 81 Now I have my Lint room full of gin Cotton. **1866** W. REID *After the War* 284 In the lint-room were stacks of muskets.

* **Lion.**

+**1.** =COUGAR. Also attrib.

*c***1613** in Smith *Works* (1884) I. p. cvi, Ther be in this cuntry [Va.] Lions, Beares, woulues [etc.]. **1635** *Relation of Md.* iii. 23 In the upper parts of the Countrey there are Bufeloes, Elkes, Lions, . . . and Deare. **1681** SEWALL *Diary* II. 16 Newes is brought of Mr. Deans son . . . Killing a Lion with his Axe at Andover. **1840** EMMONS *Mass. Quadrupeds* 35 The Puma, or American Lion . . . preys . . . upon all the animals weaker than itself. **1894** EGGLESTON in *Century Mag.* April 849 The panther was long called a 'tyger' in the Carolinas, and a 'lyon' elsewhere. **1903** *Chicago Chronicle,* 11 April 1/2 (*caption*), Roosevelt on a Lion Hunt. *Ib.,* The lion they have used for the purpose is one captured by Buffalo Jones last month.

+**2.** *fig. Lion of the West,* a frontier ruffian or rowdy. *Obs.*

1831 PAULDING (*title*), The Lion of the West. **1848** COOPER *Oak Openings* I. 37 The time is at hand when the Lion of the West will draw his own picture.

+**Lion dollar.** Also **lyon dollar.** =DOG DOLLAR. *Obs.* {*a*1725} — **1697** *Va. State P.* I. 52 Dollers, commonly called Lyon or Dog Dollers, have no vallue ascertained whereby they may pass currantly amongst the inhabitants of this Country. **1720** *Amer. Wkly. Mercury* 1 Dec. 2/1 An Act appointing the Value Lyon Dollars shall pass current for. **1723** *Doc. Hist. N.Y. State* I. 714 The Current Cash being wholly in the Paper Bills of this Province and a few Lyon Dollars. **1889** *Cent.* 1725/1 *Lion dollar,* . . . a Dutch (Brabant) coin in circulation in the province of New York in colonial times.

Lion's-ear. (See quotations.) {1835–} — **1861** WOOD *Botany* 558 *Leonotis.* Lion's-ears. **1890** *Cent.* 3471/1 *Lion's-ear,* . . . a plant of the genus *Leonotis.* **1901** MOHR *Plant Life Ala.* 706 *Leonotis nepetaefolia.* . . . Lion's Ears. . . . Waste places, roadsides, perfectly naturalized.

***Lion's-foot.** +A plant of the genus *Prenanthes,* as the gall of the earth (*P. serpentaria*) or the rattlesnake-root (*P. altissima*). Cf. GALL[2] I. — **1814** PURSH *Flora Amer.* II. 499 *Prenanthes Serpentaria* . . . is known by the inhabitants under the name of Lion's-foot, and is in high esteem as a specific in curing the bite of the rattlesnake. **1850** S. F. COOPER *Rural Hours* 283 These plants are sometimes called lion's-foot, rattlesnake-root, &c., but the name of Bird-bell is the most pleasing.

+**Lion's-heart.** =DRAGONHEAD a. — **1789** MORSE *Amer. Geog.* 415 Lyons hart . . . is a sovereign remedy for the bite of a serpent. **1795** WINTERBOTHAM *Hist. View* III. 200 Among others [*i.e.,* herbs] are the ginseng; Virginia snake root; . . . lion's heart. **1847** WOOD *Botany* 426 *P[hysostegia] Virginiana.* . . . Lion's Heart. . . . A beautiful plant, native in Penn., S. and W. States!

Lion skin. {1805–} A heavy woolen cloth. Also attrib. — **1803** *Lit. Mag.* (Phila.) Nov. 153 Three of them wore lion-skin great-coats, the other had a coattee and boots on. **1812** *Niles' Reg.* II. 9/1 The *flushings* or *lion skins* for great coats . . . are nothing more than good tweeled blanketing. **1850** JUDD *R. Edney* 139 He wore a blue, shaggy lion-skin overcoat margined with black.

Lion('s)-mouth. Any one of various long-lipped flowers as snapdragon, foxglove, etc. {1706–} — **1773** *Hist. Brit. Dom. N. Amer.* II. 189 The flower called lion's-mouth . . . forms a sweet nosegay of itself, and is worthy the gardens of kings. **1892** *Amer. Folk-Lore* V. 101 *Antirrhinum majus,* lion-mouth. Mansfield, O.

* **Lip.** +*To keep a stiff upper lip,* to maintain one's courage or resolution. *colloq.*

1815 *Mass. Spy* 14 June (Th.), I kept a stiff upper lip, and bought [a] license to sell my goods. *c***1845** W. T. THOMPSON *Chron. Pineville* 150 Keep a stiff upper lip. **1867** LOCKE *Swingin' Round* 198 [He] wuz determined to keep up a stiff upper lip over it. **1896** FREDERIC *Damnation of T. Ware* 508 You mustn't be afraid of things. Just you keep a stiff upper lip. **1910** SANGER *70 Yrs. a Showman* 183 It was an awful predicament, but I managed to keep a stiff upper lip all the same.

+**Lipan.** [Amer. Indian.] (See quot. 1907.) Also attrib. — **1845** T. J. GREEN *Texian Exped.* 167 They were visited in prison by some Americans and Lipan Indians, who were not permitted to speak with the men. **1854** BARTLETT *Personal Narr.* I. 106 A little experience will enable him to distinguish the tribe, whether Comanches, Lipans, or Apaches. **1865** PIKE *Scout & Ranger* (1932) 65 They belonged to the tribe of the Lipans. **1907** HODGE *Handbook* I. 768 *Lipan.* . . . An Apache tribe . . . which at various periods roamed from the lower Rio Grande in New Mexico and Mexico eastward through Texas to the Gulf coast. . . . The name has probably been employed to include other Apache groups of the southern plains, such as the Mescaleros and the Kiowa Apache.

+**Lip stick.** A pomade or rouge in sticks for use on the lips. — **1880** E. JAMES *Negro Minstrel's Guide* 4 Prepared burnt cork, ready for use, 25 and 50 cents per box; lip sticks, 25 cts. *Ib.* 8 An application of lipstick . . . around the natural part of the lips will extend that feature to a size quite remarkable. **1919** WILSON *Ma Pettingill* 93 Metta was even using a lip stick!

* **Liquidambar.** Also †**liquid-amber.** The copalm or sweet gum tree, *Liquidambar styraciflua.* {1731– (Miller *Gard. Dict.* s.v. *Styrax*)}

1756 KALM *Resa* II. 273 Sassafras, *Liquidambar.* **1797** IMLAY *Western Territory* (ed. 3) 277 The liquidambar, copalm, or maple-leaved storax . . . affords a balm, the virtues of which are infinite. **1802** ELLICOTT *Journal* 286 Sweet gum, (liquid-amber,) . . . in great abundance in some parts of the Mississippi Territory. **1850** S. F. COOPER *Rural Hours* 210 The sweet-gum, or liquid-amber, is unknown here. **1900** KEELER *Our Native Trees* 162 The starry five-pointed leaves of the Liquidambar suggest the Sugar Maple.

Liquidator. {1858–} +*Liquidator of vessels,* (see quotations). — **1884** *Harper's Mag.* June 58/1 The accounts of each vessel are put into the hands of a class of officials known as liquidators of vessels. . . . They examine the accounts of the liquidators of entries. **1909** *Cent. Suppl.* 737/1 *Liquidator of vessels,* one of a number of officials belonging to the New York Custom-house.

Liquid fire. {1604–} +Whisky. *colloq.* — **1836** EDWARD *Hist. Texas* 81 The faces of the Men are made pale by the dying struggles of liquid fire. **1857** *Lawrence* (Kan.) *Republican* 28 May 4 Having just opened a commodious shop for the sale of 'liquid fire,' . . . on Saturday next I shall commence the business.

* **Liquor,** *n.* Also *colloq.* **licker.**

* **1.** An alcoholic or spirituous liquid; whisky.

1654 R. WILLIAMS *Letters* (1874) 286 From him have the Indians been furnished with store of liquors. **1663** *East-Hampton Rec.* I. 199 Mr. Gardiner shall give A quart of licker a peece to the cuters of every whale. **1691** *Boston Rec.* 209 Gasker . . . is aproued of by ye select to sell wine and liquors by retayle out of dore. **1716** *Mass. H. Rep. Jrnl.* I. 101 An Act for Granting unto His Majesty an Excise upon Wines, Liquors, and other Strong Drink Sold by Retail. **1756** *Lett. to Washington* I. 280, I sent a Serjeant to him desiring him at his Perril not to sell Liquor to the Soldiers. **1842** *Diplom. Corr. Texas* III. (1911) 1420 The use of the wines of France would be, more salubrious . . . than the stronger liquors now used. **1871** DE VERE 217 The worst of lickers . . . is called Chain-lightning, from its terrible strength and stunning effect. **1912** NICHOLSON *Hoosier Chron.* 196 Wasn't he satisfied to take his licker or let it alone?

2. *attrib.* **a.** Designating places of business where liquor is sold or drunk. (See also LIQUOR STORE.)

1826 FLINT *Recoll.* 86 A vast flat boat . . . in which there were families, liquor-shops, drunken men and women. **1849** G. G. FOSTER *N.Y. in Slices* 79 We believe the Liquor Groceries (by which we mean family groceries where grog is retailed) are the most pernicious. **1851** *Polly Peablossom* 61 About forty men . . . entered the liquor room. **1866** *Rep. Indian Affairs* 247 It is to be regretted that . . . the surroundings of their reservation should be dotted with liquor stalls. **1873** *Newton Kansan* 12 June 2/3 The board of councilmen of Emporia passed an ordinance licensing liquor saloons.

b. Designating persons, interests, organizations, etc., that control or promote the sale of liquor. (See also LIQUOR DEALER, MAN, etc.)

1850 JUDD *R. Edney* 81 He broke the bottles of the liquor-pedler with a religious zeal. 1859 WILMER *Press Gang* 172 The 'Liquor League,' the avowed object of which is to 'put down' the friends and advocates of temperance. *Ib.*, The Liquor Trade has become a moneyed and political power. 1884 *Century Mag.* Nov. 126 Something in the past history of a public man is supposed to give him the best chance to capture the 'soldier' vote . . . or the liquor or the anti-liquor interest. 1910 C. HARRIS *Eve's Husband* 148 There was less excuse for his running on the liquor ticket. *c*1919 in Bryan *Memoirs* 466 Your voice . . . has sent the shock of alarm throughout the ranks of the liquor forces.

c. Designating legal instruments for the control of the liquor traffic. (See also LIQUOR LAW, LEGISLATION.)

1856 MACLEOD *F. Wood* 214 In addition to your usual Sunday liquor report, please make returns of any daguerreotype-rooms . . . illegally open on Sunday. 1884 WELLS *Practical Economics* (1885) 174 The number of those who take out similar liquor licenses in those States where prohibition has been engrafted on the constitution . . . appears to increase.

* **Liquor,** *v.* Also *colloq.* **licker.** +*intr.* To drink alcoholic liquor. Also with *up. slang.*

1831 *Maysville* (Ky.) *Eagle* 12 July, Let's liquor and then I'll explaterate more. *c*1845 *Big Bear Ark.* 43 Suppose we licker agin, and then fill that case-bottle up there. 1850 A. W. THAXTER *Poem before Iadma* 7 Hast 'liquored up' at Parker's? 1882 SALA *Amer. Revisited* (1885) 59 Swearing fealty to the Republic by *'liquoring up.'* 1904 *McClure's Mag.* Feb. 359/1 'Let's liquor,' he said.

+**Liquor dealer.** One engaged in the buying and selling of spirituous liquor. — 1856 MACLEOD *F. Wood* 262 He has issued a kind and courteous circular to the liquor-dealers. 1875 'MARK TWAIN' *Old Times* iv. 14 The wholesale liquor-dealer's son became a barkeeper on a boat. 1884 *Century Mag.* June 315/1 The sad experiences in work among liquor-dealers and liquor-drinkers naturally led . . . to this idea of prevention through education. 1894 *Voice* 1 Feb., All the laws, good and bad, are so mis-executed by Tammany as to give it a clutch upon . . . liquor dealers.

Liquorice. Variant of LICORICE.

+**Liquorite.** One who approves of the use and sale of liquor. *Obs.* — 1888 *Voice* 19 Jan. 8 The Democracy of the State will hold only the rabid liquorites and the debauched element of the Negro race. [1895 *Ib.* 19 Sept. 3 It has even been admitted by pro-liquorites that the voters of New Jersey would . . . adopt county, municipal, and township local option.]

+**Liquorize,** *v.* **1.** *intr.* To drink liquor. *slang. Obs.* **2.** *tr.* To supply with liquor. — (1) 1833 J. E. ALEXANDER *Transatlantic Sk.* II. 6 Here is the Bar, you must liquorise. 1839 TOWNSEND *Narrative* 130 Refusing the landlord's polite invitation to *'liquorize,'* we marched from the house. 1840 *S. Lit. Messenger* VI. 510/2 Friends, you liquorize too freely —it is a bad thing. (2) 1895 *Nat. Temp. Advocate* Jan. 6/1 The proposition to invest saloons with a legal right to liquorize the community on Sundays.

Liquor law. A law regulating the manufacture or sale of intoxicating liquor. — 1852 *Boston Bee* 29 July (B. '59), The Life Boat . . . takes the Bee to do, for its course in relation to the Liquor law. 1856 MACLEOD *F. Wood* 43 It was before the passage of the Prohibitory Liquor Law. 1871 *Rep. Indian Affairs* (1872) 181 We organized temperance Societies, and had a liquor law. 1885 WELLS *Pract. Economics* 233 The prevalent . . . delusion, that liquor laws can be made different in principle from all other laws.

Liquor legislation. Legislation relating to the manufacture, sale, or use of liquor. — 1883 *Century Mag.* July 337/2 The effect of the liquor legislation is that a man who would ordinarily be satisfied with a mug of beer must buy a whole bottle. 1891 *Cycl. Temperance* 207/2 [The high-license] policy of American liquor legislation . . . [requires] that individual liquor-sellers shall pay relatively large annual fees. 1914 *Cycl. Amer. Govt.* II. 356/1 The temperance movement has set a lasting mark upon all modern liquor legislation.

+**Liquor man.** One who favors or is interested in the liquor business. — 1884 *Century Mag.* April 861/2 The liquor men . . . pay the taxes of their colored allies in order that their votes may be counted. 1891 *N.Y. Wkly. Witness* 11 Nov. 4/4 The liquor-men will hold on to the bitter end.

+**Liquor question.** The political issue arising out of efforts to prohibit the liquor traffic. — 1882 *Nation* 14 Sept. 221/2 The moral power of the nation 'is not, on the liquor question, arrayed against a few thousand brewers and rumsellers' simply. 1884 *Century Mag.* April 864/2 Another issue which is deeply agitating the Southern States is the liquor question. 1893 *Voice* 14 Sept., The utter demoralization of the Republican and Democratic parties is again manifest in their attitude toward the liquor question. 1918 STELZLE *Why Prohibition!* 291 Michigan was about to vote on the liquor question.

Liquor-seller. One whose business is selling alcoholic liquors. — 1855 BARNUM *Life* 359 The liquor-seller, the moderate drinker, and the indifferent man. 1886 ROOSEVELT in *Century Mag.* Nov. 79/2 It is this that gives the liquor-sellers their enormous influence in politics. 1919 *Maine My State* 331 The burly mate of a coaster . . . [was] hired by some liquor sellers to horsewhip Neal Dow.

Liquor store. A store in which intoxicating liquors are sold. {1815 at Port Royal, Jamaica} — 1825 PICKERING *Inq. Emigrant* 31 The roads leading to a town in America are full of houses on their sides, called 'taverns,' or 'liquor' . . . or 'grocery,' stores. 1869 BREWER *Rocky Mt. Lett.* 10 'Sample-rooms,' 'liquor stores,' 'lager beer,' etc., furnish most of the signs on the places of business. 1894 *Harper's Mag.* Oct. 698/1 The full-fledged liquor-stores . . . are on the side-street corners. 1916 WILSON *Somewhere* 190 He [didn't] . . . lead a double life by stopping in at the Family Liquor Store for a gin fizz.

Liquor traffic. The business of manufacturing, buying, selling, or transporting alcoholic liquors. {1901–}

1848 J. MARSH (*title*), A Discourse on the Extent and Evils of the Sunday Liquor Traffic in Cities. 1872 *Newton Kansan* 7 Nov. 2/1 At Sterling, Illinois, they have hit upon a novel mode of regulating the liquor trafic [*sic*]. 1885 *Century Mag.* Oct. 973 The laws placing restrictions upon the liquor traffic have had only a semblance of enforcement in the city of Boston. 1911 *Okla. Session Laws* 3 Legisl. 165 Any person violating any provision of the laws of this state for the suppression of liquor traffic shall be guilty [etc.]. 1915 BRYAN *Memoirs* 434 [Mr. Bryan told the German-Americans] that the brewers and distillers were connecting them with the liquor traffic to their detriment.

Liriodendron. [Bot. L. (Linnaeus).] A tree of a genus of the magnolia family; the tulip tree, *L. tulipifera.* — 1802 CUTLER in *Life & Corr.* II. 104 [We] went to Mr. Holt's garden and collected a number of trees, magnolias, bignonias, Liriodendrons, etc. 1841 *S. Lit. Messenger* VII. 38/1 The tall Liriodendrons . . . bear their flowers too high to be rifled by the passer by.

Lisbon. *attrib.* Designating articles imported from Lisbon, Portugal. {1767–}

1654 *Essex Probate Rec.* I. 185 Lisbourn waire & other erthen vessells. 1705 *Boston News-Letter* 10 Dec. 4/2 To be Sold in Boston . . . , new Lisbon Salt at 23s. per Hogshead. 1761 ROWE *Letters* 391 Its not in my power to Send you Either port or Lisbon Wine. 1769 *Boston Chronicle* 1 June, Wine to be sold . . . , viz. Old Sterling Madeira, Lisbon, Teneriff, [etc.]. 1790 *Columbian Centinel* 15 Sept. 3/3 At One o'clock, will be sold by publick Vendue, . . . ten bags Lisbon Feathers.

Lisle-thread. *attrib.* Designating articles made of a hard twisted thread originally manufactured in Lille, (formerly Lisle), France. {1851–} — 1863 'G. HAMILTON' *Gala-Days* 201 The gloves your lovers find will be sure to be Lisle-thread. 1908 MCGAFFEY *Show-Girl* 70 Turning my back in maidenly modesty to the court, I dug down in the lisle-thread bank and came up with a hundred dollar bill. 1913 LONDON *Valley of Moon* I. ix, [She] delayed a moment longer to put on her tan lisle-thread gloves.

Lisle. *attrib.* [*Lisle*, now Lille, France.] =prec. {1858–} — 1882 LATHROP *Echo of Passion* v, A pair of Lille gloves only half drawn on. 1922 COURTENAY *Physical Beauty* 49 Pay more for your stockings (silk, lisle or silk and wool) rather than risk infection.

Lisse. *attrib.* Made of lisse, a kind of silk gauze. {1864–} — 1852 *Harper's Mag.* VI. 143 Bonnet of lisse crape trimmed with blonde and marabouts. 1923 WYATT *Invis. Gods* 4 The family barouche . . . containing his mother's black veil and lisse ruche.

* **List,** *n.*[1] *Agric.* +A ridge of earth thrown up by a moldboard plow or hoe.

1768 WASHINGTON *Diaries* I. 267 Began to cross gd. at Muddy hole . . . , having Run only a single furrow for a list. 1786 *Ib.* III. 57 Began at the first to cross the lists in order to Plant corn. 1814 J. TAYLOR *Arator* 104 A deep and wide furrow is to be run by a large plough . . . to form . . . a neat ridge or list on which to plant the corn. 1833 SILLIMAN *Man. Sugar Cane* 20 The cotton beds are shaved down into the alleys, covering the trash, &c. and forming a wide list. 1886 *Amer. Philol. Ass. Trans.* 40 *List*, 'a bed,' . . . (of a cotton row) . . . is common in South Carolina.

List, *n.*[2] {1602–} +An enumeration or description of property subject to taxation. — 1646 *Va. Statutes* I. (1823) 329 To the prejudice of many who have duely and according to law presented their lists. 1655 *Conn. Rec.* I. 279 Sea-Brooke is fyned forty shillings for not sending ye Lists of theire estates to the Courte. 1779 *Va. State P.* (1823) 295 The listers . . . [shall] warn all the inhabitants . . . to give in to them their respective lists. 1809 KENDALL *Travels* I. 187 The listers or assessors are to retain the lists in their possession till the last day of December annually.

* **List,** *v.*[1] +*tr.* To record or enter for purposes of taxation. (Cf. LIST *n.*[2]) — 1658 *Va. Statutes* I. (1823) 454 All negroes imported . . . and Indian servants . . . being sixteen years of age, to be listed and pay leavies as aforesaid. 1676 *Conn. Rec.* II. 294 Stoneington, for one fowrth part of their improved land by tillage, moweing and English pasture, to be listed twenty shillings pr acre. 1877 BURROUGHS *Taxation* 214 Assessors are to list such lands only as are situate [etc.].

* **List,** *v.*[2]

+**1.** *Agric. tr.* and *absol.* To form lists or ridges on (land), usually with a moldboard plow, while cultivating, or preparatory to planting, a crop. (Cf. ENLIST *v.*[2] and LIST *n.*[1])

1768 WASHINGTON *Diaries* I. 267 Began plowing at Doeg for Corn—that is to list. 1770 *Ib.* 374 Finished listing Ground for Corn at Muddy hole. 1814 J. TAYLOR *Arator* 139 If the soil is stiff or tough with turf, the first plough with four horses, ridges or lists on the old water furrow, with four furrows of the same depth and width. 1856 OLMSTED *Slave States* 432 Boys and girls, 'listing' an old corn-field with hoes.

+**2.** To plant (corn) by means of a lister.

1888 *Scientific Amer.* LVIII. 298/1 A fender for cultivators has been patented, . . . being designed more particularly for use on growing check-rowed and listed corn.

+**Listable,** *a.* Subject to enlistment for military service; taxable or assessable. — 1665 *R.I. Col. Rec.* II. 115 Their sones and sarvants that are listable, which are to be listed, and to traine. **1688** *New Eng. Hist. & Gen. Reg.* XXXIV. 371 An Accot. of the lystable Estates in the towne of Lyme. **1779** *Vt. State P.* (1823) 295 The said inhabitants . . . shall give in to the listers . . . a true account of all their listable poles, and all their rateable estate. **1895** *Columbus Dispatch* 23 Nov. 13/5 [Such certificates] will be—of a nature and form not listable for taxation.

Lister.[1] {*a*1701}

1. One who enrols for military service. *Obs.*

1678 *Conn. Rec.* III. 11 This Court [examined] whither the former immunities were stated upon the Troop as a Troop or upon those whoe were the first listers.

+**2.** One who makes out returns on taxable property; an assessor. *Obs.* (Cf. LIST *n.*[2] and *v.*[1])

1682 *Derby Rec.* 8 Dec. 130 The Town have chosen . . . John Hubbel & Abel Gun listers & rate makers. **1703** *Conn. Rec.* IV. 439 [When] any inhabitant . . . shall refuse or neglect to give in to the listers an account of his . . . rateable estate [etc.]. **1779** *Vt. State P.* (1823) 296 The listers shall add the sum total of such additions [etc.]. *c***1803** in A. E. Lee *Hist. Columbus, Ohio* (1892) I. 156 John Blair lister of taxable property in Franklin Township. **1847** in Howe *Hist. Coll. Ohio* 197 The total amount of taxable property returned by the 'listers' [in 1804], was $393.04.

+**Lister.**[2] *Agric.* A type of plow cutting a deep furrow. Used in planting corn in dry areas. — **1887** *Scientific Amer.* LVI. 6/3 When grain is planted by the so-called 'combined lister and drill,' the listing forms a ditch or furrow several inches deep, in which the seed is deposited. **1893** *Harper's Mag.* April 711/1 The lister has supplanted the hoe.

Listing. *Agric.* +**1.** The action of forming lists on land. (Cf. LIST *v.*[2] 1.) +**2.** The action of planting corn with a lister. (Cf. LIST *v.*[2] 2.) — **(1) 1805** PARKINSON *Tour* 165, I was near two months getting a plough made, therefore I hired for the listing (as they call it). **1862** *N.Y. Tribune* 19 Feb. 6/5 Manure is carted upon the land . . . , and left in heaps, . . . to be spread at the time of listing. **(2) 1887** *Scientific Amer.* LVI. 6/3 The drawback to this listing is due to the fact that close to the edges of the furrow on each side, a row of weeds springs up.

List-maker. + =LISTER *n.*[1] 2. *Obs.* — **1663** *Conn. Rec.* I. 392 The said Towne of N. London to be more carefull in their choyse of List makers, for the future. **1676** *Ib.* II. 283 What person soever shall wear gold or siluer lace . . . the list makers of the respectiue townes are hereby required to assesse such persons . . . at one hundred and fifty pownd estate. **1692** *Ib.* IV. 81 Persons . . . [are] to give in a true acct. of theire stocks . . . to the list makers according to law.

Literacy. The state of being literate; ability to read and write. {1893–} Also attrib. — **1883** *New Eng. Jrnl. Educ.* XVII. 54 Massachusetts is the first state in the Union in literacy in its native population. **1888** *New Princeton Rev.* Dec. 336 Education is more general, our literacy greatly increased, our habits and tastes more refined. **1911** PERSONS, etc. *Mass. Labor Laws* 183 No law requires duplicates of literacy certificates, and in most cases even the number is absolutely without record.

Literary, *a.* {1646–} Designating various groups and organizations interested in promoting the study of literature and in social culture. — **1879** *Harper's Mag.* Aug. 358/1 By far the most valuable fruit of the Chautauqua plan . . . will come from the Chautauqua Literary and Scientific Circle. **1883** *Ib.* Dec. 149/1 There has been no literary circle in the country like the Boston circle. **1893** *Ib.* April 654/2 The lesser circles of which I speak are bowling clubs, whist clubs, euchre clubs, poker clubs, literary guilds, musical coteries [etc.]. **1894** WISTER *Ib.* Aug. 385/1 She was president of the Ladies' Reform and Literary Lyceum.

Literary club. A social club or organization composed of those interested in literature. {1791–} — **1870** *Republican Rev.* 26 March 2/3 A literary club or reading society, to be established as soon as possible, in our town of Albuquerque. **1893** *Harper's Mag.* March 636/1 Does this mean that . . . we are to look for the young lady not in the literary club, but in the stable? **1903** *McClure's Mag.* Nov. 25/1 [We] depend upon the native talent of our literary club, which meets with song and debate every Friday evening.

Literary Emporium. A nickname for Boston, Massachusetts. — **1839** *S. Lit. Messenger* V. 629/1 Boston has been termed the 'Literary Emporium' . . . by Edmund Kean, the tragedian. **1843** *Lowell Offering* III. 24 The literati of our Literary Emporium comprises but a small proportion of its inhabitants.

Literary institution. A school, academy, or college. Often in grandiose use. — **1831** PECK *Guide* 292 Rock Spring was selected by the writer, in 1820, as a site for . . . a small literary institution. **1837** — *Gaz. Illinois* 72 A Literary Institution, modeled somewhat after the plan of the Oneida Institute . . . is in progress at Galesboro. **1849** CHAMBERLAIN *Indiana Gazetteer* 45 The following is a brief history and description of the principal Literary Institutions in the State.

Literary society. A society or club composed of those interested in self-improvement through the study of literature, public speaking, etc. Also transf. — **1857** *Lawrence* (Kan.) *Republican* 6 Aug. 4 The literary society of the town . . . now numbers over fifty members. **1864** NICHOLS *Amer. Life* I. 65 A literary society . . . makes the necessary arrangements [for the lectures]. **1881** CHASE *Editor's Run in N. Mex.* 215 Literary societies are forming, and sociables, private parties, etc., occur here as in older places. **1888** *Century Mag.* Sept. 751/1 Twin literary societies, or 'halls,' generally secret, . . . have been institutions at every leading college in the land.

Lithograph. A print produced by lithography. {1839–}

1847 *Knickerb.* XXX. 219 One [was] a lithograph of 'Old Zach.,' and the other of the 'Beauty of Arkansaw.' **1870** *Scribner's Mo.* I. 46 Maps, charts, pretty chromos and lithographs, adorn the walls. **1893** 'MARK TWAIN' in *Harper's Mag.* CIV. 601/2, I could not have believed . . . that there could be such solace to the soul in wall-paper and framed lithographs. **1899** CHESNUTT *Wife of His Youth* 159 A national flag was gracefully draped over the platform, and under it hung a lithograph of the Great Emancipator.

+**b.** *Lithograph city,* a projected city having only a pictured existence. *Obs.*

1839 BRIGGS *H. Franco* I. 90 Augustus had travelled in foreign parts, for he had drummed in Arkansas, and collected in the lithograph cities of the west. **1846** N. F. MOORE *Hist. Sk. Columbia Coll.* 23 These streets, probably, like those of many lithograph cities of recent date, existed only upon paper.

Lithographed, *a.* Produced by lithography; represented in a lithograph. {1839–} — **1839** BRIGGS *H. Franco* II. 14 Innumerable plans of lithographed towns and cities . . . were to be disposed of at auction. **1865** STOWE *House & Home P.* 96 Over each door shall hang one of the lithographed angel-heads of the San Sisto. **1877** JOHNSON *Anderson Co., Kansas* 62 On his arrival at Louisville [in 1857] he had a lithographed plat of the town made.

Lithographer. One who makes lithographs. {1842– (Timperley *Encycl. Lit. & Typogr. Anecdote* 932)} — **1828** WEBSTER, *Lithographer,* . . . one who practices lithography. **1866** *Internal Rev. Guide* 231 Productions of stereotypers, lithographers, engravers and electrotypers. **1886** *Century Mag.* May 589/1 The night classes, as in Cincinnati and St. Louis, are attended by many lithographers, draughtsmen, and engravers. **1919** *U.S. Training Service Bul.* No. 23 The data were prepared by two expert lithographers.

Lithographic *a.* {1813–} +Designating a projected city or town having only a fictitious existence. *Obs.* (Cf. LITHOGRAPH b.) — **1837** W. JENKINS *Ohio Gaz.* 147 We believe it never existed except on paper; and that the forest retains undisputed possession of a lithographic city. **1846** SAXE *Progress* (1847) 11 You deem he puffs some lithographic town.

***Little,** *a.*

1. In the names of various (1) birds, (2) fish, (3) plants, and (4) animals smaller than those denoted by the unmodified designation. (Cf. GREAT *a.* 3.)

Only a selection of examples is included.

(1) **1917** *Birds of Amer.* I. 182/1 Least Bittern. . . . [Also called] Little Bittern. **1781–2** JEFFERSON *Notes Va.* (1788) 76 *Muscicapa Caroliniensis.* . . . Little brown flycatcher. *c***1728** CATESBY *Carolina* I. 5 *Accipiter Minor.* The Little Hawk. This Bird weighs three ounces and sixteen penny weight. **1812** WILSON *Ornithology* V. 32 Little Sandpiper: *Tringa pusilla* . . . resides chiefly among the sea marshes. **1831** AUDUBON *Ornith. Biog.* I. 486 The Little Screech Owl. *Strix Asio.* **1878** *Nat. Museum Proc.* I. 163 Besides the Ibises, the Great and Little White Egrets, Louisiana and Night Herons . . . were breeding here. **1823** in James *Exped.* I. 266 *Scolopax minor*—Little woodcock.

(2) **1814** MITCHILL *Fishes N.Y.* 452 Little Herring. *Clupea parvula.* About six inches long. **1884** in Goode, etc. *Fisheries* I. 304 The Tinker Mackerel, *S[comber] pneumatophorus,* is known as 'Mackerel,' 'Easter Mackerel,' . . . 'Little Mackerel.' **1814** MITCHILL *Fishes N.Y.* 405 Little Porgee. *Labrus obliquus.* . . . Has a striking similitude to the *grunts,* but is more high-backed and gibbous. **1842** *Nat. Hist. N.Y., Zoology* IV. 11 The Little White Bass. *Labrax pallidus.* This pigmy bass . . . inhabits salt and brackish waters.

(3) **1899** GOING *Flowers* 153 The 'little panic-grass' . . . gives permanence to the coast-lines of Florida and the Gulf States. **1843** TORREY *Flora N.Y.* II. 380 *Carex stellulata.* . . . Little Prickly Sedge. . . . Wet meadows: common. **1833** EATON *Botany* (ed. 6) 336 *Serpicula canadensis,* ditch moss, little snake weed. **1821** *Mass. H. S. Coll.* 2 Ser. IX. 152 Plants . . . indigenous in the township of Middlebury [Vt., include] . . . [*Nuphar*] *kalmiana,* . . . Little yellow pond lily.

(4) **1917** *Mammals of Amer.* 239 Taylor's Deer Mouse, or Little Deer Mouse, . . . [is] one of the smallest of North American Mice. **1857** *Rep. Comm. Patents: Agric. 1856* 67 Little Red-Squirrel. . . . This pretty and active little animal is well known through the Northern States. **1842** *Nat. Hist. N.Y. Zoology* I. 34 The Small Weasel. *Mustella pusilla* . . . is usually known under the name of the *Little Weasel.*

2. Used in nicknames of various prominent persons. (Cf. LITTLE GIANT.)

1868 *N.Y. Herald* 10 July 6/5 In cutting Cass out of the vote of New York and defeating him 'Little Van' [Martin Van Buren] had full satisfaction against the regular Democratic Convention. **1869** *Congress. Globe* 18 March 136/2 'The little magician,' Martin Van Buren, had wormed himself into the confidence of 'Old Hickory.' **1871** DE VERE 250 General McClellan was *Little Mac* or *Young Napoleon,* . . . and Sheridan is still *Little Phil.*

Little Dipper. (See DIPPER 5 c.)

+**Little Giant.** (See quot. 1885.) — **1854** *Knickerb.* XLIV. 7 We will next examine into the qualities for availability that the 'Little Giant' possesses. **1865** *Congress. Globe* App. 20 Feb. 70/1 Lincoln was the giant, Douglas was the 'little giant.' **1885** *Mag. Amer. Hist.* Feb. 202/2 *Little Giant.*—A nickname for Stephen A. Douglas, who was small of stature, but of great intellect. **1901** CHURCHILL *Crisis* 135, I reckon I'll go for a walk, boys, . . . so as to be ready for the Little Giant to-morrow at Freeport.

+**Little joker.** (See JOKER 1.)

+**Little-neck (clam).** [See first quot.] A small clam of various species, esp., on the Atlantic Coast, the young of the quahog or round clam. — **1883** *Nat. Museum Bul.* No. 27, 234 Another name [for the small round clam] is 'Little Neck,' derived originally from a neck of land on the north shore of Long Island, known as Little Neck, whose clams had a superior flavor. *Ib.*, Dealers . . . [now] apply the term 'Little Neck' to all small clams. *Ib.* 241 *Chione succincta* . . . and *Chione simillima* . . . are also known in the markets [of Calif.] as 'Little-Neck' clams, but are not so abundant as *Tapes*. **1903** *N.Y. State Museum Bul.* No. 71, 5 The little-neck clam, *Venus mercenaria*, grows most abundantly below the low tide line. **1911** *Rep. Fisheries 1908* 314.

Little owl. +**1.** The screech owl (*Otus asio*) or a related bird. Also *little horned owl.* +**2.** The Acadian owl or saw-whet, *Cryptoglaux acadica.* — **(1)** *c*1728 CATESBY *Carolina* I. 7 *Noctua Aurita Minor.* The Little Owl, is about the size of, or rather less than, a Jack-daw. **1917** *Birds of Amer.* II. 109 Screech Owl. *Otus asio asio.* . . . [Also called] Little Horned Owl; Gray Owl [etc.]. **(2) 1811** WILSON *Ornithology* IV. 66 Little Owl: *Strix passerina* . . . makes up in neatness of general form and appearance for deficiency of size. **1839** PEABODY *Mass. Birds* 275 The Acadian or Little Owl, *Strix acadia*, is found in Massachusetts.

+**Little Rhody.** A nickname for the state of Rhode Island. — **1851** JOHNSTON *Notes N. Amer.* II. 326 Rhode Island [is content] with the affectionate familiarity of Little Rhody. **1860** COX *Buckeye Abroad* 444 The cry is that Rhode Island is in sight; . . . Little Rhody; in whose University so many months were passed. **1892** WALSH *Lit. Curiosities* 651.

Little Turk. {1863–} +The plum curculio, *Conotrachelus nenuphar.* — **1863** *Prairie Farmer* June 373/1 The crescent under fig. 1 is the cut made by the 'little Turk' in depositing its egg. **1890** *Cent.* 4567/1.

Little woman. An affectionate or appreciative designation for a wife. *colloq.* — **1881** *Harper's Mag.* June 110/2 When he died, his 'little woman' would be quite equal to carrying on the business. **1890** *Buckskin Mose* 218 The memory of the little woman I had left behind me in the East, or 'God's country.'

***Live,** *a.*

1. 'Chiefly *U.S.*' (*O.E.D.*). **a.** Of persons or institutions: Full of energy; wide awake; abreast of the times. {1877–}

1857 *Knickerb.* L. 456 A neighboring bath-house, kept by a live Yankee of the name of Martin. **1861** *Ill. Agric. Soc. Trans.* IV. 263 Our County Society . . . numbers among its members most of the *'live farmers'* in the county. **1875** *Chicago Tribune* 8 Dec. 12/3 The politics, or rather religion of his paper, was changed, and it became a 'red-hot,' 'live' Gentile sheet. **1893** *Publishers' Weekly* 8 April 596 (*advt.*), Good chance for a live man.

b. Of things, subjects, etc.: Possessing interest or importance; not obsolete. {1900}

1877 TALMAGE *50 Sermons* 26 In all the world of literature there is no such live book as the Bible.

+**2.** Designating varieties of trees. (Cf. LIVE OAK.)

1813 MUHLENBERG *Cat. Plants* 87 Yellow oak, or live chesnut Oak. **1818** FORDHAM *Narr. Travels* 153 The live poplar, or tulip-bearing tree, of which canoes are made, . . . grow to a prodigious size. **1856** *Mich. Agric. Soc. Trans.* VIII. 729 The sturdy oak, elm, basswood or live-ash and hickory predominate [in Ottawa Co.]. **1885** HAVARD *Flora W. & S. Texas* 510 *Rhus virens.* (Live Sumach). Shrub found in shady arroyos and on lower slopes of mountains, west of the Nueces River.

3. In special combinations.

+*Live hedge,* =LIVE FENCE; +*live gang,* +*live shout, live steam* {1889}, (see quotations).

1760 T. BROWN *Plain Narr. Sufferings* 9 The Indians made a Live-Shout, as they call it when they bring in a Prisoner alive. **1835** HOFFMAN *Winter in West* I. 184 A great many English emigrants settled upon this prairie . . . are successfully introducing here the use of live hedges instead of fences in farming. **1875** KNIGHT 1337/2 *Live-gang,* a gang-saw mill, so arranged as to cut through and through the logs without previous slabbing. *Ib.*, *Live-steam.* . . . 1. Steam from the boiler at its full pressure; in contradistinction to *dead*-steam. 2. Steam from the boiler; in contradistinction to *exhaust-steam.*

***Live,** *v.*

***1.** *To live out,* +to be employed as a domestic servant.

1841 *Lowell Offering* I. 65 Sarah . . . should 'live out.' Accordingly, a place was provided for Sarah with a Mrs. J. **1865** A. D. WHITNEY *Gayworthys* 84, I never calculated to live out, all my life. **1882** 'M. HARLAND' *Eve's Daughters* 200 The settled purpose of catching husbands whose wages will relieve them from the necessity of 'living out.'

+**2.** *Where one lives,* at the seat of one's existence, at one's most vital or vulnerable spot. *slang.*

1860 HOLLAND *Miss Gilbert* 386 When that little wife of mine says, 'Tom, you're a good feller, God bless you,' it goes right in where I live. **1883** BEADLE *Western Wilds* 602 The Mormons never got a cent of it. This hurt Brigham—right where he lived. **1886** HOWELLS in *Century Mag.* Feb. 511/1 If I could only have reached him where he lives, as our slang says!

+**Live fence.** A hedge. Also *live fencing.* — **1804** J. ROBERTS *Penna. Farmer* 84 When the hedge is full grown, then there is a perfect live fence. **1829** *Mass. Spy* 25 March (Th.), Messrs. G. Th. and Son have imported 75,000 hawthorns, for 'live fencing.' **1847** *Life B. Lundy* 57 Among this undergrowth was a species of thorn that would be excellent for live fence. **1858** WARDER *Hedges & Evergreens* 13 Live-fences, or—as they are commonly called—Hedges, are a means of inclosure that belongs to an advanced state of civilization. **1885** *Century Mag.* March 795 The cuts will be protected from snow-drifts, and long lines of 'live fences' be secured.

***Live-forever. 1. a.** The pearly everlasting, *Anaphalis margaritacea.* **b.** Any one of various plants of the genus *Sedum,* esp. *S. triphyllum.* +**2.** (See quotation.) *Obs.* — **(1) 1674** JOSSELYN *Two Voyages* 77 Live for ever, it is a kind of *cud-weed,* flourisheth all summer long till cold weather comes in. **1817–8** EATON *Botany* (1822) 456 *Sedum telephium,* orpine, live-forever. **1853** *Knickerb.* XLII. 171 Here and there a straggling red rose-bush and a patch of yellow lilies or 'live-for-ever.' **1880** *Scribner's Mo.* May 101/2 Live-forever . . . thrives and multiplies under the plow and harrow. **(2) 1859** BARTLETT 247 *Live forever,* the name of a fanatical sect in Kentucky whose principal article of faith was that those who had 'faith' would never die.

***Lively,** *a.* +**1.** Of land: Fertile, fruitful. +**2.** Of a ball: Elastic; bouncing or rebounding quickly. — **(1) 1770** WASHINGTON *Diaries* I. 426 A pretty lively kind of Land grown up with Hick[or]y. **1786** *Ib.* III. 131 The cleared part has been lively and good, but much abused and a good deal worked. **(2) 1875** *Chicago Tribune* 12 Dec. 12/4 To sum up the features of lively-ball games, it may be said [etc.]. **1885** CHADWICK *Art of Pitching* 106 A comparatively dead ball [is used] in the game, compared to the old lively rubber filled ball of years past.

+**Live oak.**

1. Any of various American evergreen oaks.

The more important species are *Quercus virginiana,* of the southern states, and various species found on the Pacific coast, as *Q. wislizenii.*

1610 *Estate of Va.* 54 Sarsafrase, liue oake, greene all the years, Cedar and Firre. **1671** *S.C. Hist. Soc. Coll.* V. 333 This Land bears very good white, red, black watr Spanish, & liue oak; Ash, Hickery [etc.]. **1709** LAWSON *Carolina* 92 Live-Oak chiefly grows on dry, sandy Knolls. This is an Ever-green, and the most durable Oak all America affords. **1791** BARTRAM *Travels* 65 After walking through a spacious forest of Live Oaks and Palms . . . [we] arrived safe at the plantation. **1832** BROWNE *Sylva* 293 This species which is confined to the maritime parts of the Southern States . . . is known only by the name of Live Oak. **1845** FRÉMONT *Exped.* 241 The prevailing tree [among the oaks in the country west of the Sierra Nevadas] was the evergreen oak, (which, by way of distinction, we shall call the *live oak*). **1901** MOHR *Plant Life Ala.* 130 On the dunes the live oak makes a more or less scrubby growth.

b. Wood or building material obtained from this.

1774 in P. L. Phillips *Notes on B. Romans* (1924) 20 There is a Scandalous illicit Trade Carried on between the inhabitants . . . & the Spanjards at Orleans the former . . . Supplying the latter with Pitch, Tarr, Charcoal, Live Oak & Cattle. **1797** *Wilmington Gazette* 30 March, A Boat, built of Live Oak and Cedar. **1814** *Ann. 13th Congress* 1 Sess. I. 668 Live oak is exclusively applied to the frame of timbers, which constitute the form and mould of the ship. **1886** *Harper's Mag.* June 4/2 This vessel . . . was built of seasoned live-oak.

2. Attrib. and comb. with reference to shipbuilding.

1735 *Georgia Col. Rec.* III. 130 [Received] four large Pieces of Live Oak Timber, sent to be tried if fit for the use of the Navy. **1831** J. Q. ADAMS *Memoirs* VIII. 322 For the live-oak plantation purchases were made of about sixteen hundred acres. **1836** *Knickerb.* VIII. 152 Here was a camp of enterprising live-oak cutters procuring timber for the navy. **1860** *36th Congress 1 Sess. H. R. Rep.* No. 621, 6 Plitt agreed to aid Swift all he could in obtaining live-oak contracts with the Navy Department.

+**Live oak tree.** A tree belonging to any one of various species of live oak. — **1695** *Duxbury Rec.* 68 A straight line to an elm or live oak tree marked. **1765** J. BARTRAM *Journal* 5 Many live oak-trees grew upon it. **1819** E. DANA *Geogr. Sk.* 226 The live oak tree appears to designate climate. **1893** *Harper's Mag.* Feb. 359/1 In remembrance of your birthday, we have planted a live-oak tree to your memory.

+**Live paper.** (See quotations.) — **1877** BARTLETT 788 *Live Paper,* a term applied to business notes-of-hand. The banks, in discounting, prefer *'live paper,'* meaning notes that will be paid at maturity, and not such as will be renewed, or their payment prolonged. **1895** E. CARROLL *Principles Finance* 299 *Live paper.* Unmatured promissory notes, in contradistinction to matured, dead, or protested paper.

***Liver.** An inhabitant or resident in a particular region or place. 'Chiefly *U.S.*' (*O.E.D.*). *Obs.* {1677} — **1678** *New Castle Ct. Rec.* 195 Hee hath forced ye people whoe are Livers wth in the Jurisdiction of this Court to pay Custome. **1765** in Chalkley *Scotch-Irish Settlement Va.* II. 452 There is many places that there is no livers in and others that doth not know their lines. **1781** WASHINGTON *Diaries* II. 210 Mr. John Flood (at present a liver at lower Salem). **1850** MITCHELL *Lorgnette* I. 41 My friend . . . is an up-town liver.

+**Liverberry.** Any one of various plants of the genus *Streptopus. colloq.* — **1894** *Amer. Folk-Lore* VII. 102 *Streptopus amplexifolius, Streptopus roseus,* liver-berry, St. Francis, Me.

+**Liverleaf.** =LIVERWORT a. — **1817–8** EATON *Botany* (1822) 304 *Hepatica triloba,* liverleaf. **1843** TORREY *Flora N.Y.* I. 10 *Hepatica triloba.* . . . Liver-Leaf. . . . A very common plant in woods, flowering frequently in the latter part of March. **1853** *Knickerb.* XLII. 172 We brought in our aprons . . . fragile anemones and bashful liver-leaf. **1875** BURROUGHS *Winter Sunshine* 125 In the woods the liverleaf and arbutus had just opened doubtingly.

+**Liver pad.** A pad worn over the region of the liver. — **1882** SWEET & KNOX *Texas Siftings* 163 The advertiser promises to send the publisher . . . an automatic cut-off double-cylinder liver pad. **1883** PECK *Bad Boy* 46, I guess the ants thought there was something to eat in the liver pad, cause they all went into it, and they crawled around in the bran and condition powders inside of it. **1889** *Internat. Ann., Anthony's Photogr. Bul.* II. 72 Used as a liver pad or a plaster that is meant for chest protection.

Liverpool. *attrib.* Designating various articles imported from Liverpool, England. (See also next.) — **1810** SILLIMAN *Jrnl. Travels England* I. 48 Most of those articles which are sold in America under the general name of Liverpool wares, are brought to this port from Staffordshire, and other interior counties. **1816** *Niles' Reg.* IX. Suppl. 185/1 [In Maine] a manufactory of fine porcelain, . . . turns out large quantities of ware, which good judges are not able to distinguish from the best *Liverpool ware.* **1873** *Maine Agric. Rep.* 126 He sows three bushels of Liverpool salt to the acre.

Liverpool coal. Coal imported from Liverpool, England. — **1818** PALMER *Travels U.S.* 443 [Price of] Coal, Liverpool [$.29-.30 bu.]. **1841** BUCKINGHAM *America* I. 164 [For anthracite we substituted] English coal, called here Liverpool coal. **1857** *Knickerb.* XLIX. 419 We . . . read and scribbled by a good Liverpool-coal fire until eleven o'clock.

***Liverwort. a.** A plant of the genus *Hepatica* having heart-shaped, three-lobed leaves. **b.** Any one of various plants having leaves shaped somewhat like the liver or reputedly useful in treating diseases of the liver. — **1622** 'MOURT' *Relation* 62 We found heere in Winter . . . Brook-lime, Liver-wort, Water-cresses [etc.]. **1784** CUTLER in *Mem. Academy* I. 458 *Anemone.* . . . Liverwort. Blossoms white, tinged with red. In woods and shady places. April. **1832** WILLIAMSON *Maine* I. 126 *Lungwort* and *Liverwort*, used as preventives, or cures of the consumption. **1869** FULLER *Flower Gatherers* 26 Those little Liverworts you were kind enough to bring me last week. **1901** MOHR *Plant Life Ala.* 285 Little more than one-half of the liverworts so far reported from the State are of a decided Southern distribution.

* **Livery.**

+**1.** =LIVERY STABLE. Chiefly attrib.

1845 F. DOUGLASS *Narrative* 16 His stable and carriage-house presented the appearance of some of our large city livery establishments. **1855** *Vermont Free Press* 8 June, The two appeared in a handsome livery buggy, paid for, we suppose, by the State of Massachusetts. **1872** *Newton Kansan* 22 Aug. 3/6 If you want to hire a good saddle horse or livery team call at A. Shuster's Livery, Sale and Feed Stables. **1888** FERGUSON *Exp. Forty-Niner* i. 15 We placed our horses in a livery on Third street. **1891** O'BEIRNE *Leaders Ind. Territory* 43/2 He has been running a large livery business, which he sold out about August 8, 1890. **1893** 'THANET' *Stories* 113 His mother . . . pays visits once a year in a livery carriage. **1902** HARBEN *A. Daniel* 29, I could 'a' gone to a livery an' ordered out a team.

+**2.** A conveyance obtained from a livery stable.

1911 LINCOLN *Cap'n Warren's Wards* 8 Of course I shall share the expense of the livery.

***Livery cupboard.** A cupboard or sideboard on the shelves of which 'liveries' (servings of food or drink) were kept for distribution. *Obs.* — **1655** *Essex Probate Rec.* I. 224 A livery cupboard . . . a featherbed. **1658** *Boston Rec.* 147 Hee is to pay fourty shillings for this sumer, and a fayre livery Cupboard for the towne house.

Liveryman. {1682-} The keeper of a livery stable. {1841-} — **1839** *S. Lit. Messenger* V. 802/2 We managed to sustain our pride . . . by imputations of ignorance to the livery-man. **1873** *Winfield* (Kan.) *Courier* 5 June 3/1 O. N. Morris, the Liveryman, has returned from Topeka. **1885** *Wkly. New Mexican Rev.* 9 April 4/6 Albuquerque livery men ran excursion wagons to Los Gregorios when the penitentes tortured themselves. **1903** ADE *In Babel* 20 She was the daughter of a livery-man.

+**Livery rig.** An equipage or conveyance kept for hire or rented out by a livery stable. — **1872** *Newton Kansan* 26 Sept. 3/2 For a good livery rig . . . go to Shuster's stable. **1880** *Harper's Mag.* May 913/2 Early that afternoon a livery rig . . . appeared at our door. **1882** PECK *Sunshine* 94 It got so that the livery rig a young man drove was an index to his thoughts. **1903** A. ADAMS *Log Cowboy* 188 Long before we reached the Mulberry, a livery rig came down the trail to meet us.

Livery stable. A public stable where horses and carriages are let. {1705-}

1708 *Boston Rec.* 3 May, The way passing on the northerly Side of Livery Stable in Justice Lynds pasture. **1799** BROWN *A. Mervyn* xviii, I was determined to prosecute my search as long as an inn or a livery-stable remained unexamined. **1839** *S. Lit. Messenger* V. 802/2 A little incident . . . occurred in this city at a livery-stable. **1873** *Newton Kansan* 22 May 3/2 A. Shuster is having a well dug in front of his livery stable. **1925** TILGHMAN *Dugout* 99 She hurried to Tremblay's livery stable.

b. Attrib. and comb. with *business, building*, etc.

1874 PINKERTON *Expressman & Detective* 115 He intended to go into the livery stable business. **1881** *Rep. Indian Affairs* 151 There is also a livery stable building now within the limits of the reservation. **1891** *Atlantic Mo.* June 807/2 The livery stable man who drove me owns several horses and carriages. **1920** COOPER *Under Big Top* 126 A yelping livery-stable owner scurried down the street.

Livery-stable keeper. One who keeps a livery stable. {1867-} — **1736** *R.I. Col. Rec.* IV. 527 Alexander Thorp, livery stable keeper, and Isaac Cusno, saddler, . . . [requested] license to keep two stage coaches for the service. **1851** CIST *Cincinnati* 346 Members of the [Cincinnati Astronomical] Society [include] Livery Stable Keepers, 3. **1879** *Cimarron News & Press* 27 Nov. 3/2 A shooting affray occurred in Otero in which Harry Bassett, the livery stable keeper, was killed. **1925** TILGHMAN *Dugout* 58 The livery stable keeper had moved his horses.

Live stock.

1. Domestic animals in general, horses, cattle, swine, etc. {in transf. sense, 1775; 1777-}

[**1660** *Springfield Rec.* I. 282 It is voted that such rates shall be raysed on the houses land & liveing Stock according to their worth.] **1742** *Georgia Col. Rec.* VI. 30 It is order'd that the said Erinkman be Supply'd with a Cow and Calf & other Live Stock. **1786** *Columbian Mag.* I. 36/1 The barn, cattle-houses, sheds, stacks, &c. are so disposed . . . as to afford the best winter shelter for live stock. **1847** RUXTON *Adv. Rocky Mts.* (1848) 203 They attacked his house, burned his mill, destroyed his grain and his live stock. **1894** ROBLEY *Bourbon Co., Kansas* 153 The show of live stock and fancy work was very good. **1918** *Nation* 7 Feb. 129/2 The transfer of live stock from areas liable to drought to those of plentiful feed.

+**2.** Negro slaves. *Obs.*

1842 BUCKINGHAM *Slave States* I. 454 Negro slaves which sold formerly at 1,000 dollars, now sell for 500 dollars. There was not so much depreciation in the value of the 'live stock,' as these are called, as in the land. **1852** STOWE *Uncle Tom* xii, The trader waked up bright and early, and came out to see his live-stock.

3. *attrib.* **a.** Pertaining to the production, exhibition, or sale of live stock.

1856 *Porter's Spirit of Times* 20 Dec. 261/3 Our live-stock markets have ruled pretty equable since our last. **1887** *Courier-Journal* 7 May 4/1 An English Consul makes a very unfriendly report to his Government concerning the live-stock interest of Texas. **1890** *Stock Grower & Farmer* 11 Jan. 3/2 Fish & Keck Co., live stock commission merchants of Kansas City. **1894** *Vt. Agric. Rep.* XIV. 95 Don't overlook the Vermont exhibit in the live-stock show. **1900** *Congress. Rec.* 16 Feb. 1893/1 Resolutions of the Kansas City (Mo.) Live Stock Exchange . . . against increasing the tax on oleomargarine. **1905** *Forestry Bureau Bul.* No. 62, 11 The method adopted for the distribution of these circulars was to secure from different live-stock associations the names of their members.

b. Pertaining to the transportation of live stock.

1858 W. P. SMITH *Railway Celebrations* 92 Equipment of the Marietta and Cincinnati Railway. . . . Cars.—Passenger, 33; . . . Live Stock, 212. **1890** *Stock Grower & Farmer* 4 Jan. 3/1 Eli Titus has resigned the position of live stock agent of the Atchison, Topeka and Santa Fe railroad.

***Living.** *attrib.* Of or pertaining to that which it is necessary for one to have in order to live, esp. *living price.*

1834 *Congress. Globe* 3 May 362/2 Mr. F[orsyth] said that . . . 70 to 76 cents was a very living price for fish oil. **1881** *Reinbeck* (Iowa) *Times* 6 Jan. 2/4 Who will make as good a Boot as can be obtained in the county, and at the lowest living prices. **1885** *Century Mag.* Jan. 475 [They] ought to be willing, to pay to their organist and choir-master 'a living salary'—a salary sufficient for all his needs. **1888** BELLAMY *Looking Backward* xxviii, Industries conducted as these are do not pay you living wages. **1894** *Congress. Rec.* 10 Jan. 662/1 Nobody pays more to ride than the farmer; let us at least give him a living chance. **1904** TARBELL *Hist. Standard Oil Co.* I. 111 Everybody declared three dollars was not a 'living price' for oil.

Living picture. A tableau in which the performers are costumed, grouped, and posed so as to suggest a picture. — **1875** *N.Y. Herald* 24 Nov. 2/4 Mr. Matt Morgan's Classical Tableaux of Living Pictures, illustrated by a Corps of Beautiful Ladies. **1895** *N.Y. Dramatic News* 7 Dec. 3/3 While the living picture, Rock of Ages, was on, one of the sisters . . . got struck squarely in the face with a hunk of liver. **1896** *Ib.* 29 Aug. 5/3 The bill . . . also included the living pictures, the Cinematographe and the Symphony orchestra.

Living room. {1825-} +A family sitting room. — **1857** VAUX *Villas* 119 Under the . . . living-room is a basement-kitchen. **1860** OLMSTED *Back Country* 237 The interior consisted of one large 'living-room,' and a 'lean-to,' used as a kitchen. **1869** TOURGEE *Toinette* 68 The 'living room,' as it is called, or sitting-room. **1883** E. H. ROLLINS *New Eng. Bygones* 167 The farmers used to sit much by the windows of their living-rooms. **1910** C. HARRIS *Eve's Husband* 310 She occupied one chair in the living room all day.

+**Liza.** [Sp.] A gray mullet. — **1883** *Nat. Museum Bul.* No. 27, 449 *Mugil brasiliensis.* . . . White Mullet; Liza. Atlantic coast from Cape Cod to South America. **1911** *Rep. Fisheries 1908* 312/2 Mullet (*Mugil cephalus* and *M. curema.*) . . . Local names are . . . 'blue-back mullet,' 'liza,' or 'josea.'

* **Lizard.**

***1.** Any one of various small, usually scaly and four-legged, lacertilian reptiles.

1602 in Smith *Gen. Hist. Va.* I. 17 [We] exchanged with them Kniues, Hatchets, Beades, Bels, and such trifles, for some Bevers, Lyzards [etc.]. **1736** CATESBY *Carolina* II. 45 The Brown Viper . . . prey[s] on Lizards, Efts, and other animals. **1780** in *Travels Amer. Col.* 649 On the head of one [war club] was the figure of a lizard. **1845** FRÉMONT *Exped.* 267 These Indians [Diggers] had long sticks, hooked at the end, which they used in hauling out lizards, and other small animals, from their holes. **1899** *Animal & Plant Lore* 38 Don't kill a lizard (salamander), or you will die within a year. Winn, Me.

transf. **1855** SIMMS *Forayers* 205 'You white livered lizard!' roared the outlaw. **1907** WHITE *Arizona Nights* 139 You have to leave town for a couple of days, and you want back that lizard [a horse] you sold me.

+**b.** A nickname for a native or inhabitant of Alabama.

1845 *Cincinnati Misc.* I. 240 The inhabitants of . . . Alabama [are called] Lizards. **1889** *Amer. Notes & Q.* III. 77 Alabama is the 'Cotton Plantation' State. Its inhabitants are called 'lizards.'

+**2.** Any one of various sledlike contrivances for hauling logs or other heavy objects.

1870 NOWLAND *Indianapolis* 16 One end was placed on a sled called a 'lizard,' to which the horse was hitched. **1905** *Forestry Bureau Bul.* No. 61, 36 A single sled used in dragging logs. One end of the log rests upon the sled. (N[orthern] F[orest].) . . . [Also called] go-devil, lizard, scoot [etc.]. **1906** in *Amer. Speech* VI. 465 Down in Texas a sledge or jumper is evidently called a lizzard. An effort is now being made to locate a lizzard made by Davy Crockett . . . in 1835.

Lizard('s)-tail. An herblike plant (*Saururus cernuus*) found in marshes. {1753-}

1791 MUHLENBERG *Index Florae* 168 *Saururus, cernuus.* Lizards-tail. **1817-8** EATON *Botany* (1822) 448. **1872** *Amer. Naturalist* VI. 728 In lower spots [of the lower Wabash Valley] the 'lizard-tail' . . . was the predominant plant. **1893** F. T. DANA *Wild Flowers* 56 The nodding, fragrant spikes of the lizard's tail abound in certain swamps from June till August. **1901** MOHR *Plant Life Ala.* 125 In the openings the shallow pools are filled with . . . *Saururus cernuus* (lizard's tail).

Llano. *S.W.* [Sp.] An extensive treeless steppe, plain, or prairie. {1613-}

1846 SAGE *Scenes Rocky Mts.* xxxiii, A continuous chain of hills . . . plainly points out the cheerless *llanos* of the Great American Desert. **1856** WHIPPLE *Explor. Ry. Route* I. 30 These appear to be the last mesa remnants of a llano, or prairie which once covered the whole region. **1867** COZZENS *Sayings* 11 They would probably have browsed on the wild grass of the llanos or plains. **1895** REMINGTON *Pony Tracks* 83 The horse herds were moved in from the *llano* and rounded up in the corral.

attrib. **1885** HARTE *Maruja* 40 Your government, Captain, handed over ten leagues of the llano land to the Doctor West.

+**b.** *Llano Estacado*, the Staked Plain, a high arid plateau of forty thousand square miles, situated in Texas and New Mexico.

1834 A. PIKE *Sketches* 42 The Llano Estacado, on whose borders we then were encamped, and which lay before us like a boundless ocean, was mentioned with a sort of terror. **1849** *31st Congress 1 Sess.* Sen. Ex. Doc. No. 64, 185 It was a vast, illimitable expanse of desert prairies—the dreaded 'Llano Estacado' of New Mexico. **1881** *Cimarron News & Press* 10 March 1/6 There is something romantic about these cañons and surrounding plains familiarly known as the 'Llano Estacado.' **1890** *Stock Grower & Farmer* 22 Feb. 8/1 The staked plains, or llano estacado, rises to the east [of the Rio Pecos].

+**L. M.** An abbreviation for LAWFUL MONEY a. *Obs.* — **1773** *Mass. Col. Soc. Publ.* VI. 115 He now promises a Reward of Ten Pounds L. M. to any who shall give Information. **1788** CUTLER in *Life & Corr.* I. 429 Oated and had my hair dressed. Bill, 9*d.*, L. M.; barber, 7*d.*, L. M.

+**Lo.** [A humorous application of Pope's well known 'Lo, the poor Indian.'] The American Indian. — **1871** *Republican Rev.* 2 Sept. 1/4 Cowardly Lo prefers to attack none but very small parties of teamsters, farmers, or lone mail riders. **1877** W. WRIGHT *Big Bonanza* 287 The Chinamen swarm the town in search of about the only kinds of work poor 'Lo' is able to do. **1879** *Harper's Mag.* Nov. 888/2 Colonel Craig . . . and his men began, not unsuccessfully, the repression and suppression of Mr. Lo. **1904** *Minneapolis Times* 12 June 6 The hunting is not very good and the march of civilization has convinced Lo that fighting is not as profitable as it used to be.

Loaded, *a.* {1661-} +Intoxicated, drunk. *slang.* — **1890** *Cent.* 3491/2 Loaded, . . . full of liquor; drunk. [Slang.] **1892** *Voice* 28 July, The Democratic nominee . . . came down the steps in a decidedly uncertain manner. . . . 'He's loaded' [said a bystander]. **1896** ADE *Artie* 77 You do n't mean to say that you were—loaded? **1910** E. S. FIELD *Sapphire Bracelet* 78 'Was he loaded?' 'Well, he wasn't exactly sober.'

***Loader.**

+**1.** A small measure holding just the quantity of powder suitable for charging a muzzle-loading gun: (see also quot. 1883). *Obs.*

1843 'CARLTON' *New Purchase* I. 105 A powder horn, and its loader of deer-horn. *Ib.* 199 A black, surly looking rifle, with the appurtenances of horns, pouches, loaders, tomahowks and knives. **1883** KNIGHT *Suppl.* 552/1 *Loader*, an instrument for re-loading cartridge shells.

+**2.** (See quot. 1905.)

1851 SPRINGER *Forest Life* 92 [After the swampers] come the barker and loader. **1893** *Scribner's Mag.* June 708/2 The skidway men, who are to be the 'loaders,' receive the logs brought to them by the skidding-team, and with their cant-hooks roll them into lofty tiers. **1905** *Forestry Bureau Bul.* No. 61, 41 *Loader*, one who loads logs on sleds or cars.

3. (See quotation.)

1875 KNIGHT 1337/2 *Loader*, a machine attached to a wagon, as a *hay-loader* or *stone-loader*.

***Loading.** *attrib.* +Designating various devices for putting live stock or logs aboard railroad cars. — **1890** *Stock Grower & Farmer* 25 Jan. 6/1 The loading chutes have been enlarged and remodelled. **1905** *Forestry Bureau Bul.* No. 61, 41 *Loading jack*, a platformed framework upon which logs are hoisted from the water for loading upon cars. (N[orthern] F[orest].) **1910** RAINE *B. O'Connor* 36 The loading board was lowered and the horses led from the car.

Loading tool. A device used in loading shells or cartridges for firearms. — **1874** LONG *Wild-Fowl* 20, I usually made a practice of . . . carrying an ammunition-box and loading-tools with me.

***Loadstone.** A variety of magnetite possessing polarity; a piece of this used as a magnet. — **1637** MORTON *New Canaan* 85 There are Loadstones also in the Northerne parts of the land. **1695** SEWALL *Diary* I. 413 Govr. Bradstreet . . . sent . . . a Loadstone belonging to the Publick, to the Secretary. **1781-2** JEFFERSON *Notes Va.* (1788) 31 Isinglass or mica is in several places; loadstone also. **1831** PECK *Guide* 45 [Near the Cove of Washita] the loadstone is represented to be found in great quantities.

+**Loaf,** *n.* [f. LOAF *v.*] A time spent in loafing. *colloq.* {1900}

1860 WHITMAN *Leaves of Grass* 39 The farmer stops by the bars, as he walks on a First-day loafe, and looks at the oats and rye. **1886** *American* XII. 76 A resolution I have made to enjoy a solid old-fashioned loaf this summer. **1893** *Columbus Dispatch* 5 July, The worst loaf of the meet was seen in the next half mile, the riders not knowing that there was a time limit. **1897** *Outing* XXX. 374/2 We have . . . the holiday camp, in which a restful loaf is the principal object.

b. *Loaf day*, a day when regular work is not done; a holiday.

1881 *Scribner's Mo.* XXII. 217/2 On 'loaf-days' the hands occupy themselves with making the neat cans which it is their . . . business to fill.

+**Loaf,** *v.* [Origin unknown; cf. LOAFER and LAND LOAFER.] *intr.* To stroll or saunter aimlessly; to loiter, linger, dawdle, trifle away time. {1857-}

1837 *Harvardiana* III. 304 Tom is sure to '*loaf*' in. **1852** STOWE *Uncle Tom* xii, Men talked, and loafed, and read. **1865** *Nation* I. 174 They're too damned proud to work. Rather loaf round Richmond and Petersburg. **1890** *Boston Jrnl.* 30 June 4/1 Tennyson does the greater part of his literary work . . . between breakfast and lunch, and loafs the rest of the day. **1922** PARRISH *Case & Girl* 225 He ain't no fly cop, and just happened to be loafin' here.

b. Often followed by the adverbs *about, around.*

1844 GODLEY *Letters from A.* II. 146 There were . . . a number of people 'loafing' about. **1846** COOPER *Redskins* v, We were lounging around—loafing around is the modern Doric. **1864** in S. Longfellow *H. W. Longfellow* III. 37 You loaf about in dell and hollow. **1876** 'MARK TWAIN' *Tom Sawyer* 182 [He] fishes a little, to get money to get drunk on—and loafs around considerable. **1902** WHITE *Blazed Trail* 211 Thorpe . . . engaged four axmen whom he found loafing about.

***Loaf bread.** *local.* Bread in the form of a loaf. {now *dial.*} Also attrib. — **1635** R. MATHER *Journal* 11 Many went on shoare . . . and brought . . . loafe bread, fresh fish, &c. **1682** *Boston Rec.* 156 To inquire into ye midle price of wheate, . . . & to publish the same to ye loafe bread bakers. **1775** in Pusey *Road to Ky.* (1921) 42 We git some good loaf Bread & good Whiskey. **1835** *S. Lit. Messenger* I. 338 Cold greens or turnips, with loaf bread baked a month ago . . . form the traveller's supper.

+**Loaf cake.** A cake baked in the form of a loaf. — **1828** LESLIE *Receipts* 62 Loaf Cake. **1844** *Knickerb.* XXIV. 423 The biscuit would not rise, her loaf-cake was heavy. **1878** COOKE *Happy Dodd* 344, I've give one boy . . . three doughnuts, a big slice o' loaf-cake and two cookies. **1906** *Springfield W. Repub.* 29 March 7 Sipping hot tea and tasting a large piece of loaf cake.

+**Loafer.**[1] [App. related to LAND LOAFER.] One given to loafing; an idler or lounger; one too lazy to work.

1835 *Knickerb.* VI. 63, That species of the *genus homo* . . . which Custom has christened with the expressive appellation of *Loafer!* **1862** *Trial C. M. Jefferds* 50 She called him a loafer, and said he deserved hanging. **1889** BRAYLEY *Boston Fire Dept.* 198 A gang of stout boys and loafers . . . had followed the firemen. **1925** TILGHMAN *Dugout* 94 In these times he became a sort of genteel loafer.

b. Attrib. and comb. with *class, ridden, wise.*

1842 HONE *Diary* II. 144 The amusement of prize-fighting . . . has become one of the fashionable abominations of our loafer-ridden city. **1850** JUDD *R. Edney* 395 Clover had been at Green Mill frequently of late, loafer-wise. **1888** BRYCE *Amer. Commonw.* II. III. lvii. 397 The 'loafer' class . . . have votes but no reason for using them one way more than another.

+**Loafer.**[2] (See quotations.) — **1891** O'BEIRNE *Indian Territory* I. 209 The 'loafer,' or large mountain wolf, is very plentiful. **1912** HOUGH *Story of Cowboy* 225 The great gray wolf [is] known as the timber wolf, buffalo wolf, 'loper,' 'loafer,' or 'lobo' wolf. **1913** BARNES *Western Grazing Grounds* 382 *Loafer.*—Western corruption of the Spanish Lobo; a wolf.

+**Loaferdom.** An aggregation of loafers; the state of being a loafer. — **1862** *Richmond Examiner* 10 July 2/6 Why cannot the authorities, among all loaferdom around Richmond, both black and white, secure a sufficient burial force for the cemeteries? **1894** *Forum* May 276 The steps from enforced idleness down into loaferdom, drunkenness, vagrancy, and crime, are short and near together.

+**Loaferess.** A female loafer. — **1840** C. E. LESTER *Glory & Shame of England* I. 40 The revised statutes of English *etiquette* have legalized these exactions of 'loafers' and 'loaferesses,' to use a very expressive Americanism. **1885** *Advance* 16 July 458 The loafers and loaferesses . . . stared at her with unanimous admiration.

+**Loaferish** *a.* Of, pertaining to, or like a loafer. — **1866** HOWELLS *Venetian Life* xix, Four pleasant ruffians in the loaferish postures which they have learned as *facchini* waiting for jobs. **1872** *Chicago Tribune* 14 Oct. 1/4 His language is a bit rough at times, and his style somewhat loaferish. **1893** *Scribner's Mag.* Feb. 262/2 A mere loaferish breach of the peace.

+**Loaferism.** The practice of loafing; collect., loafers. — **1836** *Knickerb.* VIII. 407 There is a moral sublimity in . . . his calling; but it is not the sublimity of loaferism. **1851** A. O. HALL *Manhattaner* 17 [The hotel] will long remain . . . the headquarters of Creole loaferism. **1889** *Home Missionary* Dec. 362 As long as I am in charge here, loaferism and blackguardism . . . will find an unwholesome atmosphere.

***Loaf sugar.** Refined sugar molded into loaves; also, sugar in the form of small cubic or rectangular solids. — **1725** *Boston News-Letter* 8 April 2/2 At Mr. James Smith's Sugar House, . . . Loaf Sugar by the Hundred, at 2 s. per Pound. **1789** *Ann. 1st Congress* I. 142 The committee agreed to tax . . . loaf sugar three cents per pound. **1807** JANSON *Stranger in A.* 29 The principal manufactures of Boston are . . . loaf sugar, tobacco, chocolate [etc.]. **1891** *Cent.* 6046/2 *Cut sugar*, a commercial name for loaf-sugar cut into prismatic form, generally cubes. **1901** ADE 40 *Modern Fables* 207 The little Cup . . . contains Consommé and not Tea, so don't toss any Loaf Sugar into it.

***Loan,** *v. tr.* To lend; to grant a loan.

'Now chiefly *U.S.*' (*O.E.D.*).

1729 *New Eng. Hist. & Gen. Reg.* XIII. 32 Gershom Tobey loans Oxen. **a1800** TWINING *Visit* 441 Such words as *illy, vended, to loan, to enterprise*, and a few others are to be met with in the least cultivated ranks of society. **1839** BRIGGS *H. Franco* II. 37, I had his note of hand for the money I had loaned him. **1866** LOWELL *Biglow P.* 2 Ser. p. xlii, *Loan* for *lend*, with which we have hitherto been blackened, I must retort upon the mother island, for it appears so long ago as in 'Albion's England.' **1898** J. R. TRUMBULL *Hist. Northampton, Mass.* I. 564 The capital of the Public Bank was still further replenished in 1727/8 when £60,000 in Bills of Credit were loaned to the towns.

+**Loan act.** A legislative enactment providing for a loan. — **1743** *N.H. Prov. Papers* V. 668 The Loan Act for emitting £25,000 which his Majesty has condescended to approve. **1837** *Diplom. Corr. Texas* I. (1908) 267 If the loan act is altered . . . we shall soon be able to effect our desires. **1849** *Whig Almanac 1850* 37/2 The loan act of Jan. 28, 1847, pledged the unsold national estate for the payment of certain debts.

+**Loan agent.** (See quotation.) — **1884** *Milnor* (Dak.) *Teller* 5 Sept., A. Wells, the genial and enterprising land and loan agent of Forman, . . . loans money on both real and personal property, makes final proofs and attends to all business of that kind.

Loan bill. {1722}

+**1.** A bill of credit issued by a state. *Obs.*

1714 *Mass. Bay Currency Tracts* 160 The Bank Bills having a better and more certain Security than the Public Loan Bills, and more easily obtained, in Case that late Act should be Repealed. **1720** *Ib.* 266 We accept the Loan Bills, and esteem them as Mony.

+**2.** =LOAN ACT.

1814 *Ann. 13th Congress* 2 Sess. I. 1269 Mr. E. rose . . . to state . . . why the loan bill had been introduced at this stage of the session. **1842** *Whig Almanac 1843* 35/2 A Loan Bill, Treasury Note Bill, and Provisional Tariff were passed, to preserve the Treasury from dishonor. **1847** POLK *Diary* 192 The Secretary of the Treasury . . . [was] pressing members to push the speedy passage of the loan-bill. **1869** *Amer. Ann. Cycl.* 30/1 Penniless adventurers . . . have been made the recipients and beneficiaries of all the benefits of the 'loan bill,' by which some thirteen millions of dollars have been awarded.

Loan market. The phase or state of commercial activity affecting the making or securing of loans. — **1870** MEDBERY *Men Wall St.* 11 Its loan market holds the keys of trade. **1875** *Chicago Tribune* 22 July 6/1 The Approach of the Fall Trade Stiffens the Loan-Market.

Loan office. {1720-}

+**1.** One of various offices set up by the Revolutionary Continental government in various states to facilitate subscriptions to government loans.

1776 *Jrnls. Cont. Congress* V. 845 For the convenience of the lenders, a loan office [shall] be established in each of the United States, and a commissioner, to superintend such office, be appointed by the said states respectively. **1777** J. ADAMS *Works* IX. 45 The design of loan-offices was to prevent the farther depreciation of the bills by avoiding farther emissions. **1802** *Steele P.* I. 244 It may be transferred to the Books of the Loan Office in this State. **1874** BANCROFT *Hist. U.S.* X. 223 An act of a previous session [c1779] had directed debts due to British subjects to be paid into the loan-office of the state.

+**2.** An office that puts state funds out on loan.

1848 *Indiana Gen. Ass. Doc. 1848–9* II. 285 The amount of funds in the loan office is given by the Auditor of State, in his annual report to the Legislature.

3. Attrib. in sense 1 with *bill, book*, etc. (Cf. next.)

1777 *N.J. Archives* 2 Ser. I. 481 Many people object to receive the New-Jersey Paper Currency, called the Loan-office money, dated in March 1776, because . . . supposed to be of no value. **1780** FRANKLIN *Writings* VIII. 56 The Reports you tell me prevail at Cadiz that the Loan Office Bills payable in France have not been duly honoured are wicked falshoods. **1854** PIERCE in *Pres. Mess. & P.* V. 294 The amount so found due was . . . entered by his order on the loan-office books of South Carolina.

+**Loan-office certificate.** An interest-bearing certificate issued by a loan office of the Revolution. — **1778** *Mass. Spy* 29 Oct. 4/2 The Loan Office Certificates, which may issue for prizes of the second class of the lottery of the United States, shall bear an interest of six per centum per annum. **1788** *Wilmington* (N.C.) *Centinel* 18 June, Wanted, a quantity of Continental Loan-office Certificates. **1792** HAMILTON in *Ann. 2d Congress* 1064 A considerable part of the outstanding or floating Debt consists of loan-office certificates. **1794** *Ann. 3d Congress* 1430 No claim shall be allowed for the renewal of Loan Office certificates destroyed before the fourth day of March.

+**Loan officer.** One having charge of a government loan office.

1737 *N.Y. Col. Laws* II. (1894) 1040 An Act to facilitate and Explain the duty of the Loan officers in this Colony. **1797** *Ann. 5th Congress* I. 476 Mr. Hillhouse laid before the Senate the petition of William Imlay, loan officer of the State of Connecticut, praying the payment of his account for extra clerk hire. **1806** in J. T. Buckingham *Newspaper Lit.* I. 277 Benjamin Austin, Loan-Officer, . . . has circulated an infamous falsehood concerning my professional conduct.

***Lobby,** *n.*

1. A waiting room or anteroom immediately adjacent to a hall or room in which a legislative body or court of law meets. {1640-}

1690 SEWALL *Diary* I. 333 Jno. Hoar comes into the Lobby and Sais he comes from the Lord, by the Lord, to speak for the Lord. **1724** JONES *Virginia* 29 At one End . . . is a Lobby, and near it is the Clerk of the Council's Office. **1798** ALLEN *Hist. Vermont* 207 When the Court convened on this subject, Colonel Allen went into the lobby, and began to write a memorial to the Legislature of New Hampshire. **1806** *Balance* V. 51/1 In the lobby and out of doors I have heard much conversation. **1889** BRAYLEY *Boston Fire Dept.* 298 A fire caught from a defective chimney in the judges' lobby in the Supreme Court. **1911** C. B. REYNOLDS *Washington* 44 Opening off from the Hall back of the Speaker's desk are the House Lobby and the Members' Retiring Rooms.

+**2.** *collect.* Those who frequent the anteroom of a legislature to influence the actions of the legislators.

1808 *Ann. 10th Congress* 1 Sess. II. 1536 If we move to Philadelphia we shall have a commanding lobby. **1836** in Mackenzie *Van Buren* 175 Those who trade upon legislation, (the hon'ble lobby) will be blown 'sky high.' **1872** *Atlantic Mo.* Feb. 256 The lobby congratulated the miners and the miners thanked the lobby for its efficient assistance. **1884** *Century Mag.* Aug. 631/2 Only when a moneyed lobby has controlled special legislation is there any division of plunder. **1913** LA FOLLETTE *Autobiog.* 187 A powerful lobby was organized under the immediate charge of Charles F. Pfister.

+**3.** Attrib. in sense 2 with *force, fund*, etc.

1819 VERPLANCK *State Triumvirate* 44 Known chief of all the *lobby* tribe! **1844** *Knickerb.* XXIII. 299 His fame is rife among our legislators, and the 'lobby-interest' at Albany. **1871** *Scribner's Mo.* II. 272 In this mill the lobby forces at the Capitol are all the while grinding. **1882** BAILLIE-GROHMAN *Camps in Rockies* 329 The lobby system in the United States Houses of Legislature has opened the doors to 'land-grabbers.' **1890** *Stock Grower & Farmer* 25 Jan. 3/4 Suppose . . . they agree to contribute a cent for each head of cattle in the United States to form a 'lobby fund' for legislative purposes.

+**Lobby,** *v.*

1. *tr.* To solicit (a legislative body) in the lobby or elsewhere; to promote or secure (legislative action) by such means; to exert pressure on legislators in behalf of (something).

1849 LYELL *Second Visit* II. 31 A disappointed place-hunter . . . had been lobbying the Houses of Legislature. **1866** *Ill. Agric. Soc. Trans.* VI. 404 The game laws . . . he considered were lobbied through the Legislature. **1870** *Nation* 10 March 147/2 What makes it more important is, that the Governor himself 'lobbied' the whole affair. **1873** *Ill. Dept. Agric. Trans.* X. 15 A committee of six was appointed to lobby Congress upon sundry subjects. **1888** *Nation* 31 May 448/1 [This will] leave Congress to launch upon the country whatever vagaries or political jobs may be lobbied through that body.

2. *intr.* To frequent the lobby of a legislative chamber for the purpose of influencing the votes of its members.

a1848 *N.Y. Tribune* (B.), There is a quarrel in Philadelphia about Mr. W—'s appointments. Some of the Loco-focos have come out to lobby against him. **1887** J. HAWTHORNE *Great Bank Robbery* xv, The only thing to be done was to hire some one to go up to Washington and lobby against the bill. **1911** HARRISON *Queed* 297 Never believe any more that ministers can't lobby.

+**Lobby agent.** =LOBBYIST. — **1864** NICHOLS *Amer. Life* I. 260 There were lobby agents, male and female, ready to give the influence they boasted of for a consideration. **1886** POORE *Reminisc.* I. 492 A corrupt organization of Congressmen and certain lobby-agents existed.

+**Lobbyer.** =LOBBYIST. — **1841** BUCKINGHAM *Amer., N. States* II. 422 The parties employing . . . a 'Lobbyer,' to promote the passing of a bill through the Trenton legislature, . . . refused to pay him the sum he demanded. **1855** *Chicago Times* 3 Feb. 2/3 To replenish the purses . . . of the several agents, lobbyers, &c., of Washington, who are personally interested in its [*sc.*, a bill's] passage. **1882** WHITMAN *Spec. Days* 259 The members . . . were . . . lobbyers.

+**Lobbying.** Exercising influence as a lobbyist on legislators in behalf of particular measures.

1832 in Mackenzie *Van Buren* (1846) 237 Perhaps I shall have a case of congressional lobbying, by which I can make it a jaunt of pleasure and profit. **1841** in G. Combe *Notes U.S.* I. 322 Great impediments are thrown in the way of the fulfillment of imperative duties by the monstrous increase of boring and lobbying on behalf of the interests of corporate associations. **1869** BARNUM *Struggles & Triumphs* 620, I exhibited his connection with railroad reports, railroad laws, and railroad lobbyings. **1886** POORE *Reminisc.* I. 238 He never engaged in lobbying at Washington for money.

+**Lobbyist.** One who frequents the lobby of a legislative chamber in order to influence legislative action.

1863 *Cornhill Mag.* Jan. 96 There [was] a Representative listening to a lobbyist. **1868** *N.Y. Herald* 3 July 6/6 But it seems that the California Legislature has been tampered with by lobbyists. **1878** BEADLE *Western Wilds* 121 It was then I learned the miseries of a lobbyist. **1887** *Voice* 31 March, In the sense that these citizens are lobbyists, I was a lobbyist against the Crosby bill. **1900** *Congress. Rec.* 19 Jan. 994/2 A lobbyist could scarcely withstand the tide that was set in on behalf of the people for proper legislation. **1904** *N.Y. Ev. Post* 28 March 6 The sop which the President has thrown to the pension lobbyists will only whet their appetite for more.

+**Lobby member.** =prec. — **1819** VERPLANCK *State Triumvirate* 67 There is a class of men . . . generally known by the name of Lobby members. **1832** S. SMITH *Major Downing* 90 Lobby members can do as much as any on 'em on sich business as this. **1847** T. FORD *Hist. Illinois* (1854) 287 The out-door politicians . . . are called 'lobby members,' and . . . come up to the seat of government for office. **1869** *Overland Mo.* III. 63 He attended the California Legislature as a lobby member.

***Lobelia.** A genus of herblike plants widely distributed throughout the temperate zones; any one of various plants of this genus. — **1781-2** JEFFERSON *Notes Va.* (1788) 35 Lobelia of several species. **1819** E. DANA *Geogr. Sk.* 85 Divers species . . . are useful in medicine and the arts; such as . . . prickly ash, columbo, lobelia [etc.]. **1846** *Knickerb.* XXVII. 287 Dwarf cedars [were] interspersed with golden-rods, lobelias, Indian posies. **1893** *Harper's Mag.* May 843/1 The scarlet of the lobelia, and the dwarf sunflower and yellow sunbeam so dear to its watery heart.

***Loblolly.**

*1. A thick, gruel-like food, often having Indian corn as its chief ingredient. *Obs.* Also attrib.

1637 MORTON *New Canaan* 342 The Colony servant in Virginea . . . called to his wife to set on the loblolly pot. **1687** BLOME *Isles & Terr. in Amer.* 38 Loblolly [is] made of Maize mixed with water. **1709** LAWSON *Carolina* 38 They brought in great store of loblolly, and other Medleys, made of Indian grain, stewed peaches [etc.]. **1785** WASHINGTON *Diaries* II. 421 The Water is made as thick as Loblolly, or very thick cream. [**1800** BOUCHER *Glossary* p. xlix, *Lob-lolly.* . . . This is a food in use in the West Indies, made of pounded Indian corn, and differing but little from *Homony:* but, among seamen, it denotes a kind of hasty-pudding, made of oatmeal.]

+2. A miry puddle or mudhole. *colloq.*

1899 ADE *Doc' Horne* 6 In those days a mud-hole with this deceptive dry crust on top was called a 'loblolly.' **1903** A. ADAMS *Log Cowboy* 164 His ineffectual struggles caused him to sink farther to the flanks in the loblolly which the tramping of the cattle had caused. **1909** *Dialect Notes* III. 400 *Loblolly,* a mud-hole; ooze; miry road.

+**Loblolly bay.** A small evergreen ornamental tree (*Gordonia lasianthus*) of the southern states; the black laurel. (Cf. TAN BAY.) — *c***1730** CATESBY *Carolina* I. 44 The Loblolly-Bay . . . grows in Carolina; but not in any of the more Northern Colonies. **1775** ROMANS *Nat. Hist. Florida* 32 Their natural produce is a stately tree called loblolly bay. **1817** S. BROWN *Western Gaz.* 10 Between the Mobile and the Perdido, the soil is thin, timber pine, loblolly bay, cypress. **1872** POWERS *Afoot & Alone* 38 In South Carolina the planter's stately abode stands . . . deeply embowered in pine . . . and the pretty loblolly-bay. **1897** SUDWORTH *Arborescent Flora* 272 *Gordonia lasianthus.* . . . Loblolly Bay (N.C., S.C., Ga., Ala., Fla., Miss., La.).

+**Loblolly pine.** A long-leaved pine (*Pinus taeda*) that grows in swampy and sterile soils in the South; the wood of this tree. — **1760** *Georgia Gen. Ass. Acts* 219 Squared Timber . . . made of swamp or loblolly pine and Shipped or offered to Sale. **1802** DRAYTON *S. Carolina* 80 Loblolly pine. (*Pinus palustris.*) Grows in low places, in the lower country; is appropriated to common plantation uses, and for fencing rails. **1827** WILLIAMS *West Florida* 39 Pine, loblolly. *Pinus tæda*—a large tree, in valleys, has much sap. **1884** SARGENT *Rep. Forests* 197 Loblolly Pine. Old-Field Pine. Rosemary Pine. **1897** SUDWORTH *Arborescent Flora* 26 *Pinus tæda.* Loblolly Pine. . . . Common Names: . . . Frankincense Pine (lit.). **1905** *Forestry Bureau Bul.* No. 64, 7 This preservative treatment made it possible to utilize loblolly pine for cross-ties.

+**Lobo.** *W.* [Sp.] The large gray timber wolf. — **1856** WHIPPLE *Explor. Ry. Route* I. 101 Wolves (coyotes and lobos) are also numerous, and live by preying upon their weaker neighbors. **1874** COUES *Birds N.W.* 382 At nightfall the coyoté-wolves and their larger relatives, the lobos, left their hiding places. **1923** J. H. COOK *On Old Frontier* 63 One thing for which mustangs had to be on the lookout at all times was the big wolf, or 'lobo.'

+**Lobo(s) wolf.** *W.* =prec. Also transf. — **1854** MARCY *Explor. Red River* 186 Large Lobos wolf. Above Cross-Timbers. **1903** 'O. HENRY' *Heart of West* 220, I'm not one of them lobo wolves . . . who are always blaming on women the calamities of life. **1912** [see LOAFER[2]].

***Lobster.**

*1. A crustacean, +esp. an American species (*Homarus americana*), found along the Atlantic coast and prized as a sea food; also, the prepared meat of this.

1616 SMITH *New England* 30 You shall scarce finde any Baye, shallow shore, or Coue of sand, where you may not take many Clampes, or Lobsters. **1699** E. WARD *Trip New-Eng.* 58 Lobsters and Cod-fish are held in . . . disdain, by reason of their plenty. **1761** in Singleton *Social N.Y.* 364 Pickles of all sorts in small quantities, very fit for the Army, such as . . . Capers, Anchovies, etc. Pickled oysters and lobsters. **1812** *Mass. Laws* VI. 39 It shall not be lawful for any person living without the jurisdiction of this Commonwealth to take any lobsters [in Provincetown]. **1885** *Century Mag.* Oct. 840 Here his attention and hers was distracted by the passing of a wonderful preparation of lobster, served in sherry. **1911** *Rep. Fisheries 1908* 312 Lobster . . . is caught in pots and traps especially constructed for this fishery.

2. A British soldier. *slang. Obs.* {*c*1643-} Also attrib.

1770 *Mass. Gazette* Extra 21 June 2/2 The Mob still increased, . . . calling out 'come, you Rascals, you bloody Backs, you Lobster Scoundrels; fire if you dare.' **1776** MCCURTIN *Journal* (1857) 34 The Red Lobsters spied a little fire which a party of Centry made on a small hill . . . very close to Boston. **1835** THATCHER *Traits of Tea Party* 103 Mr. Pierce . . . saw him early in this tumult [the Boston Massacre, March 5, 1770] harassing and abusing the sentry, poking him rather severely with the stick, and calling him a '*lobster*'—a popular reproach. **1899** E. E. HALE *Lowell & Friends* 56 The stevedores on the wharves hated a 'nigger' as much as their ancestors in 1770 hated a 'lobster.'

3. Attrib. in sense 1 with *car, factory,* etc.

1812 *Mass. Laws* VI. 39 An act to prevent the destruction of the Lobster Fishery in the town of Provincetown. **1816** BENTLEY *Diary* IV. 398 Found the Lobster nets around Nahant as at our last visit. **1832** CHILD *Frugal Housewife* 120 Lobster Salad.—The meat of one lobster is extracted from the shell, and cut up fine. **1880** *Harper's Mag.* Aug. 352/1 He put on his lands a top-dressing of the refuse from the lobster factories. **1883** *Nat. Museum Bul.* No. 27, 116 The total value of the Lobster products . . . [was] $732,000. **1890** *Cent.* 3495/2 *Lobster-car,* . . . a box or frame in which lobsters are kept alive under water awaiting sale or transport. **1896** JEWETT *Pointed Firs* 185 A weather-beaten lobster smack . . . seemed to have been taken for a plaything by the light airs that blew about the bay.

Lobstering. Catching lobsters. — **1880** *Harper's Mag.* Aug. 347/2 Lobstering (for factories which can the lobster, chiefly for foreign markets) . . . was reduced . . . to a matter of one dollar a day. **1894** *Youth's Companion* 22 Nov. 562/3 The bulk of the eeling and quahaug clamming as well as the lobstering was done in its vicinity.

Lobsterman. One who engages in lobstering. — **1881** *Scribner's Mo.* XXII. 212/1 The lobsterman . . . ventures far out to sea. **1888** *Advance* 16 Aug., Yonder a lobsterman is mending his boat.

Lobster('s)-tail. A gastropod, esp. a chiton. — *a***1884** in Goode, etc. *Fisheries* I. 701 These shells have been called by different names, . . . such as . . . 'Rattle-snake's Tail,' 'Lobster's Tail,' 'Sea-bug,' and 'Sea-caterpillar.' **1911** *Rep. Fisheries 1908* 315/2 Sea snails (*Gasteropoda*) . . . are found on all our coasts, and are known as . . . 'wood-lice,' 'lobster tails,' 'sea-bugs,' etc.

Local, *n.* {1824-}

1. +a. A reporter or editor of local news. b. (See quot. 1879.) {1888 *collect.*}

1868 *All Year Round* 19 Sept. 351/2 We observe that Brier, local of the *News,* has on a new coat. *a***1869** W. CARLTON *Farm Ballads* 83 So long as the paper was crowded with 'locals' containing their names. **1873** *Newton Kansan* 29 May 3/3 For general locals we are personally responsible. **1879** WEBSTER *Suppl.* 1565/2 *Local,* . . . a detached item of local news for a newspaper. (*U.S. Not well authorized.*) **1885** E. W. HOWE *Mystery of Locks* 142 John Bill was so situated that he did little else than write paid locals.

+2. A train that stops at all stations in a particular district. {1902-}

1879 WEBSTER *Suppl.* 1565/2 *Local,* . . . an accommodation railway train, which receives and deposits passengers and freight along the line of the road. **1898** *McClure's Mag.* X. 399 There she stood as I came in sight—a little three-car local. **1904** *N.Y. Sun* 21 Aug. 1 The northbound local due here at 5:50 P.M. was switching some cars at Minden. **1914** GERRY *Masks of Love* 117 The only train they could get was a local, without sleeping-cars or diner.

+**3.** On a train: A passenger going to a local or intermediate point or station.

1887 George *40 Yrs. on Rail* 35 Even when tickets began to creep into use, they were at first sold only to through passengers, while the 'locals' had to pay cash.

+**4.** Postal matter bearing a local instead of an officially recognized post-office address.

1882 *Official Postal Guide* 681 Locals and nixes. Matter addressed to places which are not post offices is unmailable.

5. A local branch of a trade-union.

1890 in C. Evans *Hist. United Mine Workers* II. 20 The Secretary-Treasurer . . . shall prepare and submit to the locals a quarterly report of all moneys received. **1911** M. W. Ovington *Half a Man* 98 Strong organizations in the South, as the bricklayers, send men North with union membership, who easily transfer to New York locals.

6. *attrib.* **a.** In sense 2. **b.** In sense 1.

In some of the examples *local* partakes of the nature of an absolute used attributively, but there is also a suggestion of its originally adjectival character.

1891 *N.Y. Bd. Rapid Transit R.R. Comm. Rep.* 60, I also wish to commend the proposal . . . to locate gradients on the approaches to local stations. *Ib.* 71 The double-deck system [of subway-construction] favors the local traffic at the expense of the express. **1894** Shuman *Steps into Journalism* 151 Women have taken a permanent place in the local room —the dirty, dingy, tobacco polluted local room. **1902** MacGowan *Last Word* 11 The 'local freight' . . . pulled up at the station.

***Local,** *a.* Designating various aspects of government by small political units, as towns, school districts, counties, etc. {1776–} (Cf. Local option.) — **1688** *Conn. Rec.* III. 439 The law that doth confirm o[u]r locall lawes. **1884** *Lisbon* (Dak.) *Star* 25 July, Local politics are quiet thus far, but . . . they will be lively enough when the campaign fairly opens. **1912** Nicholson *Hoosier Chron.* 247, I tell them to . . . try to get good men on local tickets.

Local option. The right granted by a state government to the people of a town, or other small political unit, of determining by popular vote whether or not licenses shall be issued for the sale of intoxicating liquors; also, the right to forbid the sale of liquor locally; local prohibition. {1878–} Also attrib. — **1884** *Century Mag.* May 148/1 The local-option clause . . . is now well known to be an absolute failure. **1886** Z. F. Smith *Kentucky* 763 A stringent local-option law has been passed, and the sale of liquor to inebriates forbidden universally. **1887** *Courier-Journal* 11 Jan. 3/2 That judgment . . . will have the effect of restoring local option, and bringing the dispensers of corn juice . . . under the liability of fine and damages. **1891** *Cycl. Temperance* 98/2 State and National Prohibition, secured by Constitutional Amendments, . . . would be but the logical outcome of the earliest and most limited Local Option victory. **1910** C. Harris *Eve's Husband* 113 Booneville was in a 'local option' county, where it was illegal to sell liquor.

Local preacher. In the Methodist church, a layman licensed to preach in a particular district. {1772–} — **1840** *Niles' Nat. Reg.* 18 April 112/2 In the United States the Methodist episcopal church has . . . about 5,800 local preachers. **1845** *Indiana Mag. Hist.* XXIII. 20 He lived a number of years, as a member of the Methodist Episcopal church and an approved local preacher. **1888** W. Lawrence *A. A. Lawrence* 237 He was to be seen in the Methodist meeting-house listening to the local preacher, or a negro exhorter.

+**Locate,** *v.*

1. a. *intr.* To take up one's residence or quarters; to settle. {1837–} (Cf. sense 5 b.)

Some of the later examples may represent absol. uses of sense 2 a.

1652 *Virginia Mag. Hist. & Biog.* V. 35 Divers Indians from the Town of Oanancocke . . . [have] suffered us to locate upon their land. **1843** 'Carlton' *New Purchase* I. 100 Families having bought lands at the government price from Uncle Samuel, have actually *located* on it. **1870** 'O. Optic' *Field & Forest* 230 We had better move my house over to the clearing, if you will let us locate on your land. **1879** *Harper's Mag.* Sept. 517 A party of men from Tennessee 'located' on this stream. **1904** *N.Y. Ev. Post* 11 Oct. 1 He is about to move from the Rutgers Street house. He expects to locate in the immediate vicinity.

b. *reflex.* To settle down or establish residence in a place. {1807–}

1819 F. Wright *Soc. & Manners in Amer.* 176 The Dutch and the German . . . locate themselves, as the phrase is here, with wonderful sagacity. **1832** Trollope *Domestic Manners* I. 28 A squatter, who having 'located' himself close to the river's edge, proceeded to build his cabin. **1845** J. W. Norris *Chicago Directory* 99 Dr. Gibbs having located himself in Chicago is prepared to perform all operations appertaining to Dentistry. **1880** 'Mark Twain' *Tramp Abroad* xxxii. 340 We located ourselves at the Jungfrau Hotel. **1898** Westcott *D. Harum* 136, I congratulate you upon having located yourself so quickly.

c. *passive.* To live or be established in a place. {1833–}

1843 'Uncle Sam' *Peculiarities* I. 76 Where were you located when you were born? **1889** *Boston Jrnl.* 2 March 3/7 The deceased was located for many years in Manchester.

2. a. *tr.* To appoint the region or locality in which (a tract of land) is to be set apart; spec., to enter a claim to (a tract of land) by determining its exact location with reference to a survey; to take up (land).

1705 *Penn-Logan Corr.* II. 52 The locating his father's land there was doubtless a great abuse to thee. **1765** S. Smith *Hist. New Jersey* 189 Alteration in the manner of locating lands in West Jersey. **1773** Washington *Writings* II. 375, [I have written] to the Governor of West Florida expressing my hopes of obtaining this land (and more) in case you should think proper to locate it in that government. *a***1821** Dwight *Travels* II. 98 He requested, that it [the grant] might be located in the North-Western quarter of the township. **1838** *S. Lit. Messenger* IV. 653/2 He located several thousand acres of land on the river before mentioned. **1880** Ingham *Digging Gold* 296 Four companies were organized, locating two thousand five hundred and sixty acres of land. **1897** Hough *Story of Cowboy* 125 The *hidalgo* was pretty sure to locate his grant upon the best water he could find.

b. To determine the exact location, and to enter a claim thereto, of a quantity of public land granted in (a land warrant or scrip). (Cf. Land warrant 2 a.)

1754 H. Sharpe *Correspondence* (1888) I. 58 The method . . . of Locating Land Warrants by selecting the most rich and fertil Spots. **1783** in *Travels Amer. Col.* 662 Mr. Jno. May desired me to give him any warrants I had to locate and he would locate it for me. **1863** *Mass. Statutes* clxvi, To locate . . . all the land scrip.

c. *Mining.* To make and file a claim of ownership to the mining rights of (a defined area of land). Usually *to locate a claim.* Also transf.

1869 Browne *Adv. Apache Country* 485 Andrew Veatch, an enterprising explorer, . . . had discovered and located a claim called the 'Comet.' **1872** McClellan *Golden State* 246 The fortunate finder of a stranded whale generally 'locates' a 'claim' upon him. **1883** Ritch *Illust. N. Mex.* 75 In addition to gulch mining, . . . many good mines have been located in the mountains contiguous. **1901** Duncan & Scott *Allen & Woodson Co., Kansas* 70 C. L. Colman located a claim joining Geneva on the northeast.

d. To obtain ownership of (springs or streams) by filing claim to the land on which they are situated.

1883 Ritch *Illust. N. Mex.* 48 There are in many places small streams and springs, which supply water to large herds of stock. These are located under the homestead laws, or otherwise obtained, with a view to controlling the lands for miles around. **1885** *Santa Fé Wkly. New Mexican* 17 Sept. 4/4 These springs and the land adjacent were located under the homestead law some months ago.

3. To lay out or determine the line of (a road).

1739 in Parmenter *Hist. Pelham, Mass.* (1898) 26 A Comittee [was appointed] To see ye same [road] located in the most Suitable place. **1831** Peck *Guide* 317 The 'National Road' . . . is already located thus far. **1837** — *Gaz. Illinois* 63 From Vandalia, westward, the road is not yet located. **1880** *Cimarron News & Press* 18 March 3/2 Mr. Warner . . . will locate the Sonora railroad.

4. To fix or establish (a town, school, tribe, etc.) in a place.

1786 Cutler in *Life & Corr.* I. 190 Much attention ought to be paid in forming a good plan for locating the first settlements. **1813** *N.J. Hist. Coll.* II. 153 The Assembly passed an act locating the Theological Seminary permanently at Princeton. **1841** Hawthorne *Amer. Note-Books* II. 11 It is extremely doubtful whether Mr. Ripley will succeed in locating his community on this farm. **1894** Robley *Bourbon Co., Kansas* 5 About 1825 the government began locating the various tribes of the more nearly civilized Indians from the East and South on reservations. **1910** *Okla. Session Laws* 3 Legisl. (1911) 5 The Executive Mansion shall be located in the vicinity of said capital grounds.

5. a. In the Methodist ministry, to station (a minister) in a particular pastoral charge. (Cf. Circuit rider.)

*a***1814** T. Coke in Southey *Wesley* (1820) II. 464 It is most lamentable to see so many of our able married preachers . . . become located merely for the want of support for their families. **1894** H. Gardener *Unofficial Patriot* 46 He had asked the presiding elder to locate him as a married man for the next year since he was about to marry.

b. *intr.* Of a minister: To settle down in a pastoral charge. Also transf. (Cf. sense 1 a.)

1846 *Indiana Mag. Hist.* XXIII. 268 Philip Gatch, who was a traveling preacher as early as 1774, . . . traveled four years, and then located. **1853** Baldwin *Flush Times Ala.* 132 He had long felt a call to the law, and he now resolved to 'locate,' and apply himself to the duties of that . . . profession. **1859** *Ladies' Repository* XIV. 318/1 Becoming master of Hunter's Lodge, he locates! *a***1870** Chipman *Notes on Bartlett* 251 *To Locate,* . . . to cease being itinerant; to leave the itinerancy.

6. To ascertain or find out the exact location or place of (something or somebody). {1896–}

1816 *N. Amer. Rev.* Sept. 359 To locate a *noise* and locate a *quotation* . . . are expressions that violate the rules of propriety and taste. **1889** 'Mark Twain' *Conn. Yankee* xx. 245 All I need to know is . . . how to locate his vitals. **1902** Wilson *Spenders* 13 Locating old Peter Bines at this season of the year was a feat never lightly to be undertaken.

Located, *a.* {1689–} +**1.** Of land: Fixed, determined, or agreed upon as to location. (Cf. Locate *v.* 2.) +**2.** Of a Methodist minister:

Stationed permanently in a particular charge. (Cf. LOCATE *v.* 5.) — (1) **1764** in Franklin *Writings* IV. 325 The located uncultivated Lands belonging to the Proprietaries shall not be assessed higher than the lowest Rate [etc.]. **1799** J. SMITH *Acct. Captivity* 121, I took a journey westward, in order to survey some located land I had on or near the Youhogamy. **1832** WILLIAMSON *Maine* II. 287 To facilitate the meetings of '*proprieties*,' a law was passed giving them equal privileges, whether their lands were within or without a *located* township. (2) **1843** 'CARLTON' *New Purchase* I. 68 Mr. Parsons, like most *located* and *permanent* pastors of a wooden country, received almost literally nothing for ecclesiastical services. **1874** EGGLESTON *Circuit Rider* 297 [He] was directed to the double-cabin of a located preacher.

+**Locater.** =LOCATOR. — **1825** *Austin P.* (1924) II. 1016 The locaters have property that suits you. **1873** HARTE *Mrs. Skagg's Husbands* 31 The two original locaters of the great Cinnabar Lode faded from the memory of Angel's. **1875** *Chicago Tribune* 6 Nov. 3/1 But few of the mines have passed out of the hands of the original locaters. **1896** *Home Missionary* Nov. 341 Immigration into that region was greatly stimulated by the locaters of town sites.

Locating. *attrib.* Designating officials having to do with establishing a location. {1816–30} — **1835** JACKSON in *Pres. Mess. & P.* III. 129, I submit . . . evidence of certain claims to reservations . . . which the locating agent has reserved from sale. **1872** TICE *Over Plains* 143 No less than three locating committees . . . were exploring the [Colorado] Territory for the most favorable location for a colony. **1904** LYNDE *Grafters* 1 The locating engineers of the Western Pacific . . . drove their stakes along the north line of the quarter-section.

***Location.**

+**1.** The locating or fixing of the bounds of a tract or area of land.

1718 *N.J. Archives* IV. 379 Lands . . . Scituate on ye same Passaiak by an actual Survey or location before the date of that Agreemt. **1773** WASHINGTON *Writings* II. 372 Herewith you will receive Lord Dunmore's certificates of my claims . . . in the location of which in the government of West Florida I shall rely on your friendship. **1795** SULLIVAN *Hist. Maine* 159 There was no regularity in the locations of the lands. **1873** *Newton Kansan* 24 April 2/1 Would it not be well for our commissioners to look after the location of this township and county line just now?

+**b.** Surveying or laying out (a road); establishing or fixing upon a suitable site for a college, town, etc.

1808 *Ann. 10th Congress* 1 Sess. II. 2746 They have completed the location, gradation, and marking of the route, from Cumberland to . . . the Monongahela river. *a***1817** T. DWIGHT *Travels* II. 113 The object, which first demanded attention, was the location of the College. **1872** TICE *Over Plains* 10 No genius has ever appeared there [in Wall St.] equal to the task of getting up such a brilliant scheme as the location of Kansas City. **1881** AVERY *Hist. Georgia* 530 The location of the capital at Atlanta or Milledgeville was left to the people to decide by an election. **1910** *Okla. Session Laws* 3 Legisl. 2 In the contests over the location of the county seats.

+**2.** A tract or grant of land intended for occupancy by settlers.

1792 BELKNAP *Hist. New-Hampshire* III. 14 The lines of towns and locations . . . in so small a draught could not be introduced without confusion. *a***1817** DWIGHT *Travels* II. 305 There is a *location*, (*i.e.*, a grant of land, smaller than a township,) called *Wales's Gore*. **1846** FARNHAM *Prairie Land* 322 He could construct imaginary bridges where sloughs were any detriment to a fine 'location.' **1898** *Mo. So. Dakotan* I. 14 There were made more than one hundred locations of 160 acres each.

+**b.** The land or area embraced in a mining claim or in the site of a proposed oil well.

1846 *Spirit of Times* 6 June 175/1 Everywhere there were trout, apparently; but there are some choice 'locations,' as the copper speculators say. **1872** POWERS *Afoot & Alone* 293 He returned to find his location surveyed off into town lots. . . . [Men] threatened to hang him to a tree if he did not go with them and point out the rich placers. **1882** *47th Congress 1 Sess.* H.R. Ex. Doc. No. 216, 290 Little work other than assessment has been done on any of the locations of this district.

attrib. **1880** *Cimarron News & Press* 26 Feb. 1/5 Location stake notices were treated with contempt. **1883** M. H. FOOTE *Led-Horse Claim* 20 The location stakes follow the gulch, a little on this side of it. **1901** WHITE *Claim Jumpers* (1916) 232 Hustle out some paper so we can make location notices.

+**3.** The situation or position, with respect to natural advantages, of a tract of land or a town site.

1804 C. B. BROWN tr. Volney *View* 76 Considering its location, we shall perceive that it chiefly prevails in the lower basin of these two rivers. *a***1817** DWIGHT *Travels* II. 283 East-Hartford resembles East-Windsor in location, soil, agriculture. *c***1834** CATLIN *Indians* II. 1 Its location is very beautiful, and so is the country around it [Ft. Leavenworth]. **1872** McCLELLAN *Golden State* 319 It is a most difficult task to attempt a description . . . of lands in the State, so much depends upon location. **1919** HOUGH *Sagebrusher* 14 This is one of the best locations in the valley.

4. A place of settlement or residence. {1827–}

1829 COOPER *Wish-ton-Wish* i, He made his location, as it is termed in the language of the country, near the northern boundary. **1846** THORPE *Myst. Backwoods* 93 We discovered ahead of us what evinced the location of a 'squatter.' **1900** *Congress. Rec.* 2 Feb. 1457/2 If they should remove their location they should carve on a tree the name of the place to which they had gone.

+**b.** A place or site for the carrying on of a business or enterprise.

1861 *Chicago Tribune* 19 July 1/8 Wanted—A Partner with a small cash capital, to take half interest in a light and profitable business in one of the best locations in the city. **1875** *Ib.* 8 July 3/4, I have a good stock of groceries and fixtures, but not a good location.

5. In the Methodist ministry, a pastoral charge.

1846 *Indiana Mag. Hist.* XXIII. 268 [Preachers'] locations are not mentioned on the *Minutes* until the next year.

Locator. {1607–} +One who locates anything, esp. land or a mining claim.

1784 FILSON *Kentucke* 38 Prior locators may have time and opportunity to enter a caveat. **1810** in V. W. Howard *Bryan Sta. Heroes* (1932) 146 [I] transfer by Dede all my right title . . . to the ballance of my part of the tract as joint locator with Robt. Johnson. **1876** in *Cimarron News & Press* 17 Feb. (1881) 1/4 Post . . . a notice, in writing, stating thereon the name or names of the locator or locators. **1883** E. LORD *Control Mining* 98 The first locators were entitled to the exclusive possession of the section of the ledge included in their claim. **1911** J. F. WILSON *Land Claimers* 3 'Thank you,' the locator replied.

***Lock,** *n.*

***1.** A hobble or shackle for confining a prisoner. *Obs.*

1638 *Essex Inst. Coll.* VII. 186 The Court Judged him to be severly whipped & a lock vpon his ffoote. **1641** *New Haven Rec.* 57 Andrew Low junr. . . . was severely whipped, and ordered to weare a lock. **1658** *R.I. Court Rec.* 41 He had the locke put on his lege againe.

***2.** A mechanical appliance for fastening a door, window, drawer, etc.

1644 *Harvard Rec.* I. 5 For hinges, lock & nayles, 7[s] 4[d]. **1712** HEMPSTEAD *Diary* 8, I was all [day?] in Town putting on Locks & drops on 2 Cheast of Drawers. **1822** *Ann. 17th Congress* 1 Sess. I. 324 An account of . . . Chisels, augurs, locks, . . . bought at Georgetown, at high prices. **1892** M. A. JACKSON *Gen. Jackson* 189 There was no lock on the door.

***3.** On a river or canal, a structure provided with gates which may be opened or shut, in order to alter the level of the water enclosed and thus to enable vessels to move from one level to another.

1776 *Mass. H. S. Coll.* 2 Ser. VIII. 194 This great difference in the rise of the tides and time of high water . . . will make a double lock at each end of the canal necessary. **1795** *Essex Inst. Coll.* LIV. 100 If they will grant me . . . the privilege of making use of Waters Bridge or mill dam, and of constructing a lock and flood gates. **1803** *Ann. 7th Congress* 2 Sess. 405 There is no danger that this loose soil will be washed into and impede the operations of the first lock. **1835** HOFFMAN *Winter in West* I. 16 After they had gained and passed the lock, . . . I could not help rowing near [their boat]. **1900** STOCKTON *Afield & Afloat* 27 We will go into the lock and in a few minutes we shall be on the lake.

b. Attrib. with *charge, gate, house*, etc.

1788 WASHINGTON *Diaries* III. 361, 20 hands will be able to accomplish it . . . at the Great falls above the Lock Seats. **1792** *Mass. H. S. Coll.* I. 285 Should . . . the lock navigation be completed, there will not be a carrying place between New-York and Williamsburg. **1813** *Ann. 13th Congress* 1 Sess. I. 49 By increasing the height of the lock-gates one foot, [the banks will] admit a depth of nine feet of water in the canal. **1863** HALE *If, Yes, & Perhaps* (1868) 16, I would start in the morning to walk to the lock-station at Brockport on the canal. **1876** HABBERTON *Jericho Road* 20 Don't you b'leeve she could run the dam . . . , and dodge paying lock-charges? **1887** *Century Mag.* Sept. 704/2 He produced from the lock-house a white musk-rat.

4. *Lock and compass*, a design or pattern in linen weaving.

1843 *Lowell Offering* III. 90 She also had towels and table linen . . . done in patterns manifold. There was . . . diamond, bird's eye, lock and compass [etc.].

***Lock,** *v.*

1. *tr.* To furnish or equip (a canal or stream) with a lock or locks. {1892}

1792 *Mass. H. S. Coll.* 1 Ser. I. 285 There is only twenty-three miles to cut and lock, in order to carry commerce by water. **1886** Z. F. SMITH *Kentucky* 523 This was begun in surveys for locking and damming those streams. **1898** YOUNG *Jessamine Co., Ky.* 143 With swift boats operated upon the river now that it is locked and dammed, . . . a great tide of visitors will flow in.

2. To pass (a vessel) through a lock. {1840–}

1833 *Congress. Deb.* 26 Jan. 1396 It will pass very much as boats are locked up and down through a canal. **1902** WHITE *Blazed Trail* 204 They were locked through after some delay on account of the grain barges from Duluth.

3. *intr.* Of a canal: To pass *into* or *down into* through a lock or locks. {1795–}

1834 in *Atlantic Mo.* XXVI. 739 A canal . . . is to *lock* into the Conn. River. **1837** W. JENKINS *Ohio Gaz.* 161 The Wabash and Erie canal will lock down into the Maumee river, affording very considerable water power.

4. Of a boat: To pass *down* by means of a lock or locks. {1840–}

1837 W. JENKINS *Ohio Gaz.* 123 A small stream . . . affords a sufficiency of water during the greater part of the year to permit boats to lock down to the Ohio.

+5. Of the branches of adjacent cotton plants: To mingle or intertwine.

1855 *Florida Plant Rec.* 129 The cotton on the fresh Land is Locking between the Roes in places.

+**Lock box.** A box or boxlike receptacle that may be locked, esp. a mail box in a post office that may be rented by a patron. — **1880** INGHAM *Digging Gold* 228 About six hundred lock-boxes were put in the new building. **1887** *Postal Laws* 213 Individuals may provide lock boxes or drawers for their own use, under the next section. **1906** FREEMAN *Light of Soul* 384 It was not a lock box, and she had to ask the postmaster for the letter. **1916** DU PUY *Uncle Sam* 229 The writer of these letters gave his address as a lock box. . . . More letters came . . . from a lock box.

+**Lock chain.** A chain for locking the wheels of a vehicle. — **1829** ROYALL *Pennsylvania* II. 75 [They] saw nothing but a large chain, called a *lock chain.* **1843** *Amer. Pioneer* II. 121 As few of the emigrant wagons were provided with lock-chains for the wheels, the downward impetus was checked by a large log. **1859** MARCY *Prairie Trav.* 93 If there are no lock-chains upon wagons, the front and rear wheels on the same side may be tied together with ropes so as to lock them very firmly.

+**Lock-down.** (See quot. 1905.) — **1881** T. B. WALKER *Letter* 4 June, A string of logs as customarily made for rafting is when the logs are fastened together by means of poles and 'Lock Downs.' **1905** *Forestry Bureau Bul.* No. 61, 41 *Lock down,* a strip of tough wood with holes in the ends, which is laid across a raft of logs. Rafting pins are driven through the holes into the logs, thus holding the raft together. (N[orthern] F[orest].)

Lock-keeper. One having charge of a lock on a river or canal. {1794–} — **1876** HABBERTON *Jericho Road* 21 [We'll] keep up an infernal whistlin' all night so the lock-keeper'll be afraid to go to bed. **1882** *Nation* 14 Dec. 504/1 'Better not cross the lake to-day unless you are water-birds!' the lock-keeper had told us. **1886** STAPLETON *Major's Christmas* 294 She once dismissed a servant for a speaking acquaintance with a lock-keeper.

Lockout. The exclusion by an employer of the usual workers from a place of employment. {1860–}

1867 in *Penna. Bureau Indust. Statistics Rep. 1880–81,* 284 We will hold ourselves in readiness to confer, . . . thereby closing all avenues that lead to 'strikes,' 'lockouts,' etc. **1886** HOWELLS *Minister's Charge* 128 Jackson has 'struck' for twelve dollars a month, and at present there is a 'lock-out.'—I believe that's what it's called. **1888** *Century Mag.* Sept. 791/1 In every other large manufacturing village strikes and lock-outs were frequent. **1894** CARWARDINE *Pullman Strike* 16 There are strikes, lockouts and the inevitable violence. **1900** *Congress. Rec.* 8 Feb. 1640/2 There have been more panics, . . . more lockouts, more strikes . . . during the existence of the gold standard. **1908** *Lawyers Rep.* XX. ns. 319/2 An employer, . . . to effectuate the purpose of his lockout, may persuade (but not coerce) other foundrymen not to employ molders for higher wages.

***Lockram.** Also **lockrum, luckrom, lockerum,** etc. **1.** A linen fabric, often of a poor or cheap quality. *Obs.* **2.** Attrib. with *napkin, shirt.* — **(1) 1637** *Md. Archives* IV. 18 James Clofton . . . did . . . sell . . . 4 ells of lockram for the price of fourty weight of tobacco. **1666** SANFORD *Letter Book* 15, I desiere it may be Sent in good Lockerum dowles Canvice Carsey Searge and peniston. **1686** SEWALL *Letter-Book* I. 34 Please to send . . . Four peices of Lockrum att 11d. or 12d. per Ell. **1709** *Essex Inst. Coll.* VIII. 20 To 1 half pes of Luckrom. **(2) 1644** *Md. Archives* IV. 271, 1. locram shirte. **1647** *Essex Probate Rec.* I. 66, 1 dussen of lockrum napkins & a table cloth.

***Locksmith.** One whose occupation is to make or repair locks. — **1654** JOHNSON *Wonder-w. Prov.* 209 Gun-smiths, Lock-smiths, Black-smiths, Naylers, Cutlers, have left the husbandmen to follow the Plow and Cart, and they their trades. **1812** MELISH *Travels* II. 55 Professions exercised in Pittsburg . . . [include] lock-smiths, screw and hinge-makers. **1869** *Boyd's Business Directory* 34 Gun and Locksmith. Bruce George & Son, Main, Sing Sing. **1886** [see GUNSMITH].

Lock stitch. A type of stitch formed by the locking together of two threads. Also attrib. {1869–} — **1861** *Chicago Tribune* 19 July 1/9 Sloat's Elliptic Lock Stitch Sewing Machines. **1863** *Horticulturist* Sept. Advt. 5 The Grover & Baker S. M. Co. manufacture . . . the most perfect Shuttle or 'Lock Stitch' machines in the market. *Ib.* Dec. Advt. 12 Finkle & Lyon's Sewing Machines. These Machines make the lock-stitch alike on both sides, and use less than half the thread and silk that the single or double thread loop-stitch Machines do. **1880** *Harper's Mag* June 26/1 Here is a silent, lock-stitch, fully improved article.

+**Lock-tender.** =LOCK-KEEPER. — **1848** *Indiana Gen. Ass. Doc. 1848–9* II. 133 The expenditure for 'ordinary repairs,' including pay of superintendents and lock tenders, . . . [is] $34,058. **1897** *Outing* XXX. 356/2 A large fog-horn [was blown] to warn the bridge and lock tenders of the approach of the boats. **1900** WINCHESTER *W. Castle* vii. 148 [He] controlled a section of the canal and the hiring and discharging of all the lock-tenders and the laborers who kept the water-way in repair.

+**Lock tortoise.** =BOX TORTOISE. — **1842** *Nat. Hist. N.Y., Zoology* III. 25 The Common Box Tortoise, *Cistuda carolina,* . . . is designated . . . in the west by the name of *Lock Tortoise.*

Lockup. A prison or place of confinement. {1859–}

1839 *Knickerb.* XIV. 110 He was seized, and carried to the 'lock up.' **1876** *Wkly. New Mexican* 13 April 2/2 They are now in the 'lock up' awaiting an investigation. **1898** HAMBLEN *Gen'l Manager's Story* 271 We were run into a lock-up. **1912** COBB *Back Home* 86 They walked side by side . . . a short block to the lock-up.

attrib. and *comb.* **1846** CORCORAN *Pickings* 33 We perceived a prisoner whom we at once knew was above and beyond the ordinary class of lock-up prisoners. **1897** *Chicago Tribune* 18 July 12/6 Wilson had . . . attracted the attention of Lockupkeeper Goble.

Loco, *n.*[1] =LOCOMOTIVE 1. {1898–} — **1833** BRECK in *Recoll.* (1877) 274 With the *loco,* when established, he may start from one city in the morning and return again in the evening from a visit to the other.

+**Loco,** *n.*[2] =LOCOFOCO 2. *Obs.* Also attrib. — **1838** QUITMAN in Claiborne *Life & Corr.* I. 165, I thus claim to be a true Loco and Nullifier. **1842** *Niles' Nat. Reg.* 27 Aug. 405/3 Pike, the strong hold of the locos, Lies snug at the root of the tail. **1843** *Whig Almanac 1844* 42/2 The Loco Members held a jollification. **1846** *Niles' Nat. Reg.* 21 March 48/3 The loco candidates for governor and for congress will fall nearly two thousand votes short of their allied opponents. **1848** *N.Y. Tribune* 4 March (B.) The South-western and Western Locos . . . will cave in.

+**Loco,** *n.*[3] [Sp.]

1. =LOCO WEED. Also attrib.

1883 *Harper's Mag.* March 503/1 The loco, or rattle-weed, met with also in California, . . . drives them [*sc.* horses] raving crazy. **1890** *Ib.* Oct. 806/1 A slender plant of the lobelia family, with a purple blossom, which is called the *loco.* **1901** *Rev. of Reviews* XXIV. 310/1 A little green weed called 'loco' is a constant source of danger to cattle. **1909** 'O. HENRY' *Roads of Destiny* 365 Ever see a bronc that had been chewing loco? **1913** BARNES *Western Grazing Grounds* 256 The loco plant is found generally over the entire Rocky Mountain region.

b. An injurious preparation made from the loco weed or possessing the properties of this. *slang.*

1897 LEWIS *Wolfville* 59 She once saws off a thimbleful of loco on a captain in some whiskey . . . an' he goes plumb crazy. **1907** WHITE *Arizona Nights* 141 They had seen that white quartz with the gold stickin' into it, and that's the same as a dose of loco to miner gents.

c. A distemper resembling craziness manifested by cattle that have eaten loco weed. Also attrib. and transf. *slang.*

1890 *Stock Grower & Farmer* 15 March 6/2 Loco threatens to be worse than last year. Range overstocked. **1890** *Cent.* 3499/2 *Loco-disease,* . . . a disease of horses resulting from eating the loco-weed or crazy-weed. **1916** *Sunset* Jan. 29 Mrs. Vera Harkins . . . has obeyed the 'miner's loco' for thirty-three years in Colorado.

+**Loco,** *a.* Crazy. — **1887** *Outing* X. 7/1 You won't be able to do nuthin' with 'em, sir; they'll go plumb *loco,* that's what they will. **1907** WHITE *Arizona Nights* 176 He had sewn this chart in the shoulder of his coat, whence his suspicion of me and his being so loco about getting it back. **1914** 'BOWER' *Flying U Ranch* 102 You go on and tell that loco son-of-a-gun over there what he's up against. **1922** J. A. DUNN *Man Trap* 152, I figgered I was a bit loco or just hearing noises.

+**Loco,** *v. tr.* To poison with the loco weed. Usu. *past ppl.* or *ppl. a.* Also transf. — **1885** *Wkly. New Mexican Rev.* 7 May 2/6 A small dose of copperas administered three times a day is said to cure locoed horses. **1887** *Scribner's Mag.* II. 510/1 Cattle showing signs of madness are said to be 'locoed,' and so finally the word extended to human beings. **1897** LEWIS *Wolfville* 119 Wolfville intelligence is too well founded to let any law loco it or set it to millin'. **1904** *McClure's Mag.* April 618/2 Those deputies . . . were taken by surprise and 'locoed' at Adair. **1910** RAINE *B. O'Connor* 74, I'm surely plumb locoed, or else gone soft in the haid.

+**Locofoco,** *n.* [Origin uncertain. Bartlett (1859) thought *loco-* was suggested by *locomotive,* popularly thought to mean *self-moving; foco* is app. derived from It. *foco,* fire.]

1. A match or cigar capable of self-ignition. In full, *locofoco match, cigar.*

1839 HOFFMAN *Wild Scenes* i. 62 Our 'loco foco' matches would not ignite. **1844** *Lexington Observer* 1 June 3/2 The fire was caused by . . . a locofoco match . . . [a carpenter threw] on the floor. **1859** BARTLETT 252 In 1834, John Marck opened a store in Park Row, New York, and drew public attention to two novelties. One was . . . a self-lighting cigar, with a match composition on the end. These he called '*Loco-foco*' cigars. **1883** GILMAN *Amer. People* xxi. 437 When the candles had been blown out . . . they were lighted with matches then [1835] called 'locofocos.' **1891** WELCH *Recoll. 1830–40* 76 There was [*sic*] no friction or locofoco matches in those days.

transf. **1850** MATHEWS *Moneypenny* 108 The down-thrower, the tinder-box of empires—the locofoco-match of private families.

2. *Polit.* Originally, a member of the Locofoco or Equal Rights party, a faction of the Democratic party in New York state; later, used of Democrats in general. Now hist. Usually pl. (Cf. Loco *n.*[2])

The explanation of the origin of the term given in quotation 1888 is the one currently accepted.

1835 *Nat. Intelligencer* 9 Nov. 3/2 The *Agrarians*, the *Loco Focos*, and the *Ragamuffins*, are . . . the same people with whom they were . . . *glove* and *hand*—last year. **1837** *Diplom. Corr. Texas* I. (1908) 273 The two great belligerents—the Loco focos and Whigs. **1846** CORCORAN *Pickings* 154 If I find they are locofocos, I damn coon skins, log cabins, and hard cider. *Ib.* 190 'Why are you not a locofoco?' said we. . . . 'I live too near the old coon (Harrison) for that.' **1849** A. MACKAY *Western World* I. 225 'Democrats,' and 'Democratic Republicans,' are names assumed by the Democratic party, 'Loco-foco' being the nickname attached to them by their opponents. **1888** M. LANE in *America* 18 Oct. 15 *Loco-Foco.*—The term was applied to the radical wing of the Democratic party, way back in the Jacksonian days, because of a circumstance that occurred at a Democratic meeting in Tammany Hall in 1834. The discussion having become very warm, the President put out the gas for the purpose of breaking up the meeting, but one of the extremists produced some friction matches, then just coming into use under the name of loco-foco matches, and relighted the gas, when order was restored and the meeting was duly held. **1898** N. BROOKS *Boys of Fairport* 211 In those days there were only two large parties in the whole country—Whigs and Democrats. The latter was stigmatized as Loco-Focos.

b. Attrib. with *luminary*, *party*, etc.

1838 IRVING in P. M. Irving *Life W. Irving* III. (1863) 120 Those locofoco luminaries who of late have been urging strong and sweeping measures. **1844** *N.Y. Wkly. Tribune* 21 Sept. 5/2 Hon. H. C. Murphy of Brooklyn recently edified a Loco-Foco Ward Meeting in that City. **1848** *Congress. Globe* 1 March 409 [He] had riddled to flinders their young locofoco representative. **1892** WALSH *Lit. Curiosities* 654 The *Courier and Enquirer*, the Whig paper, immediately nicknamed the Anti-Monopolists the Loco-foco party. The faction thus nicknamed ultimately became dominant in the Democratic party in the State of New York.

+**Locofoco,** *a.* Imbued with the principles of the Locofoco or Equal Rights party. *Obs.* — **1837** HONE *Diary* I. 266–7 The President's message is loco-foco to the very core. **1838** *N.Y. Advertiser & Exp.* 6 Jan. 4/1 There was . . . a company somewhat less Loco Foco, Slamm, Bang-ish than was usual with the Ex-President. **1846** CORCORAN *Pickings* 61 The coat of a third, he being half whig and half locofoco, had divided, and was split up the back center seam to the collar.

+**Locofocoism.** The principles of the Locofoco party. *Obs.* — **1838** *N.Y. Advertiser & Exp.* 17 Jan. 2/1 Loco Focoism, make the best of it, is Agrarianism, Fanny Wrightism, Equality of all races, colors, breeds, and tribes. **1840** in Shields *S. S. Prentiss* (1883) 304 *Loco-focoism* has done more to break asunder the connecting links . . . which bind together the States of the Union than all other causes. **1848** *Corr. R. W. Griswold* (1898) 237 Trusting somewhat to Whig affinities, Whig associations, and even antipathies to Loco-focoism.

‖**Locofocracy.** =prec. — **1840** *Niles' Nat. Reg.* 26 Sept. 56/3 Every one present must have had a feeling of pity for the Ajax of locofocracy in Ohio [Senator Allen].

+**Locomote,** *v. intr.* To go or proceed. *slang.* {1865–} — **1834** *Knickerb.* IV. 20 Who but our author would represent him [a bard], 'locomoting' on a long, dog-trot over the bogs of his neighborhood? **1845** *Ib.* XXV. 91 We used to . . . take our skates and locomote away to a strong patch of smooth ice. **1860** *Harper's Mag.* March 566/2 [Their] attention was attracted to the parson by his peculiar style of locomoting (being partially paralysed).

Locomotive.

1. A steam engine mounted on wheels and used on a railroad for drawing trains of cars. {1829–}

1831 in Mackenzie *Van Buren* (1846) 228 We shall have our locomotive at work by the end of the week. **1849** E. DAVIES *Amer. Scenes* 188 The engine, or (as the Americans invariably say) the 'locomotive,' had got off the rail. **1879** BURDETTE *Hawkeyes* 240 There is always a wonderful fascination about railroad engineers and locomotives. **1904** *N.Y. Ev. Post* 14 May, The Pennsylvania has decided that the old way of changing locomotives at each division was the most economical.

2. An engine or motor used for the same purpose but operated by some other power, as electricity.

1850 *Scientific Amer.* 14 Dec. 97/1 Professor Page . . . is now engaged in preparation for a trial trip of a locomotive propelled by this power [electromagnetism]. **1895** *Ib.* 10 Aug. 87/2 The tunnel, for use in which this [electric] locomotive was built, runs under Howard Street. **1915** *Lit. Digest* 1 May 1016 This 2,500 horse-power double-unit locomotive takes its 600 volts direct current from the third rail.

3. Attrib. in sense 1 with *boiler*, *carriage*, *depot*, etc.

1828 *20th Congress 2 Sess.* H. R. Doc. No. 59, 19 Improved locomotive carriage, . . . William Howard, Baltimore. **1841** STEELE *Summer Journey* 25 Two fine horses . . . dragged us out of the barn into open day—up through the square, over the hill, to the Locomotive Depot. **1873** PHELPS *Trotty's Wedding* vi, They saw nothing but . . . an old locomotive boiler, rusty, and half buried in a heap of rubbish. **1883** KNIGHT 356/1 *Frame Planing Machine*, a machine with independent self-acting cross slides and tools, for planing different parts of a locomotive frame at the same time. **1883** *Harper's Mag.* Aug. 327/2 The locomotive shops turn out 100 locomotives and 73,000 wheels a year. **1891** *Atlantic Mo.* June 808/1 A list of some fifty patents taken out by colored people [includes] . . . a locomotive smokestack, a cornstalk harvester [etc.].

Locomotive engine. 1. =LOCOMOTIVE 1. {1815–} **2.** =LOCOMOTIVE 2. — (1) **1828** in *Franklin Inst. Jrnl.* VII. 346 To render the locomotive engine, or carriage, capable of travelling on a curved road, . . . two things are necessary. **1834** in Kittredge *Old Farmer* (1904) 300 A Locomotive Engine was yesterday employed in hauling gravel on the Boston & Worcester Rail Road. **1865** *Atlantic Mo.* XV. 734 Mrs. Exact is as intolerant as Torquemada or a locomotive-engine. **1884** CABLE *Dr. Sevier* lii, A locomotive engine and a single weather-beaten passenger coach, [were] moving southward at a very moderate speed. (2) **1850** *31st Congress 1 Sess.* Sen. Ex. Doc. No. 61, 4 A part of the work preparatory to building a locomotive engine [operated by electricity] has been done.

Locomotive works. A machine shop in which locomotives are built. — **1848** *Mass. Statutes* 13 March, A corporation, by the name of the Boston Locomotive Works, for the purpose of manufacturing locomotive engines. **1872** *Railroad Gazette* 3 Feb. 57/2 Baldwin Locomotive Works. The Northern Pacific has contracted for fifty new locomotives.

+**Loco weed.** *W.* Any one of various weeds, esp. one of the genus *Astragalus*, the eating of which causes stock to act drugged or intoxicated. (See also LOCO *n.*[2] 1.) — **1879** *Diseases of Swine* 211 The losses among cattle, caused by eating the poisonous loco weed, will perhaps not exceed 1 per cent. **1888** *Sanitary Era* 1 June 290/2 'Loco Weed' is said to afford a dissipation for cattle, in Kansas and Texas, where it grows abundantly. **1904** 'O. HENRY' in *McClure's Mag.* April 617/1 If you have ever seen a horse that has eaten loco-weed you will understand what I mean when I say that the passengers get locoed.

***Locust.**

+**1.** Any one of various North American species of trees of the genus *Robinia*, as the black locust, *R. pseudoacacia;* also, the honey locust, *Gleditsia triacanthos.*

[**1640** PARKINSON *Theater of Plants* 1552 The second [of the trees] is called Locus[t] by our Nation resident in *Virginia.*] **1670** DENTON *Brief Desc. N.Y.* 13 There grows black Walnut and Locust, as their doth in *Virginia.* **1709** LAWSON *Carolina* 49 Our whole Company . . . set out from the Sapona-Indian Town, after having seen some of the Locust, . . . the same Sort that bears Honey. **1782** CRÈVECŒUR *Letters* 204 The locust . . . yields the most valuable timber we have [in Mass.]. **1804** BENTLEY *Diary* III. 102 The rage for them [*sc.* Lombardy poplars] was excessive, just as it was above 30 years ago for the Locust. **1882** *Econ. Geol. Illinois* II. 105 The post-oak . . . prevails [in Clinton county] . . . together with . . . laurel oak and locust. **1905** ATHERTON *Travelling Thirds* 1 *n.*, The acacia of Europe is identical with the American locust.

b. A single tree of one or other species.

1671 ALVORD & BIDGOOD *Trans-Allegheny Region* 192 Weeds and small prickly Locusts and Thistles [grew] to a very great height. **1742** *Md. Hist. Mag.* XX. 262 The Bounded Locusts stood close by the Branch near a small ma[r]sh. **1821** COOPER *Spy* v, He would make no bad ornament, suspended from one of those locusts before his own door. **1890** *Century Mag.* Dec. 304 Above the corn shot the gaunt arm of the prickly locust, burned and bare. **1907** M. H. NORRIS *Veil* 2 Locusts, with furrowed trunks and twisted limbs, dropped their yellowing leaves like flakes of sulphur.

+**c.** A policeman's club made of locust wood. *colloq.*

*a***1882** in McCabe *New York* 381 They have too wholesome a respect for the law, for that locust, for that revolver in the pocket. **1904** *N.Y. Tribune* 19 June 4 The policemen did not carry their 'locusts.'

2. ***a.** The cicada or harvest fly.

1737 BRICKELL *N. Carolina* 166 The Locust, is an Insect or fly with a head like a Horse, six Legs and as many Wings. **1789** MORSE *Amer. Geog.* 62 Of the astonishing variety of Insects found in America, we will mention . . . Cicada or Locust. **1854** EMMONS *Agric. N.Y.* V. 145, The name locust is applied usually in this country to our harvest-fly, which is commonly called the seventeen-year locust. **1875** *Amer. Naturalist* IX. 71 The cicada (or harvest-fly), improperly called 'locust,' is so familiar that its description seems hardly necessary.

+**b.** The migratory Rocky Mountain grasshopper, *Melanoplus spretus.*

1823 FAUX *Memorable Days* 137 Grasshoppers, so called, but in fact a species of locust about the length of my little finger, swarm in countless millions. **1879** *Scribner's Mo.* Oct. 826/1 The fall of 1877 will long be remembered by the people of Minnesota, as the time when the destructive locust took his farewell meal from their wheat-fields. **1893** *Harper's Mag.* April 711/2 A succession of droughts and hot winds . . . were re-enforced by swarms of locusts, which descended from the torrid mesas of New Mexico and the sterile Piedmont of Colorado and Wyoming.

+**3.** Attrib. in sense 1 with *bush*, *log*, *stump*, *treenail.*

1700 *Md. Hist. Mag.* XIX. 352, 120 acr. Sur. . . . on the west side of Delph Creek at a Locust Stump. **1797** *Ann. 4th Congress* 2 Sess. 2791, 1,200 locust trennails, of 36 inches [were sold]. **1834** A. PIKE *Sketches* 56 The valley . . . was full of . . . mesquito [*sic*] bushes, that is, a kind of prickly, green locust bush, which bears long narrow beans in bunches. **1888** DELAND *J. Ward* 18 A spring bubbled out of the hillside, and ran singing through a hollowed locust log.

+**Locust borer.** The locust beetle (*Cyllene robiniae*) the larva of which bores into the wood of the locust tree. — **1839** *Mass. Agric. Survey 2d Rep.* 100 Locust-Borer.—Allen C. Metcalf of Lenox, washed his locust trees with spirits of turpentine, and in that way . . . compelled the borer to leave them. **1850** *New Eng. Farmer* II. 213 The locust borer is not of more than thirty years' introduction into the United States. **1871** *Rep. Comm. Agric. 1870* 73 To destroy the well-known locust-borer . . . , it has been recommended to apply soft soap to the trunks.

+**Locust post.** A post made of locust wood. — **1718** *Maryland Hist. Mag.* VI. 347 Thomas Williams brought in his Accts. for . . . setting up & painting four new Locust Posts & a new Locust Sill. **1904** STRATTON-PORTER *Freckles* 47 He climbed on the locust-post and . . . held a finger in the line of the moth's advance up the twig.

Locust tree. {1623–} + = LOCUST 1 and 1 b. — [**1640** PARKINSON *Theater of Plants* 1550 The *Virginian* Locus[t] tree . . . hath beene sent and brought us out of *Virginia*.] **1792** *N.Y. State Soc. Arts* I. 26 The locust-tree (*Robinia Pseudacacia*) is one of the most valuable trees now cultivated. . . . Their greatest use is for ship-trunnels, fence-posts, mill-cogs and fire-wood. **1843** TORREY *Flora N.Y.* I. 165 *Robinia pseudacacia.* . . . Common Locust-tree. . . . Not indigenous in any part of the State, but common about houses. **1903** FOX *Little Shepherd* xv, There were two windows in the little room—one almost swept by the branches of a locust-tree.

+**Locust year.** A year when the seventeen-year locusts are prevalent. — **1778** CARVER *Travels* 494 The years when they [locusts] thus arrive are denominated the locust years. **1800** in *S. Lit. Messenger* XXIII. 66/2 The first great locust year that I can remember, was in 1749. **1843** *Niles' Nat. Reg.* 17 June 247/3 It was confidently predicted that this [year] would also be a 'locust year.'

***Lode.** A vein of ore bearing valuable minerals. {1602–} — **1853** *Harper's Mag.* VI. 447/2 You are at a loss to know with what facility he distinguishes the lode or metalliferous portion of the rock, from the 'poor stuff' or 'country.' **1880** *Cimarron News & Press* 26 Feb. 1/6 The 'Homestake' lode so far as shown is unexampled in richness. **1901** WHITE *Westerners* 156 Thar is a lode . . . over on the J. G. fraction that's shore th' purtiest bit of quartz lead you ever see.

***Lodge.**

***1.** The den or habitation of an animal or animals, esp. beavers. (Cf. BEAVER LODGE.)

[**1744** A. DOBBS *Hudson's Bay* 40 He has seen fifteen [Beaver] of that Colour out of one Lodge or Pond.] **1804** CLARK in *Lewis & C. Exped.* I. (1904) 142 [We] found by running a pole down that we were not half way to his [the prairie dog's] Lodge. **1847** RUXTON *Adv. Rocky Mts.* (1848) 232 For the necessary timber for their lodges . . . the beaver often fells a tree eight to ten inches in diameter. **1902** W. HULBERT *Forest Neighbors* (1903) 5 Generation after generation of beavers had worked on that dam, . . . raising their lodges as the pond rose around them.

2. A local unit or branch of a secret order, as of the Masons; also, the members composing such a unit. {1686–}

1767 ROWE *Diary* 141 The officers of his Regiment marched in order first. then the Brethren of St. Andrew's Lodge. **1798** WASHINGTON *Writings* XIV. 119, I did not believe that the lodges of freemasons in this country had . . . endeavored to propagate the diabolical tenets [etc.]. **1811** *Freemason's Mag.* (Phila.) Oct. 3 The judicious selection of the officers of the lodge. **1881** *Harper's Mag.* Jan. 319/2 An Odd-fellows' lodge in Ohio had the misfortune to lose recently a very deserving member. **1912** *Hampton Mag.* April 194/1 The Elks now number 400,000 members in nearly 1,300 lodges.

***3.** A tent, shelter, etc., erected for temporary use by soldiers or woodsmen.

1748 H. ELLIS *Hudson's Bay* 177 His people, . . . had [they] built Lodges in the Woods, . . . would have suffered very little. **1805** LEWIS in *L. & Clark Exped.* II. (1904) 57 [We] were finally compelled to remove our lodge . . . to the foot of an adjacent hill. **1843** FRÉMONT *Explor.* 54 Our lodge had been planted and on account of the heat, the ground-pins had been taken out. **1885** CUSTER *Boots & Saddles* 59 Little low lodges, looking like the soldiers' shelter-tents, were used for the young men of the circle.

+**4.** = INDIAN LODGE.

1804 ORDWAY in *Journals of Lewis & O.* 172 They had a place fixed across their green from the head chiefs house across abt 50 yds to the 2 chiefs lodge. **1826** COOPER *Mohicans* xxiv, The smoke . . . ascended swiftly through the opening in the roof of the lodge. **1846** SAGE *Scenes Rocky Mts.* vii, The lodge of a mountain Indian consists of a frame work of light poles. **1881** *Rep. Indian Affairs* p. lxi, They have also quarried and hauled their own rock for chimneys, are generally abandoning their lodges. *a***1918** G. STUART *On Frontier* I. 197 They killed him and took his lodge and camp fixtures and one of his wives.

transf. **1835** SIMMS *Yemassee* I. 71 Ishiagaska has looked upon the white chief in the great lodge of his Spanish brother.

+**b.** Often used in an inclusive sense with reference to the size of an Indian population, village, party, etc.

1812 *Niles' Reg.* III. 106/2 There are on the river St. Peters and its branches, 1919 lodges of Sioux. **1834** A. PIKE *Sketches* 73 Entering the village, which consisted of about thirty lodges, we were conducted to the chief's tent. *c***1857** *Kit Carson's Own Story* (1926) 73, I discovered a large village of about 50 lodges. **1881** *Rep. Indian Affairs* 119 A party of 50 lodges of Crees passed here on their way north some days ago. *a***1918** G. STUART *On Frontier* I. 134 Just below us on the creek were camped eight lodges of Flathead Indians.

5. Attrib. and comb. +**a.** In sense 4 with *cloth, cover, covering,* etc.

1805 ORDWAY in *Jrnls. Lewis & O.* 179 The Squaws from the 1st village are cutting their lodge timber on the opposite side of the River from the Fort. **1847** PARKMAN in *Knickerb.* XXX. 234 The squaws of each lazy warrior had made him a shelter . . . by stretching . . . the corner of a lodge-covering upon poles. **1852** MARCY *Explor. Red River* (1854) 78 It is only two years since they removed from here, and their lodge-frames are still standing. **1871** *Rep. Indian Affairs* (1872) 526 The article of duck or lodge-cloth among the Indian annuities was the source of universal rejoicing. **1878** BEADLE *Western Wilds* 137 [Buffaloes] furnished them with food, clothing, lodge-covers, bow-strings, and a dozen other conveniences.

b. In sense 2 with *meeting, men.*

1897 BRODHEAD *Bound in Shallows* 224 The lodgemen surrounded [the grave]. **1903** BRADY *Bishop* 47 Most of the Churches have a week-night prayer-meeting, and the other nights are taken up with lodge-meetings.

+**Lodge fire.** A fire made in or in front of an Indian lodge. — **1837** IRVING *Bonneville* I. 111 Knots of gamblers will assemble before one of their lodge fires, early in the evening. **1848** PARKMAN in *Knickerb.* XXXI. 9, I found the ashes of an hundred and fifty lodge-fires. **1873** MILLER *Amongst Modocs* 250 In time of peace Indians never let their lodge-fires go out. **1889** *Century Mag.* Jan. 334/1 Cheyenne Indians . . . were well versed in that tribal legend which is rehearsed by the lodge fire in the long winter nights.

+**Lodge pole.** A kind of pole used, esp. by western Indians, in erecting a lodge. — **1805** LEWIS in *L. & Clark Exped* II. (1904) 88 Found a new indian lodge pole today which had been brought down by the stream. **1845** FRÉMONT *Exped.* 202 Our lodge poles were nearly worn out, and we found here a handsome set leaning against one of the trees, very white, and cleanly scraped. **1895** REMINGTON *Pony Tracks* 33 There were lodge poles . . . across the neck of land which the Sioux had proposed to defend. **1925** TILGHMAN *Dugout* 13 The women and children riding in a loose line, lodge poles trailing from the saddles.

+**Lodgepole pine.** A western tree, *Pinus murrayana,* or a similar species. — **1859** G. A. JACKSON *Diary* (MS.) 4 Cut the top off a small lodge pole pine. **1884** SARGENT *Rep. Forests* 564 The forests largely composed of the lodge-pole pine (*Pinus Murryana*) . . . cover the outlying eastern ranges of the Rocky mountains. **1905** *N.Y. Ev. Post* 29 April, The lodgepole pine, which is known in the Sierras of California as tamarack pine, and in Colorado and Montana is sometimes called white pine, . . . bears the common name of 'lodgepole' from the fact that the Indians used its long slender trunks as supports for their wigwams, or lodges. **1911** QUICK *Yellowstone Nights* 11 The moon was climbing through the lodge-pole pines.

+**Lodgepole trail.** (See quot. 1860.) *Obs.* — **1860** GREELEY *Overland Journey* 121 The Arapahoes say that a good 'lodge-pole trail'—that is, one which a pony may traverse with one end of the lodge-poles on his back, the other trailing behind him—exists from this point to the open prairie. **1876** BOURKE *Journal* 5 March, 'Lodge-pole' trails were about as numerous as yesterday.

+**Lodgepoling.** Among Indians, a thrashing or beating with a lodge pole. *Obs.* — **1848** RUXTON *Life Far West* iv. 161 [The squaws are not] so schooled to perfect obedience to their lords and masters as to stand a 'lodge-poling.' **1850** GARRARD *Wah-To-Yah* x. 131 She receives at the hands of her imperious sovereign a severe drubbing . . . or no very light lodgepoling.

Lodge room. A room in which a lodge holds its meetings. {1864–} — **1835** D. P. THOMPSON *Adv. T. Peacock* 170 Must all the world know all the didos we cut up in the lodge-room—wimen and all? **1887** *Lippincott's Mag.* Nov. 739 In addition to the secret lodge-room . . . each [fraternity] house has accommodations for from ten to eighteen students. **1911** LINCOLN *Cap'n Warren's Wards* 88, I'm more used to lodge rooms than I am to clubs.

+**Lodge skin.** The skin or hide of an animal, usually a buffalo, used in making a lodge. — **1846** SAGE *Scenes Rocky Mts.* xvii, [We were] exposed to . . . a chill storm of rain and sleet, with only a thin lodge skin to shelter us. **1852** *S. Lit. Messenger* XVIII. 414/2 The people of Fort Platte had prepared chairs and benches, backed by a curtain of elk lodge-skins. **1891** *Century Mag.* March 776/2 We had already devoured our moccasin soles, and a small sack made of smoked lodge skin.

+**Lodge trail.** = LODGEPOLE TRAIL. *Obs.* — **1845** FRÉMONT *Exped.* 114 We resumed our journey . . . following an extremely good lodge-trail. **1855** *S. Dak. Hist. Coll.* I. 391 A reconnaissance made from Chantier River to the Cheyenne, a distance by the road we took (a lodge trail) of forty miles.

+**Lodging car.** (See quotation.) — **1890** *Cent.* 3502/2 *Lodging-car,* . . . on a railroad, a car fitted with bunks, used as a sleeping- or dwelling-place for employees. (U.S.)

Lodging house. A house in which rooms or beds are rented. {1766–}

1856 SIMMS *Charlemont* 227 He returned to his room as soon as he reached his lodging-house. **1872** *Newton Kansan* 14 Nov. 1/1 A young man ran up the steps of Mrs. Porter's lodging-house. **1893** *Chicago Tribune* 24 April 2/1 Many of the boarding houses will be lodging houses only after May 1. **1908** SINCLAIR *Metropolis* 34 A maze of gin-shops, dime-museums, cheap lodging houses, and clothing stores sped past them.

b. Attrib. and comb. with *comfort, keeper, room.*

1841 TRUMBULL *Autobiog.* 261 A lodging-house keeper offered $2,200, which the executor was bound to accept. **1870** *Scribner's Mo.* I. 114 Even the newsboy . . . is so hedged about these latter days with lodging-house comforts. **1884** MATTHEWS & BUNNER *In Partnership* 147 In the privacy of his modest lodging-house room he took the handkerchief out.

Lodging room. A bedroom or room for sleeping. {1615-} — **1640** *Conn. Rec.* I. 451 In the lodgeing roome, one bedsteed. **1791** W. BARTRAM *Travels* 191 [One apartment] is the cook room and common hall, and the other the lodging room. **1860** HOLLAND *Miss Gilbert* 142 [They] crossed a spongy patch of garden to reach the lodging-room. **1906** *Springfield Repub.* 7 Feb. 2 Lodging Rooms to Let.

*** **Loft,** *n.* (See quot. 1890.)

'*Obs.* exc. *U.S.*' (*O.E.D.*).

1723 *New-Eng. Courant* 15-22 April 2/1 Some Fire was thrown into the Loft of Mr. Green's Printing-House. **1783** *Md. Gazette* 5 Sept. 4/3 To be let, A Cellar and two Rooms, and a loft of a brick warehouse. **1890** *Cent.* 3502/2 *Loft*, ... especially, in the United States, one of the upper stories of a warehouse or other mercantile building, or of a factory.

attrib. **1911** *N.Y. Ev. Post* 31 Jan. 2 They erected in the lower part of the avenue tall loft buildings to attract the wholesale garment-making trade. **1924** G. C. HENDERSON *Keys to Crookdom* 63 'Loft' burglars in New York and other big cities often loot an entire floor.

*** **Loft,** *v. tr.* To store or put away (a crop) in a loft. *Obs.* — **1785** WASHINGTON *Writings* XII. 229 The remainder of the Crop which was measured and lofted must be accted. for by the Overseer. **1786** — *Diaries* III. 136 Began to gather Corn in the Neck and at the Ferry for lofting. *Ib.* 149 The weather today prevented the Measuring and lofting it.

*** **Log,** *n.*

I. *** **1.** A section of a felled or fallen tree, cut off for use as firewood, in building, etc.

1634 *Boston Rec.* 1 Muche damage hath allreadye happened by laying of stones and logges near the bridge and landinge place. **1721** *Mass. H. Rep. Jrnl.* III. 30 A Committee, to Consider what may be the properest Methods for securing the Loggs that have been Cut in the Province of Maine. **1789** *Mass. Acts* V. 94 The laying a boom across the River Androscoggin ... for the purpose of stopping and securing logs and other lumber. **1823** JAMES *Exped.* I. 62 The houses are of one story, constructed of logs. **1877** JOHNSON *Anderson Co., Kansas* 250 In the spring of 1857 ... most of the houses were constructed of logs. **1900** *Bureau Statistics* (Treas. Dept.) *Summary* Nov. 1116 The logs can be gotten to the nearest skid road. **1912** N. M. WOODROW *Sally Salt* 303 There she sat on the log of an apple tree.

+2. (See quot. 1875.)

1875 KNIGHT 1348/1 *Log*.... (Steam-engine.) A tabulated summary of the performance of the engines and boilers, and of the consumption of coals, tallow, oil, and other engineers' stores on board a steam-vessel. **1876** INGRAM *Centennial Exp.* 351 'Logs' ... exhibit complete diagrams of the height and fluctuations of the steam within the boiler.

3. Used in sense 1 in various (usually colloq.) phrases. **+a.** *As easy as rolling* (or *falling*) *off a log*, said of something regarded as extremely easy.

1889 'MARK TWAIN' *Conn. Yankee* 20, I could ... do it as easy as rolling off a log. **1890** FREDERIC *Lawton Girl* 125 It can be fixed, as easy as rolling off a log. **1905** N. DAVIS *Northerner* 115 It will be just as easy 'as falling off a log.' **1910** MCCUTCHEON *Rose in Ring* 49 It's as easy as fallin' off a log. Joey can tell you all the tricks.

+b. In miscellaneous phrases.

To split the log, to explain a matter; *to keep the log rolling*, to keep things moving (cf. BALL *n.*[1] 1 d); *in the log*, in an unfinished state; *a bump on a log*, an inarticulate or insignificant person or a nobody.

1832 PAULDING *Westward Ho* I. 183, I'll split the log for you. **1850** H. C. WATSON *Camp-Fires Revol.* 55 We must keep the log rollin'. **1858** THOREAU *Maine Woods* 148 The largest pine belonging to his firm, cut the previous winter, ... was worth ninety dollars in the log at the Bangor boom. **1889** K. D. WIGGIN *Birds' Christmas Carol* 47 Ye ain't goin' to set there like a bump on a log 'thout sayin' a word ter pay for yer vittles, air ye?

II. *attrib.* and *comb.*

4. +a. Designating enclosures, fortifications, etc., made of logs.

See also LOG FENCE, LOG PEN 2.

1737 *N.H. Hist. Soc. Coll.* VII. 358 [In 1737 was built] a log pound, ... with a good gate. **1840** COOPER *Pathfinder* xxiv, We carried their log breastwork by storm. **1858** PETERS *Kit Carson* 14 The Carson family, with a few neighbors, lived in a picketed log fort. **1893** in Philips *Making of Newspaper* 200 They waylaid him from behind one of the old log 'blinds' they were so deadly at manufacturing. **1916** EASTMAN *From Deep Woods* 15 It was my first task each morning to bring them [*sc.* ponies] into the log corral.

+b. Designating buildings or parts of buildings made of logs.

See also LOG CABIN, etc.

1743 BRAINERD *Journal* (1902) 271 It is a log-room, without any floor, that I lodge in. **1798** ALLEN *Hist. Vermont* 22 A log Court House and Goal were erected at the latter place. **1806** PIKE *Sources Miss.* I. App. 36 [The fur-trading establishment] at Lower Red Cedar Lake ... consists of log buildings. **1823** *Baptist Mag.* IV. 74 We have a good log meeting house on Salt Creek. **1829** COOPER *Wish-ton-Wish* xxii, The log-tenement, the stacks, and the out-buildings of Reuben Ring ... were sending forth clouds of murky smoke. **1834** *S. Lit. Messenger* I. 120 The log stable belonging to Mr. Austin. **1845** JUDD *Margaret* I. 12-13 On the east side of the road was a log-barn. **1847** PARKMAN in *Knickerb.* XXIX. 313 We found the log-church and school-houses belonging to the Methodist Shawanoe Mission. *a***1861** WINTHROP *Open Air* 32 All the residents of Damville dwelt in a great log-barrack. **1874** EGGLESTON *Circuit Rider* 56 The wide old log-kitchen, with its loom in one corner. **1881** *Harper's Mag.* April 706/1 Juneau's log ware-house was the headquarters for gossip.

+c. Designating towns in which the buildings are made of logs.

[**1790** FRENEAU in *N.Y. Daily Advertiser* 19 Feb., Lines Descriptive of a Tavern at Log-Town, a small Place in the Pine Barrens of North-Carolina.] **1817** S. BROWN *Western Gaz.* 106 Vangeville,—A log city, ... has fifteen or twenty old log houses. **1836** HILDRETH *Campaigns Rocky Mts.* I. 70 The remains of a log-town long since evacuated, that had formerly been the settlement of a tribe of the Delawares.

5. +a. Designating instruments, apparatus, areas, etc., used in logging operations.

See also LOG CAR, LOG CHAIN, etc.

1779 *N.J. Archives* 2 Ser. III. 69 To be sold ... a good log waggon and four horses. **1858** THOREAU *Maine Woods* 94 Hinckley ... appeared with a truck drawn by an ox and a horse over a rude log-railway through the woods. **1878** *Lumberman's Gaz.* 5 Jan., Wyburn's improved log stamp is convenient for marking logs with the exact number of feet. *Ib.* 2 Feb. 89 He has constructed a road of ice ... on which the log-sleds slip along readily. *Ib.* 6 April, An addition to the wharf and log boom are being made. **1905** *Forestry Bureau Bul.* No. 61, 32 *Bunk*, ... a log car or truck. (S[outhern] F[orest], P[acific] C[oast] F[orest].)

+b. Designating persons engaged in logging operations. (Cf. LOGGER.)

1850 JUDD *R. Edney* xviii. 220 This flood was both spring-time and harvest for log-drivers, boom-gatherers, and lumber-men generally. **1880** *Lumberman's Gaz.* 7 Jan. 28 Next come the 'log makers,' working in gangs of three or four, each with its 'chief.' **1881** *Mich. Gen. Statutes* I. (1882) 980 Nothing in this act shall be construed as conferring upon the log interest any paramount rights. **1893** *Scribner's Mag.* June 710/2 At night he must get from the log-cutters their count for the day.

+6. Designating various utensils or articles of furniture made from a log or logs.

1816 *Ann. 14th Congress* 2 Sess. 1190 Modern contrivances, such as log stills, rectifying vats, and some other utensils. **1881** *Harper's Mag.* May 876/1 The guide is born not made.... He rolls out of his log-cradle into a pair of top-boots. **1882** THAYER *From Log-Cabin* 63 He had never undertaken to perform the feat of sitting bolt upright upon a log bench without a back.

+7. Designating types of watercraft made of a log or logs.

See also LOG CANOE.

1838 FLAGG *Far West* I. 30 The birch caïque of the Indian, and log skiffs, gondolas, and dug-outs of the pioneer [were] without name or number. **1873** in Custer *Boots & Saddles* 285 To accomplish this, Lieutenant Weston ... attempted to cross on a log-raft.

+8. Special combinations.

Log beam, (see quotation); *l. box*, a jail, humorous; *l. butting*, the end cut off in 'butting' a log; *l. camp*, =LOGGING CAMP; *l. crop*, the yield in logs of a particular area or tract; *l. crossing*, =FOOT LOG; *l. cut*, the aggregate amount expressed in board feet of lumber made from the logs cut during a particular period; *l. deck*, (see quotation); *l. dump*, (see quotation); *l. jack*, (see quotation); *l. mark*, a mark placed on a log to indicate ownership; *l.-measurer*, (see quotation); *l. pocket*, a confined body of water in which logs are accumulated; *l.-raising*, =HOUSE-RAISING; *l. rule*, (see quotation); *l. shoot, slide*, an inclined passageway down which logs are precipitated; *l. watch*, (see quotation); *l. yard*, an area where logs are assembled awaiting further transportation.

1883 KNIGHT *Suppl.* 558/2 *Log Beam*, the traveling frame in which a log lies and travels in a saw-mill. **1841** SIMMS *Kinsmen* I. 121 His friends are nigh enough to get him out of the logbox. **1879** *Lumberman's Gaz.* 15 Oct., A machine that would utilize ... Log Buttings. **1858** THOREAU *Maine Woods* 136 My companion inclined to go to the log-camp on the carry. **1879** *Lumberman's Gaz.* 7 May, The delivery of the log crop of Michigan. **1899** CUSHMAN *Hist. Indians* 227 When the spirit of a bad person arrives at the log-crossing of the fearful river, it is assailed by wakeful guards. **1882** *Uncle Rufus & Ma* 33 The log cut of 1879-'80 was 153,500,000 feet. **1905** *Forestry Bureau Bul.* No. 61, 42 *Log deck*, the platform upon a loading jack. *Ib.*, 41 *Landing*, ... a place to which logs are hauled or skidded preparatory to transportation by water or rail.... [Also called] banking ground, log dump, rollway, yard. *Ib.* 38 *Gangway*, the incline plane up which logs are moved from the water into a sawmill. ... [Also called] log jack, log way. **1859** *Michigan Rep.* VI. 270 The Mill Company had given a list of log-marks under section eight of the act. **1875** KNIGHT 1349/2 *Log-measurer*, a device for gaging logs, taking the round measure with the allowance for the squaring, and giving the results in board measure of the ascertained square in running feet of the log. **1877** *Lumberman's Gaz.* 17 Nov., A dam has been built across the river, forming a log pocket. **1897** BRODHEAD *Bound in Shallows* 169 Law, the log-raisin's and corn-huskin's they used to have! **1905** *Forestry Bureau Bul.* No. 61, 15 *Log rule*, ... a tabular statement of the amount of lumber which can be sawed from logs of given lengths and diameters. **1878** JACKSON *Travel at Home* 150 A 'log-shoot' ... is made of two split logs, laid lengthwise, close, smooth side up. Down this, logs are sent sliding into the river. **1887** HARTE *Phyllis of Sierras* 1 He would have come upon some rude wagon track, or 'log-slide,' leading from a clearing on the slope. **1905** *Forestry Bureau Bul.* No. 61, 39 *Head driver*, an expert river driver who, during the drive, is stationed at a point where a jam is feared.... [Also called] log watch (N[orthern] F[orest]). **1883** SMITH *Geol. Survey Ala.* 370 'Log-yards' are established at every convenient bluff along the river.

Log, *v.* {1699–}

+**1.** *absol.* To produce logs by cutting down timber: (see also quot. 1905).

1717 *Mass. H. Rep. Jrnl.* I. 272 Bridger [is trying] ... to compel the inhabitants ... to pay him forty shillings for each team they send to log and get timber. **1835** *Knickerb.* V. 52 [They] form companies 'to log and lumber.' **1878** *Michigan Rep.* XXXVII. 408 He was logging on the ... Manistee River. **1905** *Forestry Bureau Bul.* No. 61, 42 *Log, to*, to cut logs and deliver them at a place from which they can be transported by water or rail, or, less frequently, at the mill.

b. *tr.* To deprive (an area) of its logs; to cut (timber) into logs. Also with *up*.

[**1836** C. P. TRAILL *Backwoods of Canada* 101 After the trees have been chopped, cut into lengths, drawn together, or logged, as we call it.] **1843** *Yale Lit. Mag.* VIII. 406 What a nation sight of bother it would be to log up a clearing in these parts. **1848** THOREAU *Maine Woods* 20 Only a little spruce and hemlock beside had been logged here. **1902** WHITE *Blazed Trail* 5 We own ... five million on the Cass Branch which we would like to log on contract.

2. *To log in* (or *up*), to protect (a structure) with logs.

1786 *Md. Hist. Mag.* XIX. 268 Thomas Yates engaging to logg in, and wharf Jones's falls. **1798** *Smithtown Rec.* 351 The dam [is] to be logged up against where the saw mill shall stand. **1888** BILLINGS *Hardtack* 49 But by far the most common way of logging up a tent was to build the walls 'cob-fashion,' notching them together at the corners.

+**Loganberry.** [J. H. *Logan*, Amer. jurist and horticulturist (1841–1928).] A variety of red berry, or the plant producing it, first discovered in 1881. Regarded as either a hybrid between the western dewberry and the red raspberry or a variety of the former. Also attrib. — **1893** *Calif. Agric. Exper. Sta. Bul.* No. 103, 3 The Logan Berry ... [has] the shape of a blackberry, the color of a raspberry, and a combination of the flavors of both. **1894** *Garden & Forest* VII. 466/1 Loganberry-plants will be high-priced for a time. **1900** WICKSON *Calif. Fruits* 400 The Loganberry ... has proved a most valuable fruit in all parts of California. [**1918** *Farmers' Bul.* No. 998, 3 The Logan blackberry ... is now considered a variety of the Pacific coast species of trailing blackberry.]

+**Log bridge.** A bridge made of logs. — **1664** *Springfield Rec.* I. 316 Foure acres of low lands Northwestrly from the logg bridge. **1842** *Lowell Offering* II. 275 How natural is that rude log bridge, so carelessly thrown over the crystallized brook! **1895** *Outing* XXVI. 365/2 A very unstable log bridge ... spans the Oswegatchie river. **1915** ATKINSON *Johnny Appleseed* 185 These young pioneers knew ... how to ... build blockhouses and log bridges.

+**Log-built,** *a.* Made or constructed of logs. — **1835** HOFFMAN *Winter in West* I. 79 We stopped to breakfast at a low log built shantee. **1855** *Knickerb.* XLVI. 225 The nuptials were celebrated in the one-story 'ten-by-six' log-built mansion of the bride's father. **1902** WHITE *Conjuror's House* 111 Your work here among the Indians is rot.... You coop them up in your log-built houses. **1925** BRYAN *Memoirs* 213 The logbuilt home has vanished.

+**Log cabin.**

1. A cabin built of logs.

1770 in Summers *Ann. S.W. Virginia* 77 A log cabbin twenty four feet long and twenty wide for a Court House, with a clapbord roof. **1778** M. WASHINGTON in *Warren-Adams Lett.* II. 6 The General's appartment is very small he has had a log cabbin built to dine in. **1806** *Ann. 9th Congress* 2 Sess. 1124 At the hot springs they found an open log cabin, and a few huts of split boards. **1843** HAWKS *D. Boone* 23 A clearing in the woods was soon made, a log cabin of his own soon built. **1874** R. H. COLLINS *Kentucky* I. 24 Cincinnati has more than 100 log cabins, 12 or 15 frame houses [etc.]. **1900** *Congress. Rec.* 27 Jan. 1242/1 Go to my own State, go into ... the log cabin of the frontiersman. *a***1918** G. STUART *On Frontier* I. 24 My father built his one room log cabin in the woods a short distance from the creek.

b. *Polit.* With particular reference to the presidential campaign of 1840. Now hist. (Cf. HARD CIDER CAMPAIGN.)

1840 HONE *Diary* II. 33 Never did the friends of Mr. Van Buren make so great a mistake as when by their sneers they furnished the Whigs those powerful weapons, 'log-cabin' and 'hard cider.' **1841** *Letter from Onondaga Co., N.Y.* (MS.) 8 July, Let them wiggle with their log cabins and hard cider. **1846** CORCORAN *Pickings* 143 He looked like ... a flag-staff divested of its ensign, still standing over the ruins of a Tippecanoe log-cabin. **1888** M. LANE in *America* 11 Oct. 15 The peculiar feature of the canvass [in 1840] was the general use of 'log cabins' and 'hard cider' as drawing attractions.

2. A quilt pattern suggestive of a cabin built of logs.

1898 E. C. HALL *Aunt Jane* 57 There seemed to be every pattern that the ingenuity of woman could devise and the industry of woman put together,—'four-patches,' 'nine-patches,' 'log-cabins,' 'wild-goose chases,' 'rising suns.'

3. *attrib.* **a.** In sense 1 with *boarder*, *bonnet*, etc.

1840 *Nashville Whig* 17 Aug. (Th.), They are the representatives of a hardy race of honest log cabin pioneers. **1846** *Knickerb.* XXVIII. 360 In some of these log-cabin hotels in the west. **1856** ROBINSON *Kansas* 161 There were some with log-cabin bonnets of black silk, or cotton velvet, and dress of plain coarse stuff. **1884** *Century Mag.* March 678/2 No sooner is the 'Interocean City' of some farthest Western frontier of civilization out of the log-cabin period, than it has at once a Broadway. **1890** LANGFORD *Vigilante Days* (1912) 487 We came upon a log cabin saloon by the wayside. **1916** EASTMAN *From Deep Woods* 45 We, the log-cabin boarders, came out in Indian file.

b. In sense 1 b with *campaign*, *candidate*, etc.

1840 *Niles' Nat. Reg.* 28 Nov. 208 The Log Cabin State. We claim this title for Pennsylvania. **1840** *Boston Atlas* 11 Sept. (Th.), The log-cabin boys Of old Tippecanoe. **1840** *Picayune* 2 Oct. 2/3 A druggist is selling log cabin cologne in Boston. **1885** *Harper's Mag.* Oct. 743/1 This law grew out of the 'log-cabin, hard-cider, and 'coonskin' campaign of 1840. **1913** A. C. COLE *Whig Party in So.* 59 [The Whigs] felt the sting of the unfortunate reference to the 'log-cabin, hard-cider candidate.'

c. In sense 2 with *bedquilt*, etc.

1887 *Harper's Mag.* Dec. 36/1 She slipped her book under the log-cabin quilt. **1890** *Stock Grower & Farmer* 10 May 3/1 If Uncle Jerry will furnish our farmer's wives with a good design for a log cabin patchwork or Prairie Sunflower quilt, the deed is done. **1920** LINCOLN *Mr. Pratt* 214 Most everything was sold but a log cabin bed quilt.

+**Log canoe.** A canoe made from a hollowed-out log. (Cf. LOG *n.* 7.) — **1752** in *Travels Amer. Col.* 315 An officer and ten soldiers ... brought us in two log canoes. **1807** C. SCHULTZ *Travels* I. 129 The smallest kind of craft in use [on the Ohio R.] are simple log canoes. **1840** THOMPSON *Green Mt. Boys* I. 12 [Four men] were seen occupying a large log canoe near the eastern shore of the lake. **1923** J. H. COOK *On Old Frontier* 3 They were ... at home in a log canoe, spearing fish.

+**Log car.** A car or truck used in hauling logs, as from a boom up into a mill. — **1881** *Chicago Times* 11 June, The track upon which runs the log-car. **1897** BRODHEAD *Bound in Shallows* 218 Above the scream of the saws and the splash of the log car.

+**Log carriage.** In a sawmill, the carriage upon which the log is conveyed to and past the saw. — **1853** 'P. PAXTON' *Yankee in Texas* 251 What did that enormous saw and log-carriage mean? **1874** KNIGHT 479/2 The *log-carriage* of a sawing-machine.

+**Log chain.** A chain used principally in logging operations. Also attrib. — **1672** *Oyster Bay Rec.* I. 68, 1 loge chaine. **1741** HEMPSTEAD *Diary* 381, [I] got my Logg Chain mended. **1839** *S. Lit. Messenger* V. 325/2 They found a number of log-chains and traces. **1857** UNDERHILL & THOMPSON *Elephant Club* 233 Overdale expatiated upon [it] at some length as an extensive log-chain factory. **1914** 'BOWER' *Flying U Ranch* 191 You couldn't drag them herders across Flying U coulee with a log chain.

+**Logcock.** **1.** The pileated woodpecker, *Ceophloeus pileatus*. **2.** =IVORY-BILLED WOODPECKER. — (1) **1806** LEWIS in *L. & Clark Exped.* IV. (1905) 132 The large woodpecker or log cock, the lark woodpecker and the small white woodpecker with a read head ... are found exclusively in the timbered country. **1850** S. F. COOPER *Rural Hours* 301 The large pileated woodpecker, or log-cock, a resident in Pennsylvania through the winter, is said to [be seen]. **1884** BURROUGHS in *Century Mag.* Dec. 222/2 The log-cock, ... the largest and wildest of our Northern species, I have never heard drum. **1917** *Birds of Amer.* II. 154 Pileated Woodpecker. *Phlœotomus pileatus pileatus*.... [Also called] Logcock; Great Black Woodpecker [etc.]. (2) **1811** WILSON *Ornithology* IV. 24 The more intelligent and observing part of the natives ... distinguish them [the ivory-billed and the pileated woodpeckers] by the name of the large and lesser *Log-cocks*. **1917** *Birds of Amer.* II. 138 Ivory-billed Woodpecker. *Campephilus principalis*.... [Also called] Logcock [etc.].

+**Log college.** A school conducted in a log building. *Obs.* — **1795** FRENEAU *Poems* 374 On the Demolition of a Log-College. **1850** FOOTE *Sk. Virginia* 393 The Smiths came to Virginia to commence log colleges in the 'Ancient Dominion.'

+**Log crib.** **1.** A corncrib built of logs. **2.** =CRIB 3. — (1) [**1847** HOWE *Hist. Coll. Ohio* 240 Seventy or eighty feet of the enclosure was composed of a row of log corn cribs.] **1872** POWERS *Afoot & Alone* 66 [Alabama] is ... a land of log-cribs, high and spindling, and full of snow-white corn. (2) **1902** WHITE *Blazed Trail* 209 The steamboat ... moved slowly toward the wharf of log cribs filled with stone.

+**Log-driving.** Facilitating or expediting the passage of saw logs down a stream or watercourse. Also attrib. — **1851** SPRINGER *Forest Life* 137 We were improving [the channel of the stream] by the removal of large rocks which obstructed log-driving. **1879** *Lumberman's Gaz.* 19 Dec., The dam will be used for flowage and log-driving purposes. **1905** *Forestry Bureau Bul.* No. 61, 34 *Cut off*, an artificial channel by which the course of a stream is straightened, to facilitate log driving. (N[orthern]F[orest].)

+**Log fence.** A fence made of logs.

1651 *East-Hampton Rec.* I. 13 Those men that are behind in the Logg fence ... shall Doe their worke betweene this & the 3 of May. **1684** I. MATHER *Providences* (1856) v. 118 He hath had five rods of good log-fence thrown down at once. **1764** *N.H. Hist. Soc. Coll.* IX. 154, [I] made log fence around my young orchard. **1790** S. DEANE *New-Eng. Farmer* 89/1 In the new plantations of this country, log fences are most used. **1828** COOPER *Notions* I. 343 *n.*, The 'log-fence' ... is formed by laying the trunks of trees in a line, with their ends doubling for a couple of feet. **1880** *Scribner's Mo.* Feb. 504/2 The log fence was a structure of more substance than either the pole or brush fence. **1902** WHITE *Conjuror's House* 39 The storehouse [is] surrounded by a protective log fence.

Log fire. A fire made by burning logs. {1878} — **1828** H. FINN, etc. *Whimwhams* 198 My parents and myself were gathered around our log-fire. **1853** RAMSEY *Tennessee* 717 Never were . . . the song and the laugh, better enjoyed than . . . around the roaring log fire of the early Western settler. **1874** LONG *Wild-Fowl* 104 No one . . . ever cared . . . to go back to the old log-fire again [after using a camp stove]. **1910** TOMPKINS *Mothers & Fathers* 192 A log fire made the living room the only habitable spot.

+**Logfish.** (See quotation.) — **1884** GOODE, etc. *Fisheries* I. 334 The Black Rudder-fish—*Lirus perciformis*. This fish is also called by the fishermen 'Log-fish' and 'Barrel-fish.'

+**Log furnace.** A smelting furnace in which logs are used as fuel. — **1819** SCHOOLCRAFT *Mo. Lead Mines* 94 This furnace is called the *Log Furnace*, and is peculiar to this [Mo. lead-mining] country. It is of very simple construction, consisting of an inclined hearth, surrounded by walls on three sides, open at top, and with an arch for the admission of air below. **1850** *Western Jrnl.* IV. 412 Messrs. Tingle & McKee . . . have raised about 50,000 pounds [of ore], and are now smelting in a log furnace.

+**Logger.** One engaged in logging; a lumberman.

1734 *N.H. Prov. Papers* IV. 840 Many Towns raising a generall Contribution among the Logers for him. **1827** COOPER *Prairie* xviii, It will not be long before an accursed band of choppers and loggers will be following. **1879** HARTE *Drift from Two Shores* 32 His nearest neighbor was Trinidad Joe, a 'logger,' three miles up the river. **1890** *Boston Jrnl.* 4 Jan. 4/7 Four loggers were burned to death at Beebe's camp. **1917** GARLAND *Son of Middle Border* i, He had charge of a crew of loggers in winter.

* **Loggerhead.** Also †**log(h)er head.**

1. a. =LOGGERHEAD TURTLE 1 and 2. {1697–}

1709 LAWSON *Carolina* 133 The third [Turtle] is Logger-Head, which kind scarce any one covets, except it be for the Eggs. **1807** JANSON *Stranger in Amer.* 312 The swamps produce a variety of . . . land turtles. The natives call them loggerheads, tarapins [etc.]. **1884** [see LOGGERHEAD TURTLE 1]. **1911** *Rep. Fisheries* 1908 312 Loggerhead (*Thalassochelys caretta*).—A turtle of small economic value, found in the Atlantic as far north as Massachusetts and in the Gulf of Mexico.

+**b.** A diamond-back terrapin, or a related species. Also attrib. with *terrapin*.

1877 BARTLETT 367 *Loggerhead Terrapin*, the large fresh and salt water tortoise. *Ib.* 699 The most celebrated is the diamond-back; there are also the yellow-bellies, red-bellies, log[g]er-heads, snuff-boxes, etc.

2. A roundish or oval-shaped iron with a long handle, used, when heated, for warming beer, flip, etc. *Obs.* {1687–}

1760 *Boston Rec.* 57, 1 Loggerhead to warm Beer, 1 s. **1853** FELT *Customs New Eng.* 43 *Loggerhead.*—The name given to a long iron handle with a head. **1860** HOLMES *Professor* i. 3 In flip days . . . there were always two or three loggerheads in the fire.

+**3.** =LOGGERHEAD SHRIKE.

1803 J. DAVIS *Travels* 81 The red-bird is imitated with nice precision by the mocking-bird; but there is a bird [in S.C.] called the loggerhead that will not bear passively its taunts. **1811** WILSON *Ornithology* III. 57 [The loggerhead shrike] is generally known by the name of the *Loggerhead*. **1917** *Birds of Amer.* III. 100/1 When seen the Loggerhead is usually occupying a perch on the top of some small tree, stake, telephone pole, or fence post.

+**4.** During the Civil War, a nickname for a Federal soldier from Pennsylvania.

1888 WHITMAN *November Boughs* 70 Those [soldiers] from . . . Pennsylvania, [were called] Logher Heads.

+**5.** (See quotation.)

1890 *Cent.* 3504/2 *Loggerhead*, . . . a kind of sponge found in Florida.

+**Loggerhead shrike.** The common shrike (*Lanius ludovicianus*) of the southeastern states. — **1811** WILSON *Ornithology* III. 57 Loggerhead Shrike. . . . This species inhabits the rice plantations of Carolina and Georgia. **1831** AUDUBON *Ornith. Biog.* I. 300 The Loggerhead Shrike . . . utters a shrill clear creaking prolonged note. **1894** TORREY *Fla. Sketch-Book* 123 The loggerhead shrike is a bird of the town. **1917** *Birds of Amer.* III. 99.

Loggerhead turtle. **1.** A sea turtle, as *Caretta caretta*. {1657–, in Barbados, etc.} +**2. a.** The common snapping turtle, *Chelydra serpentina*. **b.** The alligator snapper (*Macrochelys temminckii*), valued as food. — (1) **1682** ASH *Carolina* 27 The Loggerhead Turtle, or Tortoise has neither good Shell or Flesh, so is little minded or regarded. **1766** STORK *Acct. East-Florida* 52 There are three sorts of sea-turtle common in East-Florida, the logger-head, hawk's-bill, and green-turtle. **1884** GOODE, etc. *Fisheries* I. 147 The Loggerhead Turtle . . . is commonly known in the United States as the 'Loggerhead,' *Thalassochelys caretta*, . . . in allusion to its large and thick head. (2) **1842** *Nat. Hist. N.Y., Zoology* III. 8 The Snapping Turtle . . . is one of our largest turtles. . . . In other sections, it is known under the names of Loggerhead, Alligator Turtle and Couta. **1884** GOODE, etc. *Fisheries* I. 873/1.

+**Loggery.** A log dwelling or building. *Obs.* — **1839** KIRKLAND *New Home* 261 These find no fault with their bare loggeries. **1843** 'CARLTON' *New Purchase* I. 108 The orders of cabin architecture are various like those of the Greek; for instance, . . . the *Composite Order*—i.e. loggeries with stone or brick chimneys. **1882** *Harper's Mag.* Aug. 337/2 The old 'loggery' . . . still fronts the river on the island side.

Logging.

+**1.** The cutting and getting out of logs from a forest.

1706 *N.H. Prov. Papers* III. 337 Those whose livelihood chiefly consists in Logging and working in the woods. **1845** COOPER *Chainbearer* xiii, For the heavier . . . work, such as the logging, he [the axman] called on his neighbors for aid. **1905** *Bureau of Forestry Bul.* No. 60, 7 Logging on a large scale . . . would greatly impair its beauty.

+**2.** *Polit.* =LOGROLLING 2.

1817 JEFFERSON *Writings* XV. 134 The barter of votes . . . which, with us, is called 'logging,' the term of the farmers for their exchanges of aid in rolling together the logs of their newly-cleared grounds.

+**3.** A quantity of felled logs; heavy timbers, planks, etc.

1823 COOPER *Pioneers* xvii, His piles, or to use the language of the country, his logging. **1877** WRIGHT *Big Bonanza* 451 A drift, the mouth of which they had carefully closed with 'logging' and pieces of boards. **1896** SHINN *Story of Mine* 236 The other end [of the spragg], slightly sharpened, is against heavy planks, called logging.

+**4.** The process of clearing off and piling for burning the small logs, timber, underbrush, etc., from a piece of land intended for cultivation; the area or land so cleared. *Obs.* Also transf.

1827 COOPER *Prairie* xi, Show me . . . a set of boys who will . . . sooner chop a piece of logging and dress it for the crop, than my own children. **1828** — *Notions* I. 342 With the exception of such trees as are selected for lumber, the whole are piled in heaps of sufficient size to ensure their consumption by fire. The latter process is called logging.

+**5.** Attrib. in sense 1 with *branch railroad, company*, etc.

See also LOGGING BEE, LOGGING CAMP, etc.

1838 *Knickerb.* XII. 293 The lumbermen are . . . starting into the wilderness, on a logging expedition. **1851** SPRINGER *Forest Life* 67, I have seldom taxed my judgment as severely on any subject as in judiciously locating a logging establishment. *a***1862** THOREAU *Maine Woods* 218 [We] were soon confused by numerous logging-paths. **1895** *Outing* XXVI. 393/1 We had traveled for the last twenty miles, on a logging branch railroad. **1900** BRUNCKEN *N. Amer. Forests* 79 Booms are not the only structures used on the logging rivers to facilitate the 'driving.' **1903** HART *Actual Govt.* 326 Logging companies buy up immense areas of land for timber. **1905** *Forestry Bureau Bul.* No. 61, 33 *Corkscrew*, a geared logging locomotive. (P[acific] C[oast] F[orest].) *Ib.* 42 *Logging wheels*, a pair of wheels, usually about 10 feet in diameter, for transporting logs.

+**6.** Special combinations.

Logging berth, the scene of logging operations, as a logging camp; *logging chance*, 'a forest location suitable for a single logging operation' (W. '34).

1851 *Harper's Mag.* Sept. 521/2 Such annoyances from these migrating beasts in the vicinity of logging berths . . . are of recent date. **1860** *Ib.* Feb. 296/2 An elderly man—a woodsman—came to the camp. . . . Two of his sons, he said, had started . . . to search in the woods for a 'logging chance,' and had not returned.

+**Logging bee.** =LOGROLLING 1. (Cf. LOGGING 2.) — [**1836** C. P. TRAILL *Backwoods of Canada* 192 We called a logging-bee.] **1845** COOPER *Chainbearer* xiii, 'Logging-bees' have given rise to a familiar expression known as legislative 'log-rolling.' **1857** *Quinland* I. 91 The whole neighbourhood would assemble together, in turn, to pile up the logs in a new clearing of A, B, or C; hence the 'loging [*sic*] bee.' **1893** *Advance* 16 Nov., A logging bee has been described quite in detail.

+**Logging camp.** Temporary or seasonal quarters established by loggers and lumbermen. — **1832** WILLIAMSON *Maine* I. 141 The Whetsaw . . . frequents logging camps. **1873** BEADLE *Undevel. West* 718 The lumbermen spend the long winter in the 'logging camps,' getting out and hauling the logs to the nearest stream. **1892** *Vt. Agric. Rep.* XII. 124, I have often seen traces of them . . . about the streams and logging camps. **1925** BRYAN *Memoirs* 93 He went early into the logging camps.

+**Logging crew.** A group or company of workmen engaged in logging operations. — **1878** *Lumberman's Gaz.* 9 Feb., Logging crews are coming out of the woods there, on account of lack of snow. **1900** BRUNCKEN *N. Amer. Forests* 82 He may have charge of a logging crew as foreman.

+**Logging railroad.** A railroad built to facilitate logging operations. — **1893** *Scribner's Mag.* June 711/1 Finally with a large capacity came large enterprises, great lumber-mills, logging railroads, and finally great fortunes. **1905** *Forestry Bureau Bul.* No. 60, 23 If logging railroads are constructed, . . . they can be used for nothing else.

+**Logging road.** A road made for use in logging. — **1839** *3d Rep. Maine Geol. Survey* 41 [We] walked along a logging road. **1851** SPRINGER *Forest Life* 53 Noting the surface of the land through which the logging roads are to be cut. **1902** WHITE *Blazed Trail* 6 Radway tramped the woods . . . to determine the most practical route over which to build a logging road. **1922** BROWN *Old Crow* 74 A logging road came down from the ridge, and Raven saw with interest that it had been broken out.

+**Logging sled.** A sled for use in logging. Also attrib. — **1741** *N.H. Prov. Papers* VI. 349 Sent our Baggage on loging sleds to Rochester from Cochecho. **1902** MCFAUL *Ike Glidden* 228 Cy Haines was there for the purpose of getting a logging-sled repaired. **1905** *Forestry Bureau Bul.* No. 61, 42 *Logging-sled road*, a road, leading from the skidway or yard to the landing. (N[orthern] F[orest].)

+**Logging swamp.** A swamp from which logs are obtained. — **1851** SPRINGER *Forest Life* 46 We have sometimes heard the voice of prayer even in the logging-swamps. **1860** *Harper's Mag.* March 440/2 All these are but the preparatory duties of the 'logging swamp,' to be completed before . . . winter.

+**Log heap.** Logs heaped or piled for burning. — **1819** E. DANA *Geogr. Sk.* 36 The Creoles never having before smelted, except by throwing the ore into log heaps. **1838** J. MCDONALD *Biog. Sk.* 38 When breakfast was ready, . . . he could not be found at the log-heaps. **1888** GRIGSBY *Smoked Yank* (1891) 201 He was building up a great log-heap of dry logs, with 'fat' pine for kindling. **1899** CUSHMAN *Hist. Indians* 309 Silent men . . . from whose dark features were reflected, by the light on the burning log-heaps, a thousand conflicting emotions.

+**Log house.**

1. A house built of logs.

The first group of citations indicates that log houses were originally used for prisons. The second group shows early efforts to differentiate between *log cabin* and *log house*, the tendency being to restrict the latter term to houses more pretentious than log cabins and made of logs hewn on at least two sides. In later times this sense of the term became the prevailing one.

(1) **1663** *Md. Archives* 490 Be itt Enacted . . . that A Logg howse be built Twenty foot Square . . . for a Prison. **1680** *N.C. Col. Rec.* I. 300 Ye Deponent saw ye sd Mr. Miller enclosed in a Logghouse about 10 or 11 foot square purposely built for him. **1699** *N.H. Prov. Papers* III. 88 *n.*, A strong logg house [shall] be built in the Province for a Prison. **1738** W. STEPHENS *Proc. Georgia* 248 The Magistrates committed them to the Log-House, to remain there till Monday. **1741** TAILFER, etc. *Narr. Georgia* (1835) 24 He threatned every Person . . . who . . . claim'd their just Rights and Privileges with the Stocks, Whipping-Post, and Logg-House.

(2) **1797** BAILY *Tour* 219 He must be content with a log-house for the first few years. . . . He begins then to think of erecting himself a frame-house. **1831** PECK *Guide* 126 The next step in advance [of a cabin] for a dwelling is a log house. This is made of logs hewn on two sides to an equal thickness, the ends notched together. **1835** *Knickerb.* VI. 175 [He] moved from his waggon to a log-cabin, and from a log-cabin to a log-house. **1866** 'F. KIRKLAND' *Bk. Anecdotes* 572 They were in a cleanly, well kept Virginia log-house, with old-fashioned furniture. **1894** ROBLEY *Bourbon Co., Kansas* 22 Colonel Wilson had the only store in this section of country. It was in a story and a half log house situated near what is now Market Square.

2. Attrib. with *cottage, grocery, office*, etc.

1669 *Md. Archives* II. 224 That there be a Logg house Prison Twenty ffoot Square Built . . . in the Baltemore County. **1832** WILLIAMSON *Maine* I. 605 They seemed to exult . . . in their log-house cottages. **1844** KENDALL *Santa Fé Exped.* I. 25 Our log-house quarters, however, were closely 'chinked and daubed.' **1854** *Harper's Mag.* VIII. 422/1 A little log-house grocery stood on the near bank. **1906** LYNDE *Quickening* 352 There was a sharp crisis to the fore in the old log-house office at the furnace.

+**Log hut.** A hut, cabin, shanty, etc., made of logs. Also attrib. — **1797** J. A. GRAHAM *Present State Vermont* 161 In a former Letter I mentioned the Log Hut. **1810** M. DWIGHT *Journey to Ohio* 34 We stopt at noon, at a dismal looking log hut tavern. **1835** HOFFMAN *Winter in West* I. 257 We entered a small hamlet of log huts, and drove up to the door of a frame building. **1870** EMERSON *Soc. & Solitude* 19 'Tis wonderful how soon a piano gets into a log-hut on the frontier.

+**Log jam.** A number of saw logs which, impeded in passing down a stream, have formed a compact entangled mass. (Cf. JAM *n.*) Also transf. — **1886** DORSEY *Midshipman Bob* I. 73 His father got killed in a log-jam the year Robertin . . . was born. **1900** BRUNCKEN *N. Amer. Forests* 85 A 'log jam' is formed, usually at one of the rapids with which most logging rivers abound. **1907** *Springfield W. Repub.* 14 Feb. 8 The congressional log-jam which held back all legislation for nearly a week was finally broken Thursday afternoon. **1920** LEWIS *Main Street* 204 Bjornstam told . . . [of] breaking a log-jam.

Logman. {1610-} +One engaged in getting out logs; a lumberer. — **1851** SPRINGER *Forest Life* 159 It would be a match for 'Dame Nature' to locate a handsome Pine-tree beyond the grasp of the logmen. **1904** *Springfield W. Repub.* 9 Sept. 11 The logman, as soon as he had been paid off at Mt. Tom, . . . [visited] Sobotsky's store.

‖**Logo-fogie.** =LOCOFOCO 2. *Obs.* — **1837** NEAL *Charcoal Sk.* (1838) 220 It's a logo-fogie! . . . a right down logo-fogie! *Ib.* 221, I'm pretty clear you're a logo-fogie—you talk as if your respect for me and other venerable institutions was tantamount to very little.

‖**Logo-fogieism.** Variant of LOCOFOCOISM. *Obs.* — **1837** NEAL *Charcoal Sk.* (1838) 221 You sort of want to cut a piece out of the common veal by your logo-fogieism in wishing to 'bolish laws.

+**Log pen.**

1. A log cabin, esp. a poor one. *Obs.*

1789 WEEMS *Letters* III. 418, I lodged in a log-pen. **1836** *Quarter Race Ky.* (1846) 24, I went to town last night to the confectionary, (a whiskey shop in a log pen fourteen feet square). **1853** 'P. PAXTON' *Yankee in Texas* 124 When he'd nothing else to do, [he] lazed about anybody's log-pen that he pleased.

2. A pen made of logs, esp. as a military defense or barrier.

1832 *Louisville Directory* 102 The ditch was surmounted by a breast work of log pens filled with the earth obtained from the ditch. **1836** B. TUCKER *Partisan Leader* (1861) 297 At the point where the stream . . . swept away around the shoulder of the platform, was placed a small log pen.

3. A log enclosure used as a prison. (Cf. LOG HOUSE.)

1854 SIMMS *Southward Ho* 30 The whole foraging party . . . were driven into an extemporary logpen.

+**Log perch.** =HOGFISH c. — **1882** *Nat. Museum Bul.* No. 16, 499 *P. caprodes*. . . . Log Perch; Rock-fish. **1884** GOODE, etc. *Fisheries* I. 417 [*Percina caprodes*] is known as the 'Rock-fish,' 'Hog-fish,' or 'Log Perch.' **1911** *Rep. Fisheries 1908* 311 *Hogfish* . . . is also applied to the log perch.

+**Log prison.** A log house serving as a prison. *Obs.* (Cf. LOG HOUSE.) — **1845** KIRKLAND *Western Clearings* 212, I went to prison; nothing but a log-prison. **1847** *Knickerb.* XXX. 241 A young chief and his squaw . . . were now lying in the log-prison which by courtesy was termed the guard-house.

+**Log road.** =LOGGING ROAD. — **1880** INGHAM *Digging Gold* 367 We started on a gallop up the hill on a log road. **1883** ZEIGLER & GROSSCUP *Alleghanies* 254 A net work of log roads, . . . cut by the lumbermen, branched out in every direction. **1893** *Scribner's Mag.* June 699/1 Banking-grounds [were] prepared, and log-roads made, all preliminary to the work of cutting and hauling logs.

+**Logroll,** *v. fig. Polit.* **a.** *intr.* To engage in logrolling. **b.** *tr.* To promote or carry by logrolling. (Cf. LOGROLLING 2.) — **1835** CROCKETT *Tour* 120 My people don't like me to log-roll in their business, and vote away pre-emption rights to fellows in other states, that never kindle a fire on their lands. **1854** T. FORD *Hist. Illinois* 186 The friends of the canal were forced to log-roll for that work by supporting others which were ruinous to the country. **1870** *Congress. Globe* 14 April 2700/2 If you vote for my interest I will vote for yours. That is the way these tariffs are 'log-rolled' through.

+**Logroller. 1.** One who rolls logs. **2.** *fig.* A politician who practices logrolling. — **(1) 1830** *Congress. Deb.* 10 May 932/1 The log-roller, showing the amount of his lumber. **(2)** [**1864** G. A. SALA in *Daily Telegraph* (London) 4 Aug., A professional politician, . . . lobbyer and log-roller generally.] **1883** *Century Mag.* Aug. 631/1 The caucus is fast drifting into the hands of wire-pullers and log-rollers. **1894** *Amer. Rev. of Reviews* June 648/1 [Mr. Gorman's] resources as a log-roller . . . are probably without an equal. **1901** *McClure's Mag.* Dec. 152 He is . . . a log-roller, willing to vote for this man's measure if the man will help Platt with some patronage scheme.

+**Logrolling.**

1. An occasion when a group of people assists a neighbor in piling for burning, or otherwise disposing of, logs that hinder farming operations.

1824 DODDRIDGE *Notes* 109 The standard dinner dish for every log rolling, house raising, and harvest day was a pot pye. **1847** ROBB *Squatter Life* p. ix, When he [the western squatter] encounters his fellow man at a barbecue, election, log-rolling, or frolic. **1884** HARRIS *Mingo* 234 His arm was the strongest at the log-rolling. **1904** T. E. WATSON *Bethany* 131 His flying trips to corn-shuckings, to log-rollings, to church-meetings.

2. The exchanging of assistance by political schemers or factional leaders to secure their individual ends.

1820 J. FLINT *Lett. from Amer.* 189 Much of the business . . . is privately arranged, before the questions are discussed in the house. Combinations are formed for effecting particular purposes. These are called *log rolling*. **1829** *Va. Lit. Museum* 445 A similar provision in the constitution of New York had been defeated by what had been called *log rolling*. **1860** BUCHANAN in *Pres. Mess. & P. V.* 605 A system of '*logrolling*' . . . would be inaugurated, under which the Treasury would be exhausted. **1884** *Century Mag.* March 643/2 The question of the location of the government . . . was finally settled by a curious compromise—the first recorded instance of 'log-rolling.' **1910** *N.Y. Ev. Post* 6 Oct. (Th.), He would not help his bills through the Legislature by either log-rolling or patronage.

transf. **1849** *Corr. R. W. Griswold* (1898) 246 Several clever persons in Boston have been spoiled by this log-rolling in literature.

3. Rolling logs or allowing logs to roll to a desired spot as into a river.

1848 THOREAU *Maine Woods* 15 Occasionally there was a small opening on the bank, made for the purpose of log-rolling.

4. *attrib.* **a.** In sense 2 with *branch, honesty*, etc.

1837 *U.S. Mag.* I. 23 His sense of obligation to the people . . . [was] too unbending for the log-rolling honesty of factious demagogues. **1860** MORDECAI *Virginia* 303 The log-rolling system of Virginia has diverted her energies from the completion of any one useful work. **1880** *Congress. Rec.* 27 May 3854/1 A vast number of public building provisions were grouped together on what is called the log-rolling principle. **1904** CRISSEY *Tattlings* 417, I wasn't much good in the log-rolling branch of politics.

b. In sense 1 with *frolic*.

1847 DRAKE *Pioneer Life Ky.* 36 In due time a 'log-rolling' frolic was gotten up.

+**Log-running.** Floating or guiding logs down a stream. Also attrib. (Cf. DRIVE *n.* 5 b.) — **1878** *Lumberman's Gaz.* 6 April, The Green Bay *Advocate* of March 28 says that log-running is commencing all around. **1879** *Mich. Gen. Statutes* I. (1882) 550 Each log running or booming company doing business on any waters on which the logs or timber are floated or run. **1901** WHITE *Westerners* 199 In the log running Michail Lafond was the man always called upon to skim over the bobbing logs.

+**Log scale.** (See quots. 1883, 1905.) — **1877** *Michigan Rep.* XXXVI. 168 It happens that the scale of the manufactured lumber exceeded the log scale. **1883** KNIGHT *Suppl.* 559/2 *Log-scale*, a table which gives the quantity of lumber, one inch thick, board measure, which may be obtained from a round log, the length and the diameter below the bark being given. **1905** *Forestry Bureau Bul.* No. 61, 42 *Log scale*, the contents of a log, or of a number of logs considered collectively.

+**Log schoolhouse.** A schoolhouse made of logs. — **1869** TOURGEE *Toinette* xiii. 154 She had managed to pick up . . . 'a tolerable English education,' . . . from one of the log school-houses. **1871** *Harper's Mag.* Aug. 474/1 Bishop Talbot in Nebraska . . . had occasion, as bishops and ministers often have in new and sparsely settled territories, to hold service in a log school-house. **1888** GRIGSBY *Smoked Yank* (1891) 17 A few winters at school in the old log school house of our district . . . had been my opportunities for education. **1919** HOUGH *Sagebrusher* 13 The school-ma'am . . . daily presided at the little log schoolhouse.

+**Log shanty.** A shanty built of logs. — **1847** HOWE *Ohio* 492 They fell to work . . . erecting bark huts and log shanties. **1886** ROOSEVELT in *Outing* March 611 Many of the ranches are mere . . . log shanties, stuck down in any raw, treeless spot where there happen to be water and grass. **1892** in *S. Dak. Hist. Coll.* I. 60 There came from St. Paul . . . an Ohioan, Charles Cavalier, to open the new custom house 'in a little log shanty.' **1907** LILLIBRIDGE *Trail* 7 She turned toward the rough log shanty unemotionally.

Log slate. (See quot. 1890.) — **1834** *Knickerb.* III. 83 [The mate] returned forward from adding on the log-slate another 'ditto' to the long column. **1841** DANA *Seaman's Manual* 153 It is the custom for each officer at the end of his watch to enter upon the log-slate, which usually lies on the cabin table, the courses, distances, wind and weather during his watch. **1890** *Cent.* 3506/2 *Log-slate*, . . . a double slate, marked and ruled on its inner side, like a log-book, on which the log is first recorded.

+**Log sleigh.** A heavy sleigh used in transporting logs. — **1893** *Scribner's Mag.* June 706/2 The log-sleighs have ten, twelve, and even fourteen-foot bunks. **1902** WHITE *Blazed Trail* 72 Eight log-sleighs . . . the carpenter had hewed from solid sticks of timber.

+**Log store.** A store constructed of logs. — **1873** *Winfield* (Kan.) *Courier* 11 Jan. 1/1 Millinery and Ladies Furnishing Goods. . . . One door north of Log Store. **1890** LANGFORD *Vigilante Days* (1912) 382 The central cross-beam of an unfinished log store . . . was selected for a scaffold. **1916** EASTMAN *From Deep Woods* 113 We found in a log store near by several who were badly hurt.

+**Log tavern.** A tavern built of logs. Also comb. — **1809** CUMING *Western Tour* 44 We stopped to feed our horses at a small log tavern. **1842** KIRKLAND *Forest Life* II. 107 The teamster was benighted and obliged to stop for the night at a log-tavern. **1860** GREELEY *Overland Journey* 202 The log-tavern-keeper at Weber . . . apologetically observed [etc.]. **1874** EGGLESTON *Circuit Rider* 147 Morton was conducted three miles down the river to a log tavern.

+**Log tent.** A crude temporary shelter shaped somewhat like a tent and made chiefly of logs. *Obs.* — [**1748** H. ELLIS *Hudson's Bay* 154 Some of the People were employed in cutting Fire-Wood, others in building Log-Tents.] **1755** *New Eng. Hist. & Gen. Register* XXXIII. 391 Built a Logg Tent & Coverd the Ruff.

+**Log trap.** A deadfall made of a heavy log. *Obs.* — **1784** BELKNAP *Tour White Mts.* 13 Along this road . . . we saw the culheags, or log-traps, which the hunters set for sables. **1823** JAMES *Exped.* I. 155 This was a log trap, in which one log is elevated above another at one end [etc.]. **1840** EMMONS *Mass. Quadrupeds* 41 The Pine Marten . . . is taken in a log trap, made and baited in such a way, that it cannot reach the meat without passing under the dead fall. **1851** *S. Lit. Messenger* XVII. 544/2 The skins of the game . . . caught in log-traps.

+**Logway. 1.** A sloping chute, trough, slide, or enclosed passage for logs: (see quot. 1905). **2.** A stretch of corduroy road. — **(1) 1779** in F. Chase *Hist. Dartmouth Coll.* I. 562 The Trustees . . . think fit to maintain said mills by repairing . . . the log way and necessary mill houses. **1877** W. WRIGHT *Big Bonanza* 240 Such log-ways . . . are so contrived that the logs leap from them into water of great depth. **1905** *Forestry Bureau Bul.* No. 61, 38 *Gangway*, . . . the incline plane up which logs are moved from the water into a sawmill. . . . [Also called] log jack, log way, slip. **(2) 1821** Z. HAWLEY *Tour* 94 In one place the traveller passes over a most fatiguing log-way, through which the horse occasionally thrusts his foot. **1874** B. F. TAYLOR *World on Wheels* 245 Over the old road, ran the yellow, mud-stained coach; laboring up its hills, and pitching along its log-ways.

***Logwood.**

***1.** The heartwood of a tropical American tree (*Haematoxylon campechianum*) used chiefly for dyeing.

1696 SEWALL *Letter-Book* I. 169 Inclosed is a Bill of Lading for Two Tuns and fifteen hundred of Logwood, Shipped on the Hope. **1720** *Amer. Wkly. Mercury* 12 Jan. 2/2 Price Currant at New-York. Logwood . . . 12 l. per Ton. **1790** *Penna. Packet* 2 Jan. 4/4 For Sale . . . Seneca snake root. A few tons of logwood. Bourdeaux rough hewn building stone. **1814** *Gales's N.C. Almanack* 27 To Dye Cotton Yarn Deep Blue. Take one pound of logwood chipped fine or pounded. **1890** *Cent.* 3506/2 Logwood . . . is employed in calico-printing to give a black or brown color.

attrib. **1772** ROMANS in Phillips *Notes on B. Romans* (1924) 127 No Situation on Earth is better for the Logwood Trade with Honduras and Campeachy. **1890** *Cent.* 3506/3 *Logwood-blue*, a color produced by logwood-extract on wool mordanted with alum and cream of tartar.

+**2.** The bluewood (*Condalia obovata*) of Texas.

1884 SARGENT *Rep. Forest* 4 Blue Wood, Log Wood, Purple Haw. **1891** COULTER *Bot. W. Texas* I. 58 *Condalia obovata*, . . . known as 'brasil' and 'logwood' [is] one of the common 'chaparral' plants of western Texas. **1897** SUDWORTH *Arborescent Flora* 297.

Logwork. {1725–} Construction or building by the use of logs; a structure, barricade, etc., made of logs. — **1721** in *New Eng. Hist. & Gen. Register* XXI. 57 All Hands went briskly to work, to finish ye log-work in ye Lower Block-house. **1856** OLMSTED *Slave States* 111 The chimney is . . . commonly of lath or split sticks, laid up like log-work and plastered with mud. **1895** in M. A. Jackson *Gen. Jackson* 547 Lane . . . had not placed a single picket on the right of the log works, behind which his men were then standing.

+**Logy,** *a.* [Cf. Eng. dial. *loggy*.] Dull, heavy, sluggish, slow. — **1848** BARTLETT 215 He's a *logy* man, i.e. a slow-moving, heavy man. 'He is a *logy* preacher,' i.e. dull. **1863** 'G. HAMILTON' *Gala-Days* 346 He huddled down in one corner of the cage, . . . like a logy, lumpy, country bumpkin as he was. **1903** A. ADAMS *Log of Cowboy* 16 We strung the cattle out, now logy with water.

+**Lollygag,** *v. intr.* To loiter, linger, dawdle, waste time. Also *lolly-gagging* ppl. a. *colloq.*[2] (Cf. LALLYGAG *v.*) — **1868** *Northern Vindicator* 30 Dec., The lascivious, lolly-gagging lumps of licentiousness who disgrace the common decencies of life by their love-sick fawnings at our public dances. **1870** *Ib.* 19 Feb., The weather once more is 'salubrious' and balmy, and indicates that winter will not lollygag in the lap of spring. **1902** LORIMER *Lett. Merchant* 224 The old fellows were playing poker in the smoking-room and all the young ones were lollygagging under the boats.

+**Loma.** *S.W.* [Sp.] A hill or elevation. — **1863** *37th Congress Sp. Sess.* Sen. Ex. Doc. No. 1, 20 The new road is to follow the bottom at the edge of the *lomas*. **1885** *Wkly. New Mexican Rev.* 18 June 4/1 At 8 o'clock they [the Indians] returned upon the loma, north of the city, where he [Diego de Vargas] attacked them.

Lombardy poplar. A species of black poplar, *Populus nigra italica;* also, a tree of this species. {1766–} — **1797** S. DEANE *Newengland Farmer* (ed. 2) 267 The Lombardy Poplar begins to be propagated in this country. **1805** PARKINSON *Tour* 376 The Lombardy poplar, an imported tree, grows uncommonly quick. **1860** *Ill. Agric. Soc. Trans.* IV. 447 Mr. A. R. Whitney . . . has Lombardy Poplar, six years planted. **1898** DELAND *Old Chester Tales* 8 A Lombardy poplar stood at the gate.

***London.** [*London*, Eng.] *attrib.* and *comb.*

***1. a.** Of measures: Gauged according to the standard prevailing in London.

1630 HIGGINSON *New England's Plantation* (1836) 6 Everie Hogshead holding seuen Bushels [of Indian corn] of *London* measure. **1652** *Plymouth Laws* 95 All Coopers . . . are to make all theire Caske according to London gage. **1758** in Shelton *Salt-Box House* (1900) 297, 1 London Quart Pott, 3*s.* 3*d.*

b. Made in or imported from London.

1759 *Newport Mercury* 26 June 4/3 London Nails, Tacks and Brads of all sizes. **1763** *Boston Post-Boy* 12 Dec., A few Genteel Grey and light Grey London-made Wigs, to be sold by John Crosby. **1845** *Knickerb.* XXVI. 520 He could faintly discern . . . the white tops of the Squire's 'London boots.' **1856** M. J. HOLMES *L. Rivers* 349 'Handsome as a London doll,' was her first exclamation. **1891** WELCH *Recoll. 1830–40* 379 Imported London porter was much drank.

+**2.** A city regarded as comparable to London: (see quotations).

1832 FERRALL *Ramble* 19 Having determined on quitting 'the London of the States,' as my friends the Yankees call New York, I had bag and baggage conveyed on board a steamer. **1834** C. A. DAVIS *Lett. J. Downing* 191 They used to call Philadelphy the London of America.

3. Special combinations.

London brown, a shade of brown; *London brush*, (see quotation); *London lord*, a variety of potato; *London smoke*, a color suggested by London smoke {1883}; *London stock*, (see quotation).

1805 PARKINSON *Tour* 334 There are what they call the London lords, which is a large potatoe, something like the ox-noble in England, reckoned by Americans the best potatoe for production. **1841** *S. Lit. Messenger* VII. 42/1 He pertinaciously adheres to that style of wearing the hair called the London Brush. **1854** BENTON *30 Years' View* I. 45/2 The coat, waistcoat, and pantaloons of the same 'London brown.' **1871** ROE *Army Lett.* 29 Mrs. Anderson was very handsome in an elegant gown of London-smoke silk. **1881** INGERSOLL *Oyster-Industry* 245 *London Stock.*—Oysters culled out for the foreign market; about three years old, small, round, and cup-shaped.

Lone Star.

+**1.** The single star in the flag of the Texas Republic and the state seal; also in allusive contexts.

1843 DEWEES *Lett. from Texas* 246 The lone star of Texas shall continue to wave proudly in the air as long as one brave Texan remains to defend it. **1845** POLK in *Pres. Mess. & P.* IV. Texas . . . will never have cause to regret that she has united her 'lone star' to our glorious constellation. **1846** SAGE *Scenes Rocky Mts.* xxix, Few . . . refused to enter their names upon the muster-roll, and rally beneath the banner of the Lone Star. **1886** POORE *Reminisc.* I. 315 It took him only from February 28th to April 12th to conclude the negotiation which placed the 'Lone Star' in the azure field of the ensign of the Republic. **1872** MORRELL *Flowers & Fruits* 20 Sam. Houston was then in Texas . . . intending . . . to set in motion 'a little two-horse republic under the Lone Star.'

+**b.** A nickname for Texas, derived from the Texas flag and seal. (Cf. LONE-STAR STATE.)

[**1855** PIERCE in *Pres. Mess. & P.* V. 347 Who would rejoice to hail Texas as a lone star instead of one in the galaxy of States?] **1856** *Democratic Conv. Proc.* 56 The Democracy of the 'Lone Star' do battle for that favorite, noble son of the 'Keystone of the Arch.' **1885** HOWELLS *S. Lapham* i, I got enough of the Lone Star in about three months. **1907** *Boston Transcript* 9 Nov., Little Rhody—Rhode Island. Lone Star—Texas.

2. Attrib. with *association, banner, gallantry, republic.*

1846 SAGE *Scenes Rocky Mts.* xxix, Right gladly did I hail the Lone Star Banner. **1853** *Harper's Mag.* VI. 267/1 The doctrine urged in favor of Filibustering expeditions and Lone Star Associations is also at war with some of our most popular professions. **1902** MACGOWAN *Last Word* 154 A fit example of Lone Star gallantry. **1910** J. HART *Vigilante Girl* 131 One of those veterans . . . turned over to the United States the Lone Star Republic as a Lone Star State.

+**Lone-Star State.** Texas. A nickname or sobriquet. — **1867** *Trübner's Amer. Lit. Rec.* Aug. 41/1 Texas [is popularly known] as The Love [*sic*]-Star State. **1892** *Scribner's Mag.* XI. 733/2 He was familiar with the situation in the Lone Star State. **1909** 'O. HENRY' *Roads of Destiny* 267 The Lone Star State never yet failed to grant relief [etc.].

+**Lone-Star Stater.** An inhabitant of Texas. — **1873** BEADLE *Undevel. West* 805, I am proud to find him in honor and position among the 'Lone Star Staters.'

***Long,** *n.* *Stock exchange.* One who buys commodities in expectation of their rising in price. {1890–} — **1881** *Chicago Times* 12 March, Under negotiations by the 'longs' . . . the market [*i.e.*, for pork] fell back 5c. **1881** *Harper's Mag.* April 734/2 'Spots,' 'futures,' 'longs' and 'shorts' were unknown terms.

***Long,** *a.* *Stock exchange.* +**a.** Of persons: (see quots. 1859 and 1870). **b.** Of commodities: Held for a possible rise in value. **c.** Of transactions: Based on long-term credit. Also transf.

1859 BARTLETT 225 '*Long*' means when a man has bought stock on time, which he can call for at any day he chooses. He is also said to be '*long*,' when he holds a good deal. **1870** M. H. SMITH *20 Years Wall St.* 68–69 *Long in Stocks:*—A broker buys stocks for a customer, pays the full value, and carries it. A man through his broker buys a thousand shares of New York Central at 117. The broker pays for it and keeps it. The customer is 'long' in Central. **1870** MEDBERY *Men Wall St.* 82 The bull buys, confident that stocks will be higher, and is said to be 'long.' **1882** PECK *Sunshine* 48 Millions of Bibles were shipped to this country by the firm that was 'long' on Bibles. **1892** *Courier-Journal* 1 Oct. 11/5 There was a considerable quantity of long oats thrown upon the market. **1894** *Harper's Mag.* Feb. 351/1 The ranch bookkeeper, [was] a young man 'short' on experiences and 'long' on hope. **1902** MCFAUL *Ike Glidden* 139 He bought on the short side for cash and sold on the long side on credit at twelve per cent interest.

Long arm. +(See quot. 1675.) *Obs.* — **1675** *Conn. Rec.* II. 270 Such Troopers as shall neglect to prouide themselues with long armes, viz. a carbin or muskett, . . . shall be disbanded and attend the foot company. **1695** SEWALL *Diary* I. 405 Capt. Smith of Hampton meets us with 12. by Govr. Usher's order, long Arms.

Long-billed, *a.* A qualifying term in the names of various American birds having long bills. — **1822** FOWLER *Journal* 148 We Hear for the first time Seen the long Billed Bird [*i.e.*, chaparral cock] . . . —the Bill about one foot in length. **1869** *Amer. Naturalist* III. 74 Long-billed Nuthatch. . . . Common in the Rocky Mountains. *Ib.* 186 [The] Long-billed Sparrow . . . [is] confined to the seashore [Calif.]. **1917** *Birds of Amer.* I. 205 Virginia Rail. . . . [Also called] Long-billed Rail.

+**Long-billed curlew.** (See CURLEW 3.)

+**Long-billed marsh wren.** A species of marsh-frequenting wren (*Telmatodytes palustris palustris*) or one of its regional varieties. — **1858** BAIRD *Birds Pacific R. R.* 364 Long-billed Marsh Wren. . . . North America from Atlantic to Pacific. **1884** *Amer. Naturalist* XVIII. 89 California Long-billed Marsh Wren. . . . [Their nests] were situated, mostly, just out of reach in the taller clumps of tules. **1917** *Birds of Amer.* III. 198/2 The Long-billed Marsh Wren and its regional varieties are distributed over the United States.

Long bit. +(See quot. 1877.) — **1859** A. DUNIWAY *Capt. Gray's Co.* 158 (Th.), I'd give a long bit myself to see 'em pull hair. **1877** W. WRIGHT *Big Bonanza* 354 The smallest coin in use is the bit, ten-cent piece,—sometimes spoken of as a 'short bit,' as not being twelve and one-half cents, the 'long bit.'

Long bullet. A heavy weight which competitors cast for distance; also, the game or sport of casting such weights. *Obs.* {1728–} — **1723** *Boston Rec.* 172 Throwing, Rolling or flingin of the Bullet, Commonly called Throwing the Long Bullet in the Common Training field. **1775** FITHIAN *Journal* II. 128 Some [were] throwing long-bullets. **1820** *Western Rev.* II. 34 Our Aborigines . . . [made] round balls for a game which may have been similar to long bullets.

+**Long clam. a.** The soft clam. Also *long-neck clam.* **b.** The razor clam. — **1884** GOODE, etc. *Fisheries* I. 707 Next upon the list comes the 'Soft Clam,' 'Long Clam,' or 'Nanninose' (*Mya arenaria*), dear to New Englanders. **1887** *Ib.* v. II. 614 Under the name of 'long clam,' 'knife-handle,' and 'razor-clam,' they are occasionally seen in New York market. **1903** *N.Y. State Museum Bul.* No. 71, 22 The soft or long-neck clam, Mya, is capable of locomotion only when very small. **1911** *Rep. Fisheries 1908* 308.

Long-distance. Used attrib. {1887–} with reference to telephone service between more or less distant cities. Also used ellipt. for such service. {=trunk call} — [**1884** *Whitaker's Almanack* 385/1 In America some remarkable trials of long distance telephoning have taken place, one in particular between New York and Chicago, a distance of 1,000 miles.] **1886** *Scientific Amer.* 2 Oct 208/2 There is a popular belief that the long distance telephone is crowding the telegraph to the wall. **1893** *Engineering Mag.* March 878 The reliability of the long-distance telephone service in America has become well known and appreciated. **1905** TARKINGTON *In Arena* 128, I had it by the long distance an hour ago, from your own home.

+**Long drink.** A drink requiring a glass or tumbler larger than that in which it is ordinarily served. *colloq.* {1859, in W. Indies} — **1828** *Amer. Chesterfield* 240 It has lately become common, in our Atlantic towns, and particularly at tables where light wines are used with water, as a *long drink*, to place, at convenient distances round the table, bottles of Sauterne, claret, or other light wine, (the corks previously drawn, and inserted slightly in the bottle,) and goblets of water.

+**Longe.** Variant of LUNGE. — **1866** *Vt. Acts & Resolves* 71 No person shall be permitted to take any trout or longe in this State. **1882** JORDAN & GILBERT *Fishes N. Amer.* 317 Mackinaw Trout; Great Lake Trout; Longe (Vermont). **1911** *Rep. Fisheries 1908* 311 In different localities the individuals . . . are known by the local names . . . 'reef trout,' 'longe,' etc.

Long-eared owl. The lesser horned owl, *Asio wilsonianus.* {1768– (Pennant *Brit. Zool.*)} — **1812** WILSON *Ornithology* VI. 73 Long-eared Owl: *Strix otus:* . . . is much more numerous in Pennsylvania than the White, or Barn Owl. **1839** PEABODY *Mass. Birds* 274 The Long-eared Owl, *Strix otus*, is found in Massachusetts, but is never common. **1880** *Cimarron News & Press* 23 Dec. 1/4 The species found here are the barn, great horned, screech, long-eared, . . . and burrowing owls. **1917** *Birds of Amer.* II. 101/1 The Long-eared Owl is an industrious mouser.

+**Long-eared sunfish.** One of two species of sunfish, *Lepomis auritus* or *Xenotis megalotis.* — **1884** GOODE, etc. *Fisheries* I. 406 The Long-eared Sun-fish—*Lepomis auritus.* This species . . . is found in all the coastwise streams from Maine to Louisiana. **1896** JORDAN & EVERMANN *Check-List of Fishes* 355 *Lepomis megalotis.* . . . Long-eared Sunfish. Michigan to Minnesota, South Carolina, and southward to the Rio Grande. **1903** T. H. BEAN *Fishes N.Y.* 480 The long-eared sunfish . . . is an excellent food fish.

+**Longevity pay, ration.** (See quot. 1909 and cf. FOGY *n.*) — **1879** *Congress. Rec.* 25 April 907/2 The meaning of it [the bill], then, is that the officer is to have pay allowed him computing all the time of service while in the Army . . . , in addition to what is called the fogy ration, or longevity ration? **1909** *Cent. Suppl.* 956/1 *Longevity pay*, additional pay given to officers for long service in the United States army and navy. *Army and Navy Register* XXIV. 290.

Long field. *Baseball.* The outfield. *Obs.* {of cricket, 1833–} (Cf. FIELD 3.) — **1867** CHADWICK *Base Ball Reference* 139 *A Home Run*, a run made from home to home from a hit to long-field.

Long-finned, *a.* Designating various American fish having particularly long fins. — **1842** *Nat. Hist. N.Y., Zoology* IV. 194 The Long-finned Chubsucker, *Labeo cyprinus*, . . . is common in the Susquehannah. **1884** GOODE *Fisheries* I. 188 The Long-finned Sole—*Glyptocephalus zachirus.* . . . It has been thus far noticed only in deep water about San Francisco and Monterey. *Ib.* 320 The Long-finned Tunny, *Orcynus alalonga*, . . . is taken by trolling. **1896** JORDAN & EVERMANN *Check-List of Fishes* 340 *Germo alalunga.* Long-finned Albacore; Albecor. . . . Mediterranean; San Francisco; Santa Barbara Islands.

‖**Long food.** Fodder, hay, forage. — **1823** in Commons, etc. *Doc. Hist.* I. 256 As much corn or oats and hay and fodder as our horses can destroy (usually half a bushel of grain and a rackful of long food).

‖**Long-geared,** *a.* Tall, gangling, loose-jointed. *colloq.* — **1891** *Harper's Mag.* July 208/2 One of the most successful bronco riders . . . was a long-geared, lank Texas lad.

+**Long green.**

1. (See quotation.) *Obs.*

1837 WETMORE *Gaz. Missouri* 289 The disturber known in the west by the name of 'long green' and 'blue ruin,' in Pennsylvania 'old rye' and 'cider royal,' and by the Indians appropriately named 'fire-water.'

2. Money, as in the form of greenbacks. *slang.*

1896 ADE *Artie* 110 He's . . . dug up the long green and he's puttin it out at the booze joints. **1903** A. H. LEWIS *Boss* 291 He came . . . padded with th' long green . . . an' them gams took it off him so fast he caught cold. **1910** MCCUTCHEON *Rose in Ring* 158 It's the long green he's after.

3. Home-grown, home-cured tobacco. *slang.*

1897 *Outing* XXX. 380/2 It seems that they were out of tobacco, and had been able to get only the 'long green' that the mountaineers used.

Long gun. A firearm other than a pistol or revolver. *Obs.* — **1661** *Plymouth Rec.* 44 To Thomas Morton one long gun. **1834** CARRUTHERS *Kentuckians* I. 24 When we boys of the long guns shoot, we don't turn our heads away and pull trigger in a world of smoke.

Long haul. (See HAUL *n.*)

Longhorn. {1834–}

+**1.** One of a breed of cattle formerly raised extensively in Texas and the West. Also transf.

1857 *Ill. Agric. Soc. Trans.* II. 425 The 'long horns' appeal both to our feelings and our pockets, for timely and ample preparations for food and shelter. **1898** Post *10 Yrs. Cowboy* 48 Maxwell had in this drive a good round five thousand longhorns, or Texas steers. **1901** *McClure's Mag.* 145 Tom Platt, . . . standing at the head of a drove of wild-eyed human longhorns, as if to keep them from a stampede. **1923** J. H. Cook *On Old Frontier* 32 Later, longhorns were to invade that country.

attrib. **1903** A. Adams *Log Cowboy* 353–4 There were lots of old long-horn cowmen living in the town.

+**2.** *W.* An 'old-timer'; a rustic or hayseed. *colloq.*

1905 *N.Y. Times* 28 May (Th. S.), There was a big chief on the range, an old longhorn called Abraham, and his lil' ole squaw.

Long-horned, *a.* {1777–} Of cattle: Having unusually long horns. {1846–} — **1868** *Ill. Agric. Soc.* VII. 142 The long-horned or Cherokee cattle passing through North Carolina and Virginia on their way to the Northern markets. **1874** *Dept. Agric. Rep. 1873* 128 Texas, to which is credited all the long-horned breed from the Southwest, increased her number 20 per cent. **1880** Cable *Grandissimes* 250 The long-horned oxen . . . stopped before his cabin. **1913** Barnes *Western Grazing Grounds* 23 Thousands of long-horned steers grazed their way over the grassy plains.

Long house. {1622} +Among the Indians, esp. the Iroquois, an exceptionally long wigwam or cabin serving as a communal dwelling and council house. Also transf.

1643 R. Williams *Key* (1866) 197 [In the] *Long house*, sometimes an hundred, somtimes [*sic*] two hundred foot long . . . many thousands, men and women meet. **1751** Gist *Journals* 53 The Crier . . . invited Us to the long House to see the Warriors Feather Dance. **1826** Cooper *Mohicans* Pref., One branch of this numerous people [the Delawares] was seated on a beautiful river, . . . where the 'long house,' or Great Council Fire, of the nation was universally admitted to be established. **1885** *Harper's Mag.* July 201/2 The Indians of the Long House to put out the camp fires of the Kahquahs and Eries.

Long hunter. +(See quotations.) — **1792** Imlay *Western Territory* 9 Certain men, called Long Hunters, from Virginia and North Carolina, by penetrating these mountains . . . were fascinated with the beauty. **1812** H. Marshall *Hist. Kentucky* I. 11 Nine of this company, led on by the present, Colonel James Knox, reached Kentucky; and from the time they were absent, obtained the name of the Long Hunters.

+**Long Islander.** A native or resident of Long Island. — **1637** *Mass. H. S. Coll.* 4 Ser. VI. 208 [As] for the Long Ilanders themselues & Wequashcuck, they will not medle with them. **1690** *Ib.* V. 234, I [see] no need to send commissioners, if the Long Islanders and the [re]st of their Province would do what they are capable. **1856** *Porter's Spirit of Times* 22 Nov. 193/1 Long life to the Long Islanders; and may their shadows never be less. **1894** Warner *Golden House* xviii, Perhaps it would be best to get some Long-Islander to buy it for them.

+**Long Island herring. a.** =Fall herring. **b.** ?=Bunker. — **1814** Mitchill *Fishes N.Y.* 451 Long-Island Herring, *Clupea mattowacca*, . . . is caught most commonly in autumn. **1898** *N.Y. Journal* 26 July 14/7 Thousands of bunkers, otherwise known as 'Long Island herring,' floated lifeless on the surface of the water.

Long-keeping, *a.* Of apples: Capable of being kept for a long time. — **1859** *Mich. Agric. Trans.* X. 229 It is impossible to raise winter apples in the South, and . . . it is necessary to look to the North for a supply of long-keeping varieties. **1873** *Ill. Dept. Agric. Trans.* X. 58 Janeting [apple].—A well known favorite, its long-keeping qualities recommending it wherever it is known.

Long knife. +An Indian designation for a white settler or frontiersman, esp. a Virginian: (see also quot. 1831). Now hist. (Cf. Big knife.)

1774 in Peyton *Adv. Grandfather* (1867) 141 The Indians . . . deliberately prepared to crush the force of 'Long Knives,' as they called the Virginians under Lewis. **1788** *Mass. Spy* 19 June (Th.), The squaws [*i.e.*, the white women] have taken the breech-clout, and fight worse than the long knives. **1822** in Morse *Rep. Indian Affairs* II. 246 My people have never struck the whites, and the whites have never struck them. . . . Mine is the only nation that has spared the long knives. **1831** *Illinois Mo. Mag.* 368 The amiable French, lived in peace with the Indians for a whole century; but as soon as the 'Long Knives' began to emigrate to the country, hostilities commenced. **1852** Reynolds *Hist. Illinois* 71 'Long Knives' . . . was the Indian name for the Virginians. **1923** J. H. Cook *On Old Frontier* 230 Red Cloud's popularity waned as others who were more belligerent led the young men on the trail against the 'long knives.'

Long-leaf. *ellipt.* + =Long-leaf pine. — **1860** Curtis *Woody Plants N.C.* 22 It affords a good deal of Turpentine, which is less fluid than that from the *Long-leaf*.

Long-leafed, *a.* Designating varieties of plants having especially long leaves. — **1840** Dewey *Mass. Flowering Plants* 83 *D[rosera] longifolia.* Long-leafed Sundew. . . . Blossoms in July, in swamps. *Ib.* 88 *S[tellaria] longifolia.* Long-leafed Star-grass. . . . In moist woods and swamps. **1895** *Dept. Agric. Yrbk. 1894* 433 The principal sand binders of the interior of our country . . . are the *long-leafed sand grass* . . . and *Redfield's grass*.

+**Long-leafed pine.** =next. — **1792** Pope *Tour S. & W.* 46 Notwithstanding the natural Sterility of Soil . . . the Long-leaf'd Pine, Hickory, . . . and Walnut Trees grow to their usual Height. **1814** Brackenridge *Views La.* 158 On the other side of the Mississippi, . . . the upland commences, covered, with but little variation, by the long leafed pine. **1857** *Harper's Mag.* May 745/1 These forests are of the long-leafed pine, the *Pinus palustris* of the Southern States.

+**Long-leaf pine.**

1. =Georgia pine. Also *long-leaf Georgia pine.*

1796 Hawkins *Letters* 24, [I] came to the long leaf pine and open land. **1831** Peck *Guide* 46 Up the Red river above Nachitoches, the timber is all pine—the longleaf pine. **1860** Curtis *Woody Plants N.C.* 24 Long-Leaf Pine, (*P. australis*). . . . The great value of this tree in both civil and naval architecture is . . . well known. **1904** T. E. Watson *Bethany* 8 Ours was just a plain house . . . [built] of timbers torn from the heart of the long-leaf Georgia pine.

b. Attrib. with *land, timber.*

1883 Smith *Geol. Survey Ala.* 454 A splendid growth of long-leaf pine timber, supplying some of the largest saw-mills in the State. **1905** *Forestry Bureau Bul.* No. 64, 14 'Bay galls' . . . serve as the natural drainage channels of the flat longleaf pine land.

2. *Long-leaf yellow pine*, the lumber of the long-leaf pine. Also attrib. Also *long-leaf.*

1908 *Ill. Bureau Labor Statistics Ann. Coal Rep.* 349 The head frame is built with long leaf yellow pine lumber. **1924** Croy *R.F.D. No. 3* 197 The lumber is full of knots; he sold it to me for long-leaf yellow pine. . . . Is that long-leaf?

+**Long-leaved (pitch) pine.** =Georgia pine.

1791 Bartram *Travels* 212 *Pinus palustris*, the long leaved Pitch pine, or yellow pine. **1810** Michaux *Arbres* I. 16 Long-leaved pine. **1826** Flint *Recoll.* 318 Nine tenths of the country are covered with the long-leaved pitch pine. **1865** *Nation* I. 557 Almost the only large tree to be seen was the long-leaved pine. **1894** Coulter *Bot. W. Texas* III. 554 *Pinus palustris.* Sandy soils, extending from the Gulf States as far as Trinity River. 'Long-leaved pine.'

b. One of several other species of N.A. pines.

1897 Sudworth *Arborescent Flora* 20 *Pinus ponderosa.* Bull Pine. . . . Common Names. . . . Long-leaved Pine (Utah, Nev.). *Ib. Pinus ponderosa scopulorum.* Rock Pine. . . . Common Names. . . . Long-leaved Pine (Colo.). *Ib.* 26 *Pinus rigida.* Pitch Pine. . . . Common Names. . . . Long-leaved Pine (Del.).

Long-leaved willow. {1605–} One or other species of willow having long leaves, +esp. *Salix longifolia.* Also *long-leaf willow.* — **1813** Muhlenberg *Cat. Plants* 91 *Salix longifolia*, Long-leaved willow. **1817–8** Eaton *Botany* (1822) 443 *Salix longifolia*, long-leaf willow. **1843** Torrey *Flora N.Y.* II. 207 *Salix petiolaris.* . . . Dark Long-leaved Willow. . . . Frequent in the western parts of the State. **1892** Apgar *Trees Northern U.S.* 167 Long-leaved Willow. . . . A shrub or small tree, 2 to 20 ft. high.

***Long-legged,** *a.* In the specific names of birds: (see quotations). — **1813** Wilson *Ornithology* VII. 48 Long-legged Avoset . . . arrives on the sea coast of New Jersey about the twenty-fifth of April. **1858** Baird *Birds Pacific R.R.* 770 Long-legged Duck. . . . Valley of Rio Grande, Texas. **1890** *Cent* 3512/2 *Long-legged hawk*, . . . the American sharp-shinned hawk. **1917** *Birds of Amer.* I. 84 Wilson's Petrel. . . . Other Names. . . . Mother Carey's Chicken; Long-legged Storm Petrel. *Ib.* 242 Greater Yellow-Legs. . . . Other Names. . . . Big Cucu; Long-legged Tattler; Stone-bird.

+**Long-legged sandpiper.** The stilt sandpiper (*Micropalama himantopus*) frequently found along the Atlantic coast. — **1828** Bonaparte *Synopsis* 316 The Long-legged Sandpiper . . . inhabits the middle states in summer and autumn. **1833** — *Ornithology* IV. 89 The Long-Legged Sandpiper . . . we met with . . . in the month of July, 1826, near a small freshwater pond at Long Branch. **1844** *Nat. Hist. N.Y., Zoology* II. 235 The Long-Legged Sandpiper . . . is still exceedingly rare. **1917** *Birds of Amer.* I. 230 Stilt Sandpiper. . . . [Also called] Long-legged Sandpiper.

+**Longlick.** (See quotation.) *colloq.* (Cf. Long sugar.) — **1898** F. T. Bullen *Cruise Cachalot* 6 A pot of something sweetened with 'longlick' (molasses), made an apology for a meal.

Long manure. Manure containing long undecayed straw. {long dung, 1664–} — **1839** Buel *Farmer's Companion* 198 Great economy in dung may be effected by feeding these crops with the long manure of the yards and stables, instead of summer-yarding it. **1863** Mitchell *My Farm* 237 But why don't you compost it; pack up your long manure with turf and muck.

+**Long moss.** =Black moss.

[**1744** Moore *Voy. Georgia* 105, I observed here a kind of long moss I had never seen before.] **1781–2** Jefferson *Notes Va.* (1788) 39 Long moss. *Tillandsia Usneoides.* **1814** Brackenridge *Views La.* 172 The most gloomy forests of oak, cypress and ash, upon whose boughs the long moss, or Spanish beard, is suspended. **1831** Peck *Guide* 47 The timber is all pine . . . covered with festoons of long moss. **1851** *Polly Peablossom* 128 From their branches grow in profusion the Spanish long moss. **1896** Britton & Brown *Illus. Flora Northern U.S.* I. 374.

Longneck. {1864–} +*local.* (See quotation.) — **1888** G. Trumbull *Names of Birds* 39 At Pleasantville and Atlantic City we hear Long-neck [used as a name for the pintail duck]. **1890** *Cent.* 3512/2.

+**Long-neck(ed) squash.** A variety of squash (*Cucurbita verrucosa*) having long necks and warty surfaces; a squash of this variety. — **1836** Gilman *Recoll.* (1838) 52, I send by Mr. Duncan some long-necked squashes and russet apples of my own raising. **1847** Darlington *Weeds*

& Plants 143 Warted Squash. Long-necked Squash. . . . Apt to produce worthless Hybrids among Pumpkins, when growing near them. **1868** GRAY *Field Botany* 160 *C[ucurbita] verrucosa*, Warty, Long-neck, and Crook-neck Squash, Vegetable Marrow, &c.

+Long nine. A cheap cigar. *Obs.* Also attrib. and transf. **1830** N. AMES *Mariner's Sk.* 213 The four-fold row of long-nine-smoking beaux . . . are regularly drawn up on Sunday forenoon in Market Square. **1833** NEAL *Down Easters* I. 45 He, sitting on the windlass, . . . with a long nine in his mouth. **1835** *Harvardiana* I. 157 It contained two long-nine segars. **1840** BIRD *Robin Day* 47 He demanded . . . what the devil I was doing with my long nine (meaning the duck gun). **1850** *Knickerb.* XXXV. 555 A man . . . was puffing a villanous [*sic*] 'long-nine' in the bar-room of a hotel. **1858** HOLMES *Autocrat* 53 Stable-boys smoking long-nines.

+Long-nosed gar (pike). A fresh-water fish of North America, *Lepisosteus osseus.* — **1884** GOODE, etc. *Fisheries* I. 663 The Long-nosed Gar-pike *Lepidosteus osseus* . . . is found in the Great Lakes, and throughout the Mississippi Valley, as well as in all the streams of the South from Mexico to New Jersey. **1889** *Cent.* 2453/3 *Long-nosed gar, Lepidosteus osseus*, the common garpike or bill-fish.

Long plane. A plane longer and broader than a trying plane. {1679–} — **1777** *Essex Inst. Coll.* XLIX. 106 Sold . . . long planes, at 7 s. **1875** KNIGHT 1350/2 *Long-plane*, . . . a joiner's plane used when a piece of stuff is to be planed up very straight.

Long-range, *a.* {1873–} Of a rifle: Having a range greater than usual. — **1870** KEIM *Sheridan's Troopers* 72 An old animal is killed now and then by a long-range rifle. **1885** *Rep. Indian Affairs* 66 The two Indians both had long-range rifles. **1888** SHERIDAN *Memoirs* I. 399 [It] was Butler's brigade of mounted troops, part of them armed with long-range rifles.

Long reach. +? A long-bodied wagon. — **1899** A. BROWN *Tiverton Tales* 118 Passing the window, she saw the selectmen, in the vehicle known as a long-reach, waiting at the gate.

Long room. {1722–} *Stock exchange.* +(See quotations.) — **1870** MEDBERY *Men Wall St.* 22 A chamber is provided at the Exchange, where members may bargain with members at any hour throughout the day. This is known as the Long Room. **1882** MCCABE *New York* 334 'The Long Room' . . . is devoted to the irregular sales of stocks. **1885** *Harper's Mag.* Nov. 830 On the left, or Broad Street side, is the Long Room, devoted to telegraphic apparatus and subscribers who pay $100 per annum for the privilege of using it.

+Long sauce. (See quot. 1859.) *Obs.* — **1809** IRVING *Knickerb.* III. vii, Some dashing country heiress . . . deeply skilled in the mystery of making apple-sweetmeats, long sauce and pumpkin pie. **1815** HUMPHREYS *Yankey in Eng.* 41 Long sairse and short sairse; consisting of a variety of leetle notions too tedious to mention. **1853** *S. Lit. Messenger* XIX. 666/1 Cabbages, beets, turnips, and 'long sarce' abound. **1859** BARTLETT 255 *Long Sauce*, beets, carrots, and parsnips are *long sauce.* Potatoes, turnips, onions, pumpkins, etc. are *short sauce.*

Long saw. A saw longer than most saws; a pit saw. — **1651** *Mayflower Descendant* X. 160 It[em:] one long saw, one Croscutt saw, . . . 10 [shillings]. **1875** KNIGHT 1350/2 *Long-saw*, a pit-saw; used by a man standing above the log, and one below.

+Longschat pine. (See quotations.) — **1897** SUDWORTH *Arborescent Flora* 27 Pitch pine. . . . Common names. . . . Long-leaved Pine (Del.), Longschat Pine (Del.), Hard Pine (Mass.). **1908** N. L. BRITTON *N. A. Trees* 31 Pitch Pine . . . is known by many names, such as Hard pine, Long-leaved pine, Longschat pine, Yellow pine, Black pine, [etc.].

Long session. +Before the Twentieth Amendment (1934), the session of Congress beginning on the first Monday in December of odd-numbered years. — **1886** ALTON *Among Law-Makers* 13 There is one regular session every year, commencing on the first Monday of December, thus making two regular sessions in a Congress, known as the 'long session' and the 'short session.'

***Longshanks.** +The black-necked stilt, *Himantopus mexicanus.* {1817–} — **1813** WILSON *Ornithology* VII. 50 Long-legged Avoset: *Recurvirostra himantopus*; . . . arrives on the sea coast of New Jersey about the twenty-fifth of April. . . . The name by which this bird is known on the sea coast is the Stilt, or Tilt, or Long-shanks. **1844** *Nat. Hist. N.Y., Zoology* II. 266 The Lawyer, *Himantopus nigricollis*, . . . is known under the various popular names of Tilt, Stilt, Longshanks and Lawyer. **1917** *Birds of Amer.* I. 223 Black-necked Stilt. . . . [Also called] Longshanks.

Longshoreman. One who works on a waterfront at common labor such as loading or unloading vessels.
1811 GRAYDON *Memoirs* 120 [Chester, Md.] having been a place of some trade, it was supposed there might be seamen or *long shore* men there, out of employ. **1853** *Hunt's Merchants' Mag.* May 594 In the city of New York, the 'long-shore-men have taken by force . . . the horses and labor-saving gear used for delivering cargoes. **1872** *Harper's Mag.* XLVI. 151 In New Orleans there was a 'longshoremen's strike . . . to secure $4 wages per day, instead of $3, and ten hours for the working-day. **1894** FORD *P. Stirling* 45 [Peter] would sometimes stop and chat with . . . a fruit-vender, a long-shore-man or a truckster.

‖**b.** A disreputable woman. *slang.*
1896 ADE *Artie* 80 We hadn't been in there ten minutes till Billy dug up a 'longshoreman with gold in her teeth and was buyin' beer for her.

‖**Long shorer.** =LONGSHOREMAN. — **1838** *N.Y. Advertiser & Exp.* 14 Feb. 3/5 A couple of long shorers . . . hitched an old broken winded horse . . . to the skeleton of a vehicle.

+Long short. (See quot. 1859.) *Obs.* — **1840** *Knickerb.* XVI. 22 A buxom, rosy-cheeked girl, with a blue-striped long-short . . . was busied around the fire-place. **1845** JUDD *Margaret* I. 5 A woman in a blue striped long-short and yellow skirt, comes to the door. **1859** BARTLETT 256 *Long Short*, a gown somewhat shorter than a petticoat, worn by women when doing household work.

Longspur. +Any one of several long-clawed birds, usually of the genus *Calcarius*, found chiefly in the interior plains regions of the United States. — **1874** COUES *Birds N.W.* 122 *Plectrophanes Ornatus*, . . . Chestnut-collared Bunting: Black-bellied Longspur. **1893** COUES in *Lewis & Clark Exped.* I. 349*n.*, The black-breasted lark-bunting or longspur, *Centrophanes* (*Rhynchophanes*) *maccowni.* **1917** *Birds of Amer.* III. 22 Shore Larks that feed up and down the wintry seashore of New England and the middle States have also many Longspurs among them.

Longstalk. +**1.** A variety of apple: (see quotation). +**2.** *Longstalk willow*, (see quotation). — **(1) 1709** LAWSON *Carolina* 108 The Red-streak thrives very well. Long-stalk is a large Apple, with a long Stalk, and makes good Summer Cider. **(2) 1897** SUDWORTH *Arborescent Flora* 119 *Salix occidentalis longipes.* . . . Longstalk Willow.

Long-stalked, *a.* +In the specific names of American plants: (see quotations). — **1813** MUHLENBERG *Cat. Plants* 87 *Quercus filiformis*, Long-stalk'd oak. **1814** BIGELOW *Florula Bostoniensis* 241 *Smilax peduncularis.* Long stalked Smilax. . . . A rank, herbaceous, climbing plant. . . . June. Perennial. **1833** EATON *Botany* (ed. 6) 155 *Geranium columbinum* long stalked geranium. **1843** TORREY *Flora N.Y.* II 268 *Microstylis ophioglossoides.* Long-stalked Adder's-mouth.

+Long-staple cotton. Cotton having an exceptionally long staple or fibre, esp. sea-island cotton.
1802 *Steele P.* I. 341 Black Seed or Long Staple Cotton is in demand. **1828** in Commons, etc. *Doc. Hist.* I. 269 Every successive year from 1781 saw the long staple cotton extending itself along the shores of Georgia. **1862** KETTELL *Hist. Rebellion* I. 369 The chief production is the long staple cotton, known as sea island, used for the first class of cotton goods. **1891** CHASE & CLOW *Industry* II. 7 The fibres are called staples. If they are long, the cotton is called long-staple cotton. **1900** *Congress. Rec.* 6 Feb. 1570/2, I come from a section of country that raises long-staple cotton.

+Long sugar. Molasses. *Obs.* (Cf. LONGLICK.) — **1729** BYRD *Dividing Line* (1866) 57 Their molosses comes from the same country, and has the name of 'Long Sugar' in Carolina, I suppose from the Ropiness of it.

+Long sweetening. Molasses or syrup. *colloq.* — **1714** *N.C. Col. Rec.* II. 132 Let who will go unpaid, Rum long sweet'n alias Mollasses, glystr. Sugar must be had. **1869** BOWLES *Our New West* viii. 170 The writer won his glory and victual by making the 'long-sweetening,' i.e. white sugar melted into a permanent syrup. **1886** *Harper's Mag.* June 62/1 These decoctions they mollify with home-made sorghum molasses, which they call 'long sweetening.' **1894** ROBLEY *Bourbon Co., Kansas* 68 The menu consisted of cornbread, bacon, fried potatoes and corn coffee with 'long sweetnin'.'

***Long-tailed,** *a.* +**1.** In the specific names of American birds. (See also LONG-TAILED DUCK.) +**2.** (See quotations.) — **(1) 1823** James *Exped.* I. 265 *Tetrao phasianellus*—Long-tailed grouse. **1869** *Amer. Naturalist* III. 186 [Among] the most peculiar birds [in California is] . . . the Long-tailed Mocking-bird (*Mimus caudatus*). **1873** in Coues *Birds N.W.* 230 *Parus atricapillus* var. *septentrionalis*, Long-tailed Titmouse. **1917** *Birds of Amer.* III. 163/2 The Long-tailed Chat (*Icteria virens longicauda*) of the western United States is similar to the Yellow-breasted Chat. **(2) 1857** *Rep. Comm. Patents 1846: Agric.* 95 Long-tailed Jumping Mouse. . . . *Jaculus labradorius. Ib.* 96 This animal is known as the 'Long-tailed Deer Mouse,' . . . 'Wood Mouse,' and other names.

Long-tail(ed) blue. {1899 of a butterfly}
+**1.** A blue coat having long tails.
1836 HOLMES *Poetical Works* (1895) 31/1 They did not rattle round in gigs, Or dash in long-tailed blues. **1845** *Lowell Offering* V. 148 In their eagerness to make a man of him at once they had hurried him into a 'long-tailed-blue,' though he was but about three years of age. **1860** CLAIBORNE *S. Dale* 27 The negro wore a 'long-tail blue,' the skirts flying out as he fled. **1867** MELINE *Santa Fé & Back* 295 The white man was represented, appareled in a long-tail blue, revolver in hand. **1889** *Harper's Mag.* June 139/2 The first colored gentleman to wear 'The Long-tailed Blue' was Barney Burns, who broke his neck on a vaulting board in Cincinnati in 1838.

+**2.** A dandified Negro or black-face comedian; the title of a song often sung by such an actor.
1844 'UNCLE SAM' *Peculiarities* II. 170 A dandy nigger, technically termed a 'long-tailed blue,' [is] dancing Jim Crow's pattern dance. . . . The passengers . . . are laughing at 'long-tailed blue.' **1867** *Atlantic Mo.* Nov. 610/2 'Clar de Kitchen' soon appeared as a companion piece, followed speedily by 'Lucy Long,' . . . 'Long-Tail Blue,' and so on.

Long-tailed duck. A sea duck (*Clangula hyemalis*) found in various parts of the United States as a visitor. {1766–} — **1813** WILSON *Ornithology* VIII. 93 Long-Tailed Duck. . . . This Duck is very generally known along the shores of the Chesapeake Bay by the name of South Southerly. **1839** PEABODY *Mass. Birds* 394 The Long-tailed Duck, *Fuligula glacialis*, . . . [is] seen regularly and abundantly on the shores of Massachusetts. **1884** ROE *Nature's Story* 169 Well, there is the old squaw, or long-tailed duck. **1917** *Birds of Amer.* I. 141 Old-Squaw. . . . [Also called] Long-tailed Duck; Long-tail.

Long talk. +A speech made at a conference between white people and Indians. Also used allusively. — **1832** WILLIAMSON *Maine* II. 272 'Long talks,' were followed by re-assurances from the chiefs, of their wishes to live in tranquillity. **1876** *N.Y. Tribune* 5 July 1/6 The Hon. Fernando Wood gave the 'Long Talk.'

Long tom. {1854-}

+**1.** A variety of apple. *Obs.*

1817 W. COXE *Fruit Trees* 125 Bullocks Pippin, or Sheep Nose. This is one of the finest apples in New-Jersey. . . . It is sometimes called the Long Tom. **1830** *Western Agriculturist* 318 Red fall Russet, or Long Tom, October and Nov.

+**2.** *Mining.* A trough used for washing gold-bearing dirt. (Cf. CRADLE 3.)

1850 A. T. JACKSON *Forty-Niner* (1920) 14 He says there is a new way of taking out gold by a machine called a Long Tom. **1880** INGHAM *Digging Gold* 58 The 'Long Tom' . . . is placed at an incline and a stream of water introduced into the upper end. **1896** SHINN *Story of Mine* 40 'Decomposed quartz' . . . can be panned out or washed in a rocker, long tom, or sluice box. *a***1918** G. STUART *On Frontier* I. 69 The west branch . . . rose fifty feet; sweeping away nearly all the miners' cabins . . . and all of their tools, such as long toms, rockers [etc.].

+**3.** A long cigar, esp. one of a poor quality. *Obs.*

*a***1870** CHIPMAN *Notes on Bartlett* 256 *Long Tom.* . . . (From a not wholly fanciful resemblance to a cannon.) A long cigar—usually of a quality inversely proportioned.

+**Long-toothed flounder.** (See quotation.) — **1855** BAIRD in *Smithsonian Rep.* 349 The long-toothed Flounder, *Platessa ocellaris*, . . . is generally found on sandy bottoms.

Long-wooled, *a.* Having or producing long wool. {1805-} — **1809** LIVINGSTON *Sheep* (1810) 50 The Arlington long-woolled sheep . . . were derived from the stock of that distinguished farmer, soldier, statesman, and patriot, Washington. **1850** *Rep. Comm. Patents 1849: Agric.* 161 The short and fine-wooled families of sheep do well, whilst the long-wooled do not. **1869** *Mich. Agric. Rep.* VII. 373 The call . . . for a supply of the finer kinds of long-wooled fleeces is very urgent. **1912** WING *Sheep Farming in Amer.* 58 The new Lincoln sheep . . . is a truly magnificent sheep of the long-wooled character.

Loo.

1. A card game somewhat resembling whist, played by any number of players up to seventeen. {1675-}

1773 TRUMBULL *Progress of Dulness* II. 33 His genius turn'd, with greatest skill, To whist, loo, cribbage and quadrille. **1834** NOTT *Novellettes* I. 40 They could indulge in three up, old sledge, whist, or loo. **1872** *Harper's Mag.* XLVI. 95 The Virginians were addicted to that stupid game known as shoe-maker loo. President Tyler was fond of loo.

2. Attrib. and comb. in sense 1 with *box, counter,* etc.

1810 *Columbian Centinel* 3 Feb. 4/3 James Murphy . . . offers for sale . . . 400 Loo Boxes. *Ib.* 26 Dec. 4/3 For sale . . . 50 sets Loo Counters. **1817** E. PETTIGREW *Let. to Ann Pettigrew* 7 Jan. (Univ. N.C. MS.), Myself together with four others who did not dance retired to the Loe table. **1838** *S. Lit. Messenger* IV. 327 The practice of loo-playing was then seen to decline, and was finally laid aside.

+**Lookdown.** =HORSEHEAD. (Cf. MOONFISH 2.) — **1884** GOODE etc. *Fisheries* I. 323 In the Chesapeake this fish is often called by the names 'Horse-head' and 'Look-down.' **1903** T. H. BEAN *Fishes N.Y.* 436 The lookdown is found on both coasts of tropical America and in temperate parts of the Atlantic north to Cape Cod.

***Looker.** ||**1.** An Indian watcher for buffalo. +**2.** One who is handsome or good-looking. *colloq.* — **(1) 1833** CATLIN *Indians* I. 127 [Among the Mandans] spies or '*lookers*' are kept on the hills in the neighbourhood of the village, who, when they discover buffaloes in sight, give the appropriate signal, by 'throwing their robes.' **(2) 1898** WESTCOTT *D. Harum* 322, I was alwus a better goer than I was a looker. **1904** *Springfield W. Repub.* 24 June 7 The country folk would say of the speaker that he is not much of a 'looker.' **1914** ATHERTON *Perch of Devil* 72 She's no fool—and she certainly is a looker. **1923** VANCE *Baroque* 40 Just because his daughter's one swell looker don't make father out an innocent.

Looker-out. +(See quotation.) — **1864** DICK *Amer. Hoyle* (1866) 206 *Looker-Out.*—The dealer's assistant [in faro].

***Looking-glass.** A mirror.

1640 *Maryland Archives* IV. 93 An Inventary of the ioint rights goods & chattels of xposer Martin . . . [includes] 1. looking glasse . . . 2. chests & 1. tronke . . . 1. flockbed & blanket. **1644** *Essex Probate Rec.* I. 36 Looking glass, . . . blew apron. **1715** *Boston News-Letter* 16 May 2/2 Lately arrived from England . . . new Fashion Looking-Glasses and Chimney-Glasses. **1775** *Holyoke Diaries* 90n., As to expensive furniture, such as looking glasses, . . . I shall let them abide. **1830** *Collegian* 40 We were arranging our neckcloths, as the barber presented the looking-glass to him. **1891** WILKINS *New Eng. Nun* 85 She's gone to look at her nose in the lookin'-glass, an' make sure it ain't crooked.

b. Attrib. and comb. with *factory, maker, plater.*

1809 CUMING *Western Tour* 223 Pittsburgh [has] . . . one pump maker; one looking-glass plater and maker. **1827** DRAKE & MANSFIELD *Cincinnati* 65 One Looking-glass and Picture Frame Factory.

Lookout. {1748-}

1. A station or structure affording an extensive view. {1791-}

1700 *S.C. Statutes at Large* II. (1837) 161 The Look-out formerly built on Sullivan's Island . . . is by a late storm overthrown to the ground. **1741** *S.C. Hist. Soc. Coll.* IV. 43 This Fort . . . was 4 Square, . . . and had a well and a House within, and a lookout. **1771** H. PELHAM in *Copley-Pelham Lett.* 162 Capt. Jay put up a small plain square look-out. **1854** BARTLETT *Personal Narr.* II. 213 In the afternoon our camp was filled with the . . . Indians who had discovered us from some of their look-outs. **1887** *Harper's Mag.* Feb. 354/2 On a cattle lookout near by sat three black buzzards. **1893** *Ib.* April 766/1 They had sailed down the Matanzas River (as the inlet is called) to see the old Spanish lookout.

2. One stationed as a watchman at a place of vantage. {1699-}

1711 *S.C. Statutes at Large* II. (1837) 355 The publick . . . has been at very great charge and expence to provide for and maintain great numbers of white men and Indians as watchmen and look-outs upon the sea-coast. **1830** COOPER *Water Witch* II. vi, The utmost vigilance was observed among the officers and look-outs during the rest of the night. **1870** KEIM *Sheridan's Troopers* 61 One day all except the look-out had retired to the Monitor.

+**3.** One who seeks out grazing land in advance of a herd.

1888 ROOSEVELT in *Century Mag.* Feb. 498/2 These lookouts or forerunners having returned, the herds are set in motion as early in the spring as may be.

+**4.** An attendant at a gaming table to oversee the conduct of the game. (Cf. LOOKER-OUT.)

1888 *N.Y. Ev. Post* 24 Feb. (F.), The look-outs were held in 700 dols. bail each for examination to-morrow. **1893** *Harper's Mag.* May 939/2 By each dealer's side sits the 'lookout,' . . . lazily looking on in the interests of such fair play as is consistent with professional gambling. *a***1918** G. STUART *On Frontier* I. 219 Arnett was dealing and Germagin was 'look-out' for him.

||**Look-outer.** One who looks out; a cautious person. — **1841** COOPER *Deerslayer* iii, Hutter is a first-rate look-outer, and can pretty much scent danger as a hound scents the deer.

+**Look-up.** (See quotation.) — **1844** *Nat. Hist. N.Y., Zoology* II. 226 The American Bittern [is] also familiarly known under the names of . . . Look-up, Stake-driver, and in Louisiana Garde-soleil.

***Loom.** A machine for weaving yarn or thread into a fabric.

1647 *Essex Probate Rec.* I. 77 One Lome with ye Gares belonging to it & seven Reeds. **1684** *Conn. Probate Rec.* I. 356, I give to my son Joseph both my Looms with all the Tackling. **1703** *N.H. Probate Rec.* I. 504, [I give] my Broadest Loom, with one half of all the tackleing belonging to weaveing. **1793** BENTLEY *Diary* II. 76 A Dane has been this way with plans of curious machines, which he says will . . . work many looms by one Horse. **1833** 'ELMWOOD' *Yankee among Nullifiers* 17 What right, Gentlemen, have the Yankees to the protection of their looms, their spinning jennies, their wooden nutmegs. **1890** *Century Mag.* Dec. 181 [He made] wheels for spinning wool . . . and looms, reeds, and shuttles for weaving yarn.

b. Attrib. with *bench, comb, room, work.*

1635 *Essex Probate Rec.* I. 5 A peece of tufted Holland, 6s.; 6 yds. of Loomworke, 5s. **1845** *Knickerb.* XXV. 448 After breakfast I went out to look at the loom-room. **1885** *Century Mag.* April 856/2 The ole lady . . . slid off the loom-bench. **1888** *Ib.* July 351/2 Barbara was . . . driving the threads home with the double-beat of her loom-comb.

Loom house. A house set apart and equipped for weaving operations. {1864-} — **1819** *Western Rev.* I. 303 The other two young women slept in a loom house adjoining. **1838** *S. Lit. Messenger* IV. 232/1 Besides the dwelling-house, there are negro-quarters, . . . loom-house, and kitchen. **1860** OLMSTED *Back Country* 76 We stopped at a house . . . called the loom-house, in which a dozen negroes were at work making shoes, and manufacturing coarse cotton stuff for negro clothing.

Loon.

1. a. A four-toed diving bird belonging to any one of various species of the genus *Gavia* found in the northern hemisphere. {1678-} **b.** A grebe. *Obs.* {1678-}

1634 WOOD *New Eng. Prospect* I. 31 The Loone is an ill shap'd thing like a Cormorant. **1672** JOSSELYN *New Eng. Rarities* 12 The Loone is a Water Fowl, alike in shape to the Wobble, and as virtual for Aches. **1778** CARVER *Travels* 470 The Loon is a water fowl, somewhat less than a teal, and is a species of the dobchick. **1806** LEWIS in *L. & Clark Exped.* IV. (1905) 142 There are two speceis of loons . . . the second speceis we first met with at the great falls of the Columbia and from thence down. this bird is not more than half the size of the speckled loon. *a***1861** WINTHROP *Open Air* 27 Sound has no power to express a profounder emotion of utter loneliness than the loon's cry. **1877** BURROUGHS *Birds & Poets* 70 The loon . . . is the great diver and flyer under water. **1902** W. HULBERT *Forest Neighbors* (1903) 191 The fisherman found in his net the lifeless body of a drowned loon.

attrib. and *comb.* **1869** W. MURRAY *Adventures* 107 Slight as the difference [between two styles of gun-tubes] would seem to be, it is a vital one in loon-shooting. **1902** W. HULBERT *Forest Neighbors* (1903) 193 The southland, as everybody knows, is the only proper place for a loon courtship.

+**2.** In various colloq. phrases, esp. *as crazy as a loon.*

1834 C. A. DAVIS *Lett. J. Downing* 42, I saw thru' it in a minute, and made it all as strait as a loon's leg. **1845** KIRKLAND *Western Clearings* 83

'Why, you're both as crazy as loons!' was Mr. Ashburn's polite exclamation. **1858** *Harper's Mag.* Sept. 487/2 'What do ye think he'll do,' says she, wild as a loon. **1865** 'Mark Twain' *Sketches* (1926) 163 Our reserve . . . came filing down the street as drunk as loons. **1877** Aldrich *Queen of Sheba* 67 The fellow is mad! . . . as mad as a loon. **1880** *Harper's Mag.* Dec. 35 Miss Lois had been hunting the loon with a hand-net—a Northern way of phrasing the wearing of the willow. **1888** Ferguson *Exp. Forty-Niner* 121 The next morning Costler was as crazy as a loon—the mountain fever had attacked him.

‖**Looning.** The cry of the loon. — **a1862** Thoreau *Maine Woods* 230 This of the loon—I do not mean its laugh, but its looning—is a long-drawn call.

Loon skin. The skin of a loon. — **1807** Gass *Journal* 166 Some [Indians on the Pacific coast] have robes made of muskrat skins sewed together and I saw some of loon-skins. **a1861** Winthrop *Open Air* 27 Loon-skins have a commercial value; so it is reported.

***Loop.** +In a city a somewhat circular area included within definite limits, as the main business center of Chicago circled by the elevated railroad. — [**1893** *Harper's Mag.* May 814/2 Not quite the whole of the territory (now enclosed by the lower loop of the elevated railway) which lies south of the present Battery Place [in N.Y.].] **1895** Robinson *Men Born Equal* 147 Every one who arrived from down-town brought news that it was at 'the loop' that the aspect of affairs was most threatening. **1920** Cooper *Under Big Top* 47 Through the loop district the entire cavalcade would have gone. **1923** Wyatt *Invisible Gods* 109 Her permanent abiding place was a small frame cottage . . . situated some six miles from the loop on Lake Boulevard.

***Loophole.** A hole in the wall of a stockade, fortress, etc., through which those inside may fire upon attackers. Also attrib.

1726 Penhallow *Indian Wars* 114 [One person] was in a little time shot through a loop-hole. **1812** Marshall *Kentucky* 160 Bryant's Station . . . had a bastion at either end, composed of strong logs, built in the block house form, with necessary loop holes. **1837** Bird *Nick of Woods* I. 186 Two mouldering gaps . . . showed where the narrow entrance and loop-hole windows had once existed. **1886** *Century Mag.* Nov. 14/1 Mordecai . . . saw through the loop-hole an Indian in his war-paint. **1923** J. H. Cook *On Old Frontier* 186 Loopholes [were] on all sides from which to fire.

+**Loose change.** Coins or bills of small denominations, such as one might carry loose in the pocket; money regarded as of little value. *colloq.* — **1827** Sherwood *Gaz. Georgia* 112 It would be a kind of generous charity, to leave with the tavern-keepers . . . some of the loose change. **1835** Longstreet *Ga. Scenes* 132 To give any gentleman, who might have come to the ball, encumbered with a little loose change, an opportunity of relieving himself. **1872** Eggleston *End of World* 173 Unless he means to part with all his loose change before bed-time.

+**Loose constructionist.** (See quotation and cf. Constructionist.) — **1892** Walsh *Lit. Curiosities* 656 *Loose-Constructionists*, in American national politics, those who favor a liberal interpretation of the Constitution with regard to the powers delegated by that instrument to the federal government, and who are for the reading into it of large implied sovereign powers.

+**Loose herding.** (See quotation.) — **1881** Chase *Editor's Run in N. Mex.* 109 Loose herding prevailed; that is, everybody, after putting their mark upon their animals, turned them loose upon the prairie, to run where they would.

+**Loose-hung,** *a.* Gangling, lacking firmness in build. *colloq.* — **1890** Howells *Shadow of Dream* I. i, Faulkner stooped a little, and he was, as they say in the West, loose-hung.

***Loosestrife. 1.** Any one of various plants of the genus *Lysimachia.* Also with defining adjective. **2. a.** A plant of the genus *Lythrum.* **b.** *Loosestrife family*, the Lythraceae. — **(1) 1791** Muhlenberg *Index Florae* 163 *Lysimachia*, Loosestrife. **1814** Bigelow *Florula Bostoniensis* 49 *Lysimachia thyrsiflora.* Tufted loosestrife. . . . Meadows. June, July. **1869** Fuller *Flower Gatherers* 246 Our next plant was the . . . Loose-Strife, with narrow leaves growing in whorls around the stem. **(2) 1847** Wood *Botany* 260 Loosestrife. . . . Flowers large, numerous and showy. Petals purple. **1892** Apgar *Trees Northern U.S.* 108 *Lythraceæ.* (Loosestrife Family.) **1901** Mohr *Plant Life Ala.* 631 *Lythrum alatum.* . . . Winged-stemmed Loosestrife.

***Lop,** *v. tr.* To cut off (limbs, twigs, tops) from a tree or shoot. Also *vbl. n.* — **1627** *Plymouth Col. Rec.* XI. 5 That the woods (be) ordered for felling & lopping according as the owner shall appo(int). **1695** *Boston Rec.* 221 The said Sewell . . . shall have Liberty from time to time to lop the trees. **1742** *Georgia Col. Rec.* VI. 22 That he Lops up and Clears the head of the Tree . . . that it be no Anoiance to the Road. **1794** *N.Y. State Soc. Arts* I. 137 Young oaks, walnut, or any other trees that will bear lopping, have been left. **1857** *Ill. Agric. Soc. Trans.* III. 491 All such main stems as grow top heavy and bend over, should be lopped off. **1884** Roe *Nature's Story* 158 He took the axe from his brother, who had been lopping the branches from the prostrate tree.

+**Lope,** *n.* [f. *lope* v. or Du. *loop.*] A long, swinging, galloping stride, usu. of horses. {1889–}

[**1825** Neal *Bro. Jonathan* II. 5 (Th.), [The Indian's] common pace, when he had any object in view, was a kind of loose, long, lazy trot, like that of the wolf through a light snow. Wherefore it is called in America the Indian loup.] **1833** J. Hall *Harpe's Head* 38 [The buck] came, at an easy *lope*, until he reached the top of a little knoll. **1869** McClure *Rocky Mts.* 302 The Western man always rides at a lope. **1887** *Outing* X. 115/1 The rise and fall of the perfect lope peculiar to the American broncho was observable in all its ease and beauty. **1907** Lillibridge *Trail* 72 The roan with the tiny ears had not broken its steady, swinging, seemingly interminable lope.

Lope, *v.* {a1825–, *intr.*} +*tr.* To cause (a horse, mule, etc.) to gallop at a lope. — **1885** Roosevelt *Hunting Trips Ranchman* 281 (*Cent.*), For seven or eight miles we loped our jaded horses along at a brisk pace. **1888** Cody *Wild West* 586 Soon the Indian was seen loping his pony through the grass. **1902** Wister *Virginian* 175, I loped my cayuse full tilt by Mr. Snake.

Loper. Variant of Loafer.[2]

Lop horn. A horn that grows in a downward direction; an ox having a horn of this kind. — **1850** D. Webster *Private Corr.* II. 405, I think your team a very good one; the old oxen, the starred steers, and the lop-horns. **1872** Powers *Afoot & Alone* 173 'Cut out that black fellow with the lop-horn,' he quietly orders one of the herdsmen.

+**Lopseed.** A perennial herb (*Phryma leptostachya*) having purplish flowers. — **1817–8** Eaton *Botany* (1822) 389 *Phryma leptostachia*, lopseed. **1840** Dewey *Mass. Flowering Plants* 173 Lopseed . . . grows along hedges and woods; July. **1901** Mohr *Plant Life Ala.* 696 Lopseed. . . . Alleghenian to Louisianian area.

Lord-and-lady. + =Harlequin duck. Also attrib. — **1832** Williamson *Maine* I. 142 The *Lord and Lady*, or *Noddy* is as large as a pigeon, good for food. . . . Its perpetual whiffles with the wings when flying, give it name. **1835** Audubon *Ornith. Biog.* III. 612 To the south of the Bay of Boston the 'Lord and Lady Duck' is rarely seen on our coast. **1917** *Birds of Amer.* I. 142 Harlequin Duck. . . . Rightly are its little companies called the 'Lords and Ladies' of the waters.

Lords-and-Ladies. {1760–} +The jack-in-the-pulpit, or a related plant. — **1784** Cutler in *Mem. Academy* I. 487 Arum . . . *Cuckowpint. Dragon-root. Wake-Robin. Lords & Ladies. Spatha* striped with red or black. **1832** Williamson *Maine* I. 122 [The Wakerobin's] leaves are freckled and often white streaked,—hence called 'lords and ladies.'

***Lord's day.** Sunday. Also attrib. — **1634** *Essex Inst. Coll.* IV. 89/2 To feed the cattle on the lords dayes. **1693** C. Mather *Wonders Invis. World* 141 Being in Bed, on the Lord's-day Night, he heard a scrabbling at the window. **1701** *Boston Rec.* 13 Ordered, That no person shall . . . make any coffin on the Lord's day. **1772** A. G. Winslow *Diary* (1894) 61 Last Lords day morning Mrs. Martin was deliver'd of a daughter. **1889** P. Butler *Recoll.* 193 We had meetings every Lord's day, and had frequent additions by letter and by baptism.

+**Lordy,** *interj.* An exclamation of surprise or astonishment. Also *Lordy me.* — **1853** *Southern Literary Messenger* XIX 602/2 On the sofa . . . you sank down and bounded up and said Lordy! **1857** *Knickerb.* L. 236 O Lordy me Sir! I'm so dreadful afeared you're both on you Dorrites! **1898** Westcott *D. Harum* 178 'Lordy me!' sighed Mrs. Cullom. **1901** Churchill *Crisis* 432 Lordy! how my ears ache since your damned coehorns have stopped. **1907** Field *Six-Cylinder Courtship* 126 Lordy, but it was hot!

***Lost,** *a.* +In special combinations.

Lost lover, used in designating a particular design or pattern of a quilt; *lost moon*, (see quotation); *lost river*, (see quotation); *lost salmon*, the humpbacked salmon; *lost stone*, =Lost rock.

1778 Carver *Travels* 250 Some nations among them [the Indians] reckon their years by moons, and make them consist of twelve synodical or lunar months, observing, when thirty moons have waned, to add a supernumerary one, which they term the lost moon; and then begin to count as before. **1819** McMurtrie *Sk. Louisville* 29 Fragments of primitive rock . . . are said to be found . . . in the Illinois and Missouri territories, where they are denominated *lost stones*, from the evident circumstances, of their being strangers to the soil where they are found. **1843** 'Carlton' *New Purchase* I. 58 Out come the mole rivers that have burrowed all this time under the earth, and which, when so unexpectedly found are styled out there [in Ind].—'lost rivers!' And every district of a dozen miles square has a lost river. **1881** *Amer. Naturalist* XV. 178 Hump-back. . . . [Also called] holia, lost salmon, Puget Sound salmon. **1897** Brodhead *Bound in Shallows* 169 A great scarlet-and-white quilt, pieced in the 'Lost Lover' design, was spread on stretchers in the family-room.

Lost cause. +*spec.* The cause of the South in the Civil War (1861–65).

1868 *N.Y. Herald* 2 July 4/1 'The lost cause' . . . was a decided and lamentable failure. **1879** *Scribner's Mo.* June 306/1 The South has no great love for the national flag as such, . . . [and] 'the lost cause' is still very precious to its politicians and its people. **1887** *Courier-Journal* 21 Jan. 8/4 One of the wool-dyed brethren of the 'lost cause' who believed there was no heaven for a Union man . . . became deeply affected. **1910** C. Harris *Eve's Husband* 40 He was elected . . . to the governorship of Tennessee, apparently on account of his devotion to the 'Lost Cause.' *transf.* **1905** N. Davis *Northerner* 71, I don't mind doing a little proselyting now and then, for the political 'Lost Cause'!

+**b.** The Confederate States of America; the South.

1886 Poore *Reminisc.* II. 526 They receive the representatives of 'the Lost Cause' with every possible honor. **1905** N. Davis *Northerner* 4 It is a sacred tribute to the heroes of what they call 'The Lost Cause,' meaning the under dog in the 'late unpleasantness!'

Lost rock. +(See quot. 1857.) — **1831** Peck *Guide* 136 Scattered over the surface of our prairies are large masses of rock, of granitic formation, roundish in form, usually called by the people 'lost rocks.' **1838** Flagg *Far West* II. 79, I here [=in Illinois] met with those singular granite masses, termed familiarly by the settlers 'lost rocks.' **1857** *Ill. Agric. Soc. Trans.* II. 347 'Lost rocks' . . . are found on the surface of the earth in the middle and northern sections of Illinois.

***Lot,** *n.*

+1. A tract, area, or subdivision of land, originally an allotment of public land made to a settler or colonist by local authorities. {1776–} (Cf. CORNER LOT.)

The second group of citations shows something of how lots vary in size.

(1) **1627** *Plymouth Laws* 29 Those grounds which are nearest the town in whose lott soever they fall shall be used by the whole. **1668** *Springfield Rec.* I. 366 A peece of land . . . next to the lott yt was granted to James Taylor. **1718** *N.H. Probate Rec.* II. 60 Said lot . . . running South Easterly . . . to a hemlock tree. **1791** WASHINGTON *Writings* XII. 28 The city is laid off into lots, and sale is made of these lots. **1840** *Picayune* 8 Oct. 3/5 The sixth sale of Lots . . . will commence at Austin on Monday. **1880** *Harper's Mag.* Feb. 354/2 The lots of the new town are sold on the 13th of July, 1749. **1904** *N.Y. Ev. Post* 9 May 3 The Sunday baseball decision of Justice Gaynor tempted many amateur clubs to play games in the vacant lots of Brooklyn yesterday.

(2) **1643** *Providence Rec.* II. 1, 5 an twenty Acors of ground . . . was part of his threcore Acors lot. **1667** *Ib.* I. 18 My fiue acre lot Recuied of the Towne in lewe of my Share of medow. **1672** *Derby Rec.* 22 Abell Gun hath a Lott Layed out Containeing Ten Akers more or Less wth conveinentcy of fencing. **1681** *Hartford Land Distrib.* XIV. 12 His lot on the west Side rocky Hill. the whole of it containes in bredth one Hundred & Six rod. **1698** SEWALL *Diary* I. 475, I had sold my 600. Acre Lot at Narragansett. **1709** *Boston News-Letter* 14–21 March 2/2 [There is] a good accomodation for two hundred Lotts or more, a quarter of an Acre to each Lott. **1734** *Md. Gazette* 19 July, My Lord Baltimore's Gift . . . consisting of 10,000 Acres, will . . . be divided into Lots or Farms, 50 or 100 Acres in each Lot or Farm. **1816** U. BROWN *Journal* I. 280 Lots . . . sell at $250 which is for 1/4 of an Acre. **1852** BRISTED *Upper Ten Th.* 42 A 'lot' of the ordinary size is twenty-five feet front by a hundred deep. **1866** *Rep. Indian Affairs* 296 We have thought best to clear . . . one hundred acres . . . in lots of not less than ten acres each. **1903** G. C. EGGLESTON *First of Hoosiers* 63 In the town they sought spacious 'lots,' sometimes of half an acre or more, in which to build.

+b. A burial plot in a cemetery.

1871 *Mich. Gen. Statutes* I. (1882) 1223 The said trustees . . . shall cause to be removed and again erected over the proper remains, all permanent fences around graves and lots, all tombstones and monuments. **1873** *Ib.* 668 All moneys raised for any public cemetery . . . and all moneys received from the sale of lots therein . . . shall be paid into the city treasury. **1882** MCCABE *New York by Sunlight & Gaslight* 234 At Greenwood each lot contains 378 square feet.

+c. 1. *Across lots,* by a nearer or more convenient way. 2. *To go* (or *send*) *to hell* (or *to the devil*) *across lots,* to go (or send) straight to hell (or to the devil). *colloq.*

Cf. CROSS-LOTS *adv.*

(1) **1888** BILLINGS *Hardtack* 351 [An army wagon train] was going across lots to its destination. **1903** J. HAWTHORNE *Hawthorne & Circle* 118 They were slow and methodical, never taking short-cuts across lots. (2) **1853** B. YOUNG *Jrnl. Discourses* I. 83 (Th.) [I dreamed that] I cut one of their throats from ear to ear, saying, 'Go to hell across lots.' **1857** *Speech* (B.), I swore in Nauvoo, when my enemies were looking me in the face, that I would send them to hell across lots if they meddled with me. **a1861** WINTHROP *J. Brent* xvii. 158 You may go to the devil across lots, on that runt pony of yourn, with your new friends, for all I care.

+2. An enclosure for domestic live stock, usually situated near a dwelling.

1831 PECK *Guide* 166 In autumn they [oxen] were shut up in a lot, fed with corn in the ear, . . . with water. **1880** TOURGEE *Bricks* 359 Those servants who were employed 'about the lot.' **1894** CHOPIN *Bayou Folk* 217 Near at hand, in the 'lot' that adjoined Uncle Jake's cabin, was his little creole pony. **1904** T. E. WATSON *Bethany* 10 From the open space in front of the lot, we had a view of the last spur of the Blue Ridge.

3. *attrib.* and *comb.* **a.** In sense 1 with *book, corner, holder, jumper.*

1644 *Portsmouth Rec.* 29 It is ordered that Henry Knowles shall cut his lott corner shortter. **1689** *Manchester Rec.* 33 Ye whole doo not apear fairly entered with ye return of ye severall boundarys theirof upon ye Lote books of ye town records. **1851** CIST *Cincinnati* 147 The lot-holders met and determined their right of choice in the selection of lots. **1869** *Overland Mo.* III. 63/1 Then there had been a lot jumpers' fight down at the end of the street.

b. In sense 2 with *manure, paling.*

1848 *Florida Plant. Rec.* 57, I dont think I will get done hawling out the lot manure under 3 weeks yet. **1892** HARRIS *On Plantation* 66 Here come a big pack of dogs a-chargin' 'roun' the lot-palin's in full cry.

***Lot,** *v.*

***1.** *tr.* To assign lots (of land) to individual owners. Usually with *out.* (Cf. ALLOT *v.* 1.)

1634 *Muddy River & Brookline, Mass. Rec.* (1875) 9 Hogg Island shall be lotted out unto the inhabitants and freemen of this town. **1718** SEWALL *Diary* III. 202 Novr. 10th. Lotted out the Land of Nod. **1736** in E. Hyde *Hist. Winchendon, Mass.* (1849) 75 The Committee to lot and lay out the first division. **1875** TEMPLE & SHELDON *Hist. Northfield, Mass.* 15 This tract . . . was lotted out before the planters moved upon the ground. **1891** E. CHASE *Hist. Dartmouth Coll.* I. 611 The remainder of the grant . . . was lotted, and some of it rented on long leases about 1821.

2. *local.* To divide, distribute, or apportion by casting lots. *Obs.* {1839–}

1703 SEWALL *Diary* II. 75 Mr. Banister and I Lotted our Fence on Cotton-Hill. **1723** *Ib.* III. 323 The Children's Plate and Linen is divided into Six parts, and then Lotted.

3. *To lot on* or *upon,* to count upon or expect. *colloq.* {1633–62}

'Now *U.S.*' (*O.E.D.*).

1836 GILMAN *Recoll.* (1838) 51, [I] lot upon seeing the Carolina seeds come up that you gave me. **1868** A. D. WHITNEY *P. Strong* 27 Mother's going to Europe as much as I am. 'I can't help lotting on it all the time.' **1891** COOKE *Huckleberries* (1896) 283, I do 'lot on seein' our folks in t'other world. **1899** A. BROWN *Tiverton Tales* 25 Ain't it butcher day? I've been lottin' on a piece o' liver.

+4. *To lot up,* to pen or confine (cattle) in a lot or enclosure. (Cf. LOT *n.* 2.)

1874 J. C. MCCOY *Hist. Sk. Cattle Trade* 171 In Central Illinois many of the most successful dealers in Southern cattle, feed them upon the blue grass pastures, and never lot them up.

+Lot-layer. An official appointed or selected to lay out lots. Now hist.

1636 *Ipswich* (Mass.) *Rec.* 20 Feb., Granted to Serjent French, ten acres of upland . . . to be laid out by the lott layers. **1640** *Ib.* 10 Feb., Robert Lord chosen to be a lott layer. **1669** *Rowley Rec.* 204 Its ordered that for this year that noe lot layers shall have any power to Lay out any Lands. **1682** *Essex Inst. Coll.* XXXVII. 221 The lott layers shal . . . run over and vew and bound every mans lands. **1716** *N.H. Prov. Papers* III. 654*n.*, The Proprietors . . . shall run ye lines once in two years, the same to be done by ye Lot layers of each Town or Parish. **1882** in Godfrey *Nantucket* 90 It has been customary . . . for the proprietors' agents, or 'lot layers,' to set off the land to him.

Lotment. An allotment of land. *Obs.* {*dial.*} — **1656** *1st Cent. Hist. Springfield, Mass.* (1898) I. 253 To cleare and scoure the brooke soe far as their lott or lottments is in breadth in the same meddow. **1675** *Hempstead Rec.* I. 300, [I] have sould . . . all my Right titell Intrest an Clame in and upon a lottment or parsell of Land amounting twenty two Akers. **1684** *Jamaica* (L.I.) *Rec.* I. 291 Ye above said small lotment of midow priviledg excpted. **1704** *Conn. Probate Rec.* 483 The remainder of that Lottment of Land. **1720** *Conn. Rec.* VI. 208 The Lotments in said town shall be taxed.

Lotter. {1845–} +=LOT-LAYER. *Obs.* — **1640** *Portsmouth Rec.* 16 Itt is left to the discretion of the lotters to giue [part] of his Medowe adioyninge. **1672** *Ib.* 171 The Eight acres of Land . . . is now ordered to be layd out by the Lotters.

***Lottery.**

***1.** A scheme for the distribution of property or raising of funds through the sale of tickets or 'chances' bearing numbers some of which entitle the holders to prizes.

Schemes of this kind are now prohibited throughout the United States and denied the use of the mails. Formerly, however, they were fostered by states for the purpose of raising revenue, disposing of public land, etc. It has not proved to be possible to segregate the quotations involving these uses.

[**1612** *3d Charter Va.*, We do . . . Give and Grant, unto the said Treasurer and Company, full Power and Authority, . . . to set forth, erect, and publish, one or more Lottery or Lotteries.] **1719** *Mass. H. Rep. Jrnl.* II. 174 An effectual remedy [is needed] to prevent . . . the selling of Goods, Merchandizes, and even Houses and Lands by Lottery. **1747** in Singleton *Social N.Y.* 261 At taverns . . . such lotteries are usually set on foot and drawn. **1774** FITHIAN *Journal* I. 154 They have a lottery here on foot & to be drawn in May next for to assist them in building a market-House Town-Wharf. **1808** *Ann. 10th Congress* 2 Sess. 501 Mr. Lewis presented a petition of the Vestry of the Episcopal Church, . . . praying that a law may be passed, authorizing the petitioners to raise, by way of lottery, the sum of twelve thousand dollars. **1827** SHERWOOD *Gaz. Georgia* 127 Since our repeated accessions of territory have been disposed of by *lotteries,* we have not much money to spare. **1830** A. LAWRENCE *Diary & Corr.* 91 The Directors of the Bunker Hill Monument Association have applied to the Legislature for a lottery. **1893** *Harper's Mag.* Feb. 378 The lottery being legalized, tickets are openly displayed in the shop windows [in New Orleans]. **1895** *Statutes at Large* XXVIII. 963 Any person who shall cause to be brought within the United States from abroad, . . . or carried from one State to another in the United States, any paper, certificate, or instrument purporting to be or represent a ticket, chance, share, or interest in . . . a lottery, . . . shall be punishable in the first offense by imprisonment.

2. Attrib. with *case, commissioner, grant,* etc.

1752 HEMPSTEAD *Diary* 596, I went . . . to Capt Greenmans att Westerly to See after the Lottery Mony. **1790** *Ann. 1st Congress* II. 1256 The debt . . . consists of Continental money, Loan-office certificates, lottery prizes [etc.]. **1828** *Yankee* Feb. 52/2 They are encouraging it [gaming] in every possible way, on the largest possible scale—by lottery grants. **1853** *Whig Almanac 1854* 43/1 W. Pinckney Whyte was chosen Controller,

Lemuel Roberts, Lottery Commissioner. **1895** *Statutes at Large* XXVIII. 963 An Act For the suppression of lottery traffic through national and interstate commerce and the postal service. **1903** *Chicago Chronicle* 11 April 2/1 The importance of this holding coming, as it does, upon the heels of the lottery cases cannot well be overestimated.

+**Lottery cabin.** A cabin assigned by lot: (see quotations). Now hist. — **1874** R. H. COLLINS *Kentucky* I. 518 *The First Division of Cabins*—Lottery cabins, they called them—took place in June, 1774, . . . among a company of 31 explorers under Capt. James Harrod. **1886** Z. F. SMITH *Kentucky* 29 The men dispersed . . . to build on such locations improvement cabins. These latter were known as "lottery cabins," as they were apportioned among the men by lot.

Lottery dealer. One who conducts a lottery or deals in lottery tickets. — **1856** *Porter's Spirit of Times* 20 Dec. 261/3 The lottery dealers, and the speculators in that species of 'fancy stocks,' have been done brown by a novel kind of forgery. **1872** *Chicago Tribune* 9 Oct. 1/5 All the lottery dealers in Philadelphia struck a bargain to-day with the Hartranft leaders. **1875** *Ib.* 21 Nov. 13/1 These lottery-dealers are confidence-men of the most despicable description.

Lottery office. An office where the affairs of a lottery are managed. {1772–} Also attrib. — **1777** *Penna. Post* 8 Feb. 68 The Managers of the United States Lottery are now delivering out tickets at the Lottery-Office, in Front-street. **1806** *Balance* V. 31/2 No. 17628, drawn a prize of One Thousand Dollars, in the Road Lottery, was sold at Norman's Lottery-Office. **1844** 'UNCLE SAM' *Peculiarities* II. 273 The second [gentleman] was an exchange-broker and lottery-office keeper. **1882** MCCABE *New York* 506 We may include under the head of professional criminals . . . keepers of . . . policy and lottery offices. **1894** *Harper's Mag.* July 292/2 I had often stopped to gaze . . . on the glowing pictures and transparencies with which the lottery offices were adorned.

Lottery ticket. A ticket issued to the purchaser of a chance in a lottery. {1697–}

1777 *Jrnls. Cont. Congress* VIII. 543 The agents of the Secret Committee, in South Carolina, [are ordered] to receive all the money arising from the sale of the State lottery tickets. **1788** FRANKLIN *Autobiog.* 366 Mr. Logan . . . put into my hands sixty pounds to be laid out in lottery tickets for the battery. **1850** *Mich. Gen. Statutes* I. (1882) 47 The legislature shall not authorize any lottery, nor permit the sale of lottery tickets. **1878** A. DALY in *Life* (1917) 255 Lottery Tickets at a quarter a number . . . [relieve the] visitor in New Orleans . . . of much dollars. **1892** *Harper's Mag.* Dec. 115 Mosquito-netting . . . and other general-store stock, including the accursed lottery ticket, . . . filled up the rest of the window. **1902** BELL *Hope Loring* 68, I have bought lottery tickets every year of my life.

Lottery wheel. A drumlike receptacle into which lottery tickets are placed and from which they are drawn after being shuffled by revolutions of the apparatus. {1819–} Also fig. — **1799** *Aurora* 31 Jan. (Th.), The Washington Lottery wheels remain undrawn. **1894** *Harper's Mag.* July 293/1 Upon this [platform] . . . was placed the huge lottery-wheel, all of glass except the spokes.

+**Louisiana.** [From *Louis* XIV of France.] The name of a southern state and, formerly, of a large region of which it was a part. Used attrib.

1. In the names of things made or found in, situated or existing in, Louisiana.

1834 SIMMS *Guy Rivers* II. 98, I'll go a York shilling 'gainst a Louisiana bit, that you can't tell to save you. **1843** MARRYAT *M. Violet* xxxiii, The *gourmand's* dish *par excellence* . . . [is] the Louisiana gombo. **1865** RICHARDSON *Secret Service* 35 Our road stretched out in long perspective through great Louisiana everglades. **1895** G. KING *New Orleans* 260 Indigo was the staple and profitable product of the Louisiana plantations. **1900** *Congress. Rec.* 19 Jan. 992/2 Without the use of the mails, clearly they would be powerless to survive, as was the Louisiana lottery.

2. a. In the specific names of birds found in the Louisiana area.

See also LOUISIANA HERON, TANAGER, WATER THRUSH.

1823 James *Exped.* I. 263 *Musicapa* (*Tyrannus*, Cuv.) *Ludovicianus*—Louisiana fly-catcher, Lath. **1831** AUDUBON *Ornith. Biog.* I. 78 The name of *Louisiana Flag* is the one commonly given [the blue yellow-backed warbler]. **1839** *Ib.* V. 30 Louisiana Hawk. *Falco Harrisii.* **1858** BAIRD *Birds Pacific R.R.* 325 Louisiana shrike. . . . South Atlantic and Gulf States. **1883** *Nat. Museum Bul.* No. 27, 155 Louisiana Clapper Rail. Salt-water marshes of Gulf coast. **1917** *Birds of Amer.* III. 169 Pipit. . . . [Also called] Louisiana Lark.

b. In the specific names of plants found in or adapted to Louisiana.

1827 *Western Mo. Rev.* I. 82 The kinds of cotton which are chiefly cultivated, are Louisiana, green seed, or Tennessee. **1889** VASEY *Agric. Grasses* 23 *Paspalum platycaule* . . . has sometimes been called Louisiana grass.

+**Louisiana cession.** (See LOUISIANA TREATY.)

+**Louisiana heron.** An American species of heron (*Hydranassa tricolor ruficollis*) especially abundant in the South. — **1813** WILSON *Ornithology* VIII. 13 Louisiana Heron: *Ardea ludoviciana;* . . . [is] found on the swampy river shores of South Carolina. **1828** BONAPARTE *Synopsis* 305 The Louisiana Heron . . . inhabits during the fine season, the south and south-western states. **1844** *Nat. Hist. N.Y., Zoology* II. 223 The Louisiana Heron . . . may be considered as an accidental visiter. **1917** *Birds of Amer.* I. 189/1 The Louisiana Heron ranks among the most abundant Herons in this country.

+**Louisiana Purchase.** The purchase by the United States from France in 1803 of her territorial claims in North America; the territory so obtained. — **1874** *Iowa State Hist. Soc. Tenth Rep.* 33 (*caption*), The Philosophy of the History of the Louisiana Purchase. **1887** *Amer. Hist. Assn. Papers* II. 43 The western boundary of the Louisiana Purchase was the dividing line of the Rocky Mountains. **1898** *Kansas City Star* 18 Dec. 6/2 Jefferson did not claim credit for that greatest of land trades, the Louisiana purchase. **1900** *Congress. Rec.* 30 Jan. 1313/1 There were some 30,000 people settled about the mouth of the Mississippi at the time of the Louisiana Purchase.

+**Louisiana stock.** Interest-bearing certificates issued in 1803 by the United States government in payment for the Louisiana Purchase. — **1812** *Ann. 12th Congress* 1 Sess. 1434 The Louisiana six per cent. stock is said to be generally from ½ to 1 per cent. below par. *Ib.*, It is believed that this object [bringing it back to par] would be promoted by making the Louisiana stock transferable . . . from the Treasury books to those of the Commissioners of Loans.

+**Louisiana tanager.** An American tanager (*Piranga ludoviciana*) found chiefly in the Rocky Mountain and Pacific coast region. — **1811** WILSON *Ornithology* III. 27 Louisiana Tanager. . . . This bird, and the two others . . . were discovered, in the remote regions of Louisiana, by an exploring party. **1839** AUDUBON *Ornith. Biog.* V. 90 [The] Louisiana Tanager . . . [is] common in the woods and oak groves of the Columbia. **1874** COUES *Birds N.W.* 83 The elegant Louisiana Tanager has been ascertained to breed in the vicinity of Laramie Peak. **1917** *Birds of Amer.* III. 78 [The name] Louisiana Tanager . . . is inappropriate now; for the bird is only a rare migrant in the Louisiana of to-day.

+**Louisiana territory.** The area acquired by the Louisiana Purchase, or that part of it lying outside the present limits of the state of Louisiana. — **1806** *Ann. 9th Congress* 2 Sess. 1137 Nature has marked with a distinguishing feature, the line established by Congress, between the Orleans and Louisiana Territories. **1900** *Congress. Rec.* 19 Feb. 1947/2 The Louisiana territory, Florida, Texas, California, New Mexico, Oregon, and Alaska have all been acquired under our Constitution.

+**Louisiana treaty.** The treaty (1803) between the United States and France by which the Louisiana territory was sold to the United States. Also *Louisiana cession.* — **1822** in *N. Amer. Rev.* XXIII. 408 Subjects of discussion between the two countries [France and the U.S. include] . . . *the question arising under the Louisiana treaty.* . . . I must object to uniting the Louisiana question to that of claims for indemnity. **1826** *Ib.* 410 Such is the subject of the controversy relative to the interpretation of the eighth article of the Louisiana cession.

+**Louisiana water thrush.** The large-billed water thrush or wagtail (*Seiurus motacilla*) found throughout the eastern United States. — **1831** AUDUBON *Ornith. Biog.* I. 99 The Louisiana Water Thrush. *Turdus Ludovicianus.* **1839** *Ib.* V. 287, I cannot after all distinguish between the Louisiana Water Thrush and the Common Water Thrush. **1917** *Birds of Amer.* III. 153/1 The Louisiana Water-Thrush is one of the comparatively few birds that walk.

+**Louisianian,** *n.* and *a.* **1.** *n.* A native or resident of the region or state of Louisiana. **2.** *adj.* Of or pertaining to Louisiana. — **(1) 1775** ADAIR *Indians* 240 [This will] shew our southern . . . colonies what they may still expect from the masterly abilities of the French Louisianians. **1814** BRACKENRIDGE *Views La.* 146 Louisianians, you have now become truly Americans. **1866** 'F. KIRKLAND' *Bk. Anecdotes* 454 The valiant Louisianian saved his cotton. **1922** MAGRUDER *Hist. Louisiana* 411 Louisianians are no longer necessarily of French and Spanish blood. **(2) 1835** INGRAHAM *South-West* I. 101 Americans, that is to say, Anglo Americans as distinguished from the Louisianian French. **1901** MOHR *Plant Life Ala.* 430 Asiatic or Common Day-flower. . . . [Grows in] Carolinian and Louisianian areas.

Lounge. A sofa or upholstered couch. {1895–}

1830 WATSON *Philadelphia* 183 Formerly they had couches of worsted damask . . . in lieu of what we now call sophas or lounges. **1845** *Knickerb.* XXV. 446 The hard-bottomed chairs were the same, and the lounge, and the tall mahogany clock. **1873** ALDRICH *Marjorie Daw* iii, I lie from morning till night on a lounge, staring into the hot street. **1887** N. PERRY *Flock of Girls* 227 Emily Irving flung herself back upon the pillows of the lounge and shouted with laughter. **1910** TOMPKINS *Mothers & Fathers* 62 'It's a shame,' Pauline concluded, . . . throwing herself down on a lounge.

attrib. **1890** CUSTER *Following Guidon* 252 With rough boards he made us inexpensive lounge-frames.

Lounging chair. A large comfortable chair suitable for lounging or reclining. {1841–} — **1856** STOWE *Dred* I. 157 Clayton . . . [sat] down in the large lounging-chair before the Window. **1876** *Wide Awake* 156/2 She went to a little marble alcove . . . and then sank down in a lounging-chair. **1905** N. DAVIS *Northerner* 193 Watson flung himself into his lounging-chair.

Loup-cervier. [F.] +=CANADA LYNX. — [**1744** A. DOBBS *Hudson's Bay* 41 The Loup Cervier, or Lynx, is of the Cat Kind, but as large as a great Dog.] **1804** CLARK in *Lewis & C. Exped.* I. (1904) 236, I line my Gloves and have a Cap made of the Skin of the *Louservia* (Lynx) (or wild Cat of the North). *a*1862 THOREAU *Maine Woods* 188 Loup cervier (or Canada lynx) were plenty yet in burnt grounds.

***Louse.** Any one of various small parasitic insects that live on animals and plants. — **1686** SEWALL *Diary* I. 158 Wm. Clendon . . . dies miserably, being almost eat up with Lice. **1737** BRICKELL *N. Carolina* 165 The Louse is not plenty in this Province. They are eaten by Rusticks for the Jaundice, and Consumption. **1789** MORSE *Amer. Geog.* 62 Of the astonishing variety of Insects found in America, we will mention . . . Gnat, Sheep Tick, Louse [etc.]. **1857** in Commons, etc. *Doc. Hist.* I. 277 The cut-worm and the louse are charged with many sins. **1882** *Vt. Agric. Rep.* VII. 76 He read a letter, asking how he can kill the lice on his cattle.

*****Lousewort.** Any one of various plants of the genus *Pedicularis*, +esp. the wood betony *P. canadensis*. Also with defining adjectives. — **1791** MUHLENBERG *Index Florae* 173 *Pedicularis, asplenifolia canadensis* Louse wort. **1843** TORREY *Flora N.Y.* II. 49 *Pedicularis lanceolata.* . . . Tall Lousewort. . . . Swamps; near New-York, and on Long Island and Staten Island. **1857** GRAY *Botany* 295 *Pedicularis Canadensis.* Common Lousewort. Wood Betony. . . . Copses and banks; common. May–July. **1901** MOHR *Plant Life Ala.* 52 These half parasites belong mostly to the figwort family, examples being Canadian lousewort . . . and several Gerardias.

*****Lousy,** *a. fig.* +Abounding in; teeming *with. colloq.*[2] — **1850** JACKSON *Forty-Niner* 11 Wednesday I struck a crevice in the bed-rock on the rim of the creek and it was lousy with gold. **1856** *Porter's Spirit of Times* 22 Nov. 194/2 The bed of the river is perfectly 'lousy' with gold.

*****Lovage.** Any one of various plants of the genus *Levisticum* or *Ligusticum* formerly grown in gardens for use in domestic remedies. — **1792** IMLAY *Western Territory* 207 Of herbs, &c. we have of the wild sort, . . . angelica, fennel, lovage. **1817–8** EATON *Botany* (1822) 336 *Ligusticum levisticum*, lovage, smellage. . . . Strong scented. **1840** DEWEY *Mass. Flowering Plants* 18 *Ligusticum Scoticum*, Lovage of the gardens, is naturalized near Boston and New Bedford. **1889** *Amer. Naturalist* XXIII. 667 Lovage . . . is yet to be rarely found in gardens.

*****Love apple.** A tomato. — *a***1817** DWIGHT I. 44 The fruits, which actually grow in New-England at the present time [include] . . . Gherkins, Running Blackberries, Love Apples or Tomatas. **1842** *Life in West* 267 The sickly flavour . . . being concealed under the beautiful skin of the love-apple. **1855** GOODRICH *Recoll.* I. 302 A row of tomatoes—a plant . . . producing little red balls, which bore the enticing name of love-apples! **1887** *Harper's Mag.* Jan. 309/1 To our grandmothers in this land the ruby fruit was given as 'love-apples.' **1891** WELCH *Recoll. 1830–40* 76 Never a tomato, as they were considered poisonous at that time, and only grown to ornament the kitchen garden, and known as love apples.

Love-cracked, *a.* Foolish or irrational from being deeply in love. *colloq.* — **1843** *Yale Lit. Mag.* VIII. 328 The most general opinion was, that he was love-cracked, and free blame was bestowed upon some inconsiderate hard-hearted beauty. **1867** 'LACKLAND' *Homespun* II. 259 One thin, little, sharp-featured woman . . . was reputed love-cracked. **1891** WILKINS *New Eng. Nun* 167 Christmas Jenny's kind of love-cracked.

Love-entangled. {1841} *local.* +The common stonecrop. — **1892** *Amer. Folk-Lore* V. 96 *Sedum acre*, love entangled. N. Ohio.

Love feast. {1610–} A religious service, esp. among Methodists, at which refreshments are eaten and religious experiences are related. {1738–}

1754 in Fries *Moravians in N.C.* II. 531 We kept a Lovefeast with the Journey Cakes, and afterwards a blessed Communion. **1788** MAY *Jrnl. & Lett.* 109 It was not long before we had a formal invitation to attend the love-feast in the afternoon. **1845** *Indiana Mag. Hist.* XXIII. 147 This brother . . . was on the circuit when I joined the church, and held the love feast when I was converted. **1909** CALHOUN *Miss Minerva* 96 She was always on hand at the Love Feast and the Missionary Rally.

+**b.** *transf.* A political jubilee, banquet, or occasion of common rejoicing.

1893 *Nation* 19 Jan. 44/1 On the evening of inauguration day the Populists held a 'love-feast.' **1896** *Chicago Record* 1 Feb. 13/1 While I was at Springfield at the Love Feast, some one broke into my office. **1904** *Charleston News & Courier* 1 Sept. 4 There will be a great Democratic love feast in which a thousand Democratic editors will take part.

Love knot. + =CRULLER. — **1805** *Pocumtuc Housewife* (1906) 34 Crullers, Matrimony or Love Knots.

Love-lies-(a)-bleeding. {1610} One or other species of amaranth. {1664–} — **1784** CUTLER in *Mem. Academy* I. 490 *Amaranthus.* . . . Bloody Amaranthus. Love-lies-a-bleeding. Princes Feather. Amongst rubbish. August. **1817–8** EATON *Botany* (1822) 169 *Amarantus melancholicus*, love-lies-bleeding. **1868** GRAY *Field Botany* 286 *Amarantus melancholicus*, Love-lies-Bleeding. Cult[ivated] from China or India. **1899** GOING *Flowers* 354 Some species of amaranth are cultivated in old fashioned gardens, and called 'cockscomb,' 'love-lies-bleeding,' and 'prince's feather.'

*****Lovely,** *a.* +(See quots. 1841 and 1883.) — **1832** FERRALL *Ramble* 169 The judge is a wonderfully lovely fellow. **1841** BUCKINGHAM *America* I. 236 The term *lovely man*, is as frequent as that of lovely woman, and neither of them has the least relation to personal beauty, but mean always a combination of talent, virtue, and affability, in the person to whom it is applied. **1883** M. ARNOLD in Horwill *Dict. Amer. Usage* (1935) 195, I am staying with Mrs. Fields here—a *lovely* woman, as they say here—which means not a sweetly beautiful woman, but what we call a 'very nice' woman. **1899** MUIRHEAD *Baedeker's U.S.* p. xxx, *Lovely*, loveable.

+**Love vine.** =DODDER. {1885–} — **1833** EATON *Botany* (ed. 6) 116 *Cuscuta americana*, dodder, love-vine. . . . A bright yellow leafless vine, twining around other weeds in damp places. **1892** *Amer. Folk-Lore* V. 101 *Cuscuta* sp., love-vine. Fort Worth, Tex. **1899** *Animal & Plant Lore* 103 *Cuscuta compacta*, a common dodder, is known as 'love-vine,' probably because it is used in love divinations. . . . Banner Elk, N.C. **1901** MOHR *Plant Life Ala.* 52 Of the parasites which fasten themselves upon the stems of their host, 6 are found in Alabama, all belonging to the dodders or love vines.

+**Lovey-dovey,** *a.* Insipid; namby-pamby. *colloq.* {1900, Austral.} — **1886** *Harper's Mag.* Dec. 134/1 Gray . . . I think looks lovey-dovey.

*****Low,** *a.* Designating various species of plants that do not attain the height of those denoted by the unmodified name. — **1817–8** EATON *Botany* (1822) 255 *Crataegus parvifolia*, low thorn. *Ib.* 261 *Cypripedium humile*, low ladies' slipper. **1836** LINCOLN *Botany* App. 148 *Vaccinium pennsylvanica*, low blue-berry. **1857** GRAY *Botany* 561 *P[oa] annua*, (Low Spear-Grass,) . . . [grows in] cultivated and waste grounds, everywhere. **1901** MOHR *Plant Life Ala.* 502 Low Whitlow-wort. . . . Dry sandy shores.

+**Low blackberry.** The low-bush blackberry or its fruit. (Cf. DEWBERRY.) — **1814** BIGELOW *Florula Bostoniensis* 122 *Rubus trivialis.* Low or running blackberry. Dewberry. . . . Fruit large, black, sweet. **1843** TORREY *Flora N.Y.* I. 216 *Rubus Canadensis.* . . . Low Blackberry. Dewberry. . . . Rocky barren fields; common. *a***1870** CHIPMAN *Notes on Bartlett* 257 *Low Blackberry.* The name, in Eastern Mass. for the fruit of the *Rubus trivialis.* **1898** CREEVEY *Flowers of Field* 451 Low Blackberry. . . . It is a shrubby, trailing plant, growing in the dust by roadsides or in dry fields. . . . From Newfoundland to Virginia, and westward.

Lowboy. {1715–} +A low dressing table equipped with drawers. (Cf. HIGHBOY.) — **1899** *House Beautiful* Aug. 140 [Picture of] antique mahogany chair and low-boy. **1904** *Atlantic Mo.* March 432 She spoke the strange name as . . . one should say a low-boy, or a settle, or a secretary. **1925** *Scribner's Mag.* July 92/1 Do you happen to have a lowboy? I would give anything for one.

+**Low-bush blackberry.** One or other species of dewberry. — **1857** GRAY *Botany* 122 *R. trivialis*, Michx. (Low Bush-Blackberry). **1860** HOLMES *Professor* viii. 235 Even the low-bush blackberry, the 'dewberry,' as our Southern neighbours call it. **1885** HAVARD *Flora W. & S. Texas* 512 *Rubus trivialis*, Mx. (Low-Bush Blackberry). Common at San Antonio and along the streams farther west and south. **1891** COULTER *Bot. W. Texas* I. 104 Low bush blackberry. A southern blackberry, apparently common in eastern, southern, and western Texas.

Low Church, *n.* {1702–} +A party or section of the Anglican or Protestant Episcopal church of the United States which regards as of minor importance the more formal or ritualistic aspects of Anglicanism. (Cf. HIGH CHURCH.) Also attrib. — **1835** REED & MATHESON *Visit* II. 74 The Episcopal church . . . is divided within itself, into two parts. They are here [in U.S.] denominated the Low Church and the High Church. **1864** NICHOLS *Amer. Life* I. 336 There are Episcopalian papers, High Church and Low Church, and ten or twelve Roman Catholic papers. **1883** *Harper's Mag.* Oct. 800/1 Dr. Washburn held the views entertained by the great body of Low-Church Episcopalians.

+**Low cornel.** A low plant of the dogwood family. (Cf. CORNEL.) — **1850** S. F. COOPER *Rural Hours* 85 The low-cornel is opening. **1869** FULLER *Flower Gatherers* 72 The *canadensis* is an interesting species. It is usually called Low Cornel.

*****Low country.** A region or area of comparatively slight elevation.

1797 *Last Advice of C. Pettigrew to Sons* (Univ. N.C. MS.), You may think it best to sell your possessions in this low country, and to move westwardly. **1803** *Steele P.* I. 396 This part of the County being the first healthful fertile lands above the low country. **1823** JAMES *Exped.* I. 38 Here commences the low country, which extends west to the Mississippi. **1869** TOURGEE *Toinette* (1881) 114 He came from somewhere down in the low country.

b. Attrib. with *lawyer, planter, society.*

1827 SHERWOOD *Gaz. Georgia* 170 Those who have not enjoyed your low country polite society. **1832** KENNEDY *Swallow Barn* I. 247 The law-suit . . . , having exercised the ingenuity of all the low-country lawyers . . . , has now turned into a fox-chace [*sic*]. **1893** *Harper's Mag.* Feb. 439 [The] wooden structure . . . had been built originally by a low-country planter,

*****Low-down,** *a.* +Mean, degraded, contemptible. — **1869** TOURGEE *Toinette* (1881) 242 Betty Certain, a low-down, scheming, poor-white woman, queening it at Lovett Lodge! **1884** 'MARK TWAIN' *H. Finn* 18, I was so ignorant, and so kind of low-down and ornery. **1898** CANFIELD *Maid of Frontier* 109, I've seen low-down greasers playin' three-card. **1919** HOUGH *Sagebrusher* 121 Nothing's too low down for him.

+**Low-downer.** A poor white or cracker. — **1868** *Putnam's Mag.* I. 706/1 When . . . candidates refreshed their adherents by the barrelfull [*sic*] the low-downer enjoyed his periodical benders without expense. **1871** DE VERE 45 A *corn cracker* . . . appears as *Conch* or *Low Downer* in North Carolina. **1883** STEVENSON *Silverado Sq.* 131 They are at least known by a generic byword, as Poor Whites or Low-downers.

+**Low-down people.** The crackers, poor whites, or 'white trash' in some of the southern states. — **1868** *Putnam's Mag.* I. 704 That wretched caste commonly spoken of as the 'mean whites,' . . . but in my district as the 'low-down people.' **1869** *Overland Mo.* III. 130 There are the delusive 'kettlings,' among the 'low-down' people.

*****Low Dutch,** *n.* Dutch; the language spoken by American colonists from the Netherlands. {1764–} — **1759** *Boston Gazette* 8 Oct., A white Girl . . . who talks good English, high and low Dutch. **1779** *N.J. Archives* 2 Ser. III. 610 Run away . . . a negroe man . . . talks good English and Low Dutch.

Low Dutch, *a.* +Of or pertaining to the Dutch colonists in America or their language. Also *Low Dutchman.* — **1776** *N.J. Archives* 2 Ser. I. 554 A Low-Dutchman named Peter Denny, has black curly hair. **1779**

N.H. Hist. Soc. Coll. VI. 312 The inhabitants are chiefly Low Dutch, and they worship wholly in that way. **1790** S. DEANE *New-Eng. Farmer* 34/1 The savoy, the cauliflower, and the low-dutch cabbages are common in this country. **1809** IRVING *Knickerb.* VII. vi, Peter stumped to and fro . . . whistling a low dutch psalm tune. **1823** COOPER *Pioneers* viii, The Germans, or 'High Dutchers,' as they were called, to distinguish them from the original or Low Dutch colonists, were a very peculiar people.

Lower country. A country or region of less elevation than that adjoining it. — **1789** *Ann. 1st Congress* I. 160 The people . . . in the back parts . . . consumed five times as much salt as the lower country, and would pay the tax in the same proportion. **1815** *Niles' Reg.* IX. 15/2 The same hostile disposition of the lower tribes has thrown impediments in the way in the lower country. **1837** *S. Lit. Messenger* III. 119 The lower country was indented with creeks. **1857** STROTHER *Virginia* 106 An acquaintance of mine in the lower country had a mocking-bird.

+**Lower Creeks.** *pl.* **1.** The Creek Indians living along the middle or lower Chattahoochee river on the Alabama-Georgia border. In full *Lower Creek Indians.* Now hist. **2.** The Seminole Indians. — **(1) 1734** *Georgia Col. Rec.* III. 416 He has already, by Presents, attached the Lower Creeks to the Service of your Majesty. **1739** W. STEPHENS *Proc. Georgia* 421 He had the Friendship of the Lower and Upper Creek Indians secured to us. **1800** HAWKINS *Sk. Creek Country* 56 Here is the public establishment for the Lower Creeks; and here the agent resides. **(2) 1789** *Amer. State P.: Indian Affairs* I. 15 The Creeks are principally within the limits of the United States, but some of the most southern towns of the Lower Creeks, or Seminoles, are within the territory of Spain, stretching toward the point of Florida.

***Lower house.** The popular and more representative branch of a legislative body, +as of a colonial, state, or Indian legislative assembly, or the national House of Representatives.

1666 *Md. Archives* II. 11 They would be pleased to admitt the Lower House to be present at the Piscattoway Indians Conference. **1709** *Mass. H. S. Coll.* 3 Ser. VII. 69 Several [men] then, of the lower house, were for allowing thirty pounds. **1789** MACLAY *Deb. Senate* 13 By the Constitution of Massachusetts, the Senate have a right of communicating bills to their Lower House. **1837** *Diplom. Corr. Texas* I. (1908) 194 The Committe[e] on Foreign affairs of the lower House, reported a resolution. **1891** O'BEIRNE *Leaders Ind. Territory* 205/2 [Frazier] attended the council meeting at Tuskahoma, where he was appointed journalist of the lower house. **1902** E. C. MEYER *Nominating Systems* 19 The same primary will in a city choose delegates . . . to the assembly district convention, which nominates candidates for the lower house of the state legislature.

Lower party. +During the Revolutionary War, a faction among the Americans in New York favorable to the British. *Obs.* — **1789** ANBUREY *Travels* II. 482 What are termed these Upper and Lower Parties are mostly known to each other, and possess great inveteracy on both sides. **1831** SHERBURNE *Memoirs App.* 294 We asked him 'what party?' He replied 'the lower party.'

+**Lower settlement.** **1.** *pl.* (Capitalized.) The settlements of the Cherokee Indians living in South Carolina and northeastern Georgia. **2.** *sing.* A settlement situated or regarded as being at a place lower than another or others. — **(1) 1725** in *Travels Amer. Col.* 110 The head Men of the Lower Settlements had waited upon their King. **(2) 1825** *Austin P.* (1924) II. 1209 Could the men from the lower settlements be safely drawn from there?

+**Low-flung,** *a.* =LOW-DOWN, *a. colloq.* — **1844** *Knickerb.* XXIII. 506 Who wants a parcel of low-flung, 'outside barbarians' to go in cahoot with us? **1850** LEWIS *La. Swamp Doctor* 122 [A beginning medical student] is classed with free negroes, rowdies, and low-flung draymen. **1853** BALDWIN *Flush Times Ala.* 24 [He] denounced Jefferson as a low-flung demagogue. **1893** M. A. OWEN *Voodoo Tales* 64 Time someun teach dat low-flung red-head mannehs.

Low ground. =BOTTOM LAND. {1662– (s.v. *Ground*)}

1659 *R.I. Col. Rec.* I. 464 In all meadowes, Swamps and low ground. **1687** *Ib.* III. 227. **1750** T. WALKER *Journal* 36 This night we lodged in Adam Beard's low grounds. **1796** MORSE *Univ. Geog.* I. 680 The swamps and low grounds on the rivers . . . producing naturally canes in great plenty. **1841** *S. Lit. Messenger* VII. 452/1 The level land, called in Virginia low grounds, extends in many places for more than a mile. **1898** PAGE *Red Rock* 178 The far-off call of ploughmen to their teams in the low-grounds of Red Rock.

+**b.** *Low-ground corn,* corn planted or grown in low-lying land.

1802 *Steele P.* I. 249 The squirrels eat half of the low ground corn before it was fit to Geather. **1885** *Century Mag.* April 849/1 Everybody had to complain of the ravages made by crows and blackbirds on the newly planted low-ground corn.

***Lowland.**

***1.** Low-lying land, as that along a stream. Usu. pl.

1654 *Providence Rec.* I. 89 The said house & housing with all the Landes both upland and Lowland marshes meddowes . . . whatso Ever. **1698** *Ib.* VI. 203 All the said lands both upland & lowlands. **1717** *Ib.* XVI. 333 All my Right of Low lands and meadows Lieing by Pochaset River. **1779** G. R. CLARK *Campaign in Ill.* (1869) 66 We got to the low Lands of the River Umbara, which we found deep in water. **1836** J. HALL *Statistics of West* 30 The lowlands which border on the river Ohio. **1898** *Mo. So. Dakotan* I. 110 The third [bench] blends with the second, and makes up the remaining low lands. **1913** MORLEY *Carolina Mts.* 49 One sees . . . the lowlands . . . lending a misty blue to the level landscape.

2. *attrib.* and *comb.* **a.** With *farmer, hay,* etc., in sense: Situated in, belonging to, or produced in, lowlands.

1740 *Georgia Col. Rec.* IV. 670 Many of the low Land Swamps covered with Canes. **1856** *S. Lit. Messenger* XXII. 177/1 If the mountain farmer must dig roads on sideling ground, the low-land farmer must drain his wet lands. **1872** *Harper's Mag.* June 23/1 Having driven cattle in his youth, he had recollections and anecdotes of sundry visits to the lowland towns. **1874** *Vermont Bd. Agric. Rep.* II. 412 For winter feed they will do well on all early cut, upland kinds of hay, together with most kinds of lowland hay.

+**b.** In the specific names of American plants.

1785 MARSHALL *Amer. Grove* 123 This [Water Red Oak] is generally known by the name of water or Low Land Spanish Oak. **1815** DRAKE *Cincinnati* ii. 82 The most valuable timber trees are the . . . white, black, low-land chestnut and bur oaks.

Lowlander. One who lives in the lowlands. {1692–} — **1833** *Md. Hist. Mag.* XIII. 350 We passed on the way the Country seats of several wealthy lowlanders. **1849** *S. Lit. Messenger* XV. 80/2 It was common, in old times, for Lowlanders in Virginia to spend the summer in the mountains. **1878** BEADLE *Western Wilds* 478 The lowlander, whom business or a love of novelty and wild scenery leads to climb one of the mountains around Georgetown.

+**Low maple.** A mountain maple, *Acer spicatum.* — **1813** MUHLENBERG *Cat. Plants* 95 Mountain maple or low maple. **1832** BROWNE *Sylva* 102 It is sometimes called Low Maple, from the dwarfish stature of the tree. **1897** SUDWORTH *Arborescent Flora* 282 *Acer spicatum.* Mountain Maple. . . . [Also called] Low Maple (Tenn.).

+**Low middling.** A grade used in estimating the quality of ginned cotton. — **1863** 'E. KIRKE' *Southern Friends* 53 '[Have you] any cotton?' 'Only eleven bales—low middling.' **1868** *Rep. Comm. Agric. 1867* 420 Off three acres he raised three bales, and nicely picked it so as to class a strictly 'low middling' in market. **1887** *Courier-Journal* 17 Jan. 7/6 Cotton market was dull; middling 9 1/16c; low middling 8 3/4c.

Low-neck. A gown or dress cut low in the neck. {*attrib.* 1901–} — **1885** HOWELLS *S. Lapham* xiii, I've heard that people go to dinner in low-necks. **1904** A. DALE *Wanted, a Cook* 169 Mary Ann inherits five million dollars, and becomes a society girl, in pink chiffon and low-neck.

Low-post(ed) bedstead. A bedstead the supporting posts of which are comparatively low. (Cf. HIGH-POST BEDSTEAD.) — **1813** in Rothert *Muhlenberg Co.* 32, I give and bequeath . . . the low posted bed stead. **1848** COOPER *Oak Openings* I. 80 Two common low-post maple bedsteads were soon uncorded and carried off. **1856** M. J. HOLMES *L. Rivers* 29 In the corner stood the old low-post bedstead.

Low-pressure, *a.* Of engines or boats: Operated or propelled by steam under a low degree of pressure. {1833–} — **1827** *Hallowell* (Me.) *Gaz.* 20 June 2/3 [The boat] has elegant accommodations—a good low pressure engine. **1883** 'MARK TWAIN' *Life on Miss.* l, In March, 1825, General Lafayette left New Orleans for St. Louis on the low-pressure steamer *Natchez.*

+**Low-quarter shoe.** A shoe which does not reach above the ankle; a low shoe. Also *low-quarter* — **c1862** BAGBY *Old Va. Gentleman* 73 Give me a straw hat, an oznaburg shirt, no waistcoat, . . . and a pair of low-quarter shoes, moderately thick-soled. **1880** 'MARK TWAIN' *Tramp Abroad* 275 He wore. . . very low-quarter patent-leather shoes, tied with black ribbon. **1902** G. C. EGGLESTON *D. South* 103 You want to . . . substitute low quarter shoes for your riding boots. **1912** COBB *Back Home* 15 The old judge sat at an open window with his low-quarter shoes off. **1916** *Dialect Notes* IV. 269 *Low-quarters,* Oxford shoes.

Low room. A combined living room and kitchen on the first floor. *Obs.* — **1708** *Boston News-Letter* 4–11 Oct. 4/2 A Convenient Dwelling House, having a Cellar, Low Room, Chamber and Garret, . . . to be Lett.

+**Low-studded,** *a.* Having short or low studs; built with a low ceiling. — **1854** SHILLABER *Mrs. Partington* 16 A tall man could not stand erect in the low-studded room. **1873** ALDRICH *Marjorie Daw* 155, [I] found myself in a long, low-studded bar-room. **1897** F. C. MOORE *How to Build a Home* 7 It is mistaken economy to have a low-studded cellar.

Low wine. The weak liquor that comes over first in distilling. {1641–} Also fig. — **1794** *Ann. 3d Congress* 1460 Every rectifier of low wines, or other distilled spirits, . . . shall enter at some office of inspection, all or any such low wines. **1816** *Ann. 14th Congress* 2 Sess. 1206 Distillation . . . to run off 15 gallons of low wines, which contain about 4 per cent. whiskey. **1878** BEADLE *Western Wilds* 35 They was poor as the low-wines o' pond-water.

***Loyal,** *n.* ‖=LOYALIST 1. — **1809** FRENEAU *Poems* I. 277 There, Loyals, there, with loyal hearts retire.

***Loyal,** *a.* +Faithful to or in sympathy with the North during the Civil War. Now hist. — **1863** Moore *Rebellion Rec.* V. I. 57 Hundreds of citizens of the West and other portions of the loyal States fled into 'Canada like cravens, to escape the draft.' **1866** Fleming *Hist. Reconstruction* I. 98 [These] Unionists . . . looked upon the enfranchisement of the loyal negroes as the salvation of the whole loyal element. **1876** *N. Amer. Rev.* July 240 A refuge for the patriotism forbidden loyal Kentuckians within the limits of their own Commonwealth. **1884** BLAINE *20 Years of Congress* I. 435 The line of partisan division had been practically obliterated in the Loyal States.

Loyalist. {1647–}

+**1.** During the Revolutionary War, an American who favored the British cause. Now hist.

1779 *N.J. Archives* 2 Ser. III. 291 These are worthies by Mr. Robertson, of New-York, in his Royal American Gazette of the 15th instant, called loyalists. **1790** FANNING *Narrative* 5, I was obliged now for to secret myself in the woods, and was supplied with provition by some Quakers, and other Loyalists. **1821** COOPER *Spy* ii, The loyalists . . . adopted such measures as best accorded with their different characters. **1874** BANCROFT *Hist. U.S.* X. 481 It taught the loyalists of North Carolina that they could put no trust in the promises of British generals. **1903** K. M. ABBOTT *Old Paths & Legends New Eng.* 305 The year 1776, when loyalists and patriots alike already longed for peace.

+**2.** During the Civil War, an adherent of the Union or northern side. Now hist.

1862 in Moore *Rebellion Rec.* V. II. 4 The murderous bushwhacker made an effort to deceive, by first saying they were Bill Richmond's company, a band of loyalists. **1865** RICHARDSON *Secret Service* 20 They were about equally divided into enthusiastic Secessionists . . . and quasi Loyalists. **1866** LOWELL *Writings* V. 324 We have nothing to do with the number of actual loyalists at the South, but with the number of possible ones.

Loyal League. +A secret organization fostered among the Negroes toward the close of the Civil War and immediately thereafter, seeking to secure for them their social and political rights. Now hist. — **1865** *Nation* I. 194 The colored men are forming a Loyal League, which is likely to be a numerous body. **1867** in Fleming *Hist. Reconstruction* II. 11 By means of this Loyal League these grand purposes may be realized. **1871** *Ku Klux Klan Rep.* VIII. 357 They then commenced the establishment of these Loyal Leagues, into which they got almost every negro in the country. **1877** BEARD *K.K.K. Sketches* 25 Favored by this condition of public affairs, that remarkable secret order—the Loyal League—found its way into the Southern country.

+**Loyal Leaguer.** A member of the Loyal League. *Obs.* — **1864** G. SALA in *Daily Telegraph* 23 Aug. (Th. S.), This last dirty move of the Loyal Leaguers to spite the Copperheads in view of the Chicago Convention. **1871** *Congress. Globe* 12 April 604/1 These outrages perpetrated by the Ku Klux and by the Loyal Leaguers.

+**Lubber grasshopper. 1.** A large, clumsy, short-winged grasshopper (*Rhomalea microptera*) of the Southeast. **2.** A similar grasshopper (*Brachystola magna*) of the West. — **(1) 1877** *Field & Forest* II. 160 The 'Lubber' grasshopper [is the] large grasshopper *Romalia microptera.* **(2) 1885** KINGSLEY, etc. *Riverside Nat. Hist.* (1888) II. 194 The 'Lubber Grasshopper,' or the Clumsy Locust, of the plains, *Brachystola magna*, . . . [is] confined to the central portion of North America. **1889** *Cent.* 653/2 *B. magna* is a large clumsy locust, common on the western plains of North America, where it is known as the lubber grasshopper.

Lubricator. {1756–} + = GREASER 1. *jocular.* — **1872** C. KING *Mountaineering in Sierra Nevada* 285 'String him up!' 'Burn the dog-goned lubricator.'

Lucern(e). A European fabaceous plant (*Medicago sativa*) widely cultivated in the West for forage and pasture; alfalfa; the seed of this plant. {1626–} Also attrib. — **1739** E. LUCAS *Jrnls. & Lett.* 5 Wrote my father . . . on the pains I had taken to bring the Indigo, . . . Lucern and Casada to perfection. **1760** WASHINGTON *Diaries* I. 148 The residue of them, viz. 4, was sowd with Lucerne Seed. **1781–2** JEFFERSON *Notes Va.* (1788) 40 Our grasses are lucerne, . . . greensward, blue grass, and crab grass. **1817** BRADBURY *Travels* 326 The emigrant . . . should take with him . . . a small quantity of lucerne, saintfoin, and vetches. **1848** ROBINSON *Santa Fe Exped.* 63 A species of lucerne almost ready to bloom is now furnished to us for our horses. **1883** *Harper's Mag.* Oct. 705/2 Utah would have found it as difficult to struggle into permanent existence without lucern as the early Britons without . . . acorns.

***Lucifer.** A friction match, esp. one tipped with antimony sulphide and potassium chlorate. {1831–} — **1835–7** HALIBURTON *Clockmaker* 1 Ser. xxiii. 214 Having lighted it [a cigar] by a lucifer, and ascertained that it was 'true in draft,' he resumed his reins. **1850** COLTON *3 Years Calif.* 259 [We] fired them [leaves] with a lucifer which had been given us by a traveller an hour before. **1869** J. R. BROWNE *Adv. Apache Country* 453 Here's Richmond—this crushed box of lucifers; and here's Jeff Davis—a smashed oyster! **1900** *Congress. Rec.* 5 Feb. 1521/2 They would have burned them, but the lucifers would not work well.

Lucifer match. = prec. {1831–} Also attrib. — **1843** *Amer. Pioneer* II. 251 They had not the advantage of modern lucifer matches. **1848** *Knickerb.* XVIII. 225 A little blue star hung for a moment in the air, accompanied by the sulphureous smell of a Lucifer match. **1886** POORE *Reminisc.* I. 108 Another new invention of that epoch [*c*1829] was the lucifer match-box, which superseded the large tin tinder-box with its flint and steel. **1891** WELCH *Recoll. 1830–40* 421 Then came the 'Lucifer matches,' drawn forcibly through a fold of sand paper.

+**Lucivee.** Also **leusifee, lucervee,** etc. *N.E.* [Colloq. forms of LOUP-CERVIER.] The Canada lynx, or the skin of this animal.

Cf. LUZERNE.

1791 *Mass. Laws 1780–1800* (1801) I. 509 No person . . . shall hereafter, in either of the months of June, July, August or September . . . kill any Otter . . . Fisher or Black-Cat, Leusifee [etc.]. [**1823** COBBETT *Rural Rides* (1885) I. 371 When in New Brunswick I saw the great wild grey cat, which is there called a Lucifee.] **1860** *Harper's Mag.* Feb. 302/1 'Keep still, Cap'n,' says I, 'he's after that lucive.' **1871** DE VERE 370 The *Lucyver* of Maine, a wildcat or lynx, has . . . no right whatever to a name so nearly akin to Lucifer. **1893** ROOSEVELT *Wilderness Hunter* 153 The marks which showed the loping progress of the sable, . . . the round pads of the lucivee, and many others. **1903** *N.Y. Tribune* 18 Oct., The lynx has almost entirely disappeared. In the Maine woods it is called lucervee, a corruption of the French loupcervier.

***Luck. 1.** *In luck,* fortunate. {1857–} +**2.** Attrib. with *ball, egg.* — **(1) 1835** HOFFMAN *Winter in West* I. 240 Wolves . . . come howling round the house after nightfall, and if one is 'in luck' at all, are easily shot. **1894** *Harper's Mag.* June 144/1 We're in luck to find a hotel. **1902** WISTER *Virginian* 300 We'll be in luck if we make any Sunk Creek this night. **(2) 1893** M. A. OWEN *Voodoo Tales* 169 Aunt Mymee . . . [suffered] the loss of her most powerful fetich, the luck-ball she had talked to and called by her own name. **1899** *Animal & Plant Lore* 12 The small eggs dropped at the end of the laying season are kept under the name of 'luck eggs' to bring good fortune to the owner. Maine and Northern Ohio.

Lucky. Short for LUCKY STONE b: (see quotation). — **1897** *Outing* Aug. 436 No boy cared to hook and lose a sheepshead, and none would dream of casting away the dead fish without first 'gettin' his luckies.'

Lucky bag. {1825–} +'A receptacle on a man-of-war for all clothes and other articles of private property carelessly left by their owners' (*Cent.*). — **1840** *S. Lit. Messenger* VI. 233/2 Every man-of-war, you know, has her *lucky bag,* containing a little of everything, and something belonging to everybody. **1884** S. B. LUCE *Seamanship* 310.

Lucky stone. a. A stone thought to bring good luck. {1848–, *dial.*} **b.** (See quot. 1897). — **1897** *Outing* Aug. 435 In the head of this [sheepshead] fish are two enamel-like substances, roughly circular in shape, and about the size of a nickel in the larger specimens. These were termed 'lucky stones.' **1899** *Animal & Plant Lore* 11 Smoothly polished pebbles are carried for good luck, and are called 'lucky stones.' Chestertown, Md.

+**Lucy Long.** ?A kind of minstrel dance. Also transf. — **1860** in Christy *Ethiopian Joke Book No. 3* viii, Mr. George Christy . . . danced his favourite 'Lucy Long' with such artistic grace and ease, as to draw the encomiums of the audience. **1869** *Atlantic Mo.* July 77/1 In addition to my jig, I . . . took the principal lady part in negro ballets, and danced 'Lucy Long.' **1870** in O. Logan *Before Footlights* 341 [His] wife was no other than some Lucy Long, or Coal-black Rose from Virginia.

+**Lucy's warbler.** A warbler (*Vermivora luciae*) of the Southwest and the Pacific coast. — **1869** *Amer. Naturalist* III. 476 [Among] the first birds which I could consider as probably the leaders of the summer migration, . . . [was] *Helminthophaga Luciæ,* or Lucy's Warbler. **1917** *Birds of Amer.* III. 119/1 Lucy's Warbler frequents chiefly willow and mesquite thickets.

+**Luffee.** *local.* [Cf. Du. *liefje* and Eng. *lovey.*] (See quotation.) — **1744** A. HAMILTON *Itinerarium* (1907) 90 The young men here [at Albany, N.Y.] call their sweethearts *luffees,* and a young fellow of eighteen is reckoned a simpleton if he has not a luffee.

Lug.[1] {*a*1616–} +**1.** (See quotation.) +**2.** *To put* (or *pile*) *on lugs,* to put on airs. *colloq.* — **(1) 1828** WEBSTER, *Lug,* . . . something heavy to be drawn or carried. (*Vulgar.*) **(2) 1889** MUNROE *Golden Days* 188 If you notice me . . . piling on any lugs, . . . you just bump me down hard. **1896** ADE *Artie* vi. 54 The family did n't put on no such lugs in them days. **1920** LEWIS *Main Street* 326 Oh, the lugs he puts on—belted coat, and piqué collar.

***Lug.**[2] *pl.* +The lower leaves of a tobacco plant; the poorest grade of tobacco. — **1835** J. MARTIN *Descr. Virginia* 175 An eminent tobacco manufacturer of Richmond has offered . . . to take all of their tobacco, (lugs included) at $10 a hundred. **1868** *N.Y. Herald* 1 July 1868 9/3 Lugs, per lb. [Market Quotation]. **1887** *Courier-Journal* 7 Feb. 7/1 The Spanish buyer is the principal bidder for lugs. **1896** P. A. BRUCE *Econ. Hist. Virginia* I. 442 The lowest grade [of tobacco] was known as lugs as early as 1686.

***Luggage.** Goods in general; the baggage of an army; the baggage of a traveler or passenger. Also fig.

See BAGGAGE 2, note.

1634 WOOD *New Eng. Prospect* (1865) 108 These baskets be of all sizes from a quart to a quarter, in which they carry their luggage. **1675** in I. Mather *K. Philip's War* (1862) 247 How many your honors will Alow to each Company for Cariage of Lugage and transporting souldiers. **1775** *R.I. Hist. Soc.* VI. 5 We had some sleds and oxen to assist us in carrying our Luggage. **1837** *S. Lit. Messenger* III. 233/2 On the morning of my leaving Mountain View, the Angler came for my luggage. **1843** *Knickerb.* XXII. 563 Fifteen darkeys . . . stand ready . . . to take your luggage. **1868** M. H. SMITH *Sunshine & Shadow* 315 The baggage-master . . . had charge of all luggage that came or went. **1875** *Congress. Rec.* 20 March 118/2 This resolution . . . is part of the luggage belonging to the swindle. **1910** J. HART *Vigilante Girl* 15 The passengers were descending from the steamer, and the cabin luggage was sliding out of the chutes.

b. Attrib. with *boat, car, case,* etc.

Quot. 1868 is Mrs. Hawthorne's alteration of the MS. of 1850 (1932 ed. p. 245), which read 'baggage men.'

1814 *Niles' Reg.* VI. 226/2 John L. Sullivan, of Boston, has obtained a patent for the use of steam engine power in towing luggage boats. **1841** *Knickerb.* XVII. 153 Your two pointer dogs . . . are locked up in the luggage-car. **1868** HAWTHORNE *Note-Books* II. 150 A moment passes while the luggage-men are putting on [the train] the trunks and packages. **1878** JACKSON *Travel at Home* 6 All varieties of American, I heard during thirty minutes in that luggage-shed. **1897** *Outing* XXIX. 488/2 Those not so armed carried revolvers, and had canvas luggage-cases in the diamond of their wheels.

+**Lug pole.** A pole on which a kettle is hung in a fireplace. Now hist. — **1773** *Mass. Gazette* Suppl. 4 Feb. 1/2 This Accident was supposed to be occasioned by a Defect in the Chimney, by Reason of the Wooden Lug-Pole burning out. **1842** Kirkland *Forest Life* II. 210 A huge 'lug-pole,' supported on crotches, receives the kettles. **1848** Drake *Pioneer Life Ky.* 107 The tea kettle swung from a wooden 'lug pole.' **1888** Venable *Footprints Pioneers Ohio Val.* 117 In time the lug-pole gave place to the iron crane.

***Lull,** *v. intr.* Of the wind or sea: To die down; to diminish in force. {1836–} — **1804** Clark in *Lewis & C. Exped.* I. 86 At 7 oClock the wind luled and it Commns'd raining. **1808** Pike *Sources Miss.* 10 The wind lulling, we encamped on the point of an island. **1849** N. Kingsley *Diary* 27 Wind lulled a little this morning but freshed again at noon. **1869** Parkman *Discov. Great West* xii. 144 When at length the tempest lulled, they re-embarked.

+**Lulu.** Anything of an exceptional quality; a 'honey.' Also used adjectivally. *slang.* — **1889** A. Daly *Great Unknown* 13 Oh, that's lulu! It'll suit mamma right down to the ground. **1896** Ade *Artie* 76 Mebbe you think I ain't got a lulu of a head on me this morning. **1904** 'O. Henry' *Cabbages & Kings* xvii. 301, I smelt a million violets. She was a lulu. I told her I came in a private yacht. **1911** Quick *Yellowstone Nights* 221 It was a lulu of a Society.

***Lumber,** *n.*

***1.** Anything that takes up room, or, if left lying around, gets in the way; junk. Usually collective.

1642 *Essex Probate Rec.* I. 22 Barrells & butte[r] Cherne & other lumb., 18s. **1682** *York Deeds* V. 16 In ye darie . . . tubbs trays barrells, & other Lumber. **1774** Fithian *Journal* I. 257 Fanny & Harriot by stuffing rags & other Lumber under their Gowns [etc.]. **1804** Lewis in *L. & Clark Exped.* I. (1904) 31 The Sergt. . . . [shall] see that no cooking utensels or loos lumber of any kind is left on the deck to obstruct the passage between the burths. **1900** *Congress. Rec.* 8 Jan. 690/2 The books belonging to the Congressional Library . . . were many of them piled up in their former quarter like so much old lumber.

+**b.** Articles left lying around to clutter up a road or street.

The specific meaning of this word as illustrated in sense 2 undoubtedly arose from the fact that ship masts, sawed timber, barrel staves, etc., as important but bulky commodities, once blocked or lumbered up roads, streets, and harbors of various towns. The following quotations serve to illustrate the transition from sense 1 to sense 2.

1663 *Boston Rec.* 16 Take care that noe wood logges, Timber stonnes or any other lumber be layed upon the flatts. **1665** *Springfield Rec.* I. 334 Ordered to be . . . Removed, . . . The wood & other Lumber. **1701** *Boston Rec.* 11 Nor shall any person incumber . . . any Street, lane, or Alley . . . by laying any Stones, Earth, Timber, boards, firewood or other Lumber, therein.

+**2.** *spec.* Various pieces of wood, boards, etc.; any timber rough-sawn or finished into boards, staves, joists, etc. {=timber}

Quot. 1662 may belong to sense 1.

1662 *Suffolk Deeds* IV. 50 [We] sayled in said ship, being freighted in Boston in New England wth Beames. for houses boards. pipestaues tarr and other Lumber. **1678** E. Andros in Toppan *Randolph* II. 303 The Comoditves of the Country to ye westward are wheate . . . pipe staves, timber, lumber & horses. **1708** *R.I. Col. Rec.* IV. 60 Lumber of all sorts, viz.: staves, heading hoops, board, plank, timber. **1750** J. Birket *Cursory Remarks* 11 The Exports of this province [N.H.] are Chiefly Lumber, as Boards, Plank, Joists, Staves, Shingles. **1784** Smyth *Tour* II. 77 Their method is to . . . saw or split the trees into boards, or convert them into staves, heading, or other species of lumber. **1806** *Mass. Spy* 29 Jan. (Th.), Near 32 millions feet of lumber were exported from the flourishing town of Portland [Maine] last year. **1879** *Lumberman's Gaz.* Dec. 3 Ten cars of dressed lumber have been shipped from Gowen . . . to parties in Nebraska. **1909** Casson *Life C. H. McCormick* 198 In its yard stand as many piles of lumber as would build a fair-sized city.

+**b.** A single board. *Obs.*

1775 J. Schaw *Jrnl. Lady of Quality* (1923) 184 His grand work is a saw-mill. . . . It cuts three thousand lumbers . . . a day.

+**3.** Growing timber that is suitable for lumber.

1855 in *S. Dak. Hist. Coll.* I. 411 There is no lumber on the Little Missouri River, three miles below this post.

4. *attrib.* and *comb.* +**a.** In sense 2 with *act, bill,* etc.

1694 *N.J. Archives* XIII. 215 A bill appointing officers for executeing ye lumber Bill &c. **1715** *N.H. Prov. Papers* II. 682 Mr. Treasurer Penhallow . . . has an account of the lumber mony & excise mony. **1721** *Ib.* III. 834 A message to the house . . . for repealing the lumber Act. *a***1861** Winthrop *Open Air* 21 A Maine forest after a lumber-campaign is like France after a *coup d'état:* . . . prosperous as ever, but the great men are all gone. **1865** Kellogg *Rebel Prisons* 48 We landed on a large lumber dock, where we made a stay of several hours. **1871** Grosvenor *Protection* 115 The largest works of our chief lumber-markets. **1900** Bruncken *N. Amer. Forests* 68 Twenty years ago, Saginaw [Mich.] was the centre of the greatest lumber industry in the world. **1904** Tarbell *Hist. Standard Oil Co.* I. 7 [The rock oil] came from oil springs located in Northwestern Pennsylvania on the farm of a lumber firm.

+**b.** Designating various persons engaged in the lumbering business in some capacity or other.

1775 Romans *Nat. Hist. Florida* 117 [They] planted their baronies in the pine barrens. There let the lords be lumber cutters! **1778** *Jrnls. Cont. Congress* X. 164 The Planters and Lumber Makers in the State of Georgia had large Quantities of Rice and Lumber. **1853** Fowler *Home for All* 46 One other form of outside finish has been tried with success by Mr. Thornton, lumber dealer, in Pawtucket, R.I. **1888** *N.Y. Life* 18 Feb. 27/2 One of the 'several times' a millionaire lumber 'Barons' of Michigan. **1896** *N.Y. Wkly. Witness* 30 Dec. 13/1 A famous lumber-scaler should do the hustling. **1901** Merwin & Webster *Calumet 'K'* 11 Shake hands with Mr. Max Vogel, our lumber checker. **1916** Eastman *From Deep Woods* 160 The influence of the lumber kings.

+**c.** Designating various tracts of land covered by timber suitable for lumber.

1787 in Commons, etc. *Doc. Hist.* I. 323 Great Encouragement will be given to an Overseer . . . to manage a Rice and Lumber Plantation. **1848** *N.Y. Tribune* 22 May (B.), From Petersburgh I railed it through the North Carolina . . . lumber country. **1858** *Harper's Mag.* March 564/1 In the time of the great land-speculations in Maine, several . . . were carried away with the mania of buying lumber tracts. **1896** *Vt. Agric. Rep.* XV. 82 The Maine Commissioner . . . has posted these notices of the new law, conspicuously throughout the lumber regions.

+**d.** Designating various vessels used in the transportation of lumber.

1806 Webster 17/2 *Ark,* a lumber vessel or ship. **1835** Ingraham *South-West* I. 51 These lumber vessels . . . are . . . usually loaded with shingles, masts, spars, and boards. **1848** Bartlett 123 *Droger,* lumber droger; cotton droger, etc. A vessel built solely for burden, and for transporting cotton, lumber, and other heavy articles. **1857** *Harper's Mag.* May 741/2 He visited several taverns . . . near the river, and at length found the commander of a lumber sloop. **1914** Steele *Storm* 261 The sound of a lanyard adrift on the forward shrouds of one of the lumber-boats . . . came distinctly to my ears.

e. In sense 1 with *chest, closet, garret,* etc. (Cf. Lumber room.)

1854 Cummins *Lamplighter* 39 She introduced him into the former lumber-closet. **1857** Vaux *Villas* 90 This space can be floored and fitted with a staircase, and used as a lumber garret. **1878** Pinkerton *Strikers* 242 Besides these buildings, there were numberless smaller ones, used as sand-houses, oil-houses, and lumber-sheds. **1882** 'M. Harland' *Eve's Daughters* 366 There is danger . . . of mistaking the casket in which these treasures are stored for a lumber-chest.

+**f.** Special combinations.

Lumber berth, the headquarters in the woods for lumbering operations; *l. flume,* a flume wherein lumber logs are floated; *l. shanty,* a shanty in a lumber camp; *L. State,* a nickname for the state of Maine; *l. town,* a town where lumbermen live.

1851 Springer *Forest Life* 56 Agricultural interests have invited men far into the interior in the vicinity of lumber berths. **1857** Hammond *Northern Scenes* 198 They generally keep a barrel of old rye in the lumber shanties. **1867** *Trübner's Amer. Lit. Rec.* Aug. 41 Maine is popularly known as The Lumber or Pine-Tree State. **1877** W. Wright *Big Bonanza* 240 In order to obtain a supply of water sufficient to run two lumber-flumes, a tunnel was run. **1880** *Harper's Mag.* Aug. 354/1 A cheerful little lumber town lying high among the hills.

Lumber, *v.* {1642–} +**1.** *intr.* To engage in the lumbering business. +**2.** *tr.* To cut (forest timber) and prepare it for the market. — (1) **1809** Kendall *Travels* III. 73*n.*, The verb *to lumber* . . . has also the legitimate as well as technical sense, *to procure,* or even *to manufacture lumber:* a lumberer is one that *lumbers.* **1870** *Maine Rep.* LVI. 566 The plaintiff lumbered on his township called Holeb. **1891** *Voice* 15 Oct., [I] commenced lumbering in a small way. (2) **1891** *Ib.*, We then lumbered a million and a quarter feet a year. **1893** *Scribner's Mag.* June 711/1 They bought and lumbered timber on their own account. **1905** *Forestry Bureau Bul.* No. 60, 20 About fifteen years ago some fine black cherry was lumbered on . . . Grandfather Mountain.

+**Lumber business. a.** The business of cutting down timber, cutting it into boards, and otherwise preparing it for the market. **b.** The business of retailing lumber.

1792 Belknap *Hist. New-Hampshire* III. 211 Husbandry . . . is much preferable to the lumber business, both in point of gain, contentment and morals. **1856** *Mich. Agric. Soc. Trans.* VII. 827 The lumber business of the Saginaw river and its tributaries has been developed. **1861** *Chicago Tribune* 15 April 1 The co-partnership . . . in the lumber business, is this day dissolved. **1891** O'Beirne *Leaders Ind. Territory* 83/1 In 1872 or '73 he opened a mercantile and lumber business at Stringtown. **1896** *Vt. Agric. Rep.* XV. 79 Gov. Woodbury has spent years as superintendent of the Burlington branch of J. R. Booth's gigantic lumber business.

+**Lumber camp.** A camp serving as living quarters for lumbermen. (Cf. Camp 1 d.) — **1881** *Rep. Indian Affairs* 182 The younger men find employment in the mills and lumber-camps. **1896** *N.Y. Wkly. Witness* 30 Dec. 13/1 They had sent one of their best speakers through the hundred lumber-camps. **1900** *Congress. Rec.* 16 Jan. 875/2 You do not find the Americans working on the railroad grade or in the lumber camp. **1923** Herrick *Lilla* 91 They set out on a trail that led . . . past abandoned lumber camps.

+Lumber-carrier. 1. A vessel that carries wood or lumber. 2. = LUMBER RAFT. — (1) **1700** *N.H. Prov. Papers* III. 104 Fees . . . for coasting vessels and lumber carriers going into the said Province. **1807** JANSON *Stranger in A.* 13 The vessel, too, was not accommodated for passengers, being, in fact, a lumber-carrier. (2) **1898** *Engineering Mag.* XVI. 98 Mr. Paulsen has applied for patents on his novel lumber carrier, and he expects his raft to occupy a place beside the whaleback.

+Lumber company. A company that cuts and markets lumber. — **1892** *Vt. Agric. Rep.* XII. 138 Lumber companies at Newport now own timber lands in Canada sufficient to supply their mills for the next quarter century. **1897** BRODHEAD *Bound in Shallows* 6 He was with the Jonas Lumber Company. **1904** *Springfield W. Repub.* 9 Sept. 11 The annual drive of logs down the river by the Connecticut Valley lumber company has reached its final destination.

Lumbered, *a.* {1745-} +Of land: Cut over for its lumber. — **1869** W. MURRAY *Adventures* 16 A lumbered district is the most dreary and dismal region the eye . . . ever beheld. **1905** *Forestry Bureau Bul.* No. 63, 18 The burning over of the lumbered area favors a thick growth of gray birch.

+Lumberer. One who fells forest trees and brings them to market; a lumberjack.

1809 KENDALL *Travels* III. 77 The lumberer . . . descends the river . . . to find a purchaser. **1821** W. DALTON *Travels U.S.* 217 These lumberers are, generally speaking, the most ferocious part of the population of America. **1842** *Pres. Mess. & P.* IV. 123 The hunters . . . occasionally visit the country and the lumberers . . . search it for timber. **1848** THOREAU *Maine Woods* 25 The spikes . . . the lumberers wear in their boots to prevent their slipping on wet logs. **1878** EMERSON *Fortune of Repub.* 21 In Maine, nearly every man is a lumberer. **1883** *American* VI. 297 The condition to which the lumberer and the farmer have brought the Ohio valley.

Lumber house. A building in which various things may be stored. {1728}

1720 *Mass. Bay Currency Tracts* 385 Hemp, Flax, Turpentine, Pitch, Tarr, Rozin, Fish, Oyl, Whalebone . . . to be stored up in the Lumber-house. **1769** *Virginia Mag. Hist. & Biog.* V. 134 My lumber House in Richmond [in which hemp, gunpowder, etc., were stored] was set on Fire by Lightning. **1822** *Missionary Herald* XVIII. 289/1 The missionaries have put up . . . another lumber house, 18 by 20. **1833** *Niles' Reg.* XLIV. 178/1 The foundation of an immense flour mill, is now being laid . . . , adjoining his lumber house. **1899** CUSHMAN *Hist. Indians* 162 A mill-house 34 x 30 ft, and also a lumberhouse and granary, each 18 x 20 ft.

Lumbering. {1775} +The business or action of cutting down forest trees and marketing them; the business of a lumberer.

1792 BELKNAP *Hist. New-Hampshire* III. 213 Towns adjoining the river, in which lumbering was formerly the chief employment, are fully capable of raising . . . a surplus for exportation. **1872** MCCLELLAN *Golden State* 469 Lumbering and stock-raising are carried on to considerable extent. **1884** *American* VII. 229 In Maine . . . much harm was done to the general interests of the State by reckless lumbering. **1903** *Churchman* 26 Sept. 345 Some profit there may be from reckless lumbering.

+b. Attrib. with *business, camp, party,* etc.

1832 J. MACGREGOR *British America* II. 299 Several of these people form what is termed a 'lumbering party,' composed of persons who are . . . hired by a master lumberer. **1853** *Mass. Acts & Resolves* 690 The lumbering business, from the forest to the market. **1858** THOREAU *Maine Woods* 108 Here were the ruins of an old lumbering-camp. **1885** HOWELLS *Chance Acquaintance* 44 Ha-Ha Bay is a famous lumbering port. **1893** *Scribner's Mag.* June 647/1 The out-put, for the last lumbering season, amounting to 9,000,000,000 feet. **1902** WHITE *Blazed Trail* 181 A lumbering town after the drive is a fearful thing.

+Lumberjack. A man engaged in felling trees and getting them to market. Also attrib. — **1896** *N.Y. Wkly. Witness* 30 Dec. 13/1 To lose the lumberjack vote meant to lose the election. **1902** WHITE *Blazed Trail* 41 Typical native-born American lumber-jacks powerful in frame. **1905** *Boston Transcript* 2 Sept. 22/7 Lumber jacks are . . . men, dressed in the style of a regular woodman, shoe packs, heavy flannel shirts, sombrero hats.

+Lumberman.

1. =LUMBERER; a man engaged in the lumbering business.

a1817 DWIGHT *Travels* II. 166 The lumbermen were without employment. **1838** *Niles' Nat. Reg.* 15 Sept. 48/1 The Pittsburgh Intelligencer states that lumbermen on the river estimate [etc.]. **1893** *Scribner's Mag.* 711/1 The veteran lumberman and politician, Hon. Philetus Sawyer, is a conspicuous example. **1903** *Boston Herald* 15 Aug., The lumbermen . . . have grown rich by taking dishonest advantage of the government land laws. **1910** *Springfield W. Repub.* 7 July 14 Maine lumbermen enjoy telling the casual summer visitor how great is the skill of their cant men and river drivers.

2. A boat that carries lumber.

1850 *Knickerb.* XXXVI. 261 Business-like lumbermen, from 'down-east,' loaded deep in the water. **1863** *Boston Sunday Herald* 16 Aug. 3/3 (Ernst), The pilot of the oil boat signs as gaily . . . as did the pilot of the lumberman.

+Lumber merchant. One who buys and sells lumber. — **1789** *Boston Directory* 181 Dillaway Samuel, lumber-merchant. **1825** NEAL *Bro. Jonathan* I. 23 The preacher . . . had been a wild young man—a 'store' keeper—a 'speculator'—and a 'lumber merchant.' **1834** D. WEBSTER in Benton *30 Years' View* I. 419/1 This meeting . . . was composed of carpenters, . . . lumber merchants and others. **1851** CIST *Cincinnati* 346.

+Lumber mill. A mill where lumber is sawed or finished. — **1830** *Congress. Deb.* 11 March 606/2 You will not find, in any other description of mills, such constant, unceasing labor as in our lumber mills. **1887** *Courier-Journal* 4 May 5/4 Two lumber mills have had to be closed on account of the high water. **1892** *Vt. Agric. Rep.* XII. 128 Richford has extensive lumber mills and manufactories for butter trays and boxes. **1907** *St. Nicholas* Oct. 1109/1 The lumber mills must also be told just what the orders will be so that they may get to work.

+Lumber port.[1] 'A port-hole cut in the bow or stern of a vessel for the passage of long pieces of timber' (*Cent.*). — **1838** *Yale Lit. Mag.* III. 76 [He] found that the pirates had knocked out the lumber port, with the intention of sinking [the vessel].

+Lumber port.[2] A seaport where lumber is exported. — **1883** *Wheelman* I. 333 Calais [Me.], the great lumber port of this part of the country.

+Lumber raft. A collection of logs, boards, or the like, bound together, either for support or for their conveyance downstream. — **1837** W. JENKINS *Ohio Gaz.* 62 The Hockhocking river . . . furnishes . . . a downward navigation for flat boats and lumber rafts. **1855** *Harvard Mag.* I. 70 Water, sir, was made to carry steamboats, and ships, and lumber rafts, and flat-boats. **1884** 'MARK TWAIN' *H. Finn* ix. 76 We catched a little section of a lumber-raft—nice pine planks.

Lumber room. A room where unused furniture or the like may be stored. {1741-} — **1773** *Bristol* (Va.) *Vestry Bk.* 238 A Dairy Sixteen by Ten to be built and one end to [be] fitted up Close for a Lumber Room. **1805** WEEMS *Letters* II. 312, 3 or 4000 of [your volumes] . . . will have to lie still in your lumber rooms.

+Lumber schooner. A schooner designed for transporting lumber. — **1856** OLMSTED *Slave States* 155 He had once let him go to New York as cook of a lumber-schooner. **1865** *Atlantic Mo.* XV. 535 Doctor Bowdler and he were coming down from New York on Ben Van Note's lumber-schooner. **1899** *Sat. Ev. Post* 10 June 795 Blunt-bowed, ugly lumber schooners annually bring 20,000,000 feet of pine lumber.

+Lumber sleigh. A box sleigh used for miscellaneous hauling. — **1823** COOPER *Pioneers* iv, A large lumber-sleigh, drawn by four horses, was soon seen dashing through the leafless bushes. **1827** J. HOWE *Journal* 34, [I] set off to buy a second-hand lumber sleigh. **1845** COOPER *Chainbearer* xvii, I got as handsome a load as ever you seed laid in a lumber-sleigh.

Lumbersome, *a.* Cumbrous. {1834-} — **1805** CLARK in *Lewis & C. Exped.* II. (1904) 190 To be left at this place buried, . . . a few small lumbersom articles.

+Lumber trade. 1. *collect.* Commodities made of lumber. *Obs.* 2. The business and exchange related to lumber. — (1) **1689** *Mass. H. S. Coll.* 3 Ser. I. 98 They are supplied . . . with the lumber trade, deal boards, pipe staves, &c. (2) **1809** KENDALL *Travels* III. 33 The lumber-trade precedes farming by a period of many years. **1816** *Ann. 14th Congress* 1 Sess. 809 A part of their fisheries and lumber trade gone, . . . [the people of Maine] are called upon by your tax-gatherers. **1840** *Knickerb.* XVI. 217 The lumber-trade is a business which will be introduced the moment the resources in pine, of more southerly regions, are exhausted. **1891** O'BEIRNE *Leaders Ind. Territory* 174/1 [He] engaged in the lumber trade on Red River close to the Harris Ferry.

+Lumber wagon. A springless wagon with a long box used for miscellaneous hauling.

1842 M. CRAWFORD *Journal* 5 Left Buffalo at 11 o'clock in the morning in a lumber waggon on our way to the steam boat. **1854** *Penna. Agric. Rep.* 265 A superior lumber wagon was exhibited. **1871** *Rep. Indian Affairs* (1872) 285, I have been obliged to purchase three new lumber-wagons. **1898** *Mo. So. Dakotan* I. 133 A belated lumber wagon slowly passed. **1902** BANKS *Autobiog. Newspaper Girl* 1 Gathered about the little village station in hard-seated lumber-wagons.

+Lumber wharf. A wharf especially used for handling lumber. — **1723** *New-Eng. Courant* 8-15 April 2/2 The Lumber-Wharffe belonging to the said Estate will be Attended by said Administrators. **1796** *Boston Directory* 246 Francis & Blake, lumber wharf, Fish street. **1865** *Atlantic Mo.* XV. 432 Mrs. A. . . . owned the mills and lumber-wharves adjoining. **1914** STEELE *Storm* 260 The covered passage . . . leads to Joe Smith's lumber-wharf.

+Lumberyard. A yard in which a stock of lumber is piled up for sale.

1786 *Md. Journal* 4 April (Th.), Lumber-yard, at the head of Baltimore Bason. **1790** *Penna. Packet* 27 March 4/4 The Subscribers take this method to inform the public . . . that they have opened a Lumber-Yard. **1809** CUMING *Western Tour* 223 Pittsburgh [has] . . . four lumber yards. **1838** *S. Lit. Messenger* IV. 25/1 We went on horseback, to the lumber yard of the Dismal Swamp Timber Company. **1877** JOHNSON *Anderson Co., Kansas* 180 John Ricketts opened the first lumber yard . . . in 1868. **1913** LONDON *Valley of Moon* III. iv, The wood was ordinary wood you can buy in any lumber yard.

Lummox. Also **lummux.** A stupid, clumsy person; an awkward person. *colloq.* {a1825-, '*dial.* and *U.S.*'} — **1854** PAIGE *Dow's Sermons* IV. 149 (Th.), Man in his original state is little more than a big lummux of a baby. **1889** 'MARK TWAIN' *Conn. Yankee* 382 As a rule, a knight is a lummox, and sometimes even a labrick. **1895** REMINGTON *Pony Tracks* 195 Who is the scoundrel, the lummux, humph? **1919** WILSON *Ma Pet-*

tingill 92 Oswald is a big fair-haired lummox that sings tenor in the Presbyterian choir.

***Lump,** *n.*[1] =LUMPFISH. — **1605** ROSIER *True Relation* 105 We got about thirty very good and great Lobsters, many Rockfish . . . and fishes called Lumpes, verie pleasant to the taste.

***Lump,** *n.*[2] +=LUMP COAL b. — **1859** *Rep. Comm. Patents 1858* I. 704 The screen D retains and delivers the next size to 'lump,' known as the 'egg' coal.

***Lump,** *v.* +*tr.* To put up with (something). Usu. in some variant of *if you don't like it, you can lump it. colloq.* — **1828** NEAL *R. Dyer* 70 If you don't like it, you may lump it. **1863** *Rio Abajo Press* 17 Nov. 3/2 If the natives of this Territory . . . do not like our legal and equitable views in the premises, they can 'lump' them. **1876** 'MARK TWAIN' *Tom Sawyer* i. 8 You can lump that hat if you don't like it. **1911** LINCOLN *Cap'n Warren's Wards* 318 Steve'll behave, and what he don't like he'll lump.

Lump butter. A mass of butter not put in a firkin. *Obs.* — **1795** *Columbian Centinel* 10 Jan. 1/1 He has for sale . . . firkin and lump Butter, Capers [etc.]. **1818** *Boston Selectmen* 19 Persons . . . shall not . . . receive or sell on commission at Faneuil Hall market, . . . lump butter, . . . [unless] with the express approbation of the Clerk of the Market.

+**Lump coal. a.** Coal in lumps or large chunks as taken from the mine. **b.** Screened coal of a size next larger than egg coal. — **1874** KNIGHT 579 *Coal-breaker*, a machine for crushing lump-coal as taken from the mine. **1876** RAYMOND *8th Rep. Mines* 288 The combustion is far more perfect than can be brought about with lump-coal. **1896** *Internat. Typogr. Union Proc.* 55, 13,700 lbs. Alamo lump coal . . . $34.25.

Lumper. {1781-} +**1.** (See quot. 1887.) **2.** A coarse variety of potato. {1840-, in Ireland} — (1) **1833** T. HAMILTON *Men & Manners* I. 176 There is, however, a class of men, consisting of ten or twelve, called *runners* and *lumpers*, whose duty consists in moving about the [prison] yard. **1887** *Battle Creek Moon* 17 Dec., Converse prison number is 4,234, and the position he occupies is known as a 'lumper.' His duties are to assist the forman [*sic*] of the shop in sorting and packing and putting goods in shape for shipment. (2) **1853** *Mich. Agric. Soc. Trans.* V. 208 [Among] varieties of potatoes . . . cultivated in Europe and America . . . [is] the Lumper.

+**Lump(ed) jaw.** =LUMPY JAW. *colloq.* — **1890** *Ohio Agric. Exper. Sta. Bul.* III. 107 Actinomycosis, commonly called lump jaw, or lumped jaw, is not a new disease.

Lumpfish. A clumsy marine fish, *Cyclopterus lumpus.* {1620-} Cf. LUMP and LUMPSUCKER. — **1832** WILLIAMSON *Maine* I. 156 The Lumpfish is naturally a clumsy creature and is found only in salt water, mostly about the westerly coast of the State. **1842** *Nat. Hist. N.Y., Zoology* IV. 306. **1884** GOODE, etc. *Fisheries* I. 254 The male Lump-fish is said to be very fierce in defense of its young. **1903** T. H. BEAN *Fishes N.Y.* 651 The lumpfish is found in Gravesend bay in May.

Lumpsucker. A term variously used by ichthyologists to indicate certain fish families characterized by a modification of the pelvic fin into a sucker. Also applied to individual species of these. {1766-} Cf. LUMPFISH and SEA SNAIL. — **1884** GOODE, etc. *Fisheries* I. 253 The Lump-Suckers: Lump-Fish and Sea-Snails. *Ib.*, The Lump-suckers, *Liparis lineatus* and *L. vulgaris* . . . are found on oyster and scallop beds . . . along the New England coast. **1903** T. H. BEAN *Fishes N.Y.* 649 Family Cyclopteridae. Lump Suckers. . . . *Cyclopterus lumpus.* Lumpfish; Lumpsucker. *Ib.* 652 *Neoliparis atlanticus.* . . . Sea Snail; Lumpsucker.

+**Lumpy jaw.** A disease among cattle and sheep causing suppurating tumors about the jaw. Hence *lumpy-jawed* a. *colloq.* — **1890** *Congress. Rec.* 29 May 5428/2 'Lumpy-jawed cattle' means cancerous cattle, cattle with cancer. The 'lumpy-jaw' is simply a cancer. **1913** BARNES *Western Grazing Grounds* 286 Big jaw, also called lumpy jaw and wooden tongue, is an infectious disease found generally all over the West. **1921** *Farmer's Bul.* No. 1155, 17 Actinomycosis, (Lumpy jaw, wooden tongue,) . . . is a disease rare in sheep.

+**Luna moth.** A large moth (*Tropaea luna*) with light green wings. Also attrib. — **1869** *Amer. Naturalist* II. 679/2 Luna Moth. **1876** *Field & Forest* II. 72 Mr. Rodgers . . . gives the history of the Luna moth. **1909** STRATTON-PORTER *Girl of Limberlost* 321 [He] began examining a walnut branch for Luna moth eggs.

Lunatic asylum. An institution wherein lunatics are placed and given treatment. {1828-} — **1827** DRAKE & MANSFIELD *Cincinnati* 38 He added . . . a third [petition] from himself, proposing the addition of a Lunatic Asylum. **1855** *Ill. Agric. Soc. Trans.* I. 457 The records of lunatic asylums are said to show that the percentage of insanity is greater in the United States than in . . . Europe. **1874** ALDRICH *P. Palfrey* vi, If Jack knew . . . he would be justified in placing me in the State Lunatic Asylum. **1902** WISTER in *Harper's Mag.* Feb. 467 This rendered me easily fit for a lunatic asylum.

***Lunch.**

1. A light meal, less substantial than dinner. {1829-}

American usage recognizes the following special senses: **a.** The regular midday meal, so called by those who eat dinner in the evening: (cf. DINNER HOUR, note). **b.** Food, frequently sandwiches, a piece of pie, etc., put up in a pail or package, and eaten by school children, workmen, etc., esp. at noon. **c.** A light meal eaten at any irregular time.

1840 *Picayune* 30 July 2/1 The True American was right when it spoke of the lunch on the counter of the St. Charles bar room. **1862** *Ill. Agric. Soc. Trans.* V. 197 Mrs. A., at ten and again at four o'clock, sends out a lunch to the harvesters. **1867** S. HALE *Letters* 30 You must know we handle the most stunning feed, six or eight courses at lunch and dinner. **1876** HENDERSON (*title*), Practical Cooking and Dinner Giving. A Treatise Containing Practical Instructions in . . . the Fashionable Modes of Entertaining at Breakfast, Lunch, and Dinner. **1899** *Scribner's Mag.* XXV. 106, I should like to inquire if you have any authority for your use of the word 'lunch'? As employed by the appropriating and the arrogant it has long meant a meal or a bite between breakfast and dinner; but, as used by democracy, it seems to apply to afternoon tea or late supper equally well. **1904** PRINGLE *Rice Planter* 115 They all carry their 'bittle,' as they call their lunch, in bright looking tin cans with close fitting covers. **1908** PALMER *Life A. F. Palmer* 152 Often she was unable to return till ten or eleven at night. Then she took a light lunch.

+**2.** A lunch room.

1850 S. F. COOPER *Rural Hours* 468 As for the eating-houses . . . there are some dozen of them—Lunches, Recesses, Restaurants, &c.

3. Attrib. with *bag, basket, bell,* etc.

1846 *Knickerb.* XXVIII. 558 [A] parody was found inscribed on the newspaper-board of a 'lunch-house' in Saint Louis, Missouri. **1857** OLMSTED *Journey through Texas* 53 Both pommel and cantle were hung with blankets, overcoats, ammunition-pouches, lunch-bags, et cetera. **1869** W. MURRAY *Adventures* 223 Inside I found a complete suit of flannel clothes, with a blanket, and, better than all, a lunch-basket. **1875** STOWE *We & Neighbors* 67 The ringing of the lunch bell interrupted the conversation. **1885** CRAWFORD *Amer. Politician* 39 At a lunch party . . . they sat and talked about pictures. **1897** STUART *Simpkinsville* 14 They'd give him biscuits out o' their lunch-cans. **1902** LORIMER *Lett. Merchant* 108 One of those fellows . . . goes around and makes the boys give up their lunch money to buy flowers. **1911** PERSONS, etc. *Mass. Labor Laws* 163 In the large stores, restaurants and hotels, a uniform lunch hour would cause great inconvenience. **1917** MATHEWSON *Sec. Base Sloan* 64 Then came hot coffee and fried eggs and rolls at the lunch-wagon.

Lunch box. A box in which a lunch is carried; such a box filled with food. — **1864** *Rep. Comm. Patents 1862* I. 158 Improved Lunch Box. . . . This invention consists of an arrangement of dishes, cups, &c., arranged within a case. **1881** CHASE *Editor's Run in New Mex.* 58 The lunch box is a most important part of the 'outfit.' **1914** GERRY *Masks of Love* 93 Mrs. Girard unpacked a lunch-box. **1925** BRYAN *Memoirs* 277 To prepare 2000 sandwiches and about 1000 lunch boxes.

+**Lunch counter.** A counter in a restaurant at which people, usually seated on stools, are served meals; also, a restaurant in which food is served at a counter. — **1876** INGRAM *Centennial Exp.* 701 It contained one very large room, ladies' parlor, coat and baggage room, lunch counter [etc.]. **1882** McCABE *New York* 646 Its restaurant is famous, and its lunch-counter furnishes meals to several thousand people every day. **1900** MUNN *Uncle Terry* 347 He bought a pitcher of coffee all prepared, at a railroad lunch counter. **1908** *Collier's Mag.* 17 Oct. 13/2 Mr. Bryan has . . . eaten or otherwise made way with over 1,700 meals at railroad lunch-counters.

***Luncheon.**

1. A midday meal, less substantial than dinner. {*a*1652-}

The word *luncheon* is more formal than *lunch*.

1865 A. D. WHITNEY *Gayworthys* v. 53 We're such terrible creatures, . . . talking and laughing over our luncheon. **1887** CUSTER *Tenting on Plains* 469 There were always those who . . . became experts at casual droppings in to luncheon or dinner. **1896** *Complete Bachelor* 54 Luncheons on Sunday at one or two o'clock are in New York frequently called breakfasts, because I believe many fashionable people do not want the impression to go abroad that even once a week they dine in the middle of the day. **1904** *Phila. Press* 1 June 4 Upon arriving at St. Louis the councilmanic party from this city will be taken to luncheon. **1923** WIGGIN *Garden of Memory* 112, I bought my luncheon at a different bakery every day.

+**b.** Applied to late supper.

1903 *Boston Ev. Transcript* 3 Oct. 5 At this table, from 9 o'clock until midnight, a bountiful standing luncheon was served continuously.

2. Attrib. with *basket, bell, box,* etc.

1845 *Lowell Offering* V. 211 It was so delightful under the shade of the old 'luncheon tree.' **1887** PERRY *Flock of Girls* 252 There's the luncheon bell, and you must run. **1896** JEWETT *Country of Pointed Firs* 13, I hung my hat and luncheon-basket on an entry nail. **1898** ATHERTON *Californians* 82 We owe you a great many luncheon calls. **1916** E. PORTER *David* 18, I've taken out the luncheon box.

+**Lunch pail.** =DINNER PAIL. — **1891** WILKINS *New Eng. Nun* 44 Matilda came in her voluminous alpaca, with her tin lunch-pail on her arm. **1901** MERWIN & WEBSTER *Calumet 'K'* 289 They slung their lunch pails on their arms and ate when and where they could.

+**Lunch room.** A restaurant that specializes in serving light meals. — **1884** *N.Y. Herald* 27 Oct. 7/6 Girl to learn to attend bakery, lunch room or candy store. **1887** ALDEN *Little Fishers* xxiv, There is a lunch room for young men, where they can get excellent things for just what they cost. **1914** GERRY *Masks of Love* 34 Her observations varied from the more than democratic waitresses . . . of the Woods' lunch-rooms to the discreet servility of the up-town restaurants. **1919** *Detective Story Mag.* 25 Nov. 129 He breakfasted at a hole-in-the-wall lunch room before starting out on his quest.

+**Lunch stand.** An eating place that serves light meals; a lunch wagon. — **1887** GEORGE *40 Yrs. on Rail* 79 One day Superintendent Johnson stopped at the station, and noticed this lunch-stand. **1902** *Harper's Mag.* March 618 A darky from a lunch-stand . . . passed along the line with coffee.

Lunch time. A period near midday when lunch is eaten. — **1866** A. D. WHITNEY *L. Goldthwaite* iv, It's nice that dinner is at lunch-time here. *a***1877** in Bartlett 810 As clamorous for food as the boys of a district school just let out to play at lunch-time. **1911** LINCOLN *Cap'n Warren's Wards* 171 A rather slatternly maid . . . informed the visitor that she guessed Mr. Pearson was in; he 'most always was around lunch time.

Lung disease. +=HOG CHOLERA. — **1881** *Harper's Mag.* April 768/2 Hogs are sometimes liable to an epidemic called lung disease, or hog cholera.

+**Lunge.** [Shortened from *muskellunge*.] The namaycush, *Cristivomer namaycush.* (See also LONGE.) — **1851** *Vt. Laws* 49 Such person or persons shall forfeit and pay . . . the sum of one dollar for each trout or lunge so taken. **1894** *Outing* XXIV. 368/2 It's a 'lunge.' . . . He'll weigh at least fifteen pounds.

Lungee. [Var. of *lungi*.] A kind of East Indian cloth. {1662–} Also attrib. — **1759** *Newport Mercury* 10 April 4/2 To be Sold by Simon. Pease, jun.: . . . Worsted Damask, Lungee Romals, Bandanoes [etc.]. **1761** *Ib.* 28 April 4/3 To be sold, . . . humhums, . . . silk lungee, and cotton romals.

+**Lung fever. 1.** Pneumonia. **2.** A lung disease among cattle. — **(1) 1775** in *Amer. Hist. Rev.* VI. 308 Found him extremely low with a Lung Fever. **1838** MARTINEAU *Retrospect* III. 171 Breathing the frosty air of a winter's night, after dancing, may be easily conceived to be the cause of much of the 'lung fever' of which the stranger hears. **1884** in Roosevelt *Amer. Backlogs* (1928) 14 When two years old, I had an attack of lung-fever (known now as pneumonia). **(2) 1879** *Diseases of Swine* 195 Mitchell [County, Kansas]. Murrain, black-leg, and lung-fever have prevailed to some extent among cattle.

***Lungwort.** +**1.** The Virginia cowslip, *Mertensia virginica.* ***2.** A European herb (*Pulmonaria officinalis*) cultivated in gardens. +**3.** (See quotation.) — **(1) 1791** MUHLENBERG *Index Florae* 163 *Pulmonaria, virginica.* Lungwort. **1843** TORREY *Flora N.Y.* II. 85 *Pulmonaria Virginica.* Virginian Cowslip. Virginian Lungwort. . . . Borders of Oneida creek and Fish creek, Oneida county. . . . Frequently cultivated in gardens. **(2) 1840** DEWEY *Mass. Flowering Plants* 185 *Pulmonaria officinalis.* Lungwort. Probably named from its use in pulmonary affections; a native of England. **(3) 1893** *Amer. Folk-Lore* VI. 141 *Saxifraga* (*Virginiensis?*), lungwort. Calais, Me.

+**Lunkhead.** A thick-headed person. *colloq.* — **1852** A. T. JACKSON *Forty-Niner* (1920) 150 Pard shut the book with a slam and said I was a lunkhead. **1883** *Harper's Mag.* March 647/2, I want to get a naked-eye view of the crown-heads, to compare them with the lunk-heads at home. **1895** WIGGIN *Village Watch-Tower* 50 The 'dog-goned lunk-head' wanted to starve and freeze. **1912** WASON *Friar Tuck* 73 Bein' fooled on direction wasn't any sign of Horace bein' a complete lunkhead.

+**Lunk-headed,** *a.* Slow-witted. *colloq.* — **1884** *Atlanta Constitution* Sept., Her lunk-headed admirer has to turn squarely around, blocking up the side-walk. **1889** MUNROE *Golden Days* 125 It's all my own blamed, lunk-headed fault.

***Lupine.** Also **lupin. a.** A plant of the genus *Lupinus.* **b.** The seed of this plant. — **1649** *Desc. Virginia* 4 They have store of Indian Pease, better then ours, Beans, Lupines, and the like. **1705** BEVERLEY *Virginia* II. 17 Growing upon wild vines . . . [are] Melons, Cucumbers, Lupines, and an Infinity of other Sorts of Fruits. **1784** CUTLER in *Mem. Academy* I. 471 Lupine. Blossoms blue. In corn fields, in the state of Connecticut. June–August. **1848** BRYANT *California* 135 The lupin is blooming on our camp-ground. **1913** LONDON *Valley of Moon* 370 [They] went on across wind-blown rolling sandhills held to place by sturdy lupins and nodding with pale California poppies.

Lurch. {1819–} *local.* +An inclination or penchant. — **1794** *Mass. H. S. Coll.* IV. 48 He conceived a lurch for improvement in manufacturing spanish brown. **1854** CUMMINS *Lamplighter* 118 She has a nateral lurch for it [learning], and it comes easy to her. **1878** in E. S. Phelps *A. Phelps* 219, I got from Professor Stuart and Albert Barnes . . . a lurch adverse to such work.

Lustring. A glossy silk fabric. {1697–} (Cf. LUTESTRING.) — **1726** *New-Eng. Courant* 5–12 March 2/2 Edward Carter, Silk-Dyer and Scowerer, . . . Dyes and scowers all sorts of Brocades, . . . Sattins, Lystrings [*sic*], Tabbies [etc.]. **1733** *Md. Hist. Mag.* XX. 61 A pair of womans stays of white Taby & Lined with white Lustring according to the Measure. **1784** *Mass. Centinel* 2 June 3/3 This day . . . will be sold at public vendue . . . six pieces of Lustring [etc.]. **1842** *Amer. Pioneer* I. 147 The weaving room [of the silk factory] contains six looms for the production of . . . lustring, plush for hats [etc.]. **1886** E. L. BYNNER *Agnes Surriage* 334 She must have new gowns of lustring and taffeta.

+**Lute.** [Du. *loet.*] (See quotations.) — **1875** KNIGHT 1365/1 *Lute,* . . . a straight-edge employed to strike off the surplus clay from a brick-mold. **1889** C. T. DAVIS *Manuf. Bricks* (ed. 2) 142 There is a tool used for scraping off and levelling the moulding floor. . . . It consists of a piece of light pine board, . . . set upright, with a long light handle in the centre. . . . The tool is called a 'lute.'

Lutestring. A stout glossy silk fabric; a garment of this. {1661–} Also attrib. — **1697** SEWALL *Letter-Book* I. 191 Buy for me a piece of flowered Lute string . . . to make Gowns and Petticoats for my Daughters. **1772** A. G. WINSLOW *Diary* (1894) 20 Cousin Betsey [was] dress'd in a red lutestring, . . . adorn'd with past, perls marquesett &c. **1802** BOWNE *Life* 143 Martha sent me a most elegant Indispensable, white lutestring spangled with silver. **1891** WILKINS *New Eng. Nun* 95 An' she come out bride in a blue silk dress . . . an' a white bunnit trimmed with lutestring ribbon.

***Lutheran,** *n.* One who adheres to the doctrines of Martin Luther (1483–1546); a member of the Lutheran church. (Cf. GERMAN LUTHERAN.)

*c***1680** WOLLEY *Journal in New York* (1902) 66 Two other Ministers or Domines as they were called there, the one a Lutheran, . . . the other a Calvinist. **1765** ROGERS *Acct. N. America* 72 The religious persuasions here [in N.Y.] are very numerous; there being Episcopalians, Lutherans, Presbyterians. **1831** PECK *Guide* 285 A portion of the population of this county are Germans, who . . . are subdivided into Lutherans and Dunkards. **1919** *Lutheran Church Rev.* Jan. 10 Lutherans . . . for some years have been studying the early history of their ancestors in the North.

***Lutheran,** *a.* Designating the doctrines, church, ministers, etc., that pertain to the teachings of Martin Luther. — **1670** *Doc. Col. Hist. N.Y.* XII. 473 [To the] pastor of the Lutheran Confession comonly called the Augustan . . . I have graunted my Passe. **1698** THOMAS *Penna. & N.J.* 51 The way of Worship the Sweeds use in this Countrey, is the Luthern. **1823** I. HOLMES *Account* 387 In Pennsylvania, and likewise in . . . New York, there are . . . German, Lutheran, and Dutch Reformed churches. **1881** *Phila. Record* No. 3457, 1 In today's session of the Lutheran Ministerium a report on Muhlenberg College showed a $20,000 cash endowment. **1919** *Lutheran Church Rev.* April 171 [The] Lutheran Church in America . . . [should] exert a truly Lutheran influence.

***Luzerne.** =LOUP-CERVIER. *Obs.* — **1602** BRERETON *Virginia* 13 Such commodities as we saw in the country . . . [include] Beares, . . . Luzernes, Blacke Foxes.

Lyceum. {1786–}

+**1. a.** An institution through which lectures, dramatic performances, debates, and the like are presented to a community. **b.** The association which sponsors such an institution.

1820 *Amer. Jrnl. Science* II. 366 Abstract of the proceedings of the Lyceum of Natural History, New-York. **1835** *S. Lit. Messenger* I. 273 In all the cities, and many of the larger and middling towns . . . there are Lyceums. **1842** *Knickerb.* XIX. 437 He belonged to the village lyceum and had a chance to listen to all the lectures of the season. **1865** *Atlantic Mo.* XV. 370 Our plain-speaking gentleman who makes his yearly circuit among the lyceums. **1894** WISTER in *Harper's Mag.* Aug. 387/1 'Louise, why don't you quit her outfit?' 'Resign from the Lyceum?'

+**2.** The building in which such lectures, etc., are given.

1833 COKE *Subaltern's Furlough* x, The college has . . . two chapels, and a lycæum, (in which are the recitation rooms). **1847** HOWE *Hist. Coll. Ohio* 477 On the left [are] the Cuyahoga river, the lyceum and Presbyterian church. **1889** P. BUTLER *Recollections* 11 Even in those early days Wadsworth contained . . . a lyceum where the young men discussed the questions of the day.

+**3.** The program sponsored by a lyceum.

1854 'O. OPTIC' *In Doors & Out* (1876) 306 There were balls, parties, and lyceums in Tiptop. **1858** *Harper's Mag.* April 699/2 The Lyceum—or the course of miscellaneous winter lectures in towns and villages all through the country—has now become a fixed American institution. **1877** *Ib.* Jan. 285/1, I don't care for your lyceums here winter times. **1900** BACHELLER *E. Holden* 139 Thet there is talent in Faraway township . . . no one can deny who has ever attended a lyceum at the Howard school-house.

4. A school. *Obsolescent.*

1830 WATSON *Philadelphia* 248 The simple, unassuming apellation [*sic*] of 'school' was the universal name till about the year 1795; after that time 'academies,' 'seminaries,' 'lyceums,' 'institutes,' &c were perpetually springing up in every quarter among us. **1901** STILLMAN *Autobiog. Journalist* I. 64 It was decided that I should continue my preparation for college in the Lyceum of my native town.

+**5.** Attrib. with *amusement, association, hall,* etc.

1831 *Mass. Statutes* 4 March, They are hereby made a corporation, by the name of the Lyceum Hall, . . . for the purpose of affording means and facilities for the prosecution of literary and scientific studies. **1843** 'CARLTON' *New Purchase* II. 174 The common school system, and the lyceum system. **1865** *Atlantic Mo.* XV. 363 There are library associations or lyceum associations, composed generally of young men. **1881** *Harper's Mag.* March 628/2 During the days of his lyceum lecturing, no man was more popular [than Dr. Chapin] upon the platform. **1883** *Century Mag.* Aug. 636/1 Encourage Lyceum amusement courses in the towns.

***Lye.** Also **lee, ley, lie.** A strong alkaline solution made esp. from the leaching of vegetable ashes; the commercial powder with which the solution may be made.

1705 BEVERLEY *Virginia* III. 18 Oyl of Acorns . . . they force out, by boyling the acorns in a strong Lye. **1744** FRANKLIN *Acct. Fire-Places* 28 A Lee made of Ashes and Water, with a Brush, will scour them perfectly. **1833** SILLIMAN *Man. Sugar Cane* 33 The channels and vats are also cleansed, with warm water, and finally sprinkled with lime or ley from ashes. **1850** *New Eng. Farmer* II. 66 Hominy is Indian corn shelled from the cob, divested of the yellow or outward skin by scalding in hot ley, and then winnowed and dried. **1883** ALLEN *New Farm Book* 62 Spent lye of the asheries, is the liquid which remains after the combination of the lye and grease in manufacturing soap.

b. Attrib. with *cask, leach, soap, tea.* (Cf. HOMINY 2b.)
1843 'CARLTON' *New Purchase* I. 63 A lie-cask, or rather, an inverted pyramidical box to contain ashes, resembling a hopper in a mill. **1856** M. J. HOLMES *L. Rivers* 387 From behind the ley-leach, the smoke-house, and the trees, emerged the little darkies. **1865** *Nation* I. 306 Several old women . . . were very kind in doctoring me with ley tea, pepper tea, and other villanous [*sic*] remedies. **1902** HARBEN *A. Daniel* 71 His wife sent me to 'im to carry . . . a little can o' lye-soap.

+**Lyed corn.** Corn from which the hulls have been removed by treatment with lye. Also attrib. — **1804** LEWIS in *L. & Clark Exped.* I. (1904) 33 The day after tomorrow lyed corn and grece will be issued to the party. **1814** BRACKENRIDGE *Views La.* 202 Their food consists of lied corn hominy for breakfast. **1899** CATHERWOOD *Mackinac Stories* 21 One pint of lyed corn with from two to four ounces of tallow was the daily allowance of a voyageur.

+**Lyman's long summer.** A variety of apple. — **1847** IVES *New Eng. Fruit* 48 *Lyman's Long Summer.* . . . A large and handsome American fruit introduced to notice by S. Lyman, of Manchester, Conn.

Lyme grass. Also **lime grass.** Any grass of the genus *Elymus;* wild rye. {1776-} — **1791** MUHLENBERG *Index Florae* 161 *Elymus,* Lime-grass. **1814** BIGELOW *Florula Bostoniensis* 28 *Elymus Virginicus,* Lyme Grass. . . . The large erect spikes of this grass resemble at a distance heads of barley. **1840** DEWEY *Mass. Flowering Plants* 244 *Elymus.* . . . Lime Grass. Wild Rye. **1889** VASEY *Agric. Grasses* 77 *Elymus canadensis* (Wild Rye; Rye Grass; Lyme Grass) . . . on moist prairies and banks in the west, it is quite common and is cut for hay.

+**Lynch,** *n. attrib.* passing into *adj.* Pertaining to the action of lynching. — **1811** ELLICOTT in Mathews *Life A. Ellicott* 222, I should not have asserted it as a fact [that Capt. Lynch was the originator of Lynch law] had it not been related to me by Mr. Lynch . . . together with several other Lynch-men as they are called. **1835** GARRISON in W. J. & F. J. Garrison *W. L. Garrison* I. 519 The slave States . . . have organized Vigilance Committees and Lynch Clubs. **1840** THOMPSON *Green Mt. Boys* I. 37 They formally resolved themselves . . . into a sort of tribunal, very nearly resembling, we suppose, a modern Lynch court. **1868** *N.Y. Herald* 29 July 4/5 The Indiana Lynch Murders. **1897** *N. Amer. Rev.* July 119 (*caption*), Lynch Epidemics.

+**Lynch,** *v.* [f. LYNCH LAW.] *tr.* To inflict severe bodily punishment upon (a person), as by whipping or tarring and feathering, without due process of law; to hang or otherwise kill (a person) by mob action.

Now only in latter sense.

1836 *Niles' Reg.* 1 Oct. 69/1 Some personal friend of Mr. Broux . . . proceeded to the mansion of judge Bermudez, with a view to Lynch him, or to inflict some severe punishment upon his person. **1840** SIMMS *Border Beagles* 445 Lynch 'em at Luccheso where it'll be a warning to all rogues and gamblers, and abolitionists. **1857** *Lawrence* (Kan.) *Republican* 28 May 1 The Rev. Pardee Butler had been lynched, tarred and feathered, and sent down the Missouri on a frail raft. **1882** *Nation* 5 Oct. 279/1 Rhodes, who brutally murdered an old man . . . near Charlottesville, Va., last February, was lynched near that town. **1900** *Congress. Rec.* 16 Jan. 847/2 [Colored people] are killed, lynched, and punished in all kinds of ways without law in different parts of the country.

+**Lyncher.** One who participates in a lynching.

1836 CROCKETT *Exploits* 100 Lynchers . . . seize him [an offender] and inflict such chastisement as they conceive adequate to the offense. **1847** *Harbinger* 7 Aug. 136/1 The company of lynchers once formed, they proceed to the execution of summary justice. **1882** *Advance* 22 June, No arrests of the lynchers have been made. **1906** *Boston Transcript* 28 May 8 Move to Punish Lynchers.

+**Lynching.**

1. a. The action of lynching a person.

1836 J. HALL *Statistics of West* p. xviii, The Lynching of these children in southern latitudes, is too often the terrible result of such early lessons. **1868** *N.Y. Herald* 22 July 5/2 The lynching was a premeditated affair. **1900** *Congress. Rec.* 16 Feb. 1865/2 A popular distrust is at the bottom of all the lynching that is committed in the State.

b. The treatment of being lynched.

1836 SIMMS *Mellichampe* 314 Had not Max Mellichampe pronounced me deserving of Lynching? **1840** *Picayune* 13 Aug. 2/1 If any one deserves lynching, such an infamous wretch surely does. **1900** *Congress. Rec.* 16 Jan. 847/1 Such legislation, . . . as will protect colored people from lynching and murder without the authority of law.

2. *attrib.* passing into *adj.* Designating a person or a group of persons who lynch.

1839 HOFFMAN *Wild Scenes* 112 A disbanded regulator of the Georgia guard, with a Lynch-ing corn-cracker from that state, . . . had scented the contents of my master's saddle-bags. **1858** *N.Y. Tribune* 30 Sept. (B.), As gross a violation of justice as vigilance committee or lynching mob was ever guilty of. **1887** *Courier-Journal* 11 Jan. 5/2 Two negroes . . . were arrested, and for fear of a lynching party were put aboard the Kate Adams. **1919** *30 Yrs. Lynching in U.S.* (Nat. Ass. Advancem. Colored People) 7 From 1889 to 1918 . . . 3,224 persons have been killed by lynching mobs.

+**Lynching bee.** A gathering at which someone is lynched. — **1900** *Congress. Rec.* 31 Jan. 1369/1 They have sometimes had 'lynching bees,' . . . they have sometimes lynched men for murder, for arson, for rape. **1904** HARBEN *Georgians* 62 They told me frankly that they were on the way to have a lynching-bee.

+**Lynch law.**

Named after Captain William *Lynch* (1742-1820) of Pittsylvania County, Virginia, and later of Pendleton District, South Carolina. (See A. MATTHEWS in *Mass. Col. Soc. Trans.* XXVII. 256-71 and quot. 1836 under LYNCH'S LAW, and cf. CAPTAIN 6, JUDGE LYNCH.)

1. The practice or custom by which persons are punished for alleged crimes without due process of law; the punishment so meted out.

1811 ELLICOTT in Mathews *Life A. Ellicott* 220 Captain Lynch just mentioned [residing on Oolenoy Creek, S.C.] was the author of the Lynch laws so well-known and so frequently carried into effect some years ago in the southern states in violation of every principle of justice and jurisprudence. **1835** *Md. Hist. Reg.* IX. 161 They then followed the example of the Vicksburg people in attempting to inflict the Lynch Law. **1841** BUCKINGHAM *Amer., N. States* II. 487 In this country of Lynch law, . . . tarring and feathering for mere difference of opinion is . . . often practised. **1851** *Harper's Mag.* III. 415/1 The severe code of Lynch law still continues in practical force [in California]. **1860** OLMSTED *Back Country* 102 The defense of Lynch law which is so commonly made at the South has made it notorious that the administration of criminal justice . . . is very imperfect. **1900** *Congress. Rec.* 25 Jan. 1205/1 Shall that which is equivalent in principle to lynch law be applied or not applied in this case? *c***1908** in A. H. Stone *Amer. Race Problem* (1908) 469 Lynch law does not stop arson or murder or robbery or rape.

2. Attrib. with *brother, halter, style.*

1840 GARRISON in W. P. & F. J. Garrison *W. L. Garrison* II. 365 [Several Englishmen] swore that Oxford 'ought to be strung up . . . ,' in true Lynch-law style. **1857** STIRLING *Lett. Slave States* 144 May not the Republicanism of Louisiana be characterized as a despotism tempered by Lynch-law halters? **1887** *Macmillan's Mag.* March 348/1, I could hardly recognize the complacent judge of the afternoon, in the trembling creature who tried to assure his Lynch-law brother that Cobbett and Grobe had gone East.

+**Lynch's law.** =prec. *Obs.*

In quot. 1836 the 'annexed paper' refers to an agreement by William Lynch and others to take the law into their own hands to protect their community against horse-stealing, counterfeiting, and 'other species of villany.'

1782 C. LYNCH *Let. to W. Hay* (MS.) 11 May, They are mostly torys & such as [Capt.] Sanders has given Lynchs Law too for Dealing with the Negroes &c. **1817** S. ROANE in W. Wirt *Life P. Henry* (1818) 372 In the year 1792, there were many suits on the south side of the James river, for inflicting Lynch's law. **1823** FAUX *Memorable Days* 304 The people . . . deputed four persons to inform him, that unless he quitted the town . . . , he should receive Lynch's law, that is, a whipping in the woods. **1836** POE in *S. Lit. Messenger* II. 389 Frequent inquiry has been made within the last year as to the origin of Lynch's law. . . . It will be perceived from the annexed paper, that the law, so called, originated in 1780, in Pittsylvania, Virginia. Colonel William Lynch, of that county, was its author. **1856** CARTWRIGHT *Autobiog.* 345 If you do, you will get Lynch's law.

***Lynn.** Variant of LINN.

***Lynx.**

***1.** An animal of the genus *Lynx,* +with special reference to American species. Also as pl. (Cf. LINK.)

The American lynxes include the CANADA LYNX, the BAY LYNX, and other varieties, as *L. baileyi* and *L. fasciatus* of the western states.

1791 J. LONG *Voyages* 41 The country every where abounds with wild animals, particularly bears, . . . beaver eaters, lynx, foxes [etc.]. **1838** *Mass. Zool. Survey Rep.* 27 *Felis Canadensis.* Lynx. It is valuable on account of its soft long hair and fur. It destroys sheep, pigs and other small quadrupeds. Never attacks man. *a***1862** THOREAU *Maine Woods* 242 Seeing and hearing . . . lynxes, wolves, and panthers. **1913** BARNES *Western Grazing Grounds* 330 Next to the coyote the wild cat and lynx, commonly known as 'bob cats,' cause sheepmen much loss.

2. The fur of the lynx. {1839-} Also attrib.

1789 MORSE *Amer. Geog.* 520 Their commodities are chiefly . . . lynxes and other furs. **1852** BRISTED *Upper Ten Th.* 14 The large and roomy sleigh decked with . . . lynx robes.

+**Lyscom.** A variety of apple. — **1847** IVES *New Eng. Fruit* 38 *Lyscom.*—This apple originated in Southboro', Mass. It is of medium size, rather oblong, and very regular.

M

M.A. Abbreviation for Master of Arts. {1730–} (See also A.M. and note.) — **1702** (*title*), Magnalia Christi Americana: . . . By the Reverend and Learned Cotton Mather, M.A. and Pastor of the North Church in Boston. **1733** *Boston News Letter* 18 Oct. 2/1 We hear from Springfield that last week died there of a fever Daniel Brewer, jun. M.A., schoolmaster in that town. **1764** in Peirce *Hist. Harvard* 234 That Stephen Sewall, M.A., be the Hancock Professor of the Hebrew and other Oriental Languages in Harvard College. **1912** *Yale Univ. Cat.* 22 Officers of Instruction and Administration . . . [include] John Emory Clark, M.A. . . . Addison Van Name, M.A. [etc.].

Ma'am. {1668–} *local.* +A mother. (Cf. Marm.) — **1867** Lowett in *Atlantic Mo.* Jan. 21 Your ma'am don't love no feathers clutterin' round. **1884** Jewett *Country Doctor* iii. 23 Here's her ma'am beginnin' to age. **1899** A. Brown *Tiverton Tales* 71 There's ma'am's checked apron I bought her to the fair!

+**Ma'am school.** A school conducted by a woman. *Obs.* — **1856** Goodrich *Recoll.* I. 39, I found a girl, some eighteen years old, keeping a ma'am school for about twenty scholars.

Macadam. Also **McAdam.**

1. *attrib.* Designating a road made with layers of broken stone, now usu. with some material as binder. {1824–}

1837 W. Jenkins *Ohio Gaz.* 117 Two Macadam turnpikes. **1878** *N. Amer. Rev.* CXXVI. 91 Smooth McAdam roadways before their doors. **1887** *Courier-Journal* 4 May 3/7 By grading, curbing, block-paving the gutters, and paving the carriage-way with the McAdam pavement.

+**2.** *ellipt.* A road made with successive layers of broken or crushed stone. Also fig.

1839 *Indiana H. Rep. Jrnl.* 216 Provided, . . . a good McAdam can be made on said route. **1848** *Yale Lit. Mag.* XIII. 281 Instead of plodding on foot along the dusty, well-worn McAdam of learning, why will you take nigh cuts on ponies? **1879** B. F. Taylor *Summer-Savory* 160 The streams . . . run along their rough McAdams. **1897** *Outing* May 135/2 The width of the macadam is eighteen feet, while the crushed rock is ten inches deep.

Macadamize, *v tr.* To make (a road) with layers of broken stone or similar materials. Also *vbl. n.* {1826–} — **1825** *Boston Auditor* 10 Stones for McAdamizing. **1852** *Knickerb.* XL. 198 Our road lay along a curving line of high ground, . . . which had been macadamized with shells instead of stone. **1895** *Dept. Agric. Yrbk. 1894* 520 In the central and western counties of the State there is usually an abundance of stone for use in macadamizing roads.

Macadamized road. A road built of layers of stone. {1827–} — [**1830** *Western Mo. Review* III. 481 What we now achieve, in the way of road making, is well done, and McAdamized, the only kind of road, that will stand in our deep loamy soils.] **1835** Hoffman *Life in West* II. 127 After travelling a few hundred yards on a Macadamized road, I found myself riding over paved streets . . . [in] Lexington. **1852** Marcy *Explor. Red River* (1854) 122 The road . . . is seventy miles broad, and as firm and smooth as the best McAdamized road. **1890** J. Jefferson *Autobiog.* 24 These smooth hair trunks . . . would have made slippery seats even on a macadamized road.

***Macaroni.** Wheat paste prepared in long tubes, somewhat larger than those of spaghetti; a dish in which macaroni is the principal ingredient. Also ellipt. for *macaroni pie.*

Cf. Pawnee macaroni.

1802 Cutler in *Life & Corr.* II. 71 Dined at the President's . . . [on] a pie called macaroni, which appeared to be a rich crust filled with the strillions of onions, or shallots. . . . Mr. Lewis told me . . . it was an Italian dish, and what appeared like onions was made of flour and butter, with a particularly strong liquor mixed with them. **1872** Brace *Dangerous Classes N.Y.* 194 In the same room I would find . . . women contriving still . . . to roll their dirty macaroni. **1881** *Harper's Mag.* April 682/2 A man is not . . . a pauper because he . . . likes macaroni. **1895** *Bachelor of Arts* I. 629, I have no hesitation in recommending a moderate use of macaroni, rice, tapioca, sago and custard puddings.

Macaroon. A small sweet cake made chiefly of sugar, white of egg, and ground almonds or coconut. {1611–} Also attrib. — **1828** Leslie *Receipts* 35 Break the spunge-cake and maccaroons into small pieces. **1861** *Vanity Fair* 2 Feb. 50/1 A waiter, whereon stood . . . a plate of macaroons, éclairs and sponge cake. **1893** *Harper's Mag.* Feb. 441 Ever so many nice things are all ready; chicken salad, . . . a long row of macaroon custards, each cup with *three* macaroons dissolved in madeira!

Macartney rose. (See quotation.) — **1856** *Rep. Comm. Patents 1855: Agric.* 315 The single white 'Macartney' rose, I find, in this region, forms an excellent hedge.

Maccaboy. Also **maccoboy.** A fine snuff, scented with attar of roses. {1740–} — **1819** A. Peirce *Rebelliad* 12 A box . . . fill'd with vulgar stuff, Call'd maccaboy, or headache snuff. **1838** *S. Lit. Messenger* IV. 336/2 That . . . was no vulgar sound, though not an unfrequent one since the discovery of Maccoboy. **1856** M. J. Holmes *L. Rivers* 132 She helped herself to a pinch of her favorite Maccaboy. **1891** Welch *Recoll. 1830–40* 183 It was not uncommon to see a couple of portly old gentlemen meeting on the street offering their boxes of Maccaboy, Rappee or Scotch, each to the other.

Maccaboy snuff. =prec. — **1827** *Hallowell* (Me.) *Gaz.* 20 June 4/3 (*advt.*), B. Wales Has just received . . . Lorillard's Macaboy snuff. **1854** Benton *30 Years' View* I. 420/2 He went up to Mr. Clay, and asked him for a pinch of his fine maccoboy snuff.

+**Maccarib.** [Of Indian origin.] The caribou. *Obs.* — **1672** Josselyn *New Eng. Rarities* 20 The Maccarib, Caribo, or Pohanc, a kind of Deer, as big as a Stag, round hooved.

+**McClellan.** *attrib.* [General George B. *McClellan* (1826–85).] **1.** Designating a type of saddle. **2.** Designating a kind of military cap. (1) **1866** J. E. Cooke *Surry* 83 His saddle was a plain 'McClellan tree' strapped over a red blanket for saddle cloth. **1880** Tourgee *Bricks* 94 One of them had put a 'McClellan saddle' and a gag-bit upon one of the black polled cattle. **1885** Howells *S. Lapham* ii, A burly mounted policeman, bulging over the pommel of his M'Clellan saddle, jolted by. (2) **1888** Billings *Hardtack* 277 [A] large number of the soldiers of '62 . . . did not wear the forage cap furnished by the government. They bought the 'McClellan cap,' so called, at the hatters' instead.

+**McCown's bunting.** =next. — **1856** Cassin *Illust. of Birds* 228 *Plectrophanes McCownii.* . . . McCown's Bunting. **1874** in Coues *Birds N.W.* 125 Maccown's Bunting . . . was abundant in the vicinity of Cheyenne in August.

+**McCown's longspur.** (See quot. 1917.) — **1887** Ridgway *Manual N.A. Birds* 406. **1917** *Birds of Amer.* III. 22/1 McCown's Longspur (*Rhynchophanes mccowni*) . . . is found on the interior plains of North America, east of the Rocky Mountains.

***Mace.**[1] A spice consisting of the dried covering of the nutmeg. — **1656** *Essex Probate Rec.* I. 233 Mace and Ribing, starch and poudarblu. **1759** *Newport Mercury* 26 June 4/3 Imported . . . and to be sold by Jacob Richardson, . . . new Raisins, Nutmegs, Cinnamon, Cloves and Mace. **1816** *Ann. 14th Congress* 1 Sess. 1872 Duty . . . on mace, one dollar per pound. **1923** J. M. Hill *Practical Cooking* 183 Purée of Chicken. . . . Season with salt and mace.

***Mace.**[2] A scepter or staff of office. — **1689** Sewall *Diary* I. 249 The Aldermen Came up two by two, the Mace carried before them. **1798** *Phila. Ordinances* (1812) 147 [The high constable] shall carry in his hand a short staff or mace, to distinguish him in the execution of his office. **1872** *Atlantic Mo.* March 324 As soon as he has taken his seat in the Speaker's chair [of the House of Representatives], the mace, which until that moment has lain under the table, is placed upon it.

+**MacGillivray's.** [Wm. *MacGillivray,* Scottish naturalist (1796–1852).] Used in the names of birds. — **1887** Ridgway *Manual N.A. Birds* 69 *B[ulweria] macgillivrayi.* . . . Macgillivray's Petrel. **1917** *Birds of Amer.* III. 30/2 Macgillivray's Seaside Sparrow (*Passerherbulus maritimus macgillivraii*) is found on the Atlantic coast from South Carolina to Florida and, in winter, along the Gulf coast.

+**MacGillivray's warbler.** Tolmie's warbler, *Oporornis tolmiei.*— **1839** Audubon *Ornith. Biog.* V. 75 Macgillivray's Warbler, *Sylvia Macgillivrayi,* . . . is one of the most common summer residents of the woods and plains of the Columbia. **1917** *Birds of Amer.* III. 158/1 W. Leon Dawson, the Ohio ornithologist, insists that Macgillivray's Warbler should be called 'Tolmie's Warbler.'

+**Macheer.** *W.* [Corruption of Sp. *mochila.*] The leather covering of a saddle; a flap of leather on the seat of a saddle. — **1853** Brewerton *With Kit Carson* (1930) 49 Our saddles were of the true Mexican pattern, wooden trees covered with leathers called *macheers.* *a***1861** Winthrop *J. Brent* 222 The heavy California saddle, with its macheers and roll of blankets, fell to the ground. **1873** Miller *Amongst Modocs* 50 The Prince unfastened his cloak from the macheers behind my saddle.

Machilla. (See Mochila.)

***Machine.**

+**1.** *Polit.* A party, factional, or personal organization that operates through a system of committees and individual workers in an effort to control nominations, appointments, elections, etc. {1884}

See also Political machine.

1876 *N. Amer. Rev.* Oct. 327 He encountered the combinations inside politics,—the machine. **1881** *Nation* 6 Jan. 1/2 The Conklingite Machine

[was] . . . represented by General Sharpe and the 'Anti-Machine' by Mr. Skinner. **1887** *Courier-Journal* 6 Jan. 3/2 [A] fight is being waged against the caucus idea by the most enterprising political manipulators in the State, through what is called the 'machine.' **1895** MYERS *Bosses & Boodle* 40 The 'machine' is a political trust, organized to benefit one man or a few, and to defeat an honest expression of the rank and file of a party. **1914** *Cycl. Amer. Govt.* I. 147/2 The successful boss makes use of both of the party machines as a most reliable means of deceiving the public.

2. An engine put on wheels. {a vehicle, 1687–} +**a.** 'A fire-engine' (*Cent.*). *colloq.* Hence *to run with the machine.*

***a*1859** *Yankee Notions* 259 (B.), As for the machine, why, she's a pearl of the East. **1890** *Cent.* 3560/3 *To run with the machine*, to accompany a fire-engine to a fire, either as a member of the fire-company or as a hanger-on: a phrase used when the members of fire-companies (in large cities) were volunteers, and service at fires was gratuitous. (U.S.)

b. A locomotive, a bicycle, or an automobile.

***a*1870** CHIPMAN *Notes on Bartlett* 259 *Machine*, . . . a locomotive steam-engine, is so called by R.R. engine-drivers and conductors. **1895** *Outing* XXVI. 445/2 Here we jumped off and began to push our machines up a long slanting road occupying a deep ravine. **1902** *N.Y. American* 16 Aug. 2/1 The chauffeur . . . noticed the tire of the left . . . wheel of the machine was deflated. **1922** PARRISH *Case & Girl* 275 They took me away in a machine to the yacht.

+**3.** Attrib. in sense 1 with *man, manager, ring*, etc.

1866 *Congress. Globe* 18 Jan. 308/1 Machine voting is that by which a man puts a few hundred ballots in a district and demands of certain persons a certain number of votes when the poll is closed. **1882** *Nation* 10 Aug. 102/3 In politics he is chiefly known as having . . . dissatisfied the voters of his district by his obedience to 'Machine' rule. **1882** *Ib.* 21 Dec. 519/2 With a Democrat who is a thorough partisan, a Republican Machine man can strike hands; . . . with an anti-Machine man never. **1885** *Mag. Amer. Hist.* March 295/1 The 'machine wing of the Republican party came to be known as such under the leadership of Mr. Conkling.' **1887** *Scribner's Mag.* May 625/1 If journalists and journals were in the market, . . . there would be no such widespread bolt against your machine ticket to-day. **1896** *Chicago Record* 17 Feb. 4/1 The machine managers force the holding of primaries wherein their own candidates are put in nomination. **1904** *N.Y. Ev. Post* 11 April 6 When he began his work in St. Louis as Circuit Attorney . . . he found that the criminals who were robbing the city were the machine ring.

+**Machine card.** A perforated card of wood or metal, which may be attached to a loom to cause the warp-threads to be lifted in the proper succession to produce a figured design; a Jacquard card.—**1827** *Hallowell* (Me.) *Gaz.* 20 June 4/5 S. G. Ladd has for sale Winslow's Machine Cards at Factory prices. **1844** *Lexington Observer* 25 Sept. 4/6 The subscribers have received on consignment a lot of Machine Cards for Cotton and Wool. **1853** *Mich. Agric. Soc. Trans.* IV. 108 James M. Hale, Akron, Ohio, various samples of machine cards, well got up. **1857** *Lawrence* (Kan.) *Republican* 28 May 3 Agents for the sale of James Smith & Co.'s superior Machine Cards.

Machine gun. An automatic gun which sends out a rapid, continuous fire. {1870–} Also attrib. (Cf. GATLING GUN.)

1872 *Rep. Comm. Patents 1871* II. 851/2 Operating Machine-Guns.—George O. Kinne, Hartford, Conn. **1875** KNIGHT 1454/2 The mitrailleur, or machine-gun, . . . sends a large number of small projectiles independently . . . to a considerable distance. **1886** *Harper's Mag.* Oct. 793/2 The types adopted by the United States navy are the Hotchkiss revolving cannon and . . . the smaller calibre machine guns of Gatling. **1904** *N.Y. Ev. Post* 24 Oct. 7 The casual observer wanders about such a fort without being able to see how the garrison could retire with its machine guns. **1924** *Scribner's Mag.* Dec. 652/1 He noticed a machine-gun sergeant . . . plodding through the mud.

+**Machine politician.** A politician who is a member of a political machine. — **1879** *Congress. Rec.* 25 June 2327/1 The 'machine politicians' in New York, as they are called, thought they knew better. **1886** ROOSEVELT in *Century Mag.* Nov. 74/1 Any man who perfects and uses this [political] organization is . . . a machine politician. **1906** *N.Y. Ev. Post* 1 March 8 The proposal to make Charles E. Hughes the Republican candidate for governor of New York excites no enthusiasm among machine politicians.

+**Machine politics.** Politics as practiced by a political machine. — **1882** *Nation* 16 Nov. 411/1 The President had definitively abandoned the maxims and practices of a local manager of Machine politics in New York. **1913** LA FOLLETTE *Autobiog.* 68 Never in my life have I derived benefit from the two sources of power by which machine politics chiefly thrives.

+**Machine shop.** A shop containing machines, such as lathes, planes, etc., where machines, parts of machines, or the like, are made, finished, or repaired.

1833 *Niles' Reg.* XLIV. 315/1 The edifice, in which all the machinery employed in the mills is manufactured, is termed the 'machine shop.' **1845** *Knickerb.* XXVIII. 279 He will . . . likewise do all jobs in iron, brass and steel usually done in a small machine-shop. **1860** MORDECAI *Virginia* 322 The iron foundries and machine shops in Richmond are numerous, and some of them on a large scale. **1872** TICE *Over Plains* 44 The machine shops of the Kansas Pacific railroad are located [in Brookville]. **1883** *Wheelman* I. 434, I have never had any of them [*sc.* spokes of bicycle] tightened except when visiting a machine-shop for more important repairs. **1912** RAINE *Brand Blotters* 199 The town would be a division point; the machine shops of the system would be located there. **1918** *Fed. Bd. Vocational Ed. Bul.* No. 20, 22 The machine shop should be located on the ground floor.

Machinist.

1. One who makes a machine or works in a machine shop, a mechanic; an engineer who operates a machine. {1706–}

1809 CUMING *Western Tour* 223 Pittsburgh [has] . . . one machinist and whitesmith. **1832** WILLIAMSON *Maine* I. 28 At Buxton, . . . are Salmon falls, . . . affording conveniences to the ingenious machinist. **1852** STOWE *Uncle Tom* xliii, George has found constant occupation in the shop of a worthy machinist. **1877** HOWELLS *Out of Question* IV. i, Would you tell them that he was a machinist or a steamboat engineer by trade? **1883** *Century Mag.* Oct. 954/1 The property master, the machinist, the gas engineer, the chorus master, have all to conform rigidly to their instructions. **1905** N. DAVIS *Northerner* 98 Falls was a clever machinist; . . . he knew each bolt and bar, each rod and piston.

+**2.** A machine politician. *Obs.*

An isolated English example (1799) may be found in the *O.E.D.*

1880 *Scribner's Mo.* Oct. 908/1 'This,' says the political machinist, 'is an utter misconception of the whole case.' **1882** *Nation* 2 Nov. 371/3 Office-jobbing, and trading . . . are to-day making every Machinist in the country run to ask honest men what he must do to be saved.

+**Machinize,** *v. tr.* To make like a machine; to organize into something like a machine. — **1856** EMERSON *Eng. Traits* 41 The Times newspaper, . . . by its immense correspondence and reporting, seems to have machinized the rest of the world for his [the reader's] convenience. **1901** *Congress. Rec.* 8 Jan. 738/1 The real purpose of these rules is to machinize this House; to create a one-man power; to magnify the machine and minify the member.

* **Mackerel,** *n.* Also †**mackarel, macrell,** etc.

***1. a.** An important food fish (*Scomber scombrus*) found plentifully in the North Atlantic. **b.** Less commonly, a general name for fishes specified in sense 2.

1616 SMITH *New England* 17 Holybut, Mackerell, Scate, or such like, a man may take with a hook or line. **1648** *Suffolk Deeds* I. 94 If he pay or cause to be paid . . . twelve pounds in mackerell . . . then this deed [is] to be void. **1690** SEWALL *Letter-Book* I. 3 Ship'd on board the Ketch Adventure . . . Fourty Barrels of Mackarel at 16*s.* p Barrel. **1714** *Boston News-Letter* 6 Dec. 2/2 One of them was bound from Boston to Pensilvania, with Rum, Macrell &c. **1789** MORSE *Amer. Geog.* 82 No less than five thousand barrels of mackarel, salmon, and pickled codfish, are vended annually in the city of Philadelphia. **1807** *Mass. H. S. Coll.* 2 Ser. III. 56 The mackerel passes the Sound in the spring, but does not come near Martha's Vineyard. **1844** *Lexington Observer* 5 Oct. 4/6, 100 Packages Boston Mackerel . . . in store and for sale. **1872** MCCLELLAN *Golden State* 246 A small, poor quality of mackerel is caught in and about Monterey bay. **1918** LINCOLN *Shavings* 122 Jed had bought the mackerel of the fish peddler the previous afternoon.

2. With qualifying adjectives, applied to various fishes of the superfamily Scombroidea. {*a*1672–} See also CHUB, HORSE, SPANISH, etc., MACKEREL.

1814 MITCHILL *Fishes N.Y.* 423 Spring Mackerel, *Scomber vernalis*, . . . is caught off Sandy-Hook in great numbers with the hook. **1884** GOODE, etc. *Fisheries* I. 305 The Frigate Mackerel [*Auxis thazard*] resembles, in some particulars, the common Mackerel. *Ib.* 433 The Bluefish.—*Pomatomus isaltatrix*. . . . About New York they are called 'Ship Mackerel.' **1890** *Cent.* 3561/3 *Green mackerel*, a carangoid fish, *Chloroscombrus chrysurus*. (Southern coast, U.S.) **1911** *Rep. Fisheries 1908* 308 Chub Mackerel . . . is also called . . . 'tinker mackerel,' and 'little mackerel.'

3. *attrib.* and *comb.* **a.** Designating times, activities, etc., important in catching mackerel.

1671 *Plymouth Laws* 284 If any Swine . . . do there annoy or trespass such as there Fish . . . in the Mackrel seasons. **1775** HUTCHINSON *Diary & Lett.* I. 403 The Mackerel fishery . . . began in July, or about that time. **1834** C. A. DAVIS *Lett. J. Downing* 42, I settled the first mackerel voyage of the 'Two Pollies.' **1856** *Porter's Spirit of Times* 6 Sept. 9/2 [The Spanish mackerel] is taken with the artificial squid, sailing in a mackerel-breeze. ***a*1861** WINTHROP *J. Brent* vi. 61 [He] went off on a mackerel trip.

b. Designating various instruments used in catching or preparing mackerel for the market.

1709 *Essex Inst. Coll.* VIII. 20 To 1500 of mackrell Hucks [*i.e.*, hooks]. **1715** *Boston News-Letter* 16 May 2/2 Lately arrived from England . . . a good Mackerel Saine Sixty Fathom long well fitted. **1846** CORCORAN *Pickings* 29 Isn't the curb stone 'changing partners' with the mackeral cask. **1877** PHELPS *Story of Avis* 349 Barbara was hauled in, hand over hand like a mackerel-net. **1880** N. BROOKS *Fairport Nine* i. 13 Ned Martin now dropped . . . one end of a mackerel line which he had with him. **1884** *Nat. Museum Bul.* No. 27, 821 Contents of ditty-box: . . . 1 brass-swivel; 1 mackerel-splitting knife; 1 piece cotton cloth. *Ib.* 1061 Mackerel brand-kettle. . . . Used for branding mackerel barrels.

c. Designating various boats used in catching or hauling mackerel.

1825 NEAL *Bro. Jonathan* III. 415 The fishermen say . . . a mackrel boat was coming up. **1840** DANA *Two Years* 236 Captain Faucon standing at the tiller himself, and steering her as he would a mackerel smack. **1857** *Harper's Mag.* Sept. 541/1, I can recommend a cruise in a mackerel-catcher as a certain . . . cure. **1858** THOREAU *Maine Woods* 85 Now we . . . pass near a small village-like fleet of mackerel-fishers at anchor. **1884** *Nat. Museum Bul.* No. 27, 713 Mackerel schooner A. R. Crittenden, of Gloucester.

+d. In the names of other fishes: (see quotations).

1818 MITCHILL in *Amer. Monthly Mag.* II. 322 Mackarel-Pike.—*Esox Scomberius;* an inhabitant of the fresh streams of New-York. **1842** *Nat. Hist. N.Y., Zoology* IV. 352 The Mackerel Porbeagle, *Lamna punctata.* **1897** *N.Y. Forest, Fish, & Game Comm. 2d Rep.* 238 *Decapterus macarelius,* . . . Mackerel Scad, . . . was found common at Southampton, Long Island.

+e. *Mackerel goose,* (see quotation).

1917 *Birds of Amer.* I. 218 Northern Phalarope. *Lobipes lobatus.* . . . [Also called] Mackerel Goose.

+Mackerel, *v. intr.* To fish for mackerel. — **1877** JEWETT *Deephaven* vi. 108 When we were mackereling she never give us any trouble. **1881** McLEAN *Cape Cod Folks* 62, I was going mackerellin' with ye myself that time.

Mackereler. a. One who fishes for mackerel. **b.** A boat used in mackerel-fishing. {1883–} — **1880** TOURGEE *Bricks* 430 Perhaps they were not cod-fishers but mackerelers. **1886** *Century Mag.* Oct. 824/2 The mackerelers do not keep together so much as formerly. **1889** MUNROE *Dorymates* 31 Any fishing vessel but a mackereller going out at this stormy season would have left both top-masts and her jib-boom at home.

+Mackerel gull. The common tern.

[**1796** NEMNICH *Allgem. Polygl.-Lexikon der Naturgesch.* V. 820 Mackarel gull. *Larus ridibundus.*] **1832** WILLIAMSON *Maine* I. 145 The mackerel gull is nearly as large as a goose. **1844** *Nat. Hist. N.Y., Zoology* II. 299 In Massachusetts it [the common tern] is called *Mackerel Gull,* from its simultaneous appearance with that fish. **1880** *Harper's Mag.* Sept. 504/1 The mackerel-gull swoops down from overhead. **1917** *Birds of Amer.* I. 60 Common Tern. *Sterna hirundo.* . . . [Also called] Mackerel Gull.

+Mackerel shark. [See quot. 1839.] Any of several sharks of the family Lamnidae. — **1819** *Plough Boy* I. 135 The revenue cutter brought in two very strange fish, found eating a dead horse, supposed to be mackerel sharks. **1839** STORER *Mass. Fishes* 185 *Lamna punctata.* . . . As this species is generally seen following shoals of mackerel upon which it feeds, it is commonly known among the fishermen as the Mackerel Shark. **1884** GOODE, etc. *Fisheries* I. 299 The shark known to fishermen as the 'mackerel shark' is one of the principal enemies of the Mackerel.

+Mackinaw. Also **Mackinac.**

Canadian F. *mackinac* from Ojibway *mitchimakinâk,* 'great turtle,' the name of a strait between Lake Michigan and Lake Huron, and of a city in Michigan, formerly an important Indian trading post.

1. *ellipt.* **a.** =MACKINAW BOAT.

1842 *S. Lit. Messenger* VIII. 586/2 A party of six . . . had occasion about this time to ascend the Missouri, in a Mackinaw, with the purpose of trading with the Mandans. **1880** *Scribner's Mo.* May 124/1 All available space in the overladen mackinaws needed to be reserved for the indispensable whisky.

b. =MACKINAW BLANKET.

1851 M. REID *Scalp Hunters* 22 My 'Mackinaw' . . . makes my bed by night and my great coat on other occasions. **1857** *San Francisco Call* 29 Jan. (Th.), Mac . . . was making a variety of contortions between heaven and a mackinaw.

c. A Mackinaw jacket or coat.

1902 WHITE *Blazed Trail* 375 A tall, slender, but well-knit individual dressed in a faded mackinaw and a limp slouch hat. **1908** BEACH *Barrier* 20 Her cabin deck was lined with passengers . . . still clad in mackinaw and overalls. **1920** LEWIS *Main Street* 230 He had given up roving as horse-trader, and wearing red mackinaws in lumber-camps.

2. *attrib.* **a.** In the names of various fishes. (Cf. MACKINAW TROUT.)

1838 *S. Lit. Messenger* IV. 28/1 Here I saw on the table d'hotel the Mackinaw shad, famous in those parts. **1842** *Nat. Hist. N.Y., Zoology* IV. 240 The Mackinaw Salmon, *Salmo amethystus,* . . . [is] exceedingly voracious.

b. *Mackinaw coat, jacket,* (see quot. 1907).

1902 WHITE *Blazed Trail* 16 They all wore heavy blanket mackinaw coats, rubber shoes, and thick German socks. **1903** *Outlook* 7 Nov. 586 He caught up his Mackinaw jacket and his cap and mittens and hurried me out of the camp. **1907** *Dialect Notes* III. 246 *Mackinaw coat,* a short, heavy, double-breasted plaid coat, the design of which is large and striking. Worn particularly by woodsmen, and, to a slight extent, by students of the University of Maine. **1924** CUMMINS *Sky-High Corral* 43 His second glance told him it was the reddish-brown of a mackinaw coat.

+Mackinaw blanket. A thick blanket like those formerly distributed to Indians at Mackinac: (see quot. 1891).

1827 McKENNEY *Tour to Lakes* 115, I have just been shown . . . the two stout Mackinac blankets that are to cover me. **1832** *23d Congress 1 Sess.* Sen. Doc. No. 512, II. 828 None but the Mackinac blankets, so called, will be procured for the Indians. **1850** HINES *Voyage* 128 [We found] one Mackinaw blanket, two coats, one bear-skin, and one paddle. **1870** O. LOGAN *Before Footlights* 286 The women . . . now affect the hoop-skirt, which looks 'real sweet' worn under the scantiness of a Mackinac blanket. **1891** WELCH *Recoll. 1830–40* 114n., Mackinaw blankets were those manufactured for the government to supply the Indians of the Northwest, when they assembled at Mackinaw to receive their annuities.

+Mackinaw boat. A flat-bottomed boat, sometimes with oars and sails, formerly used esp. on the upper Great Lakes. *Obs.*

1833 CATLIN *Indians* I. 73 A boat-builder . . . constructed a mackinaw-boat. **1839** *Knickerb.* XIII. 211 Our boat was . . . a Mackinac boat, of light construction, . . . provided with sails and seats, and an awning over the centre-part, and rowed by nine men. **1842** *S. Lit. Messenger* VIII. 407/2, I embarked in two 'Mackinaw' boats . . . of about three tons burthen, without deck or box, sharp fore-and-aft. **1852** J. W. BOND *Minnesota* 278 A large Mackinaw boat started for the settlements below, in quest of barley. **1876** BOURKE *Journal* 8 Sept., Daily 'Mackinaw' boats came down the Yellowstone, gliding swiftly upon the bosom of the river. These boats are rough affairs, managed chiefly by the rudder and driven along solely by the current. **1890** LANGFORD *Vigilante Days* (1912) 502 The navigation of a Mackinaw boat over this portion of the river was intensely interesting.

+Mackinaw gun. A gun of a type distributed to the Indians at Mackinac, Michigan. *Obs.* — **1824** KEATING *Narrative* (1825) I. 195 He was provided with a gun, of the kind distinguished by the name of Mackinaw gun.

+Mackinaw skiff. =MACKINAW BOAT. — **1826** FLINT *Recoll.* 102, I have seen a Mackinaw skiff, carrying five tons, which came from the lakes into the Chicago of Michigan. **1828** *Western Mo. Rev.* I. 580 The eldest son . . . took to the canoe, attached to the Mackinaw skiff.

+Mackinaw trout. A large lake trout, the namaycush. — **1840** *S. Lit. Messenger* VI. 604/1 The celebrated Mackinaw trout, so called after the town, near which they are found, is generally caught by the hook. **1842** *Nat. Hist. N.Y., Zoology* IV. 240 The Mackinaw Trout . . . exists in all the great lakes lying between the United States and the Arctic ocean. **1888** *Boston Jrnl.* 9 Nov. 2/4 The Fish Commissioner at Carson . . . [expects] 30,000 Mackinaw trout from the United States fish-hatchery.

+McKinleyism. [Wm. *McKinley* (1843–1901), representative from Ohio, later twenty-fifth president of the U.S.] The policy of high protection, as exemplified by the McKinley Tariff Act of 1890. — [**1892** *Peel City Guardian* 3 Dec. 8/6 One of the American papers . . . puts it second as a subject for congratulation on the defeat of McKinleyism.] **1896** *Congress. Rec.* 19 March 2991/2 Before McKinleyism, we imported $54,772,000 more gold than we exported.

Mackintosh. A waterproof overcoat. {1836–} — **1840** LONGFELLOW in S. Longfellow *H. W. Longfellow* I. 365 Sumner striding down Hancock Street in his white mackintosh. **1891** *Scribner's Mag.* Oct. 518/1 Leath, wearing a mackintosh reaching to his heels . . . , suddenly appeared. **1898** WESTCOTT *D. Harum* 375 A puff of wind blew the cape of his mackintosh over his head. **1912** NICHOLSON *Hoosier Chron.* 454 She watched Sylvia button her mackintosh.

+Maclura. [Wm. *Maclure,* Amer. geologist (1763–1840).] The genus of which the Osage orange (*M. pomifera*) is the single species; the Osage orange. — **1818** NUTTALL *N. Amer. Plants* II. 233 *Maclura* (Bow-wood, Yellow-wood.) **1846** BROWNE *Trees Amer.* 465 *Maclura aurantiaca.* . . . [Called in U.S.] Maclura, Osage Orange-tree [etc.]. **1857** *Ill. Agric. Soc. Trans.* II. 302 Mr. Tisdell has two hedges of the maclura growing on his farm. **1858** WARDER *Hedges & Evergreens* 32 For a fence of defence, the first in importance is the Maclura, Bodark (*Bois d'arc*) or Osage Orange; a native of Arkansas and Texas.

+Macock. Also **macocqwer, macocks,** etc. A kind of melon. Now hist.

1588 HARRIOT *Virginia* C b *Macocqwer,* according to their seuerall formes called by vs, *Pompions, Mellions,* and *Gourdes,* because they are of the like formes as those kindes in England. **1612** SMITH *Virginia* 17 [The Indians plant] a fruit like vnto a muske millen, but lesse and worse; which they call *Macocks.* **1633** Gerard *Herball* 919 The Virginian Macocke, or Pompion. **1705** BEVERLEY *Virginia* 27 Their macocks are a sort of melopepones, or lesser sort of pompion. **1896** P. A. BRUCE *Econ. Hist. Virginia* I. 98 In addition, there were muskmelons, . . . macocks or squashes, gourds [etc.].

Mad, *n.* Anger, fury, a state of anger. *colloq.*[2] {1847–89} '*Dial.* and *U.S. slang.*' (*O.E.D.*).

1834 in Bassett *Plantation Overseer* 65, I will be damde if I can do anythinge with them and they all ways in the mads. **1867** HARRIS *Sut Lovingood* 194 Tu help his mad to a head. **1876** TRIPP *Student-Life* 63 They left in a hurry; and it was lucky too, for my mad was up. **1909** STRATTON-PORTER *Girl of Limberlost* 59 'Kate,' he said, 'you needn't take out your mad over our little racket on Maggie.'

+b. *To get one's mad up,* to become angry; *to get* (someone's) *mad up,* to make (someone) angry. *colloq.*

1867 GOSS *Soldier's Story* 258 The Colonel has got his mad up, and you'll be sent into the stockade. **1891** 'THANET' *Otto the Knight* 18 He was 'round in a week; but that got my mad up, too. **1897** *Outing* XXX. 487/2 Let the pony get his mad up. **1913** LONDON *Valley of Moon* 106 When he gets his mad up it's a case of get out from under or something will fall on you—hard.

***Mad,** *a.* Angry. Often in humorous phrases. *colloq.*

'In many dialects in Great Britain and the U.S. the ordinary word for "angry"' (*O.E.D.*).

1758 in A. Tomlinson *Mil. Jrnls.* (1855) 31 They shot at a mark and our Provinshals beat them & it made them very mad. **1781** WITHERSPOON *Druid P.* No. 5, I was quite mad at him, he made me quite mad. **1816** PICKERING 128 *Mad*, in the sense of *angry*, is considered as a low word in this country, and at the present day is never used except in very familiar conversation. **1836** W. O'BRYAN *Travels* 106 Angry and bitter words are held in such abhorrence, that they call it madness. If a person speaks in an angry manner, they say he is mad. **1853** COZZENS *Prismatics* 110 The jolly sailing-master . . . departed from the place as mad as a bear with a sore head. **1859** BARTLETT *Americanisms* 524 As mad as all wrath. *a***1870** CHIPMAN *Notes on Bartlett* 260 *Mad enough to eat snakes.* Angry in a high degree.—Eastern Mass. **1888** DORSEY *Midshipman Bob* 116 He'd be as mad as Dide Tucker if he found out! **1897** BRODHEAD *Bound in Shallows* 24, I sot on a fence rail cussin' mad.

* **Mad,** *v. tr.* To anger, exasperate. *colloq.*[2]

1815 HUMPHREYS *Yankey* 106 *Mad*, (not in the usual sense, insane,) to make angry. **1816** PICKERING 129 The verb To Mad, in the sense of *to make angry* is also in use in many parts of this country; but it is considered as a mere vulgarism. **1873** M. HOLLEY *My Opinions* 249 At the same time it madded some of the Republicans. **1893** 'THANET' *Stories Western Town* 85, 'I didn't mean to mad you,' Tim grunted. **1922** A. BROWN *Old Crow* 271 The old man down the road . . . forbade secular talk in the household during a thunder shower. It 'madded' the Almighty. You might be struck.

Madagascar Negro. A Negro from Madagascar, +imported as a slave. Also attrib. — **1704** *Boston News-Letter* 26 June 2/2 Ran-away from Capt. Nathaneal Cary, of Charlestown, . . . a well set middle sized Maddagascar Negro Woman. **1723** *Amer. Wkly. Mercury* 1–8 Aug. 2/2 Run away . . . a Negro Man named Jack . . . , he is a Madagascar Negro.

* **Madam.** Also **madame.**

1. Prefixed to a surname {1703–}: **a.** A respectful or polite title given to a woman. Obsolescent except among those who affect the title.

At first its application seems to have been limited to a married woman of position, but it was later extended to a woman of any rank or position.

1704 S. KNIGHT *Journal* 9 Madm Billings . . . went wyth me to ye Tavern. **1744** A. HAMILTON *Itinerarium* 201, I find they are not quite so scrupulous about bestowing titles here as in Maryland. My landlady goes here by the name of Madam Lay. **1752** in *Travels Amer. Col.* 318 Bought a trunk of Madam Hinsdell. **1819** J. FLINT *Lett. from Amer.* 144 The wife is, of course, Mrs.; the daughter and maid servant are indiscriminately saluted Miss, or Madam. All are ladies. **1844** *Lowell Offering* IV. 191 Madam Bradshaw was evidently displeased. *a***1870** CHIPMAN *Notes on Bartlett* 260 *Madam* [is given] . . . to a widow of social eminence: as, 'Madam Mather.'

+**b.** A deceased woman of some rank or position. *Obs.*

1704 *Hist. Digest Press Mass.* (1911) 98 On Fryday died Madam Anne Paige. **1759** *Essex Inst. Coll.* XLIX. 4 Died at Danvers, Madam Hubard, mother to the Revd Mr Clarke's Lady. **1809** KENDALL *Travels* II. 44 Here [in Plymouth, Mass.], and in some of the neighboring places, it has been, and still is the practice, to prefix, to the name of a deceased female of some consideration, as the parson's, the deacon's or the doctor's wife, the title of *madam.*

c. (See quotation.)

'Now in U.S., and perh. formerly in England' (*O.E.D.*).

1849 LYELL *Second Visit* I. 129 The title of Madam is sometimes given here [in Boston], and generally . . . in the South, to a mother whose son has married, and the daughter-in-law is then called Mrs.

2. The mistress of a house. {1824}

'Now only *U.S. vulgar*' (*O.E.D.*).

1863 *Rio Abajo Press* 28 July 1/1 W. F. M. Army will . . . make a visit to Washington, for the purpose of advising Mr. Lincoln . . . and for the purpose of paying his respects to 'The Madame' in the shape of a Navajo blanket. **1879** TOURGEE *Fool's Errand* 45, I've brought back the books I borrowed of the madam the other day.

* **Madder.**

* **1.** A Eurasian climbing plant (*Rubia tinctorum*) cultivated for the dye obtained from its roots. Also attrib.

1789 MAY *Jrnl. & Lett.* 136 Madder, rhubarb, cotton, and rice grow luxuriantly. **1818** *Niles' Reg.* XV. 175/2 A vessel has arrived at Philadelphia with 433 bundles and bales of madder root, on board. **1848** *Rep. Comm. Patents 1847* 192 Madder, . . . [as a] dye plant, . . . may be made an article of profit. **1884** EGGLESTON in *Century Mag.* Jan. 434/2 Other favorite plants for experiment [during colonial times] were madder, which was tried from the extreme South to Albany, and olive trees, which were several times introduced.

* **2.** The root of this plant; also, the dye made from it. Also attrib.

1691 SEWALL *Letter-Book* I. 117 Send me also a small Cask of Madder about half a Barrell. **1759** *Newport Mercury* 26 June 4/1 Just Imported . . . Variety of Spices, Madder, Ground Redwood, white Lead [etc.]. **1777** *N.Y. State Soc. Arts* I. 368 The madder does not give so deep a red to cloth or silk as the galium. **1815** *Niles' Reg.* VIII. 56/1 Woad and madder, essential dyes in our manufactures, are already successfully cultivated. **1890** *Cent.* 3568/1 *Madder-print*, . . . cloth printed with designs in madder, or in colors of which madder forms a part; especially, cotton prints so made.

+**Mad-dog skullcap.** (See quot. 1843.) — **1821** *Mass. H. S. Coll.* 2 Ser. ix. 156 *Scutellaria lateriflora*, Mad dog scull-cap. **1843** TORREY *Flora N.Y.* II. 72 *Scutellaria Lateriflora.* . . . Mad-dog Scull-cap. . . . Wet meadows and borders of small streams; common. About twenty years ago [believed an aid] in curing hydrophobia but is now quite neglected. **1885** *Outing* Nov. 180/1 A delicate little herb with dainty, blue flowers is called mad-dog skull-cap, from its imputed power of curing hydrophobia. **1894** *Amer. Folk-Lore* VII. 96.

+**Mad-dog weed. 1.** The water plantain. **2.** =MAD-DOG SKULLCAP. — (1) **1821** *Mass. H. S. Coll.* 2 Ser. IX. 146 Plants, which are indigenous in the township of Middlebury, [Vt., include] . . . Water plantain, mad-dog-weed. **1833** EATON *Botany* 11 *Alisma . . . plantago*, . . . water plantain, mad-dog weed. (2) **1818** *Amer. Jrnl. Science* I. 371 July 17. Mad dog weed (*Scutellaria lateriflora*) and purple vervain (*Verbena hastata*) in blossom.

* **Made,** *a.* Of land: Reclaimed by drainage; filled up.

1785 *Md. Hist. Mag.* XX. 55, I have . . . laid down all the wharves and made land in the bason of Baltimore. **1789** MORSE *Amer. Geog.* 286 The land on the sea coast . . . has every appearance of made ground. **1817** S. BROWN *Western Gaz.* 195 The cotton-wood predominates on the made bottoms. **1863** *Ill. Agric. Soc. Trans.* V. 665 Made earths and puffy soils are unfit, being both too arid and liable to heave. **1898** *Boston Morning Herald* 25 Feb. 6/7 The Back Bay [of Boston] and the greater part of the South end being all made land.

* **Madeira.** also †**Madeara, Madera.**

* **1.** =MADEIRA WINE.

1687 *Doc. Hist. N.Y. State* I. 163 For every pipe of Madera, . . . Sherry & all sweet wines the summ of forty shillings [duty]. **1733** BYRD *Journey to Eden* (1901) 283 We cheer'd our hearts with three Bottles of pretty good Madeira. **1771** FRANKLIN *Autobiog.* 259 Over the Madeira he propos'd my setting up my business. **1804** *Holyoke Diaries* 145 We began upon half a quarter Cask of Madeira. **1885** HOWELLS *S. Lapham* xiv, 'I will take some of this wine,' said Lapham, pouring himself a glass of Madeira.

2. Attrib. with *bottle, grape, liquor.*

1654 JOHNSON *Wonder-w. Prov.* 208 Portugal hath had many a mouthful of bread and fish from us, in exchange of their Madeara liquor, and also Spain. **1760** WASHINGTON *Diaries* I. 145 Set out 55 cuttings of the Madeira Grape. **1835** INGRAHAM *South-West* I. 92 *Cabarets*, upon the shelves of which . . . [were] myriads of claret or Madeira bottles.

+**Madeira nut.** =ENGLISH WALNUT. — **1817–8** EATON *Botany* (1822) 321 *Juglans regia*, madeira nut. . . . It is said that this variety is indigenous to North America. **1856** *Rep. Comm. Patents 1855: Agric.* p. xiv, *The Persian Walnut*, or *Madeira Nut*, . . . appears to be well adapted to the climate of the middle and southern latitudes of the United States. **1892** APGAR *Trees Northern U.S.* 141 *Juglans regia.* (Madeira Nut. English Walnut.) . . . Hardy as far north as Boston in the East, but needs protection at St. Louis.

+**Madeira vine.** A vine with shiny leaves and white flowers, *Boussingaultia basselloides.* — **1854** *S. Lit. Messenger* XX. 622/1 Behind so impervious a screen as honeysuckle and Madeira vine, . . . I can discern you. **1899** *Animal & Plant Lore* 106 It is bad luck to have a Madeira vine growing around the house. Chestertown, Md. **1907** *St. Nicholas* May 651/1 At a little space before the 'front door,' were planted the bulbs of Maderia [*sic*] vines and seeds of moon-flowers and morning-glories.

Madeira wine. Also **Madera wine.** Wine produced on the island of Madeira. {1687–}

1676 SEWALL *Diary* I. 21, I spent 18s, 6d, in Ale, 6d in Madera Wine, etc. **1701** WOLLEY *Jrnl. N.Y.* (1860) 35 Their best Liquors are Fiall, Passado, and Madera Wines. **1714** *Boston News-Letter* 7 June 2/2 Good Madera Wine both White and Red, to be Sold by Mr. Jonathan Williams. **1733** *S.C. Gazette* 179/1 He has also . . . most sorts of Medicines, Madeira Wine, good Butter in Cask. **1790** *Ann. 1st Congress* II. 1547 Upon every gallon of Madeira wine called London particular, thirty-five cents.

+**Madeleine.** Also **Madaleine, Madeline.** [Fr.] A variety of summer pear. — **1847** IVES *New Eng. Fruit* 56 *Madaleine.*–This is the first good pear which ripens. **1851** BARRY *Fruit Garden* 300 *Madeleine.*—This is the earliest good pear we have; size medium, flesh melting, sweet and delicate. **1858** *Ill. Agric. Soc. Trans.* III. 337, I once had a tree of the Madeline attacked [by blight] eight feet from the ground.

Mademoiselle. {1642–} +(See quot. 1909.) — **1882** *Nat. Museum Bul.* No. 16, 570 *Sciæna punctata.* . . . Silver Perch; Yellow-tail; Mademoiselle. **1883** *Ib.* No. 27, 441 *Sciæna chrysura.* . . . Silver Perch; Yellow-tail; Mademoiselle. . . . Atlantic coast of the United States from Cape Cod to Florida; Gulf of Mexico. **1884** GOODE, etc. *Fisheries* I. 375 At Pensacola they [yellowtails, *Bairdiella chrysura*] are known by the name 'Mademoiselle.' **1909** WEBSTER 1294/1 *Mademoiselle*, . . . any of several sciænoid fishes which compose the genus *Bairdiella;* esp., *B. chrysura*, of the southern United States.

+**Madisonian.** A supporter of the political policies or principles of James Madison (1751–1836). Also transf. — **1809** *Ann. 10th Congress* 2 Sess. 1065 No Administration, even if composed of Adamites, Pickeronians, Jeffersonians, and Madisonians, . . . could uphold this navy system in time of peace. **1812** *Steele P.* II. 685 Clinton is the next strongest party & Madison weakest of all—and one or two of Madisonians joining the Feds. would give them the votes. **1817** *Ann. 14th Congress* 2 Sess. 795

Persons who at that time were staunch Federalists, and since that time have been staunch Jeffersonians, Madisonians, and Monroites. [**1838** *U.S. Mag.* IV. 11 The Madisonian, a paper recently established at the seat of Government, under the auspices of the Conservative party.]

+**Madison's War.** The War of 1812. — **1813** *Salem Gazette* 1 Oct. 3/3 The farms of Nantucket men were formerly upon the ocean, but Madison's war has obliged them to take land tacks on board, and pass the mountains.

Madras. [A city and province in India.] **1.** Used attrib. in the names of various articles of dress made from cloth originally produced there. {1882–} **2.** *ellipt.* =MADRAS HANDKERCHIEF; also, cloth of a kind originating in Madras. — **(1) 1840** *Knickerb.* XVI. 239 The junior stopped to brush up his whiskers, and adjust his Madras cravat, before he went. **1863** 'E. KIRKE' *Southern Friends* 59 The women wore neat Madras turbans. **(2) 1859** STOWE *Minister's Wooing* xi, Candace . . . donned the brilliant Madras which James had lately given her. **1903** *Windsor Mag.* Sept. 409/1, I was trying to sell shirts and neckties to the same crowd, but they had not been educated up to cheviots and madrasses in those days.

Madras handkerchief. A brilliantly colored handkerchief, frequently worn by Negroes as a headdress. {1833} — **1810** *Columbian Centinel* 24 Jan. 4 Just received . . . Callicoes; Bandanna and Madrass Hankerchiefs. **1847** BRIGGS *Tom Pepper* I. 122 She was a young woman, . . . with large gold rings in her ears, and a Madras handkerchief tastefully tied upon her head. **1852** STOWE *Uncle Tom* xviii, She found . . . a couple of soiled Madras handkerchiefs, some yarn and knitting-work. **1888** CABLE in *Century Mag.* Jan. 345/1 The bundles in Madras handkerchiefs had given place to traveling-bags.

Madregal. Variant of MEDREGAL.

+**Madroño.** Also **madroña.** [Sp. *madroño.*]

1. An evergreen tree or shrub (*Arbutus menzesii*) of the west coast. Also attrib.

1850 TAYLOR *Eldorado* (1862) 130 Clumps of the madrono—a native evergreen, with large, glossy leaves, and trunk and branches of light purple—filled the ravines. **1867** HARTE *Condensed Novels* 241 Occasionally the madroño shook its bright scarlet berries. **1888** *Amer. Humorist* 5 May 12/1 Here and there a madrona tree grows, with its bark peeling of[f]. **1897** *Scribner's Mag.* Nov. 609/1, I found a grove of the beautiful madrona near the home of . . . a young man. **1913** LONDON *Valley of Moon* 458 She gazed across the shimmering level of the vast Sacramento Valley. No redwoods. No hills. No forests. No manzanita. No madroños.

2. (See quotation.)

1892 *Dialect Notes* I. 249 *Madrona:* a shrub or small tree of the heath family found in the foot-hills west of the Pecos. . . . *Arbutus Xalapensis var. Texana* (Gray). [Tex.]

+**Madstone.** A stone, believed by some to be the hardened cud of a deer (see quot. 1883), popularly supposed to cure the madness caused by the bite of an animal. — **1834** *S. Lit. Messenger* I. 182 He should be able to form a concrete mass by means of beef gall and alkali, which would resemble and equal in virtue the madstone. **1864** *Round Table* 18 June 2/2 We are not so ready with an explanation of the 'mad-stone' used to obviate ill effects from the bites of rabid animals. **1883** ZEIGLER & GROSSCUP *Alleghanies* 158 The deer with a mad-stone in him is twice as hard to kill as one of the ordinary kind. **1889** *Amer. Philos. Soc. Proc.* XXVI. 336 Among the various individuals in Pennsylvania who profess ability in exorcism and charms, we occasionally find one who is reputed to possess a *mad-stone.*

Maffia. Also **Mafia.** {1875–} An Italian secret society of criminals, introduced into the United States about 1860. +Hence *Maffia affair,* the action preceding and subsequent to the lynching of eleven members of the Maffia in New Orleans in 1890. — **1891** *Nation* 9 April 296/2 The authorities at New Orleans have a knotty problem to deal with in the Mafia. **1893** *Harper's Mag.* Feb. 381/1, I had hoped to tell of the picturesque Italians . . . and their standing in the community [of New Orleans] since 'the Mafia affair.'

***Magazine.**

***1.** A storehouse or warehouse. Now rare.

1619 *Va. House of Burgesses* 11 We may . . . inforce them . . . to cure their Tobacco before they bring it to the Magazine. **1653** *Boston Rec.* 10 Begin a stocke for a publique magzine of Corne for the towne. **1755** *Lett. to Washington* I. 121, I have found it necessary . . . [to] promise a party to Walkin's Ferry to guard the Magazine of provisions there. **1792** *Ann. 2d Congress* 1022 Whatever may promote the regular establishment of magazines of ship timber, is in various views desirable. **1808** PIKE *Sources Miss.* III. App. 23 A public magazine for provisions, where every farmer brings whatever grain and produce he may have for sale.

***2.** A building or place used for the storage of arms and ammunition.

1653 *Boston Rec.* 6 The very hart & securest part of the towne . . . is the most fitt for a Magazene for Armes. **1722** BEVERLEY *Virginia* (ed. 2) 250 In his time was also built a new . . . Brick Magazine for Arms and Ammunition. **1817** S. BROWN *Western Gaz.* 203 The barracks, officer's quarters, magazine, &c. are built of logs. **1872** *Atlantic Mo.* May 532 On opening the door of the magazine, a spring-gun was discharged.

b. A quantity or supply of ammunition, powder, etc. Also attrib.

1637 *Conn. Rec.* I. 15 It is ordered that there shalbe a magacen of powder and shott in every plantacon. **1666** *Md. Archives* II. 20 The Upper House do think that the 1400 lb. powder [etc.] . . . to be very necessary to be provided as a Magazine to be distributed as in the Proposal. **1776** J. THATCHER *Military Jrnl.* 75 A *magazine* of *powder* was attached to it in such a manner as to be screwed into the bottom of the ship. **1887** *Courier-Journal* 26 Jan. 4/5 About 200 cases of giant powder exploded while . . . being transported in a magazine car [of the Missouri Pacific R.R.].

3. A periodical publication containing articles or stories by various authors. {1731–} Also attrib.

1741 (*title*), The American Magazine. **1794** *Ann. 3d Congress* 1438 If any person . . . shall receive any letter or packet, other than newspapers, magazines, or pamphlets. **1846** CORCORAN *Pickings* 81, I have contributed to the poetical department of both the dailies and the magazines. **1870** *Nation* 27 Jan. 58/1 A slang-whanging magazine or newspaper writer had only to call persons whom we all honor and admire Borgias. **1904** DERVILLE *Other Side of Story* 173 Many things [were] published in newspapers and magazines regarding the civil service clerk. **1917** SINCLAIR *King Coal* 301 Mary's eloquence was addressed . . . to a certain magazine-cover girl.

Magazinist. A writer for magazines. {1821–} — **a1849** POE *Works* XV. 90 She manages them [her literary subjects] with more skill than is usually exhibited by our magazinists. **1868** *Macmillan's Mag.* May 53/1 Holmes has almost ceased lecturing, by his own choice, since his great success as a magazinist. **1893** *Nation* 13 July 24/1 Mr. Gray the magazinist gives the lie to Mr. Gray the Congressman. **1907** *Springfield W. Repub.* 21 Nov. 1 He was more newspaper man than magazinist.

***Magic.** *Like magic,* without any apparent explanation; like lightning. — **1857** *Knickerb.* Jan. 98 Broiled chickens and oysters . . . disappeared from before us like magic. **1900** *Congress. Rec.* 9 Jan. 704/2 Germany's Chinese trade is increasing like magic.

Magic lantern. An optical instrument that projects light through a transparent slide so as to show upon a screen the image on the slide, greatly enlarged. {1696–} Also attrib.

1746 *N.Y. Ev. Post* 15 Sept. 2/1 At the House of Mr. Wood Furmans, . . . is also to be Seen, the Curious and Surprizing Magick Lanthorn, By which Friar Bacon, Doctor Faustus, and others, perform such wonderful Curiosities. **1796** A. BARTON *Disappointment* II. i, They have got magic-lanthorns, dark-lanthorns, spy-glasses. **1853** BRACE *Dangerous Classes N.Y.* 90, I have made arrangements for a lecture on the Magic Lantern to the boys of our Meeting. **1872** *Ib.* 275 He finally succeeded in subduing these wild young vagrants, . . . holding magic-lantern exhibitions, temperance meetings, . . . and the like. **1911** *Okla. Session Laws* 3 Legisl. 217 It shall be lawful for any indigent or disabled ex-Confederate or ex-Union soldier . . . residing in this state . . . to give illustrated lectures and magic lantern expositions.

***Magistrate. a.** A member of the executive government. (Cf. CHIEF MAGISTRATE, FIRST MAGISTRATE.) **b.** A judge or justice of the peace. {a1688–}

In some of the New England colonies during the seventeenth century, a magistrate of the executive council had power in church matters as well as civil.

1636 *Plymouth Col. Rec.* XI 16 To the Governmt. consisting of the Majestrates & ffreemen of this Corporacion. **1682** J. W. *Let. from New-England* 3 [The people of New Eng.] choose their own Officers, and have a Court which consists of Eighteen Magistrates, which they call a Court of Justice. **1727** in Quincy *Hist. Harvard* I. 567 The signification of magistrate in England, and even now in New England, extends to every one of his Majesty's Justices of the Peace; but in the time when the act abovesaid was made [1642], . . . the known signification extended only to those who were Assistants to the Governor in Council. **1790** *Ann. 1st Congress* I. 1109 Free white persons . . . shall [be required to] give satisfactory proof, before a magistrate, . . . that they intend to reside [in the U.S.]. **1830** COOPER *Water Witch* II. xi, Myndert . . . continued, much in the manner of a city magistrate reading a lesson of propriety to some disturber of the peace. **1854** S. SMITH *Down East* 15 The Deacon was . . . a civil magistrate, before whom most of the important causes in the place were tried. **1908** STEVENS *Liberators* 80 The boy's case was called the next morning in the Magistrate's Court.

***Magnate.** A man of eminence; +esp. one who controls large business enterprises. (Cf. RAILROAD MAGNATE.) — **1852** BRISTED *Upper Ten Th.* 17 Broadway was once the fashionable place of residence . . . and most of the city magnates lived in it. **1878** *Harper's Mag.* Jan. 234 Railway magnates more important than many kings. **1884** R. GRANT *Average Man* xiii, His relationship to the magnate had been naturally the means of connecting him with various profitable enterprises. **1898** *Kansas City Star* 18 Dec. 3/1 Nick Young's schedule called for a gathering of the club owners at 11 o'clock, but not a half dozen magnates were in sight two hours later.

Magnetic, *a.* {1632–}

1. Designating various iron ores that are attracted by, or have the properties of, a loadstone. {1796–}

1813 *N.Y. State Soc. Arts* III. 15 The ores of iron which are found in this country, are . . . magnetic iron stone, brown haematite, and bog iron ore. **1832** WILLIAMSON *Maine* I. 182 The magnetic oxide of iron . . . yields the best bar-iron. **1883** ZEIGLER & GROSSCUP *Alleghanies* 207 Outcrops of magnetic ore extend along the Iron mountains as far as Big Rock creek.

+**2.** Of a person: Possessing power to attract people.

1880 *Spectator* 3 Nov. 1437 The Americans have invented . . . a new word, intended to account for the otherwise unaccountable popularity of some politicians. They say they are 'magnetic.' **1888** BRYCE *Amer. Commw.* I. I. viii. 103 The ordinary American voter . . . likes his candidate to be sensible, vigorous, and, above all, what he calls 'magnetic.' **1898** *Daily News* (London) 16 Aug. 4/6 'He is in no sense a magnetic man,' said a capable American critic.

+**3.** Designating a practitioner who employs electrical or electrical chiropractic treatment.

1881 RITTENHOUSE *Maud* 18 The Abbots came down yesterday for Agnes to be treated by the magnetic physician. **1894** *Stone's Davenport* (Iowa) *City Directory* 345 Daniel D. Palmer, magnetic healer, room 42 Ryan blk. **1905** WIGGIN *Rose* 127 She had heard of a 'magnetic' physician in Boston.

Magnetic telegraph. A type of telegraph invented by S. F. B. Morse (1791–1852). {1845–} Also attrib. (Cf. ELECTRIC TELEGRAPH.) — **1844** *Lexington Observer* 1 June 3/2 The Baltimore papers of Saturday announce the connection of Morse's Magnetic Telegraph between Washington and Baltimore. **1848** *Whig Almanac 1849* 46/2 The trustees of the magnetic telegraph patents agreed with O'Rielly in 1845 that he should build certain lines. **1875** C. F. Wingate *Views & Interviews* 276 The practical utilization of the Magnetic Telegraph was hailed by Mr. Bennett as a means of widening the sphere of journalism.

Magnetizer. One who makes use of hypnotic power; a mesmerist. {1802–} — **1843** CHILD *Lett. New York* 254 The animal magnetizer often feels as if strength had gone out of him. **1846** *Knickerb.* XXVIII. 35 Mr. Stubbs and the magnetizer now proceeded on their walk. **1867** HOLMES *Guardian Angel* 131 It's jes' like them magnetizers,—I never heerd you was one o' them kind, Dr. Hulburt. **1891** EGGLESTON *Faith Doctor* 394 That's the way that the mesmerists and magnetizers . . . work their cures.

Magnificent distances. +*City of Magnificent Distances*, Washington, D.C. — **1835** LATROBE *Rambler in N.A.* I. 28 At Washington, 'the city of magnificent Distances,' . . . you visit the lions;—ascend to the capitol [etc.]. **1840** CHANNING *Works* (1886) 805/2 A witty foreigner observed of the city of Washington, that . . . it was a city of 'magnificent distances.' **1875** *Chambers's Journal* 13 March 172/1 Washington, the capital of the United States, is the City of Magnificent Distances.

Magnolia. [mod. L., from Pierre *Magnol*, French botanist (1638–1715).]

+**1.** A genus of large shrubs or trees of the family Magnoliaceae, noted for the beauty of their flowers and foliage; a tree of this genus.

Of the 35 or so species, about half are American, the other half Asiatic in origin. The chief American species are the evergreen magnolia, the sweet bay, the umbrella tree, the large-leaved magnolia, and the cucumber tree.

1748 *Phil. Trans.* XLV. 166 The Magnolia . . . tho' scarce in Virginia, has been since found to grow in great plenty in the North-West Parts of Pensylvania. **1784** FILSON *Kentucke* 24 Here is also found the tulip-bearing laurel-tree, or magnolia, which has an exquisite smell. **1808** ASHE *Travels* 228 Among the trees the splendid magnolia and tulip are found. **1835** A. PARKER *Trip to Texas* 114 The magnolia, celebrated for its large, splendid blossom, is an evergreen. **1860** HOLMES *Professor* x. 307 The magnolia grows and comes into full flower on Cape Ann. **1879** *Scribner's Mo.* Nov. 41/2 To one accustomed to see only young magnolias five to six feet high [etc.]. **1901** MOHR *Plant Life Ala.* 96 On the southern border of this central pine belt . . . the magnolia is found.

+**b.** With specifying adjectives.

1785 MARSHALL *Amer. Grove* 83 *Magnolia acuminata.* Long leaved Mountain Magnolia or Cucumber Tree. *Ib.*, *Magnolia glauca.* Small Magnolia, or Swamp Sassafras. This grows naturally in low, moist, or swampy ground. **1850** S. F. COOPER *Rural Hours* 476 The small Laurel Magnolia, or Sweet Bay, is found as far north as New York, in swampy grounds. **1892** APGAR *Trees Northern U.S.* 63 *Magnolia grandiflora.* (Large-flowered Magnolia. Southern Evergreen Magnolia.) . . Splendid evergreen tree.

+**2.** A flower of a magnolia tree.

1822 *Holyoke Diaries* 177 We all went to Manchester to get Magnolias. **1874** B. F. TAYLOR *World on Wheels* 131 A barefoot girl approaches you with flowers to sell—fragrant Magnolias. **1882** RITTENHOUSE *Maud* 105 Auntie Henderson sent me two glorious magnolias. **1900** *Louisiana Laws* 239 The Magnolia . . . is hereby selected and adopted as the State Flower. **1904** *Miss. Register* App. 152 Magnolia—State flower of Mississippi.

+**Magnolia warbler.** The black-and-yellow warbler, *Dendroica magnolia.* — **1887** RIDGWAY *Manual N.A. Birds* 498 Magnolia Warbler. . . . Eastern United States (west of Alleghanies). **1902** WHITE *Blazed Trail* 226 Myrtle and Magnolia warblers, oven birds, peewits . . . passed silently or noisily. **1917** *Birds of Amer.* III. 132/1 'Black and Yellow Warbler,' [was] the name formerly applied to the Magnolia Warbler.

Magnum bonum (plum). A large English plum. {1721–} — **1760** WASHINGTON *Diaries* I. 145 Grafted 12 Magnum Bonum Plums. **1850** *Rep. Comm. Patents 1849: Agric.* 448 Plum trees. . . . The varieties which are cultivated are . . . the red magnum-bonum, . . . yellow-egg, . . . Coe's golden-drop. **1851** BARRY *Fruit Garden* 339 *Magnum Bonum, Yellow.*—A very large and beautiful egg-shaped yellow plum; a little coarse, but excellent for cooking; tree vigorous and very productive. *Ib.*, *Magnum Bonum, Red.*—Large and beautiful, egg shaped, violet red; of second quality, valuable for cooking.

+**Magofer.** Also **megopher, magooffer.** [Possibly of Indian origin.] =GOPHER 1. *Obs.* — **1789** *Augusta* (Ga.) *Chronicle* 11 July 4/2 (Th. S.), [The dog] expired by the mouth of a megopher's hole. **1795** *Gazette of U.S.* (Phila.) 16 March (Th.), He must be used like a magooffer, by putting fire on his back. **1840** *S. Lit. Messenger* VI. 509/1, I'd have taken a magofer's grip upon him, and not let go.

+**Magotty bay bean.** [Perhaps from *Magothy* River, Md., or *Magotha*, Va.] A fabaceous vine that grows along the seashore: (see quot. 1829). — **1788** *Philos. Soc. Trans.* III. 228 The Eastern-Shore-bean . . . is found in all parts of Virginia and Carolina. *Ib.* [footnote], Called also the Magotty-Bay-bean. **1829** *Va. Lit. Museum* 221 Whenever a field is not in cultivation, it puts up every where a rich luxuriant crop of a sort of wild vetch, called the magotty-bay bean, which shades the land while it is growing, and, returns to it a rich coat of vegetable manure. **1855** *Amer. Inst. N.Y. Trans.* 168 On the eastern shore of Virginia there grows . . . a sort of pigeon pea, called the maggoty May [*sic*] bean. **1893** *Amer. Folk-Lore* VI. 140 *Cassia Chamæcrista*, magotty boy [*sic*] bean. N.Y.

+**Magotty bay pea.** =prec. — **1786** WASHINGTON *Diaries* III. 127 The Overseer and two or three of the Weak hands . . . were gathering the Wild (or Magity bay) Pea—a tedious operatn.

Magpie. {1605–}

+**1.** One or other of two jaylike, white-and-black-colored birds of the genus *Pica* similar to the European magpie. **a.** The species of the Rocky Mountain region, *Pica pica hudsonia;* also, a bird of this species.

[**1737** BRICKELL *N. Carolina* 180 The Rail, Jackdaw, and Magpy, are not to be met with in Carolina or any of the other Neighboring Provinces as far as I cou'd be informed.] **1807** GASS *Journal* 224 The magpie is also plenty here. **1819** E. DANA *Geogr. Sk.* 53 The *Magpie* is found in great numbers on the Missouri. **1844** *Nat. Hist. N.Y., Zoology* II. 131 The Magpie. . . . This species is very rare in this State, and has never been seen except in the western district near Niagara. **1846** SAGE *Scenes Rocky Mts.* xii, [Horses] so poor and feeble they could oppose none [*sic*] resistance to magpies, and much less to the rapacity of wolves. **1881** CHASE *Editor's Run in N. Mex.* 87 Magpies, mountain blue jays, and other birds, are plenty about the house [in Cimarron]. **1902** WISTER *Virginian* 303 Some magpies sailed down to meet them from the new country they were entering.

+**b.** The yellow-billed species of California, *Pica nuttalli;* also, a bird of this species.

1848 BRYANT *California* 121, I noticed several magpies this afternoon. **1886** *Amer. Naturalist* XX. 607 Almost any cañon which has a considerable sheep corral . . . is quite sure to have its colony of magpies.

+**2.** With specifying adjectives. **a.** *American* or *black-billed magpie*, =sense 1 a. **b.** *Yellow-billed magpie*, =sense 1 b.

1850 S. F. COOPER *Rural Hours* 409 The American magpie is more common west of the Mississippi, but even there it is much more rare than in Europe. **1858** BAIRD *Birds Pacific R.R.* 578 The restriction of the yellow billed magpie to the coast region of California . . . is an interesting fact. **1869** *Amer. Naturalist* April 80 Black-billed Magpie (*Pica Hudsonica*) . . . continued common throughout the route westward [from the Bad Lands]. **1917** *Birds of Amer.* II. 216/2 Down in the San Joaquin and Sacramento valleys of California dwells a cousin of the American magpie. His name is Yellow-billed Magpie (*Pica nuttalli*).

+**3.** *Angling.* A kind of fly.

1897 *Outing* XXX. 223/1 Useful flies: silver doctor, magpie, Cheney, Chubb, oriole, . . . and some few others.

***Maguey.** Also **maguy.** Any of the fleshy-leaved species of *Agave*, as the century plant, esp. those from which mescal or pulque is made. {Of Mexico and the West Indies}

See also ALOE, AMERICAN ALOE, and CENTURY PLANT.

1831 PATTIE *Personal Narr.* 63 It was a vegetable called by the Spanish, mascal (probably maguey). **1837** WILLIAMS *Florida* 34 The eastern side . . . is covered with luxuriant grass and herbs, among which the maguy, . . . raises her pendulous white flowers. **1844** GREGG *Commerce of Prairies* II. 88 The *maguey*, from which is extracted the popular beverage called *pulque*, is not only cultivated extensively in the fields, but grows wild everywhere upon the plains. **1869** BROWNE *Adv. Apache Country* 254 The best liquid we could place before our guests was a native production from the juice of the maguey, called mescal. **1873** COZZENS *Marvellous Country* 33 Common people built their houses of sticks set in the ground, and bound together at the top by ropes made from the fibrous leaf of the maguey. **1897** *Outing* XXIX. 425/1 The great spines of the *maguey* or century plant . . . glistened with the dew.

Maguey plant. =prec. — **1844** KENDALL *Santa Fé Exped.* II. 125 At Saenea, . . . [we] saw the celebrated maguey plant. **1858** *Texas Almanac 1859* 185 The maguey plant grows wild. **1888** SHERIDAN *Memoirs* I. 28 To prevent scurvy we used the juice of the maguey plant, called pulque. **1893** *Harper's Mag.* Feb. 392/2 There is an old dead maguey-plant in a crevice just over it at the top of the wall.

+**Mahala.** (See quot. 1877.) — **1877** BARTLETT *Mahala*, a vulgar name for an Indian squaw; a corruption of the Spanish *muger* (pron.

muher) a woman. California. **1916** WILSON *Somewhere* 338 That old mahala of mine, she not able to chew much now.

Maho. Also **moho.** Any of several small, strong-fibered trees of the family Malvaceae found in Florida. {1666–, in West Indies} Also attrib. — **1763** in W. Roberts *Nat. Hist. Florida* 96 The shore . . . [is] cloathed with . . . vanilla, moho, and cabbage-trees, &c. *Ib.* 100 They have the moho-tree, a very useful shrub, in great plenty. **1784** SMYTH *Tour* II. 12 Eminences clothed with the . . . most beautiful spontaneous productions promiscuously interspersed, as . . . vanella, maho, tupelo [etc.].

+**Mahoganize,** *v.* Also **mahoganyize.** (See quotations.) — **1848** BARTLETT 219 *To Mahoganyize,* to paint wood in imitation of mahogany. **1890** *Cent.* 3579/1 *Mahoganize,* . . . to cause to resemble mahogany, as by staining.

Mahogany. Also †**mahagony, mehogony.**

See the article by Kemp Malone in *Language* XVI. 308–18.

1. The wood of a tropical American tree (*Swietenia mahogani*) extensively used in the making of furniture. {1671–}

1738 W. STEPHENS *Proc. Georgia* 115 Mr. William McKay came up the River . . . with a Cargo of Brazilleta Wood, Mahagony [etc.]. **1773** *Mass. Col. Soc. Publ.* VI. 115 [The building was] consumed, together with . . . a large Quantity of Mahogany. **1818** FEARON *Sketches* 24 Mahogany is used for cupboards, doors, and banisters, and for all kinds of cabinet work. **1866** LOWELL *Biglow P.* 2 Ser. p. lxiv, The parson . . . annoyed him by looking into his workshop every morning, and cautioning him to be very sure to pick out 'clear mahogany without any *knots* in it.' **1883** 'MARK TWAIN' *Life on Miss.* xliii. 438 There's one thing . . . which a person won't take in pine if he can go walnut; and won't take in walnut if he can go mahogany. . . . That's a coffin.

2. Applied, often with specific adjectives, to trees or to their woods which resemble mahogany, +as the coffee tree, etc. (Cf. MOUNTAIN MAHOGANY.)

1780 in *Travels Amer. Col.* 633, I met with [the coffee tree] . . . , the bark something like a Cheery tree the wood when cut a crimson red and cald by some Mahogany. **1813** MUHLENBERG *Cat. Plants* 93 *Gymnocladus Canadensis,* coffee tree [or] mahogany. **1825** *Catawba Jrnl.* 17 May, *American Mahogany.*—A tree, the growth of which is spontaneous in Florida. is said to answer all the purposes of mahogany for cabinet work. **1897** SUDWORTH *Arborescent Flora* 208 *Cercocarpus parvifolius betuloides* (Nutt.) Sargent. Birch-leaf Mahogany.

3. *attrib.* Designating various pieces of furniture, etc., made of mahogany wood.

1756 *Boston News-Letter* 16 Dec., To be Sold, A Beautiful Eight-Day Clock, with a fine Mehogony Case. **1777** *N.J. Archives* 2 Ser. I. 251 Was put on board one of the Ferry Pettyaugers . . . a small Mahogany Box. **1838** INGRAHAM *Burton* II. 174 A portable mahogany table. **1871** STOWE *Pink & White Tyranny* 22 The heavy claw-footed, mahogany chairs . . . all spoke of days past. **1883** *Century Mag.* Sept. 786/2 Clinched with nails are the great mahogany folding-doors. **1911** FERBER *Dawn O'Hara* 207 The simple woman told the story of each precious relic, from the battered candle-dipper on the shelf, to the great mahogany folding table.

Mahogany tree. +The coffee tree. — **1785** MARSHALL *Amer. Grove* 56, [In] Kentucky . . . this tree . . . is said to grow plenty, and is called the Coffee or Mahogany tree.

+**Mahogany yard.** A lumber yard where mahogany is the chief wood sold. — **1818** FEARON *Sketches* 23 Mahogany yards are generally separate concerns.

+**Mahoneism.** The principles of Gen. William Mahone (1826–95). (See quot. 1885.) Also *Mahonist.* — **1885** *Mag. Amer. Hist.* March 295/2 *Mahonist.*—A follower of Gen. Mahone, late of the Confederate service, who organized a revolt against the 'Bourbon Democracy' in West Virginia in 1878. **1887** *Nation* 16 June 499/3 The Democratic party . . . fought a good fight against Mahoneism.

***Maid.**

***1.** A servant girl.

1655 R. WILLIAMS *Letters* (1874) 288 Mrs. Mohun and her maid stood in the pillory. **1698** CHAMBERLAIN *Lithobolia* (1914) 67 Six Stones were severally thrown into the Maid's Chamber near the Kitchin. **1704** *Boston News-Letter* 8 May 2/1 The Maid came along. **1825** NEAL *Bro. Jonathan* I. 19 There were . . . three females . . . and Miriam Brackett, a 'maid'—so called because the preacher had hired her for the 'in door work.' **1903** FOX *Little Shepherd* xi, Field-hands going to work chaffed the maids about the house and quarters.

+**2.** In the names of certain academic degrees conferred upon women. *Obs.*

1882 in *Rep. Comm. Educ. 1882–3* 691 [Degrees conferred in 1882 on women] Maid of philosophy . . . [and] maid of science. **1885** D. C. GILMAN in *N. Amer. Rev.* March 263 There are degrees devised by those who seem to think there is some incongruity in giving young ladies the title of Bachelor, viz.: . . . Maid of Philosophy, Maid of Science, Maid of Arts.

+**Maiden cane.** A creeping grass (*Panicum hemitomon*), of the southern coastal regions. — **1806** LEWIS in *L. & Clark Exped.* V. (1905) 107 Among the grasses of this country I observe a large species . . . [which] has much the same appearance of the maden cain as it is called in . . . Ge[o]rgia. **1901** MOHR *Plant Life Ala.* 346 *Panicum digitarioides.* . . . Maiden Cane. . . . Alabama: Coast plain and Littoral belt.

***Maidenhair.** Also **maiden's-hair.** Any fern having delicate fronds and hairlike stalks, as of the genus *Adiantum* or related genera, +esp. an American species, *A. pedatum.*

1676 GLOVER *Acc. Va.* in *Phil. Trans.* XI. 629 There grow wild in the Woods, . . . Yarrow, Purslan, and white Maiden-hair. **1683** *Mass. H. S. Coll.* 4 Ser. V. 112 We drink barley-water; in which boil anise-seed, liquorice, figs sliced, raisins stoned, a good quantity of maiden-hair, and pimpernel. **1778** CARVER *Travels* 515 Herbs. . . . Toad Plantain, Maiden Hair, Wild Dock [etc.]. **1814** BIGELOW *Florula Bostoniensis* 256 Few vegetables possess a greater delicacy of structure than is exhibited by the glossy stems, and fine, regular leaves of the Maidenhair. **1895** GRAHAM *Stories of Foot-Hills* 234 Some bits of maiden's-hair I had placed in reach of the cool spray yesterday were already withered in the sun. **1901** MOHR *Plant Life Ala.* 311 *Adiantum pedatum.* . . . Maidenhair. . . . Rich shady woods.

Maidenhair fern. =prec. {1833–} Also attrib. — **1879** *Scribner's Mo.* Nov. 38/1 Note the grotesque spreading branches of the gingko, with its triangular, light-colored leaves, resembling some great maiden-hair fern. **1901** HARBEN *Westerfelt* 4 [She] stood . . . holding a bunch of wild flowers and delicate maiden-hair fern leaves in her hand.

+**Maidenland.** 'Land that a man gets with his wife, and which he loses at her death. Virginia' (B. '59).

Maiden name. The surname of a woman before she is married. {1773–} — **1689** SEWALL *Diary* I. 305 Visited Cousin Powers, and Cous. Lapworth, whose maiden name was Ann Lee. **1884** 'CRADDOCK' *Where Battle Was Fought* 239 She gave him, with great particularity, the 'maiden names' of the mothers and grandmothers of his friends.

Maiden's-blush. {1648–} +A variety of apple. — **1817** W. COXE *Fruit Trees* 106 Maidens Blush. This is an apple of large size, and great beauty. **1847** IVES *New Eng. Fruit* 47 *Maiden's Blush.*—This apple is often confounded with the Hawthornden. **1863** *Rep. Comm. Agric. 1862* 168 The tree of Maiden's Blush forms a fine, round, spreading head, very productive.

***Maidservant.** A female domestic. — **1637** *Essex Inst. Coll.* VII. 129 Nicholas Cary reproued in Court for extreame corection of his mayd seruant. **1722** *New-Eng. Courant* 19–26 Feb. 2/2 A Maid Servants Time for Four Years to be disposed of on reasonable Terms. **1855** SIMMS *Forayers* 457 The coachman, cook, and one maid-servant . . . were destined to attend the ladies. **1903** BRADY *Bishop* 176 The Creegans boasted the luxury of a maid-servant.

***Mail,** *n.* Also †**mayle, male.**

As noted by Bartlett in 1859, this word has largely replaced *post* in American usage.

1. a. *Mail of letters,* a bag or sack of letters. *Obs.* {1654}

1711 *Boston News-Letter* 7 May 2/2 Capt. Ball Commander waits only for the Mayle of Letters from Boston on Saturday next per the Post. **1714** *Mass. H. S. Coll.* 3 Ser. VII. 82 The western post . . . to go alternately from Boston to Saybrook and Hartford, to exchange the mail of letters with the New York rider. **1792** *Ann. 2d Congress* 1 Sess. 62 If any person . . . shall unlawfully detain . . . any letter, packet, newspaper, bag, or mail of letters, with which he shall be entrusted [etc.].

b. *collect.* Letters, printed matter, etc., conveyed from one place to another by means of the service rendered by the post office. {1654–}

1705 *Boston News-Letter* 26 Nov. 4/2 The Southern Post carrys with him the Western Male for Connecticut and New-York. **1775** *N.H. Prov. Papers* VII. 464 A Traveller who passed this Town yesterday was the bearer of the mail. **1792** *Ann. 2d Congress* 1 Sess. 59 He shall provide for carrying the mail of the United States by stage carriages or horses. **1801** in Young *Jessamine Co., Ky.* (1898) 82 Enclosed advertisement for carrying the mails. **1815** *N. Amer. Rev.* I. 15 The rapidity with which the mail is transported, equals that of the most improved countries in Europe. **1825** *P.O. Laws* (1843) I. 5 The Postmaster General shall cause a mail to be carried from the nearest post office . . . to the Court House of any county. **1894** *Harper's Mag.* Feb. 472/2 George [Northrup] . . . was engaged in the arduous task of carrying the mail from Fort Abercrombie to Pembina. **1913** *Postal Guide* 12 The postage on fourth-class mail may be prepaid by . . . ordinary postage stamps or parcel-post stamps.

c. A consignment of such matter arriving at, or leaving, a place at a particular time. {1692–}

1705 *Boston News-Letter* 22–29 Jan. 2/2 There are two Mails due from the Eastern Post. **1778** A. ADAMS *Familiar Letters* 343 Four or five sheets of paper, written to you by the last mail, were destroyed when the vessel was taken. **1788** in Buckingham *Newspaper Lit.* II. 48 The pleasing intelligence [was] received by Saturday night's mail. **1833** in *Century Mag.* XXX. 780/1 Will you be so kind as to write by the next mail. **1842** *Diplom. Corr. Texas* III. (1911) 968 In order that this dispatch may be in time for the mail [etc.]. **1893** *Harper's Mag.* Feb. 451 'A mail in?' inquired Chase, surprised, as he saw the letters.

+**d.** A batch of letters, circulars, etc., already delivered to, or set aside for, a private individual, family, or firm; a batch of private letters, etc., to be put into the mails.

*a***1844** M. C. FIELD in Sol. Smith *Theatr. Apprent.* 204 He walks as if he had the missing mail in his pocket and an extra to issue immediately. **1852** E. F. ELLET *Pioneer Women* 332 The Colonel came in to tell his wife the express had brought them a mail, holding in his hand a letter.

1889 *Scribner's Mag.* March 264/1 [The postmaster] was opening his mail. **1906** *Harper's Mag.* March 577 Theodora took her mail and went on the back porch to read it. **1924** BLACKMAN *Business Mail* 7 When mail is held all day for the evening mailing it lies around in the way of every office duty.

2. The system by which letters, printed matter, etc., are forwarded.

1806 WEEMS *Letters* II. 349 Send them on immediately by *water*, if you can't send them very cheap by mail. **1817** *Ann. 14th Congress* 2 Sess. 854 The mail and the press . . . are the nerves of the body politic. **1848** *Whig Almanac 1849* 36/1 Of letters passing through the mails at 5 cents each, there were 36,152,556. **1888** *Amer. Humorist* 2 June 3/2 Why didn't he send his poem by mail? **1900** DIX *Deacon Bradbury* 202 He held in his hand a communication which he had evidently just received by mail.

3. A stage coach or other conveyance which carries mail. {1720–}

1817 *Ann. 14th Congress* 2 Sess. 1049 Stage coaches and expresses would supply the place of the mail. **1833** COKE *Subaltern's Furlough* vii, I again crossed the Potomac . . . and travelling in the mail . . . entered the pretty little village of Aldie. **1837** W. JENKINS *Ohio Gaz.* 1 The great eastern and western mail, via Zanesville and Lexington, passes this point daily. **1889** *Scribner's Mag.* March 267/1 The New York and Chicago Fast Mail . . . leaves New York every night at nine o'clock.

4. *attrib.* and *comb.* **a.** Designating various vehicles that carry mail.

See also MAIL BOAT, COACH, STAGE, etc.

1799 BENTLEY *Diary* II. 300, 18 weeks the Mail sleigh successively passed through Keene, N.H. **1820** *Columbian Centinel* 1 April 1/3 The Mail Carriage and driver were found . . . about 100 yards from the road. **1837** W. JENKINS *Ohio Gaz.* 468 A mail steam boat . . . plies daily to Wheeling, Va. **1848** POLK in *Pres. Mess. & P.* IV. 639 The monthly line of mail steamers from Panama to Astoria has been required to 'stop and deliver and take mails at San Diego, Monterey, and San Francisco.' **1903** A. ADAMS *Log Cowboy* 130 The mail buckboard had reported us to the sutler as camped out back on a little creek. **1903** 'O. HENRY' *Roads of Destiny* 165 One afternoon Jimmy Valentine . . . climbed out of the mail-hack.

b. Designating contrivances, tools, etc., used in handling mail.

See also MAIL BAG, BOX, KEY, etc.

1802 *Ann. 7th Congress* 1 Sess. 1366 Mail-locks, keys, pormanteaus . . . [shall be] paid for by the Postmaster General. **1821** COOPER *Spy* iv, The pedler officiously assisted to tighten the girths, and fasten the blue cloak and vallise to the mail straps. **1883** *Pat. Off. Gazette* 11 Sept. 1077/2 A mail-receptacle consisting of a box or receptacle located in a lower story, and a conductor extending thence upward to a higher story, and there provided with an inlet-opening. **1892** *Harper's Mag.* Dec. 137 The clerk [was] putting the mail-sacks in [the stage].

c. Designating various agencies, services, etc., that facilitate the dispatch of mail.

1837 *Diplom. Corr. Texas* I. (1908) 200 This Government having established regular weekly mail lines to Gaines Ferry on the Sabine River and also to Ballous Ferry on the same river, . . . you are therefore instructed to extend their mail route to each of those points. **1838** VAN BUREN in *Pres. Mess. & P.* III. 503 A moderate curtailment of mail service consequently became necessary. **1843** *P. O. Laws* 11. 1 To this [contract] office are assigned the duties of arranging the connexions of the mails . . . , making out advertisements for mail contracts [etc.]. **1853** *Knickerb.* XLIII. 442 Now I *know* you are a candidate for a mail-agency. **1860** GREELEY *Overland Journey* 199, 12 miles from Bridger—is the Mail Company's station. **1864** *Oregon State Jrnl.* 23 April 1/3 The Postmaster General had advertised for **mail lettings** on that route.

d. Designating various persons who handle or deliver mail.

See also MAIL BOY, CARRIER, etc.

1843 *P.O. Laws* 11. 30 Mail agents . . . receive letters written after the mail is closed . . . [and] hand over said letters to the proper office. **1847** ROBB *Squatter Life* 115 The mail driver now began to melt under the soft whisper floating around him. **1855** HOLBROOK *Among Mail Bags* 126 The mail messengers [are] employed to convey the mails to and from the several railroad depots at central points. **1875** *Chicago Tribune* 21 Aug. 5/3 A mail-escort that will return at once . . . with the mail. **1887** *Courier-Journal* 7 May 5/3 The snowstorms make the passage dangerous in winter, and it is seldom attempted except by mail couriers. **1907** LONDON *Road* 23 That mail-clerk relative of hers would carry me to Ogden. **1914** 'BOWER' *Flying U Ranch* 30 The mailbearer was Andy Green himself.

+**Mail,** *v. tr.* To post or send by mail. — **1827** *P.O. Laws* (1843) I. 25 And be it further enacted, That one or more pieces of paper, mailed as a letter, and weighing one ounce, shall be charged with quadruple postage. **1855** HOLBROOK *Among Mail Bags* 82 That letter . . . Marshall mailed here to go to New Haven, Ct. **1880** 'MARK TWAIN' *Tramp Abroad* 390, I was for mailing him to his widow. **1904** LYNDE *Grafters* 224 Has that letter been mailed? Because if it has, it must be stopped by wire!

+**Mailability.** The quality or condition of being mailable. — **1883** *Official Postal Guide* Jan. 664 Mailability of Doubtful Matter.

+**Mailable,** *a.* Acceptable for mailing. Esp. in phrase *m. matter.* — **1845** *Statutes at Large* V. 736 [No one shall] transport or convey, otherwise than in the mail, any letter or letters, packet or packages of letters, or other mailable matter [etc.]. **1848** BARTLETT 220 Judge Betts stated in his charge to the jury that 'any written communication between one individual and another comes within the term *mailable matter*.' **1907** *Postal Guide* 682 Any article that is mailable for delivery in the United States, is mailable . . . in Hawaii [etc.].

Mail bag. A canvas or leather bag used to carry mail.

1818 *Niles' Reg.* XIV. 48/2 [They] cut open the mail bags and *gutted* the letters of the money contained in them. **1833** COKE *Subaltern's Furlough* xiii, Carpet bags and mail bags . . . were to be seen rolling down the hill. **1854** B. J. TAYLOR *Jan. & June* 126 The mail-bag is swung up beneath the driver's feet. **1882** McCABE *New York* 658 Here are stored all the mail-bags belonging to the United States not in use. **1893** *Harper's Mag.* March 603/2 The mud-bespattered Blue Ridge stage came slowly into Asheville. . . . The mailbags were thrown out. **1907** *St. Nicholas* XXXIV. 756/2 At his funeral all the city postmen, with their mail-bags over their shoulders, were present.

+**Mail-bag catcher.** =MAIL-CATCHER. — **1867** *Statutes at Large* XIV. 393 For mail bags and mail-bag catchers, one hundred thousand dollars. **1887** *Postal Laws* 21 The Mail Equipment Division . . . is charged with . . . the furnishing of . . . mail-bag cord-fasteners, and mail-bag catchers.

Mail boat. A boat that carries mail. {1855–}

1795 in R. Putnam *Memoirs* 397 It has been suggested to me that the mail boats are much too heavy for pushing with the requisite speed. **1838** FLAGG *Far West* I. 63 A long-winded racer of a mail-boat soon after swept past us in her onward course. **1850** TYSON *Diary in Calif.* 13 Steamers . . . had left the United States to ply as mail-boats. **1899** JEWETT *Queen's Twin* 39, [I] joined my friends a little later, with two unnoticed excuses of the beauty of the morning, and the early mail boat. **1909** RICE *Mr. Opp* 17 Once a day . . . it was roused from its drowsiness by the arrival of the mail-boat.

Mail box. {1810} +**a.** A box in which mail is deposited to be collected by the postal service. +**b.** A box in which private mail is left by a carrier. — **1872** *Rep. Comm. Patents 1870* II. 751/1 In a mail-box, the arrangement herein shown and described . . . for the purpose of guiding and holding the mail matter. **1888** *Amer. Humorist* 11 Aug. (F.), His letters . . . will be carried into a United States mail box on the ground floor. **1919** HOUGH *Sagebrusher* 123 Look how he busted down my mail box. **1923** DUTTON *Shadow on Glass* 170 There were but three mail boxes on the carrier's route. **1924** *Sears, Roebuck & Co. Cat.* No. 148, 853 House Mail Box. Made of galvanized iron.

+**Mail boy. 1.** A man who carries mail, esp., in the Civil War, a Northern officer who brought mail to the soldiers. *Obs.* **2.** A clerk who sorts mail. *Obs.* — (1) **1842** in Buckingham *E. & W. States* II. 118, [I] saw descending the hill . . . the mail-boy on his horse at full speed. **a1861** WINTHROP *J. Brent* 196 Jake Shamberlain aint a hog, and his mail boys aint of the pork kind. **1862** in Higginson *Harvard Mem. Biog.* (1866) I. 112 The horrors of the battle-field I must describe to you in another letter, as the mail-boy calls for this. (2) **1874** *Congress. Rec.* 15 April 3099/1 Hitherto seven were known as mail-boys, and the others as mail-messengers.

Mail car. {1842–} A railroad car in which mail is carried. — **1855** HOLBROOK *Among Mail Bags* 124 The man who couldn't ride in the mail car, [was] rather 'chop-fallen.' **1910** *Springfield W. Repub.* 29 Dec. 9 The locomotive and tender and baggage and mail cars were thrown from the tracks.

+**Mail-carrier.** One who carries mail, as formerly from one post office to another, or recently to families on a mail route.

1790 *Ann. 1st Congress* II. 1821 Mail-carriers should be . . . exempted [from serving in the militias of the several states]. **1824** MARSHALL *Kentucky* II. 81 The mail carrier through the wilderness, was killed on Laurel river. **1855** HOLBROOK *Among Mail Bags* 195 The mail carriers . . . charged directly at the whole array of Indians. **1876** HABBERTON *Jericho Road* 43 The postmaster . . . heard the horn of the approaching mail-carrier. **1885** CUSTER *Boots & Saddles* 257 The risk and suffering of our mail-carriers during the two previous winters were . . . fresh in my memory. **1919** HOUGH *Sagebrusher* 116 The dusty figure of the mail carrier of that route came out.

+**Mail-catcher.** In a mail car, a device used for catching bags of mail suspended from posts at way stations. (Cf. MAIL-BAG CATCHER.) — **1875** *Chicago Tribune* 18 Sept. 5/3 The Post-Office Department has introduced the use of a 'mail-catcher.' **1887** *Postal Laws* 252 For the purpose of exchanging mail between post-offices at certain way and flag stations . . . the 'mail catcher' is used. **1893** CUSHING *Story of P.O.* 114 There are funds at the disposal of the division for the purchase and repair of mail bags and mail catchers.

Mail coach.

1. A stagecoach carrying mail. Now hist. {1787–}

1808 *Struggles of Capt. T. Keith* 13 They took a place in the mail coach, (or coachee, as these vehicles are here [in R.I.] termed.) **1818** J. FLINT *Lett. from Amer.* 41 The mail-coach is a large clumsy vehicle, carrying twelve passengers. **1858** *Texas Almanac 1859* 28 Requesting the establishment of a four-horse line of mail-coaches between Tyler and Waco. **1886** POORE *Reminisc.* I. 41 The mail coaches were protected by a guard.

+2. =MAIL CAR.
1889 *Scribner's Mag.* March 271/1 The fifth . . . car, is the last mail coach on the train.

Mail contractor. One who makes a contract with the government to carry the mail over a certain route. {1830} — **1830** SANDS *Writings* II. 169 Mr. Briggs and Mr. Jenks, together with the mail-contractor, were present. **1848** *Whig Almanac 1849* 47/2 There were 4,017 mail contractors. **1873** *Winfield* (Kan.) *Courier* 11 Jan. 3/2 The worthy efforts of the mail contractors to supply us with mail through the prevailing epidemic among horses will be appreciated. **1889** P. BUTLER *Recollections* 149 Captain Frederick Emory, a United States Mail Contractor, rendered himself conspicuous in Leavenworth.

+**Mail day.** In remote or not readily accessible places, a day on which mail is delivered. Chiefly in pioneer times. — **1855** *Florida Plant. Rec.* 131 People will be there [at the postoffice] every mail day. **1863** HOPLEY *Life in South* I. 75 A place of general resort for news and business; especially on 'court-days,' once a month, and 'mail-days,' twice or thrice a week. **1887** *Century Mag.* May 115/2 The next time that he saw Harp was mail day. **1900** HANDSAKER *Pioneer Life* 32 On 'mail days,' . . . the young people would 'pair off,' and mounting each a cayuse pony, take their way to the postoffice at Oakland.

+**Mailer.**

1. =MAIL BOAT.
1857 *Knickerb.* XLIX. 58 It is but a day-and-a-half to Halifax; thence by a British mailer across to those neighboring isles. **1883** *Century Mag.* Nov. 160/1 Showing the skill and good control on Transatlantic Mailers.

2. One who mails; spec., one who attends to the wrapping, addressing, etc., of newspapers for the mail.
1885 W. F. CRAFTS *Sabbath for Man* 328 Editors and compositors are kept up until the small hours on Sunday morning; pressmen and mailers for an hour or two later. **1888** *N.Y. Bureau Statistics Labor 5th Rep.* 389 Newspaper Mailers. One [strike] case reported; compromised; 55 engaged. **1896** *Typographical Jrnl.* IX. 352 A fourth vice-president . . . shall be a practical mailer. **1917** D. C. ROPER *U.S. Post Office* 196 The responsibility for this delay [at Christmas time], however, is almost invariably with the mailer who has waited till the eleventh hour.

3. A machine used for addressing mail matter.
1890 *Cent.* 3582/1 *Mailer*, . . . same as addressing-machine.

+**Mailing.** The action of sending by mail. Used attrib. to designate objects and places connected with this action.
1871 Ringwalt *Amer. Encycl. Printing* 292/2 Mailing Machines.—Contrivances of various descriptions to facilitate the operation of directing newspapers to subscribers. **1883** KNIGHT *Suppl.* 575/2 *Mailing Table*, a table at which mail matter is distributed to the mail bags for the various routes or stations. **1887** *Postal Laws* 222 The cancellation of stamps at the delivery office which were not stamped at the mailing office. **1893** Philips *Making of a Newspaper* 18 In this partial survey of the process and cost of making a 'mammoth newspaper,' no account has been taken of . . . the mailing room. **1902** LORIMER *Lett. Merchant* 16 The bottom in the office end of this business is a seat at the mailing-desk, with eight dollars [a week]. **1903** E. JOHNSON *Railway Transportation* 176 Mr. William A. Davis . . . was then chief clerk in the mailing department of the post-office.

+**Mailing clerk.** A clerk who addresses newspapers, letters, etc., for the mail. — **1866** 'F. KIRKLAND' *Bk. Anecdotes* 492 It seems that the 'mailing clerks,' at Jamestown, had neglected to furnish the Navy Department with a copy. **1902** LORIMER *Lett. Merchant* 69, [I] went for him pretty rough for having a mailing clerk so no-account as to be writing personal letters in office hours.

+**Mail key.** A key that will open the lock of a mail pouch. — **1839** *Diplom. Corr. Texas* I. (1908) 392 The Texian Post Master . . . will furnish the United States post masters . . . with a Texian Mail key, and will be furnished with a United States mail key in return. **1846** in Holbrook *Among Mail Bags* 182 You will . . . please hand over all mail matter, the mail key, and all other property belonging to the Department. **1855** HOLBROOK *Ib.* 97 The mails were in 'through bags,' and it required a mail-key to obtain access to their contents. **1887** *Postal Laws* 21 The Mail Equipment Division . . . is charged with the preparation of advertisements inviting proposals for the furnishing of . . . mail locks and keys, label cases [etc.].

Mailman. An employee of the post office who delivers mail. {1881 in Australia} — **1892** S. HALE *Letters* 275 When the mail-man came he had no mail! **1906** PRINGLE *Rice Planter* 319, I drove Ruth as hard as possible to catch the mail man.

+**Mail matter.** Letters, newspapers, etc., sent by mail. — **1839** *Diplom. Corr. Texas* I. (1908) 392 He will charge himself with all unpaid U.S. postage on mail matter on hand in the Post offices of Texas. **1846** [see MAIL KEY]. **1884** *Century Mag.* April 825/1 He arranged that no mail matter should come close to his home. **1906** *Churchman* 10 Nov. 724 All mail matter for the secretary of the convention should be addressed [etc.].

+**Mail order.** An order for merchandise, sent to a business house by mail. Also attrib.
1875 *Chicago Tribune* 8 July 6/3 Few buyers were present and the 'mail order' business also was light. **1898** *Kansas City Star* 18 Dec. 5/2 The mail orders are quite heavy for holiday stock. **1912** NICHOLSON *Hoosier Chron.* 120 She kept in her room a small library of mail-order catalogues. **1916** WILSON *Somewhere* 175 Hetty Daggett . . . orders this by catalogue, No. 3456 or something, from the mail-order house in Chicago.

+**Mail party.** *W.* A party of people traveling in a mail coach. Now hist. — **1858** PETERS *Kit Carson* 517 A fatal adventure . . . once happened to a mail party while traveling this route. **1868** in Custer *Following Guidon* 16, I send her to-night, by the mail party, to Fort Dodge.

Mail pillion. A cushion or pad on the hinder part of a saddle on which to carry luggage. Also attrib. {1639-} — **1711** BUCKINGHAM *Land Exped.* 106 An account of what I brought from home, . . . A mail pillion, Snapsack [etc.]. **1784** J. SMYTH *Tour U.S.* II. 248 All these papers were concealed in the mail pillion-sticks on which the servant carried his portmanteau. **1840** *Niles' Nat. Reg.* 8 Aug. 366/1 Each dragoon [is] to furnish himself with . . . a good saddle, bridle, mail pillion, and valise.

+**Mail pouch.** A mail bag, usually of leather and provided with a lock.
1843 *P.O. Laws* II. 57 All communications relating to portmanteaus, mail pouches and mail bags to be addressed . . . to the Inspection Office. **1855** HOLBROOK *Among Mail Bags* 100 The $40 letter . . . to be crammed into the locked mail-pouch. **1890** H. M. FIELD *Bright Skies* 62 Sometimes . . . he carries one letter, and sometimes his mail-pouch is empty! **1903** E. JOHNSON *Railway Transportation* 173 The mileage traveled by the cars containing the mail-pouches . . . [was] 24,072,558.

+**Mail rider.** A horseman charged with carrying mail; a mail-carrier. — **1835** HOFFMAN *Winter in West* I. 121, [I] was glad . . . to be overtaken by a mail-rider, with his leathern charge, on horseback. **1846** *Knickerb.* XXVII. 52 The mail-rider sank down apparently through the solid ground with his horse and saddlebags. *a***1861** WINTHROP *J. Brent* 32, I had made my arrangements to start about the first of September, with the Sacramento mailriders. **1887** *Courier-Journal* 11 Feb. 8/5 Pucket . . . [was] engaged as a mail-rider between Marion, Ky., and a rural post-office. **1893** *Harper's Mag.* Dec. 86/2 The mail-rider hev quit, 'count o' the rise in the ruver, an' thar's no way ter git word ter him.

Mail road. A road along which mail is regularly conveyed. Now hist. {1837}
1818 in Fearon *Sketches* 430 Ninety acres of land, for sale, . . . about three miles from the great mail road to Cincinnati. **1834** PECK *Gaz. Illinois* 192 [Brattleville is] on the mail road to Rushville. **1843** MARRYAT *M. Violet* xxxv, From Washington to Little Rock, the capital of the state, there is a mail-road. **1862** KETTELL *Hist. Rebellion* I. 333 General Reynolds . . . ordered the thirteenth Indiana, under Colonel Sullivan, to cut their way . . . by the mail road. **1898** YOUNG *Jessamine Co., Ky.* 82 [He wrote] urging the establishment of a mail road from Lexington.

+**Mail robber.** One who robs the mails. — **1855** HOLBROOK *Among Mail Bags* 375 The mail robber was committing depredations from day to day. **1877** *Harper's Mag.* March 614/2 A recent capture of mail robbers . . . is a signal proof of the skill that foils the most careful crime. **1882** *Nation* 28 Dec. 544/3 An important conviction of a mail robber has been secured in West Virginia.

+**Mail robbery.** Robbery of the mails. — **1820** *Niles' Reg.* XVIII. 1/1 (*caption*), Mail Robberies. **1836** *Niles' Nat. Reg.* 19 Nov. 192/2 Mail robbery. The entire mail from Cleaveland, Ohio, to Erie, was stolen from the boot of the stage. **1887** *Courier-Journal* 11 Feb. 8/5 A Kentucky Refugee Tries His Hand at Mail-Robbery in Texas.

Mail route. A route along which mail is carried, delivered, or picked up. Formerly applied to the route taken by mail coaches or mail riders. {1840} Also attrib.
1821 *Ann. 17th Congress* 1 Sess. I. 47 That the same Committee . . . inquire into the expediency of establishing a mail route from Baton Rouge . . . to Opelousas Courthouse. **1837** WETMORE *Gaz. Missouri* 44 The great western mail-route runs through Columbia, and the post-coaches pass tri-weekly. **1860** GREELEY *Overland Journey* 186 It was midnight . . . when we reached the mail-route station. **1873** *Newton Kansan* 27 Feb. 3/3 The mail route petitioned for . . . will make two trips a week. **1910** *P.O. Dept. Ann. Rep.* 34 [Legislation is recommended] to enable the Postmaster-General to make more than one extension of service on a mail route under contract.

+**Mail stage.** =MAIL COACH.
1792 *Ann. 2d Congress* 361 The mail stage passes Merrimack river, about four miles above the old ferry. **1815** *Lit. & Phil. Soc. N.Y. Trans.* I. 336 The Boston mail stage . . . reached Stratford on Thursday night, a distance of about sixty miles. **1850** *Western Journal* IV. 414 We briefly alluded . . . to the Santa Fe line of mail stages, which left this city [Independence, Mo.] on its first monthly trip. **1909** 'O. HENRY' *Options* 137 [He] caught the mail-stage back to Chico.

b. Attrib. with *line, road, route.*
1837 W. JENKINS *Ohio Gaz.* 56 The state road from Xenia . . . and the mail stage road from Cincinnati intersect at this point. **1838** HONE *Diary* I. 289 [They] go by Wilmington and Elkton,—nearly the old mail-stage route. **1839** *Indiana H. Rep. Jrnl.* 361 A memorial and joint resolution on the subject of a mail stage line from Indianapolis to Evansville.

+**Mail station.** *W.* A place along a mail route provided with food and shelter for the accommodation of the drivers, passengers, and animals of a mail coach. — **1867** in *S. Dak. Hist. Coll.* I. 451 The said bands do hereby cede to the United States the right to construct wagon roads, railroads, mail stations [etc.]. **1873** COZZENS *Marvellous Country* 185 Wells . . . had been dug at the mail stations, for the convenience of watering their stock. **1891** RYAN *Told in Hills* 130 The nearest mail station was twenty miles south.

Mail train.

1. A railroad train that carries mail. {1844}

1842 *Boston Dly. Advertiser* 14 June 4/3 The U.S. Mail train leaves Boston at 2 P.M. **1864** in Crawford *Mosby* 272 Colonel Mosby . . . destroyed a United States mail-train, consisting of a locomotive and ten cars. **1876** *Rep. Postmaster-General* p. xxiv, Over the Pennsylvania Railroad . . . a limited mail-train, with superior accommodations, was run between New York, Cincinnati, Indianapolis, and St. Louis. **1887** *Postal Laws* 253 'Catcher' pouches . . . must be returned to the mail trains at once. **1903** E. JOHNSON *Railway Transportation* 176 Over routes where the mails are heaviest 'fast mail-trains' are run composed entirely of postal cars.

+2. In the pioneer West, a party or train of wagons which carried mail.

1855 HOLBROOK *Among Mail Bags* 194 A usual 'mail train' consisted of three covered wagons, . . . each drawn by six mules, guarded by eight or ten men, and carrying perhaps as many passengers. **1858** *Texas Almanac 1859* 149 The mail train between these points consists of three men.

+Mail wagon.

1. A wagon in which mail is carried across country; a mail coach. Now hist.

1835 HOFFMAN *Winter in West* I. 240 After being detained here some days waiting for the St. Louis mail-wagon, . . . I have concluded [etc.]. **1858** PETERS *Kit Carson* 519 The curtains of the mail wagons were all fastened down, and there was no lookout kept. **1866** MOORE *Women of War* 295 She went on to General Birney's headquarters . . . in a mail wagon. **1871** EGGLESTON *Hoosier Schoolm.* 135 You can git on the mail-wagon that passes there about five o'clock. **1898** PAGE *Red Rock* 323 The mail-wagon went over in the morning after the early train. **1910** J. HART *Vigilante Girl* 16 The mail-wagons passed.

2. A horse-drawn wagon carrying mail on city streets. Now hist.

1867 *Atlantic Mo.* June 656/1 The ferry-boat . . . lies alongside of a barge to receive its enormous freight of coal-wagons, omnibuses, express-wagons, mail-wagons, carts [etc.]. **1877** *Harper's Mag.* March 615/1 The sachel [*sic*] had been stolen from a mail wagon while going from the New York post-office to Jersey City. **1904** *N.Y. Ev. Post* 17 May 3 A mail wagon that was being driven rapidly to catch a ferryboat.

+Maine law. a. A law forbidding the sale or manufacture of intoxicating liquor in Maine, enacted in 1851. **b.** Any state or local law enacted with similar provisions: (see quot. 1891).

1852 *Knickerb.* XXXIX. 575 Apropos of the 'Maine Law,' are some clever lines . . . from a friend at Newport, describing a meeting of choice 'spirits' at a well-known establishment. **1854** BROMWELL *Locomotive Sk.* 82 By the time the Maine Law is put in force in this State, the Susquehanna will probably cease to 'get high.' **1855** *Chicago Times* 3 March 3/5 [The N.Y. lawyers] oppose certain features of the Maine Law, which impose onerous duties on the Judges . . . of this city. **1891** *Cycl. Temperance* 306/2 A 'Maine Law,' then, is one prohibiting the manufacture and sale of intoxicating liquor except by specially appointed . . . agents. **1897** *Encycl. Soc. Reform* 1107/1 Vermont in 1852, New Hampshire in 1855, and Connecticut in 1854, passed the Maine Law.

attrib. **1852** CLAPPE *Lett. from Calif.* 180 We *did*, not having the fear of temperance societies or Maine-law liquor-bills before our eyes. **1855** *Chicago W. Times* 18 Oct. 1/2 He had been charged . . . with being a Maine law man, and a woman's rights man.

+Maine-lawism. The principles or supporters of the Maine law. — **1855** *Chicago W. Times* 18 Oct. 2/3 It is a party erected by the fusion of Abolitionism, Maine Lawism, and all the other isms. **1856** HAMBLETON *H. A. Wise* 252 The Democratic party in 1855 had to contend against an alliance of Maine-lawism . . . and the remnants of the old Whig party.

+Maine liquor law. =MAINE LAW. — **1852** *Knickerb.* June 570 'There is nothing new under the sun,' in the enclosed copy of a '*Maine Liquor-Law*' two hundred and sixteen years old. **1855** in Hambleton *H. A. Wise* 268 The Know-Nothing movement . . . has grown up among those who say they will trample the Bible under their feet, if it does not support the Maine Liquor Law. **1857** GRIFFITH *Autobiog. Female Slave* 295 His big nose, as red as a peony, told the story that he was no advocate of the Maine liquor law.

+Mainer, Mainite. An inhabitant of Maine. — **1857** *Harper's Mag.* Sept. 538/2, I astonished a female Mainite by my inordinate capacity for sweet milk and pumpkin-pie. **1887** *Courier-Journal* 31 Jan. 4/4 The traducers of that great prohibition State assert that the Mainers get corned as often as they can.

Main line. Of a railroad: The principal line or track, fed by branch lines. {1865} +In Philadelphia applied specifically to the main line of the Pennsylvania Railroad, running through a fashionable suburban area. — **1873** *Republic* I. 47 Roads over which Government property is transported . . . Illinois Central, main line, also Chicago branch. **1880** *Harper's Mag.* July 196/2 The main line [of the railroad] will soon have reached the Rio Grande Valley. **1900** *Congress. Rec.* 2 Feb. 1448/2 Is the track to be a switch, or a part of the main line of the road? **1916** *Rand McNally Phila. Guide* 5 The most beautiful of these suburbs may be seen along the suburban section of the Main Line of the Pennsylvania Railroad. **1919** *Lutheran Ch. Rev.* Jan. 46 It does seem almost a crime that there is no really fine Lutheran church on the entire Main Line between Paoli and West Philadelphia.

Main road. The principal road running between two places, often having short branch roads. {1878}

1687 *Penna. Col. Rec.* I. 209 A late Order for ye Viewing and Discovering a maine Road from ye Center of Philadelphia ye Shortest way to ye falls. **1716** *N.C. Col. Rec.* II. 265 The main Road from the S.W. side of Middle neck Bridge to the S.W. side of ffrylys bridge. **1817** S. BROWN *Western Gaz.* 16 The main road from Georgia to New Orleans will probably strike Mobile bay at this point. **1833** SILLIMAN *Man. Sugar Cane* 11 The sugar house and settlements are generally situated upon the main road. **1862** MOORE *Rebellion Rec.* V. II. 85 Our lines . . . were compelled to fall back to the woods across the main road. **1902** GORDON *Recoll. Lynchburg* 9 Sufficiently distant from the main road to impress the traveller . . . [are] sassafras bushes, and broom-straw.

***Mainstay.** *fig.* A chief support. {1861–} — **1787** JEFFERSON *Writings* VI. 148 The points of contact and connection with this country, which I consider as our surest mainstay under every event. **1839–40** IRVING *Wolfert's R.* (1855) 207 This maxim which has been pretty much my mainstay throughout life. **1888** SHERIDAN *Memoirs* I. 286 His firm purpose to save the army was the main-stay on which all relied.

Main street. The principal commercial street of a town. Often a proper name. {1743}

In wider use in the United States than in England where *high street* is common.

1687 SEWALL *Diary* I. 183 At night a great Uproar and Lewd rout in the Main Street. **1698** *East-Hampton Rec.* II. 434 Ten Acres of Land . . . [bound] on the west with the Maine Street of the said Town. **1717** *Narragansett Hist. Reg.* III. 279 In or through the Main street, called Hope street, in this town [Bristol, R.I.]. **1767** *York Co., Va., Rec.: Deeds* VII. 20 July, One lot . . . situate on the Main Street of Williamsburg. **1809** CUMING *Western Tour* 194 Main street, parallel to Water street, is one hundred feet wide. **1833** *Niles' Reg.* XLIV. 189/2 The procession moved up Main street. **1843** *Yale Lit. Mag.* VIII. 308 [Bodkinville] can boast of but one street, which, by way of distinction, is called Main street. **1880** INGHAM *Digging Gold* 349 Main Street is thickly studded with buildings in all stages of erection. **1903** WIGGIN *Rebecca* 20 It would be so grand to drive down a real main street.

+b. Used allusively as typical of certain small towns. Also attrib.

1889 HOWELLS *Hazard of Fortunes* I. 106 You know the kind of street Main Street always used to be in our section—half plank-road . . . and the rest mud-hole. **1916** 'BOWER' *Phantom Herd* 5 You'll have to let me weed out some of these Main Street cowboys. **1920** LEWIS (*title*), Main Street.

***Maize.** Also †**maiz, mayze,** etc. [Sp. *maíz.*] (Cf. INDIAN MAIZE.)

Not so commonly used in American speech as *corn:* (see quotations). — **1774** HUTCHINSON *Diary & Lett.* I. 171 Indian corn, or, as it is called in Authors, Maize. *a***1780** *Ib.*, Maize is the name of Indian Corn among the Europeans. **1809** KENDALL *Travels* I. 247 The planting or sowing of maize exclusively called corn, was just accomplished.

***1.** =INDIAN CORN. **a.** The grain.

[**1609** HAKLUYT *Va. Richly Valued* 13 Nothing cost them ought saue the Maiz or corne for their horses.] **1616** SMITH *New England* 16 The hearbes and fruits are of many sorts and kindes: as . . . strawberries, beans, pease, and mayze. **1683** PENN *Descr. Pennsylvania* xvi, [The Indians'] diet is maize, or Indian corn, divers ways prepared. **1784** SMYTH *Tour* I. 293 Indian corn, which is in some places called Maize, is nearly as large as horse beans. **1823** JAMES *Exped.* I. 194 Whilst the maize is yet in the milk or soft state, . . . it is collected and boiled on the cob. **1885** *Rep. Indian Affairs* 92 It is unfortunate that the Poncas do not use maize in the shape of bread.

***b.** The plant.

1666 *S.C. Hist. Soc. Coll.* V. 63 Passed through severall feilds of Maiz or Indian Corn. **1686** *Relat. Invasion of Fla.* 36 [They] went to the fields of Maes. **1794** HUMPHREYS *Industry* 10 Make the tall maize its tassell'd flag unfold. **1805** LEWIS in *L. & Clark Exped.* II. (1904) 238 [Some] Indians of the Missouri . . . do not cultivate maze. **1824** BRYANT *Summer Wind* 9 The tall Maize Rolls up its long green leaves. **1863** TAYLOR *H. Thurston* 192 The canes of maize shot the brown fields with points of shining green. **1900** *Congress. Rec.* 2 Feb. 1457/2 They were settled in a neighborhood where they still remain . . . cultivating maize and potatoes and fruits.

2. *attrib.* With *dance, ear, field, harvester,* etc.

1832 DUNLAP *Hist. Amer. Theatre* 37 No doubt they here offered to the great spirit the first fruit of their maize fields, or of their hunting. **1839** Audubon *Ornith. Biog.* V. 258 [The American Flamingo] is easily tamed, and feeds on rice, maize-meal, &c. **1851** M. REID *Scalp Hunters* 98 Your horse is standing at the maize-trough. **1855** LONGFELLOW *Hiawatha* 177 You shall bless to-night the corn-fields, . . . To protect them from . . . Paimosaid, who steals the maize-ear! **1859** *Rep. Comm. Patents 1858* I. 417 Improvement in Maize-Harvesters. **1873** COZZENS *Marvellous Country* 433 On the morrow the Zunis were to celebrate the 'Maize,' or 'Green-corn dance.' **1909** *Cent. Suppl.*, *Maize sugar*, same as glucose.

3. Attrib. in names of blights and insects that infest maize.

1849 EMMONS *Agric. N.Y.* II. 265 The maize brand . . . produces the greatest and most extensive local transformations. **1854** *Ib.* V. 262 Index, Maize-bugs, 169. [Page 169: *Lygaeus leucopterus* (Say). White-winged Lygeus.] *Ib.*, Maize-moths, 226. [Page 226: *Spilosoma orge.*] **1877** *Vermont Bd. Agric. Rep.* IV. 165 The maize smut, *Ustilago maydis*, . . . attacks all parts of the plant above ground.

Maize bird. +=MAIZE THIEF a. — **1890** *Cent.* 3584/3 *Maize-bird*, . . . an American blackbird of the family *Icteridæ* and subfamily *Agelæinæ;* one of the troopials or marsh-blackbirds: so called from its fondness for Indian corn.

Maize thief. A bird that feeds upon maize: +**a.** The red-winged blackbird, *Agelaius phoeniceus.* +**b.** The purple grackle, *Quiscalus quiscula.* — **1770** FORSTER tr. Kalm *Travels* I. 372 The laws of Pensylvania . . . have settled a premium of three-pence a dozen for dead maize thieves. **1811** WILSON *Ornithology* IV. 38 [Red-winged starlings] are known by various names . . . ; such as the Swamp Blackbird, . . . Corn or Maize Thief, Starling, &c. **1917** *Birds of Amer.* II. 267 Purple Grackle. *Quiscalus quiscula quiscula.* . . . New England Jackdaw; Maize Thief; Keel-tailed Grackle.

+**Maize whisky.** =CORN WHISKY. — **1893** LELAND *Memories* 9 Maize-whiskey could be bought then [*c*1835] for fifteen cents a gallon [in Phila.].

***Maizium.** [Latinized form of MAIZE.] Cornbread. *Obs.* — **1622** 'MOURT' *Relation* 101 We came [to Namaschet] . . . , the Inhabitants . . . giving vs a kinde of bread called by them Maizium.

***Majesty.** *His* (or *Her*) *Majesty*, in colonial usage: the king (or queen) of England. — **1699** *N.H. Prov. Papers* II. 314 Richard, Earle of Bellomont Capt Generll. and Governr. in Chief in & over his Maj'tys Province of New Hampshire. **1705** *Braintree Rec.* 62 Notifye . . . ye person that shall be . . . elected to attend Her Majesties service in ye sd great & general Court. **1721** *Mass. H. Rep. Jrnl.* III. 9 Payment of Money either to you the Governour, or to the Commander in Chief, or to any of His Majesties Council. **1756** *Md. Gazette* 28 Oct., As Thomas Frasier, Post-Rider, was coming hither with his Majesty's Mail, . . . he was knock'd off his Horse.

Major.[1] *Mil.* An officer immediately above a captain and below a lieutenant colonel in rank. {1643–} Also as title.

1648 *Charlestown Land Rec.* 99 The Creek . . . runs on the back syde of the maiors garden. **1685** SEWALL *Diary* I. 96 Mr. Dudley, Saltonstall, Buckley, to say whether they will accept their Commissions as Majors. **1724** JONES *Virginia* 62 The Gentlemen of the Country have no other distinguishing Titles of Honour, but *Colonels* and *Majors* and *Captains* of the Militia. **1788** MAY *Journal & Lett.* 45 Major Sargent and a Mr. Metcalf dined with me to-day. **1816** *Ann. 14th Congress* 2 Sess. 273 Brigade majors [shall be entitled] to the pay of a major of infantry. **1865** KELLOGG *Rebel Prisons* 306, I received . . . $5.00 in Confederate money from our kind-hearted Major. **1901** R. A. ALGER *Spanish-Amer. War* 35 In two regiments the lieutenant-colonels, and in the third the senior major, were taken from the regular army.

+**b.** As an informal title of respect.

1746 E. KIMBER *Itinerant Observ.* 36 Wherever you travel in Maryland (as also in Virginia and Carolina) your Ears are constantly astonished by the number of Colonels, Majors, and Captains, that you hear mentioned. **1852** *S. Lit. Messenger* XVIII. 680/1 Every man that ever comes from Georgia *is* a major,—repaying the honor of the commission or title by undeviating fidelity to the democratic ticket. **1873** 'MARK TWAIN' & WARNER *Gilded Age* 515 When we first came here, I was *Mr.* Sellers, and *Major* Sellers, and *Captain* Sellers, . . . but the minute our bill went through the House, I was *Colonel* Sellers every time.

Major.[2] +**1.** In certain colleges, a course of a specified length, usu. twice as long as a minor. +**2.** In some colleges and graduate schools, the subject of study to which a student devotes especial attention. — (1) **1890** in T. W. Goodspeed *Hist. Univ. Chicago* (1916) 142 A subject taken as a major requires eight or ten hours' classroom work or lecture work a week. (2) **1907** *Columbia Univ. Catalog* March, Open only to students taking a major in the Department of English.

***Major-domo.** *S.W.* +An overseer on a farm or ranch. (Cf. MAYORDOMO.) — **1836** EDWARD *Hist. Texas* 291 Having thus glanced at the Major domo, we shall take a peep at his Locum tenens. **1848** BRYANT *California* 352 We inquired for the *major domo*, or overseer. **1899** A. THOMAS *Arizona* 94 Pa . . . says you're the best Major Domo the ranch ever had.

Major general. A general officer immediately above the rank of brigadier general and below that of lieutenant general. Also as title. {1642–}

1654 JOHNSON *Wonder-w. Prov.* 207 John Endicut Esquire was chosen Major-General, which is an Officer the Freemen make a yearly choice of, all other Military Officers stand for term of life, unless any be out for misdemeanour. **1776** *Jrnls. Cont. Congress* VI. 859 Resolved, That a Disciplinarian with . . . ye Rank of Major General be appointed for ye Army of N. York. **1812** *Niles' Reg.* II. 382/1 Major-general Van Rensselear arrived . . . with his aid-de-camp. **1846** *Whig Almanac 1847* 3 Major-General of the Army—Winfield Scott, of New-Jersey. **1900** *Congress. Rec.* 16 Jan. 856/2 A gallant soldier . . . was tendered the commission of major-general during the Spanish war.

***Majority.**

1. In exact usage, more than half of a whole number {*c*1714–, in parliamentary use}; spec. in politics, more than half of the whole number of people, or of the votes cast. {absolute majority} (Cf. PLURALITY.)

1724 *Boston Rec.* 185 John Clark Esqr by the Majoritors [*sic*] of Voters is Chosen Moderator. **1777** *Jrnls. Cont. Congress* IX. 849 It was then moved . . . to insert 'provided that the nine states so assenting shall comprehend a majority of the people of the united states excluding negroes and indians.' **1787** *Constitution* ii. § 2 If no person have a majority, then from the five highest on the list the said House shall in like manner choose the President. **1825** *Niles' Reg.* XXVII. 382/2 The president of the senate then rose, and declared that no person had received a majority of the votes given for president of the United States. **1912** *Lit. Digest* 16 Nov. 889/2 Governor Wilson, altho he . . . gets a staggering majority of the electoral votes, is actually a minority President.

2. The number of votes cast for one political candidate in excess of the sum total of votes cast for opposing candidates.

In loose usage, frequently used for *plurality.*

1828 *Niles' Reg.* 25 Oct. 129/2 The electoral ticket favorable to the re-election of the present mayor . . . prevailed by a majority of 1401 votes. **1860** *Boston Transcript* 7 Nov. 2/4 Lincoln's majority in Indiana will be *twenty-five thousand.* **1888** LOWELL *Lit. & Polit. Addresses* 210, I remember an election in which the governor of a State was chosen by a majority of one vote.

+**3.** In a legislative group, the party in power. Also attrib.

1842 *Niles' Nat. Reg.* 27 Aug. 405/3 [A] description of the shape of some of the congressional districts as arranged by the majority.

***Make,** *n.* +*On the make:* Eager to 'get ahead,' intent on profit or advancement. *colloq.* {1898–}

1869 J. R. BROWNE *Adv. Apache Country* 507–8, 'I don't see what profit it is to me whether your ledge is worth two hundred thousand dollars or two cents.' 'Oh, you're on the make, are you?' . . . 'Why, yes, to be candid, I'd like to make fifty thousand or so.' **1873** BEADLE *Undevel. West* 402 They're all on the make, and in with these roughs. **1883** HAY *Bread-Winners* 150 You ain't on the make; you're fixed. **1893** *Nation* 9 March 172/2 The men who wanted offices rather than the triumph of great principles, those who were 'on the make' in politics. **1901** W. WILSON in *Harper's Mag.* April 730/1 Sir William Phips had been a ship's carpenter, a common seaman, a ship's captain,—always . . . on the make, risking everything to win his way.

***Make,** *v.*

I. ***1.** *tr.* To cure or pack (fish). *Obs.* {–1690}

1623 BRADFORD in *Hist.* (1912) I. 353*n.*, A good fishing place . . . and well stoed with fish neer at hand, and convenient places to make it. **1769** *Mass. Col. Soc. Publ.* VI. 29 Thare was not one House that he Knew off . . . except one on Damariscove an Island to make Fish on. **1809** KENDALL *Travels* II. 154 The fish, when made, is stacked in the same manner as hay. **1828** SHERBURNE *Memoirs* 54 Those benches are to be found wherever you find a fishing station in Newfoundland, and were . . . designed to make the fish upon.

+**b.** To jerk (buffalo meat).

1846 SAGE *Scenes Rocky Mts.* vi, We commenced the process of 'making meat,' . . . cutting into thin slices the boneless parts of buffalo, or other meat, and drying them in the wind or sun. **1848** RUXTON *Life Far West* i. 27 The numerous stages on which huge strips of buffalo-meat were hanging in process of cure, showed that the party had settled themselves here . . . 'to make meat.'

+**2. a.** To bring (a growing crop) to maturity; to produce (a crop). Also absol. for passive.

1714 *Boston News-Letter* 9–16 Aug. 2/2 We have had an extraordinary drought . . . which makes us apprehensive of a Scarcity of Corn, and little or no Tobacco like to be made. **1758** *Lett. to Washington* II. 323 Plese to Excuse our making So little Tobco I hope we Shall make a good Crop this year. **1763** WASHINGTON *Diaries* I. 187 Observd that my y[oun]g Corn was just beginning to show. . . . Quere, has it time to make or Ripen? **1796** HAWKINS *Letters* 18 She knew not where to fix down, and this uncertainty continued until it was too late to make corn. **1848** *S. Lit. Messenger* XIV. 635/2 Some corn and some cotton are 'made,' as the Virginians say. **1899** CUSHMAN *Hist. Indians* 222 He was allowed to return home and finish making his crop.

+**b.** *quasi-intr.* Of a crop: To amount to (a certain quantity).

1873 *Winfield* (Kan.) *Courier* 5 June 2/3 Most of the wheat over this way will make twenty-five bushels to the acre.

+**3.** *intr.* Of land: To extend in a certain direction. {1743– make out}

1780 *Ky. Petitions* 54 We have laid out . . . above the mouth of a gutt that makes into the river opposite the falls. **1785** DENNY *Journal* 58 Opposite the most prominent parts of the bottoms, hill makes in and forms what is called narrows. **1803** LEWIS in *Jrnls. of L. & Ordway* 68 The high lands make near the Mississippi below the Mouth of said River. **1869** J. R. BROWNE *Adv. Apache Country* 251 This is little better than an open roadstead, protected slightly on the north-west by a sand-spit making out into the Gulf. **1875** 'MARK TWAIN' *Old Times* iii. 46, I judge the upper bar is making down a little at Hale's Point.

+b. Of a stream: To flow or come.

1853 P. KENNEDY *Blackwater Chron.* 5 The Blackwater is a stream that makes down from the north into the Cheat river. **1885** JEWETT *Marsh Island* 94 Right over beyond the cross roads . . . where the crick makes in.

4. To arrive at or reach (a place) by land travel. {*a*1774, 1828; by water travel *c*1624–}

1784 ELLICOTT in Mathews *Life A. Ellicott* 27 About 9 O Clock we made the foot of the Allegany. **1797** F. BAILY *Tour* 339, I had *made* the banks of this river twice before. **1808** PIKE *Sources Miss.* 44 One of my men arrived: he had attempted to make the camp before, and lost himself in the prairie. **1894** WISTER in *Harper's Mag.* Sept. 515/1 They made Snake River.

+b. *Baseball.* To arrive safely at (a base).

1867 CHADWICK *Base Ball Player's Bk.* 130 When the batsman makes his first base. **1880** N. BROOKS *Fairport Nine* 35 The gallant captain hit the next ball . . . and made the first base.

+c. To get to (a place) by a certain time; to catch (a train, boat, etc.). Cf. sense 9 b.

1880 *Boston Transcript* 6 March (Th. S.), Did you make the train? **1901** MERWIN & WEBSTER *Calumet 'K'* 24 'Did you make the train?' 'Caught the caboose just as she was swinging out.' **1906** *Harper's Mag.* April 672 In a state of complete exhaustion, the three made the sloop just as she was casting off. **1916** WILSON *Somewhere* 25, I hurried home to get a bite to eat and dress and make the party.

d. Of a prize fighter: To arrive at (a certain weight) for a match.

1904 *McClure's Mag.* April 668/2 The announcer shrieked from the two sides of the ring that both men had made the required weight. **1924** T. S. ANDREWS *Ring Battles of Centuries* 3 Champions . . . should be required to make weight for their matches.

+5. *intr.* Of ice: To form.

1791 WEBSTER in E. Ford *Notes N. Webster* I. 351 Very cold; ice makes in the river. **1890** *N.Y. Tribune* 12 Dec. 3/3 Several good guides . . . will assist him in an attempt to reach Kadiak Island by crossing Alaska Peninsula before the ice makes.

6. Absol. for *to make money;* to profit.

1852 STOWE *Uncle Tom* viii, I'd 'a gin Shelby eight hundred or a thousand, and then made well on her. **1902** HARBEN *A. Daniel* 213 Ef I knowed he had made by the bu'st I'd talk different, but I don't know it!

+7. *Legal. tr.* To render or hand down (a decision).

1857 BENTON *Exam. Dred Scott Case* 4 Far from being bound by their decisions, Congress may proceed criminally against the judges for making them. **1889** *N.Y. Rep.* CXIV. 581 The word 'decision,' as used in this section, refers to a decision made by a court upon a trial of issues without a jury. **1890** *Mont. Rep.* X. 113 If the decision of the issue was made by a jury it is usually termed a 'verdict,' if made by a referee, or by the judge trying the issue without a jury, the determination of the issue of fact is usually termed the 'decision' or 'findings of fact.'

+8. Of a traveling salesman: To visit (a town) for the purpose of selling goods there.

1902 LORIMER *Lett. Merchant* 135, I hadn't more than made my first town . . . [before] I saw that business ought to be very good there. *a***1910** 'O. HENRY' *Rolling Stones* 112 When I used to sell hardware in the West, I often 'made' a little town called Saltillo, in Colorado.

II. Various phrases.

To make good, (see GOOD *a.* 6); *to make one's manners,* (see MANNER); *to make the feathers* or the *fur fly,* (see FEATHER *n.* 2 b. and FUR 2).

9. *To make it.* **+a.** In giving an order: Let it be.

1883 'MARK TWAIN' *Life on Miss.* 507 He softened, and said make it a bottle of champagne.

+b. To catch a boat or train; to get there; to succeed. (Cf. sense 4 c.)

1885 HOWELLS *Silas Lapham* 108 He jumped on board the steam-boat. . . . 'Just made it,' he said. **1890** BUNNER *Short Sixes* 160 'Put him on the train,' he said. 'There's one at twelve.' 'We can make it if we hurry.' **1895** GRAHAM *Stories of Foot-Hills* 110 It's rough walkin', . . . but I guess you c'n make it. **1896** W. A. WHITE *Real Issue* 174 The young fellows . . . put his name up as candidate for some office or other, . . . but as he saw he couldn't make it, he withdrew. **1917** SINCLAIR *King Coal* 265 He himself had to go to a dinner that evening, and would barely be able to make it.

***10.** *To make out.* **a.** To manage or make shift *to* do something. {1609}

1776 J. ADAMS *Familiar Letters* 231 Amidst these interruptions, how shall I make out to write a letter? **1797** C. PETTIGREW *Let.* 8 Oct. (Univ. N.C. MS.), I am happy to find that you have made out to settle up your accompts so much to your satisfaction. **1845** *Cincinnati Misc.* I. 127 One of our men was mortally wounded, who made out to walk to the boat, where he died in half an hour. **1864** NORTON *Army Lett.* 245 Do you make out to live upon your salary these hard times? **1885** JEWETT *Marsh Island* 36, I guess he may make out to come back if he don't like.

b. *absol.* To get along, manage, or make shift. {1861, also *dial.*}

1773 in Fithian *Journal* I. 33 It would afford you a very particular pleasure to hear that we make out well. **1788** MAY *Journal & Lett.* 87 Breck began the observances by singing, praying, and preaching. . . . Mr. Breck made out pretty well. **1816** A. PETTIGREW *Let.* 27 Dec. (Univ. N.C. MS.), Write me word how you make out housekeeping. **1850** S. WARNER *Wide, Wide World* xliv, I didn't know how you was ever going to make out at first. **1885** JEWETT *Marsh Island* 53 You just try to do all your farm work with one pair o' hands, and see how you make out. **1901** HARBEN *Westerfelt* 65 How'd you make out to-night?

***11.** *To make over.* **a.** To refashion, alter, or change (a person). {1698}

1860 *What Shall I Be?* 76, I might make a good business man after I was 'all made over' as he says. **1884** LOWELL *On Democracy* 10 We have taken from Europe . . . the most turbulent of her people, and have made them over into good citizens. **1897** ALLEN *Choir Invis.* 306 You love Kentucky, but I cannot make myself over. **1904** HARBEN *Georgians* 108 It will be a sight easier to make over a few colored people that never are troublesome . . . than to make over a race that never has been made over by nobody nur never will.

b. To refashion (old garments); to remodel (anything). Also absol.

1866 A. D. WHITNEY *L. Goldthwaite* viii, 'What do you think the third [trunk] is full of?' . . . 'Old winter dresses. To be made over. For the children at home.' **1876** *Vermont Bd. Agric. Rep.* III. 239 Many farmers have plenty of shed room that might be made over into a house for hens at small expense. **1883** HOWELLS *Woman's Reason* 254 She made over all her bonnets and dresses. **1890** WIGGIN *Timothy's Quest* 112 Aunt Hitty comes to 'make over.' **1903** — *Rebecca* 47, I have made it [a poem] over now. **1905** LINCOLN *Partners* 50 The ladies were arrayed in . . . 'dolmans' that Miss Tempy 'made over' religiously each fall.

***12.** *To make up.* **a.** To assemble (the mail) in a post office ready for dispatch or distribution.

1792 *Ann. 2d Congress* 60 All letters brought to any post office half an hour before the time of making up the mail [etc.]. **1860** *36th Congress 1 Sess.* H. Rep. No. 648, 522 There is what is called 'the foreign room,' where the foreign mails are made up and distributed.

b. To cause (the face) to assume a particular expression. {1641} 'Now U.S.' (*O.E.D.*).

1828 WEBSTER *To make up.* . . . To assume a particular form of features; as, to *make up* a face; whence, to *make up* a lip, is to pout. **1876** *Wide Awake* 295/2 She looked around, back at Janie, and 'made up a face.'

13. *To make good time,* to cover a certain distance in a relatively short time. Also fig.

1870 'MARK TWAIN' *Sketches, New & Old* 103 Vengeance Hopkins . . . made the best time on record, coming within one of reaching the Twelfth Auditor. **1887** I. R. *Lady's Ranche Life Mont.* 140 We drove to Three Forks . . . in an hour and twenty minutes. Jem calls it fourteen miles, so I think we made good time.

***Maker.** *spec.* One who makes clothes. — **1833** NEAL *Down-Easters* I. 63 'Who's your maker?' 'My maker!—Oh, I understand you—my tailor you mean?' 'Yes—who made your coat?' **1887** *Century Mag.* Jan. 438/2 Miss Faithy was a noted cutter and maker.

***Makeshift.** A shifty person, a rascal. *Obs.* {–1608} — **1848** *N.Y. Mirror* 5 June (B.), Already that city [Philadelphia] is filled with wire-pullers . . . and the whole breed of political make-shifts.

Malacontoon. (See MELOCOTON.)

Malaga. 1. *ellipt.* =MALAGA WINE. {1608–} **2.** *Malaga raisin (grape),* a sweet grape grown in Spain {1698}; a raisin made from this grape. — **(1) 1686** *Connecticut Rec.* III. 408 Every butt or pipe of Sherry, Sack, Malaga, Canary, . . . and Alicant, twenty shillings. **1778** *Jrnls. Cont. Congress* XI. 584 List of Articles [includes]: . . . white Malaga in cases; red Burgundy in cases. **1895** G. KING *New Orleans* 169 Our traveller found . . . luxuries out of keeping with so small and so new a place: Malaga, Bordeaux, Madeira [etc.]. **(2) 1769** *Amer. Philos. Soc.* I. 191 In South-Carolina, . . . the following sorts [of vines:] . . . the Alicant and Malaga Raisin Grape, the red Muscat of Alexandria. **1790** *Columbian Centinel* 29 Sept. 19/2 For sale, . . . fresh Malaga Raisins, do. Malaga Wine. **1845** *Xenia Torch-Light* 31 July 2/2, 15,000 boxes Malaga raisins . . . $33,000. **1907** *St. Nicholas* June 678/1 The little knicknack shop around the corner [sells] picture papers, spruce gum, needles and Malaga raisins.

Malaga wine. A white wine exported from Málaga, Spain. {1768} — **1683** *N.H. Hist. Soc. Coll.* VIII. 150 One butt and one quarter cask of Malaga wine . . . was lately seized. **1771** J. ROWE *Diary* 222 Mr. Edward Payne had a Quantity of Malaga Wine seized in the Heron by Sheppard. **1790** [see MALAGA 2]. **1842** *Knickerb.* XIX. 224 A gallon of whiskey . . . and a gallon of Malaga wine were placed on a large table.

Malaria. a. An unwholesome atmosphere emanating from swamps, soils, etc. {1740–, in Rome} **b.** An intermittent or remittent fever caused by a parasite in the blood.

1831 E. MARTIN *Let. to N. Webster* (N.Y. Pub. Lib. MS.), I have looked in your excellent Dictionary for the word *Malaria,* but such a word does not appear in its pages; nevertheless I am of the opinion that the word may very properly be introduced into Medical Science, if a proper meaning of it could be established. **1839** *S. Lit. Messenger* V. 209/2 The rich counties of Tennessee are not very healthy; the finest situations on the rivers are too generally infested with Malaria. **1853** 'P. Paxton' *Yankee in Texas* 59 'Hanging moss' . . . lives, and feeds, and thrives only upon malaria and vapor of the most deadly kind. **1863** Kettell *Hist. Rebellion* II. 602 The mortality from the malaria of the swamps was frightful. **1883** *Harper's Mag.* Aug. 484/1 Fires were built in each cottage every day to protect the inmates from malaria. **1907** Andrews *Recoll.* 103 Malaria had been unusually prevalent, and I had already begun to feel indications of chills and fever.

Malarial, *a.* Infected by malaria; of the nature of malaria. {1861–} — **1847** Webster 688/2 *Malarial,* pertaining to, or affected by, malaria. **1869** Beecher *Sermons* I. 319 In the malarial portions of the South, the blacks are the most prosperous class. **1883** *Harper's Mag.* Feb. 419/1 Malarial swamps made it unsafe for him to stay there. **1905** N. Davis *Northerner* 290 Betty lay, like a drooping rose, . . . convalescing from malarial fever.

‖**Malarialist.** One who studies malaria. — **1884** *Harper's Mag.* Aug. 441/2 According as one is a sanitarian, a chemist, or a malarialist will he give the credit to the hygienic, the solvent, or the antiseptic properties of *aqua pura.*

Malipi rock. [Cf. Malpais.] Basaltic lava. — **1881** *Rep. Indian Affairs* 7 The hills are covered with large stones or malipi rock.

Mall, *n.* {1644–} A walk or promenade bordered by trees, as the one in the Boston Common. {1674–, in London}

1784 *Mass. Centinel* 18 Aug. 3/1 The Mall being nearly compleated, the gentlemen . . . take the liberty to lay before the subscribers . . . an account of the expense. **1787** Tyler *Contrast* (1790) II. ii, Positively this Mall is a very pretty place. I hope the cits [of N.Y.] won't ruin it by repairs. **1801** A. Holmes *Hist. Cambridge* 6 A mall . . . made in 1792, and shaded by handsome rows of trees, is a work of neatness and taste. **1821** *Ann. 17th Congress* 1 Sess. I. 40 Praying authority to remove the course of the canal, and to convert a part of the mall [in Washington, D.C.] into building lots. **1882** McCabe *New York* 450 The Mall is the name given to the broad avenue, lined with four rows of American elms.

***Mall,** *v.* +*tr.* =Maul *v.* — **1680** *New Castle Court Rec.* 423 Two timber Trees, but that they are neither sawed nor maled. **1759** in Chalkley *Scotch-Irish Settlement Virginia* III. 58 Son, Christian, to mall 5,000 rails. **1800** Boucher *Glossary* p. l, *Fall, mall,* and *tote;* i.e. *fall,* or cut down, a tree; split, or rive it, by means of *mallets* and wedges, into rails, clapboards, staves, shingles, fire-wood . . . and then *tote,* or carry it to some pile. **1829** *Va. Lit. Museum* 56/1, I had ploughed from morning till night; had 'malled' rails in July and December.

***Mallard.** The common wild duck of the northern hemisphere, *Anas platyrhynchos* or *boscas.*

1608 Smith *Works* (1910) 13 More plentie of swannes, cranes, geese, duckes, and mallards, and diuers sorts of fowles, none would desire. **1674** *Cal. State P., Amer. & W. I.* VII. 581 [In Maine & N.H.] the islands and woods yield swarms of birds, . . . penguins, mallard, teal, and widgeon. **1737** Brickell *N. Carolina* 206 The Duck and Mallard . . . are very numerous, especially in Winter. **1768** Washington *Diaries* I. 253 Went a ducking between breakfast and dinner and killd 2 Mallards and 5 bald faces. **1846** Thorpe *Myst. Backwoods* 128 The beautiful mallard skimmed across the water. **1869** *Amer. Naturalist* III. 506 Many of the water-fowl that are now only transient visitors, as the . . . Black Duck and Mallard, undoubtedly once bred in this State [Mass.]. **1917** *Birds of Amer.* I. 115 Few Mallards breed in the East, but many winter there.

attrib. and *comb.* **1852** Glisan *Jrnl. Army Life* 102 A fine mallard duck suddenly flew up. **1874** Long *Wild-Fowl* 186 The common method of hunting them is similar to that described under the heads of morning and evening mallard-shooting. *Ib.* 214 They decoy exceedingly well to mallard decoys, and come readily to the mallard call.

***Mallow.** Also **mallows.** Any plant of *Malva* or related genera. — **1737** Brickell *N. Carolina* 20 The Pot-Herbs . . . [are] Mallows, several sorts, Tansay, Columbine, Dandelion. **1817** *N. Amer. Rev.* Sept. 316 In the western end of the pond is a high islet, . . . in which were growing the wild gooseberry, the grape, mallows [etc.]. **1843** Torrey *Flora N.Y.* I. 112 *Malva sylvestris.* High Mallow. . . . Naturalized in some parts of Westchester county. **1889** *Amer. Naturalist* XXIII. 668 Mallows. *Malva crispa.* . . . The *M. rotundifolia* . . . is the mallows of Britain and America.

+**Malpais.** *S.W.* [Sp. *mal* 'bad' and *pais* 'country.'] A rugged tract of volcanic ground; bad lands. Also attrib. (Cf. Malipi rock.)

1844 Kendall *Narr. Santa Fé Exped.* II. 384 We had crossed the mal pais, or bad country, as it is called. **1896** *Smithsonian Rep. 1895–96* 520 The Hopi took the trail through Chaves Pass, an available one for them to cross the rugged malpais of the Mogollones. **1907** White *Arizona Nights* 96 Sometimes we skipped . . . over little gullies, barrancas, and other sorts of malpais. **1919** J. S. Chase *Calif. Desert Trails* 193 The spur ran out at last in a tongue of yellowish rock of the *malpais* kind.

***Malt.**

***1.** Barley or other grain prepared for brewing.

1630 Winthrop in *Hist.* (1853) I. 454 [Get] good store of dry, Suffolk cheese, brought loose, or packed in very dry malt. **1654** *Harvard Rec.* I. 191 [Students'] payments shall be made either in currant mony or wheat; malt, butter, & fatt beasts alive. **1705** Beverley *Virginia* IV. 57 Their richer sort generally brew their Small-Beer with Malt, which they have from England, though they have as good Barley of their own as any in the world. **1804** J. Roberts *Penna. Farmer* 45 Spring barley makes the best malt. **1891** *Cycl. Temperance* 58/1 Brewing the malt . . . [involves]: (1) Crushing the malt between two iron cylinders [etc.].

2. *attrib.* and *comb.* **a.** Designating appliances or machinery used in making malt.

1643 *Essex Probate Rec.* I. 23 Halfe a mault mill, 13s. 4d. **1649** *Rowley Rec.* 57 That street which is betwene his house and his mault Kilne shall Remayne as it is now. **1662** *Essex Probate Rec.* I. 391, 1 pr. malt Milstones. **1875** Knight 1379/2 *Malt-dryer,* a device to hasten the drying of malt by artificial heat.

b. Designating liquors and other products made from malt.

1678 *New Castle Court Rec.* 312 Strong malt beare 2 gilders a gallon. **1789** *Ann. 1st Congress* I. 134, I approve as much as any gentleman the introduction of malt liquors. **1804** J. Roberts *Penna. Farmer* 44 Malt spirits, and beer, are likely to become more general in this country. **1825** Lorain *Pract. Husbandry* 120 Malt dust is also said to be a good manure. **1867** Dixon *New America* I. 231 Nearly all the malt whiskey which they had brought from Nauvoo to correct the bad water, had been seized on the road. **1897** *Voice* 8 July 1/4 As to 'malt nutrines,' 'Best's tonic,' etc. . . . they were nothing more nor less than concentrated beer.

‖**Malt coffee.** A substitute for coffee made with malt. — **1865** *Atlantic Mo.* XV. 676 The four children and herself breakfasted on bread and molasses with malt coffee.

+**Malted milk.** [A trade name coined and registered by William Horlick, Amer. manufacturer (1846–1936).] A powder made of evaporated milk and malted cereals; a drink made from this powder by the addition of water or milk, flavoring, etc. — **1887** *Pat. Off. Gazette* XLI. 358 Trade-Marks. . . . Food preparation for infants and invalids.—*Horlick's Food Company,* Mount Pleasant and Racine, Wis. . . . 'The words *Malted Milk* and the letters "M. M."' **1896** *Internat. Typogr. Union Proc.* 57/1, 200 antiseptic tablets, $1.50; 2 bottles malted milk, $7. **1920** Leach *Racine* (Wis.) 44 Horlick's, the Original Malted Milk, . . . is advertised the world round.

Maltese, *a.* Also *colloq.* **Maltee.** Of or pertaining to Malta or its inhabitants. {1781–}

1. Designating a breed of asses and a bluish gray variety of domestic cats.

1787 Washington *Diaries* III. 284 On Saturday last brot. home the 2 Maltese Jennys, and 2 Mules. **1842** *Lowell Offering* II. 25 Josephine . . . came laughing and skipping into the kitchen, followed by a little Maltese kitten. **1857** *Notes & Queries* 2 Ser. IV. 247/2 A New York merchant recently sent for a cargo of Maltese cats from that celebrated island. **1908** 'O. Henry' *Options* 189 He seemed to me to be a sort of a mixture of Maltese kitten, sensitive plant, and [actor].

2. *absol.* **a.** A Maltese cat.

1857 Hammond *Northern Scenes* 120 One great Maltese, with eyes like tea-plates, and a tail like a Bologna sausage, grinned and sputtered, and spit. **1897** Stuart *Simpkinsville* 5 Th' aint a cat in Simpkinsville, hardly, thet don't show a trace o' Jim Meredith's Maltee. **1918** Lincoln *Shavings* 45 Nate Rogers' old maltee never shed all that alone.

+**b.** The color of the Maltese cat.

1897 Stuart *Simpkinsville* 5 Maltee is a good enough color for a cat ef it's kep' true.

***Malt house.** A building in which malt is made and stored. — **1638** *Charlestown Land Rec.* 8 One homesteede . . . with one dwelling house; mault house and other outhouses upon it. **1708** Sewall *Diary* II. 242 Our Malt-House by the Mill Crick is Raised. **1776** Asbury *Journal* I. 178 We had a sudden and dreadful alarm of fire, which threatened a store-house, malt-house, and brew-house. **1884** *Century Mag.* July 327 Our biggest malt-houses are not impressive.

***Maltster.** Also †**ma(u)lster.** One whose occupation is the making of malt. Also in a place name.

1638 *Charlestown Land Rec.* 10 One dwelling house with a yard and garden, scituate . . . on the south by maulsters lane. **1657** *Ib.* 143 A mutual exchanging of a Hous and certaine parcells of Land . . . between John March, Planter, and Thomas Lynde, Malster. **1719** *N.H. Probate Rec.* II. 91 Bond of Samuel Adams, malster, with John Vifen, rope maker. **1780** *N.J. Archives* 2 Ser. IV. 211 A Maltster . . . a ditcher . . . a tutor. **1851** Cist *Cincinnati* 50 Occupations [include] . . . Maltsters, 3, Millwrights, 30. **1883** *Harper's Mag.* July 261 The maltsters [were] at work sweeping the hot iron floors. **1912** Nicholson *Hoosier Chron.* 504 Thatcher never . . . wholly escaped from the maltster's taint.

Malt tea. **1.** A tea made from malt. **2.** (See quotation.) — **(1)** *a*1821 C. Biddle *Autobiog.* 329, I believe it was with malt tea she made the cure. **(2)** **1890** *Cent.* 3598/3 Malt-tea, the liquid infusion of the mash in brewing.

***Mamelle.** +A rounded hillock. {mamelon, 1830–} Also attrib. — **1828** *Western Mo. Rev.* I. 577 Beyond him to the west, the mamelle hills of the Illinois seemed a line of domes of temples. **1849** *Western Journal* III. 46 These are the mamelles! projecting out boldly, nearly midway between the two rivers.

Mammilla. {1693–} +=prec. — **1869** Bowles *Our New West* 278 Mountains are always . . . rising and rounding out into innumerable fat mammillas.

Mammoth, *n.* {1706–} +The American mastodon, relics of which have been found in the Atlantic and central states. Also attrib.

1789 MORSE *Amer. Geog.* 55 The mammoth is not found in the civilized parts of America. . . . Skeletons of uncommon magnitude have been found at the salt licks, on the Ohio, in New Jersey, and other places. **1804–5** LEWIS in *L. & Clark Exped.* VI. (1905) 32 On the South side of this river [Osage] . . . there is a large lick, at which some specimenes of the bones of the Mammoth have been found. **1818** FORDHAM *Narr. Travels* 181, I have seen the skull of a Mammoth found in White River in Indiana—it is a Tremendous head-piece. **1834** PECK *Gaz. Illinois* 52 Bones of a huge animal, but different from the Mammoth, have been recently found in St. Clair county. **1843** *Amer. Pioneer* II. 196 The following graphic account of the mammoth mound, &c. at Grave creek, was obtained from A. B. Tomlinson, the proprietor.

Mammoth, *a.* Huge, immense. {1814–} Sometimes in proper names.

Thornton suggests that this adjectival use originated in the United States. See also quot. 1842. The reference in quot. 1802 is to the cheese sent to Jefferson at Washington in that year.

1802 *Balance* 19 Oct. 331 (Th.), No more to do with the subject than the man in the moon has to do with the mammoth cheese. **1813** *Niles' Reg.* IV. 32/2 The Mammoth bank bill passed the senate this day on a third reading. **1822** FLINT *Lett. from Amer.* 309*n.*, The great cave in Kentucky is called the Mammoth Cave, although none of the remains of that animal have been found in it. **1842** BUCKINGHAM *Slave States* II. 326 It [is] . . . the custom of this country to call every thing very large by the epithet of 'mammoth'; so that one hears of a mammoth cake, a mammoth pie, a mammoth oyster. **1868** *Rep. Comm. Agric. 1867* 305 Mr. Rogers also hybridized the Mammoth Grape (*Vitis labrusca*) with the pollen of the Black Hamburg. **1883** *Harper's Mag.* March 495/2 A large circular water-tank loomed up, . . . painted with a mammoth advertisement. **1907** ANDREWS *Recoll.* 131 Minneapolis had at this time two bridges and was building the 'mammoth dam' across the Mississippi.

b. *absol.* Anything of immense proportions.

1824 *Mass. Spy* 14 Jan. (Th.), The last load, as we Yankees say, was a 'Mammoth': . . . producing an aggregate of nearly twelve cords.

Mammoth powder. (See quotation.) — **1875** KNIGHT 1040/2 For very heavy ordnance a much larger grained powder . . . called *mammoth* powder, was introduced by the late General T. J. Rodman.

Mammoth tree. +The giant sequoia. — **1858** *Harper's Mag.* Jan. 259/1 Another grove of mammoth trees has been discovered in Mariposa County. The trees are said to average three hundred feet in height, and to measure from ten to thirty feet in diameter. **1897** SUDWORTH *Arborescent Flora* 62 *Sequoia washingtoniana*. . . . Bigtree. . . . [Also called] Mammoth-tree (Cal., and in Eng. cult.).

***Mammy.** Also †**Maum(a), Momma.** *S.* +A colored nurse; any elderly Negro woman. (Cf. AUNT 2, AUNTIE 1.)

1810 LAMBERT *Travels thro' U.S.* II. 414 An old negro woman is called *momma*, which is a broad pronunciation of *mama*. **1835** LONGSTREET *Ga. Scenes* 110*n.*, 'Aunt' and 'mauma,' or 'maum,' its abbreviation, are terms of respect commonly used by children, to aged negroes. The first generally prevails in the up country, and the second on the sea-board. **1837** *S. Lit. Messenger* III. 744/1 [Aged Negro domestics] were greeted always by the kind appellatives of 'daddy and mammy.' **1853** STOWE *Key* 34 It is often supposed . . . that young mistresses are always fond of their 'mammies.' **1884** *Century Mag.* April 859/1 This incident, which is historic, illustrates the position of the 'momma' or 'mammy' in a Southern family in the olden time. **1898** PAGE *Red Rock* 23 An old mammy in a white apron, with a tall bandanna turban around her head, suddenly appeared. **1904** LYNDE *Grafters* 81 Old Chloe . . . was my black mammy.

***Man,** *n.*

***1.** A manservant.

1639 *New Haven Col. Rec.* 31 Mr. Lamberton's man, Hen. Brasier, was freed from his chaines from hence forward. **1689** SEWALL *Diary* I. 300 At Winchester had of Mr. Edward Grace by his man Edward Hooker a bill of £20. **1825** NEAL *Bro. Jonathan* I. 18 There were two boys . . . with a 'man,' so called because he was hired by the preacher for his 'out-o' door work.'

2. In special phrases: (see quotations).

Man of color, family, (see COLOR 2 b, FAMILY 1 a). *Man of Destiny* (quot. 1885) was originally applied to Napoleon.

1885 'SIVA' *Man of Destiny* 78 Your own fame as a Man of Destiny, as you [Grover Cleveland] styled yourself . . . is the great stake for which you will play. **1888** BRYCE *Amer. Commw.* III. IV. lxxvi. 7 That representative of public opinion whom Americans call 'the man in the cars.' **1890** LANGFORD *Vigilante Days* (1912) 463 The expression 'a man for breakfast,' signifies, in mining parlance, that a man has been murdered during the night. **1914** *Cycl. Amer. Govt.* II. 390/2 *Man of the Revolution*, an affectionate nickname bestowed by the American people upon Samuel Adams . . . because of the leading part which he played in bringing about the War of Independence.

***Man,** *v. Polit.* +*tr.* (See quotation.) — **1818** FEARON *Sketches* 147 The ground was what is here called manned; that is, persons in the interest of the parties have written on their hat or breast, 'Federal Ticket,' or 'Democratic Ticket,' soliciting citizens as they approach the poll 'to vote their ticket.'

+**Manada.** *W.* [Sp.] Of horses, esp. mares, and cattle: A small drove. — **1848** BRYANT *California* xxxii. 377 We crossed in the course of the day a wide flat plain, upon which were grazing large herds of broodmares (*manadas*) and cattle. **1877** BARTLETT 382 *Manada*, . . . a herd of cattle or drove of horses. In California, it is especially applied to breeding mares. **1910** J. HART *Vigilante Girl* 195 Today the vaqueros are cutting out the manadas—what the Americans call bunches.

***Manager.**

1. *Polit.* One of a committee appointed by either house of a legislative body to confer with a similar committee from the other house. *Obs.* {1666–7–, generic sense in Parliament}

1707 SEWALL *Diary* II. 199 A Conference is agreed on: Col. Hawthorne, Col. Hutchinson, Mr. Secretary Addington, Mr. Commissary Belchar are appointed to be Managers: others may speak as they see occasion. **1789** *Ann. 1st Congress* I. 91 The managers appointed on the part of the Senate to confer on the subject of the disagreement of the two Houses . . . reported that they could not agree.

2. In specific applications: One who manages the affairs of a business, person, ball club, city, etc. {1705–}

1795 in Imlay *Western Territory* (1797) 575 The affairs and business of this [land] company shall be conducted by a board of managers, to be elected . . . by the holders of shares. **1797** *Ann. 5th Congress* I. 683 Executive[s] of every State . . . will cause the managers of every election . . . to be furnished with at least one copy. **1832** DUNLAP *Hist. Amer. Theatre* 70 The manager . . . is as careless of the tendency of the plays he adopts for his stage as the player. **1870** *Rep. Comm. Agric. 1869* 523 Thousands . . . would cheerfully invest ten, fifteen, or twenty thousand dollars in a farm, if they could find intelligent managers who would run it so that they could make seven per cent. on it. **1886** CHADWICK *Art of Batting* 64 Club managers have . . . realized very forcibly the superiority of the plan of selecting the players . . . on the basis of excellence as fielders and basemen. **1905** N. DAVIS *Northerner* 108 Carmichael . . . is Falls's uptown manager, and has his affairs generally in charge during his absence. **1922** *World's Work* April 637/1 The Council . . . has the power to appoint the [city] manager.

‖**3.** The chief of a party in one of the houses of Congress.

1905 TRENT *Southern Writers* 86 He soon showed his genius as a leader in the House, becoming a brilliant debater and for a time the Democratic manager.

Managing editor. One of the chief editors of a newspaper. — **1865** RICHARDSON *Secret Service* 18, I found the Managing Editor in his office. **1882** SWEET & KNOX *Texas Siftings* 99 Every night the managing editor calls the foreman up. **1912** NICHOLSON *Hoosier Chron.* 94 You may tell your managing editor for me that if he doesn't print more of my stuff he can get somebody else on the job here.

***Man alive.** A mild expletive. {1828 (Buckstone *Presumptive Evidence* I. ii)} — **1839** KIRKLAND *New Home* (1840) 168 Man alive! What do you put yourself into such a plaguy passion for? **1909** *N.Y. Ev. Post* 8 April (Th.), Man alive! [the wild geese] . . . know how far they have to fly to get home.

+**Mañana.** *S.W.* [Sp.] Tomorrow; the indefinite future. *Land of mañana*, a land of postponement; specifically, Mexico. — **1889** E. RIPLEY *From Flag to Flag* 165 Their *mañana* never came, never was intended to come. **1895** REMINGTON *Pony Tracks* 103 He would show you the time within fifteen minutes of right, which little discrepancy could never affect the value of a watch in the land of *mañana*. **1903** A. ADAMS *Log Cowboy* 138 Flood had had years of experience in dealing with Mexicans in the land of *mañana*, where all maxims regarding the value of time are religiously discarded.

+**Mananosay.** Variant of MANINOSE. — **1859** BARTLETT 84 The Soft Clam or Mananosay (*Mya arenaria*), obtained from the shores of tidal rivers by digging one or two feet in the loose sand. It has a long, extensible, cartilaginous snout, or proboscis, through which it ejects water. **1870** *Putnam's Mo.* May (De Vere), Even the toothsome Manonosays [*sic*] squirted water up through the sand what time the tides were out.

***Manatee.** Also **manaty, maneto, manati.** Any of various aquatic herbivorous mammals of the genus *Trichechus*, esp. *T. americanus*. Also attrib.

1672 JOSSELYN *New Eng. Rarities* 97 The Manaty, a Fish as big as a Wine pipe, most excellent Meat. **1682** ASH *Carolina* 32 Its Skin makes excellent Whips; . . . with one of these Manaty Strapps I have seen a Bar of Iron cut and dented. **1827** WILLIAMS *West Florida* 24 The Indians state that the maneto, or sea-cow, used to resort to [the river]. **1842** *Nat. Hist. N.Y., Zoology* I. 123 The Manati is still hunted for its flesh, among the keys and lagoons scattered along the southern part . . . of Florida. **1883** *Harper's Mag.* Oct. 714/2 Their facts point to a very possible monster—in fact, a fresh-water seal or manatee. **1884** GOODE, etc. *Fisheries* I. 116 The entire range . . . of the American Manatees extends over about forty-nine degrees of latitude.

+**Man car.** 'A kind of car used for transporting miners up and down the steeply inclined shafts of some mines on Lake Superior' (*Cent.*).

***Manchester.** *attrib.* Designating various textiles manufactured in Manchester, England. — **1711** *Boston News-Letter* 22 Oct. 2/2 To be Sold, . . . Ticking, Checks, Plush, Manchester Goods. **1762** in H. M. Brooks *Gleanings* 37 Flannell, Manchester Velvet. **1784** *Mass. Centinel* 19 May 3/3 Will be sold, by publick Vendue, . . . Figured Velverets, . . . Manchester Checks, Russia Sheetings. **1790** *Columbian Centinel* 6

Oct. 27/1 Just received . . . Velvets, Corduroys, Ribs of all sorts, and other Manchester Goods.

+**Mandamus counsellor.** A name opprobriously applied from 1774 to 1776 to a member of any colonial council whose appointment was by writ of mandamus. Chiefly in Massachusetts. — **1774** J. ADAMS *Works* IX. 351 Our Alva, Gage, with his fifteen Mandamus counsellors, are shut up in Boston, afraid to stir, afraid of their own shades. **1776** — *Familiar Letters* 216, I met Mr. Francis Hopkinson, late a Mandamus Counsellor of New Jersey.

+**Mandan.** *pl.* A Siouan tribe of Indians resident in the Northwest; *sing.* a member of this tribe. Also attrib.

1805 LEWIS in *Ann. 9th Congress* 2 Sess. 1064 The bridlebits and blankets I have seen in the possession of the Mandans. **1831** PECK *Guide* 21 At the Mandan villages, 1600 miles from the Mississippi, it [the Missouri] is said to be nearly as wide . . . as at St. Charles. **1841** BUCKINGHAM *America* I. 76 The 'buffalo dance' of the Mandans . . . consists of men dressing themselves in the skins of buffaloes. **1888** ROOSEVELT in *Century Mag.* May 39/1 It was the last great Indian hunting-ground across which Grosventres and Mandans . . . wandered in chase of game. **1916** EASTMAN *From Deep Woods* 41 My uncle had been on the war-path against this tribe and had brought home two Mandan scalps.

+**Mandan corn.** A type of Indian corn developed by the Mandans. — **1818** *Niles' Reg.* XV. 117/1 The Mandan corn will find itself in its own climate at the mouth of the Yellow Stone. **1824** DODDRIDGE *Notes* 90 The Mandan corn . . . ripens under the fortieth degree of north latitude; and yet the squaw and Mandan corn are not even different species. **1831** PECK *Guide* 41 A small species of maize called the Mandan corn, and produced by the Mandan and other Indians on the Upper Missouri, flourishes in this latitude.

***Mandate.** *Law.* +'The document promulgated upon the decision of an appeal or writ of error, as by the Supreme Court of the United States, directing what shall be done in the court below' (*Cent.*).

Mandolin. A musical instrument shaped like a small lute, equipped with wire strings, and played with a plectrum. {1707-} Also attrib. — **1844** KENDALL *Narr. Santa Fé Exped.* II. 93 Great numbers of the men can strum the mandolin, a species of small guitar. **1846** CHILD *Fact & Fiction* 40 The spinnet and mandolin . . . were of course banished. **1894** *Harper's Mag.* Feb. 487/1 A lady recently engaged for her reception the services of the 'Blankville Mandolin Quartet.' **1902** WHITLOCK *13th District* 30 [They] fled with relief to the banjo, the mandolin, and the coon songs that echoed . . . along the borders of Silver Lake.

***Mandrake.** +The May apple, *Podophyllum peltatum;* also, the fruit of this.

[**1778** CARVER *Travels* 118 In the country belonging to these people [the Pawnee Indians] it is said, that Mandrakes are frequently found, a species of root resembling human beings of both sexes.] **1807** C. SCHULTZ *Travels* I. 144 The only fruits I have met with, with which you are unacquainted, are the mandrake and papaw. **1839** in *Mich. Agric. Soc. Trans.* VII. 415 *Podophyllum peltatum.* Mandrake. May apple. **1850** S. F. COOPER *Rural Hours* 91 The mandrakes, or May-apples, are in flower. **1901** MOHR *Plant Life Ala.* 517.

+**Man-drowner.** (See quotation.) — **1819** in Claiborne *Life Quitman* 42 We purchased a small canoe, here called a 'dug-out,' or 'man-drowner.'

Man-eater. {1600-} +**1.** A man-eating shark, *Carcharodon carcharias.* Also attrib. +**2.** =HELLBENDER 1. — (1) **1832** WILLIAMSON *Maine* I. 161 The Shark, among fishermen, is called the 'maneater,' 'the shovel-nose,' and 'the swingle-tail;' these being varieties of the species. **1884** *Amer. Naturalist* XVIII. 940 The 'Man-eater Shark,' *Carcharodon carcharias.* . . . The various descriptions given of this species are . . . imperfect and confusing. **1884** GOODE, etc. *Fisheries* I. 671 The enormous fossil Sharks' teeth which are found in the phosphate beds of South Carolina belong to a Shark closely related to our Man-eater. (2) **1859** BARTLETT 502 In Pennsylvania and the Eastern States they [various salamanders] are called Spring-keepers and Man-eaters. **1883** *Rep. Indian Affairs* 116 The balance of this large area [on the Western Shoshoni reservation, Nev.] . . . is absolutely worthless for any purpose except as the home of the coyote, man-eater, rattlesnake [etc.].

Maneuver, Manoeuvre. {1758-} *fig.* An adroit move in politics, finance, etc. {*a*1797-} — **1774** J. ADAMS *Familiar Letters* 12 These Acts of Parliament and ministerial manœuvres will injure me. **1790** — *Works* IX. 566 When corruption shall be added to intrigue and manoeuvre in elections, . . . chance will be better than choice. **1880** CABLE *Grandissimes* 322 Was not some financial manœuvre possible which might compass both desired ends? **1909** WEBSTER 1310/2 Maneuver, manœuvre.

+**Man fashion,** *adv.* In a manly way; in the manner of a man. — **1874** *Congress. Rec.* 1 April 2682/2 [If Senator Morton] is entirely confident that his opinions are sound, why so timid? . . . Why not walk up to this man-fashion? **1877** BARTLETT 788 *Man-Fashion,* in a manly, straightforward manner. Also, riding astraddle, in distinction from the feminine use of a side-saddle.

+**Manga.** *S.W.* [Sp., 'a sleeve.'] A mantle or robe. — **1849** WIERZBICKI *California* 72 *A Serape* or a *Manga* is always accompanying its owner, be it thrown gracefully over the shoulder or slipped over the head. **1857** M. REID *War Trail* (B.), As the mustang sprang over the zequia, the flowing skirt of the manga was puffed forward. **1888** A. E. BARR *Remember the Alamo* 301 It was a grand moving picture of handsome men in scarlet and gold—of graceful mangas and waving plumes.

Manganese. **a.** A grayish white metallic element. {1783-} **b.** The oxide of this metal. {1676-} Also attrib.

*a*1817 DWIGHT *Travels* I. 35 Manganese has been discovered in Lebanon. **1819** SCHOOLCRAFT *Journal* 83, I passed a bed of black oxide of manganese. **1844** FEATHERSTONHAUGH *Slave States* 80 Zinc also and manganese are found, which last the settlers call *black tin.* **1894** *Harper's Mag.* March 590/1 The Franklinite ore of New Jersey yields excellent manganese compounds, and is therefore of great value.

+**Man gazer.** (See quotations.) — **1743** CATESBY *Carolina* App. p. xxxvii, The Grasshopper. The Man Gazer. **1789** MORSE *Amer. Geog.* 62 Of the astonishing variety of Insects found in America, we will mention . . . Man-gazer, Cock Roche, Cricket [etc.].

Mangel. *ellipt.* =next. {1877-} — **1863** MITCHELL *My Farm* 125 A closer look would reveal the delicate growth of fresh-starting carrots and mangel. **1870** *Rep. Comm. Agric. 1869* 422 One thousand eight hundred bushels of mangels have been raised from one acre, at a cost of seven and a half cents per bushel. **1883** *Harper's Mag.* April 652/1 A cow gets daily one bushel of sliced mangel.

Mangel-wurzel. Also **mangel-wurtzel.** A coarse kind of beet (*Beta vulgaris macrorhiza*), grown for cattle fodder; also, the root of this plant. {1779-} (See also MANGOLD-WURZEL.) — **1788** WASHINGTON *Diaries* III. 427, I sowed 19 Rows of the Yellow bearded Wheat between the Rows of the Mangel Wurzel and those of the Carrots. **1792** *N.Y. State Soc. Arts* I. 29 The mangel wurtzel, or root of scarcity, seems not to have succeeded among us in a degree equal to the character given of it by the French and English writers. **1817** *Niles' Reg.* XIII. 31/2 A root of the Mangel Wurzel, or large sugar beet, is now growing in the garden of Mr. James Engle, on Brooklyn Heights. **1874** *Rep. Comm. Agric. 1873* 439 Either the mangel-wurzel or the sugar-beet is superior food for hogs. **1916** *Farmers' Bul.* No. 743, 9 Of the different root crops, mangel-wurzels furnish the greatest yield per acre.

Mangle. A machine for smoothing out washed cloth, as sheets, etc. {1774-} — **1787** WASHINGTON *Diaries* III. 235 Visited a Machine at Doctr. Franklin's (called a Mangle) for pressing, in place of Ironing, clothes from the wash. **1869** *Boyd's Business Directory* 594 These Mangles are labor-saving machines, as they entirely supercede [*sic*] the use of ironing. **1876** INGRAM *Centennial Exp.* 345 Among the number of models of inventions by American women . . . were a blanket-washer, a mangle, a frame for stretching and dyeing lace curtains, etc. **1902** *Sears, Roebuck & Co. Cat.* No. 112, 548 Comparatively few people appreciate the value of a mangle.

***Mangler.** +(See quotation.) — **1875** KNIGHT 1383/2 *Mangler,* a machine for grinding meat, to render it more easy to masticate or to stew.

***Mango.** **1.** A pickled muskmelon, cucumber, etc. {1699-} ***2.** A tropical fruit of the tree *Mangifera indica.* Also attrib. — (1) **1761** in Singleton *Social N.Y.* 364 To be sold, wholesale and retail, by William Keen, . . . Pickles of all sorts . . . , such as Wallnuts, Cucumbers, Mangoes, Peppers [etc.]. **1832** CHILD *Frugal Housewife* 84 Musk-melons should be picked for mangoes, when they are green and hard. **1859** BARTLETT 263 *Mango.* We apply this name to a green musk-melon stuffed with horse-radish, mustard seed, mace, nutmeg, ginger, etc., and then pickled. (2) **1879** *Harper's Mag.* July 214 They passed to . . . the luxuries of . . . yams, mangoes, [and] apples of paradise. **1889** *Rep. Secy. Agric.* 448 The Mango . . . is one of the finest tropical fruits cultivated in the world. It has been introduced into many places in Florida. **1917** *Dept. Agric. Yrbk. 1916* 144 The investigational work incident to the building up of the mango industry in this country has occupied a prominent place in the activities of this station [at Miami].

Mango humming bird. A humming bird of the genus *Lampornis.* {1782} — **1871** DE VERE 377 The tiny *Mango* Humming-bird (*Trochilus colubris*), . . . is one of the most characteristic as well as most pleasing features of American landscapes.

Mangold-wurzel. Also **mangold-wurtzel.** = MANGEL-WURZEL. {1800-} — **1850** *Rep. Comm. Patents 1849: Agric.* 85 The Commissioner . . . desires to procure information . . . [on] turnips, carrots, beets, mangold wurtzel, artichoke. **1855** BROWNE in *Amer. Inst. N.Y. Trans.* 608 *Betterave jaune des barres* . . . some consider as a model forage beet, or mangold wurzel. **1873** *Nebraska Bd. Agric. Rep. 1871-2* 416 Either the mangold wurzel or the sugar-beet are [*sic*] superior food for hogs at any age.

Mangrove. **a.** Any tree of the genus *Rhizophora,* esp. *R. mangle.* {1613-} **b.** A tree of related genera. Usually with specifying adjective. {1683-} Also attrib.

1699 J. DICKINSON *God's Protecting Prov.* 34 [It was] surrounded with a Swamp, in which grew White Mangrove-Trees. **1722** *New-Eng. Courant* 10-17 Dec. 2/2, 3 [sloops] drove among the Mangroves into a Morass. **1833** *Niles' Reg.* XLIV. 394/2, I have seen mangrove islands . . . of several acres in extent, which did not contain one single foot of dry land. **1837** WILLIAMS *Florida* 98 The Black Mangrove covers most of the low islands and shores of the keys, as well as the southern shores of the [Florida] peninsula. **1885** *Harper's Mag.* Jan. 218/2 The mangrove . . . has had much to do with the building up of this western fringe of Florida.

+**Mangrove snapper.** **a.** =GRAY SNAPPER. **b.** The bastard snapper, *Rhomboplites aurorubens.* — **1734** *Phil. Trans.* XXXVIII. 316 The *Mangrove Snapper* . . . is esteemed pretty good food. **1884** GOODE *Fisheries* I. 397 [*Lutjanus Stearnsii*] has as yet been found only on the Gulf coasts of the United States, where it is known as the 'Mangrove Snapper.' *Ib.*, The 'Mangrove Snapper' of Charleston, called at Pensacola the 'Bastard Snapper,' . . . is less vivid, being somewhat more russet. **1897** *Outing* XXIX. 331/2 The mangrove snapper . . . is called *Lutjanus Stearnsii* by the criminal authorities, and deserves it. **1911** *Rep. Fisheries*

1908 316/2 The gray snapper or mangrove snapper (*L. griseus*), also known in Florida as 'lawyer,' is a most common species.

+**Manhaden.** = MENHADEN. Also attrib. — **1792** *N.Y. State Soc. Arts* I. 57 This addition [to making manure] has been made by green sea-weed taken directly from the creeks and bays . . . and by the fish called manhaden or mosbankers. **1807** *Mass. H. S. Coll.* 2 Ser. III. 57 The manhadon is caught, with seines only, in summer and autumn. **1868** G. G. CHANNING *Recoll. Newport* 261, I never heard of any deleterious effects from the use of the manhaden-fishery as a manure.

+**Manhattan.** **1.** Short for *Manhattan water*, the water drunk in New York City before the Croton River was used as a source of supply. **2.** A resident of New York City. **3.** A kind of cocktail. **4.** An Algonquian Indian tribe formerly resident at the site of New York City. — **(1) 1845** *Knickerb.* XXVI. 444 He abominates Croton water, and gives his preference to the delectable Manhattan, which his forefathers drank before him. **(2) 1854** SIMMS *Southward Ho* 4 My friend was a genuine Manhattan. **(3) 1894** WARNER *Golden House* v, He and old Fairfax sipped their five-o'clock 'Manhattan.' **1901** ADE *40 Modern Fables* 46 She came back by saying that she would just as soon see . . . him off in a Club . . . punishing Manhattans. **(4) 1907** HODGE, etc. *Amer. Indians* I. 800 The Manhattan had their principal village, Nappeckamack, where Yonkers now stands.

+**Manhattaner.** =next. — **1851** A. O. HALL *Manhattaner* 82 *Manhattaner.* Is litigation attended here with much formality? *Red-faced Clerk.* We do it up here as brown as they do it anywhere.

+**Manhattanese.** One who lives on Manhattan Island; a New Yorker. Usually collect. Also attrib.

1837 COOPER *France* (1928) 1 As is always done by good Manhattanese, the town house had been given up on the first of May. **1844** *Knickerb.* XXIII. 586 The pleasant smell of lobsters is already perceptible to the senses of the awakening Manhattanese. **1856** WHITMAN *Leaves of Grass* 217 But I was a Manhattanese, free, friendly, and proud! **1904** *Forum* Jan. 410 [This play] brings together a number of highly piquant Manhattanese types of to-day, sketched with captivating drollery.

+**Man hunt,** *n.* A hunt for a man, esp. a fugitive. Also in allusive use. — **1860** GREELEY *Overland Journey* 84 Should one of these countless herds take a fancy for a man hunt, our riflemen would find even the express-wagons no protection. **1873** MILLER *Amongst Modocs* 201 The man-hunt was over.

+**Man-hunt,** *v. tr.* To hunt down (a man). — **1841** *S. Lit. Messenger* VII. 769/1, I never strikes an officer—but I'll teach him how to manhunt Jim Guest. **1900** *Outing* July 345 Man-Hunting in the Pound.

Manicure, *v. tr.* To treat or care for (the hands or the finger nails), by trimming and polishing the nails, massaging the hands, etc. {1893–} Also absol. — **1889** *Century Mag.* Oct. 873/1 Where the mother's hands washed and cooked, . . . the daughter's shall . . . be soft and 'manicured' and daintily gloved. **1894** *Christian Work* 12 April, The young woman who knows how to manicure has discovered that she can make more money . . . by going to her customers at their houses. **1922** COURTENAY *Physical Beauty* 47 Before beginning to manicure your nails, soak them in hot soap water and cleanse with the nail brush.

Manicurist. One who makes a business of caring for other persons' hands and nails. {1900} — **1889** *Columbus Dispatch* 25 May, It is the usual custom with the ladies who patronize the manicurist to have their finger nails attended to once a week. **1918** OWEN *Typewriting Speed* 137 In order to have nice hands and to keep the fingers in good condition, it is not necessary . . . to ever go to a manicurist.

***Manifest.** **1.** The official list of a ship's cargo. {1706–} +**2.** A list of goods being transported by land; =GUIA. — **(1) 1719** *Mass. H. Rep. Jrnl.* II. 147 The Manifests [of Masters of Vessels] and Entries are on File in the Impost Office. **1798** *Steele P.* I. 155 A siezure was afterwards made at Boston of a qnty. of sugr. in Rice cask, entered as rice in the *coasting* manifest. **1842** *Diplom. Corr. Texas* I. (1908) 608 Texas yet maintains and reserves to herself the right to examine the Manifest of Cargo of vessels from the United States bound to said ports of Mexico. **1911** VANCE *Cynthia* 223 The cargo, by means of forged manifests, will be taken elsewhere and disposed of to the best advantage. **(2) 1872** in Tarbell *Hist. Standard Oil Co.* (1904) I. 286 The party . . . covenants and agrees . . . to make manifests or way-bills of all petroleum or its products, transported over any portion of the railroads. **1888** J. J. WEBB *Adventures* 229 Cerro Gordo was the frontier town where all trains passing from one state to the other were compelled to present their *guias*, or manifests, for inspection. **1895** E. CARROLL *Principles Finance* 299.

***Manifestation.** *Spiritualism.* The phenomenon by which the spirit is affirmed to make his presence known. {1860} — **1853** DIX *Transatlantic Tracings* 244 You can go into . . . very few communities where there are not believers in the 'manifestations' as they are termed. **1887** *Courier-Journal* 18 Jan. 1/7 Next came a spiritualistic seance which produced no 'manifestations.'

Manifest destiny. *Polit.* +The doctrine of the inevitability of Anglo-Saxon supremacy. A phrase used by those who believed it was the destiny of the United States or of the Anglo-Saxon race to govern the entire Western Hemisphere.

1858 VIELÉ *Following Drum* 104 Buildings of every description, bore the marks of inevitable progress, or go-aheadativeness, otherwise called 'manifest destiny.' **1866** LOWELL *Biglow P.* 2 Ser. p. vii, The incarnation of 'Manifest Destiny,' in other words, of national recklessness as to right or wrong. **1870** O. LOGAN *Before Footlights* 260 The large number of railways . . . is a . . . sign of the great activity of the Universal Yankee Nation, which spreads its Aegis wings over our Manifest Destiny. **1871** DE VERE 278 It was *Manifest Destiny* that conquered part of Mexico and purchased Alaska; it is *Manifest Destiny* that Cuba should be annexed and Canada ceded to the United States. **1900** *Congress. Rec.* 31 Jan. 1354/2 He discusses about the 'fogs of manifest destiny and dreams of empire which are abroad in this land.' **1923** R. MCELROY *Grover Cleveland* II. 73 On August 12th (1898), the very American flag which Grover Cleveland had caused to be hauled down was raised again [in Hawaii]. . . . 'Manifest Destiny' had triumphed at last.

+**Manifesto church.** A Boston church founded November 17, 1699. So called because of a manifesto issued by it setting forth its 'aims and designs.' — **1701** SEWALL *Diary* II. 48, I went to the Manifesto church to hear Mr. Adams.

Manil(l)a. {1697–} Short for MANIL(L)A HEMP, or for an article made of this. {1834–} Hence used attrib. with *envelope, folder, hat,* etc.

1845 *Xenia Torch-Light* 31 July 3/7 [For Sale:] Manilla and Hemp Ropes. **1850** SAWYER *Way Sketches* 107 A half-inch manila lariat forty feet long, with a picket, is wanted for each animal. **1893** *Harper's Mag.* May 942/1 The aim being to make book and letter paper, Manilas, coarse wrapping-paper, and flooring and roofing papers. **1908** 'O. HENRY' *Options* 6 Upon the colonel's desk [were] some cards, a bulky manila envelope, and a letter. **1918** OWEN *Typewriting Speed* 119 The ordinary manila folder in which is filed all the records that come under the letters of the alphabet. **1923** WYATT *Invisible Gods* 4 A short [man] . . . dressed in a light grey suit and a Manila hat.

Manil(l)a hemp. The fiber obtained from a banana (*Musa textilis*), native to the Philippine Islands. {1855–} — **1856** *Rep. Comm. Patents 1855: Agric.* 243 [Sisal hemp] readily brought within a half cent to a cent per pound as much as the best kind of Manilla hemp.

+**Maninose.** [Amer. Indian.] 'The soft clam, *Mya arenaria*' (*Cent.*). See also MANANOSAY. — **1843** *Nat. Hist. N.Y., Zoology* v. 240 *Mya arenaria* . . . in some districts . . . still retains its ancient aboriginal appellation of *Maninose.* **1877** BARTLETT 123 In Maryland the [soft clam] . . . is always called the maninose, and never soft-shell clam.

Manipulate, *v.* {1827–} +*Finance. tr.* To cause (stocks or the market) to rise or fall by dexterous contrivance. Also absol. — **1870** MEDBERY *Men Wall St.* 188 The stock . . . was most admirably manipulated, until it finally touched 152. **1888** *Nation* 9 Aug. 107/3 People do not manipulate for fun, but for profit. **1903** S. S. PRATT *Work of Wall St.* 147 A market is rigged when it is manipulated.

Manipulation. {1727–} +*Finance.* The operation of manipulating stocks or the stock market. — **1888** *Nation* 9 Aug. 107/2 Manipulation signifies a common understanding and design on the part of a clique of operators to raise or depress values in order to get other people's money. **1900** NELSON *A B C Wall St.* 141 *Fancy stocks,* new stocks quoted at high figures; highly speculative stocks that are notorious for manipulation.

Manipulative, *a.* {1836–} +*Finance.* Of or pertaining to the action of manipulating the stock market. — **1892** *Columbus Dispatch* 22 Aug., The Buffalo strike . . . does not interrupt the advance of industrial companies' shares, which have continued to climb, though manipulative assistance is discernible. [**1909** *Westminster Gazette* 8 Sept. 11/4 The powerful manipulative interests are watching [the state of health of E. H. Harriman]. . . . In the history of American finance many magnates have passed away, but many have been at hand to catch the manipulative mantle as it fell.]

Manipulator. {1851–} +*Finance.* One who manipulates stocks or a stock market. — **1888** *Economist* 17 Nov. 3/3 If the people are apathetic it is utterly useless for the manipulators to undertake to push prices up. **1900** *Congress. Rec.* 8 Jan. 691/2 The owners of the Bunker Hill and Sullivan mines . . . it is also charged, are the owners and manipulators of other similar trusts. **1904** *N.Y. Tribune* 15 May 4 Manipulators desperately endeavoring to bring back recessions which will permit them to 'get even.'

+**Manito.** Also **manitou, manetto,** etc. [Algonquian.] Among the Algonquian Indians, one of the deities or spirits, both good and bad, that dominate nature. Sometimes used allusively and figuratively.

1671 *N.J. Archives* 1 Ser. I. 74 The Manetto hath kill'd my sister & I will go & kill the Christians. **1698** THOMAS *Pensilvania* (1848) 2 They offer their first Fruits to a Maneto, or suppos'd Deity. **1701** WOLLEY *Journal N.Y.* (1902) 45 They are of opinion that when they have ill success in their hunting, fishing, &c. their *Menitto* is the cause of it. [**1773** *Hist. Brit. Domin. N. Amer.* II. 241 They assert, there are two monetoes or spirits; that the one sends all the good things they have, and the other all the bad.] **1804** C. B. BROWN tr. Volney *View* 416 They believe in a great Manito, or genius, who rules the world or universe. . . . Under this supreme power are numberless Manitos who traverse earth and air, and govern all things. **1814** BRACKENRIDGE *Views La.* 126 Perhaps some Manitou (spirit) resides here, and will not permit it! **1841** COOPER *Deerslayer* xxv, Nor do I believe there is one Manitou for the redskin, and another for a paleface. **1909** H. A. CLARKE *Longfellow's Country* 199 He has even forborne to make him scalp the Manito.

b. An image or idol of one of these deities.
1778 CARVER *Travels* 309 They place great confidence in the ir Manitous, or household gods, which they always carry with them. **1800** BOUCHER *Glossary* p. xlix, *Manitou;* an idol.

***Mankind.** *pl.* Individuals of the human species. *Obs.* — **1642** *Conn. Rec.* I. 77 Yf any man stealeth a man or mankind, he shall be put to death. **1671** *Plymouth Laws* 244 If any man Stealeth Man-kinde, he shall be put to death or otherwise grievous ly punished. **1809** KENDALL *Travels* III. 253 We have fallen in ev il times, if the government can put mankind in gaols, though there's nothing agin 'em.

Man midwife. An accou cheur. {1625–1807} — **1789** *Independent Chronicle* (Boston) 12 Feb., Mr. B——, Man-Midwife, . . . Begs leave to advertise himself as a person . . . qualified to discharge the various duties incident to this i mportant and honourable profession.

***Manna.** The exudate of the European flowering ash (*Fraxinus ornus*), used medicinally. — **1693** SEWALL *Diary* I. 383 By Dr. Oakes advice, I give her a little Manna. **1732** *S.C. Gazette* 132/2 Lately imported, and to be sold . . . sundry sorts of Druggs, viz. . . . Senna, Manna, Sperm a Ceti. **1790** *Penna. Packet* 1 Jan. 4/1 Just Imported . . . a Fresh and General Assortment of Drugs and Medicines; among which are, Opium, . . . Camphor, Rhubarb, Manna, &c.

***Manna grass.** Any grass of the genus *Glyceria.* — **1843** TORREY *Flora N.Y.* II. 464 Reed Manna-grass. . . . Wet meadows, northern and western parts of the State. . . . It is good fodder. **1849** EMMONS *Agric. N.Y.* II. 69 Manna grass, *Glyceria fluitans*. . . . As cattle are very fond of it, it may be profitable to cultivate it . . . where it is permanently wet. **1878** Killebrew *Tenn. Grasses* 231 *Glyceria Pallida*, Pale Manna Grass, . . . grows in shallow water, or very wet, boggy places. **1894** COULTER *Bot. W. Texas* III. 547 *P[anicularia] fluitans*. . . . (Manna grass.). *Ib.*, *P[anicularia] nervata*. . . . (Nerved manna grass.)

***Manner.** *To make one's manners*, to bow or pay one's respects. {1863–} — **1823** COOPER *Pilot* II. xiv, The ship is to be so cluttered with she-cattle, that a man will be obligated to spend half his time in making his manners. **1849** *Knickerb.* XXXIV. 276 He never noticed us, except to reprove us when we failed to 'make our manners to him.' **1856** GOODRICH *Recoll.* I. 127 All children were regularly taught at school to 'make their manners' to strangers.

+**Mannersbit.** (See quotation.) — **1859** ELWYN *Glossary* 73 *Mannersbit.* A portion of a dish left by the guests, that the host may not feel himself reproached for insufficient preparation. . . . This still exists in New England.

Manoeuvre. Variant of MANEUVER.

+**Man-of-the-earth.** **1.** The American morning-glory, *Ipomoea pandurata.* **2.** =MANROOT. — (1) **1833** EATON *Botany* (ed. 6) 105 *Convolvulus panduratus*, mechoacan, wild potato vine, man of the earth. . . . A mild cathartic, and resembles rhubarb in its effects. **1843** TORREY *Flora N.Y.* II. 97 *Convolvulus panduratus*. . . . Man of the earth. Wild Potato-vine. . . . Dry fields and borders of woods; southern part of the State. **1847** WOOD *Botany* 442 Wild Potato. Man-of-the-earth. . . . In sandy fields, N.Y. to Ga. **1868** GRAY *Field, Forest, & Garden Botany* (1879) 264 Wild Potato-Vine or Man-of-the-Earth. Sandy or gravelly soil, Conn. to Ill. & S. (2) **1871** *Rep. Comm. Agric. 1870* 407 *Wild potato vine*, (*Ipomœa leptophylla*.)—This showy plant of the dry deserts of the West is commonly called man root, or man of the earth. . . . The Cheyennes, Arapahoes and Kioways roast it for food when pressed by hunger.

* **Man-of-war.** Also **man-o'-war.**

***1.** An armed fighting vessel of a recognized navy.
1643 *Suffolk Deeds* I. 50 Richard Parsons doth Covenant . . . that he sufficiently furnish the said vessell to sea for a man of warre. **1666** *R.I. Col. Rec.* II. 184 In the time of the Dutch man of warr being on this coast. **1704** *Boston News-Letter* 28 Aug. 2/1 We dayly expect a Fleet of Men of War, and some Land Forces from England. **1776** A. ADAMS *Familiar Letters* 163 It is rumored here that Admiral Hopkins is blocked up in Newport harbor by a number of men-of-war. **1815** *Md. Hist. Mag.* I. 173 Three Men of War in Chase of us. **1862** *N.Y. Tribune* 13 March (*Cent.*), A wooden man-of-war is now as worthless as an eggshell; more so, for it is a death-trap. **1898** *Scribner's Mag.* Aug. 186/2 The American flag was thrown out against the sky, and the sailors on the men-of-war, the Cubans and our own soldiers, . . . shouted and cheered.

2. a. =sense 3. {1657–, in Barbados} **b.** The parasitic jaeger, *Stercorarius parasiticus.*
1796 WANSEY *Excursion U.S.* 194 Of some kinds of birds they have great plenty [in N.J.], such as robins, swallows, cat birds, and king birds, or men of war, as some call them. **1917** *Birds of Amer.* I. 35 Parasitic Jaeger. . . . Man-o'-war.

3. *Man-of-war bird, falcon, hawk*, the frigate bird, *Fregata aquila.* {1707–, in Jamaica}
1850 TYSON *Diary in Calif.* 16 Two beautiful tropical birds, denominated by sailors 'skim-o'er-the-seas,' were also observed, and a 'man-of-war falcon' silently poised above. **1871** *Harper's Mag.* XLIII. 194/2 The birds we have most noticed are the 'man-o'-war hawks,' or 'frigate-birds'—*Tachypetes aquila.* **1917** *Birds of Amer.* I. 106 The Man-o'-war-birds, . . . The larger (*Fregata aquila*) . . . visits more or less regularly the coasts of California, Texas, and Florida.

Man-of-war's man. A sailor serving on a man-of-war. {1875} — **1774** J. ANDREWS *Letters* 79 The Marines . . . are ten times more dissolute . . . than the marching regiments—partaking of the extreem ill qualities of a soldier as well as that of a man-of-war's man. **1840** DANA *Two Years* 200 [He] was a singular mixture of the man-of-war's-man and Puritan. **1925** *U.S. Navy* (Office Naval Intelligence) 222 Enlisted men in the Navy are generally designated as '*men*', as also . . . 'man-o'-war's-men.'

* **Manor.** Also †**mannor, manner,** etc.

* **1.** A tract of land whereon the tenants pay a fee-farm rent to the proprietor. Chiefly in colonial times.
The relationship between the proprietor and the tenants of a manor was of a feudal character, the proprietor having the right to exact certain fees, fines, etc. In New York the manor was established either by patent granted by the king, or by confirmation of grants formerly made by the States-General of Holland to the patroons. Since the Revolution the rights of the proprietors have gradually diminished.
1635 *N.H. Probate Rec.* I. 8 All the Rest & residue of all & Singuler my Mannors Messuages, Lands Tenemts & hereditements. **1650** *Md. Council Proc.* 259 Any one transporting five men into this Province were to have 1500 acres of Land to be erected into a Mannor. **1661** *Portsmouth Rec.* 391 His manner of East Grenwich in the County of kent. [**1682** *Charter & Laws of Penna.* (1879) 89 Wee give and Grant Licence vnto the said William penn . . . to erect any parcells of Land within the p[ro]vince aforesaid, into Mannors . . . , and in every of the said Mannors, to haue and to hold a Court Baron.] **1730** *Brookhaven Rec.* 121 All that was intended by the Town to grant Coll. Smith, was nothing else but paying rates & doing other duty within his manour. **1785** WASHINGTON *Diaries* II. 398 The possessors of them (on a Manner belonging to Chs. Carroll, Esqr. of Carrolton, who holds in one Tract, 12 or 14,000 Acres) are Tenants at will. **1830** COOPER *Water Witch* xiii, 'It is vain to contend with the inclinations,' returned the proprietor of the manor, sighing. **1884** *Encycl. Brit.* (ed. 9) *Amer. Suppl.* I. 198/2 The *manors*, as the grants of the early Dutch rulers of New Netherland were called, have disappeared under the pressure of republican institutions.

b. Attrib. with *land, troubles.*
1639 *Md. Archives* 63 Any Mannour Lands or Tenements within this Province. **1846** COOPER *Redskins* ii, Others . . . had in view a project to get rid of the rents altogether. Out of this combination grew what have been called the 'manor troubles.'

+**2.** *transf.* A plantation in the South.
1843 *Knickerb.* XXII. 3 The lordly owners of these manors pass the winter months in superintending the affairs.

Manor house. +The house on a manor plantation. Usu. *S.* — **1843** *Knickerb.* XXI. 42 He has but to call at the door of the manor-house next at hand . . . to receive all the kindness of an invited guest. **1869** STOWE *Oldtown Folks* p. iv, A full description of the old manor-house which in this story is called the Dench House. **1883** 'MARK TWAIN' *Life on Miss.* xl, Now and then you see a pillared and porticoed great manor house. **1897** *Outing* XXX. 70/1 He had heard of a manor-house back on the Rappahanock, in which lived a young girl.

+**Manor plantation.** *S.* The principal plantation of a landowner in the South. — **1788** *Edenton* (N.C.) *Intelligencer* 9 April, The Manor Plantation will be Sold so as to contain between two and three hundred Acres. **1806** *Will Rev.C.Pettigrew, Pettigrew P.* (Univ. N.C. MS.), I leave my dearly & well beloved Wife Mary Pettigrew in the full possetion of my House & mannor plantation.

+**Manroot.** The long-rooted ipomoea (*Ipomoea leptophylla*) of the dry western plains. — **1846** EMORY *Military Reconn.* 13 The principal growth is the buffalo grass, . . . and very rarely that wonderful plant, the Ipomea leptophylla, called by the hunter man root. **1871** [see MAN OF THE EARTH 2]. **1890** *Cent.* 3616/2 *Manroot* . . . [is] found on the dry plains of Colorado and in adjacent regions.

Mansard. =next. {1734} — **1873** ALDRICH *Marjorie Daw* 17 One may be familiar for years with the reception-room of his neighbor, and never suspect what is directly under his mansard.

Mansard roof. A hipped roof having two sections on each end and side of different slope or pitch; a hipped curb roof. {1842–}
1868 BEECHER *Norwood* 66 The ancient New-England architects seem to have had a vague idea of a Mansard roof. **1875** *Chicago Tribune* 8 Oct. 8/4 The two story frame house with Mansard roof, . . . is located at No. 700 Michigan avenue. **1882** MCCABE *New York* 147 On the west side of Broadway, is the marble front of the Grand Central Hotel . . . surmounted by a mansard roof. **1902** BELL *Hope Loring* 193 The mansard roof gave it a low ceiling and slanting walls.
fig. **1880** 'MARK TWAIN' *Tramp Abroad* 50 [Foreign youths] go to the university to put a mansard roof on their whole general education.

+**Man school.** A school taught by a man. — **1769** *Essex Inst. Coll.* XXI. 238 Voted to carry two Papers one for a man Scool and one for a woman Scool the most Signers to haue the use of the house. **1838** *U.S. Mag.* I. 404 [Kendall] went to a 'woman school' each summer for about two months, and to a 'man school' in the winter.

* **Manservant.** **a.** A male servant. +**b.** A male indentured servant. *Obs.*
1636 *Plymouth Laws* 45 That each person . . . have peece, powder and shott . . . for himself and each man servant he keepeth able to beare armes. **1643** *Md. Hist. Mag.* V. 170 For transporting himself into the Province, and 2 men Servants in the year 1638. **1705** *Boston News-Letter* 8 Oct. 2/2 Ran away from his Master, . . . an Indian Man Servant, aged about 26 Years. **1727** *New Eng. Wkly. Journal* 11 Sept., Ran-away from

his Master . . . A Young Negro Man-Servant, about 20 Years of Age. **1816** Clipping in *Pettigrew P.* (Univ. N.C. MS.), The said man servant . . . being of a middling stature. **1842** KIRKLAND *Forest Life* II. 51 An excellent man-servant . . . had been Mr. Sibthorpe's factotum. **1904** *N.Y. Ev. Post* 9 Jan. (Horwill), An ever-ready man-servant reaches out obsequious hands to take coat and stick and hat.

* **Mansion.** A large dwelling house; a stately residence.

Cf. FAMILY MANSION.

1648 *Suffolk Deeds* III. 306, [I] Doe bargaine Graunt & Sell vnto Henry Rashley of the sajd Boston the mansion or dwelling house scittuate in the north end of the sajd Boston. **1720** *Providence Rec.* XVI. 357, I give . . . unto my beloved Daughter . . . my manshon Where I now dwell. *a***1817** DWIGHT *Travels* II. 97 Mr. Geyer has erected a large elegant mansion, fronted towards the river. **1877** *Harper's Mag.* April 689/2 There is always something sorrowful about a fine private mansion which has been turned to a public use. **1907** ANDREWS *Recoll.* 118, I remember the 'elegant mansion' of Mr. Dayton on what is now Dayton's bluff.

+**b.** The residence of the president or of a state governor.

Governor's mansion, particularly, is widely used.

1846 POLK *Diary* (1929) 128 He had not been in my office or at the President's mansion for many weeks. **1892** M. A. JACKSON *Gen. Jackson* 473 We were . . . driven through the most retired streets to the governor's mansion. **1923** M. N. STANARD *Richmond* 144 A Temperance Society is born [*c*1840] in Richmond whose pledge seems to presage the death knell of the free punch-bowl at the Governor's Mansion.

* **Mansion house. a.** A dwelling house. *Obs.* **b.** A large country house; a manor house. **c.** Any imposing or stately residence. Sometimes an official residence.

In sense c 'now only U.S.' (*O.E.D.*).

1641 *Wyllys P.* 19, [I] doe hereby give & graunt . . . all my mansion howse Landes & Tenementes in Hartford. **1695** *Providence Rec.* VI. 156 All my mansion houses lands meadows. **1700** SEWALL *Letter-Book* I. 231 Madam Usher obtaind a Judgment for her Dower in the Mansion-House over against the Town-House yesterday. **1746** E. KIMBER *Itinerant Observ.* 37 A Negro Quarter, is a Number of Huts or Hovels, built at some Distance from the Mansion-House. **1765** ROGERS *Acct. N. America* 65 The Governor's mansion-house [is] within the fort. **1812** *Niles' Reg.* III. 9/2 The majority then retired to the Mansion house on the banks of the North River. **1832** WILLIAMSON *Maine* II. 461 He built his elegant mansion-house in Thomaston: . . . Its style of building, its piazzas, its balconies, its farm, summer, and out-houses, . . . formed a seat which far surpasses . . . any other in the State. **1860** HOLMES *E. Venner* v, In this street were most of the great houses, or 'mansion-houses,' as it was usual to call them.

Man slave. A slave of the male sex. — **1642** *Md. Archives* IV. 189 John Skinner . . . bargained to deliver unto the said Leonard Calvert, fourteene negro men-slaves, & three women slaves. **1704** *Boston News-Letter* 13 Nov. 2/2 Ran-away on Wednesday last, the 8th. Currant from his Master in Boston, a Sirranum Indian Manslave, named Prince. **1734** HEMPSTEAD *Diary* 278, 10 negro men Slaves taken & secured in Prison last night for being out unseasonably in a frolick at old Rights.

Manta. [Sp., 'blanket.']

1. Among Spanish Americans and Indians: +**a.** A blanket. **b.** A shawl used for street wear. {1697-, in Spanish-speaking countries}. **c.** A fabric.

[**1828** IRVING in P. M. Irving *Life W. Irving* II. 306 They [Spanish travelers to Malaga] . . . lie on the mantas of their mules and horses.] **1848** *Santa Fe Repub.* 16 Aug. 2/4 He also has on hand a well Assorted Stock of Merchandize, consisting of Lienzos, Manta, Prints [etc.]. **1866** *Rep. Indian Affairs* 139 [The Mescalero Apaches'] mode of living is in huts of hides, manta or grass, which they remove from time to time. **1869** J. R. BROWNE *Adv. Apache Country* 63 [An Indian chief wears] the usual girdle of manta upon his loins. **1876** HARTE in *Scribner's Mo.* XI. 382/2 They slyly slipped aside vail or *manta*, to peep furtively at the Donna Maria entering chapel. **1887** *Outing* X. 5/1 We had some scrambling and sliding which cost me 200 pounds of flour, . . . and one manta, or pack cover. **1910** J. HART *Vigilante Girl* 163 The women of my race never wear hat or bonnet, and always have a veil, or *manta*, or *mantilla* on their heads and wrapped around their chins.

2. *Mining.* **a.** (See quot. 1860.) +**b.** A mineral placer.

[**1860** *Eng. & Foreign Mining Gloss.* Span. Terms 109 *Manta*, a blanket, or horse cloth, used to contain ores or tools.] **1874** RAYMOND *6th Rep. Mines* 318 They pass through three rich streaks or *mantas*. **1890** *Cent.* 3617/1 *Manta*, . . . in mining, a blanket or sack of ore; a placer in situ. (Western U.S.)

Man tailor. A tailor who makes clothes for men. Used esp. of women. *Obs.* — **1789** *Boston Direct.* 204 Woodman Abigail, stay-maker & man-taylor, Creek-lane. **1796** *Ib.* 228 Bowns Martha, man-taylor, Sheaf street.

+**Manteca.** [Sp.] Lard; butter; fat. (Although in *O.E.D.* as 'a kind of butter' {1660-1748}, this word represents a new borrowing.) — **1845** GREEN *Texian Exped.* 264 These sixty-two chunks . . . are boiled in water with six ounces of manteca, lard, with a sufficiency of salt and red pepper. **1890** *Century Mag.* Dec. 165 He brought me . . . a handful of *manteca*, which is used by Mexicans instead of lard.

***Mantel.** Also **mantle.** Used attrib. in sense: MANTELPIECE 1 and 2.—**1841** CIST *Cincinnati* (*advt.*), Astral, Mantel, and Suspending Lamps. **1846** *Knickerb.* XXVII. 262 We have been sitting to-night for a full hour, by the mantle-clock of our goodly sanctum. **1852** in Stowe *Key* 136 Estate Sale of Furniture, . . . [including] Carpets, Rugs, Andirons, Fenders, Shovel and Tongs, Mantel Ornaments. **1865** — *House & Home P.* 86 Now come the great mantel-mirrors for four hundred [dollars] more. **1881** *Art Interchange* 27 Oct. 93/1 Mantel scarfs . . . could be of double-faced Canton flannel, finished with fringe and floss apples.

***Mantelet.** Also **mantelette.** A short, sleeveless cape or cloak for the shoulders. — **1742** *Md. Hist. Mag.* XX. 178 One Blew Velvet manteelet lined with silk & Trimed with blew silk Snail Loops. **1851** *Harper's Mag.* June 143/1 Mantelets are more in vogue than the gossamer-like shawls of July. **1856** *Porter's Spirit of Times* 22 Nov. 194/1 We have observed mantelettes, or cloaks, for the season.

Mantelpiece. Also **mantlepiece. 1.** The structure of stone, brick, wood, etc., around a fireplace. {1686-} **2.** =MANTELSHELF. {1827-} — (1) **1744** FRANKLIN *Acct. Fire-Places* 17 The Mantle-piece or Breast of the Chimney. **1833** *Knickerb.* I. 179 Take your feet from the mantle-piece. **1893** *Scribner's Mag.* June 787/1 Several of the mantel-pieces are hideous. (2) **1807** IRVING, etc. *Salmagundi* xiii. 321 He would . . . contemplate the little shepherdesses on the mantel-piece for a few minutes. **1838** INGRAHAM *Burton* II. 194 On the mantelpiece was a New Testament. **1854** M. J. HOLMES *Tempest & Sunshine* xxi, The waxen flowers . . . filled the vases on the mantel-piece. **1905** N. DAVIS *Northerner* 171 Falls laid the key and his own pistol upon the mantelpiece.

+**Mantelplace.** *S.* =MANTELSHELF. — *a***1870** SIMMS *Last Wager* (De Vere), You have a very singular ornament for your mantle-place.

Mantelshelf. The part of a mantelpiece, above the fireplace, which serves as a shelf. {1833-} — **1828** WEBSTER *s.v.*, *Mantle-Shelf*, the work over a fire-place, in front of the chimney. **1880** CABLE *Grandissimes* 84 They stood beneath their lofty mantel-shelf, each with a foot on a brazen fire-dog. **1891** WILKINS *New Eng. Nun* 91, I had gilt vases as tall as that on my parlor mantel-shelf. **1911** HARRISON *Queed* 152 The balled-up veil and gloves [were] on the mantel-shelf.

Mantilla. A shawl or veil, often of lace, worn over the head and shoulders, esp. by Spanish-American women; a light cape worn by a woman. {1717-}

1844 *Lexington Observer* 25 Sept. 2/6 In our stock may be found . . . Shawls, Mantillas and Scarfs. **1850** GARRARD *Wah-To-Yah* 179 The women . . . [wear] the *reboza* or *mantilla*—a scarf of cotton and silk, five to six feet in length by two or more in width. **1860** E. COWELL *Diary* 141 Bought a black silk, 'Bedouin' mantilla for me—$22. **1883** *Harper's Mag.* Sept. 510/1 Elderly ladies consulted her seriously as to . . . the propriety of their mantillas. **1904** A. DALE *Wanted, a Cook* 187 She insisted upon wearing a lace mantilla over her head, and fastening it with a diamond brooch beneath her chin.

Mantis shrimp. A squilla: (see quotation). {1871} — **1883** *Nat. Museum Bul.* No. 27, 121 There are three common species of Mantis Shrimp (*Squilla empusa* and *dubia*, and *Coronis glabrinsculus*) living upon the eastern coast of the United States.

Mantua. {1678-} Silk cloth suitable for making a mantua. {1709-} Also attrib. — **1754** *S.C. Gazette* 21-28 May 3/1 Mathewes & Lloyd Have just imported . . . mantuas and other silks, grandurells [etc.]. **1790** *Holyoke Diaries* 121 Bought my Black Mantua Silk Gown.

Mantuamaker. a. One who makes mantuas or loose gowns worn by women. *Obs.* {1694-} **b.** A dressmaker. {1841-}

1767 *Holyoke Diaries* 67 Mantua maker here. **1776** *Boston News-Letter* 22 Feb., Masks will be prepared, and sold by almost all the Milliners and Mantua Makers in Town. **1803** BOWNE *Life* 157, I have a mantua maker here making you a gown. **1844** *Lowell Offering* IV. 131 Miss Smith was the tailoress and Miss Jones was the mantua-maker. **1871** *Harper's Mag.* XLIII. 385/2 She was killing herself trying to earn a living in a mantua-maker's shop. **1905** VALENTINE *H. Sandwith* 100 After Wednesday evening prayer-meeting it had been his heroic duty to escort home . . . the little lame Mantua-maker.

***Manual.** +=JEFFERSON'S MANUAL. — **1900** *Congress. Rec.* 1 Feb. 1375/2 That is the only restriction which is laid down in the Manual, and there is no rule, of course, of the Senate relating to the matter.

***Manualist.** +One who uses manual methods to teach the deaf. — **1883** *Amer. Annals Deaf & Dumb* April 79 In the judgment of most manualists there can be no question that this fact alone, of prior speech, establishes such an important difference.

***Manual labor.** +*attrib.* Of or pertaining to a system of education embodied in manual labor schools. — **1835** HOFFMAN *Far West* I. 6 The latter is a *Manual labour institution* (a term I need hardly explain to you), recently incorporated. **1837** W. JENKINS *Ohio Gaz.* 406 Here is a literary institution . . . on the manual labor plan in successful operation, where the silk culture is extensively engaged in. **1849** CHAMBERLAIN *Indiana Gazetteer* 48 From the beginning the manual labor system had prevailed, and the students . . . had paid a great part of their expense by their own labor. **1881** *Rep. Indian Affairs* p. lviii, The entire agency farm and mission manual-labor tract were inclosed in a substantial post and board fence.

+**Manual labor college.** =MANUAL LABOR SCHOOL 1. — **1839** *Indiana H. Rep. Jrnl.* 210 [Resolved to appropriate] five hundred dollars . . . to aid the trustees of the Wabash manual labor college in the purchase of a library. **1853** *Harper's Mag.* Sept. 563/1 A cat . . . mischievously scratched up the corn and other seeds planted by the students of a manual-labor college situated in the neighborhood.

+Manual labor school.

1. A school in which students pay for their education in whole or part by doing manual labor.

1835 *S. Lit. Messenger* I. 274 *Manual Labor Schools* (on the Fellenberg plan) have not multiplied there [in New England], or grown in esteem, as might have been expected. **1843** *Lowell Offering* III. 214 There are now several Female Manual Labor Schools in New England. **1895** *Dept. Agric. Yrbk. 1894* 87 Between 1830 and 1840 there was much talk about 'manual labor schools.'

2. An Indian school similarly conducted: (see quot. 1866).

1850 HINES *Voyage* 95 At noon we arrived at . . . Chemekete, where the Oregon mission have commenced erecting mills, and where it is in contemplation to establish the Mission Manual Labor School. **1866** *Rep. Indian Affairs* 78 The 'manual labor' schools— . . . where the Indian children are separated from their savage parents, housed, clad, and taught not only the contents of the spelling-book and the Testament, but the elements of agriculture, mechanic and domestic arts. **1871** *Ib.* (1872) 180 The Creeks have thirty-two neighborhood schools, and two manual-labor schools, filled with pupils. **1910** *Indian Laws & Tr.* III. 440 For support of two manual-labor schools, . . . ten thousand dollars.

+Manual training. *Educ.* A course of training for the hands, esp. training in wood and metal work, basket-making, etc. Also attrib. — **1893** *Harper's Mag.* April 667/2 Manual training, as an adjunct to the schools, for the training of the eye and hand, he concluded to be . . . important. **1899** *Mo. So. Dakotan* I. 167 Manual training is the training of the hand in the use of tools. **1909** *Indian Laws & Tr.* III. 398 For equipment of manual training school, two thousand five hundred dollars. **1920** LEWIS *Main Street* 44, I believe in manual training, but Latin and mathematics always will be the backbone of sound Americanism.

Manufactory. {a1618–}

1. An establishment in which goods are manufactured. {1692–}

1760 *Post Boy* 31 March 2/2 To be let or sold the Sperma-ceti Manufactory in Weymouth. **1797** *Ann. 4th Congress* 2 Sess. 2124 The iron used was from our own mines; the guns from our own manufactories. **1814** *Niles' Reg.* V. 380/2 The eastern papers teem with notices of new manufactories. **1832** CLAY *Speeches* (1842) 185 Who has not been delighted with contemplating the clock-work regularity of a large cotton manufactory? **1862** CUMMING *Hospital Life* (1866) 54/2 Manufactories have arisen where before the war they were not known. **1898** YOUNG *Jessamine Co., Ky.* 272 In conjunction with his farm [he] operated a hemp manufactory.

+2. *attrib.* Designating currency issued by the manufacture bank; pertaining to the manufacture bank. *Obs.*

1741 *Manchester Rec.* II. 34 Voted that manefactory mony shall pay town charges if it hath a Corincey. **1742** in Felt *Mass. Currency* (1839) 113 Some of our fellow-partners . . . have not nor will pay in their several shares and parts of the said Land Bank or Manufactory Bills. **1767** HUTCHINSON *Hist. Mass.* II. 392 A general dread of drawing in all the paper money . . . disposed a great part of the province to favor . . . the land bank or manufactory scheme.

+Manufactural, *a.* Pertaining to industrial production through factories. {1852–} — **1789** MORSE *Amer. Geog.* 91 Pennsylvania has confessedly taken the lead . . . in manufactural improvements.

***Manufacture,** *n.*

1. A branch of productive industry that makes use of mechanical power, machinery, etc. {1683–}

1706 *N.C. Col. Rec.* I. 631 These Independent Colonies do turn the Course of Trade to the promoting and encouraging Woolen and other Manufactures. **1792** *Ann. 2d Congress* 971 The expediency of encouraging manufactures . . . appears at this time to be pretty generally admitted. **1816** *Ann. 14th Congress* 2 Sess. 12 It is to be regretted that a depression is experienced by particular branches of our manufactures. **1832** BENTON in *30 Years' View* I. 245/2 Why have the two bills reported by the Committee on Manufactures . . . [been] abandoned? **1882** Brockett *Our Country's Wealth* 162/1 Mr. [Samuel] Slater, the father of American cotton manufactures.

2. An article produced by manual labor, with or without the aid of machinery. {1611–}

1740 in Felt *Mass. Currency* (1839) 105 We Promise for ourselves and Partners to receive this Twenty Shilling Bill of Credit, . . . and after ye expiration of twenty yeares to pay ye possessor ye value thereof in Manufactures of this Province. **1768** FRANKLIN *Writings* V. 126 If our manufactures are too dear, they will not vend abroad.

Manufacture, *v.* {1683–} *spec. tr.* To grind (grain). *Obs.* — **1771** WASHINGTON *Diaries* II. 12 Began to Manufacture my Wheat with the Water of Piney Branch. **1774** FITHIAN *Journal* I. 111 Mr. Carter's Merchant Mill begins to run to-day—She is calculated to manufacture 25,000 Bushels of Wheat a Year. **1834** PECK *Gaz. Illinois* 273 Lebanon has two steam mills, one for sawing lumber, and the other for manufacturing grain.

+Manufacture bank. The Massachusetts land bank of 1740. So called because its bills were to be redeemed chiefly in manufactured products: (see MANUFACTORY 2 and cf. LAND BANK 1.) — **1742** Felt *Mass. Currency* 113 We the subscribers were partners in that unlucky and unfortunate scheme, called the Land or Manufacture Bank.

+Manufactured tobacco. Tobacco that has been processed. — **1835** *S. Lit. Messenger* I. 259 Among the items brought down may be enumerated . . . 2,230,900 lbs. of manufactured tobacco. **1862** *Statutes at Large* XII. 463 On tobacco, cavendish, plug, twist, fine cut, and manufactured of all descriptions . . . [there shall be a tax of] thirty cents per pound. **1884** HARRIS *Mingo* 87 'Manufactured' tobacco, in contradistinction to the natural leaf.

Manufacturer. {1719–} One who manufactures goods, esp. the owner of a factory. {1752–} — **1767** *Boston Gaz.* 23 Nov., The Manufacturers of Paper at Milton. **1790** *Ann. 1st Congress* II. 1549 A petition from the manufacturers of cordage . . . praying that a further duty may be imposed on the importation of foreign cordage. **1888** *Atlantic Mo.* Sept. 19/1 The central portion of the factory village . . . is still owned by the manufacturers. **1908** LORIMER *J. Spurlock* 62 The American manufacturer must be left free to run his own business.

Manufacturing. {1690–} *attrib.* **a.** Designating establishments that produce manufactured goods. **b.** Designating places where the chief industry is manufacturing.

1792 *Ann. 2d Congress* 982 Women . . . are rendered more useful . . . by manufacturing establishments, than they would otherwise be. **1819** MCMURTRIE *Sk. Louisville* 138 There are at this moment, in Louisville . . . one steam manufacturing mill, two breweries, two distilleries. **1840** *Niles' Nat. Reg.* 11 April 96/3 Norwich and Worcester railroad. . . . This road passes over the most extensive manufacturing district in Connecticut. **1855** in A. Lawrence *Diary & Corr.* 148 An old friend . . . was on a visit at Lowell, to inspect the works of the Middlesex Manufacturing Company. **1881** *Harper's Mag.* Jan. 185/2 Wilmington . . . is now a manufacturing centre of the first importance. **1894** *Ib.* Nov. 964/1 Labor troubles existed in many manufacturing towns.

+Manufactury. =MANUFACTURE *n. Obs.* — **1721** *Mass. H. Rep. Jrnl.* II. 372 Encouraging the Produce and Manufacturies of the Province. **1778** *N.H. Hist. Soc. Coll.* IX. 287 That all kinds of American manufacturies & internal produce . . . be estimated at rates not exceeding 75 per Cent advance.

***Manumission.** The action of formally freeing a slave; an instance of this.

1671 *Md. Archives* II. 272 Where any Negro or Negroes Slave or Slaues being in Servitude or bondage . . . shall become Christian . . . the same . . . shall [not be] . . . taken to be . . . a manumicion or . . . discharging any such Negroe or Negroes Slave or Slaues. **1716** *Mass. H. Rep. Jrnl.* I. 134 If this Court will indemnify him from the Law relating to the Manumission of Negroes. **1796** MORSE *Univ. Geog.* I. 231 Societies for the manumission of slaves have been instituted in Philadelphia, New York, Providence and New Haven. **1836** PAULDING *Slavery* 198 A case of manumission . . . occurred about three years since. **1869** TOURGEE *Toinette* xxvii, She found . . . the original deed of manumission given to Belle.

***Manumit,** *v. tr.* To release from slavery.

1671 *Md. Archives* II. 272 Negroes or Slaues . . . and the Issues of their bodies are [not] actually manumitted and made free. **1716** *Mass. H. Rep. Jrnl.* I. 135 It cannot be supposed, that he is Manumitted, by his Master, to avoid Charge in supporting him. **1790** *Ann. 1st Congress* II. 1456 Congress has no right whatever to manumit the slaves of this country. **1833** *Niles' Reg.* XLIV. 373/1 The 1st [will] directs his slaves to be manumitted, and makes provisions for their maintenance. **1869** TOURGEE *Toinette* xii, She had been manumitted according to the laws of New York.

***Manure,** *n.* A substance used as a fertilizer, esp. dung.

1660 *Watertown Rec.* I. 1. 68 He shall not cary off the p[re]mises any . . . manure. **1751** MACSPARRAN *Diary* 45 My two Negro's plowing in ye Buckwheat as Manure for English wheat. **1796** J. ADAMS *Diary* Works III. 421 B. and S. making and liming a heap of manure. **1818** J. TAYLOR *Arator* 223 Two great errours in relation to the use of corn stalks as manure, are prevalent. **1839** BUEL *Farmer's Companion* 73 Fish are converted into a valuable manure, and are a main dependence for fertility on some parts of Long Island. **1894** *Vt. Agric. Rep.* XIV. 56 If the manure be taken care of which results from the feeding [etc.].

b. *attrib.* and *comb.* Designating implements for handling manure.

1845 *Xenia Torch-Light* 31 July 3/6 A general assortment of . . .Manure and Hay Forks [etc.]. **1857** *Rep. Comm. Patents 1856* I. 302 *Improved Manure-Distributor.*—Patented October 14, 1856. . . . The amount of manure escaping through the open bottom can be regulated. **1871** *Ib. 1869* I. 535/1 *Combined Cultivator and Manure-Drag.*—January 19, 1869. **1888** *Vt. Agric. Rep.* X. 42 Implements . . . which reduce the cost of farm operating [include] . . . the hay tedder and the manure-spreader.

***Manure,** *v. tr.* To fertilize (soil) with manure. Also absol. — **1666** *Brookhaven Rec.* 18 Severall Freeholders . . . [have] Manured and Improved a considerable part [of the land]. **1787** CUTLER in *Life & Corr.* I. 288 The land very good, but the people take no pains to manure their land. **1888** *Vt. Agric. Rep.* X. 26 Manure according to your land.

+Manure tank. A cesspool. — **1857** VAUX *Villas* 46 We must . . . resort to the plan of a cess-pool or manure tank.

***Many,** *a.* Comb. with adjectives, in the specific names of plants and animals. — **1814** BIGELOW *Florula Bostoniensis* 84 *Juncus polycephalos.* Many headed rush. . . . Common in meadows and low ground. **1839** STORER *Mass. Reptiles* 249 *Salamandra dorsalis.* Harlan. The many spotted Salamander. **1840** *Niles' Nat. Reg.* 5 Sept. 16/3 The many-headed wheat is an indigenous plant of California. **1878** KILLEBREW *Tenn. Grasses* 101 [The] Many Flowered Darnel, *Lolium Multiflora*, . . . surpasses all other in showiness. **1885** HAVARD *Flora W. & S. Texas* 528 Many-eared Grama (*Bouteloua polystachya*); small, slender grass of good quality.

||**Many-millionaire.** A multimillionaire. — **1893** *Harper's Mag.* March 498 That would be but little more unexpected than that a many-millionaire should use his means in this way.

+**Manzanita.** Also (incorrectly) **manzañita, manzanito.** [Sp. dim. of *manzana* 'apple.']

1. a. Any of various shrubs of the west coast of the genus *Arctostaphylos*, esp. *A. pungens* and *A. tomentosa.* **b.** =MADROÑO.

1848 BRYANT *California* xxxii. 380 There is a growth of hawthorn, manzanita, (in bloom,) and other small shrubbery. **1857** *33d Congress 2 Sess.* Sen. Ex. Doc. No. 78 VI. III. *Arctostaphylos glauca.* ... Manzanita.... The manzanita has received the Spanish name which it bears from a fancied resemblance of its fruit to a little apple. **1871** *Rep. Comm. Agric. 1870* 413 *Manzanita,* (*Arctostaphylos tomentosa.*)—The manzañita of the Spaniards. It is a dwarf evergreen, producing a small fruit ... [which] when not fully ripe, ... tastes like an agreeably tart apple. **1899** NORRIS *McTeague* 382 Here was ... the flat overgrown with manzanita, where he once had shot three quail. **1918** MULFORD *Man from Bar-20* xvii, He pushed through matted thickets of oak brush and manzanito by main strength.

2. The fruit of one of these shrubs.

1848 BRYANT *California* xviii. 236 We have met occasionally with a reddish berry called by the Californians, manzanita.

3. Attrib. with *apple, bush, cañon,* etc.

1851 *Harper's Mag.* June 101/1 Bruin ... was seated ... in front of a manzanita bush, making a repast on his favorite berry. **1869** BRACE *New West* xi. 144 These all had Manzanita apples and acorns, for stores. **1876** MILLER *First Families* 232 Some idlers sat ... looking down the gulch as the manzanita smoke curled up from the Gopher's cabin. **1907** WHITE *Arizona Nights* 68 For the next day we planned a bear hunt afoot, far up a manzañita cañon.

***Map,** *n.*

***1.** A representation of the physical, political, or other features of a geographical area, put down on paper or other flat surfaces according to a definite scale.

1638 *R.I. Col. Rec.* I. 64 Survey all the Lands near abouts, and ... bring in a Mapp or Plott of the s'd lands. **1689** *Penna. Col. Rec.* I. 264 Ye mapp of The Province was the work of Thomas Holme, Surveyr Genell. **1755** WASHINGTON *Writings* I. 145, I herewith send you a small map of the back country. **1792** BELKNAP *Hist. New-Hampshire* III. 13 In my map, the line is inflected, so as to correspond with the last survey. **1823** *Ann, 18th Congress* 1 Sess. I. 825 The direction of the money appropriated to the purchase of books and maps for the Library of Congress. **1881–5** McCLELLAN *Own Story* 253 Attention is necessarily directed to the erroneous maps in our possession. **1911** QUICK *Yellowstone Nights* 149 The others began studying their maps to clear up this geographic anomaly.

+**b.** *fig. Off the map,* out of existence, into oblivion.

1904 W. H. SMITH *Promoters* 54 When she [Carthage] wouldn't let up, the only thing left was to wipe her off the map! **1911** SAUNDERS *Col. Todhunter* 99 A good set-to is the best way ... to put a stop to quarrelin'. It just wipes the whole thing off the map. **1920** SANDBURG *Smoke & Steel* 91 The guns blew seven millions off the map.

2. Attrib. and comb. in sense 1 with *case, maker,* etc.

1723 *New-Eng. Courant* 6–13 May 2/2 Subscriptions are also taken in by William Price, Print and Map Seller over against the Town House. **1775** ROMANS *Nat. Hist. Florida* App. 77 Our wise map-makers ... have corrupted it into *Ponio* bay. **1851** *Knickerb.* April 379 A map-peddler, in pursuance of his vocation, chanced to stop at the principal hotel. **1880** LAMPHERE *U.S. Govt.* 138/2 Force and Pay of the Coast and Geodetic Survey Service: ... 1 map mounter. **1924** *Scribner's Mag.* Dec. 652/1, I have an officer's sabre, ... three wrist watches, and a map case.

***Map,** *v. To map out.* {1619}, +to plan in detail. — **1869** 'MARK TWAIN' *Innocents* 117 We tried to map out excursions for the morrow. **1875** — *Old Times* i. 15, I set to work to map out a new career.

***Maple.** Also †**mayple, mapell, mapple.**

***1.** Any species of tree or shrub of the genus *Acer;* also, a tree of any of these species.

Particular species are often designated by qualifying adjectives. See ASH-LEAVED *a.* 2, BIRD'S EYE, CURLED, SUGAR, etc., MAPLE.

1637 MORTON *New Canaan* 65 Mayple: of those trees there is greate abundance; and these are very excellent for bowles. The Indians use of it to that purpose. **1676** B. TOMPSON *Poet. Writings* 60 Hedg'd with mighty oakes, maples and ashes. **1796** MORSE *Univ. Geog.* I. 352 The hills and mountains [of Vt.] are generally covered ... [with] birch, beach, maple, ash, elm, and butternut. **1819** SCHOOLCRAFT *Journal* 20 We have this day passed over some rich bottom lands, covered with elm, ... maple, sycamore and ash. **1839** PLUMBE *Sk. Iowa* 32 The timber ... is principally white, burr, red and black oak, ... some maple, ash, elm, birch and basswood. **1886** Z. F. SMITH *Kentucky* 184 The sugar-trough that was made to receive the sap of the maple was hewn out of half a log. **1907** *St. Nicholas* Oct. 1062/1 Mother Bear was clawing eagerly at a jagged rent in the trunk of a tall maple.

***2.** The wood of any of these trees.

1709 LAWSON *Carolina* 99 The Maple, of which we have two sorts, is used to make Trenchers, Spinning-wheels, &c. **1714** *Essex Inst. Coll.* XLIII. 51 One box of maple. **1857** CHANDLESS *Visit Salt Lake* 145 Oak, pine, cedar, and maple are the commonest, and fetch eight dollars a 'cord.' **1867** 'T. LACKLAND' *Homespun* I. 127 An uncle fetches in an armful of hickory and maple.

3. *attrib.* **a.** Designating things derived from maple trees.

1658 *Charlestown Land Rec.* 81 [The land] is boundid on the north by an oake stump ... and ffrom the sayd stump to a mapell stump. **1764** *N.H. Hist. Soc. Coll.* IX. 150 Josh Hall and my team sledded 7 loads of maple wood. **1835** *S. Lit. Messenger* I. 357 The Indians sustained great injury from the bursting of a maple log, which they had bored like a cannon. **1851** SPRINGER *Forest Life* 26 After obtaining a quantity of Maple sap, it is poured into large iron or tinned copper kettles. **1879** B. F. TAYLOR *Summer-Savory* 211 An older wearer [of the apron] ... brought apples from the orchard in it, and white maple-chips from the woodpile.

b. Designating places where maples grow.

1716 *Boston Rec.* 66 [We do] Dispose of ... Mapple Island Meadow. **1766** J. BARTRAM *Journal* 19 We saw very extensive marshes ... (with ... maple-hammocks interspersed). **1791** IMLAY *Western Territory* (ed. 3) 473 In maple plantations, it may be useful to cut down all other timber which grow intermixed with the sugar-trees. *a*1817 DWIGHT *Travels* III. 178 The land between Utica and Laird's is what in New England is called beech and maple land, and here maple and bass land.

c. Designating things made of maple wood.

1794 Buckingham *Newspaper Lit.* II. 229 My only chattels, worth the sledding, Consisting of a maple stead, a counterpane, and coverlet. **1848** COOPER *Oak Openings* v, Two common low-post maple bedsteads were soon uncorded and carried off. **1854** CIST *Cincinnati* 245 Warner B. Mahone, turner ..., executes ... walnut and maple banisters. **1899** CHESNUTT *Wife of His Youth* 49 She went to the maple dressing-case, and opened one of the drawers.

d. In the names of parasites that live on the maple.

1873 *Winfield* (Kan.) *Courier* 24 July 1/5, I find the maple worm is a peculiarly Kansas institution.... Its body is constructed like a joint snake. **1890** *Cent.* 3623/1 *Maple-borer,* ... one of the different insects which bore the wood of maples.

+**Maple beer.** A beverage consisting partly of fermented maple molasses. — **1824** *New Eng. Farmer* II. 211 Maple Beer.—To every four gallons of water ... add a quart of maple molasses. **1833** FLINT *D. Boone* 115 Persimmon and maple beer, stood them well instead of the poisonous whisky of their children. **1853** *Harper's Mag.* Dec. 22/2 The table was spread with ... cold bread and meat, fragrant glades butter, rich milk, and maple beer.

+**Maple bush. a.** A shrubby maple, esp. *Acer spicatum.* **b.** A grove of sugar maples. — **1821** SCHOOLCRAFT *Narr. Travels* 162 Bark scraped off the small red twigs of the acer spicatum, or maple bush [is used by Indians as a substitute for tobacco]. **1845** LINCOLN *Botany* App. 69/1 *Acer spicatum,* (mountain maple bush). **1881** *Harper's Mag.* April 646 Many farmers would no more part with their maple bush or orchard than with any precious heirloom.

+**Maple candy.** =MAPLE SUGAR. — **1844** *Knickerb.* XXIII. 445 Little Sue ... begged me to bring her back some maple candy.

+**Maple-leaved,** *a.* Used in the specific names of plants. — **1785** MARSHALL *Amer. Grove* 77 Maple-leaved Liquidamber Tree or Sweet Gum. **1797** IMLAY *Western Territory* (ed. 3) 277 The liquidambar, copalm, or maple-leaved storax, ... affords a balm, the virtues of which are infinite. **1813** MUHLENBERG *Cat. Plants* 48 Maple-leaved Hawthorn. **1843** TORREY *Flora N.Y.* I. 306 *Viburnum acrifolium.* ... Maple-leaved arrow-wood.... Dry open woods; very common.

+**Maple molasses.** =MAPLE SYRUP. Also attrib. — **1804** FESSENDEN *Orig. Poems* (1806) 133 The lips of my charmer are sweet, As a hogshead of maple molasses. **1832** BROWNE *Sylva* 111 Maple molasses is made by discontinuing the evaporation before the liquid is of sufficient consistence to consolidate by cooling. **1857** *Knickerb.* Jan. 38 My more ordinary dissipation didn't generally go beyond buying two or three pennies' worth of ... maple-molasses candy. **1872** *Harper's Mag.* June 26/2 There were ... hot cakes, honey, maple-molasses, and coffee.

+**Maple orchard.** An orchard or grove of sugar maples. — **1868** BEECHER *Norwood* 399 The woods and maple orchards were filled with sounds of industry. **1881** *Harper's Mag.* April 642/2 The maple orchards [of Shrewsbury, Vt.] are famous.

+**Maple sugar.** Sugar obtained by evaporating the sap of certain maples.

1720 *Phil. Trans.* XXXI. 27 Maple Sugar is made of the juice of the Upland Maple, or Maple Trees that grow upon the Highlands. **1790** *Columbian Centinel* 18 Sept. 6/2 Yesterday arrived in this city [Philadelphia], a sloop from Albany, with forty hogsheads of Maple Sugar, ... the whole of it manufactured on the waters of the Susquehannah. **1832** WILLIAMSON *Maine* I. 109 The method of making maple sugar ... is learned from the Aborigines. **1851** SPRINGER *Forest Life* 27 It is perfectly easy to make Maple sugar as white as the best double-refined loaf-sugar. **1916** EASTMAN *From Deep Woods* 169 The making of maple sugar is a leading industry.

b. Attrib. and comb. with *butternut, camp, industry,* etc.

*a*1797 in Imlay *Western Territory* (ed. 3) 151 A single family, ... on the maple-sugar lands, between the Delaware and Susquehanna, made

1800 lbs. of maple-sugar in one season. **1814** *Niles' Reg.* VI. 152/1 A Vermont statement of the maple sugar works is [etc.]. **1857** *Lawrence* (Kan.) *Republican* 11 June 4 Mr. Sloven electrified his family . . . with the announcement that he was going into the maple-sugar-making business. **1880** *Vt. Agric. Rep.* VI. 112 My object is to give a brief history of the maple sugar industry. **1884** ROE *Nature's Story* 156 We'll improvise a maple-sugar camp of the New England style a hundred years ago. **1904** WALLER *Wood-Carver* 69, I'm waiting for the 'maple-sugar-butternut' candy and the spruce gum.

+**Maple-sugar maker.** One who makes maple sugar. — **1880** *Vt. Agric. Rep.* VI. 113 The present duty of maple sugar-makers is to educate consumers up to a higher standard. **1900** *Congress. Rec.* 20 Feb. 1966/1 A petition of the Vermont Maple Sugar Makers' Association, praying for the passage of a pure-food bill.

+**Maple swamp.** A swamp in which the predominant growth is maple. — **1667** *Providence Rec.* V. 317 Standing on the west Side of a Maple Swampe. **1724** *N.H. Probate Rec.* II. 203 Twenty acres of swamp Land that was Layed out to me . . . in the mapell swamp so called. **1861** NEWELL *Orpheus C. Kerr* 326 A line about as regular as so many trees in a maple swamp.

+**Maple syrup.** A syrup made by evaporating maple sap. — **1865** A. D. WHITNEY *Gayworthys* xxiii, There are wheat-cakes and maple syrup for your breakfast. **1882** *Vt. Agric. Rep.* VII. 63 A sample of his maple syrup and sugar. **1914** 'BOWER' *Flying U Ranch* 165 With the taste of hot biscuits and maple syrup still lingering pleasantly against their palates.

***Maple tree.** A tree or species of the genus *Acer.* — **1659** *Warwick Rec.* 263 At the Northwest corner bounded by a Maple tree and by a white Oake next the brooke. **1685** *Providence Rec.* XIV. 168 A little up ye streame unto a bunch of Maple trees growing out of one Roote. **1785** MARSHALL *Amer. Grove* 1 The Maple Tree . . . hath Hermaphrodite and Male flowers upon the same tree. **1848** BRYANT *California* iv. 46 The timber on the creek consists of oak, linden and some maple trees. **1893** *Harper's Mag.* Feb. 445 In front of it extended a row of magnificent maple-trees.

+**Maple water.** The sap drawn from the sugar maple. — **1886** Z. F. SMITH *Kentucky* 84 [They] visited a neighboring sugar-camp to drink of the maple water.

+**Maqua.** A Mohawk or an Iroquois. *Obs.* — **1690** *Mass. H. S. Coll.* 4 Ser. V. 258 Five of the Maquas are dead of the small-pox. **1709** SEWALL *Diary* II. 261 Col. Hobbey's Regiment musters, and the govr orders the Maquas to be there and see them. **1826** COOPER *Mohicans* iii, Do the Maquas dare to leave the print of their moccasins in these woods?

+**Marabou.** 'The variety of negro which springs from a mulatto and a griffe' (B. '59).

+**Maracock.** [Algonquian.] The maypop or the plant that produces it. *Obs.* — **1612** SMITH *Virginia* 12 A fruit that the Inhabitants call Maracocks, . . . is a pleasant wholsome fruit much like a lemond. **1633** Gerard *Herball* 1591 Of the Maracoc or Passion-floure. . . . This Plant . . . is the same which the Virginians call *Maracoc.* **1705** BEVERLEY *Virginia* II. 17 The same Use is made also of . . . Squashes, Maycocks, Maracocks, Melons [etc.].

+**Marajuana.** Variant of MARIJUANA.

Maraschino. A liqueur distilled from the juice of the marasca cherry. {1793-} — **1840** *Knickerb.* XV. 392 Those two pet tipples of the ladies, curaço and maraschino. **1885** BAYLOR *On Both Sides* 304 Beer, sherry, champagne, claret, maraschino, and chasse-café made up a total that she had never seen a woman dispose of before.

Maraud. A raid. *On the maraud,* on a plundering expedition. — **1837** IRVING *Bonneville* I. 136 While thus encamped, they were still liable to the marauds of the Blackfeet. **1855** — *Wolfert's Roost* 18 He had an Indian's capacity in discovering when the enemy was on the maraud. **1884** *St. Nicholas* XI. 534 Certain neighboring tribes . . . make maraud upon them.

***Marble.**

***1. a.** Crystallized limestone in either its natural or its quarried state; a kind or variety of this. **b.** *collect.* Stones or slabs of this material.

1637 T. MORTON *New Canaan* 83 There is one bay in the land that beareth the name of Marble harber, because of the plenty of Marble there. **1709** LAWSON *Carolina* 42 In many Places there were great Quantities of Marble. *c*1790 T. COXE *View U.S.* 63 The produce, manufactures, and exports of Pennsylvania are very many and various, viz., . . . coal, freestone and marble. **1821** *Mass. H. S. Coll.* 2 Ser. IX. 129 The marble, in this village [Middlebury, Vt.], which is now wrought, on a large scale, and extensively diffused over the country, was discovered by Dr. Ebenezer W. Judd. **1870** *Congress. Globe* App. 26 March 225/2 The marbles of our western border have heretofore served as 'chimney rock' for the cabin of the luxurious border farmer. **1886** STAPLETON *Major's Christmas* 179 Great houses of marble and brown stone frowned down upon the beholder. **1916** *Bur. Mines Bul.* No. 106, 122 Marble is used for foundation stone and retaining walls.

***2.** A piece of masonry or sculpture made of marble, as a tombstone.

1771 FRANKLIN *Autobiog.* 236 They lie buried together at Boston, where I some years since placed a marble over their grave. **1894** ROBLEY *Bourbon Co., Kansas* 3 His countrymen will place his statue the very next to Washington's in the line of historic marbles.

3. A small spherical ball made of marble, agate, porcelain, or the like, used in various games; *pl.*, one of the games played with the marbles. {1694-}

1747 FRANKLIN *Exper. on Electricity* 10 Suspend a small cork-ball, about the bigness of a marble. **1836** in Buckingham *Amer., N. States* I. 253 The amusement of playing at marbles being at best a filthy one [etc.]. **1876** 'MARK TWAIN' *Tom Sawyer* ii, Tom was literally rolling in wealth. He had . . . twelve marbles, a couple of tadpoles [etc.]. **1905** N. DAVIS *Northerner* 111 Are we boys playing marbles—or is this a city administration?

4. *attrib.* and *comb.*

In the patent records, *marble* is frequently used in combination with participles, to designate machines or implements used in processing marble, as *marble-dressing machine.*

a. Designating things made of marble.

1775 *Essex Inst. Coll.* XIII. 185 In the *front room.* . . . A Lookg. Glass, a marble slab. **1825** WOODWORTH *Forest Rose* I. i, The geese, you must know, are mostly seen, in term time, flocking round a marble house in the park. **1838** HAWTHORNE *Notebooks* (1932) 56 The white marble grave-stones show pleasantly [among the trees]. **1844** *Lexington Observer* 25 Sept. 1/6 Girandoles, marble stand, 2 lights, from 3 to $7.00. **1860** *Ladies' Repository* XX. 40/2 With its mahogany furniture, marble center-table, and large mirror. **1868** *Putnam's Mag.* Oct. 415/2 A modest wooden house nestled shyly between two pretentious 'marble-fronts.' **1895** M. A. JACKSON *Gen. Jackson* 636, I had . . . a simple marble headstone . . . placed at the grave. **1925** *Vermont Marble* 15 Marble floors . . . must be mopped or scrubbed regularly.

b. Designating industrial plants where marble is processed.

1809 KENDALL *Travels* III. 242 The saw, . . . in this marble saw-mill, [moves] in a horizontal direction. **1856** M. J. HOLMES *L. Rivers* 385 He went straight from Mr. Douglass' to the marble factory. **1869** *Boyd's Business Directory* 356 Jamestown Marble Works, J. L. Fish, Proprietor. **1872** *Vermont Bd. Agric. Rep.* I. 663 There are twenty marble mills in Rutland county.

c. Designating persons who work with marble.

1865 *Atlantic Mo.* XV. 250/2 The tassels of the robe [of a statue] have been chiselled by Miss Hosmer's marble-cutter with . . . care. **1880** *Harper's Mag.* May 870/2 The labor of . . . superintending carpenters and joiners, marble-workers, and glass and gas fitters.

+**Marble cake.** A cake made of both light and dark batter to produce a marblelike mottle. — **1884** M. HARLAND *Common Sense in Household* 311 [Recipe for] Marble cake. Light. . . . Dark. **1903** WIGGIN *Rebecca* 290 She began to stir the marble cake. **1920** HOWELLS *Vacation of Kelwyns* 27 Three slices of pound-cake . . . and thicker slices of marble-cake, with veins of *verde antique* varying its surface of Siena yellow.

***Marbled,** *a.* +In the specific names of American (1) birds and (2) fishes: (see quots.). — (1) **1828** BONAPARTE *Synopsis* 423 The Marbled Guillemot, *Uria marmorata,* . . . inhabits the north-western coasts of America. **1839** PEABODY *Mass. Birds* 371 The Marbled Godwit, *Limosa fedoa.* . . . In August they appear in large numbers, and many are shot for the table. **1909** WEBSTER 1317/1 *M[arbled] murrelet,* a small murrelet (*Brachyramphus marmoratus*) of the Pacific coast of North America. (2) **1884** GOODE, etc. *Fisheries* I. 173 The best known species [of the devil-fishes] are the Marbled Angler, *Pterophryne histrio,* and the Sea Bat, *Malthe vespertilio.* **1896** JORDAN & EVERMANN *Check-List Fishes* 374 *Mycteroperca bonaci.* Marbled Rockfish. West Indies, Pensacola to Brazil. **1903** T. H. BEAN *Fishes N.Y.* 89 *Ameiurus nebulosus marmoratus.* . . . Marbled Cat. . . . [Found in] lowland streams and swamps from New York to southern Indiana and Florida.

+**Marblehead turkey.** [*Marblehead,* Mass.] (See quotation.) — **1859** BARTLETT 264 *Marblehead Turkeys,* codfish. So called in Massachusetts.

+**Marbleize,** *v. tr.* To color in imitation of marble. Also *ppl. a.* — **1868** *Mich. Agric. Rep.* VII. 355 J. B. Billings, Detroit, [displayed] specimens of marbleized slate, (mantels and panels). **1874** *Vermont Bd. Agric. Rep.* II. 745 [Mantels] are also painted in imitation of black walnut and other woods, and finished up as though they were marbleized. **1888** HOWELLS *Annie Kilburn* xi, The marbleized iron shelf above the stove-pipe hole supported two glass vases. **1892** *Harper's Mag.* May 936/2 Strongly scented sweet soap of a marbleized reddish color lay wrapped in tin-foil.

Marble quarry. A quarry from which marble is obtained. {1644- (Evelyn *Mem.* 19 Oct.)} — **1811** SUTCLIFF *Travels* (1815) 289 We visited the proprieter of an extensive marble quarry. **1884** *Knickerb.* XXIV. 184 The uplifted arm of labor . . . meets his eye . . . [in] the deep marble-quarry. **1883** *Century Mag.* May 155/2 This [New England] town has its railroads, its telegraphs, its marble quarries. **1916** *Bur. Mines Bul.* No. 106, 3 During 1914 Mr. Bowles personally visited 64 active marble quarries.

Marble-top, *a.* Designating a piece of furniture the top of which is made of marble. — **1886** STAPLETON *Major's Christmas* 165 She with two sets of chiny, carpets all over the house, and a marble-top set in the spare room. **1891** 'THANET' *Otto the Knight* 60 [She was] a woman of property, . . . owning two marble-top bureaus and a sewing-machine.

+**Marble yard.** A yard in which marble is stored or worked upon. — **1851** CIST *Cincinnati* 218 Seven marble yards and shops. **1855** *Chicago W. Times* 9 Aug. 1/8 The workmen were removing the plank sidewalk . . . before Wilson's marble yard. **1870** 'MARK TWAIN' *Sk., New & Old* 219

You have . . . littered up the floor with chips off your hams till the place looks like a marble-yard.

***March.**

***1.** *Mil.* The action of marching; the amount of this done continuously, as in one day.

1643 *Md. Council Proc.* 133 We are informed of your propensenes to goe a march upon the Sesquihanowes. **1790** DENNY *Journal* 144 Difficult march this day over beech roots and brush. **1867** EDWARDS *Shelby* 9, I profess simply to have given the Southern side in all accounts of battles, sieges, marches, raids, and campaigns. **1902** ALDRICH *Sea Turn* 209 That march back to Camp Blenker was a solemn business.

+b. *March to the sea,* during the Civil War, the march of General Sherman's Union army from Atlanta to Savannah, November 15 to December 21, 1864.

1865 G. W. NICHOLS *Great March* 15 The March to the Sea . . . [fills us] with admiration . . . for the gallant heroes who pushed forward day by day, bearing . . . the Stars and Stripes. **1866** *New Mexican* 3 Nov. 2/1 [He] was with Sherman in his famous 'march to the sea.' **1901** CHURCHILL *Crisis* 478 On our march to the sea, if the orders were ever given to turn northward, 'the boys' would get very much depressed.

+2. *Euchre.* (See quot. 1857.)

1857 *Hoyle's Games* (Amer. ed.) 285 In case the party who makes the trump secures . . . all five tricks, it is called a 'march,' and counts two points. **1864** DICK *Amer. Hoyle* (1866) 79 Play for a march, by leading trumps.

+3. *W.* A cattle drive.

1869 *Overland Mo.* III. 126 Two men often 'bunch' on the march, *i.e.*, unite their herds for convenience in driving.

March court. +A court session held in March. — **1836** *S. Lit. Messenger* II. 302 But if court day be thus important, how much more so is March court!

March meeting. +In New England, a town meeting that annually convenes in March. — **1728** *Boston Rec.* 222 If the Money apropriated . . . at the last march meeting be Insofficient . . . Henry Gibbon will advance and pay what falls Short. **1736** B. LYNDE *Diary* 65 Got to the fag end of a Boston March meeting. **1766** J. ADAMS *Works* II. 188 Major Miller and James Bracket, Jr. were heard, since March meeting, raving against Deacon Palmer. **1866** LOWELL *Biglow P.* 2 Ser. p. xi, Mr. Hosea Biglow's Speech in March meeting.

+Marcylite. [Gen. R. B. *Marcy* (1812–87).] A decomposed form of copper pyrites. — **1853** in Marcy *Explor. Red River* (1854) 145 On subjecting the black ore to a close investigation, it proves to be a substance hitherto undescribed, and it affords me much pleasure to name it, in honor of the very enterprising and successful explorer to whom mineralogy is indebted for the discovery, *Marcylite.*

+Mardi gras. [Fr., 'fat Tuesday.'] Shrove Tuesday, the last day of carnival as celebrated in New Orleans; also the festival ending on this day. Also attrib.

1839 *Picayune* 13 Feb. 2/1 Thus has passed 'Mardi Gras,' and may we all live to see fifty more just like it. **1884** 'CRADDOCK' *Where Battle Was Fought* 128 It was the evening of Mardi Gras and the Mystick Krewe procession was on the march. **1888** *Century Mag.* Dec. 297/2 A Voodoo . . . [created] considerable stir among the Northern attendants upon Mardi Gras. **1899** ADE *Fables in Slang* (1900) 148 His Father was too serious a Man to get out in Mardi-Gras Clothes and hammer a Ball from one Red Flag to another.

b. A carnival or festival in imitation of the annual celebration in New Orleans.

1904 *N.Y. Ev. Post* 17 Sept. 3 At a special meeting of the Coney Island business men $25,000 was subscribed to pay the expenses of the semi-centennial celebration and mardi gras on September 21.

***Mare.** The female of the domestic horse. — **1636** *Conn. Rec.* I. 4 Twoe of the mares . . . are nowe seized vppon. **1777** J. ADAMS *Familiar Letters* 235 My horse . . . clambers over mountains that my old mare would have stumbled on. **1885** HOWELLS *Silas Lapham* xviii, He turned the mare up to the curb-stone. **1900** DIX *Deacon Bradbury* 215 A second lash fell upon the mare's back.

Marèchal Niel. [f. *Marechal* Adolphe *Niel* (1802–69).] A yellow variety of the Noisette rose. {1867–} — **1869** PARSONS *On the Rose* 48 Marèchal Niel . . . is perhaps the largest and most beautiful yellow rose known, and very fragrant. **1883** RITTENHOUSE *Maud* 184 A gentleman entered the ball-room bearing a huge tray laden with roses, *real* roses, fresh, fragrant cream ones, pink ones, pure white ones, great Marshall Niels and every other variety. **1916** *Farmers' Bul.* No. 750, 9 Roses of the climbing Noisette group, represented by Marechal Niel, Lamarque, and other varieties, are suitable for culture only in the warmer sections.

***Mare colt.** A filly. (Cf. COLT.) {Now only Somerset dial.}— **1640** *Conn. Rec.* I. 448 Cattell of James Olmestead: . . . one mare colt, . . . one yoke of steeres [etc.]. **1678** *New Castle Court Rec.* 197 The Pl[ain]t[iff] demands of this def[endan]t for one mare Coult sould and delivered. **1787** WASHINGTON *Diaries* III. 155 A sorrel mare colt 1 year old, blaze in the face; A sorrel horse Colt of this spring. **1843** *Portfolio* (London) 2 Ser. II. 309 (B.), A horse-colt is simply a colt; a mare-colt, merely a filly.

+Margate fish. Any of several grunts inhabiting the waters of the Caribbean. — *c*1733 CATESBY *Carolina* II. 2 The Margate Fish. This Fish has a rounding Back, making a curved Line between the Head and Tail. **1775** ROMANS *Nat. Hist. Florida* App. 19 A little to the north hereof is a small reef . . . where vast quantities of . . . porgys, margate-fish, rock-fish, yellow-tails, Jew-fish, &c. may be taken. **1802** ELLICOTT *Journal* 255 Along the Florida Reef, and among the Keys, a great abundance and variety of fish may be taken; such as . . . margate-fish. **1911** *Rep. Fisheries 1908* 312 Margate-Fish (*Haemulon album*).—A grunt found in southern Florida; known also as 'porgy,' 'market-fish,' etc.

***Margin,** *n.*

1. *Stock exchange.* **+a.** The difference between the value of securities deposited with a lender and the amount of the loan made by him.

1848 W. ARMSTRONG *Stocks* 10 The purchaser then hands over this margin to the person with whom he hypothecates the Stock. **1870** MEDBERY *Men Wall St.* 56 The lender protects himself, first, by the margin, seldom less than ten per cent.

b. A deposit of money or securities made by a principal with his broker to cover the risk of the broker's transactions in stocks, grain, etc., on account. {1882–}

1870 MEDBERY *Men Wall St.* 56 The broker's power to buy on a margin depends upon the certainty that the collaterals will have a definite borrowing capacity. **1877** in Leavitt *Our Money Wars* (1894) 213 Money has been and still is plenty. Hence they have sent it here to be used as margins. **1880** *Harper's Mag.* Oct. 782/2 All speculated, but they did not speculate on margins. **1895** E. CARROLL *Principles Finance* 186 The amount of margin required is dependent not alone on the character of the stock, but also on the condition of the money market. **1902** WHITE *Blazed Trail* 261 If I can save my margins, I'll be all right. **1906** *Louisiana Rep.* CXVI. 22 Plaintiff . . . instructed defendant 'that he would not stand at any time loss beyond the margin to his credit, and that they must hedge when margin was about exhausted.'

+c. Transactions based upon such deposits.

1884 *N.Y. Puck* Aug., The president speculateth in margins, and then goeth to Canada for his health. **1912** NICHOLSON *Hoosier Chron.* 173 Miles hadn't found out yet that corn margins are not legitimate investments for a county's money.

+d. 'A deposit made by each of two brokers, parties to a contract, when one is "called up" (as it is termed) by the other' (*Cent.*).

2. The amount of money available on something in excess of strictly necessary expenditure; profit. {1852–, in more general sense}

1851 CIST *Cincinnati* 319 We are in the enjoyment of a clear margin, of at least, half a cent per pound, over our eastern neighbors. **1876** *Vermont Bd. Agric. Rep.* III. 159 A promising lot of salable horses, . . . that are certain to give him par value with a handsome margin, if he breeds size. **1890** *Congress. Rec.* 25 June 6499/2 When an employer feels that his margin is slipping away from him, the first thing done is to scale down the price of wages. **1902** LORIMER *Lett. Merchant* 224 There seems to be a good margin in [the export cattle business].

3. Attrib. in sense 1 b with *call, clerk.*

1886 *Harper's Mag.* July 213/2 Speculative sales of lard . . . are also made in the Call Room . . . the caller of provisions and margin clerk presiding. **1888** *Economist* 20 Oct. 3/3 Millions of dollars were sent to Chicago from New York . . . to meet losses and margin calls.

Margin, *v.* {1607–} *Stock exchange.* **+1.** *intr.* and *tr. To margin up,* to deposit more margin with a broker when a stock is falling. **+2.** *tr.* To cause the price of (a commodity) to come *down* by selling on margins. — **(1) 1889** *Amer. Economist* 29 March 176/1 The concern [had] . . . trebled its liabilities in the vain attempt to margin up after a fall begun in September, 1881. **1902** NORRIS *Pit* x, It's always better to keep our trades margined up. **(2) 1887** *Courier-Journal* 19 Feb. 7/4 Wheat is margined down under 75¢.

***Marginal,** *a.* +Of or pertaining to a margin in a stock market. — **1870** MEDBERY *Men Wall St.* 59 Nor is there any dissimilarity between the conditions of purchase in complete and in marginal transactions. *Ib.* 62 The broker . . . demands of his customer either solid deposit of money or stocks, or marginal deposit of money.

***Marigold.** Any of several plants having bright yellow or golden flowers, esp. of the genera *Calendula* and *Tagetes;* also, a flower of one of these plants. — **1709** LAWSON *Carolina* 78 Our pot-herbs [are] . . . Clary, Marigold, pot Marjoram [etc.]. **1806** in *Ann. 9th Congress* 2 Sess. 1142 Life everlasting, wild liquorice, marygold, mistletoe [etc.]. **1845** KIRKLAND *Western Clearings* 76 Beds . . . were filled to overflowing with dahlias, china-asters, and marigolds. **1891** WILKINS *New Eng. Nun* 125 Minty stopped and picked an enormous bouquet of zinnias and marigolds and balsams. **1911** C. M. SKINNER *Myths & Legends of Flowers* 174 Like other yellow flowers, the marigold was an expression of light.

+Marijuana. Also **mariguan, marajuana.** [Mex. Sp., from *maraguango,* 'any substance producing an intoxication.'] The hemp or its leaves, used as a powerful narcotic. — **1894** *Scribner's Mag.* May 596/2 [The] 'toloachi,' [and] the 'mariguan,' . . . [are] used by discarded women for the purpose of wreaking a terrible revenge upon recreant lovers. **1923** W. SMITH *Little Tigress* 102 (Bentley), The cockroach is unable to stagger around any more because he has no more marijuana to smoke. **1925** SCARBOROUGH *Wind* 90 (Bentley), Marajuana. That's a Mexican weed that has intoxicatin' properties.

***Marine,** *n.*

1. One of a body of soldiers who do service about a dock or on a warship, often used as a landing party: **a.** Such a soldier in British service. {1672–}

1703 *Mass. Prov. Press* 48 Each ship had on board 2 companies of marines. **1711** *N.C. Col. Rec.* I. 761 If you could spare us some Marines it would strike a greater Terrer in the people. **1776** LEACOCK *Fall Brit. Tyranny* IV. vii, My poor marines stood no more chance with 'em than a cat in hell without claws.

b. Such a soldier in American service.

1775 *Jrnls. Cont. Congress* III. 348 *Resolved,* That two Battalions of marines be raised. **1794** *Ann. 3d Congress* 1427 The crews of each of the said ships . . . shall consist of . . . one corporal, one drum, one fife, and fifty marines. **1812** *Niles' Reg.* II. 398/1 Among the marines was a '*back woods man.*' **1846** *Whig Almanac 1847* 25/2 A few shots were exchanged between our Marines and a handful of Mexican soldiers stationed at Tabasco. **1861** *Army Regulations* 72 Marines take the left of other infantry. **1898** *Amer. R. of R.'s* Sept. 265/2 Parties of the United States marines make landings near San Juan, [Puerto Rico]. **1907** *St. Nicholas* July 813/2 The blue-jackets stand on the port side of the quarter-deck, and the marines on the starboard, all ready for inspection.

+c. (See first quotation.)

1840 DANA *Two Years* 155 'Marine' is the term applied more particularly to a man who is ignorant and clumsy about seaman's work—a greenhorn—a land-lubber. *Ib.* 269 We knew that they were such 'marines' that they would not know whether it was our fault or not.

2. The collective naval and shipping fleet of the nation {1669–}; the merchant shipping.

1812 CLAY *Speeches* (1860) I. 24 Gentlemen fear that if we provide a marine it will produce collisions with foreign nations. **1819** *McDonogh P.* 37 Were the canal formed . . . not only would the general government be greatly benefited in relation to their marine, but it would be a source of great revenue. **1868** G. G. CHANNING *Recoll. Newport* 197 [France and England] were continually subjecting American commerce to serious interruptions, placing our 'marine' between two fires abroad.

3. Attrib. in sense 1 with *artillery, band,* etc.

1839 C. F. BRIGGS *Harry Franco* I. xvi. 154, I . . . took up the morning paper to look over the marine list, with the hope of finding the name of Captain Gunnell. **1846** POLK *Diary* I. 411 At 6 O'Clock the Marine Band performed in the grounds South of the President's House. **1862** in Moore *Rebellion Rec.* V. II. 171 Lieut. Avery, of the marine artillery, . . . accompanied the expedition. **1885** *Century Mag.* Sept. 759, I requested Admiral Porter . . . to send the Marine Brigade, a floating nondescript force.

***Marine,** *a.* Connected with the sea in matters of shipping, naval control, insurance, etc.

1744 MOORE *Voy. Georgia* 140 Having reached the south end of Cumberland, they met the periagua and marine boat at anchor. **1776** *Jrnls. Cont. Congress* V. 423 *Resolved,* That the Marine Committee be empowered to affix the names to each particular ship. **1809** KENDALL *Travels* II. 263 Merchants, Marine-insurers, sailors, ship-wrights. **1833** COKE *Subaltern's Furlough* iii, A fine Marine Asylum is building near the road to Gray's Ferry. **1883** *Wheelman* I. 298, I pedaled around the harbor this spring, on a marine bicycle. **1901** MERWIN & WEBSTER *Calumet 'K'* 213 A marine leg is the thing that takes grain up out of ships. **1913** *Harper's Mag.* Feb. 338/2 Some of the marine underwriting firms are the largest insurers of automobiles.

+Marine armor. A diver's suit. *Obs.* — **1831** *Knickerb.* Oct. 373 One of the most interesting practical exhibitions . . . was that of the 'marine armor,' off the battery. **1840** *Niles' Nat. Reg.* 4 April 80/2 Mr. Taylor, with his marine armour, has succeeded in finding the wreck of the Lexington.

+Marine corps. *Mil.* A corps made up of marines.

The Marine Corps, authorized in 1775, is the oldest military or naval force in the service of the United States.

1798 *Statutes at Large* I. 594 An act for the establishing and organizing a marine corps. **1807** *Ann. 10th Congress* 1 Sess. I. 509 He grew importunate on the subject of the Marine corps, and asked me . . . how the Marine corps stood. **1842** *S. Lit. Messenger* VIII. 96/2 An increase of the Marine Corps . . . seems to be required by the public necessities. **1902** *Statutes at Large* XXXII. 1. 686 The commandant of the Marine Corps shall have the rank, pay, and allowance of a major-general in the Army.

+Marine court. A federal district court trying a case under maritime law. (Cf. ADMIRALTY COURT.) — **1851** NORTHALL *Curtain* 35 A rather novel case was tried in the Marine Court of New York. **1855** HOLBROOK *Among Mail Bags* 119 He could not see why it was brought in the Marine Court, unless it was because the complainants were 'half seas over.' *a*1882 in McCabe *New York* 122 The Marine Court has civil jurisdiction to the amount of $1000.

+Marine hospital. A hospital established by the federal government for seamen. Also attrib. — **1798** *Statutes at Large* I. 606 Directors of the marine hospital of the United States. **1822** *Ann. 17th Congress* 1 Sess. I. 275 The resolution . . . relative to the establishment of a marine hospital at New Orleans was . . . agreed to. **1840** VAN BUREN in *Pres. Mess. & P.* III. 618 The sites for marine hospitals on the rivers and lakes . . . have all been designated. **1880** LAMPHERE *U.S. Govt.* 270/1 Original appointments of medical officers in the United States Marine Hospital Service will be made to the grade of assistant surgeon only. **1902** *Statutes at Large* XXXII. 1. 75 The Secretary of the Treasury is authorized and directed to purchase . . . [land] for a marine hospital at Savannah, Georgia.

Marine insurance. Insurance on vessels or their cargoes against loss at sea. {1810– (Hansard XV. 401)} Also attrib. — **1803** BENTLEY *Diary* III. 14 The conduct of the Marine Insurance Bank has led to a Mechanic Bank. **1809** KENDALL *Travels* II. 217 In the village is a marine-insurance office. **1811** MEASE *Philadelphia* 113 They may make all kind of marine insurances, . . . and lend money upon bottomry and respondentia. **1862** *N.Y. Tribune* 13 March 6/6 [Northern] troops . . . declare that the rates of marine insurance are immediately increased when it is learned that the boats are to run in waters where the Rebel torpedoes are planted. **1905** *Ann. Amer. Acad.* XXVI. Sept. 273 Essential to the validity of a marine insurance policy is the requirement that the insured shall actually possess an insurable interest in the subject insured.

Marine insurance company. A company that writes marine insurance. {1810– (Hansard XV. 399)} — **1803** BENTLEY *Diary* III. 12 Our Senator of Mass. contrived to have the subscription of the East Ind. Marine Insurance company one hundred thousand dollars. **1846** *Niles' Nat. Reg.* 16 May 176/1 The Marine Insurance companies of New York . . . have resolved to charge three premiums on all risks *without* the war clause. **1891** *Ann. Cycl. Insurance 1890* 294 [The] Marine insurance company of St. Louis, Missouri, was chartered January 25 [1837].

***Mariner.** Also †**marrener.** One who navigates a ship; a sailor. — **1635** *Cambridge Prop. Rec.* 15 Richard Girling Mariner. **1721** *Boston Rec.* 156 John White Marrener is Chosen as one of the Constables. **1794** *U.S. Register 1795* 39 The pay of mariners is not to exceed 10 dollars per month. **1900** STOCKTON *Afield & Afloat* 285 The whole of the estate shall be appropriated in a manner . . . which is mainly for charitable objects connected with mariners.

+Marine railway. An inclined railway running into the water, and provided with a cradle in which a vessel may be hauled. — **1849** CHAMBERLAIN *Indiana Gazetteer* 333 There are in [New Albany] one brass foundry . . . [and] a marine railway. **1874** KNIGHT 439/2 [The] Canal-lift . . . may be of the nature of the slip or marine railway, such as used on the Morris and Essex Canal, N.J.

Mariner's compass. An instrument for determining the magnetic meridian {1659– (Harvey *Mariner's Card & Compass*)} — **1730** *Md. Hist. Mag.* VI. 12 Mariners compass rectified by Mr. Wakely. **1877** W. WRIGHT *Big Bonanza* 37 It is the stuff they make compasses of—surveyors' compasses, mariners' compasses [etc.]. **1894** *Outing* July 250/1 Hanging upon the upright posts were a barometer, a thermometer, and the Professor's banjo. There was also a small mariner's compass.

+Marine society. A society interested in the sea or in the welfare of seamen; the members of such a society. — **1797** MORSE *Amer. Gaz.* s.v. *Boston,* The principal societies in the Commonwealth hold their meetings in this town, and are, the Marine Society, American Academy of Arts and Sciences, [etc.]. **1800** *Mass. H. S. Coll.* 1 Ser. VI. 239 A Marine Society was formed in 1766, which has funds, real estate, and above one hundred members. **1804** *Holyoke Diaries* 144 The Marine Society paraded. **1818** *N. Amer. Rev.* Jan. 284 The Marine Society was first established at Salem in October, 1799, and was incorporated by the Legislature, by an Act, passed the 3d of March, 1801. *a*1821 C. BIDDLE *Autobiog.* iv. 257 With Girard I had long been a manager of the Marine Society.

Marionette. {*c*1620–} +=DIPPER 1 b. — **1838** AUDUBON *Ornith. Biog.* IV. 217 Buffel-headed Duck . . . being known to these different districts by the names of . . . Marrionette, Dipper, and Die-dipper. **1917** *Birds of Amer.* I. 140 Buffle-Head. *Charitonetta albeola.* . . . [Also called] Conjuring Duck; Marionette; Dipper [etc.].

Marionette theater. A theater in which puppet shows are given. — **1878** *Harper's Mag.* Feb. 336/1 Along the beach [at Atlantic City] . . . there are photograph galleries, peep-shows, marionette theatres [etc.].

+Mariposa lily. [Sp. *mariposa* 'a butterfly.'] Any western plant of the genus *Calochortus.* — **1882** *Garden* 30 Sept. 291/1 The Mariposa Lily. **1894** *Amer. Folk-Lore* VII. 101 *Calochortus,* Mariposa lilies, Santa Barbara Co., Cal. *Calochortus Nuttallii,* . . . Mariposa lily, Deer Lodge, Mont. **1899** S. HALE *Letters* 345 Mariposa lilies, painter's brush, poppies, and dozens of others.

***Marjoram.** Any mint of the genera *Origanum* and *Majorana.* — **1709** LAWSON *Carolina* 77 Our pot-herbs and others of use . . . [are] Pot-Marjoram, and other Marjorams, Summer and Winter Savory [etc.]. **1762** *Holyoke Diaries* 56 Sowd sweet marjoram. **1784** CUTLER in *Mem. Academy* I. 462 *Origanum.* . . . Wild Marjoram. A little cotton wool moistened with it (the essential oil) and put into the hollow of an aching tooth, frequently relieves the pain. **1878** WHITMAN *Spec. Days* 123 These perennial blossoms and friendly weeds [include] . . . creeper, trumpet-flower, scented marjoram, snakeroot, Solomon's seal.

***Mark,** *n.*[1]

1. ***a.** *spec.* A sign or device put upon an animal; also, a record or drawing of this.

1636 *Plymouth Laws* 43 That every man's marke of his cattle be brought to the towne booke where he lives. **1660** *Mass. H. S. Coll.* 4 Ser. VII. 244 Bring in all your horses & mares, & brand them with this mark . . . in the sholder. **1739** W. STEPHENS *Proc. Georgia* 314 All [cattle] found without any mark, were to be judged unquestionably to belong to the Trust. **1746** *Braintree Rec.* 145 One White Ram Lamb, ye artificial Mark is a swallows tail cut out of rear (vizt.) ye left Ear & a slit in ye Right Ear. **1885** *Rep. Indian Affairs* 126 They use their own brands and marks, have their regular 'round-ups.'

*b. A character written in place of a signature by an illiterate person.

1638 *New Haven Col. Rec.* 5 Momaugin—his marke. **1648** *Charlestown Land Rec.* 104, I doe acknowledg my self to bee fully satisfied, . . . as dos apear by a bill I have delivered to him with my mark thereuntoo. **1786** in Ramsey *Tennessee* (1853) 346 We all agree to sign the above terms. . . . Old Tassel × his mark [etc.]. **1847** *Rep. Comm. Patents 1846* 290 Jonathan Bennet × his mark.

*c. A stamp, inscription, brand, or other label put upon an object to determine its ownership, quality, or the like.

1653 *Boston Rec.* 114 The seleckt men shall forthwith provide . . . ladders, . . . thes ladders to be branded with the town marke. **1671** *Plymouth Laws* 277 The choosing . . . the Print or Mark, which each Plantation shall set upon their Seals, for good or faulty Leather. **1723** *Md. Hist. Mag.* XVIII. 208 This serves to advise you of fouer Hogsheads of my Tobaccoe and under my mark on board of Capt Reed. **1787** *Phila. Ordinances* (1812) 56 The keeper of the said magazine . . . shall give receipts . . . describing the numbers and marks of the casks. **1869** W. MURRAY *Adventures* 16 The rivers are blockaded with 'booms' and lodged timber, stamped all over the ends with the owner's 'mark.'

*2. An object, as a pile of stones or a blazed tree, indicating a boundary; a landmark. (Cf. BOUND MARK.)

1650 *Conn. Rec.* I. 513 The Select men, shall . . . goe the bounds betwixt theire said Townes and renew theire markes. **1732** *S.C. Gazette* 44/1 Whereas several Pettyawgers have received great Damage for want of a proper Mark at the White Point.

3. A student's grade in a class recitation, an examination, or a course of study.

1837 *Harvard Orders & Regul.* 8 The average of the marks given by the members of the [examining] Committee. **1897** FLANDRAU *Harvard Episodes* 278 To give him . . . the lowest possible mark . . . would be to bring upon himself Prescott's everlasting anger and 'despision.' **1918** *Nat. Soc. for Study of Educ. Yrbk.* 27 In the total marks to be here considered, A was given to 8.6 percent of the class . . . D to 20 percent.

+4. A person who is the object of deception; an easy target. *slang.*

1896 ADE *Artie* 173 When that kind of a mark comes in they get out the bottle of knockout drops and get ready to do business. **1898** *Scribner's Mag.* XXIII. 450/2 What got into the boys to put up [for political office] such a mark as him, anyway? **1904** LORIMER *Old Gorgon Graham* 288 He was too easy a mark to succeed in Wall Street.

5. *To make one's mark,* to make an impression; to succeed or be a success. Also *to make a mark.*

1854 *Harper's Mag.* IX. 561/2 Jacob made his mark upon the stockbrokers and money-changers. **1871** EGGLESTON *Hoosier Schoolm.* iv. 48 He could not throw well enough to make his mark in that famous Western game of bull-pen. **1888** DORSEY *Midshipman Bob* 43 That fellow's a gentleman's son, I'll bet my hat; and he'll make his mark. **1891** O'BEIRNE *Leaders Ind. Territory* 205/2 [He] looks forward to the day when he will be fitted to make a mark among his people.

***Mark,** *n.*[2] In stating the amount of a fine: A money of account worth about 13*s.* 4*d.* *Obs.* — **1631** *Mass. Bay Rec.* I. 92 The constable of Rocksbury returnes the receipt of Mr. Shepheards ffine of 5 marks. **1644** *Conn. Rec.* I. 123 He is adiudged to pay to the County fiue marke.

***Mark,** *v.*

*1. *tr.* To trace out the line of (a road); to blaze (trees) as the line of a trail or boundary. Also *ppl. a.*

1638 *Conn. Rec.* I. 18 Willm Westwood and Nathaniell Warde shall consider of a fitting and convenient high way to bee marked and sett oute. **1647** *Watertown Rec.* I. I. 14 Mr Bisco and John Sherman shall marke certayne trees in the high-way; with a (W). **1743** *N.J. Archives* 1 Ser. VI. 158 You are to cause every tree which your random line cutts to be markt with three notches. **1785** ELLICOTT in Mathews *Life A. Ellicott* 46 We have . . . marked it . . . by falling or deadening a line of trees. **1845** KIRKLAND *Western Clearings* 3 Every mile square is marked by blazed trees. **1904** STRATTON-PORTER *Freckles* 299 The marked trees . . . are all marked something like that first maple on the line was.

*2. To put a mark or brand on (a domestic animal). Also *vbl. n.*

1657 *Md. Hist. Mag.* VIII. 33 Complaint of many . . . for common frequenting the wild gang, killing cattle, and marking of calves. **1672** *Huntington Rec.* I. 196 These farmers shall from time to time Duly mark all their calves, Lambs and Piggs within . . . 20 Days after they be fallen. **1733** *S.C. Gazette* 222/1 Stolen or Strayed out of the Pasture, . . . a grey Mare . . . , mark'd on the near Buttock CH. **1814** *Niles' Reg.* VI. 393/2 Westward of the Mississippi it is said not to be uncommon for one man to mark from one to three thousand calves in a season.

3. +a. *To mark up,* to raise (the price) of goods. b. *To mark down,* to lower the price of (goods). {1894}

(a) **1869** *Amer. Naturalist* III. 3 The prices of venison and other game was so far 'marked up' that gold . . . was charged for salmon. **1902** LORIMER *Lett. Merchant* 52 The clerks all knocked off their regular work and started in to mark up prices. (b) **1875** *Chicago Tribune* 2 July 5/6 We have selected over $30,000 of our elegant stock and marked them Down 50 per cent. **1896** HOWELLS *Impressions & Exper.* 40 She was dressed in a . . . ready-made suit, which somehow suggested itself as having been 'marked down.'

+**Mark-down sale.** A sale of goods in which prices are lowered. — **1880** (Boston newspaper), The success of our mark-down sales . . . has induced us to adopt the same means this year to introduce ourselves and stock to all new customers. **1888** *St. Paul Globe* 22 Jan., Great Mark-Down Sale. **1906** *N.Y. Ev. Post* 31 July 4 Mark Down Sale. Men's Oxford Ties. Were 6.00, 7.00, and 8.00. . . . 4.75.

***Marker.**

*1. One who marks. +a. A surveyor's helper who blazes the line on trees, sets up landmarks, etc.

1743 *N.J. Archives* 1 Ser. VI. 154 You are to employ . . . an assistant surveyor if you think proper & also proper chainbearers & markers. **1785** in *Life & Corr. Cutler* II. 431 Each surveyor shall be allowed . . . two dollars for every mile, . . . including the wages of chain-carriers, markers, and every other expense. **1813** *Steele P.* II. 702 Two common axemen who may serve as markers, 10/ each. **1843** *American Pioneer* II. 379 In running the back line of the survey, . . . I was about one hundred yards in advance of the chainmen and marker.

+b. *Stock exchange.* (See quotation.)

1870 MEDBERY *Men Wall St.* 21 The 'marker' or black-board clerk writes off the prices upon the tablet.

+2. *Agric.* An implement for marking off rows.

1859 *Rep. Comm. Patents 1858* I. 479, I am aware that markers have been previously used and arranged similar to the ones described. **1871** *Ill. Agric. Soc. Trans.* VIII. 239 After the field has been thoroughly prepared, . . . proceed to check it off from east to west with a three-rowed marker. **1874** KNIGHT 628/1 *Corn-row Marker,* a sled with a gaged width between the runners for marking out rows in which to plant corn.

+3. In contexts suggesting comparisons: Anything of importance. Usually in negative construction. *slang.*

1888 *Congress. Rec.* 12 Dec. 202/2, I can easily fancy what a cry would have been raised. . . . The waving of the bloody shirt would not have been a marker. **1895** ROBINSON *Men Born Equal* 145 It looked ugly a while back; but it ain't a marker to what's ahead. **1904** W. H. SMITH *Promoters* 366 What little I've told you isn't a marker to other things he said.

+4. A monument or stone that marks a place.

1906 *Springfield W. Republ.* 15 Feb. 16 The committee appointed to investigate the matter of a marker for the Washington elm reported in favor of a granite marker.

+5. *W.* (See quotation.)

1913 BARNES *Western Grazing Grounds* 382 Markers.—The black sheep in a herd. Every herder knows exactly how many of such he has and by running over them occasionally he feels fairly sure that if they are all there he has lost no sheep.

***Market.**

*1. The public meeting of people for the sale or purchase of commodities; the occasion of such meeting.

1639 *Plymouth Laws* 63 There shalbe a markett kept at Plymouth every Thursday. **1677** *R.I. Col. Rec.* II. 577 The markett may be removed or changed from beinge kept on the seventh day of the week. **1799** *Phila. Ordinances* (1812) 165 Market shall . . . begin at day-light and end at two o'clock in the afternoon. **1835** INGRAHAM *South-West* II. 129 Whether to attend church, class meeting or market.

*2. A particular place, as a building or an open square, where commodities are bought or sold.

1683 *Boston Rec.* 160 Candles made up for sale shall be under the cognisance of the Clarke of ye market. **1721** *Boston Selectmen* 83 The Clarks of the markit are directed to make alowance for the Biskit wel baked. **1771** FRANKLIN *Autobiog.* 255, [I] was led into the great meeting-house of the Quakers near the market. **1842** *Nat. Hist. N.Y., Zoology* I. 25 The flesh of the bear . . . was once so common an article of food in New-York, as to have given the name of *Bear Market* to one of the principal markets in the city. **1907** ANDREWS *Recoll.* 211 With the exception of three or four meat shops, the markets in summer were all out of doors.

3. *The market,* the trade and traffic in which commodities may be bought and sold; the activity of buying and selling as determined by supply and demand. {1678-}

1740 *Inquiry into Nature & Uses of Money* 47 Paper-Currency must signify certain Pieces of Paper passing current in the Market as Money. **1791** WASHINGTON *Writings* XII. 66 A great quantity of bonds, thrown suddenly into the market, . . . could not but have effects the most injurious to the credit of the U.S. **1848** RUXTON *Life Far West* iv, As there were many rival traders, . . . the market promised to be brisk. **1906** BELL *C. Lee* 247 Between ten and twelve millions of dollars would corner the turpentine market.

4. The commercial demand for commodities in a given geographical or economic area; a district, town, etc., in which there is a demand for commodities. {1615-}

1792 *Ann. 2nd Congress* 971 Regulations . . . in foreign markets abridge the vent . . . of our agricultural produce. **1847** in Stowe *Key* 187/1 The Northern freemen . . . supply their own wants with a part, and then sell the rest at a good profit in the Southern markets. **1868** *Iowa Agric.*

Soc. Rep. 1867 158 Near the river a portion [of the corn crop is] sold to grain-dealers where it finds a market at St. Louis. **1913** LONDON *Valley of Moon* 336 For the milk . . . she also had a special private market, receiving five cents more a quart than was fetched by the best dairy milk.

+**5.** *To hold the market,* (see quotations).

1870 MEDBERY *Men Wall St.* 136 Holding the market, is to buy sufficient stock at the Boards to keep the price from declining. **1900** NELSON *A B C Wall St.* 145 Holding the market. Moderate purchases skilfully distributed and designed to keep a market from declining.

6. *attrib.* and *comb.* **a.** Designating people who either work in a market place or supply it with produce, fish, etc. See also MARKET HUNTER, MAN, SHOOTER.

1695 *Mass. Acts & Resolves* I. (1869) 238 Hucksters and traders of the town shall not . . . buy of any of the market people there. **1796** *Boston Directory* 246 Franks, Margaret, market woman, Pond street. **1839** *S. Lit. Messenger* V. 272/2, I had seen . . . shin-plasters of all sorts . . . manufactured by all sorts of persons from the wealthy merchant to the market butcher. **1855** *Amer. Inst. N.Y. Trans.* 300 Mr. S. B. Halliday, an extensive market gardener, of Providence, R.I., has subsoiled extensively. **1862** *Rep. Comm. Patents 1861: Agric.* 198 Dr. Bayne . . . [has] tested more varieties than any other market grower. **1913** J. W. SULLIVAN *Markets for People* 104 The Pennsylvania markets usually get along with a single market-master.

b. Designating places where town markets are situated. See also MARKET HOUSE, PLACE, STALL.

1794 *Mass. H. S. Coll.* 1 Ser. III. 254 Besides the lower floor of Faneuil hall being used as a flesh market, a number of stalls are erected on Market square . . . and let to the market men. **1809** CUMING *Western Tour* 194 Market street, . . . in which is the market-house, a neat brick building eighty feet long. **1817** *Niles' Reg.* XII. 393/2 Harrison is a very wide street, extending northwardly from what is called the 'market-space,' or place where the principal market house of the city is located. **1921** *Dept. Agric. Bul.* No. 1002, 14 End view of good type of double overhanging market shed showing steel construction.

c. Designating vessels used to supply the markets with fish and other produce. (Cf. MARKET BOAT.)

1847 *Knickerb.* XXX. 87 Sneeden . . . deposited us upon a market-scow near the landing. **1873** C. GORDON *Boarding-School Days* 36 He had been a hand on a New York market-sloop. **1883** *Nat. Museum Bull.* No. 27, 115 The market-smacks will seldom buy Lobsters measuring less than 10 or 10½ inches in length. **1884** *Ib.* 675 Market schooner 'Mary Odell.' . . . This model represents a class of vessels employed in the mackerel fishery in summer, . . . carrying their fish, as a rule, to market in a fresh condition.

d. Designating various animals, produce, etc., raised or fitted for the market.

1817 W. COXE *Fruit Trees* 109 American Nonpareil . . . is a beautiful apple, brought from New-York . . . and is a fine market apple. **1819** SCHOOLCRAFT *Journal* 86 Cotton is also grown, but not as a market crop. **1859** BARTLETT 488 *Truck,* stuff; and especially, vegetables raised for market, called also market-truck. **1862** *Rep. Comm. Patents 1861: Agric.* 169 [The red antwerp raspberry is] the favorite market berry in many cities. **1889** WARFIELD *Cattle-Breeding* 169 New blood was constantly introduced . . . from many sources, chiefly market cows of the sturdiest type. **1898** *Kansas City Star* 20 Dec. 8/3 Little market pigs ruled fully steady, and an early clearance was made.

e. Special combinations.

Market fair, =FAIR *n.* 1; *m. sieve,* a sieve for separating broken or small rice from the whole grains; *m. slip,* a portion of a wharf where a ship serving the local market may dock.

1761 *Hist. Coll. S. Carolina* II. 202 [Rice] is then sifted from the Flour and Dust made by the pounding; and afterwards by a Wire-sieve, called a Market-sieve. **1857** *Porter's Spirit of Times* 3 Jan. 294/3 Market Fairs. . . . Why cannot such fairs be holden monthly, in each of the principal counties. **1889** MUNROE *Dorymates* 70 The crew . . . made their way at once to the market slip devoted to the use of fishing vessels.

Market basket. a. A basket for holding or displaying goods that are for sale in a market. {1884-} +**b.** A basket for carrying groceries, etc., bought in a market or store. — **1807** IRVING, etc. *Salmagundi* xii. 312 Particular description of market-baskets, butchers' blocks and wheelbarrows. **1837** NEAL *Charcoal Sk.* (1838) 37, I'll stave my fist right through you, . . . as easily as if you were an empty market basket. **1884** *Century Mag.* May 86/2 He turned back to carry her market-basket. **1912** COBB *Back Home* 74 At least twenty darkies . . . picked up a living by packing market baskets home.

+**Market boat.** A boat in which goods are taken to market; a boat from which goods are sold. {1863-} — **1780** *N.J. Archives* 2 Ser. IV. 401 Mrs. Roker, and one other woman, were going in a market boat from Philadelphia. **1839** STORER *Mass. Fishes* 76 At New Bedford, 300 pounds of fresh tautog have been sold by a single market-boat in a day. **1848** IRVING *Knickerb.* (rev. ed.) II. iv, Some bevy of country cousins, about to depart for home in a market-boat. **1853** 'P. PAXTON' *Yankee in Texas* 278 [He] bought a market-boat, and tried trading upon the bayou.

Market cart. A cart used about a market place, or for carrying produce to a market. {1833} — **1799** BROWN *A. Mervyn* xiv, Belding persisted to visit the city daily with his market-cart. **1810** *Boston Selectmen* 427 A Petition from the abutters on Ann Street praying for regulations of the market Carts usually standing in that street, was read. **1855** J. E. COOKE *Ellie* 13 The flood [of people] poured, jostling the market-carts.

***Market day.** A day fixed for holding a market. Also attrib.

1689 SEWALL *Diary* I. 303 Give the Keeper of the Roe-buck 6d. if I leave not the Horse with him on a Market day, Wednesday, Satterday. **1785** FRENEAU *Poems* (1786) 376 But your market-day mornings we cannot forget. **1798** *Phila. Ordinances* (1812) 150 On every market day, strong chains . . . shall be stretched across the passages. **1827** DRAKE & MANSFIELD *Cincinnati* 28 Market days [are] Wednesdays and Saturdays. **1864** NORTON *Army Lett.* 223 It was market day . . . and they were coming to sell the melons and other vegetables. **1913** J. W. SULLIVAN *Markets for People* 104 The Pennsylvania markets usually get along with a single market-master, assisted by a laborer or two on market days.

+**Marketer.** One who buys or sells in a market or shop.

1787 CUTLER in *Life & Corr.* I. 271 The marketers seemed to be all in and every thing arranged. **1806** LEWIS in *L. & Clark Exped.* V. (1905) 49 At 5 P.M. o[u]r marketers returned with about 6 bushels of the cows roots and a considerable quan[ti]ty of bread. **1851** *Polly Peablossom* 108 Two men from the interior, apparently marketers, halted at the corner. **1878** *Pop. Science Mo.* Aug. 430 In a butcher's shop there is a superficial sameness in the appearance of meat which it is the business of a good marketer to see through. [**1884** JAMES *Little Tour in France* xxiv, I sat down with a hundred hungry marketers, fat, brown, greasy men.]

Market fish. +Var. of MARGATE FISH. — **1884** GOODE, etc. *Fisheries* I. 394 The small ones are there [at Key West] called 'Porgies' and the large ones 'Margate-fish' and 'Market-fish.' **1911** [see MARGATE FISH].

Market garden. A garden in which vegetables, melons, etc., are raised for the market. {1840-} — **1811** MEASE *Philadelphia* 349 [There are] extensive market gardens, and several handsome summer retreats. **1862** *Ill. Agric. Soc. Trans.* V. 542 A market garden should be always located . . . near a large or compactly built city. **1882** MCCABE *New York* 34 The west side is very rural, abounding in country seats, market gardens and miniature farms. **1923** HERRICK *Lilla* 197, I can get a job in a market garden.

***Market house.** A building that houses the stalls and stands of a market, or gives shelter to those who sell in a market.

1653 *Boston Rec.* 9 The Market house is more for the conveniency of strangers & there accomodation in winter and summer in wet and dry. **1726** FRANKLIN *Writings* II. 57 There is a very neat market-house, paved with square stone. **1780** *Phila. Ordinances* (1812) 43 It shall and may be lawful for the wardens of the said city to let or demise the market houses. **1819** *Amer. Farmer* I. 223 The largest Peach I remember ever to have seen, was purchased at the Market-house. **1885** *Harper's Mag.* Feb. 458/2 The dealers in meat and vegetables are concentrated in the Market-house. **1918** J. W. SULLIVAN *Markets for People* 104 It cannot be assumed that municipal market-houses . . . may be created . . . in any and all of our cities with a probability of success.

+**Market hunter.** One who hunts wild game for sale in the market. — **1874** LONG *Wild-Fowl* 185 Blue-winged teal . . . are much sought for by market-hunters. **1888** *Outing* April 55 Pity the poor quail when the market-hunter comes along, for they are slaughtered by the hundreds.

***Market man. a.** A farmer, fisherman, or the like, who sells his produce in a market. **b.** A merchant whose stand is in a market.

1722 [see ETHIOPIAN *a.* 1]. **1724** *New-Eng. Courant* 19-26 Oct. 2/2 'Tis to be hop'd our Country Marketmen who bring bad Meat to Town, will not complain of this Piece of Justice. **1794** *Mass. H. S. Coll.* III. 254 The market men used to hawk their meat and vegetables about the streets. **1840** HAWES *Sporting Scenes* I. 112 The poor quail has to contend with . . . the coarse cupidity of the market-man. **1870** WARNER *Summer in Garden* x, The market-man shows me his peas and beets and tomatoes. **1923** WATTS *L. Nichols* 9 [He hired] out to another market man of the neighborhood.

+**Market master.** An official who administers the law respecting the market or markets of a town. — **1851** CIST *Cincinnati* 87 A city treasurer, a marshal, a wharf and three market masters are elected. **1890** HOWELLS *Boy's Town* 119 There was a market-master, who rang a bell to open the market, and if anybody bought or sold anything before the tap of that bell, he would be fined. **1913** [see MARKET DAY].

***Market place.** The place where a market is held or is situated, usually a wide open space or square.

1638 *Charlestown Land Rec.* 1 One Roode and a haulfe of grounde . . . butting south east and north east upon the markett place. **1687** SEWALL *Diary* I. 175 March'd out about one aclock to the Market place. **1728** *Boston Rec.* 225 Buying of Provisions in the Market Place . . . has Inhanced the Price of Provisions. **1843** *Knickerb.* XXI. 36 The lively hum of the market-place . . . resounds again. **1911** MUZZEY *Amer. History* 61 The high Dutch stoops and quaint market places in the villages along the Hudson.

+**Market report.** A report on trading and market conditions; spec., *pl.*, the printed reports of prices for stocks, commodities, etc., sold on an exchange. — **1866** *Oregon State Jrnl.* 5 May 3/1 We have received late numbers of *McCracken Merrill & Co's Market Report.* **1872** POWERS *Afoot & Alone* 30, I didn't read the market reports before I started. **1880** 'MARK TWAIN' *Tramp Abroad* 626 A child's handful of telegrams . . . ;

letter-correspondence . . . ; market reports. . . . That is what a German daily is made of. **1902** WILSON *Spenders* 85 They're as matter-of-fact as market reports.

+**Market reporter.** One who reports upon prices, trends, etc., in trading. — **1853** B. J. TAYLOR *Jan. & June* 83 And so, as Market Reporters have it, 'we have movements to note.'

+**Market shooter.** One who shoots wild game for the market. — **1897** *Outing* XXX. 293/2 The market-shooter . . . can sneak through the known haunts of the quail.

Market stall. A booth for the sale of commodities in a market. {1859-} — **1827** DRAKE & MANSFIELD *Cincinnati* 55 The Revenue of the Corporation is derived . . . [from] Rent of Market-stalls. **1891** HOLMES *Over Teacups* 23 The promiscuous handling . . . [of] the fruit and provisions in the market-stalls.

***Market town.** A town that has a public market; a trading center. — **1654** JOHNSON *Wonder-w. Prov.* 211 Their neerness to the chief Market Towns, makes it the more comfortable for habitation. **1743** FRANKLIN *Writings* II. 232 We shall . . . discover in every little Market-Town and Village, the 'Squire . . . [listening] to a Barber's News. **1888** CABLE in *Century Mag.* Dec. 255/2 In 1795 New Orleans was nothing but a mere market town.

Market value. The current value at which securities or commodities may be sold in the market. {1848-} — **1791** *Ann. 1st Congress* II. 1993 The rapid increase that has taken place in the market value of the public securities. **1842** TYLER in *Pres. Mess. & P.* IV. 204 The spread of a speculative mania all over the country . . . has finally ended in . . . a depreciation in the market value of real and personal estate. **1862** 'G. HAMILTON' *Country Living* 50 What do you expect will be the market value of that crop? **1913** LAFOLLETTE *Autobiog.* 463 It was avowedly for the purpose of enhancing their market value.

+**Market wagon.** A wagon in which produce is carried to a market place, often serving as a stand or booth for the sale of the produce.

1802 *Ann. 7th Congress* 1 Sess. 1027 In the State of New Jersey five hundred and forty two [of the carriages taxed] are . . . principally market-wagons. **1838** *Knickerb.* Sept. 191 They drove their long 'arks,' or market-wagons, filled with blaäing calves. **1873** *Newton Kansan* 13 Feb. 4/4 Horticulturists . . . are reported to have stoves in the rear of their maret-wagons. **1894** WARNER *Golden House* i, Here and there [was] a lumbering market-wagon from Jersey.

***Marking iron.** +**a.** A surveyor's instrument provided with a die for blazing trees. +**b.** A hammer with which a stamp can be put on a barrel, log, or the like.

1633 *N.H. Doc. & Rec.* I. 79, 1 markin iron. **1671** in Alvord & Bidgood *Trans-Allegheny Region* 191 [We] went to the first tree which we marked thus with a pair of marking irons for his sacred majesty. **1697** SEWALL *Letter-Book* I. 188, I have sent . . . four Barrels of Pork marked with marking Iron SS. **1723** *Springfield Rec.* II. 502 [We] Spotted the trees with an Axe and in the Spot Setting the Mark . . . with the Marking Iron. **1817** *Niles' Reg.* XII. 98/2 The numbers of the township and range, are marked with a marking iron (such as are used in mills and warehouses) on a bearing or other tree. **1905** *Forestry Bureau Bul.* No. 61, 42 *Marking hammer*, a hammer bearing a raised device which is stamped on logs, to indicate ownership. . . . [Also called] marking iron.

Marksman. *Surveying.* One who marks a line, as by blazing trees. {1654-} — **1816** U. BROWN *Journal* II. 220 This afternoon hunts up Chain Carriers & an Ax man or marksman.

+**Mark tree.** A tree blazed to mark a line or boundary. Also *marked tree. Obs.* — **1640** *Braintree Rec.* 8 [The way runs] as it is already set out by severall marke trees. **1677** *Portsmouth Rec.* 430 [We] owne three trees to be the true and proper Marke trees of the Southermost line of . . . David Vahans land. **1724** *Lancaster Rec.* 210 Another Hiway . . . Runeth as the mark trees direct upon to barehill. **1768** *N.C. Col. Rec.* VII. 853 From the top of Tryon Mountain beginning at the marked Trees thereon [etc.].

***Marl.** Also **marle.** A crumbling soil consisting chiefly of clay and varying amounts of calcium carbonate. Sometimes used as a fertilizer. Also attrib. — **1759** *Newport Mercury* 18 Sept. 1/1 Marle is one of the greatest Improvers of Land . . . for it is a slippery Sort of Earth. **1786** WASHINGTON *Diaries* III. 10 In my lower pasture, I put 140 Bushels of what we call Marle. **1825** *Phila. Acad. Nat. Sciences* IV. I. 16 [We] have lately returned from a short excursion to the 'Marl-pits' of New Jersey. **1883** SMITH *Geol. Survey Ala.* 112 The calcareous and gypseous marls, also abundant in the same sections of the State.

+**Marlberry.** A small tropical American tree or shrub. — **1884** SARGENT *Rep. Forests* 100 Marlberry. Cherry. . . . A small tree, sometimes 8 meters in height, . . . or often a shrub; reaching its greatest development in Florida. **1897** SUDWORTH *Arborescent Flora* 316 *Icacorea paniculata* . . . Common names [include] Marlberry, (Fla.). Cherry (Fla.).

+**Marlborough pie.** (See quot. 1893.) — **1805** *Pocumtuc Housewife* (1906) 24. **1893** HALE *New Eng. Boyhood* 115 In any old and well-regulated family in New England, you will find there is a traditional method of making the Marlborough pie, which is a sort of lemon pie.

+**Marlborough pudding.** =prec. Also attrib. — **1869** STOWE *Oldtown Folks* 340 Apple pies, Marlborough-pudding pies. **1893** HALE *New Eng. Boyhood* 115 For instance, there was always a great deal of talk about the Marlborough pies or the Marlborough pudding.

+**Marlin.** A godwit. Also with defining adjectives. — **1844** *Nat. Hist. N.Y., Zoology* II. 254 The Ring-Tailed Marlin, *Limosa Hudsonica*, . . . is not as common along our coast as the Marlin. In Boston it is called the *Goose-bird.* **1886** ROOSEVELT in *Outing* Aug. 523 Yelper, Marlin, and Yellow Legs, are all occasionally found, although not plenty. **1917** *Birds of Amer.* I. 240 Hudsonian Godwit. . . . [Also called] Ring-tailed Marlin.

Marm. A vulgar shortening of MADAM. {*c*1850-, *dial.*}

+**1.** A mother. (Cf. MA'AM.)

1835 COOPER *Monikins* xii, He could scare one by threatening to tell his *marm* how he behaved. **1839** — *Home as Found* xvi, Who taught you to call me marm! . . . Say ma', this instant. **1845** JUDD *Margaret* I. 37 Has your Marm got that done? **1859** *Harper's Mag.* Sept. 573/1 He knocked down par, and kicked marm. **1890** JEWETT *Strangers* 9 You've got real nice features, like your marm's folks.

2. =MRS.

'Obs. exc. *U.S. vulgar'* (*O.E.D.*).

1835-7 HALIBURTON *Clockmaker* 1 Ser. x. 69 Marm Pugwash is as onsartin in her temper as a mornin in April. **1887** WILKINS *Humble Romance* 107 Marm Lawson was not a duchess; but she was Marm Lawson. The 'Marm' itself was a title.

3. A woman; the mistress of a house.

1865 S. HALE *Letters* 16 The silk is seven dollars a yard, and the marm that makes it asks a great deal. **1876** TRIPP *Student-Life* 318 Why, our 'marm' charges eight dollars for meals.

***Marmalade.** Also †**marmalet.** A jam or preserve made of any of various fruits. In recent usage commonly restricted to marmalades made with citrous fruits. — **1708** SEWALL *Diary* II. 231 After dinner I carried a few of the best Figs I could get, and a dish Marmalet. **1839** *S. Lit. Messenger* V. 752/2 Poor Jacob looked aghast, when 'Miss Betsey Bud's compliments, and saucer of marmalade of her own making,' were presented to his master. **1884** OWENS *Cook Book* 339 Wild plum marmalade. . . . Take the plums that remain in the jelly-bag and rub through a sieve. **1920** HOWELLS *Vacation of Kelwyns* 86 Mrs. Kelwyn added some graces of jam and marmalade.

Marmot. a. Any of various rodents of the genus *Marmot* {1607-}, +as the woodchuck, ground hog, and whistler. (Cf. MARYLAND MARMOT.) +**b.** The prairie dog. Also attrib. and with defining adj. (Cf. PRAIRIE MARMOT.)

[**1797** *Encycl. Brit.* (ed. 3) XII. 463/1 The monax, or American marmot.] **1823** JAMES *Exped.* II. 140 The high and barren parts of this tract [between the Loup fork and the Platte] are occupied by the numerous communities of the Prairie dog or Louisiana marmot. **1875** *Amer. Naturalist* IX. 148 'Marmot' is sometimes used [for prairie dog], the present species being the tawny marmot of some writers, but this is the name of the woodchucks (*Arctomys*). **1887** *Outing* April 14/2 'Look out for the marmot furrows!' he shouted back. **1888** *Ipswich* (Mass.) *Chronicle* 15 Sept. 2/4 In Kansas, Nebraska and many other parts of the West a small marmot, which is closely allied to the prairie dog, is called a gopher. **1917** *Mammals of Amer.* 196 Eastern Woodchuck, *Marmota monax.* . . . [Also called] Eastern Marmot; Groundhog.

Maroon, *n.* Also †**meroon.**

1. A runaway Negro slave, living in the mountains, swamps, or the like. {1666-, West Indies} Also attrib.

1821 in Morse *Rep. Indian Affairs* (1822) II. 150 The maroon negroes . . . live among the Indians, on the other side of the little mountains of Latchioua. **1838** *N.Y. Advertiser & Exp.* 14 Feb. 3/3 They were joined by a number of armed 'maroons,' (run away slaves out lawed). **1858** J. R. GIDDINGS (*title*), The Exiles of Florida: or, The Crimes Committed by Our Government against the Maroons, Who Fled from South Carolina and other Slave States, Seeking Protection under Spanish Laws.

+**2.** *S.* An extended camping trip or a picnic. Also attrib.

1779 I. ANGELL *Diary* (1899) 59 Lt. Cook . . . Come from the Meroon frolick last night. **1785** *S.C. Hist. Mag.* XIII. 188 On Monday we form a maroon party to visit some saw mills. **1836** GILMAN *Recoll.* (1838) 223 Feeling the necessity of refreshment, we alighted for a while beneath a tree by the roadside, for a maroon.

Maroon, *v.* {1699-} *S.* +*intr.* To camp out for several days: (see quotation and cf. MAROONING.) — **1855** HALIBURTON *Nature & Hum. Nature* II. 283 He used to delight to go marooning. [*Footnote*:] Marooning differs from pic-nicing in this—the former continues several days, the other lasts but one.

Marooner. {1661-} +**1.** =MAROON I. **2.** (See quotation.) — **(1) 1738** BYRD *Dividing Line* (1901) 37 Not far from the inlet, dwelt a marooner. **1852** F. R. GOULDING (*title*) (Roorbach), The Young Marooners. **(2) 1890** *Cent.* 3636/2 *Marooner*, . . . one who goes marooning; a member of a marooning party.

+**Marooning party.** An extended picnic or excursion. Also *marooning expedition.* — **1777** G. FORSTER *Voyage round World* I. 165 It may be curious to know the nature of our marooning parties, as the seamen called them. **1816** PICKERING 130 A friend . . . observes, that '. . . a marooning party always carry their provisions with them: I think it always means a *party to the sea-shore.*' **1834** CARRUTHERS *Kentuckian* I. 141 He entertained me with an account of his marooning expeditions. These are their excursions upon the Sea Islands for purposes of fishing and hunting. **1856** STOWE *Dred* I. 20 How considerate of them to go off on that marooning party, and leave us to ourselves! **1890** [see prec.].

Marquee. Also †**markee.** {1690–} A large field tent, as one used by an army officer, or for a public entertainment; also, a canopy.

1776 A. R. ROBBINS *Journal* (1850) 13 Treated with great civility by Capt. Walker; supped and lodged well in our markee. **1788** CUTLER in *Life & Corr.* I. 411 General Putnam invited me to his lodgings, which is a marquee. **1845** HONE *Diary* II. 253 Tables were spread in marquees under the trees. **1920** LEWIS *Main Street* 237 She liked the plain benches, the portable stage under its red marquee, the great tent over all.

+**Marquee coop.** A hencoop shaped like a tent. — **1850** BROWNE *Poultry Yard* 122 Another kind . . . is the marquee coop.

+**Marquee tent.** =MARQUEE. — **1755** in Scull *Evelyns in Amer.* 157*n.*, They brought two markee tents, and pitched them within ten yards of the meeting-house. **1861** *Vanity Fair* 15 June 281/1, I'd like to be a great commander, and have a marquee tent away off on a hill.

* **Marriage.** *attrib.* Designating various entertainments, announcements, actions, etc., connected with getting married.

1764 *N.H. Hist. Soc. Coll.* IX. 148, [I] attended the marriage entertainment. **1778** CARVER *Travels* (1794) 137 The Indians have several kinds of dances . . . as the pipe or calumet dance, the war dance, the marriage dance, and the dance of the sacrifice. **1825** NEAL *Bro. Jonathan* II. 154 She never had sich a cold in all her life, as when she left her marriage ring off. **1840** *Boston Almanac* 125 (*advt.*), Envelopes for marriage cards. **1856** M. J. HOLMES *L. Rivers* 314 Anna . . . examined it more minutely, glancing . . . to the marriage notices. **1875** STOWE *We & Neighbors* 364 There was no question of marriage settlements, or rent and taxes. **1893** M. HOWE *Honor* 123 [The box contained] the dress in which she was wedded, . . . his marriage certificate, and one of Honor's baby curls. **1904** *Delineator* Aug. 279 The marriage service in the prayer-book of the Episcopal church is frequently used by others than Episcopalians.

***Marrowbone.** +A buffalo bone containing edible marrow. — **1837** IRVING *Bonneville* II. 181 It was a time of plenty in the camp; of . . . roasted ribs, and broiled marrow-bones. **1848** PARKMAN in *Knickerb.* Feb. 122 My friend the White Shield proffered me a marrow-bone, so skilfully laid open, that all the rich substance within was exposed to view at once. **1870** KEIM *Sheridan's Troopers* 205 A dainty dish among the savages is the marrow-bones of the buffalo.

Marrowfat, Marrow fat.

1. Any one of several varieties of late pea having rich, wrinkled seed. In full *marrowfat pea.* {1733–}

1829 *Free Press* (Tarboro, N.C.) 20 Feb., Peas. . . . Garden, Marrowfat, Early six week, Green Bunch. **1850** *Rep. Comm. Patents 1849: Agric.* 112 *Peas.*—The most esteemed varieties are the 'marrowfat,' the 'branch pea' and the 'golden-vine pea.' **1869** BROWNE *Adv. Apache Country* 72 [He] presented me with . . . a piece of pure silver about the size of a marrow-fat pea. **1904** CRISSEY *Tattlings* 404 The glare of a diamond stud about the size of a marrow-fat pea.

+**2.** A product resembling tallow or butter obtained by boiling down the marrow of buffaloes.

1833 CATLIN *Indians* I. 116 Chunks of this marrow-fat are cut off. **1846** SAGE *Scenes Rocky Mts.* viii, Marrow-fat, an article in many respects superior to butter. **1888** *Century Mag.* Oct. 898/1 Then he slicked his hair with marrow-fat from a horn.

+**Marrow gut.** The chylopoietic duct of a buffalo. *Obs.* — **1848** BRYANT *California* vii. 96 The choice pieces of a fat cow, are . . . the hump-ribs; and an intestinal vessel or organ, commonly called by hunters the 'marrow-gut.' **1894** *Harper's Mag.* Feb. 351/2 Inside of the cabin was William . . . , glowing with heat and pride over his corn cakes and 'marrow-gut.'

Marrow spoon. A long, narrow spoon for removing the marrow from bones. {1693–} — **1754** *S.C. Gazette* 5 Feb. 3/1 Just imported . . . marrow scoops and spoons, punch strainers and ladles. *c***1766** *York Co., Va., Rec.: Wills* XXI, 1 soup and 1 marrow spoon.

+**Marrow squash.** (See quot. 1864.) — **1864** WEBSTER 814/2 *Marrow-squash*, a variety of squash having a soft texture and fine grain, resembling marrow. **1875** BURROUGHS *Winter Sunshine* 29 [The] small boy . . . was as frank and simple as if he had lived on . . . marrow-squashes all his days. **1891** *Cent.* 5878/1 Other winter squashes are . . . egg-shaped and pointed at the ends, as in the (Boston) marrow, long a standard in America.

***Marry,** *v.* +*intr. To marry out* (*of meeting*), of Quakers, to marry one not of the Quaker faith. — **1842** *S. Lit. Messenger* VIII. 331/2 'Marrying out,' as the Friends call one of a different faith, is regarded by them with especial horror. **1898** HARPER *S. B. Anthony* I. 10 The Quaker was not permitted to 'marry out of meeting.'

+**Mars(e).**

1. In speech of Negro slaves: Master. Now hist. (Cf. MASSA.)

1880 TOURGEE *Bricks* 408 The old time 'Marse' was now almost universally used, and few 'niggers' presumed to speak to a white man . . . without removing their hats. **1881** — *'Zouri's Christmas* iii, [He] cursed and beat his hands, was called 'Marse,' approached with fear, and addressed hat in hand. **1899** CHESNUTT *Conjure Woman* 51 Young mars wuz in a tarrible hurry fer ter git back home.

2. Used attrib. as a title.

1869 TOURGEE *Toinette* xxviii, He gave Toinette to young Marse Geoffrey. **1883** *Century Mag.* Nov. 132/1 He always called Mr. Davis 'Marse Jeff,' and was the only one of the domestics who used that style of address. **1899** CHESNUTT *Wife of His Youth* 12 W'en I was young I us'ter b'long ter Marse Bob Smif, down in ole Missouri. **1904** 'O. HENRY' *Roads of Destiny* 350, I'm not going back on Mars' Jeff.

Marseilles. Also †**mersailles.** A strong, stiff cotton cloth first made in Marseille, France, and frequently used for summer garments. {1762–} Also attrib.

1787 *Holyoke Diaries* 118 Bought Marseilles Quilt. **1788** *Mass. Centinel* 30 April, William Scott . . . will sell . . . elegant Mersailles Bed-Quilts, Mersailles Quilting in pieces [etc.]. **1827** *Hallowell* (Me.) *Gaz.* 20 June 3/5 (*advt.*), A large assortment of . . . Dimoties; broad and narrow black Bombazines; Marseilles counterpanes. **1847** DRAKE *Pioneer Life Ky.* 68 A sufficient amount of 'fustian' to make me a 'round-about' . . . . with something else (I don't recollect, but believe it was cheap Marseilles), for an 'under-jacket.' **1860** HOLMES *E. Venner* vii, Mahogany four-poster,—come from the Jordans, I cal'late. Marseilles quilt. **1898** F. H. SMITH *C. West* 61 The bureau was covered with a freshly laundered white Marseilles cover.

b. Garments made of this.

1901 CHURCHILL *Crisis* 163 He saw the Colonel, in white marseilles, smoking a cigar.

* **Marsh.** Also †**marish.**

1. ***a.** A piece or tract of low-lying, watery land; = MARSHLAND.

1612 SMITH *Virginia* 13 In the low Marishes, growe plots of Onyons containing an acre of ground or more in many places. **1665** *Portsmouth Rec.* 130 Thomas Butts . . . [requested] this towne to Exchainge a pearcell of vpland for a pearcell of marsh lyinge in the Comon ffence. **1718** *Boston Rec.* 132 A Comittee to Consider . . . Some Expedient for Securing the Marsh at ye Lower end of ye Common. **1797** S. DEANE *Newengland Farmer* (ed. 2) 203 Marsh. . . . In this country the word is used only to signify flat land, bordering on the sea, and lying so low as to be often overflowed by the tides. **1827** DRAKE & MANSFIELD *Cincinnati* 16 A natural marsh, flooded during freshets by the neighboring streams. **1913** LONDON *Valley of Moon* II. xviii, 'I dug them [*i.e.*, clams] myself.' 'Not in the marsh?' he asked with quickened interest.

b. In place names.

1657 *Suffolk Deeds* III. 33 The high way leading to Beare marsh west. **1700** *Md. Hist. Mag.* XIX. 349 Gibsons Marsh. *Ib.* 354 Lambarts Marsh.

2. *attrib.* **a.** In specific names of various plants that grow in marshes.

Other examples can be found in books on botany.

1784 CUTLER in *Mem. Academy* I. 485 *Viola.* . . . Marsh violet. Blossoms pale blue. In moist meadows. April. **1814** BIGELOW *Florula Bostoniensis* 195 *Solidago lævigata.* Marsh Golden rod. . . . A tall, rank inhabitant of the borders of salt marshes . . . in September. **1840** DEWEY *Mass. Flowering Plants* 64 *Lathyrus palustris.* Marsh Wild Pea . . . blossoms in June, in wet meadows or low grounds, in the vicinity of Boston. **1862** *Rep. Comm. Patents 1861: Agric.* 350 Marsh blue top, a grass that is generally found around the edges of marshes. **1894** *Amer. Folk-Lore* VII. 92 *Eupatorium purpureum*, marsh milk-weed, Mass.

+**b.** In the names of certain trees and shrubs found in marshy soil.

1745 E. KIMBER *Itinerant Observ.* 10*n.*, Water Oak, Swamp Oak, Marsh Oak, Holy Oak, &c. [are to be seen]. **1785** MARSHALL *Amer. Grove* 100 *Pinus palustris*, Longest three leaved Marsh Pine, . . . is accounted equal to any for yielding tar. **1901** MOHR *Plant Life Ala.* 45 Groundsels . . . with marsh elder (*Iva frutescens*), dot here and there the salt marshes of the seashore.

* **Marshal.**

+**1.** In colonial times, an officer having various duties, as to serve writs, levy and collect fines, attend the sittings of courts, etc.

Cf. HEAD MARSHAL.

1643 *Southampton Rec.* I. 29 The sayd Marshall shall choose two Indifferent men of the ffreemen to Apprize such goods and chattels as shall bee vpon distresse. *a***1649** WINTHROP *Hist.* I. 136 We apprehended the merchant of the ship, . . . and committed him to the marshal. **1662** *Jamaica* (L.I.) *Rec.* I. 14 Richard Brutnell shall bee Marshall ffor this year. **1684** *Mass. H. S. Coll.* 4 Ser. V. 119 He ordered the Marshal to drop me at Captain Stileman's.

b. (See quotation.)

*a***1647** GORGES *Descr. New-Eng.* iv. 46, I added a Marshall for the managing of the Militia, who have for his Lievetenant a Judge-Marshall, and other Officers to the Marshall Court, where is to be determined all Criminall and Capitall matters.

+**2.** In a federal judicial district, a ministerial officer appointed by the president, with the concurrence of the Senate, to perform duties corresponding to those of a county sheriff. Also *marshal for* (or *of*) *the United States.*

1789 *Ann. 1st Congress* I. 86, I also nominate, for District Judges, Attorneys, and Marshals, the persons whose names are below. **1800** J.

ADAMS *Works* IX. 76, I have agreed to the appointment of Major David Hopkins to be marshal of Maryland. **1834** BAIRD *Valley Mississippi* xx. 257 There is . . . a Marshall for the United States. **1837** VAN BUREN in *Pres. Mess. & P.* III. 399 The marshal of the northern district of New York . . . had been directed to repair to the frontier and take all authorized measures to secure the faithful execution of existing laws. **1840** *Niles' Nat. Reg.* 21 March 47/2 A statement of the compensation received by district attorneys, clerks and marshals of the United States [was laid before the House]. **1859** in Johnson *Anderson Co., Kansas* (1877) 107 The marshal of Kansas is said to be collecting a posse of Missourians . . . to enforce the law.

b. A police officer or sheriff appointed by a territorial governor to have jurisdiction over a prescribed area.

1866 in Dale & Rader *Okla. Hist.* (1930) 363 [The governor of the territory of Oklahoma] shall have authority to appoint a marshal of said territory.

+**3.** =CITY MARSHALL.

1841 *Diplom. Corr. Texas* III. (1911) 1333 The Republic of Texas to the Sheriff . . . of the County of Travis or in defect or absence of such officer then to the Marshall of the City of Austin Greeting. **1851** CIST *Cincinnati* 87 A city treasurer, a marshal, a wharf and three market masters are elected. **1873** *Newton Kansan* 3 July 2/1 The marshall of Ellsworth receives a salary of $150 per month. **1887** F. FRANCIS *Saddle & Moccasin* 298 The prisoner . . . was now returning in charge of the Marshal of Georgetown to be tried for killing the Deputy there.

+**4.** A person appointed to take, or to direct the taking of, a census. (Cf. CENSUS MARSHAL.)

1852 *Harper's Mag.* March 561/2 In taking the Seventh Census of the United States, there have been engaged 45 marshals, and 3231 assistants. **1873** *Mich. Gen. Statutes* I. (1882) 270 That the governor appoint marshals to take the census in the unorganized territory not otherwise provided in this act.

‖**5.** *Marshal at Arms,* the sergeant at arms of the House of Representatives.

1792 CUTLER in *Life & Corr.* I. 483 The Speaker of the House sent the Marshal-at-Arms to summons them to attend the House.

+**6.** *Marshal of the day,* one charged with arranging or ordering the exercises or proceedings on a public or ceremonious occasion.

1811 *Niles' Reg.* I. 118/2 The whole was attended and regulated by the marshal of the day on horseback. **1836** in Quincy *Hist. Harvard* II. 647 Robert C. Winthrop acted as Chief Marshal of the Day, and the following gentlemen as Assistant Marshals. **1840** COOPER *Pathfinder* xi, The adjutant of the place . . . acted as master of the ceremonies, or marshal of the day. **1843** *S. Lit. Messenger* IX. 651/1 An aid to the 'marshal of the day' . . . read in a loud voice, the 'order of the day.' **1868** *Western Mag.* Jan. (De Vere), The inhabitants within a radius of ten miles were invited to a chopping-bee. . . . The work was ordered by an elected marshal of the day.

+**Marshal general.** =HEAD MARSHAL. — **1658** *Mass. Bay Rec.* IV. 326 To pay the marshall genll. three pence out of euery attachment by them [*sc.* the constables] served. **1685** SEWALL *Diary* I. 87 Marshal Genll. comes to speak with me. *Ib.* 341 Mr. Saml. Gookin is Appointed by the Governour and Council to be Marshal Generall till the sitting of the Generall Court.

+**Marshallite.** [Robert *Marshall,* Presbyterian minister.] A member of an Arian faction in the Presbyterian church in Kentucky in the early nineteenth century: (see quot. 1856). — **1847** R. DAVIDSON *Presbyterian Ch. in Ky.* 219 Mr. Stone was conspicuous . . . [in] the subsequent formation of societies, known under the various names of New Lights, Christians, Arians, Marshallites, and Stoneites. **1856** CARTWRIGHT *Autobiog.* 219 Arianism was rife through all that country [Kentucky], although they called themselves 'Christians,' and were called by the world, New Lights, Marshallites, or Stoneites. (These were two leading Presbyterian ministers, that in the time of a great revival in Kentucky, were disowned by the Synod of Kentucky.)

***Marshalship.** +The office of a United States marshal. — **1858** LINCOLN in Logan *Great Conspiracy* 74 They have seen in his round . . . face, Post-offices, Land-offices, Marshalships, and Cabinet appointments. **1881** *Nation* 26 May 362/2 They find the Administration giving marshalships . . . to persons whose sole claim to office [etc.].

+**Marshbanker.** Also **marsbanker.** [Du. *marsbanker.*] =MOSSBUNKER. — **1679** *Long Island Hist. Soc. Mem.* I. 100 Marsbanckers. **1814** MITCHILL *Fishes N.Y.* 453 Bony-fish, Hard-heads, or Marsbankers . . . [are] about fourteen inches long. **1884** GOODE, etc. *Fisheries* I. 569 New Jersey uses the New York name with its local variations, such as 'Bunker' and 'Marshbanker.'

+**Marsh blackbird.** The red-winged blackbird or starling, *Agelaius phoeniceus.* — **1811** WILSON *Ornithology* IV. 37 Starlings . . . are known by various names in the different states of the union; such as the Swamp Blackbird, Marsh Blackbird, Red-winged Blackbird. **1831** AUDUBON *Ornith. Biog.* I. 348 The Marsh Blackbird is . . . well known as being a bird of the most nefarious propensities. **1857** *Rep. Comm. Patents 1856: Agric.* 128 The red-winged starling, or red-shouldered marsh-blackbird . . . is dispersed over the whole of the United States, the fur countries, the great Western plains, the Rocky Mountains [etc.]. **1917** *Birds of Amer.* II. 248 Red-winged Blackbird. . . . [Also called] Marsh Blackbird.

+**Marsh frog.** =PICKEREL FROG. — **1745** E. KIMBER *Itinerant Observ.* 12*n.*, The Bull-Frogs, Lizards, Grasshoppers, Marsh Frogs [imitate city noises]. **1842** *Nat. Hist. N.Y., Zoology* III. 62 The Marsh Frog, *Rana palustris,* . . . occurs along salt marshes, and in wet meadows. **1899** *Animal & Plant Lore* 61 Marsh frogs, smaller frogs, *Chorophilus triseriatus.* Pike Co., Ill.

Marsh goose. {1768} +=HUTCHINS'S GOOSE. — **1890** *Cent.* 3640/1 *Marsh-goose.* . . . Hutchins's goose, *Bernicla hutchinsi.* (North Carolina.)

+**Marsh grass.** Any one of various grasses that grow in marshes, esp. those of the genus *Spartina.* (Cf. CORD GRASS.)

1785 *Md. Hist. Mag.* XX. 44 The Island . . . had flaggs or marsh grass growing on it. **1837** *S. Lit. Messenger* III. 738 The driver told us his horses were fed on . . . hay—and this too made of the marsh grass. **1849** *31st Congress 1 Sess.* H. R. Ex. Doc. No. 5, II. 844 Many of the drained beaver-ponds have become meadows, from which several tons of bluejoint or marsh grass may be annually cut. **1869** W. MURRAY *Adventures* 114 There is no use of standing here in this marsh-grass any longer. **1913** LONDON *Valley of Moon* 259 She had even roofed the hole in rough fashion by means of drift wood and marsh grass.

***Marsh ground.** =MARSHLAND. — **1634** WOOD *New Eng. Prospect* 34 On the other side of the River lieth all their Medow and Marsh-ground for Hay. **1657** *Suffolk Deeds* III. 20 William Beamsly . . . did by his deed of Sale . . . [sell] his Allotmt. of Marsh ground. **1664** *Portsmouth Rec.* 126 Richard Bulgar is to haue a pearcell of vpland laid out to him . . . in liew of a pearcell of marsh grownd. **1753** *Brookhaven Rec.* 167 Several tracts or persels of . . . marsh or morish ground situate within the township.

Marsh harrier. {1802-} +=next. — **1844** *Nat. Hist. N.Y., Zoology* II. 20 The Marsh Harrier . . . is frequently observed skimming over the marshes in search of its prey. **1867** *Amer. Naturalist* I. 41 The Marsh Harrier . . . anon skims rapidly over the snowy fields in eager quest of food. **1874** COUES *Birds N.W.* 356 The only Hawks more common were the ubiquitous Marsh Harriers and Sparrow Hawks. **1917** *Birds of Amer.* II. 64 Marsh Hawk. . . . [Also called] Marsh Harrier.

+**Marsh hawk.** The American marsh harrier or mouse-hawk, *Circus hudsonius.*

1812 WILSON *Ornithology* VI. 67 Marsh Hawk: *Falco uliginosus;* . . . is most numerous where there are extensive meadows and salt marshes. **1832** KENNEDY *Swallow Barn* I. 268 She had devoted her time to training a beautiful marsh-hawk. **1857** *Rep. Comm. Patents 1856: Agric.* 87 The marsh-hawk . . . is observed sweeping along close to the ground hunting for [meadow-mice]. **1895** *Dept. Agric. Yrbk. 1894* 220 The marsh hawk is one of the most valuable in the class on account of its abundance. **1917** *Birds of Amer.* II. 65/1 The Marsh Hawk is a bird of very wide distribution.

+**Marsh hay.** Hay made of marsh grass. — **1839** *Cultivator* VII. 33 The common, marsh hay is no better than the 'bog meadow hay' of the east. **1862** *Rep. Comm. Patents 1861: Agric.* 344 This hay . . . intelligent farmers value . . . for bedding, and the price of straw regulates the price of marsh hay. **1885** JEWETT *Marsh Island* 28 We're a cuttin' the ma'sh hay.

Marsh hen. {1802-} +**a.** Any of various American rails, as the king rail and the American coot. (Cf. FRESH-WATER MARSH HEN.) +**b.** (See first quot. 1917.) — **1709** LAWSON *Carolina* 151 Marsh-Hen, much the same as in Europe, only she makes another sort of Noise, and much shriller. **1844** *Knickerb.* XXIV. 188 Next to this [hunting the turkey] perhaps, I prefer marsh-hens. **1917** *Birds of Amer.* I. 181 Bittern. *Botaurus lentiginosus.* . . . [Also called] Indian Hen; Marsh Hen; Poke. *Ib.* 214 Coot. *Fulica americana.* . . . [Also called] Water Hen; Marsh Hen; Moor-head.

***Marshland.** Low-lying land, more or less watery, usually subject to periodic or seasonal overflow. — **1634** WOOD *New Eng. Prospect* 38 A place called Muddy-river . . . where is good ground, large timber, and store of Marsh-land, and Medow. **1665** *Portsmouth Rec.* 130 Hauinge . . . Surrendred the said marsh land vnto ye Towne. **1704** *Providence Rec.* IV. 59 The which said percell of land or Island is Marsh land. **1883** *Century Mag.* Nov. 40/1 Where marsh lands used to swelter under the sun, pavements of block stone had been laid. **1903** FOX *Little Shepherd* x, They found the earth . . . lifted above the baneful breath of river-bottom and marshland.

+**Marsh leatherwood.** A small American shrub (*Dirca palustris*) characterized by the toughness and pliability of its stem and branches. — **1785** MARSHALL *Amer. Grove* 41 Virginian Marsh Leather-wood . . . is a low shrub, growing in moist shady places. **1802** DRAYTON *S. Carolina* 68 Marsh leather wood . . . is sometimes used for cabinet work and furniture. **1815** DRAKE *Cincinnati* 78 [Plants found in Miami County include] marsh leatherwood.

+**Marsh lot.** A lot or allotment of land situated in a marsh. *Obs.* — **1638** *Essex Inst. Coll.* IV. 182/1 An acre & an half of vpland lying next to his marsh lott. **1672** *Ib.* LVI. 299 William Sargent . . . conveyed to Isaac Green . . . a marsh lot of Joseph Moyses [etc.]. **1714** *Charlestown Land Rec.* 217 We find a high way . . . att the head of the marsh lotts between the marsh and the Upland. **1740** in W. M. Sargent *Maine Wills* (1887) 530 Three Acres of Marsh to begin at the Westermost End of my Marsh lot.

***Marsh mallow.** A perennial herb (*Althaea officinalis*) found in marshy places in temperate regions. — **1775** ADAIR *Indians* 409 In the vacant ground they plant pumpkins, water-melons, marsh-mallows, sunflowers [etc.]. **1792** IMLAY *Western Territory* 207 Every part of the country abounds in a variety of natural flowers . . . marshmallows, violets, roses of different sorts, &c. **1887** BURROUGHS in *Century Mag.* July 328 The broad sedgy and flaggy spaces are sprinkled with the great marshmallow.

***Marsh marigold.** A swamp plant, *Caltha palustris*, or a related species. (Cf. COWSLIP 1 a.) — **1814** BIGELOW *Florula Bostoniensis* 134 *Caltha palustris.* Marsh Marigold. Meadow cowslip. . . . In the spring . . . its bright yellow blossoms are very common and conspicuous in meadows and wet situations. **1850** S. F. COOPER *Rural Hours* 51 We gathered . . . a bunch of the golden flowers of the marsh marigold, which enticed us off the road into a low, boggy spot. **1899** GOING *Flowers* 381 Love for the home-words . . . prompted them [*sc.* early Amer. settlers] to call the . . . marsh marigold a cowslip.

+**Marsh meadow.** A portion of marshland serving as a meadow. *Obs.* — **1638** *Essex Inst. Coll.* IV. 181/2 Granted . . . their proportions of marshe meadow. **1656** *Mayflower Descendant* X. 33, [I] bequeath unto my said sonne Jonathan . . . three acres of marsh meddow. **1689** *Norwalk Rec.* 21 North by Thomas Betts' Marsh Meadow.

+**Marsh mud.** Soil from a marsh, often valued as fertilizer. *Obs.* — **1789** MORSE *Amer. Geog.* 48 He found . . . marsh grass, marsh mud, and brackish water. *a***1817** DWIGHT *Travels* I. 183 The substance which here so rapidly accumulates is what in this country is called *marsh-mud;* the material, of which its salt marshes are composed. **1837** WILLIAMS *Florida* 107 No kind of manure has been found that will increase the quantity, without at the same time injuring the quality of the cotton, except it be sea-weeds, or marsh mud.

+**Marsh quail.** =MEADOW LARK. — **1750** J. BIRKET *Cursory Remarks* (1916) 32 Killd . . . some very pretty birds called Marsh quails, Something bigger then a field fare. **1821** *Amer. Jrnl. Science* III. 273 April 14. . . . The song of the marsh quail has been heard for a few days past. **1850** *Conn. Public Acts* 5 It shall not be lawful . . . for any person to shoot . . . [the] meadow-lark or marsh quail, fire bird or summer red bird. **1917** *Birds of Amer.* II. 251 Meadowlark. . . . [Also called] Marsh Quail.

+**Marsh rabbit.** A rabbit (*Sylvilagus palustris*), slightly larger than the cottontail, found in the coastal lowlands of the southeastern states. — **1869** *Amer. Naturalist* III. 343 It is clear that a Marsh Rabbit has passed this way. **1917** *Mammals of Amer.* 291/2 The *Marsh Rabbit* makes its home in the lowlands along rivers and the coast of the Southeastern States.

+**Marsh robin.** =CHEWINK. — **1874** COUES *Birds N.W.* 173 Ground Robin; Marsh Robin; Towhee Bunting; Chewink. . . . Eastern Province of North America to Minnesota. **1890** *Cent.* 3640/2 *Marsh-robin*, . . . the chewink or towhee-bunting, . . . so called from its haunts, and the reddish color on the sides of the breast. **1917** *Birds of Amer.* III. 58 Towhee. . . . [Also called] Marsh Robin.

Marsh rosemary. {1787-} +Any American plant of the genus *Limonium;* also, an astringent made from the root of such a plant. {1866} — **1784** CUTLER in *Mem. Academy* I. 432 Marsh Rosemary. The roots are powerfully astringent. **1814** BIGELOW *Florula Bostoniensis* 75 Marsh rosemary. . . . Very common on our salt marshes, flowering in June and after. **1861** STOWE *Pearl Orr's Isl.* I. 82 'Ma'sh rosemary is the gargle that I always use,' said Miss Roxy; 'it cleans out your throat so.' **1892** COULTER *Bot. W. Texas* II. 254.

+**Marsh snipe.** An American snipe (*Gallinago delicata*) which makes its nest in marshy ground. (Cf. JACKSNIPE.) — **1890** *Cent.* 3640/2 *Marsh snipe*, . . . the common American snipe; the meadow-snipe. (Maryland, U.S.) **1917** *Birds of Amer.* I. 227 Wilson's Snipe. *Gallinago delicata.* . . . Meadow Snipe; . . . Marsh Snipe; Bog Snipe.

+**Marsh tack(e)y.** A small wiry pony bred in marshy regions. — **1836** GILMAN *Recoll.* (1838) 131 An accident happening to my horse, I was obliged to hire one of the little animals called 'marsh tackies' to carry me over a creek. **1877** PHELPS *Story of Avis* 432 They are short clean steps, very clear and pleasant for a marsh-tackey's foot. **1890** MCALLISTER *Society* vii. 91 We all pressed through the crowd to the . . . two marsh tackeys, with their manes and tails . . . full of burrs.

Marsh tern. The gull-billed tern, *Gelochelidon nilotica aranea.* {1852-} — **1813** WILSON *Ornithology* VIII. 143 Marsh Tern: *Sterna aranea.* . . . Was first met with on the shores of Cape May, . . . darting down after a kind of large black spider. **1858** BAIRD *Birds Pacific R.R.* 859 The Marsh Tern. . . . Coast of the United States as far north as Connecticut. **1917** *Birds of Amer.* I. 54 Gull-billed Tern. *Gelochelidon nilotica.* . . . [Also called] Marsh tern; Egyptian tern [etc.].

+**Marsh tortoise.** The mud turtle. — **1848** BARTLETT 230 *Mud-turtle*, the popular name of a reptile common in all parts of the United States. Marsh Tortoise and Mud Terrapin are other names for the same.

+**Marsh wren.** Any one of various American wrens that breed exclusively in marshes, as the long-billed marsh wren, *Telmatodytes palustris palustris.*

1794 *Amer. Philos. Soc.* IV. 102 The great lark, the marsh-wren, etc., place their nests in the grass. **1839** AUDUBON *Ornith. Biog.* V. 467 Marsh wren. . . . A nest of this bird with eggs was seen in the salt marshes of Barnstable by Dr. Storer of Boston. **1844** *Nat. Hist. N.Y., Zoology* II. 56 The Marsh Wren, *Troglodytes Palustris*, . . . is chiefly found in marshes. **1874** COUES *Birds N.W.* 35 The nidification of the Marsh Wren is not the least interesting part of its history. **1917** *Birds of Amer.* III. 198/1 Marsh Wrens . . . are irrepressible songsters.

***Martagon.** +An American wild lily, *Lilium superbum.* Also attrib. — **1743** CATESBY *Carolina* II. p. xix, The Indians boil these Martagon-Roots, and esteem them Dainties. **1748** *Ib.* App. 12 The Attamusco Lily . . . is a native of Virginia and Carolina, where in particular places the pastures are . . . thick sprinkled with them and Martagons. **1784** CUTLER in *Mem. Academy* I. 433 Martagon. Curl-flowered Lily. Blossoms yellow, spotted with black. In Taunton, and very common in the state of Rhode-Island.

***Marten.** Also †**martern, martin.**

+**1.** Any one of various American long, slender-bodied animals of the genus *Martes*, of the weasel family, somewhat smaller than a house cat and valued for its fur. Also attrib.

1612 SMITH *Virginia* 14 Martins, Powlecats, weessels and Minkes we know they haue. **1674** *Cal. State P., Amer. & W.I.* VII. 581 The natural inhabitants of the woods, hills, and swamps [of N.H. and Me.], are . . . otters, mincks, martins, musquashes [etc.]. **1791** J. LONG *Voyages* 89 The Indian . . . whom I employed in hunting and making marten traps. **1805** LEWIS in *Ann. 9th Congress* 2 Sess. 1057 This country abounds more in the valuable fur animals, the beaver, otter, and marten, than any portion of Louisiana yet known. **1850** S. F. COOPER *Rural Hours* 500 The Sable, or Marten, is a small brown animal, about two and a half feet in length. **1917** *Mammals of Amer.* 114/1 The Martens in America have been given many names.

+**2.** The skin or pelt of this animal. Also attrib.

1602 BRERETON *Virginia* 9 So the rest of the day we spent in trading with them [the Indians] for furres, which are Beavers, Luzernes, Marterns, Otters . . . , blacke Foxes. **1633** *N.H. Doc. & Rec.* I. 73 Capt. Neale had . . . 17 martins, on[e] black-fox skin. **1834** NOTT *Novellettes* I. 47 On his head he wore a black martin cap.

Marten skin. Also **martin's skin.** The skin or pelt of a marten. Also attrib. — **1628** *Mass. H.S. Coll.* 3 Ser. VIII. 177, I was at a sagamore's house, and saw a martin's skin. **1633** *N.H. Doc. & Rec.* I. 72 Received by me, . . . seaventeene martin skins. **1778** *Essex Inst. Coll.* XLIX. 109 Sold . . . 250 martin skins, at 12s 6d. **1795** ELLICOTT in Mathews *Life A. Ellicott* 123, I have purchased from the Indians some fine Martin skins to replace your old Muff & Tippet. **1823** COOPER *Pioneers* iv, A fair, jolly wig furnished a neat and rounded outline to his visage, and he, as well as the other two, wore marten-skin caps.

Marthy. The American burbot. — [**1772** FORSTER in *Phil. Trans.* LXIII. 152 The second of the Hudson's Bay fish, is called, by the wild natives of that country, *Marthy.*] **1883** *Nat. Museum Bull. No. 27*, 458 *Lota maculosa.* . . . Burbot; Marthy . . . spawns in late winter or early spring. **1903** *N.Y. Museum Bull. No. 60*, 702 The American burbot . . . has received a great many names, including . . . marthy, methy, losh, eel pout, dogfish, chub eel, etc.

***Martin.** +Any one of various American swallows (esp. *Progne subis*) of a glossy steel-blue color. (Cf. BANK MARTIN, BEE-MARTIN, FIELD MARTIN.)

1709 LAWSON *Carolina* 144 Martins are here of two sorts. The first is the same as in England; the other as big as a Black-Bird. **1812** WILSON *Ornithology* V. 58, I never knew an instance of Martins eating peas. **1841** COOPER *Deerslayer* xxiii, Even the robin and the martin come back, year after year, to their old nests. **1890** HOWELLS *Boy's Town* 18 All the boys were . . . watching the martins flying down to the ground from their box in the gable. **1917** *Birds of Amer.* III. 82 Purple Martin. *Progne subis subis.* . . . [Also called] Martin; Black Martin; House Martin.

attrib. **1807** IRVING, etc. *Salmagundi* xiv. 380 Jeremy's knocking down a mouldering martin-coop with his tennis-ball. **1845** *Knickerb.* XXV. 448 The martins were . . . carefully peeping from the windows of the martin-cage. **1857** *Harper's Mag.* May 747/1 The house . . . had a lonely, dilapidated look, and even the gourds on the martin pole appeared to be tenantless.

+**Martin box.** A box set up for martins to nest in. Also fig. — **1853** B. F. TAYLOR *Jan. & June* 146 A martin-box of a house, no matter how little, provided it will hold two or so. **1862** in Moore *Rebellion Rec.* V. II. 177 Here Lieut. Phelps elevates his 'martin-box' aft. **1875** STOWE *We & Neighbors* 373 Her words . . . came so thick that they were like a flock of martins, all trying to get out of a martin-box together. **1917** *Birds of Amer.* III. 83/1 In some sections of the south there scarcely can be seen a negro's cabin but what has its Martin box.

+**Martin house.** A diminutive wooden house or houselike structure put up, usually on a pole, for martins to nest in. — **1835** BIRD *Hawks* I. 44 Here's . . . the identical old Folly, with . . . the pot in the chimney, and the old martin-house on a pole! **1850** S. F. COOPER *Rural Hours* 59 The white man builds his martin-house for these [birds]. **1867** HOLMES *Guardian Angel* 252 One of those little pony chapels, . . . if it were set up on a stout pole, would pass for a good-sized martin-house. **1884** 'CRADDOCK' *Tenn. Mts.* 40 There was a lofty martin-house, whence the birds whirled fitfully.

Martynia. [John *Martyn*, English botanist (1699-1768).] A small genus of suberect or prostrate herbs found in the warmer parts of the United States; also, a plant of this genus. {1753-} — **1847** DARLINGTON *Weeds & Plants* 222 Long-beaked Martynia. Unicorn Plant. . . . This plant . . . is cultivated for its singular fruit. **1849** EMMONS *Agric. N.Y.* II. 299 The Martynia . . . is a strong-smelling vegetable. . . . In its green state, these parts are esteemed for pickles. **1899** *Farmers' Bul.* No. 94, 20 *Martynia.* . . . The seed pods will be ready for picking in 60 to 80 days and are put up in the same way as cucumbers.

Maryland. *attrib.* [Name of a state, formerly a colony, on the Atlantic seaboard, named in 1632 by Charles I in honor of his queen, Henrietta Maria.]

+**1.** In the names of various articles originating in or characteristic of Maryland.

1777 *N.J. Archives* 2 Ser. I. 517 Two eight dollar bills, old Maryland money [were stolen]. **1834** CARRUTHERS *Kentuckian* I. 24, I gets a quid of the real Kentuck twist or Maryland kite-foot into my mouth. **1863** L. BAKER *U.S. Secret Service* (1867) 169 The property found on the persons [included] . . . Maryland and Eastern bank notes, $183.00. **1872** ROE *Army Lett.* 35 There was no April fool about the delicate Maryland biscuits. **1881** INGERSOLL *Oyster-Industry* 247 A mean quality of oysters (Maryland stock) [is sold] about the streets of Baltimore.

+**2.** In the specific names of various plants and trees found or cultivated in Maryland.

1785 MARSHALL *Amer. Grove* 8 *Andromeda mariana.* Maryland, or broad-leaved Andromeda. *Ib.* 121 *Quercus nigra trifida.* Maryland Black Oak. **1843** TORREY *Flora N.Y.* I. 163 *Clitoria mariana.* . . . Maryland Clitoria. . . . Sandy soil [near] Brooklyn. **1868** GRAY *Field Botany* 273 *S[pigelia] Marilandica,* Maryland P[ink-root]. Rich woods, from Penn. W. & S. **1760** WASHINGTON *Diaries* I. 147 Grafted 43 of the Maryland Red Strick. **1901** MOHR *Plant Life Ala.* 644 *Sanicula marilandica.* . . . Maryland Sanicle . . . [is found in the] Central Pine belt. Woods. Tuscaloosa and Bibb counties. **1856** *Rep.Comm.Patents 1855: Agric.* 166 Cob of the 'Maryland White Southern Corn' . . . weighed 290 grains.

+**Marylander.** Also †**Marilander.** A native or inhabitant of Maryland.

1665 *Mass. H. S. Coll.* 3 Ser. X. 55 A forbearance of such hostility . . . may prevent the destruction of divers dutch or English of the hither parts, or Marilanders &c. *c***1680** *Ib.* 2 Ser. I. 29 [What] moved him to take up arms . . . in the behalfe of the Marylanders his professed enemies? **1723** *Amer. Wkly. Mercury* 1–8 Aug. 2/2 Jacob Neale a Marylander about 30 Years of Age . . . Speaks prety thick. **1755** L. EVANS *Anal. Map Colonies* 14 The Sasquehannocks, after the great Defeat by the Marilanders, were easily exterminated by the Confederates. **1807** *Ann. 10th Congress* 1 Sess. I. 594 He either hated or loved Marylanders more than others. **1849** *Knickerb.* XXXIV. 219 Seen any . . . Georgians, . . . or Marylanders, or Mississippians? **1898** *Mo. So. Dakotan* I. 1 Gleason was a young and delicate Marylander.

transf. **1838** COOPER *Homeward Bound* xii, This beef is not indigestible and here is a real Marylander, in the way of a ham.

+**Marylandian.** =prec. *Obs.* — **1750** *Md. Hist. Mag.* X. 144 Most of our Marylandians do very well and they are said to be as good as any, if not the best boys in the house.

+**Maryland marmot.** An American marmot or woodchuck of the genus *Marmota* (syn. *Arctomys*) esp. *M. monax.* (Cf. GROUND HOG 1.) — [**1781** PENNANT *Hist. Quadrupeds* II. 396–8 Marmot . . . Maryland . . . Inhabits Virginia and Pennsylvania.] **1823** James *Exped.* I. 261 *Arctomys monax*—Maryland marmot. **1826** GODMAN *Nat. Hist.* II. 100 The Maryland Marmot is no where more common than in Virginia, New Jersey, Pennsylvania. **1869** *Amer. Naturalist* III. 390 The Maryland Marmot, . . . more popularly known in this locality by the common name of 'Groundhog,' is still tolerably abundant.

+**Maryland yellowthroat.** The ground warbler (*Geothlypis trichas*) of the eastern United States. — **1808** WILSON *Ornithology* I. 88 [The] Maryland Yellow-throat, *Sylvia Marilandica,* . . . is one of the humble inhabitants of briars, brambles, [and] alder bushes. **1858** *Atlantic Mo.* Dec. 866/2, I must not omit to notice . . . the Maryland Yellow-Throat (*Sylvia trichas*). **1883** *Century Mag.* Sept. 651/2 [Among the] birds on Cape Cod is . . . the Maryland yellow-throat. **1917** *Birds of Amer.* III. 161/2 There are several regional varieties of the Maryland Yellow-throat, north of the Mexican boundary.

+**Mascalonge.** =MUSKELLUNGE. (Cf. MASKINONGE.) — **1856** *Porter's Spirit of Times* 29 Nov. 209/2 The northern pike, or pickerel, is a far handsomer, as well as better fish than the mascalonge. **1863** *Rep. Comm. Agric. 1862* 55 Fishes of Maine . . . which are known to spawn in fresh water . . . [include] Mascalonge, *Esox estor;* perch, *Perca flavescens* [etc.]. **1892** SHIELDS *Amer. Game Fishes* 192 The Mascalonge, or Muskellunge, as it is usually pronounced, is a magnificent fish.

Mash, *v.*[1] +*intr.* (See quot. 1859 and MESH *v.*) *Obs.* — **1850** *Rep. Comm. Patents 1849* 155 What I claim as new . . . is . . . the shaft H, with the pinions i, mashing into racks II. **1859** BARTLETT 265 In machinery, one wheel is said to *mash* into or with another, i.e. to 'engage' with it.

Mash, *v.*[2]

1. *tr.* To ogle, flirt with, or try to attract the amorous attention of (a person of the opposite sex.) *slang.* {1883–}

The place of origin of this verb and the corresponding noun MASHER cannot be established from the evidence at present available. Cf. quot. 1889 below and the note *s.v.* MASHER.

1882 LELAND *Gypsies* 108 These black-eyed beauties by mashing men for many generations, with shafts shot sideways . . . , at last sealed their souls into the corner of their eyes. **1889** BARRÈRE & LELAND (1897) II. 44/1 About the year 1860 *mash* was a word found only in theatrical parlance in the United States. When an actress or any girl on the stage smiled at or ogled a friend in the audience, she was said to *mash* him. . . . It occurred to the writer that it must have been derived from the gypsy *mash* (*masher-ava*), to allure, to entice. **1893** CRANE *Maggie* (1896) 85 Dere wasn't a feller come teh deh house but she'd try teh mash 'im.

2. *To get mashed on,* to become suddenly smitten with sentimental affection for; to be 'gone on.'

1883 PECK *Bad Boy* 99 An aunt of his . . . got mashed on a Chicago drummer. **1894** N. BROOKS *Tales of Me. Coast* 44 How any right-sensed man could get mashed on that big gawk of a tomboy, everlastingly fetches me. **1894** HOYT *Texas Steer* (1925) III. 31 A dude who belonged to the British Legation got mashed on Dad's millions before we'd been here a week.

Masher. [MASH *v.*[2]] A man who tries to flirt with, or make advances to, women in public places. *slang.* {1882–}

'The word was common in 1882 and for a few years after. It is said to have been introduced from the U.S.' (*O.E.D.*).

1882 RITTENHOUSE *Maud* 95 Sunday-school this afternoon. Two 'mashers' in the class. **1884** NYE *Baled Hay* 211 There is no young, fair masher, strutting up and down the piazza. **1888** *N.Y. Herald* 25 March 8/6 The stage entrance to the Bijou is just above the corner, and the 'mashers' gather there to meet 'butterflies of the stage.' **1902** C. MORRIS *Stage Confidences* 163 No more vulgar term exists than 'masher.' **1904** *New Haven Register* 26 Oct. 3 'Mashers' have become such a nuisance in State street that all the dry goods stores have entered into an alliance to prosecute and drive them off the street.

attrib. **1902** C. MORRIS *Stage Confidences* 171 Now and again . . . a man really falls in love with a woman whom he has seen only upon the stage; but no 'masher' proceedings are taken in such cases.

Mashing. [MASH *v.*[2]] The action of a 'masher' or flirt. Also attrib. *slang.* — **1882** PECK *Sunshine* 130 There has got to be two parties to a mashing match, and one must be a woman. **1884** RITTENHOUSE *Maud* 306, I do try to make good honest friends but 'mashing' is altogether out of my line.

+**Mash trap.** =DEADFALL 1. *Obs.* — **1862** *N.Y. Tribune* 5 May 1/6 There is not the least danger that their precious carcasses will be caught under a mashtrap. *c***1866** BAGBY *Old Va. Gentleman* 48 [He must] set gums for 'Mollie-cotton-tails,' mash-traps and deadfalls for minks.

***Mash tub.** A tub in which malt is mashed. — **1649** *Conn. Rec.* I. 502 A copper mash tubbs, payles, treyes, &c. **1790** S. DEANE *New-Eng. Farmer* 21/2 The mash tub should have . . . a tap and fauset fixed into its bottom. **1868** *Congress. Globe* 28 March 2190/2 The stock would not starve if he . . . fed the grain . . . to the hogs without running it through the mash-tub. **1875** *Chicago Tribune* 13 Sept. 5/3 A storekeeper . . . whose duty it is to record the time of emptying and filling every mash-tub.

Masked ball. Also †**masqued ball.** A ball at which those participating wear masks. {1813–} — **1776** *Boston News-Letter* 22 Feb., On Monday, the 11th of March will be given at Concert-Hall, a Subscription Masked Ball. **1810** *Columbian Centinel* 20 Jan. 2/3 The Common Council have passed a severe ordinance against the exhibition of Masquerades, or Masqued Balls. **1895** G. KING *New Orleans* 151 With the unexpected picturesqueness of circumstance . . . that sometimes groups dancers at a masked ball, there came across to New Orleans in 1798 the royal fugitives themselves.

+**Masked bobwhite.** The Arizona bobwhite, *Colinus ridgwayi.* — **1887** RIDGWAY *Manual N.A. Birds* 189 Sonora and southern Arizona. . . . Masked Bob White. **1917** *Birds of Amer.* II. 4 The plumage of the Masked Bob-white is strikingly different from that of his eastern cousin.

+**Maskinonge.** Also †**Maskenozha.** =MUSKELLUNGE. — **1796** MORSE *Amer. Geog.* I. 351 Maskinungas, a very large species of pickerel, pout, mullet, and a fish called lake bass, are found in great plenty [in Vermont]. **1855** LONGFELLOW *Hiawatha* viii, 101 And he said to the Kenozha, To the Pike, the Maskenozha, 'Take the bait of this rude fellow.' **1870** *Conn. Public Acts* 437 No person shall . . . catch or take any pickerel, pike, black bass, or maskinonge. **1896** JORDAN & EVERMANN *Check-List Fishes* 309 *Lucius masquinongy.* . . . Muskallunge; Maskinongy; Muscalonge. Great Lakes region; Upper Mississippi Valley and northward. **1903** *N.Y. Museum Bul.* No. 60, 303 The name of this giant pike is apparently derived from the language of the Ojibwa or the Cree Indians; it is variously spelled . . . muskallunge, mascalonge and maskinonge.

***Mason.**

***1.** One who builds in stone or brick.

1633 *Mass. Bay Rec.* I. 109 Sawers, masons, . . . &c., shall not take aboue 2s. a day. **1701** *Essex Inst. Coll.* XXXVI. 82 [For] tending the mason and . . . bringing of Clay or brick. **1836** *Niles' Nat. Reg.* 10 Dec. 240/3 By the Providence Directory it appears that there are . . . 106 masons. **1881** *Rep. Indian Affairs* 7 They attended the mason, mixed all the cement for laying adobes, and carried it.

***2.** =FREEMASON. (Cf. ANTI-MASON.)

1758 *Newport Mercury* 19 Dec. 3/2 The Feast of the Antient and Honorable Society of Free and Accepted Masons, will be kept at Brother Christian Myers. **1776** A. ADAMS *Familiar Letters* 151 The Dr. was buried on Monday; the Masons walking in procession from the State House. **1809** *Steele P.* II. 600 As a Mason, as a brother, I now address you. **1869** *Boyd's Business Directory* 565, I. Pryor Tapping, . . . manufacturer of Regalia, for Masons, Odd Fellows and Good Templars. **1890** HOWELLS *Boy's Town* 118 On the Fourth of July . . . the Sons of Temperance walked in the procession with the Masons and the Odd-Fellows.

+**Mason and Dixon.** =next. *Obs.* — **1834** C. A. DAVIS *Lett. J. Downing* 36 He tell'd me Georgia would go for me, arter the Gineral, as soon as any north of mason and dickson. **1843** *Knickerb.* XXII. 185 The writer, who dwelleth near Mason and Dixon, descants upon the awful climate.

+**Mason and Dixon('s) line.** The boundary between Pennsylvania and Maryland as laid out (1763–67) by the English surveyors Charles Mason and Jeremiah Dixon. In later times regarded as the line separating the free and the slave states, or as the boundary between the North and the South. Also *Mason('s) and Dixon('s) line.*

1779 in W. B. Reed *Life & Corr. Joseph Reed* II. 134 The Virginia gentlemen offer to divide exactly the 40th degree with us.... Perhaps we [of Penna.] would be as well off with Mason and Dixon's line continued. **1781** JEFFERSON *Writings* XIX. 356 Mason's and Dixon's line shall be extended twenty-three miles with a surveyor's compass. **1833** J. HALL *Harpe's Head* 215 Of the eatables composed of bread-stuffs . . . no one who has had the misfortune to be raised north of Mason and Dixon's line, can form an adequate conception. **1858** *S. Lit. Messenger* XXVII. 446/2 The phrase, 'Mason and Dixon's Line,' has been echoing in our ears ever since 1820. **1884** BLAINE *20 Years Congress* I. 460 [West Virginia's] organization and admission to the Union would complete the chain of loyal Commonwealths on the South side of Mason and Dixon's line. **1904** *N.Y. Ev. Post* 1 Aug. 2 European immigration, which has gone to points north of the Mason and Dixon line, will soon turn southward.

Masonic, *a.*

1. Pertaining to or sponsored by freemasons. {1797–}

1819 *Niles' Reg.* XVI. 335/2 His body was returned to the dust from whence it came, with masonic honors. **1831** J. Q. ADAMS *Diary* 426 The Masonic and Anti-Masonic Controversy. **1878** COOKE *Happy Dodd* 38 The little thing had slept through many a firemen's ball or masonic dance. **1887** *Courier-Journal* 1 May 9/4 Subscriptions [are needed] for a grand prize drill of the crack companies of the United States in connection with the Masonic celebration.

2. Of articles of (ritualistic) apparel or insignia: Worn by freemasons. {1810–}

1800 *Columbian Centinel* 1 Feb. 3/2 Masonic Aprons and Gloves, May be had. **1860** E. COWELL *Diary* 10 He had given Sam a Masonic breastpin. **1862** *Trial C. M. Jefferds* 32 A masonic pin was in his breast, and I gave that also to the policeman. **1869** *Boyd's Business Directory* 685 Devereux & Luker, manufacturers of Masonic Goods, K. T. Swords, Jewels, Jewelry &c.

3. Of groups or organizations: Composed of freemasons.

1819 *Niles' Reg.* XVI. 319/1 A masonic lodge made a procession in form, to welcome the distinguished brother. **1827** DRAKE & MANSFIELD *Cincinnati* 91 The members of the different Masonic Societies of Cincinnati, are sanguine in the opinion, that the Grand Lodge of Ohio, will be removed to Cincinnati. **1885** *Harper's Mag.* March 609/2 'Lodge No. 4' of the Masonic fraternity of Fredericksburg is quite famous.

Masonic hall. A hall or building serving as the headquarters or place of meeting for a masonic lodge. — **1819** *Niles' Reg.* XVI. 56/2 That beautiful building in Chesnut street, the Masonic hall, was destroyed by fire. **1837** *S. Lit. Messenger* III. 260 The doors of the Masonic Hall were thrown open for the admission of all. **1898** PAGE *Red Rock* 156 The largest and best building there for such an entertainment was one used as a Masonic hall.

+**Masonic temple.** =prec. — **1866** *Ore. State Jrnl.* 23 June 3/5 [At] No. 10 Masonic Temple. Corner of Montgomery and Post streets. **1892** *Artistic Guide to Chicago* 112 The Masonic Temple is located at the corner of State and Randolph Streets.... When finished it will divide honors with the Auditorium. **1916** F. RIDER *New York City* 438 East of the Masonic Temple, facing the abandoned cathedral, and extending to the northwest corner of Lafayette, . . . is the recently finished Queen of All Saints' Chapel.

+**Mason jar.** A glass jar with a screw top or similar sealing device. Also *Mason screw top jar.* (Cf. FRUIT JAR.) — **1888** L. HARGIS *Graded Cook Book* 472 Quince and apple butter.... Put a little of the mixture in a plate and invert, if it adheres the butter is done. Fill Mason jars and seal. **1909** *Sears, Roebuck & Co. Cat.* No. 118 N, 3, 1 Fruit Jar Cover, to fit Mason jar. 1 Dozen Fruit Jar Rubbers, to fit Mason jar. **1920** W. S. WALBRIDGE *American Bottles* 49 Until 1857, the date of the advent of the Mason screw top jar, the only method was by sealing a jar by any process which happened to appeal to the housewife.

***Masonry.** =FREEMASONRY. {1686–} — **1779** *Essex Inst. Coll.* III. 38 [We were] desirous, for the good of Masonry, that a Lodge might be [formed]. **1798** J. ADAMS *Works* IX. 213 You are better judges than I am, whether ill uses have been or may be made of Masonry. **1831** HOLLEY *Texas* (1833) 128 There is neither masonry, anti-masonry, nullification, nor court intrigues. **1891** O'BEIRNE *Leaders Ind. Territory* 205/1 The subject of this sketch is the acknowledged father of Masonry in the Indian Territory.

Massa. =MARS(E). {1774–} — **1776** LEACOCK *Fall Brit. Tyranny* IV. iv, 'Well, my brave blacks, are you come to list?' . . . 'Eas, massa Lord.' **1816** *Niles' Reg.* IX. Suppl. 95/1 And Massa M'Donough, he sail 'em. **1835** *S. Lit. Messenger* IV. 197/1 My hack-driver solemnly assured 'Massa' that there was no other tavern in the city. **1872** POWERS *Afoot & Alone* 101 Jest a quarter, massa, fur a mighty little'll do me, 'cause I'se gwine to die right soon.

+**Massachusets.** [Algonquian, 'at or about the great hill.'] An Algonquian tribe of Indians formerly occupying the coastal region of Massachusetts Bay. Now hist. — **1616** SMITH *Desc. New England* 26 The Countrie of the Massachusets . . . is the Paradise of all those parts. **1622** 'MOURT' *Relation* 124 The Massachusets had often threatened vs. **1654** JOHNSON *Wonder-w. Prov.* 16 The Abarginny-men consisting of Mattachusets, Wippanaps and Tarratines were greatly weakned, and more especially the three Kingdomes, or Saggamore ships of the Mattachusets.

+**Massachusettensian.** A native or inhabitant of the colony or state of Massachusetts. *Obs.* — **1702** MATHER *Magnalia* (1853) I. 132 The Massachusettensians had a Winthrop for their governour. **1787** J. ADAMS *Works* IV. 392 In this society of Massachusettensians then, there is . . . a moral and political equality of rights and duties among all the individuals.

+**Massachusetts.** *attrib.* [Cf. MASSACHUSETS.] Of or pertaining to the state of Massachusetts.

1784 *Mass. Laws* I. 116 Proprietors in the said bank . . . shall be a corporation . . . under the name of The President and Directors of the Massachusetts Bank. **1787** TYLER *Contrast* II. 2, I thought, Mr. Jonathan, you Massachusetts-men always argued with a gun in your hand. **1855** in Hambleton *H. A. Wise* 295 The doctrines of Massachusetts abolitionism have . . . made rapid progress. **1883** in Hutchinson *Diary & Lett.* I. 480, A West India pine-apple . . . of which I had become proprietor for nine Massachusetts pence. **1905** SHALER *Citizen* 207 In some states the voter must also show that he can read and write the English language. This is sometimes called the Massachusetts limitation, for the reason that it originated in that commonwealth.

+**Massasauga.** Also **massassauga.** [From Ojibway *Missisauga*, place and ethnic name.] A prairie rattlesnake (*Sistrurus catenatus*) or a snake related to this. (Cf. GROUND RATTLESNAKE.) — **1840** KIRKLAND *New Home* 33 It's a rattlesnake; the Indians call them Massisangas [*sic*] and so *folks* calls 'em so too. **1857** *Rep. Comm. Patents 1856: Agric.* 87 Arvicolae are the legitimate food of the prairie rattlesnake, or massasauga (*Crotalophorus tergeminus*). **1871** *Harper's Mag.* Nov. 831 In the grass the massasauga and other venomous reptiles lurked. **1907** HODGE, etc. *Amer. Indians* I. 817 *Massassauga*, a western species of rattlesnake.

+**Massawoomics, Massawomees.** =FIVE NATIONS. *Obs.* — **1818** F. HALL *Travels* 134 The powerful Indian confederacy, known by the name of Massawoomics, or Five Nations, originally occupied the whole of the country betwixt the lakes. **1831** WITHERS *Chron. Border Warfare* 39 That portion of the state lying north west of the Blue ridge, and extending to the lakes was possessed by the Massawomees.

+**Mass convention.** An informal public meeting of political party members and leaders held primarily for discussing party interests and nominating party candidates. — **1843** *N.Y. Herald* 13 Feb. 2/2 (Ernst), The Great Tyler mass Convention on the 15th of March, will be a screamer. **1844** *Amer. Almanac 1845* 329 A great mass convention of the Whig party was held at Boston, Daniel Webster presiding. **1900** *Congress. Rec.* 25 Jan. 1172/1 The nominations had been settled at primaries or mass conventions.

+**Massena.** =next. — **1857** *34th Congress 1 Sess.* Sen. Ex. Doc. No. 108, II. Birds 23 On being shot [the bird] proved to be a male massena. **1874** COUES *Birds N.W.* 444 What has been put on record concerning the habits of the beautiful Massena.

+**Massena partridge.** [André *Masséna*, marshal of France (1758–1817).] Any of several varieties of a quail (*Cyrtonyx montezumae*) of the Southwest. — **1858** BAIRD *Birds Pacific R.R.* 647 *Cyrtonyx massena*, . . . Massena partridge, . . . [is found] chiefly on the upper Rio Grande from the high plains of the Pecos. **1887** RIDGWAY *Manual N.A. Birds* 194 *C*[*yrtonyx*] *montezumæ*. Massena Partridge. **1917** *Birds of Amer.* II. 10 Mearns's Quail. *Cyrtonax montezumæ mearnsi*.... [Also called] Messena [*sic*] Partridge; Fool Quail.

+**Massena quail.** =prec. — **1874** COUES *Birds N.W.* 443, I found no Massena Quail about Fort Whipple until a few days before my final departure. **1883** *Century Mag.* Aug. 484/1 Our partridges (viz. Bob White, the Mountain, Valley, and Massena quails, etc.) may be distinguished among American *Gallinæ*, by the foregoing characters.

Masseur. [F.] A man who practices massage. {1899} — **1879** BARTHOLOW *Materia Medica* 73 *Masseur* is a male rubber, and *masseuse* a female rubber. **1884** *N.Y. Medical Jrnl.* 21 June, A physician requiring the services of a thoroughly experienced Masseur. **1918** *Ann. Amer. Acad.* LXXX. 116 Many masseurs will be needed in these [military] hospitals.

Masseuse. [F.] A woman who practices massage. {1897} — **1879** [see MASSEUR].

Mass house. A Roman Catholic place of worship. *Obs.* {1644–} — [**1731** *Essex Inst. Coll.* XLII. 232 There are . . . in this Village [in Nova Scotia] . . . 2 Mass Houses or Churches.] **1755** *Md. Hist. Mag.* III. 3 The Mob were with Great Difficulty prevented from pulling down the Mass-House in Philadelphia. **1809** KENDALL *Travels* III. 54 On the farm are some small remains of the missionary church, called by the protestant colonists, the mass-house. **1856** WHITTIER *Poetical Works* (1894) 50/2 Is an English Christian's home A chapel or a mass-house?

+**Mass meeting.** A public meeting to which people of all classes come in great numbers.

1842 H. MANN *Oration* 4 July 64 The rival parties begin to play their game for the ignorant, and to purchase the saleable. Mass-meetings are held. **1861** E. COWELL *Diary* 302 A great Mass meeting is to be held in New York, and three more regiments are to leave. **1880** *Congress. Rec.* 1 May 2938/1 [Mr. Simonton] holds temperance mass-meetings in his district, every month. **1917** SINCLAIR *King Coal* 308 A set of demands . . . would be submitted in mass-meeting, and ratified.

transf. **1890** HOWELLS *Boy's Town* 72 If you could fool a fellow into a mass-meeting of bumble-bees, . . . it was right and fair to do so. **1899** GOING *Flowers* 39 What looks like one blossom proves on examination to be a whole floral mass-meeting.

***Mast.**[1]

***1.** A tree trunk or piece of timber suitable for or fashioned into a support for the yards, sails, rigging, etc., of a vessel.

1624 *Va. House of Burgesses* 28 [We] weare . . . wholly imployed in cuttinge downe of masts, cedar, black wallnutt, clapboarde. **1687** SEWALL *Diary* I. 189 Ride into Swamp to see a Mast drawn of about 26 Inches or 28. **1707** *Ib.* II. 207 A Letter . . . complaining of Trees cut contrary to Charter and of a great Mast ship'd. **1765** ROGERS *Acct. N. America* 50 The chief commodities exported from this province [N.H.], are, masts for the Royal navy, staves, boards, shingles, furs, &c. **1825** N. ADAMS *Annals Portsmouth* 125 Colonel Winthrop Hilton . . . was engaged in procuring masts, and . . . went about fourteen miles into the woods. **1907** *St. Nicholas* XXXIV. 781/1 [You] put a mast in with a sail or two, and have another runner at the back with a tiller for steering, and there you are.

2. Attrib. and comb. with *contract, path, swamp, team.*

1672 in M. P. Thompson *Landmarks Ancient Dover, N.H.* 140/2 On ye north side of ye Great mast path going into ye swamp. **1764** *N.H. Hist. Soc. Coll.* IX. 144 Ye mast team sat out. *Ib.* 146, [I] sent my team & brot 900 long shingles from the mast swamp. **1771** *N.H. Gazette* 30 Aug. (Ernst), Mast Contract. This to inform such persons as are desirous of contracting for white pine masts . . . to apply to me.

***Mast.**[2] The fruits of various forest trees, as oak, beech, chestnut, etc., used as food by hogs.

1670 DENTON *Brief Desc. N.Y.* 4 [Long] Island is very full of Timber, as Oaks white and red, Walnut-trees, Chestnut-trees, which yield store of Mast for Swine. **1752** MACSPARRAN *America Dissected* (1753) 10 They export Indian Corn, and Pork, fatted in the Woods, with what . . . is called Mast; that is, Acorns, Walnuts, . . . and wild Fruits. **1789** MORSE *Amer. Geog.* 352 On this mast vast numbers of swine are fed. **1849** CHAMBERLAIN *Ind. Gazetteer* 38 Such [hogs] as have become fat on the nuts or *mast* in the fall of the year. **1897** BRODHEAD *Bound in Shallows* 215 Under the beeches hogs nosed for mast.

attrib. **a1752** W. DOUGLASS *Summary* II. 375 Anno 1733, a good Mast Year, one Man . . . salted up three Thousand Barrels of Pork.

***Master.**

***1.** One who has the oversight or direction of others in performing various services, operating plants, etc.

1640 *New Haven Rec.* I. 34 The Mr. of the watch is to sett the watch an hower after sunset. **1652** *Mass. Bay Rec.* III. 261 John Hull, master of the said Mint. **1796** *Boston Directory* 221 Alker Thomas, master of duck factory, Pleasant street. **1858** W. P. SMITH *Railway Celebrations* 65 The Master of road has the general charge of all matters pertaining to the road-bed, the track [etc.]. **1889** BRAYLEY *Boston Fire Dept.* 39 The first appointment of foremen or masters, as they were then called, of engine companies is recorded under date of March 30, 1724.

***2.** A teacher or schoolmaster; a president *of* a college.

1643 *New Eng. First Fruits* (1896) 5 Every Schollar that . . . hath the Approbation of the Overseers and Master of the Colledge. **1654** R. WILLIAMS *Letters* (1874) 285 Mr. Chauncy . . . is now master of the College. **1710** *Boston Rec.* 65 We are of opinion the worke of that School do's necessarily require the Attendance of a master and an Usher. **1848** *Knickerb.* XVIII. 65 Bill Jones . . . swore he would whip the master before the week was out. **1888** SHERIDAN *Memoirs* I. 3 The village school . . . was taught by an old-time Irish 'master'—one of those itinerant dominies of the early frontier.

***3.** =MASTER OF ARTS.

1687 SEWALL *Diary* I. 181 Eleven Bachelors and seven Masters proceeded. **1734** *Harvard Rec.* I. 151 If Bachelours or Masters set an example of Idleness. **1765** ROGERS *Acct. N. America* 45 At Cambridge . . . are annually graduated, batchelors and masters, from fifty to sixty young gentlemen.

+4. Before the Civil War, an American slave owner. Now hist.

1704 S. KNIGHT *Journal* 40 Order the master to pay 40s to black face. **1795** *Mass. H. S. Coll.* V. 47 The court gave no opinion on the point, whether the emancipated negroes were to be the charge of the town, or of their late masters. **1845** DOUGLASS *Narrative* 1 It is the wish of most masters within my knowledge to keep their slaves thus ignorant. **1893** PAGE in *Harper's Mag.* Dec. 158/2 It was the fact of the former companionship with his old master which . . . made him shut his eyes to infractions of the plantation law.

+5. *Master of life,* in Indian terminology or in imitation of this, the supreme manito or ruler over the forces of nature.

1822 MORSE *Rep. Indian Affairs* II. 21 The Master of life made us Indians. **1823** JAMES *Exped.* I. 118 They say that they have never seen the Master of life, and therefore can not pretend to personify him. **1831** R. COX *Adv. Columbia River* 66 The Master of Life had sent forth the Evil Spirit from the waters to punish them for their cruelty to the white people. **1839** HOFFMAN *Wild Scenes* 88 The vengeance of the Master of Life overtook the wretch.

***6.** *attrib.* Designating one who has perfected his skill in a particular trade or line of work.

See also MASTER MECHANIC.

1622 'MOURT' *Relation* 45 Of the Ships Company there went two of the Masters Mates, Master Clarke and Master Copin, the Master Gunner. **1654** JOHNSON *Wonder-w. Prov.* 194 The Master Canoneer is an active Ingineer also. **1708** *Boston News-Letter* 2–9 Feb. 2/2 Mr. John Austin a Ship Carpenter and Master Builder, was kill'd by a piece of Timber. **1794** *Ann. 3d Congress* 1428 The said master-armorers, each, [shall receive] fifty dollars per month. **1889** *Century Mag.* Jan. 403/1 The Chicago master plumbers then devised what is known as the Chicago plan.

+7. Special combinations.

Master chopper, one in charge of a gang of log-choppers; *m. swamper,* one in charge of swampers or road-makers in logging operations; *m. wagoner,* one in charge of a wagon train.

1848 PARKMAN in *Knickerb.* Oct. 312 He told Coates, the master-wagoner, that the commissary at the fort had given him an order for sick-rations. **1851** SPRINGER *Forest Life* 92 Then [come] the choppers, meaning those who select, fell, and cut the logs, one of whom is master chopper. *Ib.*, Next [come] the swampers, who cut and clear the roads through the forest to the fallen trees, one of whom is master swamper.

Master mechanic. An employer or foreman of mechanics. — **1838** *N.Y. Advertiser & Exp.* 14 Feb. 2/3 A master mechanic . . . applied for the loan of money at various times to pay off his hands. **1843** in Commons, etc. *Doc. Hist.* VIII. 222 The master-mechanic or boss, as he is technically termed. **1878** PINKERTON *Strikers* 375 The master mechanic and division superintendent, with an engine-wiper, boarded a locomotive. **1898** *Mo. So. Dakotan* I. 105 Every man, whether he pulled the throttle, shoveled the coal, punched the ticket or twisted the brake would be at the mercy of some whimsical master mechanic or superintendent.

***Master of art(s).** In a college or university, a degree higher than the baccalaureate, granted usually in the field of the liberal arts. — **1693** *Harvard Rec.* I. 345 It was voted, That Mr. Charles Chauncey shall be Diplomated Master of Arts. **1703** SEWALL *Diary* II. 81 In the afternoon Mr. Wells of Almsbury, is made a Master of Art. **1788** FRANKLIN *Autobiog.* 386 The College of Cambridge, of their own motion, presented me with the degree of Master of Arts. **1892** *Univ. of Chicago Quarterly Calendar* June 20/1 For the degree of Master of Arts, Master of Science, or Master of Philosophy, the candidate will be required [etc.].

+Master weed. A plant thought to be useful as a cure for rattlesnake bites. (Cf. RATTLESNAKE MASTER.) — **1843** MARRYAT *M. Violet* xxiv, I removed . . . the poultice of master weed.

***Masterwort.** **+1.** The American angelica. **+2.** =COW PARSNIP. — **(1) 1796** MORSE *Univ. Geog.* I. 189 Angelica or American Masterwort (*Angelica lucida*). **(2) 1833** EATON *Botany* (ed. 6) 172 *Heracleum lanatum*, master-wort, cow parsnip. . . . A large umbelliferous plant of a white woolly appearance. . . . Meadows and other damp places. . . . Very poisonous. **1857** GRAY *Botany* 152 *H[eracleum] lanatum.* . . . A very large, strong-scented plant, . . . in some places wrongly called *Masterwort.*

***Mast-fed,** *a.* [MAST.[2]] Of hogs: Fed or fattened on mast. — **1842** *S. Lit. Messenger* VIII. 63/1 The mast-fed swine and fallow deer supply them [the settlers] with meat. **1850** *Annual of Sci. Discovery* 98 Much the larger share of this [oil] is of inferior lard, made of mast-fed and still-fed hogs. **1900** H. ROBERTSON *Red Blood & Blue* 100 The 'razor-backed' hog, mast-fed, was the only meat fit to be hung up in the smoke-house.

Mast fleet. A fleet of vessels engaged in transporting masts. *Obs.* (Cf. MAST SHIP.) — **1696** SEWALL *Diary* I. 430 The Captain . . . informs us that twas the Mast-Fleet from England. **1708** *Boston News-Letter* 19–26 Jan. 2/2 The Mast Fleet . . . design upon the breaking up of the Weather . . . to imbrace the first opportunity of Sailing for Great Britain. **1712** SEWALL *Letter-Book* II. 9 Pursue that Affair, and as speedily as may be, that the Accounts may be sent by the Mast Fleet. **1760** ROWE *Letters* 369 There is a Convoy appointed for the mast fleet which will be here in this month.

***Mastic.** Also **mastick.** A tree of Florida (*Sideroxylon mastichodendron*) valued in shipbuilding; also, the wood or fruit of this. In full *mastic tree.* {1657–, in W. Indies} — **1775** ROMANS *Nat. Hist. Florida* App. 32 The peninsula affords in this place Lignum-Vitae, Mastick and Mahogany. **1837** WILLIAMS *Florida* 34 Scattering ovino and mastic trees, give it the appearance of a plantation. **1897** SUDWORTH *Arborescent Flora* 317.

***Mastiff.** A large powerful dog of a breed valued as watchdogs. Also *mastiff dog.* — **1619** *Va. House of Burgesses* 13 That no man do sell or give . . . to the Indians, . . . any English dog of quality, as a Mastive, Greyhound, [or] Blood hounde. **1652** *Conn. Rec.* III. 475 Ninigrett bought a great mastiff dog. **1867** EDWARDS *Shelby* 475 The fox-hound has more of wind than the mastiff. **1895** *Outing* XXVIII. 74/2 A good bear dog . . . must be a mongrel; a cross of the hound with the mastiff or bull-dog is the best.

Masting. {1627–}

1. Masts. {1757–} Also attrib.

1702 C. MATHER *Magnalia* (1853) II. 84 All her masting seemed blown away by the board. **a1752** W. DOUGLASS *Summary* II. 53n., In New-Hampshire and Province of Main, much good Ship Timber and Masting Trees. **1830** COOPER *Water Witch* III. viii, The ship was so small as to need little iron-work in her masting. **1871** *Harper's Mag.* July 184.

+2. The felling of trees for masts. *Obs.* Also attrib.
1718 *Mass. H. Rep. Jrnls.* II. 109 A Proclamation for . . . the Protection of His Majesty's good Subjects in their just Rights . . . of Logging, Masting and Tember. **1726** PENHALLOW *Indian Wars* 68 Col. Hilton . . . being deeply engaged in the masting affair . . . went out with seventeen men to peel off the bark for fear of worms. **1764** *N.H. Hist. Soc. Coll.* IX. 145 At night Prince returned from masting. **1792** BELKNAP *Hist. New-Hampshire* III. 3 Persons who have been employed in surveying, masting, hunting and scouting.

+**Masting pine.** =MAST PINE. — **a1752** W. DOUGLASS *Summary* II. 52 The Pines may be subdivided into the Masting, or white Pine [etc.]. **1832** WILLIAMSON *Maine* I. 110 So literally is this erect and lofty masting-pine the greatest ornament of our forests, that it was adopted as one of the emblems in the shield of our State coat of arms.

Mast-maker. One whose occupation is making masts. {1666} — **1789** *Boston Directory* 180 Cushing Benjamin, mast-maker. **1792** BENTLEY *Diary* I. 333 Becket, James, Lieut., Mast Maker, Derby Street. **1822** *Ann. 17th Congress* 1 Sess. I. 279 The amount paid for . . . carpenters, mast makers, boat builders [etc.]. **1857** DUNLAP *Book Forms* 191 The lien exists in favor of . . . Carpenters, Blacksmiths, Mastmakers, Boatbuilders [etc.].

+**Mastman.** (See quot. 1890.) — **1839** BRIGGS *H. Franco* I. 236 All hands call him dismal Jerry, except Mike, the mast man, and he calls him Sergeant Longshanks. **1890** *Cent.* 3653/3 *Mastman,* . . . a seaman stationed at a mast in a man-of-war to keep the ropes clear and in order.

+**Mast pine.** The white pine (*Pinus strobus*) of the eastern states. — **1792** BELKNAP *Hist. New-Hampshire* III. 103 [White pines] are distinguished by the name of mast-pine. **1832** WILLIAMSON *Maine* II. 95 [In] preserving the mast pines and ship-timber, he had the patronage and aid of the Governor.

Mast ship. A ship engaged in transporting masts. *Obs.* {1666–} (Cf. MAST FLEET.) — **1688** SEWALL *Diary* I. 205 Goe to the Great Iland, saw the Mast-Ship sail. **1695** — *Letter-Book* I. 152 My Letter fell short by the Mast-Ships, and must now wait the next conveyance. **1707** — *Diary* II. 196 They might have been expected before the Mast-Ships. **1774** J. ANDREWS *Letters* 45 A mast ship had arriv'd at Portsmouth with thirty chests of tea on board. **1825** ADAMS *Annals Portsmouth* 175 The mast ships were usually stationed there to take in their cargoes.

***Mat.** +A plaited or woven article made by American Indians from bark, grass, etc., and freq. used as a covering.
1607 in Smith *Works* (1910) I. p. xlii, We found here a *Wiroans* (for so they call their kynges) who satt upon a matt of Reedes, with his people about him. **1622** 'MOURT' *Relation* 19 We found a little path to certaine heapes of sand, one whereof was covered with old Matts. **1647** ELIOT *Day-Breaking* 1 Wigwams [are] Indian houses or tents made of barks or matts. **1677** WINTHROP in *Phil. Trans.* XII. 1066 The Natives commonly Thresh it [the corn] as they gather it, dry it well on Mats in the Sun, and then bestow it in holes in the Ground. **1821** NUTTALL *Travels Arkansa* 193 [The Osages'] houses were chiefly covered with hand-wove matts of bulrushes. Their baskets and bed matts of this material, were parti-coloured and very handsome. **1866** *Rep. Indian Affairs* 83 With but few exceptions all of the Indians upon this reservation, at present, dwell in tents built of skins and mats.
attrib. **1806** LEWIS in *L. & Clark Exped.* IV. (1905) 66 The salt marshes also produce . . . Bull rushes and the Cattail flagg. of the two last the natives make great use in preparing their mat bags &c. **1807** GASS *Journal* 203 We encamped at two mat-lodges of the natives. **a1861** WINTHROP *Canoe & Saddle* iii. 33 Hickory shirts and woolen blankets are worn instead of skin raiment, mat aprons, and Indian blankets.

***Match.**

*1. *Mil.* A line or cord of hemp, flax, etc., impregnated with a preparation that causes it to burn at a uniform rate when ignited, and used in discharging guns. Now hist.
1622 'MOURT' *Relation* 53 The rest called for a fire-brand to light their matches. **1650** *Conn. Rec.* I. 544 Euery male person . . . shall bee allwayes provided with . . . two fathom of Match to euery Matchlock. **1702** *Essex Inst. Coll.* XLII. 160 Inventory of ship . . . a small parcell of Match. **1759** *Newport Mercury* 14 Aug. 3/2 List of Stores, &c. taken at Niagara. Two 14 Pounders, . . . 200 Wt. of Match, 500 Hand Grenades, 2 Cohorns and 2 Mortars, mounted.

2. =FRICTION MATCH. {1845–}
1844 *Graham's Mag.* March 133 Six for a fip! Six for a fip! Matches! Matches! **1854** *Putnam's Mag.* Sept. 247/1 He entered the house and speedily returned with a box of matches. **1898** PAGE *Red Rock* 401 Matches were only five cents a box. **1912** NICHOLSON *Hoosier Chron.* 207 He swung round . . . , fumbling in his waistcoat for a match.

3. Attrib. and comb. with *factory, holder*, etc.
1781 *Va. State P.* I. 573 The Brigs that are here, are in want of Military Stores, such as Cartridge paper, match rope, Powder & Grape shott. **1851** CIST *Cincinnati* 50 Occupations [include] . . . Match makers, 6. **1853** *Holyoke Diaries* 187 Match Factory burnt in the night. **1884** *Harper's Mag.* Dec. 134/2 A porcelain match-holder half full of matches.

Match box. {1786–} A box for friction matches. {1850– (Mayhew *Lond. Labour.*)} — **1850** JUDD *R. Edney* 211 She pointed to the mantel-piece for the match-box. **1859** *Rep. Comm. Patents* 1858 I. 734, I am well aware that match-boxes . . . [have been] arranged [etc.]. **1898** CAHAN *Imported Bridegroom* 209 He would bring . . . some useful or decorative trifle—a match-box, a towel-ring.

+**Match case.** =prec. — **1861** *Rep. Comm. Patents 1860* I. 359 Improved Portable Match Case. **1877** HOWELLS *Out of the Question* II. ii Blake takes out his match-case and strikes a light.

+**Matchcoat.** [From Chippewa *matshigoté*.] A mantle of fur, feathers, etc., worn by American Indians, or a cloth garment somewhat resembling this obtained by the Indians from white traders. Now hist.
1638 *Md. Archives* IV. 30, 1. old match coate. 1. latin pott. **1676** *Ib.* II. 488 Voted by the house tht. Match coats Corne Powder and Shott be purchased and forthwith delivered to the friend Indians. **1709** LAWSON *Carolina* 18 [The Santees'] chief Doctor . . . was warmly . . . clad with a Match-Coat, made of Turkies Feathers. **1783** FRANKLIN *Writings* IX. 138 All property, . . . except the Savage's temporary Cabin, his Bow, his Matchcoat, and other little Acquisitions . . . , seems to me to be the Creature of public Convention. **1823** DODDRIDGE *Logan* III. iv, Poor brother, he is almost naked. Here brother put this match-coat on him. **1888** HALE *Franklin in France* II. 470 'Matchcoat' was a word in familiar use among Indians on the frontier.

Matchcock. In a matchlock gun, a lever, hammer, spring, etc., that brings the match into contact with the powder. *Obs.* Also attrib. — **1636** *Plymouth Col. Rec.* XI. 14 One pound of powder and foure poundes of bullets wth. match foure fathome for eich matchcock peece. **1642** *Ib.* 180 They haue four fathom of match att all times reddy for euery matchcocke. **1661** *Plymouth Rec.* I. 44 For the use of his man John Rose one matchcock gun with a fier locke.

Match game. {1888–} +A game agreed upon and played as a test of superiority by two rival athletic teams; a match. — **1868** *N.Y. Herald* 3 July 10/3 A match game of base ball was played yesterday. **1871** BAGG *At Yale* 316 An important 'match game' is quite certain to attract a good many spectators. **1880** N. BROOKS *Fairport Nine* ix. 112, I wonder if we wont lick the White Bears, the next time we have a match game with them? **1897** *Outing* XXX. 464/1 This was the origin of the great match game.

Match girl. A girl who sells matches. {1852–} — **1852** *Knickerb.* XXIX. 165 She does not allow match-girls . . . to be begging about the basement-windows. **1863** 'M. HARLAND' *Husks* 28 You gave this match-girl no money, I hope? **1876** *Wide Awake* 217/1 Several now remembered to have seen [them] as rag-pickers and match-girls.

Matchlock. An early form of gunlock containing a match or match cord; a gun having such a lock. Now hist. {1698–} Also attrib.
1637 *Conn. Rec.* I. 16 Every military man is to have . . . one pounde of match if his peece be a match locke. **1643** *Ib.* 455 The goods of Tho. Scott: . . . 1 match locke muskett . . . 1 shreding knife. **1678** *New Castle Court Rec.* 241, 18 match Locks. **1756** *Lett. to Washington* I. 186 The French have no Match locks, powd[er] and Lead. **1832** WATSON *Hist. Tales* 35 The Indians . . . called [the Dutch] . . . Sankhicanni, the fire workers, in allusion to their use of matchlocks. **1870** *Nation* 3 March 132/2 The same mixture of curiosity and amusement with which they would watch a company of matchlock-men.

+**Match race.** A race run as a match or competition in speed. — **1836** SIMMS *Mellichampe* xviii, If by . . . a match-race on foot with an Indian runner, I could do the creature a service, I could go to work cheerfully. **1852** REYNOLDS *Hist. Illinois* 292 This race . . . was the most celebrated match race, that ocurred [*sic*] in Illinois, in early times. **1874** B. F. TAYLOR *World on Wheels* 105 The train . . . ran a match race with a train on the Michigan Central, and reached Chicago twenty-five minutes ahead.

+**Match safe.** (See quot. 1875.) — **1864** *Hist. North-Western Soldiers' Fair* 81 [Donations include] 24 bottles perfumery, 1 match safe, 1 cigar case. **1875** KNIGHT 1410 *Match-safe*, a box to contain matches for use. Usually hung up near a gas-bracket or elsewhere within ready reach. **1882** *Century Mag.* Oct. 890/1 Ornamental clay-ware . . . when finished will go to the pottery to be fired, and return as . . . grotesque monsters for match-safes. **1893** *Outing* May 124/2 A water-tight match-safe . . . should be taken.

Materialize, *v.* {1710–} +*intr.* To assume a bodily form; to become real; to appear; to come about. {1891} — **1884** MATTHEWS in *Harper's Mag.* May 911/1 [The] ghosts . . . gave dark séances and manifested and materialized. **1885** 'CRADDOCK' *Prophet* 18 Some fifteen or twenty hounds . . . suddenly materialized among the bee-hives and the althea bushes. **1887** *Boston Journal* 12 Dec. 2/6 That attack upon the Interstate Commerce law, which was predicted to occur as soon as Congress met, does not materialize. **1890** *Congress. Rec.* 31 July 7984/1, I think it will be conceded that the promised 'mule' is not likely to materialize. **1904** *Omaha Bee* 28 June 4 How soon will those elevators and mills promised last winter materialize?

+**Material train.** A train that hauls materials for construction or repair work. — **1865** *Nation* I. 174/1 He was going up the road, he said, to see about the loading of a material train. **1902** GORDON *Recoll. Lynchburg* 42 The trip had to be made on the flats of a material train.

Mathook.[1] =MATTOCK. *Obs.* {a1734–}
1646 *Essex Probate Rec.* I. 89 One crow, one andiron, one mathook. **1662** *Ib.* 378 Five axes & a mathooke. **1758** CALEB REA *Journal* 33 [The regulars'] method was to digg round ye Stumps with Mathooks cutting off ye out Side Roots, then fastening to it a Tecle. **1895** *Home Missionary* Oct. 314 [The passengers] are equipped with fishing-rods, guns, spades, and mathooks.

+Mathook.[2] A form of reaping hook. *Obs.* — **1775** ROMANS *Nat. Hist. Florida* 178, I would advise the introduction of the short scythe and hook, called in New York government segt and mat hook.

Matinee. A theatrical performance held in the afternoon or, formerly, in the morning. {1880-} Also attrib. — **1858** *Boston Ev. Gazette* 6 March, A dramatic matinee is a novel idea. Edwin Booth gave one on Thursday morning last, at Richmond, in aid of Mt. Vernon fund. **1860** E. COWELL *Diary* 223 Sam not only sings at night at the Canterbury, but also one song in the Matinee at 2 P.M. **1882** MCCABE *New York* 295 All the theatres give special performances, termed 'Matinees,' in the afternoon. **1899** VAN DYKE *Fisherman's Luck* 101 The matinée-girl is not likely to have a very luminous or truthful idea of existence floating around in her pretty head. **1904** A. DALE *Wanted, a Cook* 208 What do you say to mentioning matinée tickets once a week?

+Matlay, *n*. A pile or heap of sugar cane designed for seed placed in mats or layers and covered with earth for protection from cold during the winter. (Cf. MATTRESS 2.) — **1853** *Harper's Mag.* Nov. 756/2 In the furrow, the cane preserved in the 'matlays' is laid in two or three parallel lines, and well lapped.

+Matlay, *v. tr.* To place (sugar cane) in a matlay. — **1827** in Commons, etc. *Doc. Hist.* I. 215 Begun matlaying cane—weather too dry. **1837** in *Ib.* 221 Matlayed cane on the 4th and 5th; these cane being even then too much sprouted, kept badly.

Matriculant. A student registering or matriculating in a college. {1897-} — **1860** *Harper's Mag.* March 570/1 While I was at —— College, among a number of new matriculants was one from Green County, who was very 'green' himself. **1883** *American* V. 390 They are ready to favor the demand upon matriculants for a preliminary qualification.

Matrimony vine. A garden plant of the genus *Lycium*, esp. *L. barbarum.* {1866-} — **1817-8** EATON *Botany* (1822) 343 *Lycium barbarum*, matrimony vine. E[xotic]. **1847** WOOD *Botany* 449 *L[ycium] Barbarum.* Matrimony Vine. . . . Flowers greenish-purple. Berries orange-red. **1899** *Animal & Plant Lore* 106 Matrimony vine planted near a house and thriving means matrimonial ill luck. Cape Ann.

Matronize, *v.* {1754-} +*tr.* and *intr.* To act the part of a matron; to preside over. Also *vbl. n.* — **1877** *Rep. Indian Affairs* 7 The only individual to matronize is his family cook. **1883** *Century Mag.* May 283/1 The matronizing of a houseful of hungry school-boys. **1897** HOWELLS *Landlord Lion's Head* 204 The lady who was matronizing the tea recognized him.

Matross. {1639-} +During the Revolutionary War, an American private soldier in the artillery service. Also attrib. — **1775** *Jrnls. Cont. Congress* III. 309 Resolved, That a company of Matrosses . . . be immediately raised in New York, for the defence of Hudson's river. **1776** *Ib.* IV. 74 That the general assemblies, conventions or councils, or committees of safety . . . be desired to raise . . . one company of matrosses, consisting of forty privates, in each colony. **1777** *Ib.* IX. 822 Resolved, . . . to order the companies of matrosses in the service of the State of Maryland to join the army immediately. *c***1835** FOBES *Arnold's Exped.* 48 Two commissions were forwarded to me, one an ensign's commission in the infantry, the other a lieutenant's in a matross company. **1855** SARGENT *Braddock's Exped.* 136 A matross is an artillery soldier of a rank inferior to the bombardier or gunner.

***Mattock.** An implement provided with a long handle, used chiefly for grubbing. (Cf. MATHOOK.[1]) — **1636** *Watertown Rec.* I. I. 3 Ordered . . . every man that is Souldier or watchman to come . . . with wheelbarrow, mattock [etc.]. **1759** *Newport* (R.I.) *Mercury* 14 Aug. 3/2 250 Mattocks, . . . 12 Whipsaws, [etc.]. **1813** *Niles' Reg.* III. 296/1 [List of Military Supplies:] 250 mattocks. **1881** *Rep. Indian Affairs* 169 All the land cultivated by them is broken with mattock, spade, and hoe.

+Mattowacca. (See quotations.) — **1884** GOODE, etc. *Fisheries* I. 608 The name 'Mattowacca' is of Indian origin. **1896** JORDAN & EVERMANN *Check-List* 281 *Pomolobus mediocris.* . . . Tailor Herring; Mattowacca. **1911** *Rep. Fisheries 1908* 312 Mattowacca (*Dorosoma cepedianum*).—A poor food fish found on the Atlantic coast from Cape Cod to Florida, ascending rivers. It is called 'hickory shad' and 'hicks,' particularly in the South.

***Mattress.** Also †**matteris, mattrass.**

***1.** A sack or case, usually of some strong fabric, filled with feathers, straw, hair, moss, etc., and serving as a bed or part of a bed.

1648 *Essex Probate Rec.* I. 112 One matteris, one pillow & other beding. **1776** *Jrnls. Cont. Congress* IV. 51 Colonel Francis had left in the hands of Mr. Douw two mattrasses. **1812** *Austin P.* (1924) I. 205 You must purchase a Mattress at Orleans that you will want on your return. **1904** PRINGLE *Rice Planter* 83 A small mattress is put in the plantation wagon . . . and on that the piano is put.

2. (See quot. 1829 and cf. MATLAY *n.*)

1829 SHERWOOD *Gaz. Georgia* (ed. 2) 255 The stacks or banks in which seed cane is preserved during winter, are called mattresses. **1833** SILLIMAN *Man. Sugar Cane* 12 [Canes] are cut near the ground, and carted to the vicinity of the fields where they are to be planted; being formed . . . into long beds about fifteen feet wide, which are called *mattresses.* **1850** *Rep. Comm. Patents 1849: Agric.* 423 The cane was spoiled in the mattress, by the continued warm weather after it was mattressed.

3. Attrib. in sense 1 with *bed, cover, factory.*

1848 ROBINSON *Santa Fe Exped.* 15 They have good mattress beds, which are spread on the floors. **1889** BRAYLEY *Boston Fire Dept.* 297 This fire was discovered . . . in the mattress factory. **1908** *Sears, Roebuck & Co. Cat.* No. 118, 865 *Cretonne* . . . used for furniture coverings and draperies, and in large quantities for mattress covers.

***Mattress-maker.** One whose occupation is to make mattresses. — **1865** CUMMING *Hospital Life* (1866) 172/1 He has had comfortable cotton mattresses made by a regular mattress-maker. **1880** CABLE *Grandissimes* 336, I could be . . . a mattress-maker. **1892** *York County Hist. Rev.* 51 They are enabled to furnish this husk prepared for the mattress-maker.

Maul, *n.

***1.** A heavy mallet for pounding or hammering.

1698 CHAMBERLAIN *Lithobolia* (1914) 58 Throwing about . . . Hammers, Mauls, . . . and other Domestick Utensils. **1792** BELKNAP *Hist. New-Hampshire* III. 117 Splints of the wood of ash are obtained by pounding it with a maul. **1832** WILLIAMSON *Maine* I. 106 [The black ash] is easily cloven . . . by means of a maul.

+2. (See quotation.)

1871 DE VERE 617 *Maul and wedges*, . . . used to denote the whole of a man's possessions, his movables.

Maul, *v. Also †**mawl, mall.** +*tr.* To split (fence rails) with a maul and wedges.

1677 in *Virginia Mag.* II. 168 (Th.), [The armed men] were . . . commanded to goe to work, fall trees and mawl and toat railes. **1686** in P. A. Bruce *Econ. Hist. Virginia* (1896) I. 318*n.*, Johnson . . . doth [impower you] . . . to fall, mall, and set up . . . 400 panels of sufficient post and rails. **1751** in Chalkley *Scotch-Irish Settlement Va.* III. 297 To Archibald Stewart, contracting, mauling and laying 6700 rails. **1784** SMYTH *Tour* I. 335 *Fence rails* . . . are made out of trees cut or sawed into lengths of eleven or twelve feet, which again are mauled or split into rails from four to six inches thick. **1840** *S. Lit. Messenger* VI. 509/2 Don't you see him yonder mauling rails? **1894** in J. H. Bryant *Poems* 19 John . . . 'mauled' rails at the rate of a hundred a day.

Mauler. {1618-} +A rail-splitter. — **1788** WASHINGTON *Diaries* III. 306 The cutters and maulers had shifted to the East side of the Plantation in order to get Rails.

+Maul oak. An evergreen oak (*Quercus chrysolepsis*) found in California. — **1884** SARGENT *Rep. Forests* 146 Live Oak. Maul Oak. Valparaiso Oak. **1897** SUDWORTH *Arborescent Flora* 163 Cañon Live Oak. . . . [Commonly called] Maul Oak (Cal.).

+Mauvaise(s) terre(s). [F. tr. of Sioux *Makochi Sica* 'bad lands.'] =BAD LANDS. — **1854** E. E. HALE *Kanzas and Nebraska* 67 La Mauvaise Terre. **1855** in *S. Dak. Hist. Coll.* I. 382 Fort Pierre is situated in the country called 'Mauvaise Terre,' and for hundreds of miles around, there is no grass susceptible of being made into hay for winter food. **1857** *Harper's Wkly.* 21 March 177 The western parts of Kansas and Nebraska are, in the picturesque language of the French, who have left in their original appellation a trace of the early rule of that great nation, 'Mauvaises Terres,' or 'Bad Lands.' **1904** WHEELER *Trail of Louis & Clarke* I. 275 It is the fringes of the well-known *Mauvaises Terres* to the south, through the heart of which the Little Missouri flows,—a land weird, spectacular, fantastic, unique.

+Maverick, *n.* [From Samuel A. *Maverick*, a Texas cattle-owner who neglected to brand the calves of his herd.]

1. *W.* A calf, cow, or steer bearing no brand and hence legitimately claimed by its finder. Also attrib.

1869 *Overland Mo.* III. 127 One Maverick formerly owned such immense herds that many of his animals unavoidably escaped his rouanne in the spring, were taken up by his neighbors, branded and called 'mavericks.' **1884** NYE *Baled Hay* 73 [He] doesn't know a coyote from a Maverick steer. **1888** ROOSEVELT in *Century Mag.* Feb. 507/1 Mavericks, . . . when found on the round-up, . . . are sold for the benefit of the association. **1893** — *Wilderness Hunter* 27 On our way we came across a bunch of cattle, among which the sharp eyes of my foreman detected a maverick two-year-old heifer. **1898** POST *10 Yrs. Cowboy* 396 Any unbranded calf which is found not following a cow is called a 'maverick.' **1923** J. H. COOK *On Old Frontier* 34 You better stay here and catch mavericks.

2. *transf.* **a.** (See quotation.) **b.** (See quotation.) **c.** One entirely free to act as he pleases; an unattached person; a 'lone wolf.' *colloq.* Also attrib.

(a) 1890 *Cent.* 3666/1 *Maverick*, . . . anything dishonestly obtained, as a saddle, mine, or piece of land. (Western U.S.) **(b) 1893** *Congress. Rec.* 16 Dec. 291/1 [Mr. Raum's] successor in office . . . finds this charge as a kind of 'Maverick' wandering around, and he brands it and claims it as his own discovery. **(c) 1901** *McClure's Mag.* Dec. 147 Occasionally they found a maverick legislator, or traded for one. **1902** LORIMER *Lett. Merchant* 103 There isn't an ounce of real meanness in Ezra's whole body, but he's just naturally and unintentionally a maverick. **1903** *Critic* XLIII. 358/2, I felt as if I . . . for once was a happy maverick soul in the world at large. **1905** *Springfield W. Repub.* 20 Oct. 2 Mr. Jerome begins a telling appeal to the masses by saying: 'I am running as a maverick; I have no man's brand upon me.' **1906** 'O. HENRY' *Heart of West* 145 Here, you maverick, what are you doing in my wagon?

+Maverick. *v.* [From noun.] **1.** *tr.* (See quot. 1890.) **2.** *intr.* To stray or roam about as a maverick. — **(1) 1890** *Cent.* 3666/1 *Maverick*, . . . to seize or brand (an animal) as a maverick; hence, to take possession of without any legal claim; appropriate dishonestly or illegally: as, to *maverick* a piece of land. **1894** *McClure's Mag.* III. 115/1 Cowboys . . .

strove together eagerly and without ceasing, mavericking right and left everything they could get their hands on. **1897** LEWIS *Wolfville* 253 While he's treed an' can't come down to his claim, a passel of sharps ups and mavericks it. *a***1918** G. STUART *On Frontier* II. 167 It was only a step from 'mavericking' any calf without a brand. **(2) 1910** RAINE *B. O'Connor* 203 It hadn't penetrated my think-tank that this was your hacienda when I came mavericking in.

***Mavis.** +The brown thrasher or French mocking bird. — **1865** BURROUGHS in *Atlantic Mo.* XV. 523/2 The Mavis, or Red Thrush, sneaks and skulks like a culprit. **1917** *Birds of Amer.* III. 179 Brown Thrasher. *Toxostoma rufum.* . . . [Also called] Mavis.

+**Mawmouth.** (See quot. 1890.) Also attrib. — **1840** SIMMS *Border Beagles* I. 213 Here . . . I find you, like a cursed maw-mouth that grows blind when he sees a worm wriggle. **1856** — *Eutaw* 365, We could not withstand the bait, any more than a hungry mawmouth perch in midsummer. **1890** *Cent.* 3666/3 *Mawmouth,* . . . the calico-, grass-, or strawberry-bass, *Pomoxys sparoides,* a centrarchoid fish. (Local, U.S.)

+**Max.** (See first quotation.) *Obs.* Also attrib. — **1851** HALL *College Words* 197 At Union College, he who received the highest possible number of marks, which is one hundred, in each study, for a term, is said to *take Max* (or maximum); to be a *Max scholar. Ib.,* On the Merit Roll all the Maxs are clustered at the top. **1862** STRONG *Cadet Life W. Point* 64 [He was] working out an unmistakable 'max' in the mathematical section-room.

Maxim gun. [Sir Hiram Stevens *Maxim,* Anglo-American inventor (1840–1916).] An automatic machine gun. {1885–} — **1890** *Cent.* 3560/3 The Maxim gun is a single-barreled machine-gun invented by Hiram Maxim, an American. **1898** in *Congress. Rec.* 20 Feb. (1900) 1970/2 General Aguinaldo has now . . . 2 Maxim guns, and a dynamite gun.

***May.** [The fifth month of the year.] Used attrib. in special collocations.

May court, a session of a court that meets regularly in May; *Mayfish,* a species of killifish (*Fundulus majalis*); *May star,* the star flower (*Trientalis americana*); *May sucker,* =CUTLIPS b; *May wheat,* on the grain exchange, wheat placed on the market in May.

1836 *S. Lit. Messenger* II. 434/1 [The courthouse is] embosomed in a grove of locusts, which at the May Court fill the air with their balsamic odor. **1850** S. F. COOPER *Rural Hours* 85 The elegant silvery May-star is seen here and there; by its side the tall, slender mitella. **1884** GOODE, etc. *Fisheries* I. 614 The 'Rabbit-mouth,' 'Hare-lip,' 'Split-mouth,' or 'May Sucker' is found in abundance in many rivers of Tennessee. **1896** JORDAN & EVERMANN *Check-List Fishes* 309 *Fundulus majalis.* . . . Killifish; Mayfish; Rockfish. **1902** NORRIS *Pit* viii, I guess the visible supply of May wheat in the Chicago market is cornered.

May apple.

1. An American plant belonging to any one of various species of the genus *Podophyllum,* esp. *P. peltatum;* also, the fruit of this plant. {1733–}

1737 BRICKELL *N. Carolina* 23 The May-Apple, so call'd from its having Apples in the Month of May. **1792** IMLAY *Western Territory* 210 May-apple. This apple is produced from an annual plant which is among the first vegetables that come forward in the spring. **1814** PURSH *Flora Amer.* II. 366 *Podophyllum peltatum.* . . . The fruit is the size of a common plum, green, eatable, and known by the name of May-apple. **1878** in Summers *Ann. S. W. Va.* 1567 These hill-sides . . . abound with Indian turnips, mayapples, sweet and bitter sarsaparilla [etc.]. **1912** COBB *Back Home* 76 In summer there would be . . . heaps of the sickish-smelling May apples.

attrib. **1886** *Harper's Mag.* June 58/2 A local store-keeper told the people . . . to go out and gather all the mandrake or 'May-apple' root they could find. **1899** GOING *Flowers* 56 The circular May-apple leaves have been folded back against their stalks.

+**2.** (See quotation and cf. HONEYSUCKLE APPLE.)

1872 DE VERE 400 The same term of *May-Apple* is not unfrequently applied to a large, globular excrescence produced by the sting of a wasp on the miniature flowers of the Swamp Honeysuckle (*Azalea mediflora*), and, on account of its frequent occurrence, occasionally to the shrub itself.

+**3.** A species of mallow found in Texas.

1891 COULTER *Bot. W. Texas* I. 43 *Malvaviscus Drummondii* . . . [grows] from the Rio Grande to the Colorado and northeastward. . . . Known as 'may-apple.' The scarlet fruit, produced in late summer, is eaten both raw and cooked.

+**May basket.** A small basket of gifts, especially of flowers, left at a friend's door on May Day. Also transf. — **1869** FULLER *Flower Gatherers* 43 We found the contents of the May-baskets carefully preserved in vases on the library table. **1911** LINCOLN *Cap'n Warren's Wards* 30, I know that there must be some reason bigger than 'implicit trust' and the other May-baskets for his appointing me in his will. **1920** — *Mr. Pratt* 115 She said he could . . . hang his Maybaskets on somebody else's door —or words to that effect.

May beetle. Any of various beetles of the genus *Phyllophaga* or related genera. {1720–} — **1838** *Mass. Zool. Survey Rep.* 65 The Melolonthæ are known in England by the names of dorrs or chaffers, and in this country, by those of dorr-bugs, and may-beetles. **1871** *Ill. Agric. Soc. Trans.* VIII. 172 The manure is . . . instrumental in breeding the white-grub (May-beetle) which often ruins our meadows and strawberry beds. **1884** ROE *Nature's Story* 110 The crow . . . is the worst enemy of the May-beetle and its larvæ.

Maybird. {1864–} +**1.** In the southern states, the bobolink. +**2.** In the eastern United States, the knot or freckled sandpiper, *Calidris canutus.* — **(1)** *c***1844** *Nat. Hist. N.Y., Zoology* II. 144 The Boblink, or Bob-o'link . . . is known in others [*sc.* states] by the various names of Reed-bird, May-bird, Meadow-bird, . . . and Skunk Black-bird. **1903** PRINGLE *Rice Planter* 12 Rice planted between these seasons falls a prey to birds,—May-birds in the spring and rice-birds in August. **1917** *Birds of Amer.* II. 241 Bobolink. *Dolichonyx oryzivorus.* . . . [Also called] May-bird. **(2) 1917** *Ib.* I. 231 Knot. *Tringa canutus.* . . . [Also called] May-bird.

***May blossom.** =MAYFLOWER 2. — **1871** *Scribner's Mo.* II. 102 Tenderest of all in yonder woods, where hepatica, and May blossoms, and Quaker ladies twinkle into life.

May bug. =MAY BEETLE. {1698–} — **1835** *Harvardiana* I. 314 The multiplicity of May-bugs . . . rendered writing by candle-light highly inconvenient. **1874** *Dept. Agric. Rep. 1873* 152 The white grub of the cornfield . . . is the larva of the May-bug, *Lachnosterna.* **1882** *Vt. Agric. Rep.* VII. 72 The May or June bug which is so common makes the white grub.

May cherry. a. An early cherry or similar tree. {1664–} +**b.** = JUNE BERRY. — **1760** WASHINGTON *Diaries* I. 145 Grafted 40 Cherry—viz: 12 Bullock Hearts — (a large black May Cherry). **1797** HAWKINS *Letters* 111 Here vegetation begins to show itself and here I saw the may cherry found. **1867** *Ill. Agric. Soc. Trans.* VII. 508 Central Illinois is favorable to the production of the May Cherry. **1884** SARGENT *Rep. Forests* 84 *Amelanchier Canadensis.* . . . Service Tree. May Cherry.

Maycock.[1] (See MACOCK.)

+**Maycock.**[2] =MAYPOP. — **1709** LAWSON *Carolina* 95 The Maycock bears a glorious Flower, and Apple of an agreeable Sweet, mixt with an acid Taste.

+**Maycock.**[3] *local.* The black-bellied plover, *Squatarola squatarola.* — **1888** G. TRUMBULL *Names of Birds* 192 [The black-bellied plover is] known also at West Barnstable, Mass., as May cock. **1917** *Birds of Amer.* I. 256.

May duke (cherry). A dark-red, sour variety of the hybrid duke cherry. {1718–} — *a***1811** HENRY *Camp. Quebec* 35 The fruit was as large as a May-duke cherry. **1833** *Knickerb.* II. 346 Cherries that ripen in the fifth month, by the world's people called 'May-dukes.' **1874** *Vt. Board Agric. Rep.* II. 359 [The] May Duke, Late Duke, and other Dukes . . . are hardly less hardy than plums.

Mayflower. {1626–}

1. *Hist.* The name of the vessel in which the Pilgrim Fathers reached Plymouth, Mass., in 1620. Also attrib.

1629 in Bradford *Hist. Plym. Plant.* 296 We have allso sent some servants in ye ship called the Talbut, that wente hence latly; but these came in ye May-flower. **1669** N. MORTON *New England's Memorial* (1855) 14 Another ship was hired at London, . . . called the Mayflower. **1870** W. BOYD in *Boston Daily Times* 10 Aug., Every Mayflower native . . . may safely 'bet his pile' . . . that England won't stand still. **1885** CRAWFORD *Amer. Politician* 22 John Harrington . . . even had a teapot that had come over in the Mayflower. **1899** CHESNUTT *Wife of His Youth* 29 The memory of the governor and the judge and . . . the Mayflower pilgrim makes you strive to excel.

transf. **1887** J. KIRKLAND *Zury* 4 They are good things, these 'prairie schooners,' . . . the 'Mayflowers of the West.'

+**2.** Any one of various American spring-blooming plants, especially the trailing arbutus (*Epigaea repens*) of the eastern United States.

1778 CARVER *Travels* 520 May Flowers, Jessamine, Honeysuckles, Rock Honeysuckles. . . . I shall not enter into a minute description of the flowers above-recited. **1840** *S. Lit. Messenger* VI. 518/2 The little May-flower, earliest and sweetest of our forest-flowers, has passed away. **1867** *Amer. Naturalist* I. 154 In the books, this plant is known as the '*Epigea repens,*' but otherwise as the Trailing Arbutus, May Flower, and Ground Laurel. **1884** HOWELLS *S. Lapham* iv, The tints of her cheeks and temples were such as suggested May-flowers and apple-blossoms. **1899** GOING *Flowers* 268 First and sweetest of these is the trailing-arbutus or May-flower.

May fly. 1. A slender, fragile, neuropterous insect of the order Ephemerida. **2.** An artificial fly for anglers made to resemble this. {1651–3–} — **(1) 1854** EMMONS *Agric. N.Y.* V. 187 *Ephemeridae.* Mayfly is the common name for the insects of this family. **1884** [see EARWIG]. **(2) 1872** *Harper's Mag.* Aug. 348/1 The major's May-fly was the first that touched the mirror-like surface of the water.

+**May haw.** A small hawthorn (*Crataegus aestivalis*) common in the southern states. {1884–} — **1868** *Amer. Naturalist* II. 468 [Deer] visit the ponds in which the May-haw grows, the fruit of which is juicy with the flavor of the apple. **1884** SARGENT *Rep. Forests* 83.

***Mayor.**

+**1.** In colonial times, a member of a town or borough council chosen annually to preside over its deliberations.

Before the Revolution an American mayor was not an independent executive officer, though he was sometimes entrusted with the regulation of taverns, supervision of markets, hearing of cases at law, etc. He was appointed by the colonial governor, selected by the councilmen, or, rarely, elected by popular vote.

*a***1649** WINTHROP *Hist.* II. 219 The woman was arraigned before the mayor. **1686** in Munsell *Annals Albany* II. 71 The mayor and any three or more of the aldermen, and any three or more of the assistants . . . shall be called the common council. **1701** PENN *Phila. Charter*, The Mayor and Recorder . . . have power to take recognizance of debts. **1759** FRANKLIN *Hist. Rev. of Pa.* 292 The Mayor of Philadelphia took the Lead in this turbulent Transaction.

+**2.** The chief executive officer of a town or city, elected by direct popular vote for a term of from one to four years and serving with a council or board of aldermen.

1796 MORSE *Amer. Geog.* I. 552 A city court is held by the mayor, recorder, and aldermen [of Philadelphia] four times a year. **1812** *Ann. 12th Congress* 1 Sess. II. 2284 The corporation of the City of Washington shall be composed of a mayor, a board of aldermen, and a board of common council, to be elected by ballot. **1843** *Phila. Select Council Jrnl.* 8 June 111 The President laid before Council a communication from the Mayor. **1885** *Century Mag.* April 822 The mayor is almost certain to be infinitely superior in character to the average alderman. **1913** *World Almanac 1914* 688 The government of a city by a commission, instead of by a Mayor and other city officials, was first instituted in Galveston, Tex., in 1901.

Mayordomo. {*c*1645–} *S.W.* [Sp.] +**a.** The overseer or manager of a mission, ranch, or hacienda. +**b.** One having charge of an acequia.

Cf. MAJOR-DOMO.

1840 DANA *Two Years* 293 The mayordomo, . . . of course, refused to make any charge, as it was the Lord's gift. **1850** COLTON *3 Years Calif.* 442 It is stated, in the archives of this mission, that the mayordomo gathered 8,600 bushels of wheat from 80 bushels sown. **1863** *Rio Abajo Press* 28 April 1 He called Jose the mayordomo to the plazita, where they were soon joined by the rest of the household. **1885** *Harper's Mag.* April 692/2 The *acequias* are public works, and in each place are under the control of the highly important local official called the *mayordomo*. **1898** E. M. NICOLL *Ranchwoman in N.Mex.* 48 (Bentley), Go, and request the mayordomo to look into this affair. **1904** 'O. HENRY' *Heart of West* 14 Queen Santa had appointed as *mayordomo* of the ranch a trusty subject, named Ramsay.

***Mayoress.** +A woman who holds the office of mayor. — **1889** FARMER 10 Oskaloosa, in Kansas, has recently made a bold experiment and elected a Town Council composed entirely of women, its president being a Mayoress. **1895** *N. Amer. Rev.* Sept. 267 [One is] unable to conjecture what the results may be when women shall have become, not only *votresses*, but legisla*tresses*, mayor*esses*, and alder*women*.

***Mayor's court.** A court presided over by a mayor. — **1806** in Commons, etc. *Doc. Hist.* III. 61 Be It Remembered, that at mayor's court held at Philadelphia, for the city of Philadelphia, [etc.]. **1829** SHERWOOD *Gaz. Georgia* (ed. 2) 22 There are Mayors' Courts in the cities of Savannah, Augusta, and Darien. **1833** COKE *Subaltern's Furlough* ix, Of the public buildings, the City Hall, containing the supreme court, mayor's court, and various public offices, . . . is the most remarkable.

+**Maypop.** [Thought to be a corruption of MARACOCK, from a native word used by the Indians in Virginia.] The passion flower (*Passiflora incarnata*) found in the southern states; also, the fruit of this. Also attrib. — **1852** *Florida Plant. Rec.* 69 The Vass Place had some grass and May Pops in the Cotton. **1868** GRAY *Field Botany* 157 *Passiflora incarnata*, the fruit, called Maypops in S. States, edible, as large as a hen's egg. **1887** J. C. HARRIS in *Century Mag.* XXXIV. 713/1 An' I fotch you some Maypops too. **1902** GORDON *Recoll. Lynchburg* 120 Sometimes a crop of corn . . . with an undergrowth of 'may-pop' vines, waved its tassels immediately around the hut.

* **Mayweed.** A European weed (*Anthemis cotula*) early introduced into the United States and commonly found along roadsides. (Cf. DOG FENNEL.)

1672 JOSSELYN *New-Eng. Rarities* 86 May-weed; excellent for the Mother. Some of our English housewives call it iron-wort. **1778** CARVER *Travels* 515 Water Cresses, Yarrow, May Weed [etc.]. **1814** BIGELOW *Florula Bostoniensis* 202 May weed. . . . The road sides are full of the white blossoms of this common, annual weed. **1878** JACKSON *Travel at Home* 186 [There grows] Rabbits' foot, May-weed, shepherd's purse [etc.]. **1901** MOHR *Plant Life Ala.* 55 In its northward spread this plant [bitterweed] has largely taken the place of the mayweed (*Anthemis cotula*).

+**May wings.** =GAY-WINGS. — **1850** S. F. COOPER *Rural Hours* 86 As for the May-wings, or 'gay-wings,' they are in truth one of the gayest little blossoms we have. **1893** *Amer. Folk-Lore* VI. 140 *Polygala paucifolia*, May wings. Conn.; N.Y. gay wings. Ferrisburgh, Vt.; N.Y.

***Mazzard cherry.** A wild species of cherry bearing small black fruit. — **1782** CUTLER in *Life & Corr.* I. 90 Set out some mazzard cherries I brought from Mr. Balch's, at Newbury. **1857** *Ill. Agric. Soc. Trans.* II. 339 (*caption*), Grafting the one year old Mazzard Cherry. **1868** CHANNING *Recoll. Newport* 160 The black-heart or mazard cherry, grown on the island, was as good as the best.

+**M.C.** Abbreviation for *member of Congress*. — **1838** *N.Y. Advertiser & Exp.* 7 March 3/5 A proposition to make M.C.'s pay for their 'blanks, paper and twine,' [etc.] have been the doings in Congress during the day. **1850** *Whig Almanac 1851* 29/1 She was the daughter of Hon. Timothy Fuller, M.C. from Middlesex, Mass. **1904** *N.Y. Ev. Post* 23 Sept. 5 John Wesley Gaines, M.C., made a careful study some years ago of the evils of a President's eligibility to reëlection.

***Mead.** +(See quot. 1890.) — **1883** *Century Mag.* July 419/2 The Creole boys drink mead. **1890** *Cent.* 3671/2 *Mead*, . . . a sweet drink charged with carbonic gas, and flavored with some syrup, as sarsaparilla. **1897** ROBINSON *Uncle Lisha* 297 Refreshments of mead, spruce beer, and great cards of good old-fashioned yellow gingerbread were temptingly displayed.

* **Meadow.** Also †**medow(e), meaddow.**

1. A level, grassy lowland, esp. one which is moist or subject to inundation. {1787–, *dial.*} Chiefly New Eng.

1636 *Dedham Rec.* 21 Graunted unto Edward Alleyn . . . All that parcell of land & Medowe wch. lyeth betweene the Rivrs. . . . & the wood. **1690** *Conn. Hist. Soc. Coll.* VI. 230 So much Land throw the meadow . . . as will make a Conveniant High way. **1705** *Providence Rec.* XI. 101 To Rent a Percell of Meaddow being within their Towneshippe. **1777** J. ADAMS *Familiar Lett.* (1876) 278 The meadows, pastures, and grass-plats are as green as leeks. **1816** PICKERING 130 *Meadow*. In New England this word means exclusively grass land, which is moist or subject to being overflowed. **1881** *Maine Hist. Soc. Coll.* IX. 214 The fertility of these meadows [in N.H.] . . . attracted the adventurers of a century ago. **1902** *Harper's Mag.* April 815 [I pointed] at the incomparable, limitless prospect of meadow and salt pond and bar and sea.

+**2.** *W.* A level area of limited extent in a mountainous region, often grassy and usually dry. Freq. in place names.

1870 *Amer. Naturalist* IV. 30 The meadows are bounded by Washoe Peak, . . . by the Pea-vine mountains . . . , and a range lying to the east. **1892** O. F. WHITNEY *Hist. Utah* I. 699 The emigrants . . . went into camp at the south end of Mountain Meadows, about forty miles from Cedar [Utah]. These elevated pastures were almost on the water-shed, or 'rim of the Basin'; and . . . proved to be a pleasant, grassy spot. **1920** *Nat. Park Service Bul.: Rules & Regulations* 34 Through *Gibbon Meadow*, 4 miles from Norris, altitude 7,315 feet, are good camp sites; the next camp site is below Gibbon Falls, 5 miles farther on.

+**3.** (See quot. 1890.)

1877 [see COD]. **1890** *Cent.* 3671/2 *Meadow*, . . . a feeding-ground of fish, as cod.

4. *attrib.* and *comb.* +**a.** Designating a portion of meadow allotted to a colonist. *Obs.*

See also MEADOW LOT.

1662 *Oyster Bay Rec.* I. 9 Ye first meadow sheer at matinicuk next to ye beach. **1684** *Waterbury Prop. Rec.* 217 There should be a divition of all ye undevided meadow to each propriator according to his meadow alotment.

b. Designating an area situated in or composing a meadow.

1678 *Norwalk Hist. Rec.* 63 One parcell lyeth . . . not far distant from the West side of the cart path leading to the meadow field &c. **1700** *N.H. Probate Rec.* I. 458, I give unto my Son Joseph . . . medow marsh, and home stead with fences & buildings. **1728** *Boston News-Letter* 23–30 May 2/2 To be sold, fifty Acres of extraordinary good Meadows and Meadow Bottom Land. **1870** *Amer. Naturalist* IV. 28 A meadow tract, [is] moistened generally by artificial irrigation.

5. a. In the specific names of plants and trees that grow in meadows.

See also MEADOW BEAUTY, FESCUE (GRASS), etc.

1784 CUTLER in *Mem. Academy* I. 411 Meadow Bluebells. . . . In moist land. Not common. September. **1893** *Amer. Folk-Lore* VI. 136 *Caltha palustris*, meadow buttercup. New England. **1848** THOREAU *Maine Woods* 28 He was at this time engaged in cutting the native grass,—rush-grass and meadow-clover, as he called it. **1878** KILLEBREW *Tenn. Grasses* 183 Meadow Comb Grass forms a large constituent of the barren and mountain grasses. **1784** CUTLER in *Mem. Academy* I. 484 Meadow Cuckold. Blossoms yellow red and white. **1818** *Mass. H. S. Coll.* 2 Ser. VIII. 171 The purple sarracenia . . . is here called, meadow cups and forefathers' pitcher. **1843** TORREY *Flora N.Y.* II. 308 *Allium Canadense*. . . . Meadow Garlic. . . . Moist meadows: not common. **1818** *Amer. Jrnl. Sci.* I. 228 Meadow Oak, *Quercus Aquatica*, [grows] along the streams [in Ohio]. **1840** DEWEY *Mass. Flowering Plants* 209 *Allium Canadense*. Meadow or Wild Onion. Bears bulbs like the common onion. **1827** *Western Mo. Rev.* I. 323 Meadow pink, or honey suckle,—a shrub which fringes brooks and creeks, in the pine woods. **1817–8** EATON *Botany* (1822) 412 *Prunus chicasa*, summer plum, meadow plum. . . . The plums are yellow and reddish. *a*1817 DWIGHT *Travels* I. 43 The Meadow Strawberry of this country is the best fruit of the kind which I have seen. **1883** *Century Mag.* Sept. 727/1 The crane's-bill and the meadow-violet expend their surplus revenue in adding to their attractiveness.

b. In the specific names of birds that frequent meadows.

See also MEADOW BIRD, HEN, etc.

1893 NEWTON *Dict. Birds* 539 *Meadow-chicken* and *Meadow-hen*, names given in North America to more than one species of Rail or Coot. **1844** *Nat. Hist. N.Y., Zoology* II. 138 The Meadow Lark. *Sturnella Ludoviciana*. . . . The Crescent Meadow Starling. **1884** COUES *N. Amer. Birds* (ed. 2) 400 *Dolichonyx oryzivorus*. . . . Bobolink. Meadow-wink. Skunk Blackbird.

+**Meadow beauty.** =DEER GRASS. — **1840** DEWEY *Mass. Flowering Plants* 51 Deer Grass, Meadow Beauty, . . . flowers in July, and grows in wet meadows. **1863** *Rep. Comm. Agric. 1862* 159 The *Rhexias*, or, as our people call them, 'Meadow Beauties,' comprise the only native genus. **1887** BURROUGHS in *Century Mag.* July 327 Parts of New England have already a midsummer flower . . . in meadow beauty, or rhexia. **1901**

MOHR *Plant Life Ala.* 633 *Melastomaceae.* Melastoma Family. *Rhexia.* . . . Nine species. . . . Maryland Meadow Beauty [etc.].

+**Meadow bird.** =BOBOLINK 1. — **c1844** *Nat. Hist. N.Y., Zoology* II. 144 The Boblink . . . is known in others [*i.e.,* states] by the various names of Reed-bird, May-bird, Meadow-bird [etc.]. **1857** *Rep. Comm. Patents 1856: Agric.* 127 The 'Meadow Bird,' in Louisiana, the 'Reed Bird,' in Pennsylvania, the 'Rice Bunting,' in the Carolinas, and the 'Bob-o-link,' in New York. **1917** *Birds of Amer.* II. 241 Bobolink. . . . [Also called] Meadow-bird.

Meadowed, *a.* Provided with meadow; used as meadow. {1831-} — **a1656** BRADFORD *Hist.* 363 Some spetiall lands were granted at . . . a plase very weell meadowed, and fitt to keep & rear catle, good store. **1729** *Boston News-Letter* 6 Feb. 2/2 A Large convenient Farm containing Three Hundred Acres . . . well Meadowed and lying upon Worcester Pond. **1888** *Harper's Mag.* April 735 The Gulf has eaten three miles into her meadowed land.

Meadow fescue (grass). A species of fescue grass (*Festuca pratensis*) grown for pasturage and hay. {1762- (Hudson *Flora Anglica* 37)} — **1840** DEWEY *Mass. Flowering Plants* 241 Meadow Fescue-Grass . . . is not considered a very valuable grass. **1857** *Mass. Bd. Agric. Rep.* IV. I. 119 Among these [field or pasture grasses] might be mentioned . . . Meadow Fescue, . . . Field Barley Grass [etc.]. **1901** MOHR *Plant Life Ala.* 827 Meadow Fescue. Tennessee Valley, among meadow grasses.

Meadow foxtail. A species of foxtail grass (*Alopecurus pratensis*) somewhat resembling timothy and grown in meadows for pasturage. In full *meadow foxtail grass.* {1799-} — **1802** DRAYTON *S. Carolina* 61 Remarkable Plants . . . indigenous to the state. . . . Meadow fox tail grass. (*Alopecurus pratensis.*) **1847** DARLINGTON *Weeds & Plants* 371 The Meadow Foxtail. . . . The floret . . . [consists] of a single awned palea. **1858** FLINT *Milch Cows* 174 Meadow Foxtail . . . flourishes best in a rich, moist, and rather strong soil. **1894** COULTER *Bot. W. Texas* III. 526.

***Meadow grass. a.** Any one of various grasses of the genus *Poa*, valued for pasturage. +**b.** A grass of the genus *Glyceria.* (Cf. FOWL MEADOW GRASS.) — **1817-8** EATON *Botany* (1822) 394 *Poa pratensis*, common meadow grass, spear grass. . . . Not so good as the agrostis alba for bonnets. **1850** S. F. COOPER *Rural Hours* 124 The timothy is also an imported grass; so is the meadow-grass considered as the best of all for pasture. **1884** W. SHEPHERD *Prairie Exper.* 216 If the sage-bush is cleaned off and the land irrigated, good crops of wheat, barley, and meadow grass are gathered. **1905** VALENTINE *H. Sandwith* 255 The gale whipped the meadow-grass into leaping silver lines.

***Meadow ground.** =MEADOW 1. — **1633** *Plymouth Col. Rec.* I. 14 That Capt Myles Standish . . . devide the medow ground in the bay equally. **1697** *Derby Rec.* 302 A certain parcell of medow ground . . . at a plac Comonly Called ye uper hasacky medow. **1708** *Boston Rec.* 48 The Freeholders . . . Confirm unto us the Subscriber our heires and Assignes & Associates . . . All the upland, Beach, fflats and Meadow ground. **1794** *Belknap P.* (1877) II. 351 The Tontine Crescent [Boston, Mass.] is situated . . . in a place which, when you knew the town, was a piece of meadow ground.

Meadow hay. {1733-} *local.* +(See quot. 1879.) — **1851** SPRINGER *Forest Life* 54 Among other preliminaries which anticipate the winter operations of lumbermen is the 'putting up' of large quantities of meadow hay. **1879** WEBSTER *Suppl.* 1566/3 *Meadow-hay*, a coarse grass, or true sedge, growing on uncultivated swamp or river meadow;—used as fodder for cattle, packing for ice, and the like.

+**Meadow hen.** The American bittern or any one of various American rails and coots. — **a1841** HAWES *Sporting Scenes* I. 18 The principal inhabitants are gulls, and meadow-hens. **1863** 'G. HAMILTON' *Gala-Days* 97 You know you didn't scare a little meadow-hen. **1917** *Birds of Amer.* I. 204 Clapper Rail. . . . [Also called] Meadow Hen.

***Meadowing.**

1. A level, grassy area. *Obs.* Also attrib.

1639 *Plymouth Col. Rec.* I. 110 Mr Prence hath relinquished [the meadow land] . . . prouided he be allowed meddowing elswhere in lue thereof. **1656** *Jamaica* (L.I.) *Rec.* I. 170 [We] have reserved for ourselvs . . . twentie acres of Medowing a man. **1675** *Providence Rec.* IV. 39 Ye two shares of ye meadoing ground. **1732** *Penna. Gazette* 7 Aug. 4 A very good Plantation . . . with plentiful Meadowing fit for the Scythe.

2. The use of land as meadow; the cultivation of meadow-lands. *Obs.* {1894-} Also attrib.

1735 *Penna. Gazette* 15-22 March 2/2 Several Tracts of good Land . . . being well water'd, and good Part of it fit for Meadowing. **1796** WASHINGTON *Writings* XIII. 259, I am altogether in the farming and meadowing line;—the last of which I have much grounds proper *for.* **1798** *Ib.* XIV. 3 To improve my farms . . . by ditching and meadowing, would be more agreeable to me than immediate profit.

+**Meadowish,** *a.* Like or resembling a meadow. *Obs.* — **1668** *Springfield Rec.* II. 98 The Town granted unto Abell Wright . . . ffourteen acres of Meddowish Land up the little River. **1679** *Ib.* 253 There is granted to Jno Scott thirty acres of medowish or low land and Swamp below the Saw mill. **1687** *Lancaster Rec.* 299 Ye land . . . bounded . . . westerly partly by a brook and partly by some ministeriall meadowish Land.

Meadowland. Land used as or suitable for meadow. {1844} (Cf. MEADOW 1.)

1640 *Hartford Land Distrib.* 10 Meadow land lijng in the upper ende of that parsell of meadow. **1698** *Conn. Rec.* IV. 255 Two acrs and a halfe of meddow land. **1770** WASHINGTON *Diaries* I. 425 In it is some clear Meadow Land and a Pond. **1835** HOFFMAN *Winter in West* I. 85 [We] enjoyed a very pretty prospect of the Cayuhoga winding through a piece of rich meadow-land. **1899** JEWETT *Queen's Twin* 225 She looked eastward over a great stretch of cold meadow land.

Meadow lark. {1611-} +Any one of various American singing birds of the genus *Sturnella.* — **1775** ROMANS *Nat. Hist. Florida* 114 Meadow larks, fieldfares, rice birds, &c. &c. are very frequently had. **1811** WILSON *Ornithology* III. 22 Their general name is the Meadow Lark; among the Virginians they are usually called the Old Field Lark. **1880** *Harper's Mag.* June 80 A coy meadow-lark shows his yellow breast. **1902** WISTER xii, He had bade her listen to the meadow-lark. **1917** *Birds of Amer.* II. 252/1 The Meadowlark has . . . a just claim on the respect and affections of the people.

+**Meadow lily. a.** The Canada lily, *Lilium canadense.* **b.** The lily of the valley, *Convallaria majalis.* — **1832** WILLIAMSON *Maine* I. 126 [We have] two varieties of meadow-lilies, . . . May-lily, or 'lily of the valley;' and nodding-lily. **1894** *Amer. Folk-Lore* VII. 102 *Lilium Canadense*, . . . meadow lily, nodding lily, N.Y.

+**Meadow lot.** A lot or plot of ground in a meadow. Originally such a tract allotted to a colonist.

1637 *Dedham Rec.* 28 Graunted to Samuell Morse yt necke of medowe lying . . . towards the North to have it for a medowe Lott. **1679** *Derby Rec.* 59 One meadow lot containing: 4: acres more or les. **1692** *Waterbury Prop. Rec.* 36 A pes of lande att the est end of his medow lote in hope medow. **1728** *Lunenburg* (Mass.) *Rec.* 44 Meadow Lot, No.: 8: In Catacomog Bounded Northerly on the 10 acre of Meadow. **1878** STOWE *Poganuc People* 317 Fire-lilies in the meadow-lots and scarlet lobelias by the water-brooks.

Meadow mouse. {1801-} +Any one of various American field mice, esp. *Microtus pennsylvanicus.*—**1812** WILSON *Ornithology* VI. 59 The meadow mouse is . . . eagerly sought after by . . . great numbers of Hawks. **1857** *Ill. Agric. Soc. Trans.* II. 617 If he opens its [the snake's] stomach, it will usually be found to contain only insects, or, perhaps, meadow-mice. **1870** *Amer. Naturalist* IV. 537 Ever on the alert for wounded birds or rash Meadow-mice, they [*sc.* birds of prey] sail over the meadows from morning till night. **1895** *Dept. Agric. Yrbk. 1894* 219 Meadow mice and lemmings form the staple food of this bird.

Meadow oats. (Cf. OAT GRASS.) **1.** Oats grown in a meadow. **2.** A grass resembling oats. *pl.* — **(1) 1772** *Maryland Hist. Mag.* XIV. 279 Our Meadow Oates are so stout & Rank tht I fear they will lodge should we have Heavy Rains. **(2) 1815** *Lit. & Phil. Soc. N.Y. Trans.* I. 71 The *avena elatior*, or tall meadow oats, was imported some years ago into Pennsylvania by Dr. Muhlenburg.

***Meadow parsnip.** +**1.** The golden meadow parsnip, *Zizia aurea.* +**2.** Any plant of the genus *Thaspium* with yellow flowers. Also with defining adjective. — **(1) 1833** EATON *Botany* (ed. 6) 401 *Zizia aurea*, meadow parsnip, alexanders. **1839** *Mich. Agric. Soc. Trans.* VII. 422 *Zizia aurea.* Meadow parsnep. **(2) 1857** GRAY *Botany* 155. **1866** LINDLEY & MOORE *Treas. Botany* 1140 *Thaspium*, a genus of North American orthospermous *Umbelliferae.* . . . Its popular American name is Meadow Parsnip. **1901** MOHR *Plant Life Ala.* 642 *Thaspium pinnatifidum.* . . . Mountain Meadow Parsnip.

+**Meadow pine. 1.** The Cuban pine, *Pinus caribaea.* **2.** =LOBLOLLY PINE. — **(1) 1884** SARGENT *Rep. Forests* 202 *Pinus Cubensis.* . . . Slash Pine. Swamp Pine, Bastard Pine. Meadow Pine. **1897** SUDWORTH *Arborescent Flora* 31 *Pinus heterophylla.* . . . Cuban Pine. . . . [Also called] Meadow Pine (Cal., Fla., eastern Miss., in part). **(2)** *Ib.* 26 Loblolly Pine. . . . [Also called] Meadow Pine (Fla.).

Meadow rue. Any one of various plants of the genus *Thalictrum* having leaves resembling those of rue. {1668-} — **1817-8** EATON *Botany* (1822) 484 *Thalictrum dioicum*, meadow rue. **1843** TORREY *Flora N.Y.* I. 23 Common Meadow Rue. . . . A common tall plant in wet meadows. **1884** ROE *Nature's Story* 280 She never came to the house without bringing . . . bunches of meadow-rue from her rambles. **1901** MOHR *Plant Life Ala.* 515 Meadow Rue. . . . Temperate regions Northern Hemisphere.

+**Meadow snipe. 1.** The pectoral sandpiper, *Pisobia melanotos.* **2.** The Wilson's snipe, *Capella delicata.* — **(1) 1844** GIRAUD *Birds of Long Island* 235 To some of the residents of the Island, it is known by the name of 'Meadow Snipe.' **1917** *Birds of Amer.* I. 233/1. **(2) 1890** *Cent.* 3672/1 *Meadow-snipe.* . . . The common American or Wilson's snipe, *Gallinago wilsoni* or *delicatula. B. S. Barton*, 1799. . . . (Local, U.S.). **1917** *Birds of Amer.* I. 227.

+**Meadow swamp.** Low-lying land of a moist or marshy character, partaking of the nature of both swamp and meadow. — **1655** *Suffolk Deeds* II. 156 A parcell of meadow swamp and vpland contayneing about Six Acres. **1675** *Hartford Land Distrib.* 112 Abuts on the comon fence of the west & East on the meadow swamp. **1686** *Ib.* 91 Abutts on the meadow swamp on the east. **1720** *Amer. Wkly. Mercury* 9 June 2/2 To be Sold by Mary Willson . . . good Corn Land with several parcells Meadow Swamps.

***Meadowsweet.** +Any one of various American plants of the genus *Spiraea*, esp. *S. latifolia.* Also applied to some plants of a closely related genus. — **1784** CUTLER in *Mem. Academy* I. 415 *Lysimachia.* . . . Meadowsweet. . . . Borders of meadows, or brooks. June. **1814** BIGELOW *Florula Bostoniensis* 120 *Spiræa alba.* White Spiræa. Meadow sweet. . . . A slender shrub three or four feet high, bearing large, terminal bunches of white flowers. **1850** S. F. COOPER *Rural Hours* 169 This afternoon we . . . gathered wild flowers, meadow-sweet, white silk-weed [etc.]. **1905** *Forestry Bureau Bul.* No. 63, 11 Ferns, meadowsweet, golden-rod, . . . and trailing blackberry vines commonly make up the ground cover.

***Meal.**

***1.** The edible part of various grains ground more or less finely in a mill, +esp., in the United States, Indian corn ground in this manner.

1623 *Va. House of Burgesses* 21 The allowance . . . for a man was only eight ounces of meale and half a pinte of pease. **1659** *R.I. Court Rec.* I. 57 The Sayd Indian . . . did one time this Sumer steale a certaine percell of meals out of George Laytons Mill to the quantity of three fower or five pecks of meale. **1701** *Boston Rec.* 14 No person [shall buy] . . . any sort of grain, meal, butter ffowls [etc.] . . . before two of the clock in the afternoon. **1775** in Pusey *Road to Ky.* (1921) 42 [We] went on again to Brileys mill & suployed our Selves with meal. **1819** *Plough Boy* I. 115 A little meal of Indian corn and oats [was added]. **1852** Stowe *Uncle Tom* xiii, Simeon the second sifted meal for corn-cakes. **1894** Eggleston in *Century Mag.* April 849 'Meal' from the same historical cause is almost exclusively applied to the meal of Indian corn.

2. *attrib.* **a.** Designating containers, etc., for meal.

1650 *Essex Inst. Coll.* XLIII. 71 A meale sive. **1738** *N.H. Probate Rec.* II. 622 The Meal Chest . . . is left where it was. **1882** *Century Mag.* Sept. 765/2 Men, pouring up and down the shaft with the regularity of little meal-buckets in a great mill. **1909** *Cent. Suppl.* 329/1 *Cush,* (origin obscure) in North Carolina, the crumbs and scrapings of cracker or meal-barrels, fried with grease.

b. Designating foods prepared from meal.

1825 Neal *Bro. Jonathan* II. 156 'Thee takes thy meal with me today?' 'Meal'; thought our hero; '. . . he means a meal pudding.' **1868** G. G. Channing *Recoll. Newport* 19 The food given to us little children was bread and milk, and meal dumplings and molasses. **1898** Westcott *D. Harum* xxv, We had . . . potatoes, an' duff, an' johnny-cake, an' meal mush, an' milk emptins bread.

Meal bag. A bag for meal, +esp. one for conveying corn to, and meal from, a mill. — **1644** *Essex Prob. Rec.* I. 46 Too meal baggs. **1738** *N.H. Prob. Rec.* II. 622 He knows of no meal Bag that his son had but what he borrowed of him. **1844** Gregg *Commerce of Prairies* I. 163 The chuckling Indian set out with . . . a large quantity of meal-bags to carry in the golden stores. **1876** *Wide Awake* 72/1 She was bundled up so you would hardly have known her from one of the meal-bags.

+Mealer. One who has his meals at one place and his room or living quarters at another. *colloq.* — **1880** *Harper's Mag.* Sept. 619/2 The term 'mealer' is applied to those boarders living outside in the cottages, for whom, in wet weather, . . . [the buckboard] is sent by the hotel-keepers. **1896** *Boston Jrnl.* 24 Dec. 10/2 Boarders and mealers in this city owe a deep debt of gratitude to Dr. Harrington for his vigilance in the matter of oleomargarine. **1912** N. M. Woodrow *Sally Salt* 104 Besides the farm, I make something taking in mealers.

***Meal house.** A house serving as a storage place for meal. *Obs.* — **1733** *Boston Rec.* 53 Voted That A House be Erected . . . for a grainery or Meal House. **1739** *Ib.* 214 Voted, That there be no Person specially Appointed to give Attendance at the North Granary or Meal-House.

+Meal moth. A moth whose larva feeds on meal or flour: (see quotations). — **1842** T. W. Harris *Rep. Insects of Mass.* 343 The meal-moth (*Pyralis farinalis*), the caterpillar of which may be found in old flour-barrels, is often seen on the ceilings of rooms. **1861** *Harper's Mag.* Aug. 325/1 *Tinea Zea*—'Meal Moth.' . . . The Meal Moth is a very common, sedate-looking insect. **1902** *Bureau of Entomology Bul.* ns. No. 4, 118 The Meal Moths. Two species of moths, in addition to the clothes moths, are habitual frequenters of the household, . . . the Indian-meal moth . . . [and] the meal snout-moth.

+Mealplum vine. =Bear-berry 1. — **1882** in Godfrey *Nantucket* 36 The mealplum vine . . . gives a true richness to the commons of Nantucket.

***Meal sack.** =Meal bag. — **1865** Kellogg *Rebel Prisons* 119 The dirt was pushed back . . . in a meal sack, which we stole from the ration wagon. **1883** 'S. Bonner' *Dialect Tales* 107 He walked all the way from Mississippi to Kentucky, with his things tied up in a meal sack. **1896** Wilkins *Madelon* 98 He heaved the meal-sack from his shoulder to the floor. **1902** White *Blazed Trail* 131 They were . . . carrying each a bulging meal sack looped by a cord across the shoulders and chest.

+Meal ticket. A ticket which entitles the holder to a meal or meals. Also fig. — **1870** O. Logan *Before Footlights* 248 The rather scrubby party who occasionally purchases . . . a 'Meal Ticket,' and thus gets entrance to the festive dining hall. **1902** Wister *Virginian* xiii, You always bought meal tickets at once, else you became unwelcome. **1925** *Scribner's Mag.* Oct. 411/2 Frequently . . . a woman will marry a man so worthless . . . as to regard her simply in the light of what he calls his 'meal ticket.'

Meal trough. A long, shallow receptacle, usually of wood, in which meal or flour is made into dough and kneaded. {1623-} (Cf. Bread tray.) — **1648** *Conn. Rec.* I. 481 An Inuentory of Tho: Dewys Estate: . . . meal trow . . . a table board. **1677** *Essex Inst. Coll.* XXXVII. 93 To 3 for carrying down a meale Through [etc.] . . . 5 [shillings]. **1697** *Conn. Probate Rec.* I. 551 To my daughter Hannah . . . a table wth a Drawer in it, and a meal Trough.

Meal tub. A tub used to hold meal. {1614-} Also fig. (Cf. *cat in the meal tub*, s.v. Cat *n.* 6 f.) — **1642** *Md. Archives* IV. 100, 1 meale tubb. **1853** *La Crosse Democrat* 7 June 2/2 Notwithstanding the *Free Democrat* of May 25th, undertakes to get into the meal tub.

Mealy redpoll. {1837- (Gould *Birds of Europe* III. 193)} +(See quot. 1890.) — [**1839** Audubon *Ornith. Biog.* V. 87 On two occasions I have seen the Mealy Redpoll associated with the American Siskin, in the beginning of October in the province of New Brunswick.] **1844** *Nat. Hist. N.Y., Zoology* II. 169 The Mealy Red-Poll, *Linaria Borealis*, . . . is a northern species. **1870** *Amer. Naturalist* III. 583 *Æ. linaria*, the supposed larger Mealy Redpoll. **1890** *Cent.* 5022/3 The mealy redpoll is *Æ[giothus] canescens;* the American mealy redpoll is *Æ. exilipes*.

***Mean,** *a.*

1. Of land: Poor or unsuitable for cultivation.

1669 *Dedham Rec.* IV. 168 Much of that Lande layed out is much meaner then other Lande layed out vpon that account. **1750** Gist *Journals* 34 The Land in general from Potomack to this Place is mean stony and broken. **1881** Stoddard *E. Hardery* 111 Do you mean to say land as mean as this'll fetch twenty-five [dollars]?

+2. Vicious, hard to manage or control. Used esp. of horses. *colloq.*

1835 Longstreet *Ga. Scenes* 25 He's a monstrous mean horse, gentlemen. **1866** Gregg *Life in Army* 18 [Copperhead snakes] were considered the most poisonous, deceptive, dangerous and mean of all the snake family. **1884** W. Shepherd *Prairie Exper.* 240 Merinos are said to be particularly 'mean.' **1891** *Century Mag.* Jan. 424 Put him on the meanest horse you have.

+3. *To feel mean.* **a.** To be ashamed, feel guilty. **b.** To feel ill or uncomfortable.

(**a**) **1839** Marryat *Diary in Amer.* II. 35, I never felt so mean in all my life. **1875** 'Mark Twain' *Sk., New & Old* 88, I said I would feel mean to lie abed and sleep, and leave her to watch . . . our little patient. **1884** — *H. Finn* xli. 421 [She] tucked me in, and mothered me so good I felt mean. (**b**) *c***1849** Paige *Dow's Sermons* I. 7 He feels as mean, too, as a rooster in a thunder shower. **1867** 'Mark Twain' *Sk., New & Old* 303 Like most other people, I often feel mean, and act accordingly. **1911** J. F. Wilson *Land Claimers* 21 'Feel pretty mean?' the packer asked him kindly. 'I'm just not fit,' was the brief answer.

+4. Of whisky: Poor in quality; adulterated; cheap; harmful in effect. *colloq.*

1845 in *Tall Tales of S.W.* (1930) 6 That liquor of Sterritt's is mean enough to make a man do anything dirty. **1896** Harris *Sister Jane* 259 They had knives, pistols, bad tempers, and a good deal of mean whiskey along. **1904** *Charlotte Observer* 27 Aug. 4 There was the usual tough contingent that filled up on mean whiskey.

Meander, *v.* {*c*1612-} **+1.** *tr.* To follow the course of or explore (a river). **+2.** Of a stream: To flow through (a tract of land). — (**1**) **1831** Pattie *Personal Narr.* 13 We crossed the Missouri . . . and meandered the river as far as Pilcher's fort. **1839** Leonard *Adventures* (1904) 69 We separated, each party to meander the rivers that had been respectively allotted to them. (**2**) **1839** *Mich. Agric. Soc. Trans.* VII. 360 Branches of Swan creek meander this tract in such manner as to facilitate drainage.

***Means.** *pl. local.* +(See quot. 1800.) — **1800** Boucher *Glossary* p. xlix, *Means;* medicines:—the means whereby sickness is relieved. **1829** *Va. Lit. Museum* 30 Dec. 459 *Means.* Medicine. *South.* **1835** Longstreet *Ga. Scenes* 209 First she took the ager and fever, and took a 'bundance o' doctor's means for that.

+Means grass. =Johnson grass. — **1884** Vasey *Agric. Grasses* 51 *Sorgum halapense.* (Cuba grass, Johnson grass, Means grass, False Guinea grass, Evergreen millet, Arabian millet.) A tall perennial grass. **1887** W. J. Beal *Grasses N. Amer.* I. 171.

+Mean white. *S.* A 'cracker,' or 'clay eater'; a member of the class known as 'poor white trash.' Also attrib. — **1837** Martineau *Society* II. 146 He told me that there was great excitement among the negroes in Augusta [about a lynching]; and that many had been saying that 'a mean white person' (a white labourer) would not have been hanged. **1845** *Knickerb.* XXVI. 336 Half of the songs published as theirs [the Negroes'] are . . . the productions of 'mean whites.' **1868** *Putnam's Mag.* I. 704 That wretched caste commonly spoken of as the 'mean whites.'

***Measurably,** *adv.* +To some extent, in a measure. — **1756** Woolman *Journal* (1840) 30 The public meetings were large and measurably favoured with divine goodness. **1848** Lowell *Biglow P.* 1 Ser. p. x., If I know myself, I am measurably free from the itch of vanity. **1869** 'Mark Twain' *Innocents* xiv. 131 The ground ought to be measurably sacred by this time one would think. **1903** *N.Y. Ev. Post* 30 Oct. 16 He was measurably assisted by two circumstances.

***Measure,** *n.* Also †**measur.** A vessel of standard capacity used in measuring various commodities.

1633 *Plymouth Laws* 34 It is order that all measures be brought to the Messenger or Constable of Plym. to be sealed. **1773** in Summers *Ann. S.W. Va.* 591 Ordered that Stephen Trigg send for Weights and Measurs for the use of the said County. **1873** Howells *Chance Acquaintance* (1882) 107 There were . . . wild-looking country boys with red raspberries in birch-bark measures. **1912** *Sears, Roebuck & Co. Cat.* No. 124, 1027 Quart Measure. . . . Extra heavy tin.

Measure,** *v. tr.* +In slang expressions: (See quotations). — *a1890** *N.Y. Mercury* (B. and L.), He had been measured for a funeral sermon three times, he said, and had never used either one of them. **1890** Barrère & Leland (1897) II. 47 *Measured for a funeral sermon, to be,* . . . to be near death's door. — **1896** Farmer & Henley IV. 296/2 *To have been measured for a new umbrella.* . . . (1) To appear in new but ill-fitting clothes; whence (2) to pursue a policy of doubtful wisdom.

Measured mile. A mile by actual measurement as distinguished from one merely estimated or approximated. *colloq.* {1666–} — **1763** WASHINGTON *Diaries* I. 191 To the bridge, or Ferry over little River is 15 measured Miles. **1815** *Niles' Reg.* IX. 92/1 It is bounded . . . on the N.E. by Brandywine creek, separated at this point a measured mile. **1853** F. W. THOMAS *J. Randolph* 254 From my office to the court-house was, as the common people say, a 'measured mile.'

***Measurer.**

+1. A local officer in a town or colony who surveyed or laid out roads and land; a surveyor. *Obs.* {1616–, in general sense}

1636 *Dedham Rec.* I. 36 We doe order yt all highwayes . . . [shall] be orderly set out by our Measurer. **1649** *Plymouth Laws* 91 Survayors or Measurers of Land & such as are apointed to try & seale measures . . . shall have an oath administred. **1666** *Springfield Rec.* I. 355 The Select Men haveing agreed wth ye Measurer of Lands to meet in the house Meddow [etc.].

2. An official having oversight of measures and of the measuring of such commodities as salt, corn, wood, boards, and coal.

1641 *New Haven Rec.* I. 51 Bro: Pecke chosen measurer for the towne to fill and strike all the corne. **1659** *Boston Rec.* 152 Francis Hudson is chosen a measurer of salt aboard of ships according to law. **1680** *Ib.* 138 Chosen . . . Measurer of bords—John Barnard, John Temple, Jabesh Negus. **1692** *Ib.* 211 Measurers of Corn.—John Marshall, Robart Williams. **1789** *Statutes at Large* I. 37 It shall be the duty of the collector . . . to employ proper persons as weighers, gaugers, measurers and inspectors. **1827** DRAKE & MANSFIELD *Cincinnati* 51 The council have power to appoint . . . Measurers of wood and coal. **1851** CIST *Cincinnati* 87 They are empowered to appoint all . . . measurers of wood.

+Measuring worm. The larva of a geometrid moth; a looper. — **1843** *Nat. Hist. N.Y., Zoology* VI. 41 It walks after the manner of some caterpillars called *Measuring worms.* **1859** *Smithsonian Inst. Rep.* 186 The geometers, properly so called, or measuring worms. **1869** *Rep. Comm. Agric. 1868* 314 The larvæ [of moths of the family Geometridae] are known as span-worms, measuring worms, &c. **1899** *Animal & Plant Lore* 63 Measuring-worm, larvae of geometrid moths.

***Meat.**

***1.** Food for cattle or swine. *Obs.*

1639 *R.I. Col. Rec.* I. 88 All the meadow groundes . . . shall be layed out after the rate and proportion of twentie cowes meat to a division of three hundred acres of upland. **1674** *Conn. Rec.* II. 245 So many of those sayd cattell or swine shall be sold at an outcry as may sattisfy for their powndage, damage they have done, and charg of meat and water whilst impownded. **1691** *Conn. Probate Rec.* I. 459, I appoint my sd. son to provide winter meat for her Cow. **1738** E. PARKMAN *Diary* 67 We give the cattle dry meat and house the Cows and Calves.

***2.** The kernel of a nut. {–1613}

1775 WASHINGTON *Diaries* II. 179 Nuts . . . like the Pignut—but longer . . . and fuller of meat. **1838** HAWTHORNE *Note-Books* (1932) 46 An old man selling the meats of butter nuts under the stoop. **1900** *Boston Ev. Transcript* 29 March 7/3 [Use] English walnut meats, pecan-nut meats.

+3. (See quotations.)

1832 J. K. PAULDING *Westward Ho* I. 124 What a wild goose of a feller, not to know that nothing is called meat in these parts but salt pork and beef. *c***1845** W. I. PAULDING *Amer. Comedies* (1847) 196 The term *meat* in the West is understood to apply solely to *salt pork.* **1891** *Fur, Fin, & Feather* March 182/2 [The hunter in the Ozarks] likes the [bear] flesh if meat (*i.e.*, pork) is 'skeerse.' **1902** *Dialect Notes* II. 239 *Meat,* bacon always understood. [Pioneer dial., southern Ill.]

+4. The game or quarry which a hunter seeks or takes. Also in transferred sense. *colloq.*

1804 CLARK in *Lewis & C. Exped.* I. (1904) 145 A man had like to have Starved to death . . . for the want of Bullitts or Something to kill his meat. **1848** RUXTON *Far West* iii. 113 It felt like the old thing, they said, to be once more amongst the 'meat.' **1872** 'MARK TWAIN' *Roughing It* I. 357 Come along—you're my meat *now*, my lad, anyway. **1884** *Century Mag.* Dec. 198/2 The ram was my meat. **1902** HARBEN *A. Daniel* 141 As soon as he told me that I knew he was our meat. **1913** LONDON *Valley of Moon* 448 This young Sandow's my meat. I'll get 'm maybe in the third or fourth round.

+5. The flesh or body of a person. *slang. Obs.*

1834 CARRUTHERS *Kentuckian* I. 27 If I hadn't had so many inches, he'd have been into my meat. **1847** ROBB *Squatter Life* 59 Old Tom Jones' *yell* . . . gives my meat a slight sprinklin' of ager whenever I think on it.

+6. In colloq. phrases.

To make meat, (see quot. 1889); *to take meat,* to kill someone.

1846 MCKENNEY *Memoirs* I. 130 Red-Bird was called upon to go out, and 'take meat,' as they phrase it. **1889** FARMER 362/2 *To make meat,* is the term by which the frontiersman denotes the process of drying thin slices of animal flesh for future use.

7. *attrib.* and *comb.* **a.** Designating tools or other articles used in connection with meat.

1642 *Md. Archives* IV. 97 An apple-roster, & a meat-heater . . . 4. old hoes . . . 2 sawes. **1854** *Penna. Agric. Rep.* 80, 1 meat and root cutter. **1865** LOCKE *Struggles Nasby* 170 Where are the matrons uv Virginia? Did they not . . . plunge a meat-knife into their throbbin buzzums? **1868** *Mich. Agric. Rep.* VII. 348 R. C. Browning, 32 Courtland street, New York, [exhibited] 1 lightning meat chopper. **1883** KNIGHT *Suppl.* 591/1 *Meat rocker,* a mining knife having a handle at each end, and worked by a rocking motion. **1897** *Outing* XXX. 284/1 The two regiments would need to be supplied with . . . meat cans . . . and utensils for some kind of field cooking.

b. Designating foods made of meat.

1856 GOODRICH *G. Go-ahead* 191 A sort of meat-bread, like the beef-biscuit made in Texas. **1865** STOWE *House & Home P.* 248 Those fine, clear meat-jellies . . . form a garnish . . . palatable to the taste.

c. Designating individuals, organizations, or processes having to do with the curing or marketing of meat.

See also MEAT-PACKING.

1846 MAGOFFIN *Down Santa Fé Trail* 47 The same routine of meat drying &c. **1868** *N.Y. Herald* 7 Aug. 7/3 Our Meat Inspector should also keep a sharp look out for these animals. **1895** *Dept. Agric. Yrbk. 1894* 67 A meat-inspection tag [is attached] to each quarter or piece. **1910** LEFFINGWELL *Amer. Meat* 166 The Meat Trust, in its relations to human life and welfare, is incomparably the worst of all the combinations.

8. Special combinations.

Meat animal, an animal raised to be slaughtered for meat; *m. auction,* an auction at which meat is sold; *m. butcher, hunter,* one who hunts big game, as buffalo, and butchers it wantonly, often for commercial purposes; *m. fish,* fish suitable for food; *m. hog,* a hog raised to be butchered for meat; *m. hunt,* a hunting expedition in search of game, as buffalo; *m. man,* a member of a meat party; *m. party,* a hunting party sent out in an effort to procure meat; *m. store,* a store in which meat is sold; *m. train,* on a military expedition, a supply train carrying meat.

1774 J. ANDREWS *Letters* 23 Early this morning arriv'd in town eleven carts loaded with meat fish. **1831** R. COX *Adv. Columbia River* (1832) 261 At eleven . . . the meat-men were dispatched. **1845** FRÉMONT *Exped.* 234 The meat train did not arrive this evening. **1856** *Florida Plant. Rec.* 169 I doe not see but Verry few of the shoats that I turned out for meat hogs this year. **1856** KANE *Arctic Explor.* II. 34 We long anxiously for weather to enable our meat-party to start. **1875** in Godfrey *Nantucket* 68 Burgess's meat auction this evening! **1886** ROOSEVELT in *Outing* March 611 The brutal skin-hunters and meat-butchers of the woods and prairies have done their work. **1889** *Harper's Mag.* May 878/1 The meat-hunters are still devoting their attention to the killing of larger game. **1906** J. O. ARMOUR *Packers* 325 What I have said as to dressed beef . . . [applies] to all the other branches of raising meat animals and converting them into food for the table. **1907** J. R. COOK *Border & Buffalo* (1938) 80 In those days it was the custom of the Mexicans to go each fall to the border of New Mexico and Texas on meat hunts. **1920** HOWELLS *Vacation of Kelwyns* 187 It was the best piece of steak in the meat-store.

+Meat ax. An ax used in cutting meat. Usually in phrase: *As savage* (or *wicked*) *as a meat ax.* Also fig. — **1834** C. A. DAVIS *Lett. J. Downing* 185 Its helve is of hickory—in Kentucky parlance, 'is as savage as a meat-axe.' **1838** HALIBURTON *Clockmaker* 2 Ser. ix. 141 She was as smart as a fox-trap, and as wicked as a meat-axe. **1895** *N.Y. Dramatic News* 7 Dec. 3/2 For a lumbering, English melodrama it fills the bill, in spite of the editing Mr. Brady did with a meat-axe. **1902** LORIMER *Lett. Merchant* 41, I guess you'll see the point without my elaborating with a meat ax.

Meat bag. +Stomach. *slang.* — **1848** RUXTON *Life Far West* i. 37 Dick was as full of arrows as a porkypine; one was sticking right through his cheek, one in his meat bag. **1850** GARRARD *Wah-To-Yah* iii. 46, I bet I make you eat dogmeat . . . and you'll say it's . . . the best you ever hid in your meatbag.

+Meat barrel. A strong heavy barrel in which meat is packed. — **1778** *Jrnls. Cont. Congress* X. 249 Meat barrels, for packing beef, pork, or fish, each, 4/90ths of a dollar. **1833** A. GREENE *Yankee among Nullifiers* 84 Bring a meat barrel and a half bushel of salt.

+Meatbird. 1. =CANADA JAY. **2.** =CLARK'S CROW. — (1) *a***1862** THOREAU *Maine Woods* 220 Three large slate-colored birds of the jay genus . . . , the Canada-jay, moose-bird, meat-bird, or what not, came flitting silently . . . toward me. **1917** *Birds of Amer.* II. 225. (2) *Ib.* 234 The Clarke Crow is very fond of meat, and for this reason he has often been called 'meat bird.'

Meat biscuit. (See quot. 1889.) {1852} — **1856** KANE *Arctic Explor.* II. 169 The flour and remaining meat-biscuit were to be protected from moisture in double bags. **1865** *Atlantic Mo.* XV. 14/2 A Russian soup . . . always contains as much solid nutriment as meat-biscuit or Arctic pemmican. **1883** *Wheelman* I. 340 Some [bicycle] riders . . . carry with them some plain and simple food and drink, like a meat-biscuit and a bottle of cold tea or milk. **1889** *Cent.* 563/2 *Meat biscuit,* a preparation consisting of the matter extracted from meat by boiling, combined with flour, and baked in the form of biscuits.

Meat block. A heavy block upon which meat is cut. Also transf. — **1838** E. FLAGG *Far West* II. 59 Mr. W. . . . was on the *stump,* in shape of a huge meat-block at one corner of the market-house. **1852** *Knickerb.* XXXIX. 380 He used to appropriate a public corner of the market-house . . . and conduct Sabbatical exercises, mounted on a meat-block. **1891** 'THANET' *Otto the Knight* 59 My friend Dorothea was standing before the huge cypress log which is our meat block.

+Meat hawk. =MEATBIRD 1. — **1857** HAMMOND *Northern Scenes* 53 Small birds, of the size and general appearance of the cuckoo, save for their hooked beaks, . . . were called by our boatmen, 'meat hawks.' **1904** WHITE *Silent Places* 84 Meat-hawks . . . swooped here and there. **1917** *Birds of Amer.* II. 225 Canada Jay. *Perisoreus canadensis canadensis*. . . . [Also called] Moose-bird; Meat Hawk; Carrion Bird.

+**Meat house.** A house in which meat is kept; a smokehouse. — **1805** CLARK in *Lewis & C. Exped.* III. (1905) 284 Had the Meet house coverd and the Meat all hung up. **1822** *Missionary Herald* XVIII. 81 They also put up a meat house, and another small cabin for a cook. **1863** HOPLEY *Life in South* I. 51 These tenements are the dairy, 'meat-house,' larder, kitchen [etc.]. **a1918** G. STUART *On Frontier* I. 240, I tried to fix the meat-house so it would be fly proof.

Meat in the pot. +(See quot. 1889.) — **1869** *Overland Mo.* Aug. 126 Among names of revolvers I remember the following: Meat in the Pot, Blue Lightning, Peacemaker [etc.]. **1889** FARMER 362/2 *Meat in the pot.*—A Texan term for a revolver. The phrase is not altogether inappropriate, because on the plains of the Great Lone Star State, a man's rifle or revolver is often the only means by which he can provide and literally put *meat in the pot.*

***Meat market.** **1.** A butcher's shop. +**2.** The trade or traffic involving the buying and selling of meat. — (1) **1860** E. COWELL *Diary* 198 It is 'J. Taylor's Meat Market.' **1877** JOHNSON *Anderson Co., Kansas* 178 John S. Stowe opened the first meat market, in 1860. **1892** *York County Hist. Rev.* 86 Wm. Henry Young, Meat Market. (2) **1874** *Dept. Agric. Rep. 1873* 129 The weak and dull wool-market caused sheep to be offered for sale . . . with very little reference to the demands of the meat-market.

+**Meat-packing.** The business of slaughtering animals and preparing meat for transportation and sale. Also attrib. Hence *meat-packer.* — **1873** *Iowa Agric. Soc. Rep.* 175 The panacea for all these ills is to be found in tanneries, . . . meat packing and curing houses, glue factories [etc.]. **1892** J. J. FLINN *Chicago* 330 Meat packing is the oldest of Chicago's industries. **1903** E. JOHNSON *Railway Transportation* 131 The large meat-packers . . . own their own cars. **1906** *Okla. Governor Rep. 1905–6* 7 There are at present [in Okla.] meat-packing establishments, canning factories [etc.]. **1924** *Packing Industry* 24 Meat packing is a highly specialized business.

Meat pie. {1773–} +(See quot. a1870.) — **1860** HOLMES *E. Venner* vii, Mixed conversation chopped very small, like the contents of a mince-pie,—or meat pie, as it is more forcibly called in the deep-rutted villages. **a1870** CHIPMAN *Notes on Bartlett* 266 *Meat-pie.* A mince-pie. Occasionally, in this reference, heard in—N[ew] E[ngland]. **1894** WILKINS in *Harper's Mag.* Sept. 609/1, I dun'no' when I've eat a decent meat pie. . . . I 'ain't had a mince pie I could eat since my last wife died.

Meat platter. A large platter from which meat is served at table. — **1863** 'G. HAMILTON' *Gala-Days* 75, I decided upon a meat-platter. **1898** *Kansas City Star* 18 Dec. 11/2 Semi-porcelain Meat Platters, nicely embossed.

Meat safe. A safe or cupboard in which meat is kept. {1836–9–} Also transf. — **1861** NEWELL *Orpheus C. Kerr* I. 17 The old man put a chaw into his meat-safe, and shut one eye. **1865** *Atlantic Mo.* April 505/1 Whether he came up by the coal-bin or the meat-safe. **1869** *Boyd's Business Directory* 51 L. H. Mace & Co's Refrigerator, Meat Safe and Water Cooler Manufactory. **1887** *Century Mag.* March 740/2 We built a substantial meat-safe, with sides and top of mosquito-netting.

+**Meat saw.** (See quot. 1875.) — **1875** KNIGHT 1416/2 *Meat-saw,* a saw with a thin blade strained in an iron frame and used by butchers. **1913** BARNES *Western Grazing Grounds* 180 The points [of horns are taken] off with a pair of dehorning clippers or an ordinary meat saw.

+**Meat shop.** A butcher's shop. — **1872** *Newton Kansan* 22 Aug. 5/1 Meat Shop. Henry Mayer, West of Main street. **1873** *Ib.* 1 May 3/2 Tarbet Bros. have established a branch meat shop. **1907** ANDREWS *Recoll.* 211 With the exception of three or four meat shops, the markets in summer were all out of doors.

Meat tub. A tub for (pickled) meat. — **1779** E. PARKMAN *Diary* 171 We are unhappily low in ye Meat Tub. **1783** *Ib.* 299 Cider Barrels, Meat Tubs, & old Casks. **1875** KNIGHT 1416/2 *Meat-tub,* one for holding pickled meat.

Meaty, *a.* {1787–} +*fig.* Full of significance; weighty. {1902–} — **1865** LOWELL *Biglow P.* 2 Ser. x. 213 Their talk wuz meatier, an' 'ould stay. **1881** G. S. HALL *German Culture* 105 Any discussion of it would be likely to be rather more meaty than . . . inane speculations about the nature of the Beautiful. **1896** Advt. of *Preacher's Complete Homiletic Commentary,* The Index suggests thousands of meaty themes for sermons.

+**Mecate.** [Mex. Sp.] (See quot. 1879.) — **1879** WEBSTER *Suppl.* 1566 *Mecate,* . . . a rope of hair or of the fiber of the maguey, used for tying horses, etc. (*Southwestern U.S.*) **1919** J. S. CHASE *Calif. Desert Trails* 182 Before I left I bought of him a *mecate* or rope of plaited horse-hair, of his own making.

* **Mechanic.** One who does manual labor, now esp. one skilled in the care or use of machinery. Also attrib.

1708 *N.C. Col. Rec.* I. 687 Shoemakers and other mechanics should be appointed in their room. **1795** *Columbian Centinel* 17 Jan. 3/2 The Mechanics of this town, are requested to meet at Concert Hall. **1815** *Niles' Reg.* VII. 339/2 Mechanics of all descriptions receive nearly double the price for their labor that they get to the eastward. **1849** *Holyoke Diaries* 187 The boys went to the Mechanic fair. **1897** F. C. MOORE *How to Build a Home* 20 Plumbers and other mechanics are working with fire-pots. **1919** *Vocational Rehabilitation Series No. 11* 4 The mechanic should be able to do skilled work on all mechanical parts of any car.

b. In the names of various societies organized by or for mechanics.

1797 MORSE *Amer. Gazetteer* s.v. *Boston,* The principal societies in the Commonwealth [include] . . . Boston Mechanic Association, Society for the aid of Immigrants. **1839** A. LAWRENCE *Diary & Corr.* 172, I will give to the Charitable Mechanic Association ten thousand dollars. **1868** *Mich. Agric. Rep.* VII. 363 Mechanics' and Inventors' Association, Detroit, [exhibited] Withey's adjustable arm rest.

+**c.** *Greasy mechanic,* an opprobrious term applied during the Civil War by Southerners toNortherners.

1862 F. Moore *Rebellion Rec.* V. II. 24 A brawny Yankee, with his arm in a sling, said the 'mudsills and greasy mechanics' had been heard from, and would be again. **1864** *Rio Abajo Press* 12 July 1/3 Things that make a Patriot Mad. . . . To hear men who, were they South, would be . . . taunted as 'mudsills,' 'greasy mechanics,' etc., upholding the very men who so degrade labor. **1865** [see MUDSILL 2].

Mechanic's shop. A shop kept by a mechanic. — **a1817** DWIGHT *Travels* II. 437 [Randolph] contains . . . houses, stores, and mechanic's shops. **1831** PECK *Guide* 289 Two groceries, and various mechanic's shops. **1849** CHAMBERLAIN *Ind. Gazetteer* 389 [Spencer] contains . . . eight mechanics' shops.

***Mechlin.** A kind of lace made at Mechlin (Malines), Belgium. In full *Mechlin lace.* {1699–} — **1830** COOPER *Water Witch* xi, Half of them get their seats as clandestinely . . . as you get these rare Mechlin laces! **1850** MITCHELL *Lorgnette* I. 162 Our neighbors . . . I occasionally see . . . hanging out a bit or two of mock Mechlin to dry. **1902** *Harper's Mag.* Jan. 279 Now I suppose she sports real Mechlin on her cap.

***Mechoacan.** Also **mechoacanna.** Any of various plants of the morning-glory family having roots useful as cathartics; the root of such a plant. Also attrib. — [**1577** FRAMPTON *Joyfull Newes* 23 b, The Mechoacan is a Roote . . . brought from a countrie . . . called Mechoacan.] **1676** *Phil. Trans.* XI. 630 [In Virginia] grow two Roots, which some Physicians judg, the one to be Turbith, the other Mechoacan. **1709** LAWSON *Carolina* 143 The Mechoacan-berry . . . grows here very plentifully. **1859** BARTLETT 266 *Mechoacan.* (*Convolvulus panduratus.*) A plant growing in sandy fields and on dry banks from Connecticut to Illinois and southwards. The large root is also used for medical purposes. It is also called Man of the Earth, and Wild Potato Vine. **1894** *Amer. Folk-Lore* VII. 95 *Ipomæa pandurata,* mechoacanna, N.Y.

Mecklenburg. *attrib.* [*Mecklenburg* County, N.C.]

1. *Mecklenburg Resolves,* a series of resolutions passed May 31, 1775, at Charlotte in Mecklenburg County, North Carolina, suspending the authority of the British government and making provision for local administration.

1775 in *Amer. Hist. Rev.* XIII. 19 You'll Observe the Mecklinburg resolves, exceed all other Committees, or the Congress itself. **1907** HOYT *Meckl. Decl. Independence* 22 The Mecklenburg resolves of May 31, 1775, appeared in the *South-Carolina Gazette; and Country Journal* of Tuesday, June 13, 1775.

2. With *Declaration* (*of Independence*), etc.: Designating the resolutions (resembling those of the national Declaration of Independence of July 4, 1776) first published in 1819 as a document regarded as emanating from a convention in Charlotte on May 20, 1775.

The authenticity of this document has been questioned by many historians, who regard it as the result of false tradition based upon confusion with the Resolves (see 1 above) of May 31, 1775. Cf. W. H. Hoyt *The Mecklenburg Declaration of Independence* (1907).

1819 J. ADAMS in Hoyt *Meckl. Decl. Independence* 11 The Mecklengburg Resolutions are a fiction. **1819** in *Decl. of Indep. by Citizens Mecklenburg Co.* (1831) 16, I then proceeded on to Philadelphia, and delivered the Mecklenburg Declaration of Independence of May, 1775. **1830** *Ib.* 27, I do certify that the foregoing statement, relative to the Mecklenburg Independence, is correct. **1831** *Ib.* p. vii, The striking similarity of expression in the concluding sentences of the Mecklenburg Declaration, and the Declaration by Congress on the 4th of July ,1776, has been repeatedly urged. **1853** F. L. HAWKS in W. D. Cooke *Revolutionary Hist. N.C.* 80 Some supposed the document of May 30, 1775, to be the Mecklenburg *Declaration of Independence*. . . . It is not that declaration; but it is an authentic document, founded on that declaration. **1907** HOYT *Meckl. Decl. Independence* 15 The committee affirmed the genuineness and authenticity of the Mecklenburg resolutions. **1915** *Chicago D. News Almanac 1916* 214/2 [In] North Carolina . . . May 20 (anniversary of the signing of the Mecklenburg declaration of independence) [is a holiday].

+**Med.** (See quot. 1851.) — **1851** HALL *College Words* 198 *Med., Medic,* a name sometimes given to a student in medicine. **1853** *Songs of Yale* 16 Take . . . Sixteen interesting 'Meds,' With dirty hands and towzeled heads. **1899** QUINN *Penna. Stories* 19 The Meds waited till the visitors were opposite them.

* **Medal.** +A piece of metal, usually circular, and appropriately stamped or engraved, given by white authorities to Indians as a mark of esteem, favor, etc.

1756 *Lett. to Washington* II. 26 [Indian goods at Fort Cumberland:] 16 Let Colld. Thread. 8 s Medals. **1772** in *Travels Amer. Col.* 540 Their leader had a small Medal and spoke a little English. **1793** Jefferson *Writings* IX. 158 The British government . . . practised the giving medals, gorgets, and bracelets to the savages. **1846** Cooper *Redskins* xvii, The whole party was composed of chiefs. This was apparent by their medals. **1879** H. Phillips *Notes upon Coins* 2 Silver medals [were] given by Kings George 1st & 2d to the North American Indians.

attrib. **1808** *Ann. 10th Congress* 1 Sess. II. 2833 To each of the great Medal Mingoes, . . . five hundred dollars . . . during his continuance in office.

+**Medal chief.** An Indian chief possessing a medal given him in token of his rank, influence, etc. — **1772** in *Travels Amer. Col.* 518 [Letter] to the Great and Small medal chiefs. **1800** Hawkins *Sk. Creek Country* 27 He is one of the great medal chiefs. **1813** *Niles' Reg.* V. 270/2 At this moment a medal chief of the *Choctaw* nation is soliciting to be employed.

Medeola. [dim. fr. L. *Medea*, the enchantress.] The Indian cucumber, or the genus of plants to which this belongs. — **1784** [see Indian cucumber (root)]. **1818** *Mass. H. S. Coll.* 2 Ser. VIII. 169 Among those, that flower in June, the most interesting are . . . two species of crowfoot, the blue-eyed grass, the medeola [etc.]. **1887** Burroughs in *Century Mag.* XXXIV. 323 Indian cucumber root, one of Thoreau's favorite flowers, is named after the sorceress Medea, and is called 'medeola.'

+**Medialuna.** [Sp.] The half moon, *Medialuna californiensis.* — **1884** Goode, etc. *Fisheries* I. 395 The 'Half-moon,' more commonly known by its Spanish name, 'Medialuna,' *Scorpis californiensis*, . . . forms the greater part of the catch at San Pedro.

Medic. A student of medicine; a doctor. {1659–}

'Obs. exc. as *U.S.* college slang for "medical student" ' (*O.E.D.*).

1823 *Crayon* (Yale) 24 The slain, the Medics stow'd away. **1850** *Yale Banger* 2 Dec., And Medics sing the anthem too. **1885** *Jrnl. Nervous & Mental Disease* July 281 *Medic* is the legitimate paronym of *medicus*, but is commonly regarded as slang. **1901** Duncan & Scott *Allen & Woodson Co., Kansas* 619 The medics, in common with other professions have furnished men who could be trusted to place a hand upon the helm of state.

Medical, *n.* A medical student. *colloq.* {1834–} — **1823** Hawthorne in J. Hawthorne *N. Hawthorne & Wife* I. 111 He is the best scholar among the medicals. **1899** Quinn *Pennsylv. Stories* 19 Much joy was caused to the Medicals on the north end.

Medical, *a.* Pertaining or relating to the study or practice of medicine or to medicines. {1646–}

1779 *Essex Inst. Coll.* LVI. 30 The medical committee met in my chamber. **1814** *Niles' Reg.* VI. 36/2 A Medical Board is now sitting at the city of Washington, by order of the secretary of war. **1815** *Ib.* VII. Suppl. 89/2 In the year 1792, the board of trustees of Columbia College, organized a medical faculty, connected with the College. **1833** *Ib.* XLIV. 3/1 The whole number of students was 823—collegiate 105, medical 368 [etc.]. **1861** *Army Regulations* 286 [If] a medical officer cannot be had, . . . the enlisted man, may employ a private physician, and a just account therefor will be paid by the medical bureau. **1881** *Naval Encycl.* 491 The active list of the medical corps of the navy consists of 15 medical directors, ranking with captains; 15 medical inspectors, ranking with commanders; 50 surgeons [etc.]. **1887** *Trial H. K. Goodwin* 50 And you are the medical examiner for the district? **1888** Sheridan *Memoirs* I. 417 One medical wagon and eight ambulances were also furnished. **1900** Ade *More Fables* 161 He discovered that Alcohol was a Food long before the Medical Journals got onto it.

Medical college. A college in which the science of medicine is taught. — **1815** *Niles' Reg.* VII. Suppl. 90/1 It is not now deemed necessary to state . . . any additional facts with regard to the medical college of New-York. **1851** Cist *Cincinnati* 112 Medical College of Ohio. This Institution was first chartered, and placed in the hands of a Board of Trustees, in 1819. **1887** Alden *Little Fishers* xxiv, They will marry as soon as he graduates from the medical college. **1898** Cahan *Imported Bridegroom* 200 [She] had placed her husband in a medical college.

Medical school. A school devoted to giving instruction in the science of medicine; a medical college. — **1765** in J. Carson *Hist. Med. Dept. Univ. Penna.* 55 The institution of Medical Schools in this country has been a favorite object of my attention. **1815** *Niles' Reg.* VII. Suppl. 89/1 The recent attempts made for organizing another Medical School in New-York, . . . have completely failed. **1840** *Niles' Nat. Reg.* 21 March 48/2 A great many [doctors] . . . never received the finishing polish of a medical school. **1850** *New Eng. Farmer* II. 295 Boston Female Medical School. . . . This institution . . . is gaining favor in the public mind. **1883** *Century Mag.* July 468/2 The experience of the medical schools . . . need not discourage any one.

Medical society. An organization composed of those interested in the practice or study of medicine. {1799–} — **1785** Cutler in *Life & Corr.* I. 114, [I] forward you an extract from the Records of the Massa. Meda. Soc'y. **1805** *Holyoke Diaries* 147 Medical society met. **1872** Holmes *Poet* 72 [Florence Nightingale] had more sense in her little finger than forty medical societies. **1907** J. J. Walsh (*title*), History of the Medical Society of the State of New York. . . . In Commemoration of the Centennial of the Medical Society.

Medicinal spring. A spring the waters of which possess healing or invigorating properties. — **1783** *Mem. Academy* II. I. 43 An Account of a Number of Medicinal Springs at Saratoga in the State of Newyork. **1834** *S. Lit. Messenger* I. 91, I turned westwardly at Staunton . . . and visited the justly celebrated medicinal springs in that region. **1849** Chamberlain *Ind. Gazetteer* 246 Near this place are medicinal springs supposed to be very efficacious, called Trinity Springs.

* **Medicine.** Also †**medson, medisin.**

* **1.** A drug, physic, preparation, etc., used in treating one who is sick or injured, or as a remedy.

1678 *New Castle Court Rec.* 307 Peter Claassen Imployed him ye sd Crawford himselfe to apply the medsons to ye boy. **1726** *Md. Hist. Mag.* XVIII. 218, I likewise Expect you will Cr. me by Eight pound for medicines. **1805** Clark in *Lewis & C. Exped.* II. (1904) 165 The Indian woman verry bad, & will take no medisin what ever. **1923** Watts *L. Nichols* 223 He had carted tons of . . . magazines, clothes, and medicine to every hospital and Home in the city.

+**b.** *To take one's medicine*, to submit to something unpleasant or disagreeable. *colloq.*

1896 *Congress. Rec.* 7 Jan. 512/1, I fought . . . and was licked out of my boots. I took my medicine like a man. **1900** *Ib.* 2 Feb. 1437/2 He must walk up and take his medicine whether he wants to or not if the caucus says so. **1904** W. H. Smith *Promoters* 224 Let them take their medicine like men if the luck went against them.

+**c.** *To treat* (one) *with a dose of* (one's) *own medicine*, or variant of this: To respond or retaliate in kind, or in a tit-for-tat manner.

1894 Ford *P. Stirling* 150 'He snubbed me,' . . . explained Miss DeVoe, smiling slightly at the thought of treating Peter with a dose of his own medicine. **1898** *Kansas City Star* 21 Dec. 2/5 This measure . . . is just sharp enough to give them a little of their own kind of medicine.

+**2.** Among North American Indians: Something not understood; a mystery.

1805 Lewis in *L. & Clark Exped.* II. (1904) 177 It is probable that the large river just above those great falls . . . has taken it's name *Medicine river* from this unaccountable rumbling sound, which like all unaccountable things with the Indians of the Missouri is called *Medicine.* **1834** Baird *Valley Mississippi* ix. 93 Everything with them which is inexplicable is a 'medicine.' **1907** Hodge, etc. *Amer. Indians* I. 837/2 Among some tribes the term for medicine signifies 'mystery,' but among others a distinction is made between thaumaturgic practices and actual medicines.

+**b.** A fetish, talisman, charm, deity, patron, etc., regarded as having supernatural power or potency. Also *bad medicine, big medicine, good medicine.*

Cf. Grand, Great medicine.

1807 Gass *Journal* 44 He told them . . . that he had more medecine aboard his boat than would kill twenty such nations in one day. **1815** *Niles' Reg.* IX. 114/1 The former [Wyandotts] accuse the latter [Senecas] of administering *bad medicine.* **1817** Bradbury *Travels* 166 One of the chiefs . . . devoted his horse, or in their mode of expressing it, 'Gave it to his medicine.' **1846** Sage *Scenes Rocky Mts.* x, Here, having passed a night and a day in earnest communion with the Big Medicine [etc.]. **1849** M. Eastman *Dahcotah* xix, Each clan takes a root for its medicine, known only to those initiated into the mysteries of the clan. **1867** Richardson *Beyond Mississippi* 97 A stake at the head of the grave is carved into a rough effigy of the 'medicine' of the deceased. **1899** Cushman *Hist. Indians* 160 [When the ancient Indian] said it is 'good medicine,' he meant that the good spirit had the ascendency; and when he said it is 'bad medicine' he meant that the bad spirit had the ascendency.

transf. **1905** *N.Y. Ev. Post* 29 June 1 The coaches [were] talking 'race medicine' to the eight, who were already boated.

+**c.** = Medicine man. Also transf.

1827 Cooper *Prairie* II. xii, [The] release of the captives . . . was attributed by the hags to the incantations of the medecine. **1843** 'Carlton' *New Purchase* I. 80 Once or twice a year, our 'Medicine' put on his leather breeches. **1846** Thorpe *Myst. Backwoods* 58 The whole tribe had . . . learned to respect him, and to look upon him as a great 'Medicine.'

+**d.** *To make medicine*, to engage in an incantation or ritualistic ceremony in an effort to invoke the favor of the spirits or unseen powers.

1805 Clark in *Lewis & C. Exped.* I. (1904) 247 Some of our Men go to See a War Medeson made at the Village. **1841** Catlin *Indians* II. 248 [For] nearly every animal they hunt for, . . . they 'make medicine' for several days, to conciliate the bear (or other) Spirit, to ensure a successful season. **1866** *Rep. Indian Affairs* 280 Black Kettle informed me that the Dog Soldier Indians were . . . to make medicine. **1890** Langford *Vigilante Days* (1912) 511 'Forty-niner' made medicine over the fallen chief, and removed his scalp. **a1918** G. Stuart *On Frontier* I. 129 The musicians are usually unsuccessful gamblers, pounding and singing to make 'medicine,' so that the next time they would be lucky. **1925** [see Medicine man].

+**e.** = Medicine dance.

1805 [see Buffalo dance].

+**3.** (See quot. 1847.)

1837 Irving *Bonneville* II. 15 A small twig is then stripped of its bark, and one end is dipped in the 'medicine,' as the trappers term the peculiar bait which they employ. *Ib.*, [The beavers] can scarcely be 'brought to medicine,' to use the trapper's phrase for 'taking the bait.' **1847** Ruxton *Adv. Rocky Mts.* (1848) 235 The trap is baited with the 'medicine,' an oily substance obtained from a gland in the scrotum of the beaver. **1884**

Pop. Science Mo. XXV. 20 The 'medicine' used as bait, sometimes denominated 'barkstone,' is the product of a gland of the beaver.

+4. Attrib. and comb. (sense 2 b) with *bird, chief, dog,* etc. See also MEDICINE ARROW, BAG, etc.

1833 CATLIN *Indians* I. 158 The mourning or turtle-dove, . . . being, as they [*sc.* Mandans] call it, a *medicine-bird*, is not to be destroyed or harmed by any one. **1851** M. REID *Scalp Hunters* 312 One was the medicine chief as I could tell by the flowing white hair. **1846** SAGE *Scenes Rocky Mts.* vi, The medicine-dogs (horses), bearing fire water (whiskey). **1843** HAWKS *D. Boone* 78 Boone . . . drank the war-drink, and did not even leave the 'medicine-ground.' **1846** SAGE *Scenes Rocky Mts.* vi, Who shall then bring us medicine-irons [guns] to kill our meat? **1875** BOURKE *Journal* 28 May, An Indian medicine rag was found this evening . . . in form like a banner or 'marker,' about 14 inches by 25. . . . It had emblazoned in black upon one side the representation of over 75 horse shoes. **1869** *Amer. Naturalist* II. 646 Two squaws passed through the fire to their places beneath the two medicine rocks. **1883** 'MARK TWAIN' *Life on Miss.* App. D, You see my medicine-sack, and my war-club tied to it. **1848** PARKMAN in *Knickerb.* XXXI. 331 The pipe . . . was passing from the left hand to the right around the circle; a sure sign that a 'medicine-smoke' of reconciliation was going forward. *Ib.* 330 Close to the camp stood a line of old women singing a medicine-song to allay the tumult. **1832** CATLIN *Indians* I. 40 In one hand he shook a frightful rattle, and in the other brandished his medicine spear or magic wand. **1847** RUXTON *Adv. Rocky Mts.* (1848) 243 The Indians regard with awe the 'medicine' waters of these fountains.

+**Medicine arrow.** Among American Indians, an arrow possessing magical power. *Obs.* — **1863** J. L. FISK *Exped. Rocky Mts.* 5 Antoine Freniere described it to be a 'medicine arrow.' **1876** BOURKE *Journal* 15 June, Much solemnity is attached to the 'medicine arrows' of the medicine man who seems to possess the powers of arbitrarily stopping a march at almost any moment. **1877** W. MATTHEWS *Ethnog. Hidatsa Indians* 69 They stuck their medicine-arrows in the ground.

+**Medicine bag.** The bag in which an Indian carries his charms, fetishes, remedies, etc.

1805 CLARK in *Lewis & C. Exped.* III. (1905) 170 The Chief then directed his wife to hand him his medison bag which he opened and showed us 14 fingers . . . of his enemies which he had taken in war. **1817** BRADBURY *Travels* 116 [The medicine man] took down his medecine bag, made of deer skin, and showed its contents. **1832** CATLIN *Indians* I. 36 Every Indian in his primitive state, carries his medicine-bag in some form or other. **1877** *Harper's Mag.* Feb. 454/1 Strings of colored beads, charms, medicine-bags, and a number of quaint utensils . . . glimmered duskily here and there. **1925** TILGHMAN *Dugout* 39 The coveted chain was worn by Sah-tah-pe to support his medicine bag, and was regarded as part of the medicine.

Medicine chest. A chest in which various medicines are kept. {1828-} — **1731** in Singleton *Social N.Y.* 85 A very fine Medicine Chest with great variety of valuable Medicines. **1807** IRVING, etc. *Salmagundi* iv. 75 Five trunks, three bandboxes, a cocked hat, and a medicine chest. **1848** *30th Congress 1 Sess.* Sen. Rep. No. 75, 26 Assistant Surgeon Duvall . . . [had] volunteered to go to the camp to arrange Captain Frémont's medicine chest, and to render any assistance in his power. **1902** NORRIS *Pit* 416 Isabel sent us a wedding present—a lovely medicine chest full of homœopathic medicines.

+**Medicine dance.** Among N.A. Indians, a dance engaged in to invoke or secure magical or supernatural aid.

1808 PIKE *Sources Miss.* 132 [At] the Grand Village . . . we saw the great medicine dance. **1844** GREGG *Commerce of Prairies* II. 263 All of the frontier as well as prairie Indians . . . had many kinds of dances—the green-corn dance, the medicine, . . . and the war dances. **1877** *Rep. Indian Affairs* 59 They have to a considerable extent the same religious ceremonies, medicine-dances, feasts, and fasts. **1885** *Ib.* 79 A strange sight is their 'medicine dance'—fascinating, weird scene, their bodies naked from the waist up.

+**Medicine house.** =next. *Obs.* — **1840** *Knickerb.* XV. 398 The 'Medicine-House,' that is to say, the temple, stood in the midst of the village. **1841** CATLIN *Indians* II. 232 Council or medicine-houses . . . are always held as sacred places.

+**Medicine lodge.** Among North American Indians, a structure used for dances and formal ceremonies: (see also quot. 1852).

1814 BRACKENRIDGE *Views La.* 258 A great number of young girls were collected before the medicine lodge or temple, prizes were exhibited [etc.]. **1833** CATLIN *Indians* I. 88 One of the lodges fronting on this circular area . . . is called the 'Medicine Lodge,' or council house. **1852** MARCY *Explor. Red River* (1854) 116 In every village may be seen small structures, consisting of a frame-work of slight poles, bent into a semi-spherical form, and covered with buffalo-hides. These are called medicine-lodges, and are used as vapor-baths. **1885** *Rep. Indian Affairs* 79 A number of braves enter the 'medicine lodge.' **1904** WHITE *Silent Places* 25 In fact at this very moment the big medicine lodge raised itself in the center of the encampment.

+**Medicine man.** Among North American Indians, one who practices healing; a priest, prophet, magician, etc.

Indian healers or physicians were of two classes. One class was composed of those who made use of herbs, sweatings, and other practical remedies. The other was made up of those who depended upon charms, fetishes, exorcism of evil spirits, etc. Members of this class served also as priests, prophets, magicians, conjurors, etc. (Cf. MEDICINE WOMAN.)

1806 ORDWAY in *Jrnls. Lewis & O.* 349 Everry fiew minutes one of their warries made a Speech . . . which was all repeated by another meddison man with a louder voice. **1817** BRADBURY *Travels* 116, I was accosted by the Medicine Man, or doctor. **1847** LANMAN *Summer in Wilderness* 105 A medicine man would sooner die, than divulge the secrets of his order. **1873** MILLER *Amongst Modocs* ii, Their priest or medicine man . . . chaunts the death-song. **1891** O'BEIRNE *Leaders Ind. Territory* x/1 The dance of the 'Pashofah' . . . is carried on in front of the patient, who is placed in a house facing the east, and only accessible to the Medicine Man. **1925** TILGHMAN *Dugout* 22 The medicine men of the Cheyennes had built prayer lodges and were industriously making medicine.

+**Medicine pipe.** An Indian pipe used in various rites and ceremonies. (Cf. CALUMET 1, 3.) — **1833** CATLIN *Indians* I. 111 With medicine-pipes in his hands and foxes tails attached to his heels, [he] entered Mah-to-he-hah. **1846** W. G. STEWART *Altowan* I. 177 Amid the fumes of the medicine-pipe, they could also quaff the forbidden spirit. **1847** PARKMAN in *Knickerb.* XXX. 477 [Over] this squalid habitation . . . were suspended a 'medicine-pipe' and various other implements of the magic art.

+**Medicine pole.** (See quotations.) — **1833** CATLIN *Indians* I. 90 In the centre of the little mound is erected a 'medicine pole,' about twenty feet high, supporting many curious articles of mystery and superstition. **1876** BOURKE *Journal* 14 July, The oriflame of the tribe, the 'medicine pole' was borne along in the procession: the staff is about 12 feet long and decorated elaborately with feathers of the eagle.

+**Medicine pouch.** =MEDICINE BAG. — **1855** LONGFELLOW *Hiawatha* 205 Then they shook their medicine-pouches O'er the head of Hiawatha. **1899** CUSHMAN *Hist. Indians* 41 [The Indian] has also been ridiculed as being an idiot for carrying with him his mystic Medicine-pouch, and relying on it for safety both in seen and unseen dangers.

+**Medicine song.** A song sung by Indians as an incantation or as part of a ritualistic ceremony. — **1791** LONG *Voyages* 74 They then smoke the pipe of peace, and have their dog feast: they also sing the grand medicine song. **1809** A. HENRY *Travels* 119 In his hand, he had his *shishiquoi*, or rattle, with which he beat time to his *medicine-song*. **1923** *Bureau Ethnology Bul. No. 80*, 149 We are only told that it is the 'medicine song' of Old Dog, a prominent chief of the old days, and that he sang it before a battle.

+**Medicine stone. 1.** (See quot. 1823.) **2.** (See quotations.) — **(1)** **1805** CLARK in *Lewis & C. Exped.* I. (1904) 264 Several men of their nation was gone to consult their Medison Stone. **1823** JAMES *Exped.* I. 252 The Me-ma-ho-pa or medicine stone of the *Gros ventres*, or Minnetarees, . . . is a large, naked, insulated rock. . . . The Minnetarees resort to it, for the purpose of propitiating their Man-ho-pa or Great Spirit. **(2)** **1885** HENSHAW in *Amer. Jrnl. Archæol.* I. 110, I was told they were 'medicine or sorcery stones' used by the medicine-men [among San Buenaventura Indians] in making rain, in curing the sick, and in various ceremonies. **1890** *Cent.* 3684/3 *Medicine-stone*, . . . a smooth stone found among American prehistoric remains. It was probably used as a sinker or plummet for fishing.

+**Medicine talk.** After the Indian manner of speaking: An important discussion or conference. *Obs.* — **1859** G. A. JACKSON *Diary* (MS.) 12 Had a 'medicine talk' with them about diggings. **1907** WHITE *Arizona Nights* 6 Then there was always a big medicine talk.

Medicine tree. +A species of California pine. *colloq.* — **1851** D. B. WOODS *At Gold Diggings* 142 It is called the 'medicine-tree,' because its pitch is used as a balsam for all burns and bruises.

+**Medicine wolf.** Among Plains Indians, the small prairie wolf or coyote. *Obs.* — **1837** IRVING *Bonneville* II. 147 This little, whining, feast-smelling animal, is . . . called among Indians the 'medicine wolf.' *c***1843** O. RUSSELL *Journal* (1921) 131 The least known is little prairie or medicine wolf. **1848** RUXTON *Life Far West* iii. 117 The *wachunkamănet*, or 'medicine wolf' of the Indians, who hold the latter animal in reverential awe.

+**Medicine woman.** Among the Indians, a female healer or diviner. (Cf. MEDICINE MAN.) — **1834** *Knickerb.* IV. 372 The mother evinced her sagacity, as a diviner or medicine woman. **1849** M. EASTMAN *Dahcotah* 33 A medicine woman is a female doctor or juggler. **1877** *Harper's Mag.* Feb. 452/1 The old lady was a notable 'medicine woman,' from an Indian point of view. **1907** HODGE, etc. *Amer. Indians* 838/2 Medicine-women . . . were found among the Apache and some other tribes.

* **Mediterranean,** *a.* and *n.*

+**1.** *adj.* Designating a *duty* or *fund* formerly levied or set aside by the United States for use in defending its commerce from the Barbary powers. *Obs.*

1807 *Ann. 10th Congress* 1 Sess. I. 1208 The duties constituting what was generally called the Mediterranean fund would expire on the first of January. *Ib.* 1209 He had no objection to the continuance of the Mediterranean duties. **1811** *Ib.* II. 2052 An addition of fifty per cent. to the present amount of duties, (together with a continuance of the . . . 'Mediterranean Fund,') will be sufficient.

+**2.** *To fit like a Mediterranean pass,* (see quotation).

1848 J. MITCHELL *Nantucketisms* 40/2 'Fits like a Mediteranean [*sic*] Pass.' Fits well. A Mediteranean Pass, or Passport, is severed by the government in two pieces, the line where it is cut being undulating, the larger part, about 4/5, is issued to vessels, the small retained. When they are placed together of course they fit exactly.

3. *n.* A species of wheat introduced from the Mediterranean region. In full *Mediterranean wheat.*

1849 EMMONS *Agric. N.Y.* II. 140 Mediterranean Wheat . . . is not cultivated in Western New-York. **1850** *Rep. Comm. Patents 1849: Agric.* 204 The golden straw and Mediterranean have lately been introduced. **1856** *Ib. 1855* 192 The 'Mediterranean' is generally used for seed, and certainly answers well.

4. *Mediterranean flour moth,* the common flour moth, the larva of which feeds on flour and meal.

1895 *Dept. Agric. Yrbk. 1894* 283 The Mediterranean Flour Moth . . . has attracted much attention of recent years. **1903** *Ib. 1902* 87 The Mediterranean flour moth . . was reported as injurious in mills in new localities in California.

***Medium.**

1. Bank notes or pieces of paper currency circulating as money. In full *medium of exchange.* {1798– (s.v. *circulating* ppl. a.)}

1714 *Boston News-Letter* 16 Aug. 2 Trade . . . is very much Embarassed for want of a Medium of Exchange. **1758** in Smith *Hist. Dartmouth Coll.* (1878) 16 Difficulties . . . attend the education of youth in this Province, by reason of . . . the discredit of our medium. **1778** *N.H. Hist. Soc. Coll.* IX. 108 The Iniquitous Sinking of our Medium outbids all my hopes of Surviving the evil. **1789** MORSE *Amer. Geog.* 118 From this plenty and fluctuating state of the medium, sprung hosts of speculators.

2. A person through whom departed spirits are supposed to communicate with people on earth. {1853–}

1852 *Harper's Mag.* VI. 129/1 The *media* are . . . multiplying . . . to such an extent, that presently no live man will be sure of his side-board, and no dead man will be sure of his soul. **1865** A. D. WHITNEY *Gayworthys* 132, I assisted once at a 'table-tipping;' we were all novices, to be sure; there was no 'developed medium' among us. **1883** 'MARK TWAIN' *Life on Miss.* xlviii, One of these clients of a spiritualistic medium was a man whom the spirits . . . were teaching how to contrive an improved railway car-wheel. **1898** *Kansas City Star* 18 Dec. 6/4 Jerry . . . has become a spiritualistic medium.

attrib. **1871** in De Vere 245 A Circle is held for Medium Developments and Spiritual Manifestations at Bloomfield-street every Sunday.

+Medlar bush. A small shrub of the genus *Amelanchier,* often found in swamps. — **1817-8** EATON *Botany* (1822) 181 *Aronia ovalis,* medlar bush. **1836** LINCOLN *Botany* App. 77. **1869** FULLER *Flower Gatherers* 31 Another species of the Aronia, or Amelanchier, is known as the 'Medlar Bush.'

+Medlark, Med'lark. Short for MEADOW LARK. — **1859** *Harper's Mag.* April 603/2 He had angled for sunfish and bull-pouts, and hunted gophers and med'larks in Connecticut. **1917** *Birds of Amer.* II. 251 Meadowlark. . . . [Also called] Medlark.

+Medregal. Also **madregal. 1.** An amber fish (*Zonichthys* or *Seriola fasciatus*) of the West Indies and the southern Atlantic seaboard. **2.** The rock salmon, *Zonichthys falcata.* — **(1)** [**1884** GOODE, etc. *Fisheries* I. 331 This fish, called in Cuba the 'Medregal' and in Bermuda the 'Bonito,' has been observed in South Florida and along the coasts of the Carolinas. It is apparently exceedingly rare in the waters of the United States.] **1896** JORDAN & EVERMANN *Check-List Fishes* 344 *Seriola fasciata.* . . . Madregal. West Indies, north to Charleston, South Carolina. **(2)** *Ib., Seriola falcata.* . . . Madregal; 'Rock Salmon.' West Indies, north to Florida and Carolina.

+Medrick. Also **†medrake, madrick.** [Origin obscure.] A small gull or tern. — **1832** WILLIAMSON *Maine* I. 145 We suppose there are with us four [species of gulls] . . . 4. the swallow-tail Gull, or Medrake. **1855** LOWELL *Poet. Works* (1896) 361/2 The medrick that makes you look overhead With short, sharp scream, as he sights his prey. **1890** *Cent.* 3687/2 *Medrick, madrick,* . . . the tern or sea-swallow.

Meerschaum. Also **†meerchaum.** Short for *meerschaum pipe,* a pipe the bowl of which is made of the soft claylike silicate of magnesium known as meerschaum. {1799–} — **1835** HOFFMAN *Winter in West* I. 88 A long-bearded German [was] smoking his meerchaum. **1857** HAMMOND *Northern Scenes* 43 He knocked the ashes from his meerschaum, and refilled it. **1877** *Harper's Mag.* Feb. 454/2 He laid hold of a finely colored meerschaum. **1903** 'O. HENRY' *Cabbages & Kings* (1916) 91 [The audience's] colour was of a diversity, running from a three-days' smoked meerschaum to a patent-leather polish.

Meerstead. Variant of MERESTEAD.

Meet,** *v.* **+intr. To meet up with,* to overtake or fall in with. *colloq.* Also fig. — **1837** SHERWOOD *Gaz. Georgia* (ed. 3), *Met up with,* for overtook. **1889** MUNROE *Golden Days* 96 They'd meet up with you somewheres along Coloma way. **1900** HARRIS *On the Wing* 148 They were fortunate enough to meet up with three men belonging to Captain McNeill's Rangers. **1909** WASON *Happy Hawkins* 16 If any one was to urge me, I'd be obliged to meet up with a little food.

***Meeting.**

***1.** An assembly or gathering of people, usually for worship.

1636 *Dedham Rec.* 20 Such a fyne to be set upon him as at the next meeting after shalbe thought fitting. **1687** *Mass. H. S. Coll.* 4 Ser. V. 155 Many are forced to keep three or four horses for the necessary use of their families to ride to meeting. **1741** *N.H. Probate Rec.* III. 53 A hors he is to find his mother with to Ride on to meeting. **1772** A. G. WINSLOW *Diary* 57 Yesterday I walk'd to meeting all day, the ground very dry. **1805** *Pocumtuc Housewife* (1906) 7 Some families like to get up a great dinner on Sundays and have friends who drive to Meeting from a distance come in for the Nooning. **1891** A. M. EARLE *Sabbath* 49 It was found necessary at a very early date to 'dignify the meeting,' which was to make certain seats, though in different localities, equal in dignity. *a***1918** G. STUART *On Frontier* I. 68 We would go home from meeting, [and] climb up into the loft where we slept.

2. A congregation of Quakers, or their place of meeting; a meetinghouse. {1688–} *To turn out of meeting,* to put out of the church.

1706 G. KEITH *Journal* (1851) 44 The Quakers had formerly a Meeting [in Oysterbay, L.I.]. **1791** BARTRAM *Travels* 9 Its polite inhabitants . . . were going to Medway meeting, a very large and well constructed place of worship. **1830** WATSON *Philadelphia* 335 The Friends' Meeting, in Front above Mulberry street, built in 1685, was originally intended as an 'Evening Meeting.' **1856** MACLEOD *F. Wood* 34 He went on fighting for his native land, and was turned out of meeting by his brethren.

+3. *To speak out in meeting,* and variants of this: To express oneself frankly, regardless of circumstances; 'to speak one's mind.' *colloq.*

1830 *Mass. Spy* 23 June (Th.), O dear, I spoke out in meeting, said she. **1875** *Chicago Tribune* 20 Aug. 7/3 These are the Indians that 'spoke out in meetin'.' **1906** in *Springfield W. Repub.* 13 Sept. 8, I do not think the president will think any the less of me for speaking right out in meeting and saying that I am not for it.

4. *attrib.* Designating clothes or articles of clothing worn by persons going to church.

1775 *Broadside Verse* (1930) 141/2 He got him on his meeting clothes. **1856** M. J. HOLMES *L. Rivers* 30 Nobody'd think any better of them for being rigged out in their very best meetin' gowns. **1866** LOWELL *Biglow P.* 2 Ser. p. lxxix, Her new meetin'-bunnet Felt somehow thru' its crown a pair O' blue eyes sot upon it. **1887** WILKINS *Humble Romance* 139 An' thar was Israel in his meetin' coat, an' me in my best gown. *Ib.* 300 Hatty in her . . . white meeting-hat . . . was not pretty.

+Meeting day. The day upon which meetings, usually of a religious nature, are held. — **1644** *Portsmouth Rec.* 32 It is . . . ordered that the businesse of such metinge dayes shalbe specified. **1686** SEWALL *Diary* I. 146 Mr. Moodey exercises at our House, being our meeting-day. **1900** DIX *Deacon Bradbury* 126, An' a lie it 'd be . . . ef I stayed in th' congregation another day after nex' meetin'-day.

Meeting hall. A hall in which meetings are usually held. — **1754** in Fries *Moravians in N.C.* II. 533 We can build a house, . . . below a Meeting Hall, a dwelling room, and above a Sleep Hall. **1905** DAVIS *Northerner* 53 Falls's manager had sent in bills . . . for lighting the churches and club-rooms, and meeting-halls. **1917** SINCLAIR *King Coal* 210 In some of the camps the meeting-halls belonged to the company.

Meetinghouse.

1. A house for worship; a church. {1687–} (Cf. CHURCH *n.* 2, *note.*) Now only local or rural.

'*Church.* This word in *Johnson's* third signification (that is, a place of worship) is generally used in *New-England,* to denote the places of worship of the *Episcopalians,* as they are here called. The places of worship of the other denominations of Christians are called *Meeting-houses.* In the *Southern* States, I believe, the word *Church* is used by Christians of all denominations' (Pickering).

1632 *Cambridge Rec.* 24 Dec. 4 Euery person . . . shall [be] . . . wthin [the] meeting-house in the Afternoone. **1695** *Manchester Rec.* I. 67 Ye township of Beverly betwen Manchester & Beverly Meeting house hath cow lots. **1734** *Md. Hist. Mag.* XVIII. 14 Quaker meeting house built on Mr. Rigbie's land. **1794** *Ann. 4th Congress* 2 Sess. 2865 A place called Mingo-creek Meeting-house, in the county of Washington. **1827** DRAKE & MANSFIELD *Cincinnati* 34 The Society of Friends was formed in 1813. Their Meeting House stands near the western part of the city. **1891** WILKINS *New Eng. Nun* 26 Folks are gettin' as high-steppin' an' fussy in a meetin'-house as they are in a tavern. **1906** CHURCHILL *Coniston* 68 The high pulpit, taken from the old meeting-house, and the cricket on which he used to stand.

b. Attrib. with *gallery, hill, post, timber.*

1647 *Watertown Rec.* I. i. 11 A wrighting, shall be sett vppon the meting-house-poost to giue notice to any that will by Thomas Philpots house and Land. **1687** *Manchester Rec.* I. 32 Near Vincsons baiberry medow . . . the meeting house timber was cut. **1787** TYLER *Contrast* (1790) III. i, They shewed me . . . up to the garret, just like meeting-house gallery. **1865** *Atlantic Mo.* XV. 346/1, I was transferred from the school on the meeting-house hill.

+2. *pl.* = COLUMBINE.

1892 *Amer. Folk-Lore* V. 91 *Aquilegia Canadensis,* meeting-houses. New England.

Meetinghouse yard. The yard or grounds about a meetinghouse. {1808–} — **1712** *N.H. Probate Rec.* I. 687 Northerly on the fence by the metinge house yard. **1844** *Knickerb.* XXIII. 404 Having no house for assembling together, the inhabitants met in what they termed 'the meeting-house yard;' and there . . . determined upon the erection of the old meeting-house.

+**Meeting seed.** (See quot. 1851.) *colloq.* — **1851** *Knickerb.* XXXVIII. 372 Some people call it 'caraway' and 'anise seed,' but we call it 'meetin'-seed,' 'cause we cal'late it keeps us awake in meetin'. **1889** COOKE *Steadfast* 414 Mothers of young families distributed fragrant bunches of dried 'meetin' seed' among their flocks. **1905** VALENTINE *H. Sandwith* 25 [He] sat contentedly munching 'meeting seed' which Molly Tucker, the family seamstress, had given him as entertainment on the drive.

+**Megaphone.** [Gk. *mega* 'great' and *phōnē* 'sound.']

1. (See quot. 1890.)

1878 *Scientific Amer.* XXXIX. 111/3 Now, at last, we have a megaphone, which is to the ear almost what the telescope is to the eye. **1890** *Cent.* 3691/2 *Megaphone*, ... an instrument devised by Edison for assisting hearing, adapted for use by deaf persons or for the perception of ordinary sounds at great distances. It consists essentially of two large funnel-shaped receivers for collecting the sound-waves, which are conducted to the ear by flexible tubes.

2. A large speaking trumpet. Also attrib.

1879 G. PRESCOTT *Speaking Telephone* 561 One of the most interesting experiments made by Mr. Edison ... is that of conversing through a distance of one and a half to two miles, with ... a few paper funnels. These funnels constitute the megaphone. **1896** *Boston Jrnl.* 5 Nov. 6/4 The Society for the Suppression of Needless Noise should regulate the use of the megaphone. **1902** *Harper's Mag.* Feb. 499/1 Blasts of a whistle or fog siren, when sounded through a megaphone, can be heard many miles farther at sea than if given in the ordinary manner. **1906** 'O. HENRY' *Four Million* 201 The megaphone barks at a famous hostelry. **1907** — *Trimmed Lamp* 180 The megaphone man roars out at you to observe the house of his uncle.

+**Megopher.** Variant of MAGOFER.

+**Meikie.** Variant of MICO.

+**Melada.** [Sp.] (See quotations.) — **1875** *Statutes at Large* XVIII. 340 Melada shall be ... defined as an article made in the process of sugar-making being the cane-juice boiled down to the sugar point. **1886** *Harper's Mag.* June 93/1 'Melada' is the name of the concentrated cane juice, just on the point of graining. **1892** *Mod. Lang. Notes* Nov. 393 *Masse cuite*, or sometimes *cuite* only—a synonym of *melada* ... and much more frequently used in this country.

+**Melainotype.** Also **melanotype.** [Gr. *melano-* 'black' and *type.*] A ferrotype or tintype. *Obs.* — **1857** BRAGDON *Seaboard Towns* Advt. (Ernst), The Melainotype ... takes the place of the ambrotype. **1858** A. L. STIMSON *Hist. Express Companies* Advt. (Ernst), General Depot for every thing necessary for Operators in ambrotype, Photograph, ... Melainotype, etc. **1867** SUTTON & DAWSON *Dict. Photogr.*, Melainotype. This positive process is of American origin. **1890** *Internat. Ann., Anthony's Photogr. Bul.* III. 302 These tin or melainotypes were taken everywhere. **1890** *Cent.* 3696/1 *Melanotype*. ... Rare or obsolete.

***Melilot.** Any one of various plants or species of plants, as sweet clover and honey lotus, belonging to the genus *Melilotus*. Also attrib. — **1737** BRICKELL *N. Carolina* 20 In these Parts ... several sorts of Horehound, Melilot, Bastard-Lovage. **1784** CUTLER in *Mem. Academy* I. 473 *Trifolium*. ... The indigenous species of this genus [include] ... the Melilot Clover, the Creeping Clover. **1843** TORREY *Flora N.Y.* I. 170 *Melilotus officinalis*. ... Yellow Melilot. ... Banks of rivers; common along the Mohawk. **1862** EMERSON in *Atlantic Mo.* Aug. 248/1 [Thoreau] liked the pure fragrance of melilot.

Melocoton. Also **melocotune, malacontoon.** A large peach produced by grafting a peach scion on a quince stock. In full *melocoton peach.* {1611–1745} — **1634** *Relat. Beginnings of Md.* 21 We haue also ... Limons, Melocotunes, Apples, Peares, Potatos. **1745** HEMPSTEAD *Diary* 449, I went out to Crossmans Lot and gathered the malacontoons. **1871** *Harper's Mag.* Dec. 57/1 Annie ... helped herself as she liked to the great white-heart cherries, melocoton peaches, and the delicious greengages.

+**Melodeon.**[1] {1880–} [Alteration of *melodium* (1847), a quasi-Latin formation on *melody*.] A type of reed organ.

1850 *Rep. Comm. Patents 1849* 278 Improvement in Melodeons. **1863** MASSETT *Drifting About* 246, I had a 'Melodeon' in those days (as pianos were difficult to obtain). **1871** *Rep. Indian Affairs* (1872) 173 We have sent out supplies of all kinds, from a melodeon down to a primer. **1883** *Harper's Mag.* July 296/2 The girls had the melojun, and the boys had everything from a willow whistle to a fiddle. **1920** HOWELLS *Vacation of Kelwyns* 228 Perhaps a girl at the melodeon ... could be made very effective.

Melodeon.[2] [Gr. *melos* 'song,' *ōdeion* (Fr. *odéon*) 'music hall'.] (See quot. 1864.) *Obs.* — **1861** E. COWELL *Diary* 283 Hattie James ... was burned to death, lately at the Gayities or Melodeon. **1864** WEBSTER 827/2 *Melodeon*, ... a music-hall.

***Melon.** Also †**milion.**

***1.** The fruit of any one of various succulent annual trailing plants, as cantaloupe, muskmelon, watermelon, etc.

1652 *Mass. H. S. Coll.* 4 Ser. VII. 63, I have sent you a rariti of seeds which came from the Mouhaks, which is a kinde of milions. **1705** BEVERLEY *Virginia* IV. 56 These they dish up various ways ... Sassafras-flowers, Cymnels, Melons, and Potatoes. **1790** S. DEANE *New-England Farmer* 171/2 Of all the kinds of melons, Mr. Miller greatly prefers the canteleupe. **1819** E. DANA *Geographical Sketches* 245 Vine fruits, such as melons, pumpkins, cucumbers, and squashes, are found to be productive in this soil. **1899** JEWETT *Queen's Twin* 119 'Twas herself had a thrifle of melons planted the other side of the fince.

2. Attrib. with *bed, day, farm, vine.*

1841 WHITMAN *Spec. Days* 341 The melon-beds are found to have been completely clear'd. **1856** *S. Lit. Messenger* XXII. 176/1 For all sorts of ... vines, whether grape-vines or melon vines, ... [the Kanawha] mountains are excellent. **1893** 'THANET' *Stories* 43 But at one's elbow spreads Cavendish's melon farm. **1893** *Harper's Mag.* May 940/1 Rocky Ford, in Otero County [Colo.], is celebrated for its observance of what is called 'melon day' every year, when the idle people, tourists, and pleasure-seekers gather there to eat free melons.

Melon box. A box with a glass top for growing a melon vine and protecting it from insects. — **1855** *Amer. Inst. N.Y. Trans.* 332 Prof. Mapes ... described the *insect lamp* and the preventive principles of the *melon box*.

+**Melon patch.** A patch or area on which melons, usually watermelons, are grown. — **1800** BROWN *A. Mervyn* xxx, On the other [side was] a melon-patch. **1844** *Knickerb.* XXIII, 14 Dick was a wild, rattling scape-grace, as ever robbed hen-roost or melon-patch. **1868** A. B. CONDICT *P. Eckert* 113 Was ... some poor man's melon-patch to be rifled, Dan led on the rest. **1884** ROE *Nature's Story* 152 As ready ... as is the average youth to visit a melon-patch by moonlight.

***Melter.** +A person employed in a United States mint to melt metal used in making coins. — **1795** *Ann. 3d Congress* 1403 The Assayer ... attends and inspects the Melter and Refiner. **1805** *Ann. 8th Congress* 2 Sess. 1671 The melter and refiner, one thousand five hundred dollars. **1837** *U.S. Laws concerning Money* (1910) 501 The melter and refiner shall execute all the operations which are necessary in order to form ingots of standard silver or gold. **1880** LAMPHERE *U.S. Govt.* 72/1, 2 deposit melters, each, per diem, $5.00.

Melting ladle. A ladle used in melting operations, esp. a shallow dishlike receptacle having a long handle, used in melting lead for bullets. — **1781** *Narragansett Hist. Reg.* I. 279 Made a melting ladle for Jeffrey Champlain. **1783** in Durrett *Louisville* 147 [Military stores include] 25 melting Ladles.

***Melting pot.** A pot in which various things are melted. — **1754** *S.C. Gazette* 5 Feb. 3/1 Just imported, ... Oil stones, melting and blue pots. **1800** *Columbian Centinel* 8 Jan. 3/4 Sale at 10 o'clock ... 4 casks blue Melting Pots. **1877** W. WRIGHT *Big Bonanza* 351 In the melting-room are six furnaces ranged in a row in which are placed the melting-pots.

Melton. A strong, heavy cloth suitable for various articles of men's wear. {1823–} Also attrib. — **1875** KNIGHT 1419/1 *Melton*, a kind of broadcloth for coating. **1877** *Rep. Indian Affairs* 5 The custom ... has been to furnish blankets, and clothing made of cotton-warp fabrics, known in the markets as 'satinets' and 'meltons.' **1889** *Century Mag.* Jan. 462/2 In time we appeared in every shade from Melton gray to Georgia butternut.

+**Melungeon.** [? Fr. *melange* 'mixture.'] A member of a group of people of mixed Indian, white, and Negro blood found in some parts of the mountainous portions of Tennessee and western North Carolina. — **1889** *Boston Traveller* 13 April (*Cent.*), They resented the appellation Melungeon, given to them by common consent by the whites, and proudly called themselves Portuguese.

***Member.**

***1.** One who has joined a church. In full *member of the church.*

1636 *Conn. Rec.* I. 2 The publicke allowance of the rest of the members of the saide Churches. **1796** MORSE *Univ. Geog.* I. 274 Summary of Faith and Order for 1793. ... Members. Particular Baptists. ... 67574. **1809** KENDALL *Travels* I. 815 There was no member of the church among the upper members of this family. **1900** DIX *Deacon Bradbury* 133 Every other member of the church you're going to scandalize.

+**2.** A legislator in either branch of Congress.

1788 *Mass. Convention* 191 Shall we have a right to send members to the new Congress? **1789** *Ann. 1st Congress* I. 15 This being the day for the meeting of the new Congress, the following members of the Senate appeared and took their seats. **1854** BENTON *30 Years' View* I. 71/1 The 'member of the House' was Mr. George Kremer, of Pennsylvania. **1860** *Harper's Mag.* April 688/1 In the Senate ... a series of seven resolutions ... had been drawn up in a caucus of the Democratic Members. **1884** MATTHEWS & BUNNER *In Partnership* 119 The member from New Jersey ... engaged him in debate.

+**b.** *Member of (the) Congress*, =prec.

This term is frequently used to mean a representative as distinct from a senator. In quot. 1774 it refers to the Continental Congress.

[**1774** WASHINGTON *Writings* II. 438 Dined at the State House, at an entertainment given by the city [of Philadelphia] to the members of the Congress.] *a***1800** TWINING *Visit* (1894) 32, I asked a person in the street where the Members of Congress put up when they arrived from the different States. **1848** BRYANT *California* xv. 201 An eloquence quite as incomprehensible as that of many a member of congress. **1872** TICE *Over Plains* 33, I failed seeing a historical character, ... a member of Congress from Massachusetts. **1900** *Congress. Rec.* 15 Feb. 1847/2 Members of Congress and Senators, if given the opportunity to furnish a particular kind of man, furnish that kind.

+**3.** A participant in or delegate to a constitutional convention or a state legislature.

1788 *Mass. Convention Debates* (1856) 204, I had been a member of the Convention to form our own State Constitution, and had learnt something of the checks and balances of power. **1874** J. S. PIKE *Prostrate State* 12 [In] the House of Representatives [of S.C.] . . . sit one hundred and twenty-four members.

+4. *Member bank*, (see quot. 1914).

1914 *Federal Reserve Act* § 1 The term 'member bank' shall be held to mean any national bank, state bank, or bank or trust company which has become a member of one of the reserve banks created by this Act. **1923** *Accountant's Handbk.* 865 Member banks may rediscount short-time commercial notes with federal reserve banks.

Member-elect. +One who has been elected, as to the United States Congress or to a state legislature, but has not taken up the duties of his office. — **1889** BUTLER *Recollections* 116 He plead his privilege of exemption from arrest because he was a member-elect of Congress. **1898** *Kansas City Star* 18 Dec. 2/5 Mr. Gregory is not a popular man with any of the members-elect of the legislature. **1900** *Congress. Rec.* 10 Jan. 748/2 Hon. William L. Greene, a member of the Fifty-fifth Congress and a member-elect to the Fifty-sixth Congress.

Memorandum book. A book in which memoranda are set down. {1753-} — **1759** *Newport Mercury* 26 June 4/3 To be sold . . . Brass Clocks, Memorandum Books, Pencils, &c. **1790** *Penna. Packet* 8 May 4/4 For Sale, . . . Letter books, account current, receipt and memorandum book. **1835** J. TODD *Student's Manual* 223 When any thing is said new, valuable, or instructive, enter it in your memorandum-book. **1893** *Harper's Mag.* Jan. 210/1 Her most beautiful thoughts (she kept them written out in a memorandum-book). *a***1918** G. STUART *On Frontier* I. 24 An old memorandum book of my grandfather's . . . tells of his trading with Indians in Virginia in 1793.

+**Memorandum check.** (See quot. 1859.) — **1835** *Mass. Rep.* XXXIII. 540 The word 'memorandum,' or 'Memo.' . . . was placed there as an admission or declaration on the part of the maker, . . . distinguishing them, as memorandum checks, from other checks which were to be presented for payment. **1859** BARTLETT 267 *Memorandum Check*, a check intended not to be presented immediately for payment; such an understanding being denoted by the word '*mem.*' written on it. **1873** *Supreme Ct. Rep.* LXXXIV. 503 Memorandum checks . . . are constantly used in the settlement of accounts between merchants. **1880** *Amer. Encycl. Commerce* II. 722/2 If a Memorandum Check is indorsed, it is valid like any other check in the hands of the indorsee.

***Memorial.** A written statement of facts attached to or forming part of a petition to a legislative or other body. {1713-} — **1697** *Mass. Acts & Res.* VII. 556 The Said Committee being also directed to Consider . . . ye memorialls presented by the ministers . . . are of Opinion [etc.]. **1797** *Ann. 5th Congress* I. 656 Mr. Gallatin presented the following memorial of certain citizens, called Quakers. **1832** DUNLAP *Hist. Amer. Theatre* 64 The memorial advised as above was presented to the legislature in April. **1900** *Congress. Rec.* 3 Jan. 638/1 A memorial of the legislature of the State of Colorado, favoring the return to the Republic of Mexico of captured cannon, flags, and banners.

Memorial Day. {1836-} +A day set aside as a holiday for honoring American soldiers and sailors who served in the Civil War or in later wars by the placing of flowers on their graves and by patriotic services.

In most states May 30 is the date of this observance. The Confederate celebrations in the Southern states, however, vary in date from April 26 to June 3. (Cf. DECORATION DAY.)

1869 *G.A.R. (R.I. Dept.) 3d Encampm. Proc.* 32 Those patriotic men and women . . . gave their aid . . . to make successful this National Memorial day. **1873** *Newton Kansan* 15 May 2/1 Gen. A. E. Burnside . . . has issued an order . . . for the observance of the next memorial day. **1896** *Boston M. Journal* 26 June 3/7 The quint made its first appearance on Memorial Day. [*i.e.*, May 30.] **1905** *Springfield W. Repub.* 5 May 10 Wednesday last week [April 26] was the southern or confederate Memorial day. . . . It is claimed in the South . . . that their Memorial day antedates ours by two years, theirs having been established in 1866.

attrib. **1897** FLANDRAU *Harvard Episodes* 181, I was thinking of all the horrible . . . Baccalaureate Sermons and ghastly Memorial Day orators that are allowed to go on. **1904** *N.Y. Ev. Post* 30 May 2 Thousands of people gathered this morning to witness the Memorial Day parade of civil war veterans.

Memorialist. One who presents a petition or memorial. {1713-} — **1706** *Mass. Acts & Resolves* VIII. 721 Resolved That the sum of three hundred & fifty Pounds, be allowed & Paid out of the publick Treasury to Mr. Thomas Oakes the memorialist. **1778** *Jrnls. Cont. Congress* XI. 580 The memorialist hath produced to the Committee a promissory note. **1857** *Congress. Globe* 7 Jan. 248/1 The memorialist was struck by an escopette, or two-ounce ball, on his sword-hilt. **1899** in *Congress. Rec.* 15 Jan. (1900) 798/2 We, your memorialists, the legislature of the State of Washington, represent as follows.

Memorist. {1682} +A memorizer; one with a keen memory. — **1872** *New Cycl. Illustr. Anecdote* 9/2 Fame has given me the report of being a memorist. **1890** *Cent.* 3705/3 *Memorist*, . . . one who has a retentive memory.

Memorize,** *v. tr.* To commit to memory. 'Chiefly *U.S.*' (*O.E.D.*). — **1856** OLMSTED *Slave States* 552 His power of memorizing and improvising music. *a1870** CHIPMAN *Notes on Bartlett* 267 *Memorize. v.* To commit to memory; repeat from memory; to remember well.—N[ew] E[ng.]. **1878** W. H. DANIELS *That Boy* 140 He had even taken the pains to memorize a number of hymns and sonnets.

Menagerie. {1712-} A collection of wild animals kept for exhibition, often a part of a traveling circus. {1762-} Also attrib. — **1843** *Whig. Almanac 1844* 42/2 Davy Crockett was once attending a menagerie exhibition in Washington. **1878** DALY in J. F. Daly *Life A. Daly* 253, I have been travelling with old John Robinson's Circus and Menagerie. **1896** HARRIS *Sister Jane* 86 These immense bills were intended to inform the public at large that Robinson and Eldred's circus and menagerie would pitch its tent. **1920** COOPER *Under Big Top* 110 He took his place when the rest of the menagerie crew departed and began his vigil.

Mend, *v. To mend one's fences*, (see FENCE *n.* 2 c).

Mending basket. A basket for clothing that needs mending. Also fig. — **1863** 'G. HAMILTON' *Gala-Days* 41, I find myself in a mending-basket. **1873** PHELPS *Trotty's Wedding* vii, Poppet's mother was resting on the mending-basket, and she sat there, amazed. **1898** NICHOLS *Idyl of Wabash* 18 Taking his hose from the mending basket and darning them.

Mending day. The day on which a housewife mends the clothing of her household. — **1866** WHITNEY *L. Goldthwaite* xi, What *should* we do without our mending-day?

***Mendment.** +=AMENDMENT 2. *Obs.* — **1738** *Southampton Rec.* III. 127 The mendment of meadow belonging to No. 33, Lies on a poynt of Segg near the beach. **1745** *Ib.* 77 There is a path or passing Rode between the lot and the mendment.

+**Menhaden.** Also †**manhadden.** [Algonquian.] A marine fish of the family Clupeidae (*Brevoortia tyrannus*), abundant on the eastern coast of the United States: (see also quot. 1890).

Cf. BUNKER, MARSHBANKER, etc.

[**1643** WILLIAMS *Key* 136 Aumsûog, & Munnawhatteaûg. *A Fish somewhat like a Herring.*] **1792** TOULMIN *Descr. Ky.* 42 [In 1787 were exported from Phila.] barrels of manhadden 236. **1842** *Nat. Hist. N.Y., Zoology* IV. 259 The Menhaden, Hard-head, *Alosa menhaden.* . . . Its use as a manure is well known in the counties of Suffolk, Kings and Queens. **1867** *Amer. Naturalist* I. 224 The Finbacks feed on menhaden, and other small fishes. **1890** *Cent.* 3707/3 The name *menhaden* extends in literary use to all the other species of *Brevoortia*, of which there are several, as *B. patronus* of the Gulf of Mexico; and it is locally misapplied to the thread-herring, *Opisthonema thrissa*.

attrib. *a***1877** *Sag Harbor Express* (B.), During the last two weeks, the bunker or menhaden fishery has been very brisk. **1882** *Harper's Mag.* Sept. 588/1 A deck-load of brick for a menhaden oil-works had been dumped [on the wharf].

+**Mennist.** [Du.] =MENNONITE. Also attrib. (Cf. MENNONIST.) — **1869** *Atlantic Mo.* Oct. 474/1 The Mennists in many outward circumstances very much resemble the Society of Friends. . . . In the interior of the Mennist meeting, a Quaker-like plainness prevails. **1889** HOWELLS *Hazard of Fortunes* I. 208 Aren't they [Dunkards] something like the Mennists?

Mennonist. Also **Menonist.** =next. {1645-} — *a***1772** WOOLMAN *Journal* 122 At Monalen a Friend gave me some account of a religious society among the Dutch, called Mennonists. **1776** J. ADAMS *Works* IX. 403 At present some colonies have . . . bodies of Quakers, and Mennonists, and Moravians, who are principled against war. **1814** MCKEAN in *Ib.* X. 87 The opposition consisted chiefly of the Friends or Quakers, the Menonists, the Protestant Episcopalians. **1830** S. H. COLLINS *Emigrant's Guide* 62 The following denominations of christians are more or less numerous in the United States . . . German Calvinists or Presbyterians, Moravians, and Mennonists. **1866** H. PHILLIPS *Hist. Sk. Paper Currency* II. 72 The Menonists refuse to sell their produce unless for hard cash.

***Mennonite.** A member of a Protestant denomination originating in Friesland and organized by Menno Simons (1492-1559), from whom the sect was named.

1727 in Rupp *Relig. Denominations* (1844) 489 The Confession of Faith of the harmless and defenceless Christians, called Mennonites, is as yet little known. **1844** *Ib.* 693 Some were Lutherans, others Mennonites, and some few Methodists. **1867** DIXON *New America* II. 135 [Devotion to education] gives to the Shaker society an importance in the Union far beyond its rivals (Tunkers, Moravians, Mennonites). **1878** BEADLE *Western Wilds* 388 The German-Russian Mennonites have been pouring into Southern Dakota by thousands. **1919** *Religious Bodies: 1916* (Census) 417/1 The Mennonites . . . have often been charged with being 'clannish.'

b. Attrib. with *Baptist, book concern, colony, society.*

1844 Rupp *Relig. Denominations* 502 Reformed Mennonite Society. [Account] by the Rev. John Herr. Strasburg, Lancaster County, Pennsylvania. **1889** *Harper's Mag.* Oct. 776 He sees a smooth-shaven, long-haired people—the Mennonite Baptists— . . . speaking Pennsylvania Dutch. **1905** *N.Y. Ev. Post* 6 June 6 The young men of the Mennonite colonies in various parts of this country are breaking away from the old faith. **1919** *Religious Bodies: 1916* (Census) 431/1 A Mennonite book concern, located at Berne, Ind., issues a monthly and 2 weekly papers.

+**Menominee, Menomonee.** [Algonquian.] An Indian of an Algonquian tribe first encountered by Europeans near the mouth of the Menominee River in Wisconsin and Michigan. — **1837** VAN BUREN in *Pres. Mess. & P.* III. 391 Stipulations have been made with all the Indian tribes to remove them beyond the Mississippi, except with . . . the Six Nations in New York, the Menomonees, Munsees, and Stockbridges in Wisconsin. **1843** MARRYAT *M. Violet* ix, The Algonquin species, or family, produced twenty-one different tribes; the Micmacs, . . . Ottawas, Menomonies, Sacs [etc.]. **1907** HODGE, etc. *Amer. Indians* 842/1 *Menominee . . . meno*, by change from *mino*, 'good,' 'beneficent'; *min*, a 'grain,' 'seed', the Chippewa name of the wild rice.

+**Menominee whitefish.** A small whitefish (*Prosopium quadrilaterale*) found in northern lakes. — **1884** GOODE, etc. *Fisheries* I. 541 *Coregonus quadrilateralis*. The only name which I have heard applied to this fish is that of 'Menomonee White-fish.' **1911** *Rep. Fisheries 1908* 318/1 The Menominee whitefish . . . is also locally known as 'round whitefish,' 'frostfish,' etc.

+**Menzies spruce.** [f. Archibald *Menzies*, Scotch botanist (1754–1842)]. (See quot. 1897.) — **1869** BREWER *Rocky Mt. Lett.* 46 The trees [were] mostly Menzies spruce. **1897** SUDWORTH *Arborescent Flora* 41 *Picea sitchensis*. . . . Sitka Spruce. . . . [Also called] Menzies Spruce.

Mercantile, *a.* Designating firms or institutions conducted by merchants or in their interests. {1642–}

1823 COOPER *Pioneers* ii, A mercantile house was established in the metropolis of Pennsylvania. **1851** CIST *Cincinnati* 321 In the west, . . . his brothers were about establishing a mercantile firm. **1870** M. H. SMITH *20 Years Wall St.* 435 He was placed in a mercantile house in Boston, where he mastered the mercantile trade. **1881** *Harper's Mag.* Feb. 384/2 A group of young men like the Mercantile Library Association could set going a system of lectures. **1910** BOSTWICK *Amer. Pub. Library* 6 The 'Mercantile' type, represented by the libraries of that name in New York, Boston, and St. Louis, arose about 1820, originating in the desire to furnish good reading for the younger employees of business houses.

+**Mercantile store.** A retail store. — **1814** BRACKENRIDGE *Views La.* 123 There is a printing office, and twelve mercantile stores. **1819** E. DANA *Geogr. Sk.* 77 This town [in Ohio] . . . contains a neat court house, . . . 21 mercantile stores. **1835** MARTIN *Descr. Virginia* 143 There are 29 dwelling houses, 3 mercantile stores.

***Mercenary.** A professional soldier in the employ of a foreign government. Often with specific reference to the Hessians employed by the British government during the Revolutionary War. — **1776** *Jrnls. Cont. Congress*. IV. 369 Resolved, That . . . the said committee be directed . . . to prepare an address to the foreign mercenaries who are coming to invade America. **1776** *Decl. Independence*, [The King] is at this time transporting large armies of foreign mercenaries to compleat the works of death, desolation, and tyranny. **1867** EDWARDS *Shelby* 37 The 3d Louisiana . . . scattered his [Gen. Sigel's] German mercenaries.

Mercer. +A variety of potato. In full *Mercer potato*. — **1839** *Mass. Agric. Survey 2d Rep.* 34 The Chenango [potato], sometimes called the Mercer, or Pennsylvania Blue. **1850** *New Eng. Farmer* II. 349 The Mercer or Chenango potato is more liable to rot than most other varieties. **1855** *Mich. Agric. Soc. Trans.* VII. 637 The committee noticed a very fine lot of six varieties of potatoes, viz: White mercer, blue meshanics [etc.]. **1856** *Rep. Comm. Patents 1855: Agric.* 221 The 'Mercers' . . . find the most ready sale in market.

||**Merchandise-lumber.** Lumber that is merchantable. — **1682** *Mass. Bay Currency Tracts* 5 A Proposal for erecting a Fund of Land . . . in the nature of a Money-Bank; or Merchandise-Lumber, to pass Credit upon, by Book-Entries.

***Merchant.** One who engages in the business of buying commodities and selling them at a profit, especially one who deals in large quantities or at wholesale.

The second group of examples shows the extension of the term to retailers and shopkeepers as in Sc. and northern Eng. use.

(1) **1630** *Mass. Bay Rec.* I. 76 Those of Dorchester whoe bought certayne cattell of the merch[an]ts of Dorchester shall pay [etc.]. **1680** *Boston Rec.* 67, I, John Usher, of Boston, mercht., binde me, unto Capt. Tho. Brattle. **1704** *Boston News-Letter* 7 June 2/2 Two Negro men and one Negro Woman & Child; to be Sold by Mr. John Colman, merchant. **1833** *Niles' Reg.* XLIV. 403/1 Among the most important improvements carried on by the enterprise of the Boston merchants . . . is the splendid block now going up. **1867** EDWARDS *Shelby* 505 He was a miller, a farmer, an engineer, a drover, and a merchant. **1890** LANGFORD *Vigilante Days* (1912) 174 An attempt to rob the store of Higgins and Worden at Missoula would have succeeded, had not the merchants been apprised of it, in time to conceal their gold.

(2) **1704** S. KNIGHT *Journal* 56 [The Indians] give the title of merchant to every trader. **1784** SMYTH *Tour* I. 99 Linen-drapers, grocers, stationers, &c. are not known here; they are all comprehended in the single name and occupation of merchant, or store-keeper. **1829** *Va. Lit. Museum* 30 Dec. 459 *Merchant*. . . . In many parts of the United States, it means a retail dealer. **1853** *Harper's Mag.* Aug. 425/1 The subject, we take it, is the 'merchant' of a country-store; quite a different variety from the big bugs of the trade in the Great Metropolis. **1896** BRYAN in D. J. Brewer *World's Best Orations* (1899) II. 695 The merchant at the cross-roads store is as much a business man as the merchant of New York.

attrib. **1734** *Mass. H. Rep. Jrnl.* 77 On a motion made and seconded by divers Members respecting the Circulation of Merchant Notes so called. **1757** FRANKLIN *Writings* III. 408, I stopt my horse lately where a great number of people were collected at a vendue of merchant goods. **1875** *Chicago Tribune* 6 Oct. 8/3 John Hoffman and William Jones are two enterprising merchant-policemen in the West Division.

***Merchantable,** *a.* Suitable for market; of a good grade. **1635** *Maine Doc. Hist.* III. 60 The full weight . . . of merchantable bever skins . . . is in 3 hodgheds & a little fardell. **1674** JOSSELYN *Two Voyages* 210 When they share their fish . . . they separate the best from the worst, the first they call Merchantable fish, being sound, full grown fish and well made up. **1705** *N.C. Col. Rec.* I. 624 Seven Shillings & Six pence due by Bill payable in good Sound Merchantable Porke. **1795** WINTERBOTHAM *Hist. View* II. 116 The fish of the summer and fall fares is divided into two sorts, the one called merchantable, and the other Jamaica fish. **1833** *Niles' Reg.* XLIV. 355/1 The standard weight for merchantable wheat this season, has been fixed . . . at 58 lbs. the bushel. **1868** *Iowa Agric. Soc. Rep. 1867* 18 A gallon of sirup should furnish five pounds of merchantable sugar. **1909** *Indian Laws & Tr.* III. 403 All merchantable timber on said lands . . . shall be sold and disposed of by the Secretary of the Interior.

***Merchant adventurer.** A merchant who organized trading expeditions and established trading posts in distant territories. (Cf. ADVENTURER.) Now hist. — **1654** JOHNSON *Wonder-w. Prov.* 19 Of the first preparation of the Marchant Adventurers, in the Mattachusets. **1921** S. E. MORISON *Maritime Hist. Mass.* 44 The *Columbia's* first voyage began the Northwest fur trade, which enabled the merchant adventurers of Boston to tap the vast reservoir of wealth in China.

+**Merchanter.** Also **merchanteer.** A trading vessel; a merchantman. — **1829** MARRYAT *F. Mildmay* xiv, I'll fit out a privateer, and take some o' your merchanters. **1890** *Public Opinion* 30 Aug., A departure from the merchanteer type [of ship] was the immediate result.

Merchant marine. {1894–} +The publicly and privately owned vessels of the United States engaged in commerce. — **1855** 'P. PAXTON' *Capt. Priest* 40 Captain Job . . . embarked in our merchant marine. **1900** *Congress. Rec.* 15 Jan. 844/1 To the Committee on the Merchant Marine and Fisheries. **1914** STEELE *Storm* 151 'What's the matter, Spare Hand?' I had never addressed him by any other title (corresponding to the 'mate' of the merchant marine).

+**Merchant mill.** A mill where grain is bought, ground, and resold.

1774 FITHIAN *Journal* I. 111 Mr. Carter's Merchant Mill begins to run to-day. **1798** C. WILLIAMSON *Descr. Genesee* ii, Towards the end of summer a set of merchant mills were in considerable forwardness. **1816** U. BROWN *Journal* I. 273 He has a Merchant Mill, a Saw Mill, a Carding Mill, all on the Waters of Bath. **1851** CIST *Cincinnati* 194 It proposes to perform in a small compass, with less expense, greater safety and equal efficiency, the work of a merchant mill. **1877** JOHNSON *Anderson Co., Kansas* 252 In the spring of 1874 Chris. Bouck . . . immediately commenced the construction of a first-class merchant mill.

Merchant prince. An extremely successful and wealthy merchant. Also *humorous*. {1847–}

1841 THOREAU *Journal* 176 Among the Bedouins the richest man is the sheik, . . . and in England and America he is the merchant prince. **1853** STOWE *Key* 33/1 One of the merchant princes of Boston . . . afforded in his life a beautiful example of this truth. **1884** *Milnor* (Dak.) *Teller* 3 Oct., S. D. Bowker, the celebrated merchant-prince of Tewaukon, called at this office Wednesday evening. **1916** WILSON *Somewhere* 374 They was merchant princes from Sandusky or prominent Elks from Omaha.

Merchant service. Also **merchants' service.** Maritime commerce; the merchant marine. — **1790** *Ann. 1st Congress* II. 1549 A bill [shall] be brought in for the government and regulation of seamen in the merchants' service. **1797** *Ann. 5th Congress* I. 445 In the year 1795 there was a deficiency in that trade [fishing], owing . . . to the great demand for seamen in the merchant service. **1816** *Ann. 14th Congress* 2 Sess. 267 *Resolved*, That the Committee on Foreign Relations be instructed to inquire what alterations are necessary in the . . . regulation of seamen in the merchant service. **1840** DANA *Two Years* 4, I design to give an accurate and authentic narrative of . . . two years spent as a common sailor, before the mast, in the American merchant service.

Merchants' exchange. A place where merchants come together in furtherance of common business interests. — **1840** *Niles' Nat. Reg.* 22 Aug. 400/3 The comptroller of the state of New York . . . will cause to be sold at the Merchants' Exchange . . . the following state stocks. **1882** MCCABE *New York* 301 It was used for a number of years as the Merchants' Exchange.

***Merchant ship.** A merchantman or trading vessel. — **1747** *Md. Gazette* 13 Jan., A Merchant Ship was arrived at Boston from England. **1767** HUTCHINSON *Hist. Mass.* II. 217 Colonel Shute arrived . . . in a merchant-ship. **1880** *Harper's Mag.* July 270/1 The merchant ships made much shorter [voyages than the packet ships]. **1907** *St. Nicholas* Sept. 1047/2 He was sailing on a merchant ship named the *Rainbow*.

+**Merchants' watch.** (See quotations.) *Obs.* — **1733** *Boston Rec.* 52 The Town would alow Something toward the Charge of A watch at the Dock called the Merchants Watch which has hitherto bin Supported by a Number of Merchants. **1736** *Boston Selectmen* 301 The Watchmen supported at the Charge of the Merchants, and usually called *The Merchant's Watch*.

***Merchant tailor.** Originally a tailor who was also a merchant, dealing in or supplying the materials used in his shop, but later, esp. in American use, any tailor. (Cf. quot. 1818.) {Obs. except in guild name}

1653 *Boston Rec.* I, I Robert Keayne, Cittizen and Mrchant Taylor of London by freedome, . . . now dwelling at Boston. **1818** FEARON *Sketches* 33 Taylors are numerous: they are denominated, (in conformity with the accustomed vanity of the country,) 'Merchant Taylors.' **1841** Cist *Cincinnati* (*advt.*), James Bishop, Merchant Tailor. **1855** *Chicago Times* 16 Jan. 3/8 T. Spear, merchant tailor and dealer in cloths. **1892** *York County*

Hist. Rev. 7 David H. Welsh, Clothing Furnisher and Merchant Tailor, 13 E. Market St.

Merchant tailoring, *a.* Of or pertaining to the work or business of a merchant tailor. — **1872** *Chicago Tribune* 12 Oct. 5/3 Henry Nolte's merchant tailoring establishment. **1892** *York County Hist. Rev.* 64 Another feature and worthy of mention is the merchant tailoring department.

Merchant train. {1861–} +A train or series of wagons or pack animals conveying the goods of merchants or traders. — **1852** STANSBURY *Gt. Salt Lake* 229 A merchant-train for Salt Lake passed us during the day, from which I procured some sugar and coffee. **1860** GREELEY *Overland Journey* 206 The road, though much traversed by Mormons as well as emigrants and merchant-trains, is utterly abominable.

***Merchant vessel.** =MERCHANT SHIP. — [**1711** *Boston News-Letter* 23 April 2/1 A Wreck (a Briganteen) was found in the Latitude of 29, out of which a Merchant Vessel took a Cask of Bread, and an Anchor from the Bow.] **1797** *Ann. 4th Congress* 2 Sess. 2145 It must be the interest of Britain to diminish the number of your merchant vessels and sailors. **1836** *Diplom. Corr. Texas* I. (1908) 158 Depend not upon merchant vessels for a transmission of your correspondence with me. **1847** POLK in *Pres. Mess. & P.* IV. 554 Should the ratio of increase in the number of our merchant vessels be progressive, . . . our tonnage and commercial marine will be larger than that of any other nation in the world.

Merestead. Also **meerstead, misted, midstead, meadstead.** [Var. of *mesestead*, a messuage, through confusion with *mere* and *mead*.] A portion of land assigned or allotted to a colonist as a site for a residence. Now hist.

The forms in *meer-*, *mere-*, and *mead-* appear to be exclusively Amer.; *midstead* occurs in Yorkshire dial. (1896).

*c*1620 *Plymouth Col. Rec.* XII. 3 The meersteads & garden plotes of (those) which came first layed out 1620. **1633** *Ib.* I. 16 Richard Higgens hath bought of Thomas Little his now dwelling house and misted. **1637** *Ib.* I. 57 A midstead is graunted to George Russell in . . . Plymouth. **1640** *Ib.* 145 Willm Sherman is graunted a meadstead about the Stoney Brooke, in Duxborrow. **1858** LONGFELLOW *Poetical Works* (1893) 180/2 The men were . . . Busy with . . . garden-plot and with merestead. **1883** *New Eng. Hist. & Gen. Register* XXXVII. 277 Peter Brown, whose first house and 'meerstead' was on the south side of Leyden Street.

***Merestone.** Also **meerstone.** A stone set up to mark a bound or boundary. *Obs.*

1640 *Conn. Rec.* I. 53 The owners thereof shall bound every prticular prcell wth sufficient merestones, and so to prsearve & keepe them. **1687** *Hartford Land Distrib.* 571 One percell . . . Bounded wth. meer Stones. **1704** *Conn. Rec.* IV. 473 Running near west from a certain oak tree marked and a meerstone sett by it. **1770** *Ib.* XIII. 399 The inhabitants of said towns . . . mutually agreed to run a due east line from said meerstone one hundred and seventy rods.

Merganser. {1752–} A species of fish-eating duck of the subfamily Merginae, +esp. the fresh-water sheldrake (*Mergus americanus*); also, a bird of one of these species. Also with distinguishing adjectives.

Cf. HOODED MERGANSER.

1813 WILSON *Ornithology* VIII. 81 Red-breasted Merganser: *Mergus serrator*; . . . is frequently brought to the Philadelphia market from the shores of the Delaware. **1871** BURROUGHS *Wake-Robin* (1886) 122 A brood of the goosander, or red merganser, was the occasion of some spirited rowing. **1882** GODFREY *Nantucket* 158 There are times when the mergansers, coot, and eider furnish rare sport. **1895** *Outing* XXVII. 211/1, I killed a merganser that flew too close to me for his good. **1917** *Birds of Amer.* I. 110 Merganser *Mergus americanus*. . . . Other Names.— . . . American Merganser; Greater Merganser; . . . Buff-breasted Merganser.

+**Mergenthaler.** [f. Ottmar *Mergenthaler*, Ger.-Amer. inventor (1859–99).] **1.** *attrib.* Of or pertaining to the typesetting machine invented by Mergenthaler. **2.** One of these machines. (Cf. LINOTYPE.) — (1) **1896** *Internat. Typogr. Union Proc.* 44/2 Otis stands ready to furnish any paper with an unlimited number of Mergenthaler operators at short notice. *Ib.* 89/1 The Times is a Merganthaler office, thirteen machines being at present in operation. **1923** *Linotype Decorative Material* 1 Mergenthaler Linotype Company, 29 Ryerson Street, Brooklyn, N.Y. (2) **1896** *Internat. Typogr. Union Proc.* 29/1 The Times had just put in Mergenthalers, and would not accept the union scale. **1898** *Ib.* 54/2 There were no Mergenthalers in Quincy.

Merger. {1728–} +The merging or consolidation of different corporations or businesses into one organization. Also transf. {1902–}

In strict usage, *merger* indicates a combination in which the identity of every combining company but one is lost in that one; *consolidation* indicates a combination in which a new company absorbs the identity of every one of the combining companies.

1889 *Boston Jrnl.* 17 April 4/3 Ample powers of consolidation and merger, transfer and absorption of stock and kindred franchises are given. **1903** *Chicago Chronicle* 11 April 1/7 (*caption*), Decision Against Merger Causes Deep Concern. **1905** *Springfield W. Repub.* 1 Sept. 2 The people of Arizona are so hostile to a merger with New Mexico that they are now content to remain a territory for an indefinite period.

attrib. **1903** *Chicago Chronicle* 11 April 2 The stockholders will receive their profits from . . . the two roads, the joint stock of which is held by the merger corporation.

+**'Merican.** Short for AMERICAN *n.* 2. *colloq.* — **1761** NILES *Indian Wars* II. 408 The 'Merican's garland with much blood was won. **1850** GARRARD *Wah-To-Yah* ix. 119 The Purblos (Pueblos de Taos) was mity mad fur the 'Mericans to come in thar diggins. **1870** O. LOGAN *Before Footlights* 195 Your central Asiatic, it appears, can do nothing on earth but . . . pilfer all the Mericans he can lay hands upon.

Meridian compass. A compass especially suitable for use in establishing meridian lines. {1703–} — **1657** *Boston Rec.* 47 A nor. northwest Line . . . [was] to be run by a Meridian Compasse. **1660** *Essex Inst. Coll.* XXXVII. 229 Mr. John Gardener . . . [ran] the bounds betwixt Bostone, Charlestown and Lynn . . . by a merridian Compass. **1675** *Boston Rec.* 94, I did run a line . . . by a maridian compasse or a needle touched wch hath noe variation allowed.

***Meridian line.** +In land-surveying, a north and south line forming right angles with its corresponding base line. (Cf. BASE LINE 1.)

1761 *Holyoke Diaries* 23 Drew a Meridian line for Mr. Mascarene. **1834** PECK *Gaz. Illinois* 93 In the surveys [of new states and territories], 'meridian' lines are first established, running north from the mouth of some noted river. **1843** *Pres. Mess. & P.* IV. 244 The party of Mr. L. pursued the height of land as nearly as possible and reached the exploring meridian line. **1862** *New Amer. Encycl.* XV. 204/2 Each great survey is based upon a meridian line run due N. and S.

Merino. Also †**marino.**

1. *ellipt.* =MERINO SHEEP. {1810–} Also attrib.

(Cf. AMERICAN MERINO.)

1802 (*medal*), Presented by the Massa. Society for Promoting Agriculture to the Honle. David Humphreys . . . as a Testimony of Respect for his Patriotic Exertions in Importing into New England 100 of the Marino breed of Sheep from Spain. **1809** CUMING *Western Tour* 483 It is not uncommon at this time to give from two to three dollars per pound for the full-bred Merino wool. **1810** *Steele P.* II. 627 Pray write particularly on the subject of merinos. **1842** *Cultivator* IX. 82/2 They are common sheep, except one—a merino buck. **1850** *Rep. Comm. Patents 1849: Agric.* 88 Vermont once numbered nearly one and a half million of sheep, which have dwindled down, probably to about half a million, . . . ranging in quality from half to full-blood merino. **1871** GROSVENOR *Protection* 322 Having 100 pounds of full blood merino fleece in 1860, he could sell at 50 cents in gold. **1893** G. W. CURTIS *Horses, Cattle* 241 In the South, the Merinos are better known than any other breed of sheep.

2. A soft dress fabric originally made of the wool of Merino sheep. {1823–} Also attrib.

1820 BRECK in *Recoll.* (1877) 298 She has gone on . . . bedecking herself in merino shawls. **1850** S. WARNER *Wide, Wide World* v, Mamma wished me to look at merinoes, sir, if you please. **1856** GOODRICH *Recoll.* I. 405 In 1809, when Madison was inaugurated, his coat was made of Merino cloth from a manufactory established by Humphries. **1892** *York County Hist. Rev.* 85 The salesroom . . . carries a fine line of . . . dress goods in wool, merino and cotton goods.

b. A dress, shawl, etc., made of this fabric.

1845 NOAH *Gleanings* 16 [The lady of fashion carries] a fine merino over her arm. **1856** M. J. HOLMES *Homestead on H.* 229 Berintha . . . came down to tea in a dark, fashionably made merino. **1875** STOWE *We & Neighbors* 110 A faded merino was ripped, dyed, and . . . transformed into the stylish blue suit.

+**3.** A variety of potato. In full *merino potato. Obs.*

1849 EMMONS *Agric. N.Y.* II. 41 Merino Potato. . . . Not highly esteemed for the table. **1855** *Amer. Inst. N.Y. Trans.* 209 In Monmouth county, N.J., the potato crop is large, many farmers . . . raising the common merino potato. **1887** TOURGEE *Button's Inn* 178 He picked up the potatoes . . . —delicate white 'Kidneys' . . . and coarse red 'Merinoes.'

Merino sheep. A breed of sheep, orig. Spanish, valued for its fine long wool; also, a sheep of this breed. {1781–}

1810 *Steele Papers* II. 627, I think the Gold mine Lands the finest for merino Sheep that I ever saw. **1856** GOODRICH *Recoll.* I. 404 He sought to mend his fortune by a speculation in Merino sheep—then [1811] the rage of the day. **1873** BEADLE *Undevel. West* 464 They are about the size of those in Spain, but with . . . long hair, flocky like the Merino sheep. **1892** *Vt. Agric. Rep.* XII. 113 Addison county sustains the enviable reputation of producing the best Merino sheep in the world.

+**Merit-fish.** (See quotation.) — **1884** GOODE, etc. *Fisheries* I. 456 The Green Smelt of the Connecticut coast, *Menidia notata*, [is] also called . . . about Watch Hill the 'Merit-fish.' **1911** *Rep. Fisheries 1908* 316.

+**Merit system.** The system of making appointments and promotions in the civil service on the basis of ability to pass qualifying examinations. — **1879** *46th Congress 2 Sess.* H. R. Ex. Doc. No. 1, VII. 264 Under President Grant a trial, beginning January 1st, 1872, was made of the merit system in a limited way. **1904** DERVILLE *Other Side of Story* 169 With the Civil Service law and the establishment of what is called the merit system in the Departments, began the era of multitudinous petty and arbitrary rules. **1914** *Cycl. Amer. Govt.* II. 418/1 *Merit System*, a name which was adopted in contrast to the spoils system, and which is used to denote the method of appointment to public office in which selection is based solely upon the merit and fitness of the appointee.

*Merlin. Also †marlin. +The American pigeon hawk, *Falco columbarius*. Erroneously identified with the European merlin by some writers. Also with specifying terms in names of varieties of the Amer. bird. — **1637** MORTON *New Canaan* 72 There are very many Marlins. **1709** LAWSON *Carolina* 138 The Merlin is a small Bird in Europe, but much smaller here. **1839** PEABODY *Mass. Birds* 270 The Merlin, *Falco aesalon*, . . . is the same with the English merlin, which was formerly used in falconry. **1917** *Birds of Amer*. II. 90/1 A darker colored form of the Pigeon Hawk is the Black Pigeon Hawk or Black Merlin.

+**Merluccio.** [It.] A hake (*Merluccius productus*) of the Pacific coast. — **1884** GOODE, etc. *Fisheries* I. 243 The California Hake . . . is most commonly known along the coast by its Italian name, 'Merluccio.' **1911** *Rep. Fisheries 1908* 312.

+**Mermaid weed.** Any water plant of the genus *Proserpinaca*. — **1817–8** EATON *Botany* (1822) 410 *Proserpinaca palustris*, mermaid weed. **1840** DEWEY *Mass. Flowering Plants* 49 Mermaid Weed. Two species, *P. palustris*, and *P. pectinata*, grow in wet grounds, and round marshy places. **1891** COULTER *Bot. W. Texas* I. 111.

+**Merrimac.** *attrib.* Designating various kinds of cotton fabrics formerly manufactured at Lowell, Mass., on the Merrimac river. *Obs.* — **1843** *Knickerb*. XXI. 496 There was a dull sale for 'Merrimack blues.' **1843** *Lowell Offering* III. 166 We would willingly wear 'Merrimack print' henceforth. **1873** HOLLEY *My Opinions* 205 The 'postal Paul didn't have to buy 40 or 50 yards of merrymac calico and factory cloth every year. **1891** WELCH *Recoll. 1830–40* 354 Calicos, of which the 'Merrimac' and 'Dover' were the choice prints of that day, were then quoted at 14 cts. for 'Dover,' and 16 cts. for 'Merrimac.'

Mesa. *S.W.* and *W.* [Sp.] An elevated table-land. {1775, in Cuba}

Mesa is applied to two phenomena: an isolated flat-topped hill with abrupt and steep sides; and a comparatively flat plateau extending back from the abrupt ridges of a valley.

1844 GREGG *Commerce of Prairies* II. 47 [We] soon emerged into an open plain or *mesa* which was one of the most monotonous I had ever seen. **1856** DAVIS *El Gringo* (1857) 338 A ride of an hour and a half brought us to a *mesa* that lay in our route. **1872** BOURKE *Journal* 20 Nov., Climbed a mesa and halted for a pack train. **1887** *Scribner's Mag*. II. 505/1 The eye traverses an enormous extent of plain, mesa, and mountain. **1898** WISTER *Lin McLean* 242 With a circling sweep from somewhere out of the gloom it cut in close to the lofty mesa. **1912** HOUGH *Story of Cowboy* 19 Snow never falls at this latitude over the lower valleys and *mesas*.

attrib. **1866** *Rep. Indian Affairs* 109 A mesa formation, rising abruptly from twenty to thirty feet, and more occasionally from the bottom. **1881** *Ib*. 4 The Moquis people . . . will soon improve . . . if they can be induced to leave their old mesa homes, and settle in the valley.

+**Mescal.** *S.W.* Also **mezcal, mascal.** [Mex. Sp. *mezcal* fr. Nahuatl *mexcalli*.] {mexical 1828, in Mexico}

1. A colorless spirituous liquor made from the juice of plants belonging to one or other species of *Agave:* (see also quot. 1881). {mexical 1828, in Mexico}

[1831 Pattie *Personal Narr*. 287 It is of this juice [pulque] they make a kind of whiskey, called *vino meschal*.] **1844** KENDALL *Santa Fé Exped*. II. 126 Pulque is slightly intoxicating, but by distillation a very strong liquor is made from it, called mescal. **1881** *Amer. Naturalist* XV. 875 The main and paramount use of sotol is in the making of a spirituous liquor known as 'mescal' along the border, but in the interior of Mexico, to avoid mistaking it for a similar product from maguey, called sotol mescal. **1884** SWEET & KNOX *Through Texas* 359 He preferred whiskey to the vile mezcal on which his ancestors for hundreds of years had relied for inspiration. **1907** 'O. HENRY' *Heart of West* 188 Her father . . . herded a hundred goats and lived in a continuous drunken dream from drinking *mescal*.

2. The root or head of some variety of *Agave* prepared as food; also, the edible product of certain other plants (see quots. 1844 and 1887).

1831 PATTIE *Personal Narr*. 63, I afterwards ascertained, that it was a vegetable, called by the Spanish, mascal. **1844** GREGG *Commerce of Prairies* I. 290 Those [Apache Indians] that are found east of the Rio del Norte are generally known as *Mezcaleros*, on account of an article of food much in use among them, called *mezcal*. *Ib*., *Mezcal* is the baked root of the *maguey* (*agave Americana*) and of another somewhat similar plant. **1878** BEADLE *Western Wilds* 288 *Mescal* . . . looks when dried like a mass of soft sole-leather, and tastes much like ripe sugar-cane. **1881** *Amer. Naturalist* XV. 875 The 'mescal' of the Arizona Apaches, that is, the baked head of the *Agave palmeri* and *Agave parryi*. **1887** *Century Mag*. XXXIV. 46/2 Other native articles of diet . . . are baked *mezcal*, the bean of the mezquite tree.

3. a. One or other species of *Agave* or a plant of the species. **b.** The peyote or peyotl plant, *Lophophora williamsii*. (Cf. MESCAL BUTTON.)

1846 EMORY *Military Reconn*. 59 This afternoon I found the famous mezcal, (an agave,) about three feet in diameter, broad leaves, armed with teeth like a shark. **1856** WHIPPLE *Explor. Ry. Route* I. 86 *Agave Mexicana* is quite abundant. It is the beautiful American aloe, or Century plant, called in this country mezcal. **1866** *Rep. Indian Affairs* 110 The mescal, the few wild fruits and grass seeds of the mountains . . . together furnish but a scanty supply. **1891** *Century Mag*. March 653 Along deserts bristling with spines of the cactus, Spanish bayonet, mescal and palo verde.

4. Attrib. in senses 1 and 3 with *bibber, head*, etc.

1856 DERBY *Phoenixiana* 46 A solitary antelope, picking up mescal beans. **1869** BROWNE *Adv. Apache Country* 133 Soldiers, teamsters, and honest miners lounging about the mescal-shops, soaked with the fiery poison; . . . these are what the traveller sees. **1881** *Amer. Naturalist* XV. 875 This head, trimmed down to the white, fleshy moss, is ready for use either on the road, in the Mexican kitchen or by the mescal manufacturer. *Ib*. 876 During [the rainy season] . . . the vinata is closed, and the mescal bibber is constrained to reform. **1885** *Outing* Oct. 24/2 The old and young squaws . . . had brought down from the hillsides donkey-loads of mescal heads.

+**Mescal button.** (See quot. 1909.) — **1895** *N.Y. Dramatic News* 7 Dec. 3/2 For introducing brilliant coloring into dreams it is as efficacious as the nerve stimulant known as the mescal button, contributed to science by the Kiowa Indians. **1909** *Cent. Suppl*. 789/2 *Mescal-buttons*, . . . the dried tops of a succulent, spineless, turnip-shaped cactus growing in the arid regions of Texas and northern Mexico, known botanically as *Lophophora Williamsii*, and called by the natives in various localities *peyote, hikuli*, and *wokowi*.

***Mesh,** *v. intr.* Of cogs or gear teeth: To engage with one another. — **1875** KNIGHT 1383/2 Mangle-rack, a rack having teeth on opposite sides, engaged by a pinion which meshes with the opposite sides alternately. **1895** *Outing* XXVII. 55/1 Wooden cogs, which meshed into a horizontal wheel.

Mesmerism. Hypnotism. {1802–} — **1784** FRANKLIN in W. Pepper *Medical Side B. Franklin* 89 Some think it will put an End to Mesmerism. **1847** FIELD *Drama in Pokerville* 103 Madison is an 'awful place for revivals!' an 'awful place for Mesmerism!' **1890** HOWELLS *Boy's Town* 221 [The hall was] devoted to the purposes of mesmerism.

Mesmerizer. One who practices mesmerism. {1829–} — **1847** FIELD *Drama in Pokerville* 130 The Wolverine Mesmerizer, after astonishing a 'Hall' full, one evening, . . . returned to the tavern. **1876** 'MARK TWAIN' *Tom Sawyer* xxii. 178 A phrenologist and a mesmerizer came.

+**Mesquite.** Also **mezquite, mesquit,** etc. *S.W.* [Mex. Sp., *mezquite*, from Nahuatl *mizquitl*.]

The variant spellings of this word are of two kinds: (1) The internal variants, *mezquite, mesquit, mosquit, musquit*, etc., as illustrated throughout this and the following entries. (2) The end variant. The final *-e* of *mesquite*, of course, was pronounced in the early history of the word. This gave rise to the variant *o*-ending by analogy to the unrelated but phonetically similar word *mosquito* or *musquito*. See MESQUITO.

1. A species of deep-rooted, shrublike trees (*Prosopis juliflora*), often growing in dense clumps or thickets, or any species of this genus; also, a tree of one of these species, or the wood of these trees.

1838 'TEXIAN' *Mexico v. Texas* 70 Even where a tree appears it is sure to be a mesquite (*mimosa nilotica*). **1844** GREGG *Commerce of Prairies* II. 78 The valleys are timbered with cottonwood, and occasionally with *mezquite*. **1854** BARTLETT *Personal Narr*. II. 563 Then come the mezquit or acacia, the tornilla, the fouquiera, . . . all armed with the most terrific spikes or thorns. **1858** *Texas Almanac 1859* 185 Along the river banks there is some good timber, but the most common wood is scrubby musquite, which . . . is unfit for building purposes. **1884** SWEET & KNOX *Through Texas* 87 [The horse] caught himself by entangling a rope, that hung from his neck, in the branches of a low mesquite. **1905** 'O. HENRY' *Roads of Destiny* 130 Near the store, scattered among the mesquits and elms, stood the saddled horses of the customers.

b. *ellipt.* = MESQUITE THICKET.

1910 RAINE *B. O'Connor* 224 The Irishman . . . kept his party in the mesquit till the headlight of an approaching train was visible.

2. *ellipt.* = MESQUITE GRASS.

1852 MARCY *Explor. Red River* (1854) 43 The grass upon the Staked Plain is generally a very short variety of mezquite, called buffalo grass, from one to two inches in length. **1856** *Rep. Comm. Patents 1855: Agric*. 252 The 'mesquit' is not a native of this vicinity. **1872** TICE *Over Plains* 78 Underneath this sere covering of mesquite is a thick coating of Buffalo grass. **1899** M. GOING *Flowers* 153 The running mesquit of Arizona and the alkali-grass of the plains help to hold in place the shifting soils of the great thirst-lands.

3. (See quotation.)

1869 *Overland Mo*. Aug. 130 Texas is notable for the number of its soils. In Montgomery County there is . . . the 'mezquite,' (producing chiefly mesquite, both bush and grass) [etc.].

4. Attrib. with *flat, pasture*, etc.

See also MESQUITE BEAN, CHAPARRAL, GRASS, etc.

1844 KENDALL *Santa Fé Exped*. II. 108 We encamped . . . in a little mesquit valley. **1847** W. S. HENRY *Campaign Sketches* 24 Their residences [are] . . . nothing more than sheds partially enclosed with the crooked mesquite-wood. **1885** *Outing* Oct. 24/2 Basket-work, rendered fully waterproof by a coating of either mesquite or piñon pitch. **1905** A. ADAMS *Outlet* 16 The horses had run idle during the winter in a large mesquite pasture. **1909** 'O. HENRY' *Roads of Destiny* 145 [The] settlements feared he would come again to ride and ravage the mesquite flats.

+**Mesquite bean.** The fruit of the mesquite tree or shrub. — **1858** *Texas Almanac 1859* 143 *Mezquit beans* can also be procured sufficiently near the road to be sold to travellers. **1872** POWERS *Afoot & Alone* 162 The animals soon learned to eat mesquite beans ravenously, as all things do here [in New Mexico]. **1883** *Harper's Mag.* March 493/1 The crop of mesquit beans was so large one year as to be beyond their own unaided capacity of consumption. **1923** J. H. COOK *On Old Frontier* 27 [When] the mesquite beans and prickly pears were abundant, horses, cows, cattle, hogs and turkeys would get very fat.

+**Mesquite chaparral.** *S.W.* A clump or thicket of mesquite bushes. (Cf. CHAPARRAL.) — **1849** in *31st Congress 1 Sess.* Sen. Ex. Doc. No. 64 20 Our present camp is a mezquite chaparral in a bend of the river. **1854** BARTLETT *Personal Narr.* I. 134 [The grass] grew in tufts about the roots of the mezquit chapporal. **1865** O. W. NORTON *Army Lett.* 271 Part of the way the road lay through mesquit chaparral. **1876** COZZENS *Ariz. & New Mex.* 144 The plains around us were covered with an abundance of cactus . . . and mesquit chaparral.

+**Mesquite grass.** Also **musquit**, etc. *S.W.* Any one of various pasture grasses, esp. those of the genus *Bouteloua*, affording superior pasturage.

1823 DEWEES *Lett. from Texas* 35 The musquit grass grows very thick and about three feet high, and looks very much like a blue grass pasture. **1844** GREGG *Commerce of Prairies* II. 192 [It] is called 'mezquite grass' in Texas, from the 'mezquite tree' which grows there in the same dry regions with it. **1862** in *N.Y. Tribune* 28 June 8 Twenty acres in potatoes, and half an acre in the Texas Mosquit or Musketo Grass. **1884** SWEET & KNOX *Through Texas* 453 The principal growth is the mesquite-grass. **1916** THOBURN *Stand. Hist. Okla.* I. 5 In the western part of the state . . . [are] buffalo grass, mesquite grass and the several species of grama grasses.

+**Mesquite root.** *S.W.* The root of the mesquite tree used for fuel. — **1864** *Weekly New Mexican* 28 Oct. 1/3 [Navajos] now at the Bosque are carrying mesquit roots, on their backs, from eight to ten miles, . . . to cook their food. **1866** *Rep. Indian Affairs* 136 Mesquit root is now plenty for fuel. **1889** *Harper's Mag.* Dec. 119/2 A handful of gnarled and knotted mesquite roots blazed in the wide fireplace. **1899** *Atlantic Mo.* June 759/2 Pack burros, heavy-laden with immense bundles of fagots and mesquite roots.

+**Mesquite thicket.** *S.W.* A chaparral of mesquite. — **1845** T. J. GREEN *Texian Exped.* 32 Dawson selected his position in a musquet thicket favourable for his rifle-shooting. **1869** BROWNE *Adv. Apache Country* 52 From Pilot Knob we had a pleasant drive through the mesquit thickets bordering on the river. **1903** A. ADAMS *Log of Cowboy* 45 Suddenly in the dark we encountered a mesquite thicket.

+**Mesquite tree.** *S.W.* =MESQUITE 1. — **1827** DEWEES *Lett. from Texas* 63 The country is mostly a prairie country, the prairies being mostly covered with shrubs, musquit trees, and prickly pear. **1847** W. S. HENRY *Campaign Sk.* 25 For the first time saw the mesquite-tree, it resembles very much the wild locust, and bears a bean having a delightfully-sweet taste. **1877** H. C. HODGE *Arizona* 246 The mesquit tree . . . is probably a variety of the acacia, and like it, produces the gum arabic of commerce. **1923** J. H. COOK *On Old Frontier* 11 Such portions of the meat as were desired . . . [were] hung up in the mesquite trees.

+**Mesquite wood.** *S.W.* The hard durable wood of the mesquite tree. — [**1831** [see next].] **1847** W. S. HENRY *Campaign Sketches* 24 Their residences are . . . nothing more than sheds partially enclosed with the crooked mesquite-wood. **1903** *N.Y. Herald* 8 March (Ernst), The bed of the carreta is made of open cross sections of mesquite wood.

+**Mesquito.** Also **masketo**, etc. *S.W.* Variant of MESQUITE.

1805 LEWIS in *Ann. 9th Congress* 2 Sess. 1083 [With] a bean that grows in great plenty on a small tree resembling a willow, called masketo; the women cook their buffalo beef. *Ib.* 1103 Some small cultivated fields, fenced round with small cedar and moscheto brush. **1831** Pattie *Personal Narr.* 340 A few miserable, stinted shrubberies of a diminutive growth called musqueto wood is only found at intervals. **1834** A. PIKE *Sketches* 56 The valley was here wider, and was full of small hills interspersed with mesquito bushes. . . . We bought some meat and mesquito meal, made by grinding the bean between two stones. *Ib.* 63 We emerged from the broken hills into the mesquito.

***Mess.**

I. ***1.** A quantity *of* food, as beans, potatoes, corn, sufficient for one or more persons on a single occasion. {-1597}

'Now *dial* and *U.S.*' (*O.E.D.*).

1697 SEWALL *Diary* I. 455 Betty gets her Mother a Mess of English Beans. **1775** Rauck *Boonesborough* 179 Had a mess of snap beans. **1889** JEWETT *B. Leicester* x. 139, I told Seth Pond to run out an' pick a mess o' snap beans. **1908** FREEMAN *Shoulders of Atlas* 249, I wish you'd go out in the garden and pick a mess of green corn for supper.

+**b.** A catch or take of fish, eels, etc., sufficient for a meal.

1766 ROWE *Diary* 97 After dinner we went & caught a mess of Trout. **1775** ROMANS *Nat. Hist. Florida* 12 He told me; that his mother had an inclination to eat fish, and he was come to get her a mess. **1858** THOREAU *Maine Woods* 93 They had several messes of trout ready. **1872** *Harper's Mag.* Sept. 507/2 On being asked if she understood cooking trout, she replied, smartly, 'You'd better catch a mess first and try me.' **1880** *Ib.* Aug. 343/1 The landlord . . . was seen . . . afar on the mud flats of the cove . . . digging what he called 'a mess o' clams.' **1881** STODDARD *E. Hardery* 60, I caught a prime mess of eels last night.

***c.** The quantity of milk obtained from a cow at a milking.

1842 *Knickerb.* XIX. 557 Sally could n't hardly bring in the pail, she gave such a mess. **1872** *Vermont Bd. Agric. Rep.* I. 197, I tested their milk by weighing every mess for a month. **1873** *Ib.* II. 185 After putting her on to this hay, she gradually increased her mess to two quarts per day, which was her best performance before going dry. **1877** *Ib.* IV. 47 If I can . . . skim each mess of cream . . . I can determine . . . which is the best cow.

+**2.** A number, quantity, or amount, usu. large, *of* something. *colloq.*

1830 *Mass. Spy* 23 June (Th.), We saw yesterday a large mess of early potatoes. **1853** *Knickerb.* XLI. 502 There was wolves in the Holler—an unaccountable mess of 'em. **1872** *Vermont Bd. Agric. Rep.* I. 634 They will dress a mess of ore to any required per cent. **1890** JEWETT *Strangers* 205 A mess o' preachin' ain't goin' to alter her over.

II. ***3.** In military or quasi-military use: A group or company of persons who eat together.

1709 *Harvard Rec.* I. 388 The Steward Proposes to allow two pounds and a half to a mess. **1804** LEWIS in *L. & Clark Exped.* I. (1904) 31 The messes of Sergts. Floyd, Ordway and Pryor shall . . . form the crew of the Batteaux. **1837** IRVING *Bonneville* I. 36 In every interval there was a mess stationed; and each mess had its fire, where the men cooked, ate, gossiped, and slept. **1899** *Scribner's Mag.* XXV. 15/1 Holderman . . . for a long time acted as cook for the head-quarters mess.

+**b.** A group of Congressmen who take their meals together. *Obs.*

1821 in *New Eng. Hist. & Gen. Reg.* XXX. 191 Here a number of members [of Congress], vulgarly called a 'Mess,' put up, and have a separate table. **1830** SANDS *Writings* II. 159 The most select boarding-houses were occupied with *messes* of members of Congress. **1886** POORE *Reminisc.* I. 249 He soon became a decided favorite at the Washington 'messes,' where he was always ready to contribute freely from his fund of anecdotes.

+**4.** =MESS BEEF.

1859 *N.Y. Herald* Market Report (Hoppe), Prime mess and beef ham. **1884** *Harper's Mag.* July 299/1 [Chicago] The average weight of the class of animals used for 'mess' and 'canning' is 950 pounds. . . . The division of the carcasses] is made into . . . pieces . . . viz. loins, ribs, mess, plates, chucks, rolls, rumps [etc.]. . . . 'Extra mess' is composed of chucks, plates, rumps, and flanks.

III. 5. Attrib. in sense 3 with *fuel, pie, provision, wagon.*

1733 *Harvard Rec.* II. 607 Small meat for Pyes being .8d pr Pound, ye advance of .50. pr Cent. makes 12d one pound of Flesh being suppos'd for a Mess-Pye. **1804** LEWIS & CLARK *Exped.* I. (1904) 72 They shall allso point out what part . . . of the mess provisions are to be consumed at each stated meal. **1834** A. PIKE *Sketches* 17, [I] built me a fire of the buffalo ordure which we had gathered for mess fuel. **1897** HOUGH *Story of Cowboy* 180 The cook had his mess wagon slapped shut, and the teamster his team 'hooked up.'

***Message.** *Polit.* A formal official communication relating to matters requiring legislative consideration. {1625-}

+**1.** Addressed by a colonial or state governor to an assembly or state legislature.

1746 *Penna. Col. Rec.* V. 57 The Governor said it was equal to him when they adjourn'd, since they were not dispos'd to take His Message into their Consideration. **1758** *Memoirs of the Last War* 35 The Governor thereupon moved the Assembly in two other Messages to resume the Consideration of this Enterprize. **1800** in J. Adams *Works* IX. 90 A newspaper . . . contains a copy of the Message [of Gov. Jay]. **1874** COLLINS *Kentucky* I. 23 Gov. Shelby . . . delivers his first 'message' orally. **1898** *Kansas City Star* 18 Dec. 4/3 Governor-elect Stanley . . . has decided to divide his time between the office seekers and his message.

+**2.** Addressed to Congress by the president of the U.S.

1797 *Ann. 5th Congress* I. 305 The following Message was received from the President of the United States. **1801** HAMILTON *Works* VII. 200 Instead of delivering a *speech* to the Houses of Congress, . . . the President has thought fit to transmit a *Message*. **1845** POLK *Diary* 14, [I] was engaged in writing off a rough draft of parts of my message to be delivered to Congress at their meeting in December. **1886** ALTON *Among Law-Makers* 73 'Executive session' . . . [is] a session devoted to action upon messages from the President. **1921** *Congress. Rec.* 12 March 47/1 A message in writing from the President of the United States was communicated to the Senate.

+**3.** An official communication addressed by the mayor of a city to the aldermen.

1906 *N.Y. Ev. Post* 2 Jan. 2 Mayor McClellan in his message to the aldermen yesterday, declared [etc.].

Mess beef. Assorted salt beef put up in barrels. {1766-} — **1796** F. BAILY *Tour* 114 Lisbon salt, 4s. 3d. per bushel; Irish mess beef, 72s. per barrel. **1832** *Louisville Pub. Advertiser* 3 March, 100 bbls. No. 1 and 2, Mess beef . . . for sale. **1848** BURTON *Waggeries* 35 The charms of Bella were mixed with neats' tongues, pigs' faces, and mess beef.

+**Mess box.** A box or receptacle on a chuck wagon for storing food and cooking utensils. — **1859–60** MRS. WITTER *Letters* (MS.) 3 We had what we call a mess box which contained all our cooking utensils. **1884**

W. SHEPHERD *Prairie Exper.* 138 A mess-box was fixed into the hind-end of the waggon. **1894** WISTER in *Harper's Mag.* Sept. 515/1 He now returned to Captain Glynn and shared his mess-box. **1913** BARNES *Western Grazing Grounds* 116 One can still find the old-time 'chuck wagon' and the great mess box with its hospitable lid and cranky cook.

+**Mess chest.** A chest in which food and cooking utensils are kept; a mess box.

1830 COOPER *Water Witch* III. ix, The smaller booms, with the mess-chest and shot-boxes, were all that lay between the group . . . and the depths of the ocean. **1858** VIELÉ *Following Drum* 15 The 'worldly goods' . . . consisted of . . . a camp-kettle, mess chest [etc.]. **1875** *Fur, Fin & Feather* 107/2 Ten chances to one you were persuaded to buy a mess-chest. **1881** *Rep. Indian Affairs* 334 The latter hauled our cooking utensils, mess chest, tent and fly. **1887** CUSTER *Tenting on Plains* 466 The mess-chest was filled with a few strong dishes, . . . and a few cans of fruit and vegetables.

***Messenger.**

+**1.** In the Plymouth colony, an officer who served as constable, jailer, town crier, etc. *Obs.*

1633 *Plymouth Laws* 34 It is order that all measures be brought to the Messenger or Constable of Plym. to be sealed. **1637** *Plymouth Col. Rec.* I. 54 Josua Pratt was sworne the Messenger for the whole government. **1644** *Ib.* II. 45 That the Messenger henceforth be styled or called by the Name of Marshall.

***2.** A person employed by a representative or legislative body to convey messages.

1694 SEWALL *Diary* I. 389 Henry Ems the Baker has his name put into a Commission to be a Messenger to the Representatives when sitting. **1789** *Ann. 1st Congress* I. 17 Cornelius Maxwell was appointed Messenger [by the Senate]. **1797** *Phila. Ordinances* (1812) 133 To the messenger of the select and common councils; two hundred dollars. **1880** LAMPHERE *U.S. Govt.* 23/2 In the service of Congress: . . . 1 messenger, . . . 4 laborers in Secretary's office.

+**3.** In ecclesiastical use, esp. in the Congregational church, one sent as a delegate to a convention, synod, etc. *Obs.*

1646 *Mass. Bay Rec.* II. 155 To assemble the churches, or their messengrs., upon occasion of counsell. **1654** JOHNSON *Wonder-w. Prov.* 204 The churches of Christ should meet together in a Synod, by their Elders and Messengers to hold forth the doctrine . . . of the New Testament. **1712** SEWALL *Diary* II. 347 Declar'd that the Elders and Messengers of Churches had appointed him to give the charge. **1806** WEBSTER, *Consociation*, a convention of pastors and messengers of churches.

+**4.** [From name of stallion imported into U.S. in 1792.] A horse of a breed especially valued for riding.

1857 HERBERT *Forester's Horse & Horsemanship of U.S.* 151 It was the abiding hope of the breeder to obtain the . . . perfect symmetry of a Baronet, with the speed, power, and will of a Messenger. **1863** *Rep. Comm. Agric. 1862* 45 The Messengers were excellent horses for the road or for work. **1872** HOLMES *Poet* 325, I don't think they would quarrel with us because we made a distinction between a 'Morgan' and a 'Messenger.' **1879** TOURGEE *Fool's Errand* 61 The horse of which he spoke was a bay Messenger.

+**5.** =EXPRESS MESSENGER.

1881 BUEL *Border Bandits* 89 The messenger was forced to open the safe.

Messenger boy. A boy employed to carry messages, small parcels, etc. — **1876** INGRAM *Centennial Exp.* 713 The messenger boys were seen everywhere, conspicuous in their neat uniforms. [**1886** *Pall Mall Gaz.* 26 Aug. 11/1 A Wall-street banker . . . sent a note by a district messenger boy to the office of his broker.] **1893** POST *Harvard Stories* 26 'Rattleton,' called a messenger boy. **1911** PERSONS, etc. *Mass. Labor Laws* 199 A messenger boy employed by the Western Union Telegraph Company.

Mess hall. =DINING HALL. — **1862** STRONG *Cadet Life W. Point* 66 We were as unfortunate in the mess-hall as out of it. **1888** DORSEY *Midshipman Bob* 104 A few seconds later they . . . filed into the mess-hall, with appetites . . . well whetted by exercise.

Mess house. A house or structure in which meals are served. — **1865** *Atlantic Mo.* XV. 66 A wooden cook-house to every company, with sometimes a palmetto mess-house beside. **1885** *Rep. Indian Affairs* 179 The other head men were taking dinner at the mess house. **1914** 'BOWER' *Flying U Ranch* 47 Old Patsy came out of the messhouse, and went, with flapping floursack apron, to the woodpile.

Messmate. A companion at meals. {1746–}

1726 FRANKLIN *Writings* II. 76, I find our messmates in a better humour . . . than they have been. **1786** in *Mag. Amer. Hist.* I. 178/2 They stole [cartridges] from their messmates. **1807** J. R. SHAW *Life* (1930) 57 A certain Bill Airton . . . was a mess-mate of mine. **1865** WHITNEY *Gayworthys* 141 He was a fearless, skilful seaman; . . . but a moody messmate. **1885** *Century Mag.* June 306/2 He had been my mess-mate in the old army for more than a year.

Mess pan. A pan used in cooking for a mess. — **1813** *Niles' Reg.* III. 295/2 [Military Supplies:] Mess pans. **1856** DERBY *Phoenixiana* 47 The unpacking of the kettles and mess-pans, . . . the frizzling of the pork . . . are . . . clearly expressed by the music. **1876** BOURKE *Journal* 12 March, A huge mess-pan of boiled or baked beans, flanked by pepper and salt-bottles and several platters of hard tack. **1888** BILLINGS *Hardtack* 136 A mess pan stands about six inches high, and is a foot in diameter at the top.

+**Mess pork.** Salt pork made from the shoulders and sides of hogs and put up in barrels. {1864, Canad. (Geikie *Geo. Stanley*)} — [**1821** *Cape-Fear Recorder* 14 April, Pork, mess, North Carolina.] **1841** *S. Lit. Messenger* VII. 774/2 The meat served out to them consists generally of bacon cured on the farms, to which . . . is added Western bacon or mess pork. **1867** *Ill. Agric. Soc. Trans.* VI. 639 Mess Pork.—Shall be packed from sides of well fatted hogs, cut into strips . . . , and flanked according to diagram. **1902** LORIMER *Lett. Merchant* 33 He had better turn his attention to the stocks of mess pork.

***Messuage.** =MERESTEAD. *Obs.*

1638 LECHFORD *Note-Book* (1885) 11, [I] doe demise . . . unto Willm. Dineley . . . all those my houses, mesuages, outhouses and gardens. **1649** *Charlestown Land Rec.* 114, I William Luddington . . . weavar, have . . . sould . . . one messuage or tenement. **1678** *N.H. Probate Rec.* I. 235, [I] give unto my sone . . . all yt Tenemt or messuage wheron wee some times lived. **1704** *Ib.* 511 The Said Thomas Row have then the one halfe of all the Houses Lands Messuages Cottages Barns. **1790** *Penna. Packet* 9 Jan. 3/4 To be sold by Public Vendue, . . . That well known and Pleasantly situated large two story Brick Messuage or Public House and Garden.

+**Mestang. 1.** =MUSTANG. **2.** *Mestang court*, =KANGAROO COURT. — **(1) 1834** A. PIKE *Sketches* 74 Lewis and Irwin obtained young and unbroken wild horses, (or, as the hunters call them, mestangs). **1837** IRVING *Bonneville* I. 194 She was mounted on a mestang or half wild horse, which she managed with a long rope hitched round the under jaw by way of bridle. **1853** 'P. PAXTON' *Yankee in Texas* 120 Thar hit (it) stuck, just like one of them dern Cammanches on a mestang. **(2)** *Ib.* 205 By a unanimous vote, Judge G. . . . was elected to the bench, and the 'Mestang' or 'Kangaroo Court' regularly organized.

***Mestizo,** (fem.) **Mestiza.** Also †**mustizo.** [Sp.] A half-breed, esp. the offspring of a Spaniard and an American Indian. Also attrib.

1712 *S.C. Statutes at Large* VII. 352 All negroes, mulatoes, mustizoes or Indians, which at any time heretofore have been sold . . . for slaves, are hereby declared slaves. **1775** *S.C. Hist. Soc. Coll.* III. 141 You are hereby ordered . . . to apprehend . . . John Swan, a reputed free negro or mestizo man. **1796** *Ann. 4th Congress* 2 Sess. 2694 Free negroes, mulattoes, and mestizoes, [are taxed] at nine shillings and four pence per head. **1836** EDWARD *Hist. Texas* 117 The Mestizos, or offspring of Spaniards and Indians. **1848** BRYANT *California* xxxvi. 424 The mission of San Miguel, now occupied by an Englishman named Reed, his *mestiza* wife, and one child. *Ib.* 425 Arriving at the rancho of Don Joaquin Gomez, we found no one but a *mestiza* servant at home. **1899** *Atlantic Mo.* LXXXIII. 759/1 Perhaps you have heard or read of beautiful mestizo maidens?

***Metaphysical,** *a.* +**1.** *Metaphysical healer*, a Christian Science practitioner. +**2.** *Metaphysical healing*, =CHRISTIAN SCIENCE. — **(1) 1876** B. ALCOTT *Journals* 466 A wider acquaintance with idealism in its various phases will be serviceable to these 'Metaphysical Healers' and 'Christian Scientists' as they call their school. **(2) 1884** EDDY in *Christian Science Jrnl.* 2 Feb. 2 Metaphysical healing, or Christian Science, is a demand of the times. **1885** S. FOWLER in *Homilet. Rev.* X. 135/1 At the present time, in Boston and many other places, the so-called 'Christian Science,' or 'Metaphysical Healing,' is taking a strong hold in the communities. **1886** EDDY *Science & Health* (ed. 16) 11 In the year 1866 I discovered metaphysical healing, and named it Christian Science.

+**Metate.** *S.W.* [Mex. Sp. from Nahuatl *metlatl.*] A rectangular stone used in grinding or crushing corn, coffee, beans, etc. Also attrib. — **1857** DAVIS *El Gringo* 180 The corn . . . they grind . . . into a paste upon an oblong hollowed stone, called a *metate*. **1883** SWEET & KNOX *Through Texas* 314 [Corn] is ground into a paste on a rough flat rock, called a *metate*. **1893** LUMMIS *Land of Poco Tiempo* 49 Each brought to an appointed house her metate and sack of corn. . . . One of these *metate* songs . . . is as follows.

+**Metate stone.** Also **medatstone, metat stone.** =prec. — **1847** HENRY *Campaign Sk.* 134 The eldest was on her knees at the medatstone, grinding corn, making it up into cakes, and baking tortillas on a plate of sheet-iron. **1854** BARTLETT *Personal Narr.* II. 243 We found an immense quantity of broken pottery, metate stones for grinding corn, and an occasional stone ax or hoe. **1877** H. C. HODGE *Arizona* 60 The Indians collect large quantities of both varieties, which when dried they grind into flour on their metat stones.

***Metheglin.** Also †**mathiglin, methegler.** A spiced or medicated drink made of honey and water. Now hist. — **1633** *N.H. Doc. & Rec.* I 71 For 6 gallons of mathiglin, beaver 2 lb. **1704** KNIGHT *Journal* 55 A Gentlewoman . . . gave us . . . choice Beer and metheglin. **1789** FRANKLIN in *Century Mag.* XXXII. 271/2, I have received . . . your present of Metheglin, of which I have already drank almost a bottle. **1899** *Harper's Mag.* Sept. 504/2 Many a glass of palate-tickling 'methigler' found its easy way to the shining negroes.

Methodism. The doctrine and teachings of the Methodist church. {1739–} — **1741** W. STEPHENS *Proc. Georgia* II. 100 A notable Instance . . . of the Effect of Methodism, happening this Day, it may not be improper to take notice of it. **1824** BLAINE *Excursion U.S.* 491 Beyond the Alleghanies, Methodism exists in all its glory. **1847** COLLINS *Kentucky* 124 The early history of Methodism in Kentucky, is, to a certain extent, obscure and indefinite. **1902** ALDRICH *Sea Turn* 185–6 The New England Methodism of his youth had not hardened a very soft spot in his heart for . . . unfortunates.

*__Methodist,__ *n.* A member of a Methodist congregation or society. {1733–} — **1741** W. STEPHENS *Proc. Georgia* II. 173 The Jews, Deists, Methodists . . . profess a Dislike to our publick Way of worship. **1796** WEEMS *Letters* II. 12 Martin is a Man of great weight among that numerous and good People, the Methodists. **1807** in Commons, etc. *Doc. Hist.* II. 284 The Methodists have lately had a camp-meeting in Hancock county. **1856** P. CARTWRIGHT *Autobiog.* 56, I attended several camp-meetings among the Methodists and Presbyterians. **1906** PRINGLE *Rice Planter* 337 They are uncompromising Methodists.

Methodist, *a.* {1766–}

1. Designating a meeting, conference, etc., held by or under the auspices of Methodists. {1771–}

1797 WEEMS *Letters* II. 92 You might as well send Fiddles to a Methodist conventicle. **1811** SUTCLIFF *Travels* (1815) 122, I had the curiosity to take a view of a large Methodist meeting . . . called a camp meeting. **1831** PECK *Guide* 290 A Baptist and a Methodist society . . . keep up regular meetings. **1840** *Niles' Nat. Reg.* 2 May 136/2 Methodist general conference. This body . . . holds its sessions every fourth year. **1844** *Lexington Observer* 5 Oct. 1/3 A gang of drunken rowdies attacked a Methodist Camp Meeting.

2. Designating a church building, college, or corporation owned or operated by Methodists.

1808 ASHE *Travels* 33 Another could supply him at low price, with the workshop of a mechanic, a methodist-meeting, or a butcher's shop. **1811** MEASE *Philadelphia* 216 There are four Methodist meeting houses for whites, and two for blacks in Philadelphia. **1857** *Atlantic Mo.* I. 95/1 The little white Methodist chapel in the lane. **1882** MCCABE *New York* 148 At the corner of 10th street and Broadway, is the fine building of the Methodist Book Concern. **1925** BRYAN *Memoirs* 21 He changed his plans and entered the Methodist College.

3. Designating one who preaches or teaches Methodist doctrines. {1766–}

1815 in Mills & Smith *Missionary Tour* 17 Baptist and Methodist preachers are considerably numerous. **1833** *Trial E. K. Avery* 28 My impression was that Rev. Mr. Avery, in Bristol, was a Church minister (Episcopal,) not a Methodist clergyman. **1856** CARTWRIGHT *Autobiog.* 204, I suspect you are two Methodist ministers. **1885** *Century Mag.* March 678 He kin preach all round any o' yer Meth'dist bible-bangers 'at ever I see. **1898** YOUNG *Jessamine Co., Ky.* 259 This distinguished Methodist divine was born in Wayne County.

4. Designating bonnets or caps of a type worn by Methodist women. *Obs.*

1844 *Lowell Offering* IV. 172, I have not seen one of the old 'Simon Pure' Methodist bonnets since I have been here. **1852** EASTMAN *Aunt Phillis's Cabin* 61 She had a black-satin Methodist bonnet, very much the shape of a coal hod. **1853** STOWE *Key* 156/1 A plain Methodist cap shades her face, and the plain white Methodist handkerchief is folded across the bosom.

Methodist church. Any religious organization professing to follow John Wesley, or its edifice. — **1835** HOFFMAN *Winter in West* I. 95 There are also five churches,—a Catholic, an Episcopal, a Presbyterian, Baptist, and Methodist. **1844** in Rupp *Relig. Denominations* 461 The Methodist Protestant Church comprises all the associated Methodist churches in these United States. **1857** DAVIS *El Gringo* 53 [At Las Vegas] a teacher of the Methodist Church had just located, and was about to open a school. **1884** *Century Mag.* Nov. 151 Those who leave the Methodist Church leave it because of its inflexible discipline. **1893** 'MARK TWAIN' *P. Wilson* ii, In the colored Methodist church . . . she 'got religion.'

Methodist Episcopal church.

+**1.** The well-known American Christian denomination derived from the British organization founded by John and Charles Wesley in 1729.

1834 PECK *Gaz. Illinois* 273 There is [in Lebanon] a large society of the Methodist Episcopal Church. **1856** CARTWRIGHT *Autobiog.* 23 My mother . . . [was] a member of the Methodist Episcopal Church. **1866** in Fleming *Hist. Reconstruction* II. 252 The Freedmen's Aid Society of the Methodist Episcopal Church has been organized. **1872** MCCLELLAN *Golden State* 406 The Methodist Episcopal Church has in California one hundred and thirteen preaching stations. **1924** *M.E. General Conference Jrnl.* 201 The Twenty-ninth session of the delegated General Conference of the Methodist Episcopal Church convened in the Auditorium, Springfield, Massachusetts.

+**2.** *Methodist (Episcopal) Church, South,* the organization established in 1845 by southern Methodists, who withdrew, because of the slavery issue, from the Methodist Episcopal church. Hence *Methodist Episcopal Church, North.*

1864 in Fleming *Hist. Reconstruction* II. 240 The Methodist Church South has given no reluctant adhesion to the rebellion. **1867** DIXON *New America* II. 307 The Wesleyan body . . . parted into two great sects—a Methodist Episcopal Church North, and a Methodist Episcopal Church South. **1890** *Cent.* 3741/1 In the United States, the Methodist Episcopal Church exists in two geographical divisions, the *Methodist Episcopal Church* (*North*), and the *Methodist Episcopal Church* (*South*).

+**Methodist Protestant.** A member of a nonepiscopal church or denomination founded in 1830 by Methodists dissatisfied with the administrative organization of the Methodist Episcopal church. Also attrib. — **1831** PECK *Guide* 258 The Reformers, or Methodist Protestant church. **1836** W. O'BRYAN *Travels* 38 A convention Assembled at Baltimore, and drew up a constitution, and form of discipline, calling themselves *The Methodist Protestant church.* **1837** PECK *Gaz. Illinois* 73 The Methodist Protestant Denomination has . . . 344 members. **1844** [see METHODIST CHURCH]. **1851** in Stowe *Key* 192 Some were professors of religion—Presbyterians, Episcopal Methodists, and Methodist Protestants.

+**Métif.** Also **metiff.** [Fr.] A person of mixed blood. Also attrib. (Cf. next.)

1808 PIKE *Sources Miss.* 203 The hospitality and goodness of the Creoles and Metifs began to manifest itself. **1814** BRACKENRIDGE *Views La.* 112 The inhabitants are composed of whites, Indians, metiffs, a few civilized Indians, and negro slaves. **1821** NUTTALL *Travels Arkansa* 99 Mr. Drope remained at the Bluff, trading . . . with the two or three metif families settled here. **1845** DE SMET *Oregon Missions* (1847) 181, I was accompanied by my interpreter, and a young Metif of the Cree nation. **1884** G. P. LATHROP *True* ii. 14 She was not of octoroon or metif parentage.

+**Métis.** [Prob. pl. of prec.] Persons of mixed blood, esp. half-breeds of French and Indian extraction. — **1845** DE SMET *Oregon Missions* 98 Forty young men, chiefly *Metis,* are receiving a Christian education. **1885** *Boston Herald* 29 Nov., The paternal ancestors of the Metis were the former employes of the Hudson Bay and Northwest Fur Companies, and their maternal ancestors were indian women of various tribes. **1902** WHITE *Conjuror's House* 5 Everywhere was gay color—the red sashes, . . . the beaded moccasins and leggings of the *mètis.*

*__Metropolitan,__ *a.* Of or pertaining to a metropolis. — **1851** B. ALCOTT *Journals* 257 Metropolitan New York were fitter, or the wild West. **1874** in Fleming *Hist. Reconstruction* II. 149 The third precinct station [is] occupied by the remnant of the metropolitan brigade. **1900** *Congress. Rec.* 17 Feb. 1895/2 Is not one-half of the pay of the Metropolitan police of this city to be paid out of the revenues of the District of Columbia? **1904** A. MATTHEWS *Mass. Col. Soc. Publ.* VIII. 397 In addition to National Parks, there are in the United States various State Parks, City Parks, and, in Massachusetts at least, Metropolitan Parks. **1905** CALKINS & HOLDEN *Art of Modern Advertising* 81 Metropolitan dailies are practically the papers published in about 20 cities of the first rank in the U.S.

Metroscope. {1876–} +(See quotation.) — **1845** *Cincinnati Misc.* 270 A very ingenious instrument, called a Metroscope, . . . has been lately invented for the purpose of taking the measure of the human head so as to furnish an exact fit of hats.

+**Metump.** [Origin obscure.] (See quot. 1778.) *Obs.* Also attrib. (Cf. TUMP-LINE.) — **1754** in *N.H. Hist. Soc. Coll.* I. 279 There was next to their [Indians'] skin tied a number of small metump lines. **1778** CARVER *Travels* 331 The Indians draw these carriages with great ease be they ever so much loaded, by means of a string which passes round the breast. This collar is called a Metump.

Mexican, *n.*

1. a. A citizen of Mexico {1604–}, +esp. one residing, employed, or campaigning in territory now belonging to the United States. +**b.** A Spanish-speaking native of the Southwest.

1808 PIKE *Sources Miss.* 207 We had a dance . . . which was copied from the Mexicans, and is now danced in the first societies of New Spain. **1836** *Diplom. Corr. Texas* I. (1908) 83 An Express arrived . . . advising him of the concentration of from 1500 to 2000 Indians and a conjunction of their forces with about one thousand mounted Mexicans. **1837** IRVING *Bonneville* II. 140 The Mexicans and half-breeds of California, spend the greater part of their time in the saddle. **1844** GREGG *Commerce* II. 14 [They had] hope of 'doing' the 'Spaniards,' as the Mexicans are generally styled in the West, out of a little surplus of specie. **1852** *Harper's Mag.* Aug. 403/2 A party of five Californians were all killed by Mexicans near San Fernando. **1872** TICE *Over Plains* 181 The pasturage in their valleys is so rich that the Mexicans call them *'las vegas,'* the meadows. **1883** RITCH *Illust. N. Mex.* 66 For years the Mexicans and Indians have brought very rich specimens of copper ore from the Jemez and Nacimiento mountains. **1908** *Bur. Labor. Bul.* No. 78, 487 The proportion of Mexicans—and the term here is applied to Spanish-speaking workers from both sides of the border—was larger than previously [1905].

+**2.** = MEXICAN DOLLAR. {*c*1890–}

1827 COOPER *Prairie* v, A foal that is worth thirty of the brightest Mexicans that bear the face of the King of Spain. **1836** *Knickerb.* VIII. 580 The lad could not change the Mexican which I gave him. **1845** HOOPER *Simon Sugg's Adv.* 76 There's an old friend of mine . . . that's got three or four hamper baskets-full o' Mexicans.

+**3.** *pl. S.W.* A variety of sheep; also, wool obtained from sheep of this variety.

1878 I. L. BIRD *Rocky Mts.* 173 The flocks are made up mostly of pure and graded Mexicans. **1883** RITCH *Illust. N. Mex.* 45 Prices [of wool] this year, however, have been from 15 cents per pound for the lowest grade of Mexican, to 24 cents for the choicest. **1887** *Scribner's Mag.* II. 511/1 The season comes for the shearing of Southdowns or rough-fleeced Mexicans.

Mexican, *a.* Of or pertaining to Mexico or its inhabitants {1696–}, +or to the Spanish-speaking population of the Southwest.

1. Designating various persons.

1837 IRVING *Bonneville* II. 141 A Mexican horseman has much resemblance, in many points, to the equestrians of Old Spain. **1846** MAGOFFIN *Down Santa Fé Trail* 33 Our Mexican driver . . . would jerk the reins. **1872** McCLELLAN *Golden State* 455 The Bay and the present site of San Francisco was first discovered . . . by Governor Portala, the Mexican pioneer. **1898** ATHERTON *Californians* 302 Mrs. Polk, assisted by a Mexican maid, descended from the car. **1912** RAINE *Brand Blotters* 268 The Mexican woman could do nothing even if she would.

2. Designating articles of clothing, vehicles, tools, etc.

1858 PETERS *Kit Carson* 239 The Mexican axe . . . resembles as much the common pick of our laborers as it does the axe used by American woodsmen. *Ib.*, The most remarkable sight of all is the Mexican cart. . . The wheels . . . are at least one foot thick. **1901** *Amer. Rev. of Reviews* Sept. 313/1 The list [of provisions] includes Mexican beans, oatmeal . . . and canned tomatoes and corn. **1913** BARNES *Western Grazing Grounds* 116 The broad-brimmed Stetson or Mexican sombrero has gone. **1914** 'BOWER' *Flying U Ranch* 64 The Native Son . . . was wearing . . . Mexican spurs with their immense rowels and ornate conchos of hand-beaten silver. **1923** J. H. COOK *On Old Frontier* 59 [A man] wearing a Mexican sash about his waist and packing a pair of . . . six-shooters, would have no trouble getting something to eat.

3. a. Designating various plants and trees.

1827 *Western Mo. Rev.* I. 82 The kinds of cotton which are chiefly cultivated, are Louisiana, green seed, or Tennessee, and recently Mexican. **1836** LINCOLN *Botany* App. 117 *Mirabilis . . . dichotoma,* (Mexican four-o'clock.) **1869** FULLER *Flower Gatherers* 237 It was marked *Lobelia fulgens*, or Mexican Cardinal flower, and had retained its superb color for years. **1884** SARGENT *Rep. Forests* 128 *Morus microphylla.* . . . Mexican Mulberry. **1890** WEBSTER 272/1 *Mexican cocoa*, an American herb (*Richardsonia scabra*), yielding a nutritious fodder. Its roots are used as a substitute for ipecacuanha. **1891** COULTER *Bot. W. Texas* I. 66 *Ungnadia speciosa* Mexican buckeye. A shrub or very small tree common . . . from the valley of the Trinity through western Texas to New Mexico. **1897** SUDWORTH *Arborescent Flora* 312 *Arbutus Xalapensis,* . . . Mexican Madroña. . . . Common names. Manzanita. Madroña.

b. Designating various animals.

1827 WILLIAMS *West Florida* 26 The Mexican oppossum is very numerous. **1846** in Emory *Military Reconn.* 489 The Mexican bull, has a bunch on its back like a camel. **1873** MILLER *Amongst Modocs* 3 A narrow little pack trail, . . . barely wide enough to admit of . . . little Mexican mules, with their apparajos. **1881** CHASE *Editor's Run in N. Mex.* 83, I never saw a Mexican broncho hang his head lower. **1885** *Amer. Naturalist* Sept. 922 The Mexican badger, two specimens of which are found in Central Kansas. **1903** 'O. HENRY' *Heart of West* 250 It is well to be reasonably watchful when a Mexican lion sings soprano along the arroyos.

c. In the specific names of birds.

1869 *Amer. Naturalist* III. 473 A solitary Mexican Fly Catcher . . . gave a specimen of the summer group of migrants. **1874** COUES *Key* 28 *Catherpes Mexicanus.* . . . Mexican Wren; White-throated Wren. **1889** *Rep. Secy. Agric.* 376 The Mexican Screech Owl (*Megascops asio trichopsis*) inhabits northwestern Mexico, Arizona, New Mexico, and Colorado. **1923** J. H. COOK *On Old Frontier* 27 There were wild turkeys by the thousand; also Mexican quail.

+**Mexican bit.** (See quot. 1883.) — **1883** KNIGHT *Suppl.* 597/1 *Mexican Bit*, a stiff cheek bit, having a high port, to which is attached a large ring, which when the bit is in the horse's mouth, encircles the jaw. **1884** CABLE *Dr. Sevier* liii, A large dark horse . . . stood champing his Mexican bit in the black shadow of a great oak.

+**Mexican blanket.** A blanket made by a Mexican or similar to such a blanket. — **1845** FRÉMONT *Exped.* 272 He gave me a Mexican blanket, and I gave him a very fine one which I had obtained at Vancouver. **1894** WISTER in *Harper's Mag.* Jan. 299/1 He had parted with Pedro for forty dollars, a striped Mexican blanket, and a pair of spurs.

+**Mexican clover.** *S.* =FLORIDA CLOVER. — **1889** VASEY *Agric. Grasses* 103 *Richardsonia scabra* (Mexican Clover; Spanish Clover; Florida Clover; Water Parsley [etc.]). **1890** *Cent.* 5168/1 Mexican clover . . . appears to be of some value as a forage-plant, and perhaps of more value as a green manure. **1901** MOHR *Plant Life Ala.* 135 The so-called Mexican clover . . . furnish[es] abundant, spontaneous crops of nutritious hay.

+**Mexican dollar.** The Mexican peso. — **1854** *Harper's Mag.* April 588/1 Upon the board was displayed . . . the lure in the shape of Mexican dollars. **1873** MILLER *Amongst Modocs* 391 He had . . . raised an old Spanish galleon from Fonseca filled with doubloons and Mexican dollars.

+**Mexican eagle.** Audubon's caracara (*Polyborus cheriway auduboni*), found in the southern United States. (Cf. CARACARA EAGLE.) — **1836** HOLLEY *Texas* 100 The Mexican eagle . . . is among the smallest of the aquiline tribe. **1858** BAIRD *Birds Pacific R.R.* 45 The Mexican Eagle . . . [inhabits] Florida, Texas, Mexico.

+**Mexican hog.** The Texas peccary, *Pecari angulatus.* — **1821** NUTTALL *Travels Arkansa* 155 The *Sus tajassu* or Mexican hog, is not uncommon some distance higher up Red river. **1836** HOLLEY *Texas* 95 The Pecari or Mexican hog is even yet occasionally met with, on the frontiers, in considerable gangs. **1901** *Amer. Rev. of Reviews* Sept. 309/1 An otherwise magnificent grazing country . . . is frequented by wild Mexican hogs, panthers [etc.].

+**Mexican horse.** =BRONCO 1. — **1844** KENDALL *Narr. Santa Fé Exped.* II. 362 There is a little 'go-ahead' in a spirited, showy, well-trained Mexican horse. **1872** TICE *Over Plains* 140 The Mexican horses, or *bronchos*, will also winter out during the winter like the cattle.

+**Mexicanization.** The process of rendering Mexican; the state or condition of being Mexicanized. — **1890** *Congress. Rec.* 5 June 5655/1 Gentlemen, do you know what a single silver standard means in this country? It means Mexicanization.

+**Mexicanized,** *a.* Made to resemble Mexico or the Mexicans. — **1844** GREGG *Commerce* II. 119 To this great ball, however, no Americans were invited, with the exception of a Mexicanized denizen or two. **1872** 'MARK TWAIN' *Roughing It* 178, I had never seen such wild, free, magnificent horsemanship . . . as these picturesquely clad Mexicans, Californians, and Mexicanized Americans displayed. **1887** THWING *Serm., Foes Chr. Civ.* 8 The Mexicanized Spaniard is here, too proud to work. **1904** *Baltimore Amer.* 15 June 6 With the prospective passing of President Diaz, of Mexico, all the world will hope that his country will not revert to that condition which once led to the invention of the word Mexicanized.

+**Mexican jaçana.** *S.W.* A long-legged wading bird (*Jacana spinosa gymnostoma*) of the family Jacanidae. — **1883** *Nat. Museum Bul.* No. 27, 154 Family Parridæ.—The Jaçanas . . . Mexican Jaçana. Middle America, north to Lower Rio Grande Valley in Texas. **1887** RIDGWAY *Manual N.A. Birds* 183 *J[acana] gymnostoma.* Mexican Jacana.

+**Mexican (prickly) poppy.** A tropical herb: (see quot. 1901). — **1847** EMORY *Military Reconn.* 13 We find in the bottoms [near the Arkansas R.] . . . Mexican poppy [etc.]. **1857** GRAY *Botany* 25 *A[rgemone] Mexicana.* (Mexican Prickly Poppy.) **1901** MOHR *Plant Life Ala.* 520 *Argemone mexicana.* . . . Mexican Prickly Poppy. . . . Carolinian and Louisianian areas. Adventive sparingly in North Atlantic ports, frequent on the South Atlantic and Gulf coast.

+**Mexican saddle.** A heavy saddle having, usually, a high pommel and cantle, heavy leather skirts, and wooden stirrups. — **1848** PARKMAN in *Knickerb.* XXXI. 328 Their strong, gaunt horses were equipped with rusty Spanish bits, and rude Mexican saddles. **1865** *Atlantic Mo.* Jan. 59/2 A Mexican saddle,—out of which you can scarcely fall. **1891** 'CRADDOCK' in *Harper's Mag.* Feb. 367/1 He was a bay horse . . . [with] an old fashioned Mexican saddle. **1910** J. HART *Vigilante Girl* 345 She galloped on in her high-peaked Mexican saddle.

+**Mexican shilling.** (See quotation.) — **1889** *Cent.* 567/1 *Bit*, . . . in parts of the United States, [the name] of a silver coin formerly current (in some States called a *Mexican shilling*), of the value of 12½ cents.

Mexican tea. {1829–} +A weedy, rank-scented plant (*Chenopodium ambrosioides*) introduced into the United States from tropical America. — **1843** TORREY *Flora N.Y.* II. 135 *Ambrina Ambrosioides.* . . . Mexican Tea. . . . Road-sides and waste places; common near New-York and along the Hudson. **1847** DARLINGTON *Weeds & Plants* 272 Ambrosia-like Chenopodium. Mexican Tea. . . . Naturalized from tropical America. **1901** MOHR *Plant Life Ala.* 488 Mexican Tea. . . . Carolinian and Louisianian areas.

+**Mexican War.** The war carried on between the United States and Mexico (1846–8), occasioned chiefly by the annexation of Texas by the U.S. and the rejection by Mexico of the Rio Grande River as a boundary. Also attrib.

1850 GARRARD *Wah-To-Yah* xxiii. 276 He was . . . on a tour to Missouri at the commencement of the Mexican war excitement. **1852** EASTMAN *Aunt Phillis's Cabin* 53 Since the close of the Mexican War, he had done little else but cultivate them. **1873** *Republic* I. 31 The remaining grants . . . were made in behalf of the soldiers of 1812 and of the Mexican war. **1881** *Harper's Mag.* Jan. 258/2 The Mexican war . . . the Abolitionists declared . . . was waged to obtain new territory for the extension of slavery. **1894** LEAVITT *Our Money Wars* 82 In 1845 the Democrats . . . fought the Mexican War with Treasury notes. **1900** *Congress. Rec.* 8 Jan. 678/1 Under the Mexican war pension act the maximum is $12 a month.

+**Mexico piece.** A Spanish piece of eight, used in Mexico. In full *Mexico piece of eight. Obs.* — **1660** WINTHROP *Letters* 66 Mexico peices will passe for 5s. apeice. **1683** *Conn. Rec.* III. 119 This Court . . . doe order that for the future all peices of eight, Mexicoe, pillor and Civill peices shall pass at six shillings apeice. **1688** SEWALL *Diary* I. 240, I gave an oblong Mexico piece of Eight. **1741** *N.J. Archives* 1 Ser. VI. 118 Mexico pieces of eight, seventeen penny weight twelve grains, four shillings and six pence.

+**Miami.** Also †**Miamiha.** [Amer. Indian.]

1. *pl.* An Algonquian tribe of Indians who, when first encountered by Europeans, lived in what is now eastern Wisconsin and northern Illinois and Indiana. In full *Miami Indians.*

[**1671** *Relations des Jésuites 1670* (1858) 90/2 L'on passe ensuite chez les Miamioüek, et on arrive par de grands deserts aux Ilinois.] **1722** COXE *Descr. Carolana* 49 Near the Bottom of the Bay . . . is the fair River of the Miamihas (so call'd because upon it lives Part of a Nation bearing the same Name). **1792** *Ann. 2d Congress* 1048 [The] aggressions of the Miami and Wabash Indians . . . are solely the causes of the war. **1896** *Harper's Mag.* April 711/1 When a boy of twelve he had been captured by the Miamis.

2. *sing.* An Indian of this tribe. In full *Miami Indian.*

1808 BARKER *Indian Princess* II. iii, The insolent Miami has braved your king, and defied him with the crimson tomahawk. **1812** *Ann. 12th Congress* 1 Sess. II. 1861 It has been reported by a Miami Indian ... that twenty-four Indians of the Shawanese Prophet's band ... passed his camp. **1835** HOFFMAN *Winter in West* I. 276 The Indians that frequent the neighbourhood of Chicago ... are chiefly Pottawattamies and Ottawas, with ... a straggling Kickapoo or Miami.

3. Attrib. with *country, land, tribe, village.*

1792 *Affecting Hist. F. Manheim* 31 We arrived within a few miles of the Miami Village. **1815** DRAKE *Cincinnati* 80 Forest trees ... of the Miami country. **1838** VAN BUREN in *Pres. Mess. & P.* III. 507, I transmit, for the consideration and constitutional action of the Senate, a treaty concluded with the Miami tribe of Indians. **1840** H. CRAWFORD *Ib.* IV. 1842 The Miami lands were very valuable.

Mica. A silicate capable of being split into thin sheets, used in stove doors, lanterns, etc. {1778–} Also attrib. (Cf. ISINGLASS.) — **1832** WILLIAMSON *Maine* I. 178 *Mica* ... is seen in different parts of Maine. **1842** *Nat. Hist. N.Y., Geology* II. 420 Mica for stoves, lanterns, etc. may be obtained in Edwards. It is white, or but slightly tinged with yellowish brown. **1862** DANA *Manual of Geol.* 56 Mica ... [is] distinguished by its splitting easily into very thin elastic leaves or scales,—even thinner than paper,—and its brilliant lustre. **1880** *Harper's Mag.* Sept. 538/2 Sarah rode up to a mica mine a few miles distant. **1882** *Century Mag.* Feb. 634/1 Mica is now found in abundance in this country.

+**Micco.** Variant of MICO.

Michaelmas daisy. *local.* An aster. {1785–} — **1850** S. F. COOPER *Rural Hours* 105 Violets ... grow there, with ... Michaelmas-daisies of several kinds, perhaps the coptis, or gold-thread, and three or four ferns. **1894** *Amer. Folk-Lore* VII. 91 *Asters* of any kind, Michaelmas daisies, N.Y.

+**Michaux.** [André *Michaux*, Fr. botanist and traveler (1746–1802).] Used in possessive in specific names of plants. — **1843** TORREY *Flora N.Y.* II. 339 *Cyperus Michauxianus.* ... Michaux's Galingale. ... Borders of salt marshes: common in the neighborhood of New-York, and on Long Island. **1901** MOHR *Plant Life Ala.* 499 *Arenaria stricta.* ... Michaux's Sandwort. ... Canadian zone to Carolinian area.

+**Michigan.** [Algonquian Indian.] *attrib.* Of or pertaining to the state of Michigan, esp. with reference to fish or timber found there. — **1838** COLTON *Ind. Delineated* 26 A rail road is located from Madison to Indianapolis, and the great Michigan road through the state commences here. **1855** M. THOMPSON *Doesticks* 97 One was afflicted with the measles, and the other had the Michigan itch. **1883** *Nat. Museum Bul.* No. 27, 423 *Coregonus artedi.* ... Lake Herring; Michigan Herring. Great Lakes and northeastward. **1883** *Century Mag.* Oct. 814/1 The butts are made of Michigan oak. **1884** GOODE, etc. *Fisheries* I. 505 It is, however, the Michigan Grayling which is at present most interesting to the angler. **1922** TITUS *Timber* 12 Didn't Michigan Pine build th' corn belt?

+**Michigander.** A native or inhabitant of the state of Michigan.

1848 LINCOLN in *Congress. Globe* App. 27 July 1024/2, I mean the military tail the Democrats are now engaged in dovetailing on to the great Michigander [Gen. Cass]. **1862** in Moore *Rebellion Rec.* V. II. 91 Dana's wing was finally swung round ... his gallant Michiganders and Bay-State lads sweeping the perimeter of the circle ... with irresistible fury. **1879** *N.Y. Herald* 19 April 3/1 Mr. Conger, the eminent Michigander, was refreshingly quiet. **1898** FREDERIC *Deserter* 143 'What are you? Michiganders?' shouted the boy.

attrib. **1897** *Outing* XXX. 293/1 (*caption*), Michi-Gander Lawmakers.

+**Michigan (double) plow.** A heavy double-moldboard plow used for breaking, subsoiling, etc. — **1857** *Ill. Agric. Soc. Trans.* III. 496 For this purpose [subsoiling] the Michigan double or subsoil plow is used. **1862** *Rep. Comm. Patents 1861: Agric.* 279 This ploughing may also be done by a double team with the Michigan plough. **1863** MITCHELL *My Farm* 251 Or let him try a day at the tail of a Michigan-plough. **1864** *Ohio Agric. Rep.* XVIII. 33 Has plowing with the Michigan Double Plow been found beneficial?

+**Michigan fish.** (See quotation.) — **a1862** THOREAU *Maine Woods* 210, [I] caught several small somewhat yellowish sucker-like fishes, which the Indian at once rejected, saying that they were Michigan fish (i.e. soft and stinking fish).

+**Michiganian.** =MICHIGANDER. *Obs.* — **1813** *Niles' Reg.* V. 185 The Michiganians. **1835** HOFFMAN *Winter in West* I. 163 The pride of a Michiganian, in the beautiful land of his adoption, is ... strong. **1837** MARTINEAU *Society* I. 65 The Michiganians were in the singular position of having a state government in full operation, while they were excluded from the Union.

+**Mick.** [From proper name *Michael.*] An Irishman. *slang.* Also attrib. — **1872** 'MARK TWAIN' *Roughing It* 336 The Micks got to throwing stones through the Methodis' Sunday-school windows. **1888** *Century Mag.* March 807/1 The representative Americans of the present day ... [are] the Micks and the Pats. **1894** FORD *P. Stirling* 369 Fortunately it's a Mick regiment, so we needn't worry over who was killed. **1913** LONDON *Valley of Moon* 27 They's been too much drink, an' you know what the Micks are for a rough house.

+**Mico.** Also **meiko, micco.** [Muskogee *miko* chief.] A chief or ruler among the Muskogee Indians. *Obs.* (Cf. MINGO[3].)

1737 WESLEY *Journal* 2 Dec., Nor have they any kings or princes ... ; their meikos, or headmen, having no power either to command or punish. **1740** W. STEPHENS *Proc. Georgia* I. 565 Old Chigellie, their chief Mico at present, had of late shewn an unusual Coldness. **1800** HAWKINS *Sk. Creek Country* 68 Every town has a chief who presides over the whole; he is their Mic-co, called by the white people, 'King.' **1854** *S. Lit. Messenger* XX. 399 They had no doubts of the perfect worth of their young chief, to be the Great Mico, or King of the Catawbas!

* **Middle,** *n.*

+**1.** *Agric.* In a cultivated field, the strip of unplanted ground between the drills or rows of corn, cotton, etc.

1829 in Commons, etc. *Doc. Hist.* 238 Two Ploughs breaking middles in Popular tree cut. **1847** *Fla. Plantation Rec.* 242, 13 [slaves] plowing out middles in brickyard [field]. **1851** *Ib.* 373 Ploughs Runing around cotton and splitting cotton middles. **1907** T. F. HUNT *Forage & Fiber Crops* 352 The field is made up into alternate beds and middles or into 'back' furrows and 'dead' furrows.

+**2.** *Middle of the road,* a phrase used of the views of those members of the Populist party who in 1896 and 1900 opposed fusion with the Democratic party. Also attrib.

1892 in F. E. Haynes *J. B. Weaver* 468 Side tracks are rough, and they're hard to walk, Keep in the middle of the road. **1896** *Congress. Rec.* 10 Dec. 80/2 The only honest Populist is the 'middle-of-the-road' Populist. **1914** *Cycl. Amer. Govt.* II. 758/1 The Middle of the Road convention held [in 1900] at Cincinnati, Ohio, nominated Wharton Barker.

* **Middle,** *a.* Of land areas: Situated at the center or middle. (See also MIDDLE STATES.)

1693 *Va. Statutes at Large* III. 122 That the said college be ... built as neare the church now standing in Middle Plantation old ffields as convenience will permitt. **1792** IMLAY *Western Territory* 95 The rapidity of the settlement has driven the wild turkey quite out of the middle countries. **1812** *Niles' Reg.* II. 14/1 The middle country will experience no exemption from these particular burthens. **1839** AUDUBON *Ornith. Biog.* V. 156 [The] Cape May warbler ... seems to pass rapidly through our Middle Districts in May. **1865** *Nation* I. 208 He declared that white emigration would displace them in the middle belt, and compel them to move to the Gulf States.

Middle bachelor. (See quot. 1851.) *Obs.* {1758} — **1840** QUINCY *Hist. Harvard* II. 540 A Senior Sophister has authority to take a Freshman from a Sophomore, a Middle Bachelor from a Junior Sophister [etc.]. **1851** HALL *College Words* 207 *Middle Bachelor.* One who is in his second year after taking the degree of Bachelor of Arts.

+**Middle colonies.** *pl.* The American colonies situated between those of New England and the southern ones. Also *middle British colonies.* — **1776** (*title*), A Topographical Description of such parts of North America as are contained in the annexed map of the middle British colonies. **1781** WITHERSPOON *Druid P.* No. 7, *Chunks,* that is brands, half burnt wood. This is customary in the middle colonies. **1821** JEFFERSON *Writings* I. 19 The people of the middle colonies (Maryland, Delaware, Pennsylvania, the Jerseys and New York) were not yet ripe for bidding adieu to British connection.

Middle ground. {1801–} +(See quotation.) *Obs.* — **1784** FILSON *Kentucke* 8 The fertile region, now called Kentucke, then but known to the Indians, by the name of the Dark and Bloody Ground, and sometimes the Middle Ground.

Middleman. +**1.** An oarsman in the middle of a boat. +**2.** In Negro minstrelsy, the actor in the middle of a line or semicircle of performers. — **(1) 1839** TOWNSEND *Narrative* 355 The middle-men ply their oars. **(2) 1870** O. LOGAN *Before Footlights* 248, I give it up, Brudder Bones, as the middle man at the minstrels always does the end man's conundrums. **1880** E. JAMES *Negro Minstrel's Guide* 12 The middle and end men have to get in their jokes, gags and conundrums. **1915** MATTHEWS in *Scribner's Mag.* June 756/1 The device for immediate and boisterous laughter, this putting down of the middle-man by the end-man, the Negro minstrels appear to have borrowed from the circus.

Middle name. The name following the first name and preceding the family name. — **1835** *Harvardiana* II. 23 [He] then asks their middle names. **1880** 'MARK TWAIN' *Tramp Abroad* 440 He had all the look of an American person who would be likely to begin his signature with an initial, and spell his middle name out.

+**Middle states.** *pl.* Those eastern states, New York, New Jersey, Pennsylvania, Delaware, and Maryland, situated between the New England states and the southern states; also, sing., one of these states.

1784 WASHINGTON *Diaries* II. 326 The middle States with the Country immediately back of them. **a1800** TWINING *Visit* 398 The character of the Middle States, New York, Philadelphia, the Jerseys, and Maryland, seems to be a modification of the extremes. **1846** COOPER *Redskins* xxvi, The laboring classes of the Middle States ... use better English than thousands of educated men in New England itself. **1877** in Leavitt *Our Money Wars* (1894) 218 The failures in the Middle States are one in every 57 trading firms. **1904** *N.Y. Ev. Post* 28 Jan. 6 If there was a tariff wall separating New England from the Middle States. **1912** NICHOLSON *Hoosier Chron.* 59 A region where there had been an infusion of population from New England and the Middle States.

attrib. **1868** Beecher *Norwood* 1 If we should employ a scientific method, and speak of a Western genus, and a Southern genus, and a Middle State genus [etc.].

b. The states occupying the area between the Allegheny Mts. and the Mississippi River.

1875 *N.Y. Tribune* 17 Feb. 11/5 (*advt.*), The Great Roman Hippodrome Positively Close[s] Saturday Night, Feb. 27, to prepare for the great traveling campaign through the larger cities of the Eastern, Middle, and Western States.

+**Middle West.** The north central portion of the United States, embracing, approximately, the area north of the Ohio River and its latitude from the Rocky Mountains to the Alleghenies. — **1898** M. H. Catherwood (*title*), Heroes of the Middle West. **1903** E. Johnson *Railway Transportation* 267 The people of the middle West . . . were producing great quantities of grain and other food products. **1925** Glasgow *Barren Ground* 19 Even the prosperous James Ellgood made fun of 'the weed with the highfalutin' name from the Middle West.'

* **Middling.**

1. *pl.* Medium-sized particles sifted out of ground grain as it passes through the bolters. {1842–}

1766 *R.I. Commerce* I. 149, I shall send you the 30 Bbs. Midlings agreeable to your Order. **1770** *Md. Hist. Mag.* XIII. 69 Things sent by the wagon: . . . 3 Casks of fine Flour 1 d[itt]o midlings. **1795** Winterbotham *Hist. View* II. 407 The produce, manufactures, and exports of Pennsylvania are very many and various; viz. wheat, . . . middlings, bran, shorts, white water biscuit. **1882** *Maine Bd. Agric. Rep.* XXVI. 68 Five weeks ago I bought two shoats. . . . I set a bag of middlings by the pen, and had them fed in this way. **1896** *Vt. Agric. Rep.* XV. 59 Corn should be supplemented by . . . a combination of waste products, such as wheat bran or middlings.

+**2.** *S.* and *S.W.* The middle or side of a hog between the ham and the shoulder; pork or bacon cut from this piece.

1777 *Va. State P.* I. 288 Bakin in hams, midlings, shoulders, &c. **1821** Dewees *Lett. from Texas* 19 Our outfit was about half a middling of bacon, an old rifle gun, and our blankets. **1853** P. Kennedy *Blackwater Chron.* vii. 87 Sugar; about ten pounds of middling of bacon, to fry our trout with [etc.]. **1904** Glasgow *Deliverance* 51 She has had to fry the middling in the kitchen, and mother complains so of the smell.

+**3.** Tobacco of an intermediate grade.

1793 Washington *Writings* XII. 382 The middlings and ship stuff may be sold to answer the money calls which you will have upon you.

+**4.** Cotton which in quality comes up to the standard or basic grade upon which market quotations are based.

Cf. Low middling.

1851 in Bassett *Plantation Overseer* 229 We received . . . your crop of cotton . . . of which 56 bales are in quality a high order of 'middling' to 'good middling.' **1864** in W. Lawrence *A. A. Lawrence* 194 Cotton has sold at 165 cents a pound for 'middling.' **1887** *Courier-Journal* 17 Jan. 7/6 Cotton market was dull; middling 9$\frac{1}{16}$¢; low middling 8$\frac{3}{4}$¢.

+**Middling bread.** Bread of a middle or moderately good quality. *Obs.* — **1720** *Amer. Wkly. Mercury* 12 Jan. 2/2 White Bread, . . . Midling Bread, 18 to 19 per Hundred. **1766** *R.I. Commerce* I. 163 It was lucky I only sent you so little of the midling Bread. We distinguish it here in three sorts vizt. Ship, Midling, and White.

+**Middling cotton.** = Middling 4. — **1851** *Polly Peablossom* 144 He determined to invest . . . in a barrel of Western whiskey; paying therefor at the rate of, precisely two pounds of middling cotton for one gallon of 'ditto' whiskey.

+**Middling interest.** The middle class. Also attrib. — **1857** Stone *Life Howland* 137 He resolved on attempting to arrest this hostility by creating . . . a correct public sentiment, and by overlaying it with what is . . . denominated a 'middling interest' influence. **a1859** *Conn. Courant* (B.), Men of the middling interest class are now the best off. . . . They have felt they belonged to the middling interest.

+**Midnight appointment.** *Polit.* (See quotation.) — **1889** *Cent.* 275/3 *Midnight appointments*, in *U.S. politics*, appointments made during the last hours of an administration; specifically, those so made by President John Adams.

+**Midnight judge.** *Polit.* (See quot. 1914.) — **1855** *Congress. Globe* App. 10 Jan. 89/1 The term 'midnight judges' . . . has become a popular phrase; a phrase suggested for purposes of odium. **1914** *Cycl. Amer. Govt.* II. 430/2 Midnight Judges. A disparaging nickname bestowed by the Jeffersonian Republicans, in 1801, upon the judges whose commissions were signed by the retiring President, John Adams, just before midnight, March 3. It was again applied by the Whigs to the judges appointed by Martin Van Buren at the close of his administration, March, 1841.

* **Midway,** *n.* +A boulevard area connecting Washington and Jackson parks in Chicago, in which the amusement section of the Chicago exposition of 1893 was situated. In full *Midway Plaisance.* Also attrib.

1871 *Chicago South Park Commission Rep.* 25 The plan of the Midway Plaisance is shown on drawing No. 2. *Ib.* 26 Three streets are proposed to be carried across the Midway besides those at its end. **1884** Marquis *Handbook of Chicago* 92 Midway Plaisance extends from Jackson Park to Washington Park between Fifty-ninth and Sixtieth Streets. It was intended to connect the two parks both by boulevard and basin, the latter uniting the lake systems of the parks. **1891** *After 4 Centuries the World's Fair* (World's Columb. Exp.) 6 Jackson Park . . . has been selected as the site for the Main Exposition; . . . the Midway Plaisance and Washington Park, adjoining Jackson Park, as reserves for possible other parts. **1902** *Harper's Mag.* Dec. 163 The tents of the Midway Plaisance, that perpetual and universal gift to the State and county fairs from the great Columbian Fair at Chicago. **1909** *Guide to City of Chicago* 141 Midway Plaisance is a strip of land containing 80 acres which lies between Washington and Jackson parks and is the site of the Midway Plaisance or Side Show Section of the World's Fair.

+**b.** At a fair or exposition, a central avenue along which the chief amusement exhibits and features are located. Also attrib.

1901 *Pan-Amer. Exposition, Buffalo* (*folder*), The Midway will have the choicest of the world's amusement novelties. **1903** *N.Y. Ev. Post* 17 Oct., Out in the little 'Midway' of tents and booths, where the two-headed baby was on exhibition. **1904** *Ib.* 22 Sept., Ever since Chicago led the way, the 'Midway' features of our great fairs have threatened more and more to overshadow the mere educational features. **1906** *Springfield W. Repub.* 4 Oct. 15 There was an unusually large midway. There were five 'hit the coon' howlers . . . and many other side attractions. **1920** Cooper *Under Big Top* 12 They show the position of the 'midway' and the side show.

* **Midway,** *adv.* +*Midway of*, in the middle of.

a1811 Henry *Camp. Quebec* 192 About midway of the horn [of the moose] . . . there is a broad flat part of the horn. **1856** Cartwright *Autobiog.* 118 About midway of it there lived a Baptist minister. **1871** Harte *Luck of Roaring Camp* 152 Midway of the crossing he looked up and held his breath in awe. **1903** *Nation* 17 Sept. 234 He died midway of his 70th year.

* **Midyear,** *n.* +Short for *midyear examination*, an examination coming in the middle of an academic year. Usually pl. — **1896** Moe *Hist. Harvard* 45 Massachusetts Hall arose on the spot where it still stands, a pride to the College, and an abhorrence at the 'midyears' and 'finals.' **1897** Flandrau *Harvard Episodes* 235 The midyears were coming. . . . The examination period was well under way. **1902** Corbin *American at Oxford* 187 They had some such relation to a degree as our hour examinations, midyears, and finals.

Midyear, *a.* +Occurring at the middle of an academic or school year. — **1897** Flandrau *Harvard Episodes* 226 The midyear examinations have an unpleasant habit of disturbing the even academic tenor early in February, as their name suggests. *Ib.* 280 Thorn . . . entered the boy's midyear mark in the records as C. **1912** Nicholson *Hoosier Chron.* 218 In the midyear recess of her sophomore year she visited one of her new friends in Boston.

+**Miggle.** (See quot. 1895.) — **1895** *Stand.* 1123/1 *Miggle*, . . . a common playing-marble; in the plural, the game of marbles. **1906** *Amer. Illustr. Mag.* March 562/1 Boys garner birds' eggs, door-knobs, chalk, and miggles.

Mignonette. Any one of various plants of the genus *Reseda.* {1752–} — **1817–8** Eaton *Botany* (1822) 426 *Reseda odorata*, mignonette. **1839** 'M. Pencil' *White Sulphur P.* 82 The walks are lined with . . . pinks, mignonette, hearts-ease, ambrosias, and stork jellies. **1878** Cooke *Happy Dodd* 98 Baskets of mignonette, with here and there a late rose, and lavish branches of sweet verbena. **1901** Churchill *Crisis* 451 Virginia and he would . . . steep, as it were, in the blended perfumes of the roses and the mignonettes and the pinks.

+**Migration station.** 'A station or post for observing facts concerning the migration of birds' (*Cent.*). — **1884** *Science* IV. 374/2 Migration-stations now exist in every state and territory of the Union, excepting Delaware and Nevada.

+**Migratory pigeon.** The passenger pigeon, *Ectopistes migratorius.* Now extinct. — **1810** Wilson *Amer. Ornith.* II. 293 *Columba migratoria.* . . . Migratory Pigeon. . . . The wild pigeon of the United States.

+**Migratory squirrel.** The gray squirrel, *Sciurus carolinensis.* — **1857** *Rep. Comm. Patents: Agric. 1856* 63 The migratory squirrel . . . is the most abundant of our American squirrels.

+**Migratory thrush.** The common American robin. — **1839** Audubon *Ornith. Biog.* V. 442 American Robin or Migratory Thrush. *Turdus Migratorius.* **1844** *Nat. Hist. N.Y., Zoology* II. 70 The American Robin. *Merula Migratoria.* . . . American Robin, or Migratory Thrush. **1885** *Pall Mall Gaz.* 21 May 4/2 If you [in England] knew . . . the migratory thrush and bluebird . . . , you would try to acclimatize them. **1917** *Birds of Amer.* III. 236 Robin. . . . [Also called] Migratory Thrush.

* **Milch cow.** A cow kept for milking.

1637 *Dedham Rec.* 27 Yt medowe . . . shall become a somer pasture for milch Cowes. **1708** *Boston News-Letter* 25 Oct. 4/2 Strayed . . . out of a Pasture in North-Boston, a black Milch Cow between 3 and 4 years old. **1789** Dunlap *Father* I. i, We overtook a very modest milch-cow. **1850** Hines *Voyage* 409 Until we should get into the buffalo country, we drove twelve head of cattle besides a milch cow. **1892** M. A. Jackson *Gen. Jackson* 119 The other animate possessions of the family were . . . two splendid milch cows, and a lot of chickens.

attrib. **1638** *Charlestown Land Rec.* 9 [Thomas Lynde owns] eight milch cow common, 7 whereof fell to him in the divident.

Milch goat. A goat kept for milking. {1759–} — **1637** *Essex Inst. Coll.* IX. 42 Agreed to allowe a goatherd for keeping a whole year, 2s a milch goat. **1847** Ruxton *Adv. Rocky Mts.* (1848) 264 An old mountaineer . . . took with him a troop of milch-goats, by which to bring up the young sheep.

Mileage. {1845–} +An allowance of a fixed amount per mile to cover the expenses of traveling.

1. For members of legislative bodies.

Cf. CONSTRUCTIVE *a.* c.

1754 FRANKLIN *Writings* III. 197 Members' Pay . . . milage for travelling expenses. **1797** *Ann. 5th Congress* I. 32 Mr. Read . . . reported a bill for allowing full mileage to the members of the Senate and House of Representatives. **1840** *Niles' Nat. Reg.* 20 June 253 The bill to establish a uniform rule of mileage for members of congress coming up in the order of the business [etc.]. **1860** *Harper's Mag.* April 688/1 Mr. Sherman . . . reported a bill reducing the mileage of members from forty cents a mile to twenty. **1910** *Okla. Session Laws* 3 Legisl. 2 There is hereby appropriated . . . to pay the per diem and mileage of the contingent expenses of the Extraordinary Session [etc.].

attrib. **1850** *Whig Almanac 1851* 11/2 Mileage Reform, and several other desirable changes, were attempted.

b. *transf.* For delegates to a convention.

1874 *Internat. Typogr. Union Proc.* 41 None but delegates shall vote or receive mileage and per diem.

2. For soldiers.

1776 H. GATES in Sparks *Corr. Revol.* I. 281 The militia were promised their mileage and billeting-money. **1779** *Amherst Rec.* (1884) 76/1 Money [was] taken out of the Treasury to Pay Bounties & Mileage to soldiers. **1782** *N.H. Comm. Safety Rec.* 290 Ordered the Treasurer to pay . . . five Dollars, . . . being for milage to Soldiers. **1849** *Whig Almanac 1850* 26/2 This year $75,000 are appropriated to pay military mileage.

+**Mileage ticket.** *Railroad.* A ticket entitling the purchaser to travel a specified number of miles on a given railroad without restriction as to route or destination. — **1887** GEORGE *40 Yrs. on Rail* 255 Mileage tickets, as they are called in railroad phraseology, have been issued in many different forms. **1898** *Boston Morn. Herald* 16 April 8/3 (Ernst).

+**Mile board.** =next. Also fig. — **1857** *Harper's Mag.* Nov. 734/2 The ninth mile-board from Burnsville is past. **1894** CABLE *J. March* xxiv, If you'd made me just your first mile-board.

Milepost. One of a series of posts set up a mile apart to mark the distance from or to some place. {1812–} — **1768** *Maryland Hist. Mag.* II. 317 As we returned (besides the Mile Posts) we erected Marks on the Tops of all the High Ridges. **1869** *Mich. Gen. Statutes* I. (1882) 417 Mile posts shall be set at the close of each eighty chains. **1873** BAILEY *Life in Danbury* 164 He was standing on the platform, and had caught his coat on a mile post.

***Milfoil.** A composite herb (*Achillea millefolium*), also known as yarrow, or a plant related to this. — **1821** NUTTALL *Trav. Arkansa* 158 The common Milfoil, and sorrel . . . are as prevalent, at least the former, as in Europe. **1840** DEWEY *Mass. Flowering Plants* 49 *M[yriophyllum] ambiguum.* Nutt. Floating Millfoil . . . ; blossoms in July; found near New Bedford. **1845** FRÉMONT *Exped.* 119 *Achillea millefolium* (milfoil) was among the characteristic plants of the river bottoms to-day. **1897** *Outing* XXX. 455/2 The edges of the brook were bedecked with milfoil.

Military, *n.*

1. Soldiers in general; military forces. {1757–}

1790 MACLAY *Deb. Senate* 186 The bill for augmenting the military to sixteen hundred men came up. **1863** *Rio Abajo Press* 27 Jan. 2 The military bring the savages under wholesome restraint. **1873** MILLER *Amongst Modocs* 339, I feared . . . lest something might . . . throw me into the hands of the military, which I had just escaped. **1889** *Century Mag.* April 826/2 When the military . . . arrived . . . they were drawn up on each side.

+**2.** (See quot. 1844.) *Obs.*

1838 'UNCLE SAM' in *Bentley's Misc.* IV. 41 Are you in the military, colonel? **1844** — *Peculiarities* II. 246 The Americans designate their volunteer troops by the term 'military.'

***Military,** *a.* +Of or pertaining to land given as compensation for service in the army. — **1780** in *Travels Amer. Col.* 652, 500 acres part of a military Warrant for one thousand [acres]. **1798** PUTNAM in *Memoirs* 422 Two of the Surveyors employed in runing out the Military tract had completed there work in the woods. **1855** PIERCE in *Pres. Mess. & P.* V. 340 The aggregate amount of public land sold during the last fiscal year, located with military scrip or land warrants, taken up under grants for roads, . . . is 24,557,409 acres.

+**Military academy.** A school for boys and young men which emphasizes military training and discipline. Also attrib.

Orig. used (see first group of examples) with particular reference to the national school at West Point, New York, where officers are trained for the United States Army. (Cf. MILITARY SCHOOL.)

(1) [**1776** *Jrnls. Cont. Congress* VI. 860 Resolved, That the Board of War be directed to prepare a plan for establishing a continental Laboratory and a Military Academy.] **1802** *Ann. 7th Congress* 1 Sess. 1312 The said corps [of engineers] when so organized, shall be stationed at West Point . . . and shall constitute a military academy. **1864** 'PENNIMAN' *Tanner-Boy* 37 The Military Academy at West Point is a national institution, supported by the Government of the United States. **1877** *Harper's Mag.* March 627/1 The Military Academy Appropriation Bill was passed by the House January 12. **1892** M. A. JACKSON *Gen. Jackson* 30 A young man from the Congressional district in which he lived had received an appointment to the Military Academy at West Point.

(2) **1827** DRAKE & MANSFIELD *Cincinnati* 96 The plans of education respectively pursued at West Point, and at Captain Partridge's Military Academy, at Middletown, are generally admitted to be of the most excellent kind. **a1841** HAWES *Sporting Scenes* II. 122 Military academies and Sunday schools are extensively established among the free blacks. **1879** *Mich. Gen. Statutes* I. (1882) 303 The general government has recognized the Michigan military academy at Orchard Lake. **1925** *Harper's Bazar* July 19 New York Military Academy, a school of distinction. Cornwall-on-Hudson, New York.

+**Military bounty.** Public land given as compensation for military service. Freq. attrib. — **1792** *Ann. 2d Congress* 1036 The second reservation covers . . . grants to . . . Commissioners for laying out the military bounties; and to guards, chain-carriers [etc.]. **1812** MARSHALL *Kentucky* 105 Many surveys had been executed upon military bounty warrants, under the proclamation of George the third . . . bearing date in October 1763. **1817** *Ann. 14th Congress* 2 Sess. 44 The President communicated a report . . . concerning the progress made in surveying military bounty lands. **1831** PECK *Guide* 319 The Military Bounty Tract . . . was set aside by Congress and patented for soldiers who served in the last war.

Military chest. The treasury of an army. *Obs.* {1753–} — **1755** *Lett. to Washington* I. 80 You will be entrusted with a Military-Chest which You are to use as You see the Nature and Good of the Service requires. **1776** *Jrnls. Cont. Congress* V. 432 Resolved, That General Washington be directed to order . . . the payment out of the military chest. *Ib.* VI. 938 [The sutler shall] return to ye paymaster ye Sums supplyed him from ye military Chest.

Military fever. Typhoid fever. {1885–8} — **1790** *Penna. Packet* 26 July 3/3 Doctor Norris's Drops. Being an Effectual Cure for . . . Slow Fevers, commonly called Nervous Fevers, Military Fevers [etc.].

+**Military governor.** A military officer who administers the civil or executive affairs of a state or region occupied, usually temporarily, by military force. — **1864** LINCOLN in Fleming *Hist. Reconstruction* I. 113 Military governors will be appointed, with directions to proceed according to the bill. **1872** MCCLELLAN *Golden State* 108 Kearney, from this date, entered upon the duties of his new office as Military Governor of California. **1900** *Congress. Rec.* 25 Jan. 1172 General Ames became the military governor.

Military hospital. A hospital maintained by the army or navy to care for sick or wounded soldiers and sailors. {1799–} — **1777** *Jrnls. Cont. Congress* VII. 162 An Inspector General of the Army . . . [shall] visit the Military hospitals . . . to examine the medicines and instruments [etc.]. **1803** *Ann. 8th Congress* 2 Sess. 1508 The public buildings . . . in New Orleans . . . [include:] A military hospital. An ill-built custom-house [etc.]. **1870** O. LOGAN *Before Footlights* 220 They are going to take the house for a military hospital. **1894** WISTER in *Harper's Mag.* July 216/2 Cumnor was getting well in the military hospital at Grant.

+**Military land.** Land granted by the government to soldiers in compensation for military service. Usually pl. — **1797** *Ann. 5th Congress* I. 431 Mr. Bayard moved to strike out the exception in favor of patents for military lands. **1819** *Niles' Reg.* XVII. 159/2 No more patents can be issued until the lottery for military lands in Arkansas shall be prepared. **1835** in Howe *Hist. Coll. Ohio* 386 The unappropriated United States military lands had been brought into market during the preceding year. **1852** *Whig Almanac 1853* 14/1 This act makes all warrants for military or bounty-land . . . assignable by deed or instrument of writing.

+**Military land warrant.** A land warrant issued by the government to a soldier as payment for military service. — **1789** *Ky. Gazette* 21 Feb. 2/4 The Subscribers have now . . . likewise a quantity of military land Warrants for sale. **1803** *Ann. 7th Congress* 2 Sess. 582 The House took up the bill respecting military land Warrants. **1816** *Niles' Reg.* X. 205/1 When any soldier of the regular army having obtained a military land warrant shall have lost . . . the same [etc.]. **1865** *Chicago Tribune* 15 April 1 Military and Agricultural Land Warrants for sale and bought at best rates.

Military post. A post or station at which a military force is maintained.

1822 MORSE *Rep. Indian Affairs* I. 39 Should the Government establish a military post here it will be very important [etc.]. **1835** HOFFMAN *Winter in West* I. 99 Detroit was then a military post of the first distinction. **c1867** in Fleming *Hist. Reconstruction* I. 443 The negro population was very dense and Military Posts were established at intervals of 20 or 30 miles. **1881** *Rep. Indian Affairs* p. xxi, These penal reservations . . . should be surrounded by a cordon of military posts. **1916** EASTMAN *From Deep Woods* 11 Father had dispatched us to the nearest military post for help.

attrib. **1882** *Rep. Indian Affairs* 21 They have also worked for the military post-trader and hay and wood contractor.

+**Military reservation.** *W.* An area set aside by the government for occupation by a military force. — **1856** GLISAN *Jrnl. Army Life* 342 A plan on the part of the Indians on the military reservation here to make an attack on the fort and town [is discovered]. **1900** *Congress. Rec.* 4 Jan. 649/2, I am not able to see . . . why the military reservations should be included in [the bill].

Military road. A road made for military purposes. {1850–} — **1819** *Niles' Reg.* XVII. 287/1 The military road from Detroit to the Rapids of the Miami, has been completed by the troops. **1858** *Kansas Hist. Coll.* V. 567 These same men attacked Barnesville, quite a clever town, on the military road. **1894** ROBLEY *Bourbon Co., Kansas* 64 All freight came on ox-wagons from Kansas City, Mo., down the old military road.

Military school. = MILITARY ACADEMY.
1777 *Jrnls. Cont. Congress* VII. 288 Resolved, That a Corps of Invalids be formed . . . to serve as a Military School for Young Gentlemen. **1790** *Ann. 1st Congress* II. 1815 It had been considered as a military school for a long time. **1802** ELLICOTT *Journal* 283 An attempt was made during the administration of President Washington to form a military school. **1862** in Strong *Cadet Life W. Point* p. xv, Near by are seen the Cavalry Stables . . . belonging to the Military School. **1912** NICHOLSON *Hoosier Chron.* 478 Blackford's course at the military school he had chosen for himself.

Military station. A place at which a military force is stationed. (Cf. MILITARY POST.) — **1821** in MORSE *Rep. Indian Affairs* (1822) I. 64 An officer to be stationed at the seat of Government, . . . should have a general superintendance of . . . Education and Military stations. **1882** McCABE *New York* 95 Fort Hamilton . . . is one of the principal military stations on the Atlantic coast.

*** Militia.**

1. a. An organization, primarily for local defense, consisting, usually, of men who meet periodically for military drill and exercise. {1660–} **+b.** The whole body of adult male citizens capable of bearing arms.
1650 *R.I. Col. Rec.* I. 226 Each Towne shall order its owne militia. **1705** BEVERLEY *Virginia* IV. 34 Every Freeman . . . from Sixteen, to Sixty Years of Age, is listed in the Militia. **1744** *N.J. Archives* 1 Ser. VI. 187 The Militia, . . . in this Country, is not a select part of the people as it is in England, . . . but the whole body of the people from sixteen years of age to fifty. **1777** *S. Lit. Messenger* XXVII. 253/1 The whole militia here, lately called below, were of volunteers without a single draft. **1787** *Constitution* i. § 8 The Congress shall have Power . . . To provide for organizing, arming, and disciplining, the Militia, and for governing such Part of them as may be employed in the Service of the United States, reserving to the States respectively, the Appointment of the Officers. **1838** FLAGG *Far West* II. 165 Each district had its commandant . . . and officers of the militia. **1853** SIMMS *Sword & Distaff* 23 He was . . . wearing the costume of the woodsman, . . . though without the customary fringes which made it the military garb of the forest rangers, or militia. **1862** *Mich. Gen. Statutes* I. (1882) 282 The commander-in-chief may order out, by draft, voluntary enlistment, or otherwise, the whole, or so much of the militia of this state as the public necessity demands. **1890** *Cent.* 3761/2 *Militia*, . . . the whole body of men declared by law amenable to military service, without enlistment, whether armed and drilled or not. (U.S.)
transf. **1818** FORDHAM *Narr. Travels* 219 Some of the young men armed themselves . . . to resist the intrusion of the Militia, as the vulgar are contemptuously called.

2. Attrib. with *act, bill, claim,* etc.
1705 *Boston News-Letter* 17 Sept. 2/2 His Excellency has been pleased to fill up the Vacancy in the Militia Officers of our Regiment. **1744** *N.J. Archives* 1 Ser. VI. 187 It is fit that all these people should be trained and taught the use of arms, and it is chiefly for this that the Militia Act is intended. **1748** *Ib.* VII. 211 A Militia Bill was prepared, & passed, by the Assembly. **1798** *Ann. 5th Congress* I. 642 *Resolved,* That a committee be appointed to report whether any and what amendments are necessary to the act providing an uniform militia system throughout the United States. **1843** *Niles' Nat. Reg.* 4 March 13/3 The Massachusetts militia claims. The bill to provide for these was then taken up. **1876** *Ill. Dept. Agric. Trans.* XIII. 330 Succeeding the systems of commons and common fields came the grants of 'head rights' of 400 acres each . . . and 'militia rights' of 100 acres, under acts of congress.

Militia law. A law governing the formation, regulation, etc., of a militia. — **1744** *N.J. Archives* 1 Ser. VI. 176 The Assembly . . . [did] pass a Militia Law, and therein, besides the directions for disciplining the people, made provision for arms, ammunition, colours, [etc.]. **1778** *S. Lit. Messenger* XXVII. 259/1 Several of them associated and were in arms to oppose the execution of the militia law. **1806** *Balance* V. 259/2 Regiments to parade . . . at eight o'clock in the morning, armed and accoutred as the militia law directs. **1837** W. JENKINS *Ohio Gaz.* p. xi, The militia law was thoroughly revised, and the territorial laws on that subject were all repealed. **1897** *Outing* XXIX. 388/2 When the militia law allowed a choice in uniforms the companies [elected] . . . to keep the old dress . . . and maintain their old company designations.

Militiaman. A member of the militia. {1844–} — **1780** HAMILTON *Works* VIII. 21 The militiamen replied they were of the lower party. **1816** *Ann. 14th Congress* 2 Sess. 273 That no writ or civil process, issuing from any court of the United States, shall be served upon any militia man. **1878** PINKERTON *Strikers* 151 The engineer and fireman [were] protected . . . by armed soldiers, with still other militiamen upon the tender . . . and in the caboose. **1894** FORD *P. Stirling* 360 Only a few strikers and militia-men killed. **1915** *Alabama Rep.* CLXXXVIII. 217 A militia man is not an automaton.

+Militia muster. A gathering of militia forces for review, inspection, drill, etc. — **1809** CUMING *Western Tour* 209 On the road I met . . . above fifty horsemen with rifles, who had been in Morristown at a militia muster. **1831** *Indiana Mag. Hist.* XXII. 362 At militia muster candidates appeared, for Congress, for Governor, to the Assembly. **1847** in Howe *Hist. Coll. Ohio* 122 The first militia muster in Cuyahoga county, was held on the 16th of June, 1806. **1884** HARRIS *Mingo* 238 They could remain at home, so to speak, and attend the militia musters.

*** Milk,** *n.*

I. Phrases.

1. *In (the) milk,* of grain, in the stage immediately preceding maturity, when the kernels or seeds are soft and filled with a milky liquid. {*dial.*}
1772 HABERSHAM *Letters* 213 The Rice came up rather unequal, so that a good deal of those Fields were in Milk. **1838** *Mass. Agric. Survey 1st Rep.* 98 Late sown wheat is not likely to pass beyond that season before it gets into a condition to be injured, which is while it is in the milk. **1857** *Lawrence* (Kansas) *Republican* 23 July 4 While wheat, for instance, is in the milk, or while yet soft, there is very little woody fibre about it. **1904** PRINGLE *Rice Planter* 100 The water was brackish, and the rice was just in milk.

+b. Esp. of Indian corn.
1778 CARVER *Travels* 25 Their corn is in the milk, as they term it. **1804** ORDWAY in *Journals of Lewis & O.* 175 The Mandans . . . have a Sweet kind of corn which they Boil considerable of it when it is in the milk. **1834** *Visit to Texas* 134 The birds seized it in the milk and made great havoc. **1880** *Scribner's Mo.* Feb. 504/2 The bear . . . clambered to his feast of 'corn in the milk.' **1895** *Dept. Agric. Yrbk. 1894* 243 Green corn 'in the milk.'

+2. *The milk in the coconut,* the crux, secret, or crucial fact of a matter or situation. *colloq.*
1853 *Knickerb.* XLII. 50 The milk in the cocoa-nut was accounted for. **1870** *Congress. Globe* App. 15 June 500/2 This is the secret, this the 'milk in the cocoanut,' this the 'meat in the egg.' **1893** *Congress. Rec.* 28 Feb. 2299/1 Here is the milk in the cocoanut! A frank confession it is.

+3. *To bring* (a person) *to his milk,* to bring one to a proper realization of his duty, condition, etc. *colloq.*
1857 HOLLAND *Bay-Path* 209 There ain't anything that'll bring you to your milk half so quick as a good double-and-twisted thrashin.

II. *attrib.* and *comb.* **4.** Designating foods made of or with milk.
See also MILK SHAKE, MILK TOAST.
1629 SMITH *Travels* (1910) 886 [The Virginians'] servants commonly feed upon Milke Homini, which is bruized Indian corne pounded, and boiled thicke. **1732** *S.C. Gazette* 3 June, Milk Bisket, 2l. 10s. per Barr[el]. **1778** *Mass. H. S. Coll.* 2 Ser. II. 447, [I] drank milk Punch with Capt. Parker. **1805** *Pocumtuc Housewife* (1906) 6 Pork and apple with a milk gravy, with Irish potatoes boiled, are always handy. **1832** CHILD *Frugal Housewife* 32 Milk porridge. . . . Some people like it thicker than others. **1883** *Wheelman* I. 305 Milk tea . . . diluted with water or soda-water . . . is at once refreshing and sustaining.

5. Designating containers and storage places for milk.
See also MILK BUCKET, HOUSE, etc.
1651 *Mayflower Descendants* X. 161, 2 milk keelers & 2 other keelers. **1835** HOFFMAN *Winter in West* I. 34 A buxom country girl or two could be seen . . . bearing the milkpail to meet the cows which were coming in. **1850** E. P. BURKE *Reminisc. Georgia* 112 Even the milk-safe stood out under one great tree. **1894** ALLEN *Ky. Cardinal* xvi, I crossed the lot, near the milk-trough. **1896** Milk can [see GROWLER 2]. **1907** LONDON *Road* 70 He took the small milk-tin and climbed down the bank, while we sat above and guyed him.

6. Designating persons who deal in milk.
See also MILKMAN.
1858 FLINT *Milch Cows* 122 By feeding these substances, the milk-dairyman studies his own interest. **1870** *Rep. Comm. Agric. 1869* 449 The annual meeting of the Milk Producers' Association of Massachusetts and New Hampshire . . . was held in Boston. **1877** DOUAI *Better Times* (1884) 7 Milk-farmers in the neighborhood of New York and Philadelphia. **1879** STOCKTON *Rudder Grange* 56 She had spent the night in a wooden rocking-chair at the milk-woman's.

*** Milk,** *v.*

+1. *tr.* To tap (a pine tree) for turpentine. *Obs.*
Cf. BLEED *v.* 2.
1746 *Mass. Acts & Resolves* III. (1878) 307 Any liberty obtained . . . for cutting off any timber, wood, hay, milking pine-trees, . . . shall not be any bar. **1789** *Mass. Laws* I. 442 No liberty . . . for cutting off any wood, timber or hay, milking pine-trees [etc.].

+2. To manipulate (stocks, markets, etc.) in such a way as to obtain unfair and exorbitant financial gains. *colloq.*
1870 M. H. SMITH *20 Years Wall St.* 69 Stocks are rushed up and down rapidly. In the excitement the combination reap a golden harvest. They have milked the street. **1883** *Harper's Mag.* May 820/2 What fabulous sums besides . . . the individual managers made by the ingenious process of 'milking the market.'

Milk-and-cider. *attrib.* ? Golden brown and white. — **1832** *Cattle Sent to Range* (MS. in J. D. Davidson Coll., McCormick Hist. Assn.) 1 A Milk & cider steer 3 years old.

+Milk-and-molasses. *attrib.* Of a color between white and dark brown. *colloq.* Also fig. — **1833** NEAL *Down-Easters* I. 96 The people of this country, . . . are of two colors, black and white . . . or half-and-half sometimes at the south, where they are called milk-and-molasses. **1868** *N.Y. Herald* 2 July 5/1 Then it will be of a purer color than the platform of the radicals, which is of milk and molasses hue.

***Milk-and-water.** *attrib.* passing into *adj.* Weak, ineffective, wishy-washy. {1823–}

Thornton suggests this may be an Americanism. The *O.E.D.*, however, has a quotation for *milk-and-waterish* in 1807 and one for the substantive in 1819, both in figurative senses.

1783 *Jrnls. Cont. Congress* XXIV. 297 Change the milk-and-water style of your last memorial; assume a bolder tone. **1803** *Ann. 7th Congress* 2 Sess. 239 These milk-and-water propositions of Mr. Breckenridge will at least serve to show that something should be done. **1854** COOKE *Va. Comedians* I. 179 'A mere milk-and-water family visitor,' says Parson Tag. **1866** GREGG *Life in Army* 262 Our government . . . leaned toward mercy, compromise, and milk-and-water policy. **1907** ANDREWS *Recoll.* 206 It was the milk and water policy of the government that encouraged the southern people to act as they did.

Milk bucket. A bucket for milk, esp. one suitable for use in milking. {1830–} — **1806** *Austin P.* I. (1924) 102, 2/12 doz. Milk bucketts, wood handles, [at] $9, 1.50. **1874** EGGLESTON *Circuit Rider* 217 She persuaded her father to buy half-a-dozen tin cups and some milk-buckets.

+Milk emptins. Also **milk emptyings.** Milk, often sour, used in bread-making. Also attrib. — **1842** KIRKLAND *Forest Life* I. 23 A tumble-down loghouse, with its appropriate perfumes of milk-emptins, bread, and fried onions. **1857** YOUMANS *Household Science* 261 Milk is often used for mixing the flour, instead of water; the product is then called 'milk-emptyings bread.' **1880** *Scribner's Mo.* Jan. 426/1 The whole feminine conclave launched out into a . . . discussion of the relative merits of salt-risin's, milk-emptin's, and potato yeast.

***Milker.** A cow that gives milk. {1807–} — **1850** *Rep. Comm. Patents 1849: Agric.* 294 She was ruined as a milker, and was then fattened and killed. **1856** *Porter's Spirit of Times* 20 Dec. 262/2 It is often the case that excellent milkers are found among them [*i.e.*, Durhams, Devons, &c.]. **1901** *Vt. Dairymen's Assoc. Rep.* 66 A file of a dozen milkers marched down one of the long alleys [in a dairy].

Milk fever. {1758–} A fever which well-fed cows that are heavy milkers are subject to for a few days after calving. — **1858** FLINT *Milch Cows* 271 The diseases most to be dreaded are garget, puerperal or milk fever [etc.]. **1870** *Rep. Comm. Agric. 1869* 39 *Milk fever* has caused some loss in Livingston, Michigan, and in Lorain, Ohio. **1888** *Vt. Agric. Rep.* X. 40 [He] would give a dose of salts two or three days previous to calving . . . to avoid milk fever. **1925** SNAPP *Beef Cattle* 432 Milk fever is a disease confined largely to mature dairy cows that are particularly heavy milkers.

***Milk house.** A house in which milk and milk products are kept.

1666 *East-Hampton Rec.* I. 248 Eight boards over the Milke house. **1707** *S.C. Hist. & Gen. Mag.* XII. 6 One dwelling house, one kitchen, one barn and one dairy and milk-house. **1825** NEAL *Bro. Jonathan* I. 368 Up I gut; and off I went. . . . Off, into the milk-house, on all-fours. **1883** *Wheelman* I. 245 A milk-house, with running-water troughs to convey the refuse milk to the piggery. **1920** *3d Nat. Country Life Conf. Proc.* 155 Milk houses are isolated and located with special reference to the good of the products involved.

***Milking.** *attrib.* Of or pertaining to milking.

1638 *Md. Archives* IV. 48, 1. milking paile. **1850** *New Eng. Farmer* II. 282 Gutta percha patent milking machines are in use on Long Island. **1868** *Mich. Agric. Rep.* VII. 233 The cause of great impurities in milk, is the bad construction of milking stables. **1876** *Wide Awake* 364/2, I heard him laugh like anything down in the milking-yard. **1913** MORLEY *Carolina Mts.* 172 In some places the people still go to the 'milking gap' to milk the cows.

Milk jug. A pitcher or jug for milk. (Cf. CREAM PITCHER.) — [**1852** BRISTED *5 Years in Eng. Univ.* 60 Drowning mice in his milk jug.] **a1861** WINTHROP *Open Air* 116 There was a sugar-bowl, a milk-jug, and other paraphernalia of civilization. **1881** *Harper's Mag.* April 648/2 We were glad of the tea . . . served in a brilliant silver urn . . . with sugar bowl and milk jug to match.

***Milkman.** One who sells milk; a dairyman. — **1812** *Freemasons Mag.* (Phila.) March 459 A milk-man . . . gives me a limited credit for a pint a day. **1838** *Mass. Agric. Survey 1st Rep.* 39 Other milk men speak of trials with the common blood-beet for the feed of milch cows with great advantage. **1890** HOWELLS *Boy's Town* 242 The milkman . . . said that the people around where he lived were dying off like flies. **1920** — *Vacation of Kelwyns* 32 Kelwyn thought how promptly they had once dismissed their milkman at home for cowy milk.

***Milk pan.** A shallow pan in which milk is kept to allow the cream to rise.

1658 *Southold Rec.* I. 440 In the dyrie milk panns, churne, butter tubb. **1770** *Md. Hist. Mag.* XIII. 68, 6 Dzns. of milk pans. **1842** *Knickerb.* XX. 350 The glistening milk-pans . . . encourage him . . . to ask for a more nutritious draught. **1891** CHASE & CLOW *Industry* II. 102 The milk has therefore to be strained through sieves into the milk-pan, set away for the cream to rise. **1907** ANDREWS *Recoll.* 166 Our wash-basin was a common tin milk-pan.

+Milk pea. A plant of the genus *Galactia.* — **1843** TORREY *Flora N.Y.* I. 162 *Galactia.* . . . Milk Pea. . . . Flowers purplish. **1898** CREEVEY *Flowers of Field* 318 Milk-pea. *Galactia glabella.* . . . From southern New York to Florida, and westward to Mississippi.

Milk pitcher. A pitcher for milk, especially one from which milk is served at table. — **1855** *Harvard Mag.* I. 420 We were . . . a good deal incommoded by the diminutive size of the milk-pitchers. **1869** ALCOTT *Little Women* II. 356 Taking Teddy's little fist out of the milk-pitcher. **1894** *Harper's Mag.* Oct. 721/1 Mandy Calline, with the milk-pitcher in her hand, hurried out to the cow-pen. **1920** HOWELLS *Vacation of Kelwyns* 31 She let herself into the kitchen, with the milk-pitcher in one hand, the teapot in the other.

Milk plant. +Any one of various plants of the milkweed family; also, a plant of the genus *Galactia.* — **1836** LINCOLN *Botany* App. 99 *Galactia . . . mollis.* . . . Milk plant. Pine barrens. **1843** FRÉMONT *Explor. Rocky Mts.* 16 Along the river bottom, *tradescantia* (*virginica*) and milk plant (*asclepias syriaca,*) in considerable quantities.

***Milk pot.** A small metal or earthenware vessel, usually rounded in form, for holding milk. — **1754** *S.C. Gazette* 1 Jan. 2/1 Just imported . . . , milk pots, punch ladles [etc.]. **1780** *N.J. Archives* 2 Ser. IV. 168 Was stolen out of the subscriber's shop . . . a silver milk pot. **a1825** *Memorandum for E. Pettigrew* (Univ. N.C. MS.), Sugar dish & milkpot.

+Milk purslane. The spotted spurge (*Chamaesyce maculata*), a prostrate milky-juiced weed found in the eastern states. — **1843** TORREY *Flora N.Y.* II. 176 Milk Purselane. Small Spurge. . . . Fields, cultivated grounds and roadsides, usually in dry soils. **1847** DARLINGTON *Weeds & Plants* 288 *E*[*uphorbia*] *maculata.* . . . Spotted Euphorbia. Milk Purslane. Spotted Spurge.

+Milk ranch. *W.* A dairy farm. — **1871** DE VERE 129 A Milk-ranch has of late become the familiar Californian term for a dairy. **1899** *Mo. So. Dakotan* I. 194 [A man from Mo.] brought in a herd of cows and established a milk ranch on Slate creek.

Milk room. A room in which milk is kept. — **1836** *Knickerb.* VIII. 706 In the rear, is quite a city of additions, in the shape of bed-rooms, bath-rooms, milk-rooms, buttery [etc.]. **1856** *Porter's Spirit of Times* 20 Dec. 262/1 The breeds of his cattle and the temperature of his milk-room are . . . but slightly influential. **1871** STOWE *Sam Lawson* 157 He was laid out in the back chamber, you see, over the milk-room and kitchen. **1891** CHASE & CLOW *Industry* II. 103 The cream is generally stored in jars away from the milk-room.

+Milk route. A route along which milk is collected from producers or delivered to customers. {milk round} — **1874** *Dept. Agric. Rep. 1873* 246 The most economical method of managing the delivery of milk at the factory is by establishing milk routes. **1897** 'MARK TWAIN' *Following Equator* 464 The vested rights . . . are frequently the subject of sale or mortgage. Just like a milk-route. **1903** FREEMAN in *Harper's Mag.* Dec. 28, I'd keep cows and start a milk route.

+Milk shake. A drink made of milk, cream or ice cream, and flavoring, shaken or whipped to a frothy consistency; also, the container in which this is mixed. — **1889** 'THANET' in *Harper's Bazar* 4 May 330/3 You needs some milk shake, dat's wat you does; an' I got some nice new w'iskey to putt in. **1892** *York County Hist. Rev.* 112 During the summer a fine soda fountain is in operation and flavored drinks, milk shakes, lemonade, etc., are made to order. **1896** E. HIGGINSON *Land of Snow Pearls* 244 There, you forgot to dust that milk-shake. An' you ain't touched that shelf o' patent medicines. **1911** HARRISON *Queed* 85 You ain't feelin' good, are you, Doc? You're lookin' white as a milk-shake.

+Milk sick. =next. Also attrib. — **1819** E. DANA *Geogr. Sk.* 143 A peculiar disease among the cattle prevails here, which the people call *milk sick,* that produces in beasts strange tremulous motions, and so strongly affects them, as often to prove mortal. **1846** MCKENNEY *Memoirs* I. 141 The people . . . about these parts, were afraid of the *milk-sick;* and never used milk after early spring. **1885** 'CRADDOCK' *Prophet* 47 Baker Leal . . . let down the bars of the milk-sick pen, one day las' fall, an' druv' Jacob White's red cow in. **1889** RILEY *Pipes o' Pan* 113 They was a-havin' sich a time with the milk-sick.

+Milk sickness. A disease affecting live stock, especially cattle, that eat of certain plants, and transmitted to persons who consume the flesh or dairy products.

1823 JAMES *Exped.* I. 76 Along the Missouri R. they have a disease called the *milk sickness:* it commences with nausea and dizziness. **1835** A. PARKER *Trip to Texas* 257 The inhabitants [of Ill.] have been afflicted with a disease called *milk sickness.* **1841** *Niles' Nat. Reg.* 10 July 304/2 'Milk sickness' may be prevented by salting the cattle freely. **1874** COLLINS *Kentucky* I. 35 Legislature offers $500 reward for the discovery of the cause of . . . milk sickness. **1877** *Field & Forest* III. 41 *Eupatorium ageratoides,* by some supposed to be the cause of 'milk sickness.'

transf. **1842** *S. Lit. Messenger* VIII. 200/1 Writers . . . have inoculated a numerous population with . . . a sort of epidemic 'milk sickness,' or rather milk-and-water disease.

+Milk snake. A handsome, harmless snake (*Lampropeltis triangulum*) often found about milk houses. — **1807** *Mass. H. S. Coll.* 2 Ser. III. 54 The only snakes found on the island are the black snake . . . [and] the milk or house snake, speckled like a rattlesnake; all harmless. **1842** *Nat. Hist. N.Y., Zoology* III. 39 *Coluber eximius.* . . . Chicken Snake. . . . In this State, its most usual popular name is Milk Snake. **1857** *Rep. Comm. Patents 1856: Agric.* 88 [Meadow-mice] are also found in the stomachs of the milk-snake. **1885** HOLDER *Marvels Animal Life* 120 Many farmers . . . believe that the milk-snake . . . deprives cows . . . of their supply of milk.

Milk strainer. A strainer for milk. — **1686** SEWALL *Letter-Book* I. 33 Sent twenty duz. of cours Hair sive bottoms, . . . Five Duz. of milk strainers of the smaller sort. **1872** *Florida Plant. Rec.* 199 The milk strainer is also in bad repair.

+Milk toast. Toast that has been soaked or softened in hot milk. Also fig. — **1857** *Knickerb.* XLIX. 98 Coffee and milk-toast, waffles and honey, disappeared . . . like magic. **1864** NICHOLS *Amer. Life* I. 117 The long narrow table . . . is covered with Yankee luxuries—hot Indian-corn bread, milk-toast, hot rolls [etc.]. **1882** HOWELLS *Modern Instance* xxiv, 'I am sick of spice; and I believe that most of our readers are.' 'Cater to them with milk-toast, then.' **1903** WIGGIN *Rebecca* 258 She's just asked me for some milk-toast.

+**Milk train.** A train transporting milk to the market. — **1853** *Knickerb.* XLII. 532 The '*milk-train*' still had the right of way. **1862** *Rep. Comm. Patents 1861: Agric.* 216 The milk train reaches New York about 4 o'clock. **1873** BEADLE *Undevel. West* 795 They might have to teach the Texas Central Railroad Company how to run a milk-train fifty miles. **1910** TOMPKINS *Mothers & Fathers* 136 There is a sort of milk train we can get in half an hour.

Milk tray. ?A shallow pan or vessel in which milk is placed for the cream to rise. *Obs.* — **1651** *Mayflower Descendants* X. 39, I give her . . . halfe a Dozen of milke trayes. **1655** *Essex Probate Rec.* I. 206 Ten milk trayes & 3 cheesfats. **1684** *Hempstead Town Rec.* I. 432 Three house pailes, eight milktrayes.

***Milk vetch.** Any plant of the genus *Astragalus*, of the pea family, or related genera. — **1833** EATON *Botany* (ed. 6) 44 *Astragalus canadensis*, woody milk vetch. On the islands near Troy. **1857** GRAY *Botany* 97 *Astragalus*. Milk-Vetch. **1909** *Cent. Suppl.* 809/3 *Milk-vetch*, . . . a plant of any one of the three genera *Phaca*, *Orophaca*, and *Homalobus*, closely related to *Astragalus* and formerly included in that genus.

Milk wagon. A wagon in which milk is conveyed. — **1883** *Wheelman* April 28/1 A superannuated 'bus-driver, with a conveyance strongly resembling a milk-wagon, offered to take me to 'any part of the city' for ten cents. **1887** *Courier-Journal* 25 Jan. 6/2 The horses attached to the milk wagon . . . ran away. **1913** LONDON *Valley of Moon* 64 He couldn't rough-house a milk wagon.

Milkweed. {1706–} +Any one of various American plants, esp. of the genus *Asclepias*, having abundant latex.

1814 BIGELOW *Florula Bostoniensis* 62 *Asclepias Syriaca*, Common Silk weed or Milk weed, . . . is used as a substitute for feathers, fur, cotton, &c. **1843** TORREY *Flora N.Y.* II. 119 Milkweed. . . . The dried leaves are employed in preparing the indigo dye in woollen manufactories. **1899** GOING *Flowers* 309 The common milkweed also imprisons insects which sometimes die in captivity. **1904** STRATTON-PORTER *Freckles* 283 Milkweed, golden-rod, . . . and turtle-head stood on the very edge of the creek. **1923** CATHER *Lost Lady* 17 The silvery milkweed was just coming on.

attrib. **1869** STOWE *Oldtown Folks* 121 That's milkweed silk. . . . 'Tain't good for nothin'. **1871** — *Sam Lawson* 43 Wal, that was the reason why Jeff Sullivan couldn't come it round Ruth tho' he was silkier than a milkweed-pod.

+**Milkweed butterfly.** The monarch butterfly. — **1880** *Boston Soc. Nat. Hist. Mem.* 10 In the milk-weed butterfly the colon is somewhat pyriform in the female, . . . but is longer and more cylindrical in the male.

+**Milkweed moth.** A gray moth (*Euchaetes egle*), the larva of which feeds on milkweeds. — **1854** EMMONS *Agric. N.Y.* V. 262 Milkweed-moths, 227.

***Milkwort.** Any plant or species of the genus *Polygala*. Also with modifying term. — **1784** *Amer. Acad. Mem.* I. 470 Milkwort. This plant is generally called Low Centaury, and has, probably, been mistaken for a species of the Gentiana. **1847** DARLINGTON *Weeds & Plants* 92 Seneka Snake-root. Milkwort. Mountain Flax. . . . The root of this species is . . . valuable for its medicinal properties. **1898** CREEVEY *Flowers of Field* 418 Whorled Milkwort . . . may be known by its long, narrow leaves, whorled on the stem, scattered on the branches.

***Milky,** *a.* Of plants: Yielding a milklike juice. {1861–} — **1765** WASHINGTON *Diaries* I. 210 Note, the [mulberry] Stocks were very Milkey. **1768** *Ib.* 282 Some [wheat] whose straw and head was green but the grain of full size and Milky. **1789** MORSE *Amer. Geog.* 52 About the time that it [wild rice] begins to turn from its milky state and to ripen, they run their canoes into the midst of it.

* **Mill,** *n.*[1] Also †**milne.**

I. * **1.** A machine or apparatus for grinding grain into meal or flour; also, a building equipped with such apparatus.

1637 *Plymouth Laws* 56 Mr. John Jenney shall have liberty to erect a Milne for grinding and beating of Corne. **1751** ELIOT *Field-Husb.* iii. 55 Our Mills might have Imployment by making Rape Seed Oyl for our own Supply, as also for the West-Indies. **1813** *Niles' Reg.* V. Add. A. 9/1 This affirmant . . . built a mill . . . wherein he put a Hopper machine. **1880** *Harper's Mag.* July 176/1 Farther on they came to a mill, where a woman was the miller.

2. =SAWMILL. {1854–}

1634 *N.H. Doc. & Rec.* I. 92 A stock of iron worke to put away wth your boardes from the mill will be good. **1649** *Suffolk Deeds* I. 109 All work that hath beene done . . . towards the erecting the sd. mill. **1800** *Raleigh* (N.C.) *Register* 22 April, The Lumber can be boated, from the Mills to Georgetown. **1835** HOFFMAN *Winter in West* I. 63 The teeth of the saws in the mills adjacent were continually broken. **1888** DELAND *J. Ward* 145 The mills had no work to do, for the logs on hand . . . had been sawed into long, rough planks. **1902** WHITE *Blazed Trail* 257 He had built and equipped a modern high-efficiency mill.

3. A factory in which cotton or woolen goods are made. {1835–} (Cf. COTTON MILL.)

1823 I. HOLMES *Account* 196 These factories (or, as they are called by the Americans, mills). **1844** *Lowell Offering* IV. 237, I wish they would have a vacation in 'dog days'—stop the mills and make all the girls rest. **1860** EMERSON *Conduct of Life* 70 Success has no more eccentricity than the gingham and muslin we weave in our mills. **1873** PHELPS *Trotty's Wedding* xix, The factory-girls . . . strolled by in the evening after mills were out.

+**4.** =CANE MILL.

1833 SILLIMAN *Man. Sugar Cane* 31 When the mill is turned by cattle, the axis of the middle roller . . . has long levers fixed across it. **1835** INGRAHAM *South-West* 239 The cane . . . is placed upon a cane-carrier, so called, which conveys it to the mill. **1863** *Rep. Comm. Agric. 1862* 60 The cane produced on less than ten acres of ground is usually ground in a wooden mill.

5. An establishment or machine for working iron or steel.

1861 *Atlantic Mo.* April 431/2 The old man, like many of the puddlers and feeders of the mills, was Welsh. **1894** *Harper's Mag.* Feb. 423/2 The combination machine called the 'universal mill,' consisting of one horizontal and one vertical pair just behind it, which at the same time compress the mass laterally and vertically.

6. *Mining.* **a.** A stamping mill.

1872 RAYMOND *4th Rep. Mines* 245 Preparations were being made to transport to the mine a four-stamp mill. **1876** — *8th Rep. Mines* 329 The mill has two batteries of five stamps each.

+**b.** An excavation or passage.

1879 HARTE *Drift from Two Shores* 75 No work was done in the ditches, in the flumes, nor in the mills. **1890** *Cent.* 3763/3 *Mill*, . . . in *mining*, a passage or opening left for sending down stuff from the stopes to the level beneath.

+**7.** *W.* A circling movement engaged in by a large herd of cattle deflected from a straight course.

1897 HOUGH *Story of Cowboy* 146 By shouts and blows he did all he could to break the 'mill' and get the cattle headed properly. **1903** A. ADAMS *Log of Cowboy* xviii. 286 By the time the herd had covered a scant mile, we had thrown them into a mill.

II. *attrib.* and *comb.*

8. Designating tools or devices used in mills.

1631 WINTHROP in R. C. Winthrop *Life J. Winthrop* II. 60 Millstones . . . and rings, and mill-bills. **1633** *N.H. Doc. & Rec.* I. 79 Mill pecks 3. **1866** *Rep. Indian Affairs* 181, 1 dozen 17-inch mill files.

9. Designating streams or springs that supply water for mills.

See also MILL CREEK.

1636 *Springfield Rec.* I. 159 The lotts . . . are ordered to lye adjoining to Mill Brooke. **1644** *New Haven Col. Rec.* I. 148 Debate about the turning of the Mill River. **1647** *Suffolk Deeds* I. 83 The south side wth. the mill streame, the west wth. the millne of Bost. **1700** *Md. Hist. Mag.* XIX. 348 A bounded popular stands by the mill spring runing south.

10. Designating roads, ways, etc., leading to mills.

1641 *New Haven Col. Rec.* 52 Their upland [is] on the right hand of the mill way. **1645** *Ib.* 160 The other side of his lott towards the mill highway. **1672** *Duxbury Rec.* 26 To the mill path for the north westwardly bounds. **1704** *Boston News-Letter* 21 Aug. 2/2 At Mr. Joseph Hiller's House near the Mill-bridge in Boston, There's good Fyall Wine to be Sold. **1888** *Century Mag.* Sept. 775/1 He'd 'ave come out onter the mill-road.

11. Designating places, areas, tracts, etc., situated at or near mills.

See also MILL PRIVILEGE, MILL YARD.

1649 *Essex Prob. Rec.* I. 110 The remainder . . . of which mill land . . . and hereditaments I giue amongst my children & to their heires. **1651** *Portsmouth Rec.* 417 One great lott . . . upon the South side of the head of the Mill Swamp. **1659** *Suffolk Deeds* III. 225 Another pcell. of land on the forementioned Mill Hill, being about three acres more or lesse, with all the fruite trees & fenceing there on. **1668** *Portsmouth Rec.* 140 Two Achres . . . leuinge out the place the mill now stands on and Conveniant way to ye said mill Comon. **1713** *Southold Rec.* II. 260 There is a way through the land of Joseph Conkelyne to the mill meadows; . . . for to cart hay or otherwise. **1775** in Rauck *Boonesborough* 172 [We] camped on Otter Creek—a good mill place. **1797** *Mass. H. S. Coll.* V. 253 Charles-River furnishing several excellent mill-spots, . . . encircles a considerable part of the town.

12. Designating artificial channels or courses serving to conduct water to or away from mills.

Cf. 9 above.

1654 *Suffolk Deeds* II. 42 Henry Webb . . . doth Couenant . . . to majnetajne his said pt of the damme and all other repajrations & Charges about the mill sluces & fludgates. **1711** SEWALL *Diary* II. 319 The Rain . . . Stop'd up the Mill Canal. **1770** WASHINGTON *Diaries* I. 380 John Harvey went to Ditchg. on my Mill Race at 1/3 pr. Rod. **c1849** PAIGE *Dow's Sermons* I. 167 Minutes go past me like little killi-fish through a mill-flume.

13. Designating rooms, offices, etc., situated in or forming parts of mills.

1786 WASHINGTON *Diaries* III. 35, I was obliged to send part of it [corn] to be spread in my Mill loft. **1833** SILLIMAN *Man. Sugar Cane* 45 The length of the mill-room A is 64 feet. **1897** BRODHEAD *Bound in Shallows* 217 Dillon turned back to the mill office.

14. Designating cities, villages, or centers of population characterized by the presence of mills.

See also MILL TOWN.

1863 A. D. WHITNEY *F. Gartney* xxiii, It needs just such a man [as minister] among mill-villages like these. **1883** *Century Mag.* Sept. 694/2 Newark is . . . quite the antipodes of Paterson or any other mill city. **1911** PERSONS, etc. *Mass. Labor Laws* 57 The important mill centers in the northern part of the state . . . were not reached by the foreign laborers before 1850.

15. Designating persons employed in or about a mill.

See also MILLBOY, GIRL, HAND.

1878 PINKERTON *Strikers* 300 The mill-men, factory hands, and other artisans seemed possessed of a most devilish propensity to injure the very interests which sustained them. **1888** *Amer. Almanac* 275 Occupations of the People of the United States. . . . Oil, mill and refinery operatives. **1890** WIGGIN *Timothy's Quest* 119 The mill-folks used to say [etc.]. **1894** FORD *P. Stirling* 4 What can you expect of a son of a mill-foreman, who lives the first sixteen years of his life in a mill-village? *Ib.* 45 He usually found the statement 'my father was a mill-overseer' a way to break down the barrier. **1896** *McClure's Mag.* VI. 490/1 We did not think about the mill-people. **1911** PERSONS, etc. *Mass. Labor Laws* 53 The disappearance of the [union] organization reason may be found in the changing character of the mill workers.

16. Special combinations.

Mill boom, a boom for impounding logs at a sawmill; *m. carriage,* in a sawmill, a carlike conveyor upon which logs are brought up to and past the saw; *m. feed,* corn, oats, etc., cracked or otherwise prepared as horse feed in a mill; *m. fever,* (see quot. 1911); *m. gold,* gold occurring in a form suitable for milling; *m. plant,* all the buildings, offices, yards, etc., making up a mill; *m. refuse,* odds and ends of planks, boards, etc., found about a sawmill; *m. stuff,* mill feed.

1838 ELLSWORTH *Valley of Wabash* 95 A small portion of meal of any kind, or some one of the mill stuffs. **1868** *Iowa Agric. Soc. Rep. 1867* 133 Handle the mule when sucking; wean in September; feed on mill-feed until February. **1876** RAYMOND *8th Rep. Mines* 316 The mill-gold of these veins is usually worth $15, coin, per ounce. **1878** *Mich. Reports* XXXVI. 165 The mortgagees were to deliver at the mill-boom fifty-five million feet of merchantable pine saw logs. **1881** *Harper's Mag.* Sept. 584/1 A three-pound eel . . . leads the captor a ten minutes' dance over logs . . . and mill carriages. **1886** STAPLETON *Ma'or's Christmas* 226 Before a feeble open fire of pine edgings and mill refuse, sat a little figure. **1911** PERSONS, etc. *Mass. Labor Laws* 147 During the first week in a dusty room at either a cordage or a twine factory, an employee is likely to have what is called 'mill fever,' . . . with loss of voice, slight fever and a general feeling of weakness. **1919** HOUGH *Sagebrusher* 250 Allied with this unit of the great dam was a lesser dam operating a mill plant on the other Fork.

+Mill, *n.*[2] [f. L. *millesimum* a thousandth part.] One thousandth of a dollar; one tenth of a cent.

1791 JEFFERSON in *Harper's Mag.* LXX. 535/1 It is 8 mills per dish. **1796** *Ann. 4th Congress* 2 Sess. 2781 There is due for wastage . . . eighteen hundred and forty-five dollars ninety-five cents and five mills. **1827** DRAKE & MANSFIELD *Cincinnati* 13 Half a mill on each dollar of the grand levy of taxable property throughout the state, is to be annually assessed. **1856** *Mich. Agric. Soc. Trans.* VII. 770 The Society have received . . . the amount of the 1-10 of a mill required to be raised. **1875** HOLLAND *Sevenoaks* 15 The town of Buxton . . . pays taxes, let us say, of seven mills on the dollar. **1911** *Okla. Session Laws* 3 Legisl. 201 The city council . . . may levy a tax not to exceed two mills on the dollar annually.

***Mill,** *v.*

1. *intr.* Of a herd of cattle: To move around in a circular course. {1895} Also *ppl. a.* and transf. (Cf. MILL *n.*[1] 7, MILLING 1.)

1888 ROOSEVELT in *Century Mag.* April 862/1 The cattle may begin to run, and then get 'milling'—that is, all crowd together into a mass like a ball, wherein they move round and round. **1910** RAINE *B. O'Connor* 227 I expect you were able to make out, even if I did get the letters to milling around wrong. **1919** CODY & COOPER *Buffalo Bill* 289 Here the buffalo thundered along in their milling herd, while Will and the assembled cowboys circled them. **1924** *Scribner's Mag.* Dec. 604/2 She sat on, watching the other miners' wives mill and chafe against the barriers.

+2. To put (stale or inferior butter) into marketable condition by working and coloring it.

1877 *Vt. Dairymen's Assoc. Rep.* VIII. 79 Most grades of cheap butter and much stale old butter is now 'milled' in all the large dairy markets.

+Millage. [MILL *n.*[2]] The rate of taxation in mills per dollar. — **1891** *Columbus Dispatch* 20 Feb., As great millage as [in] Toledo is not presented in the tables.

Millboy. 1. A boy who tends or works at a mill, or who customarily takes corn to mill for grinding. **+2.** *Millboy of the Slashes,* (see quotation.) — **(1) 1850** JUDD *R. Edney* xx, Melicent wondered that a mill-boy and hack-driver should be so well informed. **1861** *Atlantic Mo.* April 443/1 People going by to church saw only a sickly mill-boy watching them. **1880** BURNETT *Old Pioneer* 10 During this time the mill-boys mostly lived on parched corn. **(2) 1885** *Mag. Amer. Hist.* March 296/1 *Mill Boy of the Slashes.*—A nickname for Henry Clay, who in his youth tended a mill in a region known as 'the Slashes,' near his birthplace.

+Mill creek. A creek upon which a mill is situated. — **1651** *Boston Rec.* 4 Granted unto Capt. John Leveret . . . free liberty of egresse and regresse in and out of the Mill Creeke. **1672** *Ib.* 69 The drawe bridge ouer the mill creeke . . . hath been veiwed by Deacon Henery Allen . . . & returned to be insufficient & dangerous. **1722** *New-Eng. Courant* 3 Sept. 2/2 One Gilcreese . . . fell out of a Canoo in the Mill-Creek, and was drown'd. **1776** *Battle of Brooklyn* II. iii, The poor souls yonder . . . attempt to cross the mill creek.

***Mill dam.** A dam placed across a stream to secure a sufficient head of water to operate a mill.

1645 *Suffolk Deeds* I. 60 Bounded wth. John Smith West, the streete south: the lane & Thomas Werdall east & the mill damn. **1715** SEWALL *Diary* III. 64 About Noon a great Breach is made in the Mill-Dam of 60 or 70 foot wide. **1790** *Ky. Petitions* 147 [We] pray that the Navigation of said River may not be obstructed by Mill Dams or Fish Dams. **1833** COKE *Subaltern's Furlough* xiii, The mill dam across Charles's River Bay is one of the most interesting objects near Boston. **1871** *Rep. Ind. Affairs* (1872) 327 The fixed property of this reservation consists of agent's quarters, 3 dwellings, . . . mill-dam and flume [etc.]. **1905** RICE *Sandy* 179, I rode [the mare] . . . round the old mill-dam, 'cross the ford.

attrib. **1650** *Rowley Rec.* 69 For maintainance of Mill dame men.

Milled, *a.* {1622–}

1. Made of milled cloth or cloth thickened by fulling. {1642–}

1639 *Md. Archives* IV. 77 It[em,] a pr. of old milld stockings. **1710** BUCKINGHAM *Naval Exped.* 80 A pair of black milled stockings. **1825** *Columbian Centinel* 5 Jan. 2/6 Tuckerman & Cushing . . . offer . . . for sale . . . milled Frocks . . . Drillings, ribbed and plain. **1891** EARLE *Sabbath* 89 The goodmen with their heavy top-boots . . . their milled or frieze stockings, . . . were dressed with a sufficient degree of comfort.

+2. *Milled butter,* (see quotation and cf. MILL *v.* 2).

1877 *Vt. Dairymen's Ass. Rep.* VIII. 79 'Milled Butter.' . . . 'The term is applied in some of the Eastern and in the St. Louis markets to butter which has been re-worked and re-colored, and put into a more marketable condition.'

***Miller.**

***1.** One who owns or operates a mill for grinding grain.

1638 *Plymouth Laws* 61 The miller shall pay for every such default . . . for every bushell. **1725** *Boston Rec.* 197 A Bill . . . to prevent the abuse of Millers in Boston upon the Inhabitants in taking Toll. **1797** *N.Y. State Soc. Arts* I. 375, I was naturally led to converse at times with my millers . . . on the economy of water in grinding. **1817** PAULDING *Lett. from South* II. 4, I borrowed a fishing-rod from a miller near by. **1883** *Rep. Indian Affairs* 106 The miller and sawyer at the Omahas . . . are Indians.

2. Any one of various moths having wings covered with dust and thus suggestive of a miller's clothes. {1668–}

1783 CUTLER in *Life & Corr.* I. 94 Tarred apple-trees to keep the millers from going up. **1845** JUDD *Margaret* I. 87 You need'nt think we are as dull as millers that fly right into your links. **1890** *Cent.* 3765/2 Common millers in the United States are *Spilosoma virginica,* a moth whose larva is one of the woolly-bear caterpillars, and *Hyphantria cunea,* the web-worm moth. **1894** *Outing* XXIV. 220/2 [The bird] never went hungry, if countless beakfuls of choicest millers and earthworms could satisfy.

+Millering. The work or occupation of a miller. Also attrib. with *business.* — **1776** *N.J. Archives* 2 Ser. I. 119 Robert Colebrook . . . says he understands the millering business. **1798** WASHINGTON *Writings* XIV. 4 To carry on the millering and distillery business . . . [would] occupy the time and attention of any one person. **1818** COBBETT *Year's Residence* III. 582 Any of the men, however, could do the millering very well.

+Millerism. [Cf. next.] The doctrines of the Millerites. Now hist. — **1843** *Niles' Nat. Reg.* 240/3 Millerism. Father Miller lately visited Rochester, New York, and devoted one whole week to dealing out exhortations. **1854** SIMMS *Southward Ho* 394 This evil spirit . . . now rages rampant through the Northern States—allied with all sorts of fanatical passions and principles—Agrarianism, Communism, Fourierism, Wrightism, Millerism, Mormonism, etc., . . . you will neither make peace nor secure union. **1872** EGGLESTON *End of World* 238 If Millerism proved a delusion, the loss of Samuel Anderson's property would leave Julia on his level. **1886** POORE *Reminisc.* I. 309 Mr. Houghton thought that Millerism (a religious craze then prevalent) should be included in the benefits of the appropriation.

+Millerite. [Wm. *Miller,* 1782–1849.] A believer in the teachings of William Miller, who predicted that the second coming of Christ would occur in 1843. Now hist.

1842 *Niles' Nat. Reg.* 6 Aug. 368/2 The Millerites held a convention at Concord . . . to consider the fulfillment of prophecies. **1849** in Wellcome *Hist. 2d Advent Message* (1874) 580 Wm. Miller, distinguished as the founder of the sect known as '*Second Adventists,* or *Millerites,*' recently died at his residence in the State of New York. **1855** HOLBROOK *Among Mail Bags* 45 One suggested that I was a Millerite, and was endeavoring to 'go up' on horseback, at the same time expressing a desire to know what I would charge for an extra passenger. **1865** *Nation* I. 330 There have been conventions of . . . teetotallers and of anti-tobacconists, of Millerites. **1883** PECK *Bad Boy* 84 They had their night shirts on and looked just like the pictures of Millerites waiting for the world to come to an end. **1895** WIGGIN *Village Watch-Tower* 107 She had good Orthodox beaux, Free and Close Baptists, Millerites and Adventists. **1906** 'MARK TWAIN' *What Is Man?* (1917) 44 Why were the Congregationalists not Baptists . . . and the Episcopalians Millerites, and the Millerites Hindoos . . . and so on?

attrib. **a1846** *Quarter Race Ky.* 60 A Millerite Miracle. By C. A. P., of Kentucky. In the following sketch is displayed in bold relief the mummeries practised by Miller, Himes, and others. **1846** *Indiana Mag. Hist.* XXIII. 411 The Millerite mania had taken such fast hold of him, that he was bereft of reason.

*__Miller's-thumb.__ +Any American fresh-water fish of the genus *Cottus.* — [**1709** LAWSON *Carolina* 160 Barbouts and Millers-Thumbs, are the very same here, in all respects, as they are in England.] **1884** GOODE, etc. *Fisheries* I. 259 In the lakes and streams of the Northern States are numerous species of *Uranidea* and allied genera, known in some localities by the English name of 'Miller's Thumb.' **1890** *Cent.* 3765/3 Miller's-thumb, . . . any fresh-water sculpin of the genus *Uranidea;* one of the little star-gazers, of which there are several species, as *U. richardsoni.*

*__Millet.__ *Panicum miliaceum,* a grass used in the United States for forage, or a similar plant. — **a1637** in Hutchinson *Hist. Mass.* I. 483 Beans, millet, and fitches and roots, which delight in a cold soil, prosper here alike [*i.e.,* poorly]. **1737** BRICKELL *N. Carolina* 16 The Millet does very well here. **1832** WILLIAMSON *Maine* I. 127 Millet has been cultivated with success as an article of bread stuff. **1895** *Dept. Agric. Yrbk. 1894* 162 Such crops also as turnips, millet, and sorghum do very well from the August rains.

*__Millet grass.__ **1.** Any grass of the genus *Milium.* **2.** The broomcorn millet, *Panicum miliaceum.* — (1) **1817–8** EATON *Botany* (1822) 354 *Milium ciliatum,* millet grass. **1843** TORREY *Flora N.Y.* II. 422 Millet Grass. Mountain meadows, and borders of streams. (2) **1884** VASEY *Agric. Grasses* 35 *Panicum miliaceum,* (Millet grass,) . . . has been cultivated to a limited extent in this country for forage, and will thrive and ripen in the Northern as well as the Southern States.

Mill girl. A girl employed in a mill, +esp. in a cotton mill. — **1856** WHITTIER *Poetical Works* (1894) 49/1 O mill-girl watching late and long the shuttle's restless play! **1865** *Atlantic Mo.* XV. 617, I never could understand how such financial marvels could be accomplished on the wages of a mill-girl. **1897** *Boston Herald* 26 Sept. 25/4 The mill girl doesn't go about with the stick protruding from her mouth.

Mill hand. A worker in a mill. — **1861** *Atlantic Mo.* April 444/2 The man wandered [among] . . . lanes and alleys and back-yards, where the mill-hands lodged. **1879** HOWELLS *Lady of Aroostook* 124 At the Mill Village . . . they have dances sometimes,—the mill hands do. **1884** W. SHEPHERD *Prairie Exper.* 205 The mill-hands, who superintend the crushing, etc., of the ore, receive six dollars a day.

*__Millhouse.__ **a.** A house in which a mill, usually for grinding grain, is located. **b.** A dwelling house connected with a mill. — **1647** *Suffolk Deeds* I. 70 Edward Gibones . . . binding himselfe to make the mill house sufficient to the towne of Braintres satisfaction. **1718** *Smithtown Rec.* 40, I leave to my son Nathaniel . . . my mill house, mill, mill dam [etc.]. **1835** *S. Lit. Messenger* I. 260 The mill house . . . is six stories high from the foundation and covered with tin. **1899** CUSHMAN *Hist. Indians* 162 A millhouse 34 x 30ft, and also a lumberhouse and granary, each 18 x 20ft.

*__Milliner.__ A person, usually a woman, who makes, trims, or sells women's hats. — **1760** ROWE *Letters* 362 You may bring me from your young Milliner a fashionable round Cap. **1810** *Columbian Centinel* 3 Oct. 2/4 Mrs. Roberts, Dress-Maker, Milliner, Pelisse and Corset-Maker. **1893** *Harper's Mag.* April 668/2 The milliners' work made of Canton flannel and farmer's satin, is often as stylish as if it was seen on Broadway. **1911** HARRISON *Queed* 151 There is your public, the readers of the *Post*—shop-clerks, stenographers, . . . drummers, milliners.

||**Millinerize,** *v. intr.* To work as a milliner. Also *vbl. n.* — **1892** 'MARK TWAIN' *Amer. Claimant* xxi, She could n't design nor millinerize with any heart for thinking of him. Never before had millinerizing seemed so devoid of interest to her.

Milliner shop. A shop kept by a milliner. {milliner's shop, 1827–} — **1827** DRAKE & MANSFIELD *Cincinnati* 66, 40 Milliner-Shops. **1872** *Ill. Dept. Agric. Trans.* 173 There are several stores, a blacksmith shop and a milliner shop. **1878** STOWE *Poganuc People* 117 Look at her new Leghorn bonnet, just home from Miss Hinsdale's milliner-shop.

Millinery. Also †**millenary.** **1.** Women's hats; the articles sold by milliners; the shop or establishment of a milliner. {1679–} Also transf. **2.** Attrib. with *box, establishment, goods,* etc. — (1) **1676** *Conn. Col. Rec.* III. 500 Millinery; disbursements for combs, mittens, gloves, thread, silk. **1760** *Boston Gazette* 30 June 4/1 Millenary of all sorts . . . French Eau de Leuce. . . . Court Plaister. **1832** KENNEDY *Swallow Barn* I. 129 Some prim old maidish poplar . . . in this sylvan millinery, coquetted with the swaggering Zephyr. **1887** *Courier-Journal* 21 Jan. 6/4 Mrs. Jett started a confectionery at Lexington and afterward . . . she established millineries. (2) **1711** *Boston News-Letter* 22 Oct. 2/2 To be Sold . . . Pipes, Sadlery, Bunting, Millenary Goods [etc.]. **1865** *Atlantic Mo.* XV. 677 Some one advertised for two men to be employed in a millinery establishment. **1880** *Harper's Mag.* June 30/2 There are about five hundred millinery houses in the city. **1883** *Ib.* Oct. 706/2, I made it [a lizard] apartments out of a large millinery box. **1898** CAHAN *Imported Bridegroom* 228 The glare of the cafés and millinery shops.

+**Millinery store.** A store or shop kept by a milliner. — **1830** WATSON *Philadelphia* 218 Millinery Stores. It is still within the memory of the aged when and where the first store of this kind was introduced into the city. **1877** JOHNSON *Anderson Co., Kansas* 182 Mrs. A. Laferty opened a millinery store . . . in 1869. **1881** RITTENHOUSE *Maud* 33 After leaving that place and a millinery store I passed him again. **1898** WESTCOTT *D. Harum* 337 When I looked 'round, there was a mil'nery store in full blast an' winders full o' bunnits.

Millinet(t). Muslin of a coarse, stiff, thin sort. — **1831** CHILD *Girl's Own Book* (1833) 126 Baskets of Millinet and Straw. . . . Pieces of millinet should be cut [etc.]. **1837** *Knickerb.* IX. 293 The two first pages were devoted to memoranda of disposed-of millinett, dimity, ribbons, gros-de-naps, and so forth. **1861** *Ill. Agric. Soc. Trans.* V. 436 Boxes covered with something like millinet . . . will certainly prove effective in warding off [attacks of cucumber beetles].

***Milling.**

+**1.** The action of a herd of cattle or buffalo in going round and round in a circle. Also transf.

Cf. MILL *n.*[1] 7, MILL *v.* 1.

1874 McCOY *Cattle Trade* 101 Drovers consider that the cattle do themselves great injury by running round in a circle, which is termed in cowboy parlance, 'milling.' **1924** *Scribner's Mag.* Dec. 607 Jack . . . stood outside the door and watched the milling of the excited, hysterical women.

+**2.** Attrib. in sense: Pertaining to the process by which stale or inferior butter is re-worked and improved.

1877 *Vt. Dairymen's Ass. Rep.* VIII. 79 The advantage of the milling process over the old hand-working is that the various batches are so broken up and mixed as to make a homogeneous mass. *Ib.,* Two or three of these milling establishments . . . have made a large amount of money.

Milling ore. Ore suitable for milling. — **1871** RAYMOND *3d Rep. Mines* 314 There is commonly a seam of first-class ore, associated with a wider belt of milling ore. **1877** H. C. HODGE *Arizona* 71 The first class milling ore gives by assay an average of $96 per ton. *Ib.* 84 Both of the last named mines are good milling ores.

Millionaire. Also **millionnaire.** One who possesses a million dollars in money or property; a person of great wealth. {1826–} Also attrib.

[**1830** *Va. Lit. Museum* 630/2 At a grand dinner party he finds a baronet loaded with debt and infamy obtain the seat of honor above an honest and rich (*millionnaire*) manufacturer.] **1838** MAYO *Polit. Sk. Washington* (1839) 22 The devil take the millionaire. **1846** HONE *Dairy* II. 269 Remarks upon acoustics from elderly millionaires who do not hear quite as well as formerly. **1881** RITTENHOUSE *Maud* 3 How lovely to be the daughter of a millionaire. **1907** *Field Six-Cylinder Courtship* 80 Latest Escapade of Millionaire Snowden.

b. (See quotation.)

1837 *Newbern* (N.C.) *Sentinel* 14 June 1/1 The Millionaires. This is the new name given to merchants who deal in millions instead of hundreds of thousands.

Millionairess. A female millionaire. {1881–} — **1887** HOLMES in *Atlantic Mo.* LX. 222 Stuffs which none but an empress or a millionairess would dare to look at. **1895** *Advance* 8 Aug. 213/2 A few millionairesses in search of titled husbands. **1906** BELL *C. Lee* 38 You'll have to go on being a millionairess, whether you will or no.

+**Millionairism.** The state of being a millionaire; the social order prevailing where millionaires are numerous. — **1865** *Atlantic Mo.* Jan. 62/1, I fancied myself rich, even to millionnairism, in Cruikshankiana. **1891** *Harper's Mag.* Jan. 320/2 Our political turmoil, our demagogism, our millionairism. **1901** *Nation* 14 March 222/1 Divisions of the book take up . . . millionairism, the spirit of social equality [etc.].

Millionary, *a.* Possessed of or pertaining to millions of dollars. {1897–} — **1816** JEFFERSON *Writings* XV. 29 All this to feed the avidity of a few millionary merchants. **1854** BENTON *30 Years' View* I. 232/1 The halls of Congress have come to be considered the proper place to lay the foundations, or to repair the dilapidations of millionary fortunes.

+**Millionism.** The state of being a millionaire. — **1858** HOLMES *Autocrat* 357 People in the green stages of millionism. **1876** GLADDEN *Working People & Employers* (1885) 183 Some of the indispensable conditions of attaining to millionism.

+**Millish.** Short for MILITIA. *colloq.* — **1862** *N.Y. Herald* 9 April (Chipman), The city 'millish,' embracing some of our very best citizens, . . . have gone into camp at the Fair-Grounds.

+**Mill log.** A log suitable for sawing in a sawmill. — **1832** WILLIAMSON *Maine* II. 564 Another act was passed, to preserve for the owners, mill-logs, masts, spars, and other timber, accidentally found floating down the rivers. **1849** NASON *Journal* 99, I asked the guide if there were any mill-logs among it. **1850** JUDD *R. Edney* i. 17 Perhaps a mill-log would be as agreeable for him to kneel upon as a hassock.

+**Millo maize.** [Bantu *maili* and *maize.*] Any of certain varieties of *Sorghum vulgare.* — **1889** VASEY *Agric. Grasses* 37 *Sorghum vulgare.* This name as at present applied includes several varieties quite different in appearance, as the variety . . . millo maize, Kaffir corn, dourra, and broom corn. **1901** MOHR *Plant Life Ala.* 135 Various kinds of sorghum, known as durrha or kafir corn, millo maize, and pearl millet, . . . furnish green forage and hay crops.

Mill-owner. One who owns a mill. {1835–} — **1712** *Boston Rec.* 178 Ordered. That the Gentlemen who are the Mill Owners, be notified [etc.]. **1850** JUDD *R. Edney* xvi, Mill-owners and log-drivers were . . . interested. **1904** PRINGLE *Rice Planter* 113 Last year I lost my engineer, he having been absorbed by a neighboring mill-owner.

Mill pond. A body of water retained by a dam for use in driving a mill. {1697–}
1647 *Suffolk Deeds* I. 70 Land bounded betweene the high way to Braintre Common, the Mill pond & the Common. **1672** *Braintree Rec.* 12 The way that goes vnto the mill pond. **1702** *Providence Rec.* V. 31 Middway betweene the sd ffalls & the . . . mill Pond on sd River. **1773** *Mass. Col. Soc. Publ.* VI. 115 It was owing to . . . the constant Supply of the Engines with Water from the Mill-Pond, that many other Wooden Buildings [were spared]. **1832** KENNEDY *Swallow Barn* I. 239 The mill-pond . . . wasted away, like a chestnut fence-rail under the united attacks of sun and wind. **1880** *Harper's Mag.* Oct. 804/1 Henderson was . . . residing a short distance from the mill-pond. **1902** GORDON *Recoll. Lynchburg* 43 Stoppin' once in a while to mend the harness, or gabble with some of his brethren who were baptized in the mill-pond yesterday.
attrib. **1686** *Braintree Rec.* 24 The Selectmen . . . was impowered by the Towne to let out the mill pond swamp it being let out to Timothy Winter.

+**b.** The Atlantic Ocean. *humorous.*
1812 PAULDING *J. Bull & Bro. Jon.* 5 He put himself in a boat, and paddled over the mill-pond to some new lands. [**1885** G. ALLEN *Babylon* 79 How was our other friend Hiram Winthrop employing his time beyond the millpond?]

+**c.** (See quotation.)
1905 *Forestry Bureau Bul.* No. 61, 42 *Mill pond,* the pond near a sawmill in which logs to be sawn are held.

+**Mill privilege.** The right to operate a mill or to use adjoining land for storing lumber; a piece of land for such a purpose. (Cf. PRIVILEGE.) — **1734** *N.H. Probate Rec.* II. 508, I also give unto my son . . . the one half of my Mill Priviledge on the southerly side of ye River. **1749** *Ib.* III. 662 [We] sett off to ye widdow . . . the Sixth part of two acres of Land Laying Convenant for a mill priveledge. **1832** WILLIAMSON *Maine* I. 59 The river St. George . . . after running south twenty-five miles, and affording a variety of mill-privileges, meets the tide in Warren. **1892** *Vt. Agric. Rep.* XII. 134 Many mill privileges with excellent water power are afforded.

+**Mill right.** The right to set up or establish a mill. — **1794** *Mass. H. S. Coll.* III. 147 The principal object of the original settlers being lumber, more attention was paid to mill-rights than to the soil. *c***1845** PAULDING *Amer. Comedies* (1847) 262 There's a man at Jack O'Lantern's that owns land and mill-rights.

Mill run, *n.* {1877–} *Mining.* +A given quantity of ore tested for its quality by actual milling; the yield of such a test. — **1874** RAYMOND *6th Rep. Mines* 292 The mill runs have been as high as 3 oz. gold with from 30 to 60 oz. in silver. **1878** BEADLE *Western Wilds* 465 This estimate is from the mill-runs—the only honest test of a mine's capacity. **1882** in Ritch *Illus. N. Mex.* 138 A millrun two months since at Pueblo, of 2,200 pounds, returned 140 ounces silver and 50 per cent. lead.

+**Mill-run,** *a.* Average, not especially selected. — **1881** *Chicago Times* 1 June, The supply of choice mill-run lumber was generally quite limited.

+**Mill-run,** *v. Mining. tr.* To yield (a stated amount) in terms of a mill run. — **1884** *Century Mag.* Nov. 57 The vein where it came from would mill-run not less than a thousand ounces.

+**Mill saw.** A saw such as is used in a sawmill. {1897–} — **1790** *Penna. Packet* 2 Jan. 4/2 To be sold by Poultney and Wistar . . . Mill, crosscut, hand, pannel, tennant, . . . compass, and keyhole saw. **1832** *Louisville Pub. Advertiser* 3 March 4/1 John D. Thorpe . . . is now opening a general and extensive assortment of Hardware; . . . [including] mill, cross cut, bastard and hand saw ½ round and 3 square files. **1856** 'MARK TWAIN' *Adv. Snodgrass* 25 Everybody was a bobbin up and down like a mill saw. **1897** BRODHEAD *Bound in Shallows* 66 All the mill saws were silent.

+**Mill seat.** A site or location for a water mill. — **1770** WASHINGTON *Diaries* I. 365 Mr. Ballendine and myself leveled Doeg Run in ordr. to fix on a Mill Seat. **1795** *Columbian Centinel* 21 Jan. 3/3 Will be sold by Public Vendue . . . a very valuable Tract of Land . . . with a Mill-seat. **1805** SIBLEY in *Ann. 9th Congress* 2 Sess. 1097 The creek . . . affords a number of good mill seats. **1855** SIMMS *Forayers* 487 They were in possession of an old mill-seat, on the Caw-caw.

+**Mill site.** =prec. — **1831** PECK *Guide* 196 There are but few good mill sites in the State. **1871** RAYMOND *3d Rep. Mines* 18 These mountains abound in timber lands, and furnish water in sufficient quantities for excellent mill-sites. **1896** SHINN *Story of Mine* 81 Water claims and mill sites were taken up almost as soon as work had fairly begun on the Comstock.

+**Mills's money.** Wildcat notes issued by a Mississippi bank, given value in Texas before the Civil War by the indorsement of R. & D. C. Mills, a rich commercial house. — **1852** GOUGE *Fiscal Hist. Texas* 235 'Mills's Money,' as it was called, was regarded as being as good as gold and silver, or even better, inasmuch as it could more readily be carried from place to place.

***Millstone.** Also †**milston.** One of a pair of thick circular stones used in a mill for grinding grain.
1631 WINTHROP in R. C. Winthrop *Life J. Winthrop* II. 60 Millstones, some two foot and some three foot over. **1713** *Mass. H. S. Coll.* 6 Ser. V. 269 Get the milston don as soon as may be. **1847** *Rep. Comm. Patents 1846* 99 Attempts have been made to drive the mill-stone at very high speed. **1900** MUNN *Uncle Terry* 364 The mill-stone [would] rumble, the big wheel splash.

b. Stone suitable for this use. Also attrib. {1661–}
1781–2 JEFFERSON *Writings* II. 43 There is great abundance . . . of stone, . . . fit for the chisel, good mill-stone, such also as stands the fire, and slate stone. **1849** CHAMBERLAIN *Ind. Gazetteer* 274 A mill-stone quarry, near Scipio, has also at times been worked extensively.

Millstone grit. *Geol.* (See quot. 1890.) {1786–} — **1837** W. JENKINS *Ohio Gaz.* 236 Great quantities of mill-stone grit are found and manufactured in the northern and central parts of this county. **1849** CHAMBERLAIN *Ind. Gazetteer* 182 A true conglomerate of mill-stone grit, consisting almost entirely of quartz, gravel and coarse sand. **1890** *Cent.* 3767/3 *Millstone grit,* . . . a silicious conglomerate rock, so called because it has been worked for millstones in England. . . . The millstone grit is an important and persistent member of the Carboniferous series both in Europe and in the United States.

+**Mill tax.** [MILL *n.*[2]] A tax of one mill per dollar of assessed valuation. — **1848** *Indiana Hist. Soc. Publ.* III. 514 The former will pay on a mill tax $200. **1853** *Mich. Agric. Soc. Trans.* VII. 293 A mill tax is annually levied to purchase books for these libraries. **1903** *Scribner's Mag.* Oct. 486 They support the Universities by a direct mill tax levied upon the assessed valuation of the State.

+**Mill town.** A town the industrial life of which centers around a mill or mills. Also attrib. — **1848** D. P. THOMPSON *L. Amsden* 199 [The paper] came into town all damp from the press of Mill-Town Emporium. **1902** WHITE *Blazed Trail* 155 He arrived out of breath in a typical little mill town. **1911** PERSONS, etc. *Mass. Labor Laws* 187 These instances are all mill or factory towns, where the number of working children is proportionately very large.

***Millwright.** An expert workman who is experienced in designing and setting up mills; a workman who sets up belting and shafting, moves machinery, etc. Also attrib. — **1640** *Portsmouth Rec.* 19 Itt is ordered that Leiftenant Baulston [find] a mill wright to builde a Mill. **1736** *Va. State P.* I. 228, [I] expect a mil wright this day to go with me to King and Queen County to build a mill. **1802** *Ann. 7th Congress* 1 Sess. 1366 For the wages of persons employed at . . . carpenter, millwright, and smith's work. **1891** O'BEIRNE *Leaders Ind. Territory* 186/1 In two years Isham learned the millwright business. **1901** MERWIN & WEBSTER *Calumet 'K'* 96 Trouble with the laborers or the carpenters or the millwrights meant loss of time and loss of money.

+**Mill yard.** An open area adjacent to a sawmill, where lumber is piled or logs assembled. — **1824** *N.H. Hist. Soc. Coll.* I. 246 A saw mill torn down and twelve thousand of boards in the mill-yard carried away. **1841** BUCKINGHAM *America* III. 49 This 'millyard,' as it was also called, had passed from the original purchasers into the possession of Sir William Pulteney.

+**Milpa.** *S.W.* [Sp. fr. Nahuatl.] A small cultivated field, usually a cornfield. — **1844** GREGG *Commerce* I. 150 The *labores* and *milpas* (cultivated fields) are often . . . without any enclosure. **1869** BROWNE *Adv. Apache Country* 164 Our houses were closely picketed in the milpas, or corn-fields, down by the river.

+**Milwaukee.** *attrib.* [*Milwaukee,* Wis.] Of or pertaining to Milwaukee. Usually with particular reference to wheat. — **1856** *Porter's Spirit of Times* 1 Nov. 149/3 Wheat is in firm market demand; sales of 33,000 bush. at $1,49 for white Michigan; and $1,31 for Milwaukie Club. **1881** *Harper's Mag.* April 710/1 Milwaukee wheat has from the first been subjected to a most rigorous and honest inspection. *Ib.* 710/2 Feeding this artery to supply the Milwaukee elevators are the Northern Pacific . . . and various other railways. **1908** *U.S. Brewers' Assn. 48th Conv.* 147 If anything can excel the quality of Milwaukee beer, it is Milwaukee hospitality.

+**Mimeograph,** *n.* [Gr. *mimeisthai* 'to imitate' and *-graph.*] A trademark name for a device for duplicating written or printed matter by the use of a stencil; in popular use, any such device. {1903–} — **1889** *Voice* 19 Sept., The 'mimeograph' and the 'autocopyist' . . . will give any number of copies of a letter.

+**Mimeograph,** *v. tr.* To reproduce (copies of an original writing, drawing, etc.) on a mimeograph or similar device. {1903} — **1895** *Advance* 6 June 1290/2 The copies were mimeographed at last, thanks to her mother's help. **1922** LEWIS *Babbitt* 36 The fortnightly form-letter, to be mimeographed and sent out to a thousand 'prospects.'

Mimosa. A genus of leguminous plants, shrubs, etc., of the family Mimosaceae, found in warm regions; also, a plant or tree of this genus. {1751–} — **1834** *S. Lit. Messenger* I. 122 Patches were here and there overspread by mimosa. **1869** *Amer. Naturalist* III. 350 The delicately branched mimosas and the loftier of the palm forms are wanting [in Fla.]. **1897** SUDWORTH *Arborescent Flora* 250 *Leucæna pulverulenta.* . . . Chalky Leucæna. . . . Common Name. Mimosa.

Minced pie. =MINCE PIE. {1607–1762} — **1694** SEWALL *Diary* I. 394 Women din'd with Rost Beef and minc'd Pyes, good Cheese and Tarts. **1723** *Ib.* III. 323 They dined with us upon Fish and Oil and very good Minc'd Py in a Dish. **1884** WARNER in *Harper's Mag.* Dec. 4/2 The minced-pie, the plum-porridge.

Mincemeat. {1663–} A cooked mixture of chopped raisins, apples, etc., usually including meat, for making mince pies. {1845–} — **1828** LESLIE *Receipts* 14 Keep your mince-meat in a jar tightly covered. **1867** 'LACKLAND' *Homespun* I. 125 Delf trays, likewise, filled nearly full with mincemeat for the pies. **1891** 'THANET' *Otto the Knight* 65 The crock of mincemeat stood underneath. **1919** *Maine My State* 289 They filled half a dozen with mince-meat.

Mince pie. 1. A pie made with mincemeat. {1600–} **2.** Attrib. with *fast, season.* — (1) **1783** *Broadside Verse* (1930) 193/1 Chesecakes, cold hams, plumb-puddings, and mince-pies! **1841** *Lowell Offering* I. 228 Abigail came in with some hot mince pies. **1876** *Wide Awake* 280/2 Between mince-pie and fruit-cake I don't think there is much difference. **1923** WATTS *L. Nichols* 146 They wound up with mince-pie opulently garnished à la mode. (2) **1857** STROTHER *Virginia* 69 It happens sometimes during the mince-pie season that Fanny enters the kitchen. **1881** STODDARD *E. Hardery* 218 The general prosperity suggested liberal preparations for what the same worthy described as 'our mince-pie fast.'

*__Mincer.__ +*Whaling.* One who cuts whale blubber into pieces from which the oil may be extracted most advantageously. — **1849** CHEEVER *Whale & His Captors* 85 The mincer, with a two-handled knife, slashes it nearly through into thin slices, which just hang together. **1851** MELVILLE *Moby-Dick* 467 A mincer . . . now comes along, and assisted by two allies, heavily backs the grandissimus.

Mincing machine. (See quot. 1875.) {1885-} — **1850** *New Eng. Farmer* II. 379 Sausage or Mincing Machine. This is a small, compact machine, remarkably strong and durable. **1875** KNIGHT 1446/1 *Mincing-machine*, a machine for chopping food into small fragments. A sausage-machine.

Mind-reader. One who professes to be able to discover from observation or by occult means the thoughts in the mind of another. Also transf. — **1887** *Courier-Journal* 18 Jan. 1 A mind-reader and spirit medium gave an exhibition of his powers at the Grand Opera-house. **1888** *Pop. Science Mo.* Dec. 154 The professional 'mind-reader' . . . takes his clew from indications which his subject is absolutely confident he did not give. **1915** CAMPBELL *Proving Virginia* 176 'Alan, I believe you're a little bit homesick.' . . . 'Mindreader, I confess that I miss the Blacks.'

+**Mind your business.** [From an inscription on the coin.] =FUGIO. — **1857** *N.Y. State Library Cat. 1856* 197 Mind Your Business, 1787 Copper.

*__Mine.__ An excavation in the earth for obtaining coal, metals, or ore.

1637 MORTON *New Canaan* II. vi, Mines of Tinne are likewise knowne to be in those parts. **1708** *Suffield Doc. Hist.* 157 Every Mine, or Mines yt do . . . appear to be in any undivided Land, within ye Township of Suffield: is . . . conserved for ye whole Town's use forever. **1819** SCHOOLCRAFT *Mo. Lead Mines* 67 The numerous mines or diggings in Washington County, are chiefly situated in the vicinity of Potosi. **1910** J. HART *Vigilante Girl* 50 Saturday was cleaning-up day for the mines.

b. Attrib. with *inspector, road, tract.*

1819 SCHOOLCRAFT *Mo. Lead Mines* 49 New-Bourbon, Caledonia, and Madansburgh, are also towns of the mine tract, but they are at present small. **1849** *Knickerb.* XXXIV. 323 A smaller road, called a tram, or mine-road, brings down little wooden car-loads of coal from Frostburg. **1911** PERSONS, etc. *Mass. Labor Laws* 231 Twenty states have separate mine inspectors.

+**Mine bank. a.** An area of ore deposits that can be worked by excavations above the water level. **b.** The ground at the top of a mining shaft. (Cf. BANK *n.*[1] 2, COAL BANK.) — **1777** *N.J. Archives* 2 Ser. I. 389 The mine bank, situated at a mile's distance from the furnace, is thought to be inexhaustible. **1807** J. R. SHAW *Life* (1930) 81, I followed working at the mine-banks. **1905** VALENTINE *H. Sandwith* 28 The iron bell that announced the arrival of ore-laden wagons from the mine banks.

*__Miner.__ One who engages in mining.

1645 in Lewis & Newhall *Hist. Lynn, Mass.* (1890) 218 Miners, founders, finers, hammer-men and colliers . . . are absolutely freed and discharged of and from all ordinary trainings, watchings, etc. **1723** *Amer. Wkly. Mercury* 18-25 July 3/2 He pretends to be a Miner. **1835** HOFFMAN *Winter in West* I. 257 Half a dozen miners in leather shirts or belted coats of Kentucky jean were lounging about. **1917** SINCLAIR *King Coal* 50 Under the state law, the miner had a right to demand a check-weighman to protect his interest at the scales.

*__Mineral.__ *attrib.* In special combinations.

Mineral entry, the filing of a claim for public land to obtain the right to any minerals it may contain; *m. knob*, a door knob made of a mineral; *m. region*, a region possessing mineral wealth or importance; *m. teeth*, ? artificial teeth made of metal or of mineral substances.

1842 TYLER in *Pres. Mess. & P.* IV. 165 The region of country . . . between Pigeon River on the north and Fond du Lac and the river St. Louis on the south and west, considered valuable as a mineral region, is thus included. **1851** CIST *Cincinnati* 220 Mineral Teeth. One factory. **1853** FOWLER *Home for All* 113 White mineral-knobs on first story, and dark colored on second story. **1908** *Indian Laws & Tr.* III. 378 Nor shall any such lands be subject to mineral entry or location.

+**Mineral belt.** [BELT *n.* 2.] An extensive stretch or strip of country in which mineral resources are abundant. Also attrib. — **1869** BROWNE *Adv. Apache Country* 507 The wonderful richness of the mineral belt could be fairly appreciated. **1882** *47th Congress 1 Sess.* H. R. Ex. Doc. No. 216, 142 There are a number of locations on the same mineral belt as the Centennial, which will be worked. **1883** RITCH *Illus. N. Mex.* 68 The usual combination of quartz and feldspar . . . [is found] within the mineral belt range proper.

+**Mineral blossom.** (See BLOSSOM 1.)

+**Mineral land.** Land that possesses considerable mineral wealth. Also attrib.

1840 *Niles' Nat. Reg.* 18 April 107/1 [Petition] by Mr. Norvell, . . . asking to be allowed to work the mineral lands of the U. States on the southern shore of Lake Superior. *Ib.* 25 July 326/3 Mr. Linn . . . moved that the report of R. Dale Owen on the mineral lands of the United States be printed for the use of the senate. **1847** *Statutes at Large* IX. 147 Said mineral lands [in the Lake Superior district] shall be offered for sale in quarter-sections. **1883** RITCH *Illus. N. Mex.* 75 Not a foot of mineral land in this county is covered by a grant. **1905** N. DAVIS *Northerner* 100 Eastern capitalists had been quick to read the South's sad astrology in . . . her empty fields, her undeveloped mineral lands.

Mineralogist. One versed in the study of minerals. {1646-} — **1803** *Lit. Mag.* (Phila.) Oct. 13 Had I been . . . a mineralogist, and found an agate or a petrifaction [etc.]. **1857** STACEY in *Uncle Sam's Camels* 21 Last night he said to Williams, the mineralogist, that 'Stacey was his right hand man.' **1876** RAYMOND *8th Rep. Mines* 349 Hogle, a practical assayer and mineralogist.

Mineral rod. =DIVINING ROD. — **1809** KENDALL *Travels* III. 101 The mysteries of the mineral-rods are many. **1849** LANMAN *Alleghany Mts.* Addenda 187 Travelling about the country under the guidance of *mineral rods* or dreams, in search of mines. **1902** MCFAUL *Ike Glidden* 184 They've sent for Squire Blunt to come up here in the morning, with a mineral rod, to assist them.

+**Mineral sperm.** (See quot. 1875.) In full *mineral sperm oil.* — **1875** *Amer. Cycl.* XIII. 371/1 Mineral sperm is the name given by Joshua Merrill, of the Downer kerosene oil company, to a petroleum product discovered by him. This is an illuminating oil. **1883** *Century Mag.* July 338/2 Obtained from petroleum by the refining process . . . [is] mineral sperm oil, a heavier oil for burning in lamps . . . employed on steamers and railroads.

Mineral spring. A spring the waters of which are impregnated with minerals. {1797-} — **1783** *Amer. Acad. Mem.* II. I. 43, I mentioned some mineral springs in the vicinity of this place [Saratoga]. **1804** CLARK in *Lewis & C. Exped.* I. (1904) 140 Several Mineral Springs broke out the water of which had a taste like Salts. **1843** *Nat. Hist. N.Y., Geology* IV. 308 In this district the only mineral springs of interest are the salines, the sulphur springs [etc.]. **1884** MATTHEWS & BUNNER *In Partnership* 150 Mineral springs may be discovered anywhere in north New York, if you only try.

*__Mineral water. a.__ Water that is impregnated with mineral salts or gases. **b.** Soda water and other drinks made in imitation of natural mineral water. Also attrib. — **1722** *New-Eng. Courant* 6 Aug. 2/2 There has lately been discover'd near Bristol . . . a Spring of Mineral Water which has effected many wonderful Cures. **1811** BENTLEY *Diary* IV. 23 These wells promise more powerful mineral water than at Spring pond. **1865** KELLOGG *Rebel Prisons* 293 A saltish kind of mineral water . . . was said to have been obtained from an Artesian well. **1893** *Harper's Mag.* May 832/2 Between us and the entrance to the park are booths and beer shops, coffee stands and mineral-water stands. **1910** C. HARRIS *Eve's Husband* 239 From Aaron . . . I learned how much mineral water our guest consumed.

+**Miners' court.** *W.* An independent court of justice set up by miners remote from long-settled regions. — **1890** LANGFORD *Vigilante Days* (1912) 139 A motion was made that the accused be tried by a miners' court. This form of tribunal grew out of the necessities of mining life in the mountains. *Ib.* 142 A very large majority were in favor of a miners' court. *a***1918** G. STUART *On Frontier* I. 232 The miners of Bonnack met and established a miners' court.

+**Miner's inch.** *W.* (See quots. 1867 and 1881.) — [**1867** J. A. PHILLIPS *Mineral. & Metall. Gold & Silver* 152 *n.*, The miner's inch of water, in California, is the quantity which will flow through an opening one inch square under a mean head of six inches.] **1872** TICE *Over Plains* 176 Mr. Charles Dabney . . . described the spring as a stream of hot water of the capacity of twenty-five 'miner's inches.' **1880** INGHAM *Digging Gold* 217 French Creek, in Custer County, of three hundred miner's inches, rises on the western rim. **1881** RAYMOND *Mining Glossary, Miners' inch*, PAC. A local unit for the measurement of water supplied to hydraulic miners. It is the amount of water flowing under a certain head through one square inch of the total section of a certain opening, for a certain number of hours daily. . . . A miners' inch in use in Eldorado County, Cal., discharges 1.39 cubic feet per minute.

+**Mingo.**[1] [Algonquian *mingwe* stealthy, treacherous.] An Indian belonging to the Iroquois or a cognate tribe: (see quot. 1907); in pl., the tribe or tribes composed of these Indians. Now hist.

[**1656** VAN DER DONCK *Descr. New Netherlands* 206 With the Minquas we include the Senecas.] **1753** WASHINGTON *Diaries* I. 51, I intend to send a Guard of *Mingo's*. **1786** in *Mag. Amer. Hist.* I. 178 Some of the Mingos (a set of vagrants living on the headwaters of the Miami) had killed two or three of our traders. **1808** ASHE *Travels* 226 The party I fell in with was a family of the Mingoes. **1840** COOPER *Pathfinder* ii, If any Mingos have seen our path below the falls, they will strike off towards this smoke. **1907** HODGE, etc. *Amer. Indians* I. 867 *Mingo*, . . . a name applied in various forms by the Delawares and affiliated tribes to the Iroquois and cognate tribes, and more particularly used during the late colonial period by the Americans to designate a detached band of Iroquois who had left the villages of the main body before 1750 and formed new settlements in Pennsylvania, on the upper Ohio r., in the neighborhood of the Shawnee, Delawares, and neighboring tribes.

attrib. **1751** GIST *Journals* 49 You send for one of your Friends that can speak the Mohickon or the Mingoe Tongues well. **1752** W. TRENT *Journal* (1871) 85 We met a Mingoe man called Powell. **1834** DRAKE *Indian Biog.* v. 41 Logan was called a Mingo chief.

b. *Little Mingoes*, the Hurons.

1750 GIST *Journals* 37 The Wyendotts or little Mingoes are divided between the French and English.

c. (See quotation.) *Obs.*

1882 WEED *Autobiog.* 268 The 'Mingoes' (as we then [1828] called Masons) were on my trail.

+**Mingo.**[2] [L. *mingo* I make water.] A chamber pot or urinal. *Obs.* — **1775** *Essex Inst. Coll.* XIII. 187, 5 Mingos and a Bed pan. **1795** C. PRENTISS in *Fugitive Ess.* (1797) 90 To him that occupies my study, I give . . . Another, handy, called a *mingo*. **1851** HALL *College Words* 207 *Mingo*. Latin. At Harvard College, this word was formerly used to designate a chamber-pot.

+**Mingo.**[3] Also **Mingco.** =MICO. Now hist.

1801 HAWKINS *Letters* 390 We commenced our conference with a full and respectable deputation from the Chickasaw nation, headed by their mingco or king. **1805** *Ann. 10th Congress* 1 Sess. I. 645, I have had some talk with both the White and Red Mingoes. **1808** *Ib.* II. 2833 One hundred and fifty dollars to each of the said Mingoes during his continuance in office. **1844** GREGG *Commerce* II. 266 With the united nation of Choctaws and Chickasaws, the executive power is vested in four chiefs, called in Choctaw *mingoes*, who are selected one from each of the districts into which the country is divided. **1859** BARTLETT 273 *Mingo* (Creek Ind.), a native king among the Creeks, Choctaws, etc.

b. In appositive construction.

1801 HAWKINS *Letters* 387 Minutes of a conference held at the Chickasaw Bluffs by . . . Commissioners of the United States, with the mingco chiefs.

***Miniature.** A portrait painted on a small scale, usually on ivory or vellum. {1716–} Also attrib. — **1769** *Copley-Pelham Lett.* 77 The Miniature you took from my Crayon Picture has been very much admir'd. **1790** *Penna. Packet* 3 Feb. 3/3 Miniature Painting. Mr. P. Henri, Miniature Painter, from Paris, . . . will do himself the honor to wait on Ladies, at their request. **1810** *Columbian Centinel* 17 Jan. 3/3 Ladies and Gentlemen may have their Miniatures executed in a correct . . . style, from 25 to 50 Dollars. **1908** 'O. HENRY' *Options* 32 Old Mr. Schrum . . . told me of a rich man in Newark who wanted a miniature of his daughter painted.

Minié. Also **Minnie.** [Claude Etienne *Minié*, Fr. inventor (1814–79).]

1. A conical bullet of a type invented by Captain Minié. In full *Minié ball, bullet.* {1859–} Now hist.

1855 *Amer. Inst. N.Y. Trans.* 576 With the balle-a-tige, or minie ball, the angle of sight must be chosen precisely. **1864** in Cumming *Hospital Life* (1866) 162/2 The shells and minies came so thick and fast, I could not mount the pony. **1866** 'F. KIRKLAND' *Bk. Anecdotes* 495, I lately saw at the head-quarters of Colonel Slack's brigade, two Minie bullets. **1884** HOWELLS *S. Lapham* i. 26 The Colonel bears embedded in the muscle of his right leg . . . a minie-ball. **1902** HARBEN *A. Daniel* 279, I feel like givin' a war-whoop an' rammin' home a minié ball.

2. =next.

1867 EDWARDS *Shelby* 59 Sure enough, flint-lock rifles and family fowling-pieces have spoken as far in the battle's van, as the costliest Enfield or the better Minnie.

Minié rifle. [Cf. MINIÉ.] A rifle designed to use the Minié ball. *Obs.* {1853–} Also attrib. — **1857** *Lawrence* (Kansas) *Republican* 13 Aug. 3 An order . . . directing a supply of Minie rifles and cavalry accoutrements to be forwarded to the Territory. **1861** NORTON *Army Lett.* 24 We are to have the short Minie rifle with sword bayonet. **1865** RICHARDSON *Secret Service* 137 A Union soldier . . . [found] his own brother, wounded by two Minié rifle balls. **1872** 'MARK TWAIN' *Roughing It* 49 By the time you have raised the hammer you see that you need a minie rifle.

***Mining.**

I. *attrib.* and *comb.* **1.** Designating areas or regions where mining is carried on.

1833 *Md. Hist. Mag.* XIII. 346 This mining land, is nothing more than the little vallies, which lie between hills. **1835** HOFFMAN *Winter in West* I. 240 It would never do to go out of this country without visiting Galena and the mining country. **1852** *Harper's Mag.* Dec. 120/2 The intelligence from the mining districts was highly satisfactory. **1866** 'F. KIRKLAND' *Bk. Anecdotes* 635/1 Do not forget to tell the people in the mining regions, as you pass through them, . . . about the development. **1871** RAYMOND *3d Rep. Mines* 2 For further particulars as to all these mining fields . . . I respectfully refer you to the accompanying report. **1876** MILLER *First Families* 243 The flat was then staked off as mining-ground by some enterprising strangers. **1890** LANGFORD *Vigilante Days* (1912) 521 Some of the band of robbers were at the different mining localities, on the lookout for victims.

2. Designating persons working in or having to do with mines.

See also MINING CAPTAIN, ENGINEER.

1869 BRACE *New West* 16 One person . . . attracted our interest, . . . a Mining Superintendent, and a self educated geologist and philosopher. **1873** RAYMOND *Silver & Gold* 13 The want of interest felt by the mining community in the labors of the Mining Commissioner and his agents. **1874** — *6th Rep. Mines* 499 He talked over the scheme with many railroad and mining-men. **1877** HODGE *Arizona* 114 Mining capitalists from abroad, both on the Pacific and Atlantic slopes, are turning their attention to Arizona. **1877** W. WRIGHT *Big Bonanza* 61 The Mining Recorder of the district . . . could hardly record the locations of mining claims as fast as they were made. **1878** PINKERTON *Strikers* 337 All the efforts of the mining 'bosses' to keep them [*sc.* miners] at work were of no avail. **1916** WILSON *Somewhere* 368, I know a slick mining promoter from Arizona.

3. Designating a community, settlement, etc., adjacent to a mine or mines.

See also MINING CAMP, MINING TOWN.

1873 RAYMOND *Silver & Gold* 15 Our mining communities have . . . been comparatively free from those unwholesome excitements. **1877** W. WRIGHT *Big Bonanza* 45 The sagacious citizens of the then mining metropolis of the country did not think much of the new strike. **1890** LANGFORD *Vigilante Days* (1912) 298 The road leading through the gulch was filled with people hastening from all the towns and mining settlements to Nevada. **1917** SINCLAIR *King Coal* 264 They went out in the mud and rain of a mining-village.

4. Special combinations.

Mining property, property, especially land, valued for its mining possibilities; *m. right*, a legal right to mine in a given area; *m. rod*, =DIVINING ROD; *m. share*, a share of mining stock; *m. shark*, a mining expert (*colloq.*[2]); *m. sluice*, an artificial channel or passage for water used in mining, cf. MINING DITCH; *m. stream*, a stream made use of in mining.

1821 *Amer. Jrnl. Science* III. 102 Permit me to suggest . . . well authenticated facts on the use of 'mining rods' in discovering fountains of water underground. **1870** MEDBERY *Men Wall St.* 20 A curious mélange of express, telegraph, mining shares . . . is enumerated as 'miscellaneous.' **1877** HODGE *Arizona* 78 Messrs Cody and Layne, who have several other good mining properties in the Cerbat Range. **1878** JACKSON *Travel at Home* 140 On all sides were old mining-sluices. **1882** *47th Congress 1 Sess.* H. R. Ex. Doc. No. 216, 12 Mining streams usually cannot carry all the *débris* washed into them. **1908** BEACH *Barrier* 10, I am supposed to see that mining rights are observed. **1923** 'BOWER' *Parowan Bonanza* 114 I'm no mining shark, but I reckon I better . . . see what you got.

+**Mining camp.** A temporary settlement composed of miners.

1866 *Rep. Indian Affairs* 119 For the purpose of securing employment they resort to the towns and mining camps in large numbers. **1872** MCCLELLAN *Golden State* 463 The noisy din of the early mining-camp is turned to social order. **1899** *Mo. So. Dakotan* I. 171, I met a notorious character well known in nearly all western towns and mining camps. **1917** *Sunset* April 23 Other Montana mining camps were a hundred miles from a railroad.

+**Mining captain.** One in charge of mining operations. — **1853** *Harper's Mag.* March 442/2 We are accompanied by Captain John Cox, the mining captain. **1872** *Vermont Bd. Agric. Rep.* I. 629 Captain Glonville, who for a year or two had been mining captain, did not understand his business. **1883** FOOTE *Led-Horse Claim* iii. 30 West [was] the mining-captain of the Led-Horse.

+**Mining claim.** An area of mining land held by a claimant by virtue of location and entry. (Cf. CLAIM *n.* 3.) — **1866** *Rep. Indian Affairs* 92 The farms and mining claims . . . are being reoccupied. **1881** RAYMOND *Mining Glossary, Assessment-work*, . . . the work done annually on a mining claim to maintain possessory title. **1890** LANGFORD *Vigilante Days* (1912) 191 Two partners in a mining claim had quarrelled. *a*1918 G. STUART *On Frontier* I. 232 A mining claim was one hundred feet up or down the creek and as far out on each side as the pay dirt extended.

+**Mining company.** A group organized for carrying on mining operations. — **1863** *Mich. Gen. Statutes* I. (1882) 1028 The president and secretary of every such mining company . . . [shall] make under their hands, a return to the state treasurer. **1872** *Harper's Mag.* Dec. 24 Either the claim owners effect a consolidation—a mining company being formed —or the capitalist steps in and purchases the whole. **1910** J. HART *Vigilante Girl* 329 A rich mining company had been buying up some of the old placer claims.

+**Mining ditch.** A ditch for conducting water used in mining. Also attrib. — **1873** RAYMOND *Silver & Gold* 45 It is made the duty of the county assessors to return each year to the surveyor general . . . a list of the quartz-mills and mining ditches. **1890** LANGFORD *Vigilante Days* (1912) 276 He had been thrown from his horse, while crossing a mining ditch. **1910** J. HART *Vigilante Girl* 90 Judge Tower is a large owner in the mining ditch properties.

Mining engineer. One versed in the science of excavating and operating mines, and in the treatment of ores; an official in charge of such work. — **1872** *Vermont Bd. Agric. Rep.* I. 629 Captain Thomas Pollard . . . had formerly been mining engineer. **1898** *McClure's Mag.* X. 572/2 We are considering life with a mining engineer. **1898** *Engineering Mag.* XVI. 121/1 He was a mining engineer, Thoroughly trained in every sphere Of knowledge scientific.

+**Mining stock.** Stock issued by a mining company. — **1870** MEDBERY *Men Wall St.* 10 Gold was the favorite with ladies. Clergymen rather affected mining-stock and Petroleum. **1893** M. HOWE *Honor* 57 It is those cursed mining stocks that have ruined me, Archer! **1903** 'O. HENRY' *Heart of West* 211 There come to the town a young chap all affluent and easy, and fixed up with buggies and mining stock.

+**Mining town.** A town that has grown up adjacent to a mine or mines. — **1869** BROWNE *Adv. Apache Country* 524 The population is one of the best I have seen in any mining town. **1890** LANGFORD *Vigilante Days* (1912) 20 Lewiston . . . grew with the rapidity known only to mining towns into an emporium. **1901** McCutcheon *Graustark* 17 They were pulling out of a little mining town built on the mountain side.

***Minister.**

***1.** A preacher, pastor, or clergyman.

1619 *Va. House of Burgesses* 13 The Ministers and Church wardens shall seeke to prevente all ungodly disorders. **1689** *Manchester Rec.* I. 35 It was Legaly voted & agreed upon by ye inhabitants of this towne for ye maintenance of a minister amongsts us if he might be procured. **1717** *Mass. H. Rep. Jrnl.* I. 217 Their Cattel and Sheep [were] taken from them from time to time, on account of their Ministers Rate. **1781** Peters *Hist. Conn.* 284 Sometimes, in quarrels between the merchants and lawyers of a particular parish, the minister is allowed to stand neuter. **1820** Dewees *Lett. from Texas* 16 There were at the camp ground, three ministers and a considerable congregation. **1881** Chase *Editor's Run in N. Mex.* 50 There have been some attempts to support a minister in Cimarron. . . . The first minister was shot, the second one was put in jail. **1920** Howells *Vacation of Kelwyns* 174 He is trying to think whether he had better be a lawyer, or a minister, or an actor.

attrib. **1792** *Mass. Spy* 31 May (Th.), Highway tax 4s. and 3q. Minister Tax, 2s. 11d. 1q.

b. (See quotation.)

1842 *Lowell Offering* II. 122 There are now three Free Chapels in Boston, and as many 'Ministers at Large,' or Ministers to the Poor.

+2. The direct diplomatic representative of the United States at a foreign seat of government. {1709–, in Europe}

In careful usage the term is applicable only to agents of the second and third classes (*ministers plenipotentiary* and *ministers resident*). Until 1893 the United States government sent no ambassadors. (Cf. Ambassador 2, Envoy extraordinary, Minister plenipotentiary, and Minister resident.)

1777 *Jrnls. Cont. Congress* VII. 8 *Resolved,* That the appointment of Ministers to the other Courts be postponed to Friday next. **1787** *Constitution* ii. § 2 The President . . . shall appoint Ambassadors, other public Ministers and Consuls [etc.]. **1790** Maclay *Deb. Senate* 233, I know not of a single thing that we have for a single minister to do at a single court in Europe. **1840** *Niles' Nat. Reg.* 26 Sept. 64/2 Major Easton, . . . late minister to Spain, . . . addressed a meeting in Wheeling. **1885** Crawford *Amer. Politician* 63 We select as our ministers a number of gentlemen who in most cases have never read a diplomatic dispatch in their lives. **1906** *N.Y. Ev. Post* 9 Jan. 2 Spencer Eddy . . . is being boomed to succeed John A. G. Leishmann as minister to Turkey.

+3. a. The horned pout, *Ameiurus nebulosus*, or a related species. **b.** (See quot. *a*1870.)

1839 Storer *Mass. Fishes* 102 The Horned Pout . . . is known in the interior of the state by the vulgar names of 'Horn pout,' and 'Minister.' **1842** *Nat. Hist. N.Y., Zoology* IV. 183 The Common Catfish, Horn Pout, or Minister . . . occurs in the great lakes, and along the Atlantic States. ***a*1870** Chipman *Notes on Bartlett* 273 *Minister*, . . . a sculpin.—Mass. **1884** Goode, etc. *Fisheries* I. 628 The common 'Horned Pout,' 'Bullhead,' 'Bull-pout,' or 'Minister' of the Northern and Eastern States is the most generally abundant and familiar representative of this family [Siluridae].

+4. (See quot. 1847.)

1847 Ives *New Eng. Fruit* 45 *Minister.*—This fine apple originated in Rowley, Mass. The size is large, the form oblong like the Bellflower. **1857** Hooper *Western Fruit Bk.* 61 Minister. . . . Better for orchard culture in the East than in the West. Needs a deep, sandy loam. **1905** W. H. Ragan *Nomenclature of Apple* 199.

***Ministerial,** *a.*

***1.** Of or pertaining to a minister of religion or to the carrying on of an ecclesiastical system.

1676 *Huntington Rec.* I. 218 An invitation . . . for his continuing to despense the word of god and what more is dutie in the ministeriall offise. **1720** Sewall *Letter-Book* II. 113 Which tract of land has been and is still known by the name of the ministerial lott or ffarm. **1845** *Indiana Mag. Hist.* XXIII. 25 The opinion of that day . . . will tolerate a ministerial boy without a beard, to marry the first or second year of his traveling. **1920** *3d Nat. Country Life Conf. Proc.* 94 [There existed] in the county . . . a County Ministerial Association.

+2. Designating the armed forces sent to this country by England early in the Revolutionary War. Freq. *ministerial army.*

1775 *Jrnls. Cont. Congress* III. 278 For the use of the ministerial army or navy in America. **1776** A. Adams *Familiar Lett.* 140 There have been some movements amongst the ministerial troops, as if they meant to evacuate the town of Boston. **1855** Irving *Life Washington* I. 453 Many still clung to the idea, that in all these proceedings they were merely opposing the measures of the ministry, and not the authority of the crown, and thus the army before Boston was designated as the Continental Army, in contradistinction to that under General Gage, which was called the Ministerial Army.

+b. Designating governmental services conducted in this country by England about the time of the Revolution.

1775 *Jrnls. Cont. Congress* III. 488 When . . . our enemies here are corresponding for our ruin, shall we not stop the ministerial post?

Ministerium. +(See quot. 1873.) — [**1748** *Hallesche Nachrichten* I. (1886) 210 (Petition from Penna.), Alle Aelteste aus denen Gemeinen . . . bitten es [den öffentlichen Gottesdienst] kürzer zu machen; überlassen es dem Ministerio was und wie selbige abzukürzen.] **1873** *Quart. Rev. of Evang. Luth. Ch.* V. 94 *Ministerium* is the term applied to the body of ordained ministers, when they hold a meeting alone, to transact business pertaining to the ministry, viz., the '*Examination, Licensure, and Ordination* of candidates *for the ministry.*' **1881** *Phila. Record* No. 3457, 1 In to-day's session of the Lutheran Ministerium a report on Muhlenberg College showed a $20 000 cash endowment. **1898** *Evang. Luth. Ministerium of Penna. Doc. Hist.* p. iv, It is hoped that the Ministerium will provide for the continuation of this work. **1918** *Lutheran Ch. Year Book* 102/1 Ministerium of New York.—Pres., Rev. Fred. H. Bosch.

Minister plenipotentiary. {plenipotentiary minister *c*1645} +A diplomatic agent of the second class, representing the United States at a foreign seat of government.

Until 1893, when the first ambassadors were sent to France, Great Britain, Germany, and Italy, the minister plenipotentiary was the highest class in the United States diplomatic service. (See also Envoy extraordinary 2, and cf. Minister 2.)

1790 *Ann. 1st Congress* I. 992 The President of the United States shall not allow to any Minister Plenipotentiary a greater sum than at the rate of nine thousand dollars per annum. **1802** Ellicott *Journal* 64 The secretary of war had consulted him . . . [about] sending Mr. Blunt to France, as minister plenipotentiary to adjust our differences with that nation. **1849** *Whig Almanac 1850* 26/1 We have three species of diplomatic representatives—the minister plenipotentiary, at a salary of nine thousand dollars; the minister resident, at a salary of six thousand dollars; and the chargé d'affaires. **1914** *Cycl. Amer. Govt.* II. 446 *Minister plenipotentiary,* a title regularly added to that of envoy extraordinary in naming diplomatic agents next below the grade of ambassador.

+Minister resident. A diplomatic agent of the third rank, representing the United States at a foreign seat of government. (Cf. Minister 2.) — **1848** *Whig Almanac 1849* 21/2 Dabney S. Carr, Md. *Minister Resident,* Constantinople, Turkey, $6,000. **1873** *Harper's Mag.* Feb. 471/2 The Senate, in executive session, . . . confirmed the nomination . . . of Julius White as minister resident to the Argentine Republic. **1893** *Statutes at Large* XXVII. 497 The minister resident and consul-general in Haiti shall also [be] accredited as chargé d'affaires to Santo Domingo.

***Ministry.** *attrib.* +Of or pertaining to the upkeep of ministers or to the maintenance of an ecclesiastical system. *Obs.* (Cf. Ministry house, Ministry land.) — **1649** *Rowley Rec.* 56 Provided that they make noe adission to the minestry Rate aboue 60 pounds. **1677** *Ib.* 204 They are yearly to pay to the ministry rate for what stocke they keepe upon the saide land. **1714** *Manchester Rec.* I. 130 John knowlton should have the minestry lott in the west Devision the 22 lott. **1751** Hempstead *Diary* 578, I was . . . Drawing Coppies &c ministry mony.

+Ministry house. A house for a minister; a parsonage. *Obs.* — **1695** *Dorchester Church Rec.* 16 Mr. Davis—where ye minestry house now stands. **1699** *Manchester Rec.* I. 85 The mony for the use aforesd namely to be Improved towards a ministry hous. **1731** *Ib.* 185 A Dead of sale . . . was formerly Completed for the minstry house & sum Land whereon it stands.

+Ministry land. Land set apart for the use of ministers or for the maintenance of a church establishment. *Obs.* Also attrib. — **1710** *Lancaster Rec.* 300 [It] butts southardly on a peice of ministry Land. **1725** *Manchester Rec.* I. 166 Poles bought & put on ye Ministry land wall, 04. 0. **1730** *Ib.* 179 Voted to Give the Revnd. Mr. Amos Chever . . . his salery, . . . Mr. Chever Relesing all his Right & intrest in the free Contrabushon & minstry Land Lying by millets swamp. **1763** *Essex Inst. Coll.* XLIX 137 Building their half fence, between the said ministry land, and lot of land given by our commoners to the poor.

+Minitari. Also **Menetaries.** [Mandan *minitari* 'they crossed the water.'] Chiefly pl.

1. The Hidatsa, a Siouan tribe of Indians. Also attrib.

1804 Clark in *Lewis & C. Exped.* I. (1904) 227 The Menetaries . . . were allarmed at the tales told them by the Mandans. **1805** *Ib.* II. (1904) 283 The *Minetarries* came in Sight, attacked & killed 4 men. **1854** Brownell *Indian Races N. Amer.* 466 The smaller Minitari tribes . . . speak the same language with the Crows. **1862** Hayden *Ethnog. & Philol. Mo. Val.* 344 [The Atsinas] have also been confounded with the Minnetarees of the Missouri.

2. *Minitari of the Prairie*, and variants, the Atsina, a branch of the Arapaho. Often confused with the Hidatsa.

1806 Lewis in *L. & Clark Exped.* V. (1905) 24 As we had not yet seen the black foot Indians and the Minnetarew of Fort de Prarie they did not think it safe to venture over to the Plains of the Missouri. **1853** Latham in *Philol. Soc.* (London) *Proc.* VI. 85 These *Arapaho* or *Atsina* Indians are . . . [also] called the *Gros Ventres*, the *Big Bellies* and the *Minitares* of the Prairie. **1862** Hayden *Ethnog. & Philol. Mo. Val.* 344 [The Atsina Indians] have received a great variety of names, as Paunch, . . . Minnetarees of the Prairie, &c.

3. *Minnetarees of (the) Knife river*, (see quot. 1907).

1805 Lewis in *L. & Clark Exped.* II. 283 Our present camp is precisely on the spot that the Snake Indians were encamped at the time the Minnetares of the Knife R. first came in sight of them five years since. **1907** Hodge, etc. *Amer. Indians* I. 870 *Minnetarees of Knife River*, an unidentified Hidatsa division. . . . Possibly the Amahami.

***Mink.** +Any one of various short-legged, weasel-like, semiaquatic American mammals of the genus *Mustela*.

See also MINX.

1612 SMITH *Virginia* 14 Martins, Powlecats, weessels and Minkes we know they haue, because we haue seen many of their skinnes. **1784** FILSON *Kentucke* 28 The waters have plenty of . . . otters, minks [etc.]. **1836** EDWARD *Hist. Texas* 75 Perhaps [one may] at times see a skunk, a weasel, or a mink. **1883** *Century Mag.* Sept. 653/2 There may still be found between Buzzard's Bay and Provincetown the mink, rabbit, fox, raccoon, and deer. **1902** WHITE *Conjuror's House* 184 A tragedy had been consummated, and the fierce little mink stared malevolently across the body of his victim.

attrib. **1866** 'KIRKLAND' *Bk. Anecdotes* 34/1 Rifle pits and mast batteries a twixt him and Richmond, thicker 'n mink traps in a Western Swomp. **1902** WHITE *Conjuror's House* 26 Louis Placide . . . reported of the trade,—so many . . . mink, otter, beaver, . . . and fisher pelts taken.

+Minkery. A place where minks are bred for commercial purposes. — **1877** COUES *Fur-bearing Animals* 182 Mr. Resseque's minkery consists of twelve stalls. **1897** *Boston Transcript* 11 Sept. 24/3 Minks have been bred for their skins in so-called minkeries.

Mink skin. +The skin or pelt of a mink. {1812–} Also attrib.— **1678** *New Castle Court Rec.* 349, 22 mincq skins great and smal. **1775** CRESSWELL *Journal* 116 Mr. Douglas gave me an Indian Tobacco pouch made of a Mink Skin adorned with porcupine quills. **1778** *Essex Inst. Coll.* XLIX. 109 Sold . . . 33 mink skins, at 6s 6d. **1867** CRAWFORD *Mosby* 169 One of the men exchanging a Confederate hat . . . and home-spun woollen gloves for his elegant fur cap and mink-skin gloves.

+Minnesotan. (See quot. 1890.) — **1890** *Cent.* 3778/1 *Minnesotan*, . . . a native or an inhabitant of Minnesota. [**1915** *Minn. History Bull.* Nov. 243 The *Minnesotan* is the title of a new Minnesota periodical.]

+Minnesotian. =prec. — **1860** *Harper's Mag.* Oct. 581 Town lot speculators striving to have the Capitol elsewhere than at St. Paul (all but Minnesotians have forgotten the name of the town now.) **1873** BEADLE *Undevel. West* 706 In May, 1859, I first became a 'gopher,'— practical Western title of the Minnesotians.

***Minnow.** Also **minow, minny.**

***1.** Any one of various species of small fishes, esp. of the family Cyprinidae; also, a fish of such a species.

1796 MORSE *Univ. Geog.* I. 222 Bony Fish [found in the U.S. include the] . . . Minow, Week fish, King fish. **1820** RAFINESQUE in *Western Rev.* II. 235 There are in the United States more than fifty species of small fresh water fishes . . . commonly called Minnies, Minnews, Bait-fish, Chubs, and Shiners. **1840** *S. Lit. Messenger* VI. 386/2 Ellen used to fish there for minnoes with a pin-hook. **1860** HOLMES *Professor* 27 She has that foolish way of dancing and bobbing like a quill float with a 'minnum' biting the hook below it. **1884** ROE *Nature's Story* 192 He would be willing to fish indefinitely for even minnows. **1911** *Rep. Fisheries 1908* 312 *Mummichog* (*Pœciliidæ*). . . . Along the eastern coast they are known as 'may-fish,' 'killifish,' . . . and in the interior as 'minnows.'

b. With a prefixed defining term.

1839 STORER *Mass. Fishes* 94 *H[ydrargira] ornata.* Le Sueur. *The ornamented Minnow.* **1842** *Nat. Hist. N.Y., Zoology* IV. 219 The Transparent Minnow. *Hydrargira diaphana*. . . . From Saratoga lake, where it is used as a bait for other fishes. *Ib.* 220 The Champlain Minnow. *Hydrargira atricada.* **1884** GOODE, etc. *Fisheries* I. 618 Its flesh spoils very quickly after the fish [*i.e.*, the shiner] is taken from the water, hence the name 'Rot-gut Minnow,' applied to it in Alabama.

2. Attrib. and comb. with *bucket, can, casting*, etc.

1835 BIRD *Hawks* I. 216 Some idlers . . . had begged pins of their cousins and sweethearts, converted them into minnow-hooks, and were already angling from the rocks. **1857** HAMMOND *Northern Scenes* 57 Nobody in them days tho't of sich contrivances as trollin'-rods, reels, and minny-gangs. **1869** *Ill. Public Laws* 188 It shall be lawful to catch minnows with minnow seines or nets. **1883** *Century Mag.* July 378/2 Ignatius . . . was fastening the strap of a small, oblong, four-quart minnow-bucket to his belt. *Ib.* 382/1 [Causing the fish to turn over in the air] can be more successfully and safely accomplished with the shorter and stiffer minnow-rod than with the fly-rod. **1888** *Outing* July 307 In the minnow casting . . . for black bass, the record was beaten fearfully. **1893** *Ib.* May 86/2 The inside of her minnow-can was lifted with care over the side of the boat into the water.

+Minny bass. The small-mouthed black bass. — **1820** *Western Rev.* II. 56 Bass Hogfish. . . . It has some similarity with . . . other River bass, wherefore it is called Minny-bass, Little-bass.

***Minor.** *Educ.* **+1.** In colleges and universities operated on the quarter system, a course of study requiring approximately half the time spent on a major. **+2.** A secondary subject of study, either graduate or undergraduate. Also attrib. — (1) **1890** in Goodspeed *Hist. Univ. Chicago* (1916) 142 The plan of majors and minors, announced in our bulletins and calendars, has been arranged in order to meet this difficulty. **1891** *Univ. Chicago Bul.* No. 1, 10 The student will select . . . two Majors and two Minors, each twelve weeks . . . until the total number . . . shall have been completed. **1893** *Univ. Chicago Register* 7/1 Courses of instruction in the University are classified as Majors and Minors. . . . The Minor, [calls] for four to five hours of class-room work, or its equivalent, each week. (2) **1909** WEBSTER 1376/3 *Minor*, . . . a subject of study, usually nearly related to the major subject, pursued by a candidate for a higher degree, less time being devoted to it than to the major subject. **1911** *Cornell Univ. Graduate Sch. Announcement* 4 Candidates for the doctor's degree are required to select a major subject and two minor subjects. **1919** *Univ. Texas Bul.* No. 1925, 105 The student will note that it is possible to arrange his minor . . . [so] as to take in effect two majors, belonging either to the same or to different groups.

***Minority.** *attrib.* **+1.** *Minority representation*, representation in a legislative body according to a procedure that allows the voter, when he has, for example, three representatives to vote for, to cast three votes for one candidate or to divide them as he sees fit. Since 1870 this has been used in Illinois. **+2.** *Polit.* With *party, platform*, in sense: Consisting of or supported by a minority. — (1) **1870** *Illinois Constitution* (Chicago, 1870) 39 (*caption*), Minority Representation. **1872** *Atlantic Mo.* Feb. 255 Calling a constitutional convention devolves this winter on the Ohio Legislature, and one of the most important subjects which will come before that body will be minority representation. (2) **1901** *N. Amer. Rev.* Feb. 271 The captors were able to defeat the minority platform. **1902** E. C. MEYER *Nominating Systems* 53 Great leaders came forward in the ranks of the minority, for the possibilities of a vigorous campaign stood out clearly. The minority party could thoroughly gauge its strength through its assembled delegates.

+Minority report. A separate report made by those members of a committee or other group who are unable to concur in the report of the majority. — **1833** *Congress. Deb.* 2 March 1927 A new set of majority and minority reports are to be launched upon the public. **1856** *Harper's Mag.* Sept. 550/1 In the House, Mr. Oliver presented a minority report on the affairs of Kansas. **1887** *Courier-Journal* 6 May 1/1 Mr. Taulbee made a spirited fight in behalf of his minority report. **1917** *Cycl. Amer. Govt.* II. 450 *Minority Report.* The minority of a legislative committee are said to make a report, since their views are filed and printed at the time that the committee makes its report.

***Minstrel.**

+1. *pl.* A group or company of theatrical performers, either Negroes or, more usually, white men in blackface, who entertain with songs, dancing, jokes, etc.

Cf. NEGRO MINSTREL.

1843 in Odell *Ann. N.Y. Stage* IV. 668 The Ethiopian Serenaders, or Boston Minstrels. **1855** *Putnam's Mo.* V. 79 Then Ethiopian Serenaders and Congo Minstrels will draw crowded houses at three dollars a seat. *c***1864** *Corsican Twins* t.-p., An Ethiopian Burlesque on the Corsican Brothers as performed by Griffin & Christy's Minstrels. **1883** RITTENHOUSE *Maud* 177 We missed the minstrels and the W. C. & L. A. entertainment and stayed quietly at home. **1902** WILSON *Spenders* 337, I got a good notion to get me one of them first-part suits—like the minstrels wear in the grand first part, you know.

+b. *sing.* A member of such a group of actors.

1904 M. MICHELSON *Madigans* 329 Kate walked with a minstrel! What shall we do?

2. Attrib. with *ballad, band, entertainment*, etc.

1865 *Chicago Tribune* 10 April 1 Buckley & Budd's minstrel house is in blast. **1870** *Ib.* 26 March, The Dearborn [is] probably the most successful minstrel entertainment in the country. **1881** *Harper's Mag.* May 818/2 The plaintive slave songs and their echoes—the plantation songs and the minstrel ballad . . . are rapidly passing away. **1882** *Sheldon* (Iowa) *Mail* 26 Jan., Sprague's Original Georgia Minstrel performance, given in this city last night, is, as a fraud and humbug, entitled to the cake. **1884** MATTHEWS & BUNNER *In Partnership* 211 A stock of musical instruments large enough to fit out a strolling minstrel troupe. **1884** *Century Mag.* June 307/2 It is hard . . . for two women of refinement and taste to stand between two members of some burnt-cork minstrel band on the Lord's Day. **1887** *Courier-Journal* 11 Jan. 5/2 The wife of . . . the minstrel performer, to-day began suit for separation against her husband.

+Minstrel show. An entertainment by minstrels or of the kind given by minstrels. Also transf. — **1872** *Chicago Tribune* 9 Oct., Its programmes present . . . minstrel shows of poor order. **1896** *Chicago Record* 12 Feb. 1/6 Give a female minstrel show. . . . The ladies of West Chicago gave their long-talked-of and much-opposed 'burnt cork' entertainment to-night. **1907** *St. Nicholas* July 815/2 With these interests and many others, such as minstrel shows, dances, . . . you can see that the forecastle is not the floating jail that it used to be.

***Minstrelsy.** +The arts or practices of Negro minstrels. (Cf. MINSTREL 1.) — **1860** *George Christy's Ethiopian Joke Book* No. 3 p. vi, The beauties of Ethiopian Minstrelsy . . . are now looked upon as the wonders of the progressive age in which we live. **1870** *Chicago Tribune* 15 March, Another week of the most remarkable success in minstrelsy ever achieved in Chicago began last evening. **1895** *N.Y. Dramatic News* 20 July 5/3 To the men of active minds and careful intelligence will the prizes be [a]warded in minstrelsy as in everything else.

***Mint.**[1] The machine or machinery used in coining money; a place where money is coined.

1652 HULL *Diaries* 145 Upon occasion of much counterfeit coin brought in the country, . . . the General Court ordered a mint to be set up. **1661** *Md. Archives* I. 414 An Acte Concerning the Setting vp of a Mint within this Province of Maryland. **1783** in D. K. Watson *Hist. Amer. Coinage* (1899) 13 On the 21st of February, 1782, Congress were pleased to approve of the establishment of a mint. **1840** *Picayune* 24 Sept. 2/3 Christopher F. Gobrecht . . . to be engraver of the mint of the United States at Philadelphia. **1868** BEECHER *Sermons* I. 402 Go with me to Philadelphia, and I will take you into the Mint there. **1900** *Congress. Rec.* 17 Jan. 922/2

The Democratic party on the floor of this House opposed the closing of the mint at New Orleans. **1918** *Statutes at Large* XL. 594 There shall be coined at the mints of the United States, silver fifty-cent pieces to the number of one hundred thousand.

attrib. **1652** *Mass. Rec.* III. 161 The mint master, for himselfe & officers, for theire paynes & labour in meltinge, refineinge, & coyninge, is allowed [etc.]. **1886** G. EVANS *Illus. Hist. U.S. Mint* 151 *Mint Mark.*—The letter or mark on the coin, designating the mint at which it was struck; as 'S' for San Francisco, 'CC' for Carson City, 'O' for New Orleans.

* **Mint.**[2] Any one of various aromatic plants, usually of the genus *Mentha.*

1698 THOMAS *Acct.Pensilvania* 21 Most sorts of Saladings, besides what grows naturally Wild in the Country, and that in great plenty also, as ... *Sage, Mint, Tanzy, Wormwood.* **1737** BRICKELL *N. Carolina* 18 The Sallads are ... Mint, the Dock or Wild Rhubarb. **1789** MORSE *Amer. Geog.* 53 Of the various aromatic and other kinds of herbs are balm, ... tansey, mint [etc.]. **1832** WILLIAMSON *Maine* I. 126 The following herbs [are] generally well known, viz. *May-flowers;* ... *Mint,* or *Spearmint* [etc.]. **1884** 'CRADDOCK' *Tenn. Mts.* 127 A mingled breath of cool, dripping water, sweet-scented fern, and pungent mint greeted him as he passed it.

attrib. and *comb.* **1711** BUCKINGHAM *Land Exped.* 106 One bottle of mint-water, and another of rum and clove water mixed together. **1765** WASHINGTON *Diaries* I. 210 Grafted 10 Carnation Cherrys on growing Stocks ... 5 of them in and about the Mint Bed. **1879** B. F. TAYLOR *Summer-Savory* 174 Mint farming seems to me pleasant though less emotional than onion-raising.

+**Mint drop.**

1. (See quot. 1872.)

In this sense 'mint' has the force of a play on MINT[1] and MINT[2].

1837 *Congress. Globe* App. 29 Sept. 339 [The money flowed to Mobile] by the aid of the far-famed Specie circular, in 'mint drops' and 'hard currency.' **1840** KENNEDY *Quodlibet* 106 [There's] Specie Circlar and Mint Drops, and the Lord knows what. **1860** *Harper's Mag.* Jan. 280/2 Old Ball ... angered his owner, who straightway swapped with his neighbor Jones, receiving as 'boot,' a 'mint drop' of the Benton stamp. **1872** DE VERE 291 When the Hon. T. H. Benton ... put his whole strength forward ... to introduce a gold currency, he accidentally called the latter mint-drops, with a slight attempt at a pun.... For many years gold coins were largely known as Benton's mint-drops.

2. A small, drop-shaped piece of candy flavored with mint. {peppermint drop, 1878–}

1876 *Wide Awake* 150/2 Red herrings and papers of mint-drops combined in attractiveness with rows of pins and a box of cheap cigars. **1905** VALENTINE *H. Sandwith* 61, I am making mint-drops and I have to count as soon as the sugar boils.

+**Mint julep.** An iced and sweetened drink made chiefly of whisky or brandy and mixed with fresh mint. (Cf. HAILSTORM 2, JULEP.) — **1809** IRVING *Knickerb.* VII. ii, The inhabitants [of Maryland] ... were notoriously prone to get fuddled and make *merry* with mint julep and apple toddy. **1839** BRIGGS *H. Franco* II. 18 He invited me into a coffee-house near by, and asked me to take a mint julep. **1889** *Harper's Mag.* Aug. 388/2 Men sat drinking mint-juleps and playing draw poker and 'old sledge.' **1908** LORIMER *J. Spurlock* xii. 297 He and the Major ... were soon deep in a learned discussion on the right way to mix a mint julep.

+**Mint sling.** A spirituous drink flavored with sprigs of mint. — **1804** *Balance* 15 March 86, 3 Mint Slings [figure in a Referees' Tavern Bill, Lancaster, Pa.] **1827** J. BERNARD *Retrosp.* 206 Mint-sling, ... as you proceeded southwardly, obtained the medicinal name of an 'antifogmatic.' **1828** *Lawrence & Lemay's N.C. Almanack* 19, October.—Now governors and mint slings are made. **1840** *S. Lit. Messenger* VI. 508/1 Alighting at a miserable looking log-hut, they called for a 'mint-sling.'

+**Mint smash.** =prec. — **1884** *Washington* (D.C.) *Critic* Sept., He proceeded to the bar-room, [and] took a mint smash. **1903** ADE *People You Know* 14 Then the atmosphere began to be curdled with High Balls and Plymouth Sours and Mint Smashes.

+**Mint stick.** A stick of candy flavored with peppermint. — *a*1855 J. F. KELLY *Humors* 187 The streets are filled by holiday-looking people, children with toys and 'mint sticks.' **1862** *N.Y. Tribune* 13 June 8/4 [Soldiers have their] hunger for dates, figs, mint-stick, ginger-cake, preserves and the other sweet stuff that the sutler keeps [for sale]. **1863** A. D. WHITNEY *F. Gartney* xxxvi, Glory resigned the boy to his mint-stick, and was saying good-by.

Minuet.

1. Music suitable for, or resembling that suitable for, the minuet, a stately dance in triple rhythm. {1686–}

1762 JEFFERSON *Writings* IV. 2 The cursed rats ... carried away ... half a dozen new minuets I had just got. **1772** WINSLOW *Diary* 58 After tea Miss Becky Gridley sung a minuet. **1898** WESTCOTT *D. Harum* 314 Mr. Fairman added a little minuet of Boccherini's.

2. The dance itself. {1673–}

1772 WINSLOW *Diary* 16, I had the honor to open the diversion of the evening in a minuet with miss Soley. **1835** LONGSTREET *Ga. Scenes* 160 Except the minuet ... and the Congo, which was only to chase away the solemnities of the minuet, it was all a jovial ... amusement. **1872** *Atlantic Mo.* Feb. 179 He had danced too many minuets in the Apollo—the great room of the old Ralegh tavern. **1915** CAMPBELL *Proving Virginia* 150 She danced the stately minuet.

***Minute.** *attrib.* +Consisting of minutemen. Now hist. — **1775** in Sparks *Corr. Revol.* I. 64 A Committee of Safety ... [for] calling the minute-battalions and drafts from the militia into service. **1775** *Md. Hist. Mag.* X. 304 To raise a Minute Company.

+**Minute-man.**

1. During the Revolutionary period, an armed citizen or militiaman who agreed to be ready for military duty the minute he was called upon. Now hist.

1774 J. ANDREWS *Letters* 60 Seven regiments ... are call'd minute men, .e., to be ready at a minute's warning with a fortnight's provision, and ammunition and arms. **1775** *Mass. Provincial Congress Proc.* (1838) 99 This Congress ... should be made fully acquainted with the number and military equipments of the militia and minute men in this province. **1775** *Jrnls. Cont. Congress* II. 188 [It is recommended] that one fourth part of the Militia in every Colony, be selected for minute men. **1903** K. M. ABBOTT *Old Paths & Legends New Eng.* 66 The regulars were picked off from the walls by the Minute-men.

b. A member of any of various groups of men organized in the South, at about the time of the outbreak of the Civil War, for the purpose of instantly resisting any forces threatening southern interests. Now hist.

1860 *Richmond Enquirer* 2 Nov. 1/6 (Th.), The formation of companies of 'Minute Men' has actually begun. **1862** in Moore *Rebellion Rec.* V. II. 281 You who belong to the regular minute-men and militia, turn out at once. **1886** LOGAN *Great Conspiracy* 104 The 'minute men' of South Carolina, and other military organizations, ... excitedly prepared throughout the South for the dread conflict at arms which they recklessly invited, and savagely welcomed. **1887** *Century Mag.* April 848/1 Some of the young men, though they wore the blue cockade, did not align themselves with the minute-men [in Ga.]. **1901** CHURCHILL *Crisis* 260 The guardians were the *Minute Men.*

2. (See quot. 1895.)

1890 WILLS *Twice Born* 70, I joined the fire department as 'minute man.' **1895** *Stand.* 1129/3 *Minute-man,* ... a fireman stationed outside of an engine-house and employed at any occupation, but subject to call.

Minx. Variant of MINK. *Obs.* {1792–} — **1683** PENN *Select Works* 1825) III. 226 The creatures for profit only, by skin or fur, ... are the ... fisher, minx, musk-rat. **1709** LAWSON *Carolina* 121 The Minx is an Animal much like the English Fillimart or Polcat.

‖**Miraculous pea.** (See quotation.) — **1709** LAWSON *Carolina* 76 We have the Indian Rounceval, or Miraculous Pease, so call'd from their long Pods, and Great Increase.

Mirage. {1812–} Any of various optical effects in hot, sunny, arid regions, as the illusion of a sheet of water, or the reflection in the sky of distant objects. {1837–} (Cf. FALSE POND.) — **1834** A. PIKE *Sketches* 15, I have seen the mirage, too, painting lakes and fires and groves on the grassy ridges near the bounds of the Missouri. **1897** HOUGH *Story of Cowboy* 18 On the horizon float the strange pictures of the mirage.

Mire hole. A hole or depression filled with mire; a bog hole. — **1822** in *Amer. Sp.* XV. 285/1 Standing about 8½ poles N 29 E from a mire-hole. **1844** *Ib.* [The] West side of the Middle fork near the Mire hole.

Miring branch, place, time. (See quots.) — **1704** in *Amer. Sp.* XV. 285 A Marked Mulberry Standing at ye Miring place on ye South Run of Quantiquart. **1899** GREEN *Va. Word-Book* 240 In the 'miring-time,' that is, in the spring when the cattle were thin and weak and apt to get stuck in the soft marshes. *Ib.* 249 'Myring-branches of a river,' were places where the bottom was so soft that animals could not cross without being stuck in the mud.

***Mirror.** A polished surface, now usually of glass backed with silver, which reflects images; a looking glass. (Cf. PIER GLASS.) — **1801** BENTLEY *Diary* II. 400 The Mirrors were large. **1854** *Penna. Agric. Rep.* 425 Two large gilt mirrors, made for the Monongahela house. **1893** *Atlantic Mo.* Feb. 199 A small warped mirror hanging outside of the bunk-house.

Mirror carp. A variety of the carp (*Cyprinus carpio*) having few scales. {1880–4} — **1878** *Rep. Comm. Fisheries 1877* 43* On the 26th of May [1877] Mr. Hessel placed there [in the ponds] 227 naked and mirror carp and 118 common carp. **1903** T. H. BEAN *Fishes of N.Y.* 168 The mirror carp has a few large scales irregularly placed.

+**Miscegenation.** [Lat. *miscere* 'to mix,' *genus* 'race.'] Mixture of races by intermarriage or interbreeding, esp. such mixture on the part of white people and Negroes. {1902–} Also fig.

1864 *Chicago Tribune* 18 March 2/1 Miscegenation. Such is the newly invented term to express the mingling of races generally, and specially the mingling of the white and black races on this continent as a consequence of the freedom of the latter. **1865** E. BURRITT *Walk to Land's End* (1868) 47 In beautiful ... contrast with this ostentatious group of Christian and pagan miscegenation is a chaste ... monument [etc.]. **1871** DE VERE 288–9, I was one ... who first publicly used the illshapen word miscegenation, and openly dared to advocate the expediency of favoring, by every agency of State and Church, the mingling of the black and white races. **1889** *Boston Jrnl.* 27 Feb. 4/4 The penalty for miscegenation is three years' imprisonment. **1900** *Congress. Rec.* 8 Jan. 674/2 The choice of a negro, by an arbitrary law, to such an office is a political marriage and miscegenation.

+Miscegenation(al)ist. One who favors miscegenation. — **1871** DE VERE 289 A *Miscegenationist*, named Williams, was tarred and feathered. **1885** *Century Mag.* Sept. 689/1 The enemies of slavery getting from us such names as negrophiles, negro-worshippers, and miscegenationalists.

Misimprove, *v. tr.* To make a wrong use of; to abuse; to fail to use. {1658–1798} Also *ppl. a.*

'Obs. or *U.S.'* (*O.E.D.*).

1666 *R.I. Col. Rec.* II. 167 The aforesayd powers and priviledges exprest in our Charter, will be so . . . neglected and misimproved, as extreemly to hazard the loss of the whole. **1681** *N.H. Hist. Soc. Coll.* VIII. 64 The estate left by his father . . . is not improved . . . but rather imperiled and misimproved. **1746** *N.H. Prov. Papers* V. 473 A large sum of money out of ye publick Treasury . . . Capt Ladd has misapply'd & misimprov'd. **1826** LONGFELLOW in S. Longfellow *H. W. Longfellow* I. 87 You either over-rate my abilities and my advantages, . . . or I have sadly misimproved them both. **1898** *Christian Herald* 26 Jan. 64/2 You may have to say . . . at the close of a misimproved lifetime: 'I did but taste a little honey.'

Misimprovement. Misuse; abuse; failure to improve. {1644–1806} — **1734** *Conn. Rec.* VII. 501 James Church . . . is authorized and impowred to take care of the said house . . . [to] prevent the abuses and misimprovements thereof by all persons whatsoever. **1774** A. ADAMS *Familiar Lett.* 48 The arm of treachery and violence is lifted over us, as a scourge and heavy punishment . . . for the misimprovement of our great advantages. **1888** SCHAFF *Hist. Christian Ch.* VI. 489 Hymnbooks with all sorts of misimprovements were introduced [in the Lutheran service in the 18th century].

+Misplay. *Sports.* A wrong play. — **1887** in H. Hall *Tribune Bk. Sports* 445 [In croquet] all balls moved by the mis-play must be returned to their former position by the umpire or adversary. **1889** *Columbus Dispatch* 1 Aug., A misplay of any kind would allow the score to be tied. **1894** *Outing* XXIV. 300/2 He was playing a steady, careful game, . . . apparently waiting for Hovey's misplays. **1907** *St. Nicholas* July 819/1 Yale had victory in her hands only to throw it away by two bad misplays in the seventh inning.

Misrepresentative. {1887} *Polit.* +One who represents his constituency badly or improperly. — **1852** *Democratic Rev.* XXX. 202/1 The misrepresentative of one of the most go-a-head districts of Kentucky, Mr. John C. Breckinridge. **1862** *N.Y. Tribune* 22 Jan. 5/2 The Senate listened to-day to a philippic from Mr. Sumner, against Mr. Bright, and to a bitter reply from that mis-representative of Indiana.

Miss.[1] {1645–} =MRS. *dial.* {1875, *dial.*}

'Dial. and *U.S.'* (*O.E.D.*).

1790 N. WEBSTER in *Amer. Mercury* 17 Nov. (Th.), The use of *Miss* for *Mistress* in this country is a gross impropriety. **1819** *Mass. Spy* 12 May (Th.), I found upon inquiry that his name was Spruce, and Miss Spruce was his wife. **1857** GUNN *N.Y. Boarding Houses* 227 Her husband always calls her 'Miss,' but we shall not adopt that Down-east peculiarity. **1912** N. M. WOODROW *Sally Salt* 36 You can do as you please, and Mis' Salt's as good to you as if you was her own mother.

***Miss.**[2] +(See quot. 1851.) *Obs.* — **1819** PEIRCE *Rebelliad* 62 Are there some who scrape and hiss Because you never give a miss. **1851** HALL *College Words* 208 *Miss*, an omission of a recitation, or any college exercise. An instructor is said *to give a miss*, when he omits a recitation. **1852** FELTON *Mem. J. S. Popkin* p. lxxvii, One of the classes applied to the Doctor for what used to be called, in College jargon, a *miss*.

+Missey-moosey. [Var. of MOOSEMISE.] (See quot. 1909.) — **1892** *Amer. Folk-Lore* V. 95 *Pyrus Americana*, missey moosey. N.H. **1909** *Cent. Suppl.* 815/3 *Missey-moosey*, . . . the American mountain-ash, *Sorbus Americana*.

***Missing.** **+1.** *To be among the missing*, to be absent. *colloq.* **+2.** *To turn up missing*, to fail to show up at all, to be absent. (Cf. *to come up missing* under COME *v.* 18.) — **(1)** **1855** HALIBURTON *Nature & Hum. Nature* 17 (B.), If a person inquires if you are at home, the servant is directed to say, No, if you don't want to be seen, and choose to be among the missing. **a1859** *Sketches of N.Y.* (B.), I don't want to see him; and think I will be among the missing. **1869** *Across the Desert* (F.), I tell you what, Jake, if this goes on I'll be among the missing before sundown. **(2)** **1888** *Mo. Repub.* 24 Feb. (F.), Finally Marie turned up missing, and she was no longer seen about the cabin of the half-breed. **1907** LONDON *Road* 32 One by one the three other survivors turned up missing, until I alone remained.

***Mission.**

+1. A permanent diplomatic establishment or institution. **1805** *Amer. State P.: Foreign Relations* II. 669 As nothing was said in my communication respecting the ordinary mission, it remains of course in force. **1833** *Congress. Deb.* App. 31 Jan. 87/1 The important papers of his mission must be kept in a tavern. **1890** *Cent.* 3798/1 The members of the British mission at Washington.

+2. A building or buildings, sometimes a whole community, serving as the center of missionary activities among the Indians; the territory served by such a mission. {in general religious sense, 1622–}

The earliest and most famous missions were those established by the Spanish friars in the Southwest.

1805 SIBLEY in *Ann. 9th Congress* 2 Sess. 1103 Similar small towns, or missions were within certain distances of each other for a great extent southwardly towards Mexico. **1838** C. NEWELL *Revol. Texas* 148 Scattered along the banks of the San Antonio, are many beautiful edifices . . . styled Missions, generally consisting of a fortress and a church. **1856** DERBY *Phoenixiana* 207 He and I . . . rode forth to the Mission, and attended a Fiesta. **1878** ROE *Army Lett.* 218 Our little entertainment for the benefit of the mission here was a wonderful success. **1890** *Century Mag.* Dec. 165/1 The next morning . . . found me starting for the mission of San José. **1899** Z. ENGELHARDT *Franciscans in Arizona* 211 Mission San Miguel de los Navajos comprises the whole territory of the Navajo tribe, located principally in northeastern Arizona, but extending into New Mexico, Utah, and Colorado. **1904** *Indian Laws & Tr.* III. 592 The lands necessary for . . . Catholic and Congregational missions are by this proclamation . . . reserved for such purposes.

3. A chapel or religious center maintained by missionary enterprise for the poor and underprivileged in a city. {1839–} Cf. MISSION SCHOOL 2.

1875 STOWE *We & Neighbors* 104 He had established his mission in one of the least hopeful neighborhoods of New York. **1887** I. ALDEN *Little Fishers* viii, The Sabbath school which she had been attending was a mission, in the lower part of the city. **1925** BRYAN *Memoirs* 456 One night . . . we went to a mission along the water front in New York City.

4. *attrib.* **a.** Employed in or belonging to a mission, especially one established among the American Indians of the Southwest.

1822 in Morse *Rep. Indian Affairs* II. 303 No person . . . would in the least suspect but that she was one of the Mission Sisters from the North. **a1861** WINTHROP *J. Brent* 16 He had . . . bought a mission farm, and established himself as a ranchero. **1871** *Rep. Indian Affairs* (1872) 444, I opened a boarding-hall for them, remodeling some of our old mission buildings for the purpose. **1883** *Harper's Mag.* Aug. 339/1 [Father Galitzin] remained in charge of the parish nearly half a century, . . . dying as a simple mission priest in 1840.

b. Resembling the simple, dark, substantial furnishings or the style of architecture characteristic of the early Spanish missions in the Southwest.

1900 *Harper's Bazar* 28 April 388/1 She stumbled upon an artistic small shop filled to overflowing with what the salesman called Mission furniture. **1911** *N.Y. Ev. Post* 1 March 8 The dignified . . . cement house, often in mission style with attractive tile roof. **1913** LONDON *Valley of Moon* 491 They . . . found the big beautiful husband lying back reading in a huge Mission rocker. **1915** CAMPBELL *Proving Virginia* 192 She was on the new back piazza in a big Mission swing.

Missionary, *n.* {1656–}

+1. One who goes or is sent to teach Christianity to the American Indians.

1720 D. NEAL *Hist. New-Eng.* I. 263 Here they maintain at present about twelve or sixteen Missionaries, part English, and part Indian, to preach the Gospel to the Nations. **1746** BRAINERD *Diary* (1902) 275 The first visit I have ever received from any near relative since I have been a missionary. **1815** *Mass. H. S. Coll.* 2 Ser. IV. 67 He was employed as a missionary to the Cherokees from A.D. 1803 to 1809 inclusive. **1877** JOHNSON *Anderson Co., Kansas* 18 These Indians had numerous missionaries . . . stationed among them. **1916** EASTMAN *From Deep Woods* 132 White men with Indian wives and missionaries, may be ordered off the reservation as 'disturbers of the peace.'

+2. =MISSIONARY BAPTIST.

1865 *Nation* I. 395 The Missionaries, they holds to free grace.

Missionary, *a.* Of or pertaining to missionaries and their work. {1644–}

In some expressions the word partakes of the nature of a noun used attributively.

1822 *Missionary Herald* XVIII. 51/1 Donations. . . . Coll. by a missionary card in Troy and Albany. **1877** JOHNSON *Anderson Co., Kansas* 17 A reservation of ten miles square had been set off near Osawatomie, as a missionary reserve for the various tribes settled on the Osage river. **1877** Missionary barrel [see BARREL *n.* 4]. **1887** RITTENHOUSE *Maud* 378 Have met with missionary meetings, but religious excitement I walk right out of. **1906** *Churchman* 20 Oct. 585 The thirty-second annual convocation of the missionary district of Sacramento was held in Trinity church, Sacramento.

+Missionary, *v. intr.* =MISSIONATE. *Obs.* — **1862** *Independent* 24 April 3/1 [The Rev. Stephen H. Tyng] was always fond of missionarying. **1883** 'MARK TWAIN' *Life on Miss.* i, In Canada the French were schooling them [*sc.* Indians] in a rudimentary way, missionarying among them. **1884** — *H. Finn* xix. 183 Preachin's my line, too, and workin' campmeetin's, and missionaryin' around.

+Missionary Baptist. A Baptist who, unlike the Primitive or Hard-Shell Baptists, supports missionary work. Also attrib. (Cf. HARD-SHELL BAPTIST.) — **1849** CHAMBERLAIN *Ind. Gazetteer* 72 A large majority of this denomination are Missionary Baptists, and the minority is rapidly diminishing. **1865** *Nation* I. 395 Most all kinds—Presbyterian, and Missionary Baptist. **1888** J. WALLACE *Carpetbag Rule in Fla.* 226 The freedmen prior to the emancipation knew nothing of any other churches than the Missionary Baptist, Primitive or foot-washing Baptist, and the Methodist Episcopal. **1891** O'BEIRNE *Leaders Ind. Territory* 184/2 He is a missionary Baptist and a good christian.

Missionary box. A box for donations of money, clothing, etc., for missionaries or missionary work. {1886–} Cf. BARREL *n.* 4. — [**1822** *Missionary Herald* XVIII. 22 Donations. . . . A miss. box kept in the room of Mr. John Blatchford of the Theo. Sem.] **1883** WILDER *Sister Ridnour* 261 Just then the missionary box comes. **1900** DIX *Deacon Bradbury* 42 After the packing of the missionary box, they met Enos Reed.

Missionary school. A school founded or maintained by missionary enterprise. — **1822** in Morse *Rep. Indian Affairs* II. 171 The missionary school [was] established in this nation by the United Brethren. **1833** NEAL *Down-Easters* I. 199 She had been so well educated as to be able to teach in a sort of missionary-school. **1845** *Knickerb.* XXV. 236 When quite a child, he was sent to a missionary school.

Missionary society. A society or organization for carrying on and promoting missionary work. {1813–} (See also HOME MISSIONARY.)

1815 DWIGHT *Remarks on Inchiquin's Letters* 175 In this country there are many Missionary, and at least sixty-five Bible Societies. *c***1852** in Stowe *Key* 218/1 It is the duty of Missionary Societies to grant aid to churches in slave-holding States in the support of . . . ministers. **1866** *Rep. Indian Affairs* 72, I do not accord with the notion of asking missionaries to be put into the service at the cost of missionary societies. **1889** P. BUTLER *Recoll.* 233 It is able to report a missionary society.

b. A specified organization of this type.

1831 PECK *Guide* 68 It is to be hoped that the Baptist Missionary Society of Massachusetts will have regard to this field as soon as possible. **1850** HINES *Voyage* 28 An Oregon Missionary Society was formed. **1877** *Harper's Mag.* March 605/2 The remainder of my property . . . I bequeath to the American Missionary Society.

+**Missionary station.** The headquarters of a missionary to the American Indians. — **1853** HANDSAKER *Pioneer Life* 52 They belong to the Omaha tribe and have a missionary station one mile from our camp. **1899** CUSHMAN *Hist. Indians* 464 She died and was buried at Monroe, the old missionary station.

+**Missionate,** *v. intr.* To do the work of a missionary. *Obs.* — **1816** PICKERING 134 *To Missionate.* . . . 'A low ecclesiastical word (says a learned clerical correspondent) used in conversation' in America. It is also used in theological publications. **1836** L. MATTHEWS *Lectures* 130 *Missionate* . . . can [hardly] be said to have the stamp of good use among us. **1896** *Home Missionary* Oct. 303 To make professional visits, or to 'missionate' to the farmer, will not serve the purpose.

Mission chapel. =MISSION *n.* 3. {1883–} — **1871** *Scribner's Mo.* I. 497 His church was only a mission chapel, supported by a richer society of the same denomination. **1875** STOWE *We & Neighbors* 119 [He] annoyed old rich saints by suggesting that it was their duty to build mission chapels and carry on mission works. **1916** EASTMAN *From Deep Woods* 109 Mr. Cook offered us the mission chapel, in which the Christmas tree still stood.

Mission church. {1792–} A church serving as the religious center of missionary work, +especially on the frontier or among the Indians. — **1869** STOWE *Oldtown Folks* 45 Our house of worship in Oldtown . . . [had] originally been built as a mission church for the Indians. **1885** *Century Mag.* Jan. 449 The little mission church of St. Mary's, with its attached group of log buildings, stands close by the village of Stevensville. **1890** HOWELLS *Shadow of Dream* II. ii, Nevil's given up his parish there, and gone . . . to Kansas, where he has charge of a sort of mission church.

+**Mission family.** A family or association of families doing missionary work in a certain locality. — **1822** MORSE *Rep. Indian Affairs* I. 78 Education Families. I give this name to those bodies which have been commonly denominated *Mission Families.* **1822** in *Ib.* II. 303 No person . . . who should enter the Mission family as a stranger [etc.]. **1850** HINES *Voyage* 14 Nearly the whole mission family were attacked with the intermittent fever, and the mission house was converted into an hospital. **1875** STOWE *We & Neighbors* 375 A few Christian people had bought a house in which they had established a mission family, with a room which they use for a chapel.

+**Mission grape.** A variety of cultivated sweet wine grape introduced into this country from Mexico presumably through the Spanish missions in California. — **1868** *Iowa Agric. Soc. Rep. 1867* 205 The Mission grape is not as much esteemed as formerly. **1869** BRACE *New West* 258 The Mission grape is really nothing more than the old Catalonian grape, brought here by the Spanish padres. **1895** GRAHAM *Stories of Foot-Hills* 139 Parker Lowe . . . says they're every one mission grapes—fer makin' wine.

Mission house. A house used in connection with a religious mission. {1839–} — [**1794** C. I. LATROBE tr. Loskiel *Hist. Mission of the U. Brethren* II. 166 On a sudden the mission-house on the Mahony . . . [was] attacked by the French Indians.] **1824** KEATING *Narrative* (1825) 150 At the time we passed at the Carey mission-house, this gentleman was absent on business. **1865** *Atlantic Mo.* XV. 440 There, to be sure, is the mission-house, conspicuous enough, quaint, and by no means unpleasing. **1877** *Rep. Indian Affairs* 53 His labors are somewhat retarded by the present dilapidated condition of the mission-house.

+**Mission Indian.** A member of any of various Indian tribes originally converted to Christianity by the Spanish Franciscan missionaries in California and governed by them until the secularizing of the missions in 1834 by the Mexican government. — **1883** *Century Mag.* Aug. 511 The Present Condition of the Mission Indians in Southern California. **1893** SANBORN *S. Calif.* 25, I can imagine even a mission Indian grunting and complaining if taken to our part of the country in the midst of a week's storm. **1903** *Indian Laws & Tr.* III. 19 Any part of the one hundred thousand dollars for the removal and support of the Mission Indians in California, . . . [may] be used for the purchase of . . . tracts of land.

+**Mission land.** Land belonging to a mission. — **1851** *Whig Almanac 1852* 18/2 The Commissioners are required to report to the Secretary of the Interior the tenure by which the Mission lands are held. *a***1861** WINTHROP *J. Brent* 7 They had been speculating in beef, bread-stuffs, city lots, . . . [and] mission lands. **1883** *Century Mag.* Aug. 528/2 These Carmel Mission lands having been rented out, by their present owner, in great dairy farms.

+**Mission school.**

1. A school for Indian children conducted by missionaries or their helpers at an Indian mission.

1822 in Morse *Rep. Indian Affairs* II. 171 There has been no particular information received from Elder Posey himself, superintendent of the mission schools at the Valley Towns. **1837** WETMORE *Gaz. Missouri* 225 The mission school is to be removed into the Osage nation. **1881** *Rep. Indian Affairs* p. xxxiii, A mission school for girls has been in successful operation for several years. **1885** *Ib.* 135 The Omahas have a mission school for girls established . . . by the Presbyterian Board of Foreign Missions. **1906** *Indian Laws & Tr.* III. 193 Mission schools on an Indian reservation may . . . receive for such Indian children duly enrolled therein, the rations of food and clothing.

2. A Sunday school at a city mission conducted by members of a church. (Cf. MISSION *n.* 3.)

1871 BAGG *At Yale* 523 One of the most approved entrances to city society lies, oddly enough, through the doors of the 'Mission schools.' **1875** STOWE *We & Neighbors* 333 Angelique and I are on a committee for buying the presents for the Christmas-tree of our mission-school. **1887** RITTENHOUSE *Maud* 387 This afternoon Harriet and I went down to the Mission-school, and I had my bright little boys once again.

+**Mission station.** A place serving as the headquarters of missionary activities, esp. among the American Indians. — [**1844** *McDonough P.* 78 One of these young men . . . is now at the mission station at Settra Kroo, Liberia, keeping a school for the native youth.] **1850** HINES *Voyage* 91 Our families found ourselves floating on the surface of the great Columbia, in two small canoes, on our way up to the mission station in the Wallamette settlement. **1871** *Rep. Indian Affairs* (1872) 535 As soon as the means are furnished to establish, permanently, mission-stations and school-houses.

+**Mississippi.** Also *dial.* **Mississip.** [Amer. Indian.] The name of a river, a former territory, and a southern state.

1. A kind of cotton.

1805 *Raleigh* (N.C.) *Register* 1 April, Common Georgia and Mississippi are quoted at 2s. to 2s. 3d.

2. *attrib.* **a.** With *Butternut, canebrake, delta,* etc.

1834 CARRUTHERS *Kentuckian* I. 218 If I was to meet that feller in a Mississip cane-brake. **1835** HOFFMAN *Winter in West* I. 68 [Pittsburgh] is now, with its adjacent villages, the third in population, wealth, and importance in the Mississippi valley. **1847** ROBB *Squatter Life* 64 Ben was an old Mississip' roarer—none of your half and half, but just as native to the element, as if he had been born in a broad horn. *Ib.* 142 A select party of river cronies . . . were seated around him upon the boiler deck of a Mississippi steamer, as she sped along one bright June night. **1866** 'F. KIRKLAND' *Bk. Anecdotes* 150 A brisk and spirited dialogue . . . took place between an East Tennesseean loyalist and a Mississippi 'Butternut.' **1868** *N.Y. Herald* 4 July 6/1 A committee of five, appointed by the Mississippi Reconstruction Convention, is in session. **1873** COZZENS *Marvellous Country* 168 To the saddles of four of the party was tied an old Mississippi yauger, of antiquated make and flint lock. **1880** CABLE *Grandissimes* 27 The pilgrim fathers of the Mississippi Delta . . . were taking wives.

b. Special combinations: *Mississippi nut,* a pecan; *Mississippi cotton tree,* a tree of the genus *Populus* common in the Mississippi region.

1775 WASHINGTON *Diaries* II. 179 Row next these 25 Mississippi Nuts —some think like the Pignut—but longer, thiner shell'd and fuller of meat. **1814** PURSH *Flora Amer.* II. 619 *Populus angulata* . . . is known by the name of Mississippi Cotton Tree.

+**Mississippian.** A native or resident of the Mississippi region or state.

1775 ADAIR *Indians* 93 'The ugly yellow French,' (as they [*sc.* Indians] term the Mississippians [*sic*]). **1835** INGRAHAM *South-West* I. 119 Creole is sometimes, though not frequently, applied to Mississippians. **1859** WILMER *Press Gang* 320 For a time shooting editors seemed to be the favorite amusement of the Mississippians. **1883** *Century Mag.* Nov. 140/2 The leader of the party was a fellow-Freemason, a Mississippian. **1900** *Congress. Rec.* 31 Jan. 1369/1 Mississippians are proud of Mississippi.

+**Mississippi bottom.** Bottom land along the Mississippi River. Also attrib. and transf. — **1818** DARBY *Emigrant's Guide* 122 The three species of soil, Mississippi bottom, bluff, and pine woods, are to be found in Claiborne and Jefferson. **1866** W. REID *After the War* 455 An investment in Mississippi bottom cotton plantations seemed to many business men very much like an investment. **1868** *Rep. Comm. Agric. 1867* 114 In De Soto are some 60 sections of 'Mississippi bottom' at $4 or less per acre.

+Mississippi kite. A kite (*Ictinia mississippiensis*) found throughout the southern states. — **1811** WILSON *Ornithology* III. 80 [The] Mississippi Kite, *Falco Mississippiensis*, . . . I first observed . . . a few miles below Natchez. **1823** JAMES *Exped.* I. 94 On a branch of the Le Mine . . . they saw four Mississippi kites. **1895** *Dept. Agric. Yrbk. 1894* 218 The Mississippi kite and its white-tailed ally devour large numbers of lizards, small snakes, and insects. **1917** *Birds of Amer.* II. 63/1 Its uniform bluish-gray plumage . . . easily distinguishes the Mississippi Kite.

+Mississippi plan. The methods followed in Mississippi, after the Civil War, for securing political supremacy for the white population by the use of terror and force if necessary. — **1877** *Congress. Rec.* 9 Jan. 501/1 The plan of intimidation or bull-dozing is frequently spoken of as the 'Mississippi plan.' **1886** LOGAN *Great Conspiracy* 657 With variations adapted to locality and circumstances, this 'Mississippi plan' soon enveloped the entire South in its mesh-work of fraud, barbarity, and blood. **1893** *Congress. Rec.* 6 Oct. 2248/1 The Mississippi plan . . . is acknowledged to be the most efficacious of all known methods for eliminating the 'unwelcome voter.'

+Mississippi rifle. A large-bore percussion rifle used by a Mississippi regiment under Jefferson Davis in the Mexican War. (Cf. KENTUCKY RIFLE.) *Obs.* — **1851** GLISAN *Jrnl. Army Life* 92 The old Mississippi rifle, carrying a half-ounce ball, is a favorite with them. **1865** PIKE *Scout & Ranger* (1932) 35 They fought us with Mississippi rifles. **1867** RICHARDSON *Beyond Miss.* 111, I have got twelve Mississippi rifles.

+Mississippi (River) steamboat. A large steamboat, often of a luxurious type, formerly in use on the Mississippi River. — **1856** *Porter's Spirit of Times* 15 Nov. 178/2 An imperialed mustached 'blood' [spoke] to a 'Hoosier' on a Mississippi steamboat. **1858** VIELÉ *Following Drum* 142 On a Mississippi river steamboat . . . he wounded . . . a fellow-passenger. **1896** SHINN *Story of Mine* 109 As distinct creations of adaptive and evolutionary genius as the . . . Mississippi River steamboat in days before railroads.

+Mississippi states. The states that border on the Mississippi River. — **1804** C. B. BROWN tr. Volney *View* p. xii, Disjunction of interests and views, and contrariety of habits, . . . separate the eastern from the southern, the Atlantic from the Mississippi states. **1890** LANGFORD *Vigilante Days* (1912) 64 The intelligence spread through the Territories and Mississippi States like wildfire.

+Mississippi Territory. A region east of the Mississippi River, embracing approximately the present states of Mississippi and Alabama, organized as a territory in 1798. Now hist. — **1802** CUTLER in *Life & Corr.* II. 98 Yesterday we attended the funeral of . . . Mr. Hunter, of the South-western or Mississippi Territory. **1817** PAULDING *Lett. from South* I. 82 Those [states] which will from time to time grow out of the Mississippi and Missouri territories. **1857** BENTON *Exam. Dred Scott Case* 47 Organizing the Mississippi Territory . . . was done by spreading the ordinance of '87 over it.

+Miss-lick. (See quot. 1859.) Also transf. — **1859** BARTLETT 273 When an axe or knife cuts out of line, it is called in the West a *miss-lick.* **1900** GARLAND *Eagle's Heart* 216 A man is liable to make a miss-lick somewhere, but that's all in the game.

+Miss-Nancyish, *a.* Prim, affected, sissified. *colloq.* — **1855** M. THOMPSON *Doesticks* 298, I could overlook the boarding-school-ism of the Miss Nancyish 'Journal.' **1888** DORSEY *Midshipman Bob* 117 He wouldn't [go to the doctor] because he didn't want to seem Miss-Nancyish.

+Miss-Nancyism. Effeminacy, fussiness. *colloq.* — **1863** 'G. HAMILTON' *Gala-Days* 117 A man's hair is shag. . . . Ceasing to be shag, it does not become beauty, but foppishness, effeminacy, Miss Nancyism. **1886** *Harper's Wkly.* 20 March 178/1 Ineffable silliness, sneering at the demand for honesty in politics as Miss Nancyism.

+Missouri. [From Illinois dialect of Algonquian, tribal name of Indians on the Missouri River.] The name of a river, a former territory, and a state in the Middle West.

1. An Indian of a tribe of the Sioux family, first encountered by Europeans near the Missouri River; also, pl., the tribe.

1807 GASS *Journal* 26 Six of them were made chiefs, three Otos and three Missouris. **1836** JACKSON in *Pres. Mess. & P.* III. 265 Treaties [are] concluded with . . . the Otoes and Missourias and Omahas, by which they have relinquished their rights in the lands lying between the State of Missouri and the Missouri River. **1847** COYNER *Lost Trappers* 55 The [Pawnee] chiefs and young men having gone to hold a council with the Ottoes and the Missouries. **1894** in *So. Dak. Hist. Coll.* I. 267 These . . . enjoyed a monopoly of the trade with the Ottoes, the Ioways and the Missourias.

2. A form of dance. *Obs.*

1846 *Sun Weekly* (N.Y.) 8 Aug., I dances notin' now but de Missouri.

3. *To be* (or *come*) *from Missouri*, to be extremely skeptical or unwilling to believe anything until it is demonstrated. *colloq.*

1900 *State Tribune* (Jefferson City, Mo.) 13 Dec. 4/1 Ex-Lieut.-Gov. Chas. P. Johnson thinks he knows the origin of the extensively-used expression: 'I'm from Missouri; you'll have to show me;' at least he can recall its use twenty years ago in Colorado. **1901** *Missouri Statesman* (Columbia) 13 Dec. 1/3 You gentlemen are from Kentucky, Texas, Tennessee and Arkansas and seem to trust each other, but 'I'm from Missouri and you must show me.' **1912** RAINE *Brand Blotters* 158, I'd say I was from Missouri and needed showing. **1912** C. MCCARTHY *Wisconsin Idea* 291 In the words of the current slang phrase, every Wisconsin legislator 'comes from Missouri' and you have to 'show him.'

4. *attrib.* **a.** Designating persons associated in some way with Missouri.

1817 BRADBURY *Travels* 41n., It is customary amongst the Missouri Indians to register every exploit in war, by making a notch for each on the handle of their tomahawks. **1818** SCHOOLCRAFT *Journal* 11 We partook of it with that keen appetite . . . felt by the wild Indian and the half-starved Missouri hunter. **1844** in *Whig Almanac 1846* 30/1 [At] Taos . . . the custom house is kept at which the Missouri caravans enter their goods.

b. Designating articles made in or characteristic of Missouri.

1824 *Mass. Spy* 4 Feb. (Th.), Randolph appears this winter in a large drab surtout, . . . and a flat Missouri fur cap. **1848** PARKMAN in *Knickerb.* XXXI. 441 A company of California emigrants . . . had determined to get rid of their very copious stock of Missouri whisky. **1850** *Western Journal* IV. 124 The better qualities of Missouri wine sell readily in St. Louis at $2 per gallon. **1873** BEADLE *Undevel. West* 649 With their big Missouri whips [they] would snap off the heads of chickens.

c. Designating birds and animals first observed in the Missouri region.

1805 LEWIS in *L. & Clark Exped.* I. (1904) 358 This bird . . . I shall henceforth stile the *Missouri Plover. Ib.* VI. (1905) 187 The only birds that I obse[r]ved during the winter at Fort Mandan was the Missouri Magpie [etc.]. **1868** *Amer. Naturalist* II. 530 Missouri Chipmunk (*Tamias quadrivittatus*). This little Chipmunk I saw in the bare rocky hills of the Mauvaise Territory.

d. Designating trees and plants found in Missouri or the region of the Missouri River.

1814 PURSH *Flora* I. 114 Oleaster, or Missouri Silver-tree. **1846** EMORY *Military Reconn.* 16 On these hills we found cedar growing, very stunted; Missouri flax; several varieties of wild currants. **1850** S. F. COOPER *Rural Hours* 117 They are extremely fond of the Missouri currant. **1883** SMITH *Geol. Survey Ala.* 546 Jute and Kentucky or Missouri hemp and India bagging are used [to fasten ties of bales of cotton]. **1897** SUDWORTH *Arborescent Flora* 125 *Salix missouriensis* . . . Missouri Willow.

e. Designating minerals found in Missouri.

1840 *Niles' Nat. Reg.* 16 May 176/2 Missouri copper. . . . Another parcel of pig copper . . . has been received. **1881** *Harper's Mag.* May 842/1 The Missouri silica . . . is naturally prepared for use.

f. Special combinations.

Missouri Act, the congressional enactment under which Missouri was admitted to the Union; *M.-bake*, (see quotation); *M. bird's-eye*, (see quotation); *M. controversy*, the controversy that arose in Congress over the admission of Missouri into the Union, (cf. MISSOURI QUESTION); *M. manufactured*, a form of plug tobacco (jocular); *M. ore blossom*, (see quotation); *M. pike*, an emigrant from Missouri; *M. raid*, a raid into Kansas during the Kansas struggle (1854–58) by Missourians seeking to influence the stand taken by that state on slavery; *M. rifle*, a heavy large-bore rifle of a type formerly used in the Missouri region; *M. ruffian*, one of those taking part in the Missouri raids; *M. toothpick*, a bowie knife or Arkansas toothpick; *M. weed*, a kind of chewing-tobacco.

1857 BENTON *Exam. Dred Scott Case* 107 It even went beyond the words of the Missouri act—entered its spirit. **1870** BEADLE *Utah* 222 Half the time our bread was 'Missouri-bake,' *i.e.* burnt on top and at the bottom, and raw in the middle. **1850** *Western Journal* IV. 123 Mr. Romel also exhibited a sample of red wine, which he calls the 'Missouri Bird's Eye.' **1854** BENTON *30 Years' View* I. 10/1 And thus ended the 'Missouri controversy,' or that form of the slavery question which undertook to restrict a State from the privilege of having slaves if she chose. **1850** GARRARD *Wah-To-Yah* xviii. 216 He kept the pipe in his mouth . . . [and] cut from a solid plug of 'Missouri manufactured' a fresh pipe of strong tobacco. **1850** *Western Journal* IV. 123 The sample chosen by the committee as the best, was a specimen of white wine, the pure juice of the Catawba grape. This is the 'Missouri Ore Blossom.' **1885** *Harper's Mag.* May 832/1 Its fifteen or twenty male inhabitants represented every class of society from the Boston lawyer down to the Missouri Pike. **1872** TICE *Over Plains* 11, I also met . . . Gen. B. F. Stringfellow, conspicuous in the Missouri raids some sixteen and more years ago. **1853** *Harper's Mag.* Aug. 323/1 Lewis . . . carried a long Missouri rifle. **1877** JOHNSON *Anderson Co., Kansas* 38 These officers were in full sympathy with . . . the Missouri Ruffians that overrun [*sic*] this county at that time. **1855** *Herald of Freedom* (Lawrence, Kan.) 9 June (Th.), We mistrust that the author of that statement saw a Missouri toothpick and was frightened out of his wits. **1847** ROBB *Squatter Life* 142 Tom squared himself for a yarn, wet his lips with a little corn juice, took a small strip of Missouri weed, and 'let out.'

+Missourian.

1. a. A native or inhabitant of the state of Missouri. **b.** =MISSOURI 1.

(a) 1820 *Ann. 16th Congress* 1 Sess. 945, I cannot believe that I, or any other man or men, are better capable of governing Missourians than they are of governing themselves. **1854** ANDREWS *Recoll.* 84 The Missourians seem to think themselves entitled to all the offices in the [Kansas] territory. **1862** KETTELL *Hist. Rebellion* I. 110 The Missourians seized on the United States arsenal at Liberty, Missouri. **1882** *Century Mag.* Oct. 869/2 Population in Montana, Idaho, Washington, and Oregon is divided into two distinct elements—the Missourians and the people from other States. (**b**) **1833** JACKSON in *Pres. Mess. & P.* III. 37 Treaty with the united bands of Ottoes and Missourians, made 21st September, 1833.

2. *The Great Missourian,* (see quotation). *Obs.*

Cf. MISSOURIUM.

1841 *Niles' Nat. Reg.* 23 Jan. 336/3, I went the other night to look at the greatest curiosity that I have ever seen. It is called *the great Missourian,* and is the skeleton of the greatest animal ever known.

+**Missouri antelope.** =ANTELOPE 1. (See also AMERICAN ANTELOPE.) — **1805** LEWIS in *Ann. 9th Congress* 2 Sess. 1046 With the addition of the skins of the Missouri antelope, (called cabri by the inhabitants of the Illinois). **c1810** *Rees's Cyclopædia* (Phila.) s.v. *Antelope,* The forked-horned, or Missouri Antelope, so called by captain Lewis.

+**Missouri Compromise.** *Hist.* In the congressional act of March 6, 1820, admitting Missouri into the Union as a slave state, a proviso stipulating that slavery should be prohibited in all other states formed from that part of the Louisiana Purchase lying north of 36° 30′ north latitude, the southern boundary of Missouri.

Cf. COMPROMISE a.

1847 POLK *Diary* 183 He further expressed his willingness to extend the Missouri Compromise west to the Pacific. **1858** DOUGLAS in Logan *Great Conspiracy* 69 [Mr. Lincoln says that] he will introduce and pass a law just like the Missouri Compromise, prohibiting Slavery again in all the Territories. **1861** in *Ib.* 177 In 1854, the repeal of the Missouri Compromise, at the instance of the South, reopened the agitation. **1886** LOGAN *Ib.* 10 The heated and protracted struggle in Congress over the admission of the State of Missouri . . . finally culminated in 1820 in the settlement known thereafter as the 'Missouri Compromise.'

attrib. **1857** BENTON *Exam. Dred Scott Case* 9 There was no necessity, in deciding upon the question of freedom or slavery to Scott and his family, to decide upon the constitutionality of the Missouri Compromise Act.

+**Missouri Compromise line.** A line extended across the area of the Louisiana Purchase at 36° 30′ north latitude and marking the southern limit of the free-state region set up in the Missouri Compromise. — **1820** in Benton *Exam. Dred Scott Case* (1857) 102 The line is . . . nominated . . . by its popular descriptive appellation of 'the Missouri Compromise Line.' **1845** in *Ib.* 109 To such State or States as shall be formed out of said Territory north of the Missouri Compromise line. **1848** POLK in *Pres. Mess. & P.* IV. 641 Under menacing dangers to the Union, the Missouri compromise line in respect to slavery was adopted.

+**Missouri question.** *Hist.* The question in Congress of the conditions under which Missouri should be admitted into the Union, and problems regarding slavery that arose in this connection. — **1819** J. ADAMS in Jefferson *Writings* XV. 236 The Missouri question, I hope, will follow the other waves under the ship, and do no harm. **1820** *Western Carolinian* 28 Nov., The *Missouri Question,* which shook the Union to its centre last winter, is again to be brought up. **1854** BENTON *30 Years' View* I. 19/2 His last speech . . . was in reply to Mr. Rufus King, on the Missouri question. **1884** BLAINE *20 Years of Congress* I. 15 The 'Missouri question' . . . formally appeared in Congress in the month of December, 1818.

+**Missouri skylark.** A variety of pipit (*Anthus spraguei*) found in the interior plains region of North America. — **1858** BAIRD *Birds Pacific R.R.* 234 *Neocorys Spraguei,* Sclater. Missouri Skylark. . . . This little known species has the general appearance of a titlark. **1874** COUES *Birds N.W.* 42 *Neocorys Spraguei.* . . . Missouri Skylark. . . . Chiefly confined to the Upper Missouri. **1917** *Birds of Amer.* III. 171/1 Sprague's Pipit, [is] called the Missouri Skylark, or sometimes the Prairie Skylark.

+**Missouri sucker.** =GOURDSEED SUCKER. — **1820** RAFINESQUE in *Western Rev.* II. 355 Black Suckrel . . . is also found in the Missouri, whence it is sometimes called the Missouri Sucker. **1884** GOODE, etc. *Fisheries* I. 615 The 'Black Horse,' . . . 'Missouri Sucker,' or 'Suckerel' is found chiefly in the river channels of the Ohio and Mississippi. **1911** *Rep. Fisheries 1908* 307 Black Horse (*Cycleptus elongatus*).—A sucker found in the larger streams of the Mississippi Valley. It is also called 'gourd-seed sucker,' 'Missouri sucker,' 'sweet sucker,' and 'suckerel.'

+**Missourium.** A specimen of the American *Mastodon giganteus* which was found in Missouri in 1840. Also fig. — **1841** in *Natural History* XXXVII. 172 The Missourium. After minute investigation . . . I have been led to conclude that the animal was a monster of the Tortoise Tribe. **1847** EMERSON *Repr. Men* (1849) 86 One of the missouriums and mastodons of literature, he [Swedenborg] is not to be measured by whole colleges of ordinary scholars.

***Misspeak,** *v.* +*refl.* (See quot. 1890.) — **1890** *Cent.* 3798/3 *Misspeak,* . . . to express improperly or imperfectly; speak otherwise than according to one's intention: used reflexively: as, I misspoke myself. (Colloq.) **1894** *Congress. Rec.* 19 Jan. 1051/1, I simply wanted to bring that matter out plainly. . . . I believe he misspoke himself.

+**Misstep. a.** A mistake in conduct.

a1800 *Spirit Farmers' Mus.* 205 The 'Squire . . . can Sit on the Sessions, and fine poor Girls for natural missteps. **1854** 'M. HARLAND' *Alone* xxi, Ida strove to keep her feet in the path, and by no misstep or fall, to cast obloquy upon the name she loved. **1892** *Harper's Mag.* June 152/2 Whatever we think of the first misstep of Tess in the immaturity of her girlhood.

b. A slip or wrongly calculated step.

1837 *Yale Lit. Mag.* III. 8 Forgetting the round door block, he made a misstep. **1878** BEADLE *Western Wilds* 483 Their narratives are full, however, of allusions . . . to frowning precipices, where one misstep was destruction. **1894** *Outing* XXIV. 363/2 One misstep might have resulted in a clear fall of three thousand feet.

Missus. Also **missis.** +=MISTIS. — **1852** STOWE *Uncle Tom* xxxiv, 'Missis,' said Tom, after awhile, 'I can see that somehow you're quite 'bove me in everything; but there's one thing missis might learn even from poor Tom.' **1894** 'MARK TWAIN' *P. Wilson* vi, Ole Missus, de house is plum jam full o' people.

Missy. {1676–} +(See quotation.) *Obs.* — **1810** LAMBERT *Travels* II. 414 An old negro woman is called *momma,* which is a broad pronunciation of *mama;* and a girl, *missy.*

***Mistake,** *v.* +*To mistake one's man,* to form an erroneous idea of the person with whom one has to deal. *colloq.* — **1794** *Mass. Spy* 16 April (Th.), If he supposes I am to be frightened by his pompous accusations, he has much mistaken his man. **1804** *Ib.* 5 Sept. (Th.), It seems that in one instance the General Committee have mistaken their man.

+**Mistflower.** A composite plant (*Eupatorium coelestinum*) widespread in the warmer parts of the United States. — **1857** GRAY *Botany* 188 *Conoclinium.* Mist-flower. [1 species:] *C. cœlestinum.* **1901** MOHR *Plant Life Ala.* 765 Mist flower. . . . A common weed in cultivated and waste places, and on roadsides.

+**Mistis.** In the speech of Negro slaves: Mistress. Now hist. — **1852** EASTMAN *Aunt Phillis's Cabin* 217 Master George, take it to mistis, and tell her de truth. **1885** *Century Mag.* Sept. 736/2, I ax your pardon, sir, but dis is *my* place, and I has my mistis' orders. **1901** JEWETT *Tory Lover* 84 Oh yis, mistis; her heart's done broke!

***Mistletoe.** A plant of the family Loranthaceae, +as the American *Phoradendron flavescens.*

Cf. AMERICAN MISTLETOE.

1737 BRICKELL *N. Carolina* 23 Misseltoe of the Oak, in great Plenty all over this Province, whereof good Birdlime is made. **1785** MARSHALL *Amer. Grove* 163 Misseltoe is most frequently found growing upon the Nyssa Sylvatica or Sour Gum, in the middle States, but to the southward upon oaks. **1817–8** EATON *Botany* (1822) 515 *Viscum album,* misseltoe. . . . On the branches of old trees. Leaves an inch long, thick and leathery. **1860** DARLINGTON *Weeds & Plants* 287 *P[horadendron] flavescens.* . . . Yellowish Phoradendron. Mistletoe. False Mistletoe. **1881** *Amer. Naturalist* XV. 214 There is a species of mistletoe which grows thickly in nearly every mesquite tree. **1905** N. DAVIS *Northerner* 202 Everywhere to-night [the drawing rooms were] wreathed and garnished with masses of holly and mistletoe.

***Mistress.** +A woman who owns or manages Negro slaves. Now hist. — **1825** J. PICKERING *Inquiries Emigrant* (1831) 20, I may just note by the way there are no mistresses or masters in this country, except for blacks. **1836** *S. Lit. Messenger* II. 279 It is this same feature too which contributes most to elevate and adorn the character of the mistress of slaves. **1852** STOWE *Uncle Tom* v, Her own room . . . was a quiet, neat apartment, on the same floor with her mistress's. **1896** WILKINS *Madelon* 301 The three went out and down-stairs, and the black woman clapped to the chamber door . . . upon her mistress.

Mistrial. {1628–} +A trial in which the jury fails to reach a verdict. — **1889** *Boston Jrnl.* 3 May 1/5 Another Mistrial. A Seven Days' Trial of a Case Results in a Disagreement of the Jury. **1889** *Phila. Press* 1 July (*Cent.*), If there had been a mistrial, the colored jurymen voting to acquit and the white jurymen to convict.

Mitchella. [John *Mitchell,* Amer. botanist (d. 1768).] A plant of the genus Mitchella, esp. the partridge berry, *M. repens.*

1785 MARSHALL *Amer. Grove* 92 Creeping evergreen Mitchella. This is a small plant, growing upon mossy, northern, shaded banks. **1818** *Mass. H. S. Coll.* 2 Ser. VIII. 169 Among those, that flower in June, the most interesting are . . . the mitchella, the red-berried gaultheria or partridge berry. **1869** FULLER *Flower Gatherers* 100 This is the Mitchella, in honor of old Dr. Mitchell of New York.

***Mite.** Any one of various small arachnids, often of a distinctive type. (Cf. HARVEST MITE.) — **1832** WILLIAMSON *Maine* I. 171 There are others, such as the deathwatch, the mite and the father-long-legs, which are not sufficiently known to be correctly classified. **1873** *Amer. Naturalist* VII. 547 An unsuspected enemy of the aphis is a little garden-mite . . . busily engaged in devouring the plant-lice on the rose-bushes. **1889** *Rep. Secy. Agric.* 341 Since the appearance of the Six-spotted Mite of the Orange in 1886, the Florida press has made frequent reference to it, . . . describing the work of the mite, and giving measures of value against it.

Mitella. *Bot.* A genus of American herbs of the family Saxifragaceae; also, a plant of this genus. — **1731** MILLER *Gard. Dict., Mitella.* . . . Bastard American Sanicle. . . . American Mitella. **1818** *Mass. H. S. Coll.* 2 Ser. VIII. 168 The latter part of May appear . . . the prostrate and two-leaved mitellas, the three-leaved arum [etc.]. **1850** S. F. COOPER *Rural Hours* 85 The elegant silvery May-star is seen here and there; by its side the tall, slender mitella. **1882** *Harper's Mag.* Nov. 853/2 Why should the starry blossom of the fringed mitella seek the snow-flake as its model?

+**Miterwort, Mitrewort. 1.** The coolwort or false miterwort, *Tiarella cordifolia.* **2.** The genus *Mitella,* or a plant of this genus. **3.** An herb of the southern states, *Cynoctonum mitreola.*— (1) **1817–8** EATON *Botany* (1822) 487 *Tiarella cordifolia,* miter-wort, gem-fruit. **1840** DEWEY *Mass.*

Flowering Plants 46 Mitre Wort. . . . Of delicate appearance, but no useful application. **1847** Wood *Botany* 280. **(2) 1857** Gray *Botany* 145 *Mitella*. Mitre-wort. Bishop's-Cap. **1898** Creevey *Flowers of Field* 363 Mitrewort. Bishop's-cap. *Mitella diphylla*. . . . Range, from New England to North Carolina. **(3) 1857** Gray *Botany* 174 *Mitreola*. Mitre-Wort. . . . [1 species:] *M. petiolata*. . . . Damp soil, from Eastern Virginia southward. **1901** Mohr *Plant Life Ala.* 669 Miter-wort. . . . Central Pine belt to Coast plain.

+**Mite society.** A society for collecting small contributions for charitable purposes. — **1822** *Missionary Herald* XVIII. 21 Female Mite So[ciety] for Cher[okee] and Choc[taw] missions [gave $]25. **1872** *Newton Kansan* 26 Sept. 3/2 The Mite Society will hold a ten cent sociable in the school room this Thursday evening. **1883** Wilder *Sister Ridnour* 262 We call upon certain poor, we attend the 'Dorcas,' the socials, the festivals, and mite societies.

***Mit(t).** A glove without fingers, or with very short ones, which covers the main part of the hand and sometimes extends to the elbow. {1765–}

1759 *Newport Mercury* 5 June 4/1 To be Sold, . . . Men's Shammy Gloves, Womens glaz'd gloves and Mitts. **1788** *Mass. Centinel* 30 April, A large quantity of silk Gloves, Mitts, and Fans. **1828** *Yankee* April 133/2 The flounces, the gown, the pelereens and the mits; they [the women] were in complete trim. **1879** *Harper's Mag.* Sept. 522 She tripped by to the store . . . her round arms covered with gray silk mitts reaching to the elbow. **1891** 'Thanet' *Otto the Knight* 97 There were diamonds and emeralds on her beautiful hands, sparkling through the meshes of her black silk mitts.

***Mitten,** *n.* Also †**mittin, mittain.**

***1. a.** A covering for the hand having a separate sheath for the thumb only. **b.** =Mit(t).

1644 *Conn. Rec.* I. 457 An Inuentory . . . of the goods of Blaynch Hunt . . . [includes] mittens & stockings. **1684** *Providence Rec.* VI. 123 One payre of Gloves, & one paire of mittins. **1722** *Mass. H. Rep. Jrnl.* III. 190, I caused to be given . . . a pair of Mittens . . . to each of the five Indians you sent. **1771** Winslow *Diary* (1894) 5, I intend to send Nancy Mackky a pair of lace mittens. **1794** *Ann. 3d Congress* 1472 There shall be levied . . . on gloves, mittens, stockings, fans, buttons, and buckles, of every kind, 5 per cent. ad valorem. **1862** Norton *Army Lett.* 124, I almost forgot the one-fingered mittens and everything else in both letters. **1905** Wiggin *Rose* 125 The boys fought for the privilege of dragging her sled up the hills, and filling her tiny mitten with peppermints. **1920** Sandburg *Smoke & Steel* 45 There ain't no law we got to wear mittens—huh—is there?

comb. **1869** *Boyd's Business Directory* 32 Glove and Mitten Manufacturers. Case Uriel, 116 Fulton.

2. a. *To get the mitten* {1884–}, to be rejected as a lover or suitor. *colloq.*

1844 Neal *Peter Ploddy* 14 Young gentlemen that have got the mitten, or young gentlemen who think they are going to get the mitten, always sythe [sigh]. **1867** 'Lackland' *Homespun* II. 181 He could tell you . . . who was likely to 'catch' this one, and who not long ago 'got the mitten' from that. **1880** *Scribner's Mo.* Jan. 428/2, I'll be darned if I haint got the mitten. **1891** Garland *Main-travelled Roads* (1922) 187 But he's goin' to get the mitten, that red-headed feller is, for I see another feller comin' up behind him.

transf. **1851** Hall *College Words* 209 At the Collegiate Institute of Indiana, a student who is expelled is said *to get the mitten*.

b. *To give the mitten*, to reject as a lover or suitor. *colloq.*

1847 *Knickerb.* July 94 What could have been the origin of the words, 'giving *the sack*' or '*the mitten*.' **1850** Mitchell *Lorgnette* I. 176 Dare say she will think I've given him the mitten. **1878** Cooke *Happy Dodd* 294 He took on so dreadful bad when you giv' him the mittin, Happy, that it kinder set me feelin' for him. **1894** Wilkins *Pembroke* 260, I wouldn't have a daughter of mine chasin' a fellar that had give her the mitten. **1902** Pidgin *S. Holton* 120 She was a great flirt, and jus' led the fellers on till they proposed to her, and then gave them the mitten.

fig. **1848** Lowell *Fable for Critics* 45 Here comes Dana, . . . Who'll be going to write what'll never be written Till the Muse, ere he thinks of it, gives him the mitten.

c. A rejection by a young lady of an offer of marriage. *colloq.*

1846 *Knickerb.* XXVII. 185 We do not affect the pinings of rejected suitors, in verse or prose. Ink is shed copiously for 'mittens' by many of our correspondents. **1871** Eggleston *Hoosier Schoolm.* 51 Young men were . . . trembling in mortal fear of 'the mitten.'

+**Mitten,** *v. tr.* To reject (someone) as a lover. *colloq.* — **1873** Carleton *Farm Ballads* (1882) 19 Once, when I was young as you, and not so smart, perhaps, For me she mittened a lawyer, and several other chaps. **1881** M. J. Holmes *Madeline* 114 When she mittened him, it almost took his life. He was too old for her, she said.

***Mixed,** *a.* +Special combinations.

Mixed breed, a crossbreed; *m. car, convention, currency*, (see quotations); *m. feed*, stock feed consisting of a mixture of corn, oats, wheat shorts, etc.; *m. forest*, (see quotation); *m. foursome*, a golf contest for two couples, each couple consisting of a man and a woman; *m. militia*, militia composed of both white men and Negroes; *m. theatrical*, (see quotation); *m. tomcod*, a variety of the tomcod or frostfish (*Microgadus tomcod*) having mixed coloring; *m. tribunal*, =Electoral Commission.

1838 *Mass. Agric. Survey 1st Rep.* 53, I have had some of the full-blood and some of the mixed breed. **1903** E. Johnson *Railway Transportation* 126 Oftentimes articles consigned to several places must be placed in the same car. Cars so loaded are called 'mixed' cars. **1902** E. C. Meyer *Nominating Systems* 15 There appeared in 1817 a new variation of our nominating machinery known as a 'mixed convention,' which was a popular convention of delegates from the counties in which the members of the legislature were to sit only in the absence of special envoys or delegates from their county. **1830** *Congress. Deb.* App. 29 March 100 A mixed currency of paper circulating with gold or silver . . . should always be exchangeable for gold and silver. **1892** *York County Hist. Rev.* 61 A fine line of fine family flour and mixed feed as well as home-made bread. **1905** *Forestry Bureau Bul.* No. 61, 15 *Mixed forest*, forest composed of trees of two or more species. **1895** *Outing* Monthly Rec. Dec. 47/2 Mixed foursomes at Brookline, on October 26, brought out fourteen couples in a handicap in which Miss W. E. Andrews and G. E. Cabot won. **1868** *N.Y. Herald* 17 July 5/2 The temper of the body is decidedly against . . . mixed militia. **1889** *Century Mag.* March 751/2 A new kind of amateur theatricals has in turn sprung up, called mixed theatricals, consisting of performances in which both professionals and amateurs take part. **1814** Mitchill *Fishes N.Y.* 369 *Gadus tomcodus mixtus*, or mixed tom cod; with yet other modifications of colours, and with variations in the rays of the fins. **1877** *Nation* XXIV. 79 The count began on Thursday at one o'clock, but the Presidential dispute was almost immediately transferred to the Mixed Tribunal, on the papers in the Florida case.

+**Mixed basis.** A basis for determining representation in Congress by taking into account the white population and amount of taxable property in a given state. *Obs.* (Cf. Federal number.) — **1830** *Va. Lit. Museum* 571/1 Mr. Doddridge moved to amend the amendment, by substituting for the federal number, the mixed basis of white population and taxation combined.

+**Mixed blood.** Descent from two or more races, as white and Indian, or white and Negro.

1817 S. Brown *Western Gaz.* 244 About one half of the Cherokee nation are of mixed blood by intermarriages with the white people. **1880** *Harper's Mag.* Dec. 31 In fact all four were of mixed blood, their mother having been a beautiful French quarter-breed and their father—William Douglas. **1899** Chesnutt *Wife of His Youth* 7, I have no race prejudice, . . . but we people of mixed blood are ground between the upper and the nether millstone.

b. A person of mixed blood. (Cf. Breed.)

1858 Thoreau *Maine Woods* 137 The two mixed-bloods . . . went off up the river. **1871** *Rep. Indian Affairs* (1872) 420 There are also connected with this agency about 20 families of mixed-bloods, individuals of almost all castes and grades. **1883** *Ib.* 73 The Osages number about 1,750, over 300 of whom are mixed bloods. **1916** Eastman *From Deep Woods* 121, I amputated the leg of a mixed blood.

+**Mixed-blooded,** *a.* Of mixed blood. — **1866** *39th Congress. 1 Sess.* Sen Ex. Doc. No. 26, 52 The committee have not discovered . . . that the mixed-blooded slave has been elevated in the moral virtues of the white race as he advanced toward it in color.

+**Mixed farming.** Farming carried on in conjunction with other pursuits of husbandry, as cattle-raising, fruit-growing, etc. — **1872** *Ill. Dept. Agric. Trans.* IX. 66 The majority of farmers, fruit-growers or others, generally succeed best by what is called mixed farming. **1876** *Ib.* XIII. 309 Wheat production, however valuable as a part of mixed farming, becomes excessively exhausting and impoverishing as a long continued staple. **1892** *Vt. Agric. Rep.* XII. 132 Our hill farms . . . produce better crops of wheat and oats, and are better adapted to mixed farming.

Mixed school. {1826–} +A school attended by white children and by colored ones. *Obs.* — **1868** *N.Y. Herald* 17 July 5/2 The temper of the body is decidedly against mixed schools. **1871** *Ann. Cycl. 1870* X. 457/1 [We] raise no questions about mixed schools.

+**Mixed ticket.** *Polit.* **1.** (See quot. 1871.) **2.** =Fusion ticket. — **(1) 1871** De Vere 270 *Sticker* is the familiar name of a candidate printed on a slip of paper with the back gummed, to be pasted over the name of another candidate by those who wish to vote a *split* ticket; the term originated in 1860 in Pennsylvania as a *mixed* ticket. **1872** *Chicago Tribune* 6 Nov. 1/6 Mixed tickets were more numerous than the unmixed, making the counting tedious, and the returns late in coming in. **1885** *Mag. Amer. Hist.* April 396/2 A 'Split ticket' represents different divisions of a party. A 'Mixed ticket' combines the nominees of different parties. **(2) 1872** *Newton Kansan* 10 Oct. 2/2 For our part we have rather favored a union or mixed ticket for our county officers.

Mixer. {1611–}

+**1.** One who mixes or prepares drinks.

1854 Longfellow *Poetical Works* (1893) 197/1 To the sewers and sinks With all such drinks, And after them tumble the mixer. **1902** Lorimer *Lett. Merchant* 236 Hired a fancy mixer to sling together mild snorts . . . for the ladies. **1919** T. K. Holmes *Man from Tall Timber* 93 [He] drank several insidious concoctions of the hotel's most famous 'mixer.'

2. A machine for mixing various things. {1876–}

1879 *Scribner's Mo.* Nov. 55/1 The charge of concrete . . . on being discharged from the mixer into an iron dumping cart. **1886** *Harper's Mag.* June 82/1 The pull of a lever raises the cask above the open mouth of the 'mixer.' **1898** *Congress. Rec.* App. 25 Jan. 223/1 They will run their flutter mills and mixers and dope the flour to suit themselves.

+**3.** A person of pleasing social qualities and affability of manner. Originally *a good mixer. colloq.*

1896 ADE *Artie* 105, I'm a good mixer. **1904** *N.Y. Ev. Post* 25 Nov. 7 As diplomacy is practised now, the really useful expert is the higher-bred 'mixer' whose good fellowship is his most conspicuous trait and who makes everybody like him and tell him the latest gossip. **1913** LA FOLLETTE *Autobiog.* 348 If pitted against brilliant talkers or good 'mixers' they might stand no show at all. **1925** *Scribner's Mag.* Sept. 249/1 He's a good mixer and a straight Republican.

Mixings. *pl.* +Materials for mixing drinks. *slang. Obs.* — **1862** LOWELL *Biglow P.* 2 Ser. i. 21 Le' 's liquor; Gin'ral, you can chalk our friend for all the mixins.

+**Mixologist.** A skilled mixer of drinks. *slang.* — **1856** *Knickerb.* XLVII. 615 Who ever heard of a man's . . . calling the barkeeper a mixologist of tipicular fixins? **1870** RAE *Westward by Rail* 201 The keeper of the 'White Pine Saloon' [at Elko, Nev.] informs his patrons that—'The most delicate fancy drinks are compounded by skilful mixologists in a style that captivates the public, and makes them happy.'

+**Mixture land.** (See quotation.) — **1859** HILLHOUSE tr. Michaux *Sylva* I. 169 In the district of Maine I have always found the Moose Wood most vigorous in mixed forests, or what are called *Mixture lands.*

Mobby. Also **mobbie, mobee.** {1638-} +The liquid, used as a beverage or for distilling, obtained by crushing apples or peaches: (see quot. 1871). Also attrib. — **1705** BEVERLEY *Virginia* IV. 699 Others make a Drink of them [*sc.* peaches], which they call Mobby, and either drink it as Cyder, or Distill it off for Brandy. This makes the best Spirit next to Grapes. **1800** BOUCHER *Glossary* p. xlix, *Mobbie;* the liquid, as first expressed from the fruit, and which is afterwards distilled, and thus becomes peach or apple brandy. **1871** DE VERE 507 *Mobee* or *Mobby* . . . is frequently applied in the South to what in England would be simply called a 'punch.'

Mobcap. A loose-fitting morning cap worn indoors by women. {1812-} — **1833** NEAL *Down-Easters* I. 151 Would you not wear a mob-cap, or say thee and thou, if it were the fashion? **1866** A. D. WHITNEY *L. Goldthwaite* xvi, Leslie Goldthwaite, in her mob-cap, quilted petticoat, [and] big-flowered calico train. **1894** *Harper's Mag.* July 221/1 That little shrivelled-up old woman in gray, with the mob-cap, is her picture here? **1907** *St. Nicholas* Oct. 1124/1 All the women's and children's hats, caps, and bonnets are started by making first the little mob cap.

+**Mobile terrapin.** [From *Mobile,* Ala.] =next. — **1882** [see next].

+**Mobilianer.** [From *Mobile,* Ala.] A fresh-water turtle (*Pseudemys Alabamensis*) of the South. — **1842** HOLBROOK *N.A. Herpetology* I. 74 [In] the New Orleans market . . . it is known under the name Mobilianer. **1882** *Nat. Mus. Bul.* No. 24, 6 *Pseudemys mobiliensis.* . . . Mobile terrapin; 'Mobilianer.' **1884** GOODE, etc. *Fisheries* I. 155 The 'Mobilianer' . . . is considered quite delicate, and is esteemed as food.

+**Mobil(l)ian.** A native or resident of Mobile, Alabama. — **1775** ADAIR *Indians* 318 [The Choctaws] killed the strolling French pedlars,—turned out against the Missisippi [*sic*] Indians and Mobillians. **1863** CUMMING *Hospital Life* (1866) 79/1 Refugeeing . . . is not the best thing in the world. But Mobilians will have to do as others have done before them. **1887** *Courier-Journal* 19 Jan. 6/1 Mobilians are jubilant over the new route cotton is taking, and have big hopes of an increase in the business.

‖**Mobite.** A member of a mob. — **1887** *Advance* 27 Oct. 674/2 The mobites, taking advantage of the opportunity offered for free discussion, came in and perverted the meeting.

Mob law. The law or rule exercised by a mob; lynch law. {1823-} —**1837** HAWTHORNE *Twice-told Tales* (1879) I. 126 Nothing saved Dominicus, either from mob law or a court of justice. **1853** 'MARK TWAIN' in *Hannibal Daily Journal* 26 May, A fellow who whips his wife . . . can be excused properly from a 'ride on a rail,' because 'cruelty to animals' is objectionable, and not because it would be 'mob-law.' **1858** DOUGLAS in Logan *Great Conspiracy* 73 To whom shall you appeal? To mob law, to partisan caucuses, to town meetings? **1887** *Courier-Journal* 7 May 4/2 Public sentiment has been awakened, and our people realize the evils of mob law.

Mob man. A member of a mob. *Obs.* — **1747** *N.J. Archives* 1 Ser. VII. 428 He discoursing with several of the mobmen, . . . has heard them [say] . . . that the King himself was unable to quell mobs in England. **1835** *Md. Hist. Reg.* IX. 160 You may see large companies of worthies marching to and fro, and a mob man, as such, cannot be seen.

+**Moccasin.** Also **mockasin, mogasheen, mockison.** [Algonquian.]

1. A soft-soled shoe, usually made of skin, of a type worn originally by American Indians. (Cf. INDIAN SHOE 1.)

1612 SMITH *Works* (1910) I. 44 *Mockasins.* Shooes. **1704** *N.H. Prov. Papers* III. 290*n.*, Every Householder . . . shall provide . . . one good pair of snow shoes and mogasheens. **1775** FITHIAN *Journal* II. 117 In these back woods . . . [men] wear Mockisons, or Indian's shoes. **1812** *Niles' Reg.* II. 383/2 The ladies having worked all Sunday to supply their husbands . . . with hunting shirts and moccasins. **1834** ARFWEDSON *United States* II. 207 [Guards at Sing Sing] wear on their feet mocassins, as they are called, which are shoes made of woollen yarn, so that their steps are never heard. **1883** *Rep. Indian Affairs* 174 An attack of pneumonia [was] brought on by wearing moccasins in wet weather. **1923** J. H. COOK *On Old Frontier* 167 One savage wore moccasins; the other had been barefoot.

b. *Moccasin Joe,* (see quotation).

1893 ROOSEVELT *Wilderness Hunter* 265 [The grizzly bear is] known to the few remaining old-time trappers of the Rockies and the Great Plains . . . as 'Moccasin Joe' . . . in allusion to his queer, half-human footprints, which look as if made by some misshapen giant, walking in moccasins.

2. =MOCCASIN SNAKE.

1784 SMYTH *Tour* I. 148 The more silent and dangerous moccossons also abound, especially in and near the swamps. **1846** in *Tall Tales of S.W.* (1930) 318 [The Irishman] would have given long odds in favor of a Stock Creek gouging, rather than face an 18 inch moccasin with 'bells on his tail,' as he termed rattles. **1851** *Polly Peablossom* 69 She got onto the whappinest, biggest, rustiest yaller moccasin. **1855** SIMMS *Forayers* 549 [Have I] had the happiness to eat of the rattlesnake, the viper, the moccasin, or the boa-constrictor? **1907** MULFORD *Bar-20* 194, I don't want to go swimmin' in no creek full of moccasins.

3. A sleight-of-hand game resembling thimblerig played by American Indians. In full *moccasin game. Obs.*

1833 CATLIN *Indians* I. 88 Groups [of Indians] are engaged in games of the 'moccasin,' or the 'platter.' **1847** LANMAN *Summer in Wilderness* 123 The younger Indians commenced playing their favorite Moccasin game. **1892** *Amer. Notes & Q.* VIII. 293 The game called Moccasin . . . was played by the use of three moccasins . . . together with the use of three leaden balls. The game was to shuffle the leaden balls and cover more than one ball with one moccasin and have it appear that each moccasin had a ball under it, when really one or more moccasins had no ball under it. This made a game of gambling among the Indians.

4. Attrib. and comb. in sense 1 with *foot, making,* etc.

1841 COOPER *Deerslayer* xxx, If he escape, blood will be in your moccasin-prints from this spot to the Canadas. **1846** SAGE *Scenes Rocky Mts.* xiii, We were variously occupied in hunting, root-digging, and moccasin-making. **1873** MILLER *Amongst Modocs* 186 He had . . . fastened his moccasin-strings over, and then dashed ahead without a word. **1899** JEWETT *Queen's Twin* 5 The old folks say that there used to be a place across a ledge where they'd worn a deep track with their moccasin feet.

+**Moccasin awl.** An awl used in making moccasins. *Obs.* — **1757** *Lett. to Washington* II. 80 Mocoson Auls . . . 16, Pounds of Thread . . . 8. **1799** J. SMITH *Acct. Captivity* 64 All the surgical instruments I had, was a knife, a mockason awl, and a pair of bullit moulds. **1806** CLARK in *Lewis & C. Exped.* V. (1905) 32 The Chopunnish . . . seem anxious always to riceve articles of utility, such as knives, axes, Kittles, blankets & mockerson awls.

+**Moccasined,** *a.*

1. Clad or encased in a moccasin.

1829 COOPER *Wish-ton-Wish* xxiv, The two chiefs left the piazza in the noiseless manner of the moccasined foot. **1845** *Knickerb.* XXV. 200 He had seen the tracks of many moccasined feet in the fresh snow beyond. *a*1861 T. WINTHROP *Canoe & Saddle* 9, I have offered indignities to the person of royalty with a moccasined toe. **1883** ZEIGLER & GROSSCUP *Alleghanies* 288 The other aborigines . . . were, with moccasined feet, threading their ways through the crowds. **1905** *N.Y. Ev. Post* 26 Aug., The lightest tread of moccasined feet starts echoes reverberating through the forests.

2. (See quotations.) *slang. Obs.*

1859 BARTLETT 275 *Moccasoned,* intoxicated. South Carolina. **1871** DE VERE 35 In the South a man made drunk by bad liquor is said to have been 'bitten by the [moccasin] snake,' or simply to be *mocassined.*

+**Moccasin flower.** Any of various American orchids, as *Fissipes acaulis,* or any American species of *Cypripedium.*

1700 PLUKENET *Opera Bot.* III. 101 *Helleborine Virginiana.* . . . The Molkasin Flower. **1705** BEVERLEY *Virginia* II. 24 Of spontaneous Flowers they have . . . the Cardinal-Flower, . . . the Moccasin Flower, and a Thousand others. **1784** CUTLER in *Mem. Academy* I. 486 Lady's Slipper. . . . Catesby says, the flowers of this plant . . . were in great esteem with the Indians for decking their hair. They called it the Moccasin Flower. **1841** *Knickerb.* March 245 What a gorgeous wreath could I now weave . . . [of] the blue larchspur, the moccasin-flower [etc.]. **1881** *Harper's Mag.* Dec. 80/2 All who love the hemlock woods will remember the common cypripedium or moccasin flower, also called lady's-slipper. **1907** *N.Y. Ev. Post* (s.-w. ed.) 27 June 6 The moccasin flower, the wild orchid, bloomed on this mountain.

+**Moccasin plant.** =MOCCASIN FLOWER. — **1850** S. F. COOPER *Rural Hours* 111 We found also a little troop of moccasin plants in flower.

+**Moccasin ranger.** (See quot. 1866.) *Obs.* — **1862** *N.Y. Tribune* 3 June 5/1 This country [of the Alleghenies] is rife with stories . . . of the strength and exploits of the 'Moccasin Rangers.' **1863** Moore *Rebellion Rec.* V. I. 6 The town of Burning Springs, in West County, Western Virginia, was burned by a party of guerrillas known as the Moccasin Rangers. **1866** 'F. KIRKLAND' *Bk. Anecdotes* 406 Among the rebel guerrilla organizations, the most noted band was that known by the name of 'Moccasin Rangers.'

+**Moccasin snake.** Any one of various pit vipers of the genus *Agkistrodon,* esp. *A. piscivorus.* Also applied to other snakes that have a superficial resemblance to serpents of this genus. — **1784** FILSON *Kentucke* 27 Serpents [include] . . . except the bull, the horned and the mockason snakes. **1826** FLINT *Recoll.* 318 The swamps, . . . are occupied by the cypress, . . . by alligators, and moccasin snakes, and musquitoes. **1852** STOWE *Uncle Tom* xxxii, Ever and anon the loathsome form of the moccasin snake might be seen sliding among broken stumps and shattered branches. **1904** M. D. CONWAY *Autobiog.* 12 A meadow we had to cross was the haunt of moccasin snakes.

+**Moccasin track.** The track or footprint of one wearing moccasins. — **1725** *Lancaster Rec.* 238 In the morning we found a mogerson tracke, and spent some time scouting after sd Tracke. **1775** Rauck *Boonesborough* 237 [They] could make no other discovery than two Moccasin tracks. **1845** HOOPER *Taking Census* 179, I kin whip any pocket-knife lawyer that ever made a moccasin track. **1865** PIKE *Scout & Ranger* (1932) 77 Moccasin tracks were plenty at the spring where they supposed I would go into camp.

+**Mochila.** Also **machilla.** [Sp.] = MACHEER. — **1856** *Harper's Mag.* Oct. 594/1 He rode a heavy black mule with bearskin *machillas.* **1862** HARTE *Luck of Roaring Camp* 210 The curves of beauty were concealed by the cumbrous *machillas* of the Spanish saddle, which levels all equine distinctions. **1900** DRANNAN *Plains & Mts.* 167 A measly redskin shot me through the calf of my leg, pinning me to the mochila of my saddle. **1913** G. D. BRADLEY *Story of Pony Express* 58 The *mochila* had four pockets called *cantinas* in each of its corners.

***Mock,** *a.* In popular or colloquial names of plants that resemble or suggest those to which the unmodified name is appropriate. (See also MOCK ORANGE.) — **1790** *Amer. Philos. Soc.* III. 234 This poisonous herb [is] called by the names of Wild-Carrot, Wild Parsnep, Fever-Root, and Mock-Eel-Root. **1815** DRAKE *Cincinnati* 78 The botanical resources [include] . . . *Hydrangea frutescens,* Mock snow ball. **1883** *Century Mag.* Sept. 643/1 In favored spots is seen the mock-cranberry's red-berried creeping vine. **1893** *Amer. Folk-Lore* VI. 138 *Silene Armeria,* mock sweet William, S. Indiana.

+**Mockbird.** = MOCKING BIRD.

1649 *Desc. Virginia* 15 We have . . . one Bird we call the Mock-bird; for he will imitate all other Birds notes. **c1729** CATESBY *Carolina* I. 28 *Turdus ruffus.* The Fox coloured Thrush. . . . This Bird is called in Virginia the French Mock-bird. . . . It sings with some variety of Notes, though not comparable to the Mockbird. **1791** W. BARTRAM *Travels* 11 Harbours and groves . . . filled with the melody of the chearful mockbird, warbling nonpareil. **1832** WILLIAMSON *Maine* I. 149 The Thrasher, or Mockbird; and . . . the Robin, are species of the Thrush family. **1917** *Birds of Amer.* III. 175 Mockingbird. . . . [Also called] Mock bird.

***Mocker.** + = MOCKING BIRD. — [**1773** *Phil. Trans.* LXIII. 286 From the attention which the mocker pays to any . . . sort of disagreeable noise, these capital notes would be always debased.] **1841** COOPER *Deerslayer* xxv, She's a noble gal, . . . [with] a voice that's as pleasant as a mocker's. **1886** *Century Mag.* Jan. 435/2 Ef a gal puts on a man's hat when she hears a mocker sing at night, she'll git married that year. **1917** *Birds of Amer.* III. 176/2 The Mocker is more or less a buffoon, but those who look upon him only as an imitator or clown have much to learn of his wonderful originality.

+**Mockernut.** Short for MOCKERNUT HICKORY; also, the nut of this. — **1814** PURSH *Flora Amer.* II. 638 *Juglans tomentosa.* . . . This is known under the name of Mocker Nut, White-heart Hickory or Common Hickory. **1832** BROWNE *Sylva* 188 The kernel is . . . difficult to extract, on account of the strong partitions which divide it; hence, probably, is derived the name of Mockernut. **1843** TORREY *Flora N.Y.* II. 182 White-heart Hickory. Mocker-nut. . . . Fertile moist woods; frequent. **1894** COULTER *Bot. W. Texas* III. 411 *Hicoria alba.* (Mocker-nut. White-heart hickory.) . . . Extending to the valley of the Brazos.

+**Mockernut hickory.** A species of hickory, *Carya alba.* — **1810** MICHAUX *Arbres* I. 20 *Mocker nut hickery* . . . dans N.Y. et N.J. **1832** BROWNE *Sylva* 187 In the parts of New Jersey which lie on the river Hudson, this species is known by the name of Mocker nut Hickory. **1871** *Ill. Agric. Soc. Trans.* VIII. 206 The Mocker-nut and Pig-nut hickories are common, but not much valued.

+**Mocking bird.** Any one of various American birds having an aptitude for mimicry, esp. *Mimus polyglottos,* found chiefly in the eastern and southern parts of the U.S.

Cf. FRENCH, GROUND MOCKING BIRD.

1676 GLOVER *Acct. Va.* in *Phil. Trans.* XI. 631 As to the Mocking-bird, besides his own natural notes, which are many and pleasant, he imitateth all the birds in the woods. **1698** THOMAS *Acct. Pensilvania* 13 That strange and remarkable fowl, call'd (in these Parts) the Mocking-Bird, that Imitates all sorts of Birds. **1709** LAWSON *Carolina* 143 The Mocking-Bird is about as big as a Throstle in England, but longer. **1744** MOORE *Voy. Georgia* 117 There are also great numbers of small birds, . . . the mocking bird, which sings sweetly, and the rice bird. **1821** NUTTALL *Travels Arkansa* 158 For the first time in my life, . . . [I] hearkened to the inimitable notes of the mocking-bird. **1877** H. C. HODGE *Arizona* 223 The most common of the birds of Arizona are . . . mocking birds, pelicans, herons, . . . and numerous quantities of vultures. **1917** *Birds of Amer.* III. 176/1 The Mockingbird stands unrivaled. He is the king of song.

b. (See quotation.) *humorous.*

1890 *Stock Grower & Farmer* 19 July 4/4 Arizona Nightingale: Otherwise 'burro,' sometimes termed 'mockingbird.'

+**Mocking thrush.** Any bird of the subfamily Miminae, esp. a thrasher. Also with defining term.

1839 AUDUBON *Ornith. Biog.* V. 336 Townsend's mocking thrush . . . [is] cinereous brown above, whitish below, with a long rounded tail. **1847** EMERSON *Poems* 144 A mocking thrush, a wild-rose, a rock-loving columbine, Salve my worst wounds. **1873** *Amer. Naturalist* VII. 329 [Illustration of] Bendire's Mocking-thrush (natural size). **1880** *Harper's Mag.* June 74 A 'mocking-thrush' he is indeed, for he mimics his own song from morn till night in all the thickets and pasture-lands. **1917** *Birds of Amer.* III. 175 Mockingbird. . . . [Also called] Mocking Thrush.

+**Mocking wren. 1.** = CAROLINA WREN. **2.** Bewick's wren, *Thryomanes bewicki.* — (1) **1874** BAIRD, etc. *Hist. N. Amer. Land Birds* I. 142 The great Carolina or Mocking Wren, is found in all the Southeastern and Southern States from Florida to Maryland. **1876** GENTRY *Life-Hist. Birds E. Penna.* I. 74 *Thryothorus ludovicianus* . . . is commonly surnamed the Mocking Wren from its remarkable powers of mimicry. **1917** *Birds of Amer.* III. 189. (2) **1890** *Cent.* 3811/1 *Mocking-wren,* . . . Bewick's wren (*T[hryothorus] bewicki*).

Mock orange. {1731–}

+**1.** The laurel cherry, *Laurocerasus caroliniana.*

[**1766** STORK in J. Bartram *Journal* 9n., There is an evergreen sort of this Bird or Cluster-cherry, which grows about 30 feet high in S. Carolina, and from the beauty of its evergreen shining leaves is called the Mock-orange.] **1860** CURTIS *Woody Plants N.C.* 57 Mock Orange. . . . It is very extensively cultivated about houses, either singly or as borders and hedges. **1893** *Amer. Folk-Lore* VI. 140 *Prunus Caroliniana,* mock-orange; wild peach. Southern States.

2. Any shrub of the genus *Philadelphus;* a syringa. {1731–}

1785 MARSHALL *Amer. Grove* 99 Syringa, or Mock Orange. **1832** S. J. HALE *Flora* 174 Carolina Syringa. . . . This species of the mock Orange is native of the Southern States. **1858** WARDER *Hedges & Evergreens* 46 The most rapid growth for a tall screen will be furnished by the mock-orange . . . , which bears a profusion of showy white flowers. **1891** COULTER *Bot. W. Texas* I. 108.

+**3.** The Osage orange, *Maclura pomifera.*

1814 BRACKENRIDGE *Views La.* 59 There is particularly one very beautiful [tree], bois jaune, or yellow wood: by some called the mock orange. **1897** SUDWORTH *Arborescent Flora* 190 *Toxylon pomiferum.* Osage Orange. . . . [Commonly called] Mock Orange (La.).

4. Any gourd that resembles an orange.

1842 *Lowell Offering* II. 68 There were apples, pears, melons, a mock-orange, a pumpkin, and a crooked cucumber. **1892** *Amer. Folk-Lore* V. 96 *Lagenaria sp.,* mock orange. N. Ohio; Central Ill.

5. The snowbell, *Styrax grandifolia.*

1860 CURTIS *Woody Plants N.C.* 101 Mock Orange. . . . A very beautiful shrub.

6. The shaddock, *Citrus maxima.*

1868 *Rep. Comm. Agric. 1867* 142 The Shaddock . . . is called . . . sometimes in this country Mock-orange, or Forbidden Fruit.

+**Mocock.** [Of Algonquian origin.] A basket or box, frequently made of birch bark, used as a container for maple sugar. — **1822** MORSE *Rep. Indian Affairs* I. 55 A Mocock of sugar, weighing about forty pounds is received for four skins. **1841** STEELE *Summer Journey* 110 Indian articles . . . are made by these poor people and sold here. Among them were small baskets called Mococks, made of birch bark embroidered with porcupine quills, stained different colors—this was filled with maple sugar. **1891** WELCH *Recoll. 1830–40* 115 Bartering tobacco . . . for their smoke-tanned deer skins, . . . baskets, mococks of maple sugar. **1905** *N.Y. Ev. Post* 6 May, An old squaw stopped to offer a small mocock, a birch-bark box, holding perhaps a pound of maple sugar.

***Mode.** = ALAMODE. *Obs.* {1766–} — **1762** *Newport Mercury* 7 Sept. 3/2 To be sold By Gideon, John & Edward Wanton . . . yellow grogorons, black figured mode. **1775** in Singleton *Social N.Y.* 247 Henry Wilmot, in Hanover Square, sells . . . a great variety of ribbons, persians, modes, sarsinets [etc.]. **1784** *Mass. Centinel* 21 July 4/2 William Gray Has For Sale, . . . Lawn Handkerchiefs, Modes, Cambricks [etc.].

* **Moderator.**

+**1.** A person selected to preside over a town meeting.

1640 in Coffin *Hist. Newbury* 20 There shall be a moderator chosen by the companie. **1698** SEWALL *Diary* I. 474 Anniversary Town-Meeting. . . . I being present, am chosen Moderator. **1723** *New-Eng. Courant* 11–18 March 2/2 Monday . . . being the Annual Town-Meeting for chusing Town-Officers for the Year ensuing, Elisha Cook Esq; was chose Moderator for that Meeting. **1733** LYNDE *Diary* 138 Town meeting; I chose moderator by written votes. **1825** NEAL *Bro. Jonathan* I. 165 The town meeting was opened with prayer. That over, a chairman or moderator, as they called him, there, was chosen. **1888** BRYCE *Amer. Commw.* II. II. xlviii. 227 The Meeting . . . is presided over by a chairman called the Moderator. **1905** *Providence Journal* 8 March 4 The annual town meeting of the town of Seekonk was called to order Monday by Town Clerk Hill, who announced that the first business before the meeting was the election of a Moderator.

+**2.** *Hist.* One of those who opposed the South Carolina Regulators (1767–69). Cf. REGULATOR.

1769 in Gregg *Hist. Old Cheraws* (1867) 182 A new set of people, who call themselves Moderators, have appeared against the Regulators.

+**b.** In Texas and elsewhere, an illegal and often criminal group organized to oppose a band of regulators.

1847 A. W. ARRINGTON (*title*), The Desperadoes of the South-West: Containing an Account of the Cane Hill Murderers, Together with the Lives of Several of the Most Notorious Regulators and Moderators of

That Region. **1853** 'P. Paxton' *Yankee in Texas* 324 A counter party is got up, nominally to keep the regulators in check. The last formed parties are called moderators, and invariably contain all the spare rascals in the county. **1855** J. Reynolds *My Own Times* 114 In the counties of Manac and Pope [Ill.] in the year 1846 . . . the citizens were kept in constant alarm and excitement by the two organized parties, known as 'Regulators,' and 'Moderators.' **1872** Morrell *Flowers & Fruits* 187 Another body of men was soon organized, to oppose the extreme measures of the Regulators, and these were called *Moderators*. **1889** Bancroft *Hist. No. Mexican States & Texas* II. 355 A society which styled itself the Moderators was organized, and a kind of vendetta warfare was carried on [with the so-called Regulators] for three years.

*__Modesty.__ **1.** An annual herb (*Bupleurum rotundifolium*) introduced into the United States from Europe. **2.** (See quotation.) — (1) **1843** Torrey *Flora N.Y.* I. 266 *Bupleurum rotundifolium*. . . . Thorough-wax. Modesty. . . . A weed about gardens and cultivated grounds; nearly naturalized in some places. June–August. **1884** W. Miller *Plant-Names* 87 Modesty of N. America, *Bupleurum rotundifolium*. (2) **1909** *Cent. Suppl.* 818/3 *Modesty*, . . . the bladder-ketmia or flower-of-an-hour, *Hibiscus Trionum*.

Modiste. A person, usually a woman, who makes women's clothes. {1852-} — **1840** *Knickerb.* XV. 387 'Modestes' [*sic*] made frocks and bonnets of the freshest patterns, for the girls. **1882** 'M. Harland' *Eve's Daughters* 320 Madame Demorest, the celebrated modiste and fashionist of New York. **1903** Burnham *Jewel* 46 Her costume was fresh from the modiste. **1911** Lincoln *Cap'n Warren's Wards* 171 In the windows above them doctors' signs alternated with those of modistes, manicures, artistes, and milliners.

+**Modoc.** [Amer. Ind. *Môatokni* 'southerners.'] An Indian of a small tribe formerly occupying a portion of the California and Oregon frontier; in pl., the tribe itself. Also *Modoc Indian*. — **1873** *Newton Kansan* 15 May 2/2 Another fight recently took place between the Modocs and a company of soldiers. **1874** B. F. Taylor *World on Wheels* I. xv. 115 Modocs seem to be excepted from any general plan of salvation but the *Quaker* plan. **1898** *Kansas City Star* 18 Dec. 4/1 The bill contains . . . items . . . for the support and civilization of the Modoc Indians. **1909** *Indian Laws & Tr.* III. 387 The Secretary of the Interior . . . is . . . directed to restore to the rolls of the Klamath Agency . . . those Modoc Indians now enrolled at the Quapaw Agency.

*__Mogul.__ +(See quotations.) — **1883** Knight *Suppl.* 613/2 The *Mogul* is generally accepted as a type of engine especially adapted to the economical working of heavy-freight traffic. **1898** *Boston Transcript* 21 June 3/6 Engines weighing eighty tons, called 'Moguls,' have long been in successful operation.

*__Mohair.__ Also †**mohaire.** A fine dress fabric made originally of the hair of the Angora goat, but later usually of a mixture of wool and cotton.

1666 *Essex Inst. Coll.* XXV. 146 A peece of mohaire & 4 yrds of holland. **1726** *New-Eng. Courant* 5–12 March 2/2 Edward Carter . . . Dyes and scowers . . . Mohairs, Poplins, Sasnets, . . . white Sasnet Hoods. **1776** *N.J. Archives* 2 Ser. I. 196 An assortment of dry goods, . . . among which are . . . paper boxes, wool cards, mohair and buttons. **1889** *Nat. Mus. Rep. 1886* II. 652 Fabrics in . . . the U.S. National Museum . . . [include] Mohair, . . . mummy cloth [etc.]. **1902** *Dept. Agric. Yrbk. 1901* 277 The durability of mohair and mohair manufactures is well known to those who are familiar with their use.

b. Attrib. with *button, overcoat, petticoat.*

1692 *Conn. Probate Rec.* I. 492, I also give to my daughter . . . my mohaire petticoat and my silk Cloak. **1721** *Mass. Col. Soc. Publ.* VI. 190 They are in 2 Trunks; Mohair Buttons, Stuffs, Silk sowing, &c. **1840** *Picayune* 28 July 3/5 Drab, olive, mohair and pilot cloth Overcoats . . . plain and ribbed cassimere d[itt]o.

Mohaicks. Variant of Mowhackees.

+**Moharra, Mojarra.** [Sp.] Any fish of the family Gerridæ, or one that is similar in appearance to these. — **1845** Storer in *Amer. Acad. Mem.* ns. II. 336 Gerres brasilianus . . . [is] called, at Porto Rico, 'Moharra.' **1884** in Goode, etc. *Fisheries* I. 276 The names 'Minny,' 'Sparada,' and 'Moharra' are also applied to the smaller species [of the surf-fish family]. *Ib.* 279 The Moharra family—Gerridæ . . . is represented on our eastern coast by four species. **1896** Jordan & Evermann *Check-List Fishes* 391 The Mojarras . . . [frequent the] Atlantic Coast of America from Carolina to Brazil, north to Long Island.

+**Mohave, Mojave.** Also †**Mohahve.** [From native name.] An Indian of a numerous and warlike tribe found along the Colorado River; in pl., occas., the tribe. In full *Mohave Indian.* Also attrib.

1845 Frémont *Exped.* 260 He had been found by a party of Mohahve (sometimes called *Amuchaba*) Indians. **1859** *Harper's Mag.* Oct. 695/2 In New Mexico the Mohave Indians have again broken out into open hostilities. *Ib.*, A fight ensued, the Mohaves charging with desperate bravery to within ten or fifteen yards of the soldiers. **1872** McClellan *Golden State* 75 On his way, at the Mohave settlements on the Colorado, all the party except Smith and two others were killed by the Indians. **1887** *Century Mag.* May 44/2 Pigments . . . are eagerly sought for temporary personal ornamentation, the Yumas and Mojaves even descending to stove-polish. **1907** Hodge, etc. *Amer. Indians* I. 920 Though a river tribe, the Mohave made no canoes, but when necessary had recourse to rafts, or balsas, made of bundles of reeds.

+**Mohawk,** *n.* Also **Mowhack, Mowhak, Moohag.** [From a native word. Cf. Narraganset *Mohowaùuck* 'they eat (animate) things.']

1. An Indian of the most easterly tribe of the Iroquois confederation, first encountered by Europeans in the Lake Champlain region; occas., also, in pl. and in sing., the tribe itself.

1634 Wood *New Eng. Prospect* II. i. 49 The very name of a Mowhack would strike the heart of a poore Abergenian dead. **1651** *Plymouth Col. Rec.* II. 169 A request was made the last winter by a messenger from the French at Canada to assist them against the Mowhakes. **1716** Church *Philip's War* 19 The Moohags made a descent upon him and killed many of his Men. **1751** *N.J. Archives* 1 Ser. VII. 598 The Susquahannah Indians only want leave from the Mohawks whom they call their Fathers in order to their accepting of a missionary. **1825** Neal *Bro. Jonathan* I. 101 The Mohawks were a terrible race of Indians; a tribe, of whom all the other savages were afraid. **1907** Hodge, etc. *Amer. Indians* I. 921/2 Like the Oneida, the Mohawk have only 3 clans.

transf. **1911** Harrison *Queed* 15 Eight sharp at the same place.—Go on you fat Mohawk you!

2. The language of the Mohawk Indians.

1754 Edwards *Works* (1808) V. 219 The question is not, whether what is said be . . . Latin, French, English or *Mohawk?* **1787** *Mohawk Prayer Bk.* t.-p., A new edition, to which is added the Gospel according to St. Mark, translated into Mohawk by Captn. Joseph Brant, an Indian of the Mohawk Nation.

3. Attrib. in sense 1 with *Indian, king,* etc.

1766 Rogers *Ponteach* II. i, The powerful Mohawk King Will ne'er consent to fight against the English. **1775** *Jrnls. Cont. Congress* III. 365 The Commissioners for transacting Indian Affairs . . . [shall] be desired to obtain from the Mohawk Indians, and the corporation of Albany, a state of the controversy between them. **1787** Mohawk nation [see sense 2]. **1870** M. H. Smith *20 Years Wall St.* 391 That is Vanderbilt, a tall, lithe, clerical looking gentleman, with nearly eighty winters upon him, yet erect as a Mohawk warrior.

b. In the names of plants. Also possessive.

1677 *Phil. Trans.* XII. 1065 In the pure Northerly parts, they have a peculiar kind called *Mohauks* Corn, which though planted in June, will be ripe in season. **1849** Emmons *Agric. N.Y.* II. 280 Early Mohawk bean. **1900** Munn *Uncle Terry* 157, I lost my boat over back here on the shore, and have had a cheerful time among the Mohawk briers.

+**Mohawking.** Masquerading as a Mohawk Indian. *Obs.* — **1825** Neal *Bro. Jonathan* I. 227 Does he ever go out 'a mohawking'? Peters alluded to a fashion—when a 'tory' was to be tarred and feathered . . . the people did it in the disguise of Indians. *Ib.* 229 Some loitering rascal who has been out a Mohawking, today.

‖**Mohawkism.** The quality of being a Mohawk; brutality. — **1855** *Chicago Times* 13 March 3/1 That new implement in modern Mohawkism brass Knuckles.

+**Mohican.** Also **Mohegin, Mohegan,** etc. [Of native origin.]

1. An Indian of an Algonquian tribe formerly living chiefly along the lower Connecticut River; in pl., occas., the tribe itself.

1660 *Mass. H. S. Coll.* 4 Ser. VII. 545 Two Mohegins . . . doe liue as seruants vnto mee for planting corne, cutting wood, &c. **1677** Hubbard *Indian Wars* 50 An hundred and fifty Mohegins, ready fixed to war on the Behalf of the English against the Narhagansets their mortal Enemies. **1722** Sewall *Letter-Book* II. 142 The Mohegins are as much a distant Nation from your English Inhabitants, as our Eastern Indians are from us. **1788** *Mass. H. S. Coll.* 2 Ser. X. 86 They, as well as the tribe at New London, are by the Anglo-Americans, called Mohegans. **1804** *Ib.* 1 Ser. IX. 75, I have nothing to add, respecting the present state of the Moheagans. **1823** Cooper *Pioneers* vii, The principal tribes . . . were, the Mahicanni, Mohicans, or Mohegans, and the Nanticokes, or Nentigoes. **1841** Trumbull *Autobiog.* 6 A small remnant of the Mohegans still exists, and they are sacredly protected in the possession and enjoyment of their favorite domain on the banks of the Thames.

transf. **1829** Royall *Pennsylvania* I. 9 Gen. E. was a Bostonian, and had now in his possession the bowl in which the punch was made presented as a treat to the Mohicans (as they were called) who threw the tea overboard, at Boston. **1913** London *Valley of Moon* 118 You're a Mohegan with a scalplock.

2. *The last of the Mohicans,* the final representatives or survivors of a noble race or class, in allusion to the title of J. F. Cooper's well-known novel.

1913 London *Valley of Moon* 155 D'ye know what we are?—we old white stock that fought in the wars, an' broke the land, an' made all this? I'll tell you. We're the last of the Mohegans.

3. Attrib. with *councilor, language, tomahawk,* etc.

1647 in Shepard *Clear Sunshine* 26 The Mohegan Counseller . . . is counted the wisest Indian in the Country. **1751** Gist *Journals* 49 You send for one of Your Friends that can speak the Mohickon or the Mingoe Tongues well. **1804** *Mass. H. S. Coll.* 1 Ser. IX. 75 The present number of the Moheagan tribe, situated between Norwich and New-London.

1832 WILLIAMSON *Maine* I. 459 That spoken by the Pawkunawkutts and the natives westward of them, is supposed to be the original *Mohegan* language. **1880** CABLE *Grandissimes* 25 The year 1682 saw a humble 'black gown' dragging and splashing his way . . . through the swamps of Louisiana, . . . backed by French carbines and Mohican tomahawks.

Moidore. Also †**moyder.** Either of two Portuguese gold coins current during the eighteenth century: **a.** A coin of 4.93 grams of fine gold. **b.** The double of this coin. {*c*1711-} — **1710** *Essex Inst. Coll.* LVI. 283 Staford Webber is . . . Cred. By a moyder gold, 2 li. **1749** FRANKLIN *Writings* II. 379, I send you also a moidore enclosed, which please to accept towards chaise hire. **1775** BURNABY *Travels* 137 [In Boston] they fabricate beaver-hats, which they sell for a moidore a piece. **1891** WELCH *Recoll. 1830–40* 168 The gold coins most popular in circulation were . . . *Moidores*, $6.00.

***Moisten,** *v.* +*intr.* To take a drink of liquor. Also *to moisten up. slang.* — **1851** *Alta Californian* 10 Aug., With his usual generous courtesy, 'Come, gents, let us moisten.' **1863** 'E. KIRKE' *Southern Friends* iii 46 You shall 'moisten up' at the doctor's.

Moke. {1848-} +**1.** A Negro. *slang.* +**2.** *College slang.* (See quotation.) — (**1**) **1856** C. WHITE *Oh, Hush!* 9 Rose, don't you interfere, I'll show dis moke a sight. **1875** *Scribner's Mo.* Nov. 142/1 'See here! my lively moke,' said he, 'you sling on too much style!' **1882** PECK *Sunshine* 53 They want to hear old fashioned negro melodies, and yet these mokes will tackle Italian opera. (**2**) **1900** *Dialect Notes* II. 46 *Moke.* 1. An easy-going fellow; one in the habit of asking favors. 2. A moderate bore. Tu[fts College, Mass.].

* **Molasses.** Also †**mollasses, molossus.**

1. * **a.** A dark, uncrystallized fluid obtained as a by-product in the manufacture of sugar. +**b.** A sweet syrup prepared by boiling down to a desired consistency any one of various vegetable juices or saps, particularly that of sugar cane. (Cf. MAPLE MOLASSES.)

'The word is now rare in British use' (*O.E.D.*). In the U.S. *molasses* has entirely supplanted *treacle*.

1666 SANFORD *Letter Book* 22 His desiere is tht by him yo would Send him five or Sixe Barrl of Rume as many of mollasses. **1701** WOLLEY *Journal N.Y.* (1902) 40 Molossus [is worth] three pence a pound, and fifty shillings a barrel in winter, that being the dearest season. **1777** CUTLER in *Life & Corr.* I. 63 Boiled some cornstalk juice into molasses. **1827** *Western Mo. Rev.* I. 84 The molasses is calculated to pay the plantation expenses and to leave the sugar net profit. **1867** EDWARDS *Shelby* 512 Broadwell gave him flour and bacon, sugar, salt, and molasses. **1925** TILGHMAN *Dugout* 21 The meal was ready; hot biscuits, coffee, molasses and meat.

transf. **1902** G. C. EGGLESTON *D. South* 136 [He advised] Arthur to have a tobacco lot cut before a rain should come to wash off the 'molasses'—as the thick gum on a ripening tobacco leaf was called.

2. *attrib.* and *comb.* **a.** Denoting foods or drinks in the preparation of which molasses is used.

See also MOLASSES CAKE, CANDY, GINGERBREAD.

1790 S. DEANE *New-Eng. Farmer* 23/1 Molasses Beer according to a method said to be practised in Philadelphia. 'Take five pounds of molasses [etc.].' **1879** HOWELLS *Lady of Aroostook* 182 Our farmer and his men stay themselves with nothing stronger than molasses-water. **1887** ALDEN *Little Fishers* xxi, [On shelves] were displayed tempting pans of ginger cookies, dough-nuts, molasses cookies, and soft gingerbread.

b. Denoting containers used for molasses.

See also MOLASSES BARREL, MOLASSES JUG.

1833 B. SILLIMAN *Man. Sugar Cane* 45, 18 inches below the tops of the cisterns . . . are the molasses cisterns, . . . made of strong four inch cypress plank, well keyed together. **1834** NOTT *Novellettes* I. 79 He was in a molasses cask. **1851** MELVILLE *Moby Dick* 116 Have an eye to the molasses tierce, Mr. Stubb. **1863** 'G. HAMILTON' *Gala-Days* 76 [He] came back with a molasses-hogshead. **1905** WIGGIN *Rose* 78 The storekeeper hung the molasses pail over Rose's right arm.

+**c.** Special collocations.

Molasses gate, (see quotation); *m. house*, a building in which molasses is made; *m. shook*, a stave of a kind used in making barrels or hogsheads for molasses; *m. stew*, a molasses candy pulling.

1875 KNIGHT 1458/2 *Molasses-gate*, a faucet with a sliding lip at the discharge end, to cut off the flow positively and prevent drip. **1864** *Ill. Agric. Soc. Trans.* V. 317 A near neighbor of mine, . . . and his two sons, have a neat molasses house, with an engine to run the crushing mill. **1820** *Columbian Centinel* 1 Jan. 3/1 Isaac Winslow & Co. . . . Offer for sale . . . Molasses Shooks, &c. **1871** DE VERE 287 The people of the South had always been fond of *molasses stews*, in which the boiling molasses was pulled or tugged out into long strings.

+**Molasses barrel.** A barrel for molasses. — **1846** CORCORAN *Pickings* 29 Isn't that cotton bale dancing a quadrille with the molasses barrel? **1865** *Atlantic Mo.* XV. 536 Inside was the usual stock of calicoes, china-ware, molasses barrels and books. **1904** TARBELL *Hist. Standard Oil Co.* I. 12 Turpentine barrels, molasses barrels, whiskey barrels . . . were added to new ones made especially for oil.

+**Molasses cake.** Cake sweetened with molasses. — **1836** SIMMS *Mellichampe* xlvii, The negro broke his molasses-cake evenly between himself and the soldier, who did not scruple readily to receive it. **1864** TAYLOR *H. Thurston* 19 Wedges of molasses-cake [were] offered by Mrs. Hamilton Bue's black-mitted hands. **1903** M. E. WILLIAMS *Elements of Cookery* 267 Mixing molasses cakes.—Mix milk and molasses and stir them into the flour [etc.].

+**Molasses candy.** Candy made from molasses.

1809 IRVING *Knickerb.* VII. iii, Each . . . he patted on the head, . . . and gave him a penny to buy molasses candy. **1847** *Knickerb.* XXIX. 8 Those who clustered round her table were no fancy children, but substantial flesh and blood, daubed with molasses-candy. **1873** PHELPS *Trotty's Wedding* xi, People sell molasses-candy in the winter without shoes. **1887** ALDEN *Little Fishers* xxii, The molasses jug was empty, and the boys had been promised some molasses candy that very evening. **1914** E. STEWART *Lett. of Woman Homesteader* 41 He had insisted on making molasses candy for her.

b. *Molasses candy pulling*, a social gathering at which those present make molasses candy. (Cf. CANDY PULL.)

1893 *Harper's Mag.* Feb. 441, I invited them all myself late this afternoon; and it is a molasses-candy-pulling.

+**Molasses gingerbread.** Gingerbread made with molasses. (Cf. GINGERBREAD.) — **1832** CHILD *Frugal Housewife* 70 A very good way to make molasses gingerbread is to rub four pounds and a half of flour with half a pound of lard [etc.]. **1864** NICHOLS *Amer. Life* I. 36 The spectators . . . ate molasses-gingerbread.

+**Molasses jug.** A jug for molasses. — **1839** *S. Lit. Messenger* V. 65/2 Behind the bar were . . . a molasses jug, a bottle of vinegar, and . . . decanters. **1877** *Harper's Mag.* March 606/1 When I filled our best customer's molasses jug with kerosene, I knew I had demonstrated my coolness. **1896** WILKINS *Madelon* 122 A man came out with a molasses-jug in hand and arms clasping parcels. **1906** LYNDE *Quickening* 111 The workmen's children . . . called her a mountain cracker when she went down to buy meal or to fill the molasses jug.

* **Mold, Mould.**[1]

1. =BULLET MOLD. {1687-}

1651 *Mayflower Descendant* X. 161, 4 moulds for bullets & shott, . . . 5 [shillings]. **1819** E. EVANS *Pedestrious Tour* 103 Around the waist was a belt with a brace of pistols, . . . and a case for moulds.

***2.** A matrix in which various articles, as candles, brick, buttons, etc., are made from liquid or plastic material by casting or pressing. Also fig.

1653 *Suffolk Deeds* I. 328 To haue and to hold the said ware hous . . . wth ye sd aleauenth thousand one hundred of Nayles and the sd twenty sett of Iran mould[s]. **1665** *Boston Rec.* 26 The law relateing to Tiles may be inlardged to Bricks, . . . that there may be a size apointed for there demensions and that there moldes may bee shod &c. **1712** *Ib.* 160 The Sel. men have Nominated . . . Capt. Timo Clark, to be veiwer of Bricks & veiwer & Sealer of Moulds. **1771** FRANKLIN *Autobiog.* 233, I was employed in cutting wick for the candles, filling . . . the molds for cast candles. **1810** *Columbian Centinel* 3 Jan. 4/1 George Connell . . . has just received . . . galloons, . . . ferrets, . . . large and small Button Moulds. **1836** in Mackenzie *Van Buren* 175 A mould for running bank charters cannot be made constitutionally. **1878** ROE *Army Lett.* 206 The brick mold was in another mold that after a while was put in cold water.

attrib. **1841** *Knickerb.* XVII. 34 A single mould candle . . . shed an uncertain light.

Mold.[2] (See MOULD.[2])

***Moldboard, Mouldboard.** The smooth, curved plate in a plow which turns over the furrow slice. — **1790** S. DEANE *New-Eng. Farmer* 128/1 A plough called a cultivator has been constructed, with two mould boards, which turn the mould both ways at once. **1814** J. TAYLOR *Arator* 104 And the large trowel-hoe plough with its two mould boards, splits the summit of the fallow ridge. **1872** EGGLESTON *End of World* 20 He cleaned his mold-board, and swung his plough round. **1896** P. A. BRUCE *Econ. Hist. Va.* I. 462 No material change had taken place in the manufacture of the plough beyond the introduction of the mould-board, an invention of the Dutch.

Moldboard plow. A plow having one or two moldboards. (Cf. DOUBLE MOLDBOARD PLOW, DOUBLE PLOW.) — **1858** *Ill. Agric. Soc. Trans.* III. 366 A bull-tongue or shovel plow put to the same depth, will raise better corn than a mouldboard plow. **1866** W. REID *After the War* 368 A good, moldboard plow seemed unheard of. **1874** KNIGHT 728/2 [In the Michigan double plow] the precedent portion . . . is a regular moldboard plow of small proportions.

* **Mole.**

***1.** Any one of various small, rodentlike, burrowing animals, usually of the family Talpidae, that live almost exclusively under ground.

1737 BRICKELL *N. Carolina* 130 The Moles . . . are not plenty here, being destroyed by Snakes. **1789** MORSE *Amer. Geog.* 55 Beasts which are the same on both continents . . . [include the] Mole, Morse, Seal. **1806** CLARK in *Lewis & C. Exped.* IV. (1905) 113 The *Mouse* and *Mole* of this neighbourhood [Fort Clatsop] are the same as those native animals with us. **1858** WARDER *Hedges & Evergreens* 74 To avoid the attacks of moles, he recommends that the ground be made dishing. **1917** *Mammals of Amer.* 303/1 The Mole is one of the most voracious of all animals.

+**b.** =GROUND MOUSE. (By error for VOLE.)

1839 BUEL *Farmer's Companion* 99 Moles or ground-mice cannot penetrate. **1857** *Rep. Comm. Patents 1856: Agric.* 84 Many persons call them [*sc.* meadow mice] 'Moles,' though they are not in the least related to that family.

+2. =MOLE DITCH. Also attrib. and comb.

1858 *Ill. Agric. Soc. Trans.* III. 361 [An engine] will do all other kinds of plowing and seeding, . . . dragging the mole drainer all over our lands. *Ib.* 368 The same mole-plow, trooping after a steam engine of some fifty horse power, . . . [will be] ditching from ten to twenty miles of our prairie soil in a single day. **1861** *Ib.* IV. 112 It was established that moles in a stiff clay soil, would make good drains. *Ib.* 249 These mole-drains may be cut either in the gang, or by the plows when used singly.

Mole cricket. A burrowing insect of the genus *Gryllotalpa.* {1714–} — **1854** EMMONS *Agric. N.Y.* V. 143 From the construction of the fore-legs, . . . and the use to which they are applied, the species has received the name of mole cricket. **1861** *Ill. Agric. Soc. Trans.* V. 441 The common mole cricket . . . is probably found here.

+**Mole ditch.** *Agric.* An underground conduit or drain. — **1868** *Rep. Comm. Agric. 1867* 232 Another mode sometimes resorted to for supplying water . . . is, *under draining* wet, heavy places, with 'mole ditches,' or blind drains. **1871** *Ill. Agric. Soc. Trans.* VIII. 83 The sloughs have all been underdrained with mole ditches, which furnish abundant stock water in fields Nos. 3, 4 and 5.

+**Mole ditching.** *Agric.* The ditching or draining of land by means of a mole or underground drain. — **1868** *Iowa Agric. Soc. Rep. 1867* 154 Under-draining by mole-ditching has been tried.

Mole shrew. {1877} +**1.** The short-tailed shrew, *Blarina brevicauda.* +**2.** The Gibbs's mole, *Neurotrichus gibbsii.* — **(1) 1884** J. S. KINGSLEY, etc. *Stand. Nat. Hist.* V. 148 The typical species, called the Mole-shrew, *Blarina brevicauda.* **1917** *Mammals of Amer.* 310 Short-tailed Shrew. *Blarina brevicauda.* . . . Other Name.—Mole Shrew. . . . Western Nebraska and Manitoba eastward to the Atlantic Coast. **(2) 1890** *Cent.* 3823/1 *Mole-shrew.* . . . The name is also applied to *Neurotrichus gibbsi.*

+**Mole tree.** The caper spurge, *Tithymalus lathyrus.* — **1847** WOOD *Botany* 487 Mole-tree. Caper Spurge. . . . Cultivated grounds and gardens. **1892** *Amer. Folk-Lore* V. 103 *Euphorbia Lathyris,* mole-tree. No. Ohio. **1899** *Animal & Plant Lore* 119 'Caper-tree,' or 'mole-tree,' . . . is supposed [in n. Ohio] to keep moles out of flower-beds if planted there.

+**Moline.** [From name of a river and a city in northwestern Illinois.] *attrib.* Designating agricultural implements and vehicles made in Moline, Ill. — **1876** *Ill. Dept. Agric. Trans.* XIII. 328 The barshare and shovel plow have been succeeded by . . . the Pekin, the Peoria, the Moline and a wonderful number of other earth turners. **1881** *Rep. Indian Affairs* 88 I used the leverage of the 50 Moline wagons and harness, as far as possible, to make every wagon represent a new farm location.

***Moll.** +The blackfish, *Tautoga onitis.* — **1884** GOODE, etc. *Fisheries* I. 269 The Tautog or Black-fish . . . is called . . . on the eastern shore of Virginia 'Moll,' or 'Will George.' **1903** T. H. BEAN *Fishes N.Y.* 598 This is better known in New York as the blackfish; farther south it is styled . . . Moll, Will George, and oyster fish.

+**Molligut.** *local.* =GOOSEFISH. — **1884** GOODE, etc. *Fisheries* I. 173 The Goose Fish or Monk Fish *Lophius piscatorius.* . . . The names of the fish are many; . . . in Eastern Connecticut [it is called] 'Molligut.' **1911** *Rep. Fisheries 1908* 310.

+**Molly cotton(tail).** =COTTONTAIL. *colloq.* — **1835** LONGSTREET *Ga. Scenes* 188 When I went into the neighborhood . . . , the common appellation of the rabbit was 'Molly Cotton-tail,' as it still is, elsewhere in Georgia. **1852** *S. Lit. Messenger* XVIII. 718/2 [I have] stopped my 'molly cotton' in her headlong flight. **1889** *Amer. Folk-Lore* II. 229 Molly-cotton.—A rabbit. 'Cotton-tail' is common at the West. **1890** *Harper's Mag.* July 231/1 Mule-eared rabbits and 'mollie-cotton-tails'; squirrels, red, black, and gray.

Molly Maguire. Also **Mollie Maguire.** {1868–} +A member of a secret organization of miners that became notorious for its criminal activities in the Pennsylvania coal region from 1865 to 1876; *pl.,* the organization composed of such members. Now hist. — **1867** DIXON *New America* II. 299 The judge who tried this murderer was elected by the Molly Maguires; the jurors who assisted him were themselves Molly Maguires. **1877** 'E. MARTIN' *Hist. Great Riots* 462 Such is the region that has become notorious throughout the Union as the country of the Mollie Maguires and the scene of their terrible crimes. **1886** STAPLETON *Major's Christmas* 86 There come among us some men that belonged to a band of murderers that called themselves Molly Maguires. **1903** *N.Y. Ev. Post* 31 Aug., He took an active interest in the politics of Schuylkill County at the time of the existence of the Mollie Maguires.

***Molton (coat).** A coat of a coarse woolen cloth made at South Molton in North Devon, England. *Obs.* — **1809** A. HENRY *Travels* 34, [I wore] a molton, or blanket coat. *Ib.* 139 The lock . . . I had carried under my molton coat. **1852** ELLET *Pioneer Women* 339 The ordinary dress of a Canadian fur trader, was . . . a 'molton,' or blanket-coat.

Monack. Variant of MOONACK.

+**Monadnock.** [Mt. *Monadnock,* N.H., from Amer. Ind. 'prominent mountain.'] *Geol.* A hill or rocky elevation on a plain worn by erosion. — **1895** W. M. DAVIS in *Geog. Jrnl.* V. 141, I have fallen into the habit of calling a residual mound of this character, a *monadnock.* **1899** — *Physical Geog.* 190 Several monadnocks are scattered over the Piedmont plain of Virginia.

Monarda. {monardus, 1712} A genus of North American mints of the family Lamiaceae, or one of its species. (Cf. BEE-BALM I.) — **1814** BIGELOW *Florula Bostoniensis* 7 *Monarda allophylla,* Soft Monarda. . . . Flowers, in terminal heads, blue or flesh coloured. **1847** WOOD *Botany* 417. **1887** BURROUGHS in *Century Mag.* July 328, I have never found it with its only rival in color, the monarda or bee-balm, a species of mint.

***Money.** Also †**monney, mony.**

***1.** Anything which passes current as a medium of payment, esp. gold, silver, copper, etc., and paper currency coined or emitted by a government.

To have money to burn, see BURN *v.* 7.

1637 *Conn. Rec.* I. 12 The payment to be made either in monney, in Wampum at fower a penny, or in good and marchantable beaver. **1682** *Mass. Bay Currency Tracts* 7 Credit pass'd in Fund, by Book, & Bills, (as afore) will fully supply the defect of Money. **1704** S. KNIGHT *Journal* 42 Mony [in Conn.] is pieces of Eight, Ryalls, or Boston or Bay shillings . . . or Good hard money. **1819** in Mackenzie *Van Buren* (1846) 156 Direct Mr. Wing to . . . request them to furnish him with small money for change, and if they refuse, to demand specie. **1868** M. H. SMITH *Sunshine & Shadow* 31 Widows and orphans who had left trust money in his hands lost their all. **1923** *Acad. Polit. Sci. Proc.* X. 158 Different banking systems make a different ratio between the gold as money in the pocket and gold as money in the bank reserves.

2. Attrib. and comb. with *box, condition, pouch,* etc.

1725 SEWALL *Letter-Book* II. 189 Two Salts. One Pepper Box. One Money-Box. **1779** FRANKLIN *Works* VI. (1888) 427 Did they take all the letters, flowers, etc., etc., except the five cases of money types which you say the Congress have taken? **1785** *Jrnls. Cont. Congress* XXIX. 500 It was Resolved, That the money unit of the United States of America be one dollar. **1855** SIMMS *Forayers* 60 We'll want you to bring out your money pouch. **1881** *Mich. Gen. Statutes* (1882) I. 394 Such meeting may vote on the amount of highway labor and money tax to be assessed. **1925** BRYAN *Memoirs* 218 The whole country had felt the stringency of money conditions.

+**3.** Special combinations.

Money act, an act dealing with money or finance; *m. bug,* a man possessing great wealth; *m.-digging,* (see quotation); *m.-loaner,* =MONEY-LENDER; *m. pay,* pay in actual money (cf. COUNTRY PAY); *m. pool,* (see quotation).

1729 FRANKLIN *Writings* II. 148 The Money-Acts in every Part [are] punctually enforced. **1904** 'O. HENRY' *Cabbages & Kings* 304 The chief had got together the same old crowd of moneybugs with pink faces and white vests to see us march in. **1848** *S. Lit. Messenger* XIV. 641/2 Joe . . . did no work; unless we dignify with that name an occasional turn at 'money digging,' a searching for hidden treasures. **1903** W. E. CURTIS *True A. Lincoln* 131 He advocated a law prohibiting money-loaners from charging exorbitant rates of interest. **1682** *Portsmouth Rec.* 215 Fifty Shillings money pay which he in the year 1676 Received for Indians. **1903** E. JOHNSON *Railway Transportation* 228 Arrangements for the division of the business were called traffic pools, those for distribution of the receipts money pools.

+**Money article.** In a newspaper, an article dealing with current quotations on stocks and bonds or financial affairs in general. — **1848** W. ARMSTRONG *Stocks* 18 Outsiders are influenced mostly by the 'money articles' in the leading papers of the day. **1854** 'O. OPTIC' *In Doors & Out* (1876) 12 The merchant, who had . . . half read a money article in his paper, turned to finish it. **1888** KIRK *Queen Money* 197 Opening the second edition of the *Hesperus,* [he] turned to the money article.

+**Money belt.** A belt having convenient pockets or folds for money or gold. — **1860** HOLMES *E. Venner* xi, Mr. Richard Venner . . . was ready to return to Rockland in less than a week, without having lightened the money-belt he wore round his body. **1867** 'E. KIRKE' *On Border* 117 He drew from his pocket a leathern money-belt such as is sometimes worn by travellers. **1908** BEACH *Barrier* 1 Some of them had money-belts weighted low with gold.

Money broker. (See quot. 1900.) {1616–} — **1809** IRVING *Knickerb.* III. ii, The cunning fox . . . skulked in the woods, where now are to be seen the dens of Gomez and his righteous fraternity of money brokers. **1838** *N.Y. Advertiser & Exp.* 7 Feb. 3/1 At that day [1808] there were but a very few Money Brokers. **1900** NELSON *A B C Wall St.* 130 *Money broker,* a dealer in coin, bullion and foreign exchange; a Stock Exchange member whose business is the lending of money on call for banks.

+**Money center.** A place of preëminent rank or importance in the financial affairs of a region or country. Freq. with reference to New York City. — **1860** HOLMES *Professor* iv. 107 What do you say to Ne' York? . . . A great money-centre. **1870** MEDBERY *Men Wall St.* 167 The money-centre of America soon became aware of the opening of a new office, with 'Fisk and Belden brokers' in flaming gilt over the doorway. **1894** LEAVITT *Our Money Wars* 113 The Law allowing the Interior Banks to keep Large Amounts of their Reserves in so-called Redemption Banks, or Banks in Money-Centers. **1900** *Congress. Rec.* 17 Feb. 1897/2 At such times gilt-edged paper can be placed in the money centers at a small per cent.

+**Money crop.** *Agric.* A readily salable crop, as cotton or tobacco, grown primarily for the market. — **1881** *Harper's Mag.* Oct. 723/1 Cotton is the money crop, and offers such flattering inducements that everything yields to that. **1892** *Vt. Agric. Rep.* XII. 130 The production of fruit . . . is attracting considerable attention, and it will soon . . . stand at the head of our money crops. **1904** T. E. WATSON *Bethany* 5 They never failed to make it their object to produce on the farm the necessary supplies: tobacco or cotton being merely the surplus crop, the 'money' crop.

+**Money-digger.** One who seeks for buried treasure or is supposed to be an adept at locating it. — **1842** *Knickerb.* XX. 306 The conjectures and suggestions . . . would have caused a money-digger's heart to leap into his throat. **1880** N. BROOKS *Fairport Nine* iii. 46 Old Tumble, too, had the reputation of being what was called 'a money-digger.' **1897** ROB-

INSON *Uncle Lisha's Outing* 227 Sam recognized an old acquaintance, one of the money diggers of Garden Island.

+**Moneyed corporation.** (See quot. 1858.) — **1834** JACKSON in *Pres. Mess. & P.* III. 43 Were they bound . . . to subvert the foundations of our Government and to transfer its powers from the hands of the people to a great moneyed corporation? **1858** *N.Y. Rev. Statutes* II. 526 The term 'moneyed corporation,' as used in this title, shall be construed to mean every corporation having banking powers, or having the power to make loans upon pledges or deposits, or authorized by law to make insurances. **1889** *Cent.* 1275/3.

+**Moneyed institution.** An institution rich in money. — **1861** *Vanity Fair* 23 Feb. 96/1 The 'Presidents of Railroads and moneyed institutions' are stealing the Post Office and Custom House monies. **1900** *Congress. Rec.* 19 Jan. 992/2 A great moneyed institution which the court said had the right under the fundamental law of Louisiana to exist.

+**Money king.** A man of great wealth who plays a dominant role in financial affairs. (Cf. KING 3 b.) — **1841** *Congress. Globe* App. 9 July 160/2 The great money kings of the age have crossed the Atlantic. **1852** *Harper's Mag.* March 566/2 The driver . . . turning to the money-king said [etc.]. **1900** *Congress. Rec.* 7 Feb. 1610/1 Where ought control of the currency to rest? . . . At present the banks and the money kings wield this power.

Money-lender. One whose business is to lend money at interest. {1780–} — **1795** *Ann. 3d Congress* 1364 The money-lender would exact exorbitant premiums. **1817** *Yankee Traveller* 76 This enviable circle consisted of a powerful pill-driver, by the name of Plaster; Gripe, a money-lender; Wax, a cobbler. **1897** HOUGH *Story of Cowboy* 331 Farmer, merchant, artisan, money lender, professional man, desperado and tenderfoot —all mingled in an eddy and boil of tumultuous, vigorous life.

***Money-maker. 1.** =COUNTERFEITER. *Obs.* {15th c.} **2.** One chiefly interested or adept in acquiring wealth. {1864–} +**3.** A thing which is financially profitable. — **(1) 1729** COMER *Diary* 65 This day came up ye case of ye money makers to trial. **1777** *N.H. Comm. Safety Rec.* 93 Ordered the R[eceiver] G[eneral] to pay Colo. Saml. Folsom nineteen pounds Eleven Shillings, for himself & 5 others apprehending Money makers. **(2) 1834–42** WHITMAN *Prose Wks.* (1892) 367 Ridman was a *money-maker.* **1893** POST *Harvard Stories* 164 If we Americans are all such narrow-minded money-makers [etc.]. **(3) 1899** ADE *Doc' Horne* 22, I expect to have an interest in the Neapolitan Dental Parlors, where I'm working now. It's a sure money-maker.

Money market.

1. A place in which the financial activity of an entire region is centered.

1791 A. HAMILTON *Works* (1850) III. 161 In Holland, the greatest *money* market of Europe, gold was to silver . . . as 1 to 14.88.] **1883** *Century Mag.* Sept. 691/2 Wall street . . . is the money market of the whole country.

2. The market or field in which those who deal in loans, stocks, etc., carry on their operations; the economic conditions governing financial transactions. {1847–}

1818 *Niles' Reg.* XIV. 226/1 The rags of three of the country banks of Maryland stand about thus in the *money*-market. **1868** BEECHER *Sermons* (1869) I. 175 That man once controlled the whole money-market of New-York. **1883** WILDER *Sister Ridnour* 169 He needed every dollar for his Winter stock of goods, and, besides, the money market was tight. **1904** PRINGLE *Rice Planter* 139 The stringency in the money market affects everything.

Money musk. [Cf. *Monymusk*, a town in Scotland.] A kind of folk dance or the tune that accompanies it. — **1843** STEPHENS *High Life N.Y.* I. 202 A set of folks come from all the four quarters of the globe . . . that didn't know how to dance an eight reel or munny-muss as it ought to be done. **1923** S. V. BENÉT *Ballad of Wm. Sycamore* 5 For I cut my teeth on 'money musk' In the Bloody Ground of Kentucky!

Money order.

1. An order for money issued, upon the payment of the sum and a small commission, by one post office and payable at another. {1802–}

1864 *Statutes at Large* XIII. 76 A money-order shall not be valid or payable unless it be drawn on a printed or engraved form. **1887** *Postal Laws* 431 Postmasters will observe that the forms for money orders and advices are numbered. **1913** LONDON *Valley of Moon* 439 Nor did she tell him of a money order inclosed with a certain blue slip of paper in a letter to Bud Strothers. **1925** *Postal Guide* 93 Domestic offices are authorized to issue money orders payable only in the United States or its possessions.

2. Attrib. with *branch, department*, etc.

See also MONEY ORDER OFFICE.

1864 *Statutes at Large* XIII. 76 The Postmaster General is hereby authorized to establish . . . a uniform money-order system. **1885** (newspaper), Another building has been rented by the government for the money order branch. **1887** *Postal Laws* 104 All Presidential and money-order postmasters are designated as disbursing officers for the payment of the salaries of . . . employés of the Railway Mail Service. **1893** *Chicago Tribune* 24 April 3/2 The first money order poster will be shown. **1900** *Congress. Rec.* 21 Feb. 2015/1 The Money-Order Department is the most useful and important adjunct to the postal service.

Money order office. {1802–} +**1.** A local post office or department thereof authorized to issue money orders. +**2.** A division of the post-office department of the U.S. government having supervision of the money order system. — **(1) 1864** *Statutes at Large* XIII. 76 [Suitable] post-offices . . . shall be designated and known as 'Money-Order Offices.' **1873** *Newton Kansan* 10 July 2/2 Peabody, Kas., postoffice is now a money order office. **1891** 'THANET' *Otto the Knight* 264 He'll sure devil the money-order office *some* way. **(2) 1865** *Postmaster Gen. Rep.* 76 The first annual report of the Money Order office embraces the period from November 1, 1864 . . . to . . . June 30, 1865.

Money panic. A comparatively brief period of widespread fear and doubt over financial affairs. — **1857** GLISAN *Jrnl. Army Life* 391 The money panic is of greater severity than has occurred for many years. **1900** *Congress. Rec.* 16 Jan. 876/1 It offers a direct premium to the bankers of New York to create a money panic.

+**Money plank.** That part of a political party's platform embodying the views of the party concerning the proper management of the financial affairs of the country. — **1894** LEAVITT *Our Money Wars* 221 February 22, 1878, the Greenback Labor Party . . . formulated an elaborate platform; the money planks of which have been much used by money reformers since then. **1900** *Congress. Rec.* 7 Feb. 1608/2 The money plank of the St. Louis convention . . . did the business.

Money power. a. The power to coin money, regulate its use, etc. **b.** The power, influence, etc., exercised by money; specifically, individuals, corporations, etc., wielding power by virtue of their wealth. — **1829** *21st Congress 1 Sess.* H. R. Doc. No. 6, 12 The application of the money power of the Government to regulate the unequal action caused by [shifts of capital, etc.]. **1831** BENTON *30 Years' View* I. 191/1 The money power of the bank is both direct and indirect. **1856** *Democratic Conv. Proc.* 24 A national bank . . . [is] calculated to place the business of the country within the control of a concentrated money power. **1875** *Chicago Tribune* 14 Oct. 1/6 Money-Power is still able in this country to throttle the people. **1913** LA FOLLETTE *Autobiog.* 466 The money power now lies in the hands of a dozen men.

+**Money price.** {1776–} The price of an article stated in terms of money rather than in commodities accepted as money. *Obs.* (Cf. COUNTRY PAY.) — **1647** *Suffolk Deeds* I. 88 Such Commodities as the sd Tho: . . . shall choose at any shopp in Boston at money prices. **1686** *Braintree Rec.* 24 Moses ffiske shall have the last yeare 90lb that is 40lb in money or corne at money prise & 50lb at Countrey rates prise. **1741** *N.H. Probate Rec.* III. 57, I give unto my Daughter Mehetiable Hains Fourty Pounds in Goods att money Prise.

Money scales. *pl.* Scales or balances for weighing money. — **1759** *Newport Mercury* 26 June 4/3 To be sold . . . walking Canes, Money Scales, Tea-chests [etc.]. **1761** in H. M. Brooks *Gleanings* 26 Money Scales, large ditto to weigh Silver, Piles of Ounce Weights, Penny Weights & Grains. **1767** *Ib.* 31 Buckle & ring brushes. Money scales & weights.

+**Money shark.** A crafty, avaricious usurer, swindler, or extortioner. *slang.* — **1844** *Congress. Globe* App. 20 Dec. 37/2 Banks . . . managed . . . by a set of irresponsible money sharks. **1900** *Congress. Rec.* 7 Feb. 1618/2 The idle few, the gold gamblers and the money sharks, may live, at the expense of the toiling masses, in idleness.

+**Money-shaver.** =prec. (Cf. NOTE-SHAVER.) — **1838** *N.Y. Advertiser & Exp.* 20 Jan. 1/3 Ten Directors of the State Bank of Missouri, a money-shaver who belongs to another State [etc.]. **1845** *Xenia Torch-Light* 23 Oct. 2/5 The abuse heap[ed] upon the tax law of last winter by the Cincinnati editors and money-shavers.

***Moneywort.** One of a number of plants suggestive in some way of money, esp. *Lysimachia nummularia.* — **1784** CUTLER in *Mem. Academy* I. 424 *Asclepias.* . . . Moneywort. Blossoms purple. In old fields. July. **1833** EATON *Botany* (ed. 6) 216 *Lysimachia ciliata*, money wort. **1869** FULLER *Flower Gatherers* 248 This plant makes a very showy appearance in garden-vases, and is often called Moneywort. **1871** *Scribner's Mo.* I. 458 Into the interstices you may tuck smaller plants—mignonette, lobelia, . . . moneywort.

***Monitor.** Also †**moneter, monotor.**

***1.** In a school or college, a student who has special duties assigned him, as teaching, recording attendance, etc.

1667 *Harvard Rec.* I. 46 The steward is from time, to tyme, . . . to allow the Monitors Account. **1790** *Harvard Laws* 56 The monitors shall be chosen by the President and the tutors. **1841** *Harvard Orders & Regul.* 4 The bills of attendance on prayers and Sabbath services shall be left at the President's study every Monday morning by the respective Monitors. **1871** BAGG *At Yale* 576 Where a whole class is assembled, that duty [*i.e.*, marking the absent or tardy students] is performed by 'monitors.' **1901** STILLMAN *Autobiog. Journ.* I. 54 Elder pupils were employed in . . . the preservation of order in the school yard. . . . I was often made 'yard monitor.' **1913** LONDON *Valley of Moon* 203 He and she had been monitors together of the composition books for one term.

+**2.** One appointed to maintain order or enforce rules:

a. In a legislative assembly. *Obs.*

1715 *Mass. H. Rep. Jrnls.* I. 3 *Ordered*, That Mr. John Sternes [etc.], . . . be Monitors of the House to take care that the Orders thereof are duly observed. **1719** *Ib.* II. 114 *Ordered*, That Capt. Chapin [etc.], . . . be Monitors of the House. **1721** *Ib.* III. 90 Voted, That Mr. John Foster [etc.], . . . be the Monitors for this Sessions.

+**b.** In a parish meeting. *Obs.*

1758 *Essex Inst. Coll.* XXI. 160 Voted that Frances Pool Joseph Thurston Junr. Nehemiah Grover be moneters for said meeting. **1766** *Ib.* 232 Said meeting Voted Joshua Gammidg Jonathan Pool Junr. Ebenezer

Grover moneters. **1786** *Ib.* XXII. 136 Chose Mr. Ebenezer Pool Mr. Joseph Thursten Mr. Ben Knights Monotors.

+**3.** An ironclad naval vessel constructed on the model of the one invented by John Ericsson in 1862. Now hist.

[**1862** ERICSSON in Church *Life Ericsson* (1890) I. 255 The iron-clad intruder will thus prove a severe monitor to those leaders [*sc.* of the Confederacy].... On these and many similar grounds I propose to name the new battery Monitor.] **1865** *Harper's Mag.* Aug. 360/1 In anticipation of a conflict with the Monitors, great numbers of military men had flocked to the city [Charleston] from all parts of the South. **1882** *Nation* 6 July 2/2 The Naval Bill ... [will] secure the completion of the monitors. **1898** *Scribner's Mag.* Aug. 144/2 There, on the silver-white water, lay the monitors Terror and Amphitrite.

+**b.** An armored railroad truck equipped with a large cannon. *Obs.*

1885 *Century Mag.* July 460 General Lee's famous railroad monitor was approaching.

+**c.** (See quotation.)

1905 *Forestry Bureau Bul.* No. 61, 33 *Catamaran*, a small raft carrying a windlass and grapple, used to recover sunken logs.... [Also called] monitor, pontoon (P[acific] C[oast] F[orest]).

+**4.** A raised roof or portion of a roof provided with openings and windows for light and ventilation. In full *monitor roof.* Also attrib.

1871 SNOW *Pathfinder* 2 'The roofs [of certain railroad passenger cars] are of the monitor pattern,' meaning slightly elevated along the centre, to make the car airy. **1875** KNIGHT 1472/1 *Monitor-car*, (*Railway*,) one having a central longitudinal raised portion in the roof, on the sides of which portion are openings for ventilation and panes for light. **1889** *Century Mag.* Feb. 574/1 A large number of factories, ... lighted with what are known as monitors, have been constructed in many parts of New England. **1923** NUTTING *Massachusetts* 294 The so called monitor roof which rises in a kind of clear story, is here and there found through the 18th century.

+**b.** (See quotation.)

1904 *Boston Sun. Globe* 28 Feb. 40/6 The monitor [of a caboose] is the square place with glass sides extending above the roof. There is a chair there ... and the rear brakeman, or the conductor, may sit in it and see what is going on and where the train happens to be.

+**5.** A nozzle capable of being turned completely around in a horizontal plane. Used in hydraulic mining.

1881 RAYMOND *Mining Glossary* 59 *Monitor*, Pac[ific slope.] A kind of nozzle used in *hydraulicking*. **1891** *Engineer* LXXII. 217/3 The monitor ... has a ball joint that permits it to be slung in any direction.

Monitorial, *a.* Pertaining to monitors, esp. with reference to the Lancasterian system of education. {1845-} — **1829** *Yankee* April 127/2 The grammar school—the monitorial schools—the Latin school—and the private schools, are now so good in themselves [etc.]. **1861** [see LANCASTERIAN]. **1886** Z. F. SMITH *Kentucky* 715 The monitorial system was founded on the plan of mutual instruction.

Monkey, *v.* +*intr.* To act mischievously; to trifle, project, tamper, fool *with* or *around. colloq.* Also *vbl. n.* — **1881** RITTENHOUSE *Maud* 39 Well, what with talking, running back and forth and general monkeying Clara slipped and fell. **1890** HASKINS *Argonauts Calif.* 282 An ex-policeman in San Francisco who had monkeyed with that style of man ... volunteered to make the arrest. **1907** STEWART *Partners* 357 There were some little yachts in a slip and a man was monkeying with the machinery of one with a monkey-wrench. **1920** LEWIS *Main Street* 338, I was brought up on a farm. And then monkeyin' round with silks!

+**Monkey business.** Deceitful or crafty carryings-on, trifling, foolish conduct. *slang.* — **1883** PECK *Bad Boy* 109 There must be no monkey business going on. **1904** *Brooklyn Standard Union* 26 Oct. 6 A warning to Russia that England will not tolerate any undue delay or any 'monkey business' whatsoever. **1910** TOMPKINS *Mothers & Fathers* 352 Father has had to work too hard ... to pay much attention to what he calls our monkey business.

Monkey flower. The genus *Mimulus*, or any plant belonging to this genus. {1789- (Aiton)} — [**1789** AITON *Hortus Kewensis* IV. 54 *Mimulus ... ringens....* Gaping Monkey-flower. *Nat.* of North America. *Ib., Mimulus ... alatus....* Oval-leaved Monkey-flower. *Nat.* of North America.] **1814** BIGELOW *Florula Bostoniensis* 153 *Mimulus ringens.* Monkey flower.... A handsome plant, fond of wet soils, where it attains the height of two feet and upward. **1840** DEWEY *Mass. Flowering Plants* 158 Monkey Flower.... A small genus, of which 4 species belong to this country and 2 to New England. **1901** MOHR *Plant Life Ala.* 719 *Mimulus....* Monkey Flower.

Monkey jacket. A close-fitting jacket or coat of coarse, stout material. {1894-} Also attrib. — **1830** N. AMES *Mariner's Sk.* 187 My wardrobe consisted of a 'monkey' jacket, bought in Gravesend ... and some other articles of clothing. **1840** DANA *Two Years* 286 One of the party produced an old pack of Spanish cards from his monkey-jacket pocket, which we hailed as a great windfall. **1880** ALDRICH *Stillwater Tragedy* viii. 77 William, thrusting his hands into the pockets of his monkey jacket. **1891** *Century Mag.* March 771 He wore a loose monkey-jacket or buckskin hunting-shirt.

Monkey rail. *Naut.* A light rail just above the quarter rail of a ship. — **1840** DANA *Two Years* 444 [We] painted ... the monkey-rail, black, white, and yellow. **1849** N. KINGSLEY *Diary* 43 Last night we shiped some terrible seas, one of which damaged our Monkey rail and stove the Galley door. **1900** *Scribner's Mag.* Sept. 290/1 Hanging over the monkey-rail in order to see as well as feel the quick answer of the vessel to her helm.

+**Monkeyshines.** *pl.* Monkeyish behavior, tricks, antics, capers, or pranks. *slang.* — **1847** BRIGGS *Tom Pepper* I. 43 (Th.), Let me catch him cutting up any monkey shines in this house, and I'll beau him. **1872** POWERS *Afoot & Alone* 61 Their own mothers was a carousin' and a cuttin' up monkey shines all night. **1890** H. PALMER *Stories of Base Ball Field* 37 Gore was ... particularly full of 'monkey-shines.' **1925** BENEFIELD *Chicken-Wagon Family* 95, I indulge in a few of those clever gymnastics which you formerly called 'piffling monkey-shines.'

Monkey show. A show or exhibition of monkeys. — **1838** FLAGG *Far West* I. 102 A redoubted 'monkey show' ... had wound its way over the mountains into the regions of the distant West. **1866** C. H. SMITH *Bill Arp* 125 Prouder to see him than a monkey show, I paddled the dug-out over in double quick.

Monkey spoon. (See quot. 1881.) Now hist. — **1749** [err. 1719] in De Vere 507 To each of the eight bearers ... a Monkey-spoon was given. **1881** *Harper's Mag.* March 530/1 A monkey-spoon. [*Note.*] Used for liquor, and so called from the figure of a monkey carved ... on the handle. It had a circular and very shallow bowl.

Monkey wrench. A straight-handled wrench one jaw of which is movable and readily adjustable. {1858-} Also fig. — **1870** 'MARK TWAIN' *Sk., New & Old* 20 You want to hang the monkey-wrench on the safety-valve! **1881** *Harper's Mag.* March 598/2 [He was] never happier than when, ... monkey-wrench in hand, he was screwing iron nuts on or off. **1907** STEWART *Partners* 104 He come and hit them on the shins with a monkey-wrench.

Monkfish. Also †**munkfish.** {1610-} **1.** The angel fish, *Squatina squatina* {1610-} or +*S. dumeril.* **2.** The angler, *Lophius piscatorius.* {1666-} Cf. GOOSEFISH. — **(1) 1672** JOSSELYN *New Eng. Rarities* 96 *Munk Fish*, a flat Fish like scate, having a hood like a Fryers Cowl. **1903** BEAN *Fishes N.Y.* 45 *Squatina squatina....* Angel fish; Monkfish.... Body raylike in shape, flat, depressed. **(2) 1832** WILLIAMSON *Maine* I. 157 Monk-fish is very plenty about Owl's-head and other bays. **1842** *Nat. Hist. N.Y., Zoology* IV. 163 The American Angler ... is not an uncommon fish in our waters. Its monstrous form has given rise to many popular names, such as Sea Devil, ... Goose-fish, Monk-fish, and various others. **1911** *Rep. Fisheries 1908* 310 Goosefish.... Local names are 'angler,' 'fishing frog,' 'monkfish,' 'bellows-fish,' ... etc.

***Monkshood.** Any of various plants of the genus *Aconitum;* also, the genus itself. — **1817-8** EATON *Botany* (1822) 155 *Aconitum uncinatum*, monk's hood.... Cultivated. **1840** DEWEY *Mass. Flowering Plants* 28 *Aconitum napellus*, Monk's Hood, is often found for ornament in gardens. **1857** GRAY *Botany* 13 *Aconitum.* Aconite. Monkshood. Wolfsbane. **1873** *Amer. Naturalist* VII. 8 Fatal mistakes have occurred when persons have eaten the root of the monkshood (*Aconitum Napellus*) in early spring ..., thinking it to be horseradish.

+**Monmouth.** *attrib.* Designating groups of citizens of Monmouth County, N.J., active in threatening or executing vengeance upon loyalists for injuries to rebels. — **1780** *N.J. Archives* 2 Ser. IV. 545 This Committee will ... retaliate on the Persons and property of the Disaffected within the County, for all Damages, & for all Injuries Sustained by any and Every of the Monmouth Associators. **1783** W. GORDON *Hist. Amer. Revol.* (1788) IV. 287 A set of vindictive rebels, known by the designation of *Monmouth retaliators*, associated and headed by one general Forman, whose horrid acts of cruelty gained him universally the name of *Black David.*

***Monmouth cap.** Also †**Munmoth, Mammouth cap.** A round, flat cap, such as was formerly worn by soldiers and sailors. *Obs.* {-1713} — **1639** *Md. Archives* IV. 82, 6 Munmoth Capps at seven pound per Capp. **1643** *Ib.* 209 Blanch oliver ... demandeth of John hollis ... 1. monmouth cap. **1744** *Md. Hist. Mag.* XXI. 246, 2 Dozn. Mammouth Caps for Negros. **1777** *Md. Journal* 22 July (Th.), [He had on a] Monmouth cap and old coarse shoes.

Monocrat. One who favors monarchic rule. +Applied *c*1790 by Jefferson and his followers to Federalists, who sympathized with England rather than France. Now hist. Also attrib.

1792 JEFFERSON *Writings* VIII. 440 Mr. Ames, the colossus of the monocrats and paper men, will either be left out or hard run. **1793** *Ib.* IX. 75 Even the monocrat papers are obliged to publish the most furious philippics against England. **1799** *Ib.* X. 124 The Anglomen and monocrats had ... artfully confounded the cause of France with that of Freedom. **1865** *Atlantic Mo.* XV. 199/1 The Federalists were aristocrats, monocrats,—lovers of court ceremonies and levees. **1883** J. T. MORSE *Jefferson* xv. 251 Here was an act, done by the great Republican doctrinaire-president, ... monarchical, beyond what any 'monocrat' had ever dared to dream of.

***Monody.** +(See quot. 1890.) — **1849** POE *Poems* (1917) 125 Hear the tolling of the bells—Iron bells! What a world of solemn thought their monody compels! **1885** 'CRADDOCK' *Prophet* 30 The vague, sighing voice of the woods rose and fell with a melancholy monody. **1890** *Cent.* 3839/1 *Monody*, ... monotonous sound; monotonousness of sound.

Monometallism. The theory or use of one metal, as gold or silver, as the only legalized standard of value in currency. {1879-} — **1881** *Nation* 23 June 434/1 [Mr. Evarts talked] of the 'intolerable burden' imposed on gold by mono-metallism. **1897** *Chicago Tribune* 9 July 6/2 So from 1792 to 1873 bimetallism and not silver monometallism was the 'American policy.' **1900** *Congress. Rec.* 18 Jan. 948/2 The adoption or rejection of gold monometallism, as proposed by this bill, [is] almost a moral question.

Monometallist. Also **monometalist.** One who favors a monometallic currency. {1886-} — **1878** *N. Amer. Rev.* Jan. 163 The monometalists denounce it [the Bland silver bill] for demonetizing the best of the two metals. **1881** *Chicago Times* 4 June, The monometallists assert, that if we succeed in bulling silver we shall also succeed in bearing gold. **1890** *Columbus Dispatch* 3 July, Unwilling to accept any of the propositions of the monometallists. **1900** *Congress. Rec.* 4 Jan. 652/2 The Democratic advocates of free coinage are not in any sense bimetallists, but silver monometallists of the most pronounced type.

+**Monongahela.** [From Lenape *Menaungehilla.*] Whisky, orig. that made in the region of the Monongahela River in Pennsylvania. In full *Monongahela whisky.* — **1829** SEALSFIELD in *N.Y. Mirror* 7 Nov. 137 The gulf of mammoth jaws just opening to swallow half a pint of Monongahela. **1842** 'UNCLE SAM' *Peculiarities* I. 43 On the outside . . . is printed the following thirsty announcement: . . . London Gin, Monongahela Whiskey, Jamaica Spirits [etc.]. **1852** REYNOLDS *Hist. Illinois* 265 Taffia, or Monongahela whiskey, was used at these husking frolics. **1897** *Congress Rec.* 27 Feb. 2466/1, I suggest that the gentleman from New York is not discussing the 'Monongahela' that he is familiar with.

Monopolist. One who has a monopoly of something or who favors monopoly. {1601-}

1798 I. ALLEN *Hist. Vermont* 46 [He] became friendly to the interests of the monopolists of New York. **1838** QUITMAN in Claiborne *Life Quitman* I. 166 The heavy commercial tribute which the states now pay to a limited number of Northern monopolists. **1872** MCCLELLAN *Golden State* 381 The completion of the Pacific and Atlantic railroad in 1869 has wrought great changes in the commercial affairs of California, . . . placing the public beyond the reach of the monopolist. **1904** TARBELL *Hist. Standard Oil Co.* I. 107 'Deserters,' 'ringsters,' 'monopolists' were the terms applied to [the refiners who had joined Rockefeller in creating a monopoly].

Monopolistic, *a.* Tending to create a monopoly. — **1883** *N.Y. Chr. Union* Aug. 30 The monopolistic 'railroad trunk-line fare-agreement.' **1892** *Nation* 25 Aug. 138/1 The spirit of trades unionism is essentially monopolistic and prescriptive.

Monotype. {1881-} +**1.** (See quot. 1890.) +**2.** The inventor's name for two machines for setting and casting in order single types. {1897-} — (**1**) [**1882** *Artist* 1 Feb. 60/1 A very interesting collection of monotypes executed by Mr. Charles A. Walker of Boston.] **1890** *Cent.* 3846/1 *Monotype*, . . . a print from a metal plate on which a picture is painted, as in oil-color or printers' ink. Only one proof can be made, since the picture is transferred to the paper. **1897** *Century Mag.* Feb. 517/1 The name 'monotype' was given to this form of art print by Mr. Charles A. Walker, of Boston who, in 1877, with no knowledge of the fact that the art was known and practised by painters in former times, discovered the process independently. (**2**) **1895** *Cyclopedic Rev. of Curr. Hist.* V. 961 The Lanston Monotype . . . marks an important advance in the development of typographical art. **1916** *Monotype Specimen Book of Type Faces* 8a Unlike other composing machines, the Monotype is built up of units which may be combined to exactly suit the requirements of any printing office.

+**Monroe (boot).** [From James *Monroe*, fifth president of the U.S.] A kind of boot or shoe. — **1828** SEALSFIELD *Amer. as They Are* 129 The dress of the planter . . . consists of a linen jacket, pantaloons of the same, Monroe boots, and a straw hat. **1845** *Xenia Torch-Light* 23 Oct. 3/6 Adams & Cooper Have just received . . . Men's Boots and Shoes: Coarse Brogans, Kip Monroes, Calf do, Calf Boots.

+**Monroe Doctrine.** *Hist.* A policy or series of policies of the United States government set forth in or deduced from President Monroe's message to Congress Dec. 2, 1823.

The most significant points in President Monroe's message were (1) that the United States would regard 'as dangerous to its peace and safety' any attempt on the part of the allied European powers 'to extend their system to any portion of this hemisphere'; (2) that the United States would view as an unfriendly act any interposition by any European power with the recently revolted Spanish American colonies for the purpose of repressing them 'or controlling in any other manner their destiny'; (3) that the United States regarded the American continents as being no longer 'subjects for any new European colonial settlement.'

[**1848** *Congress. Globe* 29 April 711 The President [Polk] had taken the opportunity of reiterating a doctrine which was said to be the doctrine of Mr. Monroe.] **1853** *U.S. Review* Feb. 188 Words . . . are introduced into the treaty at its close, invalidating the entire instrument as far as it may have been intended to carry out the principle of the Monroe doctrine. **1858** *Sun* (Baltimore) 30 Oct. 4/1, If we now fall back on the 'Monroe doctrine,' we shall see the difference between an abstraction and its application in practice. **1865** *Nation* I. 195 Gen. Thomas said at Elmira, on the 10th, that 'Maximilian would have to get out of Mexico, or we would hurry him out. The Monroe Doctrine must be enforced.' **1885** CRAWFORD *Amer. Politician* 313 [Sam & John Harrington] talked about the Monroe doctrine and the Panama canal. **1900** *Congress. Rec.* 31 Jan. 1351/1 In his dreams he [Pres. McKinley] may have again witnessed the pale and drowning features of the Monroe doctrine, to the neck of which he tied a millstone and left it to sink in mid-ocean. **1913** BRYAN in *Memoirs* 359 The first announcement of the Monroe Doctrine was intended to protect the republics of America from the political power of European nations.

+**Monroite.** A political follower of James Monroe, fifth president (1817-1825) of the United States. *Obs.* — **1816** *Mass. Spy* 11 Sept. (Th.), It has been candidly confessed by at least one of the boasted sixty-five Monroites, in caucus, that [etc.]. **1817** *Ann. 14th Congress* 2 Sess. 795 That very numerous class of persons who at that time were staunch Federalists, and since that time have been staunch Jeffersonians, Madisonians, and Monroites.

***Monstrous,** *a.* Used in the specific names of unusually large fruits. — **1817** W. COXE *Fruit Trees* 117 Monstrous Pippin, or New-York Gloria Mundi. This apple originated on Long Island, state of New-York; it is of an uncommonly large size. *Ib.* 118 Monstrous Bellflower. A very large, fair, and beautiful apple; of an oblong shape resembling the yellow Bellflower.

+**Montana.** [Sp., 'mountainous region.'] The name of a western state. Used attrib.

Montana black pine, (see quotation); *M. feathers*, hay, *jocose; M. junco, M. pheasant*, (see quotations); *M. tree*, a saddle of a type that originated in Montana.

1897 SUDWORTH *Arborescent Flora* 20 *Pinus ponderosa.* . . . Bull Pine. . . . [Also called] Montana Black Pine (var. *ambigua*) (Cal. lit.). **a1918** G. STUART *On Frontier* II. 146 A sergeant appeared at my door with an empty bed tick under his arm and told me that Mr. Athey had sent him down to have it filled with 'Montana feathers.' **1917** *Birds of Amer.* III. 47 The Montana Junco . . . is one of the slaty-hooded and brown-backed Juncos. **1895** *Outing* XXVII. 43/1 The Montana 'pheasant' (the ruffed grouse) is the same as the bird found in the mountains of Virginia and the East. [**1891** *Harper's Mag.* June 7/2 [The] saddle [of the Canadian Mounted Police] is what is known as the Montana tree.]

+**Montanian.** A native or inhabitant of Montana. — **1878** BEADLE *Western Wilds* 358 The Montanian was gone before Manson had thought to ask. **1882** *Century Mag.* Sept. 777/1 The red-faced miner or ranchman . . . brings down his fist upon the bar and says, 'I am an old Montanian.' **1894** *Harper's Mag.* Aug. 482/1 (caption), The Unterrified Montanians.

Monte. *S.W.* [Sp.] A card game of Spanish and Mexican origin, in which players bet upon a bottom and top layout of two cards each. {1836-, in Spain}

See also THREE-CARD MONTE.

1841 *S. Lit. Messenger* VII. 77/2 At a short distance were seated the proprietors of this immense herd, busily engaged in the game of Monte. **1851** KINGSLEY *Diary* 176 All kinds of gameing is going on from Faro & Monte to French Monte & Thimble-rig. **1864** DICK *Amer. Hoyle* (1866) 456 Monte . . . is the national game of the Mexicans, and is extensively played in California. **1891** SWASEY *Early Days Calif.* 37 In the bar-room a crowd of Californians were playing monte. **a1918** G. STUART *On Frontier* I. 67 All known gambling games were furnished, but monte and faro were the two favorite games.

b. Attrib. with *banker, dealer, layout, sharp.*

See also MONTE BANK, TABLE.

1844 GREGG *Commerce of Prairies* I. 240 La Tules . . . [is] now considered the most expert 'monte dealer' in all Santa Fé. **1864** DICK *Amer. Hoyle* (1866) 456 The monte banker, or dealer, must have the whole of his bank, or money which he risks at the game, in sight upon the table. **1889** MUNROE *Golden Days* 26 [A] man who doesn't know a monte lay-out from a checker-board. **a1918** G. STUART *On Frontier* I. 218 Our monte sharps are about to take the towns.

+**Monte bank.** *S.W.* A table or a place where monte is played: (see also quot. 1890).

1845 T. J. GREEN *Texian Exped.* 316 Next to the monte bank, some eight or ten were engaged in a 'bull-dance.' **a1861** WINTHROP *Open Air* 128 They seemed to see a frowzy desperado, . . . standing against a background of mustangs, monte-banks, and lynch-law. **1889** MUNROE *Golden Days* 89 A city with ships and stores, monte banks and bar-rooms. **1890** *Cent.* 3848/1 *Monte-bank*, . . . a gaming-table or an establishment where monte is played; also, the bank or pile of money usually placed in front of the dealer, and used in paying the stakes.

comb. **1846** MAGOFFIN *Down Santa Fé Trail* 120 There was 'Dona Tula' the principal *monte-bank keeper* in Sant Fé [*sic*].

+**Monterey.** [A county, city, and bay in southern California.] In special collocations.

Monterey cedar, a species of cedar found in southern California; *M. cypress*, a species of cypress (*Cupressus macrocarpa*) indigenous to the region about Monterey Bay; *M. halibut*, a flounder (*Paralichthys californicus*) found on the Pacific coast; *M. hermit thrush*, (see quotation); *M. pine*, a tall, handsome pine (*Pinus radiata*) of southern California.

1872 MCCLELLAN *Golden State* 450 The 'Monterey cedar,' a most beautiful ornamental tree, grows abundantly. **1884** SARGENT *Rep. Forests* 179 *Cupressus macrocarpa.* . . . Monterey Cypress. **1882** JORDAN & GILBERT *Synopsis Fishes N. Amer.* 821 *Paralichthys californicus.* . . . Monterey halibut; Bastard Halibut. **1917** *Birds of Amer.* III. 236/1 The Monterey Hermit Thrush (*Hylocichla guttata slevini*) is smaller, paler, and grayer than the Alaskan. California is its home and the winter is spent in Mexico and Lower California. **1884** SARGENT *Rep. Forests* 196 *Pinus insignis.* . . . Monterey Pine.

+**Monterey (Spanish) mackerel.** A kind of mackerel (*Scomberomorus concolor*) found on the Pacific coast. — **1884** GOODE, etc. *Fisheries* I.

316 The Pacific species may be called the 'Monterey Mackerel.' **1896** JORDAN & EVERMANN *Check-List Fishes* 341 *Scomberomorus concolor*. . . . Monterey Spanish Mackerel. **1911** *Rep. Fisheries 1908* 316/2 In California the Monterey Spanish mackerel . . . is a most excellent food fish.

+**Monte table.** A table or establishment at which monte is played. — **1847** RUXTON *Adv. Rocky Mts.* (1848) 190 Under the portales were numerous monté-tables, surrounded by Mexicans and Americans. **1869** BROWNE *Adv. Apache Country* 76 The city was built, bar-rooms and billiard-saloons opened, monte-tables established. **1889** MUNROE *Golden Days* 15 This influx of gold caused monte-tables, and other gambling layouts, to spring up. **1896** SHINN *Story of Mine* 63 Gold and silver were stacked up on the monte tables.

+**Montezuma.** [Nahuatl *Motecuzoma*, orig. the name of two Aztec kings of Mexico, later the name of a hero of the Pueblo Indians in New Mexico.] *Land of the Montezumas*, New Mexico. A sobriquet. — **1871** *Republican Review* 25 March 2/1 While the mineral fields of California, Colorado and Mexico have attracted whole troops of miners, the land of the 'Montezumas' has been overlooked. **1880** *Cimarron News & Press* 13 May 1/4 New Mexico. People and Climate of the Land of the Montezumas. **1885** *Weekly New Mexican Review* 8 Jan. 4/2 Journalism will henceforth prove a mighty power in the land of the Montezumas.

Monthly. A magazine or other periodical published once a month. {1856–} — **1833** *Knickerb.* I. 185 We have articles on Political Economy in the monthlys, the weeklys, and the dailys. **1851** NORTHALL *Curtain* 111 In 1836 he started the 'Gentleman's Magazine,' which soon became the popular 'monthly' of the day. **1860** MORDECAI *Virginia* 237 About 1807 or '8 . . . Seaton Grantland . . . published a thin but neat monthly, called *The Gleaner.* **1886** *Harper's Mag.* Nov. 814/1 We have had the *Galaxy*—one of the most varied and entertaining monthlies ever issued in New York.

Monthly meeting. A meeting for worship and church business held once a month by neighboring congregations of Quakers; a group of such Quaker congregations.

[**1701** *N.J. Archives* 1 Ser. II. 383 Altho' we farr exceed the Quakers parties in numbers, yet by their close contrivances at their pretended monthly, quarterly & yearly religious meetings, they outdo us in elections.] **1744** *Ib.* VI. 177 From our Monthly Meeting of Duck-Creek, held at Little Creek the 18th day of the 8th month. 1742. *a***1772** WOOLMAN *Journal* 117 A member of their meeting . . . proposed having meetings sometimes appointed for them [the slaves] on a week-day, to be attended only by some Friends to be named in their Monthly Meetings. **1849** CHAMBERLAIN *Ind. Gazetteer* 72 They have nine Quarterly meetings, about 27 Monthly meetings, and about 80 Congregations, or meetings for worship in the State.

***Monument.**

+**1.** An object fixed upon or erected by surveyors as a bound mark of a given piece of land or the limit of a survey.

1651 *Watertown Rec.* I. I. 27 Make som Dureable Monements both at the fouer angles and pert[it]ion Line. **1724** *Talcott P.* 21 All the marks and monuments erected by the surveyors in it are utterly lost. **1778** E. PARKMAN *Diary* 55 Ye Land being now cleared, the monuments are all gone. **1829** GREENLEAF *Survey of Maine* 10 *n.*, In the year 1817 the surveyors . . . erected a new monument a few feet north of the former, consisting of a square cedar post. **1885** *Rep. Indian Affairs* 147 Survey of the outward boundaries of . . . Reservations should be made and properly marked with suitable monuments.

+**2.** A milepost.

1745 HEMPSTEAD *Diary* 438, I measured ye Road from ye Court house . . . to ye Millpond bridge. . . . I made monuments at Every miles End.

+**3.** *Monument City*, =MONUMENTAL CITY.

1906 *Springfield W. Repub.* 8 March 4 Baltimore has been known for years as the 'Monument City,' and some of these monuments are in reality works of art.

+**4.** (See quotation.)

1909 *Cent. Suppl.* 827/1 *Monument*, . . . a conspicuous crag of a somewhat pillar-like and symmetrical form. (Western U.S.)

+**Monumental cactus.** =GIANT CACTUS. — **1873** COZZENS *Marvellous Country* 233 Scattered here and there, growing apparently without any soil, rose to the height of forty or fifty feet grooved columns of the *Cereus grandes*, or monumental cactus, as it is sometimes called.

+**Monumental City.** The city of Baltimore, Maryland. — **1827** *National Gazette* (Phila.) 20 Nov. 213 The brave sons of Cincinnatus at the festal board in the 'monumental city.' **1859** *Ladies' Repository* Jan. 51/1 Baltimore is the 'Monumental City,' from the great battle monument and several others of less note within its limits. **1882** *Harper's Mag.* June 20/2 No women . . . equal the fair daughters of the Monumental City. **1904** *Baltimore American* 5 Dec. 14 Detectives Hagan and Burns . . . have been working there [in Brooklyn] during the past week, and it is probable that they will return to the Monumental City to-day.

+**Mooley.** [Var. of *moiley* 'hornless.'] A cow that has no horns. Also *mooley cow.* (Cf. MULEY.) — **1838** HALIBURTON *Clockmaker* 2 Ser. iv. 47 Gives his Old Mooley a chance o' sneakin' into his neighbours' fields o' nights. **1840** *Picayune* 10 Sept. 2/6 Brought to the Pound . . . a red and white mooley cow. **1867** 'LACKLAND' *Homespun* 213 They are all so fond of patient 'mooley' too. **1902** MCFAUL *Ike Glidden* 3 The sight of poor Mooley slinking it for the woods with the cans and milk flying.

***Moon.**

***1.** The time from one new moon to another; a lunar month. +Usu. with reference to the American Indians' method of computing time.

1641 *Plymouth Col. Rec.* II. 20 Andrew Hellot shall pay Massatumpaine one fadome of beads within two moones. **1720** D. NEAL *Hist. New-Eng.* I. 30 [The Indians'] Division of Time is by Sleeps, and Moons, and Winters, and by Lodging abroad. **1756** WASHINGTON *Writings* I. 393 They proposed . . . to stay only one moon, and then to start for their nation. **1807** GASS *Journal* 210 Here some of the natives . . . informed us, that we could not cross the mountain for a moon and a half. **1872** TICE *Over Plains* 214 The Indians say that a thousand moons before they ever saw a white man's face, . . . a party of Utes . . . had spied . . . Arapahoes on the Plains. **1900** DRANNAN *Plains & Mts.* 287 [We] pulled out, telling the chief that we would be back in one moon—meaning in their language, one month.

+**2.** A large round biscuit.

1847 C. WHITE *Policy Players* (1874) 3 Get me a buttered moon and a pickle. **1883** 'MARK TWAIN' *Life on Miss.* lii, I spent my last 10 cts for 2 moons (*large, round sea-biscuit*).

+**Moonack.** Also **monack, monax, moonox.** [Virginia Indian, 'digger.']

1. The woodchuck (*Marmota monax*) or a related species.

1666 ALSOP *Maryland* (1902) 37 The Monack, the Musk-Rat, and several others (whom I'le omit for brevity sake) inhabit here in Mary-Land. **1676** GLOVER *Acct. Va.* in *Phil. Trans.* XI. 630 There are also several sorts of ravenous Beasts, as Wolves, . . . Possums, Monacks, Flying Squirrels. **1743** CATESBY *Carolina* II. p. xxviii, *Marmota Americana.* The Monax. This Animal is about the bigness of a wild rabbet. . . . They are inhabitants of Maryland, Pensilvania, &c. Their flesh is esteemed good meat. **1781–2** JEFFERSON *Writings* II. 71 There remain then the . . . wild cat, monax, bison [etc.]. **1805** CLARK in *Lewis & C. Exped.* II. (1904) 377, I have also observed some robes among them of beaver, moonox, and small wolves. **1875** BURROUGHS *Winter Sunshine* 29 In Virginia, they [*sc.* colored women] call woodchucks 'moonacks.'

2. *local.* (See quotation.)

1871 DE VERE 151–2 It is presumed, though not proven, that the *Moonack*, a mythical animal known to negroes only, is also of African origin. The beast lives, according to their belief, in caves or hollow trees, and the poor negro who meets it in his solitary rambles is doomed. His reason is impaired, till he becomes a madman, or is carried off by some lingering malady. He dare not speak of it, but old, experienced negroes say when they look at him: 'He gwine to die; he seed the *moonack.*'

+**Moonbill.** The ring-necked duck, *Nyroca* (or *Marila*) *collaris.* — **1888** TRUMBULL *Names of Birds* 61, I am told by two well-informed gunners . . . of its being known to certain South Carolina duckers as the Moon-Bill. **1917** *Birds of Amer.* I. 137 Ring-necked Duck. *Marila collaris.* . . . [Also called] Ring-bill; Moon-bill; Marsh Blue-bill.

+**Moondown.** The time when the moon goes down or sets. — **1797** HAWKINS *Letters* 276 Last evening, just before moon down, his camp had been fired on by some men supposed to be Georgians. **1861** *N.Y. Tribune* 25 Oct. (Chipman), They landed at Santa Rosa Island, at about a quarter of an hour to moondown, or 11 o'clock, P.M. **1909** CALHOUN *Miss Minerva* 147 He got 'way f'om here 'bout moon-down las' night.

Moon-eye. {1607–}

+**1.** The toothed herring (*Hiodon tergisus*) or a related species.

1842 *Nat. Hist. N.Y., Zoology* IV. 267 The Lake Moon-eye, *Hyodon clodalis*, . . . is common in Lake Erie. At Buffalo and Barcelona, it is called Moon-eye. **1845** STORER in *Mem. Academy* II. 462 *Hyodon tergisus.* . . . [This fish is] called 'Moon-eye,' 'Shiner,' 'Lake Herring,' at Buffalo. **1871** DE VERE 386 The Moon-Eye . . . [is] also known as lake and river herring. **1896** JORDAN & EVERMANN *Check-List Fishes* 280 Family LVIII. Hiodontidae. The Moon-eyes. **1911** *Rep. Fisheries 1908* 312 Moon-Eye, . . . a beautiful fresh-water food fish found in the Lake region and in the larger tributaries of the Mississippi.

2. The mooneye cisco, *Leucichthys hoyi.* Also with defining term.

1875 *Amer. Naturalist* IX. 135 This Indiana Argyrosomus appears to be quite distinct from the species found in Lake Michigan; *i.e.*, the shallow-water 'herring' . . . and the deep-water 'moon eye' (*A. Hoyi* Gill). **1884** GOODE, etc. *Fisheries* I. 541 The Moon-eye or 'Cisco' of Lake Michigan . . . is the smallest of our White-fish, rarely weighing over half a pound. **1902** *Amer. Folk-Lore* XV. 243 The lake 'moon-eye' (*Coregonus hoyi*).

Moonfish. {1646–}

+**1.** The spadefish, *Chaetodipterus faber.*

1842 *Nat. Hist. N.Y., Zoology* IV. 99 The Moon-fish, *Ephippus gigas*, . . . is rare on our coast, the mouth of the Hudson river being probably its northern limit. **1884** GOODE, etc. *Fisheries* I. 445 The Moon-fish is one of the rarer species on our coast, and . . . is one of the most highly esteemed food-fishes. **1903** BEAN *Fishes N.Y.* 603 The moonfish has occasionally been taken as far north as Cape Cod.

+**2.** The horsehead (*Argyreiosus vomer*) or a related fish.

1878 *Nat. Museum Proc.* I. 376 *Argyriosus vomer.*—Moon-fish. *Ib.*, *Selene argentea.*—Moon-fish. . . . Not common. **1903** BEAN *Fishes N.Y.* 436 Three individuals of the moonfish were obtained from Gravesend bay.

+**3.** The horsefish, *Vomer setapinnis.*

1878 *Nat. Museum Proc.* I. 376 *Vomer setipinnis.*—Moon-fish; Sunfish. **1884** GOODE, etc. *Fisheries* I. 322 [The blunt-nosed shiner, *Selene setipinnis,* is known] in North Carolina as the 'Moonfish' or 'Sunfish.' **1903** BEAN *Fishes N.Y.* 433 *Vomer setipinnis.* . . . Horsefish; Moonfish.

+**4.** The opah, *Lampris regius.*

1896 JORDAN & EVERMANN *Check-List Fishes* 350 *Lampris luna.* . . . Mariposa; Opah; . . . Gudlax; Moonfish.

+**Moonglade.** (See quotation.) — **1866** LOWELL *Biglow P.* 2 Ser. p. lviii, *Moonglade:* a beautiful word for the track of moonlight on the water.

Mooning. {1857–} +(See quotation.) — **1884** HOWELLS *Silas Lapham* 49 Her large eyes . . . were brown; they had the peculiar look of near-sighted eyes which is called mooning.

***Moonlight.** +**1.** (See quotations.) *Obs.* Also attrib. +**2.** An excursion made in the light of the moon. — **(1) 1851** HALL *College Words* 210 *Moonlight.* At Williams College, the prize rhetorical exercise is called by this name; the reason is not given. **1854** *Boston Ev. Traveller* 12 July, In the evening comes the Moonlight Exhibition, when three men from each of the three lower classes exhibit their oratorical powers. **1860** DURFEE *Hist. Williams College* 104 Those who receive the appointment to speak for the prize have always . . . been called 'Moonlights.' **(2) 1886** *Boston Jrnl.* 13 Aug. 3/7 To-night the fourth in the series of moonlights will be made.

Moonlighting. {1881–} *local.* +Exploding a charge of nitroglycerin in an oil well by night to start the flow afresh. — **1883** *Century Mag.* July 330/2 Sometimes well-owners 'torpedo' their wells stealthily by night to avoid paying the high price charged by the company. This operation is called 'moonlighting,' and many lawsuits have grown out of it.

+**Moon moth.** =LUNA MOTH. — **1868** *Amer. Naturalist* II. 187 The pale-green, satin-robed Moon-moth (*Attacus luna*). **1870** *Ib.* IV. 52 The beautiful pale green Moon-moth (*Actias Luna*).

Moonseed.

1. The genus *Menispermum*, or any plant of this genus. So called because of the crescent-shaped seeds. {1739–}

1785 MARSHALL *Amer. Grove* 85 *Menispermum.* Moonseed. . . . The Seeds are solitary, large, and kidney form. **1857** GRAY *Lessons Botany* 95 The rudiments of pistils are often found in the sterile blossoms, and rudimentary stamens in the fertile blossoms, as in Moonseed. **1869** *Rep. Comm. Agric. 1868* 205 Moonseed, (*Menispermum Canadense.*)—A small-foliaged, delicate climber; producing clusters of black fruit in autumn. **1893** CREEVEY *Flowers of Field* 444 Moonseed. *Menispermum Canadense* . . . The panicled flowers are not very noticeable.

+**2.** *Carolina* (or *Carolinian*) *moonseed*, a vine (*Cocculus carolinus*) of the moonseed family, or a related plant.

1785 MARSHALL *Amer. Grove* 86 *Menispermum carolinum.* Carolinian Moonseed. This is much smaller and weaker than the other [*M. canadense*], scarcely becoming shrubby. **1901** MOHR *Plant Life Ala.* 517 *Cebatha carolina.* . . . Carolina Moonseed.

***Moonshine.**

+**1.** =MOONSHINE WHISKY. {smuggled liquor, 1785–} Also attrib.

1886 *Century Mag.* Jan. 432/1 He had a moonshine apparatus over on Sweetwater. **1891** *Cycl. Temperance* 137/2 In this estimate no account is taken of the illicit whisky of the 'moonshine' stills. **1892** J. L. ALLEN *Blue-Grass Region* 249 The manufacture of illicit mountain whiskey—'moonshine'—was formerly . . . a source of revenue. **1924** RAINE *Land of Saddle-Bags* 127 Why do those Mountaineers make moonshine?

+**2.** *local.* A plant whose open flowers suggest moonlight.

1850 S. F. COOPER *Rural Hours* 310 Observed . . . the white silvery heads of the everlastings. The country people sometimes call these plants 'moonshine,' and really the effect in the evening upon so broad a field reminded one of moonlight. **1894** *Amer. Folk-Lore* VII. 92 *Gnaphalium polycephalum*, moonshine, Dorset, Vt.

Moonshiner. {smuggler, 1860} +One who distils spirituous liquors without a government license.

Cf. BLOCKADER 2.

1877 *N.Y. Ev. Post* 16 June 404 (B.), Nelson County, Kentucky, is the home of the Moonshiner. **1887** *Courier-Journal* 1 Jan. 4/2 The moonshiner is only a smuggler. **1893** *Harper's Mag.* March 601 'This is the country of the moonshiners, isn't it?' asked Chase, his keen eyes glancing down a wild gorge. **1899** *Caddo* (Okla.) *Herald* 19 May 1/7 A Georgia revenue man had a novel experience with a moonshiner in a suspected district. **1924** RAINE *Land of Saddle-Bags* 132 'Blockader' . . . is fully as common as 'moonshine' and 'moonshiner.'

+**Moonshine whisky.** Whisky made by individuals, usually in remote communities, having no license for distilling liquor. — **1875** E. KING *Southern St. N. Amer.* 478 Producing from his pocket a flask of 'moonshine' whiskey, [he] invited us to drink. **1894** *Harper's Mag.* Sept. 624/2 The people back in the mountains . . . do not regard it as criminal to make moonshine whiskey. **1902** LORIMER *Lett. Merchant* 217 Lem . . . ran . . . a blind tiger in the back room with moonshine whiskey.

+**Moonshining.** The illicit distilling of whisky. (Cf. BLOCKADING *n.* b.) — **1883** 'S. BONNER' *Dialect Tales* 183 You can't stop moonshinin' 's long's there's an honest man in Old Hickory's State. **1898** FOX *Kentuckians* 135 The young trusty's crime was 'moonshining.' **1911** ROLT-WHEELER *Boy with Census* 23 Most o' these hyeh feuds date back to enmities made in the Civil War an' in moonshinin'.

***Moor fowl.** +The ruffed grouse. — **1791** W. BARTRAM *Travels* 331 The wary moor fowl thundering in the distant echoing hills. **1846** *N.J. Laws* 324.

***Moor hen.** +**1.** =AMERICAN COOT. +**2.** The Florida gallinule, *Gallinula chloropus cachinnans.* — **(1) 1888** TRUMBULL *Names of Birds* 117 At Havre de Grace, Md., [the American coot, *Fulica americana*, is called] Moor-Hen, so termed by all. **(2)** *Ib.* 122 [Some gunners] distinguish the Gallinule [from the American coot, *Fulica americana*] as Rice-Hen, and again at Detroit and other points near Lake St. Clair, as Red-billed Mud-Hen, Moor-Hen . . . , and Marsh-Hen.

+**Moose.** Also †**moos, mouse.** [Algonquian.]

1. Any one of various large American forest-dwelling mammals of the genus *Alces*, esp. *A. americana;* also, an animal of this species.

[**1613** PURCHAS *Pilgrimage* (1614) 755 Captain Thomas Hanham . . . relateth of their beasts . . . redde Deare, and a beast bigger, called the Mus.] **1616** SMITH *New England* 30 [The animals here include] Moose, a beast bigger then a Stagge; deere, red and Fallow [etc.]. **1649** *Mass. H. S. Coll.* 4 Ser. VI. 278 A moose . . . was killd vpon one of your hummocks. **1707** *Ib.* 5 Ser. VI. 60* A Mooses Hide, as tough as you may Suppose it, was the best and most of her Diet. **1775** ROMANS *Nat. Hist. Florida* 174 The Moose, or American Elk, found in the higher latitudes on the river, naturally leads a life . . . nearly approaching to a state of domestication. *a*1817 DWIGHT *Travels* II. 76 The noise must have been made by the travelling of the moose through the water. *a*1862 THOREAU *Maine Woods* 232 He brought back the great-coats of moose tied up in his blanket. **1892** *Vt. Agric. Rep.* XII. 122 The last moose killed [in Essex Co.] . . . undertook a race with a railroad train on the Grand Trunk at Brighton, in 1858. **1917** *Mammals of Amer.* 22/2 The Moose is a browsing animal.

2. *attrib.* and *comb.* **a.** Designating apparel made of mooseskin.

1633 *N.H. Doc. & Rec.* I. 74, 16 mouse cootes, [£] 16. **1645** *New. Eng. Hist. & Gen. Reg.* III. 82 The said Alexander Bradford have giuen to Robert Stowton his Moose Suite & a musket & Sworde.

b. Denoting a part of a moose serving as a material or ornament.

1764 HUTCHINSON *Hist. Mass.* I. 464 Their bowstrings were made of Moose sinews. **1845** *Knickerb.* XXV. 508 His attire . . . consisted of a hunting-frock of dressed deer-skin, . . . embroidered with dyed moose-hair. **1894** *Outing* XXIII. 405/2 Moose antlers in the hall.

c. Special combinations.

Moose beat, =MOOSE-YARD; *m. dog*, a dog useful in hunting moose; *m. fly*, a blackish fly (*Haematobia alcis*) found in the northern United States and Canada; *m. ground*, a region where moose are numerous; *m. head*, a riverside plant of some kind; *m. pen*, =MOOSE-YARD; *m. shank*, (see quotation); *m. trail*, a trail made through the forest by moose; *m. trumpet*, =MOOSE HORN 2.

1838 *Knickerb.* XII. 293 The deer . . . tread the snow from around its branches [*i.e.* those of the ground hemlock], as often as it falls during the season. This spot is called the deer or moose *beat*, by the hunters. **1873** HOWELLS *Chance Acquaintance* 52 He is a moose-dog, and keeps himself in practice of catching the moose by the nose. *a*1862 THOREAU *Maine Woods* 177 While engaged in this search we made our first acquaintance with the moose-fly. **1839** HOFFMAN *Wild Scenes* 57 The broad west has no moose ground so celebrated as that in our northern counties. **1868** LOSSING *Hudson* 6 A winding and narrow river, fringed with rushes, lilies, and moose-head plants. **1854** HAMMOND *Hills, Lakes* 71 [We] had been down by the Saranac Lakes, beatin' up a moose pen. **1887** *Harper's Mag.* Feb. 458/2 'Moose shanks' are made by peeling the skin from the hind-legs of the animal. . . . The smaller end is then sewn up to form the toe; and thus a moose-hide stocking is formed. **1890** G. O. SHIELDS *Big Game N. Amer.* 37 Just as I passed the point . . . I found a Moose-trail. **1902** Moose trumpet [see MOOSE HORN 2].

+**Mooseberry.** =HOBBLEBUSH; also, the fruit of this. — **1848** THOREAU *Maine Woods* 59 The cornel, or bunch-berries, were very abundant, as well as Solomon's seal and moose-berries. **1894** *Amer. Folk-Lore* VII. 90 *Viburnum lantanoides*, moose-berry, triptoe, hobble-bush, Franconia, N.H.

+**Moose bird.** =CANADA JAY. — **1832** WILLIAMSON *Maine* I. 150 The Moose-bird, which feeds on the berries of the moose bush. *a*1862 THOREAU *Maine Woods* 220 The Canada-jay, moose-bird, meat-bird, or what not, came flitting silently . . . towards me. **1888** ROOSEVELT in *Century Mag.* June 210/1 Jays that were all of dark blue came familiarly round camp in company with the ever-present moose-birds or whisky jacks. **1917** *Birds of Amer.* II. 225.

+**Moose bush. a.** =HOBBLEBUSH. **b.** =LEATHERWOOD 1. — **1784** CUTLER in *Life & Corr.* I. 102 The ground [was] covered with an underwood of moose bush. **1832** WILLIAMSON *Maine* I. 117 *Moose-bush* [footnote: 'or "Moose-wood," *Dirca palustris*'] is a small tree or large shrub, not uncommon in the forest. **1868** *Amer. Naturalist* I. 666 Deer [in Maine] . . . browse 'moose-bush,' fir [etc.]. **1894** *Amer. Folk-Lore* VII. 90 *Viburnum lantanoides*, moose-bush, Buckfield, Me.

+**Moose call.** (See quot. 1890.) — **1890** *Cent.* 3853/2 *Moose-call*, . . . a trumpet of birch-bark used by hunters in calling moose to an ambuscade or blind. **1902** [see MOOSE HORN 2].

+**Moose deer.** =MOOSE 1. {1783–} Cf. AMERICAN ELK 1.
1672 JOSSELYN *New Eng. Rarities* 44 Water Lilly, . . . the Moose Deer feed much upon them, at which time the Indians kill them, when their heads are under water. **1743** CATESBY *Carolina* II. p. xxiv, Beasts of the same genus, but different in species from those of Europe, and the Old World [include] . . . The Panther, . . . Moose Deer, [and] Stag. **1775** BURNABY *Travels* 100 In the park I saw several American and English deer, and three or four elks or moose-deer. **1809** A. HENRY *Travels* 262 The Indians . . . killed two elk, otherwise called moose-deer. **1842** BUCKINGHAM *E. & W. States* I. 162 The moose-deer . . . is as tall as an ordinary horse.

attrib. **1805** LEWIS in *Ann. 9th Congress* 2 Sess. 1070 Brown and grizzly bear, dressed elk and moose-deer skins, muskrat skins.

+**Moose elm.** The slippery elm, *Ulmus fulva.* — **1810** MICHAUX *Arbres* I. 39 *Red Elm, . . . Slippery elm,* . . . [ou] *Moose elm,* . . . dans le haut de l'Etat de New York. **1832** BROWNE *Sylva* 311 This species of elm . . . bears the name of Red Elm, Slippery Elm and Moose Elm. **1889** *Cent.* 1881/1 The red elm, slippery-elm, or moose-elm, *U[lmus] fulva*, the inner bark of which is mucilaginous, and is used in medicine.

+**Moose flower.** The flower of the trillium. — **1850** S. F. COOPER *Rural Hours* 73 The moose-flowers are increasing in numbers. **1894** *Amer. Folk-Lore* VII. 102 *Trillium*, sp., moose-flowers.

+**Moose hide.** The hide or skin of a moose.
1736 GYLES *Mem. Captivity* 10 There [we] made Canoes of Moose-Hides. **1858** THOREAU *Maine Woods* 92 A St. Francis Indian, with his canoe and moose-hides. *a***1861** WINTHROP *Open Air* 107 Cancut . . . roofed with boughs an old frame for drying moose-hides. **1902** WHITE *Blazed Trail* 235 Injin Charley had . . . occupied odd moments in embroidering with beads and porcupine quills . . . moccasins of moose-hide.

b. Attrib. with *breeches, drum, snowshoe moccasin.*
1832 WILLIAMSON *Maine* II. 442 Some did not spare even their moose-hide breeches, moccasins and bayonet belts. **1903** WHITE *Forest* 127 In the center of the floor, . . . lay an open box from which tumbled dozens of pairs of moose-hide snowshoe moccasins. **1916** EASTMAN *From Deep Woods* 170 The moose-hide drum, stretched upon a cylinder of bass-wood, was [more than forty years old].

+**Moose horn.**

1. The horn of a moose, or a medicinal preparation similar to hartshorn prepared from this.
1672 JOSSELYN *New Eng. Rarities* 19 Moose Horns better for Physick use than Harts Horns. **1699** E. WARD *Trip New-Eng.* 13 In all Cases where Harts-horn is prescrib'd, the Moos-horn they [New England physicians] look upon to be a far better Medicine; half the Quantity being more powerful in effect. **1847** PARKMAN in *Knickerb.* XXIX. 506 The walls were plentifully garnished, he told us, with moose-horns and deer-horns, bear-skins and fox-tails. **1858** THOREAU *Maine Woods* 89, I saw a guide-post surmounted by a pair of moose-horns.

2. A trumpet, usually of birch bark, used by a hunter for calling moose within range.
1902 *Amer. Folk-Lore* XV. 249 After *moose* have been named the following: Moose-bird (the Canada jay), moose-call, moose-horn, or moose-trumpet (bark 'trumpet' used to imitate the note of the moose).

Moose-hunter. One who hunts moose. {1837–} — **1840** HOFFMAN *Grayslaer* I. 26 The moose-hunter was one of a hundred similar agents of frontier diplomacy. **1858** THOREAU *Maine Woods* 141 Ellis . . . was the most celebrated moose-hunter of those parts. *a***1861** WINTHROP *Open Air* 55 We dined with lumbermen and moose-hunters, scufflingly. **1920** *Outing* LXXVI. 304/3 The Caledonia jitney brings in another keen moose hunter.

+**Moose-hunting.** The action of searching for or pursuing moose. — **1839** HOFFMAN *Wild Scenes* 58 The deepest snows of winter of course offer the best occasion for moose-hunting. *a***1861** WINTHROP *Open Air* 36 We . . . talked of the pine-woods, of logging, . . . and of moose-hunting on snow shoes. **1886** *Outing* VII. 621 (*caption*), Moose-Hunting.

‖**Mooseling.** A young moose. — *a***1861** WINTHROP *Open Air* 56 Tame mooselings are exhibited.

+**Moose maple.** An American variety of small shrubby maple (*Acer spicatum*) found in the Maine and St. Lawrence region. — **1839** HOFFMAN *Wild Scenes* 38 We would come to a sort of plateau of swampy land, overgrown with moose maple. **1904** WHITE *Silent Places* 77 In the lucent, cool, green shadow of a thick clump of moose maples he felt . . . a certain warmth of tone.

+**Moose meat.** The flesh of the moose used as food. — **1845** *Knickerb.* XXV. 299 They ate the moose-meat which the Indians had left. *a***1861** WINTHROP *Open Air* 55 Moose-meat, combining the flavor of beef-steak and the white of turtle, appears on the table. *a***1862** THOREAU *Maine Woods* 291 He regretted that he had not taken more of the moose-meat to his family. **1920** *Outing* Sept. 271/1 The canoe . . . held about four hundred pounds of moose meat and a fine head.

+**Moose-misse.** [Algonquian. Cf. Chippewa and Nipissing *monsomish* 'moose shrub.'] **1.** (See quot. 1909.) **2.** The false wintergreen, *Pyrola americana.* — **(1)** **1893** [see INDIAN *attrib.* 14 a]. **1909** *Cent. Suppl.* 835/1 *Indian Mozemize*, the American mountain-ash, *Sorbus Americana.* **(2)** **1902** *Amer. Folk-Lore* XV. 249 *Moosemise.* A name current in certain parts of New England (Vermont) for the *Pyrola Americana* or 'false wintergreen.'

+**Moose skin.**

1. =MOOSE HIDE.
1637 MORTON *New Canaan* 29 [The Indians] make shooes of Mose skinnes. **1647** *Boston Rec.* 405 Shipped . . . 1 puncheon bever. 3 C seventy foure Moose skins. 1 pack beare skins. **1728** *Boston News-Letter* 4–11 July 2/2 To be Sold, . . . a Parcel of very good Moose & Seal Skins. **1809** A. HENRY *Travels* 69 The liquor was . . . conveyed into reservoirs or vats of moose-skin.

2. Attrib. with *belt, breeches, moccasin,* etc.
1664 *Essex Probate Rec.* I. 458 Moose skin sute. **1775** *Mass. H. S. Coll.* 2 Ser. IX. 162 Donations: . . . 1 pair moose-skin breeches. *c***1835** FOBES *Arnold's Exped.* 38 The man had some moose-skin moccasins. **1841** *Knickerb.* XVII. 30 The moose-skin belt that bound his sword, gave way. **1894** *Outing* XXIII. 405/2 The two moose-skin robes on the floor. **1896** *Harper's Mag.* April 728/1, I always walked behind my sledge, and kept my eyes on the tail of its moose-skin wrapper.

+**Moose tick.** An American tick (*Dermacentor albipictus*) found on moose. — **1868** *Amer. Naturalist* II. 559 The Moose Tick. . . . When the cow arrived in New York, her sides and back were almost covered with adult ticks. **1869** *Ib.* III. 167 We have observed that the young Moose tick lived nearly a month without food after hatching.

+**Moose tongue.** The tongue of a moose, which is prized as food. — **1675** JOSSELYN *Two Voyages* 129 Their Diet is . . . *Lobsters* rosted or dryed in the smoak, *Lampres* and dry'd *Moose*-tongues, which they esteem a dish for a *Sagamor.* *a***1862** THOREAU *Maine Woods* 289 Two or three large red chivin . . . , added to the moose-tongue, . . . made a sumptuous breakfast.

+**Moose warden.** An official appointed to enforce the game law relating to moose. Also transf., as a title. — **1853** *Maine Acts & Resolves* 24 The governor shall . . . appoint one county moose warden for each of the counties. *a***1862** THOREAU *Maine Woods* 214 The moose-wardens are not very particular. **1883** GOODE *Fishery Industries U.S.* 83 He had a canoe of birch, and on it he had burnt his name, and underneath the title 'Moose Warden,' and he said he would take care of all the moose that came within the reach of his rifle.

+**Moosewood.** Any one of various shrubs or small trees upon which the moose is accustomed to browse.

1. =LEATHERWOOD 1.
1778 CARVER *Travels* 507 The Moose Wood grows about four feet high, and is very full of branches. [**1836** TRAILL *Backwoods of Canada* 309 [In this enclosure I have] the red flowering raspberry (*rubus spectabilis*), leather-wood (*dircas*), called American mezereon, or moose-wood.] *a***1862** THOREAU *Maine Woods* 184, I found that it was a piece of dead moose-wood. **1865** A. D. WHITNEY *Gayworthys* xxxvi, The moosewood grew with its tough-grained stems and broad thick leaves. **1901** MOHR *Plant Life Ala.* 631.

2. The striped maple, *Acer pennsylvanicum.*
1792 BELKNAP *Hist. New-Hampshire* III. 163 [The moose feeds] on the leaves and bark of a species of the maple, which is called moose-wood. **1814** PURSH *Flora Amer.* I. 267 *Acer striatum.* . . . A small tree with an elegant striped bark; known by the name of Striped-maple or Moose wood. **1897** SUDWORTH *Arborescent Flora* 283.

+**Moose-yard.** An area in the forest where moose herd in winter and keep the snow trampled down for protection and feeding. — **1800** D'ERES *Memoirs* 117 The animals are overtaken in their retreats (for they herd together, sometimes a large number, just as it happens) which is called the Moose yard, formed by them in trampling down the snow. **1839** HOFFMAN *Wild Scenes* 58 The sagacious animal, so soon as a heavy storm sets in, commences forming what is called a 'moose-yard'; which is a large area, wherein he industriously tramples down the snow while it is falling, so as to have a space to move about in, and browse upon the branches of trees. **1890** *Harper's Mag.* Oct. 656/2 A moose yard is the feeding-ground of a herd of moose. **1902** *Amer. Folk-Lore* XV. 249 Moose-yard (the forest home and browsing place of the moose in winter).

+**Moot court.** A mock court held by law students to obtain practice in the conduct of cases. {1899–} — **1788** JEFFERSON *Writings* VII. 71 He gives lectures regularly and holds moot courts and parliaments wherein he presides. **1842** *Yale Lit. Mag.* VIII. 62 Another arena for improvement, . . . is the Moot Court, held once in each week, when questions of law are discussed by four students, and elaborate decisions are given by the Professors. **1888** BRYCE *Amer. Commonw.* III. VI. xcviii. 376 *n.*, In some law schools much educational value is attributed to the moot courts in which the students are set to argue cases.

***Mop.** +**1.** A snuff stick or brush. +**2.** The heavy mat of hair on the forehead of a buffalo. +**3.** A part of a dredge used by oystermen for removing starfish from oyster beds: (see quotation). — **(1)** **1860** E. COWELL *Diary* 66 Each snuff dipper has her bottle and swab stick or box and mop. **(2)** **1870** KEIM *Sheridan's Troopers* 40 On the forehead the bullet of the most powerful rifle has no effect whatever, the force being entirely expended on the immense mat or 'mop' of hair, eight or ten inches in length, between the eyes. **(3)** **1897** *N.Y. Forest, Fish, & Game Comm. 2d Rep.* 201 These mops are made of cotton twine, soft laid, and braided in ropes exactly like a mop for a kitchen floor, and, being attached to a triangle, are drawn by oyster steamers over the oyster beds.

+**Mopboard.** A baseboard or washboard where a wall joins a floor. — **1853** FOWLER *Home for All* 159 After mop or base-boards are nailed on, . . . fill in between these boards . . . with stone or mortar. **1882** HOWELLS *Modern Instance* xxii, When he sits on the sofa, and stretches out his legs, his boots touch the mop-board on the other side of the room. **1894** R. E. ROBINSON *Danvis Folks* 206 The old man was backed up to the wall with his heel against the mop-board. **1902** ALDRICH *Sea Turn* 201 Even the mop-boards were stripped off.

+**Moqui.** Also **Moquis.** *pl. S.W.* [Tribal name.] A Shoshonean tribe of Pueblo Indians, the Hopi. — **1834** A. PIKE *Sketches* 200 The Moqui (pronounced *Mokee*) and the Suni (*Sunee*) live near the Nabajo. **1873** COZZENS *Marvellous Country* 199 The Moquis, Zunis, and other Pueblo Indians in Northern Arizona and New Mexico. **1907** HODGE, etc. *Amer. Indians* I. 560 *Hopi*. . . . The name 'Moqui,' or 'Moki,' by which they have been popularly known, means 'dead' in their own language, but as a tribal name it is seemingly of alien origin and of undetermined signification.

Moral dialogue. +A theatrical performance. A term used to disguise or make palatable dramatic exhibitions to a public opposed to the theater. Also *moral lecture.* Now hist. — *c***1761** in Odell *Annals N.Y. Stage* I. 81 [Only the astute would recognize Othello . . . in shape of] a Series of Moral Dialogues, in Five Parts, Depicting the Evil Effects of Jealousy and Other Bad Passions. *a***1789** in E. B. Lee *Sketches N. Eng. Village* 101, I have been to the theatre, or rather to the moral lecture, as they have named it here. . . . This was . . . a very amusing play, called the 'School for Scandal.' **1853** W. W. CLAPP *Rec. Boston Stage* 8 'Love in a Village,' 'Romeo and Juliet,' 'Hamlet,' were also performed, as moral lectures.

Moral reform. Social uplift; improvement in morals. Also attrib. — **1837** *S. Lit. Messenger* III. 473 'Tis not alone in teaching . . . or getting subscribers to Moral-Reform newspapers that these ladies excel. **1842** *Niles' Nat. Reg.* 21 May 180/3 Female Moral Reform Society. *c***1848** WHITCHER *Bedott P.* xii. 123 A spell ago she was wide awake against Sabbath-breakin', and dident talk about nothin' else—then 't was moral reform—next come Millerism.

Morass. Also †**morast.** A marsh, bog, or fen. {1655-} — **1675** *Doc. Col. Hist. N.Y.* XII. 532 By ordr. of the shiriff & magistrates of this towne to dispose of a parcele of morast or flye formerly belonging to Capt. Carr. **1732** BYRD *Progress to Mines* (1901) 348 Neither this nor the South Branch run up near so high as the Mountains, but many Miles below them spread out into a kind of Morass. **1798** *Amer. Philos. Soc.* IV. 440 The Dismal swamp, much of which is a bog or morass. **1867** EDWARDS *Shelby* 54 Pope's column was saved from destruction only by the interposition of night and a deep morass.

Moravian, *n.* A member of an evangelical sect, known also as the Renewed Church of the United Brethren, which came to the United States from Germany in the eighteenth century. {1746-}

1737 W. STEPHENS *Proc. Georgia* 22, I should be present to hear what passed betwixt him and some of the Moravians. **1776** J. ADAMS *Works* IX. 403 At present some colonies have . . . bodies of Quakers, and Mennonists, and Moravians, who are principled against war. **1811** SUTCLIFF *Travels* (1815) 101, I come this day to Bethlehem, a town inhabited almost entirely by Moravians. **1871** LONGFELLOW in S. Longfellow *H. W. Longfellow* III. 173 Meditating a third play, . . . the scene to be among the Moravians at Bethlehem, Pennsylvania. **1890** *Cent.* 3857/1 The Moravians are especially noted for their energy and success in missionary work.

Moravian, *a.* Of or pertaining to the religious sect known as Moravians. {1745-}

1739 W. STEPHENS *Proc. Georgia* 393 An heavy Complaint being exhibited against the Moravian Brethern. **1777** J. ADAMS *Familiar Letters* 236 Yesterday we had the pleasure of seeing the Moravian mills in New Jersey. **1788** FRANKLIN *Autobiog.* 413, I inquir'd concerning the Moravian marriages, whether the report was true that they were by lot. **1826** FLINT *Recoll.* 10 Our journey from the beautiful Moravian settlements in Pennsylvania had been rendered sometimes tedious. **1835** HOFFMAN *Winter in West* I. 18 [Bethlehem, Pennsylvania] is a place of considerable interest, . . . on account of . . . the Moravian institutions which have rendered it so celebrated. **1919** *Census: Religious Bodies 1916* II. 524/2 The philanthropic institutions under Moravian auspices include . . . a home for the widows of Moravian ministers, at Bethlehem, Pa.

+**Moravian Indian.** An Indian converted by or under the influence of Moravian missionaries. *Obs.* — **1779** *N.H. Hist. Soc. Coll.* VI. 320 This place was settled by a denomination of people called Moravian Indians, by the Moravians having missionaries among them. **1831** WITHERS *Chron. Border Warfare* 232 The revengeful feelings . . . towards the Moravian Indians . . . were yet more deeply radicated by subsequent events.

+**Moravian town.** A town composed chiefly of Moravian missionaries and their Indian converts. *Obs.* — **1791** WASHINGTON *Diaries* IV. 186 Arrived at Salem, one of the Moravian towns. **1807** J. R. SHAW *Life* (1930) 56 [We] took a rout [*sic*] by the Moravian towns. **1815** *Niles' Reg.* VIII. 36/1 The places usually called the Moravian towns, were mere collections of Indian huts and cabins. **1831** WITHERS *Chron. Border Warfare* 160 Intelligence was conveyed to General Hand at Fort Pitt, by some friendly Indians from the Moravian towns.

+**Moray.** Also †**moreray, muray, murrey.** [App. from Port. *moreia.*] Any one of various species of eels of the family Muraenidae, found in warm seas. — **1624** SMITH *Gen. Hist. Va.* v. 172 Some of them yet knowne to the Americans, as the Purgoose, the Cauallo, the Gar-fish, Flying-fish and Morerayes. [*c***1733** CATESBY *Carolina* II. 20 The Muray [is found in the Bahama Islands].] **1884** GOODE, etc. *Fisheries* I. 629 The Morays—Murænidæ. On our Southern coasts are several species of eel-like fishes belonging to this family. **1897** *Outing* XXIX. 330/1 The murrey is not large, as Florida fishes go, but he is very red and excessively freckled.

Moreen. A strong fabric of wool or wool and cotton; also, a variety or grade of this textile. {1691-} Also attrib. — **1784** *Mass. Centinel* 19 May 3/3 Will be sold by publick vendue, at Russell & Clap's Auction-room . . . English and Raven's Duck, Moreens. **1812** *Niles' Reg.* II. 9/1 Much [wool] . . . may be wrought into . . . moreens. **1823** COOPER *Pioneers* vii, Her petticoat of green moreen. **1839** BRIGGS *H. Franco* I. 53 He took me . . . into a long room with green walls and red moreen curtains.

Morel. An edible fungus, *Morchella esculenta*, or a related fungus. {1672-} — **1855** *Rep. Comm. Patents 1854: Agric.* 364 Morel. (*Phallus esculentus.*) This vegetable is a native of this country, and closely related to the mushroom, from which it is distinguished by the cap being hollow within. **1885** *Rep. Comm. Agric.* 105 *Morchella esculenta*. . . . [Known also as] *Phallus esculentus, Helvella esculenta, &c.* . . . The morel is found in April or May in grassy places. . . . In the United States it is little known, although it grows in several of the States. **1898** *Dept. Agric. Yrbk. 1897* 467 Among the best edible fungi are the morels. **1917** *Farmers' Bul.* No. 796, 18 The morel has long been considered, both here and abroad, an excellent edible species.

More'n, Mor'n. Short for *more than.* Also ellipt. for 'no more than.' *colloq.* — **1850** GARRARD *Wah-To-Yah* xviii. 214 You have more'n enough for all. **1885** W. L. ALDEN *Adv. J. Brown* 203 There was mornascuttleful [*sic*] of big lumps of coal in the yard in the morning. **1886** *Harper's Mag.* July 323/2 But he (mor'n you and I with all our might) Could not here always remain. **1903** WIGGIN *Rebecca* 8 We've only just started on it, . . . it's more'n two hours.

+**Morgan.**[1] =MORGAN HORSE. Also attrib.

1843 *Knickerb.* XXI. 331 The stage generally being able to work its own way, drawn by horses of the Morgan breed. **1857** *Ill. Agric. Soc. Trans.* III. 463 Our best roadsters are produced from a cross of the thoroughbred or Morgan stallions with grade mares. **1862** *Rep. Comm. Patents 1861: Agric.* 548 Almost every breed or strain may find a representative; . . . nearly every one, and more especially the Morgan, improves on the western prairies. **1893** G. W. CURTIS *Horses, Cattle* 66 The Morgans we have already mentioned as taking the name and excellence of old Justin Morgan. **1906** CHURCHILL *Coniston* 22 The tough little Morgans of that time . . . have all but disappeared.

+**Morgan.**[2] *Hist.* In allusive contexts with reference to William Morgan, of Batavia, New York, alleged to have been murdered by the Freemasons. Also attrib. (Cf. GOOD-ENOUGH MORGAN.) — **1828** *Western Mo. Rev.* II. 253 There are [in Rochester] . . . plenty of Morgan excitement, soda fountains, concerts, shows. **1849** *Commercial* (Wilmington, N.C.) 5 May 2/2 (Th.S.), The *Standard* has got it up as a 'very good Morgan' for political effect.

Morgan horse. A superior breed of horses developed in Vermont by Justin Morgan {1747-1798}; also, a horse of this breed.

1849 *New Eng. Farmer* I. 314 There has never been a stock of horses in New England which has proved so generally useful as the Morgan stock of the original Morgan horse, raised by Justin Morgan, of West Springfield, Mass., in 1793. **1862** *Rep. Comm. Patents 1861: Agric.* 550 Being a Vermonter, I have known Morgan horses as long as I have known any. **1883** HAY *Bread-Winners* 77 If you don't want to talk, a team of Morgan horses couldn't make you. **1892** *Vt. Agric. Rep.* XII. 113 The Morgan horse is one of the productions that the State is justly proud of.

Morgen. =HOLLANDS ACRE. {1845-} — [**1626** *Doc. Col. Hist. N.Y.* I. 37 The Island Manhattes . . . [is] 11,000 morgens in size.] **1688** in Munsell *Annals Albany* II. 101 Granted him two flatts or plains upon both sides of ye Maquase river . . . containing about eleven morgen. **1744** A. HAMILTON *Itin.* (1907) 73 We met several Dutchmen on the island [near Albany, N.Y.], who had rented morgans of land upon it.

Morgue. [Fr.] +**1.** A place for the bodies of the dead, esp. one in which corpses are exposed in order that they may be identified and claimed. {1821, in Paris} +**2.** In a newspaper office, a file of clippings or reference collection of items of miscellaneous information, as biographical notes for use in writing obituaries, etc. — **(1) 1850** LEWIS *La. Swamp Doctor* 134 The morgue, in this institution [a hospital], was directly under the lecture room. **1869** J. H. BROWNE *Great Metropolis* 282 Two or three days pass without the entrance of a corpse into the morgue. **1899** in *Congress. Rec.* 10 Jan. (1900) 748/2 The body was removed to the morgue. **(2) 1925** BENEFIELD *Chicken-Wagon Family* 94, I have written a column of assorted obituaries after having dug up enough material in the 'Transcript's' 'morgue' for six columns.

+**Mormon.**

I. 1. The alleged prophet and author of the writings published in 1830 by Joseph Smith, the founder of the Mormon church.

1830 (*title*), The Book of Mormon. **1851** *Harper's Mag.* June 64/2 It professes to be an abridgement of the records made by the prophet Mormon.

+**2.** A member of the Church of Jesus Christ of Latter-Day Saints.

1830 *Massachusetts Spy* 22 Dec. (Th.), Elder Rigdon, one of the early Mormons, is described as having been 'a Campbelite leader of some notoriety.' **1846** T. H. JAMES *Rambles U. S.* 129 There are the *Davidites* . . . ; the *Fourrierites*, in Massachusetts; the *Mormons*, at Nauvoo. **1849** PARKMAN in *Knickerb.* XXXIII. 108 We were soon beset by a swarm of Mormons and Missourians. **1883** RITCH *Illust. N. Mex.* 57 The Mormons have also gained a foothold on its [New Mexico's] domain. *a***1918** G. STUART *On Frontier* I. 50 Our horses were greatly in need of rest so we stayed with . . . the Mormons . . . for several weeks.

+**b.** *transf.* A man with more than one wife. *colloq.*[2]

1887 *Courier-Journal* 17 Feb. 6/7 A Dusky Mormon. Three Women Claim Richard Woods for a Husband. . . . Officers . . . arrested Richard Woods, colored.

II. *attrib.* and *comb.*

3. Designating persons or groups of persons of the Mormon faith.

See also MORMON MISSIONARY.

[**1842** CASWALL *City of Mormons* 6 Houses . . . occupied . . . by Mormon emigrants. **1863** *All Year Round* 14 March 69/1 Such, exclaims our Mormon pilgrim, are the miracles which religious faith performs.] **1872** 'MARK TWAIN' *Roughing It* xii. 106 [We] took supper with a Mormon 'Destroying Angel.' 'Destroying Angels,' as I understand it, are Latter-Day Saints who are set apart by the Church to conduct permanent disappearances of obnoxious citizens. **1884** *Century Mag.* May 114 It was a Mormon elder, come to preach in that conservative, comfortable-minded village the strange doctrines of the Latter-Day Saints. **1892** GUNTER *Miss Dividends* 213 Then this Mormon fanatic is upon him.

4. Designating various aspects of conflicting interests of Mormons and non-Mormons.

See also MORMON WAR.

1847 PARKMAN in *Knickerb.* XXIX. 499 The St. Joseph emigrants were as good Christians and as zealous Mormon-haters as the rest. **1872** MC-CLELLAN *Golden State* 584 The 'Mormon rebellion' . . . had assumed alarming proportions. **1885** BAYLOR *On Both Sides* 224 Curious problem that, the Mormon one, and growing more serious every day, I hear. Perhaps history will be talking of the Mormon conquest in earnest some day. **1900** *Congress. Rec.* 23 Jan. 1104/1, I stand here to-day elected by the gentile votes of Utah, rather than by the Mormon votes. **1913** LONDON *Valley of Moon* 430 Clara's father had . . . ridden as far east with his troop as Salt Lake City, of which place he had been provost marshal when the Mormon trouble flared up.

5. Designating various aspects of commerce and public relations under the control or supervision of Mormons.

*a***1850** FORD *Hist. Illinois* (1854) 404 The Mormon press . . . and the anti-Mormon papers . . . kept up a continual fire at each other. [**1863** *All Year Round* 14 March 69/1 Liverpool is the point of departure for European Mormon emigrations. In that city, the Church has a special agency, which usually freights a whole ship for each voyage.] **1871** RAYMOND *3d Rep. Mines* 218 Far into the mining districts of other Territories went the Mormon trading-trains, carrying grain and vegetables. **1882** COYNER *Hand-Book of Mormonism* 90 Under the direction of the Church, 'Co-operative Mercantile Institutions' have been established . . . for the purpose of depriving Gentile and apostate Mormon merchants of the Mormon trade. **1888** ROE *Army Lett.* 385 Mormons . . . can purchase only at the mormon store, where the gentiles are ever cordially welcomed also.

6. Special combinations.

Mormon Battalion, a company of soldiers enlisted from the Mormon camps in the territory of Iowa for service in the Mexican War; *M. City*, Salt Lake City, Utah; *M. expedition*, the troops sent in 1857–8 to compel the Mormons in Utah to submit to federal laws; *M. Station*, (see quotation); *M. Temple*, a building dedicated to the administration of Mormon ordinances.

1848 *Santa Fe Repub.* 27 June 1/4 Capt. Hunt of the Mormon battalion, has left the Ciudad de Los Angelos for the Salt Lake. **1878** BEADLE *Western Wilds* 39 We got to the Mormon City all beat out. **1858** GLISAN *Jrnl. Army Life* 397 Our military friends of the Mormon expedition are perhaps barely sheltered under canvas tents on the snow-covered plains of Utah. **1877** W. WRIGHT *Big Bonanza* 20 To all who crossed the Plains, on their way to the gold-fields of California, in the early days, Genoa [Utah] was known as 'Mormon Station,' a name it continued to bear for some years. **1849** (title in Sabin XII. 384), An Authentic History . . . Including a full Exposure . . . of the Seven Degrees of the Mormon Temple.

+**Mormon Bible.** Those writings, alleged by Joseph Smith to have been discovered and translated by him, recognized as having divine authority by the Church of Jesus Christ of Latter-Day Saints; the Book of Mormon. — **1838** WHITTIER in W. P. & F. J. Garrison *Life W. L. Garrison* II. 221 A discussion of the merits of animal magnetism, or of the Mormon Bible, would have been quite as appropriate [as a debate over the question of admitting women to membership on an anti-slavery committee]. **1845** *S. Lit. Messenger* XI. 476/1 These facts were withheld from the world for the nine years which intervened from the first publication of the Mormon Bible. *a***1873** in Beadle *Undevel. West* 540, I'll take, to prove myself sincere, My 'davy' on a Mormon Bible.

+**Mormon church.** The common but unofficial name for the Church of Jesus Christ of Latter-Day Saints. — **1853** *Harper's Mag.* April 607/2 Persecution began with the first organization of the Mormon church. **1884** *Century Mag.* May 115/1 All the elder's efforts to converse on . . . the doctrines of the Mormon Church, he repelled. **1893** in *Congress. Rec.* 23 Jan. (1900) 1081/2 Polygamy had been forbidden by the Mormon Church.

Mormondom. The region over which Mormonism prevails; Mormon country. {1860–} — **1862** *N. Amer. Rev.* July 222 We cannot discover any Jews in Mormondom. **1878** BEADLE *Western Wilds* 314 All that part of the Mormondom south of the rim of the Great Basin is called Dixie. **1887** *Courier-Journal* 21 Jan. 1/2 His experience in Mormondom satisfies him that the Latter Day Saints are a thoroughly incorrigible people.

‖**Mormoness.** A female Mormon. — *a***1861** WINTHROP *J. Brent* 99 'What are those vermin about?' said Brent. 'Selecting, perhaps, a Mormoness to kidnap to-night or planning a burglary.'

+**Mormon flower.** (See quotation.) — **1878** JACKSON *Travel at Home* 19 This sunflower is called the Mormon flower, and is said to spring up wherever Mormons go.

+**Mormon fly.** (See quotation.) — **1847** C. LANMAN *Summer in Wilderness* 34, I noticed on . . . [the upper and lower rapids of the Miss. R.] a certain fly or miller which is found at the evening hour flying about in immense numbers. They are called the Mormon fly and I was told were found on these rapids alone.

+**Mormonism.** The doctrines and church polity of Mormons. {1845–}

1831 *Niles' Reg.* 16 July 353/1 Mormonism. . . . Certain knaves . . . started a new religion. **1844** 'UNCLE SAM' *Peculiarities* I. 65 Mormonism is a religion invented to raise the price of land in the smiling but partly unwooed valley of the Mississippi. **1872** *Newton Kansan* 28 Nov. 1/4 The object . . . is to resuscitate Mormonism. **1884** W. SHEPHERD *Prairie Exper.* 259 Polygamy to the outsider stands prominently as an ugly feature, on which the whole of Mormonism is based.

+**Mormonite.** A member of the Mormon church; also, in pl., the sect or entire body of believers in Mormonism. {1882–} — **1831** *Columbian Reporter* (Taunton, Mass.) 24 Aug. 1/5 The Mormonites. We learn from the Painesville Gazette, that this infatuated people are again in motion. **1835** ABDY *Journal* III. 40 The Kentuckian was well acquainted with the Mormons, or Mormonites. **1838** FLAGG *Far West* II. 83 He imparted to me some facts respecting that singular sect styling themselves Mormonites. **1848** BARTLETT 228 The Mormonites, or Latter-day Saints, are a religious sect which derive their name from the 'Book of Mormon.'

+**Mormon missionary.** One who attempts to make converts to Mormonism. — [**1863** *All Year Round* 14 March 72 He abstained, and accepted the office of Mormon missionary to France.] **1881** in Coyner *Hand-Book of Mormonism* (1882) 40 There is not a country on the globe where a Mormon missionary cannot be found.

+**Mormon state.** **a.** A state dominated by Mormons. **b.** (Both words usually capitalized.) Utah. — **1881** CHASE *Editor's Run in N. Mex.* 109 Grant appointed Axtell governor, who . . . went so far as to lay plans to import Mormons and get the territory [of N. Mex.] admitted into the Union as a Mormon state. **1893** L. WAGNER *More about Names* 35 Utah, otherwise The Mormon State, is called by the Mormons themselves Deseret.

+**Mormon trail.** The route followed by the Mormons in their emigration from the territory of Iowa to Utah in 1847. — **1850** G. K. WILDER *Diary* (MS.), We struck the old Mormon trail at this place. **1868** 'MARK TWAIN' *Curious Dream* 45 The post route from Indian Gulch . . . changed partly to the old Mormon trail.

+**Mormon war.** *Hist.* **1.** The disorders in Illinois (1844–6) caused by the enmity between the neighboring population and the Mormons in Nauvoo. **2.** The conflict between the Mormons of Utah and the troops sent (1857–8) to compel them to recognize the authority of the federal government. — (1) **1844** *Lexington Observer* 5 Oct. 3/5 Mormon War.—Military movements. **1845** *Niles' Reg.* 25 Sept. 64/3 Mormon war. The latest intelligence from the disgraceful scene in Illinois [etc.]. (2) *a***1918** G. STUART *On Frontier* I. 121 The best thing we could do would be to . . . come back in the spring, as the Mormon war would probably be over then.

+**Mormon-weed.** The American jute or Indian mallow, *Abutilon theophrasti*. {1896–8–} — **1872** *Ill. Dept. Agric. Trans.* IX. p. ix, The Indian Mallow . . . [is] variously known as . . . 'velvet leaf,' 'butter print,' 'Mormon weed,' etc. **1892** *Amer. Folk-Lore* V. 93 *Abutilon Avicennæ*, sheep-weed; Mormon-weed; velvet-weed. Quincy, Ill.

***Morning.** *attrib.* Designating various articles of clothing worn in the morning or during the day. {1620–} (See also MORNING CAP.) — **1678** *New Castle Court Rec.* 362, 2 wemens morning Coates. **1711** *Boston News-Letter* 26 Nov. 2/2 An old Morning Gown, dark colour'd Flower'd Damask on one side, and green on the other, and several other things were taken out of the House. **1852** *Harper's Mag.* Dec. 2/2 He found her in her morning-dress attending the flowers in her garden. **1856** STOWE *Dred* II. 46 Anne Clayton, in a fresh white morning-wrapper, . . . looked like a queenly damask rose.

+**Morning boat.** A steamboat that begins a trip or passage early in the morning. (Cf. DAY BOAT.) — **1857** WILLIS *Convalescent* 153 Taking the 'morning boat' which starts down the river, at seven, we disembark, an hour after, at West Point. **1871** HOWELLS *Wedding Journey* ii. 40 You had better go by the morning boat.

+**Morning business.** In the United States Senate, legislative matters dealt with in the period immediately following the reading of the journal. — **1870** *Congress. Globe* 21 April 2862/3 After the privileged morning business shall have been concluded, the Calendar shall be taken up. **1900** *Congress. Rec.* 3 Jan. 632/2 Senators about me suggest that the bill might be called up to-morrow immediately after the morning business.

Morning cap. (See quot. 1890.) — **1784** *Mass. Centinel* 14 July 4/2 Millenary . . . for sale, . . . consisting of Dress, Half-Dress, and Morning-Caps [etc.]. **1824** COOPER *L. Lincoln* II. 15 The airy band of her morning cap waved aside. **1875** STOWE *We & Neighbors* 131 Our modern Eves wear jaunty little morning caps and fascinating wrappers and slippers. **1890** *Cent.* 3861/3 *Morning-cap*, . . . a cap worn during the day, on other than ceremonial occasions; especially, a cap worn by women in the morning to cover and protect the hair.

+**Morning-glory.** Any one of various plants of the genus *Ipomoea* or related genera; also, the blossom of this.

1814 PURSH *Flora Amer.* I. 146 *Ipomoea Nil.* . . . Flowers beautiful pale blue, only open early in the morning, from which it has been called Morning-glory. **1846** *Knickerb.* XXVII. 171 [She bent down] to look after some stray 'morning-glory.' **1873** ALDRICH *Marjorie Daw* 57 Dew . . . had been left from the revels of the fairies overnight in the cups of the morning-glories. **1905** WIGGIN *Rose* 169 There was an open back door to this kitchen, a door framed in morning-glories.

attrib. **1871** STOWE *Sam Lawson* 75 She sat down in the mornin'-glory porch, quite quiet, and didn't sing a word. **1883** THAXTER *Poems for Children* 91 All clothed in bells of lovely blue, a morning-glory vine.

b. *Morning-glory stove*, a make or kind of stove for heating.

1885 ROE *Driven Back to Eden* 74 A morning-glory stove gave out abundant warmth and a rich light which blended genially with the red colors of the carpet.

Morning hour. {1634–} +One of the stages in the regular order of business in the Senate and the House of Representatives: (see quotations 1889 and 1911). — **1876** *Congress. Rec.* 10 Feb. 1003/1, I desire to make a suggestion . . . that the morning hour for reports from committees for this day be dispensed with. **1886** ALTON *Among Law-Makers* 57 After the 'morning hour,' the Senate generally devoted itself to the consideration of those measures which lead to the great debates of Congress. **1889** *Century Mag.* March 793/1 In those days there used to be what was called a 'morning hour,' wherein committees reported bills and put them on their passage. **1911** C. A. BEARD *Amer. Govt. & Pol.* 286 To this morning hour are assigned by rule certain public measures relating to such matters as the judiciary and interstate and foreign commerce, and carrying no appropriations.

Morning paper. A newspaper designed to reach its subscribers or the news stands in the early morning. {1862–} In full *morning newspaper*.

1809 *Ann. 10th Congress* 2 Sess. 1330 He had seen in a morning paper, that the Committee of Claims had reported. **1861** *Atlantic Mo.* April 445/1 In the police-reports of the morning paper you can find a dozen such tragedies. **1870** 'F. FERN' *Ginger-Snaps* 74 A lady who studiously avoids flashy apparel does not care to read in the morning paper that 'she appeared in a yellow gown trimmed in pink.' **1888** *Harper's Mag.* Oct. 679/2 The New York and Washington wire . . . gathers the cream of the 'exclusive' news to be found in the offices of the great New York morning newspapers. **1915** R. H. DAVIS *With Allies* 10 We would study the morning papers and . . . from them try to dope out the winners.

Morning room. A parlor or sitting room for the women of a household. {1822–} — **1845** KIRKLAND *Western Clearings* 122 Her morning-room—indeed, her only parlour—was fitted up [etc.]. **1872** *Atlantic Mo.* Jan. 21 Mrs. Washington's morning-room at Mount Vernon,—that room which was so 'nicely fixed for all sorts of work.' **1923** WATTS *L. Nichols* 230 The morning-room was a warm, nest-like place with an atmosphere essentially feminine.

Morocco. Leather, usually of goatskin, of a kind originally produced in Morocco, or an imitation of this. {1634–} Also attrib. and comb. — **1815** *Niles' Reg.* VIII. 141/2 [There are] 8 tanneries; 1 morocco factory; 7 tinners and coppersmiths [etc.]. **1876** INGRAM *Centennial Exp.* 631 [Among Delaware's industries are] those of iron ship-building, morocco manufacturing and car-building. **1885** *Harper's Mag.* Jan. 278/1 'Morocco' manufacture deals with the little goat and sheep skins for ladies' wear. **1891** CHASE & CLOW *Industry* II. 69 Fine morocco, for coach furniture and cabinet work, is made from the skin of the goats.

+**Morocco-head.** = DUN DIVER a. — **1888** TRUMBULL *Names of Birds* 65 To some Atlantic City gunners, [the goosander is known as] Morocco-Head. **1890** *Cent.* 3862/1 *Morocco-head*, . . . the American sheldrake or merganser, . . . (New Jersey.) **1917** *Birds of Amer.* I. 110 Merganser. *Mergus americanus*. . . . [Also called] Morocco-head (female).

+**Morocco-jaw.** The surf scoter, *Melanitta perspicillata.* — **1888** TRUMBULL *Names of Birds* 103 At Bellport, L.I., Morocco-Jaw and White-Head. **1917** *Birds of Amer.* I. 151 Surf Scoter. *Oidemia perspicillata*. . . . [Also called] Plaster-bill; Morocco-jaw; Goggle-nose.

+**Morocco millet.** = JOHNSON GRASS. — **1889** VASEY *Agric. Grasses* 36 *Sorghum halepense* (Johnson Grass; Mean's Grass) . . . has been called . . . Australian Millet, and Morocco millet.

Morocco shoes. Shoes made from morocco leather. — **1822** *Ann. 17th Congress* 1 Sess. I. 320 Women's morocco shoes . . . cost about seventy-five and eighty seven and a half cents per pair. **1833** *New England Mag.* IV. 58 A pair of Morocco shoes. **1843** *Lowell Offering* III. 92 Cousin Mary would sit and wait for him . . . with her pink calico gown on . . . and her best morocco shoes.

+**Morrisite.** A follower of Joseph Morris, the leader of a group of Mormons who seceded from the orthodox church about 1860. — **1863** J. L. FISK *Exped. Rocky Mts.* 31 On entering the mountains to the north of the Mormon settlements, we passed 'Soda Springs,' a small town of 'Morrisites,' seceders from Mormonism. **1870** BEADLE *Utah* 417 The Morrisites could only reply with their ducking-guns. **1878** — *Western Wilds* 340 He, too, longed for a living prophet, and in a month was as zealous a 'Morrisite' as he had once been a Brighamite. **1883** Schaff *Relig. Encycl.* II. 1579/2 In Utah there have been Morrisites, reproaching Brigham that he was so barren of 'revelations.'

Morse. *attrib.* [S. F. B. *Morse*, Amer. inventor (1791–1872).] Designating telegraphic inventions made by Morse or things pertaining to these. — **1858** G. B. Prescott *Telegraph* 191 We work with Morse Key and detector. **1862** in Moore *Rebellion Rec.* V. II. 535 The following letter . . . gives an interesting account of the services of the Morse telegraph to the army. **1880** *Harper's Mag.* Oct. 727/2 Buyers . . . rap out their bids with the Morse instrument. **1890** *Ib.* Feb. 429/1 The expertness . . . made him one of the 'knights of the key,' as manipulators of the Morse alphabet delighted to call themselves.

***Mortar.** Also †**morter.**

***1.** A vessel in which various things are beaten up or pounded with a pestle.

1638 *Md. Archives* IV. 48, 1. litle brasse morter & pestle. **1705** BEVERLEY *Virginia* III. 15 The Kernels of the Hiccories they [*sc.* Indians] beat in a Mortar with Water. **1797** HAWKINS *Letters* 252, I will give . . . each a pestle and mortar, a sifter and riddle and fanner. **1819** *Penna. Gazette* 22 June 2/3 [The Seminoles] use a root called coonty, as a substitute [for corn]. . . . They beat it in a mortar. **1894** *Congress. Rec.* 12 Dec. 236/1 The real Indian . . . raises, in a very rude way, some corn on these 2 or 3 acres. He pounds it in a stone mortar.

+**b.** *Mining.* (See quot. 1881.)

1881 RAYMOND *Mining Gloss.*, *Mortar*, . . . the receptacle beneath the stamps in a stamp mill, in which the dies are placed, and into which the rock is fed to be crushed. **1882** *47th Congress 1 Sess.* H. R. Ex. Doc. No. 216, 588 The gold goes in and out of the mortars continuously.

***2.** A short piece of large-bore, heavy ordnance designed to throw shells at high angles. Orig. *mortar piece*.

*c*1695 MILLER *Desc. of New York* (1843) 35 Two or three mortar pieces. **1745** SHIRLEY *Correspondence* (1912) I. 277 Cross fires from the Cannon and Mortars and even from our Musquetry rang'd thro' the Houses and Streets. **1756** *Doc. Hist. N.Y. State* I. 504 The Garrison on their side continued to fire above 4 hours with 12 Guns and 4 Mortars whereof one of the latter burst. **1838** INGRAHAM *Burton* II. 148 The cannonading . . . became spirited, occasionally mingled with the roll of musketry, and the dull, heavy report of a mortar. **1889** *Cent.* 448/3 *Barbed shot*, a shot having barbs or grapnels. It is fired from a mortar to carry a life-line to a wreck.

3. Attrib. in sense 2 with *boat, fleet, flotilla*, etc.

1862 NORTON *Army Letters* 62 Our mortar-fleet had taken New Orleans. **1863** in Moore *Rebellion Rec.* V. I. 86 Sabine Pass, Texas, was this day attacked and captured by the United States steamer Kensington . . . assisted by the mortar-boat Henry Janes. **1865** RICHARDSON *Secret Service* 225 The mortar-rafts, with tremendous explosions, began to throw their ten-inch shells. **1885** *Century Mag.* April 924/2 A naval expedition was to be fitted out . . . with a powerful mortar-flotilla.

Mortar bed.[1] {1842–} +**a.** A shallow box or boxlike receptacle in which mortar for use in building is mixed. **b.** A layer of mortar or stratum of rock resembling mortar. — **1853** FOWLER *Home for All* 21 Throw the stuff, namely, grayish, reddish sand, and stones, right into your mortar beds, mix with lime, and then shovel into the wall. **1857** *Ill. Agric. Soc. Trans.* III. 472 The back yard . . . [is] filled with rags, bones, chip piles, broken hoe handles, . . . refuse shingles, old mortar beds, ash barrels [etc.]. **1862** *Ib.* V. 168 The soil a light chalky one, . . . in the wet season forming a perfect mortar bed. **1905** *Forestry Bureau Bul.* No. 66, 8 In western Kansas and southwestern Nebraska there are extensive bodies of irregular, coarse-grained, mortarlike rock of Tertiary formation, locally known as 'mortar beds' or 'magnesia.'

Mortar bed.[2] {1769–} *Mining.* The inclined bottom of a stamp used in crushing ore. — **1871** RAYMOND *3d Rep. Mines* 340 The battery-box is . . . cast in one piece with the mortar-bed. **1874** — *6th Rep. Mines* 353 The mortar-beds constitute a series of inclined terraces . . . ; and the pulp passing through the screens of one battery is discharged immediately into the one next in front, to be crushed still finer.

***Mortgage.**

***1.** *Law.* A legal instrument that operates as a lien or claim upon specific property given by a debtor to a creditor as security for money.

1636 *Plymouth Laws* 43 That all sales exchanges gifts morgages leases or other conveyances of houses & lands, the sale to be . . . committed to publick record. **1703** *Mass. H. S. Coll.* 3 Ser. VII. 61 Col. Hamilton . . . was necessitated to take a mortgage of said Patents, else have nothing. **1796** *Ann. 4th Congress* 2 Sess. 2696 Taxes . . . must be paid out of the assets in the hands of executors, prior to any judgments, mortgages, or debts whatsoever. **1862** *Huntington Rec.* III. 473 To pledge . . . mortgages or other vouchers belonging to the Town of Huntington, as collateral security for the payment of said loan. **1881** CARLETON *Farm Festivals* 128 And for that [ground] and some down-money put a mortgage on my farm. **1912** N. M. Woodrow *Sally Salt* 335, I'll foreclose the mortgages I hold on your patches of ground.

b. *First* (or *second* or *third*) *mortgage*, a conveyance of this kind which is the first (or second or third) given and outstanding on a particular property. Also attrib.

1855 *Huntington Rec.* III. 418 In payment we will give assigned mortgages (first mortgages) on real estate, principally in the town of Huntington. **1873** *Republic* I. App. p. ii, Each subscriber to it was entitled to receive as a bonus an equal amount of first-mortgage bonds. **1882** *Nation* 17 Aug. 144/3 The Western Farm Mortgage Co., Lawrence, Kansas, [issues] First Mortgage Loans. **1884** Matthews & Bunner *In Partnership* 109 There was nothing new on the place except a third mortgage. **1898** Westcott *D. Harum* xvii, That afternoon I sent over to the county seat an' got a description an' had a second morgidge drawed up fer two hundred dollars.

2. Attrib. with *bond, deed, lien, limitation, man.*

1657 *Suffolk Deeds* III. 7 The said premisses . . . to be bargained and sold . . . wthout any former mortgage limitation. **1672** *Essex Inst. Coll.* LVI. 304 Mortgage deed, Theoder Atkinson, sen., of Boston, merchant and felt maker. **1708** *R.I. Col. Rec.* IV. 50 The said committee . . . there heard the claims and pretended titles of those gentlemen, called the mortgage men. **1871** *Mich. Gen. Statutes* I. (1882) 990 After such mortgage-lien shall have attached to such interest in such canal and water-power, the secretary of such association shall make a certificate in writing. **1909** *Cent. Suppl.* 830/1 *Mortgage-bond* . . . , a bond secured by a mortgage.

+**Mortician.** An undertaker. — **1895** *Columbus Dispatch* 14 Aug. (*advt.*), We, Mauk & Webb, are the only Morticians in the city who do not belong to the Funeral Directors' Protective Association. **1921** Mencken *Amer. Language* (rev. ed.) 144 [The Englishman] never calls an undertaker a *funeral director* or *mortician.*

***Mortise.** Also †**mortis, mortoise.** *attrib.* Designating tools used in making mortises. — **1676** *Essex Inst. Coll.* XLII. 146 An Inventory of Jonathan Wilds estate . . . a mortis Auger. **1789** *Ky. Gazette* 30 Jan. 1/4 To be sold . . . Turning, Mortoise and Socket Chisels. **1875** Knight 1085/1 *Heading-chisel.* A chisel for cutting down the head of a mortise. A mortise-chisel.

Mortising ax. Also †**mortessing, mortissing axe.** An ax of a type used in cutting mortises. *Obs.* — **1655** *Essex Probate Rec.* I. 201 Mortising axe, 2s, a pair of tow cards, 1s.; hatt bruish, 6d. **1663** *Old Eliot* I. 180 Working Towles [include] 1 mortessing axe, 2 adges. **1678** *Maine Wills* 82, I do giue unto my sonn . . . my mortissing axe & my sword.

+**Morus multicaulis.** =Multicaulis. — **1833** *Niles' Reg.* XLIV. 332/2 A succession of crops of silk . . . can, by the Chinese *moras multicaulis*, be repeatedly cultivated and distributed throughout in this part of the new world. **1839** *S. Lit. Messenger* V. 752/2 From the hitherto barren enclosure, was seen to sprout a flourishing young plantation of the morus multicaulis. **1847** Darlington *Weeds & Useful Plants* 295 About twenty years ago, a variety of the White Mulberry—of smaller stature, and much larger leaves, (well known by the name of *Morus multicaulis*), was introduced, as being still better adapted to the feeding of Silk-worms.

+**Morus plantation.** A plantation of white mulberry of the variety of multicaulis. — **1839** *S. Lit. Messenger* V. 753/1 She busied herself more than ever with her morus plantation.

+**Mosbyite.** During the Civil War, one of the guerrilla fighters under the leadership of the Confederate colonel, John S. Mosby (1833–1916). — **1867** J. M. Crawford *Mosby* 286 In those expeditions he [a Northern officer] did nothing very damaging to us, except here and there picking up a Mosbyite and a horse or two.

+**Mose.** A 'b'hoy.' In allusion to a character in *A Glance at New York*, a play first acted in 1848. *slang. Obs.* — **1851** Northall *Curtain* 92 Mose, instead of appearing on the stage, was in the pit, the boxes, and the gallery. **1856** M. Thompson *Plu-ri-bus-tah* 222 Yunga-Merrakah determined To put off his Bowery notions, . . . To have done with Mose and 'Syksey.'

***Moses.**

1. A ship's boat of a certain kind: (see quot. 1769). *Obs.*

This is possibly short for Moses boat.

1759 *Essex Inst. Coll.* II. 286/1 The Capt. sent our Moses (Boat) after them. [**1769** Falconer *Dict. Marine* (1776) F4v A moses is a very flat broad boat, used by merchant-ships amongst the Carribee-islands, to bring hogsheads of sugar off from the sea-beach to the shipping.] **1774** Romans in P. L. Phillips *Notes on B. Romans* 19 It must Blow very hard before the Water begins to be too Rough for a Small Moses.

2. +**a.** *To give particular Moses*, to scold or handle severely. **b.** In various oaths. {1855–}

1850 Lewis *La. Swamp Doctor* 52 The way a number ten go-to-meetin' brogan commenced givin' a hoss particular Moses, were a caution to hoss-flesh. **1858** Holmes *Autocrat* 298 The parson . . . stopped perplexed At what the—Moses—was coming next. **1869** 'Mark Twain' *Innocents* v. 52 The suffering Moses!—there ain't enough money in the ship to pay that bill. **1871** De Vere 595 An effective ejaculation and moral waste-pipe for interior passion or wrath is seen in the exclamation, *By the Ever-Living Jumping Moses.*

+**Moses boat.** *N. Eng.* [Origin uncertain.] A ship's boat constructed with a keel: (see quots. and cf. Moses 1). *Obs.*

1706 *Boston News-Letter* 3 June, There was Stole, a Little Moses Boat from the side of the Sloop Larke. **1766** *Mass. Gazette* 16 Oct. (Ernst), A Moses Boat, about fourteen Foot long, having a Turpentine Bottom, her sides paid with Spanish Brown. **1770** *Boston Gaz.* 23 April 3/2 Taken from Long Side a Schooner at the North-End, the 13th Inst. a Moses Boat, 16 Feet. **1795** *Columbian Centinel* 12 Oct. 4/4 (Ernst), Found, In Medford-River, adrift, a Moses-Boat, about 10 feet keel. **1812** *Boston Gazette* 26 Oct. Suppl. (Th.), On Saturday was picked up, on Dorchester Flats, a small Moses boat.

+**Moses-built boat.** A boat built in the manner of a moses boat. *Obs.* — **1753** *S.C. Gazette* 5 Feb., Stolen, a New-England moses-built boat. **1770** *Boston Gazette* 12 March 3/2 (*advt.*) (Ernst), A Moses built Boat.

+**Mosey,** *v.* [Perhaps from *vamose.*]

1. a. To move along slowly; to go along *with. slang.* **b.** As an understatement: To move along fast; to be lively. *slang.*

1829 *Va. Lit. Museum* 30 Dec. 459 *Mosey.* To move off. *Kentucky.* **1837** Neal *Charcoal Sk.* (1838) 13 If your tongue wasn't so thick, I'd say you must mosey. **1851** *Polly Peablossom* 169 But you jist git rite up an mosey. **1876** *Wide Awake* 21/2 'Everybody hurry now!' Nellie 'mosied,' and everybody hurried. **1885** 'Craddock' *Prophet* 238 Hurry 'long, D'rindy, . . . you-uns ain't goin' ter reel a hank ef ye don't mosey. **1889** Munroe *Golden Days* 26 Even if you should . . . mosey with the outfit, I'd be willing to let it go for the sake of the experience. **1903** Ade *People You Know* 74 'That will be about all from you,' said the Man. 'Mosey! Duck! Up an Alley!'

2. With adverbs. **a.** With *around, off*, etc.

1836 *Phila. Publ. Ledger* 2 Dec. (Th.), You'r not going to smoke me. So mosey off. **1880** 'Mark Twain' *Tramp Abroad* xxvi. 269 Tomorrow I'll be up bright and early . . . and mosey off to Tennessee. **1901** White *Claim Jumpers* 245, I'll mosey up to the shack and see about supper. **1923** J. H. Cook *On Old Frontier* 36 When that hyena comes to camp, you kind o' mosey around till he puts his gun down.

b. *To mosey along.* Also fig.

1870 'Mark Twain' *Curious Republic of Gondour* (1919) 57, I hain't got time to be palavering along here—got to . . . mosey along. **a1877** *N.Y. Tribune* (B.), I'll get a room nicely furnished, and my wife and I will jes mosey along till the election trouble is over, an' den dere'll be a powerful sight of whitewashin' to be done. **1897** Clover *Paul Travers' Adv.* 271 But say, let's mosey along and get some breakfast. **1913** Biggers *7 Keys to Baldpate* 94, I got a little business here, and then we'll mosey along.

+**Mosey sugar.** (See quotations.) — **1849** W. Duane *Let. to Bartlett* 22 Jan. (MS.), *Sugar Mosey* or *Mosey Sugar*, the name of a cake made of sugar, for children, in Harrisburgh Pa. **1870** *Nation* July 56/2 'Mosey-sugar' . . . was a black molasses candy—not cake, as Bartlett says—scalloped at the edges like our cakes of maple-sugar.

+**Moshay.** (See quotation.) — **1877** Bartlett 408 *Moshay*, a slave who came from Florida at the beginning of the late civil war states that this is the name given there to the keeper of bloodhounds.

***Mosquito.** Also **muske(e)to, muscato,** etc.

Of the variant spellings of this word, *musketo* and *musquito* have been the most common until recent times.

***1.** Any of certain insects of the family Culicidae, esp. of the genera *Culex, Aëdes*, and *Anopheles.*

1622 'Mourt' *Relation* 109 What with . . . fleas within doores, and Muskeetoes without, wee could hardly sleepe. **1630** Higginson *New-England* 17 Musketoes, . . . except they be smoaked out of their Howses are troublesome in the night season. **1682** *Hist. Coll. S. Carolina* II. 136 There are few Insects in Carolina that can reasonably be complain'd of, except a sort of Gnats, which they call *Muscatoes.* **1785** Ellicott in Mathews *Life A. Ellicott* 41 We are much pestered with Muskeetoes and Knats. **1788** Asbury *Journal* II. 37 The Gnats are almost as troublesome here, as the mosquitoes in the lowlands of the seaboard. **1829** *Va. Lit. Museum* 221 Their only annoyances seem to be a few musquetoes, a good many gnats, and now and then a bilious, or an intermittent fever. **1884** *Boston Jrnl.* 23 Sept., More to be grateful for is the freedom from the pests of camps—mosquitoes. **1920** Lincoln *Mr. Pratt* 96 As for the live stock, that was seven thousand hop-toads . . . and green-heads and mosquitoes forever and ever, amen.

2. *attrib.* and *comb.* +**a.** Designating places or areas infested with mosquitoes. Sometimes in place names.

1668 *Oyster Bay Rec.* I. 42 Joseph Carpenter of Muskeeto Cove. **1778** Carver *Travels* 106 All the wilderness between the Mississippi and Lake Superior is called by the Indians the Moschettoe country. **1837** W. Jenkins *Ohio Gaz.* 323 Musketoe creek . . . was so called by the original surveyors of the Western Reserve, on account of the great numbers of Musketoes. **1847** Robb *Squatter Life* 70 Hoss Allen's Apology; or, The Candidate's Night in a Musquito Swamp!

b. Designating various devices for protection against the mosquito.

1826 Cooper *Mohicans* xiv, The mists of Horican are not like the curls from a peace-pipe, or the smoke which settles above a mosquito-fire. **1843** *Nat. Hist. N.Y., Geology* 1. 233n., Although provided with thick gloves and musquito veils, myself and lady were much annoyed. **1857** *Rep. Comm. Patents 1856* 317 *Mosquito Canopy.* . . . The rods 8 and 9 which support the canopy [etc.]. **1866** *Ib. 1863* I. 294 An expanding mosquito frame formed of bars fitted so as to be increased or decreased in length to fit the window. **1867** *Ib. 1866* I. The deep frame . . . , [and] the narrow fringe or edging . . . forming a mosquito guard for the face. **1870** *Ib. 1868* II. 145/2 *Mosquito Killer*. . . . The head-piece is made of thin board covered with cloth of a loose nap.

+**Mosquito bar.** (Cf. BAR *n.*[3])

1. A framework covered with mosquito netting that may be fitted like a tent over a bed to protect the sleeper from mosquitoes.

1809 *Ann. 11th Congress* 2448 Ninety-five musquito bars, at 4½ and 7 dollars each. **1819** LATROBE *Journal* 237 The mosquito bar is a kind of a box without a bottom. **1850** TYSON *Diary in Calif.* 55 The former . . . we found lying under a rude sort of mosquito bar. **1907** *Harper's Mag.* Jan. 218 The canvas top of his mosquito-bar protected him from the torrent from above.

2. The mosquito netting that serves this purpose; any mosquito netting. Also attrib.

1828 J. HALL *Lett. from West* 227 The musquitoe bar . . . is a curtain, of the thinnest gauze, . . . which admits the air, and excludes the musquitoe. **1863** *Rep. Comm. Patents 1861* 443 Improved Mosquito-Bar Frame. . . . Frames of wood or other material . . . [which] when covered by a proper material . . . may be used as a protection against mosquitoes or as a tent. **1869** *Rep. Comm. Agric. 1868* 329 Lay a strata of wet moss in the bottom of the box, and cover the same with a fold of the gauze called 'musquito bar.' **1888** CABLE in *Century Mag.* Dec. 260/1 From a sort of dais escaped the folds of an embroidered bobbinet mosquito-bar. **1904** STUART *River's Children* 37 Mammy . . . tucked the mosquito-bar snugly around her.

+**Mosquito bear.** =prec. *Obs.* (Cf. BEAR *n.*[3]) — **1804** ORDWAY in *Jrnls. Lewis & O.* 87 Got mosquetoes bears from Capt. Lewis to sleep in. **1806** CLARK in *Lewis & C. Exped.* V. (1905) 323 My Musquetor Bear has a number of small holes worn through [which] they [mosquitoes] pass in.

+**Mosquito bier.** =MOSQUITO BAR. *Obs.* (Cf. BIER *n.*[1]) — **1805** LEWIS in *L. & Clark Exped.* II. (1904) 228, I sent a man to the canoes for my musquetoe bier . . . as it is impossible to sleep without being defended against the . . . insects. **1821** NUTTALL *Travels Arkansa* 191 Two very handsome young men of the Osages . . . endeavoured, though ineffectually, to hook off a musquetoe bier.

+**Mosquito box.** A box lined with dark blue or black cloth used to trap mosquitoes. Used fig. — **1887** N. PERRY *Flock of Girls* 224 Here you are in this poky little mosquito-box.

Mosquito curtain. A mosquito net or gauze used around a bed as protection against mosquitoes. {1819} — **1803** *Lewis & Clark Exped.* VII. (1905) 234 Camp Equipage [includes]: . . . Muscatoe Curtains, 2 patent chamber lamps & wicks. **1829** B. HALL *Travels in N.A.* III. 356 The beds were enclosed in mosquito curtains. **1852** STOWE *Uncle Tom* xxxviii, Marie disposed herself on a lounge, under a silken mosquito curtain. **1863** WHITMAN *Spec. Days* 42 The mosquito-curtains of the adjoining cots obstructed the sight.

+**Mosquito hawk.**

1. A night hawk.

1709 LAWSON *Carolina* 144 *East-India* Bats or Musqueto Hawks, are the Bigness of a Cuckoo, and much of the same Colour. **1789** ANBUREY *Travels* II. 228, [I] am apt to conclude, that the Musquito hawk and whipper-will are the same bird. **1850** *Conn. Public Acts* 5 It shall not be lawful . . . for any person to shoot . . . the robin, blue-bird, swallow, . . . night or mosquito-hawk, whip-poor-will [etc.]. **1873** *Ill. Dept. Agric. Trans.* X. 352 No person shall . . . kill any . . . swallow, martin, mosquito hawk, whip-poor-will [etc.]. **1917** *Birds of Amer.* II. 172.

2. *S.* A dragon fly: (see quotations).

1737 BRICKELL *N. Carolina* 163 The Muskeetoe-Hawks, are Insects, so called, from their continually hunting after Muskeetoes, and killing and eating them. **1837** WILLIAMS *Florida* 70 Musquito Hawk. . . . Called by some the dragon fly. **1842** BUCKINGHAM *Slave States* II. 39 Another . . . destroyer is common here, called the mosquito-hawk, a large insect of the moth species. **1899** *Animal & Plant Lore* 63 Mosquito-hawk, dragon-fly.

Mosquito net. A net or screen for keeping out mosquitoes, used on beds, windows, etc.; also, =next. {1764} Also attrib.

1745 E. KIMBER *Itinerant Observ.* 13 [The people of Georgia] scorn Umbrellas and Musketto-Nets, as *Jamaican* and *Carolinean* Effeminacies. **1775** ROMANS *Nat. Hist. Florida* 189 Where musketoes are plenty, have a close covering, . . . made in form of a musketo net, to put up over your bed. **1804** LEWIS in *L. & Clark Exped.* VII. (1905) 299, I send you . . . 16 musquetoe nets and our shirts. **1868** *Rep. Comm. Patents 1867* II. 1046/2 *Mosquito Net Frame*. . . . The upright bow is attached to the head posts of the bed-stead [etc.]. **1885** JACKSON *Zeph* iv, There ain't a window nor a door out to Greenhills that hasn't got mosquito net in it. **1894** CABLE *J. March* xxix, One dark hand lifted back the white mosquito-net.

Mosquito netting. A coarse fabric with open meshes out of which mosquito nets are made; also, a mosquito net. {1840–} Also attrib.

1854 BOYNTON & MASON *Journey through Kansas* 56 The musquito netting was ingeniously hung. **1866** A. D. WHITNEY *L. Goldthwaite* viii, You might tie up a branch with mosquito-netting. **1894** *Harper's Mag.* July 242/2, I sank down among the soft and caressing covers and drew the mosquito-netting together. **1905** WIGGIN *Rose* 78 He opened the mosquito netting door to let her pass out. **1912** N. M. WOODROW *Sally Salt* 133 He took the mosquito netting off the bust.

+**Mosquito proof,** *a.* Of persons: Immune to mosquito bites. — **a1656** BRADFORD *Hist.* 196 They are too delicate . . . that cannot enduer the biting of a muskeeto; we would wish such to keepe at home till at least they be muskeeto proofe. **1818** FORDHAM *Narr. Travels* 216, I thought I was mosquito proof last year.

***Moss.** Also †**morse.**

+**1.** The plant *Tillandsia usneoides* of the southern states, which hangs on trees like tufts of long gray hair. Freq. with defining terms.

See also BLACK, HANGING, LONG, NEW ORLEANS, SPANISH MOSS.

1733 *Ga. Col. Rec.* III. 381 There is no Morse on the Trees, tho' in most Parts of Carolina they are covered with it. **1803** J. DAVIS *Travels* 119n., This moss . . . is bought [in Charleston] to stuff mattresses, and chair-bottoms. **1850** LEWIS *La. Swamp Doctor* 197 The swamp moss was flowing around him in long, tangled masses. **1882** J. SMITH *Dict. Pop. Names of Plants* 277 American or New Orleans Moss. **1896** Florida moss [see FLORIDA 2 b]. **1907** *St. Nicholas* July 847/1 Then there is the hanging beard 'moss' that drapes the oaks.

***2.** *collect.* Any one of several bryophytic plants of the class Musci, with small and leafy stems; also, any one of numerous lichens or other plants that resemble these.

1850 LEWIS *Louisiana Swamp Doctor* 181 Here you sit, like a knot in a tree, with the moss commencing to grow on your back. **1888** M. LANE in *America* 18 Oct. 16 Mossback . . . seems to have originated in the swamps of North Carolina, where a particular class of the poor whites were said to have lived among the cypress until the moss had grown upon their backs. **1905** *Forestry Bureau Bul.* No. 61, 42 *Moss*, to fill with moss the crevices between the logs in a logging camp.

3. *attrib.* and *comb.* **a.** In the specific names of plants.

1817–8 EATON *Botany* (1822) 172 *Andromeda hypnoides*, moss bush . . . small, creeping. **1861** WOOD *Botany* 486 *Cassiope*. Moss-plant. . . . Small, alpine, moss-like or heath-like shrubs. **1898** Moss milion (melon) [see MOSS BERRY].

b. In the specific names of birds.

1880 CABLE *Grandissimes* 237 The red-bird, the moss-bird, the night-hawk and the Chuckwill's widow. **1888** TRUMBULL *Names of Birds* 75 The colored women often use a large bunch of 'Florida Moss' . . . as a cushion for the heavy loads they carry upon their heads, and I am inclined to believe that 'Moss-head' [as a name for the hooded merganser, *Lophodytes cucullatus*] was suggested by this practice, rather than by any direct resemblance to moss in the bird's crest. [S.C.]

Moss agate. An agate of mosslike appearance. {1845} Also attrib. — **1869** BOWLES *Our New West* 124 Over the river . . . was the famous 'moss agate patch.' **1876** CROFUTT *Trans-continental Tourist* 53 The manufacture of moss agate jewelry has grown into an extensive trade. **1879** B. F. TAYLOR *Summer-Savory* 34 You see rich displays of Colorado 'specimens,' from tiger-cats to moss-agates. **1897** LEWIS *Wolfville* 175 He ain't tender now; he's as hard as moss-agates, an' as worthless.

+**Mossback.** [See MOSS 2, quots. 1850, 1888.]

1. A person who is behind the times; a conservative partisan in politics. *colloq.*[2]

1885 *Boston Jrnl.* 5 March 2/3 Everybody rejoices over the passage of the bill . . . except a few intense mossbacks, who were known during the war as copperheads. **1887** *Nation* 12 May 403 The mossback reigns in unquestioned supremacy. **1890** *Pomona Times Courier* 7 June 4/6 Several old moss-backs who have been in their holes for some time have crawled out and raised a howl over Waterman's proposition. **1900** *Congress. Rec.* 1 Feb. 1408/1 There has never occurred a change . . . without arousing the hostility of some old mossback. **1912** C. MCCARTHY *Wisconsin Idea* 138 Some mossback whose theoretical learning was acquired by carefully keeping away from the only laboratory which could be of any service to him.

b. A member of a conservative faction of Ohio Democrats.

1885 *Mag. Amer. Hist.* March 296/1 *Mossbacks.*—A subdivision of the Democratic party in Ohio. **1895** MYERS *Bosses & Boodle* 187 The Washington end of the Ohio Democracy . . . wanted a 'Mossback' nominated upon a platform of National issues.

c. 'In the southern United States, during the civil war, one who hid himself to avoid conscription' (*Cent.*).

Cf. MOSSYBACK and MOSSY-BACKED RANGER.

2. (See quotation.)

1884 W. SHEPHERD *Prairie Exper.* 102 Three old bull buffaloes, 'moss backs,' from the faded tint of their shaggy manes, were feeding quietly with the tame herd in front of the ranch.

3. 'A large and old fish, as a bass: so called by anglers, in allusion to the growth of seaweed, etc., which may be found on its back' (*Cent.*).

+**Moss-backed,** *a.* Extremely conservative or reactionary. *colloq.* — [**1900** *Speaker* 17 March 644 A few malcontents and mossbacked mugwumps.] **1904** *N.Y. Globe* 28 March 3 It breaks the monotony of being looked at all day, and keeps them from getting 'moss backed.' **1911** HAR-

RISON *Queed* 223 How could he ever do anything, with a lot of mossbacked trustees tying his hands?

+**Mossbackism.** The rule of the mossbacks. — **1887** *Courier-Journal* 15 Feb. 6/6 The day of Mossbackism is over in Kentucky.

+**Moss bass.** =LARGE-MOUTHED (BLACK) BASS. — **1883** *Century Mag.* July 376/2 Black bass . . . have received names somewhat descriptive of their habitat, as, lake, . . . bayou, moss, grass, and Oswego bass. **1911** *Rep. Fisheries 1908* 307 Black Bass . . . is known in the Great Lakes region as 'Oswego bass,' in Indiana as 'moss bass,' in Kentucky as 'jumper.'

Moss berry. The European or small cranberry. {1732-} — **1784** CUTLER in *Mem. Academy* I. 438 *Vaccinium*. . . . The Craneberry, or Mossberry. These berries make an agreeable tart. **1869** *Rep. Comm. Agric. 1868* 178 Among them [*sc.* small fruits] may be noted red and black currants . . . [and] mossberries. **1898** BRITTON & BROWN *Illus. Flora* III. 574/3 (Index), Moss-milion (melon). [In text, II. 581:] *Oxycoccus Oxycoccus*. . . . Small or European Cranberry. . . . In cold bogs, Labrador to Alaska, New Jersey, Michigan and British Columbia. . . . Also called . . . Moss-, Bog-, Fen- or Moor-berry.

+**Mossbunker.** Also **mosbanker, mossbonker.** [f. MARSHBANKER.] The menhaden. Also attrib. (Cf. BUNKER.)

1792 HOMMEDIEU in *Amer. Assoc. Proc.* XXVIII. 436*n.*, The fish called menhaden or mosbanker. **1839** *Knickerb.* XIII. 499 Mossbonkers and horse-feet had been strewn over it [*i.e.*, the farm], to enrich it. **1842** *Nat. Hist. N.Y., Zoology* IV. 259 The Mossbonker. . . . On the coast of Massachusetts, they are used as bait for mackerel, cod, and halibut. *c***1849** PAIGE *Dow's Sermons* I. 206 Under the surfaces, and inside the exteriors of all these [smooth characters], there may be found as many asperities as there are bones in a moss-bunker. **1881** in Goode, etc. *Amer. Fishes* 112 These smacks are engaged in the . . . 'mossbunker' fishery for the oil-rendering and fish-scrap works on Barren Island. **1904** *Newark Ev. News* 13 June 6 The pound nets drive away bluefish by decimating the schools of mossbunkers upon which the blues feed.

+**Moss pink.** A mosslike plant (*Phlox subulata*) bearing white or pink flowers. — **1857** GRAY *Botany* 332 Ground or Moss Pink. . . . Dry rocky hills and sandy banks, S. New York to Michigan and southward. **1898** CREEVEY *Flowers of Field* 295 It is often cultivated under the familiar name of moss-pink.

Moss rose. 1. A variety of the cabbage rose (*Rosa centifolia muscosa*) having a mossy calyx. {1776-} Also attrib. **2.** *W.* A false mallow, *Malvastrum coccineum*. — **(1) 1817-8** EATON *Botany* 433 *Rosa muscosa*, moss rose. **1854** CUMMINS *Lamplighter* 264 Kitty, whose hair was adorned with moss-rose buds. **1884** RITTENHOUSE *Maud* 315, I kept some beautiful roses for my personal adornment and a lovely little moss-rose-bud for Mr Hough. **(2) 1898** BRITTON & BROWN *Illus. Flora* III. 574/3 (Index), Moss-rose. [In text, II. 421:] *Malvastrum coccineum*. . . . Red False Mallow. . . . Prairies, Manitoba to Nebraska and Texas, west to British Columbia and New Mexico.

+**Mossyback. 1.** =MOSSBUNKER. **2.** =MOSSBACK 1 C. — **(1) 1871** DE VERE 67 In the State of New York the same fish appear under the name of *Mossy Back* or *Mossbunkers*. **(2) 1871** DE VERE 283 The Mossybank [*sic*] . . . was the man of the South, who secreted himself in a remote forest, or an inaccessible swamp, in order to escape conscription.

+**Mossy-backed ranger.** (See quotation and cf. MOSSBACK 1 C.) — **1876** *Congress. Rec.* 13 Jan. 411/1 [In the cotton states] those too cowardly to fight . . . were known as 'mossy-backed rangers' during the war, but came out fully fledged 'Union men' after the war.

+**Mossy-cup (white) oak.** =BUR OAK 1. — **1810** MICHAUX *Arbres* I. 21 Q[uercus] muscosa, *Mossy cup oak. Mossy cup oak*, nom donné par moi à cette espèce, qui se trouve dans le Gennessée, (Etat de New-York) et près Albany. **1832** BROWNE *Sylva* 277 The flowers are succeeded by acorns of an elongated, oval form, and are inclosed in cups of nearly the same configuration. . . . From this peculiarity is derived the name of Mossy-Cup Oak. **1875** *Field & Forest* I. 40 The noble Live Oak fails to reach us from the south, and the grand Mossy-cup Oak from the north. **1897** SUDWORTH *Arborescent Flora* 155 *Quercus macrocarpa*. Bur Oak. . . . Mossycup White Oak (Minn.).

***Mote,** *n.* +*spec.* A broken cotton seed in ginned cotton. Also attrib. — **1842** in Bassett *Plantation Overseer* 166 The gin dos not doo good work it draws too many motes through. **1847** *Rep. Comm. Patents 1846* 64 Others have substituted for the rotating mote brushes stationary brushes, through which the saws carry the fibres to be stripped of the motes. **1854** *Fla. Plantation Rec.* 96 The bresting [of the gin] was worn so that the Seed and moates went throu.

***Mote,** *v.* +**1.** *tr.* To pick out broken seeds from (ginned cotton). Also *vbl. n.* +**2.** *intr.* Of cotton in the process of ginning: To accumulate broken seeds. — **(1) 1829** B. HALL *Travels in N.A.* III. 222 These stray particles are afterwards separated by hand—a process which is called moting. One hand can mote from twenty to thirty pounds per day. **1854** in Commons, etc. *Doc. Hist.* I. 273 The cotton is 'moted' as it comes from the gin, namely; all particles of broken seed, and every speck which may have escaped detection in the 'sorting' are carefully removed. **(2) 1880** *MS. Cotton Rep. U.S. Census* (*O.E.D.*), The lint rating about the same from old or fresh land, the former motes worse in ginning.

***Moth.** Any of certain nocturnal or crepuscular insects of the order Lepidoptera, forming the division, Heterocera, esp. the clothes moth. Also attrib. — **1682** ASH *Carolina* 5 The Dust and Shavings of Cedar, laid amongst Linnen or Woollen, destroys the Moth and all Verminous Insects. **1737** BRICKELL *N. Carolina* 160 The Moth . . . differs in nothing from those in Europe, being as . . . destructive to Woollen Cloth and Books. **1861** E. COWELL *Diary* 407 In the evening, . . . thousands of moths filled our room. **1906** PRINGLE *Rice Planter* 417 They are all sewed up in homespun bags in the spring with camphor or moth balls.

***Mother.** +In special phrases.

Mother of Commonwealths, Virginia; *Mother of her Country*, Martha Washington (1731-1802); *Mother's Day*, the second Sunday in May, celebrated in honor of mothers.

1879 *Congress. Rec.* 10 Jan. 413/2 If it affords that gentleman any pleasure . . . to pour out the vials of his impotent wrath upon the 'Mother of Commonwealths,' . . . let him enjoy it. **1876** *Wide Awake* 158/1 She knew the couple in advance to be the Father and Mother of their Country, George and Martha Washington. **1912** *Ladies' Home Jrnl.* May 3 In the Month of May Comes Mothers' Day.

Mother Carey's chicken. One of various petrels, esp. the stormy petrel. {1767-} Also transf. — **1807** J. R. SHAW *Life* (1930) 147, [I] was introduced to a fine parcel of ladies [prostitutes] (all mother Carey's chickens). **1844** *Nat. Hist. N.Y., Zoology* II. 290 This little Petrel, or *Mother Carey's Chicken*, occurs commonly along our coast from Mexico to high northern latitudes. **1883** *Nat. Museum Bul.* No. 27, 175 *Procellaria pelagica*. Stormy Petrel; Mother Carey's Chicken. . . . North Atlantic, south to Newfoundland Banks. **1917** *Birds of Amer.* I. 87 Storm Petrel. *Thalassidroma pelagica*. . . . [Also called] Mother Carey's Chicken. . . . Occasionally found on the Newfoundland Banks and off the coast of Nova Scotia.

***Mother Church.** +The central church of the Christian Science denomination; =FIRST CHURCH OF CHRIST, SCIENTIST 1. — **1889** EDDY in *Christian Science Jrnl.* April 13, I want to say, too, to my students everywhere . . . that they can become members of the 'mother church' here in Boston, and be received into its communion by writing without their personal presence. **1895** *Baltimore American* 14 Jan., The dedication in Boston last Sunday of the Christian Science church, called The Mother Church, which cost over two hundred thousand dollars, adds interest to the Baltimore organization. **1906** *Boston Transcript* 9 June III. 7/6 The First Church of Christ, Scientist. The Mother Church. June 10th services will be held in the new church edifice. **1916** *Ib.* 3 June 9/5 The First Church of Christ, Scientist. The Mother Church. Falmouth, Norway and St. Paul sts., Boston, Mass. Sunday services, 10.45 A.M. and 7.30 P.M.

***Mother country.** In specific applications.

1. England. {1732-}

[**1617** ROBINSON & BREWSTER in Bradford *Hist.* 42 We [the Leyden Pilgrims] are well weaned from ye delicate milke of our mother countrie.] **1747** FRANKLIN *Writings* II. 339 We have Numbers of the same Religion with those who of late encouraged the *French* to invade our Mother-Country. **1774** J. ADAMS *Works* IX. 338 The treatment we receive from our mother country . . . begins to discourage persons here from making any applications to her. **1854** BENTON *30 Years' View* I. 217/1 The terms of the enjoyment are questions for the mother country. **1891** *Harper's Mag.* July 215/2 The last tie of colonialism which bound us to the mother country is broken. **1900** *Congress. Rec.* 20 Feb. 1995/2 The States that originally formed this Union were certain colonies which had revolted against the oppression of the mother country.

+**2.** Any of various countries considered at one time or another as the source of certain American populations: Spain, the Netherlands, the United States, Mexico.

1808 PIKE *Sources Miss.* 229 Malgares . . . deprecated a revolution or separation of Spanish America, from the mother country. **1809** IRVING *Knickerb.* II. v, The accumulating wealth and consequence of New Amsterdam and its dependencies, at length awakened the serious solicitude of the mother country. **1836** *Diplom. Corr. Texas* I. (1908) 75 Please repair . . . to Washington City and there unite your exertions with those of our Commissioners in procuring a recognition from the government of our mother country. **1848** *Santa Fe Repub.* 3 May 1/2 [New Mexico] was but a colony . . . devoted by the mother country to none of those branches of industry that foster the . . . growth of the people. **1885** *Santa Fé Wkly. New Mexican* 9 July 1/2 Mexico is in trouble. . . . Will those of New Mexico . . . come to their mother country's relief now and at once!

+**Mother ditch.** The canal from which lateral irrigating ditches get water. — **1844** GREGG *Commerce of Prairies* I. 151 One *acequia madre* (mother ditch) suffices generally to convey water for the irrigation of an entire valley. **1857** DAVIS *El Gringo* 197 The secondary canals are provided with flood-gates, to regulate the flow of water into them from the mother ditch. **1870** *Rep. Comm. Agric. 1869* 603 A large portion of the elevated plateaus bordering the Rio Grande may be irrigated from this stream, but this will require a considerable outlay in constructing the *acequia madre*, or mother ditch.

Mother England. England, the mother country. — **1721** *Boston News-Letter* 28 Aug., People will take it for granted, they are a New Club set up in New-England, like to that in our Mother England. **1817** PAULDING *Lett. from South* I. 203 It is the production of one of the good ladies of Mother England.

Mother Hubbard. 1. A kind of loose, full garment once popular with women. {1883-, of a cloak} Also attrib. +**2.** *Mother Hubbard overalls*, loose-fitting overalls. *humorous.* — **(1) 1878** ROE *Army Lett.* 186, I made a Mother Hubbard apron of white paper-cambric. **1885** RITTENHOUSE *Maud* 340 Locust Street [presents] a long panorama of . . . well dressed papas leading small specimens in Mother Hubbard wraps. **1888**

KIRK *Queen Money* 125, I determined to have . . . a wife, and at least three beautiful little angels in white embroidered Mother Hubbard frocks. **1894** *Outing* XXIV. 271/1 Six years ago the finest dress to be seen was a calico Mother Hubbard. (2) **1897** *Ib.* XXX. 555/2 The Doctor in brown 'Mother Hubbard' overalls.

+**Mother lead.** =next. — **1874** RAYMOND *6th Rep. Mines* 342 The Mother lead is . . . taken up and named, on the supposition that it is the *mother-vein* of the country from which the ores of the Silver Flat and the Chloride districts are derived.

+**Mother lode. a.** The principal vein of ore in a given place. **b.** The great quartz vein which runs from Mariposa to Amador in California. — **1883** BEADLE *Western Wilds* 561 What miners call a 'mother lode' is often like a tree in its upward development. **1901** *Science* ns. XIII. 950/2 Mother-Lode (Cal., Ransome) exhibits parts of the uplifted and dissected peneplain of the Sierra Nevada

+**Mother of eels. 1.** The American burbot, *Lota maculosa.* **2.** =CONGER EEL 2. — (1) **1884** GOODE, etc. *Fisheries* 236 Professor Jordan gives the names 'Aleby-trout' and 'Mother of Eels' as in use in the Upper Great Lake region. **1903** T. H. BEAN *Fishes N.Y.* 702. (2) **1911** *Rep. Fisheries 1908* 313 Mutton-fish (*Zoarces anguillaris*). . . . It is also called the . . . 'mother-of-eels.'

***Mother-of-pearl.** The hard pearly substance of the inner lining of certain shells. Also attrib. — **1850** TAYLOR *Eldorado* (1862) 174 The avelone . . . furnishes the finest mother-of-pearl. **1872** MCCLELLAN *Golden State* 245 The 'mother-of-pearl oyster' is found in the bays on the lower coast.

+**Mother of Presidents.** The state of Virginia, which furnished seven of the first twelve Presidents of the United States. — **1827** A. SHERWOOD *Gaz. Georgia* 98 James Monroe . . . was born in Va., the mother of Presidents. **1850** *Congress. Globe* App. 13 May 563/3 Virginia, the mother of Presidents, the Old Dominion. **1868** *Ib.* 17 Dec. 132/2 He spoke of Virginia, the proud mother of Presidents, become a breeder of slaves for the southern market. **1904** *N.Y. Tribune* 12 June 8 Virginia concluded not to indorse any candidate. The 'Mother of Presidents' is a trifle particular.

+**Mother of States.**

‖**1.** The state of Connecticut.

1838 *Yale Lit. Mag.* III. 86 But to thee, Land of Steady Habits! to thee, Mother of States! to thee, good old Connecticut, do our praises most belong.

2. The state of Virginia.

In allusion either to its being the first settled of the original states, or to the fact that numerous states have been carved out of its original territory or settled by its people.

1855 *S. Lit. Messenger* XXI. 675/1 Virginia . . . [was] hailed as 'the Mother of States,' . . . for where in all the West can we go without finding her children. **1861** *Chicago Tribune* 19 July 1/6 He went to Virginia, 'the mother of States.' **1875** *Chambers's Jrnl.* 13 March 171/2 Virginia is . . . the Mother of States, and also the Mother of Presidents. **1896** *Congress. Rec.* 9 June 6342/2, That grand old Commonwealth of Virginia, the mother of States and statesmen, the mother of Presidents.

***Motherwort.** Any of various mintlike plants of the genus *Leonurus.*

1784 CUTLER in *Mem. Academy* I. 462 *Leonurus.* . . . Motherwort. Blossoms purplish. Among rubbish. July–August. **1814** BIGELOW *Florula Bostoniensis* 145 *Leonurus cardiaca.* Motherwort. . . . The herb has a strong, pungent odour, and is a popular remedy in considerable request. **1840** DEWEY *Mass. Flowering Plants* 178 *Mother Wort.* A well-known plant about houses and gardens . . . still considerably used as a popular drink for the relief for colds. **1894** R. E. ROBINSON *Danvis Folks* 230 The moist soil . . . [was] dotted with green tufts of young motherwort and catnip. **1901** MOHR *Plant Life Ala.* 56 *Leonurus cardiaca* (motherwort).

+**Moth miller.** A moth or miller. — **1871** *Harper's Mag.* June 29 In this cocoon the worm eats its fill, and then lies dormant until a new life comes to it in the shape of a moth-miller. **1885** JEWETT *Marsh Island* 162 Don't flitter about so, mother; you make me think of a singed moth-miller. **1899** — *Queen's Twin* 207, I'd looked more'n twenty times to see if there was any more moth-millers.

***Moth mullein.** A mullein (*Verbascum blattaria*) naturalized in America. — **1784** CUTLER in *Mem. Academy* I. 419 Moth Mullein. Blossoms yellowish white. By the road sides in Lynn. July. **1898** CREEVEY *Flowers of Field* 212 Moth-mullein. . . . The white and yellow varieties often grow side by side.

Motion picture. {1891–} =MOVING PICTURE 2. {1908–} Also attrib. — **1896** *Boston Ev. Transcript* 7 Nov. 16/4 The cinematographe motion picture programme will be augmented daily. **1907** *Pearson's Mag.* Jan. (*advt.*), It Pays Big To Amuse The Public With Motion Pictures. **1916** DU PUY *Uncle Sam* 200 The Lily Maid might read the lips of those unconscious motion picture actors. **1923** WATTS *L. Nichols* 201 He was loitering at the entrance to the Dreamworld motion-picture house.

+**Motocycle.** A horseless carriage or automobile. *Obs.* {1895} Also attrib. — **1895** *Daily News* (London) 22 Nov. 2/2 The American inventor says 'motocycle,' the American newspaper editor follows his example, and the word has passed into the American language, and we must take it and like it. **1897** *Boston Transcript* 4 Sept. 24/4 The principal obstacle to motocycle use is really our wretched American street pavements and roads. **1899** *Chicago Record* 2 Jan. 17/4 Horseless carriages or moto-cycles, by whatever name known, do not seem to be 'moting' very satisfactorily.

***Motor.**

1. An apparatus or machine for supplying motive power. {1881–} Also attrib.

1856 EMERSON *Eng. Traits* 91 They adopt every improvement in rig, in motor, in weapons. **1872** *Ill. Dept. Agric. Trans. 1871* p. viii, More than twenty parties . . . are experimenting upon the steam plow and motor. **1882** *Nation* 31 Aug. 169/1 He is able to construct one of the motors without the assistance of the inventor. **1907** *Engineering Mag.* Oct. 195/1 Motor Buses in New York City. . . . About a year ago the service [operating horse-drawn buses] began to experiment with motor buses.

2. An automobile. {1900–} Also attrib.

1900 *Congress. Rec.* 15 Jan. 802/1 It proposes to extend to June 3, 1902, the time for completing the construction of a wagon and motor bridge across the Missouri River. **1908** GALE *Friendship Village* 169 We heard the questioning horn of a motor. **1923** HERRICK *Lilla* 209 One Sunday Lilla packed them both off in the motor for a ride.

Motor car. +**1.** (See quotation 1890.) **2.** An automobile. {1895–} Also attrib. — (1) **1890** *Cent.* 3874/3 *Motor-car,* . . . a car which carries its own propelling mechanism, as an electric motor. . . . Many such cars have sufficient power to draw other cars attached to them. **1898** *Boston Morn. Herald* 22 April 7/1 A number of new open cars . . . are to be used as trailers, and in their way are as interesting as the motor cars by which they are drawn. **1903** *N.Y. Ev. Post* 4 Sept., As a crowded 6-car train was leaving the 16th Street station, the motor-car was discovered to be afire. (2) **1900** *Boston Transcript* 11 Aug. 12/6 Rolled partinium is now used for the bodies of motor cars. **1903** *Motoring Annual* 294 The Automobile Club of America . . . has started a Motor-car Servants' Register. **1922** PARRISH *Case & Girl* 39 Occasionally a belated motor car passed along the road.

Motorcycle. A two-wheeled, motor-driven vehicle. {1896–} — **1897** *Pat. Off. Specifications* I. 91 This invention relates to power-transmitting mechanism for motor-cycles or self-propelled vehicles. **1917** *Scientific Amer. Suppl.* 2 June 342/3 For the transportation of machine guns a powerful and rugged motorcycle is required, and for this use our American machines are without doubt the best in the world.

+**Motorman.** A man who operates a car or train on an electric railway. — **1890** *Boston Jrnl.* 12 April 4/4 Has it . . . become the established policy of the West End road, from the late vice president to the motormen, that the public must learn that the electric cars cannot be fooled with? **1900** *Congress. Rec.* 12 Feb. 1731/1 The railroad is fighting . . . all efforts for protecting the motormen or accommodating the passengers in the night. **1911** HARRISON *Queed* 174 He was a motorman on the suburban line.

+**Motorneer.** [By analogy with *engineer.*] (See quot. 1890.) *Obs.* — **1890** *Boston Jrnl.* 22 Nov. 2/3 Somebody has coined the word 'motorneer,' to designate the person who manages the motor on an electric car. **1893** 'THANET' *Stories* 4 [She sobbed,] in too distracted agitation to heed the motorneer of the passing street-car who stared after her at the risk of his car.

+**Motte.** Also **mot(t).** *S. & W.* [Fr., 'hillock.'] A clump or small grove *of* trees on a prairie. (Borrowed before 1600 in sense 'hill' the word is now obsolete in English use. The American use is apparently a new borrowing.) — **1844** G. W. KENDALL *Narrative Santa Fé Exped.* I. 41 All that was necessary was to keep a bright look-out . . . while passing the different *mots* and ravines scattered along our trail. **1852** *S. Lit. Messenger* XVIII. 435/2 About twenty Camanches . . . had got into a mot of timber in the prairies. **1886** Z. F. SMITH *Kentucky* 267 Hardin selected a motte of timber situated in a prairie. **1902** 'O. HENRY' *Roads of Destiny* 150 A stone's cast away stood a little mott of coma trees; beneath it a *jacal* such as the Mexicans erect.

+**Mottled grampus.** (See quotation.) — **1884** *Nat. Museum Bul.* No. 27, 639 *Grampus Stearnsii.* Mottled or White-headed Grampus. Pacific coast of North America.

Mottled owl. An American screech owl with its plumage in the gray phase.

[**1781** LATHAM *Gen. Synopsis Birds* I. I. 126 Mottled Owl. . . . The length of this species is eight inches and a half. The bill is brown: irides yellow. . . . Inhabits North America.] **1811** WILSON *Ornithology* III. 17 [The] Mottled Owl, *Strix Naevia,* . . . is a native of the northern regions. **1878** *Nat. Museum Proc.* I. 134 *Scops asio.*—Little Mottled Owl; Screech. This Owl is quite abundant at Stockton. **1917** *Birds of Amer.* II. 109 Screech Owl. . . . [Also called] Mottled Owl.

***Motto.** +A piece of candy wrapped in a paper inscribed with a motto or a line of verse. — **1835** *S. Lit. Messenger* I. 358, I only ate . . . a few macaronies and mottoes. **1856** COZZENS *Sparrowgrass P.* 42 That lady who prized confectionery above good-breeding, . . . went home with her pockets well stuffed with mottoes.

+**Motto candy.** =prec. — **1876** *Wide Awake* 90/2 [He] gave her motto-candies with the most complimentary verses he could pick out.

+**Motto mug.** A mug with a motto inscribed upon it. — **1859** *Texas Almanac 1860* 248 Toilet Ware, in sets and separate; Ornaments, Vases, Motto-Mugs, Card-Trays, etc.

Mould[1], Mouldboard, Mouldboard plow. Variants of MOLD[1], etc.

+**Mould.[2]** [Back formation.] Short for MOLDBOARD. — **1858** *Ill. Agric. Soc. Trans.* III. 367 In fall-plowing we run the share and mould of the plow under the soil and invert it. **1861** *Ib.* IV. 249 The moulds used on this plow will . . . be the best, that . . . can ever be made. **1868** *Iowa Agric. Soc. Rep. 1867* 266 There is no clogging, and the mould and lay are so hardened that they scour readily.

***Mound.** Also †**mond.**

*1. A hedge or other fence. *Obs.*

1640 *Wyllys P.* 7 Sticklinge . . . doth Covenant . . . to keepe the sayd house and housinge and moundes belonginge to the sayd homelotte . . . in good repayre. **1654** *Suffolk Deeds* II. 38 Cotton flacke & Jeane his wife . . . [do sell] all the trees Tymber Rayles Pales and Monds to the same belongeing. **1659** *Ib.* III. 427 Wth. all & singular houses . . . mounds pailes [etc.].

+2. *Archaeology.* A kind of extensive earthwork erected by the Mound-Builders.

Chiefly in the Ohio and Mississippi valleys, the Gulf states, and the Great Lakes region. (See also INDIAN MOUND and cf. MOUND-BUILDER and MOUNT 3.)

[**1791** W. BARTRAM *Travels* 350 The council-house, which was a very large dome or rotunda, situated on the top of an ancient artificial mound. **1819** in Schoolcraft *Mo. Lead Mines* 291 The pious custom [among the Indians] of collecting the relics of the dead . . . explains the origin of the artificial mounds in our vicinity.] **1837** W. JENKINS *Ohio Gaz.* p. xvii, The most prominent antiquities are the numerous mounds and forts of earth, in the State of Ohio. **1884** COLANGE *Nat. Gazetteer* 674/2 Moundsville, W.Va. . . . Its name is derived from a remarkable mound in the vicinity, one of the largest of the ancient mounds in the U. States.

+**Mound-Builder.** *Ethnology.* One of the aboriginal Indians who built burial and fortification mounds.

Once supposed to have preceded the Indians as inhabitants of the Mississippi basin and adjacent areas, the mound builders are now known to have been of the same stock as the Indians.

1839 C. MATHEWS *(title)*, Behemoth: A Legend of the Mound-Builders. **1847** SQUIER & DAVIS *Ancient Monum. Miss. Valley* 188 Among the mound-builders the art of pottery attained to a considerable degree of perfection. **1871** *Amer. Naturalist* V. 148 He found the identical flint arrowhead that the *Mound builders* used. **1893** *Harper's Mag.* April 697/1 Mysterious colonizations of strange races of men—the Aztecs, the mound-builders, the cave-dwellers—whose genesis is unknown, appeared upon the fertile plains and perished. **1916** EASTMAN *From Deep Woods* 52 The college grounds [in Beloit, Wis.] covered the site of an ancient village of mound-builders.

Mound-building. +The action of building an Indian mound. — **1853** LAPHAM *Antiq. Wisconsin* (1855) 89 These later tribes continued the practice of mound-building so far as to erect a circular or conical tumulus over their dead.

+**Mound City.** St. Louis, Missouri. So called from the Indian mounds that once occupied its site. Also attrib. — **1854** M. REID *Hunter's Feast* i. 5 On the western bank of the Mississippi . . . stands the large town of St. Louis, poetically known as the 'Mound City.' **1859** *Ladies' Repository* XIX. 51/1 St. Louis, Missouri, is the 'Mound City,' from the ancient mounds within and near the city. **1896** *Typographical Jrnl.* IX. 68 Mound City Craft Notes. At the last meeting of No. 8 a proposed amendment . . . was taken up.

+**Mound prairie(s).** A region in the state of Washington covered with moundlike formations. — **1867** *Ore. State Jrnl.* 5 Jan. 1/3 The following extract is a description of the Mound Prairies which are in a few reach [*sic*] from Olympia. **1917** *Wash. Geol. Survey Bul.* No. 17, 204 Mound Prairie. A prairie of several hundred acres, northeast of Grand Mound, in southwestern Thurston County. **1923** E. S. MEANY *Origin of Wash. Names* 173 Mound Prairie. . . . Many geologists have given differing theories about the origin of the mounds which caused the name of this prairie.

+**Mound region.** (See quotation.) — **1873** BEADLE *Undevel. West* 38 [Boscobel] is the centre of the 'Mound Region' of Wisconsin—so called from the many Indian mounds scattered about the valley.

***Mount,** *n.*

*1. A more or less conical hill or mountain. Obs. except in place names.

*a***1649** WINTHROP *Hist.* I. 73 They came to another high pointed rock, having a fair ascent on the west side, which they called Mount Feake. **1784** ELLICOTT in Mathews *Life A. Ellicott* 17 [We] are now living very comfortably on the Top of the highest Mount in this part of the World. **1872** TICE *Over Plains* 190 The towns . . . along the flank of the Rocky Mountains, are as high above the sea as the top of Mount Washington.

+2. A square tower fitted up for a sentry. *Obs.*

1724 in Temple & Sheldon *Hist. Northfield, Mass.* 202, 1 day's warding for a soldier which did work at the mount. **1744** in G. Sheldon *Hist. Deerfield, Mass.* I. 529 Voted to build Mounts at one house in Green River and at four Houses in the Town. **1748** J. NORTON *Redeemed Captive* 6 He kept two Men in the Northwest Mount, and some in the Great House.

+3. =MOUND 2. *Obs.*

1732 *Georgia Col. Rec.* III. 406 Half a Mile from Savannah is a high Mount of Earth, under which lies their chief King. **1742** *Travels Amer. Col.* 219 We Camped at Ocmulgas River where are three Mounts raised by the Indians over three of their Great Kings. **1772** *Ib.* 504 These Mounts are Artificial but the Indians cannot give any Account of the Reasons of their being made. **1792** *Amer. Philos. Soc.* III. 217 On the low grounds of the Mississippi . . . is a very large mount encompassed by a number of smaller ones.

***Mount,** *v.* +*tr.* To beat or overcome (a person). *slang.* — **1835** HOFFMAN *Winter in West* II. 185 Little John never insulted anybody, but he knows how to mount them that don't treat him like a gentleman.

***Mountain.** Also †**mountayn, mounteing.**

I. *1. A natural, more or less abrupt, and impressively high elevation of the earth's surface.

The word has sometimes been applied, esp. in place names, to elevations of moderate altitude. (See HILL note.)

1608 SMITH *Works* (1910) 6 The north side [of the river is] high mountaines. **1651** *Conn. Rec.* I. 223 In this rocky country, amongst these mountaines and stonye hills, there are probabilities of mynes of mettals and minneralls. **1669** *Springfield Rec.* II. 99 The ledge of Mountaynes is to be the bounds. **1697** *Conn. Probate Rec.* 562 My Lott at the Mountains. **1738** *Southampton Rec.* III. 94 He or they shall have liberty to go round ye said hills or mountains. **1756** in Winsor *Miss. Basin* 217 Its head-springs interlocked on a neighboring mountain. **1806** CLARK in *Lewis & C. Exped.* VI. (1905) 73 To Hungary Creek from the right passing on a Dividing Mounteing. **1836** NICKLIN *Peregrination* 60 The goods destined to the West, are taken from the boats and placed in Burthen Cars which are to carry them over the mountains. **1900** *Congress. Rec.* 24 Jan. 1148/1 The men of the mountains never demanded it and never will.

+b. *Over the mountain(s)*, a phrase used on the eastern seaboard to designate a location west of the Appalachians.

1800 TATHAM *Agric. & Commerce* 150 Which (in common language) is called *over the mountains, universally*, by all the people who inhabit the Atlantic states. **1832** KENNEDY *Swallow Barn* I. 12 The generations . . . had been broken up, or, what in his conception was equivalent, had gone 'over the mountain.'

+2. *The Mountains*, (see quotation).

1866 A. D. WHITNEY *L. Goldthwaite* ii, 'The Mountains' in New England means always, in common speech, the one royal range of the White Hills.

II. *attrib.* and *comb.*

3. +a. Designating pieces of land in or next to the mountains, used in farming, stock-raising, etc. Also fig.

1700 *Waterbury Prop. Rec.* 52 Six acers on ye easter sid of his land on ye hill or mountain lot. **1883** *Century Mag.* Sept. 718 The miserable little mountain farm . . . produces nothing salable. **1906** *N.Y. Ev. Post* 8 Sept. 3 The educational needs of 3,000,000 people of pure Anglo-Saxon blood inhabiting the 'mountain backyards' of eight Southern States. **1908** LORIMER *J. Spurlock* 306 Uncle Bill . . . runs a mountain ranch—one of those natural parks back in the range.

b. Designating various dwellings or places in the mountains where people live or visit.

1835 *Harvardiana* II. 6 Catskill mountain-house is about two thousand feet above the level of the ocean. **1881** PIERSON *In the Brush* 142 The Bishop found at a mountain-inn a Methodist circuit-rider. **1893** *Harper's Mag.* March 495 [They] now go to the so-called piny woods and mountain resorts of Georgia and the Carolinas. **1907** LONDON *Road* 129, I ran into him first at the mountain town of Truckee.

c. Designating various regions, political divisions, etc., that are mountainous.

1860 CURTIS *Woody Plants N.C.* 75 Gray Willow. . . . I have met with this insignificant plant only in the mountain counties. **1863** KETTELL *Hist. Rebellion* II. 504 It was finally determined to annex Eastern Tennessee and Kentucky to the department of Western Virginia, and erect it into 'the mountain department.' **1869** MCCLURE *Rocky Mts.* 285 [Helena, Mont.] boasts of . . . more go-aheadativeness generally, than any other city in the mountain mining-regions. **1894** *Harper's Mag.* Sept. 616/2 The mountain districts of West Virginia are as strange in their primitive population as in their tossed and tumbled surface.

4. Designating various substances found in the mountains.

1734 *Doc. Hist. N.Y. State* I. 734 We have a great many Iron mines both of the bogg, and of the Mountain Oar. **1775** ADAIR *Indians* 234 The Indians . . . forbid them [the patients] . . . every kind of flesh-meat, applying mountain allum, as the chief ingredient. **1848** THOREAU *Maine Woods* 68 The continual bathing of our bodies in mountain water . . . made this walk exceedingly refreshing. **1853** RAMSEY *Tennessee* 1 He recollects to have seen his chieftain . . . perpetuating the annals of his tribe in rude hieroglyphics upon the mountain granite. **1861** MCCLELLAN in *Own Story* 58 We are well up in the hills and have the mountain air.

5. Designating physical and topographical features of the mountains.

1800 ASBURY *Journal* II. 470 We passed Montgomery-town and court-house among the mountain barrens. **1830** *Mass. Spy* 25 Aug. (Th.), 'Mountain slides.' An account of four of them. **1838** *S. Lit. Messenger* IV. 231/2 Next day we crossed mountain-spurs and ridges. **1851** GLISAN *Jrnl. Army Life* 73 Today several friends and myself rode to the summit of several of these mountain peaks. **1851** J. F. W. JOHNSTON *Notes N. Amer.* I. 257 The mountain-ridge, as it is called, formed by the outcrop of the Niagara limestone, has been long known to the inhabitants of western New York. **1868** H. M. FLINT *Railroads* 12 'The Glades' are the mountain meadows, a region on the high table land at the summit of the Alleghany mountains. **1879** STOCKTON *Rudder Grange* xvii, The road crosses the ridge of the mountain-range. **1883** *Harper's Mag.* Sept. 628/2 Clouds walled in the mountain plateau. *a*1892 in M. A. Jackson *Gen. Jackson* 391 The general and his army would pass over the mountain gap near by to Eastern Virginia.

6. Designating various persons or groups of people who live or work in the mountains.

See also MOUNTAIN BOY, MAN, TRAPPER.

1839 TOWNSEND *Narrative* 271 He preferred the 'free and easy' life of a mountain hunter and trapper. **1846** SAGE *Scenes Rocky Mts.* ii, A mountain company generally comprises some quaint specimens of human nature. **1847** ROBB *Squatter Life* 143 Old Fecho had been a mountain trader . . . and looked wicked as a tree'd bear. **1890** LANGFORD *Vigilante Days* (1912) 319 [They] were joined by William Page, an old mountain teamster. **1891** *Harper's Mag.* Jan. 219/2, 'I be a yerb doctor, by the grace o' God,' returned the mountain practitioner. **1894** *Ib.* Sept. 613/1 All the mountain folk knew her or knew about her. **1898** PAGE *Red Rock* 533 Steve was represented as every species of brigand, from the sneaking law-breaker who entered houses under cover of night to the dashing, bold, mountain robber and desperado. **1910** J. HART *Vigilante Girl* 116 What class of men make up the Mountain Vigilantes? **1924** RAINE *Land of Saddle-Bags* 19 [The people living in the Appalachian region] usually call themselves 'Mountain People.'

7. a. Designating various roads or routes in the mountains.

1843 FRÉMONT *Exped.* 201 The mountain trail from the Dalles joined that on which we were travelling. **1846** SAGE *Scenes Rocky Mts.* iv, The mountain road strikes the above stream. **1866** A. D. WHITNEY *L. Goldthwaite* x, They overtook the Routh party at the beginning of the mountain-path. **1883** *Harper's Mag.* Sept. 523/1 The first trip on the mountain railroad was made in July, 1882.

+b. Designating various vehicles used in the mountains.

See also MOUNTAIN SCHOONER, MOUNTAIN WAGON.

1880 *Cimarron News & Press* 26 Feb. 2/1 A strongly built mountain carriage . . . to which were hitched a pair of sturdy Mexican ponies. **1896** SHINN *Story of Mine* 109 The wagons . . . were in their way as distinct creations of adaptive and evolutionary genius as the mountain stagecoach of the period. **1897** *Outing* XXX. 135/2 The mountain-chaises and the stage-coaches. **1910** J. HART *Vigilante Girl* 127 Their vengeance will probably take the practical form of . . . holding up the mountain stages for the express boxes.

+8. Designating diseases prevalent in the mountains.

See also MOUNTAIN FEVER.

1884 *Century Mag.* Oct. 928/1 The horrors (not too strong a word) of mountain-sickness. **1903** FOX *Little Shepherd* ii, The mountain cholera had carried off the man and the woman who had been father and mother to him.

9. +a. Designating various wild animals, fishes, and insects that live in the mountains. Often in specific names.

See also MOUNTAIN BISON, BOOMER, BUFFALO, etc.

1884 *Century Mag.* Dec. 193/2 As a popular name mountain antelope or antelope-goat might be suggested. **1890** *Cent.* 3877/1 *Mountain-beauty*, . . . the California mountain-trout. **1884** J. S. KINGSLEY, etc. *Stand. Nat. Hist.* V. 121 The 'Showt'l' or 'Sewellel' of the aborigines . . . [is] known to more prosaic hunters and trappers as the 'Boomer' or 'mountain Beaver.' **1882** BAILLIE-GROHMAN *Camps in Rockies* 48 A scourge . . . swept down upon us when we struck the timbered foothills of the Rockies, i.e. the dreaded mountain flies—a species of mosquito. **1819** *Western Rev.* I. 235 Black-tail fox, *Canis melanurus*, . . . is more like the mountain fox (*Canis alopex*). **1842** *Nat. Hist. N.Y., Zoology* I. 38 The hunters in the north of the State have described . . . [the] Mountain Mink, which is small and black. **1737** BRICKELL *N. Carolina* 159 The *Mountain-Spider*, so called, for its being found commonly in the Woods near the Mountains. **1857** *Rep. Comm. Patents 1856: Agric.* 67 This pretty and active little animal is well known through the Northern States, under the names of 'Red-Squirrel,' . . . and, sometimes, 'Mountain Squirrel.' **1858** PETERS *Kit Carson* 22 The flesh of the mountain wolf, when cooked, has something of the smell and taste of mutton.

+b. Designating domestic animals that live or range in the mountains.

1847 PARKMAN in *Knickerb.* XXX. 475 Their mountain-horses were turned to graze in the meadow among our own. **1869** BRACE *New West* 82 Buy a mountain-mustang at one of the towns in the Foot Hills.

+c. Designating birds that live in the mountains. Often in specific names.

See also MOUNTAIN CHICKADEE, COCK, GROUSE, etc.

1917 *Birds of Amer.* III. 245/1 The Mountain Bluebird [*Sialia currucoides*] presents a general appearance very similar to that of its eastern relative. **1881** CHASE *Editor's Run in N. Mex.* 87 Magpies, mountain blue jays, and other birds, are plenty about the house [in Cimarron]. **1917** *Birds of Amer.* I. 142 Harlequin Duck. *Histrionicus histrionicus*. . . . [Also called] Mountain Duck. **1856** SIMMS *Charlemont* 316 Her eye [was] no longer uplifted like that of the mountain-eagle. **1846** SAGE *Scenes Rocky Mts.* xv, The mountain fowl . . . is rather larger than our domestic hen, and of a grayish brown color. **1886** *Outing* IX. 44/2 The mountain magpie had sent his grating note abroad, when I awoke to find it day. **1858** BAIRD *Birds Pacific R.R.* 347 *Oroscoptes Montanus*, . . . Mountain Mocking Bird. **1869** *Amer. Naturalist* III. 75 Mountain Titmouse . . . [was] seen . . . at Fort Dalles, Oregon. **1883** ZEIGLER & GROSSCUP *Alleghanies* 56 A mountain turkey is no small game. **1828** BONAPARTE *Synopsis* 82 The Blue Mountain Warbler, *Sylvia montana*. . . . Inhabits the United States during summer.

+10. In the specific names of American plants.

See also MOUNTAIN CRANBERRY, GRAPE, HOLLY, etc. Other examples for senses 10 and 10 b can be found in books on plants.

1847 WOOD *Botany* 369 *Vaccinium uliginosum*. Mountain Blueberry. . . . A low, alpine shrub, White Mts. . . . Berries oblong, deep-blue. **1850** *Rep. Comm. Patents 1849: Agric.* 138 Peas are cultivated for the table, market, stock. . . . The 'mountain crowder' and 'black-eyed' are the most common varieties. **1833** EATON *Botany* (ed. 6) 304 *Ribes rigens*, mountain currant. . . . Canada. Wachuset. Monadnok. White Mts. **1841** FARNHAM *Travels Prairies* (1843) II. 74 The mountain flax was very abundant and ripe. **1817** S. BROWN *Western Gaz.* 322 [In n.e. Ohio are found] woodbine, . . . whortleberries, . . . mountain ivy, mountain laurel [etc.]. **1860** CURTIS *Woody Plants N.C.* 100 Mountain Pepper-Bush. (*C[lethra] acuminata.*) —Quite an ornamental shrub, 10 to 15 feet high, growing in the mountains from Ashe to Cherokee. **1844** LEE & FROST *Oregon* 122 Toiling through immense tracts of mountain sage, or, more properly, wormwood. **1889** VASEY *Agric. Grasses* 41 Mountain Foxtail . . . is called in some localities mountain Timothy. . . . It is of little value for grazing. **1760** WASHINGTON *Diaries* I. 136 An order on Hunting Creek Warehouses for 7 Hhds. of my Mountain Tob[acc]o. **1785** MARSHALL *Amer. Grove* 132 *Ribes oxycanthoides*. Mountain Wild Gooseberry.

b. +In the specific names of American trees.

See also MOUNTAIN ASH, CHERRY, CHESTNUT OAK, etc.

1843 TORREY *Flora N.Y.* II. 203 *Alnus viridis*. . . . Mountain Alder. . . . Along the mountain streams of Essex county. **1785** MARSHALL *Amer. Grove* 113 *Prunus-cerasus montana*. Mountain Bird-Cherry-Tree. **1884** SARGENT *Rep. Forests* 34 *Ximenia Americana*. . . . Wild Lime Tallow Nut. Hog Plum. Mountain Plum. **1813** MUHLENBERG *Cat. Plants* 32 *Rhus copallinum æstivale*, (mountain sumach). **1884** SARGENT *Rep. Forests* 143 *Quercus Douglasii*. . . . Mountain White Oak. Blue Oak. **1872** *Harper's Mag.* Dec. 32/2 The mountain willow (*Salix phylicifolia?*) . . . is only abundant on the lowlands of the frozen North.

+11. Special combinations.

Mountain barometer, a barometer for use in high altitudes; *m. engine*, a mountain locomotive (q.v. below); *m. feud*, among southern mountaineers, a continued state of strife between families (cf. FEUD 2); *m. lamb*, (see quotation); *m. law*, customs with the force of law among mountain people; *m. locomotive*, a heavy locomotive esp. fitted for climbing mountains; *m. park*, an amphitheaterlike valley between mountain ranges; *m. saddle*, (see quotation); *m. shad*, (see quotation).

1852 MARCY *Explor. Red River* 15 Captain McClellan was so unfortunate as to break his mountain barometer last night. **1877** 'E. MARTIN' *Hist. Great Riots* 130 The mountain engine was backed out of the round house. **1903** FOX *Little Shepherd* v, That night they tied up at Jackson—to be famous long after the war as the seat of a bitter mountain feud. **1902** CLAPIN 281 Mountain-lamb. In parts of New England, especially New-Hampshire, a common term for deer killed out of season. **1851** M. REID *Scalp Hunters* 269 They believe themselves, according to mountain law, in the right. **1880** *Cimarron News & Press* 3 June 2/5 Mountain locomotives have two enemies—the falling rock and the snow slide. **1883** RITCH *Illus. N. Mex.* 40 Excepting in several of the mountain parks, irrigation is more or less, a necessity. **1848** PARKMAN in *Knickerb.* XXXI. 357 Though aided by the high-bowed 'mountain-saddle,' I could scarcely keep my seat on horseback. **1883** ZEIGLER & GROSSCUP *Alleghanies* 48 Some 'varmint' . . . [had eaten] a fine hundred-pound hog (otherwise known as a mountain shad).

* **Mountain ash.** +Either of two species of trees having characteristics of the true ash: The American mountain ash, *Sorbus americana*, or the western mountain ash, *S. decora;* a tree of either of these species.

1785 MARSHALL *Amer. Grove* 144 *Sorbus*. The Service Tree, Quickbeam, or Mountain Ash. **1818** *Mass. H. S. Coll.* 2 Ser. VIII. 169 The mountain ash is a very ornamental tree. Its leaves, resembling those of the sumach, are . . . succeeded by bunches of red berries, which hang on during the winter. **1848** ROBINSON *Santa Fe Exped.* 18 Pine and mountain-ash are the growth. **1868** BEECHER *Norwood* 351 A fine mountain ash relieved its cluster of berries against the dark green. **1904** WALLER *Wood-Carver* 49, I noticed . . . some fine specimens of mountain-ash.

+**Mountain bison.** (See BISON 1 b.)

+**Mountain boomer.** *S.E.* =BOOMER[2] 1. — **1858** [see BOOMER[2] 1]. **1870** *Amer. Naturalist* IV. 394 The inhabitants are well acquainted with [*Sciurus Hudsonius*] . . . under the name of the 'Mountain Boomer.' **1883** ZEIGLER & GROSSCUP *Alleghanies* 62 Over all broods a slumberous silence, unbroken but for . . . the singing of the mountain boomer, or the howl of wolves.

Mountain boy. +1. A member of an informal military company of Vermont during the Revolution. (Cf. GREEN MOUNTAIN BOY.) +2. A member of other military companies made up of men living in the mountains. — (1) **1777** HAMILTON *Works* VII. 522 Nixon's brigades, and Colonel Warner's mountain boys, to remain in and about Albany. **1815** *Niles' Reg.* IX. 171/1 In their hats [were] sprigs of ever-green, the ancient badge of the mountain-boys. (2) **1787** *Amer. Museum* II. Chron. 6/1 We may shortly expect to hear of . . . a new display of gallantry of the Mountain Boys. **1815** *Niles' Reg.* VIII. 39/2 At the most gloomy period of the war, these mountain boys of *Pennsylvania*, . . . organized themselves into a company.

+**Mountain buffalo.** **1.** =MOUNTAIN SHEEP. **2.** (See quot. 1884.) — (1) **1868** *Amer. Naturalist* II. 538 'Mountain Buffalo.' . . . The Bighorn is sometimes called so. (2) *Ib.*, I saw no difference in the skulls, indicating a different species, or 'Mountain Buffalo' of the hunters. **1884** DE VERE in *Encycl. Brit.* (ed. 9) *Amer. Suppl.* I. 540/2 Buffaloes long inhabiting other localities than the open plains, their natural homes, acquire distinguishable varietal characters. They are known as 'wood-buffalo' and 'mountain-buffalo.'

+**Mountain cat.** **a.** The cougar. **b.** The bobcat. **c.** *Calif.* The cacomistle, *Bassariscus astutus.* — **1709** LAWSON *Carolina* 118 The Mountain-Cat, so call'd, because he lives in the Mountainous Parts of America, . . . is a Beast of Prey, as the Panther is. **1789** ANBUREY *Travels* II. 433 At the very instant, a ferocious animal . . . called the mountain cat, was going to spring upon him. **1832** WILLIAMSON *Maine* I. 135 The *Wild-Cat*, or mountain cat, is much heavier and fiercer than any of the domestic species. **1842** *Nat. Hist. N.Y., Zoology* I. 51, I suppose the Mountain Cat described by Loskiel as having reddish or orange-colored hair, with black streaks, to have been the Bay Lynx. **1872** MCCLELLAN *Golden State* 239 The wild cat and mountain cat . . . are found in the mountains and hillsides of the State. **1890** LANGFORD *Vigilante Days* (1912) 92 To the agility of a mountain cat he added the quick, sharp eye of an Indian.

+**Mountain cherry.** Any of several wild cherries: (see quotations). — **1813** MUHLENBERG *Cat. Plants* 48 *Prunus montana*, . . . mountain cherry. **1871** *Harper's Mag.* Oct. 707 We must . . . gather mountain cherries (*Prunus cerasus*). **1893** *Amer. Folk-Lore* VI. 140 *Prunus Chicasa* mountain cherry. Md. **1909** WEBSTER 1413 Mountain cherry. A wild cherry (*Prunus angustifolia*) of the eastern United States.

+**Mountain chestnut oak.** The chestnut oak, *Quercus prinus.* — **1801** MICHAUX *Histoire des Chênes* 6 Chêne Chataignier (des montagnes). Mountain Chesnut Oak, Roky Oak. **1815** DRAKE *Cincinnati* 83 [The] fox grape and mountain-chestnut oak are still scarcer. **1821** NUTTALL *Travels Arkansa* 15 Much of the *Quercus Prinos monticola* (or mountain chestnut oak) presents itself on the mountain.

+**Mountain chickadee.** A western titmouse (*Penthestes gambeli*) having a white stripe over the eye. — **1874** COUES *Birds N.W.* 22 Mountain Chickadee. . . . Common in various coniferous mountainous tracts in New Mexico and Arizona. **1878** *Nat. Museum Proc.* I. 400 *Parus montanus.*—Mountain Chickadee. This is a very common resident of Big Trees.

Mountain cock. {1802} +**1.** A grouse similar to the European capercaillie. +**2.** =COCK OF THE PLAINS. — (1) **1791** W. BARTRAM *Travels* 290 *Tetrao lagopus;* the mountain cock, or grous [is found in Pennsylvania]. (2) **1805** LEWIS in *L. & Clark Exped.* II. (1904) 124 [We] saw . . . a flock of the mountain cock, or a large species of heath hen with a long pointed tail which the Indians informed us were common to the Rockey Mountains.

+**Mountain cranberry.** **1.** An evergreen shrub (*Vaccinium vitis-idaea*); the dark red berry of this shrub. **2.** =BEAR-BERRY 1. — (1) **1848** THOREAU *Maine Woods* 22 Mountain cranberries (*Vaccinium Vitis-Idaea*), stewed and sweetened, were the common dessert. **1869** FULLER *Flower Gatherers* 120 There are . . . four species, one of which is a shrub . . . called the Bush, or Mountain Cranberry. **1892** TORREY *Foot-Path Way* 72 Broad patches of bearberry showing at a little distance like beds of mountain cranberry. (2) **1894** *Amer. Folk-Lore* VII. 93 *Arctostaphylos Uva-ursi*, mountain cranberry, Southern Me.

+**Mountain Day.** At certain colleges, an annual holiday, devoted by students to mountain-climbing. — **1845** *Williams Mo. Misc.* I. 555 Some, not content with a mountain day, carried their knapsacks and blankets to encamp till morning on the summit. **1854** *Boston Ev. Traveller* 12 July, 'Mountain day' . . . comes at the beginning of the summer term. **1887** *Springfield D. Repub.* 14 Oct. 6/4 Yesterday was mountain day at Smith college and many students spent the day in the woods and upon the mountain.

Mountain deer. A deer that inhabits the mountains; +*spec.*, the mule deer. *Obs.* — **1820** EASTBURN & SANDS *Yamoyden* 18 He led them, fleet as mountain deer. **1832** in W. Kennedy *Texas* (1841) I. 189 Two of the mountain deer [were] killed to-day. **1834** A. PIKE *Sketches* 122 Around the tent two or three skins of the grizzly bear and of the mountain deer were stretched.

Mountain dew. {1816–} +Illicit strong whisky distilled in the mountains; moonshine. *colloq.*

1878 in Summers *Ann. S.W. Va.* 1617 Each armed with a revolver . . . and a bottle of 'mountain dew.' **1888** *Century Mag.* XXXVI. 766/1 Pine tags and even potato peelings went into the impromptu still to come out pure 'mountain dew.' **1913** MORLEY *Carolina Mts.* 66 Corn is not only the principal food of the mountaineer, but supplies as well . . . 'mountain-dew.'

Mountaineer.

1. **a.** A native or inhabitant of the mountains. {1610–} +**b.** *spec.* A person native to the mountains or hills of the South.

1721 *Mass. H. Rep. Jrnl.* III. 111 [A letter bearing] the signature of the nations of the Abnaquoise, and of . . . The Mikemaks, The Mountaniers on the North-side. **1834** NOTT *Novellettes* II. 144 The farmers occasionally employed the mountaineers to lend a hand at harvest, shuck corn [etc.]. **1843** *Knickerb.* XXII. 431 The rough mountaineer of New Hampshire has as much right to calculate upon the good old age of eighty-six [etc.]. **1859** *Harper's Mag.* Sept. 569/1 [His] coon-skin cap and patchwork coat of many colors proclaimed him to be a mountaineer. **1898** J. FOX *Kentuckians* 52, I'll send you a feudsman, if you are getting interested in mountaineers. **1913** [see MOUNTAIN DEW].

+**2.** *W.* =MOUNTAIN MAN 2.

1837 IRVING *Bonneville* I. 25 A totally different class has now sprung up, 'the Mountaineers,' the traders and trappers that scale the vast mountain chains. **1846** SAGE *Scenes Rocky Mts.* xxviii, Having occasion to camp out at night, like a genuine mountaineer, he took his saddle for a pillow. **1857** DAVIS *El Gringo* 318, [I] made the acquaintance of Kit Carson, the celebrated mountaineer. **1864** *Rio Abajo Press* 5 July 1/3 [Frémont] obtained the sobriquet of 'Pathfinder,' in finding paths well known to Kit Carson and other mountaineers, who guided him. **1904** *Chicago Ev. Post* 23 Aug. 7 In it [a dunnage bag] the aspiring mountaineer may pack fifty pounds of necessities.

+**Mountain fever.** Any of various fevers contracted in the mountains. {1875}

Malaria and typhoid fever have not infrequently been diagnosed by mountain settlers as mountain fever.

1850 SAWYER *Way Sketches* 56 Some of our men have been sick with mountain fever. **1869** BROWNE *Adv. Apache Country* 522 An attack of mountain fever laid me on my back. **1878** BEADLE *Western Wilds* 331 He fell from his horse in a paroxysm of that dread disease, mountain fever. **1890** *Buckskin Mose* 84, I was taken sick with that terrible disease, emigrants have named the mountain-fever. **a1918** G. STUART *On Frontier* I. 51 A severe attack of mountain fever . . . laid me on my back in the wagon.

+**Mountain goat.** A goatlike animal (*Oreamnos montanus*) of the northwest mountains; the Rocky Mountain goat.

1833 CATLIN *Indians* I. 113 His dress from head to foot was of the skins of the mountain-goat. **1844** LEE & FROST *Oregon* 98 These [moccasins] are of dressed skins of the deer, antelope, mountain-goat, and sheep. **1888** *Outing* May 121 The rarest mammal in America . . . is, probably, the mountain goat. **1907** *St. Nicholas* XXXIV. 752/2 Would you also tell me what the mountain goats and deer eat in winter?

attrib. **c1837** CATLIN *Indians* II. 196 His leggings and shirt were of the mountain goat skin.

Mountain grape. {1756–} +One of two grapes found in Texas: **1.** The sweet mountain grape, *Vitis monticola.* **2.** The sand grape, *Vitis rupestris.* — (1) **1862** *Rep. Comm. Patents 1861: Agric.* 485 *Vitis monticola* . . . is called the 'White or Mountain grape;' differs from *V. rupestris* in its trailing habit and long, slender branches. (2) **1885** HAVARD *Flora W. & S. Texas* 511 *Vitis rupestris*, Scheele, (Mountain Grape.) . . . Said to grow on the hillsides of the Limpio and other mountains. **1891** COULTER *Bot. W. Texas* I. 63 In the Valley of Devil's River and westward into the mountains of the Pecos. Also called 'mountain grape.'

+**Mountain grouse.** =FRANKLIN'S (SPRUCE) GROUSE. — **1858** PETERS *Kit Carson* 362 Mountain grouse and prairie chickens helped to complete the load. **1887** *Century Mag.* March 747/1 [In California] there is a bird called the mountain grouse which can be found on Pine Mountain. **1917** *Birds of Amer.* II. 16 Franklin's Grouse. . . . [Also called] Mountain Grouse.

+**Mountain hemlock.** One of various hemlocks that grow in the mountains: (see quotations). — **1884** SARGENT *Rep. Forests* 572 The timber on these ridges [in Shoshone Co., Idaho] was often small and scattered . . . with larch and red fir, balsam, hemlock, and sometimes the mountain hemlock (*Tsuga Pattoniana*). **1892** APGAR *Trees Northern U.S.* 182 Mountain-hemlock. . . . Wild, but scarce, in the higher Alleghanies, south. **1909** WEBSTER 1413 *Mountain hemlock*, . . . a hemlock (*Tsuga mertensiana*) of the western United States.

+**Mountain herring.** *local.* The Rocky Mountain whitefish, *Prosopium williamsoni.* — **1884** GOODE, etc. *Fisheries* I. 542 This species [the Rocky Mt. whitefish] is usually known as the White-fish; in Utah as the 'Mountain Herring.'

+**Mountain holly.**

1. The Oregon grape of the genus *Mahonia.*

1806 LEWIS in *L. & Clark Exped.* IV. (1905) 274 Near the river we find . . . two speceis of mountain holley, & common ash. **1807** GASS *Journal* 135 There is also a small bush . . . which bears a bunch of small purple berries. Some call it mountain holly; the fruit is of an acid taste.

2. Either of two shrubs of the eastern United States: **a.** An obovate-leaved shrub, *Nemopanthus mucronata.* **b.** An upland holly, *Ilex dubia monticola.*

1817–8 EATON *Botany* (1822) 317 *Ilex canadensis*, mountain holly. . . . A shrub 3 to 5 feet high. **1843** TORREY *Flora N.Y.* II. 5 *Nemopanthes Canadensis*, Mountain Holly, . . . [is found] on the Catskill mountains. **1901** MOHR *Plant Life Ala.* 71 Mountain holly (*Ilex monticola*) . . . extend[s] northerly on the lower of the western Alleghenian ranges to southeastern Kentucky.

Mountain howitzer. A howitzer specially fitted for use in the mountains. {1812} Also attrib. — **1843** TYLER in *Pres. Mess. & P.* IV. 274 I transmit herewith a communication . . . 'on the subject of the "mountain howitzer" taken by Lieutenant Fremont on the expedition to the Oregon' [Territory]. **1864** *Rio Abajo Press* 2 Feb. 1/1 Colonel Carson has taken the mountain howitzer battery to Chelle, where it will . . . be used with good effect against the Navajoes. **1894** *S. Dak. Hist. Coll.* I. 303

Sibley got away from Fort Ridgeley . . . with 2,000 infantry, 800 cavalry, and some mountain howitzers.

+**Mountain jack.** A kind of card game. — **1877** CAMPION *On Frontier* 25 Cards [were] brought out; seven-up, mountain-jack, and euchre had each their turn.

+**Mountain jay.** The high-crested blue jay (*Cyanocitta stelleri*) of the West. — **1872** *Amer. Naturalist* VI. 398 The great-crested, Woodhouse's and the Canada jays were of frequent occurrence in the mountains, the former being familiarly known as the 'mountain jay.' **1917** *Birds of Amer.* II. 219 Steller's Jay. . . . [Also called] Mountain Jay; Pine Jay; Conifer Jay.

+**Mountain laurel.**

1. a. =GREAT LAUREL b. **b.** A glossy-leaved, evergreen shrub (*Kalmia latifolia*), with rose-colored and white flowers.

The shrub of sense b is also called *American laurel, calico bush, mountain ivy*, etc.

1759 MILLER *Gard. Dict.* (ed. 7) s.v. *Kalmia*, Ever-green Rose Laurel . . . commonly called in America Mountain Laurel. **1785** MARSHALL *Amer. Grove* 127 *Rhododendrum maximum*. Pennsylvanian Mountain Laurel. This grows to the height of about six or eight feet. **1832** BROWNE *Sylva* 191 The Mountain Laurel is a large shrub, which indifferently bears the name of Mountain Laurel, Laurel, Ivy, and Calico Tree. **1850** *New Eng. Farmer* II. 109/1 The Mountain Laurel, or Calico Bush, is a fine evergreen shrub, found in Gloucester. **1880** *Harper's Mag.* June 80 The mountain laurel, with its deep green foliage and showy clusters peers above that rocky crag. **1906** J. A. HARRISON *G. Washington* 91 The bluish-pink masses of the mountain-laurel.

2. The California laurel (*Umbellularia californica*), having aromatic evergreen foliage.

1884 SARGENT *Rep. Forests* 120 Mountain Laurel. California Laurel. Spice Tree. **1889** *Cent.* 3373/1 The California laurel or bay-tree, the mountain-laurel of the West, is *Umbellularia Californica*.

+**Mountain lion.** The cougar. — **1859** G. A. JACKSON *Diary* (MS.) 2 Killed a mountain lion today. **1872** *Harper's Mag.* Dec. 30/2 The mountain lion—which is here [in Colo.] sometimes met with—is the panther or cougar of the Eastern States. **1880** INGHAM *Digging Gold* 405 The mountain lion of the Rockies is a large and ferocious beast, of heavier build than the panther, and resembling the African lion, except that it has no mane and beard like the latter. **1913** BARNES *Western Grazing Grounds* 330 Wolves and Mountain Lions.—These animals do more damage to cattle and horses than to any other class of domestic animals.

+**Mountain mahogany.**

1. The sweet birch (*Betula lenta*), common in the eastern United States.

1810 MICHAUX *Arbres* I. 26 *Sweet birch*, [ou] *Mountain mahogony*, dans Virginia. **1814** PURSH *Flora Amer.* II. 622 *Betula lenta* . . . is known by the name of Mountain Mahogany, Black Birch, Cherry Birch, and Sweet Birch. **1832** BROWNE *Sylva* 118 Black Birch: . . . [is known as] Mountain Mahogany in Virginia.

2. *W.* Any of various western shrubs of the genus *Cercocarpus*, having gray bark and reddish wood.

1860 GREELEY *Overland Journey* 268 There is a . . . small tree which a driver termed a mountain-mahogany and a passenger called a red haw. **1870** *Amer. Naturalist* IV. 35 At seven thousand feet . . . the sage yields to the western juniper . . . and mountain mahogany. **1884** SARGENT *Rep. Forests* 9 The mountain mahogany . . . with the nut pine . . . characterizes this region. **1913** BARNES *Western Grazing Grounds* 43 In the foothills there are several varieties of edible bushes like Mountain mahogany . . . and the catclaw and mesquite found elsewhere.

3. *W.* The Pacific yew, *Taxus brevifolia*.

1897 SUDWORTH *Arborescent Flora* 103 *Taxus brevifolia*. . . . Pacific Yew. . . . Mountain Mahogany (Idaho).

Mountain man.

1. A man who lives in the mountains; =MOUNTAINEER 1. {1691, of the Scotch Cameronians}

1781 *Va. State P.* I. 494, A late pressing application of General Greene for the aid of the Mountain Men, will not be so effectually answered. **1856–7** D. D. OWEN *Geol. Survey Ky.* (B.), We even hear the inhabitants of this part of Kentucky frequently styled 'Blue-grass men' in contradistinction to the 'mountain men,' residents of the adjacent hill and mountain country. **1917** COMSTOCK *Man* 117 A mountain man might still love his woman even if he beat her.

+**2.** A man skilled in going through, or living in, the mountains, as a mountain guide, trapper, or trader: (see quot. 1910).

1847 RUXTON *Adv. Rocky Mts.* (1848) 217 The depreciation in the value of beaver-skins has thrown the great body of trappers out of employment, and there is a general tendency among the mountain-men to settle in the fruitful valleys of the Rocky Mountains. **1852** STANSBURY *Gt. Salt Lake* 74 Major James Bridger, one of the oldest mountain-men in this entire region, . . . has been engaged in the Indian trade . . . for the last thirty years. **1871** RAYMOND *3d Rep. Mines* 215 Gillette is one of the best mountain-men of the party, and . . . he may bring some tidings of the missing man. **1910** DOUGLAS ed. Parkman *Oregon Trail* 338 *Mountain-men*, a well-defined class of backwoodsmen, . . . versed in everything pertaining to life upon the plains and in the mountains.

+**Mountain maple.** One of several shrublike maples found in mountainous areas, as *Acer spicatum* of the eastern states and *A. glabrum* of the Rocky Mountains. Also with defining terms.

1785 MARSHALL *Amer. Grove* 2 *Acer pennsylvanicum*, Pennsylvanian Dwarf Mountain Maple, . . . grows naturally upon the mountains in the back parts of Pennsylvania. **1815** DRAKE *Cincinnati* 83 [The] mountain maple, red berried elder and witch hazle I have only found at the falls of the Little Miami. **1832** BROWNE *Sylva* 102 The mountain maple seldom rises above 20 feet in height, and it often blooms at an elevation less than six feet. **1860** CURTIS *Woody Plants N.C.* 53 Mountain maple (*A. spicatum*). . . . Its leaves and fruit have the common characters of a Maple, the latter being rather small. **1897** SUDWORTH *Arborescent Flora* 284 *Acer glabrum*. Dwarf Maple. . . . Mountain Maple (Colo., Mont.).

Mountain mint. {1671} +**1.** Oswego tea, *Monarda didyma*. +**2.** An American mint of the genus *Pycnanthemum*. — (1) **1817–8** EATON *Botany* (1822) 356 *Monarda didyma*, mountain mint. (2) *Ib.* 415 *Pycnanthemum incanum*, wild basil, mountain mint. **1840** DEWEY *Mass. Flowering Plants* 182 Mountain Mint. . . . Rather handsome. **1892** COULTER *Bot. W. Texas* II. 334.

+**Mountain mutton.** The flesh of the mountain sheep. — **1836** IRVING *Astoria* II. 165 Here they encamped for the night, and supped sumptuously upon their mountain mutton. **1847** COYNER *Lost Trappers* 152 What is commonly called mountain mutton . . . is very delicate and sweet.

+**Mountain oak.** Any of various upland oaks: (see quotations).

1817–8 EATON *Botany* (1822) 421 *Quercus montana*, rock oak, chestnut oak, mountain oak. **1821** *Mass. H. S. Coll.* 2 Ser. IX. 155 Plants, which are indigenous in the township of Middlebury, [Vermont, include] . . . *Quercus montana*, Mountain oak. **1883** SMITH *Geol. Survey Ala.* 296 On the high lands . . . are found . . . the mountain or tan-bark oak [etc.]. **1897** SUDWORTH *Arborescent Flora* 153 *Quercus gambelii*. . . . Mountain Oak (Nev., Oreg.). **1901** MOHR *Plant Life Ala.* 84 Oaks form the predominating forest growth of these highlands—white oak, mountain oak, and fine black oak.

+**Mountain partridge.** **1.** =RUFFED GROUSE. **2.** =MOUNTAIN QUAIL. — (1) **1781–2** JEFFERSON *Notes Va.* (1788) 74 Pheasant. Mountain partridge. **1789** MORSE *Amer. Geog.* 60 American Birds [include the] . . . Pheasant or mountain Partridge, Water Pheasant, [and] Pelican. (2) **1887** RIDGWAY *Manual N.A. Birds* 191 Pacific coast district, from San Francisco north to Washington Territory. . . . *O. pictus*. Mountain Partridge. **1917** *Birds of Amer.* II. 5 Mountain Quail. *Oreortyx picta picta*. . . . [Also called] Mountain Partridge.

Mountain pine. +Any of several tall pines, as the western *Pinus monticola*. Also attrib. — **1814** *Niles' Reg.* 21 May 194/1 The mountain-pine . . . cradles the eagle. **1850** GARRARD *Wah-To-Yah* xiii. 180 The hard bread, *bescoche*, is . . . a perfect luxury with a cup of coffee by a mountain-pine fire. **1892** APGAR *Trees Northern U.S.* 173 *Pinus monticola*. (Mountain-pine.) . . . Pacific coast.

+**Mountain plover.** A small plover of the upland prairies of the West, *Eupoda montana*. — **1858** BAIRD *Birds Pacific R.R.* 693 Mountain Plover . . . is only known to inhabit the western countries of North America. **1872** *Amer. Naturalist* VI. 272 The so-called 'mountain' plover was . . . seen on the dry prairies far away from the streams and sloughs. **1883** *Nat. Museum Bul.* No. 27, 147 *Podasocys montanus*. Mountain Plover. . . . Western United States, north to British Provinces. **1917** *Birds of Amer.* I. 267 Mountain Plover. . . . Nest: On the open prairies; a depression in the ground, lined with leaves and grass.

+**Mountain quail.** A partridge of the west coast, *Oreortyx picta palmeri*. — **1858** BAIRD *Birds Pacific R.R.* 642 Plumed Partridge; Mountain Quail. . . . Mountain ranges of California and Oregon towards the coast. **1869** *Amer. Naturalist* III. 185, I have heard of the Mountain Quail . . . as occurring on this spot. **1910** J. HART *Vigilante Girl* 200 The open roasting fires, before which slowly revolved . . . saddles of lamb, mountain quail, canvas-back. **1917** *Birds of Amer.* II. 5 The Mountain Quail rarely raises more than one brood in a season but its broods are large.

+**Mountain ram.** The Rocky Mountain sheep or bighorn, *Ovis canadensis*. — **1804** CLARK in *Lewis & C. Exped.* I. (1904) 169, I also Saw a Spoon Made of a horn of an Animell of the Sheep Kind (the mountain ram of Argalia). **1807** GASS *Journal* 74 We packed the boxes full of skins, buffaloe robes, and horns of the Mountain ram, of a great size for the president. **1886** ROOSEVELT in *Outing* May 131 One of my foremen shot a mountain ram.

Mountain rat. {1753} +A pack rat (*Neotoma cinerea*) of the West. (See also ROCKY MOUNTAIN RAT.) — **1885** *Outing* VII. 51/2 If the mountain rats hadn't eaten up my copy of Shakespeare, . . . I should have the very best of company. **1897** HOUGH *Story of Cowboy* 41 Small birds twitter and flit about the ranch house, . . . and the mountain rats appear from their nests.

Mountain rice. +Any of various grasses of the genus *Oryzopsis*, as the Rocky Mountain species, *O. hymenoides*. Also with defining term. — **1817–8** EATON *Botany* (1822) 370 *Oryzopsis asperifolia*, mountain rice. Woods and bushy fields. **1843** TORREY *Flora N.Y.* II. 432 *Oryzopsis melanocarpa*. . . . Black-fruited Mountain-rice. . . . Rocky woods, in the western and northern parts of the State. **1869** *Amer. Naturalist* III. 155

The Mountain Rice . . . I found in flower and about two feet high by the latter part of May. **1894** COULTER *Bot. W. Texas* III. 517 *O[ryzopsis] membranacea*. . . . (Mountain rice.) . . . Mountain regions of western Texas and northward.

+**Mountain schooner.** A covered wagon or prairie schooner fitted up for travel through the mountains. — **1869** BRACE *New West* 188 Coaches, wagons, and the stream of 'mountain-schooners' pour into it unceasingly. **1882** HARTE *Flip* 2 Anxious faces yearned toward it . . . from the blinding white canvas covers of 'mountain schooners.'

+**Mountain sheep. a.** The bighorn (*Ovis canadensis*), ranging in the high mountains of the West. **b.** A generic term for varieties of this animal.

See also ROCKY MOUNTAIN SHEEP.

1805 *Lewis & Clark Exped.* VII. (1905) 125 At noon Capt. Clark killed a mountain Sheep, on the Side of a Steep redish hills or clifts. **1807** GASS *Journal* 82 We saw some Mountain sheep, which the natives say are common about the Rocky mountains. **1846** SAGE *Scenes Rocky Mts.* xiv, In size the mountain sheep is larger than the domestic animal of that name, and its general appearance is in every respect dissimilar—excepting the head and horns. **1872** MCCLELLAN *Golden State* 241 In many parts of the Sierras is found the mountain-sheep. **1893** ROOSEVELT *Wilderness Hunter* 17 The bighorn, or mountain sheep is found . . . from the Coast and Cascade ranges to the Bad Lands of the western edges of the Dakotas. **1917** *Mammals of Amer.* 56 Stone's is a dark form of Mountain Sheep living in the northern Rockies.

***Mountain snow.** + =SNOW-ON-THE-MOUNTAIN. — **1888** 'CRADDOCK' *Despot* 159 He mechanically noted . . . how the blooming 'mountain snow' brushed his mare's fine coat. **1913** BRITTON & BROWN *Illus. Flora* II. 469 *Euphorbia marginata*. . . . In dry soil, Minnesota to Colorado, south to Texas. Introduced into waste places in the Central and Atlantic States. Snow-on-the mountain. . . . Mountain-snow.

+**Mountain tea. 1.** The wintergreen, *Gaultheria procumbens*. **2.** A beverage made from steeping the leaves of this plant. — **(1) 1785** MARSHALL *Amer. Grove* 53 *Gaultheria procumbens*. Canadian Gaultheria, or Mountain Tea. . . . The leaves have been used as a substitute for Bohea Tea, whence the name of Mountain Tea. **1819** *Western Rev.* I. 94 On the Cumberland mountain . . . Common Laurel, and . . . Mountain tea, grow. **1891** RYAN *Pagan* 65 As they reached the level above the cliff, the level carpeted with mountain-tea and rabbit-berries, . . . the mountaineer halted. **(2) 1832** WILLIAMSON *Maine* I. 121 This 'mountain tea' [from chequer-berries] promotes mammillary secretions. **1886** *Harper's Mag.* June 62/1 Another beverage is 'mountain tea,' which is made from the sweet-scented golden-rod and from winter-green.

+**Mountain time.** The standard time of the Rocky Mountain area west of the 105th meridian. Also attrib. — **1883** *N.Y. Herald* 18 Nov. 12/3 In the United States the standards will be known as the 'Eastern,' 'Central,' 'Mountain' and 'Pacific' times. [**1909** *Westm. Gaz.* 8 March 3/1 At Broadview another change of an hour is made to Mountain time.] **1923** *Daily News* (Chicago) *Almanac 1924* 48/1 Between mountain and Pacific time zones the line is fixed following [etc.].

+**Mountain trapper.** A man who traps animals in the mountains. — **1837** IRVING *Bonneville* II. 61 Peak after peak had they to traverse, struggling with difficulties and hardships known only to the mountain trapper. **1848** PARKMAN in *Knickerb.* XXXI. 334 When winter sets in, . . . the mountain-trappers, returned from their autumn expeditions, often build their rude cabins in the midst of these solitudes. **1872** PARKMAN *Oregon Trail* (ed. 4) p. viii, The mountain trapper is no more.

+**Mountain trout. a.** A trout that lives in a mountain stream {1898, in Australia}, as the brook or rainbow trout. **b.** In parts of the South, the black bass.

1805 LEWIS in *L. & Clark Exped.* II. (1904) 150 These trout . . . resemble our mountain or speckled trout. **1820** RAFINESQUE in *Western Rev.* II. 177 Alleghany Trout . . . has the manner of the small Brook-trouts, and is called Mountain-trout, Creek-trout, &c. **1872** TICE *Over Plains* 126 She had just finished catching a fine mess of mountain trout. **1883** *Harper's Mag.* Sept. 625/2 He had gone into the kitchen, and finding some bacon and fresh mountain trout, had set about cooking dinner. **1884** GOODE, etc. *Fisheries* I. 401 In Alabama, according to Professor Jordan, it [the small-mouth black bass, *Micropterus dolomieu*] is called the 'Mountain Trout.' *Ib.* 475 The Black spotted Trout—*Salmo purpuratus*. This fish is known as the 'Trout,' 'Mountain Trout,' 'Spotted Trout,' 'Black Trout,' 'Silver Trout,' etc., in the mountains, but when in the ocean, full grown, as 'Salmon Trout' or 'Steel-head.' **1911** *Rep. Fisheries 1908* 307.

+**Mountain wagon.** A wagon or carriage used in the mountains: (see esp. quot. 1873). — **1867** DIXON *New America* I. 170 On my return through the Bitter Creek country, I had the honour of riding in the mountain waggon with an old road-agent. **1873** BEADLE *Undevel. West* 255 We change from the coach to a 'mountain-wagon'—so called—a street hack with three seats and no springs. **1896** SHINN *Story of Mine* 108 These trains of mountain wagons . . . contained dry goods, provisions, tools, machinery, and merchandise.

Mounted harness. Harness ornamented with brass, silver, or the like. — **1892** *York County Hist. Rev.* 80 Here is displayed light and heavy, single and double, plain and mounted harness.

Mounted infantry. *Mil.* Infantry which moves from place to place on horseback, but fights dismounted. {1882–} — **1792** *Ann. 2d Congress* 1134 General Harmar . . . detached . . . the mounted infantry, part of the cavalry, and a detachment of militia. **1847** BAKER *Ohio* 235 The novel expedient of charging through the British lines with mounted infantry. **1858** tr. Domenech *Missionary Adv. Texas & Mex.* 177 The Indians were once nearly taking prisoners a whole company of mounted infantry (as they are called).

Mounted police. A police squad on horseback. {Mounted Police organized in Canada 1873} — [**1864** *Ladies' Repository* April 200/2 The 'Light Horse,' a mounted police, were our only dependence in an emergency.] **1882** MCCABE *New York* 375 Special detachments . . . do duty as a Mounted Police. *Ib.* 400 The Mounted Police . . . constitute a distinct squad.

+**Mounted ranger.** A man who ranges on horseback to patrol or protect an area. — **1812** *Ann. 12th Congress* 2 Sess. 195 [The Indiana Territory] had not enjoyed one hour of security and repose, from the protection of the one company of Mounted Rangers, which had been allotted for its defence. **1852** GOUGE *Fiscal Hist. Texas* 73 Treasury notes should be issued only to defray the expenses of the civil department, and those of the gun-men and mounted rangers.

***Mounting.** *attrib.* +Designating the left side of a horse. *Obs.* — **1732** *S.C. Gazette* 5 Feb. 4/2 (Th. S.), A dark colour'd Horse, branded with M and a cross a top, on the mounting shoulder: . . . also a bay Horse . . . branded with H on the mounting buttock. **1737** *Ib.* 26 Feb. 3/1 (Th. S.), [He is] branded on the Mounting shoulder with a Diamond. **1794** *Ib.* 29 July 1/1 (Th. S.), A black gelding, . . . branded on the Mounting buttock C.

***Mourner.**

***1.** One who mourns the death of a relative or friend; one who attends a funeral out of respect for the deceased.

To crowd the mourners, (see CROWD *v.* 5 a).

1687 SEWALL *Diary* I. 179 The mourners went into the Schoolhouse. **1775** *Jrnls. Cont. Congress.* III. 303 This Congress will attend their funeral as mourners, with a crape round their left arm. **1863** A. D. WHITNEY *F. Gartney* xxi, There ought to be somebody to stay a while and cheer up the mourners. **1904** PRINGLE *Rice Planter* 59 Sitting on top of . . . [the cart were] the chief women mourners, veiled in crêpe.

+**2.** At a revival or camp meeting, one who publicly repents his sins. (Cf. ANXIOUS BENCH, ANXIOUS SEAT.)

1845 HOOPER *Simon Suggs' Adv.* 121 Having thus deposited his charge among the mourners, he started out, summarily to convert another soul! **1853** *S. Lit. Messenger* XIX. 217/2 The courthouse was as solemn as a camp-meeting when they are calling up the mourners. **1883** SWEET & KNOX *Through Texas* 110 Around in front of the preacher's stand was an open space fenced off by a row of reserved seats for the mourners. **1901** HARBEN *Westerfelt* 252 When they begin to call up mourners she commences to clap 'er hands an' shout.

+**3.** (See quotation.)

1904 *N.Y. Ev. Post* 10 March 12 The rush of people to the Tax Department to swear off taxes has set in. Yesterday the 'mourner's lines,' which ordinarily contains 10 or 15 persons, extended out into the corridor.

+**Mourners' bench.** At a revival or camp meeting, a front seat reserved for the mourners. Also transf. Also *mourner's seat*. — **1845** HOOPER *Adv. Simon Suggs* 126 'Bimeby I felt so missuble, I had to go yonder' —pointing to the mourner's seat. **1848** *Ladies' Repository* VIII. 102 She loves the mourner's bench, for there she found peace and pardon. **1856** CARTWRIGHT *Autobiog.* 403 You must go to the Methodists' despised mourners' bench. **1864** 'MARK TWAIN' *Sketches* (1926) 129 He goes through the camp-meetings and skirmishes for raw converts, whom he brings to the front and puts them in the corral, or the mourner's bench, as they call it in that section. **1902** LORIMER *Lett. Merchant* 149 The first thing Josh knew he was out from under cover and a-hallelujahing down between the seats to the mourners' bench. **1904** *Charlotte Observer* 27 July 4 In the city police court a motley crowd of prisoners filled the mourners' benches

***Mourning,** *n.*

1. *Half mourning*, mourning dress lightened by white, gray, or lavender. {1848–}

1829 *Va. Lit. Museum* 312 The other [woman] wore that particular dress . . . which, though termed *half mourning*, commonly tells the world that 'Time the Comforter,' has already done his part.

2. *attrib.* **a.** Designating various articles of clothing, pieces of jewelry, etc., worn in mourning.

*a***1649** WINTHROP *Hist.* II. 273 The captain gave every one of them an eln of black taffeta for a mourning robe. **1663** *Dorchester Antiq. & Hist. Soc. Coll.* No. 3, 103 [Thomas Lake's will directs that his body] shall be buried in the North burying-ground, without any solemnity of souldiers, mourning ribbon, wines and cakes. **1709** SEWALL *Diary* II. 254 Being Artillery day, and Mr. Higginson dead, I put on my Mourning Rapier. **1720** *Ib.* III. 249 Judge Dudley in a mourning Cloak led the Widow. **1732** *S.C. Gazette* 48/1 Lost a Mourning hair Ring, engraved on the Inside, March 3d E. L. Deceas'd 1731. **1814** J. BEASLEY *Will Pettigrew P.* (Univ. N.C. MS.), To my Cousin Ebenezer Pettigrew I give & bequeath a mourning breast pin. **1857** *Lawrence* (Kan.) *Republican* 28 May 3 Mrs. M. P. Canfield will keep constantly on hand . . . French and American Hats; Mourning Bonnets [etc.]. **1900** MUNN *Uncle Terry* 75 Her sweet face, sheltered by a mourning-hat on Sunday at church, was a magnet.

b. Designating various things used in connection with mourning.

1688 SEWALL *Diary* I. 203 On Satterday Feb. 11, the mourning-cloth of the Pulpit is taken off and given to Mr. Willard. **1695** *Ib.* 404 The mourning Guns are fired at the Castle and Town for the Death of our Governour. **1698** *Ib.* 470 Mourning Coach also and Horses in Mourning. **1812** *Austin P.* I. (1924) 209 Mourning Poles were up. When an indian died his wives or relations put up a long Poll [*sic*] hung with hoops or wrethes of grape vine.

Mourning, a.* In the specific names of plants or trees. — **1813 MUHLENBERG *Cat. Plants* 91 *Salix tristis*, Mourning willow, Pens. **1817–8** EATON *Botany* (1822) 381 *Pelargonium triste*, mourning geranium. . . . Flowers dark-green. **1880** HOWELLS *Undiscovered Country* 300 Here is bachelor's button, and mourning bride, and marigolds, and touch-me-not. **1896** E. HIGGINSON *Land of Snow Pearls* 49 An' such flowers as she ust to have, . . . bach'lor's-buttons, an' mournin'-widows, an' pum-granates.

+**Mourning cradle.** (See quotation.) — *c***1836** CATLIN *Indians* II. 133 A *mourning cradle*. . . . If the infant dies during the time that is allotted to it to be carried in this cradle, it is buried, and the disconsolate mother fills the cradle with black quills and feathers, in the parts which the child's body had occupied, and . . . carries it around with her wherever she goes for a year or more, with as much care as if her infant were alive and in it.

+**Mourning dove.** The Carolina turtledove, *Zenaidura macroura carolinensis*, or an allied bird of the West. — **1833** CATLIN *Indians* I. 158 The mourning or turtle-dove, . . . being, as they [*sc.* Mandans] call it, a *medicine-bird*, is not to be destroyed or harmed by any one. **1850** E. P. BURKE *Reminisc. Georgia* 138 The mourning dove is a solitary bird nearly as large as the robin, and of a light brown color. **1850** *Conn. Public Acts* 5 It shall not be lawful . . . to kill, or destroy . . . [the] mourning-dove, meadow-lark or marsh quail [etc.]. **1917** *Birds of Amer.* II. 47/1 Probably all of the 'Passenger Pigeons' reported during the past twenty years have been Mourning doves.

+**Mourning granite.** (See quotation.) — **1872** *Vermont Bd. Agric. Rep.* I. 669 Below this [black marble] is a layer of grey, or as has recently been named, mourning granite.

+**Mourning piece.** A pictorial memorial of a person who has died, often showing a tomb, weeping willows, etc. — **1843** *Knickerb.* XXII. 189 The parlor . . . was ornamented . . . [with] the indispensable family mourning-piece. **1845** *Lowell Offering* V. 256 Over the fireplace is a 'mourning-piece,' representing a short chubby red-cheeked girl, in a short black gown. **1876** *Wide Awake* 78/2 Over the fireplace hung . . . a mourning-piece, which her great-grandmother painted when she was young. **1894** WILKINS in *Harper's Mag.* March 504/1 She worked a mourning-piece, and after that a great picture, all in cross-stitch.

Mourning ring. A particular kind of ring worn in memory of a person who has died. {1703–} — **1744** *N.H. Probate Rec.* III. 197, I give my said Son Jonathan ten Shillings Lawfull Money to buy him a Mourning Ring. **1751** *Boston Ev. Post* 4 Feb., A gold mourning ring with 3 stones. **1830** BRECK in *Recoll.* (1877) 17 He died the 16th of February, 1713, aged thirty-two, as appears by the inscription on our family mourning rings distributed at his death. **1868** ALCOTT *Little Women* I. 280 [There were] the jet mourning rings and pins . . . and weeping willows made of hair inside.

+**Mourning warbler.** A warbler (*Oporornis philadelphia*) of the East. — **1810** WILSON *Ornithology* II. 101 [The] Mourning Warbler, *Sylvia Philadelphia*, . . . was shot in the early part of June, on the border of a marsh. **1844** *Nat. Hist. N.Y., Zoology* II. 81 The Mourning Warbler derives its name from its peculiarly melancholy notes. **1917** *Birds of Amer.* III. 157/1 The Mourning Warbler is a quiet Thrush-like bird.

* **Mouse, *n.***

* **1.** A small rodent of one of various genera, as *Mus, Peromyscus, Microtus*, etc.

In the United States as in England, the word is applied, not only to the common house mouse (*Mus musculus*), but also to other rodents, some of which do not belong to the family Muridae: see DEER, FIELD, HARVEST, JUMPING, KANGAROO, etc., MOUSE.

1637 MORTON *New Canaan* II. 83 Mise there are good store, and my Lady Woodbees black gray-malkin may have pastime enough there. **1709** LAWSON *Carolina* 213 The Mice . . . were the busiest in eating their Corn in the Fields, when it lightned the most. **1737** BRICKELL *N. Carolina* 131 The Mice, whereof there are four sorts, viz. the House-mice, the Shrew-mice, the Dor-mice, and the Bat, or Rear-mouse. **1784** CUTLER in *Mem. Academy* I. 431 The green leaves [of Elder] are said to drive away mice. **1804** CLARK in *Lewis & C. Exped.* I. (1904) 187 Those people gave us to eate . . . Corn & Beans boild. a large Been (of) which they rob the mice of the Prarie. **1880** *Scribner's Mo.* May 100/2 If they catch the Colorado beetle of us it will go far toward paying them off for the rats and the mice. **1903** *Chautauquan* Nov. 285 The red squirrel . . . keeps his keen eye on chipmunks and mice hoping to find where they store their food. **1917** *Mammals of Amer.* 240 Occasionally several Mice will occupy the same nest.

+**2.** A pad for a woman's hair.

1866 *Ore. State Jrnl.* 30 June 1/4 Such little things as 'waterfalls,' 'nets' and 'mice,' and other head fixings we were prepared for. **1888** *Century Mag.* Sept. 769/1 The crescent shaped pillows on which it [hair] was put up, the startling names of which were 'rats' and 'mice.'

Mouse, v.* +*To mouse over* (a book), to read studiously. — **1808 IRVING, etc. *Salmagundi* xx. 546 With . . . a table full of books before me, to mouse over them alternately. **1864** TAYLOR in *Life & Lett.* II. 422, I have Little and Brown's 'British Poets' complete now, so you'll have wherewithal to mouse over. **1889** GRETTON *Memory's Harkb.* 137 He was . . . always 'mousing' over books.

Mouse bird. {1822–} +A shrike: (see quotations). — **1857** *Rep. Comm. Patents 1856: Agric.* 87 The Southern shrike, (*Lanius ludovicianus*,) . . . breeds largely in the prairie districts [of Ill.]. . . . Its destruction of arvicolae in summer is well known, and has gained for it the name of 'Mouse Bird,' in Central Illinois. **1917** *Birds of Amer.* III. 101 The White-rumped Shrike, or Mouse-bird (*Lanius ludovicianus excubitorides*) . . . is found in the arid districts of western North America.

* **Mouse-ear.** The name of various plants that have soft hairy leaves. Also with defining term.

1778 CARVER *Travels* 515 Herbs. . . . Mullen, Wild Pease, Mouse Ear [etc.]. **1784** CUTLER in *Mem. Academy* I. 480 *Gnaphalium*. . . . Cats foot. Woolly Mouse-Ear. Blossoms yellowish white. Road sides. **1791** MUHLENBERG *Index Florae* 169 *Cerastium*, Mouse-ear. **1872** *Vermont Bd. Agric. Rep.* I. 268 The tiny mouse-ear blooms beneath the snows of spring. **1892** *Amer. Folk-Lore* V. 91 *Hepatica triloba*, mouse-ears. Mason, N.H.

+**b.** An American species of everlasting, *Antennaria plantaginifolia*.

1833 EATON *Botany* (ed. 6) 159 *Gnaphalium plantagineum*, mouse ear, early life-everlasting. **1855** *Harvard Mag.* I. 233 About the middle of April we may often see in pastures and on dry hill-sides the Mouse-ear. **1869** FULLER *Flower Gatherers* 314 One species of the Everlasting, the Mouse-ear, blooms in early spring.

Mousehawk.* + =MARSH HAWK. — **1812 WILSON *Ornithology* VI. 67 Marsh Hawk[s] . . . are usually known by the name of the Mouse Hawk along the sea coast of New Jersey. **1884** *Harper's Mag.* March 620/1 The marsh-hawk . . . is often called the mouse-hawk. **1917** *Birds of Amer.* II. 64.

+**Mouseproof, *a.*** Safe against mice. — **1895** *Outing* XXVI. 365/2 A mouse-proof locker. **1897** F. C. MOORE *How To Build a Home* 47 The Store-Room . . . may be made rat- or mouse-proof at small expense.

+**Mouse squirrel.** A small squirrel-like rodent, as the chipmunk. — **1674** JOSSELYN *Two Voyages* 86 There are three sorts, the mouse squirril, the gray squirril, and the flying-squirril. **1677** WINTHROP in *Phil. Trans.* XII. 1066 If two or three [grains of corn] grow, it may do well. For some of them are usually destroyed by Birds, or Mouse-Squirrels. **1725** T. SYMMES in Kidder *Exped. Lovewell* (1865) 36 They then caught two Mouse-Squirrels, which they roasted whole, & found them a sweet morsel. **1796** MORSE *Univ. Geog.* I. 203 The Striped Squirrel Linnaeus confounds . . . with a striped mouse squirrel.

Mousing, *a.* {1605–} +Of a person: Thorough and patient in searching for something. — *a***1862** FELTON *Greece: Anc. & Mod.* II. 521 The dialects . . . will have become . . . obsolete curiosities for the researches of the mousing antiquarian. **1883** LODGE *D. Webster* 107 One Parker Noyes, a mousing, learned New Hampshire lawyer.

Mousquetaire. {1706–} *attrib.* Designating various articles of female attire supposedly like the dress of the French mousquetaire. {1883–} — **1891** HOWELLS *Imperative Duty* vi, She came back pulling on one long mousquetaire glove. **1896** *Boston Jrnl.* 3 Dec. 5/2 Showing the long mousquetaire sleeves of the gown.

Mousseline. Also †**mouselain.** A fine muslin or a garment made of this. {1696–} Also attrib. — **1847** in J. Hawthorne *N. Hawthorne & Wife* I. 311 The dark purple mousseline which I wore in Boston I had to give up. **1855** COOKE *Ellie* 568 Lizzie was still more eloquent upon the subject of her best blue mouselain, with open sleeves. **1863** A. D. WHITNEY *F. Gartney* v, She sees the tidy parlor-maid come, . . . holding up her pretty printed mousseline dress with one hand.

Mousseline (de) laine. Muslin made of wool or of wool and cotton. {1835–} — **1840** *Picayune* 18 Oct. 2/6 The subscribers have received . . . printed mousseline laines. **1867** 'LACKLAND' *Homespun* 167 The girls flock . . . to finger, for the twentieth time, the limited stock of berages, prints, and mousselin de laines.

Mouth, n.* **1. *To make up one's mouth* {1606–}, +fig., to prepare one's mouth *for*; to be ready to accept. +**2.** *To shoot off one's mouth*, (see SHOOT *v.*). — **(1) 1843** STEPHENS *High Life N.Y.* I. 110 Tu save my life, I couldn't make up my mouth to it. **1890** *Harper's Mag.* Oct. 715/2 No one who has his mouth made up for a laugh is prepared to relish a dose of reason. **1890** *Cent.* 3587/3 His mouth was made up for a chicken salad.

Mouth, v.* +*College slang.* (See quot. 1851.) — **1835 J. TODD *Student's Manual* 115 Should you allow yourself to think of going into the recitation-room, and there trust to 'skinning,' as it is called in some colleges, . . . or 'mouthing it,' as in others. **1851** HALL *College Words* 211 *Mouth*, to recite in an affected manner, as if one knew the lesson, when in reality he does not.

Mouth organ. {*a*1668–} A small wind instrument played by the mouth, consisting of two sets of free metallic reeds, one set being sounded by blowing, the other by inhaling; =HARMONICA 2. — **1866** LOCKE *Struggles Nasby* 314 He wuz . . . playin 'Hail to the Chief' on a mouth organ. **1887** *Scientific Amer.* 19 Feb. 120/3 The mouth organ, or harmonica, is a familiar example of a simple reed instrument. **1921** PAINE *Comr. Rolling Ocean* 75 A banjo and a mouth-organ were tearing off dance music for a dozen couples.

+**Mouthroot.** =GOLDTHREAD. — **1784** CUTLER in *Mem. Acad.* I. 457 Mouth Root. . . . The roots are astringent. **1795** WINTERBOTHAM *Hist. View* III. 398 Among the native and uncultivated plants of New-England . . . [we find the] Golden thread, or mouth root [employed for medical purposes]. **1860** DARLINGTON *Weeds & Plants* 31 *C[optis] trifolia*. . . . In some places it is a domestic remedy for the sore mouths of children; whence the name 'Mouth-root.'

+**Movable mill.** (See quotation.) — **1898** N. E. JONES *Squirrel Hunters of Ohio* 26 Movable mills. [Note:] Mills erected on two boats, separated at an angle, with water wheel near the bow. The natural current of the stream passing between the boats turned the wheel that moved the machinery of the mill.

***Movables.** *pl.* Personal property that can be moved. Now rare. — **1653** *Boston Rec.* 18 My whole estate lying cheifly in . . . houshold stuffe, plate & divers sorts of tooles & moveables. **1702** *Maine Wills* 138, I do giue . . . my louing Wife all the rest of my Estate it being Mouables. **1818** FLINT *Lett. from Amer.* 48 The father pushed a wheel-barrow, containing the moveables of the family. **1846** THORPE *Myst. Backwoods* 115 Some Indians . . . launched a canoe that lay among their movables.

***Move,** *n.* +*To get a move on,* to hurry or make haste; to get started. *colloq.* — **1893** *Columbus Dispatch* 7 July, Now is the time for the mover of dead animals 'to get a move on himself.' **1896** *N.Y. Dramatic News* 29 Aug. 2/3 The political campaign seems . . . to be somewhat slower than usual in 'getting a move on.' **1923** WATTS *L. Nichols* 83 [Mr. Schulte ordered] him to hunt up Nichols, with a further recommendation to get a move on!

* **Move,** *v.*

1. *tr.* **a.** To get (a crop) out of the fields. **b.** To get (a crop) to a market or place of storage.

1712 HEMPSTEAD *Diary* 7, I was att work att home all day movening and fenceing hay. **1869** *Congress. Globe* 25 March 273/2 When we want money to move our wheat we understand we can go down there and borrow it. **1870** *Nation* 21 April 250/2 We must have . . . cheap gunny-bags to move corn, which heats in a cotton, flax, or hemp bag.

+**2.** *intr.* To go into new territory to make a home; to migrate. Often with *out.*

1753 WASHINGTON *Diaries* I. 55 They had heard of some Families moving-out. *c***1785** S. PEARS *Narrative* (MS.) 13 Stephen Lowry . . . was prepareing to move out with a waggon. **1810** M. DWIGHT *Journey to Ohio* 39 They say there has been a heap of people moving this fall. **1818** FEARON *Sketches* 237 When you arrive in Ohio, its inhabitants are 'moving' to Missouri and Alabama. **1835** *Knickerb.* V. 274 Farmer Powers 'moved' to Ohio when Hiram was thirteen.

***Movement.** +The activity of a commodity or stock in the market. — **1847** *Knickerb.* XXX. 165 The over-reaching 'movements' in flour which were every moment vibrating between New-York and Buffalo. **1886** *49th Congress 2 Sess.* H. R. Ex. Doc. No. 2, I. 58 The total movement of bonds held for national banks was $87,967,300. **1895** *Stand.* 1158/3 An upward movement in stocks.

* **Mover.**

+**1.** An emigrant moving west to settle; a person participating in the tide of western migration.

Cf. EMIGRANT 2.

1810 M. DWIGHT *Journey to Ohio* 47 We are at a baker's, near a tavern which is fill'd with movers & waggoners. **1834** BAIRD *Valley Mississippi* 87, I would caution travellers and 'movers,' against much journeying in September and early October. **1842** BUCKINGHAM *E. & W. States* II. 293 [Along the emigrants' road to the West] we saw several houses by the road-side, expressly for their use, with the signs 'Moovers' Accommodation'—others with more correct orthography, had 'House for Movers.' **1878** BEADLE *Western Wilds* 327 Reluctantly the 'movers' consented to his remaining for the night. **1886** Z. F. SMITH *Kentucky* 148 The tide of 'movers' once set in seemed to swell into the flow of a mighty stream. **1906** PITTMAN *Belle Blue Grass Country* 261 The emigrants, or 'movers' were kindly invited to occupy the old log house.

+**2.** 'One whose business is to move furniture and other household goods, as from one place of residence to another' (*Cent.*). {=remover}

1894 *Boston Directory* 1944 J. W. Cook & Son, . . . Movers of Piano-fortes, Furniture, etc. *Ib.* 1947 T. G. Buckley, Piano and Furniture Mover.

+**3.** *spec.* A tenant farmer who exhausts the natural richness of a piece of land and then moves on to repeat the process again and again.

1913 LONDON *Valley of Moon* 434 The 'movers' . . . lease, clean out and gut a place in several years, and then move on.

+**Mover's wagon.** A wagon in which a mover migrates west. (Cf. EMIGRANT WAGON.) — **1883** HOWE *Country Town* (1926) 3 The building stood on the main road where the movers' wagons passed. **1889** *Harper's Mag.* Dec. 121/2 A mover's wagon with dingy cover was creeping slowly townward along the white road.

+**Moving day.** A day on which leases expire and people who have not renewed theirs move to other residences.

1832 WATSON *Hist. Tales N.Y.* 123 'Moving day' was, as now, the first of May. **1841** *S. Lit. Messenger* VII. 661/2 A sudden light bursts upon me! 'tis 'moving day'—the dreaded 'first of May!' **1855** *Knickerb.* XLV. 585 In the southern part of New-Jersey, one who rents or purchases a house or farm usually takes possession . . . on the twenty-fifth day of the present month [March], which is therefore denominated 'moving-day.' **1897** *Scribner's Mag.* XXII. 58/2 In every city there are what are called 'moving days,' when old leases expire and new ones begin. **1910** *Nation* 22 Sept. 259/2 A September Labor Day on which no manual labor is performed is less characteristic of us than our October moving day, . . . not without its realistic exhibits and its impressive parade.

Moving picture.

1. A pictorial view or exhibition in which objects move by mechanical control; a panorama. {1710}

1715 *Boston News-Letter* 14 March 2/2 The Italian Matchean, or Moving Picture, wherein are to be seen, Wind-Mills and Water-Mills moving round, Ships Sayling on the Sea, and several curious Figures, . . . to be daily shewn. **1787** *Penna. Packet* 12 Jan. 1/3 Mr. Peale will only continue his Exhibitions of Moving Pictures with Changeable Effects, for a short time. **1859** *S. Lit. Messenger* XXIX. 151/1 What is most improperly called a 'Panorama,' a long moving picture of striking scenery or imposing events, . . . is now a popular entertainment in our cities.

2. A series of pictures representing objects or people in successive positions slightly changed, projected upon a screen in rapid succession. {1899–} Usually pl. Also attrib.

Cf. MOTION PICTURE.

1898 *N.Y. Tribune* 30 Oct. 8/3 The always interesting moving pictures in the biograph at Keith's will include this week four new scenes. **1903** 'O. HENRY' *Four Million* 3 He cursed the moving pictures. **1907** *Pearson's Mag.* Jan. (*advt.*), Moving Picture Machines. **1913** LONDON *Valley of Moon* 400, I don't care if I never see movin' pictures again. **1923** WATTS *L. Nichols* 239 It was past belief that she would pick him . . . at the moving-picture theatre.

+**Moving van.** (See quotation.) — **1898** *Kansas City Star* 21 Dec. 9/2 The moving vans and pie-wagons of New York are changing their pictures. Before the war of 1898 these vehicles were moving panoramas of scenes and incidents of the Revolutionary or the Civil War.

* **Mow.** **a.** A stack of hay, corn, etc., often in a barn. **b.** The place in a barn where such a stack is stored. {1755–}

Cf. HAYMOW.

1695 SEWALL *Diary* I. 398 An undermined Mow in the Barn . . . fell upon him and kill'd him. **1708** *Boston News-Letter* 19–26 April 2/2 The Thunder [was] so extraordinary that it . . . killed a Horse in a Leanto under a Mow of Hay. **1825** NEAL *Bro. Jonathan* I. 420 When you caught me asleep in the mow, [you] wouldn't steal a kiss. **1847** DRAKE *Pioneer Life Ky.* 66 We had no . . . mow, and both wheat and hay were stacked out. **1872** EGGLESTON *End of World* 29 She climbed from mow to to mow gathering the eggs. **1884** *Vt. Agric. Rep.* VIII. 284, I begin husking as soon as the corn is dry and the fodder cured off so it will not be injured by packing in the mow. **1907** *St. Nicholas* Sept. 978/1 'Be careful what you say,' interrupted Chub, sliding down from the top of the mow.

+**Mow bird.** A gull. *Obs.* {**mow(e)*, now dial.} — **1781–2** JEFFERSON *Notes Va.* (1788) 77 Besides these, we have The Royston crow, . . . Mow-bird, [and] Blue peter. **1789** MORSE *Amer. Geog.* 60 American Birds [include the] . . . Mow Bird, Purple Martin, [and] Nightingale. **1792** IMLAY *Western Territory* 227 We have besides, the duck and mallard, . . . water pheasant, mow bird, blue peter [etc.].

* **Mower.**

***1.** One who cuts grass, weeds, etc., with a scythe.

1633 *Mass. Bay Rec.* I. 109 Tylars, joyners, wheelwrights, mowers, &c, shall not take aboue 2s. a day. **1663** *Oyster Bay Rec.* I. 10 Noe man or men are to mowe any of the bove sayd medows befor ye 15th day of sixt mo. . . . and then but one mower a day for a lot. **1709** *N.H. Hist. Soc. Coll.* III. 54 Joseph Pitman slain by the Indians as he was guarding some mowers. **1780** E. PARKMAN *Diary* 249 The mower, Mr. Warrin dind with us. **1863** MITCHELL *My Farm* 140 The mowers complain that the broken limbs,—are a pest. **1895** *Dialect Notes* I. 372 A mower, when rain was coming on: 'I reckon we'll have to hang up for all day.'

2. =MOWING MACHINE.

Cf. LAWN-MOWER.

1857 *Lawrence* (Kan.) *Republican* 9 July 4 All cannot have a mower, and the scythe will answer a good purpose yet. **1863** *Rep. Comm. Agric. 1862* 9 A large number of our farmers now use mowers for cutting their grasses. **1883** KNIGHT *Suppl.* 795/1 To show to what immense proportions the manufacture of binders, reapers, and mowers has grown in the United States, we give . . . the dimensions of the establishments of one of the great firms. **1898** *Mo. So. Dakotan* I. 87 The alternate rattle and hum of the mower . . . had a cheering influence. **1920** HOWELLS *Vacation of Kelwyns* 43 Kite had his team hitched to his mower.

+**Mow fly.** An insect destructive to wheat. — **1859** *Harper's Mag.* Dec. 47/1 Next comes a very pretty Mow fly. . . . You will find her oftenest depositing her eggs near the joints [of wheat].

+**Mowhackees.** *pl.* Also †**Mohakes, Mohaicks.** Dark wampum beads, twice as valuable in Indian trade as the regular white variety. Now hist. — **1634** WOOD *New Eng. Prospect* II. iii. 65 The Narragansets . . . are the most curious minters of their Wampompeage and Mowhakes, which they forme out of the inmost wreaths of Periwinkle-shels. **1672** JOSSELYN *New Eng. Rarities* 36 A kind of Coccle, of whose Shell the Indians make their Beads called Wompampeag and Mohaicks. **1910** HODGE

Handbk. Amer. Ind. II. 908/2 The Dutch applied the name *Sewan hacky*, 'Wampum land,' to Long Island, perhaps in imitation of the natives. . . . In New England *mowhackees*, 'black beads,' was used.

***Mowing.**

***1.** The action of cutting grass, etc., with a scythe.

1649 *Conn. Rec.* I. 204 Hee shall haue . . . six acres of planting ground, and libberty of feed and mowing. **1759** *Holyoke Diaries* 20 First mowing of my Oats. **1856** OLMSTED *Slave States* 43 Wheat [is] sown with herd's grass . . . and clover, which is to remain, for mowing and pasture, as long as the ground will profitably sustain it. **1918** *Farmers' Bul.* No. 987, 3 If mowing is done in the morning and raking in the afternoon, more men and horses than usual will be required.

+**2.** *ellipt.* Land on which hay is grown; a mowing field.

1741 *N.H. Probate Rec.* III. 71 One peice of Woodland . . . with about an Acre of mowing. **1778** *Mass. Spy* 15 Oct. 4/3 To be Sold, A farm, . . . contain[in]g Ploughing, Mowing, and Pasturing. **1838** *Mass. Agric. Survey 1st Rep.* 11 A considerable amount of this land . . . has been converted into profitable mowing. **1874** *Vermont Bd. Agric. Rep.* II. 206 He thought the American custom of robbing the pasture to enrich the mowing a ruinous policy.

+**b.** *English mowing*, land that produces English grass (q.v.).

1807 *Mass. H. S. Coll.* 2 Ser. III. 51 In Chilmark . . . upland English mowing . . . yields about eighteen hundred to an acre; the salt marsh, a ton; and the black grass marsh, a ton and a half.

+**3.** *attrib.* Designating pieces of land on which grass is grown for hay.

1799 WASHINGTON *Writings* XIV. 231 Although I am not sanguine enough to expect, that it will make good mowing meadow, I shall be much disappointed if it does not produce grass. **1819** E. EVANS *Pedestrious Tour* 145 How many of our mowing fields are . . . shamefully poached and grubbed by horses and sheep!

+**Mowing ground.** **a.** Natural grass-producing ground set aside by the early colonists for mowing. **b.** Ground on which a hay crop is produced. **c.** (See quot. 1790.)

1634 *Cambridge Prop. Rec.* 1 [The constable] shall make a surueyinge of the Houses backsids Corne ffeilds Moweing grounds and other lands. **1652** *Southampton Rec.* I. 86 Thomas Halsey . . . shall lay ovt Saga-ponack & Seponack mowing ground for a present supply of the Inhabitants of this towne for this yeare. **1703** *N.H. Probate Rec.* I. 504, I give unto my son, Josiah, the use & Improvement of all my other marsh, & mowing ground. **1790** DEANE *New-Eng. Farmer* 179/2 *Mowing-Ground*, a name commonly given in this country to land, which being fit for either mowing or tillage, is alternately used for the one and the other. **1800** *Mass. H. S. Coll.* 1 Ser. VII. 245 [The Isles of Shoals] lie in common, except a few small inclosures for gardens and mowing ground.

+**Mowing land.** Land productive of grass to be mowed; land used to produce a hay crop.

1640 *Hartford Land Distrib.* 357 One parsell Called Swamp Now mowing land. **1663** *Conn. Rec.* I. 402 They are to improue the mowing land as formerly. **1689** *Conn. Probate Rec.* 478 One acre of mowing Land and one acre of plowing Land Lyeing in ye Slipe. **1745** *Boston News-Letter* 28 March, To be Sold . . . a Farm . . . which will make good Pasture and Mowing Land, and yields about 200 Cocks of Hay annually. **1816** *N. Amer. Rev.* III. 428 At the distance of five or six miles it [the Sugar River in N.H.] begins to wind gently through large tracts of fine rich mowing land. **1858** FLINT *Milch Cows* 169 The grasses differ widely; and their value as feed for cows will depend . . . on the management of pastures and mowing-lands.

+**Mowing machine.** A machine that mows grass, alfalfa, weeds, etc. {1850- (*Imperial Dict.* II. 201)}

1823 *17th Congress 2 Sess.* H. R. Doc. No. 36, 6 Improvement in the mowing machine, Feb. 13, [1822,] Jeremiah Baily. **1838** ELLSWORTH *Valley of Wabash* 47, I have a plan . . . to introduce the mowing and grain-cutting machine into this State. **1862** NORTON *Army Lett.* 106 Mowing machines are rattling over the meadows, and the barns are filling up. **1885** *Rep. Indian Affairs* 26 The Indians have also purchased from the trader 6 mowing machines . . . at $75 each. **1916** THOBURN *Stand. Hist. Okla.* I. 328, 5,000 tons of hay were burned, together with wagons and mowing machines.

Mowing scythe. A scythe for cutting grass, etc.: (see also quot. 1874). — **1779** *N.J. Archives* 2 Ser. III. 478 For sale, . . . a few dozen of mowing scythes. **1874** KNIGHT 641/2 *Cradle-scythe*, . . . a broad scythe to be fitted in a grain-cradle, as distinguished from a *grass* or *mowing* scythe. *a***1918** G. STUART *On Frontier* I. 184 Last Sunday Granville lent Dempsey's employees a mowing scythe.

+**Mow land.** =MOWING LAND. — **1845** JUDD *Margaret* II. 214 Women . . . [were] turning hay among alders and willows, that yet flourished in their best mow-lands. **1874** *Vermont Bd. Agric. Rep.* II. 411 The breeding of wrinkled sheep is like a farmer who ridges up his level mow-land and seeds the ridges with an inferior grass.

+**Mow lot.** A lot where grass grows for mowing. — **1845** JUDD *Margaret* II. 325 They let me take the Colt; I kept him here in the mow-lot, made considerable of him, groomed him [etc.].

Moy. A measure for salt. *Obs.* {1535, 1538 *Sc.*} — **1756** *Essex Inst. Coll.* XLVI. 331 To the amount of 240 Moyes of Salt on the Sea Nymph.

Mozambique. [Named after Portuguese territory in Africa.] (See quot. 1875.) — **1861** *Chicago Tribune* 15 April 1 Cheap Dry Goods. . . . Mozambiques, 6¼ cts. Yd. **1875** KNIGHT 1493/1 *Mozambique*, . . . an open dress-goods having a chain in which the cotton threads are associated in pairs, and the woolen filling is soft and fleecy. **1896** *Godey's Mag.* April 436/1 A new material of mohair and silk is known as Mozambique, it is semi-transparent and in rather straggling all-over designs; two tones are generally employed, such as brown and reseda.

+**Mozemize.** (See MOOSE-MISSE.)

M.P. {1809-} +Abbreviation for *Metropolitan Police. slang.* — **1872** BRACE *Dangerous Classes N.Y.* 176 They [street boys] could dodge an 'M.P.' as a fox dodges a hound.

***Mr.** [Orig. an abbrev. for *master.*] A prefixed title for a man; mister.

In early usage *Mr.* was a title only for men above a certain undefined rank: (cf. GOODMAN). It is now used before the names of all men unless a title like Prof. or Dr. is used. Before other titles *Mr.* is now used vocatively only, as 'Mr. President,' 'Mr. Chairman.'

1640 *New Haven Col. Rec.* 33 Liberty granted to Mr. Gregson, bro: Andrewes and Goodm[a]n Warde to lett their timber lye in the woods. **1703** SEWALL *Diary* II. 81 Coming home I order'd Mr. Sheriff to take up a Scurvy post out of the middle of the High way. **1711** *Boston Rec.* 149 Voted, that in case ye Town be Nonsuited . . . Mr. Attorney be desired to renew ye suit. **1806** SILLIMAN in G. P. Fisher *Life B. Silliman* I. 160 I should much rather have preferred to pass simply as *Mr.*, being sufficiently conscious that my years—not to say my attainments—hardly justified the appellation of Professor. **1884** BLAINE *20 Yrs. of Congress* I. 480 Mr. Gallatin had conceived an intense hostility to Mr. Chase, and inspired Mr. Brooks to make . . . some unfounded charges against the Secretary. **1900** *Congress. Rec.* 6 Feb. 1537/2 Mr. President, that creates a state of facts which rendered the Filipino government such that it could have been recognized as an independent republic.

Mrs. [Orig. an abbrev. for *mistress.*] {*a*1612-} **a.** A title prefixed to a married woman's name. {1615-} **b.** To an unmarried woman's name. {*c*1645-1791} *Obs.*

1646 *Conn. Rec.* I. 142 Robert Bartlett, for his grosse misdemeanor in slaundring Mris Mary Fenwicke, is to stand on the Pillory, Wensday. **1702** C. MATHER *Magnalia* (1853) I. 484 He was married in England to Mrs. Sarah Brown, the eldest daughter of Mr. Joseph Brown. **1726** SEWALL *Diary* III. 381 Moses Gerrish marries Mrs. ——— Perce, *virginem*, at Newbury. **1872** TICE *Over Plains* 55, I looked doubtfully at Mrs. T. who had been looking out for the same object on the opposite side of the cars. **1923** HERRICK *Lilla* 262 [She thought] 'I am to all intents and purposes a widow. . . .' So the mail box . . . bore the legend, Mrs. Lilla Vance James.

Mrs. Goff. (See quot. 1851.) *Obs.* — **1819** PEIRCE *Rebelliad* 21 Mrs. Goff has deign'd to weep. **1851** HALL *College Words* 211 *Mrs. Goff.* Formerly a cant phrase for any woman.

Much, *n.* (See MUTCH.)

Much, *v. tr.* To make much over. *colloq.*² {*dial.* 1736} — **1848** LOWELL *Fable for Critics* 61 As soon as she's touched it, And, (to borrow a phrase from the nursery,) *muched* it. **1868** S. HALE *Letters* 60 They all 'muched' me and I was a heroine. **1887** *Century Mag.* May 119/1, I never cud much her like I cud t'other gells. **1896** HARRIS *Sister Jane* 143 Man . . . come 'long take de chil' in he arms an' much im, an' den he gi' 'im sump'n t'eat.

***Much,** *adv. Not much*, certainly not; I should say not. *colloq.* — **1886** *Harper's Mag.* Dec. 148/1 'Go home?—explain?' he began, more calmly. 'Not much.' **1887** GEORGE *40 Years on Rail* 141, 'I could best of all this group be spared. I'll try it.' 'Not much,' replied the man who at first had suggested it. **1904** *Pittsburgh Gazette* 31 Oct. 4 Can anyone suppose Russia would apologize in the face of so grave a violation of neutrality? Not much.

+**Muchacho.** [Sp.] A boy; a male servant. Also transf. — **1863** MASSETT *Drifting About* 127 A young 'Muchacho' fresh from the diggings came up to the counter. **1877** HARTE *Story of Mine* 412 Father Pedro had taken a muchacho foundling for adoption. **1894** *Harper's Mag.* March 528/2 Go on, dar, you muchac[h]os; specks we ever get to Bavicora dis yar gait?

+**Muche.** [Du. *mutsje.*] A liquid measure of about one fifth of a pint. *Obs.* — **1673** *Hempstead Rec.* I. 291 If any man shall Refuse to: go: . . . he shall pay six muches of Rume to them that gose [*i.e.*, to run the bounds of the town].

***Mucilage.** +A sticky solution of gum or similar adhesive substance. {=gum} Also attrib. — **1859** *La Crosse Union* 15 Oct. 3/3 Mucilage, sealing wax, playing cards. **1868** *Rep. Comm. Patents 1867* II. 989/1 Mucilage Stand. . . . The reservoir mucilage stand has a supply fountain. **1876** *Wide Awake* 306/2 Dip a wire in mucilage, and coat the insides of the eyelids. **1887** FREDERIC *Seth's Brother's Wife* 125 The use of scissors and mucilage brush was painfully unfamiliar to his clumsy fingers. **1898** FORD *Tattle-Tales* 227 What a pity some glue company can't buy those two [men] and melt them down into mucilage! **1923** WIGGIN *My Garden of Memory* 112, I bought pencils, crayons, and mucilage of the local stationers.

+**Mucilaginous elm.** =AMERICAN ELM. *Obs.* — **1818** DARBY *Emigrant's Guide* 34 *Ulmus Americana*, Mucilaginous elm. **1819** E. DANA *Geogr. Sk.* 245 A list of the most valuable forest trees growing . . . [includes] sycamore, white oak, black oak, linden, locust, mucilaginous elm and red elm.

*** Muck.**

*** 1.** Barnyard manure or manure mixed with decomposing vegetable matter. *Obsolescent.*

1660 *Watertown Rec.* I. 1. 68 He shall not cary off the p[re]mises any compost, muck or manure. **1698** *Conn. Probate Rec.* I. 578, I give to my son David Porter my Dwelling house and Barn, . . . the muck in the Yard belonging to it. **1780** E. PARKMAN *Diary* 227 Ben Wood helps in harrowing and getting out muck.

+2. a. Vegetable matter used as fertilizer. **b.** The slimy ooze that accumulates in the bottoms of ponds, etc., used as fertilizer. **c.** Peat; soil composed of peat. **d.** (See quot. 1914.)

1825 LORAIN *Pract. Husbandry* 147 The muck could not have generated the seeds of the May weed. **1843** *Nat. Hist. N.Y., Geology* I. 10 If the water flowing into lakes . . . be loaded with earthy matter, the ooze (or muck, as it is frequently called by our farmers) will probably predominate. **1849** CHAMBERLAIN *Ind. Gazetteer* 305 The soil is a black muck, based on clay. **1862** DANA *Manual Geology* 614 *Muck* is another name for peat, . . . especially when the material is employed as a manure. **1868** BRACKETT *Farm Talk* 113 You can also make several cart-loads of the very best kind of manure, if you keep the yard and pen supplied with muck, . . . and other vegetable rubbish. **1874** *Vermont Bd. Agric. Rep.* II. 547 The opinions of men vary in regard to the desirableness of burning off the scurf, duff, or muck, of soft wood land. **1889** *Century Mag.* Dec. 217/2 The soil proved to be a wet muck, overlaying sand with boulders. **1914** ATHERTON *Perch of Devil* 148 His . . . hands were white with 'muck,' a mixture of rock-dust and water.

+3. Attrib. in sense 2 b and 2 c: Designating pieces of land that produce muck.

1848 *Rep. Comm. Patents 1847* 358 They have been planted the present year, on deep muck lands. **1862** *Ill. Agric. Soc. Trans.* V. 202 Mr. M. has a large pond or muck hole lying near the grove. **1863** 'G. HAMILTON' *Gala-Days* 49 [Like stagnant water, you] go oozing along . . . , subsiding with entire satisfaction into a muck puddle. **1870** *Rep. Comm. Agric. 1869* 270 The soil was . . . black mud or muck swamp, five feet deep, containing a mixture of sand. **1874** *Vermont Bd. Agric. Rep.* II. 553 Do not wantonly destroy a good muck bed.

+Muckawis. (See quotation.) — **1837** WILLIAMS *Florida* 74 Muckawis. . . . This bird resembles the Whippoorwill in every thing but his note.

+Muck bar. *Iron-smelting.* A bar of iron that has gone only through the muck rolls. — **1866** *Internal Revenue Guide* 104 On Steel made directly from muck-bar, blooms, slabs, or loops, a tax of three dollars per ton. **1894** *Harper's Mag.* Feb. 421/2 The 'muck bar' is broken up, bunched together, raised to a welding heat, and again and again carried through the rolls.

+Mucker.[1] [Ger.] **1.** A fanatical reformer. **2.** A young townsman in a college town as distinguished from the college students. *slang.* **3.** An unrefined or boorish person. *slang.* — **(1) 1891** *Cycl. Temperance* 269/1 The saloon-keepers then resolved to make 'the muckers take their own medicine,' and insisted that the Mayor should enforce the Sunday law against 'common labor.' **(2) 1893** POST *Harvard Stories* 75 On the first corner . . . were stationed three or four small boys (the occasionally useful Cambridge muckers) employed as vedettes. **(3) 1899** ADE *Fables in Slang* 108 They were not Muckers; they were Nice Boys, intent on preserving the Traditions of dear old *Alma Mater.* **1902** BELL *Hope Loring* 220 Get off my feet, you mucker! **1904** *Phil. Public Ledger* 4 June 6 Cheering by the side benefited [by a misplay] was distinctly out of order; it was, in the elegant language of the campus, 'muckerish,' and the college which practiced it was composed of 'muckers.' **1921** PAINE *Comr. Rolling Ocean* 99 He grumbles about the food and says the officers are dubs and most of the boys muckers.

Mucker.[2] **+1.** A workman who removes gravel, hardpan, etc., in a mine or other excavation. **+2.** A workman who handles muck bars. — **(1) 1899** *Harper's Weekly* 20 May 498/1 [The] Company . . . paid $3. for miners and $2.50 for 'muckers,' or underground laborers. **1907** *N.Y. Ev. Post* (s.-w. ed.) 11 Feb. 6 The 'sand hogs,' or 'muckers,' are the common laborers of the tubes. **1916** SANDBURG *Chicago Poems* 21 Twenty men stand watching the muckers. Stabbing the sides of the ditch . . . for the new gas mains. **(2) 1906** LYNDE *Quickening* 122, [I'll] go to work in the iron plant and be a mucker all the rest of my life, I reckon.

+Mucket. (See quotation.) — **1862** NORTON *Army Lett.* 64 Each of us has a small tin kettle holding three pints or so, fitted with a tight cover. We call them muckets for want of a better name. . . . I believe almost any of us would throw away a blanket before he would his mucket, they are so indispensable.

***Mucky,** *a.* +Of land or soil: Consisting of decomposing vegetable matter or peat. — **1840** HOFFMAN *Greyslaer* I. 61 He had laid the logs right down on a piece of deep, mucky soil, made up of old roots, rotten leaves [etc.]. **1855** *Mich. Agric. Soc. Trans.* VI. 219 New land with a rich, mucky, or vegetable mould. **1874** *Vermont Bd. Agric. Rep.* II. 548, I have about five acres of mucky meadow that was mostly covered with alders.

*** Mud,** *n.*

I. *1. Wet, soft earth: **a.** Used as mortar or building material. {1839-}

1837 *S. Lit. Messenger* III. 217 A plain building of sawed logs, *crammed*, as we say in Virginia, with mud. **1847** PALMER *Rocky Mts.* 86 Fort Hall is built of mud or adobes. **1870** KEIM *Sheridan's Troopers* 247 The Witchitas . . . lived in regular houses, similar in form to an ordinary wigwam, but constructed of thatch and mud. **1895** *Outing* XXVI. 36/1 A shanty built of logs chinked with mud, a slanting roof of slabs discarded from the saw mill.

+b. *To pull mud,* to travel. *slang.*

1884 *Century Mag.* Dec. 284 We took up our line of march, or, as Wad Rider expressed it, 'began to pull mud.'

II. *attrib.* and *comb.*

2. a. Designating fortifications made of earth or mud.

1777 *Md. Hist. Mag.* V. 217 The Landing in front & Rear of our Mud or Grand Battery is also very good. **1861** NEWELL *Orpheus C. Kerr* I. 343 An orderly . . . [was] sent to demand the surrender of a rebel mud-work in front. **1867** EDWARDS *Shelby* 486 Sabine Pass, at that time, had a mud fort manned with four guns.

b. Designating various structures or groups of structures made of clay, adobe, or some other kind of soil.

See also MUD FENCE, HOUSE, HUT, WALL.

1808 PIKE *Sources Miss.* 207 Several little mud walled villages . . . had round mud towers. **1836** *Diplom. Corr. Texas* I. (1908) 134 Their titles must not be adjudged defective . . . for any failure to comply with formal and unessential requisitions, such as . . . erecting Stone or mud corners. **1849** F. ROBINSON *Calif. & Gold Regions* 31 The Indians . . . crush the ore between rocks, and then melt it in rude mud furnaces, producing what is called fire silver. **1865** KELLOGG *Rebel Prisons* 177 [We] went to work with the rest of the boys to build a mud stove. **1872** POWERS *Afoot & Alone* 165 Here there is a mud-coop, there a mud oven. **1873** COZZENS *Marvellous Country* 154 [We] spread our blankets on the mud floor, and cooked our food in the mud fire-place. **1885** *Rep. Indian Affairs* 168 The brush and mud-hovel is a thing of the past. **1891** C. ROBERTS *Adrift Amer.* 120, I selected one [house] that had a mud chimney and fireplace. **1894** *Harper's Mag.* March 526/2 He had concluded . . . to create a business in a little mud town down the big road.

3. Designating footgear worn for protection against the mud.

1840 *Picayune* 12 Aug. 2/2 Dressed out in his *mud pumps,* hunting shirt, and Mexican chapeau. **1850** LEWIS *La. Swamp Doctor* 22 We mount a canoe, a pair of mud boots, sometimes a horse, and traverse, unmindful of exposure or danger, the sullen slough or angry river.

4. Designating various natural objects composed of mud or soft earthy substances.

See also MUD BANK, LUMP[2], VOLCANO.

1842 *Knickerb.* XX. 309 [He] knew a great deal more about the inconveniences of groping about among mud-shoals in the dark. **1851** SPRINGER *Forest Life* 61 We clamber, under our heavy burdens, over rocks, . . . and through mud-sloughs. **1852** STANSBURY *Gt. Salt Lake* 112 Following the western edge of the mud-plain at the foot of the range . . . , we came to the southern point of the mountain. **1882** *Century Mag.* Aug. 510/2 Back of these mud buttes . . . are immense stretches of grazing country. **1884** W. SHEPHERD *Prairie Exper.* 229 It was very difficult to prevent the band from rushing into a mud-spring not fifty feet across in which a little water stood in holes.

5. Designating persons or actions concerned with besmirching people's characters.

See also 7 below, *mud press.*

1884 *Lisbon Star* 22 Aug., Campaign Lies and Mud Slinging Fail to Carry the Day. **1888** *Voice* 28 June, Gen. Fisk is just the kind of a man we like to see the mud-flingers attack. **1895** CHAMBLISS *Diary* 276 They were willing to resort to the most detestable methods of 'mud-throwing.' **1896** *Advance* 17 Sept. 366 Noble [profession of journalism] indeed; and one which the swarm of caricaturists, libelers and party mud-slingers ought to enter.

6. a. In the names of various American birds.

See also MUD COOT, DIPPER, GOOSE, etc.

1903 *Forest & Stream* 21 Feb. 150/2 [Call ducks] are a cross between the mallard and ordinary mud duck. **1917** *Birds of Amer.* I. 235 Least Sandpiper. *Pisobia minutilla.* . . . [Also called] Mud-peep. *Ib.* 256 Black-bellied Plover. *Squatarola squatarola.* . . . [Also called] Gray Plover (autumn); Mud Plover; Palebelly (young). **1809** IRVING *Knickerb.* vi. ii Squatting himself down on the edge of a pond catching fish for hours together, . . . [Dirk Schuiler bore] no little resemblance to that notable bird ycleped the Mud-poke. **1917** *Birds of Amer.* I. 112 Hooded Merganser. . . . Other Names. . . . Mud, Pickax, or Summer, Sheldrake. **1897** *N.Y. Forest, Fish, & Game Comm. 2d Rep.* 322 Popular synonyms [for the Woodcock, *Philohela minor*]: Bog-sucker; mud snipe; blind snipe. **1917** *Birds of Amer.* I. 122 Green-winged Teal. *Nettion carolinense.* . . . [Also called] Winter Teal; Mud Teal.

b. In the names of various American animals and fishes.

See also MUD BASS, CAT, CATFISH, etc.

1827 WILLIAMS *West Florida* 28 A livid looking mud asp, that has sometimes been mistaken for an eel, has . . . proved fatal to those who expose themselves by wading in muddy creeks. **1877** BARTLETT 410 *Mud-Dabbler,* a species of small fresh-water fish, of the same appearance as the *sucker,* although much smaller. **1883** *Nat. Museum Bul.* No. 27, 470 *Um-*

bra pygmæa. . . . Mud Dace; Pigmy Dace. **1823** WEEMS *Letters* III. 353 The British . . . fairly chased our militiamen across Broad River, to the huge amazement of the mud eels and cats. *c***1862** BAGBY *Old Va. Gentleman* 92 [The water is] full of all manner of nasty and confounded 'mud-kittens,' 'snap'n turtles,' and snake doctors. **1839** STORER *Mass. Fishes* 198 *A[mmocoetes] bicolor*. The Mud Lamprey. **1870** *Amer. Naturalist* IV. 386 [The] Mud Pike (*Esox porosus*) [is found in the Delaware at Trenton, N.J.]. **1843** MARRYAT *M. Violet* xliv, Among these [phenomena of rivers and bayous] is the mud vampire, a kind of spider leech.

7. Special combinations.

Mud ball, a building material (see quotation); *m. mortar*, mortar made of mud; *m. pike*, (see quotation); *m. pipe*, a clay smoking pipe; *m. press*, a newspaper that besmirches people's characters; *m. rake*, (see quotation); *m. runner*, a race horse that runs well on a wet track; *m. scoop*, (see quotation); *m.-snoot*, a depreciative epithet; *m. stick*, a pole with a forked or widened end used in punting against a muddy bottom.

1877 *Harper's Mag.* April 706/1 The chimney, built of mud balls kneaded up with straw, . . . stands outside one end of the mansion. **1831** PECK *Guide* 126 The chimney . . . [is] built of sticks of wood . . . laid up with . . . mud or clay mortar. **1860** MORDECAI *Virginia* 302 Some of them [*sc.* roads] soon acquired the name of *mud pikes*, the demand of toll being the only distinction by which to know them from country roads. **1870** KEIM *Sheridan's Troopers* 140 He never failed to enjoy . . . lighting an old cob or mud pipe. **1846** MCKENNEY *Memoirs* I. 197 Jonathan Elliot, . . . had printed a paper in Washington, the quality of which had secured for it the title of 'the mud press.' **1890** *Cent.* 3887/2 *Mud-rake*, . . . oyster-tongs with long poles or handles. (New Jersey.) **1905** *N.Y. Ev. Sun* 17 Aug. (*Cent. Suppl.*), All the races . . . were won by the product of stallions that in their day were famous mud runners. **1877** BARTLETT 411 *Mud-Scoop*, a dredge; a dredging-machine or boat used in taking mud from the bottom of rivers. **1873** BAILEY *Life in Danbury* 34 Reubens was prompted to call him a mud-snoot, a new name just coming into general use. **1874** LONG *Wild-Fowl* 142 Now, you see, this mud-stick or setting-pole as we call it, which I have exchanged the oar for, comes into use.

***Mud,** *v.* +*tr.* To put clay or mud into (the chinks of a log building); to chink (a log house or cabin) with mud. — **1818** BIRKBECK *Lett. from Illinois* 30 This cabin is built of round straight logs, . . . the intervals between the logs 'chuncked,' . . . and 'mudded,' that is, daubed with a plaister of mud. **1842** KIRKLAND *Forest Life* II. 86 Even the house whose neat rustic appearance so charms her, has to be 'chunked and mudded.' **1862** L. BAKER *U.S. Secret Service* (1867) 143 All the quarters at this point were well constructed, being made of logs and mudded in and out. **1905** *Forestry Bureau Bul.* No. 61, 42 *Mud*, to fill with soft clay the crevices between the logs in a logging camp. (N[orthern] F[orest].)

+**Mud-and-stick.** *attrib.* Designating walls or chimneys made by plastering a frame of laths or sticks with mud. — **1817** S. BROWN *Western Gaz.* 65 Some [houses] have . . . a frame skeleton filled up with mud and stick walls. **1869** *Overland Mo.* III. 286 They build mud-and-stick chimneys. **1912** C. DAWSON *Pioneer Tales* 94 The chimney was a mud-and-stick construction.

Mud bank. A bank of mud in a river or harbor that obstructs navigation or the flow of water. — **1774** *Virginia Gazette* 17 March 2/2 A Sloop . . . ran aground on a Mud Bank, a little Way up the Creek. **1791** WASHINGTON *Diaries* IV. 167 Wilmington . . . has a Mud bank . . . over which not more than 10 feet water can be brought at common tides. **1832** WILLIAMSON *Maine* I. 38 From both [islands] a mud bank extends to the main shore. **1889** DELAND *Florida Days* 165 The canoe has to be pushed from a mud-bank on which it has grounded.

+**Mud bass. 1.** =MUD SUNFISH 1. **2.** In Indiana, the large-mouthed black bass. — **(1) 1884** GOODE, etc. *Fisheries* I. 405 The Mud Bass—*Acantharchus pomotis*. This species is found only in the coastwise streams of the lowlands from New Jersey to North Carolina. **(2) 1909** WEBSTER 1417/3 *Mud bass*, . . . the large-mouthed black bass. . . . *Indiana*.

Mud boat. {1824} **1.** =MUD SCOW. {1838} +**2.** *Logging*. (See quotation.) — **(1) 1868** *Rep. Comm. Patents 1867* I. 558 The mud boat has several vats resting on two boats. **(2) 1905** *Forestry Bureau Bul.* No. 61, 43 *Mudboat*, . . . a low sled with wide runners, used for hauling logs in swamps. (S[outhern] F[orest], N[orthern] F[orest].)

+**Mud brick.** *S.W.* An adobe brick. — **1808** PIKE *Sources Miss.* II. App. 7 [Because of shortage of wood] houses [along the Kansas, Platte, and Arkansas rivers] would be built entirely of mud-brick (like those in New Spain) or of the brick manufactured with fire. **1848** BRYANT *California* xxii. 279 This is a square, containing about two hundred yards in each front, formed of a weak wall made of mud-bricks. **1881** *Amer. Naturalist* XV. 979 All of the houses [in Tucson] are built of . . . sun-dried mud bricks.

+**Mud cat. 1.** An edible catfish: **a.** Of the Mississippi valley and of the South, *Opladelus olivaris*. **b.** Of the Carolinas and Georgia, *Ameiurus platycephalus*. **2.** An inhabitant of Mississippi. — **(1) 1820** *Western Rev.* II. 361 Toad Mudcat, *Pylodictis limosus*, . . . bears the name of Mudcat, Mudfish, Mudsucker, and Toadfish. It is good to eat and bites at the hook. **1835** MARTIN *Desc. Virginia* 347 [The New River] is also remarkable for its fine fish, particularly the mud and blue cat. **1883** 'MARK TWAIN' *Life on Miss.* liv, He didn't really catch anything but only just one small useless mud-cat. **1897** *Outing* XXX. 439/1 The small 'mud-cat,' or bull-head, also had these weapons [*i.e.*, spikes in the fins] with a complete knowledge of their use. **(2) 1871** [see MUD-CAT STATE].

+**Mud catfish.** The bullhead, *Ameiurus nebulosus*. — **1842** *Nat. Hist. N.Y., Zoology* IV. 187 The Mud Catfish, *Pimelodus nebulosus*, . . . [is] recognized by the scarified and clouded appearance of its skin. **1870** *Amer. Naturalist* IV. 386 [The] Mud Cat-fish (*Amiurus DeKayi*) [is found in the Delaware near Trenton, N.J.].

+**Mud-Cat State.** A nickname for Mississippi. — **1871** DE VERE 660 Mississippi is occasionally spoken of humorously as the *Mudcat State*, the inhabitants being quite generally known as Mud-cats, a name given to the large catfish abounding in the swamps and the mud of the rivers.

+**Mud clerk.** (See quot. 1903.) — **1872** EGGLESTON *End of World* 171 It was natural enough that the 'mud-clark' on the old steamboat Iatan should have taken a fancy to the 'striker.' **1875** 'MARK TWAIN' *Old Times* i. 14 Boy after boy managed to get on the river. . . . The doctor's, and the post-master's sons became 'mud clerks.' **1903** *Dialect Notes* II. 321 *Mud-clerk*, the second clerk of a river steamer. So called because it is his duty to go on shore (often at a mere mud bank,) to receive or check off freight. (Not facetious.) **1912** COBB *Back Home* 103 Even her two mud clerks, let alone her captain and her pilots, wore uniforms.

+**Mud coot.** (See quotations.) — **1890** *Cent.* 3886/3 *Mud-coot*, the common American coot, *Fulica americana*. **1917** *Birds of Amer.* I. 214 Coot. *Fulica americana*. . . . [Also called] Pond Hen; Mud Coot; Ivory-billed Coot.

Mud crab. Any of several marine crabs of the genus *Panopeus* or related genera. {1713} — **1843** *Nat. Hist. N.Y., Zoology* VI. 5 This species is commonly known . . . by the names of Mud Crab and Oyster Crab. It is . . . almost invariably found on oyster beds. **1883** *Nat. Museum Bul. No. 27*, 111 The Mud Crabs (*Panopeus*) . . . are also used as bait, especially on the coast of the Southern States. **1883** *Ib.* 128 *Panopeus Herbstii*. . . . Mud Crab. Atlantic coast, Cape Cod to Brazil; shore. Used as food and bait. **1911** *Rep. Fisheries U.S.* 308.

+**Mud cracker.** 'A name given by boys to a fire-cracker which explodes with a dull report' (B. '77).

+**Mud-dauber.**

1. Any of various wasps of the genus *Sceliphron*, or related genera, which construct their cells of mud.

1856 *Zoologist* XIV. 5030 The species of the genus *Pelopæus* are popularly known as mud-daubers in America. **1867** *Amer. Naturalist* I. 137 An investigation of the extensive family of Mud Daubers would be an interesting and instructive study. **1886** EBBUTT *Emigrant Life* 169 Wasps are plentiful, also another insect, very similar, but black, and termed 'mud-daubers,' from their practice of building nests of mud all over the place. **1899** *Animal & Plant Lore* 63 Mud-dauber, a black and yellow striped wasp, genus *Pelopæus*. *Pike Co., Ill.*

2. A swallow that builds a nest of mud.

1899 *Animal & Plant Lore* 34 The building of the mud-daubers, or swallows, on the barn or house is a sign of prosperity to the occupants. . . . Kansas.

+**Mud devil.** =HELLBENDER 1. (Cf. MUD PUPPY.) — **1825** *Amer. Jrnl. Science* XI. 278 *Menopoma Alleghaniensis*. . . . Hell-bender. Mud-devil. **1859** BARTLETT 283.

+**Mud dipper.** The ruddy duck. — **1888** TRUMBULL *Names of Birds* 110 [The ruddy duck, *Erismatura rubida*, is known] at Eastville, Va., [as] Mud Dipper. **1917** *Birds of Amer.* I. 152.

***Muddle,** *v. tr.* (See quotation.) — **1890** *Cent.* 3886 *Muddle*, . . . to mix; stir: as, to *muddle* chocolate or drinks.

Muddler. {1885-} +(See quot. 1883.) — **1855** *Chicago Times* 16 Jan. 4/1 Butter moulds and stamps, ladles, rolling pins, potato mashers, muddlers . . . wholesale and retail at Hollister's Bazaar. **1883** KNIGHT *Suppl.* 621/2 *Muddler*, a churning stick for chocolate. A smaller one for mixing toddies.

+**Muddling stick.** =prec. — **1839** BRIGGS *H. Franco* I. 65 After a great display of nutmeg graters and muddling sticks, and of sousing and flourishing of tumblers, . . . the juleps were mixed.

***Muddy,** *a.* In allusion to BIG MUDDY. Also absol. — **1877** HALE *G. T. T.* 216, I have been reading La Salle's account of this very 'Muddy' River, Pekatonoui they called it, which means muddy. **1884** 'MARK TWAIN' *H. Finn* xvi. 130 When it was daylight, here was the clear Ohio water inshore, sure enough, and outside was the old regular Muddy!

+**Muddy breast.** *local.* =GOLDEN PLOVER. — **1888** G. TRUMBULL *Names of Birds* 196 At Newport, R.I., [the golden plover is called] Muddy-breast. **1917** *Birds of Amer.* I. 257.

Muddying. {1713-} *S.* +'A mode of fishing in which attendants stir up the muddy bottom of a lake or stream' (*Cent.*). — **1877** HALLOCK *Sportsman's Gaz.* 371 The season for muddying begins.

Mud fence. +**1.** An adobe wall. +**2.** *As ugly as a mud fence*, very ugly. — **(1) 1844** GREGG *Commerce* I. 150 Mud-fences, or walls of very large *adobes*, are also occasionally to be met with. **(2) 1893** *Harper's Mag.* March 646/2 It is the custom . . . to speak of the bride as beautiful, even if she is as ugly as a mud fence. **1907** *Dialect Notes* III. 190 Very ill-favored. . . . N.W., Ark., *ugly as a mud fence stuck with tadpoles*.

***Mudfish.** One of various fishes that burrow in the mud or live in muddy water. Also with defining term.

Mudfish is most commonly applied to the bowfin, the killifish (*Fundulus heteroclitus*), and the small goby (*Gillichthys mirabilis*).

1704 *Boston News-Letter* 13 Nov. 2/2 Capt. Laurence's Prize . . . will be exposed to Sale, together with . . . her Loading of Mud Fish and Salt. **1767** HUTCHINSON *Hist. Mass.* II. 445 The French find their account in taking what they call their muid or mud fish when the English cannot. **1791** W. BARTRAM *Travels* 176 The mud fish is large . . . ; his meat white and tender, but soft and tastes of the mud. **1842** *Nat. Hist. N.Y., Zoology*

IV. 269 The Western Mud-fish, *Amia occidentalis*, . . . is found in Lake Erie and Ontario. **1855** BAIRD in *Smithsonian Rep.* 342, The Mud-Fish. *Melanura pygmaea*. . . . I have caught the Mud Fish . . . on the American shores of all the great lakes except Lake Superior. **1870** *Amer. Naturalist* IV. 99 Other streams, sluggish and thick, . . . are paradisiacal to the mud fish (*Melanura*). **1884** GOODE, etc. *Fisheries* I. 659 The Bowfin or Johnny Grindle—*Amia calva*. . . . Though not considered eatable in the North, it is very highly esteemed by the negroes of the South, who say 'there is nothing sweeter than a Mud-fish.' **1886** *Nat. Museum Proc.* VIII. 204 *Cobitis heteroclitus*. . . . The editor . . . has evidently been misled by the common name 'mud-fish' in referring number eleven to *Amia calva*.

Mud flat. A low, flat area frequently covered with water. {1871–} — **1813** WILSON *Ornith.* VII. 45 The Red-breasted Snipe arrives on the sea coast of New Jersey early in April. . . . They frequent the sand bars and mud flats at low water, in search of food. **1870** BEADLE *Utah* 437 In most cases the water supply is so scant that these 'sinks' become entirely dry in summer, and are then known as 'mud flats.' **1882** WAITE *Adv. Far West* 65 There are vast prairies, dreary and treeless, sandhills, mud-flats. **1910** J. HART *Vigilante Girl* 28 Where he made his biggest clean-up was in buying some mud-flats.

+**Mud goose.** =HUTCHINS'S GOOSE. — **1844** *Nat. Hist. N.Y., Zoology* II. 352 Hutchins's Goose . . . is not uncommon on the eastern part of Long island . . . and is known under the name of Mud Goose. **1917** *Birds of Amer.* I. 161 Throughout its range it [Hutchins's goose, *Branta canadensis hutchinsi*] is variously known also as Goose-brant, . . . Short-necked Goose, or Mud Goose.

Mudhead. {1886} +'A nickname applied to the natives of Tennessee' (B. '59). *Obs.* — **1838** HALIBURTON *Clockmaker* 2 Ser. xix. 289 There's the hoosiers of Indiana, . . . the mudheads of Tenessee [etc.].

Mud hen. {1611} +Any of various American birds of the family Rallidae, as the American coot.

1813 WILSON *Ornithology* VII. 110 [The Virginia rail] is known to some of the inhabitants along the sea coast of New Jersey, by the name of the Fresh-water Mud Hen. *Ib.* IX. 62 [The] Common Coot . . . is known in Pennsylvania by the name of *Mud-hen*. **1835** AUDUBON *Ornith. Biog.* III. 291 In Louisiana, this species [*Fulica Americana*] is named *Poule d'Eau* . . . In all other parts of the Union, it is known by the names of Mud Hen and Coot. **1874** LONG *Wild-Fowl* 77 Mud-hens often cause the duck-shooter considerable annoyance. **1917** *Birds of Amer.* I. 204 Clapper Rail. *Rallus crepitans crepitans*. . . . [Also called] Mud Hen; Sedge Hen. *Ib.* 212 Florida Gallinule. *Gallinula galeata*. . . . [Also called] Red-billed Mud Hen; Water Hen.

+**Mudhole.**

1. A soft, muddy place in a road or street; a hole or depression filled with mud.

1760 in Commons, etc. *Doc. Hist.* I. 310 As Soon as one Gets out It Rains on him or he Is In a large due or in a mud hole. **1784** ELLICOTT in Mathews *Life A. Ellicott* 26 Snow . . . hid the Mud-Holes and rendered Traveling not only tedious but dangerous. **1848** BRYANT *California* iii. 36 The travelling has been very fatiguing to our oxen, the wagons frequently stalling in the mud-holes. **1854** BARTLETT *Personal Narr.* I. 87 We passed a mud-hole, marked on the map as the 'Mustang Ponds.' It was a slight depression in the prairie. **1872** MCCLELLAN *Golden State* 137 The mud-holes and gulches were filled up with boxes of choice tobacco. **1899** ADE *Doc' Horne* 6 When a mud-hole dries rapidly a cracked and flaky crust forms on top.

2. 'A soft spot in granite due to decomposition. (Quarrymen's slang.)' (*Cent. Suppl.*)

1898 *19th Rep. Geol. Survey* VI. (II). 230 Knots, streaks, and 'mud holes' must be carefully avoided in a conscientious selection of stock for monumental work.

Mudhook. **1.** An anchor. *slang.* {1884} +**2.** A person's foot. *slang.* — **(1) 1827** COOPER *Red Rover* I. 48 He would . . . fasten her [a ship] to the spot with good hempen cables and iron mud-hooks. **1862** *N.Y. Tribune* 23 May 12/4 We soon let go our mud-hook. . . . In the morning, the sea had gone down. **1905** LINCOLN *Partners* 230 He wrote to Captain Titcomb, giving the 'ranges' as near as he could remember them, and the partners agreed to undertake the job of recovering the lost 'mudhook.' **(2) 1850** GARRARD *Wah-To-Yah* xx. 245 This 'mudhook' . . . hasn't a moccasin on for nuthin'. **1884** *Century Mag.* Dec. 283 The [soldier] boys called their feet 'pontons,' 'mud-hooks,' 'soil-excavators,' and other names not quite so polite.

***Mud house.** **a.** A house in which the main building material is mud. +**b.** *S.W.* An adobe house. — **1834** A. PIKE *Sketches* 38 The sole inhabitants of the Old Village now, are rattlesnakes, of which we killed some two or three dozen about the old mud houses. **1846** EMORY *Military Reconn.* 81 It was the remains of a three-story mud house, 60 feet square, pierced for doors and windows. **1881** CHASE *Editor's Run in N. Mex.* 114 We found the Penitente church, a mud house, some eight feet high, surrounded by a mud wall. **1889** BRAYLEY *Boston Fire Dept.* 3 Mud houses were known in the early days, but they were very few.

+**Mud iguana.** The siren (*Siren lacertina*) of the South. *Obs.* — **1766** J. ELLIS in *Phil. Trans.* LVI. 189 The natives [of S.C.] call it Mud-Inguana [*sic*]. **1796** MORSE *Univ. Geog.* I. 224 The *Siren* or *Mud-iguana*, a fish of the order, *Branchiostegi*.

Mud lark. **1.** A hog. *slang.* +**2.** (See quot. 1917.) — **(1)** [**1796** GROSE *Dict. Vulgar Tongue* (1931) 238 *Mud Lark*, a hog.] **1833** J. NEAL *Down-Easters* I. 47, I should like to know . . . what upon irth he means by . . . pone bread, an' mud-larks that's made into Virginny-ham. **1869** *Overland Mo.* III. 129 A hog clandestinely killed outside of [a Confederate] camp and smuggled in . . . was called a . . . 'mud-lark.' **(2) 1917** *Birds of Amer.* II. 251 Meadowlark. *Sturnella magna magna*. . . . [Also called] Medlark; Mudlark; Medlar.

+**Mud lick.** A mudhole or seep impregnated with salt. — **1779** in *Amer. Sp.* XV. 287/2 Crossing a branch to a red oak near a mud lick. **1824** *Ib.*, On the bank of the Bee tree branch, about 200 yards above the mud lick. **1849** *Ib.*, To a white Oak and poplar near a mud lick.

+**Mud lump.**[1] =LUMPFISH. — **1832** WILLIAMSON *Maine* I. 156 There are two varieties, if not species; the *mud* or *green*, and the red lump.

+**Mud lump.**[2] A mound of mud or soft spongy land rising in the shallow water of a muddy stream, esp. in the lower Mississippi River. (Cf. MUD VOLCANO 1.) — **1868** *Putnam's Mag.* May 591/2 Small islands of bluish clay suddenly emerge from the water. . . . These are the famous *mud-lumps* of the Mississippi. **1874** *Congress. Rec.* 5 June 4623/2 The mud-lump must necessarily by its constitution rise in shallow water. **1879** *Scribner's Mo.* Nov. 48/2 Lying in front of each of these passes is found a peculiar formation called 'mud lumps.' **1902** *Smithsonian Rep. 1901* 71 Within the region [lower Colo. Valley] lie a number of 'mud volcanoes,' apparently analogous to the 'mud lumps' of the Lower Mississippi.

+**Mud machine.** A machine for dredging a river or harbor. — **1806** *Balance* V. 162/3 The Mayor and Corporation of the city of New York will man their mud-machine. **1868** PAULDING *Book of Vagaries* 152 There was likewise an incorporated company, to build a mud-machine for deepening the river.

+**Mud minnow.** Any small, pickerel-like fish of the genus *Umbra*, as *U. limi* of the Mississippi Valley. — **1870** *Amer. Naturalist* IV. 386 The Mud Minnow (*Melanura limi*) [is found in the Delaware at Trenton, N.J.] **1886** *Ib.* XX. 824 The young mud-minnow leaves the egg on the sixth day. **1897** *N.Y. Forest, Fish & Game Comm. 2d Rep.* 229 *Umbra limi*. . . . A number of mud minnows were shipped in wet moss from Caledonia, N.Y.

+**Mud ore.** (See quotation.) — **1804** *Mass. H. S. Coll.* IX. 256 There is another kind found in bogs and swamps, which the workmen call swamp or mud ore; it is a ferruginous earth, or glebe, resembling black mould, externally destitute of any metallick appearance; but being washed with water, small granulated particles of iron subside to the bottom.

+**Mud oven.** An open-air oven made of clay or adobe. — **1850** GARRARD *Wah-To-Yah* xv. 180 In front of many dwellings is a mud oven, in shape like a cupping glass. **1872** POWERS *Afoot & Alone* 165 Here there is a mud-coop, there a mud oven.

+**Mud plantain.** A North American plant (*Heteranthus reniformis*) that grows in marshes. — **1817–8** EATON *Botany* (1822) 304 Mud-plantain . . . [is found] in muddy overflowed places. Very abundant in South Bay, below Hudson City. **1894** COULTER *Bot. W. Texas* III. 441 *Heteranthera* (Mud Plantain.)

+**Mud pot.** =MUD VOLCANO 2. — **1897** *Outing* XXX. 164/2 The bank was honeycombed with miniature geysers and mud-pots. **1912** A. HAGUE *Geol. Hist. Yellowstone Park* 21 The number of geysers, hot springs, mudpots, and paintpots scattered over the park exceeds 3,000.

+**Mud pout.** A catfish. — **1804** FESSENDEN *Orig. Poems* (1806) 132 Like an otter that paddles the creek, In quest of a mud pout, or sucker. **1859** BARTLETT 72 [The catfish, genus *Prinelodus*] is also called by the name of Horned-pout, Bull-head, Mud-pout, Minister, or simply Cat.

+**Mud puddle.** A wet and muddy place. — **a1841** HAWES *Sporting Scenes* I. 183 [The woodcock] arrives here from the South . . . just as soon as the thawing mud-puddles will yield to his hungry mandible. **1873** PHELPS *Trotty's Wedding* xx, The mud-puddles lay in the school-house yard. **1890** HOWELLS *Boy's Town* 72 It was perfectly good form . . . to get a boy, if you could, to shut his eyes, and then lead him into a mud-puddle.

+**Mud puppy.** Any of various American salamanders, as the hellbender. — **1882** *Amer. Naturalist* XVI. 325 Vitality of the Mud Puppy. —The observations on the Menopoma [etc.]. **1897** *Outing* XXX. 439/2 The mud-puppy . . . is a repulsive-looking water-lizard. **1899** *Animal & Plant Lore* 62 Mud-puppy, salamander. Lawrence, Ky.

+**Mud road.** An ungraveled dirt road. — **1830** *Congress. Deb.* 30 March 717/2 A mud road can [not] be of any use after it is made. **1887** *Courier-Journal* 2 Feb. 1/1 They will arrive home as soon as the wretched state of the mud roads will permit.

+**Mud scow.** A barge or flatboat used in dredging. — **1766** *Mass. Gazette* 20 Oct. 1/3 To Be Sold, a new Mud-Scow, 24 Foot long, and can carry 12 or 14 Tons Weight. **1837** HAWTHORNE *Notebooks* (1932) 9 Running along the gunnel of a mud-scow, jumping into a skiff, . . . [a man was] put on board. **1894** *Outing* XXIV. 325/1 Charlie Thayer . . . could manage any kind of a boat from a crack yacht to a mudscow.

+**Mud shad.** The gizzard shad, *Dorosoma cepedianum*. — **1883** *Nat. Museum Bul.* No. 27, 455 Gizzard Shad; Mud Shad; Hickory Shad. . . . The species has no commercial value. **1884** *Ib.* 476 Mud Shad; Gizzard Shad. . . . The species is scarcely fit for food, and yet it is sold rather freely in Washington markets. **1884** GOODE, etc. *Fisheries* I. 610 The 'Mud-Shad' . . . is abundant in brackish waters along the coast from Delaware Bay southward to Mexico.

Mudsill. Also †**mudsell.**

1. The lowest sill or timber of a structure as of a house or bridge. Also fig. {1741–}

1685 *Boston Rec.* 178 The middle of the wall to lie even with northerlie or outward side of the said Simkins Mudsell in the old Celler. **1718** *Lan-*

caster Rec. 183 Ye Neck Bridge . . . should have 5 Trussells . . . to brace into ye Posts above ye caps & Down into yee Mudsells. **1858** *Congress. Globe* 4 March 962/1 In all social systems there must be a class to do the mean duties, to perform the drudgery of life. . . . Such a class . . . constitutes the very mud-sills of society and of political government. **1868** T. D. PRICE *Diary* (MS.) 16 Oct., Drew a load of mud-sills for bridge on road. **1905** *Forestry Bureau Bul.* No. 61, 43 *Mudsill,* . . . the bed piece or bottom timber of a dam which is placed across the stream, usually resting on rocks or in mud.

+**2.** A member of the laboring classes. Applied opprobriously during the Civil War by Southerners to Northerners.

1860 STODDARD in *Vanity Fair* III. 269/1 White niggers, mudsills, Northern scum, Base hirelings, hear me, and be dumb. **1865** KELLOGG *Rebel Prisons* 65 Talk no longer about 'mudsills,' and 'greasy mechanics!' **1878** *N. Amer. Rev.* May 500 In Southern political articles of faith it was declared that the black laborer was a 'chattel,' and the white laborer a 'mudsill.' **1910** J. HART *Vigilante Girl* 125 They affect to look down on us of the North, and call us 'Yankees' and 'mudsills.'

+**b.** With the adjective *Northern.*

1863 TROWBRIDGE *Cudjo's Cave* 12 You don't act as if your heart was in this yer act of dooty we're performin', any more'n as if you was a northern mudsill yourself! **1863** *Ladies' Repository* Jan. 60/1 We should not be surprised if that boy—an excellent specimen of our Northern mudsills—were destined to hoist the American flag to its old place on the capitol at Richmond.

+**c.** (See quotation and cf. next.)

1885 *Mag. Amer. Hist.* March 296/1 *Mudsill.* . . . Assumed by certain political associations in California in 1858.

+**Mudsill club.** (See quotation.) — **1859** BARTLETT 284 *Mud-Sill Clubs.* The miners and working-men of California who support Broderick in his opposition to the Administration, are preparing for a vigorous campaign, and are already organizing themselves into associations which they style 'Mud-sill Clubs.'—*New York Evening Post,* 1858.

+**Mudsucker.** Any of various American fresh-water fishes of the family Catostomidae, which feed in the bottoms of streams, ponds, etc. — **1820** [see MUD CAT]. **1870** *Amer. Naturalist* IV. 113 The Mud-sucker (*Hylomyzon nigricans*). **1884** GOODE, etc. *Fisheries* I. 615 Although called the 'Mud Sucker' in the books, it [the stone-roller, *Catostomus nigricans*] is most characteristically a fish of the running streams. **1911** *Rep. Fisheries 1908* 317 The different species [of sucker] are known as 'May sucker,' 'mud sucker' [etc.].

+**Mud sunfish. 1.** The fresh-water sunfish, *Acantharchus pomotis.* **2.** (See quot. 1909.) — **(1) 1870** *Amer. Naturalist* IV. 102 Professor S. F. Baird, during the summer of 1854, discovered, in New Jersey, . . . the Mud Sunfish. **1883** *Nat. Museum Bul.* No. 27, 462 Mud Sun-Fish. Eastern United States from New York to South Carolina in sluggish streams. **(2) 1909** WEBSTER 1418/1 *Mud sunfish,* . . . the warmouth.

+**Mud swallow.** =CLIFF SWALLOW. Also transf. and attrib. — [**1873** LELAND *Egypt. Sketch-Bk.* 43 Those curious mud-swallow nests of little villages.] **1898** DELAND *Old Chester Tales* 181 Mud-swallows had built their nests in the corners. **1917** *Birds of Amer.* III. 84 Cliff Swallow. *Petrochelidon lunifrons lunifrons.* . . . [Also called] Barn Swallow; Mud Swallow; Republican Swallow.

+**Mud terrapin.** (See quotations.) — **1842** *Nat. Hist. N.Y., Zoology* III. 23 The Musk Tortoise or Mud Turtle, Mud Terrapin or Stink-pot, . . . is to be found in most of our ponds and ditches. **1859** BARTLETT 284 *Mud-Turtle.* (*Sternothœrus odorata.*) The popular name of a reptile common in all parts of the United States. Marsh Tortoise and Mud Terrapin are other names for the same.

+**Mud tortoise.** A mud turtle, esp. of the genera *Sternotherus* and *Kinosternon.* — **1839** STORER *Mass. Reptiles* 210 *Sternothaerus odoratus,* the mud Tortoise, . . . is found burying itself in the mud in ditches and small ponds. **1842** *Nat. Hist. N.Y., Zoology* III. 21 The Mud Tortoise, *Kinosternon pennsylvanicum,* . . . inhabits ditches and muddy ponds, and often takes the hook. **1890** *Cent.* 3887/3 *Mud-tortoise,* . . . same as *mud-turtle.*

+**Mud turtle.**

1. Any of various fresh-water turtles, esp.: **a.** A turtle of the genus *Kinosternon.* **b.** The snapping turtle *Chelydra serpentina.*

1796 *Aurora* (Phila.) 17 May (Th.), The crocodile throat of the gentle snappers or mud tortles in the Jersey market. **1848** BURTON *Waggeries* 10 While the darkey was . . . snorin' himself sober, a mud tortle, about the size of our capting's epillitts, crawls right slick into his open mouth. **1869** 'MARK TWAIN' *Innocents* xlvii. 490 He was . . . throwing a clod at a mud-turtle which was sunning itself on a small log in the brook. **1897** *Outing* Aug. 439 The last heave would surely reveal either a mud-turtle or a mud-puppy.

2. Used as food. Also attrib.

1854 M. J. HOLMES *Tempest & Sunshine* 69 What kind of soup? Beef soup or mud-turkle? **1884** 'MARK TWAIN' *H. Finn* viii. 69 You ain't had no meat nor bread to eat all this time? Why didn't you get mud-turkles? **1893** *Harper's Mag.* March 593 He will give them cider and mud-turtle, but he will see to it that the sly old lobbyist . . . and the experienced Senator . . . are served with French champagne and veritable terrapin.

3. Used in comparisons and figurative contexts.

1857 STROTHER *Virginia* 32 'Looks more like he was embalmed,' cried another. 'A mummy! or a mud-turtle lying on his back!' **1866** C. H. SMITH *Bill Arp* 129, I run like a mud turkel, lookin ahead of me at every step. **1875** 'MARK TWAIN' *Old Times* i. 19 You dash-dash-dash-*dashed* split between a tired mud-turtle and a crippled hearse-horse! **1891** C. ROBERTS *Adrift Amer.* 239 In the creeks were plenty of mud turtles. . . . If disturbed they drop into the water instantly, giving rise to a saying to express quickness, 'like a mud turtle off a log.'

Mud volcano. +**1.** =MUD LUMP.[2] **2.** An eruption of the earth which spouts mud. {1817–} — **(1) 1868** *Putnam's Mag.* May 591/2 *Mud-lumps,* or more properly Mud-volcanoes, have been known to rise to the height of twenty-five feet. **1902** [see MUD LUMP[2]]. **(2) 1872** MCCLELLAN *Golden State* 228 Hot springs, and mud volcanoes, point unmistakably to the fact that the tremendous forces . . . are here still asserting themselves. **1890** LANGFORD *Vigilante Days* (1912) 493 It is surrounded by innumerable warm and hot springs, sulphur deposits, and mud volcanoes.

+**Mud wagon.** An inferior stagecoach: (see quot. 1868). — **1835** LATROBE *Rambler in N.A.* II. 259 We had to put up with an open 'mud-waggon,' with spring seats. **1868** WATERS *Life among Mormons* 43 The inferior coaches, commonly known on the plains as 'mud wagons.' **1896** SHINN *Story of Mine* 117 [Stage drivers of the Nevada-California lines] drive 'mud-wagons' for the most part, that two or four horses can manage.

***Mud wall.** A wall made of clay or of materials held together with mud; +an adobe wall. Also attrib. — **1696** *Massachusetts* 40 In their Mud-wall Meeting House . . . [the number] was so small, as a Child might have told the whole Assembly. **1844** GREGG *Commerce of Prairies* I. 109 [San Miguel, N.Mex.] consists of irregular clusters of mud-wall huts.

+**Mud wasp.** A wasp that uses mud in the construction of its cells, esp. the mud-dauber. — **1824** *Old Colony Memorial* (Plymouth) 6 March (Th.), [He was] a sort of would-be dandy; having the bottom of his waist pinched up to the size of a quart pot, and thus resembling in shape what we call a mud wasp. **1860** *Ladies' Repository* XX. 263/1 The mud wasp makes its abode in the loose, sandy ground. **1869** *Amer. Naturalist* III. 391 The Spider and Mud-wasp. . . . A very large spider was attacked by one of the small blue mud-wasps, or dirt-daubers. **1881** *Ib.* XV. 443 Baron Osten Sacken . . . records the breeding of *A[rgyramœba] cephus* and *A. fur* from the nest of a Texan mud-wasp.

***Muff,** *n.*[1]

***1.** A pillowlike cover open at opposite ends into which the hands may be thrust for warmth.

Cf. FOOT MUFF.

1644 *Essex Inst. Coll.* L. 322 Mr:es Noris shall have my mufe. **1709** LAWSON *Carolina* 125 [Foxes'] Furs, if in Season, are used for Muffs and other Ornaments. **1740** in Earle *Sabbath* 89 [Lost, a] sableskin man's muff. **1767** *Boston Gazette* 19 Oct., Elizabeth Courtney . . . designs to teach the making all sorts of French Trimmings, Flowers, and Feather Muffs and Tippets. **1875** *Chicago Tribune* 12 Dec. 9/2 Muffs, Boas, Caps, and Gloves, the largest and finest stock in the West. **1904** STRATTON-PORTER *Freckles* 293 Her hands were in a muff as big as her body.

2. Attrib. and comb. with *box, lining, maker, stand.*

1724 *New-Eng. Courant* 20–27 Jan. 2/2 John Arno Muff-maker next to the Three Crowns, Boston. **1868** *Mich. Agric. Rep.* VII. 363 Henry Fowler, Detroit, [exhibited] . . . 1 dozen muff and collar boxes, combined in one. **1874** *Rep. Comm. Patents 1873* 14 Berghold, L., Buffalo, N.Y. Muff-stand. *Ib.* 27 Butterworth, C. F. Troy, N.Y. Muff-lining.

Muff, *n.*[2] {1837–} +In baseball or football, a failure to handle the ball properly. — **1868** CHADWICK *Base Ball* 64 In the . . . score sheet . . . to the left the initials represent the words Runs, Outs, Times, Bases, Muffs, Balks, Left, Home. **1880** N. BROOKS *Fairport Nine* ii. 38 Captain Sam . . . inwardly groaned 'he'll make a muff!' **1886** ALTON *Among Law-Makers* 255 General Garfield . . . was constantly exclaiming: 'Good catch!' 'Fine hit!' 'Oh! what a muff!' **1893** CAMP *College Sports* 125 As a punt may traverse a distance of fifty yards, a muff may mean a loss of that distance.

Muff, *v.* {1857–} +*Baseball. tr.* To fumble (the ball). — **1868** CHADWICK *Base Ball* 43 Any ball 'muffed' by the catcher . . . is recorded as a passed ball. **1880** N. BROOKS *Fairport Nine* 40 Joe went for the first base as fast as his legs could carry him, . . . and Pat Adams muffed the ball. **1912** MATHEWSON *Pitching* 162, I muffed fly after fly.

Muffetee. Also †**muf(f)tee, muffotee.** {c1706–} A muff or a mitten. {1808–} — **1749** in Singleton *Social N.Y.* 248 Elizabeth Boyd . . . follows as usual . . . making and mending of silk gloves, mittens, muftees. **1830** WATSON *Philadelphia* 174 Gentlemen in the olden time used to carry mufftees in winter. It was in effect a little woollen muff of various colours. **1855** COOKE *Ellie* 532 Little girls . . . tripped from side to side with diminutive hands, covered with muffotees. **1892** *Harper's Mag.* Jan. 282/2 She had thought of making Willie a nice pair of muffetees.

Muffin.

1. A kind of flat dish. {1885}

1820 *Columbian Centinel* 12 Jan. 3/6 An extensive assortment of Crockery, Glass, and China Ware, viz. . . . Twifflers and Muffins [to be auctioned off]. **1864** WEBSTER 865/2 *Muffin,* . . . an earthen table plate of several different sizes, not exceeding seven inches in diameter.

2. A kind of bread made with baking powder or a similar agent and baked in the form of a cup cake; a gem. {an English muffin, 1703–} Also attrib.

1835 LONGSTREET *Ga. Scenes* 36 Waffles were handed to Ned, and he took one: . . . and so on of muffins, rolls, and corn bread. **1848** JUDSON *Mysteries N.Y.* III. 91 The muffin-man has been here. **1887** *Century Mag.* Nov. 16/2 A procession of little darkies [came in] . . . supporting plates of hot batter-cakes, muffins, Sally Lunns, rice waffles. **1896** *Internat. Typogr. Union Proc.* 64/1, 2 biscuit pans, 55¢; 4 muffin pans, $1.40.

+**3.** *Baseball.* (See quotations.) Also attrib. *Obs.*

Cf. MUFF *v.* and MUFF *n.*[2]

1867 *Ball Players' Chronicle* 26 Sept. 3/4 Balls were muffed, picked up clumsily, and allowed to run through legs in real muffin style. **1868** CHADWICK *Base Ball* 42 Muffins.—This is the title of a class of ball players who are both practically and theoretically unacquainted with the game. . . . 'Muffins' rank the lowest in the grade of the nines of a club. **1871** BAGG *At Yale* 317 'Muffins,' or clubs which make no pretence to good playing, [use the practice ground]. **1875** *Chicago Tribune* 26 Sept. 12/2 The muffin character of the game renders it entirely unworthy of a detailed account.

+**Muffinism.** Poor playing at baseball. *Obs.* — **1867** *Ball Players' Chronicle* 26 Sept. 1/4 Martin and Akin rivalling each other in muffinism. **1868** CHADWICK *Base Ball* 97 The alleged muffinism of the Excelsiors . . . did not benefit their opponents much.

+**Mufflejaw.** Any of various American fresh-water fishes of the genus *Cottus*, as *C. ictalops* of the East, *C. semiscaber* of the Rocky Mountains, etc.; =MILLER'S-THUMB. — **1882** *Nat. Mus. Bul.* No. 16, 696 *U[ranidea] richardsoni.* . . . Miller's Thumb; . . . Muffle-jaw. . . . Middle and Northern States. **1884** GOODE, etc. *Fisheries* I. 259 In the lakes and streams of the Northern States are numerous species of *Uranidea* and allied genera, known in some localities . . . [as] 'Bull-heads,' 'Goblins,' 'Blobs,' and 'Muffle-jaws.' **1911** *Rep. Fisheries 1908* 315 Sculpin . . . in the lakes and streams of the Northern states [are called] . . . 'goblins,' 'blobs,' 'muffle-jaws,' etc.

* **Muffler.**

* **1.** A wrap or scarf for the neck or throat.

1655 *Essex Probate Rec.* I. 202, 5 croscloths and a mufler. **1699** SEWALL *Diary* I. 508, I left off my Muffler but this day and yet find no inconvenience. **1847** *Knickerb.* XXX. 14 The preacher came up . . . a red-and-yellow muffler about his neck and face. **1893** MATTHEWS in *Harper's Mag.* Dec. 29/1 Little groups of young people passed, the girls with . . . mufflers of orange and black. **1904** 'O. HENRY' *Cabbages & Kings* (1915) 168 The outfit [consisted of] . . . Arctic overshoes, fur cap and earmuffs, with elegant fleece-lined gloves and woollen muffler.

2. *spec.* The mechanism that deadens or muffles the sound of the exhaust of a gasoline motor. Also fig.

1896 *Cosmopolitan* XX. 420 The noise of the exhaust is stifled in a muffler. [**1903** *Motoring Ann.* 206 Muffler: required at all times on public highways [in R.I.].] **1916** 'BOWER' *Phantom Herd* 310 Luck's heart began to pound so that he half expected his neighbors to tell him to close his muffler.

* **Mug.** Also †**muge, mugg.**

* **1.** A small cylindrical vessel for holding liquids; esp. a drinking vessel with or without a handle.

[**1689** SEWALL *Diary* I. 291 Mugg, [£] 2.2.0. . . . Fish Tackle, [£] 1.4.6.] **1722** *New-Eng. Courant* 8–15 Jan. 1/2 The Servants . . . within this Three Weeks have broke Fourteen earthen Mugs and a Looking-Glass. **1779** *York Co., Va., Rec.: Wills* XXII. 28 April, 4 plates, 2 mugs, a tea pot 6/8/0. **1857** *Knickerb.* XLIX. 42 Bringing out a bottle, and two tumblers, and a china mug, [he] invited us to draw what water we required. **1896** JEWETT *Pointed Firs* 46, I'm goin' right down to get us each a mug o' my beer.

+**2.** A loving cup put up as a prize. Also comb. *contemptuous. Obsolescent.*

1883 *Harper's Mag.* Aug. 443/2 To the extreme mug-hunters [at yacht races] it [speed] meant [everything]. **1890** *Ib.* Sept. 593/1 The cruise is done and the mugs have escaped them. *Ib.*, He may be bitten by the tarantula of matches, be possessed of the fury of mug-hunting.

‖**Muggin.** A mug. — **1872** *Congress. Globe* 20 March 1824/2, I, if I knew how to manufacture my little muggin of rum on Lake Michigan, had my drawback equally with the Yankees in New England.

Muggins. 1. One of various card games in which the object is to give an opponent all of one's cards. {1876} **2.** (See quot. 1864); a fool or simpleton. {1884} **3.** A kind of game at dominoes. {1881} — (**1**) **1864** [see sense 2]. **1889** RITTENHOUSE *Maud* 447 Mr Mayne was expected to show Miss McKee how to manage her hand at Muggins. **1896** ADE *Artie* ii. 10 You didn't think this was a game o' muggins, like you boys play up at your little old cycle club. (**2**) **1860** HARTE *Stories & Poems* (1914) 45 J. B. expressed his opinion that I was a Muggins. **1864** MARK TWAIN' *Sketches* (1926) 123, I have been playing the noble game of 'Muggins.' In that game, if you make a mistake of any kind, however trivial it may be, you are pronounced a muggins by the whole company. **1884** — *Huckleberry Finn* xxviii. 292 Why, you talk like a muggins. (**3**) **1868** ZINCKE *Last Winter in U.S.* 268 The other [Am. lady] took her husband's absence . . . very philosophically, consoling herself with a kind of dominoes she called 'muggins.'

***Mugwort.** +Any of several American species of the genus *Artemisia*, which resemble the European species. — **1784** CUTLER in *Mem. Academy* I. 480 Mugwort. . . . A decoction of it is taken by the common people to cure the ague. **1792** IMLAY *Western Territory* 207 Of herbs, &c. we have of the wild sort . . . mugwort, ox-eye, mother-wort. **1901** MOHR *Plant Life Ala.* 56 [Among] escapes from the gardens of potherbs, medicinal herbs, and otherwise useful plants . . . [is] *Artemisia vulgaris* (mugwort).

+**Mugwump,** *n.* [Algonquian *mugquomp*, 'a chief.']

John Eliot (1604–1690) used the word in his Indian Bible (1663–1), e.g. in Gen. 36:15.

1. An important person; the high-muck-a-muck. Used ironically.

1832 in *Nation* LII. 414/3 The secret bulletin . . . has extensively circulated among the Knights of Kadosh and the Most Worshipful Mugwumps of the Cabletow. **1865** in *Amer. Notes & Q.* I. 204 One other political bruiser we like to have forgotten . . . is 'Uncle Nat Eaton,' formerly of Calais, but now 'Mugwump' No. 2, of Middlesex. **1867** *Atlantic Mo.* May 589/2, I've got one of your gang in irons,—the Great Mugwump himself. **1877** *N.Y. Tribune* 16 Feb. 4/4 John A. Logan is the Head Center, the Hub, the King Pin, the Main Spring, Mogul, and Mugwump of the final plot. **1925** *N.Y. Times* 10 May, The royal red Indian mugwump, the chief, was copiously red-blooded.

transf. **1835** D. P. THOMPSON *Adv. T. Peacock* 6 This village, I beg leave to introduce to the reader, under the significant appellation of *Mugwump*, . . . used at the present day, vulgarly and masonically, as synonymous with greatness and strength.

2. *Polit.* A member of the Republican party who bolted the party's presidential nominee, James G. Blaine, in 1884; more generally, any independent Republican. Now hist.

1884 *N.Y. Ev. Post* 20 June (*Cent.*), We have yet to see a Blaine organ which speaks of the Independent Republicans otherwise than as Pharisees, hypocrites, dudes, mugwumps, transcendentalists, or something of that sort. **1885** *Boston Jrnl.* 25 April 2/2 Does it mark the turning point in Mr. Cleveland's course toward the Mugwumps? Is he at the end of his concessions to their peculiar and frequently-repeated demands? **1887** *Courier-Journal* 8 May 16/2 The Mugwumps represent the same thing in politics that the letter x does in algebra. **1904** *Dallas Morning News* 20 July 6 The two great parties should be kept as nearly equal to each other as possible. The one force by which they can be kept in this safe condition is the independent, detached, free, unterrified, contingent of mugwumps.

b. A person who withdraws his support from any group or organization; an independent; a chronic kicker.

[**1884** *Sat. Rev.* 22 Nov. 659/1 It may be that in a few years . . . a little group of British Mugwumps . . . will arise in their might [etc.].] **1888** BILLINGS *Hardtack* 286 [The mule's] reputation as a kicker is world-wide. He was the Mugwump of the service. **1894** FORD *P. Stirling* 302, I'd have believed anything but that you [a Democrat] would be a dashed Mugwump!

3. Attrib. in sense 2.

1887 *Courier-Journal* 8 Jan. 4/5 The Mugwump War Department is a horse-power to the Republican machine. **1888** S. HALE *Letters* 202 If the Reps. win, . . . 't will be terrible facing the mugwump Churches and Democrat Osborns. **1904** *Grand Rapids Ev. Press* 7 June 4 The Democratic and mugwump press is making the most of it.

+**Mugwump,** *v. Polit. intr.* To bolt a party or candidate. — **1889** *N.Y. Tribune* 10 March 1/6 E. D. Graves . . . 'Mugwumped to Cleveland,' in 1884 because he 'could not conscientiously support James G. Blaine.' **1911** *Springfield W. Repub.* 2 Nov. 3 The Bay State voters do not mugwump very deep.

+**Mugwumpcy.** *Polit.* =next. — **1887** *Ohio State Jrnl.* 17 Aug., The people have resolved that Democracy and mugwumpcy must go!

+**Mugwumpery.** *Polit.* The views and practices of the mugwumps (sense 2). — **1885** *Boston Jrnl.* 25 April 2/2 Has he [Cleveland] thrown this bombshell into the very citadel of Mugwumpery? **1887** *Courier-Journal* 5 Jan. 3/1 The above instance shows what a grip 'Mugwumpery' has on this Administration. **1904** *N.Y. Ev. Post* 29 July 6 Despised Mugwumpery never had a finer tribute than in the competition of the two parties this year for the favor of the citizen who is sworn to neither party.

+**Mugwumpian,** *a. Polit.* Believing in the principles of the mugwumps. — **1885** *Boston Jrnl.* 21 Jan. 4/1 The college . . . must speak manly English and must not be too mugwumpian in its proclamation of free trade. **1887** *Voice* 1 Sept., Our esteemed Mugwumpian contemporary, the New York Times, is very solicitous for the Republicans to make concessions to the Prohibitionists.

+**Mugwumpian Democrat.** *Polit.* A Republican who supported Grover Cleveland for president in 1884. — **1885** *Boston Jrnl.* 21 Jan. 2/4 There is a row . . . between a Democrat and a mugwumpian Democrat.

+**Mugwumpism.** *Polit.* Independent action in politics; mugwumpery. — **1886** *Congress. Rec.* 31 March 2968/1 That maudlin political sentiment which we recognize, for want of a better, under the name of 'Mugwumpism.' **1887** *Nation* 14 April 305/3 The municipal election in Jacksonville, Fla., last week was another victory for nonpartisanship, and showed that Mugwumpism is growing in the South as well as in the West.

+**Mulada.** *S.W.* [Mex. Sp. f. *mulo* 'a mule.'] A drove or caballada of mules. — [**1847** RUXTON *Adv. Rocky Mts.* (1848) 154 A caballero . . . invited me to take up my quarters with him for the night, and place the mulada in his stables.] **1858** *Texas Almanac 1859* 143 We keep a mulada at Fort Yuma for our changes. **1902** CLAPIN 282 *Mulada,* . . . in Texas, a drove or herd of mules.

∗Mulatto. Also †**malatta, melatto,** etc. A person who is the offspring of a Negro and a white person; a Negro with some white blood.

1658 in Neill *Virginia Carolorum* (1886) 365*n.*, Two mulattoes offered to go rather than remain eternally in prison. **1692** SEWALL *Diary* I. 366 The Court of Oyer and Terminer is opened at Boston to trie a French Malatta for shooting dead an English youth. **1722** *Boston Rec.* 170 [The selectmen shall] take Espesial care to keep the Indians, Negroes, & Melattoes in Good Order, and Se that the Province Law Respecting them be Attended. **1796** *Ann. 4th Congress* 2 Sess. 2694 Free negroes, mulattoes, and mestizoes, [are taxed] at nine shillings and four pence per head. **1831** PECK *Guide* 72 The number of mulattoes seen in every direction, is a melancholy proof of the irregularities that prevail. **1877** JOHNSON *Anderson Co., Kansas* 36 On the proposition in the constitution, for the expulsion of negroes and mulattoes, there were 25 votes for and 18 against. **1884** 'MARK TWAIN' *H. Finn* vi. 43 There was a free nigger there from Ohio—a mulatter, most as white as a white man. **1890** HARTE *Heritage of Dedlow Marsh* 14 Six years ago Boone Culpepper had . . . brought to it his wife—variously believed to be a gypsy, a Mexican, a bright mulatto, a Digger Indian.

Mulatto. Also †**molatto.** *attrib.* and *adj.*

1. Designating persons of mixed Negro and white blood. {*a*1704–}

See also MULATTO MAN, SERVANT, etc.

1707 in Sheldon *Hist. Deerfield, Mass.* I. 341 To pay for the Redemption of a molatto Captive, . . . 40 pieces of 8s, 8d. **1759** *Newport Mercury* 9 Oct. 3/3 Run away, . . . a Molatto Man Slave, 36 Years of Age. **1779** *N.J. Archives* 2 Ser. III. 530 Ran away from the subscriber, . . . a likely, stout Mulatto lad, . . . American born. *c***1822** in Claiborne *Life Quitman* I. 77 Does every master keep his mulatto concubine, and his harem of darkies? **1852** in Stowe *Key* 177/2 Ran Away . . . , a Dark Mulatto Girl. **1883** *Century Mag.* Nov. 130/2 Our party consisted of Mrs. Davis, Miss Howell . . . , the four children, Ellen (the mulatto maid-servant), and James Jones (the mulatto coachman). **1897** HOWELLS *Open-eyed Conspiracy* xi, There were some mulatto ladies present as stylish as their white sisters, or step-sisters.

+2. Designating soils of a brownish color. Also absol.

See also MULATTO LAND, MULATTO SOIL.

1788 JEFFERSON *Writings* XVII. 260 The soil [is] a barren mulatto clay, mixed with a good deal of stone, and some slate. **1837** WILLIAMS *Florida* 82 The surface is covered with a mulatto or chocolate colored loam. **1858** *Texas Almanac 1859* 65 The mulatto or copper colored prairies are more kindly and easily cultivated. **1869** *Overland Mo.* III. 130 There is the 'chocolate' prairie, and the 'mulatto,' and the 'mezquite,' . . . and the 'hummock,' (yielding principally small honey-locusts). **1883** SMITH *Geol. Survey Ala.* 371 The lowlands of the . . . Terrapin and other creeks, embrace a small proportion of black alluvial soil and close mulatto and coarse white sand.

+Mulatto land. =MULATTO SOIL. (Cf. MULATTO *attrib.* 2.) — **1741** in *Amer. Sp.* XV. 287/2 A Tract of rich Mulattoe Land, lying in that County. **1784** SMYTH *Tour* I. 77 There is some very good land on this river, both low grounds and high; it is what is called mulattoe land by the planters, from its colour. **1789** MORSE *Amer. Geog.* 447 The mulatto lands are generally strong and yield large crops. **1827** SHERWOOD *Gaz. Georgia* 86 Its soil, the real mulatto land, is very rich in its virgin state. **1883** SMITH *Geol. Survey Ala.* 435 The red or mulatto lands are much the best for cotton.

Mulatto man. A servant of mixed Negro and white blood. — **1711** *Boston News-Letter* 11 June 2/2 Ran-away from William Gardner of Kingstown in the Colony of Rhode-Island . . . a Molatto Man of middle stature. **1719** *Amer. Wkly. Mercury* 29 Dec. 2/2 Run away. . . . A Mallato Man named Johney, but of a very White Complexion. **1831** *Georgian* (Savannah) 5 April 3/3 For Sale, A Bright Mulatto Man. **1866** 'F. KIRKLAND' *Bk. Anecdotes* 305 A mulatto man, who was a servant of one of the officers of the Union forces, was brought.

Mulatto servant. A servant or slave of mixed Negro and white blood. — **1677** *New Castle Court Rec.* 91 The Pl[ain]t[iff] declares as p[e]r declaration for the upholding & detayning of this pl[ain]t[iff]s molatto servant In Maryland, demands for damage 3000 lb of tobacco. **1705** *Boston News-Letter* 3 Sept. 2/2 The several Constables . . . to walk the Streets . . . after 9 at Night, . . . to see if after that time, any Indian, Negro or Molatto Servant or Slave is found abroad, unless upon some Errand of their Masters. **1739** W. STEPHENS *Proc. Georgia* 344 His most visible Foible, was keeping a Mulatto Servant (or Slave).

+Mulatto slave. A slave of mixed Negro and white blood. — **1705** *Boston News-Letter* 25 June 2/2 It will be necessary to pass an Act . . . to punish Negro, Indian and Mallatto Slaves, and to prevent them from running away. **1738** *Va. Gazette* 22 Sept., Ran away . . . Mulatto Slave. . . . Had on an old Felt Hat. **1839** *Diplom. Corr. Texas* III. (1911) 1260 No negro or mulatto slave, can be brought into Texas except from the United States and North America.

+Mulatto soil. Brownish-colored, fertile land.

Cf. MULATTO *attrib.* 2 and MULATTO LAND.

1789 MORSE *Amer. Geog.* 447 It changes into what is called the mulatto soil, consisting of a black mould and red earth. **1819** E. DANA *Geogr. Sk.* 190 A skirt of rich pine land, dark mulatto soil, with hickory. **1861** *Ill. Agric. Soc. Trans.* IV. 112 [He] would not choose the dark prairie mold, but that kind of soil best known in the west as the 'mulatto soil.' **1883** SMITH *Geol. Survey Ala.* 417 The mulatto soils of this formation are much the best.

Mulatto woman. A woman of mixed Negro and white blood. — **1674** ALVORD & BIDGOOD *Trans-Allegheny Region* 214 They have two Mullatto women. **1852** EASTMAN *Aunt Phillis's Cabin* 102 She is a tall, dignified, bright mulatto woman, named Phillis. **1907** ANDREWS *Recoll.* 104 They got for me an experienced [nurse], . . . a married mulatto woman.

+Mulattress. A female mulatto. {1845} — **1805** *Amer. Pioneer* II. 234 The chief of the audience is formed of mulattresses and negresses. **1873** STOWE *Palmetto Leaves* 23 Our handmaiden, a pretty, young mulatress, occasionally brings to us a whole dish of roses. **1889** CABLE in *Century Mag.* Jan. 367/2, 'I will come to see you, Celeste,' replied Alix to the young mulattress.

∗Mulberry.

∗1. Any tree of the genus *Morus* or its fruit.

Native American species include the red mulberry (*M. rubra*) and the Mexican mulberry (*M. microphylla*). The former is sometimes called the black or Virginian mulberry. The white mulberry (*M. alba*), widely introduced into the United States, is perfectly naturalized in many localities. (See BLACK, ITALIAN, RED, etc., MULBERRY.)

1607 in Smith *Works* (1910) I. p. xlii, Now they had gotten mulberyes, little sweete nuttes like Acorns . . . , wheate, beanes and mulberyes sodd together and gave vs. **1685** BUDD *Penna. & N.J.* 31 Fruits that grow natural in the Countries are Strawberries, . . . Mulberies [etc.]. **1705** BEVERLEY *Virginia* II. 15 Our Mulberries are of Three sorts, two Black and one White; the long Black sort are the best. **1781–2** JEFFERSON *Notes Va.* (1788) 40 The silk-worm is a native, and the mulberry, proper for its food, grows kindly. **1839** PLUMBE *Sk. Iowa* 97 In 1837, the writer introduced the mulberry and sugar beet into Du Buque county [Wis.]. **1897** *McClure's Mag.* X. 161, I frequently met soldiers coming into camp with buckets full of mulberries, blackberries, and red and yellow wild plums. **1910** *Dept. Agric. Yrbk. 1909* 193 Foremost in attractiveness to birds among cultivated fruit-bearing plants are mulberries.

+2. *local.* Any of various American raspberries or blackberries of the genus *Rubus*.

1672 JOSSELYN *New Eng. Rarities* 93 Raspberry, here called Mulberry. **1832** WILLIAMSON *Maine* I. 114 High bush Blackberry is sometimes called '*Mulberry.*' *Rubus villosus.* **1892** *Amer. Folk-Lore* V. 95 *Rubus triflorus*, mulberry. Washington Co., Me.; N.B.

3. *attrib.* and *comb.* **a.** In sense 1 with *mania, orchard, timber, wood.*

1743 *Md. Hist. Mag.* XX. 373 In case he will putt Mulberry Timbers in I will give him five Pounds more. **1817** S. BROWN *Western Gaz.* 126 The sandy and most sterile soil . . . is very useful for the cultivation of peach and mulberry orchards. **1823** JAMES *Exped.* I. 89 The boat's crew were employed in taking on board a supply of dry mulberry wood. **1839** *S. Lit. Messenger* V. 115/2 If the mulberry mania should continue, we may have silk-worms fed on that . . . land.

b. In the names of insects.

1854 EMMONS *Agric. N.Y.* V. 262 (Index), Mulberry beetles, 93. [93. In Italy, the branches of the *Morus multicaulis* are perforated by the *Apate sexdentata.*] **1862** *Rep. Comm. Patents 1861: Agric.* 614 The mulberry tree in Pennsylvania has an enemy in . . . *Dorcaschema wildii*, (Uhler,) or 'mulberry borer.' **1909** *Cent. Suppl.* 836/3 *Mulberry-wing*, an American hesperiid butterfly, *Poanes massasoit*, occurring in the eastern and middle United States, Texas, Nebraska, and Colorado.

∗Mulberry tree. A tree of the genus *Morus*: (see MULBERRY 1, note).

1612 SMITH *Virginia* 11 By the dwelling of the Savages are some great Mulberry trees; and in some parts of the Countrey they are found growing naturally in prettie groues. **1619** *Va. House of Burgesses* 10 About the Plantation of Mulberry trees be it enacted that every man, . . . doe for seven yeares together every yeare plante & maintaine in growth sixe Mulberry trees at the least. **1671** in Neill *Virginia Carolorum* 334 We have begun to make silk, and . . . many mulberry trees are planted. **1724** H. JONES *Virginia* 60 Mulberry Trees and Silkworms thrive there to Admiration. **1787** SARGENT in *Mem. Academy* II. I. 159 Mulberry Trees, growing on bottoms and rich uplands, eighteen inches diameter. **1838** C. NEWELL *Revol. Texas* 168 The mulberry tree grows remarkably well in the West of Texas. **1872** MCCLELLAN *Golden State* 340 The mulberry tree, upon the leaves of which the silk-worm feeds, grows in every county in California. **1901** ROBERTSON *Inlander* 126 The mulberry-tree beyond the elm was hung with pink fruit.

∗Mule.

I. ∗1. The offspring of an ass and a horse, usually of a jack and a mare.

1738 BYRD *Dividing Line* (1901) 197 Horses are very improper animals to use in a long Ramble into the Woods. . . . I should much rather recommend Mules. **1787** WASHINGTON *Diaries* III. 277 In one [plow] I put the She Mule which worked very well. The horse Mule is intended also for this Plantation. **1796** *Ann. 4th Congress* 2 Sess. 2686 The tax on horses and mules is estimated to have produced, $15,154.95. **1831** PECK *Guide* 166 Mules are brought into Missouri, and find their way to Illinois, from the Mexican dominions. **1836** HOLLEY *Texas* 98 Mingled with the herds of mustangs are often found jacks, jennies, and mules. **1844** GREGG *Commerce of Prairies* I. 179 Mules [are] . . . to the Mexican, . . . invaluable for the transportation of freight. **1864** CUMMING *Hospital Life* (1866) 127/1, I have been told that nearly all of the mules and carriage horses at the wedding were taken by an impressing officer. **1898** *Boston Transcript* 26 Nov. 26/1 The 'croppers' work the land on shares, . . . but Mr. Summerall furnishes farming implements, fertilizer, horses or mules. **1912** COBB *Back Home* 104 The black draymen . . . would whirl their mules down the levee at a perilous gallop.

2. A machine for spinning cotton, wool, etc., invented by S. Crompton in 1779. {1797–}

1796 WANSEY *Excursion U.S.* 84 [In N.Y.] they have the machine called the mule, at which they have spun cotton yarn. **1847** *Rep. Comm. Patents 1846* 69 Letters patent have been granted this year for an improved self-acting mule. **1888** *Boston Jrnl.* 22 Dec. 4/1 Edward Hayes was caught in a mule at one of the mills in Lewiston on Tuesday and badly crushed about the leg.

+**3.** (See quotation.) *slang. Obs.*

1842 BUCKINGHAM *Slave States* I. 240 The first offspring of this young mother, produced after seven months' gestation, was 'a mule!' . . . This was a cant phrase [in Ga.] to denote a 'coloured child.'

+**4.** A tractor or locomotive for towing canal boats.

1903 *Elect. World & Engineer* 14 Nov. 795/2 The 'electric mule' . . is a vehicle closely resembling a 'hog-back' mine locomotive.

II. *attrib.* and *comb.* **5.** Designating various paths or routes over which mules travel.

1834 A. PIKE *Sketches* 25 They would find a mule-path leading from the ford of the Canadian. **1849** LANMAN *Alleghany Mts.* 58 The distance from Hubbard's Cabin . . . in a direct line, is eight miles, but by the ordinary mule-route it is thirteen. **1850** TYSON *Diary in Calif.* 24 [Down] the only pass . . . was a narrow mule-way. **1880** 'MARK TWAIN' *Tramp Abroad* 445 We followed the mule-road, a zigzag course, now to the right, now to the left, but always up.

6. Designating various vehicles or loads drawn or carried by mules.

1847 PARKMAN in *Knickerb.* XXX. 228 Our little mule-cart was but ill-fitted for the passage of so swift a stream. **1849** *N.Y. Ev. Express* 17 Feb. 1/6 The conveyances used [on the route from Vera Cruz to Cal.] were generally mule stages. **1888** BILLINGS *Hardtack* 315 Another invention for the transportation of the wounded from the field was the *Cacolet* or *Mule Litter.* **1900** STOCKTON *Afield & Afloat* 53 Slowly the mule-car trundled along the shaded avenue. **1911** QUICK *Yellowstone Nights* 309 A puncher . . . scooted through the British aristocracy, . . . on the strength of a gold prospect an' the diamond hitch to a mule-pack.

7. Designating various trappings, instruments, etc., used in connection with mules.

1848 BRYANT *California* viii. 122 The ground is so hard that it is with difficulty that we can force our mule-pickets into it. **1849** AUDUBON *Western Journal* 48 February 19th was spent in running all over New Orleans, ordering horse and mule shoes. **1884** CABLE *Dr. Sevier* lviii, The stillness yields to . . . the tinkle of a mule-bell where in the distance the softly rumbling street-car invites one to the center of the town's activities.

8. Designating various persons who handle mules.

1850 GARRARD *Wah-To-Yah* xxiv. 300 A faint cry . . . reached those nearest the muleguard, and by them it was repeated. **1867** in Custer *Tenting on Plains* (1887) 537 Teams of luggage, dogs, horsemen, mulemen, cross and recross at will. **1889** MUNROE *Golden Days* 279 [The] mule owners . . . were carrying freight at from thirty to fifty cents per pound. **1923** J. H. COOK *On Old Frontier* 153 One of these was Arthur Sparhawk, an expert cargador or mule-packer.

9. Designating various parts of a mule (sense 2).

1869 *Overland Mo.* III. 9 [Here] is a cotton-gin . . . and ponderous wooden wheels, and the mule-sweep underneath. **1874** KNIGHT 824/2 The faller is an arm on a mule-carriage, operating the faller-wire, whose duty it is to depress the yarns when the carriage is about to run back. **1891** CHASE & CLOW *Industry* II. 19 The mule frames move forward and draw out the thread.

+**Mule bear.** The grizzly bear. So called in the mistaken belief that he feasted on mules. *Obs.* — **1824** DODDRIDGE *Notes* 21 Being in the woods, he saw an old mule bear winding along after him.

Mule bird. {1768} + ?A kind of field sparrow. — **1867** MELINE *Santa Fé & Back* 8 The road is alive with the mule-bird, whip-poor-will, doves, plover, and meadow lark.

+**Mule cavalry.** During the Civil War, a jocular name for the mounted infantry (q.v.). — **1862** MOORE *Rebellion Rec.* V. II. 599 The mounted infantry, or 'mule cavalry,' proved an entire success. . . . They move with the celerity of cavalry, yet fight as infantry.

Mule colt. A young mule. — **1788** WASHINGTON *Diaries* III. 400 Turned . . . the two yearling Mule Colts . . . into the Clover Paddock. **1856** *Rep. Comm. Patents 1855: Agric.* 40 At weaning time, breeders generally sell their mule colts to men who buy up lots every fall for raising. **1885** *Rep. Indian Affairs* 11 The increase has been 8 horse and mule colts, 50 calves, and 150 pigs.

+**Mule deer.** A long-eared deer of the West, *Odocoileus hemionus*, syn. *Cariacus macrotis.* (See BLACK-TAILED *a.* 1.) — **1805** LEWIS in *L. & Clark Exped.* II. (1904) 21 With the mule deer the horns consist of two beams. **1814** BRACKENRIDGE *Views La.* 57 The black tailed, or mule deer; remarkable for very long ears, and tails almost without hair. **1872** MCCLELLAN *Golden State* 241 There are several varieties: the mule-deer, black-tail, antelope, and white-tail. **1893** ROOSEVELT *Wilderness Hunter* 16 The common blacktail or mule deer, which has likewise been sadly thinned in numbers, . . . extends from the great plains to the Pacific.

+**Mule-driver. a.** A teamster who drives a mule team. **b.** One of the drivers of a caballada of pack mules. — **1862** in Brewster *Life J. D. Whitney* 215 Averill acts as mule-driver, commissary, barometrical observer, etc. **1882** *Wheelman* I. 176 The caution . . . administered to me . . . by a mule-driver, whose aspect was as uncouth and forbidding as that of the ideal tramp. **1888** BILLINGS *Hardtack* 294 Another soldier, a mule-driver, remembers of seeing a mule-team which had run off the corduroy road into a mire of quicksand. **1909** 'O. HENRY' *Roads of Destiny* 192 He had been mule-driver, cowboy, ranger, soldier, sheriff, prospector, and cattleman.

+**Mule-killer. 1.** *W.* (See quot. 1847.) **2.** Chiefly *S.* Any of several arthropods supposed to kill stock by their stinging. — **(1) 1847** PARKMAN in *Knickerb.* XXIX. 161 Almost hidden in this medley, one might have seen a small French cart, of the sort very appropriately called a 'mule-killer.' **1852** *Fla. Plantation Rec.* 67, I would call the New Waggon a nother Mule killer. **(2) 1890** *Cent.* 3890/3 *Mule-killer,* . . . the whip-tailed scorpion, *Thelyphonus giganteus.* Also called *nigger-killer* and *grampus.* (Florida.) **1899** *Animal & Plant Lore* 63 Mule-killer, devil's war-horse, praying mantis. *Kansas.*

+**Mule load.** A load of a size and weight that a mule is able to carry. — **1808** PIKE *Sources Miss.* III. App. 4 There are taken, to be coined, 100 mule-loads of bullion in gold and silver monthly. **1846** SAGE *Scenes Rocky Mts.* xxi, Wood too, being two *rials* (25 cents) per mule-load. **1880** 'MARK TWAIN' *Tramp Abroad* 491 We had plenty of company, in the way of wagon-loads and mule-loads of tourists—and dust.

+**Mule meat.** The flesh of a mule used as food. — **1846** SAGE *Scenes Rocky Mts.* xxx, We ended our fast of nearly seven days' continuance with a feast of mule meat. **1863** in *Century Mag.* XXX. 771/2 Rice and milk is my main food; I can't eat the mule-meat. **1891** *Ib.* March 774 We made our Christmas and New Year's dinner on mule meat.

+**Mule rabbit.** (See quotation.) — **1859** BARTLETT 218 Jackass Rabbit (*Lepus callotis*) . . . is known also by the names of Mule Rabbit, Texan Hare, and Black-tailed Hare.

+**Mule-skinner. 1.** *W.* A mule driver; a freighter who drives with mules. **2.** A long whip for driving mules. — **(1) 1870** BEADLE *Utah* 224, I took to the plains with the train . . . in the capacity of a 'mule-skinner.' **1888** *Century Mag.* Feb. 499 These prairie schooners usually go together, the brawny teamsters, known either as 'bull-whackers' or as 'mule-skinners,' stalking beside their slow-moving teams. **1896** SHINN *Story of Mine* 167 The fine old silver freighter, in Nevada slang the mule-skinner, [and] the bull-puncher, . . . went their ways into the unrailroaded distance. **1910** RAINE *B. O'Connor* 217 Mule-skinners freighted supplies in to feed Uncle Sam's pets. **(2) 1912** WASON *Friar Tuck* 58 He would stand up an' yell, crack his mule-skinner, and send the ponies along on a dead run.

Mule spinner. A workman who operates a mule or spinning jenny. {1835–} — **1814** *Niles' Reg.* VI. 199/2 The mule spinners alone will do more work extra in the time saved from snuffing candles, than will pay the whole expense of light for the factory. **1866** in Persons, etc. *Mass. Labor Laws* (1911) 111 The mule spinners of New England . . . will not work more than ten hours per day or sixty per week. **1890** *Boston Jrnl.* 11 Feb. 4/7 A committee from the mule-spinners of the Nashua Corporation claim that their position has been misrepresented. **1911** PERSONS, etc. *Mass. Labor Laws* 91 The mule spinners struck for higher wages.

Mule team. A team of mules. — **1846** MAGOFFIN *Down Santa Fé Trail* 25 His mule team (some eighteen or twenty) were . . . passing the little wet creek. **1885** *Century Mag.* Sept. 762 Thirty wagons also, counting two two-horse or mule teams as one, will be allowed to transport such articles as cannot be carried along. **1904** GLASGOW *Deliverance* 7 Zebbadee Blake passed me yestiddy drivin' his own mule-team.

***Muleteer.** A driver of mules, +esp. one who helps drive a mule train. — **1843** FARNHAM *Travels* I. 3 A Mexican Spaniard, as chief muleteer, mounts the right-hand wheel mule. **1844** GREGG *Commerce of Prairies* I. 182 The *Arrieros*, or muleteers, harness and adjust the packs of merchandise upon their beasts. **1858** PETERS *Kit Carson* 380 The muleteers, as they walked beside their teams, . . . held in one hand their rifles, while in the other were their whips. **1872** MCCLELLAN *Golden State* 48 Companies of soldiers, with muleteers, herds, and flocks, were to proceed overland from Lower California. **1891** *Century Mag.* March 779 Having hired muleteers and a train of mules, . . . we set out for Santa Fé.

+**Muleteering.** The action of freighting goods with mules. — **1847** RUXTON *Adv. Rocky Mts.* (1848) 183 Muleteering is the natural occupation of the Mexican.

+**Mule train. a.** A train of wagons drawn by mules. **b.** A train of pack mules.

1866 *Rep. Indian Affairs* 125 The goods for the coming year [forwarded] by early mule trains . . . reached this point early in September. **1869** BROWNE *Adv. Apache Country* 268 The fresh tracks of mule-trains and wagon-wheels . . . showed how profitable this sort of enterprise must be to the Sonoranians. **1873** *Newton Kansan* 12 June 1/1 The people were gathered at the express and post-offices to await the arrival of the semi-weekly mule-train. **1876** *Congress. Rec.* 19 June 3885/2 Those expeditions are accompanied by immense wagon-trains, and by mule-trains carrying provisions. **1910** J. HART *Vigilante Girl* 123 He stood . . . looking beyond the moving mass of coaches, freight-wagons, and mule-trains.

+**Mule wagon.** A heavy-built freight wagon drawn by mules. — **1847** PARKMAN in *Knickerb.* XXX. 229 Seeing the mule-wagon wheeling from the track, he began to turn his own team in the same direction. **1854**

Harper's Mag. April 589/1 He was seated upon the driver's box of a heavy mule-wagon. **1873** *Newton Kansan* 12 June 2/1 Seventeen Modoc captives . . . were murdered . . . while the captives were being conveyed south in a mule wagon. **1885** CUSTER *Boots & Saddles* 66 It seemed to me preferable to die from accident, surrounded with friends, than to expire alone in the mule-wagon.

+**Mule-whacker.** =MULE-DRIVER. — **1873** BEADLE *Undevel. West* 88 The streets were thronged with motley crowds of railroad men . . . and mulewhackers. **1888** *Century Mag.* Nov. 159/2 Ah! you called him 'mule-whacker.' **1889** O'REILLY *50 Years on Trail* 357 The town was full of cow-punchers, mule-whackers [etc.].

∗**Muley.**

∗**1.** A cow; +spec., a hornless cow or ox. Also fig.

Cf. MOOLEY, MULEY COW.

1838 *N.Y. Advertiser & Exp.* 24 Feb. 4/1 Mr. Van Buren has quieted the *Wolves* and the *Muleys* in Pennsylvania, after the manner he quieted the scramblers for the Collectorship of New York. **1852** *Mich. Agric. Soc. Trans.* IV. 67 No. 305. James Smith, Detroit, muleys entered as one year old, but are poor in quality. **1903** A. ADAMS *Log Cowboy* ii. 25 There were a number of muleys among the cattle. **1913** BARNES *Western Grazing Grounds* 180 Bulls should not be dehorned so close as to make them muleys, as they need their horns as a means of defense against steers or stags.

attrib. **1903** A. ADAMS *Log. Cowboy* vi. 83 That muley steer, the white four year old, didn't like to bed down amongst the others.

+**2.** =MULEY SAW. Also attrib.

1864 WEBSTER 865/3 *Muley*, a stiff, long saw, not stretched in a gate, and moved much more rapidly than an ordinary gate-saw. **1875** Muley head [see MULEY SAW]. **1883** *Harper's Mag.* Jan. 208/2 If the log is of large size, it is sent at once against a 'muley,' or straight rip-saw, working perpendicularly, which splits it in two. **1887** *Courier-Journal* 22 Jan. 4/3 Sawyer goes to the Senate again from Wisconsin. Sawyer doesn't cut his logs with a muley.

Muley cow. Also **mulley cow.** =MULEY 1. {moiley coo, 1824–, *dial.*}

1848 BARTLETT 230 *Mulley cow*, a name used for a cow chiefly among children, or by parents when speaking to children. **1861** *N.Y. Tribune* 14 Aug. 3/3 [The hippopotamus] is no more vicious than a good-natured muley cow. **1867** HARRIS *Sut Lovingood* 178 Like ontu a white faced muley cow. **1872** POWERS *Afoot & Alone* 115 P'raps you mout 'a seen a red mulley cow somewhar. **1893** CURTIS *Horses, Cattle* 201 The best 'muley,' or polled cows were selected from among the common or native herds in the central-western and Mississippi Valley portions of the United States. **1907** WHITE *Arizona Nights* 132 In comes a little Irishman . . . with more upper lip than a muley cow.

+**Muley saw.** (See quot. 1875.) Also attrib. — **1852** *Mich. Agric. Soc. Trans.* III. 487, 1 reaction water wheel and mully saw gearing. **1871** *Rep. Comm. Patents 1869* II. 165/2 Muley-Saw Mill. . . . The inclined guides D [etc.]. **1875** KNIGHT 1495/2 *Muley-saw*, a mill-saw . . . which is not strained in a *gate* or *sash*, but has a more rapid reciprocating motion, and has guide-carriages above and below, called *muley-heads*. **1881** *Hist. Washington Co.* (Minn.) 196/2 May 13th, 1839, [a group of men] began work . . . , and in the fall of the same year, started their muley saw, thus becoming the pioneers in lumber in the St. Croix Valley.

Mull, *n.* A thin plain cotton fabric. {1798–} — **1810** *Columbian Centinel* 27 Jan. 4/4 Plain mull and cob-webb Muslins . . . are for sale. **1897** *Outing* XXX. 377/1 It is not a bad plan to take a few yards of Swiss mull, in case insects prove troublesome.

Mull, *v.* [Perhaps fig. application of ∗*mull* v. 'to pulverize, grind, squeeze.'] +**a.** *tr.* To think (a thing) *over;* to consider (a subject) thoroughly. +**b.** (See quot. 1879). — **1873** FISKE in J. S. Clark *Life John Fiske* I. 488 [Huxley] hopes I will add the chapter on 'Matter and Spirit' which I have been mulling for a year back. **1879** WEBSTER *Suppl.* 1568/3 *Mull*, . . . to work steadily without accomplishing much. **1907** *Chicago Tribune* 8 May 8 Mr. Bonaparte has been mulling over the constitution, and it is no secret he discovered grave objections to many of its provisions. **1920** LEWIS *Main Street* 444, I like a little privacy and mulling things over by myself.

∗**Mullein.** Any plant of the genus *Verbascum*, esp. the common mullein, *V. thapsus.*

See also MULLEN and cf. MOTH MULLEIN.

1709 LAWSON *Carolina* 78 Harts-Tongue; Yarrow abundance, Mullein the same, both of the Country. **1802** DRAYTON *S. Carolina* 63 Hoary white and red flowered mullein. (*Verbascum lychnitis.*) Grows in sandy pine land; blossoms in May and June. **1814** BIGELOW *Florula Bostoniensis* 52 *Verbascum Thapsus.* Common Mullein. . . . Every body knows this tall, woolly, and very common plant. **1863** MITCHELL *My Farm* 139 Here and there [was] a mullein lifting its yellow head, and domineering over the lesser wild growth. **1911** STRATTON-PORTER *Harvester* 5, I remain at home to harvest the golden seal, mullein, and ginseng.

attrib. **1846** in Emory *Milit. Reconn.* 386 The meadow lark, [was] perched on some tall mullein weed. **1854** SHILLABER *Mrs. Partington* 41 Mullein-stalks . . . grow rankly by the gate. **1886** *Harper's Mag.* Nov. 879/2 A vesper song from a mullein-top.

+**Mullein foxglove.** An American herb: (see quotation). — **1857** GRAY *Botany* 292 *S[eymeria] macrophylla.* (Mullein-Foxglove.) . . . Shady river-banks, Ohio, Illinois, and southwestward.

Mullein pink. The rose campion, *Lychnis coronaria.* — **1840** DEWEY *Mass. Flowering Plants* 87 *Agrostemma coronaria.* Mullein Pink. Named from its woolly leaves, bearing white or red flowers, . . . a native of Italy. **1850** S. F. COOPER *Rural Hours* 108 Thus the corn-cockle bears a fine flower, not unlike the mullein-pink of the garden.

+**Mullein tea.** A tea made from the leaves of mullein. — **1887** HARRIS in *Century Mag.* Aug. 551/2 She sent me word to make me some mullein tea. **1905** PRINGLE *Rice Planter* 275 Ruth's leg and foot . . . must be bathed twice a day with hot mullein tea and then rubbed dry.

∗**Mullen.** =MULLEIN. Also attrib. Chiefly U.S.

1778 CARVER *Travels* 515 *Herbs.* . . . Wake Robin, Betony, Scabious, Mullen, Wild Pease [etc.]. **1832** KENNEDY *Swallow Barn* II. 213 The tall and beautiful mullen . . . [is] almost the first plant that puts forth in the spring. **1856** A. CARY *Married* 260 We found ourselves in a green, quiet lane, bordered with . . . gray mullen stalks, all starry with flowers. **1897** BRODHEAD *Bound in Shallows* 193 A small herd of common cattle was . . . cropping the bearded blade and nosing the scattered mullen.

+**b.** *To go to grass and eat mullen*, to go to the devil. (Cf. GRASS 3.)

1833 S. SMITH *Major Downing* 108 As for going to South Carolina to fight such chaps as these, I'd sooner let nullification go to grass and eat mullen.

∗**Muller.** *Mining.* +A stone or pestle used for pulverizing ore; a bucking iron. {1889} — **1869** BRACE *New West* 198 The great object of the 'muller,' or grinder, is to grind thoroughly the material, and to bring all the particles in contact with the quicksilver. **1872** 'MARK TWAIN' *Roughing It* xxxvi. 252 The mass of pulp in the pans was kept constantly stirred up by revolving 'mullers.' **1896** SHINN *Story of Mine* 80 Quartz that has been broken into small pieces by a sledge hammer is . . . ground to dust by the dragging of a large 'muller' or slab of granite over the quartz-covered pavement.

∗**Mullet. a.** Any fish of the family Mugilidae, as the striped mullet, *Mugil cephalus.* **b.** Any fish of the family Mullidae. +**c.** Any fish of the family Catostomidae, as the sucker. *colloq.*

1612 SMITH *Virginia* 15 Of fish we were best acquainted with . . . mullets, white Salmonds, Trowts, Soles, . . . Cocles, and Muscles. **1682** ASH *Carolina* 26 Mullet, a delicious sweet Fish, of whose Roes or Spawn Botargo is made. **1750** T. WALKER *Journal* 44 We saw Perch, Mullets, and Carp in plenty, and caught one of the large Sort of Cat Fish. **1799** ELLICOTT in Mathews *Life A. Ellicott* 186 A great abundance and variety of fish may be taken: such as . . . mullets, bone-fish, [and] amber-fish. **1808** ASHE *Travels* 282 The Mississippi yields turtle of a peculiar sort, . . . mullets, herring, carp [etc.]. **1839** STORER *Mass. Fishes* 84 [Suckers] are occasionally brought into the city by the cartload, and palmed off upon the ignorant, as the mullet. **1869** *Amer. Naturalist* III. 401 From the wharves [in Fla.], at the proper tide, many fish are caught, principally Sheep's-head . . . and Mullet. **1884** GOODE, etc. *Fisheries* I. 614 The common 'Red Horse' or 'Mullet' abounds in most streams westward and southward of New York. **1890** *Boston Jrnl.* 26 March, Two fishermen [at Tampa] ran into a lot of tarpons that were jumping and chasing mullet, and became . . . frightened.

+**Mullethead.** A flat-headed, fresh-water fish. — **1873** BEADLE *Undevel. West* 102 A fish called the mullet-head, . . . cannot be intoxicated by any amount of liquor. It can even swim in that fluid. **1893** FORBES-MITCHELL *Great Mutiny* vi. 110 That fish, my son, is called a mullet-head: it has got no brains.

+**Mullet-headed,** *a.* Stupid. — **1884** 'MARK TWAIN' *H. Finn* xxxix. 370 They're so confiding and mullet-headed they don't take notice of nothing at all.

+**Mullet sucker.** (See quotation.) — **1842** *Nat. Hist. N.Y., Zoology* IV. 201 The Mullet Sucker, *Catostomus aureolus*, . . . at Buffalo passes under the various names of Mullet, Golden Mullet, and Red Horse.

Mulley cow. Variant of MULEY COW.

+**Mulling.** Excitement, stir: (see quotation 1866). — **1845** JUDD *Margaret* I. 170 There has been a pooty consid'rable mullin goin on 'mong the doctors ever sen the Nommernisstortumbug come out. **1866** LOWELL *Biglow P.* 2 Ser. p. lvii, We have always heard *mulling* used for *stirring, bustling*, sometimes in an underhand way.

Mully saw. Variant of MULEY SAW.

+**Multicaulis.** [L., 'many-stemmed.'] A variety of white mulberry, grown esp. during the 1830's in expectation of making profits in the silk industry. *Obs.* Also attrib.

See also MORUS MULTICAULIS.

1833 *Niles' Reg.* XLIV. 332/2, I had the first opportunity of receiving from Paris, . . . three rooted trees of the Chinese multicaulis. **1840** *Knickerb.* XV. 508 Such fevers are exceedingly prevalent in this new country [near Pottsville, Pa.]. Now it is a township in Maine; . . . now coal, now multicaulis; and the soberest heads of the commonwealth have been demented under these influences. **1850** *Rep. Comm. Patents 1849: Agric.* 136 [He] who calculates on making general and sudden changes in national pursuits, will be the dupe of something like the multicaulis humbug. **1860** MORDECAI *Virginia* 294, I saw on one occasion a wagon load of multicaulis plants brought all the way from Tennessee.

+**Multicaulised,** *a.* (See quotation.) *slang. Obs.* — **1840** *Alexander's Wkly. Messenger* (Phila.) 27 May 1/5 New Word.—Multicaulised.—Run out—good for nothing—dished.

Multiflora. =next. {1852-} — **1852** STOWE *Uncle Tom* xiv, His poor, foolish heart would be turning backward to . . . the little cabin, overgrown with the multiflora and bignonia.

Multiflora rose. A garden rose derived from a Japanese species. — **1829** *Western Mo. Rev.* III. 57 It is literally embowered in vines of the multiflora rose. **1839** 'M. PENCIL' *White Sulphur P.* 82 A small arbor is covered with the multiflora rose and honey-suckle. **1890** *Harper's Mag.* Jan. 282/1 A multiflora rose, entangled with honeysuckle, clambered up the squat chimney.

+**Multimillionaire.** A person having two or more million dollars. Also attrib. — **1858** HOLMES *Autocrat* 288 The multi-millionaires sent him a trifle, it was said, to buy another eye with. **1879** RANOUS *Diary of Daly Débutante* 103 Hart Conway . . . has some curious Spanish music in his character of Don Jannario Something-or-other, a Brazilian planter and multi-millionaire. **1893** *Advance* 3 Aug., On a salary of $5,000 per annum, [the Congressman] has become the multi-millionaire owner of a marble palace. **1906** LYNDE *Quickening* 176 It had been his good fortune . . . to have gained . . . a speaking acquaintance with the multimillionaire iron king.

Multiplication.* +*Multiplication, Division, and Silence*, (see quotation). — **1885 *Mag. Amer. Hist.* March 296/2 *Multiplication, Division, and Silence.*—Ascribed to William M. Tweed (*circa* 1872), as his definition of the proper qualifications of a contractor, under the administration of the 'Ring.'

Mumble-the-peg. Also **mumble-peg, mumblety-peg.** A boys' game in which the players try to throw a knife from a series of positions in such a way as to make the blade stick in the ground. {1627-}

The name is derived from the penalty, originally imposed on an unsuccessful player, of drawing out with the teeth a peg or pin driven into the ground by the others.

1845 JUDD *Margaret* I. 130 Two boys sat . . . playing mumble-the-peg. **1863** *Rio Abajo Press* 30 June 1/3 You might see him two minutes after one of these skin-flaying operations . . . playing marbles, or mumble the peg, with the first scaramouch he met. **1882** SWEET & KNOX *Texas Siftings* 75 When other boys were engaged in mumble-peg and leap-frog pursuits, he was absorbed with division [etc.]. **1920** LEWIS *Main Street* 147 While you're playing mumblety-peg with Mrs. Lym Cass, Pete and me will be rambling across Dakota.

+**Mumchimmee.** ?=next. — **1807** *Mass. H. S. Coll.* 2 Ser. III. 57 The mumchimmee, a small fish, four or five inches long, resembling an eel in shape, is caught in summer.

+**Mummichog.** Also **mummychog, mummachog.** [Narraganset: '*Moamitteaūg*, A little sort of fish' (1643 Williams *Key* 141).] A name applied in the East to various killifishes.

1787 PENNANT *Arctic Zoology Suppl.* 149 Inhabits New York, where it is known by the Indian name of Mummy Chog. **1842** *Nat. Hist. N.Y., Zoology* IV. 219 [To] the Barred Killifish, *Fundulus zebra*, . . . is applied the indian name of Mummachog. **1883** *Nat. Museum Bul.* No. 27, 451 *Fundulus majalis*. . . . Mummichog. . . . Atlantic coast of the United States. **1911** *Rep. Fisheries 1908* 312 Mummichog (*Poeciliidae*).—These fish are found in the brackish waters along the Atlantic, Pacific, and Gulf coasts.

Mummy-cloth. Also **momie-cloth.** {1843-} +**a.** A modern fabric used especially as a base for embroidery, made in imitation of the cloths used by the Egyptians for wrapping mummies. +**b.** (See quot. 1890.) — **1881** *Art Interchange* (N.Y.) 27 Oct. 93 Mantel scarfs . . . could be of . . . cretonne, momie cloth, plush [etc.]. **1887** *49th Congress 2 Sess.* H. R. Mis. Doc. No. 170, II. 652/2 [Textile fibers and fabrics in the U.S. National Museum include] Mummy cloth. **1890** *Cent.* 3897/3 *Mummy-cloth*, . . . a fabric resembling crape, having the warp of either cotton or silk and the weft of woolen: used for mourning when black on account of its lusterless surface.

+**Mum social.** A party at which everyone tries to keep silent until a certain hour. — **1883** RITTENHOUSE *Maud* 253 Thursday night was the sociable here—a 'mum social'. I found the silence appalling and flew for refuge to my room, where I wrote poetry till Mr Davenport walked me down.

+**Mung news.** False or out-of-date news. *Obs.* — **1844** *Spirit of Times* (Phila.) 26 Sept. (Th.), Mung News [the heading of an item concerning news a year old]. **1849** *N.Y. Ev. Express* 17 Feb. 2/5 As there are many of our citizens who intend to go to California, who may possibly base their arrangements upon this kind of 'mung news,' we conceive it our duty to state, . . . that most of these letters are the silliest fictions.

Mungo. {1752-} ‖ *Brown mungo*, an animal similar in appearance to the mongoose of India. — **1806** LEWIS in *L. & Clark Exped.* IV. (1905) 185 This robe is made most commonly of the skins of a small animal which I have supposed was the brown Mungo.

+**Mungo bass.** ?=BLACK BASS 1. — **1832** WILLIAMSON *Maine* I. 158 *Mungo Bass* is both smaller and much better fish [than the bass];—fat and fine flavoured as a salmon.

***Municipal,** *a.* Pertaining to the corporate government of a town or city.

1822 *Ann. 17th Congress* 1 Sess. I. 70 The Federal judiciary has assumed guardianship over the States, even to the controlling of their peculiar municipal regulations. **1828** *Yankee* April 124/2 For the head of our municipal court . . . we want . . . a man of great energy of character. **1840** *Niles' Nat. Reg.* 26 Dec. 260 The Boston municipal election took place on the 14th inst. **1883** *Harper's Mag.* Sept. 610/1 The municipal debt . . . had risen to 698 millions. **1887** *Nation* 14 April 307/3 New York is better known . . . [for] municipal rings than for anything else. **1911** *Okla. Session Laws* 3 Legisl. 238 Any incorporated city or town . . . [may] exempt from municipal taxation . . . the personal property mentioned in section 1 of this act.

b. Designating persons or groups of persons authorized to act for, or employed by, a municipality.

1832 DUNLAP *Hist. Amer. Theatre* 128 The municipal authorities criminally suffered this nuisance to exist. **1857** *Harper's Mag.* Aug. 402/1 A larger number of the municipal police had been assembled in the hall, and a contest ensued. **1889** *Electrical Rev.* 26 Jan. 12 Any contract let hereunder will require the approval of the Municipal Assembly [of St. Louis] by ordinance. **1911** *Okla. Session Laws* 3 Legisl. 158 The books shall be opened to the inspection of any officer of this state, whether such an officer be a state, county, or municipal officer. **1921** F. M. TODD *Story of Exposition* V. 233 There was . . . music by the Municipal Chorus and the Municipal Band.

Municipal bond. A bond issued by a city or a local government. — **1870** MEDBERY *Men Wall St.* 9 Through these subtle influences, over even the municipal and county bonds, . . . the paramount money-mart exercised peculiar control. **1877** JOHNSON *Anderson Co., Kansas* 160 People . . . have adopted the system of aiding railroad companies in the construction of their roads by voting and issuing municipal bonds of the county.

+**Municipal corporation.** An incorporated town. — **1855** in Hambleton *H. A. Wise* 306 Let the States and your municipal corporations, pass such laws as they please. **1870** *Ill. Revised Statutes* 68 All municipal corporations may be vested with authority to assess and collect taxes. **1877** JOHNSON *Anderson Co., Kansas* 174 On the 7th day of October, 1861, Charles Hidden, probate judge of Anderson county, . . . declared the town of Garnett a municipal corporation.

Municipality.

1. A town, city, or district with the power of local self-government. {1790-}

1867 *Nation* IV. 434 Municipalities have a 'natural right' to govern themselves. **1877** *Penna. State Rep.* LXXXV. 411 This act concerns a municipality—a division of the state for governmental purposes. **1883** *Harper's Mag.* Sept. 611/2 The State should interfere with the municipalities through the exercise of its central authority. **1901** DUNCAN & SCOTT *Allen & Woodson Co., Kansas* 9 It was in the acts of this legislature . . . that Allen county first appears as a recognized municipality. **1911** *Okla. Session Laws* 3 Legisl. 183 [Any] contracts . . . shall not be charged against the municipality.

+**2.** In New Orleans between 1836 and 1852, any of the three districts into which the city was divided, each having a distinct local government.

1840 *Picayune* 8 Aug. 2/6 The Police Prison of the Second Municipality. **1883** *Century Mag.* June 222/1 The city boundaries had been extended to take in both these faubourgs; and the three 'municipalities,' as they were called, together numbered one hundred and two thousand inhabitants.

+**Municipality paper.** Certificates of indebtedness issued by one of the municipalities of New Orleans. — **1840** *Picayune* 28 July 1/4 A small Pocket-Book, containing $75 in city bank notes, $7 or $8 in Municipality paper, two $10 bills on the Canal Bank.

+**Municipal ownership.** The state or condition of ownership by a municipality, esp. of a public utility. — **1891** *Advance Club* (Providence, R.I.) *Leaflets* No. 1, 12 Mayor Sargent of New Haven recommended with powerful arguments in his inaugural, municipal ownership of electric lighting. **1899** E. W. BEMIS *Municipal Monopolies* 19 In the last six years the tide has set the other way, and municipal ownership [of waterworks] has been on the increase. **1906** *N. Amer. Rev.* June 855 Thoughtful citizens may well hesitate to favor the present Socialistic fad of municipal ownership. **1918** A. M. TODD *Municipal Ownership* 6 Our general judgment, considering the political and industrial conditions in this country, is in favor of municipal ownership.

***Murder.** (See DEGREE 2.)

***Murderer.** A small cannon. *Obs.* — **1622** in Arber *Story of Pilgrim Fathers* 507 He took away of the Owners, a Newshett cable, an anchor, two murderers with their chambers [etc.]. **1634** *Relation of Beginnings of Md.* 20 We haue built a strong Fort & Palizado, & haue mounted vpon it one good piece of Ordnance, and 4 Murderers. **1644** *Conn. Rec.* I. 267 George Fenwick Esqr doth . . . convey . . . one Murderer, with two chambrs, and two hammered peeces.

Murre. One of various guillemots. {1602-} — **1674** *Cal. State P., Amer. & W.I.* VII. 581 The islands and woods [of Maine] yield . . . brants, murrs, penguins, mallard, teal, and widgeon. **1844** *Nat. Hist. N.Y., Zoology* II. 279 The *Foolish Guillemot*, or *Murre*, is a northern species. **1917** *Birds of Amer.* I. 25 Murre. *Uria troille troille*. . . . Other Names.—Foolish Guillemot; Guillem, or Gwilym.

+**Murrelet.** Any of several small sea birds of the family Alcidae, found chiefly on the Pacific coast. — **1872** COUES *Key to Birds* 344 *Brachyrhamphus marmoratus*. . . . Marbled Guillemot, or Murrelet. **1887** RIDGWAY *Manual N.A. Birds* 15 Southern California to Cape St. Lucas. . . . *B[rachyramphus] hypoleucus*. . . . Xantus's Murrelet. **1917** *Birds of*

Amer. I. 22 Ancient Murrelet. *Synthliboramphus antiquus*. . . . Other Names.—Gray-headed Murrelet; Black-throated Murrelet. . . . *Ib.* 23/2 The Ancient Murrelet is another of the diving birds which fairly swarm on many of [the] islands along the southern coast of Alaska.

***Muscadine.** Also †**muskedine.** +The southern fox grape, *Muscadinia rotundifolia.*

In the earliest quots. 'fox grape' appears to mean the northern species.

*c***1785** SARAH PEARS *Narrative* (MS.) 4 Greenbrier berreys, honey locust pods, muskedines, a fruit like to fox graps [etc.]. **1800** HAWKINS *Sk. Creek Country* 24 In some of the rich flats there are fox grapes and muscadines. **1829** *Western Mo. Rev.* II. 523 The Muscadine of the south will prove equally valuable. **1847** DARLINGTON *Weeds & Plants* 84 Fox-Grape, of the Southern States; also called 'Muscadine,' and 'Bullet- or Bull-Grape.' **1885** M. THOMPSON *Byways & Bird Notes* 100 Along the banks of the streams of Georgia and South Carolina grows a grape, known by the musical name of muscadine. **1899** CUSHMAN *Hist. Indians* 484 [Autumn brought] prodigal abundance of hickory nuts of several varieties, walnuts, pecan[s], huckle berries, wild plums, persimmons, wild grapes, muscadines, all of excellent flavor.

Muscadine grape. {1611–} +=prec. — **1797** IMLAY *Western Territory* (ed. 3) 266 Muscadine grapes, of an amber colour, of a very good kind, and very sweet, have been found upon declivities of a good exposure, even so far north as lat. 31. **1837** WILLIAMS *Florida* 79 Muscadine grape. *Vitis rotundefolia*—heads of small streams, thick skin.

+**Muscallonge.** Also **muscalinga, muscalunge, muscalonge.** =MUSKELLUNGE.

1815 *Lit. & Phil. Soc. Trans. N.Y.* I. 496 The muscalinga, a species of pike, is greatly esteemed. **1857** HAMMOND *Northern Scenes* 43 He will be among the black bass, the pickerel, muscalunge, and striped bass, in the greatest abundance. **1893** *Outing* XXII. 160/1 'Twas the last vain plunge of a muscallonge As my boatman's gaff struck home. **1905** *Springfield W. Repub.* 1 Dec. 16 Three large muscalonges were caught in Moody's cove last week.

***Muscle.** Variant of MUSSEL.

1612 SMITH *Virginia* 15 Of fish we were best acquainted with . . . Crabs, Shrimps, Creuises, Oysters, Cocles, and Muscles. **1676** GLOVER *Va.* in *Phil. Trans.* XI. 625 There are also in some places great store of Muscles and Cockles. **1709** LAWSON *Carolina* 161 The Muscles in Carolina have a very large shell, striped with dents. **1791** J. LONG *Voyages* 46 Wampum is of several colours, but the white and black are chiefly used; the former is made of the inside of the conque or clam shell, the latter of the muscle. **1808** PIKE *Sources Miss.* 11 The two soldiers had been six days without anything to eat, except muscles. **1848** BRYANT *California* xvi. 208 In the bed of the stream we found large quantities of muscles. **1855** GLISAN *Jrnl. Army Life* 249 [The Indians near Port Orford, Washington Terr.] are also very fond of shell-fish, such as oysters, clams, muscles, etc.

b. Attrib. with *bank, bed, man,* etc.

1634 WOOD *New Eng. Prospect* (1865) 47 The Bay . . . will be all flatts for two miles together, upon which is great store of Muscle-banckes, and Clam bancks. **1774** J. ADAMS *Familiar Letters* 18, I long more still to see the procuring more sea-weed, and muscle mud, and sand, etc. **1817** PAULDING *Lett. from South* I. 177 Honest little Dennis Callaghan . . . is neither muscleman, nor oysterman. **1838** *Mass. Agric. Survey 1st Rep.* 35 The manure very generally applied, where attainable, is muscle-bed.

Muscle shoals. *pl.* Shoals where the shells of mussels accumulate, +esp. those on the Tennessee River. — **1779** in Ramsey *Tennessee* (1853) 200 After running until about 10 o'clock, [we] came in sight of the Muscle Shoals. **1812** *Niles' Reg.* III. 52/2 Above the muscle shoals, extends south-eastwardly towards Coosahatcha, a branch of the Alabama. **1921** *Scientific Amer.* 7 May 364/1 The Federal Government finally decided to build a great nitrate plant at Muscle Shoals.

Muscovado. Also **muscavada, muscovade.** Unrefined cane sugar obtained by evaporating the cane juice and draining off the molasses. In full *muscovado sugar.* {1642–}

1652 *Suffolk Deeds* I. 45 Forty parcells Barbadoes muscavadoes [*sic*] sugr. . . . cometh as per Invoice and bill of ladinge. **1666** SANFORD *Letter Book* 22 His desiere is tht . . yo would Send him . . . one hhds of good muscovado Sugr. **1723** *Doc. Hist. N.Y. State* (1849) I. 715 We import . . . from Jamaica . . . the best Muscovada Sugar for the consumption of the Country. **1761** in H. M. Brooks *Gleanings* 26 Choice Muscovado best Powder and brown Sugars, by the Hogshead or Barrel. **1787** CUTLER in *Life & Corr.* II. 398 The sap . . . is granulated, by the simple operation of boiling, to a sugar equal in flavor and whiteness to the best Muscovado. **1812** *Niles' Reg.* II. 86/2 Mr. Spalding, Mr. Cooper and Mr. Grant, all made small parcels of Muscovado sugar last year. **1851** A. CARY *Clovernook* 74 Every day in winter she used to feed them [the bees] maple sugar, if she had it—and if not, a little Muscovade in a saucer. **1886** *Harper's Mag.* June 93/1 'Muscovado' sugar is that cured by simple drainage.

Muscovy duck. The domesticated Brazilian or musk duck, *Cairina moschata.* {1657–} — **1792** IMLAY *Western Territory* 88 The provision consist of . . . Muscovy ducks, turkeys, geese, dunghill fowls and pidgeons. **1843** *Knickerb.* XXI. 257 From rats he naturally slid upon coon-hunting, from coons to foxes, from foxes back to coon, geese, chickens, roosters, and Muscovy ducks. **1896** HARRIS *Sister Jane* 293 While these two decrepit old women were nodding their heads together like two muscovy ducks, Mrs. Beshears was growing more and more talkative.

Museum. {1615–}

1. A building or a part of a building wherein various objects of some permanent interest are housed and exhibited; also, the collection of these objects. {1683–} Also attrib.

1797 *Boston Chronicle* 19 Dec., Late Additions to the Columbian Museum, at the Head of the Mall, Boston. **1833** COKE *Subaltern's Furlough* vii, The museums in the states are generally good, but the owners . . . possess a strange taste for collecting such a quantity of trash and childish trifles,—as pieces of old shells, . . . grapeshot, &c. **1893** M. HOWE *Honor* 320, I was expected to give ten thousand to the Art Museum. **1910** BOSTWICK *Amer. Pub. Library* 232 Elaborate work rarely pays, except with 'museum' books. **1916** WILSON *Somewhere* 374 Find a male and female born here and have 'em stuffed and mounted under glass in a fire-proof museum.

+**2.** A show place wherein curious objects and freaks are exhibited. Also attrib.

See also DIME MUSEUM.

1844 *Gem of Prairie* 30 Nov., The museum is open every day and evening where every lover of the curious . . . cannot fail to be pleased with the figures, birds, relics etc. it contains. **1846** *Chicago Jrnl.* 8 June, Mr. J. B. Gilbert with his theatrical corps make their second appearance this evening at the Museum Saloon. **1851** NORTHALL *Curtain* 121 Clarke, the popular manager of the museum, consented to his own absence for a single evening. **1864** *Statutes at Large* XIII. 277 Any person, firm, or corporation . . . having the care or management of any theatre, opera, circus, museum, or other public exhibition.

Mush. {1686–, of iron ore}

+**1.** Porridge or hasty pudding made of corn meal.

[**1671** J. HARDY *Descr. Last Voyage to Bermudas* 11 Indian corn . . . Which being groun'd and boyl'd, Mush they make Their hungry Servants for to slake.] **1676** B. TOMPSON *Poetical Works* 50 Merchants car'd not a rush For other fare than Jonakin and Mush. **1717** *N.C. Col. Rec.* II. 310 My family have had little else for sometime, but a little boiled corn . . . and now and then mush, alias hasty Pudding made of Indian Meal. **1775** CRESSWELL *Journal* 95 Bargained with the old Woman for as much mush as we all could eat. **1814** BRACKENRIDGE *Views La.* 202 Their food consists of . . . a pot of mush for supper. **1839** TOWNSEND *Narrative* 280 We purchased a large bag of Indian meal, of which we made a kettle of mush. **1873** PHELPS *Trotty's Wedding* ix, And tell them how, one morning, the Princeton student had hot mush for breakfast. **1901** GRINNELL *Gold Hunting in Alaska* 4 Once I landed a big platter of mush upside down on the deck.

+**b.** *Mush and milk,* mush with milk poured over it.

1745 E. KIMBER *Itinerant Observ.* 34 The meaner Sort you find little else but Water amongst, when their Cyder is spent, *Mush* and Milk, or Molasses, *Homine,* Wild Fowl, and Fish, are their principal Diet. **1797** F. BAILY *Tour* 352 If we could get a mess of mush and milk, some fried bacon, or some fresh meat of any kind, it was as much as we expected. **1817** *Essex Inst. Coll.* VIII. 244 [The settler's family] gave me a supper of mush and milk. **1850** LEWIS *La. Swamp Doctor* 126 'What are its [calomel's] effects upon the system?' 'The free use of coffins, spit-boxes, mush-and-milk, and the invention of new oaths.' **1894** 'MARK TWAIN' *P. Wilson* iv, Chambers got mush and milk, and clabber without sugar.

attrib. and *fig.* **1866** 'MARK TWAIN' *Lett. Sandwich Isl.* (1938) 151, I'm disgusted with these mush-and-milk preacher travels.

+**c.** *Mush and molasses,* mush sweetened with molasses.

1745 [see prec.]. **1810** *Mass. Spy* 24 Jan. (Th.), They have mush and molasses twice a day. **1815** *View N.Y. State Prison* 36 [The convicts'] suppers consist of mush and molasses, or bread and molasses. **1848** *Indiana Gen. Ass. Doc.* 1848–9 II. 77, [I] suggest . . . mush and molasses, in lieu of bread, for supper. **1908** SINCLAIR *Metropolis* 162 [Common people] ate mush and molasses.

+**d.** *Fried mush,* mush allowed to cool, and then sliced and fried.

1869 E. PUTNAM *Receipt Bk.* 312 Children's Breakfast. Boiled hominy, fried mush, boiled mush. **1886** EBBUTT *Emigrant Life* 81 We lived principally on . . . Johnny cake and fried mush, both made from Indian corn meal. **1909** *N.Y. Ev. Post* (s.-w. ed.) 11 March 4 Losing a good school-ma'am because she would not eat the fried mush where she was requested to board.

+**2.** Any other food mixture of the same thick consistency.

1850 GARRARD *Wah-To-Yah* xxi. 254 With unbolted Mexican flour and bacon greases, a thick mush was manufactured. **1857** *Harper's Mag.* Sept. 538/2 Flummadiddle . . . is a kind of *mush,* baked in the oven. **1864** *Sufferings in Rebel Prisons* (Sanitary Comm.) 37 To render the [corn] bread eatable, they grated it, and made mush out of it. **1887** I. R. *Lady's Ranche Life Mont.* 65 For breakfast we have porridge (which Americans call 'mush'), eggs, fried potatoes.

+**b.** 'Fish ground up; chum; pomace; stosh' (*Cent.*).

3. *fig.* Anything soft and yielding; effusive sentiment, twaddle. {1856–}

1841 EMERSON *Friendship* Ess. 1 Ser., I hate, where I looked for . . . a manly resistance, to find a mush of concession. **1852** *Gleason's Pictorial Drawing Room Companion* III. 61/1 Uncle Tom's Cabin has had a large sale, but the book is a perfect 'mush.' **1904** *Life* 26 May 500 That sort of

Bible defense is mere mush. **1918** in *Liberty* 11 Aug. (1928) 8/2 Some bright baby with stars on his shoulders and mush in his head . . . ordered us to march on a reservoir five miles from camp with picks.

+**4.** Attrib. in sense 1 with *pan, pot.*

1847 ROBB *Squatter Life* 59 Betsy Jones' Tumble in the Mush Pan. **1847** HOWE *Hist. Coll. Ohio* 432 Johnny, who wore on his head a tin utensil which answered both as a cap and a mush pot, filled it with water and quenched the fire.

+**Mush ice.** Water only partly frozen. — **1815** *Niles' Reg.* IX. 201/2 You may . . . take a pole sixty feet long, and . . . run it down the whole length, and find no termination of what is called the mush ice. **1907** LONDON *White Fang* 202 The fall of the year, when the first snows were falling and mush-ice was running in the river.

***Mushmelon.** =MUSKMELON. *colloq.* — **1775** J. HARROWER *Diary* 101 My Plantation for my Amusement consists of the following Articles Vizt. Watermelons, mushmelons, Cucumbers, Pumpkins [etc.]. **1855** *Amer. Inst. N.Y. Trans.* 314 His sweet mush melons lay in abundance on the ground. **1884** 'MARK TWAIN' *H. Finn* xii. 102 We talked it over . . . , trying to make up our minds whether to drop the watermelons, or the cantelopes, or the mushmelons.

+**Mushmelon bonnet.** (See quot. and cf. MUSKMELON HOOD.) *Obs.* — **1830** WATSON *Philadelphia* 176 The 'mush-mellon' bonnet, used before the Revolution, had numerous whale-bone stiffeners in the crown, set at an inch apart in parallel lines and presenting ridges to the eye, between the bones.

***Mushroom.** In popular language, any edible fungus of the orders Agaricales or Lycoperdales, esp. the field mushroom, *Agaricus campestris.*

1737 BRICKELL *N. Carolina* 19 Mushrooms, good and in great Plenty all over the Fields. **1850** S. F. COOPER *Rural Hours* 303 Mushrooms are not much eaten in our country neighborhood; people are afraid of them. **1884** F. E. OWENS *Cook Book* 25 Cook the mushrooms in water, with salt to flavor. . . . A few mushrooms will flavor a large dish. **1907** *St. Nicholas* July 801/2 The representative simply dotes on beefsteak and mushrooms.

+**Mushroom town.** A town that has sprung up rapidly, esp. along a railroad line. — **1862** in Moore *Rebellion Rec.* V. II. 309 One of those railroad mushroom towns, located in the pine woods of St. Helena parish—was to be the base of our operations. **1872** TICE *Over Plains* 11 Atchison . . . is not a mushroom town, but its growth has been gradual, steady and permanent. **1880** *Harper's Mag.* May 908/2 He who has never lived . . . in one of the many mushroom towns . . . along the lines of our new Western railways, has missed a novel and interesting experience. **1909** 'O. HENRY' *Options* 302 Paloma was a new town on the line of the Southern Pacific. A reporter would have called it a 'mushroom' town.

+**Mush sugar.** Crystalline sugar precipitating in or mixed with syrup. — **1868** *Iowa Agric. Soc. Rep. 1867* 178 When sugar is contemplated, White Imphee is . . . the best, as all I have made went to thick mush sugar immediately.

+**Mush syrup.** =prec. — **1863** *Rep. Comm. Agric. 1862* 131 We have taken from one gallon of mush sirup . . . eight pounds of sugar.

Mushy, *a. colloq.* **1.** Soft, sentimental, insipid. {1876} **2.** Of the consistency of mush. {1883} — (1) **1839** *S. Lit. Messenger* V. 209/2, I soon recognized old *Noth Calinur* in their nasal mushy pronunciation. **1870** *Nation* 3 Feb. 67 The death penalty is disappearing . . . before a kind of mushy and unthinking doubt of its morality. **1909** *Springfield W. Repub.* 11 March 3 The new president is affable, but he is not mushy. **1921** PAINE *Comr. Rolling Ocean* 71, I don't like the idea of losing you. Sounds sort of mushy, . . . but I'm hoping we'll be buddies again. (2) **1862** *Harper's Mag.* June 35/2 He has a leetle soft spot right here [on his head], and it is mushy all round it. **1880** 'MARK TWAIN' *Tramp Abroad* 267 [He] said a buggy was just the trick to skim along mushy, slushy early spring roads with.

***Music.** Also †**musick.**

***1.** Any succession of melodic or harmonic sounds; the art or science of producing these sounds.

1689 [see MUSICIAN]. **1760** WASHINGTON *Diaries* I. 126 Musick and Dancing was the chief Entertainment. **1802** ELLICOTT *Journal* 135 The natives of the southern part of the Mississippi . . . have a natural turn for mechanics, painting, music, and the polite accomplishments. **1843** *Niles' Nat. Reg.* 10 June 234/2 Instruction in vocal music has been successfully introduced into the common schools of New York. **1883** *Rep. Indian Affairs* 18 Music is very attractive to them [*sc.* Indians], and a great incentive to other duties as well as a means of recreation. **1924** *Outlook* 29 Oct. 331/1 The time is at hand when music as a profession for Americans will no longer entail financial sacrifice.

+**2.** *local.* Liveliness, fun: (see also quot. 1890).

1859 BARTLETT 285 Jim is a right clever fellow; there is a great deal of music in him. **1890** *Cent.* 3907/3 *Music,* . . . diversion; sport; also, sense of the ridiculous. . . . (New Eng.).

+**3.** *To face the music,* to meet an ordeal or rigorous test without flinching; to accept the consequences of one's action without hesitation; to face facts. {1897}

1850 *Congress. Globe* App. 4 March 324/3 There should be no skulking or dodging— . . . every man should 'face the music.' **1854** *Alta California* 4 Feb., President Walker . . . concluded by exacting a promise from the 'men' . . . to put an end to the unsoldierlike practice of growling whenever called upon to 'face the music.' **1862** in Moore *Rebellion Rec.* V. II. 21 Troops of less experience and hardihood would have flinched where these faced the music. **1893** *Nation* LVI. 466/2 The President's first duty . . . is to get the two houses in session and make them face the music. **1897** *Outing* XXX. 564/2 Out of fifty yachts entered only twenty-seven faced the music when the starting signal was given at 11:35. **1918** C. WELLS *Vicky Van* 31, 'I shall remain and face the music,' I heard Mrs. Reeves saying.

4. *attrib.* and *comb.* **a.** Designating various places where music is performed.

1740 SEWARD *Journal* 6 Some Gentlemen threaten'd to Cane me for having taken away the Keys of the Assembly-Room, Dancing-School, and Musick-Meeting. **1856** M. J. HOLMES *Homestead* VII. viii, [He] led her to the music-room, where some one was playing the piano. **1863** MASSETT *Drifting About* 27 The fashionable music stores and lounges for musical people, . . . were Atwill's Music Saloon, . . . Millett's, . . . [and] Firth and Hall. **1882** McCABE *New York* 423 In the centre is a tasteful music pavilion, where concerts are given by the city band.

b. Designating persons who make, sell, or take care of music or musical instruments.

1848 *Knickerb.* XXXI. 450 Mr. Joseph F. Atwill, one of our most popular music-publishers . . . is issuing . . . a musical publication of rare interest and value. **1851** CIST *Cincinnati* 50 Occupations [include] . . . Music dealers, . . . Musical instrument makers. **1860** E. COWELL *Diary* 107 Bade farewell to Mrs. Clare, the music-seller, etc. **1887** *Nation* 28 April 372/1 Mr. Thomas Goodwin was a music-librarian in this city [New York].

c. Designating various devices for holding or handling sheet music or music books.

1855 *Knickerb.* XLV. 136 You hide behind the music-rack while Miss Mince passes. **1872** *Rep. Comm. Patents* 1871 II. 510/1 Music-Leaf Holder. An improved article of manufacture . . . for the purpose of holding up and clasping the leaf. **1873** *Pat. Off. Gazette* III. 88/2 Music portfolio . . . [patented by] J. C. Koch.

d. Special combinations.

Music blackboard, (see quotation); *m. committee,* in a church congregation, a committee responsible for the musical program and especially the engagement of musicians; *m. repository,* music store; *m. stool,* a piano stool; *m. stroller,* an organ-grinder.

1873 *Pat. Off. Gazette* IV. 652/2 Music-Blackboard. . . . The board inclines slightly backward, and the characters used—notes, bars, rests, &c. —are adjusted in or removed from grooves representing the lines and spaces, at pleasure. **1882** McCABE *New York* 635 The 'Music Committee' ask only for good voices, and do not trouble themselves about the daily lives of the choristers. **1819** McMURTRIE *Sk. Louisville* 138 There are at this moment, in Louisville, . . . Five tobacco factories, one sugar refinery, one music repository. **1857** *Ladies' Repository* XVII. 72/2, I saw Kate jump up from the music-stool and put her hand to her forehead. **1841** *Knickerb.* XVII. 331 One poor Italian music-stroller, with his organ-box before him, labored hardest and longest.

***Musical,** *a.*

+**1.** Of persons: Having a sense of humor; amusing; good humored. *colloq. Obs.*

1816 PICKERING 135 In some towns in the interior of New England, . . . they would say of a man of humour, He is very musical. **1819** *Mass. Spy* 12 May (Th.), [They declared him to be] a nice man, and very musical, that is to say, good-humoured and polite. **1835** THOMPSON *Adv. T. Peacock* 122 'My horse will trot as slow as common horses will stand still!' 'You are a musical fellow,' said the master. **1846** WHITCHER *Bedott P.* vi. 61 Old Green's a musical old critter, you know.

+**2.** Of a story or situation: Funny, amusing, strange. *colloq. Obs.*

1842 *Life in West* 281 The rule is to 'gammon a stranger' who persists in asking questions, telling him something 'awfully musical.' **1878** COOKE *Happy Dodd* 344, I don't blame 'em none as I know of, but it's musical to see 'em do it. **1881** — *Somebody's Neighbors* 242 Why . . . I can't be left to do what I darn please is musical to me.

3. Special combinations.

Musical burletta, a comic sketch with music; *m. clock,* a clock that chimes at regular intervals {1747}; *m. club,* a society which sponsors music; *m. farce,* a farcical show set to music; *m. magazine,* a periodical that publishes music or articles on music; *m. saloon,* a room for musical entertainment; *m. sardine box,* a flute harmonica, a wind instrument shaped like a small box, with a mouthpiece at one end and equipped with keys; *m. steam engine,* a calliope.

1895 *Boston Transcript* 1 Jan. 5/7 A Continuous Stage Show from 1 to 11 P.M. No waits. A Great Variety Bill. Funny Musical Burletta. **1774** in Singleton *Social N.Y.* 325 The unparallel'd Musical Clock, made by the great master of Machinery David Lockwood. **1872** ROE *Barriers Burned Away* xxii, No one could join our musical club at college who could not read anything placed before him. **1832** DUNLAP *Hist. Amer. Theatre* 94 Hallam and Henry opened the theatre . . . with Reynolds' new comedy of the Dramatist, and the musical farce of the Padlock. **1786** (*title*), American Musical Magazine [New Haven, Conn.]. **1840** *Knickerb.* XVI. 413 Pen may not fully portray . . . the blooming women in the musical saloon, or the crowd in the crush-room. **1880** E. JAMES *Negro Minstrel's Guide* 4 Flute harmonicas, or musical sardine box, $3.50. **1856** *Porter's*

Spirit of Times 27 Sept. 55/3 There was the musical Steam Engine discoursing 'Pop goes the weasel' on a big scale.

Musical box. 1. =MUSIC BOX. {1840–} +**2.** (See quotation.) — (1) **1829** ROYALL *Pennsylvania* I. 10 A small wooden musical box . . . by mechanical invention produced the name of any capital town you called for. **1842** HAWTHORNE *Note-books* (1932) 145 Mr. Thorow (*sic*) has twice listened to the music of the spheres, which, for our private convenience, we have packed into a musical box. **1865** *Atlantic Mo.* XV. 27 I wind up my little musical box. **1872** *Rep. Comm. Patents* 1870 II. 622/1 Musical Box. . . . A series of cylinders arranged upon a rotating shaft [etc.]. (2) **1871** DE VERE 283 The *Musical-box* of the Confederates was also known as *Jeff Davis' Box*: it was the humorous name given by the men to the lumbering, ill-built army-wagons, which were apt to creak horribly for want of greasing.

+**Musical comedy.** A type of theatrical composition in which the plot is subordinated to musical numbers, comic dialogue, dancing, and similar vaudeville features. — **1898** *Opera Glass* Aug. 116/2 The Herald Square will offer The French Maid as the opening attraction, to be followed by The Hotel Topsy Turvey, a new musical comedy. **1901** *Theatre* July 5/2 Messrs. Klaw & Erlanger will produce Mr. Harry B. Smith's new musical comedy, 'The Liberty Belles.' **1908** SINCLAIR *Metropolis* 145 The entertainment was another 'musical comedy' like the one he had seen a few nights before.

+**Musicale.** [Fr. *soirée musicale.*] A social affair with music as the main feature; a private concert. — **1872** ROE *Barriers Burned Away* xxx, He soon found himself involved in a round of sociables, musicales, and now and then a large party. **1883** RITTENHOUSE *Maud* 191 We went to the social musicale at Temperance Hall, where I turned Alice's music. **1888** *Battle Creek Moon* 21 Jan., A musicale was given at the residence of Mrs. D. H. Rust last evening. **1907** *St. Nicholas* Oct. 1087/2 Now that the plans for the musicale were running steadily on, every one would have been happy if . . . they had only known what they should attempt to earn a living.

Musical party. =MUSICALE. — **1878** *Decorum* 173 Thus the words 'musical party' . . . should be inserted. **1885** CRAWFORD *Amer. Politician* 7 Those women who . . . are invited . . . as an element of success to every dinner, musical party, and dance in the season.

Music book.** A book of musical compositions. — **1757** in Singleton *Social N.Y.* 290 Lost; a musick-book, the principal fiddle of twelve concertos, entitled Dominico Scarlatti's Lessons. **1833** *Knickerb.* I. 157 Allow me to adjust the music-book. *a1861** WINTHROP *Open Air* 11 The parlor . . . [was] furnished with a map of the United States and an oblong music-book open at 'Old Hundred.'

Music box. {1773} A box or case containing a mechanism by which a tune or different tunes may be played. {1849} — **1844** EMERSON *Poet* Ess. 2 Ser., A man of subtle mind, whose head appeared to be a music-box of delicate tunes and rhythms. **1876** SCUDDER *Dwellers* 140 A good music-box is certainly a very companionable little fellow. You wind it and it plays a little air with great accuracy, then rests a moment and plays another. **1890** *Augusta* (Me.) *Fireside Visitor* 15 Nov. 13/1 The sweet airs of the Music Box are always pleasing . . . and we are now selling a superior two-tune box, at . . . $1.15. **1907** 'O. HENRY' *Roads of Destiny* 71 A mushy black man with whiskers like the notes on a Swiss music-box cylinder.

Music-grinder. One who grinds a barrel organ; an organ-grinder. {1852} — **1840** *Picayune* 5 Aug. 2/2 Dancing monkeys, perambulating dandies, music grinders and flash loafers are not to be seen at the present writing in New Orleans. **1857** WILLIS *Convalescent* 210 An Italian music-grinder who chanced to be on board played vigorously at the bowsprit.

Music hall. A hall or auditorium used for concerts, vaudeville, etc. {1885–} Also attrib. (Less frequent in the U.S. than in England in sense of *vaudeville house.*) — [**1842** DICKENS *Amer. Notes* I. 71 The pupils all repaired . . . to a spacious music-hall, . . . and listened . . . to a voluntary on the organ.] **1872** HOLMES *Poet* 61 Many deaths have happened . . . from that well-known complaint, *Icterus Invidiosorum*, after returning from a visit to the Music Hall. **1896** *N.Y. Dramatic News* 4 July 13/2 In Gay New York is a powerful competitor of the music halls, and the attendance at the Casino is always very large. *a***1918** G. STUART *On Frontier* I. 69 In the larger towns of Marysville and Sacramento were the magnificent gambling houses, saloons, dance halls, music halls, theaters [etc.].

***Musician.** One who sings or who plays a musical instrument; a composer or a professional performer of music.

1689 SEWALL *Diary* I. 260 Three musicians Came in, two Harps and a Violin, and gave us Musick. **1802** *Statutes at Large* II. 134 Every non-commissioned officer, musician and private . . . shall receive . . . one coarse linen frock and trowsers for fatigue clothing. **1852** *N.Y. Tribune* 23 Dec. 1/2 The entertainments offered by this celebrated company of Musicians and Ethiopian Delineators cannot be equaled by any other band in the United States. **1921** *Lit. Digest* 4 June 33/2 Most of the recitals given are given for show and at a loss to the musician.

Music stand. 1. A rack for holding sheet music or music books. {1762–} +**2.** A platform where music is performed; a band stand. — (1) **1850** *Rep. Comm. Patents 1849* I. 170, I claim as my invention . . . the combination and arrangement of an apparatus with the music or book stand. **1882** RITTENHOUSE *Maud* 59 Our piano is in the spare room, also . . . a music stand. (2) **1861** *Ill. Agric. Soc. Trans.* IV. 17 A ring, well inclosed with posts and two planks . . . with music stand two stories high. **1880** *Cimarron News & Press* 30 Sept. 3/3 Sauntering down the street I found a square or plaza containing many fine, large trees and a music stand.

+**Music store.** A store in which sheet music, musical instruments, etc., are sold. — **1829** ROYALL *Pennsylvania* I. 83 Near this office there is a music store. **1860** E. COWELL *Diary* 80 The Concertina, which Mr. Hicks had been trying with the piano at the Music store. **1898** *Kansas City Star* 18 Dec. 10/2 Splendid Leather Music Rolls, music store price 98¢.

Music teacher. One who gives instruction in music. — **1854** M. J. HOLMES *Tempest & Sunshine* 248 Kate . . . is fine looking and appears well, even if she is a music teacher. **1872** MCCLELLAN *Golden State* 456 There were [in San Francisco in 1870] . . . 30 photographic galleries, 450 physicians, . . . 100 music teachers. **1883** *Century Mag.* June 196/1 The music teachers are chosen mainly for their knowledge of notation. **1908** GALE *Friendship Village* 7 She is a little rosy . . . music teacher.

+**Muskanounge.** Also **muskinunge.** =MUSKELLUNGE. — **1798** I. ALLEN *Hist. Vermont* 13 Lakes and rivers in Vermont . . . are abundantly stored with fish . . . particularly sturgeon, salmon, salmon-trout, muskinunge, pike, &c. **1840** *S. Lit. Messenger* VI. 604/1 Spring lured the sturgeon and muskanounge from their deep blue homes in the Lake. **1847** LANMAN *Summer in Wilderness* 74 The only two desirable kinds [of fish in the Mississippi R. near Crow Wing, Minn.] are the muskanounge and a very large pike.

Musk beaver. =MUSKRAT 1 a. — **1771** PENNANT *Synopsis Quadrup.* 259. **1842** *Nat. Hist. N.Y., Zoology* I. 75 The Musquash. *Fiber zibethicus.* . . . Musk Beaver.

Muskeg. Also **muskegg.** [Canad. Eng. from Algonquian; cf. Ojibway *mashkig.*] A marsh or bog usually filled with sphagnum. {1865–, in Canada} — **1898** S. B. GREEN *Forestry in Minn.* 297 *Muskeg*, a term commonly applied to sphagnum swamps by the Indians and woodsmen of northern Minnesota. **1916** EASTMAN *From Deep Woods* 167 The great inland seas of northern Minnesota and the Province of Ontario are surrounded by . . . the immense bogs called 'muskeggs' filled with tamaracks.

+**Muskellunge.** Also **muschilongoe, muskalonge,** etc. [Ojibway *mashkinoje* 'great pike.'] **a.** A large pike (*Esox masquinongy*) of the Great Lakes. **b.** Either of two other forms of this fish, *E. m. ohiensis*, of Chautauqua Lake and the tributaries of the Ohio River, or *E. m. immaculatus*, the great northern pike of Wisconsin and Minnesota.

The variant spellings of this word are numerous: see MASCALONGE, MASKINONGE, MUSCALLONGE, MUSKANOUNGE.

1794 S. WILLIAMS *Hist. Vermont* 122 The Pike or Pickerel abounds much in Lake Champlain. It is there called by the name of Muschilongoe. **1809** CUMING *Western Tour* 441 The streams abound with a variety of excellent fish, muschelongir, cat-fish, sturgeon, pike, white and black bass. **1834** *Ind. Q. Mag. Hist.* XV. 257 The pike is probably the same as the pickerel, only the larger ones here are called pike or muskalonge. **1842** *Nat. Hist. N.Y., Zoology* IV. 222 The Muskellunge, *Esox estor*, . . . occur[s] as far north as Lake Huron. **1868** *N.H. Laws* 133 No person shall . . . take, catch, kill or destroy any . . . pickerel, pike, or muskallonge. **1884** GOODE, etc. *Fisheries* I. 464 At Milwaukee the Muskellunge occurs in the lake but rarely. **1911** *Rep. Fisheries 1908* 312 Muskallunge . . . is caught in pound nets, with hook and line, and by trawling.

***Musket.** Also †**muskett, musquet.**

***1.** A hand firearm.

Musket has been applied successively to different types of weapons gradually developed from the heavy and clumsy matchlock musket. The tendency is now to restrict the word to obsolete forms of the weapon: (cf. 1 b, and SMOOTHBORE MUSKET). The CARBINE, FIRELOCK, FLINTLOCK, FUSIL, MATCHLOCK, etc., are species of the musket.

1622 'MOURT' *Relation* 13 Sixteene men were set out with every man his Musket, Sword, and Corslet. **1634** WOOD *New Eng. Prospect* 53 Whosoever shall carrie over Drummes and English Colours, . . . Pickes, Muskets, Bandelerous, with Swords, shall not neede to feare good gaine for them. **1646** *Essex Probate Rec.* I. 75 A muskett with a fyrelock. **1677** HUBBARD *Narrative* 103 The Indian having an old Musket with a large touch-hole. **1744** *N.J. Archives* 1 Ser. VI. 192 Every person of a Foot Company shall be armed with a good musket or fusee, well fixed, and a bayonet. **1787** *Ky. Gazette* 18 Aug. 4/3 Every non commission officer and private, is by law directed to furnish himself with a good clean musquet, containing an ounce ball. **1817** *Ann. 14th Congress* 2 Sess. 905 But why, then, do they not throw away their muskets in war? **1863** *Rio Abajo Press* 6 Oct. 3/2 Juan José Jaramillo . . . loaded his musket with a heavy charge of powder and slugs. **1883** *Century Mag.* Sept. 687/2 My father . . . armed me with an old musket and sent me to shoot chipmunks around the corn.

b. *Large* (or *long*) *musket*, a musket with a long barrel.

1835 LONGSTREET *Ga. Scenes* 222 In olden time the contest was carried on chiefly with *shot-guns*, a generic term which in those days, embraced three descriptions of fire-arms—*Indian-traders*, . . . *the large Musket*, and the *Shot-gun*, properly so called. **1837** IRVING *Bonneville* II. 141 On the pommel of his saddle, he carries a long musket, with fox-skin round the lock.

c. A smoothbore, single-shot gun, as distinguished from a rifle.

1851 *Harper's Mag.* Jan. 268/1 The Governor says that during the year he has purchased largely of muskets and rifles. **1857** *Lawrence* (Kan.) *Re-*

publican 11 June 2 Their arms were muskets, double barrelled shot guns and rifles.

2. Attrib. with *bullet, cap,* etc.

1647 *Essex Probate Rec.* I. 92 One Fowlinge peece, one muskett rest and sword. **1676** *N.H. Hist. Soc. Coll.* III. 98 The young man was wounded in his shoulder by a musket Bullet. **1757** *Lett. to Washington* II. 74 Nine Waggons ... will be sufficient to bring to Lancaster ... 100 Barrells Gunpowder, 12000 Musquet Flints. **1780** *Va. State P.* I. 385 I Recd.... 7 barrels of powder, 4 boxes of musket Cartridges & he says 500 flints. **1867** EDWARDS *Shelby* 411 Musket caps were fearfully scarce in the department and none anywhere in reach nearer than St. Louis.

Musket ball. A ball or bullet that may be shot from a musket. {1725} — **1761** NILES *Indian Wars* II. 426 Colonel Armstrong, receiving a wound in his shoulder by a musket-ball, ordered their houses to be set on fire. **1825** NEAL *Bro. Jonathan* III. 109 A musket-ball had gone thro' both legs. **1898** *McClure's Mag.* X. 352 Soon the musket balls and the cannon shot began to reach the place where we stood.

***Musketeer.** Also **musketier, musketer.** A soldier armed with a musket. *Obs.* — **1622** 'MOURT' *Relation* 93 Instantly came our Governour with Drumme and Trumpet after him, and some few Musketiers. **1643** *Suffolk Deeds* I. 7 Mounseir Latour doth promise at his owne propper Cost to provide ... pouder and shott for twenty muskiteers. **1785** FRANKLIN *Poor Richard's Almanac* 1786 22 A visible Army of 20000 *Musketers* will land, some in *Virginia.*

Musketo. Variant of MOSQUITO.

Musketoon. Also **musquetoon.** A short musket, usu. with a large bore. Now hist. {1650-} — **1729** *Boston News-Letter* 8 May 2 To be Sold by John Osborne & Company, choice Musquets and Musquetoons for Shipping. **1812** IRVING *Knickerb.* II. iv, He seized a musquetoon that lay at hand, and ... fired it. **1835** SIMMS *Yemassee* I. 37 The stranger ... carried a light-musketoon, or smoothbore, ... richly ornamented with drops of silver. **1866** MOORE *Women of War* 257 She marched in the dusk beside the soldiers, with a musketoon upon her shoulder.

Musk hog. The collared peccary of the Southwest, *Pecari angulatus.* {Mexican musk hog, 1773} Cf. MEXICAN HOG. — **1865** PIKE *Scout & Ranger* (1932) 23 We hunted deer, wild turkey, and musk hogs. **1917** *Mammals of Amer.* 62/1 In the middle of the back the Peccary has a large gland containing an oily substance smelling somewhat like musk; hence the animal is sometimes called the Musk Hog. **1923** J. H. COOK *On Old Frontier* 20 When trying to run the wild cattle into the decoy herd, we stampeded bunches of musk hogs or peccaries.

***Muskmelon.** Also †**muskemelon, muskmillion,** etc. Either the fruit or the vine of different varieties of the plant, *Cucumis melo.* Sometimes restricted to the nutmeg melon, *C. m. reticulatus.* (See also MUSHMELON.)

In the United States no clear distinction has usually been made between *muskmelon* and *cantaloupe*, except that the latter term is the one generally applied to the netted-rind varieties.

[**1580** FLORIO tr. Cartier in *Hakluyt's Voyages* III. 276 They have great store [of] ... other fruits, as musk mellons, and very great cucumbers.] **1610** *Estate of Va.* 13 What should I speake of cucumbers, muske melons, pompions, potatoes, parsneps, carrets, turn vps. **1634** WOOD *New Eng. Prospect* (1865) 15 The ground affoards very good kitchin Gardens, for Muskmillions, Isquouterquashes, Coucumbers. **1709** LAWSON *Carolina* 77 Of Musk-Melons we have very large and good, and several Sorts, as the Golden, Green, Guinea, and Orange. **1774** FITHIAN *Journal* I. 230, I bought & sent her however this evening a present a large Musk Melon. **1796** HAWKINS *Letters* 21 They made beans, ... watermelons, musmelons collards and onions. **1840** DEWEY *Mass. Flowering Plants* 113 One variety of the Muskmelon is commonly called *canteleup*, or, as often written, *cantelope*, a very delicious fruit. **1884** ROE *Nature's Story* 293 Musk-melons formed one of their breakfast dishes. **1913** LONDON *Valley of Moon* 252 One flood tide she found the water covered with muskmelons.

+**Muskmelon hood.** =MUSHMELON BONNET. — **1891** EARLE *Sabbath* 91 The good wives' heads bore ... hoods of all kinds and descriptions, from ... 'muskmelon hoods,' to the warm quilted 'punkin hoods' worn within this century in country churches.

Muskrat. {1681-} [See quot. 1778.] Cf. MUSQUASH.

1. +**a.** An aquatic rodent (*Ondatra*, syn. *Fiber, zibethicus*), having a long, laterally compressed tail.

In view of the interval between the first two quotations, it is possible that the first one should go under MUSQUASH 1.

1607 in Smith *Works* I. (1910) I. p. lxix, There are Beares, ... Muskats [*sic*], and wild beasts vnknowne. **1701** WOLLEY *Journal N.Y.* 33 A Musquash or a Muskrat's-skin [is worth] six shillings and sixpence. **1778** CARVER *Travels* 455 The Musquash or Musk-rat, is so termed for the exquisite musk which it affords. **1821** NUTTALL *Travels Arkansa* 51 [In northern Ark.] I also saw a few skins of the musk-rat (*Arctomys monax*, L.) which are never met with further to the south. **1876** *Wide Awake* 55/1 Muskrats always ... select a site for building purposes in a swamp, or the shallow parts of a pond, or on a marsh in the bend of a river. **1905** *Springfield W. Repub.* 4 Aug. 7 He experienced much trouble with muskrats in his chicken yard. **1917** *Mammals of Amer.* 253/1 A few days later the boy set traps at the mouth of the Musk-rats' burrows in the bank of the pond.

+**b.** In Florida, a large ratlike rodent resembling the common muskrat, but having a round tail, *Neofiber alleni.*

1917 *Mammals of Amer.* 256 While called a Musk-rat, this less familiar animal occupies a group by itself, intermediate between the smaller Mice and its big cousin the common Musk-rat.

+**2.** The fur or pelt of the common muskrat.

1666 ALSOP *Maryland* I. 66 Furrs and Skins, as Beavers, Otters, Musk-Rats, ... were first made vendible by the Indians of the Country, and sold to the Inhabitant [*sic*]. **1678** *New Castle Court Rec.* 349, 6 musk Rats. **1822** in McKenney *Memoirs* I. 288 Mr. Kennerly sold, of the parcel which was destined to this market, ... rackoon, muskrat, and beaver. **1883** *Rep. Indian Affairs* 25 These peltries consist principally of muskrat, fox, polecat, and badger, and are obtained on the reservation [in Dakota].

+**3.** A nickname for an inhabitant of a low-lying district; spec., a resident or native of Delaware.

1845 *Cincinnati Misc.* I. 240 The inhabitants of ... Delaware [are called] Muskrats. **1888** WHITMAN *November Boughs* 406 Those from ... Delaware ... [were called] Muskrats. **1890** *Century Mag.* July 369/2 Her grandmother ... [had] a profound contempt for the 'muskrats' as the Flats people [near Detroit] are generally called.

4. *attrib.* and *comb.* +**a.** In sense 1 a with *burrow, colony, house,* etc.

1642 *Md. Archives* IV. 99, 2. musk-rat-skins. **1835** HOFFMAN *Winter in West* I. 170 Some of the men were cleaning their weapons, and others were arranging their bundle of muskrat-traps. **1837** IRVING *Bonneville* I. 174 About the beginning of April, they encamped upon Godin's river, where they found the swamp full of 'muskrat houses.' *a***1861** WINTHROP *Open Air* 78 Our muskrat-hunters ... were visited with indescribable Nemesis. **1870** *Amer. Naturalist* IV. 385 This fish, when the bank was carelessly approached, would withdraw to a deserted muskrat burrow. **1882** PECK *Sunshine* 261 Ask this red-headed muskrat trapper to sit on the other side of me. **1907** *St. Nicholas* Sept. 1041/2, I was sitting on the margin of a stream where there is a muskrat colony.

+**b.** In sense 2 with *cap.*

1916 EASTMAN *From Deep Woods* 101 We saw that they were colored troopers, wearing buffalo overcoats and muskrat caps.

‖**Muskrateer.** One who hunts or traps muskrats. — *a***1861** WINTHROP *Open Air* 73 One of the muskrateers had relieved Cancut of his head-piece, and shot the lower rush of water.

+**Musk tortoise.** =next. — **1842** HOLBROOK *N. Amer. Herpetology* I. 134 *Sternothærus Odoratus.*... Musk tortoise, or mud tortoise, *Vulgo.* **1884** GOODE, etc. *Fisheries* I. 154 Of the six species of Musk Tortoises inhabiting the United States, three are found only in Arizona and the Sonoran region generally, one in the Southern States, except lower Florida and Texas, and the remaining three in the Eastern and Southern States, and the central States westward to the extremities of the tributaries of the Mississippi.

+**Musk turtle.** Any of various fresh-water turtles of the genus *Sternotherus* (formerly *Aromochelys*), esp. the stinkpot, *S. odoratus.* Recent classifications place some of the so-called musk turtles in the genus *Kinosternon* as well as in *Sternotherus.* — **1868** *Amer. Naturalist* II. 330 The Turtle which you sent ... is the 'Musk Turtle,' *Aromochelys odoratus.* **1885** *Ib.* XIX. 1228 A representative of the musk turtle ... is interesting in that it is a giant of its species. **1923** STEJNEGER *Rehabil. of Overlooked Species of Musk Turtle* 2 Three full-grown specimens of a musk turtle ... [proved] to be true *Sternotherus carinatus.*

+**Musky.** Short for MUSKELLUNGE. — **1894** *Outing* XXIV. 453/1 We were then all ready for old musky to begin his real fight. **1902** *Scribner's Mag.* XXXI. 534 To begin with, call him by the familiar term, with which sportsmen have come to know him, the musky.

***Muslin.** Also †**muzlin.**

1. A fine and delicately woven cotton cloth, used for women's dresses, curtains, etc. {1609-}

Muslins vary from the very thin, plain fabrics imported from India to fabrics of different thicknesses and patterns made by modern manufacturers.

1693 SEWALL *Letter-Book* I. 137 One p[iec]e of Ell-wide Muzlin fine and thick. **1732** *S.C. Gazette* 5 Aug., Lately imported ... suits of Diaper, Muslins, Cambricks. **1770** *Md. Hist. Mag.* III. 146 We will not hereafter ... import or cause to be imported ... Lace, Cambrick, Lawn, Muslin, Kenting, Gauze. **1807** IRVING, etc. *Salmagundi* v, Will thundered down the dance ... making sad inroads into ladies' cobweb muslins. **1877** *Harper's Mag.* March 565 In Easter-week Dolly was married, and in trailing robes of India muslin. **1891** WILKINS *New Eng. Nun* 122 Tonight she had on a flimsy blue muslin with a good many flowers, and a deal of wide cotton lace. **1925** TILGHMAN *Dugout* 57 She unrolled a mass of soft white flannels, fine muslin [etc.].

+**2.** Stout cotton cloth used esp. for underwear and bedding.

1792 *Ann. 2d Congress* 1000 Great quantities of ... jeans and muslins ... are made in the household way. **1830** S. H. COLLINS *Emigrant's Guide* 176 Calico [in the English sense] is called muslin, and prints are called calicoes here. **1851** J. F. W. JOHNSTON *Notes N. Amer.* II. 420 *n.*, Something of the still youthful character and primitive habits of the females of New England and of New York State may be gathered from the fact, that our twopenny or threepenny calico is usually called *muslin* among them. **1871** DE VERE 71 A gentleman in Philadelphia ... ordered muslin shirts in Boston ... meaning cotton-shirting. **1887** I. ALDEN *Little Fishers* vi, Unbleached muslin makes about as pretty a curtain as a body could have. [**1899** MUIRHEAD *Baedeker's U.S.* p. xxx, *Muslin*, cotton cloth.]

3. A noncotton fabric similarly woven.

1723 HEMPSTEAD *Diary* 135, I Recd of G. Buttolph 17 yds of Silk Muslin.

4. *attrib.* and *comb.* **a.** Designating garments, etc., made of muslin.

1695 *Essex Inst. Coll.* LVI. 288 Jno. Hobs . . . an account of his Close being leftt abord . . . 1 whitte hancacher & 1 fringed muslin neckcloth [etc.]. **1711** *Boston News-Letter* 19 Feb. 2/2 Stolen or carried privately away . . . , two white Muslin Hoods. **1848** *Rep. Comm. Patents 1847* 201 [Milk] is strained through a perfectly clean muslin strainer. **1852** EASTMAN *Aunt Phillis's Cabin* 29 Her muslin three-cornered handkerchief, [was] pinned precisely at the waist. **1855** COOKE *Ellie* 425 For the gay garlands glitter, flower on flower, And muslin dresses hang out in the sun. **1857** M. J. HOLMES *Meadow-Brook* i, The gentle breeze . . . came through the open window, lifting the folds of the muslin curtain. **1907** *St. Nicholas* May 641/1 You can use a white muslin sheet for the wigwam. **1910** C. HARRIS *Eve's Husband* 318, I exclaimed, amazed at the lavender glory of the old muslin gown.

b. In combinations, indicating other uses to which muslin is sometimes put.

1878 JACKSON *Travel at Home* 104 Not that you cannot . . . live decently and with sufficient comfort for weeks in the muslin-walled bedroom. **1879** *Mich. Gen. Statutes* I. (1882) 432 Such map shall be made on sheets of good muslin-backed paper.

Muslin ceiling. A ceiling covered with muslin. — **1865** *Atlantic Mo.* Jan. 14/2 [We] found ourselves at last in a low room with a shaky floor and muslin ceiling. **1879** *Scribner's Mo.* Oct. 822/1 As to interiors, there are all the grades from a mud floor and rough-rock fire-place, . . . to the elaborate structure with muslin ceiling and calico walls.

Muslin delaine. =MOUSSELINE (DE) LAINE. {1862} — **1844** *Lexington Observer* 10 Dec. 4/3 Their assortment of Cashmeres, Crapes and Muslin de Lanes comprises new and elegant patterns of all qualities and latest styles.

Muslinet. A thick variety of muslin. *Obs.* {1787–} — **1768** FRENEAU *Poems* I. (1902) 17 All that would suit man, woman, girl, or boy; Muslins and muslinets, jeans, grograms, corduroy. **1790** *History of Congress* (1834) 377 All velvets, velverets, satins, . . . muslins, muslinets . . . 5½ per centum ad valorem. **1797** *Ann. 4th Congress* 2 Sess. 2327 Velvets and velverets, . . . and all muslins and muslinets, two and a half per cent. [duty].

+**Musquash,** *n.* Chiefly *N.* [Algonquian.]

Variant spellings of this word are numerous: *musquassus, mussascus, mushquash*, etc.

1. =MUSKRAT 1 a.

1616 SMITH *New England* 17 Fitches, Musquassus, and diuerse sorts of vermine, whose names I know not. **1624** — *Gen. Hist. Va.* II. 27 A Mussascus is a beast of the forme and nature of our water Rats, but many of them smell exceeding strongly of Muske. **1637** MORTON *New Canaan* 81 The Muskewashe, is a beast that frequenteth the ponds. **1672** JOSSELYN *New-Eng. Rarities* 53 There is a little Beast called a *Mushquash*, . . . their Cods scent as sweet and as strong as Musk. **1682** ASH *Carolina* 22 There are Bevors, Otters, Foxes, Racoons, Possums, Musquasses, Hares and Coneys. **1701** WOLLEY *Journal N.Y.* (1902) 37 The Skins of . . . Rackoons, Foxes, Otters; Musquashes, Skunks, [etc.] . . . they bring upon their backs to New-York. **1791** *Mass. Laws* (1801) I. 509 No person . . . shall hereafter, in either of the months of June, July, August or September . . . kill any . . . Musquash or Wolverin. **1842** *Nat. Hist. N.Y., Zoology* I. 75 The Musquash or Muskrat is so called from its strong musky odor. **1881** *Harper's Mag.* Sept. 588/2 The keen eyes of a half-grown boy, roving in search of a 'Musquash.' **1903** W. J. LONG *Beasts of Field* 187 No plash of musquash or leaping trout sends its vibrations up into the air.

b. *To talk musquash*, (see quotation).

1892 *Harper's Mag.* March 491/1 Talking business in the fur trade has always been called 'talking musquash.'

2. Attrib. with *cabin, fur, hole*, etc.

1633 *N.H. Doc. & Rec.* I. 72 Received by me . . . three racoon skins, and fourteene musquash skins. **1835–7** HALIBURTON *Clockmaker* 1 Ser. xxiii. 222, I thought it was like Uncle Peleg's musquash hole, and that no soul could ever find the bottom of. **1848** THOREAU *Maine Woods* 27 The Millinocket is a small shallow, and sandy stream . . . lined with musquash cabins. *a***1862** *Ib.* 212 What increased the resemblance, was one old musquash house almost afloat. **1876** GOODE *Anim. Resources U.S.* 74 Musquash fur used in felting.

+**Musquash,** *v.* Also **mushquash.** *intr.* To hunt or trap for muskrats. — **1833** S. SMITH *Life J. Downing* 25 This was most capital fun, but it want quite equal to musquashing. **1843** STEPHENS *High Life N.Y.* I. 137 He mushquashed round in the woods till he got tired of that kind of fun.

+**Musquash root.** The water hemlock, *Cicuta maculata.* — **1807** *Mass. Spy* 22 July (Th.), Five children were lately poisoned in Scipio (Newyork) by eating Wild Parsnip, or *Musquash Root.* **1821** *Mass. H. S. Coll.* 2 Ser. IX. 148 Plants, which are indigenous in the township of Middlebury, [Vermont, include] . . . Water carpet [and] Musquash-root. **1891** COULTER *Bot. W. Texas* I. 147 *C[icuta] maculata.* (Spotted cowbane. Musquash root. Beaver poison.) . . . Throughout the United States.

+**Musquash weed.** The fall meadow rue, *Thalictrum polygamum.* — **1767** *Mass. Gazette* 21 May 3/1 Persons (especially Children) would do well to beware of this Weed: It is called wild Hemlock by some, and Musquash Weed by others: It grows in low Lands, especially by running Water. **1892** *Amer. Folk-Lore* V. 91 *Thalictrum polygamum*, muskrat-weed; musquash weed.

Musquit(e). (See MESQUITE and following entries.)

Musquito. A common variant of MOSQUITO. (See also MESQUITO.)

Muss, *n.* {1838–, n. Cy. *dial.*} *colloq.*

1. A disturbance; a quarrel; a fight. {cf. *muss*, a scramble, 1591—*a*1734}

1838 *N.Y. Advertiser & Exp.* 17 Feb. 4/6 The complainant testified that there was a 'muss' in Chatham street. *c***1845** PAULDING *Amer. Comedies* (1847) 194 We'd have one of the awfulest musses that ever did take place. **1857** BORTHWICK *In California* 153 I got into a muss down at the store last night, and was whipped. **1873** 'MARK TWAIN' & WARNER *Gilded Age* 267 That gentleman delivered the young aspirant for a muss one of his elegant little left-handers. **1903** LEWIS *Boss* 19 It was nothin' but a cheap muss on the pier.

b. *To kick up a muss* (or variants of this), to start a quarrel or fight.

1840 HOFFMAN *Greyslaer* II. 206 That's jist what I told Red Wolfert when he showed signs of kicking up a muss. **1848** JUDSON *Mysteries N.Y.* IV. 65 'Then I expect, you'll have to raise a muss,' said Whitmore. **1878** BEADLE *Western Wilds* 303 They've been kicking up such a muss about polygamy. **1883** SHIELDS *S. S. Prentiss* 81 We shall soon see what a 'muss' was stirred up.

2. A state of confusion or untidiness; a mess.

1840 HOFFMAN *Greyslaer* II. 142 All this muss is of Wat Bradshawe's cooking. **1856** M. J. HOLMES *L. Rivers* 291 Did she think she was spiting her by showing what muss she could keep the 'best chamber' in if she chose? **1870** WARNER *Summer in Garden* i, Women always did, from the first, make a muss in a garden. **1908** FREEMAN *Shoulders of Atlas* 132 My hair is all in a muss.

Muss, *v. tr.* To make untidy; to confuse. {Suffolk *dial.*} — **1848** BARTLETT 231, I hate to ride in an omnibus, . . . it musses my clothes. **1892** *Boston Jrnl.* 19 Dec. 1/7 [A clothes-tree] keeps your clothing from all wrinkles, dries and ventilates it, and preserves it from being 'mussed.' **1907** *Springfield W. Repub.* 10 Oct. 5 Guilty persons could probably find ways to muss the psychological process beyond all possibility of repair.

***Mussel.** Also †**mussle, musstle.** (Cf. MUSCLE.)

***1.** Any of various bivalve mollusks: **a.** The marine mollusks of the family Mytilidae. (Cf. HORSE MUSSEL.) **b.** The fresh-water mollusks of the genera *Unio, Anodonta*, etc.

1622 'MOURT' *Relation* 4 We found great Mussles, and very fat and full of Sea pearle, but we could not eat them, for they made vs all sicke that did eat. **1674** *Cal. State P., Amer. & W.I.* VII. 581 [In] Maine . . . there are infinite quantities of fish, such as bass, . . . mussels, cockles, and scallops. **1764** HUTCHINSON *Hist. Mass.* I. 23 Many were obliged to live upon clams, mussels and other shell-fish. **1804** CLARK in *Lewis & C. Exped.* I. (1904) 110 This creek [near modern Dakota City, Neb.] is Crouded with large Musstles verry fat. **1869** *Amer. Naturalist* III. 369 Von Baer observed an adult *Hydrachna concharum* living parasitically on the gills of the fresh-water mussel, Anodon. **1881** MCLEAN *Cape Cod Folks* 208, I could distinguish Madeline wandering lightly about among the rocks, scraping off mussels with her hoe. **1913** LONDON *Valley of Moon* 376 As the tide grew lower, they gathered a mess of mussels.

2. Special combinations.

+*Mussel cripple*, a low-lying area in which mussels thrive; *m. duck* {1864}, +(see quotation); +*m. eater*, (see quotation).

1678 *New Castle Court Rec.* 305, 800 acres Called the mussel Cripple. **1917** *Birds of Amer.* I. 135 Scaup Duck. *Marila marila.* . . . Other Names.—Mussel Duck; . . . Flock Duck; Shuffler. **1890** *Cent.* 3911/1 *Mussel-eater*, . . . the buffalo perch, *Aplodinotus grunniens*, of the Mississippi valley.

+**Mussy,** *a.* Untidy, disheveled. Hence *mussiness.* — **1859** BARTLETT 287. **1869** *Independent* 25 March (*Cent.*), A general appearance of mussiness, characteristic of the man. **1890** *Harper's Mag.* Dec. 139/1 He had kind o' light, reddish-yeller hair, not very slick, but mussy an' rough like. **1904** *N.Y. Times* 9 May 4 A washing is all the most mussy of them need to render them things of beauty.

+**Must.** Newspaper matter that must be printed. Also attrib. — **1892** *Dial. Notes* I. 205 An article marked with the word *must* is spoken of as a *must*, or emphatically—if there is absolutely no way of keeping it out of the paper—as a *dead must.* Moreover, as the word is usually accompanied on the copy with the initials of the man who makes the order, there follows a gradation, so that one hears of 'Mr. X's must,' 'Mr. Y's must.' **1912** NICHOLSON *Hoosier Chron.* 180 His gratification at being able to write 'must' matter for both sides of a prominent journal [etc.].

Mustafina. (See quotation.) {*a*1818–, in W. Indies} — **1858** *Sun* (Baltimore) 3 Sept. 4/2 A mulatto is the offspring of a white and a negro; . . . and a mustafina, of a white and a mustee, being one-sixteenth black.

+**Mustang.** [Sp. *mestengo*, 'wild, having no master,' said of horses and cattle. Cf. the more correct form MESTANG.]

1. One of the wild horses of the western prairies and the Southwest.

Horses introduced by the Spaniards into the Southwest were the ancestors of the mustang: (see quot. 1913). Cf. BRONCO.

1808 PIKE *Sources Miss.* 273 [We] passed several herds of mustangs or wild horses. **1820** DEWEES *Lett. from Texas* 18 We discovered a large herd of Mustangs searching for water. **1836** CROCKETT *Exploits* 129 The mustangs . . . are taken by means of a lazo, a long rope with a noose, which is thrown around their neck. **1842** *Civilian & Galveston City Gaz.* 1 Oct. 1/3 Caught from the Mustangs, on the 2d of July, one bay mare branded on the shoulder OM. **1895** REMINGTON *Pony Tracks* 130 We 'cut the trail' of a big band of mustangs, or wild horses. **1913** BARNES *Western Grazing Grounds* 98 The true mustang was a small-boned inbred under-sized pony, generally of an 'off' color, mean of temper and narrow between the eyes.

b. (See quotation.)

1836 EDWARD *Hist. Texas* 108 Hence the figure of speech so often used by the inhabitants of Texas, to denote any wild and uncultivated person: as wild as a mustang!

2. a. A horse of this breed broken to the saddle or harness. **b.** Any tough, sturdy pony of the West; a cow pony.

1835 IRVING *Tour on Prairies* 248 The hardy Indian horses . . . are generally mustangs, or a cross of the wild breed. **1847** HENRY *Campaign Sk.* 25 For the first time had the pleasure of riding a mustang with complete though rude Mexican rigging. **1851** D. B. WOODS *At Gold Diggings* 22We were mounted on 'mustangs,' a small and hardy horse, peculiarly adapted to the mountains over which we were to travel. **1883** SWEET & KNOX *Through Texas* 169 The horses are hardy mustangs, called cow-ponies. **1897** *Outing* XXIX. 596/1 My pursuers . . . imparted a prodigious lashing to their winded mustangs.

3. *transf.* 'An officer entering the U.S. navy from the merchant service, after serving through the Civil War' (F. and H.). *slang.*

4. =MUSTANG GRAPE.

1854 LONGFELLOW *Poetical Works* (1893) 196/2 The red Mustang, Whose clusters hang O'er the waves of the Colorado. **1862** *Rep. Comm. Patents 1861: Agric.* 482 The Mustang is not a good table grape, but promises to be of great value for wine.

5. *attrib.* **a.** (See quotation and cf. 1 b above.)

1831 HOLLEY *Texas* (1833) 89 These wild horses are called . . . Mustangs, and hence the figure of speech to denote anything wild and uncultivated, as a mustang girl, applied to a rude hunter's daughter.

b. In senses 1 and 2 with *cavalry, colt, horse,* etc.

1836 EDWARD *Hist. Texas* 79 [The people of Texas] have more . . . milk than they know how to dispose of, except they are well stocked with farrow sows, or have around them pet mustang colts. *Ib.* 108 The mustang horses . . . [the Comanches] catch and tame for service, or kill for subsistence. **1841** *Picayune* 8 June 2/3 The Indian trail discovered a few miles west of Austin, is likely to turn out nothing but a mustang trail. **1849** *31st Congress 1 Sess.* Sen. Ex. Doc. No. 64, 207 This lake I have called 'Mustang pond.' **1861** *Harper's Mag.* June 11/2 Horses then [in 1849] became valuable, and the mustang hunters made a good business of it. **1872** POWERS *Afoot & Alone* 118 Ox-driving Eastern Texas furnished to the Confederacy several infantry regiments who were worth more than all the mustang cavalry together. **1923** J. H. COOK *On Old Frontier* 67, I never took any part in 'mustang hunts' of this type, but I watched the performance a few times.

+**Mustanger.** One who makes a business of catching wild mustangs. — **1857** OLMSTED *Texas* 443 The business of entrapping them [*sc.* mustangs] has given rise to a class of men called 'mustangers,' composed of runaway vagabonds, and outlaws of all nations, the legitimate border-ruffians of Texas. **1883** SWEET & KNOX *Through Texas* 583 These men were called mustangers.

+**Mustang grape.** A woody grapevine (*Vitis candicans*) of the Southwest; the light-colored, pungent grapes of this vine. — **1848** *Rep. Comm. Patents 1847* 198 He speaks of the great mustang grape in very high terms. **1862** *Rep. Comm. Patents 1861: Agric.* 482 The Mustang grape abounds in rich soils throughout a large portion of Texas. **1891** COULTER *Bot. W. Texas* I. 62 Mustang grape. Along streams from the Colorado to the Rio Grande and west to the Pecos. **1903** A. ADAMS *Log Cowboy* i. 6 Along the [San Antonio] river grew endless quantities of mustang grapes.

+**Mustang pony.** =MUSTANG 1 and 2. — **1846** THORPE *Myst. Backwoods* 15 Before the ox has recovered from its astonishment, a hair rope has been passed through his nose, [and] secured to the mustang pony's tail. **1858** VIELÉ *Following Drum* 84 A light wagon and a pair of mustang ponies were provided for us. **1873** MILLER *Amongst Modocs* 3 Mexicans drive mules or herd their mustang ponies. **1890** GUNTER *Miss Nobody* v, Sure-footed as these mustang ponies generally are. **1922** T. A. MCNEAL *When Kansas Was Young* 188 The Texan 'called' with . . . fourteen Texas mustang ponies and the deed to a tract of land.

+**Mustang wine.** Wine made from mustang grapes. — **1862** *Rep. Comm. Patents 1861: Agric.* 483 Mustang wine is made in Texas by gathering the grapes in July, and passing them through a cog or cane-mill, or else they are placed in a cask open at one end and pounded. **1882** SWEET & KNOX *Texas Siftings* 45 The contents of the bottle was not the vile stuff called 'home-made mustang wine.'

* **Mustard.**

***1.** Any of various plants of the genus *Brassica,* esp. the white and black mustards; any of several other plants of the mustard family, Brassicaceae.

1698 THOMAS *Penna. & N.J.* 21 Besides what grows naturally Wild in the Country, and that in great plenty also, as Mustard, Rue, Sage, Mint. **1737** BRICKELL *N. Carolina* 20 The Pot-Herbs . . . are . . . Bastard Saffron; and several sorts of Mustard. **1838** *Mass. Agric. Survey 1st Rep.* 70 Charlock or Cadluc. This pernicious and troublesome weed, known by some, as the wild turnip or mustard, prevails to some extent. **1872** POWERS *Afoot & Alone* 259 The whole valley is now utterly parched and dry, ragged with . . . weeds and mustard.

b. With specifying adjectives.

1784 CUTLER in *Mem. Academy* I. 468 *Sinapis siliquis glabris tetragonis.* . . . Black Mustard. Blossoms pale yellow. Common about barns. **1814** BIGELOW *Florula Bostoniensis* 159 *Sinapis nigra.* Common mustard. . . . Very common in cultivated and waste grounds. **1843** TORREY *Flora N.Y.* I. 53 *Turritis stricta.* . . . Straight Tower Mustard. . . . On rocks, Watertown, Jefferson county. **1847** DARLINGTON *Weeds & Plants* 47 These two species, known as Black and White Mustard, . . . are naturalized in many places, having escaped from gardens. **1857** GRAY *Botany* 35 *E[rysimum] cheiranthoides.* (Worm-seed Mustard.) . . . Banks of streams, New York, Penn., Illinois, and northward: apparently truly indigenous.

***2. a.** The ground-up seeds of the black or white mustard. **b.** The paste made from this by the addition of vinegar, water, etc., used as a condiment or as a counterirritant.

1812 *Niles' Reg.* II. 147 Among the luxuries . . . for which we have principally been dependent on foreign countries, is the article of *Mustard.* **1860** *Ladies' Repository* XX. 41/1 The pie underdone, the castor destitute of mustard, and the coffee not fit to drink. **1875** STOWE *We & Neighbors* 68 Doctors apply mustard to the feet, to divert the too abundant blood from the head.

+**3.** *To be the (proper) mustard,* to be the genuine article or the main thing; *to be all* (or *so much*) *to the mustard,* to be very important.

Cf. CUT *v.* 25 i.

1903 A. ADAMS *Log Cowboy* 237 For fear they [two dogs] were not the proper mustard, he had that dog man sue him in court for the balance, so as to make him prove the pedigree. **1903** 'O. HENRY' *Cabbages & Kings* 101, I'm not headlined in the bills, but I'm the mustard in the salad dressing just the same. **1907** — *Trimmed Lamp* 217 Why don't you invite him if he's so much to the mustard? **1922** SANDBURG *Slabs Sunburnt West* 7 Kid each other, you cheap skates. Tell each other you're all to the mustard.

4. Attrib. and comb. in sense 2 with *foot bath, grinder, manufactory,* etc.

1674 *Harvard Rec.* I. 62 Kitchins Utensils . . . 1 Mustard-querne [etc.]. **1789** *Boston Directory* 196 Rumney Edward, chocolate and mustard-grinder. **1793** *Mass. Spy* 19 Sept. 4/3 The following articles of plate were stolen: . . . One Pepper Box, One Mustard Pot, A pair of Salts. **1796** *Boston Directory* 279 Rumney, Edward, mustard manufactory, Back street. **1885** CABLE *Dr. Sevier* 283 He lifted his great feet and lowered them into the mustard foot-bath. **1890** HOWELLS *Boy's Town* 33, I do not know just what it was they did with a mustard-mill that was there.

Mustard plaster. *Med.* A plaster made of mustard spread out on a cloth. {1866} — **1858** VIELÉ *Following Drum* 32 Apply a uniform to a man, and like a mustard plaster, it seems to draw all that is inflammable to the surface. **1879** BURDETTE *Hawkeyes* 51 It's a ninety days' note, and it's down in the bank now, drawing interest like a horse race or a mustard plaster. **1905** PRINGLE *Rice Planter* 141, I sent her out at once with . . . a mustard plaster I made, and told her to see it put on.

***Mustard seed.** +=next. — **1874** COUES *Field Ornithol.* 9 A small bird . . . may be riddled with mustard-seed and yet be preservable.

+**Mustard-seed shot.** Very small bird shot. — **1809** FESSENDEN *Pills Poetical* 8n., Her single great gun loaded with mustard seed shot. **1834** *S. Lit. Messenger* I. 182 He might as well attempt to batter the rock of Gibraltar with mustard seed shot as to attack the yellow fever with alkali. **1846** THORPE *Myst. Backwoods* 180 A charge of mustard-seed shot, or a poke with a stick when at bay, will cause it [the 'cat'] to desert its airy abode.

Mustee. {a half-caste, 1699-} **a.** The offspring of a quadroon and a white person. {1796-} **b.** Loosely, the offspring of an Indian and either a white person or a Negro. {1712-}

In English use chiefly with reference to the East Indies.

1720 *S.C. Statutes* III. 109 The Captains . . . shall form and compleat a list of such negroes, mulattoes, mustees and Indian slaves, as they . . . shall judge serviceable for the [militia]. **1724** H. JONES *Virginia* 37 Such as are born of an Indian and Negroe are called Mustees. **1741** *S.C. Hist. Soc. Coll.* IV. 14 In 1706 the Spaniards at St. Augustine joined the French from Martinico in making up a Fleet of ten sail, with 800 men, whites, mustees and negroes, and 200 Indians. **1768** *Smithtown Rec.* 107 No Squaw Mustee or Mulatto female shall after the first day of May next have any house or cellar, or wigwam, standing in the bounds of said Smithtown. **1806** *Balance* V. 53/1 The expression 'people of color,' means mulattoes, mustees, costees, etc. all colors from black to white. **1817** *Niles' Reg.* XII. 60/1 The assembly of New York . . . has passed the bill declaring all negroes and mulattoes and mustees within that state, to be free after the 4th of July 1827. **1861** NEWELL *Orpheus C. Kerr* I. 211 A

South Carolina gentleman. . . . You trace his genealogy, and not far back you'll see A most undoubted octoroon, or mayhap a mustee.

attrib. **1732** *S.C. Gazette* 11/2 Run away, . . . a Mustee Wench about 18 Years of Age. **1761** *Newport Mercury* 19 May 3/3 A Likely Mustee Boy, aged 13, will be sold for ten Years. **1797** *Wilmington Gazette* 7 Sept., A Mustee fellow named Josh, the property of Craik's estate, well known in town as a fidler. **1832** *Congress. Deb.* 2 June 3247 The people in the neighborhood of the Menomonee village . . . he denominated mustee French, and pronounced incapable of self-government.

***Muster,** *n.*

***1.** The action of assembling soldiers, recruits, etc., for inspection, ascertainment of numbers, drill, etc.; the occasion of such action.

See also GENERAL MUSTER.

1658 *Md. Council Proc.* 345 They do appoint sett times and places for the next Muster before they depart from euery meeteing to Trayne and Exercise. **1775** *Jrnls. Cont. Congress* III. 333 Every officer . . . shall, upon notice given to him by the commissary of the musters, . . . assemble the regiment. **1838** *S. Lit. Messenger* IV. 638/2 Stout boots—worn only upon grand occasions,—such as musters, county courts, and elections. **1898** PAGE *Red Rock* 233 There was to be a great muster of Leech's 'new militia.'

+2. *transf.* A group of race horses assembled at the starting line.

1836 *Quarter Race Ky.* (1846) 13 The muster at the stand was slim.

3. Attrib. in sense 1 with *day, field, ground,* etc.

1777 *N.H. Comm. Safety Rec.* 68 Made out a Form of orders for the Muster orders. **1780** ASBURY *Journal* I. 380, [I] had about sixty people, it being a muster-day. **1798** *Ann. 5th Congress* 1707 At the muster ground on the Commons of Portsmouth, the 5th of May, 1798, the following proceedings took place. **1838** DRAKE *Tales & Sk.* 179 Our sons . . . assembling in the 'muster field,' divide themselves into armies, and pelt each other with Buckeye balls.

***Muster,** *v.*

+1. *To be mustered into the service,* to be enrolled into military service. Also *to be mustered in.*

1848 *30th Congress 1 Sess.* Sen. Rep. No. 75, 36, I was present when the California battalion was mustered into the service of the United States. **1861** *Chicago Tribune* 26 May 1/6 Five companies of the regiment . . . were mustered into service for three years. **1865** *Mich. Gen. Statutes* I. (1882) 298 All officers, non-commissioned officers, musicians and privates, who may be mustered into the service of this state . . . shall be privileged from arrest. **1911** *Okla. Session Laws* 3 Legisl. 217 Before any ex-Confederate or ex-Union soldier or sailor shall be entitled to any of the privileges, he shall make an affidavit in writing that he was properly mustered in and served as a soldier or sailor in the army or navy of the Confederacy or United States prior to the year 1866.

+2. *To be mustered out,* to be summoned to a muster in order to be discharged from service. Also in active voice.

1834 WAKEFIELD *Hist. Black Hawk War* (1907) 145 Lieutenant Anderson, of the United States army, . . . mustered us all out of the service of the United States. **1865** in W. Lawrence *A. A. Lawrence* 205 The officers put on their civilian dress the next day after they are mustered out. **1877** JOHNSON *Anderson Co., Kansas* 134 Crawford was selected as captain of the company, and after five months' service it was mustered out and re-organized. **1883** HAY *Bread-Winners* 242, I wouldn't muster out that army of yours till to-morrow. **1903** FOX *Little Shepherd* xxvii. 27 Chad got permission straightway to go back to Ohio and be mustered out with his old regiment.

+b. *fig.* To be killed in action.

1866 'KIRKLAND' *Bk. Anecdotes* 629 The simple epitaph [read:] . . . A Soldier of the Union Mustered Out.

***Mustering.** *attrib.* +Designating articles of dress worn by soldiers or sailors on the occasion of a muster. — **1841** *S. Lit. Messenger* VII. 768/1 Who should I see . . . but Mr. Jim Guest himself, in . . . mustering jacket and trowsers, and tarpaulin hat. **1894** *Outing* XXIV. 468 [Picture showing] Enlisted Men in Mustering Uniform.

+Mustering day. A day on which a muster is held. — **1745** HEMPSTEAD *Diary* 442 The 1st & 2d Company are viewing Arms &c. mustering Day through the Colony. **a1846** *Quarter Race Ky.* 174 Now take my advice and have it altered by next mustering day.

+Mustering-in. The action by which men are mustered into service. — **1869** *Overland Mo.* III. 129 At the mustering-in no member was of a lighter weight than a hundred and eighty pounds.

Mustering officer. {1758} =next. Also transf. — **1861** *Army. Reg.* 497 The mustering officer will give his particular attention to the state and condition of the public property: such as quarters, camp-equipage [etc.]. **1864** 'PENNIMAN' *Tanner-Boy* 95, [I] appoint you on my staff, with the position of mustering-officer of volunteers for the State. **1884** *Boston Jrnl.* 6 Sept., Stirring speeches were made by . . . District Commander Atwood of Plymouth county and Mr. Chas. Penniman, Chief Mustering Officer of the Sons of Veterans of Minnesota.

***Muster master.** (See quot. 1918.)

1636 *Mass. Bay Rec.* I. 187 Each regiment shall have one muster master. **1775** *Mass. Prov. Congress* (1823) 199 Muster masters in the Massachusetts army, whose business it shall be to pass muster on every soldier that shall be enlisted into said army. **1779** E. GERRY in *Warren-Adams Lett.* II. 124 The Departments of the Muster and Barrack Masters are abolished. **1918** FARROW *Dict. Mil. Terms* 401 *Muster Master.*—One who takes an account of troops, and of their equipment; a mustering officer or inspector.

Muster master general. The chief of the muster masters. {1662–} *Obs.* — **1640** Neill *Va. Carolorum* 149 Following your Majesties orders and directions by your letters in speedy appointing a Muster Master General and Marshall. **1650** *Md. Archives* I. 292 The Mustermr. Generall of this province shall haue yearely allowed him . . . ffower pounds of Tob[acco] and Caske uppon every taxable person. **1776** *Jrnls. Cont. Congress* V. 460 Resolved, That General Washington be empowered and directed to nominate and send a deputy muster master general to Canada.

+Muster-out. The action of discharging a soldier or soldiers from service. Also attrib. — **1888** *Century Mag.* May 95/1 The muster-out rolls of this gallant regiment furnish the names from which the following abstract is made. **1899** *Statutes at Large* XXX. 1073 All enlisted men . . . shall be paid two months' extra pay on muster out and discharge from the service. **1903** FOX *Little Shepherd* xxv, The Commandant . . . ordered the muster-out of all State troops then in service.

Muster roll. An official list or register of the officers and men of a soldiers' or ship's company present or accounted for at a muster. {1605–}

On this list has sometimes been kept the record of the soldiers' accounts and days of service. Hence the sense: a record of a company's accounts.

1705 *Boston News-Letter* 12 Nov. 2/1 Whosoever . . . shall apprehend and return such Deserters . . . shall be at all times paid their just Charges therein out of the wages of such Souldier so restored . . . to be Assigned by the Governour, out of their next Muster-Roll, wherein such Deserters names are, and payment accordingly. **1720** *Mass. H. Rep. Jrnls.* II. 305 In which muster-roll Thomas Brown, was put down for Eleven weeks Two days. **1721** *Ib.* III. 73 The Committee . . . have taken the same out of the Amount of the Muster-Roll, being *l.* 329—13—7. **1800** *Essex Inst. Coll.* X. III. 62 Forwarded my despatches to the Navy Office, consisting of a muster roll [etc.]. **1812** MARSHALL *Kentucky* 235 By means of tythe lists, and muster-rolls, the number of the males of each county, could be ascertained with tolerable accuracy. **1861** *Army Regulations* 127 Extra-duty pay of the saddler in a mounted company will be charged on the company muster-roll. **1900** *Congress. Rec.* 22 Jan. 1033/2 An examination of the muster rolls discloses the fact that not a member of the legislature which submitted the proposed amendment participated in that struggle.

***Mutch.** Also **much.** *local.* A woman's cap: (see quot. 1704). *Obs.* — **1680** *New Castle Court Rec.* 404 His wyfe had stole a mutch or Capp. **1704** S. KNIGHT *Journal* 54 The Dutch . . . women, in their habitt go loose, were French muches wch are like a Capp and a head band in one, leaving their ears bare.

***Mutton.**

***1.** The flesh of sheep used as food.

1630 J. WINTHROP in Winthrop *Life & Let.* II. 54 Though we have not beef and mutton etc., yet . . . we want them not; our Indian corn answers for all. **1681** *Penna. Mag.* VI. 175 That which is most scarce is Mutton and Beef, because you must kill it yourself, I mean of your own. **1701** *Boston Rec.* 14 No person . . . [shall buy] any sort of . . . mutton, veal, . . . or any other sort of provision. **1761** *Holyoke Diaries* 25 Mutton sent to the poor @ Thanksgiving. **1863** *Rep. Comm. Agric. 1862* 47 Many farmers began to raise other breeds which were more hardy and better fitted for the production of mutton. **1909** *Indian Laws & Tr.* III. 419 [Granted] for the purchase of beef, mutton, wheat, flour, beans, and potatoes, . . . thirty thousand dollars.

+b. *To fix one's mutton,* (see FIX *v.* 6 b).

2. *attrib.* **a.** Designating various kinds of cooked foods made with or consisting of mutton.

1769 WASHINGTON *Diaries* I. 353 Had a Mutton Chop at Mrs. Campbell's. **1787** FRENEAU *Misc. Works* 426 He longs to have hold of the bak'd mutton pye. **1828** H. FINN, etc. *Whimwhams* 132 He was a sickly, feeble wight, . . . Living on viands acetose, Weak gruels—mutton soup. **c1866** BAGBY *Old Va. Gentleman* 48 A true Virginian . . . must have . . . potatoes, June apples, . . . milk and peaches, mutton stew, dewberries [etc.]. **1883** H. P. SPOFFORD in *Harper's Mag.* Aug. 463/2, I should like mutton broth and gumbo every day. **1892** GUNTER *Miss Dividends* 232 She's got three beefsteak pies, two mutton-hash pasties.

b. *Mutton cane,* young, tender sprouts of cane: (see quotation).

1901 MOHR *Plant Life Ala.* 103 These simple sprouts, which are known as 'mutton cane', are tender and sweet and afford the best of pasturage.

Mutton fish. {1882–} **+1.** The pargo, *Lutianus analis.* **+2.** =CONGER EEL 2. **+3.** (See quotation.) In full *mutton-fish thimble.* **+4.** The mojarra, *Diapterus olisthostomus.* — (1) [**c1735** CATESBY *Carolina* II. 25 *Anthea quartus Rondeletii.* . . . The Mutton Fish. . . . For the excellency of it's Tast it is in greater Esteem than any other at the Bahama Islands.] **1911** *Rep. Fisheries 1908* 313/1 Mutton-fish (*Zoarces anguillaris*). The name is also given to the snapper . . . of Florida. (2) **1884** GOODE, etc. *Fisheries* I. 247 The Mutton-fish . . . is often seen near the shore north of Cape Cod. **1897** *N.Y. Forest, Fish, & Game Comm. 2d Rep.* 245 Mutton-Fish . . . never endures the warm water in summer. **1911** [see 1 above]. (3) **1885** J. S. KINGSLEY, etc. *Stand. Nat. Hist.* I. 93 One of the most abundant medusæ at times in the neighborhood of the Florida

Keys is a Discophore, called by naturalists *Linerges*, and known to fishermen there as the 'thimble-fish,' 'mutton-fish thimble' [etc.]. *Ib.*, Index, Mutton-fish 93. (4) **1896** JORDAN & EVERMANN *Check-List Fishes* 392 *Gerres olisthostoma*. . . . Irish Pompano; Mutton-fish. West Indies, north to southern Florida.

Mutton ham. {*a*1791–} +A certain kind of sail used on a fishing smack. Hence *mutton-ham boat*. — **1899** *Atlantic Mo.* Aug. 197 In a Mutton-Ham boat. *Ib.*, [The boat's] mutton-ham fluttered as white as new cotton around her single mast. I more than once sought to learn why Albemarle and Pamlico fishing smacks call their huge sails 'mutton-ham.'

+**Muttonhead.** A stupid person. *colloq.* — **1804** FESSENDEN *Terrible Tractoration* 159 And couldst thou, pertinacious Bradley, But maul these mutton heads, most sadly. **1825** NEAL *Bro. Jonathan* I. 99 Peace, muttonhead! **1912** RAINE *Brand Blotters* 238 You'd *savez* it now, if you weren't a muttonhead.

+**Muttonize,** *v. tr.* (See quotation.) *colloq.*[2] — **1895** *Voice* 17 Oct. 7/5 'Muttonize' is the latest word in sheep-breeding. It means the introduction of the blood of meat-growing sheep into the wool flocks.

Mutton-leg. *attrib.* +**1.** *Mutton-leg sleeve*, a sleeve fashioned in the shape of a leg of mutton. {leg-of-mutton s., 1840–} +**2.** *Mutton-leg sail*, =MUTTON HAM. — (1) **1845** *Lowell Offering* V. 201 Here is a piece of the first dress I ever saw, cut with what were called 'mutton-leg' sleeves. (2) **1880** *Harper's Mag.* May 856/2 The 'mutton-leg' sails have no provision for reefing.

* **Mutual,** *a.*

+**1.** Designating various insurance companies in which the policyholders constitute the shareholders and elect the officers.

1798 *Mass. Statute* 1 March, The Massachusetts mutual fire insurance Company . . . shall have power to choose . . . fifteen Directors . . . to manage the concerns of the said Corporation. **1810** in Marshall *Kentucky* II. 470 A mutual assurance society against fire on buildings in this commonwealth. **1865** *Atlantic Mo.* Jan. 86/1 [In New York City] there existed at the same date [Dec. 31, 1863] twenty-one mutual fire-insurance companies. **1881** *Harper's Mag.* Jan. 279/2 Insurance . . . companies should be strictly mutual. **1912** E. V. FRENCH *1860–1910: Arkwright Co.* 5 The Mutual Companies, beginning among the textile mills of New England, found the average mill a substantial structure of stone or brick.

+**2.** Designating various other societies organized so that the members are of assistance to each other.

1833 COKE *Subaltern's Furlough* iii, There are . . . above one hundred and fifty mutual benefit societies, on the principle of the English clubs. **1864** NICHOLS *Amer. Life* I. 64 The mutual improvement and debating societies had their day. **1887** *Courier-Journal* 1 May 12/1 [By] a kind of mutual benefit association, . . . season tickets could be obtained here cheaper than in any city where the National Opera Company has played. **1891** *Atlantic Mo.* June 814/1 The colored people have developed . . . Good Samaritan societies, and mutual benefit organizations.

Mutual admiration society. An ironic designation for any group of persons whose chief concern appears to be demonstrating approval of each other. {1880} — **1858** HOLMES *Autocrat* 4 Who can tell what we owe to the Mutual Admiration Society of which Shakespeare, and Ben Jonson, and Beaumont and Fletcher were members? **1859** *Ladies' Repository* XIX. 508/2 The Boston *literati* constitute a kind of 'mutual admiration society.' **1873** COZZENS *Marvellous Country* 396 The 'brave man's dance' proved to be the assembling together of a body of Indians who evidently belonged to a 'mutual admiration society.' **1894** *Nation* 22 March 211/2 They are members of a mutual-admiration society . . . and have periodical dinners.

+**Mux,** *n.*[1] [?Amer. Ind.] Any sharp-pointed, metal instrument that may be used, according to its design, for boring holes, spearing fish, etc. *Obs.* — **1648** *Southampton Rec.* I. 51 In consideracon of twentie Coats, . . . one hundred Muxes, . . . we do give vp . . . all our right and interest in the sayd land. **1650** *Smithtown Rec.* 1 In consideration of which land we the aforesaid Partyes do promise to pay . . . Six Kettles, one hundred Muxes. **1653** *Oyster Bay Rec.* I. 671 He is to receaue . . . thirty Aulnblades, or muxes, twenty Kniues, three shirts. **1658** *Huntington Rec.* I. 17 Huntington . . . shall pay . . . twenty dutch howes, twenty duch knivis, two hundred of muxes.

+**Mux,** *n.*[2] [f. next.] A disordered condition; a mess. *New Eng.* — **1848** J. MITCHELL *Nantucketisms* 41 'In a mux.' Confused, disarranged. **1865** E. STODDARD *Two Men* 28 (*Stand.*), I knew you would come back. Now we are in a mux. **1890** *Cent.* 3916/3 *Mux*, . . . work performed in an awkward or improper manner; a botch; a mess: as, he made a mux of it.

+**Mux,** *v. tr.* To make disorderly; to mess up. {1867} — **1806** *Balance* 26 Aug. 272 (Th.), To do observance, make obliging mention, Wink lovingly, mux chastity away. **1859** BARTLETT 287 *To Mux* is much used in New England for *muss;* as, 'Don't *mux* my crinoline.' **1877** J. M. BAILEY *They All Do It* 22 (B.), Stop muxin' that bread! . . . I shan't have you muxing and gauming up the victuals.

Muxy, *a.* {1746–, *dial.*} Of a meadow: Slushy, muddy. *Obs.* {1855– (s.v. *mucksy*)} — **1665** *Springfield Rec.* II. 218 And it is Ordered yt the Said six acres, . . . is soe to run to thorow along by the fence side to cover the muxy meddow. **1688** *Ib.* 275 Thomas Cooper desires . . . that the Town would grant him Ten acres on this side the muxy medow for conveniency of fencing. **1715** *Ib.* 325 [The] Land is situate and Lyeth on the back side of Muxy medow.

Muzzle-loader. A gun that is loaded through its muzzle. {1858–} — **1874** LONG *Wild-Fowl* 24 For a muzzle-loader, a slight increase in the gauge will admit of larger charges being used for flock shooting. **1880** *Harper's Mag.* May 918/2 When game was plenty, in the days of the old muzzle-loaders, every boy learned to shoot. **1902** LORIMER *Lett. Merchant* 31 Thirty years ago, you could take an old muzzle-loader and knock over plenty of ducks in the city limits [of Chicago].

Muzzle-loading rifle. A rifle loaded at its muzzle. — **1856** *Porter's Spirit of Times* 22 Nov. 192/1 A muzzle smaller than the chamber is a disadvantage to an ordinary muzzle-loading rifle, an advantage to a breech-loading piece. **1871** *Rep. Indian Affairs* (1872) 405 Nearly all the men are supplied with muzzle-loading rifles and Colt's revolvers. **1925** BRYAN *Memoirs* 36 We began the afternoon before . . . moulding the bullets for a muzzle-loading rifle.

Mynheer. {1652–} **a.** A Dutchman. {1782–} +**b.** A generic name for Dutchmen, or loosely, for the Germans of Pennsylvania.

1701 WOLLEY *Journal N.Y.* (1902) 69 *Frederick Philips* the richest *Miin Heer* in that place . . . was said to have whole Hogsheads of Indian Money or *Wampam*. **1784** FRENEAU *Poems* (1786) 407 Had his sword and his title been equally slender In vain had they summon'd Mynheer to surrender. **1862** in Moore *Rebellion Rec.* V. I. 81 [The Southern soldiers would] teach the Dutch farmers and graziers, who have been clamorous for this war, what invasion really is. . . . Mynheer will cry aloud for peace in a very short time. **1882** MCCABE *New York* 135 The portly 'mynheers' turned out their cows to graze. **1890** *Century Mag.* Nov. 46/1 It gave the good mynheers inexhaustible food for reflection.

* **Myrtle.** Also †**mirtle.**

1. ***a.** Any shrub or tree of the family Myrtaceae, esp. *Myrtus communis*. **b.** Any shrub or tree of the genus *Myrica*, +esp. the wax myrtles, *M. cerifera* and *M. carolinensis*.

See also CANDLEBERRY MYRTLE and WAX MYRTLE and cf. BAYBERRY.

1634 WOOD *New Eng. Prospect* 13 In the woods, without eyther the art or the helpe of man, . . . [grow] mirtle, saxifarilla, bayes, &c. **1682** ASH *Carolina* 6 There are many other Fragrant smelling trees, the Myrtle, Bay and Laurel. **1705** BEVERLEY *Virginia* II. 22 The Myrtle, bearing a Berry, of which they make a hard brittle wax. **1778** CARVER *Travels* 509 The myrtle . . . bears small berries, which are generally called Bay Berries. **1821** NUTTALL *Travels Arkansa* 232 The pomegranate, and the myrtle, grow and fruit almost as in their native climate. **1868** GRAY *Field Botany* 149 *Myrtus communis*, Common Myrtle, from the Mediterranean region. **1897** SUDWORTH *Arborescent Flora* 117 *Myrica californica*. . . . Myrtle (Nev.).

attrib. **1696–8** *Mass. H. S. Coll.* 1 Ser. V. 127 There is great store of the myrtleberries, which being boiled up to a wax, make as good candles as the best wax candles whatsoever.

2. Any of various other plants: +**a.** The trailing periwinkle, *Vinca minor*. +**b.** =MOUNTAIN LAUREL 2.

See also BLUE MYRTLE.

(**a**) **1890** *Cent.* 3923/3 Running myrtle, more often simply *myrtle*, a name of the common periwinkle. **1892** *Amer. Folk-Lore* V. 100. (**b**) **1897** SUDWORTH *Arborescent Flora* 203 *Umbellularia californica*. . . . Myrtle (Oreg.).

+**Myrtle bird.** =MYRTLE WARBLER. — **1810** WILSON *Ornithology* II. 139 Thro the whole of the lower parts of the Carolinas, wherever the myrtles grew, these birds [*sc.* yellow-rumped warblers] were numerous. . . . In those parts of the country they are generally known by the name of Myrtle-birds. **1844** *Nat. Hist. N.Y., Zoology* II. 88 The Myrtle-Bird . . . feeds on . . . the myrtle-wax berries. **1917** *Birds of Amer.* III. 128.

Myrtle grass. The sweet flag, *Acorus calamus*. — **1791** MUHLENBERG *Index Florae* 167 *Acorus, Calamus*. Myrtle-grass.

+**Myrtle warbler.** (See quot. 1917.) — **1892** TORREY *Foot-Path Way* 95 Myrtle-warblers . . . manifest a particular fondness for the immediate vicinity of houses. **1902** WHITE *Blazed Trail* 296 Myrtle and magnolia warblers, oven birds, peewits . . . passed silently or noisily. **1917** *Birds of Amer.* III. 128.

+**Myrtle wax.** A wax obtained from the berries of the wax myrtles.

1700 *Va. State P.* I. 68, 26 pounds of Mirtle-wax, 01. 06. 00. **1726** *Md. Hist. Mag.* XVIII. 215 Inclosed is bill Loading for one Case Conta[ining] 1 Hundred weight Myrtle & bees wax. **1789** MORSE *Amer. Geog.* 414 The exports . . . [are] myrtle-wax, and a few other articles. **1837** WILLIAMS *Florida* 114 Some of the most important productions of the country indeed, require to be manufactured on the spot; such are, sugar, indigo, myrtle wax [etc.]. **1880** CABLE *Grandissimes* 414 He removed the lid and saw within . . . the image, in myrtle-wax.

attrib. **1766** STORK *Acct. E. Florida* 48 The myrtle-wax shrub is, without doubt, the most useful of the spontaneous growth of America. **1770** PITTMAN *Present State* 23 The different articles are indigo, cotton, rice, maiz, beans, myrtle wax-candles, and lumber. **1797** IMLAY *Western Territory* (ed. 3) 271 The myrtle wax tree is one of the greatest blessings with which nature has enriched Louisiana.

+**Mystic testament, will.** *La.* [Fr. *testament mystique*.] A testament or will made under seal. — **1839** BOUVIER *Law Dict.* II. 435/2 A mystic testament is also called a solemn testament, because it requires more formality than a nuncupative testament. **1891** *Amer. & Eng. Encycl. Law* XVI. 111 *Mystic Will*. In *Louisiana*, a mystic will is a will under seal.

N

N. A. *abbrev.* +**1.** For *National Academician* or *Academy.* **2.** (See quotation.) — **(1) 1883** *Harper's Mag.* Nov. 843/2 [G. H. Boughton] enjoys . . . the unusual distinction of being an N.A. and an A.R.A. **1924** *Who's Who in Amer.* XIII. 1706/1 Inness, George, Jr., painter; . . . A.N.A., 1895, N.A., 1899. **(2) 1890** *Cent.* 3927/1 *N.A.* An abbreviation . . . of *North America,* or *North American.*

Nabob. {1612–}

+**1.** (See quot. 1804.) *Obs.*

1803 E. S. Bowne *Life* 151 Silk nabobs . . . are much worn. **1804** Fessenden *Orig. Poems* (1806) 36 Misses, squires, and gentlefolks, Call for Nabobs, hats, and cloaks. [Note:] Nabobs were a kind of outside garment formerly worn by the dashing belles of America.

+**2.** A wealthy or aristocratic southern plantation owner. {1764–, in more general sense}

1830 Royall *Southern Tour* I. 39 The nabobs of highborn Virginia would run before an old woman. **1856** M. J. Holmes *L. Rivers* xxxvii, She went off to Virginia to teach music, and so married a nabob. **1863** 'E. Kirke' *Southern Friends* 113 You Southern nabobs do nothing but waste. **1891** Welch *Recoll. 1830–40* 157 This southern travel mostly consisted of the sugar 'Nabobs' of Louisiana and rich planters from the 'Cotton States.'

Nabobess. {1767–} ||The wife of a southern nabob. — **1864** in *Amer. Speech* V. 478, I find these Southern nabobs, yes, and nabobesses, who were going to die in the last ditch, are quite willing to swear any amount of oaths in order to taste the sweets of Uncle Sam's pantry.

***Nag.** A small horse or pony, especially one used for riding. — **1704** S. Knight *Journal* 18, I gave reins to my Nagg. **1829** Cooper *Wish-ton-Wish* ii, His little nag stopped of itself on a small eminence. **1881** *Rep. Indian Affairs* 168, I have . . . frequently made application . . . for permission to dispose of our four old nags and purchase a good active team. **1910** J. Hart *Vigilante Girl* 367 We come mighty near forgettin' Strang's nag.

***Nail,** *n.*

***1.** A slender metal spike, usually pointed, designed to be driven into two or more pieces of wood, etc., to hold them together.

1634 Winthrop in *Hist.* I. 462 Yourself . . . may consider accordingly . . . store of sail cloth, nails, cordage, pitch. **1716** *Mass. Bay Currency Tracts* 174 Nails, & other small Works . . . at present cannot be made at the price for want of a Slitting Mill, to slit the Iron into suitable Rods. **1813** *Niles' Reg.* IV. 294/2 We have tons of nails, cut or drawn, with spikes, brads, sprigs and tacks. **1907** *St. Nicholas* July 780/1 Many of the old joists and plank, however, were too rotten to hold nails.

+**2.** *Nail City of the West,* Wheeling, W.Va.

1890 *Congress. Rec.* 9 May 4433/2 Down through the thriving city of Wheeling—the Nail City of the West—I could hear the rattling roll of machinery.

3. Attrib. and comb. in sense 1 with *manufactory, mill, tool, works.*

1779 *Narragansett Hist. Reg.* I. 97 Made nail tools and hammer. **1809** *Ann. 11th Congress* 2248 There are now in this vicinity [near Boston] extensive nail manufactories. **1850** *Rep. Comm. Patents 1849: Agric.* 93 Within . . . [the] present limits [of Bristol Co., Mass.] are about . . . seven rolling, slitting, and nail mills. **1913** London *Valley of Moon* 269 Saxon recognized . . . the shipyards, the nail works, Market street wharf.

+**Nail,** *v. carpentry.* ||*intr.* To work as a carpenter. — **1885** Whitman in *N. Amer. Rev.* Nov. 434, 1st Conductor [of a horse car], 'What did you do before you was a snatcher?' Answer of 2d Conductor, 'Nailed.' (Translation of answer: 'I worked as carpenter.')

Nail-cutter. 1. One whose occupation is cutting nails. **2.** =next. — **(1) 1851** Cist *Cincinnati* 50 Occupations [include] . . . Nail cutters, . . . Nail makers. **(2) 1875** Knight 1505/2 The American nail-cutter was the first to cut the nails and swage the heads at one operation.

+**Nail-cutting machine.** A machine that makes cut nails. — **1816** *Mass. H. S. Coll.* 2 Ser. VII. 70 There were in the county of Hillsborough, in 1810 . . . 5 nail cutting machines, making 10 tons per annum. **1818** Darby *Emigrant's Guide* 227 Already have been erected [in Cincinnati] a nail cutting machine, many flour mills, . . . and several saw-mills. **1819** Flint *Lett. from Amer.* 125 The manufactories are . . . a grist-mill, a nail-cutting machine, . . . and a white-lead factory.

Nail-driver. +In figurative applications: **1.** A cannon that shoots accurately. **2.** A straight-running horse. — **(1) 1823** Cooper *Pilot* viii, The cannon, above which were painted the several quaint names of 'boxer,' . . . 'exterminator,' and 'nail-driver.' **(2) 1878** Hickman *Brigham's Destroying Angel* 54, I had a nail-driver very swift and no end to his bottom.

***Nailer.** Also †**nayler, nailor.**

***1.** A nail-maker.

1643 *Suffolk Deeds* I. 52 Thomas Cartter . . . granted unto Edward Jackson of Cambridge nayler, his Meddowe at the Pines. **1716** *Mass. Bay Currency Tracts* 174 If the Souldiers at the Castle had Nailers to instruct them, many of them might be imployed in [nail-making]. **1780** *Va. State P.* I. 402 It will be of advantage to the State to engage those nailers for some time longer, on account of the heavy demand . . . for nails. **1809** Cuming *Western Tour* 173 He has nailors, coopers, chairmakers, turners, and stone cutters.

2. A machine for driving nails.

1892 *York County Hist. Rev.* 92 [A cigar-box factory] is fitted out with the latest approved machinery, planers, tackers, nailers, presses etc.

Nailery. A place or factory where nails are made. {*a*1798–} — **1798** Jefferson *Writings* VII. (1896) 271, I had been here for six months advancing for all the nail rods for my nailery without . . . receiving any thing from it. **1815** *Niles' Reg.* VIII. 141/2 There are [in Pittsburgh] . . . 3 trunk makers; 2 gun smiths; 6 naileries.

Nail factory. A factory in which nails are made. — **1809** *Ann. 11th Congress* 2250 At Dover . . . [is a rolling and slitting mill] owned by the Boston iron and nail factory. **1817** *Niles' Reg.* XII. 78/2 Mr. Werwag's extensive nail factory, not far from Dowingstown, Pa. was partially destroyed by fire on the 14th inst. **1840** *Niles' Nat. Reg.* 16 May 168/3 A nail factory is . . . in Lincoln county, manufacturing the article from the iron ore found in that part of the state [N.C.]. **1864** Cumming *Hospital Life* (1866) 127/1 He said that he paid a visit to a nail factory.

+**Nail file.** (See quot. 1875.) — **1875** Knight 1506/2 *Nail-file,* a small, flat, single-cut file for trimming the finger-nails. **1902** *Harper's Mag.* Jan. 256/2 [She] took from her dressing-table several small articles and put them out of sight: a nail-file on the floor under the bed; a pair of nail-scissors under the bureau. **1922** Courtenay *Physical Beauty* 47 Finish with emery or a steel nail file.

+**Nail grab.** An implement with nipping claws for grasping a nail and withdrawing it. Also fig. — **1851** Hooper *Widow Rugby* 44 His mouth . . . looked as if it had been . . . made by gouging a hole in his face with a nail-grab! **1852** 'Mark Twain' in *Hannibal Jrnl.* 16 Sept., 'Thar he sot,' . . . his 'nail-grabs' grasping a pew like grim death.

Nail keg. Also *dial.* **nail kag. 1.** A small barrel for shipping and storing nails. +**2.** *transf.* A hat resembling this in shape. — **(1) 1869** Browne *Adv. Apache Country* 402 Adobe-bricks, mud, . . . whiskey-barrels, nail-kegs, and even canvas, are the component parts [of chimneys]. **1885** Howells *S. Lapham* xxiv, He pulled up a nail-keg . . . and sat down. **1905** Wiggin *Rose* 65 You can't drownd a Wiley, not without you tie nail-kags to their head an' feet an' drop 'em in the falls. **(2) 1869** 'Mark Twain' *Innocents* 269 [Americans] wear a comical hat termed a 'nail-kag.'

Nail machine. A machine for making nails. {1853–} — **1797** *Essex Inst. Coll.* LIV. 110 My Nail Machine consists of a cutting lever of the common form, which vibrates to cut, head & pound. **1819** E. Dana *Geogr. Sk.* 77 Zanesville is on the east branch of the Muskingum, . . . whereon various mills are erected . . . [including] an oil mill, nail machine, and woolen factory. **1831** *21st Congress 2 Sess.* H. R. Doc. No. 50, 145 Briggs, Saml., sr. & jr., Philadelphia, Pa., Nail machine, Aug. 2, 1791. **1859** *Rep. Comm. Patents 1858* I. 548 Improved Nail Machine. **1883** *Century Mag.* Sept. 792/2 In mechanical trades there is a fear that such teaching will unfit the boy for tending a nail machine or a shoe-pegging machine.

***Nail-maker.** One whose trade is nail-making. — **1776** *N.J. Archives* 2 Ser. I. 112 John Clarke, late a regular soldier, . . . by trade a nail maker. **1781** *Va. State P.* I. 473 A very large quantity of nails wanted for the public building—nailrod received from Fredericksburg, but nail-makers are wanting. **1841** Child *Lett. New York* (1846) 64 The third [visitor] . . . asked if there was a nail-maker on board. **1851** [see Nail-cutter 1].

Nail plate. A plate or sheet of iron from which nails are cut. {1810–} Also comb. — **1797** *Essex Inst. Coll.* LIV. 107 Cutting every kind of rods and dubble for iron hoops or nail plates. **1859** *Rep. Comm. Patents 1858* I. 549 The nail-plate . . . is put in at the upper end of the sheath. *Ib.* 550 Improved Nail-Plate Feeder.

Nail rod. A rod or strip of iron from which nails are made {1761–}; also, the material of which these rods or strips are made. {1892–}

1777 *Jrnls. Cont. Congress* VII. 33 [Certain men shall] be directed, with all possible despatch, to procure . . . three tons of steel and five tons of nail rods, for the use of the army. **1789** *Ann. 1st Congress* I. 157 Every State can manufacture them [*sc.* nails], although they cannot make nail rods. **1813** *Niles' Reg.* V. 190/1 Of iron. . . . Nail rods and nails, implements of husbandry, etc. **1869** *Rep. Comm. Agric. 1868* 433 The most convenient method of destroying the bugs is by using a pair of tongs made of nail-rod.

attrib. **1796** *Boston Directory* 243 Ellis, Jonathan, paper and nail-rod manufacturer, Newbury street.

Nainsook. Also †**nansouk.** A soft, fine muslin originally made in India. {1804-}

1790 *Penna. Packet* 19 Oct. 3/2 Richard and James Potter are rapidly disposing of their Fall Importation. . . . Alliballies Nainsooks Conjevrams. **1852** *Harper's Mag.* July 288/1 The skirt has nine graduated openings . . . through which is seen a nansouk petticoat. **1866** *Wkly. New Mexican* 22 Feb. 1/2 Dry goods. . . . Hoop Skirts, Corsets, . . . Nainsooks. **1875** *Chicago Tribune* 26 July 1/1 We are offering splendid Bargains in . . . Swisses, Books, Nainsooks, Jacienets, etc. **1887** *Courier-Journal* 23 Jan. 1/6 We have just received four splendid bargains in White Checked Nainsook for aprons.

b. A dress made of this.

1876 *Wide Awake* 358/2 Miss Clarissa came back in a white nainsook.

Naked fallow. (See FALLOW *n.* 3.)

+**Naked wood. 1.** ? The wild cinnamon, *Canella winterana.* **2.** (See quot. 1884.) **3.** (See quot. 1884.) — **(1) 1837** WILLIAMS *Florida* 98 Wild Cinnamon.—Called by the inhabitants, Naked Wood. **(2) 1884** SARGENT *Rep. Forests* 42 *Colubrina reclinata.* . . . Naked Wood. Semi-tropical Florida, Umbrella Key, on the North end of Key Largo, and sparingly on the small islands south of Elliott's Key; through the West Indies. **1897** SUDWORTH *Arborescent Flora* 300. **(3) 1884** SARGENT *Rep. Forests* 88 *Eugenia dichotoma.* . . . Naked Wood. Semi-tropical Florida . . . ; in the West Indies. **1897** SUDWORTH *ArborescentFlora* 304 *Anamomis dichotoma.* . . . Naked Stopper. . . . Naked-wood (Fla.).

+**Namaycush.** Also **naymacush.** [Algonquian Indian.] A large trout (*Cristovomer namaycush*) found in North American lakes. — [**1787** PENNANT *Arctic Zool.* Suppl. 139 Naymacush. Inhabits the lakes of Hudson's Bay.] **1829** RICHARDSON *Fauna Bor. Amer.* III. 179 The namaycush is the tyrant of the lakes. **1884** GOODE, etc. *Fisheries* I. 486 The Lake Trout of the East is identical with the Mackinaw Trout, or Namaycush. **1911** *Rep. Fisheries 1908* 311 *Cristivomer namaycush.* . . . The individuals vary greatly in color, size, and shape, and are known by the local names 'salmon trout,' 'namaycush,' 'togue,' 'tuladi' [etc.].

***Name,** *n. By the name of,* named. {1676-}

'Now *colloq.* and *U.S.*' (*O.E.D.*).

1796 *Mass. Spy* 13 July 4/2 Some wags . . . fabricated a story of the capture of an American by the name of Figsby, of the brig Fan Fan. **1818** *Norfolk* (Va.) *Beacon* 18 Nov. 3/2 (Th. S.), His father is a ship carpenter, by the name of Harry Hall. **1859** BARTLETT 62 *By the name of.* Some persons will say, 'I met to-day a man by the name of Smith.' An Englishman would say 'of the name,' etc.; except in such phrases as 'He went by the name of Smith.' **1896** *Congress. Rec.* April 3863/2 This lady married a man by the name of Madigan in 1846 or thereabouts.

***Name,** *v.*

***1.** *tr.* To appoint or assign (a person) to an official position.

'The verb *name* is rarely used in Eng. but commonly in Am. in the sense of *appoint*' (Horwill).

1799 JEFFERSON *Writings* X. 111 In the meantime, a *consul general* is named to St. Domingo. **1821** *Ib.* I. 153 All the other Ministers having resigned, a new administration was named. **1905** *N.Y. Ev. Post* 4 Dec. 3 Mr. King has been named consul at Aix la Chapelle.

2. *To name for* (see FOR *prep.*).

Nankeen, Nankin.

1. a. A durable yellow cotton cloth formerly brought from Nanking, China; an imitation of this. {1755-} **b.** A kind or variety of these. {1797-}

1754 *S.C. Gazette* 21–28 May 3/2 Wooddrop & Douxsaint have just imported . . . brown hollands and nankeens. **1784** *Mass. Centinel* 15 May 3/3 Fine Nankins of the best quality at 9/6 per piece. **1826** COOPER *Mohicans* i, His nether garment was of yellow nankeen. **1845** SIMMS *Wigwam & Cabin* 2 Ser. 131 His pantaloons were of very excellent nankin. **1891** *Century Mag.* March 735 The middle and lower half had been supplanted by another vest and trousers of faded nankeen.

+**2.** =NANKEEN COTTON.

1796 HAWKINS *Letters* 30 The cotton grew well. . . . I saw he had not thinned it sufficiently, nor toped any part and that it was mixed with the Nankin. **1865** *Notes & Queries* 3 Ser. VII. 474/2 A new species of cotton, called Nankeen, of a bright yellow colour and fine texture, is now raised in the United States.

3. *pl.* Trousers made of nankeen. {1806-7-}

1807 *Ann. 10th Congress* 1 Sess. I. 667 There was something about . . . clothing his soldiers with nankeens, which he had brought from Philadelphia. **1839** *Knickerb.* XIII. 40 July 27th. . . . Warm; so I mounted a pair of nankins; found great comfort therefrom. **1851** A. O. HALL *Manhattaner* 43 [January] is at New Orleans as capricious and teasing as a village flirt: . . . now asking your Blucher trowsers, and next bringing your nankeens from their last autumn resting place.

4. *attrib.* Designating garments made of nankeen.

1825 NEAL *Bro. Jonathan* I. 149 The corporal wore . . . a pair of nankeen pantaloons, rather tighter than his own skin. **1863** DAVIS *Young Parson* 89 He used to wear striped cotton trousers that didn't come much below his knees, and a nankeen roundabout. **1882** PECK *Sunshine* 26 He had to put on a pair of nankeen pants and hide his cassimeres in the boat house.

Nankeen cotton. A variety of naturally yellow cotton from which nankeen cloth was first made. {1797-} — **1802** DRAYTON *S. Carolina* 128 Nankeen cotton, is principally grown in the middle and upper country, for family use. It is so called from the wool, resembling the colour of nankeen or *Nam-king* cloth. **1829** SHERWOOD *Gaz. Georgia* (ed. 2) 266 The nankin cotton was introduced at an early period. **1838** *S. Lit. Messenger* IV. 638/2 *'The Forsythe cotton'*; then [during the Revolution] as common as any other kind, under the title of *'nankeen-cotton.'* **1842** BUCKINGHAM *Slave States* II. 43 The nankeen cotton . . . produces a brownish-yellow wool, and can be made up without dying, so as to look like dark nankeen.

+**Nanninose.** Variant of MANINOSE. — **1884** GOODE, etc. *Fisheries* I. 707 Next upon the list comes the 'Soft Clam,' 'Long Clam,' or 'Nanninose' (*Mya arenaria*), dear to New Englanders.

+**Nanny berry.** A small North American tree or shrub: (see quotations). — **1884** SARGENT *Rep. Forests* 94 *Viburnum Lentago.* . . . Sheepberry. Nannyberry. **1894** *Amer. Folk-Lore* VII. 90 *Viburnum nudum,* nanny-berry, West Va., Livingston Co., N.Y., Ferrisburgh, Vt. **1897** SUDWORTH *ArborescentFlora* 339 *Viburnum prunifolium.* Stagbush. . . . [Also called] Nannyberry (N.J.).

+**Nanquitoche.** [App. from Amer. Indian.] A variety of tobacco formerly grown in Florida. *Obs.* — **1775** ROMANS *Nat. Hist. Florida* 149 There are present but two sorts [of tobacco] produced viz *Nanquitoche* and *Pointe coupée,* the first infinitely superior to the second.

Nanticoke. Also †**Nanticoack.** [Name of an Algonquian tribe in Maryland.] A variety of bean, or its seed, native to the eastern states. — **1709** LAWSON *Carolina* 76 These are latter Pease, and . . . are very good; and so are the Bonavis, Calavancies, Nanticokes, and abundance of other Pulse . . . which we found the Indians possess'd of. **1737** BRICKELL *N. Carolina* 17 The Nanticoacks are another kind of Pulse, and resemble the Calivances.

+**Nantucket.** *attrib.* Belonging to or associated with the island or the town of Nantucket, Massachusetts. Often humorous. — **1707** *Boston News-Letter* 7 April 2/1 The Nantucket Whale-boats came up with a Sloop that was overset. **1848** *Knickerb.* XXXI. 225 Who has not seen the eyes of the boarding-school boy almost suffused with tears as he gazed upon the cod-fish dinner, alias 'Nantucket owls?' **1882** GODFREY *Nantucket* 69 The Cape-Codders and the Vineyarders retaliated by calling the Nantuckers 'Scrap Islanders,' or 'Nantucket Scraps.' **1891** *Cent.* 5692/2 *Nantucket sleigh-ride,* the towing of a whale-boat by the whale.

+**Nantucketer.** An inhabitant of Nantucket. — **1857** WILLIS *Convalescent* 260 Hair still brown and thick, with the stubborn vitality of the un-killable Nantucketer. **1882** GODFREY *Nantucket* 24 The Nantucketers seem to have a mania for bell-ringing.

‖**Nantucketism.** A word or phrase characteristic of the natives of Nantucket Island. — **1848** J. MITCHELL *Nantucketisms* 39/2 We have collected some words & phrases. . . . I do not claim them as Nantucketisms, except a very small part of them.

***Nap.** +**1.** A cloth having a nap or pile on it. *Obs.* {1888.} +**2.** In phrases, as *to bring* (or *get*) *up one's nap:* Temper, anger. *colloq.* (Cf. DANDER.) — **(1) 1760** *Newport Mercury* 1 Jan. 3/2 To be Sold by King & Hagger, . . . Naps of different Colours, . . . Gimp and small Trimmings. **1776** *Jrnls. Cont. Congress* IV. 51 Goods purchased for the said treaty [with the Indians]: . . . 2 pieces of white Nap. **1790** *Penna. Packet* 2 Jan. 1/3 A further supply of Seasonable Goods . . . Consisting of . . . Flannels Naps Frizes Halfthicks. **(2) 1845** HOOPER *Taking Census* 155 This information brought our nap right up. **1849** NASON *Journal* 112 The bootblack, having got his nap up, came round very cautiously.

+**Napa.** [Name of a county and town in California.] Leather prepared from the skins of sheep or goats by a special tawing process. Also attrib. — **1897** C. T. DAVIS *Manuf. Leather* (ed. 2) 275 The staking machine . . . can be adjusted to any kind of leather, including napa. **1903** FLEMMING *Pract. Tanning* 49 The making of Napa leather. The cheapest tannage by which sheepskins are tanned is the Napa tannage, so called because it originated in Napa, Cal.

***Naphtha.** Also (*colloq.*) **naptha.**

***1.** Petroleum.

1806 *Ann. 9th Congress* 2 Sess. 1132 Several drops of petroleum, or naptha, rose and spread upon the surface. **1818** FLINT *Lett. from Amer.* 76 In the mouth of a creek, I observed that the surface of the water was tinged with the oil of naphtha. **1837** IRVING *Bonneville* I. 223 The bituminous oil, called petrolium [*sic*] or naptha . . . is called Seneca Oil [in N.Y.].

2. Any of several volatile inflammable liquids, refined from petroleum or distilled from various organic substances, and used as solvents in dry cleaning, as fuels, etc.

1859 *Rep. Comm. Patents 1858* I. 702 Neither do I claim the use of benzole or naphtha for carbonizing air or gas. **1879** *Mich. Gen. Statutes* I. (1882) 867 No passenger car on any railroad shall be lighted by naphtha, or by any illuminating oil or fluid made in part of naphtha. **1903** *Forest & Stream* 21 Feb. ix/4 For Sale: Duck shooters' complete outfit. . . . [Includes] one 6½ h.-p. naptha launch. **1904** TARBELL *Hist. Standard Oil Co.* I. 20 They were making naphtha, gasoline, and benzine for export.

***Napkin.** A small cloth, usually linen, used at meals for wiping the fingers and mouth and protecting the clothes. Also attrib. — **1636** *Essex Inst. Coll.* L. 221 Napkins, 7 s.; a yd. of Canvis, 1 s. **1724** *New-Eng. Courant* 5–12 Oct. 2/2 To be sold by John Ruck Esq; at his Warehouse ... Tabling and Napkin Diaper, and sundry Sorts of other Linens, lately imported from Ireland. **1865** *Atlantic Mo.* XV. 182 Not one has slipped the napkin from his chin. **1907** *St. Nicholas* Sept. 1019/2 [She] lifted her plate to release an edge of the napkin.

Napoleon. {1814–, from Napoleon I} +A brass field gun adopted in France about 1856, under Napoleon III. In full *Napoleon gun. Obs.* — **1862** in Moore *Rebellion Rec.* V. II. 405 [I propose] that the ... smoothbores ... be exclusively the twelve-pound gun of the model of 1857, variously called 'the gun-howitzer,' the 'light twelve-pounder,' or the 'Napoleon.' **1880** *Harper's Mag.* May 917/1 The artillery is almost entirely the old brass Napoleon. **1881–5** McCLELLAN *Own Story* 117 The shrapnel and canister from the Napoleons was always most destructive to the hostile infantry at close range. **1897** *Outing* XXX. 80/1 These gun companies were each supplied with one 12-pounder Napoleon gun and one Gatling gun (new), and the men were armed with sabers.

Nappy. A small, shallow dish for serving fruit, preserves, etc.: (see also quot. 1895). {1808, *Sc.*} — **1864** WEBSTER 874/2. **1873** A. D. WHITNEY *Other Girls* xxxiii, Kate, ... producing some nice little stone-ware nappies hot from the hot closet, transferred the food from the china to these. **1895** *Dialect Notes* I. 391 *Nappy:* round shallow crockery dish used for baking pies, Gloucester, Mass. (A square vegetable dish was billed as a 'nappie' from R. H. Macy & Co., New York, in July, 1895.) **1922** *Sears, Roebuck & Co. Cat.* No. 145, 840 Individual round nappies ... per doz. $1.75. *Ib.* 854 Extraordinary bargain in glassware.... This 50-piece assortment contains 2 6-Inch Handled Nappies.

***Narcissus.** A well-known genus of bulbous plants of the family Amaryllidaceae, having linear leaves and showy flowers with large, cup-shaped coronas; also, a plant or a flower of this genus.

1737 BRICKELL *N. Carolina* 22 Narcissus, Daffodil, Snow-Drops, Wall-Flowers, Bloodwort, the white and red Lillie, Stargrass [are found here]. **1779** FRENEAU *Poems* (1786) 103 The Primrose there, the violet darkly blue, Daisies and fair Narcissus ceas'd to rise. **1852** *Horticulturist* VII. 424 No object amongst our early spring flowers, is more beautiful than the Narcissus. **1883** C. THAXTER *Poems for Children* 52 Think ... Of the breath of the rich narcissus waxen-pale. **1910** [see HYACINTH].

b. With modifying terms.

1836 LINCOLN *Botany* App. 118 *Narcissus poeticus,* (poet's narcissus). **1868** GRAY *Field Botany* 330 *Narcissus biflorus,* Two-flowered Narcis sus, or Primrose Peerless of the old gardeners, has two white or pale straw-colored flowers.

+**Narraganset(t).** Also †**Narrohigganset, Narhaganset,** etc. [Algonquian *Naiaganset* 'people of the small point (of land).']

1. An Indian of an Algonquian tribe formerly prominent in New England, especially in Rhode Island; often, pl., the tribe of such an Indian. In full *Narraganset Indian.*

1622 'MOURT' *Relation* 118 Massasoyt was put from his Countrey by the Narrohiggansets. **1637** R. WILLIAMS *Letters* (1874) 27 The news of the cutting off three hundred Narragansetts and all the English held still for current. **1677** HUBBARD *Narrative* I. 142 An hundred and fifty Mohegins, ready fixed to war on the Behalf of the English against the Narhagansets their mortal Enemies. **1682** M. RAWLINSON *Narr. Captivity* 11, I was sold to him by another Narrhaganset Indian. **1764** HUTCHINSON *Hist. Mass.* I. 138 At first, the Naragansets gave kind words to the messengers ... but they soon changed their tone. **1809** IRVING *Knickerb.* v. iv, He had been secretly endeavoring to instigate the Narrohigansett (or Narraganset) ... Indians. **1832** J. PEIRCE (*title*), The Narraganset Chief; or the Adventures of a Wanderer.

2. A small, hardy horse, valued chiefly for riding, of a breed developed in Rhode Island in the region of Narragansett Bay; also, pl., the breed of such a horse.

1826 COOPER *Mohicans* ii, A breed of horses ... were once well known in America by the name of the Narragansets. They were small, commonly of the color called sorrel in America. **1845** JUDD *Margaret* III. 398 Nimrod ... made us a purchase of some beautiful Narragansetts with draught and carriage horses.

3. A hog of an inferior breed.

1852 *Mich. Agric. Soc. Trans.* III. 332 About 10,000 things which Wolverine audacity have denominated swine—variously known as narragansetts, alligators, ... and flea breeders.

+**Narraganset(t) pacer.** A breed, or one of a breed, of pacing horses developed in the region about Narragansett Bay in Rhode Island. Also *Narragansett pacing mare.* Now hist.

1777 J. ADAMS *Familiar Letters* 272 Narraganset pacing mares. **1809** IRVING *Knickerb.* v. iv, Two lean sided hungry pettifoggers, mounted on Narraganset pacers. **1832** WATSON *Hist. Tales N.Y.* 163 The Narraganzet pacers of Rhode Island were in such repute that they were sent for ... by some few who were choice in their selections. **1884** *Century Mag.* Jan. 445/1 The natural pacer, was known in Virginia not later than the first quarter of the eighteenth century. The 'Narragansett pacers' of Rhode Island came into request at about the same time. **1886** *Harper's Mag.* July 166/2 Colonial aristocracy ... [were] perhaps best known for their breed of Narragansett pacers.

***Narrow,** *n.* +**1.** The narrowest part of a neck of land or of an island. +**2.** A narrow pass or way between mountains. *Obs.* Usually pl. (Cf. GAP 2, NOTCH *n.* 3.) — **(1) 1668** in *Amer. Speech* XV. 288/1 To an oake marked on three sides standing in the narrow of yt neck. **1747** STITH *Hist. Virginia* 122 Sir Thomas Dale ... pitched upon a Place for his new Town, on the Narrow of Farrar's Island, in Varina Neck. **(2) 1788** CUTLER in *Life & Corr.* I. 403 We passed the narrows or gaps of two ranges of high mountains. **1808** PIKE *Sources Miss.* 175 We followed [the creek] through narrows in the mountains for about six miles. **1870** POLLARD *Va. Tourist* 141 Following the stream a few miles, ... we come to the 'Narrows,' where it passes through Peters' Mountains.

***Narrow,** *a.* +In specific names of plants and trees: (see quotations). — **1784** CUTLER in *Mem. Academy* I. 436 *Rumex floribus hermaphroditis: valvulis dentatis nudis, pedicellis planis reflexis.* ... Narrow Dock.... The fresh roots bruised and made into an ointment, or decoction, cure the itch. **1785** MARSHALL *Amer. Grove* 124 *Quercus phellos angustifolia,* Narrow willow-leaved oak. **1801** MICHAUX *Histoire des Chênes* 6 *Quercus prinus* (*acuminata*), Chêne chataignier (des Illinois). Narrow Live Chesnot Oak. **1897** SUDWORTH *Arborescent Flora* 25 *Pinus attenuata.* Lemmon. Knobcone Pine.... [Also called] Narrow-cone Pine (Cal. lit.).

+**Narrow ax.** An ordinary ax primarily for chopping, as distinguished from a broadax for hewing. *Obs.*

1641 *Conn. Rec.* I. 444 A broad axe, 2 narrow axes, wimbell & chessells. **1679** *Maine Wills* 78, I bequeath unto the aforesd Peter Grant ... my great broad axe & a narrow axe. *c***1728** *Inventories Toxhall's Estate, Bertie Co.* (N.H. Hist. Comm. MS.), A Broad ax and Two Narrow axes. **1755** *Lett. to Washington* I. 136 Broadaxes are wanted, narrow axes I have been obligd to order some to be made. **1854** THOREAU *Walden* 46, I went on for some days cutting and hewing timber, and also studs and rafters, all with my narrow axe.

Narrow gauge. {1841–}

+**1.** (Usually hyphened.) *ellipt.* = NARROW-GAUGE (RAIL)-ROAD; also, a narrow-gauge train.

The early British *narrow gauge* of 4 ft. 8½ in. (as opposed to their early *broad gauge* of greater width) became the standard gauge of Great Britain. Contrariwise, the American *broad gauge* of 4 ft. 8½ in. (so called since the Civil War in contradistinction to the *narrow gauge* of lesser width) has become the standard gauge. In the early history of American railroading, *broad gauge* was also applied to gauges wider than the standard gauge.

1872 TICE *Over Plains* 24 Amongst those under contract and in a state of progress, the most important is a narrow gauge to Denver, thence to Santa Fe. **1883** *Harper's Mag.* Aug. 330, I came down the narrow-gauge in an observation car. **1885** *Wkly. New Mexican Review* 23 April 3/6 The Denver & Rio Grande railroad ... is now operating 1,317 miles of road in Colorado and New Mexico.... It is the longest narrow-gauge in the world. **1909** 'O. HENRY' *Roads of Destiny* 205 Watch our front window after the narrow-gauge gets in.

2. Attrib. passing into adj. **a.** With *car, line, locomotive,* etc.

1871 *Republican Rev.* 6 May, The Denver and Rio Grande Railway is the longest narrow gauge line yet projected in this country. **1881** M. ALEXANDER *Going West* 94 Travelers who are used to palace sleeping cars find an all night ride in a narrow gauge car very tiresome. **1883** *Phila. Times* No. 3023, 3 A narrow gauge train derailed. **1897** *McClure's Mag.* X. 82 Little narrow-gauge locomotives puff their way in and out between the buildings. **1903** 'O. HENRY' *Heart of West* 246 The sandy road ... ran parallel to the narrow-gauge track.

+**b.** Small-minded; insignificant; provincial; limited in view or vision. *colloq.*

Cf. BROAD-GAUGE 2 b.

1872 *Harper's Mag.* March 637/2 This infamous proposition was combated by a narrow-gauge member from the 'outsquirts' of the Territory. **1902** WISTER *Virginian* xii, That young come-outer, and his fam'ly that can't understand him—for he is broad gauge, yu' see, and they are narro' gauge. **1906** BELL *C. Lee* 249 His ideas were on too narrow-gauge a plan to admit the suggestion now.

c. *Polit.* Designating members of the Prohibition party in 1896 who favored restricting the platform to the liquor issue, with no free-silver plank.

1896 *Prohibition Party Campaign Text-Book* 21 Governor St. John ... wanted to see the platform as narrow as the narrow gauge men wanted it.

Narrow-gauge (rail)road, railway. A railroad having a width between the rails of less than the usual standard of 4 ft. 8½ in. {1889} — **1872** *Harper's Mag.* Dec. 149/2 In California ... the want of more abundant and cheaper means of transportation is severely felt. As a remedy it is proposed to build narrow-gauge railroads. **1873** *Ib.* April 790/1 An important means for the cheapening and extension of transportation facilities ... is the construction of narrow-gauge railways. **1898** *Boston M. Herald* 19 April 12/1 South Carolina's 'Jim Crow car law' ... shall not apply to nurses on trains, to narrow gauge roads, ... nor to officers or guards transporting prisoners.

Narrow-leaf. *attrib.* In plant and tree names: (see quotations). — **1804** LEWIS in *L. & Clark Exped.* VI. (1905) 145 The narrow leaf willow . . . is male and female, the female bearing it[s] seed in a small pod. **1811** *Boylan's N.C. Almanack*, Cancer [Remedy]. . . . Let the roots of Sour Dock (sometimes called Narrow-Leaf Dock) be washed clean and put into a moderate quantity of water. **1817–8** EATON *Botany* (1822) 415 *Pycnanthemum lanceolatum*, narrow-leaf virginian thyme. **1901** MOHR *Plant Life Ala.* 767 *Lacinaria graminifolia*. . . . Narrow-leaf Blazing Star. . . . Flowers pale rose; September.

Narrow-leaved, *a.* Also **narrow-leafed.** In plant and tree names: (see quotations). {1629–}

Many other examples may be found in books on botany.

1785 MARSHALL *Amer. Grove* 72 Narrow-leaved or Glaucous-leaved Kalmia. **1805** LEWIS in *L. & Clark Exped.* II. (1904) 303 The underwood consists of the narrowleafed or small willow, . . . allso . . . a species of dwarf burch. **1843** TORREY *Flora N.Y.* I. 110 *Claytonia Virginica*. . . . Narrow-leaved Spring Beauty. . . . Low moist grounds, and damp woods. April–May. **1845** FRÉMONT *Exped.* 287 The narrow-leaved cottonwood (*populus angustifolia*) . . . was the principal tree. **1869** *Amer. Naturalist* III. 408 Narrow-leaved Poplar (*Populus angustifolia*). This peculiarly western poplar . . . I believe to be the most common species in the mountains. **1915** ARMSTRONG & THORNBER *Western Wild Flowers* 106 Narrow-leaved Umbrella-wort. *Allionia linearis*. . . . The flowers are fragile and pretty, of various shades of pink.

Nary, *a.* Also **narra,** etc. [*Ne'er a.* Cf. ARY.] Not any; neither; never a. *illit.* or *humorous.*

'The form is typically U.S., but app. occurs in some Eng. dialects, and is occas. used imitatively by English writers' (*O.E.D.*).

1746 in *New Eng. Hist. & Gen. Reg.* II. 209 There was no 'spile dunne on nary side.' **1795** DEARBORN *Columbian Grammar* 137 Improprieties, commonly called Vulgarisms, . . . [include] Narra one for None. **1830** S. SMITH *Major Downing* 28 They pulled and grinned all day, but nary side couldn't pull up tother. **1848** LOWELL *Biglow P.* 1 Ser. ix. 128 To nary one on 'em I'd trust a secon'-handed rail. **1858** *N.Y. Ev. Post* 1 Sept. (B.), The Atlantic Cable and the White Mountains,—both monuments of God's power, but nary one alike. **1873** *Ill. Dept. Agric. Trans.* X. 168 The jay does feed largely upon the larvæ and eggs of insects, but nary a potato bug. **1891** 'THANET' *Otto the Knight* 5 An' he ain't got nare nuther pa'r on earth, nur nuthin' ter mend 'em with 'cept pins! **1909** WASON *Happy Hawkins* 288 Here they was with a wall of ice between 'em an' nairy a lovin' glance to melt it down.

b. *Nary red (cent)*, not a cent.

1856 DERBY *Phoenixiana* 125 Playin at billiards and monte Till they've nary red cent to ante. **1857** *N.Y. Herald* 27 May 5/2 As regards the old cents, there will be 'nary red' to be seen. **1876** *Wide Awake* 236/2 These young folks . . . talk about the 'cops,' and 'plug-uglies,' say 'nary red,' and 'going on the straight,' like the low roughs.

+**Nasaump, Nausamp.** [Narraganset Ind.] =SAMP. *Obs.* — **1643** WILLIAMS *Key* (1866) 40 Nasàump, a kind of meale pottage, unpartch'd. From this the English call their Samp, which is the Indian corne, beaten and boild, and eaten hot or cold with milke or butter. **1764** HUTCHINSON *Hist. Mass.* I. 465 *n.* The Indian corn boiled, after being a little broken, they called Nasaump. The English call it Samp. **1832** DURFEE *Whatcheer* 23 Waban's nausamp and venison shall be free, . . . when his store shall fail.

+**Nashville warbler.** [See quot. 1917.] A plain olive-green yellow-breasted warbler (*Vermivora ruficapilla*) common in eastern North America. — **1811** WILSON *Ornithology* III. 120 [The] Nashville Warbler, *Sylvia Ruficapilla*, . . . [was] shot in the state of Tennesee, not far from Nashville. **1831** AUDUBON *Ornith. Biog.* I. 450. **1892** TORREY *Foot-Path Way* 16 Nashville Warblers were especially numerous . . . upon the White Mountains. **1917** *Birds of Amer.* III. 120 The Nashville Warbler was discovered by Alexander Wilson at Nashville, Tennessee, and . . . has ever since borne the name Nashville Warbler.

***Nasturtium.** Also †**nasturtion.** Any one of various trailing plants of the genus *Tropaeolum*, esp. *T. majus* or *T. minus;* a blossom of one of these plants. {1704–, in transl.}

Cf. CANARY BIRD 2.

1806 B. MACMAHON *Amer. Gardener's Calendar* 318 The *Tropæolum majus*, or large Nasturtium, is very deserving of cultivation. . . . There are, of the nasturtium, a major and minor kind; the former, being of a large running growth, and the most productive, is the proper sort for the above purposes. **1835** BIRD *Hawks* I. 19 One corner of the porch . . . supported festoons of nasturtions and morning-glories. **1875** STOWE *We & Neighbors* 23, I have been so busy with my parlor ivies . . . and some perfectly seraphic hanging baskets, gorgeous with flowering nasturtiums. **1890** HOWELLS *Boy's Town* 224 One of them at least had beds of tulips and nasturtiums, and borders of flags and pinks. **1916** E. PORTER *David* 135 Two huge granite posts topped with flaming nasturtiums marked the point.

***Nasty,** *a.*

***1.** Foul, dirty; offensive to touch or smell.

Nasty is not as freely used in the U.S. as it is in England. The common English sense of 'unpleasant' or 'annoying' is not, however, unknown here.

1758 *Essex Inst. Coll.* XII. 140 The Dutch here have a nasty practice of yarding their cows in ye Street before their doors. **1835** LONGSTREET *Ga. Scenes* 57 You nasty, good-for-nothing, snaggle-toothed gaub of fat. **1871** DE VERE 509 *Nasty* . . . denotes in America something disgusting in point of smell, taste, or even moral character, and is not considered a proper word to be used in the presence of ladies. **1895** *Outing* XXVII. 209/1 Our game was dragged into the boat, and a nastier looking and smelling thing I never rode with.

+**2.** Superior, first-class, excellent. *slang.* Also comb.

1834 *Knickerb.* III. 37 *'Sling a nasty foot,'* means to dance exceedingly well. *Ib., 'She is a nasty looking gal,'* implies she is a splendid woman. **1912** MATHEWSON *Pitching* 68 Hoblitzell is a nasty hitter.

***Nation,** *n.*[1]

+**1.** A tribe of American Indians.

See also FIVE NATIONS, SIX NATIONS.

1650 *Md. Council Proc.* 260 The Ports adjoyning are very much pestered with great Concourse of Indians of several nations. **1671** *Doc. Col. Hist. N.Y.* XII. 484 Hee saith the whole Nation of the Indyans of whom these Murderers are, consists of about 50 or 60 persons. **1709** LAWSON *Carolina* 199 Two Nations of Indians here in Carolina were at war together. **1722** COXE *Descr. Carolana* 49 Near the Bottom of the Bay . . . is the fair River of the Miamihas (so call'd because upon it lives Part of a Nation bearing the same Name). **1805** LEWIS in *L. & Clark Exped.* III. (1905) 6 The dress of these people is quite as desent and convenient as that of any nation of Indians I ever saw. **1866** *Rep. Indian Affairs* 250 All personal acts of chiefs, councillors, or private individuals, in such matters as affect the general interests of the nation, shall be considered null and void. **1900** *Congress. Rec.* 2 Feb. 1455/2 The work of survey . . . for the two great nations—the Choctaw and Chickasaw nations—could be completed within the next year.

+**b.** The territory occupied by Indians.

See also CHEROKEE 4 (2), CREEK[2] 2 (b).

1725 in *Travels Amer. Col.* 98 The said Sharp . . . went to one of the Towns in the said [Cherokee] Nation. **1775** ADAIR *Indians* 333 [The Muskohge] would be ashamed to allow the latter to carry those captives, who were their friends, through their nation to Charles-town. **1814** *Niles' Reg.* VI. 264/1 Our own troops are on the point of marching into the nation. **1873** BEADLE *Undevel. West* 355 My first Sabbath in the 'Nation' [*i.e.*, the Indian Territory] was bright and clear. **1923** J. H. COOK *On Old Frontier* 6 We saw plenty of Indians all the way through the Indian Territory, or 'Nation,' as it was called, but we had no trouble with them.

+**2.** The United States of America. Usu. with *the.*

1847 LOWELL *Biglow P.* 1 Ser. iv. 50 We're the original friends o' the nation, All the rest air a paltry an' base fabrication. **1864** LINCOLN in Fleming *Hist. Reconstruction* I. 113, I am . . . sincerely hoping and expecting that a constitutional amendment abolishing slavery throughout the nation may be adopted. **1894** *Outlook* 20 Jan. 111/1 This Nation has accepted the Provisional Government as the lawful government of the Hawaiian Islands. **1916** F. D. ROOSEVELT in *Outlook* 28 June 495/1 The majority of people in the Nation have kept silent [on the question of military defense].

Nation, *n.*[2] [A euphemistic shortening in colloq. speech of DARNATION or *damnation.*] *A nation*, a great deal. (Cf. next.) *The nation*, =DARNATION. {1897, *dial.*}

1775 *Yankee Doodle* in *Broadside Verse* (1930) 141/1 A swamping gun . . . makes a noise like father's gun, Only a nation louder. **1789** DUNLAP *Father* II. i, I guess she did mean so; for the nation knows she doesn't look much like hopping. **1872** 'MARK TWAIN' *Letters* (1920) 117 Where in the nation can I get that portrait? **1880** *Cimarron News & Press* 23 Dec. 1/7 'Well, I've got the g.b.' 'The geebee, Thomas! What in the nation is that?' 'I've got the grand bounce.' **1918** LINCOLN *Shavings* 213 Now how in the nation did I get it Wood?

Nation, *a.* [See NATION *n.*[2]] Large or great. {1828–, *dial.*}

1765 *Moving Times & No Friends* 4 (B), I believe, my friend, you're very right: They'll get a nation profit by't. **1815** HUMPHREYS *Yankey* 19 You were a nation deal wiser than brother Jonathan.

+**b.** *A nation sight*, a great deal.

1809 WEEMS *Marion* (1833) 121 Besides them plaguy guns, they have a tarnal nation sight of pistols. **1810** LAMBERT *Travels* (1813) II. 512 We have lost a nation sight of money by her. **1838** HALIBURTON *Clockmaker* 2 Ser. xviii. 262 The whole world . . . [could not] produce such a factory stand as Niagara Falls; what a 'nation sight of machinery that would carry, wouldn't it? **1843** *Yale Lit. Mag.* VIII. 406 What a nation sight of bother it would be to log up a clearing in these parts.

Nation, *adv.* [See NATION *n.*[2]] Very, extremely, greatly, etc. {1785–, *dial.*}

1800 *Aurora* (Philadelphia) 14 Aug. (Th.), He'll read a speech—reads 'nation bad. **1829** SANDS *Writings* II. 148, I guess you've been a nation long time a writing that 'are answer. **1843** STEPHENS *High Life N.Y.* I. 195 The pockets are nation handy. **1872** 'MARK TWAIN' *Roughing It* 30 It's so nation dark I should 'a' gone by unbeknowns if that air thorough-brace hadn't broke. **1884** — *H. Finn* xix. 186, I'm nation sorry for you.

National, *n.* {1653–} +**1.** A member of the Hard-Shell faction of the Democratic party, so called because sectional differences were minimized by this faction. Also attrib. +**2.** A soldier of the Union army during the Civil War. *Obs.* (Cf. NATIONAL *a.* 6.) — **(1) 1853** *N.Y. Tribune* 2 April 3/6 A Hard shell . . . favors the execution of the Fugitive Slave

Law and goes for a distribution of the offices among the Nationals. *Ib.*, The Hards embrace the Cass Hunkers of 1848 of the National School of politics, while the Softs are composed of the remnants of the Van Buren and Adams party of 1848, and such Hunkers as Secretary Marcy and Gov. Seymour. (2) **1863** in Moore *Rebellion Rec.* V. I. 38 A company of guerrillas . . . were captured by a body of Nationals belonging to Col. Boone's regiment.

***National,** *a.*

+1. Pertaining or belonging to a nation of Indians.

1754 *Mass. H. S. Coll.* 3 Ser. V. 31 [We] recommend to and expect it from you, for your own safety, to collect yourselves together, and dwell in your national castles. **1822** in Morse *Rep. Indian Affairs* II. 169 The Cherokee Nation is governed by the acts of one National Council, held on[c]e a year by a national Committee, and members of Council. **1853** RAMSAY *Tennessee* 169 This tower was used . . . as a place for celebrating the green corn dance and other national ceremonials. **1866** *Rep. Indian Affairs* 248 A national jail shall be built on the public grounds, upon which the councilhouse is now situated. **1891** O'BEIRNE *Leaders Ind. Territory* 37/1 During the administration of Gov. Jonas Wolf he was appointed National Interpreter, and National Treasurer in the Byrd administration of 1888.

+2. In the debate over the Constitution: Constituting a government which would eliminate the powers of the separate states. Now hist.

1788 [see FEDERAL *a.* 1]. **1824** in *Congress. Deb.* 25 Jan. (1830) 49/1 When the American colonies redeemed themselves from British bondage, and became so many independent nations, they proposed to form a national union. **1830** *Ib.* 49/1 [The union desired by the Federalists was] not a federal union . . . but a national union. **1847** [see FEDERAL *a.* 1].

+3. Founded by or conducted under the auspices of the federal government.

1794 *Ann. 3d Congress* 1428 There shall be established, at each of the aforesaid arsenals, a national armory. **1840** *Niles' Nat. Reg.* 7 March 11/1 [A memorial from Mr. Henderson] asking for the establishment of a national hospital at Vicksburg. **1870** *Rep. Comm. Agric. 1869* 15 The large collection of plants . . . are now arranged in suitable cases for convenient study and reference, constituting the nucleus of a national herbarium. **1873** *Newton Kansan* 3 April 2/1 The Secretary of War under an act of Congress has designated Rock Island as the location of the national military prison. **1910** BOSTWICK *Amer. Pub. Library* 29 Dr. Putnam . . . has endeavored to make the institution [Library of Congress] in fact what it should be in name—the National Library.

+4. Of persons: Concerned with the interests of the United States as a whole rather than with those of a party, faction, or region.

1801 J. ADAMS *Works* IX. 585 Mr. Jefferson's administration . . . is too strongly infected with the spirit of party, to give much encouragement to men who are merely national. **1859** in W. Lawrence *A. A. Lawrence* 136, I am the son of Amos Lawrence, . . . who brought me up to be a 'national' man, as we understand that term.

+5. In the names of political parties: (see quotations).

See also NATIONAL DEMOCRATIC PARTY, NATIONAL REPUBLICAN.

1855 in Hambleton *H. A. Wise* 303 [The Know-Nothing party] professes now to be the only true National Conservative Union party. **1868** *Republican Platform* in K. Porter *National Party Platforms* 68 The National Union Republican Party of the United States . . . make the following declaration of principles. **1876** *N.Y. Tribune* 18 May 1/1 Two National and five State Conventions were held yesterday, namely: Those of the National Greenback and Prohibition parties [etc.]. **1884** *Greenback National Platform* in K. Porter *National Party Platforms* 125 We, the National party of the United States, in national convention assembled. **1884** *Boston Jrnl.* Aug., Seven regularly nominated tickets in the field . . . are the Democratic, Republican, . . . National Christian, Anti-Monopoly [etc.]. **1896** in McKee *National Conventions* (1901) 320 The National Party [of seceders from the Prohibition convention] . . . presents the following declaration of principles. **1896** *National Silver Platform* in K. Porter *National Party Platforms* 193 We, the national silver party, . . . hereby adopt the following declaration of principles.

+6. With reference to the Civil War: Belonging to the Union.

Cf. FEDERAL *a.* 6.

1863 in Moore *Rebellion Rec.* V. I. 52 One hundred and twenty-five rebels attacked seventy-five National troops at Ozark, Mo. **1893** *Nation* LVI. 85/2 The differences between National and Confederate writers have greatly diminished with the progress of time.

+7. In special uses.

National banking law, the law enacted by Congress in 1863, amended in 1864, under which the present national banking system operates; *n. banking system,* the framework of national banks under the national banking law; *n. chairman,* the chairman of a national (party) committee; *N. Covenant,* (see quotation); *n. day,* =INDEPENDENCE DAY; *N. Grange,* =GRANGE I; *n. holiday,* a holiday observed throughout the nation as opposed to a state or local holiday; *n. representative,* a member of Congress; *n. turnpike,* spec., =NATIONAL ROAD 2.

1883 *Century Mag.* July 398/1 A man's opinions on the protective tariff, or the national banking law, . . . were no test of his fitness to collect taxes. **1900** *Congress. Rec.* 10 Jan. 736/1 The national banking system . . . should be abolished. **1904** *Forum* April 483 As national chairman he [Mark Hanna] conducted the campaign which carried McKinley to the White House. **1864** *Rio Abajo Press* 14 June 1/2 The American women are organizing a society, under the style of the *National Covenant*. . . . They are pledging themselves, for three years or during the war, not to purchase any foreign article when an American one can be substituted. *a***1918** G. STUART *On Frontier* I. 248 We celebrated the national day by having a fine dinner with trout as the principal dish. **1868** in Commons, etc. *Doc. Hist.* X. 79 The State Granges are in unity with the National Grange. **1866** MOORE *Women of War* 492 On the recurrence of the national holidays, as Thanksgiving and Independence, she was specially active in securing provisions. **1811** *Agric. Museum* I. 244 The meeting of the national Representatives in the fall of the year, affords an opportunity of receiving . . . whatever is rare or useful in our own extensive territory. **1822** WOODS *English Prairie* 52 From the north branch of the Potomac river, we passed a very hilly country, to a new road, called the National Turnpike.

National anniversary. +=INDEPENDENCE DAY. — **1840** *Niles' Nat. Reg.* 11 July 290/2 The national anniversary. The fourth of July just passed has been observed throughout the country as a general holiday. **1884** BLAINE *20 Years of Congress* I. 437 Two great States held their conventions [in 1862] on the National Anniversary.

+National bank.

1. In discussions and debate over the advisability of establishing a bank instituted by the federal government: A bank similar to the banks of sense 2.

1790 MACLAY *Deb. Senate* 270 Yesterday, the Secretary's report on the subject of a national bank was handed to us, and I can readily find that a bank will be the consequence. **1790** HAMILTON in *Ann. 1st Congress* II. 2049 The principles upon which a National Bank ought to be organized. **1814** *Ann. 13th Congress* 1 Sess. 873 [The subscribers] are desirous of establishing a National bank. **1815** MADISON in Leavitt *Our Money Wars* (1894) 47 If the operation of the State banks cannot produce this result [a stable and sufficient currency], the proper operation of a National bank will merit consideration. **1841** TYLER in *Pres. Mess. & P.* IV. 63 The power of Congress to create a national bank to operate *per se* over the Union has been a question of dispute from the origin of the Government. **1856** *Democratic Conv. Proc.* 24 The Democratic party [declares] . . . That Congress has no power to charter a national bank.

2. a. The first Bank of the United States, chartered by Congress in 1791 for a period of twenty years.

1797 *Monthly Mag.* III. 199 Besides the said four funded stocks, a national bank is established at Philadelphia. **1799** WELD *Travels* 41 As soon also as the seat of government is fixed there [in Washington, D.C.], the national bank . . . will be established at the same time.

b. The second Bank of the United States, chartered by Congress in 1816 and expiring by the limitation of its charter in 1836.

1837 JACKSON in *Pres. Mess. & P.* III. 301 The establishment of a national bank by Congress, with the privilege of issuing paper money receivable in the payment of the public dues, . . . drove from general circulation the constitutional currency and substituted one of paper in its place. **1842** *Whig Almanac 1843* 31/2 The National Bank had now been destroyed.

3. Any of numerous commercial banks chartered under the federal government in accordance with the banking acts of 1863–64, empowered to receive, lend, and transmit money, and to issue currency notes; a building that houses such a bank. (Cf. STATE BANK.)

1864 *Wkly. New Mexican* 3 June 1/4 The house ways and means committee will report a bill having adopted the amendment permitting states to tax the national banks. **1865** *Atlantic Mo.* XV. 85/2 The national banks will go far towards increasing the total metropolitan banking capital. **1880** *Harper's Mag.* July 192/2 Instead of . . . long lines of canvas-topped wagons I saw . . . churches, and national banks. **1891** S. CLARK *Northampton First Church* 5 [Samuel Wright's] home lot lay between King and Market streets. On it are, The First National Bank, The Smith Charities and other buildings. **1904** *N.Y. Ev. Post* 10 May 11 A certified check on a National Bank for five per cent of the bonds bid for must accompany each proposal. **1914** *Polit. Science Q.* June 268 Membership [in the Federal Reserve system] is voluntary, and is open to state banks and trust companies as well as to national banks.

4. Attrib. in sense 3 with *act, circulation, examiner, note.*

1864 *New Mex. Press* 2 Aug. 1/1 We have seen several National Bank notes of the denomination of ten dollars. They are more picturesque than the greenbacks. **1874** *Statutes at Large* XVIII. III. 123 An act to provide a national currency secured by a pledge of United States bonds, and to provide for the circulation and redemption thereof . . . shall hereafter be known as 'the national-bank act.' **1880** LAMPHERE *U.S. Govt.* 88/2 National Bank Examiners are allowed compensation. **1882** *Nation* 23 Nov. 436/2 Before the end of 1883 the Government will . . . have paid off . . . some $30,000,000 held by the Treasury as security for national-bank circulation.

+National bird. The bald eagle, regarded as an American patriotic symbol. — **1859** *Harper's Mag.* May 860/2 Those of you who know the habits of the national bird know full well that he never feeds upon carrion! **1894** ALDRICH *Two Bites* 63 The starry shield, supported by two crossed cannon cut out of tin and surmounted by the national bird in the same material, . . . hung proudly over the transom.

+**National cemetery.** A cemetery created by Act of Congress chiefly for those members of the military or naval forces of the United States who die in battle or after having been mustered out of service or honorably discharged. — **1866** *Statutes at Large* XIV. 310 To establish national cemeteries, and to purchase sites for the same . . . fifty thousand dollars [is appropriated]. **1884** 'CRADDOCK' *Where Battle Was Fought* 10 It was the flag-staff, and the flying flag above the National Cemetery across the river. **1900** *Congress. Rec.* 17 Jan. 893/2 Authorize needed repairs of the graveled or macadamized road from the city of Newbern, N.C., to the national cemetery near said city.

+**National committee.** The 'permanent' committee at the head of a political party, chosen at each national convention for a period of four years.

[**1848** *General Taylor's Two Faces* (Dem. Natl. Com. 1848–52) 1 Published under authority of the National and Jackson Democratic Association Committee.] **1852** *Dem. Convention Proc.* 3 It has been assigned to me, as chairman of the Democratic National Committee, appointed by the last convention, to call this convention to order. **1856** (*title*), Philadelphia [Republican] National Convention. Circular of the National Committee, Appointed at Pittsburg on the 22d of February, 1856. **1891** *Boston Jrnl.* 12 Nov. 3/2 Two weeks hence the Republican National Committee will meet to determine at what time and place the next Republican National Convention shall be held. **1896** (*title*), Prohibition Party Campaign Text-Book. . . . Issued by the Prohibition National Committee, Albion, Michigan. **1914** *Cycl. Amer. Govt.* I. 362 With the opening of the convention, the national committee is dissolved to give place to this supreme organ of the party by which is appointed a new national committee.

+**National committeeman.** A member of the national committee of a political party. — **1856** *Democratic Conv. Proc.* 72 It is intended to send the question of the selection of a National Committeeman to the next State Convention to be held in New York. **1899** *Mo. So. Dakotan* I. 184 At the Chicago convention he [Gov. Mellette] was chosen national committeeman for Dakota territory. **1904** *Hartford Courant* 25 June 8 The La Follette convention, whose delegates were so summarily ordered to hit the pike by the national committeemen at Chicago.

National convention. {1792, of France} *Polit.* +A convention held by the delegates of a political party (now representing the states, territories, and possessions of the United States) to nominate candidates for president and vice president and to formulate a party policy.

1834 *Indiana Democrat* 4 Jan., The Hoosier State like true democrats have taken the lead in appointing delegates to a National Convention. **1840** *Niles' Nat. Reg.* 11 April 96/1 The abolitionists have had a national convention in Albany, six states being represented. **1855** in Hambleton *H. A. Wise* 202 We adhere as firmly as ever to the Compromise of 1850 and the platform laid down by the National Convention of 1852. **1876** *N.Y. Tribune* 18 May 1/1 Two National and five State Conventions were held yesterday, namely: Those of the National Greenback and Prohibition parties [etc.]. **1882** *Nation* 27 July 63/2 The 'time-honored' two-thirds rule . . . used to enable the politicians of the slave States, though in a minority, to control national conventions. **1904** *Utica Observer* 23 June 6 Telegraphing it [the ultimatum to the Sultan of Morocco] to the National Convention at Chicago made it look very much like a grand stand play. **1925** BRYAN *Memoirs* 97 It so happened that the Democratic National Convention . . . was held in St. Louis.

National council. +A congress of representatives of an Indian nation. — **1792** PUTNAM in *Memoirs* 292 The War Club . . . belongs to the Charokees, a Ba[n]ditte of out Casts . . . not admited into the National Councils. **1820** in Morse *Rep. Indian Affairs* (1822) II. 161 It is out of our power to see you, in any short time, on account of the National Council. **1871** *Rep. Indian Affairs* (1872) 179 They have a commodious brick capitol of . . . suitable accommodations for the sessions of the two houses of their national councils. **1891** O'BEIRNE *Leaders Ind. Territory* 61/1 Sylvester Durant . . . at the time of his death was a member of the House of Representatives of the National Council.

National debt. {1721–} +The federal debt (q.v.), esp. that which is funded.

Cf. DEBT, FLOATING DEBT, FUNDED DEBT.

1784 (*title*), A Statement of the National Debt, with a Requisition of Congress, on the United States. **1818** J. BRISTED *Resources U.S.* 72 The national debt of the United States at present does not amount to one hundred and twenty millions of dollars. **1875** *Southern Mag.* July 74 Our National debt at the beginning of July 1860 aggregated only sixty-four millions. **1880** *Cimarron News & Press* 26 Feb. 1/7 The National debt is getting boiled down to only a little over $2,000,000,000. **1900** *Congress Rec.* 12 Feb. 1722/2 My amendment provides that the national debt shall be discharged, and very rapidly. **1914** *Cycl. Amer. Govt.* I. 548 Since 1902 the national debt has slightly increased standing at $1,027,575,000 in 1912.

+**National Democratic party.** (See quot. 1914.) — **1896** (*title*), Proceedings of the Convention of the National Democratic Party, held at Indianapolis, Indiana, September 2 and 3, 1896. **1914** *Cycl. Amer. Govt.* II. 85/1 The free silver element got control of the Democratic national convention at Chicago [in 1896], and nominated William J. Bryan on a free coinage platform. In September a convention of gold Democrats . . . met at Indianapolis, took the name of National Democratic Party, and nominated John M. Palmer of Illinois and Simon B. Buckner of Kentucky for President and Vice-President. . . . With the passage of the gold standard act of March 14, 1900, the activity of the gold Democrats terminated.

+**National flag.** =FLAG *n.*[2] 4. — **1841** *Pres. Mess. & P.* IV. 25 The national flag will be displayed at half-staff; at dawn of day thirteen guns will be fired. **1890** LANGFORD *Vigilante Days* (1912) 94 He procured a National flag, hired a drummer and fifer, and followed them, waving the banner, through the streets of the town, greatly to the disgust of the secessionists.

National game. + =BASEBALL *n.* 1. — **1856** *Porter's Spirit of Times* 15 Nov. 176/2 We feel a degree of old Knickerbockic pride, at the continued prevalence of Base Ball as the National game. **1868** *N.Y. Herald* 9 July 5/6 The National Game. Base Ball Notes. **1871** *Harper's Mag.* Sept. 635/2 The youth of the country are rampant with the 'national game.' **1887** *Outing* June 283/2 The Staten Island athletic club . . . are doing good service in promoting the welfare of the grand old national game.

National government. + =FEDERAL GOVERNMENT. — **1792** HAMILTON *Works* VIII. 264 A disposition on my part towards a liberal construction of the powers of the national government. **1816** *Ann. 14th Congress* 1 Sess. 964 Should the National Government not afford them [*sc.* Amer. manufacturers] protection, the dangers which . . . threaten them will destroy all their hopes. **1883** *Harper's Mag.* Nov. 936/1 Within the U.S. are four great [R.R.] routes all subsidized by the national government with grants of land, money, or both.

National Guard. {1797–, of France} +(See quot. 1918); also, a member of the National Guard.

Cf. MILITIA 1 a.

1847 *Santa Fe Repub.* 18 Dec. 3/1 Some National Guards that were at San Antonio had a small fight. **1857** *Harper's Mag.* Aug. 402/1 The National Guard, a military company, . . . were drawn up in front of the Hall. **1868** *N.Y. Herald* 4 July 6/1 The First division of the National Guard will parade. **1882** MCCABE *New York* 499 The military organizations of the City of New York constitute the First Division of the National Guard of the State of New York. **1894** *Outing* XXIV. 392/2 The respective States supplying the uniforms, as is now done in the case of the various divisions of the National Guard. **1909** *World To-day* Oct. 1099 While many of the American states designate their amateur soldiery as 'National Guards,' the venerable Bay State still sticks to the thoroughly Yankee caption of 'militia.' **1918** FARROW *Dict. Mil. Terms* 404 *National Guard.*—A body of militia, or a local military organization. In the United States, the regularly commissioned and enlisted militia of the various states, organized, armed and equipped as provided for the corresponding branches of the service in the Regular Army.

+**National highway. 1.** A highway built by or with the assistance of the federal government. **2.** A railroad. — (**1**) **1816** *Ann. 14th Congress* 2 Sess. 28 That the Secretary of this Department shall execute the orders of the President in relation to . . . The National Highways. **1818** FLINT *Lett. from Amer.* 80 This [road] being a national highway, on which no tolls are to be levied, . . . a great increase of trade is . . . anticipated. **1900** *Congress. Rec.* 10 Jan. 736/1 The national highways should be open to the use of all on equal terms. (**2**) **1865** *Nation* I. 616/1 The National Highways. . . . The safety of travellers ought not to be trusted to the railroad companies.

Nationalism. {1836–} +**1.** (See quotation.) *Obs.* +**2.** A form of socialism based on national control of all business; the ideal set forth by Edward Bellamy in his sociological novel *Looking Backward* (1888), and made the objective of a movement. *Obs.* — (**1**) **1846** WORCESTER 476/2 *Nationalism*, a national idiom or phrase. *Hamilton.* (**2**) **1889** *Nationalist* Sept. 180 This noble ship Nationalism will be freighted with the hopes of future millions. **1892** BELLAMY in *N. Amer. Rev.* June 745 Greenbackism was strongly tinctured with the sentiment of Nationalism.

Nationalist. {1715–} *attrib.* +Of or pertaining to the theory of nationalism (q.v., sense 2). *Obs.* — **1889** *Nationalist* Sept. 171 The growth of the Nationalist movement is so phenomenal that [etc.]. *Ib.* 178 (*caption*), Address . . . at August Meeting of Boston Nationalist Club.

+**National park.**

1. An area having exceptional interest or value because of its scenery, history, forests, etc., usually owned by the federal government and managed chiefly for public recreational purposes. Also *national public park.*

In June, 1864, Congress granted the Yosemite Valley to California on condition that the area should 'be held for public use, resort, and recreation.' This area, later included within Yosemite National Park provided for by Congress in 1890, was the first to which the term *national park* was applied as shown in the first group of examples. See A. Matthews, 'The Word Park in the United States,' in *Mass. Col. Soc. Publ.* VIII. 373–399.

(1) **1868** J. D. WHITNEY *Yosemite Book* 22 The Yosemite Valley . . . has been made a National public park and placed under the charge of the State of California. **1872** C. NORDHOFF *California* 78 Who goes to California will certainly visit the Yosemite; and a corporation . . . could very well afford to . . . spend . . . two hundred thousand dollars in beautify-

ing this 'National Park.' **1880** BUNNELL *Discovery of Yosemite* 221 When this is done, this National Park will be esteemed entirely worthy of this great republic and of the great golden State that has accepted its guardianship.

(2) **1872** *Mass. Col. Soc. Publ.* VIII. 377 Congress, by an act approved March 1, 1872, has set apart a tract of land near the head-waters of the Yellowstone River, in the Territories of Montana and Wyoming. . . . The reservation so set apart is to be known as the 'Yellowstone National Park.' **1876** CROFUTT *Trans-continental Tourist* 89 A bill has passed Congress setting apart a tract of country 55 by 65 miles in extent [about Yellowstone Lake] as a great national park. **1900** *Congress. Rec.* 3 Jan. 628/2 A petition . . . praying for the enactment of legislation prohibiting sheep to enter upon the national parks and forest reserves in that State [California]. **1920** *World Almanac* 350 The Yellowstone is the largest national park . . . with an average elevation of about 8,000 feet.

2. *National Military Park*, any one of various celebrated battlefields of the Civil War set aside for public commemorative purposes by the federal government.

1890 *Statutes at Large* XXVI. 333 An act to establish a national military park at the battlefield of Chickamauga. **1892** *Ib.* XXVII. 376 To enable the Secretary of War to complete the establishment of the Chickamauga and Chattanooga National Military Park . . . one hundred and fifty thousand dollars. **1894** *Ib.* XXVIII. 597 The battlefield of Shiloh, in the State of Tennessee, is hereby declared to be a national military park, . . . and the area thus enclosed shall be known as the Shiloh National Military Park.

3. *National Zoological Park*, a tract of rough, picturesque land near Washington, D.C., set aside by Congress for preserving a representative collection of American animals.

1890 *Statutes at Large* XXVI. 78 The National Zoological Park is hereby placed under the directions of the regents of the Smithsonian Institution.

+**National platform.** *Polit.* A statement or series of resolutions agreed upon by party delegates at a national convention as embodying the political principles for which the party stands. — **1856** *Democratic Conv. Proc.* 25 The Democratic party of the Union, standing on this national platform, will abide by . . . the Compromise measures. **1900** *Congress. Rec.* 10 Jan. 736/1 Both great political parties are no doubt getting ready in their next national platform to denounce the evil. *Ib.* 17 Jan. 904/2 It was a declaration in the national platform of the lack of power on our part to control our own affairs.

+**National Republican.** *Polit.*

1. A member of a political party which in the campaigns of 1828 and 1832 supported John Quincy Adams and Henry Clay respectively for president. Also attrib.

After their defeat in 1832 the National Republicans joined with other elements to form the Whig party.

1828 *Address to Electors of Middlesex Co.* (Conn.), [Signed by] Committee on behalf of the National Republicans of the town of Middletown. **1830** S. SMITH *Major Downing* 6 There was a majority of . . . national republicans in the Legislater. **1831** J. Q. ADAMS *Memoirs* VIII. 437 [Henry Clay] was nominated by the National Republican Convention at Baltimore yesterday for the Presidency. **1838** *Whig Almanac* 3 The Whig party comprised . . . those who, under the name of National Republicans, had previously been known as supporters of Adams and Clay. **1854** BENTON *30 Years' View* I. 47/2 Mr. Clay . . . joined the Whigs (then called national republicans). **1884** BLAINE *20 Years of Congress* I. 106 The supporters of Adams called themselves National Republicans.

b. Hence *National Republican party.*

1888 BRYCE *Amer. Commw.* II. III. liii. 333 The National Republican, ultimately the Whig party, represented many of the views of the former Federalists.

2. *attrib.* Pertaining to the modern Republican party.

1872 (*title*), National Republican Grant and Wilson Campaign Song-Book.

+**National road.**

1. =NATIONAL HIGHWAY.

1817 *Niles' Reg.* XII. 13/2 On the subject of national roads, the first that presents itself, and of primary importance, is a turnpike from Maine to Louisiana. **1858** W. P. Smith *Railway Celebrations* 6 This Great Railroad is located nearly upon the line formerly traveled by the National Road, running between the Cities of Washington and Baltimore.

2. *spec.* The old Cumberland Road, built by the federal government from Cumberland, Maryland, to Ohio and eventually on into Illinois.

[**1822** WOODS *English Prairie* 53 This grand national road is intended to connect all the western country with the seat of government, as there is water communication from Cumberland to the city of Washington.] **1831** WITHERS *Chron. Border Warfare* 59 The present National Road from Cumberland to Brownsville via Uniontown, differs in direction but little from Nemacolin's Path. **1842** ALLARDICE *Agric. Tour* 83 The communication from those cities is maintained, first by the several lines of railroad emerging from them, to Frederick, in Maryland, and from thence, by what is called 'the great national road,' across the Alleghany mountains. **1906** *Springfield W. Repub.* 16 Aug. 2 The old National road, often referred to as the Cumberland road, was the main highway of traffic across the Alleghany mountains in the first quarter of the 19th century.

+**National treasury.** The department of the federal government which has charge of the nation's finances. — **1845** *Xenia Torch-Light* 31 July 3/1 The National Treasury is open to any and all demands made as the price of Texas Annexation. **1854** PIERCE in *Pres. Messages & P.* V. 261 Applications for appropriations would have perverted the legislation of Congress, [and] exhausted the National Treasury. **1874** WELLS *Pract. Economics* (1885) 7 The national treasury was first established, so far as the election of a treasurer could establish it, in November, 1835. **1884** BLAINE *20 Years of Congress* I. 269 The seventh [section of an 1861 amendment] provided for the payment from the National Treasury for all fugitive slaves whose recapture is prevented by violence.

+**National university.** A university projected but never established at Washington, D.C. *Obs.* — **1796** *Ann. 4th Congress* 2 Sess. 1600 Mr. Madison presented a memorial from the Commissioners of the Federal City, stating the many advantages that would result from the building of a National University at the said city. **1803** *Ann. 7th Congress* 2 Sess. 345 An appropriate and characteristic equestrian statue of the original founder of the National University, as a beautiful centre piece for the entire plan, . . . may be built. **1816** *Niles' Reg.* X. 18/1 A bill for the establishment of a National University . . . [is] reported by the select committee of the house of Representatives.

***Native.**

+**1.** An American Indian.

1636 *Conn. Rec.* I. 1 None . . . shall trade w[i]th the natiues or Indians any peece or pistoll or gunn. *a***1772** WOOLMAN *Journal* 193 My meditations were on the alterations in the circumstances of the natives . . . since the coming in of the English. **1807** GASS *Journal* 82 On the top of the highest [bluff] we saw some Mountain sheep, which the natives say are common about the Rocky mountains. **1846** SAGE *Scenes Rocky Mts.* xxxiii, Skins furnish to the natives a favorite material for arrow-cases.

+**2.** *ellipt.* =NATIVE AMERICAN. *Obs.* Also attrib.

1845 *Whig Almanac 1846* 4 *n.*, Whigs in Italics; Locos in Roman; Natives in Small Caps. Total Whigs 76; Locos, 135; Natives, 6; Vacancies, 4. **1845** *Congress. Globe* 18 Dec. 44/1 In six weeks the Native flag was hauled down, the Native press was driven to an abandonment of the faith. **1848** *Ib. 1849* 59/2 The aggregate vote for Members of XXXth Congress was . . . Native, 6,374.

+**3.** A Spanish-speaking inhabitant of the Southwest.

1846 MAGOFFIN *Down Santa Fé Trail* 92 My veil was ingenuously drawn down . . . for the better protection of my face from the wind and constant stare of '*the natives*.' **1863** *Rio Abajo Press* 14 July 1/1 He excited the fanatic prejudices of the natives against the Americans as heretics and offscourings of the earth. **1873** ARNY *Items New Mex.* 28 Oak of a diameter reaching 8 inches and hackberry (called 'anzanita' by natives) of 12 inches diameter are sometimes found in small quantities. **1883** RITCH *Illus. N. Mex.* 59 Only a few of the natives can understand or speak the English language.

4. A domestic animal of native breed: (see also quot. 1884).

1856 OLMSTED *Slave States* 6 The cows are . . . a few imported Ayrshires and Alderneys, and some small black 'natives.' **1858** FLINT *Milch Cows* 50 Perhaps the whole class of animals commonly called 'natives' would be better described as grades. **1876** *Vermont Bd. Agric. Rep.* III. 102 Some extra cows, claimed as natives, were made up of crosses of foreign breeds. **1884** *Century Mag.* Feb. 515/1 The sheep of the United States were the descendants of the English breeds, mixed and intermixed till they had lost the distinctive characteristics of their long-wooled, well-fleshed ancestors, and were known as 'natives.'

5. A Negro. {1848}

1863 'E. KIRKE' *Southern Friends* 106 [He] held in his hand the ordinary slouched hat worn by the 'natives.'

+**6.** *To astonish* (or *startle*) *the natives*, to shock or make a powerful impression on public opinion. *humorous.* {1852}

1807 IRVING *Salmagundi* xii. 298 Unfortunate Straddle! may thy fate be a warning to all young gentlemen who come out from Birmingham to astonish the natives. *c***1835** CATLIN *Indians* II. 37 The *natives* are again 'to be astonished.' **1865** RICHARDSON *Secret Service* 154 On the way here, they indulged in a number of freaks which startled the natives. **1901** RYAN *Montana* 96 Much of her afternoon was spent there under that lady's surveillance, fashioning a party gown with which to astonish the natives.

Native American.

+**1.** A member of the Native American party. Now hist.

1844 GODLEY *Letters from A.* II. 167 The establishment of a party in New York, who call themselves 'Native Americans.' Their professed object is to counteract the growth of Irish influence. **1854** *S. Lit. Messenger* XX. 541 They declare themselves Native Americans; meaning by that term to advocate a repeal of all naturalization laws, and the elevation of none but American-born citizens to office. **1886** POORE *Reminisc.* I. 500 The Native Americans and the Republicans flattered themselves that the Democratic party had been reduced to a mere association of men.

2. *attrib.* and *adj.* In names of organizations: Representing political opposition to aliens and foreign-born citizens and to Catholics.

1835 *Niles' Reg.* 7 Nov., Native American Democratic Association. **1841** W. KENNEDY *Texas* I. p. xlvi, Societies . . . for excluding foreign settlers in the States from the benefits of naturalization . . . have been organized in New Orleans and elsewhere, under the name of 'Native American Associations.' **1843** MARRYAT *M. Violet* xxxvii, The Yankee philosopher will to-morrow run for a seat in legislature; if he fails, he may turn a Methodist preacher, . . . a member of the 'Native American Society,' or a mason. **1884** BLAINE *20 Years of Congress* I. 205 In 1854 James Pollock was chosen governor by the sudden uprising and astounding development of the Native-American excitement.

+**Native Americanism.** Hostility towards all but native-born, Protestant Americans, especially as forming one of the basic principles of the Native American party (q.v.). Now hist. — **1844** *Whig Almanac 1845* 4/1 Native Americanism, . . . inculcated by Mr. Polk's partisans, . . . struck us a hard blow. **1854** in Hambleton *H. A. Wise* 55 Native Americanism . . . is no recent thing in this country. It is a hoary and oft punished abomination of the Federal party. **1922** McCORMAC *J. K. Polk* 279 'Native Americanism' was said to have cost the Democrats votes in Pensylvania.

+**Native American party.** A short-lived political party which arose about 1845, characterized chiefly by opposition to foreigners, foreign-born citizens, and non-Protestants. Now hist. (Cf. AMERICAN PARTY.) — **1845** *Congress. Globe* 18 Dec. 43/3 This Native American party had been generated . . . by the corruptions of our great cities. **1852** *Harper's Mag.* Sept. 544/2 A National Convention of the Native American party was held at Trenton on the 5th of July, at which Mr. Webster was nominated for President.

***Native-born,** *a.* +Born in the United States, as contrasted with *immigrant* or *naturalized.* — **1817** PAULDING *Lett. from South* II. 212 The people in the neighbourhood were obliged to get up a society for the protection of native-born citizens, against Pat. **1834** PECK *Gaz. Illinois* 95 Any person, whether a native born citizen, or a foreigner, may purchase forty acres of the richest soil, and receive an indisputable title, for fifty dollars. **1862** Moore *Rebellion Rec.* V. II. 203 The 'Order' contains two oaths: one, applicable both to the native-born and to such foreigners as have not claimed and received a protection from their government. **1900** *Congress. Rec.* 18 Jan. 968/1, 98 per cent of them [*sc.* inhabitants of Okla.] are native-born American citizens.

+**Native pony.** A mustang. Also attrib. — **1873** ARNY *Items New Mex.* 61 We have . . . the wild native ponies of the country. **1883** *Gringo & Greaser* 1 Sept. 2/3 Races every day. Native pony and burro races.

+**Native son.** A native of a certain place. — **1850** *31st Congress 1 Sess.* Sen. Ex. Doc. No. 76, 3 The native sons of the United States living in New Mexico knew their right to equality of privileges. **1864** *Wkly. New Mexican* 25 Nov. 3 Lieut.-Colonel Chaves . . . is one of New Mexico's favorite native sons. **1916** 'B. M. BOWER' *Phantom Herd* 27 [He] backed out of the way of the Native Son, who sprawled himself over the table corner.

+**Nativism.** Also **nativeism.** A policy favoring native as opposed to foreign-born citizens, especially with reference to political movements. Now hist. (Cf. NATIVE AMERICAN PARTY.) {1887–, in philosophy}

1844 *Whig Almanac 1845* 4/2 Thousands were Naturalized expressly to oppose Nativism, and voted the Polk ticket mainly to that end. **1854** in Hambleton *H. A. Wise* 55 The men who shaped and penned the odious alien law, sought to engraft 'Nativeism' upon the organic law of the country. **1864** NICHOLS *Amer. Life* II. 90 The conspiracy of nativism or know-nothingism . . . failed, because neither of the existing political parties could hope to succeed without the Catholic vote. **1867** *Congress. Globe* App. 12 July 12/2 The naturalized citizen, enjoying his rights largely through the opposition of Andrew Johnson to Nativism and Know-Nothing-ism. **1880** *Lib. Universal Knowl.* VII. 341 The [Hartford] convention's views on amending the federal constitution savored of that nativism that afterwards developed into a great but short-lived American party.

+**Nativist.** *Polit.* One who believes in or advocates nativism. Also attrib. — **1855** *Chicago W. Times* 29 March 3/4 '"Pure Americanism!" you call this Know nothing chicken of yours!' 'We do,' replied the nativist. **1864** NICHOLS *Amer. Life* II. 78 The nativist party, with its secret organization. **1885** LALOR tr. Von Holst *Const. Hist. U.S.* V. 436 Fillmore . . . was chosen by the Nativists of Philadelphia as their standard-bearer. **1892** *Nation* 24 March 231/1 The 'nativist' constituency of the city [of New York] was so transformed as to present a majority which was foreign by birth or extraction. **1894** *Forum* July 534 [The South] was full of nativist feeling in its best form.

+**Nativistic,** *a.* Of or pertaining to nativism. — **1880** *Nation* 22 April 311/1 The nativistic tendencies of the Whig party drove them [*sc.* German Americans] almost to a man into the ranks of the Democracy.

***Natural,** *a.* +Savage or wild. — **1832** KENNEDY *Swallow Barn* II. 125 Ned Hazard's a pretty hard horse to ride, too; only look at his eye,—how natural it is!

+**Natural bridge.** **1.** =FLOATING BRIDGE 2. **2.** The name of a natural arch formation suggestive of a bridge, esp. the one near Lexington, Virginia. — (1) **1806** in *Ann. 9th Congress* 2 Sess. 1136 About fifty leagues above this natural bridge [on the Red R.], is the residence of the Cadeaux. (2) [**1775** BURNABY *Travels* 35 Sixty miles southward of Augusta court-house, [there is] a natural arch, or bridge, joining two high mountains.] **1817** PAULDING *Lett. from South* II. 63 Oliver, whose impatience to see the Natural Bridge very naturally increased as we approached its neighbourhood **1838** *Knickerb.* XII. 32, I am the only surviving witness of that most adventurous exploit of climbing the Natural Bridge in Virginia. **1872** *Atlantic Mo.* March 331 The Natural Bridge, eighty miles from Monticello, was upon one of the tracts now added to their property. **1895** CRITTENDEN *Yellowstone Nat. Park* 244 At the northwest of the [Yellowstone] lake, a trip of a mile will take the tourist to . . . a *Natural Bridge* over a small tributary of Bridge Creek.

+**Natural gas.** **1.** Inflammable gas formed naturally in the earth and obtained for commercial purposes usually by boring. **2.** Attrib. with *company, country, well.* — (1) **1845** SOL. SMITH *Theatr. Apprent.* 102 Many of the stores and shops in the village are lighted with natural gas! **1854** *N.Y. & Erie R.R. Guide* 171 Ere long, 'natural gas,' as it is commonly called, will be brought into more general use. **1883** *Century Mag.* July 336/2 Bradford and some of the smaller towns in the oil regions are lighted with natural gas from wells which fail to yield oil. **1909** *Nat. Conservation Congress Proc.* 58 Natural gas is a very important natural resource of Louisiana. (2) **1885** *Century Mag.* Jan. 466 Natural gas wells have been common in the oil country for years. **1888** KIRK *Queen Money* 395 If there were . . . working natural-gas companies . . . behind the stocks, why should all these brilliant financiers [etc.]? **1889** HOWELLS *Hazard of Fortunes* I. 105 Well, the natural gas country is worth seeing.

***Naturalization.** The act of conferring citizenship upon an alien; the state of being naturalized.

Besides the usual individual process of naturalization for alien immigrants, a group process has on occasion been employed for whole populations, as for the French of Louisiana after the Louisiana Purchase.

1658 *Va. House of Burgesses* 118 It is ordered accordingly that a Commission of Naturalizacon shall be granted him. **1705** BEVERLEY *Virginia* IV. 45 The Method of obtaining Naturalization is thus; the Party desiring it goes before the Governor, and tenders his Oath of Allegiance. **1787** *Constitution* i. § 8 The Congress shall have Power . . . To establish an uniform Rule of Naturalization. **1850** *Whig Almanac 1851* 17/1 No alien shall be entitled to a patent to land . . . until he shall produce . . . record evidence that his naturalization as a citizen of the United States has been completed. **1910** J. HART *Vigilante Girl* 388 Before securing naturalization a man must take out his first papers, under the law, and then remain in the country for five years.

attrib. **1798** *Ann. 5th Congress* II. 1566 The Committee for the Protection of Commerce and the Defence of the Country . . . were instructed to inquire and report whether any and what alterations were necessary in the naturalization act.

+**Naturalization law.** A law prescribing the conditions and processes of naturalization. — **1812** *Ann. 12th Congress* 1 Sess. II. 1571 The House resolved itself into a Committee of the Whole, on the bill supplementary to the naturalization laws. **1840** *Niles' Nat. Reg.* 7 March 10 [Memorial] by Mr. Mouton, from citizens of Louisiana, asking a repeal of the naturalization law. **1859** WILMER *Press Gang* 142 The validity of our Naturalization laws may be called in question. **1916** *Atlantic Mo.* Feb. 231/1 Most of the questions arising under the naturalization laws have had reference to the duty of the United States to extricate its newly made citizens from difficulties . . . in other countries.

+**Naturalization papers.** *pl.* The papers or documents recording an application for naturalization or certifying completion of naturalization. — **1856** *Porter's Spirit of Times* 15 Nov. 181/2 There has come to light one case . . . of forging naturalization papers. **1866** *Wkly. New Mexican* 21 July 2/1 We hadn't taken out our naturalization papers. **1870** O. LOGAN *Before Footlights* 555 Carl Rosa, the violinist, took out naturalization papers in New York last winter. **1900** HANDSAKER in *Pioneer Life* 44 He handed 'em back and ast for my naturlaziation papers.

***Naturalize,** *v. tr.* To invest (an alien) with citizenship. {1605–} Also *ppl. a.* Also transf.

1686 Munsell *Ann. Albany* II. 80 No person or persons, shall be made free . . . but such as . . . shall be naturalized by act of general assembly. **1717** *N.J. Archives* 1 Ser. IV. 293 An act to naturalize Jacob Arents and his three children. **1775** *Mass. Spy* 3 May 1/3 If we are not annexed to the realms we are aliens, and no charter, grant, or other act of the crown can naturalize us, or entitle us to the liberties and immunities of Englishmen. **1808** *Ann. 10th Congress* 2 Sess. 24 They [*i.e.*, captured British goods] would be brought in, condemned, and then naturalized, as Irishmen are now naturalized. **1891** 'THANET' *Otto the Knight* 306 She came in—behind her a young man with the aspect of a 'naturalized American.' **1906** *Statutes at Large* XXXIV. I. 596 Exclusive jurisdiction to naturalize aliens as citizens of the United States. **1916** *Atlantic Mo.* Feb. 223/2 If a Mongolian were permitted to be naturalized in the United States, he would be as much a Mongolian after naturalization as before.

b. With reference to Indians.

1865 *Atlantic Mo.* XV. 157 The United States could naturalize Indians. **1872** TICE *Over Plains* 13 Chief Parthe . . . had himself been naturalized, and was influencing his people to become both civilized and naturalized.

+**Natural road.** (See quots. 1824 and 1869). *Obs.* — [**1824** BLANE *Excursion U.S.* 104 The road is a *natural* one, that is to say, it is a track left open and cleared, but which has never had a single cart load of gravel or stones thrown upon it.] **1835** REED & MATHESON *Visit* I. 110 Towards evening we got on the greensward, or natural road. **1869** BREWER *Rocky Mt. Lett.* 12 The road is what is called here 'a natural road,' that is, the hand of man has done nothing except to build bridges across the streams.

* **Nature.** Also *dial* or *colloq.* **natur, nater.**

1. *All nature,* +'all creation,' everybody, everything. *colloq.* (Cf. CREATION 2.)

1819 *Mass. Spy* 3 Nov. (Th.), Father and I have just returned from the balloon—all nature was there, and more too. **1857** G. RILEY *Puddleford P.* (1875) 369 All nater couldn't stop Puddleford having ten thousand inhabitants 'fore 'nother census. **1862** LOWELL *Biglow Papers* 2 Ser. vi. 158 But I don't love your cat'logue style,—do you?—Ez ef to sell all Natur' by vendoo. **1878** STOWE in *Atlantic Mo.* Oct. 472/2 Cuff would prance round . . . and seem to think he . . . had the charge of *all natur'*.

+**2.** *Like all nature,* like the dickens. *colloq.*

1824 *Woodstock* (Vt.) *Observer* 17 Feb., They said too 'twould shoot like *all nater,* 'Tis singlar what stories they tell. **1840** HOFFMAN *Greyslaer* III. 254 The poor critter would have been sucked under . . . and dragged off like all natur.

+**3.** *To beat all nature,* to excel superlatively, to surpass 'all creation.' *colloq.*

1825 NEAL *Bro. Jonathan* II. 93 Hurra for you—that beats all nater! **1838** *Poor Will's Almanack 1839* 1 And puddings! it does beat all nater! **1847** LOWELL *Biglow P.* 1 Ser. ii. 21 The sort o' trash a feller gits to eat doos beat all nater. **1852** H. C. WATSON *Nights in Blockhouse* 47, I know summut about redskins. This 'ere beats all natur.

+**Nauvoo legion.** [f. *Nauvoo,* Ill.] *Hist.* A military organization composed of Nauvoo Mormons. — **1843** MARRYAT *M. Violet* xxxix, In the winter of 1840, they applied to the . . . state for several charters, . . . one for the Nauvoo legion. **1844** J. SMITH in Rupp *Relig. Denominations* 409 That portion of the citizens subject to military duty are organized into a body of independent military men, styled the 'Nauvoo Legion.'

+**Navajo, Navaho.** Also †**Nanahaw, Nabebo,** etc. [Sp. *Apaches de Navajó* from Tewa *Navahú* 'a large field.']

1. =NAVAJO INDIAN; also, pl., the tribe of such an Indian. (Cf. JOHNNY NAVAJO.)

Although the spelling *Navaho* is preferred by modern authorities, the Spanish spelling *Navajo* has been much more common. The forms *Nanahaw* and *Nabebo* are probably misreadings for *Navahaw* and *Nabeho.*

[**1629** ZÁRATE SALMERÓN in *Archaeol. Inst. of Amer. Papers* (Amer. Ser.) IV. 294*n.*, La nacion de los Indios Apaches de Nabaju.] **1808** PIKE *Sources Miss.* III. App. 9 The Nanahaws are situated to the north-west of Santa Fe . . . and are supposed to be 2000 warriors strong. **1822** J. FOWLER *Journal* 137 We Ware Informed that Spanish army Had Returned . . . three old Horses that Ware So poor the Nabebo Cold not drive them up the mountains. **1846** ROBINSON *Journal* (1932) 40 A friendly Nebajo, named Sandeval, goes with us, as a guide to their country. **1863** *Rio Abajo Press* 10 Feb. 2/3 The Navajos have as yet committed no depredations in this vicinity [Fort Wingate, N.M.]. **1875** *Scribner's Mo.* Dec. 213/1 There are two great bodies of Indians in this country who are intruders—the Navajos and Apaches. **1886** *Century Mag.* May 592/1 A rude art has been applied . . . to metal-work by the Navajos for hundreds of years.

2. The area inhabited by Navajos.

1844 GREGG *Commerce* I. 284 Of such character are the ruins of Pueblo Bonito, in the direction of Navajó, on the borders of the Cordilleras.

3. The language of the Navajos.

1873 BEADLE *Undevel. West* 524 Nearly all the employes understood a little Navajo, but not enough to interpret. **1918** MULFORD *Man from Bar-20* 99, I can only swear in English, Spanish, Navajo, an' Ute.

4. *ellipt.* =NAVAJO BLANKET.

1909 WASON *Happy Hawkins* 26 The cook said I should roll up in the Navajos he'd brought. **1914** 'BOWER' *Flying U Ranch* 12 His blanket was a scarlet Navajo, and his rope a rawhide lariat.

5. Attrib. with *bread, burro, country,* etc.

1847 PARKMAN in *Knickerb.* XXX. 235 Richard committed our horses to a Navaho slave. **1847** *Santa Fe Republican* 17 Sept. 2/4 Maj. Walkers Battalion was to have left the Rio Del Norte . . . for the Navajoe country. **1863** *Rio Abajo Press* 11 Aug. 2/1 Two hundred and fifty more mounted volunteers are called for especially for the Navajo War, to serve in the First New Mexico. **1873** BEADLE *Undevel. West* 528 For the last three days we lived on Navajo bread, coffee, and 'commissary butter,' straight. **1878** — *Western Wilds* 256 The little feet of Navajo burros have cut the trail into a groove two inches deep. **1884** *N. Mex. Terr. Rep.* 86 Five companies are on the line of the A. & P. R. R., near the Navajo reservation.

+**Navajo blanket.** A blanket made by a Navajo woman. — **1834** A. PIKE *Sketches* 99 An Indian girl with her Nabajo blanket, black, with a red border. **1858** PETERS *Kit Carson* 124 Navajoe blankets are very celebrated in the far west of America. **1873** BEADLE *Undevel. West* 545 My horse, bridle, saddle, lariat, gun . . . and two Navajo blankets cost me two hundred dollars. **1912** N. M. WOODROW *Sally Salt* 275 There was a table with books, [and] a couch covered with a bright Navajo blanket.

+**Navajo Indian.** An Indian of an important Athapascan tribe now occupying a large reservation in Arizona, New Mexico, and Utah; also, pl., the tribe of these Indians. — **1822** J. FOWLER *Journal* 123 Ward and Duglass . . . state that the Spanierds have sent 700 men against the Nabeho Indeans. **1857** DAVIS *El Gringo* 412 The Nabajo Indian is seldom seen on foot, a horse being as indispensable to him as to an Arab of the desert. **1868** *N.Y. Herald* 15 July 5/3 The government troops having in charge the remainder of the Navajoe Indians crossed with them and their stock into the new territory. **1890** *Stock Grower & Farmer* 15 Feb. 6/2 Neither Governor Prince nor the commander at Fort Marcy have received any information of serious trouble between the Navajo Indians and the whites.

Naval, *n.* Variant of NAVEL.

* **Naval,** *a.* Of or pertaining to a navy, spec. that of the U.S. See also NAVAL ACADEMY, NAVAL SCHOOL.

1791 *Ann. 1st Congress* II. 1753 The trade of the United States to the Mediterranean cannot be protected but by a naval force. **1797** *Ann. 5th Congress* I. 57 The Naval Establishment must occur to every man who considers the injuries committed on our commerce, the insults offered to our citizens [etc.]. **1822** *Ann. 17th Congress* 1 Sess. I. 47 The petition of the mayor, aldermen, and inhabitants of the city of New Orleans, praying that a portion of the plot of the naval arsenal may be granted to the said city. **1884** *Century Mag.* April 812/1 A few of the most important offices, such as foreign missions, high posts in the military and naval service [etc.]. **1894** *Harper's Mag.* July 252/1 The great establishment that, in its entirety is known as the Naval Gun Factory. **1907** *St. Nicholas* July 815/1 Our blue-jackets are probably the finest naval gunners in the world.

Naval academy. A school for training men for naval service; spec., the United States Naval Academy, at Annapolis, Maryland. Also attrib.

1814 *Amer. State P.: Naval Affairs* I. 323, I would also respectfully suggest . . . the establishment of a naval academy. **1850** (*title*), Rules and Regulations for the Government of the Naval Academy at Annapolis, Md. **1872** BARNARD *Military Schools* (rev. ed.) 935 The aggregate expense of . . . the Naval Academy at Annapolis . . . is not represented by the specific sums [etc.]. **1900** BENJAMIN *U.S. Naval Academy* 368 Uniforms [of the cadets] . . . must be obtained from the Naval Academy storekeeper. **1916** F. D. ROOSEVELT in *Outlook* 28 June 501/1 There is no reason . . . why a graduate of the Naval Academy should be taken away from more important duties to be placed in command of a patrol-boat.

Naval officer. {1769–} +A government official, now a member of the United States Treasury Department, on duty at a customhouse in a large port to estimate duties, countersign clearances, etc. — **1739** *Boston Gazette* 17 Dec., John Boydell . . . was appointed . . . naval officer for the port of Boston. **1789** *Ann. 1st Congress* I. 59 My nomination of Benjamin Fishbourn for the place of naval officer of the port of Savannah not having met with your concurrence, I now nominate Lachlan McIntosh for that office. **1882** MCCABE *New York* 302 Offices . . . are used by the Collector of the Port, the Naval Officer, and the Surveyor of the Port. **1914** *Cycl. Amer. Govt.* II. 499/1 In certain customs districts where a daily accounting with the Treasury Department is impracticable, a treasury official known as a naval officer acts concurrently with the collector in estimation of duties.

Naval school. A school in which men are trained for service in the navy. — **1842** *Niles' Nat. Reg.* 2 April 74 Mr. Mangum, on leave, introduced a bill for the establishment of a naval school. **1845** BANCROFT in *29th Congress 1 Sess.* Sen. Doc. No. 1, 843, I leave you . . . to prepare and lay before this department . . . a plan for the organization of the naval school at Fort Severn, Annapolis. **1849** TAYLOR in *Pres. Mess. & P.* V. 5 The military and naval schools, sustained by the liberality of Congress, shall receive the special attention of the Executive.

Naval stores. *pl.* Materials used in shipping or in the navy; *spec.*, tar, pitch, and other resinous products. {1678–}

1707 *Boston News-Letter* 3 Nov. 2/2 The Briganteen . . . is loaden with Naval Stores. **1728** *N.J. Archives* 1 Ser. V. 209 During the time that the bounty upon naval stores subsisted. **1789** *Ann. 1st Congress* I. 169 Very considerable quantities of ginseng, naval stores, lumber, and provisions, were shipped. **1812** STODDARD *Sk. Louisiana* 126 Various articles, usually denominated naval stores, are produced here; such as hemp, pitch, tar, turpentine, and shipping timber. **1843** HONE *Diary* II. 194 This ship has taken out to England a cargo consisting of articles all (with the exception of the naval stores) of Northern production. **1896** *Pop. Science Mo.* Feb. 472 The different resinous products of trade, which go under the name of 'naval stores.'

+**Navarino.** [*Navarino,* Greece, made famous by a battle there in 1827.] A bonnet of a style popular about 1845. In full *Navarino bonnet.* Also *Navarino scoop.* — **1846** FARNHAM *Prairie Land* 101 A capacious sugar-loaf Navarino scoop which had once vied with the raven hair. *Ib.* 103 [The monkey] winked a little quicker when he faced the Navarino. **1863** TAYLOR *H. Thurston* 345 We wore Navarino bonnets then, and sleeves puffed out with bags of down. **1865** A. D. WHITNEY *Gayworthys* xxiii, I know when old Mrs. Gibson has had the bows turned on her black Navarino.

* **Navel, Naval.** +An orange having a small navel-like depression at its apex. In full *navel orange.* Also attrib. — **1882** *Harper's Mag.* Dec. 58/2 He can go into his orchard and concern himself about his Navel or Brazilian varieties . . . without let or hindrance. **1891** *Ib.* Jan. 170/1 The prices for fruit in the spring of 1890 [were] $1.60 per box for seedlings and $3 per box for navels. **1898** *Kansas City Star* 18 Dec. 5/2 Oranges . . . sold very freely, and there were some fine navals in from Southern California. **1915** H. H. HUME *Citrus Fruits* 33 In Florida the navel oranges have not been a success, owing to the small crops usually produced.

+**Navel orange tree.** A tree producing navel oranges. — [**1846** BROWNE *Trees Amer.* 58 Navel Golden-fruited Orange-tree. The author of the present work claims the honour of first introducing this variety [from Brazil] into the [U.S.].] **1900** E. J. WICKSON *Calif. Fruits* 355 (*caption*), Budded Navel Orange Tree, about Five Feet High.

+**Nave wood tree.** ?A tree having tough wood suitable for making naves for wheels. *Obs.* — **1685** *Springfield Rec.* II. 175 We marked . . . A Nave wood Tree O.O. in a Swamp or run of water. *Ib.* 179 In the Swamp [is] a Nave wood Tree marked, S P on the North side for Springfield.

***Navigate,** *v.* +*intr.* To move, walk. Used esp. of intoxicated persons. *colloq.* — **1846** *Spirit of Times* (N.Y.) 11 July 234/3 Well, by this time I began to think of navigating. **1881** Cooke *Somebody's Neighbors* 88 What are you navigating round me for so glib? **1904** *N.Y. Sun* 9 Aug. 10 She was so drunk that she could barely navigate. **1908** Lorimer *J. Spurlock* 117 While he could navigate successfully . . . he could only just stuttah.

***Navigation.** Shipping; ships collectively. {1605–1772} Also attrib. — **1705** *Boston News-Letter* 25 June 2/1 Unless effectual care be taken in that matter, . . . our Navigation will be entirely ruined. **1742** *Md. Hist. Mag.* XX. 180 Certificate of Goods Imported if required to Clear a Navigation Bond abroad. **1808** in *Niles' Reg.* XV. 51/2 Mr. Weston, then engineer to the western navigation companies of the state of New-York. **1850** Cheever *Whale & Captors* 28 Six hundred and ten [ships were in the American whale fishery, 1849], . . . nearly one tenth of the navigation of the Union.

***Navy.**

+**1.** The ships of war of the United States, considered collectively, or the personnel engaged in their operation and maintenance.

[**1777** *Jrnls. Cont. Congress* IX. 920/1 The United States, in Congress assembled, shall have authority to . . . build and equip a navy. **1796** *State P.* (1819) II. 108 These considerations invite the United States . . . to set about the gradual creation of a navy.] **1800** J. Adams *Works* IX. 77 We do so much of this in the army, [and] navy . . . that it frequently gives me great anxiety. **1842** *Whig Almanac 1843* 21/1 In less than two years our gallant Navy became the terror even of British fleets. **1872** *Atlantic Mo.* Feb. 253 The navy is chiefly engaged in maintaining the department at Washington and the various navy-yards throughout the country. **1916** F. D. Roosevelt in *Outlook* 28 June 495/2 The size of our navy . . . [depends on] the amount which the American people are willing to spend on the construction of fighting ships.

+**2. a.** ?A sword of a type used in the navy. **b.** A pistol or revolver of a type used in the navy. Also attrib.

Cf. Navy revolver, Navy six(-shooter).

(a) 1777 Wayne in W. H. Smith *St. Clair P.* I. 388 Lieutenant Henry defended himself with great bravery . . . , dangerously wounding two of the Indians with his navy. **(b) 1873** Miller *Amongst Modocs* 312 Was it possible that this man . . . could still live with a navy bullet through his body fired at two feet distance! **1873** *Harper's Mag.* Jan. 274/2 They fought . . . with navy pistols, and young Key was killed at the first fire. **1875** 'Mark Twain' *Sk., New & Old* 122 She turned on that smirking Spanish fool like a wild cat, and out with a 'navy' and shot him dead in open court! **1881** *Harper's Mag.* Dec. 956/2 Judge put hand under pillow, drew out 'navy' and fired—*through a looking glass!*

+**3.** =Navy plug.

1876 Tripp *Student-Life* 399 Hawes had smoked 'navy' in it all the year of Sam's probation. **1877** Burdette *Rise of Mustache* 96 He begged a big 'chaw' of navy, and when he went to bed he tucked it snugly away in his cheek. **1889** Riley *Pipes o' Pan* 40, I draw my plug o' navy, and I climb the fence.

4. Attrib. in sense 1 with *bread, biscuit, gun,* etc.

1800 *Steele P.* I. 188 The purser at Boston . . . said the accounts must be settled at the Navy office. **1840** *Niles' Nat. Reg.* 28 March 59 A statement of all the sums of money belong[ing] to the navy pension fund which have at any time been invested in stocks of the several states. **1841** *S. Lit. Messenger* VII. 12/1 The report too is current among Navy officers. **1842** *Ib.* VIII. 90/1 Judge Upshur has given his countrymen an earnest of what they may expect from him as a Navy Secretary. **1848** *Rep. Comm. Patents 1847* 374 The 'navy bread' is usually made out of the coarser particles of the meal. **1867** 'Lackland' *Homespun* 216 The people not only want the Word, but they want it as hard and dry as a navy biscuit. **1875** *Chicago Tribune* 5 Oct. 5/5 With reference to the defalcation of the Navy Paymaster's clerk in San Francisco, it is currently reported [etc.]. **1885** *Century Mag.* Sept. 758 Admiral Porter, however, supplied us with a battery of navy-guns of large caliber. **1917** *Lit. Digest* 3 March 556/1 Emergency Detachments of Nurses . . . can be quickly mobilized and used to supplement the service of both the Army and Navy Nurse Corps.

Navy agent. {1814–} +A naval disbursing officer; a paymaster. *Obs.* — **1846** Polk *Diary* I. 293 Received notes . . . requesting me to withhold the Commission of Mr. Isaac H. Wright as Navy Agent of Boston. **1860** *36th Congress 1 Sess.* H. R. Rep. No. 621, 21 When articles are needed not embraced in a contract a requisition is made out by the master workman . . . and sent to the navy agent.

+**Navy bean.** A small white bean so called from its use in the navy. — **1856** Kane *Arctic Explor.* II. 94 Coffee . . . ; one part of the genuine berry to three of navy-beans. **1897** Wickson *Calif. Vegetables* 176 *Small White Bean.*—This is the accepted local name for the variety which is called the Navy bean at the east. **1909** 'O. Henry' *Options* 143, I care not one parboiled navy bean for your education. **1918** Findlay *Practical Gardening* 182 The Boston Navy or Pea bean and the Dwarf Horticultural are the two best for small gardens.

Navy board. {1695–} An administrative board in charge of naval affairs; +spec., the board of commissioners in the Navy Department (1815–42). — **1777** J. Adams *Works* IX. 464, I had the boldness to make a motion that a navy board should be established at Boston. **1778** *Jrnls. Cont. Congress* X. 15 A letter of the 26 December, from the navy board, at Bordentown, . . . was read. **1842** *S. Lit. Messenger* VIII. 90/1 The Secretary . . . has already satisfied himself that the Navy-Board is an irresponsible power, which should give place to a system of proper responsibility. **1872** *Harper's Mag.* Dec. 94/1 For years the old Navy Board controlled the service in every respect.

+**Navy Department.** The department of the federal government charged with the control, supervision, and maintenance of the navy.

Immediately after the Revolution, United States naval affairs were administered by the War Department, but in 1798 the Department of the Navy was created.

1779 *Journals Continental Congress* XV. 1216 Congress took into consideration the report of the Marine Committee respecting the navy department. **1798** *Ann. 5th Congress* II. 1545 [Mr. Gallatin] did not think it necessary to establish a Navy Department. **1808** *Ann. 10th Congress* II. 1960 We had just navy enough . . . to give rise to the dignified style of 'the Navy Department,' which had dwindled down to a department of gunboats. **1821** *Ann. 16th Congress* 2 Sess. 757 When, and why, the agency of the Treasurer of the United States for the War and Navy Departments was first established. **1850** *Pres. Mess. & P.* V. 67 The circumstances of these cases will appear by the inclosed correspondence, taken from the files of the Navy Department. **1898** *Kansas City Star* 18 Dec. 4/5 The Navy Department Will Take No Chances of Losing a Warship.

Navy jacket. A jacket of the type worn in the navy. — **1840** Mathews *Politicians* II. i, [He] had boasted out of doors he could and would save his life with a word, as easily as hem-stitch a navy-jacket! **1864** *Md. Hist. Mag.* XXI. 300 [He] had on his navy jacket with bright buttons and pants of the same dark blue.

+**Navy plug.** A strong, dark-colored, plug tobacco, or a piece of this. — **1869** Aldrich *Bad Boy* (1870) 245 Between the beer and the soothing fragrance of the navy-plug, I fell into a pleasanter mood. **1871** in McNeal *When Kansas Was Young* (1922) 37 [The Texas cattle herder's] diet is principally navy plug and whiskey. **1879** *Scribner's Mo.* June 243/2 Randall, taking a piece of navy-plug out of his waistcoat pocket, and with his penknife shaving off a piece. **1904** 'O. Henry' *Roads of Destiny* 357 It seems that the only maritime aid I am to receive from the United States is some navy-plug to chew.

+**Navy Register.** An official list of the officers and ships in the United States Navy. — **1841** *S. Lit. Messenger* VII. 4/1 Statistics . . that are furnished by the Navy Register will show [etc.]. **1869** W. T. Sherman in *Sherman Lett.* (1894) 327 Boyd asked me for army and navy registers, past surveys, and railroad surveys. **1924** *Navy Register* 2 In this issue of the Navy Register all officers on the active list of the Navy have been credited in the column headed 'Previous service' only with that service [etc.].

+**Navy revolver.** A heavy, large-caliber revolver of a type used in the navy. (Cf. Navy six(-shooter).) —*a*1861 Winthrop *Canoe & Saddle* 26 This machine . . . is called a Six-shooter, an eight-inch navy revolver. **1872** 'Mark Twain' *Roughing It* 42 The man wore . . . a great long 'navy' revolver (slung on right side, hammer to the front). **1884** Matthews & Bunner *In Partnership* 225 [He] spread on the table a pair of navy revolvers, a pair of shot-guns, a pair of duelling swords, and a couple of bowie-knives. **1911** Vance *Cynthia* 241 It contained a heavy Navy revolver.

+**Navy six(-shooter).** =Navy revolver.—**1865** Pike *Scout & Ranger* (1932) 27, I was advancing rapidly, with . . . my right [hand] on the stock of my 'Navy Six.' **1872** 'Mark Twain' *Roughing It* 57 He might have to enforce it [an order] with a navy six-shooter and so he always went 'fixed' to make things go along smoothly. **1882** Percy *Williams Bros.* 78 They put the twenty-four shots of a couple of pairs of Colt's navy sixes within the space covered by the palms of one's two hands. **1884** Cable *Dr. Sevier* 401 The hand that rested a moment on the cantle as he rose grasped a 'navy-six.'

Navy yard. {1771} A dockyard owned and operated by the federal government where government vessels are built and serviced and where munitions and naval stores are laid up.

'Now *U.S.*' (*O.E.D.*).

1796 *Ann. 4th Congress* 2 Sess. 2786 The cannon for the gun-deck are all in the navy-yard. **1813** Bentley *Diary* IV. 200 Lately a sloop of war has been launched at Charlestown Navy Yard. **1845** Polk *Diary* I. 126 In company with the Secretary of the Navy visited the Navy Yard at Washington. **1887** *Courier-Journal* 1 May 9/3 A member of one of the newly organized regiments which had just been quartered at Washington . . . stumbled into the navy-yard. **1907** C. C. Andrews *Recoll.* 80 The courthouse was guarded by United States marines from the Charleston navy-yard.

***Nay.** A negative vote in a deliberative body. — **1774** *Vermont Hist. Soc. Coll.* I. 8 Passed in the affirmative—all yeas, no nays. **1804** *Essex Inst. Coll.* XXXIX. 325 Ye majority won against us—Yeas 67—Nays 65. **1840** *Niles' Nat. Reg.* 11 July 303/2 Mr. Cave Johnson moved to lay it on the table and on this motion he demanded the yeas and nays. **1896** *Omaha*

Bee 18 Feb. 3/5 The members had taken the alarm and numerous 'nays' came back in response to the roll call.

N.E. +Abbreviation for NEW ENGLAND. Also attrib. — **1645** *Plymouth Laws* 80 The Smyth to make a seale of two Roman letters namely N.E. to seale the measures besides the P. **1667** *Ib.* 153 The charge of the printing of the History of Gods dispensations towards N.E. **1832** CHILD *Frugal Housewife* 26 Balm-of Gilead buds bottled up in N.E. rum, made the best cure in the world for fresh cuts and wounds.

***Neap.** The tongue or pole of a cart. *dial.* {-1659} (Cf. CART NEAP.) — **1828** WEBSTER, *Neap*, the tongue or pole of a cart, sled or wagon. *N. England.* **1877** WARNER *Being a Boy* 2, I rode on the neap of the cart, and drove the oxen . . . to the cider-mill.

***Near about(s),** *adv.* Almost, nearly. *colloq.* {1881-, *dial.*} — **1702** *Boston Rec.* 20 The front of the Old house . . . is neer abt Eleven foot from the Street. **1708** *Ib.* 81 The mouth of the Said creek bears Neer about North East from ye Knowl of Trees. **1834** CARRUTHERS *Kentuckian* II. 206 Yes, I believe everybody's married, nearabouts, as far as I can learn. **1890** JEWETT in *Harper's Mag.* Dec. 103/1 We'll have some o' your clam fritters, and near about stuff him to death.

Near-by, *a.* Neighboring; close at hand. {1858} 'Chiefly *U.S.*' (*O.E.D.*). — **1862** *Independent* 1 May 8/4 The near-by trade and Western dealers are buying moderately. **1891** *Boston Jrnl.* 25 Sept. 2/3 One of our near-by farmer citizens on paying a bill at a store [etc.]. **1906** FREEMAN *By Light of Soul* 417 Many had their luncheons at a near-by restaurant.

Neat cattle. *Agric.* =CATTLE 2. {1753-}

1619 *Va. House of Burgesses* 13 No man with out leave from the Governour shall kill any neat cattle whatsoever. **1667** *Plymouth Col. Rec.* XI. 219 Indians [shall] be prohibited to make any use of any horses neat cattle or hoggs appertaining to the English. **1694** *Huntington Rec.* II. 171 If any creaturs found Doing Damage shall be brought to the pound the owners . . . shall pay . . . for Neatt cattell four pence per head [etc.] **1751** *Duxbury Rec.* 306 A petition to the General Court to make an act to prevent all sorts of neat cattle going upon, or feeding upon Duxborough beach. **1808** *Ann. 10th Congress* 1 Sess. II. 2825 For horses and neat cattle, other than those in teams, . . . six cents and a quarter each. **1850** HINES *Voyage* 415 Eight hundred persons who emigrated principally in ox-wagons, and drove before them fifteen hundred head of neat cattle. **1886** *Century Mag.* Nov. 25/2 About the time . . . when Lincoln grew to manhood, garments of wool and of tow began to be worn . . . , and the hides of neat-cattle began to be tanned.

***Neatherd.** **1.** A cowherd. **2.** (Two words.) A herd of cattle. *Obs.* — **(1) 1636** *Essex Inst. Coll.* IX. 41 Its agreed with Roger Marie Neatherd that he shall begin the keeping of all this Towns Catle. **(2) 1654** JOHNSON *Wonder-w. Prov.* 142 They are not above 50. or 60. families [in the town of Sudbury, Mass.], and about 80. souls in Church-fellowship, their Neatheard about 300.

***Neat's-foot oil.** A pale yellow oil obtained by boiling the feet and shin bones of neat cattle. — **1790** *Penna. Packet* 11 May 3/4 Richard Hicks, Parchment & Glue-maker. . . . Neats Foot Oil. **1810** *Columbian Centinel* 26 Dec. 1/2 Neat's-foot oil, constantly kept for sale per cask or single gallon. **1889** *Century Mag.* March 706/1 The kind of oil used is mentioned in 155 cases, viz.: . . . neat's-foot oil, 2; olive oil, 2; cocoanut oil, 1; tea oil, 1; and refined petroleum, 9.

Neat stock. =CATTLE 2. (Cf. NEAT CATTLE.) — **1850** *Rep. Comm. Patents 1849: Agric.* 94 It is estimated that there are in this county . . . fifteen thousand two hundred and eighty five neat stock. **1863** *Maine Bd. Agric. Rep.* VIII. 13, I have had no little experience in the breeding of animals, particularly of neat stock. **1882** *Ib.* XXVI. 265 The way is to fence off such a piece, and allow no neat stock or horses to run in it at any time.

+**Nebraska.** [Name of the former territory including the present state of Nebraska.] Attrib. with *bill, measure*, in sense: Providing for the erection of the territory of Nebraska. (See also KANSAS-NEBRASKA BILL.) — **1854** *S. Lit. Messenger* XX. 178/1 We are happy to find from his late speech on the Nebraska Bill, that he does occasionally cast all doubts and fears to the winds. **1854** *N.Y. Tribune* 27 Sept. 4/6 The 'Hards' support the Nebraska measure because it is infamous. **1858** LINCOLN in Logan *Great Conspiracy* 58, I have always hated it [slavery], but I have always been quiet about it until this new era of the introduction of the Nebraska Bill began.

+**Nebraskaism.** **1.** A locution peculiar to Nebraska. **2.** The principles underlying the Kansas-Nebraska Bill. — **(1) 1860** *Harper's Mag.* Jan. 282/2, 'I have seldom (if ever) met with a Nebraskaism,' says a Northwestern[er], 'in the [Editor's] Drawer.' **(2) 1887** *Century Mag.* April 858/1 One or two . . . Whigs in central Illinois declared their adherence to Nebraskaism.

+**Nebraskan.** A native or resident of Nebraska. — **1898** *Kansas City Star* 18 Dec. 3/3 Bryan . . . May Be Sent to the Senate Soon After the Holiday Recess—The Nebraskan Talks Guardedly About the Colonial Policy. **1900** *Congress. Rec.* 27 Jan. 1241/2 He aided in the nomination of Mr. Bryan for President, and was an enthusiastic supporter of the brilliant Nebraskan.

Necessary house. A privy. *Obs.* {1611-1828} — **1723** *Amer. Wkly. Mercury* 4 July 3/2 A new Brick House and Lot, with a good Kitchin, . . . half of a Well, Necessary House and a handsome Garden. **1780** *N.H. Hist. Soc. Coll.* IX. 234 Severl Wooden Necessary Houses are to be duge and the Troops Injoined to use them. **1788** WASHINGTON *Diaries* III. 318 In my Botanical Garden, next the Necessary house, was sown 3 Rows of Grass-seeds.

***Neck,** *n.*

1. ***a.** A narrow strip of land, usually an area lying between two bodies of water, rivers, etc. +**b.** 'A corner or triangular district' (*Cent.*). In full *neck of land.* +**c.** (See quot. 1829.)

1608 SMITH *Works* (1910) I. 10 The Towne adioyning to the maine by a necke of Land of sixtie yardes. **1677** *Conn. Rec.* II. 302 The inhabitants that dwell aboue the ferry upon that Neck. **1683** [see POINT *n.* 2]. **1684** in *Amer. Speech* xv. 289/1 A neck or Island bounding Easterly by Machepongo river Westerly . . . part by Cattaile marshes. **1720** *Mass. H. Rep. Jrnl.* II. 233 A Petition . . . praying that he may have leave to purchase . . . a Neck of Up Land. **1747** *Georgia Col. Rec.* VI. 200 Five hundred Acres of Land . . . being a Neck bounded on two sides by the Ogeechee & River Midway. **1770** WASHINGTON *Diaries* I. 422 The River (Ohio) running round it in the nature of a horse shoe, forms a Neck of flat Land. **1829** *Virginia Literary Museum* 228/1 Both rivers are shallow, so shallow that the water leaves innumerable necks bare in every part of the channel. **1857** BRAMAN *Texas* 29 It is a delightful place, located in a neck of prairie, connecting with the Grand Prairie. **1858** HAWKS *Hist. N. Carolina* II. 217 The land was cut up by the rivers and their tributary creeks into 'necks,' as they were termed, or peninsulas. **1903** *Critic* XLIII. 305*n.*, The Horseneck is a curving neck of sand barely three miles long and three quarters of a mile wide.

2. In place names.

1640 *Md. Hist. Mag.* V. 373 Robert Huett & Henry Bellamy pray to have confirmed to them the neck called Crany neck. **1665** *Essex Inst. Coll.* LVI. 299 The meadow lot I bought of Mr. Saml. Hall, butting upon great Neck and little River. **1707** *N.C. Col. Rec.* I. 662 There is an old field Known at this day by the name of Weyanoake neck. **1793** *Mass. H. S. Coll.* 1 Ser. III. 1 The natives . . . inhabit a part of said town, known by the name of Betty's-neck. **1830** *Va. Lit. Museum* 632/2 With these recommendations, she had been the most celebrated belle in the Northern Neck. **1919** *Maine My State* 337 In the tall, old-fashioned house behind the spruces on Harpswell Neck, lives Rev. Elijah Kellogg.

||**3.** The inhabitants of a neck.

1669 *Lancaster Rec.* 81 The Cages . . . shall be set down vpon the nekes Charge.

4. In phrases: **a.** *Neck of meadow*, a strip of meadow.

1637 *Dedham Rec.* 28 Graunted to Samuell Morse yt necke of medowe lying next unto ye medowes graunted unto Edward Alleyn. **1663** *Oyster Bay Rec.* I. 11 All the medows on the est of the bever swamp river except the neck of medow all ready granted to Anthony wright are all to remaine common. **1698** *Providence Rec.* VI. 200 A percell of Meadow which . . . is scituate in a neck of Meaddow on the north side of Pautuxett River.

+**b.** *Shot in the neck*, partly intoxicated. *slang.*

1833 GREENE *Dod. Duckworth* II. 176 He was seldom downright drunk; but was often . . . shot in the neck. **1855** *Brooklyn Jrnl.* 18 April, Some of the prisoners' attorneys got as often 'shot in the neck,' as the Under-Sheriff did in the head. **1870** *Picayune* 17 March (De Vere), When I tried to help him up he offered to fight me, saying that he was not drunk, but only shot in the neck.

c. *Neck of (the) woods* {1780}, +a neighborhood or community. *colloq.*

'From this use of neck in neck of meadow may have come another Americanism, neck of woods, meaning region, section, settlement in the woods' (Krapp *Eng. Lang. in Amer.* I. 83).

1851 *Polly Peablossom* 49 The big black customer that circumlocutes down in our neck o' woods beats 'em all hollow. **1856** A. CARY *Married* 137 Tell her she is welcome to the hospitalities of this neck of woods. **1904** 'O. HENRY' *Cabbages & Kings* 50 Why, Central Park ain't in it with this neck of the woods. **1919** T. K. HOLMES *Man from Tall Timber* 154 Of all the old blow-hards that ever come into this neck o' woods.

+**d.** *To get it in the neck*, to get the worst of it; to be hard hit. *slang.*

1887 *Courier-Journal* 20 Jan. 6/4 Dem dubs is goin' to git it in de neck in a minit. **1896** *Typographical Jrnl.* IX. 502 Suffice to say that we 'got it in the neck' (a la Thanksgiving turkey) on a large majority of the points arbitrated upon. **1902** W. IRWIN *Love Sonnets* Epilogue, . . . Humble Virtue gets it in the neck. **1905** D. G. PHILLIPS *Plum Tree* 26 You'll soon be used to getting it in the neck if you stay in politics.

5. Attrib. in sense 1 with *bridge, fence, gate*, etc.

1640 *New Haven Col. Rec.* 32 The gates att the ends of the neck bridge and the way to itt [shall] be made convenient forthwith. **1647** *Ib.* 333, 35 acrs. of upland . . . lying on[e] end butting upon the necke highway, the other end butting upon the mill highway. **1649** *Ib.* 470 Henry Humerston . . . mett Mr. Westerhousen within ye necke gate. **1656** *Dorchester Rec.* 80 The Selectmen Do order and appynt that all the p'prietors of the neckelande doe meete att the meting howse by 9. **1689** *Hartford Land Distrib.* 121 One parcell of land which . . . abuts north on land belonging to Andrew Sandford . . . & east [on the land] comonly Called the neck fence. **1695** *Ib.* 325 One parcell of Land w[hi]ch . . . is abutted East on the great River west, on the Neck lotts.

***Neck,** *v.* +*tr.* To seize or catch by the neck; to tie neck to neck. — **1857** GUNN *N.Y. Boarding-Houses* 133 The landlady . . . *necked* the dog and bore him vengefully into the passage. **1857** BRAMAN *Texas* 73 The usual practice of farmers, whenever they want work oxen, is to go to the prairie, and neck together, with ropes, as many pair of three and four-year old steers as they desire. **1923** J. H. COOK *On Old Frontier* 21 Each of them had to be 'necked' to a gentle one, to be led for a time.

Neckcloth. A kerchief for the neck. {1639-} — **1638** *Md. Archives* IV. 30 The Inventory of John Bryants goods [includes] . . . 2. neck-clothes, 1. band, 1. cap. **1693** *Conn. Probate Rec.* I. 508 A Caliminco Jacket & Breeches and 2 paire of Stockings and white Neck Cloth to be divided amongst the rest of my Estate. **1758** R. EASTBURN *Captivity* 6 [They] stripped me of my Cloathing, Hat, and Neckcloth. **1818** FLINT *Lett. from Amer.* 7 Washing and dressing of shirts, neckcloths, &c. costs a dollar and a half per dozen.

+**Necked calf.** A calf being weaned by being tied up; a calf roped by the neck. — **1890** *Stock Grower & Farmer* 15 March 5/3 If some passing puncher should hear the peculiar bawl that a 'necked' calf makes, he is dead sure to investigate. **1907** WHITE *Arizona Nights* 153 'No more necked calves,' they announced.

+**Necked pine.** A variety of strawberries. — **1851** CIST *Cincinnati* 295 Necked Pine—highest flavored. **1861** *Ill. Agric. Soc. Trans.* 469, I have a bed of Necked Pine so thickly matted that a mouse could not get through them.

Neck handkerchief. A neckerchief. {1712-} — **1642** *Md. Archives* IV. 95, 9. plaine neckcloths & 5 plaine neckhandkerchiefes. **1683** *Conn. Probate Rec.* I. 376 She gave to her gr[and]child . . . a Neck Handkercheire. **1835** LONGSTREET *Ga. Scenes* 218, I believe mammy's got a neck-handkerchief now, that daddy won on your shooting at Collen Reid's store. **1871** *Atlantic Mo.* Nov. 574 Fifty or sixty teamsters inserted their dusty heads in buckets of water [and] turned their once white neck-handkerchiefs inside out.

Necking. {1804-} +(See quotation.) — **1890** *Stock Grower & Farmer* 15 March 5/3 The method [of weaning calves] generally followed in a hilly country is as follows, and is known as 'necking.' You drive the calf off, four or five miles and tie it up short to a bush.

+**Necklace poplar.** The cottonwood, *Populus balsamifera.* — **1847** WOOD *Botany* 507 *P[opulus] monilifera.* Necklace Poplar. . . . Near Troy, N.Y. . . . A tree 60-70 f[t.] high. **1884** SARGENT *Rep. Forests* 175 *Populus monilifera,* . . . Cottonwood. Necklace Poplar. Carolina Poplar. Big Cottonwood. **1897** SUDWORTH *Arborescent Flora* 135 *Populus deltoides* . . . Yellow Cottonwood. . . . [Also called] Necklace Poplar (Tex., Colo.).

+**Necklaceweed.** The white baneberry. — **1817-8** EATON *Botany* (1822) 155 *Actaea alba,* necklace weed, white beads. . . . Berries white. **1821** *Mass. H. S. Coll.* 2 Ser. IX. 146.

Neck ribbon. A ribbon worn around the neck. — **1851** A. CARY *Clovernook* 97 She selected a white muslin, which she thought would do if she only had a new neck-ribbon. **1877** PHELPS *Story of Avis* 371 The baby had pulled down Avis' pink neck-ribbon and her bright hair. **1883** *Century Mag.* Aug. 572/2 Partly to rescue the rest of her raiment from the shower which had ruined her neck-ribbon.

+**Necktie party.** A lynching or hanging. Also *necktie sociable. slang.* — **1878** BEADLE *Western Wilds* 46 He had the pleasure of presiding at a 'neck-tie sociable' where two of the men . . . were hanged. **1882** in *Nat. Geogr. Mag.* LVI. 247 If Found within the Limits of this City after Ten O'Clock P.M. this Night, you will be Invited to attend a Grand Neck-tie Party. **1900** DRANNAN *Plains & Mts.* 390 A new log house . . . had been prepared for this neck-tie party by placing four dry goods boxes in a row in the house. **1920** SANDBURG *Smoke & Steel* 20 Two of them croaked on the same day at a 'neck-tie party.'

+**Neck-twister.** A kind of spirituous drink. *slang. Obs.* — **1859** CORNWALLIS *New World* I. 300 Cold punch, gum ticklers, and neck twisters, drinks of Yankee concoction.

Neckwear. (See quot. 1879.) {1910-} — **1879** WEBSTER *Suppl.* 1569/1 *Neck-wear,* a collective term for cravats and collars. (*Colloq.*) **1887** *Harper's Mag.* May 947/2 He waited at the corner of the block, . . . affecting an interest in the neckwear of a furnisher's window. **1896** *Harper's Mag.* April 701/1 Grant . . . [loitered] before a shop window, but [was] wholly unconscious of the spring neck-wear therein displayed. **1918** RIDEOUT *Key of Fields* 284 He had found . . . a new shirt, new boots, and very noble neckwear, lying on his bed.

***Neckweed.** +The purslane speedwell, *Veronica peregrina:* (see also quot. 1833). — **1833** EATON *Botany* (ed. 6) 386 *Veronica agrestis,* field speedwell, neckweed. **1843** TORREY *Flora N.Y.* II. 42 Neck-weed. . . . Formerly considered a valuable remedy for scrophulous affections, but probably of little value. **1901** MOHR *Plant Life Ala.* 723 Neckweed . . . [is found] throughout the continent.

Neck yoke. {1688} +A bar, usually of wood, connecting two draft animals working abreast, and supporting the end of the pole or tongue of the vehicle which they draw. — **1868** WOODRUFF *Trotting Horse* 349 The neck-yoke came off the pole, and he got loose. **1870** T. D. PRICE *Diary* 26 Feb. (MS.), Neckyoke to have turned. **1877** JOHNSON *Anderson Co., Kansas* 159 The neck yoke became detached, the pole dropped to the ground, and the horses became frightened. **1891** C. ROBERTS *Adrift Amer.* 200 Picking up an old buggy neck yoke, I laid him out with it.

Nectarine. Also †**necterine.**

1. A peach or variety of peach having a very thin, smooth skin and firm pulp. {1676-}

1709 LAWSON *Carolina* 110 We have likewise very fair Nectarines, especially the red, that clings to the Stone. **1792** IMLAY *Western Territory* 92 Kentucky produces . . . apricots and nectarines. **1858** VIELÉ *Following Drum* 53 The piles of pineapples, bananas, pomegranates, and nectarines, seemed entirely to take from the stern reality of roast beef. **1924** *Farmers' Bul.* No. 1435, 2 On peaches and nectarines . . . the cracking [of the skin] is more severe.

2. The tree bearing this fruit. {1616-} In full *nectarine tree.*

1743 CATESBY *Carolina* II. p. xx, *Nusipersica.* The Necterine-Tree. **1800** HAWKINS *Sk. Creek Country* 67 He has a peach orchard of fine fruit, and some fine nectarines. **1836** CROCKETT *Exploits* 68 The cultivated fruit trees are the apple, pear, peach, plum, nectarine, cherry, and quince. **1862** *Rep. Comm. Patents 1861: Agric.* 541 Nectarines and peaches do better in pots than apricots or plums. **1924** *Farmers' Bul.* No. 1435, 2 Bacterial spot is an orchard disease which affects fruits, twigs, and leaves of the peach, apricot, nectarine, and plum.

Ned.

+**1.** =OLD NED. Also transf.

1850 GARRARD *Wah-To-Yah* x. 140 Numerous were the curses showered on the 'Neds,' by the mountain men of our party. [Note:] Among many farmers, pork is familiarly called 'Ned,' and as pork forms a principal portion of the government rations, the United States employees were so termed, by the mountain men, in derision. *Ib.* xxi. 253 They were entitled every day to three-fourths of a pound of messpork or 'Ned.'

2. (See quotation.) *cant.*

1859 MATSELL *Vocabulum* 58 *Ned,* a ten-dollar gold piece. **1882** MCCABE *New York* 510.

+**3.** *To raise (promiscuous* or *merry) Ned,* to stir up trouble; 'to raise Cain.' *colloq.* (Cf. CAIN 1, JACK *n.*[1] 7.)

1848 LOWELL *Biglow P.* 1 Ser. v. 69 Your fact'ry gals . . . 'll go to work raisin' promiscoous Ned. **1870** in O. Logan *Before Footlights* 165 We are real smart girls . . . and can raise ned and keep folks A laughing. **1901** MERWIN & WEBSTER *Calumet 'K'* 134 It's the little work that can raise Ned with you. **1906** QUICK *Double Trouble* 223 You've been raising merry Ned, Florian, in your Brassfield capacity.

+**4.** *By Ned,* a mild oath. *colloq.*

1853 'P. PAXTON' *Yankee in Texas* 227 'By Ned,' says he, 'if it aint that owdacious critter of Miss Mash's.'

***Needle.**

***1.** A slender, pointed instrument used in sewing.

1633 *N.H. Doc. & Rec.* I. 77, 1 small bagg containing aules, great needles, hob nayles, and sparables. **1772** A. G. WINSLOW *Diary* 22, I cannot so well manage the needle. **1886** *Congress. Rec.* 17 June 5836/1 It was supposed that the sailors would want [ditty boxes] . . . to hold their needles and tobacco and pipes and such things. **1914** STEELE *Storm* 189 The warm air stung like a rain of needles.

b. The art of sewing.

1752 HEMPSTEAD *Diary* 584 The celebrated School-mistress who taught Reading, writing, & Arithmetick & the Needle to the female.

+**2.** =CYPRESS KNEE.

1853 'PAXTON' *Yankee in Texas* 60 Around the foot of each tree are standing a number of those singular conical-shaped shoots, termed needles, resembling so many grave-stones.

Needlefish. {1601-} Any one of various American fishes of the family Belonidae, esp. those of the genus *Tylosurus.* — **1883** *Nat. Museum Bul.* No. 27, 450 Needle-fish. . . . In Washington market it is occasionally offered for sale without the head; but the green bones make it unpopular. **1903** BEAN *Fishes N.Y.* 318 The silver gar, also called soft gar, billfish and needlefish, is found along our coast from Maine to Texas.

Needle gun. A breech-loading rifle in which the cartridge is discharged by a comparatively long needlelike firing pin. {1865-} — **1867** *Wkly. New Mexican* 11 May 2/2, I fired a needle gun. **1875** *Chicago Tribune* 20 July 2/1 The needle-gun that the soldiers carry only shoots once without reloading. **1904** STEEDMAN *Bucking Sagebrush* 86 They were what were called needle guns, or old Springfield rifles that probably had been issued towards the end of the Civil War. **1922** MCNEAL *When Kansas Was Young* 18 One of our party carried a three-band Sharp's needle gun and a belt full of cartridges.

Negative, *v.* {1778-}

+**1.** *tr.* To reject (a person proposed for an office). Also *ppl. a.* used absolutely.

1706 SEWALL *Diary* II. 162 In stead of the Negativ'd were chosen B. Brown, 55. Ephr. Hunt, 42. **1720** *Ib.* III. 255 The Govr. Consented to the Choice of the Councillours, having Negativ'd Col. Byfield and Dr. Clarke. **1823** TUDOR *Otis* 7 Colonel Otis, as he was generally called, was several times negatived as a Councillor, by Governor Bernard. **1876** BANCROFT *Hist. U.S.* IV. 6 Negativing six of the ablest 'friends of the people in the board.'

+**2.** To veto (a bill or law).

1749 *Conn. Rec.* IX. 453 It would . . . invest the Governor . . . with a power to negative all acts that should be passed in our Assembly. **1834** D. WEBSTER in *Congress. Deb.* 18 March 992/2 We passed a bill for such a recharter, through both Houses, but it was negatived by the President. **1882** BANCROFT *Hist. U.S.* VI. III. 271 Madison put forth all his strength to show that a power of negativing the improper laws of the states is the most . . . certain means of preserving the harmony of the system.

***Neger.** Also **neager, negur.** [Fr. *nègre.*] =NEGRO. *Obs.* — **1650** *Conn. Rec.* I. 532 The Magistrates . . . [shall] deliuer vp the Indian seized to the party or partyes endammaged, either to serue or to bee shipped out and exchanged for neagers. **1701** SEWALL *Diary* II. 43 Mr. Cotton Mather . . . talked very sharply against me as if I had used his father worse than a Neger. **1787** TYLER *Contrast* (1790) II. ii, Servant! Sir, do you take me for a neger,—I am Colonel Manly's waiter. **1819** B. HALL *Travels in N.A.* II. 77 The white lords of creation . . . would as soon think of sitting down to eat . . . chopped pumpkins, with their cattle, as of entering into social intercourse with a 'negur.' **1885** *Harper's Mag.* Oct. 774/1 She had abused the 'neager' Anthony, and the other servants.

Negligee. 1. A loose gown formerly worn by women. *Obs.* {1756–; now *hist.*} +**2.** A woman's dressing gown or robe, usually made of silk and trimmed with lace, ruffles, etc. (Cf. DRESSING GOWN.) — **(1) 1755** *Boston Ev. Post* Nov., Horsehair Quilted Coats to wear with Negligees. **1775** *Jrnls. Cont. Congress* II. 40 She missed the following things: . . . one rich brocade gown, called a negligée, one lutestring gown [etc.]. **1830** J. F. WATSON *Philadelphia* 177 Robes or negligees, as they were called, were always worn in full dress. **(2) 1862** *Harper's Mag.* Oct. 720/1 The morning negligée is of white . . . Cashmere. **1871** STOWE *Pink & White Tyranny* 40 She lay in a loose negligé on the bed. **1903** BURNHAM *Jewel* 186 She came finally in her white negligée into her mother's room.

Negress. A female Negro. {1786–}

*a***1800** TWINING *Visit* (1895) 33, I observed that the maid-servant who assisted . . . was a negress. **1831** in Peck *Guide* 62 Then such crowds . . . of *Negresses* and Quatre-unes, . . . carrying [cakes and fruit] on their *bandanaed* heads. **1855** R. GLISAN *Jrnl. Army Life* 191 We saw a few negresses handsomely dressed. **1880** CABLE *Grandissimes* 15 The crew was a single old negress . . . [who] rowed the barge with a tea-spoon. **1896** WILKINS *Madelon* 296 Elvira Gordon . . . entered the room past the sullen negress.

***Negro.**

In informal speech, esp. in the South, *Negro* is often pronounced as if spelled *nigger*. In main entries as NEGRO BOY, NEGRO BUSINESS, NEGRO CABIN, etc., the conventional spelling *Negro* is used in the entry word even though the examples show both the *Negro* and the *Nigger* spellings. (Cf. NEGER, NIGGER *n.*)

***1.** A person, especially a male, belonging to the black or African race; also, collectively, the Negro race.

1653 *Suffolk Deeds* I. 262 He is engaged with me to Mr. Adam Winthrop for delivery of a Negro in may next. **1678** *Doc. Col. Hist. N.Y.* XII. 607 That Liberty of traede may bee granted us with the neighbouring Collony of Maryland for the Suppplying us with negros. **1700** SEWALL *Diary* II. 16 There is a Motion by a Boston Committee to get a Law that all Importers of Negros shall pay 40s. per head, to discourage the bringing of them. **1724** H. JONES *Virginia* 36 The Negroes live in small Cottages called Quarters, in about six in a Gang. **1792** tr. Brissot de Warville *New Travels* (1794) 344 The Quakers . . . have no slaves; they employ negroes as hired servants. **1830** WATSON *Philadelphia* 479 Once they submitted to the appellation of servants, blacks, or negroes, but now they require to be called coloured people. **1858** DOUGLAS in Sparks *Lincoln-Douglas Debates 1858* (1908) 95, I do not question Mr. Lincoln's conscientious belief that the negro was made his equal, . . . [but] I do not regard the negro as my equal. **1890** *Congress. Rec.* 23 Aug. 9092/2 What relief do you propose to give the negro? **1920** *3d Nat. Country Life Conf. Proc.* 41 The negro became the largest single factor in cotton production.

+**2.** English as spoken by Negroes in the United States. *Obs.* (Cf. NEGRO ENGLISH, NIGGER *n.* 2.)

1704 S. KNIGHT *Journal* 38 You speak negro to him. I'le ask him. **1884** *Amer. Philol. Soc. Trans.* XVI. App. 32 Such parasynetic forms as *sparrer-grass* for *asparagus* . . . are common enough in Negro.

3. *attrib.* (passing into *adj.*) and *comb.* **a.** Pertaining to the traffic in Negroes as slaves.

See also NEGRO BUSINESS.

1724 *Va. St. P.* I. 206 This Duty must have been a great hindrance to the Negroe Trade, as well as a Burthen upon the Poore Planters. **1860** in W. Lawrence *A. A. Lawrence* 164 Negro dealing is carried on here by 'gentlemen' of family who have been unfortunate in other business. **1866** MOORE *Women of War* 308 Before the war he had lived at Memphis and on the river, following the cognate and equally infamous branches of business, negro-trading and river gambling.

b. Denoting things, usually cloth or articles of clothing, designed or reserved for Negro slaves. *Obs.*

See also NEGRO CLOTH, CLOTHING, etc., and NIGGER *n.* 6.

1732 *S.C. Gazette* 1 April, He had on . . . a brown Coat . . . and blue Negro Boots. **1834** SIMMS *Guy Rivers* 414 [He kept] three hundred and odd dollars . . . ready to be expended for . . . wooden combs, knives, and negro-handkerchiefs. **1835** *S. Lit. Messenger* I. 260 The fabrics are heavy —negro shirtings 29 inches wide [etc.]. **1841** *Picayune* 3 March 3, 300 pair of Negro Blankets, in Store and for Sale. **1841** in W. J. & F. L. Garrison *Life W. L. Garrison* III. 27 We recommend to abolitionists as the most consistent and effectual method of abolishing the 'negro pew,' to take their seats in it, wherever it may be found, whether in a gentile synagogue, a railroad car, a steamboat, or a stage-coach. **1853** SIMMS *Sword & Distaff* 69 The wagon was mostly filled with . . . negro clothes.

c. Designating places, troops, etc., inhabited by or composed of Negroes.

See also NEGRO QUARTER and cf. NIGGER *n.* 7.

1739 *Georgia Col. Rec.* IV. 677 In the Negro Colonies, the Hire of White Men is more than that of Negroes. **1798** BENTLEY *Diary* II. 270 A Negro town has been encouraged on the Hill south of the road to the Bridge. **1833** *Niles' Reg.* XLIV. 410/1 This habitation . . . [was] undisturbed but by the little bustle in the neighboring negro camps. **1865** CUMMING *Hospital Life* (1866) 168/1 Negro regiments . . . have been turned loose on the helpless inhabitants.

d. Designating those having to do with Negroes in slavery or as recently freed.

See also NEGRO-CATCHER, NEGRO-DRIVER, etc.

1741 *Georgia Col. Rec.* IV. 678 This exposes them to the Envy and Hatred of our Negro-Mongers. **1748** *Ib.* VI. 215 The two Petitioners have for several Years past been Negro Overseers in South Carolina. **1780** J. JONES *Letters* 47 The negro holders in general already clamour against the project. **1831** in Stowe *Key* 6/2 Write to me about . . . any mark the fellow has who says he got away from the negro-buyer. **1843** MARRYAT *M. Violet* xxxi, Labour had fallen so low, that thousands of individuals had abandoned their farms to become horse-thieves and negro smugglers. **1845** F. DOUGLASS *Narrative* 73 Mr. Covey enjoyed the most unbounded reputation for being a first-rate overseer and negro-breaker. **1853** STOWE *Key* 5/2 The trader, the kidnapper, the negro-catcher, the negro-whipper, and all the other . . . appendages of what is often called the 'divinely-instituted relation' of slavery. *Ib.* 130/2 Where there are negro-hunters advertising in a paper, there are also negro-hunts. **1856** OLMSTED *Slave States* 30 The negro-dealers had confidential servants always in attendance. **1866** *Congress. Globe* App. 14 Nov. 33/3 Bands of 'guerrillas' and 'negro regulators' soon increased in numbers and audacity.

e. Designating persons belonging to the Negro race.

See also NEGRO BOY, FELLOW, etc., and cf. NIGGER *n.* 5.

1836 PAULDING *Slavery in U.S.* 193 A negro preacher rose and thanked the gentleman kindly for his discourse. **1852** *Harper's Mag.* Aug. 335/2, I could not help laughing at the important procession of negro-waiters stamping in with the different courses. **1860** MORDECAI *Virginia* 213 Gilbert Hunt, a negro blacksmith, possessed naturally a powerful frame. **1870** *Scribner's Mo.* Dec. 115/1 A negro newsboy would be as great a rarity in New York as a black swan. **1883** *Century Mag.* July 423/1 Strange arch-way and door-way groups of beggar and lady, . . . fruit-peddler, negro porter, priest, [etc.]. **1895** G. KING *New Orleans* 317 There was one year of simple existence and endurance of the new condition of things; negro soldiers, negro policemen, negro officials, and hired negro menials.

f. Designating stories, songs, etc., arising among or emanating from Negroes.

See also NEGRO SONG, SPIRITUAL.

1775 CRESSWELL *Jrnl.* 53 A couple . . . begins to dance a jig (to some Negro tune). **1840** DANA *Two Years* 158 [He] amused us often with queer negro stories. **1846** FARNHAM *Prairie Land* 170 A negro dance or a lofty flight of admiration for the works of nature . . . were executed with nearly equal excellence. **1886** *Harper's Mag.* Aug. 483/1 The following bayou version of one of the negro folk-lore stories is translated by a lady on Petite Anse Island, Louisiana. **1908** *S. Atlantic Quarterly* Oct. 332 Gullah: a Negro Patois . . . spoken in the mainland and island regions, bordering the South Atlantic Seaboard. **1919** *Outlook* 17 Sept. 84 Two Negro Lullabies. By Leigh Richmond Miner. **1922** *Amer. Folk-Lore* July 248 The prolongs peculiar in much of the Negro folk-songs, are touchingly beautiful.

g. Designating activities performed or carried on, or resembling something performed or carried on, by Negroes.

1844 J. COWELL *Thirty Years* II. 66 [Tom Blakeley] was the first to introduce negro singing on the American stage. **1851** *Knickerb. Mag.* XXXVII. 191 We wonder whether he ever attended a negro-camp-meeting at the South! **1871** *Ku Klux Klan Rep.* VIII. 233 Sheriff Barber and Mr. Coffin . . . went out to a negro-baptizing about five miles from town. **1899** HARTE *Hamlin's Mediation* 102 The dancing of the girl suggested a negro 'break-down' rather than any known sylvan measures.

h. Pertaining to political rule or government conducted or dominated by Negroes. Usually with reference to conditions in the South just after the Civil War.

1877 BEARD *K.K.K. Sketches* 25 The governments in the South—State, district, and municipal—were negro governments. **1884** *Century Mag.* April 861/2 It was the period of negro supremacy—the reign of terror. *Ib.* 862/1 The methods which overturned the carpet-bag and negro dynasties find their justification . . . in the instinct of self-preservation. **1885** *Mass. H. S. Proc.* 2 Ser. VI. 402 We visited several Southern cities . . . during the period of 'carpet-bag' government and negro legislation. **1887** *Harper's Mag.* March 635/2 To be a Republican . . . was to be identified with the detested carpetbag government and with negro rule. **1890** *Congress. Rec.* 2 June 5545/1 To rid themselves of what they are pleased to term 'negro domination,' [they] habitually count out the negro vote. **1898** in *Congress. Rec.* 6 Feb. (1900) 1555/1 The only way to rid the country of the negro ballot is [etc.]. **1900** *Ib.* 23 Jan. 1064/1 The people broke into fierce energy and overthrew the negro-carpetbag domination.

4. In special combinations.

Negro auction, an auction or sale of Negro slaves; *N. cellar*, a low dive frequented by Negroes; *N. pen*, an enclosure or place of security for Negroes awaiting sale as slaves; *N. problem*, the problem of satisfactory adjustment of Negroes as a race to their social and political environment; *N. yard*, a Negro pen.

1856 OLMSTED *Slave States* 31 This must not be taken as an indication that negro auctions are not of frequent occurrence. **1849** G. G. FOSTER

N.Y. in Slices 28 The Five Point negro-cellar, with its tallow candle stuck in a bottle. **1851** in Stowe *Key* 122/2 Suppose now, for a moment, that your daughter . . . was in these hot days incarcerated in a negro-pen. **1920** *3d Nat. Country Life Conf. Proc.* 137 Could a better method for indefinitely perpetuating our 'negro problem' be devised? **1806** *Balance* V. 53/2, I am informed that there are several negro-yards in Savannah, where slaves imported into South Carolina are kept for sale.

Negro boy. A boy or an adult male of the Negro race, before 1865 usually a slave. {1625–} Cf. Boy 1.

1675 *Va. State P.* I. 10 Mrs. Beazley . . . did order . . . that yo[u]r pet[itione]r by the then name of negro boy Phillip, should serve her cousin. **1701** Wolley *Journal N.Y.* (1902) 50, [I] ordered my Negro boy about 12 years old to tye them [*sc.* two bear cubs] under the Crib by my Horse. **1763** *Huntington Rec.* II. 464 To my son Isaac [I give] my negro man named Tom & my negro boy named Ned. **1835** Kennedy *Horse Shoe Robinson* II. 99 This was a diminutive negro boy, . . . gaudily bedecked in a . . . pair of loose white linen trowsers. **1840** *Picayune* 30 Sept. 2/6 His negro boy . . . is very black, about 40 years of age. **1852** in Stowe *Key* 136/2 A Likely Negro boy, about twenty-one years old, a good wagoner and field hand. **1894** Allen *Ky. Cardinal* xvi, This morning I took a negro boy and set him to picking the berries. **1922** Stribling *Birthright* 172 A negro boy going off and doing what you have done—extraordinary.

+**Negro business.** The business of trading in Negro slaves; business concerning Negroes; the acting of Negro roles. *colloq.* — **1853** Stowe *Key* 91/2 The justice introduces the business as follows:—Now, about this nigger business. **1869** Dumont *Benedict's Congress Songster* 9 Lew met with a hearty reception and concluded to adopt the 'negro business' as his profession. **1877** Habberton *Jericho Road* 150 That's better than we done when we was in the nigger business.

Negro cabin. A cabin occupied by a Negro or Negroes, +esp. one in the Negro quarter of a plantation. — **1790** Bentley *Diary* I. 180 There is . . . a group of Negro Cabins on the west side. **1833** J. Hall *Harpe's Head* 18 Still further back were the negro-cabins, and beyond them the stables. **1862** 'E. Kirke' *Among Pines* 227 Two of these structures (log shanties) were negro-cabins. **1906** Bell *C. Lee* 62 In her imagination the rows upon rows of negro cabins were rebuilt and whitewashed anew.

+**Negro car.** =Jim Crow car. — **1860** Abbott *South & North* 103 He was thrust into the negro-car, and sent out of the State. **1874** Pinkerton *Expressman & Detective* 50 A German . . . took his seat in a car called, in the South, the 'nigger car.' **1881** *Century Mag.* Nov. 126/2 The conductor came into the negro car to collect tickets.

+**Negro-catcher.** One who made a practice of catching runaway Negro slaves. Also *Negro-catching*. *Obs.* — **1853** [see Negro 3 d]. **1861** *Winsted Herald* 22 Nov. (Chipman), He was no 'nigger-catcher.' **1862** 'E. Kirke' *Among Pines* 171 The business of nigger-catching, then, is brisk, just now? **1899** Chesnutt *Wife of His Youth* 198 They got the notion somehow that Grandison belonged to a nigger-catcher.

+**Negro cloth.** A strong coarse cloth frequently used for the garments of Negro slaves. *Obs.* Also attrib. — **1732** *S.C. Gazette* 17 June 4/1 (Th.), Just imported, white and blue Negro Cloth. **1760** *Ib.* 15 Nov. 3/1 A short new negro fellow . . . has on new white negro cloth jacket and breeches. **1797** Hawkins *Letters* 253 The goods he wants are . . . 1 piece striped cotton homespun, 1 piece negro cloth [etc.]. **1840** *Niles' Nat. Reg* 18 April 100/2 The beautiful machinery recently erected in the Louisiana penitentiary at Baton Rouge . . . made last week 1,600 yards of superior negro cloth. **1872** Powers *Afoot & Alone* 88 Their only garments, I judge, are kirtles of coarse negro-cloth, once almost white.

+**Negro clothing.** Clothing for Negro slaves or material for making this. *Obs.* — **1764** Habersham *Letters* 21, I hope this will find you very active, in providing our Negroe Clothing. **1797** *Wilmington Gazette* 26 Oct., White Napt Negro Cloathing. **1810** T. Trotter *Letter* 28 Oct. (Pettigrew P.), She is oblidged she says to see about Negro cloathing.

+**Negro cotton.** Cotton cloth intended for the use of Negro slaves. *Obs.* Also attrib. — **1776** Fithian *Journal* II. 170 Wrapping him in a thin blanket made of what is called here Negro cotton, they tied him to a tree. **1788** *Edenton* (N.C.) *Intelligencer* 4 June, He carried off with him a blanket, negro cotton coat and jacket. **1803** *Ann. 7th Congress* 2 Sess. 349 Wool hats . . . kerseys, negro cottons, flannel . . . pay an extra duty. **1818** *Norfolk Beacon* 19 Dec. 1/4 Negro Cottons. 10 Bales just received.

+**Negro dog.** A dog trained to trail down and assist in the capture of escaped Negro slaves. Now hist. — **1845** in Stowe *Key* 109/1 The undersigned having bought the entire pack of Negro Dogs (of the Hay and Allen stock), he now proposes to catch runaway negroes. **1856** Olmsted *Slave States* 161, I have since seen a pack of negro-dogs. . . . They were all of a breed, and in appearance between a Scotch stag-hound and a fox-hound. **1877** Beard *K.K.K. Sketches* 147 Uncle Jack had been the proud proprietor of the largest and best known pack of 'nigger dogs' in the 'Goober State.' **1898** Harris *Tales of Home Folks* 47, I'm going to get me a nigger dog and run old Shade down and catch him.

+**Negrodom.** The area or territory in the United States in which Negroes were formerly held in bondage; Negroes collectively. {1876– (s.v. *Niggerdom*)} — **1847** *Congress. Globe* App. 13 Feb. 376/1 Our measures have given all that wide region to be the empire of negrodom. **1862** Hawthorne in Bridge *Personal Recoll.* (1893) 173, I ought to thank you for a shaded map of negrodom, which you sent me a little while ago. **1866** C. H. Smith *Bill Arp* 24 That eventful period which you have fixed when . . Niggerdom is to feel the power of your proclamation.

Negro-driver. One having direct oversight or supervision of Negro slaves at their work; an overseer or subordinate overseer. *Obs.* {1771–} Also transf. (Cf. Driver 4, 4 b.)

1798 Fessenden *Orig. Poems* (1806) 56 With many a southern negro driver. **1809** Cuming *Western Tour* 300 Overseers [are] . . . made use of literally as negro drivers, to keep those unfortunate wretches in the field. **1840** Dana *Two Years* 128 You've got a driver over you! Yes, a *slave-driver*—a *negro-driver!* **1862** *N.Y. Tribune* 13 Jan. 7/2 The Commissary Department on the works . . . is in the hands of John Hazan, the negro-driver.

||**Negro drunk,** *a.* Dead-drunk. *slang. Obs.* — **1830** *Mass. Spy* 24 Feb. (Th.), I have never been right 'negro drunk,' though I have been pretty 'tipsey.'

+**Negro election.** (See quot. 1894.) *Obs.* — **1868** S. Smith *Autobiography* 12 We chased all the niggers off the Common, as was usually done on occasions of gatherings, except on what was termed 'nigger 'lection,' which I don't know the meaning of to this day. I only know that on that day the colored people were permitted to remain unmolested on Boston Common. **1894** Earle in A. G. Winslow *Diary* 118*n.*, Boston had two election days. On Artillery Election the Ancient and Honorable Artillery had a dress parade. . . . The other day was called 'Nigger Lection,' because the blacks were permitted to throng the Common.

+**Negro English.** The English used by Negroes in the United States. — **1808** Ashe *Travels* 79 The husband . . . had lived long enough in Virginia to pick up some Negro-English. **1862** 'E. Kirke' *Among Pines* 132 Not to weary the reader with a long repetition of negro-English, I will tell in brief what I gleaned from an hour's conversation with the two blacks.

+**Negro equality.** Social and political equality of Negroes with white people. Also attrib. — **1858** Douglas in Logan *Great Conspiracy* 54, I am opposed to Negro equality. **1865** *39th Congress 1 Sess.* H. R. Ex. Doc. No. 70, 402 Having before them the fear of 'negro equality,' [most white laborers in the South] do what they can to oppose their freedom. **1880** Tourgee *Bricks* 256 We can't stand no such nigger-equality schools as you are running at Red Wing. **1905** N. Davis *Northerner* 52 You think I might be nice to Mr. Falls, negro equality and all?

Negro fellow. A male Negro, usually a slave. *Obs.* — **1760** Washington *Diaries* I. 155 Mr. Barnes's Davy brot home my Negroe fellow Boson. **1783** *S.C. Gazette* 3 June 1/2 A negro fellow named Fortune . . . can talk pretty good English. **1845** Green *Texian Exped.* 157 A negro fellow . . . swindled all who dealt with him for *chilē, tortillas, frijoles,* &c. **1860** Claiborne *Sam. Dale* 28 [We] bought an old Continental uniform coat, the best in the fort, for the negro fellow.

+**Negro gallery.** A gallery reserved for Negroes in a church or theater. — **1844** 'Uncle Sam' *Peculiarities* II. 99 The 'nigger gallery'—the only part of an American theatre where men with the slightest tinge of African blood can be admitted. **1869** Stowe *Oldtown Folks* 48 Several other colored families . . . also found seats in the negro gallery. **1894** 'Mark Twain' *Those Twins* viii, It usurped the place of pious thought in the 'nigger gallery.'

Negrohead. {1781–} (See also Niggerhead.) *ellipt.* = next. {1839–} Also attrib.

1843 Lumsden *Amer. Memoranda* 14 My next communication will probably contain full details of the methods adopted by the Virginian planters in the manufacturing of the nigger-head, . . . pig-tail, honey-dew, and other varieties of the stimulating and soothing herb. **1845** Green *Texian Exped.* 163 Some were chewing and eating negro-head and prickly-pear leaves, to produce moisture in their mouths. *a***1855** J. F. Kelly *Humors* 355 [He] knocked the ashes out of his pipe—filled it up with 'nigger-head,' dipped it in the embers [etc.]. **1884** 'Mark Twain' *H. Finn* xxi. 194 You borry'd store tobacco and paid back nigger-head.

+**Negrohead tobacco.** A low grade of strong, dark-colored tobacco. {1892, in Canada}

1833 *Congress. Deb.* 26 Jan. 1407 Virginia has been purchased by a patent to manufacture bituminous coal, pigtail and negro head tobacco. **1836** Weston *Visit* 112 The sugar . . . is in reality nearly as dark as negro-head tobacco. *a***1855** J. F. Kelly *Humors* 353 Tantabolus would . . . treat all hands to another stifling with his old calumet, and nigger-head tobacco! **1876** Harte *G. Conroy* 248, I've heerd that the smell of nigger-head terbacker do git inter the strings of a pianner and kinder stops the music. **1891** Welch *Recoll. 1830–40* 125 Using cut 'nigger-head' tobacco instead of the fragrant 'Havana' of the earlier days.

||**Negro hound.** One who tries to capture and return fugitive slaves. — **1862** *N.Y. Tribune* 9 May 12/5 It has been found by them that Schenk, Piatt, and the rest, are not negro-hounds.

Negro house. A house for Negroes, +especially one for slaves in a Negro quarter. *Obs.* — **1790** in Winterbotham *Hist. View* III. 275 In this route he takes an opportunity to stop at the negroe houses. **1796** Wansey *Excursion U.S.* 100, I observed several negro houses, (low buildings of one story) detached from the family house. **1844** in Commons, etc. *Doc. Hist.* I. 169 Prepare . . . good framed negro houses, with brick chimnies. **1858** *Texas Almanac 1859* 85 He should see that . . . his negro-houses are made close and comfortable.

Negro hut. =Negro cabin, Negro house. — **1793** Bentley *Diary* II. 38 Mr W. Browne . . . removed a building . . . upon land below the east meeting House, near the place, where many Negro huts had been erected. **1820** Flint *Lett. from Amer.* 205 The inferior buildings, as stables, barns, (and negro huts in slave States,) are unseemly log cabins.

1845 *Cincinnati Misc.* I. 241 The mother determined to go down to the negro hut, and wake up her negro man Dan. **1864** NICHOLS *Amer. Life* I. 169 The tavern would take the lead, and all the little stores and negro huts could follow in its wake.

||**Negroic,** *a.* Of a Negro or Negroes. — **1855** *Putnam's Mo.* Jan. 75/1 Melancholy reminiscences of negroic childhood fill the places once allotted to the grand old ballads of former days.

Negroidal, *a.* Like or resembling Negroes. *Obs.* — [**1878** STANLEY *Dark Continent* I. 113 They were truly negroidal in hair and colour.] **1881** CABLE *Mme. Delphine* 7 Comely Ethiopians culled out of the less negroidal types of the African live goods.

+**Negroish,** *a.* Like a Negro; characteristic of a Negro. {1861} (See also NIGGERISH *a.*) — **1789** MORSE *Amer. Geog.* 65 The children, by being brought up, and constantly associating with the negroes, ... contract a negroish kind of accent and dialect.

Negroism. {niggerism, 1844–}

1. a. The principle of establishing equal rights between the Negroes and the white people. {1851–} +**b.** A set of beliefs or opinions favorable to Negro slavery. **c.** Negro domination. **d.** The qualities or characteristics of Negroes.

1847 *Congress. Globe* App. 8 Feb. 323/2 [The Wilmot Proviso] smelt rank of negroism. **1862** *N.Y. Tribune* 14 April 8/4 Several of the conservative prisoners, ... born in the North, deplored the effects of Slavery. ... Most of the common soldiers had been reared among negroes, had become infused with negroism, and knew nothing beyond it. **1871** *Ku Klux Klan Rep.* VII. 608 [White people] would not submit to negroism in [Georgia]. **1900** *Congress. Rec.* 5 Feb. 1507/2 As a fresh manifestation of negroism, of what the negro's attitude is toward the white man, ... its significance should not be allowed to escape us.

2. A word, expression, pronunciation, etc., characteristic of the speech of Negroes. {1864–}

1859 BARTLETT p. viii *n.*, The term 'Americanisms,' as used in this Dictionary, may then be said to include the following classes of words: ... Indian words, ... Negroisms [etc.]. **1878** BEADLE *Western Wilds* 19 This [Hoosier] language is the result of a union between the rude translations of 'Pennsylvania Dutch,' the negroisms of Kentucky and Virginia, and certain phrases native to the Ohio Valley. **1884** *Amer. Philol. Ass. Trans.* XVI. App. p. xxxi, The wonderful figure-speech, specimens of which will be given later under the head of Negroisms.

||**Negroized,** *a.* Given over to Negroes. — **1888** *Voice* 23 Aug., The only party that stands between the people and a Negroized government.

+**Negro kitchen.** The kitchen, as on a plantation, where food was prepared for the Negro slaves. *Obs.* — **1815** *Austin P.* I. (1924) 248 You will see that the Cook in the negro Kitchen keeps it in proper order. **1860** ABBOTT *South & North* 209 She will work ... with no remuneration but such fare and dress as a scullion can find in a 'nigger kitchen.'

+**Negro labor.** Labor performed by Negroes; Negro laborers collectively. — **1868** *Rep. Comm. Agric. 1867* 417 It has been declared by representative southern men that negro labor is the best on the continent. **1906** BELL *C. Lee* 243 Half the time this cheap negro labour ... is drunk or striking.

+**Negroless,** *a.* Not possessing Negro slaves. *Obs.* — *c***1859** in Morison *Hist. U.S.* II. (1927) 145 Is it to be lands for the landless or niggers for the *niggerless?* **1862** GREELEY in *N.Y. Tribune* 3 April 4/4 Go to Baltimore, and you will find the negroless majority hearty devotees of the Union. **1866** RICHARDSON *Secret Service* 140 If you gentlemen who own negroes attempt to take the State of Missouri out of the Union, in about six months you will be the most—niggerless set of individuals that you ever heard of.

Negroling, Niggerling. {1842–} A Negro child. *Obs.* — *c***1845** W. T. THOMPSON *Chron. Pineville* 20 The little niggerlings sprang into the air. **1857** STROTHER *Virginia* 294 Just then they passed a group of negrolings huddled in a fence corner.

Negro man. A man of the Negro race. {1686–}

1689 *Boston Rec.* 146 Thomas Baker, 1 negro man. **1707** *Boston News-Letter* 27 Oct. 2/2 A great Clap of Thunder and Lightning ... struck a lusty Negro man that sat in the Chimney Corner. **1759** *Va. Gazette* 30 Nov. 3/2 Committed to the publick Gaol in Williamsburg, a Negro Man named Tom. **1822** *Ann. 17th Congress* 1 Sess. I. 67 The petition of Francis Larche ... praying compensation for a negro man. **1884** HARRIS *Mingo* 5 Upon a bench ... sat an old negro man.

+**Negro meeting. 1.** A meeting of Negroes for religious services. **2.** A meeting for a lecture or discussion concerning the slavery issue. *Obs.* — **(1) 1823** in Mathews *Memoirs* III. 350 The pranks that are played in the 'nigger meetings,' as they are called, are beyond belief—yelling, screeching, and groaning. **1863** 'E. KIRKE' *Southern Friends* 111, I asked Preston if the old black led the services at the negro meetings. **(2) 1858** G. K. WILDER *Diary* 20 July (MS.), We were 'at nigger meeting in the evening.'

+**Negro minstrel.**

1. One of a group of comedians, usually white men in blackface, who give a performance consisting of Negro songs, dances, jokes, etc.; also, any blackface comedian who uses Negro material. {1864} Cf. MINSTREL 1.

1857 *Ladies' Repository* July 421/2 The negro minstrel may have a large audience. **1869** BREWER *Rocky Mt. Lett.* 43 He built a theater and hired a band of nigger minstrels on his own hook. **1884** *Century Mag.* March 681/1 At that time the negro-minstrel was not a black-faced singer of sentimental songs and propounder of satirical conundrums, but a man (Dan Rice) who sang and jumped Jim Crow, alternating this *chanson de geste* with 'Clar de Kitchen' and other genuine plantation songs. **1915** B. MATTHEWS in *Scribner's Mag.* June 754 Time was when the Negro-minstrels held possession of three or four theatres in the single city of New York and when a dozen or more troupes were travelling from town to town.

2. Attrib. with *entertainment, humor, troupe.*

1889 MUNROE *Golden Days* 74 In one [gambling house] they found ... a negro minstrel troupe. **1890** HOWELLS *Boy's Town* 102 The negro-minstrel entertainment ... is to follow. **1895** *N.Y. Dramatic News* 23 Nov. 10/1 For negro-minstrel humor is like Rider Haggard's 'She.'

Negro minstrelsy. {1864–} +The entertainment provided by Negro minstrels. — **1868** *N.Y. Herald* 28 July 5/4 The 'bill of fare' was immense. Dancing, the light drama, gymnastic feats, negro minstrelsy and a variety entertainment. **1915** B. MATTHEWS in *Scribner's Mag.* June 754/1 Negro-minstrelsy is ... absolutely native to these States.

+**Negro party.** *Polit.* **1.** A party of slaveholders. **2.** A party sympathetic to the interests of Negroes. — **(1) 1857** *Lawrence* (Kan.) *Republican* 2 July 2 Although the number of Free State men, perhaps, treble the Nigger party, the election must be carried by the latter. **(2) 1895** G. KING *New Orleans* 322 The carpet-bag and negro party ... saw itself becoming hopelessly overmatched by the civil and social power organized against it. **1900** *Congress. Rec.* 22 Jan. 1035/2 The South Carolina Republicans are still denounced as belonging to the 'nigger party.'

+**Negrophilist.** A Negro-lover; one interested in Negroes. Usu. derogatory. {cf. negrophil, 1803–} — **1842** in S. Longfellow *H. W. Longfellow* I. 449 When the Eastern negrophilists are prepared to pay a tax, they will have a right to dispose of the property of their Southern brethren. **1857** *S. Lit. Messenger* XXIV. 25/2 Of course he sides with the anti-slavery movement and desires the success of the Negrophilists. **1874** *Congress. Rec.* 13 Jan. 616/2 This sudden change from an old State-rights Democrat to what Caleb Cushing used to call a negrophilist. **1899** *Pop. Science Mo.* LV. 178 The most infatuated negrophilist would not stultify himself.

Negrophobia. A dislike or hatred for Negroes, regarded as a disease. {1833–} — **1819** *Niles' Reg.* XVI. Suppl. 173/2 The gentleman from Kentucky ... has charged us ... with being under the influence of *negrophobia.* **1857** WILLIS *Convalescent* 173 His hatred of colored people amounted to a negro-phobia. **1863** PHILLIPS *Speeches* 528 The North has a second element, Negrophobia. **1898** T. J. MORGAN *Negro in Amer.* 125 It would not be fair to say that ... there exists well-defined Negrophobia among us.

+**Negro property.** Property consisting of Negro slaves. *Obs.* — **1797** *Last Advice of C. Pettigrew to Sons* (Univ. N.C. MS.), I became possessed of a negro property by my union with your mother. **1825** *Austin P.* II. (1924) 1020 There has been a parragraph ... of Nuse paper publication ... which precludes the introduction of negro property into the Mexican Republick. **1853** STOWE *Key* 181/2 Negro property is decidedly 'brisk' in this county [*i.e.*, in Shelby Co., Ky.].

+**Negro quarter.** The group of buildings occupied by Negro slaves on a plantation. Often pl. Now hist.

1734 *N.Y. Gazette* 18–25 March 1/1 Coll. Thomas L—d keeps at some Miles distance from his dwelling House, Negro-quarters (as they are called). **1775** CRESSWELL *Journal* 55 This morning saw a Negro Quarter of Mrs. Marsden's burnt down. **1848** DRAKE *Pioneer Life Ky.* 183 'Negro quarters' replace the humble habitations of happy families. **1881** PIERSON *In the Brush* 228 In the 'negro quarters,' ... they all thought I must be a 'nigger-trader.' **1895** G. KING *New Orleans* 258 The electric car of today speeds through the cane-fields, negro quarters, ... and pastures of these old plantations.

||**b.** = NEGRO CABIN.

1888 GRIGSBY *Smoked Yank* (1891) 60 We were guarded in a negro quarter or hut.

+**Negro question.** The social and political question or problem created by the existence of a Negro population in the United States. — **1832** *Congress. Deb.* 2 April 2348 [If] the South must be threatened with the negro question, and with having their throats cut if they attempted to resist, he would ask, on whose side was the bullying? **1859** *Harper's Mag.* Dec. 137/2 Sir, in 1850–'51 you were a Compromise man; ... then again you were 'soft' on the 'nigger question.' **1866** CARPENTER *At White House* 83, I was brought to the conclusion that there was no dodging this negro question any longer. **1906** *Outlook* 1 Dec. 844 (*caption*), The Negro Question Again.

Negro race. {1842–} The African branch of the black race. — **1840** in W. J. & F. L. Garrison *Life W. L. Garrison* II. 365 The whole 'nigger race' [should be] made to suffer for so foul an act. **1852** STOWE *Uncle Tom* xvi, The negro race, no longer despised and trodden down, will, perhaps, show forth some of the latest and most magnificent revelations of human life. **1869** BEECHER *Sermons* I. 320 The judgment of men of the North ... in regard to the negro race ... has proved to be more accurate ... than the judgments of the men that lived among them. **1904** PAGE in *McClure's Mag.* March 549/1 [It is a] singular fact that two sections of the same race, with ... the same historical relation to the Negro race, should regard so vital a question from such opposite points.

+**Negro school.** A school for Negroes. — **1740** W. SEWARD *Journal* 2, I am, moreover, to collect Subscriptions for a Negroe School in Pensilvania. **1833** in *Century Mag.* XXX. 786 The Deputy Sheriff . . . presented me with five indictments for a panegyric upon their virtuous and magnanimous actions, in relation to Miss Crandall's *nigger school* in Canterbury, [N.Y.]. **1866** W. REID *After War* 30 Half the residences are filled with army officers, or . . . used for Negro schools. **1875** in Fleming *Hist. Reconstruction* II. 206 You have set up a nigger school in the settlement which we will not allow you to teach.

Negro servant. A servant, usually a slave, who is a Negro.

1664 *R.I. Court Rec.* II. 29 [There was] some debate in this Court Concear[n]ing the Death of a young neger sarvant to Mr Benidict Arnold now govenor. **1700** SEWALL *Diary* II. 22 [They] come to Speak to me about the Marriage of Sebastian, Negro serv[an]t of said Wait, with Jane, Negro servant of said Thair. **1750** FRANKLIN *Writings* III. 4 We conclude to sell them both the first good Opportunity, for we do not like Negro Servants. **1838** INGRAHAM *Burton* II. 32 A negro servant was holding two or three horses at the gate. **1852** STOWE *Uncle Tom* xxix, We hear often of the distress of the negro servants on the loss of a kind master. **1893** *Harper's Mag.* Feb. 449 The negro servant . . . returned no answering smile.

+**Negro shoe.** A shoe of a type provided for Negro slaves. *Obs.* — **1770** *Md. Hist. Mag.* XIII. 69 Things sent by the wagon [include] . . . 24 Pair of negro shoes. **1817** *Cape-Fear Recorder* 5 April, 80 pair Negro Shoes. **1852** *Fla. Plantation Rec.* 84, I saw Mr. Livingston the Man that [ma]kes your Negro Shoes.

Negro slave. A slave who is a Negro. *Obs.* {1719-}

1666 *Md. Hist. Mag.* I. 74 All Lands Tenements or hereditaments that are or may be belonging unto me with five nigroe Slaves, three white Servants [etc.]. **1709** LAWSON *Carolina* 75 The Negro-Slaves . . . in many Places, eat nothing but this Indian Corn and Salt. *a*1772 WOOLMAN *Journal* 134 Some Friends . . . this summer (1758) had bought negro slaves. **1871** STOWE *Sam Lawson* 81, I've ben a drivin' and workin' all day like a nigger-slave. **1894** ROBLEY *Bourbon Co., Kansas* 66 At this time [1857] there were in Fort Scott and Bourbon County about thirty negro slaves.

Negro slavery. +The institution of Negro slaveholding in the United States. Now hist. — **1789** *Ann. 1st Congress* I. 216 If the pernicious effects of New England rum have been justly lamented, what can be urged for negro slavery? **1831** HOLLEY *Texas* 87 The question of negro slavery . . . is one of great importance. **1855** *Kansas Hist. Coll.* V. 175 They must, to preserve their own consistency, advocate the introduction of negro slavery into the states where they reside. **1868** *N.Y. Herald* 2 July 3/2 It is very strange that the same Congress which abolished negro slavery should at the same time re-establish the old colonial laws.

+**Negro song.** A song composed or sung by Negroes or in the Negro manner. — **1851** *Knickerb.* XXXVIII. 181 'E.P.,' whose port-folio appears especially rich in 'negro-songs,' sends us the following. **1858** WILLIS *Convalescent* 392 By its frequent mention in negro songs, this fruit [persimmon] has become classic. **1882** PECK *Sunshine* 53 Along toward the end of the programme they will sing some old nigger song. **1922** *Amer. Folk-Lore* XXXV. 223 Swing Low, Sweet Chariot! . . . is one of the old and now exceedingly popular Negro songs.

+**Negro speculator.** One whose business was the buying and selling of Negro slaves for gain. *Obs.* — **1835** A. PARKER *Trip to Texas* 91 Among our passengers, there were twenty-three negro slaves, men and women; bought in Kentucky by negro speculators. **1860** OLMSTED *Back Country* 239 So we sold them to the first nigger-speculator that come along.

+**Negro spiritual.** A religious song of folk character, originating among American Negroes. — **1867** HIGGINSON in *Atlantic Mo.* June 685/1, I had for many years heard of this class of songs under the name of 'Negro Spirituals.' **1899** *Century Mag.* Aug. 577/1 The education of the negro in the South is gradually abolishing . . . the old negro 'spirituals.' **1922** *Amer. Folk-Lore* July 223 The Negro spirituals of slavery times . . were inspired by some sad or awe-inspiring event.

+**Negro state.** Before the Civil War, a state in which Negro slavery was legal. *Obs.* — **1780** *Essex Inst. Coll.* XIII. 220 You did not carry home contemptible Ideas enough of the negro States or of this great Braggadocio. **1809** *Congress. Deb.* 20 Jan. 1152 The Potomac the boundary—the Negro states by themselves! **1827** J. BERNARD *Retrosp.* 240, I have smallish faith in these chaps from the nigger states, upon principle. **1867** LOCKE *Swingin' Round* 49 Kentucky alone—the only nigger State in the North—wood hev bin helpless.

+**Negro-stealer.** One who steals or kidnaps Negro slaves in order to resell them; also, one who assists Negro slaves to escape from their masters. *Obs.* — **1827** *Western Mo. Rev.* I. 69 It will be the refuge of Negro-stealers and the Elysium of rogues. **1840** BIRD *Robin Day* 43 The third [swore] that I was 'a kidnapper, a Georgeye nigger-stealer.' **1859** JONES *Southern Scenes* 180 It is less than one-tenth the value of the slaves your negro-stealers have deprived us of. **1883** 'MARK TWAIN' *Life on Miss.* xxix, 311 This was a colossal combination of robbers, horse-thieves, negro-stealers.

+**Negro-stealing.** The stealing of Negro slaves; also, the assisting of Negro slaves to escape from their masters. *Obs.* — **1819** *Niles' Reg.* XVI. 160/1 Sentence of death has been pronounced on a fellow in North Carolina, for negro stealing. **1843** MARRYAT *M. Violet* xxxvi, Mr. Courtenay related to me a case of negro stealing by the same General John Meyer. **1862** 'E. KIRKE' *Among Pines* 39 Why have you elected a president who approves of nigger-stealing?

+**Negro suffrage.** The right of the Negro to vote; the enfranchisement of the Negro. Usually with reference to the Negroes in the South after the Civil War. Also attrib.

1867 *Atlantic Mo.* Jan. 113/1 Negro suffrage is the measure to arrest and put an end to that dreadful strife. **1868** *N.Y. Herald* 2 July 4/1 It is instructive to know how they look upon the negro suffrage question. **1888** BRYCE *Amer. Commw.* II. III. lxxv. 621 Negro suffrage produced, during the few years of 'carpet-bagging' and military government which followed the war, incredible mischief. **1914** *Cycl. Amer. Govt.* II. 519/1 The fundamental hostility to negro suffrage has never been the dislike of an ignorant electorate, but goes back to a race feeling intensified by the former servile condition of the negroes.

+**Negro thief.** =NEGRO-STEALER. *Obs.* — **1842** tr. Sealsfield *Life in New World* 315 Cowhides would do just as well to drive off a few horse-thieves, and cow-thieves, and nigger-thieves. **1853** SIMMS *Sword & Distaff* 499 Here's the box; it's got the pretickilar papers to convict him and to hang him, the villain, and the nigger thief, and murderer. **1862** *N.Y. Tribune* 13 Feb. 8/1 The jail was . . . under the superintendency of a negro-thief named Wise. **1877** JOHNSON *Anderson Co., Kansas* 24 Some came for political purposes— . . . some, to drive out the 'cursed Yankees,' whom they regarded as negro thieves.

+**Negro trader.** A trafficker in Negro slaves. Now hist. — **1825** *Catawba Journal* 24 May, The numerous negro traders . . . are almost daily passing with their gangs through this section of country. **1834** in Bassett *Plantation Overseer* 66 He sayes that they shall stay heare or he will sell them to negro trader. **1877** BAGBY *Old Va. Gentleman* 1 The stage rattled along, . . . the driver and the negro-trader, both drunk, on top. **1884** 'MARK TWAIN' *H. Finn* viii. 60, I noticed dey wuz a nigger trader roun' de place considable lately.

+**Negro vote.** *collect.* The votes cast by Negroes; the Negro voters. — **1871** SOMERS *Southern States* 228 By dexterously 'fugling' the negro vote, [the governor] got himself advanced to this high position. **1882** *Nation* 26 Oct. 349/2 The Southern papers contain every day longings for white immigrants to help them to solve the political problem created by the size of the negro vote. **1900** *Congress. Rec.* 22 Jan. 1027/2 In the fourteenth amendment the power to reject the negro vote is admitted in favor of the States.

Negro wench. A Negro girl or woman, especially one held as a slave. {1761-} — **1715** *Boston News-Letter* 23 May 2/2 A Likely Negro Wench aged about Eighteen Years, to be Sold by Mr. John Vrieling. **1746** *N.H. Hist. Soc. Coll.* IX. 141, [I] bought a negro wench of Capt Clough. **1835** BIRD *Hawks of Hawk-H.* I. 16 [She] had even obtained a little negro wench to dwell with Elsie as a domestic. **1866** KIRKLAND *Bk. Anecdotes* 421 The mail agent . . . said that Mr. Walker 'was no gentleman for traveling with a nigger wench.'

Negro-worshiper. A disparaging term for a person who favored the abolition of slavery or was interested in the welfare of the Negro. *Obs.* — **1857** *Lawrence* (Kan.) *Republican* 9 July 2 There is not a 'border ruffian' or 'nigger worshipper' in Kansas who would not be put to flight by such a document. **1865** RICHARDSON *Secret Service* 313 His opponents found their old cries of 'Abolitionist' and 'Negro-worshipper' hollow and powerless. **1879** TOURGEE *Fool's Errand* 130 My children are insulted every now and then as 'nigger-worshipers.'

***Neighborhood.** +*In the neighborhood of*, approximately, about. {1893-} — **1854** *Fla. Plantation Rec.* 100, I have about in the neighborhood of 40 packed bales of Cotton. **1871** RAYMOND *3d Rep. Mines* 208 The length of the ditch would be in the neighborhood of forty miles. **1905** A. ADAMS *Outlet* 310 It was in the neighborhood of ninety miles across to the mouth of the Yellowstone.

+**Neighborhood road.** A road maintained locally which passes through or serves a rural neighborhood or community. — **1843** 'CARLTON' *New Purchase* I. 89 Notice here, a neighborhood road does not imply necessarily much proximity of neighbours. **1855** SIMMS *Forayers* 457 He was to travel only by night; to . . . use neighborhood roads or open pine woods when he could. **1860** MORDECAI *Virginia* 303 [Railroads] are like neighborhood roads on an extended scale. **1884** CABLE *Dr. Sevier* 395 The buggy was moving at a quiet jog along a 'neighborhood road.' **1903** *Dialect Notes* II. 306.

+**Neighborhood school.** A school, usually an elementary rural one, situated in and serving the needs of a neighborhood. — **1842** *S. Lit. Messenger* VIII. 65/1 As this was what was called a 'neighborhood school,' the pupils necessarily came from a great distance. **1871** *Rep. Indian Affairs* (1872) 180 The Creeks have thirty-two neighborhood schools. **1887** *Harper's Mag.* Feb. 353/2 There is a neighborhood school where English is taught.

+**Nelson's (sharp-tailed) finch.** =next. — **1880** *Nuttall Ornith. Club Bul.* V. 32 Nelson's Sharp-Tailed Finch.—'Took a beautiful adult male, May 8, 1879; flushed him from a timothy meadow.' **1917** [see next].

+**Nelson's (sharp-tailed) sparrow.** [f. Edward W. *Nelson*, Amer. naturalist (1855-).] A variety of the sharp-tailed sparrow. (Cf. prec.) — **1887** RIDGWAY *Manual N.A. Birds* 413 *A[mmodramus] caudacutus nelsoni.* . . . Nelson's Sparrow. **1917** *Birds of Amer.* III. 30 Nelson's Sparrow (*Passerherbulus nelsoni nelsoni*), also known as Nelson's Finch and as Nelson's Sharp-tailed Sparrow, is decidedly smaller than the Sharp-tailed Sparrow.

Nelumbo. Also **nelumbium.** A water lily or a genus of water lilies of the family Nelumbonaceae having large leaves and yellow flowers. {1818- (Abel *Narr. Journey in China* 103, 121)} — [**1836** SEALSFIELD *Gesammelte Werke* XII. 162 Er schaut Millionen der Nelumbo.] **1850**

S. F. COOPER *Rural Hours* 275 It is chiefly in our western waters that the Nelumbo is found. **1853** *Harper's Mag.* Nov. 751/2 The broad prairies ... are also diversified by lakes, their surfaces shaded from the hot sun by the broad-leafed nelumbium. **1857** GRAY *Botany* 21 *Nelumbium*, Nelumbo. Sacred Bean.

Nemophila. A genus of annual herbs of ornamental appearance; any plant of this genus. {1838-} — **1857** GRAY *Botany* 327. **1883** *Harper's Mag.* Jan. 284/2 During the afternoon Jim Barker had picked a bunch of delicate nemophilas and handed them to Alice Winthrop. **1898** A. M. DAVIDSON *Calif. Plants* 119, I have seen Nemophilas that, as early as February, had climbed to the top of a high fence, and were looking over for something else to grasp.

+**Nephite.** According to the Book of Mormon, a member of the nation founded by Nephi, who, with his father and brothers, fled from Jerusalem to America about 600 B.C. — **1830** *Book of Mormon* (1920) 108/2 Now the people which were not Lamanites were Nephites. ... Those who are friendly to Nephi I shall call Nephites, or the people of Nephi. **1843** MARRYAT *M. Violet* xxxvii, The lost tribes ... afterwards had quarrels and contentions, and separated into two distinct nations, one of which is denominated Nephites, and the other Lamanites.

Nervine. {1730-} +Any species of *Cypripedium*, supposed to be a tonic for the nerves. — **1882** *Harper's Mag.* Feb. 435/2, I saw that she had been searching for nervine and sassafras.

Nervy, *a.* {1607-}

1. Jerky or jumpy; sudden.

1884 CABLE *Dr. Sevier* xxviii, The nervy, unmusical waking cry of the mocking-bird. **1885** — in *Century Mag.* April 918/2 The movements were quick, short, nervy.

+**2.** Cheeky, impudent, bold. *colloq.*

1896 ADE *Artie* 75, I just received your nervy letter. **1904** E. ROBINS *Magn. North* II. 118 It is a little 'nervy,' as the Boy had said, to walk into another man's house uninvited.

+**3.** Requiring nerve or courage.

1897 *Outing* XXX. 481/2 It takes nerve, and lots of it, to play polo. It's the nerviest game played. **1898** *Columbus Dispatch* 19 March 1/4 Two colored farm hands performed a nervy job at the residence of A. W. McDonald.

4. Nervous, excited. *colloq.* {1906-}

1891 COOKE *Huckleberries* (1896) 319, I expect I be sort o' nervy, what with takin' a journey and the thought o' seein' Melindy.

+**Nesselrode pudding.** [Named for Count K. R. *Nesselrode*, Russ. diplomat (1780-1862).] A frozen dessert flavored with nutmeats, citron, other fruit, etc. — **1876** HENDERSON *Cooking* 312 Nesselrode Pudding. ... Ingredients: Forty chestnuts, one pound of sugar, ... one pint of cream, the yolks of twelve eggs [etc.]. **1919** FRANDSEN & MARKHAM *Manuf. of Ice Creams & Ices* 110 Nesselrode Pudding [requires] 4 gal. French cooked cream, 6 oz. vanilla, 2 lbs. candied cherries, 2 lbs. raisins [etc.].

Nest box. {1660-} A box provided for a domestic fowl to nest in. — **1850** BROWNE *Poultry Yard* 88 Every poultry house ... should be provided with nest boxes. **1871** LEWIS *Poultry Book* 112 Under these dropping boards are the nest-boxes, where the fowls lay.

Nester. Also **nestor.** {1895-} *W.* +An opprobrious term for one seeking to settle down permanently as a homesteader, farmer, small rancher, etc., in a cattle-grazing region. — **1880** *Ft. Griffin* (Tex.) *Echo* 3 Jan., [A sheep man is] a tramp, an ingrate, a 'Nester,' and a liar. **1897** HOUGH *Story of Cowboy* 264 The term 'nester' was one applied in half contempt by the cattle men of the Southwest to those early squatters and homesteaders. **1904** 'O. HENRY' in *McClure's Mag.* April 611 The nesters [in Colorado] ... had taken up the land and elected officers who were hard to get along with. *a***1918** G. STUART *On Frontier* II. 158 The cattle men were encroaching on the Indians as well as small ranchers or 'nestors' as they were called.

***Net.**

***1.** An openwork fabric made of twine and used for catching fish.

1630 HIGGINSON *New-England* 12 Our Fishers take many hundreds [of bass] together, ... yea, their Nets ordinarily take more then they are able to hale to Land. **1707** *N.H. Probate Rec.* I. 552, I give my sonn ... ½ of ye new fishing craft as nets, Lines, *hookes* and Lead. **1845** FRÉMONT *Exped.* 148 Several families of Root Diggers ... appeared very busy about several weirs or nets which had been rudely made of canes and rushes for the purpose of catching fish. **1911** *Rep. Fisheries 1908* 310 Eels are caught in weirs, nets, traps [etc.].

2. A loose mesh covering to protect a horse from flies; a horse net.

1760 ROWE *Letters* 365 Please to send me a pair of Netts for Horses, Let them be Large.

Nether Dutch, *a.* =LOW DUTCH *a. Obs.* — **1686** in Munsell *Annals Albany* II. 81 The Nether-Dutch nation. **1689** *Ib.* 110 Resolved, yt ye fall of waters on ye Bevers kill or creek ... be sold to ye deakons of ye Netherdutch church.

+**Netop.** Also **neetup.** *New Eng.* [Algonquian; cf. Narraganset *netoup* 'my friend.']

1. A friend; companion, dear one. *Obsolescent.*

[**1643** WILLIAMS *Key* (1866) 155 *Nétop Kunnatótemous.* Friend, I will aske you a Question.] **1662** *New Haven Col. Rec.* 461 The Indian ... shooke her ... by ye hand, and asked her where her netop was. *c***1707** in G. Sheldon *Hist. Deerfield, Mass.* I. 362 She spake, saying, 'Netop, Netop, my master.' **1890** *Amer. Notes & Q.* IV. 237 *Netop.* Fifty years ago, in New England, this word was not very uncommon among the older people. It meant a close friend, a chum, a companion. **1898** WESTCOTT *D. Harum* 289 'Mr. Harum and I are great "neetups," as he says.' ... 'It means "cronies," I believe, in his dictionary.'

2. An Indian. *Obs.*

1704 S. KNIGHT *Journal* 38 You speak negro to him. ... Hah! says Netop, now me stomany that. **1716** CHURCH *Philip's War* 19 Mr. Churches hands were fastned in the Netops hair. **1760** NILES *Indian Wars* I. 229 Mr. Wheelwright ... should be such a netop's servant.

***Nettle.** Any plant of the genus *Urtica* or of the family Urticaceae, or any of various stinging plants of other genera. (Cf. DEAD NETTLE, STINGING NETTLE.) — **1780** in *Travels Amer. Col.* 637 The Nettles growing very tall and strong, when broke and spun makes a strong thread when wove makes a strong coarse cloth. **1817** S. BROWN *Western Gaz.* 336 [The timber land in Erie Co., Pa., is] covered with a luxuriant and troublesome growth of nettles, the genuine *Urtica Whitlowi.* **1886** Z. F. SMITH *Kentucky* 186 The wool of the buffalo, and the bark or rind of the wild nettle were used in the manufacture of cloth.

***Nettle tree.** The genus *Celtis*, or a tree of this genus, +esp. *C. occidentalis.* — **1770** FORSTER tr. Kalm *Travels* 69 In the woods which are nearest to Philadelphia ... [is] the nettle tree, in the fields. **1785** MARSHALL *Amer. Grove* 29 *Celtis.* The Nettle-Tree. The Hermap[h]rodite flowers are solitary and superior. **1821** NUTTALL *Trav. Arkansa* 64 [In the canebrake] I found abundance of the *Celtis integrifolia* (entire-leaved nettle tree). **1897** SUDWORTH *Arborescent Flora* 184 *Celtis occidentalis.* Hackberry. ... [Also called] Nettle Tree (R.I., Mass., Del., Mich.).

+**Nettle weed.** A plant of the nettle family. — **1843** 'CARLTON' *New Purchase* I. 159 [Settlers in Indiana] gathered a peculiar species of nettle, (called there nettleweed,) which they succeeded in dressing like flax. **1867** 'LACKLAND' *Homespun* 18 Their blackened skeletons ..., overgrown with the nettleweeds and long grasses.

***Network,** *n.* A complex, netlike system {1839-}, as of railroads or telegraph lines. — **1851** CIST *Cincinnati* 331 The network of railroads ... will connect us shortly with every important point. **1865** *Atlantic Mo.* XV. 619/2 We [women] may travel unattended over the vast network of railroads. **1870** KEIM *Sheridan's Troopers* 10 Opulent cities and thriving towns and villages, linked together by a net-work of iron highways and electric wires. **1885** *Harper's Mag.* July 215/1 He who tries to drive out into the country is held fast in a net-work of railway tracks.

+**Network,** *v. tr.* To cover (an area) with a network of railroad lines. — **1887** *Courier-Journal* 24 Jan. 8/1 It is only a question of time when railroads will net-work the Pan-handle. **1914** *Cycl. Amer. Govt.* III. 139/1 Whole regions are networked, and one can go by trolley car from the Atlantic to the Middle West.

***Neutral.** In the colonial wars between France and England, a French-speaking resident of Nova Scotia, subject to British rule; an Acadian. Also, pl., *neutral French. Obs.*

1756 *Boston News-Letter* 22 Jan. 2/2 The French Inhabitants of Nova-Scotia, commonly call'd Neutrals. **1761** *Nova Scotia Archives* (1869) 315 The ancient Inhabitants of this Province, who called, or had been taught to call themselves neutrals. **1761** NILES *Indian Wars* II. 373 Not to omit the tragical downfall, exit, and unparalleled massacre that befell the very noble, heroic Colonel Noble, ... through the perfidy and treachery of the Neutral French (as they were called) at Menis, we must, in this narrative, turn back to ... 1746. **1764** COLDEN in *N.Y. Hist. Soc. Coll.* IX. 334 These Accadians were neither treated as Subjects in Rebellion nor as Prisoners of War, & for that reason I suppose they obtain'd the name of Neutrals, neither Subjects nor Enemys.

Neutral ground. {1857-} +**1.** A zone between Spanish Texas and the United States declared neutral in 1806. Now hist. +**2.** (See quotation.) — **(1) 1836** *Diplom. Corr. Texas* I. (1908) 83 The object of the concentration of forces at Jessup is to protect the frontier and the Neuteral [*sic*] Ground also to keep the Indians in check. **1856** YOAKUM *Hist. Texas* I. 133 Until the question of boundary between the two governments was settled, all the territory between the Sabine and the Arroyo Honda should be a *neutral ground*, not to be occupied by either party. *Ib.* 151 The territory ... left as neutral ground by the agreement between Wilkinson and Herrera, had become the rallying point and refuge of a large number of desperate men. **(2) 1844** *Knickerb.* XXIII. 775 The Government of the United States ... have laid out between them [the Sioux and Sac and Fox Indians] a strip of country forty miles in width, denominated the 'Neutral Ground,' and on to which neither nation is permitted to extend their hunting excursions.

Neutrality act, law. A law prescribing the obligations resting upon neutrals during a war.

Washington's neutrality proclamation of 1793 with reference to the war then beginning between France and England, and the neutrality enactments of 1794 and 1818 initiated this type of legislation in the United States.

[**1794** HAMILTON in *Ann. 3d Congress* 1286, I transmit herewith a schedule of rules concerning sundry particulars which have been adopted by the President, as deductions from the laws of neutrality, established and received among nations.] **1840** *Niles' Nat. Reg.* 16 May 163/1 Convictions for violation of the neutrality law. **1851** *Harper's Mag.* June 127/2 The offense with which they were charged was the violation of the Neutrality Act of April 20, 1818. **1858** *Ib.* Feb. 399/1 When . . . it was rendered probable that a new expedition against Nicaragua was on foot, orders were issued to carry into effect the Neutrality Laws of 1818. **1883** SWEET & KNOX *Through Texas* 562 When the Rio Grande is booming, sixty feet deep, and five miles wide, the Mexicans uphold rigidly the neutrality laws.

+**Nevada.** [f. Sierra *Nevada* Mts.] One of the western states of the United States: Used attrib. — **1876** J. J. POWELL *Nevada* 15 [Mormon leaders issued] an edict, in 1855, recalling their Nevada settlers to Salt Lake. **1897** SUDWORTH *Arborescent Flora* 18 *Pinus monophylla.* Singleleaf Piñon [is also called] Grey Pine (Nev.), Nevada Nut Pine (Cal.). **1901** *Independent* 18 April 888/1 Existing conditions are not the fault of the Nevada people. **1903** *Harper's Wkly.* 20 June 1027/2 The government has already turned its attention to a portion of this vast Nevada desert. *Ib.* 1029/2 Examples of what can be done with Nevada lands under sensible irrigation systems.

***New,** *a.* +Recently settled or available for settlement by white people. (Cf. OLD TOWN.)

1817 BRADBURY *Travels* 331 In the early settlements . . . of new country, its progress in improvements is slow. **1823** COOPER *Pioneers* viii, ['Patent'] was a term in common use throughout the *new* parts of the state. **1828** — *Notions* I. 341 The Americans call all that portion of their territory which has been settled since the revolution 'new.' If the state has been created since that period, it is a 'new state.' **1832** DUNLAP *Hist. Amer. Theatre* 74 Returning to Massachusetts, he became involved in pecuniary difficulties, and retired to Vermont, then a *new country.* **1871** DE VERE 176 When the immigrant . . . must go to what is called *New Lands,* he has to be careful in his selection. **1880** *Cimarron* (N.M.) *News & Press* 15 April 2/4 Nelson W. Starbird, an enterprising young hackman, was driving along from the new to the old town.

Newark. *attrib.* +Produced or originating in or near Newark, New Jersey. — **1817** W. COXE *Fruit Trees* 120 Newark King, or Hinchman Apple. This is a large, fair, and handsome apple; called the Newark King in East-Jersey. *Ib.* 133 Newark Pippin. Called the French Pippin in East-Jersey. **1870** TOMES *Decorum* 136 Never invite a plain-spoken person to dinner, for he will be sure to detect the Newark cider in your Champagne bottle. **1910** BOSTWICK *Amer. Pub. Library* 45 In the type of two-card [charging] system known as the 'Newark' system from its use in the free library at Newark, N.J., an additional record of the date is made on a flap attached to the inside of the book.

+**New-corn dance.** Among American Indians, a ceremonial dance at the time of harvesting Indian corn. (Cf. CORN DANCE, GREEN-CORN DANCE.) — **a1820** in *Western Rev.* II. 161 There are a number of other [Indian] dances, such as the . . . Turkey dance, the new corn dance, the pipe dance.

+**New Court party.** *Hist.* In Kentucky, a party which supported the creation of a new state supreme court when the old court opposed certain relief legislation: (see COURT PARTY 2). — **1826** *Spirit of '76* I. 14/1 The people declared at the polls at the last August election, . . . That the New Court party have not redeemed their promises. **1847** L. COLLINS *Kentucky* 208 The intensely exciting contest of three years duration [c1825], between the 'Relief' or 'New Court,' and the 'Anti-Relief' or 'Old Court' parties.

New deal. [From the term as used in card-playing.] +A new arrangement or system for obviating disadvantages in an existing order.

1863 [see DEAL[1] 2]. **1873** *Newton Kansan* 30 Jan. 2/2 It is the first card [*i.e.*, event] in a new deal. **1882** *Nation* 16 Nov. 416/3 He could see nothing wrong there which could not be cured by a 'conference' or a 'new deal.' **1910** PINCHOT *Fight for Conservation* 142 The people of the United States demand a new deal and a square deal.

New departure. +The new regime in the South after the Civil War and Reconstruction; spec. (both words capitalized), the policy, supported by the Democrats and the Liberal Republicans in the campaign of 1872, of regarding reconstruction as completed, and of granting universal amnesty. Also attrib. — **1871** *Ku Klux Rep.* VIII. 425 The white people in our country, though they may accept what is known as the 'new departure,' are at heart unalterably opposed, in my opinion, to negro suffrage. **1871** *Harper's Mag.* Aug. 474/1 The following, [is] told by way of illustrating the significance of the 'new-departure' movement. **1872** J. SHERMAN in *Sherman Lett.* 335 There were five or six Republicans who . . . were inclined to support Cox as an Anti-Grant or new departure candidate.

+**New Divinity.** A system of Calvinistic theology originating with certain New England divines, esp. with Jonathan Edwards and his son. (Cf. EDWARDSISM.) — **1883** Schaff *Religious Encycl.* II. 1634/2 [New England divines] announced a few principles, which were called 'New-Light Divinity,' or 'New Divinity.'

New England. [Named by Capt. John Smith in 1614.]

I. 1. That part of the present area of the United States lying east and north of the state of New York; =NEW ENGLAND STATES.

1616 SMITH *New England* 4 That part wee call *New England* is betwixt the degrees of 41. and 45. **1646** *Charlestown Land Rec.* 102 An Acknowledgment of a sale by William Roberts of wapping in ould England unto William Kilcop of charltowne in new England. **1789** *Ann. 1st Congress* I. 215 What, then, ought to be the language of the people of New England on a proposal for taxing an article equally as useful to them as fruit is to the Southern States? **1831** PECK *Guide* 7 The mountainous parts of New-England. **1870** *Scribner's Mo.* I. 143 New England is divided from the rest of the country. **1903** *Boston Herald* 19 Aug., Colonial teas, Thanksgiving celebrations and other occasions . . . seek to recall the early history of New England.

+**b.** *New England of the West,* (see quotation).

1871 DE VERE 660 Minnesota is known as the New England of the West, on account of the number of New England people to be found there. **1907** *Boston Transcript* 9 Nov.

+**2.** Short for NEW ENGLAND RUM.

1827 J. HOWE *Journal* 12, I told him I would take some New England and molasses. **1848** *Knickerb.* XXXII. 276 In a certain town in New-Hampshire, a certain inhabitant thereof required for his comfortable enjoyment at least a pint of 'white-faced New-England,' daily. **1857** *Lawrence* (Kan.) *Republican* 2 July 4, I'll come down and take a little New England with you.

II. *attrib.* +**3.** Designating persons native to, living in, or coming from New England.

1654 JOHNSON *Wonder-w. Providence* 10 It may seeme a meane thing to be a New England Souldier. **1686** DUNTON *Lett. from New.-Eng.* (1867) 26 Yet he had some smatterings of Divinity (as most of the New England Captains have). **1704** SEWALL *Diary* II. 95 He was a Right New-England Christian. **1776** *Battle of Brooklyn* I. ii, The New England Colonels are in a mutiny and say they will not fight. **1854** BANCROFT *Hist. U.S.* IV. 299 There were the six hundred New England rangers, dressed like woodmen; armed with a firelock and a hatchet. **1868** *N.Y. Herald* 3 July 4/6 Most of the New England delegates to the New York Convention are in this city to-day. **1880** *Harper's Mag.* Dec. 35/2 She was a comparatively new Episcopalian, having been trained a New England Congregationalist of the severest hue.

+**4.** Designating various productions, institutions, etc., identified with New England.

1655 *Suffolk Deeds* II. 166 Thirty quintalls he receiued . . . was New England fish. **1696** *Boston Rec.* 137 [He shall fix] sd Roofe Strong and Substantiall fitt to beare New England Slates. **1711** *Boston News-Letter* 17 Sept. 2/2 One New-England Ship [was lost], but all her men sav'd. **1788** *Wilmington Centinel* 18 June, N. England Cheese 10 d to 16 d. **1831** PECK *Guide* 233, I have not yet seen half a dozen cases of the genuine New England consumption in all my travels, and but few of asthma. **1839** *S. Lit. Messenger* V. 112/2 Noah Webster . . . will ere long succeed in giving us a New England tongue which shall not be intelligible in Britain. **1899** GOING *Flowers* 347 The little pink-tipped English daisy, so tenderly reared in New-England gardens, is in its own country a troublesome lawn weed.

+**b.** *spec.* Designating currency and financial institutions of New England.

1715 SEWALL *Diary* III. 56 Gave Mr. Short's daughter a New-England Shilling. **1831** SLOCOMB *Amer. Calculator* 86 The dollar is reckoned in . . . New England, Virginia, and parts of Ohio, Kentucky, and Tennessee, 6s.od.=3/10 New-England currency. **1835** A. PARKER *Trip to Texas* 88 A New-England *ninepence* is called a *bit* [along the Mississippi R.]. **1894** LEAVITT *Our Money Wars* 46 The New England banks [were] . . . as deeply involved in this conspiracy to destroy the credit of these Treasury notes as they are now.

+**5.** In the specific names of plants and trees identified with New England.

See also NEW ENGLAND ASTER.

1846 BROWNE *Trees Amer.* 350 *Cornus florida,* The Flowery Dogwood. . . . [Also called] New England Box-wood. . . . Flowers greenish-yellow, and very large. **1674** JOSSELYN *Two Voyages* 80 *Umbilicus veneris,* or *New-England* daisie, it is good for hot humours. **1855** *Harvard Mag.* I. 232 Most admired of our spring flowers is the Ground Laurel, *Epigaea repens,* commonly called Trailing Arbutus, or New England Mayflower. **1672** JOSSELYN *New Eng. Rarities* 54 A Plant like Knavers-Mustard, called New-England Mustard. **1843** TORREY *Flora N.Y.* II. 399 *Carex Novæ-Angliæ.* . . . New England Sedge. . . . Mount Marcy, Essex county, on the Adirondack river.

+**New England aster.** A perennial aster having purplish flowers, common in the East. — **1814** BIGELOW *Florula Bostoniensis* 199 *Aster Novæ Angliæ.* New England Aster. . . . A tall, and very beautiful plant. Stem three feet high, brown, very hairy. **1840** DEWEY *Mass. Flowering Plants* 134 New England Aster, the most beautiful of our species, . . . has a fine aromatic odor. **1850** *New Eng. Farmer* II. 12 The Trumpet Weed, and the New England Aster, having fine, sweet-scented, aromatic flowers, attract many insects.

+**New England Confederation.** 'The union effected by the colonies of Massachusetts Bay, Plymouth, Connecticut, and New Haven in 1643, suggested by the need of a common defense against the Dutch and the Indians. It was discontinued in 1684' (*Cent.*).

New Englander. A native or resident of New England. {1637–}

1638 *Mass. H. S. Coll.* 3 Ser. VI. 41 The New-Englanders, therefore, advanced the weal public all they could. **1693** C. MATHER *Wonders Invis. World* (1862) 13 The New-Englanders are a People of God. **1775** JEFFERSON *Writings* IV. 244 The New-Englanders are fitting out light vessels of war. **1815** DWIGHT *Remarks on Review of Inchiquin's Lett.* 14

I am a federalist, and a New Englander; a Yankee, as a multitude of your countrymen choose to style us. **1865** LOWELL *Writings* II. 15 The only things a New-Englander was ever locked out of were the jails. **1916** EASTMAN *From Deep Woods* 66, I absorbed much of the New Englander and his peculiarities.

+**New Englandish,** *a.* Characteristic or typical of New England. — **1863** HAWTHORNE *Our Old Home* 25 A respectable-looking woman, . . . decidedly New-Englandish in figure and manners, came to my office. **1892** *Advance* 8 Dec., The pews were filled with a quiet orderly New Englandish audience. **1904** *N.Y. Ev. Post* 17 Aug. 5 Poe may have been the least New Englandish of American writers, but he was born in Boston.

+**New Englandishness.** The quality of being New Englandish. — **1896** *Advance* 9 Jan. 51/1 There is a still more striking New Englandishness in the people themselves.

+**New Englandism.** A word or expression peculiar to New England; the tone or culture characteristic of New England. — **1835** *S. Lit. Messenger* I. 423 This is a New England-ism not confined to the vulgar. **1845** COOPER *Chainbearer* xvii, Foreigners often mistake New Englandisms for Americanisms. **1858** H. W. BEECHER *Life Thoughts* 27 New Englandism is but another name for Puritanism in the Independent sense. **1895** WILLIAMS *Princeton Stories* 229 On Sundays the little tutor went to the principal church of the place, and a kind of essay that seemed to him nothing but washed-out New Englandism was thrown out to him.

+**New Englandize,** *v. tr.* To imbue with New England qualities. — **1883** T. SILLOWAY & L. POWERS *Cathedral Towns of England* 332 New-Englandize it [Ireland], and the Irish millennium would come. **1887** *Advance* 17 March 169/3 Be sure to watch with peculiar interest the development of this grand work of new-englandizing that Southeasternmost State of the Union [*i.e.*, Florida].

‖**New Englandly,** *adv.* In the manner of New England or a New Englander. — *a***1886** DICKINSON *Further Poems* (1929) 60 Without the snow's tableau Winter were lie to me—Because I see New Englandly.

+**New England man.** A man who resides in New England.

1638 UNDERHILL *Newes from Amer.* (1837) 5 Let the clamor be quenched . . . , that New England men usurp over their wives, and keep them in servile subjection. **1686** DUNTON *Lett. from New-Eng.* (1867) 302 Our Captain . . . (like a right New-England-Man) went to prayers duly twice a Day. **1714** *New. Eng. Hist. & Gen. Reg.* III. 297 Mr. Couch . . . demanded his Living again of the Intruder, one Edward Rawson, a New-England-Man, and a violent Presbyterian. **1789** MACLAY *Deb. Senate* 49 Lee led, Ellsworth seconded him, the New England men followed. **1845** COOPER *Chainbearer* xxix, The supercilious feeling of the New England-man can very easily be traced to his origin in the mother country.

b. A New England vessel.

1776 in *S. Lit. Messenger* XXVII. 326/2 A tender came last week to Hobbs' Hole and took a New England man, loaded with grain and flour, from the wharf.

+**New England pine.** A pine (*Pinus strobus*) found in the eastern part of the United States and valued for its soft light wood. — **1785** MARSHALL *Amer. Grove* 101 New-England, or White Pine . . . is allowed to out top in growth most of our other trees. **1847** DARLINGTON *Weeds & Plants* 336 New England Pine . . . is also a most valuable tree,—furnishing an immense amount of lumber.

+**New England Primer.** A primary school book, probably compiled by Benjamin Harris, published in Boston about 1689, and frequently reprinted. — *c***1689** (*title*), The New-England Primer. **1780** *N.J. Archives* 2 Ser. IV. 630 New-England Primers To be sold by the Thousand or smaller Quantity at the Printing-Office, in Trenton. **1894** FORD *New-Eng. Primer* 38 No copy of this first edition of the New England Primer is known.

+**New England rum.** Rum manufactured in New England.

1740 *Mass. Hist. Soc. Proc.* V. 112 But the New-England rum is not so valuable as West-India. **1784** SMYTH *Tour* II. 30 New England takes off a great quantity of molasses raw, and from thence is distilled there, a very inferior ill-tasted spirit, named New England or Yankee Rum. **1817** *Yankee Traveller* 75 Wrangle . . . drove a lucrative trade in the sale of potatoe whisky, and adulterated New-England rum. **1857** GUNN *N.Y. Boarding-Houses* 51 They made our room-mate drunk on New England rum with tobacco in it. **1891** EARLE *Sabbath* 123 This bi-annual celebration of the Lord's Supper . . . was followed on Monday by cheerful thanksgiving and social intercourse, in which, as in every feast, our old friend, New England rum, played no unimportant part.

+**New England states.** *pl.* The northeastern states of the United States: New Hampshire, Vermont, Massachusetts, Rhode Island, Connecticut, and, after 1820, Maine. — **1787** CUTLER in *Life & Lett.* I. 195 [You are] acquainted with the institution of a Company in the New England States by the name of the Ohio Company. **1817** PAULDING *Lett. from South* I. 87 In Connecticut, and probably in nearly all the New-England states, . . . there has been little growth in numbers, since the western States became objects of attention. **1882** THAYER *From Log-Cabin* 87 The New England States presented a scene of enthusiasm without precedent, and the interest spread into north-eastern Ohio. **1900** *Congress. Rec.* 15 Feb. 1856/2 The examination for engineer in the particular section of country . . . is of the same sort as is required in the New England States. **1925** BRYAN *Memoirs* 218 In the New England States . . . the Grange . . . [demanded] the issuance of greenbacks by the Federal Government.

+**New England whiting.** (See quotations.) — **1884** GOODE, etc. *Fisheries* I. 240 The Silver Hake, or New England Whiting. *Merlucius Bilinearis*. . . . The Silver Hake commonly inhabits the middle depths of ocean. **1911** *Rep. Fisheries 1908* 316 Silver Hake (*Merluccius bilinearis*). —It is also called 'New England whiting.'

+**New Englandy,** *a.* Suggestive of New England; in the manner of New Englanders. — **1861** TUCKERMAN in J. Hawthorne *N. Hawthorne & Wife* II. 275 For the book . . . I claim little, but that it is New Englandy (I hope).

+**New English,** *a.* Of or pertaining to New England.

1632 *Mass. H. S. Coll.* 4 Ser. VI. 184 Tis a ridle as yet to me whether you meane any Elder in these New English churches. **1655** *Suffolk Deeds* II. 175 Receiued of mr. michell martyn . . . two Caske of new English Spirrits. **1701** SEWALL *Diary* II. 49 That Church . . . renounce the Cross in Baptisme, Humane Holydays &c. as other New-english Churches does **1725** T. SYMMES in Kidder *Exped. Lovewell* (1865) 38 This Action Merit' a Room in the History of our New-English wars. **1863** 'G. HAMILTON. *Gala-Days* 211, I had a pleasant New-English feeling of self-gratulation, **1870** LOWELL *Among My Books* 1 Ser. 234 All their unconscious training by eye and ear, were *New English* wholly.

+**b.** *absol.* The people of New England.

1643 WILLIAMS *Key* (1866) 25 To that great Point of their [*i.e.* the Indians'] Conversion so much to bee longed for, and by all NeW-English so much pretended. **1647** ELIOT *Day-Breaking* 25 Cutting their Haire in a modest manner as the New-English generally doe.

***New-found,** *a.* Of lands: Recently discovered or reclaimed, +esp with reference to a tract or island in the Dismal Swamp. — **1588** T. HARRIOT (*title*), A Briefe and True Report of the New Found Land of Virginia. **1763** WASHINGTON *Diaries* I. 192 The Inhabitants of what they call new found land, which is thick settled, very rich Land. **1860** MORDECAI *Virginia* I. 26 A German, named Widewilt, whose trumpet called the troops to horse, procured a land warrant and located it on this new-found land.

***Newfoundland.** [A large island at the mouth of the St. Lawrence River. {1611–}]

1. Short for NEWFOUNDLAND DOG. {1845–} Also attrib.

1827 *Hallowell* (Me.) *Gaz.* 20 June 3/4 They report to have seen . . . 2 greyhounds, 1 newfoundland, 50 French dogs. **1852** STOWE *Uncle Tom* v, Old Bruno, a great Newfoundland, who slept at the end of the porch, rose, with a low growl. **1872** *Atlantic Mo.* May 552 He has a couple of Newfoundland pups for sale. **1907** LONDON *Road* 55 As that big Newfoundland behaved at the plate of my dog Punch, so behaved I at the table of those two maiden ladies of Harrisburg.

2. Attrib. with *bank, cuff:* (see quotations).

1635 New-fondland banke [see BANK, *n.*[1]]. **1884** *Nat. Museum Bul.* No. 27, 793 Woolen Mittens. Known to the fishermen as 'Newfoundland cuffs.' Made of very heavy woolen cloth, called 'swan's skin,' with a heavy nape [*sic*]. Used . . . by the fishermen of Gloucester.

Newfoundland dog. A large dog of a breed which originated in North America. {1824–} — **1809** IRVING *Knickerb.* v. vii, Kildermeester . . . had cherished . . . a rugged mop of hair, not a little resembling the shag of a Newfoundland dog. **1850** MATHEWS *Moneypenny* 131 [He] encountered . . . a large black and white Newfoundland dog. **1875** STOWE *Deacon Pitkin's Farm* 39 She knows that Bill . . . obeys all her mandates with the faithful docility of a good Newfoundland dog. **1907** LONDON *Road* 55 A visitor had ridden over . . . and with him had come a Newfoundland dog as big as a calf.

+**New ground.** Ground which has just been cleared for cultivation. (Cf. NEW LAND.)

1624 SMITH *Gen. Hist. Va.* IV. 126 We haue ordinarily foure or fiue [barrels of produce an acre], but of new ground six, seuen, and eight. *a***1656** BRADFORD *Hist.* 123 For the Indeans used then to have nothing so much corne as they have since ye English have stored them with their hows, and seene their industrie in breaking up new-grounds therwith. **1769** WASHINGTON *Diaries* I. 333 That piece of New Ground containing 14 Acres next the widow Sheridine's. **1800** TATHAM *Tobacco* 6 The condition of soil of which the planters make choice, is that in which nature presents it when it is first disrobed of the woods. . . . This is termed *new* ground, which may be there considered as synonymous with *tobacco* ground. *c***1866** BAGBY *Old Va. Gentleman* 53 A negro boy is running up from the 'new ground' to take your horse. **1902** G. C. EGGLESTON *D. South* 89 Let's ride to the tobacco new grounds at once.

b. Attrib. with *corn, patch,* etc.

1771 *Md. Hist. Mag.* XIV. 134 Our new ground tob[acc]o Here has been Housed 3 or 4 days past. **1800** BOUCHER *Glossary* p. l, *New-ground patch:* a piece of ground that had never been cultivated before. **1902** *Dialect Notes* II. 240 *New-ground* (with strong accent on first word). . . . Newly cleared land, the first crop on which is called [in Illinois] 'New-ground corn,' or 'Nêew-ground taters.'

+**New Hampshire grants.** *pl. Hist.* Land grants made (1749–64) west of the Connecticut River by the royal governor of New Hampshire.

These grants, embracing 131 townships in what is now Vermont, were in a region claimed by both New Hampshire and New York. The King, by an order in council on July 20, 1764, decided the controversy in favor of New York, but some settlers under the leadership of Ethan Allen maintained by force the legality of their New Hampshire titles. (See GREEN MOUNTAIN BOY.)

1776 *Vt. Hist. Soc. Coll.* I. 16 The Humble Address, Remonstrance and Petition of that part of America being situated south of Canada line, . . . commonly called and known by the name of the N[ew] Hampshire Grants. **1798** [see GRANT *n.* 1]. *a***1817** DWIGHT *Travels* II. 113 Vermont was then [in 1775] regarded as a part of New-Hampshire; and in customary language was styled *the New-Hampshire grants.* **1863** *New Amer. Cycl.* XVI. 73/2 The country west of the Connecticut was only known at that time [1760] by the name of 'New Hampshire grants.'

+**New Haven.** [A city in Connecticut.] Used attrib. to designate the theological system of Taylorism (q.v.). — **1884** Schaff *Religious Encycl.* III. 2306/1 The 'New-Haven Theology' . . . was one of the most influential of the types of so-called 'New-School Divinity.' *Ib.*, The peculiarities of 'New Haven Divinity' as it existed in the generation among whom Dr. Taylor was a prominent leader [1822–58]. **1889** *Cent.* 1707/2 *New Haven Divinity*, a popular title for a phase of modified Calvinism, deriving its name from the residence of its chief founder, N. W. Taylor (1786–1858) of Yale Theological Seminary in New Haven, Connecticut.

+**New Jersey.** *attrib.* [The name of one of the Middle Atlantic states.] Designating plants and other natural features of New Jersey.

See also NEW JERSEY TEA and JERSEY 5 b.

1770 FORSTER tr. Kalm *Travels* 69 [Trees] which grow spontaneously in the woods which are nearest to Philadelphia [include] . . . *Pinus tæda*, the New Jersey fir tree, on dry sandy heaths. **1832** BROWNE *Sylva* 234 New Jersey Pine. *Pinus Inops.* **1870** *Rep. Comm. Agric.* *1869* 410 Whatever may be said in . . . depreciation of the productive value of 'New Jersey sands' [etc.]. **1882** MCCABE *New York* 313 The building is constructed of New Jersey sandstone. **1897** *Congress. Rec.* 18 May 1137/2, I have never been in New Jersey, but I know the reputation of the New Jersey mosquito.

+**New Jersey tea.** =AMERICAN CEANOTHUS. Used as a substitute for tea during the Revolution. Also attrib. (Cf. JERSEY TEA.) — **1785** MARSHALL *Amer. Grove* 27 American Ceanothus, or New-Jersey Tea-tree, . . . is a low shrub, growing common in most parts of North America. **1815** DRAKE *Cincinnati* 77. **1877** *Vermont Bd. Agric. Rep.* IV. 159 Riley recommends persons . . . to plant a small patch of New Jersey Tea . . . as a decoy near the strawberry bed. **1901** MOHR *Plant Life Ala.* 610 New Jersey Tea. Red Root. . . . Used medicinally.

New Jerusalem church. A church that accepts the doctrines of Emanuel Swedenborg. — **1842** BUCKINGHAM *E. & W. States* I. 181 There are six churches in Bath [Me.]; two Calvinist Congregationalists, one Methodist, one Baptist, one New Jerusalem or Swedenborgians, and one Universalist. **1845** SOL. SMITH *Theatr. Apprent.* 35, [I] played the organ in the New Jerusalem church three times every Sunday, and every Thursday evening.

‖**New Jerusalemite.** A member or supporter of the New Jerusalem church. — **1845** SOL. SMITH *Theatr. Apprent.* 35, [I taught] a whole lot of young New Jerusalemites the art of psalmody two evenings each week.

***New land.** +Land newly brought under cultivation. (Cf. NEW GROUND.) — **1763** WASHINGTON *Writings* II. 196 The arm of Dismal, which we passed through to get to this new land (as it is called) is 3½ miles measured. **1825** LORAIN *Pract. Husbandry* 346, I have seen grass seeds fail almost entirely . . . from no other cause than the loose, open, spongy texture of the new land. **1833** SILLIMAN *Man. Sugar Cane* 13 The Crab Grass . . . which comes up abundantly on new land, is cut with hoes. **1871** *Rep. Indian Affairs* (1872) 330 It is my intention, during the coming season, to plow as much new land as possible. **1881** *Ib.* 31 The improvements . . . consist of the erection of houses, stables, fences, corrals, &c., and the breaking of new land.

New Light. {1650–}

1. +**a.** A member of a group in sympathy with the revival of religious zeal in eighteenth-century America, as one of the Presbyterians who seceded in 1741 from the Philadelphia synod. Now hist.

1743 HEMPSTEAD *Diary* 407 All come to settle the disorders that are subsisting among those called New Lights which follow Mr. Davenport. **1750** J. BIRKET *Cursory Remarks* 22 There is Nineteen different places of Worship in the Town (to wit) thirteen of the Independents Presbyterians & newlights &Ca. **1764** WHITEFIELD *Works* III. (1771) 317 From that place [Newburn] to this [New Brunswick, N.C.], I have met with what they call New-lights almost every stage. **1776** FITHIAN *Journal* II. 175 They are most of them 'New Lights' as the term used to be. **1815** ASBURY *Journal* (1821) III. 378 Bohemia manor was formerly the field in which the Whitefield Methodists, called New Lights, laboured with success. **1830** WATSON *Philadelphia* 519 This church was formed of the Presbyterians who went off from the first church in High street, as seceders—receiving the name of 'New Lights.'

+**b.** A member of a religious group which about 1803, under the leadership of Barton W. Stone, John Marshall, and others, left the Presbyterian church; a Campbellite or Disciple of Christ. *Obs.*

1807 MCNEMAR *Ky. Revival* 29 These . . . taught as an important truth, that the will of God, was made manifest to each individual . . . by an inward light, which shone into the heart.—Hence they received the name of 'New-Lights.' **1824** R. H. BISHOP *Hist. Church Ky.* 130 The people of whom we propose to give a short sketch in the following article, had their origin at the second meeting of the Synod of Kentucky, which was in Sept. 1803. . . . They have assumed to themselves the exclusive name of 'The Christian Church.' They have usually been called 'New Lights, or Stoneites.' **1847** R. DAVIDSON *Presbyterian Ch. in Ky.* 219 In the Great Revival, Mr. Stone was conspicuous . . . [in] the subsequent formation of societies, known under the various names of New Lights, Christians, Arians, Marshallites, and Stoneites. **1856** CARTWRIGHT *Autob.* 219 Arianism was rife through all that country [Kentucky], although they called themselves 'Christians,' and were called by the world, New Lights, Marshallites, or Stoneites. **1871** EGGLESTON *Hoosier Schoolm.* 121, I don't know whether you're a Hardshell . . . or a Campbellite, or a New Light. **1889** *Cent.* 780/3 The Campbellites were also called New Lights.

+**2.** =CAMPBELLITE 2.

1877 JORDAN in *Nat. Museum Bul.* No. 9, 21 *Pomoxys annularis.* . . . Throughout Kentucky it is known as the 'New Light,' and sometimes as 'Campbellite.' **1885** J. S. KINGSLEY, etc. *Standard Nat. Hist.* III. 235 It is known as the crappie, new-light, Campbellite, and bachelor, and is an abundant fish in the Mississippi river. **1911** *Rep. Fisheries 1908* 308.

+**3.** Attrib. with *church, Divinity, doctrine*, etc., in senses 1 a and b.

1742 HEMPSTEAD *Diary* 402, 2 of them Newlight Exhorters begun their meeting. **1744** EDWARDS *Works* (1834) I. p. cxviii/1 To attend the ministry of those that are called New Light ministers. **1749** *Ib.* 524 The New Light party have an other house they go to. **1781** PETERS *Hist. Conn.* (1829) 139 A most thundering preacher of the new-light order. **1784** SMYTH *Tour* I. 102 Here I . . . had to defend myself against the formidable attacks of a new-light itinerant preacher. **1807** MCNEMAR *Ky. Revival* 46 Taking what is called the *New-light* doctrine, as the rudiments of divine truth, they proceeded to consider the nature of justification, reconciliation to God, etc. **1837** JENKINS *Ohio Gaz.* 373 There are in this county . . . eight christian (or newlight) . . . and five dunkard churches. **1883** New-Light Divinity [see NEW DIVINITY].

b. *transf.* Newfangled, novel.

1833 WYETH *Oregon* 25 What the *new-light* Doctrine of Phrenology calls the disposition bump of *Inhabitiveness*.

+**New Lightism.** The ideas and beliefs of the New Lights. — **1755** *Essex Inst. Coll.* LII. 78 He seems a grave, close, heavy Man, not given to talk & deeply immerged in New Lightism. **1838** FLAGG *Far West* II. 87 The priest was politely advised to decamp before the doctrine should get unsavoury. Thus ended the glorious discovery of New-lightism! **1845** JUDD *Margaret* I. 42 The town underwent and survived . . . antinomianism, New-lightism, Scotch Presbyterianism. **1856** CARTWRIGHT *Autobiog.* 32 B. W. Stone stuck to his New Lightism.

New measure. *attrib.* +Denoting a sect in the Presbyterian church composed of those in accord with the teachings of the Rev. Charles Finney (1792–1875). *Obs.* — **1837** PECK *New Guide* 343 *Oberlin Institute* has been recently established in Lorrain County [Ohio], under the influence of 'new measure' Presbyterians.

+**New Mexican,** *n.* A native or resident of New Mexico. — **1834** A. PIKE *Sketches* 170 Even the New Mexicans call him a great rascal. **1844** GREGG *Commerce of Prairies* I. 96 Every year, large parties of New-Mexicans . . . drive out into these prairies to procure a supply of buffalo beef for their families. **1854** *Harper's Mag.* April 582/1 To that hard-headed animal, the goat, the New Mexicans are indebted . . . occasionally for the very raiment which they wear. **1893** LUMMIS *Land of Poco Tiempo* 10 If the Neo-Mexicanized Saxon were . . . as the un-Saxonized New Mexican, he would have one chief fetich in the territory of his adoption—the burro.

+**New Mexican,** *a.* Of or pertaining to New Mexico. — **1846** *30th Congress 1 Sess.* Sen. Ex. Doc. No. 23, 57 Acoma is the most western of the New Mexican towns. **1850** GARRARD *Wah-To-Yah* xiii. 183 The New-Mexican plows, for the most part, are of the primitive kind. **1883** RITCH *N. Mex.* 72 The history of the world contains no parallel in this New Mexican mine. **1893** LUMMIS *Land of Poco Tiempo* 294 Twenty miles south of the New Mexican hamlet of Manzano, and the riddle of its ancient apple-trees, is the noble ruin of the pueblo of Abó.

New Negro. A Negro slave newly brought from Africa. *Obs.* — [**1701** WOLLEY *Journal N.Y.* 32 In Barbados (new Negro's i.e. such as cannot speak English,) are bought for twelve or fourteen pound a head.] **1775** *Amer. Archives 4 Ser.* III. 1367 He is a new negro, and by his actions he sometimes diverts your people; but I defy you to point out a single instance of dissatisfaction on that score. **1785** C. PETTIGREW *Let. to M. Blount* (Univ. N.C. MS.), I purpose to replace them in New Negroes if I can. **1860** MORDECAI *Virginia* 350, I do not speak of the New Negros, as the imported Africans were called, but of their descendants.

Newness.** +*The Newness*, New England transcendentalism. *Obs.* — **1865** LOWELL *Writings* I. 363 There was a much nearer metaphysical relation . . . between Carlyle and the Apostles of the Newness, as they were called in New England, than has commonly been supposed. *c1870** in *Century Mag.* XXXIX. 124/1 By the 'Newness' I mean a very singular intellectual and spiritual movement which broke out like an epidemic in New England some forty years ago, and ran its course for about ten years. **1889** *Ib.* 129/1 Next to Brook Farm, Concord was the chief resort of the disciples of the 'Newness.' Here lived Emerson, Thoreau, and Bronson Alcott.

+**New Orleans boat.** (See quot. 1812.) *Obs.* — **1807** C. SCHULTZ *Travels* I. 132 Kentucky and New-Orleans boats from one dollar to one and a half a foot. **1812** MELISH *Travels* II. 85 *Kentucky* and *New Orleans* boats are flats, with sides boarded like a house, about six or seven feet high, over which there is an arched roof.

+**New Orleans molasses.** Molasses comparatively light in color and high in sugar content, obtained as a by-product in the manufacture of sugar. — **1849** FOSTER *N.Y. in Slices* 82 The grocery-keeper . . . buys a barrel of common New Orleans molasses at twenty-five cents per gallon, and retails it to his customers at sixpence the pint. **1859** *Rep. Comm. Patents* (1858) I. 689 Mix one quart of the best New Orleans molasses, which should be previously boiled for ten or fifteen minutes. **1885** *Buckeye Cookery* 99 In making ginger-bread . . . always use New Orleans or Porto Rico molasses, and never syrups.

+**New Orleans moss.** The long moss, *Dendropogon usneoides.* — **1877** BARTLETT 789 *New Orleans Moss*, . . . a moss which hangs from the boughs of trees in Louisiana, giving to the landscape a weird-like appearance, . . . is used in the South . . . for mattresses, cushions, &c.

+**New Orleans syrup.** =NEW ORLEANS MOLASSES. — **1898** *Kansas City Star* 18 Dec. 5/2 New Orleans Syrup, per gal, 19¢.

+**Newport.** [Name of a city in Rhode Island.] **1.** *attrib.* Identified with Newport, Rhode Island, as a fashionable resort. **2.** *Reverse Newport*, a kind of ballroom dance. — **(1) 1863** 'M. HARLAND' *Husks* 187 It was the 'grand hop' night at the head-quarters of Newport fashion. **1894** BROWNELL *Newport* 14, I can fancy . . . people who preferred a Jamestown barrack to a Newport cottage at the same price, maintaining that life was freer in Jamestown. **1924** VAN RENSSELAER *Social Ladder* 243 The seasoned member of the Newport colony enters into the cruel game of quashing the pride of the stranger with great glee. **(2) 1883** RITTENHOUSE *Maud* 179, I danced the reverse Newport with George Corliss for the first time and got it to perfection.

New potato. A potato of the incoming harvest or crop. — **1837** HAWTHORNE in *U.S. Mag.* I. 33 Behind comes a 'sauceman,' driving a wagon full of new potatoes, green ears of corn [etc.]. **1862** NORTON *Army Lett.* 115 If we didn't have . . . new potatoes and green corn, it was because we were too lazy to get them. **1924** I. E. LORD *Everybody's Cook Book* 766 New potatoes are often served with a rich Cheese Sauce.

New purchase. +Any one of various large areas or tracts of land purchased by individuals or by a company from Indians or the federal government for resale to settlers. *Obs.* (Cf. PURCHASE.) — **1775** FITHIAN *Journal* II. 37, I met on the road, a tinker on the way to what is called the 'New Purchase.' **1809** CUMING *Western Tour* 441 The New Purchase is situated on the western side of the Tuskarawas river . . . forty-four miles west of New Lisbon. **1834** PECK *Gaz. Illinois* 374 *Flint Hill*, a town site on the west side of the Mississippi . . . has been recently commenced. . . . The country back called the 'New Purchase,' is rapidly settling. **1843** 'CARLTON' *New Purchase* II. 12 A New Purchase is not the most pleasant place in the world for boarding-school young ladies.

New rich, *n.* and *a.* [tr. of Fr. *nouveaux riches.*] **1.** *n.* Those who have recently become wealthy. **2.** *adj.* (Hyphened.) Resembling the new rich; showy or ostentatious. — **(1) 1886** *Harper's Mag.* Oct. 795/2 The sons of the 'new rich' . . . are like men drunk with new wine. **(2) 1923** 'BOWER' *Parowan Bonanza* 157 You've never seen *me* look new-rich, have you, Bill?

***News.** In special combinations: +*News hallow*, among American Indians, a shout to announce news; *n. item*, an item of news in a newspaper; *n. service*, an agency or organization that supplies news to papers and other periodicals; *n. whoop*, a news hallow. — **1765** TIMBERLAKE *Memoirs* 83 The News Hallow was given from the top of Tommotly town-house. **1844** *Knickerb.* XXIV. 179 News-items, matters of information; actual discoveries. **1893** in Philips *Making of a Newspaper* 16 Certain excellent local newspapers . . . , satisfied with the outside news-service of the press associations, pay for telegraph-tolls. **1775** ADAIR *Indians* 301 The others [*sc.* Indians] . . . told me . . . to be sure to call them, by sounding the news-whoop, as soon as he arrived at camp.

+**News agency.** **1.** A company that distributes periodicals; a news company. **2.** A company that supplies news to newspapers and other subscribers. — **(1) 1873** F. HUDSON *Journalism* 521 News agencies . . . branched out and extended into colossal news companies as a . . . necessity of the age. **1881** *Rep. Postmaster-General* 8 Newspapers and periodicals mailed to regular subscribers from known offices of publication, and from news agencies. **1887** *Postal Laws* 147 In admitting second-class publications sent from a news agency, postmasters will observe the following [rules]. **(2) 1900** NELSON *A B C Wall St.* 154 *News agency.* Two companies, the New York News Bureau and Dow, Jones & Co., supply Wall St. with news. Each uses a ticker service. **1905** PHILLIPS *Plum Tree* 190 He attended to the subsidizing of news agencies that supplied thousands of country papers with boiler-plate matter to fill their inside pages. **1925** BENEFIELD *Chicken-Wagon Family* 98 'Flimsy' is the thin mimeographed copy that comes in from news agencies that cover the city and suburbs.

News agent. A news dealer. {1851–} — **1861** *Chicago Tribune* 15 April (*advt.*), News Agents and Booksellers, Attention. We . . . are now prepared to furnish News Dealers and Booksellers with Every Paper, Periodical and Book [etc.]. **1865** *Atlantic Mo.* XV. 470/1 Cheap postage, and the establishment of news-agents all over the country, enable the people to get papers at less cost. **1887** *Postal Laws* 147 News agents are persons, including newsboys, engaged in business as news dealers or sellers of second-class publications. **1892** GUNTER *Miss Dividends* 247, I've spoilt my voice hollerin' as news-agent, an' I can't bring it down!

+**News boat.** A boat which meets incoming vessels to obtain news of events abroad and other information. — **1833–5** E. LESLIE in *Casquet Lit.* V. 25/1 We were visited by a news-boat. **1838** COOPER *Homeward Bound* xxxi. [A boat] had been lying-to, to take in stores sent from the town and to communicate with a news-boat. **1841** *Knickerb.* XVII. 258 Though the vessel in which they came had been boarded by all the news-boats, nothing transpired to satisfy public curiosity. **1855** I. C. PRAY *Mem. J. G. Bennett* 134 In 1827, the journals had but one news-boat. *a***1882** WEED *Autobiog.* 56 The 'Courier' had no news boat.

Newsboy. A boy who delivers or sells newspapers. {1812–}

1764 *Broadside Verse* (1930) 205 The News-Boy's Christmas and New-Year's Verses. **1839** in Brewster *J. D. Whitney* 33 Every sweep and coal-seller and newsboy in the city seems to redouble his exertions as he comes under my window. **1874** B. F. TAYLOR *World on Wheels* 125 With the steam comes the newsboy, the boot-black, . . . and—peanuts. **1902** NORRIS *Pit* x, The musical Gregorians of the newsboys chanting the evening's extras from corner to corner of the streets rose into the air.

b. Attrib. with *class, euphemism, rapidity.*

1877 BEARD *K.K.K. Sketches* 191 To reach a superlative . . . we . . . adopt the beautiful newsboy euphemism, hunky-dory. **1882** MCCABE *New York* 515 The pickpockets are largely recruited from the newsboy class. **1892** GUNTER *Miss Dividends* 240 Into this Elysium, Buck Powers . . . breaks with news-boy rapidity.

+**News bureau.** =NEWS AGENCY 2. — **1898** *Scribner's Mag.* Nov. 540/1 The few assignments he got were, for the most part, . . . to run down stories which the news-bureaus sent in. **1900** NELSON *A B C Wall St.* 154 The news slips of the New York News Bureau are known as the 'yellow slips.' **1902** MACGOWAN *Last Word* 182 You look like the head of a news bureau.

New school. {1844–}

+**1.** (Both words usually capitalized.) The less conservative of the two factions into which the Presbyterian church was divided from about 1825 to 1869. Now hist.

1837 W. JENKINS *Ohio Gaz.* 317 The public buildings consist of . . . two presbyterian churches, one of the old, and one of the new school. **1842** BUCKINGHAM *Slave States* II. 269 The Presbyterians are thought to be the most extensive . . . ; but the late schism, which has divided them into Old School and New School, the former being rigid Calvinists, and the latter inclining to Arminianism, has divided the body. **1846** COOPER *Redskins* xiv, What 'new-school' means, in a spiritual sense, . . . I suppose . . . to be some improvement on some other improvements of the more ancient and venerable dogmas of the sect to which it belongs.

‖**2.** (See quotation.)

1837 *S. Lit. Messenger* III. 107, I once read medicine . . . under a disciple of the '*new school*' (vulgarly called steam doctors).

+**3.** *attrib.* **a.** Of or pertaining to the Anti-federalists and their political philosophy.

Cf. ANTI-FEDERAL *a.* and *n.* and ANTI-FEDERALIST.

1806 FESSENDEN *Democracy Unveiled* I. 113 That were not justice in arrears, These New School folks would lack their ears. *Ib.* II. 35 Among our new-school rights and duties, There's no monopoly of beauties.

+**b.** In sense 1 with *divinity, general assembly, man.*

See also NEW SCHOOL PRESBYTERIAN.

1853 STOWE *Key* 220/1 A large body of New-School men, and many Old-School, are decided anti-slavery men. **1853** *Harper's Mag.* July 266/1 The 'New School' General Assembly met at Buffalo, also on May 19, and was opened by a discourse from the Rev. William Adams. **1884** New-School Divinity [see NEW HAVEN].

+**New School Presbyterian.** **1.** A member of the New School faction in the Presbyterian church. Now hist. (Cf. prec.) **2.** Attrib. with *church, minister.* — **(1) 1837** PECK *Gaz. Illinois* 72 The Illinois college at Jacksonville is [identified] with the 'New School' Presbyterians. **1849** CHAMBERLAIN *Ind. Gazetteer* 281 The other public buildings are . . . churches . . . for the Methodists, . . . Old and New School Presbyterians [etc.]. **1872** MCCLELLAN *Golden State* 406 The Old and New School Presbyterians have . . . 2,600 members and 3,500 Sunday-scholars. **(2) 1847** HOWE *Hist. Coll. Ohio* 360 [Piqua] contains 1 New and 1 Old School Presbyterian, 1 Methodist Episcopal, . . . and 1 Disciples church. **1857** QUINLAND I. 306 [The teacher] is a 'new-school' presbyterian minister, and prays from twenty to forty minutes every morning at the opening of the school.

+**News company.** A firm acting as a wholesale dealer in newspapers and periodicals. — **1872** *Chicago Tribune* 9 Oct. 3/3 Newsmen will supply their counters from the Western News Company. **1884** *Tenth Census* VIII. I. 159 The American News Company . . . involved the consolidation of several of the largest newsdealing firms of New York City.

News dealer. A dealer in newspapers; a news agent. {1868–} — **1861** [see NEWS AGENT]. **1870** *Scribner's Mo.* I. 115 The news-dealer near St. Patrick's Cathedral, . . . , stocks his stand . . . with the latest issue of the Catholic World. **1911** PERSONS, etc. *Mass. Labor Laws* 215 The local newsdealer who hires a crowd of small boys to sell papers for him on commission . . . [has] been free from responsibility for violations of the law.

+**News depot.** A news stand or shop at which newspapers are sold. — **1873** *Winfield* (Kan.) *Courier* 15 May 3/2 Latest publications at Webb's news depot. **1877** HODGE *Arizona* 154 Tucson has . . . one news depot, . . . four feed and livery stables.

News editor. An editor on a newspaper staff who edits local or foreign news or has general charge of collecting and editing news. — **1868**

BAGBY *Old Va. Gentleman* 190 Pollard he declared was 'the best news editor in the whole South.' **1894** SHUMAN *Steps into Journalism* 19 On the larger papers the work of the managing editor is divided, giving him an assistant, the managing news editor.

New-settled, *a.* Newly occupied by settlers. *Obs.* — **1718** *Mass. H. Rep. Jrnl.* II. 56 The House Request . . . that meet Persons be appointed . . . in the Eastern and new settled parts of the Province. **1797** F. BAILY *Tour* 307 All these new-settled places, and, in fact, almost all colonies, are filled with adventurers.

News-gatherer. {1712–} +A newspaper reporter. *literary.* — **1842** 'UNCLE SAM' *Peculiarities* I. 27 We were here boarded by . . . the 'news gatherer' to the New York press. **1877** *Harper's Mag.* Dec. 48/1 The staff included any number of other really able descriptive writers and news-gatherers. **1892** A. E. LEE *Hist. Columbus, Ohio* I. 459 The war developed newsgatherers just as it developed generals. **1907** GIVEN *Making a Newspaper* 196 A star newsgatherer chancing to be sent to a small tenement-house fire will search the house from top to bottom.

+**News girl.** A girl who sells newspapers. — **1868** *Putnam's Mag.* I. 518/1 A few years ago, a news-girl was as rare a sight as a Dodo. **1870** *Scribner's Mo.* I. 124 Here is a little newsgirl . . . exclaiming lustily, 'Extra Commercial! Defeat of the French!'

New South. +The South, with the activities, institutions, and spirit of its people reshaped in conformity with the changes necessitated by the Civil War and Reconstruction. — **1884** *Century Mag.* April 864/1 Opposed to these errors is the spirit of the New South, a phrase which this magazine first made current. **1887** *Ib.* March 769/2 The New South is connected far more closely with the new life and labor of the white man of the South than with the emancipation and labor of the freedmen. **1900** *Congress. Rec.* 1 Feb. 1404/1 That spirit to-day animates every son of the old and of the new South. **1905** N. DAVIS *Northerner* 101 The New South was born: first-fruit of the union of the East and South.

Newspaper.

1. A periodical publication, usu. weekly, semi-weekly, or daily, the chief or ostensible purpose of which is to give recent news. {1670–}

1704 *Boston News-Letter* 14 Aug. 2/2 Here is a person apprehended & secured, . . . supposed to be Thomas Odell mentioned in the NewsPaper for Counterfeiting the Massachusetts-Bay's 20. *s.* bills of Crdit. **1771** FRANKLIN *Autobiog.* 246, I remember his being dissuaded by some of his friends from the undertaking, . . . one newspaper being, in their judgment, enough for America. **1800** JAY in J. Adams *Works* IX. 90 A newspaper . . . contains a copy of the Message. **1821** *Ann. 17th Congress* 1 Sess. I. 22 After adopting the usual orders for supplying the members with newspapers, &c., the Senate adjourned to Monday. **1857** *Ladies Repository* XVII. 99/2 The patriot cherishes his newspaper as almost a necessity of life. **1907** *St. Nicholas* June 681/1 His first venture into the world of literature [was made] through the columns of a friendly local newspaper.

2. *attrib.* and *comb.* **a.** Designating an editor, employee, or part-time worker on a newspaper.

See also NEWSPAPER CORRESPONDENT, MAN, REPORTER.

1801 *Ann. 6th Congress* 919 A few printers, and a few miserable newspaper scribblers have fallen victims to [the Sedition Law]. **1809** *Ann. 10th Congress* 2 Sess. 1084 Notwithstanding the licentiousness of newspaper editors, he was against any law for curbing them. **1851** CIST *Cincinnati* 50 Occupations [include] . . . Newspaper publishers, 9; Newspaper carriers, 23. **1894** SHUMAN *Steps into Journalism* 65 One of the most prolific newspaper hacks in Chicago once remarked that he did not consider a man . . . a reporter unless he could make good reading out of anything. **1913** LA FOLLETTE *Autobiog.* 144 The letter impressed me as a precaution taken to forestall newspaper interviewers.

b. Designating material appearing in or taken from a newspaper.

1798 *Ann. 5th Congress* II. 2107 The gentleman from Connecticut . . . had communicated to the House . . . a number of newspaper paragraphs. **1799** *Ib.* III. 2724 Mr. T. Claiborne did not wish to depend upon newspaper reports. **1838** Newspaper clipping [see CLIPPING 2]. **1844** S. M. FULLER *Summer on Lakes* 185 Has ever Art found out a richer theme, . . . sketched carelessly, In the newspaper column of to-day? **1877** *Harper's Mag.* March 564/1 She read and re-read the old newspaper story. **1907** *St. Nicholas* May 641/1 Let them cut out large colored newspaper pictures and paste them around the lower part of the wigwam. **1913** LA FOLLETTE *Autobiog.* 142 The further fact that he was my brother-in-law and my partner in the firm . . . was also the subject of newspaper comment.

c. In special combinations.

Newspaper bag, a mail pouch for newspapers; *n. bulletin*, a notice posted in a conspicuous place by a newspaper, containing the latest news about some matter of exceptional public interest; *n. English*, English of the quality found in newspapers; *n. exchange*, =EXCHANGE 3; *n. file*, an orderly collection of issues of a newspaper; *n. stand*, a booth or station at which newspapers are sold; *n. support*, support given, as to a political candidate, by a newspaper; *n. syndicate business*, the business of selling news or features, provided by a single organization, to appear simultaneously in a number of newspapers.

1872 'MARK TWAIN' *Roughing It* 30 Right here is the very direction which is wrote on all the newspaper-bags. **1883** *Harper's Mag.* Nov. 956/2 Our correspondent recalls the cholera in 1832–3, and the crowds of anxious faces peering at the newspaper bulletins, upon which were posted the reports of the Board of Health. **1888** *Ib.* May 962/2 The phrase 'newspaper English' has come to have a significance which is not flattering to newspapers. **1873** *Newton Kansan* 5 June 2/1 The Postmaster General has decided that the law forbids the free transmission of newspaper exchanges. **1913** LA FOLLETTE *Autobiog.* 332 Newspaper files of that day will record the fact. **1893** POST *Harvard Stories* 31 At a newspaper-stand he bought all the picture papers. **1913** LA FOLLETTE *Autobiog.* 70 Insurgents or Progressives . . . have won their victories . . . often without newspaper support. **1889** HOWELLS *Hazard of Fortunes* II. 120, I told 'em I hadn't much practice with Go-devils in the newspaper syndicate business.

Newspaper correspondent. One who contributes news, criticism, etc., to a newspaper, especially one sent to a particular place or scene of action to report news regularly. {1868–} Also *newspaper war correspondent.* — **1880** 'MARK TWAIN' *Tramp Abroad* 263 Riley and I were newspaper correspondents in Washington, in the winter of '67. **1886** POORE *Reminisc.* II. 65 Among them were several newspaper correspondents. **1897** C. A. DANA *Recoll. Civil War* 215 The newspaper correspondent who was responsible for the misstatement was with us. **1907** *St. Nicholas* June 679/1 He gave up his other work to become for a time a newspaper war correspondent.

Newspaper man. A man engaged in reporting or writing for newspapers. {1806–} — **1850** MATHEWS *Moneypenny* 38 You newspaper men know every thing. **1872** *Harper's Mag.* Dec. 140 Charles Nordhoff is a 'newspaper man,' and . . . understands what people want to know. **1898** *Kansas City Star* 22 Dec. 1/4 He left San Francisco for Cuba, where he was a newspaper man in the field. **1923** HERRICK *Lilla* 201 You had better stay here and explain your story to the newspaper men.

Newspaper office. In general, the quarters in which a newspaper is edited and printed; more specifically, the editorial or business office of a newspaper. — **1872** *Newton Kansan* 10 Oct. 4/2 The following notice is posted conspicuously in a newspaper-office out West. **1881** *Harper's Mag.* May 868/1 He had returned to New York and to his desk in a newspaper-office. **1891** *Ib.* Dec. 44/2, I came to a newspaper office, where I cornered a Directory. **1912** NICHOLSON *Hoosier Chron.* 89 In no other place can a young man so quickly attain wisdom as in a newspaper office.

Newspaper postage. Postage required for sending newspapers through the mail. — **1808** *Postal Laws & Reg.* 65 (Ernst). **1812** *Niles' Reg.* I. 361/1, [I] admit your publication to be a newspaper and to be rated at Newspaper Postage. **1833** *Amer. State P.: Post office* 355 In April, 1816, Congress established the rates as they now stand, to wit: . . . Newspaper postage continued as before, except that the postage was reduced to one cent, though conveyed more than one hundred miles.

Newspaper press. The collective aggregate of the newspapers published in a country, state, etc. {1840–} — **1841** in Buckingham *America* II. 333 The newspaper press of this country is distinguished from that of Europe in several essential particulars. **1859** WILMER *Press Gang* 383 Such, in effect, is that financiering system which is upheld by our newspaper press. **1872** MCCLELLAN *Golden State* 464 In its newspaper press California is at the head of every community in the world.

Newspaper reporter. One who collects news for a newspaper. — **1862** in *Sherman Lett.* (1894) 140 Take my advice, be hopeful, cheerful, polite to everybody, even a newspaper reporter. **1875** STOWE *We & Neighbors* 293 With not even a newspaper reporter to tell the people what they were talking about. **1883** BUNNER in *Century Mag.* Sept. 788/1 The newspaper reporter . . . measures the interest of a divorce case with a column-rule. **1910** 'O. HENRY' *Strictly Business* 87 The newspaper reporters dug out of their trunks the old broad-brimmed hats and leather belts.

Newspaper wrapper. A piece of strong paper, usually gummed and having a stamp embossed upon it, used for placing around newspapers sent by mail. — **1879** *Postal Laws* 69 The law allows no compensation to postmasters for the sale of postage-stamps, stamped-envelopes, newspaper-wrappers, or postal-cards. **1887** *Ib.* 23 [To] the Office of the Third Assistant Postmaster-General . . . is assigned . . . the care of the manufacture of adhesive stamps, postal cards, stamped envelopes, and newspaper wrappers. **1898** H. S. SCOTT *Roden's Corner* ii, A large table littered with newspaper wrappers.

+**Newspaporial,** *n.* A newspaper item. *Obs.* — **1787** *Mass. Centinel* 18 July 4/1 (*caption*), English Newspaporials. **1800** *Boston Commercial Gazette* 3 Feb. (*caption*). **1882** *Jrnl. Education* 27 April 274/1 *Newspaporial.*—We have received the first three numbers of the Alabama Progress, a weekly educational paper.

+**Newspaporial,** *a.* Of or pertaining to a newspaper. — **1794** *Columbian Centinel* 14 May 2/4 Newspaporial rule of three. **1853** in A. E. Lee *Hist. Columbus, Ohio* I. 474 In this day of newspaporial dearth, anything above the mud level will create a sensation.

‖**Newspaporialist.** A newspaper man; an editor. — **1871** *Vt. Hist. Gazetteer* II. 721/1 The Rev. Joshua Butts, . . . one of the Editors of the 'New York World,'—the popular newspaporialist.

Newsroom. a. A public room where newspapers can be consulted or news, esp. shipping news, can be obtained. {1817–} +**b.** A part of a newspaper office: (see quot. 1923). — (**a**) **1844** 'UNCLE SAM' *Peculiarities* II. 254 A grocery store . . . serves as a news-room and tavern. **1851** HAWTHORNE *Twice-told Tales* II. 172 Peter had long absented himself from his former lounging-places, at insurance-offices, news-rooms, and bookstores. **1873** F. HUDSON *Journalism* 189 On the establishment of the Merchants' News-room in the old State House . . . , much of the shipping intelligence of the port of Boston was collected by Samuel Topliff . . . [and]

placed on his books. (**b**) **1896** *Internat. Typogr. Union Proc.* 29/1 The Daily Democrat changed hands the first of June, and after a conference with the new publishers, they put a union foreman in their newsroom the first week in July. **1923** G. C. BASTIAN *Editing Day's News* 9 Inside the News Room . . . [we find the] Managing Editor, . . . Makeup Editor, . . . City Editor, . . . Telegraph Editor [etc.].

+**News stand.** A stand, usually in the lobby of a large building or on a street corner, at which newspapers are sold. — **1871** EGGLESTON *Hoosier Schoolm.* 77 You can buy trap-doors . . . dirt-cheap at the next news-stand. **1883** *Century Mag.* Aug. 572/1 Cheap weeklies . . . load every news-stand in the country. **1891** WELCH *Recoll. 1830–40* 251 Hawks was allowed the use of a space within the . . . lobby of the Post Office, where he placed a table . . . which he called a 'News-Stand.' **1904** 'O. HENRY' *Roads of Destiny* 294 At the age of eight he managed a news-stand for the Dago that owned it.

New state. +A state in the United States recently settled or formed. — **1790** PUTNAM in *Memoirs* 246 The New States forming in the western quarter. **1839** PLUMBE *Sk. Iowa* 59 They can make a better figure in the new states.

+**New tenor.** (See quot. 1891.) Also attrib. (Cf. OLD TENOR.) — **1738** *Duxbury Rec.* 262 Fifty pounds in bills of credit . . . , of the new tenor, for one year's service in the work of the Ministry. **1832** WILLIAMSON *Maine* II. 208 By act passed in March 1742, the new tenor bills were a tender, except in written contracts. **1891** *Cent.* 6233/1 *New tenor.* (*a*) In the financial history of Massachusetts and Rhode Island, a form of paper currency of the public issues which began in 1737 in the former colony and in 1740 in the latter, and of which each bill bore a declaration that it should be equal in value to a stated amount of coined silver or of gold coin. (*b*) In Massachusetts, a new form of such currency, issued in accordance with an act of the year 1741 and subsequent years, and differing but slightly from that above described.

||**Newtowner.** =NEWTOWN PIPPIN 2. — **1846** COOPER *Redskins* i, Their *poire beurrée*, here at Paris, . . . will not compare with the Newtowners we grow at Satanstoe.

+**Newtown Pippin.** Also **Newton Pippin.** [Newtown, Long Island, N.Y.]

1. The tree which bears the Newtown Pippin or Yellow Newtown apple. In full *Newtown Pippin tree.*

1760 WASHINGTON *Diaries* I. 147 Grafted 10 of the New Town Pippin. **1785** *Ib.* II. 435 Received two New Town and 2 Golden Pippin trees.

2. A variety of highly prized yellow winter apple; also, an apple of this variety.

1770 *Md. Hist. Mag.* XIII. 69 Things sent by the wagon 4 Barrills of Apples Russetins, Golden Pippins, Newtown Pippins & Parmains. *a***1817** DWIGHT *Travels* I. 43 The varieties of apple trees are: . . . Janneting, Newton pippin, Fall pippin. **1856** *Rep. Comm. Patents 1855: Agric.* 295 The winter varieties [of apples] are the 'Newtown Pippin,' 'Green Pippin' [etc.]. **1875** BURROUGHS *Winter Sunshine* 153 The youth recognizes . . . the bonny-cheeked Newton pippin. **1913** LONDON *Valley of Moon* 364 Every year he goes to England, and he takes a hundred carloads of yellow Newton pippins with him.

+**Newtown Spitzenburg.** Also **Newton Spitzemberg.** A Spitzenburg apple originally grown at Newtown, Long Island. — **1817** W. COXE *Fruit Trees* 126 Newton Spitzemberg. This apple is in some parts of this State called the English, or Burlington Spitzemberg: it was brought from Newton on Long-Island. **1847** IVES *New Eng. Fruit* 43 *Newtown Spitzenburg.*—The size is large, the form round and regular. **1863** *Rep. Comm. Agric. 1862* 168 Newtown Spitzenberg. . . . A very hardy tree; good bearer; fruit of superior quality; keeps and bears transportation well.

+**New Virginia.** Land west of the Allegheny Mountains, formerly a part of Virginia and now in West Virginia. *Obs.* — **1797** PRIEST *Travels* 155, I observed one of my fellow travellers . . . take every opportunity of singing forth the praises of New Virginia. **1817** PAULDING *Lett. from South* I. 112 The people [west of the Blue Ridge] call those east of the mountain Tuckahoes, and their country Old Virginia. They themselves are the Cohees, and their country New Virginia. **1822** WOODS *English Prairie* 231 A man, who boarded a short time at my house, said, he was born in Old Virginia; that he removed, with his father, over the mountains into New Virginia.

***New World.** The land in the Western Hemisphere, especially that part of it which became the United States of America. Also attrib.

1624 SMITH *Gen. Hist. Va.* I. 1 (*caption*), How Ancient Authors Report, the New-VVorld, Now Called America, was Discovered. **1837** *S. Lit. Messenger* III. 644 She would have paused before taking ship for the new world. **1867** HOLMES *Guardian Angel* 216 There is a double proportion of oxygen in the New-World air. **1872** McCLELLAN *Golden State* 33 The growth of civilization and colonization in what is termed the New World presents many striking features of interest. **1900** *Congress. Rec.* 11 Jan. 772/1 It was the silver of the New World which revolutionized the Old and broke up the feudal system. **1901** *Munsey's Mag.* XXIV. 530/1 These and other causes have acted and reacted to bring about, in this new world metropolis, . . . a crowding together of the poor.

New-Year cake. A cake prepared for New Year's Day. — **1809** IRVING *Knickerb.* VII. vi, He was the first that imprinted new year cakes with the mysterious hieroglyphics of the Cock and Breeches. **1850** S. WARNER *Wide, Wide World* viii, There's a very fine beefsteak, . . . cheese, preserved quinces,—with the usual complement of bread and toast and muffins, and doughnuts, and new-year cake.

+**New-year cookie.** A cookie made for new-year festivities. — **1808** IRVING, etc. *Salmagundi* xx. 522 These notable cakes, hight new-year-cookies, . . . originally were impressed on one side with the burly countenance of the illustrious Rip. **1850** S. F. COOPER *Rural Hours* 433 Cake-jars are filling up . . . with raisined olecokes, with spicy, New-Year cookies, all cakes belonging to the season. **1881** *Harper's Mag.* March 532/2, 'I want a dozen New-Year cookies,' she screamed.

***New Year's.** +Short for New Year's Day. — **1845** *Knickerb.* XXV. 128 He did not call New Year's, and we will not invite him. **1865** *Atlantic Mo.* XV. 450/1 [Fifteen dollars will] leave somethin' over for Almiry, who's always wantin' fresh ribbons about New Year's. **1883** *Harper's Mag.* Jan. 282/2 We got to give him a log-rollin'. . . . We'll have it on New Year's. **1909** *Springfield W. Repub.* 4 Nov. 1 The general elections are not now expected until after New Year's.

New Year's call. A social call made on New Year's Day. — **1861** [see CALLING]. **1870** TOMES *Bazar Book of Decorum* 240 New-Year's calls are very much like other visits, except that they are made exclusively by the male sex [etc.]. **1890** LANGFORD *Vigilante Days* (1912) 216 On New Year's day he . . . broke jail, and went to the sheriff's house, as he said upon entering, 'to make a New Year's call.'

New York. A city (named in 1664 after the Duke of York, previously called New Amsterdam) and a state, formerly a colony, in the eastern United States: Used attributively.

+**1.** Designating persons living in or identified with New York.

1862 NORTON *Army Lett.* 48 The Twenty-fifth New York is composed of New York roughs, Bowery boys, 'Dead Rabbits,' etc. **1868** *N.Y. Herald* 24 July 4/5 How . . . aware the New York pickpockets have become. **1881** *Harper's Mag.* May 859/1 You can tell a New York girl at a glance when you meet her in the West or the South. **1894** ROBLEY *Bourbon Co., Kansas* 7 These various tribes of New York Indians, consisting of the remnants of the Senecas, Onondagas, Cayugas [etc.] . . . were called the 'Six Nations.' **1905** *Independent* 30 Nov. 1279/2 This is the New York Jew as he is, with his faults and his virtues.

2. + **a.** In the names of fruits and other plants.

1817 W. COXE *Fruit Trees* 117 Monstrous Pippin, or New-York Gloria Mundi. This apple originated on Long Island, state of New-York; it is of an uncommonly large size. **1849** *New Eng. Farmer* I. 214 The first is a very large apple, resembling what was called, forty years ago, the *New York Greening.* **1843** TORREY *Flora N.Y.* II. 497 *Aspidium Noveboracense.* . . . New-York Shield-fern. Moist woods and thickets. **1771** *Copley-Pelham Lett.* 157, I mentioned in a former letter . . . some fine Large New York Water Melons.

+**b.** In the names of fishes and oysters.

See also NEW YORK SHINER.

1818 *Amer. Monthly Mag.* II. 295 New-York Black-Fish. . . . The black-fish is one of the excellent edible fishes of the New-York market. **1875** *Chicago Tribune* 1 Sept. 5/4 The luscious New York counts, and all the other choice varieties [of oysters], will be kept through the season. **1855** BAIRD in *Smithsonian Rep.* 349 The New York Flat-Fish. Winter Flounder. *Platessa plana.* **1814** MITCHILL *Fishes N.Y.* 439 New York Gudgeon. *Esox flavulus.* . . . A pretty little fish. **1842** *Nat. Hist. N.Y., Zoology* IV. 301 The New York Plaice . . . is considered as a delicate article of food. **1839** STORER *Mass. Fishes* 30 *Gasterosteus Noveboracensis.* The New York Stickleback.

+**c.** In the names of animals.

1842 *Nat. Hist. N.Y., Zoology* I. 36 The New-York Ermine. *Putorius Noveboracensis.* . . . [This animal destroys] hordes of mice. **1842** *Ib.* I. 140 (Index), New York Weasel, 36.

+**d.** In the names of birds.

1844 *Nat. Hist. N.Y., Zoology* II. 263 The New-York Rail, *Ortygometra noveboracensis*, . . . is distributed through the United States in the interior to the Rocky mountains. **1839** PEABODY *Mass. Birds* 306 The New York Thrush, *Turdus Noveboracensis.* **1917** *Birds of Amer.* III. 154 New York Warbler. . . . By some observers, the song of this species is considered more musical than that of the Louisiana Water-Thrush. **1844** *Nat. Hist. N.Y., Zoology* II. 78 The New York Water Thrush. *Seiurus Noveboracensis.* . . . This musical little bird . . . is partial to the neighborhood of brooks, in search of insects.

+**3.** In special combinations.

New York cracker, a kind of hard biscuit made in New York; *N.Y. money*, =NEW YORK CURRENCY; *N.Y. price*, the price which a commodity will bring on the New York exchange.

1846 W. G. STEWART *Altowan* I. 141 Their contents consisted of . . . the biscuit root, tasting exactly like a New York cracker newly baked. **1731** HEMPSTEAD *Diary* 232 In the Eve I put up into my portmantle . . . £58 in our bills of Cr. . . . [and] about 5 or £6 N york Mony. **1872** TICE *Over Plains* 136, $2.04 cents per bushel . . . was about New York price for prime white wheat.

+**New York bat.** The red bat (*Nycteris borealis*), common in eastern North America. — **1771** PENNANT *Synopsis* 367 New York Bat with a head shaped like that of a mouse, top of the nose a little bifid: ears short, broad, and rounded. **1826** GODMAN *Nat. Hist.* I. 68 New York Bat. . . . This species is found in the state of New York, Pennsylvania, New Jersey, on the Missouri, &c. **1842** *Nat. Hist. N.Y., Zoology* I. 6 The New-York Bat . . . is the most common species in our State.

+**New York currency.** Currency used in New York before the adoption of the Constitution and current for some years afterward. (Cf. NEW YORK SHILLING.) — **1756** ROGERS *Jrnls.* 14 According to the General's orders, my company was to consist of sixty privates, at 3s. New York currency *per* day. **1831** SLOCOMB *Amer. Calculator* 86 The dollar is reckoned in New York and N. Carolina 8s. od.=4/10 New York currency.

+**New Yorker.** A native or inhabitant of the city or state of New York.

1756 WASHINGTON *Writings* I. 315 The Jerseys and New Yorkers, I do not remember what it is they give [to their soldiers]. **1792** POPE *Tour S. & W.* 28 At 10 o'Clock espied a Shingle roofed House, occupied by a Family of New-Yorkers. **1833** J. E. ALEXANDER *Transatlantic Sk.* II. 119 They must be blockaded, I swear, said a New Yorker to me. **1884** MATTHEWS & BUNNER *In Partnership* 127 'Are you a New Yorker, sir?' 'From the north of the State.' **1916** WILSON *Somewhere* 398 The New Yorker was now sunk deep in a trance.

‖**New Yorkeress.** A female New Yorker. — **1871** HOWELLS *Wedding Journey* i. 10 The New-Yorkeress was stylish, undeniably effective.

+**New Yorkese.** A variety of English regarded as characteristic of residents of New York City. (Cf. BOSTONESE 2.) — **1894** *Harper's Mag.* Oct. 695/1 'Café' . . . is New-Yorkese for dram-shop. *a***1910** 'O. HENRY' *Rolling Stones* (1915) 178 'Address' is New Yorkese for 'home.'

‖**New Yorkish,** *a.* Characteristic of New York. — **1894** HOWELLS in *Harper's Mag.* May 822/2 The Nation was always more Bostonian than New-Yorkish by nature.

+**New-Yorkize,** *v. tr.* To give (something or someone) the character or appearance of the institutions or people of New York City. — **1867** *Atlantic Mo.* March 342/2 What a reproach to Tammany, that a politician in far-off Chicago should have been the first to see the mode of New-Yorkizing the politics of the South! **1871** HOWELLS *Wedding Journey* i. 33 Broadway had filled her length with . . . that easily distinguishable class of lately New-Yorkized people from other places.

+**New York shilling.** A coin of the New York currency. — **1834** *Knickerb.* III. 349 A levy was a coin; corresponding . . . to a New York shilling. **1836** CROCKETT *Exploits* 19 [The barkeeper] knew that a coon was as good a legal tender for a quart in the west, as a New York shilling, any day in the year.

+**New York shiner.** The golden shiner (*Notemigonus crysoleucas*), a silvery fish common in the eastern United States. — **1814** MITCHILL *Fishes N.Y.* 459 New York Shiner. *Cyprinus crysoleucas*. . . . Lives in the ponds. **1839** STORER *Mass. Fishes* 89 The New York Shiner . . . is generally taken for pickerel bait, and is the best bait for that fish. **1842** *Nat. Hist. N.Y., Zoology* IV. 204 The New York Shiner . . . is common in all the fresh-water streams of this and adjoining States. **1856** *Porter's Spirit of Times* 20 Dec. 253/2 [Pike-perch] can also be trolled for, successfully, with a frog, a New York shiner, or a minnow on spinning tackle.

+**New York Stock Exchange.** An organization of brokers in New York for buying and selling securities according to established rules; also, the place where this trading is done. Also attrib. (Cf. EXCHANGE 1.)

The New York stock exchange is the oldest of its kind in the United States. On May 17, 1792, twenty-four brokers met on a spot across from 60 Wall St., and drew up a working agreement. Formal organization was effected in 1817.

[**1842** (*title*), Report of the Committee of the New York Stock and Exchange Board.] **1862** *Amer. Ann. Cycl. 1861* 307/2 The highest, lowest, and average quotations for 1859, 1860, and 1861, at the New York Stock Exchange for the stocks most largely dealt in. **1865** H. HAMON (*title*), New York Stock Exchange Manual. **1900** NELSON *A B C Wall St.* 141 New York Stock Exchange seats command . . . $40,000. **1925** (*title*), Constitution of the New York Stock Exchange. Adopted . . . June 10, 1925.

Next man. +Anyone taken at random; the next comer. Usually in comparative phrases introduced by *as*. — **1857** *Lawrence* (Kan.) *Republican* 18 June 2 The Judge . . . will probably talk as long to a crowd without tiring them as the next man. **1902** S. G. FISHER *True Hist. Amer. Revol.* 146 We do not surrender our property to the next man who is an abler business manager. **1908** *N.Y. Ev. Post* 29 June 4 Mr. Bryan knows this as well as the next man.

+**Nez Percé.** [Fr. 'pierced nose,' though there is no proof that the Nez Percé Indians practiced nose-piercing.] An Indian of the principal tribe of the Shahaptian family, discovered by Lewis and Clark in 1805 in what is now western Idaho; also, pl., the tribe. (Cf. PIERCED NOSE.)

*c***1836** CATLIN *Indians* II. 108 The *Nez Percés* who inhabit the upper waters and mountainous parts of the Columbia, are a part of this tribe [Iroquois], though they are seldom known to flatten the head. **1837** IRVING *Bonneville* I. 169 In another part of the field of action, a Nez Percé had crouched behind the trunk of a fallen tree, and kept up a galling fire from covert. **1843** MARRYAT *M. Violet* x, We were divided into four war-parties: one which acted . . . against the Cayuses and Nez-percés, at the forks of the Buona Ventura and Calumet rivers. **1855** KIP *Diary of Indian Council* 11 The Nez Perces, or pierced-nose Indians, received their name from the early traders and trappers, but they call themselves by the name of Chipunish. **1884** BARROWS *Oregon* 121 The Rev. Mr. Parker joined himself to the Nez Percés, and under their . . . protection, threaded his way to Walla Walla.

b. Attrib. with *Flathead, Indian, prisoner,* etc.

1844 LEE & FROST *Oregon* x. 109 Four Indians, from beyond the Rocky Mountains, belonging to . . . the 'Nez Percé' tribe, accompanied some of the white trappers. **1845** FRÉMONT *Exped.* 183 A small town of Nez Percé Indians gave an inhabited . . . appearance to the station. **1877** in *Century Mag.* XXVIII. 142/1 On account of the cost of transportation of the Nez-Percé prisoners to the Pacific coast, I deem it best to retain them. **1884** BARROWS *Oregon* 121 [Whitman and Parker] met the Nez Percé Flat-Heads. **1910** HODGE *Amer. Indians* II. 67/1 Practically the only rupture in these relations was the Nez Percé war of 1877.

N.G., *n.* and *a.* Abbreviation for 'no go' or 'no good.' *colloq.* (Cf. GO *n.* 5.)

1840 *St. Louis D. Pennant* 20 June (Th.), The bells, boys, and engines tried to get up a fire last night, but it was N.G. **1888** *Cincinnati W. Gazette* 22 Feb. (F.), Hill claims . . . that he will make the farmers sweat who have been asserting that his claim was N.G. **1896** *N.Y. Dramatic News* 4 April 8/1 Willoughby's N.G. Check. **1898** *Congress. Rec.* App. 11 Jan. 37/2 John F. Atkinson, discharged July 1, 1894. N.G.; lives in Indiana. **1904** *N.Y. Times* 14 May 9 The store people sent the check to the bank, and were astonished when it was sent back with the ominous letters 'N.G.' marked across it.

+**Niagara.** [Iroquoian. Name of a river and a famous waterfall between Lakes Erie and Ontario.]

1. In transferred uses.

1843 STEPHENS *High Life N.Y.* II. 243 The winders were . . . kivered from top tu bottom with a hull Niagara of red silk. **1872** 'MARK TWAIN' *Roughing It* 530 The flaming torrent . . . remains there [in the Hawaiian Islands] to-day all seamed, and frothed, and rippled, a petrified Niagara. **1889** — *Conn. Yankee* 224 An amazing kind of a surprise party it was, too . . . [with] cyclones of frantic joy, and whole Niagaras of happy tears. **1912** COBB *Back Home* 321 Rivers of red pop had already flowed, Niagaras of lager beer and stick gin had been swallowed up.

2. *attrib.* **a.** With *cane, frontier, roar.*

1871 HOWELLS *Wedding Journey* 28 Down the swarming length of Broadway . . . the Niagara roar swelled and swelled from those human rapids. **1881** *Harper's Mag.* March 538/2 In the war of 1812 . . . [Stephen Van Rensselaer was] a general on the Niagara frontier. **1891** WELCH *Recoll. 1830–40* 147 He wore a short, drab brown, sack coat, the prevailing fashion of those days, his hands stuck in his low coat pockets, his right hand holding a crooked neck Niagara cane, wrong end up, handle in the pocket.

b. In specific names: (see quotations).

1916 ALWOOD, etc. *Chemical Comp. Amer. Grapes* 6 [Grapes tested by government analysts include] Niagara, North Bass, Ohio. **1842** *Nat. Hist. N.Y., Zoology* IV. 394 The Niagara Gudgeon. *Gobio cataractae*. . . . Body elongated and rounded. **1843** TORREY *Flora N.Y.* II. 67 *Micromeria glabella*. . . . Niagara Thyme. . . . On calcareous rocks, about the Falls of Niagara; Goat Island, and on Table Rock.

***Nibbler.** +=CONNER. (Cf. BLUE PERCH and NIPPER 3.) — **1842** *Nat. Hist. N.Y., Zoology* IV. 173 The Bergall has various popular names: Nibbler, from its vexatious nibbling at the bait thrown out for other fishes [etc.]. **1859** BARTLETT 58 *Burgall, (Ctenolabrus ceruleus)*. . . . Other names . . . are Nibbler, . . . and in New England, those of Blue Perch and Conner.

+**Nicholite, Nicolite.** A member of a religious sect in some respects resembling Quakers. In full *Nicholite Quaker. Obs.* — **1786** *Md. Journal* 21 Feb. (Th.), Not a Presbyterian, Baptist, Methodist, Dunker, Menonist, Nicolite nor even the peaceable old Quaker can now be prevailed with to contribute a single farthing towards the good design. **1804** DOW *Journal* (1814) 196 At night I lodged with one of the Nicholites, a kind of Quakers who do not feel free to wear coloured cloaths. *a***1870** CHIPMAN *Notes on Bartlett* 292 *Nicholites, Nicholite Quakers*. A sect in and about Delaware, about 1750–90.

***Nick.**[1]

1. A notch made in the ear of an animal as a mark of ownership. *Obs.*

1652 *Md. Archives* X. 304 One Cowe calfe . . . the right Eare being cropt and the left Eare underkeeled with a nick in the Said Eare above. **1698** *N.C. Col. Rec.* I. 495 Ralph ffletcher Sener Recorded His Marke being on ye Right Eare a Slet . . . and ond ye Left a nick. **1709** *Portsmouth Rec.* 261 Two nicks . . . under the right ear. **1799** in Rothert *Muhlenberg Co.* 44 Peter Lyons' stockmark: two smooth crops and a nick under each ear.

2. An instance of crossbreeding in which a superior offspring results.

1889 WARFIELD *Cattle-Breed* 26 This thing of a 'nick,' or a successful cross, is as difficult as determining beforehand how much an animal will inherit from one or the other of its parents. **1897** *Outing* XXIX. 484/1 In time Star, a good one in the field, was bred to Druid, and Mr. Wells made a record with this nick.

+**Nick.**[2] Short for NICKEL 2. *colloq. Obs.* — **1857** *N.Y. Herald* 27 May 5/2 The bags containing the 'Nicks' were neat little canvass [*sic*] arrangements, each of which held five hundred [of the new coins].

Nickel.

1. A hard whitish metal closely related to cobalt {1755–}; +esp. used in the manufacture of coins. Also attrib.

[**1857** *Statutes at Large* XI. 163 The said cent shall be composed of eighty-eight per centum of copper and twelve per centum of nickel, of such shape and device as may be fixed by the director of the mint.] **1866** *Wkly. New Mexican* 18 Aug. 1/4 At Philadelphia . . . the nickel three and five cent coins, can be had in exchange for gold and silver coins. **1883** in Wells *Pract. Economics* (1885) 126 A single establishment in Connecticut uses of nickel annually three times the amount that has been imported into this country.

+**2.** One of various coins made in part of nickel. (Cf. THREE-CENT *a.*) **a.** A one-cent piece authorized in 1857 and discontinued in 1864. *Obs.* (Cf. NICKEL CENT.)

1857 *N.Y. Herald* 27 May 4/6 'Nary red' will soon be an obsolete phrase among the 'boys,' and 'nary nickel' will take its place. **1858** HOLMES *Autocrat* 257 A picture as big as a copper, or a 'nickel,' rather. **1863** *Chicago Tribune* 1 May 2/3 The heavy coinage of 'nickels' still continues, the number last week made at the mint in Philadelphia being 53,000.

+**b.** A five-cent piece made of three parts copper and one part nickel; also, a trifling sum of money. Also fig.

See also FIVE-CENT NICKEL and FIVE-CENT PIECE, note. Cf. HALF-DIME.

1881 CHASE *Editor's Run in N. Mex.* 111 Stock men will not make money by selling victuals or squeezing nickels. **1882** *Century Mag.* Feb. 566/1 The South will learn . . . the difference between a cent and a nickel. **1894** FORD *P. Stirling* 341 It is not fair, because a man's pockets are filled with nickels instead of eagles, that he shall not have the same right . . . to drink at any time. **1903** ALDRICH *Ponkapog P.* 120 Reaching out with some other man's hat for the stray nickel of your sympathy.

attrib. **1896** SHINN *Story of Mine* 1 Pistols and bandits abound in a nickel-novel atmosphere. **1914** LOWRY *Himself* 165 Ragged and dirty children attending 'nickel shows' and buying quantities of cheap candy.

+**Nickel cent.** A one-cent coin made in part of nickel. *Obs.* (Cf. NICKEL 2 a.) — **1863** 'G. HAMILTON' *Gala-Days* 305, I shall by and by throw you a paltry nickel cent for your tropical dreams. **1872** *Harper's Mag.* Aug. 347/1 To make amends, he gave it a handful of nickel cents.

+**Nickel-in-the-slot machine.** A machine in which, by the insertion of a nickel in a slot, certain gears are, or may be, moved, thereby releasing a bar of candy, gum, etc. (Cf. SLOT MACHINE.) — **1893** *Harper's Mag.* March 494 [In Jacksonville] there were the same . . . nickel-in-the-slot machines [as in Asbury Park]. [**1895** *N.Y. Dramatic News* 26 Oct. 5/1 A nickle in the slot chewing gum machine had fallen from a six-story window.] **1914** *Calif. Appellate Rep.* XXIII. 769 The statute under discussion relates only to gambling machines, and does not purport to make the business of manufacturing 'coin operating machines commonly known as nickel-in-the-slot machines' unlawful.

+**Nickelodeon.** [f. NICKEL 2 b.] **a.** A theater or show making an admission charge of five cents. **b.** (See quot. 1913.) — **1888** *Boston Transcript* 26 Nov. 5/7 Austin's Nickelodeon. . . . Open Day and Evening. Shows Hourly. **1908** *World To-day* Oct. 1053/1 There is no town of any size in the United States which does not contain at least one nickelodeon [moving-picture show]. **1913** *Stand.* 1673/2 *Nickelodeon*, . . . a place of amusement generally charging no admission fee, containing various automatic machines, such as cinematographs, graphophones, etc., which may be used by patrons for a small charge.

Nicker tree, Nickar tree. {1707–, in W. Indies} +The Kentucky coffee tree, *Gymnocladus dioica*. (Cf. KENTUCKY 4 a.) — **1785** MARSHALL *Amer. Grove* 56 The Species with us, *Guilandina dioica*, Canadian dioiceous Bonduc, or Nickar Tree, . . . is said to grow plenty [in Kentucky], and is called the Coffee or Mahogany tree. **1890** *Amer. Notes & Q.* IV. 286 The name Nickar Tree is locally given in the United States to the Kentucky coffee tree. **1897** SUDWORTH *Arborescent Flora* 255 *Gymnocladus dioicus*. . . . Coffeetree. . . . [Also called] Nickertree (Tenn.).

Nick-tailed, *a.* Of a horse: Having the tail nicked. — **1841** *S. Lit. Messenger* VII. 219/1 Brenda, mounted on Paul Clifford, nick-tailed sorrel pacer. **1852** *Ib.* XVIII. 753/2 The horse, a nick-tailed trotter, Tom had raffled off. **1867** G. W. HARRIS *Sut Lovingood* 19 A nick tailed, bow necked, long, poor, pale sorrel horse.

+**Nifty,** *a.* [Origin obscure.] Neat, stylish, smart. Also comb. *slang.*

1865 HARTE *Poems* (1871) 103 Here comes Rosey's new turn-out! Smart! You bet your life 'twas that! Nifty! (short for *magnificat*). **1872** 'MARK TWAIN' *Roughing It* 334 He was always nifty himself, and so you bet his funeral ain't going to be no slouch. **1897** LEWIS *Wolfville* 88 Take it all over, he's a nifty-lookin' savage. **1902** *Boston Globe* 15 Sept. 6/6 'Nifty' is slang and means 'Good in style and appearance.' **1913** *Emporia Gazette* 6 Sept., A nifty little phrase it was.

Nig, *n.* {1879–} +**1.** Short for NIGGER 1. *slang.* +**2.** *All right on the nig*, holding views favorable to slavery. *slang.* (Cf. GOOSE 3, 5 b.) — (1) **1840** *Picayune* 20 Sept 2/2 Two little nigs . . . had a most scientific set-to at the corner. **1869** in Dumont *Benedict's Songster* 49, I'm a piccaniny nig, I am somewhat on a jig. **1872** *Fla. Plantation Rec.* 198 Perhaps it would pay to get some common whiskey for the nigs. **1905** PRINGLE *Rice Planter* 160 Her manner is what the 'nigs' call 'stiff.' (2) **1856** *Porter's Spirit of Times* 25 Oct. 132/3 The once all-absorbing 'goose question' has completely 'gin in,' and the only thing now necessary to know is, 'Is your man all right on the *nig?*'

+**Nig,** *v. intr.* Colloquial contraction of RENIG *v.* — **1829** *Mass. Spy* 10 June (Th.), If you hadn't a nig'd . . . you might have had better luck. **1859** *Harper's Mag.* March 568/2 If you have got any trumps you had better play them and not undertake to nig any more!

Nigger, *n.* Also **niger, niggur.**

I. 1.=NEGRO 1. *colloq.* and *S.* {1786–}

The pronunciation indicated by the spelling *nigger* is often the result of carelessness or ignorance, but as a rule it carries with it a derogatory implication. (Cf. NEGRO, note, and quots. 1834 and 1866.)

1700 SEWALL *Diary* II. 19 *n.*, 'Tis to be feared, we have no other kind of Title to our *Nigers*. **1834** LIEBER *Lett. to Gentleman in Germany* 90 A negro boy under my window [in Phila.] calls a lad of the same race, by way of reproach, '*nigger*.' **1838** COOPER *Homeward B.* xxvii, Them niggers . . . have had their fingers in everything. **1866** *Atlantic Mo.* July 79/1 When they call each other 'nigger,' the familiar term of opprobrium is applied with all the malice of a sting. **1884** 'MARK TWAIN' *H. Finn* 8 That nigger was corked up and had to take a back seat. **1921** PAINE *Comr. Rolling Ocean* 141, I drifted in for a minute to listen to a nigger with a bully voice.

+**b.** *transf.* A servant; one who performs drudgery.

1843 'CARLTON' *New Purchase* I. 63 Right hard to get gals here, mam—folks has to be their own niggurs, mam. **1846** THORPE *Myst. Backwoods* 122 The rifle won't make a man a living now—he must turn nigger and work. **1883** HAY *Bread-Winners* 20, I wasn't born to make a nigger of myself. **1896** HARRIS *Sister Jane* 135 'She is doing what she wants to do—cooking and helping around.' . . . 'She's dar playin' de nigger.'

+**2.** A quality, manner of speech, etc., characteristic of Negroes.

1825 NEAL *Bro. Jonathan* I. 414 Cotch!—I reckon!—clear nigger that. **1853** 'PAXTON' *Yankee in Texas* 61 Huntin' and fishin' on that day [Sunday] wer *clar* nigger, and went agin him. **1894** 'MARK TWAIN' *P. Wilson* x, He found the 'nigger' in him involuntarily giving the road.

+**3.** *transf.* A term of opprobrium applied to persons of other races. Also in comb.

1840 SIMMS *Border Beagles* II. 85 They're afraid of me, the niggers. . . . D—n 'em, I don't mind half-a-dozen of them, fair front and no dodging. **1850** GARRARD *Wah-To-Yah* viii. 109 Did they touch you, the darned niggurs? *Ib.* xviii. 217, I *cached*—I did—an' the niggurs made fur the prairie with my animals. **1881** MCLEAN *Cape Cod Folks* 146 The Indians rather set themselves up above the benighted Wallencampers, . . . while they, in turn, made derisive allusions to the 'Nigger-camp' minister.

+**4. a.** (See quot. 1875.) **b.** A fault or defect in the insulating covering of an electrical conductor which may cause a short circuit. *colloq.* **c.** A steam ram or plunger used in a sawmill for turning or adjusting a log on the carriage.

1875 KNIGHT 1526/2 *Nigger*, . . . a steam-engine employed in hoisting; especially on shipboard and on the Western and Southern rivers. **1886** *Scientific Amer.* LIV. 308/3 The consequence of neglect might be that what the workmen call 'a nigger' would get into the armature, and burn it so as to destroy its service. **1910** WHITE *Rules of Game* 32 When the car had flown back to its starting-point, the 'nigger' rose from obscurity to turn the log half-way round.

II. *attrib.* (passing into *adj.*) and *comb.*

5. Designating persons belonging to the Negro race. (Cf. NEGRO 3 e.)

1825 NEAL *Bro. Jonathan* III. 207 Nobody there, I guess—but a nigger boy. **1837** *Knickerb.* IX. 270 The fair damsel . . . was none other than a nigger wench, baking cassaba bread on an old rusty griddle. **1852** STOWE *Uncle Tom* xv, A vest like this . . . does for a poor nigger-fellow like me. **1865** TROWBRIDGE *Three Scouts* 146 The Abolition generals don't object to nigger body-servants. **1867** LOCKE *Swingin' Round* 17, I see horrid visions! On the Camden and Amboy, nigger brakesmen! **1884** HARRIS *Mingo* 198 When I got out there, I saw a great big nigger man. **1900** *Congress. Rec.* 5 Feb. 1507/1 It is bad enough that North Carolina should have the only nigger Congressman.

6. Designating articles used by or in connection with Negro slaves. (Cf. NEGRO 3 b.)

1861 NEWELL *Orpheus C. Kerr* I. 78 Last summer at the North I bought, Some nigger hats and shoes. **1862** *Ill. Agric. Soc. Trans.* V. 507 There is no reason why we cannot compete with the bar-share plow, the nigger-hoes, and the unskillful labor of the Southern cotton States. **1867** LOCKE *Swingin' Round* 151 He generally stood over em with a nigger whip.

7. Designating places, groups of people, etc., inhabited by or composed of Negroes. (Cf. NEGRO 3 c.)

1863 NORTON *Army Lett.* 142 He says there is a nigger regiment near him with black commissioned officers. **1898** PAGE *Red Rock* 226, I'll turn 'em out in the road and make their place a nigger settlement. **1902** HARBEN *A. Daniel* 94 They put a ball an' chain to one of his ankles an' sent 'im out with the nigger gang.

8. In the specific names of (1) fishes, (2) birds, and (3) plants.

(1) **1859** BAGBY *Old Va. Gentleman* (1938) 294 Great Ketching of Flat-Back, Mullet, and Nigger-Knockers in the Appomattox. **1884** GOODE,

etc. *Fisheries* I. 618 The 'Cut-lips,' 'Day Chub,' or 'Nigger Chub,' . . . [is] found in abundance only in the basin of the Susquehanna. **1888** GOODE *Amer. Fishes* 321 Next in importance . . . comes the Flat Fish, *Pseudopleuronectes Americanus*. . . . New York anglers call it the 'Nigger Fish.' **1896** JORDAN & EVERMANN *Check-List Fishes* 265 Cut-lips; Nigger Chub; Nigger Dick. . . . Abundant in the basins of the Susquehanna, Hudson, Potomac, James, Roanoke, and Kanawha.

(2) **1876** *Fur, Fin, & Feather* Sept. 101/2 The gray-duck, shell-drake and teal . . . are obliged to tolerate in their society that . . . stupid, tough, shot-resisting thing, which is vulgarly called 'nigger duck.' **1917** *Birds of Amer.* I. 97/2 The Cormorants have many local names, such as 'Shag,' 'Lawyer,' and 'Nigger Goose.'

(3) **1894** *Amer. Folk-Lore* VII. 92 *Eupatorium purpureum*, nigger-weed, queen-of-the-meadow, Ind. *Ib.* 103 *Carex.* sp., nigger-wool, Neb.

+**9.** In special combinations.

Nigger corner, a portion of a church or hall reserved for the use of Negroes; *n. crib*, =NEGRO CAR; *n. talk*, credulous gossip or exaggeration emanating from Negroes; *n. teacher*, a white person, usually from the North, serving as a teacher for Negroes in the South.

1894 'MARK TWAIN' *P. Wilson* xxi, In the 'nigger corner' sat Chambers. **1849** A. MACKAY *Western World* I. 102 'But where have you put him [a Negro]?' . . . 'Put him?—in the nigger crib, to be sure.' **1866** C. H. SMITH *Bill Arp* 105 All else was rumor and nigger talk. **1880** TOURGEE *Bricks* 163 A good many gentlemen called in to see the school . . . , merely desirous to see the pretty Yankee 'nigger teachers.'

III. Phrases and expressions.

10. *To let off a little nigger*, to act in the manner of a Negro. *colloq. Obs.*

1828 *Yankee* May 175/1 You would swear from the words and sounds . . . that the fellow was going to tear somebody limb from limb. . . . No such thing . . . he is only letting off a little nigger.

+**11.** *To work like a nigger* (or variant of this), to work very hard. *colloq.*

1836 GILMAN *Recoll.* (1838) 189, I have toiled night and day, I've worked like a nigger, and more than a nigger. **1880** 'MARK TWAIN' *Tramp Abroad* 40 He laid into his work like a nigger. **1901** MERWIN & WEBSTER *Calumet 'K'* 20, I'd been working like a nigger 'most five months.

+**12.** *A nigger in the woodpile* (or *fence*), a concealed or inconspicuous but highly important fact, factor, or 'catch' in an account, proposal, etc. *colloq.*

1861 in Moore *Rebellion Rec.* I. III. 21 He soon discovered 'the nigger in the woodpile.' **1876** *Congress. Rec.* 4 Aug. 5153/1 If some one should say . . . that there was some 'nigger in the wood-pile,' some 'cat in the bag,' some motive to actuate me. *a*1882 WEED *Autobiog.* 477, I'll find out in the course of the day what this means. There's a nigger in the fence somewhere. **1884** HARRIS *Mingo* 186 Once 'twas the nigger in the woodpile; now it's the nigger in the steeple. **1900** *Congress. Rec.* 6 Feb. 1571/2 Louisiana sugar planters had found a new 'nigger in the wood pile,' who was not as useful as the one they have now. **1904** *N.Y. Herald* 13 Feb. 8 There is evidently a 'nigger in the woodpile'—and he should be smoked out. **1911** QUICK *Yellowstone Nights* 286 He's always looking for a nigger in the fence.

+**Nigger,** *v.*

1. *To nigger off*, to burn (a log) in two, or to burn off a piece or length of a log. Also *vbl. n. colloq.*

1833 S. SMITH *Life J. Downing* 22 He laid sticks across the large logs that were too heavy to move, and *niggered* them off with fire, and then roolled them up in piles and sot fire to 'em again. **1843** 'CARLTON' *New Purchase* I. 188 In addition to the 'niggering off,' it became necessary as the cold increased, to chop off logs. *Ib.*, Niggering belongs mainly to very large timber, and pertains rather to the science of log-rolling than of preparing fuel. **1887** J. KIRKLAND *Zury* 38 This [tree-trunk] he would measure off in about twenty-foot lengths, and at the end of each length he would build a fire, which . . . would sever the log at that point, leaving it in lengths which could be hauled by a stout team over the snow to the place where they might be needed. This method of severing logs is called in the vernacular 'niggering them off,' whether because of its laziness, or of the blackness of the resulting heads.

2. *To nigger out*, (see quotation.) *Obs.*

1859 BARTLETT 292 To *nigger out* land, signifies, in Southern phraseology, to exhaust land by the mode of tilling without fertilization pursued in the slave States.

3. *To nigger it*, to live meagerly or barely.

1857 J. HYDE *Mormonism* 120 Many of the people express satisfaction in seeing these 'better-dressed fellers' obliged to 'nigger it' as well as themselves. **1878** BEADLE *Western Wilds* 349 Was it not more of an honor to be the 'bishop's fourth' . . . than the 'slavey' of a poor mechanic, to 'nigger it on love and starvation?'

Nigger baby. +**1.** (See quotation.) +**2.** *pl. local.* (See quotation.) — (1) **1871** DE VERE 117 Among the cant words produced by the late Civil War, nigger babies also became very popular; the term originated with the veterans serving under the Confederate General Hardee, who gave that name to the enormous projectiles thrown into the city of Charlestown by the Swamp Angel of General Gillmore, as his monster-gun in the swamps was ironically called. (2) **1901** JEPSON *Flora of Western Middle Calif.* 129 *S[isyrinchium] bellum.* Blue-eyed grass. Nigger-babies. . . . Very common throughout California. Mar.–April.

+**Nigger-chaser.** A squiblike form of fireworks which when ignited zigzags over the ground. *colloq.* — **1883** PECK *Bad Boy* 22, I had a lot of rockets and Roman candles, and six pin-wheels, and a lot of nigger chasers. **1921** MULFORD *Bar-20 Three* xvi. 217 Most likely they'll be nigger-chasers, th' way some folk'll be steppin' lively to get out of th' way.

+**Nigger-engine.** =NIGGER *n.* 4 a. — **1878** BEADLE *Western Wilds* 378 Then oaths, spars, 'nigger-engine' and all the other available machinery were set in operation. **1882** *Harper's Mag.* Jan. 175/2 One of the 'nigger' engines is suddenly called into service to tighten a two-inch rope, or wind up a discarded cable.

+**Niggerhead.** (See also NEGROHEAD.)

1. A stone or rock: (see quot. 1886).

1847 HOWE *Hist. Coll. Ohio* 569 It was a saw mill, with a small pair of stones attached, made of boulders, or 'nigger heads,' as they are commonly called. **1886** *Smithsonian Inst. Rep.* II. 523 *Nigger head.* (1) The black concretionary nodules found in granite; (2) Any hard, dark, colored rock weathering out with rounded nodules or bowlders; (3) Slaty rock associated with sandstone. A quarryman's term. **1916** SANDBURG *Chicago Poems* 41 A boy passes and throws a niggerhead that chips off the end of the nose [of a statue].

+**2.** (See quot. 1871.) *Obs.* Also attrib.

1868 *N.Y. Herald* 6 July 3/2 The d—d radical party, with its niggerhead Congress. **1871** DE VERE 281 They were Democrats, and retorted upon violent Union men by calling them Niggerheads.

+**3.** (See quot. 1859.)

1859 BARTLETT 292 *Nigger Heads*, the tussocks or knotted masses of the roots of sedges and ferns projecting above the wet surface of a swamp. South. **1892** A. E. LEE *Hist. Columbus, Ohio* I. 274 Hummocks, called in the borough dialect 'nigger-heads,' formed by tufts of swamp grass. **1908** BEACH *Barrier* 75 Five men wound up the valley . . . emerging from sombre thickets of fir to flounder across wide pastures of 'nigger-heads.'

+**4. a.** The black-eyed Susan *Rudbeckia hirta.* +**b.** The greenbrier, *Smilax rotundifolia.*

1899 COULTER *Flora of Indiana* 984 *R[udbeckia] hirta.* Black-eyed Susan. Meadow Cone Flower. Nigger-head. . . . Flowers from early in June until the late frosts. **1913** BRITTON & BROWN *Flora N.A.* III. 470 Black Eyed Susan. . . . Prairies and plains. . . . [Also called] Nigger- or darkey-head. **1923** CLUTE *Dict. Amer. Plant Names* 15 *S[milax] rotundifolia* [is called] Cat-brier, greenbrier, . . . nigger-head, devil's hop-vine [etc.].

+**5.** A cactus of the genus *Ferocactus.* Also attrib. with *cactus.* (Cf. BARREL CACTUS.)

1877 H. C. HODGE *Arizona* 244 The kind [of cactus] commonly called the nigger head is round, of the size of a cabbage, and covered with large, crooked, catlike thorns. **1881** *Amer. Naturalist* XV. 984 Another species of the family is one commonly called the 'nigger-head' or 'barrel' cactus, a Mammalaria. **1923** *Stand. Plant Names* 293 Niggerhead cactus.

‖**Niggerheadism.** [NIGGERHEAD 2.] The policy or views of those favoring equal rights for Negroes and white persons. An opprobrious term. — **1868** *N.Y. Herald* 7 July 6/2 It demanded . . . a final settlement of all the vexed questions of copperheadism and niggerheadism.

+**Nigger heaven.** (See quot. 1912.) *colloq.* — **1878** DALY in J. F. Daly *A. Daly* 249 There is a 'Nigger Heaven' (as the third tier is called in Troy) here, & as 'tis very capacious I have been liberal with my pencilled passes. **1912** THORNTON 608 *Nigger heaven*, the gallery of a theatre or place of entertainment. Common in Boston in 1888–91.

+**Niggerish,** *a.* Like or characteristic of a Negro or Negroes. A derogatory term. Also comb. — **1825** NEAL *Bro. Jonathan* II. 67 Ye great niggerish lookin', wap-sided, haw. **1866** *Atlantic Mo.* XVIII. 79/1 Aunt Judy's piety was in no respect the niggerish kind; when I say 'colored,' I mean one thing, respectfully; and when I say 'niggerish,' I mean another, disgustedly.

+**Nigger-jockey.** A sharper who trades in Negro slaves. *Obs.* — [**1838** HALIBURTON *Clockmaker* 2 Ser. 32 A nigger-jockey, sir, says I, is a gentleman that trades in niggers,—buys them in one state, and sells them in another, where they arn't known.]

+**Nigger-killer. 1.** One who maltreats Negro slaves. *Obs.* **2.** (See quot. 1889.) *colloq.* — (1) **1856** OLMSTED *Slave States* 108 If a man does not provide well for his slaves, . . . he gets the name of a 'nigger killer.' (2) **1889** *Cent.* 2596/1 The whip-tailed scorpion, *Thelyphonus giganteus.* Also called . . . *nigger-killer*. . . . (Florida.)

+**Nigger luck.** Unexampled and unexpected good luck. *colloq.* — **1851** GLISAN *Jrnl. Army Life* 90, I occasionally made him a little envious by my nigger-luck, as he is pleased to term it. **1869** HARTE *Luck of Roaring Camp* 31 When a man gets a streak of luck,—nigger-luck,—he don't get tired. **1888** *Critic* 14 April (F.), I am cussed . . . if any darned rebel can have such nigger luck and enjoy it while I live. **1900** SAVAGE *Midnight Passenger* 135 It has been a great stroke of nigger luck.

+**Nigger-shooter.** A sling shot. *colloq.* — **1883** SWEET & KNOX *Through Texas* 339 Just about the time people have got used to tops buzzing about their ears, the 'nigger-shooter' mania breaks out. **1901** ADE *40 Modern Fables* 172 All you wanted to do was to tear out with those Toughs and kill Birds with Nigger-Shooters. **1903** 'O. HENRY' *Cabbages & Kings* (1916) 95 He went at the chocolate team like a bean out of a little boy's nigger shooter.

+**Nigger show.** (See quot. 1890.) *colloq.* — **1884** 'MARK TWAIN' *H. Finn* xxvi. 261 They never see a holiday from year's end to year's end; never go to the circus, nor theater, nor nigger shows, nor nowheres. **1890** HOWELLS *Boy's Town* 105 [There was] a Nigger Show, or a performance of burnt-cork minstrels.

+**Niggertoe. 1.** A variety of potato. **2.** A Brazil nut. — **(1) 1853** *Mich. Agric. Soc. Trans.* V. 208 Some of the more approved [kinds of potatoes] are . . . the Niggertoe, the Meshannock, the Cumberland Kempt. **(2) 1896** *Dialect Notes* I. 421 *Nigger toes:* for *Brazil nuts.* N.Y.c., n., w., O. n., Pa. s.e.

Night-blooming cereus. A cactus (*Selenicereus grandiflorus*) that blooms about midnight, or a cultivated species of this. {1835–} Also *night-flowering cereus.* {1789– (Aiton *Hortus Kewensis* II. 152)}

1810 CUTLER in *Life & Corr.* II. 342 Saw the cactus grandiflora, or night-flowering cereus. **1863** GRAY *Botany* p. li, *Cereus grandiflorus,* Night-blooming Cereus, . . . is only occasionally met with in conservatories. **1883** HAY *Bread-Winners* 117 My night-blooming cereus has her coming-out party to-night. **1890** *Harper's Mag.* March 613/1 My wife has a sweet face of her own, but one bearing the same relation to Miss Jasmine's as that existing between a sprig of mignonette and a night-blooming cereus. **1905** VALENTINE *H. Sandwith* 11 He recognized that the object of admiration in the cottage was a night-blooming cereus.

+**Night city editor.** On a big city newspaper, the editor in charge of the gathering and editing of local news at night. (Cf. CITY EDITOR.) — **1892** *Harper's Wkly.* 9 Jan. 42/4 The night city editor . . . has also had to send out reporters to look after matters brought to his attention after nightfall. **1899** J. L. WILLIAMS *Stolen Story* 227 He told the night city editor all about it with eloquence. **1916** SEITZ *Training for Newsp. Trade* 81 When night city editor of the New York *Recorder,* I sent him to Bloomingdale asylum to verify a tip that a patient had been scalded to death.

+**Night clerk.** A clerk on duty at a hotel receiving desk at night. — **1882** SWEET & KNOX *Texas Siftings* 25 The night clerk is not so gorgeous or inclement as the day clerk. **1887** *Courier-Journal* 2 Feb. 1/1 She placed her diamonds and jewelry . . . in the hands of Charles Talbott, night clerk at the Gayoso house. **1902** HARBEN *A. Daniel* 28 The sleepy night-clerk rose from his lounge behind the counter in the office. **1923** WYATT *Invisible Gods* 21 The sleepy night clerk . . . was catching a nap with his head buried on his arm.

+**Night editor.** A newspaper editor who is on duty at night; on a morning newspaper, the editor supervising final make-up. — **1870** MAVERICK *Raymond & N.Y. Press* 326 One assistant [to the chief editor], placed in charge of the news, is known as the Night Editor. **1894** SHUMAN *Steps into Journalism* 20 On all morning papers, we have another very important functionary—the night editor. **1920** COOPER *Under Big Top* 40 The telegraph editor of the Kansas City Star looked up from his desk, toward the night editor.

Night-flowering cereus. (See NIGHT-BLOOMING CEREUS.)

+**Night flutterer.** A term applied to an American moth of some species. — **1784** J. BELKNAP *Hist. New Hamp.* II. 182 Insects . . . [include] Night flutterer, *Sphinx.* Owl moth, many new species. Moth, or miller, *Phalæna.* **1832** WILLIAMSON *Maine* I. 172.

Nighthawk, *n.* {1611–}

+**1.** Any one of various American goatsuckers of the genus *Chordeiles.* Occasionally confused with the whippoorwill.

Cf. BULLBAT, GOATSUCKER, MOSQUITO HAWK 1.

1778 CARVER *Travels* 466 The Night Hawk. This Bird is of the hawk species. **1793** W. BENTLEY *Diary* II. 48 We observed a great number of the birds, called here [Charleston, N.H.] night hawks, playing in the air. **1812** WILSON *Ornithology* V. 65 Three species only, of this genus, are found within the United States; the Chuck-will's-widow, the Whip-poor-will, and the Night-hawk. **1882** GODFREY *Nantucket* 243 On the first of October come the night hawk, pigeon, and sparrow hawk. **1917** *Birds of Amer.* II. 173 An old delusion—which is still a belief of many ignorant people, especially in the South—is that the Nighthawk and the Whip-poor-will are identical.

2. ? A dish of some kind.

1784 *Mass. Centinel* 10 July 3/3 Will be sold, by Public Vendue, . . . 3 doz. Dishes, 1 do. small do., 6 Nighthawks, 2 doz. black Bowls, 4 do. large Porringers.

+**3.** A member of a local unit of the Ku-Klux Klan who acted as a scout or courier. *Obs.*

1867 in Lester & Wilson *Ku Klux Klan* 136 The officers of this . . . shall consist of . . . a Grand Cyclops of the Den and his two Night Hawks. **1877** BEARD *K.K.K. Sketches* 75 There were from four to six scouts belonging to the Den, who performed courier duty, and to whom was applied the titular distinction of Night-Hawks. **1884** *Century Mag.* July 405 The Grand Cyclops of the Den and his two Night Hawks.

+**4.** A cab which is operated at night. *colloq.*

1890 DAVIS *Gallegher* 3 He knew several drivers of 'night hawks.' **c1895** NORRIS *Vandover* (1914) 284 Occasionally a belated coupé, a nighthawk, rattled over the cobbles. **1898** *Scribner's Mag.* XXIII. 443/2 Standing at the curb . . . are a few 'night hawks.'

‖**Nighthawk,** *v. intr.* To go about at night. — **1878** STOWE *Poganuc People* 14 Little girls like you must go to bed early. They can't be up 'night-hawkin',' and goin' round in the cold.

Night heron. {1785– (Latham *Gen. Syn. Birds*)} The American quawk or black-crowned night heron, *Nycticorax nycticorax hoactli.* Also with defining term. (Cf. QUA-BIRD.)

[**1785** PENNANT *Arctic Zool.* II. 451 Night Heron. . . . Inhabits New York. . . . Is common to Europe.] **1813** WILSON *Ornithology* VII. 105 The food of the Night Heron, or Qua-bird, is chiefly composed of small fish, which it takes by night. **1839** PEABODY *Mass. Birds* 363 The Night Heron, *Ardea nycticorax,* . . . is said to be as good as . . . the pigeon. **1867** *Amer. Naturalist* I. 343 The species was the Night-heron or Quawk (*Nyctiardea Gardeni*). **1882** GODFREY *Nantucket* 241/1, I have met with the following specimens, . . . Night Heron (*Nyctiardea Gardeni*). . . . Black-Breast Plover (*Squatarda Helvetica*). **1917** *Birds of Amer.* I. 194/1 The Black-crowned Night Heron feeds chiefly in the evening. *Ib.* 195/1 The Night Heron moves about briskly, holding its head lowered and its neck curved.

***Nightingale.** +Any one of various American birds noted for their singing, as the cardinal and the white-throated sparrow. Also attrib.

See also VIRGINIAN NIGHTINGALE.

1649 *Perfect Descr. Va.* 15 The Mock-bird . . . will imitate all other Birds notes, and cries both day and night-birds, yea, the Owels and Nightingalls. **1709** LAWSON *Carolina* 144 The Nightingales are different in Plumes from those in Europe. **1775** BURNABY *Travels* 17 In the woods [of Va.] there are . . . the mocking-bird, the red bird or nightingale, [and] the blue-bird. **1804** CLARK in *Lewis & C. Exped.* I. (1904) 38 Passed a Small Creek . . . Which we named Nightingale Creek from a Bird of that discription which sang for us all last night. **1836** EDWARD *Hist. Texas* 75 Among the songsters are the thrush . . . [and] the nightingale. **1902** WHITE *Blazed Trail* 139 Down in the thicket, fine, clear, beautiful, . . . came the notes of the white-throat—the nightingale of the North.

+**Nightingale sparrow.** The song sparrow, *Melospiza melodia.* — **1828** *Western Mo. Rev.* I. 520 Nightingale sparrow, *fringilla melodia,* a very diminutive sparrow, with plain plumage, but pours from its little throat a powerful song, like that of the nightingale.

+**Night key.** A key for unlocking a night latch. — **1837** NEAL *Charcoal Sk.* (1838) 136 The owner of the dog . . . took out his night-key, and walked up the steps. **1856** M. THOMPSON *Plu-ri-bus-tah* 131 'Twas midnight, . . . Ere he reached his modest mansion; Which he entered with his night-key. **1870** A. S. STEPHENS *Married in Haste* 306 Constance heard the night-key turned in the lock. **1894** WARNER *Golden House* i, In one of the noble houses . . . sat Edith Delancy . . . listening for the roll of wheels and the click of a night-key.

Night latch. (See quot. 1875.) {1862} — **1853** FOWLER *Home for All* 113 The front door . . . secured with two barrel-bolts and a suitable sized front-door lock, with a night-latch and two keys. **1875** KNIGHT 1527/1 *Night-latch,* a form of door-lock in which the spring-latch may be opened by a key from the outside, or may be fastened shut so as to be immovable from the exterior of the door. **1907** M. H. NORRIS *Veil* 5 The irony of the modern nightlatch seemed to vaunt their security.

Night line. A line provided with one or more baited hooks set for catching fish at night. {1848–} — **1800** MAUDE *Niagara* 108 The River abounds with fish, principally cat-fish, which are taken with night-lines. **1872** *Penna. Laws* 729 It shall not be lawful for any person or persons to take . . . any fish, by means of nets of any kind, . . . night-lines, swimmers or floating lines. **1925** TILGHMAN *Dugout* 50 We don't get much time, so we mostly set night lines.

Night liner. {1902} (See quotation.) — **1890** *Cent.* 3992/3 *Night-liner.* . . . **1.** One of a line or class of public vehicles which stand all night in the streets to pick up passengers.—**2.** The driver of such a conveyance. (Colloq. in both senses.)

***Night owl.** *transf.* +A person who is commonly up or abroad late at night. *colloq.* — **a1846** *Quarter Race Ky.* 163 Do I know it, you no-souled, shad-bellied, squash-headed, old night-owl you! **1880** 'MARK TWAIN' *Tramp Abroad* 270 He calculated to get his claim through and be off before night-owls like me have turned out of bed. **1891** in Rankin *K. Chapin* (1932) 220 What night-owls we are. **1893** *Chicago Tribune* 24 April 7/1 [They] failed to notice the attention which they attracted from a few other night-owls prowling in the vicinity of the White House.

+**Night partridge.** *local.* =AMERICAN WOODCOCK. (Cf. NIGHT PECK.) — **1888** TRUMBULL *Names of Birds* 153 At Pocomoke City (Worcester Co.), Md., and Eastville (Northampton Co.), Va., [the woodcock is called] Night Partridge. **1917** *Birds of Amer.* I. 225.

Night pasture. A pasture in which animals are kept at night. *Obs.* Also attrib. — **1652** *Lancaster Rec.* 20 Hermon Garret vs John Hall for takeing away part of their night pasture fence. **1654** *Boston Rec.* 45 Foure accres and a halfe more or lesse in the night pasture. **1673** *Groton Rec.* 46 Near to the night pasture wading place. **1698** *Boston Rec.* 233 [The line is to run] from thence . . . to a great Rock in Col: Shrimptons ground called the night pasture.

+**Night peck.** *N.C.* =AMERICAN WOODCOCK. (Cf. NIGHT PARTRIDGE.) — **1888** TRUMBULL *Names of Birds* 153 The woodcock is known . . . in portions of North Carolina as the Night Peck. **1917** *Birds of Amer.* I. 225.

Night rider.

+**1.** A horseman who rides on sinister missions at night; *spec.* a member of a secret organization formed by southern white men just after the Civil War to overawe and keep in subjection the newly freed Negroes; sometimes, in pl., one of these organizations.

Cf. KU-KLUX KLAN.

1879 *Congress. Rec.* 20 May 1480/2 There was much said . . . of kuklux, white leagues, and night-riders. . . . There are . . . no night-riders in the State of Louisiana. **1880** TOURGEE *Invisible Empire* iii, A huge joke which certain pretended ghostly night-riders were playing upon the ignorant freedmen of the South. **1887** *Courier-Journal* 13 Feb. 9/3, I should like to have . . . anecdotes that would show the humor and give side-lights upon the character of that bold young night-rider. **1898** PAGE *Red Rock* 580 He had done much to break up later the organization of night-riders.

+**2.** *pl.* A group of Kentucky tobacco-growers who (*c*1906–1909) used violence in their efforts to perfect an association of tobacco producers. Now hist.

1907 *Lit. Digest* 28 Dec. 976 The first appearance of the night riders was in November, 1906, when they destroyed some tobacco-barns and small factories in Todd County with a loss of about $10,000. **1909** *N.Y. Ev. Post* 15 April (Th.), The Presbyterian Church at Fredonia, Caldwell Co., Ky., was burned last night, and 'night-riders' are suspected. **1909** *Ib.* (s.-w. ed.) 4 Oct. 4 He advises the anti-pool tobacco growers to form liberty leagues for the purpose of waging war against the night-riders.

Night riding. +The action of horsemen who ride at night to intimidate or terrorize. Also attrib. (Cf. NIGHT RIDER.) — **1875** *Chicago Tribune* 6 Nov. 3/6 To-night . . . there is to be a 'night riding' and shooting. It is not on the programme to do bodily harm to any person during these rides, but merely to arouse a degree of uneasiness in the darky's mind and cause him . . . not to go to the election. [**1909** *Chambers's Jrnl.* Feb. 104/1 The first night-riding adventure . . . gave evidence of careful planning.]

***Nights,** *adv.* At night. {–1601}

'Now *dial.* and *U.S.*' (*O.E.D.*).

1786 *Exchange Advertiser* (Boston) 19 Oct. (Th.), Not a flute that has a hole in it, but that is employed very successfully nights. **1846** *Spirit of Times* 6 June 171/1 The river was low, and it was not thought advisable to 'run nights'—at any rate until we got below Memphis. **1878** BEADLE *Western Wilds* 185 [He] onloosed a regular old English bull that he kept in the store nights. **1918** LINCOLN *Shavings* 39 Nights now when I'm walkin' around in that house alone I meet myself comin' round every corner.

Night school. A school held at night. Also attrib. — **1780** *N.J. Journal* 22 Nov. 4/2 Wanted, to be bound, a Boy; . . . he shall be . . . sent to night school if required. **1837** WETMORE *Gaz. Missouri* 333, I have refrained from change of place and occupation; . . . teaching night-school and singing-school in winter. **1871** *Scribner's Mo.* I. 609 On the register of one night school for girls are recorded the names of fifty as 'errands' for a single large dry goods firm. **1925** *Scribner's Mag.* July 84/2 Along with my night-school course in pedigrology, . . . I had to learn a lot about heraldry too.

***Nightshade.**

***1.** Any one of various plants of the genus *Solanum* or the family Solanaceae.

See also BLACK NIGHTSHADE and cf. BITTERSWEET 1.

1709 LAWSON *Carolina* 78 Night-Shade, several kinds; Harts-Tongue. **1832** WILLIAMSON *Maine* I. 127 Nightshade, or banewort, belongs to the multiform *Solanum* genus. **1901** MOHR *Plant Life Ala.* 712 *Solanum nigrum.* . . . Common Nightshade.

+**2.** =DITCH STONECROP. *Obs.*

1743 CLAYTON *Flora Virginica* 51 *Penthorum.* . . . Night-shade.

+**3.** =GARGET. Also *American nightshade.*

1784 CUTLER in *Mem. Academy* I. 447 *Phytolacca.* . . . Garget. Cunicum. Skoke. American Nightshade. Blossoms white, tinged with red. Berries black. Common by road sides. July. **1835** HOFFMAN *Winter in West* I. 144, I could fancy the glossy leaves of the nightshade, with its white blossoms and poisonous berries.

Night shift. A crew of workers who are on duty at night {1839–}; also, the turn of service of such a crew. {1860–} — **1882** *47th Congress 1 Sess.* H. R. Ex. Doc. No. 216, 16 It is intended first to prepare a place to store the *débris*, loosened during the night shifts. **1889** 'MARK TWAIN' *Conn. Yankee* 295, I took along a night shift of monks. **1901** MERWIN & WEBSTER *Calumet 'K'* 20, I'd been working like a nigger 'most five months . . . and the last three weeks running night shifts and Sundays. *a***1918** G. STUART *On Frontier* I. 82 Part of us worked on day shift and the others on night shift.

Nightshirt. A long, shirtlike garment usually worn at night in bed. {1857–} — **1850** LEWIS *La. Swamp Doctor* 72, I found the old gentleman . . . standing up in his night-shirt and making whiskey-toddy in a teapot. **1872** *Atlantic Mo.* April 401 The lieutenant . . . hurried on deck in his night-shirt. **1882** PECK *Sunshine* 103 There was a long female night-shirt, clapboarded up in front with trimming and starch. **1896** E. HIGGINSON *Land of Snow Pearls* 217 She bent over the canton flannel night-shirt she was making for Mr. Wincoop.

+**Night stick.** A stick or club carried by policemen at night. Also attrib. — **1893** CRANE *Maggie* (1896) 98 The officer made a terrific advance, club in hand. One comprehensive sweep of the long night stick threw the ally to the floor. **1905** *N.Y. Times* 15 July (*Cent. Suppl.*), San Juan Hill and the Gut were under nightstick law until early this morning. **1911** ROLT-WHEELER *Boy with Census* 337 There was a brief struggle and nightsticks were drawn.

Night train. A train that runs at night. {1885–} — **1865** *Nation* I. 287 Luxurious sleeping cars accompany each night train. **1873** *Newton Kansan* 10 July 3/3 Those desiring to run directly through without any stopping, can take the night train. **1909** 'O. HENRY' *Options* 291 Why did you spend your summers there for the last four years, even sneaking away from town on a night train?

Night watchman. One employed to keep watch at night as a guard or policeman. {1874–} — **1863** A. D. WHITNEY *F. Gartney* xxviii, A man employed as night-watchman in Mr. Rushleigh's factory, had a sick wife and child at home. **1873** *Mich. Gen. Statutes* I. (1882) 664 The council of any city may provide by ordinance for . . . such number of policemen and night-watchmen as they may think necessary for the good government of the city. **1890** LANGFORD *Vigilante Days* (1912) 469, I want you . . . to aid me in getting the position of night-watchman in this city. **1907** *St. Nicholas* June 677/2 Night-watchmen arrived and speedily collared the boys and marched them off to the lock-up.

+**Night willow-herb.** The evening primrose, *Œnothera biennis.* — **1791** MUHLENBERG *Index Florae* 168 *Oenothera*, Night-willowherb. **1847** DARLINGTON *Weeds & Plants* 136 *Biennial Œnothera.* Evening Primrose. Night Willow-herb.

+**Night wrangler.** One who has charge of horses by night. — **1893** [see DAY WRANGLER].

Nigh wheeler. In a team, the animal on the left of the tongue or in the lead. — **1873** BEADLE *Undevel. West* 98 The writer seated on his 'nigh-wheeler,' and wielding a 'big-bellied blacksnake' over the backs of six mules. **1887** TOURGEE *Button's Inn* 90 He checked up the nigh-wheeler lest he should drink too freely. **1903** A. ADAMS *Log Cowboy* 131 The nigh wheeler in Joe Jenk's team . . . was missing.

+**Nimble Will.** A slender American grass (*Muhlenbergia schreberi*) which spreads rapidly in uncultivated fields and in the woods. (Cf. DROP-SEED GRASS.) — **1817** S. BROWN *Western Gaz.* 109 A short, nutritious grass called 'nimble will' . . . has completely overspread with astonishing celerity, almost every spot of waste or uncultivated ground. **1843** TORREY *Flora N.Y.* II. 435 Drop-seed Grass . . . is a very abundant grass in the Western States, and is the '*Nimble Will*' of Kentucky farmers. **1878** KILLEBREW *Tenn. Grasses* 155 Nimble Will, *Muhlenbergia diffusa.* . . . In woods, . . . in the fall, . . . it carpets the earth with living green. **1894** COULTER *Bot. W. Texas* III. 523 Nimble Will. . . . Dry hills and woods, northern Texas and northward.

Nimshi. +(See quot. 1848.) *colloq.* — **1848** BARTLETT 233 *Nimshi.* A foolish fellow, or one who habitually acts in a foolish manner. **1853** *Turnover* 60 (Th.), Why, any nimshi can jump acrost that little crick.

***Nine.** *collect.* +The nine players making up a baseball team. (See also FRESHMAN NINE.) — **1867** CHADWICK *Base Ball Reference* 81 The captain of a nine should be a good general player. **1880** N. BROOKS *Fairport Nine* 23 The White Bears, with all their muscle, were not very much better in the base-ball field than the Fairport Nine. **1904** *N.Y. Ev. Post* 27 Oct. 5 Men cheer for their own baseball nine. **1923** FOSTER *Beachcomber in Orient* 269 Out at the Ball Park Filipino nines regularly worsted the teams from the American regiments.

+**Ninebark.** Any of various American shrubs of the genus *Physocarpus*, with bark which separates readily into thin layers.

1785 MARSHALL *Amer. Grove* 146 Guelder Rose-leaved Spiraea, or Nine-Bark. This rises with many shrubby branching stalks . . . to the height of five or six feet. **1806** LEWIS in *L. & Clark Exped.* IV. (1905) 49 The seven bark or nine bark as it is called in the U' States is also common [near Ft. Clatsop]. **1832** KENNEDY *Swallow Barn* I. 226 Morasses . . . now over-grown with thickets of arrow-wood, nine-bark, and various other shrubs. **1860** CURTIS *Woody Plants N.C.* 104 Nine Bark . . . is found upon river banks in the western part of the State. **1901** MOHR *Plant Life Ala.* 538.

attrib. **1789** MORSE *Amer. Geog.* 461 The prevailing growth of timber [includes] . . . plumb trees, nine bark spice, and leatherwood bushes. **1847** DARLINGTON *Weeds & Plants* 120 Opulus-leaved Spiræa. . . . A very showy ornamental species. . . . Sometimes called 'Nine-Bark Syringa.'

***Nine hole.** *fig.* +*In the nine hole(s)*, in a difficult situation. *colloq.* — **1863** 'E. KIRKE' *Southern Friends* 76 He owned har [the slave] till he got in the nineholes one day, and sold har ter the Gin'ral. **1877** *Congress. Rec.* 3 Nov. 230/1 We have put the gentleman in the 'nine-holes;' and there we intend to keep him. **1887** *Courier-Journal* 8 Feb. 1/2 His friends have been placed in the nine-hole by the Speaker. **1890** *Congress. Rec.* 12 June 6002/1 This bill . . . has passed the Senate, and, to use a Western expression, it will put me 'in the nine-hole' if I do not get it through.

Nine-killer. {1678, 1801–} +=NORTHERN SHRIKE. (Cf. BUTCHERBIRD.)

1778 in *Amer. Philos. Soc.* IV. 126 This bird of prey called the nine-killer . . . is said to have the habit of sticking beetles or other insects, and perhaps sometimes nine of them in succession, upon thorns. **1795** *Ib.* IV. 125 These grasshoppers were stuck up by a small bird of prey, which the Germans [in Pa.] called *neun-toedter* (in English, *Nine-killer*); that this bird had a practice of catching and sticking up nine grasshoppers a day. **1844** *Nat. Hist. N.Y., Zoology* II. 128 The name of *Nine-killer* is derived from the popular belief that it catches and impales nine grasshoppers in a day. **1900** HARTE *Treasure of Redwoods* 220 He's a 'butcher bird'—wot they call a 'nine-killer'—kills nine birds a day! **1917** *Birds of Amer.* III. 99 Northern Shrike. *Lanius borealis.* . . . [Also called] Nine Killer.

Ninepence. {1606–} +The Spanish real, having a value of about 12½ cents, or a coin of approximately its value. *Obs.* (Cf. BIT *n.* 3.) — **1828** *Yankee* 14 May 157/2 A *ninepence* in New-England . . . is a *shilling* in New York. **1845** COOPER *Chainbearer* ii, No one could have imagined that I had only a York shilling, which is a Pennsylvania 'levy,' or a Connecticut 'ninepence,' in my purse. **1865** RICHARDSON *Secret Service* 175 The people of these mountain regions [in W.Va.] use the old currency of New England, and talk of 'fourpence ha'pennies' and 'ninepences.' **1892** A. E. LEE *Hist. Columbus, Ohio* I. 398 The coin in circulation at that time [c1821] was almost entirely Spanish, consisting of the silver dollar and its half, quarter, eighth and sixteenth, the last two being known as 'four pence-ha'penny' or 'fippeny bit,' and 'nine-pence' respectively. *Ib.*, The last two of these pieces being scarce, their place was supplied by cutting a quarter into two or four pieces, which passed for a 'ninepence' or a 'fip' respectively, and were known in popular parlance as 'sharp shins.'

Ninepin alley. A place provided with the equipment used in playing ninepins. {1756–} — **1831** *Ohio Rev. Statutes* I. 448 Any keeper of a public house . . . [who] shall establish any ball or ninepin alley [etc.]. **1844** *Knickerb.* XXIII. 46, [I] lounged up to the nine-pin alley to close up the 'unfinished business.' **1877** *Mich. Gen. Statutes* I. (1882) 546 If any person shall keep . . . any nine-pin alley, or any alley to be used in the playing of nine-pins . . . for hire, gain, or reward [etc.].

***Ninepins.** A game in which a ball is rolled in an effort to knock down as many as possible of nine wooden pins stood on end. (Cf. TENPINS.) — **1825** J. PICKERING *Inquiries of Emigrant* (1831) 15 Almost every tavern keeps a bowling-alley, where the idle resort to play at ten pins (nine pins having been prohibited by law!). **1846** *Spirit of Times* 4 July 218/2 [We] tried our hands at nine-pins, but with little success. **1886** POORE *Reminisc.* II. 35 He rolled several games of nine-pins with the pupils.

Nine-spotted, *a.* +Designating a variety of ladybird or ladybug the specimens of which have nine spots on the back. — **1861** *Ill. Agric. Soc. Trans.* IV. 347, I found numerous specimens of a nine-spotted lady-bird (*Coccinella novemnotata*, Herbst,) under dry cow-dung. **1867** *Amer. Naturalist* I. 278 The nine-spotted Lady Bug . . . is one of a large group of beetles, most beneficial from their habit of feeding on the plant-lice.

+**Ninety-day gunboat.** [See quot. 1883.] One of a number of heavily armed, rapidly built, screw gunboats added to the Federal navy during the Civil War. — **1883** J. R. SOLEY *Blockade & Cruisers* 19 Some of them within four months from the date of contract, were afloat, armed, and manned. . . . From their rapid construction, they were commonly known as the 'ninety-day gunboats.' **1886** *Harper's Mag.* June 7/1 The 'ninety-day gun-boats,' and the 'double-enders' were added to the navy list.

+**Ninseng, Ninsin.** =GINSENG 1. — **1748** CATESBY *Carolina* App. 16 *Aureliana Canadensis R. P. Lafiteau.* The Ginseng, or Ninsin, of the Chinese. An accurate description [of the plant] . . . gave light to the discovery of the same plant in Canada and Pensylvania. **1784** CUTLER in *Mem. Academy* I. 492 Ninsin. From the quantity that grows in this country, . . . we have reason to hope it will become a valuable export. **1790** DEANE *New-Eng. Farmer* 203/1 Panax, Ginseng, or Ninseng. . . . This plant is a native of our country, and is become a considerable article of commerce.

+**Nip and tuck.** Also **nip and chuck,** etc. A close approximation to equality in racing or other competition; neck and neck. *colloq.*

1832 PAULDING *Westward Ho!* I. 172 There we were at rip [?misprint] *and* tuck, up one tree and down another. **1836** *Quarter Race Ky.* 16 It will be like the old bitch and the rabbit, nip and tack every jump. **a1846** *Ib.* 123 Then we'd have it again, nip and chuck. **1869** *Putnam's Mag.* Jan. (De Vere), It was nip and tuck all along, who was to win her. **1888** CODY *Wild West* 337 For several minutes it was nip and tuck which should reach the Platte River first. **1911** WILSON *Land Claimers* 114 It was nip and tuck whether he'd get her relinquishment filed before she was buried.

attrib. **1890** Shields *Big Game N. Amer.* 92 It was a nip-and-tuck race. **1912** MATHEWSON *Pitching* 113 The Giants were having a nip and tuck game with the Cubs in the early part of last summer, when Devore came to the bat . . . and shot a three bagger over third base.

***Nipper.**

***1.** *pl.* An instrument, usually of metal, having two jaws suitable for seizing and holding fast an object.

Other uses can be found in the technical and scientific dictionaries.

1702 *Essex Inst. Coll.* XLII. 162 Inventory of Ship Providence. . . . 1 file & pr Nippers. **1812** *Niles' Reg.* II. 9/2 The rods are at the beginning drawn through the holes by a pair of nippers fastened to a glide. **1905** VALENTINE *H. Sandwith* 5 The heavy iron nippers of the crane for dragging cinder scabs dangled from the roof like an instrument of torture.

+**2.** A thick mitten or glove used by New England cod fishermen to protect their hands and wrists.

1840 *Niles' Nat. Reg.* 15 Aug. 376/3 An article, neither mittens nor gloves, which he [Bay of Fundy fisherman] wears upon his hands, he calls '*nippers.*' **1884** *Nat. Museum Bul.* No. 27, 794 Fishermen's Nippers. Knit of woolen yarn and stuffed with woolen cloth. Gloucester, Mass. . . . Used on the hands of fishermen to enable them to grasp and hold a fishing-line better than they otherwise could do. **1897** KIPLING *Capt. Courageous* 56 A heavy blue jersey well darned at the elbows, a pair of nippers, and a sou'wester.

+**3.** =CONNER.

1884 GOODE, etc. *Fisheries* I. 273 At Salem they are called 'Nippers,' and occasionally here and elsewhere 'Bait-stealers.' **1911** *Rep. Fisheries 1908* 308 Chogset (*Tautogolabrus adspersus*).—This fish . . . is also called . . . 'nippers.'

***Niter, Nitre.**

***1.** Potassium nitrate or saltpeter. Also attrib. and comb.

1775 *S.C. Hist. Soc. Coll.* II. 66 If he was assisted with a sufficient sum, . . . he says he could bring the nitre works to a great degree of perfection. **1817** BRADBURY *Travels* 248 In those [caves] which produce the nitre, . . . [the earth] is strongly impregnated with it, and visible in needle-form crystals. **1833** WYETH *Oregon* 40 Nitre is found wherever there are suitable caves and caverns for its collection. **1869** *Rep. Comm. Agric. 1868* 397 One of these niter-producing caves exists on the farm of Dr. Lee.

+**2.** A precipitate of malic acid formed in making maple sirup.

1872 *Vermont Bd. Agric. Rep.* I. 219 The gritty sediment from maple syrup, commonly termed 'nitre.' **1874** *Dept. Agric. Rep. 1873* 475 Our sirup . . . percolates into the settling tub, leaving upon the strainer most of the substance spoken of as 'niter.' **1882** *Vt. Agric. Rep.* VII. 65 The higher the [sugar maple] tree is tapped the more of nitre or malate of lime is found.

+**Nitweed.** The orange grass, a plant with yellow flowers, *Sarothra gentianoides.* — **1817–8** EATON *Botany* (1822) 380 Nit-weed, false john's wort. . . . On the sandy plain west of Ball's spring, New Haven. **1843** TORREY *Flora N.Y.* I. 89 Ground Pine. Nitweed. Pine-weed.

Nix. Also **nixie, nixy.** {1789–} +(See quot. 1883.) Also attrib. with *clerk.* — **1879** *Postal Laws & Regul.* 113 Misdirected second-class matter ('nixes'). **1883** *Postal Guide* 733 'Nixes' is a term used in the railway mail service to denote matter of domestic origin, chiefly of the first and second class, which is unmailable because addressed to places which are not post offices, or to States, etc., in which there is no such post office as that indicated in the address. **1901** *Congress. Rec.* 17 Jan. 1145/2 Mailing clerks, . . . directory, and nixie clerks . . . [shall receive] from $600 to not exceeding $1,400 per annum. **1904** *Springfield Repub.* 29 Oct. 4 He was made what is known in the office as a 'nixy' clerk—one who looks up misdirected letters. **1905** *N.Y. Ev. Post* 8 Feb. 5 What the railway postal clerks most dread is the class of mail matter they know as 'nixies.'

***No.** A negative response or vote. (Cf. NAY.) — **1722** SEWALL *Diary* III. 300 'Twas voted it should be done in that manner. Were 11. Yeas, 3 Nos. **1812** *Niles' Reg.* I. 376/2 On the question, the ayes and noes were called. **1871** *Ill. Agric. Soc. Trans.* VIII. 7 The ayes and noes being called for.

+**No-account,** *a.* Of no account, value, or use; worthless, insignificant. *colloq.* Also absol. (See also NO-'COUNT *a.*) — **1845** HOOPER *Simon Sugg's Adv.* 39 The land I'm after is a d—d little, no-account quarter section, that nobody would have but me. **1850** GARRARD *Wah-To-Yah* iii. 53 Caballadas are mostly led by a no-account mare or mule. **1907** *St. Nicholas* May 600/2 There's only about a dozen fellows over there and they're the no-accountest lot I ever did see. **1924** MULFORD *Rustlers' Valley* x, Th' no-accounts are gettin' restless up Los Altos way.

Noah's ark. {1611–} +(See quots. 1890, 1898.) — **1826** DARLINGTON *Florula Cestrica* 95 C[*ypripedium*] *pubescens.* . . . Noah's Ark. Yellow Mocasin [*sic*] flower. **1890** *Cent.* 4002/1 *Noah's ark.* . . . In *bot.*, the larger yellow lady's-slipper, *Cypripedium pubescens.* **1898** CREEVEY *Flowers of Field* 296 Stemless Lady's Slipper. Noah's Ark. Moccasin-flower. *Cypripedium acaule.*

***Noble,** *n.* An obsolete British gold coin formerly current in the American colonies. — **1640** *Conn. Probate Rec.* I. 28 Mr. Michell . . . was fyned twenty Nobles for undertaking the office [of recorder of Wethersfield]. **1646** *Essex Probate Rec.* I. 53 Abigail and Israell have 20 nobles each, when twenty-one. **1651** *Ib.*, The other three children . . . are to have 20 nobles, to make good to them the 8 li. apiece. **1662** *R.I. Col. Rec.* I. 503 Ordered, that William Harris's bill be received without paying his noble.

***Noble,** *a.* +In specific names of trees. (See also NOBLE LIVERWORT.) — **1846** BROWNE *Trees* 411 *Laurus nobilis*, The Noble Laurel-tree. **1858** WARDER *Hedges & Evergreens* 257 *Picea nobilis*, Noble Silver Fir. . . . This majestic tree forms large forests in the northern part of California. **1892** *Amer. Folk-Lore* V. 100 *Chimaphila umbellata*, noble pine; bitter-sweet. N.H. **1897** SUDWORTH *Arborescent Flora* 57 *Abies nobilis.* Noble Fir.

***Noble liverwort.** A species of liverleaf, *Hepatica triloba.* — **1778** CARVER *Travels* 515 Herbs [include] . . . , Wild Dock, Rock Liverwort, Noble Liverwort, Bloodwort [etc.]. **1836** EDWARD *Hist. Texas* 42, I can give but few examples [of the herb varieties], such as . . . the noble-liverwort, the wild liverwort [etc.]. **1893** *Amer. Folk-Lore* VI. 136 *Hepatica triloba*, noble liverwort. Buckfield, Oxford Co., Me.

+**Nocake.** Also †**nokaeg, nokake.** [Algonquian.] The meal of parched Indian corn, or food made from this. Now hist. (See also NOKEHICK and cf. HOECAKE.)

1634 WOOD *New Eng. Prospect* 68 *Nocake* (as they [=Indians] call it) . . . is nothing but Indian Corne parched in the hot ashes; the ashes being sifted from it, it is afterward beaten to powder, and put into a long leather bag. **1674** GOOKIN in *Mass. H. S. Coll.* 1 Ser. I. 150 This meal they call nokake. **1723** *New-Eng. Courant* 4 Feb. 2/2 A Cake or two of Bread, with a Pot of Nokaeg, were likewise put into the Coffin. **1790** DEANE *New-Eng. Farmer* 141/1 When they eat it they reduce it to a paste with water. . . . It is called *nocake.* **1832** DURFEE *Whatcheer* 25 In trays the nocake, and the joints of deer. **1907** *Springfield W. Repub.* 21 March 13 A sweet meal or grits was made [by the Indians of New England] of parched corn and known as 'nocake.' This often furnished the only food of the traveler for days together.

+**No-'count,** *a.* Short for NO-ACCOUNT *a.* Also absol. *colloq.*[2] — **1853** 'P. PAXTON' *Yankee in Texas* 282 Yes, Massa, dern no 'count calves done fool me agin. **1884** HARRIS *Mingo* 248 To think that sech a no-'count old creetur as that should be a-ha'ntin' the face of the earth! **1897** BRODHEAD *Bound in Shallows* 265 Don't you go back to that no 'count, triflin' scamp! **1917** COMSTOCK *Man* 9 Nella-Rose is a little no-count—that's what I say.

*****Nodding,** *a.* In specific names of plants. {1789-} — **1814** BIGELOW *Florula Bostoniensis* 85 *Trillium cernuum.* Nodding Trillium. . . . In shady thickets. **1817-8** EATON *Botany* (1822) 362 *Neottia cernua,* nodding ladies' tresses. **1843** TORREY *Flora N.Y.* II. 385 *Carex gracillima.* . . . Slender Nodding Sedge. . . . Moist meadows. **1894** COULTER *Bot. W. Texas* III. 548 *Festuca nutans.* . . . (Nodding Fescue.) . . . Rocky woods and hills, central Texas to Illinois and Pennsylvania.

*****Noddy. a.** =NODDY TERN. +**b.** Applied to other birds regarded as foolish or stupid: (see quotations).

1789 MORSE *Amer. Geog.* 60 American Birds [which] have been enumerated [include the] . . . Noddy, Nuthatch, Oyster catcher. **1828** BONAPARTE *Synopsis* 356 The noddy, *Sterna stolida,* . . . inhabits all parts of the tropical seas, migrating occasionally to the North American coasts. **1835** [see NODDY TERN]. **1888** TRUMBULL *Names of Birds* 112 At Newberne, N.C., [the ruddy duck, *Erismatura rubida*] is called Paddy and Noddy. **1917** *Birds of Amer.* I. 80 Fulmar. *Fulmarus glacialis glacialis.* . . . [Also called] Noddy.

Noddy tern. The tern, *Anoüs stolidus.* — **1835** AUDUBON *Ornith. Biog.* III. 516 The Noddy Tern. *Sterna Stolida.* . . . About the beginning of May, the Noddies collect from all parts of the Gulf of Mexico, and the coasts of Florida. **1874** COUES *Birds N.W.* 710 Noddy Tern. . . . South Atlantic and Gulf coast of North America. **1883** *Nat. Museum Bul.* No. 27, 172 Noddy Tern. Intertropical seas; also South Atlantic and Gulf coasts of United States. **1917** *Birds of Amer.* I. 69/1 There is more or less similarity in the appearance, habits, and habitat of the Noddy and Sooty Terns.

Nodhead. {1652} +=JEWETT RED. — **1849** *New Eng. Farmer* I. 54 The Nodhead . . . has done poorly with me as yet. **1859** ELLIOTT *Western Fruit Book* 149 Jewett's Red. . . . Nodhead. . . . Best adapted to strong clay soils North.

Nog, Nogg. {1693-} +=EGGNOG(G). — **1851** A. O. HALL *Manhattaner* 10, I tremble to think of the juleps, and punches, and nogs, and soups. **1858** *Harper's Mag.* May 729/1 At our meeting during Christmas week . . . I read a funny essay. . . . Nog was handed round. **1881** TOURGEE *'Zouri's Christmas* viii, Just one glass of foamy nogg stood by each plate. **1896** *Harper's Mag.* April 783/2 Mrs. Raker was holding a foaming glass to the sick man's lips. 'There; take another sup of the good nog,' she said.

+**Nogal.** *S.W.* [Sp.] A walnut tree; a pecan tree. — **1869** BROWNE *Adv. Apache Country* 262 We returned to our pleasant camping-place under the wide-spreading nogales, or walnut-trees, by the margin of the creek. **1892** *Dialect Notes* I. 192 *Nogal:* properly the walnut tree, in Texas the pecan tree. . . . The hickory is called *nogal encarcelado.*

Noggin.

1. a. A small wooden cup or bowl. {1630-} +**b.** A pail or small tub: (see also quot. 1890). *local.*

1766 in Chalkley *Scotch-Irish Settlement Va.* I. 127 Four wooden noggins, also . . . one Dutch blanket. **1785** *Lower Norfolk Co., Va., Antiquary* I. 136, 4 Tubs (washing) 8/, . . . 1 noggin 2/. **1824** DODDRIDGE *Notes* 109 The furniture for the table . . . consisted of a few pewter dishes, . . . but mostly of wooden bowls, trenchers and noggins. **1843** *Amer. Pioneer* II. 424 For bowls or basins they made *noggins;* these were small vessels shaped like a pail, made from small cedar staves, and held about a quart. **1865** *Atlantic Mo.* XV. 545/1 She would be asleep now, . . . her pipe and noggin of tea on the oven-shelf. **1885** 'CRADDOCK' *Prophet* 175 Mirandy Jane, seated on an inverted noggin, listened tamely to the conversation. **1890** *Cent.* 4007/2 *Noggin,* . . . one end of a keg that has been sawn into halves, used for various purposes on shipboard.

+**2.** A person's head. *colloq.*

1893 M. A. OWEN *Voodoo Tales* 23 Lemme scratch dis hyeah ole noggin. **1902** HARBEN *A. Daniel* 77 He made a business o' feelin' o' heads. . . . When he got to Pole's noggin he talked fer a good hour.

No go. (See GO *n.* 5.)

No how. {1775-} +*No how you can fix it,* (see FIX *v.* 5 e).

Noisette (rose). A class or group of handsome garden roses: (see quot. 1917). {1830-} — **1870** WOOD *Amer. Botanist & Florist* IV. 110 *R. Indica.* . . . Other var. *Noisette,* . . . *Cloth of Gold* (sulphur yellow), and the favorite *Tea Roses.* **1916** [see MARÉCHAL NIEL]. **1917** BAILEY *Stand. Cyclop. Hort.* V. 2988 The Noisette rose was raised about 1816 by John Champney, of Charleston, S.C. . . . From the seed of this, . . . Philippe Noisette, a florist at Charleston, obtained a rose which was afterward distributed as Blush Noisette by his brother Louis Noisette of Paris.

+**Nokehick.** Also **nuichicke,** etc. =NOCAKE. *Obs.*

1637 R. WILLIAMS *Letters* (1874) 30 They brought this present week divers baskets of their nokehick and chestnuts to Canonicus towards his wars. **1691** C. MATHER *Life J. Eliot* 71 [The Indians'] Diet has not a greater dainty than their *Nokehick,* that is, a spoonful of their parch'd meal, with a spoonful of water, which will strengthen them to travel a day together. **1720** D. NEAL *Hist. New-Eng.* I. 27 When Fishing and Hunting fails, they [Indians] live upon nothing but *Nokohick.* **1764** HUTCHINSON *Hist. Mass.* I. 465 A small pouch of . . . Nuichicke, which is well enough translated Nocake, would support them several days in their travelling. **1803** J. DAVIS *Travels* 257 The Indians dwell in wigwams. . . . Their principal diet is Nokehick. **1832** WILLIAMSON *Maine* I. 510 Their nokehike was corn parched and pounded.

+**Nolle,** *n. Law.* Short for NOLLE-PROS *n.* — **1871** EGGLESTON *Hoosier Schoolm.* 214, I now enter a *nolle* in his case . . . and I ask that this court adjourn. **1878** BEADLE *Western Wilds* 507 He had been indicted along with the others, and a *nolle* entered.

+**Nolle,** *v. Law. tr.* Short for NOL(LE)-PROS *v.* — **1888** *Battle Creek Jrnl.* 7 March, The prosecution stated that it would be impossible to secure a conviction in either case, and he asked that they be nolled. **1896** *Watertown Repub.* 18 Nov., The criminal libel suit pending against W. J. Rambusch was nolled. **1899** CHESNUTT *Wife of His Youth* 309 The case would not have been prosecuted if the judge had not refused to allow it to be nolled. **1910** *Springfield W. Repub.* 24 Nov. 10 Case Against Haskell Nolled.

+**Nolle-pros,** *n. Law.* Short for *nolle prosequi,* an acknowledgment or declaration of record by the plaintiff or his representative that a suit or indictment will be prosecuted no further. — **1895** *Denver Times* 5 March 1/3 John Doyle was dismissed on a nolle pros in both cases.

+**Nol(le)-pros,** *v. tr.* To drop (a suit) by a nolle-pros. — **1880** G. A. PIERCE *Zachariah* 436 Judge Spalding informed Zach. . . . that the case could be 'nolle prossed' when it came up. **1883** *N.Y. Ev. Post* 13 May, All of the indictments were nolle-prossed late last evening. **1897** HOUGH *Story of Cowboy* 322 The prosecution for the State *nolle prossed* the cases. **1905** *Springfield W. Repub.* 15 Dec. 2 The court heard petitions for a new trial, and upon these being granted the cases were nol prossed and the brothers set free.

*****No man's land.** An area not included or clearly embraced in any established jurisdiction. Often applied as a proper name. +**a.** A small island near Martha's Vineyard, Massachusetts. Also attrib.

1675 in C. E. BANKS *Hist. Martha's Vineyard* I. 35 That no man presume to land any goods any where at Marthas Vineyard, . . . Nomans Land, or Elizabeth Isles, unless at the places appointed. **1884** *Nat. Museum Bul.* No. 27, 695 No Man's Land Fishing Boat. . . . The boats built from this model are employed in the shore fisheries about Vineyard Sound and No Man's Land.

+**b.** The area of the present panhandle of Oklahoma. Now hist.

Until 1890 this area, which had been ceded to the United States by Texas in 1845, was not assigned to any state or territory. It was proposed that it should form a separate territory of Cimarron.

1885 *Santa Fé Wkly. New Mexican* 16 July 3/2 Nearly 50,000 cattle . . . have been forcibly stopped and prevented from passing over the common trail . . . through the Indian country, the Cherokee strip and no man's land. **1891** O'BEIRNE *Leaders Ind. Territory* 66/2 James became restless for adventure, and determined to go to Mexico, but never got farther than 'No Man's Land' north of the Indian Territory. **1896** *Congress. Rec.* 16 May 5338/2 From the Sabine to the Rio Grande, and from No Mans Land to the Gulf of Mexico he [W. H. Crain] was known to all.

+**c.** (See quotation.)

1892 WALSH *Lit. Curiosities* 806 *No Man's Land.* . . . Locally, the name is also given to a strip of territory on the boundary between Pennsylvania and Delaware. According to the official surveys, it seems to belong to Pennsylvania, but by habit and custom of the people to Delaware.

*****Nominate,** *v.*

1. *tr.* **a.** To propose (someone) as a candidate for an elective office. {1601-} **b.** *spec.* To choose (someone) in a caucus or convention to run as a candidate for a political office.

1828 WEBSTER, Any member of the assembly or meeting *nominates,* that is, proposes to the chairman the name of a person whom he desires to have elected. **1831** J. Q. ADAMS *Memoirs* VIII. 437 He was nominated by the National Republican Convention at Baltimore yesterday for the Presidency. **1872** *Newton Kansan* 19 Sept. 2/1 The Missouri Republicans have nominated ex-senator John B. Henderson for Governor. **1906** *Springfield W. Repub.* 5 July 1 The prohibitionists have nominated Mr. Berry for governor and have failed to fuse on other nominations.

+**2.** Of the president of the United States: To appoint (someone) to a particular office, subject to confirmation by the Senate.

1894 *Harper's Mag.* May 967/1 Senator Edward D. White was nominated by President Cleveland to be Associate Justice of the Supreme Court. **1900** *Congress. Rec.* 3 Jan. 633/2 Edward H. Banks . . . was nominated [to be collector of customs] and confirmed by the Senate . . . as Edward Banks.

+**Nominating convention.** A party convention of delegates chosen to nominate candidates for political office. (Cf. CONVENTION *n.* 2 a, quot. 1817.) — **1866** 'F. KIRKLAND' *Bk. Anecdotes* 54 The following jaunty account is told of an interview with the Cabinet chiefs, just after the Baltimore Republican Nominating Convention. **1882** McCABE *New York* 123 They will not attend the primary meetings or the nominating conventions. **1902** E. C. MEYER *Nominating Systems* 7 The introduction of these meetings of delegates which took to themselves the name of 'nominating conventions,' . . . is the most important landmark in the third era of the development of our nominating machinery.

***Nomination.** +(See quot. 1806.) *Obs.* — **1806** WEBSTER 203/1 *Nomination*, . . . in Connecticut, a list of men selected by choice as candidates for council or congress. **a1817** DWIGHT *Travels* I. 254 At the same time, and place, they vote, also, for twenty persons as a Nomination for the Council of the ensuing year.

Nomination paper. A nominating petition. — **1897** F. W. DALLINGER *Nominations for Elective Office in U.S.* 180 In Massachusetts and Colorado nomination papers must be accompanied by the written acceptance of the candidate. **1914** *Cycl. Amer. Govt.* II. 552/1 The names of persons with nomination papers complete are placed on an official ballot.

Nominee. {1664–} +One who has been nominated by a political party to run as a candidate in an approaching election.

1848 LOWELL *Biglow P.* 1 Ser. ix. 126, I didn't like at fust the Pheladelphy nomernee. **1852** *Harper's Mag.* Nov. 833/2 The Hon. Wm. A. Graham, Whig nominee for the Vice Presidency. **1877** *Ib.* March 627/2 The Republican nominee for that office is Benjamin F. Prescott. **1900** *Congress. Rec.* 17 Feb. 1901/1, I want to see Ohio cast its electoral vote for the Democratic nominee for President. **1916** THOBURN *Stand. Hist. Okla.* II. 694 The populist nominee was Ralph Beaumont.

Noncommissioned officer. *Mil.* An enlisted man appointed to the rank of sergeant or corporal not by a commission, but by the Secretary of War or the commanding officer of the regiment. {1703–}

1777 *Jrnls. Cont. Congress* VIII. 426 *Resolved*, That the clothier general furnish each non-commissioned officer and soldier . . . with the articles of cloathing enumerated by a resolution of Congress. **1846** *Whig Almanac 1847* 19/1 This command of Captain Thornton's consisted of . . . sixty-one privates and non-commissioned officers. **1874** GLISAN *Jrnl. Army Life* 453 The wives of the private soldiers and non-commissioned officers are denominated camp-women. **1884** *Century Mag.* May 141/1 Every officer or non-commissioned officer who wore a badge of rank was killed or wounded, save one.

+**Noncommittal,** *n.* A refusal to commit oneself on a matter. *rare.* {1876–} — **1833** *Congress. Deb.* 30 Dec. 82 This message was a non-committal. The President does not announce clearly his own opinion. **1840** HALIBURTON *Clockmaker* 3 Ser. xii, Not lettin' on as if I know'd that he was there, for there is nothin' like a non-committal.

+**Noncommittal,** *a.* Not committed on a particular issue; neither assenting nor dissenting. {1890–} — **1829** ORNE *Lett. Columbus* 18 The non-committal system prevailed. **1851** *Fraser's Mag.* Sept. 287/2 A successful politician here [in New York] is . . . a 'non-committal' man, who says everything to everybody, and never gave an intelligible, manly, straightforward opinion in his life. **1879** J. HAWTHORNE *Laughing Mill* 112 It was written in an ordinary business hand, quite characterless and non-committal.

+**Noncommittalism.** A policy or practice of being uncommitted on a particular question or in general. {1891–} — **1838** *U.S. Mag.* I. 52 The Democratic party was determined to explode at least that portion of the plan of their opponents which involved a present non-committalism on the question of a National Bank. **1845** *Congress. Globe* App. 11 Jan. 295/3 We have had bold messages from the land of abstractions [Va.]; this is a message from the headquarters of non-committalism. **a1848** *N.Y. Commercial Advertiser* (B.), On many points he either avoids the expression of opinion, or expresses his opinion with so many qualifications as to subject himself to the charge of *non-committalism*.

+**Noncommittally,** *adv.* In a noncommittal way. — **1885** HOWELLS *Silas Lapham* 148 'She's a pretty girl,' said Corey, non-committally. **1890** — in *Harper's Mag.* March 515/2 'Oh, yes,' she said, non-committally.

+**Nonconcur,** *v. tr.* To reject; to refuse to agree to. Also absol.

1703 SEWALL *Diary* II. 83 Bristol Business is Non-concurr'd by the Deputies. **1721** *Mass. H. Rep. Jrnl.* III. 39 The Council have oftimes Non-Concurred Bills, that the House have been very Sollicitous to have Passed into Acts. **1790** *Mass. Spy* 23 Dec. (Th.), The house then non-concurred that part of the message. **1823** TUDOR *Otis* 239 The Council non-concurred this resolve [from the House, Boston, 1766]. **1911** PERSONS, etc. *Mass. Labor Laws* 53 The House went on record as favorable to the resolution. The State nonconcurred.

b. Also with *in* and *with.* Usu. *intr.*

1855 *Chicago Times* 3 March 3/5 The House non-concurred with the Senate amendment appropriating $30,000 to purchase Camels for army use. **1862** *Congress. Globe* 9 July 3214/1, I hope the House will non-concur in that amendment of the Senate. **1871** *Harper's Mag.* June 150/2 The Senate amendments were non-concurred in by the House, and a conference committee was appointed. **1907** *Springfield W. Repub.* 20 June 1 The Senate has nonconcurred with the House amendments.

Nonconductor. *Phys.* A substance or material that has little or no conductivity with respect to heat, electricity, etc. {1759–} Also fig. — **1751** FRANKLIN *Writings* III. 36 The terms *electric* . . . and *non-electric*, should be laid aside as improper . . . ; the terms *conductor* and *non-conductor* may supply their place. **1842** *Nat. Hist. N.Y., Geology* II. 420 *Non-conductors for Safes.* Asbestus occurs in only limited quantities in the northern district. **1857** *Ill. Agric. Soc. Trans.* II. 179 Nail on the outside plank first, edge to edge, and as you advance with the outside let the teamster be filling in with the nonconductor. **1875** STOWE *We & Neighbors* 201 When you intend to produce real acquaintance that shall ripen into intimacy, it is necessary that there should be no non-conductors to break the circle. **1876** INGRAM *Centennial Exp.* 276 These articles are said to be water-proof, non-conductors, durable, and undoubtedly capable of a fine finish.

+**Nonconsumption.** *Hist.* A refusal to consume, as in the policy announced in 1774 by the American colonies of refusing to consume tea and other products imported from England or English possessions. Also attrib. — **1774** J. ADAMS *Works* IX. 347, I believe we shall agree to non-importation, non-consumption, and non-exportation. **1774** *Jrnls. Cont. Congress* I. 53 A plan for carrying into effect, the non-importation, non-consumption, and non-exportation resolved on. *Ib.* 77 A non-consumption agreement . . . will be an effectual security for the observation of the non-importation.

+**Nondo.** [Origin obscure.] The angelico, *Ligusticum canadense.* — **1791** W. BARTRAM *Travels* 45, I observed . . . the carminative angelica lucida. [Note:] Called nondo in Virginia: by the Creek and Cherokee traders, white root. **1857** GRAY *Botany* 155 *L[igusticum] actæifolium.* . . . Nondo. Angelico. . . . Rich woods, Virginia, Kentucky. **1889** *Cent.* 210/2 *Angelico*, . . . an umbelliferous plant of North America, . . . resembling the lovage. Also called *nondo*.

None-so-pretty. Braid or tape used for ornamental purposes. *Obs.* {*c*1700–1759} Also as adj.

1754 *S.C. Gazette* 2/2 Just imported, . . . silk watch strings, none-so-pretties, star and scarlet gartering. **1759** *Newport Mercury* 26 June 4/3 To be Sold by Jacob Richardson, . . . Worsted Caps, striped Tapes, Nonesopretties, &c. **1771** in Earle *Costume Col. Times* (1894) 173 None-so-Pretty Tapes. **1772** *Ib.*, Blue & white, Red & white, Green & white Furniture checks with None-so-Prettys to match. **1804** CLARK in *Lewis & C. Exped.* VI. (1905) 271 For Indians Presents . . . 10 pieces Nonsoprettys.

***Nonesuch.** Also **nonsuch. 1.** =BLACK MEDICK. {1668–} **2.** A variety of apple. {1676–} — **(1) 1814** BIGELOW *Florula Bostoniensis* 174 Nonesuch. . . . When cultivated it is said to form a valuable grass, especially for sheep. **1843** TORREY *Flora N.Y.* I. 172 Black Medick, or Nonesuch. . . . Fields and cultivated grounds, road-sides, etc. **1860** *Darlington's Weeds & Plants* 100. **(2) 1846** B. ALCOTT *Journals* 176, I set out six apple trees. . . . They were Hubbard Stone, Nonesuch, Bell Flower, and Hood's Early Sweeting. **1859** ELLIOTT *Fruit Garden* 190 Nonsuch. English Nonsuch. Foreign. . . . October, November. [Superseded.] **1862** THOREAU *Excursions* 291, I have no faith in pomological gentlemen. . . . Their 'Favorites' and 'None-suches' and 'Seek-no-farthers' . . . commonly turn out very tame and forgetable.

+**Nonexportation.** *Hist.* A lack, stoppage, or refusal of exportation. Also attrib. — **1774** HUTCHINSON *Diary & Lett.* I. 323 They had agreed upon Non-Importation, Non-exportation, and Non-Consumption. **1774** *Jrnls. Cont. Congress* I. 76 We are of opinion, that a non-importation, non-consumption, and non-exportation agreement . . . will prove the most speedy, effectual, and peaceable measure. **1813** *Steele P.* II. 704 The Senate declined acting on . . . the Licence and non-exportation Bills.

+**Nonimportation.** *Hist.* The cessation of the process of importing goods; a policy advocating such cessation. {1833, in general sense}

1. Applied to the action taken by the American colonies in the Nonimportation Agreement (q.v., sense 2).

1774 [see NONEXPORTATION]. **1774** in *Mag. Amer. Hist.* I. 441 The Congress met and considered non-importation and non-exportation. **1775** in Johnston *N. Hale* 153 Their Resources are many, and so large that the Americans' Nonimportation & exportation will be like the lightdust of the Ballanca.

2. Applied to the policy of the United States government at the time of the nonimportation act (q.v.).

1809 *Steele P.* II. 617 Thus after running the destructive round of embargo—non-intercourse & non importation—we come back to the same place from which we started.

+**Nonimportation Act.** *Hist.* A law passed by Congress on April 18, 1806, prohibiting the importation of specified articles from Great Britain, as a measure of reprisal for British violations of American commercial rights. — **1811** *Salem Gazette* 29 Nov., The most odious measures of democracy in Congress, such as the Forcing Act, Non-importation Act, &c. have been prepared at midnight. **1812** *Niles' Reg.* III. 10/1 The non-importation act being still in force, must, in every respect, be carried into effect.

+**Nonimportation agreement.** *Hist.* **1.** An agreement not to import British goods, made by merchants of colonial America as retaliation for the Townshend Acts (1767). **2.** (See quotation 1889.) — **(1) 1770** in *Pennsylvania Mag.* VI. 118/2 A majority of your city have determined to break your Non-Importation Agreement. **(2) 1774** in *Copley-Pelham Lett.* 276 [The] Committee Men, have now enter'd upon their department to put the Non Importation agreem't in force. **1783** (*title*), The Constitutions of the Several Independent States of America. . . . To Which Are Now Added, the Declaration of Rights; the Non-importation Agreement [etc.]. **1889** *Cent.* 117/2 *Non-importation agreement*, an agreement made between the American colonies at Philadelphia, Oct. 20, 1774, not to import anything from or manufactured in Great Britain or Ireland or the West Indies. This action was taken by way of retaliation for the passage by Parliament of certain acts for raising revenue in America.

+**Nonimportation Law.** =NONIMPORTATION ACT. — **1807** *Ann. 10th Congress* 1 Sess. I. 1172 Mr. Quincy presented twenty-two memorials . . . praying for the modification, suspension, or repeal of a law commonly called the non-importation law. **1811** *Niles' Reg.* I. 103/2 One of the first acts of Congress will be—to enforce the non-importation law.

+**Nonintercourse.** {1826, in general sense} *Hist.* The suspending of commercial relations; a policy advocating such suspension.

+**1.** Between the United States and Great Britain, or between the United States and both Great Britain and France.

1807 *Ann. 10th Congress* 1 Sess. I. 13 A five years' state of non-intercourse with Great Britain will establish the manufactures of America on a foundation which no return of peace will ever shake. **1809** JEFFERSON *Writings* XII. 265 We have substituted for it [the embargo] a non-intercourse with France and England and their dependencies, and a trade to all other places. **1813** S. MORSE in *N. Amer. Rev.* CXCVI. 123 The measures of the embargo, non-intercourse, and war I consider as just measures against this country [England].

+**2.** Between the North and the South.

1851 in Claiborne *Life Quitman* II. 122 Non-intercourse with abolition states . . . may also be recommended. **1859** in Harper *S. B. Anthony* I. 184 Measures are in progress . . . to establish non-intercourse with you and to proscribe all articles of northern manufacture or origin, including New England teachers.

+**Nonintercourse law.** Also **Nonintercourse act.** *Hist.* A law suspending commercial intercourse between nations, esp. a retaliatory law or act passed by Congress in 1809, cutting off commercial relations with England and France and prohibiting British and French vessels from entering United States ports.

Since the 1809 quot. in the *O.E.D.* does not correspond to anything in the original French text, it may be reflecting American usage.

1800 JEFFERSON *Writings* XVIII. 216 The continuance of the non-intercourse law for another year, and the landing of our commissioners at Lisbon, have placed the opening of the French market . . . at such a distance that I thought it better to sell our tobacco at New York. **1809** *Ib.* 259 The non-intercourse law will be past. **1810** *Steele P.* II. 645 [The President] has issued his proclamation in favor of France in direct contradiction to his own construction of the power given to him by the last non-intercourse law. **1812** *Niles' Reg.* II. 119/2 In the memorial of sundry merchants of this city to Congress, praying a modification or suspension of the non-intercourse law, it is stated [etc.]. **1832** JACKSON *Statesmanship in Writings* 236 The excise law in Pennsylvania, the embargo and nonintercourse law in the Eastern States, the carriage tax in Virginia, were all deemed unconstitutional. **1835** C. P. BRADLEY *I. Hill* 27 This, it is to be remembered, was immediately after the renewal of the non-intercourse act.

Nonintervention. {1831–} *Hist.* The policy on the part of Congress of allowing territorial governments to decide the slavery question for themselves. Also attrib. (Cf. POPULAR SOVEREIGNTY.)

1854 BENTON *Exam. Dred Scott Case* (1857) 191 Here again might be found a case for the non-intervention principle; but of that I say nothing. **1861** DOUGLAS in Logan *Great Conspiracy* 172 Congress must and could prohibit Slavery in the Territories. The issue for ten years was between Non-intervention on the part of Congress, and prohibition by Congress. **1864** GREELEY *Amer. Conflict* I. 312 'Non-Intervention' with 'Popular Sovereignty' was the original and established Democratic doctrine with regard to Slavery in the Territories. **1913** A. C. COLE *Whig Party in So.* 156 [The Whigs] had advanced to the abandoned ground of non-intervention, of 'popular sovereignty' as understood in the South at this time.

b. A policy of non-interference with the political affairs of other countries except as provided for by the Monroe Doctrine. {1831–, in general sense}

1852 *Congress. Globe* 2 Feb. 439/3 Would not the establishment of the principles of non-intervention as the law of nations, be in direct opposition to the principles declared by Mr. Monroe in relation to the continent? **1852** *Harper's Mag.* April 692/1 Further debate has been had upon the resolutions on the subject of non-intervention. **1898** *Amer. Acad. Pol. Sci. Ann.* May 66 The Monroe Doctrine, if it applies to Cuba, commits us to a policy of non-intervention with regard to that island as long as Spain continues even in nominal possession.

+**Nonny.** [From NONPARTISAN *a.*] A nonpartisan voter. *slang.* — **1888** *Voice* 9 Feb., The Work of Spiteful Nonnies.

***Nonpareil.** +The painted bunting (*Passerina ciris*) of the southern and southwestern states.

[**1758** G. EDWARDS *Gleanings* I. 132 The Painted Finch . . . , more generally known to the curious in London by the name of Nonpareil and Mariposa.] **1811** WILSON *Ornithology* III. 68 Painted Bunting. . . . This is one of the most numerous of the little summer birds of Lower Louisiana, where it is universally known . . . by the Americans [as] the *Nonpareil.* **1847** *Knickerb.* XXIX. 493 The sun-light quivered through the leafy branches, disclosing the rainbow-hued nonpareil, as it flitted from limb to limb. **1887** WARNER in *Harper's Mag.* Feb. 349/2 There [in La.] was the lively little nonpareil, which seems to change its colour, and is red and green and blue. **1917** *Birds of Amer.* III. 73.

Nonpartisan, *a.* Not connected with a political party; free from party affiliation. Also absol. — **1885** *Century Mag.* April 823 A citizens' ticket, largely non-partisan in character, was run for certain local offices. **1888** *Voice* 9 Feb., The non-partisans have for some time been making Mr. Johnson's position very uncomfortable for him. **1900** *Congress. Rec.* 16 Jan. 874/1 The Department's action so far has been patriotic and non-partisan. **1925** BRYAN *Memoirs* 285 The [Chautauqua] movement is supported and guaranteed by a large local committee, unsectarian and non-partisan.

***Nonresident,** *n.* One whose residence is outside a specified area, esp. an owner of property who resides elsewhere. {1819–}

1713 SEWALL *Diary* II. 409 Henry Farwell of Dunstable talks with me about a Meeting at Woburn of the Non-residents. **1803** *Ann. 7th Congress* 2 Sess. 1291 There are large bodies of unproductive land owned by non-residents. **1840** KIRKLAND *Western Clearings* 6 They hated . . . him who aided by his local knowledge the immense purchases of non-residents. **1881** *Mich. Gen. Statutes* I. (1882) 571 If such owner be a non-resident of such county, then . . . within five days, Sunday excepted, from the date of said notice, . . . [he shall] effectually remove or destroy said hives. **1906** *Indian Laws & Tr.* III. 191 The said lands and the improvements thereon shall be appraised by three disinterested appraisers, who shall be non-residents of the county wherein the land is situated.

***Nonresident,** *a.* Not residing permanently within a particular or specified jurisdiction. — **1721** *Mass. H. Rep. Jrnl.* III. 29 This Court did impower them to Levy a Tax on the Lands of the Resident and Non-Resident Proprietors of said Town. **1787** *Mich. Gen. Statutes* I. (1882) 29 In no case shall non-resident proprietors be taxed higher than residents. **1885** *Calif. Supreme Ct. Rep.* LXVII. 382 A person who was born in another country and . . . is here residing . . . temporarily . . . [is] a non-resident alien.

+**Nonresident land.** Land owned by one who does not reside upon it, or within the community where it is located. — **1849** CHAMBERLAIN *Ind. Gazetteer* 313 The large amount of non-resident lands has hitherto retarded improvements. **1869** *Mich. Gen. Statutes* I. (1882) 326 If the tax be assessed on real estate, such real estate shall be returned in the same manner as if the same were non-resident lands. **1881** *Ib.* 385 Such notice to owners of such non-resident lands, shall be served by posting up the same in three public places.

+**Nonslaveholder.** One not an owner of Negro slaves. Now hist. — *c***1841** in Stowe *Key* 149 The burden of this defence . . . is to fall upon the less wealthy class of our citizens, chiefly upon the non-slaveholder. **1850** in Claiborne *Life Quitman* II. 37 A large proportion of the population are non-slaveholders. **1862** in Logan *Great Conspiracy* 418 [The Border States] calculated largely . . . upon the repugnance of Non-Slaveholders in those States to a Free Negro population. **1880** TOURGEE *Bricks* 275 That struggle which the non-slaveholders fought . . . in the interest of the slaveholding aristocracy.

+**Nonslaveholding,** *a.* Not believing in, practicing, or permitting slavery. Now hist. — **1853** STOWE *Key* 208/2 Here we have the Presbyterian Church, slave-holding and non-slaveholding, virtually formed into one great abolition society. **1854** BENTON *30 Years' View* I. 18/1 Including the extinction in Texas consequent upon its cession to a non-slaveholding power. **1865** in Fleming *Hist. Reconstruction* I. 117 The outrages are mostly from non-slave holding whites against the negro, and from the negro upon the non-slaveholding whites.

+**Nonslaveholding state.** A state in which slavery is not practiced or permitted. Now hist.

1819 *Ann. 15th Congress* 2 Sess. II. 1235 A line . . . shall divide the slave-holding from the non-slaveholding States. **1835** JACKSON in Benton *30 Years' View* (1854) I. 575/1 The deep-rooted attachment of the people of the non-slaveholding States, to the Union. **1846** *McDonogh P.* 88 If the senators . . . from your state, a non-slaveholding state, would bring forward such a law. **1860** in Logan *Great Conspiracy* 230 There ought not have been . . . any irrepressible conflict between the Slaveholding and the non-Slaveholding States. **1886** LOGAN *Ib.* 87 All 'open or covert attacks [on slavery] . . . ,' made either by the Non-Slave-holding States or their citizens.

Nonunion, *a.* {1890–} Not belonging to a trade union; not employing union labor. — **1874** *Internat. Typogr. Union Proc.* 22 Attempt to force non-Union printers upon Union printers. **1896** *Columbus Dispatch* 22 Dec. 1 Several others made uncomplimentary remarks about the non-union driver. **1898** *Mo. So. Dakotan* I. 106 Did you ever notice non-union concerns parade the fact? **1906** *Outlook* 9 June 784/1 The non-union shop from which unionists are completely excluded . . . [is] very strongly represented [in the United States].

Nonunion man. A man who does not belong to a labor union. {1863–} — **1872** *Chicago Tribune* 9 Oct. 3/1 There are enough non-union men to do all the work that is offered. **1887** *Courier-Journal* 29 Jan. 5/1 Non-union men employed at the Ward line docks struck for union rates. **1904** *McClure's Mag.* Feb. 371/2 The union has even offered money to non-union men working in the *Times* offices to induce them to desert.

Noodle. A thin strip of dough, of varying widths, usually made with egg. {1779–} Usually pl. — **1812** MELISH *Travels* II. 75 We did not much like the appearance of the dish, which was called *noodles*, but, on tasting it, we found it to be very palatable. **1871** DE VERE 144 *Noodles*, also, derive their name from the German *Nudeln*, and differ from the vermicelli of Italy only in the addition of eggs. **1885** *Outing* VII. 71/2 Each plate adorned with a pair of extraordinary 'noodles'—two tiny twists of a delicious paste, tied together by a strip of the same. **1904** *N.Y. Herald* 30 Oct., Fresh noodles are made daily for consumption in the German quarter.

+**Noodlejees.** *pl. local.* =prec. — **1848** BARTLETT 235 *Noodlejees.* (Dutch.) Wheat dough rolled thin and cut into strings like maccaroni. It is used for the same purpose. **1871** DE VERE 83 *Noodlejees*, an humble imitation of maccaroni and used like them for dumplings and in soup, retain in New York at least their old Dutch name, but are hardly known elsewhere. **1896** *Dialect Notes* I. 383 *Noodeljees*, . . . 'noodles.' [N.J.]

***Nook.** A triangular piece or corner of land; a point or neck. In full *nook of land*. — **1638** *Essex Inst. Coll.* IX. 80 Henry Bayly desires a little nooke of land next Mr. Conants howse at Catt Cove. **1716** *Boston Select-men* 4 The Select men . . . Do consent . . . that the S[ai]d Mr. Davenport do Inclose and add unto his Land . . . as far Southerly as the S[ai]d corner or nook of Land. **1769** *Va. House of Burgesses* 196 The Inconveniences complained of . . . preceed from the Form of the Parish, running up Appomattox River in a very long and narrow Nook.

***Noon,** *n.*

+1. *Big noon, little noon*, (see quotation). *Penna.*

1870 *Nation* 28 July 56/2 Recess, as we say now, the young 'micher' of fifty years ago called 'little noon,' while 'big noon' was the interval between the forenoon and afternoon sessions of the school.

2. *attrib.* In special combinations.

Noon basket, a small basket in which a pupil carries lunch to school; *n. camp*, a camp or halt made by travelers at noon; *n. time*, the time of noon recess at school; *n. train*, a train that starts its run at noon.

1865 A. D. WHITNEY *Gayworthys* vi, Don't you remember what we used to say at school, when we opened our noon-baskets? **1850** GARRARD *Wah-To-Yah* i. 17 We reached the Grand Arkansas for noon camp. **1834** *Knickerb.* III. 283 [They] would sit and read for hours together from the same story book, during 'noon time' and 'play time,' . . . in front of the school-house. **1904** STRATTON-PORTER *Freckles* 347, I'm going to take Freckles to Chicago on the noon train.

+**Noon,** *v. intr.* To spend the noon hour; to halt for rest and lunch at noon. Also with *it*. {*dial.*}

1805 LEWIS in *L. & Clark Exped.* II. (1904) 9 We nooned it just above the entrance of a large river. **1834** A. PIKE *Sketches* 66 We fell off from the prairie into a bottom of good land. . . . Here we nooned. **1883** SWEET & KNOX *Through Texas* 84 'Nooning it' means stretching a rope out on the prairie . . . ; it means gathering an armful of wood and buffalo chips . . . ; it means a dinner . . . ; it means a long nap [etc.]. **1894** WISTER in *Harper's Mag.* Sept. 515/1 'We'll noon here,' said the General. *a***1918** G. STUART *On Frontier* I. 84 Nooned on the divide between American and Indian valleys, and camped for the night down in Indian valley.

+**Noon halt.** A halt in a journey for rest and refreshment at noon; also, the place where such a halt is made. — **1843** FRÉMONT *Explor.* 15 At our noon halt, the men were exercised at a target. **1854** BARTLETT *Personal Narr.* II. 395 On our return we made a noon halt on the banks of the river. *a***1918** G. STEWART *On Frontier* I. 115 John Dickey rode ahead from our noon halt to try to kill a sage hen.

+**Noon hour.** A period used for rest and lunch at noon. — **1889** *Charity Organisation Rev.* Aug. 341 He asked a few men to call every day at his noon hour at the place where he worked. **1902** WISTER *Virginian* xxx, Saving the noon hour, I had been in the saddle since six.

+**Noon house.** *New Eng.* A house adjacent to a church for the convenience of those from a distance who wished to attend both morning and afternoon services. Now hist. — **1845** JUDD *Margaret* I. 110 Several elderly men and women went to what was called a 'Noon House,' a small building near the Schoolhouse, where they ate their dinner and had a prayer. **1887** EGGLESTON in *Century Mag.* April 906/2 Some parishes in Massachusetts, and perhaps elsewhere, had a common 'noon-house' for all comers to rest in. **1891** EARLE *Sabbath* 102 There might have been seen a hundred years ago, by the side of many an old meeting-house in New England, a long, low, mean, stable-like building, with a rough stone chimney at one end. This was the 'noon-house,' or 'Sabba-day house,' or 'horse-hows,' as it was variously called. It was a place of refuge in the winter time, at the noon interval between the two services.

***Nooning.**

1. A meal at noonday. *Obsolescent.* {*a*1652–1849}

'Now *dial* and *U.S.*' (*O.E.D.*).

1805 *Pocumtuc Housewife* (1906) 7 Some families like to get up a great dinner on Sundays and have friends who drive to Meeting from a distance come in for the Nooning. **1880** 'MARK TWAIN' *Tramp Abroad* 359 A German gentleman and his two young lady daughters had been taking their nooning at the inn. **1889** COOKE *Steadfast* 416 He was alone in the study with his friend, waiting for Esther to prepare their simple 'nooning.'

2. A rest taken at noon {1552 only, 'Now *U.S.*'}; +a period for rest and refreshment at the middle of the day.

1847 PARKMAN in *Knickerb.* XXX. 231 We stopped for a short nooning at the side of a pool of rain-water. **1850** LOWELL *Letters* I. 193, I mean to take a nooning and lie under the trees looking at the sky. *a***1861** WINTHROP *Canoe & Saddle* iv. 63 There must be a long nooning, that the horses . . . might recruit. **1882** 'M. HARLAND' *Eve's Daughters* 145 Fifteen minutes of the hour's 'nooning' is consumed by the rapid run homeward. **1904** MABIE *Backgrounds of Lit.* 186 There is time for luncheon and a quiet nooning for the horses.

+b. =NOON RECESS.

1865 *Atlantic Mo.* Feb. 148/1 Two school girls—home for the nooning—are idling over a gateway. **1876** 'MARK TWAIN' *Tom Sawyer* xviii. 157 She said she would look at pictures all through the nooning. **1882** *Harper's Mag.* Feb. 434/2 At nooning next day, too, the school-children were full of [stories].

c. *New Eng.* The noon interval between morning and afternoon church services.

1865 WHITNEY *Gayworthys* 285 In the nooning Say joined herself to Blackmere again. *Ib.* 289 She reached the vestry just vacated by the Sunday School children, out now for their short 'nooning.' **1891** EARLE *Sabbath* 60 Not only could these men of authority keep the boys in order during meeting, but they also had full control during the nooning.

+3. (See quotation.)

1884 W. SHEPHERD *Prairie Exper.* 161 Through the heat of the day the sheep do not care to feed or to travel; if full they will lie down, seeking some shade, or drooping their heads under the shadow of each other's bodies. This is called nooning; it may begin as early as eight o'clock in the height of summer, and last till four or five in the evening.

+4. Attrib. in sense 2 with *hour, meal, sleep*, etc.

1856 *Porter's Spirit of Times* 20 Sept. 39/1 'Twas noonin' time, an' thar was niggers enough roun' an' about that field to skear the deer to death. **1863** A. D. WHITNEY *F. Gartney* xxiii, Luther Goodell . . . [got] into the way of straying up the field-path in his nooning hours. **1865** — *Gayworthys* v, Baskets were opened and the simple nooning meal, that needed intervention of neither knife nor fork, was eaten. **1867** 'LACKLAND' *Homespun* 290 The workers . . . eat and drink their forenoon fill, not unmindful of the coming dinner and the nooning spell. **1890** PHILLIPS in C. Martyn *Wendell Phillips* 443 A picture of a dozen sailors, taking their nooning sleep. **1895** WIGGIN *Village Watch-Tower* 59 It was used as a 'nooning' tree by all the men at work in the surrounding fields.

+**Nooning place.** A place, usu. one having such natural advantages as water, grass, shade, etc., for a noon stop or halt in a journey. — **1687** in *Amer. Speech* XV. 290 At ye head of a bottom tending to ye aforesaid Nooning place. **1849** PARKMAN in *Knickerb.* XXXIII. 5 As we approached our nooning place we saw five or six buffalo. **1884** BOURKE *Snake Dance of Moquis* 77 A sorcerer [was] killed near this very nooning-place.

+**Noon mark.** A mark made to indicate the position of noon shadows; hence, noon. Also fig. and transf. — **1854** B. J. TAYLOR *Jan. & June* 131 The sun has driven the shadows around under the west and north walls; it has reached the noon-mark on the threshold. **1880** COOKE in *Harper's Mag.* Sept. 585/2 Noon-mark was straightened out by the great gnomon of a tulip-tree on the turf dial where the shanty stood. **1889** — *Steadfast* 275 Goodness! 'tis most noon-mark and I haven't took a step towardst dinner. **1891** EARLE *Sabbath* 77 The time of the day was indicated to our forefathers in their homes by 'noon marks' on the floor or window-seats.

+**Noon recess.** A school recess at noon. — **1871** EGGLESTON *Hoosier Schoolm.* 38 Then the master walked out . . . to spend the noon recess in the woods. **1903** FOX *Little Shepherd* xii, Georgie Forbes . . . brought out the terrible charge in the presence of a dozen school-children at noon-recess one day.

+**Noon spell.** A period at noon for rest and lunch. — **1839** KIRKLAND *New Home* (1840) 319 Even the 'noon-spell' shines no holiday for the luckless subjects of her domination. **1886** HOWELLS *Minister's Charge* 167 At the noon-spell some of them sat with their arms round one another. **1897** *Outing* XXIX. 419/1 We'll make one [stop] every night, an' git lunches for noon-spells.

+**Nootka cypress.** Also **Nootka Sound cypress.** [*Nootka Sound*, harbor on Vancouver Island, British Columbia.] An evergreen tree of the Pacific coast (*Chamaecyparis nootkatensis*) valuable for its hard, yellow wood. — **1892** APGAR *Trees Northern U.S.* 195 Nootka Sound Cypress. . . . Tree 100 ft. high in Alaska. **1897** SUDWORTH *Arborescent Flora* 79 Yellow Cedar. . . . [Also called] Nootka Cypress (Cal. lit.). Nootka Sound Cypress (cult. Eng.).

+**Nootka fir.** [See prec.] The Douglas fir, *Pseudotsuga taxifolia.* — **1803** LAMBERT *Descr. Genus Pinus* 51 Nootka Fir. . . . A specimen . . . was discovered on the North-west coast of America [by Menzies]. **1813** MUHLENBERG *Cat. Plants* 89 *Pinus taxifolia*, Nootka fir.

Nopal, *a.* The cochineal cactus (*Nopalea coccinellifera*), or a related species. {1730–, in Central and Spanish America} **b.** A prickly pear. (Cf. INDIAN FIG.)

1823 JAMES *Exped.* II. 209 The nopals are considered characteristic of warm and dry climates. **1837** WILLIAMS *Florida* 111 [At maturity the Cochineal insect is] scraped off the nopal with a feather, and exposed to a hot sun for twenty successive days, on a piece of polished tin or other metal. **1863** *Rep. Comm. Agric. 1862* 61 The Cochineal insect is a native of Florida. The Nopal, on which the insect feeds, is also a native plant. **1875** BOURKE *Journal* 30 May, A plant, plentiful in this country [along the South Cheyenne R.], called the nopal, or Tuna cactus, plate cactus, or Indian fig is employed with success to clarify water for drinking purposes. **1891** *Century Mag.* Jan. 386 More Nopal hedges were planted, and the old ones extended.

+**No-party.** *attrib.* Not belonging to a political party; nonpartisan.— **1828** *Yankee* 16 July 230/3 Wo to the no-party-man, who is fed of both parties. **1842** *Amer. Pioneer* I. 276 History informs us that since the struggle of 1799–1800, there presided a no-party-president. **1848** in *Scribner's Mo.* XIX. 60/1 Hall wanted it a no-party call.

‖**No-partyism.** The condition of being unaffiliated with any political party.— **1848** in Shields *S. S. Prentiss* (1883) 407, I am not ready to abandon such a party and such principles for the chimera of independent no-partyism.

+**Nope,** *adv.* No. *colloq.* — **1888** *Chicago Tribune* (F.), 'I suppose you will be a literary man . . . when you grow up.' 'Nope,' said the little boy . . . , 'literary nuthin'!' **1891** BUNNER *Zadoc Pine* 85 'Was you at the Sweatmans' sociable?' she inquired. 'Nope,' said Mr. Cargill. **1905** *N.Y. Ev. Post* 7 March 14 'Got your life insured?' . . . 'Nope, I'll take a chance.' **1923** 'BOWER' *Parowan Bonanza* 14 'Nope, I'm a never-was,' Bill retorted shamelessly.

***Norfolk.** *attrib.* [Name of a county in England.] Designating varieties of turnips. — **1765** WASHINGTON *Diaries* I. 212 The upper part of [the garden] . . . is the Norfolk Turnep. **1788** *Ib.* III. 396 Sowed Turnips yesterday in a square below the Stables—Norfolk Globe. **1805** PARKINSON *Tour* 338 A few of the Norfolk lily-white, and some of the Norfolk green-top [turnips are in use].

Normal, *a.* {1650–} +Erected for or devoted to the training of teachers. (Cf. NORMAL SCHOOL.) — **1857** *Ill. Laws* 298 The Board of Education of the State of Illinois . . . [shall] establish by-laws and alter or repeal the same as they shall deem necessary for the government of the normal university hereby authorized to be established. **1878** *Harper's Mag.* April 677/1 The Normal College of New York City . . . contains . . . a library, a calisthenium, two drying-rooms. **1881** *New Eng. Jrnl. Educ.* XXIV. 347 Prof. P. J. Williams to the deanship of the Normal department. **1894** *Educator* Nov. 166/2 The normal classes at Washington and Northampton have been created by a demand. **1901** DUNCAN & SCOTT *Allen & Woodson Co., Kansas* 597 The normal institute . . . is, in Kansas, the educational Chautauqua of the school teacher.

Normal school. {1834–, with reference to Continental schools, tr. of Fr. *école normale*}

+**1.** A school for training teachers, usually state-supported and forming part of the system of public education.

1839 *Mass. Acts & Resolves* 30 Said board may occupy the premises, and establish and maintain a Normal school therein, and have the entire management and control of the same. **1854** *Penna. Agric. Rep.* 230 Normal schools are founded for the express purpose of training teachers and assistants for the agricultural schools. **1872** BRACE *Dangerous Classes N.Y.* 181 We chanced on a teacher of singular ability . . . , a graduate of the best Normal School in the country. **1900** *Congress. Rec.* 24 Jan. 1130/2 She attended a normal school . . . and she is now employed as a teacher in a church academy. **1910** *Okla. Session Laws* 3 Legisl. 2 Any act for the removal or location of the state capital or any normal school or other educational or charitable institution.

2. Attrib. with *building, fund, ground,* etc.

1854 *Mass. Acts & Resolves* 437 That the sum of five hundred dollars be appropriated for repairs and improvements to be made upon the State Normal School-house at Westfield. **1865** *Nation* I. 779 The largest school, held in the old Normal School building, contains nearly eight hundred pupils. **1875** *Mich. Gen. Statutes* I. (1882) 182 All money . . . placed to the credit of . . . the normal school fund. **1881** *Harper's Mag.* April 664/1 A party of excursionists landed on the Normal School grounds. **1920** *3d Nat. Country Life Conf. Proc.* 47 Young people who have had the advantage of normal-school and college training . . . appreciate the value of these things.

***North.** *collect.* +The population of the northern states. Used esp. in reference to the sectional struggle between the North and South.

1796 WASHINGTON in *Pres. Mess. & P.* I. 215 The North, in an unrestrained intercourse with the South, . . . finds in the productions of the latter great additional resources. **1842** *Whig Almanac 1843* 28/2 War with her [S.C.] would, beyond doubt, soon become a war between the North and the South. **1855** PIERCE in *Pres. Mess. & P.* V. 344 [The] groundless allegation that the South has persistently asserted claims and obtained advantages in the practical administration of the General Government to the prejudice of the North. **1865** PIKE *Scout & Ranger* (1932) 132 Every proposition of the North was treated with disdain. **1907** *Springfield W. Repub.* 2 May 4 The men who fought in the civil war beneath the banners of the North or the cross-barred flag of the confederacy.

North America. That part of the continent of North America occupied by European, especially British, colonists. *Obs.* — **1715** *Boston News-Letter* 17 Jan. 2/2 Robert Mompesson, Esq., Barrister at Law, . . . was esteemed the best Lawyer in North-America. **1719/20** *Boston Gazette* 11 Jan. 1 John Hamilton, Esq., Deputy Post Master General of North-America. **1766** Buckingham *Newspaper Lit.* I. 294 What else can be the meaning of his barefaced Falsehood, in representing North-America as in a state of absolute rebellion against the best of Kings?

North American, *n.* **a.** A person of European descent living in North America, esp. in the United States. **b.** An Indian of North America.

(a) 1766 FRANKLIN *Writings* III. (1887) 501 Did ever any North-American bring his hemp to England for this bounty? **1769** OTIS in Tudor *Life J. Otis* 361 William Burch, and John Robinson, Esquires, have frequently . . . treated the characters of all true North Americans in a manner that is not to be endured. **1775** *Jrnls. Cont. Congress* III. 316 The Inhabitants of Passamaquaddy in Nova Scotia, having chosen a committee of Safety, and having, by their petition, applied to the Congress to be admitted into the association of the North Americans, for the preservation of their rights and liberties. **1838** C. NEWELL *Revol. Texas* 20 The notorious and, more than all, odious law of the 6th of April, 1830, prohibiting the farther emigration of North Americans to Texas, except in so far as regarded the fulfilment of existing contracts. **(b) 1775** ADAIR *Indians* 197 Any English reader [of Spanish writers] . . . will not only find a wild portrait, but a striking resemblance and unity of the civil and martial customs, the religious rites, and traditions, of the ancient Peruvians and Mexicans, and the North Americans. **1825** NEAL *Bro. Jonathan* II. 1 The Man of America—the Original North American: . . . the 'Indian,' as he is called.

North American, *a.* Of or pertaining to North America, esp. the United States.

1770 OTIS in Tudor *Life J. Otis* 476 My humble North American word of honour for it, my lord, these volumes will hurt neither thee, nor thy master. **1783** (*title*), The North-American Calendar. **1837** *S. Lit. Messenger* III. 695 A declaration of the independence of the North American States. **1838** C. NEWELL *Revol. Texas* 23 It must be perfectly evident that Mexican soldiers and North American citizens could not live together without collision. **1864** 'PENNIMAN' *Tanner-Boy* 17 Some of the most bitter enemies of the United States are to be found in the British North-American provinces. **1874** COUES *Birds N.W.* p. vii, To give it a distinctive character apart from the several North American Ornithologies published . . . , it seemed necessary to restrict its scope.

North American Indian. An Indian of North America.

1775 ADAIR *Indians* 197 We can trace a near agreement between the civil and martial customs . . . of the ancient Peruvians and Mexicans, and those of the present North-American Indians. **1788** FRENEAU *Poems* (1903) II. 369 *n.*, The North American Indians bury their dead in a sitting posture. **1835** CHANNING *Works* (1886) 720/2 The African . . . watches the life of a master, whom the North-American Indian, in like circumstances, would stab to the heart. **1880** CABLE *Grandissimes* 23 She had . . . the nerve of the true North American Indian. **1887** ALDEN *Little Fishers* xxiv, If he had asked them to say he was a North American Indian I believe they would have done it.

+**b.** In the Texas republic: An Indian in United States territory. *Obs.*

1837 *Diplom. Corr. Texas* I. (1908) 261 The prairie Indians are unskillful in the use of fire arms, who, without the guidance of N. American Indians, would be comparatively harmless.

Northbound, *a.* Bound for the north; going north. {1903–} — **1882** SWEET & KNOX *Texas Siftings* 23 He does not know whether the North-bound train leaves at 3 P.M. **1904** HARBEN *Georgians* 217 The young man was at the seven-o'clock north-bound train when it stopped in the . . . car-shed.

+**North Carolina.** *attrib.* Belonging to or identified with the state of North Carolina. — **1769** *Boston Chronicle* 6 Feb. 43/1 The North Carolina Regulators . . . drove a gang of villains back. **1826** in Benton *30 Years' View* (1854) I. 83/2 By the North Carolina convention, the same amendment was recommended. **1834** C. A. DAVIS *Lett. J. Downing* 110 He shook like a North Carolina ague. **1867** Goss *Soldier's Story* 61 The Buffaloes, as the North Carolina companies were called, escaped in some cases by swimming the river. **1868** *N.Y. Herald* 4 July 6/1 In the North Carolina Senate yesterday a resolution was introduced.

+**North Carolinian.** A native or inhabitant of North Carolina.

1787 in Ramsey *Tennessee* 392 A body of about fifteen hundred veterans, embodied themselves to rescue their governor . . . out of the hands of the North-Carolinians. **1800** *Steele P.* I. 197 As a North Carolinian and Native of the same State with yourself, I am ready [etc.]. **1852** in Commons, etc. *Doc. Hist.* VIII. 71 Where is the man, abstractionist, North Carolinian, Virginian, or citizen of any other State, who [etc.]? **1869** *Overland Mo.* III. 129 When you see a man . . . get a cold boiled sweet potato . . . and a piece of cane-brake cheese, . . . you may be certain he is a North Carolinian. **1873** *Winfield* (Kan.) *Courier* 17 July 1/5 The word 'galoot' does not mean us North Carolinians.

Northeaster. Also **nor'easter.**

1. A violent wind blowing from the northeast. {1836–48, nor'easter}

1774 FITHIAN *Journal* I. 235 This is a true August Northeaster, as we call it in Cohansie. **1787** in Brayley *Boston Fire Dept.* (1889) 90 The wind was a dry Northeaster and had prevailed two days. **c1840** NEAL *Beedle's Sleigh Ride* 34 One stormy day, I put my head down against a North-easter, and set my feet agoing. **1865** *Atlantic Mo.* XV. 546 A bleak morning wind mingled with the fierce, incessant nor'easter. **1887** WILKINS *Humble Romance* 180 Jackson Reed . . . had wildly and fruitlessly patched some of the worst places, off and on, after a hard 'northeaster.' **1891** WELCH *Recoll. 1830–40* 375 Occasionally a sleighing party would get snowed in, by an old fashioned 'North-easter.'

+**2.** A waterproof cap or hat worn in stormy weather.

1838 *Yale Lit. Mag.* III. 9 A large tarpaulin North Easter was the covering of my head.

+**Norther.** A furious cold wind from the north, esp. one blowing over Texas, the plains of the Southwest, or the Gulf of Mexico: (see also quot. 1891).

1820 DEWEES *Lett. from Texas* 17 A heavy storm of rain and sleet, together with a furious 'norther' overtook us. **1849** *31st Congress 1 Sess.* Sen. Ex. Doc. No. 64, 212 The cold 'norther' has had an effect upon our animals which I did not anticipate. **1857** OLMSTED *Journey through Texas* 169 These northers upon the open prairies are exceedingly trying. **1871–3** *Texas Almanac* 97 The people here in Texas divide these winter storms into 'wet northers' and 'dry northers.' **1891** *Scribner's Mag.* X. 283 The weather along the Pacific highway has been uniformly pleasant, for northers are infrequent. **1897** HOUGH *Story of Cowboy* 12 Such a storm is called a 'norther'; by which we may know that we are upon a Southern ranch or one manned by Southern cowmen. **1920** COOPER *Under Big Top* 177 It was in the autumn, and the carnival was rounding out its season in the south, only to be caught in a 'norther.'

+**b.** *Blue (Texas) norther*, a particularly violent norther.

1871–3 *Texas Almanac* 98 There is evidently in these dry 'blue northers' (as they are called) a state of high electrical condition of the atmosphere. **1872** MORRELL *Flowers & Fruits* 234 A blue Texas norther whistled around my ears. **1878** BEADLE *Western Wilds* 430 Warm, moist weather [in southern Texas] is generally followed very suddenly by a 'blue norther' that pinches one fearfully. **1905** 'O. HENRY' *Strictly Business* 93 It's a comfortable town. It's different from the plains in a blue norther.

***Northern,** *a.*

+**1.** Of persons or groups: Living in or coming from the northern colonies or states.

See also NORTHERN DEMOCRACY, NORTHERN DEMOCRAT.

1789 *Ann. 1st Congress* I. 227 Are the Northern people made of finer clay? **1790** *Steele P.* I. 69 Yourself and my other northern Friends may readily account why they have been so long without hearing from me. **1853** STOWE *Key* 476 This Methodist Church subsequently broke into a Northern and Southern Conference. . . . The Northern Conference has still in its communion slave-holding Conferences and members. **1855** in Hambleton *H. A. Wise* 343 We shall endeavor to . . . make some extracts from it for the benefit of its Northern Freesoil readers. **1867** DIXON *New America* I. 21 A Northern Emigrant Aid Society was founded in Massachusetts. **1881** *Harper's Mag.* April 720/2 The day scholars dressed with the exquisite simplicity of Northern school-girls. **1890** *Rep. Secy. Agric. 1889* 126 Most [varieties of apples were] . . . unknown to Northern orchardists.

+**2.** Of lakes, woods, etc.: Situated in the northern portion of the United States.

1814 *Ann. 13th Congress* 1 Sess. I. 1142 The crews of the fleets in the service of the United States, upon the Northern Lakes. **1865** *Atlantic Mo.* May 521/1 [The winter wren] is one of those birds of the deep Northern forests, that . . . only the privileged ones hear. **1889** DELAND *Florida Days* 170 One misses the silken rustle of the Northern woods. **1897** HOUGH *Story of Cowboy* 75 On the northern range the cow horse was called a 'cayuse.'

+**3.** Of various products: Made in or coming from the northern states. Also absol.

Cf. NORTHERN-MADE *a.*

1821 *Cape-Fear Recorder* 14 April, 10 barrels Northern Whiskey. **1829** *Free Press* (Tarboro, N.C.) 23 Jan., Cheese, northern butter, apples. **1843** HONE *Diary* II. 194 This ship has taken out to England a cargo consisting . . . of Northern productions, and the 'Ashburton,' which sailed a day or two since, has not a Southern article on board. **1847** *Florida Plantation Rec.* 335 Catherine 4½ Northern [Note:] 'Northern' means cloth from some northern factory.

+**b.** Of publications: Issued in the northern states.

1883 'MARK TWAIN' *Life on Miss.* xlvi, If one take up a Northern or Southern literary periodical of forty or fifty years ago, he will find it filled with wordy . . . 'eloquence.' **1900** *Congress. Rec.* 6 Feb. 1548/2 The Washington Post . . . understands the peculiar social and industrial conditions of our section better than any other Northern paper.

+**4.** Of activities or attitudes: Characteristic of or prevailing in the northern states, esp. with reference to the sectional differences underlying the Civil War.

1835 HOFFMAN *Winter in West* I. 68 The varied products of Northern industry. **1844** *Lexington Observer* 25 Sept. 4/5 The following rates . . . are so low as to make it the interest of the farmer to seek the Northern Market. **1857** BENTON *Exam. Dred Scott Case* 41 People of the slave States have a prejudice against that ordinance [of 1787] as being a northern measure, put upon them by the North, and from hostility to slavery. **1865** PIKE *Scout & Ranger* (1932) 127, I heard nothing now, but clamor about 'Northern aggression,' and 'Southern rights,' wherever I went. **1870** *Nation* 6 Jan. 4/1 The foul-mouthed organs of Northern Copperheadism. **1879** MOTLEY in Holmes *John Lothrop Motley* 108, I hammered the Northern views into him as soundly as I could.

+**5.** In specific names. **a.** Of trees and plants.

See also NORTHERN SPY.

1850 *New Eng. Farmer* II. 12/2 The name of some of these plants are the . . . Oak-leaved Gerardia, Northern Calla, and Northern Dracena. **1846** BROWNE *Trees Amer.* 265 *Cerasus borealis.* . . . The northern cherry is found in a common soil from Newfoundland to the northern parts of the Rocky Mountains. **1894** *Amer. Folk-Lore* VII. 101 *Clintonia borealis*, Northern lily, Penobscot Co., Me. **1892** APGAR *Trees Northern U.S.* 178 Gray or Northern Scrub Pine . . . [is] a straggling shrub, sometimes a low tree, found wild in the extreme Northern States. **1813** MUHLENBERG *Cat. Plants* 44 *Arbutus Acadiensis*, Northern strawberry tree. **1901** MOHR *Plant Life Ala.* 85 The Northern yellow wood (*Cladrastis tinctoria*) . . . reaches here its extreme southern station.

+**b.** Of birds and animals.

See also NORTHERN PHALAROPE, NORTHERN SHRIKE.

1917 *Birds of Amer.* II. 81/2 In northwestern Alaska . . . and the Great Lakes occurs . . . the Northern Bald Eagle (*Haliæetus leucocephalus alascanus*). **1813** WILSON *Ornithology* IX. 84 Great Northern Diver, or Loon: *Colymbus glacialis:* . . . is said to be restless before a storm. **1842** *Nat. Hist. N.Y., Zoology* I. 50 The Northern Lynx . . . is a timid animal. *Ib.* 47 The Northern Panther, *Felis concolor*, . . . is an animal of undoubted strength and ferocity. **1858** BAIRD *Birds Pacific R.R.* 142 Northern Swift. . . . This remarkable swift was first indicated as North American by Dr. Kennerly, in the proceedings of the Philadelphia Academy. **1828** BONAPARTE *Synopsis* 437 The Northern three-toed Woodpecker, *Picus tridactylus*, . . . inhabits the north of both continents. **1842** *Nat. Hist. N.Y., Zoology* III. 71 The Northern Tree-toad, *Hyla versicolor*, lives almost exclusively on trees. **1870** *Amer. Naturalist* III. 579 Northern Wax-wing. . . . The visits of this beautiful northern species so far south are very infrequent, and in only a few instances has it been recorded from [Mass.]

c. Of fishes.

1851 HERBERT *Frank Forester's Fish & Fishing of U.S.* 154 The Northern Pickerel is taken up to the weight of sixteen or seventeen pounds. **1856** *Porter's Spirit of Times* 1 Nov. 142/3 The northern pike, . . . in point of capacity, . . . ranks next to the muscalonge among our lake fishes.

Northern army. +During the Revolution and after, an army operating in the northern department. — **1775** *Jrnls. Cont. Congress* III. 341 A committee will be appointed to procure as much hard money as will be necessary to be transmitted to the deputy pay master general in the northern army, to be used in Canada. **1777** CUTLER in *Life & Corr.* I. 63 Mustering men to go the Northern Army. **1780** J. JONES *Letters* 10 Col. Grayson has mentioned to me his receiving a letter from Genl. Weedon desiring to serve in the northern army, if any employment can be carved out for him. **1814** *Niles' Reg.* VI. 37/2 General Harrison has received instructions from the war department, to return to the northern army.

+**Northern Democracy.** *Polit.* The northern wing or faction in the Democratic party. — **1854** BENTON *30 Years' View* I. 10/1 [The Missouri question led to] a federal movement, . . . sweeping all the Northern democracy into its current.

+**Northern Democrat.** A Democrat of or from the North. — **1845** *Xenia Torch-Light* 23 Oct. 2/2 The Administration project of reduction of the tariff by the votes of the Northern Democrats. **1881–5** MCCLELLAN *Own Story* 37 If they [=Southerners] had chosen to draw near the Northern Democrats again, seeking their remedy and protection within the Union, . . . they would have retained the right on their side. **1910** J. HART *Vigilante Girl* 293 These Chivs have been bullying us Northern Democrats long enough.

Northerner. {1863– M. Howitt, tr. Bremer *Greece.*} +A native or inhabitant of the northern states. — **1831** in Peck *Guide* 60 You may see [in New Orleans] . . . much beautiful shrubbery, such for beauty and splendor and fragrance the Northerners have never seen. **1852** STOWE *Uncle Tom* xix, I have no patience with the unutterable trash that some of your patronizing Northerners have made up. **1885** *Harper's Mag.* Sept. 547/2 One of the strongest impressions made upon a Northerner who visits the extreme South now . . . is the extent to which it suffered in the war. **1914** *Cycl. Amer. Govt.* I. 230/2 *Carpetbagger.* . . . By extension the term was often applied to any unpopular northerner living in the south.

Northern-made, *a.* +Made in the northern states. — **1828** *Free Press* (Tarboro, N.C.) 24 Oct., I have a northern made Cotton Gin. **1865** *Atlantic Mo.* April 512/1 What, with those new Northern-made pantaloons on?

***Northern man.** +A man living in or coming from the North.

1803 J. DAVIS *Travels* 209 There was a perpetual conflict of opinions between these southern and northern men. **1828** COOPER *Notions* II. 224 He is also a northern, or, as it would be expressed here [in Washington, D.C.], an eastern man (coming from New England). **1865** PIKE *Scout & Ranger* (1932) 132 The President was hung in effigy, and treated with indignity, simply because he was a Northern man, and was elected by free State votes. **1881** *Phil. Record* No. 3459, 2 The 'solid South' is a protest against carpet-bagism, whether in the form of Northern men going down in person to take charge of Southern politics or staying at home and trying to do the same thing by pulling wires. **1887** *Century Mag.* May 114/2 Northern men . . . had bought the plantation.

+**Northern phalarope.** A bird (*Lobipes lobatus*) of the family Phalaropodidae that breeds in northern Alaska and the far north. (Cf. PHALAROPE.) — **1858** BAIRD *Birds Pacific R.R.* 706 Northern Phalarope . . . one of the handsomest and most graceful of the wading birds. **1874** COUES *Birds N.W.* 470 In the interior of the United States the Northern Phalarope is nowhere so abundant as Wilson's, and appears to be of less general dispersion. **1882** GODFREY *Nantucket* 241/2, I have met with the . . . Northern Phalarope (*Phalaropus hyperboreus*). **1917** *Birds of Amer.* I. 219/1 Like the Red Phalarope, the Northern Phalarope breeds in the extreme north. . . . I have seen many flocks on the ocean, well off the shore of the New England coast, during August and September.

+**Northern shrike.** A shrike (*Lanius borealis*) found in the northern part of North America. (Cf. BUTCHERBIRD, NINE-KILLER.) — **1857** *Rep. Comm. Patents 1856: Agric.* 86 One of their greatest enemies in this vicinity [n. Ill.] is the Northern shrike, or butcher-bird, (*Lanius borealis*,) the food of which consists almost wholly of arvicolæ and a few white-footed prairie mice. **1867** *Amer. Naturalist* I. 42 The savage Butcher Bird or Northern Shrike . . . , which seems but a hawk in miniature, . . . is one of our regular, but not very numerous visitors [in Mass.]. **1869** *Ib.* III. 35 Northern Shrike. . . . I shot a specimen, the only one I saw, at Fort Dalles [Mont.], October 15th,—early in the season for it to appear even at that latitude. **1874** COUES *Birds N.W.* 101 Butcher Bird; Northern Shrike. . . . 'Quite common in Colorado, in October, about the Middle Park, and during the winter along the edge of the plains.'

+**Northern Spy.** A variety of hardy, red, winter apple; also an apple of this variety.

1847 IVES *New Eng. Fruit* 46 *Northern Spy.*—This new native fruit, originated near Rochester, N. York. It is a fine winter apple, and is one of the most popular fruits in New York. **1855** *Ill. Agric. Soc. Trans.* I. 361 Apples . . . Ladies' Sweeting, Northern Spy. **1863** B. ALCOTT *Journals* 360 Send apples to Anna for her winter use—Baldwins, Sweetings, and Northern Spys. **1875** BURROUGHS *Winter Sunshine* 150 Becoming to the centre-table in winter . . . [is] a bouquet of spitzenbergs and greenings and northern spies. **1903** *Dept. Agric. York. 1902* 246 In New York and New England the Northern Spy, Roxbury *Russet*, Tolman, and Arctic are among the least susceptible [to sun scald].

attrib. **1850** *New Eng. Farmer* II. 404 Northern Spy Apple. We had hoped to be able to test the qualities of this apple ourselves.

+**Northern state.**

1. A state in the northern part of the United States; spec., pl., the states lying north of Mason and Dixon's line and the Ohio River.

1780 MADISON *Writings* I. (1900) 64 It appears from sundry accounts from the frontiers of New York and other Northern States, that the savages are making the most distressing incursions. ***a*1800** TWINING *Visit* 397 [Unfriendly spirit assumes] almost the character of fixed antipathy between the Northern and Southern States. **1834** *S. Lit. Messenger* I. 85 The general rule of deference towards the sex, which prevails to the south —can scarcely be said to prevail, in the northern states. **1857** *Rep. Comm. Patents 1856: Agric.* 63 In the Northern States, the migratory squirrel replaces the *Sciurus carolinensis*, of the South.

2. *pl.* The states north of the middle states; the New England states.

1828 COOPER *Notions* I. 430 Religion . . . [is] inculcated . . . in all the northern and middle, and some of the southern states of America. **1852** EASTMAN *Aunt Phillis's Cabin* 260 In the Middle and Northern states free blacks are in a degraded condition.

***Northman.** + =NORTHERN MAN. — **1836** *S. Lit. Messenger* II. 111 The Southron . . . calls that a *Hare* which the North-man eats under the title of *Rabbit.* **1862** Moore *Rebellion Rec.* V. II. 281 No regiments calling themselves Mississippians are marching with the Northmen.

Northward, *n.* or *quasi-n.* {1624–} +The northern colonies or states. Usually *at* or *from the northward. Obs.* — **1764** HABERSHAM *Letters* 20, I was lately at the Northward to visit two of my sons at New Jersey College. **1797** C. PETTIGREW *Let. to J. Pettigrew* 8 Oct. (Univ. N.C. MS.), If your Cousin . . . should be returned from the Northward, I shall probably see him. **1800** [see NORTHERN COLONIES]. **1817** T. TROTTER *Let.* 25 July (Pettigrew P.), I cannot get any Cast Iron from the northard.

***Northward,** *a.* +Made in or native to the northern part of what is now the United States. *Obs.* — **1765** CROGHAN *Journal* 139 Southern Indians, who are always at war with the northward Indians. **1820** *Western Carolinian* 25 July, *Candles.* Northward, (mould Tallow) 18 *a* 20 cents. **1853** POYAS *Peep into Past* 114 It will be necessary to have a Northward man that's used to that business for an Overseer.

***Northwest.** +**a.** The region lying north and west of the settled or occupied portion of the United States. +**b.** The area lying in the northwest part of what is now the United States.

As the frontier of the United States was pushed westward, the term *northwest* progressively designated areas farther and farther from the Atlantic seaboard. The region north and west of the Ohio River was the first 'northwest' (see quots. 1789 and 1886), but was usually designated as the *Northwestern Territory* or *Northwest Territory* (qq. v.).

[**1789** *Ann. 1st Congress* I. 51 A message from the House of Representatives brought up a bill to provide for the government of the territory northwest of the river Ohio.] **1818** *Niles' Reg.* XIV. 208/2 From the north west we have unpleasant news anticipating hostilities with the Indians. **1856** *Democratic Conv. Proc.* 47 New Hampshire . . . went heartily for the champion of the North West [Douglas]. **1876** CROFUTT *Trans-continental Tourist* 41 In Nebraska . . . the traveler will find a better field for observing the rapid growth and great natural resources of the North-west. **1886** LOGAN *Great Conspiracy* 7 The first Federal Congress . . . at once enacted a law . . . prohibiting Slavery in the Territories of the North-west. **1913** *Dialect Notes* IV. 26 By the Northwest is meant the states of Washington, Oregon, Idaho, Montana, and Wyoming.

Northwester. Also **norwester.** A violent wind or gale blowing from the northwest. {norwester, 1703–} Also transf., a tall tale.

1733 BYRD *Journey to Eden* (1901) 297 Towards the Evening, a strong Norwester was so kind as to sweep all the Clouds away, that had blacken'd our Sky. **1777** E. DRINKER *Journal* 57 Cloudy all day, and rain ye greatest part, but now, near 10 o'clock, it seems to be clearing with a Northwester. **1807** IRVING, etc. *Salmagundi* 388 The brisk north-westers, which prevailed not long since. **1855** in A. Lawrence *Diary & Corr.* 123 A long trot . . . in the face of a keen winter north-wester, would severely tax their . . . strength. **1884** MATTHEWS & BUNNER *In Partnership* 74, I told him two or three North-westers, just as well as I could in French, and then . . . he told me about the glass which broke when poison was poured into it.

+**Northwestern,** *n.* (See quotation and cf. NORWESTER.) — **1701** WOLLEY *Journal N.Y.* 27 A thick winter Coat there [in N.Y.] is commonly called a North-western.

Northwestern, *a.* {1612–} +**1.** Of or belonging to those regions situated northwest of the earlier European settlements in North America. +**2.** *spec.* Designating a gun of a type sold by fur traders to Indians of the Northwest. (Cf. INDIAN TRADER 2 and NOR'WEST FUSIL.) — (1) **1789** *Ann. 1st Congress* I. 39 A report from the Secretary of War, on the negotiations of the Governor of the Western Territory with certain northern and northwestern Indians. **1807** *Ann. 10th Congress* 1 Sess. I. 16 Among our Indian neighbors in the Northwestern quarter, some fermentation was observed. **1814** *Niles' Reg.* VI. 37/2 The council which he [Gen. Harrison] is now holding at Dayton, with the several Indian chiefs of the north-western tribes. **1859** *Harper's Mag.* Feb. 399/1 Constructing the railroad, he would choose a path which would be a continuation of the road that our great Northwestern emigration had hitherto followed. (2) **1859** *Congress. Globe* 16 Feb. 1069/1 The arms furnished to the Indians are what are called northwestern guns. They are little popguns, with which nothing can be killed but the buffaloes.

Northwesternmost, Northwestmost, *a.* Situated furthest to the northwest. — **1782** Poyas *Peep into Past* (1853) 223, I give Robert the Northwestmost part of the tract of land I now live on. **1818** *Niles' Reg.* XV. 116/1 Calculate the immense extent of unappropriated territory . . . which stretches into the north-westernmost angle of the United States. **1837** W. JENKINS *Ohio Gaz.* 487 *York*, the northwesternmost township of Morgan county.

+**Northwestern states.** Those states in the northwestern part of the United States.

Cf. NORTHWEST, note.

1835 INGRAHAM *South-West* I. 106 Produce of all kinds, brought from the 'Upper country,' (as the north western states are termed here). **1848** BURTON *Waggeries* 171 The land speculator, hastening to the various sales expected to take place in the north-western states. **1870** *Nation* 10 Feb. 86/2 The whole discussion of the bill hinged upon the urgent need in the Southern and South-western and North-western States of more currency and banking facilities. **1893** PAGE in *Harper's Mag.* Dec. 22/2 [Virginians] are to be found in every Western and Northwestern State, where they begin as cowboys on ranches.

+**Northwestern Territory.** *Hist.* The region, about 266,000 square miles in extent, east of the Mississippi River, north of the Ohio, west of Pennsylvania, and south of the Canadian border. Also attrib.

The United States acquired this region from Great Britain at the close of the Revolution. New York, Virginia, Connecticut, and Massachusetts relinquished to the federal government their claims to parts of the region and in time the states of Ohio, Indiana, Michigan, Illinois, and Wisconsin were formed from it.

1796 in R. Putnam *Memoirs* 411 A vacancy [will be created] by this appointment on the judicial bench of the north western territory. **1798** *Ann. 5th Congress* I. 1045 A petition had been this morning presented . . . on the subject of the Northwestern Territory lands. **1802** ELLICOTT *Journal* 17 Cincinnati was at that time the capital of the North western Territory. **1834** NOTT *Novellettes* II. 190 He was [killed] . . . on his way to the north-western territory. **1857** in Benton *Exam. Dred Scott Case* 34 The ordinance was intended for the government of the Northwestern Territory.

+**Northwest Territory.** The Northwestern Territory: (see also quot. 1873). Also attrib. — **1802** CUTLER in *Life & Corr.* II. 105 Spent [today] on N.W. Territory State Bill. It is a most palpable violation of the Constitution. **1857** BENTON *Exam. Dred Scott Case* 32 The new-born Congress . . . adopted . . . the famous ordinance of 1787, for the government of the North-West Territory. **1873** *Republic* I. 54 During the last year the States of what is known as the northwest territory . . . produced three-quarters of all the cereals raised in the entire country. These eleven States . . . [are] Ohio, Kentucky, Indiana, Illinois, Missouri, Kansas, Nebraska, Iowa, Minnesota, Wisconsin, Michigan. **1900** *Congress. Rec.* 19 Feb. 1948/2 The Northwest Territory . . . was bounded by the Mississippi River, opening a market to the world by way of the Gulf.

Northwestwardly, *a.* and *adv.* Situated in, or extending toward, the northwest; in a northwesterly direction. — **1769** *Fitchburgh, Mass., Rec.* (1898) 60 Laid out a two Roade Rode begining at the Northwesterly Corner of Cornet Thos Carters Land. **1796** MORSE *Univ. Geog.* I. 223 Doubled Cape Horn, and then pursued a northwestwardly course.

1839 *S. Lit. Messenger* V. 209/1 The country slopes north-westwardly from the mountains. **1860** MORDECAI *Virginia* 301 The Brook Turnpike, towards the north, was the first one constructed; then north-westwardly the Richmond Turnpike, in the line of Broad street. **1863** A. D. WHITNEY *F. Gartney* xxvi, Looking off, northwestwardly, across the head of the Pond, the long windows . . . let in all the light.

+**North woods.** Any one of several heavily timbered regions in the northern part of the United States or in Canada. Also attrib. — **1881** *Harper's Mag.* May 867/1, I came out of the Adirondacks, or North Woods, free from cough, . . . with greater physical vigor than I had known for years. **1902** WHITE *Blazed Trail* 258 The old-fashioned, picturesque ice-road sleigh haul will last as long as north-woods lumbering. **1912** NICHOLSON *Hoosier Chron.* 61 Ware's references to the North woods had touched lightly some dim memory of her own.

Norway fir. (See NORWAY SPRUCE.)

Norway haddock. (See quot. 1911.) {1847-} — **1838** STORER *Mass. Fishes* 26 *S[ebastes] Norvegicus.* The Norway Haddock. . . . With us, this is not a common species. **1883** *Nat. Museum Bul.* No. 27, 498 *Sebastes marinus.* . . . Norway Haddock. **1911** *Rep. Fisheries 1908* 314 Rosefish (*Sebastes marinus*).—A brilliantly colored fish found off the north Atlantic coast. . . . It is also called . . . 'redfish,' 'Norway haddock,' [and] 'snapper.'

Norway maple. A European maple (*Acer platanoides*) planted in the United States for shade and ornament. {1797-} — **1846** BROWNE *Trees Amer.* 80 [The] Norway Maple . . . is a handsome tree, of the first rank, . . . introduced into the United States by the late Mr. Prince, of Flushing, New York, prior to 1820. **1859** HILLHOUSE tr. Michaux *Sylva* I. 165 This species of maple . . . is most multiplied in Sweden & Norway, whence it has received the name of Norway maple. **1879** *Scribner's Mo.* May 52/1 We accomplished the effect . . . by planting . . . three deciduous shade-trees, namely, a Norway maple, a scarlet maple, and a liquid amber. **1892** APGAR *Trees Northern U.S.* 87 Norway Maple. . . . The leaves resemble those of the Sycamore. . . . Flowers a little later than the leaves in spring, in stalked corymbs, less drooping than the Sugar-maple.

Norway pine. {1829- (Loudon *Encycl. Plants* 804)} +The American red pine (*Pinus resinosa*) found in New England, northern Wisconsin, and Minnesota; also, the wood of this. Also attrib.

1784 CUTLER in *Life & Corr.* I. 99 We rode five miles over pitch and Norway-pine plains, with very low shrubs. **1817-8** EATON *Botany* (1822) 392 *Pinus resinosa*, yellow pine, Norway pine, red pine. . . . Bark of a reddish colour. . . . Often grows very tall and straight. **1838** COOPER *Homeward B.* xvi, [He] applied his knife to try the quality of the wood, and pronounced the Norway pine of the spars to be almost equal to anything that could be found in our own southern woods. *a*1862 THOREAU *Maine Woods* 282 On the mainland were Norway pines, indicating a new geological formation. **1896** WILKINS *Madelon* 1 There were evergreens—Norway pines, spruces, and hemlocks—bordering the road.

Norway rat. The common brown house rat (*Rattus norvegicus*) introduced into the United States from Norway. {1759-} (Cf. BROWN RAT.) — **1826** GODMAN *Nat. Hist.* II. 78 The common, brown, or Norway rat . . . [is] extensively diffused over this country. *a*1830 — in *Waldie's Select Library* II. 90/2 The brown or Norway rat . . . [is] addicted to all sorts of mischief.

Norway spruce. Also **Norway fir.** A north European spruce (*Picea abies*) grown in the U.S. for ornament. {Norway [fir], 1670- (s.v. *Spruce*); 1797-} — **1847** DARLINGTON *Weeds & Plants* 338 Tall or Lofty Abies. Norway Spruce or Fir. . . . Cultivated. **1892** APGAR *Trees Northern U.S.* 180 *Picea excelsa.* Link. (Norway Spruce.) . . . Abundant in cultivation. **1900** MUNN *Uncle Terry* 15 A small house almost hid by luxuriantly growing Norway spruce.

Norwegian. {1605-} +A fishing boat of a type used on the Great Lakes. — **1873** *Rep. Comm. Fisheries 1872-3* 9 At Milwaukee, for a time, the most of the boats were the sloop-rigged 'Norwegians,' afterwards abandoned, and the square stern adopted. *Ib.*, The 'Norwegian' is a huge, unwieldy thing, with flaring bows, great sheer, high sides, and is sloop-rigged. . . . She is only used by the Scandinavian fishermen.

Norwester. {1703-} +An oilskin or waterproof coat worn chiefly by seafarers in rough weather. In full *norwester coat.* — **1690** *Long Island Wills* (1897) 46 My Will is that my norwester Coat . . . may be given to Christopher Leaming. **1853** KANE *Grinnell Exped.* 296 A still more sentimental song sung in seal-skin breeks and a 'norwester.'

+**Nor'west fusil.** Also **Nor'west fusee.** A light, cheap musket of the type sold to Indians by fur traders. (Cf. INDIAN TRADER 2.) — **1850** GARRARD *Wah-To-Yah* i. 16 The pursuer changed tack, only to be shot by one of the teamsters with a Nor'west fusil (Hudson Bay Company trade gun). *Ib.* ix. 119 A Purblo, *cached* behint a pile of dobies, shot him with a Nor'west fusee twice.

***Nose. 1.** A projecting or overhanging part of a hill or mountain. +**2.** *A nose for news*, an innate ability for ferreting out the news. — **(1) 1791** in *Amer. Speech* XV. 290/1 Thence . . . to two black Oaks on the nose . . . thence . . . to two hickories & 2 W. Oaks on the top of the nose at the path. **1912** WAYLAND *Hist. of Rockingham Co.* 29 A typical exposure of this quartzite is found at the nose of Peaked Mountain. **(2) 1875** Wingate *Views & Interviews* 196 The 'nose for news,' by which is meant unwearying alertness . . . for something 'ahead of the other papers.' **1893** in Philips *Making of a Newspaper* 54 Some managing editors are born with a 'nose for news.' **1916** SEITZ *Training for Newsp. Trade* 63 The reporter . . . is ubiquitous and versatile, possessing a heaven-born quality called 'the nose for news.'

Nose bag. A bag of strong canvas and leather for suspending from a horse's head in a way that enables him to eat from it. {1796-} (Cf. FEED BAG.) — **1812** *Niles' Reg.* II. 131/1 The purveyor of public supplies advertises for . . . 3000 nose or feeding bags. **1882** *Rep. Indian Affairs* 438 Bags, nose, dozen, 8½. **1888** *Century Mag.* Jan. 447/2 The horses munched their oats and corn in their nose-bags. **1897** LEWIS *Wolfville* 127 They sends over to the corral an' gets a nose-bag for to deposit the votes.

***Nosebleed.** Any one of various plants, as trillium, painted cup, etc., reputedly capable of causing bleeding when placed at the nose. 'There is no clear evidence of the name being actually current [in England] after 1600' (*O.E.D.*). — **1869** FULLER *Flower Gatherers* 102 Old Rose said it was '*Nose-bleed*,' and an aged squaw who used to bring around roots for small beer, called it *Indian pink*. **1894** *Amer. Folk-Lore* VII. 102 *Trillium erectum* . . . nosebleed, N.Y.

+**No-see-'em.** In Indian speech or in imitation of this: A minute biting fly or midge of the family Chironomidae; a punkie. *colloq.* — **1848** THOREAU *Maine Woods* 2 In the summer myriads of black flies, mosquitoes, and midges, or, as the Indians call them, 'no-see-ems,' make travelling in the woods almost impossible. *a*1864 *Ib.* 228 Here first I was molested by the little midge called the No-see-em (*Similium nocivum*). **1902** HULBERT *Forest Neighbors* (1903) 129 The mosquitoes and black-flies and no-see-'ems had bitten him until his skin was covered with blotches and his eyelids were . . . swollen.

Nose glasses. (See quot. 1890.) — **1890** *Cent.* 4020/2 *Nose-glasses*, . . . eye-glasses connected by a spring by which they are held on the nose; . . . a pince-nez. **1901** ADE *40 Modern Fables* 22 He said 'Whom,' and wore Nose Glasses. **1902** 'O. HENRY' *Roads of Destiny* 186 He was short in stature, but strongly built, with . . . smooth, determined face, and aggressive, gold-rimmed nose glasses.

+**Nose paint.** Intoxicating liquor. *slang.* — **1881** HAYES *New Colorado* 158 We saw . . . a sign, in which the name which I have never encountered elsewhere was given to stimulating beverages. This sign was '*Nosepaint and Lunch*.' **1897** LEWIS *Wolfville* 195 One of them reeconciliations . . . is mighty condoosive to the sale of nose-paint.

+**No sir-ee,** *adv.* An emphatic form of *no.* (Cf. YES SIR-EE and BOB, *interj.*) — **1851** *Knickerb.* XXXVIII. 496 'Can you take two to Whitlockville by five o'clock?' . . . 'No, Sir-*ee*!' **1863** NORTON *Army Lett.* 135 No, siree, I wouldn't take a discharge now if I could get it. **1883** *Wheelman* April 2/2 No, sir-e-e, you can't have any of my boats. **1921** MENCKEN *Amer. Lang.* (ed. 2) 107 Examples [of the use of intensifying suffixes] are *no-siree* and *yes-indeedy*.

***Notary.** A public officer legally authorized to take acknowledgment of or attest deeds, affidavits, depositions, etc. In full *public notary* or *notary public.*

1639 *New Haven Col. Rec.* I. 21 Tho. Fugill was chosen publique notary. **1685** SEWALL *Diary* I. 102 Having occasion this day to go to Mr. Hayward the Publick Notary's House, I speak to him about his cutting off his Hair. **1720** *Mass. H. Rep. Jrnl.* II. 255 The vote of the House, passed the 19th. currant, respecting Public Notaries. **1797** *State P.* (1819) III. 192 The subscriber, notary publick of the commonwealth of Massachusetts for the county of Hancock. **1881** STODDARD *E. Hardery* 134 His wife had yet to call with him at the notary's, and acknowledge the deed of that bit of land to Esau Hardery. **1908** PUTER *Looters of Public Domain* 18 They would appear before Fred W. Bell, a notary public, and execute an acknowledgement of a blank deed. **1924** RAINE *Troubled Waters* 298 She's a notary, ain't she? . . . Get her. I want to make a sworn statement before witnesses.

***Notch,** *n.* Also †**noch.**

+**1.** An indentation made in the ear of a domestic animal to indicate ownership. *Obs.*

Cf. NICK[1] 1 and OVERBIT.

1636 *Plymouth Rec.* I. 1 The top of the right eare cut of and two notches cut out of each side hether eare. **1641** *Suffolk Deeds* I. 21 A Gelding [was] taken vp . . . with a starr in his forehead with two Round notches Cutt in his neere eare. **1743** *Braintree Rec.* 148 One [ram] . . . Marked with an ell—of ye neer ear and a noch ond[e]r ye off ear.

+**2.** A cut made in a tree to denote that it stands on a boundary line or beside a way or road.

Cf. BLAZE n.[1] 2.

1641 *Md. Hist. Mag.* VI. 366 That Poynt of Land . . . ffrom the Poynt, to a great white oak marked wth. three notches wth. an Axe. **1680** *Plymouth Col. Rec.* VII. 228 Ephraim Morton . . . did deface the bound markes of the said land of the said Ellis and Dotey, being a pyne tree, marked with two noches on the one syde, and three noches on the other syde. **1769** *Fitchburgh, Mass., Rec.* I. 60 Markt the trees on the south side of said Roade with two notches mening two two Rods wide. **1821** W. T. HARRIS *Remarks* 139 *n.*, The tracks or roads from one settlement to another in the woods [in Ill.], are marked by one notch in the bark of the trees for a foot-path, two for a bridle-road, and three for a waggon route.

+**3.** A narrow passageway or defile between mountains, or the narrowest part of such a passage. Also attrib.

Cf. GAP 2.

1718 Sewall *Diary* III. 195 Lodg'd . . . at Olcot's, about ½ way between the Notch of the Mountains and Hartford. **1792** Belknap *Hist. New-Hampshire* III. 57 The head of Saco river, is in the White mountains, at the western pass, commonly called the notch. **a1821** Dwight *Travels* II. 147 The Notch of the White Mountains is a . . . narrow defile, extending two miles in length between two huge cliffs. **1879** J. E. A. Smith *Taghconic* 249 Mr. Thoreau ascended the mountain, from North Adams through 'The Notch,' a savage cleft between Greylock peak and a lower hill upon the east. **1888** Stockton *Dusantes* 12 The other road pursued its way along a valley or notch in the mountain. **1906** Churchill *Coniston* 2 Coniston Mountain, with its notch road that winds over the saddle behind the withers of it. **1914** Steele *Storm* 144, I saw it a quarter of an hour later in the notch where the Province Land boundary stone lies.

+**4.** A cut made on a stick or a weapon to signify the killing of someone. {1580–, in general sense}

1817 J. Bradbury *Travels* 41*n.*, It is customary amongst the Missouri Indians to register every exploit in war, by making a notch for each on the handle of their tomahawks. **1848** Cooper *Oak Openings* I. 109 This notch on a stick was the Indian mode of gazetting a warrior; and a certain number of these notches was pretty certain to secure for him a sort of savage brevet. **1867** Edwards *Shelby* 233, [I remember] Ingram and Pat Marshall filing notches in their pistol-butts for Federals killed in manly combat. **1902** *Wyoming Derrick* 9 Oct. 1/3 As a scout, the hunter of train robbers and outlaws and the regulator of cattle thieves, he has put a good many notches in his gun.

+**5.** *fig.* A mark or degree; a standard or measure of achievement. *colloq.*

1836 Crockett *Exploits* 54 Everything was cooked to the notch precisely. **1853** Kane *Grinnell Exped.* 349 We . . . tumbled over, no matter how often; but we hit the ships to a notch. **a1861** Winthrop *J. Brent* 295 Here we are three weeks or more behind them, . . . full three weeks to the notch.

+**b.** (*Up*) *to the last notch* or variants of this: (Up) to the proper standard or manner; up to all expectations; to the peak or highest point possible. Also *to the lowest notch,* to the extreme limit.

1790 Tyler *Contrast* v. i, Ho, ho, ho! There the old man was even with her; he was up to the notch—ha, ha, ha! **1843** 'Carlton' *New Purchase* I. 135 It's my sentimental opinyin this stranger's acted up, clean up, to the notch, and is most powerful clever. **1887** J. Hawthorne *Great Bank Robbery* xvi, You've been getting out of bed wrong-end first, John,—you ain't up to your notch! **1891** *Century Mag.* March 656 Baggage was cut down to the lowest notch. **1897** *Outing* Aug. 466/2 When you have girded yourself up to the last notch, so to speak.

***Notch,** *v.*

+**1.** *tr.* To cut notches in (trees) to indicate a way or road. Also *ppl. a.* and transf. of a road.

1726 *N.J. Archives* 1 Ser. V. 115 To return to my Path & Barrier . . . 20 foot wide will be Sufficient and the Trees Knotched on both Sides of Said path. *Ib.*, Such paths or Rhoads is what all the People in Virginia & Maryland Travell by & in paths with Knotcht Trees, And many paths not 20 foot wide. **1883** Sweet & Knox *Through Texas* 119 There are notched roads and blazed roads.

+**2.** To make notches in the ends of (logs), esp. preparatory to fitting them into a house wall. Also *ppl. a.*

1768 C. Beatty *Journal* 72 *n.*, Some of the houses . . . are made of logs of wood laid upon one another, notched at the corners into each other. **1791** W. Bartram *Travels* 192 The other half of this building is closed on all sides by notched logs. *Ib.* 459 [We] cut down a White-Oak sapling, and by notching this at each end, bent it up, which formed the keel, stem and stern post of one piece. **1831** Peck *Guide* 126 The first buildings put up are of logs, slightly hewn on two sides, and the corners notched together. **1837** — *New Guide* 123 Four stout men with axes, are placed on the corners, to notch the logs together.

***Note.**

1. A written promise to pay a certain sum at a given time. {1683–} See also Note of hand.

1667 *Suffolk Deeds* II. 208, I doe hereby acknouledge this 25th Aprill 1667 by a Receite of a noate from Serjant Wm. Cotton . . . for the payment of seventy pounds in mony [etc.]. **1847** A. Lawrence *Diary & Corr.* 36 My honored father brought to me the one thousand dollars, and asked me to give him my note for it. **1905** Pringle *Rice Planter* 150, I wrote a note for it at 6 per cent.

2. A short, written notice given to a minister to be read by him to the congregation. Usually *to put up a note.*

1685 Sewall *Diary* I. 68, I put up a Note to pray for the Indians that Light might be communicated to them. **1688** *Ib.* 211 After the Notes [he] said such an Occasion was by the Governour recommended to be given Thanks for. **1720** *Ib.* III. 256, I put up a Note to this purpose; Samuel Sewall, depriv'd of his dear Wife by a very sudden and awfull Stroke, desires Prayers.

3. A bank note or a similar form of paper money issued by a government. {1696–}

1714 *Mass. Bay Currency Tracts* 121 The Sovereign has been pleased to indulge us with the Priviledges of Emitting Publick Notes for the defraying the necessary Charge in the Defence . . . of the Government. **1761** in H. M. Brooks *Gleanings* 29 Articles . . . which they will sell . . . at very low Prices for Cash or Treasurer's Notes. **1790** *Ann. 1st Congress* II. 2055 The bills and notes of the bank . . . which shall have become payable on demand in gold and silver coin, shall be receivable in all payments to the United States. **1817** S. Brown *Western Gaz.* 112 The notes of this bank are in excellent credit. **1884** Blaine *20 Years of Congress* I. 474 Any persons . . . can receive United States notes in such denominations as may be desired. **1910** J. A. Mitchell *Dr. Thorne's Idea* 35 He noticed the roll was composed of one-hundred-dollar notes.

+**4.** A surprise or thing of great importance. *colloq.*

1849 Kingsley *Diary* 32 This morning, the greatest note that has taken place yet come out. **1863** P. S. Davis *Young Parson* 211 '[You] may be glad enough if I do not yet have you before the vestry to testify in the case.' 'That would be a great note.' **1911** Lincoln *Cap'n Warren's Wards* 167 Do you tell me that? That's a note, I must say.

Note of hand. =Note 1. {1766–}

1734 *Mass. H. Rep. Jrnl.* XII. 93 For . . . the Bills of this Government were never brought to so low an Ebb as at present, nor are those Notes of Hand (as they are sometimes called) any ease at this Day to the Trading Part of the Province. **1741** *N.H. Probate Rec.* III. 30, I give to my Beloved Wife . . . two noats of hand of her Brother Richard. **1776** *N.J. Archives* 2 Ser. I. 91 Joseph Archer . . . has this day obtained of me . . . a note of hand of twelve pounds proclamation money for a horse. **1853** *Knickerb.* XLII. 433 A man 'hereabouts,' having obtained a note-of-hand of his preceptor, . . . handed it to the newly-fledged lawyer to bring suit upon. **1875** *Chicago Tribune* 31 Oct. 2/4, He can't have de money unless he gives me his note of hand!

+**Note-shaver.** One who makes a business of discounting notes, warrants, etc.; a usurer. *slang.* (Cf. Shaver.)

1816 *Mass. Spy* 4 Sept. (Th.), We have too many note-shavers; too many gentlemen. **1828** *Yankee* I. 52/1 [Bank directors can keep] our laboring community . . . forever at work . . . for the *note shavers* and *Bank proprietors.* **1847** Briggs *Tom Pepper* I. 141 He was a note shaver, besides being a negotiator of paper of all kinds. **1869** Barnum *Struggles & Triumphs* 410 A note-shaver . . . held a thousand dollar note, which it seemed he had bought for seven-hundred dollars. **1887** *Courier-Journal* 14 Jan. 6/3 Because the City Book-keeper . . . neglected to register the vouchers and stamp them, 150 men . . . are . . . forced to sell their claims to the note-shavers. **1911** Saunders *Col. Todhunter* 113 Don't you forget that old Eph Tucker was a note-shaver long before he was a politician.

+**Note-shaving.** The practice of discounting notes at an excessive rate. Also attrib. — **1828** *Yankee* I. 52/1 [By] the system of note-shaving that prevails here . . . the industrious and active are held in a state of bondage to the more wealthy and more lazy. **1862** *N. Amer. Rev.* July 113 This Wall-Street note-shaving life is a new field, a very peculiar field. **1869** Barnum *Struggles & Triumphs* 65, I had used the term 'usury,' instead of extortion, or note-shaving, or some other expression which might have softened the verdict. **1911** Saunders *Col. Todhunter* 113 He's got note-shavin' in his blood bigger 'n a mule.

***Nothing.**

+**1.** *No nothing,* nothing whatsoever. *colloq.*

1835 Cooper *Monikins* xxiv, In this happy land, there was no registration, no passports, 'no nothin' '—as Mr. Poke pointedly expressed it. **1884** *Harper's Mag.* March 516/2 There is no store, no post-office, no sidewalked street—no nothing.

+**2.** In emphatic or exclamatory expressions: By no means; not at all. *colloq.*

1888 [see Nope *adv.*]. **1898** Nicholas *Idyl of Wabash* 175 'My account —nothing!' was her scornful ejaculation. **1909** Calhoun *Miss Minerva* 42 'Don't you think she looks pale, Jimmy?' 'Pale, nothing!' **1923** Wyatt *Invisible Gods* 66 'It is disloyal.' 'Disloyal nothing!'

+**3.** *Nothing to nobody,* beyond adequate description or setting forth. *slang.*

1835 Longstreet *Ga. Scenes* 166 The way them women love punch is nothing to nobody! **1838** Drake *Tales Queen City* 37 Well now the way these ere steam captains do things, is nothing to no body, no how. **a1859** *N.Y. Spirit of Times* (B.), The way she would make Indian cakes, and the way I used to slick them over with molasses, was nothing to nobody.

Nothingarian. {1820–} +One who subscribes to no particular religious faith, creed, or denomination. *Obs.*

1789 Morse *Amer. Geog.* 206 There is a considerable number of the people who can be reduced to no particular denomination, and are, as to religion, strictly Nothingarians. **1803** *Mass. H. S. Coll.* IX. 205 There are a few persons who pretend to be a sort of Quakers, but who in fact are nothingarians. **1815** in B. P. Smith *Hist. Dartmouth Coll.* 95 This comprises all the professed friends of liberal religion, most of the Baptists and Methodists, and all the nothingarians. **1845** Lyell *Second Visit* I. 139 A Nothingarian . . . was indifferent whether he attended a Baptist, Methodist, Presbyterian, or Congregationalist church, and was often equally inclined to contribute money liberally to any one or all of them. **1882** *Home Missionary* April 340, I find only two families that avow themselves to be freethinkers or infidels. Many are 'nothingarians'; several are Catholics.

b. One who has no special occupation or interest. Also attrib. or as adj.

1817 *Mass. Spy* 2 April (Th.), Office-hunters, brokers, clerks, stay-tape and buckram gentry, speculators, and nothingarians, crowd to the President's every Wednesday evening. **1889** *Open Court* 3 Jan. 1393 (*Cent.*), The blessed leisure of wealth was not to him the occasion of a nothingarian dilettantism, of idleness or selfish pursuits of vanity, pleasure or ambition.

∗**Notify,** *v. tr.* To inform or give notice to (a person or group).

From the end of the seventeenth century this use of *notify* has apparently been more common in this country than in England. It has sometimes mistakenly been regarded as of American origin: (see quots. 1781, 1829).

1697 *Boston Rec.* 226 The Selectmen are to be notified thereof that they may be present. **1726** in Peirce *Hist. Harvard* App. 99 The Corporation being duly notified who the said successor is. **1781** WITHERSPOON *Druid P.* No. 5, To notify the publick; or the people had not been notified. By this is meant inform and informed. In English we do not notify the person of the thing, but notify the thing to the person. **1795** *Maine Hist. Soc. Coll.* IV. 305 Preached from John 12:35 to an assembly, rather small, people not being sufficiently notified. **1829** *Va. Lit. Museum* I. 459 To *notify*. 'To inform.' This is an American signification; and, hence, 'to *notify* him of it,' is common. The real interpretation of the word is 'to make known;' and the sentence ought to be 'to notify it to him.' This error is universal. **1875** TEMPLE & SHELDON *Hist. Northfield, Mass.* 226 A committee . . . notified the petitioners to meet at Concord. **1895** WINSOR *Miss. Basin* 83 Pontchartrain notified the new governor of his appointment.

∗**Notion.**

+**1.** *pl.* Small articles of trade, usually of domestic manufacture, as tinware, clocks, wooden bowls, etc., such as were formerly sold by Yankee peddlers.

See also YANKEE NOTION.

[**1796** *Aurora* (Phila.) 1 Feb. (Th.), Parentheses one within the other, like a nest of Boston boxes, commonly called notions.] **1811** *Mass. Spy* 10 July (Th.), Our codfish and notions would settle commotions. **1833** A. GREENE *Yankee among Nullifiers* 48 Among other 'notions,' which he contrived to manufacture, were wooden Jewsharps. **1853** 'P. PAXTON' *Yankee in Texas* 28 He was a . . . shrewd thorough-going Yankee peddler, who had brought with him . . . a large stock of clocks and other notions. **1886** *Harper's Mag.* July 174/2 People brought in . . . fancy shops for the sale of all manner of cheap and bizarre 'notions.'

+**b.** *pl.* A miscellaneous assortment of various wares making up a cargo.

[**1805** SOUTHEY in *Ann. Rev.* III. 31 The Americans . . . , finding no longer a market there for their lumber cargoes, or notions, as they call them.] **1815** *Niles' Reg.* VIII. 139/2 Nor does the lady, while sipping her tea, . . . dwell on the thought, whether it . . . was brought hither, via Salem, in a schooner with 'notions.' **1840** DANA *Two Years* xxxv. 441 She proved to be the brig Solon, . . . from New York, bound to the Spanish Main, with a cargo of fresh provisions, mules, tin bake-pans, and other notions. **1872** *Atlantic Mo.* April 398 Give a Yankee captain, in time of war, a schooner full of 'fish and notions,' a flag of truce to the enemy, and a free range of the seas.

+**c.** *pl.* Various useful articles, as ribbon, thread, hooks and eyes, etc.

The first quotation may belong to the primary meaning of sense 1.

1869 BARNUM *Struggles & Triumphs* 63 We stocked the 'yellow store,' as it was called, with a full assortment of groceries, hardware, crockery, and 'notions.' **1884** *Lisbon* (Dak.) *Star* 10 Oct., Ten thousand dollars worth of dry goods, notions, clothing, hats and caps [etc.]. **1892** *York County Hist. Rev.* 47 Each line of goods is large, commencing from dry goods and notions, dress goods and trimmings, piece goods in cloths, cassimeres, silks and satins. **1902** LORIMER *Lett. Merchant* 135, I was traveling out of Chicago for Hammer & Hawkins, wholesale dry-goods, gents' furnishings and notions.

2. *To take a notion*, to make up one's mind to do a particular thing. Also fig.

1776 in F. Chase *Hist. Dartmouth Coll.* I. 347 Ther was Ten Regt ordert to march for Newyoark, and I toock a notion to go with them. **1810** M. DWIGHT *Journey to Ohio* 4 This morning Susannah came & invited us to attend meeting—we at first refused but I afterwards chang'd my mind, & 'took a notion' . . . to go. **1824** *Nantucket Inquirer* 5 Jan. (Th.), Bimeby he took notion to hab my darter. **1885** 'CRADDOCK' *Prophet* 40 There was tobacco, too, placed . . . where it was hoped it would take a notion to grow.

+**3.** Attrib. and comb. with *counter, house, peddling*, etc.

1809 IRVING *Knickerb.* IV. iii, He swore that he would have nothing more to do with such a squatting, bundling, . . . notion-peddling crew. **1839** *Chemung* (N.Y.) *Democrat* 17 April (Th.), A 'Notion seller' was offering Yankee clocks, &c. **1844** M. C. HOUSTON *Texas* (1845) 78 Outside a great many of the 'notion' stores, I saw just such figures hanging up. **1887** *Courier-Journal* 21 Jan. 7/2 The wholesale notion houses were pretty fully employed. **1891** S. FISKE *Holiday Stories* (1900) 152, I went to the store . . . and recognised her . . . at the notion counter. **1898** *Kansas City Star* 18 Dec. 10/2 Greater attractions every day come to the Notions stocks. **1902** GHENT *Our Benev. Feudalism* 18 This tendency is pronounced in the notion trades and in the manufacture of women's ready-made wear.

∗**Notional,** *a.* +Full of notions or whims; overparticular or fastidious.

1791 *Gazette of U.S.* 9 Feb. (Th.), If a man is a little odd in his ways, his friends say he is a notional creature, or full of notions. **1819** *Niles' Reg.* XVI. 224 A somewhat similar occurrence [took place] among the *notional folks* of Boston. **1877** JEWETT *Deephaven* 154 The cap'n was a first-rate seaman and died rich, but he was dreadful notional. **1904** *Hartford Courant* 1 July 10 The 'New York Evening Post,' fantastically notional about the use of English, announced last night that in a collision a surgeon had been 'painfully hurt.'

‖**b.** Inclined to think.

1823 COOPER *Pioneers* ix, I'm glad if the Judges is pleased; but I'm notional that you'll find the sa'ce overdone.

Notionate, *a.* Notional, foolish, sensitive, stubborn. *colloq.* {1871–, Sc.} — **a1848** in Northall *Yankee Hill* 127 Samuel Winston . . . was considered a 'notionate critter,' and one of his notions was Cabala. **1867** A. J. EVANS *Vashti* xxvi, She is as notionate as a child, and no one but my poor mother could ever manage her. **1880** *Scribner's Mo.* May 21/1 She's mighty still an' sits an grieves a heap, but she aint never notionate. **1896** HOWELLS *Idyls in Drab* 119 That young woman has made you blame yourself for nothin'. You're perfectly notionate about it.

+**No-top.** A buggy having no covering or top. In full *no-top buggy*. — **1827** *Harvard Reg.* Oct. 247 He who desires to be a big-Bug, rattling in a natty gig, No-top, or chaise, or tandem. **1830** *Collegian* 199 He may ride in the rattling gig, Or flourish the no-top gay. **1894** CHOPIN *Bayou Folk* 14 [At] Natchitoches . . . they found Pierre's no-top buggy awaiting them.

+**Novanglian,** *a.* and *n.* Also **Novanglican. 1.** *adj.* Of or pertaining to New England. *Obs.* **2.** *n.* A native or inhabitant of New England. *Obs.* — (1) **1679** *New Eng. Hist. Reg.* IV. 130 Nov-Anglian Heroes universall call, Did Constitute him major Generall. **1752** J. MACSPARRAN *Amer. Dissected* 31 The Novanglian clergy of our Church . . . have introduced a Custom [etc.]. **1862** TAYLOR *At Home & Abroad* 2 Ser. (1864) 339, I rather admire this stolid self-reliance and Novanglican assumption. (2) **1752** J. MACSPARRAN *Amer. Dissected* 31 The Novanglians in general, the Rhode-Islanders in particular, . . . have hit on the Art of enriching themselves by running in debt. **1813** J. ADAMS *Works* X. 49 You may find something upon correspondences, whig and tory, federal and democratic, Virginian and Novanglian, English and French.

∗**Novelty.** *attrib. Theat.* +Designating groups employed or active in variety or vaudeville. — **1875** *Boston Transcript* 17 Aug. 1/7 Tony Pastor's Novelty Troupe . . . present . . . Sanford and Wilson in an Ethiopian sketch. **1887** *Courier-Journal* 31 Jan. 8/4 [The] proprietor and manager of the Andy Hughes American and European Novelty Company . . . was arrested. *Ib.* 6 Feb. 3/7 Comprising Twenty Frolicsome Queens of the Novelty World.

∗**November.** The eleventh month of the year, +as the time when general elections are held. (Cf. FIRST TUESDAY AFTER THE FIRST MONDAY.) — **1856** *Democratic Conv. Proc.* 29 Kentucky . . . could promise . . a majority in November next. **1872** *Statutes at Large* XVII. 28 The Tuesday next after the first Monday in November . . . is hereby fixed . . for the election . . . of Representatives and Delegates to the Congress. **1900** *Congress. Rec.* 2 Feb. 1464/1 The Republican party will need every vote it can muster or buy to make even a decent showing on the election-night bulletin boards next November.

N.T. ‖(See quotation.) *Obs.* — **1879** TOURGEE *Fool's Errand* 46 One of the 'N.T.'s' became so full of the spirit of the occasion, that she kissed one of the colored boys who waited at the table. . . . ('N.T.,' you know, is Southern euphemism for *Nigger Teacher*.)

∗**Nub.** +The gist or crux of a matter; the point or moral of a story. — **1834** C. A. DAVIS *Lett. J. Downing* 210 That's pretty much the *nub* of the business. **1870** 'MARK TWAIN' *Curious Republic of Gondour* (1919) 32 The 'nub' or moral of the burlesque . . . escapes notice. **1884** NYE *Baled Hay* 51, I would be so pleased to follow up an anecdote till I had reached the 'nub.' **1903** SHUMAN *Pract. Journalism* 61 The beginner cannot go far wrong if he gets the nub of the whole story into his first paragraph.

Nubbin. {1851–, *dial.*} +A stunted or dwarfed ear of Indian corn.

1692 *Md. Hist. Mag.* XIII. 209 Jones saw him buy one beaver skin . . . for thirty ears and nubbins of corn. **1838** DRAKE *Tales* 150 A handfull of salt and a few nubbins of corn, were procured. **1872** EGGLESTON *End of World* 272, I'm afeard they'll be a heap of nubbins not wuth the shuckin'. **1894** ROBLEY *Bourbon Co., Kansas* 159 Corn was raised, in some instances as much as five bushels to the acre, of little wormy-ended nubbins. **1906** PRINGLE *Rice Planter* 419 There is scarcely a fifth of a crop—all the big ears gone, leaving only nubbins.

b. *transf.* Something small or poorly developed.

1857 *Harper's Mag.* Feb. 399/2 They served me, at the 'American,' with a little hard *nubbin* of steak. **1868** BEECHER *Norwood* 127 They drove little nubbins of horses, tough and rough. **1880** *Harper's Mag.* Nov. 863/2 In a corner by themselves we see the pile of 'vinegar nubbins'—a tanned and soft variety of apple. **1888** KIRKLAND *McVeys* 59 There must always be a 'nubbin' of ground in one corner or in the middle, where short furrows come together and plague him.

Nubia. Also **nube, nuby.** A wrap, usually crocheted or knitted, for the head and neck. {1881-} — **1856** *Harper's Mag.* Sept. 448/2 The lake was entirely hidden by a thick coverlet of white mist, which lay upon its surface almost as palpable as if it had been . . . an extensive worsted nube. **1864** *Hist. North-Western Soldiers' Fair* 126 [Donations include] 1 elegant worsted nubia [etc.]. **1904** GLASGOW *Deliverance* 29, 'The same evening that I got this pink crochetted nuby.' She touched a small pointed shawl about her shoulders. **1908** GALE *Friendship Village* 234 Her bare shoulders [were] wound in the rosy 'nubia' that had been her mother's.

'Nuf sed, Nuf(f) ced. A colloquial or jocular shortening of *enough (has been) said.* — **1850** NORTHALL *Yankee Hill* 38 'Nuff ced,' exclaimed the Captain, 'and now let us liquor.' **1854** *La Crosse Democrat* 28 March 1/5 (*signature of article*), 'Nuf Ced.' Truly, R. E. G. **1923** *Dialect Notes* V. 232 'Nuf sed.

Nugget. A small lump or mass of native gold. {1852-} Also attrib. — **1855** *Chicago Times* 16 Jan. 2/3 The California *nugget*, as big lumps are called, is now at New Orleans. **1872** MCCLELLAN *Golden State* 129 Excitement . . . [was] caused by the discovery of . . . nuggets in the gulches. **1877** HODGE *Arizona* 64 A few men took out, in less than three months, $108,000 in nugget gold, from the size of a pin head to that of five or six hundred dollars in value. **1884** *Century Mag.* Oct. 842/1 Pritchard is alive and still digging for the yellow nuggets. **1923** 'BOWER' *Parowan Bonanza* 33, I've got a nugget in my shirt pocket that I didn't show you.

Nullification. {1630-} *Hist.*

+**1. a.** Action, based upon the doctrine of state sovereignty, taken by a state to abrogate within its limits the operation of a federal law. **b.** *spec.* Action taken or threatened by South Carolina in her opposition to the tariffs of 1828 and 1832. Also *South Carolina nullification.*

The right of a state to nullify acts of Congress regarded by it as unconstitutional was affirmed in the Kentucky Resolutions of 1799 (see KENTUCKY 6). In 1828 South Carolina, in a set of resolutions, protested the unconstitutionality of the tariff, and accompanied the resolutions with Calhoun's 'South Carolina Exposition,' setting forth the theory of nullification. In 1832 a state convention in South Carolina passed an ordinance of nullification, which was rescinded in 1833.

1798 JEFFERSON *Writings* XVII. 386 Where powers are assumed which have not been delegated, a nullification of the act is the rightful remedy. **1799** *Ky. Resolutions* in Elliott *Debates* IV. (1836) 545 A nullification, by those sovereignties, of all unauthorized acts done under color of that instrument, is the rightful remedy. **1830** *Mass. Spy* 27 Oct. (Th.), In Columbia (S.C.), the seat of Government, and the very focus of Nullification, two Nullifiers, and two anti-Nullifiers are chosen to the Assembly. **1832** CLAY *Speeches* (1842) 198 The ranks of those who, unfurling the banner of nullification, would place a state upon its sovereignty. **1839** BROTHERS *United States* 187 It was what was termed the South Carolina Nullification; that is, the state of South Carolina refused to pay any more taxes to the general government. **1850** *Whig Almanac 1851* 28/2 [John C. Calhoun] was the most formidable champion of Slavery, Free Trade and Nullification that our country has ever known. **1854** BENTON *30 Years' View* I. 299/1 The ordinance of nullification reached President Jackson in the first days of December. **1877** *Harper's Mag.* March 628/2 Mr. Tyler, with many distinguished Southern statesmen, had been hard bitten with the rabies of 'nullification.' **1886** LOGAN *Great Conspiracy* 464 Including within the scope of States Rights, the threats of Nullification, Disunion and Secession, . . . small wonder is it that, in those days [*c*1824-45], every fresh demand made by these political autocrats was tremblingly acceded to.

2. Attrib. with *candidate, law, newspaper, tariff,* etc.

1830 J. Q. ADAMS *Memoirs* VIII. 210 Mr. Calhoun will be the Nullification candidate. **1833** *Niles' Reg.* XLIV. 20/1 Mr. John C. West . . . has been required by governor Hayne to take the nullification test oath. **1857** BENTON *Exam. Dred Scott Case* 181 All the nullification newspapers opened for secession for that new cause. **1859** Nullification times [see NULLIFIER 2]. **1860** in Logan *Great Conspiracy* 112 We earnestly recommend the repeal of all Nullification laws. **1871** GROSVENOR *Protection* 230 The production has . . . increased little more . . . than it increased in eight years under the 'South Carolina nullification tariff.'

+**Nullification party.** In South Carolina, the political party or faction composed of those who favored nullification of the high protective tariffs of 1828 and 1832. *Obs.* — **1832** HONE *Diary* I. 70 These appointments prove the strength of the 'Nullification' party. **1846** MANSFIELD *Winfield Scott* 231 The name of the party of the majority was known as the nullification party, and that of the minority as the Union party.

+**Nullificator.** =next. *Obs.* — **1830** *Mass. Spy* 27 Oct. (Th.), It is to be hoped that, if the Nullificators do move, it will be to Mexico, or beyond the Rocky Mountains. **1833** *Niles' Reg.* XLIV. 33/2 The 'nullificators' believe that they have obtained a glorious victory.

+**Nullifier.**

1. An advocate of nullification, especially with reference to the action of South Carolina in 1832. Now hist.

Cf. NULLIFICATION.

1830 *Mass. Spy* 7 July (Th.), This argument was considered by all the nullifiers as overwhelming. **1832** IRVING in P. M. Irving *Life W. Irving* (1866) III. 44 Preston . . . is a member of the Legislature, and one of the leaders of the nullifiers. **1857** BENTON *Exam. Dred Scott Case* 172 Open arms to all deserters from all ranks! nullifiers and disunionists preferred! and this continued to be the rule of action during the whole Pierce administration. **1913** BASSETT *Short Hist. U.S.* 410 On February 1 [1833] the leading nullifiers met and decided to suspend the execution of the ordinance of nullification.

+**b.** *Great Nullifier,* John C. Calhoun.

1882 H. VON HOLST *J. C. Calhoun* 104 Hundreds of eyes closely scrutinized the face of the 'great nullifier' as he took the oath to support the Constitution.

2. (See quot. 1859.)

1840 *Picayune* 20 Sept. 2/3 His understandings [shoes] could not be legitimately called boots, brogans or nullifiers. **1859** BARTLETT 298 *Nullifier* . . . was also applied to a sort of shoe, made like a decapitated boot, brought into fashion in the 'nullification' times.

***Nullify,** *v.* +*tr.* Of a state or state authority: To refuse to enforce or uphold (a federal law). Now hist. Also absol. — **1798** JEFFERSON *Writings* XVII. 387 Every State has a natural right in cases not within the compact . . . to nullify of their own authority all assumptions of power by others within their limits. **1833** A. GREENE *Yankee among Nullifiers* 20 Why the case is perfectly clear: Nullify; I say nullify. **1837** CALHOUN *Works* III. 57 The State of South Carolina . . . declared the act to be unconstitutional, and as such null and void. In a word, we nullified. **1877** *Harper's Mag.* March 595/2 The statesmen of South Carolina insisted upon the right of the State to nullify an unconstitutional act of Congress.

Nulling. *Furniture.* Knurling; the making of bosses or similar ornaments. — **1851** CIST *Cincinnati* 245 All kinds of turning used by cabinet makers, including nulling of every pattern, furnished at the shortest notice. **1914** EBERLEIN & MCCLURE *Pract. Bk. Period Furniture* 63 Nulling, made up chiefly of beading, cabling and hollows, is often used to ornament the bulbous legs of Jacobean furniture.

+**Nully.** *ellipt.* =NULLIFIER. *colloq. Obs.* — **1833** *Niles' Reg.* XLIV. 384/1 War upon the proclamation . . . is now the order of the day with the nullies, under the lead of Messrs. Calhoun and Hamilton. **1835** in E. J. Hooper *Address Lit. Soc. Pittsborough,* The Gineral you know wants to keep a sharp look out upon them nullies in South Carolina.

***Number.** *To get, have,* or *take one's number* {1880-}, to form a judgment about or gain a revealing insight into a person's character, ability, class, etc. *colloq.* — **1889** 'MARK TWAIN' *Conn. Yankee* 459 That was the sort of master we had. I took his number. **1913** LONDON *Valley of Moon* 101 He got your number, Charley Long. **1921** PAINE *Comr. Rolling Ocean* 129 Do you remember . . . when he made that crack at you? . . . I had his number right then.

+**Number-one,** *a.* Fine, first-rate; of highest quality. *colloq.* Also absol. (Cf. A No. 1.)

1843 MARRYAT *M. Violet* xxviii, After having drained half-a-dozen cups of 'stiff, true, downright Yankee No. 1,' we all of us took our blankets. **1848** *Corr. R. W. Griswold* (1898) 242, I have some beautiful poems by me by Mrs. Barnes. . . . They are No. 1, full of passionate feeling and eminently worthy of a place. **1855** *Mich. Agric. Soc. Trans.* VI. 495 Wheat first-rate; peas also; oats number one. **1872** EGGLESTON *End of World* 78 This walk seems the shortest, when I'm in superfine, number-one comp'ny. **1896** JEWETT *Pointed Firs* 85 What Mrs. Todd proudly called a full 'kag' of prime number one salted mackerel. **1925** TILGHMAN *Dugout* 57, I just told the storekeeper's wife to put up a number one outfit.

Number six. +A household medicinal remedy. *Obs.* — **1842** KIRKLAND *Forest Life* I. 71 We stick to thoroughwort,—balmony,—soot tea,—'number six,'—and the like. **1853** 'P. PAXTON' *Yankee in Texas* 122 His old woman doctored me, and give me 'number six.'

Numbheaded, *a.* Stupid, foolish. *colloq.* {1892, *dial.*} — *c***1847** WHITCHER *Bedott P.* x. 98 The old coot was so awful numbheaded I couldent beat anythin' into him.

Numerous,** *a.* +Superior, first-rate, pre-eminent. *slang.* — *c1845** *Big Bear Ark.* 23 In bar hunts I am numerous. **1860** HOLLAND *Miss Gilbert* 172 He sort o' stands round, and spreads, and lets off all the big talk he hears. Ain't he rather numerous, though? *Ib.,* 'It had occurred to me that he might be in a public position.' 'Well he does look numerous, that's a fact.'

***Nunnery.** The residence of a community of nuns; spec., a community of Seventh-Day German Baptists. — **1744** *Mass. H. S. Coll.* 1 Ser. VII. 181 The Governor, the honourable the commissioners, and several other gentlemen, went to the Dunkers' nunnery, about twelve miles from [Lancaster, Penna.]. **1835** HOFFMAN *Winter in West* I. 54 The golden tints of sunset . . . freshened the white outline of a long, low-built nunnery, standing on a sudden elevation back from the river. **1878** *N. Amer. Rev.* CXXVII. 56 When crossed in love they would prefer a nunnery to an Owen phalanstery. **1907** ANDREWS *Recoll.* 183 One of the buildings to be guarded was a nunnery.

Nun's Holland. A kind of fine Holland cloth. *Obs.* Also shortened to *Nuns.* — **1745** in Watson *Philadelphia* 179 Nuns, bag and gulix. **1756** *Lett. to Washington* I. 362 Tandem & Nuns Hollands from 27/— to 52/— some of these exceeding fine.

Nun's thread. A fine, white, linen thread suitable for lace-making. *Obs.* {1766-} — **1691** SEWALL *Letter-Book* I. 118 Send me . . . a pound of very fine Nuns Thred. **1746** *Md. Hist. Mag.* XXI. 381 Invoice of Goods. . . . 1 pound nun's thread sorted. **1810** *Columbian Centinel* 3 Jan. 4/3 John Tappan . . . offers for sale . . . 3 cases Nuns Thread.

∗**Nurse.** **a.** A woman who cares for a child. **b.** One who attends to the needs of the sick.

1642 *Plymouth Laws* 73 If the nurse educator physicon or Chirurgeon take not sufficient securyty of the person to be nursed. **1674** SEWALL *Diary* I. 3 To the Nurse 2d., for a pair of sizers 4 d. **1767** HUTCHINSON *Hist. Mass.* II. 107 She prevailed upon the nurse and the English boy to join with her in the destruction of the Indian family. **1835** INGRAHAM *South-West* II. 92 The Africans . . . whom they have had for their nurses, play-fellows, and 'bearers.' **1890** *Century Mag.* Nov. 46 The old darky nurse . . . had educated him to a gruesome terror of that ancient Church. **1907** *St. Nicholas* Aug. 879/2 Promptly at three the little guests began to arrive, some of them in charge of nurses, but most of them brought by their mamas. **1918** *Lit. Digest* 3 Aug. 38/1 An army school of nurses has been established under the direction of the Army Medical Department.

∗**Nursery.** Also †**narsaree.** *Hort.* A place where trees and plants are raised for transplanting or for use in grafting; also, the collection of trees in such a place.

1675 *Jamaica Rec.* I. 125, [I] have sould . . . an acore of my home Lot . . . exept halfe ye trees that stands in ye narsaree. **1744** HEMPSTEAD *Diary* 431 [The wind] broke down the bigest part of my Choice peach Tree in the Nursery. **a1772** WOOLMAN *Journal* 91, I also had a nursery of apple-trees. **1831** PECK *Guide* 128 The black locust . . . may be raised from the seed, with far less labor than a nursery of apple-trees. **1873** *Newton Kansan* 3 April 2/2 It is every way better to sow your seed in the garden or nursery. **1908** LORIMER *J. Spurlock* 271 There were . . . dairies and henneries, and conservatories and graperies, and shrubberies and nurseries.

b. Attrib. with *catalogue, plantation,* etc.

1741 W. STEPHENS *Proc. Georgia* II. 85, I pass'd away the Forenoon at my little Nursery Plantation. **1858** WARDER *Hedges & Evergreens* 132 [Great ignorance of the principles of trimming hedges prevails, as] will be rendered apparent by inspection of the orchards, the nursery-stocks [etc.]. **1871** HOWELLS *Wedding Journey* v. 105 What is Rochester? . . . A place of . . . an unrivalled nursery trade, a university, two commercial colleges [etc.]. **1923** HERRICK *Lilla* 280 There's a bill from Glidden's, and a nursery catalogue.

Nurseryman. One who manages or cultivates a nursery. {1672–} — **c1790** *Amer. Acad. Mem.* II. I. 107 The nurseryman will perceive a perfect union of the graft and stock. **1850** *Rep. Comm. Patents 1849: Agric.* 435 Most [nurseries are] . . . either connected with, or purchasing largely of Ohio and New York nursery-men. **1868** BRACKETT *Farm Talk* 55 The nurseryman said they'd bear in six years after they were grafted. **1894** ALLEN *Ky. Cardinal* ii, I ordered from a nursery-man more trees of holly, juniper, and fir.

∗**Nut.** The fruit of certain trees and shrubs, consisting of a kernel or seed enclosed in a hard shell or outer covering.

1674 *Cal. State P., Amer. & W.I.* VII. 581 Maine [has] . . . plenty of vines, apples and pears, . . . cucumbers, small nuts, and filberts. **1709** LAWSON *Carolina* 99 Chinkapin is a sort of Chesnut, whose Nuts are most commonly very plentiful; insomuch that the Hogs get fat with them. **1787** *Amer. Acad. Mem.* II. I. 158 Beech produces a small nut in high esteem. **1838** HAWTHORNE *Notebooks* (1932) 40 They dispatch him with two or three cents to buy candy, and nuts and raisins. **1895** G. KING *New Orleans* 267 At the American theatre he saw . . . the 'Kentuckians' cracking nuts during the performance.

b. Attrib. with *bag, bowl, candy,* etc.

1778 CARVER *Travels* 55 A variety of trees [in Minn.] . . . yield amazing quantities of fruit, without care or cultivation, such as the nut-trees . . . and plum-trees. **1864** *Hist. North-Western Soldiers' Fair* 90 Miss Osborne [donated] 5 nut bags. **1869** FULLER *Flower Gatherers* 19 Skip and I were hunting a squirrel down in the nut-grove this morning. **1873** PHELPS *Trotty's Wedding* i, I'll get half a stick of nut-candy. **1907** *St. Nicholas* May 591/2 Bert, you go for the nuts; you will find the silver nut bowl on the sideboard. **1913** EMERSON *R. Fielding at Snow Camp* 102 The three boys stuck to their work . . . until there was a great bowl of nutmeats.

+**Nut cake.** A doughnut or fried cake. Chiefly *New Eng.*

1801 *Spirit Farmers' Mus.* 235 Heap the nutcakes, fried in butter. **1805** *Pocumtuc Housewife* (1906) 7 Nut cakes are expected for breakfast and some times Pye. **1837** *Harvardiana* III. 189 The traditions of those enormous nut-cakes, fried for this occasion by widow Hopkins. **1857** *Quinland* I. 36 The 'nut-cakes' are an institution of the country. Some call 'em 'dough-nuts,' and some 'fried cakes.' **1889** COOKE *Steadfast* 198 Who ever heerd tell of puttin' a reason and a bit of citron into the middle of a riz nut-cake before 'twas fried, and then callin' of it a 'oly kook'? **1897** ROBINSON *Uncle Lisha's Outing* 253 'Come right in, all of you, an' have a fried cake an some cider.' . . . 'I wouldn't go ag'in a nut cake.'

∗**Nutcracker.** Also †**nutcraker.** ∗**1.** An implement used for cracking nuts. +**2. a.** =CARDINAL GROSBEAK. **b.** =CLARK'S CROW. — (1) **1779** *York Co., Va., Rec.: Wills* XXII. 28 April, 1 key swivel and nut cracker, 0/12/0. **1828** H. FINN, etc. *Whimwhams* 105 His figure had a most striking resemblance to the Dutch nutcrackers, I have seen at the toyshops. **1876** WARNER *Gold of Chickaree* 130 Making a great and ill-adjusted effort with his nut-cracker, it slipped. (2) [**1688** HOLME *Armory* II. 242/2 The Virginian Nightingale . . . is called of some the Nut-craker, because it loves to feed on Kernells.] **1874** COUES *Birds N.W.* 207 *Picicorvus Columbianus,* . . . American Nutcracker. **1917** *Birds of Amer.* II. 234/2 The winter food of the Nutcracker is the seeds of conifers.

Nut grass. Any one of various sedges of the genus *Cyperus,* esp. *C. rotundus,* bearing small nutlike tubers. {1830, in W. Indies}

1775 ROMANS *Nat. Hist. Florida* 129 In Carolina it [*herbe au cheval*] is called *nutt* grass from a *nutt* found at its root. **1833** SILLIMAN *Man. Sugar Cane* 16 This method appears at least worthy of trial . . . on those estates not infested with the nut-grass. **1856** *Rep. Comm. Patents 1855: Agric.* p. xiv, It belongs to the same genus as the notorious nut-grass, (*Cyperus repens,*) but does not possess the power of spreading itself like that pest of Southern fields. **1883** SMITH *Geol. Survey Ala.* 293 As taking possession of the waste lands, or the cultivated soils, the following are to be mentioned: *Cyperus rotundus* (nut-grass), . . . *Panicum sanguimale* [*sic*], or crabgrass [etc.]. **1894** COULTER *Bot. W. Texas* III. 463 *Cyperus rotundus.* . . . From the South Atlantic and Gulf States to the Texan coast. . . . Often called 'nut grass.'

∗**Nuthatch.** Any one of various species of small birds of the family Sittidae that creep over trunks and branches of trees in search of insects; also, a bird of such a species. Also with defining term.

See also WHITE-BREASTED NUTHATCH.

c1729 CATESBY *Carolina* I. 22 *Sitta capite nigro.* The Nuthatch. . . . They breed and continue the whole year in Carolina. **1789** MORSE *Amer. Geog.* 60 American birds [include] . . . The Heron, . . . Nuthatch, . . . [and] Owl. **1810** Brown-Headed Nuthatch [see BROWN *a.* 1 b]. **1832** WILLIAMSON *Maine* I. 141 The Nuthatch is a small bird of the pye sort. **1875** BURROUGHS *Winter Sunshine* 28 The regular winter residents go in little bands . . . —the jays . . . in advance; the nuthatches next. **1883** THAXTER *Poems for Children* 23 Redpoll, nuthatch, thrasher, plover gray. **1902** WHITE *Blazed Trail* 38 He saw the grave nuthatch with its appearance of a total lack of humor. **1917** *Birds of Amer.* III. 202/2 The Nuthatch does no known injury but much good.

‖**Nuthatcher.** =prec. — **1862** *Ill. Agric. Soc. Trans.* V. 731 Even the Nuthatchers, are, by many, indiscriminately called Sap-Suckers.

∗**Nutmeg.** Also †**nutmege, nutmegg.**

∗**1.** A hard, aromatic kernel or nut valued as a spice, especially the seed of a tree (*Myristica fragrans*) native to the Molucca and other East Indian islands; also, spice prepared from such a kernel or nut.

1630 WINTHROP in R. C. Winthrop *Life J. Winthrop* II. 39 A little grated or sliced nutmege. **1671** *Md. Archives* II. 268 This House desired . . . Nutmeggs at 2d apiece. **1744** *Md. Hist. Mag.* XXI. 247, ½ lb Nuttmeggs. **1800** ASBURY *Journal* II. 440 C. Patton sent me a decoction of bark, rhubarb, and nutmeg, which helps me much. **1862** CUMMING *Hospital Life* (1866) 42/1 She gave us some nutmegs, which were very acceptable, as every thing of that kind is scarce, and we need them in seasoning food for the soldiers. **1892** *Amer. Folk-Lore* V. 20 In Missouri rheumatism is prevented by carrying in the pocket a nutmeg or a walnut.

+**2.** *ellipt.* =NUTMEG STATE; also, a native or inhabitant of Connecticut. Also attrib.

1866 C. H. SMITH *Bill Arp* 170 Fretman was a nutmeg skoolteacher who had gone round my naborhood with his skool artikles. **1896** *Typographical Jrnl.* IX. 367 Down Among the Nutmegs. . . . The printers of Hartford are alive to their own interests. **1907** *Boston Transcript* 9 Nov. II. 9/5 Popular names of the States: . . . New England of the West—Minnesota. Nutmeg or Wooden Nutmeg—Connecticut.

Nutmeg flower. A European annual (*Nigella sativa*) sometimes cultivated in the United States for its black, aromatic seed. — **1829** EATON *Botany* (ed. 5) 303 Exotic. *Nigella sativa,* nutmeg flower. **1836** LINCOLN *Botany* App. 119. **1868** GRAY *Field Botany* 40 Nutmeg-Flower. Cultivated in some old gardens.

Nutmeg-grater. An instrument or kitchen utensil having a rough surface, used for reducing nutmeg to a powdered form. {1695–} — **1709** LAWSON *Carolina* 159 The bones of these fish [sturgeons] make good nutmeg-graters. **1759** *Newport Mercury* 26 June 4/3 To be sold by Jacob Richardson, . . . Nutmeg Graters, Barber's Boxes and Brushes. **1879** PHELPS *Old Maid's Paradise* (1885) 47 One [package] is a patent nutmeg-grater.

+**Nutmeg hickory.** A hickory (*Carya myristicaeformis*), chiefly southern, which bears a nut about the shape and size of a nutmeg. Also *nutmeg hickory nut.* — **1810** MICHAUX *Arbres* I. 21 *J*[*uglans*] *myristicaformis,* . . . Nutmeg hickery nut . . . , nom donné par moi. **1832** BROWNE *Sylva* 177 This species . . . bears the name of Nutmeg Hickory, from the resemblance of its fruits to that of the nutmeg. **1901** MOHR *Plant Life Ala.* 101 The nutmeg hickory, when full grown, resembles the shagbark hickory in its pale, shreddy bark.

+**Nutmeg melon.** A muskmelon having a thin, netted or reticulated rind suggestive of the surface of a nutmeg. — **1822** WOODS *Eng. Prairie* (1904) 307 There are many sorts of sweet melons. . . . I have only noticed musk, of a large size; and nutmeg, a smaller one. **1854** *Mich. Agric. Soc. Trans.* V. 65 W. Smail, Detroit [exhibited] 4 nutmeg melons. **1870** WARNER *Summer in Garden* xiv, The nutmeg-melons, having covered themselves with delicate lace-work, are now ready to leave the vine.

+**Nutmeg State.** A nickname for Connecticut. In allusion to the alleged practice of the natives of making nutmegs of wood and selling them as genuine. — **1857** *Harper's Mag.* Dec. 136/2 Let us repeat a story that comes fresh from the Nutmeg State. **1868** *N.Y. Herald* 4 July 4/2 It could not be expected that . . . the Nutmeg State would send . . . a delegation . . . who would . . . tell just what they think and believe. **1894** *Congress. Rec.* 15 Jan. 824/2 My friend from the little 'Nutmeg State' of Connecticut . . . wants protection . . . upon leaf tobacco. **1903** *N.Y. Ev. Post* 14 Dec. 2 E. J. Hill, of Connecticut, . . . wants to move toward free alcohol in the arts for the use of the busy factories of the Nutmeg State.

*****Nutmeg tree.** The California nutmeg tree, *Torreya californica.* (The species referred to in the first quotation is not known.) — **1836** HOLLEY *Texas* 88 Among the underwood are found . . . the delightful magnolia, the nutmeg tree [etc.]. **1894** *Amer. Folk-Lore* VII. 100 *Torreya Californica,* . . . nutmeg-tree, Cal.

+**Nut pine.** Any one of various species of pine indigenous to the southwestern and Rocky Mountain regions (as *Pinus monophylla, P. edulis,* etc.) that bear edible nuts; also, a tree of such a species. In full *nut pine tree.*

1845 FRÉMONT *Exped.* 221 A pine tree . . . which Dr. Torrey has described as a new species, under the name of *pinus monophyllus;* in popular language, it might be called the *nut pine.* **1850** KINGSLEY *Diary* 142 The evergreen oak and Nut Pine are all the varieties of trees or timber. **1869** *Amer. Naturalist* III. 187 Junipers . . . and Nut-pines cover a few of the highest points [in southern Calif.]. **1884** SARGENT *Rep. Forests* 9 The foothills . . . are covered with the scant grove of the nut-pine. **1896** SHINN *Story of Mine* 63 The nut-pine trees were soon cut down. **1897** SUDWORTH *Arborescent Flora* 17 [Lists 5 species.]

Nut rush. A genus of sedges or a plant or species belonging to this genus. Also with specifying term. — **1843** TORREY *Flora N.Y.* II. 368 *Scleria laxa.* . . . Loose-flowered Nut-rush. . . . A common species in the pine region of New-Jersey, and in some of the Southern States. **1857** GRAY *Botany* 506 *Scleria.* Nut-Rush. [5 species listed.] **1894** COULTER *Bot. W. Texas* III. 476.

‖**Nutshelly,** *a.* Highly condensed; brief. — **1843** 'CARLTON' *New Purchase* II. 171 So nut-shelly had all books and subjects become, that all could be even cracked and devoured in infant schools.

+**Nuttall.** [Thos. *Nuttall,* Anglo-Amer. naturalist (1789–1859).] Used in possessive in specific names of birds. — **1839** AUDUBON *Ornith. Biog.* V. 335 Nuttall's Whip-Poor-Will. *Caprimulgus Nuttallii.* **1858** BAIRD *Birds Pacific R.R.* 93 *Picus Nuttalli.* . . . Nuttall's Woodpecker. . . . Coast region of California. **1917** *Birds of Amer.* I. 54 Gull-billed Tern. *Gelochelidon nilotica.* . . . Other Names.—Marsh Tern; Egyptian Tern; Nuttall's Tern. *Ib.* III. 36/2 Nuttall's Sparrow [*Zonotrichia leucophrys nuttalli*] . . . has this uninterrupted stripe.

Nutting. {1723-} +A nutting party. — **1880** *Harper's Mag.* Dec. 89/2 The younger people had their berrying frolics, . . . nuttings, and the like.

Nut weevil. A weevil whose larva infests nuts: (see quotations). {1802-} — **1838** *Mass. Zool. Survey Rep.* 83 *Balaninus* . . . signifies inhabiting a nut, . . . and the insects are called *nut-weevils.* . . . Our most common nut-weevil, *Balaninus rectus,* is found from July to October. **1854** EMMONS *Agric. N.Y.* V. 109 *Balaninus rectus.* . . . This nut weevil inhabits the Chinquapin nut, and renders useless almost the whole crop.

+**Nutwood.** Any one of various species of nut-bearing trees, as hickory, walnut, etc.; a tree or the wood of a tree of such a species. Also attrib.

1701 WOLLEY *Journal N.Y.* 75 [The Indians] had Needles of Wood, for which Nut-wood was esteemed best. **1775** FITHIAN *Journal* II. 76 These level bottoms, abound most in Walnut, Nut-wood, Locust &c. **1833** *Knickerb.* I. 205 The other [was] knitting before a cheerful nut-wood fire. **1840** COOPER *Pathfinder* i, Of this [lesser] class were the birch, . . . the quivering aspen, various generous nut-woods, and divers others that resembled the ignoble and vulgar. **1881** *Harper's Mag.* Feb. 357/1 Our [colonial] ancestors were content to dine from pewter plates . . . their few precious pieces of China being reserved for . . . display on the shelves of the . . . nut-wood parlor cupboards.

O

***Oak.**

***1. a.** A tree or shrub, or a species of tree or shrub, of the genus *Quercus*. Also collective. **b.** The wood of any of these trees.

American species of the oak are numerous: see, for instance, BARRENS, BLACK, BUR, GRAY, LIVE, RED, and WHITE OAK.

1610 *Estate of Va.* 54 The country yeeldeth abundance of wood, as Oake, Wainscot, Walnut tres. **1661** *Providence Rec.* I. 11 An oke marked neere ye ground, and Standing neere a Rocke. **1672** JOSSELYN *New Eng. Rarities* 48 There is Oak of three kinds, white, red and black, the white is excellent to make Canoes of, Shallopes, Ships, and other Vessels for the Sea. **1765** ROGERS *Acct. N. America* 42 [In Mass.] may be found plenty of oak, ash and maple. **1823** in Schoolcraft *Travels* (1825) 375 Excellent timber consisting chiefly of maple, hickory, oak, beach, walnut, white wood, bass wood. **1856** *S. Dak. Hist. Coll.* I. 416 At this point there is more timber than at any other between this and Fort Pierre, comprising oak, cottonwood, . . . and some ash. **1916** THOBURN *Stand. Hist. Okla.* I. 5 The most common species of trees in Oklahoma include oaks (of possibly a dozen species), elm . . . , cottonwood [etc.].

2. *attrib.* and *comb.* **a.** Designating articles made or consisting of oak wood.

1630 *Mass. Bay Rec.* I. 79 Sawers shall not take aboue 12d. a scoore for saweing oake boards. **1760** WASHINGTON *Diaries* I. 127 Mike and Tom . . . Cut 122 feet of oak Scantling. **1789** MORSE *Amer. Geog.* 215 The exports consist of . . . oak staves, hoops, pine boards [etc.]. **1846** THORPE *Myst. Backwoods* 142 Seizing a large oak rail, we attempted to run it down his [the alligator's] throat. **1872** *Vermont Bd. Agric. Rep.* I. 154 An experiment had been tried by a Cornwall farmer, packing butter in spruce, oak and black ash tubs. **1880** *Cimarron News & Press* 8 April 1/5 Two lots of oak ties are rotted away. **1886** STAPLETON *Major's Christmas* 245 Miss Amanda sat down in a carved oak chair and wept. **1896** WILKINS *Madelon* 350 [She] opened the carved oak chest. **1903** 'O. HENRY' *Roads of Destiny* 168 All went inside the high, carved oak railings into the banking-room.

b. Designating places where oak trees grow.

1660 *Oyster Bay Rec.* I. 1 A Deed delivered unto the townes hands Conserrning oake necke And matinecoke the A bovesayd swamp. **1702** in *Amer. Sp.* XV. 290/2 Westerly through ye oake Swamp to ye first line. **1766** J. BARTRAM *Journal* 56 Saw several good cypress-swamps and oak-hammocks alternately mixed with pine-land. **1818** SCHOOLCRAFT *Journal* 25 Instead of rich bottoms, we have a high oak-prairie. **1835** BIRD *Hawks* II. 52 His father . . . had suddenly checked his horse at the entrance of the little oak-yard. **1845** FRÉMONT *Exped.* 253 Crossing a number of dry and timbered arroyos, we travelled until late through open oak groves.

c. In special combinations.

Oak frog, plum, (see quotations); *oak poisoning,* an infection occasioned by poison oak; *oak potato,* (see quotation).

1890 *Cent.* 4050/3 *Oak-frog,* . . . a North American toad, *Bufo quercus:* so called because it frequents oak-openings. *Ib., Oak plum,* . . . a gall produced on the acorns of the black and red oaks in the United States by *Cynips quercus-prunus:* so called from its resemblance to a plum. **1866** *Ore. State Jrnl.* 23 June 3/5 For the Cure of . . . Oak Poisoning, (for which Dr. Bourne discovered the only scientific and certain cure). **1890** *Cent.* 4050/3 *Oak potato,* . . . a gall produced on the twigs of white oaks in the United States by *Cynips quercus-batatus:* so called from its resemblance to a potato.

+Oak-and-hickory, *a. S.* Of land: Having a native growth of oaks and hickories upon it. — **1735** *Ga. Hist. Soc. Coll.* II. 49 It is about thirty miles from Charleston and the land is . . . very good, being most of it oak and hickory, which is counted the best for corn and peas. **1741** TAILFER, etc. *True Narr. Ga.* 97 The Proportion of Pine Barren to either good Swamp or Oak and Hickory Land, is at least six to one. **1789** MORSE *Amer. Geog.* 429 The high-lands commonly known by the name of oak and hiccory lands, constitute the fourth kind of soil [in S.C.].

+Oak barren. A piece of ground with poor soil on which scrubby oaks grow. Usually pl. — **1811** *Niles' Reg.* I. 101/2 Our oak barrens and other wooded plains may be profitably applied to sheep. **1814** PURSH *Flora Amer.* II. 631 This shrub [*Quercus Banisteri*], about four or six feet high, covers large tracts of ground wherever it occurs, called Oak-barrens. **1835** IRVING *Tour on Prairie* 126 The soil of these 'oak barrens' is loose and unsound. **1890** *Cent.* 4120/1 Similar tracts [of scattered oak trees] in the more southern States, especially in Kentucky, are called *barrens* and *oak-barrens.*

Oak bush. A small oak tree, frequently used as a boundary mark. — **1703** *Providence Rec.* IV. 68 Bounded on the southeast Corner with a black Oake bush & stones laid about it. **1760** *Smithtown Rec.* 418 [We] have laid out a tract of meadow . . . beginning at an oak bush on the beach by Joseph Skidmores meadow.

‖**Oakery.** An oak yard. — **1836** GILMAN *Recoll.* (1838) 213 Turning suddenly, he bounded over the fence into papa's oakery.

+Oak flat. A piece of flat land covered with oaks. — **1800** HAWKINS *Sk. Creek Country* 29 Oak flats, red and post oak, willow leaved hickory . . . on its left side. **1849** CHAMBERLAIN *Ind. Gazetteer* 381 Farther west there are beech and oak flats, which are adapted only to grass.

+Oak grub. An oak bush that sprouts from a root of an oak. — **1852** ELLET *Pioneer Women* 366 The bushes which sprang in a season from their roots, called 'oak grubs,' are difficult to remove from the soil. **1853** *Mich. Agric. Soc. Trans.* IV. 365 A dense growth of hazel bush, oak grubs and willow.

+Oak land. Land covered by a growth of oak; land of rich soil once productive of oak.

1666 *S.C. Hist. Soc. Coll.* V. 84 They were rather willing to paye a greater rent for what acres of oake land they should possess. **1737** WESLEY *Journal* I. 402 Oak-land [in Ga.] commonly lies in narrow streaks between pine-land and some swamp, creek, or river. **1765** ROGERS *Acct. N. America* 135 On the north [of N.C.], towards Virginia, are some oak-lands, like those of Virginia, on which they raise tobacco. **1811** *Ann. 12th Congress* 1 Sess. II. 2116 It was a piece of dry oak land, rising about ten feet above the level of a marshy prairie. **1837** JENKINS *Ohio Gaz.* 187 The soil of Franklin is, what is generally called oak land, being a mixture of clay, sand and gravel. **1849** CHAMBERLAIN *Ind. Gazetteer* 209 The oak land is more extensive than the beech.

***Oak of Jerusalem.** The feather geranium, *Chenopodium botrys.* — **1737** BRICKELL *N. Carolina* 21 Oak of Jerusalem, Indian-purger, Swallow-wort. **1817–8** EATON *Botany* (1822) 235 *Chenopodium botrys,* oak-of-jerusalem. . . . Sweet scented. **1840** DEWEY *Mass. Flowering Plants* 97 Oak of Jerusalem. A native of this country; . . . grows on light, sandy soil; August. Tonic and antispasmodic. . . . The ashes of our species are used in the manufacture of soda.

+Oak opening. A piece of land having a few scattered oaks growing upon it. — **1835** HOFFMAN *Winter in West* I. 148 These fires . . . seize upon the large prairies, and consuming every tree in the woods, except the hardiest, cause the often-mentioned oak openings, so characteristic of Michigan scenery. **1849** CHAMBERLAIN *Ind. Gazetteer* 154 In the north-western part of the country are many oak openings, or barrens, all very fertile and easily brought into cultivation. **1868** *Iowa Agric. Soc. Rep. 1867* 175 [Sugar cane] grows well here on all our soils, high prairie, low bottom, oak openings, timber lands. **1885** *N.H. Forestry Comm. Rep.* June 30 Originally a dense forest covered our state. There were no 'parks' as in the Rocky Mountain region, or 'oak openings' and grassy plains as in the valley of the Mississippi.

Oak pin. A pin made of oak. — **1843** 'CARLTON' *New Purchase* I. 112 Now oak pins are very strong, tough and tenacious, and of most Job-like endurance. **1874** COLLINS *Kentucky* I. 516 Even the shingles being put on with oak pins.

Oak plank. A plank made of oak. Also attrib. — **1741** *Boston Rec.* 271 The Platform and Breast-Work which they propose to be of Wood, the Breast Work of Square Pine Timber, and the Platform of Oak Plank. **1838** ELLSWORTH *Valley of Wabash* 53 The floors are made of oak plank, and left to wear smooth. **1859** STOWE *Minister's Wooing* xxiv, Miss Prissy . . . was so very cautious that not the thickest oak-plank door seemed secure enough.

+Oak-pruner. A beetle (*Hypermallus villosus*) that lives on the pith of oak twigs. — **1838** *Mass. Zool. Survey Rep.* 92 *Stenocorus putator,* or the oak-pruner, so named by Prof. Peck, inhabits the white and black oaks. **1862** *Rep. Comm. Patents 1861: Agric.* 615 The black and white oak trees are infested with . . . the 'Oak-pruner.' [**1899** D. SHARP *Insects* II. 286 *Elaphidion villosum* is called the oak-pruner in North America.]

+Oak ridge. A ridge of land covered with oak growth. — **1789** MORSE *Amer. Geog.* 247 On the banks of Lake Erie, are a few chesnut and oak ridges. **1821** NUTTALL *Travels Arkansa* 164 In the evening, we encamped in the valley of the third oak ridge that separated us from Cedar prairie. *c***1835** CATLIN *Indians* II. 46 We have . . . crossed oak ridges of several miles in breadth, with a sandy soil and scattering timber.

+Oak shake. A shingle split from a piece of oak. — **1856** ROPES *6 Months in Kansas* 49 The cabin is made by . . . nailing 'oak shakes' outside, after the manner of clapboards. **1856** *Wkly. Oregonian* 27 Sept. (Th.), Oak shokes [*sic*], split out by hand, kivered the chamber floor.

Oak timber. 1. *collect.* Oaks that are growing. **2.** A piece of oak wood; lumber made of oak wood. {1767} — **(1) 1640** *N.H. Doc. & Rec.* I. 138 None shall fell any oke timber within half a mile of this part of the town except it be upon their planting lott. **1827** Drake & Mansfield *Cincinnati* 99 It abounds in fine oak, locust, and mulberry timber, suitable for ships and steam-boats. **1883** *Rep. Indian Affairs* 73 Numerous creeks . . . along which are found small rich valleys and some valuable walnut and oak timber. (2) **1696** *Boston Rec.* 136 [He shall erect] a Substantiall Timber Frame of Oake Timber . . . wch frame is to be the whole breadth of the said Shop. **1754** *Duxbury Rec.* 318 The town voted to let James Thomas and Reuben Peterson have the oak timber that was got for a new Meeting house. **1796** Morse *Amer. Geog.* I. 405 Each pier is composed of seven sticks of oak timber, united by a cap-piece.

***Oak tree.** Any tree of the genus *Quercus.* — **1637** *R.I. Col. Rec.* I. 28 The oake tree having four marks with an axe, till some other land marke be set for a certaine bound. **1679** *Conn. Rec.* III. 27 We began [the line] . . . at an oak tree by the River side. **1807** Gass *Journal* 31 Our camp is in a wide bottom, in which are large elm and oak trees. **1905** Davis *Northerner* 136 From the oak-tree came a sound of dumb straining.

Oak-tree caterpillar. One of various caterpillars that feed upon oak leaves. — **1854** Emmons *Agric. N.Y.* V. 262 (*index*), Oaktree caterpillars. [*Ib.* 240–1 *Clisiocampa Neustoria.* . . . This insect feeds upon oak leaves.] **1868** *Mich. Agric. Rep.* VII. 166 The oak tree caterpillar, larvae of the *Dryocompa senatoria*—has been even less numerous about Lansing, than in 1867.

***Oakum.** Also †**okam, ocum.** Loose fiber obtained from untwisting and picking old hemp rope. Used in calking the seams of ships and in dressing wounds. Also attrib.

1648 *Conn. Rec.* I. 507, 12 yards of okam cloath. **1711** *Boston News-Letter* 8 Oct. 2/2 Using Fire to a parcel of Ocum, Chips and other combustible Rubbish. **1797** Asbury *Journal* II. 336 [She] supports herself by picking oakum. **1814** *Niles' Reg.* V. 432/1 The fire commenced in the oakum loft. **1833** Neal *Down-Easters* I. 15 Plastering the foot all over with his furniture-polish, and wrapping it up with a bandage of loose oakum. **1889** *Century Mag.* March 706/1 Canvas bags filled with oakum saturated with oil . . . were used.

Oaky, *a.* {1631–} Covered with or consisting of oak. {*a*1849} — **1797** Hawkins *Letters* 73 The whole length of the creek is through a pine barron [*sic*], with but a small exception of some oaky land, in small quantities. **1800** — *Sk. Creek Country* 62 The good land spreads out for four or five miles on both sides of the creek, with oaky woods. **1833** J. Stuart *Three Years N.A.* II. 216 The road runs through the forest, part of which, consisting mostly of oak, they call oakey.

***Oar.** A flat-bladed, wooden lever used to propel a boat. Also comb.

1624 Smith *Gen. Hist. Va.* III. 60 We seeing them [*sc.* Indians] prepare to assault vs, left our Oares and made way with our sayle to incounter them. **1711** Hempstead *Diary* 5, I went into the woods to gitt Timber for oars. **1781** *Md. Hist. Mag.* VI. 312 Invoice of Schooner Nautilus's Materials. . . . 10 Pikes, 10 large Ores, some Langrage. **1789** *Boston Directory* 188 Hooton John, oar-maker. **1884** 'Mark Twain' *H. Finn* xvi, I buckled to my paddle and they laid to their oars. **1904** [see Oarlock].

***Oarlock.** The notch, thole-pins, fork, or other device in which an oar of a boat plays; a rowlock. {–1657} Also attrib. 'Seldom used in Eng.' (Horwill). — **1855** *Rep. Comm. Patents 1854* I. 246 Oar-Locks. . . . The oar [is provided] with a cylinder surrounded with a band and bolt forming a row-lock. **1874** Long *Wild-Fowl* 85 Both may row, if two sets of oar-lock seats are provided. **1904** *N.Y. Ev. Post* 6 July 12 Clinker-built boats, one pair ash oars and oarlocks.

+**Oarsman.** One who handles an oar; a rower. {1871–} — **1701** Wolley *Journal N.Y.* (1902) 46 Two Boats with six Men in each make a Company, *viz.* four Oars-men or Rowers; an Harpineer. and a Steers-man. **1811** *Niles' Reg.* I. 245/1 They certainly possess great dexterity as oarsmen. **1883** *Harper's Mag.* Nov. 900/1 We do not want our boys prize-fighters, . . . demon bowlers, . . . champion oarsmen. **1900** Stockton *Afield & Afloat* 419 They were packed tightly together, barely leaving room for the oarsmen to move their arms.

***Oat,** *n.* (Cf. Wild oat.)

***1.** The grain of the cereal grass, *Avena sativa;* also, the grass itself. Usually pl.

1619 *Va. House of Burgesses* 17 Proceed in . . . sending . . . greate store of all sortes of the best graine, as wheat, Barlie, Oates, and pease. **1641** *Conn. Rec.* I. 443 An acre of sumer wheat, . . . an acre of oats. **1721** *Mass. H. Rep. Jrnl.* III. 45 The Inhabitants . . . to pay the several Sums . . . in the several Species hereafter mentioned, . . . Indian Corn, Oats, Flax [etc.]. **1748** Eliot *Field-Husb.* i. 14 Oats and Peas produce a good Crop when sowed together. **1803** *Lit. Mag.* (Phila.) Dec. 172 We ordered oats for our horses. **1882** *Uncle Rufus & Ma* 50, I was shown the bunch which had produced twenty-one stalks from a single oat. **1907** *St. Nicholas* May 653/2, I went one day to the pasture to feed my pony some oats.

+**2.** *To feel one's oats,* to feel frisky or lively; to feel 'cocky'; to enjoy a sense of importance.

1833 A. Lawrence *Diary & Corr.* 126 We both 'feel our oats' and our youth. **1843** Haliburton *Attaché* 1 Ser. II. 157 You know that, and feel your oats, too, as well as any one. **1869** Barnum *Struggles & Triumphs* 33 My father . . . installed me as clerk in this country store. Of course I felt my oats. It was condescension on my part to talk with boys who did out-door work. **1890** H. M. Field *Bright Skies* 185 All this . . . is no more to be resented or criticized than the caperings of a young colt that 'feels his oats.' **1905** Davis *Northerner* 120 Rosy's beginning to feel her oats, Mr. Watson.

3. Attrib. and comb. with *box, cake, field,* etc.

1754 Hempstead *Diary* 627, I Sowed 2lb. more of Hay seed on the oat ground. **1756** *Ib.* 663 Wee Carryed 1 Ld more of oatstraw. **1834** *Knickerb.* III. 297 Their humble fare . . . consisted, as usual, of milk and oat-cakes. **1852** Mitchell *Dream Life* 68 The hard dry stubble of an oat-field. **1866** *Rep. Comm. Patents 1863* I. 439 Improved Oat Separator. . . . Consists of two perforated revolving cylinders, into the inner one of which the mixed oats and wheat are fed. **1873** Bailey *Life in Danbury* 20, I went to the oat box and filled the peck measure. **1895** *Dept. Agric. Yrbk. 1894* 420 Stinking smut of wheat and oat smut can be easily prevented.

+**Oat,** *v.* [f. the noun.] *tr.* To feed (a horse) with oats. *Obsolescent.* Also absol.

1732 B. Lynde *Diary* (1880) 26 Next morning . . . dined at Hampton; . . . thence to Greenland, where oated, and for 2 horses and drink, 2s. **1766** J. Adams *Diary* Works II. 240 Oated my horse, and drank balm tea at Treadwell's in Ipswich. **1778** Cutler in *Life & Corr.* I. 65 Oated and had my hair dressed. . . . After oating, we went on to Martin's two miles. **1787** *Ib.* 314 We oated again at another wretched little tavern. **1848** *Knickerb.* XXXI. 32 Having 'oated the horses' at Williamstown-Centre, we started to pay our respects to Madam. **1855** Barnum *Life* 70 Old 'Bob' was duly oated and watered.

Oat bag. A horse's nose bag for oats. {1882} — **1851** A. O. Hall *Manhattaner* 5 It was a modest commercial plain . . . with . . . bits of machinery, and ploughs, and oat bags, and hay bales. **1898** Deland *Old Chester Tales* 76 She got the oat-bag from the back of the buggy.

***Oat grass. a.** Any of several wild oats of the genus *Avena.* **b.** Any grass of several allied genera, as *Arrhenatherum, Danthonia,* and *Trisetum.* Often with descriptive terms.

See also Black oat-grass.

1795 Winterbotham *Hist. View* III. 401 The States of New-England abound with . . . Millet, . . . Fescue grass, . . . Oat grass. **1802** Drayton *S. Carolina* 61 Oat grass. (*Avena Caroliniana.*) Grows in rich tide lands. **1825** Lorain *Pract. Husbandry* 292 The speargrasses grown on the farm . . . consisted principally of timothy, orchard, and green grasses, with some little oat grass. **1840** Dewey *Mass. Flowering Plants* 237 *Avena flavescens.* Yellow Oat Grass. Recently introduced. **1878** Killebrew *Tenn. Grasses* 109 Meadow Oat Grass is one of the few grasses that do best on a dry soil. **1884** Mohr in Vasey *Agric. Grasses* 92 *Uniola latifolia.* (Broad-flowered Fescue grass.) . . . It is called by some *wild fescue* or *oat grass.* **1901** — *Plant Life Ala.* 372 *Trisetum pennsylvanicum.* . . . Swamp Oat Grass. . . . Alleghenian and Carolinian areas.

***Oath.**

***1.** A statement or promise solemnized by an appeal to God as witness.

1623 *Plymouth Laws* 28 Twelve honest men to be impanelled . . . in forme of a jury upon their oath. **1789** *Phila. Ordinances* (1812) 65 Every alderman . . . shall, before he enters on the execution of his office, take a solemn oath. **1862** *Trial C. M. Jefferds* 94 Let me call your attention to the sanctity of the oath which you took on entering the jury-box. **1905** *Indian Laws & Tr.* III. 608 Any person [wishing to establish a townsite must state] . . . fully and under oath the necessity or propriety of founding or establishing a town at that place.

2. Special oaths, as *oath of abjuration, allegiance, fidelity, office.* (Cf. *amnesty oath* s.v. Amnesty and Ironclad oath.)

1644 *Plymouth Laws* 76 That all those persons . . . yt have not taken the Oath of fidellyty . . . dep[ar]t the Government. **1718** *Mass. H. Rep. Jrnl.* II. 1 This House should . . . Take and Subscribe the Oath of Abjuration. **1777** *Jrnls. Cont. Congress* VII. 83 All the inhabitants of the said counties [Somerset and Worcester, Md., shall be directed] to assemble at appointed places, and take the oath of allegiance required by the said State. **1777** G. Clinton in Sparks *Corr. Revol.* I. 415, I have had a second call to attend at Kingston, and take the oath of office in consequence of my late appointment. **1809** Kendall *Travels* I. 73 The franchise was allowed to every Man . . . [provided] that he was an admitted inhabitant, and that he had taken the oath of fidelity. **1863** in Moore *Rebellion Rec.* V. I. 50 [He] arrested all the male inhabitants of Luray, Va., and lodged them in the court-house preparatory to administering the oath of allegiance.

***Oatmeal.**

***1.** A meal made from oats.

1623 *Va. House of Burgesses* 21 One for steelinge 2 or 3 pints of oatmeale had a bodkinge thrust through his tongue. **1677** *Boston Rec.* 112 Reced of Mr. Paul Dudley . . . 15 Barrll of oate meale, 2 Firkins of Butter. **1766** *R.I. Commerce* I. 150 Shall send you 20 firkins, with 1 Cask Oatmeal which is all there is. **1850** *New Eng. Farmer* II. 358 Oatmeal is little used as food in this country. **1901** Grinnell *Gold Hunting in Alaska* 48 They broke into the 'grub box,' and got away with . . . a sack of oatmeal and a side of bacon.

2. A porridge or mush made by boiling oatmeal in water or milk. {1708– (E. Cook *Sot-Weed Factor* 5)}

1876 *Wide Awake* 220/1 Lots of oat-meal, beef-tea, little pills, have I taken to keep me up. **1883** *Harper's Mag.* Aug. 456/2 It was a dismal breakfast . . . when dry toast preceded oatmeal, and butterless baked potato . . . brought up the rear. **1903** BURNHAM *Jewel* 185 She had, after her fruit and oatmeal, a slice of ham and a baked potato.

3. Attrib. in sense 1 with *mush, porridge.*

1882 'M. HARLAND' *Eve's Daughters* 24 The most useful milk-producing ingredients are . . . good broths, milk, really excellent ale, oatmeal porridge and cream. **1883** HOWE *Country Town* (1926) 36 If you have cold oat meal mush, or a bit of graham bread, I will refresh myself with that.

Obeah, Obi, Oby. [Of African origin.] A kind of witchcraft: (see quotations). {1760– (*Jamaica Assembly* 16 Dec. 2)} Also attrib. — **1836** SEALSFIELD *Pflanzerleben* (1843) I. 137 'He Obeah man' schreien Hannibal und Taby. **1866** *Ala. Hist. Soc. Trans.* IV. 480 A negro woman . . . says an old African hag put a snake in her four years ago, and the Obi doctor has gone to deliver her. **1893** M. A. OWEN *Voodoo Tales* 168 Des one o' dem Oby pison. . . . Hit am er powdeh mek outen de same hef' ob snails an' lizuhds an' crickits an' scorpums dry down an' beat fine.

O-be-joyful. +Alcoholic liquor. *slang.* — **1845** L. CRAWFORD *Hist. White Mts.* (1886) 45, I was loaded . . . with a plenty of what some call 'Black Betts,' or 'O-be-joyful,' as it was the fashion in those days, to make use of this kind of stuff. **1847** COYNER *Lost Trappers* 236 'O! be joyful,' as the New Englanders call it, alias, alcohol, . . . is said to be retailed at four dollars a pint. **1914** *Dialect Notes* IV. 77 *Oh-be-joyful.* Also *oh-be-rich-an'-happy.* Hard liquor.

***Obelisk.** A tapering shaft of stone: (see also quot. 1833). — **1739** W. STEPHENS *Proc. Georgia* 428 Which [grave] the General says he intends to dignify with some Obelisk. **1766** ROWE *Diary* 95 In the Common there was an Obelisk very beautifully Decorated. **1833** *Knickerb.* II. 208 *Obelisk* is the word used by stone masons in describing the sort of tomb, . . . consisting of a pedestal about three feet high, or sometimes higher, surmounted with a pyramid of about the same height, or less, and not unfrequently bearing an urn on the pinnacle.

+**Oberlinism.** A doctrine of perfectionism formulated by C. G. Finney (1792–1875) and Asa Mahan (1800–1899), both of Oberlin College, Ohio. — **1843** 'CARLTON' *New Purchase* II. 22 Would not more persons have been converted to Oberlinism, Finneyism, or Abolitionism?

+**Oberlinite.** A believer in Oberlinism. — **1867** DIXON *New America* II. 308 The Perfectionists, who declared that the world was already at an end, that the judgment had come down upon us, parted into Putneyites and Oberlinites.

+**Obflisticate,** *v.* [Humorous var. of *obfuscate* v.] *tr.* To put out of the way; to deprive of luster. Also *ppl. a. slang. Obs.* — **1832** J. HALL *Legends of West* 38 These Mingoes . . . ought to be essentially, and particularly, and tee-totally obflisticated off of the face of the whole yearth. **1833** *Sk. D. Crockett* p. v, The still more delicate repast of a constant repetition of the terms *'bodyaciously,' 'tetotaciously,' 'obflisticated,'* &c. **1840** *Crockett Almanac* 10 He looked obflisticated.

+**Obfusticated,** *a.* [Humorous var. of *obfuscated* ppl. a.] Overshadowed or eclipsed; bewildered. *slang.* — *c***1844** R. H. COLLYER *American Life* 4, I see, Doctor, you are a little obfusticated. **1848** *Knickerb.* XXXI. 175 Being completely 'obfusticated,' he was trying to 'define his position.' **1871** *Republican Rev.* 6 May 1/2 [We] speak of things and events as we find them, without dealing in far fetched theories and other 'obfusticated' nonsense.

+**Obione.** [Sp.] (See quotation.) — **1856** WHIPPLE *Explor. Ry. Route* I. 122 For camp-fires we depend upon twigs of obione, (grease-wood), or the soft pulpy stalks of the yucca.

+**Obispo pine.** [Sp., 'bishop' and *pine.*] The bishop pine of California, *Pinus muricata.* — **1884** SARGENT *Rep. Forests* 200 *Pinus muricata.* . . . Obispo Pine. Bishop's Pine. **1897** SUDWORTH *Arborescent Flora* 28 California Swamp Pine. . . . Common names [include] . . . Anthony's Prickle-Cone Pine . . . Obispo Pine (Cal.).

+**Object chart.** A chart in which objects are illustrated, used in teaching. — **1866** *Rep. Indian Affairs* 256 By the use of Wilson's object-charts, together with other expedients upon the plan of object teaching, these children are rapidly learning to speak the English language [etc.]. **1871** *Ib.* (1872) 306 A new and original series of 'object charts' gotten up expressly for the Indians of Oregon by myself.

***Objection.** +In parliamentary usage: A vocal expression of opposition to an action or measure. — **1871** *Congress. Globe* 3 March 1926/3 Is there objection to its being read again? **1900** *Congress. Rec.* 16 Jan. 885/2 If there is no objection, it will be held that he is excused. The Chair hears no objection.

Object staff. *Surveying.* A leveling rod. — **1812** *Ann. 12th Congress* 1 Sess. II. 2296 That there be not less than one surveyor, two chain carriers, and two men with object staves, employed in making the same survey.

+**Object system.** A system of teaching by use of object lessons. — **1869** BRACE *New West* 75 The improvement which we have sought so much to bring before the public in New York . . . —the 'Object System' —has already been adopted here. **1878** *Harper's Mag.* March 604/2 This school is too large for strictly Kindergarten teaching; but the 'object system' . . . was the one adopted.

+**Object teacher.** A teacher who employs the object system. — **1872** BRACE *Dangerous Classes N.Y.* 193 We trust that no Primary School in New York will be without a well-trained 'Object-teacher.'

+**Object teaching.** Teaching by means of object lessons. Also attrib. — **1860** H. BARNARD (*title*), Object teaching, and Oral Lessons on Social Science and Common Things. **1872** BRACE *Dangerous Classes N.Y.* 191 Nothing . . . impresses a child's mind like pictures, stories, or parables, or some form of 'object-teaching.' **1881** *Rep. Indian Affairs* 84 The object-teaching system has been followed throughout.

***Obligate,** *v.* Also †**oblygate.**

This word is found more frequently in American than in British usage. Its use is not uncommon, however, in English and Scottish dialects.

1. *passive.* **a.** To be under obligation, or to be required, *to do* something. {1764–}

1753 WASHINGTON *Writings* I. 33 They were obligated, according to Promise, to give the Present. **1771** *Cambridge Prop. Rec.* 365 That every person . . . [shall] become Oblygated to indemnifie him from all Demands what so ever. **1823** COOPER *Pilot* II. xiv, A man will be obligated to spend half his time in making his manners. **1888** 'CRADDOCK' *Despot* 146 The parson . . . was 'obligated' to go down to the Settlement. **1901** *Dial* 16 May 341/1 He does not consider himself in any way obligated to close his eyes to abuses on the British side.

b. To be placed in debt or under obligation *for* or *by* (a specified benefit). {1692–, in active voice}

1763 *Conn. Rec.* XII. 206 The same monies for which the said Knap and Monmouth were obligated . . . being unpaid. **1829** B. HALL *Travels* I. 286 'Even to the value of that gimlet,' said one of the [Canadian] settlers to me, 'we are obligated to the King.' **1836** GILMAN *Recoll.* (1838) 52 Sister Nancy was much obligated by the fans and basket Miss Neely sent her.

2. *reflex.* To put oneself under obligation, or under legal constraint, *to do* something.

1757 *Dudley* (Mass.) *Rec.* II. 27 We promise . . . to obligate our selves to pay ye town rates for our heads so long as the above sd prelidge is afforded to us. **1777** *New Eng. Hist. & Gen. Reg.* XLVIII. 346, I Roger Alger Have Agreaed and obligated my Self to Serve Three years in the Contenattel Servise for Ezriah Dickinson. **1826** COOPER *Mohicans* xxix, Had I that piece . . . , I would obligate myself to cut the thong. **1898** TRUMBULL *Hist. Northampton, Mass.* I. 60 The only payment the town had obligated itself to make was £14 for building the meeting house, and the sum of £30 was probably sufficient to cover all expenses.

3. *tr.* To require *to do* something. {1668}

1837 NEAL *Charcoal Sk.* (1838) 98 New fashions haven't shut up the streets yet, and obligated people to hire hackney balloons if they want to go a walkin'. **1899** *Nation* 5 Oct. 259/1 Even the treaty of peace . . . obligates the United States 'to undertake the release of all Spanish prisoners.'

Oblong. {*a*1608–}

1. A name applied to an area oblong in shape. Used in place names.

1700 *Md. Hist. Mag.* XX. 283 The Oblong, 150 acr. Sur[veyed] the 20 June 1687 for Hendrick Inlowes. **1781** PETERS *Hist. Conn.* 100 The New-Yorkers . . . in 1731, gained 60,000 acres more, called the Oblong, from Connecticut. *Ib.* 101 Connecticut was forced . . . to give up, not only Long Island and the above-mentioned twenty miles east of Hudson's river, but also the Oblong, without any equivalent. **1849** *Doc. Hist. N.Y. State* I. 750 *n.*, This tract, otherwise called 'The Oblong,' lies along the eastern line of Putnam and Dutchess counties, extending from the north line of Cortland Manor to about the south bounds of Livingston Manor in Columbia co.

+**2.** (See quotation.) *slang.*

*a***1794** in C. Mathews *Writings* ii. 233 It was a common expression among the troops to call the bank bills *oblongs.* This was more especially the case at the gaming tables.

+**Obscutely,** *adv.* (See quotation.) — **1859** BARTLETT 299 *Obscutely,* obliquely. A factitious word used in New England.

***Observation.** +**1.** *Committee of observation,* one of the early local committees of the Revolution. +**2.** *Observation locomotive,* ? a railroad locomotive used for inspection of the track, bed, etc. +**3.** *Observation platform,* an open-air platform on an observation car. — **(1) 1775** *Md. Hist. Mag.* X. 302 A meeting of the Freemen of the middle district of Frederick County at the Court House on the 12th of September 1775, . . . the following Gentlemen were chosen a Committee of Observation. **(2) 1905** *Springfield W. Repub.* 7 July 12 Edward J. Pitchetson and a pair of horses he was driving were instantly killed . . . by the Boston & Albany observation locomotive Berkshire. **(3) 1906** LYNDE *Quickening* 29 At the rear of the string of Pullmans was a private car, with a deep observation platform. **1916** DU PUY *Uncle Sam* 46 They came tumbling among the chairs of the observation platform.

+**Observation car.** A railroad car designed to give passengers a better view of the scenery than is afforded by an ordinary coach; one of the cars of an observation train. — **1872** *Harper's Mag.* May 876/1 You look out of the open 'observation car' as you sweep down from a height of 7000 feet. **1882** *Uncle Rufus & Ma* 37 The party rapidly gathered on the rear platform of the observation car. **1901** MCCUTCHEON *Graustark* 35 You were reading over my shoulder in the observation car. **1904** *N.Y. Ev. Post* 30 June 1 In the observation cars spectators were talking and laughing and waiting.

Observation hive. A beehive with glass sides permitting direct observation of the bees. — **1883** *Century Mag.* Oct. 815/2 On the outside wall of the cabin is fastened an observation hive, with glass sides.

+**Observation train.** A train run along a watercourse to allow the passengers to watch a boat race. — **1893** POST *Harvard Stories* 294 The 'gang' had got seats in the same car on the observation-train and were waiting for it to start. **1904** *N.Y. Ev. Post* 30 June 1 The finish was so close that nobody on the observation train could decide which crew had won.

Observatory.

1. A building or place equipped with instruments for making observations of natural, esp. astronomical, phenomena. {1676–}

1784 ELLICOTT in Mathews *Life A. Ellicott* 17 Our Observatory is in good order, and Well Stored with Instruments. **1800** — *Journal* (1814) App. 127 The meridian was extended south from the observatory the distance of 99.12 perches. **1819** *N. Amer. Rev.* VIII. 205 It has long been considered as very desirable to have an Observatory at Cambridge, connected with the University. **1851** CIST *Cincinnati* 107 Such is the character of the position selected for the erection of the first great Astronomical Observatory ever erected by the *people.* **1872** HOLMES *Poet* ii. 68 He passes most of his time in a private observatory, it appears; a watcher of the stars. **1921** *Univ. of Chicago Off. Publ.: Yerkes Obs.* 3 The establishment of a large observatory for astrophysical research . . . was the conception of George E. Hale.

attrib. **1802** ELLICOTT *Journal* 179 Our observatory tent being worn out by the military, . . . I was now under the necessity of erecting a wooden building for that purpose.

+2. A building in a prison yard from which a watch can be kept on the prisoners.

1829 B. HALL *Travels in N.A.* II. 346 In the centre of the [prison] yard is erected what is called an observatory.

+3. A tower room, deck, or open balcony on top of a house where a wide view may be commanded.

1838 HAWTHORNE *Note-Books* I. 78 An old man . . . sits on a hill-top, or on the observatory of his house, and sees the sun's light. **1853** FOWLER *Home for All* 112 Cornice all around the house, with brackets as per elevation, with an observatory on top. **c1870** BAGBY *Old Va. Gentleman* 297 The tops of houses, church steeples, the 'observatories,' . . . were alive with human beings. **1893** 'CRADDOCK' in *Harper's Mag.* Dec. 85/2 A great flimsy white building, with its many pillars, its tiers of piazzas, its 'observatory,' its band-stand. **1906** LYNDE *Quickening* 26 There were houses, . . . hip-roofed, with a square balustered observatory on top.

attrib. **1857** VAUX *Villas* 182 The observatory room is intended to be both useful and ornamental.

+4. (See quotation.)

1870 MEDBERY *Men Wall St.* 314 This tendency toward sharp and unscrupulous bear tactics was largely due to the presence of new men, known popularly as the 'Observatory,' who had come from the West with large accumulations of capital.

***Obsidian.** Smoke-colored volcanic glass, +used by the Indians for arrowheads and spearheads. Also attrib. — **1837** IRVING *Bonneville* II. 45 Their weapons were bows and arrows; the latter tipped with obsidian, which abounds in the neighborhood. **1854** BARTLETT *Personal Narr.* II. 365 We found nothing but broken pottery, an obsidian arrow-head, and some small marine shells. **1873** COZZENS *Marvellous Country* 119 His only weapon was a spear, the head made of obsidian. **1909** STRATTON-PORTER *Girl of Limberlost* 89 'What does he pay [for arrows]?' 'Ten cents for any common perfect one, . . . a dollar for obsidian.'

+Obsquotulate, *v. intr.* =ABSQUATULATE 1. — **1870** *Northern Vindicator* (Estherville, Iowa) 12 March, Mr. O. C. Bates . . . obsquotlated [*sic*] on Mulroney's stage last Monday.

Obstructionist. One who makes a practice of obstructing the adoption of any measure, esp. in Congress. {1846–} — **1870** *Nation* 6 Jan. 6/1 Mr. Edmunds, of Vermont, is a professional obstructionist, and may . . . be depended upon to oppose any measure, good or bad, wise or foolish. **1886** ALTON *Among Law-Makers* 166 The 'filibusters' . . . are styled by their more dignified antagonists, 'obstructionists'. **1898** *Kansas City Star* 18 Dec. 2/5 Whitecotton . . . is looked upon as an obstructionist.

+Ocala platform. A platform drawn up by the Farmers' Alliance Congress in 1890 at Ocala, Florida. It provided for the abolition of national banks, free coinage of silver, a graduated income tax, etc. — **1892** *Congress. Rec.* 28 May 4802/1 The Ocala platform [was] repudiated by the regular rock-ribbed Democrats. **1897** *Ib.* 26 March 357/1, I see that I have the attention of my friend from Kansas [Mr. Simpson], the great apostle of the Ocala platform.

***Occamy.** Also **ocome, ockumy, -imy.** A metal imitating gold or silver. Also attrib. *Obs.* (Cf. ALCHEMY.) — **1639** *Md. Archives* IV. 77 It[em] 8 ocome spoones. **1648** *Conn. Rec.* I. 489 An Inventory of the Goods of Robert Day. . . . 6 ockumy spoons. **1696** SEWALL *Letter-Book* I. 167 Item; 30 Dozen of Ockimy Spoons.

***Occasion,** *v. local.* +*intr.* (See quot. 1859.) — **1845** *Knickerb.* XXVI. 416 Ne'er a village nor a city in the land they have not 'occasioned' at, nor a mile of road between Kennebec and California which they have not wandered over. **1859** BARTLETT 299 *To Occasion,* or *'Casion,* to go about asking for work; i.e. to ask if employers have any occasion for one's services. Maryland.

***Occidental,** *a.* +Belonging to the western United States. — **1846** *Knickerb.* XXVII. 471, 'I. L. of this vicinity,' writes an occidental correspondent, 'had carried the knife for a long time.'

+Occidental plane (tree). =BUTTONWOOD 1. — **1809** KENDALL *Travels* II. 28 Among the natural forest-trees, are the button-wood or occidental plane, the spruce-fir and the locust-tree. **1823** JAMES *Exped.* I. 21 The occidental plane tree is, perhaps, the grandest of the American forest trees.

+Occident ant. (See quot. 1884.) — **1882** H. C. McCOOK (*title*), The honey ants of the Garden of the Gods and the occident ants of the American plains. **1884** *Amer. Naturalist* XVIII. 334 The occident ant (*Pogonomyrmex occidentalis*) was in Dakota confined to the bottom lands along the Missouri river.

***Occupation.** The actual holding of land by a military force: **+a.** With special reference to territory acquired from Mexico.

1846 *Whig Almanac 1847* 17/2 The Army of Occupation remained at Corpus Christi for about six months, entirely unmolested and unmolesting. **1848** *Santa Fe Repub.* 24 Aug. 2/2 We date the prosperity of New Mexico from the occupation of the country by the U. States forces. **1883** RITCH *Illust. N. Mex.* 33 Since the American occupation, (1846) . . . , the net production in precious metals . . . [has reached] a total of $13,972,000. **1898** ATHERTON *Californians* 156 It was the first dance he had attended since the one given by Thomas Larkin to celebrate the Occupation of California by the United States.

+b. With special reference to Oregon. Also attrib.

1846 *Whig Almanac 1847* 7/1 The long-standing Joint Occupation of Oregon would terminate at the expiration of the stipulated twelve months' notice. **1846** *Niles' Nat. Reg.* 23 May 192/2 Oregon Occupation Bill.—The subject come [*sic*] up in the U.S. senate yesterday.

+Occupation tax. 1. A tax levied upon persons or firms engaged in certain occupations. **2.** A tax for the Indians levied upon settlers who took up land in Indian Territory. — **(1) 1869** *Texas Constitution* 37 Occupation tax. . . . The Legislature shall have power to levy an income tax, and to tax all persons pursuing any occupation, trade or profession. **1885** *Texas Rep.* LXIV. 276 It is a tax imposed on a named business which may be carried on by natural persons or by corporations . . . and such as is designated in the constitution an 'occupation tax.' **1888** BRYCE *Amer. Commonw.* II. II. xliii. 134*n.*, License taxes or occupation taxes may be imposed . . . [on] grocery keepers, liquor dealers, insurance, vendors of patents [etc.]. **1919** *Okla. Rep.* LXXXI. 135. **(2) 1900** *Congress. Rec.* 2 Feb. 1458/2 The Five Civilized Tribes, with their great trust fund, with their great income from occupation tax, and especially from their income by way of royalties.

+Occupying claimant. A settler who bases his claim to a piece of land upon the fact of occupation. Also attrib. — **1821** *Ann. 17th Congress* 1 Sess. I. 24 The Occupying Claimant Law [of Ky.] . . . the object of which was the settlement of conflicting land claims. **1859** BARTLETT 299 *Occupying claimant,* one who claims land by virtue of occupation of the same under the land systems of various States.

***Ocean.** *attrib.* Designating commercial and social activities and services connected with the ocean.

1852 *Mass. Acts & Resolves* 281 An essential reduction on present rates of ocean postage will remove a very serious restraint [etc.]. **1859** *36th Congress 1 Sess.* H.R. Rep. No. 648, 663, I submit to you a brief of all the laws of the United States relating to 'ocean mail service.' **1873** BEADLE *Undevel. West* 761 They only want the road to the head of Willamette Valley to serve as a 'feeder' to their ocean line. **1874** *Jrnl. of Soc. Science* July 116 The necessity of . . . assigning fixed limits to the routes of the steamships, was first considered as early as the year 1855. . . . I think it was then that the expressive designation of 'ocean lanes' was introduced. **1896** *N.Y. Dramatic News* 29 Aug. 12/2 An ocean pier is very handy to sink it [a fortune] from.

b. Designating various seagoing vessels.

See also OCEAN FERRY.

1890 Ocean greyhound [see GREYHOUND 2]. **1893** PAGE in *Harper's Mag.* Dec. 24/1 [Virginia's] coal produces the highest speed in the ocean racers. **1915** CAMPBELL *Proving Virginia* 330 Even if a whale could swallow one of them ocean liners he couldn't belch it up again.

Ocean cable. A telegraphic cable laid on the ocean floor. Also attrib. {oceanic cable, 1858} — **1860** HOLMES *Professor* i. 32 The following poem is my . . . only contribution to the great department of Ocean-Cable literature. **1879** *Scribner's Mo.* Sept. 653/2 The importance of this telegraph station has somewhat decreased since the ocean cable came into use. **1883** *Popular Science Mo.* Dec. 255 A prominent department of the electrical engineer's work is the localizing of faults in ocean-cables.

‖**Oceaner.** An ocean liner. — **1879** WHITMAN *Spec. Days* 136 Characteristic [of a] New York scene . . . [was] the proud, steady, noiseless cleaving of the grand oceaner down the bay.

+Ocean ferry. 1. A sea lane for transoceanic steamers. **2.** A transoceanic passenger boat. — **(1) 1882** in McCabe *N.Y. by Sunlight & Gaslight* 361 In addition to these great ships that ply over the ocean ferry to Europe, there are lines to South and Central America. **(2) 1885** *Lippincott's Mag.* Nov. 491/2 Fussy custom-house officers [get in the way of] . . . the newly-landed passengers from the ocean-ferries. **1892** *Congress. Rec.* App. 27 April 273/1 The ocean ferries ply unceasingly every day in the week between this country and Europe.

Oceanic, *a.* {1656–} In the specific names of fishes. — **1842** *Nat. Hist. N.Y., Zoology* IV. 178 The Oceanic Catfish. *Galeichthys marinus.* . . . Its flesh has been represented to me . . . as having an exquisite flavor. *Ib.* 378 The Sea Devil, or Oceanic Vampire, . . . is known to seize the cables of small vessels at anchor. **1883** *Nat. Museum Bul.* No. 27, 499 *Orcynus pelamys.* . . . Oceanic Bonito.

Ocean telegraph. A telegraph operated over an ocean cable. Also attrib. — **1857** *Lawrence* (Kansas) *Republican* 11 June 1 He yet thinks enough has been done to show that the Ocean Telegraph project is feasible. **1859** J. B. JONES *Southern Scenes* 487 The agents had found access to him with dispatches from his Government, transmitted by the Ocean Telegraph. **1871** *Harper's Mag.* XLIII. 15/1 The steamer starts on her voyage . . . and, by means of the ocean telegraph, that fact is instantly known on this side of the Atlantic.

Ocelot. A large American spotted cat (*Felix pardalis*) of the Southwest. {1774} Cf. LEOPARD CAT. — **1836** EDWARD *Hist. Texas* 111 He told them . . . that they should be scattered by the white men, with the rapidity of the ocelot. **1867** *Amer. Naturalist* I. 286 Two other species of true long-tailed cats may possibly exist, particularly in the southeastern portions [of Ariz.]. These are the Ocelot . . . and the Jaguar. **1917** *Mammals of Amer.* 152 If one talks with hunters or ranchmen about Ocelots, the probability is that they will refer to them as Leopard Cats or Spotted Cats.

***Ocher, Ochre.** Also †**Oaker.** Any of various native ferruginous clays, often used as pigment. Frequently with adj. designating color. — **1709** LAWSON *Carolina* 82 Good Bricks and Tiles are made, and several sorts of useful Earths, as Bole, Fullers-Earth, Oaker, and Tobacco-pipe-Clay, in great plenty. **1782** CRÈVECŒUR *Letters* 162 The western point of this island [Nantucket], abounds with a variety of ochres of different colours. **1829** WEEMS *B. Franklin* 184 Painted in red ochre, and decked in all the savage pomp of wild skins and feathers. **1881** *Art Interchange* (N.Y.) 27 Oct. 93/1 In painting a flesh tint with water colors, use yellow ochre, vermilion and rose madder for the general tone.

‖**Ocochilla.** =next. — **1864** *Harper's Mag.* Nov. 697/2 Passing through some dense thickets of mesquit and ocochilla, the struggling family found themselves at the foot of a rocky bluff.

+**Ocotillo.** [Sp. dim. of *ocote*.] A candlewood of the Southwest, *Fouquieria splendens*. Also attrib. (Cf. JACOB'S STAFF 2.) — **1883** *Harper's Mag.* March 502/2 The ocotilla is simply a wattle of sticks, fifteen and twenty together, waiting to be cut down and turned into palings. **1893** *Nation* 7 Sept. 169/3 Walking-sticks [are] made of the porous ocotillo cactus. **1917** BAILEY *Cycl. Hort.* III. 1271/1 Ocotillo . . . is a conspicuous object in the deserts from Texas westward, standing on the open exposed places and slopes, the rod-like stiff canes looking like lifeless sticks in dry weather and in its season crowned with masses of showy bloom.

+**October state.** A state that has its general state election in October instead of November. — **1885** *Century Mag.* Jan. 461 Skillful correspondents were sent out by the 'great dailies' to write up the preliminary struggles in 'the October States.' **1895** MYERS *Bosses & Boodle* 77 Until 1887, Ohio was an 'October' state. Under the first and second Constitutions, the election for state officers took place in October, while the Federal elections were held in November.

Octoon. [*Octo* and *oon* on the analogy of *quadroon*.] One eighth part. — **1840** DANA *Two Years* xiii. 97 The least drop of Spanish blood, if it be only of quatroon or octoon, is sufficient to raise them from the rank of slaves.

Octopus. {1758-} *fig.* +A powerful commercial organization with extended ramifications and influence; a trust. — **1878** in Tarbell *Hist. Standard Oil Co.* I. 182 One refiner after another . . . fell shivering with dislike into the embrace of this commercial octopus. **1893** *Columbus Dispatch* 15 May, They could not succeed against the suburban enterprise were it not aided and assisted by the Consolidated octopus. **1900** *Congress. Rec.* 23 Jan. 1097/1 What would happen . . . to New Jersey, which is now the breeding ground of trusts and octopuses? **1901** NORRIS (*title*), The Octopus.

Octoroon. Also **octroon.** [*Octo* and *roon* on the analogy of *quadroon*. Cf. OCTOON.] A person of one-eighth Negro blood. {1891} Also attrib.

1861 in F. Moore *Rebellion Rec.* I. III. 133 That octoroon—who made you jealous, love— . . . is so pale a thing. **1887** *Harper's Mag.* Jan. 200/2 Her father was Spanish, her mother was an octoroon. **1891** HOWELLS *Imperative Duty* vi, She was an octoroon. **1895** *N.Y. Dramatic News* 20 July 5/3 His Octoroon company . . . will comprise in its entirety most of the principal singers of the colored race. **1922** G. D. JOHNSON *Bronze* 36 The Octoroon. One drop of midnight in the dawn of life's pulsating stream Marks her an alien.

Octroi. {1614-} +In Utah, a local tax on imported merchandise. Now hist. — **1862** *N. Amer. Rev.* July 214 The *octroi* and the water tax, which are local and municipal, . . . meet the special expenses of the city governments [in Utah]. Every hundred pounds of merchandise which comes from the East pay $20, and every hundred pounds from the West, $25.

Odd Fellow. A member of a secret order or lodge organized for mutual aid and for social purposes. {1811-}

The American lodge was at first affiliated with the British lodge, but in 1842 it was separated.

1819 *Baltimore American* 13 Feb., A few members of the Society of Odd Fellows will be glad to meet their brethren for consultation upon the subject of forming a lodge. **1835** MARTIN *Descr. Va.* 368 There are 2 academies, . . . 2 common schools, . . . a lodge of masons, and 1 of odd fellows. **1857** DAVIS *El Gringo* 166 The Odd Fellows have erected a new hall for their order, one square from the Plaza [in Santa Fe]. **1889** BRAYLEY *Boston Fire Dept.* 439 He is a member of the Boston Veterans, Grand Army of the Republic, and the Odd Fellows. **1907** C. E. JOHNSON *Poet Wildey* 11 It is the Independent Order of Odd Fellows, or if you like the term better, American Odd Fellowship.

b. Used in the possessive to designate buildings, social functions, etc.

1851 CIST *Cincinnati* 313 E. C. Middleton, dealer in books, etc., . . . Odd Fellows Building. **1856** DERBY *Phoenixiana* 272, I see by your card . . . that you live on Seventh Street, opposite the Odd Fellows' Hall. **1860** E. COWELL *Diary* 72 We got out, and went to see the Oddfellows graveyard, and the Firemen's Do. **1872** MCCLELLAN *Golden State* 399 The Odd Fellows' library of San Francisco is perhaps the best supplied of any in the United States. **1883** *Century Mag.* Aug. 574/2 She sometimes went to the social gatherings affected by her father's friends, Odd Fellows' and Druids' balls.

***Odds.**

1. *By* (*all*) *odds*, +in every way; by far.

1799 WASHINGTON *Writings* XIV. 234 [This] would be the cheapest and by odds the most convenient mode. **1816** U. BROWN *Journal* I. 350 Too sick by odds to travel any farther, [he] puts up at John Smiths gets some more soop. **1866** HOWELLS *Venetian Life* 50 By all odds, the loungers at Florian's were the most interesting. **1883** BAGBY *Old Va. Gentleman* 152 But by odds the best of our troops were the Texans.

+**2.** *To ask* (or *beg*) *no odds*, to seek no favor; to ask for no advantage.

1806 *Baltimore Ev. Post* 5 March 2/2 (Th.), No odds he begs Of any beast that walks upon four legs. **1836** *Quarter Race Ky.* (1846) 23, I ask no man any odds further than civility. **1857** H. C. KIMBALL in *Jrnl. Discourses* V. 32/2 (Th.), I ask no odds of them, no more than I do of the dirt I walk on. **1894** *Congress. Rec.* 29 May 5447/1 Give us equitable laws and fair play, and South Dakota asks no odds of any State of the Union.

Odist. A writer of an ode {1797-}, +esp. for a graduation exercise. — **1876** TRIPP *Student-Life* 470 Lyman is on the Class-Day committee, and Lewis is odist.

Odometer. {1824-} An instrument attached to a wheel or bearing that records the revolutions of the wheel: **a.** Used to measure the distance traversed by a wheeled vehicle. **b.** Used on a light wheel trundled along by hand to measure distances in a survey. — **1791** JEFFERSON in *Harper's Mag.* LXX. 536/1 Pd. Leslie for an odometer 10 D[ollars]. **1853** MARCY *Expl. Red River* p. iii, The positions thus deduced have been corrected by . . . observations of courses and distances with the compass and odometer. **1858** *35th Congress 1 Sess.* H. R. Ex. Doc. No. 124, 1 This itinerary gives distances as they exist, . . . every turn of our wheels recorded by the odometer attached. **1885** CUSTER *Boots & Saddles* 127 Some officer wished to measure the distance of a day's march, and having no odometer elected his wife to that office.

Oekology. Also **oikology.** {1873-} +The science of home economy; domestic science. *Obs.* — **1892** *Columbus Dispatch* 8 Dec., The latest Boston Science is oekology. . . . It is from the Greek oikos, meaning a house, and the familiar termination, logy, from logos. **1896** *Advance* 23 Jan. 128/3 The chair of paidology and perhaps oikology will soon be founded in our universities. **1898** *Pop. Science Mo.* LII. 534 *Oikology* . . . includes also family life or homekeeping.

Oenothera. A genus of annual or biennial herbs, chiefly American, having mostly nocturnal flowers. {1601-} — **1817** BRADBURY *Travels* 82 I observed a number of large white flowers . . . belonging to a species of oenothera. **1846** EMORY *Military Reconn.* 14 We find in the bottoms . . . several varieties of solidego, oenothera, and helianthus. **1863** *Life in South* II. 304 Splendid phloxes, oenotheras, mimosas . . . crowded upon the trees.

+**Of,** *v.* A way of writing *'ve*, unstressed form of the verb *have*. *colloq.* — **1844** *S. Lit. Messenger* X. 486/2, I never would of married in the world, ef I couldn't of got jist exactly suited. **1854** M. J. HOLMES *Tempest & Sunshine* 115, I don't see why in the old Harry he couldn't of lived. **1897** BRODHEAD *Bound in Shallows* 155 If I'd of got at it sooner maybe matters 'd be different. **1919** HOUGH *Sagebrusher* 214 Like enough we both ought to of been shot for it.

***Of,** *prep.* +**1.** In expressing the time: Before. {=to} **2.** *Of the same date*, dating from the same day. '*Sc.* and *U.S.*' (*O.E.D.*). {1866 in Scotland} — **(1) 1857** M. J. HOLMES *Meadow-Brook* v, Five minutes of nine, and round the corner at the foot of the hill appeared a group of children. **1879** STOCKTON *Rudder Grange* 10 We ceased to call it a boat at about a quarter of eleven. **1887** *Harper's Mag.* June 99/2 'What time is it now?' . . . 'It's a quarter of one.' **1922** PARRISH *Case & Girl* 28 It was a few moments of seven, and she would undoubtedly be waiting for him. **(2) 1882** SCHOULER *Hist. U.S.* II. 284 All interdictions against Great Britain would cease of the same date.

***Off,** *a.*

In the following senses, *off* retains something of its character as an adverb and is used only in the predicate.

1. No longer binding, out of force, at an end. {1760-}

1720 *Amer. Wkly. Mercury* 8 Dec. 2/2 The Bargain made by the three Quakers for that Province [S.C.] is off, the Lords Justice having interposed. **1808** *Ann. 10th Congress* 1 Sess. 181 If our embargo was off we should have more trade than would be enjoyed by us, if all the world were at peace. **1874** EGGLESTON *Circuit Rider* 79 In case it should prove to be 'all off' between him and Patty. *a***1882** in McCabe *New York* 102 Vessels from domestic ports are permitted to go to the city . . . the quarantine regulations for them being declared 'off' during that interval.

+**2.** Opposed, out of agreement; wide of the mark.
1809 *Ann. 10th Congress* 2 Sess. Jan. 1185 Mr. W[illiams] hoped these [expenditures] were not intended to enforce the embargo. If they were, he was entirely off. **1887** *Presbyterian Banner* Oct., The leader . . . is not merely off on the subject of future probation, but also with regard to the Lord's day.

+**3.** Of a horse or athlete: Not up to his usual form. Also *off form*, ellipt. for *off in form*.
1846 *Spirit of Times* 18 April 91/1 He had endurance and speed enough to make a good race in any crowd, when 'all right,' but then, he [the horse] was liable to be oftener 'off' than otherwise. **1868** WOODRUFF *Trotting Horse* 300 It is assumed, not that the loser was 'off,' but that the winner is greatly superior. **1912** MATHEWSON *Pitching* 142 The Chicago pitchers were away off form in the series.

+**4.** Finished with one's work for the time being. (Cf. OFF WATCH.)
1882 McCABE *New York* 384 Then begins five hours' patrol . . . after which he is 'off.'

Off, *v.* {1642-} +*tr.* To take off (a garment). *colloq.*[2] or *slang.* — **1834** C. A. DAVIS *Lett. J. Downing* 32 As there was an eend of the dance, all the galls off shoes and stockins, and went hum. **1843** STEPHENS *High Life N.Y.* II. 187 The captin, he offs coat and boots and gin a dive at the wash bowl.

***Offal.** In specific senses: **1.** The bran and shorts of ground grain. **2.** (See quotation.) — **(1) 1850** *Rep. Comm. Patents 1849* 303 What I claim . . . is the process of re-grinding the offal of wheat. **1850** *Western Jrnl.* IV. 279 After the 'offal' is thus ground or severely scoured, it is then passed into the lower bolts, or dusters. **1872** T. D. PRICE *Diary* (MS.) 9 Jan., Bro. Josiah came for his grist, pays me $1.20 a bu. for it, and I have offal. **(2) 1912** A. E. TANNER *Tobacco* 107 This refuse tobacco consists of the midribs of the leaves, called 'stalks,' broken pieces, dust, cigarette waste or 'smalls,' and damaged tobacco—all classed under the general term of 'offals.'

Off color. (See COLOR 7.)

Off day. {1848-} A day on which one's performance is not up to the usual standard. (Cf. OFF *a.* 3.) — **1880** *Chicago Inter-Ocean* 28 May 8/3 Peters had an 'off' day.

***Offer,** *v.* +**1.** *intr.* To stand as a candidate for office. +**2.** *reflex.* To make an offer of marriage; to propose. — **(1) 1803** *Steele P.* I. 405 The Gentlemen who prevailed upon me 'to offer' as they call it, consisted principally of the moderate men of both parties. **1835** LONGSTREET *Ga. Scenes* 234 Then lowering his voice to a confidential but distinctly audible tone, 'what you offering for?' continued he. **(2) 1874** ALDRICH *P. Palfrey* xviii, The afternoon before he went away, . . . he offered himself to me. **1885** HOWELLS *S. Lapham* xvii, There's nothing the matter. Only, Mr. Corey offered himself to me last night. **1891** — *Imperative Duty* xi, I offered myself to her in Liverpool before she sailed.

+**Offering book.** A book in which a record is made of notes and other bills of credit offered as security for a loan. — **1811** *Steele P.* II. 658 In short this is intended to furnish as a day book all the results which do not and cannot appear on the face of the offering book. **1858** J. S. GIBBONS *Banks of New-York* 29 No objection is made [to discounting someone's note], and the President scores opposite to it, on the Offering Book, the letter A—which means, *accepted*.

‖**Off-hand ox.** The off ox. — **1845** F. DOUGLASS *Narrative* 58 He told me which was the in-hand ox, and which the off-hand one.

* **Office,** *n.*

***1.** A position of trust, duty, or authority, esp. in the service of the government, conferred upon an individual either by election or appointment.
1632 *Plymouth Laws* 30 If now or hereafter any were elected to the office of governor and would not stand to the election [etc.]. **1666** *Md. Archives* II. 132 No . . . Sheriff or Clarke of those Courts wherein they bear office shall plead as Attorney for or in behalf of any person. **1776** *Decl. Independence*, He has erected a multitude of new offices, and sent hither swarms of officers to harass our people, and eat out their substance. **1796** *Tenn. Constitution* Art. VI. Sec. i, There shall be appointed in each county, by the county court, . . . a sufficient number of constables, who shall hold their offices for two years. **1834** C. A. DAVIS *Lett. J. Downing* 154 Folks about us here don't feel it [lack of money], for they have all got fat offices. **1868** *Mich. Agric. Rep.* VII. 465 He shall leave his post-office address with the county clerk, and shall enter upon the duties of his office. **1900** GOODLANDER *Fort Scott* 65 Some of the county and city officers of the present day . . . appear to farm the offices they hold for all they are worth.

b. In non-specific uses in such phrases as *a candidate for office, to be in office, the attractions of office, the spoils of office, to run for office.*
1816 PICKERING 76 We sometimes see this word [declension] used in our news-papers, in speaking of a person's declining to be a candidate for office. **1830** ROYALL *Lett. from Ala.* 203 Every blue skin of them is still in office. **1837** *U.S. Mag.* I. 89 One remarkable trait . . . is the elevation of his ambition above the attractions of office. **1860** *N.Y. Herald* 8 Nov. 4/1 Now that Lincoln is elected, an irrepressible conflict will commence about the distribution of the spoils of office. **1876** FISHER *Californians* 116 The man who 'runs for office' will find it overshadowing, not only himself, but his children. **1912** NICHOLSON *Hoosier Chron.* 54, I'd go into their counties and spend every cent I've got fighting 'em if they ever ran for office again.

***2.** A room or set of rooms where private or public business is transacted; a place where the clerical work of a concern is done; +the reception desk of a hotel; +the business quarters of professional men, as dentists, lawyers, etc. (Cf. HOTEL OFFICE.)
1711 *Boston News-Letter* 26 Nov. 2/2 Several Files of Papers belonging to the Court of Admiralty . . . were taken. . . . If any one will discover where the same are to the said Edward Weaver, at his Office, . . . they shall be satisfyed. **1816** U. BROWN *Journal* II. 233, I then offer'd to shew him on the spot or in his office; he did not incline to accept of my offer. **1849** E. DAVIS *Amer. Scenes* 16 The waiter stared, and said he had none to take us to, except I would first go to the 'office' [the clerk's desk in a hotel]. **1864** NICHOLS *Amer. Life* I. 344 While in the office, as the American lawyer's chambers are called, a younger brother and partner told me they had a third brother. **1874** ALDRICH *P. Palfrey* xiii, It was after bank hours, and the office was deserted. **1882** McCABE *New York* 145 The upper floors are devoted mainly to offices. **1922** AITKEN *Automatic Telephone System* I. 3 The switch room, or office, was very generally known . . . as the exchange.

+**b.** The bar of a saloon. *facetious.*
1842 *Knickerb.* XX. 571 He ushered me into the bar-room—I beg pardon, into the office. **1855** HOLBROOK *Among Mail Bags* 62 We went up to what was then the bar, but in these temperance times would be called the 'office.'

+**c.** *spec.* An executive's office, as in a college or school. Also transf.
1897 FLANDRAU *Harvard Episodes* 278 He would be upheld . . . if he gave Prescott an E, and brought the heavy hand of the Office down on him. **1902** G. M. MARTIN *Emmy Lou* 102 One day Miss Jenny was sent for. When one was sent for, one went to the office.

3. *attrib.* and *comb.* **a.** Designating various things used in connection with an office.
1715 *Boston News-Letter* 11 April 2/2 All Masters . . . to make a fair Alphabetical List of the Names and Number of Letters in his Bagg, which List hung up at the Office Door, would soon resolve any Person if they had any Letters by such a Ship. **1869** TOURGEE *Toinette* (1881) 404 The old surgeon laid down his pen, . . . and turned his office-chair round toward his visitor. **1871** *Lippincott's Mag.* Nov. 475/2 Charlotte came and lighted the office-lamp, and then Squire Grimmer came in to see the doctor. **1890** LANGFORD *Vigilante Days* (1912) 419 While seated by the office stove, in conversation with some old friends, the clerk came. **1913** LA FOLLETTE *Autobiog.* 143 It was written on office-stationery of ex-treasurer Harshaw.

b. Designating persons or actions associated with the holding of public office, the making of appointments thereto, etc.
See also OFFICE BEGGAR, HOLDER, HOLDING, etc.
1814 *Ann. 13th Congress* 2 Sess. 1576 Unless the honesty and intelligence of the nation shall confederate into one great American party, disdaining petty office-keeping and office-hunting views [etc.]. **1817** IRVING in P. M. Irving *Life W. Irving* I. 392, I should not like to have my name hackneyed about among the office-seekers and office-givers at Washington. **1880** CABLE *Grandissimes* 138 One act of summary vengeance upon a few insurgent office-coveters has branded him . . . as Cruel O'Reilly. **1884** *Century Mag.* April 863/2 Office-getting is coming more and more into the control of rings. **1892** *Nation* LIV. 307/1 He voluntarily . . . put himself into stalemate on the chess-board of Federal politics, so far as Federal office-bearing was concerned.

c. Designating persons who work or loiter in an office.
1874 ALDRICH *P. Palfrey* xvii, The young minister was in the habit of absenting himself for several days together without notifying the office-clerk. **1879** B. F. TAYLOR *Summer-Savory* 90 [The bustler] degrades me in the sight of the bell-boys, the porters, the chambermaids, and the office loungers. **1902** LORIMER *Lett. Merchant* 215 Besides keeping in touch with your office men, you want to feel your salesmen all the time. **1911** *Okla. Session Laws* 3 Legisl. 27 The board of county commissioners may allow such jail guards as are necessary and one office deputy.

d. In sense 2 with *patient.*
1897 STUART *Simpkinsville* 94 Even the doctors . . . are wont to receive their 'office patients' in this comfortable fashion.

***Office,** *v.* ‖*intr.* To keep one's office or offices in a certain place. — **1891** *Nation* LIV. 303/2 An attorney officing in the same building.

+**Office beggar.** A person who asks to be appointed to a political office. — **1857** *Lawrence* (Kansas) *Republican* 2 July 2 How does it come that he can select no person for the office in Kansas but hungry office-beggars? **1882** *Nation* 9 Nov. 401/1 The abominable system which has converted our Government . . . into a mere machine for the use and the abuse of a horde of loaferish and hungry office-beggars.

Office boy. A boy who does odd jobs in an office.
1846 *Knickerb.* XXVII. 457 No songs for you, my sad street-sweeper! . . . nor for you, melancholy office-boy! **1870** *Scribner's Mo.* I. 47 He was installed as office-boy. **1897** *Outing* XXX. 585/1 The office-boy opened the door and handed me a telegram. **1912** HASKIN *Amer. Govt.* 71

Large business houses felt the loss from the petty grafting of stamps by office boys.

+**Office building.** A building used for an office; a building in which the rooms are rented out as offices. — **1840** *Niles' Nat. Reg.* 23 May 182/1 The Free Trader office building has been crushed in and much shattered. **1868** *Mich. Agric. Rep.* VII. 422 The property of the Society . . . consists of . . . a grand stand, and a good office-building for the Secretary and Treasurer. **1883** *Century Mag.* Sept. 786/2 Brief-hungry young lawyers and shabby speculators in the skyward stories of tall office buildings. **1900** STOCKTON *Afield & Afloat* 173 The boy had . . . found this dipsy lead . . . in a gutter in Decatur Street, just back of the office buildings.

+**Office force.** A group of workers in an office. — **1900** SAVAGE *Midnight Passenger* 7 Certain gray-bearded bookkeepers, a couple of brisk stenographers [etc.] . . . were the office force besides the travelling manager. **1900** *Congress. Rec.* 17 Feb. 1903/2 A gentleman . . . has had an insufficient office force and has by reason of that fact been compelled to do more.

+**Office girl.** A girl who works in an office. — **1863** A. D. WHITNEY *F. Gartney* xi, Faith looked up, and remembered the poor office-girl of three years since. **1912** NICHOLSON *Hoosier Chron.* 560 The telephone provides a welcome companionship for the office girl.

+**Office-holder.** One who holds public office, esp. through political patronage.

1818 FEARON *Sketches* 143 Every federalist has an opportunity . . . of resisting those dangerous abuses in government, introduced by office holders. **1832** DUNLAP *Hist. Amer. Theatre* 59 The ignorant are the same at all times, and the office-holder ever prone to the assumption of airs of superiority. **1860** CLAIBORNE *Sam. Dale* 206 If we could every where turn out our lazy office-holders, and substitute their pretty wives and daughters, probably business would go on better. **1882** *Nation* 31 Aug. 168/1 Federal Officeholders from Virginia are also receiving a circular, calling on them for a contribution of five per cent. **1909** G. F. PARKER *G. Cleveland* 54 He took a strong position in favor of reform in the Civil Service, and against assessments upon office-holders.

+**Office-holding,** *a.* Designating a person or persons in public office. — **1835** CROCKETT *Tour* 106 The office-holding gentry [at Washington] . . . will meet with their match in an indignant people. **1857** BENTON *Exam. Dred Scott Case* 148 The Convention at Cincinnati was gorged with office-holding retainers of the administration for that purpose. **1880** TOURGEE *Bricks* 469 He did not come of an office-holding family.

Office hour. The time during which a person stays in his office; the hours during which an office is kept open. Usu. pl. {1852} — **1802** *Steele P.* I. 326 He receives in addition thereto, 300 Dollars for services termed extra, but wholly performed during the usual Office hour. **1833** CATLIN *Indians* I. 141 Amongst a people who have no office hours to attend to . . . it would be strange if they did not practice many games and amusements. **1873** PHELPS *Trotty's Wedding* iv, The Doctor was called out of 'office hours.' **1885** CRAWFORD *Amer. Politician* 101 We Americans . . . are content to surround ourselves with the paraphernalia of pleasure when office hours are over. **1904** *Southwestern Reporter* LXXXIII. 855/2 Citation may be served on the president of a corporation . . . by leaving a copy of the same at the principle office of the company during office hours.

+**Office-hunter.** =OFFICE-SEEKER. — **1806** *Balance* V. 83/1 Every Burrite in this state is a disappointed office hunter. **1832** HONE *Diary* I. 48 The company consisted, as usual, of all the varieties of rank and station—foreign ministers and shopkeepers, . . . senators and office-hunters. **1846** MACKENZIE *Van Buren* 213 A Tammany Office-Hunter in the dumps.

+**Office-hunting.** =OFFICE-SEEKING *n.* Also attrib. — **1814** [see OFFICE *n.* 3 b.]. **1824** *Niles' Reg.* 20 March 37 *Office-hunting*. The decease of Col. Freeman, late fourth auditor of the treasury, the salary of which is $3,000 a year, has caused a great stir at Washington. **1830** *Congress. Deb.* Feb. 159/1 The downward tendency of our countrymen to a spirit of universal office hunting, servility, and corruption . . . has been remarked with patriotic regret. **1845** *Knickerb.* XXV. 276, I heard a good joke to-day touching 'Office-Hunting.'

***Officer.**

***1.** One who holds a public or civil office.

1620 *Plymouth Laws* 19 [We] do enact, constitute and frame such just and equal laws, . . . constitutions and officers, from time to time, as shall be thought most meet. **1654** JOHNSON *Wonder-w. Prov.* 14 To elect and set up all sorts of Officers, as well Superior as Inferior. **1772** *R.I. Col. Rec.* VII. 65, I then instanced what had been the fate of one made by the officers of the port a little before. **1796** *Boston Directory* 224 Bancroft, James, custom house officer, Nassau street. **1802** HAMILTON *Works* VII. 233 The first officer of the government . . . speaking in his official capacity. **1879** *Mich. Gen. Statutes* I. (1882) 235 The governor may remove all county officers . . . chosen by the electors of any city or village, when he shall be satisfied . . . that such officer is incompetent to execute properly the duties of his office. **1882** *Nation* 3 Aug. 81/1 Congress in a very important statute has treated the word 'officer' as embracing both Senators and Representatives. **1920** *3d Nat. Country Life Conf. Proc.* 209 Rural health officers should be continued.

***b.** A sheriff or sheriff's deputy; a constable; a member of a city police force.

1647 *R.I. Col. Rec.* I. 169 [If a] constable, or other officer that hath arrested a man, . . . lets him goe at libertie, . . . the blame shall wholly lie upon the officer. **1851** NORTHALL *Curtain* 133 Officer Bowyer, of the Chief's Bureau, . . . was standing beside the veteran manager. **1885** CABLE *Dr. Sevier* 208 The arresting officer mounts to the witness-stand. **1917** COMSTOCK *Man* 7 It will be a mighty reasonable trick fur this here officer of the law to be somewhere else till Burke settles with his friends an' foes.

***2.** A person who holds an office in a private organization, as a church, school, or corporation.

In certain New England colonies, because of the close association of church and state, some of the early officers of the church exercised public and civil functions.

1648 *Platform Church-Discipline* (1772) 29 Officers for the church are justly accounted no small parts, they being to continue to the end of the world. **1654** JOHNSON *Wonder-w. Prov.* 105 The Churches of Christ in New England, and their Officers have hitherto been . . . far from imbracing the erronious Doctrines of these times. **1854** *Harper's Mag.* IX. 273/1 There are no dryer wits or 'sly humorists' than many presidents and subordinate officers of our American colleges. **1872** *Vt. Bd. Agric. Rep.* 630 The officers and stockholders . . . began to sue and enjoin one another in a vein that proved a rich deposit for the lawyers. **1897** FLANDRAU *Harvard Episodes* 255 Now you're a great, haughty Ph. D. person, an 'Officer of Instruction and Government,' announced in the prospectus to teach in two courses. **1901** *N. Amer. Rev.* Feb. 261 The excessive loaning of a bank's funds to its officers and directors.

***3.** *Milit.* A person holding a position of authority or command in an army, navy, or marine corps.

Cf. COMMISSIONED and NONCOMMISSIONED OFFICER.

1705 *Boston News-Letter* 25 June 2/1 That a Sum may be provided sufficient to pay One Hundred Fuzileers, and Fifty Out scouts, with their proper Officers, to be sent to Albany. **1756** *Lett. to Washington* I. 313 Wishing You, Officers and Soldiers of your Regiment good Health. **1816** *Ann. 14th Congress* 2 Sess. 271 Officers of experience shall be detailed by the Executives . . . , who shall . . . organize the militia. **1862** in F. Moore *Rebellion Rec.* V. II. 187 We are returning with eighty prisoners, including a number of prominent officers. **1894** C. H. HOYT *Texas Steer* (1925) III. 31 A Captain is all very well on the frontier, but he doesn't cut much of a figure among the officers in Washington. **1912** NICHOLSON *Hoosier Chron.* 48 She was introduced first to Admiral Martin, a retired officer of the Navy.

+**Office relation.** The relation of a preacher or minister to a congregation or of a tutor or instructor to a college. *Obs.* — **1670** MATHER *Life R. Mather* 74 For some years after his accepting Office-Relation in Dorchester, he was in much Spiritual distress by reason of uncertainties concerning his own Eternal estate. **1686** SEWALL *Diary* II. 21 Since his being in Office-Relation . . . he is . . . charged with speaking such words as are scandalous breaches of the Third Commandment. **1742** in Peirce *Hist. Harvard* App. 86 [The] Overseers of Harvard College did . . . vote the removal of Mr. Nathan Prince (one of the Fellows and Tutors of said College) from all office-relation thereto.

+**Officer tree.** A saddletree designed for a cavalry officer. — **1894** *Harper's Mag.* Feb. 350/1, I carefully adjusted my Whitman's officer-tree over a wealth of saddle blanketing.

+**Office-seeker.** One who is striving to get a political appointment to public office.

1813 *Ann. 12th Congress* 2 Sess. 582 It would augment the office-seekers, who, with the friends of the Administration, were continually haunting the Executive. **1841** in MacLeod *F. Wood* 71 Was it made the issue by that illustrious convention of office-seekers who nominated the successful candidate at Harrisburg? **1853** *Harper's Mag.* VI. 420/2 Washington, the papers tell us, is even now filling up with the firstlings of that tribe of office-seekers, who will presently overrun the capital. **1871** *Harper's Mag.* XLIII. 18/1 The popular idea of the business of a Collector of the port of New York is that he is created to distribute political rewards to needy office-seekers. **1910** J. HART *Vigilante Girl* 125 She belongs to the ultra Southern circle. . . . Their men are all office-seekers and office-holders.

+**Office-seeking,** *n.* and *a.* **1.** *n.* The action of seeking appointment to a public office. **2.** *adj.* Of persons: Who seek public office. {1884-} — **(1) 1860** GREELEY *Overland Journey* 68 If he will work right ahead, . . . keeping clear of speculation and office-seeking, he can hardly fail to do well. **1885** CRAWFORD *Amer. Politician* 65 We are sick with the foul disease of office seeking. **(2) 1857** ALGER *Genius & Posture of Amer.* 4 An indiscriminate glorification of the country, office-holding partisans, office-seeking demagogues, slavery, and all. **1877** *Harper's Mag.* Dec. 54/2 Among [the editor's callers are] . . . office-seeking politicians who want recommendations.

***Official,** *a.*

1. In the capacity of a public servant as distinct from a private person. {1607-}

1790 *Ann. 1st Congress* II. 2116 No mode of inquiry into his official conduct has hitherto been put in operation. **1797** in *Ann. 5th Congress* App. 3337 Cards of hospitality were sent to us and our secretaries, in a style suitable to our official character. **1868** *Trial of Andrew Johnson* I. 145 The higher officers are not liable to prosecution in the ordinary courts for *official* misdemeanors. **1911** *Southwestern Reporter* CXXXV. 709/2 [When] that officer willfully misdates his file mark, he commits an act which is a fraud upon the other party and constitutes gross official misconduct.

2. Authorized or supported by a government; having the sanction of a person in office. {1854–}

1791 *Ann. 1st Congress* II. App. 2121 An official paper from the bureau of the balance of commerce of France. **1795** *Ann. 3rd Congress* 1 Sess. App. 1300 The Secretary of State [reports] . . . that he has had an official communication of a Decree rendered by the National Assembly of France. **1805** *Ann. 8th Congress* 2 Sess. 1038 An examination of the official documents upon our tables will evince [that] these claims have been recognized. **1872** *Newton Kansan* 21 Nov. 2/1 Official returns from all counties in Virginia, but one gives Grant 1,975 majority.

+3. *Official family*, the president's cabinet.

1903 W. E. CURTIS *True A. Lincoln* 193 It was perfectly natural for the President to select a member of his official family from a State of such importance.

Officiary. {1611–} +A body of officials. — **1888** *Voice* 5 April, It would be next to impossible . . . to get a city officiary in sympathy with the law. **1889** *Christian Union* 10 Jan., The virtual contract between officiary and pew-holder.

+**Offish,** *a.* Inclined to be aloof; distant. {1874–} — **1831** S. SMITH *Life J. Downing* 146, I find some [folks] . . . ready to shoulder their guns and march to-morrow if I say the word, and others are a little offish. **1854** — *Down East* 243 The deacon was a good deal offish. **1873** 'MARK TWAIN' & WARNER *Gilded Age* xlii. 377 Do not be offish and unsociable. **1907** *St. Nicholas* Aug. 905/2 It was so hard for loyal, fun-loving Rob to be 'offish' with one who was so kind to those she loved.

+**Offishly,** *adv.* In an offish manner. — **1861** *N.Y. Tribune* 17 June 6/6 A majority of the people in our neighborhood regard us very offishly.

+**Off-islander.** *local.* A visitor to the island of Nantucket; one who is not a native. — **1883** J. G. AUSTIN (*title*), Nantucket Scrapes: being the experiences of an off-islander, in season and out of season, among a passing people. **1916** *Dialect Notes* IV. 335 He was a great soldier and a great statesman, but he was an off-islander. **1921** F. M. ANDERSON (*title*), An Off-Islander; a story of Wesquo by the sea.

Off lead. =next. — **1897** *Outing* XXX. 254/1 Take the off-lead and off-wheeler's reins in right hand.

Off leader. The right hand horse of the forward pair of a team. — **1823** COOPER *Pioneers* iv, I knew just the spot where to touch the off-leader. **1877** ALDRICH *Queen of Sheba* 270 Here the driver leaned forward, skilfully touching the ear of the off-leader with the tip of his lash. **1897** *Outing* XXX. 254/1 Take up about six or seven inches of your off-leader's rein. **1910** J. HART *Vigilante Girl* 140 An iron 'jockey-stick' ran from the near leader's hames to the off leader's bit.

+**Off market.** (See quot. 1870.) — **1870** MEDBERY *Men Wall St.* 137 An 'off' market, is where prices have fallen either in a week, a day, or even an afternoon. **1885** *Harper's Mag.* Nov. 842/1 He rejoices in an 'off' market when prices fall. **1900** NELSON *A B C Wall St.* 154.

+**Off ox. a.** In a yoke of oxen, the right-hand beast. **b.** *fig.* A clumsy or unmanageable person.

1807 *Balance* 25 Aug. 267 (Th.), We behold a clumsy awkward off ox trying the tricks of a kitten. **1819** *Amer. Farmer* I. 315 Take out the off ox's bow. **1848** LOWELL *Biglow P.* 1 Ser. 90 Ez to the answerin' o' questions, I'm an off ox at bein' druv. **1899** *Mo. So. Dakotan* I. 176 [He] walked slowly 'round and lovingly rubbed the brockeled face of the off ox.

* **Offset,** *n.*

1. Something that counterbalances or cancels out something else {1792–}; +a cancellation.

1769 *Conn. Rec.* XIII. 207 The petitioner and petitionee have executions against each other now in the hands of Ezekiel Williams, . . . upon which the petitioner prays for an off-set. **1825** *Austin P.* (1924) II. 1214 He cannot pretend to have any off setts against this claim. **1841** *Week in Wall St.* 95 Their claims on each other were so nearly balanced, that they settled it by offset.

2. +**a.** A mountain terrace.

1864 WEBSTER 909/2 *Offset*, . . . a flat surface or terrace on a hill-side. **1873** BEADLE *Undevel. West* 284 We . . . now must make a wide detour to scale the cliff, or first offset, which frowns two thousand feet above us.

+**b.** *Mining.* A stepwise or terraced excavation for extracting ore.

1872 *Vt. Board Agric. Rep.* I. 627 It consists in taking out the ore in successive offsets or stopes.

+**c.** A fence built at right angles to a main fence.

1903 A. ADAMS *Log Cowboy* 54 The cattle . . . after following down the fence several miles had encountered an offset, and the angle had held the squad.

Offset, *v.* 'Chiefly *U.S.*' (*O.E.D.*).

1. *tr.* To balance (one thing) against another thing; to cancel.

1673 *Portsmouth Rec.* 179 The towne doe thereupon offsett the Said Sums and doe allow it him. **1792** N. CHIPMAN *Rep. & Diss.* I. (1871) 85 The demands of both plaintiff and defendant must be mutual, . . . or they will not be allowed to offset one against the other. **1877** *Scribner's Mo.* XV. 196/1 He had lost twenty-four Whig votes to offset the twenty-five Democratic votes which Lathers received. **1911** HARRISON *Queed* 333 You considered my companionship as fully offsetting the difference in the money we paid.

2. *intr.* To project as a terrace or offset.

1853 KANE *Grinnell Exped.* 371 Ridges, offsetting from the higher range, project in spurs laterally.

Offside, *n.* {1675–} +**1.** The wrong or difficult side. **2.** *Football.* Formerly, any position taken by a player in respect to the ball from which play was defined as illegal; +now, an action in which a player moves beyond the line of scrimmage before the ball is put into play. {c1868–, in English football} Also attrib. — **(1) 1870** 'F. FERN' *Ginger-Snaps* 299 The off-side of a question has such an unconquerable attraction for him. **1901** JEWETT *Tory Lover* xii, There was some o' them fools that likes to be on the offside that went an' upheld him. **(2) 1881** in P. H. Davis *Football* (1911) 469 The referee shall disqualify a player whom he has warned three times for intentional off-side playing. **1899** QUINN *Penna. Stories* 24 During the excitement, claims of 'off-side' were freely made and repudiated by the captains. **1925** *Kansas City Star* 22 Nov. 16/4 The ball was called back and Kansas was penalized five yards for off-side.

Offside, *adv. Football.* In a position where play is illegal {1867–}; +in the modern game, beyond the line of scrimmage before play has begun. — **1876** in P. H. Davis *Football* (1911) 463 Every player when off side is out of the game and shall not touch the ball. **1887** *Century Mag.* Oct. 889/2 No player has legal rights when he is between the ball and his opponents' goal; he is then 'off-side.' **1925** *Kansas City Star* 16/6 Kansas was penalized five yards for being off side.

+**Off watch.** On a boat, the watch that is off duty. — **1875** 'MARK TWAIN' *Old Times* 25 The 'off-watch' was just turning in, and I heard some brutal laughter from them.

Off wheel. The right-hand or front right-hand wheel of a vehicle. {1764–} Also attrib.

1762 in Brooks *Gleanings* 128 The off-wheel [of the chaise] has two Gripes thereon. **1828** NEAL *R. Dyer* 126 He had not gone above six rods . . . in his cart, before the off-wheel sunk into a hole. **1868** BRACKETT *Farm Talk* 94 A main travelled road should always be wide enough for loaded teams to meet and pass each other without any danger of running the off wheel into the gutter. **1897** *Outing* XXX. 254/2 Let go off-wheel rein, and the team will straighten out.

Off wheeler. The horse or mule of a team nearest the off wheel. — **1887** CUSTER *Tenting on Plains* 354 The old reliability of a mule-team is the off-wheeler. **1897** *Outing* XXX. 254/2 This . . . leaves the right hand free to use the whip on off-wheeler if he happens to be sluggish.

+**Off year. 1.** In politics, an election year in which a president is not elected. Also attrib. **2.** A year that is below standard in some respect. — **(1) 1882** *Congress. Rec.* 14 Dec. 277/2 It is true this was in the off year, and not the Presidential year. **1906** *N.Y. Ev. Post* 5 Nov. 4 It would be contrary to all precedent if, in this off-year election, the party in power did not suffer a considerable diminution in its strength. **(2) 1898** WILKINS *People of Our Neighborhood* (1901) 105 All the other orchards yielded . . . little fruit, for it was an unusually 'off year.'

+**O.F.M.** Abbreviation for 'Our first men.' *Obs.* — **1840** HALIBURTON *Clockmaker* 3 Ser. x, Jeremiah Sterling . . . is an O.F.M. as we call Our First Men among us. **1847** *Knickerb.* XXIX. 279 Here comes one of 'O.F.M.'

+**Ogeechee lime.** [Named after the *Ogeechee* River in Georgia.] A southern species of tupelo (*Nyssa ogeche*); the acid fruit of a tree of this species or, pl., the preserves made from it. Also attrib. — **1785** MARSHALL *Amer. Grove* 97 The Ogeche Lime Tree. . . . The fruit is nearly oval, of a deep red colour of the size of a Damascene Plumb. **1821** NUTTALL *Travels Arkansa* 71 In this swamp, I also observed the *Nyssa aquatica, N. pubescens* (Ogechee lime, the fruit being prepared as a conserve). **1868** GRAY *Field Botany* 169 *Nyssa capitata*, Ogeechee Lime; so called from the acid fruit. **1890** *Cent.* 3457/1 Its large acid fruit is made into a conserve called Ogeechee limes. **1897** SUDWORTH *Arborescent Flora* 311 Sour Tupelo. . . . Common Names. . . . Ogeechee Lime (S.C., Fla.). Gopher Plum (Fla.).

+**Ogling-glass.** A monocle. *humorous.* — **1843** *Knickerb.* XXII. 111 There he was promenading, . . . an ogling-glass lifted to his eye.

+**O-grab-me.** [*Embargo* spelled backwards.] A facetious name applied to the embargo acts of 1807 and following years. Also attrib. Now hist. — **1808** *Balance* 7 June 92 (Th.), As soon as O grab me! shall let go his end, I'll haste to relate the sweet tidings to you. **1810** LAMBERT *Travels* II. 506, I guess I shall soon be on the opposite side of the Line, in spite of their ograb-me laws. **1858** *S. Lit. Messenger* XXVII. 466/1 The war of 1812, and the famous 'O-Grab-Me,' as the wags of that day ana-grammatized the embargo measures of Mr. Madison.

+**Ohian.** =OHIOAN. *Obs.* — **1819** in Flint *Lett. from Amer.* 128 The Ohian is in many cases growing up to manhood. **1836** C. R. GILMAN *Life on Lakes* 54n., I use this word [Ohian] out of respect for Mr. Senator Ewing of Ohio, with whom, I believe, it originated. . . . He himself is the very man of all the world who should be called Buck Eye and not Ohian. **1839** C. A. MURRAY *Travels* I. 152 The Ohians are a quiet, industrious, peaceable people.

+**Ohio.** [Perhaps from Iroquois *Oheo* 'beautiful.'] The name of a river, of a region, and of a state. Used attrib.

1. Designating land or territory within the limits of the Ohio country.

Cf. OHIO COMPANY, FEVER, GRANT.

1788 *Mass. Spy* 3 April 2/4 Several families from the State of Massachusetts are already on their way to the Ohio purchase. *Ib.* 20 Nov. 3/4 Ohio Land. Two shares in the Ohio Company, containing 3000 acres, to be sold, or exchanged.—Apply to the printer.

2. Designating things produced in Ohio.

1835 HOFFMAN *Winter in West* I. 245 The frontiersman, knocking the ashes from his tomahawk-pipe, passed me a flask of Ohio whiskey. **1853** FOWLER *Home for All* 148 My material was composed of one part Blake's black Ohio paint, to six parts fine beach sand. **1864** *Ohio Agric. Rep.* XVIII. 25 A premium of $20 shall be offered for the best three samples of pure Ohio wine, made from the Catawba, Virginia Seedling or Delaware grape. **1865** *Chicago Tribune* 10 April 1 Pure Ohio Apple Cider . . . for sale. **1881** *Harper's Mag.* April 711/1 Lime stone . . . and gray Ohio sandstone are much used in construction.

3. In the specific names of fish.

See also OHIO SHAD.

1820 *Western Rev.* II. 173 Ohio Gold Herring. *Notemigonus auratus.* . . . Not uncommon in the Ohio, Kentucky, Miami, &c. *Ib.* 171 Ohio Goldshad. *Pomolobus chrysochloris.* . . . It seldom goes as far as Pittsburgh. **1889** *Cent.* 2809/3 *Ohio herring*, the skipjack, *Clupea chrysochloris.* **1856** *Porter's Spirit of Times* 40/3 The Pike-perch, *Lucioperva americana*, variously known as the Glass-Eye, the Ohio Pike, the Yellow Pike, and possibly also, as the Ohio salmon. **1820** *Western Rev.* II. 54 Ohio Red-eye, *Aplocentrus calliops. Ib.* 362 Ohio Toter, *Hypentelium macropterum.*

4. In the specific names of fruits and plants.

See also OHIO BUCKEYE.

1868 *Rep. Comm. Agric. 1867* 136 Ohio Beauty [a variety of cherry]. . . . Size, large; form, round, obtuse heart-shaped, sometimes nearly round. **1842** KIRKLAND *Forest Life* II. 142 A beautiful perennial here [in Mich.] called the Ohio bluebell, a far larger plant than the one we know by that name. **1862** *Rep. Comm. Patents 1861: Agric.* 166 The Ohio ever-bearing raspberry is not the only one . . . to produce an autumnal crop of fruit: the same tendency is often observed in . . . [the] Black-cap. **1819** *Western Rev.* I. 93 The trees and plants peculiar to this region and giving a decided character to its vegetation: *Platanus occidentalis*, Sycamore or Button wood, *Hesperis pinnatifida*, Ohio Wall Flower [etc.].

+Ohioan. A resident or native of the state of Ohio.

1817 FORDHAM *Narr.* 165, I do not choose the risk of being insulted by any vulgar Ohioans. **1861** *Ill. Agric. Soc. Trans.* IV. 117 The learned Colonel has told all we Ohioans know about it. **1868** *N.Y. Herald* 4 July 4 [The Mich. delegates to the convention] seemed to be, however, very much like all the Western States, greatly in favor of the Ohioan. **1900** *Boston Jrnl.* 11 March 11. 6/5 We don't care for the term 'Ohioan,' but, as President McKinley employs it, we think it best to let it pass, out of courtesy. **1922** *Daily Maroon* (U. of Chicago) 14 Nov. 3/1 Maroons defeat Ohioans in third Big Ten victory. Harry Thomas individual star.

+Ohio boat. A flat-bottomed river boat used on the Ohio River. — **1852** STOWE *Uncle Tom* xii, A few days saw Haley, with his possessions, safely deposited on one of the Ohio boats.

+Ohio boatman. A boatman on the Ohio River. — **1820** J. HALL *Lett. from West* 47 Eight or ten of those 'half horse and half alligator' gentry, commonly called Ohio boatmen.

+Ohio buckeye. [See quot. 1832.] The common buckeye, *Æsculus glabra.* — **1810** MICHAUX *Arbres* I. 38 Esculus ohioensis, *Ohio buck eye* . . . , nom donné par moi. **1832** BROWNE *Sylva* 227 We have denominated it Ohio Buckeye, because it is most abundant on the banks of this river. **1884** SARGENT *Rep. Forests* 42. **1901** MOHR *Plant Life Ala.* 46 The characteristic trees [of Alabama include] . . . *Diospyros virginica* (persimmon), *Aesculus octandra* (Ohio buckeye) [etc.].

+Ohio Company.

1. A land company controlled by Virginians, which was formed to colonize a tract of land south of the Ohio River, granted to them in 1749 by George II.

1748 in K. P. Bailey *Ohio Company of Va.* 298 Petition of John Hanbury to the King on behalf of the Ohio Company, 1748. **1751** *Ib.* 99 [Carved on a rock:] The Ohio Company Feby 1751 by Christopher Gist. **1778** *Ib.* 325 The said Ohio Company was always intended to consist, and doth at present consist of twenty Shares. **1831** WITHERS *Chron. Border Warfare* 52 England gave to an association of gentlemen in Great Britain and Virginia, (under the title of the Ohio Company,) liberty to locate and hold in their own right, 600,000 acres of land within the country then claimed by both England and France.

2. A land company formed in 1786 for the purchase and colonization of a tract of land between the Ohio River and Lake Erie.

1787 CUTLER in *Life & Corr.* I. 204 Settled the principles on which I am to contract with Congress for lands on account of the Ohio Company. **1792** in *Ib.* I. 475 The Ohio Company . . . opened the sale of lands in the Western Territory by becoming the first purchasers of any considerable tract.

+Ohio fever. A desire to move west to Ohio. (Cf. CALIFORNIA FEVER 3.) — **1835** *Knickerb.* V. 274 Such of them as some fifteen years since happened to reside in any part of New-England where what was called the 'Ohio fever' prevailed. **1882** THAYER *From Log-Cabin* i. 28 Abram Garfield took the 'Ohio fever,' . . . and he, too, started for the West. **1904** in Thwaite *Travels* VIII. 57*n.*, The 'Ohio fever' became a well known expression for this desire to move West.

+Ohio flour. A flour made of wheat grown in Ohio. — **1832** *Louisville Pub. Advertiser* 3 March, 350 barrels fresh Ohio Flour . . . for sale. **1850** SIMMS *Charlemont* 342 Biscuits hot, of best Ohio flour, are smoking on his plate.

+Ohio grant. A grant of land west of the Allegheny Mountains originally made over to the British Crown by the Six Nations in 1768, but purchased in 1773 by the Grand Ohio Company, a rival of the early Ohio Company. — **1774** T. HUTCHINSON *Diary & Lett.* I. 185 He told me a final stop was put to the Ohio Grant. **1775** *Ib.* 421 The Tho. Walpole concerned in the Ohio Grant, I saw the first time.

+Ohio(h)ian. =OHIOAN. — **1832** FERRALL *Ramble through U.S.* 68 Close by the granary, on which the young 'Ohiohians' and 'buck-eyes'—the lasses of Ohio are called 'buck-eyes'—seated themselves in pairs. **1845** *Xenia Torch-Light* 31 July 2/6 They succeeded in reaching the bank on this side of the river, where a large number of Ohioians were standing.

+Ohio idea. A scheme sponsored by Ohio Democrats between 1868 and 1876 whereby United States notes and bonds would be paid off with greenbacks. Also used allusively. — **1880** in S. Leavitt *Our Money Wars* (1894) 244 The defeat of Ewing will finally dispose of the Ohio Idea. **1881** *Congress. Rec.* 13 April 276/2 The Ohio idea is the absolute equality of all men before the law. **1886** POORE *Reminisc.* II. 349 Mrs. Hayes brought with her from her rural home what was known as 'the Ohio idea' of total abstinence from intoxicating drinks, and she enforced it at the White House.

+Ohion. =OHIOAN. — **1837** PECK *New Guide* 226 These shades of character will become blended, and the next generation will be Ohions, or to use their own native cognomen, Buckeyes.

‖**Ohionian.** =OHIOAN. — **1817** S. BROWN *Western Gazetteer* 148 Here [in New Orleans] in half an hour you can see . . . Kentuckians, Tennesseans, Ohionians, Pennsylvanians [etc.].

+Ohio shad. **a.** The blue herring, *Pomolobus chrysochloris.* **b.** A species of shad, *Alosa ohiensis.* — **(a) 1820** *Western Rev.* II. 171 Ohio Goldshad. . . . Its vulgar names are Ohio Shad, Gold Shad, Green Herring, &c. **1883** *Nat. Museum Bul.* No. 27, 455 *Clupea chrysochloris.* . . . Ohio shad; Skipjack; Blue Herring. **(b) 1902** *Rep. Comm. Fisheries* XXVII. 277 It at once became evident that the Ohio shad was an undescribed species.

+Oidonia. [Origin uncertain.] (See quotation.) — **1750** J. BIRKET *Cursory Remarks* 10 The wine most commonly Drunk here [in Portsmouth, N.H.] is from the Canaries & Western Islands—called Oidonia, tis of a pale collr. tasts harsh and is inclined to look thick.

***Oil.** Also †**oyle, oile,** *dial.* **ile.**

I. 1. A viscid, inflammable, liquid substance, of a characteristic smoothness and stickiness. ***a.** Vegetable or animal oil.

1612 SMITH *Virginia* 10 A sweete oyle, which they keep in goards to annoint their heads and ioints. **1656** *Plymouth Laws* 100 The country hath received great damage by a defect in the order about the barrell of oyle due for every whale taken on drift or cast on shore. **1767** CUTLER in *Life & Corr.* I. 19 Captain Pease arrived with 260 barrels of oil from the Western Islands. **1804** CLARK in *Lewis & C. Exped.* I. (1904) 93 A quart of Oile Came out of the surpolous fat of one of these [cat] fish. **1857** OLMSTED *Journey Texas* 7 Let us pray for the day when honest wine and oil shall take the place of our barbarous whisky and hog-fat. **1911** *Rep. Fisheries 1908* 315 The seal tribe embraces the walrus, eared seals, and earless seals. . . . They are captured for their oil, skins, and flesh.

b. Mineral oil or petroleum. {oyle petrolium, 1526; petroleum oil, 1799–}

The first commercial production of oil in this country was from the Drake well in Pennsylvania in 1859. (Cf. SENECA OIL.)

1832 B. DAVENPORT *Gazetteer* 272/1 The celebrated Oil Springs . . . rise from the bed of Oil creek [Penn.], and afford an inexhaustible supply of oil. **1865** *Atlantic Mo.* XV. 393/2 The fortunate borer has nothing more to do than to put down a tubing of cast-iron artesian pipe, lead the oil from its mouth into a tank. **1904** TARBELL *Hist. Standard Oil Co.* I. 15 On the flood or freshet the flatboats loaded with barrels of oil were floated down stream.

+2. *To strike oil*, to reach a pool of oil as a result of sinking a well.

1861 *Appleton's Ann. Cycl.* 580/1 The oil, when first struck, has . . . been known to burst forth with great violence. **1870** RAE *Westward by Rail* 60 A Spiritualist has a communication to the effect that if he sank a well in a particular locality he would 'strike oil.' **1885** *Wkly. New Mexican Rev.* 23 April 3/6 Mr. Moore returns . . . with the determination to 'strike oil' if there is any there.

+b. *fig.* To make a lot of money; to strike it rich.

1879 WEBSTER 1580/1 *To strike oil*, . . . to make a lucky hit, especially financially. **1888** LOWELL *Lit. & Polit. Addresses* 207 We are a nation which has struck ile, but we are . . . sure the well will never run dry. **1890** *Harper's Mag.* Oct. 727/2 Should he not have 'struck oil' by the time the money reached him, he should use it in paying off his debts.

II. *attrib.* and *comb.* **3. a.** Designating fabrics and goods made waterproof with oil.

See also OILCLOTH, OILSKIN.

1683 *Hempstead Rec.* I. 445, I doe ffully and absolutly give grant and bequeath unto my true and well beloved brother . . . five oyle leather sckins. **1744** *Md. Hist. Mag.* XXI. 247 One Yard Green oil Case or oile Cloth. **1851** MELVILLE *Moby Dick* 253 That worthy, . . . buttoned up in his oil-jacket, was now calmly smoking his pipe. **1892** *York County Hist. Rev.* 71 In the depot building is carried . . . the finest line of . . . caps, trunks, valises, oil-clothing [etc.].

b. Designating containers for oil or places where oil is stored.

*c***1760** in Singleton *Social N.Y.* 180 Shaving equipage containing razors, scissars, penknives, combs, hones, oil bottle [etc.]. **1782** Crèvecœur *Letters* 196 [The men of Nantucket] employ themselves in . . . making bungs or spoyls for their oil-casks. **1797** *Ann. 4th Congress* 2 Sess. 2048 For the repairs requisite at Reedy Island, and the oil vault, &c. at Cape Henlopen, [$]4,500. **1820** *Boston Selectmen* 122 The committee appointed . . . to confer with Mr. Black on the subject of new invented oil buckets & lamp burners. **1851** *Rep. Comm. Patents 1850* 162 Improvement in Oil Cans . . . [is claimed by] David G. Starkey. **1852** *Knickerb.* XL. 457 Before you know it, he has sucked your eggs, gnawed your hams, or emptied your oil-betty. **1865** *Atlantic Mo.* XV. 392/1 [The driver's] less placid wife sat upon a throne of oil-barrels.

4. Designating various processes, products, pieces of equipment, etc., connected with extracting oil from vegetable and animal substances.

See also Oil cake, factory, mill.

1851 *Rep. Comm. Patents 1850* 139 Improvement in Oil Presses. **1868** *Mass. Bd. Agric. Rep.* I. 105 Fish manures, the product of the oil-fisheries on our coast, . . . sell at about forty-five dollars per ton. **1881** in Goode *Amer. Fisheries* (1888) 112 These smacks are engaged for the oil-rendering and fish-scrap works on Barren Island. **1882** *Harper's Mag.* Sept. 588/1 A deck-load of brick for a menhaden oil-works had been dumped there. **1883** *Century Mag.* Oct. 819/2 The process of oil-making [from olives] is an interesting spectacle. **1887** *Courier Journal* 24 Jan. 6/3 Then feed [the calves and sheep] fattening food, oil meal or corn.

5. Pertaining to mineral oil or petroleum. +**a.** Designating geological phenomena, land areas, etc., connected with the discovery or production of oil.

See also Oil belt, land, region, etc.

1862 *Scientific Amer.* 122/1 This oil district [in Penna.] is peculiar in many respects. **1883** *Century Mag.* July 324/1 The oil stratum lies on a level. *Ib.* 330/1 When the oil-sand is struck, the oil, mingled with gas, spurts up with great force. **1885** *Wkly. New Mexican Rev.* 16 April 3/5 An old Pennsylvania oil prospector had located a spring which bore every indication that the flow of water came from the vicinity of an oil lead. **1899** Tarkington *Gent. from Ind.* xviii, The 'Herald' boomed the oil-field. **1903** *McClure's Mag.* Nov. 109 The bulk of the oil country was for it.

b. Designating machinery, vehicles, and watercraft used in the production and marketing of petroleum.

1863 *Boston Herald* 16 Aug. 3/3 (Ernst), The pilot of the oil boat sings as gaily . . . as did the pilot of the lumberman. *Ib.* 3/3 (Ernst), You see, in close proximity on every side, oil depots, oil refineries, oil derricks, oil tanks, oil shippers. **1865** *Atlantic Mo.* XV. 403 On one side of the street, crowded with oil-wagons, the freight of each worth thousands of dollars, stand . . . dwellings. **1867** *Rep. Comm. Patents 1865* II. 681 Oil drill, . . . a drilling apparatus which will remove broken and pulverized rock from the bore of a well, etc. **1876** Ingram *Centennial Exp.* 336 The oil . . . was loaded by gravity upon oil cars. **1877** 'E. Martin' *Hist. Great Riots* 143 The railroad authorities took the first opportunity to move an oil train which was standing near the depot.

c. Designating persons connected with the production or marketing of petroleum and its products.

See also Oilman, Oil-well operator.

1865 *Atlantic Mo.* XV. 403 Crowds of oil-speculators, oil-dealers, oil-teamsters, . . .—such is Oil City. **1880** in Tarbell *Hist. Standard Oil Co.* I. 277 The oil refiners of Cleveland came to affiant as a representative of transportation. **1886** Winchell *Walks & Talks* 137 All of these principles were disregarded by a majority of the oil-prospectors.

+**d.** Designating something connected with the production or marketing of petroleum or its products.

See also Oil business, company, exchange.

1862 *Scientific Amer.* 22 Feb. 122/1 An 'oil fever' affected the community [in western Penna.]. **1865** *Atlantic Mo.* XV. 392/2 In the beginning of the oil speculation . . . [many of the land owners] sold out at moderate prices to shrewd adventurers. **1880** Ingham *Digging Gold* 299 In a few days over one hundred locations had been made, and a miniature oil city created. **1888** in Tarbell *Hist. Standard Oil Co.* II. 117 Is there a Standard Oil Trust in this country or not? **1904** Tarbell *Ib.* I. 97 The report was received with 'approbation and delight' and put an official end to the 'Oil War.' **1907** *St. Nicholas* June 718/1 Enterprise had been threatened with an 'oil boom.' **1909** A. C. Rice *Mr. Opp* 269 What did you go and buy Widow Green's oil-shares back for?

6. In special combinations.

Oil brick, (see quotation); *oil-burner*, a ship that uses oil as fuel; *oil-distributor*, a device to spread oil over the surface of the water; *oil-filler*, (see quotation); *oil-smeller*, (see quotation).

1844 *S. Lit. Messenger.* X. 41/2 They are of the species styled oil-bricks, so called from the oil used in moulding them. **1860** *Harper's Mag.* June 8/1 New Bedford is the chief seat of the whaling interest. . . . Here the gaugers, clerks, supercargoes, oil-fillers [etc.] . . . ply their busy offices. **1889** *Century Mag.* March 714/2 For pilot-boats oil-distributers are valuable when boarding vessels in breaking seas. **1921** Paine *Comr. Rolling Ocean* 160 That ship of his . . . is an oil-burner. **1890** *Cent.* 4098/1 *Oil-smeller* . . . a person who pretends to be able to locate oil-bearing strata, and to locate positions for successful well-boring, by the sense of smell, and who makes a profession or trade of this pretension.

Oil bearing, *a.* {1770–4} +Of certain subterranean soils or rock: Productive of mineral oil. — **1880** Ingham *Digging Gold* 298 The experienced Oil City men were thoroughly at home among the immense beds of oil-bearing shale. **1883** *Century Mag.* July 323/1 It must not be supposed that the oil-bearing sandstone stratum underlies all this region.

Oil beetle. Any beetle of the genus *Meloe.* {1658–} — **1832** Williamson *Maine* I. 171 *Meloe Proscarabaes*, Oile Beetle. **1868** *Amer. Naturalist* II. 199 The Oil-beetle, *Meloë angusticollis*, . . . is a large dark-blue insect. **1881** *Harper's Mag.* Dec. 72/2 When touched, it exudes from every joint a yellowish liquid, from which habit it is commonly known as the 'oil-beetle.'

+**Oil belt.** A stretch of country yielding oil. — **1885** *Century Mag.* Jan. 466 The term 'gas line' has now all the attractions of the 'oil belt' of former days. **1894** *Congress. Rec.* 31 Jan. 1743/2 The great oil belt in this country commencing in New York, running through Pennsylvania, West Virginia, Ohio, and Kentucky, has its beginning in my district.

+**Oil business.** The business of producing and marketing petroleum. — **1883** *Century Mag.* July 324/2 In the early days of the oil business, all wells were sunk in valleys. **1891** in B. S. Heath *Labor & Finance Revol.* p. xviii, We met my uncle, Judge Hall, of Titusville, Penn., who was deeply engrossed in the oil business. **1903** *McClure's Mag.* Nov. 111 Mr. Rockefeller's chief concern in the oil business for the next twenty years was to keep his would-be competitors from reaching the sea with their own pipes.

Oil cake. A mass of compressed seed as linseed, cottonseed, etc., from which oil has been pressed out. {1757–} — **1800** Tatham *Agric. & Commerce* 142 Oil-cake, considered as an offal of the American oil-mills. **1819** *Plough Boy* I. 115 Her food . . . was chopped straw, scalded and seasoned with salt, . . . and a small allowance of oil cake, or boiled flax-seed. **1863** *Rep. Comm. Agric. 1862* 119 The oil-cake is in great demand for fattening stock. **1887** *Century Mag.* March 772/2 A ton of cotton-seed produces . . . seven hundred and fifty pounds of oil-cake.

Oil can. A can used to hold oil, esp. one with a long nozzle or funnel. {1839} Also fig. — **1879** *Scribner's Mo.* Nov. 146 A lamp, an oil-can, and a quart of oil cost so many cents. **1898** *McClure's Mag.* X. 215, [I] handed the engineer oil-cans, wrenches, and lights for his pipe. **1912** N. M. Woodrow *Sally Salt* 71 It was the engine-room and oil-can for hers.

Oilcloth.

1. Any fabric made waterproof by treatment with oil, paint, etc., and used for garments, table and floor coverings, wrappings, etc. {1697–}

1744 [see Oil 3 a]. **1790** *Penna. Packet* 1 Jan. 1/3 Vanuxem & Lombaert Have for Sale, . . . Oil cloth for wrappings. **1814** *Western Gleaner* I. 109 This establishment has been since permanently removed to Philadelphia . . . as a manufactory of oil-cloth. **1871** *Rep. Indian Affairs* (1872) 442 The houses without tables are the exceptions, and these tables are often covered with oil-cloth. **1895** Wiggin *Village Watch-Tower* 205 She had oilcloth on her kitchen to save the floor. **1920** Howells *Vacation of Kelwyns* 127 [As the van] drew nearer it showed, gaily painted, a frame-work of wood under a dark tenting of oilcloth.

2. A piece of such fabric.

1802 Ellicott *Journal* 223 It began to rain, but we soon made such a covering with . . . some oil cloths, that our people and their arms were kept dry. **1843** *Postal Laws* II. 51 If the mail be carried on horse-back, he will see that it be covered with an oil-cloth or bear-skin. **1887** *Courier-Journal* 17 Jan. 3/4 The office of the Auditor of the Texas and Pacific begins the new year with a brand-new oil-cloth on the floor. **1913** London *Valley of Moon* 6 On the frayed oilcloth, a supper waited.

b. *pl.* Garments made of oilcloth.

1884 *Nat. Museum Bul.* No. 27, 821 Contents of ditty-box: . . . 1 piece cotton cloth for mending oil clothes; 1 ball woolen yarn and needle.

3. *attrib.* and *comb.* **a.** Designating various garments, covers, etc., made of oilcloth.

1796 Hawkins *Letters* 26, I had prepared for a shelter in time which was covered with a blanket, bear skins and oilcloth cloak. **1837** *S. Lit. Messenger* III. 685 Those who wish to pass under the sheet of water . . . are here furnished with oil-cloth caps and dresses. **1840** Dana *Two Years* x. 79 We had on oil-cloth suits and south-wester caps. **1879** Burdette *Hawkeyes* 101 The man . . . always carries an old-fashioned, oil-cloth carpet-bag with him. **1883** *Harper's Mag.* Nov. 951/1 Nothing there [in the boat], except a heap of regulation blankets and an oil-cloth overcoat. **1900** Bacheller *E. Holden* 6 Then he put a woolen shawl and an oilcloth blanket on the bottom [of the basket].

b. Designating persons who help process oilcloth.

1837 Jenkins *Ohio Gaz.* 318, 3 bakers, 1 oil-cloth-painter, 8 saddlers. **1889** Brayley *Boston Fire Dept.* 498 He is an oil-cloth printer by trade.

+**Oil company.** A company that drills for, refines, or markets petroleum. — **1865** *Atlantic Mo* XV. 399 Another young fellow, originally employed in a very humble position by one of the oil companies, suddenly acquired a fortune. **1890** [see OILER 4]. **1904** TARBELL (*title*), The History of the Standard Oil Company.

+**Oildom.** [Analogous to *kingdom*.] The world that is interested in the production and marketing of petroleum: (see also quot. *c*1870). — *c***1870** CHIPMAN *Notes on Bartlett* 301 *Oildom.* The Petrolean manufactures; the oil or petroleum part of Pa. **1880** *Harper's Mag.* Dec. 63 Huge shops ... send ... iron tanks into the oil regions to hold the surplus of Oildom. **1904** TARBELL *Hist. Standard Oil Co.* I. 71 The rise [in freight rates] which had been threatening had come.... At the news all oildom rushed into the streets.

***Oiled,** *a.* +Inebriated. *slang.* {1916–} — **1737** *Penna. Gazette* 13 Jan. 2 He's Oil'd. **1924** P. MARKS *Plastic Age* 252 It was soon apparent that some of the couples had got at least half 'oiled' before the dance began.

Oiled paper. Paper rendered waterproof by being treated with oil. {oil paper, 1836–9} — **1835** *S. Lit. Messenger* II. 53 The holes, ycleped windows, covered with oiled paper to keep out the air. **1891** EARLE *Sabbath* 9 The earliest meeting-houses had oiled paper in the windows to admit the light. **1907** *St. Nicholas* June 730/2 Have ready a square of confectioner's oiled paper.

***Oiler.**

+**1.** An oil can with a nozzle used to oil machinery.

1856 OLMSTED *Slave States* 54 He did not give himself the trouble to elevate the outlet of his oiler, so that a stream of oil ... was poured out upon the ground. **1881** *Rep. Indian Affairs* 432 Oilers, zinc, medium size, dozen, 20½.

+**2.** A garment made of oiled cloth.

1889 *Scribner's Mag.* V. 681 Some of the more daring, still stick to their chairs and with oilers and rubber boots defy the waves. **1900** MUNN *Uncle Terry* 295 He had donned a suit of oilers.

+**3.** 'A vessel engaged in the oil-trade, or in the transportation of oils' (*Cent.*). *rare.*

+**4.** A well that brings in oil, as opposed to one that brings in gas.

1890 *Columbus Dispatch* 24 May, The Ohio Oil Co. ... drilled in an oiler ... that will be the largest one in this field.

+**Oil exchange.** An exchange where petroleum or petroleum securities are bought and sold. — **1883** *Century Mag.* July 337/2 The oil exchanges at Bradford and Oil City are noisy and animated places. **1887** *Courier-Journal* 8 May 12/6 This afternoon the tickers were put back on the floor of the Oil Exchange, whence they were removed nearly a year ago. **1904** TARBELL *Hist. Standard Oil Co.* I. 95 The Oil Exchange passed votes of censure, and the Producers' Union turned them [oil brokers] out.

+**Oil factory.** A factory where oil is extracted from animal or vegetable substances, esp. from whales and fish. — **1841** *Niles' Nat. Reg.* 9 Oct. 96/1 The oil factory of the Staten Island Whaling company was burnt ... with $30,000 worth of oil. *c***1849** PAIGE *Dow's Sermons* I. 267 All the odors of cavendish and camphor that now vivify your oil-factories must vanish forever. **1849** *Holyoke Diaries* 187 Oil Factory burnt two o'clock at night. **1914** STEELE *Storm* 81 I looked away at the dock and the oil-factory, black, desolate, dusty.

+**Oil house. 1.** A shed or building where oil was extracted from whales or fish and stored. **2.** A storehouse for lubricating oil. — **(1) 1678** *N.H. Probate Rec.* I. 211, I doe give unto my Son ... my storehouse, oyle house. **(2) 1877** 'E. MARTIN' *Hist. Great Riots* 108 The railroad buildings were destroyed as follows: Two round houses, ... three or four oil houses.

Oil lamp. A lamp that burns oil, esp. kerosene. {1831} — **1852** *Knickerb.* XXXIX. 152 The room was lighted, or rather darkened, by four or five oil-lamps, with tin shades. **1882** LATHROP *Echo of Passion* xi, The shuttered windows made dark spaces on the walls, in the dim light of a few oil-lamps. **1897** BRODHEAD *Bound in Shallows* 246 Several men sat smoking in the moderate glow of an oil-lamp on the office table. **1923** HERRICK *Lilla* 6 Her father didn't want the gas thing, oil lamps were good enough for him.

+**Oil land.** Land presumed to have oil. — **1865** *Chicago Tribune* 15 April 1 Oil Lands for Sale. **1872** *Harper's Mag.* Feb. 371/2 The family supposed very naturally that the enterprise alluded to was digging a well for oil, or speculating in 'oil lands.' **1909** A. C. RICE *Mr. Opp* 157, I've got a nice lot of gentlemen on board, going down to your place, ... to buy up all your oil-lands.

***Oil man.** +A man engaged in the business of producing or marketing petroleum. — **1865** *Atlantic Mo.* XV. 388 She was still considering her probable success in finding an oil-man to take her down the Creek. **1883** *Century Mag.* July 323/2 Oil men talk a great deal about the forty-five degree line. **1919** R. S. MCBETH *Oil* 5 New fortunes are now being made with a rapidity that almost dizzies one by oil men, ranchmen and farmers.

***Oil mill.** A machine that crushes and presses seeds, as linseed, cottonseed, etc., for the extraction of oil; also, a factory employing such machines.

1694 *N.J. Archives* XIII. 220 A petition by Isaac Lancer for liberty to Erect an oyl mill & to prohibite all others ye Space of 17 years. **1747** FRANKLIN *Writings* II. 310 We have many Oil-Mills in this Province, it being a great Country for Flax. **1789** MORSE *Amer. Geog.* 217 Oil mills, of a new and very ingenious construction, have been erected in several parts of the state [of Conn.]. **1818** DARBY *Emigrant's Guide* 253 Some saw mills, grist mills, a furnace, forge, oil mill, ... have been erected. **1873** *Iowa Agric. Soc. Rep.* 175 The panacea for all these ills is to be found in tanneries, oil-mills, ... butter factories, candle factories [etc.].

Oil nut. A nut or large seed which yields oil {1707–, in Jamaica}; +esp. the buffalo nut and the butternut; also, the tree or plant producing any of these nuts. Also attrib.

1694 *Topsfield Rec.* 86 From thence on a straight line to an oylenut tree which is Isaac Burtons tree marked. **1758** *Essex Inst. Coll.* XII. 147 Observed the leaves begin to fall ... chiefly from ye Oyl Nutt tree. **1778** CARVER *Travels* 500 The Butter or Oilnut.... The tree grows in meadows, where the soil is rich and warm. **1813** MUHLENBERG *Cat. Plants* 96 Oil nut, or Elk nut. **1817–8** EATON *Botany* (1822) 298 *Hamiltonia oleifera*, oil-nut.... Flowers small. **1832** BROWNE *Sylva* 173 In Massachusetts, New Hampshire and Vermont, it [the butternut] bears the name of Oil Nut. **1897** SUDWORTH *Arborescent Flora* 108 Butternut.... Common Names.... Oil Nut (Me., N.H., S.C.). Buttnut (N.J.).

Oil refinery. A plant where petroleum is refined into gasoline, benzine, etc. — **1863** [see OIL 5 b.]. **1865** *Atlantic Mo.* XV. 387/1 Here is also a large oil-refinery belonging to Mr. Downer of Boston. **1904** TARBELL *Hist. Standard Oil Co.* I. 39 Many a man in Cleveland tried his luck in an oil refinery.

+**Oil region(s).** An area productive of petroleum, esp. the oil country in Pennsylvania. — **1862** *Prelim. Rep. 8th Census* 72 The Pennsylvania oil region ... has thus far been the principal source [of petroleum]. **1868** J. D. WHITNEY *Life & Lett.* 265, I got them to make a topographical survey of the oil region. **1890** H. O. WILLS *Twice Born* 75, I now went to the oil-region to take charge of oil-wells. **1904** TARBELL *Hist. Standard Oil Co.* I. 3 A strip of Northwestern Pennsylvania, not over fifty miles long, [is] known the world over as the Oil Regions.

Oil shark. +(See quot. 1896.) — **1883** *Nat. Museum Bul.* No. 27, 420 The oil shark is valued for the oil in its liver. **1896** JORDAN & EVERMANN *Check-List Fishes* 215 *Galeorhinus zyopterus*.... Oil Shark; Soupfin Shark. Coast of southern California.

Oilskin.

1. A wrapping or garment made of oilcloth. {1812–}

1850 LEWIS *La. Swamp Doctor* 79 At length she came to the last [covering], the oil-skin. **1897** *Outing* XXX. 363/2 The men on deck, though clad in oilskins and sou'westers, were wet to the skin. **1913** LONDON *Valley of Moon* 355 They saw a gray-bearded man clad in streaming oilskins.

2. *attrib.* Designating objects made of oilcloth.

1877 *Harper's Mag.* Feb. 454/2 This [meerschaum] he filled with some fragrant tobacco from an oil-skin bag. **1883** *Ib.* Sept. 627/1 Lucy, peeping through the oil-skin blind, could see ... the young countryman. **1887** *Ib.* June 121/2 The fluid pulp is spread over this 'wire' ... by an 'apron' ... or oil-skin cloth. **1902** WISTER *Virginian* xxx, I had thrown off my long oilskin coat.

+**Oil spring.** A place where petroleum issues from the ground.

1765 ROGERS *Acct. N. America* 177 About 150 miles up this river [in N.Y.], are those remarkable springs, greatly esteemed by the Indians as a remedy for almost every disease; they are called the oil-springs. **1808** CUMING *Western Tour* 377 There are many springs called oil-springs, where the Petroleum and Seneca oil is gathered in abundance. **1818** *Niles' Reg.* XV. 139/2 A letter, written in Ohio, asserts that an *oil spring* has lately been discovered on the banks of Duck creek. **1847** COLLINS *Kentucky* 540 A tar or American oil spring, from which tar or oil constantly flows, in considerable quantities. **1890** *Harper's Mag.* Oct. 724/1 Oil springs were known near the present town of Cuba [N.Y.].

***Oilstone.** A fine-grained whetstone, lubricated with oil; also, the stone of which this is made.

1754 *S.C. Gazette* 5 Feb. 3/1 Just imported ... oil stones, melting and blue pots. **1821** NUTTALL *Travels Arkansa* 117 From ... the surveyor, I obtained two small specimens of the oil-stone, or hone of the Washita. **1853** O. BYRNE *Handbook for Artisan* 17 The amateur is most strenuously counselled to polish the tool upon the oilstone. **1878** *Harper's Mag.* Jan. 204 In commerce, under the name of the Arkansas whetstone or Ouachita oil-stone, [novaculite rock] has almost eclipsed its Turkish rival.

+**b.** (See quot. 1806.)

1799 J. SMITH *Acct. Captivity* 38, I asked [him], what was the use of the beaver's stones, or glands, to them;—as the she beaver has two pair, which is commonly called the oil stones, and the bark stones? **1806** LEWIS in *L. & Clark Exped.* III. (1905) 319 The male beaver has six stones, two [of] which ... resemble small bladders, contain a pure oil of a strong rank disagreeable smell, and not unlike train oil, these are called the oil stones.

Oil stove. A stove that burns kerosene or some other oil product {1884} Also attrib. — **1880** *Harper's Mag.* Aug. 400 Oil stoves are objectionable because of the unpleasant odor of the fuel. **1891** 'THANET' *Otto the Knight* 213 She an' Lida have got an oil-stove up, and some hot biscuits and coffee. **1897** *Outing* XXX. 113/1 Under the forward seat stood the oil-stove boxes.

+**Oil tank.** A tank in which petroleum is stored. Also attrib. — **1864** *Rep. Comm. Patents 1862* I. 189 Claim:—Constructing an oil tank with an open bottom in combination with buoys or floats. **1884** MATTHEWS & BUNNER *In Partnership* 154 A forethought ... of reeking oil-tanks, filling the air with petroleum, sent him down the embankment to wait.

1923 H. S. BELL *American Petroleum Refining* 293 Corrosion in oil tanks occurs at three points.

+**Oil territory.** A territory productive of, or presumed to be productive of, petroleum. — **1865** *Chicago Tribune* 15 April 1 The subscriber has secured a very advantageous lease of oil territory adjoining a large oil well. **1886** WINCHELL *Walks & Talks* 136 The trends of 'oil territory' must conform to the trends of formations. **1898** WESTCOTT *D. Harum* 301 That section of country . . . wa'n't in the oil territory them days, or wa'n't known to be, anyway.

+**Oil well.** A well drilled for oil or petroleum; a well that produces oil.

1847 COLLINS *Kentucky* 249 The American Oil well is situated three miles above Burksville, on the bank of the Cumberland river. **1864** *Appleton's Ann. Cycl.* 668/1 Oil wells are at present sunk in the sandstones of the N.W. Pennsylvania region, by contract, at $3 per foot. **1880** INGHAM *Digging Gold* 300 There are no oil wells successfully worked in all the trans-Missouri region. **1897** *Boston News Bureau* 22 June 1/1 An oil well is expected to pay for itself out in one year, and all the production after that is 'velvet.' **1918** *Bureau of Mines Bull.* No. 151, 3 New oil wells producing many million feet of gas under high rock pressure . . . are often brought in, in the Mid-Continent and California fields.

fig. **1878** B. F. TAYLOR *Between Gates* 241 [The whale was] a floating oil-well.

+**Oil-well operator.** One whose business is to operate or look after oil wells. — **1870** *9th Census* I. (1872) 682. **1888** *Amer. Almanac* 275 Occupations of the People of the United States. . . . Oil-well operators and laborers, . . . Organ-makers.

Oily grain. (See quotations.) {1753–} — **1829** EATON *Botany* (ed. 5) 390 *Sesamum indicum*, bene-benni, oily grain. **1840** DEWEY *Mass. Flowering Plants* 172 Oily-grain. Introduced from the East, . . . seeds used in cookery, contain much excellent oil.

+**Ojo.** *S.W.* [Sp.] A spring. Often *ojo caliente*, hot spring. — **1844** *Commerce of Prairies* II. 73 To procure water for our thirsty animals, it is often necessary to . . . drive them to the *Ojo del Muerto* (Dead Man's Spring), five or six miles to the westward. **1849** *31st Congress 1 Sess.* Sen. Ex. Doc. No. 64, 68 They concluded he must have gone down the *Ojo Caliente!* (one of the hot springs I have already described). **1872** POWERS *Afoot & Alone* 143 West of the Pecos there begin to occur those peculiar desert springs, the Spanish ojos, the eyes which weep brackish tears. **1885** *Wkly. New Mexican Rev.* 16 April 4/3 The city of Socorro has been restrained by a writ of injunction from using or interfering with the ojo caliente or warm spring there.

+**O.K.,** *n.* Also **okeh.** [See O.K. CLUB and note under O.K. *a*]

1. A member of the O.K. Club (q.v.). Now hist.

1840 *N.Y. Daily Express* 9 April 2/2 The Whig young men have a grand rally tomorrow night. On Friday, come the Indomitables—O.K.'s. **1840** *Boston Transcript* 15 April 2/1 When the Registry Law was first spoken of, the tail of the Democratic party, the roarers, buttenders, ringtails, O.K.'s, (flat burglary this latter title) and indomitables, talked strong about nullification and all that.

2. The letters 'O.K.' **a.** The watchcry of the O.K. Club.

1840 *N.Y. Daily Express* 3 April 2/2 About 9 o'clock a procession from the 10th and other up town wards marched down Center street headed by a banner inscribed 'O.K.' **1840** *Nat. Intelligencer* 7 Nov. 1/1 The Irish Locofocos in the 6th Ward [of N.Y.C.] have been parading the streets with shillelahs, swearing 'O.K.' &c.

b. An alleged abbreviation of 'all correct.' (Cf. O.K. *a.*, second quot. 1840.)

1840 *Nat. Intelligencer* 7 April 1/2 The Locos translate 'O.K.' *oll korrect*, (Locofoco orthography, of which they are proud!) **1840** *Atlas* 18 June 2 The band [of the Barre Whig Association] rode in a stage, which had a barrel of hard cider on the baggage rack, marked with large letters, 'O.K.'—*oll korrect.*

c. Used allusively and humorously: (see quotations).

1840 *Picayune* 30 Sept. 2/4 O.K.—These initials, which in party parlance are understood to mean *All is correct*—viz. 'Oll Korrect'—are used now for *'Orful Katastrophe.'* **1840** *Lexington Intelligencer* 9 Oct. 3/2 O.K. Perhaps no two letters have ever been made the initials of as many words as O.K. . . . When first used they were said to mean *Out of Kash*, (cash;) more recently they have been made to stand for *Oll Korrect, Oll Koming, Oll Konfirmed*, &c. &c. **1841** *Congress. Globe* App. 5 Feb. 141 Jeremiah, of olden times, would be ashamed of his lamentations, were he here to hear the modern Whigs mourning over the distresses of the people, on account of a weak Treasury. O.K. Orful Kalamity.

d. An endorsement denoting approval.

*c***1849** PAIGE *Dow's Sermons* I. 273 [Fortitude] infuses new life into his soul, while Hope adds an O.K. to his condition. **1896** *Congress. Rec.* 5 March 2507/1 The deputy marshall . . . would send word to the prose-cuting attorney asking for an 'O.K.' **1901** MERWIN & WEBSTER *Calumet K* 273 A formal permit . . . bearing the O.K. of the general manager. **1925** *Dollar Mag.* Dec. 207 To find new and more vivid forms of expression . . . in the hope that they will, in time, receive the okeh of the reading public.

+**O.K.,** *a.* [Origin uncertain: see note below.] 'All correct'; all right; satisfactory.

Two alleged uses of O.K., one in the Mass. Archives of 1757 (XCV. 552), the other in the Sumner County, Tenn., Court Minutes of 1790, have been examined in manuscript and photostat by Albert Matthews, Miss Isabel Howell of Vanderbilt University, and others. Both are clearly misreadings. (Cf. O.R.)

The 'ok' of the following quotation, which is interlined in the MS., may not be the modern expression at all. No satisfactory counter-explanation of its meaning, however, has been suggested: 'Arrived at Princeton, a handsome little village, 15 miles from N Brunswick, ok & at Trenton, where we dined' (1815 Wm. Richardson *Diary* 21 Feb.).

The adjective may be an extension of the noun in senses 1 and 2a, but the 'flat burglary' quotation of sense 1, as well as the *particular* Whig explanation (see second quot. 1840 below), suggests a previous usage.

See *American Speech*, April, 1941, pp. 85 ff., and *Sat. Rev. of Lit.*, 19 July, 1941, pp. 3 ff.

1840 *N.Y. Daily Express* 9 April 2/2 The Locos having gone into Masonic Hall O.K., and come out K.O. (Kicked out), the O.K.'s have changed their name. **1840** *Atlas* 19 Aug. 2/4 These initials, according to Jack Downing, were first used by Gen. Jackson. 'Those papers, Amos [Kendall], are *all correct*. I marked them O.K.' (oll korrect). The Gen. was never good at spelling. **1840** *Lexington Intelligencer* 27 Nov. 4/4 Old Tip is O.K. in Pennsylvania. **1846** *Spirit of Times* (N.Y.) 11 July 232/1 That's it. O. K. Now I have got you. Go ahead. **1873** E. S. PHELPS *Trotty's Wedding* xiii, So we had an O.K. time till we went to bed. **1883** *Gringo & Greaser* 1 Sept. 2/2 The little Jesus doing well, the virgin mother ditto and holy liable to pull thro O K. **1900** GOODLANDER *Fort Scott* (Kansas) 116 If my bid in my own name was not the lowest he would take the straw bid that was lower than the Jew and Frenchman, and I was to guarantee the bid O.K. **1923** WATTS *L. Nichols* 86 'Machine all O. K.?' 'Yeh, I give her th' once-over.'

+**O. K.,** *v. tr.* To mark with the letters 'O. K.'; to approve. — **1888** *Missouri Republican* 25 Jan., Please O. K. and hurry return of my return. **1895** CHAMBLISS *Diary* 220 The chairman ordered the secretary to 'O. K.' everything. **1904** *Brooklyn Standard Union* 25 June 6 The inspectors who O.K'd the rotten hose and useless life 'preservers.' **1912** DREISER *Financier* 49 Making out bills, O. K.-ing vouchers, transferring accounts, and maintaining the bank balances, was drudgery.

+**O.K. Club.** A Democratic club of New York City in 1840, said to be short for 'Old Kinderhook Club' in allusion to Kinderhook, New York, birthplace of Martin Van Buren. — **1840** *Nat. Intelligencer* 7 April 1/2 Already the Locofocos have got out their banners and procession, and 'the Butt-enders' and 'Point-enders' are marching at night through our streets, led by the so-called 'O.K.' club, which is just now a cant phrase in Tammany.

+**Oklahoma.** [Choctaw 'beautiful land.'] The name of a former territory and of one of the states.

1. A light, temporary hut or shanty. *Obs.*

In allusion to such huts used in Oklahoma during the rush of 1889. (Cf. EIGHTY *a.* 3.)

1889 *N.Y. Post* 21 Sept., A light fall of snow here [in Johnstown, Pa.] yesterday gave the people living in the Oklahomas a foretaste of what winter will be like in their shells.

2. *attrib.* Of or pertaining to Oklahoma.

1883 *Rep. Indian Affairs* p. xxiii, Notwithstanding his repeated expulsion from the Indian Territory, Payne and his party of 'Oklahoma Colonists' have twice during the present year made attempts at settlement in that country. **1891** O'BEIRNE *Leaders Ind. Territory* 98/1 Being struck, however, by the Oklahoma fever in 1889, he incautiously moved his herd to the promised land. **1897** DALE & RADER *Okla. Hist.* (1930) 775 Secretary of the Oklahoma Live Stock Association. **1920** Dale in *Amer. Hist. Assn. Rep.* (1925) 320 Little newspapers grew up near the border, established apparently for the . . . purpose of 'booming' the opening of Oklahoma lands to settlement. **1923** *Chronicles of Okla.* I. 176 The old time Oklahoma pioneer had his vision.

Okra. A tall, malvaceous plant (*Abelmoschus esculentus*) grown extensively in the South; the mucilaginous pods of this plant used in making gumbo soup. {1707–, West Indies}

1770 FORSTER tr. Kalm *Travels N.A.* I. 58 The Hibiscus esculentus, or Okra, is a plant which grows wild in the West Indies, but is planted in gardens here [in Penna.]. **1781–2** JEFFERSON *Notes Va.* (1788) 64 The gardens yield musk melons, water melons, tomatas, okra, pomegranates, figs, and the esculent plants of Europe. **1818** DARBY *Emigrant's Guide* 182 Another vegetable, the okra, of the same class and order with cotton, is cultivated in Louisiana as an article of food. **1855** *Amer. Inst. N.Y. Trans.* 417 The poorest negro would think himself poor, indeed, if he could not get okra for his gumbo soup. **1905** W. R. BEATTIE *Okra* 5 The principal use of okra is in soups and various culinary preparations in which meats form an important factor, as in the so-called gumbo soups.

attrib. **1845** SIMMS *Wigwam & Cabin* 361 It was a confident faith among the old ladies that okra soup was always inferior if cooked in any but an Indian pot. **1903** *Outlook* 7 Nov. 584 A row of tall okra stalks growing beside the path.

+**Okra cotton.** A variety of short-staple cotton. Also attrib. — **1840** *Niles' Nat. Reg.* 8 Aug. 368/1 Okra cotton. This species of cotton has now established amongst the planters of that part of Alabama where it was first discovered and most extensively cultivated, an undisputed superiority over all other varieties of the short staple. **1853** in J. A. Turner *Cotton Planter's Manual* (1865) 126 Next, in the year 1837 or '38, the

Twin or Okra cotton seed came up; seed sold at various prices, from $5 a quart to $160 per bushel.

***Old,** *a.*

American usage of this adjective does not differ from British usage. The following categories are illustrated because of their special American contexts.

1. Formerly; first in existence.

Applied to organizations, institutions, etc., to distinguish them from more recent organizations, etc., of the same general or specific name. (See also OLD BAPTIST, OLD SCHOOL BAPTIST, OLD SCHOOL PRESBYTERIAN, etc.)

1735 in C. Hazard *Thomas Hazard* 226 We the Subscribers, Teaching Elders or Pastors of the first gathered (com[mon]ly called the Old) Church in Boston New England [etc.]. **1809** *Ann. 10th Congress* 2 Sess. 1420 The Old Republican party of 1798 . . . is broken down. **1834** *Atlantic Mo.* XXVI. 488 Three divisions among the Presbyterians—Old Calvinistic—Newlights, rather evangelical—and a third, whose characteristic Mr. C. did not know. **1840** KENNEDY *Quodlibet* 48 What was generally . . . denominated and known by the appellation of the Old Federal Party. **1849** CHAMBERLAIN *Ind. Gaz.* 175 Presbyterians, Methodists, United Brethren, Christian, . . . Old Christian, (or new Light) and Baptists. *c*1864 in S. Leavitt *Our Money Wars* (1894) 67 In the days of the old United States Bank, the Democracy broke the Bank and bankrupted the country.

2. Of alcoholic liquors: Aged or allegedly aged.

1831 PECK *Guide* 60 Occasionally some [boats] are to be found which are full of . . . 'Old Monongahela.' **1834** *S. Lit. Messenger* I. 158 A cask of 'old corn,' for the refreshment . . . of the *corps militaire.* **1851** *Polly Peablossom* 180 I'll take a little of the 'Old Bourbon.' **1861** *N.Y. Tribune* 22 Nov., Why not send them brandy in bombs? and Old Wheat under a flag of truce? **1875** MILLER *First Families* (1876) 126 All of the following popular drinks, that is Old Tiger, Bad Eye, Forty Rod, [etc.], . . . were all made from the same decoction of bad rum, worse tobacco, and first-class cayenne pepper. **1882** 'M. HARLAND' *Eve's Daughters* 115 Mamie . . . thinks a glass of old sherry would give her a relish for the dinner she does not care to taste.

3. Of grain or a crop: Harvested a year or more ago.

1854 *Florida Plant. Rec.* 92, I New it would Not doe to give all my old Corn Away and to feed the Mules on New Corn. **1913** CATHER *O Pioneers* 66 The thing to do is to sell our cattle and what little old corn we have.

+4. *Old Dominion,* a sobriquet for Virginia: (see also quot. 1837).

'Dominion' was used by English sovereigns in referring to the possessions in America. In the course of time Virginia was known as the Ancient Dominion (see under ANCIENT *a.* 2), then the Old Dominion. (See A. MATTHEWS in *Notes & Queries* 2 Ser. XII. 31.)

1778 *Va. State P.* I. 311, I should not see the old Dominion this winter. **1806** FESSENDEN *Democracy Unveiled* I. 137 The blustering old dominion frets Because she has to pay her debts. **1835** J. HALL *Sk. of West* II. 94 This district [*i.e.*, Kentucky] . . . was considered rather an expansion of the *Old Dominion,* than as the formation of a new community. **1837** PECK *New Guide* 183 There are fewer slaves, less wealth, more industry and equality than in the 'old dominion,' as Eastern Virginia is sometimes called. **1840** *Niles' Nat. Reg.* 27 June 268/1 Our enemies shall not separate the whigs of the Old Bay state from the whigs of the old Dominion. **1886** POORE *Reminisc.* I. 245 But he never abjured the political doctrines of the Old Dominion. **1905** *N.Y. Ev. Post* 16 May 7 The Old Dominion is unlikely to send anybody else until his [Lee's] statue has been received there.

attrib. **1861** *Vanity Fair* 25 May 246/2 We will wrap the flag of our fathers around the 'Pan Handle' of Virginia, and upset the entire dish of Old Dominion Secession. **1883** *Harper's Mag.* Dec. 110/2, [I had] passed across the boundaries of the Old Dominion State.

+5. In various specific and familiar names: (see quotations).

See also OLD ABE, OLD BULLION, OLD HICKORY, etc.

1864 *Ore. State Jrnl.* 16 April 1/3 The General [*i.e.*, Gen. Halleck] . . . enjoys the sobriquet of 'Old Brains.' **1860** *Richmond Enquirer* 13 March 2/1 (Th.), Shakespeare died, and 'Old Buck' [Pres. Buchanan] was born, on the twenty-third of April. **1912** THORNTON II. 622 *Old Chapultepec.* General Winfield Scott (1786–1866). He won the battle of Chapultepec, Sept. 1847. **1882** *Century Mag.* March 783/2 The 'Old Commoner' [Thaddeus Stevens] undoubtedly inaugurated this method. **1884** ROE *Army Lett.* 322 For two nights our camp was in the fine forest back of 'Old Faithful,' and that gave us one whole day and afternoon with the geysers. **1882** MCCABE *New York* 196 The descendants of the original Dutch settlers of New York . . . style themselves 'the Old Knickerbockers.' **1871** *N.Y. Herald* 6 Sept. 6/6 It seems as if 'the Old Man of the Mountains' [*i.e.*, Brigham Young] meant to fight every step of the federal government for the supremacy of Utah. **1881** *Harper's Mag.* March 538/2 The 'old Patroon' [Stephen Van Rensselaer] was a member of the Congress that elected John Quincy Adams President. **1846** *Congress. Globe* 26 May 865 Col. [Zachary] Taylor . . . had won for himself by his gallant conduct in the field the soubriquet of 'Old Rough and Ready.' **1888** M. LANE in *America* 25 Oct. 15 *Old Tecumseh,* General W. T. Sherman. **1868** *Congress. Globe* 17 Dec. 131/1 With his own supporters . . . 'Old Thad' was a phrase of endearment; while even his foes spoke of him [Thaddeus Stevens] with pride as the 'great Commoner.' **1888** M. LANE in *America* 25 Oct. 15 *Old Three Stars,* General Ulysses Grant. **1885** *Mag. Amer. Hist.* March 297/1 *Old Whitey.*—The name of the horse ridden by Gen. Taylor during the war with Mexico. This animal was popular as a political symbol during the presidential campaign of 1849 [*sic*], which resulted in Taylor's election to the presidency. **1880** *Congress. Rec.* 28 Jan. 584/1 The name of Zachariah Chandler, or 'Old Zach,' as he was more commonly called, was familiar in every household.

6. In the specific names of birds.

1917 *Birds of Amer.* I. 141 Old-Squaw . . . Other Names.—Long-tailed Duck; Long-tail; Swallow-tailed Duck; South-southerly; Old Wife; Old Injin; Old Granny; Old Molly; Old Billy.

7. *Any old thing,* something or other. A term expressing indifference.

1900 ADE *More Fables* 205 An Author was sitting at his Desk trying to . . . grind out Any Old Thing that could be converted into Breakfast Food.

8. In special combinations.

Old Curiosity Shop, a parlor game; *Old Defenders' day,* (see quotation); *Old Family Coach,* a parlor game; *Old Granite State,* =GRANITE STATE; *Old Home week,* (see quotation); *old master,* the former master of a slave; *old mother state,* Virginia; *old ore,* (see quotation); *old Oregonian,* one of the early shiftless settlers of Oregon; *old trimble toes,* a dance step; *old witch,* (see quotation).

1850 S. WARNER *Wide, Wide World* xxix, They played the Old Curiosity Shop; and Ellen thought Mr John's curiosities could not be matched. **1903** *N.Y. Ev. Post* 12 Sept., To-day . . . is a holiday by legislative act. The day is known [in Md.] as Old Defenders' Day, in memory of the battle of North Point in 1814, in which the Maryland militia defeated an invading British army. **1850** S. WARNER *Wide, Wide World* xxix, They played the Old Family Coach, . . . and Ellen laughed till she was tired; she was the coach door. **1900** C. WINCHESTER *W. Castle* i. 18 In the infinite mercy of God, a mighty revival visited that section of the 'Old Granite State.' **1904** *Boston Herald* 2 Aug. 6 In . . . Massachusetts this first week in August is being observed as Old Home Week, and preparations have been made for welcoming back . . . the visitors who return to their native, or earlier, home to renew acquaintance with former scenes and companions. **1872** POWERS *Afoot & Alone* 61 Negroes everywhere . . . seemed to think they were not free unless they left the old master. **1866** 'F. KIRKLAND' *Bk. Anecdotes* 142 Had R. M. T. Hunter's famous pronunciamento to the people of Virginia been accompanied with those last two lines, it . . . would have saved the 'old mother State' from plunging into a four years' war. **1839** in *Mich. Agric. Soc. Trans.* VII 368 The deposit [of ore] is mostly of inferior quality, being what is technically known as an old ore. **1882** *Harper's Mag.* Oct. 766/2 This unenterprising class of farmers, locally spoken of as 'the old Oregonians,' has declined in influence. *a*1846 *Quarter Race Ky.* 178 When my time came [in the dance], therefore, I . . . commenced 'the double shuffle,' . . . and finally finished off on 'old trimble toes'—a rare and difficult movement. **1881** *Harper's Mag.* Jan. 184/2 The young folks . . . played at 'prisoner's base' or 'old witch by the way-side.'

+Old Abe. A sobriquet for Abraham Lincoln. Also *Honest Old Abe.* — **1860** *Congress. Globe* App. 19 June 462/2 They call him 'Uncle Abe,' 'Old Abe,' 'Honest old Abe,' 'The old rail-splitter,' 'The flat-boatman,' &c. **1864** *Ore. State Jrnl.* 23 April 1/2 We abandon 'Honest Old Abe' as a hopeless case. **1867** GOSS *Soldier's Story* 110 Those so employed [as teamsters] were always men that were loudest in blaming our government and 'Old Abe.'

+Old Baptist. (See quot. 1889.) — **1845** *Indiana Mag. Hist.* XXIII. 18, I see nothing awaiting the 'old Baptist' churches but utter annihilation. **1889** BUTLER *Recollections* 252 'Hardshell' Baptists . . . wish to be known as Old Baptists, or United Baptists.

+Old Bay State. =BAY STATE. — [**1838** *S. Lit. Messenger* IV. 164 Certain self-styled philanthropists of the good old Bay-State.] **1866** 'F. KIRKLAND' *Bk. Anecdotes* 309 As noble a fellow as ever wore the uniform of the Old Bay State, was Timothy Crowley. **1899** E. S. BROOKS *Old Bay State* Pref. 5 The Old Bay State has built itself into the very bone and sinew of the republic.

+Oldberg. [A shortening of *Oldenberg.*] A variety of apple. (Cf. *Duchess of Oldenberg* and *Oldenburgh* s.v. DUCHESS(E).) — **1895** *Dept. Agric. Yrbk. 1894* 211 In this zone we enter the true agricultural part of our country, where apples (Oldberg, Baldwin, Greening . . .), attain their highest perfection.

Old boy. {1601–} The devil. {1869–, Irish} — **1802** *Balance* 14 Oct. 317 (Th.), The devil has been nick-named the old boy. **1815** HUMPHRIES *Yankey* 29 Perfectly at home! entirely at his ease! yet cunning (as he would say) as the old Boy. **1847** BRIGGS *Tom Pepper* I. 14 If he were to meet the 'old boy' himself, he would take hold of his horns. **1854** M. J. HOLMES *Tempest & Sunshine* 203 Where the old boy is your mistress? **1896** HARRIS *Sister Jane* 25 The Old Boy's done took possession of him.

+Old Bullion. (See quot. 1892.) — **1850** *Commercial* (Wilmington, N.C.) 30 May 2/2 (Th. S.), Old Bullion [in a caricature] looks like an enraged Buffaloe Bull, tearing his hide open in front, daring a Camanche to fix an arrow deep in his panting breast. **1884** 'CRADDOCK' *Where Battle was Fought* 211 His views on specie payment would have graced the days of 'Old Bullion.' **1892** WALSH *Lit. Curiosities* 841 *Old Bullion,* a sobriquet of Colonel Thomas Hart Benton (1782–1858), . . . given to him for his persistent advocacy of a gold and silver currency.

Old clothes. {1781–} +Everyday clothes. *colloq.* — **1788** MAY *Jrnl. & Lett.* 18 After breakfast met numbers of people going to meeting, in their old clothes, it being fast day. **1865** *Atlantic Mo.* XV. 73/1, I felt like some anxious mamma whose children . . . have accidentally appeared at dancing school in their old clothes.

+**Old Colony.** Plymouth Colony. Also attrib. (Cf. COLONY 6.) — **1798** *Columbian Centinel* 29 Dec. 3/1 The following toasts evinced that the spirit of the *Old Colony* patriots had been bequeathed to the inheritors of their soil. **1858** LONGFELLOW *Courtship M. Standish* 7 In the Old Colony days, in Plymouth the land of the Pilgrims, To and fro in a room . . . Strode . . . Miles Standish. **1914** A. MATTHEWS in *Mass. Col. Soc. Publ.* XVII. 362 This restriction, however, of the terms Pilgrims and Pilgrim Fathers exclusively to the Plymouth settlers is recognized at the present time only in the Old Colony itself.

+**Old comer.** (See quotations and cf. FIRST COMER and FOREFATHER 1.) — **1849** in *Mass. Col. Soc. Publ.* XVII. 363 These later pilgrims [*i.e.*, those who came on the Anne and Little James] are reckoned with those who came in the Mayflower and Fortune, as the *Old Comers* or *Forefathers.* **1898** W. E. GRIFFIS *Pilgrims in 3 Homes* 161 Those who reached New Plymouth in the Mayflower, Anne, and Little James were called the 'Old Comers,' or 'Forefathers.'

+**Old Congress.** The Congress under the Articles of Confederation.

1804 *Ann. 8th Congress* 1 Sess. 1062, I believe the Territorial government, as established by the ordinance of the Old Congress, the best adapted to the circumstances of the people of Louisiana. **1822** *Ann. 17th Congress* 1 Sess. I. 97 The Old Congress turned their attention to this subject as early as February 1781. **1857** BENTON *Exam. Dred Scott Case* 39 So indispensable was the Old Congress to the Convention, that it not only sat as long as the Convention did, but longer. **1886** ALTON *Among Law-Makers* 119 The new Union and government came into existence and the First Constitutional Congress of the United States assembled in the City of New York on March 4, 1789, pursuant to a resolution of the Old Congress of the Confederation.

+**Old continental. 1.** A former soldier of the Continental army. **2.** =CONTINENTAL *n.* 3. — **(1) 1807** IRVING, etc. *Salmagundi* xi, The great crowd of buzzards, puffers, and 'old continentals' of all parties, who throng to the polls, to persuade, to cheat, or to force the freeholders into the right way. **1845** [see CONTINENTAL *n.* 1]. **(2) 1828** JOHN NEAL *Bro. Jonathan* I. 159, I ins with my hand arter that; and I outs with a handful o' the right stuff; old continental. **1838** *U.S. Mag.* I. 13 This revival of the 'Old Continental,' by the present hard-money reform Administration, was indeed unexpected.

Old coon. (See COON 2 and 3.)

+**Old country.** The British Isles or any part of Europe.

1796 F. BAILY *Tour* 172 The scenery . . . [was] so very different from what we had been used to in the old country. **1808** A. GRANT *Memoirs Amer. Lady* II. 6 Many of those new comers were ambiguous characters, originally from the old country, (as expatriated Britons fondly call their native land). **1823** COOPER *Pioneers* xxiv, I wouldn't be helping to such a sinful kind of fishing for the best rifle that was ever brought out from the old countries. **1850** J. THORNTON *Diary* 89 Everything here shows Anglo-Saxon origin and bears the impress of 'the old country,' as they term England. **1902** CLAPIN 293 *Old Country,* At first, applied solely to England, but now meaning the Old World generally, and of course more especially Europe. **1908** GALE *Friendship Village* 112 The secretary's in the old country on a pleasure trip. **1924** SUCKOW *Country People* 34 She looked as if she might just have come from the old country.

+**Old countryman.** A man from the old country: (see esp. quot. 1848). *Obs.* — **1828** PICKERING in *Amer. Q. Rev.* IV. 211 Even the illiterate in our country will distinguish an Englishman by his pronunciation, and will designate him as an 'old countryman,' as we have often heard them do. **1842** 'UNCLE SAM' *Peculiarities* I. 294 These old-countrymen . . . keep come, come, coming over the water. **1848** BARTLETT 239 *Old countryman.* A native of England, Scotland, Ireland, or Wales. The term is never applied to persons from the Continent of Europe.

+**Old court party.** *Ky. politics.* =COURT PARTY 2. (Cf. NEW COURT PARTY.) — **1826** *Spirit of '76* I. 320/2 The struggle is over, and the party denominated the old court party, have succeeded in electing their candidates in this county. **1847** COLLINS *Kentucky* 208 The intensely exciting contest of three years duration [*c*1825], between the 'Relief' or 'New Court,' and the 'Anti-Relief' or 'Old Court' parties. **1901** Z. F. SMITH *Hist. Kentucky* 512 The result [in 1825] was the triumph of the old-court party by a large majority.

+**Old dirt.** *Placer mining.* Dirt that has already been washed. — **1851** *Alta Californian* 19 Aug., At Grizzly Bear Bar they are engaged in washing 'old dirt,' that is, the dirt that was passed through the cradle last year. **1878** BEADLE *Western Wilds* 107 In places [we] pass hundreds of acres of 'old dirt,' which has been washed out and abandoned.

+**Old driver.** The devil. — **1877** BARTLETT 437 *Old Driver,* euphemism for the devil. **1895** WIGGIN *Village Watch-Tower* 68 Pitts' relations or not, they're all wuss'n the Old Driver.

Old England. England. {1647-}

Used in contradistinction to New England (q.v.), but in later usage there is a blend of the sense: Good old England.

1631 *N.H. Hist. Soc. Coll.* IV. 243 Wee were free enough in Old England, to turne our in sides outwards. **1680** *New Castle Court Rec.* 397, I: bequeath itt to my brother & sister in ould England. **1740** W. STEPHENS *Proc. Georgia* 588 Dispatching his Friend, Mr. Seward, first to Old-England, before he himself visited the New. **1775** *Mass. H. S. Coll.* 3 Ser. V. 87 Thus stands the matters betwixt Old England and America. **1840** *S. Lit. Messenger* VI. 241/1 More of Old England is left in the hearts of the Old Dominion than in all the states beside. **1884** *Boston Journal* 30 Dec. 2/4 Our goods are crossing the water to keep alive old England.

***Old English,** *a.* +Of or pertaining to England, as distinguished from New England. — **1632** *Mass. H. S. Coll.* 4 Ser. VI. 184 Tis a ridle as yet to me whether you meane any Elder in these New English churches, or . . . old English. **1647** ELIOT *Day-breaking* 16 Now all see it [New-English ground] to bee scarce inferiour to Old-English tillage.

+**Oldermost,** *a. W.* Oldest. *Obs.* — **1843** 'CARLTON' *New Purchase* II. 70 Ain't that oldermost stranger a kinder sort a preacher? **1856** CARTWRIGHT *Autobiog.* (De Vere) Where is your oldermost child, said the man to the unfortunate father?

Old field.

+**1. a.** A field cultivated by the Indians before the coming of the whites. (Cf. INDIAN FIELD.) **b.** A field worn out, esp. by tobacco and cotton culture; a field allowed to lie fallow.

1635 in *Amer. Speech* XV. 290/2 Northerly on Cugleyes ould field. **1656** *Braintree Rec.* 7 A highway layd out in the old feild for goodman Hoydin to bring his corne out. **1686** *Jamaica Rec.* I. 299 The afore sd. John Rodes is to have . . . twenty seaven acres more lying eastward . . . in ye old field. **1761** *Descr. S.C.* 6 There are dispersed up and down the Country several large Indian old fields, which are lands that have been cleared by the Indians, and now remain just as they left them. **1771** in *New Eng. Mag.* ns. XII. 348/2 [I] crossed over an old field. **1801** W. STRICKLAND *Agric. U.S.* 38 [There is] a repetition of the same [crops], as long as the land will bear any thing; after which it is laid by without seed for old-field. **1853** F. W. THOMAS *J. Randolph* 203 We . . . struck off into what was called an 'old field,' an uninclosed place, where tobacco had been tilled, until the soil was exhausted. **1905** *Bureau of Forestry Bul. No. 63* 5 This study has to do mainly with the life history of second-growth white pine on old fields and pastures in New England.

+**2.** *attrib.* **a.** Designating areas constituting old fields or things associated with such land.

1690 *Huntington Rec.* II. 70 A black oak by ye south cornar by a rock by ye ould feld fence side. **1741** *Brookhaven Rec.* 148 A certain piece of Thatch or thatch bed, lying between the little neck & the old field beach. **1772** *Md. Hist. Mag.* XIV. 278 Our Corn . . . is very good at all the Quarters, some of this old Field ground . . . Excepted. **1835** *S. Lit. Messenger* I. 582, I could . . . only remember that every untrimmed *old field* colt was a regular descendant of Eclipse. **1883** ZEIGLER & GROSSCUP *Alleghanies* 175 It is not wise to select 'old field land,' with a view to raising it to a good state of cultivation.

+**b.** Designating things grown on an old field.

1771 *Md. Hist. Mag.* XIV. 128 Nothing but Rain is wanting to make the Oldfield tob[acc]o before the House very good. **1829** in Commons, etc. *Doc. Hist.* I. 240 Ploughs . . . started in old field corn. **1883** ZEIGLER & GROSSCUP *Alleghanies* 170 Smaller tracts are covered with what is known as old field growth—scrub oak and pines. **1887** *Harper's Mag.* Sept. 588/2 She been goin' out before day, and between times, and gatherin' old-field plums, and, arfter always givin' me the pick, sellin' the balance for what she can git.

+**c.** *Old-field preacher,* an old-fashioned rural preacher.

Cf. OLD FIELD SCHOOLMASTER.

1904 T. E. WATSON *Bethany* 168 The tremendous emphasis with which the old field preacher uttered the words . . . I shall never forget.

+**Old-field birch. a.** The American gray birch, *Betula populifolia.* **b.** The paper birch, *B. papyrifera.* — **1810** MICHAUX *Arbres* I. 26 *White birch* [ou] *Old field birch,* (Bouleau des terreins secs.) **1814** PURSH *Flora Amer.* II. 621 *Betula populifolia* . . . is known by the name of White Birch or Old Field Birch. **1832** BROWNE *Sylva Amer.* 123 In the state of Maine, . . . [the name] Old Field Birch is . . . employed to distinguish the white birch from the canoe birch. **1884** SARGENT *Rep. Forests* 159 *Betula alba.* . . . White Birch. Old-field Birch. Gray Birch.

+**Old-field lark.** *S.* A meadow lark. — **1805** LEWIS in *L. & Clark Exped.* II. (1904) 180 There is a kind of larke here that much resembles the bird called the oldfield lark with a yellow brest and a black spot on the croop. **1811** WILSON *Ornithology* III. 22 Their general name is the Meadow Lark; among the Virginians they are usually called the Old Field Lark. **1917** *Birds of Amer.* II. 251 Meadowlark. . . . Other Names.—Common Lark; Old Field Lark; Field Lark [etc.].

+**Old-field pine.** Chiefly *S.* **a.** =LOBLOLLY PINE. **b.** The sandpine (*Pinus clausa*) of Florida and Georgia. **c.** The shortleaf pine, *P. echinata.*

1797 HAWKINS *Letters* 89, The whole grown up with old field pine, some of them a foot and an half diameter. **1841** *S. Lit. Messenger* VII. 452/1 The old-field pine had not intruded so largely on the domain of the ploughman and reaper. **1856** OLMSTED *Slave States* 89 Cannot some Yankee contrive a method of concentrating some of the valuable properties of this old-field pine, so that they may be profitably brought into use in more cultivated regions? **1877** BARTLETT 363 *Loblolly Pine.* Sometimes called, in the Southern States, 'Old-field Pine,' and in Southern Virginia, 'White Pine.' **1883** ZEIGLER & GROSSCUP *Alleghanies* 177 Those . . . are what we call old field pine. **1894** COULTER *Bot. W. Texas* III. 554 *Pinus Taeda.* A tree 15 to 45 m. high. . . . Extending from the Gulf States to the valley of the Colorado. 'Loblolly pine.' 'Old-field pine.' **1897** SUDWORTH *Arborescent Flora* 28 Sand Pine. . . . Oldfield Pine (Fla.). *Ib.* 29 Shortleaf Pine. . . . Oldfield Pine (Ala., Miss.).

+**Old-field school.** A school situated in an old field, esp. a rural elementary school.

Cf. *Cornfield school* under CORNFIELD 2 c.

1806 WEEMS *Washington* (1867) 12 The first place of education to which George was ever sent, was a little 'old field school.' **1829** SHERWOOD *Gaz. Georgia* (ed. 2) 141 An academy supposes instruction in the higher branches of education; but some are no better than 'old field schools.' **1853** *S. Lit. Messenger* XIX. 68/2 The master of the old field school was one of the regular faculty, who had great faith in the old medicines for the eradication of moral diseases. **c1866** BAGBY *Old Va. Gentleman* 49 He must now go to old-field school, and carry his snack in a tin bucket. **1887** *Harper's Mag.* May 842/2 At that time the only educational facilities in the rural districts were offered by the old-field schools.

+**Old-field schoolmaster.** A schoolmaster in an old-field school. — **1853** BALDWIN *Flush Times Ala.* 106 He had been an old-field schoolmaster.

+**Old flag.** The American flag, the symbol of union, esp. during the Civil War. — **1861** *Chicago Tribune* 26 May 1/4 States wor dropping away from the old flag just like the shooting stars of the firmament. **1864** *Santa Fe New Mexican* 24 June 2/1 It is hoped he will . . . become faithful to the Union and the old flag. **1894** *Harper's Mag.* May 949/1 The flames leap round the flag-staff. 'Now you'll see that old flag go down!' cries a boy. **1900** *Congress. Rec.* 9 Feb. 1674/2 My position . . . possibly may be used to influence some old soldier to keep on voting for the old flag and increased appropriations.

+**Old gay,** *adv.* To a comfortable degree; very well. *slang. Obs.* — **1863** NORTON *Army Lett.* 177 We are living 'just old gay' now. The commissary issues soft bread enough to keep us all the time.

+**Old glory.** The flag of the United States of America. — **1862** W. DRIVER in *Salem* (Mass.) *Register* 10 March, I carried my flag, 'Old Glory,' as we have been used to call it, to the Capitol, presented it to the Ohio 6th and hoisted it with my own hands on the Capitol. **1865** BOUDRYE *Fifth N.Y. Cavalry* 270 The moment we beheld the Old Glory, three enthusiastic cheers burst from one and all. **1878** B. F. TAYLOR *Between Gates* 97 They cheer 'old glory' with the ardor of a perennial Fourth of July. **1896** *Boston Journal* 30 Oct. 8/4 Patriotic citizens . . . wanted one or more specimens of 'Old Glory' for use on that day. **1910** *Boston Sunday Globe* 3 July 32/1 'Old Glory,' the affectionate sobriquet applied to the flag, . . . was chosen offhand by a Massachusetts skipper, Captain William Driver of Salem, who sailed from the port of the Witch City in December of 1831.

+**Old ground.** Ground that has been some time in cultivation, as contrasted with new ground (q.v.). Also attrib. — **1769** WASHINGTON *Diaries* I. 331 Got over the old ground Corn at the same place with the Hoes. **1871** *Lawrence* (Kansas) *Republ. Jrnl.* 21 March, As to pulverizing the soil, all 'old ground' in Kansas is apt to pulverize itself.

Old guard. +**1.** *fig.* The conservative, dependable element in an organization; the old stand-bys. {1894} +**2.** (See quotation.) — **(1) 1852** QUITMAN in Claiborne *Life Quitman* II. 164 What shall we of the strict state-rights school, what shall the 'Old Guard' do? **1875** *Chicago Tribune* 8 Dec. 1/5 'Here we are again!' . . . Ex-Senator Dilworthy and the Old Guard of Treasury-plunderers from the South. **(2) 1900** *Congress. Rec.* 16 Feb 1880/2 The regiments and the companies from Maryland . . . distinguished themselves throughout the Revolutionary war as . . . the Old Guard of the Continental forces.

+**Old Hickory.**

1. A nickname for General Andrew Jackson (1767–1845). Also transf.

Cf. HICKORY 8.

1827 *Hallowell* (Me.) *Gaz.* 20 June 2/2 He was in favor of amending the Constitution, so as to let the people vote for Old Hickory. **1833** *Niles' Reg.* XLIV. 3/1 We wish the house would pass it [Clay's land bill], only to see how quick old Hickory would veto it. **1880** *Harper's Mag.* Aug. 355/1 There is always some Old Hickory to rule Pennsylvania . . . because there are so many Hoevens in the hills who are glad to pay him with office to do their thinking for them. **1907** *Springfield Repub.* 24 Oct. 8, I should not say that Old Hickory was faultless, but Andrew Jackson was as upright a patriot as ever any nation had.

2. (See quotation.)

1858 VIELÉ *Following Drum* 225 [Scouts' shirts] are composed of a dark blue check material, warranted to last a week. . . . They are termed 'Old Hickories.'

+**Old Hunker.** [Origin uncertain, but see quot. *a*1848.] A name applied esp. by the Barnburners to a member of the conservative element of the New York Democratic party *c*1840–50; also, any conservative Democrat. (See also HUNKER.)

1844 *Congress. Globe* 21 March App. 632 (Th.) The 'Old Hunkers,' as the drill sergeants of the party are styled, expect to be, and are, rewarded with appointments to office. **1847** *Whig Almanac 1848* 32/1 The bill met with considerable opposition from the 'Old Hunkers,' among whom was one old gentleman from the Western Reserve. **a1848** in Bartlett 26 'Old Hunker' . . . was also intended to indicate that those on whom it was conferred had an appetite for a large *hunk* of 'the spoils.' **1866** GREGG *Life in Army* 268 [The negro] won't vote for old hunkers; he won't forget who the copperheads were. *transf. & attrib.* **1910** *Springfield Repub.* 15 Dec. 2 This will shock republicans of the old hunker type, if any such exist in this time of political upheaval.

+**Old Ironsides.** The United States frigate 'Constitution,' launched in 1797; also, transf., the nickname for the commander of this ship during the war of 1812.

1815 *Niles' Reg.* IX. Suppl. 90/2 Old *Ironsides,* once more now rides, In search of English cruizers. **1830** HOLMES *Poet. Works* (1899) 3 (*caption*), Old Ironsides. **1833** *Niles' Reg.* XLIV. 267/2 That [dock] at Charlestown is . . . for the reception of 'Old Ironsides.' **1890** *Congress. Rec.* 9 May 4383/1 Like the famous frigate Constitution, [Admiral Charles] Stewart received the appellation of 'Old Ironsides.' **1900** *Congress. Rec.* 8 Feb. 1656/1 The frigate *Constitution,* better known as 'Old Ironsides,' is now moored to a wharf at the Boston Navy-Yard.

+**Old issue.** *attrib.* Designating a Negro born or made free before the Civil War. — **1879** TOURGEE *Fool's Errand* 87 The meeting was led . . . by a mulatto man named Robert, who was what is now called an 'old-issue free nigger.' **1899** CHESNUTT *Wife of His Youth* 214 Wright came of an 'old issue' free colored family, in which, though the negro blood was present in an attenuated strain, a line of free ancestry could be traced beyond the Revolutionary War.

Old ladies' home. A home or institution for aged women. — **1893** HOWELLS *Coast of Bohemia* 68 There are homes of all kinds; . . . old ladies' homes, and young girls' homes, and destitute females' homes, and children's homes, where they can go for the night. **1908** GALE *Friendship Village* 111, I got off an' went up an' visited the Old Ladies' Home. **1910** 'O. HENRY' *Strictly Business* 14 No Old Ladies' Home or Retreat for Imprudent Actresses for me.

Old lady. A man's wife. *colloq.*[2] — **1871** EGGLESTON *Hoosier Schoolm.* xvii. 134 Here's the old lady and Shocky. **1873** 'MARK TWAIN' & WARNER *Gilded Age* xxvii. 245 You make yourself perfectly comfortable, old lady. **1884** NYE *Baled Hay* 88 If I thought so it would kind o' harden me and the old lady and make us sour on all creation.

Old land. {1784–} +**a.** Worn out land. (Cf. OLD FIELD 1 b.) +**b.** Land in cultivation for a long time. — **1715** in *Amer. Sp.* XV. 290/2 At the Corner of the said Jones's old land. **1748** J. ELIOT *Field-Husbandry* 11 The Third sort of Land I would speak of is our old Land which we have worn out. **1833** SILLIMAN *Man. Sugar Cane* 10 [Violet cane] prefers old land, and that which is rather dry. **1871** *Rep. Indian Affairs* (1872) 330 It is my intention, during the coming season, to . . . summer-fallow as much of the old land as can be spared from cultivation.

Old light. {1785–} A conservative member of a church body divided by the religious revival of the eighteenth century. (Cf. NEW LIGHT.) — **1781** PETERS *Hist. Conn.* 288 (Th.), The Old Lights held that the civil magistrate was a creature framed on purpose to support ecclesiastical censures. **1819** J. M. DUNCAN *Travels U.S.* II. 359 At the period of this rupture there were two synods, that of New York, and that of Philadelphia; the New England party . . . were the dominant power in the former and the others, who gloried in the name of Old Lights, in the latter.

+**Old line,** *a.* In agreement with traditional doctrines and principles; conservative. Applied esp. to a political party member.

1856 *Congress. Globe* 9 Jan. 180 Have they offered us one of my colleagues, an old-line Whig? **1860** *36th Congress 1 Sess.* H.R. Rep. No. 621, 7 Mr. Swift . . . had a number of old-line whig friends in Massachusetts. **1884** R. GRANT *Average Man* 259 The old line Democrats are madder than blazes. **1890** *Stock Grower & Farmer* 22 March 3/1 The 'old line' commission men must bestir themselves or they will find their occupation gone. **1922** MCCORMAC *J. K. Polk* 214 Old-line politicians such as Buchanan, Calhoun, Benton, and Blair were doing their utmost to ruin Polk's prospects.

+**Old liner.** A member of the old guard; a conservative and dependable member of a party. — **1855** in Hambleton *H. A. Wise* 419 Endorsed thus by two 'old liners,' he was most cordially received. **1884** *Boston Journal* 25 Sept. 2/2 The old-liners appear to be out of the fight. **1903** *N.Y. Ev. Post* 31 Oct. 5 The old-liners quietly backbite him for taking up a 'fanatic' like Johnson.

+**Old line state.** Maryland. So called because its northern boundary coincided with the Mason-Dixon line. — **1871** DE VERE 660 Maryland bears the proud title of *Old-Line State* from the *Old-Line* regiments which she contributed to the Continental Army in the War of the Revolution—the only state that had regular troops of 'the line.' **1904** *Americana* XI. *Old Line State,* a popular name for the State of Maryland, which in the early colonial days was the dividing line between the Crown land grants of William Penn and Lord Baltimore.

* **Old maid.** +**1. a.** The Indian mallow of the East Indies, *Abutilon theophrasti.* **b.** A garden variety of zinnia, *Z. elegans.*

1839 *S. Lit. Messenger* V. 751/2 A particular spot in his garden was appropriated to the culture of old maids. **1880** *Scribner's Mo.* May 101/2 In my section an annoying weed is *Abutilon,* or velvet-leaf, also called 'old maid.' **1888** *Century Mag.* Oct. 896/1 There were no pigs to disturb the flower-garden overrun with prince's feathers, bachelor's-buttons, four-o'clocks, old-maids, and sunflowers.

+**2.** In the possessive in the names of flowers.

1892 *Amer. Folk-Lore* V. 92 *Saponaria officinalis,* old maid's pink. **1894** *Ib.* VII. 92 *Coreopsis,* sp., old maid's breastpin, Plymouth, O.

***Old man.**

1. A familiar term applied to men in various relationships.

The term is seldom used in the presence of 'the old man.' It is not limited in application to elderly men and it usually connotes affectionate regard.

a. A father or the head of a family. {1892}

1792 BRACKENRIDGE *Adv.Capt.Farrago* xxiii. 113 You are welcome, Sir, if you wish to stop, . . . though, since my old man's time, we don't take in strangers for common. **1832** F. TROLLOPE *Domestic Manners* I. 140 Mr. Trollope was . . . constantly called 'the old man.' **1844** *Corr. R. W. Griswold* (1898) 160, I . . . have frequently heard his sons say that the 'old man' (as they called him) had written much better things. **1887** *Lisbon* (Dak.) *Star* 30 Dec. 3/1 The old man had much higher views for his daughter. **1901** WHITE *Claim Jumpers* 4, I believe he's been pestering the old man to send him West. Old man doesn't approve.

+b. A master, foreman, or overseer; the boss.

1837 *S. Lit. Messenger* III. 86, I say, darkie, the old man keeps good liquor, and plenty of belly timber, don't he? **1844** *Knickerb.* XXIII. 83 The 'old man' himself came to the door, and looking down at his apprentice, shook his head sorrowfully. **1887** GEORGE *40 Yrs. on Rail* 167 All 'the boys' on the road will swear by their superintendents, and . . . they feel that if they can only lay it [a grievance] before the 'old man' it will be properly dealt with. **1898** N. BROOKS *Boys of Fairport* xiii. 172 You had better be careful how you call the master 'Old Man' so near the school-house. **1914** 'BOWER' *Flying U Ranch* 58 He had worked for the Flying U when it was strictly a bachelor outfit, and . . . he held . . . his beloved 'Old Man,' as but a degree lower than that mysterious power which made the sun to shine.

c. The master of a ship. {1865}

1840 DANA *Two Years* xxxi. 374 The 'old man' did not mean to be frightened in broad daylight, and was determined to carry sail till the last minute. **1872** EGGLESTON *End of World* xxvi. 179 There is only one 'old man' on a steamboat. **1895** CHAMBLISS *Diary* 334 The captain of a ship is always referred to by the rest of the ship's company as 'the old man.'

+d. Any old man. Used as a substitute for 'Old Mr. —.'

1843 'CARLTON' *New Purchase* I. 92 It ain't more nor a mile to ole-man Sturgisses. **1873** 'MARK TWAIN' & WARNER xl. 359 Old man Bolton's behind him. **1902** MCFAUL *Ike Glidden* 126 There is old man Spencer who had always been poor. **1914** ATHERTON *Perch of Devil* 1 'Old Man Compton' . . . had been . . . a hayseed.

+e. A middle-aged Negro: (see quotation).

1856 OLMSTED *Slave States* 207 'Well, now, old man,' said I, 'you go and cut me two cords to-day.' 'Oh, Marsa! two cords! Nobody couldn do dat.' *Ib. note*, 'Old Man' is a common title of address to any middle-aged negro in Virginia, whose name is not known. 'Boy' and 'Old Man' may be applied to the same person.

+f. Among the Indians, a wise man or seer.

1903 WHITE *Forest* 208 Certain individuals gain a remarkable . . . respect for wisdom, or hunting skill. . . . These men are the so-called 'old-men' often mentioned in Indian manifestoes.

2. The southernwood, *Artemisia abrotanum.* {1824-}

1839 *S. Lit. Messenger* V. 751/2 Bachelor's hat with southern wood or old man, were conspicuous embellishments to almost every parterre. **1853** HANDSAKER *Pioneer Life* (1908) 58 Here [in the vicinity of Wyo.] may be seen acres of that beautiful shrub, old man. **1898** DELAND *Old Chester Tales* 90 Here and there [one sees] a low bush of old-man, or musk, or clove-pink.

+3. A grizzly bear. *colloq.*

1886 *Outing* IX. 108/1 You've got more sand than I thought you had to tackle the old man on the open plain.

Old man eloquent. {c1645} +A sobriquet for John Quincy Adams (1767-1848). — **1848** *Congress. Globe* 24 Feb. 388/3 Let not the grave of the old man eloquent be desecrated by unfriendly remembrances. **1900** *Congress. Rec.* 25 Jan. 1208/1 John Quincy Adams, the 'Old Man Eloquent,' expressed very happily what we now . . . believe.

Old man's beard. **1.** The Spanish moss. **+2.** =FRINGE TREE. **+3.** The black gum, *Nyssa silvatica.* — **(1)** [1756 P. BROWNE *Jamaica* 193 Old-Man's-Beard . . . is frequently imported from North America for the use of sadlers and coachmakers.] **1836** LINCOLN *Botany* App. 144 *Tillandsia usneoides*. . . . Parasitic. From its peculiar appearance, suspended from trees to which it has fastened itself, it is called *old man's beard.* **1877** BARTLETT 790 *Old Man's Beard*, a moss hanging from the boughs of most trees in Louisiana and Texas. **(2)** **1855** SIMMS *Forayers* 485 Don't forget the 'wake robbin,' and the 'old man's beard,' the leafy green look of the one, and the snow-white fringes of the other. **1884** SARGENT *Rep. Forests* 113 *Chionanthus Virginica*. . . . Fringe Tree. Old Man's Beard. **1901** MOHR *Plant Life Ala.* 668 Fringe tree. Old Man's Beard. . . . New Jersey, . . . south to Florida and Texas. **(3)** **1894** *Amer. Folk-Lore* VII. 90 *Nyssa sylvatica*, old man's beard, Lincolnton, N.C.

+Old Mexico. Mexico. So called in contrast to New Mexico. — **1863** *Rio Abajo Press* 28 April 1/3 Those whose business called them to Old Mexico were often obliged to camp out. **1882** *47th Congress 1 Sess.* H.R. Ex. Doc. No. 216, 328 As many of those engaged in the gulch diggings . . . were Mexicans, a considerable portion of [gold] . . . found its way into old Mexico. **1890** *Stock Grower & Farmer* 11 Jan. 6/2 The sign riders cut the trail, going in the direction of Old Mexico.

+Old Molly. A common sea duck, the old squaw, *Clangula hyemalis.* — **1841** *S. Lit. Messenger* VII. 220/1 An old molly has her nest in the inside. **1917** [see OLD *a.* 5].

+Old money. =OLD TENOR. — **1780** *Va. State P.* I. 377 Fix my pay on the first footing of ten shillings old money, or fifty pounds of Tobacco pr: day.

+Old Ned. *S.* [See quot. 1869.] Salt bacon.

1833 J. E. ALEXANDER *Transatlantic Sk.* II. 83 A snow-white cloth was spread, on which were placed bacon, or 'Old Ned,' as it is called in Tennessee. **1857** STACEY *Journal* 83 We have mutton every day instead of 'Old Ned,' in other words, salt bacon. **1869** *Overland Mo.* Aug. 129 Southern smoke-cured pork, in distinction from the Northern salted article, in allusion to the famous negro song, was termed *'Old Ned,'* from its sable appearance. **1872** POWERS *Afoot & Alone* 122 We squatted on the grass around the biscuits and the rashers of 'Old Ned.'

+Old North State. North Carolina. Also attrib. and transf.

?**1845** in Bartlett (ed. 4) 438 W. A. Graham . . . will be elected governor by the largest majority ever before given . . . in the Old North State. **1861** JACKSON in M. A. Jackson *Gen. Jackson* 192 Whose dear face I can still see, though she is 'way down in the Old North State. **1872** POWERS *Afoot & Alone* 31 The Old North State is not in repute for hospitality. **1884** BLAINE *20 Years of Congress* I. 90 Willie P. Mangum . . . represented the steadfast Union sentiment of the 'Old North State' Whigs. **1893** *Harper's Mag.* Feb. 445 The Asheville hotel bore the name 'The Old North State,' the loving title given by native North Carolinians to their commonwealth.

Old one. The devil. *Obs.* — **1787** TYLER *Contrast* v. ii, Is the old one in you? **1825** NEAL *Bro. Jonathan* I. 253 His Master . . . the Old One. **1859** MATSELL *Vocabulum* 61.

+Old orchard. Cider. *Obs.* — **1810** *Farmer's Alm.* (Boston) Sept., Come, ye lovers of Old Orchard, let us take a walk into the fields. . . . O, this is a pleasant month not only to cider drinkers, but to all. **1844** *Lowell Offering* IV. 68 Tea, coffee and 'old orchard' served to wash down the good things. **1851** *Knickerb.* XXXVII. 557 One of them . . . was quite importunate in his demands for 'old orchard.'

+Old planter. One of the earliest settlers of a colony, esp. in New England: (see quot. 1871).

1624 *Va. House of Burgesses* 34 We, the old Planters, relieved them. **1635** *Essex Inst. Coll.* IV. 93/1 That place where the old planters do move from. **1640** *Mass. H. S. Coll.* 4 Ser. VI. 144, I shall . . . call the old planters together assoone as convenientlie I can. **1871** DE VERE 165 In New England the first settlers were known as *planters*, and distinguished select families as *Old Planters*.

+Old Probabilities. *pl.* (See quot. 1877.) Also fig.—**1874** *Congress. Rec.* 1 April 2679/1 A certain politician . . . seemed to have a political 'Old Probabilities' who foretold for him the political atmosphere. **1877** BARTLETT 496 *Old Probabilities*, a term applied to the superintendent of the bureau at Washington, from which the weather reports are issued. **1888** *N.Y. Herald* 4 Nov. 8/4 As a rule Old Probabilities has been rather kindly disposed to both parties and has vouchsafed tolerable marching weather . . . [for both] republicans and democrats.

Old river. ?The former bed of a river which has cut itself a new channel. — **1694** *Derby Rec.* 171 The Land which Thomas woster has Reserved . . . is bounded . . . west with the old River & East with the new River. **1787** in *Amer. Speech* XV. 291/1 Beginning at the Roaring hole on the Old River. **1825** *Ib.*, To two sycamores at the mouth of the Old River.

Old Roman. +A sobriquet for Andrew Jackson (1767-1845). — **1839** *Congress. Globe* App. 22 Feb. 371 Often has he [Andrew Jackson] been styled the Old Roman, upon this floor and elsewhere. **1846** F. WYSE *America* I. 87 To administer to the vanity, and appease the wounded pride of the 'old Roman,' as President Jackson was familiarly termed.

+Old rye. Whiskey made from rye. — **1835** INGRAHAM *South-West* II. 56 The painful effects of 'old rye' in the abstract upon the body. **1848** BURTON *Waggeries* 64 The boss has cooled off a bit. . . . Hand us over the old rye. **1890** *Buckskin Mose* xvii. 243 He continued, lifting the Old Rye to his lips, 'here's long life to you.'

Old Sam. +The devil. *Obs.* — **1834** CARRUTHERS *Kentuckian* I. 60 I believe I was in Old Sam's hands last night. **1840** *Knickerb.* XVI. 185 Some darnation accident has played Old Sam with the saw-mill!

Old school. {1798- (*Monthly Mag.* Feb. 127)}

+1. In Pennsylvania, a third party of conservative Democrats. Now hist. (Cf. OLD-SCHOOL MAN.)

1817 *Niles' Reg.* XII. 16 At the late election for state treasurer [of Penna.] the joint ballot of the legislature stood thus—for . . . James Brady, 'fed.' 20; James Whitehill, 'old-school,' 10.

+2. A church group adhering to a traditional interpretation of doctrine.

Cf. OLD SCHOOL BAPTIST, OLD SCHOOL PRESBYTERIAN.

1842 BUCKINGHAM *Slave States* II. 269 The late schism, which has divided them [Presbyterians] into Old School and New School, the former being rigid Calvinists, and the latter inclining to Arminianism. **1849** CHAMBERLAIN *Ind. Gazetteer* 62 This institution [New Albany Theol. Seminary] is under the care of seven Synods of the Presbyterian Church,

(Old School). **1853** STOWE *Key* 212/1 We cannot hold our churches in the union; they will divide, and go to the Old School. **1900** *Congress. Rec.* 17 Jan. 916/2 The old hard-shell Presbyterian of the old school took occasion in his remarks . . . to say that the Lord had ordered everything.

3. *attrib.* or *adj.* +**a.** In sense 1 with *democrat, democratic candidate.*

1815 *Niles' Reg.* IX. 120/2 The federal and 'old school' democratic candidate for Congress, . . . has been elected. **1816** *Ib.* XI. 108 The highest federal vote in the city and county of Philadelphia was, 4449. . . . 'Old school' democrats, 2595.

+**b.** In sense 2 with *assembly, branch.*

1853 *Harper's Mag.* VII. 266/1 The General Assembly of the 'Old School' branch of the Presbyterian Church held its annual session at Philadelphia. **1853** STOWE *Key* 211/1 The course of the Old-School Assembly after the separation, in relation to the subject of slavery, may be best expressed by quoting one of their resolutions.

+**Old School Baptist.** An extremely Calvinistic branch of the Baptist church, dating from about 1835. (Cf. HARD-SHELL BAPTIST.) — **1867** DIXON *New America* II. 308 In a very short time this body was divided into Old School Baptists (called by their enemies Anti-effort Baptists), Sabbatarians [etc.]. **1873** 'MARK TWAIN' & WARNER *Gilded Age* vii. 80 Grandmother . . . was an Old-School Baptist. **1878** BEADLE *Western Wilds* 183 The Old School Baptisses never went nigh the Methodis' meetin' house.

+**Old-school man.** (See quot. 1818.) Now hist. — **1818** FEARON *Sketches* 139 The moderate democrats, [are] called by the several names of 'Independent Republicans,' 'Democrats of the Revolution,' and 'Old Schoolmen.' **1819** *Niles' Reg.* XVII. 224/1 The senate of this state [Penna.] is composed of 23 republicans, 6 federalists, and 2 'old school' men. **1835** H. C. TODD *Notes* 34 The names of their political parties are *Patent Democrats, Old Schoolmen, Hartford Conventionalists,* and *Blue-light Men.*

+**Old School Presbyterian,** *n.* and *a.* **1.** *n.* A conservative Presbyterian opposed to the views of the New School Presbyterian (q.v.). **2.** *adj.* Adhering to the opinions of such a Presbyterian. — **(1) 1837** PECK *Gaz. Illinois* 72 McDonough College . . . is identified with the interests of the 'old school' Presbyterians. **(2) 1847** H. HOWE *Hist. Coll. Ohio* 274 The first church, the old school Presbyterian, . . . was built about 1817. **1898** HARPER *S. B. Anthony* I. 218, I recommend that you form an acquaintance . . . with some well-settled Old-School-Presbyterian clergyman.

+**Old settler.**

1. One of the first or earliest settlers in a community; a first settler.

1838 *S. Lit. Messenger* IV. 294 How powerful a motive with an old settler and locator of land-warrants, is the hope of securing a title. **1847** *Santa Fe Republican* 4 Dec. 3/1 Gen. Taylor was stationed here [Fort Crawford] for several years, from '31 to '38, and I have made many inquiries of the old settlers here in relation to him. **1860** BUCHANAN in *Pres. Mess. & P.* V. 611 The 'old settlers' . . . are public benefactors. This class have all paid for their lands the Government price, or $1.25 per acre. They have constructed roads, established schools, and laid the foundation of prosperous commonwealths. **1873** *Winfield* (Kansas) *Courier* 27 May 2/3 Mr. and Mrs. Kellogg . . . will long be remembered by the old settlers of Arkansas City, and Winfield.

2. A member of that part of the Cherokee nation that settled west of the Mississippi prior to 1819.

1839 *26th Congress 1 Sess.* H. R. Ex. Doc. No. 129, 15 The President of the United States, and many of the principal men of the old settlers, do not recognise this as the settled government of the Cherokee Nation. **1843** TYLER in *Pres. Mess. & P.* IV. 225 A memorial from the Old Settlers, or Western Cherokees, . . . recently presented, is not transmitted. **1846** POLK *Diary* (1929) 138 About one o'clock the Cherokee chiefs, including those of the Ross Party, the Treaty party, and the Old Settlers, called in a body to take leave of me.

+**Old-side Baptist.** =OLD SCHOOL BAPTIST. — **1847** POLK *Diary* III. 25 They were from several States of the Union, and belonged to . . . the old side-Baptists as they are sometimes called. **1862** in F. Moore *Rebellion Rec.* V. II. 20 At the Cheesecoke Church, an antiquated building used by the 'Oldside Baptists,' erected in colonial times, . . . the divisions parted.

+**Old-sided Baptist.** =prec. — **1858** *Harper's Mag.* May 853/1, I profess to be, what is vulgarly called, an 'old sided Baptist,' and have been for a number of years.

+**Old sledge.** All-fours or seven-up. — **1834** NOTT *Novellettes* I. 40 They could indulge in three up, old sledge, whist, or loo. *a***1846** *Quarter Race Ky.* 83 He hates a circuit rider, . . . loves a woman, old sledge, and sin in eny shape. **1857** STROTHER *Virginia* 45 In the centre was the eternal party at 'old sledge.' **1888** *Congress. Rec.* 6 Aug. 7263/2 A fellow in my country [N.C.] was caught once with an extra jack in his sleeve when playing a game of old sledge.

***Old soldier.**

+**1.** A soldier who has served in one of the early American wars. Also collect. and attrib.

1787 R. TYLER *Contrast* 81, I came hither to solicit . . . that a number of my brave old soldiers may be put upon the pension-list. **1815** *Niles' Reg.* VII. 381 [Many] old soldiers who now hold commissions in the army of the United States . . . entered the revolutionary army as privates. **1852** GOUGE *Fiscal Hist. Texas* 166 Nothing the Legislature could do . . . would afford any relief to the old soldiers. **1885** *Santa Fé Wkly. New Mexican* 10 Dec. 1/3 Evidently the smut machines that have concentrated their mud-slinging at the senator don't have much weight with the old soldier element. **1898** *Kansas City Star* 18 Dec. 4/3 Governor-elect Stanley [of Kans.] . . . will give the places that come within his patronage to old soldiers. **1900** *Congress. Rec.* 9 Feb. 1676/1 Over $2,400,000,000 have been paid to the old soldier, and the increase still goes on. **1923** *World's Work* XLV. 467/1 Young women . . . have haunted these institutions [old soldiers' homes], seeking to wheedle old soldiers into matrimony.

+**2.** (See quotation.)

1835 J. HALL *Sk. of West* II. 141 The appellation of *old soldier,* was always associated with the idea of a hard drinking man.

+**3.** The end of a used cigarette or cigar, or a quid of used tobacco.

1845 GREEN *Texian Exped.* 272 The most usual bet was an old soldier. **1867** 'MARK TWAIN' *Amer. Drolleries* 41 Killikinick . . . is composed of equal parts of tobacco stems, chopped straw, 'old soldiers,' . . . and any refuse . . . that costs nothing and will burn. **1869** — *Sk., New & Old* 45 There was a wooden box of sand, sprinkled with cigar stubs and 'old soldiers.' *a***1877** in Bartlett 438 Ladies who swab our sidewalks, . . . And . . . Haul off old soldiers lying there at rest.

+**Old South.** (See quot. 1889.) — **1888** *Miss. Valley Lumberman* May (F.), The people [of Grenada, Miss.] . . . have enough of the hospitality and friendliness of the Old South to make their town a haven of rest to the visitor. **1889** FARMER 400 *Old South,* . . . the South before the war, and previous to the enfranchisement of the negro. **1925** in Bassett *Plantation Overseer* 169 It is to be explained only by recalling the utter lack of a sense of inferiority in the poorer whites of the Old South.

+**Old squaw.** A common sea duck of the Northern Hemisphere, *Clangula hyemalis.* — **1844** *Nat. Hist. N.Y., Zoology* II. 329 The Old-wife, or Old-squaw, is one of the most common and least valued of the genus. They appear on our coast in the autumn. **1870** *Amer. Naturalist* IV. 49 The same kind of food that our Coot and Old Squaw live on. **1892** TORREY *Foot-Path Way* 41 The cliffs . . . offer an excellent position from which to sweep the bay in search of loons, old-squaws, and other sea-fowl.

Old state. +*pl.* States for some time a part of the Union as distinguished from a state or states recently admitted. — **1790** R. PUTNAM in *Memoirs* 237 The intrest of the old States and theirs . . . is inconsistent with each other. **1839** PLUMBE *Sk. Iowa* 70 Farmers of Pennsylvania and elsewhere, in the old States read this. *a***1861** WINTHROP *J. Brent* 14 He was an American horse,—so they distinguish in California one brought from the old States. **1898** CANFIELD *Maid of Frontier* 29 He owed me a grudge back in the old states.

+**Old state line.** In west Tennessee, a line north of lat. 35° supposed until 1832 to be Tennessee's southern boundary. — **1862** in F. Moore *Rebellion Rec.* V. II. 271 The same division . . . moved forward about two miles and a half, in the direction of Corinth, to the crossing of the 'Old State Line' with the 'Purdy and Farmington road.'

+**Old tenor.** In the colonies, esp. in Massachusetts, a form of paper currency issued before the issuance of other paper currency intended to be of more stable value. (Cf. NEW TENOR quot. 1891). Now hist.

1738 *Boston Rec.* 201 We enjoin you . . . That the Funds be laid in Paper Bills of the Old Tenor, and not in Bills of the New Tenor. **1743** *Suffield Doc. Hist.* 290 Voted to allow Mr. Abraham Burbank . . . Nine pounds Two shillings and Four pence Old Tenor for so much Remaining Due to him. **1751** ELIOT *Field-Husb.* iii. 55 There are so many Oyl Mills in this Government [New England], . . . the whole Number Amounts to the Sum of Ten Thousand Pounds, Old Tenor. **1753** *Essex Inst. Coll.* XXI. 153 Voted the Parish Rate to be this year 460=00=00 old tenner. **1763** *Holyoke Diaries* 60 Paid Sarah Cloutman 40/ Old Tenor for muff. **1776** M'ROBERT *Tour* 23 They have [in New York] two denominations of currency, *viz.* Old tenor, and lawful money. Old tenor is of very small value.

+**Old Thirteen.** The original thirteen states of the Union. — **1845** *S. Lit. Messenger* XI. 584/2 Charleston . . . [was] the chief commercial city of the 'Old Thirteen.' **1856** *Democratic Conv. Proc.* 50 As Pennsylvanians, the representatives on this floor of a State, which . . . is inferior to none in the Union—one of the 'Old Thirteen'—[we] are proud [etc.]. **1894** *Harper's Mag.* July 290/1 The Fourth of July was celebrated . . . when a salute of thirteen guns was fired in honor of the 'Old Thirteen.'

Old-time, *a.* Belonging to, in the tradition of, or characteristic of a former time; of long standing. {old-times, *a*1824–; 1888–}

1865 *Atlantic Mo.* XV. 146/1 Their gambrel-roofed houses [were] odorous with traditions of old-time visits by some worthies of the Colonial period, or of the Revolution. **1877** BAGBY *Old Va. Gentleman* 12 There was . . . a fine old-time staircase leading to the guest-chambers. **1887** PERRY *Flock of Girls* 144 You are regarding a young girl . . . decked out for some fancy dress-party in this old-time dress. **1893** *Harper's Mag.* May 974/1 He was an 'old-time darky,' and to this owed his position. **1899** *Amer. Missionary* Nov. 391 The . . . hysterical old time religion among the negroes. **1911** *Sears, Roebuck & Co. Cat.* No. 123, 628 This Round Drop Leaf Extension Table is an old time favorite. **1922** *Commoner* Feb. 11/3 [Bryan] launched into a glowing tribute of the farm bloc in congress—its work as compared to the 'old-time Wall Street bloc.'

+Old-timer.

1. A person who has been in a place or position for a long time; an experienced person.

1866 *New Princeton Rev.* V. 122 Most of us old timers . . . are poor now. **1879** *Cimarron News & Press* 20 Nov. 3/2 A tenderfoot can sling his heels higher at a baile than the average old timer. **1887** *Courier-Journal* 25 Jan. 2/4 Senator McClure is an old-timer. He has been a member of the Senate or House almost continuously for the past forty years. **1891** *Atlantic Mo.* June 815/2 In religion the 'old-timer' is giving way to the educated preacher. **1901** WHITE *Westerners* 146, I was an old timer when the first house was built. **1912** NICHOLSON *Hoosier Chron.* 319, I don't want these fellows who are old-timers in state conventions. **1920** C. R. COOPER *Under Big Top* 229, I'm an old-timer on this line, and I've seen it go to pieces mile by mile.

2. Anything that has been around for a long time.

1894 *Outing* XXIV 34/1 A cutter of some six to eight tons . . . , a regular old-timer, built in the days when the cod's head and mackerel tail model embodied the highest ideas of yacht architecture.

+Old-timey, *a.* Characteristic of old times. — **1850** A. J. DOWNING in *Horticulturist* V. 265 The terraced garden, too, is quaint and 'old-timey.' **1879** STOCKTON *Rudder Grange* xvii. 206 Things that were apparently so 'old-timey' . . . that David Dutton did not care to take them with him. **1887** *Courier-Journal* 8 May 19/8 We are old-timey people, too.

Old town. +**1.** 'A tract of clear land formerly the site of an Indian village' (*Amer. Sp.* XV. 291). +**2.** In towns formerly Spanish or French: The old section of town as distinguished from the American-built section. — (1) [**1635** in *Amer. Speech* XV. 291/1 Beginning on Wly. side of an old Indian Towne.] **1699** *Va. State P.* I. 65 The English intend to take up land and seat upon a place—called then old Town. **1707** *Virginia Mag. Hist. & Biog.* V. 48 The Waynoak Indians . . . settled upon the South side of the Black Water Swamp, at a place now called the old town. (2) **1880** *Cimarron News & Press* 15 April 2/4 Starbird, an enterprising young hackman, was driving along from the new to the old town. **1883** *Century Mag.* June 230/1 However, the suburban lands [in New Orleans] were sold, old town and down-town property was sinking in value. **1885** *Wkly. New Mexican Rev.* 9 April 3/3 Albuquerque . . . has an old town like nearly all of the New Mexico cities.

+Old Virginia. A term applied to Virginia, esp. the eastern portion of it. Also ellipt., Virginian tobacco. — **1624** SMITH *Gen. Hist. Va.* A 3 A Map of the old Virginia, with the figures of the Salvages. **1817** ROYALL *Letters from Ala.* (1830) 21 Foreigners often distinguish it [eastern and western Virginia] by the terms Old Virginia and New Virginia. **1850** GARRARD *Wah-to-Yah* xiii. 169 We reclined on out-spread saddle blankets, . . . thoughtfully puffing 'Old Virginia,' from time-worn clay pipes. **1894** 'MARK TWAIN' *P. Wilson* xii, In Missouri a recognized superiority attached to any person who hailed from Old Virginia.

+Old Virginia breakdown. A kind of rollicking rustic dance.— **1867** J. L. PEYTON *Adv. Grandfather* 170 Graceful minuets, Scotch reels or as they are sometimes called 'Old Virginia break downs,' were the order of the night.

+Old Virginian. A Virginian of older times. — **1800** TATHAM *Agric. & Com.* 87 The inhabitants [of certain Spanish colonies] . . . partake . . . of the habits of that ancient order of happy and liberal people the *old Virginians.* **1893** PAGE in *Harper's Mag.* Dec. 10/2 [In Richmond] met, year after year, the old Virginians, . . . to enjoy the gay life of the capital of the Old Dominion.

+Old Whig. A member of the Whig party opposed to Henry Clay's leadership; a strict constructionist Whig. — **1835** C. P. BRADLEY *I. Hill* 166 It is said the old Whigs are most averse to a reform. **1856** *Democratic Conv. Proc.* 68, I am proud to avow that I belong to those old Whigs who, revering the Constitution of our country, look alone to its principles as the true safeguard of the Union. **1900** *Miss. Hist. Soc. Publ.* III. 78 A tabular view of the [Mississippi constitutional] convention [1868] . . . shows that it [included] . . . 2 Henry Clay Whigs, 4 Old Whigs.

***Old wife.**

1. Any of several fishes as the alewife, menhaden, fall herring, etc.

1588 HARRIOT *Briefe Rep. Va.* D 3 There are also Troutes: Porpoises: Rayes: Oldwiues: Mullets: Plaice. **1671** *S.C. Hist. Soc. Coll.* V. 336 Fish there are in both riuers multitudes, As Bass, mullets, Old Wiffes; &c. **1705** BEVERLEY *Virginia* II. 31 The Old-Wife, a Fish not much unlike an Herring. **1709** LAWSON *Carolina* 160 Old-Wives . . . are a bright, scaly Fish, which frequent the Swamps, and fresh Runs. **1805** LEWIS in *L. & Clark Exped.* II. (1904) 143 The other species is precisely the form and about the size of the well known fish called the *Hickary Shad* or *old wife.* **1911** *Rep. Fisheries 1908* 314 Other species [of pompano] found on our eastern coast are the 'old-wife,' . . . the 'round pompano,' or 'Indian River permit.'

+2. =OLD SQUAW.

1634 WOOD *New Eng. Prospect* (1865) 34 The Oldwives be a foule that never leave tatling day or night, something bigger than a Ducke. **1709** LAWSON *Carolina* 147 Old Wives are a black and white pied Gull with extraordinary long Wings, and a golden colour'd Bill. **1794** *Mass. H. S. Coll.* 1 Ser. III. 199 Sea fowl are plenty on the shores and in the bay; particularly the . . . sea duck, old wife, . . . widgeon, and peep. **1813** WILSON *Ornithology* VIII. 93 Long-Tailed Duck. . . . On the coast of New Jersey they are usually called *Old Wives.* **1856** *Porter's Spirit of Times* Dec. 242/2 The noisy, long-tailed ducks, old-wives or south-southerlies . . . are none of them worth the powder and shot that kills them. **1883** THAXTER *Poems For Children* 8 The old-wives sit on the heaving brine, White-breasted in the sun. **1917** *Birds of Amer.* I. 141 Old-Squaw. . . . [Also called] Old Wife.

+Old witch grass. The common panic grass, *Panicum capillare.* — **1847** DARLINGTON *Weeds & Plants* 403 Old-witch grass. . . . Sandy pastures, cultivated grounds: throughout the United States. **1863** *Ill. Agric. Soc. Trans.* V. 867 Old Witch-grass, is found in sandy pastures. **1878** in Killebrew *Tenn. Grasses* 220 Old Witch Grass. . . . Cattle will not touch it. **1894** COULTER *Bot. W. Texas* III. 508 Old witch grass. . . . Annual. . . . In cultivated land everywhere.

***Old woman.** A wife. *colloq.* or *vulgar.* {1859–, *dial.*}

*c***1775** BOUCHER *Glossary* p. l, Could my *old woman,* whilst I labour'd thus At night reward me with a *smouch,* or buss. **1834** W. G. SIMMS *Guy Rivers* I. 68 There's not one of my neighbors . . . that can't tell all about the rotten prints he put off upon my old woman. **1851** J. J. HOOPER *Widow Rugby* 43 Mr. Wallis and his 'old woman' were from home when we got there. **1884** SWEET & KNOX *Through Texas* 97 The old woman is down with the chills.

transf. **1886** *Outing* IX. 104/2, I heerd a cracklin', an' . . . 'long come the old woman with a cub follerin' behind.

+Old woman's smock. (See quotation.) — **1789** ANBUREY *Travels* II. 451 The leaves [of the tulip tree] grow in a very peculiar shape; from whence the tree has, in some places, the appellation of the old woman's smock.

Old world. {1712–} The Eastern Hemisphere, esp. Europe.

1789 MORSE *Amer. Geog.* 55 Beasts of different genus from any known in the old world; of which are the opossum, the racoon [etc.]. **1856** *Democratic Conv. Proc.* 26 In the view of the condition of popular institutions in the Old World . . . a high and sacred duty is devolved . . . upon the Democratic party [etc.]. **1883** *Century Mag.* Sept. 689/2 The Old World has left many of its once imperial centers literally buried in the track of its westward-moving vortex.

b. Attrib. with *custom, folk, man, origin.*

1844 *Knickerb.* XXIII. 181 We profess to have lopped from our democratic tree the old-world customs of hereditary title and patrimonial honor. **1860** HOLMES *Professor* (1902) 50 If he were a superior fellow . . . I think I would let out the fact of the real American feeling about Old-World folks. **1862** LOWELL *Biglow P.* 2 Ser. ii. 68 Thou, skilled by Freedom an' by gret events To pitch new States ez Old-World men pitch tents. **1880** *Scribner's Mo.* May 101/1 Of Old World origin, too is the curled leaf-dock . . . that is so annoying about one's garden.

+Old Zack. A nickname for General Zachary Taylor (1784–1850), twelfth president of the United States. — **1847** *Santa Fe Republican* 18 Dec. 2/2 Old Zack and the U.S. Volunteers—Their names speak volumes. **1848** LOWELL *Biglow P.* 1 Ser. 125 So I edvise the noomrous friends . . . [to] make fer the safest port they can, wich, *I* think, is Ole Zack.

***Oleander. a.** A plant of the East Indies (*Nerium oleander*), cultivated for its handsome red and white flowers. **b.** Any plant of the genus *Nerium.* Also attrib.

1845 *S. Lit. Messenger* XI. 182/1 The solid comforts of the hot-house and grapery would pay for the geraniums, oleanders and camelias. **1853** 'PAXTON' *Yankee in Texas* 232 Great numbers of flowering plants . . . grow to a large size . . . such as the various kinds of jessamine, the tube rose, the oleander. **1865** *Nation* I. 682 Beaufort is a quiet town, with . . . abundance of orange trees, and oleanders, and pomegranates. **1890** WIGGIN *Timothy's Quest* 114 She's . . . got enough [shells] left for a pile in one corner, where she's goin' to set her oleander kag. **1912** N. M. WOODROW *Sally Salt* 85 He stood, tall and sedate, awaiting her between two great tubs of blooming oleander.

Oleo. [Abbreviation of OLEOMARGARINE.] Oleomargarine. {1884–} — **1886** *Stat. at Large* XXIV. 209 Certain manufactured substances . . . shall be known . . . as 'oleomargarine,' namely: All substances heretofore known as oleomargarine, oleo [etc.]. **1890** *Stock Grower & Farmer* 15 March 4/2 If farmers would join in the demand for a removal of the oleo tax, . . . that would help. **1898** *Kansas City Star* 18 Dec. 10/6, 3 lbs. Oleo . . . 25¢. **1923** [see OLEOMARGARINE].

Oleomargarine. {1882–} A mixture of oleo oil, neutral lard, etc., churned with milk to make a substance like butter; artificial butter. {=margarine} Also attrib.

1873 *Scientific Amer.* 18 Oct. 246 Description of the manufacture of artificial butter by the 'Oleomargarine Manufacturing Company.' *a***1877** [see BUTTERMAKER]. **1883** *Gringo & Greaser* 1 Dec. 2/1 It is butter all the same, and none of your dog-on butterine or oleymargerine. **1892** *Penna. Dept. Agric. Rep.* 121 In many tests made I have never observed a normal butter to behave as oleomargarine. **1900** *Congress. Rec.* 3 Jan. 628/1 Mr. Allen presented a petition of the Nebraska Dairymen's Association . . . praying for the enactment of legislation taxing all oleomargarine colored in semblance to butter. **1923** *Treasury Dept. Bul.* No. 9 24 Oleo, oleomargarine-oil, . . . and all mixtures and compounds of tallow, beef-fat, [etc., are] . . . taxable as oleomargarine.

+Oleo oil. An oil expressed from animal fat and often used in making oleomargarine {1893–, rare; usu. called *oleomargarine*} — **1882** *Missouri Rep.* LXXVII. 114 The proper butterfat is separated by a scientific process from the natural fat into oleo oil, which . . . is churned into butter. **1902** LORIMER *Lett. Merchant* 7 Does it pay to take a steer . . . and feed him corn till he's just a solid hunk of porterhouse steak and oleo oil? **1906** E. H. RICHARDS *Food Materials* 58 Oleomargarine and butterine are prepared in a similar manner from oleo oil (beef fat) or neutral lard and milk by churning and salting and coloring to imitate butter.

Olio. {a1643–} **a.** A musical performance in which a miscellaneous collection of pieces is given. Also attrib. +**b.** The vaudeville part of a minstrel show; a variety show. Also attrib.

1809 S. BRECK in *Recoll.* (1877) 271 We . . . rode round to Mr. Brent's, . . . with whose family we took tea, and afterward accompanied them to an olio concert. **1840** *Picayune* 18 Sept. 3/2 The evening's entertainments will commence with the farce of the Irish Tutor. . . . After which—A Musical Olio. **1856** C. WHITE *Oh, Hush!* (t.p.), An Operatic Olio, In One Act, and Three Scenes. **1870** *N.Y. Herald* 13 Oct. 9/6 (*advt.*), Great success of the new olio and burlesque. All the great star company appear. **1887** *Courier-Journal* 19 Feb. 8/1 In the olio Frank McNish did his inimitable 'Silence and Fun' as well as usual. **1895** *N.Y. Dramatic News* 23 Nov. 4/4 Ida Siddons in her snake dance, two Italian pantomimists and the breathing paintings stood out in the olio like warts on a fat man's face. **1898** *Boston Transcript* 29 Aug. 5/7 Wm. H. West's Big Minstrel Jubilee Grand Array of Vocalists and Olio Artists.

***Olive.**

***1.** The oval fruit of the tree *Olea europaea.*

1711 *Boston News-Letter* 12 March 2/2 Luke Olives, Currants, Raisins of the Sun and Smirna, Good Cinnamon, . . . To be Sold by Zabdiel Boylston. **1720** *Amer. Wkly. Mercury* 28 April 3/2 Very Good Olives and Capers, to be sold by David Evans. **1790** *Columbian Centinel* 29 Sept. 19/3 [For sale,] Fresh jar Olives, Lemons, Sweet Oil [etc.]. **1868** *Rep. Comm. Agric. 1867* p. x, Florida is destined to be a winter garden, yielding . . . oranges, figs, and olives, and other fruits of sub-tropical climes. **1883** *Century Mag.* Oct. 819 The olives are first dried in trays with slat bottoms. **1907** 'O. HENRY' *Roads of Destiny* 343 He got along fine with the olives and celery and the bluepoints.

***2.** The tree that produces this fruit.

1816 W. DARBY *Geogr. Desc. La.* 150 That the olive has never yet been brought into general use in southern Louisiana, excites astonishment. **1833** SILLIMAN *Man. Sugar Cane* 17 Olives [have been obtained] which sustain a severer cold than those of France. **1849** WIERZBICKI *California* 11 The olive, the currant, the gooseberry and various other berries are found here. **1855** *N.Y. Amer. Inst. Trans.* 624 In 1769, the olive was introduced into Florida, by a colony of Greeks and Minorcans, . . . who founded a settlement called 'New Smyrna.' **1883** *Century Mag.* Oct. 819/2 California has as much land suited to the olive as Italy has.

3. *attrib.* and *comb.* **a.** With *cultivator, farm,* etc.

See also OLIVE TREE.

1883 *Century Mag.* Aug. 555/2 At a late meeting of the State Horticultural Society in San Francisco, it was stated that one olive farm yielded $2200 to the acre. **1883** *Ib.* Oct. 819/2 The leading industry of this ranch is to be the making of olive oil. **1889** *Rep. Secy. Agric. Rep.* 197 One of the leading olive cultivators of California . . . [says that] the olive oil of the United States is sold to dealers in its original purity. **1893** SANBORN *S. Calif.* 155 Pomona is the head-quarters of the olive industry.

b. In the specific names of birds.

See also OLIVE BACK, OLIVE-BACKED THRUSH, OLIVE-SIDED *a.*

1917 *Birds of Amer.* III. 159 Maryland Yellow-Throat. . . . Other Names.—Olive-colored Yellow-throated Wren. **1827** WILLIAMS *West Florida* 30 Little Olive do. [*sc.* flycatcher]. **1904** WHITE *Silent Places* 4 The white-throats and olive thrushes called in a language hardly less intelligible. **1917** *Birds of Amer.* III. 123 Olive Warbler. . . . Fore parts, orange; upper parts, olive-green and gray.

+**Olive back.** =next. — **1845** JUDD *Margaret* I. 148 The olive-backs trolled and chanted among the trees. **1892** TORREY *Foot-Path Way* 19 The moment the road entered the ancient forest [on Mt. Lafayette], the olive backs began to make themselves heard. **1917** *Birds of Amer.* III. 233 The food of the Olive-back is similar to that of other small Thrushes.

+**Olive-backed thrush.** A common thrush (*Hylocichla ustulata swainsoni*) having a back of olive-brown color. — **1844** *Nat. Hist. N.Y., Zoology* II. 74 The Olive-Backed Thrush is closely allied to the [hermit thrush]. **1870** *Amer. Naturalist* IV. 541 The Olive-backed Thrush . . . makes its appearance in May. **1892** TORREY *Foot-Path Way* 99 Two birds dashed by me—a blackpoll warbler in hot pursuit of an olive-backed thrush. **1917** *Birds of Amer.* III. 232 Olive-Backed Thrush. . . . Upper parts, olive-brown.

+**Olive-sided,** *a.* In the specific names of birds: (see quotations). — **1839** AUDUBON *Ornith. Biog.* V. 422 Olive-Sided Flycatcher, *Mus[c]icapa Cooperi,* . . . has never been observed in South Carolina, although I met with it in Georgia. **1844** *Nat. Hist. N.Y., Zoology* II. 118 The Olive-Sided King-Bird. *Tyrannus cooperi.* . . . This plain-colored species was discovered by William Cooper (from whom it derives its name) in 1829.

***Olive tree.** **a.** =OLIVE 2. +**b.** =AMERICAN OLIVE TREE. +**c.** (*Wild*) *olive tree,* the tupelo gum, *Nyssa aquatica.* — **1785** MARSHALL *Amer. Grove* 98 *Olea.* The Olive-Tree. **1812** STODDARD *Sk. Louisiana* 168 These swamps produce olive trees, so called, because they bear a fruit similar in appearance to the real olive. **1846** BROWNE *Trees Amer.* 426 Whitish-Leaved Nyssa. . . . *Large Tupelo-tree, Wild Olive-tree,* of the Anglo-Americans. **1883** *Century Mag.* Oct. 818 [In a] ranch in California . . . [are] five thousand olive, two thousand fig and domestic fruit trees. **1897** SUDWORTH *Arborescent Flora* 312 *Nyssa aquatica.* . . . Wild Olive-tree (La.) . . . Olivetree (Miss.).

Olla. [Sp.] {1622–, in Spain} +*S.W.* An earthen pot or jar used esp. as a container for water.

An independent borrowing in the Southwest from the Spanish.

1846 MAGOFFIN *Down Santa Fé Trail* 94 A cheese . . . and two earthen *jollas* (*ollas*—jugs) of a mixture of meat, *chilly verde* (green pepper) and onions boiled together completed course No. 1. **1854** BARTLETT *Personal Narr.* II. 360 In all [mounds] that have been excavated, there have been found jars (cantaros), pitchers, ollas, etc., of pottery. **1872** POWERS *Afoot & Alone* 231 Under this hangs the great olla, full of water. **1881** *Amer. Naturalist* XV. 455 One of the finer specimens is an olla or meal bowl from Laguna. **1899** A. THOMAS *Arizona* 88 An olla of drinking water hangs outside the door. **1912** RAINE *Brand Blotters* 75 She was disposing of her flowers in ollas when Jim Budd . . . appeared in the hall.

+**Olykoek.** Also **olikoëk,** etc. [Du. *oliekoek*] A cake fried in deep fat; a fried cake or cruller. Chiefly *N.Y.*

1809 IRVING *Knickerb.* III. iii, The table . . . was always sure to boast an enormous dish of balls of sweetened dough, fried in hog's fat, and called dough nuts, or oly koeks. **1845** *Knickerb.* XXV. 447, I had long before discarded Dutch 'crullers,' and olikoëks. **1850** S. F. COOPER *Rural Hours* 433 Cake-jars are filling up . . . with doughnuts, dark, full, and round; with raisined olecokes, with spicy, New-Year cookies, all cakes belonging to the season. **1864** *Rio Abajo Press* 24 May 1/2 He would call for olykrocks [*sic*], krollers, rollitjes, &c., with a cup of tea. **1889** R. T. COOKE *Steadfast* 78 Refreshing him with hot flip, oly keoks, or Indian preserves and arrack punch.

+**Omaha.** A member of a Siouan tribe of Indians in Nebraska or, in pl., the tribe itself. — **1823** JAMES *Exped.* I. 190 Several of the Pawnee *caches* . . . had been broken open and robbed of their corn by the Omawhaws. **1854** SIMMS *Southward Ho!* 406 The Pawnees and the Omahas were neighboring but hostile nations. **1883** *Rep. Indian Affairs* 105 Each year new land was broken and the farms increased in size until this year the Omahas have about 6,000 acres under cultivation. **1900** G. B. GRINNELL *Indian of To-Day* 12 He killed one more Omaha.

+**Omish,** *a.* Variant of AMISH. — **1844** RUPP *Relig. Denominations* 560 Omish or Amish, is a name which was, in the United States, given to a society of Mennonites. **1867** W. H. DIXON *New America* II. 309 No sect escaped this rage for separation, for independence, for individuality; neither Unitarian, nor Omish, nor River Brethren.

Omnibus, *n.*

1. A large, four-wheeled, public conveyance with seats usually arranged on both sides of an aisle, and entered, esp. before the advent of motor power, from the rear; a bus. {1829–}

1833 *Boston Transcript* 4 May 3/1 The Gov Brooks, Omnibus, Will leave Roxbury, on the arrival of the Brookline Stage. **1842** *Knickerb.* XIX. 46 The rumbling and ponderous omnibus and clattering cab . . . passed on. **1857** *Lawrence* (Kansas) *Republican* 28 May 3 Arrangements are being made to place a daily line of omnibuses between this point and Topeka. **1882** MCCABE *New York* 153 The lights of omnibuses and carriages dart to and fro . . . like myriads of fire-flies.

2. *transf.* Anything that carries a number of miscellaneous items, esp. a legislative bill or one of its sections.

[**1831** IRVING in P. M. Irving *Life W. Irving* II. 455 The great reform omnibus [the English Reform Bill] moves but slowly.] **1842** *Congress. Globe* App. 5 July 661/1 These two articles [tea and coffee] . . . were caught in the omnibus, or dragnet section, in the rear of the bill. **1846** *Spirit of Times* 25 April 108/2 Burton has been running 'an Omnibus' lately in shape of a [theatrical] piece which embraces all the large and small incidents of American History. **1850** *Whig Almanac 1851* 10/2 Mr. Clay . . . assented to the combination of the Admission of California, the Organization of the Territories, and the adjustment of the Texas Boundary, all in one bill, which thence obtained the nickname of 'the Omnibus.' **1868** *Congress. Globe* 16 June 3205/2 [This appropriation bill] may be set down, to begin with, as an omnibus that a great many people can ride in.

3. Attrib. in sense 1 with *company, driver, horse,* etc.

1837 NEAL *Charcoal Sk.* (1838) 106 Shouted an omnibus driver, . . . Don't stand all day a blockin' up the gangvay. **1844** HOLMES *Poetical Works* (1895) 34 Poor drudge of the city! . . . He holds in his fingers an omnibus straw. **1854** CUMMINS *Lamplighter* xviii, Are you sure you know the way from the omnibus-office? **1868** *N.Y. Herald* 15 July 5/4 The Omnibus Companies . . . have suffered very heavily. **1870** *Rep. Comm. Agric. 1869* 372 Horse buyers and shippers for eastern and southern markets are regularly obtaining desired supplies of . . . street-car animals, and heavy dray or omnibus horses. **1870** M. H. SMITH *20 Years Wall St.* 379 The habits of a stable, and the training of an owner of an omnibus line, . . . do not always fit a man for refined society. **1925** *N.Y. Division of Franchise Rep.* No. 184, 5 Resolved, That the Board of Estimate and Apportionment approve the omnibus routes recommended by the Board of Transportation.

+**Omnibus bill.** A legislative bill containing many dissimilar or unrelated items. {1884–} — **1850** *Congress. Globe* App. 8 May 524/1, I am opposed to all omnibus bills. **1854** Hambleton *H. A. Wise* 371, I refused to support the celebrated omnibus bill in 1850. **1888** *Boston Jrnl.* 15 Dec. 2/5 The Omnibus Bill. . . . Mr. Randall . . . to-day reported to the House the Legislative, Executive and Judicial Appropriation bill for the fiscal year 1890.

+**Omnibus sleigh.** A sleigh used as a public conveyance. — **1860** *Boston Auditor's 48th Ann. Rep.* App. 323 City property [includes] . . . One Covered Omnibus Sleigh, One Box Top Sleigh.

Omnibus ticket. 1. A bus ticket. +**2.** A ticket admitting a number of persons. — **(1) 1863** HALE *If, Yes, & Perhaps* (1868) 3 One hundred dollars . . . would pay, in cash, the butcher, and the grocer, and the baker, . . . and would buy the omnibus tickets. **(2) 1868** *Iowa Agric. Soc. Rep. 1867* 408 Some . . . tender hearted friends would take in their settlement and then proceed to some hole . . . in the fence and hand his 'omnibus ticket' to some other parent.

*****On,** *quasi-adj.* +**1.** Aware; possessing full knowledge or understanding. *colloq.*[2] +**2.** Fashionable. — **(1) 1885** *Santa Fe Wkly. New Mexican* 9 July 2/2 He hoped to sell the cavalry a large lot of supplies, but Major Van Horn was 'on.' **1910** TOMPKINS *Mothers & Fathers* 11 You would be so *on*, Bessie Trent. **(2) 1887** RITTENHOUSE *Maud* 403 He looked so good to my eyes standing there in his dark suit, . . . even the tie I preferred—a small dark one instead of the big flashy things that are 'on' now.

*On, *prep.*

+1. *On yesterday*, yesterday. *colloq.*

1848 *S. Lit. Messenger* XIV. 636/2 'On' yesterday, (another Southern emendation of the Queen's English, which is funny enough,) I was so unfortunate [etc.]. **1852** *N.Y. Tribune* 9 Jan. 6/1 It was the intention to send in the Treasury Report . . . on yesterday. **1922** LODGE in *Congress. Rec.* 27 Dec. 942, I took occasion to ask the Secretary of State on yesterday.

+2. *To be on it*, to be ready for something; to be prepared to fight. *slang. Obs.*

1866 'MARK TWAIN' *Lett. Sandwich Isl.* (1938) 70 In San Francisco sometimes, if you offend a man, he proposes to take his coat off, and inquires, 'Are you on it?' **1873** MILLER *Amongst Modocs* 95, I hope the Indians are 'on it' . . . and that they will receive the wretches warmly as they deserve. **1884** SWEET & KNOX *Through Texas* 247, I'm *on* it, I want you to know. I'm no feather-bed soldier.

3. +a. Of a joke or a laugh: Against or at the expense of. *colloq.*

1885 HOWELLS *S. Lapham* vii, If you try to get off any more of those things on me. **1894** WISTER in *Harper's Mag.* April 784/2 She tore out fer the coast, and the joke's on her! **1906** *Nation* 6 Dec. 478 The people rejoiced that the laugh was on those whom they consider their natural enemies. **1912** NICHOLSON *Hoosier Chron.* 205 It's one on Ed Thatcher, that's all!

+b. At the cost of. *colloq.*

1905 BEACH *Pardners* ii, 'Bout to-morrer evening we'll be eating hog-bosom on Uncle Sam. **1922** TITUS *Timber* 183 The board . . . trooped to the Commercial House to eat with Jim and on Jim.

+c. *To have nothing on a person*, to have no advantage over him. *colloq.*[2]

1912 MATHEWSON *Pitching* 7 'Hans' Wagner, of Pittsburg, has always been a hard man for me, but in that I have had nothing on a lot of other pitchers. **1913** BIGGERS *7 Keys to Baldpate* 171 You have nothing on me there.

4. *On board*, (see BOARD *n.* 5).

*Once, *adv.* +*Once in a while*, occasionally. {1877} Also *once and a while.*

1781 WITHERSPOON in *Penna. Jrnl.* 23 May 1/3 He will *once in a while*, i.e. *sometimes*, get drunk. [Used in] the middle states. **1820** E. HOWITT *Select. from Lett.* 69 '*Once in a while*,' to use an American phrase, is left a peep-hole to see the water. **1842** COOPER *Wing-and-Wing* II. 97 Spies is nothing to us, though it might teach 'em manners to keel-haul one, once-and-a-while. **1883** *Harper's Mag.* June 162/2 'Once in a while,' replied the boy. **1895** WINSOR *Miss. Basin* 309 This Virginia governor once in a while hurt his prospects by an imperious air. **1869** STOWE *Oldtown Folks* 116 If he could come down here once and a while after work-hours, 't would kind o' reconcile her.

Ondatra. [Amer. Ind.] A muskrat. {1774–, in Canada} — **1867** *Amer. Naturalist* I. 400 The Musk-rat, or Ondatra (*Fiber zibethicus*), so extensively diffused over North America.

*****One,** *a.* In the names of various games similar to one-old-cat (q.v.). — **1850** *Knickerb.* XXXV. 84 [We] never indulged in a game of chance of any sort in the world, save the 'baseball,' 'one' and 'two-hole-cat,' and 'barn-ball' of our boyhood. **1875** BURROUGHS *Winter Sunshine* 210, I could not only walk upon the grass, but lie upon it . . . or play 'one catch all' with children . . . upon it. **1888** *Cosmopolitan* Oct. 443 'One-cornered cat' . . . was, therefore, forced to give way to a further development called 'three-cornered cat.' **1891** *Amer. Folk-Lore* IV. 231 One o' Cat.

+**One-and-a-half-story house.** A house of one story with a low second story. — **1867** 'T. LACKLAND' *Homespun* 66, We came near the . . . lane that led to the good man's little brown one-and-a-half story house. **1879** *Scribner's Mo.* June 260/1 Three hundred acres of moderately good ground, a neat one-and-a-half story house, with piazza.

*****Oneberry.** +**1.** =INDIAN TURNIP 1. +**2.** =CHECKERBERRY b. — **(1) 1877** BARTLETT 319 Jack-in-the-Pulpit. (*Arisæma triphyllum*). . . . In Connecticut, it is called *One-berry.* **(2) 1892** *Amer. Folk-Lore* V. 100 *Gaultheria procumbens*, one-berry.

+**One-cent piece.** A coin worth one cent. — **1873** *Statutes at Large* XVII. 427 The minor coins of the United States shall be a five-cent piece, a three-cent piece, and a one-cent piece. **1894** S. LEAVITT *Our Money Wars* 126 A pound of this metal [copper, tin, and zinc] coins 160 one-cent pieces.

+**One-dollar.** *attrib.* Designating types of money having the value of one dollar. — **1838** *N.Y. Advertiser & Exp.* 10 Jan. 3/4 He dwelt upon the One Dollar Bill Act. **1890** *Statutes at Large* XXVI. 485 From and after the passage of this act the coinage of the three-dollar gold piece, the one-dollar gold piece, and the three-cent nickel piece be, and the same is hereby, prohibited. **1907** *St. Nicholas* Sept. 1007/2 In her pretty pocket-book . . . she had found a crisp one-dollar bill.

One-horse, *a.*

1. Drawn or operated by a single horse; having only one horse. {1750–}

1789 FRENEAU *Poems* (1795) 321 A pensive Printer in a one-horse-chair (Dragg'd slowly on by sullen sleepy steed.) **1818** FLINT *Lett. from Amer.* 50 Emigrants carry their moveables in one horse carts, or two or four horse waggons. **1838** *Knickerb.* XII. 202 What does he do, but get up his one-horse wagon, and drive post-haste, four miles to . . . Flushing. **1858** *Ill. Agric. Soc. Trans.* III. 522 One man, . . . with one horse, and a one horse mill, expressed 50 gallons of juice per hour. **1858** HOLMES *Autocrat* 295 Have you heard of the wonderful one-hoss shay, That was built in such a logical way? **1914** *Dialect Notes* IV. 155 *Express-wagon*, a four-wheeled, one-horse wagon, lighter than a farm-wagon.

+2. Small or petty; unimportant; limited in capacity.

1854 *N.Y. Jrnl. Commerce* (Th.), I'm done with one-horse bedsteads, I am. **1860** GREELEY *Overland Journey* 36 The twin curses of Kansas . . . are land-speculation . . . and one-horse politicians. **1880** *Harper's Mag.* Nov. 950/1 This story of life at 'a one-horse college.' **1887** FREDERIC *Seth's Brother's Wife* 217 If an engineer on this one-horse line should ever get a train through on time I believe he'd have a fit. **1920** LEWIS *Main Street* 319 Now I'm going to start something in these rotten one-horse lumber camps.

+**One-horse town.** A small and unimportant town. Usually disparaging. — **1855** *Knickerb.* XLVI. 106 In this 'one-horse' Town, . . . as our New-Orleans neighbors designate it. **1861** *Vanity Fair* 6 April 161/2 We, sir, of Boston . . . are a one-horse town, *but* moral. **1880** *Cimarron News & Press* 30 Sept. 1/7, I was just in the condition to chaw up half the police force of this one-horse town. **1912** NICHOLSON *Hoosier Chron.* 23 It had accepted meekly the rebuke implied in its designation as a one-horse town.

+**Oneida.** An Indian of an Iroquoian tribe formerly dwelling in New York, now scattered in N.Y., Canada, and Wis.; in pl., the tribe. Also attrib. — **1666** *Mass. H. S. Coll.* 3 Ser. X. 63 Hereof the Mohawkes and the Oneiades have given assured notice; insomuch that he takes it for a truth. **1722** SEWALL *Diary* III. 311 The Messenger of the Oneidas was buried in the South Burying place. **1778** *Mass. Spy* 15 Oct. 2/2 This day I expect our Oneida friends will strike a blow on the tory inhabitants at Tunadilla. **1840** COOPER *Pathfinder* i, There must be Oneidas or Tuscaroras near us, Arrowhead. **1907** *St. Nicholas* July 834/2 Joined by a couple of friendly Oneidas, they so frightened St. Leger's Indian allies that they decamped at once.

+**Oneida communism.** A type of communism practiced by the Oneida Community. — **1876** *Galaxy* Dec. 817/1 Mr. Noyes . . . introduced this kind of discipline in the Bible class at Putney, Vermont, which was the root of the Oneida communism.

+**Oneida Community.** A community established by J. H. Noyes (1811–86) at Oneida, N.Y., in 1847–48, which practiced a type of communism of which a system of 'complex marriage' and 'mutual criticism' were prominent features. — **1848** in G. W. Noyes *John Humphrey Noyes* 388 The original four-square nucleus of the Putney Community . . . will give tone to the Oneida Community. **1876** *Galaxy* Dec. 815/1 'Mutual criticism' in the Oneida Community . . . is the trial of any person by his social intimates. **1879** *Nation* 4 Sept. 154 Dissensions within and public opinion without have combined to force the abandonment of 'complex marriage' on the Oneida Community. **1900** ESTLAKE *Oneida Community* 1 It was not a fanatical proceeding . . . when he founded the Oneida Community and declared it to be the Kingdom of Heaven.

One-man, *a.* Exercised or done by one man alone. +Freq. *one-man power*, (see quot. 1892). {1882–} — **1848** POLK in *Pres. Mess. & P.* IV. 663 The Executive veto is a 'one-man power,' despotic in its character. **1887** *Nation* 10 March 206 The necessity of leadership has developed into one-man power, but unaccompanied by one-man responsibility. **1892** W. S. WALSH *Literary Curiosities* 845 *One man power*, a term by which Americans personify a subject of their rooted jealousy, the government by, or great power lodged in, any single individual. **1925** BRYAN *Memoirs* 245 We want no one-man power.

+**One-night stand.** *Theater.* **a.** A single night performance of a show in a given town. Also attrib. **b.** A theater that houses such performances. Also attrib. — **1880** RANOUS *Diary of Daly Débutante* 189 This coming week . . . is to be what they call 'one-night stands.' **1895** *N.Y. Dramatic News* 6 July 3/4 The Baldwin Theatre, Springfield, Missouri, made a record last season as one of the best one-night stands in the country. **1896** *Chicago Record* 12 Feb. 4/4 The high class one night stand shows . . . have failed. **1900** *Ib.* 7 May 5/5 The first formidable effort the 'one-night-stand' manager had ever made to protect himself against the imposition of cheap shows. **1904** CRISSEY *Tattlings* 199 A minstrel show that was making one night stands through Missouri and Arkansas. **1918**

SANDBURG *Cornhuskers* 74 A little [clock] . . . carried . . . by an actress . . . is under her pillow in a sleeping-car between one-night stands.

+One-old-cat. A form of baseball similar to one-two-three, wherein the batsman, if he hits the ball, tries to run to a base and back home without being put out. (Cf. CAT *n.* 4 and ONE *a.* 1.) — **1860** *Harper's Mag.* July 195/1 Mrs. Tyler Todd caught the toss, like a skilful player at 'one old cat,' on the edge of her . . . bonnet. **1888** *Cosmopolitan* Oct. 443 By easy gradations . . . this primitive pastime was developed into the simple game of 'one-old-cat.' **1894** P. L. FORD *P. Stirling* 49 Here 'cat' and 'one old cat' render bearable many a wilting hour for the little urchins. **1912** DREISER *Financier* 5 Frank . . . liked to play 'one old cat,' the new baseball game coming into vogue at that time.

Onery. =ORNERY. *dial.* {*dial.*} — **1860** M. J. HOLMES *Maude* v. 63 She pronounced her 'not quite so *onery* a white woman as she at first took her to be.' **1894** B. MATTHEWS in *Harper's Mag.* Sept. 590/1 She's very clever, if she is onery.

One-seeded, *a.* In the specific names of plants. {1812– (Withering *Brit. Plants* I. 70)} — **1813** MUHLENBERG *Cat. Plants* 96 *G. monosperma,* One-seeded honey locust. **1821** NUTTALL *Travels Arkansa* 63, I found the woods almost impenetrably laced with green briars . . . and the one-seeded locust. **1846** BROWNE *Trees Amer.* 215 *Gleditschia monosperma,* The One-seeded Gleditschia.

One-sided, *a.* {1833–} In the specific names of plants: (see quotations). — **1813** MUHLENBERG *Cat. Plants* 49 *Cratægus unilateralis,* One-sided hawthorn. *a***1862** THOREAU *Maine Woods* 309 The prevailing flowers and conspicuous small plants . . . [were] *Pyrola secunda* (one-sided pyrola), . . . small *Circœa* (enchanter's nightshade) [etc.]. **1817–8** EATON *Botany* (1822) 416 *Pyrola secunda,* one-sided shin-leaf. **1814** BIGELOW *Florula Bostoniensis* 105 *Pyrola secunda.* One sided Winter green. . . . The flowers all tend to one side of the stem.

One-storied, *a.* =next. {1861} — **1821** WIRT in Kennedy *W. Wirt* (1849) II. 132 It is a small, red, hip-roofed, one-storied old house. **1832** KENNEDY *Swallow Barn* II. 8 A small one-storied frame house, the very tenement now in possession of Sandy Walker.

One-story, *a.* Of a building: Consisting of a single floor or story, with or without a basement and an attic.

1833 SILLIMAN *Man. Sugar Cane* 64 The bagasse houses at Demerara are high one story buildings. **1844** *Knickerb.* XXIII. 558 A mile and a half below, stood a couple of one-story houses, the logs of which they were built newly hewed. **1877** JOHNSON *Anderson Co., Kansas* 180 Bruns & Fabricius built a one-story brick house for a furniture store and factory in 1868. **1907** LILLIBRIDGE *Trail* 191 There, like kernels of seed scattered on fallow ground, [was] a sprinkling of one-story houses. **1924** MULFORD *Rustlers' Valley* 38 The street was a busy one in front of a line of lighted buildings, frame, one-story shacks all.

+One-term, *a.* Of or pertaining to a single term for the President. — **1845** *Congress. Globe* App. 13 Jan. 122/2 The North had been taunted with the fact that it never had had any but one-term presidents, democratic or federal. **1873** *Harper's Mag.* May 942/1 Belonging to the unfinished business [is] . . . the joint resolutions for the election of the President and Senators by the people, and for a one-term amendment to the Constitution.

+One-two-three. 1. A game in which each player, after every out, changes his position until he earns the right to bat. **2.** (See quot. 1868.) Also attrib. with *order.* — **(1) 1867** CHADWICK *Base Ball Reference* 138 *One, Two, Three.*—Another preliminary practice game in which all the positions of the field are occupied alternately. **1891** *Amer. Folk-Lore* IV. 232 One, Two, Three! This game is similar to 'One o'Cat,' except that the players call out numbers, 'one, two, three, four,' etc. instead of the names of their positions. **(2) 1868** CHADWICK *Base Ball* 43 One, Two, Three . . . refers . . . to the order of going out, when the first three batsmen in an inning retire in succession. **1875** *Chicago Tribune* 24 Aug. 5/6 The White Stockings were retired in one, two, three order. **1886** CHADWICK *Art of Batting* 50.

One while, *adv.* {1882} +A long time. — **1835–7** HALIBURTON *Clockmaker* 1 Ser. xvi. 136 You'll search one while . . . afore you'll find a man that . . . is equal to one of your free and enlightened citizens. **1897** 'MARK TWAIN' *Following Equator* liii. 511 If India knows about nothing else American, she knows about those, and will keep them in mind one while.

***Onion.**

The following examples illustrate dialectal pronunciations: **1794** DRAYTON *Letters* 58 [Boston school children] are taught to pronounce the word first in its proper way, and then to contrast it with the mode in which it is miscalled. . . . Onions [are called] Onions, [and not] *Inions.* **1825** NEAL *Bro. Jonathan* II. 84 Ingyons are proper good, when ye're sick. **1888** STOCKTON *Dusantes* 120 We'll plant inyans for ye on the shears, on the stocks, or in the dry dock.

+1. =WILD ONION.

1612 SMITH *Virginia* 13 In the low Marishes, growe plots of Onyons containing an acre of ground or more in many places. **1791** J. LONG *Voyages* 20 We were . . . living chiefly on . . . onions, which grow in great abundance. **1806** LEWIS in *L. & Clark Exped.* V. (1905) 88 One of the men brought me today some onions from the high plain of a different speceis from those near the borders of the river.

***2.** A well-known esculent garden plant, *Allium cepa,* or its bulbous root.

1652 *Suffolk Deeds* I. 259 Shipped . . . by me Hesekiah Vsher of Boston . . . one hogshead of oynions three hogsheads of biskitt. **1709** LAWSON *Carolina* 77 The Garden-Roots that thrive well in Carolina, are . . . Onions, Shallot, Garlick [etc.]. *c***1790** COXE *View U.S.* 62 The produce, manufactures, and exports of Pennsylvania are very many and various, viz. . . . spelts, onions, potatoes [etc.]. **1818** SCHOOLCRAFT *Journal* 40 No cabbages, beets, onions, potatoes, turnips, or other garden vegetables are raised. **1880** 'M. HARLAND' *Common Sense* (1884) 165 In my own kitchen I usually put in the onion, considering a suspicion of garlic a desideratum in roast duck.

3. Attrib. and comb. with *crop, growing, patch,* etc.

See also ONION FISH, FLY, etc.

1809 IRVING *Knickerb.* IV. i, [The Yankees] planted the onion-patches of Weathersfield under the very walls of Fort Goed Hoop. **1843** STEPHENS *High Life N.Y.* II. 28 Jonathan Slick, if you haint broke your onion string now! **1851** *Polly Peablossom* 168 It attained at least the size of an ordinary onion-bed. **1862** *N.Y. Tribune* 8 March 4/6 Onion-growing in Connecticut. **1863** in *Century Mag.* XXX. 768 An onion salad, dressed only with salt, vinegar, and pepper, seemed a dish fit for a king. **1874** *Rep. Comm. Agric. 1873* 13 Onion-rust, pear-blight, orange-blight, and other diseases have been thoroughly studied. **1877** *Phila. Sunday Gaz.* 8 April, Onion peeler. Potato Parer. **1879** *Congress. Rec.* App. 23 June 120/1, I do not know just what the onion crop of South Carolina was in 1878. **1886** *Harper's Mag.* Oct. 708/2 'Onion sets' . . . are produced by sowing the ordinary black seed very thickly on light poor land. **1909** *Farmers' Bul.* No. 354, 12 All stable manure used on onion land should be well composted.

Onion fish. {1854–} +(See quotation.) — **1884** GOODE, etc. *Fisheries* I. 244 The Grenadiers, or, as the fishermen frequently call them, on account of the size and shape of their eyes, 'Onion-fishes,' inhabit the deep parts of the ocean.

Onion fly. Any one of several insects, as *Hylemyia antiqua,* the larva of which is injurious to onions. {1882–} — **1868** *Amer. Naturalist* II. 203 The young of another fly allied to Anthomyia, of which the Onion-fly is an example. **1870** *Dept. Agric. Rep. 1869* 224 Another cause of failure in the culture of the onion is the onion fly, (*Anthomyia ceparum.*)

Onionskin. **+a.** (See quot. 1890.) **+b.** *attrib.* Designating a ballot on thin or onionskin paper used for fraudulent purposes. — **1879** *Congress. Rec.* App. 23 June 120/1 The term 'onion skin' or 'tissue ballots' had obtained a generic and well-defined meaning synonymous with 'stuffing the ballot-boxes.' **1890** *Cent.* 4113/1 *Onion-skin* . . . , a kind of paper: so called from its thinness, translucency, and finish, in which respects it resembles the skin of an onion.

+Onondaga. [Iroquois *Ononta' gé,* a place name meaning 'on, or on top of, the hill.'] An Indian of an important tribe formerly living in the present Onondaga county, New York; freq. in pl., the tribe itself. Also attrib.

1684 *Mass. H. S. Coll.* 4 Ser. IX. 187, I haue perswaded all the considerable Indians, the Maquas, Sineques, Onondages, . . . to give up their lands. **1765** *Doc. Col. Hist. N.Y.* VII. 719 The Onondagas . . . intended speaking to the Senecas, and Delawares. . . . The Onondaga Speaker *Tyawarunt* spoke as follows. **1832** DUNLAP *Hist. Amer. Theatre* 50 The allies of the English arms, the Mohawks, Senecas, Onondagos, and other supporters of his majesty's honour. **1840** [see CAYUGA]. **1874** B. F. TAYLOR *World on Wheels* I. 31 The painted Senecas and the smoky Onondagas went gliding about like vanishing shadows. **1894** ROBLEY *Bourbon Co., Kansas* 7 These various tribes of New York Indians, consisting of the remnants of the Senecas, Onondagas, Cayugas, Tuscaroras, [etc.] . . . , were called the 'Six Nations.'

+Onondaga salt. Salt obtained from the region formerly occupied by the Onondaga Indians. *Obs.* — **1843** *Niles' Reg.* 10 June 240/3 Onondaga salt . . . can now be delivered in New York for twenty-five cents the bushel of 56 pounds. **1849** *New Eng. Farmer* I. 144, 1000 parts of Onondago coarse salt contain pure salt 991 parts.

Onto, *prep.* {on to, 1581–}

1. To a position that is on or upon. {1819–}

1715 *Duxbury Rec.* 105 [A] place gutted away by the rain down onto Mr. Wiswells land. **1758** PUTNAM *Journal* 62 Capt. Nixon's men . . . fell a tree onto some men as they were in another camp. **1788** MAY *Jrnl. & Lett.* 75, I put powder-horn and shot-bag onto him, and a gun in his hand. **1841** *Knickerb.* XVII. 460 When Mr. Chipp comes onto the stage, you must greet him. **1886** *Narrag. Hist. Reg.* V. 331 A party of six . . . rode through the swamp onto the island.

+2. *To be onto,* to have knowledge of. (Cf. ON *quasi-adj.* 1.) *colloq.*[2]

[**1888** *N.Y. Mercury* 21 July (Farmer), A wife poisoner . . . ought to have for his wife a woman who is on to him, and who can meet his poison advances.] **1893** *Scribner's Mag.* June 756/1 They're not onto it at all. **1897** ADE *Pink Marsh* If you went to throwin' a million dollars around don't you s'pose the police'd be onto you? **1917** MCCUTCHEON *Green Fancy* 251 We don't want them to get onto the fact that she's here.

+Ontocycle. *Biol.* The development that takes place in a cycle, earlier characteristics reappearing in the organism in its decline. — **1893** *Boston Soc. Nat. Hist. Proc.* 109 It is proposed to use in this way ontocycle or ontocyclon for the ontogeny, meaning the cycle of the individual. **1899** HYATT *Biol. Lectures* 134 (*Cent. Suppl.*), The whole cycle of the ontogeny or ontocycle.

Oodles. *pl.* A large quantity or supply. Freq. in phrase *dead oodles. slang.* {1892, ?*Irish dial.*}

1869 *Overland Mo.* III. 131 A Texan never has a great quantity of any thing, but he has 'scads' of it, or 'oodles,' or 'dead oodles.' **1882** SWEET & KNOX *Texas Siftings* 73 Just a very small piece of the pigeon, but bring dead oodles of the *a la Jardinere.* **1894** F. T. CLARK *On Cloud Mt.* 12 'They's ranches 'round 'ere, ain't they?' 'Dead oodles o' 'em.' **1900** H. ROBERTSON *Red Blood & Blue* 280 'Oodles' of money had been spent for bunting and fire-works. **1923** WATTS *L. Nichols* 178 Isn't it ridiculous, though? Our having such oodles of money.

+**Oolachan.** Variant of EULACHON.

Oolong. A drink prepared from a commercial variety of dark, cured tea. In full *oolong tea.* {1852–} — **1850** JUDD *R. Edney* 340 [He] drank two strong cups of oolong. **1896** JEWETT *Pointed Firs* 90 Our guest had so frankly demanded the Oolong tea.

***Ooze.** A decoction, obtained from bark that contains tannin, which is used in tanning leather. — **1656** *Conn. Rec.* I. 286 Nor shall [any person] put any leather into any hott or warme oozes w[ha]tsoever. **1806** B. HAWKINS *Letters* 430 The handler is a vat of ooze to colour the leather. **1867** G. W. HARRIS *Sut Lovingood* 86 He puts in tan ooze, in what [whiskey] he sells.

+**Opeidoscope.** *Physics.* An instrument used for demonstrating and exhibiting the air vibrations caused by speaking and singing. — **1873** A. E. DOLBEAR in Prescott *Sp. Telephone* (1879) 262 While engaged in making a manometric flame capsule, I invented the opeidoscope.

***Open,** *n.* +(See quot. 1846 and cf. OAK OPENING.) — **1846** W. G. STEWART *Altowan* I. 42 All openings of natural clearings are called 'opens' by the half-breeds of the Indian country. **1902** WISTER *Virginian* 407 The basin . . . lay below us, a great cup of country,—rock, woods, opens, and streams.

***Open,** *a.*

1. Of a conveyance or vehicle: Having no top or covering. {1854–}

1771 *Conn. Rec.* XIII. 514 Every open chair and other open top riding wheel-carriage [shall be rated] three pounds. **1873** HOLLAND *A. Bonnicastle* iii, We saw before us a light, open wagon drawn by two gray horses. **1884** RITTENHOUSE *Maud* 319 Mr. Butler came here and we were both whirled off in an open carriage. **1889** BRAYLEY *Boston Fire Dept.* 323 One open buggy, one top-buggy, and water-tower were purchased during the year. **1907** LILLIBRIDGE *Trail* 269 Upon the scene . . . appeared a traveller in an open road waggon.

2. Of a region or area: Having no trees or other impediments to prevent access. {1725–} (Cf. OPEN COUNTRY.)

1783 in *Amer. Speech* XV. 291/1 To three dead white oak Saplins in open or clear Ground. **1805** LEWIS in *Ann. 9th Congress* 2 Sess. 1045 A great proportion of this country is open plains, interspersed . . . with groves of timber. **1825** DOUGHERTY *Light to People of Ky.* 1 Most of the open land was cleared. **1883** HOWELLS *Woman's Reason* xvii, The open lots stretched brown and bare. **1917** *Birds of Amer.* I. 267 [The nest of the mountain plover is] on the open prairies.

+**3.** Of an office or shop: Hiring without discrimination both union and nonunion workers.

1896 *Typographical Jrnl.* IX. 445 Our next efforts were directed to the Morning Leader, also an 'open' office. **1904** *N.Y. Ev. Post* 15 Aug. 2 The Exposition is conducted along the lines of an 'open shop,' by permitting the employment of both union and non-union labor. **1923** *Lit. Digest* 2 June 18/2 There is no occasion for the Republican party . . . to advocate either the 'closed shop' or the 'open shop.'

4. In special combinations.

Open convention, a political convention free from factional or 'machine' domination; *o. front,* (see quotation); *o. furnace,* a furnace of a type used in smelting iron; *o. note,* (see quotation); *o. rate,* a regular published railroad rate as distinguished from a 'special rate'; *o. road,* (see quotation); *o. running,* in football, running through a field of players out of their regular positions and widely scattered; *o. shelf, style* (see quotations); *o. trail,* a trail not impeded or blocked by ice, snow, etc.

1904 *N.Y. Ev. Post* 5 Sept. 1 The governor still asserts that the Republicans will have an 'open convention,' but the belief is general that he has decided to nominate Lieut-Gov. Higgins. **1881** RAYMOND *Mining Gloss., Open-front,* the arrangement of a blast furnace with a fore-hearth. **1814** BRACKENRIDGE *Views La.* 150 The three modes of smelting, to wit, the *open furnace,* the *ash furnace,* and the air furnace, . . . have all been introduced since the Americans took possession of the country. **1879** in Tarbell *Hist. Standard Oil Co.* I. 331 Do you know what the open rate, the published rate is to the seaboard by the barrel? **1817** FORDHAM *Narr.* 100 The trees on each side are notched at convenient distances, to distinguish the State road from private ones to Plantations, and this is then called an open road. **1907** *St. Nicholas* Sept. 1013/2 Players of this fall will be obliged to perfect themselves in forward passing, open running, kicking, and catching. **1910** BOSTWICK *Amer. Pub. Library* 38 Practically all small and moderate sized American libraries are now 'open-shelf,' which means that the user is allowed to go personally to the shelves and select his book. **1903** *Churchman* 10 Oct. 447 The notes are of the open (or, as our English friends term it, minim or semibreve) style. **1901** WHITE *Westerners* 47 At Pierre he announced open trail.

***Open,** *v. tr.*

1. To clear or render fit for cultivation (a plantation or other area). {1617} Also with *up.*

1809 F. CUMING *Western Tour* 290 The country here is well opened and inhabited to a little beyond Uniontown. **1814** BRACKENRIDGE *Views La.* 208 Stopped a few moments at the cabin of a Frenchman, who is beginning to open a plantation. **1846** T. B. THORPE *Myst. Backwoods* 141 A gentleman . . . 'opening a plantation,' [in La.] found . . . that in the centre of his land was a boggy piece of low soil. **1879** *Scribner's Mo.* Nov. 132/1 What miles and miles of . . . emerald prairies where the plows are going! But there are liberal intervals not yet 'filed upon' or 'opened up.'

+**2.** To make (public land) available for entry and settlement.

1871 *Rep. Indian Affairs* (1872) 180 The influences at work to 'open' this lost home of the race are powerful, representing great and diversified interests. **1906** *Indian Laws & Tr.* III. 615 A nontransferable certificate . . . will entitle him [*sc.* the applicant for land] to go upon and examine the lands to be opened hereunder.

+**3.** *Poker. To open the pot,* to place money in (a jackpot), thereby opening it for play.

1880 DICK *Amer. Hoyle* 202 The blind now deals, and any player in *his regular turn* may *open* or *break* the pot, provided he holds a pair of Jacks or better. **1887** KELLER *Draw Poker* 35 If in opening a pot a player finds in his hand a pair and a four flush, or four straight, he may break his pair and draw to the straight or the flush. **1922** T. A. MCNEAL *When Kansas Was Young* 187 Three deals were made before either could open the pot.

Open and shut, *n.* and *adj.* +**1.** *n.* The essence of simplicity; a simple matter or operation. +**2.** *adj.* Free from complexity, straightforward. *colloq.* — (1) **1848** DURIVAGE & BURNHAM *Stray Subjects* 128 That chap's snoring beat *all* the high-pressures he *ever* heerd—jest as easy as open and shet! **1857** *Harper's Mag.* Sept. 568/1, I can take and heave you across that river yonder, just like open and shet. **1904** W. H. SMITH *Promoters* 162 It seems as if it was a dead open and shut that we've got to stay with 'em. (2) **1893** *Harper's Mag.* May 975/2 The case was a dead open-and-shut one. **1902** HARBEN *Abner Daniel* 153, I 'lowed we was going to make a open-and-shut trade that we could be proud of.

+**Open board.** An association that transacts small dealings in options not permitted by the local stock exchange or board of trade. — **1870** MEDBERY *Men Wall St.* 15 The consolidation of the Government and the Open Boards with the old historic Stock Exchange. **1902** LORIMER *Lett. Merchant* 113 She's the daughter of old Job Dashkam, on the open Board.

Open communion. Among Baptists, communion in the Lord's supper with Christians other than those who have been immersed. Also attrib. (Cf. CLOSE COMMUNION.) — **1794** MORSE *Amer. Geog.* (ed. 3) 223 Except those who are styled 'open communion baptists,' . . . they refuse to communicate in the ordinance of the Lord's Supper with other denominations. **1824** *Baptist Mag.* IV. 412 It has been said that the practice of open communion would be politic.

Open country. A region unimpeded by barriers, esp. woods or forests, or remote from towns and cities. {1818–} Also attrib. — **1807** GASS *Journal* 22 This is the most open country I ever beheld, almost one continued prairie. **1898** CANFIELD *Maid of Frontier* 128 He was willing, too, to go back to the open country . . . and anxious to escape from the oppressive flavor of the county town. **1903** A. ADAMS *Log of Cowboy* 193 The prairie section of the State left its indelible imprint on the cattle bred in the open country. **1920** *3d Nat. Country Life Conf. Proc.* 173 In the open-country churches of the South there was an unwillingness to engage in the actual reorganization of parish lines.

***Open court.** A court organized and in session for the transaction of judicial functions; a court open to the public. — **1656** *R.I. Court Rec.* 22 Joyned by the atturnies this caues is Ended by the concents of boath parties in open court. **1678** *Conn. Rec.* III. 18 John Wheeler being complayned of for contemptuous carriage . . . in saying to the court, in open court [etc.]. **1881–5** MCCLELLAN *Own Story* 137 He had convicted Halleck of perjury in open court. **1900** *Congress. Rec.* 25 Jan. 1184/2 In 1887 he pleaded 'guilty' in open court to the crime of unlawful cohabitation.

***Opener.** *Poker.* +The person who begins the betting; also, pl., the cards, a pair of jacks or better, with which a player may open the jackpot. — **1880** DICK *Amer. Hoyle* 203 After all the players who determine to go in have made good the bet of the player who opened the Jack Pot, . . . then the opener of the pot makes the first bet. **1887** *Courier-Journal* 24 Jan. 2/4 Fortune varied one way and then another and finally they played a jacker in which the opener was promptly raised $500. **1909** WASON *Happy Hawkins* 114, I didn't hold openers. **1920** MULFORD *J. Nelson* ii, A round or two had been played when Big Tom drew his first openers.

Open-gaited, *a.* Of a horse: Having a gait, especially in trotting, in which the hind feet overreach the outside limits of the forward ones. — **1872** *Vermont Bd. Agric. Rep.* I. 206 A good sized, rangy, open-gaited and enduring horse of a good color. **1894** *Vt. Agric. Rep.* XIV. 97 His sire being Allen, his dam Lady Alice, . . . he is a pure open-gaited trotter.

Open-hearth. *attrib.* Of or pertaining to a process or method of making steel involving regenerative gas-heating in a furnace of a reverberatory type. {1885–} — **1883** *Harper's Mag.* Aug. 333/2 At Johnstown may be seen . . . the puddling process, the Bessemer system; and the Pernot open-hearth method of oxidation. *Ib.* 334/2 You look into a peep-hole of the open-hearth caldrons . . . and see the iron there melted into a dead white wrinkled semi-liquid. **1894** *Ib.* Feb. 412/1 It may be crucible, Bessemer, or open-hearth steel.

***Opening.**

+**1.** A place in a swamp where it may be crossed. *Obs.*

1663 *Providence Rec.* V. 206 The place comonly Called the first opening of the great swampe. **1678** *Hempstead Rec.* I. 319 To John Bedell all the comon medow betwen the hether-must spring at the first oponing and the spring at Cos medow. **1704** *Providence Rec.* IV. 178 On the south side of the place in the . . . great swampe which is Called the first opening. **1839** in *Mich. Agric.Soc.Trans.* VII. 358 Ridges of sandy 'openings' and detached prominences or *islands* . . . are intersected by long bands of marsh.

2. An area in a forested region which is by nature treeless or only slightly timbered. {1745–} Cf. OAK OPENING.

1798 C. WILLIAMSON *Descr. Genesee* iv, The openings, or large tracts of land, found frequently in this country free of timber, and showing great signs of having once been in a state of cultivation, are singularly curious. **a1817** DWIGHT *Travels* IV. 58 These grounds are also termed *Openings.* **1852** E. F. ELLET *Pioneer Women* 377 The original site of the village . . . was a burr oak opening. **1900** BRUNCKEN *N. Amer. Forests* 9 There were also light groves, called openings, in many places in the uplands.

+3. A cleared field or site for a settlement. *Obs.*

1800 TATHAM *Tobacco* 6 Thus the planter is continually cutting down *new* ground, and every successive spring presents an additional field, or *opening* of tobacco. **1831** PECK *Guide* 180 All confined places should be avoided . . . unless an opening can be made immediately. **1837** *Knickerb.* X. 491 Like thousands of others . . . he 'kept bachelor's hall,' until he had 'made an opening, and reared his rustic cot.'

4. The public ceremony or occasion on which a business formally begins operations for the first time or for the season.

1872 *Chicago Tribune* 27 Dec. 5/1 Our wondering citizens have seen 'opening' after 'opening' announced. **1892** *Courier-Journal* 2 Oct. 10/4 Six months ago we had our first millinery opening. **1903** *N.Y. Ev. Post* 19 Sept., This is the first week of the annual fall openings in all the shops.

+5. The action by the federal government of throwing open for settlement land not previously available for settlers.

1889 in Thoburn *Oklahoma* (1916) II. 645 Owing to the press of other business upon Congress at the time the bill for the opening of the land was passed, there was no provision for territorial government made by Congress. **1906** *Indian Laws & Tr.* III. 618 The opening of said unallotted lands was extended to the fifteenth day of August. **1914** *Cycl. Amer. Govt.* II. 577 [Oklahoma] was rapidly expanded by subsequent 'openings' until in the year 1901, its limits touched the Kansas and Texas lines.

Open kettle. +(See quot. 1892.) — **1887** *Courier-Journal* 20 Jan. 7/3 Sugars—We quote . . . open kettle, 5¼ c, and granulated, 6⅞ @ 6¾ c **1892** *Mod. Lang. Notes* Nov. 393 *Open Kettle*—open pan in which the syrup is reduced until it begins to crystallize. . . . Also a trade name for sugar manufactured by this process.

Open policy. (See quot. 1895.) {1848–} — **1836** *Diplom. Corr. Texas* I. (1908) 88 The Offices having also issued Open Policies by Vessel or Vessels at and from any Port in Mexico to this in the belief that the American Flag would be respected by Texian Cruizers [etc.]. **1895** E. CARROLL *Principles Finance* 300 *Open policies.* (Marine Insurance) Policies in which the value of goods insured is not specified.

+Open prairie. A stretch of open, level country usually covered with grass. (See PRAIRIE.)

1819 E. DANA *Geogr. Sk.* 272 In this region, three-fourths of the banks, of the Mississippi consist of open prairas. **1835** LATROBE *Rambler in No. Amer.* I. 214 We always hailed the prospect of entering upon a tract of open prairie with delight. **1846** SAGE *Scenes Rocky Mts.* xv, We camped in a small open prairie. **1877** JOHNSON *Anderson Co., Kansas* 57 The party engaged George Partridge to guide them up the South Pottowatomie, across the open prairie. **1887** I. R. *Lady's Ranche Life Mont.* 9 [We] struck off across the open prairie for the Great Divide.

+Open range. *W.* A range or extent of grazing country not enclosed or intersected by fences. Also attrib. — **1890** *Stock Grower & Farmer* 15 March 6/3 The cow men of the open ranges will make money. **1905** *Bureau of Forestry Bul.* No. 62, 9 The great bulk of the western stockmen are definitely in favor of the Government control of the open range. *Ib.* 52 Under the open-range system the honest and law-abiding cattleman was at a great disadvantage. **1913** BARNES *Grazing Grounds* 116 The advent of the barbed wire fence probably did more to improve the condition of the open range stockman than any one thing that has come to him.

+Open stove. =FRANKLIN STOVE. — **1788** FRANKLIN *Autobiog.* 370 [I] invented an open stove for the better warming of rooms. **1830** WATSON *Philadelphia* 186 Doctor Franklin first invented the 'open stove,' called also 'Franklin stove.' **1835** HOFFMAN *Winter in West* I. 28 A blazing fire of seasoned oak in a large open stove sputters and crackles before me.

+Open timber. A forested area on which there is no undergrowth. — **1884** *Century Mag.* Feb. 500/1 The ground in his front was, first, open timber. **1907** ANDREWS *Recoll.* 154 Two lines of our own cavalry [were] approaching us . . . through the open timber.

Open top. *attrib.* Designating a vehicle the top of which is open. — **1771** [see OPEN *a.* 1]. **1856** *Mich. Agric.Soc.Trans.* VII. 61 John Patton . . . [exhibited an] open top buggy.

Opera.

1. A dramatic composition or performance in which music plays an essential part. {1644–} Also in collective sense.

1761 *N.Y. Post-Boy* Dec. 31 The original Overture to be performed, and the Opera to conclude with a Dance by the characters. **1796** DUNLAP (*title*), The Archers, or Mountaineers of Switzerland; An Opera in Three Acts. **1851** NORTHALL *Curtain* 113 Operas, Vaudevilles, and the everlasting Ravel Family, occupied the theatrical saloon. **1883** *Harper's Mag.* Nov. 877/1 The interest in opera is at least three parts social to one part musical. **1895** *N.Y. Dramatic News* 19 Oct. 2/4 The audience had listened to a part of one of the worst sung operas it had ever been called upon to endure. **1921** *Lit. Digest* 2 July 29/2 New York went without its opera once, a dozen years ago.

b. With a modifying term. Freq. applied in colloq. or slang use to other forms of theatrical entertainment.

1863 *Chicago Jrnl.* 10 June 4/2 'Canterbury Hall' and the 'Dearborn Street horse opera' having subsided [etc.]. **1882** MCCABE *New York* 580 The metropolis has a warm corner in its heart for the 'burnt-cork opera.' **1895** *N.Y. Dramatic News* 26 Oct. 14/3 A One Man Opera. . . . Leopolo Fregoli . . . has remarkable control over his voice and can sing soprano, alto, baritone and bass. **1899** *Chicago Tribune* 13 Feb. 3/6 *By the Sad Sea Waves.* A rag time opera in three acts, produced under the direction of Dunne & Ryley . . . at the Grand Opera-House.

+2. A cigar somewhat shorter than usual that was formerly popular with gentlemen attending the opera. In full *opera cigar. Obs.*

1857 *Lawrence* (Kansas) *Republican* 16 July 3 We do semi-occasionally puff an 'opera,' if we find one that suits. **1892** *Harper's Mag.* Feb. 486/2 I am also the man who introduced 'opera' cigars.

3. *attrib.* **a.** Designating individuals or groups engaged in the performance of opera.

1855 W. B. WOOD *Recoll. Stage* 307 The French opera corps of New Orleans produced a version of this opera. **1856** *Porter's Spirit of Times* 264/2 Mr. Forrest and a German Opera Company succeed Mr. Lorraine. **1860** E. COWELL *Diary* 5 We went . . . to the Tremont Hotel . . . where also some of the Opera Troupe were staying. **1890** *Boston Jrnl.* 12 March 1/9 The woman . . . who gave the name of May Casey, an opera singer, was found this morning by another policeman.

b. Designating articles of apparel worn at or to the opera.

1855 M. THOMPSON *Doesticks* 315 Lorgnettes, Opera-hoods, and white kids are not exhibited here in such profusion as in some other places of amusement. **1856** STOWE *Dred* I. 7 That's my opera-hat. **1864** *Hist. North-Western Soldiers' Fair* 149 [Donations include] 1 opera cap, 2 aprons. *Ib.* 74 An opera shawl. **1878** *Decorum* 282 Either black or white lace may be adopted with advantage in an opera-dress. **1892** *York County Hist. Rev.* 110 The shoe department . . . [handles] all grades, from the heavy brogan to that of a fine opera slipper.

+Opera chair. A chair for use in theaters and public halls the seat of which may be turned up, affording more space between rows of seats. — **1872** *Chicago Tribune* 13 Oct., The parquet and dress circle are seated with opera chairs; the upper circles with sofas. **1890** J. JEFFERSON *Autobiog.* 29 Folding opera-chairs were unknown [in Chicago c1840]. **1895** *N.Y. Dramatic News* 6 July 3/4 Bargains in Opera Chairs.

Opera cloak. A fine cloak or wrap worn by women attending the opera, evening parties, etc. {1872} — **1856** *Porter's Spirit of Times* 74/1 Some newly arrived opera cloaks, the materials being light green, blue, and pink merino. **1865** *Chicago Tribune* 15 April 1 Opera Cloaks and Mantles, . . . in all the latest Paris Shapes. **1908** 'O. HENRY' *Options* 84 Nevada [pulled the letter] . . . out from beneath her opera-cloak.

Opera glass. {1738} A small binocular telescope for use at the opera or the theater. {1842–} — **1841** *Knickerb.* XVII. 459 His next movement was to take out a kind of opera-glass. **1862** BROWNE *A. Ward His Book* 112 Sevral opery glasses was leveld at me. **1898** *Kansas City Star* 18 Dec. 1/2 Gold spectacles, eye glasses, opera glasses at lowest prices. Julius Baer, optician.

Opera goer. A frequenter of the opera. — **1850** MITCHELL *Lorgnette* I. 20 Girls, who would not make it a material objection to a lover, that he was an Opera-goer. **1856** *Porter's Spirit of Times* 152/1 Your paper of yesterday contained a communication, signed 'Opera Goer.' **1881** *Harper's Mag.* Jan. 305/2 The true opera-goer leaves his mind and conscience at home.

Opera house. A theater in which operas are given; a grandiloquent name for any theater. {1720–}

1829 *New York Evening Post* 20 May, American Opera House. **1851** NORTHALL *Before Curtain* 109 A few years after this a splendid Opera House was erected on the site of the old establishment. **1870** *Chicago Tribune* 1 March, The Opera House was again filled last evening . . . with a very large audience. **1885** *Wkly. New Mex. Rev.* 28 May 3/7 Utilizing the building for the two-fold purpose of opera house, skating rink and public hall. **1904** A. DALE *Wanted, a Cook* 98 Just after I had heard the conversation about the Metropolitan Opera House on Wagner nights, an old . . . person came in. **1917** MCCUTCHEON *Green Fancy* 17 They started out the back way of the opery house and nobody missed 'em till next mornin' except the sheriff.

attrib. **1869** *Boyd's Business Directory* 71 Patent Opera House Chairs, with seats to turn up, for Theatres and Public Buildings. **1882** RITTENHOUSE *Maud* 131 David Lansden met me at the Opera House entrance, and took my boxes and me around to the greenroom door around the corner.

Operate, *v.* {1606–}

1. *tr.* To work or direct the workings of (a machine, snowplow, boat). {1876–}

1864 WEBSTER 914/2. **1865** *Atlantic Mo.* XV. 175 The first tailor ... found no difficulty in having ... girls taught to operate [the machines]. **1872** *Omaha Bee,* The monster [steam snow plough] ... will be operated by three of the heaviest engines on the road. **1903** W. E. CURTIS *True Abraham Lincoln* 24 When he was 16, he operated a ferry-boat.

2. To manage or have supervision over (a railroad or steamship line, telegraph system, etc.) {1891–}

1880 *Travellers' Off. Guide U.S. & Canada* July 91 The Roads owned and operated by the Pennsylvania Railroad. **1887** *Lit. World* 6 Aug. 248/1 How long is it to be before the government of the United States will operate the telegraph system of the country as it operates the mails? **1891** *Scribner's Mag.* Sept. 275/2 Some of the other long lines operated by this efficient organization ... are those between Bremen and the United States. **1902** W. J. GHENT *Our Benevolent Feudalism* 50 Something more than every third farm in the United States is operated by a tenant.

+3. *intr.* To follow a career of crime; to engage in political machinations. *colloq.*

1884 SWEET & KNOX *Through Texas* 16 This high-toned and honorable desperado 'operated' in one of the inland cities of Texas two years ago. **1901** W. A. WHITE in *McClure's Mag.* Dec. 147 Platt and Payn, operating with less than half a score of legislators, went down to Albany to take in the senatorial election.

***Operation.** A business transaction, esp. one of a speculative character. {1832– (*Congress. Deb.* App. Aug., 1833, 107)}

1845 *Knickerb.* XXV. 409 A beautiful operation may be made of it. **1855** 'PAXTON' *Capt. Priest* 249 Jacob went into—what in the vernacular of brokers is termed—'an operation.' **1893** M. HOWE *Honor* 119 Those who profited by it preferred to refer to the same [a mining transaction] by the less offensive title of 'operation.' **1911** LINCOLN *Cap'n Warren's Wards* 178, I judged ... that you were well enough acquainted with Wall Street to know that queer operations take place there.

***Operator.**

+1. One who owns or directs the operations of a coal mine or other industrial plant or institution.

1838 *Niles' Nat. Reg.* 13 Oct. 112/2 Our trade ... is brought nearly to a stand again, by a collision between the dealers, operators and boatmen, as regards the price of freight. **1851** CIST *Cincinnati* 170 The largest operators in this line [manufacturing alcohol], are Lowell Fletcher & Co. **1857** *Harper's Mag.* Sept. 459/1 The leases of the operators usually covered a 'run' upon the out-crop ... of from fifty to seventy yards. **1875** *Chicago Tribune* 30 Sept. 2/4 The operators on the Pan-Handle Railroad have been paying 2½ cents per bushel for mining over 1¼ inch screen. **1904** TARBELL *Hist. Standard Oil Co.* I. 27 He became interested in the oil business in 1862 ... as an operator in West Virginia.

+2. a. One who sends and receives telegraphic communications. **b.** One who operates a typesetting machine. **c.** One who handles telephone calls at a telephone switchboard.

1858 HALE *If, Yes, & Perhaps* (1868) 119 It is not the business simply of 'operators' in telegraphic dens to know this Morse alphabet. **1879** BURDETTE *Hawkeyes* 95 When you go to a railway station ... you look into the telegraph office and see the operator. **1893** M. Philips *Making of Newspaper* 133 The full-sweep letter of credit that was laid before the operator. **1896** *Internat. Typogr. Union Proc.* 17/1 Members of the International Association of Machinists shall not hold positions as operators on typesetting machines. **1900** *Everybody's Mag.* II. 410/2 Let me advise you to go up to the operating room at the central office and watch the operator work. **1916** DU PUY *Uncle Sam* 204 The message was given to the operator.

***Opinion.** *Law.* The formal judgment or decision of a court, as the Supreme Court of the United States. — **1803** MARSHALL *Marbury* v. *Madison* 154 In rendering the opinion of the court, there will be some departure in form ... from the points stated in that argument. **1857** BENTON *Exam. Dred Scott Case* 70 The present Supreme Court, in pronouncing its 'Opinion,' has noticed this decision of its predecessor. **1900** *Congress. Rec.* 25 Jan. 1162/2 The supreme court of the State of Mississippi delivered a very able opinion upon that subject, and that opinion was affirmed by the Supreme Court of the United States.

***Opium.** A narcotic drug obtained from the unripe capsules of a species of poppy, *Papaver somniferum.* — **1729** *Md. Hist. Mag.* XVIII. 333. **1782** CRÈVECŒUR *Letters* 210 A singular custom prevails here [in Nantucket] among the women ... of taking a dose of opium every morning. **1835** SIMMS *Partisan* I. 103 If a Dorchester granny loves one thing more than another, after opium, it is brandy. **1916** DU PUY *Uncle Sam* 124 The smuggling of opium and of Chinamen was known to go hand in hand.

Opium den. =next. {1897–} — **1882** MCCABE *New York* 590 Here are the headquarters of the Mongolians, their gaming houses and opium dens. **1886** *Starry Flag* (San Francisco) May 2/1 The first place we entered was an opium den on Sullivan alley.

+Opium joint. A low dive or resort frequented by those addicted to the use of opium. Also transf. — **1884** *Boston City Council Minutes* XIX 375/1 A committee of five [to] be appointed to ascertain and report whether or not the Chinese headquarters, commonly known as the 'Opium Joints,' are prejudicial to the health and detrimental to the morals of our city. **1890** *Stock Grower & Farmer* 3 May 7/4 The Denver Chinese drug peddlars are former laundrymen, cooks and keepers of opium joints. **1903** *N.Y. Ev. Post* 4 Sept., Four men were arrested this morning in an alleged opium joint.

Opium-smoker. One addicted to the smoking of opium. — **1860** GREELEY *Overland Journey* 259 [The Chinaman] is an inveterate gambler, an opium-smoker, ... and a devotee of every sensual vice. **1883** *Harper's Mag.* Nov. 944/2 A young man about thirty eight years of age, known to me for some years past as an opium smoker.

Oporto (grape). A variety of the frost grape, *Vitis cordifolia.* — **1846** HUGHES *Diary* 67 About two miles below San Filipe we encamped—Abundance of the fine Oporto Grape, the finest in the world. **1870** *Rep. Comm. Agric. 1869* 85 The most promising varieties are the Clinton, Franklin, Huntingdon, Taylor, and Oporto.

+Opossum. Also †**apossoun, opassum, opposom.** [Algonquian.] Any one of various American marsupials about the size of a house cat and belonging to the family Didelphidae, esp. *Didelphis virginiana.* (Cf. POSSUM.)

1610 *Estate of Va.* 29 There are Arocouns, and Apossouns, in shape like to pigges. **1687** BLOME *Isles & Terr. in Amer.* 138 The Opassum [is] about the bigness of a Cat, with a sharp Snout. **1765** R. ROGERS *Acct. N. Amer.* 263 The Opposum is a remarkable animal in this country, having under its belly a bag or false belly, in which they breed their young. **1791** BARTRAM *Travels* 7 Opposoms are here in abundance, as also pole-cats, wild-cats, rattle-snakes. **1817** BRADBURY *Travels* 261 The quadrupeds ... of which the flesh is eaten, are bear, deer, hares, racoon, opossum, and a variety of squirrels. **1884** Z. F. SMITH *Kentucky* (1886) 122 The great dish of the occasion was an opossum baked whole. **1904** STRATTON-PORTER *Freckles* 255 Crones ... eternally sucking a corncob pipe and stirring the endless kettles of stewing coon and opossum.

attrib. **1806** *Balance* V. 29/3 Many ... should be permitted to quit their ... hoes and spades, hog, hominy and opossum fat. **1832** KENNEDY *Swallow Barn* II. 193 Nothing takes off the load from the mind like an opossum hunt. **1877** JOHNSON *Anderson Co., Kansas* 138 Four of the braves had each nail kegs, covered with opossum skins.

***Opposed,** *a. To be opposed to,* to be averse to or against. {1844–} — **1789** FRANKLIN *Writings* X. 77 The Word *opposed* ... I find used in a new Manner, as, 'The Gentlemen who are *opposed* to this Measure; to which I have also myself always been opposed.' **1816** PICKERING 144 To be *Opposed to* for To *Oppose*.... I shall *be opposed* to that measure.

‖**Opticist.** One who is versed in optics. — **1884** *Pop. Science Mo.* XXIV. 814 The real cause ... is now thoroughly understood by physiological opticists.

***Option.** *Mining.* +(See quotation.) — **1882** *Harper's Mag.* May 897/1 The large land-owners have adopted the policy of granting 'options'; that is, signing an agreement that if any person shall uncover a bed of ore on his land, the finder shall be entitled to a certain interest, generally one-third.

+Optional, *n. Educ.* An optional or elective course or study. *Obs.* (Cf. ELECTIVE *n.*) — **1855** *Songs, Biennial Jubilee* (Yale), For optionals will come our way. **1857** *Yale Lit. Mag.* XXII. 291 (Th.), What was never known since the establishment of optionals, the number pursuing the study of Hebrew is nine.

Optional, *a.* {1765–} *Educ.* (See quot. 1856.) — **1856** HALL *College Words* (ed. 2) 340 During another portion of the course, he is allowed to select from certain branches those which he desires to follow. The latter are called *optional* studies. **1871** BAGG *At Yale* 695 'Optional' or 'elective' studies, too, do not always realize the expectations of their advocates. **1880** *Harper's Mag.* July 254/1 In the German universities the studies are all elective and optional.

Opuntia. {1601} A genus of cactus indigenous to America; a species or plant of this genus. (Cf. PRICKLY PEAR.) — **1766** STORK *Acct. E. Fla.* 48 Of the opuntia, or prickly pear, are different species in East-Florida. **1838** 'TEXIAN' *Mexico v. Texas* 10 Hardly can one find, here and there, a sturdy *agave,* or a half withered *opuntia* sadly vegetating in the rocky crevices. **1896** *Garden & Forest* 1 Jan. 2/2 This large Cactus ... has a much more extended range than any of our cylindrical Opuntias.

+Oquassa (trout). *local.* [Abnaki Indian.] A small, somewhat slender, lake trout (*Salvelinus oquassa*) found in Maine. — **1884** *Nat. Museum Bul.* No. 27, 427 *Oquassa Trout; Blue-Back Trout.* Lakes in Western Maine. **1890** *Cent.* 4134/3 *Oquassa,* ... the blue-backed trout, *Salmo oquassa.* (Rangeley Lake, Maine.) **1896** JORDAN & EVERMANN *Check-List Fishes* 293.

+O.R. An abbreviation for *Ordered recorded. Obs.* — **1790** *Sumner Co.* (Tenn.) *Court Minutes* (MS.) 27, July 7, 1790 Power of attorney from Alex Dever to Joseph McElurath is duly acknowledged & O.R. *Ib.* 30, October 6, 1790 Andrew Jackson, Esqr. proved a bill of Sale from Hugh McGary to Kasper Mansker for a negro man which is O.R. **1796** *Ib.* 105, April 6, 1796 Deed of conveyance ... is duly proved by oath of Jno. Daveson and O.R.

Oral. {1885–} +*Educ.* Short for *oral examination.* — **1876** TRIPP *Student-Life* 18 Do something splendid on the mathematics and the 'orals,' and I will wager any thing you will pass clear.

‖**Oralism.** The method by which deaf-mutes are taught lip reading. — **1883** *Amer. Ann. Deaf & Dumb* April 90 So far as oralism ... is concerned.

***Orange.**

***1.** The large globose fruit of the orange tree.

1634 *Relat. Beginnings of Md.* 21 We haue also English Peasen, & French-beanes, Cotten, Oringes, Limons. **1709** Lawson *Carolina* 5 These more Southerly Parts will afford Oranges, Limons, Limes, and many other Fruits. **1791** Bartram *Travels* 303 A feast of Water mellons and Oranges, the Indians having brought a canoe load of them to the trading-house. **1837** Williams *Florida* 115 Our exports consist of . . . hides, horns, tallow, bees-wax, peltries and oranges. **1908** *Bur. Plant Industry Bul.* No. 123, 17 A 'Fancy' orange is supposed to have a deep orange color.

2. = Orange tree. {1615–} Also collect.

1775 Burnaby *Travels* 99 In the gardens is a very large collection of citrons, oranges, limes, lemons, . . . and other tropical plants. **1834** Baird *Valley Miss.* (ed. 2) 265 The orange grows here, but is often injured by the climate. **1847** Longfellow *Evangeline* 86/1 Through the Golden Coast, and groves of orange and citron, Sweeps with majestic curve the river away to the eastward. **1880** Cable *Grandissimes* 193 [The houses] were seen by glimpses . . . above their groves of orange or down their long, over-arched avenues of oleander.

3. *attrib.* and *comb.* **a.** Designating persons engaged in the sale or cultivation of oranges.

1722 *New-Eng. Courant* 3 Sept. 2/1 Some are Orange-Merchants, others Coal-Merchants, and some very good Gentlemen are contented to be called Rag-Merchants. **1842** *Knickerb.* XX. 472 The orange-girl is generally allowed to enter [an auction-store], for auctioneers are mortal, and sometimes eat oranges. **1871** Howells *Wedding Journey* 178 The stevedores . . . joked in a kindly way with the orange-women. **1874** *Dept. Agric. Rep. 1873* 201 The following letter [will] . . . prove of interest to orange-cultivators. **1889** *Secy. of Agric. Rep.* 17 Despondency has given way to hope and confidence among California orange-growers.

b. Denoting a part of an orange or orange tree.

1740 W. Stephens *Proc. Georgia* 521 An Experiment . . . of putting some Hundreds of good Orange-Seeds into the Ground. **1785** Marshall *Amer. Grove* 150 [The flowers] have somewhat the fragrance of an Orange flower. **1836** Gilman *Recoll.* (1838) 25 An orange leaf . . . was laid on every finger bowl. **1852** Stowe *Uncle Tom* ii, Her mistress herself adorned the bride's beautiful hair with orange-blossoms. **1865** *Atlantic Mo.* XV. 506 Reason with love! As well with orange-boughs for bearing orange-buds.

c. Designating foods and flavorings prepared from oranges.

1723 *Amer. Wkly. Mercury* 23 May 4/2 Lemon and Orange-Peel, very well made. **1809** E. S. Bowne *Life* 229, I send . . . a tumbler of Orange Marmalade for Mother. **1828** E. Leslie *Receipts* 17 [A recipe for making] Orange Pudding. **1867** *Common Sense Cook Book* 28 Orange Sauce for Game. **1878** *Amer. Home Cook Book* 161 Orange Cream. **1908** 'O. Henry' *Options* 62 A kind of cocktail they make along the P. R. R. . . . —dry gin, French vermouth, one squeeze of a lime, and a good dash of orange bitters.

d. Denoting areas where oranges are grown.

See also Orange grove, Orange orchard.

1869 Browne *Adv. Apache Country* 246 The city [of Hermosillo] lies spread at your feet, with its vineyards and orange gardens. **1885** Baylor *On Both Sides* 187 My son has an orange-plantation in Florida. **1895** *Dept. Agric. Yrbk. 1894* 198 Phosphoric acid . . . is a very necessary element of fertilization on Florida orange lands.

4. a. In the names of birds, fishes, etc.: (see quotations).

See also Orange-crowned warbler.

1839 Peabody *Mass. Birds* 313 The Orange-colored Warbler, *Sylvia celata*, probably passes through our State on its way to the eastern parts of Maine. **1874** Coues *Birds N.W.* 70 Golden-crowned thrush; Orange-crowned Accentor. . . . It is one of our most abundant woodland birds in summer. **1890** Ballard *Among Moths* 142 The common name in Florida for this caterpillar [the larva of the orange-tree butterfly] is 'the orange dog,' from a fancied resemblance of its most curious head to that animal. **1884** Goode, etc. *Fisheries* I. 171 The Orange File Fish, *Alutera Schoepfii*, . . . is rather common in Southern New England. **1858** Baird *Birds Pacific R.R.* 67 Orange-headed parrot. . . . Head and neck all round gamboge yellow. **1884** Goode, etc. *Fisheries* I. 265 Orange Rock-fish. . . . This species is usually called simply 'Red Rock-cod' or 'Red Rock-fish.' **1839** Peabody *Mass. Birds* 309 The Orange-throated Warbler, *Sylvia auricollis*, . . . makes us a passing call on its way to Canada.

b. In the names of plants and vegetables: (see quotations).

1787 Washington *Diaries* III. 199 The Northernmost of which was sowed with the large Orange Carrot Seed. **1882** E. K. Godfrey *Nantucket* 36 The orange-grass with its fragrance, now greeting us at every turn. **1817–8** Eaton *Botany* (1822) 306 *Hieracium aurantiacum*, orange hawkweed. **1709** Lawson *Carolina* 77 Of Musk-Melons we have very large and good, and several Sorts, as the Golden, Green, Guinea, and Orange. **1859** A. Van Buren *Sojourn in South* 133 The orange myrtle, with its glossy green foliage, trimmed in the shape of a huge strawberry. **1790** Deane *New-Eng. Farmer* 224/2 Orange potatoe, so called from its colour.

Orange crop. The harvest or yield of oranges for a season. Also transf. — **1840** *Niles' Nat. Reg.* 21 Nov. 192/2 The Apalachicola, Florida Advertiser of the 31st October says:—The Orange crop of this year, raised in this territory, will be worth $200,000. **1860** Holmes *E. Venner* viii, The failure of the morning's orange-crop and the deficit in other expected residual delicacies were not very difficult to account for. **1883** *Century Mag.* Oct. 807/1 The main orange crop ripens from January to May.

+Orange-crowned warbler. A small American warbler (*Vermivora celata*) widely distributed throughout the United States. Also with a specific defining term. — **1825** Bonaparte *Ornithology* I. 45 During winter, the Orange-crowned Warbler is one of the most common birds in the neighborhood of St. Augustin, Florida. **1844** *Nat. Hist. N.Y., Zoology* II. 87. **1878** *Nat. Museum Proc.* I. 404 *Helminthophaga celata*, [var.] *lutescens*, Californian Orange-crowned Warbler. **1917** *Birds of Amer.* III. 121 The Orange-crowned Warbler is a bird of the far Northwest.

Orange grove. A grove of orange trees.

1766 J. Bartram *Journal* 56 [We] encamped at a great orange-grove. **1826** Flint *Recoll.* 314 There are some very pleasant plantations, gardens, and orange groves, on the Bayou St. John. **1863** *Rep. Comm. Agric. 1862* 64 Old fields abounding in peach and persimmon orchards and wild orange groves. **1883** Rittenhouse *Maud* 166, [I] never have seen an orange grove, or swampy forests covered with Spanish moss. **1898** *Dept. Agric. Yrbk. 1897* 504 The velvet bean [is a widely grown forage crop] for Florida orange groves.

+Orange orchard. A grove of orange trees, regularly planted and cultivated. — **1872** *Harper's Mag.* May 881/1 You should drive to the Mission San Gabriel, where are the finest orange orchards. **1883** *Century Mag.* Oct. 808/2 It has . . . one hundred and fifty [acres] in orange orchards, fifty of almond trees, sixty of walnuts. **1889** Deland *Florida Days* 196 Low shores, where orange-orchards stretch, dark and still, across the level land.

+Orange riot. *Hist.* An outbreak of violence in New York, July 12–14, 1871, between Protestant and Catholic Irishmen. — **1872** Brace *Dangerous Classes N.Y.* 30 No one doubted . . . during the Orange riot of 1871, the existence of 'dangerous classes' in New York. **1882** McCabe *New York* 500 [The National Guard] have promptly and bravely responded to every call upon them . . . checking the Orange riots in 1871; and overawing the mob in the Railroad riots, in 1877.

+Orange root. = Goldenseal. — **1817–8** Eaton *Botany* (1822) 310 *Hydrastis canadensis*, orange root. **1857** Gray *Botany* 14. **1884** *Rep. Comm. Agric.* 132 Orange-root . . . is a perennial herb, seldom growing more than a foot high.

Orangery. A place where oranges are cultivated. {1664–} — **1791** Bartram *Travels* 76 On the right hand was the Orangery, consisting of many hundred trees, natives of the place. **1837** Williams *Florida* 123 The orangery and out houses have been suffered to go to ruin. **1888** Cable *Bonaventure* 201 [She] mentioned the small sugar-farm and orangery of the kinsman Robichaux.

***Orange tree.** A rather low, thickly branching evergreen tree of the genus *Citrus* having fragrant white flowers and bearing oranges.

[**1623–4** *Va. House of Burgesses* 36 A ship alsoe was sent to the Summer Islandes for such commodities as that place afforded, as Potatoes, Fig Trees, Orange and Lemon Trees.] **1666** *S.C. Hist. Coll.* II. 13 They have . . . Orange, Lemon, and other Fruit-trees. **1737** Brickell *N. Carolina* 24 There being only some few Rose-Trees, Bead-Trees, Orange-Trees, [in the gardens of N.C.]. **1792** Pope *Tour S. & W.* 93 Without Cultivation the Orange and Lemon Trees attain a proper Size. **1844** Kendall *Santa Fé Exped.* II. 124 Here, for the first time, we saw the orange tree in full bearing. **1882** *Wheelman* I. 171 To lazily pluck the yellow fruit from an overladen orange-tree in a sleepy garden of Mobile [etc.]. **1915** *Dept. Agric. Bul.* No. 256, 1 The fork-tailed katydid . . . is also responsible for a certain amount of injury to orange trees.

attrib. **1874** *Dept. Agric. Rep. 1873* 206 Many letters have been received by the Department from intelligent orange-tree cultivators in Florida.

Orate, *v.* **1.** *intr.* To deliver an oration or lecture; to 'speechify.' *colloq.* {*c*1600–} 'This word is occasionally instanced since *c*1600, but has only recently come into more common use, as a back-formation from *oration*, app. first in U.S. *c*1860' (*O.E.D.*). **2.** *tr.* To deliver (a speech) in a bombastic or declamatory manner. *colloq.* — **(1)** **1864** Sala in *Daily Telegraph* (London) 18 Nov., General Banks . . . has been 'orating' in New York. *a***1881** Diman in Hazard *Mem. J. L. Diman* 231 You see my time this summer is much taken up with 'orating.' **1902** Lorimer *Lett. Merchant* 166 Wore a silk hat and a Prince Albert coat all the time, except when he was orating. **(2)** **1900** *Congress. Rec.* 17 Jan. 914/2, I should hate exceedingly to have the present speeches of the gentleman from Pennsylvania orated around over the country as mine.

***Orator.** +A student in college or high school selected to deliver a speech on a public occasion. — **1737** *Harvard Rec.* II. 661 Voted, . . . that Mr Flynt Dr Wigglesworth & Mr Rogers be desired to appoint an Orator and Respondents among the Candidates for their Second degree. **1871** Cutting *Student Life Amherst* 40 For the Exhibition, four orators are now chosen in each society from the Senior class. **1923** *Breeze* (Albion, Mich.) [24] Charles Rogers. Advertising Manager Breeze. Class orator.

***Orchard.**

See also Old orchard.

***1.** An enclosure in which fruit trees are grown; also, collect., the trees themselves.

1639 *R.I. Col. Rec.* I. 89 Mr. Coddington shall have six acres for an Orchard. **1697** *Derby Rec.* 301 My dwelling house barn orchard and hom lot containing two acres more or les. **1724** *Providence Rec.* XVI. 393 [The] Lands Adjoyneing with the fenceing buildings Orchard and Improvements there on. **1845** *Knickerb.* XXV. 448 The guinea-hens were screaming down in the orchard. **1887** *Outing* X. 12/1 Back of its hacienda is a fine orchard and vegetable garden, watered by an acequia. **1907** *St. Nicholas* May 603/1 Harry pointed out, at a distance, the stables and barns and the orchard beyond.

2. Attrib. and comb. with *culture, ground, house,* etc.

See also ORCHARD GRASS, LAND, etc.

1655 *Suffolk Deeds* II. 151 The orchard meadow before the Doore with fowre acres of vpland. **1689** SEWALL *Diary* I. 298 There are Seven Closes, two very fair ones besides the Orchard Ground. **1843** HAWTHORNE *Notebooks* (1932) 178 The orchard-path is still deeply covered with snow. **1862** *Rep. Comm. Patents 1861: Agric.* 538 By an orchard house is meant a house where fruit trees are grown under glass. **1874** *Dept. Agric. Rep. 1873* 428 Orchard-culture of the pear is limited.

b. In the specific names of insects injurious to orchards.

1854 EMMONS *Agric. N.Y.* V. 262 Orchard caterpillars. *Ib.* 241 They [*Clisiocampa neustoria*] differ from those of our common orchard moth named by Dr. Harris *Clisiocampa Americana.* **1895** *Dept. Agric. Yrbk. 1894* 272 (*caption*), Remedies for Orchard Scales.

Orchard grass. {1765-} +=COCKSFOOT (GRASS) a.

1781-2 JEFFERSON *Notes Va.* (1788) 73 Our grasses are lucerne, st. foin, burnet, timothy, ray and orchard grass. **1805** PARKINSON *Tour* 47, I had not yet seen any grass; except a few bunches of orchard-grass. **1880** *Vt. Agric. Rep.* VI. 34 Other varieties, such as orchard grass, blue grass, etc., [should] be added. **1901** MOHR *Plant Life Ala.* 384 *Dactylis glomerata* . . . *Orchard Grass.* . . . Alleghenian to Louisianian area.

attrib. **1785** WASHINGTON *Diaries* II. 420 Plowed up a Cow pen in order to sow the ground with Orchard Grass seeds.

+**Orchard hangnest.** =ORCHARD ORIOLE. — **1844** *Nat. Hist. N.Y., Zoology* II. 140 The Orchard Oriole. *Icterus Spurius.* . . . Orchard Hangnest. **1917** *Birds of Amer.* II. 256 Orchard Oriole. . . . [Also called] Orchard Hang-nest.

Orcharding. {1664-}

1. Land upon which fruit trees are grown. {1721-}

1654 *Conn. Prob. Rec.* 155 One halfe of all my howsing, Barnes & orcharding. **1710** *Lancaster Rec.* 300 Six acres . . . together with all the orcharding fencing on sd land. **1850** *Rep. Comm. Patents 1849: Agric.* 275 From an acre of orcharding of forty trees, . . . one hundred barrels of fruit would be a small crop. **1863** *Maine Bd. Agric. Rep.* 142 One acre of orcharding on suitable soil . . . will produce three times the amount in value of any other crop.

2. The cultivation and management of an orchard. {1664-}

1753 *Boston News-Letter* 27 Dec. 2/2 Eighty [acres] . . . are under Improvement in mowing, pasturing and plowing and good Orcharding. **1861** *Ill. Agric. Soc. Trans.* IV. 321, I have had more than half a century's experience in orcharding. **1892** *Boston Jrnl.* 16 Jan. 1/4 An interesting address . . . upon 'The Advances of Orcharding in New England.' **1913** *Boston Post* 23 Nov. 41 She has had 2000 young trees set out this month, as a starter in orcharding.

Orchardist. One who cultivates or manages an orchard. {1794-} — **1822** J. THACHER (*title*), The American Orchardist. **1857** *Rep. Comm. Patents 1856: Agric.* 85 Careless orchardists allowing grass to grow about the roots of their fruit-trees [etc.]. **1891** *Boston Jrnl.* 23 Sept. 2/3 If California shall hold the place she now occupies in the market, it will be by the productions of the orchardist of few acres. **1915** E. ATKINSON *Johnny Appleseed* 24 The orchardist must know how to wait.

Orchard land. Land suitable for or devoted to fruit growing. — **1687** *Southampton Rec.* II. 55 One acre is for his orchard land. **1796** *Ann. 4th Congress* 2 Sess. 2648 Orchard land, . . . at one shilling and sixpence per acre. **1865** *Atlantic Mo.* XV. 77 A country . . . consisting chiefly of the richest grazing, grain and orchard-land.

+**Orchard oriole.** An oriole (*Icterus spurius*) resembling the Baltimore oriole but slightly smaller and of duller plumage. — **1808** WILSON *Ornithology* I. 71 The Orchard Oriole . . . is no sneaking pilferer. **1857** *Rep. Comm. Patents 1856: Agric.* 130 The orchard oriole enters the Southern States from South America early in March, and continues there until October. **1878** *Nat. Museum Proc.* I. 135 This small race of the Orchard Oriole is found rather plentifully from the latter part of March until August. **1917** *Birds of Amer.* II. 257 The Orchard Oriole seldom visits the ground.

+**Orchard starling.** =prec. — **1865** *Atlantic Mo.* XV. 516, I love his [the robin's] note and ways better even than those of the Orchard-Starling or the Baltimore Oriole. **1882** *Century Mag.* Jan. 361/2 The English . . . have no songsters to match our oriole, our orchard starling, our cat-bird. **1917** *Birds of Amer.* II. 256 Orchard Oriole. . . . [Also called] Orchard Starling.

Orchestarion. A musical instrument, probably one attempting to simulate the various instruments of an orchestra. — **1872** in Odell *Ann. N.Y. Stage* IX. 356 [Robert Spice] inventor and player on the Orchestarion.

***Orchestra.**

1. A band of musicians who play various musical instruments; esp. a group which includes a string section and is capable of playing operas, symphonies, etc. {1720-}

1797 *N.Y. Advertiser* 8 June, The days of performance only, the Garden, in which is an Orchestra, will be decorated. **1812** *Niles' Reg.* I. 329/1 Mr. Taylor [was] the last of the musicians who quitted the orchestra. **1835** WILLIS *Pencillings* I. 10 The balls . . . would go on if there were only musicians enough left to make an orchestra. **1907** *St. Nicholas* July 797/2 Fritzi has taken my place in the orchestra.

+**2.** A section of the auditorium of a theater, now usually the forward part or all of the main floor. Also attrib.

1856 *Porter's Spirit of Times* 20 Dec. 262 Laura Keene's Theatre . . . Reserved Orchestra Seats, 75 cents. . . . Seats in orchestra stalls, $1 each. **1872** *Chicago Tribune* 28 March, The interior will contain an orchestra and three circles. **1872** *Chicago Jrnl.* 18 July, The house is divided into an orchestra circle which includes the entire main floor, (Mr. McVicker having decided to discard the names parquet and parquet circle) orchestra and orchestra chairs and dress circles of first and second balcony circle. **1895** *N.Y. Dramatic News* 19 Oct. 3/4 You wouldn't know the orchestra seats were $1, . . . the scale 75, 50, 25 being displayed everywhere. **1911** *World's Work* Sept. 14840/1 They were accustomed, when they went to the theatre, to pay an extra half dollar for seats in the front rows of the orchestra. **1924** D. LAWRENCE *True Story Woodrow Wilson* 117 A President . . . cannot sit in the orchestra or in the balcony.

Orchid. Any one of various plants of the family Orchidaceae or a flower of such a plant. {1845-}

1847 WOOD *Botany* 529 Orchidaceæ.—Orchids. . . . Many of its species are cultivated for ornament. **1868** *Amer. Naturalist* II. 342 The Orchids . . . are royal in their incomparable and exhaustless world of beauty. **1893** M. HOWE *Honor* 169 She carried in her hand a bunch of orchids. **1899** *Animal & Plant Lore* 103 The orchid (*Aplectrum hiemale?*) locally known as 'Adam and Eve' is used for love divination. **1907** *St. Nicholas* Aug. 938/1 What is an orchid? . . . There are over fifty species native to the United States.

attrib. **1886** MITCHELL *R. Blake* 141 The orchid-grower wiped his spectacles, and readjusted them.

***Orchis.** Any one of various plants or a genus of plants of the family Orchidaceae. Often with a defining term.

1784 *Mem. Academy* I. 486 Red-Winged Orchis. Blossoms red or purple. **1818** *Mass. H. S. Coll.* 2 Ser. VIII. 170 In July the lover of plants is gratified with . . . the broad and narrow-leaved kalmias, the brilliant fimbriate orchis, [etc.]. **1825** BRYANT *Poetical Works* (1903) 93 The brier-rose and the orchis died amid the summer glow. **1843** TORREY *Flora N.Y.* II. 272 *Orchis spectabilis.* . . . Showy Orchis. . . . Woods, in rich vegetable mould. **1855** SIMMS *Forayers* 485 Here, at this very season, you will find the yellow orchis. *a***1886** E. DICKINSON *Works* (1924) 112 The orchis binds her feather on.

***Order,** *n.*

I. 1. In the specific names of various fraternal societies. {of orders of knighthood, 1387-}

1856 *Porter's Spirit of Times* 15 Nov. 178/2 Do you belong to the Order of Odd Fellows? **1873** SNYDER *Good Templars' Hand-Book* 9 The Independent Order of Good Templars does not, as an organization, rank among the venerable institutions of antiquity. **1896** *Founders & Patriots of Amer. Reg. 1902* 28 Charter Members of the Order of the Founders and Patriots of America. **1913** A. C. COLE *Whig Party in So.* 308 A secret nativist order known to its members as the 'Order of the Star Spangled Banner' or the 'Order of the Sons of the Sires of '76.'

2. A direction or commission for certain goods or commodities from a purchaser; an indication of the food desired by a customer in a restaurant. {1845-}

1879 GEORGE *Progress & Pov.* 242 Manufacturers find orders falling off. **1902** *Rep. of Librarian of Congress* 97 Orders even of moderate size can not be filled as promptly as desired. **1902** LORIMER *Lett. Merchant* 216 We are making goods for which we need orders. **1904** 'O. HENRY' *Four Million* 253 And all this while she [the waitress] would be performing astounding feats with orders of pork and beans, pot roasts [etc.].

II. Phrases. **3.** *Order of* (or *in*) *council* {1785-}, +an enactment or decree passed by a colonial governor and his council. *Obs.*

1685 *Penna. Col. Rec.* I. 129 Whether this following Writing should be the foreamble to the Order of Councill. **1715** *Boston News-Letter* 28 March 2/2 There was no Order of Council for Inserting the same [notice]. **1746** *N.J. Archives* 1 Ser. VI. 369 An Embargo on all Vessels in this Province for the Space of one Month unless his [*sc.* the president's] Order in Council shall be first Obtained for the Sailing of any Vessel.

4. *Order of the day* {1792-}, in the U.S. Congress, the business planned to be taken up on a particular day; also, a statement or listing of such business.

1775 *Jrnls. Cont. Congress* II. 53 Agreeable to the order of the day, the Congress resolved itself into a committee of the whole. **1789** MACLAY *Deb. Senate* 55 The *impost* bill, being the order of the day, was taken up. **1798** *Ann. 5th Congress* II. 1837 Mr. Gallatin called for the order of the day on the bill providing for the assessment and collection of direct taxes. **1840** *Niles' Nat. Reg.* 2 May 142/1 The hour of one having arrived, the speaker announced the special order of the day.

transf. and *fig.* **1795** WASHINGTON in Sparks *Life G. Morris* III. 66 Peace has been (to borrow a modern phrase) the order of the day. **1815** *Niles' Reg.* IX. 111/2 A cattle show and fair . . . was to be held at Pittsfield. . . .

The following [was the] 'order of the day.' **1840** DANA *Two Years* xxvi. 289 Industry was the order of the day.

5. *To call to order*, to open (a convention, meeting, etc.) in order to begin formal proceedings. Also *vbl. n.*

1830 SUTHERLAND *Legislative Practice* 115 The Speaker . . . [shall] call the members to order. **1888** BRYCE *Amer. Commw.* II. III. lxix. 545 Business begins by the 'calling of the convention to order' by the chairman of the National Party committee. **1905** *Providence Jrnl.* 8 March 4 The annual town meeting of the town of Seekonk was called to order Monday by Town Clerk Hill. **1923** ROBERT *Parliamentary Practice* 4 The member who calls the meeting to order may say, 'I move that Mr. Jones act as chairman.'

+**6.** *In short order* (or variants), without delay, summarily. *colloq.*

1834 SIMMS *Guy Rivers* I. 204 Be off now in a hurry, or I shall fire upon you in short order. **1840** HOFFMAN *Greyslaer* II. 28, I cut out in quick order from the hollow, and made clean tracks for camp. *c***1850** WHITCHER *Bedott P.* xxv. 307 If ever you dew it agin you'll git your walkin'-ticket on short order. **1861** NORTON *Army Lett.* 26 A field of potatoes, five acres, was emptied of its contents in short order. **1902** E. BANKS *Autobiog. Newspaper Girl* 27, I dressed myself in short order.

***7.** *In order*, +appropriate, suitable, befitting the occasion. *colloq.*

*a***1861** WINTHROP *J. Brent* 85 If the gent has made a remark what teches you, apologies is in order. **1873** BEADLE *Undevel. West* 233 He is a being with whom written contracts are quite in order. **1880** INGHAM *Digging Gold* 382 In the evening . . . stories and songs were in order. **1905** *N.Y. Times* 4 Sept., Good-byes were in order on the Erin last night.

***Order,** *v.* +*To order up*, in euchre, to ask an opponent who is dealing to take up the trump and discard. Also *vbl. n.* — **1847** ROBB *Squatter Life* 129 His antagonist ordered the king up. **1864** W. B. DICK *Amer. Hoyle* (1866) 62 *Ordering Up.*—Requiring the dealer and his partner to play the trump as it has been turned. **1899** CHAMPLIN & BOSTWICK *Cycl. Games & Sports* (ed. 2) 298 If the player that orders up . . . fails to win three tricks he is euchred and his opponent scores two points.

Orderly. A soldier assigned to a superior officer, usually as a messenger. {1800–} — **1781** *Va. State P.* I. 453 The orderly, his wife and negro woman at York . . . have never received one single shilling. **1853** SIMMS *Sword & Distaff* 12 The orderly . . . looked about the room for his superior. **1881–5** MCCLELLAN *Own Story* 588, I rode along the whole front . . . accompanied by . . . a couple of orderlies. **1897** C. A. DANA *Recoll. Civil War* 115 My orderly stuck to me like a veteran.

Orderly book. A book kept by a military company or regiment for the entry of general or regimental orders. {1815–} — **1755** *Lett. to Washington* I. 120 Orderly Books, being lost I could not get an authentick copy that was proper. **1837** *S. Lit. Messenger* III. 609 It was discovered that he had taken his baggage, arms, and orderly book.

Orderly sergeant. The first or senior sergeant in a company or other military unit. {1727–} — **1757** *General Orders* 126 Each Corp is to have an Orderly Searj[ean]t Ready for ye Earl of London. *c***1805** R. PUTNAM *Memoirs* 26, I did orderly Sarjents duty untill the 26th of July. **1862** NORTON *Army Lett.* 130 My orderly sergeant was killed in the charge. **1867** J. M. CRAWFORD *Mosby* 121 Horace Johnson of Warrenton . . . was appointed orderly sergeant.

***Ordinance.**

***1.** A local law or regulation passed by the governing body of a municipality.

1701 *Phila. Ordinances* (1812) 7 The said mayor, recorder, aldermen and common council men . . . shall have power . . . [to make] good and reasonable laws, ordinances and constitutions. **1790** *Ib.* 119 An ordinance for the suppression of nuisances. **1802** in C. Cist *Cincinnati* (1841) 193 For a blank-book to record ordinances, 8 [dollars]. **1885** *Century Mag.* Oct. 973 Out of every sixty arrests made by the police of Boston last year . . . only one [was] for infringing the ordinances of the city. **1904** *Atlantic Mo.* March 295 An ordinance was adopted in Buffalo to limit the height of billboards to seven feet.

+**2.** A decree, law, or enactment passed by the United States Congress under the Confederation. Now hist.

1781 *Jrnls. Cont. Congress* 1187 An ordinance to incorporate the subscribers to the bank of North America. **1787** *Old South Leaflets* I. No. 13, 1 An Ordinance for the Government of the Territory of the United States Northwest of the River Ohio.

+**3.** *Ordinance of 1787*, an Act of Congress of July 13, 1787, providing a system of government for the Northwest Territory.

[**1787** CUTLER in *Life & Corr.* I. 342 Was furnished with the ordinance establishing a government in the Western Federal Territory.] **1847** *Whig Almanac 1848* 33/2 The imperishable principle set forth in the ever-memorable Ordinance of 1787. **1857** BENTON *Exam. Dred Scott Case* 9 Scott had been carried by his owner from Missouri into the State of Illinois, where the ordinance of '87 against slavery was admitted by the Court to be in full force.

+**4.** *Ordinance of secession*, an enactment passed by a representative body in a seceding state signifying the intention of the state to withdraw from the federal Union. Now hist.

1865 *Atlantic Mo.* XV. 744 On the 17th of April, 1861, Virginia in Convention passed an Ordinance of Secession. **1866** 'F. KIRKLAND' *Bk. Anecdotes* 60/2 The General drew forth a large fac-simile of the Ordinance of Secession, and pointed to the signature. **1884** BLAINE *20 Years of Congress* I. 458 Five hundred staunch Union men . . . denounced the Ordinance of Secession.

***Ordinary.** A tavern or inn. *Obs.* (Cf. HOUSE OF ENTERTAINMENT.)

Properly (as in England) one at which meals were provided, but also locally applied to any public house or tavern.

1637 *Essex Inst. Coll.* IX. 55 Mr. John Holgraue . . . hath undertaken to keep an ordinary for the entertainment of strangers. **1650** *Md. Archives* 294 Except Wine or other Provisions to bee expended in any Ordinaries within this Province. **1704** S. KNIGHT *Journal* 47 [We] took up our Lodgings at an ordinary, wch a French family kept. **1774** CRESSWELL *Journal* 20 Breakfasted at Rollin's, a Public House, but in this Country called Ordinaries. **1816** U. BROWN *Journal* II. 230 Thence to an orniary took a Cut refreshed & fed $0.50.

attrib. and *comb.* **1662** *Md. Archives* I. 447 The Sheriff . . . appoynted by such Ordinary Keeper, to collect or gather up such Ordinary debts. **1710** *Providence Rec.* X. 113 Anne Tirpin tooke a licence for Ordinary Keeping and gave bond.

+**Ordinary-keeper.** The proprietor of an ordinary. *Obs.* — **1645** *Essex Inst. Coll.* IX. 136 Md. to prouide for a ordinarie keeper. **1665** *Conn. Rec.* II. 14 Jonathan Sellick is approued for Ordnary keeper at Standford. **1712** SEWALL *Diary* II. 340 John Rickard, Ordinary-keeper, our quondam Landlord dyes this day.

***Ordination.** The action or ceremony of appointing a person to a position in a religious body. Also attrib.

1652 *Roxbury Land & Ch. Rec.* VI. 197 A church gathering & ordination at Medfield. **1666** *Conn. Rec.* II. 55 Whether the laying on of hands in ordination of Elders belong to Presbiters or Brethren. **1722** *New-Eng. Courant* 9–16 April 2/2 An Ordination Sermon Preached . . . when the Reverend Mr. Joseph Emerson was Ordain'd Pastor. **1781** S. PETERS *Hist. Conn.* 315 Numerous as the ceremonies are in a minister's ordination, there are but few judged necessary in dismissing him. **1815** DWIGHT *Remarks Rev. Inchiquin's Lett.* 56 In order to . . . be admitted to ordination, they must . . . pass through the Associational or Presbyterial examination. **1860** *Harper's Mag.* Nov. 789/2 Among the hoarded treasures of this last little box . . . was an ordination *Ball Ticket*. . . . 'An ordination ball! . . . who ever heard of such a thing?' *Ib.* 791/2 The ordination council said there hadn't been such an examination passed by a young candidate for many a year. **1861** LOWELL *Biglow P.* 2 Ser. 14 They laid an' snoozed ez . . . Meek ez digestin' deacons be at ordination dinners.

***Ordnance.**

***1.** A heavy gun or cannon. Freq. *piece of ordnance.*

1636 WINTHROP in R. C. Winthrop *Life J. Winthrop* II. 156 We had nine pieces of ordnance to the Rebecca her side; but all the means could be used could not get one into her. **1792** *Ann. 2nd Congress* 1126 He moved out with the Federal troops . . . together with Captain Ferguson's company of artillery, and three pieces of ordnance. **1812** *Niles' Reg.* I. 373/1 The bill authorizing the purchase of ordnance and ordnance stores. **1823** THACHER *Military Jrnl.* 43 Our privateers had fortunately captured some prizes with cannon and other ordnance. **1858** D. PETERS *Kit Carson* 294 This force set out, taking with them a piece of heavy ordnance. **1890** *Century Mag.* Dec. 168 This ordnance Sutter conveyed up the Sacramento River on the launch to his colony.

2. Attrib. with *bureau, corps, department*, etc.

1758 *Essex Inst. Coll.* XII. 138 Ordnance stores from Albany [were] stored on road. **1836** *Pres. Mess. & P.* III. 229 Whether any increase or improvement of organization is needed in the Ordnance Corps. **1861** *Army Regulations* 26 An Ordnance Sergeant in charge of ordnance stores . . . shall be held responsible for the safe-keeping of the property, and he shall be governed by the regulations of the Ordnance Department in making issues of the same. **1873** *Newton Kansan* 3 July 2/1 The War Department will send to West Point from the Ordnance Bureau . . . the first gun fired in the late war.

***Ore.**

***1.** A metal-bearing mineral occurring in nature.

*c***1644** *Mass. H. S. Proc.* 2 Ser. VIII. 13 This place well viewed & considered of by the workemen, both for the ore & the conveniency of waters for furnass. **1731** *Md. Hist. Mag.* XIX. 192 By the Appearance of the Oar sent by Mr. Lee find it to be no other than Iron. **1814** BRACKENRIDGE *Views La.* 148 The ore is what is called potter's ore, or galena, and has a broad shining grain. **1875** *Chicago Tribune* 11 Sept. 4/1 Car-load after car-load of ore is dumped on our docks and in our depots. **1901** WHITE *Claim Jumpers* (1916) 27 He and Davidson climbed down shafts, and broke off ore, and worked the gold pan.

2. *attrib.* and *comb.* **a.** Designating areas or geological formations where ore is found.

1787 CUTLER in *Life & Corr.* I. 205, I arrived at the ore-beds at 12 o'clock. **1804** *Mass. H. S. Coll.* IX. 255 Bog ore abounds in swamps and other low places, . . . particularly in the vicinity of the several ore ponds. **1817** PAULDING *Lett. from South* II. 258 The ore-bank is excavated sixty or seventy feet, and is still unexhausted. **1871** RAYMOND *3d Rep. Mines* 25 This vein has shown thus far three separate ore bodies. **1905** VALEN-

TINE *H. Sandwith* 238 On coming to central Pennsylvania he had invested in ore lands.

b. Designating machines and appliances used in reducing ore.

1859 *Rep. Comm. Patents 1858* I. 556 Improved Ore Separator. **1871** RAYMOND *3d Rep. Mines* 47 A new concentrating machine . . . called the Rawlins & Stephens slime ore-concentrator. **1876** — *8th Rep. Mines* 447 From the ore-breaker the ore went through a chute to the first set of steel rolls below. *Ib.* 48 Automatic ore-feeders are coming into general use. **1882** *47th Congress 1 Sess.* H. R. Ex. Doc. No. 216, 597 There should be no mistakes made as to the value of new ore-crushing machines. *Ib.* 569 The ore table is stationary, not having any side or end shake of any kind.

c. Pertaining to the transporting and marketing of ore.

1871 RAYMOND *6th Rep. Mines* 292 The effect on the ore-market of Clear Creek County would be very great. **1876** — *8th Rep. Mines* 200 Ore-transportation from mine to mills, (11 miles), [$]34,073.14. *Ib.* 203 This estimate of 'base bullion and ores' is, however, too low, the ore shipments from Atlanta . . . having evidently been omitted. **1883** M. H. FOOTE *Led-Horse Claim* 27 [He] looked across to . . . the procession of ore-teams loading at the dumps.

d. Designating persons interested or engaged in the mining or handling of ore.

1876 RAYMOND *8th Rep. Mines* 26 The ore-sorters constitute quite a large force. **1883** WELLS *Practical Economics* (1885) 95 In unison with the ore-miners and wire-manufacturers [etc.]. **1896** SHINN *Story of Mine* 2 Maybe they'll die there, and some ore freighter will put them under the sand. **1901** *N.Y. Comm. Advertiser* 11 April (*Cent. S.*), The merchant oremen made the decision, which is generally regarded as conservative.

Ore car. A small car for hauling ore in a mine. — **1877** W. WRIGHT *Big Bonanza* 302 Our speed is probably not half that at which the cage is lowered when its only load is an empty ore-car. **1896** SHINN *Story of Mine* 218 Let us follow the course of an ore car from the mouth of the shaft. **1907** *St. Nicholas* Oct. 1145/1 We had to cross several tracks where small electric ore cars run to and from the smelter.

+**Ore chimney.** =CHIMNEY 3. — **1882** *47th Congress 1 Sess.* H. R. Ex. Doc. No. 216, 195 The ore chimney is from 250 to 300 feet in length, and the ore is all taken out above the tunnel. **1896** SHINN *Story of Mine* 225 The general tendency of air currents in the Comstock is in the same direction as the slopé of the ore chimneys.

+**Ore chute. a.** A channel, shaft, or trough through which ore is conveyed from a higher to a lower level. **b.** =CHUTE 4. — **(a) 1874** RAYMOND *6th Rep. Mines* 32 The entire product of the mine will be run out through this tunnel, in cars, . . . to the ore-chute. **(b) 1896** SHINN *Story of Mine* 146 The rich ore chutes near the surface had been worked out.

+**Oregon.** [Origin obscure, but see Hodge II. 146/2.] The name of a western region and state. In attrib. uses.

1. Designating persons, places, articles, etc., living in, associated with, or characteristic of, Oregon.

1844 LEE & FROST *Oregon* 209 Torrents, . . . from the Oregon Alps, dashed along to impede and prevent their progress. **1845** *Whig Almanac 1846* 17 The clearest and best account we have seen of the Oregon Boundary controversy is given in the following article. **1851** *Polly Peablossom* 110 'What, you hev never seen a *live* Grizzly?' exclaimed an old Oregon gold-digger. **1872** POWERS *Afoot & Alone* 303 His flitch of Oregon bacon [was] gone. **1884** BLAINE *20 Years of Congress* I. 8 Texas was also included in the transfer but the Oregon country was not. **1889** *Century Mag.* Jan. 341/1 A strain of horses early imported into Montana from the West and known as the Oregon horse. **1913** BARNES *Western Grazing Grounds* 368 The diamond hitch is rather a professional tie to be used with an aparejo. . . . One is apt to get mixed on it and end up with what is frequently called an 'Oregon wind.'

2. In the specific names of birds.

See also OREGON SNOWBIRD.

1889 MUNROE *Golden Days* 118 They might think we was Oregon ducks, and go for us. **1858** BAIRD *Birds Pacific R.R.* 631 Oregon Grouse. . . . Rocky mountains to Pacific coast of Oregon and Washington. **1869** *Amer. Naturalist* III. 31 Oregon Robin (*T[urdus] nævius*). I found this beautiful thrush common near the summit of the Cœur d'Aleñe Mountains. **1837** *Phila. Acad. Nat. Sci. Jrnl.* VII. 188 [The] Oregon Snow-finch . . . is nearly related to the common snow-bird. **1891** *Cent.* 6406/3 *Oregon towhee*, a black, white, and chestnut towhee bunting, *Pipilo maculatus oregonus*, with spotted scapulars. **1917** *Birds of Amer.* III. 24 [The Vesper Sparrow and the Western Vesper Sparrow] are replaced in the Pacific coast district by the Oregon Vesper Sparrow.

3. In the specific names of plants, trees, etc.

See also OREGON ASH, GRAPE, etc.

1874 GLISAN *Jrnl. Army Life* 480 Thus the Coast Range [of Oregon] . . . is covered with evergreen forests . . . intermixed at places with Oregon alder, balsam tree, . . . Oregon ash. **1869** *Amer. Naturalist* III. 407 Oregon Bearwood (*Frangula Purshiana*). This species of Beechthorn occurs in both slopes of the Coeur d'Aleñe Mountains. **1884** SARGENT *Rep. Forests* 179 Port Orford Cedar. Oregon Cedar. White Cedar. **1849** *New Eng. Farmer* I. 368 Oregon corn . . . resembles the many-rowed corn of the south, excepting the ear is shorter. **1884** SARGENT *Rep. Forests* 73 Oregon Crab Apple. . . . A small tree, sometimes 9 meters in height. **1845** WILKES *U.S. Explor. Exped.* IV. 434 The seed of the Balsamoriza (Oregon sunflower), is also used here, being pounded into a kind of meal. **1897** SUDWORTH *Arborescent Flora* 54 Great Silver Fir. . . . Common names. . . . Oregon White Fir (Cal.), Western White Fir [etc.].

+**Oregon ash.** A western ash (*Fraxinus oregona*) valued for its hard, light wood. — **1869** *Amer. Naturalist* III. 407 Oregon Ash. . . . This first appears at the Dalles [Mont.]. **1874** [see OREGON 3]. **1884** SARGENT *Rep. Forests* 111.

+**Oregonese.** =OREGONIAN *n.* Also pl. — **1848** BRYANT *California* xv. 197, I think the Oregonese had a little the advantage of us in this respect. **1860** WHITMAN *Leaves of Grass* 350 One from Maine or Vermont, and a Carolinian and an Oregonese, shall be friends triune.

+**Oregon grape.** A small evergreen shrub (*Mahonia aquifolia*) of the Pacific coast; also, the fruit of this. — **1859** BARTLETT 304 *Oregon Grape.* Frequently mentioned by explorers in Oregon. **1869** BOWLES *Our New West* 107 They call it [the mahonia holly] here the Oregon grape, for it bears a little berry. **1893** *Amer. Folk-Lore* 136 *Berberis aquifolium*, Oregon grape. Ore. **1915** PIPER & BEATTIE *Flora of Northwest Coast* 164.

+**Oregonian,** *n.* A native or inhabitant of Oregon.

1845 *Phila. Public Ledger* 26 March 2/1 The Oregonians could govern themselves at home under the Federal Government as well as they could without it. **1873** BEADLE *Undevel. West* 772 No Oregonian will eat of salmon caught above the mouth of the Willamette. **1894** *Outing* XXIV. 351/1 No Swiss can feel greater pride in their Alps than all Oregonians do in Mount Hood. **1913** J. B. ELLIS *Lahoma* 214 A year . . . ago, they might have been New Yorkers, Californians, Oregonians, but now all were westerners.

+**Oregonian,** *a.* Of or pertaining to Oregon. — **1873** BEADLE *Undevel. West* 762 There is a distinctly Oregonian look about all the natives and old residents. **1883** *Harper's Mag.* Nov. 943/2 Californian or Oregonian flour . . . can hardly surpass that of Utah. **1902** A. MACGOWAN *Last Word* 156 Washington . . . fell something short of the Barcan desert, or the Oregonian woods.

+**Oregon jargon.** =CHINOOK 4. — **1851** *32d Congress Spec. Sess.* Sen. Ex. Doc. No. 4, 169 The agent communicated with one of them, familiar with the Tchinook language, or Oregon jargon, through Mr. Gibbs. **1910** HODGE, etc. *Amer. Indian* II. 146/2 Oregon jargon, Oregon trade language.

‖**Oregonly,** *adv.* In the manner of an Oregonian. — **a1861** WINTHROP *J. Brent* 243 Armstrong's opinion was only my own, expressed Oregonly.

+**Oregon pea.** (See quot. 1855.) — **1855** BROWNE in *Trans. Amer. Inst. N.Y.* 597 [The] Oregon pea . . . greatly resembles, if it is not identical with the oleaginous pea (*dolichos viridis*) lately introduced into France from China. **1856** *Rep. Comm. Patents 1855: Agric.* 259 The 'Oregon' pea was cultivated here [in Penna.] both in 1854 and 1855.

+**Oregon pine.** =DOUGLAS(S) FIR. — **1845** *No. Amer. Rev.* LX. 166 One of those gigantic Oregon Pines . . . whose prostrate trunk Douglas found to be two hundred and fifty feet in length. **1884** SARGENT *Rep. Forests* 209. **1894** *Amer. Folk-Lore* VII. 99 *Abies Douglasii.* Oregon pine, San Francisco, Cal.

Oregon question. *Hist.* The dispute, settled in 1846, over the boundary line between U.S. and British territory in the Northwest. — **1846** *McDonogh Papers* 113 A gentleman saw him in Havana discussing in a theater the Oregon . . . and other questions. **1846** POLK in *Pres. Mess. & P.* IV. 455 A statement of the propositions for the adjustment of the Oregon question previously made and rejected by the respective Governments. **1848** BRYANT *California* xv. 196 They all manifested great interest in the 'Oregon question.'

+**Oregon snowbird.** A handsome, black-headed finch (*Junco oregonus*) found on the north Pacific coast. — **1852** BAIRD in Stansbury *Gt. Salt Lake* 316 [The] Oregon Snowbird . . . occurs abundantly in Oregon and California. **1869** *Amer. Naturalist* III. 77 *Oregon Snowbird.* . . . I saw no Snow-birds until September 1st. **1874** COUES *Birds N.W.* 142 Oregon Snow-bird. . . . The Oregon species resides in summer . . . down to the 35° parallel.

+**Oregon Territory.** The region west of the Rocky Mts. and between California and Alaska. Now hist. — **1840** *Niles' Nat. Reg.* 7 March 10/2 [A petition], from two hundred and thirty-eight citizens of Ohio, asking the aid of congress in making a settlement in Oregon territory. **1845** *Whig Almanac 1846* 39/2 It was agreed that the arrangement made in 1818, allowing each nation freedom to . . . settle in the Oregon Territory, should be extended. **1846** POLK *Diary* (1929) 111 The proposal is substantially that the Oregon territory shall be divided between the parties by the 49° latitude.

+**Oregon Trail.** *Hist.* The old emigrant route (*c*1805–50) beginning at Independence, Missouri, and leading for about 2000 miles through parts of Kansas, Nebraska, Wyoming, and Idaho into the Oregon country.

1847 PARKMAN in *Knickerb.* XXIX. 310 (*title*), The Oregon Trail. **1860** GREELEY *Overland Journey* 193 Five miles beyond this, the old and well-beaten Oregon Trail strikes off to the northwest. **1903** SEMPLE *Amer. Hist. & Geog. Conditions* 211 The dust of travel thickened on the Oregon Trail. **1912** C. DAWSON *Pioneer Tales* 47 The two remaining ends, or head and tail, of the Oregon Trail continued to wiggle spasmodically a few years longer.

+**Ore house.** *Mining.* A house in which ore is stored. (Cf. ORE SHED.) — **1876** RAYMOND *8th Rep. Mines* 272 A portion of the ore-house and concentration-works was carried away by a snow-slide. **1910** J. HART *Vigilante Girl* 330 The rattle and roar of rock was heard . . . as it slid down the dump to the little stamp-mill and the ore-house below.

+**Oreodon.** The typical genus of *Oreodontidae*, fossils of which are found in the western states. — **1851** *Phila. Acad. Nat. Sci. Proc.* V. 238 Neither of these fossils Dr L[eidy] suspected belonged to Merycoidodon. ... For the first he proposed the name of Oreodon. **1877** LE CONTE *Elem. Geology* (1879) 505 The Oreodon is another very remarkable animal, intermediate between the hog, the deer and the camel, which at this time inhabited the whole Continent from Nebraska to Oregon.

+**Ore shed.** *Mining.* A shed in which ore is stored. (Cf. ORE HOUSE.) — **1883** FOOTE *Led-Horse Claim* 26 [He] looked across to the Shoshone's shaft-houses, its new ore-sheds. **1906** F. LYNDE *Quickening* 384 He meant to fire from where he stood under the eaves of the ore-shed.

+**Ore wagon.** A wagon in which ore is hauled from a mine. — **1896** SHINN *Story of Mine* 109 They were not prairie schooners, or ... square-built ore wagons. **1905** VALENTINE *H. Sandwith* 156 She passed a string of ore-wagons returning from the mines—great clumsy conveyances drawn by gaunt mules.

+**Ore-washer.** (See quot. 1881.) — **1859** *Rep. Comm. Patents 1858* I. 520 Improved Ore Washer. **1881** RAYMOND *Mining Gloss., Ore-washer,* a machine for washing clay and earths out of earthy brown-hematite ores. **1900** *Engineering Mag.* XIX. 777/2 The La Bella Power Plant, Goldfield, Colo., ... [was] built to supply ... water for ore washers nearby.

* **Organ.**

1. * **a.** A wind musical instrument consisting essentially of a number of pipes, a bellows for supplying air to these, and keys for sounding them. +**b.** A reed organ.

1711 *Essex Inst. Coll.* X. I. 90, [I] heard ye organs and saw strange things in a microscope. **1766** J. ROWE *Diary* 95 After church the Vestry met abo[ut] cleaning the Organ & voted it to be cleaned. **1802** *Holyoke Diaries* 142 We went to Doct Oliver's to hear the Organ. **1875** *Cimarron News & Press* 7 Aug. 3/2 Persons contemplating the purchase of Organs or Sewing Machines [etc.]. **1880** E. PROUT in *Grove Dict. Mus.* I. 61 The American organ under its present name ... was first introduced by Messrs. Mason and Hamlin of Boston, about the year 1860. **1907** *St. Nicholas* May 637/1 Then, after a pause, they heard a fine organ.

2. Attrib. and comb. with *bellows, blower, builder,* etc.

1763 *Md. Hist. Mag.* X. 40 An Account of Mr. Victors for Blowing the Organ Bellows one year. **1827** DRAKE & MANSFIELD *Cincinnati* 66 One Organ Builder. **1872** HOLMES *Poet* 351 The organ-blower works harder with his muscles ... than the organ-player. **1881** *Harper's Mag.* May 814/1 Piano and organ recitals have long been fashionable. **1907** *St. Nicholas* Sept. 1016/1 He was quite close to the player, though separated by the panels of the organ-case.

+**Organ cactus.** =GIANT CACTUS. — **1883** *Harper's Mag.* March 502/2 The enormous saguaras, the organ-cactus which ... bristle over the landscape like masts or columns.

Organdy. Also †**organdi, organdie.**

1. A fine translucent muslin, plain or figured, used for women's dresses. {1835–} Also attrib.

1851 *Harper's Mag.* Feb. 432/2 A very pretty pattern for an Evening Dress is made of a material called Organdi. **1871** *Scribner's Mo.* II. 209 Fluted ruffles of French organdy edged with footing. **1879** RANOUS *Diary of Daly Débutante* 9 In the third and last act we girls are to wear white organdie and lace summer costumes. **1904** GLASGOW *Deliverance* 76 The girl, dressed daintily in a faded muslin, with an organdy kerchief crossed over her swelling bosom. **1919** *Sears, Roebuck & Co. Cat.* No. 138, 436 Organdies are very popular and in this number is offered a cotton cloth of beautiful sheerness.

2. A dress made of this material.

1863 'M. HARLAND' *Husks* 60 A certain organdie which had formed a part of Lucy's wardrobe the previous summer. **1898** ATHERTON *Californians* 89 Her mother's present was ... a white organdie. **1919** T. K. HOLMES *Man fr. Tall Timber* 167, I don't know but I'd better put on my figgered organdy.

Organ-grinder. An itinerant street musician who operates a hand organ. {1806–} — **1841** *Picayune* 27 May 2/3 An organ grinder yesterday accidentally let his monkey loose in the street. **1869** *Overland Mo.* III. 53 Who has not met graduates of the German Gymnasia, all through this country, in the capacity of wood-sawyers, organ-grinders [etc.]? **1872** BRACE *Dangerous Classes N.Y.* 202 The term '*pianist*' is ironically applied to newly-landed organ-grinders. **1920** HOWELLS *Vacation of Kelwyns* 151 One morning ... there came a family of organ-grinders.

+**Organic Act.** An act of the U.S. Congress conferring the powers of government upon a territory. (Cf. ENABLING ACT.) — **1857** in Johnson *Anderson Co., Kansas* 73 We will use all legal means to resist every attempt to force upon us a Territorial government, ... which is in violation ... of the organic act of the Territory. **1867** *Wkly. New Mexican* 17 Aug. 2/2 In the organic act it is defined who shall be voters at the first election after its passage. **1913** J. B. ELLIS *Lahoma* 211 Congress made them wait five months ... before approving the Organic Act.

Organic law. +The basic or fundamental law by virtue of which a government exists as such; also, =prec. — **1847** *Santa Fe Republican* 30 Oct. 2/1 This organic law provides for the appointment of various officers from Governor down. **1863** *Rio Abajo Press* 3 March 2/1 More than twelve years since Congress enacted our Organic Law; yet no steps are taken for its entering the Union as a State. **1880** *Cimarron News & Press* 9 Sept. 2/1 Under our organic law each 16th and 32d section of public land is reserved for school purposes. **1900** *Congress. Rec.* 6 Feb. 1544/1 The fifteenth amendment ... is a part of the organic law of this Republic.

* **Organist.** One who plays an organ, esp. one employed to play in a church — **1689** SEWALL *Diary* I. 296 Got the Organist to give us some Musick. *a***1841** W. HAWES *Sporting Scenes* II. 94 The hired organist and bellows blower, have each his quota of duty to perform. **1885** *Century Mag.* Jan. 475 The average salary now paid to organists is not so large as was paid five or ten years ago. **1917** H. T. COMSTOCK *Man* 247 The organist was in his place, his music discriminately chosen.

* **Organization.**

+**1.** The drawing up or establishing of the laws and regulations in accordance with which a township or territory functions as a governmental unit.

1861 *Mich. Gen. Statutes* (1882) I. 195 All the requirements as to notice, petition, and applications for the organization of such township shall be the same as are now required. **1890** LANGFORD *Vigilante Days* (1912) 224 Previous to the organization of the Territory of Idaho on the third of March, 1863 [etc.].

+**2.** The body of officials, committee members, etc., that direct the affairs of a political party.

1873 *Republic* I. 3 The Republican organization had become effete and corrupt. **1903** HART *Actual Government* 98 Those persons, often very few in number, who control the regular routine of party action, take upon themselves the name of 'the organization'; by their opponents, within or without their party, they are habitually called 'the machine.' **1904** *Booklovers Mag.* Oct. 439 Editors are called in frequent consultation so as to be in close touch with the organization.

‖**3.** Physical build or set-up.

1890 LANGFORD *Vigilante Days* (1912) 456 She was of powerful organization, and having passed her life upon the borders, knew how to use the rifle.

* **Organize,** *v.*

+**1.** *intr.* To effect or achieve an organization, esp. of political bodies; to elect a presiding officer, appoint committees, etc., preparatory to the orderly discharge of business.

1816 PICKERING 144 *To Organize.* ... Used in speaking of political bodies. **1829** *Va. Lit. Museum* 30 Dec. 459 *Organize.* ... This word has a restricted sense, being applied to political and other bodies; as, 'have you organized?' **1894** REED *Man. Parliamentary Law* 18 Those assemblies the membership of which can not be in dispute ... can organize permanently at once. **1911** *N.Y. Ev. Post* 9 Jan. 3 The Legislature of New Jersey will organize to-morrow for the 135th time.

+**b.** *tr.* To prepare (a body of representatives or a political party) for proper functioning through the election of officers, committees, etc.

1840 *Niles' Nat. Reg.* 5 Dec. 218 Both houses [in S.C.] being organized, the governor ... transmitted his message on Tuesday the 24th. **1860** *Harper's Mag.* May 860/2 Uncle Davie ... was giving Colonel B— 'fits' because the Republicans didn't 'organize the House.' **1905** *McClure's Mag.* XXIV. 346 Brayton ... 'organized' the Republican party; ... he organized the General Assembly and ran it.

+**2.** To found or establish (unions or granges); to systematize or form (labor or laborers) into a union. Also used of a locality.

[**1832** *Congress. Deb.* 15 June 3575 A former Secretary of the Treasury ... urged upon Congress ... to imitate the Pacha, by 'organizing the whole labor of the country' in order to produce 'the greatest aggregate of national wealth.'] **1871** *Atlantic Mo.* May 557/1 The 'National Labor Union' was organized at Baltimore in 1866. **1872** *Chicago Tribune* 27 Dec. 4/2 Farmers' 'Granges,' or clubs, are being organized quite extensively in Illinois and Iowa. **1887** *Courier-Journal* 29 Jan. 5/1 Delegates are actively engaged in organizing every branch of labor about the piers and docks. **1896** *Internat. Typogr. Union Proc.* 18/2 There is still a great field for the organizers and their deputies in helping us to organize German printers. **1899** *Ib.* 112/1, I dispatched them organizing literature and letters, with a view to organizing their respective localities. **1903** J. MITCHELL *Organized Labor* 431 Trade unionism in the United States is still in its infancy; American labor is still far from being organized.

b. *intr.* To unite in forming a union.

1874 in C. Evans *Hist. United Mine Workers* I. 52 Organize secretly if you are not permitted to do so publicly, but do organize. **1887** McNEILL *Labor Movement* 81 The merchants at this time [1832, denied] ... the right of the workingmen to organize for protection. **1921** J. R. COMMONS *Trade Unionism* 563 Workers everywhere should insist upon their right to organize into trade-unions.

+**3.** *tr.* To set up or prescribe for (a county, territory, or territorial government) fundamental laws and regulations.

1851 FILLMORE in *Pres. Mess. & P.* V. 127 Some difficulties have occurred in organizing the Territorial governments of New Mexico and Utah. **1861** *Mich. Gen. Statutes* (1882) I. 195 Said board may, in their discretion, set off and organize the attached territory into a separate township. **1868** *Congress. Globe* 22 July 4344/2 When the Territory of Montana was organized, ... [I] gave it the name of Wyoming.

Organized labor. Workingmen who are organized in labor unions. Also attrib. — **1885** in C. Evans *Hist. United Mine Workers* I. 131 To organized labor . . . and to the generous and sympathetic public . . . we return our sincere and heartfelt thanks. **1896** *Internat. Typogr. Union Proc.* 4/1 There is no disposition to minimize the desirability of workingmen, and especially those identified with organized labor, advancing and defending their interests. **1924** WOLMAN *Growth of Amer. Trade Unions* 82 The number of wage earners . . . would not be considered by some a thoroughly fair base for measuring the achievement in size of an organized labor movement.

Organizer. {1849-} +A member of a labor union whose duty it is to persuade other workmen to join a union. — **1874** in C. Evans *Hist. United Mine Workers* I. 60 One or more competent persons in each state embraced in the organization who shall be known as 'organizers,' and whose duties shall be to organize new lodges or branches. **1898** *Kansas City Star* 21 Dec. 5/1 Organizers are to be sent into the South to enlighten the negro upon the benefits to be derived from unionism. **1917** SINCLAIR *King Coal* 81 A letter which certified him to be Thomas Olson, an organiser for the United Mine-Workers.

Oriental, a.* In the specific names of trees and plants: (see quotations). — **1818 DARBY *Emigrant's Guide* 185 Oriental bhené . . . is known in Louisiana, but much neglected. **1846** WOOD *Botany* 431 *Borago orientalis*, Oriental Borage, . . . an ornamental garden plant. . . . Flowers blue, appearing in the spring months. **1892** APGAR *Trees Northern U.S.* 139 *Platanus orientalis* . . . (Oriental Plane.) Leaves more deeply cut, smaller, and sooner smooth than those of the American Sycamore. *Ib.* 181 *Picea orientalis*. . . . Eastern or Oriental Spruce. . . . A beautiful, conical, slow-growing, compact tree.

+Original package. *Law & Commerce.* The package in which goods are transported from one state into another; spec., an unopened bottle of liquor. Also attrib. — **1855** *Chicago Times* 21 June 2/4 The city court decided that a bottle of champagne was an 'original package,' and discharged a complaint based on the drinking of it. **1890** *Congress. Rec.* 9 May 4374/2 An attempt was made . . . to introduce liquors [into Me.] in the original package. *Ib.* 18 July 7436/2 Cities like Topeka, in Kansas, where the school-boys never saw saloons and where the jails are empty, now have these original-package saloons in full blast. **1891** *Voice* 31 July, With infinite 'gall,' he opened an office for the sale of 'original packages' only a few feet away.

+Original states. *collect.* The thirteen states united under the Articles of Confederation and later under the Federal Constitution. (Cf. CONFEDERATION 3.) — **1802** *Ann. 7th Congress* 1 Sess. 1349 An act . . . for the admission of such State into the Union, on an equal footing with the original States. **1835** JACKSON in *Pres. Mess. & P.* III. 186 Such State should be admitted by its delegates into the Congress of the United States on an equal footing with the original States in all respects whatever.

+Orignal, Original. Also **aurignial.** [Can. Fr.] The American moose or elk. *Obs.* — **1775** J. ANDERSON *Essays Relating to Agric.* 462 In North America they have a species of deer, called by the natives Orignial or Aurignial . . . probably the Moose-deer. **1781-2** JEFFERSON *Notes Va.* (1788) 57n., It were to be wished, that naturalists . . . would examine well the animals called there [in northern Amer.] by the names of grey and black moose, caribou, original [*sic*], and elk.

***Oriole.** +Any one of various American birds of the family Icteridae, closely allied to the finches. {1792, in Antigua}

[**1782** LATHAM *General Synopsis of Birds* I. 417 Oriole. . . . These birds are inhabitants of America, except in a few instances.] **1831** J. Q. ADAMS *Memoirs* VIII. 426 The oriole of Baltimore is the fiery hang-bird. **1845** *Knickerb.* XXV. 443 The oriole flitting among the trees over my head . . . was the same that sang there twenty years before. **1865** *Atlantic Mo.* XV. 518 May is the month of the Swallows and the Orioles. **1880** *Harper's Mag.* June 70 Now we see the fiery Oriole in his gold and jetty velvet flashing in the morning sun. **1920** HOWELLS *Vacation of Kelwyns* 59 The song of the bobolinks and orioles in the fields and dooryards.

+b. With a defining term.

See also BALTIMORE 1, BULLOCK'S ORIOLE, etc.

1844 *Nat. Hist. N.Y., Zoology* II. 139 The Golden Oriole. *Icterus Baltimore.* **1858** BAIRD *Birds Pacific R.R.* 542 Audubon's oriole . . . *Hab.* Valley of the Lower Rio Grande of Texas, southward. **1917** *Birds of Amer.* II. 256 Orchard Oriole. . . . [Also called] Brown Oriole; Basket Bird.

+Orleanese, a. Residing in New Orleans. — **1808** JEFFERSON *Writings* XII. 185 If the Orleanese Creoles would but contemplate these truths, they would cling to the American Union.

Orleans.

1. a. A variety of grape. **b.** Short for 'New Orleans sugar.'

1769 *Amer. Philos. Soc.* I. 190 The vines proper for these countries [N.H., R.I., & Conn.] are, 1. The black Auvernat, 2. The black Orleans [etc.]. **a1846** *Quarter Race Ky.* 83 He gives Jim Smith . . . *warnin* to fetch . . . sum 'Orleans' for sweetnin.

+2. *attrib.* Designating things found in or associated with New Orleans, Louisiana.

1867 G. W. HARRIS *Sut Lovingood* 87 Gin em a rale Orleans fever in five minits. **1883** *Practical Housekeeping* 100 Ginger Cakes. One quart Orleans molasses, pint lard or butter [etc.]. **1895** KING *New Orleans* 293 Many a good story of the fathers . . . and elder brothers of the young gentlemen at the Orleans college. *Ib.*, The great lantern of the Orleans theatre.

+3. *Orleans territory*, that part of the Louisiana purchase which in 1812 became the state of Louisiana.

1806 in *Ann. 9th Congress* 2 Sess. 1137 Nature has marked with a distinguishing feature, the line established by Congress, between the Orleans and Louisiana Territories.

+Orleans boat. 1. (See quot. 1817.) *Obs.* **2.** A Mississippi River steamboat bound for New Orleans. — **(1) 1797** F. BAILY *Tour* 225 An Orleans boat (as it is here called) stopped at the town. **1817** FORDHAM *Narr. Travels* 79 These flat boats or Orleans boats as they are called in the Western Waters are from 12 to 25 feet wide, and from 30 to 90 feet long. **1843** *Amer. Pioneer* II. 63 *Kentucky boats*, as they were called, in contradistinction to the *Orleans boats*, which were of a larger and better finished kind, having a longer voyage to undergo. **(2)** 'MARK TWAIN' *H. Finn* xxiv. 241 She's a big Orleans boat, and I was afeard she mightn't stop there.

+Orneriness. Meanness, the state of being 'ornery.' *colloq.* — **1899** TARKINGTON *Gent. from Ind.* iv, Sometimes they . . . let loose their deviltries just for pure orneriness.

Ornery. Also **ornary.** [Variant of *ordinary.*] Low, mean, contemptible; cantankerous, hard to manage. *local.* {dial.} (Cf. ONERY.)

1830 *Mass. Spy* 28 July (Th.), You ornery fellow! do you pretend to call me to account for my language? **1855** *Harper's Mag.* XI. 290/2, I tuck a notion to come back to this or'nary country agin. **1897** *Boston Globe* 26 Dec. 7/5 The burro is such a cussed ornery crittur that he'll try and get away from you every time. **1921** PAINE *Comr. Rolling Ocean* 90 Am I ornery enough to lie to you, after what had happened on deck last night?

+Ornithoid, a. Resembling or approaching the structure found in birds. — **1858** HITCHCOCK *Ichnol. New Eng.* 105, I attach the Typopus to the ornithoid Lizards. **1895** *Pop. Science Mo.* Sept. 693 Ornithoid lizards or batrachians.

+Oronoco (tobacco). Also **†Arronoca, Aranoko, Oronooko,** etc. [From the *Orinoco* River in South America.] A variety of strong-scented tobacco.

1660 *Va. State P.* I. 5 Two thousand five hundred pounds of good, sound, bright and large Arronoca Tobacco. **1688** CLAYTON *Va.* in *Phil. Trans.* XVII. 943 The richer the Ground, the better it is for Aranoko Tobacco. **1708** E. COOK *Sot-Weed Factor* 23 Broad Oronooko bright and sound. **1800** W. TATHAM *Tobacco* 4 The different species of the genus have been in former days distinguished in Virginia by the names of Oronoko, sweet scented, and little Frederic. **1859** *Harper's Mag.* Dec. 81/1, [I] began diffusing the fumes of fragrant Oronoka prodigally through the apartment. **1896** P. A. BRUCE *Econ. Hist. Va.* I. 436 Between the sweet-scented and the Oronoco, . . . there are several varieties

***Orphanage.** =next. {1865-} — **1870** *Republican Review* 29 Oct. 2/2 An orphanage and hospital belonging to the Sisters of Charity. **1883** *Harper's Mag.* Oct. 701/1, I refuse to permit her to open an orphanage for you. **1906** PRINGLE *Rice Planter* 306, I went to the orphanage to see him.

Orphan asylum. An institution for the care of orphans.

1835 J. MARTIN *Descr. Va.* 162/2 There are [in Petersburg] . . . a Masonic Hall, female orphan asylum, several common schools and one free school. **1850** A. LAWRENCE *Diary & Corr.* 285 The manifest pleasure you felt in visiting our Female Orphan Asylum yesterday has left a sunbeam on my path. **1873** *Mich. Gen. Statutes* (1882) I. 533 Children in any orphan asylum where the officers thereof desire to surrender them to the care of the state. **1902** LORIMER *Lett. Merchant* 163 His mother disinherited him, and left her money to an orphan asylum. **1916** E. PORTER *David* 91 There's the orphan asylum, or maybe the poorhouse—if they'd take him.

b. In the names of benevolent organizations interested in the care of orphans.

1811 *Freemasons Mag.* (Phila.) Nov. 97 The other proclaims its benevolent character in its name, 'The Orphan Asylum Society.' **1828** *Yankee* Jan. 3/1 The society shall be called the Female Orphan Asylum of Portland, . . . being strictly a charitable institution.

Orphan house. =ORPHAN ASYLUM. *Obs.* {1832}

[**1711** C. MATHER *Diary* II. 150, I am again writing to the University of Halle, . . . sending a present of Gold for the Orphan house there.] **1738** WHITEFIELD *Works* (1771) I. 44 What I have most at heart, is the building an orphan-house [in Georgia]. **1741** *Ga. Hist. Soc. Coll.* II. 259 The frame of the Orphan-House is up. **1792** BENTLEY *Diary* I. 388, I went this evening . . . to settle the affairs of the Orphan House in Georgia. **1834** NOTT *Novellettes* I. 7 Pack the brat off to the orphan-house.

+Orphans' court. (See quot. 1914.)

1713 *Penna. Col. Rec.* II. 565 An act for Establishing Orphan's Courts. **1784** *N.J. Archives* XXIII. p. lxxi, An Act to . . . Establish an Orphan's Court in the Several Counties of this State. **1808** *Md. Laws* 87 The Proceedings of the Orphans' Court of Saint Mary's County. **1850** *Penna. Rep.* XIII. 124 The record of the orphans' court was in evidence by the plaintiff. **1914** *Cycl. Amer. Govt.* I. 504 In New Jersey, Pennsylvania, Delaware and Maryland the probate of wills, the administration of decedents' estates and supervision of minor heirs is vested in orphans' courts. Their jurisdiction and powers are similar to those of probate courts in other states.

attrib. **1873** *Penna. Rep.* XIII. 121 An Orphans' Court sale is a judicial sale.

Orphan('s) home. =ORPHAN ASYLUM. — **1898** *Kansas City Star* 18 Dec. 2/4 Contributions to the Christmas fund for the children of St. Joseph's Female Orphan home . . . may be left at Altman's store. *Ib.* 4/3 One reform the new governor has in mind is a law that will enable authorized orphans' homes to rescue young children from vicious or criminal families.

Orrery. An apparatus for illustrating by means of small spheres and wheelwork the relative size, position, and movements of bodies in the solar system. {1713-} — **1748** FRANKLIN *Exper. on Electricity* 31 These wheels may be applied . . . to the . . . moving of light-made Orreries. **1816** *Ann. 14th Congress* 1 Sess. 607 That great palladium of our independence had been compared to that miniature representation of the planetary system called an Orrery. **1860** OLMSTED *Mech. Heavens* 110 The machinery of the heavens is much simpler than that of an orrery.

***Orris.** A plant of the genus *Iris;* also, the powder prepared from its fragrant root. — **1737** BRICKELL *N. Carolina* 22 Oris, Water-lillies, Peony, Male and Female, Solomons-Seal, Agarick. **1870** R. TOMES *Decorum* 72 A powder of starch or arrowroot, which it would be well to perfume with bitter almonds, orris, or some other no more intrusive odor. **1905** E. W. PRINGLE *Rice Planter* 184 The orris of commerce is the root of the iris.

***Orthodox,** *a.* +Of or pertaining to the evangelical or conservative section of Quakers as contrasted with the more liberal Hicksites. — **1833** *Niles' Reg.* XLIV. 372/2 The court of errors and appeals . . . [considered] the important case between the two parts of the society of Friends commonly called Orthodox and Hicksites. **1839** MARRYAT *Diary Amer.* Ser. 1. III. 95 The Friends . . . have been separated into Orthodox and Hicksite. **1841** PARK *Pantology* 158 The Hicksites, who have seceded from the Orthodox Quakers, incline to the doctrines of the Socinians. **1882** Schaff *Religious Encycl.* I. 839/2 About the year 1827 the society [of Friends] in America was divided into two bodies,—evangelical or 'orthodox,' and liberal or 'Hicksite.'

+**Ortley (pippin).** A winter eating apple. — **1847** IVES *New Eng. Fruit* 42 Ortley Pippin.—The size sometimes large, the form oblong; the skin, when ripe, a bright yellow. **1856** *Rep. Comm. Patents 1855: Agric.* 292 Winter apples [include] . . . Small Romanite, Ortley, or White Bellefleur, Baldwin.

***Ortolan.** {1656-} +**a.** =CAROLINA RAIL. +**b.** =BOBOLINK 1. (The author of quot. 1836 seems to be confusing the American with the English bird.) — **1836** HOLLEY *Texas* 100 Ortolans, which form so celebrated a dish in Europe, are abundant in Texas. **1874** COUES *Birds N.W.* 538 *Porzana Carolina,* . . . Carolina Rail; Sora; 'Ortolan.' **1903** *Baltimore Sun Almanac* 29 Sora, Water Rail or Ortolan. **1917** *Birds of Amer.* I. 207 Sora. *Porzana carolina.* . . . Other names. . . . Ortolan; Mud Hen. *Ib.* II. 241 Bobolink. . . . Other Names. . . . Meadow-bird; American Ortolan; Bob-lincoln.

+**Osage.** Also †**Ozage.** [From tribal name *Wazhazhe* 'war people.']

1. a. An Indian of the most important southern Siouan tribe west of the Mississippi River, first encountered by Europeans along the Osage River in Missouri. **b.** Freq. in pl., the tribe itself.

1698 tr. Hennepin *New Discovery* I. 141 Several Savages of the Nations of the Osages, Cikaga, and Akansa, came to see us. **1722** COXE *Descr. Carolana* 16 The Yellow [River] is called the River of the Massorites, from a great Nation inhabiting in many Towns near its juncture with the River of the Ozages. **1807** *Ann. 10th Congress* 1 Sess. I. 575 The health of the Osages . . . [is] now generally restored. **1821** NUTTALL *Travels Arkansa* 211 The Indian councils now pending betwixt the Osages and Cherokees filled the fort with a disagreeable bustle. **1842** *S. Lit. Messenger* VIII. 63/2, I found everything in possession of a party of ten or twelve Osages. **1906** *Indian Laws & Tr.* III. 253 The principal chief of the Osages shall . . . file with the Secretary of the Interior a list of names.

2. *attrib.* **a.** Designating places or groups composed of or inhabited by Osage Indians.

1804 CLARK in *Lewis & C. Exped.* I. (1904) 36 They had letters from the man Mr. Choteau Sent to that part of the Osage Nation settled on Arkansa River. **1821** J. FOWLER *Journal* 6 We set out early along the road leading to the Osage vilege. **1843** N. BOONE *Journal* (1917) 200 The horses taken were picketed . . . so near the Osage camp that no Pawnees would ever come there for them. **1906** *Indian Laws & Tr.* III. 253 All lands belonging to the Osage tribe of Indians . . . shall be divided among the members of said tribe.

b. Designating persons belonging to the Osage tribe.

See also OSAGE INDIAN.

1808 PIKE *Sources Miss.* 125 A Sac . . . was married to an Osage femme and spoke French *only.* **1822** *Missionary Herald* XVIII. 148 We are daily talking among ourselves about the way to obtain more of the Osage children. **1835** IRVING *Tour on Prairies* 48 Osage hunters had recently crossed the river, on their way to the buffalo range. **1836** IRVING *Astoria* I. 161 By the Osage warriors, Mr. Hunt and his companions were again to be warned to be on their guard.

c. Designating the shrub or tree of the Osage orange.

1856 *Rep. Comm. Patents 1855: Agric.* 316 The Osage plant has, at all periods of its growth, a tap-root, longer and thicker than the top or stem. **1869** *Rep. Comm. Agric. 1868* 251 Specimens of the single-row Osage thorn . . . had much the appearance of a line of brush with tops all outward.

3. In special combinations.

Osage buhr, a form of silicious rock suitable for millstones; *Osage hedge,* a hedge made of Osage orange; *Osage hunting trail,* a trail between the Arkansas and Missouri Rivers made by the Osage Indians on their hunts; *Osage prairie,* an extensive prairie region between the Arkansas and Missouri rivers formerly occupied by the Osage Indians; *Osage reserve,* an area of about one and a half million acres in Oklahoma set apart by Congress in 1870 for the Osage Indians; *Osage trace,* (see quotation).

1837 WETMORE *Gaz. Missouri* 73 An excellent substitute for the French buhr has been quarried in this county. . . . It is commonly called the Osage buhr. **1902** WHITE *Blazed Trail* 102 An osage hedge and a board fence respectively bounded the side and back. **1843** BOONE *Journal* (1917) 192 Followed until 2 o'clock the great Osage hunting trail. **1821** NUTTALL *Travels Arkansa* 171 About eight miles from the Arkansa, commences the great Osage prairie, more than 60 miles in length. **1901** DUNCAN & SCOTT *Allen & Woodson Co., Kansas* 582 This strip began at the state line and ran westward beyond the surveys, while on the south it joined the Osage Reserve. **1818** SCHOOLCRAFT *Journal* 52 In pursuing up the valley of Swan Creek, . . . we fell into the Osage trace, a horse path beaten by the Osages in their hunting excursions.

+**Osage apple.** =OSAGE ORANGE. — **1804** LEWIS in *L. & Clark Exped.* VI. (1904) 172 No appearance of the buds of the Osage apple. *Ib.* VII. 296. **1817** *Amer. Mo. Mag.* II. 57 Mr. Rafinesque read an interesting paper . . . on the Osage Apple.

+**Osage Indian.** An Indian of the Osage tribe; also, pl., the tribe of these Indians. Also attrib.

1820 DEWEES *Lett. from Texas* 15 The Osage Indians . . . are very hostile to us. **1843** FRÉMONT *Exped.* 107 Maxwell . . . entered the camp at full speed at the head of a war party of Osage Indians. **1868** *N.Y. Herald* 18 July 6/2 The Osage Indian land swindle still hangs fire in the Senate. **1900** *Congress. Rec.* 1 Feb. 1396/1, I do not think it includes the Osage Indian war. **1901** DUNCAN & SCOTT *Allen & Woodson Co., Kansas* 9 They found about four hundred lodges of Osage Indians encamped in the timber.

+**Osage orange.**

1. An American tree (*Maclura pomifera*) native to Arkansas and adjacent regions; also, the hard, flexible wood of this tree.

The wood of this tree was prized by the Indians for making bows, hence the French name BOIS D'ARC and the American corruptions BOWDARK, BODOCK. The tree is also valuable as a hedge shrub.

1817 BRADBURY *Travels* 160 *n.,* It bleeds an acrid milky juice when wounded, and is called by the hunters the Osage Orange. **1849** *New Eng. Farmer* I. 82 Some of our friends have made inquiries as to the value of the Osage orange for hedges. **1852** MARCY *Explor. Red River* (1854) 106 Their bows are made of the tough and elastic wood of the 'bois d'arc,' or Osage orange. **1870** KEIM *Sheridan's Troopers* 159 Everywhere along the stream there was an abundance of wood, . . . box elder, Osage orange and some locust. **1891** *Harper's Mag.* Sept. 579/2 There was a hedge of Osage orange on one side of the yard. **1898** E. C. HALL *Aunt Jane* 86 A tall hedge of Osage orange bordered each side of the road.

2. Attrib. with *bush, hedgerow, plant,* etc.

See also OSAGE ORANGE HEDGE.

1846 BROWNE *Trees Amer.* 465 *Maclura aurantiaca,* The Osage Orange-Tree. **1855** *Chicago Times* 29 March 3/2 Over 3,000 bushels of Osage orange seed was brought into the western market last year from Texas. **1857** *Ill. Agric. Soc. Trans.* II. 23 The practicability of successfully cultivating the osage orange plant into a protective hedge. **1859** MARCY *Prairie Trav.* 26 Wheels made of bois d'arc, or Osage-orange wood, are the best for the plains, as they shrink but little. **1892** ALLEN *Blue-Grass Region* 28 A pleasure it is, too, to come occasionally upon an Osage orange hedge-row. **1902** HARBEN *Abner Daniel* 282 It was a sequestered spot, well hidden from the rest of the road by an old hedge of Osage orange bushes.

+**Osage orange hedge.** A hedge formed of Osage orange trees or bushes. — **1855** *Chicago W. Times* 29 March 3/2 The introduction of the Osage orange hedges, as a substitute for fences on the Western prairies, . . . is becoming very general. **1870** *Rep. Comm. Agric. 1869* 433 This farm . . . is entirely surrounded by an Osage orange hedge, from one to two years' growth. **1883** ZEIGLER & GROSSCUP *Alleghanies* 248 Osage-orange hedges line the path to it under the cluster of noble trees. **1896** *Typographical Jrnl.* IX. 51 Stone fences and osage orange hedges . . . inclose breeding establishments of fine stock on every road.

+**Osage plum.** (See quot. 1804.) *Obs.* — **1804** CLARK in *Lewis & C. Exped.* I. (1904) 46 Wild plumb of a Superior . . . quallity, Called the Osages Plumb Grows on a bush the hight of a Hasel. **1826** FLINT *Recoll.* 125 The trees about the house were literally bending under their loads of apples, pears, and the yellow Osage plum. **1827** *Western Mo. Rev.* I. 323 Some of them, especially the yellow Osage plum, are among the most delicious fruits, we have ever tasted.

+**Oscine,** *a.* Of or pertaining to oscines or singing birds. — **1883** *Nation* 29 March 281 *Boot* . . . is used to denote the continuous front sheath of the tarsus of most oscine or singing birds, like the robin. **1885** *Library Mag.* Aug. 97 Those liquid bird-phrases . . . have been the same since first an oscine throat was filled with music.

*** Osier.** Any one of various willows having tough, pliant boughs used in making basketwork, furniture, etc.; also, a bough or shoot of this. (Cf. BASKET-WILLOW.)

1779 FRENEAU *Poems* (1786) 104 There cedars dark, the osier, and the pine, Shorn tamarisks, and weeping willows grew. **1806** in *Ann. 9th Congress* 2 Sess. 1119 The islands are skirted with osier. **1835** HOFFMAN *Winter in West* II. 19 The wigwam was formed of . . . mats of woven rushes, subtended around a frame-work of osiers. **1847** DARLINGTON *Weeds & Plants* 328 *S[alix] viminalis*. . . . Osier. Basket Willow. . . . This species, the common Osier of Europe, is cultivated to some extent for its long flexible branches which are wrought into baskets. **1914** *Farmer's Bul.* No. 622, 9 Both the white and black osier . . . are worthless in the Eastern, Central, and Southern United States, though both may do well in the Northwest.

b. Attrib. and comb. with *basket, growing, holt, island.*

1815 *Mass. H. S. Coll.* 2 Ser. IV. 274 Before the ice is yet broken up, the swan finds an open resting place among the ozier holts. **1852** *Harper's Mag.* April 643/1 You see the broad arm of a river, with little swampy osier islands upon it. **1889** *Rep. Secy. Agric.* 288 A few figures regarding the profit of Osier growing, obtained from the neighborhood of Syracuse, may be of interest. **1890** RYAN *Told in Hills* 146 The fish that they smoke, dry, and pack in osier baskets for the winter.

*** Osnaburg(s).** Also †**Ozenbrig, Osnabrug,** etc. Coarse linen cloth of a kind made originally at Osnaburg (*Osnabrück*), Germany; strong, durable cloth somewhat similar to this but made of cotton.

1660 *Suffolk Deeds* III. 382 Three smale packetts conteining three peices of ozenbrigs. **1709** LAWSON *Carolina* 88 The Commodities, which are necessary to carry over to this Plantation . . . are . . . Linnens of all sorts, but chiefly ordinary Blues, Osnabrugs, Scotch and Irish Linnen. **1792** *Ann. 2d Congress* 1026 It would . . . be good policy to raise the duty . . . on the following articles: . . . osnaburgs . . . and upon all other linens. **1817** *Cape-Fear Recorder* 5 April, 27 packages German Goods, consisting of a handsome assortment of Linens, . . . Ticklenburgs, Osnaburgs, Browns, and Burlaps. **1856** *Fla. Plantation Rec.* 519 Recived . . . 17½ yards Cotton osnaburgs from Alistena. **1902** G. C. EGGLESTON *D. South* 153 Telling Moses to send me all the blankets and all the cloth he has of every kind, from calico and osnaburgs to heavy woollen goods.

b. Attrib. with *breeches, cloth, gown,* etc.

1681 *New Castle Court Rec.* 493 Twoo Remnants of osnabriggs Linnen. **1704** *Boston News-Letter* 19 June 2/2 A tall lusty Indian Man . . . , with a black Hat, brown Ozenbridge Breeches and Jacket. **1720** *Amer. Wkly. Mercury* 28 April 3/2 A Servant Man . . . [wore] a new Ozenbrig Shirt a pair of Leather Breeches. **1772** *Md. Hist. Mag.* XIV. 151 Mrs. Darnalls had an Osnabrigs Petticoat stolen from them. **1835** INGRAHAM *South-West* I. 274 The indigo matter . . . is put in a wooden frame, with a loose Osnaburg cloth between it and the frame. **1863** 'E. KIRKE' *Southern Friends* 99 She still wore the tattered red and yellow turban, and the thin Osnaburg gown.

+**Osophy.** [From phil*osophy*, the*osophy*, etc.] A new or strange doctrine or theory. *contemptuous.* — **1865** E. BURRITT *Walk to Land's End* (1868) 28 Hampton Court . . . is a parliament in which the idiosyncracies, *isms* and *osophies* of race and nation . . . are represented in a pleasant and instructive manner. **1897** *Advance* 28 Oct. 574/2 That man would be hard to please who could not find . . . some variety of doxy, or osophy, or ism, which would come within hailing distance of his theory of life and destiny.

*** Osprey.** +A large American hawk, *Pandion haliaëtus carolinensis*, having the head and under parts white and the upper parts dark brown.

See also AMERICAN OSPREY and cf. FISH HAWK, FISHING EAGLE.

1612 SMITH *Virginia* 14 Hawkes there be of diuerse sorts as our Falconers called them, Sparowhawkes, Lanarets, Goshawkes, Falcons and Osperayes; but they all pray most vpon fish. **1672** JOSSELYN *New Eng. Rarities* 11 The Osprey . . . in this Country is white mail'd. **1812** WILSON *Ornithology* V. 13 Fish-hawk, or Osprey: *Falco hallætus* . . . [is a] formidable, vigorous-winged, and well known bird. **1895** *Outing* XXVII. 60/2 A splendid osprey circled in the sunlight on the look-out for breakfast. **1917** *Birds of Amer.* II. 96/1 Kingfishers seize their prey with their bill but the Osprey, like other raptorial birds, uses its feet only.

+**Ostend Manifesto.** *Hist.* A statement issued in 1854 by the United States ministers to Spain, France, and Great Britain, meeting at Ostend, Belgium, recommending the purchase or, if Spain refused to sell, the seizure of Cuba by the United States. Also *Ostend Circular.* — **1856** in H. H. Smith *Republican Nat. Conventions* (1896) 13 *Resolved,* That the highwayman's plea, that 'might makes right,' embodied in the Ostend Circular, was in every respect unworthy of American diplomacy. **1884** BLAINE *20 Years of Congress* I. 241 He was led by Mason and Soulé into the imprudence of signing the Ostend Manifesto. **1914** *Cycl. Amer. Govt.* I. 533/2.

***Ostentate,** *v. tr.* To show off or display in a boastful or ostentatious manner. {–1676} — **1702** C. MATHER *Magnalia* (1853) II. 546 This proud Thraso would in his preaching ostentate skill in Latin, and in Greek. **1886** *American* XII. 264 The Viburnums ostentate their cymes of fruit. **1889** *Ib.* 21 Dec. 192/1 San Marco . . . ostentates upon the upper portion of its façade all the florid detail of the Venetian manner.

+**Osteopath.** [f. OSTEOPATHY.] One who practices osteopathy. — **1897** *Columbus Dispatch* 26 March, The [Iowa] house to-day passed the senate medical practice act, . . . driving out osteopaths . . . unless they pass examinations the same as physicians. **1922** *Atlantic Mo.* July 75/2 Osteopaths have established research laboratories in California and Chicago.

+**Osteopathic,** *a.* [f. next.] Of or pertaining to osteopathy. {1899–} — **1897** A. T. STILL *Autobiography* 114 During the winter of 1878 and 1879 . . . I treated partly by drugs, as in other days, but also gave Osteopathic treatments.

Osteopathy. {1857–} +A school of medicine which adopts the theory that structural derangement, especially of the spinal column, is the principal cause of disease, and stresses the restoration of normal structure by manipulation. — **1891** A. T. STILL in *Kirksville* (Mo.) *Graphic* 16 Jan. 1/5 Its name [*i.e.*, of 'the new science of health'] is and will be osteopathy. **1897** *Mo. Laws* 206 The system, method or science of treating diseases of the human body, commonly known as osteopathy, . . . is hereby declared not to be the practice of medicine and surgery [etc.]. **1905** STILL in *Independent* 9 Nov. 1097/2 The first postulate of Osteopathy [is]: 'An unobstructed, healthy flow of arterial blood is life.' **1922** *Atlantic Mo.* July 75/1 Osteopathy was founded in 1874, by Dr. A. T. Still who at that time was practising medicine in a small town in Kansas.

Ostrich fern. A tall fern of the genus *Matteuccia.* {1882–} — **1833** EATON *Botany* (ed. 6) 358 *Struthiopteris pennsylvanica*, ostrich fern. **1843** TORREY *Flora N.Y.* II. 486 *Struthiopteris Germanica.* . . . Common Ostrich-fern. . . . Low grounds and borders of rivers. **1868** *Amer. Naturalist* II. 528 [In] the majestic Ostrich Fern, beauty, elegance, grace and novelty will be found.

+**Oswego bass.** [*Oswego* River, N.Y.] =LARGE-MOUTHED (BLACK) BASS. — **1758** C. REA *Journal* (1881) 34 The Lake affords plenty of a Fish call'd Oswego Bass, also Perch, Roche, Trouts &c. **1803** *Mass. H. S. Coll.* 1 Ser. IX. 124 In the river, shad are caught in the spring: also a fresh water fish called Oswego bass, which weighs from four to twelve pounds. **1840** COOPER *Pathfinder* ix, Even the major himself . . . will sometimes swear that an oatmeal cake is better fare than the Oswego bass. **1897** *N.Y. Forest, Fish, & Game Comm. 2d Rep.* 176 There are two species of black bass, the small mouth, with the Latin name, . . . and the large mouth, . . . improperly called 'Oswego' bass.

+**Oswego tea.** =BEE-BALM 1. — **1806** MCMAHON *Amer. Gardener's Cal.* 604 *Monarda dydima.* . . . Oswego-Tea. **1843** TORREY *Flora N.Y.* II. 58 *Monarda didyma.* Oswego Tea. . . . Moist fertile meadows and borders of streams. **1850** S. F. COOPER *Rural Hours* 117 Humming-birds . . . are partial to the bee larkspur also, with the wild bergamot or Oswego tea.

+**Otaheite cane.** Sugar cane of a variety obtained from the island of Otaheite, now Tahiti. *Obs.* — **1812** *Niles' Reg.* II. 86/2 The former will have fifty acres in Otaheite cane this year. **1833** SILLIMAN *Man. Sugar Cane* 10 A second variety is called the Otaheite Cane, from its having been brought to Antigua, and afterwards to the Continent, from Otaheite. **1856** *Rep. Comm. Patents 1855: Agric.* 274 The 'Otaheite' cane originated in the Society Islands.

+**Otaheite corn.** Indian corn, or a grain resembling this, obtained from the island of Otaheite, now Tahiti. *Obs.* — **1805** in *Commun. to Mass. Soc. for Promoting Agric.* (1806) 26 A singular kind of grain, . . . Otaheite corn, . . . [was] distributed . . . to several gentlemen of this town [Boston], who raised it in their gardens. **1837** WILLIAMS *Florida* 111 The Guinea corn, Otaheite corn, and Millet, succeed very well.

+**Otarian,** *a.* Of or pertaining to otaries or eared seals. — **1880** J. ALLEN *N.A. Pinnipeds* 2 The walruses are really little more than thick, clumsy, obese forms of the Otarian type, with the canines enormously developed.

+**Otary.** Any one of various eared seals. — **1847** WEBSTER 781/1 *Otary*, Eared seal; a name given to all those animals of the seal family which have external ears. **1880** J. ALLEN *N. A. Pinnipeds* 225 The largest species of the Otaries . . . are Hair Seals, while the smallest . . . are Fur Seals.

+**Otoe.** Also †**Ottoe.** ['From *Wat'ota,* "lechers"' (Hodge).] A member of a Siouan tribe of Indians; also, pl., the tribe. Also attrib. — **1806** LEWIS in *L. & Clark Exped.* V. (1905) 20 We left the Ottoes on the river Platte. **1817** *Indian Laws & Tr.* II. 139 There shall be perpetual peace and friendship between all the citizens of the United States of America and all the individuals composing the said Ottoes tribe. **1854** *Ib.* 660 The Ottoe and Missouria Indians cede to the United States all their country west of the Missouri River, excepting [etc.]. **1906** *Ib.* III. 234 The Secretary of the Interior . . . [shall] pay, out of the funds of the Otoe and Missouri Indians, of Oklahoma Territory [etc.].

+**Otologist.** One who has specialized in diseases of the ear. — **1874** ROOSA *Diseases of Ear* (ed. 2) 47 The high character of the work that has been done by American otologists. **1876** BARTHOLOW *Materia Medica* (1879) 549 Glycerine is used by otologists to soften cerumen.

+**Otology.** (See quot. 1842.) {1899–} — **1842** DUNGLISON *Medical Lexicon, Otology.* . . . The part of anatomy which treats of the ear. **1874** ROOSA *Diseases of Ear* (ed. 2) 17 Formerly known as aural medicine and surgery, but . . . better designated by the term Otology. **1880** (*title*), American Journal of Otology, A Quarterly Journal of Physiological Acoustics.

+**Otsego bass.** A variety of whitefish (*Coregonus clupeaformis*) found in Otsego Lake, New York. — **1822** DE WITT CLINTON in *Amer. Med. Philos. Reg.* III. 188 (*caption*), Account of the *Salmo otsego* or the Otsego basse. **1850** S. F. COOPER *Rural Hours* 376 It is a shad-salmon, but is commonly called the 'Otsego Bass,' and is considered one of the finest fresh-water fish in the world. **1911** *Rep. Fisheries 1908* 318/1 The common whitefish . . . is known . . . also as 'Otsego bass' in the neighborhood of Otsego Lake, N.Y.

+**Ottawa.** [Can. Fr. *Otaua, Otawa,* from a native Indian word meaning 'trader.'] An American Indian of a tribe found chiefly in Michigan and around the Great Lakes; also, pl., the tribe. Also collect.

[**1640** *Relations des Jésuites* (1858) 34/2 Au Sud . . . est vne Isle . . . habitée des Outouan.] **1799** J. SMITH *Acct. Captivity* 30 The company . . . was composed of Cauglanewagas, and Ottawas. **1833** JACKSON in *Pres. Mess. & P.* III. 38, I transmit . . . a treaty concluded between the commissioners on the part of the United States and the united nation of Chippewas, Ottawas, and Potawatamies, at Chicago. *c***1836** CATLIN *Indians* II. 100 [The Potawatomis] have formerly been a part of the great tribe of Chippeways or Ot-ta-was. **1910** HODGE, etc. *Amer. Indians* II. 171/1 There were 197 Ottawa under the Seneca School, Okla.

b. The language of the Ottawa Indians.

1799 J. SMITH *Acct. Captivity* 37, I could not, at this time, talk Ottawa or Jibewa well.

c. Attrib. with *Indian, nation.*

1789 *Ann. 1st Congress* I. 42 The Wyandot, Delaware, Ottawa, Chippawa, Pattiwatima, and Sac nations . . . [inhabit] part of the country northwest of the Ohio. **1836** JACKSON in *Pres. Mess. & P.* III. 225, I transmit herewith . . . a treaty concluded with the Ottawa and Chippewa Indians.

***Otter.**

+**1.** A well-known amphibious fur-bearing mammal (*Lutra canadensis*) found throughout the United States.

The first quotation may belong under sense c.

1602 BRERETON *Virginia* 16 Beares, Otters, Wolves . . . and squirrels . . . [are] accounted very rich furres. **1676** GLOVER *Va.* in *Phil. Trans.* XI. 626 There likewise keep in the rivers Bevers and Otters. **1701** WOLLEY *Journal N.Y.* (1902) 37 The Skins of . . . Otters . . . they bring upon their backs to New-York. **1791** LONG *Voyages* 41 The country every where abounds with wild animals, particularly . . . otters, martins, minx. **1807** GASS *Journal* 56 Two of the hunters . . . had killed a buffaloe and an otter. **1835** HOFFMAN *Winter in West* I. 171 One old fellow . . . was occupied in flaying an otter, but just taken. **1902** HULBERT *Forest Neighbors* 29 One of the [beaver] children was killed by an otter before the summer was over.

+**b.** As a generic term or in collective sense.

1637 MORTON *New Canaan* 78 The Otter of those parts, in winter season, hath a furre so black as jett. **1683** PENN *Works* (1782) IV. 304 The creatures for profit only, by skin or furr, and that are natural to these parts, are the wild cat, panther, otter. **1764** HUTCHINSON *Hist. Mass.* I. 155 Pay such custom as hereafter is expressed, viz. all skins of beaver, otter, moose, etc. two pence per skin. **1832** *N.H. Hist. Soc. Coll.* III. 92 The Otter is now nearly if not entirely extinct here. *a***1862** THOREAU *Maine Woods* 188 His game had been, beaver, otter, black cat [etc.]. **1881** *Harper's Mag.* April 748/1 Has he come to hunt the bear and deer, To trap the otter?

+**c.** An otter skin or otter skins.

1602 [see MARTEN 2]. **1634** in Winthrop *Life J. Winthrop* II. 126 [They] offered us a great present of wampompeag, and beaver, and otter. *a***1656** BRADFORD *Hist.* 269 If you please to sell us any beaver, or otter. **1777** *Ill. Hist. Coll.* I. 296 He bartered [rum] to them [the Indians] for beavers, otters, etc. **1832** WILLIAMSON *Maine* II. 337, I have seen one of the flanker-rooms as full as it could be well stowed, with the first quality of furs, beaver, otter, sable, &c.

+**2.** =SEA OTTER.

1870 *Amer. Naturalist* IV. 71 It is estimated that the best shooters average at least twenty-five shots to every otter killed. **1917** *St. Nicholas* Nov. 78/2 There was a time not so very long ago when these otters were found in the Pacific Ocean in countless herds.

3. Attrib. with *cap, oil, pelt,* etc.

1634 in *Amer. Speech* XV. 291/2 Along the side of the Pocoson or great Otter pond soe called. *Ib.*, Two hundred acres of land . . . to begin at a little Otter damm. *a***1861** WINTHROP *J. Brent* 205 Brent looked a fit chieftain . . . [with] his otter cap and eagle's plume. *a***1862** THOREAU *Maine Woods* 288 He remembered how good the yellow-lily roots were, made into a soup with the otter oil. **1873** MILLER *Amongst Modocs* 92 There was not a saloon . . . that did not have a sheaf of feathered, flint-headed arrows in an otter quiver. **1902** WHITE *Conjuror's House* 26 So many . . . mink, otter, beaver, . . . and fisher pelts [had been] taken in return.

4. In special combinations.

Otter board, a form of trawl in which two boards are used to keep the net spread; *otter breed,* the breed to which otter sheep belong; *otter canoe,* a canoe of a type used in hunting sea otter; *otterman,* a fisherman who uses an otter tackle; *otter slide,* a smooth declivity down which otters slide.

1901 *Field* 5 Jan. 19/2 The otter-board was only employed . . . upon those lakes where the trout were indifferent to the angler's flies. **1811** D. HUMPHREYS in *Phil. Trans.* CIII. 88 Hence proceeded a strongly marked variety in this species of animals, before unknown in the world. It has been called by the name of the Otter breed. **1870** *Amer. Naturalist* IV. 69 An 'otter canoe' is fifteen feet long, nearly five feet wide, and eighteen inches deep. **1901** *Field* 5 Jan. 19/2 The otterman must chuckle inwardly when he sees a perspiring and jaded angler . . . with one or two fish in his basket. **1842** *Nat. Hist. N.Y., Zoology* I. 40 These otter slides . . . form one of the most interesting peculiarities in the history of the animal.

‖**Otterbein Methodist.** A Methodist in sympathy with the religious views of Philip William Otterbein (1726–1813). (Cf. UNITED BRETHREN.) — **1856** CARTWRIGHT *Autobiog.* 204 This gentleman was an *Otterbein Methodist.*

+**Otter sheep.** A variety of sheep having short crooked legs resembling those of an otter. (Cf. ANCON.) — **1809** KENDALL *Travels* I. 309 [In Conn.] some of the farmers are partial to a remarkable variety of sheep, which they call the otter-sheep. **1863** RANDALL *Pract. Shepherd* 42 A family of them, the Otter Sheep—so termed from their short, crooked, rickety legs. **1873** *Amer. Naturalist* VII. 742 The otter sheep . . . originated on the farm of Seth Wright, near Charles River, Mass. **1884** *Century Mag.* Feb. 516/1 There were also the Otter sheep, said to have originated on some island on our eastern coast.

***Otter('s) skin.** +The skin of an American otter.

1634 WOOD *New Eng. Prospect* 86 When they [=Indians] play [certain games] country against country, there are rich Goales, all behung with Wampompeage, Mowhackies, Beaver skins, and blacke Otter skinnes. **1646** *Mass. H. S. Coll.* 4 Ser. VI. 334 Wequash Cooks brother tooke from him and his aunt severall things, as an otter skyn, 2 *s.* 6 *d.* in wampum [etc.]. *a***1656** BRADFORD *Hist.* 130 This ship (caled ye Fortune) was . . . laden with . . . 2. hoggsheads of beaver and otter skins. **1701** WOLLEY *Journal N.Y.* 39 A black Otter's-skin, if very good, is worth Twenty Shillings. A Fisher's-skin three shillings. **1785** in Ramsey *Tennessee* 297 It shall . . . be lawful for the aforesaid land tax, . . . to be paid in the following manner: . . . cased otter skins, six shillings; uncased ditto, five shillings. **1805** *Lewis & C. Exped.* III. 54 The men [wore their hair] Cewed [queued] with otter Skin on each side falling over the Sholders forward. **1832** WATSON *Hist. Tales N.Y.* 13 They collected and exported 4,700 beaver and otter skins, valued at 27,125 guilders or 11,300 dollars. **1856** *Rep. Comm. Patents 1855: Agric.* 395 Articles of merchandise, of domestic growth and manufacture, exported from St. Marks, Florida, [include] . . . Otter skins, . . . Pitch, . . . Potatoes.

b. Attrib. with *coat, collar, pouch, quiver, strap.*

1660 *Mass. H. S. Coll.* 3 Ser. III. 137 Some Otter-skin coats, and Beaver, and skeins of wampum. **1775** ADAIR *Indians* 84 The American *Archimagus* wears a breast-plate, made of a white conch-shell, with two holes bored in the middle of it, through which he puts the ends of an otter-skin strap. *Ib.* 239, I took the foot of a guinea-deer out of his shot-pouch—and another from my own partner, which they had very safely sewed in the corner of each of their otter-skin-pouches. **1805** LEWIS in *L. & Clark Exped.* II. (1904) 378 The center of the otterskin collar is also ornamented with the shells of the perl oister. **1847** PARKMAN in *Knickerb.* XXX. 236 An Indian bow and otterskin quiver . . . garnished the walls.

Ottoman. An upholstered seat somewhat like a sofa but having no arms, and usually without a back; a cushioned footstool. {1806–} Also attrib.

1837 *S. Lit. Messenger* III. 487 The lover ventures to seat himself upon the ottoman but on the opposite side to that of the child. **1852** EASTMAN *Aunt Phillis's Cabin* 199 'No,' said Ellen, looking up from the ottoman at Miss Jarrett's feet, where she was seated. **1864** *Hist. North-Western Soldiers' Fair* 88 [Donations include] 2 ottoman covers and material for working them. **1894** FORD *P. Stirling* 371 She went upstairs to her room and sank down by an ottoman which stood in the middle of the floor. **1917** COMSTOCK *Man* 44 Draw up the ottoman; so long as you have a spine, rely upon it.

+**Ouch,** *interj.* [G. *autsch.*] A cry expressive of pain or annoyance.

1837 NEAL *Charcoal Sk.* 38 'Ouch!' shrieked Dabbs; 'my eye, how it hurts!' **1843** 'CARLTON' *New Purchase* I. 9 The tiers becoming all vocal with 'bless my soul's'—'my goodness!'—and vulgar 'ouches!' **1876** 'MARK TWAIN' *Tom Sawyer* iv. 46 [He] stuck a pin in another boy, presently, in order to hear him say 'Ouch!' **1898** DELAND *Old Chester Tales* 205 'Ouch—ain't it cold!' she said. **1921** PAINE *Comr. Rolling Ocean* 82 Ouch! That's my nose you're pushing against.

+**Ouija board.** [Fr. *oui* yes and G. *ja* yes and *board.*] A board used with a planchette for spelling out mediumistic messages. — **1895** RITTENHOUSE *Maud* 590 Once or twice he had referred to something a Ouija-board in Chicago had said, and how it had spelled my name in full. **1904** *Pop. Science Mo.* Jan. 195 The '*Ouija*-board,' and certain other devices for making our muscles . . . liable to escape from control. **1911** W. JAMES *Memories & Studies* 189 Most of us reveal such a tendency whenever we handle a ouija-board.

+**Oulachan.** Variant of EULACHON.

***Ounce.**[1] +The Canada lynx or wildcat. *Obs.* — **1634** WOOD *New Eng. Prospect* 23 The Ounce or the wilde Cat, is as big as a mungrell dog. **1699** E. WARD *Trip New-Eng.* 14 Of the Wild-Cat, Which the Indians call the Ounce. Tis as tall as an English Bull-dog; and as fierce.

***Ounce.**[2] **1.** *S.W.* The Spanish 'onza,' a coin worth about $16.00. *Obs.* {1799–} **2.** *attrib.* Designating shot of the weight of an ounce. — (1) **1853** BREWERTON *With Kit Carson* (1930) 188 Upon the board was displayed the lure in the shape of Mexican dollars and Spanish doubloons, or 'ounces,' as they are called in that region. **1873** COZZENS *Marvellous Country* 183 We witnessed . . . a regular Spanish 'cock-fight,' at which silver ounces freely changed hands. (2) **1778** *Jrnls. Cont. Congress* X. 270 The cartridge boxes [are] to be made to hold at least 29 rounds of cartridges when made up with ounce-balls, and the cover of good substantial leather. **1848** BRYANT *California* xi. 153 Several trades were made, generally at the rate of twelve charges of powder, and as many ounce-bullets, for a large elk or deer skin well dressed.

Out, *n.* {1622–}

1. In printing, an omission or something that is left out.

1784 FRANKLIN *Writings* IX. 263 [Your compositors'] *Forms* . . . are continually pester'd by the *Outs* and *Doubles*, that are not easy to be corrected. **1864** WEBSTER 926/3 *To make an out*, to omit something in setting up copy.

‖**2.** Permission to go out.

1845 JUDD *Margaret* II. 198 [She] gave them [*sc.* pupils] their outs, rapped . . . on the window to call them in.

+**3.** *Baseball.* The putting out of a player; a player put out.

1868 CHADWICK *Base Ball* 95 Williams was next, and as he began by tipping out, the result was two outs and no runs. **1878** *De Witt's Base-Ball Guide* 31 Up to a late period, scoring in base-ball matches was confined to the simple record of the outs and runs. **1886** CHADWICK *Art of Pitching* 15 Mere speed costs more in wild pitches, and called and passed balls than it yields in outs or strikes. **1910** [see INFIELD 3].

+**4.** A flaw, defect, or blemish.

1885 PHELPS *Old Maids* II. 48 Sound as sense! Hadn't an out about him. **1893** SANBORN *S. California* 69 Are there no 'outs,' no defects in this Pasadena? **1901** *Scribner's Mag.* April 418/1 There were horses of every kind—except the right kind. Each one had his own peculiar 'out.'

5. In phrases: +**a.** *To make an out* or variant: To attain a specified result in doing something. *colloq.*

See also sense 1, quot. 1864.

1845 NOAH *Gleanings* 148 He slipped the fatal jack of diamonds from the bottom of the pack, and claimed the money then in stake. . . . I at first thought him in jest, and laughed at him for making so bungling an out. **1853** BALDWIN *Flush Times Ala.* 31, I might have made a pretty good *out* of it, if I had thrown myself upon the merits of my case. **1859** G. K. WILDER *Diary* (MS.) 1, I don't believe we will make much of an out. **1904** HARBEN *Georgians* 176 Warren . . . actually tried to pray; but he made a pore out.

+**b.** *At outs (with)*, not in harmony or agreement. Also *on the outs.*

1884 *Congress. Rec.* 23 April 3326/1 His church and the Unitarians [were] very much at outs. **1901** MERWIN & WEBSTER *Calumet 'K'* 251 He was still in the mistake of supposing that Peterson and the boss were at outs. **1904** *N.Y. Sun* 24 Aug. 3 She was at outs with her parents because of her marriage, so she went to live with her aunt. **1917** MCCUTCHEON *Green Fancy* 87 My daughter and I are—er—what you might say 'on the outs' at present.

***Out,** *a.* Situated on the frontier or in a rural region at considerable distance from older and more established settlements.

It is impracticable to distinguish *out* in its purely adjectival use from *out-* as an adverbial combinative element. (See also OUTCAMP, OUTLAND, etc.)

1653 *Boston Rec.* 6 The very hart & securest part of the towne (& noe out or by place) is the most fitt for a Magazene for Armes. **1677** HUBBARD *Narrative* I. 128 Doing some small Mischief upon some Out-dwellings of Springfield. **1725** in *Travels Amer. Col.* 161 Four of the Enemy . . . went in the dead of Night to the Out Fortification. **1779** *Bristol* (Va.) *Vestry Bk.* 259 To Duke Bonner for horse block's at the Out Church, [£]6. **1849** in *Worcester City Docs. 1849–56* No. 1, 33 Most of the schools in the out-Districts, have been conducted . . . under the new order. **1887** EGGLESTON in *Century Mag.* April 905/2 The common lands came to be more and more divided, and farms and out-hamlets were settled.

***Out,** *adv.* In phrases.

To be out of one's head, see HEAD *n.* 7.

+**1.** *From this out*, from now on, henceforth. *colloq.*

1882 HOWELLS *Modern Instance* xiv, Will you manage the bargaining from this on? . . . I'll take a back seat from this out. **1884** *Boston Jrnl.* 25 Oct. 2/4 He says that from this out he will oppose monopoly. **1893** 'MARK TWAIN' *P. Wilson* iii, You's young Marse *Tom* fum dis out. **1905** H. CORKRAN *Lucie & I* 36 From this out I will think of you as a young *diablesse.*

2. *To be out* {1605–}, +of Indians, to be on the war-path.

1877 CAMPION *On Frontier* 67 The Kiowas and the Cheyennes were certainly on the war-path, the Sioux probably 'out.' **1882** BAILLIE-GROHMAN *Camps in Rockies* 381 In '62, when the Sioux and Soshoné were 'out,' he had 'a couple o' months scouting.' **1923** J. H. COOK *On Old Frontier* 184 Had it not been for his heroic work, Geronimo would probably have been 'out' for some time.

+**3.** *To be out for* (something), to be intent upon getting or achieving (a specified thing). Also *to be out* (to do something). *colloq.*

1892 *Boston Jrnl.* 7 Aug. 4/3 The Bourbon Democrats are out for wild-cat currency. **1901** MERWIN & WEBSTER *Calumet 'K'* 13 They're mostly out for results up at the office. Let's see the bill for it. **1901** WHITE *Westerners* 272 When they are out to have a good time, . . . they want somebody they can have their sort of fun with. **1903** LEWIS *Boss* 95, I'll give you a flash of what I'm out to do an' why I'm out to do it.

+**4.** *To get out from under*, to escape from a system, danger, etc. *colloq.*

1875 *Scribner's Mo.* Nov. 124/2 The system is rotten, root and branch, and, if the nation cares for its life, the quicker it gets 'out from under' the better. **1925** J. AUSLANDER in *Amer. Mercury* Aug. 401 You traveled Like the devil to get out from under.

5. *To have out*, +to have harvested or picked (cotton) from the field.

1854 *Fla. Plantation Rec.* 94, I Suppose I have about 10 or 12 bales more out and will send a nother Load off on Satterday 2nd of Septr.

Outbat, *v. Baseball.* +*tr.* To excel (opponents) at batting. — **1873** *N.Y. Herald* 13 July 5/3 The New Yorkers outbatted the Brooklyn boys. **1886** *Outing* June 365/2 The Browns outbatted and outfielded the League nine, but the latter bunched their hits.

Outbuilding. =OUTHOUSE. {1626–} — **1788** *Mass. Spy* 3 April 3/4 About 90 acres of . . . Land, with a good House, Barn, and other Out Buildings thereon. **1829** COOPER *Wish-ton-Wish* ii, The surfaces of the meadows immediately around the out-buildings, were of a smoother and richer sward. **1867** 'LACKLAND' *Homespun* 325 [He] runs about the barns and out-buildings for some implement that has mysteriously gone astray. **1883** *Rep. Indian Affairs* p. xxxviii, The pupils of those schools will have to be crowded into barns, bakeries, and outbuildings. **1916** THOBURN *Stand. Hist. Okla.* I. 261 There were numerous outbuildings, including the smoke-house.

+**Outcamp.** A camp at some distance from the main or principal encampment. — **1844** *Knickerb.* XXIII. 116 The Sioux . . . would not fail to attack, according to their custom, the out-camps.

Outcrop, *n.* A portion of a stratum of coal or vein of ore that appears on the surface of the ground. {1805–} — **1840** in *Mich. Agric. Soc. Trans.* V. 325 The out-crops of this coal, within that part of the State under consideration, are of small extent. **1865** *Atlantic Mo.* XV. 311/1 Mining was done by surface openings along the line of the outcrop of the vein. **1876** RAYMOND *8th Rep. Mines* 278 The Hidden Treasure is now developed to a depth of 1,100 feet below its outcrop. *a***1918** G. STUART *On Frontier* I. 223 Granville found the out crop of coal in Pikes Peak gulch.

Outcrop, *v.* {1848–} ‖*tr.* To excel (one) in making a crop. — **1770** *Md. Hist. Mag.* XIII. 73 He assures me th[a]t . . . Rigges never out cropped Him.

Outcropping, *n.* =OUTCROP *n.* {1882–} — **1853** KANE *Grinnell Exped.* 135 The bright red outcroppings of the feldspar. **1869** BROWNE *Adv. Apache Country* 507 Never was there any thing so fabulously rich!— . . . outcroppings three hundred dollars to the ton! **1877** H. C. HODGE *Arizona* 100 One mile north from the Peck Mine . . . is a heavy outcropping of copper, eight hundred feet in length. **1923** 'BOWER' *Parowan Bonanza* 13 Outcropping of lively looking rock, Jim.

Outcropping, *a.* Emerging or becoming visible at the surface of the ground. — **1845** *Amer. Jrnl. Science* April 299 Brine springs . . . issue, at the outcropping edges of the siliceous portion of the mass. **1849** *31st Congress 1 Sess.* H. R. Ex. Doc. No. 5, II. 850 This iron ore bed is . . . quite variable in richness in different portions of its outcropping surface. **1853** KANE *Grinnell Exped.* 134 We could distinctly see outcropping faces of red feldspathic rocks. **1892** in A. E. Lee *Hist. Columbus, Ohio* I. 678 In the high land . . . [shale] is still found as an outcropping rock.

***Outcry.** An auction or public sale. {*c*1600–} *Obs.* — **1640** *Md. Archives* 96 All uncertaine goods to which no party Justly claymeth shall be Sould att an Outcry. **1686** *Huntington Rec.* I. 467 It was voated and agreed by the towne that the medowe in ye east neck should bee sould at an outcry or vandue. **1715** HEMPSTEAD *Diary* 51, I bought 18 lb. Leather yt was Sold at an outcry p[er] Jno Morgan Collector. **1743** *Ib.* 416, I was . . . at ye Sign Post to See the Sheriff Sell Mr Winthrops Land at an outcry or vendue.

+**Outcurve.** *Baseball.* A pitched ball that curves away from a right-handed batter. (Cf. INCURVE.) — **1881** *N.Y. Herald* 29 July 6/5 Reipslaugher, . . . not being used to the difficult delivery of Bond, found great difficulty in handling the in-shoots and out-curves. **1886** CHADWICK *Art of Pitching* 18 With the rotary motion imparted to it, . . . it would curve to the left, making what is known as the 'out-curve.' **1887** *Outing* May 98/2 The 'out curve' [is] the one most easily attained by a right-hand pitcher.

***Outdone,** *a.* +Nonplused; exhausted; disgusted. *colloq.* — **1816** U. BROWN *Journal* I. 362 Now again we feel out done in finding it has left the Books & for what Cause we know not. **1884** 'CRADDOCK' *Tenn. Mts.* 260 Tony air mightily outdone 'kase the gran' jury let him off. **1886** STOCKTON *Mrs. Lecks* 123, I was gettin' pretty well outdone with you.

Outdoor life. Life spent chiefly outdoors or in the open. — **1885** *Rep. Indian Affairs* 165 The out-door life which they lead during the summer strengthens and fortifies their systems against the depressing effects of the long, dreary winters. **1892** M. A. JACKSON *Gen. Jackson* 28 It was hoped that the out-door life and horseback exercise would invigorate him. **1918** ROOSEVELT in *Maine My State* 17 The vigorous out-door life was just what I needed.

+**Outdoors,** *n.* Also *colloq.* **ou'doors, owdoors.**

1. A region, or the world, outside the limits of a dwelling.
1857 WILLIS *Convalescent* 121 The 'down party' . . . were enjoying the river from the uncommon out-doors of Mr. Grinnell's broad prairies. **1896** WILKINS *Madelon* 336 Well used to all the wild disorder of out-doors was Lot Gordon. **1922** A. BROWN *Old Crow* 449 She stopped to breathe in the wood fragrances, coming now like a surprise. She had almost forgotten 'outdoors.'

2. *All outdoors*, the whole wide world; everybody. Often in comparisons. *colloq.*
1830 S. SMITH *Life J. Downing* 64, I had a letter from him t'other day, as long as all out doors, in the Boston Advertiser. *a***1861** WINTHROP *J. Brent* 22 Thar ken be stuff made out er grapes what'll make all owdoors stan' round. *Ib.* 296 The Pallis [was] blowin' her whistle like all outdoors. **1862** LOWELL *Biglow P.* 2 Ser. i. 23 Ourn's the fust thru-by-daylight train, with all ou'doors for deepot. **1893** 'THANET' *Stories* 209 It would have been enough for Esther's mother to know that anything was for my interests; it wouldn't have to help all out-doors, too! **1918** RIDEOUT *Key of Fields* 296 That picture must be big as all outdoors.

+**Outdoors,** *adv.* In the open air; out of doors. {1882-} — **1817** S. BROWN *Western Gazetteer* 113 The chimney is sure to be placed out doors. **1851** JUDD *Margaret* (ed. 2) I. 112 She could see nothing out doors but great tremulous masses. **1865** *Atlantic Mo.* XV. 110/2 Out-doors [one sees] nothing but bare branches and shrouding snow. **1913** STRATTON-PORTER *Laddie* xiii, What you learn there [in school] doesn't amount to a hill of beans compared with what you can find out for yourself outdoors.

Outdoor sport. A field sport, or athletic contest, played or held out of doors. Also transf. — **1886** *Boston Jrnl.* Nov., A New England city could . . . provide all the desired attractions for a festival of out-door sports. **1921** PAINE *Comr. Rolling Ocean* 2 The oldest living graduate pushed a baby carriage as his favorite outdoor sport.

+**Outdrift.** A passageway for cattle; an outlying pasture area. *Obs.* (Cf. DRIFTWAY 1.) — **1676** *Doc.Col.Hist.N.Y.* XII. 556 Capt. Cantwell took away ye privilege of ye Sayd way & outdrifft from ye widdow of ye Sayd Mr. Block. **1697** in Munsell *Ann. Albany* III. 34 They will give him 50 acres . . . with free outdrift for his cattle. **1779** *N.J. Archives* 2 Ser. III. 71 This tract, besides the great advantage of out drift for cattle forever in the mountains adjacent, is exceedingly well watered.

+**Outdrop.** *Baseball.* A drop ball which curves away from a right-handed batter. (Cf. DROP *n.* 6.) — **1893** *Harper's Wkly.* 8 July 657 Colby's best ball is his outdrop, which is very quick and deceptive.

Outer field. + =OUTFIELD 2. *Obs.* — **1865** *N.Y. Herald* 11 July 5/4 The Empires batted well also, but their outer field was not as well attended to as it might have been. **1868** CHADWICK *Base Ball* 41 The batsman tosses the ball up and tries to send it to the outer field, and the player catching it on the fly takes the bat. **1886** — *Art of Pitching* 9 To hit at a ball so as to send it high to the outer-field.

Outfence. =OUTSIDE FENCE. *Obs.* {1769-} Cf. CROSS FENCE. — **1653** *Cambridge Prop. Rec.* 340 The Marsh . . . [receives] as much benefit by the out fence as the upland. **1662** *Portsmouth Rec.* 116 All out fences that are fower foout and a halfe high shall be Judged sufitient.

Outfield, *n.* {1637-}

+**1.** A field at a considerable distance from a homestead or group of these.
1676 *Conn. Rec.* 464 The sending of thirty men to be a Guard while you gather in your harvest from your out-fields. **1724** *Talcott P.* 12 Six men allowed to guard their laborers at Farmington in their out-fields. **1746** in *N.H. Hist. Soc. Coll.* IV. 202 Returning to an out field, about half a mile from the Fort—there tracked an Indian. **1879** *Diseases of Swine* 215 A farmer here recently rented an out-field to hog down.

+**2.** *Baseball.* The part of the playing field beyond or outside the base lines. {1851-, in cricket (Bolland *Cr. Notes* 136)}
Cf. INFIELD.
1868 CHADWICK *Base Ball* 73 The Irvingtons . . . took an out-fielder from his regular position, . . . and placed the substitute in the out-field. **1886** — *Art of Batting* 63 In running bases on fly balls caught in the outfield, the moment such high ball is hit, . . . [the player] should hold the base he occupies. **1893** POST *Harvard Stories* 86 He slipped his collar and ran into the out-field to congratulate the centre-fielder. **1917** MATHEWSON *Sec. Base Sloan* 290 Overhead the long flies arched to the outfield.

+**b.** The players, namely the right, center, and left fielders, stationed in the outfield.
1867 CHADWICK *Base Ball Reference* 138 The Out-Field—The out-fielders are the left[,] centre and right-field positions. **1868** — *Base Ball* 17 The out-field being neither active in their movements, or sure catchers. **1897** *Outing* May 203/1 Rand and Burgess, with Lynch, . . . make up the outfield.

+**Outfield,** *v. Baseball. tr.* To excel (opponents) in fielding. — **1875** *Chicago Tribune* 17 Aug. 5/6 The Browns were outbatted and outfielded.

Outfielder. *Baseball.* +A player stationed in the outfield. — **1867** CHADWICK *Base Ball Reference* 138 The out-fielders are the left[,] centre and right-field positions. **1887** *Outing* May 102/1 It is among the possibilities for the intelligent outfielder to predict the direction. **1897** *Ib.* May 204/1 Stagg has the problem of finding a catcher, a second baseman, short stop, third baseman, and a couple of . . . outfielders. **1924** *Lit. Digest* 21 June 57 The first and third basemen and the outfielders are mighty important factors in the play of any ball club.

Outfit, *n.* {1769-}

+**1.** The articles, equipment, etc., required by a minister or other governmental representative upon assuming duties in another country.
1787 JEFFERSON *Writings* VI. 238, I believe there is no instance of any nation sending a minister to reside anywhere without an outfit. **1798** *Ann. 5th Congress* I. 716 An outfit for him on his appointment as Chargé d'Affairs. **1814** *Columbian Centinel* 24 Dec. 2/3 The salary of a Plenipo. is 9000 dollars per year, and 9000 dollars outfit. **1841** *Diplom. Corr. Texas* III. (1911) 1352 This appointment would have been made long before this—but hitherto it has been wholly impossible to pay your outfit. **1849** *Whig Almanac 1850* 25/2 About $520,000 were voted to diplomatic agents, nearly $160,000 of which was for outfits.

2. The equipment, supplies, etc., required for a journey or expedition. {1848-}
1809 A. HENRY *Travels* 11 On the 15th of June, [I] again arrived in Montreal, bringing with me my outfits. **1822** *Ann. 17th Congress* 1 Sess. I. 324 An outfit of goods was furnished by Mr. Erwin. **1844** LEE & FROST *Oregon* 113 An opportunity was given us to forward the necessary outfit for the commencement of our mission. **1880** *Harper's Mag.* March 551/2 Next . . . he may procure tent and general 'outfit.'

+**3.** The things pertaining to or making up a person's dress or costume.
1852 STOWE *Uncle Tom* v, Saying these words, she had tied and buttoned on the child's simple outfit. **1858** VIELÉ *Following Drum* 55 A beaver hat, with a broad gold band and cockade, complete their stylish outfit. **1875** *Scribner's Mo.* Dec. 286/1 The comfortable dress for the mother or flannel outfit for the baby, can be sent under cover of a Christmas greeting.

+**4.** Used colloquially in a variety of applications.
The broad signification given to *outfit*, esp. in western terminology, is shown in the following group of examples.
1863 *Rio Abajo Press* 10 Feb. 2 There is a paper published at Albuquerque. . . . Why don't you send one as a sample of the outfit? **1867** MELINE *Santa Fé & Back* 74 This word 'outfit' is on duty night and day, without relief, from the Missouri River to California. To cross the plains, or go to the mountains, every one must get an outfit; and having outfitted, you become yourself an outfit. . . . The saddler who sold me my saddle assured me it was the best outfit he had furnished for some time. Bought a hat, and was told, 'Well, Sir, I call that a good outfit.' **1869** MCCLURE *Rocky Mts.* 211 Everything is an 'outfit,' from a train on the plains to a pocket-knife. It is applied almost indiscriminately,—to a wife, a horse, a dog, a cat, or a row of pins. **1882** BAILLIE-GROHMAN *Camps in Rockies* 1 'Outfit,' it may at once be mentioned, is an expressive Western term, covering every imaginable human, animate, and inanimate being or article. **1924** MULFORD *Rustlers' Valley* xi, You ain't believin' everythin' *this* outfit [*i.e.*, person] tells you, are you?

+**a.** A group or company of travelers, miners, hunters, etc., associated in a common undertaking.
1869 S. BOWLES *Our New West* 163 With a mounted escort of about twenty gallant young miners . . . we made up a grand 'outfit.' **1883** 'MARK TWAIN' *Life on Miss.* ii, In that day, all explorers traveled with an outfit of priests. **1897** *Outing* XXX. 190/2 The outfit from Maine, log-cabin, brush-camps, guides and all, was busy at the old stand. **1902** WISTER *Virginian* 303 It's part of that outfit that's been hunting. **1908** STEVENS *Liberators* 200 We used their decision . . . against this reform outfit. **1923** VANCE *Baroque* 41 You'd have a grand time makin' me believe you wasn't in with this outfit clean over your ears.

+**b.** A group of cowboys, together with the horses, teams, wagons, etc., used by them in range work. Often preceded by the name of the cattle ranch to which the group is attached.
1876 Whilldin *Descr. W. Texas* 15 Twenty-five men are about as many as can work to an advantage in one gang, and for this number one large four-mule wagon, laden with provisions, camp equipage, a very little baggage, and about one hundred horses, make up 'the out-fit.' **1890** *Stock Grower and Farmer* 15 March 6/3 John Donahue, range foreman for the G-bar-outfit, came in on Monday. **1894** WISTER in *Harper's Mag.* Jan. 295/1 You must have slept at the Sand Hill outfit coming down. **1905** A. ADAMS *Outlet* 81 As the outfit rode away to relieve the last guard, every mother's son was singing. **1924** MULFORD *Rustlers' Valley* x, He had an outfit that gladdened his heart, and it was needful that he exercise care in the examples he set it.

+**c.** A herd of cattle.
1897 LEWIS *Wolfville* 226 When mixed cattle is in a bunch . . . an' you-all is ridin' through the outfit cuttin' out, y'ear-marks is what you goes by. **1903** A. ADAMS *Log of Cowboy* 23 About half our outfit grazed them around on a large circle.

+**5.** A supply, stock; a large number.
1901 GREENOUGH & KITTREDGE *Words & Their Ways* 1 The sum-total of our retrospect accounts for only the minutest fraction of our whole outfit of words and phrases. **1904** *Hartford Courant* 2 Dec. 8 What under the canopy does little, poverty-stricken Greece want with an outfit of warships? **1907** *St. Nicholas* May 641/1 If you do not happen to have

enough newspapers on hand for the entire outfit of tepees and costumes, you can use a white muslin sheet for the wigwam.

Outfit, *v.*

1. *tr.* To fit out (someone or something); to supply with an outfit. {1847-}

a1861 WINTHROP *J. Brent* 192 They outfitted me with a pistol, and this ere horse. **1876** RAYMOND *8th Rep. Mines* 19 Certain San Francisco capitalists and miners . . . purchased the largest and most promising claim, . . . [and] proceeded to outfit it in first-rate style. **1890** LANGFORD *Vigilante Days* (1912) 422 Old miners . . . were to share with those who 'outfitted' them in all their discoveries. **1910** RAINE *B. O'Connor* 39 Get together at once posse of four and outfit same for four days. **1923** J. H. COOK *On Old Frontier* 25, I was soon outfitted with another saddle and rope from the home ranch, and was once again ready for more sport with the playful longhorns.

+2. *intr.* To get or purchase an outfit.

1860 *Harper's Mag.* Oct. 584/1 The lodges around the fort are those of Indians, come in from their hunts to spend their proceeds or outfit anew. **1866** *Wkly. New Mexican* 4 Aug. 2/2 [He] had to come to this side of the river to 'outfit.' **1884** *Century Mag.* Dec. 194 Here I 'outfitted,' and . . . we were in a few days on our way. **1902** WHITE *Blazed Trail* 160 Thorpe . . . returned at once to a boarding-house off Fort Street, where he had 'outfitted' three months before. **1923** 'BOWER' *Parowan Bonanza* 8 One day in spring Bill Dale walked behind his burros into Goldfield and outfitted for a long trip.

+**Outfitting point.** A town or trading center where outfits are usually procured. — **1848** E. BRYANT *California* i. 13 Independence, Mo., . . . has been for some years the principal outfitting point for the Santa Fé traders. **1864** *Rio Abajo Press* 5 April 4/3 Albuquerque is the Outfitting Point for persons from the East and North.

Outfort. {1625-} +A fort on the frontier or other remote region. *Obs.* — **1715** *Boston News-Letter* 11 July 2/1 The Indians had surprized an Out Fort wherein were about Twenty White Men and Ten Negroes. **1756** *Lett. to Washington* II. 27 Not knowing Your Numbers in those Out-Forts I gave general Orders to call them all in. **1757** *Ib.* 219 For every bushell of Salt that Shall be deliver'd him . . . at any the Outforts the Sum of Ten Shillings.

+**Outgarrison.** A garrison at an outpost or outfort. *Obs.* — **1711** *N.C. Col. Rec.* I. 826 Captain Brice detached from our out-garrisons fifty men. **1758** *Lett. to Washington* II. 291 Untill that time I do not see in what manner you can get in your Out Garrisons.

Outgrounds. *pl.* The outlying grounds of an estate or farm. — **1856** *Mich. Agric. Soc. Trans.* VII. 811 To have the yard and outgrounds beautifully adorned with here and there the majestic oak.

Outhouse.* A house or building, as a barn, smokehouse, crib, etc., adjacent to a residence. — **1635 *Cambridge Prop. Rec.* 2 One Dwelinge House with other out houses. **1708** *Boston News-Letter* 7 June 2/2 A good Dwelling House, a Ware-house, two Barns, with other Out-houses convenient. **1803** *Lit. Mag.* (Phila.) Nov. 155 His out-houses consisting of two stables and a corn-house . . . were all reduced to ashes. **1904** GLASGOW *Deliverance* 327 He took his hoe from an outhouse and went to 'grub' the young weeds from the tobacco.

Outhousing. A collection of outhouses. {1630-} — **1635** *Essex Inst. Coll.* VIII. 252, I John Woolcott of Salem haue Bartered and sould . . . also all the out housing. **1679** *Ib.* XXXVII. 212 The Dwelling house, bakehouse & out housing & the land they stand on. **1701** *N.H. Probate Rec.* I. 490, I give unto my beloved son Joshua Gilman my dwelling house and out housing. **1745** *Ib.* III. 311, I Give and Bequeath unto my Other Two Sons . . . Barns Outhouseing Edifices ffences and all Other Appur[t]-enances.

Outkitchen. A kitchen erected as a separate building near a house; a back kitchen. {1722-} Cf. KITCHEN 1 b. — **1776** *N.J. Archives* 2 Ser. I. 33 On the lot are a good stable, chair house and out kitchen.

***Outland.** +In a colonial town, land lying outside the inner bounds of the town jurisdiction. — **1645** *New Haven Col. Rec.* 198 All such who are admitted planters into howselotts freely, but have had noe outland formerly allotted to them, they shall each of them have 6 acres of upland to plant in. **1701** *Groton Rec.* 121 Any man . . . should have liberty to brake up any out land in the town. **1731** *R.I. Col. Rec.* IV. 442 An Act for erecting and incorporating the out-lands of the town of Providence, into three towns. **1875** TEMPLE & SHELDON *Hist. Northfield, Mass.* 219 [At] the first meeting of the town to act upon the apportionment of undivided lands, . . . it was voted to distribute the more desirable outlands to the inhabitants by choice.

***Outlaw,** *n.*

***1.** A roving criminal who lives in defiance of law.

1842 tr. Sealsfield *Life in New World* 42 The trappers are generally outcasts or outlaws, who have escaped the arm of the law. **1847** *Santa Fe Republican* 17 Sept. 2/2 He has been seen long since the massacre, among a band of outlaws, and . . . he appeared to be their leader. **1877** HARTE *Story of Mine* 296 They already knew him as a gambler, outlaw, and desperado. **1893** *Harper's Mag.* March 640/1 A band of outlaws . . . burned a Mexican barrack, killed several soldiers, and returned to Texas. **1910** RAINE *B. O'Connor* 19 The outlaw turned on his heel.

+2. (See quot. 1904.)

1885 ROE *Army Lett.* 337 Many a fine, spirited animal is ruined, made an 'outlaw' that no man can ride, just by the fiendish way in which they are first ridden. **1904** STEEDMAN *Bucking Sagebrush* 75 An outlaw, or spoiled horse, is one that is incorrigibly vicious, either by temperament or because he has been made so from unskilful or brutal handling when being broken. **1923** J. H. COOK *On Old Frontier* 76 [He] was riding an outlaw (spoiled horse).

***Outlaw,** *v. tr.* and *intr.* for *refl.* (See quot. 1864.) {1647-a1661} ('Now only in U.S.' *O.E.D.*) — **1854** *Congress. Globe* 13 July 1717/2 [They] came to this country so long ago that the sin of their '*immigration*' ought . . . to be outlawed. **1864** WEBSTER 927/2 *Outlaw*, . . . to remove from legal jurisdiction or enforcement; as, to *outlaw* a debt or claim; to deprive of legal force. **1883** 'MARK TWAIN' *Life on Miss.* 433 A debt . . . outlawed by the statute of limitations. **1895** — in Paine *Biog.* II. 1007 Honour is a harder master than the law. It cannot compromise for less than a hundred cents on the dollar, and its debts never outlaw.

***Outlet.** A pasture or common. *Obs.* {1793-} — **1723** *Amer. Wkly. Mercury* 4 July 4/1 A Dwelling House and a good large Barn, and an Orchard lying at the eastern end of the Loadstones Barren, very convenient for an Out-let or Liberty. **1752** J. MACSPARRAN *Amer. Dissected* 13 The Climate is benign, and their Outlets or Commonages large.

Outlie, *v.* {1873-} +*intr.* To remain out in the forest or prairie as a scout or marauder. — **1826** COOPER *Mohicans* xviii, We are not about to start on a squirrel hunt, . . . but to outlie for days and nights, and to stretch across a wilderness. **1827** — *Prairie* xii, Here has the live-long night gone by, and he out-lying on the prairie. **1840** — *Pathfinder* ii, It is war-time, and no red-skin is outlying without using his senses.

Outlier. Also **outlyer.** {a1658} +One who lies out or camps in the forest as a bushwhacker or marauder. — **1812** MARSHALL *Kentucky* 226 Some out-lyers of the Chuckamoggas, committed depredations on the wilderness road, upon the travelling emigrants. **1827** COOPER *Prairie* xxii, The outliers of the accursed tribe drove us to the caves on the island. **1836** SIMMS *Mellichampe* xii, My force in a short time will be adequate to clear the country in this quarter of the troop of outliers that haunt it. **1854** — *Southward Ho* 269 It is to hunt up these outlyers—to protect you from their annoyances, that I am here now.

+**Outline.** *Fishing.* A trot-line. — **1872** *Penna. Laws* 729 It shall not be lawful for any person or persons to take . . . any fish, by means of . . . outlines, night-lines, swimmers or floating lines.

+**Outliver.** One who lives on the frontier or remote from others. *Obs.* — **1675** *Doc. Col. Hist. N.Y.* XII. 535 The Towne paying double to what the Outlivers. **1675** *Conn. Rec.* II. 268 That all out livers . . . doe take a speedy and effectuall course to get their women and children . . . to places of the most hopefull securety.

+**Outlot.** In early times, a lot or piece of ground situated outside a town or other jurisdiction. Now hist. — **1643** *New Haven Col. Rec.* 94 Mris Eldreds out lotts. **1774** in Durrett *Louisville* 134 An out-lot of ten acres, contiguous to the town, shall be laid off for such as desire the same at an easy rent. **1815** DRAKE *Cincinnati* 130 Several persons have since divided out-lots, or tracts adjoining to the first town plat. **1886** Z. F. SMITH *Kentucky* 29 [They gave] to each man a half-acre lot and a ten-acre outlot.

‖**Outlying,** *n.* The action, or an instance, of remaining or living out in the forest as a scout. *Obs.* — **1827** COOPER *Prairie* xxii, Often have I talked the matter over with the Great Serpent of the Delawares, in the more peaceful hours of our out-lyings. **1840** — *Pathfinder* II. iii, I loved to think of my scoutings, and of my marches, and out-lyings, and fights.

Outlying, *a.* {1663-}

1. Of domestic animals: Remaining away at night from the enclosures provided near the owner's residence. {1663-, of deer}

1676 *New Castle Court Rec.* 34 They fetch in their old out Lying hoghs. **1740** *Georgia Col. Rec.* IV. 668 There not being Horses or Men sufficient to drive up the young and out-lying Cattle. **1786** WASHINGTON *Diaries* III. 3, I had been to cut Straw . . . to feed their outlying Horses.

+2. Of persons: Remaining or living in the forest for purposes of scouting or marauding.

1755 *Lett. to Washington* I. 117 In our way Discover'd two outlying men one of which was taken. **1839** HOFFMAN *Wild Scenes* 129 He had been on a long tramp, through woods alive with out-lying Indians. **1840** COOPER *Pathfinder* ii, I have come up the other [side of the river], in order to scout for the outlying rascals.

Out-of-door(s). {1856-} +(*As*) *big as all out-of-door(s)*, without parallel in size; extremely large. *colloq.* (Cf. OUTDOORS *n.* 2.) — **1825** NEAL *Brother Jonathan* I. 111 Stuffy feller, . . . big as all out o' doors. **1842** 'UNCLE SAM' *Peculiarities* I. 218 They reckon they are as big as all-out-of-door—they estimate they are giants. **1855** HAWTHORNE *Eng. Note-Books* (1870) I. 299 [He] felt that he was in a great public building,—as big, nearly, as all out of doors.

+**Outoven.** (See quot. 1875.) — **1875** KNIGHT 1583/1 The *out-oven* . . . is so called because built out of doors; not a *house*-oven. It has a domed chamber, is built of brick, and is heated by means of light wood or sticks burned inside. **1913** STRATTON-PORTER *Laddie* i, They went to bring wood for the cookstove, outoven, and big fireplace.

+**Outparty.** A military detachment that operates at a distance from the main body, as on the frontier. *Obs.* Also transf. — **1756** ROGERS *Jrnls.* 18 A party of 220 French and Indians were preparing to invest the outparties at Fort Edward. **1757** *General Orders* 23 All offrs Mounting Guard Detachments out Partys &c. are . . . to Examen their Mens Ammunition.

1758 *Lett. to Washington* II. 275, I hope you will keep your Out Parties in a readiness to rendesvous on a short Notice. **1841** COOPER *Deerslayer* ix, He could only account for it . . . by their having out parties, of the existence of which he was ignorant.

+Outplantation. A plantation outside the limits of a township or province. *Obs.* — **1669** *R.I. Col. Rec.* II. 283 There are severall out plantations in this Colony, which are not included in any towneship. **1691** *Mass. H. S. Coll.* 4 Ser. V. 298 The Indians . . . are breaking in upon outplantations. **1740** W. STEPHENS *Proc. Georgia* I. 593 A small Boat . . . [stopped] at one of our Out-Plantations. **1765** ROGERS *Acct. N. America* 112 The out-plantations upon this were deserted, their corn and cattle destroyed, great difficulties ensued to the colony.

Outpost. A post at a considerable distance from the main body of an army; an advance guard. {1779–}

1757 WASHINGTON *Writings* I. 478 The uncertain and difficult communication with the out-posts. **1789** MORSE *Amer. Geog.* 225 Putnam was on a visit to his out-post. **1836** CROCKETT *Exploits* 169 A military outpost was established at this spot by the Spanish government in 1718. **1888** SHERIDAN *Memoirs* I. 171 Skirmishes between outposts on this line were of frequent occurrence, etc.

b. Attrib. with *duty, guard, work.*

1776 *Battle of Brooklyn* II. i, We are the remains of the out post guard, your honours. **1870** KEIM *Sheridan's Troopers* 206 This simple means is also resorted to by the troops on outpost duty. **1887** *Courier-Journal* 7 May 1/4 What most strikes the regular soldier . . . [is] how badly the staff and outpost work generally was performed on both sides.

+Outpublish, *v. New Eng. tr.* To publish the marriage banns of (a couple) in church for the last time. *Obs.* — **1719** SEWALL *Diary* III. 232, I was Out-published on the Thanksgiving-Day. **1722** *Ib.* 305 S.S. and M.G. were Out-published. **1727** *Canton* (Mass.) *Rec.* 22 The Names . . . haue ben out published as the Law directs, By me Joseph Tucker town Clerk.

***Outrage.** +One who is outrageous in conduct or appearance. *colloq.* — **1869** 'MARK TWAIN' *Innocents* 35 Who is that smooth-faced animated outrage yonder in the fine clothes? **1904** 'O. HENRY' *Roads of Destiny* 351 This old medical outrage floated down to my shack when I sent for him.

+Outrank, *v. tr.* (See quot. 1864.) — **1842** *Phila. Spirit of Times* 1 Sept. (Th.), It won't be long before he fills the place of some one of the drones and cakes who now outrank him. **1864** WEBSTER 928/1 *Out rank,* to take the precedence of, or be superior to, in rank; to rank. **1884** *Harper's Mag.* Jan. 296/2 Your husband . . . could compel some other officer, whom he outranked, to move. **1898** N. BROOKS *Boys of Fairport* 182, I told you that we would get into a scrape along of you fellers being so pernickerty about outranking each other.

+Outreach. The act of reaching out. — **1870** WHITTIER *Poetical Works* (1895) 206/1 No proof beyond this yearning, This outreach of our hearts, we need. **1884** P. BROOKS *New Starts in Life* v. 80 What a different thing this life and this outreach toward man becomes.

Outréness. The state or quality of being *outré* or peculiar. — **1832** MOTLEY *Correspondence* I. 19 The University towns [in Germany] are the homes of 'outré-ness.' **1882** HAWTHORNE *Dr. Grimshawe* viii, A certain seemly beauty in him showed strikingly the . . . outréness of the rest of their lot.

***Outride,** *v. W.* +*tr.* (See quotation.) — **1874** J. C. MCCOY *Sk. Cattle Trade* 375 He does not herd his cattle but designates certain bounds within which the employees permit the stock to range at will. This manner of holding stock is termed 'out riding' the country.

***Outrider.** +A cowboy who rides beside a herd of cattle to prevent straying or stampeding. — **1892** *Scribner's Mag.* XI. 740/2 Outriders were necessary to watch for these enemies [buffalo] and turn their course from the trail. **1907** WHITE *Arizona Nights* 117 We saw in clarity the whole herd and the outriders and the mesas far away.

Outsentry. A sentry on outpost duty. *Obs.* {1691–} — **1741** *Ga. Hist. Soc. Coll.* II. 116 This deponent . . . [was] bound with ropes . . . for refusing to cry 'all is well,' when he was an out-sentry. **1757** *General Orders* 12 That No Man Go without ye Out Sentrys without His Arms. **1775** *Jrnls. Cont. Congress* III. 318 Three hundred watch coats . . . [shall be] kept for the use of the outcentries.

Outsettlement. A settlement on the frontier or other outlying region. *Obs.* {1761–, in Nova Scotia, etc.} — **1740** W. STEPHENS *Proc. Georgia* 621 Matters here and there among our Out-Settlements. **1747** *Boston News-Letter* 16 July 2/1 The Indian . . . went out . . . to annoy the French in their Out-Settlements at Canada, with thirty odd Indians. **1782** CRÈVECŒUR *Letters* 81 [The] dialogue passed at an out-settlement, where I lately paid a visit.

+Outsettler. One who lives on the frontier or other remote region. *Obs.* {1852} — **1756** *Boston News-Letter* 15 April 2/1 Cruel and barbarous outrages [were committed by Indians] on the four Outsettlers of those Parts. **1775** ADAIR *Indians* 250 It would have been much better for . . many hundreds of our unfortunate out-settlers. **1824** MARSHALL *Kentucky* I. 196 Horses were stolen, and the out settlers kept in fear, by skulking parties, who dared not attack any place of strength.

Outshoot. {1613–} +**1.** *Baseball.* =OUTCURVE. **2.** The action of thrusting out quickly. — (1) **1887** *Courier-Journal* 5 May 6/3 He has a queer drop and out-shoot on which McQuaid failed to give him strikes **1903** BARBOUR *Weatherby's Inning* 230 Then followed an out-shoot and a drop, neither of which did Joe take to. (2) **1897** *Outing* XXX. 237/1 A smart out-shoot of the hands before commencing the swing forward [in rowing].

Outside, *a.* +In special combinations.

Outside board, =OPEN BOARD; *o. camp,* a camp for convicts at a distance from a state penitentiary or other prison; *o. corner,* in baseball, the corner of the home plate nearest to first base; *o. Whig,* (see quotation and cf. OUTSIDER 1).

1870 MEDBERY *Men Wall St.* 305 The 'outside' Board was becoming a power. **1880** in *Century Mag.* XXVII. 593/2 The most usual mode of punishment practiced at outside camps is by stocks. **1912** MATHEWSON *Pitching* 159 A right-handed hitter will naturally push a curve over the outside corner of the plate toward right field. **1913** A. C. COLE *Whig Party in So.* 321 Former Whigs [were] divided into Democrats, 'outside Whigs,' anti-Know Nothings, and Know Nothings.

Outside, *adv.* {1813–}

+**1.** *Outside of,* with the exception of, except. *colloq.*

1859 ELWYN *Glossary* 82 *Outside.* This word is frequently used by writers in newspapers in a sense not known to the language. In a *Ledger* of a late date, there is a phrase . . . '*outside* of the Secretary of War,' for 'no one but that official.' **1889** FARMER 405/1 Outside of the tradesmen there was no one at the meeting. **1890** *Century Mag.* 127/2, I do not often see anybody outside of my servants, being not at all given to visiting. **1916** SANDBURG *Chicago Poems* 61 Outside of a few bankers and higher-ups among the con men of Jerusalem everybody liked to have this Jesus around.

+**2.** *To get outside,* (see quotation). *colloq.*

1889 FARMER 405/1 *To get outside a thing* is to understand it, or to use an expression very common in the West Indies, to get to the windward of it.

+**3.** *To be outside of* (something), to have (something) in the stomach as a result of having eaten it. *colloq.*

1890 G. O. Shields *Big Game N. Amer.* 521 My wife said she knew, from his [*sc.* a raccoon's] full stomach and his sneaking look, that he was outside of her pet turkey.

Outside broker. (See quot. 1900.) {1894–} — **1888** KIRK *Queen Money* 71 When Conway failed . . . Kendal went into business as an 'outside broker.' **1900** NELSON *A B C Wall St.* 130 *Outside Broker.*—A member of no exchange who trades in miscellaneous securities.

Outside chimney. A chimney on the outside of the house which it serves. — **1866** W. REID *After the War* 14 Bricks . . . were built up into little outside chimneys for these cabins of the Freedmen. **1884** *Century Mag.* April 825/2 Jones's house at this time was . . . one story high, with a door in the middle, an outside chimney at each end, and a small kitchen.

Outside fence. A fence separating an inclosed tract from an unfenced area. — **1658** *Boston Rec.* 145 All outside fences aboutt pastures or cornfeilds shall bee substantially fenced. **1669** *Groton Rec.* 28 All the out sid fences about all cornfeilds orchards and gardens in the towne shalbe a sufficient fiue Raill fence.

Outsider. {1800–}

+**1.** One outside the ranks of a regular political party.

1848 *N.Y. Mirror* 10 June (B. '48), With the outsiders of all descriptions, Barnburners, and everybody else with a spark of independent patriotism, the nomination of General Taylor is equally a source of delight. **1848** *Lowell Jrnl.* (B. '59), A large number of outsiders have gone to the free-soil convention at Buffalo.

+**2.** (See quotations.)

1848 W. ARMSTRONG *Stocks* 7 Outsiders are those of all ranks and classes who dabble in Stocks to a greater or less extent—they never buy or sell personally, but employ a Commission Broker for that purpose. **1888** *Economist* 27 Oct. 8/2 The insiders still hold the stocks, and the outsiders refuse to come in to any considerable extent.

+**3.** An Indian assigned to, but not remaining within the limits of, a reservation.

1866 *Rep. Indian Affairs* 165 The only way he could properly feed the outsiders and obtain the requisite receipt from the chiefs of the bands properly under his charge.

+**4.** (See quot. 1875.)

1875 KNIGHT 1582/1 *Out-sider.* (*Locksmithing.*) A pair of nippers with semi-tubular jaws, adapted to enter a keyhole and grasp the pin of a key, so as to turn it and unlock the door from the outside. **1896** *Columbus Dispatch* 15 Jan. 1/8 The burglary must have been well planned. Three of the doors . . . were opened by means of outsiders.

5. An outside passenger on a stage or bus.

1882 MCCABE *New York* 159 The number of 'outsiders' is carefully counted by 'spotters' or spies placed along the route.

+Outstock. Domestic livestock allowed to run at large on the range. *colloq.* — **1852** *Fla. Plantation Rec.* 70 The Plough team is in Verry good work order also the out Stock is in good Living order. *Ib.* 78 The out stock look Verry well.

+Outtown. **1.** In colonial times, a town on the frontier or away from a well-settled area. *Obs.* **2.** Attrib. in sense: Out of town; not included within the corporate limits of a town. — (1) **1688** *Conn. Rec.* III. 438, I lately wrott you abt Watching and Warding in yor out townes. **1689** *Mass. H. S. Coll.* 4 Ser. V. 203 Some parties of our friend[ly] Indians . . . [can serve] as a flying army to scout upon the heads of the out towns and plantations. **1690** *Andros Tracts* II. 216 No suitable Provision was made for our out-Towns and Frontiers. (2) **1856** MACLEOD *F. Wood* 181 How far the out-town railroad lines, entering the city, are subject to municipal regulations, I am not at this time enabled to advise.

‖**Outtownsman.** One who resides beyond the limits of a town. — **1714** *Topsfield Rec.* I. 182 If any out Townsmen shall Joyn with them, they shall pay to the ministers Rate as our Towns young men do.

+**Outward inhabitant.** A frontier inhabitant. *Obs.* — **1713** *Va. State P.* I. 168 Foreign Indians . . . [have] Killed and carryed off at least twenty of our outward Inhabitants and Tributary Indians. **1758** *Lett. to Washington* II. 313, I expect to hear of Some murder Committed by them when they Get to the outward Inhabitants.

+**Out West,** *n.* and *adv.*

1. *n.* A region west of older or earlier settled areas. Also attrib. (Cf. FAR WEST and note.)

1835 HOFFMAN *Winter in West* II. 119 Old Kaintuck . . . whips all 'Out-West' in prettiness. **1848** *Corr. R. W. Griswold* (1898) 243 The 'out West Editor' would inform her, in due time, as to who he is. **1887** GEORGE *40 Years on Rail* 62 New York State was considered 'out West' then.

2. *adv.* In or within a region of this kind.

1857 *Lawrence* (Kan.) *Republican* 4 June 2 But any one who has spent any time in farming 'out West,' will see that this is a mistake. **1880** *Scribner's Mo.* March 768/1 For New Sharon, let me hasten to explain, was what was known out West as 'a cattle-town.' **1898** FORD *Tattle-Tales* 205 As they say out West, it's come to stay and grow up with the country.

Outwharf. *spec.* +A sea wall and wharf projected in 1673 and erected in Boston Harbor, to defend the town from attack by sea, and to encourage maritime trade; ?also, any section of this wall, or any wharf built out from it. Now hist. — **1710** *Boston Rec.* 66 The proposalls . . . will be a means to have the Out wharves brought into good repaire. **1728** *Ib.* 220 A Committee [shall] be appointed to Inspect the Ruenous Condition the Out wharfs . . . are in. **1731** *Ib.* 25 The Wharf Latly Rebuilt . . . upon the Southerly End of the Out Wharf or Barricado . . . of Right belongs to the Town of Boston. **1880** WINSOR *Memorial Hist. Boston* I. 227 *n.*, This 'out-wharf,' as it was sometimes called, . . . ran pretty nearly in the direction of the present Atlantic Avenue.

Outwork. An outer defense or stronghold of a fortification. {*c*1615–} — **1678** *Doc. Hist. N.Y. State* I. 89 [There is] a wooden redout & out worke at Pemaquid. **1758** *Lett. to Washington* II. 368 Here with you . . . have the agreeable News of taking all the Outworks at Lewisburg. **1813** J. Q. ADAMS *Diary* (1929) 111 Allies had taken one of the outworks. **1888** SHERIDAN *Memoirs* I. 393, The failure of Wilson's column to get possession of the outwork which commanded the pike necessitated my crossing at Meadow Bridge.

+**Out-Yankee,** *v. tr.* To outwit, surpass, get the better of, as in a trade. *colloq.* — **1846** MATHEWS *Writings* II. 308 (Th.), Let any Yankee take a journey south on a real good horse, and when he returns see if the beast he rides does not show he has been out yankeed. **1854** *Harper's Mag.* VIII. 583/1 A Mexican is a shrewd talker, and in this particular instance they out-Yankee'd me completely. **1868** LOWELL *Writings* I. 350 Is it not that he out-Yankees us all? that his range includes us all?

***Oven.**

***1.** A chamber or container for baking and roasting, often forming part of a cookstove.

1654 JOHNSON *Wonder-w. Prov.* 49 Our last peck of Meale is now in the Oven at home a baking. **1717** HEMPSTEAD *Diary* 68, I was at home in ye foren[oon] mending my Oven. **1790** *Penna. Packet* 3 April 3 To be Sold . . . a large brick biscuit bake house, well constructed, with two good ovens. **1820** *Columbian Centinel* 1 Jan. 4/5 The fire [of the cookstove] passes round the Oven, Boilers Tea-Kettle or under the Griddle. **1892** *York County Hist. Rev.* 14 The bake house is . . . provided with four excellent ovens and all the latest and best improved machinery. **1903** FOX *Little Shepherd* v, Chad . . . built an oven of stones, where coffee could be boiled and bacon broiled.

attrib. and *fig.* **1654** *Essex Probate Rec.* I. 192 An Ioron oven peale. **1859** STOWE *Minister's Wooing* xvii, Candace, armed with a long oven-shovel, stood before the open door of the oven. **1878** B. F. TAYLOR *Between Gates* 256 The limbs [of the yucca are] . . . sometimes oven-brooms for the wind to swing.

+**2.** *New Orleans.* An oval or ovenlike sepulcher or tomb in which the dead are buried above ground. Also attrib.

1851 WORTLEY *Travels U.S.* 126 New Orleans has several peculiarities. . . . The dead are buried in sepulchral houses, which are termed here 'ovens.' **1865** RICHARDSON *Secret Service* 46 New Orleans is two feet lower than the Mississippi. . . . In the cemeteries the tombs are called 'ovens.' **1921** *Chambers's Jrnl.* Aug. 511/1 There was no system in the arrangement of the 'ovens.'

attrib. **1893** *Harper's Mag.* Feb. 374/1 The tombs are houses built upon the ground, and provided with cubby-hole or drawerlike compartments, to be sealed with a marble slab as each coffin is put in place. The term 'oven tombs' describes them well.

Ovenbird. {*a*1825–} +The golden-crowned thrush (*Seiurus autocapillus*), which builds an ovenlike or dome-shaped nest. — **1831** AUDUBON *Ornith. Biog.* I. 121 Children name this warbler the *Oven-bird.* **1868** *Amer. Naturalist* June 182 Its curious nest has long been known; from it, it derives the name of 'Oven-bird.' **1886** *Harper's Mag.* Nov. 877/2 The oven-bird, or golden-crowned thrush . . . on this occasion was but a nameless spirit to me. **1902** WHITE *Blazed Trail* 296 Myrtle and magnolia warblers, oven birds, peewits . . . passed silently or noisily.

Over, *adv.* +Until a later time or season. — **1861** *Ill. Agric. Soc. Trans.* IV. 317 Old bugs live over, and produce eggs the following season. **1883** HAY *Bread-Winners* 172, I am so glad you resolved to stay over. **1898** NICHOLAS *Idyl of Wabash* 53 We don't want to winter them steers over.

***Over,** *prep.* +*Over* (one's) *signature,* etc., with one's signature subscribed to what is written. {1857} — **1806** *Spirit of Public Jrnls.* 96 (Th.), A writer over the signature of Zanga, is another buckram expression. Custom justifies, and therefore requires us to say, a writer under such a signature. **1829** *Mass. Spy* 9 Dec. (Th.), I took up a newspaper, and found the following advertisement over your name. **1839** *Congress. Globe* App. 15 Feb. 187/2 The first time I ever saw it in print, over a responsible signature, was in a letter signed by the Senator from New York. **1875** STEDMAN *Victorian Poets* 261 Who relieved his eager spirit by incessant poetizing over the pseudonym of 'Spartacus.' **1908** *N.Y. Ev. Post* 10 Dec. (Th.), Mr. Fox, in a statement issued over his signature, says [etc.].

+**Overall(s).** *pl.* Trousers of strong cloth or leather, worn by soldiers, hunters, and others engaged in outdoor work; in later use chiefly a garment worn by farmers, mechanics, factory workers, etc. {1807–} Sometimes sing. in attrib. use.

The first group of examples illustrates the variety of styles in overalls. They are worn either as outer garments or as a protection over one's usual clothes.

(1) **1845** JUDD *Margaret* 358 He wore . . . a pair of overalls buttoning from the hip to the ankle. **1861** *Army Regulations* 488 *Canvas overalls for Engineer soldiers*—of white cotton; one garment to cover the whole of the body below the waist, the breast, the shoulders, and the arms. **1865** *Atlantic Mo.* XV. 61 Don insisted on my assuming . . . the leathern *chapareros* or overalls.

(2) **1776** *Jrnls. Cont. Congress* V. 855 A suit of cloaths [shall] be annually given each of the said officers and soldiers, to consist, . . . of two linen hunting shirts, two pair of overalls [etc.]. **1781** DENNY *Journal* 35 They are chiefly all light infantry, dressed in frocks and over-alls of linen. **1799** *Ky. Gazette* 22 Jan., Jonathan Halter . . . had on . . . a drab colored outside jacket and waistcoat, and leather overalls. **1805** CLARK in *Lewis & C. Exped.* I. (1904) 269 [He] had received . . . from M. Chaboillez . . . 1 Brace of Scarlet a par Corduroy overalls. **1886** Z. F. SMITH *Kentucky* 184 Deerskins were extensively used . . . to compose the hunting-shirt, the overalls, and the soft and pliable moccasins. **1904** ATHERTON *Rulers of Kings* 3 The boy wore overalls on other days [than Sunday]. **1923** J. H. COOK *On Old Frontier* 86, I jumped down, pistol in hand, holding up my overalls with the other hand.

attrib. **1884** *Harper's Mag.* Aug. 402/2 A manufactory for canvas 'overall' clothing. **1885** HOWELLS *Silas Lapham* iv, She was followed by the carpenter, with his rule sticking out of his overalls pocket.

+**Over-and-over stitch.** A stitch used in joining two pieces of carpet, cloth, etc., by drawing the thread through and over the edges which are laid together. — **1876** INGRAM *Centennial Exp.* 380 [The carpet machine was] intended to sew the breadths of carpets together by the 'over and over' stitch. **1898** HARPER *S. B. Anthony* I. 22 There is also a bed quilt the pieces sewed together with the fine 'over-and-over' stitch.

Over-arm, *a.* {1887–} *Cricket.* +Performed with the arm raised above the shoulder. — **1864** *Realm* (London) 13 July, We have long been discussing at our cricket meetings the lawfulness of overarm bowling.

***Overbear,** *v.* +*intr.* To bear too much fruit. — **1863** *Horticulturist* XVIII. 295/2 You can now point out every tree that was allowed to overbear. **1866** *Maine Agric. Soc. Returns 1865* 40 This third year . . . the vine will show a great disposition to overbear. **1872** *Vermont Bd. Agric. Rep.* I. 118 The Bartlett and Louise Bonne de Jersey commence bearing young, and are inclined to over bear.

+**Overbill,** *v. tr.* To 'bill' or advertise to excess. *colloq.* — **1890** J. JEFFERSON *Autobiog.* 229 My engagement in San Francisco was an unmistakable failure. . . . I had been 'over-billed,' as it is technically termed,

+**Overbit.** A notch or semicircle cut in the upper edge of an animal's ear to denote ownership. — **1887** *Scribner's Mag.* Oct. 508/2 Marks signifying ownership [of cattle] are [called] *over-bit, over-hack* [etc.].

***Overcast.** +In levying rates or taxes, an overestimate or excessive computation. *Obs.* — **1771** *Conn. Rec.* XIII. 482 There was an overcast made by the listers upon the grand levy of the year 1761, of the sum of £427 00. **1772** *Ib.* XIII. 579 Abatements for over-cast of the list . . . shall be made and certifyed by the listers.

+**Overcoat.** =GREATCOAT 1. {1848–}

1807 IRVING, etc. *Salmagundi* xix. 507 Observing it to be dressed in a man's hat, a cloth overcoat, and spatterdashes, I framed my apology accordingly. **1834** J. VAN BUREN in Mackenzie *Van Buren* 253 For G—d's sake send me my over coat. **1856** GLISAN *Jrnl. Army Life* 305 We countermarched about a mile, and then encamped for the night—with neither tents, blankets or overcoats. **1875** *Chicago Tribune* 5 Dec. 3/6 He is jeered at by small boys, who expressed their disgust at his brand-new overcoat. **1907** *St. Nicholas* June 700/1 You know a thief . . . stole papa's winter overcoat and a lot of silverware, and they never got him!

attrib. **1856** CARTWRIGHT *Autobiog.* 201 My pistol . . . was in my overcoat pocket. **1868** *Mich. Agric. Rep.* VII. 352 For best piece of overcoat cloth, 14 ounces or over, first premium [was] awarded to H. R. Gardner, Jonesville Woolen Mills.

***Overcome,** *v. tr.* To pass over or traverse (a space) {–1697} — **1835** LONGSTREET *Ga. Scenes* 7, I had overcome about half the space which separated it from me.

***Overcomer.** [Cf. Rev. 2:3.] +A member of a communistic religious sect founded in Chicago *c*1880. — **1884** Schaff *Religious Encycl.* III. 1889/1 More recent developments of the same kind [as the Irvingites and the Millerites] may be instanced in the so-called 'Overcomers' of America.

+**Overcrop,** *n.* A crop that is excessively large. — **1878** *Lumberman's Gaz.* 26 Jan., The fears entertained . . . that there would be a ruinous over-crop of logs . . . harvested this winter may be dismissed. **1879** *Harper's Mag.* July 198/2 Scarcely less dreaded by the peach-growers than a failure is an over-crop, when the superabundant fruit ripens too fast to be plucked.

***Overcrop,** *v.* +*refl.* (See quot. 1859.) Also fig. *colloq.* — **1859** BARTLETT 305 A planter or farmer is said to *overcrop* himself when he plants or 'seeds' more ground than he can attend to. **1866** C. H. SMITH *Bill Arp* 27 General Hunter tried it your way and over-cropped himself.

+**Overcup.** *absol.* Any one of various oaks the acorns of which are almost entirely covered by their cups, as the overcup oak and the overcup white oak. — **1817** BRADBURY *Travels* 288 Of the oak only, there are fourteen or fifteen species, of which the over cup (*Quercus macrocarpa*) affords the best timber. **1831** PECK *Guide* 122 The growth of the bottom lands [of Ill.] consists of . . . over cup, bur oak, swamp or winter oak [etc.] **1854** GLISAN *Jrnl. Army Life* 152 The following are some of the principal trees observed along our route. . . . Sweet-gum, over-cup, cottonwood. **1874** *Ib.* 480 A few cotton-woods along the bottoms of the larger rivers; and overcup, pecan, sycamore, . . . and red elm, along the tributary streams.

+**Overcup oak.** Any one of various trees, esp. *Quercus lyrata*, producing acorns deeply imbedded in their cups.

1806 in *Ann. 9th Congress* 2 Sess. 1114 The margin of the [Ouachita] river begins to be covered with such timber as usually grows on inundated land, particularly a species of white oak, vulgarly called the over-cup oak. **1814** PURSH *Flora Amer.* II. 633 This oak is from eight to fifteen feet high, and known under the name Over-cup Oak, Swamp-post Oak, and Water White Oak. **1832** BROWNE *Sylva* 272 The name of Over-Cup Oak is the most common in South Carolina. **1882** *Econ. Geol. Illinois* II. 22 The principal growth of timber is the swamp white oak, scaly-bark hickory, black walnut, ash, over-cup oak. **1901** MOHR *Plant Life Ala.* 46 The overcup oak . . . prefers the shallow lagoons of the alluvial lands in the center of the state.

+**Overcup white oak.** The mossy-cup oak, *Quercus macrocarpa*. (Cf. BUR OAK, MOSSY-CUP (WHITE) OAK.) — **1795** MICHAUX *Journal* 15 June, Quercus glandulibus magnis, capsula includentibus, nommé *Overcup White Oak.* **1814** PURSH *Flora Amer.* II. 632 *Quercus macrocarpa.* . . . A large tree, called Overcup White Oak by the inhabitants. **1859** A. L. HILLHOUSE tr. Michaux *Sylva* I. 35. **1897** SUDWORTH *Arborescent Flora* 155 *Quercus macrocarpa.* . . . Overcup White Oak (Vt.).

+**Overcut.** ‖**1.** A short or direct way as over a hill. **2.** A cut from above. — **(1) 1636** *Boston Rec.* 13 All the ground lying betweene the two brooks . . . and soe to the other end unto shortest overcut beyond the hill towards the north west. **(2) 1883** *Harper's Mag.* Jan. 202/1 The axes were laid aside, and the spring-boards inserted in new mortises behind the tree, and a big two-handed saw [was] set at work to make the overcut.

+**Overglaze,** *n. Ceramics.* An additional glaze applied to a porcelain surface already glazed; also, painting or decoration applied after pottery has been glazed. — **1880** *Harper's Mag.* Nov. 904/1 The over-glaze, that is, painting in mineral colors on either pottery or porcelain which has already received a fire glaze or enamel, so that the article is equally fit for use before as after decoration. **1884** *American* VII. 217 Enthusiastic amateurs have grappled with the pottery question, and the mysteries of 'overglaze' and 'underglaze' have engrossed [etc.].

+**Overglaze,** *a.* On or upon a glazed surface. — **1881** *Harper's Mag.* May 835/1 It was unquestionably the most . . . satisfactory exhibit of amateur overglaze decoration made. **1883** *Ib.* July 259/1 The overglaze painting of tea-cups.

Overhand, *v. Sewing. tr.* To sew over and over. Also *vbl. n.* — **1871** BURROUGHS *Wake-Robin* (1886) 155 The mouth [of the Baltimore oriole's nest] is hemmed or overhanded with horse-hair. **1897** *Advance* 8 April 452/2 All little maids in our grandmother's day . . . [learned] the art of hemming and 'overhanding,' stitching and felling.

Overhaul. {1826–} ‖A severe scolding or reprimand. — **1797** J. PETTIGREW *Let.* 27 June (Univ. N.C. MS.), The steward has provided very poorly untill lately, when the Trustees gave him a severe over-hall, and I believe threatened him severely.

Overhauls. *pl.* =OVERALL(S). *colloq.*? — **1797** BAILY *Tour* 342 Their clothes . . . consisted only of a pair of overhauls and a coarse hunting shirt. **1850** JUDD *R. Edney* 117 A pair of denim over-hauls mated it on the other. **1911** J. F. WILSON *Land Claimers* 72 Overhauls and a blue shirt'll beat the rest of it.

Overhill, *a.* +**1.** Situated or dwelling beyond a hill or hills. {1901–} +**2.** Brought by way of, or involving a route across, the hills. — **(1) 1765** TIMBERLAKE *Memoirs* t.-p., Illustrated with an Accurate Map of their Over-hill Settlement. **1784** JEFFERSON *Writings* III. 452 It would be to our interest to have an agency kept up with the Overhill Cherokees, and Martin the agent. **1835** BIRD *Hawks* I. 83 From the time of the massacre of the over-hill Moravians . . . until the end of the year, Indians were ever prowling in the woods. **(2) 1816** WEEMS *Letters* III. 164, I am just arrived from my overhill excursion. **1895** WINSOR *Miss. Basin* 183 A Scotch baronet . . . was sent hither to prepare the way for a revival of this over-hill trade.

+**Overkeel,** *n.* A mark of identification or ownership made in the ears of cattle or hogs. *Obs.* — **1677** *New Castle Court Rec.* 79 In each Eare a swallow forke and in the Right Eare an overkeel. **1693** *N.C. Col. Rec.* I. 388 Diana ffoster records her marke an undr keele and over keele on the right ear [etc.].

+**Overkeel,** *v. tr.* To mark (the ears of cattle) with an overkeel. *Obs.* — **1647** *Md. Archives* IV. 310 One red heyfer Calfe . . . [with] both eares overkeeld.

Overland, *n.* {1769–} +Short for *overland stage* or *overland train.* — **1872** 'MARK TWAIN' *Roughing It* 76 The place to keep a man 'huffy' was down on the southern Overland, among the Apaches. **1893** *Chicago Tribune* 26 April 10/5, I drove seven year' on the overland. **1907** LONDON *Road* 5, I wanted to take the westbound overland that night.

Overland, *a.* {1800–}

+**1.** Of or pertaining to a journey, communication, etc., across the great plains to or from the Far West.

1837 *S. Lit. Messenger* III. 61 In the course of this over-land journey, the most practicable line of communication would be explored. **1856** *Democratic Conv. Proc.* 27 The following is the resolution with respect to overland communication with the Pacific. **1877** HARTE *Story of Mine* 83 He telegraphed to San Francisco, and . . . secured an overland passage to Washington. **1883** RITCH *Illust. N. Mex.* 41 This home market . . . receives natural protection from eastern competition by an overland transportation of hundreds of miles intervening. **1890** LANGFORD *Vigilante Days* (1912) 122 The Northern Overland Expedition, as it was called, left St. Paul on the sixteenth of June, 1862.

+**2.** Denoting a road or railroad across the great plains.

1862 KETTELL *Hist. Rebellion* I. 194 Frederick W. Lander . . . became superintendent of the overland wagon-road, in 1859 and 1860, to California. **1872** MCCLELLAN *Golden State* 412 The completion of the overland railroad brought . . . a great influx of professional thieves.

+**3.** Of an individual or group: Engaged in or having to do with crossing the great plains.

1877 *Harper's Mag.* Dec. 85/1 The newspapers . . . gave me my first information of the sufferings of Mr. Fremont's overland party. **1880** in Buel *Border Outlaws* 238 Majors Russell and Waddell, the greatest overland freighters the world has ever produced, lived in Independence. **1907** ANDREWS *Recoll.* 94 The Sioux Indians . . . [have trespassed] on the property of overland emigrants.

+**Overland coach.** A stagecoach operating across the western plains, esp. one used on the overland mail route. Now hist. — **1867** *Wkly. New Mexican* 4 May 1/3 It is rumored that some of the Overland coaches have been attacked. **1901** DUNCAN & SCOTT *Allen & Woodson Co., Kan.* 17 The little mule gave way to a two horse hack, then a jerky, or two horse stage, and finally an imposing Overland coach which, in its turn was succeeded by the passenger train.

+**Overland mail.**

1. Mail that is carried overland; an overland mail system or service. Also attrib.

1841 *Niles' Nat. Register* 6 Feb. 353/2 The news from China and India we have received by the overland mail. **1845** POLK in *Pres. Mess. & P.* IV. 397 An overland mail is believed to be entirely practicable. **1858** *Texas Almanac 1859* 28 Requesting the establishment by Congress of a weekly overland mail. **1865** *Oregon State Jrnl.* 16 Dec. 3/3 The above is a very important section of the overland mail route.

2. *spec.* The mail or the mail service overland between St. Louis and San Francisco. Also attrib.

In 1857 Congress authorized the establishment of an overland mail line to California. The semi-weekly carrying of mail by stage coach between St. Louis and San Francisco was begun in 1858. The service so performed was finally entirely superseded upon the completion of the transcontinental railroad in 1869. See LeRoy R. Hafen, *The Overland Mail* (1926).

1856 *Congress. Rec.* 15 Dec. 117/3 Mr. Houston gave notice of his intention to ask leave to introduce a bill providing for the establishment of a mail route and carrying a semi-weekly overland mail from the Mississippi river to San Francisco. **1863** *Rio Abajo Press* 17 March 3/1 The property known as the Overland Mail Company's house. **1865** PIKE *Scout & Ranger* (1932) 7 As we passed through, we met the overland mail stage, coming at full speed. **1866** *Rep. Indian Affairs* 157 The overland mail road was being constructed through their hunting grounds. **1867** DIXON *New America* I. 9 The Overland Mail . . . has ceased to run by the Platte route. **1873** COZZENS *Marvellous Country* 85 An overland mail coach was occasionally attacked.

Overland route. {1857–} +A route across North America from the Atlantic to the Pacific, esp. any one of various routes between the Mississippi Valley region and California.

1850 *31st Congress 1 Sess.* Sen. Doc. No. 64, 50 El Paso, from its geographical position, presents itself as a resting-place on one of the great overland routes between the seaports of the Atlantic on one side and those of the Pacific on the other. **1850** *Whig Almanac 1851* 35/1 The emigrants to California by the overland route have been exposed to incredible sufferings from famine and disease. **1867** G. A. CUSTER in E. B. Custer *Tenting on Plains* 572 The Superintendent called to consult with me regarding the protection of the Overland Route. **1869** J. R. BROWNE *Adv.*

Apache Country 28 Charles D. Poston, . . . had just arrived from the East by the overland route through Salt Lake.

+**Overland stage. 1.** A stagecoach operated on an overland route to the Far West. Now hist. **2.** Attrib. with *company, line, route.* — **(1) 1863** J. L. FISK *Exped. Rocky Mts.* 32, I left Salt Lake by the 'overland stage.' **1872** 'MARK TWAIN' *Roughing It* 20 Not much packing up was necessary, because we were going in the overland stage from the Missouri frontier to Nevada. **1880** *Harper's Mag.* March 556/1 He told . . . of the overland stages. **(2) 1866** *Rep. Indian Affairs* 157 The overland stage line had just completed a survey for a new route. **1890** LANGFORD *Vigilante Days* (1912) 441 He was intrusted with the care of one of the divisions of the Great Overland Stage route in 1859. *Ib.* 443 Those associated with him as employees of the Overland Stage company.

+**Overland trade.** Trade or commercial dealings carried on across the great plains of the West or Southwest. — **1844** GREGG *Commerce of Prairies* I. 17 The overland trade between the United States and the northern provinces of Mexico, seems to have had no very definite origin. **1883** RITCH *Illust. N. Mex.* 25 The overland trade amounted . . . in 1876 to $2,108,000.

+**Overland train.** A railroad train on a western overland route. Also *overland passenger train.* — **1889** CUSTER *Tenting on Plains* 357 The overland trains became an every-day sight to us. **1907** WHITE *Arizona Nights* 262 The overland train brought him from Tucson the five thousand dollars in double eagles. **1913** LONDON *Valley of Moon* 427 Now and again an overland passenger train rushed by in the distance.

***Overlook.** +A superior height or elevation from which a view of a scene may be secured; a view from such a place. — **1861** L. L. NOBLE *Voyage Icebergs* 37 Paths wound among rocky notches and grassy chasms, and led out to dizzy 'over-looks,' and 'short-offs.' **1884** *Lit. World* 23 Feb. 51/3 High overlooks upon the smiling valley.

***Overlooker.** An overseer or superintendent. *Obs.* — **1772** in Commons, etc. *Doc. Hist.* I. 328 His brother, the overlooker there, may be miffed at it. **1792** WASHINGTON *Writings* XII. 255 All the articles in the world would not enforce the measure longer than he himself was under the observation of an overlooker. **a1846** *Quarter Race Ky.* 82 He's a squire, a school comishoner, overlooker of a mile of Nob road. **1854** HAWTHORNE *Eng. Note-Bks.* (1870) I. 96 About in the centre of the garden there was an actual, homely-looking, small dwelling-house, where perhaps the overlookers of the place live.

‖**Overmountain country.** Land west of the Allegheny Mountains. — **1831** WITHERS *Chron. Border Warfare* 52 The English colonists early wanted the over-mountain country watered by the Ohio.

***Overnight.** The preceding evening.

'Now chiefly *U.S.*' (*O.E.D.*).

1705 in Perry *Hist. Coll. Amer. Col. Ch.* I. 170 Came to Town the over night before that general meeting. **1770** WASHINGTON *Diaries* I. 423 After much Councelling the overnight, they all came to my fire. **1803** LEWIS in *Jrnls. L. & Ordway* 46 The morning was clear and having had every thing in readiness the over night we set out before sunrise. **1865** A. D. WHITNEY *Gayworthys* 129 Fastening something else, also, back in her own knowledge, for the over-night, at least. **1871** HOWELLS *Wedding Journey* 21 The air, . . . freshened by the over-night's storm.

+**Overpitch.** *Baseball.* (See quot. 1867.) *Obs.* — **1862** *N.Y. Sunday Mercury* 13 July (Nichols). **1867** CHADWICK *Base Ball Reference* 139 An Over-Pitch.—A ball pitched over the head of the catcher on which bases are made. **1868** — *Base Ball* 126 By an over-pitch Fred got to his second.

***Overplus.** +Superabundance, excess. — **1850** TAYLOR *Eldorado* (1862) 14 An idea of the splendid overplus of vegetable life within the tropics. **1874** *Internat. Typogr. Union Proc.* 23 They received more than the sum needed to pay the fines and costs of Court; and the overplus was returned. **1888** *Economist* 3 Nov. 6/2 The available wheat supplies . . . have gone into consumption so rapidly as to change an overplus . . . into a deficiency.

‖**Overplussage.** An overplus or amount in excess. — **1874** *Vermont Bd. Agric. Rep.* II. 636 When a full supply [of moisture] comes [from the roots], they open the portal and send out the overplussage.

***Overrun,** *v. Baseball.* +*tr.* To run past or beyond (first base) along the foul line. — **1880** *Brooklyn Daily Eagle* 20 Aug. (Nichols). **1886** CHADWICK *Art of Batting* 77 The rule allowing the first base to be overrun was adopted in 1870. **1910** *Spalding's Base Ball Guide* 373 If, after overrunning first base, he attempt to run to second base [etc.].

***Overseer.**

+**1.** In a colonial town, an official chosen to have oversight of the general public business; a selectman. *Obs.*

1636 *Boston Rec.* 14 Not above one dwelling house shalbe built upon any one lott without the consent of the Townes overseers. **1669** *Southampton Rec.* II. 55 We the Cunstable and overseers of the same [etc.], . . . authorize and appoint Samuel Daiton to make a final Ishue . . . about the drift whales that come on the beach within our bounds. **1682** *N.H. Hist. Soc. Coll.* VIII. 93 The trustees or overseers, hitherto called selectmen. **1688** *Springfield Rec.* II. 196 It was voted & concluded to have Six Select men Townesmen or Overseers.

2. A town official chosen for a specific duty.

Often in specific phrases, as *overseer of the fence*, etc.

+**a.** One charged with the supervision and inspection of fences. *Obs.*

Cf. FENCE-VIEWER.

1633 *Dorchester Rec.* 4 If the overseers aforesayde do upon vewe find any pales of the feilds aforesayde defective [etc.]. **1640** *Boston Rec.* 56 Our brother Thomas Grubb and our brother Garrett Bworne are appoynted overseers of the fence at muddy river. **1668** *Cambridge Rec.* 176 Samuel Goffe, & Thomas Longhorne are appoynted overseers of the fences about the necke.

+**b.** One having supervision of roads and highways, or charged with the upkeep of a particular road or section of road.

See also ROAD OVERSEER.

1637 *Essex Inst. Coll.* IX. 67 There are appointed 3 men for overseers. **1668** *Springfield Rec.* I. 361 As overseer to take care for ye repairing of ye Highways & calling men to sd. worke. **1704** *N.C. Col. Rec.* I. 607 Wm. Jackson presents George Gordon overseer of the High Wayes in his Room for the year Ensuing. **1733** *Md. Hist. Mag.* XV. 218 Charles Wells is appointed overseer of the roads . . . from the fording place of Davis's Run to Moale's Point. **1828** COOPER *Notions* I. 346 The overseers of the highway are the men who lay out the ordinary roads of the town. **1858** *Texas Almanac 1859* 23 It is made the duty of overseers to set up posts every mile on the road in their precincts. **1861** *Mich. Gen. Statutes* I. (1883) 259 [A copy of the township laws may be supplied] to each of the several township officers, and the overseers of the highways.

c. An official, originally of a town, chosen to look after the relief of the poor. {1601–}

1647 *R.I. Col. Rec.* I. 185 Each Towne shall provide carefully for the releife of the poore, . . . and shall appoint an overseer for the same purpose. **1686** in Coffin *Hist. Newbury* 147 Deacon Nicholas Noyes, deacon Robert Long and deacon Tristram Coffin were . . . chosen standing overseers of the poore for the town of Newbury. **1702** *Boston Rec.* 23 Elisha Hutchinson Esqr., Penn Townsend Esqr. . . . together with the Overseers of the poor are chosen a committee. **1760** *Boston Gazette* 13 Feb., Yesterday there was a general Visitation of the Town by the Justices of the Peace, Selectmen and Overseers of the Poor. **1827** DRAKE & MANSFIELD *Cincinnati* 20 Each county is subdivided into a number of townships, in which trustees, overseers of the poor, with other local officers, are annually elected. **1854** 'O. OPTIC' *In Doors & Out* (1876) 53 She ought to go to the poorhouse; the overseers offered to take her. **1885** *Harper's Mag.* Jan. 266/1 There are chosen . . . overseers of the poor, constables, [etc.].

+**d.** An official chosen to inspect chimneys. *Obs.*

Cf. CHIMNEY VIEWER.

1654 *Rowley Rec.* I. 91 All thached Chimnies in the towne shall be swept . . . and the overseers are reqvered to vew the day after. **1691** *Boston Rec.* 207 Ouerseers of Chimnies chosen.

+**e.** A town official having supervision over the swine and sheep running at large. *Obs.*

1659 *Boston Rec.* II. 151 Richard Gridley is chosen overseer for the swine, and to levy two shillings, sixe pence by distress for every swine either unyoaked or unrung. **1681** *Cambridge Rec.* 257 The select men doe Alsoe appointd Abraham holman to bee ouerseer of the flocke. **1690** *Groton Rec.* 101 Ouer seeres of swine Jonathan Lawrenc Samll. Woods senr [etc.].

+**f.** One chosen to have oversight of fields and woodlands owned by a colonial town. *Obs.*

1667 *Charlestown Land Rec.* 164 Lift. Richard Sprague, William Dadie, Thomas Rand, and John Cutler, [were chosen] to ioyne with the overseers of the feild . . . to settle [etc.]. **1682** *Cambridge Rec.* 261 Chose this day . . . Samll. Chamne to be ouerseer ouer the hundred achers on the South side the riuer. **1697** *Providence Rec.* XI. 31 Joseph Whipple & Phillipp Tillinghast are Chosen Overseers . . . of all the Gennerall ffields.

+**g.** A person having other special supervisory duties: (see quotations).

1679 *Boston Rec.* 127 Ouerseers of Corders of Wood. **1681** *Ib.* 144 If the ouerseers of wood cordrs. finde any corders unfaithfull or defective [etc.]. **1682** *Plymouth Laws* 194 The Overseer of the Indians in each Towne shall . . . make Inquiry from time to time whoe of the said Indians have procured any English armes and seize the same. **1719** SEWALL *Diary* III. 234 Mr. Oliver in the name of the Overseers [of the meetinghouse] invites my Wife to sit in the Fore-Seat.

***3.** A person appointed to supervise or assist in carrying out the provisions of a will. *Obs.*

1639 *Conn. Rec.* I. 44 This present day there was returned into the Court by Mr. Gaylard, one of the overseers, a coppy of the estate of the children of Thomas Newbery. **1665** *Charlestown Land Rec.* 161 Anna March, relict of John March, did Acknowledge the Legall sale of the two Akers of Land . . . with the aprobation of Richard Kettle and John Cutler, overseers of the will of John March. **1695** *N.H. Probate Rec.* I. 411 That the Over Seers of my Will Should See Meet to advise the Sale.

+**4.** One of a number of officials chosen to have oversight of or to manage the affairs of a college, esp. Harvard.

1643 *New Eng. First Fruits* (1896) 2 Over the Colledge are twelve Overseers chosen by the generall Court. **1685** C. MATHER *Diary* I. 105 What Service may I do for the Lord Jesus Christ, as I am an Overseer of Harvard-College? **1723** in Peirce *Hist. Harvard* 115 The memorial of the Overseers of Harvard College. **1832** WILLIAMSON *Maine* II. 563 Its government was committed to a board of 13 Trustees, including the President, and a supervisory body of 45 Overseers. **1872** *Atlantic Mo.* Feb. 256 The Hare system has been in force in the nomination of overseers at Cambridge for two or three years. **1902** CORBIN *Amer. at Oxford* 274 The Overseers were not in sympathy with the Teutonized faculty.

+**5.** One having immediate charge or supervision of Negro slaves on a plantation or other estate. Now hist.

Cf. NEGRO-DRIVER.

1705 BEVERLEY *Virginia* IV. 37 An Overseer is a Man, that having served his time, has acquired the Skill and Character of an experienced Planter, and is therefore intrusted with the Direction of the Servants and Slaves. **1724** H. JONES *Virginia* 36 The Negroes live in small Cottages called Quarters, in about six in a Gang, under the Direction of any Overseer or Bailiff. **1770** *Md. Hist. Mag.* XVIII. 275 Mr. William Elson overseer of Mr. Stephen West . . . was murdered by negroes on the 14th instant. **1810** WEEMS *Washington* (ed. 10) 211 Long before the sun peeped into the chambers of the sluggard, Washington was on horseback, and out among his overseers and servants. **1866** W. REID *After the War* 497 The overseer rarely left the field. **1894** *Wm. & Mary Coll. Quart.* III. 52 There were many persons who while not owning slaves, were dependent upon that species of property, such as overseers, store-keepers, physicians etc.

attrib. **1865** *Atlantic Mo.* April 509/2 Their conversation [was] a languid mixture of Cracker dialect and overseer slang. **1884** *Century Mag.* April 826/1 Born poor, somewhat of the overseer class, . . . he was eminently made to obey instructions and to keep faith.

+**6.** An officer in a Quaker society or group.

1832 WILLIAMSON *Maine* II. 699 Each society [of Quakers] has at least four Overseers, two males and two females.

7. One who has supervisory duties in a mill or factory.

1844 *Lowell Offering* IV. 16 Martha Stillman must take the new boarder . . . to the mill, and show her the overseers and counting-room folks, and help her get a place. *Ib.* 48 The hours of labor average within a few moments of twelve for overseers and weavers. **1891** *Century Mag.* Feb. 485/1 So long as a quart of meal, a slice of bacon, and a plug of tobacco remain, the overseer implores in vain and the whirl of the spindle ceases.

+**8.** The supervisor or manager of a ranch or cattle range.

1885 JACKSON *Zeph* iv, If he's going to be my overseer 'n' run that ranch, . . . he's just got to be my overseer 'n' nothin' else. **1895** *Dept. Agric. Yrbk. 1894* 118 How can we tell the isolated overseers of cattle ranges in Wyoming of the approach of a blizzard? **1907** LILLIBRIDGE *Trail* 154 The overseer did not seem surprised or offended.

+**Overseer('s) house.** A house for an overseer of Negro slaves. *Obs.* — **1785** WASHINGTON *Writings* XII. 225 Sowed millet in eleven rows three feet apart, opposite to the overseer's house in the Neck. **1803** *Steele P.* I. 396, I have an Overseer with a few Hands, a good Overseer House. **1825** in Commons, etc. *Doc. Hist.* I. 252 Upon the premises there is . . . a good kitchen, Overseer's house, cotton house [etc.]. **1838** *S. Lit. Messenger* IV. 232 Besides the dwelling-house, there are the negro-quarters, . . . overseer's house [etc.]. **1869** TOURGEE *Toinette* (1881) 22 You and Hulda shall have the overseer's house then.

Overshirt. A shirt worn over another; an outer shirt. {1869–} — **1805** LEWIS in *L. & Clark Exped.* II. 159 The weather being warm I had left my leather over shirt and had woarn only a yellow flannin one. **1822** Morse *Rep. Indian Affairs* II. 262 [The women] were employed in making an over shirt for Tom's burial. **1880** *Cimarron News & Press* 26 Feb. 3/1 A large assortment of Gent's Woolen Overshirts, Fine Cheviot Shirts [etc.].

+**Overshoe.** A shoe or shoelike covering, usually of India rubber, worn over ordinary shoes for protection from mud, cold, etc. {1862–} (Cf. GALOSH, GUM n.[1] 4.)

1823 *Salem Observer* 29 Jan., 200 pair Rubber Over Shoes. **1851** MELVILLE *Moby-Dick* 41 Hat and coat and overshoes were one by one removed. **1873** BAILEY *Life Danbury* 177 The principal manufacturing is in rubber goods, such as over-shoes, boots, belting, and the bottom crusts of store pies. **1891** WELCH *Recoll. 1830–40* 173 When the first specimens of rubber overshoes appeared they were hideous devices to look upon, or to utilize. **1910** TOMPKINS *Mothers & Fathers* 356 [He] was down on one knee, humbly removing the overshoes that covered Mr. Hammond's patent leathers.

comb. **1851** HALL *Manhattaner* 51 Overshoe-shod I have paddled the causeways of various cities.

***Overshot mill.** A mill operated or driven by an overshot wheel. Also *overshot gristmill.* — **1659** *New Haven Col. Rec.* 391 The ground through wch. the water must run for an overshott mill. **1790** *Penna. Packet* 2 Feb. 3/3 To Be Sold, A Valuable 20 feet over-shot Grist Mill and Plantation. **1806** in *Ann. 9th Congress* 2 Sess. 1126 The whole quantity of hot water delivered from the springs . . . might work an overshot mill. **1837** SHERWOOD *Gaz. Georgia* (ed. 3) 203 The largest warm spring . . . [makes] a stream sufficiently large to turn an over shot mill one mile from the spring.

Overskirt. A skirt worn over another; an outer or upper skirt usually shorter than the dress skirt and draped. — **1873** 'G. HAMILTON' *Twelve Miles* 264 The ruffles are on one chair and the over-skirt on another. **1875** STOWE *We & Neighbors* 473 Your little dress-maker has made it over with an over-skirt. **1883** *Phila. Press* 7 June 597 Underskirt concealed, or very nearly concealed, by a light overskirt. **1891** WILKINS *New Eng. Nun* 39 The waist and over-skirt were trimmed with black velvet ribbon.

Overslaugh, *n.* {1772–} +A sand bar or succession of islands which obstructs navigation in the Hudson River below Albany.

In this sense evidently from a local use of Du. *overslag.*

1776 C. CARROLL *Jrnl. Visit to Canada* (1845) 42 Having passed the overslaugh, had a distinct view of Albany. **1795** WINTERBOTHAM *Hist. View* II. 298 Ship navigation to Albany is interrupted by a number of islands, six or eight miles below the city, called the *Overslaugh.* **1835** *Harvardiana* II. 5 If perchance you did not get on the overslaugh, you might get to New Amsterdam in a week. *a***1842** S. WOODWORTH in *N.Y. Post* (1877) March (B.), The overslaugh alone For weeks detained a few. **1901** STILLMAN *Autobiog. Journalist* I. 29 The 'overslough' [*sic*] or bar formed in the Hudson . . . prevented the steamers of greater draught from getting up to the wharf at Albany.

Overslaugh, *v.* {1768–} [Du. *overslaan.*]

+**1.** *tr.* To pass over (someone) in favor of another; to ignore the rights and claims of (someone).

1846 *N.Y. Comm. Advt.* 21 Oct. (B.), It was found that public opinion would not be reconciled to overslaughing Taylor, and he was nominated. **1849** *N.Y. Tribune* 20 Dec. (B.), If the conspiracy of the Calhounites with the doughfaces of the North to overslaugh him [Benton] succeeds, it will render him the stronger in Missouri. **1866** *N.Y. Herald* Jan., He was overslaughed in the great topic of reconstruction between Congress and the President. **1874** J. S. PIKE *Prostrate State* 55 This legislation . . . was intended to overslaugh and crowd out the blacks. **1888** KIRKLAND *McVeys* 270 Now she would see whether or not she was to be overslaughed like dirt!

+**2.** To hinder, bar, thwart, or overwhelm.

1858 *Congress. Globe* 21 May 2293/2 Gentlemen on the other side of the House . . . hold their hands up in holy horror because the Private Calendar is to be overslaughed. **1872** W. MATHEWS *Getting On in World* 89 Society is everywhere overslaughed with institutions. **1903** *N.Y. Ev. Post* 28 Dec. 1 The spirit of commercialism will overslaugh every less practical consideration.

Overslope. +A mark or cut made in the upper part of an animal's ear to denote ownership. — **1869** *Overland Mo.* Aug. 126, I had seen a brown-and-white-pied calf, with an overslope and a slit in the right, and a swallow-fork in the left. **1887** *Scribner's Mag.* Oct. 508/2 Marks signifying ownership [of cattle] are . . . *over-slope, swallow-fork, under-bit.*

Overstock, *v.* {1649–} +*tr.* To oversupply (a range) with livestock; also, in passive (quot. 1846), to be supplied with an overabundance of livestock.

1846 *Spirit of Times* 18 April 89/3 It is the worst policy imaginable for farmers to be '*overstocked,*' as it is called. **1888** *Century Mag.* Feb. 507/2 A range may be in reality overstocked when to an Eastern and unpracticed eye it seems hardly to have on it a number [of cattle] worth taking into account. *Ib.* 510/1 The man who overstocks his own range damages his neighbors as much as himself. **1898** *Farmers' Bul.* No. 72, 9 In his eagerness to get rich fast he greatly overstocked the range. **1905** *Forestry Bureau Bul.* No. 67, 56 Nearly all of this reserve affords excellent pasture, but it has been overstocked by outside sheep. **1917** *Dept. Agric. Bul.* No. 588, 18 This range was considered overstocked at least 25 per cent for the quantity of feed it produces.

***Overthrow.** +*Baseball.* (See quot. 1885.) — **1862** *N.Y. Sunday Mercury* 13 July (Nichols). **1868** CHADWICK *Base Ball* 42 Over-throws.—An over-thrown ball is rated as an error of fielding, and, of course, detracts from a batsman's score of bases on hits. **1875** *Chicago Tribune* 24 Aug. 5/6 A furious overthrow by Beals at second . . . tallied three unearned runs. **1885** CHADWICK *Art of Pitching* 139 Any fielder throwing a ball out of the reach of the player he is throwing to is said to be charged with an 'over throw.'

Overtrousers. Trousers worn over one's usual trousers. — **1852** *Harper's Mag.* April 707/1 My duck over-trowsers . . . were beginning to be rather tender in certain places. **1894** *Scribner's Mag.* May 604/1 [The Rio Grande Mexican] must wear 'chapparejos,' or over-trousers, of sheep- or goat-skin.

***Owl.**

***1.** Any one of various nocturnal birds of prey of the family Aluconidae or Stringidae.

See also AMERICAN BARN-OWL, *Barred owl* (s.v. BARRED *ppl. a.* 1), BURROWING OWL, etc.

1637 MORTON *New Canaan* 71 There are Owles of divers kindes: but I did never heare any of them whop as our doe. **1709** LAWSON *Carolina* 145 Of Owls we have two sorts; the smaller sort is like ours in England. **1778** CARVER *Travels* 469 The only sort of owls that is found on the banks of the Mississippi, is extremely beautiful in its plumage. *c***1830** *Waldie's Select Library* II. 86/1 Field-mice . . . passed to the stream in search of food or drink, unseen by their enemies, the hawks and owls. **1898** CANFIELD *Maid of Frontier* 40 The sharp cluck-cluck of some bird disturbed by the passage overhead of the slow-flapping owl. **1907** *St. Nicholas* May 655/1 So far as sight is concerned, the face of an owl or a hawk is not very different from ours.

attrib. **1812** WILSON *Ornithology* VI. 64 [The hawk owl] is a connecting link between the Hawk and Owl tribes. **1845** T. J. GREEN *Texian Exped.* 317 [The Mexicans] danced to poor 'Tecolote's' music, who, at the conclusion of every set, would . . . give his inimitable owl-whoop.

+**2.** In various figurative expressions, esp. *like a boiled owl*, or variants of this.

1831 H. J. FINN *Amer. Comic Annual* 106 Sly Cato hurried back, As solemn as an owl in black. **1831** S. SMITH *Life J. Downing* 125, I want to make them are chaps stare like an owl in a thunder shower. **1846** THORPE *Myst. Backwoods* 24 The way 'the dear creeters [the ladies] could pull music out of it [a piano] was a caution to hoarse owls.' **1857** *Harper's Mag.* Aug. 367/1, I felt, to use a certain figurative expression, 'like a boiled owl.' **1892** *Amer. Folk-Lore* V. 60 To feel like a stewed owl, or like a stewed monkey. More idiomatically, like a biled owl. **1906** 'O. HENRY' *Trimmed Lamp* 33 Babbitt was in last night as full as a boiled owl.

+**Owl car.** A street car that runs late at night. — **1889** FARMER 405/2 *Owl-car*, a tram-car plying late into the night. **1897** *Chicago Tribune* 20 Sept. 3/5 A Deputy Sheriff, was waiting for an 'owl' car at 3 a.m. **1901** ADE *40 Modern Fables* 296 It seemed rather strange to realize that he could stay out as late as the Owl Cars. **1916** DU PUY *Uncle Sam* 144 The owl car of the trolley line that ran through the village had deposited its last late revelers at eleven-thirty. **1923** WATTS *L. Nichols* 218 Them old owl-cars don't run but once an hour.

||**Owl line.** =OWL TRAIN. — **1866** *Congress. Globe* 26 March 1641/2 He is expected to take the owl-line, the midnight line, as it passes his house.

+**Owl's-clover.** One or other species of wild flower of the genus *Orthocarpus* found in the West. Also with defining term. — **1898** A. M. DAVIDSON *Calif. Plants* 142 Another member of this family is the owl's-clover, or the painter's brush. **1915** ARMSTRONG & THORNBER *Western Wild Flowers* 498 Yellow Owl's Clover . . . often makes patches of bright color. *Ib.* 500 Owl's Clover . . . [is] an interesting annual plant, quite pretty, about a foot high.

+**Owl train.** A train that begins its run late at night. — **1868** *N.Y. Herald* 23 July 4/2 [He] despatched to Washington, by the owl train, the discreet and trusty John D. Van Buren. **1876** WARNER *Gold of Chickaree* 248 Must take the morning train. It's not quite an 'owl train'—but comes along, I believe, by eight o'clock. **1882** McCABE *New York* 190 The Third avenue [elevated] line runs its trains all night. . . . These are 'the Owl Trains,' and carry home the late workers. **1910** *N.Y. Ev. Post* 22 Dec. 3 The engine of the 'owl train'—for by this term the one leaving New York after midnight is called—went off the track.

***Ox.**

I. ***1.** A castrated male of domestic bovine stock, raised for use as a draft animal or for food.

1636 *Watertown Rec.* I. 1. 3 If any Oxen or Steers be found . . . it shall be lawful . . . to drive them to pound. **1714** *Boston News-Letter* 1-8 Nov. 2/1 The Troops in Arms were entertained with Wine and Bisket and an Ox Roasted whole. **1837** *Yale Lit. Mag.* II. 149 Star's an all-fired good ox —he'll draw more'n any two oxen in town. **1908** *Springfield W. Republican* 17 Sept. 10 As to the novelty of the barbecue, a pair of white-faced oxen were the chief features. **1920** HUNTER *Trail Drivers Texas* I. 162 Many times I have seen the heel-flies attack a yoke of oxen.

||**b.** *To drive the wrong ox*, to make a mistake.

1837 *Harvardiana* III. 237 They drove the wrong ox, when they sent me on this business.

II. *attrib.* and *comb.* **2.** Designating structures erected for the care of oxen.

1657 *Suffolk Deeds* III. 41 The half of the oxehowse next and Adjoyning to the west end of the Barron. **1665** *Dorchester Rec.* 129 William Trescots request . . . to haue some small parcell of Land . . . for English grass about the Ox pen. **1858** THOREAU *Maine Woods* 129 Grant's barn . . . was said to be . . . the biggest ox-nest in the woods. **1872** FLAGG *Good Investment* 45/1 Near it are a log corn-crib and ox-stable, both under one roof.

3. Designating the flesh or specific parts of an ox used as food.

1731 J. SECCOMB *Father Abbey's Will* xiii, My Pouch and Pipes, Two Oxen Tripes, An Oaken Dish well carved. **1771** FRANKLIN *Autobiog.* 253 [She] gave me a dinner of ox-cheek with great good will, accepting only of a pot of ale in return. **1878** *Amer. Home Cook Book* 5 Ox-Beef, when it is young, will have a fine open grain.

4. Designating things used in caring for or working oxen.

1740 *N.H. Probate Rec.* III. 1, I give and bequeath unto my three sons . . . all my ox tackling. **1810** *Austin P.* 1. (1924) 168, 1 Ox Ring and Staple. **1836** *Knickerbocker Mag.* VIII. 681 His father kept a long ox-gad to whip him with. **1837** BIRD *Nick of Woods* I. 228 It looked less like a canoe than an ox-trough. **1845** F. DOUGLASS *Narrative* 59 Before I could get hold of my ox-rope, the oxen again started. **1881** *Rep. Indian Affairs* 420 Cards, ox.

5. Designating vehicles, implements, etc., drawn or operated by means of oxen.

1754 ELIOT *Field-Husb.* v. 103 With a common Ox Plow, turn of[f] a Furrow from the Ridge. **1817** in *Ill. State Hist. Soc. Trans. 1910* 150 An inclined Wheel ox Saw Mill with two saws. **1823** *New-Eng. Farmer* II. 9 The most expeditious, effectual, and economical mode of making a drain would undoubtedly be to use oxen, and a scraper or ox-shovel, as it is sometimes called. **1831** PECK *Guide* 196 Ox tread mills, on the inclined plane, . . . are very common. **1835** HOFFMAN *Winter in West* I. 246 Our sleigh, a low clumsy pine box on a pair of ox-runners, was soon after at the door. **1854** in Commons, etc. *Doc. Hist.* I. 212 Three ox carts hauled 10 tons of guano from the River. **1858** WILLIS *Convalescent* 386, I saw about to be performed—the unloading of an immense trunk of a tree from a cumbrous ox-drag. **1904** PRINGLE *Rice Planter* 71, I climbed into the ox jumper with the maid and told Marcus to drive home as quickly as possible.

6. Designating one having to do with oxen.

1828 ROYALL *Black Book* II. 114 He was one of your right down flat-footed ox-drivers. **1874** B. F. TAYLOR *World on Wheels* 43 You meet now and then a 'freighter,' as the ox-expressmen of plain and prairie are called. **1889** *Century Mag.* Feb. 603/1 'Tis n't the new ox-hand, is it?

7. In special combinations.

Ox balm, =HORSE BALM; *o. chip*, a piece of dried ox dung (cf. BUFFALO CHIP); *o. frame*, a frame or brake in which an ox is placed for shoeing; *o. gadfly*, =GADFLY; *o. noble*, a variety of potato; *o. power*, power exerted or furnished by oxen; *oxproof*, of a fence, strong enough to restrain oxen; *o. road*, a road for ox-drawn vehicles; *o. work*, work carried on slowly or laboriously, as if by oxen.

1853 *Mich. Agric. Soc. Trans.* V. 130 The plants were very numerous, among which were oxbalm . . . and marsh grass. **1857** CHANDLESS *Visit Salt Lake* 1. 122 Some one pitched on an old camping-place studded with 'ox-chips.' **1844** *Knickerb.* XXIII. 155 An ox-frame standing by the door, and at one side a shed. **1832** WILLIAMSON *Maine* I. 172 Oestrus; *Ox-Gadfly*, (size of a common bee.) **1819** *Plough Boy* I. 170 Some of that useful fraternity at Lebanon . . . brought to our market a most excellent potatoe called the Ox Noble. **1831** PECK *Guide* 199 There is a spinning machine in Bond county, of one hundred and sixty spindles, . . . carried by ox power, on an inclined plane. **1886** S. W. MITCHELL *R. Blake* 21 'A hell-fence?' 'Yes, sir, that's what they call 'em here,—pig-tight, ox-proof, hoss-high, stumps upside down.' **1886** *Ib.* 20 They came upon a deserted ox-road which led out into a rather more open and rolling country. **1868** *Congress. Globe* 16 May 2490/1, I do not see why we cannot . . . go forward with the regular ox-work (if I may be permitted to use a country term) of legislation.

Oxalis. One of various species of wood sorrel of the genus *Oxalis*. Also with defining term. {1706-} — **1821** *Jrnl. Science* III. 283 Black cherry tree, and white flowered oxalis in blossom. **1863** S. HALE *Letters* 15 The ground [was] carpeted with Linnaea . . . little Oxalis, Pyrola, and all matter of moss. **1880** *Harper's Mag.* July 178/2 Huge trees, fallen a century before, lay in gigantic round furrows on the ground; furrows of deep moss . . . and of trailing myriads of pink oxalis.

+**Oxammite.** An oxalate of ammonium found in guano. — **1870** *Amer. Jrnl. Science* L. 274 Oxalate of Ammonia, which Professor Shepard names Oxammite. **1884** DANA *Mineralogy* (ed. 10) 433 *Oxammite.*—Ammonium oxalate . . . from the Guanape Islands.

***Oxbird.** +=FALL SNIPE. — **1839** PEABODY *Mass. Birds* 367 The Red Backed Sandpiper, *Tringa alpina*, is called . . . in this country the Red-back, or the Ox-bird. **1917** *Birds of Amer.* I. 237 Red-backed Sandpiper. *Pelidna alpina sakhalina*. . . . [Also called] Lead-back; Ox-bird, Fall Snipe.

***Oxbow.**

***1.** A piece of wood bent into the shape of the letter U and serving as the collar for an ox.

1736 HEMPSTEAD *Diary* 299, I was at home al day making ox Bows. **1831** S. SMITH *Life J. Downing* 106 A farmer ort to stick to his ox bows and goard sticks. **1846** SAGE *Scenes Rocky Mts.* iii, An extra quantity of ox-bows, axle-trees . . . as a resource in case of accidents or breakage. **1878** *Rep. Indian Affairs* 370 [38½ doz.] ox-bows.

b. *transf.* (See quotation and cf. next.)

1882 *Harper's Mag.* Jan. 172/1 The curves succeed each other until the river is a huge ox-bow.

+**2.** A river bend similar in shape to a bow for an ox, or the land enclosed in such a bend. Usually in proper names.

1797 GRAHAM *Pres. State of Vt.* 148 In this town [Newbury, Vt.] are those extensive intervales known by the name of the great Ox-Bow, which form the River assumes in its course at this place. **1838** *2d Rep. Maine Geol. Survey* 31 Having reached a curve called the Oxbow, we found that the Indians had there held an encampment. **1841** BARBER & HOWE *Hist. Coll. N.Y. State* 201 Oxbow, on the Oxbow of the Oswegatchie river, . . . has about 30 dwellings. **1854** E. F. JONES *Stockbridge, Mass.* 251 The Housatonic River winds among the meadows. . . . Its curves are often beautiful, particularly one called the 'Ox Bow.' **1888** BITTINGER *Hist. of Haverhill, N.H.* 25 The [Connecticut] river flows in a very winding direction through the Town . . . forming in the northern part the famous Ox Bow. *Ib.* 33 These intervals now known as Great Ox Bow in Newbury, Vermont, and Little Ox Bow in Haverhill, had been cultivated at times by the Indians.

3. *attrib.* +**a.** With *bend, curve, lake.*

1867 RICHARDSON *Beyond Miss.* 63 It was at the extreme point of an oxbow curve. **1875** TEMPLE & SHELDON *Hist. Northfield, Mass.* 12 The high plain here . . . turns the course of the Connecticut so that it makes an ox-bow bend. **1904** CHAMBERLIN & SALISBURY *Geology* I. 181 If it [an abandoned channel curve] contains standing water and has the proper form, it is called an ox-bow lake.

+**b.** In special combinations.

Oxbow cut-off, (see CUT-OFF 1); *o. key*, a pin for preventing an oxbow from coming out of the yoke; *o. stirrup*, a stirrup shaped like an oxbow.

1882 *Rep. Indian Affairs* 480 Ox bow keys, 2 inch. **1907** WHITE *Arizona Nights* 5 Uncle Jim sat placidly on his white horse, his thin knees bent to the ox-bow stirrups, smoking.

Oxcart. A cart drawn by oxen. {1877–} — **1749** HEMPSTEAD *Diary* 526 No ox Carts in these parts & very few Horse Carts. **1785** WASHINGTON *Diaries* II. 441 A good Oxe Cart—2 Oxe yokes. **1844** *Lexington Observer* 25 Sept. 2/7 At the same time and place will be sold . . . an Ox-cart, and a Six Horse Wagon. **1884** 'CRADDOCK' *Tenn. Mts.* 160 The ox-carts rumbled slowly down the steep hill. **1907** ANDREWS *Recoll.* 255 There [we saw] a porter carrying an empty dry-goods box as big as an ox-cart.

Ox chain. A chain used in working oxen as draft animals. — **1785** WASHINGTON *Diaries* II. 441 [1] Oxe Chain. **1817** PAULDING *Lett. from South* I. 128 Next came three men, bare-headed, half naked, and chained together with an ox-chain. **1842** KIRKLAND *Forest Life* I. 120 A 'variety store' offering for sale . . . ox-chains, tea-cups [etc.]. **1866** *Rep. Indian Affairs* 292, I also repaired 20 wagons, 15 ox chains, [and] 15 grain cradles.

+**Ox common.** Land owned by a colonial town and set aside for pasturing oxen. *Obs.* — **1651** in G. W. Chase *Hist. Haverhill, Mass.* 73 The ox-common . . . shall be for the use of them who live upon the east side of the mill brook. **1655** *N.H. Probate Rec.* I. 30 Two shares of Cow com'ons and one of ye Oxe Common. **1727** *Ib.* II. 309, I give and Bequeath unto my son . . . my shear of marsh on the great ox Common.

∗**Oxeye.**

∗**1.** Any one of various plants having flowers suggestive of the eye of an ox, +esp. such a plant of the genus *Heliopsis.*

1790 DEANE *New-Eng. Farmer* 313/2 Of the upland-weeds those which have proved to be the most troublesome are . . . the greater-daisy, ox-eye, or piss-abed [etc.]. **1792** IMLAY *Western Territory* 207 Of herbs, &c. we have of the wild sort . . . mugwort, ox-eye, mother-wort. **1817–8** EATON *Botany* (1822) 302 *Heliopsis laevis*, ox-eye. . . . Tall resembling the sunflowers, for which it is often mistaken by botanists. **1829** *Ib.* (ed. 5) 143 *Buphthalmum frutescens*, ox-eye. **1854** *S. Lit. Messenger* XX. 618/1 Sprigs of feather-grass, red-top, and ox-eye.

+**2.** Applied to various North American birds, esp. the mud peep or least sandpiper.

1612 SMITH, etc. *Virginia* I. 15 In winter there are plenty of . . . Oxeies, Parrats, and Pigeons. **1832** WILLIAMSON *Maine* I. 147 The *Oxeye* is a little tottering shore-bird, large as a martin. **1842** *Knickerb.* XX. 360 One of those diminutive snipe, about the size of your thumb, denominated ox-eyes, . . . went off with a whistle. **1844** *Nat. Hist. N.Y., Zoology* II. 244 This little sandpiper commonly known as the Peep, from its usual note, and as the Oxeye, from the size and brilliancy of its eye, is one of our most abundant species. **1849** *Knickerb.* XXXIV. 554 All the varieties of long-billed birds, including ox-eyes and sand-snipe, as well as wild ducks and tame geese. **1896** P. A. BRUCE *Econ. Hist. Va.* I. 115 There was . . . the duck in all those varieties so well known to modern sportsmen, the canvas-back, the red head, . . . the dottrell, the oxeye. **1917** *Birds of Amer.* I. 256 Black-bellied plover. *Squatarola squatarola.* Other names.—Black-breast; Black-breasted Plover; . . . Ox-eye; Four-toed Plover; Gump.

Oxeye(d) daisy. a. The whiteweed, *Chrysanthemum leucanthemum.* {1753–} +**b.** Any one of various American flowers of the genus *Heliopsis.* **c.** The black-eyed Susan, *Rudbeckia hirta.* — **1817–8** EATON *Botany* (1822) 236 *Chrysanthemum leucanthemum*, ox-eyed daisy. . . . Fields. **1850** *Rep. Comm. Patents 1849: Agric.* 374 In southern Pennsylvania . . . the 'ox-eye daisy,' a species of wild camomile, . . . [is] very often nipped by cows when the herbage is scarce. **1894** *Amer. Folk-Lore* VII. 92 *Rudbeckia hirta*, . . . ox-eye daisy, somewhat general in Mass. **1903** ADE *People You Know* 29 He was too large to sit around and count the Petals of the Ox-Eye Daisy.

Oxfly. Any one of various flies that trouble cattle, as the ox warble fly. {1601–} Also transf. — **1737** BRICKELL *N. Carolina* 160 The Ox, or Gad-flies, are so called, from their tormenting the Cattle in the Summer time. **1835** BIRD *Hawks* II. 222 Oh, you old ox-fly! would you have sucked the poor young feller's blood? [**1897** G. YOUNG *Manitoba Memories* 59 Our horses were tormented occasionally by a large fly—called 'bull-dogs' out here. They are larger than our Canada ox fly.]

Oxford mixed. Woolen cloth predominantly black but having a slight trace of white. *Obs.* Also attrib. or as adj. {Oxford mixture, 1837–} — **1826** *Harvard Coll. Laws* 25 By black-mixed (called also *Oxford mixed*) is understood, black with a mixture of not more than one twentieth, nor less than one twenty-fifth part of white. **1855** *Harvard Mag.* June 263 It has disappeared along with Commons, . . . the Oxford-mixed uniform and buttons of the same color, fines for cutting recitations, and other old college customs. **1856** HALL *College Words* (ed. 2) 171 The black-mixed, otherwise called *Oxford Mixed* cloth, is explained under the latter title.

∗**Oxgate.** +An amount of pasture sufficient for an ox. *Obs.* — **1650** *Rowley Rec.* 64 Euery ox gate two rale lengths and euer aker of medow foure and a half. **1660** *Hempstead Rec.* I. 98 There is this Day Leet to Edward Titus the Towene Oxe Gatts for the Sume of A Leavene Shillings. **1662** *Ib.* 101 Also the same Day was lett to William Yeates two Oxe gates in the East Oxepaster for 5s to bee paide in Corne.

Oxheart. +A sweet cherry of any one of several varieties. Also attrib. — **1852** *Knickerb.* XL. 190 From aloft ox-hearts and black-hearts nodded in the passing wind a kindly invitation. **1856** COZZENS *Sparrowgrass P.* 150 Our cherry-tree put out quite a respectable show of oxhearts. **1870** LOWELL *Poetical Works* (1896) 408/1, I perched, Dappled with noonday, under simmering leaves, And pulled the pulpy oxhearts. **1884** ROE *Nature's Story* 267 The moist sultriness of the Fourth finished the ox-heart cherries. **1903** ADE *In Babel* 189 The ox-heart tree which had blossomed so sturdily, showed not a cherry.

∗**Oxhide.** The skin of an ox. Also attrib. — **1804** CLARK in *Lewis & C. Exped.* VI. (1905) 278 Necessary stores [include] . . . 1 Watch Coat, 2 pr ox hide Shoes. **1855** SIMMS *Forayers* 333 They found good Mrs. Travis, sitting calmly in her rustic rocker, . . . with a square of undressed oxhide stretched across the seat. **1876** INGRAHAM *Centennial Exp.* 201 Among these was an immense ox-hide, tanned and finished for belt leather. **1903** FOX *Little Shepherd* xxii, Hunt had seen . . . men wearing ox-hide buskins.

∗**Oxhorn.** The horn of an ox used as a powderhorn, blowing horn, etc. — **1823** COOPER *Pioneers* i, Over his left shoulder was slung . . . an enormous ox-horn, so thinly scraped as to discover the powder it contained. **1876** INGRAHAM *Centennial Exp.* 201 A very handsome pair of ox-horns. **1889** MUNROE *Golden Days* 37 At each end of these dangerous places were hung ox-horns, upon which warning blasts must be sounded before the passage was attempted.

+**Ox mill.** A mill the motive power for which was supplied by oxen. *Obs.* — **1826** FLINT *Recoll.* 211 Steam-mills arose in St. Louis, and ox-mills on the principle of the inclined plain [*sic*], or treadmill. **1831** PECK *Guide* 318 Vandalia contains . . . one water grist mill, one water saw mill, one ox mill, one horse mill, and two schools. **1837** — *Gaz. Illinois* 33 Ox mills on the inclined plane, and horse mills by draught, are common throughout . . . the state.

∗**Ox pasture.** A pasture for oxen. Also attrib. — **1635** *Cambridge Prop. Rec.* 36 All the right title and Intrest w[hi]ch he hath in the ffresh Meaddows and the Ox pastuer. **1658** *Hempstead Rec.* I. 50 Ye East ox-pasture shal be made vp wth A sufficient 3 raylde fence round Aboute. **1708** *Conn. Hist. Soc. Coll.* VI. 291 A Highway, from the Ox pasture hill, to the Town Common. **1713** *Mass. H. S. Coll.* 6 Ser. V. 279 As to the ox-pasture, thay can do nothing.

Ox-shoeing. The putting of shoes on oxen. Also attrib. — **1856** *Porter's Spirit of Times* 4 Oct. 71/3 Ox-shoeing. . . . We frequently find oxen, especially the large oxen, lamed by shoeing. **1890** LANGFORD *Vigilante Days* (1912) 226 We sat down upon an ox-shoeing frame, and talked over the whole matter.

+**Ox sled.** A sled drawn by an ox or by oxen. — **1844** *Knickerb.* XXIII. 445 Let us ride . . . home on the ox-sled. **1854** SHILLABER *Mrs. Partington* 20 Slides down-hill on the ox-sled runners, in winter, that the boys hauled up to the summit. **1878** STOWE *Poganuc People* 90 The roads, through which the ox-sleds of the farmers crunched and squeaked their way. **1904** WALLER *Wood-Carver* 82 Uncle Shim is driving the ox-sled down the Pent Road to Gilead.

∗**Ox team.** A team composed of oxen.

1776 *Huntington Rec.* III. 17 Carting Genll Tryons Baggage from Huntington to Jamaica with an Ox team. **1855** BARNUM *Life* 21 My grandfather paid me ten cents per day for riding the horse which preceeded the ox-team in ploughing. **1896** WILKINS *Madelon* 119 An ox-team drawing a sled laden with cedar logs. **1913** LONDON *Valley of Moon* 297 The chest of drawers . . . had crossed the Atlantic by sailing ship and the Plains by ox team.

attrib. **1864** *Ohio Agric. Rep.* XVIII. p. xxiii, Ox team spaders. Two other spaders are used, drawn by three yoke of oxen each.

+**Ox train.** *W.* A number of freight wagons traveling together, drawn by oxen. Now hist. (Cf. BULL TRAIN.) — **1850** GARRARD *Wah-To-Yah* 72 Overtaking a United States ox-train, with which I traveled and stayed all night. **1852** STANSBURY *Gt. Salt Lake* 27 In the morning we passed a government ox-train, laden with provisions for the new post. **1889** CUSTER *Tenting on Plains* 357 There is no picture that represents the weariness and laggard progress of life like an ox-train bound for Santa Fé or Denver. **1892** in *S. Dak. Hist. Coll.* I. 75 The visitor—still inquiring for the 'wild west'—gazed with wonder upon the ox-train that conveyed the machinery for a stamp-mill.

Ox wa(g)gon. A wagon, especially one used for carrying heavy freight, drawn by oxen. {1895–} — **1831** PECK *Guide* 135 From twelve to fifteen large ox waggons are employed . . . in hauling it [*sc.* coal] to market. **1894** ROBLEY *Bourbon Co., Kansas* 64 All freight came on ox-wagons from Kansas City, Mo., down the old military road. *a***1918** G. STUART *On Frontier* II. 17 William Young with a company of ninety-four men left Virginia City . . . on foot, with their luggage hauled in ox wagons.

Ox whip. A whip used in driving oxen. {1831–} — **1850** S. WARNER *Wide, Wide World* ix, There stood a large, strong built man, with an ox-whip in his hand. **1869** *Overland Mo.* III. 127 The 'cow-whip' is a very long lash with a very short stock . . . but the 'ox-whip' has both parts as long as they can be managed. **1876** CROFUTT *Trans-continental Tourist* 42 How many blows from the ox-whip have fallen on the sides of the patient oxen as they toiled along, hauling the ponderous wagons of the freighters? **1884** ROE *Nature's Story* 254 A man ploughing near had come to the rescue with a heavy ox-whip.

∗**Ox yoke.** Also †**ox yoak(e).** A yoke for oxen used as draft animals.

1678 *New Castle Court Rec.* 361 An ox yoake wth. a Ring and 2 hookes. **1724** HEMPSTEAD *Diary* 139, I made an ox yoak. **1809** *Austin P.* I. (1924) 164 One Plough one Harrow . . . and two Ox yokes. **1868** *Rep. Comm. Agric. 1867* 335 Is the ox-yoke, as used with us, a natural or an absurd implement of draught? **1879** B. F. TAYLOR *Summer-Savory* 138 Awkward H's like a pair of leaning bar-posts with one bar, and B's like ox-yokes.

***Oyster,** *n.*

I. +1. A well-known edible bivalve mollusk (*Ostrea virginica*) found along the Atlantic and Gulf coasts of North America.

1612 SMITH, etc. *Virginia* I. 15 Creuises, Oysters, Cocles, and Muscles. **1661** *Plymouth Laws* 132 Five shillings shalbee payed to the Countrey upon euery barrell of Oysters that is carryed out of the Govrment. **1704** S. KNIGHT *Journal* 39 There are great plenty of Oysters all along by the sea side. **1790** *Phila. Ordinances* (1812) 122 No oysters . . . shall be sold . . . in any other manner, than by count, or tale. **1826** MITCHILL *Discourse on Jefferson* 27 A project has been started for carrying oysters to the Arkansa, for propagation. **1892** M. A. Jackson *Gen. Jackson* 393 A bucket of oysters came from down the river. **1911** *Rep. Fisheries 1908* 315 *Seekonks.*—Oysters (mainly seed) growing in the Seekonk River, Rhode Island.

b. A mollusk of a related species (*O. lurida*) native to the Pacific coast.

1872 MCCLELLAN *Golden State* 245 Oysters are scarce and small, mussels and clams plenty.

+2. In various figurative expressions.

1843 *Knickerb.* XXII. 83 Every place was shut as tight as an oyster. **1863** NORTON *Army Lett.* 139, I found Alf well, enjoying himself like an oyster in the mud. **1889** Dumb as an oyster [see CLAM *n.* 3]. **1922** SANDBURG *Slabs of Sunburnt West* 6 You ain't got the sense God Gave an oyster.

II. *attrib.* and *comb.* **3.** Designating persons having to do with the taking or selling of oysters.

1726 FRANKLIN *Writings* II. 58 The oyster-merchants fetch them . . . from other places. **1777** *Narragansett Hist. Reg.* I. 73 Honourable Nickolas Cooke, Esq., Governor; Oyster Pickler. **1835** LONGSTREET *Georgia Scenes* 41 We were received by the oyster-vender, in a small shop, which fronted upon the street. **1859** *Huntington Rec.* III. 441 Resolved, that Tobias Dillon and Warren Lewis be appointed to serve notices on the oyster planters. **1870** *Scribner's Mo.* I. 167 When she was gone he would sink back into Dick Dort, clam and oyster trader. **1872** *Ninth Census* I. 682 Occupations. . . . Needle-makers, . . . Oyster-packers, . . . Paper-hangers. **1876** *7th Rep. Mass. Labor Bur.* 9 Wage Workers from whom Schedules were received. . . . Oysterman, Oyster Opener, Packer (of merchandise). **1885** *Rep. Indian Affairs* 190 The Shoalwater Bay Indians . . . secure employment with the oyster-gatherers of that vicinity. **1907** LONDON *Road* 104 He was a huge, illiterate brute, an ex-Chesapeake-Bay-oyster-pirate, an 'ex-con' who had done five years in Sing Sing.

4. Designating shallow places or obstructions in waters where oysters abound.

1827 WILLIAMS *West Florida* 16 St. George sound, between the island and the main, is a pleasant inland passage, but is obstructed about midway by an oyster bar. *Ib.*, The entrance to this bay [Ocklockney] is obstructed by sand bars and oyster shoals. **1882** G. C. EGGLESTON *Wreck of Red Bird* 175 'Where on earth are you?' 'Here,' answered Ned, 'out here on the oyster reef.'

5. Denoting foods made with oysters.

See also OYSTER PATTY, SOUP, STEW, etc.

1839 GRUND *Aristocracy in A.* II. 64 We *admire* roast beef, and dote on oyster pies. **1867** *Common Sense Cook Book* 72 [Recipe for] oyster curry. **1890** *Opelousas* (La.) *Democrat* 20 Dec. 2/1 Oyster Gumbo at Mrs. A. J. Perrault's restaurant every Wednesday and Saturday. **1893** *Harper's Mag.* Feb. 378/1 'Oyster loaves' . . . are among the queer edibles of [New Orleans].

6. Designating activities connected with oysters as a commercial product.

1854 SIMMS *Southward Ho* 21 Perhaps, the most exciting of recent events is the oyster war between the Gothamites and Jerseyites. **1861** *N.Y. Tribune* 20 Dec. (B.), The great Virginia Fundum. Reopening of the Oyster Trade. **1870** *Rep. Comm. Agric. 1869* 600 Oyster fishing is carried on to some extent at Shoalwater Bay, in Washington Territory, and at Yaquina Bay in Oregon. **1879** *Harper's Mag.* June 64/1 Along the water's edge . . . [are] the oyster packing houses. **1884** *Nat. Museum Bul.* No. 27, 1064 Oyster cannery. **1887** GOODE, etc. *Fisheries* II. 275 The oyster fisheries of Taunton and Cole's River are of considerable importance. **1891** *Scribner's Mag.* X. 469 Bivalve is the safe port of entry for the majority of the vessels employed in the New Jersey oyster traffic. *Ib.* 475 The oyster-laws stop the planting June 15th. **1914** *Cycl. Amer. Govt* II. 595 Oyster Commissions. Commissions formed in a number of coastwise states for the control of the oyster and other shellfish industries.

7. Designating boats of various types used in gathering or cultivating oysters.

See also OYSTER BOAT, OYSTER SCOW.

1860 E. COWELL *Diary* 70 All three were sailors on board the oyster-schooner. **1883** *Nat. Museum Bul.* No. 27, 266 Shell-Fish Fishery. Vessels and Boats. . . . Model of an oyster pinkie. *Ib.*, Model of a Chesapeake oyster-pungy. *Ib.* 267 Model of a Chesapeake oyster-canoe. . . . Used in 'tonging' oysters in Chesapeake Bay. **1891** *Scribner's Mag.* X. 469 Captain Robert C. Lore, commander of the fast sailing, light-burthen oyster sloop Mail.

8. Designating social gatherings at which the eating of oysters is the chief attraction.

See also OYSTER SUPPER.

1861 *Vanity Fair* 9 Feb. 62/1 You'll have enough to do . . . when I give my oyster parties. **1897** *Ore. State Jrnl.* 10 April 5/2 After the meeting adjourned a number repaired to the Bonboniere where they were served to an oyster banquet. **1906** BELL *C. Lee* 326 Aunt Angie was to give an oyster roast on the shore.

9. Denoting places where oysters are cultivated or grow naturally.

1864 NICHOLS *Amer. Life* I. 270 Gentlemen living upon the rivers, sounds, and inlets in the vicinity of New York, have their oyster-plantations as regularly as their gardens. **1870** *Scribner's Mo.* I. 60 His oyster and clam farms, in which he had at last become master and director of other men. **1888** *Amer. Anthropologist* I. 297 The oyster field . . . would supply a bounteous repast.

10. Designating places at which oysters are sold or served.

See also OYSTER CELLAR, HOUSE, etc.

1872 *Newton Kansan* 22 Aug. 5/5 Parties, balls and socials . . . will be supplied with Fresh Oysters at all times at the old oyster depot. **1875** *Chicago Tribune* 1 Sept. 5/5 Wilson's is decidedly the handsomest and most convenient oyster parlor in the city. **1901** ADE *40 Modern Fables* 208 And he got out and went into an Oyster Bay. **1903** H. HAPGOOD *Autobiog. of Thief* 66 In those days he 'hung out' in an oyster shanty.

11. In special combinations.

Oyster drill, a snail (*Urosalpinx cinerea* or a related species) that destroys oysters by boring through their shells and feeding on them; *o. grass*, (see quotation); *o. lime*, lime obtained by pulverizing oyster shells; *o. season*, the time, principally during the fall and winter, when oysters are gathered; *o. wagon*, a wagon from which oysters are peddled.

1907 *St. Nicholas* June 747/2 But the snail-like oyster-drill astonishes us more by the large size of the hole which it makes. **1881** INGERSOLL *Oyster-Industry* 246 *Oyster Grass.*—The kelp and other sea-weeds which attach themselves to oysters and mussels, or grow on the beds (Cape May). **1853** *Whig Almanac 1854* 39/1 All lands on which the clover or the grasses are grown, must either have lime in them naturally, or the mineral must be artificially supplied . . . in the form of stone lime, oyster lime, or marl. **1866** 'F. KIRKLAND' *Bk. Anecdotes* 181/2 [He] traded up and down the James and York rivers, especially during the oyster season. **1849** G. G. FOSTER *N.Y. in Slices* 18 The massive Exchange . . . is supported on one side by the inevitable fancy soap and shaving-cream man, and on the other by an oyster-wagon.

+Oyster, *v. intr.* To take or gather oysters. — **1767** *Brookhaven Rec.* 186 The Trustees of the Town of Brookhaven shall have liberty . . . to grant liberty to the inhabitants of the town . . . to fish, oyster or clam anywhere within the bounds of the premises. **1840** *Niles' Nat. Reg.* 18 April 112/3 The large oyster taken by Xavier Francois, while oystering on Monday last, was brought up from the wharf. **1896** *Voice* 13 Feb. 3/3 Being near the Gulf some would oyster and fish.

Oyster bank. A shallow area in a river, bay, etc., where oysters breed or are cultivated. {1831–}

1612 SMITH, etc. *Virginia* II. 102 Others complained hee . . . forced them to the oyster banks, to liue or starue. **1624** *Va. House of Burgesses* 28 We weare forced . . . to disperse the wholl Collony, some amongst the Salvadges but most to the Oyster Banks. **1637** MORTON *New Canaan* 90, I have seene an Oyster banke a mile at length. **1705** BEVERLEY *Virginia* III. 59 The Indians . . . found them [*sc.* pearls] in the Oyster Banks, which are frequent in this Country. **1802** ELLICOTT *Journal* 197 The bay and mouth of the river, being full of shoals and oyster banks, it appears only adapted to the coasting trade. **1843** *Knickerb.* XXI. 174, I had just stepped ashore from the boat of the Timoleon, which lay on an oyster-bank a mile or two below.

+b. A pile or heap of oyster shells.

1832 WILLIAMSON *Maine* II. 541 The Oyster banks in this town . . . consist of oyster shells from 12 to 15 feet in height.

***Oyster bed.** An oyster bank, esp. a cultivated one. — **1798** [see INDIAN *attrib.* 10]. **1848** BURTON *Waggeries* 18 They're playin' old hub with my garding grounds and oyster beds. **1870** *Rep. Comm. Agric. 1869* 615 This industry is fostered by the government, a grant of ten acres being made to each person who will plant an oyster-bed. **1879** STOCKTON *Rudder Grange* i, The oysterman . . . had an oyster-bed out in the river, and he made cider in the winter. **1911** *Rep. Fisheries 1908* 317 [The starfish] is of importance only on account of the great damage it does to oyster beds.

***Oyster boat. a.** A boat of a type used in taking or cultivating oysters. **+b.** (See quot. 1890.)

1776 *Remembrancer* (1777) III. 89/1 General Putnam has been pleased to order, that a person should be appointed there, to give permits to oyster-boats. **1814** *Niles' Reg.* VII. 284/2 A British tender . . . gave chase to an oyster boat in the neighborhood of Blackstone's island. **1860** MORDECAI *Virginia* i. 24 At the mouth of the creek, where the gas holders now rise and fall, was a wharf, . . . where oyster boats and small craft resorted. **1882** *Harper's Mag.* Aug. 359/1 [The ship] was both a fruiterer and an oyster-boat, prosecuting these callings at different seasons. **1890** *Cent.* 4219/2 *Oyster-boat*, . . . a large establishment or floating house, constructed on a raft. . . . These houses are usually moored together, and kept in constant communication with the wharf by means of a swinging bridge, which rises and falls with the tide. **1891** *Scribner's Mag.* Oct. 472/2 The deck of an oyster-boat must be trimmed for its work.

+**Oyster can.** (See quot. 1881.) — **1881** INGERSOLL *Oyster-Industry* 246 *Oyster can.*—The tin receptacle, holding from one pint to four quarts, in which oysters are packed for shipment. These may be square, or round, and of various shapes. **1883** PECK *Bad Boy* p. iii, He will tie an oyster can to a dog's tail to give the dog exercise. **1899** 'O. HENRY' *Roads of Destiny* 321 Blinky, pass the empty oyster-can at your left to the empty gentleman at your right.

+**Oyster-catcher.** {1773–} Any one of various American shore birds of the genus *Haematopus*, esp. *H. palliatus*.

1731 CATESBY *Carolina* I. 85 The Oyster-Catcher. . . . I have seen them on the Sea Coasts both of Carolina and the Bahama Islands. **1789** MORSE *Amer. Geog.* 60 American Birds [which] have been enumerated . . . [include] the Heron, . . . Nuthatch, Oyster catcher [etc.]. **1813** WILSON *Ornithology* VIII. 17 The Oyster-catcher will not only take to the water when wounded, but can also swim and dive well. **1844** *Nat. Hist. N.Y., Zoology* II. 217 The Oyster-catcher . . . feeds on oysters and other marine bivalves. **1870** *Amer. Naturalist* III. 232 The Oyster-Catcher, a Southern coast-bird, . . . occasionally wanders as far north as Marshfield. **1917** *Birds of Amer.* I. 271/1 Oyster-catchers . . . carry about with them each its oyster-knife, in order to be able to feed upon the oysters.

+**Oyster cellar.** A shop, originally one in a basement, where oysters are sold or served. {1889–} (Cf. OYSTER HOUSE.) — **1830** WATSON *Philadelphia* 220 Oyster Cellars . . . did not at first include gentlemen among their visiters. **1853** BALDWIN *Flush Times Ala.* 161 He used to boast that he and D.L. had never failed to break an oyster cellar in Tuscaloosa whenever they made a run on it.

Oyster crab. A small crab living commensally with an oyster in the shell of the latter. {1756–} — **1843** *Nat. Hist. N.Y., Zoology* VI. 12 The *P. depressum* of Say, is . . . the male, or as we suppose the young, of the Common Oyster Crab. **1881** INGERSOLL *Oyster-Industry* 246 *Oyster-Crab.*—The female of the *Pinnotheres ostreum*, found parasitic in the gills of oysters from Massachusetts southward. **1902** WILSON *Spenders* 131 Now the oysters will be due—fine fat Buzzard's Bays—and oyster crabs.

+**Oyster cracker.** (See quotation 1890.) — **1890** *Cent.* 4219/2 *Oyster-cracker*, . . . a small kind of cracker or biscuit served with oysters. **1898** WESTCOTT *D. Harum* 110 Mr. Elright's ravagement of the larder had resulted in . . . some chunks of soft white cheese, and a plate of what are known as oyster crackers. **1908** *Sears, Roebuck & Co. Cat.* No. 118, 115, 20-lb. box Oyster Crackers.

Oyster fish. 1. The toadfish, *Opsanus tau.* {1611–} +**2.** =BLACKFISH 2. +**3.** (See quotation.) — **(1) 1855** BAIRD in *Smithsonian Rep.* 340 The toad-fish, or, as it is called at Beesley's point, the oyster-fish, . . . is one of the fisherman's pests. **1884** GOODE, etc. *Fisheries* I. 251 The Toad-fish, *Batrachus tau*, called also on the coast of New Jersey and in some parts of the Southern States 'Oyster-fish,' is one of the most repulsive looking fishes upon our coast. **(2) 1878** *Nat. Museum Proc.* I. 374 *Tautoga onitis.*—Oyster-fish. Rather common. **1903** T. H. BEAN *Fishes N.Y.* 598 This is better known in New York as the blackfish; farther south it is styled . . . Moll, Will George and oyster fish. **(3)** *Ib.* 656 *Gobiosoma bosci.* . . . Naked Goby; Mud Creeper; Oysterfish.

+**Oyster fritter.** An oyster dipped in stiff batter and then cooked in hot fat. — **1867** *Common Sense Cook Book* 10 Oyster Fritters . . . are made the same way as the fritters of soft clams. **1891** *Amer. Notes & Q.* VI. 179 The terms fritters and flat-jacks are very common to Pennsylvania at the present time, and especially to the county of Lancaster. . . . There are few persons who are not familiar with 'apple-fritters' and 'oyster-fritters.'

+**Oysterhouse.** A restaurant which specializes in serving oysters. (Cf. OYSTER CELLAR.) — **1834** NOTT *Novellettes* I. 94 He can escape from the empty pageant to the substantial and homely comforts of a beefsteak or oyster house. **1875** *Chicago Tribune* 1 Sept. 5/4 The St. Charles is the oldest oyster-house in Chicago. **1882** McCABE *New York* 254 All along the avenue are . . . oyster-houses in which no decent person ever sets foot. **1902** *Harper's Mag.* May 964/1 The most brilliant shop on the 'Avenoo' . . . was an oyster-house, and a very unusual, almost wonderful one of its kind.

+**Oystering.** Taking, gathering, or fishing for oysters, esp. for commercial purposes. {1860, in Australia} (Cf. OYSTER *v.*)

1662 *Virginia Stat.* (1823) II. 140 The poore Indians whome the seating of the English hath forced from their wonted conveniences of oystering. **1755** *Brookhaven Rec.* 178 The Indian propriators of the South Bay . . . [sell] the profits, advantages and previliges of Fishing, Fowling, Oystering and other previliges. **1798** *Huntington Rec.* III. 195 No person or persons not being an Inhabitant or Inhabitants of this Town shall Practice Fouling Fishing Claming or Oystering in the Town of Huntington. **1824** *Ib.* 314 Trustees of Sd town . . . [reserve] the privilege of fishing fowling claming oystering [etc.]. **1881** *Rep. Indian Affairs* 169 These Indians have always made their living by oystering on the bay during the oyster season.

Oyster knife. A knife specially adapted to opening oyster shells. {1694–} Also transf. — *a***1841** HAWES *Sporting Scenes* II. 120 Oyster-knives and blood become well acquainted. **1861** NEWELL *Orpheus C. Kerr* I. 236 Ef I don't make a doctor's two-wheeler outer that ere wagon, then bleed me to death with a oyster-knife! **1873** BAILEY *Life in Danbury* 124 He took all these off with an oyster knife in the afternoon. **1891** *Scribner's Mag.* X. 469/1, A great glass case . . . [contained] an oyster knife. **1917** [see OYSTER-CATCHER].

***Oysterman.**

***1.** One who gathers or cultivates oysters.

1753 Singleton *Social N.Y.* 350, I am informed that an oysterman, industriously employed, may clear eight or ten shillings a day. **1817** *Niles' Reg.* XIII. 18/1, I know a person that once was an oysterman, in the Delaware bay. **1839** IRVING in *Knickerb.* Oct. 344 The Communipaw oystermen . . . declared that they had more than once seen him suddenly disappear, canoe and all, as if they plunged beneath the waves. **1855** *Knickerb.* XLVI. 222 In the sounds, 'hard-shell' clam-catchers, fishermen, and oyster-men steadily ply their different callings. **1879** STOCKTON *Rudder Grange* i, This boat we soon found was inhabited by an oysterman and his family. **1891** *Scribner's Mag.* X. 469 A great glass case . . . [contained] the weather-beaten costume of a New Jersey oysterman.

+**2.** One who keeps an oyster cellar or oysterhouse.

1853 FOWLER *Home for All* 23 Those persons who would economize, have only to order those very shells which the oyster-man has to pay to have carted from his cellar, on to your building spot. **1857** *Lawrence* (Kan.) *Republican* 23 July 1, I went through a narrow street or alley in which was an oysterman's shop.

Oyster patty. A small pie made with oysters. — **1828** LESLIE *Receipts* 26 For oyster patties, the oysters are prepared in the same manner. [**1869** STOWE *Oldtown Folks* 517 Debby, put an oyster-*paté* on Horace's plate.] **1883** WILDER *Sister Ridnour* 149 The oyster patties, the quahaug pies, the roasted ducks, and the Saratoga potatoes.

Oyster plant. {1858–} +The salsify (*Tragopogon porrifolius*), having an edible fusiform root. — **1824** 'SINGLETON' *Lett. South & West* 72 [Virginians] also cherish the salsify, or oyster-plant, so called from its flavour when fried. **1868** GRAY *Field Botany* 206 *T[ragopodon] porrifolius*, Common S[alsify] or Oyster-plant, . . . [has] deep violet-purple flowers. **1884** ROE *Nature's Story* 186 Will your nose become *retroussé* if I ask you to aid me in planting parsnips, oyster-plant, carrots, and . . . onions?

Oyster-planting. The placing of oysters on submerged areas suitable for their propagation. Also attrib. — **1845** SOL. SMITH *Theatr. Apprent.* 87, [I] dug into the oyster-planting scheme. **1891** W. K. BROOKS *Oyster* 106 The drawback to East River oyster-planting, . . . is the abundance of enemies with which the beds are infested.

+**Oyster police (force).** A police force established by Maryland and Virginia to regulate oystering in the waters of those states. — **1870** *Md. Code: Suppl.* 69 The commanding officer of the 'state oyster police force' is hereby charged with the enforcement of the provisions of this article [on fines]. *Ib.* 112 It shall be the duty of . . . the oyster police of the state . . . to examine the licenses of all boats or vessels engaged in taking or catching oysters. **1879** *Harper's Mag.* June 65/2 An oyster police was instituted by Virginia.

+**Oyster pond.** Also †**oyster pound.** A pond in which oysters grow or are grown. Also attrib. — **1655** *Southold Rec.* I. 27 The above said ffower acres and a halfe of meadowe more or lesse in the Oysterpounds. **1658** *Ib.* 48 Which meadow was exchanged . . . for his Seller meadow at the Oysterponds. **1731** COMER *Diary* 116 [We] anchored at Southhold harbour, by ye oyster ponds on Long Island. **1870** *Huntington Rec.* III. 592 Over and across the cove to the old oyster pond dam.

+**Oyster rake.** A long-handled rake used for gathering oysters. — **1705** *Providence Rec.* VI. 247 Oyster Rake 3 hammer and a hand Bill. *c***1863** in Billings *Hardtack* 72 If I'm not here when you awake, Just hunt me up with an oyster rake. **1884** *Nat. Museum Bul.* No. 27, 856 Oyster-rake or toothed dredge. Galvanized-iron frame; 12 teeth; net of iron-mesh.

+**Oyster room.** An oyster cellar or an oysterhouse. — **1883** *Century Mag.* Nov. 41/1 American life is invading the thoroughfare, . . . multiplying flashy saloons and cheap restaurants, cigar stores and oyster-rooms. *a***1889** W. D. O'CONNOR *Three Tales* 14 The street-floor of one of my houses in Hanover Street lets for an oyster-room.

+**Oyster saloon.** =OYSTERHOUSE. — **1833** *Knickerb.* I. 117 Certain fiery and bulbous excrescences [noses] to be seen about taverns and oyster-saloons. **1850** *New Eng. Farmer* II. 99 The young lad strays away . . . to the oyster saloon. **1870** O. LOGAN *Before Footlights* 255, [I confined] myself to the perusal of a fracas in an oyster saloon. **1894** CABLE *J. March* xix, The two Rosemonters were about to walk past an open oyster saloon hard by the capitol.

Oyster sauce. A sauce made of oysters, butter, milk, flour, and seasoning. {1816–} — **1775** *Essex Inst. Coll.* L. 100, I dined at Prentices on boil'd turkey & oyster sauce. **1817** PAULDING *Lett. from South* II. 148, [I] would like very much to dine on a turkey and oyster sauce. **1867** *Common Sense Cook Book* 31 [Recipe for making] Oyster Sauce. **1869** *Boyd's Business Directory* 713 Goodell & Haskells, Sole Agents for . . . American Oyster Sauce.

+**Oyster scow.** A scow used as an oyster boat. Also attrib. — **1824** *Nantucket Inquirer* 26 Jan. (Th.), He wore a hat of the new oyster-scow cut, with a long piece of crape hanging to it. **1844** *Knickerb.* XXIV. 293 I am told of a coalition between two oyster-scows which are covered over with the shell of an ordinary boat.

***Oyster shell.**

***1.** A shell of an oyster.

1654 JOHNSON *Wonder-w. Prov.* 194 The country affords no Lime, but what is burnt of Oyster-shels. **1797** HAWKINS *Letters* 87 At the lower part of [the bluff] . . . is a bed of oyster shells. **1817** PAULDING *Lett. from*

South I. 62 There are large masses of oyster-shells along the banks. **1895** *Dept. Agric. Yrbk. 1894* 520 In the counties bordering the coast excellent roads can be built and maintained by the use of oyster shells. **1907** *St. Nickolas* June 747/2 But the snail-like oyster-drill astonishes us more by the . . . hardness of the substance (the oyster shell) through which it drills.

2. Attrib. with *bank, field, lime, plain.* Formerly used in place names.

1642 *New Haven Col. Rec.* 62 The comon feild called the oyster shell feild. **1723** *Providence Rec.* XII. 68, 89 acres upon oyster Shell plains. **1855** *Knickerb.* XLVI. 542 He was intercepted . . . by a party of skirmishers, advantageously posted on an oyster shell bank. **1885** Eggleston in *Century Mag.* April 874/1 Oyster-shell lime was the material most commonly in use for plastering.

+**Oyster-shell bark louse.** A scale insect (*Lepidosaphes ulmi*) very injurious to certain trees and plants. — **1868** *Rep. Comm. Agric. 1867* 73 The oyster shell bark louse or scale insect, *Aspidiotus conchiformis*, is said to be exterminated by washing the tree with a mixture [etc.]. **1870** *Ib. 1869* 536 The most troublesome insect at present, however, in Michigan, is the oystershell bark-louse, (*Aspidiotus conchiformis* of Gmelin.) **1877** *Vermont Bd. Agric. Rep.* IV. 150 Dr. Worcester has also shown me a branch covered with . . . oyster shell bark-louse. **1895** *Dept. Agric. Yrbk. 1894* 253 One form . . . for many years has been considered a true enemy of the oyster-shell bark louse of the apple.

+**Oyster-shell scale.** =prec. — **1877** *Vermont Bd. Agric. Rep.* IV. 150 The insect is shorter and stouter than that of the oyster shell scale.

Oyster shop. A shop or restaurant where oysters are sold or served. — **1830** Holmes *Poetical Works* (1895) 330/1 Now they keep an oyster-shop for mermaids down below. **1842** Buckingham *Slave States* II. 450 The name of Victoria has been appended to almost every thing, from Mr. Sully's portrait of the Queen, down to the last new oyster-shop opened in New York. **1894** Aldrich *Two Bites* 159, I had thrust my hand under his arm, and was dragging him towards a small oyster shop.

Oyster soup. Soup made of oysters and milk, cream, etc. — **1799** Weld *Travels* 96 A couple of dishes of salted meat, and some oyster soup, formed the whole of the dinner. **1866** 'F. Kirkland' *Bk. Anecdotes* 606 He then rushed frantically up stairs and drowned his sorrow in a flowing bowl of oyster soup. **1907** Harris *Tents of Wickedness* 227 She had assimilated the oyster-soup, the turkey [etc.]. **1908** 'O. Henry' *Options* 26 You can make oyster-soup without oysters, turtle-soup without turtles, coffee-cake without coffee.

+**Oyster stand.** A stall or booth where oysters are served. — **1845** Sol. Smith *Theatr. Apprent.* 133 The mischievous actors contrived . . . to substitute *pepper vinegar*, from an oyster stand. **1849** *Knickerb.* XXXIV. 85 There is a street-sign also of an oyster-stand. **1851** A. O. Hall *Manhattaner* 7 Oyster stands, where dirty mouths and flickering tallow candles grinned ghostly satisfaction.

+**Oyster stew.** =Oyster soup. — **1846** Corcoran *Pickings* 128 Mrs. Smith was never known to have an oyster stew of an evening that she did not divide it with Mrs. Jones. **1868** Condict *P. Eckert* 152 An oyster stew, with a little something to wash it down, will start you all right again, my boy! **1902** C. Morris *Stage Confidences* 171 One would think that the democratic twenty-five cent oyster stew . . . would taste better [etc.].

+**Oyster supper.** A supper, usually a festive or social occasion, at which oysters constitute the major part of the meal. — **1791** Maclay *Deb. Senate* 285 Mr. Brown . . . told me that Muhlenberg was very busy in giving oyster suppers, etc. **1835** Longstreet *Georgia Scenes* 41, [I] propose that we go out and take an oyster supper before we retire to rest. **1860** Olmsted *Back Country* 213 He amused me much with a humorous account of an oyster supper to which he had been invited in town. **1896** Frederic *Damnation of T. Ware* 10 The oyster suppers given by their Ladies' Aid Society . . . had established rank among the fashionable events in Tecumseh's social calendar.

+**Oyster tongs.** (See quot. 1875.) — **1716** *Providence Rec.* VI. 161 To Iron Teeth for Oyster Tongs and Carpenters. **1804** *Mass. H. S. Coll.* IX. 254 A man . . . in a small boat, with an instrument similar to oyster tongs, can raise from its watery bed about half a ton of this ore in a day. **1875** Knight 1589/1 *Oyster-tongs*, an instrument having two rake-shaped jaws and a pair of long handles, to grapple oysters in their beds and lift them to the surface. **1891** *Scribner's Mag.* X. 473 A pair of oyster-tongs will serve.

Ozenbrig(s). Variant of Osnaburg(s).

P

+**Paas.** Also **Paus.** *N.Y.* [Du. *Paasch.*] Easter. *Obs.* Also attrib. (The term here represents an independent borrowing from Dutch.) — **1809** IRVING *Knickerb.* VII. i, Under his [Stuyvesant's] reign was first introduced the custom of cracking eggs at Paas or Easter. **1830** COOPER *Water Witch* I. i, Thou canst lighten thy heart in the Paus merry-makings. **1859** BARTLETT 307 *Paas Bloomachee*, i.e. Easter flower. (*Narcissus pseudo-narcissus.*) Not the Pasque Flower of botanists, but the common Yellow Daffodil. *Ib. Paas Eggs.* Hard-boiled eggs cracked together by New York boys at the Easter season. They are often dyed of various colors in boiling.

+**Pac, Pack.** [Lenape *paku, pacu*, a kind of shoe.] (See quot. 1875); also used of a heavy half-boot worn by lumbermen in winter. — **1875** KNIGHT 1590/1 *Pac; Pack.* A moccasin having a sole turned up and sewed to the upper. Though now made of leather of various kinds, the pac, as used by the Indians of the Six Nations, for instance, was made of hide boiled in tallow and wax; or of tawed hide subsequently stuffed with tallow or wax. **1893** *Scribner's Mag.* June 715 Logger's Footgear. . . . Old-fashioned boot-pack. Modern rubber-soled boot-pack.

Paccan. Also †**pacan, packawn.** *Obs.* = PECAN 1 and 2. Also *paccan nut.* (Cf. ILLINOIS NUT.)

1773 in Hutchins *Va., Penn., Md., & N. Car.* 52 The timber, Bois Connu, or Paccan, Maple, Ash, Button Wood. **1786** JEFFERSON *Writings* V. 243 Procure me two or three hundred paccan-nuts from the western country. **1805** *Ann. 9th Congress* 2 Sess. 1100 Then for about one league, left side, is a beautiful grove of pacans, intermixed with no other growth. **1806** *Ib.* 1107 There are generally seen willows growing on one side, and on the other a small growth of black oak, packawn, hickory, elm, &c. **1838** 'TEXIAN' *Mexico v. Texas* 218 He brought also a handkerchief full of pacans. **1844** GREGG *Commerce of Prairies* II. 198 About the streams we find an intermixture of elm, hackberry, paccan (or pecan), ash [etc.].

***Pace.** *Baseball.* +The speed of a pitcher's delivery. Also *dropping the pace.* — **1867** CHADWICK *Base Ball Reference* 138 *Dropping the Pace.* —Sending in a slow ball suddenly after having pitched swiftly for some time. **1868** — *Base Ball* 44 *Pace.*—This is a term applied to the speed of a pitcher's delivery. **1886** *Outing* June 365/1 But his pace is useless, as no one could stand the punishment involved in facing such a delivery behind the bat.

***Pacer.**

1. A horse that paces {1661–}, +esp. one that racks.

See also NARRAGANSET(T) PACER.

1741 FRANKLIN *Poor Richard's Almanac 1742* 1 Will her next Colt be a Pacer? **1829** COOPER *Wish-ton-Wish* xviii, Put the spur smartly into the pacer's flank. **1857** H. W. HERBERT *Forester's Horse & Horsemanship* II. 70 The 'Narragansett Pacer' . . . [moved] without inclining the rider from side to side, as the common racker or pacer of the present day. **1897** J. H. WALLACE *Horse of America* 192 In many sections of the country the pacer is called a racker. **1897** *Outing* XXX. 85/2 Eighty-one of his daughters had ninety-one trotters and twenty-nine pacers in the same lists. **1902** MCFAUL *Ike Glidden* 20 Run across a fellow what had a pacer, pretty good built one, looked sound and smooth.

2. *Natural pacer*, a horse that paces without having been trained to do so.

1776 *N.J. Archives* 2 Ser. I. 103 Strayed from a meadow . . . a Horse, . . . a natural pacer, but can trot. **1785** WASHINGTON *Diaries* II. 441 Grey [horse]—natural pacer. **1799** PARMENTER *Hist. Pelham, Mass.* 488 Also entered . . . a Yearling horse colt. . . . Neatrel paser. **1884** EGGLESTON in *Century Mag.* Jan. 445/1 That delightful American eccentricity, the natural pacer, was known in Virginia not later than the first quarter of the eighteenth century.

+**Pache, 'Pache.** Short for APACHE. *colloq.* — **1850** GARRARD *Wah-To-Yah* xiii. 168 The Paches (Apaches) took my beaver. **1912** RAINE *Brand Blotters* 282 Even in the daytime it would take a 'Pache, but at night—well, here's hoping the luck's good.

***Pacific,** *a.*

In the following quotations the term derives from the attrib. use of *Pacific* in *Pacific Ocean.*

+**1.** Designating railroads, mail, and express crossing the continent to the Pacific coast or carried to or from that region.

1854 *La Crosse Democrat* 17 Jan. 2/3 Gov. Stevens' exploring expedition has discovered large quantities of gold on the Yenass river, on the route of the proposed Pacific Railroad. **1856** *Porter's Spirit of Times* 11 Oct. 95/1 Pacific Express.—We are indebted to this prompt and vigilant establishment for early and full files of California papers. **1857** *Harper's Mag.* Feb. 403/1 The most important measures now under consideration are those relating to . . . the Pacific Railway. **1868** *N.Y. Herald* 2 July 6/1 The alleged Pacific Mail perjury case . . . was continued before the Supreme Court.

2. In specific names. +**a.** Of birds found on or near the Pacific coast.

1874 COUES *Birds N.W.* 723 The Pacific Diver, as its name indicates, is confined to the West. **1839** AUDUBON *Ornith. Biog.* V. 331 Pacific Fulmar. *Procellaria Pacifica.* **1917** *Birds of Amer.* I. 240 The Pacific Godwit . . . [is] included in check-lists of North American airfauna.

+**b.** Of fishes and animals found in the Pacific.

1917 *Mammals of Amer.* 116 Pacific Fisher.—*Martes pennanti pacifica.* . . . Various parts of the Pacific slope, California to Alaska. **1884** *Nat. Museum Bul.* No. 27, 639 *Orca atra*, Cope. Pacific Killer. *Ib.* 632 The common Pacific Porpoise, *P. vomerina*, . . . [is] esteemed by the Indians . . . [and] pursued by them with considerable vigor. **1911** *Rep. Fisheries 1908* 316/1 The Pacific smelt (*O[smerus] thaleichthys*) is found from San Francisco to Alaska. **1884** GOODE, etc. *Fisheries* I. 223 The Pacific Tom Cod . . . [is] found in California.

+**3.** In special combinations.

Pacific canal, the projected Isthmian or Panama canal; *P. guano*, (see quotation); *P. time*, time as reckoned in the Pacific time belt or as prevailing on the 120th meridian west of Greenwich.

1900 *Congress. Rec.* 1 Feb. 1407/2 Build the Pacific canal . . . and you will make the Pacific slope the counterpart of our Atlantic seaboard. **1883** SMITH *Geol. Survey Ala.* 118 'Pacific guano' is an artificial product made of a mixture of South Carolina phosphates, and the bodies and other refuse of fish. **1883** *N.Y. Herald* 18 Nov. 12/3 In the United States the standards will be known as the 'Eastern,' 'Central,' 'Mountain' and 'Pacific' times.

+**Pacific coast.** That part of North America, esp. of the U.S., that borders on the Pacific Ocean. Also attrib. Also *Pacific coaster.* — **1872** MCCLELLAN *Golden State* 523 The Pacific coast . . . contains an area equal to one-half of the whole territory of the Republic of America. **1883** *Harper's Mag.* 9 Nov. 943/1 [The completion of the Union Central route has not] given that 'boost' to California that the 'Pacific coasters' so fondly dreamed of. **1890** *Ib.* Oct. 705 They have an expression on the Pacific coast which conveys a world of meaning. **1917** *Birds of Amer.* III. 211/2 The Oregon Chickadee . . . is found in the Pacific coast district from the Columbia River to British Columbia.

+**Pacific slope.** The region in North America, esp. that part in the United States, lying west of the Continental divide. Also *Pacific sloper.* — **1845** FRÉMONT *Exped.* 274 [We were] now about to turn the back upon the Pacific slope of our continent. **1856** WHITTIER *Poetical Works* (1895) 326/1 Down the Pacific slope the evil Fate Glides like a shadow to the Golden Gate. **1871** RAYMOND *3d Rep. Mines* 2 The labor question . . . has received, in many localities of the Pacific slope, a peaceful . . . adjustment. **1883** *Harper's Mag.* March 648/1 'Well,' said the Pacific sloper, 'ef it's a private funeral, what do they call it a reception for?' **1890** LANGFORD *Vigilante Days* (1912) 110 One who had been for many years a resident of the Pacific slope. **1915** H. B. NIVER *Elem. Geography* 167/1 By means of irrigation, the Pacific Slope has become one of the greatest fruit-growing sections of the world.

+**Pacific states.** *pl.* States in the Pacific slope region. — **1820** TUDOR *Lett. Eastern States* 57 When the future Pacific states come to be represented in congress . . . it may be difficult to get over this inconvenience. **1874** *Rep. Comm. Agric. 1873* 30 In the Pacific States and in the Territories . . . the winter might be considered a mild and pleasant one. **1883** WELLS *Practical Economics* 84 Bright, sharp Yankees . . . are now scattered all over the West, the South, and the Pacific States. **1900** *Congress. Rec.* 16 Jan. 857/1 In the Pacific States, according to the same authority, 44 per cent of the national banks organized have failed.

Pacing, *n.* {1706–} A racking gait of horses; racking. — **1848** RUXTON *Life Far West* (1849) 192 The horses moving with the gait peculiar to American animals, known as 'pacing' or 'racking,' in Indian file. **1882** J. D. B. STILLMAN *Horse in Motion* 114 This pace is called *racking*, or *pacing*, in America, and *ambling* in England.

Pacing, *a.* Also **paceing.** That paces or pertains to pacing. Used esp. of horses. {1652–}

1688 *East-Hampton Rec.* II. 224 Nathaniell Baker hath sold one litle black naturall Paceing horse with a star on his forehead. **1718** HEMPSTEAD *Diary* 83 Rid my pacing mare. **1772** in *Travels Amer. Col.* 557 His daughter loved a little paceing horse of mine. **1830** BRECK in *Recoll.* (1877) 189 He would hitch his pacing nag to the railing of the Presidential Palace. **1879** *N.Y. Ev. Express Almanac* 370 (Ernst), Pacing race . . . time, 2:18.

1893 G. W. CURTIS *Horses, Cattle* 68 The idea of 20 years ago, that pacing blood was of no value in a trotting pedigree, has gone, and gone to stay.

***Pack, *n*.**

+**1.** A bundle or package containing the belongings of an Indian. {*in general sense}

1674 Alvord & Bidgood *Trans-Allegheny Region* 216 An Indian lett his pack slip into ye water. **1707** *Boston News-Letter* 25 Aug. 2/2 We took 24 of their Packs, and drove them off their ground. **1726** PENHALLOW *Indian Wars* 59 [The Indians] dropped their packs, in which were three scalps. **1792** *Ann. 2d Congress* 1134 They fell in with two Indians on foot who threw off their packs, and . . . made their escape.

+**2.** A bundle or package of skins, esp. beaver skins.

[**1744** A. DOBBS *Hudson's Bay* 39 He had four Packs of Beaver of 40 each.] **1809** A. HENRY *Travels* 238 They had a sort of trading-house at its mouth, and annually drew from it a hundred packs of beaver. **1814** BRACKENRIDGE *Views La.* 93 He was joined by Mr. Henry and all his party, who brought about forty packs of beaver. **1831** R. COX *Adv. Columbia R.* 194 Our returns are about ninety-five packs. **1846** SAGE *Scenes Rocky Mts.* xvii, The boat was freighted with some sixty packs of robes.

3. A number of wolves hunting or congregating together. {1795–}

1807 GASS *Journal* 105 We also saw 25 wolves in one gang or pack. **1848** COOPER *Oak Openings* II. 33 The wolves . . . are often seen in packs, pressing upon the heels of the antelope, deer, and other creatures of that family. **1852** GLISAN *Jrnl. Army Life* 98 The noise proceeded from a pack of rascally wolves. **1902** HULBERT *Forest Neighbors* 136 Earlier in the day the men had crossed the trail of a pack of wolves.

4. *attrib.* and *comb.* **a.** Designating various articles used for tying or securing packs.

1805 CLARK in *Lewis & C. Exped.* III. (1905) 47 We Purchased pack cords . . . & Set out on our rout. **1895** REMINGTON *Pony Tracks* 180 The 'commissaries' . . . were spread out on a pack canvas. **1902** WISTER *Virginian* xxxvi, Twice the steepness loosened the pack ropes. **1902** WHITE *Blazed Trail* 113 The solitary man with the packstraps across his forehead and shoulders had never seen so many [woods creatures]. **1905** COLE *Early Oregon* 62 Half a dozen pack covers, half a dozen lash ropes, a hatchet and some nails were taken.

b. In special combinations.

Pack-broken, of a pony, trained to carry a pack; *p.-carrier*, a device used in carrying a pack; *p. company*, a company that engages in packing or transporting goods by means of pack animals; *p. jack*, a jackass or donkey used for carrying a pack; *p. master*, one in charge of the packs of a company or organization; *p. rack*, (see quotation); *p. road*, a road suitable for use by pack animals (cf. PACK TRAIL).

1925 TILGHMAN *Dugout* 23 We got ten ponies. . . . Three of 'em I know are pack-broken. **1924** *Scribner's Mag.* Dec. 649/2, I'll take me pack, pack-carrier, [and] mess-kit. **1852** STANSBURY *Gt. Salt Lake* 30 The pack company from Boston . . . had passed us on the route. **1869** BOWLES *Our New West* 102 Even the top-heavy pack jacks,—mountains on molehills, indeed,—carried their burden and themselves unharmed to the top. **1894** WISTER in *Harper's Mag.* Sept. 509/1 His name was Jack Long, and he was pack-master. **1884** *Nat. Museum Bul.* No. 27, 985 *Pack-rack*, an old-fashioned angler's pack-rack, which can be strapped to the back and loaded with blankets and other outfit. **1852** WATSON *Nights in Block-House* 383 He avoided the pack-road which had been opened by Boone, and, pursuing an untrodden route, reached the settlement in safety.

***Pack, *v*.**

+**1.** *tr.* Of persons: To carry or convey (goods, etc.), usually on the back. Chiefly *W*.

1805 CLARK in *Lewis & C. Exped.* III. (1905) 181 Set all hands packing the loading over the portage which is below the grand shute. *Ib.* 280 Proced up the 1st. right hand fork 4 miles & pack the meat from the woods to the canoes from 4 mile to 3 miles distance all hands pack not one man exempted from this labour. **1845** *Big Bear Arkansas* 144 Did you pack him in? **1851** *S. Lit. Messenger* XVII. 46/2 This man will kill his deer every day . . . and pack off the saddle on his shoulders. **1872** *Harper's Mag.* Sept. 503/2 Some fellers packed so much ammunition and cold victuals that they broke down before they found any game. **1891** RYAN *Pagan* 85 She can't trapse over the mountain after cattle and pack that squaller at the same time. **1906** 'O. HENRY' *Heart of West* 53, I take a little claret with my meals, but I'm not in the habit of packing a jug of it into the brush and raising Cain.

+**b.** To carry (liquor). *colloq.*

a1846 *Quarter Race Ky.* 103 The captain used to boast that he could pack a gallon without its setting him back any.

+**c.** To wear or carry as a part of one's regular equipment, esp. to carry (a pistol). *colloq.*

1890 LANGFORD *Vigilante Days* (1912) 436 No man that ever packed a star in this city can arrest me. **1902** LEWIS *Wolfville Days* v, When he finds this person ain't packin' no gun. **1923** *Dialect Notes* V. 216 *Pack*. . . . To carry, especially a firearm. 'He's a-packin' a gun.' [McDonald Co., Mo.] **1924** R. CUMMINS *Sky-High Corral* 17 He's from the border country, where men who pack guns know how to use 'em.

+**2.** Of animals: To transport or carry (goods, commodities, etc.).

1816 U. BROWN *Journal* II. 360, I let him know that I . . . meant to hire a horse of him to pack our provisions. **1869** J. R. BROWNE *Adv. Apache Country* 123 Mr. Lennan's body was wrapped up in a blanket and packed on his own saddle-mule as far down as the junction of the Salinas and Rio Verde. **1880** INGHAM *Digging Gold* 38 In the early days of California . . . provisions, clothing, and tools had to be 'packed' on the backs of mules. **1891** *Harper's Mag.* Nov. 890/1 He was to be 'packed' to Sproat's Landing on a mule at the company's expense.

+**3.** *intr.* and *absol.* To travel with one's belongings or equipment in packs.

1842 M. CRAWFORD *Journal* 14 Some of the company preparing to pack from here. **1848** BRYANT *California* vii. 97 If mules could be obtained for packing, our design was to abandon our oxen and wagons. **1857** CHANDLESS *Visit Salt Lake* 264 Waggoning through the settlements . . . and thence 'packing' to California. **1904** STEEDMAN *Bucking Sagebrush* 47 Each bought a horse to ride and one to 'pack'—that is, to carry our blankets and also serve as a spare horse. **1911** J. F. WILSON *Land Claimers* 1 It isn't much fun packing along that trail.

+**b.** *To pack it*, to betake oneself, to go. *colloq.*

Perhaps the idea of carrying a load is retained in this phrase.

1852 WHITMORE *Diary* 14 Dec., P. M. went over to the Cherokee Flat to look up Tom. Packed it home. **1873** COZZENS *Marvellous Country* 152 If we lose the wheels again, you'll have to pack it, I'm afraid.

+**4.** To cohere or settle into a compact or solid mass.

1844 in *Rep. Comm. Patents 1846* 34 [Cotton] does not pack and become hard. **1887** TOURGEE *Button's Inn* 200 [The storm] filled the road with a slippery mealy mass, which did not cling or pack. **1890–3** TABER *Stowe Notes* 8 The snow packs so readily that I can walk without much difficulty up and down the sides of boulders.

Package. {1611–} In special combinations.

Package man, one engaged in hauling or transmitting packages (cf. EXPRESSMAN 2); *p. office*, a railroad office where packages to be forwarded are accepted; *p. paper*, strong coarse paper used for wrapping packages; *p. sale*, a sale of assorted goods in packages; *p. service*, a service for forwarding or transmitting packages; *p. trade*, trade involving the sale of goods, especially dry goods, in packages.

1888 DELAND *J. Ward* 2 They were at the mercy of Phibbs, the package man, who brought their wares in his slow, creaking cart over the dusty turnpike from Mercer. **1859** *Harper's Mag.* Sept. 504/1 More and more parcels [are] addressed to the 'package-office of the Harlem Railroad.' **1768** *R.I. Col. Rec.* VI. 548 One paper mill, at which is manufactured wrapping, package and other coarse paper. **1821** *Ann. 16th Congress* 2 Sess. 1526 Package sales . . . by the assortments of merchandise they combine, excite most interest. **1896** ERNST in *Bostonian Soc. Proc.* (1897 25 Our word 'express,' denoting a systematic package service, has become a true Americanism. **1887** *Courier-Journal* 21 Jan. 7/2 Staple cotton goods were more active in first hands and a fairly good package trade . . . was done by leading jobbers.

+**Package express.** A system or service for transmitting or forwarding packages. Also attrib. — **1840** *Boston Directory*, Harnden's New York package express. **1903** E. JOHNSON *Railway Transportation* 166 It is also argued that the Government could do the package-express business better than private companies can.

Pack animal. A beast of burden used for transporting food, clothing, or other commodities. {1884–} — **1847** *Santa Fe Republican* 16 Oct. 2/2 They left their wagons and took pack animals, and ten days' provisions, and proceeded to Zuni and the Red Lake. **a1861** WINTHROP *Canoe & Saddle* 66, I chose first for my pack animal a strawberry roan cob, a 'chunk of a horse.' **1890** LANGFORD *Vigilante Days* (1912) 206 The great stampede with its numerous pack-animals, penetrated the dense alder thicket. **1904** *N.Y. Sun* 7 Sept. 6 In a newly settled country or the backwoods . . . pack animals are used.

+**Pack basket.** (See quotation 1891.) — **1891** *Fur, Fin, & Feather* March 196 A pack basket is the Adirondack substitute for trunk, valise, gripsack, and knapsack. **1895** *Outing* XXVI. 365/1 By the time Sydney came over with the pack-basket, our duffle was all collected. **1900** BACHELLER *E. Holden* 6 [He] stooped so that I could climb into the basket —a pack basket, . . . the top a little smaller than the bottom.

+**Pack burro.** A burro used as a pack animal. — **1885** *Wkly. New Mexican Rev.* 23 April 4/4 He will . . . haul the product of their mines to Santa Fe on pack burros. **1908** M. AUSTIN in *Century Mag.* April 926/2 The horse-pistol was in the saddle-bag on the pack-burro that fed forward with the flock.

***Packer.**

+**1.** An official of a colonial town chosen to pack or supervise the packing of various merchantable articles, as beef, pork, tobacco, etc. *Obs.*

An extension of an earlier English use.

1652 *Mass. Bay Rec.* III. 284 The searcher & packer . . . are hereby enjoyned to set there seuerall markes on them. **1662** *East-Hampton Rec.* I. 195 Each Towne in this Colony shall chose an abell Inhabitant to the office of packer whoe shall pack and repack all meat transported out the towne. **1677** *New Castle Court Rec.* 94 The Court have this day appointed Cornelis Post to bee viewer & packer of Tobbacco in this Towne and pr[e]cincts. **1706** *N.C. Col. Rec.* I. 653 Orderd That John Parish Francis Beesley & Saml Phelps be packers for this pr[e]cinct. **1744** *Mass. Province Laws* III. 130 No pork or beef . . . shall be exported beyond sea that shall not first have been certified by the packer to have been packed by him or re-packed according to law.

+**2.** One engaged in the business of preparing and marketing meat and meat products.

1778 *Essex Inst. Coll.* XLIII. 15 A scheme of some packers of Beef [was] this way; in the fall of the year they barrill'd it [etc.]. **1830** *Congress. Deb.* 12 May 9721 The packers who pickled a barrel of pork in foreign salt, at Cincinnati, New Orleans, or Boston. **1868** *Ill. Agric. Soc. Trans.* VI. 323 The live stock of the great North-West is . . . delivered into the hands of the Chicago packer. **1890** *Stock Grower & Farmer* 25 Jan. 3/2 [Make] it a conspiracy . . . for 'packers' to form a combination to raise the price of dressed meats beyond reasonable figures. **1903** *N.Y. Times* 28 Sept. 5 The packers will grant the wage increases if the men will agree to do 10 per cent more work.

+**3.** One who transports goods by means of pack animals. Chiefly *W*.

1788 CUTLER in *Life & Corr.* I. 402 Here we met a Packer with ten pack-horses. **1843** *Amer. Pioneer* II. 162 The packers, who had been the lions of the day, were succeeded by . . . the keel boatmen. **1857** BORTHWICK *In California* 192 A packer has in his train from thirty to fifty mules. **1885** *Wkly. New Mexican Rev.* 25 June 3/8 Tom Moore, the veteran packer who steered pack trains for Crook and Custer years ago up in the Sioux country, passed down the road Sunday with a complete packing outfit. **a1918** G. STUART *On Frontier* I. 80 When the pack train got in with the flour the packers swore that they would not make another trip that winter.

+**b.** A peddler or dealer who transports his goods on pack animals.

1804 *Md. Hist. Mag.* IV. 5 A tolerable track is beaten for us, however by a description of peddlars who pass by the name of 'packers.' **1809** CUMING *Western Tour* 46 Packers with from one to twenty horses, selling or trucking their wares through the country. **1850** N. KINGSLEY *Diary* 148 A load of provisions came in to night brought by packers to sell. **1911** J. F. WILSON *Land Claimers* 19 'Want any supplies today?' said the packer, coming forward.

+**4.** One skilled in arranging a pack on a pack animal.

1871 *Scribner's Mo.* II. 4 The dexterity with which a skilful packer will load and unload his horses is remarkable. **1887** ROOSEVELT in *Century Mag.* XXXVI. 202/2 The Missourian was an expert packer. **1900** GARLAND *Eagle's Heart* 291, 'I'm no packer,' growled Dan. **1923** 'BOWER' *Parowan Bonanza* 111 Government men—but I didn't like the look of their packer.

Packery. {1891} +=PACKING HOUSE. — **1880** *Lib. Universal Knowl.* X. 447 Broom factories, pork packeries, soap-works [are found in Nebraska]. **1890** *Stock Grower & Farmer* 22 March 5/2 Then the party took in a Wichita hog killing and in Whittaker's big packery saw the fat porkers swing down to death.

***Packet,** *n.* A boat on a regular schedule carrying either mail or passengers or both. {1709–} +**a.** A passenger boat operating along the coast.

1806 WEBSTER 213/2 *Packet,* . . . in America, a coasting vessel for passengers. **1836** *Diplom. Corr. Texas* (1908) I. 144 A Packet at this season going North will I am assured have constant head winds. **1889** *Century Mag.* April 810/2 Late Wednesday evening [in 1789] the packet . . . arrived at Warwick Neck in Rhode Island [from N.Y. City].

+**b.** =PACKET BOAT 2. Now hist.

1848 BURTON *Waggeries* 91 The satellites of the judge tied the unresisting Quaker to the tow-rope of the packet, and hauled him across the canal and back again. **1874** B. F. TAYLOR *World on Wheels* 28 It was the aristocrat of canal craft, the packet was. **1901** STILLMAN *Autobiog. Journalist* I. 11 The Erie Canal was the quickest channel of communication westward, with its horse 'packets' traveling at the creditable speed of four miles an hour.

attrib. **1879** BAGBY *Old Va. Gent.* 237 The little fellow in the upper berth . . . would listen to the . . . packet-horn, as we drew nigh the locks. *Ib.* 239 No well-regulated packet-hand was ever allowed to say plain 'bridge.' *Ib.* 244 The effect of the Canal was soon seen in the array of freight-boats, the activity and bustle at the packet landing.

+**c.** A steamboat engaged in river traffic.

1851 HALL *Manhattaner* 182 There is little card-fleecing nowaday on the Mississippi first-class packets. **1880** *Harper's Mag.* Dec. 53 The Ohio is plied by a line of Cincinnati and Pittsburgh packets, and by smaller craft. **1894** 'MARK TWAIN' *P. Wilson* viii, She took the little local packet at Cairo.

Packet, *v.* {1621–} +*intr.* (See quotations.) *Obs.* (Cf. PACKETING.) — **1806** WEBSTER 213/2 *Packet,* to ply with a packet [*i.e.*, coasting boat]. **1816** PICKERING 148 *To Packet.* 'To ply with a packet.' *Webst. Dict.* I have never known this verb used in *America;* nor is this signification given in the English dictionaries. It is probably a *local* use of the word.

‖**Packetarian.** A member of the crew of a packet. — **1882** *Harper's Mag.* July 281/1 The typical 'Jack' of the pre-propeller age—the 'packetarian,' and the able seaman of the clipper-ship fleet—has, however, utterly vanished.

Packet boat.

1. An ocean-going or coasting boat carrying mail, passengers, goods, etc., on regular schedule. {1641–} Now hist.

1711 *Boston News-Letter* 19 March 2/2 On the 24th of February Freebody met the Pacquet Boat bound hither from Bristol. **1763** *Md. Gazette* 19 May, A Mail will be . . . made up at this Office upon the second Saturday of every Month . . . and the Packet-Boats in Turn will Sail therewith directly. **1797** in *Boston Pub. Lib. Bul.* XI. 73 We arrived at North Point where the Packet boat which was to carry us across the bay was waiting for us. **1836** GILMAN *Recoll.* (1838) 162 We strolled to the cove to observe the arrival of the packet-boats, bringing from the city their customary motley group.

+**2.** A long, narrow boat or towboat of light draft designed especially for carrying passengers and mail on canals. Now hist. (Cf. CANALBOAT.)

1828 *Western Mo. Rev.* II. 250, I . . . made an exchange, incomparably for the better in every way, in a packet boat. **1833** FINCH *Travels* 68 The packet-boats are seventy feet long, and are fitted out in a very good style, drawn by four horses, and travel one hundred miles in twenty-four hours. **1841** BUCKINGHAM *America* I. 494 [The boat] in which we embarked was one adapted for passengers only, and as such was called a packet-boat. **1847** Howe *Hist. Coll. Ohio* 455 Notwithstanding the recent and bloody defeat sustained in the packet-boat, a fresh crew was immediately procured.

+**Packeting.** Transporting by means of packets. *Obs.* Also attrib. (Cf. PACKET *v.*) — **1813** *Boston D. Advertiser* 9 March 3/4 Regular New York Packets. The subscribers respectfully inform the Publick that they continue the Packeting Business between Providence and New York. **1868** G. G. CHANNING *Recoll. Newport* 140 During the period of 'packeting,' it was no unusual thing . . . for the best sloops to reach Peck Slip, New York, in sixteen to seventeen hours.

+**Packet line.** A number of packets or packet boats under one management, operating regularly in series between certain places or ports. (Cf. LINE 6 a, b.) — **1839** *S. Lit. Messenger* V. 5/1 The packet line was a sort of hobby to Jeremiah Thompson. **1873** *Newton Kansan* 13 March 2/1 The various packet lines of the Upper Mississippi have agreed upon a basis of consolidation. **1883** 'MARK TWAIN' *Life on Miss.* xxiii, It would be necessary to go from place to place by the short packet lines.

+**Packet ship.** An ocean-going vessel engaged in carrying mail, goods, and passengers, usually sailing at stated intervals. Now hist.

1782 MORRIS in Jay *Correspondence* II. 349 Joshua Barney . . . [is] now commanding the Packet Ship *General Washington.* **1838** COOPER *Homeward B.* ii, The assembling of the passengers of a packet-ship is at all times a matter of interest. **1846** *Spirit of Times* 9 May 121/1 As you are in no hurry and 'go in for comfort,' take your passage in one of our first rate packet ships. **1880** CABLE *Grandissimes* 381 To ascend into the drawing-rooms seemed . . . like going from the hold of one of those smart old packet-ships of his day [*c*1803] into the cabin.

+**b.** =PACKET *n.* a.

1883 *Harper's Mag.* Dec. 166/1 [We were] writing in the cabin of a packet-ship bound from New York to Charleston, South Carolina.

+**Packet steamer.** A steamboat, esp. one engaged in river traffic, operating as a packet. (Cf. PACKET *n.* c.) — **1863** KETTELL *Hist. Rebellion* II. 463 These two vessels had been packet steamers, running to New York. **1874** COLLINS *Kentucky* I. 189 Explosion . . . [of the] packet-steamer Magnolia. **1883** EGGLESTON *Hoosier School-Boy* 115 The little packet-steamer was landing at the wharf.

***Pack horse.** A horse used as a pack animal.

1725 in *Travels Amer. Col.* 99 [We] were Obliged to Encamp for this Night (the Pack horsses being very much gauled). **1772** *Ib.* 554 Sent a Servant with a packhorse to the Geehaws to Carry my baggage to this place. **1802** ELLICOTT *Journal* 182 On the way I halted a few days at Darling's Creek, for the purpose of refreshing our pack horses. **1835** J. HALL *Sk. of West* II. 40 The enterprising trader conducted his train of pack-horses . . . over their steep acclivities. **1892** in *S. Dak. Hist. Coll.* I. 56 Thither went the pack horses, the wagon trains, the stage coaches, from the ferries of the Missouri River. **1924** MULFORD *Rustlers' Valley* vi, Matt led the pack horse to the cook shack and went in.

b. Attrib. and comb. with *department, driver,* etc.

1725 in *Travels Amer. Col.* 207 Sd hodge Being a Pack horse Driver. **1792** *Ann. 2d Congress* 1141 [He] never heard an individual . . . point out any defects, except in the commissary and pack-horse departments. **1813** *Niles' Reg.* IV. 418/1 They have actually received therefrom '100 pack-horse loads' of supplies. **1895** WINSOR *Miss. Basin* 168 The Virginians already . . . had a considerable pack-horse traffic with the Cherokees.

+**Pack-horse man.** One in charge of pack horses. — **1725** in *Travels Amer. Col.* 133 Issued to Capt Wm. Hatton . . . additional Instructions . . . forbiding his two Packhorse men to Trade. **1792** BRACKENRIDGE *Mod. Chivalry* (1937) 83 The captain took him for what is called a pack-horse man, that was carrying salt or sugar to some place of market. **1852** E. F. ELLET *Pioneer Women* 202 The other two teams went to an old tavern stand, well known to the early pack-horsemen and borderers of that region.

+**Pack-horse path.** A path or trace followed by pack horses. — **1792** PUTNAM in *Memoirs* 288 There is now a pack horse path the whole distance which has ben much used by Indian war parties. **1842** *S. Lit. Messenger* VIII. 5/2 There was nothing but a packhorse path across the mountains.

***Packing.**

+1. The wadding or 'patching' used in a muzzle-loading gun.

1831 *N.Y. Tribune* 31 Dec. (Chipman), A piece of hickory shirting . . . was used for packing.

+2. The transporting of goods by pack animals, or by individuals serving as carriers.

1843 *Amer. Pioneer* II. 162 Merchandise . . . was principally carried on pack horses until after 1788. Packing continued to be an important business in Kentucky until 1795. **1884** *Harper's Mag.* June 106/2 The mines can now only be reached from the coast by 'packing.' **1897** *Boston Ev. Globe* 4 Aug. 5/2 (Ernst), Prices for packing across the pass have risen to 25 and 27 cents per pound.

3. *attrib.* passing into *adj.* +Pertaining to or engaged in the packing and preservation of foodstuffs, esp. meat.

1834 C. A. DAVIS *Lett. J. Downing* 24 Zekil is a knowin cretur; he keeps a packin-yard, and salts down more fish than any man in three counties round. **1844** *Lexington Observer* 2 Oct. 1/4 The Undersigned . . . has taken the Slaughtering and Packing Establishment. **1873** *Vermont Bd. Agric. Rep.* II. 72 A good supply of pure dairy salt and well prepared spruce packing tubs are kept constantly on hand. **1890** *Stock Grower & Farmer* 8 Feb. 3/4 With the larger meat shops . . . dependent as they are on a central packing city for their supplies, . . . the cattle man's hopes will not be realized so soon. **1893** *Harper's Mag.* May 942/1 At the stock-yards . . . there are two large packing companies.

Packing box. A strong box in which articles and commodities are packed for transportation. {1842-} — **1774** *Copley-Pelham Lett.* 284. **1847** FIELD *Drama in Pokerville* 21 There was an altar, sure enough, a packing box set up on end. **1885** CUSTER *Boots & Saddles* 112 The man who could get a packing-box for the body of his sleigh was a Croesus. **1925** TILGHMAN *Dugout* 2 The door was a stout affair made from the boards of a packing box.

+Packing house. A house or establishment where meat and meat products are prepared for transportation and the market.

1835 HOFFMAN *Winter in West* II. 115 One of the packing-houses, built of brick, and three stories high, is more than a hundred feet long, and proportionably wide. **1861** *Chicago Tribune* 26 May 1/8 Docking Lot, near Hough's Packing House. **1880** INGHAM *Digging Gold* 203 Does such pork ever get into the barrels we buy in the East branded from Chicago packing-houses? **1902** LORIMER *Lett. Merchant* 19, I make every hog which goes through my packing-house give up more lard than the Lord gave him gross weight. **1921** GREER-PETRIE *Angeline at Seelbach* 23 Hit was a right smart piece out to the packing houses.

attrib. **1890** *Stock Grower & Farmer* 3 May 4/2 One thousand packing house men by a unanimous vote decided to go out on a strike. **1895** *Dept. Agric. Yrbk. 1894* 76 Packing-house pork has seldom been accused of causing [trichinosis]. **1903** E. JOHNSON *Railway Transportation* 131 The large meat-packers in Chicago, Omaha, and other centers of the packing-house business own their own cars.

+Packing room. 1. The room in a cotton gin where ginned cotton is packed into bales. **2.** A room in which articles or commodities of various kinds are packed for shipment. — (1) **1854** *Harper's Mag.* March 456/1 The 'packing-room' is the loft of the gin-house. (2) **1857** *Ib.* March 443/1 We might now take a walk through the extensive cooperage and packing-rooms [of the fisheries]. **1887** *Trial H. K. Goodwin* 17, I was on my way to the office and had got as far as the packing-room. **1892** *York County Hist. Rev.* 44 The shipping room, packing room, as well as the office, is on the 1st floor.

+Packing screw. A large screw of wood or metal used for exerting great pressure in packing or compressing various objects, as cotton. — **1803** *Mass. H. S. Coll.* 1 Ser. IX. 114 All these various operations, with a packing screw, are performed by water. **1861** in Logan *Great Conspiracy* 136 [The cotton] is carried to the packing screw. **1884** HARRIS *Mingo* 259 He found that a wagon had been driven to his packing-screw.

Packing season. The season or time of year when meats, fruits, etc., are packed or put up for preservation and transportation. — **1851** CIST *Cincinnati* 286 The stranger here, during the packing, and especially the forwarding season, of the article [*i.e.*, pork], becomes bewildered. **1874** *Rep. Comm. Agric. 1873* 135 The Chicago Commercial Bulletin gives the following items from the last two packing seasons in that city. *Ib.* 280 During the packing season 200 girls and 25 men were employed. **1888** *Economist* 20 Oct. 8/2 The shortage may be considerably increased before the close of the packing season.

Packman. {a1625-} +One engaged in transporting goods, usually by pack animals. (Cf. PACKER 3.) — **1849** *31st Congress 1 Sess.* H. R. Ex. Doc. No. 5, II. 627 Two of Judge Burt's packmen arrived today for provisions to take to the parties south. **1853** RAMSEY *Tennessee* 64 The traders and packmen generally confined themselves to the path. **1889** *Internat. Ann., Anthony's Photogr. Bul.* II. 220 There were six of us all told, myself and an assistant, with four guides and packmen. **1894** WINSOR *Cartier to Frontenac* 326 There were suspicions that English packmen were following [the Indians].

+Pack mule. A mule used as a pack animal. Also attrib.

1839 LEONARD *Adventures* (1904) 61 We now scattered over a considerable range of country for the purpose of hunting, leaving ten or twelve men only to bring on the pack-mules. **1849** *31st Congress 1 Sess.* Sen. Ex. Doc. No. 64, 64 The troops will remain here . . . until the assistant quartermaster . . . can perfect his arrangements for a change from wagon to pack-mule transportation. **1855** KIP *Diary of Indian Council* 27 We set off . . . with two boys, whose business it was to drive the pack mules. **1884** *Century Mag.* Oct. 842 To the snow-shoe and toboggan mode of transportation succeeded the pack-mule trail. **1888** FERGUSON *Experiences of Forty-Niner* 28 The camp was thrown into a state of excitement by the approach of a solitary horseman leading two pack mules. **1923** J. H. COOK *On Old Frontier* 130 We took all game killed into camp on pack mules or horses.

+Pack peddler. One who sells from house to house various articles of merchandise, esp. dry goods, carried about in a pack. — **1880** *Harper's Mag.* Nov. 892/1 There was a pack peddler with smuggled shawls and laces at the door. **1917** SINCLAIR *King Coal* 250 Betty . . . [was] working at the Harrigan family task of making the children of a pack-peddler into leaders in the 'younger set.'

+Pack pony. A pony used for carrying packs. — **1870** KEIM *Sheridan's Troopers* 201 [The Indians] drive the herds and pack-ponies, or else on foot lead them. **1885** *Century Mag.* June 223/2 Sometimes the ponies . . . would commit some other of the thousand tricks which seem to be all a pack-pony knows. **1899** CUSHMAN *Hist. Indians* 236 Long accustomed to their duty, the faithful little pack-ponies seldom gave any trouble. **1923** J. H. COOK *On Old Frontier* 98 We used pack ponies on the return trip.

+Pack rat. A wood rat of the genus *Neotoma*, esp. *N. cinerea*, the trade rat of the Rocky Mountain region. — **1885** ROOSEVELT *Hunting Trips* 13 These rats were christened pack rats, on account of their curious and inveterate habit of dragging off to their holes every object they can possibly move. **1893** — *Wilderness Hunter* 69 The big pack-rats . . . are handsome, with soft gray fur, large eyes, and bushy tails. **1912** WASON *Friar Tuck* 176 We had the blamedest time with a pack-rat I ever did have. **1923** J. H. COOK *On Old Frontier* 163 Metal buttons and buckles, and even parts of clothing, stored near by by the pack-rats, often added their mute testimony.

***Packsaddle.** A saddle of a type used on a pack animal.

The examples in the first group indicate something of the construction of such saddles.

(1) **1847** W. S. HENRY *Campaign Sketches* 162 The pack-saddle is an immense pad, stuffed with hay or wool, tightly girted on, weighing from thirty to forty pounds; on the top some matting is placed. **1854** BARTLETT *Personal Narr.* I. 359 The *aparejo* or pack-saddle, is a heavy, clumsy affair, stuffed with hay.

(2) **1747** *Va. State P.* 241 Horse bell and pack saddle £3. **1792** *Ann. 2d Congress* 1107 Complaints were made of fatal mismanagements and neglects . . . , particularly as to . . . pack-saddles. **1806** ORDWAY in *Jrnls. Lewis & O.* 355 Most of our horses and pack Saddles were Safe, but Some of boath had been [made] use of by the admittance of the head chief. **1846** SAGE *Scenes Rocky Mts.* xxxiii, Carefully hung . . . [were his] 'pack saddles,' with his halters . . . and all needful *materiel* for camp and travelling service. **1890** LANGFORD *Vigilante Days* (1912) 119 They at once set to work to manufacture pack-saddles and other gear. *a***1918** G. STUART *On Frontier* II. 105 Thomas Irvine had a good saddle horse and a pack mule with two pack saddles.

attrib. **1868** *Ore. State Jrnl.* 8 June 1/1 Also Riding and Pack Saddle-Trees made to order. **1894** *Harper's Mag.* Feb. 351/2 William had put the 'grub' on a pack-saddle blanket.

***Packthread.** Strong thread suitable for sewing or tying up packs or bundles. Also attrib.

1745 FRANKLIN *Poor Richard's Almanac 1746* 15 Mad Bulls, are not to be held by . . . packthread. **1767** in Singleton *Social N.Y.* 226 Children's pack thread stays from one to eight years old. **1789** *Ann. 1st Congress* I. 149 It was agreed to lay . . . on twine or pack-thread, one hundred cents per 112 pounds. **1813** *Niles' Reg.* V. 190/1 Cordage, twine and pack-thread. **1839** F. A. KEMBLE *Journal* 28 Our sole mode of summoning our attendants is by a packthread bell-rope suspended in the sitting-room. **1899** VAN DYKE *Fisherman's Luck* 29 The great fish . . . broke the line as if it had been a pack-thread.

+Pack trail. A narrow trail suitable for pack animals. — **1853** *Knickerb.* XLII. 433, I brought [it] all the way over the pack-trail. *a***1918** G. STUART *On Frontier* I. 81 We found the snow instantly becoming deeper, but here was a well beaten pack trail.

+Pack train. A train of horses, mules, etc., loaded with packs. — **1856** WHIPPLE *Explor. Ry. Route* 75 Taking an early start, the pack-train following the guide . . . , we proceeded about eleven miles over a slightly undulating prairie. **1871** *Scribner's Mo.* II. 6 General Washburn detailed four of our company to guard the pack train. **1890** LANGFORD *Vigilante Days* (1912) 58 The pack-train was always a lively feature in the gigantic mountain scenery of Oregon and Idaho. **1923** J. H. COOK *On Old Frontier* 15 Our pack train generally carried a plentiful supply of black navy plug tobacco.

***Paddle,** *n.*

1. A comparatively short oar having a broad blade at one end or both ends and used to propel a canoe or other small boat. {1712-}

1624 SMITH *Gen. Hist. Va.* II. 32 Instead of Oares, they [*sc.* Indians] use Paddles and sticks. **1684** I. MATHER *Providences* i. 15 Meeting with some thin boards of ceiling, . . . they made paddles therewith. **1701** WOLLEY *Journal N.Y.* (1902) 56 [The Indians] row [their canoes] with long paddles. **1726** PENHALLOW *Indian Wars* 90 [The Indians] knocked them [*sc.* ducks] down with billets and paddles, and sold a great number of them to the English. **a1811** HENRY *Camp. Quebec* 56 What skill in boatmanship! What aptitude with the paddle was here exhibited. **1897** *Outing* XXX. 544/1 A full equipment of paddles consists of a nine-foot, for shoving through grass and in shoal water, a six-foot for paddling in deep water, and a short paddle, about four feet long, for 'creeping' on ducks. **1916** THOBURN *Stand. Hist. Okla.* I. 27 Kneeling, paddle in hand, in the bottoms of their canoes, . . . they laboriously ascended the courses of the rivers.

+**b.** The distance traversed in a specified time by one paddling a canoe.

1894 *Outing* XXIV. 187/1 There was fly-fishing to be had within a five-minutes paddle of our landing.

2. Denoting various things used or shaped more or less like a paddle: +**a.** A perforated, paddle-shaped ferule used in punishing Negro slaves; a blow from this. *Obs.*

1828 *Cherokee Phœnix* 10 April (B.), Should any negro be found vending spirituous liquors, without permission from his owner, such negro so offending shall receive fifteen cobbs or paddles for every such offence. **1856** OLMSTED *Slave States* 281 The paddle is a large, thin ferule of wood, in which many small holes are bored; when a blow is struck, these holes, from the rush and partial exhaustion of air in them act like diminutive cups.

+**b.** A small wooden instrument shaped like a boat paddle, used in working butter.

1876 *Vermont Bd. Agric. Rep.* III. 97 To smooth the top of butter, a wooden paddle, well prepared, should be used.

+**c.** A battling stick used in washing clothes.

1884 'CRADDOCK' *Tenn. Mts.* 3 The garments, laid across a bench and beaten white with a wooden paddle, would flutter hilariously in the wind. **1886** *Amer. Philol. Ass. Trans.* 36 *Battling-stick* is the name of the 'paddle or mallet' with which the clothes are battled.

+**d.** A hornbook.

1886 Z. F. SMITH *Kentucky* 691 The smaller children were furnished with a paddle, which had their letters and a, b, c's printed upon it. When the paddle was finished, the children could then own a Dilworth speller.

+**e.** 'The long flat snout of the paddle-fish' (*Cent.*).

+**f.** *Tanning.* A tank having a revolving paddle in it.

1897 C. T. DAVIS *Manuf. Leather* 558 Large paddles or reels are used in the paddle method, in which as many as twenty-five dozen skins or more are dyed in one bath.

Paddle, *v.* {1697-}

1. *intr.* To move over water in a canoe or other small boat by the use of a paddle. Also said of a canoe. {1719-}

1677 HUBBARD *Narrative* 129 He accidentally met with a Canooe . . . . by which means he padled . . . out of the harbour. **1726** PENHALLOW *Indian Wars* 33 From hence, they paddled to Penobscot. **1788** CUTLER in *Life & Corr.* I. 423 In a few minutes we saw the canoe paddling up very close to the shore. **1840** COOPER *Pathfinder* xxii, What do then?—couldn't paddle six—ten—eight mile! **1876** *Wide Awake* 238/2 For hours he would sit quietly in the stern, paddling first on one side and then on the other. **1902** WHITE *Conjuror's House* 181 Then, heedless of what he was saying, she began to paddle straight from the shore.

+**2.** *tr.* To propel (a canoe, boat, etc.) by means of a paddle; to transport (a person) in a canoe.

1784 BELKNAP *Jrnl. Tour to White Mts.* (1876) 20 Our horses swam after a canoe, in which we put our saddles and bags; an old woman paddled us over. **1841** COOPER *Deerslayer* xvi, I dares to say, the Delaware can paddle a canoe by himself. **1876** *Wide Awake* 238/2 It was sport for John even to paddle a boat for Uncle Sim. **1908** 'O. HENRY' *Options* 73 I've paddled a canoe down Little Devil River.

+**b.** *To paddle one's (own) canoe,* to get on or make one's way by individual effort.

1828 J. HALL *Lett. from West* 261 The Lady of the Lake . . . 'paddled her own canoe' very dexterously. **1840** HOFFMAN *Greyslaer* II. 228 Let every man paddle his own canoe his own way. **1854** *Harper's Mag.* May 854/1 Whate'er your lot may be, Paddle your own canoe. **1874** *Vermont Bd. Agric. Rep.* II. 200 Shoemakers, even, have their own organization, and paddle their own canoe. **1887** *Harper's Mag.* March 547/1 They couldn't see how he was to paddle his canoe all alone by himself.

+**3.** To beat or spank (a person) with, or as with, a paddle.

1856 OLMSTED *Slave States* 189, I thought it was nothing but damned sulkiness so I paddled him, and made him go to work. **1904** *Hartford Courant* 23 June 8 A secret society of girls 'initiated' some neophytes by blindfolding them, . . . paddling them, and then rolling them down a steep hill. **1907** *Springfield W. Republican* 22 Aug. 6, 'I'll paddle you!' is the threat used by despairing mothers and teachers [in Texas] in case of necessary discipline; and sure enough they do, with a regular wooden paddle constructed for the purpose.

Paddle boat. A boat propelled by paddles; a paddle steamer. — **1874** LONG *Wild-Fowl* 78 The size and shape of a paddle-boat . . . must depend . . . upon the locality intended for its use. **1891** *Scribner's Mag.* X. 13 She was a paddle boat, built of wood, and was 207 feet long. **1909** *Nat. Conservation Congress Proc.* 131 Seattle was reached by a steamer, the old paddle-boat, 'North Pacific.'

+**Paddlefish.** A fish of the family Polyodontidae, esp. *Polyodon spathula*, found chiefly in the streams of the Mississippi Valley. — **1807** JANSON *Stranger in A.* 191 The paddle-fish . . . is four feet and four inches in length. The snout resembles in shape the paddle used by Indians in crossing rivers. **1880** *Lib. Universal Knowl.* XI. 168 *Paddle-fish, Polyodon folium*, a fish inhabiting the Mississippi river and its tributaries. **1884** GOODE, etc. *Fisheries* I. 660 The 'Paddle-fish' or 'Duck-billed Cat,' *Polyodon spathula*, is one of the most characteristic fishes of the rivers of the Western and Southern States. **1911** *Rep. Fisheries 1908* 313/1 Paddle-fish. . . . It is a poor food fish, but the roe is extensively used for caviar.

Paddler. One who paddles a canoe. {1799-} — **1841** COOPER *Deerslayer* ix, I can easily bring down the paddler. **a1861** WINTHROP *Canoe & Saddle* ii. 20 The tariff of canoe-hire on Whulge is equally simple,—a blanket for the boat, and one for each paddler. **1892** *Nation* 29 Sept. 247/1 We there made a dugout of a green log, and, with two half-breed paddlers, navigated it all the way to St. Louis.

Paddling. {1719-}

+**1.** Beating, thrashing, or spanking with, or as with, a paddle; a beating.

Cf. PADDLE *v.* 3.

1851 HOOPER *Widow Rugby* 96 What a devil of a paddlin' the old woman gin him with the battlin'-stick. **1856** OLMSTED *Slave States* 189, I sent them word to give him a good paddling, and handcuff him. **1862** *N.Y. Tribune* 13 Jan. 4/4 All the starving, paddling, and pickling in the world will not insure good crops. . . . Let Bleeding Africa go.

+**2.** Attrib. with *boat, canoe,* in sense: Propelled by a paddle or by paddles.

1894 *Outing* XXIV. 422/1 A small fleet of paddling canoes and row-boats had gathered together. **1905** PRINGLE *Rice Planter* 144 She jumped into her paddling boat . . . [and] paddled herself across.

Paddy.[1]

1. An Irishman. *nickname.* {1780-}

1784 J. BELKNAP in *Belknap P.* II. 168 By yours of the 10th I find you have some knowledge of *Paddy* the Socinian, though he has none of you. **1852** BRISTED *Upper Ten Th.* 220 By Jove! you should have seen the Paddies scud! **1856** OLMSTED *Slave States* 551 If the Paddies are knocked overboard, . . . nobody loses anything! **1872** ROE *Barriers Burned Away* iv, Strength is not what is needed, but experience. Ours is not the kind of work for Paddies.

+**b.** (See quotation.)

1889 MUNROE *Golden Days* 304 He watched the steam excavators, or 'paddies,' tearing down and levelling the tall hills.

+**2.** (See quot. 1818.) *Obs.* Also transf.

1818 FEARON *Sketches* 369 In Washington, on last St. Patrick's day, according to custom, a figure was stuffed similar to our Guy Faux, and called Paddy. . . . In Philadelphia a gentleman informed me that there were numerous Paddies exhibited in the same style. **1823** *Niles' Reg.* XXIV. 72/1 A much respected old gentleman . . . every morning of the 17th March, was sure to find a 'Paddy' at his door—he took it into his house and proclaimed a feast in honor of the saint. **1843** *Knickerb.* XXII. 51 He may light upon a stuffed Paddy some six feet high.

+**3.** *local.* The ruddy duck, *Erismatura jamaicensis.*

1895 RIDGWAY *Ornith. Illinois* II. 1. 185 Ruddy Duck . . . [is called] Hickory-head, Greaser, Paddy, Noddy, Paddy-whack, [etc.]. **1917** *Birds of Amer.* I. 152 Other names [of the ruddy duck are] . . . Paddy-whack; Stub-and-twist; . . . Dinky; Dickey; Paddy.

Paddy.[2] Rice in the straw; unhusked rice. {1623-} — **1829** B. HALL *Travels in N.A.* III. 164 Rice with the husk on, or what is technically called Paddy—a word borrowed from India—will keep fresh and good. **1850** *Rep. Comm. Patents 1849: Agric.* 154 For the want of mills or a market for the rough rice or paddy it is fed mainly to stock. **1868** *Rep. Comm. Agric. 1867* 174 The captain . . . presented him with a bag of 'paddy' or 'rough rice.'

Paddywhack. {1811-} +=PADDY[1] 3. — **1895, 1917** [see PADDY[1] 3].

+**Padgo.** [La. F. *pategau*, var. of O.F. *papegau, papegaut.*] A figure of a bird set up as a target for marksmen. *dial.* Also transf. (Cf. PATGO.) — **1848** *S. Lit. Messenger* XIV. 482/1 The padgo was already in position. **1888** CABLE *Bonaventure* 68 For 'Thanase there was . . . the *papegaie*, or, as he called it, *pad-go*—the shooting-match.

***Padlock.** A lock having a jointed or pivoted shackle for passing through a staple or ring. — **1654** *Essex Probate Rec.* I. 180 Too padlocks & small things. **1727** *Md. Hist. Mag.* VIII. 67 A pad lock to the gate. **1820** *Columbian Centinel* 12 Jan. 3/5 Hooks, . . . Pad Locks, . . . pair Sugar Tongs. **1888** STOCKTON *Dusantes* 128 [He appreciated] the advantage of having the key of the gate's padlock in his pocket.

+**Padre.** *S.W.* [Sp.] A priest or monk.

An independent borrowing from the Spanish.

1844 GREGG *Commerce of Prairies* I. 263 A large portion of the *pastores*, the padres themselves, are foremost in most of the popular vices of the country. **1869** J. R. BROWNE *Adv. Apache Country* 58 Two Jesuit Padres, attached to the Arizona command, had previously secured the attention of the principal Señoritas in the neighborhood. **1918** WHITE *Forty Niners* 3 The original *padres* were almost without exception devoted to poverty.

b. Used as a title.

1854 Bartlett *Personal Narr.* II. 320 Padre Pacheco and another gentleman dined with me today. **1867** *Wkly. New Mexican* 6 April 2/3 It is reported here, that C. P. Clever will not accept the nomination . . . and that padre Gallegos will probably be taken up and run in his stead. **1871** *Republican Rev.* 15 July 2/2 If we are not mistaken, Padre Gallegos presided at one of the largest and most enthusiastic of their meetings.

Paduasoy. Also †**paddisway,** etc. A corded silk fabric, or a garment made of this. {1663–} Also attrib. — **1714** Sewall *Letter-Book* II. 37 Good black paddisway, enough to make two womens suits. **1773** *Holyoke Diaries* 81 Sent . . . 12 small peices of Blue Padusoy to Be Dyed Bloom. **1851** S. Warner *Wide, Wide World* xxv, Go in that fur closet and bring me my paddysoy that hangs there. **1860** Holmes *Professor* 330 She must have been of some consideration, for she was dressed in paduasoy and lace with hanging sleeves. **1889** Cooke *Steadfast* 44 It was like a picture to see her, stately in her paduasoy gown.

+**Paducah.** Also **Padouca, Padduca.** (See quot. 1885 and cf. Comanche.) — [a**1726** L'Isle *Atlas Nouveau* (Carte de la Louisiane et du Cours du Mississipi), Pays des Apaches et des Padoucas.] **1804–5** *Lewis & Clark Exped.* VI. (1905) 108 Padoucas. . . . This nation live in Villages on the heads of River Platt & Arkansaws. **1821** J. Fowler *Journal* 54 Kiawas and Padducas the[n] Continu to Increes. **1885** J. S. Kingsley, etc. *Stand. Nat. Hist.* VI. 188 The Comanchee tribe is one of the most important in North America. In the older works they figure as the Paducahs, the name applied to them by the Osage.

***Pagan.** +An American Indian. *Obs.* — **1643** Williams *Key* (1866) 21 [The English call the Indians] Wild-men, (so the Dutch call them Wilden) Abergeny men, Pagans, Barbarians, Heathen. **1648** *Md. Archives* 233 Noe Inhabitant of this Province shall deliver any Gunns or Ammunition to any Pagan for the killing of meate.

***Page.** +A messenger or errand boy serving a legislative body. Also attrib. — **1863** Hopley *Life in South* I. 24 'Pages' . . . were leaning and lolling restlessly on the steps at his feet. **1886** Alton *Among Law-Makers* 1 When quite a small boy I was appointed a page to the Senate of the United States. *Ib.* 153 During my page career, I saw a great deal of the Supreme Court. **1910** C. Harris *Eve's Husband* 118 Occasionally . . . [an influential citizen] got his little boy appointed as a 'page' in the hall of Representatives.

+**Paid fire department.** A fire department the members of which are regularly employed and paid. — **1858** [see Fire department]. **1866** *Harper's Weekly* 16 June 371/1 The question of a paid Fire Department in a large city no more admits of serious discussion than that of a paid police. **1881** *Harper's Mag.* Feb. 380/2 The Paid Fire Department was organized. **1889** [see Fire department].

***Pail.**

***1.** A vessel, usually of tin or wood, having a bail and used as a container for water, milk, etc.; a bucket.

1622 'Mourt' *Relation* 36 We found . . . also an English Paile or Bucket. **1706** *Boston News-Letter* 7 Jan. 2/2 To be Sold . . . 12 Pales, one Hogshead with a Copper Cock, 5 Iron Doors, Two great Shovels. **1846** Farnham *Prairie Land* 129 The best ewer I could get was an old pail. **1891** Chase & Clow *Industry* II. 102 [Milk] is carried to the dairy in shining pails, kept clean and sweet by scalding and scrubbing. **1907** *St. Nicholas* Aug. 886/2 Several of the women carried pitchers and pails.

attrib. **1847** Howe *Hist. Coll. Ohio* 329 Maumee City . . . now contains . . . 1 pail factory. **1905** *Forestry Bureau Bul.* No. 63, 15 The lumber . . . is always in demand at good prices for match blocks, pail staves, and box boards.

+**2.** =Dinner pail.

1880 *Harper's Mag.* June 68/1 Through the uncertain twilight we see the little knots of workmen with their swinging pails. **1886** Stapleton *Major's Christmas* 177 There are the laborer with his pail; the female and male clerks with their genteeler dinner baskets. **1887** Alden *Little Fishers* i, No wonder, poor man; always having to eat his dinner out of a pail.

+**Pain-killer.** Any one of various medicines or remedies for abolishing or relieving pain. — **1853** *La Crosse Democrat* 7 June 2/4 Ayer's Cherry Pectoral, Perry Davis' Pain Killer, Jew David's Honey Coated Pills. **1873** Aldrich *Marjorie Daw* 60 A guerilla warfare with itinerant vendors of furniture polish, and pain-killer, and crockery cement. **1884** Wells *Practical Economics* 159 Another manufacturer who made a 'pain-killer,' [bought] 41,195 gallons [of alcohol]. **1902** Lorimer *Lett. Merchant* 249 [He] stuffed himself . . . and then howled for painkiller.

Paint, *n.* {1602–}

1. Any one of various opaque mixtures of a pigment and some suitable drying or thinning liquid, applied to a surface in order to preserve or beautify it. {1712–}

1673 *N.J. Archives* 1 Ser. I. 111 We doe acknowledge to have rec[eive]d one-halfe anker of drinke, two match-coates, . . . [and] some painte. **1750** Franklin *Writings* II. 439, I had a mind to lay a coat of paint over the filletting of gold on the cover of a book. **1841** Lowell *Offering* I. 212 [The old home] had neither paint nor plaister, without or within. **1883** Howells *Woman's Reason* xvi, I don't suppose . . . that you would know the place now; . . . fresh paint and paper everywhere. **1907** *St. Nicholas* Aug. 920/1 The cost of the bridge was . . . eighty-five cents for paint.

2. A pigment, as vermilion, used by American Indians for embellishing their faces and bodies.

1806 Lewis in *L. & Clark Exped.* V. (1905) 97 In swiming the horse lost a dressed Elk skin of Lapages and several small articles, and their paint was distroyed by the water. **1823** James *Exped.* I. 168 [The Canadians] were adorned with paint after the Indian manner. **1885** *Rep. Indian Affairs* 179 Unquestionably, paint, feathers, and pride make an Indian appear to as good advantage as a metropolitan belle.

+**3.** Short for Paint horse.

1893 G. W. Curtis *Horses, Cattle* 94 Spotted ponies—'paints'—are frequently found [among the mustangs].

4. *attrib.* and *comb.* **a.** In sense 2 with *bag, pouch.*

1805 Ordway in *Jrnls. Lewis and O.* 199 We found some little notions which Some Indian had hung up. Viz. a Scraper a paint bag with ½ an ounce in it. **1870** Keim *Sheridan's Troopers* 198 The [Indian] women wear belts . . . suspended from which are an awl-case and paint-pouch.

b. In special combinations.

Paint clay, clay used in making paint; *p. king,* one who has made a fortune in paints or the paint industry (cf. King 3 b); *p. knife,* a knife used in scraping or removing paint; *p. oil,* oil used in making paint; *p. ore,* (see quotation); *p. store,* a store which specializes in selling paints.

1882 *Econ. Geol. Illinois* II. 55 There is a local deposit of paint clays underlying the true northern drift. **1884** Howells *Silas Lapham* 244 She might be expected at least to endure the paint-king and his family. **1877** Hale *G. T. T.* 142 With a paint-knife [they] cut off the mud which still clung to the overshoe. **1863** *Maine Bd. Agric. Rep.* 12 It would take a great breadth from our bread-producing acres to yield so much flax seed as to supply our wants for paint-oil. **1843** *Nat. Hist. N.Y., Geology* IV. 419 A stratum or bed of argillaceous oxide of iron [which] extends through Wayne county . . . has been ground for paint, and hence receives the name of *paint ore.* **1840** *Niles' Nat. Reg.* 11 April 96/2 Dennis Spurrier, paint store.

***Paint,** *v.*

1. *tr.* Of Indians: To cover or coat (the face or body) with paint; to apply (paint); to decorate (something) with paintings or drawings. Also *ppl. a.*

1622 'Mourt' *Relation* 95 All his followers likewise, were in their faces, in part or in whole painted. **1666** Alsop *Maryland* (1869) 72 The Indians paint upon their faces one stroke of red, another of green, another of white, and another of black. **1743** Catesby *Carolina* II. p. xiii, The Chigasaws . . . were painting their faces. **1805** in *Ann. 9th Congress* 2 Sess. 1083 The dress of the [Comanche] women is a long loose robe, . . . made of neatly dressed leather, on which they paint figures of different colors and significations. **1831** Buttrick *Travels* 45 Five hundred Indians . . . were marching in Indian file, painted and in their war dress.

+**2.** *To paint the town red,* to go on a riotous or reckless spree. *slang.*

1884 *Boston Jrnl.* 13 Sept., A 'spectrophotometric study of pigments,' by Professor Nicolls, is recommended to young men who intend to 'paint the town red.' **1888** Clampitt *Echoes Rocky Mts.* 134 Sometimes buildings would be burned and valuable lives would be lost, when resisting the efforts of these lawless pirates to 'paint the town red,' as was their favorite expression when engaged in making such a raid. **1892** *Harper's Mag.* Jan. 255/1 You stay on here and Roberts will paint the town red for you. **1921** Paine *Comr. Rolling Ocean* 108 He thinks it's smart to paint the town red.

Paint box. A box or case containing colors or coloring materials. — **1725** *New-Eng. Courant* 8–15 Feb. 1/2, I would oblige every Sign-Painter to serve seven Years at College, before he presum'd to handle Pencil or Paint-Box. **1863** 'M. Harland' *Husks* 18 [Are] your paint box, and your easel . . . such good company that you are contented and happy? **1907** *St. Nicholas* June 736/1 So she bought a paint-box with two little saucers in it for 10 cents.

***Painted,** *a.* Used in the names of birds, fish, etc., characterized by brilliant markings. {1811–} (See also Painted bunting, cup, etc.) — **1840** Dewey *Mass. Flowering Plants* 214 *Trillium pictum.* Painted or Variegated Wake Robin. **1883** *Nat. Museum Bul.* No. 27, 260 *Calista gigantea.* . . . Painted Clam. . . . Southern coast of the United States. **1819** Rafinesque in *Western Rev.* I. 375 *Calliurus.* Painted Tail. Calliure. . . . Vulgar names, painted-tail or bride-perch.

+**Painted bunting. 1.** =Nonpareil. **2.** Smith's longspur, *Calcarius pictus.* Also *painted lark bunting.* — **(1) 1811, 1839** [see Bunting[1]]. **1917** *Birds of Amer.* III. 74/1 The Painted Bunting is a southern bird of such a quiet manner that he is not very well known. **(2) 1874** Coues *Birds N.W.* 121 *Plectrophanes Pictus.* Painted Lark Bunting. **1890** *Cent.* 4234/1 *Painted bunting,* . . . a very common longspur of western and northwestern America, of many variegated colors.

Painted cup. {1787–} +A North American plant (*Castilleja coccinea*) with bright-colored bracts, or a related species. Also with defining term. (Cf. Indian paintbrush.) — **1821** Nuttall *Travels Arkansa* 143, I was pleased to see the Painted Cup of the eastern states. **1857** Gray *Botany* 294 *C[astilleia] septentrionalis.* (Mountain Painted-Cup.) . . . Alpine region of the White Mountains, New Hampshire, and Green Mountains, Vermont. **1882** *Harper's Mag.* Nov. 853/2 What elf took pity on the painted-cup, and decked its leaves with the brilliant scarlet denied its hidden flower? **1901** Mohr *Plant Life Ala.* 52 These half-parasites belong mostly to the figwort family, examples being Canadian lousewort, . . . painted cup (*Castilleja canadensis*), and several Gerardias.

+**Painted finch.** =Nonpareil. — c**1730** Catesby *Carolina* I. 44 *Fringilla tricolor.* The Painted Finch: . . . They breed in Carolina and affect much to make their nests in Orange-Trees. **1789** MORSE *Amer. Geog.* 59 American Birds [include the] Bahama Finch, American Gold-Finch, Painted Finch [etc.]. **1831** AUDUBON *Ornith. Biog.* I. 279 Few vessels leave the port of New Orleans during the summer months, without taking some Painted Finches. **1917** *Birds of Amer.* III. 73 Painted Bunting. *Passerina ciris.* . . . [Also called] Painted Finch.

+**Painted goose.** The emperor goose. — **1872** [see EMPEROR GOOSE]. **1897** J. H. STUDER *Birds of N. Amer.* 162 Painted Goose; Emperor Goose. (*Philacte canagica.*) A species that is quite common . . . on the Northwest coast of the United States. **1917** *Birds of Amer.* I. 163 Painted Goose. . . . This is the 'least known and the most beautiful' of all the wild geese which make their summer home in the Far North.

+**Painted salamander.** A salamander characterized by bright-colored markings. — **1839** STORER *Mass. Reptiles* 251 *Salamandra picta.* . . . The painted Salamander. **1842** *Nat. Hist. N.Y., Zoology* III. 75 The Painted Salamander. . . . Inhabits shallow streams. **1869** *Amer. Naturalist* III. 158 Our common *Desmognathus fuscus*, or Painted Salamander, was observed by me in Maine.

+**Painted tortoise.** A brilliantly marked turtle or terrapin (*Chrysemys picta*) found in ponds and slow streams throughout the United States. — **1839** STORER *Mass. Reptiles* 208 *Emys picta.* . . . The painted Tortoise. **1842** *Nat. Hist. N.Y., Zoology* III. 12 The Painted Tortoise. . . . For the variety and beauty of its markings, this is unquestionably the handsomest of our fresh-water species.

+**Painted trillium.** A showy perennial herb (*Trillium undulatum*) especially common in New England. — **1855** *Harvard Mag.* I. 236 The Painted Trillium (*pictum*) is by far the most delicate of the species. *a*1862 THOREAU *Maine Woods* 320 *Trillium erythrocarpum* (painted trillium).

**Painter.*[1] A workman who applies paint to the surface of wood, iron, etc.

1652 *Suffolk Deeds* I. 194, [I] have Given Graunted Bargained & sould . . . vnto Augustine Clements of the same Dorchester, Painter, one peece of ground. **1681** *Boston Rec.* 71 Samuel Shrimpton became surety to the town for Daniel George, painter. **1724** *New-Eng. Courant* 22–29 June 2/2 Ran away from his Master, Mr. John Gibbs, Painter, in Boston, a Negro Boy. **1786** BENTLEY *Diary* I. 36 On friday morning at 4 o'clock a fire was discovered in a painter's Shop. **1820** FLINT *Lett. from Amer.* 213 There are . . . five painters and glaziers; two brush-makers. **1878** in Summers in *Ann. S.W. Va.* 1558 We have . . . any number of carpenters, painters, shoemakers, tailors [etc.]. **1907** *St. Nicholas* July 853/2 The house was fresh in May, We have but paid the painter's fee.

+**Painter.**[2] *colloq.*

1. =PANTHER.

[**1764** REUTER *Wachau* 577 *Painter*, or *Panther*, has the color of a Deer.] **1823** COOPER *Pioneers* xxxi, I say, Master Oliver, we'd like to have had a bad job of that panther, or painter's work. **1832** VIGNE *6 Mos. in Amer.* II. 85 The principal tenants of the forest are the cougar or painter (panther), as it is very improperly termed [etc.]. **1869** STOWE *Oldtown Folks* 356 The painters (panthers) used to come round their log cabin at night. **1893** ROOSEVELT *Wilderness Hunter* 335 No animal of the chase is so difficult to kill by fair still-hunting as the cougar . . . known in the East as panther and painter. **1913** LONDON *Valley of Moon* 320 An' panthers! —all the old folks called 'em painters an' catamounts an' varmints.

b. Attrib. with *blanket, hop, kitten, yell.*

1840 HOFFMAN *Greyslaer* II. 255 By the everlasting hokey, if he hasn't got one foot in a painter trap. **1850** LEWIS *La. Swamp Doctor* 170 Don't you want some bar-meat or painter blanket? *Ib.* 171 Please, Mr. Bar-Grave, cotch me a young bar or a painter kitten. **1867** HARRIS *Sut Lovingood* 54 Sum ove the wimmin fotch a painter yell.

2. In figurative expressions.

1845 KIRKLAND *Western Clearings* 124 When I saw she was coming to life, I ran like a painter. **1846** *Quarter Race Ky.* 85 Don't holler so! you are no worse nor a painter. **1849** *Knickerb.* XXXIII. 171 If you should see me now, you would grin like a 'painter.'

Painter's brush. {1685–} +=INDIAN PAINTBRUSH. — **1869** BOWLES *Our New West* 104 The painter's brush, as familiarly called here, is a new flower to me. **1899** S. HALE *Letters* 345 Mariposa lilies, painter's-brush, poppies, and dozens of others.

+**Paint horse.** *W.* [Perhaps from Sp. Cf. PINTO.] A piebald horse or one of conspicuous coloration. — **1868** G. A. MCCALL *Lett. from Frontiers* 110, I recognized the dashing Pierre Le Rocher . . . by his well-known pied or 'paint' horse. **1869** *Overland Mo.* III. 126, I had seen . . . a black-and-white-paint horse, fifteen hands high. **1903** 'O. HENRY' *Roads of Destiny* 96 Sam Kildrake's old paint hoss . . . killed hisself over-drinkin' on a hot day.

Paint keg. A keg for paint. — **1855** 'P. PAXTON' *Capt. Priest.* 54 In the sheds, connected with the main building, were to be found all kinds of . . . paint-kegs. **1869** *Mich. Agric. Rep.* VII. 184 Thirty-one beetles . . . he buried in an old paint keg. **1894** *Harper's Mag.* April 806/2 I shows her an old paint-keg thet I kep' rusty bolts in.

Paint shop. A shop where paint is made or where paint and painters' supplies are sold; a place in which various articles are painted. — **1866** *Ore. State Jrnl.* 23 June 3/4 Enquire of W. W. Winter, at paint shop under picture gallery. **1888** STOCKTON *Dusantes* 129 You stop at that paint-shop . . . , an' pay for the paint. **1899** *Sat. Ev. Post* 10 June 795 Eight hundred tons of white lead are ground in the paint shop every twelve months. **1911** PERSONS, etc. *Mass. Labor Laws* 283 The third floor is used as a paint-shop and for storing lumber.

Pair.* +1.** *Pair of falls*, in a stream, a rapid involving two or more definite descents. +**2.** *Pair of verses, pair of bars*, (see quotations.) — (1) **1770** in F. Chase *Hist. Dartmouth Coll.* I. 133 It is in . . . a very narrow place in the great river for a bridge; and it is by a long pair of falls. **1775** THAYER *Journal* (1867) 16 We sat out and pass'd three pair of Falls, went one mile and Encamp'd. (2) **1833** NEAL *Down-Easters* I. 108 And then ye koted some varses, pair o' varses we call 'em—about fools and adminstations. **1880** *Scribner's Mo.* Feb. 511/1 The bar-way (in Yankeeland 'a pair of bars') seems to belong to the stone wall, rail and stump fences.

+**Paisano.** *S.W.* [Sp.]

1. a. A fellow countryman. **b.** A rustic, peasant, or countryman.

1844 KENDALL *Narr. Santa Fé Exped.* II. 230 [He] invariably called me his paisano, or country man. **1893** LUMMIS *Land of Poco Tiempo* 88 Every one was out, but they were no longer the friendly paisanos we had known.

2. =CHAPARRAL COCK.

[**1844** GREGG *Commerce of Prairies* I. 195 There is to be found in Chihuahua and other southern districts a very beautiful bird called *paisano* (literally 'countryman'), which, when domesticated, performs all the offices of a cat in ridding the dwelling-houses of mice and other vermin.] **1858** BAIRD *Birds Pacific R.R.* 73 [*Geococcyx*] is represented in the United States by a single species known as the Paisano, Chapparal [*sic*] Cock, or sometimes Road Runner, on account of its frequenting public highways. **1885** *Harper's Mag.* Feb. 423/1 This bird . . . is popularly known [on the west coast] under several other names, such as road-runner, chaparral cock, and paisano. **1917** *Birds of Amer.* II. 126.

Paisley, *a.* Of fabrics and patterns: Made in Paisley, Scotland, or resembling the cloth made there. Freq. applied to shawls. Also absol. — **1843** *Knickerb.* XXI. 408 My good Paisley blanket . . . cost but five [dollars] . . . and looks as well as anybody need wish. **1850** *Harper's Mag.* Oct. 621/2 She will be forever talking of her fortune . . . and buying very extravagant Paisleys. **1885** BAYLOR *On Both Sides* 247 Parsons, looking quite as respectable as her neighbors, in her best black silk, her velvet bonnet, her handsome Paisley shawl, but still Parsons! **1905** VALENTINE *H. Sandwith* 112 She draped her admirer with a Paisley shawl borrowed from Mrs. Hamilton.

+**Paixhan gun.** A howitzer cannon shaped along lines suggested by Henri Joseph Paixhans (1783–1854), a French general. *Obs.* — **1857** HAMMOND *Northern Scenes* 150 The buck . . . sent him like a ball from a Paixhan gun, head foremost into the chaff. **1886** *Harper's Mag.* Oct. 782/2 The guns were shaped in accordance with the form adopted by General Paixhans . . . ; from this circumstance they obtained the title of Paixhan-guns.

**Palace.*

+**1.** *S.W.* The official residence and seat of government in Santa Fe, New Mexico, of the former Spanish and Mexican rulers, and of the New Mexico territorial government.

In this sense a rendering of PALACIO.

1808 PIKE *Sources Miss.* 212 The public square is in the centre of the town; on the north side of which is situated the *palace* (as the[y] term it) or government house, with the quarters for guards, &c. **1855** *Santa Fe Gazette* 8 Dec., The legislative Assembly of the Territory of New Mexico convened in the Palace, in Santa Fe, on Monday. **1870** *Republican Rev.* 7 May 1/4 T. B. Catron, Attorney General of the Territory of New Mexico said to me he desired me to look at a room in the Palace in which he wanted some alterations and repairs. **1872** *Ib.* 3 Feb. 1/3 The Governor's House, or 'Palace' as it is here called, is by no means a credit to the Territory. **1885** *Wkly. New Mexican Rev.* 22 Jan. 4/6 The old palace, the only palace known as such in the land, was seared with age before Europeans ascended the Allegheny mountains.

+**2.** The residence of the president of the U.S. *Obs.*

1809 QUINCY in E. Quincy *Life J. Quincy* 185 Dawson, a man of the palace, has moved to postpone the subject indefinitely. **1833** *Md. Hist. Mag.* XIII. 280 There are other lions in the city [Washington, D.C.]—especially the 'roaring Lion' up in the Palace as they call the President's House here.

+**b.** *Palace troops*, the supporters of President Jefferson's administration; *Palace in the Wilderness*, (see quotation).

1809 QUINCY in E. Quincy *Life J. Quincy* 174 The result [of the voting] was astonishing to Campbell and the leaders of the Palace troops. **1872** *Harper's Mag.* Dec. 42 The books . . . were assigned a room in the 'Palace in the Wilderness,' as the unfinished Capitol was then derisively styled by those who preferred New York or Philadelphia as the seat of government.

+**3.** =PALACE CAR.

1877 HALE *G. T. T.* 220 A belated baggage agent came into the palace for orders. **1877** *Harper's Mag.* March 580/2 Up to the Yellow Springs platform came two unusual palaces, especially engaged.

+**4.** *attrib.* and *comb.* Designating any one of various conveyances fitted out with superior accommodations for passengers.

See also FLOATING PALACE, PALACE CAR.

1844 *Knickerb.* XXIV. 192 Pleasant was the fishing-excursion . . . on board the matchless palace-steamer Knickerbocker. **1869** BREWER *Rocky Mt. Lett.* 9 Took a palace sleeping car, and were off. **1870** Palace day car [see COACH]. **1874** B. F. TAYLOR *World on Wheels* 162 The wounded lay . . . packed away in the box-cars. But you heard less complaint than is made any day on a palace-train. **1880** INGHAM *Digging Gold* 19 To cross the continent . . . is, with the aid of the palace-coach and sleeper, but the pleasure-trip of a week.

+**Palace car.** *Railroad.* A passenger car or coach fitted out with superior accommodations; a sleeping car. Also attrib. and fig. — **1869** BREWER *Rocky Mt. Lett.* 10 We took a palace car, paying $4 each for the privilege, but it was very pleasant. **1876** CROFUTT *Trans-continental Tourist* 41 All cannot afford to ride in Palace Cars. **1884** *Century Mag.* Oct. 945/1 One of our leading palace-car companies, . . . is said to pay its porters only fifteen dollars a month. **1895** *N.Y. Dramatic News* 7 Dec. 2/4 What a burst of vivid fancy it was that came to the mind of George M. Pullman when he christened his sleeping coach a palace car. **1898** N. E. JONES *Squirrel Hunters of Ohio* 297 No manufacturer of personal or political enthusiasm, even of palace-car order, ever obtained that intensity.

+**Palacio.** *S.W.* [Sp.] *spec.* A governor's palace, esp. the palace at Santa Fe, New Mexico. — **1844** GREGG *Commerce of Prairies* I. 203 These bricks are called *adobes*, and every edifice, from the church to the *palacio*, is constructed of the same stuff. **1847** *Santa Fe Republican* 20 Nov. 2/2 The citizens met together at the Palacio last night to make arrangements for the reception of General Price. **1885** *Wkly. New Mexican Rev.* 18 June 4/1 There he created a palacio.

Palatinate.** *Hist.* +An American colony, as Carolina, Maine, Maryland, the proprietors of which had palatine rights. — [**1669** *Fundamental Constit. Carolina* xxxv, It shall not be lawful to put the seal of the Palatinate to any writing, which is not signed by the Palatine. *c1680** *Maine Hist. Soc. Coll.* I. 400 Your Majesty's father . . . by his letters patent bearing date at Westminster in the fifty-first year of his reigne, did grant unto Sir Ferdinando Gorges . . . that tract of land called the Province of Maine, making the same equal with the Palatinate of Durham.] **1840** *Penna. Hist. Soc. Mem.* IV. I. 141 The chronicler of the Palatinate of New Albion signs himself Beauchamp Plantagenet. **1879** SCHARF *Hist. Maryland* I. 60 The province of Maryland was in fact a palatinate, and enjoyed the peculiar immunities attached to that species of government.

***Palatine.**

See A. Matthews, 'The word palatine in America,' in *Mass. Col. Soc. Publ.* VIII. (1902–04), 203–224.

+**1.** The title of the senior proprietor of the Carolina colony; also, the holder of this title. *Obs.*

[**1669** *Fundamental Constit. Carolina* i, The eldest of the Lords Proprietors shall be Palatine; and upon the decease of the Palatine, the eldest of the seven surviving proprietors shall always succeed him.] **1682** *Hist. Coll. S. Carolina* II. 20 To the Right Honourable William Earl of Craven Pallatine, and the rest of the true and absolute Lords and Proprietors of the Province of Carolina. **1705** *N.C. Col. Rec.* I. 627 Mrs. Juliana Lakar assumes to be indebted unto his Excellency the palatine & the Lords Proprietrs. **1726** *S.C. Hist. Coll.* II. 144 (The Governor) represented the Palatine, and the others the rest of the Lords Proprietors.

+**2.** An American colonist from the Lower or Rhenish Palatinate. Now hist. {1709–, in Britain}

1710 *Boston News-Letter* 26 June 2/2 The three Transports that are arrived with Palatines are the Fame, Baltimore and Town Frigor. **1726** PENHALLOW *Indian Wars* 79 The Jesuits . . . at last did influence them [*sc.* Indians] to make a descent on the borders of Virginia, where they murdered a great many of the Palatines. **1772** *Md. Hist. Mag.* XIV. 363 The Palatines by agreement have severall days to looke out for Masters & to make the Best terms they Can. **1784** WASHINGTON *Diaries* II. 307 Govr. Johnson of Maryland . . . has settled two or three families of Palatines. **1884** W. H. BROWNE *Maryland* 181 The 'Palatines,' or German fugitives from the Palatinate . . . did not enter Maryland in any numbers until towards the middle of the eighteenth century.

attrib. **1722** *New-Eng. Courant* 22–29 Oct. 2/1 The Ship Hanover from Holland, but last from Cowes, . . . having on Board above 130 Palatine Passengers, who are come to settle in this Country.

+**Palatines' court.** A court made up of the palatine and proprietors of the Carolina colony. *Obs.* — [**1669** *Fundamental Constit. Carolina* xxviii, Ye Palatine's court, consisting of the palatine and the other seven proprietors.] **1694** *N.C. Col. Rec.* I. 401 Ordered that . . . ye other [be] reteined to longr Time or be delivered by the Palatines Court.

***Pale,** *n.* **a.** A stake or bar of wood used in making a fence or barricade. Also attrib. **b.** A paling or palisade. *Obs.*

1624 *Va. House of Burgesses* 32 Against a domistic [enemy there was] noe other [fortification] but a pale inclosinge the Towne to the quantitye of four acres. **1661** *Springfield Rec.* I. 204 He which felled ye Trees may take his owne tyme for cross cutting of ye tymber or Cleaving Bolts, Rayls & Pales. **1789** MORSE *Amer. Geog.* 454 Land . . . [shall be] fenced round with a worm fence, or pales, six feet high. **1836** DUNLAP *Mem. Water Drinker* (1837) I. 12 It was . . . a ricketty wooden pale-gate drawn back by a chain and bullet. *Ib.* 19 They had now entered within the fence (then of wooden pales) which separated our magnificent public walk . . . from the street. **1871** *Rep. Indian Affairs* (1872) 484 The corn is . . . stored with pumpkins and beans in pale-cribs.

Pale,** *a.* +In specific names: **1.** Of fishes. **2.** Of plants. — **(1) 1883** *Nat. Museum Bul.* No. 27, 431 *Paralichthys squamilentus.* . . . Pale Flounder. Pensacola Bay, Florida. **1814** MITCHILL *Fishes N.Y.* 407 Pale Labrus. (*Labrus palladus.*) . . . A deep fish, and shaped much like the pond sun-fish, or *labrus auritus.* Caught near New-York. **1842** *Nat. Hist. N.Y., Zoology* IV. 200 The Pale Sucker, *Catostomus pallidus*, . . . is a common species, and is taken about the beginning of April. **(2) 1843** TORREY *Flora N.Y.* II. 321 *Prosartes lanuginosa.* . . . Pale-flowered Prosartes. *a1862** THOREAU *Maine Woods* 311 Shrubs and small trees in swamps: . . . *Kalmia glauca* (pale laurel), . . . *Prunus Pennsylvanica* [etc.]. **1901** MOHR *Plant Life Ala.* 91 Pignut hickory and pale-leaf hickory (*Hicoria villosa*), a tree of medium size, lately distinguished. **1843** TORREY *Flora N.Y.* II. 403 *Carex pallescens.* . . . Pale Pubescent Sedge. . . . Wet meadows; not common. **1901** MOHR *Plant Life Ala.* 493 Pale Umbrellawort. . . . Central Prairie region.

+**Pale disease.** A disease affecting sheep. — **1870** *Rep. Comm. Agric. 1869* 42 In Ohio several reports of death from 'pale disease' are received.

***Paleface.**

+**1.** A white man as distinguished from an Indian. A term usually employed by Indians or in imitation of them.

1826 COOPER *Mohicans* xi, The arms of the pale-faces are long, and their knives sharp! **1840** — *Pathfinder* ix, No Christianizing will ever make even a Delaware a white man; nor any whooping and yelling convart a pale-face into a red-skin. **1851** *Harper's Mag.* July 218/2 Nothing could seem less inviting than what the pale face called heaven. **1872** MCCLELLAN *Golden State* 604 The murderous Apache . . . raise the bloody tomahawk for the scalp of the 'pale face.' **1885** *Santa Fé Wkly. New Mexican* 17 Dec. 1/3 The noble savage . . . calling rum 'fire water' and me a 'pale face' fails to reconcile me to him. **1890** *Boston Jrnl.* 22 Nov. 2/1 They go with the profound conviction that the time has come when they are to drive the pale faces back from the hunting-grounds of their ancestors.

+**b.** Attrib. with *brother, law, maiden, squaw.*

1841 COOPER *Deerslayer* xi, 'This is the paleface law,' resumed the chief. **1850** GLISAN *Jrnl. Army Life* 18 The right and wrong of these cruel encounters will . . . [rest at] one time with the red man—at another with his pale-face brother. *a***1861** WINTHROP *Canoe & Saddle* 240 He had even condescended to take lessons in cookery from the pale-face squaws of the Willamette. **1899** CUSHMAN *Hist. Indians* 464 The young warrior resolved in the coming future to make the pale-face maiden his wife.

+**2.** Whisky. *slang.*

1846 *Spirit of Times* (N.Y.) 11 July 234/3 Provided pretty well with bread, meat, and a bottle of pale-face, which were stowed away in a pair of leather saddle bags.

***Pale-faced,** *a.* +White-skinned; belonging to the white, as distinguished from the red or Indian race. — **1832** DURFEE *Works* (1849) 68 Confounding pale-faced friends with warring foes. **1881** *Rep. Indian Affairs* 113 They compare favorably with their pale-faced brothers. **1901** DUNCAN & SCOTT *Allen & Woodson Co., Kan.* 311 The Red Man . . . thought little of the encroachment of his pale-faced brother. **1902** *Atlantic Mo.* Dec. 803/2 The pale-faced missionary and the hoodooed aborigine are both God's creatures.

Pale fence. A fence made of pales. — **1664** *Conn. Hist. Soc. Coll.* VI. 143 Ther shall be a suffishant palle fens set up Round about the sd. bering yard. **1839** *S. Lit. Messenger* 67/2 A handsome pale-fence skirted the lawn on the roadside. **1886** STOCKTON *Mrs. Lecks* 73 Of all the foolish things that ever came under my eye, the buildin' a wall around a garden, when a pale fence would do just as well, is the foolishest.

***Paling.**

***1.** =PALING FENCE.

1806 *Balance* V. 231/1, 1,200 feet of new cypress paling from around Captain Randolph's lots blown down. **1839** *S. Lit. Messenger* V. 751/1 Before the door was a . . . row of trees . . . fenced in by a white paling along the top of which ran a cornice. **1851** A. CARY *Clovernook* 63 The paling around the yard was to be straightened up. **1863** A. D. WHITNEY *F. Gartney* xii, A white paling that fenced in a grassy door-yard. **1890** HOWELLS *Shadow of Dream* I. vii, Some former proprietor had built a paling of slender strips of wood ten or twelve feet high.

b. *pl.* =PALING FENCE. {1834–}

*c***1845** W. T. THOMPSON *Chron. Pineville* 167 You've broke the major's palins down. **1884** 'CRADDOCK' *Tenn. Mts.* 195 There was a figure leaning against the palings. **1896** HARRIS *Sister Jane* 19, I don't want to be put on my cooling-board on account of driving a new set of nails in the front palings. **1920** HOWELLS *Vacation of Kelwyns* 161 She got him a dish to pick them in, and while he mounted the tree she praised him over the palings to Parthenope in undertone.

fig. **1850** *Rep. Comm. Patents 1849* 595 By gallantly dashing through the palings which some savans had imprudently raised before them, oceanic steamers have read the learned a lesson about laying out boundaries for science.

2. =PALE, *n.* a. Usu. pl.

1858 WARDER *Hedges & Evergreens* 156 All fields and inclosures shall be inclosed with a fence, sufficiently close, composed of posts and rails, posts and palings—or of turf. **1885** *Century Mag.* April 835 [He] had fenced in with palings a bit of a door-yard. **1898** POST *10 Yrs. Cowboy* 19 A fence of 'palins,' thin strips of timber split from some straight grained ash or oak tree, and pointed at the end, was . . . erected. **1903** J. HAWTHORNE *Hawthorne & Circle* 71 The palings, instead of being upright, were criss-crossed over one another.

Paling fence. A fence made of pales. {1805–} — **1843** *Amer. Pioneer* II. 308 A strong body occupied the yard of Ebenezer Zane, . . . using a pailing fence as a cover. **1873** 'Mark Twain' & Warner *Gilded Age* 60 Hawkins put up the first 'paling' fence that had ever adorned the village. **1895** *Outing* XXVI. 40/2 [We] leaned [our bicycles] . . . against a paling fence. **1925** Bryan *Memoirs* 17 Our yard was enclosed in the old-fashioned paling fence with a baseboard about a foot high.

Palisade. Also †**palizide.** (See also Palisado.)

1. *Mil.* A fencelike barrier or fortification made of tree trunks sharpened and set upright in the ground; one of the stakes or timbers used in such a structure. {1600–}

1622 'Mourt' *Relation* 22 We found the remainder of an old Fort, or Palizide, which as we conceiued had been made by some Christians. **1777** *Md. Hist. Mag.* V. 215 After they have knock'd down our Pallisades & destroy'd our Block Houses they will attempt a Storm. **1803** in *Ann. 8th Congress 2 Sess.* 1510 The fortifications at New Orleans . . . consist of five ill constructed redoubts, with a covered way, palisade, and ditch. **1852** *Harper's Mag.* Feb. 294/2 The fort was to be built of palisades. **1893** *Ib.* May 816/1 It is deemed necessary to enclose the city with breast-works and palisades.

attrib. **1725** *Md. Hist. Mag.* VII. 277 Makeing one pair of ffolding Palisadee Gates. **1815** *View N.Y. State Prison* 13 The upper yard . . . is separated from the lower yard . . . by a pallisade fence running parallel with the east side of it to the extremity of each wing of the prison.

+2. *pl.* A line of bold, precipitous cliffs along the western bank of the Hudson River north of Fort Lee, New Jersey; a similar formation elsewhere.

1838 Willis *Amer. Scenery* I. 14 The Palisades—Hudson River. . . . This singular precipice varies in height from fifty to two hundred feet, and presents a naked front of columnar strata, which gives it its descriptive name. **1849** *Knickerb.* XXXIV. 323 Precipitous palisades, down which they slide lime-stone, crags of flint-stone. These were subjects which kept the eyes and ears well occupied during that ride of nine miles. **1861** *Ladies' Repository* XXI. 699/1 Hidden by the mural cliffs of the Palisades . . . and along the slopes of the Catskills are many quiet nooks. **1907** White *Arizona Nights* 20 The cliffs and palisades near at hand showed dimly behind the falling rain.

Palisaded, *a.* {1890} Enclosed within a palisade. — **1804** C. B. Brown tr. Volney *View* 356 Five pallisaded forts . . . were the only stages in this journey. **1894** Winsor *Cartier to Frontenac* 31 Cartier and his companions were led to a gate in a circular palisaded village. **1916** Thoburn *Stand. Hist. Okla.* I. 49 The new post was typical of the frontier fortifications of that day, consisting of a ten-foot palisaded enclosure.

***Palisado.** Also †**palazado, pallisado,** etc.

***1.** =Palisade 1.

1622 'Mourt' *Relation* 49 One part . . . was incompassed with a large Palazado, like a Church-yard. **1675** *Plymouth Rec.* 146 The pallasadoes to be 10 foot and one halfe longe. **1809** Irving *Knickerb.* II. iv, A number of huts soon sprung up in the neighborhood, to protect which, they made an enclosure of strong pallisadoes. **1829** Cooper *Wish-ton-Wish* ii, About half-way up the sides of the eminence . . . was an unbroken line of high palisadoes, made of the bodies of young trees.

attrib. **1663** *Providence Rec.* I. 37 A pallesadoe Stake Butting on the high way West ward. **1679** *East Hampton Rec.* II. 88 Darvall . . . is to sett up . . . A good sofisient pallasadoe fence of five footh in hight.

b. An area enclosed by a palisade.

1853 Cozzens *Prismatics* 104 Certain Indians . . . were attacked . . . in the palisado called Fort Neck.

+2. *pl.* =Palisade 2.

1835 *Harvardiana* II. 4 The Palisadoes are a massive pile of rocks a few miles above Weehawken. **1840** *Penny Cycl.* XVI. 179/2 From Tappan to a distance of about 8 miles from the town of New York, the Palisadoes, as they are called, extend along the river.

Palisadoed, *a.* =Palisaded *a.* {1611–} — **1624** Smith *Gen. Hist. Va.* III. 60 They conducted vs to their pallizadoed towne. **1675** in Easton *Indian War* 75 A Block House or some stockadoed or palisadoed House or Place. **1753** Washington *Writings* I. 16 They also acquainted me that there was a small pallisado'd Fort on the Ohio. **1814** Brackenridge *Views La.* 185 Remains of palisadoed towns are found in their vicinity.

Pallbearer. Formerly, a pallholder {1707–}; +now one of those who carry the coffin. — **1727** Comer *Diary* (1893) 32 [She] exchanged this world for a better . . . , and I was chosen a pall bearer. **1828** Sherburne *Memoirs* 252 He was one of the pall-bearers. **1882** McCabe *New York* 232 The best of kid gloves must be furnished to the pall bearers. **1898** *Kansas City Star* 19 Dec. 1/4 The pallbearers were: W. K. Boone, Walter Ritchie, S. S. Wheeler.

Pallet bed. 1. A small or inferior bed or couch. {1707–} **+2.** A quilt or blanket spread on the floor as a bed; a pallet. — **(1) 1696** Sewall *Diary* I. 427 Our two old Nurses got my Wife on the Pallat-Bed. **1702** *Ib.* II. 51 My wife gets on to the Pallat Bed in her Cloaths, and there keeps, while Linen Curtains are put up within the Serge. **1715** *Ib.* III. 55 Visit Cousin Higginson sitting on her Pallet Bed. **(2) 1863** in *Century Mag.* XXX. 772/1 An eighty-pound Parrott . . . had entered through the front, burst on the pallet-bed, which was in tatters.

Pallholder. One of those who at a funeral hold up the corners and edges of the pall. *Obs.* — **1769** Rowe *Diary* 184, I went to the funeral of Henry Vassall. . . . I was a Pallholder. **1787** Bentley *Diary* I. 78 The Patient . . . talked of his Pall holders. **1807** *Holyoke Diaries* 149 My Papa Pall holder to Madam Oliver. **1817** Bentley *Diary* IV. 450 It was the first time the Hearse appeared in the Eastern part of Salem without pall holders.

***Palm. 1.** Any one of various ornamental plants or trees of the family Arecaceae, found chiefly in the southern states and California. (See also Cabbage palm, etc.) **+2.** =Hemlock. — **(1) 1699** J. Dickenson *God's Protecting Providence* 37 [There] came in Indian-Women loaden with Basketts of Berries, mostly of the Palm. **1791** Bartram *Travels* 65 After walking through a spacious forest of Live Oaks and Palms, . . . I and my fellow traveller arrived safe at the plantation. **1850** Tyson *Diary in Calif.* 19 The graceful and shadowy palm and cocoanut. **1901** Mohr *Plant Life Ala.* 423. **(2) 1791** Long *Voyages* 44 [Near L. Superior] the palm, birch, ash, spruce, and cedar grow large.

+Palma. *S.W.* [Sp.] Any one of various American palms, or a plant or tree resembling this. — **1838** 'Texian' *Mexico v. Texas* 64 At the foot of a large palma . . . the stranger assisted by the villagers began to dig. **1872** Powers *Afoot & Alone* 138 It is only the palmas, in their grimly sleepless vigils . . . [on] the Staked Plain.

***Palma Christi.** Also **palma Christa.** =Castor-oil plant. — **1737** Brickell *N. Carolina* 21 Palma-Christi, several sorts of Mint, Red-Dock, Jamestown-Weed, so called from its being so very plenty in Virginia. **1831** Peck *Guide* 158 The *Palma christi*, or castor oil bean, is produced in larger quantities in Madison, Randolph, and other counties [in Ill.]. **1856** *Rep. Comm. Patents 1855: Agric.* 276 The pea-nut, or pindar, the palma-christa, the bene, or other leguminous plants, adapted to the climate, and valuable for their productions. **1868** Gray *Field Botany* 295 *Ricinus*, Palma-Christi, Castor-Oil Plant. . . . *R. communis*, the only species.

***Palmer worm.** +The larva of a tineid moth, *Dichomeris ligulellus*, which in the eastern states is especially destructive to apple leaves. — **1668** *New Eng. Hist. & Gen. Reg.* XXXIV. 298 It pleased God to restrain the Palmer worm amongst vs in ye Bay and to spare our fruit trees. **1737** Brickell *N. Carolina* 167 The Caterpillar, Palmer or Canker-worm, is the same in Carolina as . . . in Ireland. **1815** *Lit. & Phil. Soc. N.Y. Trans.* I. 65 The ravages of the . . . canker worm, palmer worm, grass worm, and rose bug, are incalculably injurious. **1925** Herrick *Man. Injurious Insects* 113 The palmer-worm is an old pest, serious in certain seasons mainly in the northeastern United States, although the insect occurs from Maine to Texas.

***Palmetto.** Also †**palmeto, palmeta.**

The spelling *palmetto* may be of American origin as the earliest English evidence for this form is 1760. The 1746 edition of Thomson's 'Summer,' the first edition of the poem in which the word appears, has *palmeto*.

1. A plant or tree belonging to one or other species of American fan palm. {1746–, of the tropics}

1742 in *Travels Amer. Col.* 232 They had pulled the Palmettoes up by the Roots to eat. **1814** Brackenridge *Views La.* 172 The wind here became too strong, and we were compelled to put to shore on a little point of land overgrown with palmettoes. **1855** Glisan *Jrnl. Army Life* 188 The surrounding country is studded with palmettos and cocoanut trees. **1891** *Harper's Mag.* Sept. 594/2 Hunters . . . have seen smoke rising above the tops of the tall oaks and palmettoes far within. **1906** Bell *C. Lee* 169 Six or eight negro boys and men . . . had been asleep in the shade of a dusty palmetto.

b. The trunk or leaves of such a plant or tree, esp. as a building or thatching material.

1740 *S.C. Hist. Soc.* IV. 172 A House built of Palmetto, with several out Houses of the same work. **1745** E. Kimber *Itinerant Observ.* 6 The Huts are built generally of Clapboards and Palmetto's. **1776** *S.C. Hist. Soc.* III. 262 The Council issued orders for the following payments: . . . for rafting Palmettos to Charles-Town. **1829** *La. Acts 1828–29* 78 Every new levee . . . shall be fascined on the side of the river, either with palmetto or otherwise with picquets. **1839** *S. Lit. Messenger* V. 375/2 Several smoky huts, thatched with palmetto, peeped from among the underbrush.

***2.** Any one of various species of fan palms found especially in the South.

See also Blue, Cabbage, Fan palmetto and cf. Cabbage palm, Fan palm, Fan plant.

1765 Bartram *Jrnl.* 13 The hammocks of . . . palmettos are generally surrounded . . . with swamp. [**1808** Pike *Sources Miss.* III. App. 27 From the river Nassus to the east there is the palmetto. . . . Its wood . . . is of the same species as that of the same name in the southern states.] **1847** Henry *Campaign Sk.* 13 You miss, however, the palmetto and pine. **1879** Bishop *4 Months in Sneak-Box* 298 With their venison these men served a very palatable dish made from the terminal bud of the palmetto known as the 'cabbage.' **1899** Going *Flowers* 126 The palmettos . . . are not found in a wild state north of the Carolinas.

b. With a qualifying term.

1766 J. Bartram *Journal* 40 The small palmetto or chamaerops yields a small white bud no bigger than one's finger, which is eaten by men, bears, and horses. **1872** Powers *Afoot & Alone* 25 Here [is] . . . the row-palmetto.

+3. The palmetto as a state or party emblem or badge in South Carolina.

Cf. PALMETTO BUTTON, FLAG, STATE.

[**1833** *Md. Hist. Mag.* XIII. 367 The island is . . . covered with the Palmetto, formerly known as the Cabbage tree, and the chosen emblem of Nullification.] **1833** *Niles' Reg.* XLIV. 139/1 Then taking the flag . . ., he shook open the folds, and displayed the arms of the state, and Carolina's palmetto. **1844** EMERSON *Poet* Ess. 2 Ser., The cider-barrel, the log-cabin, the hickory-stick, the palmetto, and all the cognizances of party. **1847** *Whig Almanac 1848* 23/1 Lieut. Col. Dickinson . . . was bearing the Palmetto proudly amid the storm.

+4. Short for PALMETTO HAT.

1852 STOWE *Uncle Tom* xxx, Mr. Skeggs, with his palmetto on, . . . walks around to put farewell touches on his wares.

5. *attrib.* a. Designating structures, shelters, etc., built of the trunks or leaves of the palmetto.

1739 W. STEPHENS *Proc. Georgia* I. 480, I found them well covered from bad Weather, by a strong Palmetto Hut. **1741** *S.C. Hist. Soc.* IV. 42 [The army] came to Some Palmetto Houses, where they Halted about one Hour. **1744** MOORE *Voy. Georgia* 114 These palmetto bowers were very convenient shelters being tight in the hardest rains. **1820** *Amer. Naturalist* III. 458 With a palmetto cabin, plenty of oysters, game and fish, he lives a free and easy life.

b. Designating parts of palmetto trees or plants.

1741 *Ga. Hist. Soc. Coll.* II. 118 This deponent and the rest of their company were reduced to the necessity of feeding on palmetto roots to keep themselves from starving. **1776** *S.C. Hist. Soc.* III. 229 Palmetto logs for the use of the fortifications. **1812** *Niles' Reg.* III. 237/1 [We] threw up breast works between two ponds, living upon gophers, alligators and palmetto stocks.

c. Designating areas or regions in which palmetto is the prevailing growth.

1744 MOORE *Voy. Georgia* 124 The Indians were prevailed upon to return to the Palmetto ground. **1853** 'P. PAXTON' *Yankee in Texas* 55 A wolf skin, or the nearest palmetto brake, furnishes him with a hat. *Ib.* 56 The '*marais*' or slough, . . . according to my friend Joe's account, changed into a 'branch:' then after running through a cypress brake or two, ultimately assumed the form of a palmetto swamp, and in that guise joined the river.

+d. With reference to the use in South Carolina of the palmetto as a badge or emblem.

1840 *Niles' Nat. Reg.* 4 April 77/2 Mr. Everett said he had yielded the floor for explanation, not for a palmetto speech. **1846** MANSFIELD *Winfield Scott* 248 Sullivan's Island . . . was daily visited by respectable citizens, . . . most of whom wore the palmetto cockade. **1850** in Claiborne *Life Quitman* II. 38 May I hope that Mississippi will . . . allow the Palmetto banner the privilege of a place in her ranks. **1861** *Vanity Fair* April 201/1 The bold Palmetto men, Sumter stormed.

e. In special combinations.

Palmetto cabbage, =CABBAGE PALMETTO; *p. fan,* =PALM-LEAF FAN; *p. juice,* a liquid obtained from the esculent portions of the palmetto.

1802 DRAYTON *S. Carolina* 6 Their soil is of very sandy nature; producing . . . palmetto cabbage, palmetto royal, silk grass. **1865** *Nation* I. 240 A negro man-servant waited at the table, over which presided the landlady, with a palmetto fan in her hand. **1845** GREEN *Texian Exped.* 162 Several were left on the road exhausted for the want of water and here they commenced unfortunately, the use of the palmetto juice as a substitute.

Palmetto bush. A young or dwarfed plant of one or other species of southern palmetto. — **1784** HUTCHINS *Hist. Narrative La. & W. Fla.* 34 The whole is . . . covered with thick wood, Palmetto bushes, &c. **1812** *Niles' Reg.* III. 237/1 Many more must have been slain, but were hid from our view by the thick and high Palmetto bushes. **1901** *Scribner's Mag.* April 433/1 Narrow grooves have been worn in the hillsides, divided one from the other by . . . pyramids of earth and clay, crested with the stunted stems and roots of palmetto bushes.

+**Palmetto button.** A button worn as a badge or emblem by nullifiers in South Carolina. *Obs.* (Cf. PALMETTO FLAG, PALMETTO STATE.) — **1833** *Md. Hist. Mag.* XIII. 356, I saw the Nullification badge very frequently in S.C. that is the blue cockade and the small palmetto batton [*sic*]. **1846** MANSFIELD *Winfield Scott* 243 The palmetto cockade and the palmetto buttons distinguished the *nullifiers* from the *Unionists*.

+**Palmetto City.** Charleston, South Carolina. A nickname. — **1857** *Harper's Mag.* June 1/1 Our artist has possessed himself of the Palmetto City—Charleston, South Carolina. **1859** *Ladies' Repository* Jan. 51/1 Charleston, South Carolina, is called the 'Palmetto City,' on account of the abundance of palmetto-trees in and around it.

+**Palmetto flag.** Any one of various flags used in or adopted by South Carolina which made use of the palmetto as a device. (Cf. PALMETTO 3.) — **1860** in Logan *Great Conspiracy* 98 [He would] unfurl the Palmetto flag. **1862** KETTELL *Hist. Rebellion* I. 91 The palmetto flag was raised over the post-office and custom-house at Charleston. **1868** BEECHER *Norwood* 382 Nowhere in the city or harbor, except at Fort Sumter, is the flag of the United States flying; everywhere it is the Palmetto flag! **1894** *Harper's Mag.* May 946/2 The streets [of Charleston, S.C.] bloomed with palmetto flags, and with a great variety of mottoes.

+**Palmetto hat.** =PALM-LEAF HAT. — **1747** *N.J. Archives* XII. 364 The woman . . . [wore] blue worsted stockings, palmeta hat, scarlet red cloak [etc.]. **1853** 'P. PAXTON' *Yankee in Texas* 19 [His face] beamed forth from beneath the overshadowing of a home-made palmetto hat. **1877** PHELPS *Story of Avis* 410 She looked very young and girlish that day in her palmetto hat and white linen dress. **1889** CABLE in *Century Mag.* Feb. 516/2 Before the end of the month all the women in St. Martinville were wearing palmetto hats.

Palmetto leaf. The leaf of the palmetto, freq. used for covering or thatching houses. {1662–} Also allusive. — **1709** LAWSON *Carolina* 7 One side of the Roof of his House was thatch'd with Palmeto-leaves, the other open to the Heavens. **1797** IMLAY *Western Territory* (ed. 3) 246 Care must be taken to have ready a hanger (or tobacco-house) . . . [built in] the form of a house of an oblong square . . ., and covered with cypress bark, or palmetto leaves. **1837** *Yale Lit. Mag.* II. 9 Others were endeavoring to arrange shelters, by means of sticks covered with palmetto leaves. **1880** CABLE *Grandissimes* 89 On it [the floor] were . . . white mats woven of bleached palmetto-leaf. **1891** *Harper's Mag.* Dec. 47/1 Mrs. Wattles was such an uncompromising patriot. . . . Perhaps the colonel would not wave the palmetto leaf too vigorously.

Palmetto royal. {1756–} +The Spanish dagger, *Yucca gloriosa.* — **1741** *South Carolina Hist. Soc.* IV. 43 This Fort . . . [had] a Ditch without on all sides, Lined round with Prickly Palmetto Royal. **1786** WASHINGTON *Diaries* III. 34 Sowed . . . all the seed I had of the palmetto royal. **1802** DRAYTON *S. Carolina* 67 Palmetto royal. (*Yucca gloriosa.*) Grows only on sea islands; or lands immediately connected with salt water. **1813** MUHLENBERG *Cat. Plants* 35 *Yucca gloriosa.* Broad-leaved (palmetto royal) Car.

+**Palmetto scrub.** The saw palmetto, *Serenoa serrulata.* — **1880** *Scribner's Mo.* July 423/2 The palmetto scrub rustled, the shambling feet shuffled away. **1894** TORREY *Fla. Sketch-Book* 5 White-eyed chewinks were at home in dense palmetto scrub. **1905** N. DAVIS *Northerner* 292 Before him was a stretch of dazzling sand, the feathery green of palmetto scrub and the blue waters seen through a burning mist.

+**Palmetto State.** South Carolina. A nickname. — **1843** *Knickerb.* XXI. 222 The merry days of good old Christmas are still observed in the Palmetto State. **1856** in P. Butler *Recollections* 106 It is not reported that these emigrants from the Palmetto State seek out a claim. **1875** in Fleming *Hist. Reconstruction* II. 405 The means to be adopted to overthrow negro rule in the Palmetto State may not be precisely the same as that which proved successful in Mississippi.

+**Palmetto-thatched,** *a.* Thatched or roofed with palmetto leaves. — **1888** CABLE *Bonaventure* 86 On a bank of this bayou . . . [stood] the palmetto-thatched fishing and hunting lodge. **1895** G. KING *New Orleans* 34 There is absolutely no seeing of Bienville's group of palmetto-thatched huts by the yellow currents of the Mississippi.

***Palmetto tree.** 1. Any one of various American fan palms. Also with defining term. +2. *transf.* The banner or flag of South Carolina. (Cf. PALMETTO FLAG.) — (1) **1709** LAWSON *Carolina* 101 The Palmeto-Tree I have not yet met withal in North-Carolina. **1796** MORSE *Univ. Geog.* I. 677 The palmetto or cabbage tree, the utility of which, in the construction of forts, was experienced during the war. **1884** *Century Mag.* April 806/2 The gilded niches where stand dwarf palmetto trees. (2) **1865** 'G. HAMILTON' *Skirmishes* 172 If he is concocting . . . rebellion, can he not go on just as blithely under the Stars and Stripes as under the Palmetto-tree?

+**Palmilla.** *S.W.* [Mex. Sp.] Any one of various plants whose bulbs or roots are used for soap. — **1844** GREGG *Commerce of Prairies* I. 160 Among the wild productions of New Mexico is the *palmilla*—a species of palmetto . . ., whose roots . . ., when bruised, form a saponaceous pulp called *amole*, much used by the natives for washing clothes. **1847** RUXTON *Adv. Rocky Mts.* (1848) 217 After leaving this creek we passed a barren rolling prairie with scanty herbage and covered with the palmilla, or soap-plant. **1851** M. REID *Scalp Hunters* 125, I could only see the long bayonets of the picturesque *palmillas*.

Palm leaf. {1660–}

+1. =PALM-LEAF HAT.

1852 STOWE *Uncle Tom* vi, Sam's palm-leaf had been ingeniously disentangled from all pretensions to braid. **1854** M. J. HOLMES *Tempest & Sunshine* 15 He gave his old palm-leaf three flourishes round his head. **1857** — *Meadow-Brook* xviii, A gust of wind lifted the old palmleaf from his woolly head.

+2. =PALM-LEAF FAN.

1852 *Knickerb.* XXXIX. 153 Fans, of all sorts and sizes, were in constant use, from nine-penny palm-leafs to two-shilling paper-spreads. **1912** NICHOLSON *Hoosier Chron.* 163 He fanned himself in a desultory fashion with a palm leaf.

3. *attrib.* Designating articles of apparel made of, or suggestive of, palm leaves.

1864 *Hist. North-Western Soldiers' Fair* 148 [Donations include] palm leaf collar, cuffs and bib. **1895** A. BROWN *Meadow-Grass* 89 The Widder Poll, clad not only in the Tycoon rep, but her best palm-leaf shawl, her fitch tippet, and pumpkin hood.

+**Palm-leaf fan.** A fan made of a leaf of the fan palm. — **1860** HOLLAND *Miss Gilbert* 132 Then Mrs. Puggles helped herself to a palm-leaf fan. **1881** M. J. HOLMES *Madeline* 322 Mrs. Noah sat with her for a time, fanning her with a palm-leaf fan. **1890** WIGGIN *Timothy's Quest* 59 She could keep the flies off her by waving a palm-leaf fan. **1912** NICHOLSON *Hoosier Chron.* 328 'Who is that preposterous fat man?' demanded Mrs. Owen, plying her palm-leaf fan vigorously.

+**Palm-leaf hat.** A summer hat made of the leaves of the fan palm or saw palmetto. — **1820** *Boston Daily Advertiser* May 18 2/6 (Ernst). **1835** INGRAHAM *South-West* I. 58 Our summer garments and palm-leaf hats. **1854** THOREAU *Walden* 40 Gradually leaving off palmleaf hat or cap of woodchuck skin. **1880** TOURGEE *Bricks* 451 The man . . . fans himself with a palm-leaf hat.

***Palm tree.** =PALM 1. Also attrib. — **1775** ROMANS *Nat. Hist. Florida* App. 17 It is remarkable on account of the immense number of palm trees whence it has acquired the name of *Palmar de Ais*, or the palm grove of Ais. **1791** BARTRAM *Travels* 115 The palm-trees here seem to be of a different species from the cabbage tree. **1858** VIELÉ *Following the Drum* 69 As its palm-trees . . . passed from my sight, I felt that with them a dream had vanished. **1905** *World Today* Jan. 26/2 One might pass along the edge of the desert . . . and never know that there was a canyon here, or a luxuriant palm tree growth.

+**Palm warbler.** The American warbler, *Dendroica palmarum* or subspecies *D. p. hypochrysea*. — **1828** BONAPARTE *Ornithology* II. 12 [The] Palm Warbler, *Sylvia Palmarum*, . . . is found during winter in Florida . . . and in other parts of the territory wherever the orange-tree is cultivated. **1874** COUES *Birds N.W.* 68 The Palm Warbler is an extremely abundant bird in the Southern States in winter. **1917** *Birds of Amer.* III. 150/1 The Palm Warbler nests in the very northern part of Minnesota and farther north to the Great Slave Lake and west of Hudson Bay.

Palm wine. The fermented juice or sap of any one of various palms. {1613-} — **1704** *Boston News-Letter* 31 July 2/2 Brought in two Spanish Prizes a Setty and a Sloop, on board of which are . . . 30 Pipes of Palm-Wine. **1717** *Mass. H. S. Coll.* 6 Ser. V. 352 Shall send som gallons of Palm wine for present occation. **1865** *Atlantic Mo.* XV. 340/1 The bread is very good, palm wine being used for yeast.

+**Paloverde.** *S.W.* [Sp. *palo* 'wood' and *verde* 'green.']

1. Either of two species (*Cercidium torreyanum* and *C. floridum*) of green-barked acacia.

1854 BARTLETT *Personal Narr.* II. 188 The vegetation consisted of mezquit and palo verde. **1869** J. R. BROWNE *Adv. Apache Country* 225 Our trail over the mesa . . . was pleasantly diversified by groves of palo-verde and bunches of cactus. **1877** HODGE *Arizona* 57 A fair supply of other wood and timber, such as ash, black walnut, . . . palo verde, alder, willow. **1881** *Amer. Naturalist* XV. 982 The 'Palo[v]erde' of the Mexicans . . . is the *Parkinsonia torreyana*. . . . It grows to be some fifteen or twenty feet high [near Tucson, Ariz.]. **1897** SUDWORTH *Arborescent Flora* 256 *Cercidium floridum*. Greenbark Acacia. . . . Palo Verde (Tex., Ariz., N. Mex.).

2. (See quotation.)

1897 SUDWORTH *Arborescent Flora* 255 *Parkinsonia microphylla*. Small-leaf Horse Bean. . . . Palo Verde (Cal.).

Pamela. A style of women's hats. Used attrib. — **1856** *Porter's Spirit of Times* 18 Oct. 116/1 The first [bonnet] was of the Pamela shape, in rice straw. *Ib.*, Another Pamela bonnet was of Leghorn.

Pampas grass. Also **pampa grass.** An ornamental garden grass (*Cortaderia argentea*), introduced from South America. {1850-} — **1868** GRAY *Field Botany* 358 *Gynerium argenteum*, Pampas Grass. Tall reed-like grass, from S. America, planted out for ornament. **1886** ALCOTT *Jo's Boys* v, Plumy pampas-grass . . . pleased the girls. **1900** NORRIS *Blix* 26 Balancing the tuft of pampa-grass to the left, was an inverted section of a sewer-pipe painted blue and decorated with daisies.

+**Pampas rice.** *S.* (See quotation.) — **1890** *Cent.* 4252/3 *Pampas-rice* . . ., a variety of the common sorghum, *Sorghum vulgare*, with a drooping panicle: grown to some extent in the southern United States.

***Pamphlet.** A short argumentative or factual treatise printed as a separate work and published unbound, with or without paper covers. Also attrib. — **1654** JOHNSON *Wonder-w. Prov.* 120 Many pamphlets have come from our Countreymen of late, to this purpose, namely, scurrillously to deride all kind of Scholarship, Presbytery, and Synods. **1757** *Narragansett Hist. Reg.* IV. 145 The Honb' Stephen Hopkins Esqr and Mr. Samuel Currie . . . began a Dispute about a pamphilit which Mr. Samuel Ward had Published against the Said Hopkins. **1837** *Diplom. Corr. Texas* I. (1908) 176 The tables of the Members have groaned with pamphlets written by the abolitionists for the purpose of injuring and calumniating Texas. **1901** *Book Buyer* Nov. 280/1 The Department of Agriculture and the various experiment stations offer good examples of the timely dissemination of special news through pamphlet publications.

***Pan,** *n.*

***1.** A broad and shallow metal vessel used about a household for cooking, etc.

1652 *Conn. Rec.* III. 474 Some other of the Sachems' men . . . took from them much goods, trays, pots, pans &c. **1768** J. LEES *Journal* 10 [In Providence, R.I.] a good many Potts, Pans, Anchors, and such work is manufactured. **1850** S. WARNER *Wide, Wide World* xxxv, Ellen . . . got the pans ready for the evening milk. **1897** *Outing* Aug. 438 A very beautiful fish, excellent for the pan and dearly loved by the small boy, was the sunfish or pumpkin-seed.

b. An open vessel used for evaporating or boiling down sugar, salt, etc. {1674-}

1708 *N.J. Archives* 1 Ser. III. 345 Ye Salt that the Pans produce will be a constant Supply. **1850** S. F. COOPER *Rural Hours* 26 The syrup . . . [is then] placed in tin pans to cool and form the 'grain.' **1896** *Vt. Agric. Rep.* XV. 36 For boiling I prefer an evaporator . . . because . . . the average results are of a better quality than is secured with pans [in making maple sugar].

2. A hard substratum of the soil through which water does not easily permeate. {1786-} Also attrib.

Cf. HARD PAN 1.

1751 ELIOT *Field-Husb.* iii. 63 [Plowing] will effectually break up the Pan-bottom, so that the Water will Soak away. **1784** *Belknap P.* II. 180 [The water] descends to the hard stratum, commonly called the pan. **1830** *Illinois Mo. Mag.* I. 57 This limestone pan is generally but a few feet below the surface.

+**3.** =FIRE PAN b.

1845 W. T. THOMPSON *Chron. Pineville* 162 His pan [was] upon one shoulder and his musket on the other.

+**4.** *Placer mining.* **a.** A shallow circular metal vessel used in washing gold from gravel, etc. **b.** The contents of such a pan; a panful.

1850 TYSON *Diary in Calif.* 9 You will soon become accustomed to the mode of proceeding, either with a shovel, pickax, pan, or washer. **1865** *Wkly. New Mexican* 20 Oct. 1/3 Gold prospected in the bed of the stream from one cent to one dollar per pan. **1885** *Wkly. New Mexican Rev.* 25 June 3/7 All he has to do there [at Golden] is to step out into his door yard with a pan and gather it up! **1890** LANGFORD *Vigilante Days* (1912) 34 The veteran gold searcher . . . with pick, shovel, and pan, a magnifying glass [etc.]. **1899** *Mo. So. Dakotan* I. 194 The dirt being carried down the mountain in sacks and washed out with rocker and pan.

5. *Metallurgy*. A vessel in which ores are ground and amalgamated. {1839}

1869 BROWNE *Adv. Apache Country* 396 The Real del Monte contains . . . thirty-six Wheeler pans, and other machinery in proportion. **1872** 'MARK TWAIN' *Roughing It* 255 We got the pulp out of the pans and batteries. **1896** SHINN *Story of Mine* 218 The Consolidated Virginia mill as built in bonanza days has . . . forty pans, four agitators, and twenty settlers.

+**6.** *Whaling.* The broad posterior part of a whale's lower jawbone.

1883 *Nat. Museum Bul.* No. 27, 293 These cases contain the 'pans' (posterior portions of the jaw-bone of the sperm-whalc). **1887** GOODE, etc. *Fisheries* v. II. 232 *n.*, Canes made full length from the ivory of the 'pan' of the sperm whale.

7. *To shut pan*, to be silent, to close one's mouth. *slang.* {1833}

1799 *Mass. Spy* 2 Jan. (Th.), Instead of saying grace decently, as he used to do, he called out attention—handle arms—and for grace after dinner—now shut pans. **1840** *Crockett Almanac* 33 Says I 'have you shut pan?'

8. *attrib.* and *comb.* **a.** In senses 1 and 1 b with *jerker, man, stone.*

1833 SILLIMAN *Man. Sugar Cane* 82 The panman further tests the purity of the liquor. **1857** *Harper's Mag.* Sept. 448/2 The boilers . . . have become thickly coated with a sedimentary deposit. . . . This incrustation, sometimes called pan-stone, is principally composed of the sulphates of lime and soda. **1878** PINKERTON *Strikers* 55 The 'pan-jerkers'—all that large class of loafers who subsist by rendering some slight service about restaurants.

b. In senses 4 and 5 with *amalgamation, amalgamator, charge*, etc.

1871 RAYMOND *3d Rep. Mines* 392 The Washoe Pan Amalgamation. **1874** — *6th Rep. Mines* 21 These tailings . . . will yield, under pan-washing, a fair prospect, and very often a notable quantity of gold. *Ib.* 415 The worn-out pan-shoes and dies . . . have quicksilver sticking to them. *Ib.* 429 The first building contains . . . Dodge's pan-amalgamator and settler. **1882** *47th Congress 1 Sess.* H. R. Ex. Doc. No. 216, 651 The pan-charge is drawn into the settlers and thinned down. **1888** *Chicago Inter-Ocean* 8 March, On their way to inspect the California pan mill. **1896** SHINN *Story of Mine* 88 The term 'tailings' as here used includes all the ore residues, or waste, whether slimes, pan tailings, or concentrates. **1901** WHITE *Westerners* 208 He showed them . . . hanging walls, country rock, pan tests.

Pan, *v.* {a1825-}

I. +**1. a.** *absol.* To wash auriferous dirt in a miner's pan. **b.** *intr.* Of gravel or soil: To produce gold. Hence, fig., to pay.

(a) 1850 KINGSLEY *Diary* 123 About 200 Indians & squaws came down and began to pan all around us. **(b) 1848** DANA *Mineralogy* 317 Gravel or soil . . . is said to *pan well* or *pan poorly* according to the result. **1882** BAILLIE-GROHMAN *Camps in Rockies* 19 Out here them tony chin music don't pan worth a cent.

+**2.** *tr.* **a.** To wash (auriferous soil) in a miner's pan. **b.** To wash out the soil of (a gulch) in a miner's pan.

(a) 1875 BOURKE *Journal* June 12 Interest . . . was keenly excited by the discovery of a fleck of gold in some dirt panned by one of Prof. Janney's servants. **1923** 'BOWER' *Parowan Bonanza* 33 Rock so rich that he could break it up by hand and pan it in the spring. **(b) 1880** *Cimarron*

News & Press 2 Sept. 2/5 The gold placers supply a living now for many Mexicans who pan the richest gulches.

+**3.** To wash (gold) from auriferous soil by means of a pan.

1883 RITCH *Illust. N. Mex.* 88 Gold can be panned from the sands of any of the streams and arroyas running down from the mountains.

+**4.** *transf.* To capture.

1887 GOODE, etc. *Fisheries* V. II. 477 The crew 'panned' about 10,000 seals, but did not succeed in putting them on board.

II. With adverbs. ||**5.** *To pan* (something) *off on*, to palm off on.

1884 *Gringo & Greaser* 15 Feb. 2/3 The dirty lie he was trying to pan off on the public for the truth.

6. *To pan out.* +**a.** =sense 2 a. Hence, fig., to examine closely; to separate into its elements.

1852 CLAPPE *Lett. from Calif.* 212 Of course they immediately prospect it, which is accomplished by panning out a few basinfuls of the soil. **1859** G. A. JACKSON *Diary* (MS.) 3 Panned out two cups. no gold in either. **1879** *Harper's Mag.* Sept. 510 The population, like the dirt, was slowly panned out. **1880** INGHAM *Digging Gold* 89 William Fairweather went to the gulch and panned out a little gravel. **1890** LANGFORD *Vigilante Days* (1912) 189, I have panned that fellow out and could n't get a color. **1907** WHITE *Arizona Nights* 164, [I] panned out some dust, so I camped a while.

+**b.** To obtain (gold) by washing ore in a miner's pan; hence, fig., to produce (anything).

1873 *Newton Kansan* 16 Jan. 2/1 [Franklin's father's] business failed to 'pan out' enough profit. **1874** CODMAN *Mormon Country* 35 Poor men and Chinamen . . . 'pan out' the gold in the primitive way. **1875** *Chicago Tribune* 19 Aug. 2/5 The Athletics . . . struck upon a very rich lead of batting, and panned out seven base hits. **1880** *Cimarron News & Press* 24 June 3/1 Mr. E. Platt Stratton returned from Ute Creek . . . [with] a 34 dwt nugget that one of the miners had panned out at the head of the creek. **1889** MUNROE *Golden Days* 109 In washing with a pan, or 'panning out gold,' an ordinary hand-basin . . . or a shallow iron pan constructed especially for the purpose, is used. **1891** RYAN *Told in Hills* II. 25 All it panned out for me was empty pockets.

+**c.** Of a mine or mineral-bearing soil: To produce gold or mineral.

1872 *Kansas Mag.* I. 558/2 No amount of scientific effort could make it [the dirt] 'pan out' better. **1874** ALDRICH *P. Palfrey* vii, Though it did not yield so bounteously as the silver lode, it panned out handsomely. **1878** BEADLE *Western Wilds* 41 The diggins begun to pan out rich.

d. Of any enterprise, person, or thing: To yield results; to come out.

When the construction is without an adjective or adverb, the phrase frequently means: To succeed; to show up advantageously; to be satisfactory.

1871 HAY *Pike County Ballads* 13, I don't pan out on the prophets And free-will and that sort of thing. **1875** *Scribner's Mo.* X. 277 A good business is said to 'pan out well.' **1879** HARTE *Drift from Two Shores* 116 That depends pretty much on how things pan out. **1885** *Wkly. New Mexican Rev.* 15 Jan. 2/5 Taylor informed the doctor that he had lost his hat in the Rio Chiquito and desired another, but this wouldn't 'pan out' with Dr. Alexander. **1887** *Courier-Journal* 27 Jan. 2/1 Sam came up here with an idea of being a candidate for United States Senator himself, but his idea did not pan out. **1890** *Stock Grower & Farmer* 15 Feb. 6/2 This delightful winter is about to pan out too dry for stock. **1917** MATHEWSON *Sec. Base Sloan* 193 Sure! That is, if you pan out like I think you will.

***Panada.** Bread boiled in water to a pulp and variously flavored. — **1784** CUTLER in *Amer. Mem. Academy* I. 415 The leaves give a grateful flavour to cakes and panadoes. **1850** S. WARNER *Wide, Wide World* xxi, I have got quite tired of gruel, and panada I can't bear. **1866** MOORE *Women of War* 196 [She] prepared . . . a large supply of hot ginger panada for the pickets.

Panama. =PANAMA HAT. {1885-} — **1873** MILLER *Amongst Modocs* 44 He could not push his panama any further back. **1876** *Wide Awake* 268/1 Ruby Gilbert . . . settled a broad panama upon her head. **1904** A. FRENCH *Barrier* 109 A monkey in a Panama, saying foolish things.

Panama canal. The proposed and actual ship canal across the isthmus of Panama.

American interest in this canal began with the acquisition of California. Decisive action for its construction, however, was not taken until 1903-4. It was ready for use in 1914.

1880 *Nation* 5 Feb. 90 The United States government and the Panama Canal. **1889** *Atlantic Mo.* March 350/1 It is as reasonable to maintain that the Panama Canal is to constitute part of the coast-line of Mexico as of that of the United States. **1903** *Rev. of Reviews* Nov. 525/1 [The merchants at Panama] see plainly that . . . their business is ruined if President Roosevelt . . . drops the idea of the Panama Canal. **1910** *Outlook* 1 Oct. 256 Should the Panama canal be fortified? **1914** *Yale Review* July 708 The Panama Canal is about to open a new highway between the Atlantic and the Pacific.

Panama fever. Either yellow fever or malaria contracted in the Panama region. {1890} — **1850** TYSON *Diary in Calif.* 29 The so-called *Panama fever* rarely occurs, unless previous disease has wasted the powers. **1868** *Overland Mo.* 1 Ser. I. 561/1 After hearing all about how she felt, his diagnosis was a mild case of fever—Panama fever.

Panama hat. A hand-plaited hat made in Central and South America of the young leaves of the jipijapa; an imitation of this. {1833-} — **1848** *Knickerb.* XVIII. 224 It is little matter of astonishment that the appearance of a gentleman wearing . . . a Panama hat . . . should be an object of attention. **1861** NEWELL *Orpheus C. Kerr* I. 31 A Southerner sat, A-twisting the band of his Panama hat. **1885** HARTE *Snow-bound* 29 A man's broad-brimmed Panama hat . . . protected her from the sun. **1908** *Harper's Wkly.* 26 Sept. 33 The Passing of the Panama Hat.

+**Pan-American,** *n.* A delegate to a Pan-American congress; one interested in Pan-American affairs. — **1890** *Ann Arbor Reg.* 3 March 6 The Pan-Americans. . . . The delegates to the International American conference are beginning to talk about final adjournment. **1891** *Harper's Mag.* June 3/2 Our own ignorance . . . respecting our South-American neighbors, despite even the Pan-Americans [is culpable].

+**Pan-American,** *a.* Of or pertaining to North, Central, and South America as a whole. — **1889** *N.Y. Ev. Post* 27 Sept. 4/3 European Opinion on the Pan-American Congress. **1890** *World Almanac* 60 [A] Pan-American Conference . . . assembled at Washington, October 2, 1889, to consider . . . the formation of an American Customs Union. **1901** *Atlantic Mo.* July 90 Electricity plays, indeed, the predominant part in the Pan-American Exposition [at Buffalo]. **1907** *Am. Pol. Sci. Rev.* Feb. 192 The American governments to appoint . . . a permanent commission on Pan-American affairs.

+**Panamite.** (See quotation.) — **1835** TODD *Notes* 23 Pennsylvanians are also called *Panamites*, and a justice denominated *squire*.

Panax. A plant belonging to a genus (*Panax*) of perennial herbs of real or supposed medicinal value. {*c*1617-} Cf. GINSENG. — **1790** S. DEANE *New-Eng. Farmer* 203/1 *Panax, Ginseng, or Ninseng* . . . is a native of our country, and is become a considerable article of commerce. **1818** *Mass. H. S. Coll.* 2 Ser. VIII. 168 The latter part of May [in Plainfield, Mass.] appear . . . the beautiful three-leaved panax and the common ginseng.

***Pancake.**

***1.** A flat, thin cake made of batter fried on a griddle; a griddlecake; a flapjack. Also attrib.

1682 M. RAWLINSON *Narr. Captivity* 25 He gave me a Pancake, about as big as two fingers. **1748** ELIOT *Field-Husb.* i. 5 A soft Mud of the Consistence of Pan-cake Batter. **1805** *Pocumtuc Housewife* (1906) 6 In summer fried pudding is too heating. Pancakes with Cider and Sugar are better. **1886** EBBUTT *Emigrant Life* 81 We lived principally on fried pork and flap-jacks,—the latter a kind of pancake. **1903** 'O. HENRY' *Heart of West* 66 Mr. Judson, did you ever taste the pancakes that Miss Learight makes?

+**b.** A tortilla.

1872 POWERS *Afoot & Alone* 201 Mexicans . . . [live] on pancakes, beans, and red pepper.

+**2.** A cap shaped like a pancake.

1875 NADAL *Impressions of London Social Life* 143 The cap [pictured in McGuffey's Second Reader] was peculiar, though about the year '56 we had something like it called the 'Pancake.'

***Pandora's box.** A medical device. — **1721** *New-Eng. Courant* 7-14 Aug. 1/1 That they [inoculators] be compleatly armed with Incision-Lancet, Pandora's-Box, Nut-Shell and Fillet.

+**Pandowdy.** [Origin unknown.] A deep apple pie or pudding, seasoned usually with molasses. — ?**1805** *Pocumtuc Housewife* (1897) 25 (Ernst). **1830** S. SMITH *Life J. Downing* 101 You dont know how queer it looks to see . . . politics and pan-dowdy . . . jumbled up together. **1873** *Harper's Mag.* March 593/2 He should relish an old-fashioned pandowdy, such as his mother used to make forty years ago. **1893** LELAND *Memoirs* I. 74 Pan-dowdy—a kind of coarse and broken up apple-pie. **1895** COFFIN *Daughters of Revolution* 55*n.*, Pandowdy was a compote of apples, with several layers of pastry, made from rye meal, baked in a deep earthen dish and eaten with milk.

***Panel.** Also †**panell, pannel.**

***1.** A section of a fence, as the rails between two posts.

1661 *Southampton Rec.* II. 214 The said three partners . . . [shall] set up a panell of convenient barres that may be fit for footmen or horsemen, or cartes to goe through. **1686** in P. A. Bruce *Econ. Hist. Virginia* (1896) I. 318*n.*, Johnson . . . doth [impower you] . . . to fall, mall, and set up . . . 400 panels of sufficient post and rails. **1787** WASHINGTON *Diaries* III. 186 In the Neck 105 Pannels of Post and rail fencing . . . was compleated. **1833** *Niles' Reg.* XLIV. 263/1 Additional fencing was required, of about 1,800 pannels. **1856** *Mich. Agric. Soc. Trans.* VII. 808 Some farmers never stop to put up a panel that has blown or fallen down. **1898** PAGE *Red Rock* 187 He indicated the panel where Steve stood. **1909** *Dialect Notes* III. 355 *Panel* is never used in the sense of a single fence-rail in the South.

***2.** A list of jurors.

1705 BEVERLEY *Virginia* IV. 23 They give their Sheriff order the Morning before, to provide his Pannel. **1833** *Trial E. K. Avery* 9 The juror was affirmed, and put on the panel. **1890** LANGFORD *Vigilante Days* 107 The regular panel of jurors was exhausted.

+**Panel crib.** A prostitute's room provided with a secret entrance whereby a thief can enter; a house containing such rooms. — **1848** JUDSON *Mysteries N.Y.* I. 14 We will leave her to seek a victim for her panel-crib, for she has long been an active panel-thief. **1892** WALSH *Literary*

Curiosities 854 The lair of a panel-thief is called indiscriminately a panel-house, panel-crib, or panel-den.

Panel door. A door made of thin boards set into a framework. — **1742** *N.H. Hist. Soc. Coll.* II. 86 We now agree to have them [*sc.*, doors] done otherwise, even framed, or pannel doors. **1851** CIST *Cincinnati* 237 Every other building article, panel doors, . . . flooring-boards and plank, etc., will exhibit a proportionate saving.

+**Panel fence.** A fence constructed in sections. — **1800** TATHAM *Tobacco* 10 The *worm* or *pannel* fence, *originally of Virginia*, consists of malled rails. **1858** WARDER *Hedges & Evergreens* 113 A half-acre lot, with a seven-foot panel-fence on one side and a hedge on the other.

+**Panel game.** The trick or game of stealing by means of the panel crib. — **1868** M. H. SMITH *Sunshine & Shadow* 155 You lost your money in bad company by the panel game. **1910** J. HART *Vigilante Girl* 309 When the required deviltry is a little too raw—such as poisoning, or the panel-game—then big wigs like Bell or Tower hire thugs.

+**Panel house.** =PANEL CRIB. — **1848** JUDSON *Mysteries N.Y.* II. 44 This is a panel house, and I have led a bad, bad life for many a year. **1873** F. HUDSON *Journalism* 523 Descriptions of panel-houses and bagnios have since been published. **1882** MCCABE *New York* 487 Many of the street walkers are in the regular employ of the 'panel houses.'

Panel saw. A fine-toothed saw used in cutting out panels. {1815-} — **1754** *S.C. Gazette* 1 Jan. 2/2 Thomas Evance Has just imported . . . tenent, pannel and compass Saws. **1790** *Penna. Packet* 2 Jan. 4/2 To be sold by Poultney and Wistar . . . hand, pannel, tennant, . . . compass, and keyhole saw.

+**Panel thief.** One who participates in the panel game. — **1848** [see PANEL CRIB]. **1868** M. H. SMITH *Sunshine & Shadow* 306 The evidence showed that she was one of the most notorious panel-thieves in New York. **1882** MCCABE *New York* 488 If discovered, the panel thief endeavors to disable the victim.

Panelwork. {1847-} Woodwork consisting of thin boards set into a moulding or frame. {1874-} — **1813** *Ann. 13th Congress* 2 Sess. 2723 There shall be levied . . . on every coachee having pannel work in the upper division thereof, the yearly sum of ten dollars. **1851** CIST *Cincinnati* 160 The furniture of the chapter room is of mahogany, with Gothic open panel work, on a rich crimson satin ground. **1879** TAYLOR *Summer-Savory* 67 You see little square clearings set deep in the woods here and there, like panel-work. **1896** WILKINS *Madelon* 85 The high white panel-work around Dorothy's mantel was carved with curving garlands and festoons of ribbon and flowers.

+**Pan fish.**

1. A fish of such size and quality as to be suitable for frying in a pan.

1805 ORDWAY in *Jrnls. Lewis & O.* 272 [We] made a fish drag of willows and caught 520 fine pan fish. **1833** WATSON *Hist. Tales of Phila.* 49 Before the house flows a small but deep creek, abounding in pan-fish. **1851** SPRINGER *Forest Life* 57 The hooking of beautiful trout, pickerel, and other delicious pan-fish, afford agreeable relief. **1903** *N.Y. Ev. Post* 21 Sept., The catfish . . . is one of the best pan fishes.

2. 'The kingcrab, *Limulus polyphemus*' (*Cent.*).

Panhandle.

+**1.** Any arm of land or territory suggesting the shape of the handle of a pan, as the panhandle of West Virginia or of Texas.

1861 *Vanity Fair* 25 May 246/2 We will wrap the flag of our fathers around the 'Pan Handle' of Virginia, and upset the entire dish of Old Dominion Secession. **1873** *Newton Kansan* 13 March 2 Another road is proposed . . . to the pan-handle of Texas. **1881** HAYES *New Colorado* 157 One was . . . 'Flapjack Bill, the Pride of the Pan-handle.' **1897** J. STEELE *Klondike* 9 An arm of it [Alaska] runs southward in a long 'panhandle' about six hundred miles long, and of an average width of fifty miles. **1904** *St. Louis Globe-Dem.* 19 Nov. 8 Dunklin county, in the panhandle of the south-east corner of Missouri. **1917** GITTINGER *Formation of Okla.* 5 The Osage tribe relinquished to the United States all the land now included in Oklahoma except the Panhandle.

+**2.** A Pittsburgh-St. Louis railroad that runs across the panhandle of West Virginia. A nickname.

1868 FLINT *Railroads of U.S.* 125 The Pennsylvania Railroad Company has recently purchased the Pan-Handle, or Steubenville Railroad, extending from Pittsburg to Newark in Ohio. **1915** *Chicago D. News Almanac 1916* 632 Pittsburgh, Cincinnati, Chicago & St. Louis (Pan Handle).

+**3.** *attrib.* **a.** In sense 1 with *beat, country*, etc.

1851 J. J. HOOPER *Wid. Rugby's Husb.* 121, 'I want his hide . . . ,' said a fellow from Pan-Handle Beat. **1890** *Stock Grower & Farmer* 29 March 5/3 The panhandle country is settling up rapidly. It is a fine wheat country. **1894** *McClure's Mag.* III. 112/1 Its domain, including portions of nine Panhandle counties as big as small States, was taken by the company in payment for the Texas Capitol building. **1899** C. GRAHAM *Ipané* 178 Like . . . some Pan Handle town during the progress of a bar-room fight. **1902** 'O. HENRY' *Roads of Destiny* 256 The Pan-handle solon winds his muffler above his well-buttoned overcoat.

+**b.** In sense 2 with *engine, flyer, road.*

1875 SIPES *Penna. R. R.* 18 The Pittsburg and Steubenville Railroad . . . is commonly called the 'Pan-handle road,' from the fact that it runs through the strip of Western Virginia wedged in between the State of Pennsylvania and the Ohio river. **1877** 'E. MARTIN' *Hist. Great Riots* 78 This work was done by Pan-Handle engines. **1903** *N.Y. Times* 11 Dec. 3, 15 injured and one dead resulted from the wrecking of the east-bound Panhandle flyer this evening.

+**c.** *Panhandle (State)*, (see quotation).

1907 *Boston Transcript* 9 Nov., A list of the popular names of the States. . . . Panhandle—West Virginia.

+**Panhandler.** A beggar. *colloq.* — **1899** ADE *Doc' Horne* 255 He had 'sized' the hustler for a 'pan-handler' from the very start. **1903** *N.Y. Tribune* 27 Sept., A large number of pan-handlers . . . have been arrested for begging. **1925** *Lit. Digest* 11 July 50/2 You encourage the street panhandler and thieving idler to come here.

Panharmonicon. 'A mechanical musical instrument of the orchestrion class, invented by J. N. Maelzel in 1800' (*Cent.*). {1848-} — **1811** *Salem Gazette* 29 Nov., Sometimes the variety of nasal twangs produced a concert as entertaining as that of the Panharmonican [*sic*].

Panic. {1627-} A widespread fear concerning the financial and commercial soundness of a community; a business and financial depression. {1757-} — **1839** *Diplom. Corr. Texas* I. (1908) 413 This all makes the money market there gloomy and creates quite a stir—a panic here in the commercial community. **1877** JOHNSON *Anderson Co., Kansas* 192 The company has labored earnestly for the completion of the road, but the panic in money matters in 1873, and the active opposition . . . have prevented its success. **1900** *Congress. Rec.* 16 Jan. 881/2 During the late panic banks in New York loaned money as high as 100 per cent. **1911** *Dept. Agric. Yrbk.* 81 When the boll weevil came, bankers and business men lost confidence and extensive local panics resulted.

Panic grass. Any grass of the genus *Panicum;* also, the genus itself. {1668-} Often with defining term.

1791 MUHLENBERG *Index Florae* 160 *Panicum*, Panicgrass. **1814** BIGELOW *Florula Bostoniensis* 19 *Panicum sanguinale*, Purple panic grass. . . . Cultivated grounds. July, August. Annual. **1843** TORREY *Flora N.Y.* II. 425 *Panicum latifolium*, Broad-leaved Panic-grass. . . . Woods and moist thickets. **1894** COULTER *Bot. W. Texas* III. 501 *Panicum*. . . . (Panic-grass.) . . . The largest genus of grasses in Texas and having a larger number of species there than in all North America beside. **1901** MOHR *Plant Life Ala.* 355 Wiry Panic-Grass. . . . Exposed places in light soil.

Panicled, *a.* {1677-} In the specific names of plants: Having pedicels which form a panicle. — **1785** MARSHALL *Amer. Grove* 7 *Andromeda paniculata*. Panicled Andromeda. This shrub grows in boggy wet ground, rising from two or three to six or seven feet high. **1814** BIGELOW *Florula Bostoniensis* 39 *Cornus paniculata*. Panicled Cornel. . . . The berries or drupes are white. **1821** *Mass. H. S. Coll.* 2 Ser. IX. 149 *Cornus paniculata*, Panicled dog-wood [is indigenous to the township of Middlebury, Vt.]. **1843** TORREY *Flora N.Y.* I. 180 *Desmodium paniculatum*, Panicled Desmodium. . . . Dry woods, copses, and hill-sides.

+**Panic session.** The first session of the Twenty-third Congress. So called because of the financial distress which prevailed at the time. — **1854** BENTON *30 Years' View* I. 369/2 On the second day of December, 1833, commenced the first session of the Twenty-third Congress, commonly called the Panic session.

+**Panisee.** [Amer. Ind.] 'An Indian medicine-man or haman' (Hodge). — **1624** WINSLOW *Good Newes* 41 This caused one Pecksnot who was a *Pinese*, being a man of a notable spirit to come to Hobbamock. **1844** WHITTIER *Poetical Works* 27/1 For that chief had magic skill, And a Panisee's dark will, Over powers of good and ill.

+**Pan miner.** One who mines or separates gold with a miner's pan or rocker. — **1880** INGHAM *Digging Gold* 69 The gold [was] too unevenly distributed through them to pay the ordinary pan miner to wash it.

Panning. +The action of washing auriferous dirt in a pan. Frequently with *out.* Also attrib.

1848 DANA *Mineralogy* 317 The operation of hand washing is called in Virginia *panning*. **1850** AUDUBON *Western Journal* 211 These diggings . . . were completely riddled . . . by the hurried, superficial 'panning out' of the lucky American who came first and reaped his fortune. **1850** KINGSLEY *Diary* 122 Stoped down to day and made a panning trough to pour quicksilver from the riffler into. **1872** 'MARK TWAIN' *Roughing It* 443 '*Panning out*' refers to the washing process by which the grains of gold are separated from the dirt. **1880** INGHAM *Digging Gold* 54 The Panning Process, consists of a tin or sheet-iron pan [etc.]. **1882** *47th Congress 1 Sess.* H. R. Ex. Doc. No. 216, 568 F. A. Huntinton, of San Francisco, manufactures this rocking and panning amalgamator for saving fine gold and floured mercury. **1908** E. S. MEADE *Story of Gold* 39 A small amount of gold is still taken out by the simple process of panning.

+**Panoche.** [Mex. Sp. *panocha.*] **1.** A Mexican sugar made from cane. **2.** A kind of brown-sugar candy. — **(1) 1848** BRYANT *California* xxxv. 408 A large amount of sugar cane is grown, from which is made panoche, a favorite sugar with the natives. **1854** BARTLETT *Personal Narr.* I. 269 Each man . . . [carries] half a pound of panoche, the coarse brown sugar of the country. **1887** *Outing* April 10/2 It is ordinarily made of corn, roasted and crushed and slightly sweetened, the most common sweetening being *panoche*, a crude sugar. **(2) 1871** *Rep. Indian Affairs* (1872) 359, I doubt the good policy of issuing bread, and at times candy (panoche,) to the pupils. **1921** M. L. MATTHEWS *Foods & Cookery* 274 Panocha. . . . Mix sugar, milk, and salt. Boil until it reaches the 'soft-ball' stage.

Panorama. A long picture which is exhibited by being rolled out a part at a time; a cyclorama or long picture which encircles the spectator. {1796-} Cf. MOVING PICTURE 1. — **1854** *Holyoke Diaries* 188 Hitty & I went to see Panorama of Niagara falls. **1859** *S. Lit. Messenger* XXIX.

151/1 What is most improperly called a 'Panorama,' a long moving picture of striking scenery or imposing events. **1865** *Atlantic Mo.* XV. 39/1 Suppose we let Eunice take the children to the panorama to-morrow. **1871** 'MARK TWAIN' *Sk., New & Old* 296 There was a fellow traveling around . . . with a moral-religious show—a sort of scriptural panorama.

+**Pan pie.** =PANDOWDY. — **1805** *Pocumtuc Housewife* (1906) 25. **1862** 'G. HAMILTON' *Country Living* 70 No pan-pie with hot brown bread on Sunday morning. **1882** *Maine Bd. Agric. Rep.* XXVI. 403 You have all heard of the pan-dowdy, or pan-pie, the pride of our grandmothers.

+**Pansaje.** Also **pansage.** *Texas.* [Mex. Sp.] A barbecue serving the middle part of an animal. — **1893** *Galveston News* 11 Feb. (Th.), A pansaje where all could refresh the inner man. **1902** CLAPIN 300 *Pansage.* In Texas, a feast or 'barbecue' for men exclusively, in which the 'pauza' [*sic*], or body of the animal is barbecued.

***Pansy.** A cultivated garden plant (*Viola tricolor hortensis*), with variously colored flowers; the flower of this plant. — **1817-8** EATON *Botany* (1822) 514 *Viola tricolor*, garden violet, hearts-ease, pansy. **1832** S. J. HALE *Flora* 119 Pansey, *Viola, tricolor.* . . . A European species of the violet but cultivated here. **1877** *Harper's Mag.* March 561/2 Here was a peculiarly lovely child . . . coming up the little yard like a fashionable Flora, with . . . clusters of velvet pansies. **1913** LONDON *Valley of Moon* 190 She saw the strikers leaping the fence, trampling her few little geraniums and pansies into the earth.

Pantalets. Also **pantalettes, pantaletts.** *pl.*

1. a. Long loose drawers, worn by girls and women, esp. in the period 1830–1850, having a frill or ruffle at the bottom of each leg {1857-}; hence, any bloomers, trousers, or the like worn by women. **b.** A detachable ruffle used to lengthen the legs of a pair of drawers.

1834 *Knickerb.* IV. 117 In their blushing girlhood, they assume the *pantalettes*, or little pantaloons. **1838** *S. Lit. Messenger* IV. 28/1 Two pretty sisters, in pantalettes, waited on table. **1854** H. H. RILEY *Puddleford* 25 Most of the women had something frizzled around their shoes, which were called pantalettes. **1882** *Harper's Mag.* March 557/2 All the women [on Beaver Island, a Mormon kingdom] were compelled to wear the short skirts and ample pantalets of the Bloomer costume.

2. In transf. or allusive senses.

1846 T. B. THORPE *Myst. Backwoods* 21 Said traveller stated he had seen a piano somewhere in New England with pantalettes on. **1853** B. F. TAYLOR *Jan. & June* 85 Hens with Camwood-colored pantalettes. **1883** *Harper's Mag.* July 246/1 Each [chimney] ending in a violent mitred decoration, reminding one of nothing so much as of the paper pantalets which adorn the broiled lamb chop. **1884** NYE *Baled Hay* 138 The full . . . swell and broad cincha of the chaparajo have given place to the tight pantaletts [a pair of chaps].

Pantaloonery. {1821-} +'The particular description of fabrics from which pantaloons are made' (B. '59). — **1857** *Seaboard Towns* (Ernst), A good stock of cloths, pantaloonery, vestings &c.

***Pantaloons.** *pl.* **a.** 'A species of close long trowsers extending to the heels' (W. '28), sometimes fastened by straps running under the shoes or boots. {pantalooned, 1798; 1806-7-} +**b.** Any pair of trousers. *Obs.*

'In U.S. . . . this use [sense b] may have been independently taken directly from F. *pantalon*, a1800' (*O.E.D.*).

1803 *Austin P.* I. (1924) 89, 2 Silk pattern pantaloons. **1805** *Ann. 9th Congress* 2 Sess. 1083 The dress of the men is, close leather pantaloons, and a hunting shirt, or frock of the same. **1817** PAULDING *Lett. from South* I. 56 One pair of pantaloons, so immeasurably wide and loose you could hardly tell whether they were petticoats or not. **1820** *Niles' Reg.* XVII. 335/1 Proposals are issued for furnishing 1000 coats, 2000 pair of pantaloons, 4000 shirts, . . . and 1000 do. trowsers. **1839** LEONARD *Adventures* (1904) 77 Some of the men had the front part of their pantaloons lined with deer skin. **1852** *Knickerb.* XXXIX. 163 He wore . . . the tight pantaloons which were in vogue at that date. **1855** BRISTED in *Cambridge Ess.* 65 Pantaloons for trousers, and hat for bonnet, are obvious Gallicisms (pantalon and chapeau). **1865** *Atlantic Mo.* XV. 55 His dandies wear straps to their tight pantaloons in lieu of pegtops. **1887** CUSTER *Tenting on Plains* 206 The regulation white pantaloons, . . . being of duck, are easily creased. **1916** EASTMAN *From Deep Woods* 21 Their pantaloons belonged neither to the order *short* nor to the *long*.

Panter.** [Var. of PANTHER.] + =PANTHER 1. *dial.* Also fig. and attrib. — **1845** HOOPER *Simon Suggs' Adv.* 47 We didn't make quite as much noise as a panter and a pack of hounds. *a1846** *Quarter Race Ky.* 95 I'd a gin you a touch of panter fistcuffs—a sort of cross of the scratch on the bite—and a powerful strong game it is, in a close fight. **1848** W. T. THOMPSON *Major Jones's Sk. Travel* 114 (Th.), I staggered up agin the lamp-post, and held on to [the baby], while it kicked and squalled like a young panter.

***Panther.**

See also PAINTER, PANTER.

+**1. a.** The cougar. **b.** Less commonly, the jaguar.

1683 PENN *Works* (1782) IV. 304 The creatures . . . that are natural to these parts, are the wild cat, panther, otter, wolf [etc.]. **1709** LAWSON *Carolina* 26 Numbers of Panthers, Tygers, Wolves, and other Beasts of Prey . . . take this Swamp for their Abode in the Day. **1714** *N.J. Archives* XIII. 552 An Act for Encourageing the Killing of Woolves Panthers and Red Foxes. **1764** H. GRACE *Hist. Life & Sufferings* 35 The Panther is a very furious Creature, and will lie upon the Branch of a Tree till Deer come by, when he will jump on them. [**1774** GOLDSMITH *Hist. Earth* III. 252 The Jaguar or Panther of America.] **1836** EDWARD *Hist. Texas* 74 The panther a species of the tiger, and the spotted leopard, are not so very shy. **1846** *Spirit of Times* (N.Y.) 11 July 230/3 The animal is the Couga or Puma, (*Felis concotor*) commonly called in this country the Panther, and is the largest and most formidable of the Cat kind in North America. **1872** *Harper's Mag.* Dec. 30/2 The mountain lion—which is here [in Colo.] sometimes met with—is the panther or cougar of the Eastern States. **1901** *Rev. of Reviews* XXIV. 311/2 The panther is occasionally seen.

+**2.** Attrib. with *ledge, skin.*

1842 *Nat. Hist. N.Y., Zoology* I. 48 The Panther . . . prefers for its usual retreat, ledges of rocks inaccessible to man, which are known familiarly to the hunters under the name of *panther ledges.* **1846** SAGE *Scenes Rocky Mts.* viii, Taking from him his bow, arrows, and panther-skin quiver.

+**Panties.** *pl.* [Diminutive of PANTS.] A pair of drawers. — **1845** *Knickerb.* XXVI. 433 If your panties weren't sheeted home at the bottom, you'd out-jump a monkey. **1848** BURTON *Waggeries* 19, I hadn't on nothin' . . . only a blue cotting shirt and sail-cloth pantys.

Pantile. A curved roofing tile. {1640-} — **1687** *Doc. Hist. N.Y. State* I. 163 Upon all other merchandizes imported into the province . . . the summ of forty shillings . . . for every hundred pounds valued at the prime cost except . . . Salt, Brick, Pan-tyles, Coals [etc.]. **1691** *N.Y. Gen. Assembly Jrnl.* I. 7/2 All Merchandizes exported, to pay Two *per Cent.* prime Cost, except Salt, Bricks, Pantiles, Coals. **1749** in Singleton *Social N.Y.* 31 Several houses in this town have been tiled with very good pantiles made at Albany, as cheap as they could be had from Holland.

***Pantomime.**

1. A dramatic piece or performance in which the story is told, at least in part, by dumb show. {1739-} Also attrib.

The pantomimes which are a traditional feature of the English stage at Christmas time are practically unknown in the United States.

1739 *N.Y. Wkly. Jrnl.* 5 Feb. 4/2 On Monday the 12th of February will be performed A New Pantomime Entertainment . . . call'd the Adventures of Harlequin and Scaramouch or the Spaniard Trick'd. **1750** *New York Post-Boy* 5 Nov., This Evening Sir *Harry Wildair* will be perform'd, with the Pantomime. **1809** IRVING *Knickerb.* I. iv, I have often beheld the clown in a pantomime . . . [gaze] in stupid wonder at the extravagant gambols of a harlequin. **1832** DUNLAP *Hist. Amer. Theatre* 56 This clause prohibited the erecting of any 'playhouse, stage, or scaffold' for the purpose of acting any kind of dramatic work, enumerating them from the tragedy to the pantomime. **1879** ROE *Army Lett.* 218 Her pantomime, 'John Smith,' . . . was far and away the best part of the entertainment. **1917** N. A. SMITH *Plays, Pantomimes & Tableaux for Children* Pref.,The miniature plays, pantomimes and tableaux which compose this little book were written . . . for an equally miniature stage.

+**2.** *Pantomime dance*, a ceremonial entertainment performed by certain Indian tribes.

1765 TIMBERLAKE *Memoirs* 80 [The Cherokees] are likewise very dexterous at pantomime dances; several of which I have seen performed that were very diverting.

***Pantry.** A room or closet in which provisions, sometimes plate and linen, are kept. — **1654** *Harvard Rec.* I. 208 The building . . . [contains] a Pantry & small corne Chamber. **1710** *N.J. Archives* 1 Ser. IV. 13 A pantry with dressers and shelves . . . is under lock and key. **1831** PECK *Guide* 247 A boarding-house, including a dining hall, fifteen feet by thirty, two kitchens, a pantry, and two chambers for the use of the family. **1907** *St. Nicholas* Aug. 958/1 Annie had put the pies in the pantry to cool.

Pants. *pl. colloq.*

1. Pantaloons; trousers. {1853-} Also attrib.

'Chiefly U.S.' (*O.E.D.*).

1840 *Picayune* 12 Aug. 2/6 A dark mulatto boy named Bob . . . had on a pair of black pants, taking a pair of white ones with him. **1843** *Knickerb.* XXII. 594 It irks us, however, to encounter in a description of Mr. Legare's dress the term 'pants' instead of pantaloons. **1863** NORTON *Army Lett.* 137, I was sitting by the fire smoking a cigar, when I felt something twitch at my pants' leg. **1896** *Boston Jrnl.* 16 Feb. 145 About 1500 pantsmakers held a meeting in New Irving Hall yesterday afternoon. **1920** SANDBURG *Smoke & Steel* 25 He wore cool cream pants.

+**2.** =PANTALETS 1.

1851 *Washington Telegraph* in *Illustr. London News* 19 July 86/1 Garments as graceful and becoming as are the 'frock and pants' [*i.e.*, the bloomer costume].

***Pap.**[1] +Political patronage; revenue from public office. Also comb. — **1841** *Congress. Globe* App. 29 Jan. 300/2 The very new *States* are nursed from their chrysalis territorial condition into existence upon Federal pap from the Executive spoon. **1856** CARTWRIGHT *Autobiog.* 503 What do they care, if they can ride triumphantly into office and suck the public pap? **1863** *Rio Abajo Press* 17 Feb. 2/2 Our good-for-nothing, Government pap-sucking goslings. **1894** *Voice* 6 Sept., The Prohibition Party is the only party that is not controlled by public pap-seeking politicians and the debauching power of the saloon.

+**Pap.**[2] An abbreviation of *papa. dial.* — **1844** *Knickerb.* XXIII. 15 They said, pap wasn't at home. **1872** *Harper's Mag.* March 551/1 Your good-for-nothing pap's bound to let him have it, too, unless you stop him. **1899** *Mo. So. Dakotan* I. 200, I reckon an' you'll be welcome to come an' spark her or argy with her pap. **1925** TILGHMAN *Dugout* 51 But she died, and Pap said a girl shouldn't know books anyhow.

+**Papabotte.** *La.* [Creole origin.] (See quot. 1917.) — **1887** *Harper's Mag.* Feb. 349/2 There was . . . the papabotte, a favorite on New Orleans tables in the autumn. **1917** *Birds of Amer.* I. 247 Upland Plover. *Bartramia longicauda.* . . . [Also called] Prairie Snipe; Papabotte; Quaily.

***Papaw.** Also †**papau.**

See also PAWPAW.

+**1.** The oblong, edible, yellowish fruit of the American papaw tree.

Cf. CUSTARD APPLE a.

1728 *Boston Rec.* 224 No Person or Persons what soever [shall] Presume to play . . . with Shells, or Papaws or any thing of that nature. **1792** IMLAY *Western Territory* 211 Papaw. This fruit . . . is in shape more like a seed cucumber than any thing else. **1807** C. SCHULTZ *Travels* I. 144 The only fruits I have met with, with which you are unacquainted, are the mandrake and papaw. **1822** WOODS *English Prairie* (1904) 308 Papaws, or pawpaws, grow in clusters of three or four on a shrub 20 feet high. **1885** M. THOMPSON *Byways & Bird Notes* 100 Next to the muscadine among wild fruits I rate the papaw as best. **1897** W. E. BARTON *Hero in Homespun* 335 Bringing with her the first ripe papaws.

+**2.** = PAPAW TREE.

1709 LAWSON *Carolina* 105 The Papau is not a large Tree. **1785** WASHINGTON *Diaries* II. 347 Planted my Cedars, all my Papaw, and two Honey locust Trees in my Shrubberies. **1819** E. EVANS *Pedestrious Tour* 284 The papaw resembles the locust. **1834** PECK *Gaz. Illinois* 13 The undergrowth are redbud, papaw, sumach [etc.]. **1894** TORREY *Fla. Sketch-Book* 125 One of the smaller papaws, or custard-apples, a low shrub, just then full of large, odd-shaped, creamy-white, heavy-scented blossoms.

+**b.** The wood or bark of the papaw tree.

1886 *Harper's Mag.* June 58/2 Traces are made of hickory or papaw, as also are bed-cords.

3. Attrib. with *bush, whistle.*

See also PAPAW TREE.

1785 WASHINGTON *Diaries* II. 444 Sent to Mr. Digges for Papaw Bushes to replace the dead ones in my Shrubberies. **1872** EGGLESTON *End of World* 77 As for papaw whistles, why, I say Jericho wouldn't a-tumbled for no such music.

Papaw tree. {1704–} +Any one of various North American trees or shrubs of the genus *Asimina*, esp. *A. triloba.* — **1733** BYRD *Journey to Eden* (1901) 314 We also saw in this place abundance of papa trees, the wood whereof the Indians make very dry on purpose to rub fire out of it. **1785** MARSHALL *Amer. Grove* 9 Papaw Tree, or Custard Apple. **1801** *Hist. Review & Directory* I. 10 At a place call Musquito Inlet, the high lands are covered with Cabbage, Papaw trees, and other Tropical plants. **1842** BUCKINGHAM *Slave States* II. 364 The papaw tree . . . is sometimes called the Indian fig-tree. The fruit is something like a cucumber.

***Paper,** *n.*

I. ***1.** A substance made into thin flexible sheets from various fibrous materials, as rags, wood, bark, etc.

1676 *Conn. Rec.* III. 500 Disbursements for paper, wax, books. **1698** THOMAS *Penna. & N.J.* 42 All sorts of very good Paper are made in the German-Town. **1771** FRANKLIN *Autobiog.* 308, I sometimes brought home the paper I purchas'd at the stores thro' the streets on a wheelbarrow. **1839** *Mass. Acts & Resolves* 6 [They] are hereby made a corporation . . . for the purpose of manufacturing paper from beach grass. **1903** *Scientific Amer.* 14 Nov. 340/2 A manufacturer of paper [informs us] that the average spruce tree yields a little less than half a cord of wood, which is equivalent to 500 pounds of paper.

b. Special forms of this suited to different uses, as for covering a wall or wrapping a package. {1712–}

1764 in E. Singleton *Social N.Y.* 43 The Dining-Room is 14×19, hung with genteel Paper; the Entry or Passage from the Door, is hung with the same. **1771** *Copley-Pelham Lett.* 152 Only get the neet low prised papers . . . and with the Border the Rooms will look well. **1867** *Rep. Comm. Patents 1865* I. 558 Cigarette paper coated on one side with an adhesive substance, dried. **1883** *Century Mag.* Oct. 819/2 [Olive oil] is filtered through six layers of cotton batting, then through one of French paper, before it is bottled.

c. *On paper*, as set down in writing or print; in theory; merely planned.

1788 *Amer. Museum* III. 336/2 The form of [the Dutch] constitution, as it is on paper, admits not of coercion. But necessity introduced it in practice. **1791** MORRIS in Sparks *Life G. Morris* II. 144 They muster an army, on paper, of 100,000 men. **1884** *Harper's Mag.* May 879/1 As yet the railroad is all 'on paper.'

+**2.** A ballot made of paper. *Obs.*

Cf. PAPER VOTE.

1643 *Plymouth Laws* 74 In every Towne there [shall] be three or foure men chosen by writing their names in papers as the majestrates are chosen to rate all the Inhabitants. *a***1649** WINTHROP *Hist.* I. 143 The inhabitants of Boston met to choose seven men who should divide the town lands among them. They chose by papers. **1660** *Springfield Rec.* I. 267 And ye Moderator shall always be chosen by Papers.

3. A printed or written essay or article on some particular subject. {1669–}

1671 SEWALL *Letter Book* I. 18 Sir Bayly tells me, that Mr. Wheelwright read the printed paper on a Lecture-day. **1744** FRANKLIN *Acct. Fire-Places* 2 The New Fire-Places are a late Invention . . . of which this Paper is intended to give a Particular Account. **1874** *Vt. Bd. Agric. Rep.* II. 200 Few . . . of the hard-handed farmers could be induced to prepare and read papers at the meetings.

4. A newspaper. {1642–}

1690 *Publick Occurrences* (Boston) 25 Sept. 1/1 The Publisher of these *Occurrences* . . . will in this Paper . . . expose the Name [of the spreader of a false report]. **1719** *Amer. Wkly. Mercury* 22 Dec. 2/2 This Paper will be Publish'd Weekly, and shall contain an Impartial account of Transactions, in the Several States of *Europe, America,* &c. **1789** *Low Politician Outwitted* I. i, There's never anything in this paper but what's on your side of the question. **1866** 'F. KIRKLAND' *Bk. Anecdotes* 226/2 Leading Republican papers also loudly denounced him. **1900** *Congress. Rec.* 31 Jan. 1368/2 A paper in Mississippi said it was sorry to see the campaign starting off with such acrimony. **1917** SINCLAIR *King Coal* 250 Bert Atkins . . . the papers referred to as a 'club-man.'

5. +**a.** = PAPER CURRENCY a. **b.** = PAPER CURRENCY b. {*a*1674–}

*c***1720** *Mass. Bay Currency Tracts* 380 A paper bank can't be as good as the bank of England or Holland til paper is as good as Silver. **1767** FRANKLIN *Writings* V. 10 Then the rising of Silver above Paper to that Height of additional Value . . . may be called a Depreciation of the Paper. **1797** *Ann. 5th Congress* I. 410 Mr. Otis supposed that at least two-thirds of the whole amount of paper issued by the banks, returned and were reissued every year. **1819** in Mackenzie *Life Van Buren* 162 The credit of the paper is very low in this country—hardly any one takes it at par. **1840** *Picayune* 28 July 4/1 All . . . will be sold cheap for cash or approved paper. **1860** *Ill. Agric. Soc. Trans.* IV. 37 A resolution was passed loaning Mr. Fawkes $1,000 on his own paper. **1872** POWERS *Afoot & Alone* 102, I gave her a small piece of the current paper of the Republic. **1900** *Congress. Rec.* 17 Feb. 1897/2 At such times gilt-edged paper can be placed in the money centers at a small per cent.

6. +**a.** A playing card.

1842 *S. Lit. Messenger* VIII. 412/1, I found myself . . . around a table in a corner, and the 'papers' in motion. **1862** NORTON *Army Lett.* 41 Those whose tastes incline them that way are playing with the 'spotted papers.' **1894** MASKELYNE *Sharps & Flats* 43 In America . . . one may still find 'saloons' which are stocked entirely with this kind of 'paper' as the cards are called.

b. A poster or placard.

1878 *Harper's Mag.* March 599/2 Struggling families who have 'one room to let,' or . . . a modest paper in a window 'Boarders wanted.' **1896** *N.Y. Dramatic News* 18 July 12/1 Car No. 6 . . . was here July 7–8, posting very attractive paper, which reads 'coming soon.'

7. *pl.* Curl papers. {1876}

1854 M. J. HOLMES *Tempest & Sunshine* 201 Father's beard will probably be long enough to do up in papers. **1873** PHELPS *Trotty's Wedding* i, Miss Merle Higgins's mother did up Miss Merle's hair in papers over night.

II. *attrib.* and *comb.* **8. a.** Designating things cut out, or intended to be cut out, of paper.

1687 SEWALL *Diary* I. 173 Some officers have red paper Crosses fastened to their Hats. **1866** A. D. WHITNEY *L. Goldthwaite* xiii, Her rosy little face and wilful curls came out of each [dress] prettier than the last, precisely as a paper dolly's does. **1879** HOWELLS *Lady of Aroostook* 7 She stood upright, the slim and elegant shape . . . clothed with the stylishness that instinctive taste may evoke, even in a hill town, from study of paper patterns.

b. Designating containers made of paper.

1780 *N.J. Archives* 2 Ser. IV. 193 To be sold, . . . a quantity of excellent Lamp Black, in neat paper barrels. **1869** *Boyd's Business Directory* 12 Howlett Brothers, paper bags. **1869** *Rep. Comm. Patents 1868* I. 818/2 Paper Cask. . . . Each edge of the paper cylinder has a metallic band [etc.]. **1872** *Pat. Off. Gazette* 30 April 424/1 Paper Pail. . . . A water-pail or other like vessel made of paper-pulp.

c. Designating garments and household articles, etc. made of paper, or fabrics similar to paper.

1809 IRVING *Knickerb.* VI. viii, Little urchins . . . followed in droves after the drums, with paper caps on their heads. **1812** *Niles' Reg.* I. 328/1 Many . . . have ordered their floors to be immediately covered with paper carpets. **1840** *Knickerb.* XVI. 18 Our hero . . . took particular notice of . . the green paper curtains at the windows. **1852** *Ib.* XXXIX. 153 Fans . . . were in constant use, from nine-penny palm-leafs to two-shilling paper-spreads. **1867** *Rep. Comm. Patents 1866* II. 692 A new article of manufacture, a paper shirt. **1870** MEDBERY *Men Wall St.* 23 A broker cannot . . . innocently fling a 'paper dart' at a neighbor without being amerced ten dollars. **1878** ROE *Army Lett.* 186 Then I made a Mother Hubbard apron of white paper-cambric. **1885** *Harper's Mag.* Feb. 455/1 The Allen Paper Car-wheel Company claims a capacity of fifteen thousand paper car-wheels a year. **1888** *N.Y. Mercury* 21 July (F.), Paper garments for ladies is the very latest.

+**9.** Designating various phenomena arising from the use of paper as money.

1691 C. MATHER in *Mass. Bay Currency Tracts* 17 If neither Silver can be had, nor Corn brought in without loss both to the Government and People, what remains but Accounts, Bills, or such like Paper-pay? *c*1720 Paper bank [see PAPER *n.* 5]. **1820** FLINT *Lett. from Amer.* 193 A run on the paper shops commenced; and a suspension of specie payments soon became general. **1838** *N.Y. Advertiser & Exp.* 11 April 3/1 The cry . . . of the Loco Focos in this City is, 'Rag Barons—no paper aristocracy . . . Andrew Jackson and Thomas Humbug Benton.' **1876** *Scribner's Mo.* Jan. 432/2 The good sense of the people and the good faith of the people will have a voice, and the 'paper lie' will go into everlasting disgrace. **1900** *Congress. Rec.* 18 Jan. 944/2 The people of the United States will be upon a paper basis in part at least, and that will be paper issued by the banks.

10. Designating various things, persons, or actions related to the manufacture of paper.

1766 in Buckingham *Newspaper Lit.* I. 35 The Bell Cart will go through Boston before the end of next month, to collect Rags for the Paper-Mill at Milton, when all people that will encourage the Paper Manufactory, may dispose of them. **1820** FLINT *Lett. from Amer.* 196 Many of the paper manufacturers were obliged to suspend specie payments. **1842** *Niles' Nat. Reg.* 12 March 29 Mr. Simmons presented a memorial from paper manufacture[r]s, asking for protection. **1858** HALE *If, Yes, & Perhaps* (1868) 120 The child had been building cob-houses out of lucifer-matches in a paper warehouse. **1867** HOLMES *Guardian Angel* 297 [The poems go] to the paper factory, where they have a horrid machine they call the devil, that tears everything to bits. **1891** CHASE & CLOW *Industry* II. 93 The sisters saw their stems or straws carried away to the straw-workers and paper-makers, or sold for bedding for the cattle.

11. Designating various articles used in handling or holding office papers, letters, or the like.

1857 *Rep. Comm. Patents 1856* II. 348 Improved Paper Clip. . . . The outer cylinder is made to slide over the inner cylinder [etc.]. **1859** STOWE *Minister's Wooing* xxvii, [He] took the letter, . . . laid it on the table, and put a heavy paper-weight over it. **1861** WINTHROP *C. Dreeme* 200 The antique dagger you use for a paper-cutter has rust marks. **1866** *Rep. Comm. Patents 1864* I. 617 This invention consists of an ornamental paper fastener. **1875** KNIGHT 1621/2 Paper-file, a device to hold letters or other papers in a pack. **1880** 'MARK TWAIN' *Tramp Abroad* 389 That hat was as stubborn as any paper-knife could have been.

12. Special combinations.

+*Paper boom*, a boom promoted by schemes and plans that exist only on paper; +*p.-carrier*, a person who delivers newspapers; +*p. farmer*, a person who has theories on farming and farm problems, but no practical experience; *p. hunt*, a game in which certain players drop bits of paper to aid others in attempting to trail them down {1871}; *p. sand*, sand suitable for sandpaper.

1887 *Courier-Journal* 8 Jan. 4/4 [The article] was a general description of how paper booms are worked by sharpers upon fools. **1855** COOKE *Ellie* 22 In all their occupations, as newsboys, paper-carriers, errand-runners, . . . Beau Sam or Sam Beau . . . was easily the chief and leader. **1873** *Winfield* (Kan.) *Courier* 22 May 2/2 The 'Grange' organizations and 'paper farmer's club' are good enough in their way. **1893** *Harper's Mag.* April 680/1 Country clubs and hounds, aniseseed bags and beagles, paper hunts and al fresco breakfasts—all these made the poor old picnic . . . seek the deep shadows of a remote and somewhat impecunious past. **1819** SCHOOLCRAFT *Mo. Lead Mines* 67 The ore . . . is sometimes used in this state as paper-sand, for which it is an elegant substitute.

***Paper**, *v.*

1. *tr.* To put wall paper on the walls and ceiling of (a room or house). {1774–}

1763 in H. M. Brooks *Gleanings* 34 Benjamin Russell . . . undertakes Papering Rooms and Stair-Cases in the best Manner. **1771** *Copley-Pelham Lett.* 151, I should be glad, that you would instruct me . . . about painting and papering the [house]. **1786** WASHINGTON *Diaries* III. 114 Began to Paper the yellow room this day. **1912** *Ladies' H. Jrnl.* Aug. 17/2 The other rooms took longer. Some of them I painted and papered myself.

2. To supply with paper.

1883 *N.Y. Ev. Post* 13 May, The paper-manufacturers are able to paper the country for a year in something less than a year.

+**3.** *To paper out*, to keep (the cold wind) out by the use of paper.

1855 ROPES *6 Mos. in Kan.* 87 We must paper out the cold wind.

Paper bill. {1670–} +A piece of paper currency, esp. one issued by the colonial and the continental governments. — **1716** *N.J. Archives* 1 Ser. IV. 270 If paper bills were made, to the vallue of twenty thousand pounds [etc.]. **1738** *Boston Rec.* 201 We Injoin You . . . That the Funds be laid in Paper Bills of the Old Tenor, and not in Bills of the New Tenor, redeemable in Silver and Gold. **1740** in *Mass. Hist. Soc. Proc.* V. 123 Paper bills . . . are issued by the Governor and Council. **1786** D. HUMPHREYS, etc. *Anarchiad* (1861) 15 Fraud, tendry, paper bills, whate'er thy name; That medium . . . By which great villains flourish. **1796** MORSE *Univ. Geog.* I. 323 [The introduction of a plentiful supply of specie] accelerated the depreciation of paper bills.

+**Paper birch.** =CANOE BIRCH. — **1810** MICHAUX *Arbres* I. 25 *Paper birch* (Bouleau à papier). **1832** BROWNE *Sylva* 121 This tree . . . is known to the Americans . . . [as] Paper Birch. **1861** WINTHROP *Open Air* 49 The white-birch, paper birch, canoe-birch, grows large in moist spots near the stream where it is needed. **1903** WHITE *Forest* 193 Farther along there would be a point of high land and delightful little paper-birches.

+**Paper blockade.** A blockade that is proclaimed but not made effective. — **1803** *Ann. 7th Congress* 2 Sess. 129 Paper blockades were substituted for actual ones, and the staple commodities of our country lay perishing in our store-houses. **1812** *Ann. 12th Congress* 1 Sess. 2206 The extension on paper, for whatever purpose intended, favors the principle of paper blockades. **1814** *Ann. 13th Congress* 2 Sess. 1479 It was their *paper* blockades against which this Government contended. **1862** KETTELL *Hist. Rebellion* I. 124 [Jefferson Davis] denounced the proclamation of the United States in relation to Southern ports, as a mere paper blockade.

Paper box. A box made of paper. Also attrib. — **1757** *Lett. to Washington* II. 80 Paper Box of Tarsils . . . 1. **1869** *Boyd's Business Directory* 460 H. Lettington, Manufacturer of Paper Boxes. **1913** LONDON *Valley of Moon* I. xi, As if I didn't know . . . how long you worked in . . . the paper-box factory.

+**Paper city.** A town or city, sometimes existent only on a promoter's map, represented to be larger or more important than it is; a town planned but not built. (Cf. CITY 2.) — **1860** GREELEY *Overland Journey* 36 The manufacture of paper-cities and bogus corner-lots [in Kan.] . . . is not half so mischievous as the grasping of whole townships [etc.]. **1861** *Ladies' Repository* Oct. 640 The majority [of the cities on the upper Mississippi], however, are of that species extensively known as 'paper cities.' **1871** GROSVENOR *Protection* 38 Loans and paper-money alike had corner lots in paper cities for their only security. **1878** BEADLE *Western Wilds* 365 The Pacific Railroad was pushing westward, and paper cities were springing up along its way.

Paper collar. A collar made of paper in imitation of linen. Also attrib. — **1872** BRACE *Dangerous Classes N.Y.* 356 There are from one thousand five hundred to two thousand children . . . employed in . . . the manufacture of paper collars. **1888** BILLINGS *Hardtack* 105 He is the paper-collar young man, just from the recruiting station.

Paper credit. Credit given on some written security; an instrument of credit, as an I.O.U. or a bank draft. {*a*1697–} Also attrib. — **1739** W. DOUGLASS *Discourse Currencies* 5 Depreciating of the Value . . . by a late Contrivance of a depreciating Paper-Credit-Currency. **1846** *Georgia Messenger* 24 Dec., Those carpet-bag gentry . . . are wandering through upper Georgia with the view of forcing into circulation the *paper credits* of the Carolina Banks. **1858** HOLMES *Autocrat* 42 Life would be nothing without paper-credit and other fictions.

+**Paper currency. a.** Paper money issued by a government; legal tender notes. **b.** Negotiable documents, esp. bank notes, that pass from hand to hand as money.

1723 *Amer. Wkly. Mercury* 7 Nov. 2/2 The natural Situation of these Counties and the Practice of our Neighbours, has laid us [of Penna.] under the necessity of coming into a Paper Currency. **1739** *Boston Rec.* 225 Our neighboring Governments, especially Rhode Island, are daily Rivalling of Us in Our Trade, and Medium of Paper Currency. **1752** *Md. Gazette* 30 July, At his Store in Annapolis . . . may be had, great Variety of European and East India Goods, . . . for Bills of Exchange, Gold, Sterling, Paper Currency, or Tobacco. **1776** *Battle of Brooklyn* I. i, He has been my evil genius, ever since I was concerned with him in counterfeiting paper currency. **1807** A. BANCROFT *Life Washington* (1808) 218 The depreciation of the paper currency had reduced the pay of the American officers to a pittance. **1839** VAN BUREN in *Pres. Mess. & P.* III. 542 An irredeemable and depreciated paper currency is entailed upon the people by a large portion of the banks. **1857** BUCHANAN in *Pres. Mess. & P.* V. 437 So long as the amount of the paper currency . . . of the country shall be left to the discretion of 1,400 irresponsible banking institutions. **1900** *Congress. Rec.* 4 Jan. 653/1 With the habits of our people and their preference for the use of paper currency wherever possible instead of gold and silver coinage [etc.].

+**Paper dollar.** A piece of paper money bearing a face value of one dollar. — **1778** *N.H. Hist. Soc. Coll.* IX. 108, I have been for Some time receiving old Silver Debts paid numerically in paper Dollars which for some time past has been but a quarter & now not more than one fifth of their true value. **1796** MORSE *Univ. Geog.* I. 323 The depreciation continued . . . until seventy, and even one hundred and fifty nominal paper dollars, were hardly an equivalent for one Spanish Milled dollar. **1870** M. H. SMITH *20 Years Wall St.* 423 The common necessaries of life were exorbitantly high, and a paper dollar was worth only thirty-six cents in coin.

Paper flower. 1. A flower made of paper. **2.** (See quotations.) — **(1) 1854** *Penna. Agric. Rep.* 176 The first premium on paper flowers, is awarded to No. 177. **(2) 1892** *Amer. Folk-Lore* V. 99 *Xeranthemum*, [and] *Helichrysum*, paper-flowers. N. Ohio. **1915** ARMSTRONG & THORNBER *Western Wild Flowers* 542 Paper Flowers. *Psilostrophe Cooperi*. Yellow. Spring. Southwest.

+**Paper fog.** Depreciated paper money such as post notes. *slang. Obs.* — **1813** *Columbian Centinel* 7 April 2/2 His next resort [to obtain cash] must be *Paper Fog*. **1816** *Niles' Reg.* X. 216/1 It is asserted that the treasury of the United States has nearly two millions of *paper fog* in its vaults, at this moment.

Paper-folder. An instrument for folding paper; a paper knife. — **1781** *Salem Gazette* 3 July, Isaac Greenwood . . . [makes] Paper-Folders, Sand-Boxes, Bannisters for Stair-cases. **1871** STOWE *Pink & White Tyranny* 98 Lillie took a paper-folder, and cut the leaf out quite neatly. **1884** CABLE *Dr. Sevier* xxxi, Picking up his paper-folder and shaking it argumentatively.

Paper-hanger. A workman whose business is to put up wall paper. {1809-12-} — **1851** CIST *Cincinnati* 346 [Members of the Cincinnati Astronomical Society include] Lockmakers, . . . Paperhangers, . . Stonemasons. **1871** GROSVENOR *Protection* 117 Nor can masons, . . . whitewashers, paper-hangers, . . . be protected in their industry. **1892** *York County Hist. Rev.* 10 His reputation as a paper hanger, painter and interior decorator is of the highest character. **1904** *McClure's Mag.* Feb. 375/2 The paper-hangers' wages were $4 a day.

Paper-hanging.

1. *pl.* Paper used for covering or adorning the walls of a room; wall paper. {1693-}

1760 *Newport Mercury* 7 June 2/2 Just Imported . . . a Variety of Paper Hangings. **1790** *Columbian Centinel* 15 Sept. 4/2 The largest and most general assortment of Paper-Hangings, . . . as well executed as any ever imported. **1807** JANSON *Stranger in A.* 29 The principal manufactures of Boston are, . . . pot and pearl-ashes, paper-hangings, plate and common glass. **1830** WATSON *Philadelphia* 186 As early as the year 1769, we see that Plunket Fleeson first manufactures American paper hangings at corner of Fourth and Chesnut street. **1887** *Courier-Journal* 30 Jan. 1/3 We invite an inspection of the largest stock of Paper Hangings ever shown in this city.

attrib. in *sing.* **1845** J. W. NORRIS *Chicago Directory* 128 Ornamental painting, wall coloring and paper hanging business.

2. The process of putting wall paper on the walls of a room.

1873 *Winfield* (Kan.) *Courier* 11 Jan. 1/2 Painting, Sign-writing, Kalsomining, Paper hanging and all kinds of work in the painting line. **1892** *York County Hist. Rev.* 10 Mr. Sterner is prepared to execute general house painting and paper hanging in a manner that cannot be otherwise than satisfactory.

+**Paper hornet.** =PAPER WASP. — **1870** *Amer. Naturalist* III. 52 The Paper Hornet (*Vespa maculata*) often enters my nucleus hives, when I am rearing Italian queen bees. **1886** *Pop. Science Mo.* XXVIII. 642 The positions of the paper-hornets' nests . . . are variously asserted to be indicative of a 'hard' or 'open' winter.

Papering. 1. Paper-hanging. Used attrib. {1825-} +**2.** Wall paper. +**3.** The action of examining a ship's papers. *slang.* +**4.** *Papering system*, the practice of securing an audience for a theatrical performance, etc., by issuing free tickets. — **(1) 1771** *Copley-Pelham Lett.* 156 He would be much obliged to you for your employ, in the Glazeering, Papering and Plumbing Business's. **(2) 1883** *Harper's Mag.* Feb. 365/1 This room remains in its original state, with the exception of the papering. **1893** S. HALE *Letters* 282, [I] came home with brooms, . . . bread, dish-towels and papering for Fullum's room. **(3) 1883** *Congress. Rec.* 1 Feb. 1911/1 The whole extent of the official force . . . [is engaged] in the papering of vessels and the care and control of the issuing of the papers. **(4) 1895** *N.Y. Dramatic News* 26 Oct. 5/3 The 'papering' system has been indulged in too freely in some quarters.

Paper light. A paper-covered window; a paper window. — **1698** CHAMBERLAIN *Lithobolia* (1914) 70, I also found many Stones . . . to fly in, breaking the Glass-Windows, and a Paper-Light.

* **Paper maker.** A person whose business is to make paper.

1776 *N.J. Archives* 2 Ser. I. 81 Wanted, One or two journeymen, paper-makers. **1784** FRANKLIN *Autobiog.* 324 She assisted me chearfully in my business, . . . purchasing old linen rags for the paper-makers, etc., etc. **1790** *Penna. Packet* 27 March 4/3 Wanted, A Journeyman Paper-Maker, who is a good Vatman, and capable of making best kinds of Writing Paper. **1822** *Ann. 17th Congress* 1 Sess. I. 60 So long as this operates as a protection to the paper maker it is a tax on the book maker. **1892** *York County Hist. Rev.* 70 An immense amount of blanketing felt for the paper maker . . . is turned out.

Paper medium. A medium of exchange consisting of paper currency. — **1720** *Mass. Bay Currency Tracts* 353, I can see no likelihood of our having a Silver *Medium*, but by having a *Paper Medium*. **1809** in *Scribner's Mo.* XI. 578/1 It will be a long time before the evil of a paper medium will be corrected. **1841** TYLER in *Pres. Mess. & P.* IV. 83 The task of furnishing a corrective for derangements of the paper medium with us is almost inexpressibly great.

* **Paper mill.** A mill in which paper is made.

1724 *New Eng. Courant* 8-15 June 2/2 Some Gentlemen design to set up a Paper-Mill in New-England. **1778** *N.H. Hist. Soc. Coll.* IX. 108 You would not think [such garments] worth taking from the floor unless for a papermill. **1795** WINTERBOTHAM *Hist. View* III. 213 One paper mill has lately been erected at Salem [N.C.], by the Moravians. **1812** *Emporium Arts & Sci.* (Phila.) May 75 The paper mills amount to 190 [enumerated in the census of 1810]. **1873** *Harper's Mag.* March 562/2 Pleasant times we girls had in the old paper-mill. **1909** *Nat. Conservation Congress Proc.* 61 The largest paper mills in the world are on one of our rivers, the Connecticut.

Paper money. {a1697-}

1. +**a.** Legal-tender notes issued by some of the colonies; province bills. +**b.** =CONTINENTAL MONEY. **c.** Any negotiable document that passes current for money, as a bank note or a greenback.

1691 C. MATHER *Considerations on Bills of Credit* 2 Our countrymen . . . Refuse to accept that, which they call Paper-money. **1714** *Mass. Bay Currency Tracts* 101 The poorest Country-Man in the Province, is not convinced to this Day, but that Silver . . . is preferable to the finest Paper-Money that ever was seen. **1738** BYRD *Dividing Line* (1901) 81 Paper-money . . . is the only Cash that will tarry in the Country. **a1756** *Mass. H. S. Coll.* 2 Ser. IV. 99 Some time about the year 1703, upon the occasion of the Indian War, came forth 'Province Bills,' which we call Paper Money. **1771** FRANKLIN *Autobiog.* 293 Being employ'd to print some paper money in New Jersey, which would require cuts and various types that I only could supply. **1782** PAINE *Let. to Abbé Raynal* (1791) 24 The paper money having now ceased, . . . the war will now be carried on by taxation. **1818** FLINT *Lett. from Amer.* 108 There is here [in Cincinnati, Ohio] much trouble with paper money. **1836** EDWARD *Hist. of Texas* 131 The people are afraid of paper money. **1894** LEAVITT *Our Money Wars* 29 Never until 1862 was the power of the Government to make its paper money, or that of the banks, legal tender for all payments to the United States denied. **1900** *Congress. Rec.* 7 Feb. 1605/2 Our paper money, outside the gold and silver certificates and a very few currency certificates, is composed of $346,681,016 in United States notes.

2. Attrib. with *act*, *contract*, *disease*, etc.

1740 *Col. Rec. Penna.* IV. 441 The Paper-Money Act . . . was a low Composition for the Quit-Rents due to them instead of Sterling Money. **1790** *Kentucky Petitions* 160 In some instances paper money contracts were not distinguished from specie. **1793** *Mass. H. S. Coll.* 1 Ser. III. 169 Not among their number was ever yet found, either a tory, a paper money man, or insurgent. **1830** *Va. Lit. Museum* 526/1 The federal did not intend that the state governments should issue paper money, but meant that this should be a 'hard money government,' and yet it is a 'paper money government.' **1837** JACKSON in *Pres. Mess. & P.* III. 306 The paper-money system and its natural associations—monopoly and exclusive privileges—have already struck their roots too deep. **1852** GOUGE *Fiscal Hist. Texas* vi, The paper-money disease is hereditary with us Americans.

+**Paper-money colony.** A colony that issued paper money. — **1738** *Virginia Gaz.* 4-11 Aug., A caution to the Paper-Money Colonies. **1739** W. DOUGLASS *Discourse Currencies* 19 We see . . . in our Paper Money Colonies, the Currencies have incredibly depreciated from Sterling.

Paper mulberry. An Asiatic tree (*Broussonetia papyrifera*), grown as a shade tree in the United States. {1777-} Also attrib. — **1811** SUTCLIFF *Travels* (1815) 256, I assisted in planting several paper-mulberry trees. **c1850** BAGBY *Old Va. Gentleman* 253 The white palings in front enclosed a little yard, green with a patch of sward on either side, and a little paper-mulberry tree in the centre of each patch. **1871** *Harper's Mag.* Oct. 704/1 The paper-mulberry foliage above and the dust below. **1892** APGAR *Trees Northern U.S.* 138 *Broussonetia papyrifera.* (Paper-mulberry.) . . . Hardy north to New York.

+**Paper rind.** An orange with a thin skin. Also attrib. — **1882** *Harper's Mag.* Dec. 58/2 He can go into his orchard and concern himself about . . . his paper-rind St. Michaels. **1891** WARNER in *Ib.* Jan. 180/1 But there are many excellent varieties [of oranges]— . . . the paper rind [etc.].

+**Papershell.** A thin-shelled variety of something; a firecracker in a paper case. — **1884** GOODE, etc. *Fisheries* I. 776 The terms 'Soft Crab,' 'Paper-shell,' and 'Buckler' denote the different stages of consistency of the shell. **1889** *Century Mag.* April 832/2 In the two hours' interval was a display of . . . crackers, serpents, paper-shells. **1911** *Rep. Fisheries 1908* 309/1 While growing a new shell, [edible crabs are called] 'soft-shell,' 'paper-shell,' 'buckler,' and 'hard-shell.' **1912** *Bur. Plant Industry Bul.* No. 251, 46 With reference to the pecan, the term 'papershell' has been extended in its application until it is now practically without significance.

***Paper-stainer.** A maker of paper hangings. {1756-} — **1789** *Boston Directory* 192 May, Wm., paper-stainer, No. 43, Marlborough-street. **1857** VAUX *Villas* 19 Self-supporting schools of design for . . . modelers, carvers, paper-stainers, etc., must follow in due course.

+**Paper title.** A title or claim to land based upon a document of some kind. — **1794** *Ann. 4th Congress* 2 Sess. 2803 The decisions of the State courts, . . . discountenanced improvement titles, and gave the preference to paper titles. **1843** *Amer. Pioneer* II. 25 Pennsylvania and Virginia had also their paper titles upon parts of the same territory. **1845** *Ill. Rev. Statutes* 104 Every person in the actual possession of lands or tenements . . . shall be held and adjudged to be the legal owner . . . to the extent and according to the purport of his or her paper title.

+**Paper town.** =PAPER CITY. — **1819** EVANS *Pedestrious Tour* 228 On this river too is General Simcoe's paper town called London. **1856** W. A. PHILLIPS *Conquest of Kan.* 118 [He went] to Lecompton, then merely a paper town without a house. **1877** JOHNSON *Anderson Co., Kan.* 257 These paper towns have failed to bring forth the future profit. **1887** *Courier-Journal* 29 Jan. 4/3 If the new South . . . is satisfied with mere 'paper towns,' . . . the Courier-Journal is its relentless enemy.

+**Paper vote. a.** =PAPER *n.* 2. **b.** Voting by ballots. — **1692** *Boston Rec.* 210 Ouerseers of the poore Chosen by papor Votes. **1706** *Ib.* 38 Voted that One Collector be chosen . . . by a Paper Vote.

+**Paper wasp.** Any wasp, as a yellow jacket, that makes a nest out of paperlike material. — **1854** H. H. RILEY *Puddleford* 216 The 'paper-wasp' was gathering wild cotton and flax. **1898** DELAND *Old Chester Tales* 181 A gray ball showed that the paper-wasps liked the crumbling shelter.

∗Papist. A Roman Catholic. Sometimes used derogatorily. — **1629** Neill *Virginian Carolorum* 66 No Papists have been suffered to settle their aboade amongst us. **1666** *Md. Archives* II. 55 The sd Erbery did call the whole howse Papists, Rogues, Turdy rogues, etc. **a1817** DWIGHT *Travels* III. 532 So far as they [*sc.* Irish colonists] know anything concerning religion, they are generally Papists.

+Papoon corn. A sweet corn. — **1884** *Vt. Agric. Rep.* VIII. 278 A few ears . . . were brought to Plymouth [1779] from the region of the Susquehanna river, and [it] was described as having a white shriveled grain when ripe, with a red cob, and called 'pa-poon corn.' But not till within a few years . . . has it been generally cultivated for culinary purposes.

+Papoose, *n.* Also †**pappouse,** etc. [Algonquian *papoos.*]

1. An Indian baby or young child.

1634 WOOD *New Eng. Prospect* (1865) 108 This little Pappouse travells about with his bare footed mother to paddle in the Icie Clammbankes. **1648** SHEPARD *Clear Sun-Shine* 10 [He] desired to know . . . what God would do with him and his *Squaw* and *Papooses.* **1711** *N.H. Prov.Papers* III. 477*n.*, Voted, That for . . . every minor or Papoose [slain], fifteen pounds be payd out of the Treasury. **1755** *Essex Inst. Coll.* LII. 81 Gave a papous 5d. **1846** *Knickerb.* XXVII. 211 Squaws, papooses, men and missionaries were there to partake of their dinner. **1858** VIELÉ *Following the Drum* 204 They had with them several little copper-colored papooses strapped down . . . to a shingle. **1890** CUSTER *Following Guidon* 103, [I] was looking . . . at a papoose that was strapped to a board and lay in a corner as quiet as a mouse. **1903** *N.Y. Tribune* 20 Dec., The cutest thing of human kind is the papoose.

2. A white man's child. Used either jocularly or in imitation of the Indians' speech.

1871 *Republican Rev.* 16 Sept. 1/4 White squaws and papooses are the best to commence practising on. **1899** *Mo. So. Dakotan* I. 199 Tepee go, pony go, white squaw and papooses be lost.

3. Attrib. in sense 1.

1633 *N.H. Doc. & Rec.* I. 74, 5 papoose cootes. **1648** SHEPARD *Clear Sun-Shine* 14 He was soon snib'd by the other Indians, calling it a *Papoose* question. **1839** TOWNSEND *Narrative* 196 Several of these women have little children tied to their backs, sewed up papoose fashion, only the head being seen. **a1918** G. STUART *On Frontier* II. 49 The infants are strapped to a papoose board and this board hung over the pommel of the mother's saddle.

‖**Papoose,** *v. tr.* To confine or bind like a papoose. — **a1861** WINTHROP *Canoe & Saddle* 204 This fashionable martyr was being papoosed in a tight-swathing wicker-work case.

+Papoose root. =BLUE COHOSH; a medicine made from this. — **1815** DRAKE *Cincinnati* 85 Poppoos root. **1816** *Analectic Mag.* VII. 263 A dose and a half of his papoose root. **1843** TORREY *Flora N.Y.* I. 33 *Leontice thalictroides* . . . Blue Cohosh. Pappoose-root. . . . The root of this plant is in some repute as a diuretic and bitter. **1859** BARTLETT 309.

Parade. {1656–} ‖**1.** *pl.* Troops that take part in a formal march or procession. **2.** A formal march or procession participated in by a large number of people of the same profession or of kindred interests. — **(1) 1847** *Santa Fe Republican* 25 Dec. 4/1 The Washington correspondent . . . says the landing of Parades will have no pernicious influence on the conclusion of the treaty. **(2) 1871** BAGG *At Yale* 504 On Saturday, October 30, 1841, was held the annual parade of the City fire-department. **1881** *Harper's Mag.* Jan. 192/2 If we had a parade, we paid the expenses ourselves. **1888** BRYCE *Amer. Commonw.* II. III. lxxi. 580 When a procession is exceptionally large, it is called a Parade. *Ib.* 581*n.*, In the Cleveland Business Men's parade it was alleged that 1500 lawyers had walked.

Parade cap. A cap of a type worn by a soldier or cadet on parade. — **1866** HALE *If, Yes & Perhaps* (1868) 256, I was . . . looking for an old parade cap of mine. **1880** LAMPHERE *U.S. Govt.* 181/2 Cadets, immediately after their admission, will supply themselves with . . . 1 parade-Cap [price] $4.10.

Parade ground. An extent of open level ground, usually within or adjacent to a fort, where soldiers are accustomed to parade.

1724 in Temple & Sheldon *Hist. Northfield, Mass.* 200 The soldiers will be safe, even if the enemy get within the parade ground. **1815** *Lit. & Phil. Soc. N.Y. Trans.* I. 284 The parade-ground of the fort was said to have settled . . . below its former level. **1868** WATERS *Life among Mormons* 9 Fort Kearney . . . consists simply of a number of two story frame buildings, arranged in the usual way around a parade ground. **1888** SHERIDAN *Memoirs* I. 110 Just inside the limits of the garrison, . . . on the parade-ground, . . . they killed her. **1902** ALDRICH *Sea Turn* 295 He flung back the flap and looked down upon the parade-ground with its radiating white-walled streets.

attrib. **1892** *Harper's Mag.* Dec. 137 Both dismounted at the parade-ground gate.

Parade rest. The position of rest for a soldier when standing motionless and silent in ranks. — **1862** STRONG *Cadet Life W. Point* 65 We were formed . . . into two ranks at *parade rest.* **1889** *Century Mag.* Jan. 465/1 Not a man moved from the military posture of 'parade-rest.'

Paragraphist. A writer of paragraphs, esp. one employed by a newspaper. {1798–}

1790 *Gazette of U.S.* 27 Nov. 655/1 A paragraphist in the General Advertiser of Thursday last, reprobates in very forcible terms, the mode of voting *viva voce.* **1792** JEFFERSON *Writings* VIII. 406 One of its principal ministers enlists himself as an anonymous writer or paragraphist. **1816** *Ann. 14th Congress* 2 Sess. 268 European orators and paragraphists . . . said the Yankee cockboats were to be speedily driven from the ocean. **1849** WILLIS *Rural Letters* 192 There are passable paragraphists by scores. **1893** *Advance* 20 July 560/4 The statement . . . that Mrs. Humphry Ward is writing a new story . . . to be a 'companion work' to *David Grieve* and *Robert Elsmere* has . . . been evolved from the paragraphist's own brain.

Pará grass. [*Pará,* Brazil.] {1858–} A forage grass (*Panicum barbinode*) introduced into the southern states from South America. {1871} — **1889** VASEY *Agric. Grasses* 26 *Panicum barbinode* (Para Grass.) . . . Dr. Charles Mohr, of Mobile, Ala., states that it has been some years introduced in that vicinity. **1894** COULTER *Bot. W. Texas* III. 504 *P[anicum] barbinode.* . . . (Para grass.) . . . Introduced and cultivated throughout the State in moist soil.

Paraguay tea. A South American plant (*Ilex paraguayensis*), or tea prepared from its leaves. — **1818** *Ann. 15th Congress* 1 Sess. 1976 The Paraguay tea is a great article of trade throughout the country.

∗**Parakeet.** Also †**parrakeeto,** etc. +The Carolina parrot, *Conuropsis* (syn. *Conurus*) *carolinensis.* (See also PAROQUET.) — **1649** *Perfect Descr. Va.* 15 We have most rare coloured Parraketoes. **1709** LAWSON *Carolina* 142 The Parrakeetos are of a green Colour, and Orange-Coloured half way their Head. **1804** CLARK in *Lewis & C. Exped.* I. (1904) 59 In the Point above the Kansas Kanzas River I observed a great number of Parrot queets this evening. **1858** BAIRD *Birds Pacific R.R.* 67 *Conurus Carolinensis.* . . . Parakeet; Carolina Parrot. . . . Southern and southwestern States, as far west as the Missouri.

∗**Parallel,** *v. tr.* To provide with a parallel street, etc.; to go or run parallel with. {1899–} 'Chiefly *U.S.*' (*O.E.D.*). — **1885** *Harper's Mag.* April 695/1 Railroad Avenue has been paralleled by another . . . business street named Gold Avenue. **1891** *Cosmopolitan* XII. 52/2 Ribbons of greenest turf, . . . paralleled on both sides by shaded promenades. **1903** A. ADAMS *Log Cowboy* 40 For the next few days we paralleled the coast. **1905** *N.Y. Ev. Post* 4 April 13 The Big Four will parallel the tracks of the Chicago and Eastern Illinois.

+Parara. Also **pararee.** =PRAIRIE. — **1789** MORSE *Amer. Geog.* 463 A parara . . . is an extensive, rich plain without trees, and covered with grass. **1816** U. BROWN *Journal* II. 148 If those Pararees was in Pennsylvania or Maryland I should Call them Abominable Swamps with high rough grass. **1832** VIGNE *6 Mos. in Amer.* II. 44 These barrens, it is supposed by many, were originally Prairies, or 'Pararas,' as they are called by the lower class of Americans. **1858** *Harper's Mag.* March 439/2 At nightfall you see parties of emigrants making their way in slow lines across the rolling prairie (or 'parara,' as the borderers like to call it).

+Parasitic jaeger. A species of jaeger, *Stercorarius parasiticus.* (Cf. MAN-OF-WAR 2 b.) — **1887** RIDGWAY *Manual N.A. Birds* 22. **1917** *Birds of Amer.* I. 36 The Parasitic Jaeger is a robber and lives largely on what it can take by force from its smaller brethren.

Parasol. {1616–} A small, light umbrella carried by women as a protection against the sun. {1660–}

1797 *Columbian Centinel* 12 April, A new-invented Parasol, fixed on an angle, convenient for riding in chaise, or walking in the sun. **1823** COOPER *Pioneers* xxvi, Where is thy parasol, girl? **1877** 'E. MARTIN' *Hist. Great Riots* 103 Bundles of umbrellas, fancy parasols, hams, . . . laces and flour, were mixed together in the arms of robust men. **1904** GLASGOW *Deliverance* 136 With her white parasol over her bared head, she started for a restless stroll.

attrib. **1888** *Amer. Almanac* 275 Occupations of the People of the United States. . . . Umbrella and parasol makers, . . . Upholsterers.

Parasolette. A small parasol. *Obs.* {1842–} — **1845** *Xenia Torch-Light* 31 July 4/5 Adams & Cooper Have just received a large stock of Spring and Summer Goods [including] . . . Parasoletts, and sun Shades. **1848** *Boston Directory* App. 24 Geo. W. Robbins, Manufacturer and dealer in umbrellas, parasols, and parasolettes.

∗**Parcel.** Also †**parcell, parsel(l).**

∗**1.** A tract or portion of land. In full *parcel of land* or *parcel of ground.*

1624 in *Amer. Sp.* XV. 292/1 Northward upon another p[ar]cell of the the said John Bush his devident. **1635** *Cambridge Prop. Rec.* 15 All his parcells of land lyeing and beeing in Newtowne. **1682** *Conn. Hist. Soc. Coll.* XIV. 99 One parcell . . . whose ends abutt on a drift High way. **1704** *Charlestown Land Rec.* 174 Charls Chambers . . . lets unto the said Stephen Williams one Certaine Track or parcel of Land. **1798** *Phila. Ordinances* (1812) 92 Sundry religious societies . . . have been induced to purchase certain pieces and parcels of ground. **1819** E. DANA *Geogr. Sk.* 224 Some parcels are second rate lands. **1906** *Indian Laws & Tr.* III. 174 Such tract or parcel shall revert to the tribe.

b. Such an area of a specified kind of land.

1640 *Boston Rec.* 55 The parcell of marsh ground unallotted at hogg Island . . . is now resigned up to our Brother Marshall. **1646** *Conn. Probate Rec.* I. 16, 1 p[a]rcell of meado Cont 3 roods. **1655** *Mayflower Descendant* X. 16 Mr. William Paddy . . . hath freely . . . sould unto the said John Cooke a certaine p[ar]cell of upland meddow. **1675** *Conn. Rec.* II. 256 There was a parcell of beach of twenty-fower acres.

∗**2.** A collection or aggregation of domestic animals. {of people and animals in general}

a1656 BRADFORD *Hist.* 251 They bought allso a parcell of goats, which they distributed at home as they saw neede & occasion. **1679** *New Castle*

Court Rec. 297 A parcell of small swyne. **1757** *Lett. to Washington* II. 200, I agreed, for a parcel of Beeves. **1775** C. MARSHALL *Diary* (1877) 37 The transports . . . [brought] (a) parcel of hogs, one thousand pounds of cheese, &c. **1798** *Wilmington* (N.C.) *Gazette* 8 March, A parcel of Breeding Mares and Colts. **1834** C. A. DAVIS *Lett. J. Downing* 321 A parcel of dogs belongin to other folks yelpin and barkin.

3. A number or quantity of things: (see quotations). *Obs.* {1645–}

1639 *Md. Archives* IV. 78 A p[ar]cell of latin ware . . . 2. small kettles. **1677** *Hempstead Rec.* I. 353 He helped Cornelus Mott Get a parsell of Posts. **1679** *York Deeds* V. I. 33 A Parcell of flints. **1705** *Boston News-Letter* 8 Oct. 2/2 To be Sold . . . , a parcel of the best Jamaica Sole-Leather. **1714** *Ib.* 9 Aug. 2/2 A Parcel of Tobacca and Painters Colours, condemn'd at the Court of Admiralty, To be Sold. **1720** *Amer. Wkly. Mercury* 21 July 3/1 Lately Imported from England a choice parcell of very good fowling Peices. **1758** *Lett. to Washington* II. 326 Capt. Feilos Came to my house With A parceil of Wagins said to belong To A Sutler. **1778** *Essex Inst. Coll.* LV. 164 At Farmington there was the finest parcel of Cannon I ever saw & the Town very pleasant. **1805** LEWIS in *L. & Clark Exped.* II. (1904) 163 Ordered them . . . to set about making a parsel of truck wheels in order to convey our canoes and baggage.

b. Used with reference to timber, trees, or lumber.

1679 *York Deeds* V. I. 43 An Inventory of the Estate of John Moor: . . . a parcell of Timber. **1685** *Ib.* IV. 85 There is a parcell of firr trees growing . . . neare a little Hill. **1753** *Boston Post Boy* 31 Dec. 2/2 To be sold . . . a parcel of choice lumber. **1771** HAMILTON *Works* VII. 472 She has on board . . . a parcel of lumber for yourself. **1806** LEWIS in *L. & Clark Exped.* V. (1905) 153 An excellent horse of Cruzatte's snagged himself . . . badly in the groin in jumping over a parsel of fallen timber.

c. Used of fish. *Obs.*

1678 *York Deeds* V. I. 33 One Parcell of Cod. **1683** *Ib.* 22 A P[a]rcell of fish at Twenty foure shillings. **1686** *Ib.* IV. 64 A Parcell of fish formerly receiued. **1759** *Essex Inst. Coll.* XIX. 188 They Caught a good Parsell of fish. **1806** LEWIS in *L. & Clark Exped.* IV. (1905) 201 They had taken a fine parcel of sturgeon.

Parcel(s) post. {1837–} A government system of carrying parcels by mail, as a branch of the regular United States postal service. Also attrib. — **1887** *Statutes at Large* XXV. 1407 William F. Vilas . . . and Sir Ambrose Shea . . . have agreed upon the following articles for the establishment of a parcels post system of exchanges between the two countries [the U.S. and the Bahamas]. **1893** CUSHING *Story of P.O.* 1024 Very many persons have been in favor of a limited parcels post, or a fuller transportation of packages by the Post Office Department. . . . This country has a full parcels post with foreign countries. **1900** *Congress. Rec.* 21 Feb. 2015/1 Legislation to provide for . . . the establishment of a parcels-post system. *Ib.* 13 Feb. 1744/1 A memorial . . . against the passage of the so-called parcels-post bill. **1912** *Statutes at Large* XXXVII. I. 559 For the purpose of a further inquiry into the subject of the general parcel post, a joint committee of six persons (Members of Congress) . . . is constituted.

***Parched,** *a.* Roasted, preparatory to being used as food. — **1622** 'MOURT' *Relation* 36 Two or three Baskets full of parched Acornes. **1817** *N. Amer. Rev.* IV. 177 [We] drank coffee made of parched beans, and black pepper. **1837** IRVING *Bonneville* II. 189 The old house-wife . . . produced a pot of parched flour and a string of biscuit roots. **1866** 'F. KIRKLAND' *Bk. Anecdotes* 484/1 Putting his hand into his pocket and hauling out a handful of parched coffee.

+**Parched corn.** Indian corn roasted for use as food. Hence *parched-corn flour.*

1648 SHEPARD *Clear Sunshine* 21 It is no small part of Religion . . . to crave a blessing with affectionate hearts upon a homely dinner, perhaps parcht Corne or Indian stalks. **1807** GASS *Journal* 132 After eating a few grains of parched corn, we set out at 8 o'clock. **1820** *Amer. Antiq. Soc. Trans.* I. 283 The knapsack is an old blanket, and contains some parched corn flour, jerked meat, and leather. **1836** IRVING *Astoria* I. 183 He filled his shot pouch with parched corn, . . . and set off to cross the neck on foot. **1890** CUSTER *Following Guidon* 50 Officers and men subsisted on parched corn and horse-flesh.

b. (See quotation.) *Obs.*

1800 BOUCHER *Glossary* p. l, *Ebo-Nan,* and *Parch'd Corn;* two favourite tunes, or jigs, among the negros are so called.

c. Hominy or pop corn.

1828 COBBETT *Treatise on Corn* § 20 The parched corn talked of here, means that which is called homany, in Virginia and the Carolinas. **1850** S. F. COOPER *Rural Hours* 388 Besides these different ways of cooking the maize, we should not forget parched or 'popped' corn, in which the children delight so much. **1876** HALE *P. Nolan's Friends* xi, Travelers of to-day, solicited in palace cars to buy sugared parched-corn, do not know, perhaps, that this is the food of pioneers in front of Apaches.

+**Parched meal.** Meal made by pounding parched or roasted Indian corn in a mortar. *Obs.* — **1643** R. WILLIAMS *Key* (1866) 39 *Nókehick.* Parch'd meal which is a readie very wholesome food, which they eate with a little water, hot or cold. **1797** IMLAY *Western Territory* (ed. 3) 237 Parched meal . . . is a very nourishing food, and is an excellent provision for travellers. **1805** LEWIS in *Ann. 9th Congress* 2 Sess. 1039 [We] have thus been enabled to reserve the parched meal, portable soup, and a considerable proportion of pork and flour.

Parche(e)si. {pacheess, pachisi, etc., 1800–} A game, somewhat resembling backgammon, adapted from an Indian game called *pachisi.* — **1884** CHADWICK *Sports & Pastimes* 253 Parcheesi . . . , as played in America, has a regular card-board field. **1893** *Amer. Folk-Lore* VI. 215 *Pachisi* . . . was introduced from India to the United States, where it was first published in 1860 under the name of *Parchesi,* and has become very popular. **1900** *McClure's Mag.* Oct. 497 One of their earliest attempts at diversion was in the contrivance of a make-shift game of parchesi.

+**Parching corn.** Corn suitable for parching, as pop corn. — **1845** *Knickerb.* XXV. 199 Over head hung bunches of parching-corn.

***Parchment.**

***1.** The skin of a sheep, goat, etc., prepared for writing upon, or for similar purposes.

1645 *Essex Inst. Coll.* L. 336 Books, parchment & other things in a chest, 2 li. **1666** *Md. Archives* II. 54 Seaven coppys of the lawes made this Assembly [shall] be fairely transcribed into parchm[en]t. **1771** FRANKLIN *Autobiog.* 307, I had also paper, parchment, chapmen's books, etc. **1789** *Ann. 1st Congress* I. 58 After a bill shall have passed both Houses, it shall be duly enrolled on parchment. **1813** *Niles' Reg.* V. 190/1 Gloves, muffs and tippets, parchment and glue.

+**2.** The dried hide of an animal, as an elk or buffalo. In full *parchment hide. Obs.*

1805 LEWIS in *L. & Clark Exped.* III. (1905) 12 Roots of three different kinds . . . were foalded in as many parchment hides of buffaloe. **1823** JAMES *Exped.* III. 50 These traders offered various articles . . . in exchange for horses and mules, bison-robes, and parchment or parfleche.

+**b.** *In (the) parchment,* said of a hide in a dried, undressed condition to distinguish it from a green or a dressed hide.

*c*1785 S. PEARS *Narrative* (MS.) 4 [Except] one elk skin in the parchment . . . we had not anything to live on. **1805** LEWIS in *Ann. 9th Congress* 2 Sess. 1043 Deer and elk tallow, elk skins dressed and in parchment.

+**3.** A diploma received upon graduation from college; an official certificate.

1851 *Knickerb.* XXXVIII. 93 [The boy] had just obtained his 'parchment' from an eastern college. **1856** CARTWRIGHT *Autobiog.* 59 This permit to exhort was all the license I ever received from the Church to preach until I received my parchment of ordination. **1896** MOE *Hist. Harvard* 73 Three of these lusty young feed-casters were not given their parchments for *thirty-two years.*

+**4.** In special combinations.

Parchment proprietor, in those parts of the United States formerly held by Spain, one who holds or owns land by virtue of an old Spanish grant; *p. right,* a right granted by or contained in an official document.

1791 *Ann. 1st Congress* II. 1915 The deviation from charters, and the infringement of parchment rights . . . had been made on different principles from those now mentioned. **1870** *Republican Rev.* 22 Oct. 2/1 Some lineal (?) descendant of a defunct parchment proprietor, draws forth his Spanish Grant and imperatively demands an immediate possession.

+**Parchment money.** Official currency made of parchment. *Obs.* — **1723** *New-Eng. Courant* 3 June 2/1 On Tuesday last a Woman try'd at our Superior Court for counterfeiting the Parchment Money of this Province, was brought in guilty. **1727** COMER *Diary* (1893) 25 This month in Boston the authorities made parchment money, i.e., a penny two pence, and 3 pence.

+**Pard.** Short for PARDNER. *slang.* — **1850** A. T. JACKSON *Forty-Niner* (1920) 18 It makes a lot of difference having a pard with you. **1872** 'MARK TWAIN' *Roughing It* 336 Cheese it, pard; you've banked your ball clean outside the string. **1885** *Outing* Oct. 51/2 Douglass and Williams were old 'pards' of theirs. **1923** J. H. COOK *On Old Frontier* 106, I rode at the top speed of my horse in order to reach the lead cattle and help my pard swing them.

+**Pardener.** =next. *colloq.* — **1795** DEARBORN *Columbian Grammar* 137 Improprieties, commonly called Vulgarisms, . . . [include] Pardener for Partner. **1837** NEAL *Charcoal Sk.* (1838) 203 Grigsby's 'pardeners' . . . are quiet lads. *a***1861** WINTHROP *J. Brent* 71, I don't mean sech. I mean jolly dogs, like me and my pardener.

+**Pardner.** [Var. of *partner.*] A close associate, partner or chum. Hence *pardnership.* — **1837** SHERWOOD *Gaz. Georgia* (ed. 3) 71 *Pardner,* for partner. **1849** *Knickerb.* XXXIII. 175 David Graham, and Arphaxed his 'pardner,' might . . . help to put an end to this utterly ridiculous formula. **1862** LOWELL *Biglow P.* 2 Ser. iii. 99 Thet is, to hev the pardnership under th' ole name continner. **1876** 'JOAQUIN' MILLER *First Families* 55 That evening Limber Tim [told] . . . what a hero his 'pardner' had become. **1925** TILGHMAN *Dugout* 70 But we're neither of us going back on you, pardner.

+**Parfleche.** Also **parflesh, parflash.** [Can. Fr.] A hide, usually of a buffalo, that has been haired and dried, or an article, as a robe, made of this. Also attrib. — **1844** FRÉMONT *Exped.* 237 Some of us had the misfortune to wear moccasins with parflêche soles, so slippery that we could not keep our feet. **1870** KEIM *Sheridan's Troopers* 168 Opposite the chief . . . lay several very fine robes and parfleshes finely painted. **1882** R. I. DODGE *Our Wild Indians* 254*n.*, Among almost all the Plains tribes, the common name for a skin so prepared is 'parfleche,' and almost everything made of it is also 'parfleche.' *a***1918** G. STUART *On Frontier* II. 40 [The medicine man] usually had a highly ornamental parflash, in which he kept one or more fetishes.

Parietal, *n.* {1706–} +**1.** A demerit or deduction affecting a student's standing made by a parietal board or committee. *Obs.* +**2.** A member of a parietal board or committee in a college. *Obs.* — (1) **1836** *Harvardiana* III. 44 What is 't ye do? Beware the parietals! **1848** *Oration before H[arvard] L[odge] I.O.O.F.* (Hall), Reckon on the fingers of your mind the reprimands, deductions, parietals, and privates in store for you. **1851** HALL *College Words* 223 The deductions made by the Parietal Committee are also called *Parietals*. (2) *Ib.*, The members of the [parietal] committee are called, in common parlance, *Parietals*.

***Parietal,** *a.* +Resident within the walls or buildings of a college; of or pertaining to the discipline administered by an officer or committee residing on a college campus. — **1836** *Harvardiana* III. 98 Had I forgotten, alas! the stern parietal monitions? **1849** *Oration before H[arvard] L[odge] I.O.O.F.* (Hall), I see them shaking their fists in the face of the parietal tutor. **1851** HALL *College Words* 223 At Harvard College the officers resident within the College walls constitute a permanent standing committee, called the Parietal Committee. They have particular cognizance of all tardinesses at prayers and Sabbath services, and of all offences against good order and decorum. **1878** *N. Amer. Rev.* CXXVI. 15 One instance in which the Parietal Board [at Harvard] took him in hand. **1893** *Nation* 5 Jan. 16/1 One might call it, in college phrase, a style of parietal admonition.

***Paring.** +=next. — **1887** *Century Mag.* Dec. 331/1 There was nothin' wuth declarin', 'Cept I'd kissed her onct or twice, At a huskin' or a parin'.

+**Paring bee.** =APPLE-BEE. Also attrib. — **1845** *Lowell Offering* V. 269 When we were about to have a paring bee we sent our invitations a day or two previous. **1850** *Knickerb.* XXXV. 24 Give me the real paring-bee reels and jigs. **1857** *Quinland* I. 191 Went this evening . . . with the young people to a paring-bee at Squire Carter's. . . . Some pared, some quartered, some cored, some strung. **1896** *Vt. Agric. Rep.* XVI. 97 The old fashioned husking and paring bees have been done away with.

***Paris.** *attrib.* Designating materials and articles of apparel made in Paris, France, or after the Paris style.

1759 *Newport Mercury* 26 June 4/3 To be sold by Jacob Richardson, . . . plain Gauze, Parisnets, gimp and floss Garland. **1847** RUXTON *Adv. Rocky Mts.* (1848) 231 The curse of the trapper is levelled against all the new-fashioned materials of the Paris hats. **1853** FELT *Customs New Eng.* 119 They were at first called *sombreros*, . . . *slouches*, and *California hats*, . . . but latterly, by some, the *Paris felts*. **1869** STOWE *Oldtown Folks* 307 I declare I forgot a package of gloves that I brought over . . . —the very best Paris kid. **1889** *Harper's Mag.* April 827/1 It is indisputable that the woman in any company who has on a Paris gown . . . 'takes the cake.'

Paris green. A vivid green powder of aceto-arsenite of copper, used as an insecticide. Also attrib. — **1874** *Rep. Comm. Agric. 1873* 154 Paris-green was extensively used [to destroy beetles] in some counties with varying success. **1881** *Amer. Naturalist* XV. 821 Weight for weight London purple is more efficacious than Paris green as an insecticide. **1887** *Ib.* XXI. 482 Spraying will fully compensate for the small expense of the Paris-green application. **1892** KELLOGG *Kansas Insects* 7 Paris green, or arsenite of copper, containing 55 per cent. to 60 per cent. of insoluble arsenic, retails at drug stores at about 23 cents a pound.

***Parish.**

+**1.** In some southern states, formerly a district or subdivision of a county serving as the ultimate political unit in local government; in Louisiana, =COUNTY.

In the South, as well as in New England, this term was originally ecclesiastical, but it quickly took on a political aspect which gained precedence and has persisted in Louisiana (see second group of examples), where the parish corresponds to the county in other states.

(1) **1641** in Neill *Virginia Carolorum* 165 Resolved, That the county of Upper Norfolk be divided into three distinct parishes. **1655** *Va. House of Burgesses* 98 It is ordered that in each parish of the said county a monthly court be held. **1705** BEVERLEY *Virginia* IV. 9 Besides this Division into Counties, and Parishes, there are two other Sub-divisions. **1829** SHERWOOD *Gaz. Georgia* (ed. 2) 12 The separate sections of the settled parts of the State were denominated Parishes . . . ; *now* they were called counties. **1864** in Fleming *Hist. Reconstruction* I. 119 The provisional governor shall, by proclamation, declare the number of delegates to be elected by each county, parish, or election district. **1879** G. CAMPBELL *White & Black* 341 A parish [in S.C.] is a mere popular term for a tract of country; it is not now a real division, civil or ecclesiastical. **1891** *Harper's Mag.* June 111/2 The Virginians preserved the parish, but its boundary lines were often coterminous with those of the county, while in more than one instance a parish included more than a single county.

(2) **1839** *Penny Cycl.* XIV. 174/1 For political and civil purposes Louisiana is divided into thirty-one parishes. **1868** *Rep. Comm. Agric. 1867* 100 In Union parish, Louisiana, the damage was 'slight—1,000 head.' **1880** CABLE *Grandissimes* 221 Down in the rich parish of St. Bernard . . . lay the plantation. **1900** *Congress. Rec.* 5 Feb. 1498/2 The subdivisions of my State instead of being called counties are called parishes.

+**2.** In New England, an ecclesiastical district possessing certain powers of local self-government.

a1647 GORGES *Descr. New-Eng.* 48 Every parish [shall have] one Constable. **1654** *Suffolk Deeds* II. 5 Wm. Halsey of Pullin point in the parisshe of Boston aforesd. **1684** I. MATHER *Providences* (1856) X. 226 Four other parishes were much endamaged, multitudes of chimneys beaten down. **1716** *Mass. H. Rep. Jrnl.* I. 145 To Consider of and Report the most suitable Place, for the Setting the Meeting House in the upper Parish in Kittery. **1772** *Amherst Rec.* 60/1 The Vote taken respecting the Dividing of the Disstrict into two Districts or parishes was paist in the Negative. **1781** PETERS *Hist. Conn.* (1829) 145 The township . . . is divided into seven parishes, three of them episcopal. **1832** WILLIAMSON *Maine* II. 77 The northern settlements of Kittery, denominated 'the parish of Unity,' and the 'precinct of Berwick,' . . . [have] been successfully defended through the late war.

+**3.** (See quotations 1828 and 1875.)

1828 WEBSTER s.v. *Society* 7 In *Connecticut*, a number of families united and incorporated for the purpose of supporting public worship, is called an *ecclesiastical society*. . . . In Massachusetts, such an incorporated society is usually called a *parish*, though consisting of persons only, without regard to territory. **1841** PARK *Pantology* 156 The Congregationalists, are so called because they believe each church or parish to be entirely independent of all others; its members having a right to select and ordain their own minister. **1875** IERSON ed. Lamson *Church First 3 Cents.* VII. ii. 308 The term 'parish' is applied in America to congregations, considered as the minister's 'cure of souls' without the reference to local limits with which in England it is associated. **1891** WILKINS *New Eng. Nun* 119 This poor parish had no settled preacher.

4. *attrib.* **a.** In sense 1 with *country, levy, prison.*

1713 *N.C. Col. Rec.* II. 37 All Friends that do suffer . . . Either for not bearing arms or Refusing to pay Parish Levies . . . [should] keep a true act. of the sum they suffer. **1853** SIMMS *Sword & Distaff* 58 They had just passed an ancient Clubhouse, such as may be found, to this day, throughout the parish country of South Carolina. **1891** *Atlantic Mo.* June 805/1 The convicts in the chain gang in the New Orleans Parish prison and the Birmingham mines.

b. In sense 2 with *affair, church, committee,* etc.

1654 JOHNSON *Wonder-w. Prov.* 1 By Proclamation throughout their Parish churches. **1753** *Essex Inst. Coll.* XXI. 153 Voted the Parish Rate to be this year 460=00=00 old tenner. **1758** *Ib.* 159 The be hindments of Parish taxes for years Past. **1773** *Ib.* 271 The Parish Committe shall . . . beuld a good pare of bars to go into the yard. **1785** *Ib.* 288 A Comitte for To Sottle all parish afaers that lyes un Sattled. **1788** FRENEAU *Misc. Works* 371 She would have killed the parish schoolmaster with the churn-stick.

+**Parish court.** *La.* A court having certain jurisdiction within a parish. — **1834** BAIRD *Valley Mississippi* 273 The Parish Courts [in La.] hold a regular session in each parish on the first Monday in every month, **1840** *Picayune* 9 Aug. 3/3 To file a tableau of distribution in the Parish Court. **1853** STOWE *Key* 74/1 The parish court [in La.] decreed that she should recover 1200 dollars.

+**Parish judge.** (See quot. 1826.) *Obs.* — **1826** FLINT *Recoll.* 350 The 'parish judge' . . . decides probate affairs, and holds a parish court, which takes cognizance of a great variety of causes. **1851** HALL *Manhattaner* 95 Forgetful of the . . . duties of Parish Judge (a historical office now) . . . , [he] is drinking the liquid notes.

+**Parish library.** A library serving the needs of a parish. — **1854** THOREAU *Walden* 119 Let the village . . . not stop short at a pedagogue, a parson, a sexton, a parish library, and three selectmen, because our pilgrim forefathers got through a cold winter once on a bleak rock with these. **1910** BOSTWICK *Amer. Pub. Library* 5 Church or parish libraries [were] established in many of the colonies.

***Park,** *n.*

1. Used in place names, esp. with reference to the grounds immediately adjacent to the city hall in New York City.

1643 in *Amer. Sp.* XV. 292/1 That parcell of land at Dunn Park. **1678** *Md. Hist. Mag.* XX. 284 James Park, 200 acr Sur[veyed] the 30 May 1678 for Thomas James Lyeing on the South side of Midle river. **1836** WESTON *Visit* 55 The City Hall . . . is situated in a small enclosure called The Park, on the east side of Broadway. **1852** *Harper's Mag.* V. 392/2 We have just returned from the Park and City-Hall. **1882** McCABE *New York* 424 The *City Hall Park*, or 'The Park' as it is termed by old residents, is located about a mile above the Battery. **1903** *N.Y. Sun* 26 Nov. 9 (*captions*), Evacuation Day Kept. Flag Raised at the Battery and in the Park as When the British Left.

+**b.** (See quot. 1895.)

1808 PIKE *Sources Miss.* (1895) II. 380 Passed the *Park*, which is ten miles round, and not more than three quarters of a mile across. **1895** COUES in *Ib.* 381*n.*, Near the N.E. corner of St. Clair Co. and the S.E. corner of Henry Co. [Missouri]. The Park is a narrow, somewhat rectangular loop of the Osage, including some bold bluffs in its bight.

2. *Mil.* A unit or company of artillery. {1799–}

1755 WASHINGTON *Writings* I. 160 The remaining companies of the Provincial troops, and the whole park of artillery were ordered to hold themselves in readiness to march. **1807** *Ann. 10th Congress* 1 Sess. I. 480 A park of artillery . . . was also to be seized. **1864** 'PENNIMAN' *Tanner-Boy* 162 The governor of the State of Mississippi sent forward a park of artillery.

+**3.** *W.* =CORRAL *n. Obs.*

1805 LEWIS in *L. & Clark Exped.* I. (1904) 313 There was a park which they had formed of timber and brush, for the purpose of taking the cabrie or antelope. **1839** LEONARD *Adventures* (1904) 224 After travelling a short distance we arrived at a large pen, enclosing about three-fourths of an acre, which they call a park or correll.

4. A tract of ground, usually in or near a city, usu. artificially beautified with trees, flowers, etc., and set apart for public recreation. {1663–}

Cf. NATIONAL PARK.

1825 WOODWORTH *Forest Rose* I. i, The geese, you must know, are mostly seen, in term time, flocking round a marble house in the park. **1855** GLISAN *Jrnl. Army Life* 175 The poor . . . are holding large meetings in the park to hear exciting speeches from fanatical demagogues. **1882** *Wheelman* I. 112 The opening of parks and drives that, until a recent date, were closed to wheelmen, speaks for itself, and needs no comment. **1891** WELCH *Recoll. 1830–40* 271 The 'Potters Field' and the Catholic burying grounds, have recently been discontinued, the remains of their occupants removed and the place transformed into a public square or park. **1908** *Indian Laws & Tr.* III. 382 The Secretary of the Interior is hereby authorized . . . to survey, lay out, and plat into town lots, streets, alleys, and parks, not less than forty acres of said land.

+**5.** An area occurring naturally in a forest or unsettled region resembling an artificial park or pleasure ground.

1834 CLAY in Benton *30 Years' View* I. 418/1 It was a most beautiful country [near Lexington, Ky.]—all the land in it, not in a state of cultivation, was in parks (natural meadows).

+**6.** In the Rocky Mountains, esp. in Colorado and Wyoming, an elevated valley shut in by high hills or mountains.

For a full discussion of the word in this sense see A. Matthews in *Mass. Col. Soc. Publ.* VIII. 387 ff.

1845 FRÉMONT *Exped.* 281 The Platte, the Arkansas, and the Grand River fork of the Rio Colorado of the gulf of California . . . and the three remarkable mountain coves, called Parks, in which they took their rise. **1859** PETERS *Kit Carson* 51 There are two of these natural Parks in the Rocky Mountains. To distinguish them they are called the Old Park and the New Park. **1872** *Amer. Naturalist* VI. 67 [In the mountains of Colo. are] high table-lands known as 'parks.' They are verdant valleys walled in by snowy mountains. **1913** BARNES *Western Grazing Grounds* 66 Open prairie-like areas known as parks . . . [are found] especially in Colorado.

+**7.** =PARKING 3.

1900 *Congress. Rec.* 17 Feb. 1894/1 There are hundreds of little parks at the intersection of streets.

+**8.** Short for BALL PARK.

1917 MATHEWSON *Sec. Base Sloan* 217 Which way is the park from here, please?

9. *attrib.* **a.** Designating idlers in parks.

1861 *Vanity Fair* 13 April 173/1 A brutal looking young park-loafer . . . 'shied' a stone . . . at the superior biped with wings. **1909** 'O. HENRY' *Options* 260 When I was twenty feet away the park-bencher called to me.

b. Designating individuals or groups having to do with the upkeep or maintenance of parks (sense 4).

1868 *Mich. Agric. Rep.* VII. 395 Holding the Annual Exhibition on the grounds of the Park Association. **1882** MCCABE *New York* 447 The remainder of the building is taken up with the offices of the Park Commission and officials. *Ib.* 468 The Park police are uniformed in gray. **1898** *Kansas City Star* 19 Dec. 1/3 Mr. Monroe . . . often turned prisoners over to the park commissioner. *Ib.* 21 Dec. 1/3 Engineer Kessler submitted to the park board . . . a year's work in the survey and systematic plan of improvement of Swope park. **1911** *Springfield W. Repub.* 19 Jan. 16 Quick work on the part of the park employees and firemen saved the collection of more than 100 birds.

+**c.** Designating a region which contains a park (sense 5).

1880 INGHAM *Digging Gold* 217 Custer City is situated on this stream at a point before it leaves the beautiful park country we have described.

+**d.** *Park chair*, (see quotation).

1771 in *Harper's Mag.* LXXXI. 207/2, [I] have determined to send to England for . . . a Park Chair, painted green, full large enough to carry two people, & constructed with four wheels, an exact Phaeton, . . . drawn by one horse only.

***Park,** *v.* +*tr.* To put, set, or draw up in a particular place and leave temporarily (a wagon, train, automobile, etc.). {cf. military use, 1812–} — **1864** BILLINGS in F. H. Garrison *John S. Billings* 95 The trains are parked along the edge of the river. **1880** HAYES *New Colorado* 148 A motley crowd from all parts of the earth 'dwelt together in unity' where the wagons were 'parked.' **1911** *N.Y. Ev. Post* 29 Nov. 16 The train was parked near the Union Station and was visited by hundreds of townsfolk and countrymen. **1924** CROY *R.F.D. No. 3* 2 Where once the horses and mules had stood were now rows of cars parked at an angle.

+**Parkerism.** The theological views and teachings of Theodore Parker (1810–60). *Obs.* — **1850** B. ALCOTT *Journals* 227 Groton Conventions, . . . Parkerism, Conversations, and Emerson—these were significant aspects of the time.

***Parking.** +**1.** The setting of a house well back from the front line of a building lot. **2.** A strip of land, usually turfed and planted with trees, about a building, beside a street, etc. **3.** In Washington, D.C., an open space, beautified with grass, flowers, etc., from which several streets radiate. — **(1) 1884** *Century Mag.* March 649/2 In Washington, however, the streets were wide enough to permit this without sacrificing any private property, and the system of 'parking' thus became the rule, and not the exception. **(2) 1885** E. INGLE *Local Insts. Va.* 109 Spaces were left [in Williamsburg, Va.] for a market place, court-house green and parking for the palace. **1893** *Congress. Rec.* 20 Feb. 1856/2 It is not an usual thing to find parking around manufacturing establishments in the heart of cities. **(3) 1900** *Congress. Rec.* 17 Feb. 1895/1 The little plats of ground at the intersection of streets which are generally denominated 'parkings.'

+**Parkman('s) wren.** [f. George *Parkman*, Boston physician (1791–1849).] (See quot. 1917.) — **1839** AUDUBON *Ornith. Biog.* V. 310 Parkman's Wren. *Troglodytes Parkmanii.* . . . I have named it after my . . . friend, George Parkman. **1874** COUES *Birds N.W.* 231 This bird, . . . though merely a geographical race, may well be designated as Parkman's Wren, in distinction from the typical House Wren. **1917** *Birds of Amer.* III. 194/2 The Western House Wren, or Parkman Wren (*Troglodytes aëdon parkmani*), as he is called.

+**Parkway. a.** A boulevard. **b.** =PARKING 2. — **1896** *Godey's Mag.* April 350/1 The 'League of American Wheelmen' . . . began as a fraternity of young men banded together for mutual protection and for the attainment of the right to travel upon the public roads and parkways. **1898** *19th Cent.* April 585 'Park-ways,' to connect the great outlying woodlands . . . with the Metropolitan Parks of Boston and the surrounding townships. These park-ways are broad boulevards with margins of grass, wood, and river. **1903** *N.Y. Times* 16 Aug., He must tear up the parkway again, rebuild it with proper earth, and plant in it trees that will give shade.

+**Parlay,** *v.* Also **parlee.** [Fr., f. It. *paroli.*] *tr.* To wager (money) on a horse race, cards, etc., and to continue to wager the original stake plus the winnings on subsequent races, cards, etc. — **1892** J. P. QUINN *Fools of Fortune* 194 Almost all [faro] bankers will allow a player to 'parlee,' as the percentage is largely in favor of the bank. **1895** *How to Make Money on Small Cap.* 63 Were he, however, to what is termed 'parley' his money—that is to say, if . . . he put his $5 on his choice on the first race, and, if the horse should win, put all the winnings and his original $5 on the next race, and so on. **1895–** *Stand.* and later dicts. **1903** ADE *People You Know* 110 He wanted to parlee a $2 Silver Certificate and bring home enough to pay the National Debt.

***Parlor, Parlour.**

***1. a.** A family sitting room. **b.** =BEST ROOM.

1640 *Conn. Rec.* I. 57 A true Inuentory: . . . In the parlour, a fetherbed. **1783** Griswold *Republ. Court* 74, I was writing in the parlor quite *en dishabille.* **1841** STEELE *Summer Journey* 149 Upon returning to the parlor we found a centre table containing annuals, and several excellent volumes of the best authors. **1870** NOWLAND *Indianapolis* 299 A parlor . . . is a room where young ladies see their beaux when they come 'sparking.' **1900** DIX *Deacon Bradbury* 279 After greetings on all sides, the four found themselves in the quiet little parlor. **1923** 'BOWER' *Parowan Bonanza* 132 He was just married today—this morning upstairs in the parlor.

+**2.** A place of business, usually one where personal services are rendered and freq. fitted out in an elegant or showy manner.

See also HAIR-DRESSING PARLOR, ROOM.

1904 A. DALE *Wanted, a Cook* 348 An adjacent ice-cream parlor sent me in a large bill for ice-cream sodas. **1908** *Harper's Wkly.* Oct. 22/1 Scene.—The 'beauty parlors' of a large department store. There are a number of booths divided off by wooden partitions. **1908** WHITE *Riverman* 60 They supported row upon row of saloons, . . . refreshment 'parlours,' where drinks were served. **1911** PERSONS, etc. *Mass. Labor Laws* 212 It has become the usual thing for bootblacks to open a 'parlor.' **1923** WATTS *Luther Nichols* 68 Some [of the buildings had been] made over into tenements with saloons, barber-shops and boot-blacking 'parlors' on the first floors.

3. *attrib.* **a.** Designating parts of a parlor, or those parts of a house connected with the parlor.

1647 *Boston Rec.* 89 Wm. Davice . . . shall have leave to sett up a payll afor his hall window and parlor window. **1851** *Knickerb.* XXXVIII. 178 The great clusters of Isabella-grapes, . . . shut in the parlor-piazza. **1869** ALCOTT *Little Women* II. 104 She found the vases paraded on the parlor chimney-piece. **1875** STOWE *We & Neighbors* 55, I noticed a broom in the parlor closet not hung up.

b. Designating articles used in or making up the furnishings of a parlor.

1759 *Newport Mercury* 26 June 4/3 Imported . . . and to be sold by Jacob Richardson, . . . Parlor and Kitchen Bellows [etc.]. **1827** *Harvard Reg.* Dec. 298 The book is lying on the parlor-table. **1839** KIRKLAND *New Home* (1840) 260 A sober neighbor . . . took my husband to task on the appearance of the ghost of a departed parlor carpet. **1856** *Porter's Spirit of Times* 15 Nov. 173/3 They are equally well adapted to public houses and parlor centre-tables, and are as ornamental as they are convenient. **1896** *New Eng. Mag.* Nov. (*advt.*), Rare Japanese Bronzes for library and parlor lamps. **1902** NORRIS *Pit* 334 The men were buying buggies again, the women parlor melodeons, houses and homes were going up. **1907** *St. Nicholas* Aug. 958/1 The water went right in the window and all over the parlor cushions.

c. Designating social gatherings or amusements taking place in a parlor.

1850 MITCHELL *Lorgnette* I. 162 One of our little parlor-soirées . . . came off not long since. **1864** STOWE *House & Home P.* 50 He is . . . a good tenor in a parlor-duet. **1889** CUSTER *Tenting on Plains* 501 A game of parlor croquet was proposed. **1903** WIGGIN *Rebecca* 184 In that event we could hold a parlor meeting.

+**Parlor car.**

1. A railroad passenger car equipped with superior accommodations, as individual chairs, sofas, etc. Formerly applied to a sleeping car; now usually to a chair car.

1868 H. M. FLINT *Railroads of U.S.* 406 We left Albany ... in a Pullman's saloon parlor car. **1881** *Harper's Mag.* Dec. 119/1 The only drawback to his perfect enjoyment was the fact that on this train there was no parlor-car. **1902** LORIMER *Lett. Merchant* 122 Mose Greenebaum ... got into the parlor car with them. **1920** BOK *Americanization* 251 For in those days, twenty years ago, the decoration of the Pullman parlor car was atrocious.

b. Attrib. with *passenger, seat, traffic.*

1892 HOWELLS *Quality of Mercy* 89 Impossible to identify parlor-car passengers. **1898** *Boston Herald* 3 July 14/8 (Ernst), The Pullman method for affixing the war tax stamps to parlor car seats is to have the conductors put them on when the ticket is lifted. **1903** E. JOHNSON *Railway Transportation* 146 The profits ... from the parlor- and sleeping-car traffic are really smaller than those obtained from the day coach service.

2. *Parlor cattle car,* a cattle car of a superior type.

1881 *Chicago Times* 30 April, The first parlor cattle-car left to-night for New York.

Parlor chair. A chair designed for use in a parlor. — **1863** 'G. HAMILTON' *Gala-Days* 423 You shall see ... a restive horse evoked from a passive parlor-chair. **1868** *Mich. Agric. Rep.* VII. 353 Detroit Chair Factory, [exhibited] 1 set cane seat parlor chairs. **1892** *York County Hist. Rev.* 83 A novel and original idea with him is to construct parlor chairs out of the old fashion[ed] spinning wheel.

Parlor furniture. Furniture for use in a parlor. — **1859** *Ladies' Repository* Jan. 53/2 Two wax-dolls, and sets of parlor and chamber furniture. **1864** STOWE *House & Home P.* 10 Our parlor-furniture ... began to show marks of ... decay. **1882** RITTENHOUSE *Maud* 104 The 'parlor furniture,' a sofa and six chairs all very elegant, were left vacant.

+**Parlor girl.** A housemaid. — **1863** A. D. WHITNEY *F. Gartney* iii, The parlor-girl made her appearance with her mop and tub of hot water, to wash up the silver and china. **1875** STOWE *We & Neighbors* 323 Maggie was parlor-girl and waitress, and a good one too. **1883** HOWELLS *Woman's Reason* xviii, I've never seen distinctions in society so awful as the distinction between shop-girls and parlor-girls.

+**Parlor grand.** [Short for *parlor grand piano.*] — **1856** *Porter's Spirit of Times* 8 Nov. 168/2 Chickering's Pianos at the Boston Fair—carried away the palm of excellence, as by far the best instruments exhibited, whether Grand, Semi-Grand, or Parlor Grand. **1883** WILDER *Sister Ridnour* 168 Mrs. Kendrick has a new 'parlor grand' that is perfectly magnificent.

Parlor mantel. A mantelpiece in a parlor, usually above a fireplace. — **1875** HOWARD *One Summer* ii, The lamp still stood upon the parlour mantel. **1883** WILDER *Sister Ridnour* 190 Every Christmas she had this text, made in evergreen, over the parlor mantle.

+**Parlor match.** A friction match containing little or no sulphur. — **1898** *Kansas City Star* 20 Dec. 9/2, 12 boxes Parlor Matches ... 5¢. **1902** *N.Y. Herald* 15 Nov. 5/1 Parlor matches can be ignited by striking them anywhere. **1904** *N.Y. Ev. Post* 5 Feb. 5 In striking a parlor match the head flew off.

+**Parlor organ.** A musical instrument having metal reeds acted upon by currents of air set in motion by a bellows, and controlled from a keyboard like that of a piano. Also transf. — **1845** *Cincinnati Misc.* I. 179 'I was on a visit to Vermont a few weeks since,' said he, 'and intended to buy a parlor Organ.' **1879** HOWELLS *Lady of Aroostook* 33 That lady had ... heard Lydia sing at her parlour organ in the old homestead. **1882** MCCABE *New York* 365 We should probably find ... all the comforts for a small family, even to parlor organs and sewing machines. **1908** 'O. HENRY' *Options* 11 This Southern parlor organ [a magazine] you've been running has never played a note that originated above Mason & Hamlin's line.

+**Parlor set.** A set or suite of matched furniture suitable for a parlor. (Cf. PARLOR SUIT.) — **1873** *Winfield* (Kan.) *Courier* 24 July 2/3 Better to use the old cane-seated chairs ... than to tremble at the bills sent him from the upholsterers for the most elegant parlor set ever made. **1898** CAHAN *Imported Bridegroom* 242 [A] rocking-chair ... proved to be the gift of a family who had been set down for nothing less than a carpet or a parlor set. **1920** HOWELLS *Vacation of Kelwyns* There was a parlor set of black walnut.

Parlor stove. A stove for use in a parlor. — **1835** *Stimpson's Boston Directory* 11 Stoves, Counting Room and Parlor. **1872** *Newton Kansan* 5 Sept. 4/6 Sold for a less price than any Sheet Iron Parlor Stove. **1898** CAHAN *Imported Bridegroom* 1 She sat in her rocker, in front of the parlor stove, absorbed in 'Little Dorrit.'

+**Parlor suit.** =PARLOR SET. — **1875** *Chicago Tribune* 21 Nov. 1/4 Parlor Suits. It will pay you to compare prices before buying. **1887** *Courier-Journal* 20 Jan. 5/6 We have a full line of Parlor Suits. **1892** *York County Hist. Rev.* 99 In the furniture department are all kinds of cabinet ware, bedroom and parlor suits.

Parochial school. {1791– (Sinclair *Stat. Acct. Scotl.* I. 457)} +A school, usually of elementary rank, maintained by a church, esp. the Roman Catholic church.

1817 DWIGHT *Travels* I. 16 [In Mass., N.H., & Conn.] what may be called parochial schools are everywhere established. **1851** CIST *Cincinnati* 58 Parochial Schools. The Catholic schools are the only ones which are strictly parochial. **1903** HART *Actual Govt.* 549 The withdrawal of hundreds of thousands of children into parochial schools is unfortunate because the public school is the greatest democratic influence in our country. **1911** JENKS & LAUCK *Immigration Problem* 289 Of course, the races of the Roman Catholic religion have much larger numbers in the parochial schools than do the races with the Protestant religion or especially the Hebrews.

attrib. **1904** CRISSEY *Tattlings* 263 When he [the Governor] was renominated the parochial school teachers camped on his trail and made it some hot for him.

Parole, *n.* {1616–} + ?A certificate given an Indian chief by a government representative in token of his being regarded as the legal head of his tribe. *Obs.* — **1804** CLARK in *Lewis & C. Exped.* I. (1904) 129 To the Grand Chief we gave a Flag and the parole (certificate).

Parole, *v.* {1716–} +*tr.* To release (a prisoner) on his pledge to observe certain conditions. — **1790** D. FANNING *Narrative* 32, I then parolled the prisoners, except 30, which I sent to Wilmington. **1865** BOUDRYE *Fifth N.Y. Cavalry* 269 We are going to be paroled when these rolls are finished. **1888** *Troy* (N.Y.) *D. Times* 7 Feb. (F.), The defendant was paroled on his own recognisance. **1888** *N.Y. Herald* 29 July 15/2 He was paroled until August 8. **1911** *Missouri Reports* CCXXXII. 586 The court shall have no power to parole any person after he has been delivered to the warden of the penitentiary.

+**Parole camp.** Any one of several camps established by the federal government for Northern soldiers who had been captured and paroled by the Confederacy but who were not yet regularly exchanged. *Obs.* — **1867** Goss *Soldier's Story* 53 Three months followed in the parole camp, where I regained strength. **1888** BILLINGS *Hardtack* 307 Our government established what were known as parole camps, where such prisoners [those paroled] were required to remain until duly exchanged. **1892** *Congress. Rec.* 18 March 2220/1 It was necessary for this man to get a pass from this parole camp when he left?

Paroled, *a.* Placed on parole. — **1865** BOUDRYE *Fifth N.Y. Cavalry* 196 It is remarkable how readily paroled Rebel soldiers affiliate with us. **1867** Goss *Soldier's Story* 252 The Colonel and Adjutant were very jealous of any of the paroled men having communication with the other prisoners. **1925** *Scribner's Mag.* Oct. 410/1 A large proportion of paroled prisoners have been reclaimed from their evil ways by this judicious system.

***Paroquet.** Also **parroquet.** Variant of PARAKEET. — **1775** CRESSWELL *Journal* 77 Saw several Buffalo tracks and a flock of Paroquets. **1792** IMLAY *Western Territory* 115 The blackness proceeds from the incisions made in the bark by the pecking of the parroquet, and other birds. **1835** HOFFMAN *Winter in West* I. 236, I sat down upon a fallen tree ... and watched a flock of green parroquets fluttering among the wych-elms. **1894** TORREY *Fla. Sketch-Book* 147 He had seen two flocks of paroquets during the winter. **1917** [see PARROT].

Parquet. Also **parquette.** {1816–} +The main floor of a theater, or that part of it extending back from the orchestra as far as the parquet circle.

1835 INGRAHAM *South-West* I. 221 The pit or parquette, as it is here termed, which is considered the most eligible and fashionable part of the house. **1851** NORTHALL *Curtain* 176 In the more fashionable theatres in the city, the good old pits appear under another name, and are called parquettes. **1877** *Harper's Mag.* Feb. 466/1 If the destruction of the hapless people in the upper galleries of the theatre was a 'judgment' upon them for going to the play, was the escape of those in the parquet a sign of approbation? **1891** WELCH *Recoll. 1830–40* 369 The parquet, or pit seats are now thought to be the choicest for both seeing and hearing, thus driving out the pit rowdies. **1917** MCCUTCHEON *Green Fancy* 343 Parquet $217.50, dress circle $105.

attrib. **1842** *Chicago American* 18 Aug., Parquet tickets 50 cents. **1880** CABLE *Grandissimes* 1 They had laid a temporary floor over the parquette seats.

+**Parquet circle.** Also **parquette circle.** That part of the main floor of a theater beneath the galleries. — **1854** E. Tompkins *Boston Theatre* (1908) 15 Persons who purchase Tickets ... for either the Parquette, Parquette Circle, Balcony [etc.]. **1882** RITTENHOUSE *Maud* 104 In the middle I saw a photographer turn his camera at me from the hall back of the parquet circle. **1896** BIRKMIRE *Planning of Amer. Theatres* 62 The parquette circle ... is arranged in steps.

***Parrot.** Also †**parrat.** +A North American representative of the parrot family Psittacidae: (see quot. 1917).

See also CAROLINA PARROT.

1588 HARRIOT *Brief Rep. New Found Land of Va.* D3 Foule [found in Va. include] ... Stockdoues: Partridges: ... Parots, Faulcons, & Marlin haukes. **1612** SMITH, etc. *Virginia* 1. 15 In winter there are great plenty of Swans, ... Oxeies, Parrats, and Pigeons. *c*1728 CATESBY *Carolina* I. 11 *Psittacus Caroliniensis.* The Parrot of Carolina. This Bird is of the bigness [of], or rather less than a Black-bird. **1779** in *Travels Amer. Col.* 621 Here was several flocks of Parrots flying about. **1821** NUTTALL *Travels Arkansa* 58 Flocks of screaming parrots were greedily feeding. **1874** COUES *Birds N.W.* 296 In Iowa, according to Mr. Trippe, the Parrot still occurs. **1917** *Birds of Amer.* II. 122 [Of] the species of typical Parrots ... only one, the Carolina Paroquet, is a resident of the United States, and but one other, the Thick-billed Parrot [*Rhynchopsitta pachyrhyncha*], casually crosses the international boundary at the south.

Parrott. + =next. Also attrib. — **1862** Moore *Rebellion Rec.* V. II. 528 All Loomis's pieces were ... thundering away with the sharp, quick, deadly report which rifled Parrotts always make. **1863** — *Women of War*

276 Soon the fierce screech of the Parrott shells from our gunboats mingled with the din. **1865** RICHARDSON *Secret Service* 296 Half way up the mountain, you rest your panting horse among . . . black solemn Parrotts, with iron-banded breech, and shining howitzers of brass. **1891** *Century Mag.* Jan. 411 Our Parrotts also fell into the hands of the enemy. **1901** CHURCHILL *Crisis* 422 His cap is fanned off by the blast of a Parrott six feet above his head.

+**Parrott gun.** [Robt. Parker *Parrott*, Amer. inventor (1804–77).] A muzzle-loading, cast-iron, rifled gun having the breech reinforced with a band of wrought iron.

1862 NORTON *Army Lett.* 72 A little way on the other side a battery of Parrott guns. **1865** *Atlantic Mo.* April 423/1 Major Strong was in command upon . . . an army gunboat, carrying a thirty-pound Parrott gun, two ten-pound Parrotts, and an eight-inch howitzer. **1872** MCCLELLAN *Golden State* 366 The friction of the blow fired a fifteen-inch Parrott gun at the Golden Gate. **1904** *McClure's Mag.* Feb. 427, [I] came upon a battery of small *Parrott guns* at work amid the wreck of corn-stalks.

attrib. **1865** BOUDRYE *Fifth N.Y. Cavalry* 33 Our company and company E were ordered to cover the parrot gun battery.

+**Parsley haw.** A small tree (*Crataegus apiifolia*) found in the southern states: (cf. next). — **1884** SARGENT *Rep. Forests* 81. **1897** SUDWORTH *Arborescent Flora* 232 *Cratægus apiifolia.* . . . Parsley Haw (N.C., Ala., Fla. Miss., La.). . . . Parsley-leaved Haw (S.C.).

+**Parsley-leaved,** *a.* Used in specific names, esp. of the parsley haw (q.v.), in sense: Having leaves similar to sprigs of parsley. — [**1785** MARSHALL *Amer. Grove* 166 *Vitis laciniosa.* Canadian Parsley-leaved Vine. . . . The leaves are cut into many slender segments, somewhat in manner of a Parsley-leaf.] **1813** MUHLENBERG *Cat. Plants* 49 *Crataegus apiifolia.* Parsley-leaved hawthorn. Car. Cherok. **1860** CURTIS *Woody Plants N.C.* 83 Parsley-leaved Haw. . . . The fruit is red and about 1/4 inch long. **1892** APGAR *Trees Northern U.S.* 105 *Crataegus apiifolia.* (Parsley-leaved Thorn.) . . . Virginia and south, in moist woods. **1897** [see prec.].

***Parsnip.** A well-known erect biennial plant (*Pastinaca sativa*), the taproot of which is used as food.

1610 *Estate of Virginia* 13 What should I speake of cucumbers, muske melons, pompions, potatoes, parsneps, carrets, turn vps. **1649** *Desc. Virginia* 4 They have Roots of severall kindes . . . Parsnips, Onions, and Hartichokes. **1709** LAWSON *Carolina* 77 The Garden-Roots that thrive well in Carolina, are Carrots, Leeks, Parsnips, Turneps. **1794** DENNY *Journal* 200 There have been very fine gardens here; parsnips, currant bushes and many other things growing wild. **1809** BENTLEY *Diary* III. 451 The Parsnip was not so common as heretofore. **1885** *Rep. Indian Affairs* 126 Each farmer raised a small patch of vegetables, such as . . . carrots, parsnips, onions, etc.

b. In the names of insects: (see quotations).

1867 *Amer. Naturalist* I. 220 Early in the month the Parsnip Butterfly (*Papilio Asterias*) may be seen flying over beds of parsnips. **1925** HERRICK *Man. Injurious Insects* 283 The Parsnip Webworm. *Depressaria heracliana.* . . . This imported pest occurs in southern Canada and the eastern United States.

***Parson.**

***1.** A minister or clergyman.

1704 S. KNIGHT *Journal* 59 One Church of England parson officiated in all these three towns. **1827** COOPER *Prairie* xxxi, Some think it is enough to say yes and no, to the questions of the magistrate, or of the parson if one happens to be handy. **1884** J. HAWTHORNE in *Harper's Mag.* Feb. 433/2 You must get up early to get the better of a man who has been a parson. **1920** BOK *Americanization* 357 The parson was given a parsonage.

b. Used as a title.

1773 J. ADAMS *Diary* Works II. 320 Spent this evening at Wheelwright's, with Parson Williams of Sandwich. **1825** NEAL *Bro. Jonathan* I. 105 Darn it all, parson Harwood, can't ye let a feller get his breath? **1871** STOWE *Sam Lawson* 78 'Why, Parson Carryl,' says Mis' Deakin Blodgett, 'how you've come it over us.' **1896** JEWETT *Pointed Firs* 110 Parson Dimmick was a vague person.

+**2.** (See quotation.)

1816 in G. Shaw *Gen. Zool.* IX. 407 [The indigo bunting] is called in Carolina the Parson.

***Parsonage.** Also †**parsonadge, parsonag.**

***1.** A house belonging to a parish or church for the use of the resident minister.

1739 *Duxbury Rec.* 262 A vote was asked of the town whether they would buy Seth Bartletts farm for a parsonage. **1832** WILLIAMSON *Maine* II. 78 In the old parish at Kittery-point, a parsonage, provided as early as 1669, . . . was occupied. **1874** ALDRICH *P. Palfrey* v, Prudence . . . reached the gate of the parsonage without accident. **1908** *Indian Laws & Tr.* III. 365 The Episcopal parsonage and church building.

2. Attrib. with *home, house, kitchen,* etc.

1672 *Huntington Rec.* I. 186 The towne hous or parsonadge hous and land and fence. **1684** *Manchester Rec.* I. 19 The west corner bounds of the parsonag land and from thence norwesterly to a heap of stons. **1706** *Topsfield Rec.* 154 William Averell shall have the benefit of ye frute of ye parsonage orchard. **1865** *Atlantic Mo.* May 594/2 The proposed introduction of the young stranger from abroad to the advantages of the parsonage home did not weigh upon his thought greatly. **1891** EARLE *Sabbath* 89 The eight godly, shivering souls wished profoundly that one of their number had . . . permitted the seven others and the minister to have the sermon in comfort in the parsonage kitchen.

+**Parsonage lot.** A lot adjacent or belonging to a parsonage. — **1690** *Huntington Rec.* II. 66 Their shall bee laid out sixty acars of land . . . to bee reserved for a parsonage lott. **1706** *Manchester Rec.* I. 112 It the 19th Lot is the parsonage lot.

***Part.** +(See quot. 1890.) — **1890** *Cent.* 4302/2 *Part.* . . . The parting of the hair. (U.S.) **1895** *Century Mag.* Aug. 489/1 His straight, smooth hair, with its definite part.

Parterre. {1639–} +The lowest tier of boxes in the Metropolitan Opera House, New York City. {1711–56, in sense of 'pit,' as in French} Also attrib. — **1883** *Harper's Mag.* Nov. 884/1 Over this [the half-tier] in succession, are the parterre, the first and second tiers, and then the balcony and the gallery. **1896** BIRKMIRE *Planning of Amer. Theatres* 5 The hangings between the *parterre* boxes and the nineteen in the *grand* tier [of the Metropolitan Opera House] are of a maroon tint.

+**Partialism.** A religious view that does not take into account all the facts bearing upon a subject. — **1872** BEECHER *Yale Lectures on Preaching* I. 26 Your mode of presenting the truth will be imperfect. Your partialisms are full of danger. **1897** *Advance* 2 Dec. 779/3 The Gospel also is in danger . . . from partialism, because men do not fully realize what Christ is in his three offices of prophet, priest, and king.

***Partialist.** +One who holds a partial theory or is inclined toward partialism. Also *partialistic* a. — **1844** EMERSON *Nominalist & Realist* Ess. 2 Ser., Very fitly, therefore, I assert, that every man is a partialist. **1874** BEECHER in *Chr. World Pulpit* VI. 239/1 We are all of us ignorant; we know in part; we are partialists. **1896** GLADDEN in *Ohio Ch. Hist. Soc. P.* VII. 141 The whole partialistic scheme of a rulership which is for a portion of mankind and against the rest.

***Particular,** *a.* Much in excess of the usual. *slang.* (See also FIT *n.*[1] 1.) — **1846** [see JESSE 1]. **1851** BYRN *Life Ark. Doctor* 51 (Th. 494) I'll give you particular thunder one time, and then perhaps you will stay out of here. **1856–** [see FIT *n.*[1]]. **1871** *Harper's Mag.* Oct. 690 Ef *Pat* Role, or any other consarned Irishman, kicks up a muss 'bout these yer diggins, he'll kotch *par*tic'lar lightnin'.

Particularist. {1727–} *Hist.* +An adherent of the policy of states' rights; one who favors strict construction. Also attrib. or as adj. — **1876** *N. Amer. Rev.* Oct. 338 During the administration of Washington the particularist tendencies were mostly quiet. **1885** *Mag. Amer. Hist.* March 297/1 *Particularists.*—A wing of the post-revolutionary Whigs. . . . They were also known later on as 'Anti-Federals.' **1913** A. C. COLE *Whig Party in So.* 7 With evidences of friendship from President Jackson . . . the southern particularists had very natural hopes of strengthening their position. *Ib.* 8 Jackson had led many to believe that he was decidedly friendly to the particularist cause.

+**Parting line. 1.** A boundary line between two properties. *Obs.* **2.** (See quotation.) — (1) **1699** *Boston Rec.* 233 The way shall [run] . . . to the gate in the parting line between Mr. Winthrops land and Major Townsends farm. *Ib.*, [The way is] to run . . . through the gate in the parting line between John Tuttle & Jonathon Tuttle. (2) **1875** KNIGHT 1460/1 The *parting-line* is, as a general rule, that line upon the pattern, as it lies in the sand, above and below which the sides of the pattern run inward from the perpendicular.

***Partisan.**

+**1. a.** A chief or a leader among the Indians. *Obs.* **b.** The chief or one in charge of a band of trappers. *Obs.*

1761 NILES *Indian Wars* II. 565 Monsieur Longville . . . was a famous partisan or partner with [the Indians]. **1827** COOPER *Prairie* xx, What tribe or nation has not felt the blows of the Dachotahs? Mahtoree is their partisan. **1837** IRVING *Bonneville* I. 66 [The trappers] were headed by Mr. Fontenelle, an experienced leader, or 'partisan,' as a chief of a party is called, in the technical language of the trappers. **1844** LEE & FROST *Oregon* 29 [The trader] had been a partisan under General Wayne, in his Indian wars. **1847** PARKMAN in *Knickerb.* XXX. 490 The White Shield, their partisan, rode in gorgeous attire at their head.

attrib. **1861** *Harper's Mag.* March 451/1 Captain Dalzell, who had won great renown as a partisan warrior with Putnam, proposed . . . a night surprise of Pontiac's encampment.

2. During the Revolutionary War, and in the South during the Civil War, a member of a body engaged in petty or guerrilla warfare. Also attrib.

1781 WASHINGTON *Diaries* II. 244 A house . . . out of view, I conceive, of the crossing place most favorable to a partizan stroke. **1835** SIMMS (*title*), The Partisan: A Tale of the Revolution. **1862** *N.Y. Tribune* May (Chipman), We publish the recent act of [the Confederate] Congress, authorizing the raising and bringing into service of partisan rangers. Now is the time for free fighters, the men of dash and daring. **1867** CRAWFORD *Mosby* 63 Mosby received his commission as captain in the Confederate States army, and authority to wage a partisan ranger war on the enemy.

Partition fence. A fence on the boundary between two farms or properties. — **1639** *Dedham Rec.* III. 51 Ordered. . . . That may both be a particion fence in ye same: as also may serue for a Course vnto a water mill. **1641** *Mass. Bay Rec.* I. 333 Where farmes ioyne, the partition fence is to bee run betwixt the owners. **1780** *Phila. Ordinance* (1812) 45 An act for regulating party walls and partition fences. **1870** *Rep. Comm. Agric.* 1869 395 Partition fences must be proof against sheep.

Partition line. A boundary line. Also attrib. — **1717** *N.Y. Col. Laws* I. 988 The Charge of Running . . . and Ascertaining the Partition Line Limitt betweene this Colony and the Colony of New Jersey. **1743** *N.J. Archives* 1 Ser. VI. 146 The Partition line would nearly run South forty seven degrees east according to the magnetick compass. **1858** WARDER *Hedges & Evergreens* 145 If upon the partition-line, there has been a valid division.

Partition wall. A partition in a building. — **1698** CHAMBERLAIN *Lithobolia* (1914) 72 The pressing-Iron clattered against the Partition Wall between the Hall and the Chamber beyond it. **1801** *N.H. Hist. Soc. Coll.* V. 58 The library . . . was arranged against the partition wall directly behind the fire place of that house. **1877** *Rep. Indian Affairs* 40 Main building . . . with a partition-wall through center.

+**Partnership fence.** A fence owned commonly or jointly by neighbors. — **1845** *Indiana Senate Jrnl.* 20 Sess. 335 A bill to provide for the dissolving of partnership fences.

***Partridge.**

+**1.** *S.* The bobwhite, *Colinus virginianus.*

See also AMERICAN PARTRIDGE, NIGHT PARTRIDGE.

1588 HARRIOT *Briefe Rep. Va.* D2 Stockdoues: Partridges: Cranes: Hernes: & in winter great store of Swannes & Geese [are found in Va.]. **1612** SMITH, etc. *Virginia* I. 15 Patrridges there are little bigger than our Quailes, wilde Turkies are as bigge as our tame. **1676** GLOVER *Va.* in *Phil. Trans.* XI. 631 The Fowls that keep the Woods are, wild Turkies, Turkie Buzzards, Turtle-Doves, Partridges, Hawks of several sorts. **1709** LAWSON *Carolina* 67 The woods [were] stor'd every where, with . . . great Store of Partridges, Cranes, and Conies. **1775** BURNABY *Travels* 16 Pheasants, woodcocks, and partridges, are in the greatest abundance [in the forests of Va.]. **1812** WILSON *Ornithology* VI. 26 The Quail, as it is called in New England, or the Partridge, as in Pennsylvania, is nine inches long. **1872** *Fur, Fin & Feather: Game Laws* 182 The Germantown (Penn.) Telegraph says that partridge (quail) were never known to be so plentiful in that vicinity as they are this year. **1897** *N.Y. Forest, Fish, & Game Comm. 2d Rep.* 317 Popular synonyms [for the bobwhite]. . . . Virginia quail; partridge or colin.

+**2.** The ruffed grouse, *Bonasa umbellus.*

1630 HIGGINSON *New-England* 15 And [I] my selfe . . . sprung a Partridge so bigge that through the heauinesse of his Body could fly but a little way. **1701** WOLLEY *Journal N.Y.* 40 They have great store of wildfowl, as Turkys, Heath-hens, Quails, Partridges, Pigeons. **1792** BELKNAP *Hist. New-Hampshire* III. 171 The partridge is very common in our woods. **1812** WILSON *Ornithology* VI. 45 Ruffed Grous. . . . This is the Partridge of the eastern states, and the Pheasant of Pennsylvania and the southern districts. **1856** GOODRICH *Recoll.* I. 98 The *partridge* of New England is the *pheasant* of the South, and the *ruffed grouse* of the naturalists. **1918** ROOSEVELT in *Maine My State* 19, I also remember . . . the meals of venison, trout or partridge.

+**Partridge berry.**

1. a. A trailing plant (*Mitchella repens*) common throughout the eastern United States. **b.** The wintergreen, *Gaultheria procumbens.* (Cf. CHECKERBERRY b and c.)

1714 *Phil. Trans.* XXIX. 63 Another Plant, . . . Partridge-berries, excellent in curing the Dropsy; a Decoction of the Leaves being drank several days as a Tea. **1784** CUTLER in *Amer. Acad. Mem.* I. 410 *Mitchella*. . . . Partridgeberry. The stems trailing. . . . Blossoms white. In thick woods and swamps. **1814** BIGELOW *Florula Bostoniensis* 101 *Gaultheria procumbens*. Partridge berry. . . . A plant universally known for its pleasant, aromatic flavour. **1858** *Harper's Mag.* March 495/1 The shining foliage of the partridge-berry cover[s] the earth with a gay, fragrant mosaic. **1892** COULTER *Bot. W. Texas* II. 160 *Mitchella* (Partridge-berry.) A smooth and trailing small evergreen herb. **1905** *Forestry Bureau Bul.* No. 60, 14 The ground cover is chiefly partridge berry, club moss, wood sorrel, ferns, and mosses.

2. The fruit of the partridge berry.

1810 in Wilson *Ornithology* III. 109 A favourite article of their diet is the heath-hen plum, or partridge-berry. **1814** PURSH *Flora Amer.* I. 283 Berries red, eatable, and known by the name of Partridge-berries. **1850** JUDD *R. Edney* 277 He filled their baskets with box-berries and partridge-berries. **1905** WIGGIN *Rose* 112 Partridge-berries glowed red under their glossy leaves.

+**Partridge berry vine.** =PARTRIDGE BERRY 1 a. — **1868** BEECHER *Norwood* 91 Here the little queen took on airs, and sent her Ethiop . . . [for] some partridge-berry vines from the edge of the wood. **1878** JACKSON *Travel at Home* 196 There is not a single unillumined moss stem . . . where moss and Linnæa, and partridge-berry vines are so inextricably tangled. **1892** TORREY *Foot-Path Way* 242 Like the lowly partridge-berry vine, I would be always the pine-trees' neighbor.

+**Partridge bush.** =PARTRIDGE BERRY 1 b. — **1843** *Amer. Pioneer* II. 125 The vivid green leaves and bright scarlet berries of the 'Partridge bush,' or 'Checkerberry.'

+**Partridge hawk.** =GOSHAWK. — **1895** *Dept. Agric. Yrbk. 1894* 231 From the persistency with which this species hunts the ruffed grouse in many of the Northern States, it has received the name 'partridge hawk.' **1917** *Birds of Amer.* II. 68 Goshawk. *Astur atricapillus atricapillus*. . . . [Also called] Blue Darter; Partridge Hawk; Dove Hawk.

+**Partridge pea.** A sensitive pea of the genus *Chamaecrista*, esp. *C. fasciculata.* — **1817–8** EATON *Botany* (1822) 226 *Cassia chamoecrista*, cassia, partridge pea. . . . A most elegant plant, . . . dry sand. **1836** LINCOLN *Botany* App. 85. **1873** *Harper's Mag.* April 751/1 The partridge-pea, with its crimson hood, Is scattered about like drops of blood.

+**Partridge plant.** =PARTRIDGE BERRY 1 b. — **1850** S. F. COOPER *Rural Hours* 105 Violets . . . grow there, with . . . squaw-vine, partridge-plant, pipsissiwa. **1894** *Amer. Folk-Lore* VII. 93 *Gaultheria procumbens*, partridge-plant, N.Y.

+**Partridge plum.** =PARTRIDGE BERRY 2. — *c***1876** STOWE *First Christmas* 121 Little Love gathered stores of bright checker berries and partridge plums.

+**Partridge run.** A run, dash, or dance step suggestive of the quick running away of a partridge. *Obs.* — **1807** IRVING *Salmagundi* xvii. 460 [Rigadoon] gave a short partridge run, and with mighty vigor and swiftness did bolt over the walls with a somerset. **1825** PAULDING *J. Bull in Amer.* 113 Several . . . were seen cutting pigeon wings and taking the partridge run with all the alacrity imaginable.

+**Partridge trap.** A trap in which partridges are taken.— **1832** KENNEDY *Swallow Barn* II. 223 The model by which boys build partridge-traps. **1839** *S. Lit. Messenger* V. 113/1 [There] is the log-hovel, . . . its chimney not unlike a tall partridge trap, ever tottering to its fall. **1858** *Ib.* XXVI. 254/2 Like the figger 4 trigger to a imments partrich trap.

+**Partridge vine.** =PARTRIDGE BERRY 1 a. — **1880** *Harper's Mag.* Nov. 864/1 Here are soft beds of rich green moss studded with scarlet berries of wintergreen and partridge vine. **1907** *N.Y. Ev. Post* (s.-w. ed.) 6 May 5 In the basket was one growing plant, with moss and a bit of partridge vine.

***Party.**

1. Any one of various American political organizations which seek to influence the course of government by electing their candidates to office. {in general sense, 1689– (s.v. *Tory* a. 1)}

1802 JEFFERSON *Writings* X. 321 Candid federalists acknowledge that their party can never more raise its head. **1830** J. Q. ADAMS *Memoirs* VIII. 240 What with Anti-Masonic and Jackson men, parties were all broken up. **1884** *Century Mag.* April 863/2 The State offices within the gift of party are too few to 'go round.' **1900** *Congress. Rec.* 19 Jan. 980/1 This great [Populist] party grew out of the fact that the Republican party is given to empire and to the destruction of republican form of government. **1909** PARKER *G. Cleveland* 202 He saw the party lose its regular or occasional footholds in one State after another.

2. *attrib.* and *comb.* **a.** Of or pertaining to political parties in general. {1711–}

1806 *Balance* V. 148/2 We ask democrats to divest themselves of party-prejudice. **1830** *Congress. Deb.* 9 Feb. 149/2 The provisional power of removal from office by a President . . . [should not] be exercised . . . in the corrupting spirit of 'party discipline.' **1838** MAYO *Polit. Sk. Washington* (1839) ix, Each [candidate for election is] endeavouring . . . to substitute some plausible dogmas, regardless of their consistency, or good keeping with the cognomen of his party banner. **1858** *N.Y. Tribune* 3 Aug. 5/5 (Th.), Mr. Elmore . . . has strong enemies in the ranks of the Democracy, he having 'bolted' party nominations at pleasure. **1870** *Nation* 24 Feb. 113/2 Those who hold that the nomination to places in the public service is party 'plunder,' or 'spoils.' **1873** *Harper's Mag.* Jan. 273/1 Cilley was a sacrifice to the rancor of party strife. **1879** *Congress. Rec.* 14 June 2000/1 In filling the box, the names of men who are fittest for jurymen . . . are to be placed there without reference to party affiliation. **1885** CRAWFORD *Amer. Politician* 355 Trample under your free-born feet the badges of party bondage, the ignoble chains of party slavery, the wretched hopes of party preferment. **1913** LA FOLLETTE *Autobiog.* 171 In order to bring about the desired party harmony H. C. Thom was elected.

b. Designating particular members or types of members of political parties.

See also *party hack* s.v. HACK[1] 2.

1838 MAYO *Polit. Sk. Washington* (1839) 12 These mock reforms have resulted in the engenderment of abuses and enormities; such as . . . sinecures, party pensioners, and charity incumbents. **1855** I. C. PRAY *Mem. J. G. Bennett* 79 It led to a train of consequences which ultimately surrounded Mr. Bennett's progress as a party journalist with difficulties and embarrassments. **1864** 'PENNIMAN' *Tanner-Boy* 140 Gen. Grant has never been assailed by any but traitors, . . . party politicians, and their aiders and abettors. **1865** *Atlantic Mo.* March 370/2 A thousand times have party-speakers and party-organs . . . washed their hands of all responsibility. **1868** *N.Y. Herald* 10 July 6/2 The party jugglers of this Tammany Hall Convention had a different game to play. **1883** *Century Mag.* Sept. 704/1 Such men will not sink their convictions at the bidding of party managers. **1881–5** MCCLELLAN *Own Story* 149 They then saw clearly that it would not be possible to make a party tool of me. **1885** CRAWFORD *Amer. Politician* 353 Would any of us remember this day without shame if we disgraced those who trust us, by giving our votes to a mere party candidate? **1888** BRYCE *Amer. Commw.* II. III. lxiv. 470 Certain salaries and fees in local offices are kept notoriously high, so that the incumbent may freely 'bleed' for party use, or, what is the same thing, for the use of party 'bummers.' **1892** *Courier-Journal* 2 Oct. 1/7 The 'party workers' . . . were well represented.

c. Designating groups serving political parties.

1881 *Nation* 7 July 4/3 The slipshod method in which the Vice-President is commonly chosen by party conventions. **1882** THAYER *From Log-*

Cabin 390 Garfield . . . was nominated by acclamation at the party caucus, and unanimously elected. **1883** *Century Mag.* July 469/1 The party Committees and associations shall be re-organized so as to admit the leaders of both factions. **1895** MYERS *Bosses & Boodle* 118 The primaries are manipulated by the 'Bosses,' large and small, of party 'rings.'

Party dress. A dress worn to social parties; a best dress. — **1875** STOWE *We & Neighbors* 38 What are you going to do about the girls' party dresses? **1901** RYAN *Montana* 99 Presenting herself to his notice in all the glory of her party dress. **1908** BEACH *Barrier* 42 It's my first party-dress, you know. **1923** WATTS *L. Nichols* 257 That's a party-dress, isn't it?

Party feeling. Feeling inspired by belonging to a political party. {1823-}

1808 *Ann. 10th Congress* 1 Sess. 356 Patriotism . . . [should] enable us to make a willing sacrifice . . . of all local and party feelings. *a***1817** DWIGHT *Travels* I. 262 The zeal and party-feeling, so commonly found in free States. **1843** *Whig Almanac 1844* 19/2 The earnestness and depth of conviction on the part of those who had shared in the experience of the country without as well as with a Bank . . . nearly overbore the mountain of prejudice and party feeling arrayed against that institution. **1881** MCCLELLAN *Own Story* 27 Up to within a brief period, party feeling has run so high that the pathway for the truth has been well-nigh closed. **1913** LA FOLLETTE *Autobiog.* 159 Party feeling and party loyalty were still strong.

Party gown. =PARTY DRESS. — **1899** TARKINGTON *Gentleman from Ind.* xvii, It was a Rouen 'party-gown' wherewith she chose to abash poor John Harkless. **1904** LOVETT *R. Gresham* 65 The girls wore . . . faded party gowns.

+**Party line. 1.** A political tenet regarded as a bound beyond which the party or a loyal party member can not go. **2.** A telephone circuit serving more than one subscriber. — **(1) 1834** BENTON *30 Years' View* I. 431/2 Look at the vote in the Senate, upon the adoption of the resolution, also as clearly defined by a party line as any party question can ever be expected to be. **1860** CLAIBORNE *Sam. Dale* 218 Party lines were strictly drawn, and there was a U.S. senator to elect. **1884** BLAINE *20 Years of Congress* I. 277 It was not only a sharp division on the party line but almost equally so on the sectional line. **1913** LA FOLLETTE *Autobiog.* 172 I did not propose that those nominally in control of the party organizations should for any reason blacklist and put me outside of party lines. **(2) 1902** *Encycl. Brit.* XXXIII. 237/2 A number of subscribers can be placed upon a single circuit or 'party line.'

+**Party machinery.** The leaders, advisers, committees, etc., engaged in carrying on the work of a political party. — **1829** ORNE *Lett.Columbus* 71 (Ernst), Gen. Jackson was also less embarrassed by party machinery than any other candidate ever was. **1913** LA FOLLETTE *Autobiog* 53, I knew nothing about the underlying forces which at that time controlled and in large measure still control, party machinery.

Party man. {1701-} A man definitely and dependably attached to an American political party. — **1729** FRANKLIN *Works* II. 110 The Author is no Party-Man, but a general Meddler. **1830** in Claiborne *Life Quitman* I. 95 You are not regarded strictly as a party man. **1877** JOHNSON *Anderson Co., Kansas* 41 Violent party men . . . commenced the work of persecution. **1900** *Congress. Rec.* 11 Jan. 783/1 There are many strict party men there.

+**Party platform.** A formal statement of the principles and policies of a political party. — **1848** LOWELL *Biglow P.* 1 Ser. viii. 111 It gives a Party Platform, tu, jest level with the mind Of . . . honest folks thet mean to go it blind. **1873** *Newton Kansan* 15 May 4/3 It cannot be made a predominant issue in any party platform. **1888** M. LANE in *America* 11 Oct. 15 *Kickers*, . . . disaffected politicians who refuse . . . to support the party platform regularly adopted.

Party politics. {1773-} Political affairs, activities, interests, etc., engaged in or considered from the standpoint of an American political party. — **1807** IRVING, etc. *Salmagundi* xv. 406 He pledged himself never to engage in party schemes, or party politics, but to stand up solely for the broad interests of his country. **1863** LINCOLN in Logan *Great Conspiracy* 519 Among the Commanders who hold these views are some who have never had an affinity . . . with 'Republican party politics.' **1884** *Century Mag.* April 864/2 [The introduction of the liquor question] into party politics is to be deprecated. **1900** *Congress. Rec.* 25 Jan. 1176/2 Every member of this House, regardless of party politics, . . . should vote now as he thinks is right.

+**Party question.** A question or subject upon which political parties differ as a matter of party policy. — **1803** *Ann. 7th Congress* 2 Sess. 337 This ought not to be made a party question. **1830** in Benton *30 Years' View* I. 165/2 The extent of the jurisdiction of Georgia, and the policy of removing the Cherokees . . . , have become party questions.

+**Party rig.** A dress or costume suitable for wearing to a social party or gathering. *colloq.* — **1865** STOWE in *Atlantic Mo.* July 105/2 Holloa, Bess! is that your party-rig? **1881** RITTENHOUSE *Maud* 24 Here I sit in party-rig waiting for Elmer.

+**Party ticket. 1.** A list of the candidates for office put forward or endorsed by the leaders or representatives of a political party. **2.** A printed ballot containing such a list. — **(1) 1843** *Niles' Nat. Reg.* 176/3 The party ticket nominated at Tammany Hall was generally voted and was generally successful. **1913** LA FOLLETTE *Autobiog.* 233 These old machine leaders thus came to the support of the party ticket in 1900. **(2) 1886** ROOSEVELT in *Century Mag.* Nov. 77/1 Before election day, many thousands of complete sets of the party ticket are printed, folded, and put together, or, as it is called, 'bunched.'

+**Party vote. 1.** A vote, as in Congress, along strictly party lines. **2.** The collective vote polled by a political party. — **(1) 1846** *Whig Almanac 1847* 10/2 It has been re-enacted in substance by the present Congress, by a strict party vote. **1868** *Ore. State Jrnl.* 25 July 2/4 The bill [was] passed by a strict party vote. **(2) 1904** *Brooklyn Eagle* 9 June 4 One unable to hold his straight party vote in his own city would be a calamity.

+**Party whip.** The pressure exerted by a party upon its members in a legislature. — **1880** *Scribner's Mo.* Oct. 908/2 The vigorous cracking of the party whip is a pretty sure sign that corruption has crept into the management. **1900** *Congress. Rec.* 29 Jan. 1259/2 Executive influence was brought to bear; the party whip was cracked. *Ib.* 8 Feb. 1641/1 Every vote that can be obtained by the party whip, by threats, and by cajolery will be obtained to pass [the bill].

+**Parula (warbler).** [Dim. fr. L. *parus* 'titmouse.'] A small American warbler (*Compsothlypis americana*) having a brownish-yellow patch on the back. — **1887** RIDGWAY *Manual N.A. Birds* 491 Eastern United States and Canada, breeding throughout. . . . *C. americana*. Parula Warbler. **1917** *Birds of Amer.* III. 123 The Parula Warbler has been called the Blue Yellowback, but the name 'Parula,' . . . was given it because of the Chickadee-like habit of searching for its food. *Ib.*, If one watches long enough he is pretty sure to see the Parula hanging from a limb.

Par value. The face value of bonds, stocks, etc. {1861-} — **1807** *Phila. Ordinances* (1812) 213 No purchase of six per cent stock shall be made at a higher price than the par value. **1848** W. ARMSTRONG *Stocks* 5 The par value is commonly $100 or $50. The first is called 'full stock,' and the latter 'half stock.' **1870** MEDBERY *Men Wall St.* 14 The par value of annual sales, made at the boards and 'over the counter.' **1906** *Indian Laws & Tr.* III. 180 No improvement script shall be issued or sold for less than its par value.

Pasilaly. A universal language. — [**1805** *Annual Rev. & Hist. Lit.* III. 14 It appears that the Indians have invented what a recent French writer calls a *pasilaly*, a method of talking to people of all languages, without understanding theirs.] **1869** *Overland Mo.* III. 131 A Texan goes forth . . . [not] to pay his devoirs to his Amaryllis, . . . but (employing a word worthy of a place in the pasilaly of mankind) his jimpsecute. **1890** *Cent.* 4311/2 *Pasilaly*, . . . a language adapted for universal use; universal speech.

Paspalum. A genus of grasses, chiefly American, some species of which are valuable for hay or pasturage; a plant or species of this genus. Freq. with specifying term. {1830- (Loudon *Hort. Brit.* 23)} — **1845** LINCOLN *Botany* App. 137/1 Creeping paspalum, joint-grass. **1857** GRAY *Botany* 575 Paspalum. . . . Said to have been a Greek name for Millet. . . . *P. fluitans*. River-swamps, Virginia, S. Ohio, Illinois and southward. **1901** MOHR *Plant Life Ala.* 341 *Paspalum*. North America, 28 species, all east of the Rocky Mountains, and chiefly south of the Ohio Valley.

***Pasque flower.** A plant of the genus *Pulsatilla*, +esp. *P. ludoviciana*. — **1857** GRAY *Botany* 4 *Pulsatilla*. Pasque-flower. . . . (Derivation obscure. The popular name was given because the plant is in blossom at Easter.) . . . *P. Nuttalliana*. . . . Prairies, Wisconsin. **1863** *Rep. Comm. Agric. 1862* 157 There are many pretty species [of anemones]: one, the 'Pasque flower,' . . . a large blue flower, is common in Illinois.

***Pass,** *n.*[1] A narrow passage or way through a mountainous country or across a mountain.

1720 *Va. House of Burgesses* 271 It is necessary for the defence . . . That ffort's be built at the Two passes thro' the Great Ridge of Mountaines. **1755** EVANS *Anal. Map. Colonies* 10 The Pass through the Mountains . . . is from my own Observations. **1775** BURNABY *Travels* 32 The pass at Ashby's Gap, from the foot of the mountain on the eastern side to the Shenando, . . . is about four miles. **1830** WATSON *Philadelphia* 716 Colonel Spotswood . . . had happily discovered passes in the Allegheny mountains. **1897** *Boston Globe* 4 Aug. 5/2 (Ernst), There are 500 people now at Dyea waiting to get over the pass. **1912** RAINE *Brand Blotters* 174 You'll have to cross the dead line to get over the pass.

b. In the names of particular places of this kind.

1848 *Santa Fe Republican* 24 July 2/1 The 'Lagima Pass' of the Sierra that divides the vallies of the Del Norte, and the Colorado of the west. **1865** *Wkly. New Mexican* 15 Sept. 1/4 The best passes over the backbone of the Continent (the Rocky Mountains) . . . [are] Guadalupe Pass and . . . 'Apache Pass.' **1869** A. B. STREET *Indian Pass* 5 At ten o'clock, one bright September day, I found myself at Scott's, ten miles due north from the Indian Pass. **1883** RITCH *Illus. N. Mex.* 23 The general direction of the road from the Colorado State line at Raton Pass to Rincon Junction is nearly south. **1916** in E. S. Meany *Mount Ranier* 319, I explained the phenomenon and the place was called St. Elmo Pass.

***Pass,** *n.*[2] Also †**passe.**

1. Written permission or authorization: **a.** A permit issued by proper authority to a colonist to pass out of a colonial jurisdiction. *Obs.*

1642 *Md. Archives* I. 160 A passe may not be granted to any one untill he have sett up an note at the usuall place. **1663** *Plymouth Laws* 140 [The constable shall give] them a passe to depart the government. **1704** *Boston News-Letter* 24 July 4/2 On the 11th a Proclamation was issued, appointing all Persons that go beyond Sea to take Passes.

+**b.** A document authorizing an indentured servant to go on a journey. *Obs.*

1767 *Penna. Chronicle* 9-16 March 32/2 Run away . . . a Dutch indented Servant Man, named Phillip Nold. . . . [He] may perhaps produce some old Pass. **1771** *Ib.* 13 June 4/1 Run away . . . William King, a native of Ireland. . . . [He] writes a good hand, and may forge a pass.

+**c.** A permit given a Negro to go about, esp. at night, away from his usual abode. *Obs.*

1841 BUCKINGHAM *America* I. 322 No coloured person can go at large in the city of Washington after ten o'clock, without a pass from a justice of the peace. **1856** OLMSTED *Slave States* 161 When the hunters take a negro who has not a pass, or 'free papers,' . . . they confine him in jail, and advertise him. **1870** O. LOGAN *Before Footlights* 42 Colored persons are liable to be confined [in the guardhouse] if they are found in the streets after a certain hour without a 'pass.' **1880** CABLE *Grandissimes* 121 [She was] fortified against the street-watch with her master's written 'pass.' **1893** [see PAT(T)ER(R)OLLER].

d. A permit entitling the holder to free railroad transportation. {railway pass, 1871–}

See also FREE PASS.

1873 *Winfield* (Kan.) *Courier* 26 June 4/2 A member of the legislature . . . who was on a deadhead excursion out on the plains, lost his pass. **1879** BURDETTE *Hawkeyes* 136 And you have to either sit on the wood-box or have a timid quarrel with some man traveling on a pass or a half-fare ticket. **1885** CUSTER *Boots & Saddles* 196 The railroad officials were good enough to give us passes. **1890** *Stock Grower & Farmer* 11 Jan. 3/2 But few, if any railroads, have adhered to the agreement made not to issue passes to shippers.

+**2.** *Amer. football.* The transferring of the ball from one player to another on the same side. {1891–, of Rugby}

See also FORWARD *a.* 2.

1893 POST *Harvard Stories* 26 A bad pass by the Harvard quarterback . . . might turn the result. **1921** *Kansas City Star* 3 Jan. 12/1 The 'Buckeyes' were helpless before the long passes of the accurate 'Brick' Muller [of Calif.].

+**Pass,** *n.*[3] [From El Paso, Texas]. (See quot. 1844.) In attrib. uses. *Obs.* — **1840** *Picayune* 6 Sept. 2/4 The wild American youths . . . were highly excited with pass whiskey, which they had been drinking at some fandango. **1844** GREGG *Commerce of Prairies* II. 77 The inhabitants [of the El Paso valley] manufacture [from grapes] a very pleasant wine, somewhat resembling Malaga. A species of *aguardiente* (brandy) is also distilled from the same fruit. . . . These liquors are known among Americans as 'Pass wine' and 'Pass whiskey.' **1854** BARTLETT *Personal Narr.* I. 186 Brandy, or *aguardiente*, is also made from the grape. It is of a light color, and is known in New Mexico as 'Pass Whiskey.' **1866** *Wkly. New Mex.* 21 July 1/4 They immediately staked their little all, if not their whole kit, at a licensed table of pass monte.

* **Pass,** *v.*

+**1.** *tr.* To omit or fail to pay (a dividend).

1870 MEDBERY *Men Wall St.* 137 To 'pass' a dividend. . . . A dividend is said to be passed when the directors vote against declaring it. **1885** *Harper's Mag.* Nov. 843/2 To 'pass a dividend' is not to pay it. **1895** E. CARROLL *Principles Finance* 295 *To pass a dividend*, to fail to make an expected dividend. **1903** *Forum* Oct. 209 Concerns which not only passed dividends but went bankrupt.

+**2.** *intr.* (See quotation.)

1889 *Amer. Folk-Lore* II. 155 In New England the ordinary term used to express the throwing and catching of a ball by two or more persons is *pass*. 'Let's go out and *pass*.'

+**3.** *Baseball. tr.* To permit (a batter) to reach first base on balls.

1912 MATHEWSON *Pitching* 102 In the ninth he passed a couple of men, and a hit tied the score. *Ib.* 304 Once I started to pass 'Hans' Wagner in a pinch to take a chance on the next batter.

***Passage boat.** A passenger boat that plies regularly between two points; a ferryboat. — **1647** *Boston Rec.* 89 It is ordered that George Halsoll shall kep and imploy a passag boatt betweene his wharfe and the ships wher the ships rid. **1738** *N.J. Archives* XI. 529 He also keeps a Passage-Boat to ply between New-York and Amboy. **1760** *Ib.* XX. 472 Francis Bernard . . . the next Morning proceeded from thence to Providence in a Passage-Boat provided for that Purpose. **1820** *Niles' Reg.* XVII. 396/1, I have returned the passage-boat belonging to you, which was taken by my boats on the 5th inst.

+**Passage wagon.** (See quot. 1774.) — **1774** J. ADAMS *Diary* Works II. 357 [Near Phila.] we saw two or three passage wagons, a vehicle with four wheels, contrived to carry many passengers and much baggage. **1860** GREELEY *Overland Journey* 106 The express-line . . . has run out some thirty passage wagons from Leavenworth.

Passageway. a. A way, road, or route over ground. **b.** A passage or hallway in a building. {1878–}

'Chiefly *U.S.*' (*O.E.D.*).

1649 *Boston Rec.* 98 Wm. Franklin is fined 20s. for disablinge the passage way. **1715** *Cambridge Prop. Rec.* 276 It is neither needful nor convenient for to have a passage way thru Said Dickson's lot. **1797** *Ib.* 328 [We] are of opinion, that a passage way thrô said lots is necessary to be laid out. **1889** BRAYLEY *Boston Fire Dept.* 151 A fire originates in narrow passageways, where engines cannot operate to advantage. **1908** 'O. HENRY' *Strictly Business* 182 There was a long hallway (or 'passageway,' as they call it in the land of the Colonels) with one side latticed running along the rear of the house.

Pass book. {1828–} **1.** (See quot. 1839.) +**2.** A book kept by a soldier or sailor in which articles of clothing, etc., are checked off as issued to him by the storekeeper or supply officer. — **(1) 1839** BOUVIER *Law Dict.* 230/2 *Pass-book*, . . . a book used by merchants with their customers, in which an entry of goods sold and delivered to a customer is made. It is kept by the buyer and sent to the merchant whenever he wishes to purchase any article. **1864** WEBSTER 954/3. **1893** *Harper's Mag.* Jan. 282/2 The grocer twirled between his finger and thumb a clean new pass-book. **(2) 1880** LAMPHERE *U.S. Govt.* 181/2 [Cadets] will supply themselves with . . . 1 pass-book. **1907** *Naval Acad. Regulations* 75 After the requisitions are served, they shall be entered in the pass books of the midshipmen, by the storekeeper.

+**Passed ball.** *Baseball.* (See quot. 1889.) — **1861** *N.Y. Sunday Mercury* 10 Aug. (E. J. Nichols). **1867** CHADWICK *Base Ball Reference* 139 A passed ball is one muffed by the catcher on which a base is run. **1875** *Chicago Tribune* 15 July 5/5 Higham . . . then scored an unearned run on a passed ball. **1889** CAMP *College Sports* (1893) 177 A 'passed ball' is a pitched ball which by an error of the catcher is allowed to go behind him so that a runner is advanced a base. **1912** MATHEWSON *Pitching* 201 Herzog . . . tried to advance on a short passed ball.

* **Passenger.**

+**1.** *To wake (up) the wrong passenger* (or variant), to wake or call a passenger other than the one requesting such service; fig., to misjudge an adversary or the person with whom one has to deal.

1851 *Polly Peablossom* 33 He had awakened the wrong passenger. **1856** WHIPPLE *Explor. Ry. Route* I. 30 It was evident to the Doctor that, in Western parlance, 'he had waked the wrong passenger.' There was to be a struggle [with the rattlesnake]. **1862** 'E. KIRKE' *Among Pines* 53 Extending his hand to me, he said: 'I see, sir, I've woke up the wrong passenger.' **1886** POORE *Reminisc.* I. 38 The large brass door knockers were vigorously plied, and sometimes quite a commotion was caused by 'waking up the wrong passenger.'

2. *attrib.* and *comb.* **a.** Designating vehicles or means of conveyance for passengers. {1836–}

1851 KINGSLEY *Diary* 178 No mercy is shown as a general thing in a passenger ship especially in a little Hermaphrodite Brig like this. **1865** *Atlantic Mo.* Jan. 82/1 The night-tows . . . [consist] of a few cattle, produce, and passenger barges attached to a steamer. **1877** 'E. MARTIN' *Hist. Great Riots* 227 An engine with a postal car attached was coupled to two passenger coaches. **1879** *Harper's Mag.* July 165 A bustling little locomotive with one passenger-carriage comes whistling down the valley. **1880** INGHAM *Digging Gold* 331 Our train was detained by an accident. . . . But one passenger truck left the track, and no passengers were hurt. **1886** *Standard Guide of Washington* 205 The building . . . is furnished with passenger-elevator, steam-heating, deposit-vaults, speaking tubes. **1924** *Railway Rev.* 16 Feb. 294/1 Window sills and arm rests in all-steel passenger cars are generally made of wood.

b. Denoting one who works on a passenger train.

1872 *Newton Kansan* 17 Oct. 3/2 W. J. Hobbs, passenger conductor to Ft. Dodge, has rented S. Lehman's house on Broadway. **1913** LONDON *Valley of Moon* 196 He's got one son, Jack, a passenger engineer.

c. In special combinations.

Passenger engine, a railroad engine designed for passenger service (cf. FREIGHT ENGINE); *p. house*, a building at a railroad depot or station for the convenience of passengers; *p. law*, a law prescribing the conditions under which a railroad or other common carrier may carry passengers; *p. mile*, the transporting of one passenger a distance of one mile (regarded as a unit in transportation accounting); *p. railroad*, a railroad for passenger rather than for freight service; *p. tax*, (see quotation).

1843 *Mass. H. R. Rep. Western R.R.* 26 Have the Lowell passenger engines cost more in '42 than in '40, per mile? **1862** STRONG *Cadet Life W. Point* 249 His wife had hesitated on the platform of the passenger-house, . . . while the nurse . . . had entered the cars. **1865** *Atlantic Mo.* Feb. 159/2 His opinions . . . on the liquor and passenger laws . . . will soon be all forgotten. **1903** E. JOHNSON *Railway Transportation* 140 This is shown by dividing the total number of miles traveled by all passengers (the passenger miles) by the miles of railroad. **1887** *Courier-Journal* 19 Feb. 4/3 The place to build passenger railroads is in the South. **1849** *Western Journal* III. 86 The passenger-tax is for the privilege of coming within the territory where, if he [*i.e.*, a passenger from a foreign port] remained, in due season, he would be subject to pay the other tax [*i.e.*, the poll tax].

+**Passenger car.** A railroad car for carrying passengers. — **1832** *Phila. Advertiser* 26 Nov., (Ernst). **1834** *Amer. Traveller* 22 Aug. 3/2 (Ernst), The passenger cars . . . [will] be despatched daily from the Depot. **1858** W. P. SMITH *Railway Celebrations* 92 Cars.—Passenger, 33; Express and Mail, 9. **1880** *Harper's Mag.* July 194/2 We saw it from the rear platform of a single passenger-car at the end of a long freight train. **1913** *N.Y. Ev. Post* 28 Aug. 1/7 Freight Train Sideswipes Passenger Car on Vandalia line.

+**Passenger depot.** =DEPOT 2. — **1856** WHIPPLE *Explor. Ry. Route* II. 64 Engine-houses and passenger depots, $250,000. **1882** PANGBORN *Picturesque B. & O.* 46 The fashion in the Monumental City being to term passenger-depots 'stations,' prefixing the name of the street they are located upon.

Passenger list. A list of names of passengers. Also transf. — **1869** 'MARK TWAIN' *Innocents* 199 We had the whole passenger-list for company, but their room would have been preferable, for there was no light, there were no windows, no ventilation. **1901** MCCUTCHEON *Graustark* 98 Why is she not in the passenger list? **1907** HARRIS *Tents of Wickedness* 19 His name was not on the passenger-list, owing perhaps to his late arrival.

+**Passenger pigeon.** A wild pigeon (*Ectopistes migratorius*) formerly quite common over the greater part of North America but now extinct.

[**1802** BINGLEY *Anim. Biog.* (1813) II. 225 Passenger Pigeons visit, in enormous flocks, the different parts of North America.] **1823** JAMES *Exped.* I. 265 *Columba migratoria*—Passenger pigeon. (*C. Canadensis* is the female, Temm.). **1857** *Rep. Comm. Patents 1856: Agric.* 148 The passenger pigeon, or wild pigeon, . . . is very rarely met with except in communities of millions or billions. **1894** ALLEN *Ky. Cardinal* vi, He took himself off with a silence and speed that would have done credit to a passenger-pigeon. **1917** *Birds of Amer.* II. 44 The last passenger pigeon. She died in the Cincinnati Zoological Park in 1914. **1923** J. H. COOK *On Old Frontier* 4 The passenger pigeon has disappeared from view.

Passenger train. A train that carries passengers, as distinguished from a freight train. {1846-} — **1845** *Xenia Torch-Light* 31 July 3/7 On and after Tuesday, the 8th inst., . . . a Passenger Train will leave the Depot on Front street daily, at 8½ A.M. **1876** CROFUTT *Trans-continental Tourist* 42 Passenger trains stop here, both from the east and the west, for dinner. **1920** COOPER *Under Big Top* 1 There under the train sheds it stands at the end of a south-bound passenger train.

***Passing.** *attrib.* +Designating things through or over which one passes. *Obs.* — **1698** *East-Hampton Rec.* II. 417 Whosoever shall presume to Leave open any fence; or pasing barres or gate or gates . . . shall [be fined]. **1716** CHURCH *Philip's War* 84 Maj. Church . . . ask'd the French men where their passing Place was? **1740** *Ib.* IV. 113 The roads and paths here under mentioned are to be and remain for passing highways, so that one cart may pass another. **1804** *Southampton Rec.* III. 386 In case the said Commissioners of highways shall think proper to lay out a passingroad through the said David Burnets land, for the footmen, men on horseback, teams and carriages to pass and repass.

Passion flower. Any one of various plants of the genus *Passiflora* or a related genus; also, the flower of such a plant. {1633-} Also attrib.

Cf. MAYPOP and MARACOCK.

1802 ELLICOTT *Journal* 287 The China root . . . and passion flower . . . are abundant in the rich grounds. **1840** DEWEY *Mass. Flowering Plants* 80 Order 131. Passifloreæ. The Passion Flower Tribe. **1873** *Harper's Mag.* May 854/2 A stately girl with . . . a scarlet passion-flower quivering just above the low straight forehead. **1893** SANBORN *S. Calif.* 174 Most effective of all was the cachuca, danced by a girl of pure Castilian blood, who was dressed to symbolize the scarlet passion-flower.

***Passover.** +A pass or way over a hill. *Obs.* — **1839** LEONARD *Adventures* (1904) 230 [We] continued all day without any interruption, and in the evening encamped at the foot of the passover.

+**Pass shooting.** (See quotation.) — **1877** C. HALLOCK *Sportsman's Gaz.* 204 Another method is pass shooting; that is, standing . . . in belts of woods, over which the birds fly when travelling in their afternoon flights to the roosting and feeding grounds.

+**Pass system.** The system of giving passes over railroad lines. — **1873** *Newton Kansan* 3 July 2/1 J. Edgar Thompson . . . thinks the effort of the railways to abrogate the pass system will prove a failure. **1874** B. F. TAYLOR *World on Wheels* 113 When people who held 'complimentaries' were asked to hold their tongues . . . , there began to be a lull in the pass-system. **1903** E. JOHNSON *Railway Transportation* 154 There is, moreover, evidence of a growing moral sense in the public mind against the pass system.

Passway. 1. A way, road, or route. {1825-} +**2.** =PASS *n.*[1] — **(1) 1835** LONGSTREET *Georgia Scenes* 99 These were the only passways to the interior. **1874** LONG *Wild-Fowl* 161 There is a good passway for flight shooting. **1884** 'CRADDOCK' *Where Battle Was Fought* 63 The driver loudly and fervently insisted on a pass-way. **1889** *Harper's Mag.* Aug. 390/2 Our family carriage . . . is left out in the streets along with many others to block up the passway. **(2) 1886** *Ib.* June 66/1 We stood in the passway, amid the deepening shadows of the twilight.

Paste blacking. Blacking in paste form. Also attrib. — **1835** *Stimpson's Boston Directory* 24 Bell's Paste Blacking Warehouse, Over 88 State Street. **1855** BARNUM *Life* 208 [Proler] was a manufacturer of paste-blacking, . . . Cologne water, and bear's grease. **1871** *Harper's Mag.* Oct. 798/1 He found it necessary to take a seat behind a pyramid of paste-blacking and write up his notes.

***Pasteboard.** Also †**pastboard.**

***1.** A stiff, firm material made by compressing and rolling sheets of paper or paper pulp.

1748 FRANKLIN *Exper. on Electricity* 43 Take two round pieces of pasteboard two inches in diameter. **1789** MORSE *Amer. Geog.* 90 Of the long list of articles which we now make ourselves, we will mention . . . pasteboard. **1843** *Yale Lit. Mag.* VIII. 124 Thumbing the corners of what seemed a quadrangular card of pasteboard, the President 'opened his mouth and spoke.' **1876** MILLER *First Families* 225 Two sun-bonnets, made of paste-board and calico. **1923** WATTS *L. Nichols* 301 Mr. Levin distributed a number of small green chips of pasteboard to the breeze.

+**b.** A ticket for entrance to a game or a ride on a railroad. {1901} *colloq.*[2]

1873 BEADLE *Undevel. West* 771 The call of 'Tickets, gents,' showed one man without the pasteboard. **1898** *N.Y. Tribune* 13 May 11/2 Mr. Hoy is supposed to stand near the ticket-box and see to it that the pasteboards are dropped into the box.

2. A board on which pastry dough is rolled out. {1858-}

1828 LESLIE *Receipts* 65 Throw some flour on your paste-board. **1867** [see PASTRY].

3. *attrib.* (passing into *adj.*) and *comb.* In sense 1 with *box, flower stand, mask,* etc.

1689 SEWALL *Diary* I. 288 Three Pasteboard Boxes, with Hats. **1759** *Boston Gazette* 13 Aug., Black Sattin Bonnetts and Hatts, Pastboard Stomachers. **1807** IRVING, etc. *Salmagundi* vii, In your pasteboard skirts, your broidered waistcoats and your plaited shirts. **1841** BACHE *Fire-Screen* 169 To these were now added an old filigree basket, a crushed pasteboard flowerstand [etc.]. **1851** MELVILLE *Moby-Dick* 181 All visible objects, man, are but as pasteboard masks.

Paster. {1737-} +(See quot. 1885.)

1870 *Congress. Globe* 13 April 2659/3 There were ten tickets . . . which were scratched and had pasters with the name of Caleb N. Taylor. **1885** *Mag. Amer. Hist.* March 297/2 *Pasters.*—Narrow slips of paper gummed on the back and bearing printed names of candidates . . . are distributed by local political leaders prior to or during an election, so that voters may readily re-arrange ballots to suit their own individual preferences. Pasters . . . reduce 'scratching' . . . to a system. **1889** *Columbus Dispatch* 19 Sept., Persons may paste slips over names, providing the names so substituted by pasters are printed or written in red ink. **1906** *N.Y. Ev. Post* 5 Nov. 7 The ballots to be used to-morrow must bear pasters with McMillan's name on them.

+**b.** A slip of paper which is pasted over some part of a printed bill, circular, etc.

1882 *Nation* 6 July 7/2 The Erie and Central Railroads have made the attempt to rid themselves of all liabilities . . . by putting a 'paster' on their bills of lading.

***Pastor.**[1] A minister in charge of a church.

The early quotations here may belong under sense b.

1632 *Mass. Bay Rec.* I. 100 Mr. Batchelr. is required to forbeare exerciseing his guifts as a pastr. or teacher publiquely, in o[u]r pattent. **1640** *Dedham Rec.* III. 72 Fifteene acres all to lye near about our Pastors Farme. **1678** *Mass. H. S. Coll.* 4 Ser. V. 15 About two months before our pastor's death. **1714** *Boston News-Letter* 17-24 May 2/1 The Reverend Mr. George Curwin was Ordained Pastor of the Church in [Salem]. **1738** *Duxbury Rec.* 260, I have also received . . . the sum of three hundred and thirteen pounds in full for my salary as Pastor of the said town. **1831** PECK *Guide* 260 There is a society of Seceders . . . and another of Covenanters, both supplied with pastors of their own orders. **1898** *Kansas City Star* 19 Dec. 1/4 The services were conducted by the pastor . . . at the Market Street Presbyterian church. **1907** GOODELL *Pastoral & Personal Evangelism* 135 The purpose of this book is to help every pastor to become his own evangelist.

+**b.** In the Congregational churches of early New England: (see quot. 1648). *Obs.*

1629 in Bradford *Hist.* 317 So Mr. Skelton was chosen pastor [of Salem], and Mr. Higgison to be teacher. **1648** *Platform Church-Discipline* (1772) 30 The pastors special work is, to attend to exhortation, and therein to administer a word of wisdom: The teacher is to attend to doctrine, and therein to administer a word of knowledge. **1654** JOHNSON *Wonder-w. Prov.* 41 The Officers of this Church are at this day one Pastor, and one Teacher, one Ruling Elder, and three Deacons. **1670** ELIOT *Brief Narr.* 21 Ordained . . . to do the Office of a Teacher and Pastor. **1735** in C. Hazard *T. Hazard* 226 The Subscribers, Teaching Elders or Pastors of the first gathered . . . Church in Boston.

+**Pastor.**[2] [Sp.] A sheep-herder. (A new borrowing.) — **1849** *31st Congress 1 Sess.* Sen Ex. Doc. No. 64, 132 The flock [of sheep] was under Mexican and not Navajo control, and, from my conversation with the *pastor*, became assured that our apprehensions were groundless. **1857** DAVIS *El Gringo* 362 When a boy he tended sheep and goats upon the mountains, and grew up a *pastor*. **1865** *Wkly. New Mexican* 10 March 1/4 575 They will furnish him with full information . . . as to the number of *pastores* who have been the victims of [the Navajos].

Pastorage. {1662} A parsonage. {1897} — **1884** HARTE *In Carquinez Woods* 40 The 'pastorage' . . . [was] the only 'fireproof' structure in town.

***Pastry.** Attrib. with *cake, crust, plate,* etc.

1674 *Harvard Rec.* I. 230 Kitchen utensills . . . 4 wood pastry-platts. **1676** TOMPSON *Poetical Writ.* 70 A tribe of female hands, but manly hearts Forsake at home their pastry-crust and tarts. **1844** 'UNCLE SAM' *Peculiarities* II. 256 In pastry-stores . . . peppermint-cakes and mince-pies . . . give a relish for seasoning and palate-tickling food. **1855** *Herald of Freedom* (Lawrence, Kan.) 13 Oct. 4/1 We soon shall arrive in the land of the dairy Where apples are plenty and pastry-slabs used. **1863** A. D. WHITNEY *F. Gartney* xx, Some pastry-cakes that Faith's fingers had shaped. **1867** *Rep. Comm. Patents 1866* II. 1464 Pastry Roller. . . . The paste-board is revolvable. The roller is moved by a crank [etc.]. **1876** M. F. HENDERSON *Cooking* 266 Pastry Ramekins.

Pastry cook. One whose business is to cook pastry, esp. for public sale. {1712–} — **1771** FRANKLIN *Autobiog.* 243 My light repast . . . often was no more than a bisket or a slice of bread, a handful of raisins or a tart from the pastry-cook's, and a glass of water. **1796** *Boston Directory* 292 Wentworth, Mary, pastry cook, Marshall's lane. **1857** *Harper's Mag.* March 457/1 'Bob Thompson' . . . was quite celebrated as a pastry-cook.

***Pasturage.** Also †**pastorage, pastureage.** Grass or other plants for live stock to feed on.

1707 *Boston News-Letter* 24 March 2/2 It contains . . . good Pastorage, Meadow and Commonage. **1750** T. WALKER *Journal* 75 Mr. Johnston . . . sent my Horses to Mr. David Stewards who was so kind as to give them Pastureage. **1823** JAMES *Exped.* I. 131 The prairies, for many miles on each side of the Missouri produce abundance of good pasturage. **1880** *Vt. Agric. Rep.* VI. 25 Many thousands of acres of pasture lands within the limits of Vermont . . . once afforded the best and most abundant pasturage. **1925** TILGHMAN *Dugout* 22 For the grass was now good pasturage, and it was time to go on the warpath.

***Pasture,** *n.* Also †**pastar, pastur.**

***1. a.** A grass-covered piece of land used or suitable for grazing; grass land. **b.** Grass or other growing herbage eaten by livestock.

See also BIG PASTURE.

1624 Smith *General Hist. Virginia* IV. 108 Two new Forts . . . command a great circuit of ground, containing Wood, Pasture and Marsh. **1626** *Va. Mag. of Hist.* XXVI. 241 [The inhabitants shall so] fence their cattle ground as the pasture & field of the cattle bee not taken from them. **1644** *New Haven Col. Rec.* 126 None should fence the springs in the neck from the comon when it is layd for a pasture. **1670** *Derby Rec.* 15 A soficyent high way down to his pastar. *c***1700** *Md. Gen. Assembly Acts* (1723) 11 The Ascertaining of the Bounds and Limits of the said Town Pasture and Common. **1749** ELIOT *Field-Husb.* ii. 42 When he had washed his Sheep, he did not shear them . . . but laid them in a clean Pasture five or six days. **1811** SUTCLIFF *Travels* (1815) 163 It consisted of what are called prairies, or pastures. **1814** J. TAYLOR *Arator* 126 The rotation of corn, wheat and pasture, or the three shift system. **1866** *Rep. Indian Affairs* 140 The fuel and pastures . . . were sufficient to last at least thirty years. **1889** *Harper's Mag.* June 158/2 A farmer . . . found an estray cow in his pasture. **1925** TILGHMAN *Dugout* 106 There white-faced Herefords graze in the fenced pastures.

+**2.** *W.* A large, fenced-in part of a cattle range: (see quot. 1897).

1890 *Stock Grower & Farmer* 12 April 4/3 Jesse H. Pressnal sold Jim Lane . . . 2000 head of beeves from his Hondo pasture. **1897** HOUGH *Story of Cowboy* 16 A 'pasture' is an inclosed tract of land perhaps forty or fifty miles square. **1907** WHITE *Arizona Nights* 156 Fifty head of beef steers found asylum . . . in the mile-square wire enclosure called the pasture.

+**3.** (See quotations.) Also attrib.

1884 GOODE, etc. *Fisheries* I. 201 There are also certain local schools of fish which have names of their own; for instance, . . . the 'Pasture School' of Cape Ann. **1890** *Cent.* 4323/1 *Pasture*, . . . one of the compartments of a deep-water weir . . . ; that part of the weir which the fish first enter. **1895** *Stand.* 1290/3 *Pasture*, . . . an inshore spawning-ground for codfish.

4. *attrib.* ***a.** Designating areas used as pasture.

1658 *Suffolk Deeds* III. 150 So much of that pasture close . . . as is almost surrounded wth. the great Riuer and a litle Creeke. **1662** *Hartford Land Distrib.* 66 One percell of land . . . being pasture land. **1668** *Ib.* 21 All that percell of pasture Ground lyeing on the east Side. **1741** in *Amer. Speech* XV. 293/1 One hundred acres of Pasture Marsh adjoining the land. **1782** in Summers *Ann. S.W. Va.* 766 He ought to be paid the sum of 30/ for the use of his pasture field for the Washington Militia. **1899** JEWETT *Queen's Twin* 55 It was the wildest, most Titanic sort of pasture country up there.

b. Designating plants that grow in pasture land. {1806–}

1891 *Amer. Folk-Lore* IV. 149 All ferns we knew as *Brakes*, and the common pasture brake we called Polypod [in N.H.]. **1839** in *Mich. Agric. Soc. Trans.* VII. 415 *Poa trivialis.* Pasture-grass. **1815** *Mass. H. S. Coll.* 2 Ser. IV. 124 There are large quantities of fine ship timber of pasture oak in the vicinity. **1847** DARLINGTON *Weeds & Plants* 196 *C[irsium] pumilum.* . . . Low or Dwarf Cirsium. Pasture Thistle.

***Pasture,** *v.* +*intr.* Of bees: To gather honey *upon* a certain place. — **1880** *Harper's Mag.* Oct. 777/2 One of our modern apiaries, with its bees pasturing upon acres of carefully cultivated honey plants.

Pasture fence. A fence that closes in a pasture. — **1727** *N.H. Probate Rec.* II. 298, I geive to my sun . . . thirty akers of Land beginning at the head of my pasture where my pasture fence now is. **1885** *Rep. Indian Affairs* 85 It is no uncommon thing for a herder, in his daily ride around the pasture fence, to find it cut in one or more places. **1904** GLASGOW *Deliverance* 223 [I've] mended the pasture fence.

+**Pasture lot.** A plot of land used as a pasture. — **1693** *Norwalk Hist. Rec.* 85 To Elnathan Hanford for his part and portion out of his father's estate . . . : To pasture lott [£]18. **1873** *Winfield* (Kan.) *Courier* 7 Aug. 1/5 Many farmers who live in the creek bottoms have open pasture lots fenced with a stock or open post and rail fence. **1902** MCFAUL *Ike Glidden* 111 Chase Yourself up 'crost the pasture lot.

Pasture man. {1621} ‖A cattleman who leases grazing land. — **1895** *Congress. Rec.* 15 Jan. 997/2 The first names of the pasture men that I see upon my list are [etc.].

+**Pasture range.** An expanse of open country suitable for grazing stock. — **1860** GREELEY *Overland Journey* 325 A broad expanse of dried-up pasture range . . . [shows] the protracted fierceness of the summer drought. **1869** J. R. BROWNE *Adv. Apache Country* 273 The first part of our journey . . . lay along a series of foot-hills to the left, with a fine pasture range to the right. **1872** MCCLELLAN *Golden State* 472 Throughout the county there are many rich valleys and wide pasture-ranges.

***Pat,** *v.* +*intr.* To beat time for dancing by clapping the hands, tapping the feet, etc. Also *patting* vbl. n. — **1861** G. F. BERKELEY *Eng. Sportsm. W. Prairies* 349 Asked them who could 'pat' as an accompaniment to a dance and song. **1869** *Atlantic Mo.* July 74/2, I was made to dance 'Juba' to the time which the comedian himself gave me by means of his two hands and one foot, and which is technically called 'patting.'

***Patch,** *n.*

+**1.** A plot of farm land; a small cultivated field.

This sense is an extension of the general English sense of 'a small piece or area of . . . ground' {1577–}, but it no doubt was also suggested by the appearance of cultivated plots of land outlined by virgin forest or prairie: (see quot. 1724). See also CORN PATCH, COTTON PATCH, etc.

1653 in *Amer. Speech* XV. 293/2 To begin at the head of the Southermost Branch [of] little neck & soe upon a line to the middle patch. **1698** *N.J. Archives* III. 490 Their Surveyor pinching here a bitt, & there a patch out of the land of honest men. **1724** JONES *Virginia* 10 All the Country is but one continued Forest, with Patches of some hundred Acres here and there cleared. **1775** Rauck *Boonesborough* 177, [I] am just going to our little plant patches in hopes the greens will bear cropping. **1800** TATHAM *Tobacco* 8 The beds, or patches, as they are called, differ in size. **1836** CROCKETT *Exploits* 26 The same as a patch of land for which he had the patent. **1856** OLMSTED *Slave States* 689 On most plantations, . . . the slaves cultivate 'patches,' and raise poultry for themselves. **1863** 'E. KIRKE' *Southern Friends* 55 The poor trash who scratched a bare subsistence from a sorry patch of beans and collards. **1884** *Century Mag.* April 859/2 Many of the thrifty negroes are acquiring the ownership of the 'patches' they cultivate. **1904** PRINGLE *Rice Planter* 97 They plant a field of corn, a patch of rice, a patch of cotton, and one of tobacco.

***2.** A small piece of black court-plaster or silk worn on the face to heighten the beauty of the skin or to hide a defect; a beauty spot. Now hist.

1732 *S.C. Gazette* 120/2 To be Sold . . . papers of patches, . . . brown, white, & blue ozenbrigs. **1739** in Singleton *Social N.Y.* 387 Gloves, patches, fans, shoes. **1759** *Newport Mercury* 17 April 4/1 To be Sold by Simon Pease, . . . Superfine Patches. **1853** FELT *Customs New Eng.* 111 Catharine Mariott, of Boston, advertises, in 1737, patches for sale. The custom of wearing them . . . prevailed in New England till sixty years since.

+**3.** A piece of cloth or leather used, when greased, to wrap a rifle ball in order to make it fit the bore. {1846–}

1799 WELD *Travels* 67 The grease and the bits of rag, which are called patches, are carried in a little box. **1824** DODDRIDGE *Notes* 289 Get patches one hundred finer than those you commonly use, and have them well oiled. **1837** WETMORE *Gaz. Missouri* 48 While the men were firing, the women made it their business to cast balls and cut patches, so as to keep up the defence. **1894** *Harper's Mag.* Sept. 624/2 Slung from his neck . . . [was] his shot-pouch (with its . . . bent-wire hook crowded with cotton 'patches' to wrap around the bullets).

+**4.** (See quotation.)

1877 'E. MARTIN' *Hist. Great Riots* 460 The whole population of the coal regions living in cities, towns and small settlements, are often called 'patches.'

+**5.** Attrib. in sense 3 with *box, leather.*

1807 GASS *Journal* 13 March, Each man has also a sufficient quantity of patch-leather. **1855** HOLBROOK *Among Mail Bags* 231 A post-office clerk . . . had crammed the stolen notes into the 'patch-box' of the rifle.

Patch,** *v.* +*tr.* To fit a patch about (a rifle ball). (Cf. PATCH *n.* 3.) — **1843** 'CARLTON' *New Purchase* II. 255 Therefore, we at last ventured on *patching* the balls separately. *a1846** *Quarter Race Ky.* 138 The bar . . . was hunting about for me, when, just as I was patching my ball, he again saw me. **1877** HALLOCK *Sportsman's Gazetteer* 545 If the bullet is the right size and properly patched, the patch will not be torn in putting the cartridge into the chamber.

+**Patchhead (coot).** *local.* The surf scoter, *Melanitta perspicillata.*— **1888** TRUMBULL *Names of Birds* 103 Surf Duck. . . . In Maine, . . . Patch-Head; in Massachusetts . . . and at Stonington, Conn., Patch-Polled Coot. **1917** *Birds of Amer.* I. 151 Surf Scoter. . . . Other Names. . . . Patch-head; Patch-head Coot.

***Patching.**

+**1.** Material for rifle patches.

1835 LONGSTREET *Ga. Scenes* 286 [He] drew out his patching, found the most even part of it [etc.]. **1887** *Harper's Mag.* June 61/1 In the bullet-pouch were carried . . . the cotton 'patching' . . . and the precious extra flints.

+**2.** *Not a patching to*, in no way comparable to. *colloq.* {not a patch on, 1860–}

1851 *Polly Peablossom* 52 All the sailors an' French parrots in Orleans ain't a patchin' to him. **1872** EGGLESTON *End of World* 236 The devil a'n't a patchin' to her. **1898** FOX *Kentuckians* 114 Why, I'm not a patchin' to Sherd Raines. **1921** GREER-PETRIE *Angeline at Seelbach* 2 The Phoenix Hotel . . . ain't a-patchin' to Miss Seelback's place.

+**Patch-polled coot.** =PATCHHEAD (COOT). — **1888** [see PATCHHEAD (COOT)]. **1917** *Birds of Amer.* I. 151.

+**Patch quilt.** =PATCHWORK QUILT. Also fig. — **1850** LEWIS *La. Swamp Doctor* 95 Untying the scrap-bag of memory, [she] proceeded to make a patch-quilt for me, of a case that resembled the one we were ministering to. **1881** *Harper's Mag.* March 528/2 The patch-quilt was a most marvelous affair.

Patchwork. {a1692–}

1. Any article, esp. a quilt, that consists of small pieces of different kinds of cloth sewed together by the edges. {1726–}

1772 A. G. WINSLOW *Diary* 62, I exchanged a piece of patchwork . . . for a pair of curious lace mitts with blue flaps. **1830** *Va. Lit. Museum* 598/1 One of Margaret's sisters having made herself a fine bedquilt of patch work, she was indulged with a quilting frolic. **1890** *Stock Grower & Farmer* 10 May 3/1 If Uncle Jerry will furnish our farmers' wives with a good design for a log cabin patchwork . . . , the deed is done.

2. *attrib.* Designating various articles made of patchwork.

1841 BACHE *Fire-Screen* 14 The arm-chair in which he sat, was provided with a patch-work cushion. **1856** A. CARY *Married* 107 In another corner was a bed, covered with a patchwork counterpane and sheets. **1859** STOWE *Minister's Wooing* xxix, The patchwork-spread best worthy of such distinction was chosen for the quilting. **1863** LOCKE *Struggles Nasby* 105 Podhammer hed in his hand a patchwork coverlid. **1907** *St. Nicholas* July 832/1 In a short time our patchwork flag was put together.

Patchwork quilt. A quilt made of patchwork. {1840} — **1845** KIRKLAND *Western Clearings* 2 The bed is endued with the brightest patchwork quilt—the pride of the housewife's heart. **1883** 'S. BONNER' *Dialect Tales* 129 Aunt Mely sat down and went to work quietly on a patchwork quilt. **1896** JEWETT *Pointed Firs* 83, I went to the door of the bedroom, and thought how pleasant it looked, with its pink-and-white patchwork quilt.

***Patent,** *n.*

+**1. a.** A document issued by some authority, as by the king of England, a colonial proprietor, the United States government, etc., granting the right to certain land, often with specified privileges connected therewith. **b.** The right or privilege set forth in such a document.

See also LAND PATENT.

1619 *Va. House of Burgesses* 8 [He] indevoured to answere some other thinges that were objected agst. his Patente. **1654** *Md. Council Proc.* I. 299 Divers persons . . . have not Sued out their Patents in due time for the lands which they claim. **a1656** BRADFORD *Hist.* 109 The patente they had being for Virginia, and not for New-england. **1706** *N.C. Col. Rec.* I. 648 We expect . . . that any your Officers may not be permitted to disturb any that hold Lands by Virginia patents. **1797** HAWKINS *Letters* 52 The whole country was covered with old British patents. **1816** U. BROWN *Journal* II. 44 He writes to richmond . . . to know the date of John McKennys Pattent for 41,700. **1842** *Cultivator* X. 37 The purchaser receives a certificate of purchase, and afterwards obtains a patent from the President. **1890** in Dale & Rader *Okla. Hist.* (1930) 481 Each settler . . . shall, before receiving a patent for this homestead . . . pay to the United States. . . . One Dollar and Twenty-five Cents per acre. **1917** *Statutes at Large* XL. I. 248 No patent shall issue to any homestead settler who has not resided upon, improved, and cultivated his homestead for a period of at least one year.

+**2.** The territory or land conferred by a patent.

1631 *Mass. Bay Rec.* I. 88 Noe person w[ha]tsoeuer shall trauell out of this pattent, eithr. by sea or land, without leaue from the Govern[o]r, Deputy Govern[o]r, or some other Assistant. **1636** *Plymouth Laws* 36 For the ordering of a body politick within the seuerall limits of this patent. **1769** WASHINGTON *Diaries* I. 320 Run the back line of Spencer and Washington's Patent. **1789** *Smithtown Rec.* 179 The line between the two Patents to be the middle of said road. **1845** COOPER *Chainbearer* xxv, This is Mooseridge Patent, and Washington, late Charlotte County.

3. A grant issued by the government conferring upon a person the exclusive privilege of manufacturing, using, or selling a new invention for a limited time {1701–}; the invention that is so protected. {1862–}

1789 *Ann. 1st Congress* I. 796 A petition from Abraham Westervelt . . . praying an exclusive patent may be given him for manufacturing shell buttons. **1790** *Statutes at Large* I. 110 The grantee or grantees of each patent shall . . . deliver to the Secretary of State a specification in writing. **1812** *Niles' Reg.* III. 135/1, I have thought it a duty . . . to publish a few lines of information to facilitate the mode of acquiring patents. **1850** *Rep. Comm. Patents 1849* 424 There are but few patents granted for horse powers. **1860** CHRISTY *Ethiopian Joke Book No. 3* 33 Sam, I've jest got a patent out. **1870** *Statutes at Large* 203 Every patent or any interest therein shall be assignable in law. **1893** *Harper's Mag.* May 892/2 It isn't covered by any patent that I know of. **1907** *St. Nicholas* May 658/2 A 'Sure Cure' Patent.

b. *Commissioner of patents* {1852– (*Act 15 & 16 Vict.* cap. 83 § 1)}, +a government official in charge of the patent office.

1836 *Statutes at Large* V. 117 There shall be established and attached to the Department of State, an office to be denominated the Patent Office; the chief officer of which shall be called the Commissioner of Patents. **1849** *Whig Almanac 1850* 22/1 The act places under his supervision the bureau of the Commissioner of Patents. **1903** *Congress. Directory* (58th Cong., Extr. Sess.) 251 The Commissioner of Patents . . . is by statute made the tribunal of last resort in the Patent Office.

c. *Patent applied for*, a phrase sometimes put on an article to protect its use or manufacture while the issuance of the patent is pending.

1894 *Boston Ev. Transcript* 5 March 5/7 Elmer E. Vance's Marvellous Realistic Comedy Drama. 'Patent Applied For.' **1925** *Sat. Ev. Post* 18 July 129 Warner Auto-Polish. . . . Patent applied for.

4. The process of issuing a patent; admission to the rights of a patent.

1858 *Texas Almanac 1859* 24 This act extends to preemption settlers or their assigns the time to return their field-notes to the Land Office for patent. **1876** HARTE *G. Conroy* xxv, We may not even submit the grant for patent. **1906** *Indian Laws & Tr.* III. 734 Reserves under a treaty take by the treaty, not by patent from the Government.

5. Attrib. and comb. in sense 3 with *annuity, attorney, bill*, etc.

See also PATENT AGENT, OFFICE, etc.

1793 *Ann. 2d Congress* 1 Sess. 857 He saw the idea of a patent law ridiculed by some. **1860** *36th Congress 1 Sess.* H. R. Rep. No. 648, 53 There was pending . . . a private bill, well known in Congress as the Chaffee patent bill. **1877** *Harper's Mag.* Feb. 450/2 When Mrs. Danver's 'patent' annuity has been paid out of it, . . . there'll be about one hundred left over. **1886** J. A. PORTER *New Stand. Guide of Washington* 118 Business Houses of Washington, D.C. . . . [include] patent solicitors and attorneys. **1886** POORE *Reminisc.* II. 27 The defense was conducted by Edwin M. Stanton, previously known at Washington as a patent lawyer. **1893** *Harper's Mag.* Feb. 478 When we want . . . a scientific patent-examiner, . . . [we go] to a ward politician.

***Patent,** *a.* Of an invention: Protected by a patent. {1787–}

1773 *Boston Ev. Post* 4 Oct. (Ernst), A genteel curricle with patent barrel springs. **1786** *Md. Journal* 23 June (Th.), For sale, One elegant patent caboose. **1820** *Columbian Centinel* 1 July 3/3 Wm. C. Hunneman . . . continues to Manufacture his Patent Fire Engines. **1848** THOREAU *Maine Woods* 15 It looked like the balance-box of a patent hay-scales. **1875** *Chicago Tribune* 26 July 7/6 Patent Metallic Burial Cases and Caskets of Cast and Sheet Metal. **1880** *Harper's Mag.* 355/1 Corn-cribs, patent bee-hives, smoke houses and cider presses huddled about it. **1895** JEWETT *Nancy* 138 When he died he'd failed all up, owing to that patent cornsheller he'd put everything into.

Patent, *v.* Also †**patten.** {1822–}

+**1.** *tr.* To obtain a patent right to (land or a mining claim).

1675 *Va. State P.* I. 8 Major Lawrence Smith . . . did patent foure thousand six hundred acres of land. **1697** C. MATHER in *Magnalia* I. 177 All the money and moveables in the territory [of New Eng. would not] have defrayed the charges of patenting the lands. **1815** DRAKE *Cincinnati* 51 The following is the course pursued in locating and patenting these lands. **1874** RAYMOND *6th Rep. Mines* 519 When several lodes . . . may be patented in common. **1883** *American* VI. 19 Although much of it [*sc.* public land voted to railroads] is not yet patented, it is open to their claims as fast as they construct their roads.

+**2.** To grant (land) by a patent.

1789 MORSE *Amer. Geog.* 261 [They] patented away to their particular favorites a very great proportion of the whole province. **1816** U. BROWN *Journal* II. 237 It is said that William Dawsons Land was Pattened to Stephen Radcliff. **1831** PECK *Guide* 319 The Military Bounty Tract . . . was set apart by Congress and patented for soldiers who served in the last war.

3. To take out a patent on (an invention). {1822–}

1793 *Statutes at Large* I. 321 Any person, who shall have discovered an improvement in the principle of any machine, . . . which shall have been patented [etc.]. **1847** *Rep. Comm. Patents 1846* 63 Several improvements have been patented for improvements in door-knobs. **1855** *Chicago W. Times* 26 July 4/8 A man in New York has invented, patented, and introduced a paper 'dickey.' **1883** 'MARK TWAIN' *Life on Miss.* 501 The marked chart devised and patented by Bixby himself.

Patentable, *a.* Capable of being patented. {1852–} — **1817** *Niles' Reg.* XII. 283/2 The improvement relied on by Withers was not useful, and consequently not a patentable improvement under the patent law. **1858** *N.Y. Tribune* 26 April 5/4 If there be patentable improvement, of sufficient efficacy to beat the old plans, then wrong may be had. **1896** *Columbus Dispatch* 18 March 1/4 Bert Budgeon . . . says that eight years ago Edison stole from him a patentable discovery.

+**Patent agent.** (See quot. 1859.) — **1859** BARTLETT 310 *Patent Agent,* one who procures patents for inventors. **1866** *Internal Revenue Guide* 72 Every person whose business it is to . . . procure patents, shall be deemed a . . . patent agent. **1869** *Boyd's Business Directory* 83 McLellan & Benedict, Attorneys, Solicitors of Claims and Patent Agents. **1886** J. A. PORTER *New Stand. Guide of Washington* 110 Business Houses of Washington, D.C. [include] . . . claim agents, collecting agents, patent agents.

+**Patent Democrat.** A radical member of the old Democratic-Republican party. — **1818** FEARON *Sketches* 139 The political parties [in Phila.] at present range I believe as follows: 1st. The violent democrats, called 'Patent Democrats.' 2nd. The moderate democrats [etc.]. **1835** [see OLD-SCHOOL MAN].

+**Patented land.** Any land the title to which is through a patent. — **1774** *Penna. Gazette* 14 Dec. Suppl. 2/3 To be sold . . . One tract of patented land. . . . Four tracts of warranted land. **1796** *Ann. 4th Congress* 2 Sess. 2691 The revenues of this State [N.C.] are derived from taxes on . . . all patented lands, except lots in towns [etc.].

*Patentee.

+**1.** One to whom a grant of land has been made through a patent: (see also quot. 1677).

1640 *Mass. H. S. Coll.* 4 Ser. VI. 58 The Bishop caused a Quo Warranto to be sued forth in the King's Bench against our Patentees. **1677** HUBBARD *Narrative* I. 4 In the year 1630, more of the Persons interested in the said *Patent* (thence commonly called Patentees) . . . transported themselves and their Families into the said *Massachusets.* **1687** SEWALL *Diary* I. 171 To Mrs. Nowell's [funeral], the widow of Mr. Increase Nowell a Patentee. **1748** *N.J. Archives* 1 Ser. VII. 164 Who will loose if that Line should fall more northward? the Particular Pattentees, or the Province in general? **1798** I. ALLEN *Hist. Vermont* 15 The patentees or possessors after ten years were to pay ninepence sterling per annum . . . as quitrent to his Majesty. **1827** DRAKE & MANSFIELD *Cincinnati* 26 The original patentee . . . sold a part of his interest in this ground.

2. One who has received a patent on an invention. {1691–}

1790 *Statutes at Large* I. 111 In all actions to be brought by such patentee or patentees, . . . the said patents or specifications shall be *prima facie* evidence. **1812** *Emporium Arts & Sci.* (Phila.) May 76 To check any improper proceedings which may take place on the part of patentees. **1838** FLAGG *Far West* I. 135 Upon the river-bank . . . stands the 'Floating Dry Dock,' . . . the invention of a gentleman of St. Louis, and owned by a company of patentees. **1912** *62d Congress 3 Sess.* H. R. Doc. No. 1110, 288 [Whenever] a patentee has claimed as his invention or discovery more than he had a right to claim as new, his patent shall be valid for all that part which is truly and justly his own.

‖**Patenteed,** *a.* Provided with letters patent to land. — **1775** ADAIR *Indians* 144*n.*, Since the patenteed race of Daublers set foot in their land they [*sc.* Indians] have gradually become worse every year.

+**Patent flour.** The best grade of flour. — **1886** *Century Mag.* May 46/2 For three years the patent flour, as it was called, sold at the uniform price of ten dollars a barrel at the mill.

+**Patent insides.** *pl.* The inside pages of a newspaper containing syndicated printed matter. (Cf. PATENT OUTSIDE.) — **1882** RITTENHOUSE *Maud* 103 The funny places in all the old patent-insides of newspapers talk about the sweet girl graduate. **1890** *Congress. Rec.* 2 May 4144/2 Patent insides are made up first from the American newspaper, of miscellaneous matter, political, literary, and general. **1912** NICHOLSON *Hoosier Chron.* 171 Harwood . . . had little patience with . . . the 'grapevine dailies,' with their scrappy local news, patent insides, and servile partisan opinions.

+Patent leather.

1. A leather having a smooth, glossy, and hard surface, freq. made by applying to it several coats of oil varnish. {1882– (*Encycl. Brit.* XIV. 387/2)}

1836 *Mass. Laws* XIII. 734 An Act to incorporate the Boston and Roxbury Patent Leather and Cloth Company, . . . for the purpose . . . of manufacturing patent leather. **1852** MORFIT *Tanning & Currying* (1853) 453 Glazed or Varnished Leather . . . known in commerce as *patent leather* is very largely used for dress boots and shoes. **1901** NORRIS *Octopus* 286 His shoes were of patent leather.

2. Short for *patent-leather shoe* or PATENT-LEATHER BOOT.

1849 FOSTER *N.Y. in Slices* 64 Our young gentlemen . . . thus preserve their patent-leathers. **1895** RITTENHOUSE *Maud* 587, I know his beautiful patent-leathers must have suffered. **1906** 'O. HENRY' *Strictly Business* 42 He dressed himself in the Sabbath morning costume of the Canal Street importing house dray chauffeur . . . frock coat, striped trousers, patent leathers, gilded trace chain [etc.].

3. *attrib.* Designating various articles made of patent leather. (See also next.)

1867 HARRIS *Sut Lovingood* 142 One red-comb'd, long-spurr'd, dominecker feller, frum town, . . . [wore] patent leather gaiters. **1872** *Atlantic Mo.* April 428 He wore a patent-leather stock, which also suggested the soldier of former years. **1881** *Harper's Mag.* Feb. 466/1 Patent-leather pumps, . . . and a quantity of chains about his neck and pockets, served to make him . . . rather a conspicuous object. **1898** *Kansas City Star* 18 Dec. 15/3 Mr. Zangwill . . . wears a white-crowned yachting cap, with a patent-leather brim. **1899** NORRIS *McTeague* 161 He wore . . . new patent leather shoes.

+**Patent-leather boot.** A boot or shoe made of patent leather. — **1850** MATHEWS *Moneypenny* 8 Patent-leather boots in a perfect state of polish. **1897** DANA *Recoll. Civil War* 87, I believe he never went out without patent-leather boots on. **1919** SALTUS *Paliser Case* 288 It topped iron grey hair, steel-blue eyes, . . . a dark neckcloth, a morning coat, grey gloves, grey trousers, drab spats and patent-leather boots.

+**Patent line.** A boundary line of an area or district held by patent. *Obs.* — **1675** *Dedham Rec.* V. 31 [We] marked it [the line] to the patint line whear we did set vp a stake. **1685** *Plymouth Laws* 295 Plimouth, Duxbury, Scituate [etc.] . . . , together with all such places and Villages, that do or may lye between the said Towns and the Patent Line [shall] be a County.

Patent lock. 1. A lock that is patented. +**2.** Such a lock used in swindling a person out of his money. (Cf. PATENT SAFE.) — **(1) 1867** DALY *Under Gaslight* IV. iii. 41, I've got a patent lock on that door that would give a skeleton key the rheumatism to fool with it. **1898** *McClure's Mag.* X. 528/1 He used to keep his house locked up with patent locks on the doors. **(2) 1873** BEADLE *Undevel. West* 141 A score of 'smart Alecks' relieved of their surplus cash by betting on the . . . 'patent lock,' . . . and other beautiful uncertainties.

Patent medicine.

1. A medicine, the manufacture or sale of which is protected by a patent. Usually put up in a labeled package, ready for use. {1799–}

1770 *Essex Gazette* (Salem, Mass.) 17 April 4/4 To be sold by Benjamin Eaton . . . in Marblehead . . . a collection of genuine patent medicines. **1817** *Ann. 14th Congress* 2 Sess. 469 The good people of the United States suffer great impositions . . . from patent medicines, &c. **1860** OLMSTED *Back Country* 198 A Connecticut clock, and a large poster of Jayne's patent medicines, constituted all the visible furniture. **1900** ADE *More Fables* 32 He told her she had better go and get some Patent Medicine that he had seen advertised on the Fence coming out from Town. **1918** OWEN *Typewriting Speed* 134 Simple remedies are much better for you than . . . all sorts of patent medicines.

2. *attrib.* and *comb.* **a.** With *almanac, man, peddler,* etc.

1849 FOSTER *N.Y. in Slices* 107 It is quite customary to laugh at the Patent Medicine Men. **1852** *Harper's Mag.* May 847/2 Think of a patent-medicine vender rising at the head of his table . . . and proposing such a toast. **1859** WILMER *Press Gang* 341 Some other frauds in the 'patent medicine' trade . . . will become discoverable as we proceed. **1875** DALY *Pique* (1884) 47 Do I look like a patent medicine peddler? **1894** WARNER *Golden House* iv, On the bureau Edith noticed . . . a patent-medicine almanac. **1904** TARBELL *Hist. Standard Oil Co.* I. 5 The crude petroleum was put up in eight-ounce bottles wrapped in a circular setting forth in good patent-medicine style its virtues as a cure-all.

b. False; pretentious but unsound; quack.

1878 *N. Amer. Rev.* CXXVI. 499 Civil service reform . . . at its best is a mere patent-medicine remedy.

Patent office. {1696–} +A federal office from which patents are issued or where patent claims are examined. Also attrib.

1811 *Agric. Museum* I. 221 Let us turn our view to the Golconda of the United States, the *Patent Office.* **1834** *S. Lit. Messenger* I. 183 Some fellow might slip before me to the patent office, and rob me of my treasure. **1855** GLISAN *Jrnl. Army Life* 176 Made a visit to the Patent Office building. **1891** *Atlantic Mo.* June 808/1 A colored assistant examiner in the Patent Office department has . . . placed at my service a list of some fifty patents.

Patent officer. An official responsible to the patentees of an American colony or plantation. — **1721** *N. J. Archives* 1 Ser. V. 22 Patent Officers appointed in Great Britain are generally unwelcome to the Plantations.

+**Patent outside.** The printed outside pages of a newspaper, distributed to various publishers who use the inside pages for printing local items. (Cf. PATENT INSIDE.) — **1871** *Lancaster Intelligencer* 3 April (De Vere), The editor who surrenders control of one-half of his paper to some manufacturer of *patent-outsides,* may make a slight reduction in his current expenses, but in the end he will lose both money and influence. **1883** WILDER *Sister Ridnour* 204 The reading matter set before them is mostly the neighborhood news of the county paper, with a love story on the 'patent' outside. **1890** *Boston Jrnl.* 7 March 4/5 He was running his patent outsides for country newspapers.

Patent right. An exclusive right to the manufacture, sale, or use of an invented article. {1825} Also attrib. — **1805** *Ann. 8th Congress* 2 Sess. 1002 [He is] compelled to ask for the extension of his patent right, for the improvement in merchant flour mills. **1859** BARTLETT 310 In the United States an inventor takes out a 'patent right'; in England 'letters patent.' **1866** *Internal Revenue Guide* 72 Every person whose business it is to sell, or offer for sale, patent rights, shall be regarded as a patent-right dealer. **1872** *Newton Kansan* 5 Sept. 2/2 The patent-right man . . . is generally a swindler. **1885** HOWELLS *Silas Lapham* x, He had got hold of a patent right that he wanted to go into on a large scale.

Patent safe. +Attrib. and comb. with reference to a small pocket safe used in a trick to swindle a 'sucker' out of his money. — **1855** *Scientific Amer.* 11 Aug. 381/3 The sharpers who practice the 'patent safe game' are keen fellows, and try to maintain an appearance the very reverse of rogues. **1857** *N.Y. Herald* 1 Sept. (B.), Was Gen. Scott, by a sort of patent safe or Peter Funk operation, diddled out of his ten thousand? **1858** *N.Y. Tribune* 3 Nov., A flashy looking man with a black moustache, who is probably a patent safe operator.

Paterero. Also **petrara,** etc. [It. *petriero, petriere.*] A piece of ordnance formerly used for discharging stones, broken pieces of iron, etc. {1600–} — **1675** ANDROS in Easton *Indian War* 104 If I can will gett and fitt up a Petrara for Capt. Chambers, having none in the fort ready. **1689** *Mass. H. S. Coll.* 4 Ser. V. 221 On Monday last, 28th instant, we took in divers great guns and patereros into the sloop 'Resolution,' at Pemequid Fort. **1705** Boston *News-Letter* 29 Oct. 1/2 Her Majesty's Ship the Weymouth . . . brought in . . . 6 Patararo's. **1727** *Doc. Hist. N.Y. State* I. 459 The French have a Fort on the Lake at Cataraqui, where the biggest Guns they have are patereros that one man can carry about in his arms. **1775** *Warren-Adams Lett.* I. 54 They are casting Pateraras . . . and making Amuzettes.

Paternalism. {1893} A system of government in which the government regulates the whole life of the nation. — **1881** *Chicago Times* 11 June, There is nothing in the proposal that looks in the direction of paternalism, or the ownership and administration of industrial enterprises by the government. **1887** *Nation* 10 March 202/2 Mr. Cleveland has done the country a great service by taking a firm and pronounced stand against paternalism in government. **1898** *Atlantic Mo.* Oct. 563/2 Luther, the fearless champion of religious individualism, was in questions of government the most pronounced advocate of paternalism.

Paternalistic, *a.* 'Of or pertaining to paternalism' (*Cent.*). — **1893** *Voice* 23 March, There is a 'paternalistic' law on the statute books of Minnesota to which the coal combination has made itself liable.

+**Patgo.** Also **patgoe.** *S.* [Cf. PADGO.] **1.** (See quot. 1827.) **2.** The bird used in the game. — **(1) 1827** WILLIAMS *West Florida* 78–9 Patgoes are a kind of introduction to a dance. A wooden bird is fixed on a pole, and carried through the city by some slave; on presenting it to the ladies, they make an offering of a piece of riband, of any length or colour. . . . This is fixed to the bird, which thus becomes decked with an abundant and gaudy plumage. A time and place is then set apart for the fair patrons of the patgoe to assemble, who are usually attended by their beaux. . . . The patgoe is shot at; and the fortunate marksman, who first succeeds in killing it, is proclaimed king. **1868** G. A. McCALL *Lett. from Frontiers* 20 Since my last letter to you, we have had a grand '*Patgo*.' **(2) 1827** [see sense 1]. **1868** G. A. McCALL *Lett. from Frontiers* 21 On the day appointed for the fete, the Patgo or Game Bird, is mounted on a high flag-staff.

***Path.** Also **†payth.**

***1.** A way, usually narrow, incidentally formed by repeated use; a pathway; a narrow way for carts.

In early colonial development, paths were often so called, even after they had become roads. (See also FOOTPATH.)

1622 'MOURT' *Relation* 32 We found it to be onely a path made to driue Deere in. **1649** *Warwick* (R.I.) *Rec.* 83 A payth shall bee left betwixt the Indian field and their lots. **1661** *Conn. Rec.* II. 513 The north side goeth up to the path which goeth from Pagasett to New Haven. **1772** ROMANS in Phillips *Notes on B. Romans* 122 From thence to go Across the Path from Mobile to the Upper Creek Nation. **1797** F. BAILY *Tour* 354 [We] arrived . . . at what is called the Forks of the Path. **1826** BRADFORD *Kentucky Notes* 77 They crossed the Cumberland river not far below Nashville, and fell into the path from that to Kentucky. **1853** SIMMS *Sword & Distaff* 25 Take them to Moore's house, 'up the path.' **1910** TOMPKINS *Mothers & Fathers* 33 Some one was coming up the path.

+2. The warpath.

1841 COOPER *Deerslayer* xii, The dignity of a warrior on his first path, and the gravity of the circumstances in which they were placed, . . . [made] levity out of season.

3. Comb. with *breaker, cleaver, maker, walker.*

1843 *Knickerb.* XXI. 333 A new set of path-breakers arrived in sight. **1857** *Quinland* II. 169 In the woods men take any path that leads in the direction they wish to go: these are the path-makers in the wilderness of politics. **1887** *Century Mag.* Sept. 704/1 The path-walker is . . . plugging the smallest holes with sod, filling where the rain has started a gully. **1896** *Godey's Mag.* April 360/1 The indefatigable path-cleaver [Frémont] . . . crossed mountains even the Indians believed impassable.

+**Pat hand.** *Draw poker.* A hand that is played without drawing more cards. — **1868** *How Gamblers Win* 51 When quick work is to be made with a victim, 'pat hands,' in other words, hands which fall complete, as flushes, fulls, or four of a kind are given out. **1887** KELLER *Draw Poker* 72 A bold player will sometimes decline to draw any cards, and pretend to have a 'pat' hand, and play it as such, when he has none.

+Pathfinder.

1. One who discovers a way; an explorer. Also fig.

1840 COOPER (*title*), The Pathfinder. **1857** GLADSTONE *Englishman in Kansas* 112 Full of cool courage and determination as the Western pathfinder is. **1889** CUSTER *Tenting on Plains* 84 The General . . . was usually an admirable path-finder. **1904** H. W. MABIE *Backgrounds of Literature* 223 Whitman was a pathfinder, and his joy in the great new world of human experience that he explored no one would take from him. **1920** BOK *Americanization* 167 It is difficult to believe . . . that the 'Ladies' Home Journal' was a path-finder.

b. Esp. applied to John C. Frémont (1813–1890).

1850 *Living Age* XXVI. 207/2 The feet of three men have pressed the slopes of the Rocky Mountains: . . . Humboldt . . . ; Audubon . . . ; and Fremont, the pathfinder of empire. **1864** *Rio Abajo Press* 5 July 1/3 He obtained the *sobriquet* of 'Pathfinder,' in finding paths well known to Kit Carson and other mountaineers, who guided him. **1891** WELCKER *Tales 'Wild & Woolly West'* 31 Edward Bimcraw . . . was one of the many who had made the paths afterwards discovered by the great pathfinder, Fremont.

2. A publication giving routes and other items of interest to travelers.

1901 MERWIN & WEBSTER *Calumet 'K'* 28 Bannon . . . took a railroad 'Pathfinder' from his grip.

+**Path master.** An official in charge of keeping up roads and paths. — **1842** KIRKLAND *Forest Life* I. 230 So it is with regard to roads. The consultation about them, the choice of commissioner and of path-masters, . . . certainly tend to improve the faculties of those concerned. **1850** *Knickerb.* XXXV. 22 The official honors of the town-executive descended upon one man . . . who was justice of the peace, path-master, collector and town clerk. **1894** R. E. ROBINSON *Danvis Folks* 239 Hes the path-master warned ye aout tu work on the rhud in your deestrick?

Pathy. A school or method of medical practice or treatment. *humorous* or *contemptuous.* {ipathy, opathy, 1863; 1900–} — **1855** M. THOMPSON *Doesticks* 64 All the 'pathies' and 'isms' of medical Empiricism, . . . have all received from the wise ones of the nineteenth century belief and credence. **1897** *Amer. Pediatric Soc. Trans.* 6 A few works on household medicine, certain pathies, and manuals for nurses . . . were considered unworthy of mention.

***Patience.** A European dock (*Rumex patientia*) formerly eaten as a vegetable. Also *patience dock.* — **1802** DRAYTON *S. Carolina* 67 One of these [species of dock] called *patience*, is a grateful vegetable when young, not inferior to spinach. **1836** LINCOLN *Botany* App. 135 Garden-dock, patience. **1859** *Ill. Agric. Soc. Trans.* III. 513 Patience dock comes early.

+Patio. [Sp.]

1. An inner court or garden open to the sky, usually within or connected with a building. Orig. *S.W.* {1887, in S. Amer.}

[**1827** LONGFELLOW in S. Longfellow *H. W. Longfellow* I. 128 The street-door opens into a short passage through which you pass into the court,—in Spanish, the *patio*.] **1847** MAGOFFIN *Down Santa Fé Trail* 206 Outside in the patio are flour-pots, bird-cages, cats playing and pigeons eating. **1894** HARTE *Works* X. 126 Behind those blistering walls was a reposeful patio surrounded by low-pitched verandas. **1921** *Sunset Mag.* Dec. 60/2 The full possibilities of making the patio just as practical as it is attractive are only beginning to be realized by the everyday American.

2. (See quot. 1881.)

1877 W. WRIGHT *Big Bonanza* 141 This they placed upon a platform of boards, called a 'patio.' **1881** RAYMOND *Mining Gloss.*, *Patio*, the yard where the ores are cleaned and assorted; also, the amalgamation floor, or the Spanish process itself of amalgamating silver ores on an open floor.

+**Patio process.** *Mining.* A process of amalgamating silver ore by spreading it on an open floor for treatment. — **1874** KNIGHT 75/1 The Patio Process has long been in use in South America, and is now employed in Mexico, and now or lately in Nevada. **1876** RAYMOND *8th Rep. Mines* 409 The use of soluble compounds of copper . . . is the basis of the Mexican patio process and its modifications. **1896** SHINN *Story of Mine* 82 He treated them [*sc.* silver sulphurets] with the chemicals of the patio process.

Patlander. An Irishman. *slang.* {1820–34} — **1864** *Harper's Mag.* Nov. 814/2 Charley R——, as genuine a Patlander as ever left the 'ould sod,' . . . went home one day with our Postmaster. **1878** *N. Amer. Rev.* CXXVI. 259 Their success against brother Patlanders seemed doubly welcome.

Patois. A provincial or illiterate speech, esp. one varying from the French language. {1643–}

1826 COOPER *Mohicans* ix, It was easy to distinguish not only words, but sentences, in the *patois* of the Canadas. **1849** PARKMAN in *Knickerb.* XXIX. 311 Our muleteer, Delorier, brought up the rear . . . ejaculating in his prairie patois: '*Sacre enfant de garce!*' **1875** *Scribner's Mo.* July 277/1 The popular speech of San Francisco is strongly flavored with localisms. You hear the *patois* of the frontier. **1880** CABLE *Grandissimes* 312 Four men . . . were talking excitedly in the Creole patois. **1908** *So. Atlantic Quart.* Oct. 339 The vocabulary of our Gullah patois is . . . five times as great.

***Patriot.** One who is disinterestedly devoted to the well-being of his country. {1605–} Also attrib.

1765 TIMBERLAKE *Memoirs* 2, I made my first campaign in the year 1756, with a company of gentlemen called the Patriot Blues, who served the country at their own expence. **1814** *Niles' Reg.* VI. 37/2 On the tenth of January the patriots left the St. Mary's river. **1865** KELLOGG *Rebel Prisons* 247 Husbands, sons and brothers were carried [to Andersonville, Ga.], to finish . . . their careers as patriots and soldiers. **1900** *Congress. Rec.* 19 Jan. 993/2, I do not care whether he is that greatest of patriots, William Jennings Bryan.

+b. One who supported the American cause during the Revolutionary War. Also attrib.

See also PATRIOTS' DAY.

1775 *Mass. Spy* 3 May 2/1 That stupendous fabric of American independence, . . . which our patriots are struggling to preserve against the storms, the sackings and sapping of the tories. **1776** TRUMBULL *M'Fingal* 71 What pill'ries glad the Tories' eyen With patriot-ears for sacrifice! **1794** HUMPHREYS *Industry* 14 Rise then, ye Patriots! ardent rise! **1838** *S. Lit. Messenger* IV. 543 As one who . . . has a share in the heritage of glory which has descended from the patriots of the revolution. **1925** *Boston Transcript* 18 April III. 9/4 Lexington's own daring Declaration of Independence—A little known document to which the Patriots affixed their signatures in 1776.

+**Patriot army.** The American army of the Revolution. — **1783** WASHINGTON *Writings* VIII. (1835) 568 The character of those, who have persevered through every extremity . . . being immortalized by the illustrious appellation of the *patriot army.* **1881** *Harper's Mag.* Jan. 189/1 A worthy Friend, Joseph Tatnall, . . . alone dared to grind corn for the famishing patriot army.

Patriotic, *a.* {1653–} Marked by devotion to one's country; characteristic of a patriot. {1757–}

1783 WASHINGTON *Writings* X. 331 [Who] could imagine . . . that men, who came from the different parts of the continent, . . . would instantly become but one patriotic band of brothers? **1786** B. WASHINGTON *Ib.* XI. 71*n.*, We have lately instituted a society . . . called the *Patriotic Society* . . . to inquire into the state of public affairs. **1819** *Mass. Spy* 24 March (Th.), Ye who in 1816 called your patriotick Brooks to the gubernatorial chair. **1857** BENTON *Exam. Dred Scott Case* 110 These were the earnest and patriotic appeals of Mr. Polk, in favor of the two compromises. **1864** *Wkly. New Mexican* 10 June 2/3 A patriotic society was formed here [in Washington, D.C.] today, called 'The Ladies' National Covenant,' whose object is to abolish the use of foreign silks, satins, laces [etc.] . . . with a view to keep the gold in the country. **1892** *York County Hist. Rev.* 53 He is . . . a member of the Patriotic Sons of America. **1907** ANDREWS *Recoll.* 199, I have read the noble deeds of our patriotic soldiers at Mobile. **1925** *Boston Transcript* 18 April III. 9/1 [The] rider will be met at the Captain Isaac Hall House by . . . the City Government, veteran and patriotic organizations and school children.

+**Patriots' Day.** A legal holiday, April 19, celebrated in Maine and Massachusetts since 1894 as the anniversary of the battle of Lexington in 1775. — **1894** *Boston Transcript* 18 April 8/4 Lowell mill agents, having heard the indignant protest against the running of machinery in the mills Patriots' Day, have decided to reconsider their action. **1909** *Springfield W. Repub.* 22 April 11 The firing of salutes and the ringing of bells . . . ushered in the celebration of Patriots' day. . . . The day is a legal holiday in Massachusetts and Maine. **1925** *Boston Transcript* 21 April 10/1 Sesquicentennial of Patriots' Day passes into history.

Patrol. {1664–} In attrib. uses.

+*Patrol box,* a signal box used by a patrolman; +*p. district,* a district in a city constituting the beat of a policeman or policemen; +*p. judge,* a judge who moves to different parts of a race track to see that no rules of the race are broken; +*p. law,* a law that provides for the patrolling of Negroes; +*p. system,* the system involved in patrolling Negroes.

1894 STEAD *If Christ Came to Chicago* 266 The nearest patrolman who sees it [a fire] hastens to his patrol-box and sends in a fire alarm. **1882** MCCABE *New York* 371 The city was divided into separate patrol districts. **1868** WOODRUFF *Trotting Horse* xxix. 243 Sending out patrol judges, they started them for another heat. **1858** DOUGLAS in Logan *Great Conspiracy* 70 If the People of a Territory want Slavery, they will encourage it by passing affirmatory laws, and the necessary police regulations, patrol laws and Slave Code. **1880** TOURGEE *Invisible Empire* xii, The old 'patrol' system of the ante-bellum days and a devout belief in its necessity was also one of the active causes of the rapid spread of the Klan.

+**Patroller.** Also †**patroler.** One who does duty as a patrolman: (see esp. quot. 1901).

See also PAT(T)ER(R)OLLER.

1744 *Bristol* (Va.) *Vestry Bk.* 118 To Burwell Green for his Levy, Being a patroler, 50. **1796** in Summers *Ann. S.W. Va.* 467 James Bryant allowed pay for services as patroler in First Batallion for the present year. **1867** HARRIS *Sut Lovingood* 166 The pat-rollers mite cum in an' spile hit wif thar durn'd foolishness. **1880** TOURGEE *Invisible Empire* xii, This system [varied] . . . in the powers conferred upon the patrolmen, or 'patrollers' as they were popularly called. **1901** B. T. WASHINGTON *Up from Slavery* 77 The 'patrollers' were bands of white men . . . organized largely for the purpose of regulating the conduct of the slaves at night in such matters as preventing the slaves from going from one plantation to another without passes, and for preventing them from holding any kind of meetings without permission and without the presence at these meetings of at least one white man.

+**Patrolman.** A man who patrols something. In early use, a soldier; later, a policeman, life guard, etc.

1867 CRAWFORD *Mosby* 330 [They] captured five patrolmen, from whom, by the exercise of strength, awkwardness, and a mixture of deception, they succeeded in obtaining the countersign. **1878** *Harper's Mag.* Feb. 331/2 Each patrolman will carry a beach lantern. **1880** *Scribner's Mo.* Jan. 323 At the beginning of each watch two men set out from the station on patrol duty and follow their beats to the right and left respectively until they meet the patrol-men from the adjacent stations. **1890** *Electrical Rev.* 1 March 16/3 The chief lineman should . . . have charge of the carbon-setters and arc patrolmen. **1904** *N.Y. Ev. Post* 1 Feb. 2 A patrolman, attracted by the young woman's cry, elbowed his way to her. **1912** IRWIN *Red Button* 21 In the hall, she met the regular patrolman.

+**Patrol wagon.**

1. A police wagon used to carry prisoners or a squad of policemen.

1887 *Courier-Journal* 22 Jan. 3/5 The patrol wagon, filled with officers, was driven to the place at a breakneck speed. **1899** *Atlantic Mo.* June 770/1 With clamor of urgent gong, the patrol wagon rounds the corner, carrying two policemen precariously perched upon a struggling 'drunk.' **1904** *N.Y. Herald* 30 Sept. 3 Captain Bingham then telephoned to the 67th street station for its reserves, and they came down, 20 strong, in a patrol wagon. **1923** WATTS *L. Nichols* 357 The patrol-wagon . . . came churning up out of the darkness.

2. 'A light open wagon used by the underwriters' patrol in hastening to fires to protect insured goods' (*Stand.*).

+**Patrol watch.** Watchmen who patrol a district or place. — **1810** *Boston Selectmen* 426 Return of the patrole watch read. **1821** *Ib.* 227 The subject of granting permission for private patrole watches, was committed to the Chairman.

***Patron.**[1]

***1.** One who gives his support and favor to an institution.

1654 JOHNSON *Wonder-w. Prov.* 162 Mr. *Henry Dunster,* before whose coming the Lord was pleased to provide a Patron for erecting a Colledg. **1858** *Texas Almanac 1859* 22 The teachers are required to report . . . the names of the patrons of the school. **1916** THOBURN *Stand. Hist. Okla.* I. 45 [Geo. Sibley] became a founder and patron of Lindenwood College.

b. (See quotation.)

1863 HOPLEY *Life in South* II. 63, I might depend on receiving my entire salary some time or other, because his 'patrons' (as the parents of pupils are termed) were of the 'first class and very wealthy.'

+**2.** (See quot. 1851.)

1818 *N. Amer. Rev.* March 427 To provide additional security [against extravagance], the following law, requiring the appointment of a patron, has been passed. **1835** J. MARTIN *Descr. Virginia* 124 Every student . . . is required, on matriculating, to deposit with the Patron, all the money . . . which he shall have in his possession. **1851** HALL *College Words* 225 At some of the colleges in the United States, the patron is appointed to take charge of the funds, and to regulate the expenses, of students who reside at a distance.

+**Patron.**[2] [Sp. or Fr.]

A new borrowing from Spanish or French.

1. The master or steersman of a vessel; =PATROON.

1814 BRACKENRIDGE *Views La.* 206 The *patron* came to inform Mr. Lisa, they were begging him for a biscuit. **1817** BRADBURY *Travels* 192 Her crew consisted of five French Creoles, four of whom were oarsmen, and the fifth steered the boat, he is called the *patron.* **1826** FLINT *Recoll.* 217 In my trip from St. Charles to Arkansa, we went in a very large keel-boat, with an ignorant *patron.* **1849** T. T. JOHNSON *Sights Gold Region* 12 The Creoles . . . were generally the patrones or captains, and owners of the boats. **1904** *Kan. Hist. Soc. Trans.* IX. 272 The captain of the boat, called the 'patron,' did the steering.

2. *S.W.* A person who assumes some responsibility for looking after the interests of those who work for him; a landowner who employs many people.

1863 *Rio Abajo Press* 7 April 2/2 It had been given him by his 'patron.' **1895** REMINGTON *Pony Tracks* 58 You can only go there if Don Gilberto, the *patron* of the hacienda . . . will take you in the ranch coach.

***Patronage.**

1. The power arising from the right to make appointments to public office; the right of making such appointments. {1769–}

See also EXECUTIVE PATRONAGE.

1826 in Benton *30 Years' View* I. 81/1 The patronage of the federal government at the beginning was founded upon a revenue of two millions of dollars. **1865** in Fleming *Hist. Reconstruction* I. 133 Clothed with as much power of patronage as is the President, I have no doubt of his ability [etc.]. **1883** *Century Mag.* Aug. 631/1 The evils of 'patronage' are closely related to the abuses by which the tricky and unscrupulous politician secures the control of his particular district or ward. **1900** *Congress. Rec.* 15 Feb. 1849/2 The words 'spoilsman,' 'henchmen,' 'patronage,' and 'reform' were sung and echoed throughout the halls of Congress.

+**b.** The offices that are subject to this power.

1845 POLK *Diary* (1929) 28 He said that Mr. Van Buren had professed the belief that I was bestowing the patronage . . . with a view to be a candidate for a second term. *a***1882** WEED *Autobiog.* 509 President Tyler . . . found himself in a party . . . which after obtaining what patronage they could, threw him off. **1910** *N.Y. Ev. Post* 28 Nov. 1 Gov.-elect Wilson entertains no thought of parcelling out the patronage he will control in political dickering.

2. Attrib. with *list, power, system.*

1802 *Ann. 7th Congress* 1 Sess. 580 A variety of circumstances . . . gave the patronage system the preponderancy during the first three Presidential terms of election. **1887** *Courier-Journal* 5 May 4/2 If ever an Administration worked the patronage power to gain votes this one is doing it to perfection. **1899** *Chicago Record* 10 Jan. 4/1 If the president does not add a large number of positions to the patronage list he will call down upon his head the wrath of the spoilsmen.

+**Patronage night.** A night at a theater when its patrons try to be present. — **1870** M. H. SMITH *20 Years Wall St.* 395 Grace Church in the season, the opera on a patronage night, . . . cannot boast of a more fashionably or elegantly attired company.

‖**Patroned land.** Land belonging to one who helps support a church parish. — **1755** in Chalkley *Scotch-Irish Settlement Va.* II. 440 Subscribers have processioned all the *patroned* land within bounds of Cap. Wm. Christian's Company.

Patroon.[1] {1662–} Also †**pateroon, pattroon.** [Fr. and Sp. *patron.*] The master or captain of a boat; the steersman or pilot of a barge, canoe, or other boat. *Obs.* {1743–, in South Seas}

See also PATRON[2] 1.

1677 HUBBARD *Narrative* II. 57 He was forced to travel with his Pateroon four or five Miles overland to Damaniscottee. **1737** W. STEPHENS *Proc. Georgia* 8 Peter Emery, Patroon of a Canoe, being in Town from Georgia. **1775** ROMANS *Nat. Hist. Florida* 186 The vessel draws one third, the *patroon* or master, two shares of the remaining two thirds. **1808** C. SCHULTZ *Travels* II. 106 We were entirely disappointed in our expectation of obtaining a pilot, or pattroon, as they are called. **1836** in Stowe *Key* 21/2 Billy . . . is known as the patroon of my boat for many years. **1852** REYNOLDS *Hist. Illinois* 197 [The canoes] are propelled by the voyagers using paddles, and the patroon at the stern steering it also with a paddle.

+**Patroon.**[2] Also **patrone, pat(t)eroon.** [Du.]

1. A proprietor of one of the manors originally granted by the old Dutch governments of New York and New Jersey.

See MANOR 1, note.

1744 A. HAMILTON *Itin.* (1907) 74 Jeremiah Ranslaer . . . is dignified here with the title of Patroon. **1776** C. CARROLL *Journal* (1845) 42 Vast tracts of land on each side of Hudson's river are held by the proprietaries, or, as they are here styled, the *Patrones* of manors. **1781** PETERS *Hist. Conn.* 94 Messrs. Smith and Livingston, and other pateroons in New-York, will find the last determination also to have been 'founded in ignorance and fraud.' **1826** COOPER *Mohicans* xiii, Tracts of country wider than that which belongs to the Albany *Patteroon.* **1832** WATSON *Hist. Tales N.Y.* 29 [Encouragement to settlers was great,] especially to those who should go out to the 'Groot Rivier' of Hudson, with the enterprise, force, and capital of *Patroons.* . . . They were such as should undertake to plant a colony of fifty souls. **1868** LOSSING *Hudson* 120 The Patroon was invested with power to administer civil and criminal justice.

transf. **1838** *S. Lit. Messenger* IV. 305 They are addressed to a gentleman well known and highly appreciated in the annals of White Sulphur, the grand master of ceremonies for years on festive occasions, and by prescription the Patroon of the establishment.

2. Attrib. with *day, influence, system, title.*

1797 JEFFERSON *Writings* IX. 403 With the English influence in the lower, and the Patroon influence in the upper part of your State, I presume little is to be hoped. **1859** PHILLIPS *Speeches* (1863) 287 Your Barnburners said, 'Patroon titles are unrighteous.' **1885** A. JOHNSTON *Hist. U.S.* 58 The patroon system was not changed under the English. **1904** *Baltimore American* 5 Oct. 8 Now that New Yorkers can ride a mile a minute in their nice new sewer, they had better get rid of their horse-car relics of the old patroon days.

+**Patrooness.** 'A woman with the rights and privileges of a patroon; a female patroon' (*Stand.*).

+**Patroon land.** Land belonging to a patroon's manor. — **1758** in A. Tomlinson *Military Jrnls.* 13 Marched into the Paterroon Lands to Landlord Lovejoys. **1885** A. JOHNSTON *Hist. U.S.* 245 Most of the 'patroon lands' were then [*c*1844] gradually sold to the tenants.

+**Patroonry.** A system of landownership based on manorial rights. — **1858** *N.Y. Tribune* 30 Jan. 5/3 Another Blow at Patroonry.—The landholders of Rensselaer county . . . had a meeting at West Sandlake.

+**Patroonship.** A landed estate owned and governed by a patroon. — **1848** IRVING *Knickerb.* (rev. ed.) II. ix, The good Oloffe indulged in magnificent dreams of foreign conquest and great patroonships in the wilderness. **1884** *Mag. Amer. Hist.* Jan. 11 His estate would be constituted a manor, or in Dutch parlance a patroonship, with privileges similar to those of a baron in England.

+**Pattawatami.** Variant of POTAWATOMI.

***Patten.** A shoe or sandal having a sole raised a few inches from the ground by a light frame and worn in wet weather. (See also PATTOON.) — **1644** *Essex Probate Rec.* I. 46 One paire pattens, 1 s. **1690** SEWALL *Diary* I. 328 My wife was so ill could hardly get home, taking some harm in going in Pattens. **1830** WATSON *Philadelphia* 192 In those times galo shoes and pattens were necessary and resorted to by ladies. **1897** *Outing* XXX. 72/1 An ancient dame passed wearing pattens, the only time in America that I have ever seen this last-century device for keeping out of the mud.

Patteraro. Also **petteraro.** =PATERERO. *Obs.* {1693–} — **1691** *Va. Council Exec. Jrnls.* I. 157 [He] tooke from her two Petteraroes, three Musquetts. **1711** *Boston News-Letter* 17 Sept. 2/2 The Loading of the Ship . . . consisting of . . . Guns, Patteraroes, Muskets [etc.].

***Pattern,** *n.* Also †**patton.** +A quantity of material sufficient for a garment.

1695 SEWALL *Letter-Book* I. 152 Send my wife a Pattern of Silk for a gown. **1782** *Essex Inst. Coll.* XXXVIII. 54 A Patton for two Pare of overalls and two Wescoats—and a patton of White Ribed Stuf for a Wescoat & Briches. **1806** LEWIS in *L. & Clark Exped.* IV. (1905) 186 One beaver skin, or two of those of the Raccoon or tiger catt forms the pattern of the robe. **1843** 'CARLTON' *New Purchase* 109 Thrifty housewives in cutting little boy's roundabouts and trowsers always contrive out of a scant pattern of pepper and salt stuff, to leave enough for patches.

***Pattern,** *v.* +*To pattern after,* to imitate or follow as a pattern or model. — **1878** BEADLE *Western Wilds* 356 That was a nice family for us Americans to pattern after, was n't it? **1884** 'CRADDOCK' *Tenn. Mts.* 4 They dunno what he patterned arter.

Pattern-maker. One who makes patterns or counterparts of various objects that serve as guides in foundery and construction work. {1858–} — **1818** FLINT *Lett. from Amer.* 62 [Among] the manufacturing people of Pittsburg . . . [is] 1 Pattern Maker. **1851** CIST *Cincinnati* 297 He engaged in the foundery of D. A. Powell, as pattern maker.

+**Pat(t)er(r)oller.** *S.* [Variant of PATROLLER.] A person having authority to patrol roads and streets at night in order to apprehend Negroes, esp. slaves, abroad without acceptable excuse. Now hist. — **1893** *Nation* 7 Sept. 173/1 Ability to write meant ability to counterfeit passes which would outwit the ignorant midnight 'patterrollers.' **1899** GREEN *Va. Word-Book* 268 *Patteroller*, a patroller. Authority was given by the justices of the peace to hunt for thieves and nightwalkers who were punished when caught. **1899** CHESNUTT *Conjure Woman* 88 S'posen de patteroles ketch me, Aun' Peggy, w'at I gwine ter do? **1917** *Dialect Notes* IV. 385 *Pateroller.* Night-guard over negro slaves on an ante-bellum plantation. Ky.

+**Pattiwatima.** Variant of POTAWATOMI.

+**Patton stock.** (See quot. 1893.) — **1876** *Ill. Dept. Agric. Trans.* XIII. 322 Some grades of the 'Patton' stock are said to have been found in Madison. **1893** G. W. CURTIS *Horses, Cattle* 158 In 1797 some of these [shorthorn] cattle were taken across the line [from Va.] to Kentucky by a Mr. Patton, soon becoming quite well-known as the 'Patton Stock' [Durhams].

+**Pattoon.** =PATTEN. *Obs.* — **1715** *Boston News-Letter* 17 Oct. 2/2 All Persons may have Boots, Shoes, Pattoons, or any thing belonging to that Trade mended. **1725** *New-Eng. Courant* 1–8 Feb. 1/2 Those who have the Unhappiness of sitting near the Stairs . . . can hardly hear the Minister's first Prayer for . . . the Screiks of English Pattoons. **1733** *Mass. Hist. Soc. Proc.* V. 16 As to the shoes and pattoons, my spouse sends them back. **1743** *Boston News-Letter* 3 Feb., To be sold . . . Women's & Children's Shoes & Pattoons.

Pattypan. {1694–} A pan, usually of tin, in which patties or small pies are baked. {1710–} — **1758** Shelton *Salt-Box House* (1900) 298 4 pattipans, 1 pepper-pot, 1 canister. **1779** *York Co., Va., Rec.: Wills* XXII 28 April, 8 patty pans, 1 pr. scales and weights. **1828** LESLIE *Receipts* 20 You may bake it . . . in two small tin patty-pans, which, for cheesecakes, should be of a square shape. **1878** B. F. TAYLOR *Between Gates* 178 You see scalloped sheets of silver and gold, resembling the tinner's scraps when he has been cutting out the bottoms of little patty-pans.

+**Paugie, Paugy.** The scup or porgy, *Stenotomus versicolor*, syn. *chrysops.* (See also PORGY.) — **1848** BARTLETT 258 It is singular that one half the aboriginal name, *scup*, should be retained for this fish in Rhode Island, and the other half, *paug*, changed into *paugie* or *porgy*, in New York. **1884** GOODE, etc. *Fisheries* I. 386 About New York the second syllable of the abbreviated Indian name has been lengthened into 'Paugy' or 'Porgy.' **1911** *Rep. Fisheries 1908* 315/2 Scup (*Stenotomus chrysops*). . . . Common local names are 'scuppaug,' 'paugy,' 'porgy,' 'pogy,' 'fair maid,' etc.

+**Pauhagen.** Also **pohegan, poghaden,** etc. [Algonquian.] =MENHADEN: (see also quot. 1859). — *a*1838 in *Mass. Zool. Survey Rep.* 48 There are nearly three hundred and twelve thousand *pohegans* used for bait—and nearly as many thrown away, and strewed on the land for manure. **1848** BARTLETT 255 *Pohagen.* A fish of the herring species. The Menhaden of Rhode Island. *Maine.* **1859** *Ib.* 329 *Pohagen*, or *Pauhagen.* . . . The term is also applied to a kind of paste-bait for mackerel, etc., made of damaged and frequently putrid fish, chopped or ground in a cutting mill. **1890** *Cent.* 4581/3 *Poghaden*, . . . the menhaden. Also *Pauhagen.* **1910** HODGE, etc. *Amer. Indians* 212/1 *Pauhagen*, one of the New England names of the menhaden, or mossbunker. . . . Other spellings are paughaden, poghaden, pauhaugen.

Pave, *n.* Short for PAVEMENT. *Obs.* {1881–, Irish} 'Chiefly *U.S.*' (*O.E.D.*). — **1835** *S. Lit. Messenger* I. 357, I met a friend on the *pave* last week. **1851** HALL *Manhattaner* 39 Would that . . . time-honored ex-street commissioner Ewen, were in New Orleans to behold its paves and trottoirs. *a*1882 in McCabe *New York* 144 The silence and emptiness will be alone relieved by the . . . rattling of a casual carriage over the stony pave.

***Pave,** *v. tr.* To lay (a way or street) with pavement. Also *vbl. n.*

1665 *Boston Rec.* 26 Being desirous to paue the causye . . . , they haue libertye to sett vp posts. **1716** *Boston Selectmen* 3 Ye motion made by Sundry Inhabitts. abt. Paveing of Summer Street. **1790** WEBSTER in E. E. F. Ford *Notes N. Webster* I. 332, I draw up a plan for paving our Streets, or rather covering them with hard rock stone; which proves agreeable to many. **1851** ROSS *In New York* 14 The streets are generally paved with round cobble stone. **1893** HALE *New Eng. Boyhood* 3 The more important business streets of this town of Boston were paved in the middle with round stones from the neighboring beaches.

∗**Pavement.** A paved surface; a stretch of paved way or roadway.

1634 WOOD *New Eng. Prospect* 14 There is plenty of stone both rough and smooth, usefull for many things, with quarries of Slate, out of which they get covering for houses, with good clay, whereof they make Files and Brickes, and pavements for their necessary uses. **1699** *Boston Rec.* 238 That they or either of them Do forthwith repair the pavement on each side of sd. Bridge. **1790** *Phila. Ordinances* (1812) 119 Regulations should be made, suitable to prevent obstructions and nuisances being placed . . . upon the brick pavements and foot-ways. **1822** *Ann. 17th Congress* 1 Sess. I. 176 A bill authorizing and directing a durable and well finished pavement of Pennsylvania avenue. **1879** *Scribner's Mo.* May 45/1 The pavements are often defective with holes or hollows. **1891** EGGLESTON in *Century Mag.* March 665 The . . . coachman banged his way over the pavement. **1907** *St. Nicholas* Oct. 1111/1 The streets and not even the pavements can be blocked even for a few hours.

+**b.** A natural formation of flat stones, usually across the bed of a stream. Freq. *pavement of rocks.*

1747–8 WASHINGTON in *Amer. Speech* XV. 293 A certain Tract of waste & ungranted Land . . . beg: at a hickory & Walnut against a Pavement of Rocks. **1770** — *Diaries* I. 424 The pavement of Rocks are only to be seen at low Water. **1918** A. W. GILES *Country about Camp Lee, Va.* 24 The water descends by a series of cascades and rapids between granite walls and over an uneven granite pavement.

+**c.** *Mining.* The stones lining the bottom of a sluice; stone riffle blocks.

Cf. PAVING STONE b.

1880 INGHAM *Digging Gold* 77 Great care is taken to wash any particles of sand or dirt that might contain fine gold from the blocks of pavement before their removal.

∗**Paver.** Also †**pavier.** One who paves. {–1807} — **1735** *Boston Selectmen* 282 No Accounts of Work done for the Town, by Carpenters, Paviers &c. [shall] be . . . allow'd. **1769** *Phila. Ordinances* (1812) 21 A number of pavers and workmen. **1846** CORCORAN *Pickings* 207 He is a *pavier,* and . . . is ever improving the public ways. **1851** CIST *Cincinnati* 51 Paperhangers, 45. Pavers, 51. Porters, 129.

∗**Paving. a.** The construction of pavement. Also attrib. **b.** A pavement or material for this.

1678 *New Castle Court Rec.* 351, 1 paving hammer. **1689** *Boston Rec.* 197 The inconveniencie & damage that shod cart Wheeles doe, to the paueing of the streetes. **1774** *Md. Hist. Mag.* XVI. 30 Stone . . . is in general fitter for flags & Paveing. **1791** *Holyoke Diaries* 126 The Paving Brot to our Do(or). **1865** *Atlantic Mo.* Jan. 47/2 Yard-wide spaces of emerald [*i.e.* ice] . . . grew as familiar to the eye as paving-blocks to the dwellers in cities. **1873** *Mich. Gen. Statutes* I. (1882) 677 The term 'paving' shall be deemed to include the construction of cross-walks, gutters, and curbing. **1879** *Harper's Mag.* Dec. 33/1 The evidence of the 'chuck-hole' . . . is distributed throughout a mile of bad paving.

∗**Paving stone.** A stone suitable for use in paving. Also attrib.

1677 *Essex Inst. Coll.* VI. 199/1 Paueing stones reserued for the use of the towne. **1788** FRANKLIN *Autobiog.* 408 They . . . had even plac'd quantities of small paving stones between the windows of their high stone houses. **1817** BENTLEY *Diary* IV. 471 Capt. Archer . . . had taken many loads of paving stones for Salem from the neighborhood. **1913** LONDON *Valley of Moon* 501, I seen the fellow with the teamin' contract for the pavin'-stone quarry.

+**b.** *Mining.* One of the stones making up the lining of the bottom of a sluice; a riffle block of stone.

Cf. PAVEMENT c.

1880 INGHAM *Digging Gold* 77 The riffles or paving-stones are removed, commencing with the upper end of the sluice.

+**Pawaw,** etc. (See PAW(W)AW, etc.)

Pawnbroker. One whose business is to lend money on articles left as security in his care. {1687–} — **1830** WATSON *Philadelphia* 218 Pawnbrokers. Are altogether of modern establishment among us, rising in obscurity and with little notice, till they have spread like a mal-area over the morals of the community. **1882** MCCABE *New York* 203 The pawnbrokers drive a thriving trade with the ladies of position. **1901** CHURCHILL *Crisis* 387 Mr. Catherwood . . . watched the sideboard he had given his wife . . . being sold to a pawnbroker.

+**Pawnee.** Also †**Pania, Pane.** [App. from *pariki* 'horn,' with reference to a method of hairdressing in which the forelock was dressed to resemble a horn.]

1. *pl.* A Caddoan confederacy or nation of plains Indians formerly living chiefly in the valley of the Platte River in Nebraska.

See also GRAND PAWNEE. For foreign variants of earlier date see Hodge *Amer. Indians.*

1805 in *Ann. 9th Congress* 2 Sess. 1046 [The Pawnee Republicans] hunt principally on the Republican river, which is better stocked with timber than that hunted by the Panias. *c***1834** CATLIN *Indians* II. 11 At this place [Bellevue, Neb.] I was in the country of the Pawnees, . . . whose villages are on the Platte river. **1901** *Harper's Mag.* April 741/1 All the different tribes that had been attacked by him . . . came down together to fight the Pawnees. **1925** TILGHMAN *Dugout* 13 The Pawnees were late going south that year.

b. The language used by these Indians.

1806 PIKE *Sources Miss.* II. App. 48, I asked . . . [for] a Tetau prisoner who spoke Pawnee, to serve as an interpreter. **1821** FOWLER *Journal* 55 Mr. Roy—He Spoke Some Pane and (in) that language our Councils Ware Held.

2. An Indian of the Pawnee nation. In full *Pawnee Indian.*

1808 PIKE *Sources Miss.* 140 The Tetaus had recently killed six Pawnees. **1827** COOPER *Prairie* xxviii, He will never see a Pawnee become a Sioux. **1840** BIRD *Robin Day* 8, I had done a good act, and like the young Pawnee Indian, . . . I did not know it. **1889** G. B. GRINNELL *Pawnee Hero Stories* 246 The Pawnee who was disguised as a wolf could trot up close to the village of his enemy.

3. *attrib.* and *comb.* **a.** Designating individuals of the Pawnee nation.

1808 PIKE *Sources Miss.* 140, [I] met a Pawnee hunter. **1822** FOWLER *Journal* 158 The Pawne Cheef Refused to Have them killed. **1847** COYNER *Lost Trappers* 53 Two of the men went with the Pawnee warriors to their village. *a***1861** WINTHROP *J. Brent* 73 It is not for a Pawnee squaw that you go clad in skins and disdain the barber? **1868** *N.Y. Herald* 31 July 5/3 A large band of the Sioux and Cheyennes had attacked a small party of the Pawnee scouts.

b. Designating communities of Pawnee Indians, or structures built by Pawnees.

1821 FOWLER *Journal* 35 We are Camped in a pawnee fort Which appeers to Have been used about two Weakes Since. **1847** COYNER *Lost Trappers* 55 The two men sent to the Pawnee village returned about noon. **1856** BECKWOURTH *Life* (1931) 13 This is a band of the Pawnee tribe of Indians.

c. In special combinations.

Pawnee horse, a horse owned or once owned by Pawnees; *P. hunting grounds,* the hunting grounds resorted to by the Pawnee Indians; *P. rock,* (see quotation); *P. whistle,* a whistle of warning or announcement characteristic of the Pawnee Indians.

1835 IRVING *Tour on Prairies* 189 A fine Pawnee horse that had his ears slit and saddle-marks on his back. *Ib.* 58 The Osages . . . had represented to him the perils that would attend him on an expedition to the Pawnee hunting grounds. **1848** ROBINSON *Santa Fe Exped.* (1932) 11, 15 miles west of Walnut Creek [near the Arkansas R.], stands the famous Pawnee Rock, near which a hard battle was once fought between 3000 Pawnees and 60 traders. **1844** GREGG *Commerce of Prairies* II. 141 The 'Pawnee whistle' . . . was heard in every quarter.

+**Pawnee country.** A region occupied by the Pawnee Indians. — **1835** IRVING *Tour on Prairies* 103 We were in the Pawnee country. **1847** RUXTON *Adv. Rocky Mts.* (1848) 277 We were now in the outskirt of the Pawnee and Comanche country.

+**Pawnee Loup.** A member of the Skidi, an Indian tribe of the Pawnee confederacy; also, pl., the tribe. Also attrib. — **1805** in *Ann. 9th Congress* 2 Sess. 1046 Panias Loups, (or Wolves.) . . . These are also a branch of the Panias proper. **1823** JAMES *Exped.* II. 165 The camp had been occupied by a war party of Skeeree or Pawnee Loup Indians. **1826** *19th Congress 1 Sess.* H. R. Doc. No. 117, 7 The Grand Paunees and Paunee Loups, reside on the Platte, 130 miles south of the Missouri. **1847** D. COYNER *Lost Trappers* 62 As Doranto proved to be a son of a grand chief of the Pawnee Loups, he was greatly prized as a captive. **1856** BECKWOURTH *Life* (1931) 25 Six or seven Indians of the Pawnee Loup band came into our camp.

+**Pawnee macaroni.** (See quotation.) — **1894** ROBLEY *Bourbon Co., Kansas* 38 They had nothing to eat but jerked buffalo and Pawnee macarroni [*sic*]. This latter was a very succulent dish much sought after by the Pawnee Indians. It was made from the small entrails of antelope and fish-worms.

+**Pawnee Pict.** Also †**Pania Piqûe,** etc. [Fr. *Pani Piqué* 'tattooed Pawnees.'] A member of a confederacy of Indians closely related to the Pawnees; also, pl., the confederacy. Also attrib. — **1805** in *Ann. 9th Congress* 2 Sess. 1075 Pania Piqûe. . . . [Also called] Paunee Piqûe. **1823** JAMES *Exped.* II. 282 We supposed it to be the road leading from the Pawnee Piqua village on Red river to Santa Fé. **1836** HILDRETH *Campaigns Rocky Mts.* 160 The whole object of our expedition [was]—the village of the Pawnee Picts. **1856** BECKWORTH *Life* (1931) 13 The Pawnee Pics or Tattoed Pawnees.

+**Pawnee Republicans.** *pl.* A tribe of Pawnees who lived on the Republican River. (Cf. REPUBLICAN *a.* 4.) — [**1805** in *Ann. 9th Congress* 2 Sess. 1045 Panias proper and Panias Republican live in the same village.] **1808** PIKE *Sources Miss.* II. App. 14 On the La Platte, reside the grand Pawnee village, and the Pawnee loups on one of its branches, with whom the Pawnee republicans are at war.

Pawnshop. The place of business of a pawnbroker. {1849–} Also attrib. — **1882** MCCABE *New York* 436 The majority of the pawn shops are dirty and repulsive in appearance. **1887** *Harper's Mag.* March 516/1 Pawn shops—so often the 'fences' for concealing stolen goods— . . . abound most in the precincts infamous for poverty and crime. **1905** 'O. HENRY' *Strictly Business* 39 Klein sees a pair of cuff links . . . in a pawnshop window, and we all go in while he buys 'em.

Pawpaw. Also **paupaw.** [Variant of PAPAW.]

+1. =PAPAW 2.

[**1764** REUTER *Wachau* 561 *Paw-Paw* grows in the best Bottom lands.] **1787** CUTLER in *Life & Corr.* II. 397 The most useful trees are maple or sugar-tree, . . . pawpaw or custard apple [etc.]. **1815** DRAKE *Cincinnati* 120 The pawpaw grows in the fertile parts of Virginia. **1841** STEELE *Summer Journey* 205 We also observed the Chickasaw plum, the pawpaw, and cotton tree. **1875** *Amer. Naturalist* IX. 390 The pawpaw, persimmon and pecan are found more or less abundantly over the southern two-thirds of [Illinois]. **1907** *Harper's Mag.* Jan. 218 A beautiful camping-ground covered with pawpaws and fringed with wild grapes and cocoa-plums.

+b. The wood of the papaw tree.

1774 D. JONES *Journal* (1865) 47 Spent some time in getting poles for the canoe—the wood used is called paupaw, it is very light. **1880** *Scribner's Mo.* April 880/2 None of the poles were hickory or oak, but poplar, sassafras, pawpaw, or some other variety of soft wood.

+2. =PAPAW 1.

1826 FLINT *Recoll.* 328 Of wild fruits, there are the pawpaw, the persimon, the Chickasaw plum, and the pine woods grape. **1886** Z. F. SMITH *Kentucky* 27 They were reduced to a diet of wild grapes, walnuts, and pawpaws. **1891** *Amer. Notes & Q.* VII. 197 Our well-known N. American fruit, the pawpaw, has a name remarkably like that of the tropical Papaw, and the poet Bryant even calls it 'the papaya.' **1912** COBB *Back Home* 40 The woods were perfumy with ripening wild grapes and pawpaws.

+3. (See quot. 1885.) *Obs.*

1864 *Congress. Globe* 9 March 1017/3 They even accuse us radicals of speaking disparagingly of the militia of Missouri. It is false . . . except so far as relates to what are called Paw-Paws. **1885** *Mag. Amer. Hist.* March 297/2 *Paw-Paws.*—Equivalent to 'Bushwhackers' . . . current in Missouri. The paw-paw is a wild fruit of the genus *Asimina*, on which the bushwhackers are supposed to subsist.

4. Attrib. and comb. with *bark, bush, patch, shrub, wood.*

1773 in *Cincinnati Misc.* I. 265 Wednesday 6th, . . . spent some time in fitting poles of pawpawwood, which is very plenty here and very light, so that it is used chiefly for canoe poles. **1827** *Western Mo. Rev.* I. 255 A pawpaw shrub, hanging full of fruits, . . . is to us one of the richest spectacles. **1841** *S. Lit. Messenger* VII. 533/2 A grove of scrubby pawpaw bushes. **1883** EGGLESTON *Hoosier School-Boy* 64 Bob Holliday . . . took his place among the pigeon-slayers in the paw-paw patch. **1891** 'THANET' *Otto the Knight* 248 He and another guard . . . tied Looney to a gum-tree by strips of pawpaw bark like the niggers make reins out of, you know.

Pawpaw thicket. A thicket composed of papaw shrubs and trees. — **1855** *Oregon W. Times* 12 May (Th.), So out we goes to the paw-paw thicket, and pealed [*sic*] a right peart chance o' bark. **1867** HARRIS *Sut Lovingood* 224 Got in a paw-paw thicket on the bank. **1894** *Outing* XXIV. 336/1 Ten minutes' walk . . . would take one to hazel-patch or paw-paw thicket. **1912** NICHOLSON *Hoosier Chron.* 7 The paw-paw thicket where fruit for the gods lures farm boys on frosty mornings in golden autumn.

Pawpaw tree. +=PAPAW TREE. — **1787** CUTLER in *Life & Corr.* I. 273 He had the Pawpaw tree, or Custard apple. **1841** CHILD *Lett. New York* x. 72 The kindly Swiss matron, and her innocent daughter, had woven a large and beautiful Cross, from the broad leaves of the pawpaw tree. **1888** CRADDOCK *Despot* 9 An acorn dropped with a sharp thud from a chestnut oak; a locust was shrilling from a pawpaw tree.

+Paw(w)aw, *n.* Also **pawow, pawa(u).** [Var. of Powwow *n.*] *Obs.*

1. A medicine man, priest, or conjurer among the Indians.

1628 *Mass. H. S. Coll.* 3 Ser. VIII. 177 [The Indians'] pawwaws are their physicians and surgeons, and as I verily believe they are all witches, for they foretell of ill weather. **1660** *R.I. Hist. Soc. Coll.* X. 57 Mr Williams said that the Pawow asked him wherfore wee came. **1677** HUBBARD *Narrative* I. 9 This Passaconaway was the most noted Pawaw and Sorcerer of all the Country. **1714** E. MAYHEW in *New England Co. Corr.* (1896) 124 Hereupon an old Indian stood up who is Counted a Pawau among the Indians. **1809** KENDALL *Travels* I. 102 The *pawa* is the same with the *shaman* of the north-eastern parts of Asia, and with the *jongleur*, juggler, or diviner, of the French writers on the Indians of North America. **1832** DURFEE *Whatcheer* 128 Oft he thought o'er thickets brown he saw Wave the black fox-tail of the grim Pawaw.

2. A noisy ceremony or celebration, involving feasting and dancing, engaged in by Indians immediately before a council, expedition, hunt, etc. *Obs.*

*a*1652 in Quincy *Hist. Harvard* I. 53 These very Indians . . . will not be under the government of any Sagamores, but such as join with them in the observance of their pawawes and idolatries. **1778** CARVER *Travels* 270 The nations to the westward of the Mississippi, and on the borders of Lake Superior, still continue to make use of the Pawwaw or Black Dance. **1781** PETERS *Hist. Conn.* 215 An ancient religious rite, called the Pawwaw, was annually celebrated by the Indians. **1809** KENDALL *Travels* I. 102 By *pawas*, considered as rites, dances are usually understood. . . . In Pennsylvania, *pawas* appear to have received the name of canticoes apparently from their songs.

Paw(w)aw, *v.* Also **pawway, pauwaw.** [Var. of Powwow *v.*] *intr.* To hold or participate in a powwow. *Obs.*

1646 *Mass. Bay Rec.* III. 98 No Indian shall at any time pawwaw or p[er]forme outward wor[shi]pp to their falce gods. **1664** in Trumbull *Hist. Northampton, Mass.* I. 176 They shall not pawway on that place or any wher els amo[n]gst vs. **1809** FRENEAU *Poems* II. 196 All will be lost! . . . No priest shall pawwaw—and no church remain.

+Paw(w)awing. Also **pauwauing.** [Var. of POWWOWING.] The holding or performing of a powwow. *Obs.* Also attrib. — **1646** *Mass. Bay Rec.* III. 98 Such m[aste]rs of familyes as shall assist or countenance such pawwawing . . . [shall be fined] five pounds. **1650** ELIOT in *Lancaster Rec.* 27 At my first preaching at Nashaway sundry did imbrace the word, . . . and Pauwauing was wholly silenced. **1699** E. WARD *New-England* 15 At a General *Pawawing*, the Country a Hundred Miles round assemble themselves in a Body. **1751** J. BARTRAM *Observations* 32 Here was a place where the Indian had been a pawawing. **1824** DODDRIDGE *Notes* 64 We commonly had an open spell of weather during the latter part of February, denominated by [some] 'Pawwawing days,' and by others 'Weather breeders.'

+Paxton boys. *pl.* Also **Paxtang boys.** [f. *Paxton*, Pennsylvania.] A band of Pennsylvania frontiersmen, headed by Lazarus Shaw, which became a political force after the massacre of the Conestoga Indians in 1763. *Obs.* — **1764** (*title*), The Paxton Boys. **1811** GRAYDON *Memoirs* (1846) 46 The unpunished . . . massacre of certain Indians at Lancaster . . . had so encouraged their murderers, who called themselves Paxton boys, that they threatened to perpetrate the like enormity upon a number of other Indians. **1818** *Mass. Spy* 25 Feb. (Th.), The Indians fled to Philadelphia from the pursuit of the Paxton boys (as they called themselves). **1831** WITHERS *Chron. Border Warfare* 79 The Paxton boys twice assembled in the neighborhood of the city, for the purpose of assaulting the barracks and murdering the Indians. **1833** WATSON *Hist. Tales of Phila.* 66 [The Indians] were . . . massacred . . . at mid-day by an armed band of ruffians, calling themselves the 'Paxtang boys.'

***Pay,** *n.*

I. +1. An article or articles used as a medium of payment. *Obs.*

Cf. COUNTRY PAY and CURRENT *a.* 3.

1659 *Mass. H. S. Coll.* 4 Ser. VII. 233 There was only found 10 sheepewethers fitt to kill . . . [and] I sould [them] to the neighbors for other pay, excepting the skins & woole which ar kept. **1676** *Conn. Rec.* II. 276 The Generall Court recommend . . . the abatement of the sume he is fined in, and that he sattisfying in tolerable pay and in such competent time as the County Court shall set him, his estate engaged shall not become forfeited. **1680** *New Castle Court Rec.* 422, 25 gildrs. in good sound pay of this River. **1704** S. KNIGHT *Journal* 42 *Pay* is Grain, Pork, Beef, &c. at the prices sett by the General Court that Year. **1767** *Essex Inst. Coll.* XLVIII. 75 If you should purchase light pay, then proceed for Turks island.

+2. A remunerative yield of metal in a stratum or vein.

Cf. sense 6 and PAY DIRT, GRAVEL, etc.

1867 *Wkly. New Mexican* 23 Feb. 1/3 There were a good many chances to strike very good pay in rich layers. **1876** RAYMOND *8th Rep. Mines* 291 The vein shows good 'pay' in considerable quantity. **1883** RITCH *Illust. N. Mex.* 35 The pay begins at the grass roots . . . and continues to a depth already reached of fifty feet. **1904** E. ROBINS *Magn. North* II. 148 Mining up here's an awful gamble. . . . No real 'pay' outside of this little gulch.

II. *attrib.* and *comb.* **3.** Of or pertaining to the paying of those in military service.

1777 *Jrnls. Cont. Congress* IX. 1025 The inspectors general shall examine . . . the pay-books of the respective regiments. **1861** *Army Regulations* 341 An officer retiring from service must make affidavit to his pay account, and to the certificate annexed to it. **1890** *Cent.* 4339/1 *Pay-corps*, in the United States navy, the corps of paymasters. *Ib.* 4339/2 *Pay-inspector*, in the United States navy, an officer of the pay-corps, ranking with a commander. **1897** C. A. DANA *Recoll. Civil War* 21 Special commissioner of the War Department to investigate the pay services of the Western armies.

4. Designating persons who pay for a particular service.

1811 MEASE *Philadelphia* 263 Forty pay scholars are instructed by a black teacher. **1850** DANA *Two Years* 140 We sat down in the stern sheets 'as big as pay-passengers.' **1882** *Harper's Mag.* Nov. 926/2 His wife she nursed them all alike; pay patients or charity patients it made no difference to her. **1896** HARRIS *Sister Jane* 295 As pay boarders, they would receive the best of care and attention.

5. Designating services for which payment is rendered, or anything pertaining to such payment.

1861 *Atlantic Mo.* April 439/1 My duty to my operatives has a narrow limit,—the pay-hour on Saturday night. **1878** DALY in J. F. Daly *A. Daly* 255 [New Orleans] is not behind its Northern rivals in preferring the Free Show to the Pay Performance. **1884** CABLE *Dr. Sevier* 104 The Doctor had her removed to one of the private rooms of the pay-ward. **1904** *Critic* May 435 The total number of calls for each book during three months in a pay library. **1910** BOSTWICK *Amer. Pub. Library* 20 [An] increasing number of public libraries . . . have adopted the . . . 'pay-duplicate system' for popular fiction.

+6. Designating natural formations in which metals, as gold, occur in paying quantities, or a place in which such formations are found.

See also PAY DIRT, GRAVEL, etc.

1875 *Chicago Tribune* 30 Aug. 8/4 The Mountain Lion lode . . . [has] a pay vein that will compare favorably with the leading mines of Boulder County. **1876** RAYMOND *8th Rep. Mines* 107 The gold is . . . evenly distributed through the pay chimneys. *Ib.*, The first pay shoot is 150 feet . . . in length along the vein. **1877** HODGE *Arizona* 89 On the surface the pay ore is from one foot to sixteen inches wide. **1880** INGHAM *Digging Gold* 284 The nearness of the pay-ledges to the surface of the ground [gives the mines of the Black Hills an advantage]. **1901** WHITE *Westerners* 211 Lots of that is pay quartz. **1902** WILSON *Spenders* 338 All the pay-claims have been located, I guess. **1911** ROLT-WHEELER *Boy with Census* 289, I came back another way, in order to take in a little group of houses on a small pay-creek.

Pay, *v.* +In various phrases.

To pay in trade, (see quotation); *something is to pay,* something is wrong; *what is to pay?* what is the matter? what is wrong?

1820 FLINT *Lett. from Amer.* 201 Employers are also in the habit of deceiving their workmen, by telling them that it is not convenient to pay wages in money, and that they run accounts with the storekeeper, the tailor, and the shoemaker, and that from them they may have all the necessaries they want very cheap. The workman who consents to this mode of payment, procures orders from the employer . . . and is charged a higher price for the goods than the employer actually pays for them. This is called *paying in trade.* — **1877** *Harper's Mag.* Jan. 295/1 He gathered an idea . . . that 'somethin' wuz to pay,' as he expressed it to himself. **1896** WILKINS *Madelon* 102 Somethin's to pay—that girl acted queer. — **1882** THAYER *From Log-Cabin* 164 'What, then, is to pay?' urged his mother earnestly. **1884** *Harper's Mag.* Sept. 616/1 Now what's to pay? **1908** FREEMAN *Shoulders of Atlas* 80 'What is to pay now?' said she.

+**Pay car.** A railroad car carrying pay for employees, and from which payment is made. — **1872** *Newton Kansan* 3 Oct. 3/2 He was taken to Topeka on the pay car. **1879** *Scribner's Mo.* Oct. 933/2, I took the passenger back to Michigan City, to meet the pay-car there, and get my discharge. **1889** Salmons *Burlington Strike* 385 A new pay car just completed at a cost of $4,000, and six coaches, were destroyed, as were the tools of the men. **1900** 'FLYNT' *Notes Itinerant Policeman* 245 Every man on the force knows what he has to do . . . to protect the pay-car, look out for circus and excursion trains [etc.].

+**Pay department.** A department or branch of service, as in the United States Army, having to do with the paying out of money. — **1816** *Ann. 14th Congress* 2 Sess. 27 The same observation applies to the pay departments. **1847** *Santa Fe Republican* 4 Dec. 2/3 Major Spaulding, of the Pay Department, arrived here yesterday from Albuquerque in fine health. **1876** INGRAM *Centennial Exp.* 747 At the beginning of the war he accepted a position in the pay department of the United States Treasury in Washington.

+**Pay dirt.** Dirt or soil containing a mineral, as gold, in quantities sufficient to justify mining.

Cf. DIRT *n.* 2.

1857 J. D. BORTHWICK *3 Years in Calif.* 120 The miners talk . . . of stripping off so many feet of 'top dirt' before getting to 'pay dirt.' **1860** *Harper's Mag.* April 612/2, I have already described the manner of getting at the 'pay dirt' underneath a heavy layer of barren earth, by 'coyoteing.' **1873** RAYMOND *Silver & Gold* 64 The width of the channel varies from 150 to 300 feet, while the pay-dirt varies from thirty feet to the entire width of the channel. **1899** *Mo. So. Dakotan* I. 172 We prospected French creek very thoroughly . . . finding nothing that we considered pay dirt. **1918** MULFORD *Man from Bar-20* 44 They claimed there was pay dirt down there.

fig. and *transf.* **1873** *Vermont Bd. Agric. Rep.* II. 167 'Science' has paid me on the farm, and I am still working that placer, finding 'pay dirt' all the way, though not down to the 'bed-rock' yet. **1884** *Century Mag.* Nov. 60 [He] lives East in a style that proves that he has lots of pay dirt somewhere. **1903** *Nation* 1 Oct. 266 The German archaeological expedition to Babylon has now struck 'pay dirt,' and has unearthed a mass of cuneiform tablets.

+**Pay gravel.** Gravel containing a mineral, as gold, in such quantities as to justify mining. Also transf. — **1871** HARTE *Poems* 30, O, why did papa strike pay gravel In drifting on Poverty Flat? **1876** RAYMOND *8th Rep. Mines* 130 So deep and widespread are the banks of pay-gravel in this neighborhood, that [etc.]. **1884** MATTHEWS & BUNNER *In Partnership* 63 It appears the young woman had refused to have anything to do with him for a long period; but he seems to have struck pay gravel about two days before my arrival. **1899** HARTE *Mr. Jack Hamlin's Mediation* 99 Hardly a cartload of 'pay-gravel' ever arrived safely at its destination.

Paying, *a.* Profitable, remunerative. {1882–} — **1855** F. MARRYAT *Mts. & Molehills* 283 You must quarry more valueless quartz than the 'paying seam' will compensate for. **1871** *Ill. Agric. Soc. Trans.* VIII. 238 We need not expect to get a paying crop from stiff clays. **1898** WESTCOTT *D. Harum* 368 Sometimes you git a payin' well an' a dry hole only a few hundred feet apart.

+**Paying teller.** In a bank, one who cashes checks or pays out money on other collection items. — **1877** ALDRICH *Queen of Sheba* 35 A vacancy occurred unexpectedly, that of paying-teller. **1895** CARROLL *Principles Finance* 118 *Paying teller.* The paying teller is often called the 'first teller.' His duties are perhaps more exacting than those of any other officer of the bank. He is generally the custodian of the cash, and is personally responsible for the same. **1902** BELL *Hope Loring* 59 Once the paying-teller . . . asked one of them the reason.

***Paymaster.**

*1. One who makes payment of wages, salary, or similar sums.

1676 SEWALL *Diary* I. 31 He was . . . urging to make sure Lands of Mr. Broughton at Dover to my Father, and so take him Paymaster for the Annuity laid on it. **1736** *Va. State P.* I. 227 You will surely be ac-c[ounta]ble to us who are to be your Paymasters. **1742** *Georgia Col. Rec.* VI. 23 The said Thomas Ellis [agreed] to take the said Thomas Salter as his paymaster. **1836** *Dialogue betw. Strike & Steady* 4 For my part, I am working now for a merchant tailor . . . and I have always found him a kind friend, and a regular paymaster. **1921** *Lit. Digest* 5 Nov. 9/1 Nicolo Sacco and Bartolomeo Vanzetti . . . were pronounced guilty in the first degree of murdering the paymaster and guard of a Massachusetts shoe factory.

*2. *spec.* A military or naval officer whose duty is to pay soldiers, workmen, etc.

1713 *Boston News-Letter* 2 March 2/2 They are hereby Ordered . . . to apply themselves to Mr. Humphrey Huchenson Pay Master and Fire-worker to the Train here. **1792** *Ann. 2d Congress* 81 The organization of the said squadron of light dragoons shall be as follows, viz: one major commandant, . . . one quartermaster, one paymaster. **1848** *Santa Fe Republican* 24 Aug. 2/1 Maj. Weightman, Pay Master U.S.A. . . . is to remain as paymaster of this department. **1865** BOUDRYE *Fifth N.Y. Cavalry* 85 The paymaster appeared with his greenbacks. **1907** *St. Nicholas* July 813/1 When the new sailor gets his uniform from the paymaster, he often finds that it doesn't fit.

Paymaster-general. {1702–} +1. An officer in the United States Army in charge of the paying of officers and men. *Obs.* +2. (See quot. 1881.) — (1) **1775** *Jrnls. Cont. Congress* II. 94 There [shall] be a pay master general, and a deputy under him, for the army in a separate department. **1839** MAYO *Polit. Sk. Washington* p. vii, It is . . . a bureau arrangement of the paymaster-general's department. **1861** *Army Regulations* 346 The Paymaster-General shall keep in his office such record as may be necessary. (2) **1881** *Naval Encycl.* 638 *Paymaster-general.*—The chief of Bureau of Provisions and Clothing, . . . styled paymaster-general, . . . is appointed by the President from among the senior paymasters [of the Pay Corps of the U.S. Navy].

+**Payote.** Variant of PEYOTE.

+**Pay rock.** Rock containing a mineral, as gold, in such quantities as to render its mining profitable. Also fig. — **1869** BROWNE *Adv. Apache Country* 295 'Silver bricks!' and 'Pay rock!' hummed and drummed through the air. **1869** BRACE *New West* 247 The first thing for a man . . . is to live true to his convictions; if he doesn't do that, he had better sell out; there's no pay-rock in him! **1872** *Harper's Mag.* Dec. 22/2 Very little quartz mining is done in Colorado, the 'pay rock,' or ore, being principally iron and some copper pyrites. **1882** WAITE *Adv. in Far West* 265 The Capt. represents a large class who are always just going to strike 'pay rock' but never do. **1896** SHINN *Story of Mine* 157 'Bonanza' . . . means much more than merely pay rock.

Pay roll. A roll or list of those to whom pay is or may be due.

1775 *N.H. Comm. Safety Rec.* 26 Examined and allowed Capt. Crafford's pay Roll of his men. **1840** COOPER *Pathfinder* x, I have sent for you, man, to discuss anything but rosters and pay-rolls. **1860** *36th Congress 1 Sess.* H. R. Rep. No. 249 34, I think there have been as many as over four hundred on the pay-roll. **1887** GEORGE *40 Yrs. on Rail* 182 The poor fellow was dropped from the pay-roll. **1898** PAGE *Red Rock* 90 Dr. Cary summoned his hands and paid them their wages . . . , checking each name . . . on a pay-roll he had prepared.

+**Pay school.** A school at which tuition is paid; a private school. Also attrib. — **1856** MACLEOD *F. Wood* 191 The cost to us in taxation is not one fifth the usual expense for an ordinary pay-school education. **1864** NICHOLS *Amer. Life* I. 58 There were very few private or pay schools. **1883** *Rep. Indian Affairs* 90 In addition to the above there are a number of 'pay schools.'

+**Pay streak.** A streak or vein of metal, as gold, so rich as to make its mining profitable. Also transf.

1869 J. R. BROWNE *Adv. Apache Country* 488 Any new speculation that offered the slightest symptom of a 'pay-streak.' **1872** TICE *Over Plains* 112 Two men working together in sinking on a pay-streak, will raise on an average two tons of ore per week. **1890** RYAN *Told in Hills* 93 Stickin' to that old trail was a pay streak—hey? **1896** SHINN *Story of Mine* 42 On June 12th the pay streak turned and went down into a ledge. *a***1918** G. STUART *On Frontier* I. 74 The pay streak gave out and no more could be found and it was abandoned.

***Pea.** Pl. **peas,** †**pease.**

*1. The seed or fruit of any of various plants of the genus *Pisum,* or of similar or related genera; also, any one of these plants.

1616 SMITH *New England* 16 The hearbes and fruits [include] . . . strawberries, beans, pease, and mayze. **1698** THOMAS *Penna. & N.J.* 25 Their

Merchandize chiefly consists in . . . Pease, Beans, Skins. **1709** LAWSON *Carolina* 76 These are latter Pease, and require a pretty long Summer to ripen in. **1786** WASHINGTON *Diaries* III. 87 The Peas, Potatoes, and Cabbage. **1839** PLUMBE *Sk. Iowa* 30 Barley, peas, oats, . . . and also all sorts of tame grass, grow most luxuriantly. **1883** *Rep. Indian Affairs* 48 Oats, pease, and the other smaller garden vegetables were the worst injured. **1906** PRINGLE *Rice Planter* 401 There were about twenty hands. Some wanted to pick for one-third of the peas, some for money.

+**2.** In various figurative phrases.

1853 'P. PAXTON' *Yankee in Texas* 194 The whole array looked as much alike as peas from the same pod. **1871** STOWE *Sam Lawson* 44 Lawyer Dean he flew around like a parched pea on a shovel. **1902** HARBEN *A. Daniel* 206, [I] come as nigh as peas hittin' 'er in the jaw. **1913** LONDON *Valley of Moon* 343 You're as like as peas in a pod to those who yoked their oxen and held west to lands beyond the sunset.

3. Attrib. and comb. in sing. and pl. **a.** Designating foods made of peas.

1630 WINTHROP in R. C. Winthrop *Life J. Winthrop* II. 38 Pease, [*sic*] puddings & fish, beinge our ordinary diet. **1765** S. DEANE *Diary* 310, [I] found his wife warming up a mess of pea porridge, which she gave to her grandchildren to eat for breakfast. **1863** in *Century Mag.* XXX. 772/2 [The soldiers] boil . . . a kind of soup, which is easier to swallow than pea-bread. **1878** *Amer. Home Cook Book* 143 Pease pudding. One pint of peas and one potato. **1890** MCALLISTER *Society* 97 'What is pea pie?' I asked. 'Cow peas and bacon,' was the answer.

b. In special combinations.

Pea-blower, =PEA-SHOOTER; *p. coal*, a small size of coal; *p. country*, a country or region where peas abound; *p. crab*, *p.-dropper*, (see quotations); *p. fodder*, *p. haulm*, fodder or hay made of the stalks and vines of peas; *p. hook*, a hook for reaping peas; *p. lay*, (see quotation); *p. locust*, the Kentucky coffee tree (cf. KENTUCKY COFFEE 2).

1821 IRVING in P. M. Irving *Life W. Irving* II. (1862) 59 The three eldest boys kept the house in misery for two or three days by pea-blowers. **1877** BARTLETT 454 *Pea-Coal*, the smallest-sized coal of commerce, . . . obtained from sifting the larger sizes. **1853** SIMMS *Sword & Distaff* (1854) 191, I kin find as many partridges, or doves, to shoot, in a pea country, as any man can p'nt a gun at. **1864** WEBSTER 960/1 *Peacrab*, a small species of crab, not much larger than a bean, . . . which lives in muscles, oysters, and other living shells. **1876** KNIGHT 1643/2 *Pea-dropper*, . . . an implement for planting pease in hills. **1819** *Plough Boy* I. 130 It has been objected to pea-fodder that it takes too long to cure. **1863** RANDALL *Pract. Shepherd* 245 Pea-haulm . . . is highly valuable and is highly relished by sheep. **1692** *Conn. Probate Rec.* 456, I give to my son Thomas my . . . Peas Hook, and all my Casks & Barls. **1850** *Rep. Comm. Patents 1849: Agric.* 401 After this mass of vine has been turned under, you have a 'pea-lay,' over which sow a bushel and a half of wheat per acre. **1820** *Amer. Farmer* I. 398/1, I send you a pod of the 'Coffee Nut Tree,' sometimes called *pea locust*.

Peabird. {1838-} +(See quotations.) — **1872** *Amer. Naturalist* VI. 397 The black-headed grosbeak is . . . well known as the 'Pea-bird,' from its fondness for green peas. **1917** *Birds of Amer.* II. 258 Baltimore Oriole. *Icterus galbula*. . . . [Also called] Fire-bird; Pea-bird.

+**Peabody bird.** [*Peabody* Glen, N.H.] The white-throated sparrow, *Zonotrichia albicollis*. — **1897** CHAPMAN *Bird-Life* 188 Later, you will hear the sweet, plaintive notes that give to this bird the name Peabody-bird. **1903** *N.Y. Ev. Post* 24 Oct., That lovely bird, the white-throated sparrow, which under the name of 'Peabody bird' is well known in the North. **1917** *Birds of Amer.* III. 37.

+**Pea bug.** =PEA WEEVIL. — **1790** *Penna. Packet* 30 March 1/4 Damage to crops by insects; especially the Hessian-fly, . . . the pea-bug, and the corn chinch bug or fly. **1838** *Mass. Zool. Survey Rep.* 76 The *Bruchus pisi*, or pea-bug of North America, . . . has been introduced with American pease into England. **1854** EMMONS *Agric. N.Y.* V. 100 The female *peabug* deposits its eggs in the tender peapod. **1876** *Field & Forest* II. 55 The larvae . . . eat their way in, in the same manner as *Bruchus pisi* or the 'pea-bug.'

***Peace.** In attrib. uses.

+**1.** Of or pertaining to peace among the American Indians. See also PEACE BELT, PEACE PIPE.

1800 HAWKINS *Sk. Creek Country* 65 This was formerly the first among the Lower Creek towns; a peace town, averse to war. **1819** *Niles' Reg.* XVI. 160/1 Those Indians who . . . went out to England, to treat John Bull with war-dances and peace dances, . . . returned a short time since. **1827** COOPER *Prairie* xviii, We are peace-runners. The white men and the red are neighbors, and they wish to be friends . . . when the tomahawk is buried. **1847** PARKMAN in *Knickerb.* XXX. 481 The antelope is the graceful peace-spirit of the Ogillallah. **1868** *N.Y. Herald* 20 July 4/1 General Crook in Idaho has held a peace council with the Snake Indians. **1895** REMINGTON *Pony Tracks* 43 Red-Bear turned his horse in the 'peace sign,' and advanced. **1900** DRANNAN *Plains & Mts.* 42 After supper . . . we had what was called a 'peace smoke.'

+**2.** *Peace measures*, measures adopted by Congress in the Compromise of 1850. (See COMPROMISE c).

1850 *Harper's Mag.* Dec. 122/1 We recorded at the proper time, the passage by Congress of the several measures generally known as the 'peace measures' of the session.

+**Peace belt.** A belt of wampum used among North American Indians as a symbol of peace. *Obs.* — **1758** *N.J. Archives* XX. 297 Peace was solemnly ratified by a large peace belt. **1779** CLARK *Campaign in Ill.* (1869) 45, I presented them with a Peace & [a] War Belt, and told them to take their choice. **1798** HAWKINS *Letters* 312, I have received . . . from the northern nations and southern tribes a broad peace belt.

Peace commission. A board of commissioners appointed to make a peace or to promote peace. — **1866** *Rep. Indian Affairs* 180, I would recommend that a treaty be made at an early day, embracing the general provisions submitted to their representatives last summer by the peace commission. **1870** *Congress. Globe* 2 March 1643/3 Colonel Kit Carson testified before a member of the Indian peace commission. **1898** *Kansas City Star* 18 Dec. 1/3 Had Day and Moore retained their State department offices while serving on the peace commission they would have been debarred.

Peace commissioner. A member of a peace commission. — **1865** CUMMING *Hospital Life* (1866) 163/2 Lincoln has agreed to receive peace commissioners. **1873** MILLER *Amongst Modocs* 7 Peace commissioners have been killed by the Modocs. **1898** *Kansas City Star* 18 Dec. 1/3 The preliminary resignation of Mr. Day and Mr. Moore with a view to coming in for handsome fees as peace commissioners . . . arouses the admiration of politicians.

+**Peace Democrat.** *Hist.* During the Civil War, a member of the Democratic party in the North who opposed the prosecution of the war and urged instead the substitution of peaceful measures. (Cf. COPPERHEAD.) — **1864** *Ore. State Jrnl.* 16 July 1/4 The Peace Democrats or conservative fellows, as they call themselves, insisting upon the Union as it was, are thus rebuked by their Southern friends in the Richmond Whig. **1886** LOGAN *Great Conspiracy* 557 Many of these leaders . . . addressed the great gathering . . . of nearly one hundred thousand Vallandigham-Anti-War Peace-Democrats, at Springfield, Illinois.

***Peacemaker.** *local.* +=JUSTICE OF THE PEACE. *Obs.* — **1683** *Penna. Col. Rec.* I. 66 The Question was asked in Councill whether Peace Makers should sitt once a month.

Peace officer. A civil officer, as a justice of the peace, commissioned to preserve the public peace. {1714-} — **1747** *Georgia Col. Rec.* VI. 187 There would be an absolute Necessity of a Peace Officer living in the said [Creek] Nation, to preserve the Peace as well among the White Men as Indians. **1823** COOPER *Pioneers* xxx, By virtue of this warrant, and of my office, and with this peace-officer. **1854** SIMMS *Sword & Distaff* (1854) 488 Can't you relish a good army-joke, now that you're a peace officer? **1911** *Okla. Session Laws* 3 Legisl. 161 Such judge or magistrate shall, with or without any endorsement . . . of any peace officer, . . . seize all liquor.

+**Peace pipe.** A ceremonial tobacco pipe, usually having a long stem and adorned with feathers, used among North American Indians as a peace symbol.

Cf. CALUMET.

1760 CROGHAN *Journal* 105 Brother to Confirm what we have said to you I give you this Peace Pipe. **1779** G. R. CLARK *Campaign in Ill.* (1869) 45, I would defer smokeing the Peace Pipe until I heard that they had called in all their Warriors. **1808** PIKE *Sources Miss.* 85 The Chipeway chief . . . presented his peace pipe to me to bear to the Sioux. **1896** BRUCE *Econ. Hist. Virginia* I. 164 Among the most valuable treasures of each town was the peace-pipe. **1923** J. H. COOK *On Old Frontier* 228 The Professor and Red Cloud . . . were photographed with clasped hands and the peace pipe between them.

Peace policy. *Hist.* +The present Indian policy inaugurated by President Grant in 1869, providing for a board of ten commissioners to serve without compensation in regulating Indian affairs. — **1871** *Rep. Indian Affairs* (1872) 68 There are more than one-half of all the roving Apaches . . . reaping the benefit of the 'peace policy.' **1873** *Newton Kansan* 22 May 4/2 The 'peace policy' proposed to place the Indians upon reservations. **1910** HODGE, etc. *Amer. Indians* II. 219/1 For nearly 40 years the Board of Indian Commissioners has cooperated with the Government, favoring such legislation and administration in Indian affairs as by peaceful methods should put an end to Indian discontent, make impossible Indian wars, and fit the great body of Indians to be received into the ranks of American citizens. . . . A strong element of popular support [has been given] to this Peace Policy.

Peace society. A society or organization which advocates peaceful adjustment of national differences which might lead to war. Also in the names of particular groups of this kind. — **1815** in N. Worcester *Friend of Peace* I. v. 38 The name of this society shall be The Massachusetts Peace Society. **1834** *Knickerb.* III. 341 It is no slight evil which Peace Societies would remedy. **1841** *Niles' Nat. Reg.* LIX. 330/3 The following memorials and petitions were presented and appropriately referred: By Mr. Clay, from the American peace society, asking that [etc.].

+**Peace talk.** A talk or conference with or among Indians in the interests of peace. — **1789** *Steele P.* I. 51, I only mean to hold a peace talk. **1800** HAWKINS *Sk. Creek Country* 72 Peace talks are always addressed to the cabin of the Mic-co. **1809** WEEMS *Marion* 22 The Cherokees . . . sent on a deputation with their wampum belts and peace-talks to bury the hatchet. **1852** REYNOLDS *Hist. Illinois* 165 All the 'peace talks' ever presented to the red men, could not have kept them in peace.

***Peach.**

I. ***1.** =PEACH TREE.

1666 *Hist. Coll. S. Carolina* II. 12 There are many sorts of fruit Trees, as Vines, Medlars, Peach, Wild Cherries. **1807** in *S. Lit. Messenger* XXIV. 309/1 The Dog-wood and the Peach flaunted their gaudy blossoms to the sun. **1857** *Ill. Agric. Soc. Trans.* III. 492 In budding the apple, the pear, and the peach, we take out the wood. **1883** *Rep. Indian Affairs* 80 Many Indians already have thrifty orchards of peaches, apples [etc.].

*2. The fruit of the peach tree.

1681 *Penna. Mag.* VI. 175 *Peaches* as good as any in the world. **1709** LAWSON *Carolina* 38 They brought in great store of loblolly, and other Medleys, made of Indian grain, stewed peaches [etc.]. **1781–2** JEFFERSON *Notes Va.* (1788) 40 The orchards produce . . . quinces, peaches, nectarines, . . . and plumbs. **1805** PARKINSON *Tour* 613 Peaches of various sorts, chiefly distinguished by the names of clink stones and open stones. **1901** MOHR *Plant Life Ala.* 106 Peaches, plums, . . . and grapes succeed on the ridges.

+3. = PEACH BRANDY.

1809 WEEMS *Marion* (1833) 77 Suppose you take a glass of peach. **1840** SIMMS *Border Beagles* II. 130 Shall I pour you out from the jug or the piggin? I can answer for this peach—it's as good as any of Crumbaughs. **1845** HOOPER *Simon Suggs' Adv.* v, Thar's koniac and old peach and rectified, and lots I can't tell thar names. **1847** FIELD *Drama in Pokerville* 25 Mr. Major Slope, . . . having been out to get a little 'peach,' had returned just at the climax.

+4. A pretty or charming girl. *slang.*

1865 *Prairie Chicken* (Tilton, Ill.) 1 June 3/2 What is the propriety of calling a pretty girl . . . 'peaches,' etc.? **1896** ADE *Artie* 5 Don't it kill you dead to see a swell girl—you know, a regular peach—holdin' on to some freak with side whiskers and thinkin' she's got a good thing? **1900** BONNER *Hard Pan* 121 Tod said . . . that she was a 'peach,' a form of encomium that . . . he was fond of applying to every member of the other sex. **1923** WATTS *L. Nichols* 72 Your girl, I mean? . . . Why she's a peach!

b. Anything regarded as superior or extraordinary. *slang.*

1896 ADE *Artie* 9, I've got a peach of a head. **1903** A. ADAMS *Log Cowboy* 358 [The horse] was a peach. **1904** HERRICK in *Atlantic Mo.* March 354 'Now, that's what I call a peach!' Cook whistled through his closed teeth, squinting at the sketch admiringly. **1913** LONDON *Valley of Moon* 65, I've got a temper, a peach of a temper.

II. *attrib.* and *comb.* **5.** Designating foods, drinks, etc., prepared from peaches.

See also PEACH BRANDY, PEACH COBBLER, and cf. PEACHY.

1656 WILLIAMS in *R.I. Hist. Soc. Pub.* ns. VIII. 144 The Scot within named hath bene taken up, drowned . . . in going ouer in his Canow, having drunck too much Peach bear. **1709** LAWSON *Carolina* 49, I bought, for 2 or 3 Flints, a large Peach-Loaf, made up with a pleasant sort of Seed. **1796** ASBURY *Journal* II. 295 We dined on some peach-pie in the woods. **1864** *Hist. North-Western Soldiers' Fair* 139 [Donations include] 1 keg peach pickles. **1879** BISHOP *4 Months in Sneak-Box* 34 Bread and butter, with Shakers' peach-sauce . . . contributed to furnish a most satisfactory meal.

+6. Designating one having to do with peaches.

1722 *New-England Courant* 3 Sept. 2/1 A Gentleman in a neighbouring Town has been lately dignify'd with the Title of *Peach-Merchant.* **1879** *Harper's Mag.* July 197 The peach-pickers were not the specimens of 'peach-pluck' proper but farm laborers of a more respectable class.

7. In the names of trees and plants suggestive of or in some respects resembling the peach.

1790 DEANE *New-Eng. Farmer* 222/2 The peach plum, red towards the sun, with an agreeable tartness. **1817–8** EATON *Botany* (1822) 181 *Armeniaca vulgaris*, apricot . . . Var. *persicoides* (peach apricot). **1884** SARGENT *Rep. Forests* 154 *Quercus Phellos.* . . . Willow Oak. Peach Oak.

+8. In special combinations.

Peach-borer, = PEACH-TREE BORER; *p. bud* (local), a variety or type of land (cf. PEACH LAND); *p. bug*, (see quotation); *p. butter*, (see quot. and BUTTER[1] 2); *p. curl*, a leaf curl affecting the peach tree; *p. cut*, a social gathering where peaches are prepared for curing or preserving (cf. APPLE-BEE, etc.); *p.-leather*, (see quot. and cf. APPLE-LEATHER); *p.-parer*, a machine for paring peaches; *p. scale*, a scale insect that attacks peach trees; *p. wagon*, a light, open wagon, esp. adapted to carrying crated peaches.

1850 *New Eng. Farmer* II. 222 Among those matters of interest . . . , the 'peach-borer,' its ravages, and remedy, have occupied a prominent place. **1869** *Overland Mo.* III. 130 Texas is notable for the number of its soils. In Montgomery County there is what they call a 'peach-bud.' **1854** EMMONS *Agric. N.Y.* V. 262 (*index*), Peachbug, 79, 80. [*Ib.* 79–80 *Cetonia inda. Scarabaeus indus.* . . . They are charged . . . [with] feeding upon the ripening fruits: particularly do they select the best peaches.] **1877** BARTLETT 454 *Peach-Butter*, stewed peaches. **1888** *Amer. Naturalist* XXII. 738 *T[aphrina] deformans* Tul., causing the 'peach curl' of the leaves of the peach tree. **1877** BARTLETT 36 The terms apple-cut and peach-cut are also common. *Ib.* 454 *Peach-Leather*, peaches boiled, rolled out, and dried in the sun. **1876** INGRAM *Centennial Exp.* 328 The Lightning peach parer was another little ingenious machine. **1895** *Dept. Agric. Yrbk. 1894* 265 The New Peach Scale. . . . In the District of Columbia the insect is found only upon peach. **1879** *Harper's Mag.* July 194/1 At every station . . . one sees those peculiar vehicles . . . known as peach wagons, square, cumbersome, and roomy, unloading their luscious contents.

Peach and honey. ? A drink made of peaches and sweetened with honey. (Cf. PEACH BRANDY.) — **1821** QUITMAN in Claiborne *Life Quitman* I. 69 He invited me to 'peach and honey'—something I had never tasted before. **1856** *Harper's Mag.* Aug. 426/1 Old Judge Cole, of Texas, was characterized by his attachment to that seductive beverage called 'peach and honey,' and by his hatred of whisky and whisky-drinkers. **1861** NEWELL *Orpheus C. Kerr* I. 212 [The South Carolina gentleman] clears a mighty track of everything that bears the shape of . . . brandy-sour, peach-and-honey, irrepressible cocktail [etc.].

+**Peachblow.**

1. The color of a peach bloom, or an object having this color. Freq. attrib. {1886}

1829 T. FLINT *G. Mason* 32 The Red Bud in a thousand places was one compact tuft of peach-blow flowers. **1859** A. VAN BUREN *Sojourn in South* 133 The crape myrtle with its top hanging thick with long cone-shaped flowers of a peach-blow color. **1861** NOBLE *Icebergs* 176 The berg is immersed in almost supernatural splendors. . . . The blue and the purple pass up into peach-blow and pink. **1875** STOWE *We & Neighbors* 345 She dropped a knot of peach-blow ribbons from her bosom. **1886** DALY *After Business Hours* 25 Don't ask the price [of the evening costume]! It's a peach-blow! **1896** *Godey's Mag.* Feb. 212/1 The colorings are exquisite; peach-blow pink and lime green. **1904** 'O. HENRY' *Four Million* 208 Her eyes were dreamily bright, her cheeks genuine peachblow.

2. A potato having a pinkish tinge about the eyes, or the variety which produces this. In full *peachblow potato.*

***a*1849** EMMONS *Agric. N.Y.* II. 45 Peach-Blow Potato. . . . It is a good bearer, and is common in the winter in the Albany market. **1855** *Amer. Inst. N.Y. Trans.* 342 Solon Robinson exhibited two potatoes . . . supposed to be of the kind known as *Peach-blow* and old English White. **1859** *Harper's Mag.* Sept. 503/1 Mr. Johnson is appealed to . . . by the immense size of the Champion peas, and the early peach-blow potatoes. **1880** COOKE in *Harper's Mag.* Sept. 584/1 Yer ma liked them peach-blow potaters first best. **1884** *Rep. Comm. Agric.* 416 The Colorado Potato-beetle . . . appeared in greater numbers than it has done since 1881, attacking the 'Peach-blows' chiefly.

+**Peach brandy.** A spirituous liquor made from the juice of peaches. {1814}

1762 in Chalkley *Scotch-Irish Settlement Va.* III. 79 To 6 gallons peach brandy for him during his sickness, and at the funeral; paid note to John Jeremiah. **1789** MORSE *Amer. Geog.* 144 The country yields from culture . . . peaches, from which is made peach brandy. **1820** FLINT *Lett. from Amer.* 228 A rancid sort of spirit is distilled . . . , known here by the name of peach brandy. **1887** HARRIS *Free Joe* 3 He was a Virginian, he declared; and, to prove the statement, he referred all the festively inclined young men . . . to a barrel of peach-brandy in one of his covered waggons. **1903** HART *Actual Govt.* 401 Peach brandy, apple-jack, and rough corn whiskey may easily be manufactured by farmers.

+**Peach cobbler.** (See COBBLER 3.)

+**Peach land. 1.** *S.W.* **a.** Land upon which wild peach is a native growth. **b.** *Peach and cane land*, (see quot.) **2.** Land suitable for growing peaches. — (1) **1831** HOLLEY *Texas* (1833) 37 [Brazoria] is not located in a prairie . . . ; but upon a wooded elevation of peach-land. *Ib.* 51 When a colonist wishes to describe his land as first rate, he says it is all peach and cane land. (2) **1868** *Mich. Agric. Rep.* VII. 432 Mr. Stocking . . . thought the high bluffs along the western shore were the best peach lands.

+**Peach orchard.** An orchard of peach trees.

1676 GLOVER *Va.* in *Phil. Trans.* XI. 628 Here are likewise great *Peach-Orchards*, which bear such an infinite quantity of Peaches, that at some Plantations they beat down to the Hoggs fourty bushels in a year. **1758** *Va. State P.* I. 257 [We] overtook them at a peach orchard. **1794** T. COOPER *America* 51 Every farm-house in the middle and southern states has its peach orchard, and its apple orchard. **1849** *31st Congress 1 Sess.* Sen. Ex. Doc. No. 64, 103, I noticed the ordinary Navajo hut, (a conical lodge,) and close by it a peach orchard. **1906** LYNDE *Quickening* 19 It was goin' to . . . run right smack thoo' you-uns' peach orchard.

b. *Peach-orchard coal*, a variety or grade of coal.

1874 COLLINS *Kentucky* I. 210 The Peach Orchard coal, the cannel coal, and the block coal . . . are among the finest in the world.

+**Peach pit.** The pit or seed of a peach. — **1844** G. BUSH *Anastasis* (B.), You put an apple-seed or a peach-pit into the ground and it springs up into the form of a miniature tree. **1850** JUDD *R. Edney* 317 He asked Richard if they were pamphlets, and was seen to toss them, like peach-pits, into some hole or other.

+**Peach rosette.** (See ROSETTE *n.* 2.)

***Peach tree.** A well-known tree (*Amygdalus persica*) valued for its juicy, edible fruit.

1641 *Mass. H. S. Coll.* 4 Ser. VI. 368, I am prettie well storred with chirrie & peach trees. **1682** ASH *Carolina* 7 The Peach Tree in incredible Numbers grows Wild. **1724** H. JONES *Virginia* 41 At the Plantations are standard Peach-Trees, and Apple-Trees, planted out in Orchards, on purpose almost for the Hogs. **1798** C. WILLIAMSON *Descr. Genesee* iii, The peach trees . . . come to great perfection . . . near Geneva. ***a*1817** DWIGHT *Travels* II. 221 We saw a collection of peach trees on one of the hills. **1883** RITTENHOUSE *Maud* 187 When we got into Tennessee we found plum and peach trees in bloom. **1924** CROY *R.F.D. No. 3* 27 Guineas flew screaming into the tops of the peach trees with ear-splitting protests.

+**b.** *Peach-tree yellows*, = PEACH YELLOWS.

1854 EMMONS *Agric. N.Y.* V. 262 (*index*), Peachtree yellows, 113.

+**Peach-tree borer.** The larva of a moth injurious to peach trees, esp. that of the clearwing moth, *Sanninoidea exitiosa.* — **1850** *New Eng.*

Farmer II. 74 Captain George Pierce . . . said that the peach-tree borer would stand scalding-hot water. **1863** *Horticulturist* XVIII. 220 The Peach-Tree Borer. . . . The time most desirable to operate on the borer . . . [is] *early* spring. **1892** KELLOGG *Kansas Insects* 91 Peach-Tree Borer. (*Ægeria exitiosa*.) . . . The pest is an American insect, unknown on the peach trees of other countries.

+**Peach water.** A flavoring extract made from peach leaves. — **1867** DIXON *New America* II. 101 The ladies at Mt. Lebanon . . . make rose-water, cherry-water, peach-water. **1879** A. D. WHITNEY *Just How* 78 Half a teaspoonful of peach-water or essence of bitter almonds.

+**Peach worm.** A worm or caterpillar injurious to peach trees. — **a1817** DWIGHT *Travels* I. 76 The *Peach worm* has been known here about fifty years; and is now become very common. **1855** *Amer. Inst. N.Y. Trans.* 411 The lime and salt mixture around peach trees will kill peach worms. **1856** *Rep. Comm. Patents 1855: Agric.* 299 The ravages of the peach-worm have proved more extensive than usual.

‖**Peachy.** A drink made from peaches. — **1781** PETERS *Hist. Conn.* 245 They make peachy and perry; grape, cherry, and currant wines.

+**Peach yellows.** A destructive disease of the peach tree which turns its leaves a characteristic pale yellow color. — **1889** *Rep. Secy. Agric.* 22 Special attention has been given . . . to *peach yellows* in Maryland, Delaware, and other States. **1897** *Boston Jrnl.* 11 March 7/6 Does the cultivation of the peach in this State depend upon the control of peach yellows by legislation?

Pea-coat. =PEA-JACKET. {1845–} — **1790** *Penna. Packet* 4 Jan. 2/2 There are now lodged in the said Office . . . 1 pea coat; . . . 1 coatee [etc.]. **1852** *Harper's Mag.* May 843/2 The early-trout fishers upon the south shore of the island are bandaged in pea-coats. **1862** HARTE *Luck of Roaring Camp* 222, I borrow a pea-coat of one of the crew, and . . . am doubtfully permitted to pass into one of the boats.

***Peacock.** A domestic fowl, esp. the male, of the genus *Pavo.* Also attrib. — **1724** *Essex Inst. Coll.* XXXVI. 333 Saw the Peacock spread his tail. **1841** *Knickerb.* XVII. 189 Seizing her wand of peacock-feathers, [she] took her place at the tea-urn. **1844** *Nat. Hist. N.Y., Zoology* II. 201 The Common Peacock, *P[avo] Cristatus*, . . . breeds readily throughout this country. **1887** PERRY *Flock of Girls* 146 A magnificent specimen of a peacock spread its splendid court train.

Pea field. Also **peas(e) field.** A field planted in peas. — **1677** HUBBARD *Narrative* I. 24 If there were Indians in the Neck they should send them about a Peas-field not far off. **1716** CHURCH *Philip's War* 8 They then got privately and undiscovered, unto the Fence of Capt. Almy's Peasefield. **1857** *Rep. Comm. Patents 1856: Agric.* 83 [The woodchuck] never fails to visit a peafield situated near its retreat. **1897** *Outing* XXIX. 438/2 [He] flew straight across another old pea-field to seek refuge.

Peafowl. A domestic fowl or species of fowl of the genus *Pavo;* the peacock or peahen. {1804–} — **1849** *New Eng. Farmer* I. 386 Pea fowls were shown by H. L. Devereux. **1854** *Penna. Agric. Rep.* 388 Pea Fowls, best pair, J. S. Negley. **1879** *Diseases of Swine* 203 The goose and pea-fowl are the only species of domestic fowl that do not suffer with [cholera]. **1881** *Harper's Mag.* May 888/1 It was a glorious dinner—sucking-pig, pea-fowl, chicken . . . and home-cured ham.

+**Peag.** Also **peage.** [See WAMPUM.] Shells, or beads made of shells, used by N. A. Indians for ornament, and later by Indians and early colonists as a medium of exchange. Usu. collect. *Obs.*

Cf. MOHACKEES, PEAK, ROANOKE, WAMPUM.

1648 *Conn. Rec.* I. 179 No peage, white or black, [shall] bee paid or receiued, but what is strung . . . sutably, and not small and great, vncomely and disorderly mixt. **1658** *Portsmouth Rec.* 84 Eleven shillings after the Rate of Eight white peages per peny. **1677** HUBBARD *Narrative* I. p. ix, He cast off first his Blanket, then his Silver-lac'd Coat . . . , and Belt of Peag. **1697** SEWALL *Diary* III. 399 Wenoquaspouish . . . gave him a string of Peag.

b. Attrib., esp. with *belt.*

1676 I. MATHER *K. Philip's War* (1862) 146 The English . . . struck down several Indians, one of which had on a great Peag Belt. **1820** EASTBURN & SANDS *Yamoyden* 12 Their peäg belts are girt for fight. **1820** *Ib.* 24 Collar beneath and gorget shone, The peäg armlets and the zone.

+**Pea-jacket.** [Cf. Dutch *pij, pije,* 'a seaman's coat.'] A loose, double-breasted jacket of heavy woolen material, usually worn by sailors in rough weather. {1786–} — **1721** *Amer. Wkly. Mercury* 23–30 March 2/2 Cloathed with a double-breasted Pee-Jacket. **1764** HABERSHAM *Letters* 16 Mr McGillivray has imported Sailor Pea Jacket and . . . Breeches made of the same Cloth for his Men. **1850** MITCHELL *Lorgnette* I. 13, I had put on an old pea-jacket which had seen much ocean service. **1898** F. H. SMITH *C. West* 36 He had left his pea-jacket in the cabin.

***Peak.** (See quotations.) {1696–} — **1736** *Boston News Letter* (Earle), Children's Silver Peaks & Flowers, Dutch Prettys. **1737** *New Eng. Wkly. Jrnl.* 29 Sept., Children's Quilted Peaks drawn & work'd. **1894** EARLE *Costume Col. Times* 180 Peaks would appear to be pointed caps for children's wear.

+**Peak(e).** =PEAG. (Cf. WAMPUM.) — **1638** *Md. Council Proc.* I. 73 Entred by Capt. Henry fflute . . . 7 fathome of peake. **1666** *Ib.* 549 Euery Indian that shall hereafter kill any hoggs . . . shall pay for euery hogg fifty fathom of Peake. **1709** LAWSON *Carolina* 194 The general and current Species of all the Indians . . . is that which we call Peak, and Ronoak; but Peak more especially. **1738** BYRD *Dividing Line* (1901) 34 That species of conque shell which the Indian peak is made of.

+**Peaker. 1.** Short for PIKE'S PEAKER. **2.** (See quotation.) — (1) **1861** *Knickerb.* Aug. 121 Though but a few months in the country, he is as good a Peaker as the next man. **1867** MELINE *Santa Fé & Back* 89 Most of the people who have settled these farms were disappointed 'Peakers'—either those who had thrown down the shovel to take up the plough, or those who, with exhausted means, found a long mountain journey still before them after they had reached the Peak. (2) **1905** *Forestry Bureau Bul.* No. 61, 43 *Peaker.* 1. A load of logs narrowing sharply toward the top, and thus shaped like an inverted V. . . . 2. The top log of a load.

+**Peale.** [Titian Ramsey *Peale*, Amer. naturalist (1799–1885).] In possessive in names of birds: (see quotations). — **1860** BAIRD, etc. *Birds N.A.* 661 *Demiegretta pealii*, Peale's egret, . . . [is found on the] seacoast of South Florida. **1887** RIDGWAY *Manual N. A. Birds* 248 [From the] Aleutian Islands, west to Commander Islands, and south along Pacific coast to Oregon [we find] . . . Peale's Falcon. **1917** *Birds of Amer.* II. 89 Peale's Falcon (*Falco peregrinus pealei*) is a duskier slate above than the Duck Hawk.

Pealer. [Var. of PEELER.] +=PEELER 1. — **1833** S. SMITH *Major Downing* 218 Them are Pennsylvany chaps are real pealers for electing folks when they take hold. **1869** STOWE *Oldtown Folks* 117 She was spoken of with applause under such titles as 'a staver,' 'a pealer,' 'a roarer to work.'

Pea meal. Meal made from peas. {1830–} Also attrib. — **1804** J. ROBERTS *Penna. Farmer* 62 Potatoes boiled and mixed with a small quantity of Indian, pea, bean or buckwheat meal, is a good fattener. **1821** *Gales's N.C. Almanack* 13 For several years I have had red cow-peas ground into fine meal, and when the pork is taken out of the pickle . . . , run every part of it with the pea meal. **1866** 'KIRKLAND' *Bk. Anecdotes* 463/1 Pastry—pea-meal pudding. **1888** *Vt. Agric. Rep.* X. 51 If the nutritive ratio is too narrow, like pea or linseed meal, there is not sufficient of the carbo-hydrates to give digestion to all the albumen.

+**Peanut,** *n.* [PEA and NUT.]

1. The small edible nut of any one of several herbs of the genus *Arachis*, esp. *A. hypogaea;* any one of these herbs.

Cf. GOOBER, GROUNDNUT 2, GROUND PEA 1.

1807 IRVING *Salmagundi* xii. 301 Young seniors go down to the flag-staff to buy pea-nuts and beer. **1837** WILLIAMS *Florida* 112 The pea nut produces a large crop. **1856** *Rep. Comm. Patents 1855: Agric.* 259 The 'Pea-nut,' 'Pindar,' or 'Ground-nut,' (*Arachis hypogæa*,) when cultivated in this section, requires a good alluvial soil. **1881** RITTENHOUSE *Maud* 42 Nellie's aunt . . . got on with a lot of peanuts, chocolate creams etc. **1920** ALSAKER *Eating for Health & Efficiency* 20 Peanuts are rich in protein, starch and oil.

b. (See quotation.)

1893 *Harper's Mag.* May 947/2 The farm land yields, in local parlance, 'everything from peanuts to persimmons.'

2. *attrib.* and *comb.* **a.** Designating persons or things regarded as mean, paltry, insignificant, or contemptible. *slang.*

See also PEANUT POLITICS.

1836 DUNLAP *Mem. Water Drinker* (1837) II. 25 They were your peanut fellows, I suppose. **1854** *Congress. Globe* 19 May 1230/3, I know them—a set of peanut agitators and Peter Funk philanthropists. **1892** *Congress. Rec.* 18 June 5394/2 This country is not a peanut institution; it is a great country. **1910** MCCUTCHEON *Rose in Ring* 203, I suppose that peanut aristocrat friend of yours has told you it ain't swell or proper to wear tights.

b. Designating persons who sell peanuts.

1873 'MARK TWAIN' & WARNER *Gilded Age* 492 Avery Kicks, peanut-peddler. **1910** MCCUTCHEON *Rose in Ring* 56 The lowliest peanut-vender was laughing in his sleeve at the sleuth.

c. In special combinations.

Peanut brittle, a brittle candy containing roasted peanuts (cf. PEANUT CANDY); *p. bum*, a college 'jollification' at which peanuts are eaten (see quotation and cf. BUM *n.*[1] 1); *p. butter*, a spread made of peanut paste; *p.-digger*, (see quot. 1876); *p. gallery*, the last or uppermost gallery in a theater; *p. oil*, oil made from peanuts; *p.-picker*, a machine for picking peanuts; *p.-roaster*, a machine that roasts peanuts.

1903 *N.Y. Ev. Post* 2 Oct. 7 It is impossible for one man to prescribe that all records [of great eating] henceforth shall be measured in peanut brittle, or veal cutlets, or canned corn. **1871** BAGG *At Yale* 70 [At] a 'peanut-bum' . . . a sack containing one or two bushels of peanuts is emptied upon the floor, and an indiscriminate scramble is made for them. **1903** *Harper's Bazar* Oct. 981 Two [sandwiches] of wholewheat bread with peanut butter. **1876** KNIGHT 1644/1 *Peanut-digger*, a kind of plow with trailing branches, which raises from the soil the vines with the nuts attached, and leaves them . . . to be afterward gathered and picked by hand or by . . . [a] peanut-picker. **1897** BIDDLE *Shanty Town Sketches* 59 Mr. Lincoln led his beaming spouse to a seat in the 'peanut gallery.' **1900** SADTLER *Handbk. Industr. Org. Chemistry* (ed. 3) 50 Arachis oil (peanut oil, erdnuss oil). . . . The best qualities . . . are used for table oil and the inferior grades for soap-making. **1904** 'O. HENRY' *Strictly Business* 27 The whistle of a peanut-roaster puffed a hot scream into his ear.

‖**Peanut,** *v. tr.* To make small or insignificant. — **1884** *Congress. Rec.* 24 April 3356/1 The chairman of the Committee on Appropriations proposes to cut down, to cheese-pare, to peanut this whole business, so that if we should get into a war we will not be able to compete with any foreign nation.

+**Peanut candy.** Candy having roasted peanuts in it. — **1856** STOWE *Dred* I. 51 Dancing, flirting, writing love-letters, and all other enormities down to eating pea-nut candy. **1901** MATTHEWS *Notes on Speech-Making* 53 Some postprandial addresses are so thin in theme, and so thick with jokes, that they resemble the peanut candy where you cannot see the candy for the peanuts.

+**Peanut politics.** Petty politics; political action inspired by mean or narrow motives. *slang.* (Cf. PEANUT *n.* 2 b.) — **1887** *N.Y. Mail & Exp.* 27 May (F.), If the Governor would consent not to play pea-nut politics. **1888** *N.Y. Ev. Post* 6 March 4 Another glimpse at peanut-politics . . . was afforded yesterday. **1894** *Congress. Rec.* 9 Aug. 8337/2 It would be gross disrespect to a great commercial product . . . for me to denounce the course pursued by the Administration . . . as 'peanut politics.' **1909** *N.Y. Ev. Post* 4 Feb. (Th.), They used to talk about 'peanut politics' at Albany, but a peanut is too large and respectable an object to yield a comparison for yesterday's action of the State Senate.

+**Peanut stand.** A station, booth, or movable stand where roasted peanuts are sold. — **1866** GREGG *Life in Army* 139 Farther on, you come in contact with candy shops, pea-nut stands, cake wagons. **1874** *Billings' Farmer's Allminax* 30 Meet me at the pea-nut stand. **1888** *Harper's Mag.* Nov. 938/2 He began his mercantile course as the proprietor of a pea-nut stand.

+**Pea patch. 1.** A patch or comparatively small area planted in peas. **2.** (See quot. 1818.) — **(1) 1834** *Knickerb.* III. 35 Didn't I turn that pied heifer of yourn into my pea patch? **1863** 'G. HAMILTON' *Gala-Days* 34 No premonition floated over from the adjoining pea-patch. **(2) 1818** *Niles' Reg.* XIV. 15/1 Capt. Babcock, of the U.S. engineers, is advertising for a large quantity of lumber, to be used in the contemplated fortification of the Pea Patch, a marshy island in the Delaware river, below New Castle. **1833** E. T. COKE *Subaltern's Furlough* i, We . . . arrived abreast of Fort Delaware, or the 'Pea Patch,' built upon a low reedy island, which divides the river in two channels.

***Pear.**

***1. a.** The fleshy, edible fruit of any one of various trees of the genus *Pyrus*, esp. *P. communis*. **b.** =PEAR TREE.

1634 *Relat. Beginnings of Md.* 21 We haue also . . . Apples, Peares, Potatos. **1709** LAWSON *Carolina* 109 Those sorts of Pears which we have are as well relisht, as ever I eat any where. *c*1790 T. COXE *View U.S.* 63 The produce, manufactures, and exports of Pennsylvania are . . . pears, and apricots, grapes [etc.]. **1846** BROWNE *Trees of America* 287 The blossoms of the pear, which are scentless, and of a pure white, appear . . . in the southern counties of Ohio, by the middle of April. **1881** *Rep. Indian Affairs* p. xxi, Fruit (apples, pears, and peaches), of the finest quality, is very plentiful. **1909** WASON *Happy Hawkins* 306, [I] chased a flat-head clear into the Palace Hotel for throwin' a pear at me.

2. *attrib.* and *comb.* **a.** Designating various fruits or shrubs resembling or suggesting the pear.

1790 DEANE *New-Eng. Farmer* 222/2 The pear-plum, so called from its shape, which is sweet, and of an excellent taste. **1829** SANDS *Writings* II. 128, I have sent you by the bearer a basket of yellow Portugal pear-quinces. **1848** SALISBURY *N.Y. Agric. Soc. Trans.* 371 Of the Tomato or Love Apple. . . . [Subvarieties include] the *common large-lobed*, the *small*, the *pear-shaped*. **1897** SUDWORTH *Arborescent Flora* 230 *Cratægus tomentosa*. Black Haw. . . . [Called] Pear Thorn (R.I., N.J., Mich.).

b. Designating foods and drinks made from pears.

1869 STOWE *Oldtown Folks* 340 Peach, pear, and plum pies. **1892** *York County Hist. Rev.* 18 The general scope of the business includes the bottling of the various kinds of carbonated beverages, such as . . . pear cider, ginger ale, grape soda [etc.].

+**Pear blight. 1.** =FIRE BLIGHT. **2.** *Pear-blight beetle*, a beetle, as *Anisandrus pyri*, the larvae of which are injurious to pear trees. — **(1) 1854** EMMONS *Agric. N.Y.* V. 165 Atmospheric Blight . . . proves itself to be independent of the cause that sometimes produces the pear blight. **1856** *Mich. Agric. Soc. Trans.* VII. 714 The pear blight, too, is as yet unknown among us, but it is steadily marching to the west. **(2) 1854** EMMONS *Agric. N.Y.* V. 113 *Scolytus* (*Tomicus*) *pyri*. . . . Pear-blight Beetle. . . . This insect has been highly injurious to the pear tree in New-England.

+**Pear haw.** The blackthorn, *Crataegus tomentosa*. Also *pear hawthorn*. — **1884** SARGENT *Rep. Forests* 79 Black Thorn. Pear Haw. **1892** APGAR *Trees Northern U.S.* 106 Black or Pear Hawthorn; . . . wild in western New York, west and south. **1897** SUDWORTH *Arborescent Flora* 230 *Cratægus tomentosa*. Black Haw. . . . [Also called] Pear Haw (Miss., Ohio).

Pea rifle. {1862–} +=KENTUCKY RIFLE. — **1882** BAILLIE-GROHMAN *Camps in Rockies* 142 A large rack . . . held some twelve or fifteen different arms, from the Winchester repeater . . . to the antiquated Kentucky pea rifle. **1885** *Century Mag.* June 221/1 These men carried but one weapon, the long-barreled, small-bored pea rifle. **1901** WHITE *Westerners* 1 He must imagine . . . mountaineers from Tennessee and Kentucky, bearing their historic long pea rifles.

Pearlash. A form of potassium carbonate obtained from crude potash. {1727–41–}

1770 J. ADAMS *Diary* Works II. 239 Mr. William Frobisher gave me a narration of his services to the Province, in introducing the manufacture of potashes and pearlashes. **1792** in Imlay *Western Territory* (ed. 3) 552 The pot and pearl-ashes have already become an immense article of productive commerce. **1807** JANSON *Stranger in A.* 29 Pot and pearl-ashes, paper-hangings [etc.]. **1857** *Lawrence* (Kan.) *Republican* 11 June 4 If our Western friends can . . . keep the pearlash out of their bread, all the yellow people . . . will soon be restored to whiteness. **1893** M. A. OWEN *Voodoo Tales* 42 Ef yo' bile er crow-fedder wid pearlash an' sof'-soap, . . . yo' kyarn't bleach um w'ite.

b. Attrib. and comb. with *maker, works.*

1789 *Boston Directory* 183 Fairservice John, Pearl-ash-maker. **1796** *Ann. 4th Congress* 2 Sess. 2651 [The lists particularly mention] sugar-houses, pot and pearlash works, . . . and all other buildings and edifices of the value of five pounds and upwards.

Pearl barley. Barley deprived by milling of its husk and reduced to small round grains. {1710–} — **1727** *Md. Hist. Mag.* XVIII. 229 To be had of Silvanus Beven in Plough Court, . . . pearle barley. **1790** *Penna. Packet* 2 Jan. 4/2 Race ginger, Pearl barley, Sago oatmeal [etc.], . . . For Sale By John Dorsey. **1884** NYE *Baled Hay* 77 My sunny exterior was only a thin covering for bran and shorts and middlings, cracked wheat and pearl barley.

Pearl button. A button made of pearl or mother-of-pearl. {1717–} Also attrib. — **1842** *Niles' Nat. Reg.* 21 May 188/1 Manufacturers of pearl buttons in the city of Philadelphia, asking to be protected in their manufacture. **1850** MITCHELL *Lorgnette* I. 32 He will presently appear in a stout, heavy 'coachman,' with huge pearl buttons. **1898** CAHAN *Imported Bridegroom* 196 It was near seven o'clock when Boris came from the pearl-button factory.

Pear leaf. *attrib.* Designating various plants having leaves resembling those of the pear. — **1817–8** EATON *Botany* (1822) 254 *Crataegus pyrifolia*, pear-leaf thorn. *Ib.* 416 *Pyrola rotundifolia*, shin-leaf, pear-leaf wintergreen. **1821** *Mass. H. S. Coll.* 2 Ser. IX. 158 Plants . . . indigenous in the township of Middlebury, [Vermont, include] . . . *Viburnum pyrifolium*, Pear-leaf sheepberry. **1845** LINCOLN *Botany* App. 95/1 [*Cratægus*] *pyrifolia*, (pear-leaf thorn.) . . . leaves oval-ovate.

Pear-leaved, *a.* Having leaves resembling those of the pear tree. — **1785** MARSHALL *Amer. Grove* 88 *Mespilus Crus galli*. Pear leaved Thorn. **1813** MUHLENBERG *Cat. Plants* 32 *Viburnum lentago*, Pear-leaved mealy tree. *Ib.* 48 *Cratægus pyrifolia*, Pear-leaved hawthorn. **1814** BIGELOW *Florula Bostoniensis* 70 *Viburnum lentago*. Pear leaved Viburnum. . . . A tall shrub in low grounds.

+**Pearl millet. 1.** A cereal grass, *Pennisetum glaucum*. **2.** A kind of sorghum. — **(1) 1896** BEAL *Grasses of N.A.* I. 187 *P*[*ennisetum*] *typhoideum*. Pearl, Indian, African, Cat-tails, or Horse Millet. **1923** *Stand. Plant Names* 285/2. **(2) 1901** MOHR *Plant Life Ala.* 135 Various kinds of sorghum, known as durrha or kafir corn, millo maize, and pearl millet.

Pearl oyster. {1693–} +(See quot. 1911.) — **1805** LEWIS in *L. & Clark Exped.* III. (1905) 5 [Indian] men and women [in Idaho wear beads] . . . intermixed with triangular peices of the shells of the perl oister. **1883** *Nat. Museum Bul.* No. 27, 264 *Margaritiphora fimbriata*. Pearl Oyster. Head of Gulf of California to Panama. **1911** *Rep. Fisheries 1908* 313/1 Pearl oyster.—An oyster found on the California coast and in the Gulf of California. The shells are used in manufacturing various useful and beautiful articles.

Pearlwort. Any one of various plants of the genus *Sagina*. {1660–} — **1817–8** EATON *Botany* (1822) 439 *Sagina procumbens*, pearlwort. . . . At New Haven it grows only in running water, or very wet shady places, **1833** *Ib.* (ed. 6) 316 *Sagina apetala*, annual pearl-wort. **1840** DEWEY *Mass. Flowering Plants* 90 *Sagina procumbens*. Pearlwort. . . . The above species is a mere weed and troublesome. **1901** MOHR *Plant Life Ala.* 498 *Sagina*. . . . Pearlwort. About 12 species, temperate regions of Europe and North America.

+**Pearly everlasting.** An American herb of the thistle family, *Anaphalis margaritacea*. — **1857** GRAY *Botany* 229 *Antennaria margaritacea*. Pearly Everlasting. **1872** *Vermont Bd. Agric. Rep.* I. 281 Pearly everlasting, a perennial, occupies the knolls of cool, hill pastures.

***Pearmain.** Any one of several varieties of apple. Cf. BLUE PEARMAIN.

1676 GLOVER *Va.* in *Phil. Trans.* XI. 628 All sorts of English Apples, as Pear-mains, Pippins [etc.]. **1709** LAWSON *Carolina* 108 The Pearmains, of both sorts, are apt to speck, and rot on the trees. **1770** *Md. Hist. Mag.* XIII. 69 Things sent by the wagon [include] . . . Newtown Pippins & Pairmains. **1852** *Knickerb.* XL. 190 The orchard with its favorite trees, pearmain and pippin. **1880** *Harper's Mag.* Dec. 90 She stored up red pearmains in the parlor closet for Ede.

***Pear tree.** A tree that bears pears. — **1669** *Oyster Bay Rec.* I. 106 Twenty ffore Aplle trees Bearing ffruit, one peare tree. **1714** HEMPSTEAD *Diary* 38, I was at home Seting up fence by Trueman's Pare Tree. **1814** *Henderson's N.C. Almanack* 3 He had plenty of Apple Trees, Plumb Trees, Pear Trees, . . . and all sorts of Trees. **1901** CHURCHILL *Crisis* 447 I climbed out on the rotten branch of the big pear tree yonder to get you that pear.

Pea-shooter. =BEAN-SHOOTER. {1857–} — **1867** *Amer. Naturalist* I. 257 The stamens suddenly straighten and throw jets of pollen . . . like a boy's pea-shooter. **1879** BURDETTE *Hawkeyes* 20 About such a chuck as you always feel like giving a boy with a 'putty blower' or a 'pea shooter.'

Pea stick. A stick provided for a cultivated pea plant to grow upon or about. {1855–} — **1745** MACSPARRAN *Diary* 27 Harry is come home . . . & has bro't home Pea Sticks. **1837** *Crockett Almanac* 19, I went into a small grove to cut . . . pea-sticks. **1860** B. ALCOTT *Journals* 329 Pull up my pea sticks and pick the rest of my red Astrachans.

***Peat.** A carbonaceous deposit composed principally of decayed vegetable matter.

1749 ELIOT *Field-Husb.* ii. 37, I have found in the Peat where it was deep, the fibrous parts of Bark. **1792** BELKNAP *Hist. New-Hampshire* III. 119 Nature hath provided an ample store of that fossil, ligneous substance called *peat.* **1815** DRAKE *Cincinnati* 72 It is not impossible that those singular tracts will be found rich in . . . peat. **1895** *Outing* XXVII. 73 The top mold, or peat, was burned away.

b. Attrib. with *ground, land, soil.*

1817 *Niles' Reg.* XII. 99/1 The deputy surveyors are required to note . . . all lakes, ponds, swamps, peat or turf grounds [etc.]. **1838** *Mass. Agric. Survey 1st Rep.* 74 In Rowley the yield of peat land is rated at [$25 per acre]. **1879** *Scribner's Mo.* Dec. 249/2 On some peat soils the strawberry thrives abundantly.

+Pea time.

1. *fig.* The time proper or fitting for certain actions or attitudes.

1862 LOWELL *Biglow P.* 2 Ser. 11 Ther' 's ollers chaps a-hangin' roun' that can't see pea-time's past.

2. *The last of pea time(s)*, the end of the time when peas are in season; hence, fig., the last stage, or a trying or difficult time or period. *colloq.*

1834 CARRUTHERS *Kentuckian* I. 190 [He] whines it out to us like an old woman in the last of pea-time. **1834** BENTON *30 Years' View* I. 467/2 [It was] the last of pea-time. **1850** LEWIS *La. Swamp Doctor* 174 It war the last of pea-time with me, sure, if I didn't rise 'fore bar did. **1893** M. A. OWEN *Voodoo Tales* 199 'Deed my gyarden am a-lookin' mighty bad. Hit look mo' lak de las' o' pea-time den de fust o' truck-time. **1904** E. ROBINS *Magn. North* I. 63 Things looked pretty much like the last of pea time.

b. Used of persons in comparisons.

1883 'CRADDOCK' *Broomsedge Cove* 174 Ye oughter git some air an' light, Marcelly; ye look like the las' o' pea-time. **1911** SAUNDERS *Col. Todhunter* 108 'What on earth's the matter, Bill?' he asked. 'You look like the last of pea-times.'

+Peat meadow. A meadow or level area in which peat occurs. — **1836** *Niles' Nat. Reg.* 17 Sept. 48/2 A peat meadow . . . in Salem, on the old Boston road, has been burning. **1838** *Mass. Agric. Survey 1st Rep.* 74 The peat meadows in Essex are extensive, and constitute a valuable resource to the inhabitants for fuel. **1883** *Century Mag.* Sept. 650/1 In Eastham, large stumps may be discovered nearly a mile from land, and ancient peat-meadows now lie under water.

+Peat swamp. A swamp in which peat abounds. — **1839** BUEL *Farmer's Companion* 70 The inert, insoluble matter of peat-swamps is rendered soluble and enriching, by . . . manure. **1844** *Cultivator* ns. I. 92/2 A vast majority of the inhabitants of the west . . . [shake] with the ague so much . . . that they have no time to . . . drain peat swamps. **1884** ROE *Nature's Story* We make the most of our peat swamps, fallen leaves and rubbish in general.

+Peav(e)y. Also **pe(e)vy.** [Inventor's name.] +(See quot. 1905.) — **1878** *Lumberman's Gaz.* 16 March 229/3 The Best Cast Steel Pevy Made in the World! **1885** C. A. STEPHENS *Adv. Six Young Men* 109 The possessors of nothing in the world save their axes, 'peevies,' and the few dirty rags on their backs. **1893** *Scribner's Mag.* June 714/2 The banking-ground swarms with men armed with pevies (which are cant-hooks furnished with strong pikes in the end). **1905** *Forestry Bureau. Bul.* No. 61, 43 A stout lever 5 to 7 feet long, fitted at the larger end with a metal socket and pike and a curved steel hook which works on a bolt; used in handling logs, especially in driving. A peavy differs from a cant hook in having a pike instead of a toe ring and lip at the end. **1908** WHITE *Riverman* 43 This they attacked with their peavies, rolling the top logs off into the current below.

+Pea vine.

1. A clambering plant, somewhat like one or other species of the cultivated pea, found as a native growth in various parts of the United States.

Cf. WILD PEA VINE.

1675 *Penna. Mag.* VI. 89 You have Grass as high as a man's Knees, . . . interlac'd with Pea-Vines, and other Weeds that Cattel much delight in. **1796** in Imlay *Western Territory* (ed. 3) 518 In the state of Tenasee cattle at present support themselves among the reeds, pea-vines, rye-grass, and clover. **1806** in *Ann. 9th Congress* 2 Sess. 1107 The banks of the river are covered with pea vine and several sorts of grass, bearing seed. **1850** GALLAHER *Western Sketch-Book* 371 The plains and hills were covered with the rank, luxuriant pea-vine. **1892** J. L. ALLEN *Blue-Grass Region* 14 [The forest], together with cane-brakes and pea-vines, covered the face of the country.

attrib. **1870** *Amer. Naturalist* IV. 30 The meadows are bounded . . . by the Pea-vine mountains (so-called from the frequency with which the lupines or wild peas are met with on its sides). **1880** TOURGEE *Bricks* 61 Richards . . . came from up North somewhere about 1790, when everybody thought this pea-vine country was a sort of new Garden of Eden.

2. The vines of one or other species of cultivated pea.

1766 BARTRAM *Journal* 25 The last frost killed the . . . pea-vines, sunflowers [etc.]. **1850** *Rep. Comm. Patents 1849: Agric.* 151 There is much crab-grass hay and pea-vines put up for winter feed. **1870** WARNER *Summer in Garden* x, This profound truth is about the only thing I have yet realised out of my pea-vines. **1899** CHESNUTT *Wife of His Youth* 133 The peas were planted beside alternate hills of corn, the corn-stalks serving as supports for the climbing pea-vines.

attrib. **1905** PRINGLE *Rice Planter* 142 Rice flour and pea-vine hay make a perfect ration for cows.

Pea weevil. An indigenous North American weevil, *Mylabris pisorum*, that destroys peas by eating out their interiors. (Cf. PEA BUG.) — **1841** HARRIS *Insects Injur. Veget.* (1862) 62 This little insect, . . . the . . . pea-weevil, . . . is better known in America by the incorrect name of pea-bug. **1867** *Amer. Naturalist* I. 110 Many other weevils and boring-beetles, especially the Pea Weevil, . . . now abound. **1892** KELLOGG *Kansas Insects* 63 The adult Bean Weevil much resembles the Pea weevil, but is little more than one-half as large. **1925** HERRICK *Man. Injurious Insects* 355 The Pea Weevil. . . . From New York southward it is probably the most serious enemy of the garden pea.

+Pecan. Also **peccan(e), pekaun, pecaun.** [Algonquian *pakan* any hard-shelled nut.] (See also PACCAN.)

1. A species of hickory, *Carya illinoensis*; a tree of this species.

Early writers not infrequently regarded this tree as a species of the walnut, *Juglans*. Also called ILLINOIS NUT and *Mississippi nut* (see MISSISSIPPI 2 b).

1792 IMLAY *Western Territory* 212 The Carolina ground-nut grows low down on the Mississippi, and the peccane in the Illinois, in the county of Cumberland, and every where near the mouth of the Ohio. **1802** ELLICOTT *Journal* 284 Peccan, (*juglans illinoinensis,*) . . . is met with as high as the Wabash. **1814** BRACKENRIDGE *Views La.* 61 The pecanne . . . found on the low grounds . . . is a large tree resembling somewhat the hickory, but has a more delicate leaf. **1834** BAIRD *Valley Miss.* 43 The peccan with its fine fruit of the nut kind, is found in Illinois and Missouri. **1836** HILDRETH *Campaigns Rocky Mts.* I. 100 Sycamores interspersed with the cotton-wood, the coffee-nut, and pekaun. **1885** HAVARD *Flora W. & S. Texas* 458 Largest and most conspicuous of trees along the (San Antonio) river is the Pecan. **1901** MOHR *Plant Life Ala.* 100 There can be no doubt about the pecan being . . . a native of the eastern Gulf region outside of the Mississippi and Yazoo deltas.

2. The richly flavored nut of this tree. (Cf. PECAN NUT.)

1822 WOODS *English Prairie* 228 Pecan is a sort of walnut, said to be the finest nut in this country. **1837** PECK *New Guide* 278 Of nuts, the hickory, black walnut and pecaun, deserve notice. The last is an oblong, thin-shelled, delicious nut, that grows on a large tree, a species of the hickory. **1876** *Forest & Stream* 13 July 376/2 Spending a few days at Concho, gathering pecans, visiting the fine springs at Kickapoo [etc.]. **1885** BAYLOR *On Both Sides* 472 You'll find a couple of barrels of pecans at your place. **1911** *Grocer's Encycl.* 410 Among the most popular nuts of general use are . . . hickory nuts, pecans, pine nuts [etc.].

attrib. and *comb.* **1883** SWEET & KNOX *Through Texas* 270 And about pecan-shells. It is said that when they are hard, the winter is going to be cold. **1902** 'O. HENRY' *Roads of Destiny* 153 Those brigands might justly have been taken for a little party of peaceable rustics assembled for a fish-fry or pecan gathering.

+Pecan hickory. =PECAN 1. — [**1785** MARSHALL *Amer. Grove* 69 Pecan or Illinois Hickery.] **1847** DARLINGTON *Weeds & Plants* 304 C[arya] *olivæformis*. . . . Olive-shaped Carya. Pecan Hickory. Pecan nut.

+Pecan nut.

1. =PECAN 2.

1778 CARVER *Travels* 501 The Pecannut is somewhat of the walnut kind, but rather smaller than a walnut, being about the size of a middling acorn. **1797** ELLICOTT in Mathews *Life A. Ellicott* 152, I have a large Keg of Pecon Nuts put up for you. **1877** HABBERTON *Jericho Road* xiii. 125 At one time he gathered pecan nuts.

2. =PECAN 1. In full *pecan nut tree.*

1778 CARVER *Travels* 500 The Hazelnut, the Beechnut, the Pecannut, the Chesnut, the Hickory. **1821** NUTTALL *Travels Arkansa* 214 The Pecannerie, now the most considerable settlement in the territory, except Arkansas, derived its name from the Pecan nut-trees (*Carya olivaeformis*), with which its forests abound. **1836** EDWARD *Hist. Texas* 72 The Pecannut, the Chesnut [abound]. **1897** SUDWORTH *Arborescent Flora* 110.

+Pecan tree. =PECAN 1. — **1834** A. PIKE *Sketches* 70 About noon, we saw the first pecan tree which had greeted us. **1880** CABLE *Grandissimes* 43 A great rabbit-hawk sat alone in the top of a lofty pecan-tree. **1903** *N.Y. Sun* 8 Nov., The wild pecan trees of Louisiana and Texas, which grow most of the nuts.

Peccary. Also **peccari.** A hoglike mammal (*Pecari angulatus*) found in the Southwest; the collared peccary. {1613–, in S. America}

Also called *musk hog*, as well as *javalina* and *Mexican hog* (qq.v.).

1807 JANSON *Stranger in Amer.* 193 Among the quadrupeds [is] . . . the peccary, remarkable for a secretory organ on its back. **1849** *31st Congress 1 Sess.* Sen. Ex. Doc. No. 64, 52 Bear and peccary are also found in the same neighborhood; antelope on the other side of the Pecos. **1854** BARTLETT *Personal Narr.* I. 55 A tame peccari thrust his long nose against me to receive my caresses. **1907** WHITE *Arizona Nights* 209 Such trails . . . were generally made by peccaries in search of cast-up fish. **1923** J. H. COOK *On Old Frontier* 20 We stampeded bunches of musk hogs or peccaries.

*__Peck,__ *n.*[1] A dry measure of one-fourth of a bushel (q.v.). 'The imperial peck contains 554.548 cubic inches, that of the United States 537.6' (*O.E.D.*). — **1627** *Plymouth Laws* 30 Every man of the surveighers [shall] have a peck of corne for every share of land layed out. **1819** *Ann. 15th Congress* 2 Sess. 1275 The slave is . . . allowed, in many instances, but his peck of corn per week for his whole subsistence. **1860** HOLMES *E. Venner* v, Throwing a peck of potatoes up into the air. **1898** DUNBAR *Folks from Dixie* 33 An' sometimes we sells 'em; a string o' fish'll bring a peck o' co'n any time.

*__Peck,__ *n.*[2] +The action involved in striking one Easter egg against another. (Cf. EGG-PECKING.) — **1835** LONGSTREET *Georgia Scenes* 77 It was a common custom of those days with boys, to dye and peck eggs on Easter Sunday, and for a few days afterwards. . . . Our 'young operatives' sallied forth to stake the whole proceeds of their '*domestic industry*' upon a peck. Egg was struck against egg, point to point, and the egg which was broken was given up as lost to the owner of the one which came whole from the shock.

*__Peck,__ *v.* +*tr.* To strike (one Easter egg against another). — **1835** [see prec.].

+**Pecker mill.** (See quotation.) — **1802** DRAYTON *S. Carolina* 121 Three kinds of rice mills, called *pecker, cog,* and *water* mills, are used in this state. The first is the most simple; and, probably, that which was first in use. It is so called, from the pestle's striking somewhat in the manner of a wood pecker, when pecking a tree.

+**Peckerwood.** A woodpecker. Also attrib. — **1859** BARTLETT 314 *Peckerwood,* western for Woodpecker. **1866** C. H. SMITH *Bill Arp* 95 If it didn't rain any more and the entire crop was prudently gathered, he might probably make a peck to the acre of peckerwood nubbins. **1909** F. CALHOUN *Miss Minerva* 140 A big, red-headed peckerwood.

+**Pectoral sandpiper.** A small sandpiper, *Pisobia melanotos:* (see quotations and cf. JACKSNIPE). — **1828** BONAPARTE *Synopsis* 318 The Pectoral Sandpiper . . . inhabits throughout the United States and West Indies. **1844** *Nat. Hist. N.Y., Zoology* II. 242 The Pectoral Sandpiper, *Tringa Pectoralis,* . . . passes under the various names of Meadow Snipe, Jack Snipe, and Short-neck. **1883** *Nat. Museum Bul. No. 27,* 149.

*__Peculiar.__ *New Eng.* +A district or piece of land neither constituting, nor belonging to, a town; also, the owner or occupier of such land. *Obs.* — **1720** *Conn. Rec.* VI. 210 Mr. John Read, who dwells between Fairfield and Danbury, [shall] be likewise annually listed, as a peculiar to Danbury. **1739** *Ib.* VIII. 230 This Assembly being informed that a certain piece of land in the county of Windham . . . is not in any town but still remains a peculiar, . . . Be it enacted . . . That the said tract of land be annexed to the town of Voluntown. **1779** *Vt. State P.* (1823) 297. **1809** KENDALL *Travels* I. 17 Precincts or peculiars are in some cases ordered to be rated at or in certain towns, and in such cases are rated and governed by the town.

Peculiar institution(s).

+**1.** The institution of slavery. Now hist.

1842 BUCKINGHAM *Slave States* I. 216 Slavery is usually called here 'our peculiar institutions.' **1851** G. W. F. CARLISLE *Travels* 51 They have thought the policy of the North too encroaching . . . upon questions relating to what they term their peculiar institutions, which is their euphonious description of slavery. **1856** *S. Lit. Messenger* XXII. 243/1 There is a certain class of minds who see in every effort of the kind, some imaginary thrust at the 'peculiar institution.' **1861** H. JACOBS *Life Slave Girl* 69 The northern man is not welcome south of the Mason and Dixon's line, unless he suppresses every thought and feeling at variance with their 'peculiar institution.' **1865** A. JOHNSON in *Annual Cycl.* V. 801/2 A State may be in the Government with a peculiar institution, and by the operation of a rebellion lose that feature. **1904** *Nation* 12 May 375 Men . . . having no vital interest in the 'peculiar institution,' had Confederate pressure, not State loyalty, to draw them from their homes.

+**b.** *Peculiar domestic institution(s) of the South,* an expanded form of the same phrase.

c1852 in Farmer 413/2 The dangers which at present threaten the peculiar domestic institutions of the South. **1885** *Mag. Amer. Hist.* March 297/2 *Peculiar institution.*—In full 'the *peculiar* domestic *institution* of the South'—meaning negro slavery.

+**2.** In transferred use: (see quotations).

1855 *Yale Lit. Mag.* XX. 278 (Th.), Yankees do have a weakness for patent medicine. It is one of their peculiar institutions. **1857** E. STONE *Life J. Howland* 282 Judge Branch . . . welcomed the guests to all the enjoyments of a Rhode Island 'peculiar institution' [*i.e.*, a clambake].

Pedal. {1611–} A foot. *humorous.* — **1849** MELVILLE *Mardi* 304 To cool his heated pedals, he established a series of stopping-places, or stages. **1894** *Outing* XXIII. 884/2 The first two or three pairs of these stunted pedals that I noticed excited my pity.

*__Peddle,__ *v.*

+**1.** *tr.* To carry about and offer for sale; to sell in small quantities. {1880–} Also with *out.*

1831 PECK *Guide* 62 Whole rows of English and Americans are to be seen peddling those valuable little stores which one can move about in a hand-barrow, or carry in a basket. **1849** FOSTER *N.Y. in Slices* 81 If it is necessary to have . . . a 'family grocery' on every corner, there surely is no need that these establishments should . . . peddle out poison at three cents a dose. **1856** OLMSTED *Slave States* 630 Many negroes were in town, peddling eggs, nuts, brooms, and fowls. **1923** HERRICK *Lilla* 257 The woman in her . . . led her to turn to the garden patch, the bees, and the chickens, when the orchard refused to yield, peddling her produce herself.

fig. **1853** *La Crosse Democrat* 1 Nov. 2/2 Is there a man so mean as to peddle this ticket?

2. ||**a.** To parcel *out* in small quantities. **b.** To spread (a story, a piece of gossip, etc.). {1892}

1837 EMERSON *Amer. Scholar* 4 This original unit, this fountain of power, . . . has been so minutely subdivided and peddled out, that it is spilled into drops, and cannot be gathered. **1864** in *Century Mag.* XXXVIII. 703/2 Going around peddling his griefs in private ears. **1872** POWERS *Afoot & Alone* 309 There's another man peddling gab out of a boot-leg. **1900** ADE *More Fables* 196 Of course it Grieved him to be compelled to Peddle such Stories.

*__Peddler.__ Also **pedler, pedlar.**

*__1.__ One who carries about goods, farm produce, etc., for sale; a merchant who carries his goods with him.

1687 *Conn. Rec.* III. 435 Many persons have lately taken upon them the practice of peddlers and petty chapmen. **1721** *Mass. H. Rep. Jrnl.* III. 144 Mr. Wainwright, etc. [shall] be a Committee, to prepare some Addition to the Act against Hawkers, Pedlers, &c. **1767** ROWE *Diary* 139 Wee went in quest of thieves & took up one Davidson a Peddler. **1803** *Lit. Mag.* (Phila.) Dec. 169 Notwithstanding the general opprobrium heaped on the poor pedlars, . . . some of the wealthiest traders in America commenced business in this humble station. **1865** *Atlantic Mo.* Feb. 192/1 Thirty editions [of Trumbull's *M'Fingal*] were sold in shops or hawked about by peddlers. **1905** RICE *Sandy* 189 He was a peddler, you know—an Irish peddler.

b. In the possessive with *boat, cart.*

1818 FLINT *Lett. from Amer.* 80 At this place there was a pedlar's boat, a small ark, which is removed from one town to another. **1914** STEELE *Storm* 118 Gerald Duarte an' Gabe Young come ridin' up the road in a peddler's cart.

+**2.** =ESSENCE PEDDLER 2.

1858 *Harper's Mag.* Sept. 567/1 Like most Methodist ministers, he had but one good suit of clothes, and those completely saturated with essence of the peddler.

+**Peddler's wagon.** A wagon or cart in which a peddler carries his goods. — **1836** in *Jrnl. of So. Hist.* I. 370 A Yankee who has a store at Cahaba which supplies a number of Pedlars Wagons, told me that one of his wagons was going to Selma. **1876** MILLER *First Families* 226 Two sun-bonnets . . . reached far over the faces of the wearers, like the cover of a pedler's wagon. **1887** GEORGE *40 Yrs. on Rail* 153 He had the finest peddler's wagon I ever saw.

*__Peddling.__ The occupation or action of carrying goods about for sale. Also attrib. or as adj. — **1653** *Boston Rec.* 28 They are turned sellrs & pedling mrchants. **1857** *Quinland* I. 100 He invested [$300] in an old horse and wagon and Yankee clocks, and started for the interior, on a peddling tour. **1911** *Okla. Session Laws* 3 Legisl. 217 Any indigent or disabled ex-Confederate or ex-Union soldier [may] . . . engage in what is commonly known as hawking and peddling.

+**Pedicure,** *n.* (See quot. 1890.) — **1848** R. DUNGLISON *Med. Lex.* 635/2 *Pedicure,* Chiropodist. **1889** *Science* XIV. 308/1 Dentists, pedicures, trained nurses, and veterinarians. **1890** *Cent.* 4354/3 *Pedicure.* . . . 1. The cure or care of the feet. . . . 2. One whose business is the surgical care of the feet.

+**Pedicure,** *v. tr.* To treat (the feet) by removing corns, bunions, etc. Hence, *pedicuring, pedicurist.* — **1894** *Mute's Chron.* (Columbus, Ohio) 5 May, Two hot footbaths a week and a little pedicuring will remove the cause of much discomfort. **1894** *Columbus Dispatch* 25 Dec. 4/3 The art of pedicurist is very greatly in demand among society women of New York. **1896** *Ib.* 6 March 4/4 One's lower extremities are pedicured without cost. **1902** *Boston Globe* 21 Sept. 47/3 Every woman should learn the scientific care of her own feet, or the art of pedicuring.

+**Pedregal.** Also **pedragal.** *W.* [Sp., 'a stony place.'] 'A lava field' (W. '79). *Obs.* Also transf. — **1853** KANE *Grinnell Exped.* 289, I am struck more and more with the evidences of gigantic force in the phases of our frozen *pedragal.* **1881** BRYANT & GAY *Pop. Hist. U.S.* IV. 378 [Santa Anna's] position was flanked on the west by a rugged field of broken lava, called the Pedregal.

+**Pedro.** [Sp.] **1.** A variation of the game of sancho pedro in which sancho, or the nine of trumps, does not count. **2.** The five of trumps in this game or in sancho pedro. — **(1) 1880** *Cimarron News & Press* 26 Feb. 2/6 Private Rooms for those who wish to enjoy a quiet game of dr— Pedro we mean. **1907** LONDON *Road* 147, I was playing pedro with three other stiffs. **1913** — *Valley of Moon* 408 To him it was so much good time wasted that might be employed at a game of pedro, or going swimming. **(2) 1880** DICK *Amer. Hoyle* (ed. 13) 210 Pedro may be taken with any trump higher than the Five.

+**Pedro sancho.** =SANCHO PEDRO. — **1880** DICK *Amer. Hoyle* (ed. 13) 210 Pedro Sancho is played with a pack of fifty-two cards. **1899** [see SANCHO PEDRO].

Peek, *n.* A short look; a peep. {1893} — **1843** STEPHENS *High Life N.Y.* II. 41, I jest give a peak in for a minute, and streaked it upstairs. **1869** ALCOTT *Little Women* II. 300 Old Hannah . . . could not resist frequent 'peaks' through the slide. **1884** ROE *Nature's Story* vi, Their father gave them a peek into the . . . brooding-room. **1911** HARRISON *Queed* 61 Several peeks were needed . . . before she was at last convinced that she had it.

***Peek,** *v. intr.* To peer through an opening; to take a short, furtive look. {–1739; now *dial.*}

1789 *Mass. Spy* 18 June (Th.), A vain trifling curiosity to pry into secrets, to meddle with the business of others, and to peek into privacies. **1848** LOWELL *Poetical Works* (1896) 233/2 Zekle crep' up, quite unbeknown An' peeked in thru the winder. **1857** M. J. HOLMES *Meadow-Brook* v, I know too well what 'tis to be a schoolmarm, and have the hull Deestrict peekin' at you. **1887** FREEMAN *Humble Romance* 362, I peeked into the vestry, an' saw 'em both. **1918** — *Edgewater People* 157, I run in here to peek behind the lace curtains.

Peekaboo. 1.** A child's game; a cry uttered in this game. {1599} Also fig. 'Now chiefly U.S.' (*O.E.D.*). +**2.** *attrib.* Designating garments that can be seen through. — (1) *c1880** in *Notes & Queries* 10 Ser. II. 153/2 Peek-a-boo! Peek-a-boo! I see you hiding there. **1903** C. COPELAND *School of Woods* 29 Like a mischievous child playing at peekaboo. **1906** *Washington Post* 29 April 44 The budding flowers were playing peek-a-boo with one another. (2) **1906** *Springfield W. Repub.* 10 May 13 In San Francisco there is no winter suit and summer suit. The same medium-weight garment is worn the year round and the peek-a-boo waist is unknown. **1908** 'YESLAH' *Tenderfoot S. Calif.* 14 All I had in that blamed trunk of mine was some peek-a-boo underwear and drop stitched stockings.

***Peel,** *n.* Also †**peale. 1. a.** A fire shovel. **b.** A long, spadelike instrument for handling loaves of bread in an oven. +**2.** (See quotation.) — (1) **1640** *Conn. Rec.* I. 448 One peale, . . . one stupan, 3 bowles & a tunnell. **1647** *Essex Probate Rec.* I. 67, 1 fire shovell, 1 peele, 1 Jacke with some old Iron & tubs. **1684** *Essex Inst. Coll.* XXV. 155. 1 Copper. an iron peel. a hand saw. **1828** WEBSTER, *Peel*, . . . a kind of wooden shovel used by bakers, with a broad palm and long handle; hence, in popular use in America, any large fire-shovel. (2) **1876** KNIGHT 1647/2 *Peel.* (*Nautical.*) The *wash* of an oar. The end inside the gunwale is the *loom*.

***Peel,** *v.*

***1.** *tr.* To strip (the bark) from a tree or twig; to strip (a tree) of its bark.

1660 *Plymouth Rec.* I. 43 Either English or Indians peele the Rinds of cedare trees. **1694** *Huntington Rec.* II. 169 Whome soever peeleth any standing trees for bark for their use of tanning . . . shall forfit five shillings for every tree found so peeled. *a***1772** WOOLMAN *Journal* 190 Near our tent, on the sides of large trees peeled for that purpose, were various representations of men. **1843** STEPHENS *High Life N.Y.* II. 203, I was sartin that the old fox would peel me, as he would peel bark for a willow whistle, if he knew the trousers agin; for he's a mean old shote about lendin things.

+**2.** *To peel it*, (see quotation). *slang. Obs.*

1859 BARTLETT *Dict. Amer.* 314 *To Peel it*, to run at full speed. 'Come, boys; peel it now, or you'll be late.'

+**3.** *To keep one's eye peeled*, (see EYE 4).

+**Peeled stick convention.** A mass meeting in Cleveland, Ohio, before the Civil War. — **1880** *Congress. Rec.* 19 March 1708/2 Did they not meet in Cleveland in the 'peeled stick' convention, all armed and ready to resist the authority of the United States?

***Peeler.**[1]

+**1. a.** Anything of an exceptional nature, as a violent storm, a particularly attractive boat, etc.; a 'lulu.' *slang.*

1823 COOPER *Pioneers* xv, It's a peeler without, I can tell you, good woman. **1834** C. A. DAVIS *Lett. J. Downing* 331 The Captain was all the while boastin of [his boat] the 'Two Pollies;' and well he might, for she was a peeler. **1843** STEPHENS *High Life N.Y.* I. 214 Sam's fust book was a peeler, and a credit to the family. **1845** KIRKLAND *Western Clearings* 74 We're goin' straight to a bee-tree. . . . It's a real peeler, I tell ye!

+**b.** A person of extraordinary qualities. *slang.*

See also PEALER.

1835 BIRD *Hawks* II. 116 The man mought ha' shot himself; for they say he was a peeler at the bottle, for such a young un. **1843** STEPHENS *High Life N.Y.* I. 82, I was talking with a rare peeler of a gal. **1882** THAYER *From Log-Cabin* 198 He's a peeler for work too; ain't afraid to dirty himself.

2. (See quotations.) {*Sc.* and *n. Ir.* 1866–}

1877 BARTLETT 456 *Peeler.* . . . A crab just before shedding and becoming *soft*, when his shell is loose, so that it can be *peeled* off with the fingers, is called a *peeler.* **1883** *Century Mag.* July 378/2 Large craw-fish, which were about to shed their outer cases, or shells, and which for this reason are called 'shedders,' or 'peelers.' **1890** [see CRACKLER].

+**3.** (See quotation.)

1881 *Congress. Rec.* 3 May 447/1 The peelers . . . are that part of the [Va.] debt not yet funded. They are selling today at about thirty-eight cents in the dollar.

+**4.** A cowboy, esp. one who 'peels the hide' off a wild horse during the process of breaking him.

1903 A. ADAMS *Log of Cowboy* 275 The horse of some peeler, working with one of Shanghai Pierce's herds, acted up one morning. **1914** 'BOWER' *Flying U Ranch* 7 This is Mr. Mig-u-ell Rapponi, boys—a peeler straight from the Golden Gate.

Peeler.[2] A policeman. *Obs.* {1817–} — **1871** BAGG *At Yale* 515 There is a sort of traditional hostility between the students and the 'peelers'—as the city police are always called. **1874** *43d Congress 2 Sess.* H. R. Rep. No. 261, 805 The citizens were in complete possession of the city, save the Saint Louis Hotel, occupied by about a dozen peelers and a gang of negroes. **1878** *Scribner's Mo.* July 353/2 Though honest men sometimes do not seem able to put their finger upon a policeman at the instant they want him, rogues find far oftener that the 'peelers' are on hand when *not* wanted.

***Peeling.** A thin fabric used as a dress material. *Obs.* {1693–1769} — **1775** in Singleton *Social N.Y.* 247 Henry Wilmot, in Hanover Square, sells . . . persians, modes, sarsinets, peelong [*sic*]; . . . cloak trimmings, skeleton and cap wires.

***Peep.**

+**1. a.** Any of various sandpipers, esp. the least sandpiper. **b.** The Carolina rail.

1794 *Mass. H. S. Coll.* 1 Ser. III. 199 Sea fowl are plenty on the shores and in the bay; particularly the gannet, . . . widgeon, and peep. **1832** WILLIAMSON *Maine* I. 147 The *Peep* is a little land-bird, with small body, wings long and large for its size. **1853** *Knickerb.* XLII. 534 Shake a bush, and you shake out a bird, or a 'peep,' or a bug. **1898** N. BROOKS *Boys of Fairport* 208 Blackie . . . was over on the ma'ash with Sam Perkins, shooting peeps. **1917** [see PEETWEET]. **1920** LINCOLN *Mr. Pratt* 211 Blessed if he didn't come back with a dozen peep and ring-necks.

+**2.** In sense a: Used as a symbol of unsteadiness in the expressions *drunk* or *tight as a peep*, very drunk.

1855 *Knickerb.* XLV. 429 If drunk as a peep, he 'lays down.' **1864** SALA in *Daily Telegraph* 27 July, [The] New England mind . . . has long since endorsed the locution 'as tight as a peep,' to express an utter state of tipsification.

***Peeper.** +Any of certain frogs, esp. of the family Hylidae, that make peeping noises, usually the small tree toad, *Hyla crucifer.* — **1857** HAMMOND *Northern Scenes* 30 All is still now, save the piping notes of the little peeper along the shore. **1872** POWERS *Afoot & Alone* 78 At evening the 'March peepers' begin to wriggle and chirp in the scummy marsh. **1889** ELLWANGER *Garden's Story* 19 The chorus of the *Hylodes*, or peepers, . . . that piercing treble . . . that nothing—even the katydid—can equal in strident intensity. **1907** *St. Nicholas* Oct. 1063/1 The light wind; . . . peepers joining their high trebles, plainly audible [etc.].

Peep-eye. =PEEKABOO 1. — **1887** *Harper's Mag.* Dec. 79/1 He made futile efforts to play 'peep-eye' with anybody jovially disposed in the crowd.

+**Peep frog.** =PEEPER. — **1888** *Boston Jrnl.* 19 Jan. 2/3 The peet-frogs [*sic*] in the ponds serenaded their sweethearts at night.

Peep show. An exhibition of pictures or objects, seen through a peephole or magnifying glass. {1861–} — **1871** *Scribner's Mo.* II. 146 Swings, roundabouts, wild beast shows, and acrobats are . . . flanked by peep-shows, the everlasting fat lady [etc.]. **1894** 'MARK TWAIN' *Those Twins* iii, At peep-shows we pay double.

+**Peep stone.** A stone supposed to have the qualities of a divining rod. — **1870** BEADLE *Utah* 22 He began to 'divine' the locality of things which had been stolen, by means of a 'peep-stone' placed in his hat, and by the same means to point out where hidden treasures lay.

***Peerless,** *a.* +An epithet commonly applied to W. J. Bryan (1860–1925). — **1900** *Congress. Rec.* 4 Jan. 652/2 Self-seeking politicians, timorous souls, may fall away from us, but the paramount issue and the peerless candidate will remain. **1925** *Kansas City Times* 27 July 7/2 The interim between this period [1904] and the next presidential election of 1908 was occupied by Mr. Bryan, now known by many of his followers as 'The Peerless Leader.'

+**Peetweet.** [Echoic.] (See quot. 1917.) — **1839** PEABODY *Mass. Birds* 370 From its note, it is called the Peet-weet, which is its familiar name. **1858** THOREAU *Maine Woods* 135 A company of peetweets were twittering and teetering about over the carcass of a moose. **1917** *Birds of Amer.* I. 238 Spotted Sandpiper. *Actitas macularia.* . . . [Also called] Peep; Peetweet.

+**Peevy.** Variant of PEAV(E)Y.

+**Peewee, Peewee flycatcher,** etc. (See PEWEE, PEWEE FLYCATCHER, etc.)

***Peg,** *n.*

***1.** A pin, usually made of wood, used in various ways: (see quotations).

1745 HEMPSTEAD *Diary* 449, I mend my Cart. made one New Rave & New Peggs or Rounds. **1799** Rothert *Muhlenberg Co.* 45 A joint shingle roof put on with pegs. **1833** *Stimpson's Boston Directory* 13 (Ernst), Finding Store. . . . Shoe horns, pegs [etc. for sale]. **1875** HARTE *G. Conroy* II. i, Softly drawing the wooden peg that served as a bolt, Gabriel entered. **1897** MOORE *How to Build a Home* 31 Carpenters not infrequently fasten their work in process of construction by driving pegs into chimney-breasts.

2. (See quot. *c*1735.)

[*c***1735** CATESBY *Carolina* II. 39/1 Turtle are most commonly taken at the Bahama-Islands . . . by striking them with a small Iron Peg of two Inches long, this Peg is put in a Socket at the End of a Staff 12 Feet long.] **1881** INGERSOLL *Oyster-Industry* 244 In Florida the turtle-grains have only one prong and one barb (half a barb) when anything but a 'peg' is used.

3. Attrib. with *factory*, *ladder*, etc.

1849 CHAMBERLAIN *Ind. Gazetteer* 429 There are on the east fork of White Water and its tributaries, 19 flouring mills, . . . one paper mill, one peg factory. **1854** *Harper's Mag.* Nov. 849/2 Uncle G— disappeared down the peg-ladder at the corner. **1865** *Maine Board Agric. Rep.* X. 136 This stream furnishes power for a peg mill and other light machinery. **1866** *Ill. Agric. Soc. Trans.* VI. 290 Such streamlets as are made to turn at least a peg machine in Massachusetts, can be found in almost any locality.

***Peg,** *v.* **+1.** *tr.* To hang up (tobacco) by means of pegs. **2.** To throw (a ball). {1895–} **+3.** To hook (a mat or rug). — **(1) 1850** *Rep. Comm. Patents: Agric.* 321 '*Pegging*' tobacco is the neatest and best mode [of putting away tobacco]. . . . Pegs are driven in [the stalk] with a mallet, in a slanting direction, so as to hook on the sticks in the house. . . . [The tobacco is then] pulled up in the house, and there hung upon the sticks. **(2) 1862** *N.Y. Sunday Mercury* 13 July (E. J. Nichols). **1917** MATHEWSON *Second Base Sloan* 146 You peg the ball across like you were looking where you were sending it. **(3) 1898** *Boston Transcript* 16 April 14/5 To peg means [to crochet], . . . but is oftener used in relation to mats made of rags or yarn drawn through bagging—burlap.

Pegging awl. {1765–} +(See quotation.) — **1875** *Fur, Fin & Feather* (ed. 3) 119 The smaller species of loon I have heard variously called the spike-bill, the cape-race, . . . the gun-greaser, the pegging-all [*sic*], etc.

Pegging machine. A machine for putting pegs into shoe soles. — **1865** A. D. RICHARDSON *Secret Service* 62 Here was the greatest curiosity of all—the patent pegging-machine, which cuts out the pegs from a thin strip of wood, inserts the awl, and pegs two rows around the sole of a large shoe. **1871** *Scribner's Mo.* II. 495 He had the hardihood to introduce the first of Wells' pegging machines against a determined strike. **1885** *Harper's Mag.* Jan. 286/1 The pegging-machines . . . cut their own pegs before driving them.

Peg top.

1. A wooden top provided with a metal peg, and spun with a string. {1801–} Also fig.

1788 *Mass. Spy* 3 April 4/3 Children's Books. . . . Memoirs of a Pegtop. By the Author of, The Adventures of a Pincushion. **1848** LOWELL *Poetical Works* (1896) 167/1 The pockets, plethoric with marbles round, That still a space for ball and pegtop found. **1888** *Nation* 5 April 271/2 A love of marbles, or peg-tops, or hoops.

2. *pl.* A pair of trousers wide at the waist but narrowing down to the ankles. {1858–} Also attrib. in sing.

1861 *Vanity Fair* 26 Jan. 45/1 The all-round collar is no more modern than peg-tops. **1892** GUNTER *Miss Dividends* 34 His trousers . . . are cut in what was then called the 'peg-top' pattern.

Pekan. [Amer. Indian.] The fisher or black cat, *Martes pennanti*. Also *pekan weasel*. Also attrib. (Cf. FISHER 2, FISHER WEASEL.) — [**1796** MORSE *Amer. Geog.* I. 200 Fisher. In Canada he is called Pekan.] **1804** CLARK in *Lewis & C. Exped.* I. (1904) 132 [The Sioux] furnish Beaver, . . . Pekon, (*pichou*) Bear & Dear Skins. **1838** *Mass. Zool. Survey Rep.* 24 *Mustela Canadensis*, Pekan Weasel or Fisher Weasel. . . . It is very troublesome on sable lines by robbing the traps of the sable. **1840** EMMONS *Mass. Quadrupeds* 39 The fur of the Pekan is not so fine and beautiful as that of the Marten. **1917** *Mammals of Amer.* 117/1 The largest of all the Martens is an animal . . . variously designated as the 'Pekan,' 'Fisher,' . . . and 'Black Cat.'

+Pelado. *S.W.* [Sp.] A penniless person; a loafer. — **1847** RUXTON *Adv. Rocky Mts.* (1848) 207, I again packed my mules, . . . under a fusillade of very hard names from the pélados. **1863** *Rio Abajo Press* 5 May 2/2 Our enterprising men expect to make double the price, and when making their calculations they do so more like a Pelado buying sugar by the picayune's worth than men who understand business economy.

Pelage. [Fr.] The fur, hair, or wool coat of an animal. {1866–} — **1828** WEBSTER *Pelage*, . . . the vesture or covering of wild beasts, consisting of hair, fur or wool. *Bacon*. [1848 ed. marks *obs.*] **1848** S. W. WILLIAMS *Middle Kingdom* I. 156 Numerous fur-bearing animals are hunted for their pelage. **1867** *Amer. Naturalist* I. 288 At this season their pelages were thick and heavy, and a good many of the animals were killed with poison for the sake of the fur. **1876** ALLEN *Amer. Bisons* 456 A young male in summer pelage. **1912** *Univ. Calif. Publ. in Zool.* X. 125 It is thus possible to make direct comparison . . . with specimens in corresponding seasonal pelage.

+Pelefish. *Obs.* =PADDLEFISH. *Obs.* — **1609** HAKLUYT *Va. Richly Valued* 100 There was another fish [in the Miss. R.] called a pele fish: it had a snout of a cubit long, and at the end of the vpper lip it was made like a peele.

Pelerine. A mantle or cape worn by women. {1744–} — **1743** in Earle *Costume Col. Times* 180 Ladies may have their Pellerines made [at a mantua-maker's shop.] **1841** BACHE *Fire-Screen* 29 The young ladies spent two hours in animated discussions on white satin, lace veils, pelerines, . . . &c. **1853** *Harper's Mag.* Jan. 288/2 At the top of the skirt is a plain pelerine, ending at the end of the arm. **1896** WILKINS *Madelon* 321 Dorothy Fair, . . . in a white-muslin pelerine all wrought with cunning needlework, sat in the parson's pew.

Pelham bit. A bit combining the curb and snaffle in one. {1849–} — **1840** *Picayune* 28 July 1/2 Materials and tools for saddlers and coach trimmers, together with a fine assortment of Saddlery ware, such as . . . Pelham and Snaffle Bits.

***Pelican.** Any bird of the genus *Pelecanus*, +esp. the American species: (see note). Also attrib.

The white pelican (*P. erythrorhynchos*) of the West, the brown pelican (*P. occidentalis*) of Florida, and the California brown pelican (*P. o. californicus*) are the chief American species. (See BROWN, WHITE PELICAN; also FRIGATE PELICAN.)

1682 ASH *California* 22 For Prey, the Pelican, Hawk, and Eagle, &c. **1709** LAWSON *Carolina* 150 The Pellican of the Wilderness cannot be the same as ours; this being a Water-Fowl, with a great natural Wen or Pouch under his throat, in which he keeps his prey of fish, which is what he lives on. **1804** CLARK in *Lewis & C. Exped.* I. (1904) 104 Some hundreds of Pelicans were collected. **1818** FORDHAM *Narr. Travels* 149 There are Pelicans on the Wabash. **1873** *Winfield* (Kan.) *Courier* 15 May 3/2 Adlwy Davis shot a pelican on the Arkansas river last week, that measured 8 feet 8 inches from tip to tip of wing. **1917** *Birds of Amer.* I. 102/1 Through the western part of the United States, the Pelican season begins in April . . . and lasts until August or September.

fig. c**1650** *Broadside Verse* (1930) 3/1 Let Winthrops name still famous be, . . . He was New-Englands *Pelican*. **1862** *N.Y. Tribune* 20 Jan. (Chipman), [McMahon] goes on . . . to say that the South is a Pelican; that we are her progeny; that she has drained her breasts to feed us.

b. (See quotations.)

1861 MOORE *Rebellion Rec.* I. III. 12 A Committee of the Louisiana State Convention, appointed to prepare a flag and seal for that State, . . . express their opinion of that Pelican which has so long been the cherished emblem of Louisiana. **1890** *Opelousas* (La.) *Democrat* 14 June 3/2 The citizens of Louisiana are called 'Pelicans.'

+Pelican flag. The flag of Louisiana. — **1865** RICHARDSON *Secret Service* 40 There were Pelican flags, and Lone Star flags, and devices, unlike anything in the heavens above.

+Pelican State. Louisiana. A nickname. — **1859** *Harper's Mag.* May 853/2 A well-known writer in the Pelican State writes us a good thing from one of his little folks. **1877** BARTLETT 457 *Pelican State*, the State of Louisiana. **1907** *Boston Transcript* 9 Nov.

Pelisse. Also †**pelice. a.** A long outer garment of fur or with a fur lining, worn by men or women. *Obs.* {1718–} **b.** A woman's cloak reaching to the ankles, made of silk or some other fabric. *Obs.* {1755–}

1803 *Holyoke Diaries* 143 Thankful Smith altered a Pelice. **1808** ASHE *Travels* 30 The ladies cast off their fur pelisses. **1818** S. S. BRYANT in *Bryant Rec.* (1898) 97 If you have found you a piece of silk for your pelisse let us know it. **1841** MOTLEY *Correspondence* I. 73, [I] had a pelisse lined with fur. **1861** E. COWELL *Diary* 238 Cloaks, capes, pelisses of expensive velvets, silk & satin dresses trailing the *spitten* streets. **1891** WELCH *Recoll. 1830–40* 173 Cloth pelisses sometimes called a habit, generally made with plaited skirts and tight bodied jackets. **1902** L. RICHARDS *Mrs. Tree* 154 Here was Mrs. Tree again, pelisse, hat, stick, and all.

attrib. and *comb.* **1810** *Columbian Centinel* 3 Oct. 2/4 Mrs. Roberts, Dress-Maker, Milliner, Pelisse and Corset-Maker. **1820** *Ib.* 5 Jan. 3/2 20 bales of Woollens, consisting of assorted Pelisse Cloths; Navy blue Habit Cloths. *Ib.* 4/2 Constantly for sale—Bedquilt and Pelisse Wadding.

***Pellitory.** Also †**pelletory.** Any bushlike plant of the genus *Parietaria*, +esp. *P. pennsylvanica*. The plant of the first two quotations has not been definitely identified. — **1709** LAWSON *Carolina* 100 Pelletory grows on the Sand-Banks and Islands. It is used to cure the Tooth-ach. c**1729** CATESBY *Carolina* I. 26 The Pellitory, or Tooth-ach Tree, . . . seldom grows above a foot in thickness. **1817–8** EATON *Botany* (1822) 375 *Parietaria pennsylvanica*, pellitory. Hudson. . . . On rocky sidehills. **1843** TORREY *Flora N.Y.* II. 224 *Parietaria Pennsylvanica*, Pennsylvanian Pellitory. . . . Shady rocky banks, particularly in the western and northern parts of the State.

+Pelon dog. The Mexican hairless dog. — **1882** SWEET & KNOX *Texas Siftings* 61 The pelon dog is found in Austin . . . and in *tamales*.

***Pelt.**

***1. a.** The undressed skin of a fur-bearing animal. Also collective. **b.** The untanned skin, stripped of its hair or wool, of a sheep or a goat.

1697 *Md. Hist. Mag.* XV. 116 They went laden with their pelt. **1827** COOPER *Prairie* iii, With my pelts! I never took a skin from a buck, nor a quill from a goose in my life! **1881** *Rep. Indian Affairs* 137 They sell such of their wool, pelts, &c., as are not used by themselves. **1891** *Century Mag.* Nov. 62, I cannot pay for a team each year with gopher pelts as others do. **1925** TILGHMAN *Dugout* 4 [They] visited their traps and cared for the pelts they found.

attrib. **1821** NUTTALL *Travels Arkansa* 223 At one of the Quapaw or Ozark villages, . . . we found . . . a considerable number of conic fur pelt caps.

2. The hair-covered part of the head. *humorous.*

1867 'LACKLAND' *Homespun* 271 [The negro] had a queer way of lifting his entire scalp . . . which set his frizzled pelt in such comical motion that none of us could possibly resist it.

Pelter. {1827–} +A horse. A depreciatory term used in allusion to the mud thrown up by a horse's hoofs when traveling on muddy roads. — **1856** *Knickerb.* XLVIII. 314 When his earthly tenement yields his soul no shelter, May it animate the corpse of an ancient pelter. **1874** *Billings' Farmer's Allminax* 18 Porky Billings . . . alwuss had on hand an old flag-tailed pelter, with a glass eye, tew trade with ennyboddy. **1896** ADE *Artie* 4 It's like hitchin' up a four-time winner 'longside of a pelter.

+**Peltrist.** A dealer in pelts. — **1830** *Congress. Deb.* 10 May 932/1 The peltrist, with his knotted strings of account for furs. **1877** BARTLETT 791 *Peltrist*, a seller of finished peltries; a vendor of manufactured furs.

+**Peltry.** Also †**peltery.** [Fr. *pelleterie.*]

This word was formerly used in England {1436–1525} as a borrowing from Old French, but it is 'not exemplified from *c*1525 to 1700; and then first in reference to the North American fur trade' (*O.E.D.*). In American usage, it appears to be a new borrowing from the French in North America.

1. *collect.* The pelts or undressed skins of fur-bearing animals. {1771, in N. Amer.; 1861–}

1643 *Suffolk Deeds* I. 7 All which to be truly pajd . . . in peltry at the prize Currant as at the time of pajment. **1677** *New Castle Court Rec.* 81 [A bill] payable in good and merchandable winter wheat at 5 gilders or in peltery after ye first of december. **1704** *Boston News-Letter* 12 June 2/1 Laid waste several French Settlements along the Coast, taken some considerable booty of Furrs, Peltry, &c. from the Enemy. **1759** *New Amer. Mag.* Aug. 574 The Indians procure the peltry. **1796** in Imlay *Western Territory* (ed. 3) 549 In many of the frontier towns in this state, the Indians have already come in with their furs and peltry. **1815** DRAKE *Cincinnati* 149 Our imports from the Missouri Territory are lead, peltry and skins. **1860** CLAIBORNE *Sam. Dale* 45, [I] went on a trading adventure among the Creeks, bartering merchandise for cattle and hogs, peltry, hides, and tallow.

2. An individual pelt.

1804 CLARK in *Lewis & C. Exped.* I. (1904) 34 At about 10 oClock 4 *Cajaux* or rafts loaded with furs and peltries came too. **1812** *Niles' Reg.* III. 105/2 At this place are deposited the furs and peltries that are collected in the northwest. **1821** NUTTALL *Travels Arkansa* 98 This morning we met captain Prior and Mr. Richards, descending with cargoes of fur and peltries, collected among the Osages. *c***1835** CATLIN *Indians* II. 83 The Indian gets a mere shadow for his peltries. **1863** DICEY *6 Mos. in Federal States* II. 96 The Indians still come to the city at times to barter; and furs and peltries are stock articles of St. Louis commerce. **1891** *Century Mag.* March 772 He would come into the fort with a new supply of peltries. **1903** WHITE *Forest* 26 The reek . . . of the open spaces [is] in its peltries.

3. Attrib. with *standard, trade, traffic.*

1790 PUTNAM in *Memoirs* 241 When we take into consideration . . . the peltry trade [etc.]. **1805** LEWIS in *Ann. 9th Congress 2 Sess.* 1041 Their returns . . . are estimated by the peltry standard of St. Louis, which is forty cents per pound for deer-skins. **1893** *Atlantic Mo.* Feb. 148/1 If I had sons crowding your peltry traffic . . . , then you would truly see me venerated.

+**Pembina.** [Altered from Cree *nīpin* 'summer' and *minam* 'whortleberries.'] The wild cranberry; the fruit of this plant. — **1824** KEATING *Narrative* (1825) II. 48 Of the plants observed in this neigbourhood [*sic*], besides the Pembina, we can only mention the common hop; and the raspberry-bush. [Near Pembina, N.D.] [**1851** RICHARDSON *Arctic Searching Exped.* II. 298 *V. edule*, the *pembina* of the voyagers, was traced by us northwards to the Elk River.] **1877** BARTLETT 457 *Pembina*, the fruit of the *Viburnum edule*, which Michaux and Gray regard as a variety of the *V. opulus*, or Cranberry Tree of Maine.

+**Pembina buggy.** *local.* [f. *Pembina* Mts. or River, N.D.; cf. prec.] (See quotation.) *humorous.* — **1860** *Harper's Mag.* Oct. 587/2 'Pembina buggy' is the honorary title which they [homemade carts] receive from those who despair of otherwise making jolts endurable.

Pembroke. *ellipt.* A style of four-legged table having drop leaves supported on movable brackets. {1778–} — **1870** A. D. WHITNEY *We Girls* 105 Ruth . . . folded and slid back the little pembroke. *Ib.*, The little pembroke was wheeled out again.

Pemmican. Also **pemitigon.** [Cree *pimikkan.*] Among the Indians and frontiersmen, a form of prepared meat made usually of buffalo flesh or venison: (see quot. 1824). {1801–, in Canada}

1804 CLARK in *Lewis & C. Exped.* I. (1904) 168 [The Indians] then put before us the dog which they had been cooking, & Pemitigon & ground potatoe in Several Platters. **1824** KEATING *Narrative* I. 447*n.*, Pemmican is the meat of the buffalo, . . . cut into thin slices, which are jerked in the sun or smoke . . . ; it is then dried before the fire until it becomes crisp, after which it is [pounded]; . . . it is mixed up with an equal weight of buffalo grease, or marrow fat poured on when hot and liquid. . . . Sometimes, in order to give it a pleasant taste, it is mixed with a sort of wild cherry, which is pounded and introduced, stone and all. **1831** R. COX *Adv. Columbia R.* 244 Our pemmican was completely damaged by the late accident. **1880** *Scribner's Mo.* July 443/1 By 'provisions,' in the North-west everybody means pemmican, or buffalo meat preserved in a pounded and triturated state. **1904** WHITE *Silent Places* 159 Of the meat . . . most went into pemmican. *a***1918** G. STUART *On Frontier* II. 44 If pemmican, fat dogs, smoked buffalo tongue, and like delicacies were plentiful they lasted a week or until they were all eaten up.

***Pen.**[1]

***1.** An instrument for writing or drawing with ink or other fluid; also a pen point.

In modern usage, except in fig. contexts, the word does not refer to the quill pen.

1607 in Smith *Works* (1910) p. xli, So I gaue him a pen and paper. **1790** *Penna. Packet* 29 April 2/1 At 3 o'clock in the Afternoon will be Sold. . . . One long Dividers with Drawing Pen and Post Crayon. **1812** in H. M. Brooks *Gleanings* 125 A further supply of the celebrated Steel Pens. **1855** M. THOMPSON *Doesticks* 133 Pen wipers, that fill the point of a pen full of wool. **1876** SCUDDER *Dwellers* 59 A young man . . . [sat] before a little table with an exceedingly fine-nibbed pen. **1903** WIGGIN *Rebecca* 125 'Can we have a copy of the poetry?' . . . 'Yes, indeed! I'll do a clean, nice one with violet ink and a fine pen.'

2. Attrib. and comb. with *driver, point, stock,* etc.

1864 WEBSTER 966/2 *Pen-stock*, . . . the handle used with a metallic or other pen. **1867** 'LACKLAND' *Homespun* 129 Better justice [to the dinner] can be done with the knife and fork than with the pen-point. **1887** *Courier-Journal* 9 May 1/1 The man of war was badly punished by the pen-wielder. **1889** *Century Mag.* Feb. 580/1 [She] looked round on the circle of fresh-faced pen-drivers [*i.e.*, clerks] for explanation.

***Pen.**[2]

***1. a.** A small enclosure, usually thought of as having no top, for domestic animals or poultry; a corral.

1637 *Essex Inst. Coll.* IV. 114/1 The inclosing of some parte of the comon next the pen. **1672** *Oyster Bay Rec.* I. 79 Two acres of Land on ye West side of ye Mill pond beginning at his Goat pen. **1775** ADAIR *Indians* 230 They are forced to feed them in small penns. **1814** J. TAYLOR *Arator* 102 The most abundant source of artificial manure within the reach of a bread-stuff farmer is that raised in farm pens during the winter. **1850** GARRARD *Wah-To-Yah* xi. 148 A short distance beyond is a pen of logs and brush in which the *caballada* is driven, when an animal is wanted. **1878** J. MACDONALD *Food from Far West* 45 The herdboys—men on horseback—go through the ranges and gather the cattle into 'pens.' **1891** *Fur, Fin, & Feather* March 174/1 Not a single bird was lost in the blizzard of 1888, although the birds in the pens were covered out of sight with snow. **1904** PRINGLE *Rice Planter* 88 My own twenty-five pigs are kept confined in a crawl or pen for fear of their getting into the corn.

+**b.** At a camp meeting: (see quot. 1832).

1820 FLINT *Lett. from Amer.* 236 The little inclosure [at a camp meeting in the woods] . . . is by the religious called *Altar*, and some scoffers are wicked enough to call it *Pen.* **1832** F. TROLLOPE *Domestic Manners* I. 240 Such as needed their help were to come forward into 'the pen.' . . . 'The pen' was the space immediately below the preachers' stand.

c. A railed-in space in an office.

1896 PAGE *Red Rock* 269 He sat in his inner business office, with his clerks in outer pens. **1903** LEWIS *Boss* 24 Once within the room I found myself in a railed pen.

2. An enclosure used for trapping animals and birds.

1657 *Southold Rec.* I. 333 Such as are disposed to make a penn or penns to take wolves in. **1661** *Rowley Rec.* 109 Leutenant Brockellbanke [and others] . . . havinge ingaged for to make a pen for to catch wolves, had that priviledge granted that no boddy else should make any pen. **1846** THORPE *Myst. Backwoods* 68 Once was he [a gobbler] caught in a 'pen,' and got out by an overlooked hole in its top. **1870** NOWLAND *Indianapolis* 43 Turkeys were often caught by means of pens constructed for the purpose.

+**3.** The enclosure made by the walls of a log cabin.

Cf. DOUBLE-PENNED CABIN.

1846 *Xenia Torch-Light* 23 July 4/1 The rude, long pen, was the whole house. **1850** LEWIS *La. Swamp Doctor* 147 The house consisted of a double log cabin, of small dimensions, a passage, the full depth of the house, running between the 'pens.'

+**4. a.** = BULL PEN 2. Sometimes called a *Georgia pen.*

Cf. PEN.[3]

1845 SIMMS *Wigwam & Cabin* 2 Ser. 93 The 'pen' in which I was to be kept secure . . . is one well known to the less civilized regions of the country. . . . It is technically a 'bull pen,' and consists of huge logs, roughly put together, crossing at right angles, forming a hollow square,—the logs too massy to be removed, and the structure too high to be climbed. **1853** STOWE *Key* 160/1 The brothers were handcuffed, and, with their sisters, . . . put into a prison called a Georgia Pen. **1865** *Atlantic Mo.* March 286/2 'Is it a pen?' . . . 'Yes, . . . the Stockade Prison.' **1865** KELLOGG *Rebel Prisons* 353, I'd like to know if my girl has gone and married another, while I've been down in our Georgia pen. **1866** GOSS *Soldier's Story* 144 Every batch of prisoners sent into the 'pen' were accompanied by a spy in U.S. blue.

+**b.** An inclosure for Negro slaves about to be sold.

1852 STOWE *Uncle Tom* xvii, You mean to . . . put my boy like a calf in a trader's pen. **1853** THOMAS *J. Randolph* 286 You know Robinson, the nigger-dealer, who has the pen down town?

+**c.** A place of confinement in a police court.

1904 *N.Y. Ev. Jrnl.* 10 May 2 A panic was caused among the prisoners in the pen of the Ewen Street Police Court jail.

+**Pen.**[3] Abbrev. of PENITENTIARY, perhaps partly by association with PEN[2] 4 a. — **1884** 'CRADDOCK' *Tenn. Mts.* 68 He b'lieved the Pen could claim it ez convict labor. **1887** *Courier-Journal* 19 Feb. 2/3 He found an alarming state of affairs in the various pens. **1909** *N.Y. Ev. Post* 11 Jan. (Th.), The violator of his oath of office, who opens his surcharged bosom to the Voters' League, may well dream of escaping 'the pen.' **1924** Raine *Troubled Waters* 273 He escaped from the pen four days ago.

+**Penalty envelope.** A postage-free envelope for use in the transaction of government business. So called because a penalty for its unauthorized use is printed upon it. — **1879** *Postal Laws* § 147 Requisitions for . . . official penalty-envelopes are required to be made upon printed forms. **1893** Cushing *Story of P.O.* 196 Postmasters are not authorized to make use of the penalty envelope in ordering copies of the *Postal Guide* for the public. **1903** *N.Y. Times* 29 Aug., The officials of the District Government were not entitled to the use of the mails like other Federal officials who use penalty envelopes.

*****Pence.** The plural of Penny. Used only of British and colonial money. (See also Fourpence, Ninepence.) — **1633** *Plymouth Laws* 35 No beer [shall] be sold in any such place to exceed two pence the Winchester quart. **1660** *Ib.* 132 Eight pence an hundred on hogshead staues and hogshead headings [shall be paid]. **1711** *Springfield Rec.* II. 42, 14 yards of Gartering at 6 pence ye yard. **1788** *Mass. Centinel* 22 Oct. 44/2 'Seven and ten pence!' exclaimed the soldier.

*****Pencil.**

1. An instrument for writing or drawing, consisting either of a stick of graphite, lead, slate, or the like, or of a wooden stick having a core of any such substance. {1612–}

See also Lead pencil.

1684 I. Mather *Providences* (1856) ix. 214 There was cut for her upon a board, all the letters of the alphabet, so deep as . . . to follow the traces with a pencil. **1759** *Newport Mercury* 26 June 4/3 Imported . . . and to be sold by Jacob Richardson, . . . Memorandum Books, Pencils, &c. **1817** Paulding *Lett. from South* II. 192 Rummaging my pocket for a pencil to note down some of his remarks. **1866** *Rep. Indian Affairs* 252 A slate and pencil is furnished each. **1907** *St. Nicholas* May 648/1 The only materials needed for sketching from live animals in the field are two pencils, . . . a sketch-book, . . . and a soft eraser.

2. Attrib. and comb. with *maker, pusher, sack.*

1889 Rittenhouse *Maud* 502, I was showered with . . . pen-holders, paper knives, pencil-sacks etc. **1890** *Stock Grower & Farmer* 28 June 3/4 The pencil pusher [an office clerk] gazed reverently after him. **1907** *St. Nicholas* May 617/1 His father, a pencil-maker, was able, with the aid of his relatives, to send Henry to Harvard.

*****Pencil case.** A holder or case that can be fitted over a pencil or pencil lead. — **1790** *Penna. Packet* 11 Dec. 3/2 Imported, . . . Steel and silver pencil cases. **1825** in H. M. Brooks *Gleanings* 145 The self-supplying Pocket Writing Instrument . . . is manufactured in Gold or Silver, either with or without a pencil case. **1847** *Rep. Comm. Patents 1846* 260 What I claim as my invention . . . is the mode of shortening the pen or pencil-case by constructing it of two tubes or barrels. **1907** *St. Nicholas* June 681/1 The winner of the first prize was given a knife or a pencil-case.

Pencil flower. Any plant of the genus *Stylosanthes.* — **1817–8** Eaton *Botany* (1822) 482 *Stylosanthus hispida*, pencil flower. **1843** Torrey *Flora N.Y.* I. 174 *Stylosanthes elatior.* . . . Pencil-flower. . . . Sandy woods and dry gravelly hills. **1901** Mohr *Plant Life Ala.* 570.

Penciller. {1780–} ‖A writer. — **1897** *Advance* 22 July 111/1 Your penciller . . . has tarried a day to gather these scattered hints of a meeting.

+**Pencil-sharpener.** One of various devices for sharpening a pencil. — **1860** *Rep. Comm. Patents 1859* I. 258 Improved Eraser and Pencil Sharpener. **1873** 'G. Hamilton' *Twelve Miles* 30 The people . . . come around with apple-parers and pencil-sharpeners. **1876** Knight 1659/2 *Pencil-sharpener*, a device against which a lead or a slate pencil is drawn or rotated in order to sharpen the point.

*****Pendant.** The pendant part of an earring; an earbob. — **1704** S. Knight *Journal* 55 Pendants in their ears, which you should see very old women wear as well as young. **1759** *Newport Mercury* 26 June 4/3 Imported . . . a fine Assortment of the newest fashioned Necklaces, Ear-rings, and Pendants. **1775** Adair *Indians* 110 Decorated with silver ear-bobs, or pendants to their ears.

*****Pendle.** *Arch.* An overhanging projection from the wall of a building. *Obs.* (Cf. Jetty.) — **1663** *Boston Rec.* 17 Noe Jettie nor pendill yt shall be erected but shall be full 8 foot in height from the ground. **1701** *Ib.* 11 No person shall Erect or set up any Pentice, jetty or Pendal over any of the Streets, lanes or highwayes of this town.

+**Pendletonian,** *a.* Supporting the Democratic and states'-rights leader of Ohio, George Hunt Pendleton (1825–89). — **1868** *N.Y. Herald* 3 July 4/2 They are of the Pendletonian stripe, greenback and States rights men.

Pendulum. 1. a. In clocks and watches: A suspended body that swings or oscillates. {1660–} Also attrib. **b.** A clock that operates by means of a pendulum. {1664–} **2.** (See quotation.) — **(1) 1707** *Boston News-Letter* 13 Oct. 2/2 If any person or persons hath any occasion for New Clocks, or to have Old Ones turn'd into Pendelums . . . : Let them repair to the Sign of the Clock Dial. **1742** *Harvard Rec.* II. 719 The College Pendulum Watch . . . [shall] be deliver'd to Mr. Professor Winthrop, for his Use, as mathematical Professor. **1790** *Penna. Packet* 7 May 3/3 Imported . . . , verges, watch pendulum wire, steel balances [etc.]. **(2) 1885** *Harper's Mag.* March 559/1 Some blocks [of granite] are polished . . . by sinister-looking arrangements called pendulums, which are supported from above and run backward and forward over the granite.

+**Penelopize,** *v.* [*Penelope* of Homer's *Odyssey.*] *intr.* To spin out a task endlessly. — **1841** Benton in *Congress. Globe* App. 14 June 43/2 Diplomacy was still drawing out its lengthened thread—still weaving its long and dilatory web—still Penelopizing. **1853** Motley in Holmes *Life J. Motley* 72 There is nothing for it but to penelopize, pull to pieces, and stitch away again.

+**Peneplain.** [L. *paene* 'nearly.'] (See quot. 1894.) — **1894** *Nation* 9 Aug. 99/2 A lowland of moderate relief close to sea level—a *peneplain*, as I should term it. **1900** *Pop. Science Mo.* Mar. 552 Such a peneplain is characteristic of old topography.

*****Penguin.** The great auk, *Plautus impennis. Obs.* — **1674** [see Murre]. **1794** *Mass. H. S. Coll.* 1 Ser. III. 199 Sea fowl are plenty on the shores and in the bay; particularly the gannet, . . . sheldrake, penguin, gull, plover, . . . and peep. **1917** *Birds of Amer.* I. 29 Great Auk. *Plautus impennis.* . . . [Also called] Penguin. . . . It seems probable that the bird was extirpated on the coasts of North America before 1840.

+**Penicaso.** [Origin uncertain.] A kind of fabric. — **1733** *S.C. Gazette* 4 Aug., Just Imported . . . platillas and clouting diaper, . . . penicasoes, ell wide chittaes [etc.].

*****Peninsula.**

*****1.** A piece of land almost surrounded by water. +**a.** A comparatively narrow body of land between two rivers.

1608 Smith *Works* (1910) 13 A Peninsule of 4 miles ci(r)cuit, betwixt two riuers ioyned to the main by a neck of 40. or 50. yards. **1652** in *Amer. Sp.* XV. 294/1 Upon the South Side of Rappahanock river and beginneth on a Certain Creeke by which is made a Peninsula at the Eastermost End. **1814** *Va. State P.* X. 384 The whole Peninsula between James and Chickahominy is here almost a perfect plain. **1855** in *Amer. Sp.* XV. 294/1 It (Westmoreland county) occupies part of the northern neck, a peninsula formed by the Potomac and Rappahannock rivers. **1876** in *Amer. Speech* XV. 294/1 Tidewater is naturally divided into nine principal peninsulas, and these are subdivided into a great number of smaller ones.

b. The land lying in the bend of a stream.

1732 Byrd *Progress to Mines* (1901) 364 The River . . . winds in the form of a Horseshoe about Germanna, making it a Peninsula, containing about 400 Acres. **1921** Hutchins *Virginia* 171 Weyanoake plantation is a peninsula lying in a short elbow of the river.

c. Used as a specific name in different parts of the country.

1694 Sewall *Letter-Book* I. 149 Said Blackston was the first Englishman that ever dwelt upon our Boston Peninsula which I am a little fond of. **1835** Hoffman *Winter in West* I. 108 This will give you some idea of the emigration into the peninsula [*i.e.*, the upper peninsula of Mich.]. **1837** Hawthorne *Twice-told Tales* (1879) I. 249 The famous Fountain of Youth . . . is situated in the southern part of the Floridian peninsula, not far from Lake Macaco. **1862** Norton *Army Lett.* 117 Thus, I apprehend, ends the campaign on the Peninsula [between the James and York rivers, in Va.].

2. An island connected with the mainland by a narrow strip of low ground during low tide.

1653 in *Amer. Speech* XV. 294/2 Att a mark'd Elme tree Standing on ye point of a peninsula commonly called Coxes Island lying at ye mouth of ye Creeke. **1670** in *Ib.*, Begining at a peninsula, commonly called & known by the Name of a Little Island. **1726** in *Ib.*, K is a Tobacco house on the Iseland or penensula.

Peninsular, *a.* Of or pertaining to a peninsula {1612–}, +esp. in reference to specific American peninsulas, as the one in Virginia between the James and York rivers. — **1847** *Ind. Hist. Soc. Publ.* III. 439 Had we been as wise as our Peninsular sister [Michigan], we should have ultimately realized a common school fund of $3,164,800. **1866** Moore *Women of War* 38 [In] the summer of 1862 . . . the sick and wounded from McClellan's Peninsular army were brought to the northern hospitals. **1895** *Dept. Agric. Yrbk. 1894* 130 The 'peninsular district' here includes the Eastern Shore counties of Maryland and Virginia, together with the State of Delaware.

*****Penistone.** A coarse woolen cloth originally from Penistone, England; a piece of such cloth. *Obs.*

1651 *Essex Probate Rec.* I. 142 Penistone ten yards. **1667** Sanford *Letter Book* 46 When I opened my Bayles I found the penistones to be in Severall Remnants. **1686** Sewall *Letter-Book* I. 31, I received yours per Mr. Clark with the cottons and penistons and ½ doz. books. **1741** *N.J. Archives* XII. 102 He had on . . . a brown Kersey Wastecoat lined with red Peniston. **1770** *Md. Hist. Mag.* XIII. 68, 24 Yards of Green Peniston for the House Servants.

b. Attrib. with *lining, petticoat.*

1654 *Essex Probate Rec.* I. 178 One pennystone peticoat. **1685** *East-Hampton Rec.* II. 172 Send mee . . . Peniston Blewe Linning.

*****Penitent.** + = next. — **1844** Gregg *Commerce of Prairies* I. 259 As the lash was pointed only with a tuft of intwisted sea-grass, its application merely served to keep open the wounds upon the penitent's back. **1885** Baylor *On Both Sides* 176 Then followed a discussion of the Quakers, . . . the Mormons, the Penitents of New Mexico.

+**Penitente.** [Sp.] A member of a religious order of flagellants among certain Spanish American natives of New Mexico and southern Colorado, who practice self-castigation, esp. during Holy Week. Also attrib.

1838 'Texian' *Mexico v. Texas* 79 [The procession] is rendered shocking and repulsive by *penitentes*, who walk at the head of the *cortege*, naked from the waist upwards, and bare-legged. **1881** Chase *Editor's Run in*

N. Mex. 114 At the lower end of the habitations [in the Cimarron] we found the Penitente church, a mud house. **1885** *Wkly. New Mexican Rev.* 9 April 4/6 Albuquerque livery men ran excursion wagons to Los Gregorios when the penitentes tortured themselves. **1900** *Independent* 26 April 1008/1 This inversion of sensation is the basis for the extraordinary mania which shows itself . . . among those sects who call themselves Flagellantes and Penitentes.

***Penitentiary.**

1. a. A building for the safe-keeping of prisoners. **b.** *spec.* A prison, usually consisting of a building or buildings and a yard, in which persons convicted of crime are confined by the authority of the law; the organization connected with such a prison. {1816–, now rare; penitentiary house, 1777–}

This term is usually restricted to state or federal prisons.

1807 *Ann. 10th Congress* 1 Sess. I. 391 So soon as the apartments in the second story of the public jail and penitentiary shall be fit for the reception and safekeeping of Aaron Burr, he [shall] be removed thereto. **1812** *Niles' Reg.* I. 351/2 The legislature of Georgia have appropriated $10,000 towards erecting a penitentiary. **1820** *Ib.* XVIII. 448/1 The income of this penitentiary . . . has been derived from the usual sources. **1836** *Ib.* LI. 16/2 In the penitentiary there are 330 female and 237 male prisoners. **1865** KELLOGG *Rebel Prisons* 375 The Salisbury Penitentiary, in North Carolina, was originally designed as a place of punishment for Southern soldiers, guilty of military offenses. **1872** BRACE *Dangerous Classes N.Y.* 35 In the Eastern Penitentiary of Pennsylvania . . . from one-fourth to one-third of the inmates are foreigners. **1890** *Stock Grower & Farmer* 18 Jan. 5/1 Evidence has been quietly gathered against several [cattle thieves], and some of them will land in the penitentiary or meet a more deserved fate. **1905** *N.Y. Ev. Post* 27 May 4 The greater the law-created inducements to crime, the larger the number who will run the risk of the penitentiary.

+2. Attrib. with *bar, convict, establishment,* etc.

1814 *Niles' Weekly Reg.* VI. 250/1 The penitentiary establishment is an honor to mankind. **1819** *Mass. Resolves* 1 June 33 The penitentiary system can be so improved, as to accomplish more effectually than corporal punishment, the prevention of crimes. **1838** CLAY *Speeches* (1842) 343 Its author better deserved a penitentiary punishment than those against whom it is directed. **c1870** BAGBY *Old Va. Gentleman* 291 The State Guard . . . watched over the penitentiary convicts employed in grading the walks. **1911** VANCE *Cynthia* 195 Either you will carry out your undertaking with Mr. Rhode, or I'll devote my fortune to seeing that you spend the balance of your days behind penitentiary bars.

+Penitentiary offense. An offense that is punishable by imprisonment in a penitentiary. — **1855** *Chicago Times* 29 Jan. 2/2 Laws making it a penitentiary offence for the planters to *ask*, or the merchant to *make*, such pecuniary advancements. **1865** RICHARDSON *Secret Service* 383 A Virginia citizen was brought in on the charge of attempting to trade in 'greenbacks,'—a penitentiary offense under Confederate law. **1883** 'MARK TWAIN' *Life on Miss.* 223 There was a United States law making it a penitentiary offense to strike . . . a pilot.

+Penitents' pen. =PEN[2] 1 b. — **1832** FERRALL *Ramble* 71 A little in advance before the booths was erected a platform for the performing preacher, and at the foot of this, inclosed by forms, was a species of sanctuary, called 'the penitents' pen.'

***Penknife.** A pocketknife, originally used to sharpen quill pens. — **1674** SEWALL *Diary* I. 3 My brother . . . brought me an Hour-glasse and penknife. **1754** *Boston News-Letter* 23 May, Imported from London, . . . pen knives, clasp-knives, butcher's knives [etc.]. **1897** HOWELLS *Open-eyed Conspiracy* iii, He took out his penknife and clicked open a blade to begin whittling.

Penman. {1601–} A man who writes with a pen, esp. one employed to write for another, as a secretary or a copyist; an author. {1612–} — **1654** JOHNSON *Wonder-w. Prov.* 110 Mr. William Torry a good penman and skild in the Latine tongue. **1678** *Doc.Col.Hist.N.Y.* XII. 604 Should I take a pennman to writt. **1788** FRANKLIN *Autobiog.* 423, I was as active as ever in the opposition, being the penman, first, of the request to have a communication of the instructions, and then of the remarks upon them. **1924** *Scribner's Mag.* Dec. 602/2 Every pay-day Annie stopped at the corner and had the penman write a letter for her.

+Pennamite. A Pennsylvanian, esp. one engaged in the Wyoming controversy with Connecticut between 1782 and 1790. A nickname. — **1784** *Mass. Centinel* 19 May 2/1 John the Pennamitte . . . presented Joseph the ferryman with precious stones, and oil-olive. **1793** T. PICKERING in E. Ford *Notes N. Webster* I. 321 The outrages committed by the *Pennamites* in May [1784]. **1880** TOURGEE *Bricks* 383 The 'Northern' man may be . . . 'Knickerbocker,' 'Pennamite,' 'Buckeye,' or 'Hoosier.' **1896** LEONARD *Cent. of Congregationalism in Ohio* 40 The number of Pennamites [Presbyterians from Pennsylvania] and Pilgrims [Congregationalists from New England] might be nearly equal.

Pennant. {1611–} +A flag or banner awarded as the symbol of a championship in some sport, esp. baseball; also, fig., the championship thus won.

1880 N. BROOKS *Fairport Nine* 188 Billy Hetherington . . . was entrusted with the championship pennant. **1888** *Cosmopolitan* Oct. 454/1 Comisky, the captain of the St. Louis team, . . . is now in the lead for the pennant in his association. **1897** *Boston Morning Jrnl.* 8 June 4/5 (Ernst), Put McCormick behind the bat. Now . . . you'll win the pennant. **1911** FERBER *Dawn O'Hara* 103 Milwaukee's just got four more games t' win the pennant. **1915** *Lit. Digest* 21 Aug. 361/1 When I paid that eleven thousand I figured that it might help us win the pennant, and a championship would be cheap at the price.

+b. Attrib. with *class, race.*

1886 *Outing* Aug. 572/2 Questions by the dozen come in . . . in regard to the probable issue of the pennant races in the professional arena. **1915** *Lit. Digest* 21 Aug. 360/3 The New York Giants . . . are not often far from the pennant class.

+Pennite. A Pennsylvanian. A nickname. — **1872** *Harper's Mag.* Jan. 318/1 Below will be found a careful compilation of the various nicknames given to the States and people of this republic: . . . Pennsylvania, Pennites, and Leatherheads.

Pennock. A variety of apple. — **1817** W. COXE *Fruit Trees* 145 Pennock. A very large, fair, red apple, much admired as an early winter fruit. **1847** IVES *New-Eng. Fruit* 42 *Pennocks.*—This is a large apple; the form round, rather oblong; the skin a dull red.

Pennsylvania. [See note.] A middle Atlantic colony and state. +Used attrib. and as adj.

'My country was confirmed to me . . . by the name of Pennsylvania; a name the King would give it in honour of my father. . . . I proposed . . . *Sylvania*, and they added *Penn* to it' (1681 Penn in Janney *Life W. Penn* 165).

1. Found in or coming from Pennsylvania.

1789 MACLAY *Deb. Senate* 11, I mentioned a favorable disposition in some of the Maryland gentlemen to be in unison with the Pennsylvania delegation. **1840** *Niles' Nat. Reg.* 25 April 128/3 Pennsylvania bituminous coal. Supplies of this coal . . . are expected in this market in a few days. **1884** *Century Mag.* Jan. 444/2 Large droves of Carolina cattle were driven through Virginia to fatten on Pennsylvania blue grass, before going to the Philadelphia market. **1913** J. W. SULLIVAN *Markets for the People* 104 The Pennsylvania markets usually get along with a single market-master, assisted by a laborer or two on market days.

2. In the names of plants.

Cf. PENNSYLVANIAN *a.* 2.

1785 MARSHALL *Amer. Grove* 2 *Acer pennsylvanicum.* Pennsylvania Dwarf Mountain Maple. **1795** WINTERBOTHAM *Hist. View* III. 392 Pennsylvania swamp rose. **1843** TORREY *Flora N.Y.* II. 452 *Avena Pennsylvanica.* . . . Pennsylvania Wild-oat. . . . Wet meadows: rare. **1847** DARLINGTON *Weeds & Plants* 143 Pennsylvania Saxifrage. Tall Saxifrage. . . . Swampy meadows and low ground. **1869** FULLER *Flower Gatherers* 28 [The anemone] blooms later, in May and June, and is called the 'Pennsylvania Wind Flower.'

3. In special combinations.

Pennsylvania ark, =PENNSYLVANIA WAGON; *P. fireplace,* =FIREPLACE 2 b; *P. horse,* a heavy horse suitable for drawing a Pennsylvania wagon; *P. hurricane,* (see quotation); *P. mile,* a very long mile, as over the early cut-up roads of the Pennsylvania oil regions (humorous); *P. road-wagon,* =PENNSYLVANIA WAGON; *P. wag(g)oner,* a driver of a large sturdy wagon.

1891 WELCH *Recoll. 1830–40* 135 Almost any day from April to October, might have been seen passing . . . a dozen in line of Pennsylvania Arks (wagons) or 'Prairie Schooners,' so called from their rising stem and stern, with great canvas covers, sustained by curved top hoops. **1744** FRANKLIN *Writings* II. 256 To avoid the several Inconveniences, and at the same time retain all the Advantages of other Fire-places, was contrived the Pennsylvania Fire-Place. **1826** FLINT *Recoll.* 10 He rode a huge Pennsylvania horse. **1827** J. BERNARD *Retrosp.* 250 A 'Pennsylvany hurricane,' like a 'Caroliny swamper,' was, indeed, a common term, nearer home, for a sublime Munchausenism—vulgarly speaking, a long lie. **1863** *Boston Sun. Herald* 16 Aug. 3/3 (Ernst), If you take any of them [*i.e.*, roads], and travel as far as you can in a day, it will be a Pennsylvania mile. **1845** SOL. SMITH *Theatr. Apprent.* 136 The baggage was sent in a large Pennsylvania road wagon. **1810** M. DWIGHT *Journey to Ohio* 29 Among my list of cast offs, I would rank Dutchmen, a Pensylvania waggoner, ditto gentlemen—for their profanity.

+Pennsylvania blue. =MERCER. — **1838** *Mass. Agric. Survey 1st Rep.* 34 The Chenango [potato], sometimes called the Mercer, or Pennsylvania Blue.

+Pennsylvania corn. A variety of corn. (Cf. GOURD CORN.) — **1739** *Georgia Col. Rec.* III. 429 We all were disappointed by long sickness, and planting the yellow Pensilvania Corn. **1838** *Mass. Agric. Survey 1st Rep.* 24 The stover of the Pennsylvania corn, which is a gourd-seed variety would probably yield from a third to a half more than ours in weight.

+Pennsylvania currency. Currency issued by Pennsylvania before 1789. — **1775** *Jrnls. Cont. Congress* III. 279 A quantity of silver and gold, not exceeding £20,000 pensylv. curry. . . . , for the use of the army in Canada. **1780** *Virginia State P.* I. 370 He shall be paid for shot twenty five pounds pr. ton Pensylvania currency. **1831** SLOCOMB *Amer. Calculator* 86 The dollar is reckoned in . . . New Jersey, Pennsylvania, . . . 7s. 6d. =3/8 Pennsylvania currency.

+Pennsylvania Dutch, *n.*

1. *collect.* The descendants of seventeenth- and eighteenth-century immigrants to Pennsylvania from southern Germany and Switzerland.

Cf. DUTCH *n.* 4 b.

1868 BEECHER *Norwood* 468 Them Pennsylvania Dutch think more of their horses than they do of themselves. **1885** *Nation* 24 Dec. 532/2 Ever since my father boxed my ears in boyhood for saying 'Pennsylvania Dutch,' I have not liked the term. It is certainly a misnomer. . . . When folks want to be polite they say 'Pennsylvania Germans.' **1910** *Harper's Mag.* Aug. 473/1 Those strange people, the Pennsylvania Dutch, . . . after well two hundred years, have kept themselves alien amidst the other Americans.

2. A dialect of High German with English intermixed spoken by these people.

1869 *Nation* 30 Dec. 583/1 'Pennsylvania Dutch.' It is an acknowledged fact that children of German immigrants cease to speak German properly if left to themselves. **1872** S. S. HALDEMAN (*title*), Pennsylvania Dutch; a dialect of South German with an infusion of English. **1879** in *Penna.-German Soc. Proc.* XXX. p. xi, Eighteen to twenty per cent of all the words commonly used in Pennsylvania Dutch are either English or a compound of English and German. **1882** P. E. GIBBONS *'Pennsylvania Dutch'* 381 The 'Pennsylvania Dutch,' which is spoken over a large portion of our own State, . . . seems to be nearly homogeneous.

+**Pennsylvania Dutch,** *a.* Of or pertaining to the Pennsylvania Dutch. (Cf. DUTCH *a.* 2 b.) — **1882** P. E. GIBBONS *'Pennsylvania Dutch'* 401 A 'Pennsylvania Dutch' remedy for whooping-cough. **1894** ROBLEY *Bourbon Co., Kansas* 155 Mr. Miller was from Pennsylvania, of the old 'Pennsylvania Dutch' stock, and was a most excellent man and citizen. **1910** *Harper's Mag.* Aug. 474/1 We do not know how the Pennsylvania Dutch ideal of rural life was evolved.

+**Pennsylvania Dutchman.** A person of Pennsylvania Dutch stock. — **1870** NOWLAND *Indianapolis* 20 His dress was something like that of a 'Pennsylvania Dutchman.' **1873** BEADLE *Undevel. West* 403 An old Pennsylvania Dutchman, with a 'White Cherokee' wife.

+**Pennsylvania German. 1.** A descendant of a German belonging to the Pennsylvania Dutch stock. **2.** =PENNSYLVANIA DUTCH *n.* 2. Also attrib. — **(1) 1869** *Nation* 30 Dec. 584/1 Divine service among the Pennsylvania Germans is held in High German. **1895** in M. B. Lambert *Penna.-German Dict.* p. xi, It is not intended to instruct those who consider their education completed, but to aid such Pennsylvania Germans as are anxious to acquire a knowledge of the English language. **(2) 1869** *Nation* 30 Dec. 583/2 The Pennsylvania German is a South German dialect, . . . more or less interspersed with Germanized English words. **1875** A. R. HORNE (*title*), Pennsylvania German Manual.

+**Pennsylvania money.** Money issued by Pennsylvania before 1789. — **1771** FRANKLIN *Autobiog.* 286 Therefore I immediately agreed on the terms of fifty pounds a year, Pennsylvania money. **1787** CUTLER in *Life & Corr.* I. 248 Bill, 6 *s.*, 6 *d.*, Pennsylvania money.

+**Pennsylvanian,** *n.* A citizen or resident of Pennsylvania.

1698 THOMAS *West-New-Jersey* 17 Trades-Men, whose Wages are upon the same Foot with the Pensilvanians. **1747** WHITEFIELD *Works* II. (1771) 94 The Pensylvanians I am sure will soon regret the loss of you. **1782** CRÈVECŒUR *Letters* 58 Europeans . . . become, in the course of a few generations, not only Americans in general, but either Pennsylvanians, Virginians, or provincials, under some other name. **1838** *S. Lit. Messenger* IV. 165/1 Mr. Ingersoll, being a Pennsylvanian, stands impartial between the two extremes of the Union. **1862** MOORE *Rebellion Rec.* V. II. 22 Words of warm congratulation were sent to the dashing Pennsylvanian by the Commanding General. **1910** *Harper's Mag.* Aug. 473/1 Georg Schock . . . is a Pennsylvanian.

b. *pl.* In the Revolutionary War, a regiment mustered in Pennsylvania.

1776 *Battle of Brooklyn* I. i, Know, then, that the Marylanders, the Pennsylvanians, and the rife [*sic*] regiments, are mostly composed of *Europeans*.

+**Pennsylvanian,** *a.*

1. Residing in, belonging to, or characteristic of Pennsylvania.

1698 THOMAS *West-New-Jersey* 2 They (as the Pensilvanian Indians) observe the New Moons with great Devotion. **1744** B. FRANKLIN (*title*), An Account of the New Invented Pennsylvanian Fire-Places; . . . With Directions for Putting Them Up. **1825** *Wesleyan Meth. Mag.* IV. App. 455/1, I had my first view of the city of Philadelphia . . . on the Pennsylvanian shore. **1827** J. BERNARD *Retrosp.* 183 Like Pennsylvanian 'bundlers,' they passed the night in innocent conversation. **1853** BUNN *Old Eng. & New Eng.* I. 167 Mr. Nicholas Biddle . . . issued the notorious Pennsylvanian bonds.

2. In the names of various plants.

Cf. PENNSYLVANIA 2.

1785 MARSHALL *Amer. Grove* 7 *Andromeda racemosa.* Pennsylvanian Red-bud Andromeda. *Ib.* 12 *Aristolochia frutescens.* Pennsylvanian Shrubby Birthwort. **1814** BIGELOW *Florula Bostoniensis* 107 *Saxifraga Pennsylvanica.* Pennsylvanian Saxifrage. . . . A tall, green plant, of little beauty, growing in meadows. **1843** TORREY *Flora N.Y.* I. 15 *Ranunculus Pennsylvanicus.* Pennsylvanian Crowfoot. . . . Banks of rivers, in damp soils, chiefly on the Hudson River and in the northern counties. **1878** Killebrew *Tenn. Grasses* 230 *Eatonia Pennsylvanica,* Pennsylvanian Eatonia. . . . Cattle seem to prefer it to any other pickings in the woods.

+**Pennsylvania oil region(s).** A region in Pennsylvania where petroleum was first produced commercially in the United States. — **1862** *Prelim. Rep. 8th Census* 72 The Pennsylvania oil region . . . has thus far been the principal source [of petroleum]. **1867** *Atlantic Mo.* Jan. 101/1 On a recent journey to the Pennsylvania oil regions, I stopped . . . at a village [etc.]. **1884** *Boston Jrnl.* 22 Nov. 2/5 One of the most startling features in the Pennsylvania oil-region is the number of deserted villages, which have been caused by the exhaustion of oil-wells. **1888** *Chautauquan* Feb. 271/1 An oil well can be drilled . . . in less than one-tenth of the time that was required when the Pennsylvania oil regions were first explored.

+**Pennsylvania wagon.** A strong wagon, such as a Conestoga, made in Pennsylvania. — **1810** M. DWIGHT *Journey to Ohio* 39 This line is the shape of a Pennsylvania waggon. **1825** N. H. CARTER *Lett. from Europe* (1829) I. 58 The carts [of Liverpool] . . . are apparently more unwieldy than Pennsylvania wagons. **1841** R. PARK *Pantology* 462 The Pennsylvania waggon, is remarkable for its great size. **1883** ZEIGLER & GROSSCUP *Alleghanies* 237 Then would follow a strong team of horses drawing a white-covered, Pennsylvania wagon. **1891** WELCH *Recoll. 1830–40* 66 Enormous arks of the so-called 'Pennsylvania wagons,' driven with four to ten horses.

***Penny.** Also †**penie, pen(e)y.**

1. ***a.** An English coin of the value of 1/12 of a shilling; the value of this coin. **b.** One of various other coins of about the same value, as the Dutch *penning*, or coins struck in the colonies: (see also quot. 1828).

See COPPER *n.*[1] 3, note. The English coin until about 1685 was of silver; since then of copper or bronze. The quotation of 1836 may belong to sense 2.

1634 WOOD *New Eng. Prospect* 49 Foure Egges may be had for a Penny. **1649** *R.I. Col. Rec.* I. 217 Noe person . . . shall take any black peage of the Indians but at four a penny. **1655** *R.I. Court Rec.* I. 9 We find for the pla[intiff] his Bill due of twenty pounds . . . at 6 pr penie white, & 3 pr penie black marchantable [peag]. **1718** *Mass. H. Rep. Jrnl.* II. 68 The Sum of Five Pounds Six Shillings and a Peny, . . . [shall] be given to Capt. Zechariah Tuthill. **1726** PENHALLOW *Indian Wars* 90 [They] sold a great number of them [*sc.* ducks] to the English for a penny a dozen. **1787** CUTLER in *Life & Corr.* I. 308 The fish are sold alive; if they are dead they abate one penny on the pound. **1789** MORSE *Amer. Geog.* 349 Four white grains and three black ones, should pass for the value of a stiver or penny. **1789** *Ann. 1st Congress* I. 218 At this time [before the Revolution] . . . molasses paid [a duty of] one penny sterling per gallon. **1828** WEBSTER s.v. *Farthing,* The *penny* is of different value from the English penny, and different in different states. **1836** CROCKETT *Exploits* 125 If he had stolen the pennies from his grandmother's eyes in Louisiana, the people in Texas would have nothing to do with that affair.

+**2.** The American one-cent piece; an imitation of this.

'There is a bad habit, west of New England, of calling a cent a penny' (B. '77).

1861 *Vanity Fair* 15 June 281/1 [The] penny . . . came heads every time! **1876** *Wide Awake* 43/2 Two bootblacks strolled along, jingling pennies in their pockets. **1885** *Santa Fé Wkly. New Mexican* 9 July 2/2 Major Van Horn . . . had the boys . . . ride right through Tularosa, without buying a penny's worth of anything. **1903** *N.Y. Times* 12 Sept., 3,000,000,393 pennies . . . [have] been shipped from the Philadelphia mint to various parts of the country. **1910** RAINE *B. O'Connor* 22 A Lincoln penny, and a silver-plated watch. **1910** *Sunset* March 333/2 More than two generations have passed since the little penny of the 'Indian Head' was first introduced.

3. *attrib.* and *comb.* **a.** Designating an article or an amount of something costing one penny.

1647 *Portsmouth Rec.* 36 The penie loafe shall way 8 ounces. **1677** *Boston Rec.* 109 Keene to keepe cookes shopps & sell penny beere. **1840** GARRISON in W. J. & F. L. Garrison *Life W. L. Garrison* II. 418 Leavitt has started a penny daily, to advocate the third-party project. **1851** *Harper's Mag.* Jan. 151/4 The baker gave him the three penny rolls. **1857** UNDERHILL & THOMPSON *Elephant Club* 72 You will, under no circumstances, buy and smoke a 'penny grab.' **1861** *Vanity Fair* 2 March 98/1 Mr. McCrowder . . . found himself lying on the floor of a small and unknown room, at once lighted and perfumed by a penny dip. **1869** J. R. BROWNE *Adv. Apache Country* 59 Red, white, green, and gray blankets [for the Indians] . . . and penny whistles for the small fry. **1892** *York County Hist. Rev.* 32 They manufacture all kinds of stick candy and make a prominent specialty of penny goods.

b. In special combinations.

Penny ferry, a ferry that charges a penny; +*p.-pitching,* a game in which the contestants try to pitch a penny on or close to a mark; +*p. poker den,* a cheap dive; +*p. savings bank,* a savings bank that accepts deposits of as little as a penny.

1658 *Charlestown Land Rec.* 81 The highway . . . Runneth from the peney ferre to malden meting house. **1871** BAGG *At Yale* 534 Perhaps to the list of student amusements should be added the games of . . . leap-frog, . . . penny-pitching [etc.]. **1849** FOSTER *N.Y. in Slices* 29 We come upon the penny poker dens of the thieves and negroes. **1891** *Atlantic Mo.* June 814/2 A penny savings bank, chartered under state law, was organized at Chattanooga about ten months ago.

+**Penny ante.** A poker game in which the ante is limited to a penny.

1855 M. THOMPSON *Doesticks* 259 Napoleon spends most of his time playing penny 'ante' with the three Graces. **1867** L. BAKER *U.S. Secret Service* 243, I used to play penny-ante when I ran a flat-boat out West. **1883** *Century Mag.* June 273/2 They would . . . make up a little game of 'penny ante' around Armstrong's center-table. **1902** LORIMER *Lett. Merchant* 148 It was all right to play whist in the parlor if he'd give up penny-ante at the Dutchman's.

b. *comb.* Cheap.

1865 *Nation* I. 76 Look at those fellows now! . . . a'n't they a 'penny ante' lookin' lot?

Pennycress. A Eurasian plant with round and flat pods, *Thlaspi arvense.* {1713–} — **1817–8** EATON *Botany* (1822) 486 *Thlaspi arvense,* penny-cress. **1843** TORREY *Flora N.Y.* I. 64 *Thlaspi arvense.* Mithridate Mustard, or Penny Cress. . . . In the State of New-York. . . . Doubtless an introduced species in North America. **1863** GRAY *Botany* p. xc.

Penny paper. A newspaper selling for a penny; a cheap newspaper. {a paper selling for an English penny, 1711} — **1839** BRIGGS *H. Franco* II. 2 Three or four cartmen . . . were seated on their cart tails, each of them studying a penny paper. **1842** BUCKINGHAM *Slave States* I. 372 The three others are small sheets called 'Penny Papers,' though this is certainly a misnomer, as no copper coins of any kind circulate in New Orleans. **1894** FORD *P. Stirling* 297 The third [headline], printed in an insignificant little penny paper, never read and almost unknown by reading people.

Penny post. a. A service, principally local, for the conveyance of letters at a basic rate of one penny each. {1680–} +**b.** A mailman.

The official postal service, established in 1775 by the Continental Congress and maintained and improved by the U.S. government, gradually took the place of the penny post, though the phrase remained after the service was obsolete.

1730 *Md. Hist. Mag.* XIX. 187 This method I thought more convenient then running the risque of penny posts. **1753** in Singleton *Social N.Y.* 38 And all letters for persons living in town that remain uncalled for on post nights, will on Monday morning be sent out by a penny post provided for that purpose. **1788** *Deane P.* 225 Your favour of yesterday by penny Post reminds me of not acknowledging the receipt of your former favour. **1853** *Knickerb.* XLII. 628, [I] send this by the penny-post, instead of by the great leather and padlocked-mail. **1855** HOLBROOK *Among Mail Bags* 103 At about the same time, I consulted one of the Brooklyn penny-posts, whose beat took in Pat's residence. **1868** HAWTHORNE *Notebooks* I. 26 Fame! Some very humble persons in a town may be said to possess it,—as the penny-post, the town-crier.

Penny press. *collect.* Papers that sell for a penny; the persons, organizations, etc., that publish such papers. {1860–} — **1840** *Picayune* 15 Sept. 2/2 The six-penny journals have latterly grown wise enough to drop the naughty habit in which they used to indulge of swearing at the penny press. **1855** I. C. PRAY *Mem. J. G. Bennett* 175 There were other persons unfitted by temper . . . to make the necessary demonstration in behalf of the Penny Press.

***Pennyroyal,** *n.*

+**1.** A native American mint (*Hedeoma pulegioïdes*) similar to the European pennyroyal. Sometimes called *American pennyroyal.*

1630 HIGGINSON *New-England* 9 Diuers excellent Pot-herbs grow abundantly among the Grasse, as . . . Penyroyall, Wintersauerie, Sorrel [etc.]. **1698** THOMAS *Pensilvania* 21 [There are] most sorts of Saladings . . . in great plenty also, as . . . Penny-Royal and Purslain. **1795** WINTERBOTHAM *Hist. View* III. 398 Among the native and uncultivated plants of New-England, the following have been employed for medicinal purposes: . . . Horsemint, spearmint, watermint, and Pennyroyal. **1832** CHILD *Frugal Housewife* 115 Some make a decoction of indigo-weed, and other of pennyroyal, and bathe horses with it, to defend them from insects. **1847** DARLINGTON *Weeds & Plants* 232 American-Pennyroyal . . . [is] in general use as a popular diaphoretic, carminative, &c. **1883** SMITH *Geol. Survey Ala.* 350 Pennyroyal, a lime-loving plant, is found in most of the fence corners where this [red or yellow clayey] soil predominates.

attrib. **1847** *Knickerb.* XXX. 562 They didn't help me any more than it would to turn a colt into a penny-royal pasture.

b. *Oil of pennyroyal,* a commercial oil used as a medicine or an insectifuge.

1815 *Niles' Reg.* IX. 94/2 Oils, of mint, sassafras, worm and penyroyal [*sic*] and castor, . . . are to be found in our druggists' shops. **1897** *Outing* XXX. 377/1 As good a mixture as I know of [for an insectifuge] contains: Three ounces pine-tar, one ounce oil of pennyroyal, and two ounces castor oil.

c. A medicine or insectifuge made from pennyroyal.

1854 S. SMITH *Down East* 103, I give her sage, . . . and cammermile, and pennyryal, and motherwort, and balm. **1884** *Century Mag.* Nov. 109 Jack! Jack! you've forgotten to take your pennyroyal. **1903** WHITE *Forest* 106 [Each] heralds the particular merits of his own fly-dope. [There are] eager advocates of the advantages of . . . pennyroyal.

+**2.** One of various other plants, as a species of mountain mint.

See also FALSE PENNYROYAL.

1784 CUTLER in *Mem. Academy* I. 463 *Trichostema.* . . . Wild Lavender. Great Pennyroyal. . . . In old fields. **1806** CLARK in *Lewis & C. Exped.* V. (1905) 110, I observe here . . . water penerial (pennyroyal), elder, coalts foot [etc.]. **1894** *Amer. Folk-Lore* VII. 96 *Pycnanthemum lanceolatum,* . . . pennyroyal, Minn.

+**3.** =PENNYROYAL HYMN.

1905 *Methodist Rev.* LXXXVII. 704 The attitude to take toward the sort of tune . . . variously denominated, 'gospel song,' 'spiritual song,' 'pennyroyal,' has cost the Commission a good deal of vexation of spirit.

+**Pennyroyal,** *a.* (See quot. 1902.) — **1864** *Ohio Agric. Rep.* XVIII. 21 If the gentleman has any Pennyroyal cattle I hope to see them at the Fair. **1902** CLAPIN 304 *Pennyroyal,* in the West, used adjectively to describe inferior stock. 'A pennyroyal steer or bull.'

+**Pennyroyal hymn.** (See quot. 1850.) — **1850** JUDD *R. Edney* 274 He sang one, popularly known as a pennyroyal hymn,—a measure that combines unction and vivacity. **1895** WIGGIN *Village Watch-Tower* 115 It was pennyrial hymns she used to sing mostly.

+**Pennyroyal tea.** A tea steeped from the leaves of pennyroyal. — **1841** *Knickerb.* XVII. 391 A little penner'yal tea would be good for Burks. **1874** B. F. TAYLOR *World on Wheels* 99 They give penny-royal tea to bring out the measles. **1894** R. E. ROBINSON *Danvis Folks* 5 It would be a good thing for her tu take a leetle pennyr'yal tea.

***Pennyweight.** A unit of Troy weight equal to 1/20 of an ounce. — **1704** *Boston News-Letter* 19 June 2/1 He also Seiz'd 45 Ounces and Seven Penny weight of Gold of the said Pirates. **1792** *Ann. 2d Congress* 71 Cents; each . . . to contain eleven pennyweights of copper. **1843** *Niles' Nat. Reg.* 192/3 A gold mine has been lately discovered . . . out of which two hands obtained, in one week, about eighty pennyweights of the precious metal. **1883** ZEIGLER & GROSSCUP *Alleghanies* 320 The stream through Heddin's property . . . was worked at the rate of ten pennyweight a day per man.

Pennywinkle(r). =PERIWINKLE. {*dial.*} — **1881** INGERSOLL *Oyster-Industry* 246 *Pennywinkle; Pennywinkler.*—The mollusks of the genera *Fulgur* and *Sycotypus,* interchangeably. **1883** *Nat. Museum Bul.* No. 27, 193 *Littorina littorea.* . . . Pennywinkle. This species is not an indigenous one, having been introduced from Europe.

***Pennywort. 1.** Any species of the genus *Hydrocotyle.* +**2.** An herb with white or purplish flowers, *Obolaria virginica.* — **(1) 1791** MUHLENBERG *Index Florae* 165 *Hydrocotyle americana,* Penny-wort. **1843** TORREY *Flora N.Y.* I. 262 *Hydrocotyle umbellata.* . . . Many-flowered Marsh Penny-wort. . . . Overflowed boggy places and shallow ponds. **1875** *Amer. Naturalist* IX. 388 In the water, beside many of the grasses and sedges, are found pennywort [etc.]. **(2) 1817–8** EATON *Botany* (1822) 364 *Obolaria virginica,* penny-wort. **1901** MOHR *Plant Life Ala.* 672.

Penologist. A person versed in the science or practice of penology. {1838–} — **1885** *American* XI. 23 Much less is it near the standards of our own American penologists. **1892** *Advance* 15 Dec., Major McClaughery, of Chicago, formerly prison warden, and still one of the leading penologists. **1912** NICHOLSON *Hoosier Chron.* 356 The indeterminate sentence law—was praised by penologists all over the country.

***Pension,** *n.* Also †**pention.**

***1.** A periodical money payment made to a person for past services, or as a bounty or emolument; +esp. such a payment by the national government to an old soldier, his widow, or his minor children left orphans.

1717 *Mass. H. Rep. Jrnl.* I. 189 And that an Annual Pension for Life may be Settled upon him, having no hopes of being otherwise than a Creeple all his Days. **1792** *History of Congress* (1834) 539 They would be entitled to pensions as invalids. **1839** *Diplom. Corr. Texas* I. (1908) 414 He then assured me that if (it) became necessary he would not only restrain the Indians within the limits of the U. States by force, but that he would withhold their pensions and supplies which would entirely incapacitate them from doing us any injury. **1840** *Niles' Nat. Reg.* 18 July 320/2 A friend of ours lately met an old soldier of the revolution . . . [seeking] evidence to substantiate his claims to a pension. **1865** *Atlantic Mo.* Feb. 237/1 The immense collection of back pay, bounties, pensions, and prize-money . . . is Special Relief. **1890** WIGGIN *Timothy's Quest* 118 Joel Whitten's widder's just drawed his pension along o' his bein' in the war o' 1812. **1900** *Congress. Rec.* 3 Jan. 638/1 A bill . . . granting pensions to the survivors of the war of 1861 and 1865.

2. Attrib. with *act, attorney, bureau,* etc.

1749 *N.H. Probate Rec.* III. 733, I give . . . all my Waidges Prize money Pention money [etc.]. **1839** *S. Lit. Messenger* V. 314/1 What has America done to reward her warriors and statesmen? . . . A few tardy pension acts . . . [are] the tributes their worth has received. **1886** ALTON *Among Law-Makers* 38 She was a soldier's widow and had what is known as a 'pension claim' against the Government. **1887** *Courier-Journal* 4 Jan. 1/2 (*caption*), Commissioner Black's Determined and Energetic Prosecution of Bogus Pension Claimants. **1888** *Nation* 2 Feb. 84/1 It is impossible to imagine Gov. Hill vetoing the pension grab or issuing the tariff-reform message. **1893** *Harper's Mag.* Jan. 235/1 The increased expenditures arising from the pension legislation of the Fifty-first Congress have attracted general notice. **1898** *Kansas City Star* 18 Dec. 5/3 Assistant Secretary Webster Davis . . . is urged by all who fancy that his extremely liberal pension views would be put in practice, to the delight of the pension attorneys and with an immediate increase of the pension vote. **1900** *Congress. Rec.* 8 Jan. 676/2 The other amendment urged by the Grand Army . . . is that in estimating disabilities the Pension Bureau shall aggregate minor disabilities so as to give a soldier under that act a pensionable status. *Ib.* 19 Jan. 1004/1 Of the money awarded to the soldiers . . . over two-thirds, or one-half, went to the pension sharks of Washington.

Pension, *v.* {1642–} *tr.* To provide with a pension. {1702–} — **1832** KENNEDY *Swallow Barn* I. 47 [She] is supposed to have pensioned out several poor families; besides being a stirring advocate of the scheme for colonizing the negroes. **1900** *Congress. Rec.* 29 Jan. 1265/2 It is not proposed to pension them beyond eight or twelve dollars. **1923** *World's Work* XLV. 466/2, I do not recognize any public obligation to pension women who now, nearly sixty years after the Civil War, become the wives of veterans of that war.

Pensionable, *a.* Entitling a person to a pension; qualified for a pension. {1892} — **1882** *West Chester* (Pa.) *Local News* II. No. 19, 1 Those who incurred pensionable disabilities. **1889** *Atlantic Mo.* June 797 Our brevet martyrs speedily reduced themselves to a pensionable condition. **1893** *Harper's Mag.* Jan. 237/2 In 1886 the eight-dollar rate of widows, minors, and other pensionable dependents of enlisted men was increased to twelve dollars. **1900** *Congress. Rec.* 8 Jan. 676/2 She is not pensionable under this act.

+**Pension agent.** One who acts as agent for getting a person a pension. — **1848** *Whig Almanac 1849* 28/2 There are 43 Pension Agents, who charge $2 on every $100 they pay out. **1884** *Century Mag.* July 433/2 This document goes to the Pension Agent for the district where the claimant lives. **1892** *York County Hist. Rev.* 10 Mr. Strayer has been a resident of York for 35 years, and is Pension Agent. **1902** HANDSAKER in *Pioneer Life* 38 There was no necessity to employ a pension agent ('sharks,' they were called).

+**Pension bill.** A legislative bill authorizing the payment of a pension to designated persons. *Private pension bill,* such a bill authorizing a pension for a particular person. — **1868** *N.Y. Herald* 10 July 6/1 In the evening session a long list of private pension bills was passed. **1887** *Courier-Journal* 6 Feb. 1/7 The United States Senate ... ground out sixty-six more pension bills. *Ib.* 7 Feb. 4/4 He has recently signed a Mexican 'service' pension bill.

***Pensioner.** One who receives a pension, esp. for past military service. (See also INVALID PENSIONER.) — **1819** *Niles' Reg.* XVII. 99/2 A certain pensioner had deposited the whole amount of his pension in the savings bank! **1840** *Picayune* 24 Oct. 2/4 Died in Boston. . . . Mr. Wm. Pierce, aged 96 years, . . . a pensioner of the Revolution. **1848** *Whig Almanac 1849* 28/2 The number of pensioners of all classes on the rolls of the Pension Office, is twenty-three thousand and nineteen. **1900** *Congress. Rec.* 16 Feb. 1889/1 It is in the matter of the unjust pensioner that the American people feel they are being outraged.

+**Pension-grabber. 1.** One who is quick to claim a pension right. **2.** A congressman who votes for bigger and more pensions. — **(1) 1887** *Courier-Journal* 10 Feb. 4/5 It is not so hard a fate, after all, that keeps the Confederate soldier from appearing as a pension grabber. **(2) 1900** *Congress. Rec.* 16 Feb. 1886/2, I hope it will do some good in stopping the greyhound speed which some of you pension grabbers want to make in giving pensions to soldiers.

Pension law. A law authorizing pension payments. — **1838** *S. Lit. Messenger* IV. 796 When the revolutionary pension-law was enacted, a majority of the war-worn veterans had travelled . . . beyond the reach of human reward. **1893** *Harper's Mag.* Jan. 235/2 Disability, within the meaning of the pension laws, may be defined as the effect of any disease.

Pension list. A list of soldiers qualified for or receiving pensions. {1816}

1787 TYLER *Contrast* IV. 1, I came hither to solicit the honourable Congress, that a number of my brave soldiers may be put upon the pension-list. **1797** *Ann. 5th Congress* I. 677 A bill passed that House . . . for placing certain persons on the pension list. **1803** *Ann. 7th Congress* 2 Sess. 520 Every man in that state (Connecticut) was on the pension list who ought to be placed there. **1819** *Niles' Reg.* XVII. 99/2 The pension list of the United States is of a formidable length. **1848** *Whig Almanac 1849* 40/1 Among the results of the War with Mexico may be mentioned an increase . . . of the Federal Debt and the Pension List. **1893** *Harper's Mag.* Jan. 235/1 Is the pension list a roll of honor? All patriotic citizens agree that it ought to be.

Pension office. A federal office that administers the pensions granted by the government. — **1778** *Jrnls. Cont. Congress* X. 19 *Resolved,* . . . That a Pension Office be forthwith opened, and kept in the Place where Congress shall from Time to Time hold its Session. **1834** JACKSON in *Pres. Mess. & P.* III. 114 Information has from time to time been communicated to the Pension Office questioning or denying the right of persons placed upon the pension list to the bounty of the country. **1893** *Congress. Rec.* 16 Dec. 290/1 It is a chilly day when a Congressman goes to the Pension Office. **1898** *Kansas City Star* 21 Dec. 3/4 A new section was inserted, making the chief of the record and pension office a brigadier general.

***Pension roll.** =PENSION LIST. — **1828** SHERBURNE *Memoirs* xi. 242 This gentleman . . . forwarded to me the certificate of the continuation of my name on the pension roll. **1893** *Harper's Mag.* Jan. 238/1 The last Revolutionary soldier borne upon the pension roll died in 1869. **1900** *Congress. Rec.* 19 Jan. 1009/1 The pension roll of the United States to-day is . . . the grandest record of brave and patriotic soldiery that the world has ever known.

Penstock. {1607–} +**a.** One of various tubes, pipes, or open troughs used for the conveyance of water. Also attrib. +**b.** An open trough or cistern which contains a supply of water. +**c.** (See quot. 1864.)

1799 *Amer. Philos. Soc.* IV. 349 Let ABCD Fig. 1 represent a large cistern or penstock, and MKLN an orifice made in one of its sides. **1828** WEBSTER *Penstock,* a narrow or confined place formed by a frame of timber planked or boarded, for holding or conducting the water of a mill-pond to a wheel, and furnished with a flood gate which may be shut or opened at pleasure. **1846** EMMONS *Agric. N.Y.* I. 265 The penstock water of the city [of Albany] contains, of Soluble matter, per gallon, 4.64; Organic matter, 8.00. **1851** CIST *Cincinnati* 103 Here the first fire-plug,—a wooden pent-stock [*sic*]—was placed. **1864** WEBSTER 966/2 *Pen-stock,* . . . the barrel of a wooden pump. **1886** *Leslie's Mo.* XXI. 745/1 A never-failing penstock offers refreshment to thirsty beasts. **1894** *Pop. Science Mo.* XLV. 613 A penstock . . . is a great tube, usually . . . of boiler plate, . . . conveying water under head into the wheel-case in which the turbine revolves. **1898** HARPER *S. B. Anthony* I. 7 In the other end were the sink and the 'penstock' which brought water from a clear, cold spring.

Pentado(e). (See PINTADO.)

***Penthouse.** Also †**pentice.** Any of various subsidiary structures, usu. having a sloping roof.

1651 *Dedham Rec.* III. 197 He shall . . . shingle the penthouse ouer the Bell [of the meetinghouse]. **1701** *Boston Rec.* 11 No person shall Erect or set up any Pentice, jetty or Pendal over any of the Streets, lanes or highwayes of this Town. **1790** *Phila. Ordinances* (1812) 127 Any person . . . [who shall] suspend them [*sc.* goods] from the pent-house of any house . . . [shall pay] two dollars. **1876** W. M. FISHER *Californians* 13 Two engineers sit in front in their little pent-house, . . . one with hand on a long lever by the furnace-door. **1921** *Country Life* April 65/1 Two of the elevators were designed to run to the roof, where a pent-house . . . was being built.

Pen trap. A trap consisting of a pen into which something can be enticed or driven. — **1884** *Nat. Museum Bul.* No. 27, 1017 Pen Traps. Pocket Traps. Fishslide or Trap. . . . Made of wooden slats set in a sloping frame, with box at upper end. **1902** WHITE *Conjuror's House* ii, Then a little movement brought the scene flashing before her—the white snow, . . . the little square pen-trap.

Pentstemon. [Named, 1748, by John Mitchell, Amer. botanist.] A genus of herbs, chiefly American, of the family Scrophulariaceae; a plant of this genus. — **1843** TORREY *Flora N.Y.* II. 35 *Pentstemon Pubescens.* . . . Pubescent Pentstemon. . . . Hills and borders of woods; north and west of Catskill. **1883** *Century Mag.* XXVI. 808/2 From whatever side one approaches Santa Anita in May, he will drive through a wild garden . . . [of] scarlet pentstemons, blue larkspur [etc.]. **1915** ARMSTRONG & THORNBER *Western Wild Flowers* 478 There are a great many kinds of Pentstemon and some of our handsomest and most conspicuous western flowers are included among them.

+**Pent way.** *New Eng.* 'A road, not public, and generally kept closed' (B. '77).

+**Peon,** *n.* [Sp.] {1828–, in S. America}

The early use of *peon* in India is presumably borrowed from Portuguese and French, and has no connection with the American borrowing from Spanish.

1. *S.W.* **a.** A person held in serfdom by a landlord or creditor; a servant. Also transf. **b.** A common laborer.

1826 DEWEES *Lett. from Texas* 56 The Peons, or lower class, are a sort of slaves, who are employed by the aristocracy. **1848** *Santa Fe Repub.* 12 Feb. 1/4 A good looking Mexican girl . . . was held in servitude as a peon, having been sold by her father to pay a debt. **1857** DAVIS *El Gringo* 412 A Nabajo never sends his wife to saddle his horse, but does it himself if he has no peon. **1882** CHASE *Editor's Run in N. Mex.* 107 Maxwell's force . . . [consisted] of two or three whites, a few Mexicans in his service, and a few peons, or Mexican young men bought and owned, according to a custom then [1856] prevailing in the Territory. **1890** *Stock Grower & Farmer* 25 Jan. 3/4 The dressed beef man wired instructions to his Wyoming peon.

2. Attrib. with *class, dog, labor,* etc.

1847 HENRY *Campaign Sk.* 134 This 'peone' system is fully equal to our slavery. **1865** *Wkly. New Mexican* 22 June 1/3 The peon law [has] been overthrown. **1869** J. R. BROWNE *Adv. Apache Country* 203 Down in a beautiful little valley . . . stand the reducing works, store-houses, and peon quarters of the Mowry Silver Mines. **1874** RAYMOND *6th Rep. Mines* 332 Peon labor was but a trifling expense to the employer. **1890** *Stock Grower & Farmer* 10 May 3/3 The former peon class needs industrial education. **1902** CLAPIN 304 *Peon-dog,* in Texas, a name sometimes given to the hairless Mexican dog.

+**Peon,** *v. tr.* To reduce (one) to the status of a peon. *colloq.* — **1895** REMINGTON *Pony Tracks* 92 The Mexican punchers . . . are mostly *peoned,* or in hopeless debt to their *patrons.*

+**Peonage.** {1870} A form of servitude involving the holding of peons or dependents for service, esp. in payment of debts. — **1849** *31st Congress 1 Sess.* Sen. Ex. Doc. No. 64, 49 From this cause, and the miserable system of 'peonage' that prevails, the products of agriculture are barely sufficient to support the inhabitants [north of El Paso]. **1888** J. J. WEBB *Adventures* 101 The system of peonage, or voluntary servitude, was a fixed institution. **1893** LUMMIS *Land of Poco Tiempo* 20 Peonage in disguise is still effective in New Mexico.

+**Peonism.** =prec. *Obs.* — **1850** D. WEBSTER *Works* V. 351, I understand that *peonism,* a sort of penal servitude, exists [in Calif.]. **1857** DAVIS *El Gringo* 231 Another peculiar feature of New Mexico is the system of domestic servitude called peonism, that has existed, and still exists, in all the Spanish American colonies.

***Peony.** Any one of various plants of the genus *Paeonia,* or the flower of such a plant.

1777 CUTLER in *Life & Corr.* I. 63 Planted out in my borders in a great alley . . . early and late Daffies, and Peonies. **1840** DEWEY *Mass. Flower-*

ing Plants 29 *Pæonia officinalis* is the well-known peony of our gardens. **1880** *Harper's Mag.* Dec. 87/2 There was a 'bow-pot' of great red peonies, . . . set under the chimney in the well-whited fire-place. **1923** Wyatt *Invis. Gods* 16 An aster bed in the center of its lawn surrounded by the rosy foam of peonies, the sprays of bleeding heart.

+**b.** A tea made from the peony.

1886 *Outing* Dec. 229/2 Among her other remedies were anise seed, peony and chamomile.

***People.**

+**1. a.** The Negro field hands on a plantation. **b.** The body of Negro slaves on a plantation or under one owner. *Obs.*

1771 *Md. Hist. Mag.* XIV. 135 You will have it that my People are not well fed, it is true they do not live so well as our House negroes, But full as well as any Plantation negroes. **1833** A. Ferguson *Notes Tour U.S.* 209 We walked out to see what Mr C—— called his *people*, or, in other words, the slaves, of whom he possesses about 200. **1851** in Bassett *Plantation Overseer* 190 Youre people are all well at present. **1858** in Commons, etc. *Doc. Hist.* I. 145 Favouring and siding in any difficulty with the people, against the Drivers. **1863** Hopley *Life in South* I. 44 'My own people,' I repeated to myself, then they *are* slaves.

2. *People of color*, (see Color 2).

People's party. +A political party thought of as including or representing everybody; spec., the official designation of the Populist party (q.v.). Also attrib.

1811 *Niles' Reg.* I. 9/2, I will attach myself, as an editor, to no party but the People's Party, whose wish is '*peace, liberty and safety.*' **1880** *Cimarron News & Press* 26 Aug. 2/2 The convention of the People's Party met at the Court House . . . last Saturday. **1896** *Congress. Rec.* 15 May 5297/2 It may be, sir, that this People's Party has 'fanatics' in it; it may be that we are 'wild-eyed lunatics.' **1900** *Ib.* 25 Jan. 1169/1 A statement . . . entitled 'A reply to the People's Party Handbook.'

***Pepper.**

***1.** A well-known pungent condiment.

1640 *Conn. Rec.* I. 453 The Inuentory of Tho. Johnson . . . a shute of apparrell . . . halfe a pownd of peppr, a seefe bottom. **1715** *Boston News-Letter* 21 Feb. 2/2 The following Goods were stolen out of the Ware-House Seller . . . viz 13 Cheshire Cheeses, . . . a considerable quantity of Pepper, some Candles and Brimston. **1851** Melville *Moby-Dick* 73 That smoking chowder was made of small juicy clams, . . . the whole enriched with butter, and plentifully seasoned with pepper and salt.

+**2.** Any species of Capsicum or its fruit. Also with specifying term.

See also Bird pepper, *Cayenne pepper* s.v. Cayenne, Green pepper, etc.

1756 Kalm *Resa* II. 209 Capsicum annum. . . . Kallades här Peppar. **1760** *Boston Rec.* 61 Pickled cucumbers & peppers. **1858** *Texas Almanac 1859* 186 The finest white onions and Chili pepper are also raised here. **1862** *Ill. Agric. Soc. Trans.* V. 543 The balance of the bed you may sow with peppers and celery. **1878** *Harper's Mag.* Jan. 272/2 Of these the guisado of the country would be made, which answers to the *pot au feu* of the French, only more warmly flavored with this pepper. **1887** *Harper's Mag.* Jan. 310/1 The pepper is another hot-blooded vegetable that shivers at the suggestion of a frost. **1911** *Grocer's Encycl.* 99 There are many species of Capsicum, all native to the warm parts of America. . . . The small fruited types . . . are best known popularly as 'Chilies,' and the larger as 'peppers.'

+**3.** *ellipt.* =Pepper tree.

1893 Sanborn *S. Calif.* 116 There are several handsome avenues shaded with peppers. **1897** *Outing* March 582/1 The peppers throve and the magnolias didn't.

4. Attrib. and comb. with *bag, plant, pod, shaker.*

1787 Tyler *Contrast* III. i, I should like to take a sling with him, or a drap of cyder with a pepper-pod in it. **1850** Hawthorne *Scarlet Letter* 32 The Custom-House marker imprinted [my name] . . . on pepper-bags, and baskets of anatto. **1855** *Amer. Inst. N.Y. Trans.* 314 We examined pepper plants set out . . . since the commencement of the drought. **1900** *Century Mag.* Feb. 644/2 [We] sprinkled a little Cayenne pepper on the sticky side with a pepper-shaker.

b. In special combinations.

Pepper ball, a ball made of or containing pepper (in fig. context); *pepper-brand*, a disease of wheat; *p. porridge*, porridge flavored with pepper; *p. vinegar*, vinegar in which peppers have been steeped (cf. Pepper sauce).

1870 *Nation* 5 May 280/2 The *Tribune* threw shells, pepper-balls, and stink-pots. **1850** *Rep. Comm. Patents 1849: Agric.* 393 Another uredo called bunt, or pepper-brand, seizes on the grain of wheat. **1804** Fessenden *Terrible Tractoration* 185 All piping hot, as pepper-porridge. **1845** Sol. Smith *Theatr. Apprent.* 133 The mischievous actors contrived . . . to substitute *pepper vinegar*, from an oyster stand.

Pepper-and-salt.

1. Woolen cloth evenly dotted or speckled with black or dark gray and white or light gray spots; a garment made of this. {1774–} Also attrib. or as adj.

1834 *S. Lit. Messenger* I. 73 His dress was a pepper-and-salt frock, vest and trowsers. **1862** *Trial C. M. Jefferds* 15 The Coroner showed the witness two coats—one a common brown linen, the other a 'pepper-and-salt,' darker than the first. **1898** Westcott *D. Harum* xiii, He was dressed in a sack coat of dark 'pepper-and-salt,' with waistcoat and trousers to match. **1920** Lewis *Main Street* 412 When Carol saw him with his uniform off, in a pepper-and-salt suit and a new gray felt hat, she was disappointed.

+**2.** (See quot. 1890.)

1861 Wood *Botany* 384 *Erigenia*, Pepper-and-Salt. **1890** *Cent.* 4384/1 *Pepper-and-salt*, the plant harbinger-of-spring: so named from the mixture of white petals and dark stamens.

***Pepperbox.**

***1.** A small container having a perforated top used for sprinkling ground pepper.

1707 *Boston News-Letter* 17 Feb. 2/2 One Peppar Box, a large Porringer. **1754** *S.C. Gazette* 1 Jan. 2/1 Just imported . . . , salts, pepper boxes and castors. **1845** *Knickerb.* XXV. 445 The silver pepper-box [was set out]. **1882** Howells *Modern Instance* xiv, Besides the caster, there was a bottle of Leicestershire sauce on the table, and salt in what Marcia thought a pepper-box.

+**2.** A pistol of a type invented by Ethan Allen. Often *Allen's pepperbox*. Also attrib.

1850 Jackson *Forty-Niner* (1920) 28 Donovan . . . jumped a claim, and when the rightful owner warned him off he drew an Allen's pepper box. **1864** *Ore. State Jrnl.* 23 April 1/5 The counsel for the prisoner insisted that an Allen's pepper-box was not a deadly weapon. **1888** Ferguson *Experiences of Forty-Niner* 95 Others had *Allen's pepper-boxes*, as the early style of revolvers was called. **1890** Harte *Waif of Plains* 99 An old-fashioned 'six-shooter'—whose barrels revolved occasionally and unexpectedly—known as 'Allen's Pepper Box,' on account of its culinary resemblance. **1901** Churchill *Crisis* 280 Out of his coat pocket hung the curved butt of a big pepper-box revolver.

Pepper bush. {1832–} +**1.** The privet andromeda, *Xolisma ligustrina.* +**2.** =Sweet pepper bush. — (1) **1784** Cutler in *Amer. Acad. Mem.* I. 443 *Andromeda.* . . . White Pepperbush. . . . Common in swamps. **1833** Eaton *Botany* (ed. 6) 17 *Andromeda paniculata*, white bush, pepper bush. . . . A shrub running into several varieties. **1860** Curtis *Woody Plants N.C.* 96 Pepper-Bush. (*A*[*ndromeda*] *ligustrina.*)—This occurs in all the Districts. (2) **1869** Fuller *Flower Gatherers* 231 Father calls it a 'Pepper-bush.'

Pepper caster, Pepper castor. 1. A small bottle or metal container, usu. one of the casters of a cruet stand. {1676–} Also attrib. ||**2.** A revolver. — (1) **1842** *Knickerb.* XX. 355 The table was soon spread and garnished, from pepper-castor to cold-slaw. **1855** M. Thompson *Doesticks* 120 The old-fashioned country meeting-house, with a 'steeple,' either of the extinguisher or pepper-castor pattern. (2) **1890** J. Jefferson *Autobiog.* 72 Badger and I would trudge to our room, . . . each armed with a Colt's patent 'pepper-caster.'

***Peppercorn.** The berry of the black-pepper plant, formerly often stipulated for as a nominal rent. — **1653** *Suffolk Deeds* I. 268 John Tuttell doth [grant] . . . house & lands at the yerely rent of one pepper Corne. **1756** *Southampton Rec.* III. 1756 The said land is for the building of a store house and tan yard, rent one pepper corn if it be lawfully demanded. **1796** J. Dabney *Address* 60 Plunge the chick into cold water, . . . and force down one whole pepper corn. **1833** *Niles' Reg.* XLIV. 423/1 He has executed an indenture of lease for ten years to that institution, at the nominal rent of a pepper corn, per annum. **1878** *Amer. Home Cook Book* 22 Add them, with the peppercorns and herbs.

***Peppergrass.** Any one of various plants of the genus *Lepidium.* {–1760}

1784 Filson *Kentucke* 24 The Shawanese sallad, wild lettuce, and pepper-grass, and many more, . . . have excellent virtues. **1806** Lewis in *L. & Clark Exped.* V. (1905) 192 Saw the common small blue flag and peppergrass. **1859** *Ill. Agric. Soc. Trans.* III. 505 Cress, Pepper Grass, Tongue Grass.—The seed of this plant is sown for an early salad. There are two varieties—the curled and the broad leaf. **1898** M. Leonard *Big Front Door* 19 The long grass was cut down, and with it those patches of pepper grass that had seasoned many a feast.

attrib. **1889** *Harper's Mag.* Oct. 695/1 They'd jest . . . put a pepper-grass poultice to the soles o' their feet.

+**Pepperidge.** Also **piperidge,** etc.

1. The black or sour gum *Nyssa sylvatica;* also, a tree of this species.

The origin of the name is obscure. In English *pepperidge* occurs only as a late and rare dialect variant of *pipperidge*, the barberry.

1810 Michaux *Arbres* I. 30 *Peperidge*, fréquemment usitée par les Hollandois du New Jersey. **1826** Cooper *Mohicans* vi, A trencher, really carved from the knot of the pepperage. **1828** Webster s.v., The *piperidge* of New England is the *nyssa villosa*, a large tree with very tough wood. **1866** *Ill. Agric. Soc. Trans.* VI. 390 Do you want a Sweet or Sour Gum, give your order for *Liquidamber*, but do not be so vulgar as to call it 'peperage.' **1885** *Century Mag.* Oct. 916 [The Hudson R.] gleams over the flattened top of some pepperidge. **1901** Mohr *Plant Life Ala.* 651 Highland Black Gum. Pepperidge. . . . A tree of large size.

attrib. **1743** Hempstead *Diary* 406 Wee Sawed of a pr Peperage wheels for my Stone Cart. **1821** Cooper *Spy* ix, A lieutenant of cavalry . . . whose captain is as tough as a peperage log.

+**2.** The pepper vine of the southern states.

1901 MOHR *Plant Life Ala.* 611 Woody climbers. . . . Pepperidge . . . [is] frequent, on bushes, or ascending high trees.

+**Pepperidge tree.** =prec. — **1689** *Huntington Rec.* II. 56 A piperage tree marked faceing eastward and south ward. **1772** *Southampton Rec.* III. 272 A peperidge tree, originally marked . . . now . . . stands two rods and three feet to the northward of Capt. Stephens fence. **1859** BARTLETT 316 Pepperidge (*Nyssa multiflora*), a name given in the South and West to the Black or Sour Gum, also called Tupebo [*i.e.*, tupelo]. **1876** *Field & Forest* I. 66 This parasitic shrub has been found growing on several Pepperidge or Sour-gum trees (*Nyssa Multiflora*).

Peppermint.

1. A pungent herb (*Mentha piperita*) of the mint family. {1696-}

1805 LEWIS in *L. & Clark Exped.* II. (1904) 186 Great quantities of mint also are here . . . [resembling] the pepper mint in taste and appearance. **1817-8** EATON *Botany* (1822) 352 *Mentha piperita*, peppermint. . . . E[xotic]. **1882** THAYER *From Log-Cabin* 149 This Mr. Smith was a farmer, and his land, on the Chagrin Flats, was adapted to the cultivation of peppermint, which he raised for the market in large quantities. **1891** WILKINS *New Eng. Nun* 9 She used to occupy herself . . . distilling . . . essences from roses and peppermint and spearmint.

2. The oil or essence obtained from this plant. {1836-}

1811 *Austin P.* I. (1924) 186, 1 Bottle Peppermint. **1839** *S. Lit. Messenger* V. 65/2 There's nothing there but a few drops of peppermint . . . and some of the patent hive-syrup. **1856** CARTWRIGHT *Autobiog.* 49, I had a phial of peppermint in my pocket.

+**3.** =PEPPERMINT CANDY.

1883 *Harper's Mag.* Sept. 534/2 The windows were decorated . . . with rows of glass jars in which were sticks of striped candy, the half-moist peppermint, and the brown sugary squares.

4. =PEPPERMINT DROP. {1899-}

1835 TODD *Student's Manual* 281 A handful of hot peppermints. **1884** QUINCY *Figures of Past* 176 [He] produced just the stimulant required in the form of a package of peppermints. **1907** *St. Nicholas* Oct. 1067 And from her silken bag she takes A peppermint or two.

5. Attrib. with *essence, oil*, etc.

1820 *U.S. Pharmacopœia* 85 In the same manner are prepared peppermint water, . . . spearmint water, . . . [and] rose water. **1873** *Mich. Gen. Statutes* I. (1882) 268 The number of pounds of peppermint oil manufactured the preceding year. **1898** *N.Y. Jrnl.* 16 Sept. 11/6 Each contained . . . chamomile and peppermint teas, . . . pipe, smoking and chewing tobacco. **1905** *N.Y. Ev. Post* 4 Aug. 7 The introduction of peppermint and checkerberry essences has almost resulted in driving carraway seeds out of the pharmacopoeia of the family. **1908** 'O. HENRY' *Strictly Business* 181 She had a wide mouth that kept the peppermint-pepsin tablets rattling like hail from the slot-machine.

+**Peppermint candy.** Candy flavored with peppermint. — **1843** *Knickerb.* XXII. 46 Her red lips contrast with her white skin as do red stripes with the white in Stewart's peppermint candy. **1898** WESTCOTT *D. Harum* xx, We done the hull programmy—gingerbread, . . . pop corn, peanuts, pep'mint candy, cin'mun candy. **1916** WILSON *Somewhere* 355 He's having a high old time with a sack of peppermint candy and a copy of the *Scientific American*.

Peppermint drop. A small roundish piece of candy flavored with peppermint. {1878-} — **1843** STEPHENS *High Life N.Y.* I. 248 She and the 'pothecary sidled about, eat peppermint drops and talked soft sodder to one another. **1877** *Harper's Mag.* March 606/1 To the feminine imagination matrimony on the income of seventy-five thousand is naturally a less 'solemn ordinance' than on a precarious salary of eight dollars a week, and nothing found but peppermint drops. **1907** *St. Nicholas* May 615/2 To the popcorn they soon added fudge, yellow molasses candy, peppermint drops, and several other kinds of candy unknown to French children.

Pepper pot. a. A thick, highly seasoned stew composed chiefly of meat or fish and vegetables. {1704-} +**b.** (See quot. 1890.)

1791 MACLAY *Deb. Senate* 277 When the Senate adjourned, he asked me to go and eat *pepper-pot* with him. **1803** J. DAVIS *Travels* 45 An old negro-woman was passing at the same moment with some pepper-pot on her head. **1840** *Knickerb.* XVI. 26 None but a Creole could ever make a pepper-pot. **1883** *Harper's Mag.* Aug. 456/1 He considered pepper pot a dish fit for the gods. **1890** *Cent.* 4384/2 *Pepper-pot*. . . . Tripe shredded and stewed, to the liquor of which small balls of dough are added, together with a high seasoning of pepper. (Pennsylvania.)

+**Pepperroot.** The crinkleroot (*Dentaria diphylla*), or any other species of *Dentaria*. (Cf. TOOTHWORT.) — **1814** PURSH *Flora Amer.* II. 439 *Dentaria diphylla*. . . . The roots of this plant . . . are used by the natives instead of mustard; in the mountains it is generally known by the name of Pepper-root. **1839** in *Mich. Agric. Soc. Trans.* VII. 405. **1857** GRAY *Botany* 31 Toothwort. Pepper-root. . . . Rootstocks of a pleasant pungent taste. **1915** ARMSTRONG & THORNBER *Western Wild Flowers* 174 Pepper-root . . . is one of the loveliest of the early spring flowers in the Coast Ranges and usually found in damp spots.

+**Pepper tea.** A tealike medicinal preparation containing a liberal amount of pepper. — **1841** *S. Lit. Messenger* VII. 38/1 The pepper-tea done me heap of good. **1865** *Nation* I. 306 There were several old women who were very kind in doctoring me with ley tea, pepper tea, and other villanous remedies. **1905** LINCOLN *Partners* 23 'Pepper tea' was a new prescription for the boy, and he watched . . . while Miss Tempy turned some milk into a bowl, flooded it with boiling water, added a spoonful of sugar, and vigorously shook the pepper box over the mess. **1925** TILGHMAN *Dugout* 33 They poured the tobacco into the barrel; strained the pepper tea and added it.

Pepper tree. {1691-2-} +An evergreen tree or shrub (*Schinus molle*) found in the warmer portions of the United States. — **1784** FILSON *Kentucke* 23 The pepper-tree . . . is a soft wood, bears a fine fruit much like a cucumber in shape and size, and tastes sweet. **1890** *Internat. Ann., Anthony's Photogr. Bul.* III. 339 At Pasadena there are . . . many pretty streets shaded by beautiful pepper trees. **1902** *Harper's Mag.* May 882/1 Speranza, neighing joyfully from the shade of the pepper-tree to which she was tethered, greeted him at the little terminal station.

+**Pequot.** Also †**Pecoat, Pequoitt, Pequod, Pequit.** [App. a contraction of *paquatanog* 'destroyers.'] An Indian of a warlike Algonquian tribe at one time holding sway over most of southern New England; also, pl., the tribe. Also attrib.

1631 *N.H. Hist. Soc. Coll.* IV. 226 Wee heare their numbers exceed any but the Pecoates and the Narragansets. **1637** *Conn. Rec.* I. 10 To parle w[i]th the bay aboute o[u]r settinge downe in the Pequoitt Countrey. **1654** JOHNSON *Wonder-w. Prov.* 109* The English sought by all meanes to keepe these [fighting men] at least from confederating with the Pequods. **1673** *Ib.* II. 213 Moween . . . was secured in the common goale upon suspition of murthering a Pequit girle. **1714** SEWALL *Diary* III. 12 Commissioners met to give Govr. Saltonstall an Opportunity to vindicate himself relating to the Pequot and Mohegan Indians. **1848** HOLMES *Poetical Works* (1895) 30/1 He heard the Pequot's ringing whoop.

||**b.** The language of the Pequot Indians.

1848 LOWELL *Biglow P.* 1 Ser. p. xiii, Colds in the head . . . Transformed the helpless Hebrew thrice a week To guttural Pequot or resounding Greek.

***Perambulate,** *v.* Also †**perambelate, preambulate.**

1. *intr.* To make perambulation of boundaries.

1653 *Watertown Rec.* I. I. 37 Christefer Grant and one of the Deacon stones Sonnes are Chosen to perambelate this yeare. **1708** SEWALL *Diary* II. 222 Capt. Culliver and others perambulating for Baintrey and Milton, went with us.

2. *tr.* To go around (the boundaries of a town) by way of establishing or preserving officially its limits. *Obs.* {1757}

1772 *Amherst Rec.* 58/2 Voted that the Select Men be Directed to Preambulate the Line between Hadley and Amherst. **1798** I. ALLEN *Hist. Vermont* 25 Some Patents which began in New York on perambulating and re-measuring the line, were extended into the towns of Pownal, Bennington, &c. **1858** EMERSON *Soc. & Solitude* 134 The selectmen have once in every five years perambulated the boundaries, and yet, in this very year, a large quantity of land has been discovered and added to the town.

***Perambulation.** The action of traversing officially the limits of a town to assert or preserve its boundaries. — **1654** *Boston Rec.* 119 Mr. James Oliver and Rob[er]tt Turner are appoynted to run the line betwixt Cambridge and Rocksbury, and the towne of Boston in perambulatyon. **1664** *Muddy River & Brookline Rec.* 39 Mr. Tho. Brattle . . . [and] John White are chosen for perambulation between Muddy Ryver and Cambridge. **1674** *Boston Rec.* 87 Capt Huchinson & his sonn with Mr. Tho: Brattle were ready to proceed on ye p[er]ambulation aboue. **1732** *Boston Selectmen* 222 The Return of the Perambulation between Boston and Roxbury august the 23rd 1732.

Perambulator. {1611-}

+**1.** One who performs a perambulation for establishing or preserving the boundaries of a town. *Obs.* {1815}

1667 *Muddy River & Brookline Rec.* 39 Mr. John Hull . . . [and] Peter Aspinwall are chosen perambulators for the bounds between Muddy River and Roxbury. **1669** *Boston Rec.* 47 Capt Edward Huchinson & Mr. Elias Mauericke p[e]rambulators to run the line betweene Charlestowne & Bostone. **1696** *Ib.* 223 Hugh Floid, and Joseph Hasey were chosen Perambulatours for to meet Malden messengers those from Lin and those from Reading to run the line of the bounds. **1708** SEWALL *Diary* II. 222 So took leave of the perambulators.

2. A baby carriage. {1857-} Also attrib.

1893 WIGGIN *Cathedral Courtship* 136 There are often two youngsters of a perambulator age in the same family at the same time. **1905** RICE *Sandy* 62 Sandy had announced his intention of putting on baby clothes and being wheeled in a perambulator.

Percaline. A glossy cotton cloth of a kind originally made in France. Also attrib. — **1893** *Chicago Tribune* 23 April 44/3, 50 pieces 36-inch Fine Percaline Lining, all staple shades. **1898** *Voice* 20 Jan. 7/2 Sateen and alpaca skirts are lined through the upper part with flannel for winter and percaline below.

+**Percent,** *v. Educ. tr.* To rate or evaluate (a student or examination) in terms of per cent. *Obs.* — **1883** *Student* 286 When students are found obtaining help of others they are not percented at all. **1883** *Cincinnati Bd. of Educ. Rep.* No. 53, 71 As in Physics so in United States History, there is no percented written examination.

***Perch.**[1]

+1. Any one of various American fish or species of fish of the genus *Perca*, esp. *P. flavescens.*

1637 MORTON *New Canaan* 91 There are in the rivers, and ponds, very excellent . . . Perches, Tenches, Eeles, and other fishes. **1698** THOMAS *Pensilvania* 13 And for Fish, there are prodigious quantities of most sorts, *viz.* . . . *Roach, Eels, Perch.* **1705** BEVERLEY *Hist. Va.* II. 32 Those [fish in Virginia] which I know of my self, I remember by the Names. Of Herrings, Rocks, . . . Conger-Eels, Perch, and Cats, &c. **1797** PRIEST *Travels* 70 [The Susquehanna R.] abounds in cat-fish, perch, jack, eels, and a great variety of others. **1808** PIKE *Sources Miss.* 3, [I] caught three cat-fish and one perch. **1895** *Outing* XXVI. 62/1 We passed on, seeing schools of sunfish, perch, rock bass, and croppies, which kept the water in constant commotion. **1911** *Rep. Fisheries 1908* 313 Perch (*Perca flavescens*).—This fish, the true perch, is found throughout the Great Lakes region and the rivers of New England and the states east of the Alleghenies as far south as Georgia.

+b. On the Pacific coast, a surf fish of the family Embiotocidae.

1884 GOODE, etc. *Fisheries* I. 276 The general name 'Perch' is applied to these fishes everywhere along the coast. **1911** *Rep. Fisheries 1908* 307/1 Alfione (*Rhacochilus toxotes*). . . . It is also called 'perch' and 'sprat.' . . . It is the most important of the surf-fishes.

2. Attrib. and comb. with *fisherman, hook, minnow, pool.*

1836 *Knickerb.* VIII. 152, I have known her to catch turtles . . . with a fish-hook not larger than a perch-hook. **1897** *Outing* XXIX. 343/2 At this time of the year the lake is dotted in many places with the little box-like shanties of the perch and pickerel fishermen. **1906** LYNDE *Quickening* 58 His lip curled stiffly at the thought of a girl . . . dividing the sovereignty of . . . the perch pools in the creek with him. **1910** C. HARRIS *Eve's Husband* 235 It is much easier to get perch minnows and lettuce seed out of the Government than an appropriation.

Perch.**[2] A measure of length now equal to 5½ yards, but formerly variable. (Cf. POLE, ROD.) — **1640** *Conn. Hist. Soc. Coll.* XIV. 78 Two acres & two Roodes & tenn parches of medow. **1679** *Doc. Col. Hist. N.Y.* XII. 636 The plantation of the said John Glovear . . . [begins] at a Bounded poplar by the Branch Running vp the Branch Southwest three hundred perches to the Land of William Steuens. *c1805** R. PUTNAM *Memoirs* 46 The yasou river is about 25 perches wide, a dead streme, bad water,—with many Allegators. **1867** MITCHELL *Rural Studies* 130 Every rod of them shaded a good perch of grain-land.

Percheron. A draft horse of a breed developed in Perche, a former district in northern France. {1875–} Also attrib. and transf. — **1876** INGRAM *Centennial Exp.* 673 There were quite a number of the imported Percheron stallions and brood mares. **1893** G. W. CURTIS *Horses, Cattle* 12 The Percheron Society requires that all animals imported after January 1st, 1884, must be recorded in the Percheron Stud Book of France. **1894** *Vt. Agric. Rep.* XIV. 100 For heavy draft purposes the Percherons seem to give satisfaction. **1902** LORIMER *Lett. Merchant* 279 Of course, I was in the Percheron class, and so I just stood around with a lot of heavy old draft horses.

+Percosan. Also †**percoarson, perkoson.** =POCOSIN. Also attrib. — **1709** LAWSON *Carolina* 9 As we row'd up the [Santee] River, we found the Land . . . scarce any Thing but Swamp and Percoarson, affording vast Ciprus-Trees. **1737** BRICKELL *N. Carolina* 12 There are likewise Perkosons and Swamps, which are good Pasturage for Cattle. **1859** G. W. PERRY *Turpentine Farming* 9 Every kind of turf should be turned over, such as low bush huckleberry, gallberry, percosan bush.

***Percussion.** *attrib.* Designating firearms having percussion locks. {1844–} — **1853** *33d Congress 1 Sess.* Sen. Ex. Doc. No. 1, III. 275 Operations at this armory during the year [include] . . . 500 percussion musketoons, . . . 4,120 hammers for percussioning muskets. **1861** *Army Regulations* 447 One pair percussion pistols.

Percussion cap. A metal cap containing fulminating powder which explodes upon being struck. {1823–}

1839 *Diplom. Corr. Texas* I. (1908) 411 [They] explode, after they strike the vessel, . . . by a percussion cap, which goes off from the jar or concussion by the striking of the vessel. **1850** *Annual of Sci. Discovery* 47 There is now in operation at the Arsenal in Washington, a machine for making percussion caps, which is spoken of as being superior to any other in use. **1886** POORE *Reminisc.* I. 171 The percussion-cap exploded without discharging the pistol. *a***1918** G. STUART *On Frontier* I. 33 It was a small-bore rifle fired with percussion caps placed on the nipple.

transf. and *attrib.* **1840** HONE *Diary* II. 17 The 'young idea' [was] first beginning to put on its percussion-caps. **1866** 'MARK TWAIN' in *Harper's* Dec. 108/1*n.*, A piece [of biscuit] the size of an ordinary percussion-cap box.

Percussion gun. A gun having a percussion lock. {cf. next} — **1827** *Franklin Inst. Jrnl.* IV. 283 The slowest powder was much the safest in the percussion gun with the hammer in any other way than at half cock. *a***1861** WINTHROP *Open Air* 54 Since percussion-guns and friction cigar-lighters came in, flint has somewhat lost its value.

Percussion lock. A gunlock designed for use with percussion caps; a gun having such a lock. {percussion gun lock, 1819; 1845–} Also attrib. — **1829** in *Congress. Deb.* (1830–1) p. xcii/2, I have used the percussion locks but little, but believe them admirably well constructed for general use. **1867** CRAWFORD *Mosby* 35 Old flint-locks were converted into percussion-locks. **1879** B. F. TAYLOR *Summer-Savory* 118 The lid [of the eye] does not shut down so much like a percussion lock, nor fly open so easily. **1884** *N. Mex. Terr. Rep.* 88 The Territory now has four hundred old style percussion lock Austrian muskets.

+Percussion table. (See quot. 1876.) — **1876** KNIGHT 1666/1 *Percussion-table.* . . . A form of ore-separating apparatus consisting of a slightly sloping table on which stamped ore or metalliferous sand is placed to be sorted by gravity. A stream of water is directed over the ore, and the table is subjected to the concussion at intervals. **1876** RAYMOND *8th Rep. Mines* 310 This apparatus presents features which have been superseded in the best modern percussion-tables.

***Per diem.** +An amount or allowance of so much a day, usu. with reference to members of Congress or of state legislatures. In full *per diem allowance.*

1809 *Ann. 10th Congress* 2 Sess. 350 Officers of the United States . . . have received . . . the per diem allowance fixed by law. **1812** *Niles' Reg.* I. 361/2 The *per diem* of the members has been raised to *four* dollars. **1846** McKENNEY *Memoirs* I. 192, I referred to him the making up of my account for my per diem allowance. **1848** *Wilmington* (N.C.) *Commercial* 24 Aug. 2/4 (Th. S.), The per diem will hardly pay a gentleman for soiling his hands with it. **1903** HART *Actual Govt.* 131 Many of the constituencies limit the length of session to 40 or 60 days, and it is very common to cut off the per diem at the expiration of the specified time.

***Peregrine falcon.** +The duck hawk, *Falco peregrinus anatum.*

The name is sometimes applied to an allied variety, Peale's falcon, *F. p. pealei.*

1831 WILSON & BONAPARTE *Amer. Ornith.* I. 51 *Falco peregrinus.* . . . Great Footed Hawk, or Peregrine Falcon. . . . Our hawk . . . is not migratory. **1850** S. F. COOPER *Rural Hours* 410 The Duck-hawk, or Peregrine Falcon, is chiefly found on the coast. **1871** *Amer. Naturalist* V. 80 The *Falco peregrinus* Wilson . . . is very commonly called the Peregrine Falcon. . . . There seems to be some diversity of opinion as to the identity of this and the European species. **1880** *Cimarron News & Press* 23 Dec. 1/5 Of the falcons we have the lanier, peregrine, pigeon, Richardson's and rusty-crowned falcon or sparrow hawk. **1917** *Birds of Amer.* II. 87 Duck Hawk. *Falco peregrinus anatum.* . . . [Also called] Peregrine Falcon; American Peregrine.

Perennial, *a.* In the names of plants that remain alive through a succession of years or indefinitely. {1672–} — **1843** TORREY *Flora N.Y.* II. 141 *Salicornia ambigua.* . . . Perennial Saltwort. . . . Seabeach and borders of salt-marshes, Glencove, Long Island. **1855** BROWNE in *Amer. Inst. N.Y. Trans.* 618 Cow Grass, or Perennial clover (*trifolium medium vel perenne*), from England, usually sown among other grass seeds for permanency. **1890** *Cent.* 3469/3 Perennial flax is a very handsome blue-flowered species abundant in the northern parts of the United States. **1901** MOHR *Plant Life Ala.* 388 Perennial Ray Grass. . . . Valuable for pasture and lawn.

+Perfecting press. (See quot. 1875.) — **1858** *Printer* I. 95 This wonderful achievement . . . the perfecting press. **1876** KNIGHT 1666/2 *Perfecting-press,* . . . one in which the paper is printed on both sides during one passage through the machine.

Perfectionist. {1657–83–} +A member of a communistic religious sect founded by John Humphrey Noyes. (Cf. BIBLE COMMUNIST, ONEIDA COMMUNITY.) — **1834** (*magazine title*), The Perfectionist. **1867** DIXON *New America* II. 208 Perfectionists . . . profess to base their theory of family life on the New Testament, most of all on the teachings of St. Paul. **1874** J. H. BLUNT *Dict. Sects, Perfectionists,* a . . . sect of Antinomian Communists, established about the year 1845 by John Humphrey Noyes. **1875** *N. Amer. Rev.* CXX. 227 The success that he ascribes to the Shakers, the Perfectionists, and the rest.

+Perfecto. [Sp., 'perfect.'] A cigar unusually large in the middle and small at both ends. — **1895** WILLIAMS *Princeton Stories* 57 Bring some Perfectos, Jackson—please pardon me, I forgot entirely that you smoked. **1897** *Outing* XXX. 326/2, I forgot to light my cigar—and it's a perfecto at that. **1904** 'O. HENRY' *Four Million* 75 He always looked in for five minutes, smiled at the girls and handed out real perfectos to the delighted boys.

Periagua. Also **periauger,** etc. [Var. of *piragua.*] A small flat-bottomed sailing boat; a canoe made of a tree trunk. {1630–, in W. Indies, etc.}

See also PERIOGUE, PEROGUE, PETTIAUGER, PIROGUE.

1609 HAKLUYT *Va. Richly Valued* 119 The periagua overset. **1696** *S.C. Statutes at Large* II. 105 Any person . . . [who] shall steal, take away, or let loose any boat, perriaguer or canoe . . . shall be liable to corporal punishment. **1704** *N.C. Col. Rec.* I. 603 A pond of five miles broad, and nothing to carry one over but a small perryauger. **1770** JEFFERSON *Writings* IV. 20 Your periagua . . . will meet us, automaton-like, of its own accord. **1802** ELLICOTT *Journal* 189 They had a sufficient depth of water to float loaded periaguas and canoes. **1887** EGGLESTON in *Century Mag.* April 904/2 In the Middle and southern colonies . . . boats, small periaugers, and canoes were favorite vehicles for travel.

attrib. **1732** *S.C. Gazette* 135/2 Run away from his Master John Richards, a Perriauger-Man belonging to Winyaw.

b. (See quotation.)

1744 MOORE *Voy. Georgia* 112 These periaguas are long flat-bottomed boats, carrying from twenty to thirty-five tons. . . . They have two masts . . . and sails like schooners. They row generally with two oars.

Periodical. A magazine or miscellany which comes out at regular intervals. {1798–}

1839 LOWELL *Letters* I. 46 [To] get paid for contributions to periodicals. **1862** NORTON *Army Lett.* 115 He was the editor of an agricultural periodical. **1902** BANKS *Newspaper Girl* 277 Only once during my several years' connection with his periodical has he been under the necessity of writing to ask me for a contribution.

b. Attrib. with *press, reading room, store.*

1854 BENTON *30 Years' View* I. 122/1 The incessant action of the daily and periodical press. **1878** *Harper's Mag.* Jan. 192 He used to look into the windows of the periodical stores, and read the titles of the dime novels with delight. **1910** BOSTWICK *Amer. Pub. Library* 282 In some New York branches periodical reading rooms may be used as assembly rooms.

Periogue. =PEROGUE. (See also PERIAGUA, PIROGUE.) — **1799** in CUMING *Western Tour* 329 [The general] ordered a periogue to convey us down to our boat. **1843** HAWKS *D. Boone* 132 The light-hearted Frenchmen swept up the river in their fleets of periogues on their hunting excursions. **1874** COLLINS *Kentucky* I. 17 [They] in periogues, or large canoes, descend the Ohio to the Falls.

+**Perique.** [Louisiana Fr. perhaps fr. *Pierre* Chenet, tobacco grower.] A tobacco of strong flavor and tough fiber raised in Louisiana. In full *perique tobacco.* — **1882** *Congress. Rec.* 6 April 2642/2 Perique tobacco may be sold by the manufacturer or producer . . . in the form of carottes . . . without the payment of tax. **1885** CUSTER *Boots & Saddles* 84 The officers gave this chief tobacco—Perique I think it is called. **1897** *Outing* XXX. 63/2, I fill up the pipe called Dick with a certain black abomination known as perique tobacco.

***Periwig.** Also †**perriwigg, perriwig.** A wig or peruke. — **1642** *Md. Archives* IV. 99 Some trading fishooks in a small lether bagg[,] a periwig. **1685** *N.H. Hist. Soc. Coll.* VIII. 266 My coat, periwig, and stockings were burnt. **1707** *Boston News-Letter* 31 March 2/2 He commonly wears a Perriwigg, his Right leg is crooked. **1764** HUTCHINSON *Hist. Mass.* I. 152 Perriwigs . . . in New-England . . . did not generally obtain until about the time of the revolution.

***Periwig-maker.** One who makes periwigs. — **1686** SEWALL *Diary* I. 158 This day Wm. Clendon the Barber and Perriwig-maker dies miserably. **1714** *Boston News-Letter* 16–23 Aug. 2/2 Ran away from his Master Richard Hall Perriwigg Maker in Kingstreet, Boston. **1723** *Amer. Wkly. Mercury* 14–21 Mar. 2/2 Ready Money, and a good Price for all sorts of light and gray Hair, By Georg Sheed, Perywigg-Maker in the Front-Street.

***Periwinkle.**[1] Any of various sea snails or shells, esp. those of the genera *Litorina* and +*Busycon*, or the whelk *Buccinum undatum.*

Cf. PENNYWINKLE.

1624 SMITH *Gen. Hist. Va.* VI. 216 Oisters, Clamps, Periwinkels, and diuers others. **1643** WILLIAMS *Key* (1866) 173 Their owne [money] is of two sorts; one white, which they make of the stem or stocke of the Periwincle. **1709** LAWSON *Carolina* 162 Wilks, or Periwinkles, are not so large here, as in the Islands of Scilly, . . . though very sweet. **1806** CLARK in *Lewis & C. Exped.* IV. (1905) 173 The Periwinkle both of the river and ocian are similar to those found in the same situation on the Atlantic. **1817** *N. Amer. Rev.* V. 317 We found the murex caniculatus, a shell confounded by the inhabitants of this part of the Commonwealth with the murex carica, under the common name of perriwinkle, which properly belongs to neither. **1883** *Nat. Museum Bul.* No. 27, 197 *Lunatica heros* and *Neverita duplicata* . . . are frequently confounded one with the other, and are usually known . . . as 'Sea-Snails,' and sometimes as 'Winkles' or 'Periwinkles.' **1884** GOODE, etc. *Fisheries* I. 694 *Buccinum undatum*, the Cape Ann 'Periwinkle,' might well serve as food, since in Europe it has long been thus utilized. *Ib.*, Two of the largest mollusks on the Atlantic coast north of the tropic—*Fulgur carica* and *Sycotypus canaliculata.* North of New Jersey these two are confused under the general names of 'Periwinkle,' 'Winkle,' and 'Wrinkle.' **1911** *Rep. Fisheries 1908* 313/2 *Periwinkle.*—A common name for the sea snail (*Littorina*) and whelk (*Fulga*), which are used for bait and sometimes for food on the north Atlantic coast.

attrib. **1701** WOLLEY *Journal N.Y.* 29 Their Money is called Wampam and Sea-want, made of a kind of Cockle or Periwinkle-shell, of which there is scarce any, but at Oyster-bay.

***Periwinkle.**[2] Any one of various plants of the genus *Vinca.* (Cf. MYRTLE 2 a.) — **1737** BRICKELL *N. Carolina* 20 Perewinkle growing in great plenty in most parts of the Woods. **1850** S. F. COOPER *Rural Hours* 22 The periwinkle is almost in blossom: this is one of the very earliest flowers to open with us. **1904** GLASGOW *Deliverance* 390 He turned from her, throwing himself upon the carpet of periwinkle.

Permanent camp. A camp designed for occupancy over an extended period. — **1884** *Century Mag.* Feb. 592/1 Every 'permanent camp' [of convicts working away from the penitentiary, in the South] has a hospital, a physician, and a chaplain. **1897** *Outing* July 374/2 Camping . . . can be done in many ways. . . . We have the hunting camp, the fishing camp, . . . the permanent camp, the family camp [etc.].

Permit.[1] {1714–} +A license or written order giving an Indian, or one dealing with Indians, permission to do certain things.

1682 *Plymouth Laws* 194 Noe foraigne Indian of other Collonies or Plantations shalbe suffered to hunt in any Towne or Plantation of this Collonie without a p[er]mitt from a Majestrate. **1740** W. STEPHENS *Proc. Georgia* 578 Conferring with some Indian Traders, and adjusting Matters with them, in order to obtain new Licences, or Permits. **1867** *Wkly. New Mexican* 8 June 2/4 To Parties trading with Comanches.—All Persons pretending to trade on 'permits' claimed to be given by me are hereby warned that they do so at their Peril. **1873** BEADLE *Undevel. West* 399 [An Indian] can pay a license and take out a 'permit' for his white employés, and the 'Nation' takes the responsibility. **1881** *Rep. Indian Affairs* p. viii, A Lieutenant of the United States Army . . . gave a written permit to three Indians at this agency. **1906** *Indian Laws & Tr.* III. 202 If any adult member of the Nez Perce Tribe of Indians in Idaho believes himself or herself competent to make leases and transact his or her affairs, such member may file a request with the Commissioner of Indian Affairs for a permit to lease the lands.

+**b.** A fee paid by an Indian for a permit. Also comb.

1891 O'BEIRNE *Leaders Ind. Territory* 101/2 He pays permits for twenty-five renters. *Ib.* 155/2 He became Permit Collector, and still holds that position.

+**Permit.**[2] [Corruption of Sp. *palometa.*] **a.** The great pompano, *Trachinotus goodei.* **b.** *local. Permit of Indian River* or *Indian River permit*, the round pompano, *Trachinotus falcatus.* — **1884** GOODE, etc. *Fisheries* I. 329 The African Pompano—*Trachynotus goreensis.* . . . In the Gulf of Mexico it is not unusual, being known at Key West as the 'Permit.' **1896** JORDAN & EVERMANN *Check-List Fishes* 348 *Trachinotus falcatus.* . . . Round Pampano; Palometa; Permit of Indian River. East coast of United States, Cape Cod to Florida. **1911** *Rep. Fisheries 1908* 314/1 Other species [of pompano] found on our eastern coast are the 'old-wife' . . . ; the 'round pompano,' or 'Indian River permit;' the 'permit' or 'great pompano.'

Perogue. Also **perrogue, peroque.** A large canoe; a dugout. (Cf. PERIAGUA, PERIOGUE, PIROGUE.) — **1787** DENNY *Journal* 102 A party of Indians, about fifteen in number, attacked three perogues. **1807** C. SCHULTZ *Travels* I. 129 The smallest kind of craft in use [on the Ohio R.] are simple log canoes; next follow perrogues, which are a larger kind of canoes. **1832** WYETH *Journal* 213, I was here supplied with a peroque traded from the Blackfeet. **1853** RAMSEY *Tennessee* 187 Perogues and canoes were immediately made from the adjacent forest.

***Perry.** A beverage made from pears. *Obs.* — **1671** *Md. Archives* II. 296 Six pence per gallon Syder Perry and Quince drink. **1716** *Mass. H. Rep. Jrnl.* I. 118 The Excise upon Cyder, and Perry, [shall] be but One Shilling, per Barrel. **1792** BELKNAP *Hist. New-Hampshire* III. 139 Perry is still made in the old towns, bordering on Pisctaqua river. **1885** EGGLESTON in *Century Mag.* April 884/2 People of delicate tastes ground pears to make perry.

***Persian,** *n.* A thin, soft silk used chiefly for linings. Now hist. {1696–} — **1759** *Boston Gazette* 13 Aug., Indian Taffities, Grograms, Persians, black and colour'd Sattins. **1770** *Penna. Chronicle* 10–17 Sept. 138/2 An English servant girl . . . took away with her . . . a black sattin bonnet lined with blue persian . . . and a pair of old black worsted shoes. **1891** EARLE *Sabbath* 91 The goodwives' heads bore . . . 'hoods of crimson colored persian,' . . . 'scarlet gipsys' [etc.].

***Persian,** *a.* Imported from or associated with Persia.

1761 in Singleton *Social N.Y.* 242 My design was to have appeared . . . in a blue Persian silk long robe. **1789** *Md. Hist. Mag.* XXI. 234 If you can recollect the confus'd mixture of . . . beads, Persian feathers and Lace, . . . you will have the best idea I can give you of Miss Garnetts Hatt. **1832** CHILD *Frugal Housewife* 69 Rhubarb stalks, or the Persian apple, is the earliest ingredient for pies, which the spring offers. **1884** JAMES in *Century Mag.* Aug. 575/2 Her drawing-room embraced neither festoons nor Persian rugs, nor plates and *plaques* upon the wall. **1892** KELLOGG *Kansas Insects* 9 Persian Insect Powder, California Buhach, Dalmatian Insect Powder, are other names for pyrethrum.

***Persicaria.** Any one of various plants or a genus of plants of the buckwheat family. — **1766** J. BARTRAM *Journal* 42 We were nearly stopped by the pistia and persicaria growing all in a matt. **1806** in *Ann. 9th Congress* 2 Sess. 1142 Trees, shrubs and plants, growing in the vicinity of the Washita . . . [include] ipecacuanha, persicaria, Indian turnip. **1843** TORREY *Flora N Y.* II. 150 *Polygonum Pennsylvanicum.* . . . Hairy-stalked Persicaria. . . . Low moist places, banks of ditches, and cultivated grounds.

Persico. (See quot. 1724.) *Obs.* {1709–} — **1724** H. JONES *Virginia* 126 From Peaches is distilled an excellent Spirit in very great Plenty, very difficult to be distinguished (when well made) from *Citron Water.* This they call *Persico.* **1822** WOODS *English Prairie* 279 Beer, peach-brandy, and persico, are also frequently to be purchased.

+**Persimmon.** Also †**putchamin, posimon,** etc. [Algonquian.]

See also BLACK PERSIMMON, SIMMON.

1. The edible, plumlike fruit of the persimmon tree.

1612 SMITH, etc. *Virginia* I. 12 The fruit like medlers; they call Putchamins, they cast vppon hurdles on a mat, & preserue them as Pruines. **1670** DENTON *Brief Desc. N.Y.* (1845) 3 The Fruits natural to the Island are Mulberries, Posimons, . . . Huckelberries. **1724** JONES *Virginia* 52 Some Planters, &c. make good small Drink with Cakes of *Parsimmons* a kind of Plumbs, which grow there in great Plenty. **1785** BELKNAP in Cutler *Life & Corr.* II. 235, I inclose you the seeds of the Persimmon, a fruit natural to Pennsylvania, and the Pomegranite of Carolina. **1813** in Young *Jessamine Co., Ky.* 120 He was in the habit of letting the young women have my horses to hunt grapes and persimmons on Hickman creek. **1898** DUNBAR *Folks from Dixie* 77 Ike was happy, for the frost had turned the persimmons. **1916** THOBURN *Stand. Hist. Okla.* I. 5 Of wild fruits there are a number of species, including plums, . . . persimmons, and strawberries.

2. =PERSIMMON TREE.

1709 LAWSON *Carolina* 102 Persimmon is a Tree, that agrees with all Lands and Soils. **1815** DRAKE *Cincinnati* 83 The chestnut, persimmon, . . . and mountain-chestnut oak are still scarcer. **1896** P. A. BRUCE *Econ. Hist. Virginia* I. 94 A fruit tree that aroused unusual interest in the first adventurers was the persimmon. **1901** MOHR *Plant Life Ala.* 68 Shrubby hawthorns, . . . persimmon, and black gum . . . [were] entangled with the tough vines of bamboo briers.

3. In various colloq. phrases.

Expressions such as the typical examples here given were formerly exploited as established features of frontier vernacular.

a. *A huckleberry to a* (or *one's*) *persimmon,* a doughnut to a dollar; nothing in comparison with something.

1832 PAULDING *Westward Ho!* I. 80 If the horn gets broadside to the current, I wouldn't risk a huckleberry to a persimmon that we don't every soul get treed, and sink to the bottom. **1856** SIMMS *Eutaw* 553 My larning . . . ain't a huckleberry to your persimmon.

b. *To be a huckleberry over* (someone's) *persimmon,* to be beyond (someone's) capacity; *to be a hickory* (or *huckleberry*) *over* (or *above*) (someone's) *persimmon(s),* to surpass or be greatly superior to (someone).

1834 CROCKETT *Narr. Life* 70 But to do this, and write the warrants too, was at least a huckleberry over my persimmon. **1836** *Quarter Race Ky.* 17 One of the nominees . . . was a hickory over anybody's persimmon in the way of ugliness. **1844** *Spirit of Times* (Phila.) 24 Aug. (Th.), She's a great gal that! . . . She's a huckleberry above most people's parsimmons. **1885** D. D. PORTER *Incidents Civil War* 204 'I am the fleet-surgeon of the Mississippi squadron!' . . . 'I'm a huckleberry above that persimmon, 'cause I'm the chief cook.'

c. *To be a jump above* (someone's) *tallest persimmons,* to be beyond (someone's) immediate comprehension or understanding.

1845 *Knickerb.* XXV. 425 Wall now, that are's a jump above my tallest persimmons.

d. *To bring down the persimmon,* to win the prize; *to rake up the persimmons,* (see quot. 1871).

1857 *Porter's Spirit of Times* 3 Jan. 294/2 The lad that goes a sparking on a spanking horse of his own, is the one that 'brings down the persimmon!' **1871** DE VERE 50 To *rake up the persimmons* is a frequent term for 'pocketing the stakes.'

4. Attrib. with *bark, bush, pond, time.*

1626 in *Amer. Speech* XV. 294/2 Extending Southerly . . . towards the pursimond ponds. **1786** WASHINGTON *Diaries* II. 102 A parcel of small Persimon bushes. **1832** KENNEDY *Swallow Barn* II. 164 *'Possums* in general were not to be followed till persimmon time. **1865** KELLOGG *Rebel Prisons* 324 One of the principal remedies for diarrhea was prepared from oak, sweet gum, and persimmon bark.

+**Persimmon beer.** *S.* A beer made of persimmons.

1737 BRICKELL *N. Carolina* 38 The following are made in the Country, *viz.* Cyder, Persimon-Beer, made of the Fruit of that Tree [etc.]. **1784** SMYTH *Tour* I. 151 [In the Carolinas] they brew a fermented liquor, which is called persimmon beer. **1833** FLINT *D. Boone* 115 Persimmon and maple beer stood them well instead of the poisonous whisky of their children. **1898** HARRIS *Tales of Home Folks* 19 The colonel insisted on having some yam-potatoes roasted in the ashes to go along with persimmon beer. **1904** STUART *River's Children* 71 Toasts, drunk in ginger-pop and persimmon beer innocent of guile, were offered.

+**Persimmon tree.** An American tree (*Diospyros virginiana*) common throughout the South.

1737 WESLEY *Journal* I. 402 In the moistest part of this land [in Ga.] some persimmon-trees grow (which bear a sort of yellow, clear, luscious plum). **1785** WASHINGTON *Diaries* II. 409 Corn . . . had been planted under the Persimon trees in the fields. **1817** FORDHAM *Narr. Travels* 143 I found today a beautiful prisimon tree, about fifty feet high, and a great quantity of fruit upon it. **1883** *Harper's Mag.* Sept. 645/1 Climb the persimmon tree and git yer breakfast. **1902** BELL *Hope Loring* 29 Hope . . . did not stop until she reached a tall persimmon-tree which overhung the roof of the side porch.

Personal. {1678-} +**a.** One of a series of short advertisements concerning individuals, their whereabouts, their personal problems, etc. +**b.** A local news item concerning a person. — **1873** F. HUDSON *Journalism U.S.* 472 Take the 'personals' of the *Herald* any day, and they will set one to thinking. **1875** HOLLAND *Sevenoaks* 103 His eye was attracted, among the 'personals,' to an item [etc.]. **1889** CUSTER *Tenting on Plains* 411 Her son declared . . . that he had caught her reading the 'personals.'

Personal liberty. The freedom of an individual to do as he pleases so long as he does not violate the laws of organized society. {1765-} +Freq. used in connection with Negro slavery in the United States. Also attrib.

1849 *Ill. Laws* 99 When any such prisoner is about to be removed beyond the limits of this state . . . , [he] shall at all times be entitled to reasonable delay for the purpose of . . . availing himself of the laws of this state, for the security of personal liberty. **1857** *Harper's Mag.* June 117/2 The Legislature of Maine has passed a 'Personal Liberty Bill,' declaring all slaves brought into that State to be free. **1864** J. SHERMAN *Sherman Lett.* 237 All the clamor the Copperheads can make about personal liberty doesn't affect the people, if they can only see security and success. **1887** *Independent* 17 Nov. 11/2 The Saloon played a conspicuous part in the elections of last week, particularly in New York and Pennsylvania, where it appeared in the guise of 'Personal Liberty.' **1899** CUSHMAN *Hist. Indians* 267 He seized his bottle of whiskey, that 'bright insignia' of the white man's 'Personal Liberty.' **1914** *Cycl. Amer. Govt.* II. 673/1 The earliest personal liberty laws were statutes enacted by northern states to secure the benefit of trial by jury to alleged fugitive slaves.

+**Personal Liberty party.** A political party in New York and Pennsylvania in 1887 which opposed legislation aimed against saloons and the liquor traffic. — **1887** *N.Y. Tribune* 12 Oct. 2 The alliance of the Democratic party and of the Personal Liberty party, to pass a law to open the liquor stores from 2 P.M. until midnight on Sunday, is alarming the clergymen of the State. **1887** *Public Opinion* 29 Oct. 58/1 The Personal Liberty party believe that they ought to be able to spend their Sundays as they see fit.

Personnel. {1834} The body of persons engaged in some service or employed by some institution. {personal, 1818-; personnel, 1857-} Also attrib. — **1819** W. T. TONE *Necessity of Improving Our Nat. Forces* 97 Everything relative to the personnel and materiel of the artillery. **1862** MCCLELLAN in *Own Story* 485 In case our front is broken, I will still make every effort to preserve at least the *personnel* of the army. **1922** *Factory* Feb. 177/2 Under personnel records comes all clerical work incidental to keeping necessary information on the personnel.

+**Person of color.** A Negro or a person of Negro blood. (Cf. COLOR 2 b 2.) — **1808** *Phila. Ordinances* (1812) 222 Free persons of colour. **1817, 1840, 1844, 1888** [see COLOR 2 b 2].

***Persuader.** +A cannon or revolver. — **1844** DICKENS *Martin Chuzzlewit* xxxiv, I didn't admire his carryin' them murderous little persuaders, and being so ready to use 'em. **1862** *N.Y. Tribune* 3 June (Chipman), In the South heavy guns are called persuaders. **1913** LONDON *Valley of Moon* 355, I've got my little persuader with me.

Peruke-maker. One who makes perukes. *Obs.* {1697-1817} — **1743** FRANKLIN *Writings* II. 232 Alexander Miller, Peruke-maker, . . . takes Opportunity to acquaint his Customers, that he intends to leave off the Shaving Business after the 22nd of August next. **1761** *Boston Gazette* 18 Feb., Joshua Davis, Peruke-Maker, . . . has Remov'd his Shop from the Head of the Long Wharf. **1790** *Penna. Packet* 16 Oct. 3/4 The highest Wages will be given to a Journeyman Peruke-Maker and Hair-Dresser, who understands his business.

Peruvian bark. The dried bark of any one of various trees of the genus *Cinchona.* {1663-} — **1776** *Jrnls. Cont. Congress.* IV. 324 Resolved, That the Secret Committee be directed to send two hundred pounds of Peruvian bark to the commanding officer. **1806** LEWIS in *L. & Clark Exped.* V. (1905) 243, I had last evening applyed a poltice of peruvian barks. **1856** *Fla. Plantation Rec.* 163, I have him on aprepration of Steeal dust, Copras, Pruvian barks and Salt peater and Whiskey.

Peruvian guano. Guano obtained from places on or near the Peruvian coast. (Cf. GUANO.) — **1852** *Horticulturist* VII. 144 Bone dust and Peruvian guano advertised by New-York dealers. **1858** C. FLINT *Milch Cows* 198 The best of the concentrated manures . . . is, unquestionably, Peruvian guano. **1863** *Rep. Comm. Agric. 1862* 98, I applied 125 pounds of Peruvian guano. **1889** *Cent.* 2644/2 The Peruvian guano of commerce formerly came from the Chincha islands; but in recent years the chief sources of supply are Pabellon de Pica, Punta de Lobos, Huanillos, and other places on or near the Peruvian coast.

+**Peskily,** *adv.* In a pesky or vexatious manner. *colloq.* — **1834** C. A. DAVIS *Lett. J. Downing* 139 The Post Office accounts was the next bother; and that puzzled all on us peskily. **1835-7** HALIBURTON *Clockmaker* 1 Ser. xxi. 188 When he seed that, he grew most peskily ryled. **1877** *Atlantic Mo.* July 77/2 It doos rile him peskily; he dono how on airth to put up with it.

+**Pesky,** *a.* and *adv. colloq.* [Origin obscure.]

1. *adj.* Mean; annoying; disagreeable.

1775 DEANE *Correspondence* 224 What reply, think ye, these heroes of five companies of the invincible Royal Irish, gave to this pesky Yankey? **1830** *Mass. Spy* 13 Oct. (Th.), I'm plagued most to death with these ere pesky sore eyes. **1880** N. BROOKS *Fairport Nine* 14 'Those pesky boys,' sighed Grandmother Boffin. **1923** J. H. COOK *On Old Frontier* 146 We had better send the man back to camp . . . while we tried to kill the pesky varmint that had tampered with our meat cache.

2. *adv.* 'Darned.' An intensive with derogatory implications.

1833 SMITH *Life J. Downing* 193 They called each other some pesky hard names. **1845** JUDD *Margaret* II. 305 So pesky slow, we sha'nt get through teu night. **1855** HALIBURTON *Nature & Hum. Nature* II. 64 Don't be so pesky starch. **1901** *Harper's Mag.* Dec. 228 Pesky few Democrats ever I see who—.

***Peso.** *S.W.* +**a.** =MEXICAN DOLLAR. +**b.** A name occasionally given the American dollar. — **1840** *Picayune* 18 Sept. 2/5, I'll give a heap of *paysos* for Santa Fe just for your sakes. **1885** *Wkly. New Mexican Rev.* 19 March 4/6 One of them [an Indian] whittled out a bowie-knife out of a pine stick, . . . swore to Jake Gold that it was a relic of his ancestors, demanding 'tres pesos' for it. **1900** *Congress. Rec.* 15 Feb. 1824/2 The valuation of a peso in 1899 in American money was 46 cents on the dollar. **1907** WHITE *Arizona Nights* 255 'Here Tony,' said he with a slight laugh, 'here's a peso.'

Pesthouse. A house or hospital for those having infectious or contagious diseases. {1611–} — **1718** *Boston Rec.* 127 The Select men [shall] be impowered to Lease out a peice of Land on Dere Island . . . to be improved for the Erecting an Hospitall or Pest House there for the reception & entertainmt of Sick persons comeing from beyond Sea, and in Order to prevent the Spreading of Infection. **1790** BENTLEY *Diary* I. 211 Odell's funeral from the Pest House was without a single man in the procession but myself. **1856** GOODRICH *Recoll.* I. 42 In the year 1798, . . . my father's house was converted into a hospital, or, as it was then called, a 'pest-house,' where . . . I was inoculated for this disease [smallpox]. **1898** *Kansas City Star* 18 Dec. 4/2 A pest house [for smallpox patients] has been built at Stroud [Okla.].

***Pestle.** Also †**pestill.**

***1.** An instrument, usually club-shaped, used for pounding or grinding substances in a mortar.

1633 *N.H. Doc. & Rec.* I. 77, 1 pestle and morter. **1688** SEWALL *Letter-Book* I. 90 Send so much Lignum Vitae as may make two or three very fair Mortars and pestills. **1729** *Md. Hist. Mag.* XVIII. 333, 2 glass pestles, 15[s.]. **1898** CANFIELD *Maid of Frontier* 213 Large stone with a hollow scooped in the center, that has a pestle for grinder.

+**2.** *spec.* A pestle used in preparing corn for use as samp or hominy.

1655 *Mayflower Descendant* XI. 18 One samp morter one pestle one Dressing board. **1731** HEMPSTEAD *Diary* 231, I was at home al day. fixt my Samp Morter made a Pestill &c. **1827** COOPER *Prairie* ii, Others [were engaged] in plying the heavy pestle of a movable hominy-mortar. **1856** CARTWRIGHT *Autobiog.* 25 [We] beat our meal and hominy with a pestle and mortar.

+**Pet bank.** (See quot. 1914.) Now hist. Also attrib. — **1834** C. A. DAVIS *Lett. J. Downing* 353 Mr. Van Buren . . . didn't say nothin about hard money in the place [of bank bills]. . . . The *safety fund* banks and the *pet* banks couldn't drink that toast no how. **1838** CLAY *Speeches* (1842) 355 The senator from South Carolina reminds us that we denounced the pet bank system. **1852** GOUGE *Fiscal Hist. Texas* p. vii, Does the deep experience of the evils we have suffered under both a national bank and a league of 'pet banks' incline us to separate bank and State? **1914** *Cycl. Amer. Govt.* II. 674/2 *Pet Banks.* Term derisively applied by the opponents of President Jackson to the state banks which Amos Kendall and Secretary Taney selected in 1833 in which to place the government deposits, in place of the Second United States Bank.

Peter, *v.*[1] {1812–} +*intr.* To fail, become exhausted, or give out. In full *to peter out.* Also *ppl. a.*

1854 H. H. RILEY *Puddleford* 84 He 'hoped this 'spectable meeting war n't going to Peter-out.' **1869** *Overland Mo.* III. 127 After a long desert journey the oxen become much 'petered.' *c*1873 DE VERE *MS. Notes* 308 Petered out, carries no sense of disapproval or dislike w[ith] it. A person, or mine or anyth[in]g alive may be 'petered out' but never a lifeless object. **1884** *Century Mag.* Dec. 194 We'll have a blank good time, . . . anyhow, as long as the whisky don't peter out. **1902** LORIMER *Lett. Merchant* 246 After they have told you what they propose to do and get right up to doing it, they simply peter out. **1911** ROLT-WHEELER *Boy with Census* 10 The real ol'-time feud is peterin' out, an' it's mainly due to the schoolin'. **1913** LONDON *Valley of Moon* 377 The road . . . peters out altogether farther down.

+**Peter,** *v.*[2] [f. next.] 'To run up a thing at an auction sale' (B. '77).

+**Peter Funk.** A swindler; a by-bidder at an auction. Also fig. and attrib. — **1834** GREENE *Perils of Pearl St.* 51 Peter Funk . . . is the very imp of deception; . . . his name is sometimes used figuratively to signify any thing which is employed for the purpose of deception. **1862** BROWNE *A. Ward His Book* 230 Then advisin him to keep away from the Peter Funk auctions of the East. **1867** *Congress. Globe* 19 July 737/3 [This lottery swindler] has an office in this city where he claims to have the pictures exposed, as Peter Funks generally do. **1893** *Chicago Tribune* 19 April 11/4 It is rarely that any one gets a fair equivalent for his money in one of these so-called 'Peter Funk' shops.

***Peter's-wort.** (See also ST.-PETER'S-WORT.) +**a.** A plant of the genus *Ascyrum*, esp. *A. stans* of the southeastern states. +**b.** The snowberry (*Symphoricarpos racemosus*) or a related species. — **1813** MUHLENBERG *Cat. Plants* 68 *Ascyrum*, Andrew's cross, Peter's wort. **1817–8** EATON *Botany* (1822) 186 *Ascyrum crux-andreæ*, peter's wort. **1819** SCHOOLCRAFT *Mo. Lead Mines* 29 There are also some plants from which colours have been extracted for dyeing; such are peterswort[,] crab-apple, shumac [etc.]. **1833** EATON *Botany* (ed. 6) 360 *Symphoria racemosa*, peter's wort.

+**Petitionee.** The person against whom a petition is made. — **1764** *Conn. Rec.* XII. 262 The said Wheeler refused . . . to give the petitioner any further day of payment thereon, unless the petitioner would . . . execute notes of hand to the petitionee for the whole added together. **1767** *Ib.* 618 Under the circumstances the petitioner ought not in equity to be holden to answer the same to the petitionee.

Petit juror. A member of a petit jury. (Cf. PETTY JUROR.) — **1742** *Boston Rec.* 305 The Town proceeded to Choose Six Grand Jurors and draw Ten Petit Jurors out of the Box. **1774** J. ANDREWS *Letters* 36 The Grand-jurors gave in their reasons in writing and the petit-jurors by a bare negative. **1809** KENDALL *Travels* I. 182 The petit-jurors are chosen by the justices of the peace, selectmen, constables, grand-jurors conjointly. **1845** *Indiana Senate Jrnl.* 29 Sess. 366 A bill for summoning grand and petit jurors in the counties of Madison and Hancock.

***Petit jury.** A jury of twelve men that decides upon the facts involved in a case brought before it; a trial jury. (See also PETTY JURY and cf. GRAND JURY.) — **1641** *Mass. Liberties* 221 Whether it be a grand or petit Jurie, It shall have libertie to give a non Liquit, or a spetiall verdict. **1737** *Boston Rec.* 167 The Select Men, having taken a List of the Names of the Inhabitants, liable by Law, and qualified to serve on the Petit Jury, laid the same before the Town. **1802** *Ann. 7th Congress* 1 Sess. 1341 Nor shall he [*i.e.*, the clerk of the district court] cause to be summoned or returned a petit jury to such sessions of the said district court. **1877** JOHNSON *Anderson Co., Kansas* 89 Judge J. Y. Campbell . . . had both grand and petit juries.

Petit juryman. =PETTY JURYMAN. — **1670** *Portsmouth Rec.* 155 Chosen pettit jury men for the Court of Tryalls aforesayd.

Pet lamb. +**1.** =FIRE ZOUAVE. *Obs.* +**2.** (See quotation.) *Obs.* — (**1**) **1861** *N.Y. Tribune* 18 July 3/4 A Pet Lamb Astonishes the Secessionists.—The Richmond papers tell of a Fire Zouave who was caught and taken to Fairfax. (**2**) **1892** M. A. JACKSON *Gen. Jackson* 224 The malcontents left their posts . . . and taunted 'Jackson's pet lambs,' as they called the Stonewall Brigade.

Petrara. (See PATERERO.)

+**Petrified forest.** Logs of trees in which the organic substance has been changed to mineral matter; an area where such petrified trees may be found. — **1872** MCCLELLAN *Golden State* 484 [In] Calistoga . . . are located the hot springs and petrified forests. **1873** COZZENS *Marvellous Country* 76 We came upon the remains of a petrified forest, . . . converted by some chemical process into specimens of variegated jasper. **1915** ARMSTRONG & THORNBER *Western Wild Flowers* 506 Desert Innocence . . . grows in the dreadful sandy wastes of the Petrified Forest.

+**Petrified wasp('s) nest.** A madreporite or fossil coral: (see quot. 1824). — **1814** *Amer. Mineral. Jrnl.* I. 4 The marine production, commonly called 'petrified wasp's nest,' or 'honeycomb.' **1818** *Amer. Jrnl. Science* I. 385 These fossils are known by the name of petrified wasp-nests, from the resemblance they bear to the nests of those insects. **1824** BLANE *Excursion U.S.* 116 In one part [of the rapids near Louisville, Ky.], there is a large reef of coral and madreporite, which latter substance, from its singular appearance, the people call 'petrified wasps' nests.'

+**Petrolatum.** A tasteless, odorless, pharmaceutical substance consisting essentially of the refined residue resulting from the distillation of petroleum. — **1887** *Scientific Amer.* 7 May 293/3 With a silk handkerchief apply petrolatum evenly. **1890** WEBSTER 1073/2 *Petrolatum* is the officinal name for the purified product. *Cosmoline* and *vaseline* are commercial names for substances essentially the same.

***Petroleum.** Also †**petrolium.** A heavy, dark-colored, inflammable, mineral oil occurring in nature; rock oil.

1805 T. M. HARRIS *Journal* 46 The *Seneca Indian Oil* in so much repute here is *Petroleum.* **1837** IRVING *Bonneville* I. 223 Petrolium, or naptha, . . . is found . . . in some places in the United States. **1890** *Stock Grower & Farmer* 25 Jan. 5/3 During 1889 the United States exported 400,000,000 gallons of petroleum. **1913** *Bureau of Mines Bul.* No. 71, 5 The United States produces all of the fuller's earth used for refining petroleum within its borders.

b. Attrib. with *oil, people, stove, torch.*

1868 *Mich. Agric. Rep.* VII. 349 D. Kellogg, Detroit, [exhibited the] best petroleum stove. **1889** *Scribner's Mag.* Aug. 192/2 A vessel of high-boiling petroleum-oil like the well-known 'astral oil.' **1894** CABLE *J. March* ix, Viewing matters impartially in the clear, calm light of petroleum torches. **1914** *Cycl. Amer. Govt.* II. 675/2 *Petroleum People*, a name given by the newspapers about 1864 to the ostentatious newly rich who had gained their wealth from the oil wells of western Pennsylvania.

Petteraro. (See PATTERARO.)

Pettiauger. =PERIAGUA. {1703–} — **1732** *S.C. Gazette* 28/1 Tuesday Night last a Pettyawger laden with a considerable Quantity of Rice, was unfortunately lost. **1741** *N.C. Laws* (1791) 77 This Act . . . [shall not] be construed to extend to any Person who shall press any Boat, Canoe, or Pettiaugua, by public Authority. **1791** W. BARTRAM *Travels* 92 The trunks of these trees, when hollowed out, make large and durable pettiaugers and canoes. **1813** *Niles' Reg.* IV. 75/1 A large petiauger . . . was intercepted by the above pilot-boat.

***Petticoat.** A skirt or underskirt worn by women and girls.

1644 *Conn. Rec.* I. 457, 2 Cloath petticoats. **1697** SEWALL *Letter-Book* I. 191 Buy for me . . . fourty yards to make Gowns and Petticoats for my Daughters. **1707** *Boston News-Letter* 14 July 2/2 A Servant Maid . . . having on a green damask Gown and Petticoat. **1798** in Hawkins *Letters* 500 Emautlau Haujo takes with him 2 women's petticoats, 1 woman's jacket [etc.]. **1807** GASS *Journal* 165 The women have a kind of fringe petticoats, made of filaments or tassels of the white cedar bark. **1891** WILKINS *New Eng. Nun* 86 She had on nothing but a woollen petticoat and a calico waist. **1907** *St. Nicholas* July 832/1, I rushed around, . . . finally securing . . . an old red cloth petticoat from the wife of one of our soldiers.

+**b.** (See quot. 1890.) Also attrib.

1884 *Nat. Museum Bul.* No. 27, 796 *Petticoat barrell.* 'A very useful garment to fishermen, better serving the purpose of pants in warm weather, by permitting the free circulation of air around the body of wearer.' **1890** *Cent.* 4429/3 *Petticoat*, . . . a garment worn by fishermen . . . , made of oilcloth or coarse canvas, very wide and descending to the calf of the leg, generally with an insertion for each leg, but sometimes like a woman's petticoat.

+**Petticoat pipe.** (See quotations.) — **1864** Webster 977/3 *Petticoat pipe*, . . . one of a series of short, conical pipes, in a smoke-box, to equalize the draught. **1876** Knight 1676/2 *Petticoat-pipe*, . . . a pipe (*a*) in the chimney (*b*) of a locomotive, which comes down over the exhaust-nozzle (*c*), and conducts the escaping steam and the smoke and sparks which follow the induced current into the arrester *d*. **1888** *Scientific Amer.* LIX. 369 Most of our engines are still run with a diamond stack and short smoke-box, with the petticoat-pipe for leading the steam into the stack.

Petticoat trousers. {1867-} +**1.** Wide, baggy trousers. *Obs.* **2.** =Petticoat b. {1867} — (1) **1753** *N.J. Archives* XIX. 291 He took with him . . . two Pair of Petticoat Trowsers. **1761** *Ib.* XX. 597 An English servant lad . . . [had] long petticoat trowsers, much worn. (2) *a***1870** Chipman *Notes on Bartlett* 318 *Petticoat-trowsers*, trowsers, very short but of great width, worn by fishermen.—Essex Co., Mass. **1881** *Harper's Mag.* Jan. 190/1 One day two sailors, dressed in petticoat trousers, . . . arrested the attention of a young girl.

Petty juror. =Petit juror. — **1691** *Duxbury Rec.* 182 The town made choice of Ensign Barker and Josiah Holmes to serve as petty jurors.

Petty jury. =Petit jury. {1711-} Also attrib. — **1686** *Duxbury Rec.* 175 The Town made choice of Seth Arnold & John Soule to serve on the petty jury. **1694** *N.C. Col. Rec.* I. 401 Ye Petty Jury . . . found ye Priso[ne]r guilty of Petty Larceny. **1709** *Md. Hist. Mag.* IV. 385 The petty Jury room Twelve foot long and sixteen foot wide.

Petty juryman. A member of a petit jury. — **1663** *Portsmouth Rec.* 124 Graund Jury men . . . Pettey Jury men. **1690** *Plymouth Laws* 223 All persons concerned . . . in any Case Civill or Criminal witnesses Grand and Petty-jurymen and Constables are to attend sd Court.

***Petty morrell.** +The American spikenard, *Aralia racemosa*. Also attrib. — **1778** Carver *Travels* 511 *Spikenard*, vulgarly called in the colonies Petty-Morrell, . . . appears to be exactly the same as the Asiatick spikenard. **1789** Morse *Amer. Geog.* 53 Besides these are several other roots and plants of a medicinal kind, such as . . . spikenard or petty-morrell. **1832** Child *Frugal Housewife* 28 Petty morrel-root, and horse-radish, well steeped in cider, are excellent for the jaundice. **1892** *Amer. Folk-Lore* V. 97 *Aralia racemosa*, Indian root; life of man; petty morrell. N.H.

Petunia. An herb of the genus *Petunia* of the potato family, esp. *P. hybrida*, the common garden petunia; also, the showy flower of such an herb. {1825-} Also attrib. — **1842** *Lowell Offering* II. 290 Unless, indeed you could find a daisy, snow-ball, petunia, or rose hiding itself in the shrubbery. **1865** A. D. Whitney *Gayworthys* 311 They placed flowers about; . . . colorless asters and petunias. **1879** Stockton *Rudder Grange* ii, The boarder was there, standing by the petunia bed. **1909** 'O. Henry' *Options* 284 She thought she saw some petunias . . . just like some she used to raise down in the old Virginia home.

***Pew.** Also †**pue.** In a church auditorium, a long bench or seat with a back; formerly, often, a compartment provided with seats, usu. for the members of a family.

1701 Sewall *Diary* II. 39, I was in the Lt. Governours Pue. **1745** *N.H. Probate Rec.* III. 237, I give unto my Son Nathaniel Webster my Pew & Chairs in the Meeting house. **1847** Robb *Squatter Life* 99 Jake Simons, sittin' close bang up agin Sofy, in the same pew with her daddy! **1891** Earle *Sabbath* 37 The seats were, until well into this century, almost universally hung on hinges, and could be turned up against the walls of the pew. **1908** Lorimer *J. Spurlock* 69 A pew costs ten thousand a year.

b. Attrib. and comb. with *chair, holder, seat, tax.*

1845 *Lowell Offering* V. 18, I can see no alternative unless our ministers consent to live in a less expensive manner, and thereby diminish our pew-tax. **1868** G. G. Channing *Recoll. Newport* 28 Upon trial, it was ascertained that only one pew-holder wished the privilege of contributing weekly. **1876** Knight 1676/2 *Pew-chair*, a seat affixed to the end of a pew so as to occupy a part of the aisle when seats in excess of the pew accommodation are required. **1891** Earle *Sabbath* 80 In the middle of his petition the minister usually made a long pause in order that any who were infirm or ill might let down their slamming pew-seats and sit down.

Pew cushion. A cushion for use on the seat of a church pew. — **1879** Burdette *Hawkeyes* 56 The woman's aid society . . . had been unable to fulfill their pledge to pay for the pew cushions. **1885** *Century Mag.* Aug. 612/1 The condition at . . . improvised hospitals was improved next day by the offerings from many churches of pew-cushions, which, sewn together, made comfortable beds. **1907** Wiggin *Old Peabody Pew* 36 There are only twenty pew-cushions and six hassocks in the whole church.

+**Pewee.** Also **peewee.** [Echoic.] **a.** =Chewink. **b.** Any of various small flycatchers, as the phoebe bird, *Sayornis phoebe.* **c.** (See quot. 1917.)

See also Wood pewee.

1796 Morse *Univ.Geog.* I. 210 Towhe Bird, Pewee, Cheeweeh. *Fringilla erythrophthalma.* **1806** Lewis in *L. & Clark Exped.* VI. (1905) 214 At the rock fort camp saw the prarie lark, a species of the peawee. **1839** Irving in *Knickerb.* XIII. 434 The Pewit, or Pe-wee, or Phœbe-bird . . . is called by each of these names. **1858** *Atlantic Mo.* Dec. 870/2 In the open field . . . as well as in the wood we find the Pewee, or Phoebe, (*Muscicapa nunciola*,) one of our most common and interesting birds. **1877** *Harper's Mag.* April 659/2 [The wood pewee] is . . . even more familiar than its cousin, the common pewee, or Phoebe-bird. **1893** *Scribner's Mag.* June 765/2 The plain, dull-colored pee-wee or phœbe, . . . catching insects. **1917** *Birds of Amer.* I. 225 Woodcock. *Philohela minor*. . . . [Also called] Bogbird; Pewee; Whistler.

+**Pewee flycatcher.** The phoebe bird (*Sayornis phoebe*) or a related bird. — **1823** James *Exped.* I. 263 *Musicapa fusca*—Pewee fly-catcher, Wilson. **1839** Audubon *Ornith. Biog.* V. 424 Common Pewee Flycatcher, *Muscicapa Fusca*, . . . is found in every portion of the United States. **1885** M. Thompson *Byways & Bird Notes* 9 He was sure I should find every evidence that a mocking-bird was a soulless monster, murdering little pee-wee fly-catchers and warblers. **1917** *Birds of Amer.* II. 203 Wood Pewee. *Myiochanes virens*. . . . [Also called] Pewee Flycatcher.

***Pewit.** Also **peewit.** +**a.** =Chewink. +**b.** =Pewee b.

1832 Williamson *Maine* I. 143 The Pewit, or Cheeweeh, lives in the summer months about barns and out buildings. **1872** *Maryland Laws* 664 It shall be unlawful . . . to shoot or trap . . . any of the following named birds: . . . wren, pewit, goldfinch, sapsucker [etc.]. **1902** White *Blazed Trail* 296 Myrtle and magnolia warblers, oven birds, peewits . . . passed silently or noisily. **1917** *Birds of Amer.* II. 203 Wood Pewee. *Myiochanes virens*. . . . [Also called] Pewit; Pewee; Pewee Flycatcher.

+**Pewit flycatcher.** The phoebe bird, *Sayornis phoebe*. — **1810** Wilson *Ornithology* II. 78 [The] Pewit Flycatcher, *Muscicapa Nunciola*, . . . I overtook . . . in the low swampy woods of North and South Carolina. They were feeding on smilax berries. **1839** Peabody *Mass. Birds* 293 The Pewit Flycatcher, *Muscicapa atra*, commonly known by the name of phoebe, is a familiar and welcome bird. **1874** Coues *Birds N.W.* 241 *Sayornis Fuscus*. . . . Pewit Flycatcher; Phoebe-bird. **1917** *Birds of Amer.* II. 198.

Pew rent. The rent paid for a pew. {1840-} — **1840** Mathews *Politicians* iv. viii, No taxes, pew-rents, ground-rents, assessments. **1894** 'Mark Twain' *Those Twins* ii, Pew-rent is on the same basis, but at peep shows we pay double. **1904** Glasgow *Deliverance* 38, I go to church like clockwork, and pay my pew-rent.

***Pewter.** Also †**puter.**

***1.** *collect.* Pewter ware.

1639 *Conn. Rec.* I. 444 Brasse and pewter. **1699** *N. H. Probate Rec.* I. 449 My puter and bras I give to my three dofters. **1745** *Ib.* III. 320, I give to my welbeloved Daughter Sarah King all my Pewter which is Fouer Platers Six Plates one Bason. **1790** *Columbian Centinel* 29 Sept. 19/3 [For sale,] mahogany Chairs with hair bottoms, . . . copper Sauce-Pans, some Pewter, Feather-Beds, &c. **1885** Eggleston in *Century Mag.* April 878/2, I must content myself with a passing mention of the ancient 'dresser' of the earlier colonial time, with its stock of pewter. **1905** *Smithsonian Inst. Ann. Rep. 1904* 708 As by a process of natural evolution pewter has ousted wood from the kitchen, so china in its turn has inevitably supplanted pewter.

***2.** *attrib.* passing into *adj.* Made of pewter.

1624 Smith *Gen. Hist. Va.* I. 3 Granganameo taking most liking to a Pewter dish, made a hole in it, [and] hung it about his necke for a brest-plate. **1684** *Essex Inst. Coll.* XXV. 154 A bason, six Pewter platters, a bed pan. **1701** *N.H. Probate Rec.* I. 486, I give unto my grand child William marston one gun and one puter platter. **1784** Franklin *Autobiog.* 324 My breakfast was a long time bread and milk (no tea), and I ate it out of a twopenny earthen porringer, with a pewter spoon. **1830** Watson *Philadelphia* 184 Pewter platters and porringers, made to shine along a 'dresser,' were universal. **1898** I. H. Harper *S. B. Anthony* I. 15 Along the edge of the pantry shelves hung rows of shining pewter porringers. **1901** Churchill *Crisis* 482 Two candles were burning in pewter sticks on the bare mahogany table.

***Pewterer.** One who makes various articles of pewter. — **1654** Johnson *Wonder-w. Prov.* 209 Weavers, Brewers, . . . Pewterers, . . . are orderly turn'd to their trades. **1685** *Boston Rec.* 178 Thomas Clarke pewterer, hath libertie gra[n]ted to dig vp the towne ground. **1710** *Ib.* 67 Mr. Thomas Clark of Boston Pewterer . . . Signified his request. **1800** *Columbian Centinel* 11 Jan. 2/3 The procession . . . [included] lightermen, limners, . . . pewterers [etc.].

+**Peyote.** Also **payote.** *S.W.* [Mex. Sp. from Nahuatl *peyotl*.] A cactus, as *Lophophora williamsii*, or a food or drink prepared from this. (Cf. Mescal 3 b.) — **1849** Audubon *Western Journal* 186 Out of these acorns the Indians make their 'payote,' a kind of paste, which they dry, and then put into water in flakes, no doubt to allow the acrid matter to escape. *Ib.* 213 The food of these Indians is chiefly the 'payote' made from the acorns into a kind of gruel. **1892** *Dialect Notes* I. 193 *Peyote:* a plant of the cactus family, sometimes called 'dry whiskey,' as it is said to produce intoxication when chewed (*Mamillaria fissurata*, Engelm., or *Anhalonium fissuratum*, Lemaire). Probably of Mexican origin. [Tex.]

+**P. G.** Abbreviation for *public gaol:* (see quot.). — **1748** *Va. Statutes at Large* V. 554 The said keeper shall cause a strong iron collar, with the letters P. G. stamped thereon, to be put on the neck of every runaway.

+**Phacelia.** A genus of American plants of the waterleaf family or a plant of this genus. Also with specifying term. — **1817-8** Eaton *Botany* (1822) 386 *Phacelia bipinnatifida*, phacelia. **1898** A. M. Davidson *Calif. Plants* 119 There are many kinds of Phacelias; the flowers vary much in size and in color and form, but they always grow in clusters that last a long time. **1915** Armstrong & Thornber *Western Wild Flowers* 402

There are many kinds of Phacelia. *Ib.* 410 Arizona Phacelia ... [is] a little desert plant, not very pretty.

***Phaeton.**

1. A light, four-wheeled carriage or buggy, usually with two seats, with or without a top. {1742-}

There were different styles of the basic design of this carriage.

1759 *Penna. Gazette* 19 Nov. 1/3 (Ernst), Landaus, phaetons, two and four wheeled chaises. **1794** *Ann. 3d Congress* 1452 There shall be levied ... for and upon every phaeton and coachee, six dollars. **1838** *U.S. Mag.* Jan. 152 Judge Cushing always travelled in an open phaeton and pair. **1884** *N.Y. Herald* 27 Oct. 1/2 Extension Top Phaetons, $100 up. **1907** *St. Nicholas* Aug. 880/2 And very lovely they all looked, especially the lady dolls in their broughams, Victorias, and phaëtons.

+2. A two-seated, open automobile.

1908 *Internat. Motor Cycl.* 367/1 *Phaeton.*—An open carriage, frequently provided with a top and a single seat (for two) for the owner, and, generally, a servant's seat fixed at the rear and entered from both sides. **1922** *Automotive Industries* XLVII. 759/1 In the 1906 Handbook [of the Association of Licensed Automobile Manufacturers], Packard, Walters and Stevens-Duryea used the name 'phaeton.'

Phalanstery. [Fr. *phalanstère.*] In Fourier's scheme of society, a socialistic community, or the set of buildings occupied by a community. {in fig. senses 1850-} — **1846** *Knickerb.* XXVIII. 16 And are all your slaves productive workers? This is contemplated, I believe in all the *Phalansteries* of Unitative Associationists. **a1850** M. FULLER *Life Without* 148 Visions of phalansteries in every park. **1852** HAWTHORNE *Blithedale Rom.* 153 One of our purposes was to erect a Phalanstery ... after Fourier; ... where the great and general family should have its abiding-place.

***Phalanx.** A community of Fourierists. {1843} — **1843** *Mass. Acts & Resolves* 489 George Ripley, Charles A. Dana, and Lewis H. Ryckman, their associates and successors, are hereby made a corporation, by the name of the Brook Farm Phalanx. **1845** *Xenia Torch-Light* 31 July 2/4 Numerous "Phalanxes" have been established throughout the country, but in no instance that has fallen under our eye has one of them stood the test of experience.

Phalarope. Any of several small snipelike birds of the family Phalaropodidae {1776-}, +as the red phalarope and Wilson's phalarope. (See also NORTHERN PHALAROPE.) — **[1813** WILSON *Ornithology* IX. 72 The Phalaropes constitute one of the links between the Waders and the Web-footed tribes.] **1835** AUDUBON *Ornith. Biog.* III. 400 My son procured two specimens of this [Wilson's] Phalarope out of a flock of five, on the rocks at the rapids of the Ohio below Louisville. **a1852** THOREAU *Cape Cod* 103 One little bird not larger than a sparrow,—it may have been a Phalarope,—would alight on the turbulent surface where the breakers were five or six feet high. **1883** *Nat. Museum Bul.* No. 27, 153 *Phalaropus fulicarius* (Linn.) Red Phalarope.... Northern hemisphere, breeding far northward. **1917** *Birds of Amer.* I. 217 The baby Phalaropes are covered with down at birth.

Pharmaceutist. A pharmacist. {1836-} — **1849** *Amer. Jrnl. Pharmacy* XV. 213 This work ... is designed to instruct the pharmaceutist. **1885** WELLS *Practical Economics* 231 Artisans, manufacturers, and pharmaceutists ... formerly consumed untaxed alcohol in great quantities.

Pharmacist. One who compounds medicinal prescriptions; one skilled in compounding drugs. {1834-} Cf. DRUGGIST. — **1869** *Pharmacist* (Chicago) I. 76 The conscientious pharmacist is often compelled to keep on hand the preparations of several manufacturers. **1884** *Ill. Bd. of Pharmacy Rep.* III. 5 Popular opinion today demands from the pharmacist more than the ordinary routine knowledge of dealing in drugs. **1892** *York County Hist. Rev.* 7 R. William Ziegler, Pharmacist, 400 W. Market St. **1918** *Amer. Jrnl. of Pharmacy* XC. 838 Any educational institution should be proud of the opportunity of training both pharmacists and druggists.

***Pharmacy.** A drug store. {1833-} — **1858** VIELÉ *Following Drum* 149 A billiard room, an eating saloon, a bakery and even a 'pharmacie' ... are found here. **1880** CABLE *Grandissimes* 92 That evening at the pharmacy—was there a tall handsome gentleman standing by the counter. **1916** WILSON *Somewhere* 21 She says to Mrs. Judge Ballard and Mrs. Martingale and me in the Cut-Rate Pharmacy [etc.].

Phase, *v. tr.* Variant of FAZE *v.* {1898} — **1852** *Oregonian* 25 Dec. (Th.), The 18 lb. shot struck [General Scott] in the pit of the stomach, and never phased him. **1876** 'MARK TWAIN' *Tom Sawyer* x. 94 You might take and belt him over the head with a church and you could n't phase him. **1904** *Buffalo Commercial* 28 Sept. 6 Don't be phased by democratic predictions and boasting! **1915** WILSON *Ruggles* v, I got one sheath skirt ... that just had to be looked at. Never phased them, though.

+Ph.B. [Abbrev. for L. *Philosophiae Baccalaureus.*] Bachelor of Philosophy. Also attrib. — **1883** *Century Mag.* May 158/1 They gave me a diploma which ... didn't have a lot of letters after my name like his—A.B. or Ph.B. or whatever they are. **1903** *Univ. Chicago Pres. Rep. 1892-1902* 112 Students in Commerce and Administration receive the Ph.B. degree. **1911** MONROE etc. *Cycl. Educ.* II. 286/1 A.B. (Bachelor of Arts) ... Ph.B. (Bachelor of Philosophy).

+Ph.D. [Abbrev. for L. *Philosophiae Doctor.*] **1.** A Doctor of Philosophy. **2.** The academic degree granting a person the status of a Doctor of Philosophy. Also fig. — **(1) 1869** *Atlantic Mo.* Jan. 89/2 His cousin, the Ph.D. from Göttingen, cannot help despising a people who do not grow loud and red over Aryans and Turanians. **1911** HARRISON *Queed* 218 There were only three Ph.D.'s among them. **(2) 1903** W. JAMES *Memories & Studies* 331 A Ph.D. in philosophy would prove little ... as to one's ability to teach literature. **1925** *Scribner's Mag.* Oct. 2/2 He awards Barnum a Ph.D. in humbugology.

***Pheasant.** Also **†pheisant, pheysant, phesant.**

+1. a. The ruffed grouse, *Bonasa umbellus.* Also comb.

'The Ruffed Grouse (called "Partridges" in most of the northern States) ... is popularly but quite inaccurately called "Pheasant" in the southern, and also in some of the northern States, notably Ohio and Pennsylvania' (1917 *Birds of Amer.* II. 34).

1637 MORTON *New Canaan* 70 There are a kinde of fowles which are commonly called Pheisants, but whether they be pheysants or no, I will not take upon me to determine. **1674** *Cal. State P., Amer. & W.I.* VII. 581 [In] Maine ... the islands and woods yield swarms of birds, turkeys, pheasants, heath-hens [etc.]. **1698** THOMAS *Pensilvania* 13 There are an Infinite Number of Sea and Land Fowl, of most sorts, *viz.*... Turkies, ... Pheasants, Partridges [etc.]. **1768** WASHINGTON *Diaries* I. 303 Went a Pheasant Huntg. **1775** CRESSWELL *Journal* 63 Shot some Pheasants, which have made a good supper. **1834** *Indiana Mag. Hist.* XV. 255 The thick woods are well stocked with game such as deer, turkeys, foxes, rabbits or pheasants as they are called here. **1895** *Outing* XXVII. 43/1 The Montana 'pheasant' (the ruffed grouse) is the same as the bird found in the mountains of Virginia and the East generally. **1917** *Birds of Amer.* II. 17 Ruffed Grouse. *Bonasa umbellus umbellus.*... [Also called] Birch Partridge; Pheasant; Drumming pheasant.

+b. Any of several other American grouse: (see quotations).

1805 LEWIS in *L. & Clark Exped.* II. (1904) 295 As I passed these mountains I saw a flock of the black or dark brown phesants [Richardson's grouse]: ... this bird is fully a third larger than the common phesant of the Atlantic States. **1806** *Ib.* IV. (1905) 129 The large black and white pheasant [Franklin's grouse] is peculiar to that portion of the Rocky Mountain watered by the Columbia river. **1808** PIKE *Sources Miss.* 168 Some distance up we found buffalo, higher still the new species of deer and pheasants [dusky grouse].

***2.** Any of certain bright-colored birds of the family Phasianidae; the true pheasant, esp. *Phasianus colchicus.*

The first successful introduction of this bird into the United States was in Oregon in 1880. See also GOLD 4, quot. 1786.

1885 *Forest & Stream* XXV. 104/1 The method of rearing the pheasants as now pursued [at Pierre Lorillard's farm in N.J.] is to keep the old imported birds in coops. **1889** *Rep. Comm. Agric. 1888* 484 Four flourishing colonies of introduced Pheasants now exist in the Pacific Coast region. **1896** *Outing* Sept. 596/2 The first day of September marks the beginning of the open season on pheasants, grouse, and quail in Oregon. **1909** *Farmers' Bul.* No. 390, 13 More than a hundred years ago, Richard Bache, ... who married the only daughter of Benjamin Franklin, imported from England both pheasants and partridges. **1924** *S.D. Dept. Game & Fish 16th Rep.* 5 In November, 1924, the game and fish commission declared an open season on cock pheasants.

+Pheasant chicken. ?A pinnated grouse. — **1854** *Penna. Agric. Rep.* 205 E. Culbertson, for best pair Pheasant chickens.

Phebe. (See PHOEBE.)

+Phi Beta. *ellipt.* =next. Used attrib. — **1845** C. T. BROOKS *Poem* 11 Him no dread honors wait— ... no Phi Beta days! **1883** *Harper's Mag.* Sept. 636/1 The Phi Beta address of Mr. Adams was but another voice of the spirit [etc.].

+Phi Beta Kappa. An honorary Greek-letter society, orig. a secret society founded at William and Mary College in 1776, having chapters in many American colleges. Also attrib., esp. with *society.*

The name is derived from the initial letters of the Greek words φιλοσοφία βίου κυβερνήτης 'philosophy the pilot (or guide) of life.'

1776 in *Wm. & Mary Coll. Quart.* IV. 214 A list of Members who have been Initiated into the S. P. *alias* ΦBK Society. **1836** HOLMES *Poetical Works* (1895) 15/1 Poetry. A Metrical Essay, Read before the Phi Beta Kappa Society, Harvard University, August, 1836. **1847** *Cat. Harvard Chapter* ΦBK (1912) 168 A petition ... presented from certain members of the graduating class at Amherst College, praying for the establishment of a Chapter of the ΦBK Society in that institution. **1883** *Harper's Mag.* Sept. 635/2 The address of Charles Francis Adams, Jun., before the Phi Betta Kappa Society ... commanded serious attention. **1894** B. MATTHEWS in *Harper's Mag.* June 34/1, I've got to read the Phi Beta Kappa poem at Harvard next week. **1912** NICHOLSON *Hoosier Chron.* 278 Sylvia ... just walked through everything and would be chosen for the Phi Beta Kappa.

Philadelphia. A city in Pennsylvania, founded and named by William Penn in 1682. Used attrib.

+1. Designating things issued or produced in Philadelphia.

1723 *Amer. Wkly. Mercury* 22-29 Aug. 2/2 William Bradford of New-York takes Philadelphia Paper Money, upon Reasonable Terms. **1733** Philadelphia gamon [see PHILADELPHIA FLOUR]. **1758** *Newport Mercury* 26 Dec. 3/2 Choice Flour, Ship Bread and Philadelphia Butter by the Firkin. **1759** *Ib.* 20 Nov. 4/3 A Handsome Philadelphia Fire Stove, to be sold by Peter Bours. **1790** *Columbian Centinel* 18 Sept. 8/4 Joseph Blake ... [sells] Philadelphia Iron, English Goods, &c. **1834** NOTT *Novellettes* I. 10 He drank a pint of Philadelphia beer qualified with a gill of New-England rum. **1844** M. C. HOUSTON *Texas* (1845) 84 The buffalo-tongues are very praiseworthy, and so are the Philadelphia hams, which they assert . . . 'whip the Westphalia by a long chalk.' **1869** TOURGEE *Toinette* (1881) 17, I have a new edition of Blackstone. . . . It's a Philadelphia edition, and just out.

+**2.** Designating things, actions, or persons that exist in, or come from, Philadelphia.

1813 *Salem Gazette* 22 Oct. 3/2 Last evening arrived, the tandem Philadelphia pilot boat [jocular term for a freight wagon] . . . from a three weeks cruise in Rhode-Island and Connecticut. **1868** *N.Y. Herald* 30 July 6/5 A Philadelphia democrat . . . offers the following. **1894** LEAVITT *Our Money Wars* 80 When the Phila. Bank of the United States failed, in 1841, that institution was largely in debt to the Bank of England. **1894** *Harper's Mag.* June 17/2 In Philadelphia cricket the prize is a place on the eleven which is to uphold the honor of the town against an opposing English or Australian team of players.

+**3.** In special combinations.

Philadelphia raspberry, a variety of raspberry; *P. system*, a method of prison discipline based on the solitary confinement of the prisoners.

1842 BUCKINGHAM *E. & W. States* II. 306 The system of discipline pursued here, is that which is called the Auburn, or Silent System, in contradistinction to the Philadelphia, or Solitary System. **1874** *Dept. Agric. Rep. 1873* 389 The Philadelphia raspberry was regarded as the best berry for profit.

+**Philadelphia brick.** (See quot. 1909.) — **1807** *Indep. Chronicle* 21 Sept. 3/2 The Subscriber has been at considerable expense for several years past in the improvement of Face Bricks . . . superior to the Philadelphia Bricks, both for appearance and for turning water. **1882** *Century Mag.* March 792/2 If a Philadelphia brick is employed for the exterior, the deep contrasting color will produce a pleasing effect. **1909** *Cent. Suppl.* 164/2 *Philadelphia brick*, a fine quality of hard smooth-faced brick of a deep red color.

+**Philadelphia flour.** A bolted flour manufactured in Philadelphia. — [**1723** *New-Eng. Courant* 4 Feb. 2/2 The best new Philadelphia Town-boulted Flower, to be sold by Mr. William Clark.] **1733** *S.C. Gazette* 16 June, Just imported . . . jamaica lime-juice, philadelphia gamons, and flower. **1761** in H. M. Brooks *Gleanings* 26 Choice new Raisins by the Cask, Philadelphia Flour and Bar Iron per Quality.

+**Philadelphia greenlet.** =PHILADELPHIA VIREO. — **1892** TORREY *Foot-Path Way* 11 At last we had before us the rare and long desired Philadelphia greenlet. **1917** *Birds of Amer.* III. 104 Philadelphia Vireo. *Vireosylva philadelphica*. . . . Other Names.—Philadelphia Greenlet; Brotherly-love Vireo.

+**Philadelphia lawyer.** A lawyer of outstanding ability in matters involving fine points and technicalities.

The phrase arose from the eminence of the early Philadelphia bar.

1803 *Balance* 15 Nov. 363/1 It would (to use a Yankee phrase) *puzzle a dozen Philadelphia lawyers*, to unriddle the conduct of the democrats. **1839** T. BROTHERS *United States* 17, I undertook . . . to plead for myself against half a dozen '*Philadelphia lawyers*,' renowned as they are for their extraordinary cunning. **1844** 'UNCLE SAM' *Peculiarities* II. 50, I'm saving money out of my prison allowance to pay the Phillydelphy lawyers. **1896** *New York Witness* 30 Dec. 13/1 Not even a Philadelphia lawyer would have been able to pick the winners [in an election contest]. **1905** *Springfield W. Repub.* 29 Sept. 1 It would not take a Philadelphia lawyer to demonstrate this.

Philadelphian, *n.* {1656–}

+**1.** A resident or native of Philadelphia.

1789 MORSE *Amer. Geog.* 332 The Philadelphians have exerted their endeavours . . . to prevent the intemperate use of spirituous liquors. **1803** *Lit. Mag.* (Phila.) Dec. 170 A Philadelphian . . . told us, he could not, after repeated trials, find a chaise. **1817** PAULDING *Lett. from South* I. 90 When the Philadelphian is hard pushed, he boasts of his squares and his wide streets, his beef and his butter. **1841** BUCKINGHAM *America* II. 84 The Philadelphians have the reputation of being cold, formal, and difficult of approach. **1876** INGRAM *Centennial Exp.* 710 The Pennsylvania Bible Society . . . pavilion . . . was erected by special contributions from a few Philadelphians. **1894** *Harper's Mag.* 3/2 All Philadelphians have a strong feeling for their home.

+**2.** The speech spoken by Philadelphians.

1870 *Nation* 4 Aug. 73/1 'It don't signify' is pure Philadelphian.

Philadelphian, *a.* {1615–} Of or pertaining to Philadelphia. — [**1775** *Sh. View of Ld. High Admiral's Jurisdiction* 35 A Philadelphian ship might be tried with a fairer chance of condemnation at Halifax.] **1855** H. A. MURRAY *Lands of Slave & Free* I. 360 The only peculiarity in the Philadelphian mint is a frame-work for counting the number of pieces coined. **1856** MACLEOD *F. Wood* 31 So Benjamin Wood went on driving his trade in fish with his Philadelphian brethren.

+**Philadelphia porter.** A malt liquor made in Philadelphia. — **1844** 'UNCLE SAM' *Peculiarities* I. 43 Philadelphia Porter, Saratoga Spring-water [etc.]. **1845** J. W. NORRIS *Chicago Directory* 98 The bar will be furnished with the best of Liquors, such as . . . London Brown Stout, Scotch Ale, Philadelphia Porter.

+**Philadelphia vireo.** A vireo of the eastern United States, *Vireo philadelphicus*. — **1869** *Amer. Naturalist* III. 504 The Philadelphia Vireo . . . was first described . . . from a specimen taken near Philadelphia, in 1851. **1892** TORREY *Foot-Path Way* 12 The song of the Philadelphia vireo comes nearest to the red-eye's.

Philander. {1700–} +*pl.* (See quotation.) — **1828** *Yankee* 3 Sept. 288/1 *Philanders*. . . . When they play this, they all take hold of hands, excepting one who is seated in a chair in the middle of the room; round this one they all march in a circle, . . . singing the while, 'Come Philanders, . . . choose your true love now or never, and be sure you choose no other.' The person seated in a chair, if a boy, chooses a girl from the circle [etc.].

Philanthropist. a. One who works disinterestedly for his fellow men; a benevolent person. {1730–6–} **b.** One who makes gifts to educational institutions, social agencies, etc. — **1873** W. MAYO *Never Again* 314 A legion of strong-minded philanthropists, . . . all astraddle of the biggest and most rampant hobbies. **1885** CRAWFORD *Amer. Politician* 216 The Republicans mean to put in Mr. Jobbins . . . , who is . . . so good and benevolent—quite a philanthropist. **1902** WISTER *Virginian* xxv, The thought of the perennial stultification of Indian affairs at Washington, whether by politician or philanthropist, was always sure to arouse him. **1920** LYNCH *Personal Recoll. of A. Carnegie* 134 Mr. Carnegie was the most original philanthropist the world has ever known. **1922** *U.S. Bur. Educ. Bul.* No. 26, 45 The labor feature was used as an appeal to the philanthropist for support and to the parent to send his son to college.

Philippine cane. A species of sugar cane. — **1834** BAIRD *Valley Mississippi* 304 The Philippine or ribband cane is rapidly supplanting this species of cane.

Phil(o-)African, *a.* +Attached to the interests of Negroes. — **1865** WHITMAN *November Boughs* 106 [President Lincoln] will not countenance at all the demand of the extreme Philo-African element of the North. **1897** *Current History* VII. 224 The Philafrican Liberators' League is an association . . . to work for the extinction of the African slave trade.

+**Philopena, Philopoena.** Also **phillippina,** *colloq.* **phillipeener,** etc. [Corruption of G. *vielliebchen*.]

1. A two-kernel nut eaten in playing a game of forfeits: (see quot. under FILLIPEEN). Also attrib. and fig.

1839 BRIGGS *H. Franco* II. 143 There would be [at the party] . . . scandal by the wholesale, besides sugar kisses, and phillippinas. **1854** 'M. HARLAND' *Alone* ix, Will you eat a philopoena with me? **1860** *Knickerb.* Oct. 365 Nella was hunting among the almonds to find a phillipeener. **1890** *Harper's Mag.* April 715/1 Sisters is real lux'ries, . . . and when you come to a twin, a kinder phillerpener sister, why, it's like a piece o' your own self.

2. A forfeit incurred in this game. Also attrib.

See also FILLIPEENER.

1857 GUNN *N.Y. Boarding-Houses* 139 We remembering her rashly volunteering a $100 wedding-dress . . . in order to get off from paying a forfeit philopoena. **1864** *Md. Hist. Mag.* XXI. 299 He said he was trying to get something to give us for philippena. **1893** *Harper's Mag.* March 609/1 She put on her ring again, using the philopena circlet as a guard.

Philosophical apparatus. Apparatus used in the study of natural philosophy or physics. — **1792** *Ann. 2d Congress* 1000 Copper and brass wares . . . ; andirons and other articles for household use; philosophical apparatus. **1813** *Niles' Reg.* V. 190/1 Copper and brass wares, . . . — philosophical apparatus. **1815** *Ann. 14th Congress* 1 Sess. 25 Mr. Roberts presented the memorial of John Reaman Coxe, praying remission of the duties on a collection of minerals and philosophical apparatus. **1851** CIST *Cincinnati* 274 A good chemical and philosophical apparatus, have been procured.

+**Phlegm-cutter.** A drink of whisky or other liquor. *humorous* or *slang*. (Cf. ANTIFOGMATIC.) — **1806** *Balance* 13 May 146/3, I have heard of a jarum, of phlegm-cutter and fog driver. **1810** LAMBERT *Travels* (1813) II. 299 *A phlegm-cutter* is a double dose just before breakfast. **1849** A. MACKAY *Western World* II. 67 He alternated pretty frequently between the julep, the cobbler, the phlegm-cutter, and the gin-sling.

+**Phlegm-disperser.** =prec. — **1818** FEARON *Sketches* 252 Drinking . . . is effected by individuals taking their solitary 'eye openers,' 'toddy,' and 'phlegm dispersers.'

Phlox. [L. (Pliny), applied to the American genus by Linnaeus.] A large genus of American herbs of the family Polemoniaceae; a plant of this genus. {1770– (Hanbury *Compl. Body Planting* I. 708)}

1847 WOOD *Botany* 438 Phlox. . . . A highly ornamental, North American genus. . . . *P. paniculata*. Panicled Phlox. **1868** *Mich. Agric. Rep.* VII. 357 Hubbard & Davis, Detroit, [exhibited a] collection of Perennial Phloxes. **1872** TICE *Over Plains* 15 A splendid colored Phlox also abounded everywhere [in northern Kan.]. **1878** STOWE *Poganuc People* 205 Crimson and white phloxes stood ranged in midsummer ranks. **1906** BELL *C. Lee* 175 There were narrow paths bordered with . . . touch-me-nots, phlox, azaleas, and sweet-william.

+**Phoebe.** Also **phebe.** [Echoic of the bird's call.] Any of several flycatchers of the genus *Sayornis*, esp. *S. phoebe* of the eastern part of the United States.

1700 *Essex Inst. Col.* VIII. 216 Heard a Phebe and other birds sing. **1782** CRÈVECOEUR *Letters* 40 Three nests were placed almost contiguous to each other in my piazza: . . . [one was] that of a phebe. **1842** THOREAU *Journal* 331, I hear nothing but a phoebe, and the wind, and the rattling of a chaise in the wood. **1898** *Atlantic Mo.* Oct. 494/2 Two or more pairs of phœbes had settled in the neighborhood. **1908** *Ib.* Feb. 212, I am watching for the phoebes to return to the shed—they are my first birds.

+**Phoebe bird.** =prec. — **1839** IRVING in *Knickerb.* XIII. 434 The Pewit, or Pe-wee, or Phœbe-bird . . . is called by each of these names. **1844** *Nat. Hist. N.Y., Zoology* II. 115 The Phœbe-Bird. *Muscicapa fusca.* . . . This familiar and favorite little bird . . . appears with us in the latter days of March or beginning of April. **1883** *Century Mag.* Sept. 681/1 A Connecticut farmer . . . showed me a phœbe bird's nest six stories high. **1910** *Outlook* 11 June 321 The phoebe-bird who sat on Mr. Hawkins's woodshed reiterated his dismal note.

+**Phoenix City.** The city of Chicago. A nickname applied in allusion to the city's recovery after the fire of 1871. *Obs.* — **1887** GEORGE *40 Years on Rail* 206 Chicago bears to-day the title of the 'Phœnix City.'

+**Phoney,** *a.* [Origin uncertain.] Counterfeit, not genuine. *colloq.*[2] — **1900** ADE *More Fables* 138 'Overlook all the Phoney Acting by the Little Lady, Bud,' said the Fireman to the Advance Agent. **1907** A. THOMAS *Witching Hour* (1925) IV. 139 It ain't a phoney check, is it? **1916** SANDBURG *Chicago Poems* 63 You're only shoving out a phoney imitation of the goods.

Phonograph. {1835–40–}

+**1. a.** An instrument, patented by Thomas A. Edison in 1877, for the mechanical recording and reproduction of sounds. {1878–} **b.** A machine that reproduces sounds mechanically recorded on a cylinder or disc of metal, wax, or other substance.

In England the word *phonograph* in sense b has now been largely supplanted by *gramophone.* (Cf. GRAMOPHONE, GRAPHOPHONE.)

1877 *Scientific Amer.* 17 Nov. 304 Whoever may speak into the mouthpiece of the phonograph. **1880** CABLE *Grandissimes* 186 Alas! the phonograph was invented three-quarters of a century too late. **1892** RITTENHOUSE *Maud* 550 Tonight we've been listening to that wonderful phonograph at Mr Burnetts. It is the most entertaining thing! **1912** *Ladies' Home Jrnl.* March 35/3 With the Edison Phonograph you get the latest hits of Broadway's musical productions, while they are hits.

fig. **1893** *Scribner's Mag.* June 695/1 These words, which have just run off the phonograph of my memory, were spoken a quarter of a century ago.

+**2.** Attrib. with *company, plate, record.*

1879 G. B. PRESCOTT *Speaking Telephone* 305 Having provided thus for the durability of the phonograph plate, it will be very easy [etc.] **1902** LORIMER *Lett. Merchant* 214 The phonograph records of a fellow's character are lined in his face. **1907** *Pearson's Mag.* Jan. (*advt.*), Columbia Phonograph Co. . . . Stores in every large city.

Phonographer. A shorthand writer who uses the Pitman system of shorthand. {1845–} — **1866** W. REID *After the War* 71, I published that, and then sent phonographers to make a full report of the proceedings. **1887** *Harper's Mag.* Jan. 319/2 The larger number of interviewers are not phonographers.

Phosphate. }1790–1– (*Encycl. Brit.*)} *attrib.* Designating deposits, or land containing deposits, of various salts of phosphoric acid. — **1884** GOODE, etc. *Fisheries* I. 671 Enormous fossil Sharks' teeth . . . are found in the phosphate beds of South Carolina. **1900** H. ROBERTSON *Red Blood & Blue* 286 He went around by Kelway, thinking to stop there a day to look after his phosphate lands.

Photo. Abbrev. for PHOTOGRAPH. *colloq.* {1870–} Also attrib. — **1863** NORTON *Army Lett.* 195, I send the promised photo, also two others. **1882** CROKER *Proper Pride* I. 105 There was a small photo of herself in a stand occupying a post of honour. **1897** *Outing* XXX. 495/1 Presuming that the photo-cyclist is ambitious enough to wish to compete with his fellows in the photographic exhibitions [etc.]. **1916** H. L. WILSON *Somewhere* v, Where's that photo album?

Photo-engraver. One skilled in the art of photo-engraving. {1902–} — **1898** *Internat. Typogr. Union Proc.* 28/1 There was but one union of photo-engravers, and their representative was treated accordingly. **1916** SEITZ *Training for Newsp. Trade* 109 The photo-engraver, a comparative newcomer, is also an important wage earner.

Photograph.

1. A picture obtained by photography. {1839–}

1859 *Harper's Weekly* III. 761 A photograph of a Winslow Homer picture of an apple-paring bee, with the title 'Fall Games—The Apple-Bee.' **1864** GEO. BANCROFT *Let. to W. C. Bryant* 28 Oct. (MS.), Brady is bent on getting a photograph of a group with yourself in the centre. **1897** *McClure's Mag.* X. 19 These photographs exhibit the great transfer railway ferryboats. **1907** *St. Nicholas* June 751/1 This photograph was taken from the side-walk, by holding the camera above the fence.

2. Attrib. with *book, plate, saloon,* etc.

1870 *Nation* 20 Jan. 45/1 Candy pedlars, photograph vendors, lung-testers, and hand-organ grinders furnish the objects of interest. **1873** HOWELLS *Chance Acquaintance* iv, Kitty knocked a photograph-book off the table. **1883** — *Woman's Reason* xv, A friend of mine . . . used to have a photograph saloon down in our place. **1887** PERRY *Flock of Girls* 54 'A photograph studio!' they exclaimed in chorus. **1897** FLANDRAU *Harvard Episodes* 205 He was very much like a supersensitive photograph plate in the hands of a bungler.

Photograph album. An album in which photographs are kept. — **1870** O. LOGAN *Before Footlights* 258 The only thing worth carrying away was a decent sort of photograph album. **1886** MITCHELL *R. Blake* 36 Somewhat listlessly, she picked up one of the photograph albums then in vogue.

Photographer. One who takes photographs. {1847–} — **1865** *Atlantic Mo.* Jan. 41/2 The wise man had brought along with him . . . a skillful photographer. **1873** ALDRICH *Marjorie Daw* x, Unluckily the photographer had spilt some acid on the plate. **1912** NICHOLSON *Hoosier Chron.* 216 The photographer didn't seem to understand that sort of millinery.

+**Photograph gallery.** A photographer's studio. — **1875** in Summers *Hist. S.W. Virginia* 655 We have . . . a photograph gallery. **1887** *Courier-Journal* 6 Feb. 5/2 Photograph gallery of C. C. Horn, value not known, no insurance. *a***1918** G. STUART *On Frontier* II. 23 The photograph gallery was as profitable as a claim in the bed of Alder gulch.

+**Photographic gallery.** =prec. — **1866** *Ore. State Jrnl.* 30 June 4/4 Ellsworth and Cardwell, Proprietors Cardwell Photographic Gallery, 89 First Street, Portland. **1873** *Newton Kansan* 13 March 3/1 There is an opening in this place for a good photographic gallery. **1877** HODGE *Arizona* 149 There are . . . two tin shops, . . . one harness shop, one photographic gallery [etc.].

Photographist. =PHOTOGRAPHER. {1843–} — **1861** *Chicago Tribune* 26 May 1/9 (*advt.*), I, Samuel M. Fassett, Photographist, . . . will continue to take . . . photographs for the low sum of one dollar, during the war. **1872** TALMAGE *Sermons* 71 There are some faces so mobile that photographists cannot take them.

Photogravure. The process of preparing a plate from a photographic negative; a print made from this plate. {1879–} Also attrib. — **1884** *American* VIII. 125/1 This will be the first specimen of photogravure made in the United States. **1885** *Harper's Mag.* March 547/1 Those engravings and photogravures . . . look well. **1898** *McClure's Mag.* Feb. 385/2 There will be ten volumes in all . . . , with several photogravure portraits.

Phrasing. {1611–} +(See quot. 1851.) — **1835** TODD *Student's Manual* 115 Should you allow yourself to think of going into the recitation-room, and there trust to 'skinning,' as it is called in some colleges, or 'phrasing,' as in others, or 'mouthing it,' as in others. **1851** HALL *College Words* 228 *Phrasing,* reciting by, or giving the words or phraseology of the book, without understanding their meaning.

Phrenologist. A practitioner of, or one skilled in, phrenology. {1815–} — **1836** HILDRETH *Campaigns Rocky Mts.* 14 Although I am no Phrenologist, yet, if there is a word of truth in the doctrine, I have the bumps of a roving disposition. **1855** *Knickerb.* XLVI. 100 Is this the place where the phrenologist 'holds out'? **1876** 'MARK TWAIN' *Tom Sawyer* xxii. 178 A phrenologist and a mesmerizer came—and went again and left the village duller and drearier than ever.

Phrenology. A body of theory based upon the assumption that the mental faculties and traits of a human being are manifested in the shape of his skull. {1815–, of the system formulated by Gall and Spurzheim. The earlier use by Rush is independent of this.} — [**1805** B. RUSH in I. W. Riley *Amer. Philosophy* (1907) 437 Very different is the state of phrenology, if I may be allowed to coin a word to designate a science of the mind.] **1845** SOL. SMITH *Theatr. Apprent.* 200, I am anxious to be thoroughly convinced regarding this science of phrenology. **1870** M. H. SMITH *20 Years Wall St.* 295 Slim, spare, with a head and face that defy phrenology and Lavater to read, he has had uniform success.

Phylaselle cloak. [Var. of *filoselle.* {*a*1605–}] A cloak made of floss silk. — **1647** *Essex Probate Rec.* I. 66, 1 phylaselle cloake lined with plush.

Physical culture. The art or science of exercising the body. Also attrib. — **1868** *Ore. State Jrnl.* 8 Aug. 2/3 Miss Flora Olney, of Portland, read an essay, 'Moral and physical culture too much neglected in our schools.' **1893** *Harper's Mag.* April 668/2 In the high-school department, . . . further instruction is given in . . . physical culture. **1898** *Kansas City Star* 19 Dec. 1/3 My papa and mama went out that evening to a physical culture exhibition. **1925** *Physical Culture* June 2/2 It is the crowning effort of Bernarr Macfadden's rich, full experience in the Science of Health and Physical Culture.

+**Physic dance.** Among certain American Indians: A ceremonial dance in the spring during which a medicine was prepared and taken. Now hist. — **1765** TIMBERLAKE *Memoirs* 77 There was to be a physic-dance at night [among the Cherokee Indians]. **1819** *Niles' Reg.* XVI. Suppl. 101/1 The physic dance was very much in use formerly [by the Cherokee Indians].

***Physician. a.** One who practices the art of healing. *Obs.* **b.** One legally qualified to practice medicine. Often distinguished from a surgeon.

1642 *Plymouth Laws* 72 If any children . . . shalbe sent . . . to a Phisician or Chirurgeon . . . they shalbe releeved . . . by the Townships whence they came. **1690** *Boston Rec.* 80 Jacob Malyne . . . became surety . . . for John Kerfbill, Physician. **1705** *Boston News-Letter* 18 June 2/2 The Reverend Mr. Michael Wigglesworth . . . was interr'd this day: Being much Lamented as a Learned and Pious Divine, and Skilful Physician. **1794** *Ann. 3d Congress* 1456 Nothing herein contained shall be construed to extend . . . to physicians, apothecaries, surgeons, or chemists. **1809** KENDALL *Travels* III. 128 In this place, too, it may be further remarked, that *physician* is the title of all medical practitioners in the United States; and that all the physicians, being regularly bred, have arrived at the academy's dignity of a doctor's degree. **1849** *Wkly. New Mexican* 28 Nov. 3/2 Dr. C. Jackson, Respectfully offers his professional services to the inhabitants of Santa Fe and the surrounding country as Physician and Surgeon. **1898** PAGE *Red Rock* 555, I am going because he is sick and I am a physician. **1922** TITUS *Timber* 150 The physician shoved back his derby wearily.

Physic nut. The seed of a small tropical American tree, *Jatropha curcas;* the tree that produces this seed. {1657–} — **1785** WASHINGTON *Diaries* II. 383, 2 Rows containing 85 of the Palmetto Nut, or acorn. Next 2 rows 87 Physic Nut. **1791** W. BARTRAM *Travels* 43, I observed . . . particularly the physic-nut, or Indian olive.

Pi. Also **pie.** Printer's type mingled in confusion. {pye, py, pie, 1659–} Also fig. — **1771** FRANKLIN *Autobiog.* 301 One of them by accident was broken, and two pages [were] reduced to pi. **c1835** CATLIN *Indians* II. 53 We were thrown into 'pie' (as printers would say,) in an instant of the most appalling alarm. **1845** SOL. SMITH *Theatr. Apprent.* 33 In a few days our 'pi was distributed,' our press put in order [etc.]. **1863** Moore *Rebellion Rec.* V. I. 49 Most of the type was knocked into 'pi,' the press injured, and much of the material was scattered outside. **1880** 'MARK TWAIN' *Tramp Abroad* 586 In our country printing-offices the apprentice . . . [learns] to sort 'pi'; then to set type.

Pianist. One who plays the piano, esp. a skilled performer. {1842–} — **1839** LONGFELLOW in S. Longfellow *H. W. Longfellow* I. 336 Hear that Schlesinger, the great pianist in New York, is dead. **1881** *Harper's Mag.* May 814/1 Very few American pianists have adopted the concert-room as their field of labor. **1907** *St. Nicholas* May 595/2 Everybody except the pianist and the dignified young conductress, was whispering and giggling.

+**Piankashaw.** An Indian of a tribe related to the Miamis, originally settled in the Middle West; in pl., the tribe. Also attrib. — **1757** *Doc. Col. Hist. N.Y.* VII. 268 There came several of the Chiefs of the Wawioughtanes and Pianguisha Nations. **1824** *Missouri Intelligencer* 12 June 2/3 A remanant of the Piankashaws on the head waters of the Black River. **1852** in B. DRAKE *Tecumseh* 160 All the neighboring tribes, the Piankishaws excepted . . . , are either intruders upon them, or have been permitted to settle in their country. **1883** *Indiana Geol. Rep. 1882* 42 A band of the Miami tribe, who occupied the country along the waters of the Vermillion, were called 'Pi-auk-e-shaws.'

Piano.

1. =PIANOFORTE. {1803–}

1807 IRVING, etc. *Salmagundi* x. 264 It is certainly much more agreeable to hear a lady give lectures on the piano, than . . . in the usual discordant measure. **1848** BRYANT *California* xxvii. 336 The parlor was furnished with . . . a fine piano, the first I have seen in the country. **1908** 'O. HENRY' *Options* 146 There is . . . a piano with an automatic player.

2. *attrib.* and *comb.* **a.** Designating places where pianos are made or sold.

1827 DRAKE & MANSFIELD *Cincinnati* 66, 2 Piano Factories. **1885** CUSTER *Boots & Saddles* 216 One of the band, who had been in a piano-house before enlisting, kept the instrument in order.

b. Designating things forming parts of, or used in connection with, pianos.

1859 *Rep. Comm. Patents 1858* I. 542 Improved Piano Lock. **1864** STOWE *House & Home P.* 108 The window-shades, the table-cover, and the piano-cloth, all repeated the same colors, in the same cheap material. **1876** INGRAHAM *Centennial Exp.* 256 [The] exhibit of the State of New Hampshire . . . [included] specimens of manufactured woods in . . . piano sounding-boards [etc.]. **1897** *McClure's Mag.* Nov. 57 The soft, yellow light from the shaded piano-lamp fell about her.

c. Designating persons who have to do with pianos.

1881 *Harper's Mag.* May 813/1 The generous rivalry between the great piano manufacturers [Steinway and Chickering] has resulted in a gain to the city of two fine halls. **1887** *Courier-Journal* 12 Jan. 6/7 S. W. Poole, the piano tuner, was arrested yesterday on a disorderly conduct warrant. **1889** BRAYLEY *Boston Fire Dept.* 659 He began life as a piano-polisher. **1902** *Harper's Mag.* May 976 The blanket was . . . held against the jamb of the front door, according to the piano-man's instructions.

Piano case. The case or exterior housing of a piano. Also attrib. — **1850** *Rep. Comm. Patents 1849* 300 What I claim . . . is a piano case or trunk lock. **1864** *Hist. North-Western Soldiers' Fair* 170 [Donations include] one 6 octave piano case melodeon. **1876** INGRAM *Centennial Exp.* 344 Another very creditable piece of work was a rosewood piano-case, carved by Miss Agnes Pitman. **1882** PECK *Sunshine* 259 That little shrimp . . . would sit on the piano keys, and knock his boots against the piano case.

Pianoforte. A well-known musical instrument in which tones are produced by hammers operated from a keyboard and striking upon metal wires. {1767–} Also attrib. — **1773** in Singleton *Social N.Y.* 295 [Rivington had] spinets, piano fortes; guitars [etc.]. **1785** JEFFERSON *Writings* V. 147, I had almost decided, on his advice, to get a piano-forte for my daughter. **1829** ROYALL *Pennsylvania* I. 103 You hear the violin or Piana Fort, of an evening, almost in every house. **1852** HALE *If, Yes, & Perhaps* 14, I was at work as a veneerer in a piano-forte factory at Attica. **1887** *Courier-Journal* 25 Jan. 3/3 This cultivated lady . . . comes to our city with the highest testimonials . . . as to her . . . method of teaching the use of the piano forte.

+**Pianola.** A trade name for a form of mechanical piano-player; a player piano. Also attrib. — **1899** *Boston Transcript* 3 June 12/7 The Pianola may be seen any day at the warerooms. **1901** ADE *40 Modern Fables* 4 Then he would wish that a white-haired Old Lady . . . might come along and Adopt him and put him in a white and gold Suite with a Pianola and a Man-Servant. **1903** — *People You Know* 96 Unless he could raise the Wind, it meant . . . the Pianola to the Hock-Shop. **1915** *Chicago D. News Almanac 1916* 615/2 The Coe music collection . . . [contains] 560 pianola rolls.

Piano-maker. One who makes pianos. — **1882** SWEET & KNOX *Texas Siftings* 159 Awards of merit may be given to all the . . . piano makers in the country. **1885** *Harper's Mag.* Feb. 399/1 His first occupation . . . was that of a piano-maker.

Piano stool. A stool upon which one sits while playing a piano. — **1863** A. D. WHITNEY *F. Gartney* ii, She withdrew a little . . . , brought forward a piano stool, and seated herself thereon. **1877** PHELPS *Story of Avis* 335 Barbara Allen sat on the piano-stool. **1891** 'THANET' *Otto the Knight* 198 Ossie sat on the piano-stool making aimless half-circles of motion and looking dejected.

***Piazza.** Also †**peazer.** +A veranda or porch. {1796, in S. Amer.}

The transition from the British to the American sense is indicated in the following example (see A. Matthews 'Piazza' in *Nation* 1 June 416): — **1699** *Va. Statutes at L.* (1823) 421 The two parts of the building shall be joined by a cross gallery of thirty foot long, and fifteen foot wide each way, . . . raised upon piazzas, and built as high as the other parts of the building.

1724 JONES *Virginia* 26 It is a lofty Pile of Brick Building adorn'd with a *Cupola*. . . . There is a spacious *Piazza* on the *West* Side, from one Wing to the other. **1771** *Copley-Pelham Lett.* 131, I would have the Windows put in the north side of my Rooms as above, for should I not add the Wings I shall add a peazer when I return. **1804** *Mass. Spy* 20 June (Th.), The back piazza of Mr. Taylor was destroyed. **1854** CUMMINS *Lamplighter* 491 In a moment steps were heard crossing the piazza. **1887** WILKINS *Humble Romance* 27 Their cottage was one of those which had its piazza across the front. **1920** HOWELLS *Vacation of Kelwyns* 157 He would put a piazza all round it.

attrib. and *comb.* **1835** INGRAHAM *South-West* I. 197 A little piazza-girted cottage . . . stood on the banks of the river. **1883** HOWELLS *Woman's Reason* xix, Helen descended the piazza steps and sauntered past the beds of foliage-plants across the grass with her charge. **1906** J. A. HARRISON *George Washington* 198 The piazza politician, sipping his toddy, spreading his legs, and discussing constitutional questions on the spacious verandahs of open-air Virginia.

+**Piazza chair.** A chair suitable for use on a piazza or porch; a porch chair. — **1876** A. D. WHITNEY *Sights & Insights* I. 8 There were settees, and regular piazza chairs. **1903** BURNHAM *Jewel* 324 Mr. Evringham took the doll from her arms, and . . . deposited it in a piazza chair.

Piazzaed, *a.* {1698–} +Of a house: Provided with a piazza. — **1838** COOPER *Home as Found* ix, Still its inns were of respectable size, well piazzaed, to use a word of our own invention, and quite enough frequented. **1873** C. GORDON *Boarding-School Days* 161 A glance of a long, brown, piazzaed house, with wild, luxuriant vines growing up its sides. **1891** WILKINS *New Eng. Nun* 191 In the distance she could see the Tenney house—white-painted and piazzaed, a village mansion.

+**Pic.** Short for PICAYUNE *n.* — **1841** STEELE *Summer Journey* 159 In paying for them I found a new currency here, my shillings and sixpences being transformed into *bits* and *pics* or picayunes. **1850** LEWIS *La. Swamp Doctor* 51 The animal didn't mind him a pic. **1855** M. THOMPSON *Doesticks* 202 A stranger must disburse an avalanche of 'bits,' 'pics,' and 'levys,' before he can get even a plate of cold victuals.

+**Picacho.** *S.W.* [Sp.] A large isolated hill or butte. — **1873** COZZENS *Marvellous Country* 245 Our guides pointed to a thin, blue, vapory smoke ascending from among a range of low *picatchos*, which seemed to form a portion of the Florida range. **1877** HODGE *Arizona* 234 The southern portion of the Territory has numerous sugar-loaf mountains, which rise abruptly from the surface of the great plains and valleys to a height of hundreds and thousands of feet, and are called there picachos. **1903** KING *Apache Princess* 207 (Bentley), Not a sign, except Stout's signal blazes at the pichacho.

Picaillon. Also **pickalion, piccalu.** [Fr.] =PICAYUNE. — **1832** PAULDING *Westward Ho!* I. 124 And then he put his hand in his pocket, and gave her a *pickalion*. **1841** *Knickerb.* XVII. 49 Haven't made a single picaillon since the Belshazzur stove her bottom. **1842** tr. SEALSFIELD *Life in New World* 106 Now not give a piccalu for it.

Picaninny. =PICKANINNY. — **1847** *Knickerbocker Mag.* XXX. 216 Forsooth, it might be very pleasant to be surrounded by half-a-dozen negro waiting-women, with their picaninnies. **1866** W. REID *After the War* 96 A few picaninnies watched our debarkation.

+**Picayune,** *n.* Also †**pecayon, picaion.** [Fr. *picaillon.*]

1. *S.* **a.** A half real. (See FIPPENNY BIT.) **b.** A coin of the value of five cents.

1805 *Amer. Pioneer* II. 228 One can't buy any thing [at New Orleans] for less than a six cent piece, called a *picayune*. **1819** *Niles' Reg.* XVI. Suppl. 160/2 Sales regular at 1 picaion per bucket full. **1834** BAIRD *Valley Miss.* 279 [In La.] the words 'piccayune' (6 1-4 cents) and 'bit'—(12 1-2 cents) fall upon the ear at every step. **1864** NICHOLS *Amer. Life* I. 195 The smallest coin in circulation is the picayune, or five-cent piece. **1866** GREGG *Life in Army* 139 The picayune is the smallest amount of money in use here, and you cannot purchase a row of pins or a needle without paying the five cents. **1894** CHOPIN *Bayou Folk* 207 Boulot and Boulotte, . . . with their quarters, their dimes, and their picayunes tied carefully in a Sunday handkerchief, descended the hill.

2. Used as a type of a small coin or slight amount.
1835 AUDUBON *Ornith. Biog.* III. 160 Their object on this occasion was to present me with some superb corals, shells . . . and a great quantity of eggs. Not a 'pecayon' would they receive in return. **1881** M. J. HOLMES *Madeline* 13 Dr. Holbrook did not care a picayune whether it was ugly or fair. **1901** CHURCHILL *Crisis* 437 These young bloods . . . don't care a picayune for anything. **1904** *N.Y. Ev. Post* 25 Jan. 6 It doesn't matter a picayune whether the justices or the members of the diplomatic corps were presented first.

3. *transf.* An insignificant person.
1903 *Scribner's Mag.* April 508 The very fathers of our country were a pack of jealous picayunes, who bickered while the army starved.

+**Picayune,** *a.* Also **picaoon.** =next.
1836 *Jrnl. of Southern Hist.* I. 351 Louisville . . . is not a *'Picaoon Place,'* as the Southerners term Cincinnati. Business is done on a larger and more liberal scale than in Cincinnati. **1853** *Knickerb.* XLII. 202 All along the Levee there are a great number of small retail, or, to use the local phrase, 'picayune,' stores, kept mainly by Israelites. **1870** *Scribner's Mo.* I. 114 His conduct brings no discredit on his older and staider confrères in the picayune traffic of the sidewalk. **1907** *Nation* 18 July 45 The whole miserable, picayune, personal baggage law ought to go. **1915** *New Republic* 31 July 336/1 They instinctively regard the critic as puny and picayune.

+**Picayunish,** *a.* Of little value; paltry, contemptible. Hence *picayunishness.*
1857 *Jrnl. of Discourses* VI. 234 (Th.), There were many picayunish fools around. **1863** *Rio Abajo Press* 19 May 2 We have often been amused at the picayunish arguments used to secure votes in other regions, but our political Utopians throw them into the shade. **1872** POWERS *Afoot & Alone* 83 Does he ask the price? No; he disdains a thing so 'picayunish.' **1887** *Springfield Republican* 14 Oct., A sad commentary on the political picayuneishness that allows [etc.]. **1905** CROTHERS *Pardoner's Wallet* 21 He contrasts his own generous and care-free nature with the picayunish prudence which he scorns.

Piccolo. A small flute an octave higher in pitch than the ordinary flute. {1856-} — **1856** DERBY *Phoenixiana* 46 A few notes on the piccolo, calls the attention to a solitary antelope, picking up mescal beans in the foreground. **1907** *St. Nicholas* May 595/2 A great twanging of strings was going on in reply to Will's insistent 'a—a—a' on the piano, and low breathing of flute and piccolo. **1923** *Sears, Roebuck & Co. Cat.* No. 146, 519 Our flutes and piccolos are carefully inspected and the keys adjusted before leaving our store.

***Pick,** *n.* A tool for digging or breaking up hard soil, rock, etc., consisting of a bar of iron, usually slightly curved, sharpened at the ends, and provided with a handle.
1645 *Conn. Rec.* I. 473 A prticuler of his goods, as followeth . . . three pickes, on auger, one draweing knife [etc.]. **1850** COLTON *Deck & Port* 401 Whenever his pick struck close upon a deposite, it was no longer there. **1884** HARTE *On Frontier* 238, *I* pitched in at once with a pick he let me have on credit. **a1918** G. STUART *On Frontier* I. 78 Taking a small pick and a gold pan, and crevice spoon, he would go down in the deep cañon.

b. In combinative expressions used attributively.
1895 REMINGTON *Pony Tracks* 193 Here they are all cavalry . . . and are not hindered by dismounted theories, or pick-and-shovel work. **1896** SHINN *Story of Mine* 78 All this resembles the simple pick-and-pan method of prospecting for placer gold.

***Pick,** *v.*

+**1.** *tr.* To gather or harvest (cotton) by plucking it from the open bolls.
1823 *Baptist Mag.* IV. 181, I helped to . . . plant, hoe, pick, gin and pack the cotton with my own hands. **1841** W. KENNEDY *Texas* I. 68 Here, the mildness of the season enables the planter to 'pick' all the cotton he can raise. **1856** in Commons, etc. *Doc. Hist.* I. 128 When Picking Cotton in the Hammock and Hickory Ridge, weigh the Tasks in the field. **1916** J. F. DUGGAR *Southern Field Crops* 361 In some localities considerable cotton is picked in December.

+**b.** To free (cotton) of its seed; to gin. *Obs.*
1807 JANSON *Stranger in Amer.* 370 Private families gin their cotton by the hand, which is called *picking,* and this work is set apart for the evening. **1834** in Bassett *Plantation Overseer* 73, I cant under take to pick a crop with them.

+**2.** To remove (ears of corn) from the stalks.
Cf. BREAK *v.* 4.
1833 SILLIMAN *Man. Sugar Cane* 13 Indian corn . . . is picked early in autumn. **1837** in Commons, etc. *Doc. Hist.* I. 221 Through breaking corn on the 18th, . . . and begun picking corn of plantation hands. **1859** *Rep. Comm. Patents 1858* I. 359 Improvement in Machine for Picking Corn. **1907** *Office of Exper. Stations Bul.* No. 173, 34 The average man picks 59 bushels of corn per day.

+**3.** (See quot. 1859.)
1859 BARTLETT 319 In the South, to *pick* the banjo or guitar, means to play upon these instruments. **1884** F. Y. HEDLEY *Marching through Ga.* (1890) 402 The other [Negro] picked a banjo, and made serious attempts to sing a plantation song. **1903** FOX *Little Shepherd* iii, Who was that a-pickin' that banjer?

+**4.** (See quotation.)
1881 INGERSOLL *Oyster-Industry* 246 *Pick.*—To gather wild oysters for seed from the muddy shores at low tide. (Georgia.)

+**5.** *To pick a* (or *one's*) *flint,* to roughen or renew the edge of a gunflint that comes in contact with the hammer; hence, fig., to get ready, to prepare for a new effort.
1833 FLINT *D. Boone* 79 Boone, picking the flint of his rifle, . . . took aim at the panther. **1835** KENNEDY *Horse Shoe Robinson* I. 87, I hold myself a match for the best man that ever picked a flint in your lines. **1846** COOPER *Redskins* xxii, Activity is the natur' of a prer-ie man, and he's always glad to pick his flint, after a spell of considerable quiet. **1871** *Northern Vindicator* (Estherville, Iowa) 8 July, The Blizzards [a baseball club] should pick their flints and try again.

***6.** *To pick at* or *on* (someone), to tease, vex, or impose upon (someone).
'Now only *dial* and *U.S.*' (*O.E.D.*).
1859 ELWYN *Glossary* 85 To *pick at;* as, 'Bill Jones kept picking at me, so I struck him,' was a common phrase, among school-boys. **1870** EGGLESTON *Queer Stories* 120 The mean fellows . . . make up for their cowardice . . . by 'picking' at little fellows or green boys. **1887** WILKINS *Humble Romance* 62, I don't see . . . what does make you girls forever pick on each other. **1896** *Cosmopolitan* XX. 430/2 But I'm always being picked at. I wish I was dead. **1897** FREEMAN *Jerome* 43 That Sim' Basset pickin' on me that way. **1914** — *Copy-Cat* 305 Say, Annie, what on earth makes them all pick on you so?

***7.** *To pick up,* +to tidy up; to put in order.
1861 *Ill. Agric. Soc. Trans.* IV. 204 We did not find 'things picked up in it'—no air of comfort about it. **1887** PERRY *Flock of Girls* 81 She mends up those little bits of things and 'picks up' after you, as you call it. **1889** FARMER 419/1 *To pick up a room,* is a New England phrase for putting it in order.

+**b.** To detect (a person) in a mistake; to show up.
1846 SOL. SMITH *Theatr. Apprenticeship* 149 The bystanders . . . were crowding around the table in great numbers to see the fun—all considering me most undoubtedly 'picked up.' **1877** HARTE *Story of Mine* (1896) 283 'That morning . . . when we were coming down the valley you picked me up twice.' . . . 'Yes—contradicted me, that's what I mean.' **1881** PIERSON *In the Brush* 44 He had to 'stand treat' all around among his companions, for being thus, in the vernacular of the country, 'picked up' by the preacher.

Pickaninny. Also **piccaniny.** A Negro child. {1657-, in W. Indies, etc.}
See also PICANINNY.
1800 BOUCHER *Glossary* p. xlix, A *Pickaninny;* a male infant: probably from the Spanish *picade nino, pequeno nino.* **1859** *Harper's Mag.* Dec. 134/2 Presently some one sent up a little pickaninny, black as the ace of spades, . . . with a dollar bill in his hand. **1883** *Ib.* Sept. 625/1, I remember when I was a baby sitting with the black pickaninnies on the ground playing with frogs. **1897** *Outing* Sept. 627/2 Fifty little dancing and singing pickaninnies have been brought directly from Kentucky and Virginia. **1905** N. DAVIS *Northerner* 289 Is it the piccaninny I rode on my shoulder?

b. Attrib. with *craft, daylight, devil.*
1871 'MARK TWAIN' *Screamers* 132 Old Mann used to own and command a pickaninny, bull-headed, mud-turtle-shaped craft of a schooner. **1873** C. GORDON *Boarding-School Days* 242 You black piccaniny debbil, I learns you p'liteness. **1903** R. BEDFORD *True Eyes* 321 By pickaninny daylight the mounted men were in motion.

‖**Pickaroon.**[1] =PICAYUNE. — **1835** A. PARKER *Trip to Texas* 88 They have some peculiarities in the calling of money. A New-England *ninepence* is called a *bit;* and the four-pence-half-penny bears the name of *pickaroon.*

+**Pic(k)aroon.**[2] [Cf. MF. *piqueron* 'a spur.'] (See quot. 1905.) — **1850** JUDD *R. Edney* 42 Richard, armed with a picaroon, descended the slip, some thirty feet, to the basin, where the logs lay in the water ready to be drawn in. *Ib.* 220 The Boy made his picaroon fast to his boat with a rope. **1905** *Forestry Bureau Bul.* No. 61, 43 *Pickaroon,* a piked pole fitted with a curved hook, used in holding boats to jams in driving, and for pulling logs from brush and eddies out into the current.

***Pickax.** A tool resembling a pick and a mattock and used for breaking up compact soil, rocks, etc.
1641 *Essex Inst. Coll.* L. 230, 3 peck axes, 3s. 6d. **1759** *Newport Mercury* 14 Aug. 3/2 List of Stores, &c. taken at Niagara. . . . 400 Pick-Axes, 250 Mattocks [etc.]. **1812** *Niles' Reg.* II. 131/1 The purveyor of public supplies advertises for . . . 2000 pick axes. **1895** M. A. Jackson *Gen. Jackson* 511 The guns, of course, had to go—prolongs and pickaxes did it.
attrib. **1812** PAULDING *J. Bull & Bro. Jon.* 119 [He] put his pickaxe hat on hind part before.

+**Picked-over,** *a.* Remaining after the best has been selected. — **1839** *Congress. Globe* App. 2 Jan. 47/2 All the emigrants went on to the new lands, where they could get first choices at $1.25 per acre, because they could not give that sum for picked-over lands in the old counties. **1886** N. SHEPPARD *Before an Audience* 124 Audiences in England outside of the Established Church . . . have a picked-over appearance. The church takes the cream, the chapel the milk of society.

+**Picked-up dinner.** A dinner prepared quickly from that which is most readily available. (Cf. PICK-UP.) — **1771** J. ADAMS *Diary* Works II. 275 We had a picked up dinner. **1867** 'LACKLAND' *Homespun* 126 A sort of 'picked-up' dinner is set before them. **1892** WILKINS *Jane Field* 102 Everything we've got is a picked-up dinner.

* **Picker.**

+**1.** One who picks cotton in the field.

1759 in Commons, etc. *Doc. Hist.* I. 115, [I] will suggest the propriety of sending a few trustworthy hands ahead of the regular pickers to gather from the early opening. **1835** INGRAHAM *South-West* II. 286 The nett weight of cotton is set down upon the slate, opposite the name of the picker. **1891** 'THANET' *Otto the Knight* 325 A far-away song [was] floating up from the cotton-fields filled with pickers.

+**2.** One who picks or sorts tobacco.

1800 TATHAM *Tobacco* 82 The *pickers* are the first gradation of subordinate officers under the rank of inspectors.

+**3.** (See quotation.)

1851 *Alta Californian* 18 Nov., 'The Pickers' is the generic name, given a year or two ago, to a class of miners in Mariposa, who, being too lazy, or not having time to sink holes themselves, would go about with a sheath knife and pan and earn their livelihood by picking among the rocks.

* **Pickerel.** +Any one of various American fish of the pike family. (Cf. PICKERING.)

1765 ROWE *Diary* 82 We caught . . . several Pickerel. **1791** LONG *Voyages* 43 At this place there is abundance of fine fish, particularly pickerill, trout, and white fish. **1814** *Mass. H. S. Coll.* 2 Ser. III. 118 The lake abounds with fish, of which the salmon trout, pickerel, eel, and cusk, or tusk, are the most plenty. **1870** *Conn. Public Acts* 437 No person shall . . . catch or take any pickerel, pike, black bass, or maskinonge. **1911** *Rep. Fisheries 1908* 315 Sauger (*Stizostedion canadense*). . . . It is known locally as . . . 'pickering,' 'pickerel,' 'horsefish,' etc.

+**b.** *Pickerel state*, South Dakota. A nickname.

1899 *Mo. So. Dakotan* I. 182, I have noticed Senator Pettigrew referred to as the 'statesman from the Pickeral [*sic*] state.'

+**Pickerel flower.** =PICKEREL WEED. — **1842** HAWTHORNE *Note-books* (1932) 155 The blue spires and broad green leaves of the pickerel-flower . . . contrast and harmonize so well with the white lilies. **1867** EMERSON *May-Day* 44 Through gold-moth-haunted beds of pickerel-flowers.

+**Pickerel frog.** The marsh frog, *Rana palustris.* — **1839** STORER *Mass. Reptiles* 238 The Pickerel Frog . . . is as frequently . . . met with about the margins of fresh water brooks and ponds, as in any other situations. **1867** *Amer. Naturalist* I. 109 Other species of Frogs found in Massachusetts . . . are the Spotted Frog, Marsh Frog, or Pickerel Frog (*Rana palustris* Le Conte); the second species of Spotted Frog [etc.].

Pickerel weed. {1653–} +Any one of various American aquatic herbs or species of herbs of the genus *Pontederia.* (Cf. PICKEREL FLOWER.) — **1784** CUTLER in *Amer. Acad. Mem.* I. 433 *Pontederia.* . . . Pickerel-weed. Blue Spike. Blossoms blue. Common on the borders of ponds and rivers. July. **1845** THOREAU *Journal* I. 383 When at length I had made one cast over the pickerel-weed, the thunder gan romblen in the heven with that grisly steven that Chaucer tells of. **1880** *Harper's Mag.* June 70 The frog pond with lush growth of arrow leaves and pickerel weed. **1910** *Atlantic Mo.* Sept. 428 Butterflies flicker in and out of the mint and the pickerel-weed and the rushes.

* **Pickering.** +Any of several species of fish, esp. one of the pike perches as the sauger. — **1842** *Nat. Hist. N.Y., Zoology* IV. 16 The Champlain Pickering . . . is [also called] the Little Pickerel, or Pickering, which is also applied to many other species. *Ib.* 18 [The Yellow Pike-Perch] is the Common Pike, Pickerel, Pickering . . . and Yellow Pike of the Great Lakes. **1884** GOODE, etc. *Fisheries* I. 424 The Sauger or Pickering of the Saint Lawrence was the original *Lucioperca canadensis* of Col. C. H. Smith. **1911** *Rep. Fisheries 1908* 315.

+**Pickeronian.** A political follower of Timothy Pickering (1745–1829). *Obs.* Also attrib. — **1800** *Aurora* (Phila.) 16 May (Th.), The three parties are now known by the designation of the Republicans, the Adamites, the Pickeronians. *Ib.* 19 May (Th.), The Pickeronian columns either led or directed every odious measure which has been brought forward. **1809** [see MADISONIAN].

+**Pickeroon.** =prec. *Obs.* — **1800** *Aurora* (Phila.) 3 Sept. (Th.), The bloody and remorseless character of the Hamiltonians and Pickeroons. **1808** *Essex* (Mass.) *Register* 2 April (Th.), Let the Lacoites, the Kitites, the Pickeroons, the Refugees, the Tories, the British, and the whole Federal fry that follows them, be convinced [etc.].

Picket. Also **picquet, piquet.** {1690–}

+**1.** *On picket*, engaged in service as a sentry; on picket duty. Also *from picket.*

1775 in Johnston *N. Hale* 158 Your being on Picquet is a sufficient excuse that you wrote no more. **1792** *Ann. 2d Congress* 1131 He also remembered very well being on picket . . . when the first men arrived. **1861** NORTON *Army Lett.* 34, I have just returned from picket. **1899** *Mo. So. Dakotan* I. 159 An accidental discharge of a gun one night in the hands of a man on picket.

2. *Mil.* A soldier or a small body of soldiers, usually on sentinel or outpost duty. {1761–}

1776 *Md. Hist. Mag.* III. 105, I march'd with a Piquet by the way of New Ark to one Peck's. **1792** *Ann. 2d Congress* 1127 A standing order directed the pickets to turn out small parties and drive in every horse. **1881–5** MCCLELLAN *Own Story* 339 His advanced guard had communicated with Franklin's pickets.

+**3.** A portion of a tree trunk set upright in the ground to form part of a stockade or barrier, esp. as a defense against hostile Indians.

1785 DENNY *Journal* 59 All hands set to work chopping, clearing &c., and preparing timber for block-houses and pickets. **1791** in Jillson *Dark & Bl. Ground* 107 The pickets are round logs of oak, grown near by, and all of them more than a foot in diameter. **1807** GASS *Journal* 42 The pickets are 13½ feet above ground. **1843** HAWKS *D. Boone* 57 The fort consisted of several cabins, surrounded by pickets ten feet high, planted firmly in the ground.

+**b.** The stockade formed by such timbers.

1833 CATLIN *Indians* I. 81 The piquet is composed of timbers . . . eighteen feet high, set firmly in the ground at sufficient distances from each other to admit of guns and other missiles to be fired between them. **1835** HOFFMAN *Winter in West* I. 97 The river on one side, and the high picket on the other, would have hedged the remainder in. **1838** INGRAHAM *Burton* I. 219 In advance . . . , about two hundred yards, stood a blockhouse protected by a picket.

4. =PICKET PIN. {1702–}

1806 LEWIS in *L. & Clark Exped.* IV. (1905) 301 His horse . . . was not to be found when I ordered the others to be brought up and confined to the picquits. **1848** PARKMAN in *Knickerb.* XXXII. 504 The horses and mules loosened from their pickets, were feeding on the neighboring meadow. **1870** KEIM *Sheridan's Troopers* 155 One of the volunteers, tying his horse to the picket, was somewhat astounded to find the animal jerk away from him.

+**5.** A thin, narrow strip of wood used as a lath or as a paling for a fence.

Cf. PICKET FENCE.

1853 FOWLER *Home for All* 109 All the outside walls or inclosing to be of pickets or strips of common refuse stuff, about four inches wide. **1871** EGGLESTON *Hoosier Schoolm.* 92 Miss Martha Hawkins, . . . leaning over the palings—pickets she called them—of the garden fence, talking to the master. **1897** BRODHEAD *Bound in Shallows* 102 The pickets of the Morrows' fence struck white upon the road-side shadows.

6. *attrib.* and *comb.* **a.** In sense 2 with *duty, fight, firing,* etc.

1816 *Niles' Reg.* X. 361/1 It was customary for officers commanding regiments, battalions, or companies, to volunteer for what was then called 'piquet fights.' They always terminated in driving the piquets of the enemy. **1861** MCCLELLAN in *Own Story* 170 In front of us the enemy remain quiet, with the exception of occasional picket-firing. **1862** *Ib.* 635 The other portion of my command, now absent on picket duty, has horses which are about in the same condition. **1862** NORTON *Army Lett.* 59 We pitched our picket tents which we carry with us on the ground lately occupied by a *secesh* regiment. **1895** in M. A. Jackson *Gen. Jackson* 546 The Thirty-third North Carolina Regiment was . . . deployed . . . about two hundred and fifty or three hundred yards in front of the picket guns or the log works of the Twelfth Corps.

b. In sense 5 with *header, paling, yard.*

1845 *Big Bear Ark.* 60 'Twarnt but a little squar picket yard. **1857** *Atlantic Mo.* I. 97/1 It is a square area of two acres in extent, inclosed by a mossy picket paling. **1883** *Harper's Mag.* Jan. 208/2 The capacity of these mills is from twenty to forty thousand feet of lumber a day, and to them are attached planers, shingle machines, picket headers, and so on.

c. In sense 3 with *corral, stockade.*

1860 CLAIBORNE *Sam. Dale* 110 Fort Wayne—a mere picket stockade, garrisoned by only one company—resisted for several days a combined attack led by Tecumseh. *a***1918** G. STUART *On Frontier* II. 127 They have a picket corral of box elder logs . . . where they corral their horses every night.

d. In sense 4 with *stake.*

1894 WISTER in *Harper's Mag.* April 789/2 The emigrants attended to their affairs, watering the horses and driving picket stakes.

Picket boat. A boat on picket duty. {1885–} — **1866** *Ore. State Jrnl.* 13 Jan. 1/4 For the capture of the Albermarle [*sic*], by Lieu[t]. Cushing's picket-boats, the crew netted $100 per man. **1887** *Appletons' Cycl. of Amer. Biog.* II. 41 With his usual good luck, he [Lt. Cushing] found a picket-boat.

Picket cord. A cord or rope for picketing a horse. — **1778** *Jrnls. Cont. Congress* X. 312 For each trooper a pair of boots, a saddle, halters, curry-comb and brush, portmantle, picket cord, and pack saddle. **1812** *Niles' Reg.* II. 131/1 The purveyor of public supplies advertises for . . . 7000 yards of picket cord, 3000 valises, also woollen and other usual supplies.

Picketed, *a.* {1818–} Surrounded or protected by a stockade of pickets. {1885–} Cf. PICKET 3. — **1745** *Jrnl. Siege of Louisbourg* in Shirley *Letter* (1746) 18 A Blockhouse was erected on Canso Hill, . . . picketted without, and defended by eight Cannon. **1852** E. F. ELLET *Pioneer Women* 163 The term 'station,' in the frontier vocabulary of those times, meant a blockhouse, picketed so as to shelter several families.

+Picket fence. A fence made of pickets. Also fig. (Cf. PICKET 5.)

[**1800** *Boston Carpenters' Rules* 32 (Ernst), Plain picket open fence.] **1817** S. BROWN *Western Gazetteer* 66 Almost every house [in Vincennes, Indiana] has a garden in its rear, with high, substantial picket fences to prevent the thefts of the Indians. **1888** STOCKTON *Dusantes* 125 From the gate of the picket-fence in front of the yard a brick-paved path led up to the house. **1906** F. LITTLE *Lady of Decoration* 85 She had surrounded herself with a regular picket fence of creed and dogma. **1917** SINCLAIR *King Coal* 27 It was an unpainted, three room cabin, . . . with bare dirt and cinders about it, and what had once been a picket-fence, now falling apart.

+Picket fort. A fort having for its outer defense a stockade made of pickets. (Cf. PICKET 3.) — **1775** *Mass. H. S. Coll.* 2 Ser. II. 230 This fort consists of two large block-houses, and a large barrack, which is enclosed with a picket fort. **1779** *N.H. Hist. Soc. Coll.* VI. 316 The two regiments . . . move about three miles up stream and encamp . . . near a large picket fort. **1827** MCKENNEY *Tour to Lakes* 141 The old fort . . . was only a *picket*-fort, and on the water's edge. **1846** — *Memoirs* I. 127 The old picket fort standing on the plain.

Picket guard. *Mil.* A detail of soldiers kept in readiness for instant service at any desired spot; a picket performing guard or sentry duty. {1703-}

1756 ROGERS *Journals* 35, I at length discovered two men, centries to the piquet guard of the French army. **1778** *Essex Inst. Coll.* LII. 16, I found that a party of soldiers had gone out into the rebel encampment & had taken . . . one of their picket guard. **1872** *Atlantic Mo.* March 317 A picket-guard, in 1813, posted on the Potomac to watch for the expected British fleet. **1916** THOBURN *Stand. Hist. Okla.* I. 328 The picket guards of the defenders were driven back to the stockade.

attrib. **1862** McClellan *Own Story* 292 Capt. Nicholson says he found a good picket-guard house for cavalry, stables, etc., within the Box.

+b. Short for *picket-guard duty.*

1861 NEWELL *Orpheus C. Kerr* I. 47 Jim . . . was out on picket-guard the night before.

Picketing. {1753-} +A stockade or palisade made of pickets. (Cf. PICKET 3.) — **1755** *N.H. Hist. Soc. Coll.* V. 254 Seven men . . . [were] getting a few poles to complete the new picketing of the fort. **1813** *Niles' Reg.* IV. 12/2 An order was given to retreat within the picqueting. **1838** DRAKE *Tales Queen City* 104 Several breaches in the picketing [were] rapidly repaired. **1860** CLAIBORNE *Sam. Dale* 25 These forts were merely a number of log cabins built round a small square, . . . the whole surrounded by a rough picketing.

+Picket pin. An iron pin or wooden stake to be driven into the ground for tethering a horse.

1847 RUXTON *Adv. Rocky Mts.* (1848) 211 The half-frozen animals, standing over their picket-pins and collapsed with cold. **1875** *Fur, Fin & Feather* (ed. 3) 106 Early morning finds you out on the prairie pulling at the picket pin of your horse. **1889** MUNROE *Golden Days* 164 His mustang . . . had succeeded in drawing his picket-pin, and was no where to be seen. **1920** COOPER *Under Big Top* 128 The herd had broken from its picket pins.

transf. **1897** LEWIS *Wolfville* 26 The fact's done pulled its picket-pin an' strayed from my recollections.

Picket post. A post occupied by a picket or sentry; the soldiers on duty at such a station. — **1863** A. D. WHITNEY *F. Gartney* xxviii, Sentinels have lain down at picket-posts. **1867** CRAWFORD *Mosby* 74 Ames being perfectly familiar with all the picket-posts, . . . Mosby took him on this raid. **1888** SHERIDAN *Memoirs* I. 175 He had come in . . . pell-mell with our picket-post stationed about three miles out on the Ripley road.

+Picket rope. A rope used in picketing a horse or mule.

1848 BRYANT *California* xvii. 225 Our mules were greatly alarmed several times during the night, breaking their picket-ropes. **1864** *Wkly. New Mexican* 21 Oct. 2/3 Indians . . . cut the lariet that held two horses to the picket rope. **1886** *Outing* Dec. 230/1 Mr. Rios rode ahead, his horse helping pull, by means of a lariat or picket rope fastened to the horn of his saddle and to the pole of the wagon. **1923** J. H. COOK *On Old Frontier* 47 Some Indian had . . . cut the picket-rope of this horse.

attrib. **1874** G. C. EGGLESTON *Rebel's Recoll.* 37 One young gentleman . . . [found] himself assigned to a picket rope post, where his only duty was to guard the horses.

+Picket work. A stockade or barricade made of pickets. (Cf. PICKET 3.) — **1804** CLARK in *Lewis & C. Exped.* I. (1904) 208 The [Mandan] Village . . . containes houses in a kind of Picket work. **1834** J. HALL *Sk. of West* (1835) I. 189 The garrison was removed to a spot about a mile further up, . . . where a picket-work and block-houses were erected. **1842** *Amer. Pioneer* I. 236 This horn-work, as well as the fort itself, was a mere stockade or picket work.

Pick handle. A handle or helve for a pick. — **1850** KINGSLEY *Diary* 156 Tinkered a little at Pick handles, putting door in the tent [etc.]. **1868** *Maine Agric. Rep.* 113 In California the miner can find no wood for a lever or a pick-handle, better than a pine limb. **1873** MILLER *Amongst Modocs* 64 Some decanters . . . and a long white pole, perhaps a sort of pick-handle, . . . are all that I remember.

***Picking.** *attrib.* +Of or pertaining to the harvesting of cotton or to the removal of seed from cotton. — **1807** JANSON *Stranger in Amer.* 370 Private families gin their cotton by the hand. . . . Sometimes they invite their acquaintances to what they call 'a picking frolic,' at which, after the visitors have duly performed their task, they are regaled with a supper, and the evening concludes with a reel or country dance. **1835** INGRAHAM *South-West* II. 285 'Picking time' . . . continues where full crops are made until the first of December. **1856** *Fla. Plantation Rec.* 522 Cloath to make Cotton Pickin Bages.

***Pickle.**

1. A vegetable, esp. a cucumber, fruit, etc., preserved in brine or vinegar. {1707-} Sometimes collect. and freq. pl.

1715 *Boston News-Letter* 16 May 2/2 At the Store-House No. 28, . . . are to be Sold . . . Cases of Pickle on reasonable terms. **1761** in Singleton *Social N.Y.* 364 Pickles of all sorts . . . such as Wallnuts, Cucumbers, Mangoes, Peppers, Capers, Anchovies, etc. **1845** KIRKLAND *Western Clearings* 212 They gi'n me nothing to eat but stale corn bread and pork rinds; not even a pickle to make it go down. **1847** DARLINGTON *Weeds & Plants* 140 [The cucumber is] . . . universally cultivated for the young or green fruit. The young fruit (sometimes called Gherkins) is much used for Pickles. **1883** *Practical Housekeeping* 254 Many think that mustard-seed improves pickles, especially . . . mangoes. **1903** *Harper's Bazar* Oct. 980 A bottle of olives, with one of small sweet pickles. **1914** E. STEWART *Lett. of Woman Homesteader* 281 The young tender ones [*i.e.*, squashes] make splendid pickles.

***2.** Brine or vinegar, spiced or unspiced, in which meats, vegetables, etc., are placed to cure.

1761 *Holyoke Diaries* 23 Tongues 12 put into Pickle. **1775** *Jrnls. Cont. Congress* III. 381 The Captain is . . . [to have] the flesh casks [examined], and if any of the pickle be leaked out, to have new made. **1834** PECK *Gaz. Illinois* 42 Few families in the west and south put up their pork in salt pickle. **1902** LORIMER *Lett. Merchant* 3 You can cure a ham in dry salt and you can cure it in sweet pickle.

3. Attrib. in sense 1 with *bottle, caster, dish,* etc.; in sense 2 with *kettle, tub.*

1664 *Brookhaven Rec.* 12, 4 Sherts, 3 peckle kettels. *c*1766 *York Co., Va., Rec.: Wills* XXII, 2 pickle saucers and stone milk pot. **1855** M. THOMPSON *Doesticks* 187 The ball-room . . . was so full already that each cotillon had only a space about as big as a pickle-tub. **1884** HARRIS *Mingo* 143, 'I wish you'd take keer this pickle-bottle, Cap,' he continued, drawing a revolver from his coat-tail pocket and placing it on the table. **1898** *Kansas City Star* 18 Dec. 10/2 Tea Pots, Syrup Pitchers and Pickle Casters. **1901** ADE *40 Modern Fables* 217 When you . . . begin to Swap duplicate Pickle-Dishes and Lamps for something you can use in the Kitchen, I may look in on you.

***Pickled,** *a.*

***1.** Of fruits and vegetables: Preserved in brine or vinegar.

1760 *Boston Rec.* 61 Pickled cucumbers & peppers. **1788** M. DEWEES *Journal* (MS.) fol. 8 Those who chose had a dish of cold ham and pickled beats. **1805** *Pocumtuc Housewife* (1906) 39 Pickled Cabbage. **1885** *Buckeye Cookery* 268 Pickled Raisins. Leave two pounds raisins on stem, add one pint vinegar and half pound sugar; simmer [etc.].

***2.** Of shad, salmon, etc.: Cured by being immersed in brine for a suitable length of time.

1761 in E. Singleton *Social N.Y.* 364 Pickled oysters and lobsters. **1778** *Jrnls. Cont. Congress* X. 249 Each assistant purchasing commissary shall receive . . . for purchasing . . . pickled shad, per barrel, 12/90ths of a dollar. **1797** PRIEST *Travels* 34 On the table . . . [were] hung beef, sugar, pickled salmon, butter [etc.]. **1869** 'MARK TWAIN' *Innocents* 94 Pickled pigs' feet— . . . *any thing* in the world that can stay a Christian stomach! **1883** *Harper's Mag.* Aug. 456/1 A cold pickled shoulder of pork he thought good enough to invite the king to partake.

Pickled beef. Beef cured by being cut into pieces of convenient size and submerged for a time in pickle or brine. — **1775** *Amer. Husbandry* I. 59 Exports of this province [New Eng.] since the peace. . . . Pickled beef and pork, 19,000 barrels. *c*1790 T. COXE *View U.S.* 62 The produce, manufactures, and exports of Pennsylvania are very many and various, viz. . . . pickled beef, . . . shad, herrings.

Pickled fish. Fish cut up, well salted, packed in water-tight containers, and allowed to cure.

[**1778** *R.I. Commerce* II. 47 We tooke another Schooner from Hallifax . . . , her cargo consists of sixty four hogsheads and eight tierces of Codfish eighty five barrells of Pickled Fish and seventeen hundred feet of Lumber and Staves.] **1789** *Ann. 1st Congress* I. 168 A duty of fifty cents per dozen was imposed on wool cards . . . ; and on every barrel of pickled fish, seventy-five cents. **1804** *Ann. 8th Congress* 2 Sess. 1591 In 1791, there were . . . 57,424 barrels of pickled fish exported from the United States. **1844** *Knickerb.* XXIV. 471 We discussed at large the merits of dun-fish, pickled fish, pollock . . . and trout.

Pickled pork. Pork cured by being cut into hams, shoulders, etc., and immersed in brine for a time. Also *pickle pork.* — **1750** J. BIRKET *Cursory Remarks* 52 They have a good Trade here in Pickled porke And Hams which they Send to the city of Philadelphia for Exportation to the West Indies. **1823** DEWEES *Lett. from Texas* 31 They appeared to have plenty of pickled pork, coffee, and such things. **1852** in Bassett *Plantation Overseer* 196, 1200 lbs of bakin or pickkle pork.

Pickle jar. A jar for pickles. {1899-} — **1838** *S. Lit. Messenger* Jan. 28/1 At this log-house in the prairie, . . . [were] tin canisters, teapot, pickle-jar [etc.]. **1872** *Atlantic Mo.* May 536 She would rob the pickle-jar. **1908** 'O. Henry' *Strictly Business* 12 Bob Hart's sketch was not destined to end in a pickle jar.

||**Picklesome,** *a.* Troublesome, mischievous. — **1885** *Century Mag.* July 380/2 Violet Carmine was a pickle. . . . The stimulating atmosphere of New York had not by any means tended to make her less picklesome.

+**Pickleworm.** The larva of a moth (*Diaphania nitidalis*) of the family Pyralididae: (see quotation). — **1870** *Amer. Naturalist* IV. 614 A new pest to the cucumber in the West, the Pickle worm, . . . is a caterpillar which bores into the cucumbers when large enough to pickle, and it is occasionally found in pickles.

Pickling. {1691–} *attrib.* Designating receptacles in which various things are pickled. {1812–} — **1775** *Essex Inst. Coll.* XIII. 187, 5 Greese Pots, pickling Tubs, . . . etc. **1844** *Lexington Observer* 25 Sept. 2/5 Preserve and Pickling jars of all sizes. **1879** A. D. Whitney *Just How* 271 Then place in your pickling-kettle alternate layers of vine-leaves and pickles.

Pick-up. {1877–} +(See quot. 1859.) Also attrib. or as adj. with *dinner* and *lunch.* (Cf. Picked-up dinner.) — **1848** Bartlett 249 A *pick-up*, or *a pick-up* dinner, is a dinner made up of such fragments of cold meats as remain from former meals. The word is common in the Northern States. **1878** Stowe *Poganuc People* 231 We shall just have a pick-up dinner. **1889** Cooke *Steadfast* 275 The deacon's gone over to New Haven to-day, so you and me can have a pick-up. **1902** Norris *Pit* 53 Just a pick-up lunch—coffee, chops. I thought we wouldn't bother to-day.

Pictorial. An illustrated paper or magazine. {1880–} — **1844** *Knickerb.* XXIII. 197 The handsome 'Lady's and Gentleman's Magazine' hight '*The Columbian*' . . . is to run a brisk competition . . . with the other 'pictorials,' *Godey's*, *Graham's*, and *Snowden's*. **1872** *Congress. Globe* 27 May 3909/1 Other pictorials might be published on paper a little smaller or a little larger. **1887** *Courier-Journal* 2 May 5/3 The work of death that the wicked author does in a whole book the bad engraver may do on a half side of a pictorial.

***Picture.** Also *colloq.* **pictur, picter, pictar.**

+**1.** In profane or strongly condemnatory expressions, such as *consarn* or *confound his picture*, etc., in the sense: Damn him. *slang.*

1825 Neal *Bro. Jonathan* III. 387 Young Bob's dad—con-sarn his pictur! spry as a cat. **1843** *Yale Lit. Mag.* IX. 79 Is that the way the Britishers larnt ye to treat a gal, blast your infarnal pictur! **1845** W. T. Thompson *Chron. Pineville* 181 You'll get waked up worse than you ever was afore—drat your infernal picters. **1852** *Daily Morning Herald* (St. Louis) 28 Dec. (Th.), Bill Jones . . . kissed me; and, confound his picture, I told him everybody would find it out. **1875** Winans *Reminiscences* 63 Consarn yer picter, young feller—see what you've done.

+**2.** A person's face. *slang.*

1847 Robb *Squatter Life* 137, I jest swar a bible oath, I'd spile his pictur' so he couldn't enjoy campmeetin' much. **1848** Durivage & Burnham *Stray Subjects* 168 Ef I could only come across that ere Vermonter which I was took in by, if I wouldn't spile his picter, bust my boots and gallowses!

3. *pl.* Playing cards. *slang.*

1853 Simms *Sword & Distaff* (1854) 275, I hev' the pictars in my own hand. **1855** — *Forayers* 506 Flirting the cards at 'old sledge' from well-thumbed and greasy packs of 'pictures.'

+**4.** *To be high up in the pictures* or *to be in the picture*, to be highly successful; to be in keeping with the occasion.

1851 *Polly Peablossom* 147 He was gettin' too high up in the pictures enny how. **1902** C. Morris *Stage Confidences* 202 Oh, well, I feel that I am in the picture, when I wear black during Lent.

5. In special combinations.

Picture card, (see quotation); *p.-collector*, one who collects pictures, as for a picture gallery; *p. nail*, a strong nail for picture hanging having a detachable ornamental head.

1887 Perry *Flock of Girls* 92 It was, to be sure, a childish game,—a game of picture-cards, each card bearing the face of some king or queen in English history. **1886** *Century Mag.* May 577/1 Cincinnati was the first of the Western cities to become known as a home of picture-collectors. **1909** Wason *Happy Hawkins* 285 The ol' man's face turned grey an' his eyes stuck out like picture nails.

Picture book. A book, usu. for children, consisting wholly or chiefly of pictures. {1854–} Also fig. — **1859** *Ladies' Repository* Aug. 466/2 A little girl entertains a doll, almost as large as herself, with a gayly-painted picture book. **1870** 'F. Fern' *Ginger-Snaps* 34 There are mothers whose pockets contain alleviations for this juvenile restlessness, in the shape of sugar-plums, or picture-books. **1875** Emerson *Lett. & Soc. Aims* 20 A man's action is only a picture-book of his creed. **1891** Wilkins *New Eng. Nun* 176 There were picture-books and cards, and boxes of candy, and oranges.

+**Pictured rocks.** Rocks upon which quaint designs have been produced by weathering. Usually applied to sandstone cliffs about three hundred feet high in Alger County, Michigan, along the shore of Lake Superior. — **1827** McKenney *Tour to Lakes* 225 The Doric rock . . . is about two miles from the line of towers and battlements which compose this grand display of the Pictured rocks. **1847** Lanman *Summer in Wilderness* 132 That portion of the coast . . . is low, and with the exception of the Pictured Rocks, uninteresting. **1857** Chandless *Visit Salt Lake* 121 Travelling . . . over steep ridges, beside pictured rocks (on the right hand, never on the left). **1902** Hulbert *Forest Neighbors* 158 From Lake Huron to the Pictured Rocks.

Picture frame. A frame, more or less ornamental, in which a picture is mounted for protection or display. {1668–} Also attrib. — **1725** *New-Eng. Courant* 10–17 July 2/2 At the same Place may be had all Sorts of Picture-Frames made. **1774** *Copley-Pelham Lett.* 280, I inclose a rough sketch for a picture frame. **1827** Drake & Mansfield *Cincinnati* 65 One Looking-glass and Picture Frame Factory. **1888** *Amer. Almanac* 275 Occupations of the People of the United States. . . . Miners, . . . Mirror and picture frame makers. **1905** N. Davis *Northerner* 197 Turning from Falls, [he] adjusted a picture-frame upon the mantelpiece.

Picture gallery. A hall or room where pictures are exhibited; a collection of pictures. {1761–} Also transf. and fig. — **a1841** Hawes *Sporting Scenes* I. 178 [Wild geese are] willing to wait for the wooden devices which we have anchored in the shallow feeding-grounds, as a picture-gallery of their uncles, cousins, and sweet-hearts. **1864** Nichols *Amer. Life* I. 158 There are . . . several large publishing houses, libraries, picture-galleries [etc.]. **1887** Perry *Flock of Girls* 88 Louise . . . went out with her mother . . . to visit the picture-galleries. **1923** J. H. Cook *On Old Frontier* 213 Occasionally I can look back into that picture-gallery of my brain and see again the weather-beaten faces of those old Indians.

Picture man. One who makes or sells pictures; one conversant with pictures. — **1771** Rowe *Diary* 216 Mr. Price the Picture man died on Fryday. **1881** Whitman *Spec. Days* 81, I stood long and long before 'the Sower.' I believe what the picture-men designate 'the first Sower,' as the artist executed a second copy, and a third.

Picture paper. A newspaper or similar publication consisting wholly or chiefly of pictures. — **1869** Aldrich *Story of Bad Boy* (1877) 233 [In] the little knicknack shop . . . they sell picture-papers. **1885** *Wkly. New Mexican Rev.* 16 April 4/6 The Albuquerque Journal has also begun to publish a picture paper. **1898** Westcott *D. Harum* xxxviii, She grudged me even to look at a picture paper. **1907** *St. Nicholas* June 678/1 The little knicknack shop around the corner [sells] picture papers, spruce gum, needles and Malaga raisins.

Picture shop. A shop where pictures are sold. {1732–} — **1722** *New-Eng. Courant* 13–20 Aug. 2/2 To be sold at the Picture-Shop . . . , an exact Prospect of the City of New York. **1856** *Harper's Mag.* Dec. 46/1 We had three hours upon our hands, which we pleasantly filled by visits to a studio and a picture-shop.

Picture show. A showing or exhibition of pictures; a motion picture show. — **1881** Carleton *Farm Festivals* 69 'Twas a picture-show, a lecture, and a sermon—all united. **1912** Irwin *Red Button* 3 They all sang the foolish ephemeral songs of the picture-shows. **1925** *Scribner's Mag.* Oct. 430/1 There's young people and parties, and a picture-show every night.

+**Picture store.** A store at which pictures are sold. — **1872** Roe *Barriers* xxvii, Mr. French, proprietor of another large picture-store. **1883** Howells *Woman's Reason* xiii, She stopped a moment on her way home at the window of a picture-store. **1884** *Century Mag.* Oct. 874/2, I went to see the landscapes at Radfield's picture-store.

+**Pided,** *a.* [Var. of *pied.*] Parti-colored; marked with different colors in patches or blotches. *dial.* — **1757** *S.C. Gazette* Suppl. 23 June, A black and white pided cow . . . a red and white pided heifer. **1845** Hooper *Simon Sugg's Adv.* 144 The old feller looked as pided as a rattle-snaik. **1921** Greer-Petrie *Angeline at Seelbach* 14 [He] was so mad he was plum pided.

***Pie.**[1]

***1.** A baked dish made of fruit, vegetables, or meat, inclosed, or partially inclosed, in pastry.

Cf. Apple pie, Berry-pie, etc.

1676 B. Tompson *Poetical Works* 70 Like Christmas pyes, Their pastry by degrees on high doth rise. **1746** *S.C. Gazette* 29 Dec., All sorts of Pyes, Tarts, Cakes. **1775** Fithian *Journal* II. 68 We have . . . boil'd potatoes, & huckleberry-pie. **1805** *Pocumtuc Housewife* (1906) 8 Pie and gingerbread and custards are good enough for common use. **1882** F. Owens *Cook Book* 144 Green apples should be stewed before making into pies. **1925** Tilghman *Dugout* 50 Can you cook . . . pies and doughnuts and the like?

+**b.** *fig.* In comparisons.

1847 Paige *Dow's Sermons* I. 21 (Th.), Let her alone and in five minutes the storm will be over, and she as good as pie again. **1878** Cooke *Happy Dodd* 178 (Th.), We've been awful good; good as pie, hain't we? **1891** *Harper's Mag.* Sept. 579/1 Ain't he as polite as pie to her? **1917** McCutcheon *Green Fancy* 275 He is as nice as pie this afternoon.

+**2.** In various figurative expressions, freq. in the sense of the acme of goodness or of a cinch. *slang.*

1866 'Mark Twain' *Lett. Sandwich Isl.* 77 In the sorrowful expression of its deserted halls . . . and its decayed magnificence, it seems to proclaim, in the homely phrase of California, that it has 'got enough pie.' **1876** — *Tom Sawyer* x. 97 Tom Sawyer, you're just old pie, 'longside o' what *I* am. **1883** — *Life on Miss.* xxiv, You dredge an alligator once and he's *convinced*. . . . He wouldn't come back for pie. **1895** *Outing* XXVI. 436/1 Green dogs are pie for [the raccoon]. **1901** *N. Amer. Rev.* Feb. 166 Is it good? Sir, it is pie. It will bring into camp any idiot that sits in darkness anywhere.

+**3.** Political patronage or graft. *slang.*

1879 *Daily Telegraph* (Lond.) 26 Dec., Men may come and men may go; the Grant 'Boom' may be succeeded by the Sherman 'Boom;' but Pie goes on for ever. **1898** PAGE *Red Rock* 229 Does he want to keep all the pie for himself? Why don't he pay that rent to the State for the railroad him and his crowd leased? **1910** *Richmond W. Times-Dispatch* 17 Aug. 10 Representative Slemp was looked upon as the dispenser of the patronage in Virginia because of the promise of the President that he would allow the pie to be handed out by the men who did the fighting.

+**4.** *To cut a pie*, to meddle in a matter.

1843 HALIBURTON *Attaché* Ser. xi, By gosh, Aunty, . . . you had better not cut that pie: you will find it rather sour in the apple sarse, and tough in the paste.

5. *attrib.* and *comb.* **a.** Designating things used in pies. See also PIEPLANT, PIE RHUBARB.

1859 *Mich. Agric. Soc. Trans.* X. 623 Best pie melon, [exhibited by] H. T. Young. **1867** DALY *Legend of 'Norwood'* 73 Miss Agate, here's the pie fruit.

b. Designating various utensils used in making, serving, or eating pies.

1869 E. PUTNAM *Receipt Bk.* 85 Flour the birds . . . [and] lay them into a pie-dish. **1873** BAILEY *Life in Danbury* 37 A bed-quilt comes out first, then a pie-tin, next a piece of cold ham. **1875** STOWE *We & Neighbors* 474 Of course the reader knows that there were the usual amount of berry-spoons, and pie-knives, and crumb-scrapers. **1887** GEORGE *40 Years on Rail* 187 An exquisite set of pie forks, of English make, and valued at seventy-five dollars.

c. Pertaining to political 'pie' (sense 3 above).

1912 NICHOLSON *Hoosier Chron.* 470, I'm in the ranks of the patriots and not looking for the pie counter.

d. In special combinations.

Pie buggy (facetious), a ranch wagon sent to town for supplies; *p.-hunter*, a political adherent or follower motivated by a desire for 'pie' or graft (cf. sense 3 above); *p.-marker*, *p. print*, the fruit of Indian mallow; *p. wagon*, the wagon of an itinerant showman.

1890 *Stock Grower & Farmer* 28 June 3/4 Why I have seen half a hundred 'pie buggies' standing on our streets in one day, waiting for a chance to get up to a grocery to load up with swine bosom, flour, canned goods, etc. **1898** *Kansas City Star* 20 Dec. 5/1 Early arrivals talked of abolishing unnecessary offices and reducing the number of appointments. This smoked out the pie-hunters of both parties. **1899** *Animal & Plant Lore* 120 *Abutilon Avicennæ* is called 'butter-print,' 'pie-print,' and 'pie-marker,' because its pods are used to stamp butter or pie crust. Ohio, Illinois, Iowa, and Missouri. **1898** *Kansas City Star* 21 Dec. 9/2, 90 per cent of the pie-wagons had pictures of Washington crossing the Delaware.

+**Pie.**[2] Variant of PI.

+**Pie-biter.** An adept at biting through pies. *slang.* Also transf. — **1871** *Harper's Mag.* June 159/2 The 'Great American Pie-Biter' . . . lately put in his appearance at one of the saloons of Helena, and gave out that he could bite through more pies than any other one man in the world. **1884** NYE *Baled Hay* 215 By his strict attention to the duties of his office, [the Indian chieftain] made for himself a name as a warrior and a pie biter. **1890** LANGFORD *Vigilante Days* (1912) 308 [Hilderman] was the original of the story of 'The Great American Pie-biter.' This feat of spreading his jaws so as to bite through seven of Kustar's dried-apple pies, had been frequently performed by him. **1902** WISTER *Virginian* ix, You're a plumb pie-biter.

***Piece,** *n.*

***1.** A firearm, e.g. a musket or rifle.

1619 *Va. House Burg.* 13 That no man do sell or give any Indians any piece shott or poulder. **a1649** WINTHROP *Hist.* I. 118 The Indians took such pieces as they found there ready charged, and bent them at the English. **1709** LAWSON *Carolina* 45 Some of our Company shot several times, at one Turkey, . . . the Pieces being loaded with large Goose-shot. **1823** JAMES *Exped.* I. 69 There was no time for reloading their pieces after they had discharged them. **1884** *Century Mag.* Feb. 500/2 Others fled headlong down the further slope, the national soldiers not waiting to reload their pieces, but driving the enemy with stones.

***2.** A field or limited portion *of* land.

1624 in *Amer. Speech* XV. 294/1 Upon a peece of ground called the blockhouse field. **1677** *Derby Rec.* 55 That little pece of land betwen the Rock and the gully or Creke. **1707** *Boston News-Letter* 7 July 2/2 A Convenient double Brick House and Garden . . . , with a piece of Land near to that which was Sir William Phipps. **1898** WESTCOTT *D. Harum* 170 My father farmed a piece of about forty to fifty acres. **1924** CROY *R.F.D. No. 3* 33 Decker's 'piece' must be threshed in a day.

3. A short distance; a part of the way between two places. *colloq.*[2] {1612–1817}

1776 *Battle of Brooklyn* II. i, We was standing by the end of a side of an Indian cornfield, up yonder a piece. **1807** *Ann. 10th Congress* 1 Sess. 457 Captain Bissel told me to get six men, with the Clinker boat, to take him down the river a small piece. **1884** 'MARK TWAIN' *H. Finn* vii. 51 So I took the gun and went up a piece into the woods. **1912** COBB *Back Home* 312 Out from shore a piece, in the current, floating snags were going down.

4. An article or item of baggage: (see also quot. 1809). 'Chiefly *U.S.*' (*O.E.D.*).

1809 A. HENRY *Travels* 15 The freight of a canoe . . . consists in sixty *pieces*, or packages, of merchandize, of the weight of from ninety to a hundred pounds each. **1890** *Railways of Amer.* 253 The cases in which pieces go astray are astonishingly rare. **1914** STEELE *Storm* 274 The man on the steps had taken up his luggage, but now he put the two pieces down again.

+**5.** (See quotation.)

1847 LANMAN *Summer in Wilderness* 106 By one piece they [*i.e.*, Indian medicine men] mean a blanket, a pair of leggings, a knife, a gun, or any other useful article.

6. A poem or prose passage selected for public recital {1875–, *dial.*}; *to speak* (one's) *piece*, to recite a memorized poem or passage; +hence (often with depreciatory implication), to unburden one's self of one's opinions or views.

1865 BROWNE *A. Ward His Travels* 128, I have spoken my Piece about the Ariel. **1879** *Congress. Rec.* 16 May 1380/2, I expect to read to-morrow [in the papers] that I spoke a piece, that is the way they print it sometimes, in favor of slavery. **1890** *Harper's Mag.* Dec. 139/2 Don't you want to hear me speak my piece? **1902** G. M. MARTIN *Emmy Lou* 115 Emmy Lou had to learn a piece for Friday. It was poetry, but you called it a piece. **1902** 'O. HENRY' *Heart of West* 167, I spoke my piece, explaining how the Brazilian diamonds and the fire kindler were laying up sufficient treasure to guarantee the happiness of two.

7. *All to pieces.* +**a.** Through and through; completely. **b.** Badly.

(a) **1839** C. F. BRIGGS *H. Franco* I. 27 'Do you know the name of that individual who helped you to steak?' . . . 'I know him all to pieces,' replied the gentleman. **1863** 'E. KIRKE' *Southern Friends* 86 Oh! I know you Yankees all to pieces; I've lived among you. **(b)** **1898** CANFIELD *Maid of Frontier* 184 He had been shot all to pieces. **1911** HARRISON *Queed* 155 He was shot all to pieces, but they patched him together.

8. *attrib.* Designating a scale or system of payment for work. (See also PIECEWORK.)

1896 *Internat. Typogr. Union Proc.* 25/2, I compromised it on a piece scale of 13 cents per 1,000 on machines, instead of $21 per week. *Ib.* 43/2 The piece system is . . . vastly more satisfactory in its results to all concerned.

***Piece,** *v.* +*tr.* To make (a quilt) by sewing together small pieces or scraps. — **1884** WILKINS in *Harper's Mag.* July 304/2 They won't . . . hev to piece quilts fur a livin'. **1887** WILKINS *Humble Romance* 79 She did odd housewifely jobs for the neighbors, wove rag-carpets, [and] pieced bed-quilts. **1888** 'CRADDOCK' *Despot* 395 The quilts she had 'pieced' . . . were piled high on the 'corner-shelf.'

+**Piece bag.** A bag for small pieces or odds and ends of cloth. — **1869** ALCOTT *Little Women* II. 11 So rich a supply of dusters, holders, and piece-bags. **1878** COOKE *Happy Dodd* 324 An old drugget that had been Mrs. Dodd's was fresh bound with some bits of scarlet flannel from the piece-bag. **1896** JEWETT *Pointed Firs* 109 What did she do for clothin' when she needed to replenish, or risin' for her bread, or the piece-bag that no woman can live long without? **1900** DIX *Deacon Bradbury* 251 Mr. Bradbury . . . sought his wife, who was upstairs sorting over her piece-bag.

Piece goods. *pl.* Fabrics woven in lengths suitable for retail sale by linear measure. {1665–} — **1784** *Mass. Centinel* 21 Aug. 1/1 To be Sold, . . . Boltingcloths, with a variety of other piece goods. **1833** *Boston Mercantile Jrnl.* 26 Sept. 4/3 How & Jones . . . have for sale, an extensive assortment of seasonable Foreign and Domestic Piece Goods. **1892** *York County Hist. Rev.* 68 A fine line of piece goods of unique design and shade . . . [is] carried in stock.

Piece of eight. The Spanish peso. Now hist. {1610–1748} (Cf. DOLLAR 1.) — **1646** *Suffolk Deeds* I. 80 The summe of one hundred pound to be payd in pieces of eight. **1694** *Mass. H. S. Coll.* 4 Ser. I. 106 In this place, and so throughout this Province, pieces of eight pass for 6 shillings and 9 pence. **1704** *N.C. Col. Rec.* I. 597 The ten pounds in pieces of eight . . . shall be sent to Boston. **1771** FRANKLIN *Autobiog.* 261, I gave them a piece of eight to drink.

Piecework.

1. Work done or paid for by the piece. {1830–} Also attrib.

1795 WASHINGTON *Writings* XIII. 58 The new [commissioners of the Federal City] have gone more into the execution of it [*i.e.*, business] by contracts, and piece work. **1860** *36th Congress 1 Sess.* H. R. Rep. No. 249 90 The committee . . . [should] compel the employing printer to pay the journeyman by the piece for all work for which he received pay in the proportion of piece-work. **1882** *N.Y. Tribune* 7 Aug. 1/5 The blockers . . . quit work . . . , owing to dissatisfaction with the prices paid for piece-work. **1906** 'O. HENRY' *Trimmed Lamp* 3 Lou is a piece-work ironer in a hand laundry.

+**2.** *Piecework bedquilt*, a bedquilt made up of small pieces of cloth sewed together.

1842 KIRKLAND *Forest Life* I. 90 No gorgeous piece-work bed-quilts exhibiting stars of all magnitudes and moons in all quarters.

Pieceworker. One who does piecework. {1891–} — **1884** *Harper's Mag.* Sept. 625/1 With a piece-worker, time is literally money. **1898** *Scribner's Mag.* June 739/1 They were piece-workers all of them, earning fifteen dollars a week at the very least. **1913** LONDON *Valley of Moon* 114 By three in the afternoon the strain of the piece-workers in the humid, heated room grew tense.

***Piecrust.** +*As short as piecrust*, impatient, testy, snappish. *colloq.* — **c1849** PAIGE *Dow's Sermons* I. 287, I feel as short as pie-crust. I mean to put it to all the women in creation, in the hardest kind of style. **1851**

NORTHALL *Curtain* 174 None of them will speak to you, or if they do, they are as short as pie-crust.

+**Pied-bill dobchick, dopchick.** =next. — **1731** CATESBY *Carolina* I. 91 The Pied-Bill Dopchick. . . . These Birds frequent fresh water-ponds in many of the inhabited parts of Carolina. **1789** MORSE *Amer. Geog.* 59 The Pied bill Dobchick. **1828** BONAPARTE *Synopsis* 418 The Pied-bill Dobchick, *Podiceps carolinensis*, . . . inhabits the whole continent of America.

+**Pied-billed grebe.** The American dabchick, *Podilymbus podiceps.* — **1839** PEABODY *Mass. Birds* 377 The Pied-Billed Grebe, or Dobchick, *Podiceps Carolinensis*, comes to us from the north early in autumn. **1874** COUES *Birds N.W.* 737 Pied-billed Grebe; Dabchick; Water-witch. **1917** *Birds of Amer.* I. 8 The Pied-billed Grebe . . . is a more accomplished swimmer than any duck of which I have knowledge.

+**Pied duck.** A black duck (*Camptorhynchus labradorius*) with white head and markings. Now extinct. — **1637** MORTON *New Canaan* 68 Ducks there are of three kindes, pide Ducks, gray Ducks, and black Ducks in great abundance. **1828** BONAPARTE *Synopsis* 391 The Pied Duck, *Anas labradora*, . . . inhabits the north of America. **1839** PEABODY *Mass. Birds* 392 The Pied Duck, *Fuligula Labradora*, is . . . called the Sand-shoal Duck. **1875** *Fur, Fin, & Feather* (ed. 3) 119 Of the various fowl called vulgarly coot, are the pied-duck, . . . the surf-duck . . . and the American scoter.

Piedmont. *attrib.* +Designating an upland region immediately east of the Blue Ridge and Appalachian Mountains and extending from New York to Alabama. — **1855** *S. Lit. Messenger* XXI. 672/2 The next breadth of country, known in several of the States as the Piedmont district, was more salubrious in its atmosphere. **1857** STROTHER *Virginia* 235 The soil of this [Amherst County, Va.], in common with many other of the *piedmont* counties, is of a bright red in many places. **1883** ZEIGLER & GROSSCUP *Alleghanies* 206 Chrome ores are found in several of the counties west of the Blue Ridge and in the piedmont belt.

Pie pan. A shallow pan with sloping sides in which pies are baked. — **1814** *Niles' Reg.* V. 318/1 Grid-irons and pye pans, cradle spits. **1846** WHITCHER *Widow Bedott P.* v. 55, I fills three of my biggest pie-pans. **1902** HARBEN *A. Daniel* 101 Into an old pie-pan he raked from the back of the fireplace a quantity of soot.

Pieplant. +The garden rhubarb (*Rheum rhaponticum*), the tender esculent leafstalks of which are used in making pies.

Cf. PIE RHUBARB.

1847 WEBSTER 825/2 *Pie-plant, Pie-rhubarb*, the garden rhubarb, used as a substitute for apples in making pies. **1864** LOWELL *Fireside Trav.* 26 His *pie-plants* . . . blanched under barrels, each in his little hermitage. **1884** NYE *Baled Hay* 91, I wrote once an article on the growth of pie plant which was copied far and wide. **1894** ALLEN *Ky. Cardinal* iv, There is one old soul who especially loves rhubarb pies, . . . and it is she who remembers me and my row of pie-plant. **1906** *Springfield W. Repub.* 15 Feb. 16 The shipping of pieplant from East Brookfield from the cellar nurseries is getting to be quite a little business.

attrib. **1884** NYE *Baled Hay* 207 Afterward pulverize and spread over the pie plant bed.

b. A preparation of rhubarb, esp. one that can be spread like butter. In full *pieplant butter.*

Cf. BUTTER 2.

1855 *Amer. Inst. N.Y. Trans.* 401 The following list of the prices of the preserved fruits. . . . Pie-plant, in square glass bottles, holding over 2 lbs. weight, [cost] $5.00 [per dozen bottles]. **1885** *Buckeye Cookery* 251 *Pie-plant Butter* . . . is a nice preserve, and children should be encouraged to eat it during the winter.

Pie plate. A shallow dish in which pies are baked; a plate on which pie is served. {1741–} Also attrib. — **1678** *New Castle Court Rec.* 361 A Pewter Py Plate. **1851** *Knickerb.* XXXVIII. 394 We see it now, as of yore it sat upon the kitchen hearth, capped with a pie-plate. **1869** *Boyd's Business Directory* 48 Pie-Plate Manufacturers, Tin. **1900** DIX *Deacon Bradbury* 5 Mrs. Bradbury . . . placed a pile of pie-plates on the sewing-table.

+**Pierced Nose.** =NEZ PERCÉ. Also attrib. — **1805** CLARK in *Lewis & C. Exped.* III. (1905) 78 They call themselves the *Cho pun-nish* or *Pierced noses.* **1831** R. COX *Adv. Columbia R.* 221 We had many reasons to suspect that the Pierced-noses . . . were actuated by feelings of hostility. **1837** IRVING *Bonneville* I. 183 A Pierced-nose chief, named Blue John by the whites. **1844** LEE & FROST *Oregon* v. 51 [Clark] found an encampment of the *Nez-Percés*, or Pierced-nose Indians.

Piercer bit. A tool for boring or piercing. *Obs.* {1703–} — **1634** WINTHROP in R. C. Winthrop *Life J. Winthrop* II. 126 [Bring] piercer bitts, sithes for grass [etc.]. **1654** *Essex Probate Rec.* I. 180 Pirser bits & braces.

Pier glass. A large tall mirror, usually placed between windows or over a pier table. {1703–} — **1732** *S.C. Gazette* 104/2 All sorts of peer Glasses. **1779** *York Co., Va., Rec.: Wills* XXII. 28 April, 1 large elegant pier glass. **1847** FIELD *Drama in Pokerville* 112 Carpets, curtains, pier-glasses, mahogany chairs, and, above all, costly side-boards. **1898** CAHAN *Imported Bridegroom* 231 As to furniture, she refused to consider any which did not include a pier-glass. **1905** 'O. HENRY' *Four Million* 18 There was a pier-glass between the windows of the room.

+**Pie rhubarb.** Any one of various plants of the genus *Rheum*, esp. *R. rhaponticum.* (Cf. PIEPLANT.) — **1817–8** EATON *Botany* (1822) 442 *Rheum tataricum*, pie rhubarb. **1848** DEWEY *Mass. Flowering Plants* 104 Pie-Rhubarb. . . . Its large, long, leaf-stalks, full of juicy acid, are often used to make tarts. **1857** GRAY *Botany* 378 *Rheum Rhaponticum* is the Pie Rhubarb, so commonly cultivated for the sake of its fleshy and acid esculent leaf-stalks.

Pier table. An ornamental table originally designed to occupy the space between two windows. — **1831** HONE *Diary* I. 29 The rooms were handsomely fitted up with mirrors, curtains, pier tables, and lamps. **1865** *Atlantic Mo.* XV. 505/1 Over the mantel-piece had been charcoaled 'Rascal'; over the pier-table, 'Abolitionist.'

***Pig.**

***1. a.** A young hog. **b.** A hog of any age. **c.** The flesh of this animal.

1634 *Maine Doc. Hist.* III. 31 The pegs ar growen to som bignes. **1666** *Md. Archives* II. 140 Every person . . . that shall Kill & carry away any young piggs . . . shall alsoe be adjudged a hogg stealer. **1767** *Boston Post-Boy* 28 Dec. (Th.), Stolen, a Pigg about 90 wt., supposed for such a Frolick as detected at New-york. **1774** FITHIAN *Journal* I. 242, I was invited this morning by Captain Fibbs to a Barbecue: . . . instead of Fish the Dinner is roasted Pig, with the proper appendages. **1834** PECK *Gaz. Illinois* 35 Wolves . . . annoy the farmer by destroying his sheep and pigs. **1846** FARNHAM *Prairie Land* 358 She nevertheless stirred about with a right hearty zeal, setting on her quail, chicken, pig, dodger, and biscuit. **1885** *Rep. Indian Affairs* 11 The increase has been 8 horse and mule colts, 50 calves, and 150 pigs. **1908** *Atlantic Mo.* Feb. 207/1 Keeping the hens, and the two pigs, the horse, the cow, . . . and the farm, for the year around, is a sure cure for winter.

2. An oblong mass of metal, now esp. iron, obtained from a furnace. {1630–; of iron, 1674–}

1657 *Mass. H. S. Coll.* 4 Ser. VII. 402 They desire youer iron to be cast in pigs, because it wil be beter to handel. **1702** C. MATHER *Magnalia* (1853) I. 173 When they saw such vast litters of silver *sows* and *pigs*, as they called them, come on board . . . , they knew not how to bear it. **1776** *Jrnls. Cont. Congress* VI. 952 The cargo . . . [included] 338 pigs of lead, 9 casks of gun flints, [and] 1 case of pins. **1789** MORSE *Amer. Geog.* 288 Iron, in great quantities, [is exported] in pigs and bars. **1816** *Ann. 14th Congress* 1 Sess. 1872 [Duty laid] on lead in pigs, bars, or sheets, one cent per pound. **1834** BAIRD *Valley Miss.* 111 Much of the iron of those counties is taken in the form of blooms and pigs to Pittsburg, Brownsville, etc. **1894** *Harper's Mag.* Feb. 418/2 When the metal cools, the larger masses are called 'sows,' and the smaller 'pigs.' . . . This iron product is contaminated with sulphur, carbon, and phosphorus.

+**3.** A type of steamer used on the Great Lakes.

1898 *N. Amer. Rev.* June 723 Whalebacks, or 'pigs,' as the lake sailors call them.

+**4.** The musk hog of the Southwest.

1917 *Mammals of Amer.* 61 [The collared peccary] is the only native 'pig' found in the United States.

5. *In less than a pig's whistle*, (see quotation).

1859 BARTLETT 320 'I'll do so in less than a pig's whistle,' that is 'in less than no time.'

6. *attrib.* and *comb.* **a.** In sense 1 with *club, drover*, etc.

1845 F. DOUGLASS *Narrative* 28 It was almost a sufficient motive, not only to make me take off what would be called by pig-drovers the mange, but the skin itself. **1845** *Cincinnati Misc.* I. 186 A stout looking fellow set his gun leaning on a pig house, and jumped in to catch some fowls. **1850** S. WARNER *Wide, Wide World* xvii, The water comes . . . from a spring at the back of the pig-field. **1857** STROTHER *Virginia* 123 They found their horses still engaged in munching some remarkably fine oats, which had been served up in an old pig-trough. **1869** STOWE *Oldtown Folks* 149 It was . . . Primus King, going on his early way to preside over the solemnities of pig-killing. **1924** CROY *R.F.D. No. 3* 53 They were members of 'pig clubs' [and] went to stock-judging shows.

b. In the names of trees.

1897 SUDWORTH *Arborescent Flora* 111 *Hicoria minima.* . . . Bitternut (Hickory). . . . Pig Hickory (Ill.). . . . Pig Walnut (N.H.).

Pig and whistle. +(See quotation.) — **1846** CORCORAN *Pickings* 75 A 'pig and whistle' is the only reg'lar eye-opener—if you can't get the ginivine article, you may fall back on a gin cocktail.

***Pigeon.** Also †**pidgeon.**

+**1.** Any native American bird of the family Columbidae, esp. the now extinct passenger pigeon.

1612 SMITH, etc. *Virginia* I. 15 In winter there are great plenty of Swans, . . . Oxeies, Parrats, and Pigeons. **1675** *Penna. Mag.* VI. 89 Every one . . . may furnish his House with excellent fat Venison, . . . Ducks, Pigeons, and the like. **1698** G. THOMAS *Pensilvania* 13 There are an Infinite Number of Sea and Land Fowl, of most sorts, *viz.* . . . Pidgeons, Heath-Birds, Black-Birds. **1709** LAWSON *Carolina* 44 You may find . . . Indian Towns . . . that have more than 100 Gallons of Pigeons Oil, or Fat; they using it with Pulse. **1782** CRÈVECŒUR *Lett.* 37 We have twice a year the pleasure of catching pigeons, whose numbers are sometimes so astonishing as to obscure the sun in their flight. **1820** FLINT *Lett. from Amer.* 275 The woods abound in pigeons, a small species of fowls which migrates to the southward in winter, and return to the north in spring. **1848** COOPER *Oak Openings* I. 173 [The white men] have become plentier than the pigeons in the spring. **1874** COUES *Birds N.W.* 389 Some years since a great flight of Pigeons occurred near Washington, where for several days, in the fall, the woods were filled with the birds. **1917** *Birds of Amer.* II. 45/1 A most remarkable attribute of the Pigeon was its disregard of the presence of human beings in its roosting and nesting places.

+**b.** *Pigeon of passage,* =PASSENGER PIGEON. *Obs.*

*c***1729** CATESBY *Carolina* I. 23 *Palumbus migratorius.* The Pigeon of Passage. . . . Of these there come in Winter to Virginia and Carolina, from the North, incredible numbers. **1781–2** JEFFERSON *Notes Va.* (1788) 74 *Columba migratoria.* . . . Pigeon of Passage. Pigeon. **1789** MORSE *Amer. Geog.* 60 American Birds . . . enumerated [include] . . . Water Pelican, Pigeon of passage, White crowned pigeon.

+**c.** With specifying adjectives.

See also BAND-TAILED *a.*, PASSENGER PIGEON, WILD PIGEON, etc., and cf. GROUND DOVE, MOURNING DOVE.

1828 BONAPARTE *Ornithology* III. 19 White-Crowned Pigeon. *Columba Leucocephala.* . . . Found in great numbers on some of the Florida keys. **1858** BAIRD *Birds Pacific R.R.* 599 White-headed Pigeon. . . . Southern keys of Florida. **1860** HOLMES *E. Venner* xxvi, A group of white fantailed pigeons had lighted on the green plot. **1917** *Birds of Amer.* II. 39 Passenger Pigeon. . . . [Also called] Blue-headed Pigeon.

***2.** A bird of the family Columbidae domestically bred.

The first two quotations may belong to sense 1.

1751 FRANKLIN *Exper. on Electricity* 63 A pigeon that we struck dead to appearance by the electrical shock, recovering life, droop'd about the yard several days. **1805** PARKINSON *Tour* 302 There are great numbers of Guinea-birds raised, and they thrive well. There are some pigeons, chiefly in boxes, by the sides of houses. **1847** MAGOFFIN *Down Santa Fé Trail* 206 Outside in the patio are . . . cats playing and pigeons eating. **1874** COUES *Birds N.W.* 388 Hundreds [of passenger pigeons] were netted, to be used instead of tame Pigeons in shooting-matches. **1907** *St. Nicholas* May 603/1, I've got a parrot, . . . heaps of pigeons, and a dog.

+**3.** *Flutter pigeon,* a decoy pigeon made to flutter.

1794 DRAYTON *Letters* 74 They then place under the sweep of the net, but upon the ground, the flutter pidgeons; (so called from being fixed to a flutter stick, which by reason of a string communicating to the skreen, they raise up and down, when the pidgeons are flying over).

4. In special combinations.

Pigeon distance, a distance at which a pigeon can be shot; *p. match,* a trap-shooting match in which pigeons are shot at; *p. nesting,* (see quotation); *p. post,* a system of communication by means of carrier pigeons; *p. stand,* a place where a hunter waits to kill wild pigeons; *p. trap,* a trap used in a pigeon-shooting match.

1840 SIMMS *Border Beagles* II. 299 The schoolmaster, . . . though a Yankee, was able to ride and shoot and had done execution more than once at pigeon-distance. **1856** *Porter's Spirit of Times* 29 Nov. 213/2 Please publish in the Spirit the result of a pigeon match, held here on the 20th instant. **1869** *Mich. Laws* I. 213 No person . . . [shall] destroy any wild pigeon or pigeons . . . where they are gathered in bodies for the purpose of brooding their young, known as pigeon-nestings. **1901** *Wide World Mag.* VI. 501/1 A regularly organized pigeon-post has been in active operation in California for several years. **1844** *Knickerb.* XXIV. 28 A pigeon-stand, built for murderous purposes. **1873** *Pat. Off. Gazette* III. 654/2 Pigeon-Trap. . . . The corners of the upper board press open the hinged flaps, and the bird thereupon escapes for the marksman.

+**Pigeon berry.** A name applied to various small fruits, or to the plants and trees producing them.

These include the pokeweed, *Phytolacca americana;* the bristly sarsaparilla, *Aralia hispida;* the service berry, *Amelanchier alnifolia;* the Cascara buckthorn, *Rhamnus purshiana;* and the blue dogwood, *Cornus alternifolia.*

1775 BURNABY *Travels* 11 Tobacco and Indian corn are the original produce of the country; likewise the pigeon-berry and rattle-snake root. **1778** CARVER *Travels* 518 Gargit or Skoke is a large kind of weed. . . . [The] red berries hang in clusters in the month of September, and are generally called pigeon berries, as those birds then feed on them. **1796** MORSE *Univ. Geog.* I. 190 Flowering Trees and Shrubs in the United States. . . . Pigeonberry (*Cissus sicyoides*)—Virginian Dogwood [etc.]. **1832** WILLIAMSON *Maine* I. 127 Its clusters, *Pigeon-berries,* are said to be poisonous. **1877** BARTLETT 478 *Poke-Berry,* the berry of the Phytolacca, from which a rich purple juice is extracted, and used as a dye. (Also called Pigeon-berry and *Pocan.*) **1894** COULTER *Bot. W. Texas* III. 372 *P[hytolacca] decandra.* (Common Poke or Scoke, Garget, Pigeon Berry.) **1894** *Amer. Folk-Lore* VII. 89 *Aralia hispida,* pigeon-berry, Buckfield, Me. **1897** SUDWORTH *Arborescent Flora* 214 *Amelanchier alnifolia.* Western Service-tree. . . . Pigeon Berry (So. Oreg.). *Ib.* 299 *Rhamnus purshiana.* Bearberry. . . . Pigeon-berry (Idaho). *Ib.* 310 *Cornus alternifolia.* . . . Blue Dogwood. . . . Pigeonberry (N.Y.).

+**Pigeon-berry bush.** Any bush that produces pigeon berries. — **1784** CUTLER in *Amer. Acad. Mem.* I. 411 *Cissus.* . . . Pigeon-Berry Bush. Pigeons feed on the berries which has been the occasion of its trivial name. **1832** WILLIAMSON *Maine* I. 115 The *pigeon-berry bush* is as tall as that of a blackberry, bears an abundance of small purple berries, the chief food of pigeons.

+**Pigeon cherry.** The pin cherry, *Prunus pennsylvanica.* — **1850** *New Eng. Farmer* II. 160/1 The small, red [,] wild cherry, often called the pigeon cherry, . . . very much resembles some of our cultivated varieties. **1884** SARGENT *Rep. Forests* 66 *Prunus Pennsylvanica.* . . . Wild Red Cherry. Pin Cherry. Pigeon Cherry. **1897** SUDWORTH *Arborescent Flora* 240 *Prunus pennsylvanica.* . . . Wild Red Cherry. . . . Pigeon Cherry (Vt., N.H., R.I., N.Y., Ont., N. Dak.).

Pigeon diver. {1694–} +=DOVEKIE. — **1839** PEABODY *Mass. Birds* 400 The Little Guillemot, *Uria alle,* sometimes called the Little Auk or Pigeon Diver, . . . are not regular visitants, but occasional, solitary wanderers. **1844** *Nat. Hist. N.Y., Zoology* II. 281 This little *Sea Dove, Sea Pigeon, Greenland Dove, Pigeon-diver,* or *Ice-bird,* is but rarely seen on our coast.

+**Pigeon falcon.** (See quot. 1917.) — **1880** *Cimarron News & Press* 23 Dec. 1/5 Of the falcons we have the lanier, peregrine, pigeon, Richardson's and rusty-crowned falcon or sparrow hawk. **1917** *Birds of Amer.* II. 89 Pigeon Hawk. *Falco columbarius columbarius.* . . . [Also called] Pigeon Falcon.

+**Pigeon grass.**

1. a. The yellow foxtail, *Setaria lutescens.* **b.** The European green foxtail, *S. viridis.*

1838 *Mass. Agric. Survey 1st Rep.* 128 There were several patches of black or pigeon grass when the dyke was built. **1852** *Mich. Agric. Soc. Trans.* III. 199 The most troublesome weeds are pigeon grass, pig weed and sorrel. **1884** VASEY *Agric. Grasses* 42 Bristle grass . . . has much the appearance of the other species which we called Pigeon grass. **1901** MOHR *Plant Life Ala.* 358.

2. The crab grass, *Digitaria sanguinalis.*

1894 *Amer. Folk-Lore* VII. 104 *Panicum sanguinale,* pigeon-grass, Hopkinton, Iowa.

+**Pigeon guillemot.** A guillemot of the Pacific coast, *Cepphus columba.* — **1883** *Nat. Museum Bul.* No. 27, 180 *Uria columba.* . . . Pigeon Guillemot. . . . North Pacific (both sides), breeding south to California. **1917** *Birds of Amer.* I. 24/1 Mr. Dawson says that the Pigeon Guillemot is 'unquestionably the most characteristic water-bird of the Puget Sound region.'

Pigeon hawk. {1885–} +Any of several small hawks, esp. the American merlin, *Falco columbarius.*

*c***1728** CATESBY *Carolina* I. 3 *Accipiter Palumbarius.* The Pigeon-Hawk. . . . It is a very swift and bold Hawk, preying on Pigeons and wild Turkeys while they are young. **1781–2** JEFFERSON *Notes Va.* (1788) 72 *Falco columbarius.* . . . Pigeon hawk. **1831** AUDUBON *Ornith. Biog.* I. 466 The Pigeon Hawk does not, I believe, raise its young within the United States, but somewhere farther to the north. **1844** *Nat. Hist. N.Y., Zoology* II. 14 The Duck Hawk, *Falco Anatum,* . . . [is] known under the various popular names of Hen Hawk, Chicken Hawk and Pigeon Hawk. **1867** *Amer. Naturalist* I. 39 A Pigeon Hawk (*Hypotriorchis columbarius* Gray). **1874** COUES *Birds N.W.* 333 *Accipiter Fuscus.* . . . Sharp-shinned Hawk; Pigeon Hawk. **1882** Godfrey *Nantucket* 241/1, I have met with the . . . Pigeon Hawk (*Falco timerarius*). **1917** *Birds of Amer.* II. 90/1 The Pigeon Hawk is a stocky, well built, impetuous miniature of the Duck Hawk, which it closely resembles in color and habits.

***Pigeon house.**

***1.** A structure provided with suitable compartments for pigeons to nest in.

1776 *N.J. Archives* 2 Ser. I. 34 To Be Sold, A house and lot . . . , wherein is . . . a barn, and other convenient out-houses, a pigeon and poultry-house. **1795** BENTLEY *Diary* II. 159 A well contrived stye, a fine pigeon house, . . . a convenient barn. **1842** HAWTHORNE *Notebooks* (1932) 152 There are sheds, and a hen-house, and a pigeon-house, and an old stone pig-stye.

transf. **1887** HARRIS *Free Joe* 165 The station consisted of a water-tank and a little pigeon-house where tickets were sold.

+**2.** *transf. La.* (See quotation.)

1849 E. DAVIES *Amer. Scenes* 90 The basement was of brick, . . . and the upper part was of wood, terminating in a pigeon house. . . . It was a place of punishment and torture for the oppressed slave. . . . Such buildings are very common, and generally pass under the euphemistic name of 'pigeon-houses.'

+**Pigeon hunt.** A hunt in which wild pigeons are trapped or shot. — **1827** *Harvard Reg.* 38, I was solicited one morning to go with him on a pigeon-hunt. **1856** GOODRICH *Recoll.* I. 100, I can recollect no sports of my youth [*c*1800] which equaled in excitement our pigeon hunts, generally taking place in September and October.

Pigeon plum. Any of the tropical sea grapes of the genus *Coccolobis,* esp. *C. laurifolia.* Also attrib. — **1743** CATESBY *Carolina* II. 94 Pigeon-Plum. . . . In December the Fruit is ripe, and is the Food of Pigeons and many wild Animals. **1775** *Mass. Hist. Soc. Coll.* 2 Ser. II. 287, I had nothing to assist Nature with, but a Tea of Piggen plumb Roots, and Spruce. **1884** SARGENT *Rep. Forests* 117 *Coccoloba Floridana.* . . . Pigeon Plum. . . . The edible and abundant grape-like fruit . . . is eagerly devoured by raccoons and other animals. **1897** SUDWORTH *Arborescent Flora* 192 *Coccolobis laurifolia.* . . . Pigeon Plum.

Pigeon roost. +A place, often of great area, used by passenger pigeons for roosting and nesting. Also a local place name.

1808 PIKE *Sources Miss.* 104 At some islands about 10 miles above Salt river . . . there were pidgeon roosts, and in about fifteen minutes my men had knocked on the head and brought on board 298. **1828** *Western Mo. Rev.* I. 522 Pigeons . . . are seen in great flocks. . . . Their places of resort are called 'pigeon roosts.' **1858** (Wash.) *States* 15 May (B.), The pigeon-roost in Decatur county, Indiana, extends over a distance of twenty-eight miles. . . . Over this vast extent of country every tree has from ten to fifteen nests. **1891** WELCH *Recoll. 1830–40* 26 Every boy knew where the pigeon roost was. **1899** CUSHMAN *Hist. Indians* 387, I first heard a sermon by Mr. Bell at the Pigeon roost about twelve years ago.

+**b.** *fig.* A multitude.

1861 STOWE in *Independent* 21 Nov. 1/1 A whole pigeon-roost of yet undreamed-of fancies.

Pigeon shoot. A contest in which the competitors shoot at pigeons as they are set free. — **1875** *Chicago Tribune* 8 July 2/1 The proposed Fourth of July pigeon-shoot at South Chicago was a failure. **1893** SANBORN *S. Calif.* 17 They have a pigeon shoot every week.

Pigeon-shooting. The action of shooting pigeons. {1793–} Also attrib. — **1823** COOPER *Pioneers* xxii, We only wait for our breakfasts, and away for the mountains and pigeon-shooting. **1875** *Chicago Tribune* 8 July 2/4 A pigeon-shooting match between A. H. Bogardus, of Illinois, and George Rimmel, champion of England, . . . was won easily by the former.

Pigeon shot. A small-sized bird shot. — **1687** SEWALL *Letter-Book* I. 64 We desire . . . six tone of shott, of which three ton Goose, two tone Duck, one tone pigeon. **1761** *Essex Inst. Coll.* XLVIII. 96 To be sold by George Deblois . . . bird, pigeon, duck and goose shot. **1846** MAGOFFIN *Down Santa Fé Trail* 15 *Mi Alma* had his rifle, loaded only with pigeon shot.

+**Pigeontail.** The pintail duck, *Dafila acuta.* — **1848** HERBERT *Field Sports* (1852) I. 128 *Anas Acuta.* . . . The Winter Duck, Sprigtail, Pigeontail, *vulgo.* **1888** TRUMBULL *Names of Birds* 39 Other aliases [are] . . . Pigeon-Tail . . . ; Sharp-Tail [etc.]. **1917** *Birds of Amer.* I. 128.

Pigeon-tailed coat. A coat having a tail shaped like a pigeon's tail. — **1889** *Harper's Mag.* Aug. 386/1 [Wearing] a pigeon-tailed coat, . . . he sat gravely and sturdily down amid his peers. **1901** CHURCHILL *Crisis* 202 He ran to his room to don for Virginia that glorious but useless full dress, —the high bearskin hat, the red pigeon-tailed coat, the light blue trousers, and the gorgeous, priceless shackle.

+**Pigeon tremex.** A horntail, *Tremex columba.* — **1879** *Scribner's Mo.* Aug. 502/2 The pigeon-tremex,—*Tremex Columba* . . . , —and a great pest it is, too. **1891** *Cent.* 6457/3 *Tremex columba* is a large and handsome North American horntail, the larva of which bores the trunks of shade-trees, particularly the maple, and is known as the *pigeon-tremex.*

+**Pigeon weed. a.** =ANGELICA TREE. **b.** A field weed, *Lithospermum arvense.* **c.** =FLORIDA CLOVER. — **1784** CUTLER in *Amer. Acad. Mem.* I 431 *Aralia.* . . . Shot Bush. Pigeon Weed. Blossoms white. Berries black. Common in new plantations. **1850** S. F. COOPER *Rural Hours* 106 The pigeon-weed of the grain-fields; the darnel, yarrow, wild parsnip. **1854** *Mich. Agric. Soc. Trans.* VI. 468 A still more troublesome pest, the 'Pigeon Weed,' . . . is making its appearance among us. **1889** VASEY *Agric. Grasses* 103 Pigeon-Weed . . . grows chiefly in cultivated grounds.

Pigeonwing, *n.* {1781–}

+**1.** *Dancing.* A fancy step executed by jumping up and striking the legs together.

1807 IRVING, etc. *Salmagundi* vii, No pigeon-wing disturbs your *contredanse.* **1835** *Knickerb.* VI. 562 One haw-buck dancer—a fellow whom I caught in several vulgar attempts to achieve a 'pigeon wing,'—came up to me with an impudent air. **1857** UNDERHILL & THOMPSON *Elephant Club* 114 You were practising some sort of an original pigeon-wing with your wooden leg. **1887** *Harper's Mag.* June 56/2 The facing lines of dancers, . . . keeping strict time, and executing the 'pigeon wing' and other intricacies, . . . make an enlivening scene. **1894** CHOPIN *Bayou Folk* 215 The spectators drew close about the couples to watch Chouchoute's wonderful performance; . . . his pigeon-wings in which his feet seemed hardly to touch the floor.

+**b.** *To cut a pigeonwing,* to execute a pigeonwing. Orig. as a movement in a dance.

1807 IRVING, etc. *Salmagundi* i, He never cut a pigeon-wing in his life. **1841** POE *Works* (1902) IV. 221 He insisted upon leaping the stile, and said he could cut a pigeon-wing over it in the air. **1868** *Putnam's Mag.* Jan. 56/1 Elkanah Dyzer . . . cut three clear pigeon-wings in the air . . . and come down lightly. **1904** W. H. SMITH *Promoters* 171 He leaped from his chair and cut a pigeon wing.

+**2.** (See quotation.)

1872 *Atlantic Mo.* Feb. 165 The miller spreads or reefs his sails, like a sailor,—reducing them in a high wind to a mere 'pigeon-wing' as it is called, two or three feet in length.

+**Pigeonwing,** *v.* **1.** *tr.* To cause (a person) to move in the manner of cutting a pigeonwing. *slang.* **2.** *quasi-tr.* To jump up. — **(1) 1826** COOPER *Mohicans* xxi, The toes are squared, as though one of the French dancers had been in, pigeon-winging his tribe. **1839** POE *Works* (1902) III. 255 The rascal . . . pigeon-winged himself right up into the belfry of the House of the Town Council. **(2) 1877** BEARD *K.K.K. Sketches* 59 The boss straggler, having eluded the individual on two sticks by pigeon-winging it through a hole in the roof, rolled upon the green sward beneath.

Pigeonwood. {1745–} *Florida.* +The porkwood, *Torrubia obtusata.* — **1884** SARGENT *Rep. Forests* 117 *Pisonia obtusata.* . . . Pigeon Wood. . . . Wood heavy, rather soft, weak, coarse-grained. **1897** SUDWORTH *Arborescent Flora* 192.

+**Pigeon woodpecker.** =FLICKER. (Cf. GOLDEN-WINGED WOODPECKER.) — **1844** *Nat. Hist. N.Y., Zoology* II. 192 This species . . . is called High-hole, Yucker, Flicker, Wake-up and Pigeon Woodpecker . . . in this State. **1899** JEWETT *Queen's Twin* 53, I caught sight of a lovely gay pigeon-woodpecker eyeing us curiously. **1917** *Birds of Amer.* II. 163 Flicker. *Colaptes auratus auratus.* . . . [Also called] Clape; Pigeon Woodpecker; Yellow-hammer.

+**Pigfish.** {1898, in Australia} Any of several fishes: (see note).

Among the fishes called by this name are: **a.** The sculpin, *Acanthocottus octodecemspinosus.* **b.** The sea robin, *Prionotus strigatus.* **c.** Any of various fishes of the genus *Haemulon.* **d.** The salt-water grunt, *Orthopristes chrysopterus.*

1807 *Mass. H.S. Coll.* 2 Ser. III. 56 The pig-fish is of the size and form of a sculpion, but with a head not so large and bony. **1814** MITCHILL *Fishes N.Y.* 380 Eighteen-spined Bullhead. *Cottus octodecem-spinosus.* . . . Called *pig fish,* from the squeaking noise he makes immediately on being taken out of the water. **1842** *Nat. Hist. N.Y., Zoology* IV. 52 The Common Bull-Head, *Cottus virginianus,* . . . is known under the various popular names of Sculpin, . . . Sea Robin, Bull-head, Sea Toad, and Pig Fish. **1859** BARTLETT 389 Sea-Robin. (*Prionotus lineatus.*) . . . From the croaking or grunting noise it makes when caught, it is sometimes called Pig-Fish. **1884** GOODE, etc. *Fisheries* I. 398 In the inshore waters of the Southern Atlantic and Gulf States occur several species of small fish belonging to the genus *Diabasis.* . . . From their habit of uttering a loud, rather melodious sound when taken from the water they have acquired the name of 'Grunt' and 'Pig-fish.' *Ib.,* A species belonging to a closely related genus is the Hog-fish, or Grunt, of the Chesapeake, called also 'Pig-fish' or 'Grunt' in the Gulf of Mexico, *Pomodasys fulvomaculatus,* and known in South Carolina as well as in Bermuda under the name of 'Sailor's Choice.' **1897** *N.Y. Forest, Fish, & Game Comm. 2d Rep.* 242 *Orthopristis chrysopterus,* . . . Pig-Fish.—Several examples were taken in Gravesend Bay, October 24, 1894. **1911** *Rep. Fisheries 1908* 310/2 *Grunt.*—The name of several small *Hæmulidæ* quite common off the south Atlantic and Gulf coasts, and sometimes found on the California coast. Different species are known as . . . 'flannel-mouthed porgy,' 'pigfish,' 'hogfish' [etc.].

Piggery. A place where pigs are kept; a pigpen. {1804–6–} — **1849** WILLIS *Rural Letters* 184 You can easily calculate the distribution of the remainder, upon the flower-garden . . . and piggery. **1854** *Alta Californian* 7 Jan., A number of persons were . . . charged with keeping a nuisance in the shape of piggeries, on the corner of Turk and Jones streets. **1882** *Maine Bd. Agric. Rep.* XXVI. 163 The waste of the dairy . . . can be profitably utilized in the piggery or calf pen. **1913** LONDON *Valley of Moon* 336 They were shown over the cattery, the piggery, . . . and the kennelry.

* **Piggin.** A small pail, esp. a wooden one having a handle made by a single stave longer than the others.

1653 *Mayflower Descendant* XI. 101, 2 bowles and 3 piggens. **1684** I. MATHER *Providences* (1856) v. 105 The man tried to save the milk, by holding a piggin side-wayes under the cowes belly. **1737** HEMPSTEAD *Diary* 323, I was at home al Day . . . putting a New bottom in to a pail & piggan. **1839** KEMBLE *Residence in Ga.* 52 A very small cedar pail—a piggin as they termed it—serves to scoop up the river water. **1886** *Amer. Philol. Ass. Trans.* 41 *Piggin,* 'a small wooden vessel with an erect handle, used as a dipper.' . . . It is common in country districts all over the South. **1912** COBB *Back Home* 297 [They] sent the piggin by a man on horseback.

Pig iron. Iron, as first reduced from the ore, cast into pigs. {1665–}

1742 *Md. Hist. Mag.* XX. 168 You have likewise Inclosed Bill Ladeing for fifty Ton Pigg Iron with the nett Proceeds of the whole Whereof you are likewise to Credit my Acctt. **1765** ROGERS *Acct. N. Amer.* 70 The commodities exported from hence [N.Y.] are . . . staves, plank, lumber, flax-seed, pig and bar-iron. **1779** *N.H. Hist. Soc. Coll.* VI. 333 At night encamp at Stirling, a place noted for making the best pig iron on the continent. **1843** 'CARLTON' *New Purchase* I. 191 Two delicate andirons in the shape of pig iron, were pushed . . . into proper position. **1880** *Harper's Mag.* Dec. 57 One-twelfth of all the pig-iron produced in the United States is wrested from the glistening ore by the furnaces of Pittsburgh. **1911** *Scientific Amer. Suppl.* 30 Sept. 218/1 The foundries of this country melt annually about 6,000,000 tons of pig iron and scrap.

b. Attrib. with *baron, product.*

1887 *Courier-Journal* 15 Feb. 2/2 Col. Colyar, . . . the original Pigiron Baron who advocates Mr. Randall's Republican views in the volunteer State, laughs with ghoulish glee. *Ib.* 1 May 5/1 The pig iron product of Alabama . . . would shortly be raised to 1,600 tons [per day].

Pig lead. Lead cast into pigs. {1825, 1832} — **1791** *Austin P.* I. (1924) 9 Take any quantity of pure pig Lead; and Melt down in Kettle. **1875** WELLS *Practical Economics* (1885) 25 Nothing could be done in the way of restraining the importation of leaden bullets in place of pig lead until Congress had provided further legislation on the subject. **1882** Brockett *Our Country's Wealth* 466 Pig, bar, and sheet lead imported . . . [in] 1870, 58,310,464 lbs.

Pig metal. Metal, usually iron, cast, or suitable for casting, in pigs. {1731–} — **1741** *N.J. Archives* 1 Ser. VI. 141 His Majesty's Province of New Jersey . . . and other the British Colonys in North America . . . are abundantly stored with iron ore . . . and proper materials for making the same into pigg mettal and barr iron. **1772** *Mass. Gazette* Sept. 3/3 Forge Masters . . . may be supplied with good pig metal. **1861** *Atlantic Mo.* April 435/1 In the neighboring furnace-buildings lay great heaps of the refuse from the ore after the pig-metal is run.

*__Pigmy, Pygmy,__ *a.* In specific names: **a.** Of plants. (See also PIGMYWEED.) **b.** Of fishes. **c.** Of birds. (See also PIGMY OWL.)

(a) 1813 MUHLENBERG *Cat. Plants* 48 *Prunus pygmæa*, Pygmy cherry tree. **1817–8** EATON *Botany* (1822) 467 *Solidago tenuifolia*, pigmy golden-rod. **(b) 1814** MITCHILL *Fishes N.Y.* 419 Pigmy Perch. *Bodianus exiguus.* A very small species, taken among the shrimp. **1842** *Nat. Hist. N.Y., Zoology* IV. 214 The Pigmy Dace. *Leuciscus pygmaeus.* **(c) 1835** AUDUBON *Ornith. Biog.* III. 444, [I have considered] the Cape Sandpiper or Pigmy Curlew as the Rarest of its genus with us. **1887** RIDGWAY *Manual N.A. Birds* 560 Western United States, north to northern border, east to, and including, Rocky Mountains, south to mountainous districts of Mexico. . . . *S[itta] pygmæa.* Pygmy Nuthatch.

+**Pigmy owl.** Any one of various owls of the genus *Glaucidium*, esp. *G. gnoma.* — **1858** BAIRD *Birds Pacific R.R.* 62 *Glaucidium Gnoma.* . . . The Pigmy Owl. . . . The smallest owl known to inhabit North America. **1880** *Cimarron News & Press* 23 Dec. 1/4 The species found here are the barn, great horned, screech, . . . pigmy and burrowing owls. **1917** *Birds of Amer.* II. 119/1 Dr. Coues gave the Pygmy Owl an excellent character.

+**Pigmyweed.** A low, tufted annual (*Tillaestrum aquaticum*) found along the Atlantic coast. — **1817–8** EATON *Botany* (1822) 487 *Tillæa ascendens*, pigmy weed. Very minute. **1843** TORREY *Flora N.Y.* I. 251 *Tillæa simplex.* Pigmy-weed. . . . On the banks of the Hudson one or two miles north of Peekskill. **1901** MOHR *Plant Life Ala.* 533 Pigmy-weed. . . . Southeastern Massachusetts to Maryland and southeastern Pennsylvania.

Pig-nose. A variety of apple. — **1807** *Mass. H. S. Coll.* 2 Ser. III. 52 The most common sorts [of apples] are the greening and the pig-nose.

Pignut. {1610–}

+**1. a.** The broom hickory, *Carya glabra.* **b.** Less often, one of various other kinds of hickories, esp. the bitternut, *Carya cordiformis.*

See the earlier evidence under PIGNUT TREE.

*c*1729 CATESBY *Carolina* I. 38 The Pignut. The Branches of this Tree spread more, are smaller, and the Leaves not so broad as those of the Hiccory. **1814** PURSH *Flora Amer.* II. 638 *Juglans ficiformis* . . . is known by the name of Pig or Hog Nut, also Broom Hickory. **1832** BROWNE *Sylva* 182 This tree is generally known in the United States by the name of Pignut. **1848** DRAKE *Pioneer Life Ky.* 73 Of the whole forest the . . . elm was the best; next to that the white elm, and then the pig-nut or white hickory. **1897** SUDWORTH *Arborescent Flora* 111 *Hicoria minima.* . . . Bitternut (Hickory). . . . Pig Nut (N.Y., W. Va., Mo., Ill., Iowa, Kans.).

+**2.** A nut of one of these trees.

1705 BEVERLEY *Virginia* II. 16 There are also several Sorts of Hickories, call'd Pig-nuts, some of which have as thin a Shell as the best French Walnuts. **1775** WASHINGTON *Diaries* II. 179 [Nuts] like the Pignut—but . . . fuller of meat. **1869** FULLER *Flower Gatherers* 305, I think pig-nuts quite good enough for squirrels. **1885** E. W. HOWE *Mystery of Locks* 72 The olives you blow about—I'd as soon eat green pignuts soaked in brine. **1892** TORREY *Foot-Path Way* 225 Our annual wild crop [includes] . . . pig-nuts (a bad name for a good thing), shagbarks, acorns, and so forth.

+**3.** =EARTHNUT a.

1847 RUXTON *Adv. Rocky Mts.* (1848) 258 A large grizzly bear [was] . . . searching for yampa-roots or pig-nuts.

+**4.** The jojoba, *Simmondsia californica.*

1897 *Amer. Folk-Lore* X. 143 *Simmondsia Californica*, pig-nut, Arizona.

+**Pignut hickory.** =PIGNUT 1. — **1785** MARSHALL *Amer. Grove* 68 *Juglans alba minima.* White, or Pig-nut Hickery. This generally grows pretty large, sometimes to the height of eighty feet or more. **1810** MICHAUX *Arbres* I. 21 *Pig nut hickory* . . . , dénomination la plus générale dans tous les États-Unis. **1832** BROWNE *Sylva* 170 Farther south it [bitternut hickory] is compounded with the pignut hickory. **1860** CURTIS *Woody Plants N.C.* 44 Pig-nut hickory. . . . The fruit is generally pear-shaped, the husk thin and green. **1901** MOHR *Plant Life Ala.* 133.

Pignut tree. + =PIGNUT 1. — **1666** *Warwick* (R.I.) *Rec.* 404 Upon a straight lyne from ye pond to a pignut tree standing upon a hill. **1877** BURDETTE *Rise of Mustache* 19 You lose this marvelous instinct for the woods, you can't tell a pig-nut tree from a pecan.

Pigpen.

1. A pen for pigs. {1833}

1803 *Lit. Mag.* (Phila.) Oct. 11 Compare every thing you saw, from the church to the pig-pen. **1845** S. SMITH *J. Downing's Lett.* 85 The deacon . . . got an armful of dry straw and threw it into the pig-pen. **1872** BRACE *Dangerous Classes N.Y.* 151 The inhabitants [of 'Dutch Hill' in N.Y.] . . . have erected shanties which serve at once for pig-pens, hen-coops, bedrooms, and living-rooms. **1902** HARBEN *A. Daniel* 246 Bishop had reached a little pig-pen in a fence-corner farther along, on his way home.

+**b.** *transf.* (See quotation.)

1872 *Harper's Mag.* April 690/2 A one-story wooden structure attached to a Tavern of only tolerable repute . . . became the rallying-place of the [Tammany] tribes. This [room], by reason of its general unsightliness, was denominated by Tammany's political adversaries the 'Pig-Pen.'

+**2.** A certain brand put on range stock.

1890 *Stock Grower & Farmer* 15 March 6/2 On all the horses recovered their hot brand was changed to a 'Pig Pen.'

Pigs in clover. 1. 'An emblem of contentment' (Th.). **2.** A parlor game the object of which is to roll marbles into special holes in a board by tilting it. — **(1) 1813** *Boston-Gazette* 7 Jan. (Th.), Canadians! then in droves come over, And live henceforth like pigs in clover. **(2) 1895** WILLIAMS *Princeton Stories* 203 With an expression on his face which reminds you of when 'Pigs in Clover' was the rage, [he] darts across the room.

Pigskin. {1855–} +A football. — **1900** *Dialect Notes* II. 48 *Pigskin*, a foot-ball. K[nox College, Galesburg, Ill.], and generally. **1902** BELL *Hope Loring* 172 That famous game destined to be . . . played over from every youngster with his first pigskin to veterans with broken noses.

*__Pigsty.__ A pigpen with a covered shelter. — **1809** IRVING *Knickerb.* III. vii, The humble log hut . . . stands hard by in ignominious contrast, degraded into a cow house or pig stye. **1840** *Knickerb.* XVI. 208 And he busied himself at a log pig-stye on the opposite side of the road, half as large as the dwelling-house. **1913** LONDON *Valley of Moon* 340, I immediately pulled down the cow barn, the pigsties, the chicken houses, everything.

Pigtail.

1. A rope or roll of twisted tobacco. {1688–1839}

Cf. LADIES' TWIST (TOBACCO).

1733 *S.C. Gazette* 230/1 To be Sold, . . . very good cut Tobacco, Scotch Snuff, and Pigtail. **1790** *Penna. Packet* 13 July 1/4 Tobacco and Snuff Manufactory Carried on by Jacob Beninghove . . . Has and always keeps, a constant supply of the best Pigtail. **1825** NEAL *Bro. Jonathan* II. 81 Wiping the offered pig tail on his cuff he . . . bit off three large mouthfuls. **1871** EGGLESTON *Hoosier Schoolm.* 41 Old Jack, having bit off an ounce of 'pigtail,' returned the plug to his pocket. **1876** MILLER *First Families* 87 A Missourian . . . lay in his bunk . . . , smoking his pipe of 'pigtail' after supper.

2. A Chinese. {1886}

1873 BEADLE *Undevel. West* 769 'Pigtails' are even more numerous on all the streets [of Portland, Ore.] than in 'Frisco.' **1889** *Harper's Mag.* June 160/1 Got two pigtails there.

Pigtail tobacco. =PIGTAIL 1. {1760} — **1748** *New Eng. Hist. & Gen. Reg.* IV. 176 She continues to sell the best Virginia Tobacco, Cut, Pigtail and spun, of all Sorts. **1779** *N.J. Archives* 2 Ser. III. 191 Bladder, plugg and pigtail tobacco by the barrel. **1834** NOTT *Novellettes* I. 10 Putting a quid of pigtail tobacco in his mouth, he . . . walked off. **1870** NOWLAND *Indianapolis* 169 He wore his wool plaited quite around his head, the plaits about two inches in length, and resembled very much the 'pigtail' tobacco so much used at that time.

+**Pig-tight,** *a.* Of a fence: Secure against a pig's getting through it. — **1871** *Ill. Agric. Soc. Trans.* VIII. 83 Each field and yard are made pig-tight, so that my pigs can follow my cattle into every field. **1886** MITCHELL *R. Blake* 21 [A fence] pig-tight, ox-proof, hoss-high, stumps up-side down. **1905** PRINGLE *Rice Planter* 177 The fence which has been put up is neither 'horse high, bull strong, nor pig tight.'

Pigweed. A name applied to various plants, esp. the goosefoot, *Chenopodium album.* {1844–}

*c*1801 FESSENDEN *Orig. Poems* (1806) 17 The hyacinth and daffodil, With now and then a big weed Of purslain and of pig weed. **1833** EATON *Botany* (ed. 6) 91 *Chenopodium album*, green pig weed. **1847** DARLINGTON *Weeds & Plants* 275 *A[marantus] hybridus.* . . . Hybrid Amarantus. Green Amaranth. Pigweed. **1865** TROWBRIDGE *Three Scouts* 8, I remember a grove of pig-weeds right before your front door, about as tall as those cedars. **1877** BARTLETT 464 *Pig-weed*, a rank weed often found about pig-sties. **1886** EBBUTT *Emigrant Life in Kansas* 75 There were great bushy plants called 'pigweeds,' which grew five or six feet high, which it was impossible for any one to pull up. **1901** MOHR *Plant Life Ala.* 487 *Chenopodium.* . . . Goosefoot. Pigweed. . . . About 8 species native in North America.

+**Pigwick.** 'A small species of duck, very numerous in the coves and rivers of the eastern shore of Maryland. It has remarkably red eyes, feeds on fish, keeps near the shore, and is a great diver' (B. '77).

Pika. {1827–} +Any one of various American rodents of the Ochotonidae family which live in the higher mountains of the West and Northwest. Also with specifying term. (Cf. CHIEF HARE, CONY 2.) — **1889** *N. Amer. Fauna* II. 11 Description of a new species of pika (*Lagomys schisticeps*) from the Sierra Nevada Mountains in California. **1899** *New Eng. Zool. Club Proc.* I. 39 Description of two new pikas from western North America. **1917** *Mammals of Amer.* 271 Colorado Pika. . . . Pale yellowish-brown mixed with black on head and back. **1924** *N. Amer. Fauna* XLVII. 1 Pikas, or 'conies,' as they are more frequently called, . . . are small, tailless, rabbitlike mammals, which on account of their shyness and the inaccessible nature of their haunts are comparatively little known.

*__Pike,__ *n.*[1]

1. a. A large, elongated, voracious, freshwater fish (*Esox estor*), possibly identical with the European species, *E. lucius.* +**b.** Any of various other fishes, some of the genus *Esox*, resembling this fish.

1637 MORTON *New Canaan* 91 There are in the rivers, and ponds, very excellent Trouts, Carpes, Breames, Pikes. **1737** BRICKELL *N. Carolina* 238 The *Jack, Pike,* or *Pickerel*, of these we have two sorts (one living in the fresh, and the other in the Salt Water). **1772** ROMANS in Phillips *Notes on B. Romans* 123 The Rivers have in Common with those of Europe the Sturgeon, the Eel, the Pike, the Chab or Chevin, here Miscalled a Trout, this last of a much finer flavour than in England, . . . But the Pike is Inferior. **1788** MAY *Jrnl. & Lett.* 32 The [Ohio] river abounds in fish, such as cat, perch, pike, buffalo, sturgeon, etc. **1816** U. BROWN *Journal* I. 349 The Monongahalea has . . . a species of pike . . . that has attacked men when in a bathing. **1836** PLUMBE *Sk. Iowa* (1839) 11 Of *Fish* there can never be any scarcity. . . . Among them may be found the pike, the pickerel, the catfish, the trout, and many other varieties. **1852** E. F. ELLET *Pioneer Women* 175 A pike weighing a hundred pounds, speared at the mouth of the Muskingum. **1896** *Outing* XXIV. 57/1 The quick 'strikes' of the 'pike' rippled the gliding surface continuously. **1902** GORDON *Recoll. Lynchburg* 117 How full were the holes of . . . daring, voracious pike.

+**2.** With distinguishing epithets.

See also BONY, GAR, GLASS-EYED, GROUND, and WALL-EYED PIKE.

1818 MITCHILL in *Amer. Monthly Mag.* II. 321 Bony-scaled Pike.—*Esox Osseus* . . . is a stout, heavy, and formidable fish. **1855** BAIRD in *Smithsonian Rep. 1854* 345 The Short-billed Pike. *Esox fasciatus*. . . . Abundant in Cedar Swamp creek. **1870** Mud pike [see MUD *n.* 6 b]. **1884** GOODE, etc. *Fisheries* I. 424 The 'Sauger,' known also as the 'Gray Pike,' 'Sand Pike,' 'Ground Pike,' 'Pickering' [etc.], . . . [is found] in the Saint Lawrence River, Great Lake region [etc.]. *Ib.* 462 The Pike . . . is sometimes known as the 'Great Lake Pike.'

***Pike,** *n.*[2] A soldier's weapon consisting of a long shaft with a pointed head and sometimes a hook; also, a half pike.

*a***1649** WINTHROP *Hist.* I. 183 They bear up near the Indians, (who stood ready armed with guns, pikes, and swords). **1669** *Plymouth Laws* 156 The Townes of this Jurisdiction respectively are to find drumes pikes halberts and Coullers att theire own charge. **1701** SEWALL *Diary* II. 42 The Pike will, I suppose, stand me in fourty shillings, being headed and shod with Silver. **1775** J. ADAMS in *Warren-Adams Lett.* I. 54 Genl. Lee and Major Gates are very fond of a Project of procuring Pikes and Pike men. **1861** *Army Regulations* 475 The pike, including the spear and ferrule, to be nine feet ten inches in length. **1888** *Century Mag.* May 60/2 The little squad of volunteers . . . were given possession of the arms,—2200 muskets . . . and 4020 pikes of the John Brown pattern.

attrib. **1655** *Essex Probate Rec.* I. 229, 2 pike heads & a halfe pike. **1775** Pike man [see above].

Pike, *n.*[3] {1827-} A turnpike road; a graded highway; a main road. {1838-, *dial.*} *To hit the pike*, to leave, to get going. *colloq.*[2]

1836 W. O'BRYAN *Travels* 69 Being informed that instead of going on the '*pike*, as they call it, I could save ten miles by crossing the Blue mountain the pine way, I took the latter road. **1852** STOWE *Uncle Tom* vii, The road . . . was an old one, . . . abandoned for many years after the laying of the new pike. **1862** Moore *Rebellion Rec.* V. II. 586 The entire command started in the direction of the river, taking a dirt road that left the pike at right angles and led to Cairo. **1894** ROBLEY *Bourbon Co., Kansas* 14 The pike, or grade, like a railroad grade, was constructed across all river and creek bottoms. **1910** RAINE *B. O'Connor* 73 Cut loose and hit the pike for yourself. **1923** WATTS *L. Nichols* 15 She must leave the house at six o'clock in order to reach the Pike, . . . and catch the station-bus.

+**b.** The midway of the Louisiana Purchase Exposition of 1904 in St. Louis.

1904 *Phila. Ev. Telegraph* 6 June 6 One of the attractions of the St. Louis Exposition is the facilities afforded by the 'Pike' . . . to witness the various amusements enjoyed by foreign nations.

+**Pike,** *n.*[4] [See note.] On the Pacific coast, a person of migratory habits; a poor white. (Cf. PIKER,[1] PUKE I.)

'Various explanations have been given of the origin of the name. The most reasonable one is, that there are in Missouri and Illinois two large counties named Pike. . . . In 1849 an immense emigration set in from these counties to California. . . . The usual question "Where are you from?" was answered, frequently, with "Pike county." . . . This led to the general impression that everybody on the road was from Pike county. . . . Hence the general name of "Pikes," as applied to emigrants' (1877 N. L. Prentis in W. E. Connelley *Doniphan's Expedition* (1907) 7-8).

1856 *Harper's Mag.* Oct. 588/2 An inhospitable coast is that of California and Oregon. . . . The men were mostly 'Pikes' of an exceedingly rough cast. *a***1861** WINTHROP *Canoe & Saddle* 18 Pikes have shaken off the fever and ague on the banks of the muddy Missouri. **1872** NORDHOFF *California* 137 The true Pike, in the California sense of the word, is the wandering, gipsy-like southern poor white. **1880** *Harper's Mag.* Sept. 535/1 Nothing could be falser than the sketches which . . . confound these uncouth but decent people with the Pikes or swaggering thieves and ruffians of the West. **1885** *Ib.* May 832/1 Its fifteen or twenty male inhabitants represented every class of society from the Boston lawyer down to the Missouri Pike.

+**Pike.** *quasi-adj.* [f. PIKE *n.*[4]] Of the nature of a Pike or poor white. — **1863** *Harper's Mag.* June 25/2 Society in San José is decidedly 'Pike' in its character.

***Pike,** *v. intr.* To go; to move off fast. *colloq.* {-*a*1825}

The widespread vogue of this word, esp. in the West during the latter half of the nineteenth century, may have been strengthened by some popular notion that it was the verb form of PIKE *n.*[3]

1864 'E. KIRKE' *Down in Tenn.* 162, I piked off for the ruin. **1871** *Republican Rev.* 27 May 2/1 Mr. Lesperance, our Humbug, . . . 'pikes' around in the meanwhile, and is making 'grub.' **1886** *Outing* Oct. 49/2 Tell ye what, jist climb onto my pony, an' we'll pike fer the spring. **1902** WHITE *Blazed Trail* 349 You get out of here! Pike! Don't you ever let me see your face again!

+**Pike County.** *quasi-adj.* Pertaining to a county in Missouri supposed to have produced a certain type of citizen. — **1856** DERBY *Phoenixiana* 206 San Diego contains at present about seven hundred inhabitants, two-thirds of whom are 'native and to the manor born,' the remainder a mixture of American, English, German, Hebrew, and Pike County.

+**Pike Countyan.** A person from Pike County, Missouri, esp. one who has emigrated to California. — **1863** MASSETT *Drifting About* 243 These 'Pike countyans' are a most extraordinary looking set of people. *Ib.* 244 Your 'Pike' countyian is not very communicative, and is apt to look upon everything and everybody with suspicion.

+**Piked,** *a.* [PIKE *n.*3] Graded *up*. — **1872** HUNTINGTON *Road-Master's Asst.* 60 How often do we see a piece of track at the foot of a steep grade, on a high embankment, *piked up* as far as possible.

Pikeman. A man who keeps a turnpike. {1857-} — **1841** *Knickerb.* XVII. 488 But the pikeman had heard the rattling of wheels, and rushed out, bare-footed, and clad only in a long shirt. **1855** *Ib.* XLV. 343 From the incivility of the surly pike-man at the bridge in Sunderland, where they paid toll, they missed their way.

Pike perch. Any of several percoid fishes resembling the true pike {1854-}, +esp. the wall-eyed pike, *Stizostedion vitreum*, and the sauger, *Cynoperca* (syn. *Stizostedion*) *canadensis*.

1842 *Nat. Hist. N.Y., Zoology* IV. 17 The Pike Perch is exceedingly voracious, and is highly prized as food. **1856** *Porter's Spirit of Times* 25 Oct. 129/1 There was not, never had been, and never could be a salmon within a thousand miles of the Kentucky River, and . . . the fish so called by the people of that State is either the pike-perch, *Luciopercea americana*, . . . or another analogous fish. **1876** *Fur, Fin, & Feather* Sept. 163/1 All along the Minnesota Division are numerous clear lakes and ponds, teeming with . . . 'wall-eyes' or pike-perch, tarred-perch [etc.]. **1884** GOODE, etc. *Fisheries* I. 417 The Pike Perches. In the interior of North America occur two species of the genus *Stizostedium*, the Wall-eyed Pike, *S. vitreum* . . . , and *S. canadense*. **1892** *Vt. Agric. Rep.* XII. 157 Our waters abound in a great variety of fish, the leading ones being . . . pike, pike perch, and pickerel. **1901** STILLMAN *Autobiog. Journalist* I. 28, I can see vividly the banks of the Mohawk, where we used to fish for perch, bream, and pike-perch.

+**Pike pole.**

1. A long pole used as a lever in raising a great weight.

1845 COOPER *Chainbearer* ix, It is our intention to put it [the meeting-house building] up this a'ternoon. . . . The pike-poles are placed, and all is waiting for the word to 'heave.' **1848** D. P. THOMPSON *L. Amsden* 214 Be ready there with pike-poles and pitch-forks to raise it.

2. *Logging.* A long pole with a spike and hook at one end, used in driving and floating logs.

1850 KINGSLEY *Diary* 139 The weeds are put down with a pike pole and the pressure of the water keeps them to their place. **1877** *Scribner's Mo.* Dec. 149 The running and rafting implements, pike-poles, etc., are made ready. **1894** ROBINSON *Danvis Folks* 241 Put in your pike-poles there. **1902** WHITE *Blazed Trail* 334 Some stood upon the logs, pushing mightily with the long pike-poles.

+**Piker.**[1] [f. PIKE *n.*[4]] *W.* A person from Missouri, esp. from Pike County; =PIKE *n.*[4]

1869 R. KEELER *Gloverson & Silent Partners* 92 He is what we call a 'Piker,' you see, . . . and he stole some of our sheep. **1873** BEADLE *Undevel. West* 763 They acknowledge their own laziness. . . . One of the better class gave me this account: 'these old Pikers don't want the country fenced up and the game scared off.' **1907** STEWART *Partners* 228, 'I'm from Missouri,' I says. 'Oh! then you are a Piker.' 'No, I ain't no Piker; don't I talk St. Louis?' I says. **1907** CONNELLEY *Doniphan's Expedition* 9 Mr. Moore says that in California in the early days Missourians were called 'Pikers' indiscriminately and generally.

+**Piker.**[2] [Of obscure origin.] A stock operator who speculates with small sums; a gambler with small means.

1898 *N.Y. Journal* 12 Aug. 1/7 (Ernst), For all that he afterward became a real estate king, John Pettit started in as a 'piker.' That's what the downtown brokers call a man who speculates with a few hundreds at a time instead of with thousands. The term is often heard on the track, too, and in gambling rooms. **1901** ADE *40 Modern Fables* 81 A Piker is one who gets into the Game on Small Capital and Lets On to be holding back a huge Reserve. **1903** *N.Y. Sun* 15 Nov., He had been hit rather heavily by pikers who had come in with a shoestring to buck the faro bank for a winter outfit. **1917** MCCUTCHEON *Green Fancy* 304, I'm not a piker, you know. . . . The stakes are always high in my game. I don't play for pennies.

b. A poor, worthless, or incompetent person; a plodder; a poor sport. *slang.*

1898 *Boston Globe* 15 May 36/4 There are two kinds of salesmen, the 'pikers,' who grind away all the time, and the men who bunch their hits, to use a baseballism. **1900** *Dialect Notes* II. 48 *Piker*, a term of reproach denoting poorness, worthlessness. [Iowa College, Grinnell, Iowa; Univ. of Mich.] **1902** LORIMER *J. Spurlock* 277 The much-advertised Digger Indians are pikers at dirt-eating beside a bunch of new rich who are trying to get in. **1920** LEWIS *Main Street* 414 The thing that distinguishes our American commonwealth from the pikers and tin-horns . . . is our Punch.

Pike road. A road that has tollgates on it. — **1897** *Outing* XXX. 385/2 The last of that 'pike' road was the worst.

+**Pikery.** A cathartic powder, hiera picra. *colloq.* — **1878** STOWE *Poganuc People* 158 He'll put it through, though; he won't go back on his tracks, but it's pikery and wormwood to him.

+**Pike's Peaker.** One who went out in 1859 to the Pike's Peak area in search for gold. — **1859** *Alta California* 17 Aug. (Th.), Gentile and Mormon, bull whacker and Pike's Peaker, all seem to mingle freely. **1859** H. VILLARD *Pike's Peak Gold Fever* (MS.) 3 The boats were crowded with 'Pike's Peakers.' **1860** GREELEY *Overland Journey* 175 We stopped for dinner . . . beside, two or three wagon's of Pike's Peakers, from whom we obtained a generous supply of fresh bread and another antelope ham. **1869** SIMONIN *Grand-Ouest* 55 Les *Pike's-pikers* ou les mineurs du pic de Pike . . . furent un instant regardé comme des rêveurs. **1873** BEADLE *Undevel. West* 467 The army . . . was largely composed of young Spanish cavaliers, who were as enthusiastic as our own 'Pike's Peakers.'

+**Pike's Peak (gold) fever.** A gold fever inspired by the discovery of gold in Colorado in 1858–9. — **1872** TICE *Over Plains* 201 When the 'Pike's Peak fever' broke out, gold hunters . . . flocked to this supposed Eldorado. **1877** JOHNSON *Anderson Co., Kansas* 270 In the spring of 1859 the inhabitants of the town . . . caught the 'Pike's Peak' gold fever, and the town was abandoned.

+**Pikish,** *a.* Characteristic of a person from Pike County. — **1869** J. R. BROWNE *Adv. Apache Country* 40 If 'George' was a little verdant and rude of speech, he . . . was by no means destitute of a dry, Pikeish sort of wit that occasionally and at very remote intervals burst upon us like a bomb-shell.

***Pilchard.** +=MENHADEN. (The meaning of the word in the first two quotations is uncertain, but it seems clear that the European pilchard is not meant.) — **1637** MORTON *New Canaan* 90 There are greate store of Pilchers. **1775** *Jrnls. Cont. Congress.* III. 503 Indian corn and fish are not to be had . . . except pilchards. **1884** GOODE, etc. *Fisheries* I. 569 In Delaware Bay, the Potomac, and the Chesapeake, we meet with the 'Alewife,' 'Bay Alewife,' 'Pilcher' (Pilchard), and 'Green-tail' [as popular names for the menhaden]. **1911** *Rep. Fisheries 1908* 312/1.

***Pile,** *n.*[1] One of the heavy pieces of timber sharpened at one end, which are driven into soft or yielding ground, esp. for the support of some superstructure, as a bridge or building.

1739 W. STEPHENS *Proc. Georgia* I. 353 Finding many Difficulties in fixing a certain Foundation in the loose sand, without Piles. **1789** MORSE *Amer. Geog.* 180 Each pier is . . . firmly secured by a single pile on each side, driven obliquely to a solid bottom. **1815** *N. Amer. Rev.* I. 447 In Old York, Maine, Major Samuel Sewall, aged 91, died, the first constructor of wooden bridges by driving piles in this country. **1875** *Chicago Tribune* 27 Sept. 4/4 They recognize . . . the neglect to reach the hard-bottom clay with piles, . . . but they do not declare the building unsafe. **1908** WHITE *Riverman* 323 'She's holding strong and dandy,' said Orde, . . . examining critically the clumps of piles.

***Pile,** *n.*[2]

+**1.** One's accumulated riches or savings; one's personal fortune.

1741 FRANKLIN *Poor Richard's Almanac* April, Rash mortals, ere you take a wife, Contrive your pile to last for life. **1849** FOSTER *N.Y. in Slices* 85 Various prices are demanded, according to the size of the immigrant's pile, from three dollars down to fifty cents a week. **1857** *Knickerb.* XLIX. 643 There was not a single seat that came down to my pile; and I felt I must . . . find a cheaper conveyance. **1866** C. H. SMITH *Bill Arp* 81 If you say so, I will send you my pile, with instructions to invest it in the first thing that gets down to the price it was the first day the bill was published. **1889** MUNROE *Golden Days* 184, I don't know nothing about the heft of his pile.

+**2.** The money of an individual player arranged at his place at a gambling table; the money wagered on a particular play. Also fig.

1844 J. COWELL *Thirty Years* 93 The bets were doubled—trebled, and he gave me a knowing, triumphant look, while glancing at his pile. **1866** C. H. SMITH *Bill Arp* 39 The Yankees had a *Strait*, which would have taken Forrest and raked down the pile. **1880** *Cimarron News & Press* 26 Feb. 1/4 Not only of this mine but of many others in the district we imagine it's the lawyers that will eventually sweep the 'pile.' **1886** HARTE *Snow-bound* 115 You kin rake down the pile.

+**3.** An amount of money, usually large.

1853 'P. PAXTON' *Yankee in Texas* 132 It's a big pile to give for a saddle mule. **1864** *Rio Abajo Press* 5 April 3/1 Our Kansas and Missouri friends had better hurry up that railroad, or they may lose a 'pile.' **1875** DALY *Big Bonanza* (1884) 20 If you want to clear a big pile—sell Bonanza!

+**4.** *To make one's pile*, to make a fortune. {1864, in Australia}

1850 SAWYER *Way Sketches* 119 Quite a large number of persons have made their piles' in this region. **1864** *Harper's Mag.* Aug. 410/1 Bill was a returned Californian, who pretended to have made his pile in the land of gold. **1893** *Harper's Mag.* March 495 Florida has become a resting-place for those who can afford to loaf at the busiest time in the year —the men who have 'made their piles,' or organized their business to run automatically. **1901** 'FLYNT' *World of Graft* 2 The professional thief goes up-town to live when he has made his 'pile' or is temporarily in luck, just as surely as the aristocrat goes down-town when his pile has been exhausted.

+**Pile,** *n.*[3] [Du. *pijl.*] 'An arrow. The word is still retained by the boys of New York' (B. '48).

***Pile,** *v.*

+**1.** *intr.* Used with adverbs or prepositions: To climb or get *in*, *off*, etc., a vehicle, obstacle, etc. *colloq.*

1843 STEPHENS *High Life N.Y.* II. 179 Then the hull on 'em begun tu pile in. **1854** M. J. HOLMES *Tempest & Sunshine* 44 Fanny, with half a dozen other girls, . . . began piling on to Bill's old sled. **1866** 'F. KIRKLAND' *Bk. Anecdotes* 333/2 Three Johnnies came 'piling' over the works into the Federal lines. **1884** 'MARK TWAIN' *H. Finn* xxxvi. 373 Here comes a couple of the hounds in from under Jim's bed; and they kept on piling in till there was eleven of them. **1919** WILSON *Ma Pettengill* 138 In comes the special [train], the officials pile off and Ben comes rushing up to Ed. **1921** PAINE *Comr. Rolling Ocean* 114 His four shipmates . . . piled into the automobile.

+**b.** *fig.* To attack; to jump *on to*. *slang.*

1894 *Outing* XXIV. 417/1 The dog . . . [will] never 'pile onto' any more bears. **1906** SINCLAIR *Jungle* 183 Like as not a dozen [policemen] would pile on to him at once, and pound his face into a pulp.

+**2.** *To pile up the agony*, to prolong the climax or effect of something to a point where it becomes painful. {1892–} Also fig.

1839 MARRYAT *Diary Amer.* 1 Ser. II. 39, I must not omit a specimen of American criticism. . . . 'I do think he piled the agony up a little too high in that last scene [of a play].' **1850** in Shields *S. S. Prentiss* 426 Their proclamations show that they are hard to beat in piling up the agony in the way of strong phrases, big words, and powerful assertions. **1875** STOWE *We & Neighbors* 219 They think there is no way but to 'pile up the agony,' to intensify the sense of danger and responsibility.

+**3.** *To pile it on*, to give (a person) all the unpleasant details; to exaggerate; to attack with every weapon at one's command. *colloq.*

1875 'MARK TWAIN' *Old Times* viii. 43 'Now I don't want to discourage you, but—' 'Well, pile it on me; I might as well have it now.' **1883** — *Life on Miss.* xliii, Pile it on and sock it to him—he won't ever holler. **1884** — *H. Finn* vi. 45 He had heard old Sowberry Hagen in his best days, and he said it laid over him, too; but I reckon that was sort of piling it on, maybe.

Pileated woodpecker. A red-crested and white-marked black woodpecker, *Ceophloeus pileatus.*

[**1782** LATHAM *Gen. Synop. Birds* I. 554 Pileated Woodpecker.] **1811** WILSON *Ornithology* IV. 24 The Pileated Woodpecker is suspected of sometimes tasting the Indian corn; the Ivory-billed never. **1874** COUES *Birds N.W.* 278 *Hylotomus pileatus.* . . . Pileated Woodpecker. . . . It varies greatly in size according to latitude. **1893** *Scribner's Mag.* June 760/2 Such purely forest birds as the pileated and ivory-billed woodpeckers. **1917** *Birds of Amer.* II. 154 Pileated Woodpecker. . . . Wooded regions of North America, mainly east of the Rocky Mountains. Next to the rare Ivory-billed, this is the largest of all North American Woodpeckers.

Pile beaver. A heavy, felted, woolen fabric with a fine hairlike nap. — **1784** *Mass. Centinel* 26 June 3/3 For Sale, . . . Cap Wire, Pile Beavers, Washing Buff [etc.].

Pile-driver.

1. A machine for driving piles into the ground, usually with a hoisted weight dropped upon the head of the pile. Often in fig. contexts. {1772–}

1842 *Amer. Pioneer* I. 259 Laborers were engaged, and the pile-driver put in operation. **1855** M. THOMPSON *Doesticks* 285, I had a powerful rival in the person of a six foot Welshman, . . . with a fist like a pile-driver. **1885** *Santa Fé Wkly. New Mexican* 30 July 3/7 A pile driver is working at the Arroyo Hondo bridge. **1909** FORT *Outcast Manufacturers* 278 On this platform were a pile-driver and a stationary engine.

b. A boat equipped with such a machine for operations in water.

1902 WHITE *Blazed Trail* 367 The tug puffed up to the booms, escorting the pile driver.

+**2.** (See quotation.)

1857 HAMMOND *Northern Scenes* 177 [A bird] known in these parts [N.Y. State] as the 'Pile-driver' . . . is about the homeliest creature in these woods. It is a small grey heron.

Pile-driving scow. =PILE-DRIVER 1 b. — **1842** *Amer. Pioneer* I. 259 The pier . . . was sufficiently extended to protect the pile-driving scow.

***Pilgrim.**

***1.** One who travels from place to place. Applied generically and in allusion to the spiritual sense (Heb. 11: 13) to those of the first settlers of Plymouth colony who had sojourned in Holland.

*a*1656 BRADFORD *Hist.* 72 So they lefte yt goodly & pleasante citie [Leyden], which had been ther resting place near 12. years; but they knew they were pilgrimes, & looked not much on those things. **1702** C. MATHER *Magnalia* (1853) I. 54 'Twas a most heavy trial of their patience, . . . this first winter of this their pilgrimage, and enough to . . . remind them that they were but Pilgrims. **1806** A. HOLMES *Discourse* (Dec. 22) 17 The opulence of the Hollanders, acquired by those means, was not seductive to men, who were literally *strangers and pilgrims on the earth.*

+**b.** *Pilgrims of Leyden,* the Plymouth fathers who had sojourned in Leyden, Holland.

1798 *Columbian Centinel* 29 Dec. 3/1 *The Pilgrims of Leyden.*—May the Empire which has sprung from their labours, be permanent as the *rock of their landing.*

+**2. a.** An early settler of Massachusetts or of Plymouth and Massachusetts jointly; a first comer to New England.

The arrangement of senses 2 and 3 is based partly upon the evidence of the attrib. quotations. A. Matthews in *Mass. Col. Soc. Publ.* XVII. (1914) 293–391 has shown that *pilgrim* was applied to 'the early Massachusetts settlers . . . a century and a half before the word was specifically applied to the Plymouth settlers.'

1702 C. MATHER *Magnalia* (1853) I. 68 These Ministers came over to Salem in the summer of the year 1629. . . . The passage of these our pilgrims was attended with many smiles of Heaven upon them. **1795** *Mercury* 16 June 4/1 Across th' Atlantic floods, The Star-directed pilgrim sails! **1820** G. SPRING *Tribute to New-England* (1821) 27 The Pilgrims of New-England were men who had pity on the heathen. **1830** HAWES *Tribute to Mem. of Pilgrims* 225 The sacred shades of the Pilgrims will testify against you. **1856** T. BRIDGMAN (*title*), The Pilgrims of Boston and their Descendants. **1893** *Harper's Mag.* April 706/1 Immigration from New England was comparatively trivial in numbers. . . . It is the ideas of the Pilgrims and not their descendants that have had dominion in the young commonwealth [Kansas].

+**b.** A settler of any other early colony or town.

1660 *Mass. Col. Soc. Publ.* XVII. 366 [New Haven colony] bounds extended neare unto Cold Spring, beyond Pilgrims Harbour. **1831** *Ib.* 371 Then and thus landed *The Pilgrims of Maryland.* **1872** J. G. WHITTIER (*title*), The Pennsylvania Pilgrim [*i.e.,* Francis D. Pastorius].

+**c.** A member of the Pilgrim Society of Concord.

1794 *Mass. Col. Soc. Publ.* XVII. 369 Toasts on the occasion, *viz.* . . . The Pilgrims in Concord.

+**3.** A settler of Plymouth colony, esp. one of those who founded the colony in 1620.

See also SONS OF PILGRIMS. Matthews, *op. cit.,* points out that *pilgrim* was not used in the celebrations of Forefathers' Day from 1769 to 1798.

1798 *Columbian Centinel* 29 Dec. 2/4 'The Heirs of the Pilgrims' Celebrated on Saturday Dec. 22, the 177th Anniversary of the landing of their Forefathers at Plymouth Rock. **1820** *Ib.* 21 June 2/3 The Anniversary of the Landing of the Pilgrims at Plymouth, in the month of December, 1620, has been publicly celebrated in that ancient town for a series of years. **1841** A. YOUNG *Chronicles of Pilgrim Fathers* 88 The term Pilgrims belongs exclusively to the Plymouth colonists. **1882** *Nation* 6 July 8/1 (*caption*), Landing of the Pilgrims—Forefathers' Day. **1911** ROOSEVELT in *Mass. Col. Soc. Publ.* XVII. 294 The coming hither of the Pilgrims three hundred years ago, followed in far larger numbers by their sterner kinsmen, the Puritans, shaped the destinies of this continent.

+**4. a.** Locally applied as a title to persons celebrating Forefathers' Day. Sometimes used sarcastically.

See also PLYMOUTH PILGRIM 1.

1798 *Columbian Centinel* 29 Dec. 2/4 Gen. Lincoln presided . . . at the board of the 'Pilgrims,' which was amply and characteristically furnished with every species of wild food. **1804** in *Mass. Col. Soc. Publ.* XVII. 344 A great number of well-fed, well-dressed Pilgrims, who had never endured penance beyond a drunken head-ache, were walking about with some impatience.

+**b.** One of the persons celebrating the 200th anniversary in 1807 of the founding of Jamestown, Virginia.

1807 in *S. Lit. Messenger* XXIV. 307/2 The sacred soil was saluted by the shouts of the *Pilgrims.* **1857** *Ib.* 311/2 On the 15th [of May, 1807], the pilgrims repaired to Williamsburg to participate . . . in the festivities held in honor of the Declaration of Independence.

+**5.** A member of a certain fanatical religious sect: (see quotations).

1821 NUTTALL *Trav. Arkansa* 226 Not far from this place [near the mouth of the Arkansas River], a few days ago were encamped, the miserable remnant of what are called the Pilgrims, a band of fanatics, originally about 60 in number. They commenced their pilgrimage from the borders of Canada, and wandered about with their wives and children through the vast wilderness of the western states, like vagabonds, without ever fixing upon any residence. **1826** FLINT *Recoll.* 275, I crossed the river to view the wretched remains of that singular class of enthusiasts, known in this country by the name of the 'Pilgrims.' **1890** *Amer. Notes & Q.* V. 257, I have by me a very brief account of a sect of fanatics called 'Pilgrims,' who about 1817 settled at Pilgrim island in the Mississippi river.

+**6. a.** A pioneer or immigrant into the West. **b.** A newcomer into the West; a tenderfoot. Often applied to miners and hunters.

1841 W. L. MCCALLA *Adv. in Texas* 46 After such an address from a citizen of that calumniated country [Texas] to a shattered old pilgrim, I took the liberty of withdrawing to another apartment. **1864** *Rio Abajo Press* 21 June 2/1 A large number of Pilgrimes are camped ten miles from here on the *Gallo.* They are en route for the Arizona Mines. **1869** F. V. HAYDEN *Prelim. Field Rep.* 73 During the gold excitement in the San Juan Mountains . . . in 1862, a large number of miners, or, as they were called in those days, 'pilgrims,' crossed the Sangre de Christo Pass. **1876** CROFUTT *Trans-continental Tourist* 140 Cars of the Trans-Continental Railroad, bound for 'Frisco'—or the 'Bay'—as the city of San Francisco is called by the older 'Pilgrims.' **1877** WRIGHT *Big Bonanza* 556 Newcomers—known as 'pilgrims' or 'greenhorns'—are much more likely to do real work when on a prospecting trip than any of the old miners. **1890** LANGFORD *Vigilante Days* (1912) 116 Some of the companies were composed entirely of 'pilgrims,' a designation given by mountain people to newcomers from the States.

+**7.** (See quot. 1887.)

1887 *Scribner's Mag.* II. 508/1 'Pilgrim' and 'tenderfoot' were formerly applied almost exclusively to newly imported cattle. **1888** *Century Mag.* Feb. 509/1 Those herds consisting of 'pilgrims,' . . . animals driven up on to the range from the south, and therefore in poor condition.

8. *attrib.* +**a.** In sense 2 a and b with *forefather, founder, people.*

1654 JOHNSON *Wonder-w. Prov.* 61 Those who were in place of civill Government . . . begun to thinke of a place of more safety in the eyes of Man, then the two frontire Towns of Charles Towne, and Boston were for the habitation of such as the Lord had prepared to Governe this Pilgrim People. **1830** J. F. WATSON (*title*), Annals of Philadelphia, . . . from the Days of the Pilgrim Founders. **1866** 'MARK TWAIN' *Lett. Sandwich Isl.* 117 A band of stern, . . . old Puritan knights . . . full of that fervent zeal and resistless determination inherited from their Pilgrim forefathers.

+**b.** In sense 3 with *anniversary, bark, mother,* etc.

1817 *Columbian Centinel* 27 Dec. 2/3 The Pilgrim Anniversary Was celebrated at Plymouth, on Monday last. **1836** Quincy *Hist. Harvard* II. 697 The name of Priscilla Mullins carries us back to our Pilgrim *Mothers.* **1849** WHITTIER *Poetical Works* 372/1 For well she keeps her ancient stock, The stubborn strength of Pilgrim Rock. **1848** L. CASS *Address* (Dec. 22) 33 The Pilgrim Puritans . . . raised an altar in the western wilderness, and died around it. **1857** WHITTIER *Poetical Works* 314/2 Come these from Plymouth's Pilgrim bark? **1862** LOWELL *Biglow P.* 2 Ser. vi. 155 Our Pilgrim stock wuz pithed with hardihood.

+**c.** In sense 7 with *cattle.*

1885 *Rep. Indian Affairs* 120 This, we think, is a very fair crop of calves considering the fact that the cattle were what is called 'pilgrim' cattle (cattle for the States that had never passed through a winter before without being housed and fed).

+**Pilgrim church. a.** The church made up of the Pilgrims who went to Leyden. **b.** The church to which all of the Pilgrims belonged. — **1806** A. HOLMES *Discourse* (Dec. 22) 10 The pilgrim church first settled at Amsterdam; but, after a few years' residence in that city, it removed to Leyden. **1897** ARBER *Story of Pilgrim Fathers* 355 Membership in the Pilgrim Church was the first qualification: intended, or actual, emigration to New England was the second. *Ib.* 357 We also speak of the Pilgrim Church: meaning by that the Scrooby Congregation in their migrations to Amsterdam and Leyden.

+**Pilgrim father.**

1. a. *pl.* The founders of Plymouth colony in 1620.

'This restriction, however, of the terms Pilgrims and Pilgrim Fathers exclusively to the Plymouth settlers is recognized at the present time only in the Old Colony itself' (1914 A. Matthews in *Mass. Col. Soc. Publ.* XVII. 362).

1799 *Columbian Centinel* 25 Dec. 3 Hail Pilgrim Fathers of our race, With grateful hearts your toils we trace. **1813** J. DAVIS *Discourse* (Dec. 22) 3 It cannot be an unsuitable employment . . . to revive, in recollection, the transactions and the toils of our pilgrim fathers, who, at such a season, first landed on these shores. **1876** CROFUTT *Trans-continental Tourist* 157 What American man, woman or child, does not feel a heart-throb of exultation as they think of the glorious achievements of Progress since the landing of the Pilgrim Fathers, on stanch old Plymouth Rock! **1898** GRIFFIS *Pilgrims in Three Homes* 161 The affectionate term 'Pilgrim Fathers,' coined by later generations, includes (1) the members of the Leyden church who voted for emigration; . . . (2) those who came from England and joined the church. **1900** *Congress. Rec.* 15 Feb. 1842/2 Their ancestors landed with the Pilgrim fathers at Plymouth Rock.

b. A single member of the Plymouth group.

1908 'O. HENRY' *Options* 89 One brother . . . came in the *Mayflower* and became a Pilgrim Father.

2. In transf. and allusive uses. Usually pl. **a.** The first settlers of any other early colony or town. Often used vaguely.

1824 HODGSON *Lett. from N.A.* II. 11, I am surprised by the proofs which are presented to me of the learning of the 'Pilgrim Fathers,' as they call the first settlers. **1837** *S. Lit. Messenger* III. 412 Individuals . . . who have had the advantage to visit the land of the pilgrim fathers—and partake . . . of the elegant hospitality of the burghers of Boston. **1842** *Mass. Col. Soc. Publ.* XVII. 371 Thus much for the public career of this great Indian benefactor to the Pilgrim Fathers of Connecticut. **1880** CABLE *Grandissimes* 27 The pilgrim fathers of the Mississippi Delta with Gallic recklessness were taking wives. **1889** *Advance* 21 March 226/2 One of the Pilgrim Fathers [of Oregon] has recently died. **1897** *Outing* XXX. 588/1 It is all so primitive here in Amogansett that you wonder you don't run into a pilgrim father. **1913** *Nation* XCVI. 149 Endecott, the Puritan Governor, . . . in common with many other Pilgrim Fathers, wished to hedge round their semi-theocracy.

b. (See quotation.)

1906 *Mass. Col. Soc. Pub.* XVII. 372 The early efforts of Josh Billings and Artemus Ward, the Pilgrim Fathers of Phonetics, . . . were not taken seriously.

+**Pilgrim Society.** **1.** A local society presumably at Concord, Massachusetts. **2.** A society organized in 1820 in honor of the founders of he Plymouth colony. — **(1) 1793** *Mass. Col. Soc. Publ.* XVII. 369 At the Anniversary Meeting of the Pilgrim Society in Concord, . . . they spent the evening in grateful and Christian conviviality. **(2)** [**1807** *Columbian Centinel* 7 Jan. 2/3 The writer would propose, that an association be formed, to be denominated the *Pilgrim Society*. The number of members to consist of 101, corresponding with the numbers of the first settlers.] **1819** *Mass. General Laws* II. 518 An Act to incorporate the Pilgrim Society.

***Pill.**

+**1.** An obnoxious person; a bore. *slang.* {1897-}

1871 BAGG *At Yale* 141 The name 'Delta Phi man' is fast becoming a synonym for 'scrub,' and 'pill,' and even the neutrals regard its members with a sort of pitying contempt. **1881** HAYES *New Colorado* 64 He was the worst-looking pill you ever saw. **1897** FLANDRAU *Harvard Episodes* 98 Miss Wolcott was the sort of Boston girl that dresses like a penwiper, and becomes absorbed in associated charities after a second lugubrious season. In the patois of her locality, she was called a 'pill.'

2. *attrib.* and *comb.* **a.** Designating persons who make, sell, or prescribe medical pills.

1817 *Yankee Traveller* 44 Corundrum . . . had a high regard for this boasting pill-driver. **1857** M. J. HOLMES *Meadow Brook* v, Why, he's a young pill-peddler, who's taken a shine to Rosa. **1882** DALY *Our English Friend* (1884) 29 No pill-grinder shall have my daughter! **1886** *Leslie's Mo.* March 306/2 Was she not the descendant of a pill-man? **1910** C. HARRIS *Eve's Husband* 159 Do you see this quack, this—this pill-person!

b. In special combinations.

Pill bottle, a facetious name for a cannon; *p.-roller*, a contrivance consisting of two grooved boards in which pills may be rolled; *p. shop*, a shop in which drugs are sold.

1861 *N.Y. Tribune* 12 July 6/4 We almost vowed that the champagne made as much noise as the reports of Uncle Sam's 'pill-bottles.' **1839** *Knickerb.* XIII. 346 Rat-traps, churns, apple-parers, pill rollers. **1850** COLTON *3 Years in Calif.* 250 Those pill-shops which slope the path to crime in the United States.

***Pillar.** +The old Spanish dollar. So called from the Pillars of Hercules, shown on the reverse. *Obs.* Usu. attrib. — **1683** *Conn. Rec.* III. 119 All peices of eight, Mexicoe, pillor and Civill peices shall pass at six shillings apeice. **1683** *N.H. Hist. Soc. Coll.* VIII. 161 Pieces of eight royals of Spain, or dollars of Seville, Mexico, and pillar, and all lesser pieces . . . shall pass in payment. **1686** SEWALL *Letter-Book* I. 30 Shipped by Saml. Sewall on the two Brothers . . . 39½ oz. Mexico and Pillar. **1741** *N.J. Archives* 1 Ser. VI. 118 Pillar pieces of eight, seventeen penny weight twelve grains, four shillings and six pence three farthings.

Pill bag. A bag in which a doctor carries medicines and instruments. — **1852** *Knickerb.* XL. 470 After procuring his degree, he had not the wherewithal to buy him pill-bags. **1873** MILLER *Amongst Modocs* 119 He came into the camp as a doctor, and had pill bags and a book or two. **1882** PECK *Sunshine* 93 The doctor got out his pill-bags and made some quinine powders.

Pill box. A box for pills. {1737-} Also transf. {1855-}

1730 *Md. Hist. Mag.* XIX. 182 From Eyre & Beecher (Druggists). . . . 12 Papers pill boxes. **1787** *Md. Gazette* 1 June 1/3 Phials and corks; gally-pots; pill-boxes. **1838** *Knickerb.* XII. 332 But some villains maltreated him sadly, . . . robbing him of his tin pill-boxes, which were full of sixpences to the brim. **1840** HALIBURTON *Clockmaker* 3 Ser. vi, Packed up in a snug pill-box in the same grave-yard. **1897** FLANDRAU *Harvard Episodes* 98 She was called a 'pill'; a girl whom Harvard men carefully avoid until it is rumored that her family shortly intends to 'give something' in the paternal pill-box.

+**Pill bug.** Any wood louse of the family Armadillididae which rolls itself into a ball when disturbed. — **1843** *Nat. Hist. N.Y., Zoology* VI. 52 *Armadillo Pillularis* . . . is known under the name of Pill-bug, from its form, in a contracted state, completely resembling a pill. **1902** JORDAN & HEATH *Animal Forms* 105 There remain the groups of the pill- or sow-bugs (Isopods) and the sand-fleas.

***Pillion.** **a.** A cushion or pad attached to the hinder part of a saddle on which a second person may ride. **b.** A woman's light saddle. *Obs.*

1648 *Conn. Rec.* I. 481 An Inuentory of Tho: Dewys Estate. . . . A saddell & pillion [etc.]. **1686** *Narragansett Hist. Reg.* III. 104 A gray mare, bridle saddle, . . . pillion, portmantle, & curry comb. **1704** S. KNIGHT *Journal* 31 Jemima . . . had Rode thirty miles that day, on a sory lean Jade, wth. only a Bagg under her for a pillion. **1727** *Mayflower Descendant* X. 15 My pillion I give to my Daughter Mary Bangs. **1830** BRECK in *Recoll.* (1877) 180 In the very front came the deacon on horseback, with a long staff in his hand, and his wife on a pillion behind. **1837** BIRD *Nick* I. 104 While secured behind the cushion or pillon (*sic*), on which she rode—for not a jot of saddle had she—was a little bundle. **1838** KENNEDY *Rob of Bowl* II. 4 The greater number . . . rode on horseback, the women seated on *pillions* behind their male escort.

Pillion cloth. A cloth placed under the pillion. *Obs.* — **1648** *Conn. Rec.* I. 508, 1 sidesaddle and pillion cloath. **1684** *Essex Inst. Coll.* XXV. 155 A sadle, pillyon and pillyon cloath. **1687** *Conn. Rec.* I. 445 His daughter Jane shall have . . . all the Beds & Bedding in the Kitchen Chamber & Pilion & Pilion Cloth.

+**Pillo.** *S.W.* [Sp.] A loafer. — **1845** GREEN *Texian Exped.* 234 This fellow also told us he had been in the United States, and knew the difference between a gentleman and a pillo.

***Pillory.** A contrivance for the punishment of persons, usually consisting of a wooden framework with holes provided to hold the neck and wrists of the offender.

1619 *Va. House of Burgesses* 12 He should stand fower dayes with his eares nayled to the Pillory. **1639** *Conn. Rec.* I. 28 Aaron Starke to stand vppon the pillory and be whipt as Williams. **1666** *Md. Archives* II. 141 Any person . . . that shall be legally convicted as a Hogg stealer shall . . . stand in the pillory . . . foure complete hours. **1729** COMER *Diary* (1893) 65 Nicholas Octis stood in ye pillory, and had his ears clipt for making money. **1771** in Earle *Curious Punishments* 52 William Carlisle was convicted of passing Counterfeit Dollars, and sentenced to stand One Hour in the Pillory, . . . to have both Ears cropped, . . . and to stand committed till Sentence performed. **1851** in Stowe *Key* III. 191/1 If I have violated the laws of North Carolina, by them I am willing to be judged, condemned, and punished; to go to the whipping-post, pillory, or jail, or even to hug the stake. **1884** *Boston Jrnl.* 25 Nov. 2/3 A curious scene was witnessed in New Castle, Del., last week. The old fashioned punishment of placing the culprit in the pillory and inflicting a castigation with the cat-o-nine tails, was performed. **1905** *Del. Laws* XXIII. 458 Standing in the Pillory as a punishment for crime in this State is hereby abolished.

***Pillow.**

***1.** A cushion for the support of the head.

1641 *Conn. Rec.* I. 444, 2 bedds and bowlsters & pillowes. **1674** *Essex Inst. Coll.* XXXVII. 98 A feather bed, bolster & 2 pillows & flock bolster 20 sh. **1767** *Ib.* II. 87/1 Sarah Vearey . . . hath one good feather Bed, one Bolster, one Piller [etc.]. **1841** in *Big Bear Ark.* (1845) 21 You can have . . . a wildcat-skin, pulled off hull, stuffed with corn-shucks, for a pillow. **1907** *St. Nicholas* May 597/2 And Jo spitefully turned off the light, leaving Fritzi to creep into bed in the dark, and cry some very salt tears upon her ruffled pillow.

+**2.** A boxing glove. *slang.*

1894 *Outing* XXIV. 443/1 Piled on a little table were four as dirty and badly-stained 'pillows' as I had ever set eyes on.

3. Attrib. in sense 1 with *fight, fustian, linen, tick.*

1663 *Essex Probate Rec.* I. 430 Sheetes and Pillow tikes, . . . Napkins. **1784** *Mass. Centinel* 3 July 3/3 A very fine assortment of goods among which are Pillow Fustians, Jeans, [and] Thicksets. **1883** RITTENHOUSE *Maud* 198 No more pillow-fights, no more ghostly wanderings in search of cards for serenaders. **1890** *Cent.* 4490/3 *Pillow-linen*, linen especially made or used for pillow-cases.

***Pillowbere.** =PILLOWCASE. *Obsolescent.* Also attrib.

1638 *Md. Archives* IV. 46 Item 4. towells & 1. pillowber. **1643** *New Haven Col. Rec.* 89 She confessed allso thatt she stole from Mrs. Gilbert, two pillow beares and a shift. **1721** SEWALL *Diary* III. 281, I gave Mr. Lewis a Lac'd Pillow-beer. **1758** in Shelton *Salt-Box House* (1900) 298, 12 Pair pillibear cases. **1875** STOWE *We & Neighbors* 168, I'm here a ironin' this 'ere pillow-bier.

Pillowcase. A washable case or cover for a pillow. {*a*1745-} Also attrib.

1724 *New-Eng. Courant* 1-8 June 1/2 You are required to demand . . . One Feather Bed, . . . one Pillow-Case, one Suit of Coat Buttons for a Coat [etc.]. **1767** *Essex Inst. Coll.* II. 87/1 Sarah Veary . . . hath one good feather-Bed, one Bolster, one Piller one Piller Case. **1835** *Stimpson's Boston Directory* Advt. 20 Benjamin Jacobs . . . keeps constantly for sale . . . 9-8 pillow-cases linens. **1863** L. BAKER *U.S. Secret Service* (1867) 165 Pillow-cases, bed-spreads, damask window-curtains . . . pillaged or stolen from Fredericksburg. **1898** HARPER *S. B. Anthony* I. 11 Lucy Anthony was considered very fortunate because she could have a few sheets and pillow-cases which were half cotton.

***Pillow coat.** =PILLOWCASE. *Obs.* {-1600; now *dial.*} — **1651** *Mayflower Descendant* X. 39, I give her the bed . . . with two paire of sheets two pillows, two paire of pillow coates. **1683** *Conn. Rec.* I. 286 An Inventory of the Estate of Susanah Bushnell: . . . 2 pillow & pillow Coats. **1727** *Mayflower Descendant* X. 15, I Give to my Granddaughter Mary Bangs A pillow-coat.

Pillow cover(ing). Probably a pillowcase. — **1644** *Essex Probate Rec.* I. 41 Two Pilcovrs and two Payer of course sheets, 10 s. **1650** *Essex Inst. Coll.* XLIII. 70 Five pilar coverings & fine napkins.

+**Pillow sham.** (See quot. 1879.) Also comb. — **1879** WEBSTER 1573/1 *Pillow-sham*, a covering, usually of embroidered linen, laid over the pillow of a bed when it is not in use. **1881** Rittenhouse *Maud* 2 Grandma gave Mama a pair of lovely pale-blue and bobinet pillow-shams which she made herself. **1884** Nye *Baled Hay* 222 Some enemy to mankind has recently invented . . . the pillow-sham holder, which is attached to the head of the bedstead and works with a spiral spring. **1903** 'O. Henry' *Roads of Destiny* 88 Pillow shams, churches, strawberry feasts and *habeas corpus* flourished.

+**Pilon.** *S.W.* [Sp.] =Lagniappe. — **1883** Sweet & Knox *Through Texas* 348 *Pelon*, was nothing more nor less than any little trifle thrown in,—a kind of voluntary commission to the customer. **1892** *Dialect Notes* I. 251 *Pilón*. . . . This is always insisted upon by the poor along the Rio Grande. **1905** A. Adams *Outlet* 189 When I drew a draft for the amount, the proprietor of the outfitting store, as a pelon, made me a present of two fine silk handkerchiefs.

+**Pilonci.** *S.W.* [Corruption of next.] =next. — **1845** Green *Texian Exped.* 264 Our cook brings us in . . . two and a half pounds of brown sugar, 'pilonci.' **1847** Henry *Campaign Sk.* 267 The juice [of sugar cane] when sufficiently boiled is run into molds in the shape of truncated cones. In this shape, wrapped around with strips of cane from which the juice is expressed, it is exposed for sale, and called pilonci.

+**Piloncillo.** *S.W.* [Sp.] A cone or stick made of brown sugar. — **1844** Gregg *Commerce of Prairies* I. 173 When short of means they often support themselves upon only a *real* each per day, their usual food consisting of bread and a kind of coarse cake-sugar *piloncillo* to which is sometimes added a little crude ranchero cheese. **1898** Canfield *Maid of Frontier* 207 'Peloncillo,' crude brown sugar, in a stick as big as Pancho's plump leg.

***Pilot,** *n.*

***1.** A steersman of a boat; spec., a person qualified to steer a boat in or out of a harbor or of any other place where knowledge of local navigation problems is needed.

See also Branch pilot.

1622 'Mourt' *Relation* 41 Robert Coppin our Pilot, made relation of a great Navigable River and good harbour. **1675** Andros in Easton *Indian War* 58, I desire you will furnish the Master of the Sloope with a Pilot. **1711** *Boston News-Letter* 4 June 2/2 A Brigt. . . . was Chased by a Sloop of the Capes . . . almost on Shore at Cape-May, where she took in a Pilot to bring her up the Eastern Chanel. **1797** *Ann. 4th Congress* 2 Sess. 1982 The House . . . resolved itself into a Committee of the Whole on the bill for the regulation of pilots within the bay and river of the Chesapeake. **1835** Ingraham *South-West* I. 247 The pilot (as the helmsman is here [on the Mississippi] termed) stands in his lonely wheel-house. **1883** 'Mark Twain' *Life on Miss.* xxiv, The pilot . . . putting his hand on a backing-bell rope. **1913** *Lit. Digest* 7 June 1272/2 The amount of line he would have to pay out would indicate the depth of channel the pilot was in and would tell him positively where he was.

2. +**a.** A guide over a land route.

1676 *Conn. Rec.* II. 444 You lead your army up to Windsor, . . . taking a pilot at Norwich to shew you that way. **1704** Sewall *Diary* II. 115 A Taunton man, Mason, overtakes us and becomes a very good Pilot to us through the wilderness. **1755** *Lett. to Washington* I. 117 Returned having went 35 miles by Computation of our Pilot. **1824** Rauck *Boonesborough* 163 Col. Boon . . . was to be our pilot and conductor through the wilderness, to the promised land. **1842** M. Crawford *Journal* 19 We should have traviled on but we was afraid of being in the night without water, this is the difficulty of traviling without a Pilot.

+**b.** A railroad conductor.

1842 Buckingham *Slave States* I. 188 Keeping up the maritime phraseology, by which the conductor is called 'the pilot,' and the sound of 'all aboard' announces that . . . all the passengers are in the cars.

3. a. Short for Pilot boat {1896}, *pilot engine*, +*p. mule:* (see sense 6 c).

1717 Hempstead *Diary* 68 Lupton Sayled. I went in her pilot for Oyster Bay. **1883** Roe *Army Lett.* 313 It requires two engines to pull even the passenger trains up, and when the divide is reached the 'pilot' is uncoupled and run down ahead, sometimes at terrific speed. **1887** Custer *Tenting on Plains* 352 [In driving a prairie schooner] a small hickory stick, about five feet long, called the jockey-stick, not unlike a rake-handle, is stretched between a pilot and his mate.

+**b.** Short for Pilot snake 1.

1782 Crèvecœur *Letters* 236 The most dangerous one is the pilot or copperhead. **1842** *Nat. Hist. N.Y., Zoology* III. 36 The Black Snake is a bold, active, wild and untameable animal. . . . In various parts of the State, they have the popular names of Racer, Pilot and Black Snake. **1860** *Harper's Mag.* April 584/1 They had been cautioned against getting into the swamps, as the deadly rattlesnake, and still more fatal 'pilot,' were frequently found in those localities.

+**c.** *Banded pilot*, =Pilot fish 2 a; *black pilot*, the rudder-fish, *Palinurichthys perciformis*.

1842 *Nat. Hist. N.Y., Zoology* IV. 118 The Black Pilot *Palinurus perciformis*. . . . This fish is an occasional visitor to our shores. . . . It has been noticed by Dr. Storer on the coast of Massachusetts. **1903** T. H. Bean *Fishes N.Y.* 415 The banded pilot is found on our east coast from Cape Ann to Cape Hatteras; it reaches the length of 2 or 3 feet.

+**4.** A cowcatcher.

1846 Wyse *America* I. 396 There is usually a 'pilot,' made of stout frame work, placed in front of the leading engine, to which it is attached. **1872** Huntington *Road-Master's Asst.* 85 Planks at road-crossings are frequently raised by frost so as to be caught by the pilot, and cause more or less damage. **1891** Ellis *Check No. 2134* 23 He came round in front of the pilot. **1904** 'O. Henry' *Roads of Destiny* 235 The train with the tiny Stars and Stripes fluttering from the engine pilot arrived.

+**5.** The black-bellied plover.

1888 Trumbull *Names of Birds* 192 On the coast of Virginia . . . the name of Pilot has been given, as it is always seen leading the large flights of birds which the rising tides drive from the shoals and oyster rocks. **1917** *Birds of Amer.* I. 256 Black-bellied Plover. *Squatarola squatarola*. . . . [Also called] Whistling Field Plover; Pilot, May Cock; Swiss Plover; Ox-eye; Four-toed Plover.

6. *attrib.* **a.** Designating places or things connected with pilots or piloting.

1819 E. Evans *Pedestrious Tour* 294 The detention [of vessels] both on the river and at the pilot ground, near its entrance into the Gulf of Mexico, is often considerable. **1833** Coke *Subaltern's Furlough* i, These proved to be rival pilot schooners, taking every advantage of flaws of wind and wet sails. **1840** *Niles' Nat. Reg.* 30 May 207/1 Mr. Hillen . . . made a report, accompanied by a bill repealing the New York pilot law. **1862** McClellan in *Own Story* 213 It is recommended that . . . a few heavy guns and some troops be left at the pilot station (at the forks of the river). **1895** *Stand.* 1341/1 *Pilot-water*, a body of water in which the service of a pilot is necessary.

b. Designating persons concerned with piloting boats.

1858 *Ore. Laws 1857–8* 52 The Legislative Assembly shall biennially elect two persons, experienced in nautical affairs, who shall constitute a board of Pilot Commissioners. **1883** 'Mark Twain' *Life on Miss.* xlix, The pilot-farmer disappears from the river annually, about the breaking of spring, and is seen no more until frost.

c. In special combinations.

Pilot cracker, a kind of hard-tack; *p. light*, (see quotation); *p. mule*, a lead mule; *p. tunnel*, (see quotation).

1880 *Harper's Mag.* Jan. 224/2 Rhene . . . watches the pilot crackers shovelled out, two to each boy. **1890** *Cent.* 4491/3 *Pilot-light*, a very small gas-light kept burning beside a large burner, so that when the flow through the main burner is turned on it will be automatically lighted by the pilot-light. **1887** Custer *Tenting on Plains* 352 A broad piece of leather . . . divides over the shoulders of the lead or pilot mule. **1895** *Stand.* 1341/1 *Pilot-tunnel*, a small sectional iron tunnel driven ahead of a main tunnel to determine its grade and direction.

Pilot, *v.* {1693–} +*tr.* To guide (a person or party) over land or about a place. {1761–}

1649 J. Eliot in *Lancaster* (Mass.) *Rec.* 16, I therefore hired a hardy man of Nashaway . . . to mark trees so that he may Pilot me thither in the spring. **1671** *Doc. Col. Hist. N.Y.* XII. 493 Peter Aldricks shall . . . pilot yor. Honor from the Navecinx. **1701** Sewall *Diary* II. 38 Mr. Clark piloted us to Squamscot. **1753** Washington *Writings* I. 11 Here I engaged Mr. Gist to pilot us out, and also hired four others as Servitors. **1816** U. Brown *Journal* I. 280 Who pilated General Braddock so well through this Mountain 50 or 60 years ago? **1891** *Century Mag.* March 777 They came upon two Indians with several old horses, and engaged them to pilot them in. **1903** *N.Y. Times Sat. Rev.* 26 Sept. 665 Designed first of all for the visitor or the Gothamite piloting friends about the city.

***Pilot boat.** A boat used by a pilot or pilots in the discharge of their duties.

1707 *Boston News-Letter* 18 Aug. 2/1 The Pilot-Boat went off, and knowing the Sloop, was going on Board her. **1779** *Boston Gazette* 30 Aug. 4/2 The Pilot-Boat Hero, burthen ab. 15 Tons, with her Guns, Swivels, Small-Arms, & Ammunition. **1806** *Balance* 6 May 138/3 A pilot boat, full of volunteers, well-armed, sailed in quest of the vessls . . . previously captured at the Hook. **1833** in *Century Mag.* XXX. 785/2, I shall . . . go down the river in a pilot-boat and overtake her. **1885** Baylor *On Both Sides* 132 A certain florist . . . had been ordered by telegraph to send off [roses] . . . by the pilot-boat, to greet the strangers before they had so much as set foot on American soil.

attrib. and *comb.* **1806** *Ann. 9th Congress* 2 Sess. 1015 Pilot-boat built schooners. **1808** *Ann. 10th Congress* 2 Sess. 286 Virginia pilot-boat schooner arrived there with 750 barrels of flour.

transf. **1813** *Salem Gazette* 22 Oct. 3/2 Last evening arrived, the tandem Philadelphia pilot boat [a wagon] . . . from a three weeks cruise in Rhode Island and Connecticut.

+**Pilot bread.** A kind of ship biscuit; pilot crackers. {1858–, in W. Ind.} — **1788** *Md. Jrnl.* 7 March (Th.), The subscriber has just begun to bake Ship, Pilot, and Cag Bread. **1796** F. Baily *Tour* 114 Pilot bread, 50s. per barrel. **1821** *Ann. 17th Congress* II. 2497, 2910 pounds of pilot bread, for the officers, ladies, and their children. **1849** T. T. Johnson *Sights Gold Region* 191 We saw old miners . . . with one month's supply of provisions, consisting of 75 lbs. of pork and 75 lbs. of pilot bread. **1862** Norton *Army Lett.* 50 We now have our soft bread baked in the regiment, but we have eaten a great many of the crackers, or pilot bread, as it is called. **1894** *Outing* XXIV. 252/2 He quickly wrapped up some pilot-bread and . . . tied the package under the balloon.

+**Pilot cloth.** A kind of coarse, blue cloth used for overcoats and sailors' garments. Also attrib. — **1840** *Knickerb.* XV. 140 His winter clothing is usually a peet jacket and trowsers, of strong pilot cloth. **1846** Corcoran *Pickings* 134 Both of them chewed tobacco freely, wore pilot cloth great coats, had shocking bad hats, and carried a long whip across the left arm. **1889** BRAYLEY *Boston Fire Dept.* 193 Coats of pilot-cloth were then made which proved entirely satisfactory.

Pilot coat. A pea jacket. — **1865** A. D. WHITNEY *Gayworthys* 151 The stout, manly-grown figure . . . stood there, in the rough pilot coat. **1885** CRAWFORD *Amer. Politician* 211 Enormous Irishmen in pilot coats, comforters, and india rubber boots, . . . were struggling to keep the drifts from the pavement.

Pilot fish.

1. A pelagic, carangoid fish (*Naucrates ductor*) that is often seen near a shark. {1634–}

1751 WASHINGTON *Diaries* I. 17 Catched . . . a Shark at 11 and a one of his pilot fish. **1819** E. EVANS *Pedestrious Tour* 359 The pilot-fish, which attends the shark, is only a few inches long; and like the jackall, accompanying the lion, seems to cater for prey, and to partake of the spoil. **1842** *Nat. Hist. N.Y., Zoology* IV. 112 The New York Pilot-fish. *Naucrates noveboracensis*. . . . Four transverse blue bands, and four spines before the dorsal. **1911** *Rep. Fisheries 1908* 313/2 Pilot-fish (*Naucrates ductor*).—A pelagic fish of no economic importance, and seldom taken on our coast.

2. a. A banded amber fish, *Seriola zonata.* **+b.** The Menominee whitefish, *Prosopium quadrilaterale.*

1880 *Harper's Mag.* Sept. 503/2 The tiny pilot-fish, perhaps a kind of fugleman for the mackerel, but more likely his prey, like the rest, came first. **1903** T. H. BEAN *Fishes N.Y.* 221 Other names are Menominee whitefish, roundfish, shad-waiter, pilotfish and chivey. **1911** *Rep. Fisheries 1908* 318/1 The Menominee whitefish . . . [is] also locally known as . . . 'shad-water,' 'pilot fish,' 'chivey' [etc.].

+Pilot house.

1. A house on land in which a pilot lives or stays while waiting for incoming or outgoing boats.

1812 STODDARD *Sk. Louisiana* 160 On the south side of the east pass, about three miles from the bar, is the pilot house. **1827** WILLIAMS *W. Florida* 18 A small fort and pilot house formerly stood near the west end of the island.

2. A structure forward on the upper deck of a ship, esp. of a steam vessel, that shelters the steering gear and helmsman.

a1846 *Quarter Race Ky.* 127 He placed his hand upon a small brass knob at the back of the pilot house. **1849** *Knickerbocker Mag.* XXXIV. Aug. 179 [Robert L. Stevens (*c*1831)] then gave instructions that a house . . . should be immediately erected, with handsome windows in front: that was the first pilot-house. **1862** MOORE *Rebellion Rec.* V. II. 226 Two transports had also been sunk close to her, one of which had on her pilot-house 'Eliza G.' **1882** McCABE *New York* 406 [The ferryboats] are large and powerful side-wheel steamers constructed on the double-end system, with a pilot-house at each end. **1914** STEELE *Storm* 148 Crimson sat in the doorway of his pilot-house.

+Pilot snake.

1. = COPPERHEAD I.

1789 *Amer. Philos. Soc.* III. p. xx, [The Poor-Robin's-plantain is] said to frustrate the bite both of the rattle snake, and of his supposed precursor the pilote-snake. **1818** *Amer. Jrnl. Science* I. 84 He has been called sometimes *pilot-snake*, on a false supposition that he was the pilot or guide of the rattlesnake. **1859** A. VAN BUREN *Sojourn in South* 197 The pilot-snake . . . gets so full of poison in the fall that it grows blind. **1890** *Century Mag.* Aug. 615/2, I killed the large snake called the '*pilot-snake*,' from the fact that they are generally found in the vicinity of rattlesnakes.

2. The pine snake of the Atlantic coast, *Pituophis melanoleucus.*

1853 in Marcy *Explor. Red River* (1854) 211 The names of Bull, Pine, and Pilot snake, are commonly given to different species of [*Pituophis*].

3. A harmless black snake, *Elaphe obsoleta.*

1890 *Cent.* 4491/3 *Pilot-snake*, a harmless snake of the United States, *Coluber obsoletus.*

+Pilotweed. The rosinweed, *Silphium laciniatum.* — **1847** EMORY *Military Reconn.* 11 On the uplands . . . occasionally is found the wild tea . . . and pilot weed. [**1885** *Girl's Own Paper* Jan. 171/1 The compass plant—variously known, also, as the pilot weed, polar plant, and turpentine weed—is a vigorous perennial.]

Pimento. Also †**pemento, piemento.**

1. = ALLSPICE I. {1690–, in W. Indies}

1707 *Boston News-Letter* 27 Jan. 2/2 To be Sold on reasonable terms . . . Jamaica & Leeward-Islands fine Sugar, Pemento or all Spice. **1756** *R.I. Commerce* I. 65 Cocoa about £30, Coffee 6/6, Pimento 9/; Ginger wanted for the Army, the last sold at £12. Cotton wooll slow at 10/6. **1774** *Jrnls. Cont. Congress* I. 57 After the first day of December next, no molasses, coffee or piemento from the British Plantations or from Dominica . . . [shall] be imported into these colonies. **1820** *U.S. Pharmacopœia* 171 Oil of Pimento [is prepared] from Pimento. **1836** EDWARD *Hist. Texas* 132 The other agricultural products are indigo, pimento [etc.].

2. The allspice tree, *Pimento officinalis.* {1756–, in W. Indies} Also attrib.

[**1709** LAWSON *Carolina* 89 The spontaneous Shrubs of this Country, are . . three sorts of Hony-Suckle-Tree, the first of which grows in Branches, as our Piemento-Tree does.] **1775** CRESSWELL *Journal* 68 Great plenty of Wild Plum Trees and a Species of the Pimento, these are small Bushes.

3. The mild red pepper of the Spanish paprika, *Capsicum tetragonum.*

1911 *Grocer's Encycl.* 480 Pimiento, or Pimento: a large-fruited capsicum, . . . extensively used for stuffing olives, etc.

Pimlico order. Precise order. — **1843** STEPHENS *High Life N.Y.* II. 112 There the wimmen folks sat on them red benches, all in pimlico order, drinking coffee. **1864** *Congress. Globe* 15 Feb. 647/3 We should have the expenses of the Government figured out to a copper in every particular, and everything placed in such minute, Pimlico order, that everybody could understand exactly what it was.

Pimp, *v.* {1636–} +*intr.* (See quot. 1851.) — **1819** PEIRCE *Rebelliad* (1842) 33 Did I not promise those who fish'd And pimp'd most any part they wish'd! **1851** HALL *College Words* 231 *Pimp*, to do little, mean actions for the purpose of gaining favor with a superior, as, in college, with an instructor.

***Pimpernel.** One of various plants, esp. a primulaceous herb of the genus *Anagallis*, as *A. arvensis.*

1683 *Mass. H. S. Coll.* 4 Ser. V. 112 We drink barley-water; in which boil anise-seed, . . . a good quantity of maiden-hair, and pimpernel. **1784** *Amer. Acad. Mem.* I. 403 *Veronica*. . . . Pimpernel. Brooklime. Water Speedwell. Blossoms whitish or purplish. In swamps. June–July. *Ib.* 415 *Anagallis*. . . . Pimpernel. Blossoms red. In clayey ground. June. **1833** EATON *Botany* (ed. 6) 207 *Lindernia dilatata*, pimpernel. **1885** *Harper's Mag.* Nov. 820/2 The pimpernel, usually found in perfection nearer corn fields. **1901** MOHR *Plant Life Ala.* 662 *Anagallis arvensis*. . . . Common Pimpernel. . . . Adventive and partially naturalized on the Atlantic coast from Canada to Florida, Arkansas, and California.

***Pin,** *n.*

***1.** A short piece of small wire, pointed at one end and provided with a head at the other, used for fastening; also, a fancy brooch, scarfpin, etc., used for ornament.

1644 *Conn. Rec.* I. 457 An inuentory . . . of the goods of Blaynch Hunt: . . . gloues, pyns, laces [etc.]. **1711** *Boston News-Letter* 22 Oct. 2/2 To be Sold on reasonable Terms . . . all sorts of Nails, Steel, Iron Ware, . . . Manchester Goods, Pins. **1777** *Holyoke Diaries* 98 Emmerton Brought Linnen & Pins. **1857** M. GRIFFITH *Autobiog. Female Slave* 17 One gave a yard of ribbon, another a half-paper of pins. **1911** *Sears, Roebuck & Co. Cat.* No. 123, 103 Washington Needle Pointed Pins. . . . Contains 400 pins to paper.

***2.** A small round piece of wood serving as a peg or bolt.

[**1692** in Burr *Witchcraft Cases* (1914) 154 A Yellow-bird sat on my hat as it hung on the Pin in the Pulpit.] **1787** SARGENT in *Amer. Acad. Mem.* I. I. 157 The Black Locust is a very durable wood, and in use for pins and gate posts. **1824** Z. F. Smith *Kentucky* (1886) 394 Some pins, stuck in the logs at the back of the house, supported some clapboards which served for shelves for the table furniture. **1852** *Fla. Plantation Rec.* 72 White oak Makes a Splendid Pin.

+3. An ornamental badge or brooch adopted as a symbol or emblem of a fraternity, society, etc.

1871 BAGG *At Yale* 144 Its original badge was a rectangular gold plate, about the size and shape of the present Beta Xi pin. **1893** POST *Harvard Stories* 216 Freddy . . . asked me one day why Sheffield wore that funny little pin all the time. **1910** J. HART *Vigilante Girl* 19 My dear fellow, you may cast aside your Eastern frigidity—in fact, I will call it your Cambridge frigidity, for I see you wear a Harvard pin.

+b. (See quotation.)

1873 *Congress. Globe* 15 Jan. 617/3 There has been for the last seventeen years in [the Cherokee] nation a secret society called the 'Pins.' . . . The Pin Society . . . was organized five years before the war.

4. *To stick pins into* (a person) to provoke to action, stir up, or annoy. *colloq.*

1903 LEWIS *Boss* 184 This aint meant to stick pins into you.

***Pin,** *v. tr.* To fasten (a rail, frame, etc.) by means of a wooden pin or peg. — **1686** *Plymouth Rec.* I. 186 Every top raile to be pined. **1791** in Jillson *Dark & Bl. Ground* 111 Frames set in and pinned fast in holes bored in the logs. **1848** COOPER *Oak Openings* I. 29 The door was made of three thicknesses of oaken plank, pinned well together. **1883** HOWE *Country Town* (1926), 93 Jo gayly waved his hand to me from the high place to which he had climbed to pin a timber.

+Pinball. 1. A soft ball serving as a pincushion. **2.** *Pinball sight*, (see quotation). — **(1) 1803** BOWNE *Life* 176/2 We went to a room where they keep their work for sale,—pocket-books, pin balls [etc.]. **1875** STOWE *We & Neighbors* 127 Racing off at unsuitable periods like a kitten after a pin-ball. **1895** A. BROWN *Meadow-Grass* 211 Them pinballs my neighbor, Mis' Dyer, made with her own hands. **(2) 1883** KNIGHT *Suppl.* 682/1 *Pin-ball Sight*, (*Rifle*,) another name for the *bead-sight:* called also pin-head sight.

***Pincers.** *pl.* **1.** = NIPPER I. **+2.** Tongs for handling ice. — **(1) 1640** *Conn. Rec.* I. 448 An Inventory of the goods and Cattell of James Olmstead: . . . chysells, hammers, pynsers. **1783** E. PARKMAN *Diary* 298 Pair Pincers 1[*s*.]. **1840** *Picayune* 10 Oct 2/3 Mr. Blancard . . . [found] a pair of pincers used by burglars for breaking locks. **(2) 1890** *Harper's Mag.* April 746/1 [Lucilla saw] a burly ice-man, his iron pincers dangling from his hand.

***Pinch**, *n*. **1.** An especially steep or difficult part of a road or highway. **+2.** The place at which a mineral vein or bed becomes markedly thin. — **(1) 1754** WASHINGTON *Writings* I. 63 Wagons may travel now with 1500 or 1800 weight on them, by doubling the teams at one or two pinches only. **1755** in Franklin *Writings* (1840) III. 401 The expense of making the road thirty feet wide, and the principal pinches twenty, will make an expense of about eight hundred pounds. **(2) 1873** BEADLE *Undevel. West* 333 All the strange terms in mining parlance: 'true lodes, fissure-veins, pinches.' **1878** — *Western Wilds* 486 Next, perhaps, he finds the vein widening . . . ; again he encounters a 'pinch' or 'cap,' and hope almost dies out ere he gets through it.

***Pinch**, *v*.

1. *intr.* Of a vein of ore: To become narrow or thin. {1890–, in Australia}

1869 McCLURE *Rocky Mts.* 267 They know that it [the lead] may cap, or pinch, or play out entirely. **1873** BEADLE *Undevel. West* 335 [The vein] suddenly 'chambers' to some size, then 'pinches' to the thickness of a knife blade. **1880** *Harper's Mag.* Feb. 395/1 Ore is harder and more expensive to work, and the veins 'pinch' (or contract to very small dimensions).

+b. *tr.* and *intr.* (See quotation.)

1877 W. WRIGHT *Big Bonanza* 164 The miners are never discouraged so long as they find a good width of quartz. . . . What they do not like, however, is to find the walls coming together—'pinching,' as they call it. The coming together of the walls pinches out or cuts off the vein.

2. *To pinch out*, + of a vein of mineral, to run out, to end. Also transf.

1869 *Overland Mo.* III. 283 The Russian River Valley 'pinches out' at Cloverdale. **1873** BEADLE *Undevel. West* 335 He may still be only in one of the 'side fissures,' which has taken a sudden turn, 'pinching out' for a few rods. **1895** *Home Missionary* Aug. 222 The pay streak proved to be a pocket or a seam that soon pinched out. **1904** E. ROBINS *Magn. North* II. 149 Just up yonder . . . the pay-streak pinches out.

+3. *To pinch in*, to encroach *on* or *upon* so as to confine or restrict.

1873 BEADLE *Undevel. West* 346 Winter 'pinched in' on mining operations in Utah. *Ib.* 754 The spurs of the Sierras put out westward toward the Coast Range, and, in mining parlance, 'pinch in' upon the plain.

Pinchbeck. {1734–} *attrib.* or as *adj.* Made of pinchbeck. {1746–} — **1754** *S.C. Gazette* 1 Jan. 2/2 An assortment of gold, silver and Pinchbeck watches. **1782** FRENEAU *Misc. Works* 389 Men's large silver, pinchbeck and plated shoe buckles. **1841** *Knickerb.* XVII. 187 Here the chain was again attached, and thence went festooning in various directions about his vest, communicating with a pinch-beck watch. **1892** R. H. DAVIS *Silhouettes* 16 There was a general interchange of gifts: brier wood pipes, or pinchbeck scarf-pins.

+Pinch bug. Any one of various American stag beetles, esp. *Lucanus dama.* — **1856** 'MARK TWAIN' in *Iowa Jrnl. of Hist.* XXVII. 423 A tenor and bass duet by thirty-two thousand locusts and ninety-seven thousand pinch bugs was sung. **1870** EGGLESTON *Queer Stories* 74 At last we came to a log on which two of that sort of beetles that children call 'pinch-bugs,' were fighting. **1876** 'MARK TWAIN' *Tom Sawyer* v. 57 It was a large black beetle with formidable jaws—a 'pinch-bug,' he called it.

+Pin cherry. (See quot. 1897.) — **1884** SARGENT *Rep. Forests* 66 Pin Cherry. . . . The small acid fruit used domestically and by herbalists in the preparation of cough mixtures, etc. **1897** SUDWORTH *Arborescent Flora* 240 *Prunus pennsylvanica*. . . . Wild Red Cherry. . . . Pin Cherry (N.H., Vt., N.Y., Mich., Ohio, Iowa, N. Dak.). **1923** *Standardized Plant Names* 78/2.

+Pinching bug. 1. =PINCH BUG. **2.** (See quotation.) — **(1) 1850** GARRARD *Wah-To-Yah* 226 Then Noah was so hurried to git the yelaphants, pinchin' bugs, an sich varmint aboard [etc.]. **1877** BURDETTE *Rise of Mustache* 77 That Bilderback boy . . . put a pinching-bug as big as a postage-stamp down a boy's back. **1909** WASON *Happy Hawkins* 183 You'll have to do a master job of painting to make that William goat look like a pinchin' bug. **(2) 1890** *Cent.* 4495/1 *Pinching-bug*, the dobson or hellgrammite. [Western Pennsylvania.]

+Pin clover. =ALFILARIA. (Cf. PIN GRASS.) — [**1884** W. MILLER *Dict. Names of Plants* 106/2 Pin-grass, or Pin-clover, of California: *Erodium cicutarium*.] **1889** VASEY *Agric. Grasses* 102 [Alfilaria] is known as storksbill, pin clover, pin grass, and filaree. **1901** MOHR *Plant Life Ala.* 583. **1913** BARNES *Western Grazing Grounds* 39 Alfileria also is known as 'heron's bill' and 'pin clover.'

Pincushion.

1. A small cushion into which pins are stuck for future use. {1632–} Also transf.

1644 *Essex Probate Rec.* I. 45 Bonelass & thread & a pinn coshen, 1s.; a sword, 5s.; one trunk, 2s. **1784** *Md. Hist. Mag.* XXI. 28, I sent the Bride an elegant White Satin Pincushion, and garters of the same. **1845** *Knickerb.* XXV. 444 There too hung the same touch-wood pin-cushion. **1878** B. F. TAYLOR *Between Gates* 263 The cactus fences . . . slowly climbing over themselves in diagonals of serried pin-cushions. **1902** *Harper's Mag.* May 990/1 One pin-cushion has on it a wonderful robin, large as life.

2. The sweet scabious and the field scabious. {1886–} Also attrib.

1898 BRITTON & BROWN III. 290 Field Scabious . . . [is also called] blue caps, gypsy- or egyptian-rose, pincushion. **1901** JEPSON *Flora of Western Middle Calif.* 476 Mourning Bride . . . [is] called 'Pin Cushion' by children at East Oakland. **1917** BAILEY *Stand. Cycl. Hort.* VI. 3106/1 The mourning bride or pincushion flower . . . [is] among the most popular of flower-garden annuals.

Pindar. =PINDER.[2] {1756–, in W. Indies} Also *pindar pea*.— **1848** *Rep. Comm. Patents* 1847 190 The ground pea of the south, or . . . the gouber or pindar pea, is highly recommended in the Tallahassee Floridian. **1850** *Rep. Comm. Patents 1849: Agric.* 159 The 'Pindar' (ground-nut) is grown for market by the cultivator of sandy pine lands. **1903** *Southern Workman* Nov. 536 The home of the peanut or ground pea (also often called pindar and goober) is believed to be Brazil.

***Pinder.**[1] An official of a colonial town chosen to impound stray horses, cattle, etc. *Obs.* — **1642** *New Haven Col. Rec.* 82 A peny a head for goates and kids, half to the bringer in of the cattell & half to the pound, or if the pinder take all the paines he is to have all. **1660** *Hempstead Rec* I. 93 All horses and mares shall pay three shillings a heade and 2s-6d to him that bring them and 6d to the pinder. **1693** *Jamaica (L.I.) Rec.* I. 145 He [was engaged] to be pinder to ye same and to have for Every hors or maire trespasing and brought to ye pound five pence.

Pinder.[2] *S.* [Kongo *mpinda*.] The peanut or goober. — **1871** DE VERE 401 Among the negroes in Florida it [the groundnut] is . . . known as Pinders. **1877** BARTLETT 466 *Pinders*, peanuts. South Carolina. **1892** *Amer. Folk-Lore* V. 95 *Arachis hypogæa*, . . . pinders. Miss.

Pindling, *a.* {1895} +Sickly, puny, trifling. *colloq.* Also transf. — **1861** STOWE *Pearl Orr's Isl.* I. 25 [The baby is] such a pindling little thing. **1890** WIGGIN *Timothy's Quest* 115 Mis' Pennell's got a new girl to help round the house,—one o' them pindlin' light-complected Smith girls. **1895** A. BROWN *Meadow-Grass* 63 Lyddy Ann . . . looked pretty pindlin' then, mark my words; but I never see two such eyes in anybody's head. **1906** LYNDE *Quickening* 300, I know in reason it must seem mighty little and pindlin' down here to you. **1918** FREEMAN *Edgewater People* 145 Mr. Richard is kind of pindlin'.

Pindrow. 1. A kind of fir tree, *Abies pindrow.* Also *pindrow fir*. **2.** *Pindrow pine*, the Himalayan spruce, *Picea smithiana.* — **(1) 1858** WARDER *Hedges & Evergreens* 257 *Picea pindrow*, the Pindrow, . . . is hardy as far North as the Hudson River. **1890** *Cent.* 4496/1 The pindrow-fir is a variety of the king-pine. **(2) 1858** WARDER *Hedges & Evergreens* 254 The Himalayan Spruce Fir . . . has been called the Rhutrow, and has been sold as the Pindrow pine.

***Pine.**

***1.** Any one of various species or varieties of cone-bearing trees of the genus *Pinus*.

See also BLACK PINE, BROOM PINE, etc. There are thirty-five or more species or varieties of pine native to North America.

1616 SMITH *New England* 16 Firre, pyne, walnut, . . . and many other sorts. **1724** JONES *Virginia* 39 As for Timber they abound with excellent good; having . . . several Kinds of Walnut-Tree, and Hickory and Pignut, Pine, Cedar. **1800** HAWKINS *Sk. Creek Country* 59 The land up the river, above the fields, is fine for culture, with oak, hickory, blackjack, and pine. **1874** *Vermont Bd. Agric. Rep.* II. 494 He estimates the income from one acre of land planted to pine and larch to be $8920 in the course of thirty years. **1916** THOBURN *Stand. Hist. Okla.* I. 5 The most common species of trees in Oklahoma include . . . walnut, juniper (two species), pine (three species), [and] hackberry.

***b.** An individual pine tree.

1622 'MOURT' *Relation* 3 [The entrance to Provincetown harbor is] compassed about to the very Sea with Okes, Pines, Juniper, Sassafras, and other sweet wood. **1687** SEWALL *Diary* I. 191 Set an H on a sear Pine. **1708** E. COOK *Sot-Weed Factor* 19 Sturdy Oakes and lofty Pines Were level'd with Musmillion Vines. **1788** FRANKLIN *Autobiog.* 409 Two men began to cut at a pine; in six minutes they had it upon the ground. **1808** PIKE *Sources Miss.* I. App. 54 The banks of the Mississippi are still bordered by the pines of the different species. **1898** CANFIELD *Maid of Frontier* 119 He could see the bare old church amid the sweet-smelling pines.

***2.** The wood or timber of pine trees, used for burning or in building.

Cf. FAT PINE 1.

1705 BEVERLEY *Virginia* III. 12 [The Indians] generally burn Pine, or Lightwood, (that is, the fat Knots of dead Pine). **1728** *Boston Rec.* 222 No Popler, chestnut, pine, . . . or Ceder Shall be Corded up or Exposed to Sale. **1763** in H. M. Brooks *Gleanings* IV. 35 A number of Window Sashes . . . made of the best of Pine. **1866** *Rep. Indian Affairs* 295 The doors [are] to be made of clear pine, pannel style.

+3. *pl.* A region covered with pines, esp. an extensive area in New Jersey extending from Lakewood to Cape May County.

1871 *Harper's Mag.* Aug. 474/1 The answer that another missionary of the society, exploring 'The Pines' in New Jersey, got from the wife of a hunter. **1873** *Ib.* March 639/1 Very much of the pine wood which gave name to the region so long known as the Pines of New Jersey has been cut and taken away. **1875** *Amer. Naturalist* IX. 1 In the 'pines' of southern New Jersey, which probably is the northern limit of the species, is a notable serpent. **1895** *Outing* XXVI. 34/2 All the roads in the Pines are alike; the majority of them lead nowhere.

4. *attrib.* and *comb.* **a.** Designating areas, regions, etc., covered with pine trees. Also in place names.

See also PINE BARREN, PINE BLUFF, etc.

1640 *Hartford Land Distrib.* 24 [The] cowpasture abutteth on the westfeild . . . & on the pinefeild. **1667** *Conn. Probate Rec.* I. 192, I bequeath too . . . my gr. Child all my Lott lying at Pine Meadow. **1741** *N.H. Probate Rec.* III. 70 One peice of Plowland lying Near about fifty Rods from the Dwelling house on a Pine nole. **1789** WASHINGTON *Diaries* IV. 31 The Inclosures have but indifferent fences; wood or stone according as the Country abounds with the latter—of which it is full after passing the pine levels. **1815** *Mass. H. S. Coll.* 2 Ser. IV. 290 The pine commons of Wareham, Sandwich, and Plymouth, are very extensive and contiguous, affording a wide range for sheep. **1883** SMITH *Geol. Survey Ala.* 243 The soils along this gravelly belt are not materially different from those of the other parts of the Oak and Pine Uplands. **1906** LYNDE *Quickening* 346 The rough wood road . . . led off to the Pine Knob settlement.

b. Designating streams flowing through or situated in pine forests.

1647 *New Haven Col. Rec.* 314 Wm. Andrewes propowned that . . . [he] might have a neck of land . . . beyond the pine river. **1652** *Ib.* 105 All the land from that wch is commonly called the pine brooke by the English. **1800** HAWKINS *Sk. Creek Country* 22 There are several pine creeks on this side. **1821** *Amer. Jrnl. Science* III. 41 A little above the pine bayou . . . there is a large quantity of blind coal.

c. Designating things made of pine.

1663 *Plymouth Rec.* I. 62 Lott is . . . bounded with a pyne stake at the west side. **1715** HEMPSTEAD *Diary* 51 Moses & Josh fetched ye pine plank from Wilsons. **1777** *Jrnls. Cont. Congress* VII. 100 There is due to Gerard Hopkins, for six chairs and a pine table . . . , the sum of 24 60/90 dollars. **1816** *Austin P.* I. (1924) 263, 1 Pine Buckett. **1891** O'BEIRNE *Leaders Ind. Territory* 218/1 He owns several pine houses, and a stock ranch and a range which are scarcely equaled in that portion of the country. **1909** 'O. HENRY' *Options* 275 In the village I found a pine hotel called the Bay View House.

+**d.** In the names of birds.

Pine goldfinch, =PINE FINCH; *p. jay*, =MOUNTAIN JAY; *p. sparrow*, any one of various sparrows or sparrowlike birds, as the pine siskin, that frequent pine woods.

1878 *Nat. Museum Proc.* I. 414 *Chrysomitris pinus.*—Pine Goldfinch. **1917** *Birds of Amer.* II. 219 Steller's Jay. *Cyanocitta stelleri stelleri.* . . . [Also called] Mountain Jay; Pine Jay; Conifer Jay. **1903** WHITE *Forest* 91 You will hear . . . purple finches or some of the pine sparrows warbling high and clear.

e. In special combinations.

Pine almond, the seed of a pine; *p. beer*, beer made from or flavored with the twigs and leaves of the black spruce, spruce beer; *p. cannon*, a Quaker gun made of a pine log; *p. cedar*, =CEDAR PINE; *p. corner*, a pine tree serving as a corner (cf. CORNER *n.* 3); *p. gum*, the dried sap of a pine; *p. holding*, a tract of pine forest held or owned by a lumber company; *p. mast*, the edible seed of a pine tree (cf. PINE NUT); *p. oil*, any one of various oils, as oil of turpentine, obtained from pine trees; *p. overcoat* (facetious), a pine box serving as a coffin (cf. PINE BOX); *p. quill*, =PINE NEEDLE; *p. settlement*, a settlement in a region covered with pines; *p. spill*, *p. tassel*, =PINE NEEDLE; *p. water*, water in which pieces of pine wood have been steeped; *p. work*, work of an ornamental nature made of pine wood or pine bark.

1842 THOREAU *Journal* I. 338, I need not think of the pine almond or the acorn and sapling when I meet the fallen pine or oak, more than of the generations of pines and oaks which have fed the young tree. **1863** B. ALCOTT *Journals* 360 In spring comes the hop and pine beer, and I take cocoa with my meals. **1862** NORTON *Army Lett.* 59 The three terrible forts at Centreville were mounted with pine cannon and sheet iron mortars, so the great Manassas humbug is exploded. **1805** LEWIS in *L. & Clark Exped.* II. (1904) 248 The pine cedar and balsum fir grow on the mountains in irregular assemb[l]ages or spots mostly high up on the sides and summits. **1799** *Herald of Freedom* (Edenton, N.C.) 27 March, Beginning at a pine corner of his own survey. **1855** SIMMS *Forayers* 434 A leetle pine-gum plaister on that head of yourn will stop up the sore places. **1902** WHITE *Blazed Trail* 5 We expect to cut this year some fifty millions, which will finish our pine holdings in the Saginaw waters. **1879** *Diseases of Swine* 214 Some old stock-raisers say that this disease [thumps] is always worse after a heavy pine mast, which my own experience confirms. **1859** *12th Rep. Penna. R.R.* 114 Articles of the third class . . . camphene and pine oil. **1896** *Congress. Rec.* 20 Jan. 796/2 The bill provides that the Committee shall . . . get as cheap a coffin as it can bargain for . . .—perhaps what they call in the army a pine overcoat. **1873** MILLER *Amongst Modocs* 180 On that side where only grass has grown and pine-quills fallen, . . . the ground is often broken. **1836** GILMAN *Recoll.* (1838) 51 Our summers were usually passed at Springland, a pine settlement. **1901** *Harper's Mag.* Dec. 45/2, I ain't goin' to have . . . [honey] full o' dry bark an' pine spills, dead bees, an' all them sorts o' trollick. **1858** WILLIS *Convalescent* 393 The wilderness [is] covered thick with a compost of pine-tassels and dead leaves. **1888** *Whitewater* (Wis.) *Reg.* 23 Feb., Oftentimes the simplest remedies, such as pine-water or shuck-tea, were made to serve a timely and efficient turn. **1868** *Mich. Agric. Rep.* VII. 357 Joseph Krusch, Detroit, [exhibited] pine work, horn of plenty.

* **Pineapple.**

1. The juicy, edible fruit of the tropical, agavelike plant *Ananus sativus*, or the plant itself. {1664–}

[**1686** *Relat. Invasion of Fla.* 11 They have a fruit there which they call Ananas, of the Shape and bigness of a Pine-apple, which hath a very good taste.] **1771** *Copley-Pelham Lett.* 145 With regard to the Pine Apples, [we] are very Glad you have had such plenty. **1850** TYSON *Diary in Calif.* 20 The citron, the pineapple, were scattered around in rich profusion. **1862** *Rep. Comm. Patents 1861: Agric.* 403 In this locality [tropical Florida] the cocoa-nut, date, guava, pineapple, banana, . . . and coffee, are all growing. **1905** BEACH *Pardners* i, I'd picked up a basket of tomatoes, a gunny-sack of pineapples, and a peck of green plums on the way.

attrib. **1842** 'UNCLE SAM' *Peculiarities* I. 43 Pine-apple Cider. **1882** RITTENHOUSE *Maud* 106 There we found music and flowers, and two tables set in arbors, with ice cream and pineapple ice. **1899** *Dept. Agric. Yrbk. 1898* 266 One of the most important problems in pineapple culture is to secure sorts with large fruits . . . and resistant to disease, especially pineapple blight.

2. A variety of cultivated strawberry. In full *pineapple strawberry.* {the fruit, 1860–}

1817–8 EATON *Botany* (1822) 282 *Fragaria grandiflora*, pineapple-strawberry. **1853** FOWLER *Home for All* 140 The Virginia seedling is an early variety (of strawberry). . . . The Pine-apple comes on later . . . , and on this account is valuable. **1863** GRAY *Botany* p. xlvii, *F[ragaria] Virginiana*, . . . and its crosses with the next have given origin to the Pineapple, and the greater part of the large sorts.

+**Pineapple bush.** ?The strawberry shrub. — **1881** *Harper's Mag.* April 744/1 There were [on Lost Island, La.] . . . pine-apple bushes bursting with blossoms; stiff magnolias half hiding their haughty flowers.

+**Pineapple cheese.** A cheese molded in the shape of a pineapple and suspended in netting to give the surface a reticulated appearance. — **1862** NORTON *Army Lett.* 104 The pineapple cheese was the great curiosity. **1893** HOWELLS *Coast of Bohemia* 204 Pine-apple cheese was Philistine.

+**Pineapple squash.** (See quotation.) — **1890** *Amer. Naturalist* XXIV. 732 The *Pine Apple* squash . . . was introduced in 1884. . . . It is a winter squash, creamy white when harvested, of a deep yellow at a later period. It belongs to *Cucurbita pepo.*

Pine bark. The bark of a pine tree, used for roofing or covering. — **1709** LAWSON *Carolina* 177 They make use of Pine-Bark [in making their Cabins]. **1800** HAWKINS *Sk. Creek Country* 71 These are covered with clay, and that with pine bark; the wall, six feet from the octagon, is clayed up.

+**Pine barren.** Chiefly *S.*

1. A tract of sandy or peaty land upon which the prevailing native growth is pine.

Cf. BARREN, OAK BARREN.

1735 *Ga. Hist. Soc. Coll.* II. 57 We rode about four miles on a direct course through an open pine barren, when we came to a large cane swamp. **1789** MORSE *Amer. Geog.* 429 The pine-barren . . . is valuable only for its timber. **1806** *Ann. 9th Congress* 2 Sess. 1112 These high lands are reported to be poor, and badly watered, being chiefly what is termed pine barren. **1893** *Harper's Mag.* April 753/2 The veiled forest had been left behind; the rest of the way lay over the pine-barrens. **1901** MOHR *Plant Life Ala.* 779 *Sericocarpus bifoliatus.* . . . Mouse Ears. . . . Common in the pine barrens of the Coast Pine belt.

transf. **1830** PAULDING *Chron. Gotham* 26 Mr. Puddingham . . . had so over-cultivated a thin-soiled intellect, that he . . . turned it into a pine-barren.

b. With particular reference to the quality of soil in a region of this kind.

1737 WESLEY *Journal* I. 401 The land [in Ga.] is of four sorts—pine-barren, oak-land, swamp, and marsh. **1812** STODDARD *Sk. Louisiana* 122 In the two Floridas are to be found a variety of soils. . . . The first is denominated pine barrens, which extend over almost the whole of the peninsula. **1842** BUCKINGHAM *Slave States* I. 38 The sixth is the pine barren.

2. Attrib. and comb. with *country*, *land*, *pond*, etc.

1743 CATESBY *Carolina* II. p. iv, The third and worst kind of Land is the Pine barren Land, the name implying its character. **1832** WATSON *Hist. Tales N.Y.* 39 [Schenectady] derived its Indian name from its situation, as placed in a surrounding pine-barren country. **1868** GRAY *Botany* 682 [The sedge (*Carex glaucescens*) grows in] pine-barren ponds from Portsmouth, Virginia . . . southward. **1901** MOHR *Plant Life Ala.* 125 Descending from the rolling hills to the flats of the coast plain the pine-barren streams overflow their low banks of shifting sands and gravel.

b. In special combinations.

Pine-barren beauty, the pyxie (*Pyxidanthera barbulata*), a small creeping evergreen; *p.-b. sundrop*, a species of sundrop of the genus *Kneiffia* found in pine barrens in the South; *p.-b. terrapin*, (see quotation).

[**1884** W. MILLER *Dict. Names of Plants* 106/2 Pine-barren Beauty. *Pyxidanthera barbulata.*] **1901** MOHR *Plant Life Ala.* 638 *Kneiffia linearis.* . . . Pine-barren Sundrops. . . . Southern Virginia along the coast to Florida, west to Louisiana. **1884** GOODE, etc. *Fisheries* I. 158 The Carolina Box Turtle [*Cistudo carolina*]. . . . In the Southern States it is known as the 'Pine-barren Terrapin.'

Pine-blank, *adv*. Point-blank. *colloq*. — **a1871** in De Vere 624 His temper was sharp and high, but steady; as it never fell into feebleness, so it never rose into rage; the percisely and pineblank tone of feeling, ever present, kept him too well balanced for that. **1889** RILEY *Pipes o' Pan* 45, I ast her Pine-blank, ef she ever missed me!

+**Pine bluff.** A bluff overgrown with pines. — **1766** J. BARTRAM *Journal* 41 We rowed . . . by some oak and pine-bluffs. **1821** NUTTALL *Trav. Arkansa* 100 [We] came in sight of another pine bluff of about 100 feet elevation. **1868** LOSSING *Hudson* 12 We drew our boats upon a pebbly shore at twilight, at the foot of a pine-bluff.

Pine board. A board made from a pine tree. {1825, in Jamaica}. Also collect.

1638 *Dedham Rec.* III. 39 To alowe for saweing Pyne board 5 s. **1696** *Boston Rec.* 137 He . . . [shall] lay both chamber and garrett Floore with good plained Seasoned pine boards. **1706** *N.H. Probate Rec.* I. 556 Five or Six thousand ffoot of merch[an]table pine boards at the Currant money price. **1806** *Balance* V. 156/1, 17,000 feet of pine boards. **1899** JEWETT *Queen's Twin* 107 Johnny would unload a few feet of clean pine boards from the freight train.

attrib. **1843** *Knickerb.* XXII. 325 'The fortifications' . . . consisted of a pine-board enclosure. **1847** *Ib.* XXX. 207 No more pine-board and calico-gown religion would be done by Mrs. Wiggins. **1872** 'MARK TWAIN' *Roughing It* 43 The rocking-chairs and sofas . . . were represented by two three-legged stools, a pine-board bench four feet long, and two empty candle-boxes.

+**Pine-borer.** Any one of various insect larvae that bore into pine trees. — **1862** *Rep. Comm. Patents 1861: Agric.* 614 The larvæ [*sic*] of this insect is evidently a pine-borer, for I have found it about saw-mills. **1884** *Rep. Comm. Agric.* 379 The Common Longicorn Pine-Borer . . . is destructive to the white pine.

Pine box. A box made of pine boards, +esp. one used as a coffin. — **a1846** *Quarter Race Ky.* 86 *Ar* you a goin to tum-tum all nite on that pot-gutted old pine box of a fiddle? **1867** HOLMES *Guardian Angel* 406 The long pine boxes came by almost every train,—no need of asking what they held! **1890** LANGFORD *Vigilante Days* (1912) 533 A company of twenty or more men approaching the station, bearing in their midst a long pine box. **1907** 'O. HENRY' *Strictly Business* 50 Standing on a pine box a head higher than his flock of goats, the Preacher exhorted whatever transient and shifting audience the north wind doled out to him.

Pine brush. Pine bushes or boughs cut from pine trees. — **1703** *Manchester Rec.* I. 103 It is voted to work two Days in a year to cut Down pine and hemlock brush. **1874** *Dept. Agric. Rep. 1873* 169 Some planters . . . plowed between the rows with pine-brush fastened to the swingle-tree in order to sweep off the caterpillars from the plants on to the ground.

Pine bullfinch. =PINE GROSBEAK. — **1828** BONAPARTE *Ornithology* III. 17 The female Pine Bullfinch is eight and a half inches long. **1844** *Nat. Hist. N.Y., Zoology* II. 181 The Pine Bulfinch . . . visits sparingly the Atlantic district of this State during the autumn and winter. **1917** *Birds of Amer.* III. 3 Pine Grosbeak. *Pinicola enucleator leucura*. . . . [Also called] Pine Bullfinch.

+**Pine bur.** =next. — **1800** HAWKINS *Sk. Creek Country* 77 They collect old corn cobs and pine burs. **1804** CLARK in *Lewis & C. Exped.* I. (1904) 149 They Saw as well as my self Pine *burs* & Sticks of Birch in the Drift wood up [the White R.]. **1836** SIMMS *Mellichampe* xx, You should be pelted with pine-burs, and I will undertake your punishment before the day is well over. **1899** GREEN *Va. Word-Book* 276 *Pine-burr*, the cone of the pine-tree.

Pine cone. The cone or fruit of the pine tree. {1695-} Also attrib. — **1839** EMERSON in *Western Messenger* VII. 230 Pine-cones and acorns lay on the ground. **1883** *Harper's Mag.* Oct. 711/1 Can't you throw something at it to make it fly! Try a pine cone. **1899** JEWETT *Queen's Twin* 20 There's always a new fashion o' frames comin' round; first 'twas shell-work, and then 'twas pine-cones, and bead-work's had its day. **1909** 'O. HENRY' *Strictly Business* 134, I looked around for the portrait of Andrew Jackson and the pine-cone hanging basket.

+**Pine creeper.** =PINE WARBLER. — **c1730** CATESBY *Carolina* I. 61 *Parus Americanus lutescens*. The Pine-creeper. . . . They creep about Trees; particularly the Pine- and Fir-trees; from which they peck Insects, and feed on them. **1789** MORSE *Amer. Geog.* 59 American Birds . . . enumerated [include] . . . Pine Creeper, Yellow throated Creeper, Dove. **1837** WILLIAMS *Florida* 74 There are many birds in Florida . . . [including the] Pine Creeper. **1917** *Birds of Amer.* III. 148 Pine Warbler. *Dendroica vigorsi*. . . . [Also called] Pine-creeping Warbler; Pine Creeper.

+**Pine creeping warbler.** =PINE WARBLER. — **1811** WILSON *Ornithology* III. 25 [The] Pine-Creeping Warbler . . . inhabits the pine woods of the Southern states, where it is resident. **1866** J. G. WOOD *Homes without Hands* 267 The Pine-Creeping Warbler is found in the pine-woods of the Southern States. **1868** *Amer. Naturalist* II. 170 The Pine-creeping Warbler . . . affects, principally, the evergreen woods, but is often met with in other places. **1917** [see prec.].

+**Pinedrops.** A stout, purplish brown plant (*Pterospora andromedea*) found in stiff clay soil on the roots of pine trees. (Cf. *Albany beech-drops* under ALBANY.) — **1857** GRAY *Botany* 261 *Pterospora*. Pine-drops. . . . *P. Andromedea*.—Hard clay soil, parasitic on the roots apparently of pines, from Vermont, Peekskill and Albany, N.Y., and N. Pennsylvania northward and westward: rare. **1890** *Cent.* 4826/2 *P*[*terospora*] *andromedea*, known as 'pine drops,' is a slender, purplish-brown herb. **1899** GOING *Flowers* 260 In July pine-roots give a home and a maintenance to some curious parasitic plants—'pine-drops,' 'pine-sap,' and 'Indian-pipe' or 'ghost-flower.'

Pine finch. {1894-} +A small North American bird, *Spinus pinus*. (Cf. PINE LINNET, PINE SISKIN.) — **1810** WILSON *Ornithology* II. 133 [The] Pine Finch . . . seeks the seeds of the black alder, on the borders of swamps, creeks and rivulets. **1828** BONAPARTE *Synopsis* 111 The Pine Finch . . . inhabits the northern regions. **1871** BURROUGHS *Wake-Robin* (1886) 96, I observed several pine finches, a dark brown or brindled bird, allied to the common yellow-bird. **1917** [see PINE SISKIN].

+**Pine flat.** A level tract of land covered with pines. (Cf. FLAT *n.* 2 c, OAK FLAT.) — **1807** IRVING, etc. *Salmagundi* xvi. 421 Some . . . enjoy the varied and romantic scenery of burnt trees, . . . pine flats [etc.]. **1819** E. DANA *Geogr. Sk.* 196 Along the Tensaw . . . are cane swamps, interspersed with pine flats, covered with soil suitable for sugar, cotton or corn. **1866** W. REID *After the War* 416 Between New Orleans and Jackson, one saw little to admire in the pine flats that lined the railroad for nearly its whole length.

Pine forest. A forest of pine trees. {1822-} — **1799** C. B. BROWN *A. Mervyn* ii, Betty Lawrence was a wild girl from the pine-forests of New Jersey. **1839** HOFFMAN *Wild Scenes* 28 The demolition of the pine forests . . . will rapidly clear the country. **1877** ALDRICH *Queen of Sheba* 10 Almost any one might mistake . . . the agreeable rustle of her garments for the wind blowing through the pine forests. **1913** LONDON *Valley of Moon* 472 Vainly Saxon's eye roved the pine forest in search of her beloved redwoods.

Pine grosbeak. A large fringilline bird, *Pinicola enucleator*. (Cf. PINE BULLFINCH.) — [**1772** *Phil. Trans.* LXII. 402 [The] Pine Grosbeak . . . visits the Hudson's Bay settlements in May, on its way to the north, and is not observed to return.] **1808** WILSON *Ornithology* I. 80 [The] Pine Grosbeak . . . is perhaps one of the gayest plumaged land birds that frequent the inhospitable regions of the north. **1839** PEABODY *Mass. Birds* 331 The Pine Grosbeak . . . comes to us at irregular intervals, either in winter or when that season is nigh. **1890** *Atlantic Mo.* Aug. 255/2 [I] saw with perfect distinctness . . . two pine grosbeaks in bright male costume, —birds I had never seen before except in winter. **1917** *Birds of Amer.* III. 5 In western North America are several varieties of the Pine Grosbeak.

+**Pine grouse.** The dusky grouse (*Dendragapus obscurus*) of the Rocky Mountain region. — **1860** SUCKLEY & COOPER *Nat. Hist. of Wash. Terr. & Oregon* 220 This bird, called generally in Oregon the blue Grouse, also known as pine grouse, dusky grouse, &c., I met, for the first time, when our exploring party reached the main chain of the Rocky mountains. **1917** *Birds of Amer.* II. 12 Dusky Grouse. *Dendragapus obscurus obscurus*. . . . [Also called] Blue Grouse; Pine Grouse; Pine Hen [etc.].

Pine hen. =prec. — **1883** *Harper's Mag.* Oct. 711/1 The 'pine hen' immediately commenced hopping up from branch to branch farther into the tree. **1917** [see prec.].

Pine hill. A hill overgrown with pines. — **1654** *Boston Rec.* 16 The land running northward upon a straite line untill it cometh to range even with north side of the shop . . . and pine hill south. **1693** *Waterbury Prop. Rec.* 38 A pes of land at the pin hill. **1772** in *Cincinnati Misc.* I. 245/2 Here we have pine hills, but they do not appear too poor to raise good wheat. **1846** SAGE *Scenes Rocky Mts.* xii, Undulating prairie, bounded on either side by pine hills.

attrib. **1857** STROTHER *Virginia* 203 He was the acknowledged cock of the walk, and *preux chevalier* of the pine-hill country.

+**Pine knot.**

1. A knot of pine wood. (Cf. KNOT.)

1670 *Plymouth Rec.* 119 There shalbe noe pine knot picked. **1761** NILES *Indian Wars* II. 421 Throwing pine-knots and other combustible matter against the walls. **1823** COOPER *Pioneers* xxxviii, The kearless fellows . . . had thrown the lighted pine-knots in the brush. **1897** *Outing* XXX. 69/2, I held a pine-knot for him to make the entry in our log-book. **1917** COMSTOCK *Man* 5 Conning Truedale stretched his long legs out toward Jim White's roaring fire of pine knots and cones.

transf. **1856** MACLEOD *F. Wood* 48 That human pine-knot John C. Calhoun. **1876** WARNER *Gold of Chickaree* 360 Relaxation! . . . When you know as well as I do, that you are a pine knot for endurance.

2. In fig. expressions with reference to the toughness, compactness, or hardness of pine knots.

1812 PAULDING *J. Bull & Bro. Jon.* 5 Jonathan, though as hard as a pine-knot, . . . could bear it no longer. **1850** WATSON *Camp-Fires Revol.* 31 But we stuck to them close as pine-knots, sending one after another out of misery. **1904** STRATTON-PORTER *Freckles* 95 He was as tough as a pine-knot and as agile as a panther.

+**Pine-knot fire.** A fire made of pine-wood knots. — **1830** *Mass. Spy* 26 May (Th.), At night parties collect by a pine-knot fire, and play cards for the earnings of the day. **1853** 'P. PAXTON' *Yankee in Texas* 310 We stood confessed with the bright light of a pineknot fire shining full upon us. **1894** *Harper's Mag.* Oct. 714/1 A pine-knot fire was soon kindled on the hearth.

+**Pine-knot torch.** A burning pine knot used as a torch. — **1808** BARKER *Indian Princess* III. i, [She] lit me with her pine-knot torch to bedward. **1877** HALE *G.T.T.* 111 From the depths appeared two great pine-knot torches.

+**Pineland.** Land upon which pine is the prevailing or characteristic growth. (Cf. HICKORY LAND, OAK LAND.)

c1660 *Lancaster Rec.* 271 Thare is another peice of upland . . . which buts northerly upon Common Land Sum part pine Land partly oak Land. **1709** LAWSON *Carolina* 68 [We] found some Tracts of good Ground . . . but backwards some two Miles, all Pine Land. **1784** CUTLER in *Life &*

Corr. I. 97 We traveled fifteen miles in Rochester—plain, pine land, thin soil, houses low and poor. **1821** NUTTALL *Travels Arkansa* 99 The pine land is here, as every where else, poor and unfit for cultivation. **1883** SMITH *Geol. Survey Ala.* 540 With the use of guano these pine lands bring very fair crops. **1916** EASTMAN *From Deep Woods* 160 The Ojibways have much valuable pine land, aggregating millions of dollars.

attrib. **1845** SIMMS *Wigwam & Cabin* 2 Ser. 105 'Possum Place' . . . consisted pretty evenly of reclaimed swamp-land . . . and fine high pine-land hammock, on which he raised his corn. **1903** PRINGLE *Rice Planter* 53 Drove S—— to church in our little pine-land village; she seemed to enjoy the very simple service.

+**Pinelander.** One who lives in pinelands. — **1839** KEMBLE *Residence in Ga.* 75 He gave me a lively and curious description of the Yeomanry of Georgia, more properly termed pine-landers. **1890** *Harper's Mag.* April 790/1 Quaint and indolent pine-landers and degraded swamp-dwellers, have all supplied our literary comedians with unique characters.

Pine leaf. =PINE NEEDLE. — **1834** WHITTIER *Poetical Works* (1894) 496/2 In the pine-leaves fine and small, Soft and sweetly musical. **1856** STOWE *Dred* I. 102 No sound was heard but the shivering wind, . . . through the long pine-leaves. **1885** *N.H. Forestry Comm. Rep.* June 83 Mulching with sphagnum, chaff, sawdust, or pine-leaves, will preserve a more uniform degree of humidity.

+**Pine linnet.** =PINE FINCH. — **1874** COUES *Birds N.W.* 115 Pine Linnet. . . . The erratic movements of this species . . . render it difficult to define its limits with precision. **1899** GOING *Flowers* 269 The brooding silence of the evergreen woods is broken . . . by the tremulous whistle of the pine-linnet, or the bell-like notes of the hermit-thrush. **1917** [see PINE SISKIN].

+**Pine lizard.** =FENCE LIZARD. — **1842** *Nat. Hist. N.Y., Zoology* III. 33 From its abundance in pine forests, [the brown swift] has obtained the name of Pine Lizard. **1895** *Outing* XXVI. 34/2 A pine lizard ran up the trunk of a cedar tree.

Pine log. A log consisting of or obtained from the trunk of a pine tree.

1694 *Mass. H. S. Coll.* 4 Ser. I. 105 Ye town is incompass'd with a fortification, consisting of pine-logs. **1807** IRVING, etc. *Salmagundi* x, Floating bridge made of pine logs fastened together by ropes of walnut bark. **1865** KELLOGG *Rebel Prisons* 180, I quietly shouldered a *pine log*, which lay invitingly near the road-side. **1902** WHITE *Blazed Trail* 266 The instant necessity was to get thirty millions of pine logs down the river.

attrib. **1869** ALDRICH *Bad Boy* 14 He proceeded at once to knock down all my pine-log houses. **1873** MILLER *Amongst Modocs* 73 The principal saloon . . . was the 'Howlin' Wilderness'; an immense pine-log cabin.

b. In a place name.

1747 *Georgia Col. Rec.* VI. 199 John Hencock petitioned for two hundred and fifty Acres of Land at a place called Pine Logg Bluff.

+**Pine lot.** A lot or area upon which pine trees grow or are grown. — **1840** *Knickerb.* XVI. 206 These [land-lookers] met you at every turn, ready to furnish 'water-power,' 'pine-lots,' . . . or any thing else, at a moment's notice. **1905** *Forestry Bureau Bul.* No. 63, 16 This map is not designed to show the merchantable pine lots in New England.

+**Pine lumber.** Lumber obtained from pines. — **1803** *Ann. 8th Congress* 2 Sess. 1506 The country on the east side of Lake Pontchartrain . . . would, however, afford abundant supplies of pitch, tar, and pine lumber. **1837** WILLIAMS *Florida* 115 Our exports consist of . . . pine lumber, staves, . . . bees-wax, peltries and oranges. **1890** Langford *Vigilante Days* (1912) 499 In three days our craft was completed. She was as stanch as pine lumber and nails could make her.

Pine marten. {1768–} The American marten, *Martes americana*, or a related species. — [**1768** PENNANT *Brit. Zoology* (1776) I. 78 Pine Martin. . . . This species is found in Great Britain. . . . North America abounds with these animals.] **1826** GODMAN *Nat. Hist.* I. 201 The pine marten resembles the ermine weasel in habits and disposition. **1838** *Mass. Zool. Survey Rep.* 25 *Mustela Martes.* Pine Marten. . . . Is found in the vicinity of Williamstown. The fur is beautiful and much esteemed. **1917** *Mammals of Amer.* 113 American Marten. *Martes* (=*Mustela*) *americana* (Turton). Other Names.—Pine Marten, American Sable.

+**Pine mouse.** A reddish brown vole, *Microtus pinetorum*, found often in pine barrens. — **1851** AUDUBON *Quadrupeds N. Amer.* II. 216 *Arvicola Pinetorum.* . . . Leconte's Pine-Mouse. . . . This species bears some resemblance to Wilson's Meadow Mouse. **1885** *Amer. Naturalist* XIX. 895 On the 13th of June, 1884, at my home in Lewis county, New York, I caught a female pine mouse. **1917** *Mammals of Amer.* 249/1 From their homes in woods and thickets Pine Mice invade fields, orchards, nurseries, dooryards, and gardens, passing always through underground runways.

Pine needle. The long needlelike leaf of the pine. — **1866** Higginson *Harvard Mem. Biog.* I. 410 The dry leaves and pine-needles are as luxurious to lie on. **1898** *Outing* April 24/1 We wheeled down the road a short distance and pitched camp in a quiet nook where a soft carpet of yielding pine-needles covered the ground. **1901** WHITE *Westerners* 175 The pine needles were soft and slippery and fragrant underfoot. **1909** 'O. HENRY' *Options* 150 Up the faint pathway, slippery with its carpet of pine-needles, toiled Beatrix.

***Pine nut.** +The edible seed of various low-growing pines, as the piñon, found in the western and southwestern parts of the United States. — **1845** FRÉMONT *Exped.* 222 A party of twelve Indians came down from the mountains to trade pine nuts, of which each one carried a little bag. These seemed now to be the staple of the country. **1866** *Rep. Indian Affairs* 114 They also obtain quantities of pine-nuts from the groves of the piñon, which in places cover the mountain sides. **1898** HARTE *Stories in Light & Shadow* 46 We had to grub on pine nuts and jackass-rabbits.

+**Pine oak.** ?Error for PIN OAK. — **1835** IRVING *Tour on Prairies* 184 There is a pine-oak which produces an acorn pleasant to the taste.

+**Pine plain.** A plain covered with pine trees. (Cf. PINE BARREN, PINE FLAT.) — **1665** *Lancaster Rec.* 79 A slipe of medow ground Runing through the most part of a great pine plaine. **1725** Kidder *Exped. Lovewell* (1865) 76 Capt. Lovewell's men being between the brook and the Pond, it being a Pine Plain. **1789** WASHINGTON *Diaries* IV. 30 For the first 8 miles rid over an almost uninhabited Pine plain; much mixed with sand. *a***1817** DWIGHT *Travels* II. 37 The road after leaving Providence lay for two or three miles on a pine plain; and was tolerably good. **1860** GREELEY *Overland Journey* 111 The surrounding prairies—sterile as 'pine plains' are apt to be.

Pine plantation. A tract or area upon which pines are grown. {1775–} — **1870** EMERSON *Soc. & Solitude* 144 In Massachusetts we fight . . . the blowing sand-barrens with pine plantations. **1874** *Dept. Agric. Rep. 1873* 283 Valuable pine-plantations have also been formed in other towns on [Cape Cod].

Piner. {1891–} *local.* +A resident of the Pines of New Jersey. (Cf. PINE 3.) — **1894** *Dialect Notes* I. 332 *Piners:* those who live in the Jersey pines,—the 'ridge' sections (eastern and southern) of the state. **1894** *Harper's Mag.* Aug. 337/1 The term 'piners' is synonymous with the term 'poor whites' in the South.

+**Pine ridge.** A ridge overgrown with pines. Also as a place name. (Cf. OAK RIDGE.) — **1802** ELLICOTT *Journal* 184 On one of the pine ridges I saw a few stones. **1821** NUTTALL *Travels Arkansa* 164 In the course of the afternoon, we passed over three pine ridges, and two creeks. **1851** HOOPER *Simon Suggs' Adv.* ix, Soon they had reached the long, straight pine ridge upon which the game was to be played. **1889** VASEY *Agric. Grasses* 26 Para Grass . . . makes a heavy growth on the high pine ridges of Florida. **1916** EASTMAN *From Deep Woods* 119, I found at Pine Ridge no conveyance for the doctor's professional use.

Pinery. {1758–} A large tract or area of pine forest {1831–}, +esp. one in which lumbering operations are carried on. Also attrib. — **1822** *Mass. Spy* 30 Jan. (Th.), [We] found a continued pinery for about a mile. **1857** *Lawrence* (Kan.) *Republican* 23 July 4 That traveler, in the pineries of North Carolina, . . . entered a cabin. **1882** *Harper's Mag.* Dec. 12/1 When the timber shall have been stripped from the pineries of Maine, Michigan and Wisconsin, the magnificent fir forests of the northwest coast will prove a great source of supply. **1906** *Wausau* (Wis.) *Pilot* 24 July, In a month or so they [the cattle] would be fat enough for pinery beef. **1907** ANDREWS *Recoll.* 276 The great region of pineries had not yet been surveyed, much less sold by the government.

+**Pinesap.** Any one of various herbs of the genus *Hypopitys*, esp. *H. lanuginosa*, false beech-drops. Also attrib. (Cf. BEECH-DROPS 3.) — **1840** DEWEY *Mass. Flowering Plants* 108 *M[onotropa] lanuginosa.* Pine Sap. . . . By many the plant is considered a parasytic, deriving nourishment by its roots from the roots of other plants. **1857** GRAY *Lessons Botany* 35 Other parasitic plants, like the Beech-drops and Pine-sap, fasten their roots under ground upon the roots of neighboring plants. **1869** FULLER *Flower Gatherers* 190 It is an oddity of the species, which is '*Monotropa hypopytis*,' or Pine Sap. **1901** MOHR *Plant Life Ala.* 652 Monotropaceae. Pinesap Family. . . . *Hypopitys hypopitys.* . . . Pinesap.

+**Pine savanna.** A savanna with a scattered growth of pines. (Cf. PINE BARREN, FLAT, PLAIN.) — **1735** *Ga. Hist. Soc. Coll.* II. 43 We rode about two miles farther, where we came to a large pine savannah. **1791** W. BARTRAM *Travels* 208 The cattle which only feed and range in the high forests and Pine savannas are clear of this disorder.

+**Pine shingle.** A shingle made of pine. Also attrib. and fig. (Cf. CEDAR SHINGLE, CYPRESS SHINGLE.) — **1836** NICKLIN *Peregrination* 20 The roofs are in general of cedar, cypress or pine shingles. **1855** M. THOMPSON *Doesticks* 217, [I] admired the easy and graceful scenery painted on the 'drop,' which looks as if it was whittled out of a pine shingle. **1869** STOWE *Oldtown Folks* 445 You think the universe will go to pieces if we upset your pine-shingle theology. **1876** 'MARK TWAIN' *Tom Sawyer* x. 95 He picked up a clean pine shingle . . . and painfully scrawled these lines.

+**Pine siskin.** =PINE FINCH. — **1887** RIDGWAY *Man. N.A. Birds* 400 Northern North America, breeding from northern United States northward, and south in Rocky Mountains; south, in winter, to Gulf States and Mexico. . . . Pine Siskin. **1917** *Birds of Amer.* III. 16 Pine Siskin. . . . [Also called] Pine Finch; Pine Linnet; American Siskin.

+**Pine slab.** The rough board or puncheon first sawed from a pine log in working it up into planks; an outer portion split or slabbed from a pine log in hewing it. — **1666** *East-Hampton Rec.* I. 248 A Pine slab by the well with my lath bench. **1800** HAWKINS *Sk. Creek Country* 71 The fire is made, of . . . dry old pine slabs. **1881** *Chicago Times* 16 April, About everybody who keeps house in Chicago has paid $7 per cord for pine slabs for kindling-wood. *c***1908** CANTON *Frontier Trails* 95 We built breastworks at the ranch building from heavy pine slabs.

+**Pine snake.** Any one of various harmless snakes of the genus *Pituophis*, esp. *P. melanoleucus*, commonly found in pine woods in the Atlantic coast region. (Cf. BULL SNAKE, GOPHER SNAKE.) — **1791** W. BARTRAM *Travels* 276 The pine or bull snake is very large, and inoffensive with respect to mankind. **1837** WILLIAMS *Florida* 67 The Pine Snake is long and slender also. **1875** *Amer. Naturalist* IX. 6 There is nothing sibilant in this blowing of the pine snake. **1895** *Outing* XXVI. 39/2 A pine snake, bloated and glistening, wriggles across the road.

+**Pine squirrel.** A squirrel found in coniferous forests, esp. *Sciurus hudsonicus*, the common American red squirrel. (Cf. CHICKAREE.) — **1857** *Rep. Comm. Patents 1856: Agric.* 67 This pretty and active little animal is well known through the Northern States, under the names of Red-Squirrel,' 'Chickaree,' 'Pine Squirrel,' and, sometimes, 'Mountain Squirrel.' **1873** MILLER *Amongst Modocs* 187 Little foxy-looking pine squirrels with pink eyes, stopped from their work of hoarding them [*sc.* pine nuts] for winter, to look or chatter at us. **1897** *Outing* XXX. 456/2 The nimble pine-squirrel has his home in a tufty bough of the tallest, most tapering pine-tree. **1917** *Mammals of Amer.* 168 Eastern Red Squirrel. *Sciurus hudsonicus.* . . . [Also called] Chickaree, Pine Squirrel. *Ib.* 171 Fremont's Chickaree. *Sciurus fremonti.* . . . [Also called] Pine Squirrel.

+**Pine straw.** Dried pine needles. Also attrib. — **1832** KENNEDY *Swallow Barn* I. 295 The ground was strewed with a thick coat of pine-straw. **1845** SIMMS *Wigwam & Cabin* 1 Ser. 178 His negro-houses . . . [were] temporary shanties, covered with poles and thatched with bark and pine-straw. **1884** CABLE *Dr. Sevier* lvii, Mary Richling . . . still had on the pine-straw hat. **1905** PRINGLE *Rice Planter* 217 The stables not cleaned, no pine straw hauled for bedding.

+**Pine stump.** The stump of a pine tree. Also attrib.

1659 *Watertown Rec.* I. i. 65 Abram Brownes Land . . . begins ten rod from Rich. Bloyse his lott, & soe apon a straite line to a pine stump. **1684** *Manchester Rec.* 15 And from s[ai]d burtch stump to a pine stump. **1729** *Ib.* 177 Near the pond aGoing Down the hill . . . thence to a pine stump with stones about it. **1816** *Niles' Reg.* IX. Suppl. 178/1 Many a farmer . . . dreaded the pine stump as an enemy which would survive himself and annoy his heirs. **1894** *Home Missionary* Oct. 328 This pine-stump land . . . is proving to be the best potato land in the world. *Ib.* 329 Another of these pine-stump country churches granted twenty-three letters last year to members who have gone into the cities.

+**Pine swamp.** A swamp in which pines grow. (Cf. CEDAR SWAMP, CYPRESS SWAMP.) — **1635** *Cambridge Prop. Rec.* 6 The pine Swamp on the north east. **1699** *Boston Rec.* 236 A small tree called Dogg-wood right against a great pine swamp. **1705** *Providence Rec.* XVII. 207 At the south End of a Piece of Meaddow & a Pine Swampe. **1756** *Doc. Hist. N.Y. State* I. 483 The enemy . . . had possessed themselves of a thick Pine Swamp. **1862** NORTON *Army Lett.* 62 We are bivouacked in a pine swamp.

+**Pine-swamp warbler.** The black-throated blue warbler, *Dendroica caerulescens.* — **1812** WILSON *Ornithology* V. 100 The Pine-swamp Warbler is four inches and a quarter long, and seven inches and a quarter in extent. **1828** BONAPARTE *Synopsis* 85.

+**Pine tag.** *S.* (See quot. 1899 and cf. PINE LEAF, NEEDLE, STRAW.) — **1851** *S. Lit. Messenger* XVII. 226/2 We made [a bonfire] of dead boughs and 'pine-tags.' **1881** *Harper's Mag.* Nov. 868/2 At night they [*sc.* mountain people] lie down on their pine-tag beds. **1899** GREEN *Va. Word-Book* 276 *Pine-tag*, the needle or leaf of the pine-tree.

Pine tar. Tar obtained from pine wood. Also attrib. — **1880** *Harper's Mag.* Oct. 806/1 My pine-tar balsam . . . drives a cough away. **1903** WHITE *Forest* 106 Eager advocates of the advantages of pork fat, kerosene, pine tar [as an insectifuge], . . . will assure you . . . that his is the only true faith.

Pine thicket. A thicket of pine trees or shrubs. — **1836** *Southern Hist. Jrnl.* I. 367, I have been lost nearly all day . . . , wandering about in pine thickets—cane thickets, and all sorts of thickets. **1855** SIMMS *Forayers* 430 Moving rapidly through an open pine thicket. **1867** J. M. CRAWFORD *Mosby* 109 The recruit . . . overtook Ab Wren and Walker Whaley converging from the dense pine thicket, leading horses. **1888** HARRIS *Free Joe* 12 Major Frampton sauntered into a convenient pine thicket, and blew out his brains.

Pine top. +(See quot. 1899.) *slang.* — **1858** *S. Lit. Messenger* XXVII. 463/2 A rough, but hearty frolic, characteristic of the time and place, with . . . profusion of 'pine-top' succeeded. **1869** *Overland Mo.* III. 130 'Pinetop' is a kind of mean turpentine whisky of North Carolina. **1883** *Congress. Rec.* 1 Feb. 1898/2 A man in this country can not take a drink of American whisky, be it the Cincinnati bust-head or the North Carolina pine-top, however distilled, without paying 200 per cent. on it. **1899** GREEN *Va. Word-Book* 276 *Pinetop*, cheap, adulterated whisky, said to be made of pinetags.

Pine torch. A torch made of pitch pine wood. — **1825** NEAL *Bro. Jonathan* II. 71 All carrying great pine torches. **1852** WATSON *Nights in Block-House* 135 Blazing pine-torches are affixed to the wall on two sides of the room. **1896** HARRIS *Sister Jane* 36 By the dim light of the pine-torch . . . [I] saw a woman huddled in one corner.

***Pine tree.**

*1. A tree belonging to the genus *Pinus.*

1630 HIGGINSON *New-England* 16 Yea our Pine-Trees that are the most plentifull of all wood, doth allow vs plentie of Candles. **1700** *Providence Rec.* IV. 141 Northeast Corner is a pine tree marked standing in a swampe. **1749** *N.H. Probate Rec.* III. 751 The Remender . . . is to be Made up from the Marked pine tree on the fare Huckellberry hill streght to the head of allon andorsons uper Meadow. **1834** A. PIKE *Sketches* 28, I reached a clump of eight or ten pine trees. **1891** RYAN *Pagan* 96 She had halted a moment, leaning, panting and tired, against one of the pine-trees. **1916** PORTER *David* 62 If you've only heard them daytimes, you don't know a bit what pine trees really are.

+2. In special combinations.

Pine-tree beetle, =PINE-BORER; *pine-tree cod*, (see quotation); *pine-tree currency*, =PINE-TREE MONEY; *pine-tree flag*, the flag of the colony of Massachusetts, (see quotation); *pine-tree rattlesnake*, a rattlesnake found in pine woods.

1854 EMMONS *Agric. N.Y.* V. 262 (*index*), Pinetree beetles, 82, 83 [etc.]. **1884** GOODE, etc. *Fisheries* I. 201 In Southeastern Maine the name 'Pine-tree Cod' is also in use [as a name for the cod]. **1893** HALE *New Eng. Boyhood* 76 Old-fashioned New Englanders will to this hour speak of seventy-five cents as 'four-and-six-pence,' or of thirty-seven and a half cents as 'two-and-threepence.' These measures are in pine-tree currency. **1896** *Peterson Mag.* ns. VI. 288/2 These vessels all sailed under the pine-tree flag. This flag was of white bunting, on which was painted a green pine-tree, and upon the reverse the motto: 'Appeal to Heaven.' **1887** CUSTER *Tenting on Plains* 139 The most venomous of snakes, called the pine-tree rattlesnake.

+**Pine-tree money.** (See quot. 1864.) Now hist. — **1864** WEBSTER *Pine-tree money*, money coined in Massachusetts in the seventeenth century, and so called from its bearing a figure resembling a pine-tree. **1894** LEAVITT *Our Money Wars* 3 In 1652 a mint was set up in Boston to coin silver into what was called 'Pine Tree' money.

+**Pine-tree shilling.** A silver shilling coined in Massachusetts (1652–*c*1684) having a device of a tree, presumably a pine, in a field surrounded by a circle of dots. Now hist. Also attrib. — **1857** *Amer. Notes & Q.* July (B.), The wide-awake citizens of Boston have been sadly bitten by a bogus issue of the old 'Pine-tree Shilling currency.' **1885** BAYLOR *On Both Sides* 208 The coins now rare and no longer in use, such as the Continental paper money, the pine-tree shillings, [etc.]. **1889** COOKE *Steadfast* 140 She wasn't left so much as a pine-tree shillin' in't. **1902** S. G. FISHER *True Hist. Amer. Revol.* 20 [The colonists of Mass.] coined their own money, and issued the famous pine-tree shilling.

+**Pine-Tree State.** The state of Maine. A nickname. — **1860** *Harper's Mag.* March 454/2 The 'Pine-tree State,' like a Yankee clock with wooden works, would cease to run without its *main-spring* [*i.e.*, the lumber industry]. **1883** *Wheelman* I. 333 This was not because there are no good roads in the Pine Tree State. **1896** *Vt. Agric. Rep.* XV. 81 In Maine, 'the Pine-tree State,' the pine as a lumber tree is already a thing of the past. **1906** *Churchman* 2 June 898 There are no more pine trees in the 'Pine Tree State.'

+**Pine warbler.** A small, migratory, insectivorous bird (*Dendroica pinus* or *vigorsi*) inhabiting pine woods throughout eastern North America. (Cf. PINE CREEPER, PINE CREEPING WARBLER.) — **1839** PEABODY *Mass. Birds* 310 The Pine Warbler . . . is not much known, because it resides in deep, evergreen forests. **1868** *Amer. Naturalist* II. 171 Soon after the pine-warbler has arrived, . . . the Yellow Red-polled Warbler . . . makes his appearance. **1892** TORREY *Foot-Path Way* 191, I came upon . . . three goodly throngs, including . . . black-throated blue warblers, pine warblers [etc.]. **1917** *Birds of Amer.* III. 149/1 The Pine Warbler is a well-named bird, because its nesting sites are always in pine trees.

+**Pineweed.** 1. Orange grass, *Sarothra gentianoides.* 2. Corn spurry, *Spergula arvensis.* — (1) **1814** BIGELOW *Florula Bostoniensis* 73 *Sarothra gentianoides.* Pine weed. . . . A small, erect, branching plant. **1843** TORREY *Flora N.Y.* I. 89 *Hypericum sarothra.* . . . Ground Pine. Nitweed. Pine-weed. . . . Sandy fields and road-sides. (2) **1891** *Amer. Folk-Lore* IV. 148 *Spergula arvensis* was very fittingly named *Pine Weed.*

+**Pine weevil.** Any one of various weevils injurious to pine trees. — **1862** *Rep. Comm. Patents 1861: Agric.* 605 *Hylobius pales* . . . is the common 'pine weevil' of the north and the south. **1867** *Amer. Naturalist* I. 110 The Pine Weevil (*Pissodes strobi*), and *Hylobius pales* and *Hylurgus Terebrans*, also infesting the pine, now [in April] abound. **1868** *Ib.* II. 165 Another Pine-weevil (*Hylobius pales*, Fig. 4) also abounds in May.

Pine wood.

1. A forest of pine trees. Usually pl. {1813–}

1694 *Mass. H. S. Coll.* 4 Ser. I. 105 Our whole company came to Greenbush, a place so called from those pine-wooods [*sic*]. **1790** *Penna. Packet* 11 Oct. 3/4 A ganninipper is a kind of large horse-fly frequent in pine woods. **1826** FLINT *Recoll.* 263, In dry and hilly pine woods, far from streams and stagnant waters, it [*i.e.*, Spanish moss] almost wholly disappears. **1894** WILKINS in *Harper's Mag.* March 501/1 Then the horses leapt forward, and the whole was out of sight behind the spray of pine woods. **1906** A. BROWN in *Ib.* Oct. 707/1 She had lived alone in this little clearing, backed by pine woods, for over thirty years.

2. *attrib.* a. With *bluff, country, hog,* etc.

1688 CLAYTON *Va.* in *Phil. Trans.* XVII. 945 That which is called Pine-wood Land. **1805** *Ann. 9th Congress* 2 Sess. 1093 The house is on a point of a high pine woods bluff. **1851** *Polly Peablossom* 81 Having been transferred from a level pine-woods country, . . . the novelty of mountain scenery and a pure bracing atmosphere seemed to inspire him. **1872** MCCLELLAN *Golden State* 204 These hogs . . . are somewhat like the North Carolina pine-woods hogs. **1894** TORREY *Fla. Sketch-Book* 6 One of the three novelties which I knew were to be found in the pine lands . . . [was] the pine-wood sparrow.

b. *Pine-wood knot*, =PINE KNOT.

1836 SIMMS *Mellichampe* 423 The heavy pine-wood knot was lifted above the head of the tory.

+**Pine-wood(s) grape.** The turkey grape (*Vitis linsecomii*) of the southeastern United States. — **1826** FLINT *Recoll.* 255 They are common through the pine-woods of Louisiana, and known by the name of the pine-woods grape. **1862** *Rep. Comm. Patents 1861: Agric.* 485 'Post-oak grape,' 'Pine-wood grape,' *Vitis Linsecomii*, (new species.) . . . Grows in eastern and middle Texas and western Louisiana. **1923** *Standardized Plant Names* 526/1.

Piney, *a.* =PINY. — **1686** *Providence Rec.* XVII. 74 Grant mee . . . 20 Acres of low land and it being piney. **1751** J. BARTRAM *Observations* 72 We rode over some stony poor land, then piney, white oak, and some middling land. **1789** WASHINGTON *Diaries* IV. 48 Good and bad lands—cultivated and in woods—some high and barren, and others low, wet and piney. **1819** 'AGRICOLA' *Ess. Agriculture* 182 Our piney barrens are also to be converted into cultivation, or into some kind of grass adapted to such soil. **1879** TOURGEE *Fool's Errand* 334 It's like Northern farming in a piney old-field,—looks well enough, but don't pay.

+Piney wood(s).

1. *S.* A region of pine woods. (Cf. PINE WOOD.)

1803 PETTIGREW *Let. to Mrs. Tunstall* (Univ. N.C. MS.), The children are enjoying the health & soundness so peculiar to the piney woods. **1841** *S. Lit. Messenger* VII. 441 Our piney-wood's Esculapius . . . enjoins perfect quiet, with the rigorous enaction of gum-tea. **1882** SWEET & KNOX *Texas Siftings* 12 A man saw a drummer in the piney woods of North Carolina camping out under an umbrella. **1887** HARRIS in *Century Mag.* XXXIV. 543/2, I tested the piney woods of Georgia thoroughly years ago.

2. Attrib. with *county, fight, tory, village.*

1809 WEEMS *Marion* (1833) 127 Had this savage spirit appeared among a few poor British *cadets*, or *piney wood* tories it would not have been so lamentable. **1835** LONGSTREET *Georgia Scenes* 128 *He* could not be reconciled, until he fretted himself into a pretty little *piney*-woods fight, in which he got whipt. **1870** *Rep. Comm. Agric. 1869* 380 This [flock of sheep] was the scrub stock of the 'piney wood' counties of Georgia. **1887** HARRIS in *Century Mag.* Aug. 544/1 Azalia, the little piney-woods village which Dr. Buxton had recommended as a sanitarium.

+Pinfish. 1. The sailor's-choice, *Lagodon rhomboides.* **2.** A small sparoid fish, *Diplodus holbrooki.* — **(1) 1878** *Nat. Museum Proc.* 378 *Lagodon rhomboides.*—Robin; Pin-fish. Excessively abundant everywhere in the harbor [Beaufort]. **1911** *Rep. Fisheries 1908* 315/1 Sailor's Choice. . . . It is also called 'robin,' 'pinfish,' 'salt-water bream,' [etc.]. **(2) 1884** GOODE, etc. *Fisheries* I. 386 The Pin-fish . . . is abundant at Charleston and about Beaufort, North Carolina.

***Pinfold.** A place for confining stray animals; an inclosure for horses, cows, etc. — **1654** *Rowley Rec.* 91 Fourpence to the keeper of the pinnefold. **1837** BIRD *Nick* I. 84 His mouth war a-watering after the new beasts in the pin-fold. **1888** 'CRADDOCK' *Despot* 153 The cattle slept as he went out to the pinfold by the light of the stars.

+Pin grass. =ALFILARIA. (Cf. PIN CLOVER.) — **1850** COLTON *3 Years Calif.* 346 Here . . . [Nature] presents a pingrass, on which the cattle thrive. **1889** FARMER 10/2 *Alfilaria* (*Erodium cicutarium*). Also known as Storksbill, Pin-grass, Filaree, etc. A valuable forage plant of the dry regions from Colorado and New Mexico to Southern California.

Pinhead. {1662-} **+1.** A small minnow. **+2.** A dull, stupid person. *colloq.*[2] — **(1) 1845** JUDD *Margaret* I. 18 Minnows and pinheads were flashing and skirting through the clear, bright stream. **(2) 1896** ADE *Artie* 168 There's just as many pin-heads on State Street as you'll find anywhere out in the woods. **1924** DAWES in *Glasgow Herald* 14 Jan. 9 There are too many 'pinheads' throwing mud.

Pinhead sight. (See PINBALL 2.)

+Pin hook. A fishhook made of a bent pin. Also attrib. — **1840** *S. Lit. Messenger* VI. 386/2 Ellen used to fish there for minnoes with a pin-hook. **c1866** BAGBY *Old Va. Gentleman* 48 [He must] fish for minnows with a pin-hook, and carry his worms in a cymling. **1897** *Outing* Aug. 439 With the shiner and young perch, [the sunfish] ranks among the first victims of pin-hook wiles.

***Pinion, Pinyon.** =PIÑON 1. Also attrib. — **1831** PATTIE *Personal Narr.* 43 A nut of the shape and size of a bean . . . grows on a tree resembling the pine, called by the Spanish, pinion. **1846** SAGE *Scenes Rocky Mts.* xxi, Groves of pine, pinion and cedar. **1875** *Chicago Tribune* 11 Dec. 3/7 Mountains rose with gradual slopes, covered with a dense growth of the pinion tree. **1897** LEWIS *Wolfville* 280 Thar's bands of [turkeys] . . . a-eatin' of the pinyon-nuts.

***Pink.**[1] A small sailing vessel, usually employed in fishing or in coastwise trade. (Cf. PINKIE.) — **1636** *Mass. H. S. Coll.* 4 Ser. VII. 54 When the pinckes comes downe I hope the[y] will bringe hay. **1680** *Conn Rec.* III. 299 In Standford, 1 Pinck of 80 tunn. **1705** *Boston News-Letter* 30 April 2/1 Barbadoes, March 22. . . . On the 15th Instant, arrived here William Card in a Pink from Boston.

***Pink.**[2] (See also CAROLINA PINK, INDIAN PINK.)

***1.** Any one of various plants or species of plants of the genus *Dianthus.*

Cf. CARNATION.[1]

1737 BRICKELL *N. Carolina* 24 There being only some . . . Clove Gilly-Flower, Pinks of several sorts, Sweet-William, Cowslips. **1785** *Holyoke Diaries* 114 Pinks in bloom in our Garden. **1839** 'M. PENCIL' *White Sulphur P.* 82 The borders of the walks are lined with the prettiest flowers, pinks, mignionette [etc.]. **1893** M. A. OWEN *Voodoo Tales* 6 The onions were in bed with the pinks. **1910** C. HARRIS *Eve's Husband* 299, I passed up the path between clumps of sweet jimson and borders of balsam and pinks.

b. The flower or blossom of such a plant.

1837 HAWTHORNE *Notebooks* (1932) 17 A lady gave him a nosegay of roses and pinks. **1898** E. C. HALL *Aunt Jane* 45 My Jane had put a bunch of honeysuckles and pinks on the organ. **1901** *Harper's Mag.* April 672/1 Them pinks must have come from a greenhouse.

2. In fig. expressions with reference to the appearance of a pink.

1819 NOAH *She Would Be a Soldier* I. i, You look as pretty and as rosy as a field of pinks on a sunshiny morning. **1859** A. CARY *Country Life* 13 [They are] bright as a row of pinks. **1881** *Harper's Mag.* April 742/2 You look as fresh as a pink in yo' clean dimity frock.

+Pink curlew. 1. The scarlet ibis, *Guara rubra.* **2.** The roseate spoonbill, *Ajaia ajaja.* — **(1) 1858** BAIRD *Birds Pacific R.R.* 683 *Ibis Rubra.* . . . Red or Scarlet Ibis; Pink Curlew. . . . Mr. Audubon saw it but once, when a flock of three passed high over his head in Louisiana. **(2) 1917** *Birds of Amer.* I. 175/1 Formerly the Spoonbills, or 'Pink Curlews,' as the Florida hunters know them, were extensively shot and their feathers shipped to Jacksonville where they were made into fans to sell to winter tourists.

+Pinkerton. [Allan *Pinkerton* (1819–1884), organizer of a detective bureau in Chicago in 1850.] A member of a Pinkerton detective agency; a private detective or law enforcement officer. Usually pl.

1889 SALMONS *Burlington Strike* 387 The switchmen found out that their company was not desired by the Pinkertons. **1901** 'FLYNT' *World of Graft* 182 Take the Pinkertons. . . . I'd rather put the case in their hands than in the hands o' the Boston police. **1910** *N.Y. Ev. Post* 13 Dec. 8 But let the employer arm; let his Pinkertons or deputy sheriffs shoot to uphold the law, and the welkin rings with protests. **1913** LONDON *Valley of Moon* 186 Saxon . . . saw a dozen scabs, conveyed by as many special police and Pinkertons.

attrib. **1887** *Courier-Journal* 21 Jan. 2/5 Thomas Hogan . . . was shot and killed by one of the Pinkerton men. **1892** *Congress. Rec.* 7 July 5827/2 The Republican party . . . deals with such forces, and not with Pinkerton mercenaries. **1906** C. D. WRIGHT *Battles of Labor* 131 The immediate occasion of the fighting was the approach of a body of Pinkerton detectives.

‖**Pinkertonism.** The employment of private police. — **1891** *Voice* 26 Feb. (Th. MS.), You can't make men moral by law and Pinkertonism.

Pink eye.

1. A potato or variety of potato having pinkish eyes or buds. In full *pink-eye potato.* {1795-}

1849 EMMONS *Agric. N.Y.* II. 49 Pinkeye Potato. . . . Color orange gray; eyes purple. **1855** *Mich. Agric. Soc. Trans.* VI. 153, I harvested 65 bushels . . . of the common large round pinkeye. **1856** *Rep. Comm. Patents 1855: Agric.* 220 The 'Mercer,' the 'Pinkeye,' the 'Galena,' and the 'Long Reds,' are the principal [varieties cultivated in Allegheny Co., Pa.].

+2. A contagious form of conjunctivitis characterized by the pinkish color of the eyeball. {1882-}

1855 *Amer. Inst. N.Y. Trans.* 359 An opthalmic disease, called the pink eye, . . . attacks horses from the country, and injures their sale. **1884** *Rep. Comm. Agric.* 445 The disease known as pinkeye has prevailed more extensively than any other. **1895** *Denver Times* 5 March 1/7 Topeka Citizens Are Afflicted by the New York Disease. . . . Pinkeye, noted as being prevalent in New York city, has reached Topeka.

Pinkey-stern. (See PINKSTERN.)

Pinkie, Pinky. +A vessel having a high, narrow-pointed stern, used in the cod and coast fisheries. (Cf. PINK,[1] PINKSTERN.) — **1840** *Niles' Nat. Reg.* 15 Aug. 376/3 Chebacco boats and small schooners are known to him as '*pinkies*,' '*pogies*,' and '*jiggers*.' **1843** *Knickerb.* XXII. 187 The 'pinkie' is a schooner-rigged craft, sharp at both ends, a short peak running up aft, and designed for a chasing sea. **1886** *Leslie's Mo.* Feb. 223/1 In the days of the old pinkies and of the still earlier chebacco-boats. **1891** COOKE *Huckleberries* 234, I'd ruther sail a pinky round Pint Judy pint in a sou'easter.

Pinking iron. A sharp tool used in cutting out pinked borders. {1780-} Also in allusive context. — **1761** in Singleton *Social N.Y.* 242 [I] have ever since been so scrupulous an observer of it [*i.e.*, taste] that I never was the mark of a pinking-iron behind it. **1878** *Rep. Indian Affairs* 394 Hardware. . . . Pinking-irons [2]. **1881** *Ib.* 432.

‖**Pinkling.** A pink-cheeked adolescent boy. — **a1861** WINTHROP *J. Brent* 294 Biddulph, once a sentimental pinkling, now a bronzed man of the wilds.

+Pinkroot. The root of an herb of the genus *Spigelia*, esp. *S. marilandica*, used as a vermifuge; the plant or species of plant producing this. (See also CAROLINA PINKROOT.) — **1764** *Ann. Register 1763* 54/1 Produce of South Carolina . . . , Pink-root, 1 cask. **1795** WINTERBOTHAM *Hist. View* III. 395 The following have been employed for medicinal purposes: . . . Pink root, . . . Senna [etc] **1802** DRAYTON *S. Carolina* 63 Pink root, or Indian Pink. (*Spigelia Marilandica.*) . . . [It] has become a profitable article of trade with the Cherokee Indians . . . and is used in worm cases, with much success. **1889** FARMER 124/2 The *Pink Root* of Maryland which, further South, is popularly known as the *Carolina pink*, . . . bears beautiful flowers. **1913** BRITTON & BROWN *Illust. Flora* II. 730 Indian or Carolina Pink. . . . May-July. Pink-root. Worm-grass.

+Pink saucer. A small saucer containing pink coloring matter; also, the coloring matter itself. — **1864** WEBSTER 989/2 *Pink-saucer*, a small saucer, the inner surface of which is covered with a pink coloring matter, used in giving color to small articles. **1888** *N.Y. World* 22 July (F.), Flesh tights . . . are colored with what we call pink saucer in the profession, a kind of stuff you buy at the druggists.

+**Pinkster.** Also **Pinxter** [Du.].

1. *N.Y.* Whitsunday or Whitsuntide. Also attrib. Now hist.

1821 COOPER *Spy* xxix, Upon my word, you'd pass well at a pinkster frolic. **1848** IRVING *Knickerb.* (rev. ed.) v. ii, Whitsuntide or Pinxter also flourished in all its bloom. **1881** *Harper's Mag.* March 525/2 The Pinkster festivities commenced on Monday after Whitsunday, and now began the fun for the negroes, for Pinkster was the carnival of the African race. **1896** EARLE *Colonial Days N.Y.* 196 There was one old-time holiday beloved of New Yorkers whose name is now almost forgotten,—Pinkster Day.

b. (See quotation.)

1895 *Dialect Notes* I. 392 *Pinxter*, Easter. [Used by] negroes in N.Y.

2. In regions of former Dutch influence, esp. New York, used attrib. in the names of various flowers that bloom about Whitsuntide, esp. the wild honeysuckle, *Azalea nudiflora.*

With quots. 1817–8 and 1881 cf. *blummechies* and *blummies* in Bartlett (1859).

1743 CLAYTON *Flora Virginica* 21 *Azalea*. . . . Pinkterbloem. **1817–8** EATON *Botany* (1822) 149 *Azalea nudiflora*, . . . early honeysuckle, pinxter blomachee. . . . Woods. **1857** GRAY *Botany* 257 *Azalea nudiflora*. Purple Azalea. Pinxter-Flower. **1881** *Harper's Mag.* March 526/1 [The Pinkster king] and his followers were covered with Pinkster *blummies*—the wild azalea, or swamp-apple. **1896** EARLE *Colonial Days N.Y.* 200 Various wild flowers were known as Pinkster flowers.

Pinkstern. Also **pinkey-stern.** =PINKIE. {1759–} Also attrib.— **1859** BARTLETT 76 *Chebacco boat*, a description of fishing vessel employed in the Newfoundland fisheries. They are also called Pinksterns, and sometimes Tobacco Boats. **1880** *Harper's Mag.* Sept. 510/2 Apart from an occasional 'pink-stern,' there was little picturesqueness in the hulls. **1884** *Nat. Museum Bul.* No. 27, 681 Pink-stern fishing schooner. . . . Sharp stern with a raised 'pink.' . . . A few old ones still survive at Gloucester and fishing ports in Eastern Maine. **1903** *N.Y. Tribune* 25 Oct. 14 On another occasion the Houghton ran into a pinkey-stern schooner.

+**Pink tea.** A gay or frivolous social gathering attended largely by women; an inconsequential and harmless occasion. Also attrib.

1887 *Harper's Mag.* Jan. 204/1 Protestant ladies assist at Catholic fairs, and the compliment is returned by the society ladies of the Catholic faith when a Protestant good cause is to be furthered by a bazar or a 'pink tea.' **1902** BELL *Hope Loring* 152 An old pink tea to introduce a girl to society! **1906** *N.Y. Ev. Post* 17 Nov. 1 From all accounts these [football] battles of the early eighties and late seventies were no 'pink tea' affairs.

Pinky. (See PINKIE.)

***Pin-maker.** One whose business is to make pins. — **1714** *Boston Rec.* 108 Samll Plummer & William Down Pin-maker, are Chosen to Serve as Scavingers for the year ensuing. **1788** FRENEAU *Misc. Works* 352 Set the pin-maker to build a house, or the carpenter to make a needle, and they are equally awkward and helpless. **1903** *Sci. Amer. Suppl.* 31 Jan. 22638/2 With the new tariff law of 1842, . . . the pin-makers of America entered upon a career of prosperity.

***Pinnace.** A small, light, sailing vessel; a row-boat forming part of the equipment of a ship. — **1619** *Va. House of Burgesses* 14 No man shall trade into the Baye either in Shallop pinnace or ship wth out the Governours License. **1704** *Boston News-Letter* 19 June 2/1 Major Stephen Sewall who attended with a Fishing Shallop, and the Fort Pinnace, offered to go. **1840** DANA *Two Years* xxiii. 225 There were five boats belonging to the ship—launch, pinnace, jolly-boat, larboard quarter-boat, and gig. **1871** *Scribner's Mo.* II. 573 His little army sailed in pinnaces down Narraganset Bay.

+**Pinnated grouse. a.** The prairie chicken, *Tympanuchus cupido americanus.* **b.** =HEATH HEN 1.

Cf. PRAIRIE CHICKEN, PRAIRIE HEN.

1812 WILSON *Ornithology* VI. 45 In those open plains called the barrens of Kentucky, the Pinnated Grous was seen in great numbers. **1838** *Mass. Zool. Survey Rep.* 32 The Pinnated grous, formerly so common that domestics stipulated not to be fed with it too often, is met with in small numbers in Martha's Vineyard. **1858** BAIRD *Birds Pacific R.R.* 628 *Cupidonia Cupido*. . . . Prairie Hen; Prairie Chicken; Pinnated Grouse. . . . Western prairies and plains . . . ; Long Island, and eastern coast. **1870** *Mass. Acts & Resolves* 224 [Whoever] takes or kills any of the birds called pinnated grouse, or heath hens, . . . shall forfeit for every such bird twenty-five dollars. **1894** *Outing* XXIV. 385/2 There is no game bird in America equal to the pin-tailed grouse. His habits are much like those of his brother, the pinnated grouse, or prairie chicken. **1917** *Birds of Amer.* II. 24 Prairie Chicken. . . . [Also called] Pinnated Grouse.

+**Pinning blanket.** A blanket suitable for pinning around a baby. — **1895** WIGGIN *Village Watch-Tower* 113, I wish to the land the moths had eat the pinning-blanket. **1906** LYNDE *Quickening* 24 So now we see to what high calling Thomas Jefferson's mother purposed devoting him while yet he was a helpless monad in pinning-blankets.

+**Pin oak.**

1. The swamp Spanish oak, *Quercus palustris.*

1813 MUHLENBERG *Cat. Plants* 87 Swamp or Pin Oak. **1832** BROWNE *Sylva* 278 These small limbs die as the tree advances, which gives the tree the appearance of having pins or trunnels driven into it: whence the name of Pin Oak. **1859** HILLHOUSE tr. Michaux *Sylva* I. 83 [The name] Pin Oak . . . is indicative of a characteristic arrangement of the branches. **1894** COULTER *Bot. W. Texas* III. 417 Swamp Spanish or Pin oak. . . . Low grounds.

b. Various other oaks: (see quotations).

1897 SUDWORTH *Arborescent Flora* 153 *Quercus gambelii*. Gambel Oak. . . . Pin Oak (Ariz.). *Ib.* 156 *Quercus acuminata*. . . . Chinquapin Oak. . . . Pin Oak (Kans.). *Ib.* 159 *Quercus breviloba*. . . . Durand Oak. . . . Pin Oak (Tex.). **1901** MOHR *Plant Life Ala.* 100 On these rich uplands [in the prairie region of Ala.] the Texas white oak (*Quercus breviloba*), commonly known in this section as pin oak, is found most frequent.

2. Attrib. with *ridge, tree.*

1847 COYNER *Lost Trappers* 23 The young trapper was relieved by the arrival of two of the company, one of whom climbed a pin-oak tree, that stood in the edge of the brush. **1897** *Outing* XXIX. 516/1 The acorns rolling down from the pin-oak ridges are accessible.

+**Pinochle.** [Origin unknown.] A card game resembling bezique but played with two packs from which all cards below the nines are left out. {1892} — **1864** DICK *Amer. Hoyle* (1866) 137 Bezique . . . is known among our German brethern as *Peanukle*. **1875** *Chicago Tribune* 14 Oct. 2/2 [If] he could . . . take a hand at penuckle or sixty-six, his chances would be infinitely increased. **1913** LONDON *Valley of Moon* 406 Billy played at cutthroat pedro, horrible fives, bridge, and pinochle.

‖**Pinochler.** One who plays pinochle. — **1894** *Harper's Mag.* Oct. 698/2 The Pinochlers were dumfounded.

+**Pinole.** *S.W.* [Mex. Sp., fr. Nahuatl *pinolli*.] Flour made from various seeds, as the mesquite bean, or from parched Indian corn or wheat. (Cf. COLD FLOUR.) — **1844** GREGG *Commerce of Prairies* I. 280 Some of the wilder tribes make a peculiar kind of *pinole*, by grinding the bean of the mezquite tree into flour, which is then used as that of corn. **1858** *Harper's Mag.* Sept. 458/1 The white powder he had used was found to be 'pinole,' the flour of parched corn. **1869** J. R. BROWNE *Adv. Apache Country* 30 A jewel of a White is he in his native element of sage-deserts and Indians, pork and beans, adobe hovels and pinole. **1919** J. S. CHASE *Calif. Desert Trails* 78 Mixed with flour it [*i.e.*, chia seed] becomes the famous *pinole* of the Mexicans, the staff of life of the common people.

+**Piñon, Pinon.** [Sp.]

1. Any of several low-growing pines of the West producing edible, nutlike seeds, as *Pinus parryana, P. cembroides,* and *P. edulis;* a tree of one of these species. Also collect.

Cf. NUT PINE.

1844 GREGG *Commerce of Prairies* I. 158 A kind of Scrub pine called *piñon* . . . grows generally to the height of twenty or thirty feet, with leaves ever-green and pine-like, but scarcely an inch long. **1865** *Wkly. New Mexican* 27 Oct. 1/3 There is a sufficiency of water, an abundance of timber, pine, oak, cedar and piñon. **1885** *Santa Fé Wkly. New Mexican* 15 Oct. 4/1 Toppy Johnson, the 'topper out' of cattle in Sierra county, . . . started for the distant pinons. **1897** HOUGH *Story of Cowboy* 19 Back of these [foothills] are mountains, . . . sometimes black with the heavy growth of piñons. **1910** J. HART *Vigilante Girl* 351 The cactus and sagebrush found themselves met by chaparral and occasional *piñon.*

ellipt. **1849** *31st Congress 1 Sess.* Sen. Ex. Doc. No. 64, 64 [The Jemez Indians wore] around their arms, above the elbow, . . . a green band, decked with sprigs of *piñon*. **1881** CHASE *Editor's Run in N. Mex.* 206 The common fuel is pinon, the best fire-place wood in the world, full of pitch, and burns like a pine knot.

2. A nutlike seed produced by the tree.

In pl. usually *piñones.*

1848 BRYANT *California* xviii. 236 The burrs of the pine, which have fallen to the ground, . . . contain a nut, (*piñon*,) which, although it is said to be nutritious, is not agreeable to the taste. **1849** *31st Congress 1 Sess.* Sen. Ex. Doc. No. 64, 131 A large portion of the inhabitants are at this time away [from Laguna], gathering *piñones*, an edible fruit of the piñon, the common scrub pine of the country. **1885** *Santa Fé Wkly. New Mexican* 24 Dec. 3/5 Montezuma was born . . . of a young virgin, to whom was given three pinones.

3. Attrib. with *forest, pitch, woods.*

1846 MAGOFFIN *Down Santa Fé Trail* 76 Took a walk this P.M. through the pinon woods adjacent &c. **1875** *Cimarron News & Press* 7 Aug. 4/3 Colfax county has not less than 1,000,000 acres of pine, spruce, cedar, hemlock and pinon forests. **1885** *Outing* Oct. 24/2 Opposite are two old crones filling 'ollas' of basket-work, rendered fully water-proof by a coating of either mesquite or piñon pitch.

+**Piñon jay.** A western, bluish, corvine bird (*Cyanocephalus cyanocephalus*) that feeds on piñon nuts. — **1889** *Cent.* 1419/3 [The] piñon jay . . . is abundant in the mountainous regions of the West, especially where the piñon tree grows. **1917** *Birds of Amer.* II. 235/1 The Piñon Jay is a loosely clothed, fluffy bird that combines the form of a Crow with the color and habits of a Jay.

+**Piñon mouse.** The large-eared deer mouse, *Peromyscus truei truei.* — **1885** HAVARD *Flora W. & S. Texas* 408 True's Piñon mouse differs then from the common white-footed mouse, *Hesperomys leucopus*, in the fact that it chooses a different character of the country where it is found, as its home; in its more robust form; in its extraordinarily large ears.

+**Piñon nut.** =PIÑON 2. — **1864** *Rio Abajo Press* 9 Feb. 3/1 Two women [Navajoes] . . . had been ten days travelling, during which time their food was cedarberries and piñon nuts. **1873** BEADLE *Undevel. West*

658 In summer they fare sumptuously on piñon nuts. **1905** *N.Y. Ev. Post* 24 June 7 Fattening hogs on pinon nuts is the latest money-making method in Colorado.

+**Piñon pine.** =PIÑON I. Also attrib. — **1854** BARTLETT *Personal Narr.* I. 234 Several pines, among them the *Pinus edulis*, or piñon pine. **1877** HODGE *Arizona* 60 The Piñon pine . . . produces the Piñon pine nut in great quantities, which is quite an article of diet among the Indians, and is also relished by the whites. **1917** *Birds of Amer.* II. 235/2 The nuts of the piñon pines are the natural food of [the piñon jays].

+**Piñon tree.** =PIÑON I. — **1839** LEONARD *Adventures* (1904) 157 Its top is covered with the pinone tree. **1873** ARNY *Items regarding New Mexico* 28 Piñon trees . . . abound in every portion of the grant [on the Red River]. **1880** *Cimarron News & Press* 19 Aug. 2/4 No shelter other than the piñon trees is required in winter [for stock]. **1912** RAINE *Brand Blotters* 162 The girl found Antonio propped against a piñon tree, solacing himself philosophically with cigarettes.

+**Pin pool.** Any of several games of pool or billiards in which wooden pins are used. — **1864** DICK *Amer. Hoyle* (1866) 428 The game of Pin Pool is played with two white balls and one red, together with five small wooden pins. **1899** ADE *Fables in Slang* 16 The Local Editor of the Evening Paper was playing Pin-Pool with the Superintendent of the Trolley Line.

***Pint.**

***1.** A liquid or dry measure of half a quart; a container measuring this amount.

The present standard liquid pint is 28.875 cu. in. as compared with the English pint of 34.68 cu. in. The American dry pint is 33.60 cu. in.

*c*1700 *Brookhaven Rec.* 5 A pinte of Rum. **1745** *N.H. Probate Rec.* III. 283, I give to my Said Son Nathan . . . my Silver pint. **1868** BRACKETT *Farm Talk* 113 Give them a pint of rum or whiskey.

2. *attrib.* Designating vessels that measure a pint.

1659 *Conn. Rec.* I. 331 There shalbe provided for every Mill in this Collony, a Toll dish, of a just Quart, as alsoe a Pottle dish of 2 Quarts, and a pinte dish, al sealed. **1841** *Picayune* 10 Jan. 2/2 The 'Rackinsaw' man had a 'pint companion' or 'tickler' with him which he wanted filled with whiskey. **1847** RUXTON *Adv. Rocky Mts.* (1848) 236 The goods brought by the traders . . . are sold at enormous prices:—coffee, twenty to thirty shillings a pint-cup, which is the usual measure. **1856** DERBY *Phoenixiana* 148 An elderly female . . . , drawing a black pint bottle from the pocket of her dress, proceeded to take a 'snifter' therefrom.

Pintado. 1. A painted or printed cotton cloth; chintz. *Obs.* {1602-} **2.** =GUINEA FOWL. {1666-} — (1) **1633** *N.H. Prov. Papers* I. 77, 3 ruggs, 2 blanketts, 1 pentadoe. (2) **1850** *New Eng. Farmer* II. 374 The Guinea hen, or Pentado, is near an everlasting layer. **1857** *Porter's Spirit of Times* 3 Jan. 294/2 See how those ducks will *'shell out'* pretty decent eggs (where those of the hen or pintado are not to be had).

Pintado petrel. =CAPE PIGEON. {1894} — **1858** BAIRD *Birds Pacific R.R.* 828 The Pintado Petrel; The Cape Pigeon. . . . Off the coast of California. **1883** *Nat. Museum Bul.* No. 27, 175 Pintado Petrel; Cape Pigeon. . . . Southern seas; accidental (?) off coast of California.

***Pintail.**

+**1.** An American subspecies (*Dafila acuta tzitzihoa*) of a widely distributed river duck. {the European species, 1774-}

1813 WILSON *Ornithology* VIII. 72 The Pintail, or . . . the Sprigtail, is a common . . . duck in our markets, much esteemed for the excellence of its flesh. **1835** AUDUBON *Ornith. Biog.* III. 214 The Pintail . . . in the United States, is better known by the name of Sprigtail. **1858** BAIRD *Birds Pacific R.R.* 776 Pintail; Sprigtail. . . . The young male is sometimes difficult to recognize when without the long tail. **1883** *Nat. Museum Bul.* No. 27, 159 *Pintail.* Northern Hemisphere in general. . . . Coney Island, New York. . . . Mount Carmel, Illinois. **1917** *Birds of Amer.* I. 128/1 The Pintail . . . is an interesting, agile, swift-flying, hardy species.

+**2.** *local.* **a.** *W.* The sharp-tailed grouse, *Pedioecetes phasianellus.* **b.** The ruddy duck, *Erismatura jamaicensis rubida.*

(a) **1894** CRANE in *Outing* XXIV. 385/2 We found the pin-tails more frequently on the sides of hills, about the coolies in the rolling prairie. **1917** *Birds of Amer.* II. 27 Sharp-tailed Grouse. . . . [Also called] Pin-tail. (b) *Ib.* I. 152 Ruddy Duck. . . . [Also called] Pintail.

Pintail duck. =PINTAIL I. {1768-} Also *pin-tailed duck.* {1864-} — **1823** JAMES *Exped.* I. 267 *Anas acuta*—Pin-tailed duck. **1839** PEABODY *Mass. Birds* 387 The Pintail Duck . . . arrives from the north in autumn. **1870** *Amer. Naturalist* IV. 49.

+**Pin-tailed grouse.** =PINTAIL 2 a. — **1876** BOURKE *Journal* 13 March, On one occasion during our march, a small covey of 'pin tailed grouse' flew across our path.

+**Pinto,** *n. S.W.* [Sp., 'painted.'] A piebald horse. — **1890** *Stock Grower & Farmer* 26 July 6/3 We had an old pinto that was the worst bluffer that I ever saw. **1893** ROOSEVELT *Wilderness Hunter* 27 In a trice the red heifer was stretched helpless on the ground, the two fierce little ponies, a pinto and a buckskin, keeping her down on their own account. **1921** *Scribner's Mag.* March 343 'Is this Scott Lawson's dude ranch?' soberly inquired the rider of the pinto. **1924** MULFORD *Rustlers' Valley* 234, If I'd 'a' been on your cayuse, or th' pinto, I'd 'a' got him [an outlaw].

+**Pinto,** *a. S.W.* [Sp.] **1.** Of a horse: Piebald. **2.** *Pinto bean*, a mottled variety of the kidney bean. — (1) **1867** HARTE *Condensed Novels* 259 Concepcion . . . was reported to have chased the devil in the shape of a fleet pinto colt all the way from San Luis Obispo to San Francisco. **1893** ROOSEVELT *Wilderness Hunter* 416 The sheep-man . . . told me he seen a fellow in a wolf-skin coat, ridin' a pinto bronco. **1907** WHITE *Arizona Nights* 321 Goodrich sets him behind them little pinto cavallos he has. (2) **1916** 'BOWER' *Phantom Herd* 46 A girl gave me a handful of pinto beans.

+**Pinto horse.** A calico or piebald horse. — **1872** HARTE in *Atlantic Mo.* March 356 Ten minutes later, the driver of a fast Pioneer coach was overtaken by a 'man on a Pinto hoss.' **1903** A. ADAMS *Log of Cowboy* 14 There were . . . only three pinto horses in the entire cattle stock.

+**Pinweed.** Any herb of the genus *Lechea.* — **1814** BIGELOW *Florula Bostoniensis* 29 *Lechea minor.* Small Pin weed. . . . Flowers minute. **1817-8** EATON *Botany* (1822) 328 *Lechea major*, pin-weed. . . . A dull unsightly weed, in barren fields, about one foot high. **1854** THOREAU *Walden* 331 Golden-rods, pinweeds, and graceful wild grasses. **1893** TORREY *Foot-Path Way* 72 Acres and acres of horseweed, pinweed, stone clover, poverty grass, . . . and bearberry!

Pin wheel, *n.* {1704-}

1. A firework which spins about a pin as it is discharged.

1869 ALDRICH *Bad Boy* 92 Here . . . could be purchased the smaller sort of fireworks, such as pin-wheels, serpents, double-headers, and punk. **1907** *St. Nicholas* July 856/2 The crackers snap a noisy tune, The pinwheels splutter round. **1920** HOWELLS *Vacation of Kelwyns* 165 The pin-wheels caught and hung fizzing instead of revolving with a coruscation of sparks.

+**2.** *Tanning.* (See quotation.)

1885 *Harper's Mag.* Jan. 275/2 The hides next pass into a queer-looking contrivance known as a 'pin-wheel,' a stout circular wooden box, in which they are churned about in warmish water, dropping upon stout wooden pins attached to the circumference.

+**Pinwheel,** *v. Tanning. tr.* To subject (a hide) to the action of the pin wheel (sense 2). — **1885** *Harper's Mag.* Jan. 276/2 Grains and splits together are again 'pin-wheeled,' preparatory to one final soaking in strong bark liquor, the parting salute of the tan-yard.

+**Pinxter.** Variant of PINKSTER.

Piny, *a.* Of land or soil: Covered with pines or adjacent to pine lands {1627-}; +unproductive, thin.

See also PINEY.

1640 *Md. Hist. Mag.* V. 374 The Land of Richard Thompson on the South Pinie bay. **1674** *S.C. Hist. Soc.* V. 458 Ye land Piny except along ye skirts of small rivulets. **1782** CRÈVECŒUR *Letters* 146, I am at a loss to conceive on what the inhabitants [of Nantucket] live, . . . their piny lands being the most ungrateful soil in the world. **1821** W. DALTON *Travels U.S.* 215 The situation was high and healthy—the soil *piny, i.e.* not deep nor strong. **1869** *Overland Mo.* III. 9 Within a few rods one passes from the sour blue depths of the piny swamps into a broad and sunny land.

+**Pinyon.** See PINION.

Piny woods. *S.* =PINEY WOODS. Also attrib. — **1800** HAWKINS *Sk. Creek Country* 29 Broken piny woods and reedy branches on its right side. **1837** WETMORE *Gaz. Missouri* 281 When this younger son of the publican of the 'Piny woods' had nearly attained the stature of the family standard. **1893** *Harper's Mag.* Feb. 381/1, I meant to describe the charming resorts and the beauties of the piny-woods regions, the Bayou Teche country, and the shores of Lake Pontchartrain.

***Pioneer,** *n.*

***1.** One who digs a trench or pit, etc., esp. in preparation for the use of soldiers. Also transf.

1654 JOHNSON *Wonder-w. Prov.* 12 Neither shall such labourers as hee hath pickt out to be pyoneers in this Campe of his, drinke up like Spunges such meanes as hee hath sent to maintaine both Officers, and private Souldiers. **1675** *Conn. Rec.* II. 394 If any shall negligently loose or sinfully play away their armes at cardes or dice, or otherwayes, they shall be kept as pioneers or scavengers till they furnish themselues with good armes. **1741** *S.C. Hist. Soc.* IV. 22 Therein the General Enumerated everything that he thought Reasonable and Necessary . . . to assist him towards the Siege of St. Augustine, Viz: . . . 800 Pioneers (Negroes or White Men), with Tools Sufficient for that number of men, Such as Spades, Hoes, Axes and Hatchets to Dig Trenches. **1755** WASHINGTON *Writings* I. 299*n.*, I think it will be advisable to detain both mulattoes and negroes . . . , and employ them as Pioneers or Hatchetmen. **1870** KEIM *Sheridan's Troopers* 155 The pioneers were engaged in the advance, cutting a crossing [through the ice] for the [wagon] train.

+**2.** One who goes into new country to settle there; a frontiersman; an early or first colonizer. Now chiefly hist.

*a*1817 DWIGHT *Travels* II. 459 A considerable part of those, who *begin* the cultivation of the wilderness, may be denominated *foresters*, or *Pioneers*. **1829** B. HALL *Travels in N.A.* III. 127 While we were talking with this hardy pioneer of the wilderness—as these frontier settlers are well called in America. **1847** in Howe *Hist. Coll. Ohio* 366 The pioneers were forced to see the bear and the wolf leave, and make way for at least more friendly neighbors, though perhaps less welcome. **1871** *Republican Rev.* 26 Aug. 1/3 Old Joseph Walker, the old pioneer, told me . . . about the year 1845, he spent more than a year with the Navajo Indians in their own country. **1883** RITCH *Illust. N. Mex.* 103 Probably the Apache has been seen in the neighborhood for the last time, but the pioneers have not lost the habit of watching for his 'sign.' **1901** DUNCAN & SCOTT *Allen*

& Woodson Co., Kansas 10 Of these sturdy and honored pioneers not one now remains in the county. **1907** *St. Nicholas* Oct. 1145/2 My great grandmother and grandfather were pioneers.

+b. *pl.* Applied to a quasi-military band of Texans who started for Santa Fe, New Mexico, in 1841.

1842 *Picayune* 4 Jan. 2/1 The pioneers were not brought to Sante Fé, but marched along the road to the interior, which passed some miles to the eastward.

+3. A guide in unfamiliar or mountainous country.

1857 HAMMOND *Northern Scenes* 129 Our pioneer had made the entire journey the day before.

+4. Attrib. and appositive in sense 2 with *colony, expedient, farmer*, etc.

1869 *Rep. Comm. Agric. 1868* 47 The policy of growing grain for exportation, except as a pioneer expedient in opening and improving farms, is not to be commended. **1869** *Republican Jrnl.* (Lawrence, Kan.) 4 March, We have received the proceedings of the last meeting of the Pioneer Farmers' Club. **1893** *Harper's Mag.* April 701/1 The pioneer colony reached the mouth of the Kansas River July 28th. **1913** LONDON *Valley of Moon* 95 She remembered from her childhood the talk by the pioneer women of the courtesy and attendance of the caballeros of the Spanish-California days. **1916** EASTMAN *From Deep Woods* 15 He stood in front of his pioneer home with a resolute face.

Pioneer, *v.* {1780–} **+1.** *tr.* To take or lead (a person or persons) into new country. {1819–, in fig. and lit. use} **2.** To make (one's way); to occupy or open up (a place or way) as a pioneer. — **(1) 1838** *Yale Lit. Mag.* III. 86 You find him pioneering our population along the western prairies. **1882** *American* V. 87 Björn Anderson pioneered these new-comers to the Western States. **(2) 1848** *Knickerb.* XVIII. 152 He rented it [an old Dutch house] out to a numerous family that had just pioneered its way from Cape Cod. **1878** BEADLE *Western Wilds* 300 [Mormons] had pioneered all the new towns south [in Utah]. **1885** *Century Mag.* Sept. 739/1 Miners had pioneered the way some distance down the river in search of gold.

+Pioneer Day. 1. A legal holiday in Utah, July 24, commemorating the arrival of the Mormons at Salt Lake City in 1847. **2.** *Idaho Pioneer Day*, a holiday in Idaho, June 15, commemorating Great Britain's relinquishment of the Oregon country in 1846. — **(1) 1886** *Boston Jrnl.* 7 Aug. 2/4 The 'pioneer day' in Salt Lake, which celebrates the entrance of the Mormons to the valley, was rather gloomy this year. **(2) 1911** *Idaho Senate Journal* 3 Feb. 120 An Act . . . adding Idaho Pioneer Day as a holiday.

+Pioneer life. The way or manner of living of a pioneer in unsettled country. — **1845** *Xenia Torch-Light* 31 July 1/6 The Judge has been a . . . sharer in the toils, privations and dangers of western pioneer life. **1863** *Ill. Agric. Soc. Trans.* V. 866 The toils of pioneer life of our *foregones*. **1879** BISHOP *4 Months in Sneak-Box* 255 Some settlers, beguiled to this desolate region by the sentimental idea of pioneer life in a fine climate, known as 'Florida Fever,' were starving on a fish diet.

+Pioneer settler. One of the first settlers in an undeveloped area. — **1842** H. MANN *Oration* (July 4) 35 Our pioneer settlers would not have abandoned their homes, for the western wilderness. **1844** GREGG *Commerce of Prairies* I. 315 This last stroke of impudence at once roused the latent spirit of the honest backwoodsmen, some of whom were of the pioneer settlers of Missouri. **1877** ALLEN *Amer. Bison* 566 The buffaloes . . . have also often been invaluable to the pioneer settler.

+Pioneer(s') society. A society whose members are the pioneers of a given community. — **1869** DANA *Two Years* (new ed.) 439, I have already been invited to deliver the anniversary oration before the Pioneer Society, to celebrate the settlement of San Francisco. **1884** *Ore. State Jrnl.* 7 June 5/4 The members of the Lane County Pioneers' Society met here last Thursday and held their first annual re-union.

***Pipe,** *n.*[1]

I. *1. A slender tube provided with a small bowl at one end, the whole being used for smoking tobacco, etc. Often in ellipt. context.

c1618 STRACHEY *Virginia* 89 [The Indians] repose the body upon a little scaffold (as upon a tomb), laying by the dead bodies' feet, . . . his apook, and pipe. **1672** *N.J. Archives* 1 Ser. I. 84 When we had lighted our pypes, people came upon the said ground. **1708** SEWALL *Diary* II. 241 Governour calls and smokes a pipe with my wife at night. **1825** NEAL *Bro. Jonathan* III. 237 A pipe in his mouth. **1849** *31st Congress 1 Sess.* Sen. Ex. Doc. No. 64, 70 A red argillaceous rock . . . like that from which the Indians living on the head-waters of the Mississippi make their pipes. **1897** STUART *Simpkinsville* 23 My pipe has done gone out while I've been talkin'. **1905** [see DIP *v.* 3 b]. **1925** TILGHMAN *Dugout* 66 After a pipe or two, Plum Creek turned in.

+2. a. A pipe smoked by American Indians, esp. during ceremonial rites; a pipe exchanged by Indians and white men as a symbol of friendship and peace.

1643 R. WILLIAMS *Key* (1866) 82 Every man hath his pipe of their Tobacco, and a deepe silence they make, and attention give to him that speaketh. **1725** in *Travels Amer. Col.* 102 [The Indians] presented me with their pipes to Smoak out of (it being their Custom). **1765** TIMBERLAKE *Memoirs* 34 Several pipes were presented me by the headsmen, to take a whiff. **1822** Morse *Rep. Indian Affairs* II. 245 Here my Great Father, is a pipe which I present you, as I am accustomed to present pipes to all red skins in peace with us. **1849** *31st Congress 1 Sess.* Sen. Ex. Doc. No. 64, 170 On reaching the 'Grand Prairie,' you will most undoubtedly meet with the Comanches; should you do so, you will hold a 'talk' with them, and present the principal chiefs with a few pipes. **1872** EGGLESTON *End of World* 104 When an Indian has announced his intention of having a 'big talk,' he immediately lights his pipe and relapses into silence.

b. *spec.* = PIPE OF PEACE.

Cf. CALUMET 1.

1751 GIST *Journals* 50 Four Indians, two from each Tribe (who had been sent before to bring the long Pipe) . . . came in. **1760** CROGHAN *Jrnl.* 104 We then put ashore [,] shook hands and smoked with them [*sc.* Ottawas] out of their Council Pipe. **1823** JAMES *Exped.* I. 183 When the guests are all arranged, the pipe is lighted, and the indispensable ceremony of smoking succeeds. **1846** SAGE *Scenes Rocky Mts.* xxxi, All were quietly seated, and the 'pipe' performing its tireless rounds. **1848** COOPER *Oak Openings* II. 9 The smoker passing the pipe to his neighbor as soon as he had inhaled a few puffs.

+3. (See quotations.)

1847 LANMAN *Summer in Wilderness* 142 Having paddled about three pipes, (about eighteen miles,) we generally landed upon a pleasant sand-bar. *Ib.*, A 'pipe,' I should here remark, is what a sporting gentleman might call a *heat* of six miles. **1902** CLAPIN 309 In the language of the old French 'voyageurs,' a *pipe* meant two leagues, i.e. the time of smoking a pipe.

+4. Short for PIPE DREAM: (see also quot. 1902). *slang.*

1902 CLAPIN 309 *Pipe*, . . . in newspaper parlance, an assignment which a reporter knows will fail. **1908** 'O. HENRY' *Options* 170 He had a pipe that the first inhabitants of America arrived here on stilts.

II. *5. A hollow cylinder of metal, wood, or other hard substance for the conveyance of water, gas, etc. Also collect.

1652 *Suffolk Deeds* I. 137 In the yard one pumpe pipes to convey the water to the brew house. **1771** *N.H. Gazette* 30 Aug., Such persons as are desirous of contracting for . . . white oak pipe. **1799** *Phila. Ordinances* (1812) 163 Every subscriber . . . shall be entitled [to a supply of water] . . . to be taken from the street pipes or conduits. **1828** *Yankee* May 159/2 Gas-works. . . . The brick work was commenced . . . on the first of this month, and on the tenth, they had already upwards of two thousand feet of pipe laid. **1869** *Rep. Comm. Agric. 1868* 360 The best and cheapest common road culvert may be made of hard-burned terra cotta pipes. **1883** *Century Mag.* July 332/1 The refineries of Pittsburg, Cleveland, and Buffalo are supplied by pipes from the heart of the producing regions in Pennsylvania. **1905** LINCOLN *Partners* 264, I know where we can buy a complete fit-out second-hand—pumps, pipes, diver's suit and the whole business.

6. A stovepipe.

1797 *N.Y. State Soc. Arts* I. 388 The Franklin is . . . placed independent of a wall with a pipe to carry off the smoke. **1898** CAHAN *Imported Bridegroom* 226 The black aperture . . . had the day before been filled with the pipe of a little parlor stove.

III. Phrases. **7.** *To lay pipe(s)*, fig., +to bring in as voters persons not legally qualified as such; to lay a foundation *for* political preferment or office.

See PIPELAYING, note.

1848 BARTLETT 251 To lay pipe means to bring up voters not legally qualified. **1862** *Fraser's Mag.* July 28 To charge him, in the technical language of his party, with 'pulling wires,' and 'laying pipes' for the Presidency. [**1893** *Home Missionary* Oct. 305 The Irish . . . who began by laying our water-pipes . . . now lay a different kind of pipe, and make our city government.]

+8. *To hit the pipe*, to smoke opium or another drug. *slang.*

1887 *Courier-Journal* 13 Feb. 15/5 The subject of opium-smoking was discussed. The doctor himself, out of curiosity, had 'hit the pipe.' **1903** LEWIS *Boss* 373, [I] comes upon him in a joint where he's hittin' the pipe. **1906** *Washington Post* 28 May 3 They discovered Chinamen on every floor in various stages of ecstasy and captured several layouts, besides coming upon a bunch of Celestials in the act of hitting the pipe.

IV. *attrib.* and *comb.* **9.** In senses 1 and 2 with *band, bearer, case*, etc.

1776 LEACOCK *Fall Brit. Tyranny* IV. iii, There he'll get recruits enough for a hogshead or two of New-England rum, and a few owld pipe-shanks. **1810** *Austin P.* I. (1924) 168, 134 pipe bands. **1836** IRVING *Astoria* I. 196 The pipebearer . . . lighted the pipe . . . [and] handed it to the principal chief. **1847** RUXTON *Adv. Rocky Mts.* (1848) 234, I had nearly forgotten the pipe-holder, which hangs round his neck. **1881** *Harper's Mag.* March 527/2 On the wall hung the pipe-case of mahogany, with the drawer underneath for tobacco. **1889** *Century Mag.* April 888/2 Frank was taking down his pipe-rack from the space it had decorated on the parlor wall.

10. In sense 5 with *boiler, company, foundry*, etc.

c1789 in *Rep. Comm. Patents 1849* 568 *Rumsey's Pipe Boiler*, for the more ample and easy generating of steam. **1807** BENTLEY *Diary* III. 313 Father and son were pipe makers & diligent uninformed mechanics. **1838** *Mass. Statutes* xc. (Ernst), New England pipe works. **1851** J. F. W. JOHNSTON *Notes N. Amer.* I. 162 A single sample of pipe-tiles was exhibited—as a curiosity, I suppose. **1883** *Century Mag.* July 334/2 It served to show, however, that the general plan of pipe transportation was practicable, and it was not long before a number of pipe companies were formed. **1906**

LYNDE *Quickening* 319 The office building of the pipe foundry . . . burned on the night of July fifteenth.

***Pipe, *n.*²**

***1.** A large cask for liquids, esp. wine, and for other provisions, varying in size, but usually of 126 wine gallons. *Obs.*

1640 *Conn. Rec.* I. 448 One chese presse, old hogsheads & a pype. **1701** *Boston Rec.* 10 Every Householder . . . shall at all times . . . keep in thier houses yards or back sides, a pipe, hogshed or teirce full of watter. **1761** ROWE *Letters* 388, [I] am Sorry the Last Madeira was Chilly it all came out of one pipe.

***2.** A pipe full *of* something; a measure equivalent to the contents of a pipe.

1653 *Suffolk Deeds* I. 4 Seventy five pounds sterling to me pajd in three pipes of Canarje by Robert Cañnon master of the shipp charitje. **1686** *Conn. Rec.* III. 408 For every butt or pipe of Fayal wines or any other wines of the Western Islands, the sum of ten shillings. **1785** *Md. Hist. Mag.* XIX. 383 The Scocos . . . were such as carried . . . fifteen pipes of wine. **1812** *Niles' Reg.* II. 168/2 A vessel . . . has arrived at a port of the United States . . . from Amsterdam, laden with 400 pipes of gin. **1866** W. REID *After the War* 178 Do you swear positively, Mr. Wells, that you saw the pipe of whisky? **1881** *Harper's Mag.* March 529/1 In the course of the night a pipe of wine was drunk, dozens of pounds of tobacco consumed.

Pipe, *v.

+1. *intr.* To smoke a pipe.

1846 MCKENNEY *Memoirs* I. 71 These hardy adventurous fellows never rose from their paddles, nor stopped except to '*pipe*.'

+2. *Mining. tr.* To wash (dirt) away by means of a jet of water from a pipe; to supply (a claim) with water for this purpose.

1878 BEADLE *Western Wilds* 149 Worked-out mines . . . [with] all the soil 'piped' away in search of the 'pay dirt.' **1882** *47th Congress 1 Sess.* H. R. Ex. Doc. No. 216, 628 The material washed ('piped') from the bank is carried by the current . . . through sluices. *Ib.* 629 Some of the smaller claims are not piped more than one hundred to one hundred and fifty days per year.

+3. a. To put down a system of pipes in (a town) for the conveyance of water, gas, etc.

1884 *Boston Jrnl.* Jan., A special town meeting . . . to hear the report of the committee with reference to piping the town.

b. To convey (water, gas, etc.) by means of a pipe or pipe line.

[**1889** *Whitby* (Eng.) *Gazette* 27 Sept 3/2 A large Philadelphia syndicate has secured the gas rights in Indiana . . . and will pipe the natural gas to Chicago.] **1895** *Century Mag.* Sept. 677/1 A kitchen into which water was piped from a spring higher up on the mountain. [**1901** *Daily Chronicle* (London) 31 May 7/1 Fuel oil from the wells in Beaumont can be piped to Port Arthur.] **1906** BELL *C. Lee* 243 My engineer found them ladling out the crude turpentine by hand, when you know it ought to be piped. *fig.* **1904** CRISSEY *Tattlings* 334, I used to . . . lie awake nights trying to pipe lines of influence into the working department of the White House.

Pipe clay. A plastic, almost pure clay of a grayish white color, suitable for making tobacco pipes. {tobacco-pipe clay, 1758; 1806–}

1789 MORSE *Amer. Geog.* 183 Several mines of black lead have been discovered . . . and white pipe clay. **1813** *N.Y. State Soc. Arts* III. 37 Common clay is used in the manufacture of bricks, and pipe clay, which is found in Vermont, receives its name from its use. **1837** W. JENKINS *Ohio Gaz.* 321 Pipe clay, or a compound of common clay and marl, and also a *peculiar* kind suitable for crucibles, and for the manufacture of glass, are found. **1877** HODGE *Arizona* 89 The geological formation is granite, with dykes of slate, quartzites, talc, and pipe clay.

b. (See quotation.)

1874 RAYMOND *6th Rep. Mines* 15 A layer which is known as pipe-clay by the miners . . . is evidently a clay sediment deposited during periods of overflow in slow running water.

+Pipe dance. An Indian ceremonial dance in which the pipe of peace plays a conspicuous part; a Calumet dance. (Cf. PIPE-OF-PEACE DANCE.) — **1778** CARVER *Travels* 268 The Indians have several kinds of dances, . . . as the Pipe or Calumate Dance, the War Dance, the Marriage Dance, and the Dance of the Sacrifice. **a1820** in *Western Rev.* II. 161 There are a number of other dances, such as the . . . turkey dance, the new corn dance, the pipe dance, &c. **1832** CATLIN *Indians* I. 55 One of these scenes . . . appeared to me to be peculiar to this tribe [the Assiniboins], and exceedingly picturesque in its effect; which was described to me as the *pipe-dance*.

Pipe dream. A plan or daydream that has no foundation in fact or possibility. *colloq.* {1904–} — **1900** ADE *More Fables* 190 The Gigantic Enterprise which he had been Promoting got into the Public Prints as a Pipe Dream. **1913** BIGGERS *7 Keys to Baldpate* xiii, And don't have any pipe-dreams about the law. **1914** KEATE *Destruction Mephisto's Web* 87 By imbuing him with 'pipe dreams' of wealth to be acquired without labor or outlay, [he] succeeded in having Joyce accompany him to Kansas City, where he was separated from his hard-earned $5000.

Pipefish.

1. One of various slender-bodied, long-snouted, and bony-plated fishes of the family Syngnathidae {1769–}, esp. *Syrictes fuscus*. Often with specifying adjectives.

1814 MITCHILL *Fishes N.Y.* 475 Smaller Pipe-fish. *Syngnathus typhle.* . . . Is caught frequently in our salt waters during the warm season. **1839** STORER *Mass. Fishes* 162 *Syngnathus fuscus*. . . . The brown Pipe fish. Body elongated, tapering exceedingly to the tail. **1842** *Nat. Hist. N.Y., Zoology* IV. 319 The Banded Pipe-fish, *Syngnathus fasciatus*, . . . is rarely taken alive. **1855** BAIRD in *Smithsonian Rep.* 351 The Green Pipe-Fish . . . was very abundant in the sea-weed and grass near the mouths of the inlets. **1871** *Amer. Naturalist* V. 398 Pipe-fishes (*Syngnathus Peckianus*) six inches long . . . were often found. **1883** *Nat. Museum Bul.* No. 27, 430 *Siphostoma floridæ*. Florida Pipe-fish. East coast of the United States from North Carolina . . . to Florida. **1897** *N.Y. Forest, Fish, & Game Comm. 2d Rep.* 233 *Siphostoma fuscum*. . . . Pipe-Fish.—The pipe-fish is moderately common in summer in eelgrass and sea lettuce in Gravesend Bay. **1907** *Univ. Calif. Publ., Zoology* III. 183 *Syngnathus californiensis*. . . . Great Pipe Fish. *Ib.* 184 It has a longer dorsal than other Southern California pipe fishes.

+b. The sea horse, *Hippocampus hudsonius*.

1814 MITCHILL *Fishes N.Y.* 475 Sea-horse Pipe-fish. *Syngnathus hippocampus*. With thick head, subhexagonal, tuberculated body, and quadrangular finless tail.

+2. A flutemouth: (see quotations).

1842 *Nat. Hist. N.Y., Zoology* IV. 232 The American Pipe-fish. *Fistularia serrata*. . . . The species of this genus are still involved in great obscurity. *Ib.* 233 The Spotted Pipe-fish. *Fistularia tabacaria*. . . . Its geographic range is therefore from Brazil to the coast of New York.

+Pipe Franklin. A Franklin stove not built into a chimney, the smoke being carried off by a pipe. — **1797** *N.Y. State Soc. Arts* I. 388 [The close-stove method] can claim . . . but a trifling preference to the Pipe-Franklin.

+Pipe-lay, *v. Polit. intr.* To take measures preparatory to securing some desired action or event. *slang.* — **1884** MCCARTHY *Hist. Four Georges* I. 107 Bolingbroke and Oxford . . . had been 'pipe-laying,' to use an expressive American word, for the Stuart restoration during all the closing years of Queen Anne's reign. **1888** *San Francisco W. Examiner* 22 March (F.), There are not a few who are pipe-laying and marshalling forces for the fray when the conventions meet.

Pipelayer. {1851–} *+Polit.* One who manipulates an election by bringing in floaters; an intriguing politician. — **1840** *Richmond Enquirer* Nov. (Th.), The profuse use of gold, corruption of the franchise by pipe layers and yarn spinners, . . . have conspired to elect W. H. Harrison. **1841** *Congress. Globe* App. 25 Jan. 155/1, I was not defeated by voters. I was defeated by 'pipe layers.' **1864** SALA in *Daily Telegraph* 8 July, You might take them to be pipe-layers, or log-rollers, or lobbyers, or members of a municipal 'ring.'

Pipelaying. *+Polit.* The action or practice of manipulating an election, esp. by bringing in floaters. *slang.* Now hist.

The accounts of the origin of this expression are conflicting. Most accounts agree on the point that laborers from Philadelphia were imported by New York Whigs (*a*1840) and given jobs at *laying pipe* for the Croton water supply of New York City so that they could vote in the municipal election. (See also B. '48, p. 251.)

1841 *Congress. Globe* App. 26 Jan. 120/1 Others say that fraud, double voting, pipe laying, transfer of voters from one point to another, Hessians conducted by police officers and agents from city to city,—that these have done much to carry the election. **1848** *N.Y. Tribune* 30 Oct. (B.), The result of the Pennsylvania election would not be . . . doubtful, if we could be assured of fair play and no pipe-laying. **1855** *Chicago Times* 19 Feb. 2/3 The agony has commenced among the Know Nothings in their preparation and pipe laying for the coming charter election in Chicago. **1911** GOUVERNEUR *As I Remember* 12 'Pipe laying' was an organized scheme for controlling votes, and derived its name from certain political manipulations connected with the introduction of Croton water in New York City.

+Pipe line.

1. A line of pipe, usually extending across country, for the conveyance of oil, water, etc. {1891} (Cf. LINE *n.* 7 b.)

1879 in Tarbell *Hist. Standard Oil Co.* I. 354 The pipe lines owned and controlled by the parties hereto have a joint capacity for transportation. **1885** *Wkly. New Mexican Rev.* 29 Jan. 4/1 The purchase of the pipe line . . . will enable the Golden City Company to establish hydraulic works near Golden. **1900** *Congress. Rec.* 19 Jan. 995/1 One of the constituent companies . . . [charges] $1 per ton, for shipping oil through their pipe lines any distance. **1904** TARBELL *Hist. Standard Oil Co.* I. 18 The day that the Van Syckel pipe-line began to run oil a revolution began in the business. **1925** *Bur. of Mines Bul.* No. 233, 9 Main pipe lines are perforated by corrosion.

2. Attrib. with *business, company, distribution,* etc., with special reference to the oil business.

1879 *Appletons' Ann. Cycl. 1878* 618/1 A bill passed both Houses of the [N.Y.] Legislature to provide for the incorporation of pipe-line companies, and was sent to the Governor. **1883** *Century Mag.* July 334/2 The pipe line system was a thing of small beginnings and slow growth. **1894** *Cosmopolitan* May 126 The engineering difficulties in the pipe-line distribution . . . were very great. **1900** *Congress. Rec.* 19 Jan. 994/2 Whenever such charges for freight or passengers or pipe-line services shall be in excess of a fair return. **1904** TARBELL *Hist. Standard Oil Co.* I. 23 Several companies were carrying on the pipe-line business.

Pipeman. {1826-} One who attends to, works with, or lays pipes.— **1876** RAYMOND *8th Rep. Mines* 11 Gravel-miners and pipemen. **1898** *Century Mag.* Feb. 490/2 The lieutenant . . . tried to pull this unhappy pipeman with him. **1906** LYNDE *Quickening* 155 Tom waited breathless for the propitious instant when the tapping of the pipe men's hammer should drown the noise of a dash for effacement.

+**Pipe of peace.** Among the Indians, a ceremonial pipe, often decorated, smoked at a council meeting or as a sign of amity and peace; =PIPE *n.*[1] 2 b and CALUMET 1.

1705 BEVERLEY *Virginia* III. 20 They take a Pipe much larger and bigger than the common Tobacco Pipe, expressly made for that purpose . . . ; they call them the Pipes of Peace. **1760** ROGERS *Journals* 214 That evening we smoaked the calamet [*sic*], or pipe of peace, all the officers and Indians smoaking by turns out of the same pipe. **1778** CARVER *Travels* 359 The pipe of peace . . . is about four feet long. **1813** WILSON *Ornithology* VII. 14 The tail feathers of this bird [the ring-tailed eagle] are highly valued by the various tribes of American Indians for ornamenting their calumets, or Pipes of Peace. **1881** *Harper's Mag.* March 536/1 Several Indian chiefs . . . went to the 'Hoeck' . . . [to] smoke the 'pipe of peace.'

b. *transf.* and *fig.*

1872 'MARK TWAIN' *Roughing It* 173 While smoking the pipe of peace after breakfast we watched the sentinel peaks put on the glory of the sun. **1879** *Harper's Mag.* June 137/1 Why should not Mr. Folair and the other gentlemen of the play . . . smoke the pipe of peace?

+**Pipe-of-peace dance.** =PIPE DANCE. — **1841** CATLIN *Indians* II. 242 Their warriors and braves . . . dance around in a circle . . . in the '*pipe of peace dance.*'

+**Pipe organ.** An organ in which the tone is produced from pipes as opposed to a reed organ. — **1885** *Wkly. New Mexican Rev.* 9 April 4/2 The Easter offering which goes toward the purchase of a new pipe-organ amounted to $150. **1888** ROE *Army Lett.* 386 The immense pipe organ in the tabernacle was built where it now stands, and entirely by mormons. **1907** *St. Nicholas* Oct. 1120/1 The wedding party arrived at the church, and the new pipe organ for the first time gave forth the strains of the wedding march.

+**Piper's thickset.** A variety of wheat. — **1856** *Rep. Comm. Patents 1855: Agric.* 182 'Piper's Thickset,' a coarse red wheat, with thick, clustered ears, a stiff straw, and very prolific, but liable to mildew.

* **Pipe stave.** One of the wooden staves used in the construction of wine casks or pipes.

1610 *Estate of Va.* 54 The country yieldeth abundance of wood, as . . . Cedar and Firre; which are the materials . . . of Clap boards, pipe-staues. **1644** *Essex Probate Rec.* I. 34, I will have my debtes to bee payed out of the pipe staves. **1701** WOLLEY *Journal N.Y.* 33 Pipe staves are fifty shillings or three pound a thousand, . . . the best is made of white Oak. **1765** ROGERS *Acct. N. Amer.* 85 The chief articles exported from this province [Pa.], are . . . pig and bar iron, hogshead and pipe staves. **1834** CROCKETT *Narr. Life* 174, I would build two large boats, and load them with pipe staves. **1887** *Prince Society Publ.* XVII. 64 The patent recites . . . the making of clap-boards and pipe-staves.

b. *comb.* Designating persons who make pipe staves.

1640 *Mass. H. S. Coll.* 4 Ser. VI. 90 Wee are bold to intreat your . . . helpe for the suppressing pipe staff riuers and clabords in our towne. **1649** *Charlestown Land Rec.* 101, I . . . Pipe stave maker . . . [have] sould Twenty Achors of Land.

Pipestem. The tube through which tobacco smoke is drawn in a pipe; +also, transf., a thin leg. — **1727** COMER *Diary* (1893) 17 [He] fell over a log, ye pipe stem ran down his throat and broke. **1805** LEWIS in *L. & Clark Exped.* VI. (1905) 187 During the winter at Fort Mandan . . . [I observed] the beautifull eagle, or *calumet bird*, so called from the circumstance of the natives decorating their pipe-stems with it's plumage. **1850** MITCHELL *Lorgnette* I. 178 He hasn't got a leg bigger than a pipe-stem. **1883** EGGLESTON *Hoosier School-Boy* 33 Little Columbus Risdale picked himself up on his pipe stems and took his place at the end of this row.

+**Pipestone.** A soft stone of red clay. So named because the Indians carved tobacco pipes from it. Also attrib.

Cf. CATLINITE.

1804-5 LEWIS in *L. & Clark Exped.* VI. (1905) 44 The third is called *red pipe stone river.* **1809** A. HENRY *Travels* 24 We had reached the Portage du Grand Calumet, . . . which name is derived from the *pièrre à calumet*, or pipe-stone, which here interrupts the river. **1833** CATLIN *Indians* I. 234 The bowls of these [pipes] are generally made of the red steatite, or 'pipe-stone.' **1849** *31st Congress 1 Sess.* H. R. Ex. Doc. No. 5, II. 1021 This band claims the custody of the famous *wakan*, the red pipe-stone quarry, near the Coteau des Prairies. **1869** *Amer. Naturalist* II. 648 At Sioux Falls . . . a layer of Pipestone occurs intercalated with the quartzite.

+**Pipe tomahawk.** A tomahawk of which the handle is hollow and part of the head is a pipe bowl. — **1757** *Lett. to Washington* II. 129 Wm. Grymes 2 lbs. Butter & a pipe Tomahawk. **1775** CRESSWELL *Journal* 65 Some of them [*sc.* skulls] had holes broken in them about an inch diameter, suppose it to be done with a Pipe Tomahawk. **1805** ORDWAY in *Jrnls. of Lewis & O.* 308 Two canoe loads of Savages followed us and Stole Capt. Clarks pipe tommahawk which he had been Smoaking with them. **1826** *N. Amer. Review* Jan. 104 The pipe tomahawk, which alone they use, is wholly unfit for [throwing]. **1833** CATLIN *Indians* I. 236 Two of the tomahawks . . . are denominated 'pipe-tomahawk,' as the heads of them are formed into bowls like a pipe.

+**Pipevine.** The Dutchman's-pipe (*Aristolochia macrophylla*) or a related species. — **1847** DARLINGTON *Weeds & Plants* 268 The Pipe Vine, or Dutchman's Pipe, is a native of the West and South. **1869** *Rep. Comm. Agric. 1868* 204 Pipe vine, (*Aristolochia sipho*). **1886** *Century Mag.* May 237/2 Professor Gray's modest house, where wistaria, forsythia, and pipevine intertwine their varying greenery.

+**Pipeweed dynasty.** The succession of presidents from Virginia starting with George Washington. So called in allusion to Virginia as a tobacco-producing state. — **1816** 'FIDFADDY' *Adv. Uncle Sam* 21 Being the *third* of the pipeweed dynasty, he [Madison] determined to be at least the second in the philosophic regime of the family.

Pipewort. Any plant of the genus *Eriocaulon.* {1806-} — **1814** BIGELOW *Florula Bostoniensis* 215 *Eriocaulon pellucidum.* Transparent Pipewort. . . . Found in ponds, growing under water, a part of the stem only projecting above the surface, and supporting a small, flat head of obscure flowers. **1818** *Mass. H. S. Coll.* 2 Ser. VIII. 170 In August the eye is gratified with . . . the floating villarsia or spurstem, the transparent eriocaulon or pipewort, . . . and the syngenerian plants generally. **1894** TORREY *Fla. Sketch-Book* 30 Beside the railway track were blue-eyed grass and pipewort.

Piping. {1660-} +A method of mining that employs a powerful jet of water directed by a pipe or hose. — **1873** BEADLE *Undevel. West* 267 Lastly was introduced 'piping,' and complete hydraulic mining. **1881** RAYMOND *Mining Gloss.*

+**Piping plover.** A small, pale plover (*Charadrius meloda*) chiefly of the east coast. — **1828** BONAPARTE *Synopsis* 296 Ringed Plover . . . and Piping Plover. . . . Common all along the eastern sea coast of North America. **1839** PEABODY *Mass. Birds* 359 The Piping Plover, *Charadrius melodus*, so called from its pleasant, though plaintive note, is found along our whole coast in summer. *Ib.*, The piping plover is valued as game. **1858** BAIRD *Birds Pacific R.R.* 695 Piping Plover. . . . Specimens . . . collected by Dr. F. V. Hayden in the valley of the River Platte. **1869** *Amer. Naturalist* III. 231 Once numerous on the beaches of Nantasket and Chelsea, but now nearly or quite driven from them, the Piping Plover is still found along the coast of Maine. **1917** *Birds of Amer.* I. 264/1 Truly a bird of the beach-sand is the Piping Plover.

Pipit. {1768-} +**a.** =MISSOURI SKYLARK. +**b.** The common titlark, *Anthus spinoletta rubescens.* (See also AMERICAN PIPIT.) — **1869** *Amer. Naturalist* III. 183 Meadow Larks and Horned Larks, as well as the little Pipit, are so numerous in places on the bare plains [near Los Angeles] as to almost darken the air when they fly. **1893** ROOSEVELT *Wilderness Hunter* 64, I spoke above of the sweet singing of the western meadow lark and plains sky lark; neither of them kin to the true skylark, by the way, one being a cousin of the grakles and hang-birds, and the other a kind of pipit. **1917** *Birds of Amer.* III. 171 The Pipits live on the ground, and walk and run, not hop.

***Pipkin.** **1.** A small earthenware pot. +**2.** =PIGGIN. — **(1) 1638** *Md. Archives* IV. 48, 2. pipkins. **1770** *Copley-Pelham Lett.* 91 Take a Glaz'd pipkin, made long in shape thus. **1885** EGGLESTON in *Century Mag.* April 880/2 On the hearth were skillets, griddles, pipkins, and other vessels for cooking over the coals. **(2) 1855** WHITTIER *Poetical Works* (1894) 149/1 The beechen platter sprouted wild, The pipkin wore its old-time green.

***Pipperidge.** +=PEPPERIDGE. Also attrib. — **1828** WEBSTER s.v. The *piperidge* of New England is the *nyssa villosa*, a large tree with very tough wood. **1832** BROWNE *Sylva* 219 [*Nyssa aquatica*] is called indiscriminately Tupelo, Gum Tree, Sour Gum and Pipperidge. **1871** STOWE *Sam Lawson* 127 Old Black Hoss was about as close as a nut and as contrairy as a pipperage-tree.

* **Pippin.**

* **1.** A seedling apple of any one of a number of varieties.

1674 JOSSELYN *Two Voyages* 29 Mr. Luxon . . . having been ashore upon the Governours Island gave me half a score very fair Pippins which he brought from thence. **1835** HOFFMAN *Winter in West* II. 122 A large basket, containing as many of the finest pippins as we could stow about our persons, was, a moment after, brought to the road-side. **1878** *Amer. Home Cook Book* 165 Pare, core, and quarter a dozen large juicy pippins. **1892** M. A. JACKSON *Gen. Jackson* 414 A kind gentleman, Mr. Stephens, of Nelson County, sent me a barrel of select pippins.

2. With specifying adjectives: One of several varieties of apples.

See also FALL, HOLLAND, NEWTOWN PIPPIN.

1770 Golden pippin [see GOLDEN *a.* 1]. **1818** *Amer. Monthly Mag.* II. 428/2 Cider Apples [include] . . . 10. American Pippin. 11. Golden Rennet. 12. Hagloe Crab. **1868** *Rep. Comm. Agric. 1867* 130 Canada Pippin, . . . White pippin, (erroneously,) Yellow Newton Pippin, (erroneously.) **1868** *Mich. Agric. Rep.* VII. 429 The varieties of Apples now most in bearing are the Baldwin, R.I. Greening, Gale's Russet, Kirtland Pippin, Rambo, and Red Astrachan. **1871** *Rep. Indian Affairs* (1872) 565 Some of the finest varieties on the Continent have been originated in this immediate vicinity; for instance, the Shanum pippin and the Crawford pippin.

+3. *pl.* The young shoots of the checkerberry.

1891 *Amer. Folk-Lore* IV. 149 *Gaultheria procumbens* seems to have an almost endless variety of epithets. . . . Young people at Gilsum [Mass.] . . . now call the young shoots *Pippins*. **1892** *Ib.* V. 100 *Gaultheria procumbens*, pippins. Stratham, N.H.; Central Mass.

+4. An excellent or a good-looking person. *slang.*

1903 ADE *People You Know* 33 He wanted to land a Doctor's Degree. He knew that any one who aspired to this Eminent Honor had to be a Pippin. **1908** LORIMER *J. Spurlock* ii, 'I'd like to have the job which goes with that blonde,' and I pointed to a pippin who was pounding the keys just outside his door.

+Pipsissewa. Also **phipsewa, phipsissiway.** [Algonquian.] The prince's pine, *Chimaphila corymbosa;* any plant of the genus *Chimaphila*. Also attrib.

1814 BIGELOW *Florula Bostoniensis* 106 *Pyrola umbellata*, Umbelled Wintergreen, . . . [is] known by the names of *Rheumatism weed, Phipsewa* or *Wipsewog*, &c. **1818** *Mass. Spy* 25 Feb. (Th.), [On the Schuylkill, the Indians] procured the herb called by them Phipsissiway, in great plenty. . . . I informed him that we had given Phipsissiway tea, very strong, and as hot as he could drink. **1850** COOPER *Rural Hours* 433 We contributed a basket-full of ground-pine . . . with some glittering club-moss, and glossy pipsissiwa, for our share. **1893** TORREY *Foot-Path Way* 79 Lady's-slippers likewise . . . looked homelike and friendly, . . . and the pipsissewa. **1906** *Springfield W. Repub.* 5 Jan. 2 Ferns and pipsissewas, rattlesnake plantains and selaginellas, were as bright as if it were summer.

***Piracy.** Robbery or depredation on the high seas, in navigable rivers, or upon land, with the sea as a basis of operation; a single crime of this kind.

1637 *Md. Archives* IV. 4 Have them before me . . . to answere the severall crimes of sedition, pyracie and murther. **1684** *Conn. Rec.* III. 152 All treasons, piracies, roberies, murthers or confederacies commited . . . upon the sea, or any haven, creek or bay, shall be enquired . . . within this Colony. **1766** ROWE *Diary* 118 A Portugese was taken at Marblehead & brought here & put into Goal for Piracy. **1785** JEFFERSON *Writings* V. 247 The Algerines . . . have taken two of our vessels, and I fear will ask such a tribute for the forbearance of their piracies as the U.S. would be unwilling to pay. **1820** *Niles' Reg.* XVIII. 70/1 Nearly thirty convicts in the United States are at this time under sentence of death for piracy. **1842** TYLER in *Pres. Mess. & P.* IV. 167 The Government of the United States has by law declared the African slave trade piracy, and at its suggestion other nations have made similar enactments.

***Pirate,** *n.*

***1.** One who practices piracy; a sea robber.

1618 J. SMITH *Works* (1910) p. cxxii, The worst is of these 16. shippes. 2 or three of them have bene taken by Pyrates, which hath putt such feare in poore fishermen. **1684** *Plymouth Laws* 203 An act for the restraining and punnishing privateers and pirates. **1704** *Boston News-Letter* 3 July 2/1 On Fryday was carried to the Place of Execution seven Pirates to be Executed, *viz.* Capt. John Quelch, John Lambert [etc.]. **1724** *New-Eng. Courant* 11–18 May 1/1 At a Court of Admiralty held in Boston, for the Tryal of certain Pirates, a Company of Ladies of the first Quality attended during the whole Process. **1797** *Ann. 4th Congress* 2 Sess. 2202 The richest ships we have are now taken and robbed by every picaroon and pirate infesting the seas. **1820** *Niles' Reg.* XVIII. 240/2 Three persons are condemned to be executed at Boston on the 15th of June, as pirates and felons. **1865** *Atlantic Mo.* XV. 194 The United States employed him [Joel Barlow] to negotiate with the Barbary pirates, . . . to buy off the wretched cutthroats who infested the Mediterranean.

***2.** A ship employed in piracy.

1616 SMITH *New England* 226 But vnder the colour to take Pirats and West-Indie men. **1707** *Boston News-Letter* 18 Aug. 2/2 A Sloop . . . was taken by a Pyrat of 16 Guns, 50 Men, 140 Tons, under Dutch Colours. **1807** *Md. Hist. Mag.* I. 355 A French Pirate was in our Bay, boarding, plundering, and insulting several of our inward bound vessels. **1864** *N.Y. Herald* 6 July 1/1 They have sunk the Anglo-Rebel Pirate Alabama.

‖**3.** =PIRATE PERCH.

1870 *Amer. Naturalist* IV. 101 In the Assunpink Creek, where these 'pirates' it would seem must have gone to, we have also carefully searched.

4. *attrib.* Designating various ships used in piracy.

1700 *N.C. Col. Rec.* I. 518, I herewith send you a copy of what I lately received . . . concerning the taking of a pyrate ship. **1722** *New-Eng. Courant* 7–14 May 4/2 The Hector Man of War had lately taken a Pyrate Brigantine. **1723** *Amer. Wkly. Mercury* 1–8 Aug. 2/1 [Capt. Stanny] was taken by a Pirate Sloop . . . who took most of their Cargo.

***Pirate,** *v. tr.* and *absol.* To appropriate or reproduce (another's book, invention, etc.) without proper authority. {1706–} Also *ppl. a.* — **1758** *Boston W. Advertiser* 2 Jan. 2/2 They pirated the Almanack. **1774** in P. L. Phillips *Notes on B. Romans* 29 Instead of pirating from others, I have been freely communicative of my work. **1883** *American* VI. 44 The memoir . . . [was] found to be a pirated extract from a paper.

+Pirate perch. A perchlike fish (*Aphredoderus sayanus*) found in sluggish streams. — **1870** *Amer. Naturalist* IV. 107 Pirate Perch (*Aphrodedurus* [*sic*] *Sayanus*). . . . The adult fish, measuring five inches in length, has been seen frequently to swallow one of its own kind measuring an inch. **1883** *Nat. Museum Bul.* No. 27, 468 Pirate Perch. The United States from New York southward; west to and throughout the Mississippi Valley. **1903** T. H. BEAN *Fishes N.Y.* 354.

Pirogue. [Fr. ad. Sp. *piragua.*] A dugout made by hollowing out a log or by fitting together two hollowed-out logs with boards; also any of various crude open boats. {1698–, in W. Indies}

The application of this form seems to be more general than that of *piragua*. (Cf. PERIAGUA, PERIOGUE, PEROGUE.)

[**1777** ROBERTSON *Hist. Amer.* I. 376 [Indians'] *pirogues*, or war-boats, are so large as to carry forty or fifty men.] **1788** CUTLER in *Life & Corr.* I. 424 We were overtaken by the pirogue from Limestone. **1826** FLINT *Recoll.* 14 In another place are pirogues of from two to four tons burthen, hollowed sometimes from one prodigious tree. **1836** J. HALL *Statistics of West* 218 The earliest improvement upon the canoe was the pirogue, an invention of the whites. Like the canoe, this boat is hewed out of the solid log; the difference is that the pirogue has greater width and capacity. **1840** *Picayune* 10 Sept. 2/3 Charles John Theodore Snider was arrested as a suspicious person in a pirogue on the river. **1883** 'MARK TWAIN' *Life on Miss.* 595 A pirogue sometimes flits from the bushes and crosses the Red River on its way out to the Mississippi. **1894** CHOPIN *Bayou Folk* 300 The pirogue became entangled in the heavy moss that hung from the tree limbs.

Piroot, *v.* [Var. of *pirouette.*] *intr.* To go about as if performing a pirouette; to 'sashay' around. — **1863** MASSETT *Drifting About* 242 The streets were almost impassable from the mud and slush, and . . . the 'ladies' . . . would find it impossible to 'piroot' thither. **1866** C. H. SMITH *Bill Arp* 116 For four years the Confederate Horse-Stealing Cavalry have been pirooting around, preparing themselves for the frightful struggle that is to come. **1910** RAINE *B. O'Connor* 30, I've been pirootin' around this country, boy and man, for fifteen years.

Pissant. An ant. *S.* {1661} — **1770** *Md. Hist. Mag.* XII. 362 It seems the Pissants eat a great deal of Corn in the Ground. *a***1846** *Quarter Race Ky.* 84 [The girls] come pourin out of the woods like pissants out of an old log when tother end's afire. **1867** HARRIS *Sut Lovingood* 32, I felt like I'd crowded intu a ole bee-gum, an' hit all full ove pissants.

***Pistachio nut** (**tree**). A tree of southern Europe and Asia Minor (*Pistacia vera*), cultivated in the United States. — **1786** WASHINGTON *Diaries* III. 54 In box No. 9 . . . was put a pistatia Nut given to me by Colo. Mead. **1846** BROWNE *Trees Amer.* 179 The True Pistachio Nut-Tree. . . . The True Pistachio, in favourable situations, attains a height of fifteen or twenty feet. **1855** — in *Amer. Inst. N.Y. Trans. 1854* 629 Pistachio Nut, (*Pistacia vera*,) an extremely interesting tree, has been imported, . . . because it is useful and produces agreeable nuts.

+Pistareen. Also †**pisterene, pistereen.** [Prob. a popular formation on Sp. *peseta.*]

1. A small Spanish silver coin, the old peseta, once current in the American colonies and the early republic; the value of this coin.

This coin varied in value: (see quots. 1773, 1823, 1848).

1764 *Boston Ev. Post* 6 Aug. (Th.), 'New England's prospect' advertised for Two Pistareens. **1773** FITHIAN *Journal* I. 72 A Bit is a pisterene bisected; or an English six pence, & passes here for seven pence Halfpenny. **1776** *Mass. Hist. Soc. Coll.* 2 Ser. II. 296 We purchas'd some poor mutton to make Soop of at one Pistereen per pound. **1823** *Niles' Reg.* XXIV. 256/1 *Pistareens*, which hitherto passed for twenty cts. are now received at most of the banks for *seventeen* cents only. **1848** BARTLETT 252 *Pistareen*. . . . They have now become so much worn that they pass but for seventeen cents. **1860** MORDECAI *Virginia* 277 A quarter of a dollar would be radiated and subdivided into six parts, or a pistareen into five parts. **1891** WELCH *Recoll. 1830–40* 168 The common silver coin known as Pistareen . . . was worth sixteen and two-thirds cents.

2. a. *Half (a) pistareen*, the Spanish real, or one part of a bisected pistareen; a short bit.

Cf. BIT *n.* 3, CUT MONEY.

1765 *Mass. Gazette* 26 Sept. (Th.), Several persons have been committed to Goal for uttering Counterfeit Dollars, Quarter of Dollars, and half Pistereens. **1772** in F. Chase *Hist. Dartmouth Coll.* I. 262*n.*, 20 dollars and half a pistareen. **1775** *Jrnls. Cont. Congress* III. 487 That, for future works, they be allowed half a pistareen a day. **1787** BENTLEY *Diary* I. 72 Was presented by Master Lang, a Medal of Silver . . . in size below ½ a Pistareen. **1828** [see HALF *a.* 1].

b. *Head pistareen*, an old Spanish peseta with the image of a head stamped upon it.

1829 *Mass. Spy* 29 July (Th.), The head pistareens are worth 20 cents.

3. *attrib.* passing into *adj.* Petty, small.

Cf. PICAYUNE.

1860 EMERSON *Conduct of Life* 4 Now and then, an amiable parson . . . believes in a pistareen-Providence, which, whenever the good man wants a dinner, makes that somebody shall knock at his door, and leave a half-dollar. **1862** *N.Y. Observer* 12 June, 192/1 Breeders of the best imported stock will not, and ought not, to sell at the prices offered by our *pistareen* farmers.

Pistia. [Linnaeus, 1737.] Water lettuce; the genus name of a floating water herb of the family Araceae. — **1765** J. BARTRAM *Journal* 17 At the entrance of the river into the great lake there floats prodigious quantities of the pistia.

*Pistol.

*1. A short firearm having a more or less curved stock and made to be used with one hand.

1612 SMITH, etc. *Virginia* II. 69 [He] snatched the king by his vambrace . . . , with his pistoll ready bent against his brest. **1699** SEWALL *Diary* I. 502 Pole of the Calash, broken by the Horses frighted with a Pistol. **1734** *Harvard Rec.* I. 154 No Undergraduate shall keep a Gun or pistol in the College. **1794** *Ann. 3d Congress* 1448 It shall not be lawful to export from the United States any cannon, muskets, pistols, bayonets [etc.]. **1853** SIMMS *Sword & Distaff* (1854) 436 Two swords crossed in air above the victim,—two pistols, with each broad muzzle almost jammed against his own. **1867** EDWARDS *Shelby* 376 At the river he captured the horse and pistols of Colonel Ellet. **1920** HOWELLS *Vacation of Kelwyns* 156, I wonder what effect this pistol would have on the water here if I dropped it in.

2. Attrib. with *ball, belt, factory, holster.*

1783 in Durrett *Louisville* 147, 13 Pair Pistol Holsters. **1846** SAGE *Scenes Rocky Mts.* xiii, A pistol ball, fired by one of the party. **1865** *Wkly. New Mexican* 14 July 3/1 Byers & Andrews, Dealers in . . . Pistol Belts and Holsters. **1884** *Boston Jrnl.* 15 Aug., Half a dozen pistol-factories have suspended work because of lack of orders.

Pistol case. A case for a pistol or for a pair of pistols used in dueling. — **1841** BACHE *Fire-Screen* 164 Selby's pistol-case lay on a side-table. **1894** 'MARK TWAIN' *Those Twins* vi, The pistol-case was opened and the long slim tubes taken out. **1901** HARTE in *Harper's Mag.* Dec. 82/2 Colonel Starbottle, accompanied by Dick MacKinstry, his second, carrying his pistol-case.

*Pistole. Any one of various European gold coins formerly current in America, esp. the Spanish pistole worth about four dollars; the value of such a coin. (See also SPANISH PISTOLE.)

1718 *Md. Hist. Mag.* XVIII. 203 By cash 20 pistoles to be paid in bills Ster £20. **1720** *Amer. Wkly. Mercury* 28 July 3/1 Whoever will bring or send the said box to Andrew Bradford in the Second street shall have half a Pistoll reward. **1732** BYRD *Progress to Mines* (1901) 370, I gave Mr. Russel the trouble of distributing a pistole among the servants. **1760** WASHINGTON *Diaries* I. 121, [I] sent my money to pay for the Corn, viz. 37 pistoles and a Shilling. **1796** A. BARTON *Disappointment* II. ii, I hab engag'd wid Mr. Trappick . . . for a bill of exchange . . . at de rate of twenty-eight shilling de pistole.

+**Pistol gallery.** A place having facilities for target practice with pistols. — **1857** UNDERHILL & THOMPSON *Elephant Club* 61 Three-cornered wooden men . . . stand for 'pistol-galleries.' **1877** W. WRIGHT *Big Bonanza* 361 Half a dozen men went one night to a pistol gallery to practice. **1910** J. HART *Vigilante Girl* 292 When you're in a pistol-gallery you're shooting at a mark.

+**Pistol pocket.** =HIP POCKET. — **1883** PECK *Bad Boy* 22 He feels around his night shirt where his pistol pocket would be if it was pants he had on. **1884** NYE *Baled Hay* 23 The saw took a large chew of tobacco from the plug he had in his pistol pocket. **1885** E. W. HOWE *Mystery of Locks* 275 He took from his pistol-pocket a package wrapped in newspapers.

Pistol powder. Gunpowder especially suitable for use in a pistol. *Obs.* {1669} — **1666** SANFORD *Letter Book* 15 Two Barr of good fine pistole powder. **1707** *Boston News-Letter* 4 Aug. 2/2 A Parcel of Pistol Powder in small Cask. **1781** *Va. State P.* I. 505 The Baron desires you immediately to send . . . four hundr. pounds fine Pistole powder, fit for Rifles.

||**Pistolship.** Practice in using a pistol. — **1895** WISTER in *Harper's Mag.* March 537/2 The Governor, on setting foot in Idaho, had begun to study pistolship.

Pistol shot. {1645–} +One accustomed to shooting a pistol. — **1856** *Porter's Spirit of Times* 15 Nov. 177/2 This will be a match of unusual interest, both parties being acknowledged as among the very best pistol-shots in the country. **1873** MILLER *Amongst Modocs* 303 The officer and Hirst—both . . . famous pistol-shots—leapt the ditches and came darting over.

*Pit.[1]

1. A hole dug in the ground to serve as a trap in taking wolves. *Obs.* {1611–}

1653 *East-Hampton Rec.* I. 46 It is ordered that there shalbe 3 pitts Diged for the takinge of wolves. **1656** *Conn. Rec.* I. 283 W[ha]t person so ever, either Indians or English, shall take any Wolfe out of any pit made by any other man to catch wolfes in, . . . shall pay to the owner of the pit 10s. **1662** *Virginia Laws* lix. 34 For every Woolf destroyed, by Pit, Trap, or otherwise, Two hundred pounds of Tobacco.

2. The main floor, spec. the front part of this, of a theater. *Obs.* {1649–; 'now usually restricted to the part behind the stalls' *O.E.D.*}

1741 *N.Y. Wkly. Journal* 9 Feb., At the new Theatre in the Broad Way will be presented a Comedy call'd the Beaux Stratagem. . . . Boxes. 5. *s.* Pit. 2. *s.* 6. **1812** *Niles' Reg.* I. 341/2 There were in the pit and boxes 518 dollar tickets. **1854** COOKE *Va. Comedians* I. 45 There was 'box,' 'pit,' and 'gallery,' as in our own day. **1872** MCCLELLAN *Golden State* 137 Amusements were luxuries: in the circus sixty dollars for a private box, and three dollars in the pit **1890** LANGFORD *Vigilante Days* (1912) 42 Six or seven soldiers were seated side by side in the pit, a single one occupying a seat in the gallery behind them.

attrib. **1845** SOL. SMITH *Theatr. Apprent.* 24 After paying my tavern bill and purchasing a pit ticket for the theatre, not one cent remained. **1855** WOOD *Recoll. Stage* 339 How tenacious the public were of their rights, had been recently shown in the case of the pit entrance alone.

||3. (See quotation.)

1883 KNIGHT *Suppl.* 314 *Ensilage Cutter*, a machine for cutting green corn stalks or other green feed, to be stored in pits (*silos*) for winter feed.

+4. An exchange, or part of the floor of an exchange, set aside for transactions in a particular commodity, as wheat or oats. (Cf. CORN PIT, PROVISION PIT.)

1886 *Harper's Mag.* July 192/1 Back of the 'Pit' is the Call Room. **1902** NORRIS *Pit* 335 The Board of Trade vibrated with the vast trepidation of the Pit. **1903** *N.Y. Ev. Post* 25 Sept. 11 The offerings were small in all trading pits.

+**Pit.**[2] [Du.] The hard stone or seed of a fruit. (Cf. PEACH PIT.) — **1848** BARTLETT 252 *Pit.* (Dutch, *pit*, a kernel.) The kernel or nut of fruit; as, a cherry-*pit*. **1868** *Ill. Agric. Soc. Trans.* VII. 556 The peaches were all raised from the pits set out by Mr. Lane. **1873** W. MATHEWS *Getting On in World* 26 One man may suck an orange and be choked by a pit, another swallow a penknife and live. **1883** KNIGHT *Suppl.* 359/1 Hatch-pitter splits the fruit and removes the pit.

+**Pitahaya.** *S.W.* [Sp., from Haytian.] Any one of various cacti, esp. the giant cactus, or the edible fruit.

Cf. GIANT CACTUS.

[**1759** tr. Venegas *Nat. Hist. of Calif.* I. 43 And as the pitahaya is very juicy, it is chiefly found in a dry soil.] **1847** *30th Congress 1 Sess.* Sen. Ex. Doc. No. 7, 158 It [a cactus plant] is called in California *pitahaya*, but it appears that the Mexicans call by that name all large columnar cacti, the fruit of which is edible. **1885** HARVARD *Flora W. & S. Texas* 519 *Cereus stramineus.* (Strawberry Cactus; Pitahaya.) **1894** *Scribner's Mag.* May 597/1 There is an almost unvarying succession of the mesquite . . . ; the 'pitahaya,' or ice-cream cactus . . . ; the 'palo blanco,' or hackberry. **1920** BRITTON & ROSE *Cactaceae* II. 165 *Carnegiea gigantea* . . . is sometimes called pitahaya, but it is more generally known in the Southwest by the Indian name of sahuaro or saguaro.

*Pitch, *n.*[1]

*1. A thick tenacious black residue obtained by distilling coal tar, wood tar, turpentine, etc.

1610 *Estate of Virginia* 54 The country yieldeth abundance . . . of pitch and tarre, of Clap boards, Pipe-staues. **1707** *N.C. Col. Rec.* I. 663 [The North] produceth . . . Tarr & so consequently pitch. *c*1790 T. COXE *View U.S.* 75 In the settled parts of the states, rice, . . . tar, pitch and turpentine. **1807** GASS *Journal* 107 Therefore for want of tar or pitch we had . . . to haul our new boat on shore, and leave it. **1896** *Pop. Science Mo.* Feb. 474 The product called 'pitch' is the residue from the dry distillation of rosin.

attrib. **1718** HEMPSTEAD *Diary* 82, I workt at Mr Winthrops al day. Nathll & Stephen & pitch pot. **1767** HUTCHINSON *Hist. Mass.* II. 431 The lower class were beyond measure enraged and soon assembled with sticks, clubs, pitchmops, &c. **1853** SIMMS *Sword & Distaff* (1854) 282 They're people to stick like a pitch plaster, and to draw like a mustard.

*2. Resin exuded from a pine or gum tree at a cut or fracture. Also attrib.

1808 *Mass. Spy* 9 Nov. (Th.), A pine post, fat with pitch, had taken fire. **1905** *Forestry Bureau Bul.* No. 61, 43 *Pitch pocket*, a cavity in wood filled with resin. (P[acific] C[oast] F[orest]. R[ocky] M[ountain] F[orest].) *Ib.*, *Pitch streak*, a seam or shake filled with resin. **1907** *St. Nicholas* June 763/2 They took some pitch off the pine trees.

Pitch, *n.*[2]

+1. A piece of ground selected by a settler or allotted to him, usually for a house or a farm. Now hist.

1699 *Derby Rec.* 207 The laying out of John Pringles pitch upon the good hill. **1703** *Waterbury Prop. Rec.* 224 To relinquish his pich at the uper end of woster swamp. [**1888** BITTINGER *Hist. Haverhill, N.H.* 56 'Morse Meadow' got its name from that of Uriah Morse, who also at a Proprietors' meeting in 1763 was allowed to have 'pitch' No. 1 in that meadow.]

+b. *To make one's pitch*, to establish one's residence; to take up one's abode.

1764 HUTCHINSON *Hist. Mass.* I. 22 Here Mr. Nowell and some of his friends made their pitch. **1823** COOPER *Pioneers* xix, Elizabeth saw many large openings appear in the sides of the mountains, . . . where different settlers had, in the language of the country, 'made their pitch.' **1857** *Ill. Agric. Soc. Trans.* III. 408 The prairies lying near the timber were first cultivated. Very seldom would a settler make his pitch into the interior of a prairie.

2. The portion of a cape which extends farthest into the sea. {1743–}

1677 HUBBARD *Narrative* I. 5 The Sea coast from the Pitch of Cape Cod to the Mouth of Connecticut River. **1725** *New Eng. Quarterly* II. 660 They Concluded to go . . . to Ruby and there to heave down and Crean At the Pitch of Cape Florida. **1805** *Ann. 8th Congress* 2 Sess. 1673 For completing . . . the light-house at or near the pitch of Cape Lookout.

1828 SHERBURNE *Memoirs* iii. 65 We were on the eastern side of Cape St. Mary's, perhaps ten miles from the pitch, or head of the cape. **1842** COOPER *Wing-and-Wing* I. 94 Ten minutes after passing the palace, or the pitch of the promontory, the lugger opened another bay.

+**b.** The portion or tip of land extending farthest into the fork of a stream.

1694 in *Amer. Sp.* XV. 295/1 At a small naked pine Standing on the pitch of a point that makes the mouth of Quanticott creek on the North side of the creek. **1748** *Ib.*, To two red Oaks in the Pitch of the Fork of the said River. **1764** *Ib.*, A certain tract of waste and ungranted Land . . . in the pitch of the fork of Opakon & Mill Creek. **1770** WASHINGTON *Diaries* I. 410 The Fort is built in the point between the River Alligany and Monongahela, but not so near the pitch of it as Fort Duquesne stood.

+**3.** A waterfall; a rapid descent in a stream.

1786 *Mag. Amer. Hist.* I. 312 The little falls . . . is now very perceiveable as the water is very low—only one small pitch. **a1811** HENRY *Camp. Quebec* 56 [We] began to fear that he might be drawn under the pitch. **1832** WILLIAMSON *Maine* I. 87 There are also the *Great falls* . . . and several other rapids and pitches. **1871** RAYMOND *3d Rep. Mines* 201 At Shoshone City there is a cataract 100 feet high, and four miles below another, the Great Shoshone Falls, 210 feet in height, with several violent pitches in the river immediately above them.

+**4.** A steep place or declivity in a road.

1788 CUTLER in *Life & Corr.* I. 402 The road from Jennison's to this house is mostly good, some few sharp pitches. **1863** 'G. HAMILTON' *Gala-Days* 180 The pitches and holes that would fain make coaching on the common roads so precarious are entirely left out here. **1878** B. F. TAYLOR *Between Gates* 156 [The stagecoach] plunges up the pitches like a charge of cavalry.

+**5.** The game of all fours or seven-up.

1860 GEO. T. CLARK *Diary* (MS.) 10 Had a game of pitch in our tent today. **1871** *Republican Rev.* 29 July 2/3 They asked me if I could play 'pitch.' **1874** *Northern Vindicator* (Estherville, Iowa) 7 March, He can find good quarters with a jolly crowd who know how to play 'pitch.'

+**6.** *Baseball.* An act of delivering or serving the ball to the batter. {cricket, 1841–}

Cf. PITCH *v.* 4.

1886 CHADWICK *Art of Pitching* 59 Wide Pitch.—This term is applied to a ball which is pitched over the catcher's head out of his reach, or so wide of his position, on one side or the other, as to be just as much out of reach as in the first instance. **1910** *Spalding's Base Ball Guide* 383 A wild pitch is a legally delivered ball, so high, low or wide of the plate that the catcher cannot or does not stop and control it with ordinary effort. **1912** MATHEWSON *Pitching* 85 He followed the pitch through.

***Pitch,** *v.*

+**1.** *intr.* Of a roof or floor: To slope downwards.

1771 *Copley-Pelham Lett.* 137, I should have the Roof to pitch from under the Arkitraves of the Chamber Windows. **1858** *Ill. Agric. Soc. Trans.* III. 538 The roof may pitch both ways, or shed at the ends. **1897** F. C. MOORE *How to Build a Home* 94 The floor shall pitch from building to the front of piazza ½ inch to every foot of width.

+**2.** =BUCK *v.*[4] 1. *local.*

1865 PIKE *Scout & Ranger* (1932) 70, I had scarcely touched his back, when he began that species of rearing and plunging, known in Texas as 'pitching'; in California as 'spiking,' and in this country as 'bucking.' **1883** SWEET & KNOX *Through Texas* 68 The majority of Texas ponies buck, or pitch as it is sometimes termed. **1900** GARLAND *Eagle's Heart* 98 A horse that reared and leaped to fling its rider was said to 'pitch.'

+**3.** *S. tr.* To plant or sow (a crop). *colloq.*

1772 *Md. Hist. Mag.* XIV. 273 We have pitched above 9 tenths of our Crop. **1785** in *S. Lit. Messenger* XXVIII. 40/1 It has given full opportunity to the Planters to pitch their crops of Tobacco; but though many of them have repeated this operation several times, the noxious insects still threaten to abridge the prospect. **1841** FOOTE *Texas and Texans* II. 380 The planter commences *pitching* his crops—beginning with corn in the fore part of February. **1880** TOURGEE *Fool's Errand* 194 The sons were enabled to pitch a crop, the third spring after the surrender, upon their own account.

+**4.** *Baseball.* To deliver or throw (the ball) to the batter. {in cricket, 1773–; now obs.} Often absol.

1845 in *Appletons' Ann. Cycl. 1885* 77/2 The ball must be pitched and not thrown to the bat. **1868** CHADWICK *Base Ball* 60 When he [the pitcher] makes a motion to pitch and does not do so, or steps outside his ground in pitching, he makes a balk. **1890** W. CARLETON *City Legends* 37 Will you pitch or catch?

+**b.** *To pitch for* (a team), to play on (a team) in the capacity of a pitcher; *to pitch a curve,* to throw a baseball so that it curves.

1885 *Wkly. New Mexican Rev.* 21 May 3/6 A base ballist, who pitched for the Emmets of Chicago last season has been employed to play with the Albuquerque Browns. **1909** CALHOUN *Miss Minerva* 46, I can knock a home-run an' pitch a curve an' ketch a fly.

5. *To pitch in,* to start doing something vigorously. *colloq.* {1847–}

'Chiefly *U.S.*' (*O.E.D.*).

1843 STEPHENS *High Life N.Y.* I. 70 With that I pitched in, and, sez I, 'Look a here, Cuffy, none of your grinning at me.' **1856** GLISAN *Jrnl. Army Life* 342 The Indians . . . were to pitch in with their knives and clubs. **1863** *Rio Abajo Press* 17 Nov. 2/3, I must 'pitch in' and portray some of the characters now engaged in stirring up Johnny Navajo. **1867** L. BAKER *U.S. Secret Service* 218 Now is your time. Pitch in, pitch in, and take your share, while it is going! **1924** CROY *R.F.D. No. 3* 52 It was a serious thing for a girl on a farm not to pitch in and help with the work.

+**Pitched ball.** *Baseball.* A ball thrown by the pitcher to the batter. — **1886** *Outing* June 365/2 The trophy represents a ball player at the bat, in the act of striking a pitched ball. **1910** *Spalding's Base Ball Guide* 349 A batter is exempt from a time at bat . . . if he is hit by a pitched ball. **1912** MATHEWSON *Pitching* 14 Big League ball-players recognize only two kinds of pitched balls—the curve and the straight one.

***Pitcher.**[1] A vessel having, usually, an open spout or lip and a handle, which is used to hold and pour water, milk, and other liquids.

More widely used in the United States than in England and often applied to vessels that in England would be called jugs. (See also CREAM PITCHER.)

1816 *Austin P.* I. (1924) 263, 1 Pitcher. **1856** M. J. HOLMES *L. Rivers* 17 The landlord . . . [said], 'Tip-top accommodations. . . . Now-a-days we allers has a wash-bowl and pitcher; don't go to the sink as we used to when you lived around here.' **1876** *Wide Awake* 24/2 Nellie . . . [filed in] with two great pitchers of cream. **1903** BURNHAM *Jewel* 91 She poured the cream from a small silver pitcher with a neatness that won Mrs. Forbes's approval. **1923** WIGGIN *My Garden of Memory* 161 She came back with a pitcher of hot tea.

b. A vase for holding flowers.

1856 M. J. HOLMES *L. Rivers* 50 Don't you mind them little pitchers, (meaning vases,) which Master Atherton done gin you? **1903** E. O. WHITE *L. Chilton* 83 A pitcher of red lilies on the piano.

Pitcher.[2] {1707–} *Baseball.* +The player who serves or throws the ball to the batter.

1845 in *Appletons' Ann. Cycl.* XXV. 77/2 A runner can not be put out in making one base when a balk is made by the pitcher. **1871** EMERSON *Works* X. (1904) 309 They are like the baseball players, to whom the pitcher, the bat, the catcher and the scout are equally important. **1897** *Boston M. Jrnl.* 8 June 4/5 (Ernst), Everitt is a good pitcher, and ought to be given a show in the box. **1915** CAMPBELL *Proving Virginia* 101 It was that new man's last few balls that gave it to us. He's some pitcher!

attrib. **1907** *St. Nicholas* June 720/2 Raising his hands high above his head and twisting himself up in the most approved pitcher style, he tightened his grasp on the ball and let drive.

Pitcher plant. {1835–} +Any one of various plants of the American genus *Sarracenia* having leaves suggestive of a pitcher, esp. the sidesaddle flower of the northeastern states, *S. purpurea.*

1857 GRAY *Lessons Botany* 179 Dr. Sarrazin of Quebec . . . was one of the first to send our common Pitcher-plant to the botanists of Europe. **a1862** THOREAU *Maine Woods* 310 The characteristic flowers in swamps were: *Rubus triflorus* (dwarf raspberry), *Calla palustris* (water-arum), and *Sarracenia purpurea* (pitcher-plant). **1871** BURROUGHS *Wake-Robin* (1886) 101 In the margin of the pond, we found the pitcher-plant growing. **1899** GOING *Flowers* 300 The pitcher plant . . . beguiles the hapless fly to his drowning in its vase-shaped leaves, baited on the outside with nectar-bearing glands, and filled with water.

attrib. **1869** FULLER *Flower Gatherers* 185 It belongs to the rare Pitcher-plant family, and I am very glad we have one for examination.

+**Pitcher's box.** *Baseball.* The station occupied by the pitcher. (Cf. BOX *n.*[3] 6.) — **1887** *Courier-Journal* 27 May 2/4 Terry finished the game in the pitcher's box. **1897** *Outing* May 202/2 The team has a lot of seasoned material in the pitcher's box.

***Pitchfork.** A fork with a long handle, used chiefly in harvesting hay.

1641 *Essex Probate Rec.* I. 14 One pitch fork, beaving bill. **1711** *Mass. H. S. Coll.* 6 Ser. V. 252 A pitchfork you must get made there. **1841** *Congress Globe* App. Jan. 153/1 Corn dodgers and skunk skins, with pitchforks and poles. **1900** *Congress. Rec.* 24 Jan. 1120/1, I want to say to the Senator that a pitchfork seldom touches a grasshopper. **1920** HOWELLS *Vacation of Kelwyns* 138 Mr. Emerance . . . was lifting a pitchfork, with a block of wood stuck on its tines, to the roof of the barn.

b. *To rain pitchforks* {1852–}, used to express the idea of improbability.

1815 HUMPHREY *Yankey* 55, I'll be even with you, if it rains pitchforks —tines downwards. **1883** HOWE *Country Town* (1926) 27 He said it would probably come about when the sky rained pitchforks on Joe Erring's mill.

‖**Pitchfork steer.** A steer fed with hay and not allowed to graze. *colloq.* — **1890** *Stock Grower & Farmer* 2 Aug. 4/3 The 'Pitchfork' steers sold here last week at $24. They were fat.

Pitch hole. {1805–} +A hole or other defect in a road. (Cf. CAHOO.) — **1874** *Vermont Bd. Agric. Rep.* II. 659 The highways leading to our larger villages, . . . are frequently so full of pitchholes or 'cahoos' as to render them totally unfit for travel. **1890** *Harper's Mag.* Oct. 657/2 The highway was frequently interrupted by 'pitch holes.'

***Pitching.**

+1. *Baseball.* The action of throwing the ball to the batter.

1858 *N.Y. Tribune* 18 Aug. 7/3 The pitching was good on both sides. **1868** CHADWICK *Base Ball* 39 That pitching is the most effective which affords the most chances for catches or for putting players out at first base. **1886** — *Art of Batting* 22 *Base hits* are the chief criterion of effective batting, and *earned runs* off the pitching are the reward of such hitting.

+2. =BUCKING *vbl. n.*[1] Also attrib. (Cf. PITCH *v.* 2.)

1889 *Century Mag.* Jan. 335/1 [A Texas pony] does not break his legs or fall over backwards in the 'pitching' process as does the 'cayuse' of the North-west. **1890** *Stock Grower & Farmer* 26 July 6/3 When he had been saddled and allowed the length of the rope to exercise in he would give an exhibition of fancy 'pitching' that was hard to beat. **1895** REMINGTON *Pony Tracks* 198 One big animal resented carrying double, and did something which in Texas would be called 'pitching.'

+Pitch knot. The dried knot of a pine used as a torch or as fuel. (Cf. LIGHTWOOD KNOT, PINE KNOT.) — **1792** BELKNAP *Hist. New-Hampshire* III. 90 A lighted pitch-knot is placed on the outside of a canoe, which not only attracts the fish, but gives the fishermen direction where to strike. **1825** NEAL *Bro. Jonathan* I. 58 Two or three lighted pitch knots, a substitute for candles, were burning. **1850** WATSON *Camp-Fires Revol.* 157 We must have some more pitch-knots on the fire.

+Pitch-penny. A game in which players pitch pennies at a mark. Also transf. (Cf. CRACK-LOO.) — **1830** WATSON *Philadelphia* 240 'Pitch-penny' too, was frequent—to pitch at a white mark on the ground. **1861** NEWELL *Orpheus C. Kerr* I. 269 Company 3, Regiment 5, Mackerel Brigade, several members of which were engaged in the athletic game of pitch-penny. **1877** PHELPS *Story of Avis* 286 Calculating the distance ... between the baby's head and the ceiling, as he stood playing the game of human pitch-penny with the infant.

+Pitch pine.

1. Any one of various North American pitch-yielding pines, as *Pinus rigida, P. palustris,* etc.; also, a particular tree of one of these species.

Among the most valuable of the approximately twenty-four species of American pitch pines are the Georgia pitch pine and loblolly pine of the southern states and the western yellow pine. (Cf. GEORGIA PINE, LOBLOLLY PINE, LONG-LEAF PINE.)

1676 *Essex Inst. Coll.* LVI. 306, 4½ acres of land ... bounded by a pitch pine, small heap of rocks [etc.]. **1709** LAWSON *Carolina* 89 Ever-Greens are here plentifully found, of a very quick Growth, and pleasant Shade; Cypress, or white Cedar, the Pitch Pine, the yellow Pine, the white Pine with long Leaves. **1797** F. BAILY *Tour* 346 These pines are of the species which is called by the inhabitants 'pitch pine,' and grow to an enormous height and vast size. **1806** in *Ann. 9th Congress* 2 Sess. 1115 The short-leaved, or pitch pine ... is always found upon arid lands. **a1862** THOREAU *Maine Woods* 275 A peculiar evergreen overhung our fire, which ... looked like a pitch pine. **1906** *Atlantic Mo.* Aug. 212/1 He could tell a white pine (*strobus*) from a pitch pine (*rigida*) by just a cone and a bundle of needles,—one has five, the other three, to the bundle.

b. The wood of a pitch-pine tree.

Cf. LIGHTWOOD.

1771 *Copley-Pelham Lett.* 138 The floor of the Peazas except that next the kitchen should be Pitch Pine. **1804** FESSENDEN *Orig. Poems* (1806) 140 A torch-light that's made of pitch-pine. **1850** SAWYER *Way Sketches* 54 We obtained some dry pitch pine from a ravine. **1887** GEORGE *40 Yrs. on Rail* 31 Pitch pine was largely used for fuel. **1899** GOING *Flowers* 275 The needles ... of the Jersey or scrub-pine are twins, and those of the pitch-pine grow in clusters of three.

2. *attrib.* and *comb.* **a.** Designating pieces or portions of a pitch-pine tree used in construction work.

1736 *Boston Rec.* 150 Add to the South East Side Ten foot, To be Built of square Pitch Pine Timber. **1775** ADAIR *Indians* 183 Those bone-houses are scaffolds raised on durable pitch-pine forked posts, in the form of a house covered a-top, but open at both ends. **1788** *Edenton* (N.C.) *Intelligencer* 9 April, The above built with good Oak Timber and plank'd with pitch Pine plank. **1854** THOREAU *Walden* 268 A raft of pitch-pine logs with the bark on, pinned together by the Irish when the railroad was built. **1881** *Rep. Indian Affairs* 189 One of the old cavalry stables ... has been floored with the best quality of heavy pitch-pine lumber.

b. Pertaining to the use of pitch pine as fuel or kindling.

See also PITCH-PINE KNOT, TORCH.

1792 *Affecting Hist. F. Manheim* 3 Others were splitting pitch pine billets into small splinters. **1843** HAWKS *D. Boone* 21 Two people are always necessary for a fire-hunt. One goes before, carrying a blazing torch of pitch-pine wood. **1867** GOSS *Soldier's Story* 58 Throwing from her smoke-stack huge volumes of pitch-pine smoke,—she passed within a few rods of Battery Worth. **1888** GRIGSBY *Smoked Yank* (1891) 216, I was surely a pitiable object as I stood by the pitch pine fire those trusty darkies built for me.

c. Designating a region or area covered with pitch pines.

See also PITCH-PINE PLAIN.

c1805 PUTNAM *Memoirs* 39 The appearance of the country [surrounding Pensacola] ... is a pitch pine forest. **1807** *Ann. 10th Congress* 1 Sess. I. 671 The circumjacent country was a low pitch-pine barren.

+Pitch-pine knot. =PITCH KNOT. — **1824** *Mass. Spy* 15 Dec. (Th.), [He snatched] a pitch pine knot blazing from the fire. **1850** WATSON *Camp-Fires Revol.* 156 [We] have to sit up all night, over a fire of pitch-pine knots, for want of blankets to sleep in. **1893** *Outing* XXII. 93/2 Captain Joe, ... a lean, wiry North Carolinian, as tough as a pitch-pine knot from his native woods.

+Pitch-pine plain. A plain on which pitch pine is the native growth; also, the type of land found in such a plain. — **1734** *N.H. Probate Rec.* II. 508, I also give unto my sd. son ... the one half of my Thirty Acres of Land Lying between Black-Water Bridge, and the Pitch-Pine Plains. **1791** *N.Y. State Soc. Arts* I. 40 It was that species of land which is known by the name of shrub oak and pitch pine plain. **1832** WILLIAMSON *Maine* II. 136 They left [their packs] ... in a pitch-pine plain, where the trees were thin, and the brakes at that time of the year small.

+Pitch-pine torch. A torch of pitch-pine wood. — **1870** WHITTIER *Poetical Works* (1894) 99/2 Would the saints And the white angels dance and laugh to see him Burn like a pitch-pine torch? **1893** *Harper's Mag.* April 762/1 The atmosphere grew very dense with the smoke from the pitch-pine torches.

+Pitch-pine tree. A tree belonging to any one of various species of pitch pine. — **1684** *Manchester Rec.* 17 A pich pine tree marked with 4 marks. **1708** *N.H. Probate Rec.* I. 622 Beginning at a pitch pine Tree. **1883** RITTENHOUSE *Maud* 189 Such a street! Lined with ... magnolias and china-berry in full bloom, or else by the pitch-pine tree, a perfect novelty to me.

Pitch pipe. A small wooden or metal pipe sounded by blowing and used for establishing pitch for voices or instruments. {1711-} — **1773** in Singleton *Social N.Y.* 294 [Rivington had] fifes, tabors and pipes; pitch-pipes. **1826** COOPER *Mohicans* xxvi, He fumbled for his pitch-pipe, and arose with a confused intention of attempting a musical exorcism. **1856** GOODRICH *Recoll.* I. 308 In lieu of a pitch-pipe to give the key, there was a melodeon to lead the choir. **1880** E. JAMES *Negro Minstrel's Guide* 4 Pitch-pipes and tuning forks.

+Pitch wood. Resinous wood obtained from pitch pine. — **1825** NEAL *Bro. Jonathan* I. 292 The pitch wood was lighted and set in the fireplace. **1828** SHERBURNE *Memoirs* ix. 193 We then lost our course, but obtaining an abundance of excellent pitchwood, we made our way by conjecture.

Pit coal. Coal obtained from a pit or mine, as distinguished from charcoal. {1617-}

1744 FRANKLIN *Acct. Fire-Places* 32 If Pit-Coal should not be here discovered. **1796** in Imlay *Western Territory* (ed. 3) 524 In the atlantic states, pit-coal is very scarce, and is obtained with difficulty. **1801** *Hist. Review & Directory* I. 14 The interior parts of the country produce ... Quicksilver, Pit Coal, and Iron Ore. **1826** FLINT *Recoll.* 223 Vast volumes of water, and sand, and pit-coal were discharged.

+b. *Pit-coal indigo,* pit coal reputedly sold as indigo by Yankee peddlers. *Obs.*

1826 FLINT *Recoll.* 32 Fine stories about Yankee tricks ... and wooden nutmegs, and pit-coal indigo, and gin made by putting pine-tops in the whiskey. **1827** *Western Mo. Rev.* I. 85 The tin wagon, pit-coal-indigo, wooden nutmeg, and wooden clock missionaries find the harvest beginning to fall short.

***Pitfall.** A pit for taking wild animals. *Obs.* (Cf. PIT[1] 1.) — **1824** DODDRIDGE *Notes* 68 Sometimes indeed they outwitted them [*sc.* wolves] by pit-falls and steel traps. **1846** THORPE *Myst. Backwoods* 122, I shall grow as poor as a starved wolf in a pitfall.

Pitman. {1609-} +(See quot. 1876.) — **1813** *Niles' Reg.* IV. 111/2, I apply the power by means of a connecting rod or rods (or pitman, as it is called when applied in saw-mills). **1850** *Rep. Comm. Patents 1849* 361, I also claim ... connecting the pitman or pitmen with the saw gate. **1876** KNIGHT 1720/1 *Pitman.* ... The rod which connects a rotary with a reciprocating object, as that which couples a crank with a saw-gate, or a steam-piston with its crank-shaft. So called from the lower man of a pair who worked in a pit at the lower end of the saw. **1898** *Mo. So. Dakotan* I. 87 Lamoure ... was down on his knees tinkering at the pitman of the mower.

Pit saw. A large saw operated by two workmen one of whom usually stands in a pit or saw pit. *Obs.* {1703-}

1678 *New Castle Court Rec.* 361 An Iron sledge and a hand saw Iron—one Pit Saw. **1790** *Penna. Packet* 1 March 1/1 Rasps, ... pit saws, a quantity of brass furniture and escutcheons. **1850** KINGSLEY *Diary* 104 Got the pitsaw in operation ... and sawed a little with it just to get the hang of the thing. **1879** *Lumberman's Gazette* 15 Oct., An improvement over the gate saw, almost as great as was the gate over the pit saw.

attrib. Ib., Two men ... maintained a pit saw mill.

Pitter.[1] One who takes charge of gamecocks at a pit preparatory to their fighting. — **1857** *Harper's Mag.* May 751/2 The pitter ... with a pair of shears trims all the superfluous feathers from his neck, tail, and back. **1887** *Courier-Journal* 17 Jan. 2/4 His pitters oil his comb ... [and] he is ready for another fight.

+Pitter.[2] [Cf. PIT.[2]] A machine that removes the pits from fruit. — **1877** in Knight *Suppl.* 359/1 Fruit pitter.

+Pittsburg(h). *attrib.* Derived from or residing in Pittsburgh, Pennsylvania. — **1851** HALL *Manhattaner* 49 And you have never seen a fire hugged until you behold a violet lipped Creole before a blazing grate of

Pittsburg coal. **1877** 'E. Martin' *Hist. Great Riots* 170 McMunn . . . is the leader of the Pittsburgh men.

+**Pittsburg(h)er.** A native or resident of Pittsburgh, Pennsylvania. — **1835** Hoffman *Winter in West* I. 71 The Pittsburgers . . . are more bent upon increasing their 'fathers' store' than on beautifying the favoured spot in which they dwell. **1878** Pinkerton *Strikers* 241 The only Pittsburgers brave or generous enough to cast their lot with the Philadelphia troops were Captain Murphy and a small command of dismounted cavalrymen, and Captain Breck. **1880** *Harper's Mag.* Dec. 52 The care-worn Pittsburgher flees when his daily duties end, glad to escape for the time the all-pervading soot and smoke.

+**Pittsburg wagon.** A large freight wagon operating out of Pittsburgh, Pennsylvania. *Obs.* (Cf. Conestoga 1.) — **1826** Flint *Recoll.* 8 We passed hundreds of Pittsburg waggons, in the crossing. **1832** Paulding *Westward Ho!* I. 66 Occasionally they encountered one of those 'land carracks' called Pittsburg wagons.

+**Piute.** Also **Paiute.** [Cf. Hodge *Amer. Indians* II. 186/2.] (See quot. 1910.) Also attrib. — **1869** 'Mark Twain' *Innocents* xx. 205 Tahoe means . . . grasshopper soup, a favorite dish of the Digger tribe—and of the Pi-utes as well. **1877** W. Wright *Big Bonanza* 29 Miss Sarah Winnemucca, the 'Piute Princess.' **1907** London *Road* 129, I wandered over to the Piute camp. **1909** 'O. Henry' *Roads of Destiny* 351 He had the bedside manners of a Piute medicine-man. **1910** Hodge, etc. *Amer. Indians* II. 186 *Paiute*. . . . Powell states that the name properly belongs exclusively to the Corn Creek tribe of s.w. Utah, but has been extended to include many other tribes. In the present case the term is employed as a convenient divisional name for the tribes occupying s.w. Utah.

Pivot. {1611–} *attrib.* +Of or pertaining to a canal or river bridge one section of which is centrally pivoted so as to be turned to permit vessels to pass. — **1833** *Niles' Reg.* XLIV. 192/2 The rail road company shall, also, adjust the surface of that bridge to the elevation of the pivot bridge across the canal. **1872** *Statutes at Large* XVII. 398 All bridges over the Ohio River, below the Covington and Cincinnati suspension bridge, shall have . . . a pivot-draw, giving two clear openings.

+**Pivotal state.** (See quot. 1914.) — **1884** *Century Mag.* Nov. 125 The 'pivotal States' . . . sometimes make the nomination turn upon considerations of the lowest kind. **1888** *Voice* 22 Nov., What a temptation to a ring of gamblers in a pivotal state to buy votes! **1903** *Harper's Wkly.* 22 Aug., He has a prospect of regaining those pivotal States at the North which are essential to the triumph of his party. **1914** *Cycl. Amer. Govt.* II. 695/1 A doubtful state whose electoral vote is so large that it may determine the choice of a President is a 'pivotal state.'

Pivot (tooth). (See quot. 1875.) — **1842** in Koch *Hist. Dent. Surgery* I. 269 In 1811 after I came to the United States I saw a pivot tooth which had been set by Dr. Kuhn, of Lancaster, Pennsylvania. **1853** *La Crosse Democrat* 11 Oct. 4/1 Filling, Plugging, Cleansing, Extracting, inserting a Pivot or Plate. **1875** Knight 1722/1 *Pivot-tooth*, . . . an artificial crown attached to the root of a natural tooth by a dowel-pin of wood or metal occupying the nerve-canal. **1909** in Koch *Hist. Dent. Surgery* I. 258 Many pivot teeth were removed at the patient's will for the purpose of cleansing.

***Place,** *n.*

***1.** A home or residence, including the land belonging to it. Often preceded by an owner's name.

1806 Pettigrew *Let.* 26 Nov. (Univ. N.C. MS.), There is none but my mother and my Self now on the place. **1852** *Fla. Plantation Rec.* 65, I have the best stand of cotton that I Ever have had on the Place. **1884** Harris *Mingo* 195, I don't b'long on de Kendrick Place. **1894** Wilkins *Pembroke* 21 It was known as the 'old Crane place.' **1907** *Harper's Mag.* Feb. 351 Charlotte and Emory Blake lived at the old Blake place, in a vine-covered stone cottage. **1920** Howells *Vacation of Kelwyns* 225 Emerance drove to the Benson place.

+**2.** =Place kick.

1876 [see Place kick].

3. *To be in place*, +to be in a place suited to one's abilities.

1897 *Advance* 4 Feb. 138/2 If Mr. Manss were not a successful pastor, he would be very much in place as a journalist.

***Place,** *v.*

+**1.** *tr.* (See quot. 1851.) Also *vbl. n.* Now hist.

1718 in T. Clap *Hist. Yale-College* 28 Their Names should be inserted in the Class, as they were at first placed. *a***1750** *Harvard Rec.* I. p. cxli, Twenty and seven Scholars . . . were plac'd or dispos'd in the Classe by the President and Fellows. **1851** Hall *College Words* 231 *Place.* In the older American colleges, the situation of a student in the class of which he was a member was formerly decided in a measure by the rank and circumstances of his family; this was called *placing.* **1925** *Harvard Rec.* II. 869/2 *Place*, to assign a student to a certain place in his class. *Placing*, arranging students according to the social position of their fathers.

+**2.** To recall or determine who or what (a person or thing) is; to identify. {1923}

1855 *Knickerb.* XLV. 194 Who *is* our friend who writes us the following? . . . And [are] 'K. Y.' his initials? If yea, we can't 'place' him. **1886** *Century Mag.* Feb. 512/2, I've seen you before but I can't place you. **1890** *Harper's Mag.* July 291/2 He had no memory of having ever heard it before. . . . For a while he could not place it.

+**3.** *Baseball.* Of a batter: To hit (a ball) in such a way as to send it to any chosen part of the field.

1880 *Brooklyn Daily Eagle* 22 Aug. (E. J. Nichols). **1886** Chadwick *Art of Batting* 33 The highest degree of skill in scientific batting is reached when the batsman can 'place a ball'—in any part of the field he chooses.

Place-hunter. A persistent seeker for a place or position of a political nature. {1713–} — *a***1848** in Bartlett 31 Demagogues and place-hunters make the people stare by telling them how big they talked. **1854** *S. Lit. Messenger* XX. 553/1 Rapacious hordes of place hunters, would fasten themselves upon the scheme. **1884** *Century Mag.* April 803/1 Nine-tenths of a President's working hours are devoted to hearing and considering the applications of place-hunters.

Place kick. *Football.* The act of kicking a football from a fixed position. {1856–} Cf. Drop kick. — **1876** in P. H. Davis *Football* (1911) 461 A place kick, or place, is made by kicking the ball after it has been placed in a nick made in the ground for the purpose of keeping it at rest. **1887** *Century Mag.* Oct. 889/1 The ball must pass between the uprights and over the cross-bar, and must cross it from a 'place-kick.'

+**Placer.** [Sp.]

1. A deposit of sand, gravel, detritus, etc., in which gold occurs in minute particles; a place where such sand, gravel, etc., is washed for gold.

See also Gold placer and cf. Placer mine *n.*

1842 *Niles' Nat. Reg.* 8 Oct. 96/1 They have at last discovered gold [in Calif.]. . . . Those who are acquainted with these 'placeres,' as they call them, (for it is not a mine), say it will grow richer, and may lead to a mine. **1851** D. B. Woods *At Gold Diggings* 13 Such placers constitute many and the most important of the 'dry diggings.' **1890** Harte *Waif of Plains* 115 The gold had been dug out of a *placer* only thirty miles away. **1910** J. Hart *Vigilante Girl* 184 They have . . . advised me to keep my lands and my people well guarded until the rich placers . . . are worked out.

fig. **1858** Lowell *My Study Windows* 296 The Homer of Chapman . . . is a vast *placer*, full of nuggets for the philologist.

b. Used of land in which valuable minerals occur.

1880 Ingham *Digging Gold* 234 In Leadville, Colorado, it was declared—the land being placer—that as it was 'valuable for minerals,' it was not subject to entry as a town site.

2. *attrib.* and *comb.* **a.** Designating procedures involved in placer mining.

1880 *Harper's Mag.* Feb. 380 It took the 'honest miner' a long time to learn that 'placer' operations . . . were not a certainty. **1883** Ritch *Illust. N. Mex.* 129 A hydraulic company . . . is expected to have twelve miles of pipe down and arrangements completed for extensive placer washing.

b. Designating a formation or place where gold may be obtained by placer mining.

1875 *Chicago Tribune* 20 Aug. 1/7, I found gold in placer deposits on both Spring and Rapid Creeks [in the Black Hills]. **1879** *Scribner's Mo.* Oct. 802/2 One striking feature of this old placer-bar had impressed itself unpleasantly upon all the gold-seekers. **1885** *Wkly. New Mexican Rev.* 5 Feb. 2/6 Mr. Rice has returned to Golden from Chicago and commenced work upon his artesian well and placer beds with renewed vigor. *Ib.* 25 June 4/4 Col. Mason . . . will work the rich placer gulches adjacent to the San Pedro works.

c. Designating one who engages in placer mining.

1879 *Scribner's Mo.* Oct. 802/2 The few placer-washers there laughed at them for a pair of fools. **1896** Shinn *Story of Mine* 78 A more manageable tool is required than in the case of the placer prospector. **1903** A. Adams *Log of Cowboy* 352 The old placerman hesitated.

+**Placer claim.** A mining claim located on a placer deposit. — **1869** *Overland Mo.* III. 42 It is like taking out 'big pay' from a placer claim. **1896** Shinn *Story of Mine* 36 They immediately staked out four placer claims of fifty feet each. **1910** J. Hart *Vigilante Girl* 329 To stop work on a placer claim constituted abandonment.

+**Placer digging.**

1. The action of mining by placer methods.

1856 *Harper's Mag.* June 117/2 The old system of *placer* digging has ceased to exist. **1890** Harte *Waif of Plains* 116 Ye'll hev to get rid of them ther fixins if yer goin' in for *placer* diggin'!

2. *pl.* A place at which placer mining is or may be carried on.

1868 'I. Saxon' *5 Years within Golden Gate* 84 The Southern mines of California are almost wholly 'placer' or surface diggings. **1869** J. R. Browne *Adv. Apache Country* 413, I speak of the quartz ledges, . . . not of the placer diggings. **1874** Aldrich *P. Palfrey* vii, The rumors of a discovery of rich placer diggings in Montana had flown like wild-fire. *a***1918** G. Stuart *On Frontier* I. 86 Went to 'Mad Ox Canyon,' to look for placer diggings.

+**Placer gold.** Gold occurring in more or less coarse grains or flakes and obtainable by washing the sand, gravel, etc., in which it is found. Also attrib. and comb. — **1848** in Bryant *California* App. 463 The 'placer' gold is now substituted as the currency of this country. **1872** *Harper's Mag.* Dec. 22 This is 'sluicing,' a variety of placer gold digging or gulch mining. **1880** Ingham *Digging Gold* 278 A panful of this crevice matter yielded . . . gold of a very clear, bright nature, greatly resembling placer gold. **1896** SHINN *Story of Mine* 20 Trade had departed with the close of the placer-gold period of California.

+**Placer ground.** (See quot. 1884.) — **1872** C. KING *Mountaineering in Sierra Nev.* 288 In failing gold-industry, and the gradual abandonment of placer-ground to Chinamen, there is abundant pathos. **1884** *Notes & Queries* (Manchester, N.H.) Nov. 455 *Placer Ground*, ground where placer mining can be done, *i.e.* where gold can be obtained in digging up the earth and washing it for the gold. **1891** *Scribner's Mag.* Dec. 766/2 There is not . . . a hydraulic mine in New Mexico, despite the enormous areas of placer-ground.

+**Placer mine,** *n.* A mine from which a mineral, esp. gold, in particles or flakes, may be obtained by washing the sand, gravel, etc. — **1848** Bryant *California* App. 473 From all that I can learn as to similar deposits of gold elsewhere, I believe these [in upper Calif.] to be the richest *placer* mines in the world. **1876** CROFUTT *Trans-continental Tourist* 60 The placer mines were never very extensive. **1909** *N.Y. Ev. Post* (s.-w. ed.) 22 Feb. 6 A placer mine was the ideal poor man's mine from which, with the simple contrivance of a sluice box, he washed out precious nuggets of gold from the gravelly soil of the mountain gulches.

‖**Placer-mine,** *v.* [f. noun.] *intr.* To mine gold by washing the sand, gravel, etc. — **1890** *Stock Grower & Farmer* 19 July 4/4 A man who came to Arizona, . . . lived on brown beans and placer-mined on Hassayampa creek.

+**Placer miner.** One who mines gold at a placer mine. — **1871** RAYMOND *3d Rep. Mines* 199 The bars on the Snake River have long been the resort of placer-miners. **1896** SHINN *Story of Mine* 19 The placer miners in Gold Cañon were entirely indifferent to the departure of the Mormons. **1903** A. ADAMS *Log of Cowboy* 352 One of these placer miners . . . expressed some doubts about our leaving the trail.

+**Placer mining.** The separating, by means of washing, either in a gold pan or by hydraulic means, of particles of gold from the deposits or formations in which they occur. Cf. HYDRAULIC MINING.

1856 *Porter's Spirit of Times* 22 Nov. 194/2 The success of those engaged in placer mining generally, is said to be extraordinarily good. **1872** MCCLELLAN *Golden State* 258 Placer-mining is not entirely ended in California. **1896** SHINN *Story of Mine* 15 The real beginning of placer mining was early in 1850.

b. Attrib. with *day, district, region.*

1871 RAYMOND *3d Rep. Mines* 192 In the great placer-mining region of Idaho there is an underlying basis for permanent mining. **1873** *Newton Kansan* 24 April 1/1 Three of us held joint possession of a 'claim' in one of the rural districts of the placer-mining country. **1919** HOUGH *Sagebrusher* 16 Once, up in Helleny, years ago, right after the old Alder Gulch placer mining days, there was eleven millionaires.

+**Placeta.** Also **placita, plazita.** *S.W.* [Sp. *placeta*, dim. of *plaza*.] A small square or garden, usually adjacent to a residence or other building.

1847 MAGOFFIN *Down Santa Fé Trail* 211 Her house is large, . . . and the placita quite pretty, for she takes pride in raising choice fruit trees. **1863** *Rio Abajo Press* 28 April 1 He called Jose the mayordomo to the plazita. **1872** *Republican Rev.* 10 Feb. 1/3 Upon coming to Santa Fé, I found scattered around in various places about the palace and placita large quantities of manuscript documents. **1880** *Cimarron News & Press* 8 April 2/4 Rudebaugh and Allen got out of the hack and asked to be admitted to the placita of the jail. **1885** *Wkly. New Mexican Rev.* 14 May 4/3 The placita [on a ranch] was literally scattered with lead that rebounded from the walls. **1925** BURNS *Saga of Billy the Kid* 53 In every *placeta* in New Mexico, Mexican girls sing to their guitars songs of Billy the Kid.

+**Plague of the back.** (See quotation.) — **1672** JOSSELYN *New Eng. Rarities* 3 Cold . . . many times strikes the Inhabitants both English and Indian with that sad Disease called there the Plague of the Back, but with us Empiema.

***Plaice.** Also †**place.** +The summer flounder (*Paralichthys dentatus*), found on the Atlantic coast of the United States; also, any one of various other flatfishes.

1588 HARRIOT *Briefe Rep. Va.* D3 There are also Troutes: . . . Mullets: Plaice. **1612** SMITH, etc. *Virginia* I. 15 Of fish we were best acquainted with . . . Soles, Plaice, Herrings, Conyfish [etc.]. **1682** ASH *Carolina* 26 Plaice, Eels, Crabs, Prawns twice as large as ours in England. **1701** WOLLEY *Journal N.Y.* 40 Their Rivers are plentifully furnish'd with . . . Place, Pearch, Trouts [etc.]. **1807** *Mass. H. S. Coll.* 2 Ser. III. 57 The but or plaice . . . is caught during the whole year. **1814** MITCHILL *Fishes N.Y.* 389 Plaice of New York. *Pleuronectes aquosus*. . . . From his pellucidity, he is sometimes called the *watery flounder*. **1884** GOODE, etc. *Fisheries* I. 181 The common Four-spotted Flounder, *Paralichthys oblongus*, . . . occasionally finds its way to market in company with the Plaice, and is doubtless sold under the same name. *Ib.* 186 *Citharichthys sordidus* . . . is often known as the 'Plaice' in Puget Sound. **1911** *Rep. Fisheries 1908* 310/1 Flounder (*Pleuronectidæ*).—The family of flounders is composed of the turbots (*Bothinæ*), the halibuts (*Hippoglossinæ*), the plaices (*Pleuronectinæ*), and probably the soles (*Soleidæ*).

***Plaid.** A fabric of wool or cotton having a crossbarred pattern; a piece of such cloth worn as a garment.

1761 in H. M. Brooks *Gleanings* IV. 30 Diaper; Bed-Ticks; Tartans; Plaids. **1815** *Niles' Reg.* IX. 36/1 Several handsome pieces of carpeting, diaper, plaid, denim and other cotton fabrics, deserve to be mentioned. **1845** *Xenia Torch-Light* 31 July 4/5 A large lot of . . . Fancy Plaids, . . . Plain and Fancy Tweeds [etc.]. **1904** WALLER *Wood-Carver* 258 She had flung on my plaid and was off.

b. Attrib. with *cloak, cotton, domestic gingham.*

1829 SANDS *Writings* II. 202 He marched straight up to Mr. Mansfield, and fumbled under a bilious-looking . . . plaid cloak. **1852** EASTMAN *Aunt Phillis's Cabin* 61 She wore a plaid domestic gingham gown. **1872** *Atlantic Mo.* May 535 She could card and spin and weave, and her nimble fingers made up many a suit of homespun and plaid cotton for the negroes.

***Plain.**

***1.** *pl.* Plainly woven cloth, usually of wool. *Obs.*

1632 *N.H. Prov. Papers* I. 66, 158½ yards of playnes at 18s per yard. **1687** *Doc. Hist. N.Y. State* I. 163 All merchandize commonly called Indian Goods as Duffels, . . . plains, half-thicks. **1732** *S.C. Gazette* 136/2 Lately imported, and to be sold, . . . welsh plains and kendal cottons. **1790** *Penna. Packet* 2 Jan. 1/4 A considerable quantity of . . . flannels, plains, halfthicks, and duffil blankets. **1811** *Niles' Reg.* I. 292/1 White swanskins and white plains above fifty cents. **1839** KEMBLE *Residence in Ga.* 52 The allowance of clothes made yearly to each slave . . . is a certain number of yards of flannel, and as much more of what they call plains—an extremely stout, thick, heavy woolen cloth, of a dark gray or blue color, which resembles the species of carpet we call drugget.

***2.** A comparatively small, well-defined tract of level land free or nearly free from trees and readily cultivable.

1608 SMITH *Works* (1910) 10 The Towne . . . [is] pleasantly seated vpon three acres of ground uppon a plain half invironed with a greate Baye. **1636** *Dedham Rec.* III. 21 All that parcell of land . . . abutteth . . . upon the Cliffe of the Smooth playne towards the South. **1686** in Munsell *Annals of Albany* II. 93 The common council . . . [have] resolved to dispose off and sell some lotts of grounde upon ye Plain lying on ye south side of ye citty for gardens. **1704** *Providence Rec.* V. 184 Fourescore Rodd or poles . . . Eastward upon the plaine to a Rock. **1794** S. WILLIAMS *Nat. Hist. Vermont* 20 We have the wide extensive plains, of a fine level country. **1838** C. T. JACKSON *2d Rep. on Geol. of Me.* 85 Norway is a pleasant village situated on a plain or intervale. **1895** *Dept. Agric. Yrbk. 1894* 146 The soil of the 'plains,' near East Hartford, is a very light, sandy soil.

b. Preceded by a designating term.

1684 *Providence Rec.* XVII. 39 Ye playne . . . Called ye Westerne Plaine. **1704** *Derby Rec.* 361 His lott in the great hill plain. **1725** *Providence Rec.* XVI. 435 That part of my Land which Lieth Upon the Plaine Called Venter plaine and the other plaine Land there to adjoyneing. **1872** HOLMES *Poet* 23 The College plain [in Cambridge, Mass.] would be nothing without its elms.

+**3.** *pl.* An extensive region of level or rolling treeless country; prairie.

1755 L. EVANS *Anal. Map. Colonies* 13 The rest have retired beyond the woodless Plains over the Mississippi. **1806** *Ann. 9th Congress* 2 Sess. 1110 The immense plains known to exist in America, may owe their origin to this custom [of burning grass in the fall or winter]. **1848** *Santa Fe Repub.* 9 June 2/2 Major Singer . . . met with a very serious accident while crossing the plains. **1881** HAYES *New Colorado* 18 Up to the foot-hills run plains,—intersected by streams and by the 'Divide.' **1925** TILGHMAN *Dugout* 1 Far scattered over the rolling Western plains . . . the old dugouts tell their story of the past.

4. *attrib.* **a.** In sense 2 with *ground, lot, soil.* **b.** In sense 3 with *marl, travel, wagon.*

(a) **1661** *Providence Rec.* V. 285 A plaine ground betweene wayankeke & mishovosaket pond. **1670** *Derby Rec.* 15 Apece of Land lying betwen thare—plain Lottes And henary Boxfords homlot. **1895** *Dept. Agric. Yrbk. 1894* 149 The texture of this soil is similar to that of the Poquonock and of the 'plains' soil at East Hartford. **(b)** **1867** RICHARDSON *Beyond Miss.* 79 Plains-travel and frontier life are peculiarly severe upon women and oxen. **1886** ROOSEVELT in *Outing* March 614 The regular plains-wagon is perforce a stout, rather heavy affair. **1905** *Forestry Bureau Bul.* No. 66, 9 The greater proportion of the uplands in western Kansas and Nebraska is covered by deposits of very fine sand . . . and silt . . . known geologically as 'plains marl' and 'loess.'

Plain land. [Cf. PLAIN 2.] A plain or part of a plain. Sometimes with reference to the quality of soil in such an area. Also attrib.

1668 *Conn. Probate Rec.* 245 The home lotte by the plaine land side. **1678** *Derby Rec.* 34 The Town have granted . . . The uppar plain land. **1725** [see PLAIN 2 b]. **1817** WEBSTER *Let. to Pickering* 18 Meadow . . . is properly grass land, although we have extended the sense to tillage-land, and usually to plain land near rivers. **1838** *Mass. Agric. Survey 1st Rep.* 113 Perhaps the term *plain land* . . . will better convey an idea of the quality of the soil. It is altogether too light for grass. **1875** TEMPLE & SHELDON *Hist. Northfield, Mass.* 64 Plain lands . . . were then reckoned nearly worthless.

Plain people. +**1.** and +**2.** (See quotations.) +**3.** The Mennonites. — **(1)** **1871** DE VERE 281 It is said that the freedmen, in the first glow of their new rights, proposed to call the Whites *Plain People*, in return for the term *Colored People*, by which they were designated themselves. **(2)** **1900** *Congress. Rec.* 5 Feb. 1525/1 We appeal to the unofficial masses, . . . the great body of our citizenship, whom Abraham Lincoln affectionately denominated 'the plain people.' (3) **1904** H. R. MARTIN *Tillie* 113 But can't you see the inconsistentness of the plain people?

+**Plains country.** The prairie region of the central and western United States. Also *plain country.* — **1792** IMLAY *Western Territory* 52 The plain country . . . is considered as little better than barren land. **1885** *Century Mag.* June 230/2 The three hundred weary miles of treeless and barren-looking plains country. **1898** *Mo. So. Dakotan* I. 127 These breezes . . . are then known everywhere on the Plains-country as 'Hot Winds.' **1923** J. H. COOK *On Old Frontier* 61 Hundreds of bands of mustangs [were] ranging western Texas and the Plains country.

+**Plainscraft.** A knowledge of, and skill in making use of, the nature lore of the plains. — **1898** *McClure's Mag.* X. 379/1 He would use all the devices of speed and plains-craft in making the journey from the station to his house. **1899** *Scribner's Mag.* XXV. 19/1 Here their woodcraft and plainscraft, their knowledge of the rifle, helped us very much. **1901** WHITE *Westerners* 100 Billy was used to relying on his plainscraft, his courage, his skill with firearms.

+**Plains Indian.** An Indian of one of the tribes that formerly occupied the prairie region of the United States; freq. pl., these tribes collectively. — **1865** *Wkly. New Mexican* 27 Jan. 1/4 The Utes are anxious to join their white brethren in a campaign against the plains Indians. **1870** KEIM *Sheridan's Troopers* 27, I desire to contribute a few preliminary historic facts respecting the Plains Indians. **1913** LONDON *Valley of Moon* 438 A lithograph . . . of a Plains Indian, in paint and feathers, . . . gazing with wondering eye at a railroad train rushing along a fresh-made track. **1925** H. W. WHEELER *Buffalo Days* 236 [It] should be remembered as one of the most thrilling of the incidents in the warfare with the plains Indians.

Plainsman. A man accustomed to life on the plains. {1881-} — **1870** KEIM *Sheridan's Troopers* 66 [A good horse for hunting buffalo] is a treasure in the esteem of a plainsman. **1888** ROOSEVELT in *Century Mag.* Feb. 502/1 Everywhere among these plainsmen and mountain-men . . . are the cowboys. **1896** *Harper's Mag.* April 711/2 McClellan . . . a number of years afterwards became a famous plainsman and Rocky Mountain man. **1925** TILGHMAN *Dugout* 46 The plainsmen . . . came there, after weeks without sight of a house or smell of whisky.

***Plaister.** (See PLASTER.)

***Plane.** A tool used by carpenters for smoothing the surface of wood. Also attrib. and comb. — **1644** *Essex Inst. Coll.* L. 330 Playnes, Ackes & sawes. **1761** *Essex Inst. Coll.* XLVIII. 96 Plain irons, all sizes nails. **1809** CUMING *Western Tour* 223 Pittsburgh [has] . . . four plane-makers; six milliners [etc.]. **1849** *Corr. R. W. Griswold* (1898) 253 The demand for house carpenters [in San Francisco] has caused some of our young lawyers to take up the hammer and plane. **1884** *Rep. Comm. Agric.* 46 The Cane-Cutter . . . consists of a cast-iron disk, conical in shape, and carrying three knives shaped like the bit of a carpenter's plane.

***Planer.** +=PLANING MACHINE. Also attrib. — **1864** WEBSTER 995/1 *Planer-head*, . . . the slide-rest of a planing-machine, or planer. **1874** *Vermont Bd. Agric. Rep.* II. 745 This stock is . . . [taken] to the planer, a moving bed which passes under a stationary knife at the head. **1883** *Harper's Mag.* Jan. 208/2 [To] these mills . . . are attached planers, shingle machines, . . . and so on. **1900** *Engineering Mag.* Aug. 670 There will be . . . heavy planers, boring mills, and other large tools. **1904** *McClure's Mag.* Feb. 372 The employers finally proposed discharging their planer-men one at a time, substituting stone-cutters gradually.

+**Planer tree.** [I. J. *Planer*, Ger. botanist (1743-89).] A small tree (*Planera aquatica*) resembling the elm, found in wet places in the southern states. — **1810** MICHAUX *Arbres* I. 39 *Planer tree*, nom de la personne à laquelle cette espèce a été consacrée. **1832** BROWNE *Sylva* 246 The planer tree is of the second order, and is rarely more than 35 or 40 feet high. **1868** *Amer. Naturalist* II. 441 *Planera aquatica, the Planer-tree.* . . . The tree is nearly or quite lost from cultivation . . . both in Europe and in this country. **1901** MOHR *Plant Life Ala.* 46 Planer tree (*Planera aquatica*), . . . and green ash (*Fraxinus lanceolata*) are frequent inhabitants of the forest-clad swamps.

Planetarium. =ORRERY. {1805-} — **1774** J. ADAMS *Diary* Works II. 356 Here we saw . . . an orrery or planetarium, constructed by Mr. Rittenhouse, of Philadelphia. **1837** W. JENKINS *Ohio Gaz.* 485 Mr. James Russel, the ingenious inventor of 'Russel's new and improved Planetarium, or Columbian Orrery,' is a citizen of this town. **1843** in A. E. Lee *Hist. Columbus, Ohio* II. 341 Our distinguished fellow citizen and mechanic, Mr. James Russell, the inventor of the matchless planetarium.

***Plane tree.** +The American plane tree or sycamore, *Platanus occidentalis.*

Cf. AMERICAN PLANE (-TREE), BUTTONBALL, BUTTONWOOD.

[**1640** PARKINSON *Theater of Plants* 1427 *Platanus Occidentalis aut Virginensis.* The Plane tree of the West parts of Virginia.] *c***1730** CATESBY *Carolina* I. 56 The Western Plane-Tree . . . usually grows very large and tall. **1832** BROWNE *Sylva* 247 On the banks of the Ohio, and in the state of Kentucky and Tennessee, it is most frequently called Sycamore, and by some persons Plane Tree. **1897** SUDWORTH *Arborescent Flora* 206.

+**Planilla.** [Mex. Sp., dim. of *plana* 'a level.'] A cleaning floor at a mining station. — **1876** RAYMOND *8th Rep. Mines* 5 Sheds over planillas at Day tunnel and Deep Gulch tunnel. *Ib.* 7 A much larger quantity of waste vein-matter . . . has to be examined and passed over the planillas or cleaning-floors.

+**Planing machine.** A machine for planing and truing up planks. (Cf. PLANER.) — **1805** *Amer. State P.: Misc.* II. 130 Planing machine for sawing bellows boards, &c. **1853** J. W. BOND *Minnesota* 124 A shingle-saw and planing-machine will be attached. **1866** A. D. WHITNEY *L. Goldthwaite* vi, I thought it was a hay-cutter, or a planing-machine. **1875** KNIGHT 1729/1 The *cylinder planing-machine* . . . is now the usual machine.

+**Planing mill.** A mill or plant in which lumber is dressed and finished by being passed through planers, edgers, molding machines, etc. Also attrib. — **1844** *Knickerb.* XXIV. 184 The uplifted arm of Labor . . . meets his eye everywhere, in the . . . planing mill. **1883** HAY *Bread-Winners* 150 Saul's got a lot of influence among the boys in the planing-mills. **1888** *Amer. Almanac* 275 Occupations of the People of the United States. . . . Salt-makers, . . . Saw & planing mill operatives. **1905** WIGGIN *Rose* 96 When the great mass [of river ice] neared the planing mill on the east shore the girls covered their eyes.

***Plank,** *n.*

***1.** A flat piece of lumber for use in building houses, fences, boats, etc.

Cf. BOARD *n.* 1.

1626 *Plymouth Laws* 28 No man . . . [shall] sell or transport any manner of workes as frames for houses plankes boards [etc.]. **1704** *Boston News-Letter* 6 Nov. 2/2 The soot being blown into the Belfrey, fired some old Boards, and melted the Lead . . . and then Fired the Planks. **1817** S. BROWN *Western Gazetteer* 263 Houses . . . built of hewn planks neatly jointed. **1887** ALDEN *Little Fishers* viii, There's a plank across the stream down there a ways. **1907** *St. Nicholas* June 753/2 The men put weighted tubs in the water for planks to rest on.

2. =GANGPLANK.

1722 *New-Eng. Courant* 2 April 2/2 A Man belonging to the Castle, going on board a Ship at the Long Wharff, fell off the Plank, & was taken up dead the next Morning. **1852** STOWE *Uncle Tom* xxxvi, The two young men . . . walked up the plank into the boat.

+**3.** One of the declarations or statements of principles in the platform of a political party or other organization. {1891}

Cf. PARTY PLATFORM.

1848 *Boston Courier* 28 Sept. 2/2 Another plank in the platform is, no Cass or other plank to be added. **1868** *N.Y. Herald* 2 July 4/1 [They] talk with an unreasonable enthusiasm about sweeping the country from Maine to California on that plank. **1894** *Congress. Rec.* App. 26 Jan. 79/1 The very author of the tariff plank in the Chicago platform was last fall buried beneath more than 80,000 votes in that grand old 'Buckeye' State. **1896** *Internat. Typogr. Union Proc.* 47/1 The following planks were adopted: Compulsory education, . . . municipalization of street cars [etc.]. **1925** BRYAN *Memoirs* 108, I explain elsewhere the origin of the most prominent plank in the platform.

‖**4.** *To have the plank*, to have the floor. *facetious.*

Cf. FLOOR 2 b.

1832 KENNEDY *Swallow Barn* I. 185 'Silence,' said Ned, 'Mr. Walker has the plank; we can only hear one at a time!'

5. *attrib.* **a.** Designating various things made of planks.

1837 *S. Lit. Messenger* III. 390/2 Within a plank enclosure . . . the emigrants were *bivouacked.* **1867** RICHARDSON *Beyond Miss.* 29 A few pleasant white warehouses . . . and unpainted plank shanties were erected. **1884** W. SHEPHERD *Prairie Exper.* 77 The saloon may be a single-roomed plank cabin, neatly papered. **1907** *St. Nicholas* July 772/1 He sat down in the mess-tent, spread the newspaper on the rough plank table, and slowly read the head-lines.

b. In special combinations.

Plank log, a log suitable for converting into planks; *p. man*, (see quotation); *p. string*, a plank used to support the treads and risers of a stairway; *p. wagon road*, =PLANK ROAD.

1718 HEMPSTEAD *Diary* 79 In the foren[oon] I was drawing up Mr Winthrops plank Log. **1920** COOPER *Under Big Top* 12 Plank men and seat men are those who erect the seats. **1897** F. C. MOORE *How to Build a Home* 99 Stairs shall have strong plank-strings not less than 2 inches in thickness. **1901** MERWIN & WEBSTER *Calumet 'K'* 38 Turning, he walked rapidly away down the plank wagon road.

***Plank,** *v.*

+**1.** *tr.* To produce or put down (money) readily. *colloq.*

1824 *Nantucket Inquirer* 19 April (Th.), His guardy was sent for, and he planked the cash. **1838** *Knickerb.* XII. 313 'But who's to *pay* for it, Bob?' 'I am, to be sure,' replied he, 'planking' the half dollar. **1854** M. J. HOLMES *Tempest & Sunshine* 114 But you will hardly win his fair, haughty lady, unless you can plank about a million. **1877** 'MARK TWAIN' *Punch, Brothers, Punch!* 37 'Up she goes,' says I, planking the cash.

b. With *down, out, up.*

1835 CROCKETT *Tour* 59 During the last war [he] planked up more gold and silver to lend the government than Benton ever counted. **1848** BURTON *Waggeries* 65 If the nigger . . . can plank up if he's cast, I'm darned if I don't . . . sue the nigger. **1850** COLTON *3 Years Calif.* 197 Dr. S—— was the first to plank down. **1853** SIMMS *Sword & Distaff* (1854) 243 Plank down agin the heap, both on you. **1876** MILLER *First Families* 93, I move that Sandy take the chair . . . and plank down twenty ounces for the Widow. **1883** 'MARK TWAIN' *Life on Miss.* 389, I plank out your share of the dollars regular. **1894** — *P. Wilson* ix, In de fust place, you gits fifty dollahs a month; you's gwine to han' over half of it to yo' ma. Plank it out!

+**2.** To broil, or bake, and serve (fish) on a piece of board.
1877 HOWELLS *Out of Question* 134, I suppose you plank horn-pout, here. **1891** *Fur, Fin, & Feather* March 197/1 Cook the trout as Jerseymen cook shad—plank them. **1906** PRINGLE *Rice Planter* 298 The hope of getting a shad fresh from the river and having it planked.

Plank bridge. A bridge the flooring of which is made of heavy planks. — **1786** WASHINGTON *Diaries* III. 135 The Farmer having carrd. the level and staked it . . . on the No. Side from the plank bridge on Muddy hole. **1848** *Santa Fe Repub.* 24 May 2/3 There should be a plank bridge across the 'Rio Chicito' as the logs now there are becoming dilapidated. **1871** HOWELLS *Wedding Journey* 151 An elderly gentleman . . . clambered up on the plank bridge.

Planked, *a.* {1608-} +Of meat, esp. fish: Cooked and served on a piece of plank. (Cf. PLANK *v.* 2.) — **1855** *Baltimore Sun* 30 April (B.), Did you ever eat a planked shad? **1872** *Harper's Mag.* Aug. 349/1 They will cook in a few minutes with a flavor surpassing that of the famous planked shad of the Lower Potomac. **1877** HOWELLS *Out of Question* 134 [The] new fellow at the club . . . interprets one's ideas of planked Spanish mackerel with a sentiment that amounts to genius. **1902** WHITE *Blazed Trail* 171 We'll have a *bisque*. . . . Then planked whitefish, and have them just a light crisp brown. **1906** *N.Y. Globe* 27 April 7 The planked chicken was served on the plank.

+**Plank fence.** A fence made of planks. (Cf. BOARD FENCE.) — **1850** *Western Journal* III. 339 A plank fence round a forty acre lot, five feet tall. **1872** TICE *Over Plains* 257 Imagine a plank fence some seven feet high, with a support inclined at an angle of forty-five degrees, and you will have a tolerably correct idea of the appearance of a snow fence. **1892** ALLEN *Blue-Grass Region* 28 Some [limestone fences] being torn down and superseded by plank fences or post-and-rail fences.

+**Plank fencing.** =prec. — **1880** 'MARK TWAIN' *Tramp Abroad* 386 Every few hundred yards, one came across a panel or so of plank fencing. **1885** *Rep. Indian Affairs* 167 We have . . . 2 miles of plank fencing.

***Planking. 1.** A structure made of planks. +**2.** The action of preparing planked fish. (Cf. PLANK *v.* 2, PLANKED.) — **(1) 1871** HOWELLS *Wedding Journey* 266 The promenaders . . . paced back and forth upon the planking. **1883** — *Woman's Reason* xii, Helen had walked across the planking on her way to Mr. Hibbard's office. **1897** — *Open-eyed Conspiracy* xv, The dancing was to be out of doors on a vast planking, or platform. **(2) 1883** *Century Mag.* Aug. 549/2 The 'Coroner' is cleaning the shad for planking.

+**Plank road.** A road made of planks placed transversely on longitudinal supporting timbers. {1888, in Germany}
1848 *Mich. Gen. Statutes* I. (1882) 914 All corporations hereafter created for the purpose of constructing plank roads, shall be subject to the provisions hereinafter contained. **1852** *Daily Republic* (Wash., D.C.) 3 April, Plank Roads are being most extensively constructed throughout the country. **1863** *Rio Abajo Press* 26 May 3/2 Their fancy vehicles . . . do very well on MacAdamized and plank roads. **1887** *Courier-Journal* 3 May 3/8 To purchase or otherwise acquire stock in any street railroad, and turnpike and plank road, electric light company. **1899** CHESNUTT *Wife of His Youth* 314 A black man limped slowly along the old Lumberton plank road.
attrib. and *comb.* **1850** *Western Journal* IV. 93 The New York general plank road law fixed four rods . . . as the least permissible width. **1901** HARRIGAN *Mulligans* 104 He used to be a plank-road builder at Coney Island.

+**Plank-road company.** A company interested in building plank roads. *Obs.* — **1848** *Mich. Gen. Statutes* I. (1882) 918 Whenever any plank road company may wish to use any part of a public highway or street [etc.]. **1871** *Penna. Laws* 1100 The Harrowgate and Plank Road Company, . . . shall have full power and authority to sell all or any part of the real estate before mentioned. **1881** *Mich. Gen. Statutes* I. (1882) 402 The commissioner of highways of each township . . . [shall] see that all plank or gravel road companies . . . maintain their roads in . . . good and safe condition.

+**Plank sidewalk.** =BOARD SIDEWALK. — **1855** *Chicago W. Times* 9 Aug. 1 The workmen were removing the plank sidewalk. **1866** MOORE *Women of War* 395 Women were afraid to walk over the plank sidewalks where some of the prisoners had been congregated . . . through fear of vermin. **1883** 'MARK TWAIN' *Life on Miss.* xxx, Plank sidewalks on stilts four feet high were still standing. **1910** J. HART *Vigilante Girl* 327 Bursts of burlesque sympathy came from the bystanders on the weed-grown plank sidewalks.

+**Plank walk.** =BOARDWALK.
1820 *Boston Selectmen* 145 An application from the proprietors of St. Paul's Church for a portion of the street was committed to the Chairman, granting liberty on condition they . . . lay a plank walk. **1850** S. F. COOPER *Rural Hours* 379 The new-fashioned plank-walks have not yet become general here; they are convenient in muddy weather, though very ugly at other times. **1876** A. D. WHITNEY *Sights & Insights* I. 62 How could I help it, Dixon's coming down the plank-walk from the house, with that covered basket? **1902** GORDON *Recoll. Lynchburg* 98 The barrels on which a plank walk leads to the wood-pile are almost covered. **1915** G. M. WHITE *Rose o' Paradise* 105 As they reached the plank walk, the boy lagged back.

Plan of Union. +An agreement, adopted by the American Presbyterian and Congregational churches early in the nineteenth century, permitting their members in the Middle West to unite. Also *Plan of Unionism.* — **1808** in Sweet *Religion on Amer. Frontier* II. 469 It was voted unanimously, that this body acceed to the plan of union with the Presbyterian church in the United States. **1856** W. S. KENNEDY *Plan of Union* 144 The last half century has . . . developed a new type or modification of ecclesiasticism . . . which we may call co-operative Presbyterianism, Plan of Unionism, or Presbyterialized Congregationalism. *Ib.* 152 The missionary, with the Plan of Union in his hand and the love of God in his heart.

+**Planometer.** (See quot. 1864.) — **1864** WEBSTER 995/2 *Planometer,* . . . a plane, hard surface, used as a standard gauge for plane surfaces. **1876** KNIGHT 1726/2 Plane-surfaces are produced by the planing-machine, by the file, and by grinding, using an abradant. For the purpose of verifying their accuracy, the *planometer* was devised by Whitworth.

***Plant,** *n.*

1. A factory or other business establishment engaged in making or producing something. {1789-}
1875 *Chicago Tribune* 11 Sept. 4/3 The grounds [of the Union Rolling Mills] . . . contain two complete 'plants' for the Bessemer process. **1896** *Internat. Typogr. Union Proc.* 28/2 The plant was completely tied up. **1902** LORIMER *Lett. Merchant* 183 But when John L. Sullivan went through the stock yards it just simply shut down the plant. **1908** STEVENS *Liberators* 301 The first one [bill] made the same provision for other public utility plants.
transf. **1883** *Rep. Indian Affairs* 176 We can do it here only because the immense 'plant' for the negro [at Hampton Institute] makes it possible.

+**2.** (See quotation.)
1881 INGERSOLL *Oyster-Industry* 246 *Plant.*—In some localities, a young oyster, suitable for transplanting.

3. In special combinations.
Plant basket, a container for plants; *p.-cutter,* a device for cutting the taproots of plants; *p.-dropper,* one who drops plants or slips at places where they are to be transplanted; *p. stand,* a stand or support for plants.
1864 *Harper's Mag.* Dec. 40/1 She had a fanciful way of hanging plant-baskets about. **1857** *Ill. Agric. Soc. Trans.* III. 489 After the frost has completely checked the growth in the fall, the plants are to be taken up, by first running the *plant cutter* underneath and cutting them off at about eight inches deep. **1898** *Atlantic Mo.* April 504/1 The plant-droppers went ahead, . . . the main transplanting body followed, . . . and the waterer brought up the rear. **1903** WIGGIN *Rebecca* 247 She buried her face in the blooming geraniums on Miss Maxwell's plant-stand.

***Plant,** *v.*

+**1.** *tr.* To bury (a deceased person). *slang.*
1855 *Harper's Mag.* Dec. 37/1 [The yellow fever] don't take the acclimated nor the 'old uns;' . . . but let it catch hold of a crowd of 'Johnny come latelys,' and it plants them at once. **1867** 'MARK TWAIN' *Jumping Frog* 163 He died. There was not a dry eye in the crowd when they planted him. **1898** CANFIELD *Maid of Frontier* 186 They planted Chisolm in the little cemetery. **1910** RAINE *B. O'Connor* 18 Nothing left to do but plant the deceased and collect the insurance.

+**2. a.** To introduce or deposit (fish) in a pond. **b.** To deposit (oysters, oyster shells, etc.) in artificial beds. (Cf. PLANTING 3.)
(a) 1871 *Penna. Laws* 276 Fishes planted and retained in private ponds shall be at the disposal of their owners. **(b) 1881** INGERSOLL *Oyster-Industry* 246 *Plant.* . . . To place the oysters on artificial beds, intending them to survive the winter, attain full size, and spawn. . . . In Connecticut the term is applied only to southern oysters, laid down for the summer. **1883** *Nat. Museum Bul.* No. 27, 224 More attention is given to 'planting' [oyster] shells and other suitable cultch than in Rhode Island. *Ib.* 226 Citizens of the State [of Delaware] alone are permitted to 'plant' oysters.

***Plantain.**[1] Any one of various plants of the genus *Plantago,* as *P. major* and *P. lanceolata.*
See also ENGLISH PLANTAIN.
1676 GLOVER *Va.* in *Phil. Trans.* XI. 629 There grow wild in the Woods, Plantane of all sorts. **1709** LAWSON *Carolina* 78 The more Physical [herbs], are Carduus Benedictus, . . . Coriander, all sorts of Plantain of England [etc.]. **1840** DEWEY *Mass. Flowering Plants* 114 *Plantago major.* Common Plantain. One of the plants that seem to follow man in the temperate climes. **1867** *Amer. Naturalist* I. 404 The Plantain or Rib-grass (*Plantago lanceolata*), a troublesome plant which is too rapidly finding its way into meadows and waste places. **1903** FOX *Little Shepherd* xxx, The yard was running wild with plantains.

Plantain.[2] **1.** A tropical plant (*Musa paradisiaca*) closely resembling the banana. **2.** The fruit of this. {1604-} — **(1)** [**1776** FRENEAU *Poems* (1809) I. 212 The plantane and banana flourish here [in Santa Cruz].] **1837** WILLIAMS *Florida* 114 The plantain and bananna [*sic*] succeed to perfection in the southern district. **1860** ABBOTT *South & North* 212 They . . . brought their gardens into useful cultivation, with yams, bananas, plantains. **(2) 1827** DEWEES *Lett. from Texas* 66 Oranges . . . and plantains are to be found here in great quantities. **1831** Peck *Guide* 62 Negresses [in New Orleans] . . . carrying on their bandanaed heads . . . a whole table, or platform as large as a table, covered with . . . oranges, and figs, and bananas or plantains. **1885** *South Fla. Sentinel* (Orlando) 3 June 4/1 Plantains and sugar-cane have been brought in such quantities to Key West from Havana that they have glutted the market.

***Plantation.**

1. A British colony or colonial settlement in the territory now occupied by the United States. Now hist.

[**1606** *1st Va. Charter* i, James, by the grace of God, King of England, Scotland . . . etc. [do] . . . vouchsafe unto them our Licence to make Habitation, Plantation, and to deduce a Colony of sundry of our People into that Part of America, commonly called Virginia.] **1636** *Conn. Rec.* I. 2 Geo. Hubberd shall (survey) the breadth of the plantacon of Dorchester. **1695** *R.I. Col. Rec.* III. 303 Their Majesties may constitute a Chief Commander, who may have authority at all times to command . . . the forces of each Collony or Plantation. **1705** *Providence Rec.* XVII. 201 The which tree . . . is a bound Marke betweene the sd. two Plantations of sd. Providence & Warwick. **1789** in Jay *Correspondence* III. 76 Let all the English American plantations now take notice that the New Englanders in their late Revolution did but act in a quarrel wherein they and all Englishmen had an interest. **1832** WILLIAMSON *Maine* I. 53 The Sagadahock plantations, or settlements, must be called the 'Ancient Dominions' of Maine. **1903** *Amer. Hist. Review* VIII. 268 The word 'colony' merely took on a broader meaning than before, while 'plantation' remained what it had been, a local community subject to colonial government.

b. The settlers in a colony. *Obs.*

1636 *Conn. Rec.* I. 4 Every plantacon shall traine once in every moneth. **1672** *Ib.* II. 172 If Windsor plantation at their next towne meeting . . . will release their township right [etc.].

+c. *transf.* A settlement; a place occupied temporarily by a group of people. *Obs.*

1682 M. RAWLINSON *Narr. Captivity* 13 There was, as I said, about six miles from us, a smal Plantation of Indians. **1832** WILLIAMSON *Maine* I. 61 [Monhegan Island] was so noted a stage for the latter [fishermen] as to be sometimes called a *plantation*.

+2. A homestead, farm, or estate.

As a rule, in New England and the North, plantations were moderate in size, and were worked by their owners, with or without hired help. In the South plantations often embraced hundreds or thousands of acres, and were devoted to raising tobacco, cotton, rice, and sugar cane, largely by slave labor. (See also COTTON PLANTATION.)

1645 *New Haven Col. Rec.* 200 Noe planter, inhabitant or sojourner within or belonging to this towne . . . [shall] purchase any plantation or land . . . of any Indian. **1697** *Md. Hist. Mag.* XV. 116 [The Indian] comes on the Back of his Plantation, gathers his Green Corn [etc.]. **1730** *Penna. Gazette* 29 Oct., A Plantation containing Two Hundred and odd Acres, . . . in the Eastern Division of New-Jersey, . . . is fit for either Stock or Grain. **1786** WASHINGTON *Diaries* III. 43 The field intended for experiment at this Plantation is divided into 3 parts, by bouting Rows running crossways. **1817** *Ann. 14th Congress* 2 Sess. 845 The petitioner owned a plantation and house situated on the right bank of the Mississippi. **1853** *Harper's Mag.* Nov. 758/1 The various buildings necessary upon every plantation for the manufacture of cane juice into sugar. **1892** R. H. DAVIS *Silhouettes* 8 Isn't this the old Sevier plantation? **1908** 'O. HENRY' *Options* 88 Long time ago the gentlemen of the family had worn lace ruffles and carried tinless foils and owned plantations and had slaves to burn.

transf. **1904** M. MICHELSON *Madigans* 320 Everybody wanted something from Warren Pemberton, King Sammy's viceroy, in charge of his mining interests and his political plantations.

+3. (See quot. 1881.)

1881 INGERSOLL *Oyster-Industry* 246 *Plantation.*—Cultivated areas of oyster-bottom. A common and legal term in the state of Delaware. **1891** W. K. BROOKS *Oyster* 127 Before the bottom was laid out in private plantations, there were very few persons living there.

+4. *attrib.* and *comb.* **a.** Designating institutions, trade, etc., associated with the American colonies.

1645 *New Haven Col. Rec.* 191 Deputies . . . shall assist with the magistrates of this plantation in a monthly plantation court. **1677** *R.I. Col. Rec.* II. 597 Wee haveing lately taken a view of the continent and what accommodations it may afford for plantation settlements, . . . desire your speedy answer. **1696** *Mass. Province Acts & Resolves* VII. 514 All other Laws made For the Encouragemt. of navigation and Securing the Plantacon Trade [shall] be strictly put in Eexecution within this Govermt.

+b. Designating various things kept or used on plantations or farms.

1832 in Commons, etc. *Doc. Hist.* I. 129, I leave my plantation shot-gun with you. **1840** *Picayune* 28 July 1/5 Light Jersey Wagons; Drays; Plantation and City Carts. **1841** CIST *Cincinnati* Advt., Every description of plantation wagons, ox carts [etc.]. *c*1850 in Stowe *Key* 129/2 The subscriber . . . will proceed to sell, by public auction, . . . the plantation and shop tools of all kinds. **1860** ABBOTT *South & North* 324 They will do at least a third more work than they now do impelled only by the terror of the plantation-whip. **1888** CABLE in *Century Mag.* Nov. 112/1 They were only nine in all—old, yellow, ragged, torn, leaves of a plantation account-book. **1902** G. C. EGGLESTON *D. South* 58 Why, I keep the plantation book, you know.

+c. Designating life, or aspects of life, on a southern plantation.

1836 GILMAN *Recoll.* (1838) 209 Marion and my brothers wore their usual plantation dress, with hunting-coat and cap. **1852** STOWE *Uncle Tom* xix, How came you to give up your plantation life? **1856** OLMSTED *Slave States* 454 They were generally neatly dressed, . . . but in a distinctly plantation or slave style. **1869** TOURGEE *Toinette* (1881) 266 Then she thought of her heavy plantation shoes. **1884** HARRIS *Mingo* 234 His voice was the loudest at the corn-shucking, his foot was the nimblest at the plantation frolics.

+d. Designating one who serves or works on a southern plantation.

1843 *Knickerb.* XXII. 2 A kind Providence sent a fellow-being along my path, . . . my first specimen of a plantation servant. **1852** STOWE *Uncle Tom* xii, 'Why, I reckon she *is* tol'able fair,' said Haley. . . . 'Plantation hand?' said the man. **1865** PIKE *Scout & Ranger* (1932) 146 No other musician can render the piece on the violin or banjo like an Arkansas plantation darkey. **1905** PRINGLE *Rice Planter* 145 This is an old time plantation sick nurse, who, though now very old, flies to relieve the sick with enthusiasm.

e. In miscellaneous combinations.

Plantation fly, (see quotation); *p. horse,* a horse used on a plantation or suitable for such use; *p. road,* a road on or leading to a plantation; *p. store,* a store located on a plantation.

1862 *Harper's Mag.* Nov. 736/1 Here [in the middle and southern states] is another agent of Nature, the *Musca plantarium*—'Plantation Fly.' **1790** FANNING *Narrative* 64, 12 plantation Horses, three unbroke . . . [£] 96.00. **1884** 'CRADDOCK' *Where Battle Was Fought* 120 She and Marcia . . . started for an afternoon walk along the quiet plantation road. **1891** 'THANET' *Otto the Knight* 160 You can see the plantation-store and mill.

+Plantation bell. A large bell on a southern plantation for summoning and directing Negro slaves. *Obs.* — **1840** *Picayune* 18 Aug. 2/6 The subscribers . . . offer for sale . . . Plantation Bells. **1887** *Century Mag.* Nov. 112/2 Now the tones of the big plantation-bell are heard. . . . All the gangs stop work, and people and animals go trooping to the quarters for dinner.

+Plantation bitters. A medicinal liquor or tonic originally used on large plantations in the South. *Obs.* — **1867** DIXON *New America* II. 96 These people say, they want no Cherokee medicines, no plantation bitters, no Bourbon cocktails. **1868** *Ore. State Jrnl.* 6 June 1/2 All over the world people of sense and judgment have learned to use Plantation Bitters. **1877** *Harper's Mag.* Dec. 111/1, I have tracked Coldpepper's Bitters and Duck's Plantation Bitters to the fountain-head.

+Plantation dog. A dog kept on a southern plantation. (Cf. NEGRO DOG) — **1839** *S. Lit. Messenger* V. 377/1 Tommy King . . . followed by several lean, plantation dogs, brought up the rear. **1853** STOWE *Key* 186/1 The leaders of the community . . . keep this blind furious monster of the *mob,* very much as an overseer keeps plantation-dogs, as creatures to be set on to any man or thing whom they may choose to have put down.

Plantation house. A house, esp. the owner's residence, on a plantation. {1722-} (Cf. BIG HOUSE.) — **1722** *Amer. Wkly. Mercury* 15-22 March 2/2 A Tract of Land . . . together with a good Plantation-House. **1831** PECK *Guide* 55 All the plantation houses are surrounded with rich and beautiful groves. **1885** *Outing* Nov. 154/1 Katie spent much of the time . . . taking note of the old-fashioned plantation-houses. **1899** 'O. HENRY' *Roads of Destiny* 316 Dark-green groves . . . showed where the plantation-houses stood.

+Plantation manners. Rude or ill-mannered conduct. — **1857** W. R. ALGER *Genius & Posture of Amer.* 6 This slaveholder [James M. Mason] has grossly insulted our Congressional delegation . . . , carrying his insults so far . . . that our distinguished Senator . . . was forced openly to rebuke his 'plantation manners.' **1890** *Congress. Rec.* 14 May 4661/1, I was charged the other day with being guilty of plantation manners. **1897** *Ib.* 31 March 548/2 When I was a boy, . . . I used to read a great deal about what the early Republicans called 'plantation manners.'

+Plantation melody. A melody popular among the Negroes on southern plantations. — **1881** *Harper's Mag.* May 818/2 The plantation melodies and minstrel ballads have won popularity wherever the English language is spoken. **1893** *Ib.* April 802/1 Used to singing 'spirituals' and plantation melodies, they carried into the rendition of the cantata the simplicity and the primitive pathos of their musical natures.

+Plantation Negro. A Negro slave accustomed to performing unskilled field work on a plantation.

Cf. FIELD HAND, FIELD NEGRO.

1771 *Md. Hist. Mag* XIV. 135 My People . . . do not live so well as our House negroes, But full as well as any Plantation negroes. **1797** HAWKINS *Letters* 174 He is a good waggoner and active plantation negro. **1836** GILMAN *Recoll.* (1838) 81 Plantation negroes prefer to bury their dead at night or before sunrise. **1896** J. G. WILLIAMS *Ole Plantation* pref., I remember hearing the old plantation negroes before the war speak of one as a 'Gullah nigger' and another as a 'Guinea nigger.'

attrib. **1880** E. JAMES *Negro Minstrel's Guide* 4 Short crop, or plantation negro wigs, $12 per dozen.

b. A Negro tenant on a plantation.

1884 *Century Mag.* March 653/2 Unlike the plantation negroes of the South, they [*i.e.,* Northern Negroes] are provident and economical.

+Plantation slave. A Negro slave on a plantation. Now hist. — **1853** STOWE *Key* 16/2 Douglass . . . was a plantation slave in a proud old family. **1900** *Congress. Rec.* 31 Jan. 1367/1 The registrar may require every applicant for registration to prove his age. . . . A white man 50 years of age would find it exceedingly difficult to make this proof, . . . as would also the old plantation slave.

+**Plantation song.** A song often sung by plantation Negroes. — **1855** *Putnam's Mo.* Jan. 72/2 Upon his ears there fell the echo of a new plantation song. **1871** DE VERE 116 The Negro-minstrel . . . adopts the black man's manner and instrument, and recites his field and plantation songs. **1884** *Century Mag.* March 681/1 The negro-minstrel . . . sang and jumped Jim Crow, alternating this *chanson de geste* with 'Clar de Kitchen' and other genuine plantation songs.

Plant bed. {1881–} +A bed of fine, rich soil in which plants are grown from seed preparatory to transplanting. — **1833** *Niles' Reg.* XLIV. 411/1 He is clearing new grounds; preparing and burning plant-beds. **1904** GLASGOW *Deliverance* 486 If the rain had come a week later the tobacco would have been ruined. I've just been taking it up out of the plant-bed. **1907** *St. Nicholas* May 651/1 A 'running' board was put around the base and a plant bed about a foot wide made within this.

+**Plant bug.** Any one of various bugs that infest plants and suck their juices. {1864} Also attrib. — **1856** *Rep. Comm. Patents 1855: Agric.* 93 There are several insects of the 'plant-bug' species found both upon the young and the old bolls. **1860** *Ladies' Repository* June 367/2, I found a plant-bug which had plunged this thread-like sucker of his into the body of a caterpillar. **1892** KELLOGG *Kansas Insects* 80 Tarnished plant bug (*Lygus lineolaris*). . . . The blossoms of apple trees are a favorite feeding ground of this pest.

Plant cane. {1793–} +Sugar cane produced from planted seed or germs, as distinguished from ratoon or stubble cane. — **1827** in Commons, etc. *Doc. Hist.* I. 214 Most of the plant cane, and also stubbles of Creole cane in new land mark the row. **1856** *Magnolia Place Jrnl.* 17 Nov. (Univ. N.C. MS.), The last 40 acres we Planted took about 12 acres of Good Plant Cane. **1892** *Mod. Lang. Notes* Nov. 393 *Seed cane*—the seed or plant cane.

***Planter.**

+**1.** One of those who planted the earliest British colonies in the present United States. Usually *first planter. Obs.*

Cf. FIRST SETTLER, OLD PLANTER.

*c***1618** STRACHEY *Virginia* 25 Our elder planters (at their first comyng) proclaymed His Majestie king of the country at Mohominge (a neighbour village). **1659** *Dedham Rec.* IV. 230 The first planters agreed that they would entertein only sixty persons to the priveledge of house lotts. **1687** SEWALL *Diary* I. 177 This day Capt. Walker, a very aged Planter, buried at Lin. **1710** *Boston Rec.* 157 The first Planters and Inhabitants . . . did at their first Settlement . . . Sett apart, that Peice or parcell of Ground, now Known by the name of the Old burying place in Boston. **1764** HUTCHINSON *Hist. Mass.* I. 417 One great design of the first planters of the Massachusetts colony [was] to obtain . . . the liberty of worshipping God.

2. A farmer, owner, or proprietor of an agricultural holding or estate. {1647–, of W. Indies}

The word in this sense is chiefly southern. It was first used (see group 1 of the quotations) of the wealthy slaveholders of Virginia and Maryland whose chief crop was tobacco. The word in its wider use (group 2) retained its connotation of wealth, being regularly applied to the rich plantation-owners of the south, but (group 3) was sometimes applied to small proprietors.

(1) **1619** *Va. House of Burgesses* 11 Provided first that the Cape Marchant do accept of the Tobacco of all and everie the Planters here in Virginia. **1730** *Md. Hist. Mag.* XIX. 180 He is a neat planter. **1799** WELD *Travels* 89 [In Va.] those who raise tobacco and Indian corn are called planters, and those who cultivate small grain, farmers. **1800** TATHAM *Agric. & Commerce* 46 The cultivator who follows the ancient track of his ancestors, is called a *planter;* he who sows wheat, and waters meadows, is a *farmer.* **1837** *S. Lit. Messenger* III. 86 It may suit my neighbor . . . to have one of them high-headed Roanoke planters to come here.

(2) **1682** ASH *Carolina* 7 [From the peach] the Planters compose a pleasant refreshing Liquor. **1709** LAWSON *Carolina* 63 The Planters posessing all these Blessings, and Produce of great Quantities of Wheat and Indian Corn. **1799** WELD *Travels* 79 The ferry-house was one of those old dilapidated mansions that formerly was the residence perhaps of some wealthy planter. **1817** S. BROWN *Western Gazetteer* 150 The yearly income of many of the planters, amounts to 20,000 dollars. **1856** OLMSTED *Slave States* 682 We were passing a hamlet of cottages, occupied by Acadians, or what the planters call *habitans.* **1887** EGGLESTON in *Century Mag.* April 905/1 To Sheldon Church, in South Carolina, there came seldom less than sixty or seventy carriages, but a neighboring planter was accustomed to entertain the whole assembly. **1907** ANDREWS *Recoll.* (1928) 74 The fact that during the Civil War they remained peacefully toiling at the homes of the planters, so many of whom were absent, shows the kind relations that existed between master and slave.

(3) **1732** *S.C. Gazette* 97/1 Certain ill-minded Persons, having industriously endeavoured to persuade the poorer sort of Planters, that this Law was calculated for their Oppression and Ruin. **1738** BYRD *Dividing Line* (1901) 252 The poor Chaplain and two Surveyors, stoppt Ten Miles Short at a poor Planter's House. **1823** JAMES *Exped.* I. 71 The solitary planter, who has chosen his place remote from the habitation of any other family, has sometimes . . . a hand-mill. **1850** LEWIS *La. Swamp Doctor* 87 Every farmer in the South is a planter, from the 'thousand baler' to the rough, unshaved, unkempt squatter. **1870** *Scribner's Mo.* I. 157 It is, however, somewhat difficult for the Florida farmers, or planters, . . . to get their potatoes to market.

+**3.** An uprooted tree or tree trunk so planted or fixed in the channel of a river as to be a menace to navigation. Now hist.

Cf. SAWYER.

1802 ELLICOTT *Journal* 123 From the mouth of the Ohio, down to the Walnut Hills, it is not safe to descend the river in the night . . . on account of the sawyers and planters. **1812** STODDARD *Sk. Louisiana* 370 Some of them are called *planters,* because they are immoveable, and constantly expose their pointed shafts above the water. **1846** MCKENNEY *Memoirs* I. 152 Planters are trees, also; and, like sawyers, are also firm set at bottom, but are either too short to be seen above water, or have been . . . broken off. **1884** HIGGINSON in *Harper's Mag.* June 125/1 Their talk was of the dangers of the [Ohio] river; of 'planters and sawyers.'

4. An agricultural machine or device for planting seeds.

See also CORN-PLANTER 2 and SEED-PLANTER.

1850 *Rep. Comm. Patents 1849* 151 Having thus fully described my improved grain and seed planter. **1868** BRACKETT *Farm Talk* 129 They put in the corn with a planter the very first thing. **1873** *Ill. Dept. Agric. Trans.* X. 248 Mr. Smith said the clubs would meet this combination by a loaning of planters to each other.

Plant house. A greenhouse or conservatory. {1880–} — **1863** *Horticulturist* XVIII. 306 We again have the satisfaction of presenting two examples of Plant Houses; one a *Green-house*, and the other a *Cold Grapery.* **1874** *Dept. Agric. Rep. 1873* 338 The east wing, designed for a plant-house, is to be built of wood and glass.

***Planting.**

***1.** The action of placing seeds or plants in the ground preparatory to raising a crop.

1637 R. WILLIAMS *Letters* (1874) 4 The masters of families have . . . consulted about our common peace, watch, and planting. **1682** ASH *Carolina* 15 But finding a great deal of trouble in the Planting and Cure of [tobacco], . . . they do not much regard or encourage its Planting. **1784** SMYTH *Tour* I. 294 In each crossing, three grains of Corn are dropped and covered with a hand hoe; this is . . . termed *Planting of Corn.* **1814** J. TAYLOR *Arator* 233 [The planter] would be astonished to discover how often he had passed over the land, . . . in fallowing, hilling, cutting off hills, planting, replantings. **1885** JACKSON *Zeph* iv, He had left her . . . in the midst of the spring planting.

‖**b.** Ground or land upon which to plant a crop.

1643 *Portsmouth Rec.* 23 [Tha]t all theye that want plantinge be acomodated in the common fence.

***2.** A young plant or slip suitable for transplanting. {–1382}

1853 THOMAS *J. Randolph* 112 After my relative had set out his early York cabbages, we told Nat that he might have all the 'plantings' that were left.

+**3.** The placing of oysters in artificial beds.

Cf. PLANT *v.* 2.

1870 R. H. DAVIS in *Scribner's Mo.* I. 58/1 He went on for a while, calculating silently how many oysters would be needed for planting next week. **1884** *Nat. Museum Bul.* No. 27, 222 The only other branch of the industry not yet alluded to, is 'planting.'

+**4.** In special combinations.

Planting aristocracy, the wealthy slave-owning class in the South before the Civil War; *p. plan*, (see quotation); *p. region*, a region in which agriculture predominates; *p. site*, (see quotation); *p. state*, a state in which agriculture is the prevailing occupation.

1856 OLMSTED *Slave States* 272 From the beginning the planting aristocracy had merely been living on its capital. **1905** *Forestry Bureau Bul.* No. 61, 17 *Planting plan*, a detailed scheme for forest planting on a given area. **1866** *39th Congress 2 Sess.* Sen. Ex. Doc. No. 6, 144 There is a class of men, commonly known in the State as 'adventurers,' . . . swarming the planting regions like as many buzzards seeking for prey. **1905** *Forestry Bureau Bul.* No. 61, 17 *Planting site*, an area which is to be artificially stocked with forest growth. **1835** *Jamestown* (N.Y.) *Jrnl.* 7 Jan. 2/4 The great agricultural staples of the planting states are produced by a species of labor peculiar to those states.

+**Planting field.** In colonial times, a field in which crops were planted, as distinguished from one for hay or pasture. — **1636** *Cambridge Prop. Rec.* 330 Whosoeuer findes eyther horse[,] Cow, ox, goate, or Any other beast, in Any of the planting feildes . . . shall haue six pence a peice for bringing them out. **1656** *Braintree Rec.* 7 This way was . . . layed by the sid of Henry Neals planting feild one the south sid of the country way. **1684** *Providence Rec.* XVII. 39 On ye westerne part of John Scott his planting ffield a litle up the streame.

Planting ground. Ground upon which crops are planted. *Obs.* {1769–} — **1636** *Essex Inst. Coll.* IX. 28 John Abbie . . . is to haue . . . 3 acres of planting ground. **1666** *Warwick* (R.I.) *Rec.* 229 Any part or parcell of land broken up . . . for planting ground. **1740** *N.H. Probate Rec.* II. 777 A Rock between the Edge of the Mowing Ground and Planting Ground.

Planting land. Land suitable for growing crops. — **1640** *Portsmouth Rec.* 18 [He sh]all haue some planting land [granted] him. **1684** *Providence Rec.* VIII. 138 On ye westerne part of John Scot his planting land or field. **1706** *Ib.* XVII. 216 My meddow and planting Land which

Lieth in the vally. **1747** *Georgia Col. Rec.* VI. 186 He finds [the whole tract] to contain no more than about fifty Acres of good planting Land.

+**Planting lot.** A lot or small tract of land suitable for producing crops. *Obs.* — **1640** *N.H. Prov. Papers* I. 138 None shall fell any oke timber . . . , except it be upon their planting lott. **1663** *Essex Probate Rec.* I. 410 Moses is to have a planting lot. **1676** *Essex Inst. Coll.* LVI. 301 Henry Brown . . . conveyed to John Bayly . . . part of one end of my planting lott butting upon meadow of sd. Bayly.

+**Planting right.** The legal right or permission granted to or by an Indian to plant or cultivate a particular area or piece of ground. *Obs.* — **1700** *Brookhaven Rec.* 92 This planting Rite shall Descende to them & there children for Ever. **1762** *Huntington Rec.* II. 450 [We] do fully & absolutely give . . . unto them the said trustees . . . all the Soyl Right Planting and Hunting right and all the remainder.

Planting time. The time in spring when crops are planted. — **1637** *Essex Inst. Coll.* IX. 42 Mr. Ralph ffogg hath heretofore been taken of his owne imploymts. especially in planting time to attende vpon the towne occasions to his great prejudice. **1747** *N.J. Archives* 1 Ser. VII. 423 It looked barbarous to turn out people so late in the year, as it was planting time, and hard to get new places. **1845** F. DOUGLASS *Narrative* 1, I do not remember to have ever met a slave who could tell of his birthday. They seldom come nearer to it than planting-time, harvest-time [etc.]. **1877** *Rep. Indian Affairs* 59 A large tract of bottom land, hitherto cultivated, was submerged during planting-time by the Missouri.

Plant louse. (See second quot. 1890.) Also with defining terms. {1805–} — **1854** EMMONS *Agric. N.Y.* V. 264 *Aphis*, or Plantlouse. **1882** *Vt. Agric. Rep.* VII. 294 Insignificant as may be a single aphis these insects, known as 'plant lice,' are a pest everywhere that man cultivates. **1890** *Rep. Secy. Agric. 1889* 358 The Dog-wood Plant-louse (*Schizoneura corni*) is identical with a plant-louse which infests the roots of grass during summer. **1890** *Cent.* 4533/1 *Plant-louse*. . . . A small homopterous insect which infests plants; specifically, an aphid; any member of the *Aphididæ*. The members of the related family *Psyllidæ* are distinguished as *jumping plant-lice*. **1902** *Harper's Mag.* March 558/1 Instances [of parthenogenesis] are to be found in the bees, social wasps, *Bombyx psyche*, Daphnia, plant-lice, and others.

+**Plant patch.** A small area of fertile soil, well pulverized, in which plants are grown, usually for transplanting. — **1760** WASHINGTON *Diaries* I. 126 Visited my Quarters and saw a plant patch burnt at the Mill. **1775** in Rauck *Boonesborough* 177, [I] am just going to our little plant patches in hopes the greens will bear cropping. **1819** *Amer. Farmer* I. 204, I have a plantpatch, an old standing one, on a branch which we have always been able to water in the night or morning.

* **Plaster,** *n.* Also †**plaister.**

***1.** An external adhesive application consisting of a salve or other medicinal substance spread on a piece of muslin, silk, etc.

1638 *Mass. Bay Rec.* I. 224 Shee is not to meddle in surgery, or phisick, drinks, plaisters, or oyles. **1695** SEWALL *Diary* I. 408 He advises to a Plaister for the Stomach. **1772** A. G. WINSLOW *Diary* 22 Aunt Green gave me a plaister for my fingure that has near cur'd it. **1837** IRVING *Bonneville* II. 112 He stuck to the colt like a plaister, up ridges, down gullies. **1901** MCCUTCHEON *Graustark* 44 If the gentleman will allow Hedrick to trim the hair away for a plaster and then bandage it I think the wound will give him no trouble.

+**2.** Short for PLASTER OF PARIS. (Cf. GYPSUM.)

1787 WASHINGTON *Diaries* III. 222 Where the Plaister had been spread the white and red clover was luxuriant. **1816** U. BROWN *Journal* I. 264 A poor Hill Country well watered & adapted to Plaster without Doubt. **1840** *Mich. Agric. Soc. Trans.* V. 300 While he must pay for imported plaster, at the average rate of $20 per ton, the marl may be had for digging. **1880** *Harper's Mag.* June 67/2 Another glance detects the . . . farmer sowing his load of plaster across the whitening field.

3. In special combinations.

Plaster mill, a mill in which gypsum is ground for commercial use; *p.-sick*, of land, impaired in fertility from the excessive use upon it of plaster of Paris.

1839 *Mass. Agric. Survey 2d Rep.* 42 He says he knows nothing of land become, as it is termed, plaster-sick. **1846** EMMONS *Agric. N.Y.* I. 280 The material will be as useful, applied to land, as the plaster itself; besides, it is not necessary that it should be transported to a plaster mill, as it . . becomes in a few years sufficiently fine for use.

* **Plaster,** *v.* Also †**plaister.**

***1.** *tr.* To cover, overlay, or daub (laths, etc.) with builder's plaster or with clay. Also *ppl. a.*

1659 *Harvard Rec.* I. 10 Expences . . . for plaistring ye Study [one shilling]. **1674** *Md. Archives* II. 406 The Gouernour shall direct the said particions double Lathed and plaistred. **1701** *Boston Rec.* 11 Ceile two floors throughout the Sd House and plaster the Gable ends. **1750** HEMPSTEAD *Diary* 549, I was . . . plastering the broken places in the wall. **1829** T. FLINT *G. Mason* 10 [The chimney] was made of clefts, plastered with clay-mortar. **1885** *Rep. Indian Affairs* 26 The office and dwelling house are lathed and plastered, and painted inside and out.

+**2.** To treat (a crop) with plaster. Also *ppl. a.*

1814 J. TAYLOR *Arator* 155 [Bird-foot clover] among the plastered wheat will be three or four fold more luxuriant, than among the adjoining unplastered. **1839** *Mass. Agric. Survey 2d Rep.* 15 The crops are thus rated: corn without manure, but plastered. **1852** *Mich. Agric. Soc. Trans.* III. 171 As soon as the corn came up, it was plastered on the hill. **1860** T. D. PRICE *Diary* (MS.) 11 June, Finished plastering corn, put 2 barrels of plaster on the corn.

Plaster bed. A natural deposit of gypsum or plaster of Paris. — **1843** *Nat. Hist. N.Y. Geology* IV. 121 The third division, with the higher range of plaster beds, appears at Seneca falls. **1847** HOWE *Hist. Coll. Ohio* 393 On the peninsula which puts out into Lake Erie, are extensive plaster beds, from which large quantities of plaster are taken.

+**Plasterbill.** *Mass.* The surf scoter, *Melanitta perspicillata*. (Cf. BOX COOT.) — **1888** TRUMBULL *Names of Birds* 103 Surf Scoter: Surf Duck: Black Duck. . . . At Chatham, [called] Plaster-Bill. **1917** *Birds of Amer.* I. 151 Surf Scoter. *Oidemia perspicillata*. . . . [Also called] Pictured-bill; Plaster-bill; Morocco-jaw [etc.].

Plaster cast. {1825–} A plaster model or representation of a person or thing. {1859–} — **1842** *Knickerb.* XX. 468 The head of Miss Jewett is a portrait, taken from a plaster cast. **1856** STOWE *Dred* I. 18 Bronzes and plaster-casts . . . gave evidence of artistic culture. **1872** BRACE *Dangerous Classes N.Y.* 194 In the same room I would find monkeys, children, men and women, with organs and plaster-casts, all huddled together.

***Plasterer.** A workman who plasters walls, ceilings, etc. — **1659** *Suffolk Deeds* III. 433 This Indenture made . . . Betweene Richard martajne of boston . . . & mary his wife of the one parte and Thomas Cooper of the same boston Plaisterer of the other parte. **1709** LAWSON *Carolina* 167 All sorts of Handicrafts, as Carpenters, Joiners, Masons, Plaisterers, Shooemakers, . . . and most others, may . . . thrive very well in this Place. **1819** FLINT *Lett. from Amer.* 125 The more numerous part of the artizans are joiners, . . . plasterers, shoe-makers. **1907** *St. Nicholas* Oct. 1109/1 There are plumbers, electricians, plasterers, carpenters, [etc.,] . . . to be engaged.

***Plastering.** A coating of plaster on a wall, ceiling, etc. — **1741** *Md. Hist. Mag.* VIII. 359 Richard Wilkins . . . undertakes to pull down all the old Plaistering in the Church. **1777** *N.H. Comm. Safety Rec.* 79 There was . . . plastering broke down in several rooms. **1833** SILLIMAN *Man. Sugar Cane* 67 This [temperature] may be [maintained] . . . provided the room . . . is finished on the top with lath and plaistering. **1893** *Harper's Mag.* Feb. 444 From part of the wall the plastering was gone; it had fallen, and had never been replaced.

* **Plaster of Paris.** Also **plaister of Paris,** etc. Gypsum, in either its natural state or its dehydrated form. Freq. used as a top-dressing for soil. (Cf. PLASTER *n.* 2.)

1787 WASHINGTON *Diaries* III. 222 We rid to the Farm of one Jones, to see the effect of the plaister of Paris, which appeared obviously great. **1799** *Amer. Acad. Mem.* II. II. 75 A specimen of a beautiful milk white Gypsum, or plaster of paris, . . . found in large quantities in the township of Camillus and county of Onondago. **1812** *Niles' Reg.* II. 10/1 On the east side of the Cayuga lake . . . they have found a large bank of Plaister of Paris. **1830** [see GYPSUM]. **1873** *Winfield* (Kan.) *Courier* 26 June 2/3 How long will it be until Sumner and Cowley Counties will be using gypsum or plasterparis, made from their own quarries?

* **Plat,** *n.* Also †**platt, plett.**

***1.** A plan, chart, or map of a town, a river, or a piece of ground.

'Now only *U.S.*' (*O.E.D.*). See also TOWN PLAT.

*c*1640 *Cambridge Prop. Rec.* 334 A bridge is made . . . to ye new oxe-pasture soe since called as the plett of the meadow will show. **1667** *Groton Rec.* 23 At the same meetinge was a towne rate made ffor . . . him to mak two platts for the towne. **1714** *Essex Inst. Coll.* XXXVI. 330 We went to Salem & confirmed my plat by oath. **1745** *Baltimore Rec.* p. xxi, In which Book . . . shall be kept a fair Plat of said Town, neatly platted. **1785** *Md. Hist. Mag.* XX. 48 This Deponent . . . did some time afterwards see a plat of the Survey made at that time. **1806** *Ann. 9th Congress* 2 Sess. 1002 The surveyor having . . . laid down a plat of his work, showing the meanders of the Potomac and Ohio rivers. **1840** in *Mich. Agric. Soc Trans.* V. 312 The plats are now in the hands of the State Topographer, to be prepared for publication. **1877** JOHNSON *Anderson Co., Kansas* 143 The company went to work in October, . . . and had the plat and profile all made. **1893** *Scribner's Mag.* June 695/2 We ordered from the State Land Offices plats, showing the lands subject to entry. **1905** COLE *Early Oregon* 9 Plats of these new cities were made out and lots were offered for sale.

2. ***a.** An area or patch of ground, usually of small extent. +**b.** A piece of ground that has been surveyed and platted out, often of considerable extent.

1700 *Charlestown Land Rec.* 169 A plat of Marsh Land scittuate before the said Lathrops Doore, in Charlestown Already staked out. **1706** *Cambridge Prop. Rec.* 227 Sold . . . upland bounded Westerly & Southerly upon Mount Gilboa Platt. **1715** *Mass. H. Rep. Jrnl.* I. 5 A Petition of Joseph Morse Representative of the Town of Sherbourn, . . . Praying that a Plat of Four Thousand Acres of Land . . . may be confirmed to the said Town. **1773** FITHIAN *Journal* I. 77, I took a walk in the Garden; When I had gone round two or three Platts Mrs. Carter entered and walked towards me. **1834** PECK *Gaz. Illinois* 198 Each plat of ground in the common field was owned in fee simple by the person to whom granted. **1873** *Essex Inst. Coll.* XII. 110 The Plat on which the city was located was covered with large oaks. **1897** HOUGH *Story of Cowboy* 17

Some audacious hand has actually planted flowers about a small plat of precious green.

+3. An extent of level, open country; mesa land.

1814 BRACKENRIDGE *Views La.* 107 There are many fine tracts, and extensive platts. **1833** J. SCOTT *Ind. Gazetteer* 79 Half-moon Spring . . . rises in a plat of level rich land which extends some distance from the spring on all sides. **1836** IRVING *Astoria* I. 264 These lofty plats of table land seem to form a peculiar feature in the American continents. **1878** BEADLE *Western Wilds* 65 Westward a more fertile plat rose even to the foot of the Huaquetories.

**Plat, v. tr.* To make a map of (a piece of land, a town site, etc.) in accordance with a survey. {1766}

'Now only *U.S.*' (*O.E.D.*).

1703 *Cambridge Prop. Rec.* 218 Parcel of Land platted by Ensigne ffiske. **1715** *Mass. H. Rep. Jrnl.* I. 19 *Voted*, . . . That the Land Platted for a Town . . . be called by the Name of Brunswick. **1735** *Boston Rec.* 125 Voted, To proceed to the Choice of a Committee, to Inspect, Survey and Plat Three Tracts of Land, agreeable to the said Grant suitable for Town-ships. **1840** CALHOUN *Works* III. 539 About three-fourths [of the public lands] have been surveyed and platted. **1889** *Harper's Mag.* Feb. 360/1 [Bismarck, N.D.] was platted in 1872, and named in honor of Prince Otto von Bismarck. **1908** *Indian Laws & Tr.* III. 382 The Secretary of the Interior is hereby authorized . . . to survey, lay out, and plat into town lots, streets, alleys, and parks, not less than forty acres.

+**b.** *To plat down*, to plot out (a course) in order to calculate a distance.

1751 GIST *Journals* 61, I platted down our Courses and I found I had still near 200 M Home upon a streight Line.

Platan.* +The buttonwood or plane tree, *Platanus occidentalis*. In full *platan tree*. — **1698 SEWALL *Diary* I. 478 Set . . . the Poplar to the street and the Platan at the upper corner next to Charlestown. **1721** *Ib.* III. 288, [I] measured the Front of Elm Pasture, Ten Rods reach just two Rods above the Uppermost Platan Tree.

Platanus.* +=prec. — **1821 NUTTALL *Travels Arkansa* 58 On the river lands, as usual, grows platanus or buttonwood.

***Plate.**

***1.** *Building.* A strong timber put at the top of a frame; a wall plate.

1640 *New Haven Col. Rec.* 37 As for sills, beames, plates or such like timber. **1692** *Manchester Rec.* 44 It is therefore voted . . . to have a new meeting hous built . . . , the height between the sell and the plate to be sixteen foot. **1730** *Md. Hist. Mag.* VIII. 157 Mr. Philip Hammond . . . proposes further . . . to plank the Chappell below the plates with plank. **1800** HAWKINS *Sk. Creek Country* 69 Each building is a wooden frame, supported on posts set in the ground, covered with slabs, . . . the back and ends clayed, up to the plates. **1897** F. C. MOORE *How to Build a Home* 13 The studs as well as the corner posts are carried from the 'sill' . . . continuously to the wall-plate (usually called the 'plate') at the top of the wall. **1904** T. E. WATSON *Bethany* 8 Other rafters reached downward to rest upon outer plates.

***2.** A shallow vessel or dish from which food is eaten, or on which food may be placed. Sometimes made of metal, usually of earthenware.

1640 *Conn. Rec.* I. 448, 1 smale plate, . . . 2 peuter cupps, one peuter dram. **1686** SEWALL *Diary* I. 118 This day so cold that the Sacramental Bread is frozen pretty hard, and rattles sadly as broken into the Plates. **1748** WASHINGTON *Diaries* I. 11 Our Plates was a Large Chip. **1806** LEWIS in *L. & Clark Exped.* IV. (1905) 358 At dinner an indian fellow very impertinently threw a poor half starved puppy nearly into my plait by way of derision for our eating dogs. **1907** *St. Nicholas* Aug. 897/1 When the hamper from the hotel was opened, there were found knives and forks and plates and cups fitted in, in a most miraculous way.

***3.** *collect.* Domestic utensils, ornaments, harnessware, etc., made usually of silver.

1642 *Suffolk Deeds* III. 62 Tresurers Ordayned . . . to receive all such moneyes and Plate as shall be brought in. **1653** *Boston Rec.* 3 There may be a true Inventory taken of all . . . ready money, plate, rings [etc.]. **1674** *Harvard Rec.* I. 60 Only the plate [is] to be brought to the presidents house and lodged in the Colledg desks or chest there. **1680** *Conn. Probate Rec.* I. 355, I give to the South Church in Hartford £10 in plate for the use of the Sacrament. **1715** *Boston News-Letter* 17 Jan. 2/2 A Knot of Thieves . . . carry'd away Plate and other Goods. **1748** *Mayflower Descendant* X. 109 There is among my plate Two belly Cups Wrought which was belongen to my late wife when a maiden. **1833** [see PLATED WARE]. **1863** HOPLEY *Life in South* II. 257 Those who had money gave it, those who had not, gave plate and jewelry. **1889** *Century Mag.* Jan. 366/2 She took with her all her wardrobe, her jewels, the pictures from her bedroom, and part of her plate.

***4.** A thin, smooth sheet of metal of a size suitable for an inscription or writing.

1689 SEWALL *Diary* I. 261 Outside is black Velvet, and a small plate of Copper, telling time of's Death. **1882** MCCABE *New York* 233 Coffin plates of a variety of shapes . . . cast from $1 to $12. **1900** STOCKTON *Afield & Afloat* 261 Now, please look at the name on this silver plate.

+**b.** =GOLDEN PLATES.

[**1844** *S. Lit. Messenger* X. 531/1 These Records were engraved on plates which had the appearance of gold.] **1845** *Ib.* XI. 474/2 Assertions made by the late Joe Smith and his 'witnesses,' in regard to the discovery of the 'plates' upon which they pretend that the 'Book of Mormon' was written.

***5.** Bullion, esp. silver bullion; silver valued according to its weight. *Obs.*

1691 C. MATHER in *Mass. Bay Currency Tracts* 18 If the Influx of plate from the West-Indies be stopt . . . , and the Efflux in Returns for England continue [etc.]. **1720** *Amer. Wkly. Mercury* 1 Dec. 2/1 An Act for continuing the Currency of Bills of Credit to the Value of 6000 Ounces of Plate.

6. A polished sheet of metal engraved to print from {1655–}; a print made from this. {1681–}

1704 *Boston News-Letter* 31 July 2/2 And their Plate & Press is Seized, which it's hoped will put a full stop to the further progress of that wicked practice. **1719** SEWALL *Diary* III. 210 A notorious Counterfeiter of the New Twenty-shilling Bill . . . had his plate made in London, and came over in Clark. **1846** CORCORAN *Pickings* 93 The walls were ornamented with coloured plates of the fashions, cut from the monthly magazines. **1863** *Statutes at Large* XII. 670 The plates and special dies to be procured by the comptroller of the currency for the printing of such circulating notes shall remain under his control and direction. **1903** L. TAFT *Hist. Amer. Sculpture* (1925) p. ix, Plate I. Saint Gaudens. Lincoln.

+**7.** *Baseball.* =HOME PLATE.

1886 CHADWICK *Art of Pitching* 43 When the Umpire indicates the height of the ball required, the pitcher should send it in at once at the height required, but *not* over 'the plate.' **1893** *Chicago Tribune* 28 April 7/3 McGill's Inability to Get the Ball Over the Plate Brings Disaster. **1912** *Outing* LX. 34/2 The center fielder shoots back his arm for the throw to the plate. **1917** MATHEWSON *Sec. Base Sloan* 172 Ellis walked to the plate and faced Chase.

8. *attrib.* and *comb.* **a.** In sense 2 with *pan, rack, trencher*, etc.; in sense 2 or 3 with *stand.*

1642 *Md. Archives* IV. 96, 12 plate-trenchers & 11. sawcers. **1653** *Mayflower Descendant* XI. 101, 3 plate panns. **1717** *Mass. H. S. Coll.* 6 Ser. V. 365 One plate stand & two pair brass andirons. **1809** KENDALL *Travels* I. 141, I am sure that mistresses of families find *cards of invitation* . . . stuck, if not in card-racks, at least in *plate-racks*, and similar articles of kitchen-furniture. **1821** COOPER *Spy* xiii, He could see his way through the piles of reserved China and plate-warmers.

b. In sense 5 with *wreck.*

See also PLATE FLEET.

1704 *Boston News-Letter* 12 June 2/2 They took in about 10 Indian Divers, being designed in search for a Plate Wreck about Bohemia Islands.

c. In special combinations.

Plate basket, a lined basket in which silverware is kept {1838–}; +*p. boy*, a high cupboard in which plate for table use is kept.

1779 *York Co., Va., Rec.: Wills* XXII. 28 April, 1 plate basket, 1 churn, 3 funnels. **1899** *Boston Globe* 17 Sept. 33/2 Jacobean plate boys, with shelves rising nearly to the ceiling, are being especially built.

Plateau. A comparatively flat or level stretch of elevated land. {1796–} — **1853** J. W. BOND *Minnesota* 119 Henry M. Rice . . . conceived the idea of laying off the extensive plateau . . . immediately adjacent to St. Paul, into an 'addition' thereto. **1883** *Century Mag.* Oct. 921/1 [The Wilson's snipe] may be taken . . . around the edges of the alkaline lakes of the great central plateau of the Rocky Mountains. **1903** *N.Y. Ev. Post* 12 Sept., The tract consists of a bottom land along the Ohio River, and a plateau elevated 300 feet above the bottom land.

Plate button. A button made of metal, esp. silver. — **1685** *Conn. Probate Rec.* I. 377, I will and bequeath to my littel Cousen . . . my husband's platt buttons. **1737** HEMPSTEAD *Diary* 332, [I] bot . . . Some Plate Buttons of Pygan Adams.

Plated ware. Any ware covered over with a thin film of metal, esp. silver. Also comb. — **1789** *Ann. 1st Congress* I. 167 An impost of seven and a half per cent. ad valorem . . . was laid upon canes, . . . on gold, silver, and plated ware, and on jewellery and paste work. **1833** *Niles' Reg.* XLIV. 351/2 A fair of the American Institute exhibits . . . plate and plated ware, of the finest polish. **1865** *Chicago Tribune* 15 April 1 We offer also a splendid assortment of . . . Solid Silver and Plated Ware, Table Cutlery [etc.]. **1883** WELLS *Practical Economics* 125 Mr. Joseph Wharton, manufacturer of nickel in Pennsylvania, . . . protectionist, attacked certain Connecticut plated-ware manufacturers. **1893** *Harper's Mag.* April 791/2 Solid silver pots and pitchers, too. None of your plated ware.

Plate fleet. A fleet of ships used for carrying bullion. Now hist. {1625–1663, of the Spanish fleet} — **1708** *Boston News-Letter* 8–15 March 2/2 The said French Men of War [feared at Barbadoes] were gone to Convey home the Plate Fleet. **1763** W. ROBERTS *Nat. Hist. Florida* 90 Treasure out of the wreck, where the galleons, or plate-fleet, were cast away. **1774** in P. L. Phillips *Notes on B. Romans* 22 Opposite this River, perished the Admiral, commanding the Plate Flee[t] 1715.

Plate glass. A glass of fine quality cast in thick plates and rolled out with rollers. {1727–41–} Also attrib.

1844 *Knickerb.* XXIV. 287 A lanthorn, no mean apartment in itself, with its plate glass sides, twelve or fifteen feet high. **1866** *Ore. State Jrnl.* 30 June 1/1 The plate-glass, which comes from France or Germany, is first polished by means of rough brushes. **1875** STOWE *We & Neighbors* 384 They can have plate-glass windows, . . . and you pay for it all. **1877** ROE *Army Lett.* 162 That made old Hal try to pull me through an immense plate-glass mirror, in a hotel at Jackson, Mississippi. **1877** *Mich. Laws* 58 An act to allow plate glass insurance companies to do business in this state. **1885** *Century Mag.* Jan. 467/1 At the Pittsburgh plate-glass works, it [*i.e.*, natural gas] has proved especially valuable for tempering the large plates. **1900** MUNN *Uncle Terry* 252 Going to a nearby room, all mirrors and plate-glass, [he] called at the bar for brandy.

+**Plate matter.** Syndicated reading matter supplied to newspapers on stereotype plates. Also comb. (Cf. BOILER PLATE.) — **1887** W. REID in *Westminister Rev.* Oct. 862 This plate-matter became at once so popular with country publishers that new features were from time to time introduced. . . . Today one of these 'plate-matter' manufacturing firms has branch offices and foundries in New York, Boston [etc.]. . . . It furnishes matter for almost every department of a newspaper except editorial articles and local news. **1894** 'O. HENRY' *Rolling Stones* 171, I could have gotten all that from the American Press Association if I had wanted plate matter. **1907** GIVEN *Making a Newspaper* 230 Plate matter is a boon to the country editor.

Plater. An artisan who puts a thin layer or film of metal over something. {1777–} → **1719** *Boston Selectmen* 52 Richard Hanford & Joseph Watts Platers . . . [were] warned to depart.

***Platform,** *n.*

I. ***1.** A set of rules governing church discipline or doctrines, +esp. with reference to the Cambridge and Saybrook platforms (qq.v.).

1648 *Platform Church-Discipline* (1772) 5 We refer ourselves to the platform of church-discipline, agreed upon by this present assembly. *c***1680** HULL *Diaries* 246 A synod of churches . . . met at Boston. Voted the platform of discipline drawn at Cambridge, an. 1648, unanimously. **1712** *Boston News-Letter* 7 April 2/2 Reprinted and now Published, the New-England Platform of Church-Discipline, . . . agreed unto by the Elders and Messengers of the Churches, Assembled in the Synod at Cambridge, Anno 1649. **1771** BOUCHER *View of Causes of Revol.* 103 God forbid [that] this dominion [Va.] . . . shall be so degenerate and mean as to become the ape of New England in her civil institutions, and therefore too likely to follow the same wretched model in what the people of New England call the *platform* of religion! **1835–7** HALIBURTON *Clockmaker* 1 Ser. xii. 94 Why, says she, I guess I warn't brought up at all, I growed up. Under what platform, says he, (for he was very particular that all his house helps should go to his meetin,) under what Church platform? **1860** HOLMES *E. Venner* xviii, The more he read, the more discontented he became with the platform upon which he and his people were standing.

+**2.** A principle or, more commonly, a set of principles agreed upon by a group of people, usu. a political party, as a formulation of policy.

This sense appears to be primarily an extension of sense 1, but connotations of the material platform of sense 6 are usually present. Cf. the closely related sense 3 and PLANK *n.* 3.

1803 *Mass. Spy* 27 April (Th.), The platform of Federalism. **1832** *Niles' Reg.* XLIII. 1/2 Fifteen per cent. being the 'platform' on which certain interests would agree to *protect* the national industry!!! **1844** *Ib.* LXV. 408/1 These are our doctrines—this the broad platform on which we stand. **1871** *Scribner's Mo.* I. 453 All good men and women will find themselves upon a common platform. **1900** *Congress. Rec.* 19 Jan. 1006/1 There is one platform upon which we ought to be able to agree. **1921** *N.Y. Times* 11 Aug. 12/8 Communism 'will either have to revise its platform notably or be content to dwell in the barren regions of Utopia.'

+**b.** With reference to a designated issue.

1845 SUMNER in E. L. Pierce *Mem. & Lett. C. Sumner* III. 104 S. C. Phillips and W. B. Calhoun . . . will labor to bring the Whig party of Massachusetts to the antislavery platform. **1848** S. P. CHASE in *Amer. Hist. Ass. Rep. 1902* II. 135 If a popular candidate with any fair prospect of success could be brought out on the Free Territory platform we would have a fair chance of carrying Ohio. **1885** CRAWFORD *Amer. Politician* 229 We stand on the reform platform, for there is no country in the world where reform is more needed than it is here. **1890** *World Almanac* 70 Many requests were made during the last year for the publication of the Single Tax Platform. **1916** THOBURN *Stand. Hist. Okla.* I. 442 This radical temperance platform in this latitude excited our astonishment.

+**c.** A set of principles representing a single person's views.

1848 D. WEBSTER *Writings & Speeches* (1903) XIII. 367, I think he [Zachary Taylor] has made as good a platform for himself as other people, elsewhere, have made for themselves. **1849** *Knickerb.* XXXIV. 11 We have looked all through his paper and can't find one iota or scintilla of a platform. **1863** *Rio Abajo Press* 28 July 4/2 In these days of Platforms, it is necessary for everybody, and especially newspaper editors, to have a platform. **1903** 'O. HENRY' *Roads of Destiny* 166 He leaned on the desk and declared his platform to the clerk.

+**3.** A set of principles issued officially by a political party; the document stating these principles.

See also NATIONAL PLATFORM, OCALA PLATFORM, and note under sense 2.

1848 LINCOLN *Works* (1894) I. 137 There is nothing about it in the platform, nor elsewhere, that I have seen. **1857** *Lawrence* (Kan.) *Republican* 28 May 1 A free-state convention . . . adopted a platform which will be found appended to this address. **1861** MOORE *Rebellion Rec.* I. III. 23 Save the Union, and make kindling wood of all your partisan platforms. **1875** *Scribner's Mo.* Nov. 124/2 Voters, even though they have little to do with forming platforms and nominating men, can bolt. **1904** *Cincinnati Commerc. Tribune* 29 June 4 Mr. Bryan is a hefty guy when it comes to Democratic conventions and the platforms thereof. **1925** BRYAN *Memoirs* 173 The platform also laid the foundation for the currency legislation.

attrib. **1848** *Boston Courier* 26 Aug. 2/2 The Platform Candidate. . . . Mr. Van Buren . . . takes his stand upon the Buffalo platform, where he intends to 'walk delicately.' **1900** *Congress. Rec.* 5 Feb. 1527/2 He was a Chicago platform Democrat.

II. ***4.** A level place constructed as a base for artillery.

1653 *Boston Rec.* 6, I give . . . five pounds more towards the erecting of a platforme . . . in the Trayning place in Boston. **1727** *Ib.* 209 The Putting [the front wharf] . . . into a Posture fitt for a Platform of Guns would Demand a Considerable Sum of money. **1777** *N.H. Comm. Safety Rec.* 97 Wrote to Majr. Gains to procure Materials to Lay Platforms at Fort Washington.

5. ?The flooring of a meetinghouse belfry.

1657 *Watertown Rec.* I. I. 52 Looke apon the platt forme of the meeting howse, & to see wt. is to be don for the making of it thite.

6. A raised flooring, often of temporary construction, used as a speaker's stand; a place upon which distinguished guests sit at a public meeting; a stage. {1836–}

1840 *Niles' Reg.* LIX. 86/2 On the spacious platform sat some 200 ladies. **1856** *Democratic Conv. Proc.* 21 The Democratic members of the Senate and House of Representatives of the United States, who may be in Cincinnati . . . , are invited to take seats on the platform and floor of the Convention. **1895** *Amer. Art Jrnl.* 26 Jan., On the platform sat Joseph Armstrong . . . with the other members of the Christian Science Board of Directors. **1902** G. M. MARTIN *Emmy Lou* 52 The Teacher sat on the platform, and Emmy Lou loved the Teacher.

attrib. **1876** HABBERTON *Jericho Road* 56 The Squire was entitled to a platform seat at the meeting.

7. At a railroad station, a walk or floor alongside the track. {1838–}

1854 *La Crosse Democrat* 14 Feb. 2/5 [There is] but one change and that from one side of the platform to the other. **1890** *Stock Grower & Farmer* 19 April 7/4 Take a few brisk turns up and down the platform, and then go inside and eat one of Fred Harvey's meals. **1907** *St. Nicholas* Aug. 883/2 It's hot in here. Come out on the platform.

+**8.** In a railroad car, the separate floor space at the end, affording a means of entrance or exit; the corresponding part of a street car.

See also OBSERVATION 3.

1855 GLISAN *Jrnl. Army Life* 189 Some gentlemen on the platform of one car cried out that we would be run into, and sprang off. **1882** MCCABE *New York* 246 The women . . . get out on the platform before the car stops, and often have to be held back from jumping off. **1894** ALDRICH *Two Bites* 165, I hailed an approaching horse-car, and comforted myself on the rear platform with the reflection that perhaps the colonel would not wave the palmetto leaf too vigorously. **1907** LONDON *Road* 30 When the train starts, the shack rides out the blind. There is no way for him to get back into the train proper except by jumping off the blind and catching a platform where the car-ends are not 'blind.'

***Platform,** *v.* ‖*intr.* To work *for* the inclusion of something in a political platform. — **1859** LINCOLN *Works* (1894) I. 535 The point of danger is the temptation in different localities to 'platform' for something that will be popular just there.

+**Platform balance.** =PLATFORM SCALE. — **1811** *Boston Selectmen* 14 Dearborn's patent platform balance [for weighing hay, etc.]. **1860** HOLMES *E. Venner* iii, The master weighed himself at the grocer's on a platform-balance, some ten days after he began keeping the school.

+**Platform bridge.** 'A movable gangway over the space between the platforms of two railroad-cars, designed to protect passengers from falling between the cars' (*Cent.*).

+**Platform car.** A railroad freight car without either a top or sides; a flat car. — [**1843** E. H. DERBY *Two Months Abroad* 20/1 Diligences and private carriages are . . . transferred to platform cars, and at Rouen again placed on wheels, and put 'en route' for Havre.] **1858** W. P. SMITH *Railway Celebrations* 92 Cars. . . . Large Platform, 249; Lime, 10. *a***1861** WINTHROP *Open Air* 241 We are ordered to ship our howitzer on a platform car. **1878** BEADLE *Western Wilds* 52 He only had to take his store to pieces, ship it on a platform car to the next city, and set up again

+**Platform of principles.** A set of principles constituting a party platform. — **1848** *Niles' Reg.* LXXIV. 8/1 The letter of General Taylor . . . seems to be adopted by the Whigs of the country, as containing their platform of principles. **1856** (*title*), Platform of Principles of New York Know Somethings. **1887** *N.Y. Ev. Post* 20 Aug. (*Cent.*), A man does not bolt his party, but the candidate or candidates his party has put up. Sometimes, though less properly, he is said to bolt the platform of principles it has enunciated.

+**Platform scale.** A weighing machine having a platform on which objects to be weighed stand. Used esp. for weighing large objects.

1841 in Cist *Cincinnati* Advt., Platform & Common Scales. **1857** *Lawrence* (Kan.) *Republican* 28 May 3 Counter and Platform Scales, of all sizes and patterns, furnished to order by Allen & Gilmore. **1865** *Wkly. New Mexican* 8 Dec. 2/2 For Sale at the store of M. Kayser, four of Fairbank's large Platform Scales. **1876** INGRAM *Centennial Exp.* 267 In front of their exhibit was a platform scale, which had a plate-glass platform.

Platilla. A white linen fabric from Silesia. *Obs.* {1699–, in W. Indies} — **1732** *S.C. Gazette* 16 Dec., Goods lately imported, . . . Platilloes, trunks of Shoes. **1800** *Columbian Centinel* 25 Jan. 3/4 A Compleat assortment of India and Hard Ware Goods consisting of . . . Platillas and Brown Hollands. **1833** *Niles' Reg.* XLIV. 269/1 To be admitted at an ad valorem duty of 15 per cent. under the act of 14th July, 1832. Ticklenburgs, . . . Irish, Scotch and English linen sheetings: platillas.

Platilla royal. A fine kind of platilla. — **1777** *Penna Ev. Post* 18 Jan. 27/2 Russia sheetings, Dutch dowlasses, platilla royals . . . to be sold by William Sitgreaves.

Platina. =PLATINUM. *Obs.* {1750–} — [**1786** JEFFERSON *Writings* V. 241 You have heard often of the metal, called platina, to be found only in South America.] **1814** BRACKENRIDGE *Views La.* 63 A story is related of a wonderful mass of *platina*, on the Black river. **1820** *Plough Boy* I. 320 A mine of platina has lately been discovered in the state of Ohio. **1866** *Wkly. New Mexican* 6 April 2/1 The new discoveries of mineral wealth during the past year . . . in Taos county in platina and silver . . . will almost surpass human credibility.

Plating forge. A forge in which metal plates are made. — **1750** *Md. Hist. Mag.* II. 380 There was finished and is now in use . . . one Plateing Forge working with two Tilt Hammers. **1750** *Doc. Hist. N.Y. State* I. 730 There is erected . . . about twenty six miles from Hudsons River, one plateing Forge to work with a Tilt Hammer.

Plating mill. A mill in which metal is formed into plates. — *a***1817** DWIGHT *Travels* II. 16 In the two counties of Plymouth, and Bristol, there are . . . slitting and plating mills. **1876** RAYMOND *8th Rep. Mines* 358 In 1750 . . . Parliament . . . prohibited the erection in America of slitting, rolling, or plating mills, or steel furnaces.

Platinum. A heavy, ductile, metallic element of great value. {1812–} Also attrib. — **1834** DEWEES *Lett. from Texas* 152 It [a large rock of metal] is supposed to be platinum. **1865** *Wkly. New Mexican* 27 Oct. 1/4 Platinum. A rich vein of this ore has just been discovered near Taos. **1892** *Chicago Tribune* 11 Aug., It will be done by passing a current of electricity over a tiny coil of platinum wire. **1900** *Boston Ev. Globe* 18 Dec. 3/6 (Ernst), Pyrography is the art of making striking pictures upon calf and sheepskin with the red-hot point of a platinum needle.

Platman. ? A man who makes a map or plan of an area of land. — **1683** *Penna. Archives* I. 77, I shall observe what thee writes as to the platman.

Platoon.

1. *Mil.* A small body of foot soldiers or other fighting men; a subdivision of a tactical unit, as a squad or company. {1637–}

1757 *General Orders* 82 Corpll. Dorman & Lualen Rice . . . are to be Shot by a Plattoon of ye. Companys they belong too. **1788** CUTLER in *Life & Corr.* I. 420 Just as we got up with them, they began to fire by platoons. **1809** CUMING *Western Tour* 301 At Fort Adams . . . a subaltern with a platoon . . . [is] left in it, to guard the pass and prevent smuggling. **1838** J. MCDONALD *Biog. Sketches* 40 A platoon of Indians fired upon them. **1925** *Scribner's Mag.* Sept. 238/2 The second-in-command was pulled to his feet by Gunner Nice, who had taken the second platoon.

+2. A body of policemen; a police squad.

1876 INGRAM *Centennial Exp.* 614 After these [policemen] came double platoons of men. **1882** MCCABE *New York* 382 A platoon of police formed across the street was slowly retreating backward. **1898** *Scribner's Mag.* XXIII. 137/2 On election-day, the platoon which went on patrol at midnight is ordered to return to the station-house at 2.30 A.M. **1903** *Atlantic Mo.* Sept. 295 She looks out of the window and sees the platoon of policemen on a run to quell a riot.

+Platte Purchase. A triangular tract of almost two million acres of land (bounded on the west by the Missouri River north of Kansas City and included, since 1837, in the state of Missouri), purchased from the Indians in 1836 by the federal government. — **1850** GARRARD *Wah-To-Yah* xxiii. 277 Andrew . . . was from the Platte Purchase in Missouri. **1872** *Congress. Globe* 6 April 2245/1 'The Platte purchase,' which thirty-five years ago was the home of the Indian and the buffalo, . . . is now covered with beautiful farms, prosperous towns, thriving villages, and great and growing cities. **1894** ROBLEY *Bourbon Co., Kansas* 4 This territory between the due north line and the Missouri river was known as the 'Platte Purchase.'

***Platter.** A large flat dish or plate for serving meat, etc. 'Platter is nowadays a rather archaic term in Eng., but is still in current use in Am.' (Horwill).

1640 *Conn. Rec.* I. 448, 1 wooden platter, with 3 old latten pans. *c***1693** SEWALL *Letter-Book* I. 140 The bigest pewter platter not exceeding above 18 Inches over. **1745** *N.H. Probate Rec.* III. 320, I give to my welbeloved Daughter Sarah King all my Pewter which is Fouer Platers Six Plates one Bason. **1775** FITHIAN *Journal* II. 151 Large platters covered with meat of many sorts. **1858** THOREAU *Maine Woods* 147 Taking up the common platter, [the Indian] licked it clean. **1885** JACKSON *Zeph* ii, He put the beefsteak on a platter by the candlestick. **1915** *Ladies' Home Jrnl.* Oct. 48/4 The menu may include . . . a salad arranged in a platter in tiny individual portions.

+b. A game played by Indians. (Cf. MOCCASIN 3.)

1833 CATLIN *Indians* I. 88 Groups [of Indians] are engaged in games of the 'moccasin,' or the 'platter.'

Platter pie. A large fruit pie served on a platter. — **1828** *Yankee* July 227/1 A motherly quantity of lusty pumpkin and coalpit or two-story apple platter pies are provided.

***Play,** *n.*

***1.** A literary piece written for performance in a theater; a dramatic production.

1700 *Historical Mag.* April 118 The Humble petition of Richard Hunter, Sheweth That your honors Petitioner . . . [has] been at great charge and expense in providing persons and necessary's in order to the acting of Play's in this City. **1767** in H. M. Brooks *Gleanings* II. 2 (*title*), An Address to Persons of Fashion, concerning frequenting of Plays, Balls, Assemblies, Card-Tables, &c. **1784** in Dunlap *Hist. Amer. Theatre* 19 He begged the magistrates would indulge him in acting as many plays as would barely defray the expenses. **1853** A. C. M. RITCHIE *Autobiog. of Actress* 34 We would enact a standard play. **1890** HOWELLS *Boy's Town* 221 It was in this hall that he first saw a play, and then saw so many plays, for he went to the theatre every night. **1925** W. H. CRANE *Footprints & Echoes* 82 The play was a revival of *Little Nell and the Marchioness.*

+2. *Baseball.* A particular action or series of actions in which a decisive attempt is made by either side to advance its interest.

1868 CHADWICK *Base Ball* 46 A 'treble play' is made when three players are put out after the ball is hit, before it is pitched to the bat again. **1912** MATHEWSON *Pitching* 174 Most clubs try to keep an umpire from feeling hostile toward the team because, even if he means to see a play right, he is likely to call a close one against his enemies, not intending to be dishonest.

3. *attrib.* **a.** Of or pertaining to play as a recreation.

*a***1737** *Harvard Rec.* I. 401 (margin), A play-place for the Scholars. **1810** WEEMS *Washington* (1927) 38 Every day, at play-time, with corn-stalks for muskets, and calabashes for drums, the two armies [of schoolboys] would turn out. **1876** 'MARK TWAIN' *Tom Sawyer* vii. 78 She ran to the door; he was not in sight; she flew to the play-yard; he was not there. **1912** COBB *Back Home* 44 Strict church members . . . wouldn't let their children . . . go to any parties except play parties.

b. In sense 1 with *actress, book, day,* etc.

1751 WASHINGTON *Diaries* I. 25 Was treated with a play ticket by Mr. Carter. **1761** in Odell *Annals N.Y. Stage* I. 83 Those ladies who would have places kept in the boxes will please to send a sensible servant to the theatre at three o'clock on every play-day. **1845** SOL. SMITH *Theatr. Apprent.* 14 Cook's Circulating Library was ransacked for play-books. *Ib.* 14 The difficulty was how to leave home every play-night, without the knowledge of the family. **1892** *Courier-Journal* 2 Oct. 22/5 A pirate . . . is presenting a stolen version of Mr. Lacy's play. . . . Mr. Lacy threatened to prosecute theater managers who allow this play-thief . . . in their houses. **1895** *N.Y. Dramatic News* 9 Nov. 17/4 It is said by a play sharp that the source from which the Queen of Liars . . . is derived, is La Menteuse, by Daudet and Henrique. **1896** *Ib.* 4 April 19/4 Harry Lindley, the play pirate, advertises in the Clipper that J. Alexander Brown is his New York agent. **1909** STRATTON-PORTER *Girl of Limberlost* 3 But no child of mine walks the streets of Onabasha looking like a play-actress woman.

***Play,** *v.*

I. +1. *intr.* To pretend or make believe as a basis of play. {*trans. c*1386–}

1861 STOWE *Pearl Orr's Isl.* I. 147, I played their nest was a city, and I spoiled it. **1875** LOWELL *Writings* IV. 324 Children who play that everything is something else. **1890** *St. Nicholas* Oct. 1007 We played that we were gypsies.

+2. *tr.* To act as if (a person) belonged to a designated class; to take (a person) *for.*

1869 'MARK TWAIN' *Innocents* 294 Playing us for Chinamen because we are strangers and trying to learn! **1873** MILLER *Amongst Modocs* 38 Look here, what do you play me for? **1882** PECK *Sunshine* 38 How does he know but the same deacon is . . . playing him for a sardine. **1892** CRANE *Maggie* (1896) 60, I wonder if I've been played for a duffer.

3. +a. To impose (something) *on;* to play a trick; to cheat; to palm *off.* Often quasi-*tr.*

1871 HARTE *Luck of Roaring Camp* 11 It's playing it pretty low down on this yer baby to ring in fun on him that he ain't going to understand. **1884** 'MARK TWAIN' *H. Finn* ii. 23 Nothing would do Tom but he must crawl to where Jim was, . . . and play something on him. **1890** HARTE *Heritage of Dedlow Marsh* 100 The folks you trust is playing it on ye. **1894** *Outing* XXIV. 288/1 This played it on our pursuers very neatly. **1896** SHINN *Story of Mine* 249 You can't play it off any longer.

+b. *To play on* (someone), to trick.

1878 *Scribner's Mo.* XV. 812/1 Ye went back on her, and shook her, and played on her, and gave her away—dead away!

+4. To gamble on or at (cards, races, etc.).

1858 PETERS *Kit Carson* 354 The fact is . . . he'd bin playin' the papers (meaning gambling) and had lost everything. **1902** LORIMER *Lett. Merchant* 115 When he chooses a father-in-law who plays the bucket shops, he needn't be surprised if his own son plays the races. **1912** NICHOLSON *Hoosier Chron.* 180 Miles, the treasurer of Ranger County, had been playing the bucket shops with public moneys. **1914** ATHERTON *Perch of Devil* 71, I wished . . . that I'd left him to play the wheel and all the rest of it. **1916** DU PUY *Uncle Sam* 153 The assistant cashier . . . in playing the market had only executed the orders of his superior.

II. With adverbs. ∗**5.** *To play off.* +**a.** To act indifferent; to be wily.

1855 BARNUM *Life* 70 Nelson continued to importune, and my father to play off, until it was finally agreed that the horse could be had.

+**b.** To impose *on* by feigning sickness; to pretend to be *sick.*

1863 NORTON *Army Lett.* 135 If I did want one [a discharge], I fancy . . . I could play off on the doctors and get it. **1875** *Chicago Tribune* 21 Nov. 16/1 James Morgan . . . was refused any sum by the officers, who assert that he was 'playing off' sick. **1887** CUSTER *Tenting on Plains* 173 When I got better, didn't he go and say I was playin' off on him, just to get a big drink of whisky.

c. In a game or contest: To break a tie or tied game by continued play.

1880 *Chicago Inter-Ocean* 7 June 6/2 The tie game of yesterday was played off to-day, the Chicago's winning a victory over the home team. **1901** *Munsey's Mag.* Jan. 570/1 We're going to play off for the Wolcott cup.

∗**6.** *To play out.* +**a.** To weaken and come to an end; to peter out. Often in passive. (Cf. PLAYED-OUT *a.*). *colloq.* {in reflexive, 1867; 1887–}

1861 NORTON *Army Lett.* 15 Such a feeling pervades the minds of the soldiers that discipline is played out. **1872** *Vermont Bd. Agric. Rep.* I. 79 The old native fruit of our country is about playing out, as the saying is. **1884** (clipping from newspaper), This department of business that started off so brashly has played out, no teacher being able to make more than $30 a month. **1890** *Stock Grower & Farmer* 17 May 6/1 The open range is most assuredly 'playing out.' **1899** WHIPPLE *Lights & Shadows* 195 Not many years ago flogging was considered a salutary medicine for a disobedient boy; but now our boys say 'flogging is played out.'

b. In passive. Of persons or animals: To become exhausted or worn out. *colloq.*

1865 *Atlantic Mo.* March 286/1 Once you get weak in the knees, and limp in the back, . . . you're played out. **1884** *Boston Jrnl.* 29 Jan. 2/3 If men who are down at the heel and played out everywhere else continue to push into Oregon, that State will be a fool's paradise by another year. **1913** LONDON *Valley of Moon* 104 Our cattle were all played out.

III. Phrases. **7.** *To play ball,* +to play baseball; *spec.*, to start playing baseball.

1880 N. BROOKS *Fairport Nine* 30, I s'pose Pel Snelgro thinks he can play ball, but just see him whang the air every time Ned fires that ball. **1887** *Courier-Journal* 21 Jan. 8/1 Playing ball is my occupation, and I want what my services are worth. **1907** *St. Nicholas* June 720/2 The umpire . . . [said] 'Play ball.'

+**8.** *To play* (*in* or *to*) *big* (or *hard*) *luck,* to have good or bad luck.

1885 *Santa Fé Wkly. New Mexican* 9 July 3/6 These young people have been 'playing to hard luck' in the southwest. **1895** *N.Y. Dramatic News* 6 July 4/2 A certain old friend . . . was in that undesirable position that we call 'playing in hard luck.' **1914** 'BOWER' *Flying U Ranch* 158 You're playing big luck, if you only had sense enough to know it.

+**9.** *To play smash with* (something), to hit (something) with smashing or disrupting force; to affect strongly. *slang.* {'to play crash' and similar phrases, 1786– *Sc.*}

1887 *Courier-Journal* 17 Jan. 1/7 (*caption*), Plays Smash With a Passenger Train on the Fitchburg Railroad. **1902** HARBEN *A. Daniel* 43 You young bloods are a-goin' to play smash with the gals' hearts to-night.

10. In miscellaneous phrases.

To play the advantages over (someone) ,(see quot. 1839); *to p.* (*it*) *alone,* to play a game at cards without one's partner (also fig.); *to p. a bet open,* (see second quot. 1864); *to p. even,* to get even; *to p. favorites,* (see FAVORITE 2); *to p. hob,* (see HOB² 1); *to p. the hog,* to be selfish; *to p. horse,* (see HORSE 6); *to p.* a designated *limit,* to bet only up to a designated amount in a card game; *to p. pat,* (see quotation); *to p. possum,* (see POSSUM *n.* 4); *to p. sharp,* to play a trick *on; to p. a town,* to perform a play in a town.

1839 MARRYAT *Diary in Amer.* II. 235 The gamblers on the Mississippi use a very refined phrase for 'cheating'—'playing the advantages over him.' **1864** DICK *Amer. Hoyle* (1866) 62 *Play Alone.*—To play a hand without one's partner. **1873** *Winfield* (Kan.) *Courier* 24 July 3/1 The horses attached to [the] hack which runs between this place and Wellington, one day last week concluded to 'play it alone.' **1864** DICK *Amer. Hoyle* (1866) 207 *Playing a Bet Open* [in faro], is to bet a card will win, not to lose. **1877** W. WRIGHT *Big Bonanza* 427 The 'honest miner' . . . will sometimes resort to 'ways that are dark' in order to 'play even.' **1903** LEWIS *Boss* 126 He's all for playin' th' hog. **1916** WILSON *Somewhere* 372 We talked over old times and played ten-cent limit in my stateroom. **1887** KELLER *Draw Poker* 11 *Playing Pat,* playing an original hand without drawing cards. A favorite device of bluffers. **1863** NORTON *Army Lett.* 186 In testing my eyes . . . the doctor held up something and asked me what it was. I had played sharp on him by taking an inventory of the articles on the table. **1896** *N.Y. Dramatic News* 29 Aug. 11/3 A troup of barnstormers . . . are playing the smaller towns in this vicinity.

+**Playa.** *S.W.* [Sp., 'a beach or strand.'] A broad, level place that accumulates water after a rain, but is at other times dry; a dry lake. — **1854** BARTLETT *Personal Narr.* I. 246 The playas . . . seemed to have an extent of twenty-five or thirty miles. **1871** RAYMOND *3d Rep. Mines* 275 Among the 'playas' of largest extent is the valley or 'playa' of San Domingo. **1873** COZZENS *Marvellous Country* 237 Every playa [was transformed] into a beautiful lake.

Play-actor. A person who acts parts in plays. {1633–} — **1789** LOW *Politician Outwitted* IV. ii, No, you look more like a dancing-master, a fighting-master, or a play-actor, or some such flashy folks. **1845** SOL. SMITH *Theatr. Apprent.* 131 You infernal playactor! **1862** BROWNE *A. Ward His Book* 89 Ringin her hands like a female play acter. **1904** MACKAYE *Panchronicon* 3 You know players is what they called play-actors in those days, and he was a play-actor, they say.

Playbill. A bill advertising one or more plays, usually giving the time of performance and a list of the actors and their parts; a theater program. {1673–} — **1766** MONTRESOR *Journals* 358 Some Stamps as 'tis said found in the Streets were publickly burnt, at the Coffee house, together with Some play bills, all to prevent their Spirits to flag. **1835** HOFFMAN *Winter in West* II. 10 Imagine my surprise when I discovered it to be a play-bill! **1872** S. HALE *Letters* 108 The tickets are brought to this house every morning with the . . . play-bill. **1893** POST *Harvard Stories* 134 That is the play-bill of those theatricals hanging over there on the wall now.

Played, *a.* + =next. — **1872** *Republican Rev.* 16 March 2/4 The days of forked sticks for plows is about played, if farmers here want to come up to the age in which we live. **1875** *Scribner's Mo.* Nov. 142/2 He swore that something was 'too thin;' moreover it was 'played!' **1883** 'MARK TWAIN' *Life on Miss.* xliii, That's all played now. **1897** *Outing* XXIX. 421/2 He's about played.

+**Played-out,** *a.* Exhausted; worn out. *colloq.* — **1859** MATSELL *Vocabulum* 68. **1862** *Oregon Argus* 15 Feb. (Th.), The poor privilege of fawning about the skirts of a played-out codfish aristocracy. **1887** HARTE *Crusade of Excelsior* 110, I shall have a look at that played-out mine. **1910** J. HART *Vigilante Girl* 327 There was very little gold dug there now. It was a 'played-out camp.'

∗**Player.**

∗**1.** =PLAY ACTOR.

1751 in Singleton *Social N.Y.* 273 If any Gentleman or Lady has the Farce call'd 'The Intriguing Chambermaid,' and will lend it awhile to the Players, it will be thankfully acknowledged. **1789** MACLAY *Deb. Senate* 44 The play was The School for Scandal. . . . The house greatly crowded, and I thought the players acted well. **1885** *Century Mag.* Jan. 464 Some of the older players . . . are profoundly versed not only in theatrical knowledge, but in literature and art generally. **1910** *N.Y. Dramatic Mirror* 19 March 2/2 In this day the player is not without honor.

∗**2.** One who engages in a game, +esp. a baseball player.

1856 *Porter's Spirit of Times* 6 Dec. 229/1 The captains . . . shall designate the position each player shall occupy in the field. **1880** N. BROOKS *Fairport Nine* 35 With two players on the bases, it required very delicate playing. **1910** *Spalding's Base Ball Guide* 339 All ball grounds should be provided with two player's benches back of and on each side of the home plate. **1917** MATHEWSON *Sec. Base Sloan* 277 Maybe I'll try walking in past Mike at the players' gate.

Playground. A piece of ground used for play, esp. in connection with a school. {1794–} — **1835** HOFFMAN *Winter in West* I. 19 The extensive play-grounds in the rear of [the Moravian Seminary] . . . evince the attention which is paid to the health and personal habits . . . of its inmates. **1870** EGGLESTON *Queer Stories* 119 He was a great favorite on the play-ground. **1891** WELCH *Recoll. 1830–40* 27 It was a Saturday afternoon play-ground for the youngsters from up-town. **1921** *3d Nat. Country Life Conf. Proc.* 100 The community responded and during its next year equipped a fine playground.

Play hour. An hour or period in which school children play. {1857} — **1774** FITHIAN *Journal* I. 125 At the Noon play-Hours Bob & Nelson, the Boy who waits on the School, had a fight. **1877** PHELPS *Story of Avis* 39 The professor strolled about the house in the play-hour which rigorously followed meals.

∗**Playhouse.**

∗**1.** A building in which plays are acted; a theater.

1710 in Earle *Colonial Days N.Y.* 85 She shall not absent herself day or night from her Master's service without his Leave, nor haunt Alehouses, Taverns, or Play-houses. **1724** JONES *Virginia* 31 A Market Place, near which is a Play House and good Bowling Green. **1775** *Md. Hist. Mag.* X. 140 The Vestry agree that the Play house be fitted up for a place of divine worship. **1809** KENDALL *Travels* I. 164 There is no playhouse in Hartford, nor in any other place in Connecticut. **1857** *Atlantic Mo.* Nov. 80/1 The play-house was packed from top to bottom. **1893** *Harper's Mag.* Feb. 344/2 Somehow this pleasant young companion of the tea party hardly represented the wickedness of playhouses as Puritan New England loved to picture them.

+**2.** A miniature house, often of one room, in which children may play.

1857 M. J. HOLMES *Meadow-Brook* xxv, At a short distance from the house was a tall cypress . . . where now was a play-house. **1870** EGGLESTON *Queer Stories* 50 He moved to the same playhouse with the rest of the children. **1881** *Rep. Indian Affairs* 130 We need a barn and a play-house. **1907** *St. Nicholas* May 651/1 In the center of this little yard was a play-house.

***Playing card.** One of various kinds of cards used in playing card games.

1762 *Newport Mercury* 28 Sept. 3/3 Playing Cards. To be Sold at the Shop joining the Printing-office. **1807** JANSON *Stranger in Amer.* 29 The principal manufactures of Boston are . . . loaf sugar, tobacco, chocolate, and an immense quantity of playing cards. **1810** *Columbian Centinel* 3 Jan. 3/2 W. Blagrove, has just received and for sale, a quantity of *French Playing Cards*, of the first quality. **1847** *Santa Fe Republican* 27 Nov. 1/4 Hovey & Co. . . . offers for sale . . . Stoughton's Bitters, Essence of orange, 16 kegs sausages, 48 doz. playing cards. **1922** *Science* LVI. 418/2 Deal at random 25 cards from a pack of 52 playing cards.

+**Playing pasture.** A playground located in a pasture. *Obs.* — **1737** *Harvard Rec.* II. 656 Voted, . . . That the northerly part of the Land improved by the Late President and that adjoynes to the playing pasture for the Schollars be Layd open to the said playing pasture.

Playlet. A short dramatic piece. {1892} — **1884** B. MATTHEWS in *Century Mag.* Oct. 916/2 In these beautiful and witty playlets there is but the ghost of an action. **1907** *Springfield W. Repub.* 7 Nov. 16 A play-let named 'Faith' was acted at Keith's Union Square theater.

Playroom. A room for children to play in; a recreation room. — **1838** *Knickerb.* XI. 12 Seated with two or three other children in my little play-room . . . , we dressed and talked to our dolls. **1863** 'M. HARLAND' *Husks* 114 Jeannie started up to her attic play-room. **1907** *St. Nicholas* June 714/1 She flew up to the playroom and locked the door.

+**Play spell.** A time or period allotted to play. — **1845** JUDD *Margaret* II. 186 And her own play-spell comes, if, indeed, her whole life were not a play-spell. **1854** M. J. HOLMES *Tempest & Sunshine* 89 You may have a play spell the rest of the arternoon. **1878** STOWE *Poganuc People* 209 Even household disciplinarians recognized a reasonably well-behaved child's right to a Saturday afternoon play-spell.

Playwright. A professional writer of plays. {1687-} — **1806** FESSENDEN *Democracy Unveiled* I. 159 Behold the play wright Barney Bidwell. **1910** *N.Y. Dramatic Mirror* 12 March 9/4 Practically all of the new playwrights have been discovered by play-brokers.

+**Plaza.** [Sp.]

British usage {1683, 1826, of Spain and S. America} had no influence upon American usage, which represents a direct borrowing from the Spanish of the Southwest.

1. A public square or market place; an open place connected with a fort, mine, etc.

[**1836** LATROBE *Rambler in Mexico* 79 Our party entered [Zacualtipan]; wheeling . . . across the Plaza, with ringing spurs and jingling arms.] **1844** GREGG *Commerce of Prairies* II. 77 Two or three miles above the plaza there is a dam of stone and brush. **1848** *Santa Fe Republican* 15 Jan. 2/1 A man . . . round the east corner of the Plaza, met two young senoritas of his acquaintance. **1852** *Knickerb.* XL. 197 The spirit-stirring fife and drum, and the roar of cannon on the plaza [at New Orleans], announce the hour for morning parade. **1869** J. R. BROWNE *Adv. Apache Country* 203 The broad, smooth plaza in front of the works [at a silver mine] was dotted with wagons and teams. **1885** *Weekly New Mexican Rev.* 8 Jan. 2/5 The old palace . . . is in the center of the town, and opposite the plaza. **1907** WHITE *Arizona Nights* 47 A freight outfit brought him to Tucson and dumped him down on the plaza.

attrib. **1856** DERBY *Phoenixiana* 126 Every citizen . . . was aroused at 2 A.M. by the soul-stirring and tremendous report of the Plaza Artillery.

b. *Plaza publica*, a public square.

1844 GREGG *Commerce of Prairies* I. 111 On driving through the streets [of Santa Fé] and the *plaza publica*, everyone strives to outvie his comrades. **1847** HUGHES *Diary* 89 Traders have all arrived [at El Paso] and are making small sales—plaza publica fortified by wagons.

2. A place of residence; a pueblo.

1846 HUGHES *Diary* 75 Returned from the Grazing Ground to Galisteo and lodged in a Rico's plaza. **1885** *Wkly. New Mexican Rev.* 22 Jan. 4/6 Living Indians of to-day variously tell of a tradition that one of the pueblos or plazas of Santa Fe was known as 'Poga' or 'Apoga.'

Pleasant-spoken, *a.* (See first quotation.) — **1877** BARTLETT 474 'He's a pleasant-spoken man,' *i.e.* he's agreeable in conversation. **1896** *Peterson Mag.* Jan. 97/1 He is very pleasant-spoken, and invited me to come and spend the night with him.

+**Pleasurable carriage.** =PLEASURE CARRIAGE. *Obs.* — **1802** *Ann. 7th Congress* 2 Sess. 1238 The committee respectfully submit the following bill, to repeal the laws laying duties on . . . pleasurable carriages. **1806** *Phila. Ordinances* (1812) 200 The following articles . . . are hereby made taxable . . . gigs, riding chairs, chaises, and other pleasurable carriages.

Pleasure boat. A boat kept for pleasure rather than for commercial use. {1661-} — **1766** in Singleton *Social N.Y.* 265 The yacht or Pleasure Boat belonging to Captain Roddam. **1812** BENTLEY *Diary* IV. 104 Capt. G. Crowninshield's pleasure Boat we met upon our return. **1869** J. R. BROWNE *Adv. Apache Country* 332 Two enterprising Americans . . . had recently purchased the premises, with a view of getting up a splendid watering-place in the Atlantic style. Already they had bath-houses, pleasure-boats, riding-horses [etc.]. **1896** JEWETT *Pointed Firs* 132 Gay voices and laughter from a pleasure-boat that was going seaward full of boys and girls.

Pleasure carriage. A carriage kept for pleasure rather than for business. — **1827** SHERWOOD *Gaz. Georgia* 17 The permanent revenue is derived from taxes on lands and negroes, pleasure carriages, banks, . . . and retailers of spirituous liquors. **1877** *Harper's Mag.* March 518/1 A pleasure carriage, the first ever brought into [Litchfield Hill, Conn.] . . . , was in use as late as 1812. **1905** VALENTINE *H. Sandwith* 19 She was accused of having persuaded Mr. Sandwith into acquiring the mundane 'pleasure carriage' they were now riding in.

Pleasure ground. 1. A park or area laid out for pleasure and recreation. {1768-} +**2.** (See quotation.) *Obs.* — (**1**) **1836** DUNLAP *Mem. Water Drinker* (1837) I. 6 Such of the busy citizens as, in crossing this triangular pleasure-ground, find leisure to think of nature. **1882** MCCABE *New York* 424 *The Bowling Green* . . . was the first public pleasure-ground laid out in New York, and dates from 1734. (**2**) **1846** *Porter's Spirit of Times* 11 July 234/1 Since the legislative Solons of Massachusetts have prohibited trotting and racing, the Courses have taken the name of 'pleasure grounds.'

Pleasure party. A company of pleasure-seekers; a party for pleasure. — **1835** in *S. Lit. Messenger* IV. 303/1 [We] were passed and met by several vehicles, in which pleasure-parties to and from the Springs . . . were dashing along the well graded road. **1856** STOWE *Dred* I. 33 He had accomplished it during the pleasure party of the morning. **1886** *Harper's Mag.* Sept. 598 Caldwell . . . is a favorite rendezvous for pleasure parties, who leave the ground strewn with egg shells and newspapers.

+**Pleasure sleigh.** A sleigh used for pleasure. — **1836** PAULDING *S. Nicholas* 78 Pleasure sleighs, which, at that period, it was the fashion among farmers to have as fine as fiddles. **1856** *Mich. Agric. Soc. Trans.* VII. 59 Davis, Austin & Co., Jackson, [exhibited a] pleasure sleigh.

+**Pleasure wagon.** A light wagon used for pleasure rather than for business. — **1831** BUTTRICK *Travels* 41, I purchased two horses and a pleasure wagon, and proceeded to Albany in New York. **1840** *Picayune* 27 Aug. 2/5 Wanted to Purchase A Second Hand Gig, or a small pleasure wagon, with a top. **1866** A. D. WHITNEY *L. Goldthwaite* xv, How impertinent we are, rushing at the tremendousness of Washington in the way we do; scaling it in little pleasure-wagons, and never taking in the thought of it at all!

Pleb. {1865-} +A member of the freshman class at college, orig. and usu. with reference to West Point. — **1852** *Knickerb.* XXXIX. 171 The new cadets or 'plebs,' having been in the battalion but a few days, were not well enough disciplined to be detailed for guard. **1883** *Harper's Mag.* Nov. 908/1 At West Point, no matter how stooped the entering pleb, he is soon taught to carry himself as erect as any man in America. **1913** LAFOLLETTE *Autobiog.* 12, I was one of the greenest of all the 'plebs' [at Wis. U.]—a boy right from the farm.

Plebe. {1612-}

+**1.** A member of the freshman class at West Point.

1862 STRONG *Cadet Life W. Point* 116 Plebe, I want your opinions on the subject of our foreign relations. **1896** *Peterson Mag.* March 266/2 He was only a 'plebe,' as the newly entered cadet [at West Point] was termed. **1908** *Atlantic Mo.* Nov. 608 The West Point plebe enters at practically the same age as the Harvard freshman.

+**b.** *Plebeskin*, civilian dress. *slang.*

1888 *N.Y. World* 22 July (F.), The fourth class entered camp on Monday, but are still wearing their plebeskins.

+**2.** (See quot. 1890.) Also attrib.

1890 CUSTER *Following Guidon* 213 These youths [graduates from West Point] were called 'tads' and 'plebes.' **1899** T. HALL *Tales* 19 Ten to one the 'plebe' lieutenant is able to cut in ahead of the troops they are pursuing.

***Pledge,** *n.* A solemn promise not to indulge in spirituous liquors. {1846-} — **1833** *New Eng. Mag.* Aug. 141 Has he signed the Pledge? **1849** *Cincinnati Commercial* 13 Dec. 1/4 One hundred thousand had taken the pledge at his hands. **1895** GRAHAM *Stories of Foot-Hills* 167 Before I promise to marry anybody . . . he's got to sign the pledge.

***Pledge,** *v.* +*tr.* and *intr.* To promise, or cause (someone) to promise, to join a college fraternity. — **1871** BAGG *At Yale* 62 They are very attentive to his wants and do not leave him until he is 'pledged.' **1887** *Lippincott's Mag.* Nov. 741 If as the result of several such interviews he is approved, he is asked to 'pledge,' that is, to promise to join the society.

***Plenty.** Used with *a:* An abundance (*of*). {1628-}

'Now chiefly *U.S.*' (*O.E.D.*).

1700 SEWALL *Letter-Book* I. 240 We are . . . something afflicted for want of a greater plenty of Rain. **1780** *Essex Inst. Coll.* XLII. 120 They must have a plenty. **1817** S. BROWN *Western Gazetteer* 8 In which however there is a plenty of water. **1849** KINGSLEY *Diary* 62 They seem to have a plenty of everything, to live upon. **1877** *Vermont Bd. Agric. Rep.* IV. 92 Woe to the man who failed to provide finely split oven wood, and a plenty of it. **1883** HAY *Bread-Winners* 100 And as to money, he's got a plenty for two.

***Pleurisy. 1.** Inflammation of the pleura. +**2.** (See quotation.) *Obs.* — (**1**) **1730** HEMPSTEAD *Diary* 229 A Negro man died last night with the plurisee. **1772** WASHINGTON *Diaries* II. 55 Rid to the Mill Plantation to see a Negro Man sick of Pleurisy. **1865** *Atlantic Mo.* Jan. 70/2 [The Negroes'] weakness is pulmonary; pneumonia and pleurisy are their besetting ailments. (**2**) **1775** ROMANS *Nat. Hist. Florida* 249 In Georgia i saw one or two instances of a disorder among blacks, to which the people give the odd name of the pleurisy of the temple, of the forehead, of the eye, and so on; i am told they have a pleurisy for every part of the head.

+**Pleurisy root.** The butterfly weed (*Asclepias tuberosa*) or its root. (Cf. BUTTERFLY WEED.) — **1781–2** JEFFERSON *Notes Va.* (1788) 36 [Medicinal] native plants. Senna.... Pleurisy root. *Asclepias decumbens.* **1801** *Hist. Rev. & Directory* I. 144. **1901** MOHR *Plant Life Ala.* 675 The root is the 'pleurisy root' or 'Asclepias' of the United States Pharmacopœia.

Plew. *N.W.* [Canadian Fr. *plus, pêlu.*] A first-class beaver skin; also, the unit of value which is represented by such a beaver skin. — **1848** RUXTON *Life Far West* v, Beaver fetching as high a price as five and six dollars a 'plew.' **1850** GARRARD *Wah-To-Yah* xviii. 216 Goods were high—two plews a plug for bacca, three fur powder, an' so on. *a***1918** G. STUART *On Frontier* I. 179, I traded three plew of beaver skins and four buffalo tongues for [three buffalo calves].

***Pliers.** A form of pincers used for holding or manipulating small objects.

1767 in H. M. Brooks *Gleanings* IV. 31 Small sheers & plyers. Screw dividers. **1790** *Penna. Packet* 7 May 3/3 Imported and to be Sold by John Wood, Clock and Watch Maker, ... clock and watch pliers, sliding tongs. **1878** *Rep. Indian Affairs* 392. **1904** STRATTON-PORTER *Freckles* 180 His belt to which his wire-cutter and pliers were still hanging.

+**b.** *Pliers man,* (see quotation).

1897 HOUGH *Story of Cowboy* 207 Of later times the faithful cowboy who worked on a fenced ranch is sometimes called contemptuously a 'pliers man' by the rustlers who have no fences of their own.

***Plot.**

***1.** A small area or patch of ground; a burial lot. Also attrib.

1612 SMITH, etc. *Virginia* I. 21 Their houses are in the midst of their fields or gardens; which are smal plots of ground, some 20 [acres], some 40. **1685** *Providence Rec.* VII. 79 A small plot of land adjoyneing to the said house for a little Garden. **1848** THOREAU *Maine Woods* 9 More perfect specimens than any front-yard plot can show, grew there to grace the passage of the Houlton teams. **1895** M. A. Jackson *Gen. Jackson* 636, I had the plot enclosed with an iron railing, and a simple marble headstone.

***2.** A ground plan, map, or chart, of an area. {–1775}

'Obs. or *arch.* exc. in *U.S.'* (*O.E.D.*). Cf. PLAT *n.* 1.

[*c***1622** J. PORY *Descr. Plymouth Col.* 48 A Flemmish pilot ... putteth downe in his plot, a place ... which he calleth Cod Iland.] **1652** *Dedham Rec.* III. 208 Debts due ... from the Towne ... to Antho Fisher sen for helping to take a plott of the riuer. **1718** *N.H. Probate Rec.* I. 63 Any part or portion of the Sd. Lands except what falls to our Share as hereafter is expressed and Sett forth and is in the Plott or figure hereunto annexed. **1851** CIST *Cincinnati* 147 The board immediately made arrangements for obtaining a survey and plot of the grounds. **1881** *Scribner's Mag.* April 835 It will be seen on reference to the plot of the place.

***Plough,** *n.* (See also PLOW.)

In American use *plow* is now the usual spelling. For convenience the spelling *plow* is used in head words such as PLOWBOY, PLOW GEAR, etc., unless the only spelling found in our examples is *plough.*

***1.** =PLOW 1.

1644 *Conn. Rec.* I. 461 Carts, ploughs and the furniture belonging theretoo. **1671** *Plymouth Laws* 268 Lands improved by Plough or Hough, or by cutting and taking of Timber. **1792** BRACKENRIDGE *Mod. Chivalry* (1937) 8 He is a good old horse, used to the plough, and carries my weight very well. **1817** S. BROWN *Western Gazetteer* 67 For several years, they could not carry the plough or hoe a musket shot from their huts. **1885** *Harper's Mag.* June 75/1 They fled to the fort, the men leaving the plough in the furrow, the women the morning hoe-cake unbaked before the fire. **1905** PRINGLE *Rice Planter* 162, I feel just as though I had drawn the plough and the harrow as well as the three darkies.

+**b.** =PLOW 1 b.

1776 ROWE *Diary* 309 This morning Mr. Hammonds Plough began to Plough up the Pasture.

2. In special combinations.

Plough bird, (see quotation); *p. hoe,* a horse hoe; *p. plane,* a carpenter's grooving plane; *p. ridge,* a ridge of earth thrown up by a plow; *p. tackling,* =PLOW GEAR; *p. upland,* arable upland.

1898 FOX *Kentuckians* 105 'There are mountain birds up here, too'—a polyglot chat was chuckling. 'Hear that? My father used to call that the "plough-bird."' **1797** HAWKINS *Letters* 97, I wish your first care would be to have good axes and hoes ... ; I mean plough hoes. **1645** *Conn. Rec.* I. 464 Goods prysed by Gyles Smith.... One plough playne. **1891** WILKINS *New Eng. Nun* 81 Now they showed ugly plough ridges sloping over the uneven ground. **1723** *N.H. Probate Rec.* II. 194, I do give unto my said son ... my plough tackling. **1730** *N.J. Archives* XI. 226 There is also 100 Acres of Plough-Upland in very good Order.

***Plough,** *v.* +*To plough around,* fig., to get around or circumvent, as in plowing around stumps; to circulate among or associate with. — **1888** SHERIDAN *Memoirs* I. 463 General Grant had 'ploughed around' the difficulties of the situation. **1888** BRYCE *Amer. Commonw.* II. III. lxx. 557 The more skilful leaders begin (as it is expressed) to 'plough around' among the delegations of the newer ... States.

Plough factory. A factory in which plows are made. — **1827** DRAKE & MANSFIELD *Cincinnati* 65 Three Plough Factories, 11 hands. **1847** L. COLLINS *Kentucky* 319 Hickman, the county seat, ... contains two churches, ... one tan yard, one plough factory.

Plough field. A field under cultivation, as distinguished from a pasture or meadow. {1805–} — **1848** THOMPSON *L. Amsden* 6 The tops of the furrows, peering through the dissolving snows, were beginning to streak with long, faint dotted lines, the self-disclosing plough-fields. **1883** HOWE *Country Town* (1926) 24 He always made a round in the plough-field after my father had turned out.

***Plover.** Any one of various comparatively small shore birds, chiefly of the family Charadriidae.

See also FIELD, GOLDEN, GREEN PLOVER.

1610 *Estate of Va.* 30 The riuers ... are couered with flocks of ... curlews, godwights, plouers, snights, dottrels. **1682** ASH *Carolina* 23 Birds for Food, and pleasure of Game, are the Swan, Goose, Duck, Mallard, Wigeon, Teal, Curlew, Plover, Partridge. **1794** *Mass. H. S. Coll.* 1 Ser. III. 199 Sea fowl are plenty on the shores and in the bay; particularly the gannet, ... gull, plover, coot, widgeon, and peep. **1805** LEWIS in *L. & Clark Exped.* II. (1904) 260 Saw ... a species of small curlooe or plover of a brown color. **1869** *Amer. Naturalist* III. 225 Our salt marshes and our lowlands near the sea [in New Eng.] swarmed, during the spring and autumn months, with plover, snipe, godwit [etc.]. **1894** *Scribner's Mag.* May 603/2 The Rio Grande is at nearly all seasons full of ... plover. **1917** *Birds of Amer.* I. 255 Plovers' voices usually are mellow, piping whistles which have singular carrying power.

attrib. and *comb.* **1854** SIMMS *Southward Ho!* 23 They flourished their plover-guns. **1868** *N.Y. Herald* 5 Aug. 4/4 All ... are familiar with the mysteries of plover shooting.

***Plow,** *n.*

See also PLOUGH *n.* note; also DUTCH PLOW.

***1.** A farm implement drawn by one or more horses, mules, etc., and used for breaking up and stirring the soil.

1648 *Conn. Rec.* I. 508 One plow, one harrow, one grynding stone. **1805** *Ann. 9th Congress* 2 Sess. 1094 It is not more than twelve or fifteen years since they ever had a plow, or a flat to cross the river with. **1857** *Ill. Agric. Soc. Trans.* III. 433 The best lands in Kentucky, when kept under the plow for a series of years, become stiff. **1882** *Rep. Indian Affairs* 7 Aug. 11 Owing to the distribution of 30 plows ... and 60 plantation hoes, they have been able to cultivate a larger average than ever before.

attrib. **1658** *Essex Probate Rec.* I. 271, 2 plowes & plowtackle.

+**b.** *fig.* A plowman with his plow and plow animal(s).

1786 WASHINGTON *Diaries* III. 87 The Plows at Muddy hole (where 3 were at Work) had finished the East cut of Corn. **1787** *Ib.* 158, I set them to filling up gullies where the plows were at work.

2. In special combinations.

Plow gang, a group of Negro slaves who work together in plowing (*Obs.*); *p. hand,* one who plows, as a Negro slave; **plowwright,* one who makes or repairs plows; *p. yokel,* a plowboy.

1860 OLMSTED *Back Country* 47 There was also a driver of the hoe-gang who did not labor personally, a foreman of the plow-gang. **1840** in Commons, etc. *Doc. Hist.* I. 335, I am frequently compelled to work them in three separate classes, ... plow hands, hoe hands, the full grown & small hands. **1641** *Conn. Rec.* I. 65 Sufficient able Carpenters, Plow writs, Wheelewrits, ... Smithes and Coopers, shall not take aboue 20d. for a dayes worke. **1887** FREDERIC *Seth's Brother's Wife* 204 It was his fraternal feeling and generosity which had created the vast gulf between Seth the plow-yokel and Seth the editor.

***Plow,** *v.* (See PLOUGH *v.* and cf. PLOUGH *n.* note.)

***Plowboy.** A boy or man who plows; a country boy. Also transf. — **1775** FRENEAU *Poems* (1786) 76 The sport of plough boys, with their arms and arts. **1853** SIMMS *Sword & Distaff* (1854) 190 You're not to carry a good plough-boy off to find bait for you when you're a-fishing. **1885** *Santa Fé Wkly. New Mexican* 10 Dec. 1/1 Vice President Hendricks was not a 'plow boy,' nor any other kind of a poor boy, but belonged to a family of local distinction. **1904** A. DALE *Wanted: a Cook* 35, I, too, am simply starving. It must be that bracing atmosphere of Niagara. It has made plow-boys of us.

***Plowed land.** Land that has been plowed; arable land. — **1658** *Plymouth Col. Rec.* XI. 89 By Improued lands are understood meddow lands, plowed lands, and hoed lands. **1746** *N.H. Hist. Soc. Coll.* IX. 128 [I] hauled off my logs from my plowed land. **1906** *Indian Laws & Tr.* III. 254 The member ... having houses, orchards, barns, or plowed land thereon shall have the prior right to make the first selection.

***Plow gear.** The harness used on a plow animal. — **1644** *Md. Archives* IV. 279 The ploughgeare sent of Engl[and]. **1660** *Essex Probate Rec.* I. 319 One Cart and other Plowgeere. **1819** *Amer. Farmer* I. 55 Plough Gier. We have seen in use, in a particular neighborhood in this state, wooden hames or collar, as a substitute for the leathern or corn-husk collar. **1885** 'CRADDOCK' *Prophet* 15 She stepped swiftly to his horse and took off the plough-gear.

Plow ground. =PLOWLAND. *Obs.* {1895–} — **1637** *Mass. H. S. Coll.* 4 Ser. VII. 122 Its indifferent to me whether they cleare in the mowed plow ground, or in the other. **1659** *Suffolk Deeds* III. 222 Thirtie acres of Orchard plow ground & pasture.

***Plow horse.** A horse used for drawing a plow. — **1794** *N.Y. State Soc. Arts* I. 123 It was very luxuriant and cut twice before the twentieth of June for plough horses kept in the stable. **1869** *Rep. Comm. Agric. 1868* 16 The defeated warrior in a cause forever lost is patiently and cheerfully following a war-horse that is now a plow-horse. **1911** SAUNDERS *Col. Todhunter* 118 You turn me loose in a big town like this and expect me to behave like anything more'n a wall-eyed plow-horse with his tail full o' cuckle-burs.

Plowing ground. =Plow ground. *Obs.* — **1638** *R.I. Col. Rec.* I. 56, 10 acres of plowing Ground. **1755** *N.J. Archives* XIX. 483 The whole is good Meadow and Plowing Ground.

Plowing land. =Plowland. *Obs.* {1694-} — **1674** *Conn. Rec.* II. 225 There is about six hundred acres of meadow and plowing land lying on both sides of ye riuer. **1683** *Conn. Probate Rec.* I. 320, I give . . . to my son-in-law John Cole my plowing Land & Meadow & Swamp. **1726** *Boston News-Letter* 13–20 Jan. 2/2 A Farm containing about 52 Acres of very good Pasture, Mowing & Plowing Land, with a House, Barn & Orchard thereon, . . . To be Sold.

Plowing match. A contest in plowing. {1812-} — **1817** *Niles' Reg.* XIII. 147/2 There was a *ploughing match*, in which there was an interesting trial of expedition and skill. **1840** *Picayune* 24 Oct. 2/4 The annual ploughing match, . . . under the auspices of the American Institute, came off near Newark, on the 9th inst. **1852** *Harper's Mag.* VI. 121 An annual fair is now held at Sacramento, at which splendid prizes are awarded, plowing matches held, &c. **1873** *Newton Kansan* 5 June 3/2 Remember the plowing match to take place next week.

* **Plow iron.** An iron forming part of a plow, esp. a colter or share. — **1648** *Conn. Rec.* I. 491 Cartes and wheeles, & chaines & plow irons. **1697** *Conn. Probate Rec.* I. 563, I give unto my Brother . . . my Plow & Plow Irons and Timber Chain. **1731** *Md. Hist. Mag.* XVIII. 205 To a plow and plow irons. **1843** *Amer. Pioneer* II. 140 On another [horse] were packed the stores of provisions, the plough irons, and other agricultural tools.

Plow jogger. A plowman. *hum.* or *contempt.* {1605–1787} — **1722** *New-Eng. Courant* 15–22 Jan. 2/1 It will be well for the World if thou art destin'd to be a *Porter* or a *Plough-jogger.* **1772** A. G. Winslow *Diary* 25 My valentine was an old country plow-joger. **1863** *Ill. Agric. Soc. Trans.* V. 255 At least the old plow jogger will be mounted on his buggy seat, with two, and probably three horses.

* **Plowland.** Land suitable for plowing; arable land. — **1638** in H. Bond *Family Memorials Watertown Mass.* 997 All the Land lying beyond the Plowland . . . shalbe for a Common for Cattle. **1686** *Hartford Land Distrib.* 183 One parcell of Meadow . . . being partly plow land & partly grass. **1725** *Boston News-Letter* 21 Jan. 2/2 One Hundred Acres, Meadow, Pasture & Plough-land, in a suitable quality. **1845** *Cultivator* ns. II. 93 He has bought . . . 200 [acres] that is neither timber, plow land or meadow.

Plow line.

1. A line or rope used by a plowman in guiding his plow animal. Usually pl. {1886-, *dial.*}

1777 *N.J. Archives* 2 Ser. I. 516 Halters, plough-lines, bed-lacings, . . . sold by Edward Pole, . . . Burlington. **1790** *Penna. Packet* 8 March 4/2 The Subscriber . . . continues to make White Rope of all kinds, Bed-Cords, Bed-Laces, Plow Lines and Plow-Traces. **1853** Simms *Sword & Distaff* (1854) 65 But the girl was already slashing away at the ploughlines which had been used to secure the mistress. **1896** Read *Jucklins* 109 [We] waited for the negro to come with the plow-line, and presently he appeared with a new grass rope.

2. Cord or rope suitable for making plow lines. {1895-} Also attrib.

1853 Simms *Sword & Distaff* (1854) 144 The outlaws had left behind them an abundance of plough-line **1855** — *Forayers* 68 It was no pleasant arrangement . . . which found them compelled to pursue without stirrups, and with plough-line bridles. **1856** Olmsted *Slave States* 78 Saddle and bridle were removed, and she was fastened in a corner by a piece of old plow-line.

Plow-maker. One who makes plows. {1744- (Ellis *Mod. Husb.* II. I. 89)} — **1820** Flint *Lett. from Amer.* 213 A plough maker; pump and block maker; a spinning wheel factory. **1837** W. Jenkins *Ohio Gaz.* 1 It contains . . . 2 wagon and plough makers. **1883** *Rep. Indian Affairs* 194 Building for blacksmith, carpenter, wagon and plow maker.

* **Plowman.** One whose occupation is chiefly plowing; a farm laborer. — **1634** Wood *New Eng. Prospect* II. 76 The Indians . . . told the plowman, hee was . . . almost as cunning as the Devill. **1783** *S.C. Gazette* 3 June 1/1 [The slave] is also a good Sawyer and Ploughman. **1841** Emerson *Works* I. 237 My wood-chopper, my ploughman, . . . have some sort of self-sufficiency. **1880** *Harper's Mag.* June 67/2 Back and forth through the sloping lot the ploughman slowly turns the dingy sward, and in the rich brown furrow . . . we see the cackling troop of hens.

Plowpoint. A detachable share used on the front end of a plow body. — **1856** *Fla. Plantation Rec.* 478 Paid Mr. Lem Jones 50 cts. on account of '54 [1854] maid by J. Evans for 2 Plow points. **1878** *Rep. Indian Affairs* 370. **1906** Lynde *Quickening* 2 Caleb's a sight like the iron he makes in that old furnace o' his'n—honest and even grained, and just as good for plow-points and the like as it is for soap-kittles.

* **Plowshare.** The blade or cutting part of a plow.

1653 *Essex Probate Rec.* I. 157 One plow sheer, . . . one table. **1793** *Mass. H. S. Coll.* 1 Ser. II. 29 The alarm of Burgoyne's approach, urged him to lay by the plow-share and the pruning-hook. **1810** *Austin P.* I. (1924) 168 3 Plough Shears. **1881** *Rep. Indian Affairs* 93 Articles manufactured . . . by the blacksmith: Twenty-three beetle-rings, forty-eight wedges, . . . seven plow-shares.

attrib. **1780** *N.J. Archives* 2 Ser. IV. 267 To be sold, . . . A number of plow-shear moulds.

Plowstock.

1. A frame or structure consisting essentially of a strong horizontal beam to which handles and a 'foot' are securely attached.

1786 Washington *Diaries* III. 5, [I] directed them to get me . . . scantling for Plow stocks. **1856** *Fla. Plantation Rec.* 471, 1 [slave], Renty, gitten out timber for plow stocks. **1865** *Ore. State Jrnl.* 28 Oct. 4/2 Plow Stocks etc., made to order, on short notice.

+**2.** Draft animals used in plowing.

1868 *Rep. Comm. Agric. 1867* 419, I fed the plough stock. **1889** *Rep. Secy. Agric.* 259 Consumption of corn in the cotton States is always less in proportion at this date, because [of] . . . the necessity of general and late feeding of 'plow stock.'

Pluck. 1. The heart, liver, and lungs of an animal used for food. {1611-} ||**2.** One hired to pick peaches. — **(1)** **1772** A. G. Winslow *Diary* 45 One [dish] contain'd three calves heads (skin off) with their appurtinencies anciently call'd pluck. *c***1835** Fobes *Arnold's Exped.* 37 We put the pluck, jaw and tongue, together with some potatoes into the pot. **1873** *Billings' Farmer's Allminax* 31 Hash made out ov beefs pluck and sheeps liver will be charged extra for. **(2)** **1879** *Harper's Mag.* July 196 The 'plucks,' or pickers, were each supplied with a crotched stick.

Plug, *n.* {1627-}

1. A flat, rectangular piece of tobacco suitable for carrying in the pocket. In full *plug of tobacco.* {1728-}

*c***1835** Catlin *Indians* II. 66, I coaxed a young fellow up within a little distance of me, by offering him a few plugs of tobacco. **1867** Goss *Soldier's Story* 180 One of our number betrayed us to the rebel quartermaster for a plug of tobacco. **1899** Chesnutt *Wife of His Youth* 182 Here's a piece of tobacco for you off my own plug. **1905** Lincoln *Partners* 18 The stage driver produced a plug, cut off a fair-sized chunk with a big knife, and handed it down to the man.

2. Short for Plug tobacco. {1898-} Also transf.

1843 Lumsden *Amer. Memoranda* 14 My next communication will probably contain full details of the methods adopted by the Virginian planters in the manufacturing of the nigger-head, . . . plug, pigtail. **1884** 'Mark Twain' *H. Finn* xxi. 210 Store tobacco is flat black plug. **1904** Crissey *Tattlings* 130 'Big Mike' . . . allowed that a man could wear a shirt front of solid plug fringed with fine-cut if he could only give his constituents their heart's desire. **1910** McCutcheon *Rose in Ring* 61 Fine cut er plug, I don't care.

+**3.** Short for Plug hat. Also attrib.

1861 Browne in *Vanity Fair* 15 June 273/1 A noble youth . . . is attired in a red shirt and black trowsis . . . ; his hat, which it is a plug, bein cockt onto one side of his classical hed. **1883** 'Mark Twain' *Life on Miss.* lviii, Kid gloves, plug tile, hair parted behind. **1904** 'O. Henry' *Roads of Destiny* 223 He wore a high, well-kept silk hat—known as a 'plug' in Elmville.

4. +**a.** An ineffective, unskilled, or inconsequential person, perhaps in allusion to sense b. Also attrib.

1863 in Billings *Hardtack* 72 Next came General Meade, a slow old plug, For he let them away at Gettysburg. **1872** *Chicago Tribune* 15 Oct. 2/2 Such a set of Judges as they have in Arkansas can be seen nowhere outside of New York City. Several of them are plugs, with ears which stand on guard, and eyes which run into people's pockets. **1903** Fox *Little Shepherd* xxiii, Well, Woolums, you're a 'plug.' **1920** Lewis *Main Street* 308 You figure I'm just a plug general practitioner.

+**b.** An old or broken-down horse. In full *plug horse.*

'U.S. and *Colonial slang.'* (*O.E.D.*).

1869 'Mark Twain' *Innocents* 285 We bought two sorry-looking Mexican 'plugs.' **1876** Bourke *Journal* 8–22 Sept. 882 The disgust and consternation of the Indians when they arrived in the midst of our broken down plugs were very amusing to our soldiers. **1887** *Courier-Journal* 4 Feb. 3/5 Wanted—40 plug horses and mares at Lum Simon's Stables. **1898** Westcott *D. Harum* 229, I got another equine wonder an' fifteen dollars to boot fer my old plug. **1903** 'O. Henry' *Roads of Destiny* 217 He spurred his old white plug up that way.

* **Plug,** *v.*

+**1.** *tr.* To debase (a coin) by removing a portion of the metal and filling the cavity with an inferior substance. *Obs.* Also *vbl. n.* and *part. adj.*

1694 *Mass. H. S. Coll.* 4 Ser. I. 106 If a piece of eight be plugged, it will not pass. **1797** *Ann. 5th Congress* 2 Sess. I. 718 They knew the silver coin circulated by tale, the gold by weight; the value of the latter had actually diminished by various means, such as sweating, plugging, clipping, &c. **1906** *Springfield W. Rep.* 6 Dec. 16 He offered a plugged 10-cent piece to Conductor Slattery and refused to produce any good money. **1909** 'O. Henry' *Options* 312 Mr. Hinkle told me . . . you'd never taken in a lead silver dollar or a plugged one since you've been on the job.

2. a. To put (a bullet) *into* a person. **b.** To shoot (a person). {1888-}

1857 Holland *Bay-Path* 281 It goes by wind, . . . and it'll plug a bullet right into a man. **1873** *Harper's Mag.* March 639/1 Then Nigger Tom Jett . . . laid for pap and plugged him. **1905** 'O. Henry' *Roads of Destiny* 135, I got into a little gun frolic down in Laredo and plugged a white man.

1925 TILGHMAN *Dugout* 56 If I ever meet up with that galoot I'm going to plug him.

+3. To anticipate or block (a person); to thwart (a plan.) Cf. BLOCK *v.* 2.

1880 *Scribner's Mo.* Aug. 492/2 One fisherman 'plugs' another when he puts out from shore and casts in ahead of him. **1896** ADE *Artie* 110, I wouldn't like to start in and plug his game.

+4. To cut a small plug or piece from (a melon) in order to test the quality of the fruit.

1882 C. B. LEWIS *Lime-Kiln Club* 254 We would advise all members of dis Club to plug dar watermelyons befo' passin' ober dar money. **1883** PECK *Bad Boy* 49 He came over after some cantelopes for breakfast, and plugged a couple to see if they were ripe.

+5. *intr.* Of a log jam: To become stuck or impeded.

1902 WHITE *Blazed Trail* 338 Several times the jam started, but always 'plugged' before the motion had become irresistible.

+Plug hat. A man's hat having a tall, cylindrical crown. *colloq.*

1872 'MARK TWAIN' *Roughing It* 334 His funeral ain't going to be no slouch—six plumes on the hearse, and a nigger on the box in a biled shirt and a plug hat. **1883** PECK *Bad Boy* 128 Pa he cried, and said he would put on his plug hat and go to church. **1897** GARLAND *J. Edwards* 140 No other man would ever wear a plug-hat out in this wind. **1911** LINCOLN *Cap'n Warren's Wards* 155, I've always sort of thought a plug hat looked lonesome.

attrib. **1881** BUEL *Border Outlaws* 170 They were only after the 'plug hat' crowd. **1907** STEWART *Partners* 300 There was a plug-hat doctor which give a show free and sold medicine that would cure most anything.

+Plug muss. A free-for-all brawl or row. *slang. Obs.* — **1857** *Knickerb.* L. 584 The exceeding utility of a hot poker—*properly applied*—in quelling a riot or 'plug-muss.' **1861** Moore *Rebellion Rec.* I. III. 81 [His] massive under-jaw and breadth of neck indicated him 'some in a plug muss.'

+Plug tobacco. Tobacco pressed into flat rectangular cakes. {1897-} — **1814** in *Ann. 17th Congress* 2 Sess. 1218 Plug tobacco manufactured at Columbia, one shilling and three pence per pound. **1868** *N.Y. Herald* 1 July 8/1 Five hundred pounds plug tobacco found at 21 Sixth avenue. **1895** *Dept. Agric. Yrbk. 1894* 143 Different grades [of tobacco are required] for the wrappers and fillers of cigars and for plug tobacco. **1908** 'O. HENRY' *Options* 62 Out of the general results they figured up $102.30 in cash and $31 worth of plug tobacco.

+Plug-ugly.

1. A member of a gang of rowdies and ruffians formerly active in Baltimore, New York, and Philadelphia. *Obs.* Cf. BLOOD-TUBS, DEAD RABBIT.

1857 *Knickerb.* Oct. 430 There is a 'Wolverine,' there are two 'Pukes,' one 'Plug-Ugly,' and two 'Suckers.' **1858** *Ib.* Oct. 431 A distinguished 'Plug-Ugly,' of Baltimore, and a highly-talented 'Dead Rabbit,' of New York. **1861** in E. Cowell *Diary* 316 He then denounced death to the Baltimore traitor seccessionists and Plug Uglies. **1875** *Scribner's Mo.* July 267/2 'Plug uglies' from Philadelphia . . . swooped down [upon San Francisco]. **1889** *Boston Jrnl.* 24 April 1/8 Thugs, plug-uglies, and 'flash sports.'

attrib. **1872** BRACE *Dangerous Classes N.Y.* 27 The 'dangerous classes' of New York . . . are much banded together, in associations, such as 'Dead Rabbit,' 'Plug-ugly,' and various target companies. **1875** *Chicago Tribune* 4 Nov. 2/1 The Baltimore *American* has an unanswerable showing of facts of the plug-ugly element for which it was once noted.

b. A tough, a rowdy, or a roughneck. *colloq.*

1892 CRANE *Maggie* (1896) 121 And she goes off with that plug-ugly who looks as if he had been hit in the face with a coin die. **1904** *Grand Rapids Ev. Press* 16 Aug. 4 Had the escaping prisoner been a plug-ugly in appearance he would have attracted the attention of the visitors, but his neat appearance disarmed suspicion. **1913** LONDON *Valley of Moon* 242 He'll kill somebody yet, that plug-ugly of yourn, an' be hanged for it.

2. An ardent proslavery advocate in the Kansas struggle of 1854–58. *Obs.* Also attrib.

1857 *Lawrence* (Kan.) *Republican* 16 July 2 The usurpers—or, as Vaughn of the Leavenworth Times significantly terms them, the '*plug uglies*.' *Ib.* 30 July 2 Only a pitiful minority of the actual voters of Kansas, cast their votes for delegates to the plug ugly convention, soon to assemble at Lecompton.

‖**Pluguglydom.** Plug-uglies collectively. — *a*1861 WINTHROP *Open Air* 232 If the rural population did not give us a bastard imitation of Lexington and Concord, . . . all Pluguglydom would treat us *à la* Plug-ugly somewhere near the junction of the Annapolis and Baltimore and Washington Railroad.

‖**Pluguglymore.** A nickname for Baltimore. — **1861** *N.Y. Tribune* 15 July 6/4 Indeed, the number of slaves there [in Baltimore] held can scarcely be regarded as involving so much wealth as the piratic slave-trade, in which Plug-Uglymore is known to bear her part most gallantly.

***Plum,** *n.* Also †**plumb.**

***1.** The roundish, fleshy fruit or drupe of the plum tree.

1609 HAKLUYT *Va. Richly Valued* (1846) 131 There are also in Florida great store of Walnuts, and Plummes, Mulberries, and Grapes. **1622** J. PORY *Descr. Plymouth Col.* 42 Touching their fruite I will not speake of their meaner sort as of raspes, . . . strawberries, delicate plumbes and others. **1698** THOMAS *Pensilvania* 17 Cramberries, Plumbs of several sorts, and many other Wild Fruits, in great plenty, . . . are common and free for any to gather. **1705** BEVERLEY *Virginia* II. 13 Of stoned Fruits, I have met with Three good Sorts, *viz.* Cherries, Plums, and Persimmons. **1781-2** JEFFERSON *Notes Va.* (1788) 40 The orchards produce apples, pears, cherries, quinces, peaches, nectarines, apricots, almonds, and plumbs. **1804** CLARK in *Lewis & C. Exped.* I. (1904) 138 This Creek is Small it 'abounds with plumbs of a Delicious flavour.' **1892** M. A. JACKSON *Gen. Jackson* 193, I received a box of delicately flavored plums.

***2.** = PLUM TREE.

1815 DRAKE *Cincinnati* 83 The most elegantly flowering trees and shrubs [include] . . . the different species of roses, plumbs and haws. **1834** PECK *Gaz. Illinois* 13 The undergrowth are redbud, . . . sumach, plum, crab apple, . . . hazle, &c. **1885** HAVARD *Flora W. & S. Texas* 458 Of the Rose Family, the only notable arborescent members [in the San Antonio valley] are a species of Hawthorn (*Cratoegus subvillosa*) and a Plum (*Prunus americana*, var. *mollis*). **1901** MOHR *Plant Life Ala.* 61 Red plum (*Prunus Americana*) [is found] rarely along the banks of streams.

3. *Geol.* A pebble or stone embedded in a matrix of later origin.

*a*1817 DWIGHT *Travels* III. 52 He would next have inquired, how the plums, (i.e. the pebbles and other larger stones,) often exceeding twelve inches in diameter, . . . could exist in petrified vegetable matter.

4. A dark shade of bluish-purple.

1878 *Ill. Dept. Agric. Trans.* XIV. 210 [Siamese Swine] varied in color from deep rich plum to dark slate and black. **1909** RICE *Mr. Opp* 4 His trousers, of that morose hue termed by the country people 'plum,' reached to his armpits.

+5. A state or federal office obtained as a result of political 'pull.'

1887 *Courier-Journal* 13 Jan. 3/4 Senator Beck gets the credit for most of the Federal appointments in Mason county. . . . The boys enjoying the plums will support anybody who is for him and them. **1904** CRISSEY *Tattlings* 358 The machine would have to stand back and watch the young friend of the man from Buffalo hand out the official plums and give orders for future business. **1911** *N.Y. Ev. Post* 3 Jan. 8 The 'plum' is a luscious fruit in the shape of an office under the State government, which many people are on the lookout to secure.

6. *attrib.* **a.** Designating places where plum trees or bushes grow or are grown. Sometimes in proper names.

1658 *Southold Rec.* I. 56 A certen hoole like to an old seller, beinge in the west end of the plumb beach. **1677** *Derby Rec.* 36 A hom lott containing fower acres of the Half of plum meadow to the ajasent land. **1748** *Georgia Col. Rec.* VI. 226 Mr. Griffith Williams at the Upper End of the South Branch of Midway River known by the Name of Plum Orchard [desires] warrants to lay out the Same. **1846** MAGOFFIN *Down Santa Fé Trail* 28 Above these and on the side rather of the cliff, is a thick plumb grove. **1847** COYNER *Lost Trappers* 136 Our little party for the sake of greater security, went down the river to a large plum thicket, into which they crept.

b. Designating foods made of plums. See also PLUM CAKE, PLUM DUFF, etc.

*c*1847 WHITCHER *Bedott P.* ix. 88 If I should stay there to tea don't you and Kier be a lettin' into the plum sass and cake. **1850** S. F. COOPER *Rural Hours* 299 The rice-pudding, the plum tart, the apple-pie they are now eating, will no more compare [etc.]. **1869** STOWE *Oldtown Folks* 340 Peach, pear, and plum pies, custard pies, apple pies.

c. In special combinations.

Plum grape, = FOX GRAPE; *p. nectarine, peach*, (see quotation); *p. pockets*, a disease of plums in which the fruit is bloated or hollow; *p. wart*, = BLACK KNOT 1.

1817-8 EATON *Botany* (1822) 515 *Vitis labrusca*, plum grape. **1705** BEVERLEY *Virginia* IV. 78 The best sort of these [*sc.* peaches & nectarines] cling to the Stone, and will not come off clear, which they call Plum-Nectarines, and Plum-Peaches, or Cling-Stones. **1891** *Cent.* 6185/3 *T[aphrina] Pruni* [causes] the disease of plums known as 'plum-pockets.' **1851** BARRY *Fruit Garden* 364 The Plum Wart or Black Knot . . . originates . . . from an imperfect circulation of the sap, induced by violent changes of temperature.

***Plum(b),** *adv.* Completely, absolutely, quite. *colloq.* {*dial.* 1787-; now *obs.*} Also as *adj.*

'Chiefly *U.S. slang*.' (*O.E.D.*).

1845 SOL. SMITH *Theatr. Apprent.* 213 Long before the time arrived . . . the house was plum, chock full—full to overflowing. *a*1861 WINTHROP *J. Brent* 296, I paid their ticket plum through to York. **1891** RYAN *Pagan* 150 Yer a fool—a plum fool! **1906** 'O. HENRY' *Heart of West* 154 'He's a plumb buzzard,' said Buck. **1925** TILGHMAN *Dugout* 48, I'm plumb tired.

Plumbago. {1612-} Black lead or graphite. {1784-} — **1795** WINTERBOTHAM *Hist. View* II. 91 Black lead, *plumbago*, is found in large quantities (In New Hampshire). **1866** *Wkly. New Mexican* 6 April 2/1 The Pinos Altos mountains, the Organ Placer and Taos mountains, are full of rich deposits of . . . copper, plumbago, etc. **1919** *Inform. concerning Graphite* (Tariff Comm.) 9 Graphite also goes by the names 'plumbago' and 'black lead.'

Plumb bob. A leaden bob or weight used on a plumb line. {1879–} — **1835–7** HALIBURTON *Clockmaker* 1 Ser. v. 30 If he is found here after twenty-four hours, they'd make a carpenter's plumb-bob of him, and hang him outside the church steeple. **1853** FOWLER *Home for All* 186 Make a plumbob; and you are ready to begin the wall proper.

+**Plumb center.** *adv.* Centrally; absolutely in the center. *colloq.* — **1848** RUXTON *Life Far West* i, He made it throw plum-center. **1851** M. REID *Scalp Hunters* xx, Most of them [*sc.* Delawares] can hit 'plumb centre' with any of their mountain associates. **1886** *Outing* Nov. 104/2 So down I jumps an' gin her [the bear] one through the brisket, plumb-center fust shot.

+**Plumbeous vireo.** A regional variety (see quot. 1917) of the blue-headed vireo; a bird of this variety. — **1872** COUES *Key to Birds* 122 Plumbeous Vireo. Leaden-gray, rather brighter & more ashy on the crown. **1878** — *Birds Colo. Valley* 519 My suspicions that they were not the Plumbeous Vireos had at first been aroused by hearing the song. **1917** *Birds of Amer.* III. 108/2 The Plumbeous Vireo . . . of the southern Rocky Mountain Region . . . breeds from northern Nevada, northern Utah, northeastern Wyoming and southwestern South Dakota south through Arizona and southwestern Texas to the mountains of Mexico.

***Plumber.** Also †**plummer.** One who works in lead, tin, or zinc in fitting or repairing water and gas pipes, radiators, etc.

1682 SEWALL *Diary* II. 19* Wm. Allen, a Plummer, receives a blow by a piece that was used for a Scaffold falling on's head. **1789** *Boston Directory* 176 Brewer Nath. glazier & plumber. **1806** *Phila. Ordinances* (1812) 197 If any plumber . . . [shall] introduce a ferrule into any public or private pipe . . . [he] shall forfeit . . . one dollar. **1866** *Internal Revenue Guide* 78 Plumbers and gas-fitters shall pay ten dollars. **1907** LONDON *Road* 20 Her husband is a plumber—a contracting plumber.

Plum bush. A small bush or shrub which produces plums. {wild plum bush, 1902–} — **1658** *Southold Rec.* I. 54 The greate meadowe by the plum bushes. **1818** *Amer. Jrnl. Science* I. 117 Sometimes this grass is intermixed with weeds and plum-bushes. **1852** MARCY *Explor. Red River* (1854) 17 Sand-hills . . . support a very spare vegetation of weeds, grape-vines, and plum-bushes. **1875** *Chicago Tribune* 14 Oct. 7/2 [The valley of the Belle Fourche is] divided here and there by dry creeks filled with box-elder and plum-bushes.

Plum cake. A cake containing raisins, currants, etc. Now rare. {1635–} — **1643** *New Haven Col. Rec.* 84 Bakeing him a pasty and plum cakes. **1693** in S. A. Eliot *Sk. Hist. Harvard* 33 The custom taken up in the College . . . for the commencers to have plumb-cake, is dishonorable to the College. **1722** *Harvard Rec.* II. 471 Hencefore no preparation nor Provision either of Plumb-Cake or rosted, boiled or baked Meats or Pyes of any kind shalbe made by any Commencer. **1808** IRVING, etc. *Salmagundi* xx. 522 Our respectable new-year-cookies, and cherry-bounce, have been elbowed aside by plumb-cake and outlandish liqueurs. **1900** STOCKTON *Afield & Afloat* 127 Plum-cake gets better and better the longer it is kept.

Plum duff. A stiff flour pudding having raisins, currants, or prunes in it and boiled in a bag. {1851–} — **1838** [see DUFF[1].] **1840** DANA *Two Years* 63 This day was Christmas, but it brought us no holiday. The only change was that we had a 'plum duff' for dinner. **1880** *Scribner's Mo.* May 129/1 Now and then, the cook makes a plum duff to put our digestions to the test. **1900** *Boston Ev. Globe* 15 Oct. 7/4 The addition of prunes stirred into the mess makes it 'plum duff;' but prunes are expensive.

Plumed Knight. +(See quots.) Now hist. — [**1876** INGERSOLL in *Republican Nat. Convention Proc.* 74 Like a plumed knight, James G. Blaine marched down the halls of the American congress.] **1885** *Mag. Amer. Hist.* March 298/1 *Plumed knights.*—Republican campaign clubs formed during the presidential campaign of 1884, in honor of Mr. Blaine, the Republican candidate. The name 'Plumed Knight' was given to Mr. Blaine by Mr. Robert Ingersoll, who described him in an address as the 'plumed knight of the debate.' **1888** M. LANE in *America* 1 Nov. 15 *Plumed Knight.*—A name conferred upon the Hon. James G. Blaine at the National Republican Convention at Cincinnati, in 1876, by the Hon. Robert G. Ingersoll.

+**Plumed partridge.** =MOUNTAIN QUAIL. — **1839** AUDUBON *Ornith. Biog.* V. 226 Plumed Partridge. *Perdix Plumifera.* . . . This bird inhabits the dense woods along the tributary streams of the Columbia River. **1917** *Birds of Amer.* II. 5 Mountain Quail. *Oreortyx picta picta.* . . . Other Names.—Plumed Partridge; Mountain Partridge.

Plume grass. Any one of various grasses of the genus *Erianthus.* — **1861** WOOD *Botany* 807 *Erianthus,* Plume Grass. . . . Stout, erect grasses, remarkable for their large woolly or silky, tawny panicles. **1901** MOHR *Plant Life Ala.* 334.

‖**Plume-stick.** (See quotations.) — **1882** *N.Y. Tribune* 5 March, The plume-stick [among the Zuñis] is a mere twig, a little larger in circumference than a lead-pencil, having bound to one end a duck's feather. *Ib.,* The prayers . . . were addressed directly to the plume-sticks, which were placed one by one in the bottom of the hole, the feathers standing upright. . . . The sticks were then reverently covered up.

+**Plum-gouger.** A weevil (*Anthonomus scutellaris*) destructive to plums. — **1863** *Prairie Farmer* June 372/3, I have myself seen many such holes [in plums], and have little doubt that they are made by this insect. Hence I propose to call it the 'Plum-Gouger.' **1871** C. V. RILEY *3d Rep. Insects Mo.* 39 The Plum Gouger seems to be unknown in the Eastern States, or at least is not common there; but it is very generally distributed throughout the Valley of the Mississippi. **1908** KELLOGG *Amer. Insects* 296 The larva of the plum-gouger . . . bores into the stone.

Plum jelly. Jelly made of plums. — **1828** LESLIE *Receipts* 81 Plum, and green gage jelly may be made in the same manner. **1870** W. BAKER *New Timothy* 193 Plum-jelly, I found time to make last summer, she explained. **1897** 'THANET' *Missionary Sheriff* 175 Take a jar of my plum jelly to Sammy!

Plum-muss. [PLUM and Du. *moes.*] 'Plums boiled, mashed together, and dried in the form of a sheet' (B. '77).

***Plump,** *adv.* ‖*To vote plump,* ?to vote without any qualifications or directly. — **1776** in J. Adams *Works* III. 55 Our delegates in Congress, on the first of July, will vote plump [on the question of Amer. independence].

Plum pudding. A pudding containing raisins, currants, etc. {1711–} Also attrib. and transf. — **1783** [see MINCE PIE 1.] **1793** BENTLEY *Diary* II. 5 There was provision made in the Charity house for a good dinner of excellent chosen beef & plumb puddings. **1828** LESLIE *Receipts* 14. **1851** MELVILLE *Moby-Dick* 94 Some sailors . . . had just come from a plum-pudding voyage, as they called it (that is, a short whaling-voyage in a schooner or brig, confined to the north of the line, in the Atlantic Ocean only). *Ib.* 465 Plum-pudding is the term bestowed upon certain fragmentary parts of the whales flesh. **1882** RITTENHOUSE *Maud* 141 Scalloped oysters, . . . cake, plum pudding, chicken sauce, and various other modern messes fill the basement with their several odors. **1906** BELL *C. Lee* 341 Emmeline shall serve the plum pudding!

+**Plum puddinger.** A whaling boat used in short voyages in the north Atlantic Ocean; also, a member of the crew of such a boat. *slang.* — **1851** MELVILLE *Moby Dick* 95 After listening to these plum-puddingers till nearly eleven o'clock, I went up stairs to go to bed. **1874** C. M. SCAMMON *Marine Mammals* 241 Provincetown has ever been foremost with her numerous fleet of plum-puddingers, . . . which are small vessels employed on short voyages in the Atlantic Ocean.

***Plum tree.** Any one of various trees producing the edible fruit known as plums.

1616 SMITH *New England* 29 Plum tree, hazell, saxefrage, and many other sorts. **1685** *Manchester Rec.* 21 The northeast corner of said land is bounded with a plum tree. **1719** SEWALL *Diary* III. 216 Cut down the Plum-Trees at Engs's pasture, which yield a Considerable quantity of fewil. **1800** HAWKINS *Sk. Creek Country* 30 They have but a few plum trees. **1886** R. H. DAVIS *Silhouettes* 176 In the orchard . . . were her seat and work-table under the great plum-tree for thirty years.

attrib. **1854** EMMONS *Agric. N.Y.* V. 262 (*index*), Plumtree beetles, 73.

b. *fig.* The source of political offices, jobs, etc.

Cf. PLUM *n.* 5.

1904 *Newark Ev. News* 27 June 6 It is pretty tough to shut the statesmen off from one of the biggest branches of the plum tree in this summary fashion.

+**Plum weevil.** The plum curculio (*Conotrachelus nenuphar*), which is injurious to various stone fruits, as the plum, peach, and cherry. — **1850** *New Eng. Farmer* II. 252 One half of all [my Baldwin apples] that have fallen have been stung by the plum-weevil. **1867** *Amer. Naturalist* I. 112 The grubs of the Plumb Weevil often live in the wart, but they have no agency in producing it. **1874** *Vermont Bd. Agric. Rep.* II. 776 *Conotrachelus nenuphar.* This is the notorious plum weevil or curculio.

Plunder.

1. Booty, spoils, etc., taken from an enemy by force. {1694–}

1647 WARD *Simple Cobler* 59, I would not speake thus in the ears of the world, . . . for all the plunder your plunderers have pillaged. **1654** JOHNSON *Wonder-w. Prov.* 182 [The Indians] have neither plunder, nor cash to bear the charge of [war]. **1690** SEWALL *Diary* I. 323 Notice is given . . . of the Sale of the Souldiers part of Plunder taken at Port-Royal. **1705** *Boston News-Letter* 23 April 2/2 He got little or no plunder from them, but a few feathers. **1790** D. FANNING *Narrative* 14 The Rebels . . . had gone to their respective homes with their plunder. **1838** *Diplom. Corr. Texas* I. (1908) 359 [The Indians] are instigated . . . by their desire for plunder, and by the encouragement held out to them by the Mexican authorities. **1897** C. A. DANA *Recoll. Civil War* 232 It was pretty certain that they were carrying off a large amount of cattle and other plunder with them.

+**b.** Political spoils.

1870 *Nation* 24 Feb. 113/2 Nor do we see how those who hold that the nomination to places in the public service is party 'plunder,' or 'spoils,' can well object to this.

+**2.** Baggage, personal effects, household goods, etc.

In this sense perhaps from Ger., 'trash,' or obs. Du., 'household stuff.'

1805 LEWIS in *L. & Clark Exped.* II. (1904) 220, I dispatched Sergt. Ordway with 4 Canoes and 8 men to take up a load of baggage as far as Capt. Clark's camp and return for the remainder of our plunder. **1822** J. WOODS *English Prairie* (1904) 345 You have a powerful chance of plunder on your creature. **1856** S. ROBINSON *Kansas* 33 And in the midst of all this 'plunder,' as the western people say, three of us were seated, two ladies in front, and the doctor behind. **1892** C. ROBINSON *Kansas Conflict* 28 On leaving St. Louis the boat was well filled with passengers and their 'plunder.' **1902** *Dialect Notes* II. 241 *Plunder,* general term for household goods and utensils, and farm implements.

attrib. **1846** MAGOFFIN *Down Santa Fé Trail* 2, [I] received two or three visits—next I arranged my trunk 'plunder-basket.'

Plunge bath. {1896–} +A bath taken by plunging into water. — **1848** THOREAU *Maine Woods* 68 The continual bathing of our bodies in mountain water, alternate foot, sitz, douche, and plunge baths, made this walk exceedingly refreshing. **1879** B. F. TAYLOR *Summer-Savory* 188 The next thing it [the train] did was to dash across Harlem river, . . . and out it dashed as if bound for a plunge-bath in the Hudson. **1897** *Voice* 3 June 7/2 [A woman] who never fails to do her exercises before a big plunge bath, is sure to have smaller bills with the doctors.

Plunger. {1611–} +A small boat or yacht. — **1892** *Outing* March 467/1 Yachting on the Pacific coast dates from about 1869, . . . though a few small plungers and sloops had long been owned on the bay. **1900** HARTE *Treasure of Redwoods* 109, I've got him safe on that 'plunger' down at the wharf.

Plunk, *v.* {?a1800–} +*tr.* To shoot. *colloq.* — **1891** *Outing* Nov. 138/2, I would plunk the big gobbler I could distinguish from where I lay. **1916** WILSON *Somewhere* 120 Darned if he didn't up with this here air gun . . . and plunk me with a buckshot it carried.

***Plural,** *a.* +Used with reference to polygamy as formerly practiced among the Mormons. — **1894** in *Congress. Rec.* 23 Jan. (1900) 1103/1 Former polygamists . . . are utterly neglecting their former plural wives and children of those wives. **1900** *Ib.* 16 Jan. 850/1 The church has positively abandoned the practice of polygamy or the solemnization of plural marriages in this and every other State. **1900** *Ib.* 25 Jan. 1183/1 The gentleman from Utah is . . . 'up in arms to overturn society' by leading a life of open shame with plural women.

***Plurality.**

+**1.** In an election: The total number of votes obtained by the leading candidate; in exact usage, such a total number if no candidate receives a majority. {=Eng. *majority*}

In quot. 1789, since it is possible for a single candidate to secure more than half the votes, *plurality* necessarily includes the concept of *majority* (q.v., sense 1).

1789 *Ann. 1st Congress* 1 Sess. I. 21 All committees shall be appointed by ballot, and a plurality of votes shall make a choice. **1804** *Mass. Spy* 18 Jan. (Th.), In several states, many great offices are filled, and even the chief magistracy, by various methods of election. The public will is sometimes expressed by pluralities instead of majorities. **1828** WEBSTER s.v., In elections, a plurality of votes is when one candidate has more votes than any other, but less than half of the whole number of votes given. **1903** *Independent* 3 Sept. 2133 We were hasty in assuming that Vardaman had received a majority of the votes. It was only a plurality, and the combined vote of his two competitors was 19,000 more than his own. **1912** NICHOLSON *Hoosier Chron.* 404 Harwood ran ahead of his associates, . . . scoring a plurality that testified to his personal popularity.

attrib. **1851** *Harper's Mag.* July 276/1 Among the measures passed was . . . the Plurality Act, in accordance with which members of Congress at the second trial . . . are elected by a plurality of votes.

+**2.** In an election wherein there are more than two candidates: The excess of votes obtained by the leading candidate over an opponent, esp. over his nearest competitor.

The leading candidate may, or may not, also have a majority.

1860 *Boston Transcript* 7 Nov. 2/3 In Massachusetts . . . Lincoln's clear majority 42,371, Lincoln's plurality over Douglas 70,460, Lincoln's plurality over Bell 82,450. **1894** *Harper's Mag.* Jan. 318/1 In Massachusetts, F. T. Greenhalge, Republican, was elected Governor by a plurality of 30,000. **1903** *Smart Set* IX. 2/1 In six weeks followed their election by a small plurality.

***Plush.** A soft cloth of silk, cotton, wool, etc., having a nap longer than that of velvet. Also attrib. — **1639** *Md. Archives* IV. 106 A plush coate. **1806** *Ann. 9th Congress* 2 Sess. 1131 The green substance discoverable at the bottom of the hot springs . . . at first sight has the appearance of plush. **1852** STOWE *Uncle Tom* xiii, A real comfortable . . . old chair, and worth . . . a dozen of your plush or brocatelle drawing-room gentry. **1921** *New Dressmaker* (Butterick) 32 Velvet, velveteen, panne velvet, corduroy and plush, and a few wool materials like broadcloth have a distinct pile or nap.

Plymouth. *attrib.* +Of or pertaining to Plymouth, Mass. — **1654** JOHNSON *Wonder-w. Prov.* 17 Insomuch that halfe a handfull of his people landing not long after in Plimoth-Plantation, found little resistance. **1782** CRÈVECŒUR *Letters* 180 The title of these lands [on the Kennebeck R.] is vested in the ancient Plymouth Company, under the powers of which the Massachusets was settled. **1903** C. F. ADAMS *3 Episodes Mass. Hist.* I. 20 These islands the Plymouth explorers reported had been 'cleared from end to end.'

+**Plymothean.** A native or inhabitant of Plymouth, Massachusetts. *Obs.* — **1631** *N.H. Hist. Soc. Coll.* IV. 228 [The Englishmen] who survived were rescued by those of Plymouth out of the hands of Chicka Talbott and his Indians, who . . . intended to have destroyed them and the Plymotheans also. **1702** C. MATHER *Magnalia* (1853) I. 55 [Squanto had been] brought back by one Mr. Dermer, about half a year before our honest Plymotheans were cast upon this continent.

+**Plymouth pilgrim. 1.** =PILGRIM 3. **2.** A Northern soldier in a Southern prison camp during the Civil War. — **(1) 1805** *Independent Chronicle* 3 Jan. 2/4 The Plymouth pilgrims have carefully confined their approbation of John Adams to his private character. **(2) 1865** KELLOGG *Rebel Prisons* 51 Great crowds of people thronged the street corners to stare at the 'Plymouth Pilgrims,' as the city papers sarcastically called us. *Ib.* 61 The balance of the Plymouth pilgrims came in, including the remainder of our regiment.

+**Plymouth Rock.**

1. A granite boulder in Plymouth Harbor, Massachusetts, on which the Pilgrims are said to have landed in 1620.

1837 MARTINEAU *Society* I. 134 The other festival . . . was the celebration of Forefathers' Day;—of the landing of the Pilgrims on Plymouth Rock. **1848** LOWELL *Biglow P.* 1 Ser. p. xviii, If the Greek might boast his Thermopylæ, . . . we may well be proud of our Plymouth Rock. **1871** HOWELLS *Wedding Journey* 43 As for Plymouth Rock, I should have sternly resisted the blandishments of those twin sirens, Starvation and Cold, who beckoned the Puritans shoreward. **1900** *Congress. Rec.* 15 Feb. 1842/2 Their ancestors landed with the Pilgrim fathers at Plymouth Rock.

2. An American chicken or breed of chickens, the best known variety of which is characterized by long yellow legs and evenly barred feathers. Also attrib.

1849 *New Eng. Farmer* I. 386 *Plymouth Rock.*—This is a new variety, recently formed at Plymouth. **1882** *Harper's Mag.* Sept. 489/1 Here Plymouth Rocks and well-fed Brahmas cackled, oblivious to all things terrestrial but themselves. **1902** LORIMER *Lett. Merchant* 213 When you fix up a snug little nest for a Plymouth Rock hen . . . , it doesn't always follow that she has reached the fricassee age because she doesn't lay right off. **1912** N. M. WOODROW *Sally Salt* 40 A great flock of industriously pecking chickens, snow-white Leghorns, gray speckled Plymouth Rocks, buff cochin-chinas.

Pneumatic tube. A tube in which a carrier is driven by compressed air; a system using this. Also attrib. Also *pneumatic dispatch-tube.* — [**1850** GLISAN *Jrnl. Army Life* 25 My children . . . will fly through this country on the swift railroad car; and my grandchildren . . . flash across it in a pneumatic tube.] **1875** KNIGHT 1756/2 The pneumatic dispatch-tube was started by a company in London in 1859. **1893** CUSHING *Story of P.O.* 35 Propositions have been [made] . . . to have pneumatic tube service. **1900** *Congress. Rec.* 21 Feb. 2016/2 A bill . . . to authorize the laying and maintaining of a pneumatic-tube system between the Capitol and the Government Printing Office.

P.O. Abbrev. of POST OFFICE. Also attrib. — **1881** RITTENHOUSE *Maud* 18 Nearly ran over little WmSn at the P.O. and he solemnly tipped his hat. **1901** FLYNT *World of Graft* 201, I used to touch up P.O. boxes now an' then, an' I made one or two nice get-aways.

+**Pocan.** [Virginian *puccoon, pakon.*] =POKE n.³ 1. — **1866** LINDLEY & MOORE *Treas. Botany* 885/2 The Pocan, or Virginian Poke or Pokeweed, is a branching herbaceous plant, with a smooth green or sometimes purplish stem. Ib. 907/2 Pocanbush. **1877** [see PIGEON BERRY].

***Pocket,** *n.*

+**1.** (See quotation.)

1842 *Amer. Pioneer* I. 419 'Pockets' for inclosing letters are of modern mention. (Pockets are envelopes prepared and franked.)

2. *Mining.* A cavity in the earth containing rich ore, esp. of gold; an abrupt enlargement in an ore vein or lode. {1878–; in related senses, 1850–}

1848 *30th Congress 1 Sess.* H. R. Ex. Doc. No. 41, 451 The sides of the passage worn into deep rounded fissures that our host calls pockets; . . . there the richest ores are found. **1867** *Wkly. New Mexican* 23 Feb. 1/3 Some thought, that the gold in this region would be found collected in what they called pockets. **1891** *Boston Jrnl.* 22 Jan. 2/3 A pocket was recently struck in a mine at Coulterville, Cal., from which $10,000 in gold was taken from 140 pounds of rock. **1907** WHITE *Arizona Nights* 164 For a while they tried gold washing, but I had the only pocket.

transf. **1882** *Econ. Geol. Illinois* 145, I noticed . . . , at one point in the face of the bluff, a small pocket of coal, about two feet long by four inches thick at the thickest

+**3.** (See quotation.)

1862 *Congregationalist* 30 May (Chipman), The General Association of Indiana met . . . at Francisco, Gibson Co., in the 'Pocket,'—that part of the State lying south of the Ohio and Mississippi Railway.

+**4.** A cove or valley among mountains.

1874 LONG *Wild-Fowl* 215 High cypress timber . . . bordered the little coves (or pockets as they are called by the natives). **1885** *Century Mag.* March 685 These rugged peaks surrounding the little 'pocket' or valley ought not to fence in a slave or harbor a master. **1891** *Ib.* April 895/2 Through a rift they might have a fine view of the little valley, or pocket, beyond which the foothills swelled up.

‖**5.** A bag or sack into which cotton is placed in picking.

1881 *Harper's Mag.* Oct. 728/1 There is not a process to which the lint is submitted after it is thrown from the negro's 'pocket' that does not act directly on the quality of the cloth that is finally produced.

+**6.** A receptacle of strong paper pasted inside the cover of a library book to hold the charging cards.

1887 [see POCKET *v.* 4]. **1899** DANA *Library Primer* 102 Call-numbers are written on the labels, the pockets, and the book slips. **1910** BOSTWICK *Amer. Pub. Library* 45 When the book is on the shelf the book card is kept in it, in a pocket provided for the purpose.

+7. *As handy as a pocket in a shirt*, very handy or convenient. *colloq.*

1892 *Amer. Folk-Lore* V. 60.

8. *attrib.* passing into *adj.* **a.** Suitable for carrying in the pocket. {1612–}

See also POCKET BIBLE, POCKETBOOK, etc.

1776 *Battle of Brooklyn* II. iv, Behold, Joe, this pocket bottle; one-half of its contents I prescribe to your . . . restoration. **1787** *Boston Gazette* 5 March 3/3 Lost. A small Pocket Blunderbuss, or Pocket Pistol. **1827** COOPER *Prairie* vi, *Quadruped;* seen by starlight, and by the aid of a pocket-lamp, in the prairies of North America. **1840** *Knickerb.* XVI. 205 The strong, the able, but above all, the 'enterprising,' set out with his pocket-map and his pocket-compass, to thread the dim woods. **1860** PRESCOTT *Telegraph* 34 Fig. 15 represents a *pocket battery* in its case. **1876** HABBERTON *Jericho Road* 91 An' here . . . is a pocket testament—I'm afraid you haven't thought to pervide yourself with one.

b. In special combinations.

Pocket boom, (see quotation); *p.-cutter,* a pickpocket who cuts the pockets of his victims; *p. diggings,* (see quotation); *p. field,* an oil field in which a pocket or pool of oil is tapped; *p. mining,* mining that specializes in exploiting deposits of gold in pockets; *p. mouse,* (see quotation); *p. peddler,* (see quotation); *p. torch,* a flashlight; *p. vein,* a pockety ore vein.

1905 *Forestry Bureau Bul.* No. 61, 43 *Pocket boom,* a boom in which logs are held after they are sorted. **1885** *Milnor* (Dak.) *Teller* 5 June 2/3 Deck hands on the steamer Mary Morton were being robbed by pocket-cutters among the roustabouts. **1877** BARTLETT 476 *Pocket diggings,* a term used by gold-miners to denote hollow places where gold is concentrated as in a pocket. **1883** *Century Mag.* July 327/1 About ten miles from the clearing lay the little oil town of Clarendon, . . . a pocket-field, as the oil men call it, developed about ten years ago. **1872** 'MARK TWAIN' *Roughing It* 436 In that one little corner of California is found a species of mining . . . called 'pocket mining.' **1884** *Cassell's Nat. Hist.* III. 124 These animals [Saccomyidæ] . . . by American writers . . . are called 'Pocket Mice.' **1892** *Nation* 28 July 66/1 [The liquor traffic] is now largely conducted by men called pocket-peddlers—men who stand on the street corners with a bottle in one pocket and a glass in the other, and will sell you a drink in a doorway or a horse-shed. **1917** McCUTCHEON *Green Fancy* 56 Barnes found his electric pocket torch and dressed hurriedly. **1873** RAYMOND *Silver & Gold* 47 Although many so-called pocket-veins exist near to and parallel with the Mother lode, . . . it is generally believed they are outlying 'stringers' of the main lode.

***Pocket,** *v.*

+1. *Mining. intr.* Of a vein of ore: To spread out or expand into a pocket.

Cf. POCKET *n.* 2.

1873 BEADLE *Undevel. West* 336 A vein . . . 'pinching' and 'pocketing' alternately towards the interior. **1883** — *Western Wilds* 563 [The vein] may 'pocket' suddenly in a chamber the size of a keg, barrel or hogshead.

‖**2.** To become puckered or bagged.

1873 A. D. WHITNEY *Other Girls* xxv, That carpet . . . hadn't begun to pocket yet.

+3. *Polit. tr.* Of the president or a state governor: To defeat (a bill) passed in the closing days of a legislative session by retaining it unsigned.

Cf. POCKET VETO.

1848 *Congress. Globe* 24 Jan. 225/1 This House saw a President of the United States very coolly pocket a bill. **1854** BENTON *30 Years View* I. 365/1 The opposition presses and orators kept the country filled with denunciations of the enormity of his conduct in '*pocketing*' the bill—as if it had been a case of 'flat burglary.' **1895** *Kan. State Hist. Soc. Trans.* V. 136 His last attempt was to thwart it by what was called 'pocketing' the bill. To do this he decided the legal question of when a legislature expired, and retained the bill, and pertinaciously declared that it was defeated. **1898** *Ib.* VI. 63 It was his duty under the law either to sign and return it, or to return it vetoed, within three days; but he 'pocketed' it and refused to return it, attempting thus to defeat it, because the legislative term, as he erroneously asserted, had expired.

+4. To supply (a book) with a pocket for holding library cards. As *vbl. n.*

1887 *Library Notes* March 282 Among the things 'to be done' to each book [is] 'pocketing.' . . . The Acme Pocket . . . is made of strong manila, cut with a peculiar die so that the cards can be put in and taken out with the greatest rapidity, and yet are firmly held.

Pocket Bible. A small Bible suitable for carrying in the pocket. — **1743** *N.H. Probate Rec.* III. 187, I Bequeath her . . . my Pocket Bible and as many of my own other Books as she pleases. **1801** WEEMS *Letters* II. 168, I am torn to pieces for some handsome pocket Bibles. **1910** D. DE LEON *Pocket Bible* 343 The taper and the little pocket Bible which she held rolled to the ground.

Pocketbook.

1. A small book or notebook suitable for carrying in the pocket. {1617–} Also attrib.

1653 *Boston Rec.* 41 There is another booke upon the table in my closet at Boston . . . wch I call my pocket booke. **1710** *Boston News-Letter* 13 March 2/2 Intended for the Press and may speedily be Published, The Constables Pocket-Book. **1835** HOFFMAN *Winter in West* I. 246, I read over to him a slight vocabulary of words in his own language, as I had taken down the terms occasionally in my pocket-book. **1883** *Wheelman* I. 418 [He] went out and got one of those roses. He pressed it in his pocket-book with that incomplete little sketch. **1904** in Whitman *Diary* 54 Sprinkled through all Whitman's pocket-book diaries are names of men to whom he was attracted, *e.g.*, a Pullman-car conductor, a policeman, a 'bus driver.

2. a. A pocket case of leather or other material for holding paper money or papers. {1867–} +**b.** A purse.

1816 *Niles' Reg.* X. 216/1 Two methodist preachers were lately robbed of their pocket-books, containing very considerable sums in bank notes. **1835** INGRAHAM *South-West* II. 220 Pocket book in one hand, and bank bills fluttering in the other. **1861** *Atlantic Mo.* April 442/2 The roll was a small green pocket-book containing one or two gold pieces. **1882** McCABE *New York* 295 Those whose pocket-books are tightly clasped at other times, open them now. **1907** *St. Nicholas* Sept. 1007/2 In her pretty pocket-book . . . she had found a crisp one-dollar bill. **1925** BRYAN *Memoirs* 44 Noticing father's pocketbook upon the bureau, it occurred to some one of us . . . to count the money.

+3. *transf.* Money, funds. Also attrib. and in fig. context.

1894 H. H. FURNESS *Address* 4 Our ideal Provost must know the exact location in every rich man's body of the pocket-book nerve. **1904** *N.Y. Ev. Post* 10 Sept. 6 Nearly every class of apartment hotel, satisfying nearly every sized pocket-book, can now be found in Manhattan. **1924** BEARD *American Govt.* 258 The laws go deep into the pocketbooks of citizens.

+**Pocketbook dropper.** A thief who drops a pocketbook containing counterfeit money as a lure. — **1845** *N.Y. Herald* 7 May 2/2 The writer in the American Review . . . enumerates the potential agencies to which . . . Mr. Polk owes his election [as] . . . 'pocket-book droppers,' 'brothel-owners and bullies' [etc.]. **1861** *Vanity Fair* 13 April 180/2 Two pocket-book-makers have made too free with their manufactures, but no Pocket-book-dropper has disgraced himself by being arrested. **1892** WALSH *Lit. Curiosities* 457 Originally the word ['heeler'] had no political significance, but was applied to an accomplice of the pocket-book dropper.

Pocket case. 1. =POCKETBOOK 2 a. *Obs.* {1708–} **2.** A small case or container for cigars or first-aid materials. — **(1) 1722** *New-Eng. Courant* 19–26 Feb. 2/2 Lost or mislaid on Friday last, a red gilt Pocket Case, with about Forty Shillings in it in Province Bills. **1733** HEMPSTEAD *Diary* 264, I design for Boston & have put into my Pockett Case £30. **(2) 1870** 'M. HARLAND' *For Better, for Worse* 318 He was selecting some cigars from a drawer full of dainty Habañas, and refilling his pocket-case. **1904** STRATTON-PORTER *Freckles* 102 McLean . . . opened a pocket-case that he carried as regularly as his revolver and watch.

Pocket comb. A small comb to be carried in the pocket. {1848–} — **1840** *Knickerb.* XV. 140 He holds the juvenile venders of matches and pocket-combs to be his natural foes. **1869** BOWLES *Our New West* 99 We came down to 'bed-rock,' as the miners say, i.e. an extra flannel shirt and a pocket-comb. **1889** *Century Mag.* Jan. 465/1 [We] adjusted our locks in a fence corner by the aid of pocket-comb and glass.

Pocket compass. A compass that may be conveniently carried in the pocket. {1697–} — **1645** *Conn. Rec.* I. 21 A pocket compasse, a skefe & two Owyres. **1775** in Pusey *Road to Ky.* (1921) 42, I had a pocket Compas By which I got in a littel in the night. **1819** FLINT *Lett. from Amer.* 154 Not neglecting to carry with him a pocket-compass, to enable him to follow the blazed lines marked out by the surveyor. **1864** 'PENNIMAN' *Tanner-Boy* 305 'Bring me a pocket-compass,' said he [U.S. Grant], turning to an orderly.

Pocket glass. A glass of pocket size for viewing objects at a distance. — **1807** IRVING, etc. *Salmagundi* xix. 508 Resorting to my pocket glass, I discovered that it was . . . Clarinda Trollop. **1860** HOLMES *E. Venner* xxiii, With the aid of a pocket-glass he could make out persons without the risk of being observed himself.

+**Pocket gopher.** An American burrowing rodent of the family Geomyidae, having fur-lined cheek pouches opening outside the mouth. — **1873** EGGLESTON *Myst. Metrop.* 37 She would . . . explain how the pocket-gophers built their mounds. **1886** BURROUGHS in *Century Mag.* Sept. 788/2 Pocket gophers . . . are the cutest little animals, with their pockets on each side of their necks lined with fur. **1895** *Dept. Agric. Yrbk. 1894* 43 An exhaustive study has been made of the pocket gopher, the results of which will appear in a popular bulletin. **1917** *Mammals of Amer.* 267 Pocket Gophers are strict vegetarians.

Pocket handkerchief. A handkerchief carried in the pocket. {1781–} — **1645** *Essex Inst. Coll.* L. 326, 3 pocket handkerchiefs, 1 s. **1758** C. REA *Journal* (1881) 21, [I] went off in ye morn'g and left my Pocket handkerchief. **1809** IRVING *Knickerb.* II. iii, The remnant of a shirt . . . dangled like a pocket handkerchief out of a hole in his breeches. **1896** JEWETT *Pointed Firs* 122 He had picked up some round stones and things and was carrying them in his pocket-handkerchief. **1914** JAMES *Ivory Tower* 145 She bent her eyes on the . . . [cigar case], rubbing it with her pockethandkerchief.

Pocketknife. A small knife having one or more blades that fold or close into the handle, for carrying in the pocket. {1727–} — **1746** in Chalkley *Scotch-Irish Settlement Va.* III. 5 Cross-cut saw and 2 pocket-knives. **1845** *Xenia Torch-Light* 31 July 3/7 Pocket Knives, A Fine assortment, for sale by B. S. Bennett. **1898** *McClure's Mag.* X. 221, I opened my pocket-knife—it wasn't very sharp.

Pocket mirror. A small mirror suitable for carrying in the pocket. — **1837** IRVING *Bonneville* II. 188 The captain now drew forth that grand lure in the eyes of the savage, a pocket mirror. **1848** BRYANT *California* vi. 74 Once a week is as often as the most particular and fastidious exquisite of the party consults his pocket-mirror. *a***1861** WINTHROP *Canoe & Saddle* 14 A pocket-mirror shall be my meed.

Pocket pistol.

1. A small pistol that may be carried in the pocket. {1612–}

1677 *New Castle Court Rec.* 106 Mr. Johnson Complayning hee had Lost a paire of pocket pistolls for wch hee seemed to bee Troubled. **1769** *Md. Hist. Mag.* XII. 280, [I] doubt the Possibility of getting such as are called Pocket Pistols. **1807** *Ann. 10th Congress* 1 Sess. I. 434 Mr. Blannerhasset took away with him . . . a pair of pocket pistols, and a dirk. **1863** TAYLOR *H. Thurston* 249 Mrs. Babb slapped down the lid of the teapot . . . with a sound like the discharge of a pocket-pistol. **1890** *Congress. Rec.* 12 Aug. 8442/1, I was really toying and playing with the Senator, as a little boy would play with a pocket pistol.

2. A small flask for liquor. {1730–}

1851 *Polly Peablossom* 95 Tom had got a pocket-pistol, as he called it, of regular old Jimmakey, to keep off the rumatics. **1877** MINTURN *Travels West* 206 The 'pocket-pistol' and its accompanying cup do duty in lieu of hot toddy.

+**Pocket scales.** Pocket-sized scales for weighing objects. — **1876** *Wide Awake* 145/1 'He's a beauty,' said Cousin Jack, producing his pocket-scales and tape measure. **1886** *Outing* May 161/2 Out pocket-scales now! Is it a three or four or five-pound trout?

+**Pocket veto.** (See quot. 1888.) Also transf. (For the first use of the pocket veto, see *70th Congress 2 Sess.* H. R. Misc. Doc. No. 493, 2.) — **1884** Labor *Cycl. Polit. Science* III. 1065/2 This potent executive weapon, angrily called a 'pocket veto' at the time, was first employed by Jackson at the close of the summer of 1829–30. **1888** BRYCE *Amer. Commonw.* I. 1. vi. 74*n.*, If Congress adjourns within the ten days allowed the President for returning the bill, it is lost. His retaining it under these circumstances at the end of a session is popularly called a 'pocket veto.' **1897** *Pres. Mess. & P.* V. 599 The messages of February 1 and February 6, 1860, are pocket vetoes.

+**Pockety,** *a.* **1.** Of an ore vein: Characterized by pockets. {1896–} (Cf. POCKET *n.* 2.) **2.** Of the nature of a secluded hollow. (Cf. POCKET *n.* 4.) — (1) **1870** in Raymond *3d Rep. Mines* 220 The mineral veins found in the lime formations are *'pockety'* and of uncertain development. **1876** RAYMOND *8th Rep. Mines* 177 Reveille district, formerly well known on account of its rich but 'pockety' mineral deposits, . . . has again shown some life. **1914** ATHERTON *Perch of Devil* 149 You know what most mines are—pockety—yours may peter out. (2) **1893** *Columbus Dispatch* 18 May, A tiny, pockety vale whose surface is almost level on either side to the edge of noble bluffs.

+**Pocones, Pocoon.** Variants of PUCCOON. *Obs.* — **1612** SMITH, etc. *Virginia* 13 Pocones is a small roote that groweth in the mountaines, which being dryed and beate in powder turneth red; and this they vse for swellings, aches, annointing their ioints, painting their heads and garments. *a***1618** STRACHEY *Virginia* 94 Their conjurors . . . cast whesican, tobacco, copper, pocones, or such trash into the water, to pacifye that god whome they thinck to be very angry in those stormes. **1775** CRESSWELL *Journal* 72 Clark . . . showed me a root that the Indians call pocoon, good for the bite of a Rattle Snake. **1824** DODDRIDGE *Notes* 148 Indian physic, or bowman root, a species of epicacuanha was frequently used for a vomit and sometimes the pocoon or blood root.

+**Pocoson.** Also **poc(c)osin, poc(c)osson,** etc. *S.* [Algonquian.] An area of low marshy ground; a swamp.

The spelling *pocoson*, used in the earlier dictionaries, occurs much more frequently, esp. in the early records, than the form *pocosin*, adopted by the *Century Dictionary* and later works.

1634 in *Amer. Sp.* XV. 296 From that runn along the side of the Pocoson or great Otter pond soe called. **1643** *Ib.*, Nigh unto a reedy Swampe or Poquoson. **1681** *New Castle Court Rec.* 504, 74 perches to a Corner marked spannish oake standing neare a pocosen. **1713** *N.C. Col. Rec.* II. 69 John Burkett took up and surveyed . . . a certaine parcell of Land . . . beginning at a Gume by ye side of a great Swamp . . . [running] to ye pocosson [etc.]. **1799** *Herald of Freedom* (Edenton, N.C.) 27 March, 1920 acres on the north side of Trent river, including the Juniper pocosin. **1799** WASHINGTON *Writings* XIV. 224 All the hands of the farm . . . [should] be uninterruptedly employed in raising mud from the pocosons and from the bed of the creek, into the scow. **1800** TATAM *Agric. & Commerce* 65 In the cane countries and poccosins it is equally so in the winter. **1895** *Educational Rev.* Nov. 358 The various stages of sound, lagoon, salt marsh, and *pocoson* are too familiar.

attrib. **1691** in *Amer. Speech* XV. 296/2 To a small red oake by ye side of ye said pocoson swamp. **1720** *Ib.*, So Down ye Pocoson branch to William Evans his line. **1811** *Mass. Spy* 23 Jan. (Th.), A considerable extent of that kind of flat, wet pine lands, which is known in N. Carolina by the name of poccooson lands. **1883** SMITH *Geol. Survey Ala.* 522 East of Troy, . . . in the 'Pocoson' region, the valleys, which have the luxuriant growth and appearance of swamps, are surrounded on three sides by ridges of snow-white sand.

b. In proper names.

1631 in *Amer. Speech* XV. 296/2 A river called the Pocoson river. **1763** WASHINGTON *Writings* I. 194 From Suffolk to Pocoson Swamp is reckoned about 6 miles. **1836** W. B. ROGERS *Rep. Geol. Reconnoissance Va.* 23 At Pocosin, a flat swampy country, which is often inundated by the tides, this deposite is uniformly met with by digging a few feet below the surface.

+**Pod,** *n.* A flock of birds; a small herd or school of whales. {1840–} — **1832** D. WEBSTER *Private Corr.* I. 526 We saw several small pods of coots go by. **1851** MELVILLE *Moby-Dick* 487 Well, one day we lowered for a pod of four or five whales.

Pod, *v.* {1734–} +*intr.* To swell or bulge out like a pod. — **1890** *Columbus Dispatch* 9 July, Immediately twelve intelligent eyes podded until one could have snared them with grape vines.

Pod auger. An auger having a straight channel or groove. *Obs.* Also attrib. and fig. — **1833** *Niles' Reg.* XLIV. 403/1 The new twist gimblet is almost as much superior to the old English gimblet, as the screw auger is to the old pod auger. **1842** *Knickerb.* XX. 393 Not one of your big pod-auger sort. **1878** *Congress. Rec.* 15 Feb. 1123/1 A law has been worked through—and I say 'worked through' in the highest pod-auger sense that you can express by it.

+**Podunk.** [Algonquian.] Orig. an Indian place name used in Connecticut and Massachusetts; later applied in burlesque to any small or insignificant place. — **1666** *Doc. Col. Hist. N.Y.* III. 121 Yesterday there was a party of the Mowhawkes at Podunck (a place between this town [Hartford, Conn.] and Windsor). **1793** P. WHITNEY *County of Worcester, Mass.* 77 There is one large pond . . . called by the Indians Quaboag Pond; but now more generally denominated Podunk Pond, from a tract of meadow adjoining, which the Indians call Podunk. **1846** *Spirit of Times* 25 April 101/1 Podunk is a huge town, not distinguished . . . [for] climate, but for some of the characters that here do congregate. **1865** NORTON *Army Lett.* 277, I presume that just about this time of day you are sitting in one of the slips in that 'Podunk' or 'Chachunk' (what do you call it?) 'meetin' house.'

+**Podunker.** A frog. *humorous.* — **1857** HAMMOND *Northern Scenes* 30 There, hear that venerable podunker off to the right, with his deep bass.

+**Pogamoggan.** (See quot. 1805.) — **1805** LEWIS in *L. & Clark Exped.* III. (1905) 20 The Pog̃gâmog̃gon is an instrument with a handle of wood covered with dressed leather about the size of a whip handle and 22 inches long; a round stone of 2 pounds weight is also covered with leather and strongly united to the leather of the handle by a throng [*sic*] of 2 inches long; a loop of leather united to the handle passes arond the wrist. a very heavy blow may be given with this instrument. **1910** HODGE, etc. *Amer. Indians* II. 271/2 *Pogamoggan*, a club, cudgel, war-club: from Chippewa *păgămâgan* or *pâgûmâgan*, . . . meaning, literally, '(what is) used for striking.'

+**Poghaden.** (See PAUHAGEN.)

+**Pogonip.** [Paiute.] (See quot. 1870.) Also attrib. — **1870** RAE *Westward by Rail* 210 A name originally given to a thick mass of cold vapour which sometimes veils the mountain tops [of Nevada], and sometimes fills the valleys is employed to characterize these terrible storms. Tell a miner acquainted with White Pine that you have had to face the Po-go-nip and he will at once know that all your powers of endurance have been put to the test. **1880** *Harper's Mag.* Feb. 383 The Po-go-nip (icy wind) chills him to the bone. **1892** *Scientific Amer.* LXVI. 240/3 The pogonip fog is peculiar to elevated altitudes in the Nevada Sierras.

+**Pogy.** [Perh. of Algonquian origin, but cf. PORGY.]

1. a. = MENHADEN. **b.** Any of various surf fishes of the Pacific coast. **c.** The scup, *Stenotomus versicolor.* **d.** The moonfish or spadefish, *Chaetodipterus faber.*

1858 *Maine Agric. Rep.* II. 69 The fish known as menhaden, and often called along shore 'hard-heads' and 'poggies,' . . . after being boiled, are pressed . . . to extract an oil. **1884** GOODE, etc. *Fisheries* I. 276 On the coast of Oregon the large species [of the surf-fish family] (especially *Damalichthys argyrosomus*) are called 'Pogy' or 'Porgee,' in allusion to their undoubted resemblance to the scup or porgee of the East. *Ib.* 386 In New England it [*Stenotomus versicolor*] is generally called 'Scup,' while about New York the second syllable of the abbreviated Indian name has been lengthened into 'Paugy' or 'Porgy.' . . . Another Indian word, 'poghaden,' a corrupted form of the Abnaki name for the menhaden, . . . has been changed to 'pogy' and 'porgy,' thus leading to much confusion. *Ib.* 445 At Beaufort, North Carolina, . . . [the moonfish] is called the 'Porgee' or 'Pogy.' **1913** LONDON *Valley of Moon* 235 An' we used to go out on the Rock Wall an' catch pogies an' rock cod.

attrib. **1880** *Harper's Mag.* Aug. 347/1 The 'pogy' business was the catching of porgies and menhaden for their oil. **1914** W. D. STEELE *Storm* 247 The po'gie-men's got one up to St. Peter's.

+**2.** *local.* (See quot. 1840.)

1840 *Eastport* (Me.) *Sentinel* in *Niles' Nat. Reg.* 15 Aug. 376/3 Chebacco boats and small schooners are known to him [the Bay of Fundy fisherman] as *'pinkies,' 'pogies'* [*sic*] and *'jiggers.'* **1842** BUCKINGHAM *E. & W. States* I. 107. **1852** *32d Congress 2 Sess.* H. R. Ex. Doc. No. 23, 260.

+**Pogy chum.** = CHUM 1. — **1858** *Maine Agric. Rep. 1857* 69 What remains after extracting the oil, is called 'poggy chum,' and sells at twenty cents per barrel. **1863** *Rep. Comm. Agric. 1862* 57 The article which he puts up is prepared from 'pogy chum' by simply drying it in the sun.

+**Pohagan, Pohegan.** (See PAUHAGEN.)

‖**Pohano.** (See quotation.) — **1672** JOSSELYN *New Eng. Rarities* 20 The Maccarib, Caribo, or Pohano, [is] a kind of Deer, as big as a Stag, round hooved.

+**Pohickory.** (See HICKORY and PO(KA)HICKORY.)

+**Poinsettia.** [Named by Graham in 1836 after J. R. *Poinsett* (1779–1851), Amer. minister to Mexico.] A genus of tropical, alternate-leaved plants of the spurge family; a plant of this genus. {1871–} — **1868** GRAY *Field Botany* 294 *Euphorbia pulcherrima*, or Poinsettia, of Mexico. **1906** PRINGLE *Rice Planter* 302 Mr. Poinsett . . . brought many rare plants from Mexico, among others the Flor de la Noche Buena, which has borne in this country the name Poinsettia in his honor.

***Point,** *n.*

***1.** The tapering end of a piece of land that runs into the sea, a river, etc.; a neck of land bordered on each side by a river or bay; a promontory.

Elliott Coues interpreted the word *point* in quot. 1808 as 'a measure of distance,' but was 'not sure of what it means' (Pike *Sources Miss.* (1895) I. 135*n*.). Cf. POSÉ.

1622 'MOURT' *Relation* 45 A sandie poynt . . . lay within lesse then a furlong of the same. **1644** *Conn. Rec.* I. 208 To build a Fort uppon ye westerne point. **1684** *Providence Rec.* XIV. 76 A forked White Oake Tree standing upon a poynt of upland upon ye said meaddow & ye said River. **1705** *Boston News-Letter* 1 Oct. 2/1 There was a great Storm of Wind and Rain . . . , striping the Houses, and blowing the water over the Point, so that Boats might have floated. **1738** [see BLUFF *a.* 1 (2)]. **1808** PIKE *Sources Miss.* 58 We made twenty eight points in the river; broad, good bottom, and of the usual timber. **1885** JEWETT *Marsh Island* xv. 198, I set out to cross over and tell you to land on the pint where the big pitch-pine is.

+**b.** *Point of fork(s),* a point of land lying between two streams that unite.

1784 WASHINGTON *Diaries* II. 302 The Line which divides the Commonwealths of Virginia and Pensylvania crosses both these Rivers about two miles up each from the point of fork. **1789** ANBUREY *Travels* II. 405, I was detained . . . on account of the overflowing of the river, at what is termed the Point of Forks, where James River divides.

+**c.** *Points and bends,* (see quotation).

1826 FLINT *Recoll.* 258 It is the entire uniformity of the meanders of the rivers, called in the phrase of the country, 'points and bends.'

+**d.** Short for *West Point.*

1828 COOPER *Notions* I. 274 To these relics of a former age, must be added the actual and flourishing establishment at the 'Point,' which comprises a village of academic buildings, barracks, and other adjuncts.

+**2.** The tapering end of a forest or woodland that reaches down into the prairie or surrounding treeless country.

Quot. 1683 may belong to sense 1.

1637 in *Amer. Speech* XV. 297/2 Easterly butting out wth a point of wood. **1683** *Oyster Bay Rec.* I. 174 A sartaine neck or poynt of wood land. **1741** *Ga. Hist. Soc. Coll.* II. 252 A point of woods . . . stretches itself out towards the south-east. **1836** J. HALL *Statistics of West* 83 The forest has pushed long capes or points into the prairie. **1847** COYNER *Lost Trappers* 132 Joseph Cooper carried him to a point of timber where they raised a fire. **1856** CARTWRIGHT *Autobiog.* 328 We rode two miles, and the point of timber was plain in view.

+**3.** A projecting brow of a hill; a peak; an elevated piece of land above a stream.

1667 in *Amer. Speech* XV. 298 At a poynt of high ground on ye East side of ffoure Mile Creeke. **1715** *Ib.* 297 To three red oaks and a white oak upon the point of a hill. **1755** *Ib.* 298 To a Hiccory on the Point of a Ridge. **1812** J. CUTLER *Topogr. Descr. Ohio* 188 The mountains here are steep, and some of their points and sides are covered with a small growth, mostly of the spruce kind. **1854** in *Amer. Speech* XV. 298 To lynn & poplar on the foot of a point above Lewis fork.

+**4.** A lightning rod put on the roof of a building.

1766 *Essex Inst. Coll.* LII. 275 A new Meeting-House building . . . was struck with Lightning; it had Points and a Conductor as far as the Bell-free. **1775** *Ib.* XIII. 208 They have a handsome clock, points to the house, a fine walk on the top. **1870** 'MARK TWAIN' *Sk., New & Old* 22, I told him to put up eight 'points,' and put them all on the roof, and use the best quality of rod.

+**5.** On a mackinaw blanket: A short black stripe woven into the blanket to indicate usually the weight of one pound. *Obs.*

See also POINT BLANKET.

1797 HAWKINS *Letters* 347, 2 2½ point blankets, $2.25 . . . $4.50. **1803** *Austin P.* I. (1924) 88, 10 pr. 3 point blankets. **1818** MCKENNEY *Memoirs* I. 309 Northwest Company blankets—so called—three points, to measure six feet six inches long.

+**6.** *Baseball.* (See quot. 1868.) Hence *in the points,* in excellent form.

1868 CHADWICK *Base Ball* 13 An attentive study of the rules of the game, and of those special applications of them known as 'points.' **1886** — *Art of Batting* 21 A point to play on the pitcher . . . is to pretend to stand at the bat as if tired of waiting for a good ball, and yet to be on the alert to meet a quickly pitched ball. **1917** MATHEWSON *Sec. Base Sloan* 126 He never failed of a hit save when Pattern was in the points.

+**7. a.** *Stock market.* A theory, rumor, or fact upon which a speculation may be based; a tip. Hence the phrase *to deal on points.* (Cf. POINTER 5 b.)

1870 MEDBERY *Men Wall St.* 83 The first element in speculation is the 'point.' If the operator has a good 'point,' he has a 'sure thing.' **1870** M. H. SMITH *20 Years Wall St.* 556 These rumors are called points, and men who buy and sell, in consequence of them, are said to 'deal on points.' **1875** DALY *Big Bonanza* (1884) 21 When a man gives another man a point, sir, why he naturally expects [some money]. **1892** WALSH *Lit. Curiosities* 910.

+**b.** A hint or tip; a 'pointer.' *colloq.*

1877 HARTE *Story of Mine* (1896) 324 One of those officials comes up to this yer ranch . . . to get points about diamond-making. **1892** *Nation* 6 Oct. 263/2 A clever young man easily makes the mistake of supposing that he could have given Solomon points about women.

8. a. One of the scoring units bestowed on a boxer for superior boxing when no one is knocked out. {1904–}

1887 *Courier-Journal* 19 Jan. 5/1 No one calls the affair a hippodrome. The fight was to be for points, and the winner was to get 75 per cent. of the house receipts.

+**b.** In educational institutions, a unit of credit.

1903 *N.Y. Times* 29 Aug., For university credit, each 30 hours' course counts one point, and laboratory work at the rate of 60 hours to one point.

9. A unit of type measurement. {1888– (*Encycl. Brit.* XXIII. 698/2)} Also attrib.

The American standard, .013837 inch, is slightly smaller than the British.

1890 *Cent.* 4583/2 The American point was adopted by the United States Type-Founders' Association in 1883. **1924** *Publisher's Weekly* CVI. 189/2 *Point system*—The system adopted in 1886 by the United States Type Founders' Association according to which the various sizes of type characters bear a fixed and simple relation one to another.

+**10. a.** *Point man,* (see quotation).

1903 A. ADAMS *Log of Cowboy* 28 Two riders, known as point men, rode out and well back from the lead cattle, and by riding forward and closing in as occasion required, directed the course of the herd.

+**b.** *To ride point,* to ride at the head of a cattle drive or herd. (Cf. POINTER 4.)

1916 'BOWER' *Phantom Herd* 245 You see a herd drifting before a storm, . . . with your pal riding point.

***Point,** *v.* **1.** *To point with pride to,* to speak with proud satisfaction of. A political phrase. +**2.** *tr.* To guide or drive (cattle) in a particular direction. — **(1) 1894** *Congress. Rec.* 10 Jan. 667/2 Republican conventions have always 'pointed with pride' to any channel that floated boodle their way. **(2) 1903** ADAMS *Log of Cowboy* 43 Priest sent Officer to the left and myself to the right, to point in the leaders. **1916** 'BOWER' *Phantom Herd* xiv, You're trying to point the herd then . . . we'll say.

+**Point blanket.** A Mackinaw blanket marked with points. (See POINT *n.* 5.) — **1812** *Niles' Reg.* II. 9/1 It is indispensibly necessary to the right manufacture of a well knapt or coated point blanket, that the longest wool be selected. **1813** *Ib.* III. 295/1 Rose Blankets, 22,276. Point do., 17,980.

***Pointed,** *a.* In the names of plants. — **1814** BIGELOW *Florula Bostoniensis* 15 *Scirpus acutus,* Pointed bullrush. . . . This very nearly resembles the large bullrush, (*Scirpus lacustris,*) but differs in its fructification. **1878** KILLEBREW *Tenn. Grasses* 161 Pointed Slender Grass, *Leptochloa Mucronata.*

Pointed-leaved, *a.* +In the names of plants. — **1843** TORREY *Flora N.Y.* I. 176 *Desmodium acuminatum.* Pointed-leaved Desmodium. . . . Fertile woods; common. July. **1846** BROWNE *Trees Amer.* 14 *Magnolia acuminata.* Pointed-leaved Magnolia.

***Pointer.**

+**1.** A sign indicating a trail or road.

1793 BENTLEY *Diary* II. 48 There is a pointer in the Road to direct the passenger to the right in the way to Dartmouth College. **1816** U. BROWN *Journal* II. 233 There was an old rotten tree Laying there with pointers marked by some person or other.

2. A game dog of a breed that is easily trained to stand and point its muzzle in the direction of the game scented. {1717–} See also POINTER DOG.

1837 IRVING *Capt. Bonneville* I. 55 [Some] vagabond Indian dogs . . . were about the size of a large pointer; with ears short and erect, and a long bushy tail—altogether, they bore a striking resemblance to a wolf. **1856** *Porter's Spirit of Times* 22 Nov. 193/2 Where the ground is not so stony as to cut pointers' feet to pieces . . . we prefer them to setters or spaniels for ruffed grouse-shooting. **1887** CUSTER *Tenting on Plains* 191 [They] got on Armstrong's blind side forever, by giving him a valuable full-blooded pointer. **1897** *Outing* XXIX. 539/1 The drawbacks usually cited against the pointer include a dislike to cold weather and snow.

+**3.** A hog that eats large quantities of food but does not fatten.

1852 *Mich. Agric. Soc. Trans.* III. 184 One good grade sow, and two pointers. **1868** *Iowa State Agric. Soc. Rep. 1867* 423 A few pointers who never die, or cease to breed, can be found.

+4. On a cattle drive, a cowboy who rides near or at the head of the herd. (Cf. POINT *n.* 10.)

1869 *Overland Mo.* III. 126 On the march the mighty herd sometimes strings out miles in length, and then it has 'pointers,' who ride abreast of the head of the column.

+5. A bit of useful information; a hint; a tip. *colloq.*

1884 *Lisbon* (Dak.) *Star* 10 Oct. 5/2 Parties who are well informed ... are betting two to one that R. M. Davis ... will be the next sheriff.... There's a pointer for you! **1890** *Stock Grower & Farmer* 8 March 6/4 Here is a 'pointer' of value to shippers. **1906** 'O. HENRY' *Trimmed Lamp* 16, I'm not missing any pointers that I see passing around. **1910** O. JOHNSON *Varmint* 37, I promised old Fuzzy-Wuzzy to show you the lay of the land and give you some pointers.

+b. *Stock market.* A sign or piece of information upon which an operator may act.

Cf. POINT *n.* 7a.

1887 *Courier-Journal* 7 May 4/2 If one could only get a 'pointer' to the effect that such a programme is determined on there is no speculation on the Produce or Stock Exchange that could compete with it. **1892** WALSH *Lit. Curiosities* 910 A pointer ... means secret information concerning some particular stock, and by extension it has come to mean any item of reliable and important information. **1896** SHINN *Story of Mine* 153 Women ... beg every speculator to give them a 'pointer' or to carry a share of stock for them. **1900** NELSON *A B C Wall St.* 155 Pointers are worth about 30 cents a thousand.

+**Pointer dog.** =POINTER 2. — **1822** J. WOODS *English Prairie* 287 I lately saw a young pointer-dog, ... that had three days before been bitten by a rattlesnake. **1841** *Knickerb.* XVII. 153 You alight and hasten to release from chains and confinement your two pointer dogs. **1849** AUDUBON *Western Journal* 46 Some of the men had stolen a valuable pointer dog.

+**Point flow.** *Rice culture.* The second flow of water spread over a rice field: (see quot. 1859). — **1856** OLMSTED *Slave States* 473 The subsequent culture is the same as I have described, after the second or 'point' flow, in the first plan. **1859** *Harper's Mag.* Nov. 727/2 The ground [is] kept dry until the young plants appear.... At this period the water is a second time spread over the field in what is called the point flow.

***Pointing.** +The action of putting a point on a plowshare. — **1760** WASHINGTON *Diaries* I. 148 Cook Jack ... went to plowing in the 12 Acre Field, ... as did the other plow, abt. 5 oclock after Pointing. **1822** *Murphey Papers* I. 278 The Farmers calculate upon making three Crops with the same ploughs, without Pointing.

Point lace. Thread lace made wholly with the needle, as distinguished from bobbin-made lace. {1672-} Also attrib. — **1859** STOWE *Minister's Wooing* viii, The fascinating Mrs. T., whose life is a whirl between ball and opera, point lace, diamonds [etc.]. **1870** 'M. HARLAND' *For Better, for Worse* 338 An uncle, a wealthy drygoods merchant, is to give her a point-lace shawl. **1886** POORE *Reminisc.* II. 305 The bride wore a white satin dress, trimmed with point lace.

+**Point-no-point.** Something that seems to have a point, but really has none. Also attrib. — **1869** *Congress. Globe* 1 April 432/3 It may be ... that we decline to accept the 'point-no-point' policy of the party whom the gentleman from New York (Mr. Wood) in part represents here. **1878** *Congress. Rec.* 17 April 2606/1 The resolution is ... mere *brutum fulmen.* It sails for point-no-point, and it reaches no point.

+**Point shooting.** The shooting of game birds from a shelter. — **1874** LONG *Wild-Fowl* 71 For point-shooting, shooting from a blind on shore, or in the edge of the willows from a boat, a few hints may be welcome. **1876** *Fur, Fin & Feather* Sept. 90/2 Towards noon we prepared to move out into the clear water onto a bog, there get some point shooting.

***Poison,** *n.* Also *colloq.* **pison, pizon,** etc.

+1. In allusive uses and comparisons. *colloq.*

1776 *Battle of Brooklyn* II. i, Poison take the canteens; I have lost the cattle that were in Bergen's orchard. **1834** CARRUTHERS *Kentuckians* I. 63 It was as strong as *pison.* **1847** ROBB *Squatter Life* 133 Jess was hangin' arter that gal, lookin' *honey* at her, and *pizin* at the fellars who spoke pleasin' to her. **1910** W. M. RAINE *B. O'Connor* 28 They say he's part Spanish and part Indian, but all pisen.

+2. Strong alcoholic drink. *jocular.*

1805 RED JACKET in *Freemason's Mag.* (Phila.) II. 388 We gave them corn and meat; they gave us poison in return. [Editor's note:] Alluding it is supposed to ardent spirits. **1834** SIMMS *G. Rivers* II. 233 What mixture! No pizon, I hope. **1876** MILLER *First Fam'lies* 128 A true Californian of Sierras ... heads straight up to the bar, ... hoists his Poison, throws back his head, and then falls back wiping his mouth.

3. *attrib.* and *comb.* +a. In sense 2 with *factory, hitter, swilling.*

1877 *Billings' Farmer's Allminax* 15 Desaitful, and dang'rous kritter, ... And besides a pizon hitter. **1883** 'MARK TWAIN' *Life on Miss.* xxii, The multitudes of poison-swilling Irishmen had departed. **1907** WHITE *Arizona Nights* 136, I went with him to his little old poison factory [*i.e.*, saloon].

b. In the names of plants and trees. {1624-}

Passing into adj. in sense: Poisonous. See also POISON ASH, POISONBERRY, etc.

1861 WOOD *Botany* 398 *V[iburnum] pubescens....* Poison Haw. Tenn. to Ga.... and La. **1894** *Amer. Folk-Lore* VII. 92 *Porphyllus gracile,* poison flower, Colorado River. **1901** MOHR *Plant Life Ala.* 89 Box elder, ... farkleberry, and the poison laurel (*Kalmia latifolia*) shade the rocky banks of the swift mountain streams. **1909** *Cent. Suppl.* 191/2 *Poison camass, white camass,* the death camass, *Zigadenus venenosus,* a plant which causes severe losses of sheep in Montana and elsewhere.

***Poison,** *a.* +Hateful, very objectionable, extreme. *colloq.*[2] — **1839** BRIGGS *H. Franco* I. 18, 'I presume there's no occasion for hurrying,' said the driver. 'Yes there is though, you pisen critter,' said a passenger. **1850** LEWIS *La. Swamp Dr.* 152 Lizey Johnson's middle darter, Prinsanna, ... left her husband in the state of Georgy, and kum to Luzaanny an' got marred to a nother man, the pisen varmint, to do sich as that and her own laful husband. **1880** 'MARK TWAIN' *Tramp Abroad* 225 B'long to a *church!* Why boss he's ben the pizenest kind of a Free-will Babtis' for forty year. They ain't no pizener ones 'n' what *he* is. Mighty good man, pap is. **1884** — *H. Finn* xxviii. 270 The old man ... was on hand and looking his level pisonest.

+**Poison,** *adv.* Extremely; very. *colloq.*[2] — **1840** HOFFMAN *Greyslaer* I. 61 The night was pison cold, I tell ye. **1884** 'MARK TWAIN' *H. Finn* xxvii, The funeral sermon was very good, but pison long and tiresome. **1894** — *P. Wilson* xiv, You's got to be pison good, en let him see it.

Poison arrow. An arrow that has poison on its point. — **1872** McCLELLAN *Golden State* 605 In such dread do the people hold the poison-arrow, scalping-knife, and tomahawk of these 'red devils.'

Poison ash. {1760} +1. =POISON SUMAC. +2. The poison ivy, *Toxicodendron radicans.* — (1) **1763** W. LEWIS *Comm. Phil.-Technicum* 330 Mr. Catesby, in his history of Carolina, describes one, called there the poison-ash. **1785** MARSHALL *Amer. Grove* 130 *Rhus-Toxicodendron Vernix.* Varnish-Tree, or Poison Ash.... This tree ought to be handled with caution, as it is very poisonous to many people. **1897** SUDWORTH *Arborescent Flora* 276 *Rhus vernix.* Poison Sumach.... [Also called] Poison Ash (Pa.). (2) **1839** in *Mich. Agric. Soc. Trans.* VII. 417 *Rhus toxicodendron.* Poison ash.

Poisonberry. {1756-} +1. The sheep laurel, *Kalmia angustifolia.* +2. =CHINA TREE 1. — (1) **1672** JOSSELYN *New Eng. Rarities* 49 Spurge Lawrel, called here Poyson berry, it kills the English Cattle if they chance to feed upon it, especially Calves. (2) **1803** J. DAVIS *Travels* 79 The mocking-bird ... was warbling, close to my window, from a tree called by some the Pride of India, and by others the Poison-berry Tree.

+**Poison darnel.** The bearded darnel (*Lolium temulentum*), an annual grass. — **1889** VASEY *Agric. Grasses* 75 *Lolium temulentum* (Poison Darnel).... The seeds have long enjoyed a reputation of being poisonous to stock, and also to mankind when mixed in large quantity with the wheat or rye used in the making of bread. **1901** MOHR *Plant Life Ala.* 388 Poison Darnel.... Introduced with grain and sparingly naturalized in ... Oregon, California, and Eastern United States.

+**Poison dogwood.** =POISON SUMAC. — **1814** BIGELOW *Florula Bostoniensis* 72 *Rhus vernix.* Poison dogwood. Swamp Sumach.... Grows in bunches in wet swamps. **1892** TORREY *Foot Path Way* 211 As for reprobates like the so-called 'poison ivy' and 'poison dogwood,' they have perhaps borrowed a familiar human maxim 'All is fair in war.' **1897** SUDWORTH *Arborescent Flora* 276 Poison Sumach.... [Also called] Poison Dogwood.

+**Poisoned field.** A treeless or comparatively barren tract of land; a field the vegetation of which is regarded as injurious to cattle. *Obs.* (Cf. POISON FIELD.) — **1724** JONES *Virginia* 35 The whole Country is a perfect Forest, except where ... have been formerly Indian Towns, and poisoned Fields and Meadows, where the Timber has been burnt down in Fire-Hunting or otherwise. **1733** *Va. Council Exec. Jrnl.* IV. 305 Granted ... 1000 [acres] more on the poison'd or Indian Field lying on both sides the path leading from the fork of James River to Buckingham. **1748** WASHINGTON *Jrnl. of Journey over Mts.* 27 To 2 Red Oaks and W: Oak in a Poyson'd field by a Road.

‖**Poisoned oak.** =POISON OAK b. — **1807** in *S. Lit. Messenger* XXIV. 309/1 In vain did a brawny wreath of the poisoned oak ... grasp the trembling marbles, for the purpose of averting their fall.

+**Poison elder.** =POISON SUMAC. (Cf. POISONOUS ELDER.) — **1817-8** EATON *Botany* (1822) 428 *Rhus vernix,* poison sumach, poison elder.... Berries green, at length whitish.... Very poisonous.... Damp. **1893** *Amer. Folk-Lore* VI. 140 *Rhus venenata,* poison elder. Ala. **1897** SUDWORTH *Arborescent Flora* 276 Poison Sumach.... [Also called] Poison Elder.

+**Poison field.** =POISONED FIELD. Also *poison old field.* — **1694** in *Amer. Speech* XV. 298/1 To a black oak in a poyson field. **1728** *Ib.*, To two red oaks in a poyson old ffield.

+**Poison flag.** (See quot. 1909.) Also attrib. — **1840** DEWEY *Mass. Flowering Plants* 194 *Iris versicolor.* Blue or Poison Flag. Common on wet grounds, and about sluggish water. **1894** *Amer. Folk-Lore* VII. 101 *Iris prismatica,* Pursh, *Iris versicolor,* L., poison flag-root, Concord, Mass. **1909** WEBSTER 1665 *Poison flag,* any of several blue-flowered American irises, as *I. versicolor.*

+**Poison hemlock.** The common hemlock, *Conium maculatum.* — **1817-8** EATON *Botany* (1822) 247 *Conium maculatum,* poison hemlock. ... Stem very branching. **1843** TORREY *Flora N.Y.* I. 282 Common Poison Hemlock.... A native of Europe. **1901** MOHR *Plant Life Ala.* 646.

+Poison ivy.

1. Any of several vinelike sumacs, poisonous to the touch, having trifoliolate leaves, greenish flowers, and white berries.

In the central and eastern parts of the country the species is *Toxicodendron radicans* (syn. *Rhus toxicodendron*); in the Southeast, *T. pubescens* (syn. *R. quercifolia*), sometimes called *poison oak;* on the Pacific coast, *Rhus diversiloba*, usually called *poison oak*. (Cf. POISON OAK b.)

1784 CUTLER in *Amer. Acad. Mem.* I. 422 *Hedera*. . . . Poison Ivy. . . . It produces the same kind of inflammations and eruptions . . . as the poison wood tree. **1814** BIGELOW *Florula Bostoniensis* 73 *Rhus radicans*. Poison Ivy. . . . A hardy climber. . . . Berries white. **1832** WILLIAMSON *Maine* I. 130 *Poison Ivy* . . . is a dangerous medicine, though it has helped to relieve in cases of the palsy. **1869** *Rep. Comm. Agric. 1868* 204 The Poison ivy (*Rhus toxicodendron*) is sometimes mistaken for the Virginia creeper, but they can be easily distinguished by the leaf. **1876** *Field & Forest* I. 70 The pith of the Poison Ivy . . . is located from three to ten times nearer the inner side of the stem. **1891** FREEMAN *New Eng. Nun* 191 [She] saw Joseph Tenney's face through branches of pink dog-bane and over masses of poison-ivy. **1901** MOHR *Plant Life Ala.* 601 *Rhus radicans*, . . . Poison Ivy. Poison vine. . . . Alabama: Throughout. In rich damp woods. Bottom lands. Flowers white, May. **1911** *Atlantic Mo.* Jan. 6 Poison oak or poison ivy (*Rhus diversiloba*), both as a bush and a scrambler up trees and rocks, is common throughout the foothill region.

2. =MOUNTAIN LAUREL 1 b.

1897 SUDWORTH *Arborescent Flora* 315 *Kalmia latifolia*. . . . Poison Ivy (Tenn., Ala.).

+Poison oak. a. =POISON SUMAC a. **b.** Any bushlike poison ivy, esp. the species of the Pacific coast and the Southeast. (See POISON IVY 1, note).

1743 CLAYTON *Flora Virginica* 33 *Rhus*, . . . Poison-Oak. **1785** MARSHALL *Amer. Grove* 131 *Rhus-Toxicodendron toxicodendrum*. Poison-Oak. This has a low, shrubby stalk, seldom rising above three or four feet. **1814** O. O. RICH *Amer. Plants* 34 Sumach, or poison oak. **1842** BUCKINGHAM *Slave States* I. 543 Among the shrubs we were shown one that grew like a vine or creeper, called 'the poison oak,' the leaves of which exude some liquid which is particularly obnoxious to some constitutions, but does not affect others. **1851** D. B. WOODS *At Gold Diggings* 103 Captain W. is sorely afflicted with an eruption, which covers his whole body, probably the effects of having handled the 'poison oak.' **1872** MCCLELLAN *Golden State* 167 The poison oak of California exists pretty generally over the State. **1884** 'CRADDOCK' *Tenn. Mts.* 116 Jes' kicked me outn' the way like it war nuthin' more'n that thar branch o' pisen-oak. **1905** COLE *Early Oregon* 29 Having been poisoned with poison oak so that I was completely blind, the others advised me to return.

***Poisonous,** *a.* +In the names of plants and trees. (See also POISONOUS ELDER.) — **1737** BRICKELL *N. Carolina* 95 The Poysonous Vine, so called, by reason it colours the Hands of those that handle it, of a yellowish Colour. **1770** FORSTER tr. Kalm *Travels* I. 68 *Rhus vernix* the poisonous Sumach, in wet places. [Catalog of trees near Phila.] **1813** MUHLENBERG *Cat. Plants* 39 *Amyris toxifera*. Poisonous balsam tree. **1846** BROWNE *Trees Amer.* 186 *Rhus venenata*, The Poisonous Rhus. **1847** WOOD *Botany* 620 *L[olium] Temulentum. Poisonous Darnel*. . . . Remarkably distinguished from all other grasses by its poisonous seeds. N. Eng. to Penn. July.

+Poisonous elder. =POISON SUMAC. (Cf. POISON ELDER.) — **1778** CARVER *Travels* 507 The Alder or *Elder*, termed the poisonous elder, nearly resembles the other sorts in its leaves and branches, but it grows much straiter, and is only found in swamps and moist soils. **1813** MUHLENBERG *Cat. Plants* 32 Swamp s[umach] poisonous elder. **1836** EDWARD *Hist. Texas* 66 [He took the names of the shrubs] which he could designate, as . . . the Dwarf Elder, the Poisonous Elder [etc.].

+Poison sumac. A swamp-growing American sumac (*Toxicodendron vernix*, syn. *Rhus vernix, R. venenata*), poisonous to the touch, having pinnate leaves and greenish-white berries.

1832 WILLIAMSON *Maine* I. 118 The *poison Sumach* occurs in the western, but very seldom, if ever, in the eastern parts of the State. **1850** *New Eng. Farmer* II. 60 The Dogwood . . . is not to be confounded with the Poison Sumac, usually called Dogwood, which it in no way resembles. **1872** *Vermont Bd. Agric. Rep.* I. 276 *Poison Sumac* of swamps . . . should be known to all. **1901** MOHR *Plant Life Ala.* 600 Poison Sumach, Poison Elder. . . . Alleghenian, Carolinian, and Louisianian areas.

Poison tree. {1693-} +=POISON SUMAC. *Obs.* — **1756** KALM *Resa* II. 211 Poyson-tree, d. ä. det forgiftiga trä, kallades af Ängelsmän och Svänskar en art af *Rhus*. **1785** MARSHALL *Amer. Grove* 130 *Toxicodendron*. The Poison Tree.

+Poison vine. Poison ivy, esp. *Toxicodendron radicans*.

The plant of quot. 1709 cannot be identified with certainty.

1709 LAWSON *Carolina* 101 The Poison Vine is so called, because it colours the Hands of those who handle it. What the Effects of it may be, I cannot relate. **1785** MARSHALL *Amer. Grove* 131 *Rhus-Toxicodendron radicans*. Poison-vine. . . . The flowers are produced in short panicles from the sides of the branches. **1797** F. BAILY *Tour* 380 There is in this country a plant which grows wild in the woods, and which goes by the name of the *poison vine*. **1802** ELLICOTT *Journal* 212 My journey up the river was disagreeable and painful, being blistered by the rhus radicans, (poison vine,) from head to feet. **1860** CURTIS *Woody Plants N.C.* 118 Poison Vine. (*Rhus radicans*.)—Now considered by Botanists as only a variety of *Poison Oak*.

+Poisonwood.

1. =POISON SUMAC. Also attrib.

1721 DUDLEY in *Phil. Trans.* XXXI. 145 The Poyson-wood-Tree grows only in Swamps, or low wet Grounds, and . . . is by some called the *Swamp Sumach*. *c*1729 CATESBY *Carolina* I. 40 The Poison-Wood. . . . From the trunc [*sic*] of this Tree distils a Liquid black as Ink, which the Inhabitants say is Poison. **1784** CUTLER in *Amer. Acad. Mem.* I. 427 Poison wood. Swamp Sumach. . . . The poison will be communicated by touching or smelling any part of the shrub. **1897** SUDWORTH *Arborescent Flora* 276 *Rhus vernix*. . . . Poisonwood (Tenn.).

2. The bumwood (*Metopium linnaei*) of southern Florida.

1884 SARGENT *Rep. Forests* 54 Poison Wood. Coral Sumach. . . . Bum Wood. Hog Plum. **1897** SUDWORTH *Arborescent Flora* 274 *Rhus metopium*. . . . Poisonwood (Fla.).

3. The crabwood, *Gymnanthus lucida*.

1884 SARGENY *Rep. Forests* 121 *Sebastiana lucida*. . . . Crab Wood. Poison Wood. **1897** SUDWORTH *Arborescent Flora* 271 *Gymnanthes lucida*. . . . Crabwood (Fla.). Poisonwood (Fla.).

Po(ka)hickory. [Amer. Indian *pawcohiccora* 'a kind of oily liquor pressed from hickory nuts.'] (See quotations.) See also HICKORY. — *c*1618 STRACHEY *Virginia* 99 A woman goddesse . . . whoe hath . . . at all tymes ready drest greene vskathomen and pokahickory, (which is greene corne brused and boyled, and walnutts beaten small, then washed). **1896** BRUCE *Econ. Hist. Virginia* I. 167 The aborigines gathered a great abundance of hickory nuts, and placing them in mortars into which water had been poured, pounded shell and kernel until a milky liquor, known as pohickory, had been made.

+Poke, *n.*[1] Also **poake, poak, pooke.** [Virginian *uppówoc*.] The tobacco plant or some other plant similarly suitable for smoking; the cured leaves of any such plant. *Obs.*

Cf. INDIAN TOBACCO, KILLIKIN(N)ICK, KINNIKINNICK, UPPOWOC.

1634 *Relation of Beginnings of Md.* 20 After this, was brought before them a great Bagg, filled with a large Tobacco-pipe and Poake, which is the word they vse for Our *Tobacco*. **1651** in Hartlib *S. Hartlib His Legacy* (1655) 155, [I] have far greater hopes of the flourishing of this wild plant, that of Tobacco (either of that which in *New-England* is called Poak, much differing from the *Virginian*, or of that other commonly used and sown in Virginia). **1672** JOSSELYN *New-Eng. Rarities* 54 Tobacco, there is not much of it planted in New-England; the Indians make use of a small kind with short round leaves called Pooke. **1797** *Mass. H. S. Coll.* 1 Ser. V. 57 He then wishing to smoke a pipe, ransacked the island for tobacco; but, finding none, filled his pipe with *poke*, a weed which the Indians sometimes used as its substitute. [**1860** TUCKERMAN ed. Josselyn *New Eng. Rarities* 191*n*., The species intended by Josselyn [referred to by him as 'Live-for-ever, a kind of cud-weed'] is our everlasting. . . . The dried herb [was] used by the fishermen instead of tobacco, and no doubt called by them *poke*.]

***Poke,** *n.*[2] *Whaling*. +A bladder blown up with air to serve as a buoy. — **1883** *Nat. Museum Bul.* No. 27, 304 When the whale ceases its progressive motions the poke or buoy appears on the surface and the line is regained. **1887** GOODE, etc. *Fisheries* v. II. 270 When the 'pokes' are used, the officer gives the order to 'Blow up! Blow up!'

+Poke, *n.*[3] [Virginian *puccoon, pakon*, a plant used for dyeing.]

1. =POKEWEED.

The plant appears to have been misidentified in quot. *c*1729 as a species of blite. (See also VIRGINIA POKE.)

*c*1729 CATESBY *Carolina* I. 24 [Mourning doves] feed much on the Berries of Poke, i.e. *Blitum Virginianum*, which are Poison. **1737** BRICKELL *N. Carolina* 19 The Poke . . . is a kind of Mechoacan, and grows in every Field, the tender Tops whereof may be boiled and made use of as other Greens with all the safety immaginable. **1745** E. KIMBER *Itinerant Observer* 14 There is no want of HERBS for the Pot in any Wood you pass, particularly wild Spinage, or, as we call it, Poke, which is also agreeably medicinal to the Body. **1789** *Amer. Philos. Soc.* III. p. xix, *Poke*, has of late given promising experiments in the cure of cancers. **1802** DRAYTON *S. Carolina* 70 Poke. (*Phytolacca decandria*.) Grows on rich land. The young sprouts of it are used in the spring for soup. **1882** *Century Mag.* May 153/2 Mr. Robinson recommends a score or more of American plants as suitable for English woods and hedge-rows. . . . The plants and flowers named are poke, golden-rod [etc.].

2. The skunk cabbage, *Symplocarpus foetidus*. *Obs.*

The plants referred to in the following quotations are not identified with certainty. They may be the poke of sense 1, which, as Gray points out, has 'a rather unpleasant odor'; they may be the poke of sense 3, which, according to evidence under BEAR ROOT, has also been called the *skunk cabbage* (q.v.).

1778 CARVER *Travels* 518 Skunk Cabbage or Poke is an herb that grows in moist and swampy places. The leaves of it are about a foot long, and six inches broad, nearly oval, but rather pointed. The roots are composed of great numbers of fibres, a lotion of which is made use of by the people in the colonies for the cure of itch. There issues a strong musky smell from this herb. **1789** MORSE *Amer. Geog.* 53 Of the various aromatic and other kinds of herbs are skunk-cabbage, or poke, wake-robin [etc.].

3. The American or swamp hellebore, *Veratrum viride;* Indian poke.

1847 WOOD *Botany* 557 *V. viride.* . . . Poke. White Hellebore. . . . Root large, fleshy, with numerous long fibres. . . . The root is emetic and stimulant, but poisonous, and should be used with caution.

4. Attrib. in sense 1 with *juice, plant, salad, stalk.*

1834 AUDUBON *Ornith. Biog.* II. 191 When they feed on the berries of the poke-plant, the rich crimson juices . . . colour the flesh of these birds. **1871** DE VERE 405 Poke-juice is occasionally used in beverages. **1884** *Lexington Observer* 25 Sept. 3/3 It is an exceedingly common occurrence . . . to meet with poke stalks and hemp stalks elevated on gate-posts, stables, pig-sties etc. **1923** *Dialect Notes* V. 217 *Poke salat.* A salad made from the poke weed. Greens. [McDonald Co., Mo.]

+**Poke,** *n.*[4] [Origin uncertain: see SKOUK and cf. SHITEPOKE.] **1.** = GREEN HERON. **2.** =AMERICAN BITTERN. — (1) **1794** MORSE *Amer. Geog.* 165 Green Bittern. Poke. Skouk. *Ardea virescens.* **1844** *Nat. Hist N.Y., Zoology* II. 224 The Poke, Chalk-line, Fly-up-the-creek, or Schyte Poke as he was called by our Dutch progenitors, is a southern species. **1874** COUES *Birds N.W.* 522 Green Heron; Poke. . . . Occurs chiefly in the southern and eastern portions of the Missouri region. **1877** BARTLETT 801 When ponds dry up, the pokes get the pollywogs. (2) **1917** *Birds of Amer.* I. 181 Bittern. *Botaurus lentiginosus* . . . American Bittern; . . . March Hen; Poke.

Poke, *n.*[5] +A device put on the necks of cattle, horses, etc., to keep them from breaking through fences. (Cf. POKE *v.*[2]) — **1809** KENDALL *Travels* II. 198 A hog . . . by some mischance had turned his poke, so that his throat was squeezed into one of the acuter angles. **1828** WEBSTER, *Poke.* In *New England*, a machine to prevent unruly beasts from leaping fences, consisting of a yoke with a pole inserted, pointing forward. **1880** *Scribner's Mo.* Feb. 511/2 A chapter might be written of fence breakers and leapers; . . . of horses who, in spite of pokes, take fences like trained steeple-chasers.

Poke, *n.*[6] A kind of game. *Obs.* — **1824** *Nantucket Inquirer* 12 Jan, (Th.), No person shall play Foot-ball or Poke, Stick-ball or Swinger, within the compact part of the town of Nantucket.

Poke, *n.*[7] A lazy or slow person; a stupid person. *colloq.* {1886, *dial.*} (Cf. POKE *v.*[1] 1.)

1848 BARTLETT 255 *Poke*, a lazy person; a dawdle. **1856** SIMMS *Eutaw* 247 'Did you pick up any fellows?' 'A few pokes—not much; but they hev horses.' **1867** LOWELL in *Atlantic Mo.* Jan. 27 'Why, where in thunder were his horns and tail?' 'They're only worn by some old-fashioned pokes; They mostly aim at looking just like folks.' **1886** DALY *After Business Hours* 36 What a poke of a fellow he is! **1905** PHILLIPS *Social Secretary* 49 Out home all the drones and pokes and nobodies are just crazy about getting out in feathers and red plush aprons and clanking and pawing round, trying to make out they're somebody.

***Poke,** *v.*[1]

1. *intr.* To go along slowly. {to dawdle, to work in a desultory way, 1796–}

1837 IRVING *Bonneville* II. 193 [The trappers] dig out a canoe from a cotton-wood tree, and in this, poke along shore silently. **1875** 'MARK TWAIN' *Old Times* v. 16 We presently got under way and went poking down the broad Ohio. **1922** A. BROWN *Old Crow* 204 We'll blow out the candles in a minute or two and poke off home.

‖**2.** *tr.* To put (a question).

1874 EGGLESTON *Circuit Rider* 147 Well, I poked a few questions at him.

3. *To poke fun (at)*, to ridicule, to make fun (of). {1840–}

1815 HUMPHREYS *Yankey* 107 *Poke your fun*, jeer, pester, plague. **1831** S. SMITH *Life J. Downing* 140, I'll teach them are young chaps . . . that used to poke fun at me. **1835–7** HALIBURTON *Clockmaker* 1 Ser. xxii. 205 They both knowed well enough, they only made as if they didn't, to poke a little fun at them. **1843** STEPHENS *High Life N.Y.* I. 19 The critter was jest beginning to pucker up her mouth again, as if she'd found out something to poke fun at.

+**Poke,** *v.*[2] *tr.* To put a poke on (an animal). Also *ppl. a. Obs.* — **1786** *East-Hampton Rec.* IV. 256 To order the owners of all such cows or horses, to yoke, poke or fetter them. **1828** WEBSTER, To poke an ox. *New England.* **1850** *Knickerb.* XXXV. 24 Upon two 'poked' colts, which we caught and bridled with beech withes, [we] descended to the shore of the Horicon.

+**Pokeberry.** The dark purple berry of the pokeweed; also, the plant itself.

1774 FITHIAN *Journal* I. 269 To Day Harry boil'd up a Compound of Poke-Berries, Vinegar, Sugar &c to make red Ink. **1811** *Agric. Museum* I. 175 To two gallons of the juice of Poke Berries, when they are quite ripe, add half a gallon of strong Vinegar. **1839** in *Mich. Agric. Soc. Trans.* VII. 414 *Phytolacca decandra.* Poke berry. **1882** *Harper's Mag.* Feb. 435 Eyes . . . as black as pokeberries. **1901** *Munsey's Mag.* XXV. 626/1 Inside and along the fence, pokeberries, elders, sassafras, and sumac grew high and dense.

attrib. **1889** COOKE *Steadfast* 76 Old Isaac . . . had come in . . . after a dole of poke-berry rum for his rheumatism. **1914** E. STEWART *Lett. of Woman Homesteader* 40, I took the book and after a little deciphered that 'Zebulon Pike Parker was born Feb. 10, 1830,' written in the stiff, difficult style of long ago and written with pokeberry ink.

+**Pokeberry juice.** The juice of the pokeberry, used as a stain or dye: (see also quot. 1885). — **1834** CARRUTHERS *Kentuckian* II. 215 His face looks like it was boiled in poke-berry juice and indigo. **c1866** BAGBY *Old Va. Gentleman* 49 [He must] be turned out for painting his face with poke-berry juice and grinning at the school-master. **1885** *Mag. Amer. Hist.* March 298/1 *Poke-berry juice.*—A punning reference to the surname of the Hon. James K. Polk. . . . Banners and transparencies were loyally stained with the dark purple juice of the common poke-berry during the campaign which resulted in Mr. Polk's election. **1900** WILKINS *Love of Parson Lord* 18 It was the same old doll. . . . She gazed at its poor old rag face, its wide mouth painted grotesquely with pokeberry juice.

Poke bonnet. A bonnet with a projecting brim. {1820–} Cf. POKING BONNET. — **1848** BURTON *Waggeries* 74 The Queen of Palmyra ensconced her dignity in the close-fitting habit, poke bonnet, and green veil. **1870** RAE *Westward by Rail* 108 The custom seems to prevail [among the Mormons] for one or two out of the several wives who accompanied most of the men to wear 'poke bonnets,' resembling those which Quaker ladies wore in former days. **1893** *Chicago Tribune* 22 April 16/4 A little poke-bonnet of black chip recently shown is trimmed quite in the old-fashioned way, with a band of ruby velvet around the crown. **1910** MCCUTCHEON *Rose in Ring* 236 She was tying the strings of her quaint poke-bonnet under her chin.

+**Pokebush.** A pokeweed plant. — **1733** BYRD *Journey to Eden* 289 At our first Landing we were so hampered with Brambles, Vines and Poke Bushes, that our Horses could hardly force their way thro' them. **1865** *Atlantic Mo.* Feb. 172/2 He told us it was a poke-bush.

+**Poke greens.** The young shoots of the pokeweed eaten as greens. — **1848** *Knickerb.* XXXI. 222 The southern negro will dance after eating his poke-greens and bacon. **1914** E. STEWART *Lett. of Woman Homesteader* 204 So she and I talked of ash-hoppers, smoke-houses, cotton-patches, goobers, poke-greens, and shoats, until she fell asleep.

+**Poke-hooked,** *a.* Of a fish: Caught by having swallowed a hook. — **1883** *Century Mag.* April 902/1 [Many] sea-fish, and many river-fish, swallow the hook, and are caught . . . because it is fastened in their stomachs. In the Gloucester fisherman's language of to-day, a fish so captured is called 'poke-hooked.' **1897** KIPLING *Captains Courageous* 78 Help us here, Harve. It's a big un. Poke-hooked, too.

+**Pokeloken, Pokelogan.** [Algonquian, probably from Malecite *pecelâygan* 'a stopping place.'] A marshy place; a bay. — **1848** THOREAU *Maine Woods* 51 We passed what McCauslin called a pokelogan, an Indian term for what the drivers might have reason to call a poke-logs-in, an inlet that leads nowhere. **1855** HALIBURTON *Nature & Hum. Nature* II. 404 A poke-loken is a marshy place or stagnant pool connected with a river. **1858** THOREAU *Maine Woods* 100 [The moose tracks] were particularly numerous where there was a small bay, or *pokelogan*, as it is called, bordered by a strip of meadow. **1905** *Forestry Bureau Bul.* No. 61, 43 *Pokelogan*, a bay or pocket into which logs may float off during a drive. (N[orth] W[oods], L[ake] S[tates Forest].)

***Poker.**[1] A stiff metal rod designed for poking or stirring a fire. — **1779** *York Co., Va., Rec.: Wills* XXII. 28 April, 1 pr. tongs, shovel, poker and fender 6/0/0. **1839** BIRD *Robin Day* 40 One of the blackies remained on watch over me, armed with a poker. **1918** *Sears, Roebuck & Co. Cat.* No. 137, 1631 Iron Fire Tools. . . . Stand and three tools, shovel, tongs and poker.

+**Poker.**[2]

Origin uncertain, but perhaps from G. *poch, poche, pochspiel*, a game resembling poker. See Mencken *Amer. Language* (1936) 157–8.

1. Any of several varieties of a card game in which each player, at a single stage or successive stages in the dealing, meets or calls the highest bet or raise at the table, raises the bet, or withdraws from the betting. {pocher for G. *poche*, 1855}

See also DRAW, STRAIGHT, STUD, TWENTY-DECK POKER.

1836 SIMMS *Mellichampe* xviii, '*Old sledge* (or '*seven up*'), . . . in that unsophisticated [Revolutionary] period, had not given place to *brag* and *poker*. **1845** — *Wigwam & Cabin* 1 Ser. 164 You played poker with a party of five. **1873** *Winfield* (Kan.) *Courier* 15 Feb. 1/4 There has been some poker in the Manhattan Club. **1885** *Wkly. New Mexican Rev.* 15 Jan. 4/2 From Montezuma lodge he borrowed $15, and blew it in at poker. **1900** *Congress. Rec.* 2 Feb. 1464/1 They are not giving up their pink teas and poker and all that sort of thing in order to come here to vote to give pensions to soldiers. **1925** TILGHMAN *Dugout* 95 Edward could not play poker.

2. Attrib. and comb. with *clergy, club, craft*, etc.

1844 COWELL *Thirty Years* 94 He was, apparently, quietly shuffling and cutting the poker-deck for his own amusement. **a1861** WINTHROP *J. Brent* 295 He sot his white head down to the poker-table, and stuck thar. **1865** *Atlantic Mo.* April 510/1 The price of the plantation rapidly disappeared at horse races, poker-parties [etc.]. **1882** *N.Y. Times* 11 March 4/7 A Down-East ship Captain ridicules the pretense that Minister Schenck introduced poker-playing into England, . . . and says that poker-playing was carried to England in the old packet ships. **1884** CARLETON *Thompson St. Poker Club* (1889) 78 The Thompson Street Poker Club had an unusually quiet game. **1894** WISTER in *Harper's Mag.* May 912/2 He gave his name, age, and stumbled at his occupation. 'Say, poker-dealer,' sneered Toussaint's attorney. **1907** *N. Amer. Rev.* 15 March 569 He 'held the age,' as the poker-clergy say. **1910** J. HART *Vigilante Girl* 142 What fortunes in twenty-dollar pieces went back to feed the faro-banks, . . . the poker-sharps, the whiskey-sellers. **1922** MULFORD *Tex* iii, He fairly burned to turn his poker craft against this blowhard's invitation.

+**Poker chip.** A chip or counter used in playing poker. — **1879** *Cimarron News & Press* 20 Nov. 4/3 The toughest thing we have heard about any candidate for office in this section is that he got his poker chips cashed after he 'experienced religion.' **1887** KELLER *Draw Poker* 18 Poker chips . . . are made from various materials, but the best are of ivory. **1894** WISTER in *Harper's Mag.* Sept. 511/1 If you've got some cheap poker chips. **1916** WILSON *Somewhere* 114 She'd got some poker chips out of the box to buy candy with.

+**Poker dice. 1.** Dice marked with the ace, king, queen, jack, ten, and nine instead of the usual spots. **2.** A game played with five of such dice with rules taken from the game of poker. — **(1) 1890** GUNTER *Miss Nobody* vi, This young official he finds in a neighboring bar-room throwing poker dice for drinks. **(2) 1903** *McClure's Mag.* Nov. 66/1 He was a high-class salesman . . . who could drop fifty at poker dice with as seasoned a composure as a hardened sharp.

+**Poker face.** A countenance concealing the owner's real thoughts and feelings. — **1885** *Encycl. Brit.* (ed. 9) XIX. 283/2 A good *poker face* is essential; the countenance should not betray the nature of the hand. **1924** MULFORD *Rustlers' Valley* x, He glanced around the circle and found poker faces, but there was a light in Baldy's eyes that warmed him.

+**Pokerish,** *a.* [From *poker* 'a hobgoblin, devil.']

1. Of a thing or place: Having a ghostly or unearthly appearance; dreadful.

1827 *Mass. Spy* 21 Nov. (Th.), A patriarchal ram, who would fight anything but a pokerish looking ducking gun. **1833** A. FERGUSSON *Notes Tour U.S.* 228 A grave and sententious gentleman in the hotel was detailing to me the desolation of the city during the last visitation of yellow fever. . . . 'I assure you, sir,' he said, with a most portentous aspect, 'it was monstrous *pokerish.*' **1853** LOWELL *Writings* I. 36 There is something pokerish about a deserted dwelling, even in broad daylight. **1871** STOWE *My Wife & I* viii, It was a lonesome and pokerish operation to dismantle the room that had long been my home. **1888** WARNER *On Horseback* 93 At one uncommonly pokerish place, where the wet rock sloped into a bog, the rider . . . thought it prudent to dismount.

2. Of a person: Affected with a fear of something ghostly or unearthly.

1831 *Georgian* (Savannah) 22 Jan. 2/5 (Th. S.), She looked plaguy pokerish at me. **1833** *Md. Hist. Mag.* XIII. 352, I feel quite pokerish in this region. **1891** ELLIS *Check 2134* 96, I feel pokerish tonight.

‖**Pokerishness.** The quality of unearthliness. — **1845** N. P. WILLIS in *N.Y. Evening Mirror* 29 Jan. 4/1 ['The Raven' is] unsurpassed in English poetry for subtle conception, masterly . . . versification, and consistent sustaining of imaginative lift and 'pokerishness.'

+**Pokerist.** A poker-player. — **1873** *Winfield* (Kan.) *Courier* 15, 1/4 Probably Missouri and Arkansas can produce more leading pokerists than most Western or Southern States.

+**Pokeroot.** The root or the plant of: **a.** The American hellebore. **b.** The pokeweed.

1687 CLAYTON *Va.* in *Phil. Trans.* XLI. 150 Poake-root, i.e. *Solanum bacciferum*, a strong Purge, and by most deemed Poison. **1698** THOMAS *Pensilvania* 19 There grows also in great plenty the Black Snake-Root, . . . Rattle-Snake-Root, Poke-Root, called in England Jallop. **1784** CUTLER in *Amer. Acad. Mem.* I. 492 *Veratrum.* . . . White Helebore. Poke-root. Indian Poke. Common in wet meadows and swamps. June. **1795** WINTERBOTHAM *Hist. View* III. 399 Among the native and uncultivated plants of New-England, the following have been employed for medical purposes. . . . White hellebore, or pokeroot, *Veratrum album*, Moonwort [etc.]. **1811** *Mass. Spy* 8 May (Th.), [For a cancer cure] take pocoon root, finely powdered, &c. . . . Take young poke root roasted, &c. **1814** BIGELOW *Florula Bostoniensis* 246 *Veratrum viride*. Poke root. Swamp Hellebore. . . . A large, green, leafy plant, not unfrequent in meadows and swamps. **1843** *Niles' Nat. Reg.* 2 Sept. 16/3 A small quantity of *poke-root*, boiled until the juices are extracted, and that mixed with a little molasses, and placed in their track, is said to be a sovereign expedient for getting rid of [roaches]. **1896** *Cosmopolitan* Feb. 394/2 Blackberry bushes throve rank in some of the fence corners; in others poke root towered amid forests of the may-apple. **1905** VALENTINE *H. Sandwith* 65, I'm sure I'd never trust him after he nearly poisoned you all, mistaking poke-root for burdock.

+**Poker-player.** A person who plays poker. — **1844** COWELL *Thirty Years* 94 The cabin was entirely cleared . . . with the exception of one of the poker players. **1885** *Wkly. New Mexican Rev.* 21 May 2/1 There are a good many poker players in this territory. **1912** NICHOLSON *Hoosier Chron.* 137 He had the reputation of being a poor poker player, but 'a good loser.'

+**Pokeweed.** A coarse perennial herb (*Phytolacca americana*) whose roots and dark purple berries are emetic and purgative; =POKE *n.*³ 1. Also attrib.

Also called GARGET, PIGEONBERRY, POKEBERRY, POKEROOT, etc.

[**1751** *Gent. Mag.* July 306/2 The Phytolacca . . . [is] known to almost every one in America, by the name of pokeweed.] **1752** FRANKLIN in W. Pepper *Medical Side B. Franklin* 27, I am heartily glad to hear more Instances of the success of the Poke-Weed, in the Cure of that horrible Evil to the human Body, a Cancer. **1836** LINCOLN *Botany* 165 The Pokeweed . . . [is] a very common plant. **1880** ALLAN-OLNEY *New Virginians* I. 53 They had stained it pink with poke-weed berries. **1904** NESBIT *Trail to Boyland* 1 Past the pokeweeds and their berries.

Pok(e)y, *a.* {1849–} Of a person: Slow; dull. {1888–} — **1856** STOWE *Dred* iv, If religion is going to make me so poky, I shall put it off as long as I can. **1879** RANOUS *Diary of Daly Debutante* 65 Roberts . . . is a nice boy, but pokey. **1920** LEWIS *Main Street* 261, I wouldn't have your pokey old husband.

+**Pokickery.** See HICKORY.

Poking bonnet. =POKE BONNET. {poking hat, 1799} — **1798** *Mass. Spy* 5 Sept. (Th.), Their pretty faces are either obscured by a black or white fly-flapper, or wholly hidden by their poking bonnets, unless you directly face them, and close by too.

Polacca. (See POLACRE.)

***Polack.** A person of Polish stock; an immigrant from Poland; = POLE *n.*² *colloq.* — **1900** *Congress. Rec.* 7 Feb. 1625/2, I have some Polacks in my district, and . . . the blood of Pulaski, the brave Pole who fell at Savannah in the defense of American liberty, has never been avenged. **1905** BEACH *Pardners* 127 Some Polack . . . laid out the quartermaster cold. **1907** *N.Y. Ev. Post* (s.-w. ed.) 22 April 6 Polacks and Canucks have taken the places of most of the old-time American woodsmen in the Adirondacks.

Polacre. Also **polacca.** A two- or three-masted merchant ship of a type common in the Mediterranean. {1625–} Also attrib. — **1755** *Ga. Gen. Assembly Acts* (1881) 53 All Masters of Vessells . . . shall pay into the Public Treasury . . . for every Snow Brig Polacre or Sactia Twenty Two shillings and Six pence. **1781** FRENEAU *Poems* (1786) 218 In less than three months I shall send a polacca As deep as she'll swim, sir, with corn and tobacco. **1803** *Ann. 8th Congress* 2 Sess. 1524 Brigs, 63 American, 17 Spanish, 1 French; polacres, 4 Spanish. **1835** INGRAHAM *South-West* I. 59 [A] rakish looking Portuguese polacca (polaque) carrying even in so light a breeze a 'bone in her teeth,' glided swiftly along.

***Poland. 1.** A breed of chickens. Often with a distinguishing adjective. {Poland fowl, 1830} +**2.** Short for next. — **(1) 1850** BROWNE *Poultry Yard* 60 The Poland, or Polish fowl. **1856** *Rep. Comm. Patents 1855: Agric.* 63 Of all the fancy fowls, I prefer either the 'Black Spanish,' or the 'Polands.' **1871** LEWIS *Poultry Book* 50 Golden-Spangled Poland. —This variety varies in the color of its plumage. . . . The Black Polands are no strangers in this country, they having been bred as long ago as we can remember. **(2) 1895** *Bur. Animal Industry Circ.* No. 4, 3 A few instances of disease among my 'improved breeds,' Poland, Chester Whites, Durocs, and Yorkshires.

+**Poland China.** An American breed of hogs, similar to the Berkshires. Also attrib. (Cf. CHINA *n.*⁴) — **1879** *Diseases of Swine* 178 Cholera in Kansas and Nebraska seems to attack preferably the Berkshire, and the Berkshire crossed by the Poland-China. **1893** G. W. CURTIS *Horses, Cattle* 298 The Poland-China breed is one distinctively American in origin and type, originating chiefly in Warren and Butler counties, Ohio. **1900** *Farmer's Bul.* No. 117, 17 Berkshire and Poland-China blood predominates in the West. **1924** CROY *R. F. D. No. 3* 12 He dodged into the Poland China Hog Association; the pedigree he had asked for was waiting.

Polander.

1. A native of Poland. {1601–} Cf. POLE *n.*² and POLACK.

1624 *Va. House of Burgesses* 28 The second supplie was a ship the *Mary Margett*, . . . [with] sixty persons, most gentlemen, . . . except some *Polanders* to make Pitch, tarre, potashes, &c. **1809** WEEMS *Marion* (1833) 66 That impetuous Polander, the count Polaski. **1823** THACHER *Military Jrnl.* 219 This gentleman was a Polander, of distinguished rank and character.

2. =POLAND 1. {1830} Also attrib.

1850 BROWNE *Poultry Yard* 60 Polish Fowl, Polanders, Black Polish Fowl, Golden Polands [etc.]. **1856** COZZENS *Sparrowgrass P.* 86 Our great Polander is in high cluck, and we find eggs in the hens' nests. **1893** M. A. OWEN *Voodoo Tales* 247 She done sont me . . . foh er settin' o' Polandeh aigs—dem speckle-top-knot kine.

Poland oats. A variety of oats from Poland. {1764} — **1787** WASHINGTON *Diaries* III. 176 Began to sow Poland Oats with orchard and Timothy grass seeds.

+**Poland topknot.** A variety of the Poland breed of chickens. Also attrib. — **1846** *Spirit of Times* 16 May 141/2 The Poland Top-Knot fowls are highly recommended as layers. **1849** *New Eng. Farmer* I. 309 The Poland Top Knots seldom sit, and are excellent for those who keep hens expressly for eggs.

Polanisia. +The clammyweed, *Polanisia graveolens*. — **1843** TORREY *Flora N.Y.* I. 67 *Polanisia graveolens*. Heavy-scented Polanisia. . . . Gravelly banks of rivers and lakes. . . . June–August.

+**Polar plant.** The rosinweed, *Silphium laciniatum*. (Cf. COMPASS 3.) — **1843** N. BOONE *Journal* 191 Noticed on the prairie . . . the polar plant and rosin weed. **1851** M. REID *Scalp Hunt.* xxxv, We were traversing the region of the 'polar plant,' the planes of whose leaves, at almost every step, pointed out our meridian.

+**Polar wave.** A wave of cold weather. — **1888** *St. Paul Globe* 22 Jan., Another polar wave struck [Chippewa Falls, Wis.] . . . . This morning spirit thermometers indicated from 62 to 65 deg. below.

***Poldavis.** A strong, coarse canvas formerly used for sailcloth. — **1665** *East-Hampton Rec.* I. 241 Jeremiah Meachem iunior and James Diament findinge a peece of pole Davice Contayninge nere Sixty yards.

Polder. A low-lying piece of land reclaimed from surrounding water by means of dikes. {in the Netherlands, 1604–} — **1856** *Rep. Comm.*

Patents 1855: Agric. 128 Polders of three miles square, near the levees of the Mississippi, . . . could be diked and drained at a small cost compared with their subsequent value.

***Pole,** *n.*[1]

I. *1. A long, more or less cylindrical and usu. slender piece of wood.

1655 *Charlestown Land Rec.* 137, [I sell] the yeard and garden ground . . . ; with all the Rails, Poles, Posts, and fencings. **1699** SEWALL *Diary* I. 502 Pole of the Calash broken by the Horses frighted with a Pistol. **1733** BYRD *Journey to Eden* (1901) 299 That there he had found no less than ten Huts, the Poles whereof had green Leaves still fresh upon them. **1772** in *Travels Amer. Col.* 538 They hoisted an old ragged Jack on a pole telling me they had no better Collours to adorn their Square with. **1792** ASBURY *Journal* II. 177 We attended from ten till one o'clock in a house built of *poles*—here were light and ventilators plenty. **1833** NEAL *Down-Easters* I. 27 A little dapper Bostonian . . . kept a store as they call it, where every shop is a *store*, every stick a *pole*, every stone a *rock*. **1852** *S. Lit. Messenger* XVIII. 753/2 Who did I see but Tom Edmundson, . . . sitting back in an arm-chair, one thumb in his waistcoat armhole, the other hand brandishing a long switch, or rather pole. **1912** N. WOODROW *Sally Salt* 80 The kitchen looked out upon its garden of supplies— . . . tomatoes turning red in the midsummer sun, bean vines in long festoons over their poles.

b. A long piece of round timber designed for use in propelling a river boat or other craft. {pole-ground 1733}

1709 LAWSON *Carolina* 101 The Indians and English make poles, to set their Canoes along in Shoal water. **1814** BRACKENRIDGE *Views La.* 44 Oars and poles are always used for the purpose of navigating the boats. **1819** E. EVANS *Pedestrious Tour* 245 The poles are about 8 feet in length, and the bottom of them enters a socket of iron, which causes the point of the pole to sink immediately. This business is very laborious and . . . slow. **1881** *Congress Rec.* 26 Feb. 2151/1 There were appropriations in the bill for streams that never would and never could float a steam-vessel or a sail-vessel or anything more than a boat that was floated down with the current and poled up by poles.

+c. =SCALP POLE.

1804 in *Lewis & Clark Exped.* VII. (1905) 64 They took the 65 of the Mahars sculps and had them hung on Small poles. **1841** COOPER *Deerslayer* xvii, Hawkeye has stolen my wife: he must bring her back, or his scalp will hang on a pole and dry in my wigwam. **1848** — *Oak Openings* II. 18 'Have our young men taken many pale-face scalps?' 'So few that they are not worth counting. I did not see one pole that was such as an Indian loves to look on.'

+d. A fishing rod.

1832 *N.H. Hist. Soc. Coll.* III. 84 A pole of from 12 to 20 feet, with a line about the same length, is provided with a hook of three fourths of an inch bow. **1845** JUDD *Margaret* I. 8 He set himself to catch fish with a long pole. **1875** HOLLAND *Sevenoaks* 230 Ye never fished with anything but a white birch pole in yer life. **1919** HOUGH *Sagebrusher* 84 That pole of yours ain't no good, it's too limber.

***2. a.** A linear measure for land, usually 16½ or 18 feet. *Obs.*

In contexts wherein both *rod* and *pole* are used, a *pole* seems to be 18 feet.

1633 *Mass. Bay Rec.* I. 106 There is demised to Tho. Lambe, of slate in Slate Ileand, 10 poole towards the water side, & 5 poole into the land. **1659** *Providence Rec.* I. 109 His House share . . . Containeth . . . in breadth on the wes parte Eight poles . . . ; the poles being Sixteene foot and halfe. **1679** *Derby Rec.* 36 George bemans land . . . is 54: pole brode next his hom lot; the east sid line is: 38: rods long: The north east line is 25: rods long: the north west Side is 52: rods long: wch makes: ten acres: 155 polle—more or less. **1710** *N.C. Col. Rec.* I. 742 [We] found the Creeks mouth to be 20 Poles to ye southward of the place where we took the observation. **1788** *State Gazette of N.C.* (New Bern) 27 March, 640 acres of land on the north side of Cumberland river, in Davidson county, opposite the double islands, being 440 poles in front upon the river. **1842** *Amer. Pioneer* I. 427 We had progressed perhaps one hundred and forty, or one hundred and fifty poles, when our chain broke or parted. **1847** in Howe *Hist. Coll. Ohio* 373 After going about 100 poles, we were obliged to stop and rest.

b. A measure of area: The square of the linear measure, usually 272¼ square feet. *Obs.* {1637, 1660}

1638 *Charlestown Land Rec.* 11 One pole of grounde lying before his house, giuen him for A well yarde, the highway lying betwixt that and his hous. **1678** *Derby Rec.* 32 Fiftene Rods long: 18 at one eand And Three att ye other eand wch makes an acre Save thre poole. **1681** *Ib.* 123 Ye north west Side Line is: 80: rods long which: 22: acres: & ½: or 80 pole more or less. **1754** *N.H. Probate Rec.* III. 493 We have Set off to ye widow Thirty Six acres & fifty four Poles as her full third part in ye Lands of sd Deceasd.

***c.** A pole (in sense 1) of 16½ or 18 feet for measuring land or distance: (see quotations).

1662 *Providence Rec.* III. 15 Take an account of the number of the poles according to the 16 foot and a half pole. **1671** *Ib.* I. 9 Sixty Acors of Land . . . Laid out by the Eighteene foott pole being in length 220 pole. **1723** *Ib.* XII. 69 There shall be a Revisel of that highway of two poles wide by the—18—foot pole.

+3. *Horse racing.* **a.** The goal posts or other posts marking different distances about a track.

1836 *Quarter Race Ky.* (1846) 20 Crump wheeled his horse round before reaching the poles. **1868** *N.Y. Herald* 4 July 8/6 Jogging to the pole is good for a change. **1898** *Kansas City Star* 18 Dec. 3/1 Andes . . . took up the pace and led to the half mile pole.

+b. *To have* (*take* or *draw*) *the pole*, to have, etc., the inside track. Also fig.

1852 BRISTED *Upper Ten Th.* 229n., A horse that has the pole, means that he has drawn the place nearest the inside boundary-fence of the track. **1868** WOODRUFF *Trotting Horse* 207, I was forced to let them take the pole on the turn. **1898** WESTCOTT *D. Harum* 138 He'll allow that if he gits in the fust word, he'll take the pole. **1902** MCFAUL *Ike Glidden* 198 Drawing the pole was a position evidently in favor of the colt.

+4. *Lumbering.* (See quot. 1905.)

1900 BRUNCKEN *N. Amer. Forests* 97 Today he goes over the same lands and takes what he left thirty years ago, this time down to the 'pole' of eight inches and less in diameter. **1905** *Forestry Bureau Bul.* No. 61, 17 *Pole*, a tree from 4 to 12 inches in diameter breasthigh. . . . A *small pole* is a tree from 4 to 8 inches in diameter breasthigh. Syn: low pole. A *large pole* is a tree from 8 to 12 inches in diameter breasthigh. Syn: high pole.

II. *attrib.* and *comb.* **5.** Designating things or animals related to the pole or tongue of a vehicle.

See also POLE HORSE.

1760 WASHINGTON *Diaries* I. 136, [I] put the Poll end Horses into the Plow in the Morn[in]g. **1851** CIST *Cincinnati* 196 In this department are made carriage wrenches, staples, pole crabs, nuts [etc.]. **1862** NORTON *Army Lett.* 106 The driver riding the near pole mule and guiding his team with one line. **1876** KNIGHT 1761/2 *Pole-futchel*, . . . the jaws between which the hinder end of a carriage-tongue is inserted. **1886** *Outing* VIII. 65/2 If the carriage is to be held hard back by the pole-chain a slow pace is essential.

6. Designating things made of poles.

See also POLE BRIDGE, POLE CABIN, etc.

1850 GARRARD *Wah-To-Yah* xi. 149 With the aid of a half a dozen scalp-knives, its skin [*i.e.*, of a steer] was stretched on a poleframe. **1862** COLT *Went to Kansas* 48 A pole bedstead is made, corded with strips of bark. **1863** *Ladies' Repository* July 399/1 A pole stable is constructed for the horses of travelers. **1871** *Rep. Indian Affairs* (1872) 484 The corn is . . . stored with pumpkins and beans in pole-cribs, chinked and daubed with mud, and roofed with bark and skins. **1874** *Dept. Agric. Rep. 1873* 281 Mr. William Crozier . . . cures his corn-fodder (sowed corn) by stacking it on pole platforms. **1893** *Outing* May 135/2 Near by are some old shacks, or pole shanties, in which the Indians along the Columbia River place their dead. **1907** WHITE *Arizona Nights* 169 Most of the time he lay flat on his back staring at the pole roof. **1924** CROY *R. F. D. No. 3*, 78 [He] had gone to the pole barn with a rope around his waist played from the door by his wife.

+7. Designating a railroad made of poles, or the locomotive driven on it.

See also POLE ROAD.

1878 *Lumberman's Gazette* 6 April, They use on these pole railroads trucks with iron wheels. **1887** *Harper's Mag.* March 638/2 He finds in Richmond a 'pole locomotive,' made to run on logs laid end to end.

8. Designating athletic events performed with a vaulting pole.

1879 *N.Y. Ev. Express Almanac* 370 (Ernst), Duke in the pole-jump reached 96 [*sic*] ft. 5 in. **1893** *Outing* XXII. 154/2 He has . . . held the world's record in the pole vault for distance.

9. Designating persons who do various things with poles.

1892 A. E. LEE *Hist. Columbus, Ohio* I. 363 After the polesetters had done their work the [telegraph] wires were quickly strung. **1893** *Outing* XXII. 154/2 Harding . . . began training as a pole-vaulter in 1891. **1898** HAMBLEN *Gen. Manager's Story* 263 The old timers, pretty girls, and fast pickers, can cajole the pole-puller into bringing them *good* poles, *i.e.* those on which the hops grow in big, thick clusters.

+10. In special combinations.

Pole-hat, ? a top hat; *p. line*, a line of telephone or telegraph poles; *p. pruning shears*, (see quot. 1851); *p.-pulling*, an Indian ceremony celebrating the taking down of poles set up to honor the dead; *p.-raising*, a ceremony in which a liberty pole is raised; *p. wagon*, a circus wagon for carrying tent poles.

1862 *Harper's Mag.* Dec. 100/2 If we'd a coon-skin cap, . . . we was dressed up sure. We hadn't no occasion then for gloves, pole-hats, nor broadcloth. **1906** *Indian Laws & Tr.* III. 179 The right to locate . . . pole lines, and conduits . . . [shall] be allotted in severalty to any individual Indian [etc.]. **1851** BARRY *Fruit Garden* 383 *Pole Pruning Shears.*—These resemble the hand shears, but are worked by a string passing over a pulley, and are fixed on a pole of any required length. They are used in cutting scions, diseased shoots, &c., from the heads of lofty standard trees. **1824** HODGSON *Letters from N.A.* I. 216 At the celebrated ceremony of the 'pole-pulling,' the family connexions assemble from a great distance. **1878** BEADLE *Western Wilds* 38 The Whigs had a pole-raisin' along o' the election o' old Zach Taylor. **1920** COOPER *Under Big Top* 134 All eight of them, with the pole-wagon clattering along behind, ran away also.

***Pole, n.*²** A person of Polish stock; a native of Poland. Cf. POLACK, POLANDER I.

1612 SMITH, etc. *Virginia* II. 42 The hiring of the Poles and Dutch, to make pitch and tarre, . . . was most necessarie and well. **1843** *Diplom. Corr. Texas* III. (1911) 1464 Some Poles of respectability have called on me about emigrating to Texas. **1885** BAYLOR *On Both Sides* 94 And that 'Warsaw.' There must be a settlement of Poles out there. **1896** *N.Y. Herald* 13 Jan. 3/4 Under this title ['Hunks'] the Pennsylvanian includes Hungarians, Lithuanians, Slavs, Poles, Magyars, and Tyroleans. **1905** *N. Amer. Rev.* Nov. 682 The Jew ceases to be a Pole, a German, a Russian, after the first generation has graduated from the public schools.

***Pole, v.**

+1. *tr.* To finish off (certain kinds of rail fences) by running a pole from one pair of crossed stakes to another. *Obs.*

1662 *Portsmouth Rec.* 116 All out fences . . . being sufishently staked and pould.

+2. To propel (a boat or other craft) by using a pole long enough to touch bottom {1893}; to transport a boatload of (merchandise) by this method.

1774 D. JONES *Journal* (1865) 47 The canoe was poled up the stream. **1799** J. SMITH *Acct. Captivity* 25 Tontileaugo [proceeded] near the shore, sometimes paddling and sometimes polling his canoe along. **1848** E. BENNETT *Mike Fink* 13/2 Dick Weatherhead's legs . . . [are] long enough to pole a boat up the Massassip, in a high stage o' water. **1865** BROWNE *A. Ward; His Travels* 14 There was a wharf, but the enterprising Mexican peasantry, who subsist by poling merchandise ashore in dug-outs, indignantly tore it up. **1904** PRINGLE *Rice Planter* 116 At 3 o'clock . . . the last sheaf was put in the flat and so it could be poled up the river and put safely under the flat-house.

+b. *absol.* and *reflex.* To navigate by poling a boat. {1895} Also transf.

1831 R. COX *Adv. Columbia R.* 249 After pushing off, we poled away with might and main. **1843** 'CARLTON' *New Purchase* I. 90 She then poled, or 'set up stream' about 100 yards. **1849** THOREAU *Week on Concord* 271 We had poled ourselves through the canal . . . to the boatable part of the river. **1893** *Harper's Mag.* March 508/1 [The Seminole Indians] pole about the waterways in dugouts. **1900** JEWETT in *Atlantic Mo.* Aug. 162, I saw Cap'n Lorenzo polin' back up the road all alone.

+c. *tr.* To move a craft through (water) by means of a pole.

1862 HARTE *Luck of Roaring Camp* 230 We still fought our way forward, resting and rowing by turns, and oftener 'poling' the shallower surface.

+d. *To pole off*, to shove off with poles.

1873 BEADLE *Undevel. West* 703 The boat usually stuck fast for a while, till the hands could 'pole off,' when she would back out.

3. *tr.* (See quot. 1828.) Also absol. {1892-}

1779 *Narragansett Hist. Reg.* I. 92 Made hay and poled. **1828** WEBSTER, *Pole*, . . . to bear or convey on poles; as, to *pole* hay into a barn.

+4. *reflex.* To throw (oneself) over something by means of a pole.

1839 KIRKLAND *New Home* (1840) 15 The ditch on each side was filled with water and quite too wide to jump over. . . . He 'poled' himself over the ditch in a moment.

+5. *intr.* (See quot. 1851.) *College slang.*

1851 HALL *College Words* 233 *Pole.* At Princeton and Union Colleges, to study hard, e.g. to pole out the lesson. To pole on a composition, to take pains with it. **1895** WILLIAMS *Princeton Stories* 39 Others dissipate merely to the extent of cutting chapel twice in succession or pretending that they have not poled all night for an examination. **1915** POOLE *Harbor* 54 At first I honestly tried to 'pole,' to find whether, after all, I couldn't break through the hard dry crust of books and lectures down into what I called 'the real stuff.'

+Pole bean. Any climbing bean. — **1836** LINCOLN *Botany* App. 124 *Phaseolus . . . vulgaris*, (common pole-bean.) . . . From the East Indies. **1859** *Ill. Agric. Soc. Trans.* III. 503 There are many varieties of pole beans. . . . [They] should be planted in warm and rich soil. **1901** MOHR *Plant Life Ala.* 830 Kidney Bean. Pole Bean.

+Pole boat. A boat propelled by a pole. (Cf. POLE *v.* 2.) — **1827** in Commons, etc. *Doc. Hist.* I. 285, I saw three large pole boats loaded with bales of cotton. **1835** SIMMS *Partisan* 245 At this point the river ceased to be navigable even for the common poleboats of the country. **1841** — *Kinsmen* I. 163 Wherever a pole-boat had made its way, [his name had] found repeated echoes. **1881** *Congress. Rec.* 26 Feb. 2151/1 Here is a stream navigable for a pole-boat.

+Pole boating. The action or practice of using boats propelled by a pole. — **1837** SHERWOOD *Gaz. Georgia* (ed. 3) 193 A revolution in the mode and manner of transshipping goods must take place. The slow, tedious and expensive process of pole-boating will be exploded.

+Pole bridge. A bridge made of poles. (Cf. CORDUROY BRIDGE, LOG BRIDGE.) — **1809** ASBURY *Journal* III. 311 O! the rocks, roots, pole-bridges and mosquitoes. **1841** *Cultivator* VIII. 163 In crossing miles of pole bridges, one gets a vast amount of perpendicular movement without any charge. **1860** GREELEY *Overland Journey* 204 [We followed the Weber R.] some four or five miles to the shaky pole-bridge.

+Pole cabin. A cabin made of poles, freq. of young pine. (Cf. LOG CABIN.) — **1790** ASBURY *Journal* II. 75 Jesus is not always in our dwellings; and when he is not, a pole cabin is not very agreeable. **1877** JOHNSON *Anderson Co., Kansas* 58 Dewey and his party unloaded their goods in a pole cabin, 10 feet by 14 feet, roofless and floorless, on the northwest corner of what is now James Adams' farm. **1897** W. E. BARTON *Hero in Homespun* 7 [They] began life in a pole cabin, at first unchinked.

***Polecat.** Also †**pol(l)cat.**

+1. a. A skunk of the genus *Mephitis*. **b.** Any of various animals allied to the skunk of the genera *Spilogale* and *Conepatus*.

1688 CLAYTON *Va.* in *Phil. Trans.* XVIII. 124 There are [in Virginia] several sorts of Wild Cats, and Poll-Cats. **1709** LAWSON *Carolina* 119 Polcats or Skunks in America, are different from those in Europe. **1738** CATESBY *Carolina* II. 62 *Putorius Americanus striatus.* The Pol-Cat. . . . Their food is insects and wild fruit. **1784** ASBURY *Journal* I. 477 He afterward caught and eat a pole-cat. **1805** LEWIS in *L. & Clark Exped.* III. (1905) 4 Some of the dressey young men orniment the tops of their mockersons with the skins of pole-cats. **1856** J. B. JONES *Wild West. Scenes* 1 Ser. 96 The polecat (for such it was) gave its assailant a taste of its quality in a twinkling. **1888** *Ipswich* (Mass.) *Chronicle* 15 Sept. 2/4 In most parts of the Southwest a skunk is called a polecat and a polecat is called a mink—for the Western so-called mink is nothing but a polecat. **1917** *Mammals of Amer.* 132/1 The Skunk . . . is known in different localities by special names, such as 'wood-pussy,' 'essence-peddler,' and 'pole-cat.'

2. *attrib.* **+a.** With *shot, skin.*

1799 J. SMITH *Acct. Captivity* 11 [The Indians] gave me a . . . polecat skin pouch, which . . . contained tobacco, killegenico, or dry sumach leaves, which they mix with their tobacco. **a1861** WINTHROP *Canoe & Saddle* 27 Behold, also, this other double-barrelled piece of artillery, loaded . . . with polecat-shot, in case we should see one of these black and white objects skulking along shore.

+b. *Polecat tree, wood,* the buckthorn *Rhamnus caroliniana.*

1897 SUDWORTH *Arborescent Flora* 298 *Rhamnus caroliniana.* . . . Indian Cherry. . . . [Also called] Polecat-tree (Tex.). Polecat-wood (Ark.).

+Polecat dance. A kind of Indian dance, esp. among the Creeks. — **1772** in *Travels Amer. Col.* 532 The women . . . came into the Square and danced round the fire, the pole Cat dance. **1837** *S. Lit. Messenger* III. 391/1, I was informed that this was called by the Indians the *Pole Cat Dance* though our friends were disposed to distinguish it by the more agreeable . . . name of the *Shell Dance.*

+Polecat root. =next. — **1761** KALM *Resa* III. 47 De Svenske kallade henne *Björnrötter* eller *Björnblad;* men Ängelsmännerna *Polecat-rot* [tr. 1770: polecat-root].

+Polecat weed. The skunk cabbage, *Symplocarpus foetidus.* — **1743** CLAYTON *Flora Virginica* 186 Calla aquatilis odore alii vehemente prædita, radice repente, vulgo Pole Cadweed [ed. 1762: Pole-Cat-weed]. **1844** DUNGLISON *Med. Lex.*, Polecat weed, *Dracontium fœtidum.*

Pol. Econ. Among college students, an abbreviation for *Political economy.* — **1893** POST *Harvard Stories* 12, I have not been tutoring you in Pol. Econ. **1904** LOVETT *R. Gresham* 73, I've got to take on a coach to make up my Pol. Econ. from last year.

+Pole cure, *v. tr.* To cure (tobacco) by hanging it on poles. — **1899** *Soils Div.* (Dept. Agric.) *Rep.* No. 62, 30 The present method of manipulating these tobaccos after they are pole cured is quite different from what it was years ago.

+Pole fence. A fence or fencing made of poles.

A pole fence is distinguished from a rail fence in that the bars of the latter are split.

1754 HEMPSTEAD *Diary* 628 In the aftern[oon] I was setting up Pole fence next the highway over Long bridge. **1788** WASHINGTON *Diaries* III. 346 All hands were . . . finishing the Pole fence round the Barley and Pease in field No. 1. **1834** CARRUTHERS *Kentuckian* I. 79 The little fields are barely marked out with a rotten and broken down pole-fence. **1870** *Rep. Comm. Agric. 1869* 399 Pole fence must be four and a half feet high, . . . and when the stakes are placed seven feet apart there must not be less than six horizontal poles well secured to the stakes. **1880** *Scribner's Mo.* Feb. 503/2 The pole fence was laid after the same fashion of a rail fence, only the poles were longer than rail-cuts.

Pole flounder. A deep-water flounder (*Glyptocephalus cynoglossus*) of the North Atlantic. {1896} — **1879** *Rep. Comm. Fisheries* V. 5 The Pole-flounder is rare on the coast of Middle Europe . . . ; nowhere do they appear in such numbers as on the American coast. **1884** GOODE, etc. *Fisheries* I. 199 The Pole Flounder appears to be a permanent resident . . . in the deep basins of Massachusetts Bay. **1911** *Rep. Fisheries 1908* 310/1 ['Flounder'] is variously applied to the flat fishes found on all our coasts, as 'American sole,' . . . 'Greenland turbot,' 'pole flounder,' 'craig flounder' [etc.].

+Pole horse. A horse harnessed alongside the tongue of a vehicle, as distinguished from a leader. — **1823** COOPER *Pioneers* iv, The leaders were of gray, and the pole-horses of a jet-black. **1887** BILLINGS *Hardtack* 327, I saw one pole-horse shot thus. **1889** *Harper's Mag.* June 160/2 The leaders sprang upward and onward . . . , the pole-horses simultaneously crashing backward and downward.

+Pole house. A house the walls of which are made of poles. (Cf. LOG HOUSE.) — **1796** ASBURY *Journal* II. 292 At a pole-house [in S.C.] I talked a while on 1 Chron. vii, 14, and administered the sacrament. **1853** SIMMS *Sword & Distaff* (1854) 196 We must build a few pole-houses as soon as possible. **1873** BEADLE *Undevel. West* 88 The streets were eight inches deep in white dust as I entered the city of canvas tents and pole-houses.

+**Poleo.** [Sp.] ?An American plant similar to pennyroyal, *Mentha pulegium.* — **1872** POWERS *Afoot & Alone* 277 The vast mustard plains . . . stretch from Los Angeles to the sea. . . . In places this wide waste is of a dusty or coffee-green, with the little poles.

Poler. {1688–} +**1.** *College slang.* (See quot. 1851 and cf. POLE *v.* 5.) +**2.** One who tows a boat by means of a pole. — (**1**) **1851** HALL *College Words* 234 As a boat is impelled with *poles*, so is the student by *poling*, and it is perhaps from this analogy that the word *poler* is applied to a diligent student. **1895** WILLIAMS *Princeton Stories* 58 We are just amused a little bit at your posing as a heavy poler. **1915** POOLE *Harbor* 54 More pitiful still were the 'polers,' the chaps who were working for high marks. (**2**) **1895** *Outing* Oct. 71/1 A pole is attached to the bow of the lighter; the other end is held by a bare-footed negro, who walks along [the towpath]. . . . There are generally two polers to each lighter.

+**Pole road.** A railroad having rails made of barked poles; a pole railroad, used in hauling logs. — **1878** *Lumberman's Gazette* 6 April, These pole roads can be laid in the 'branch roads' direct to the skidways. **1893** *Scribner's Mag.* June 708/2 'Pole-roads' are built, where cars with wheels with concave faces run on poles instead of rails.

+**Pole trail.** A trail or way laid out with poles: (see quot. 1902). — [**1847** RUXTON *Adv. Rocky Mts.* (1848) 241, I followed a very good lodge pole-trail.] **1902** WHITE *Blazed Trail* 277 For when the snows are deep and snowshoes not the property of every man who cares to journey, the old-fashioned 'pole-trail' comes into use. It is merely a series of horses built of timber across which thick Norway logs are laid. **1908** — *Riverman* 36 The trail led through the brush across . . . a pole trail above a marsh to camp.

***Police.**

I. 1. The regulation and control of a community; the enforcement of law. {1716–}

1787 CUTLER in *Life & Corr.* I. 306 The city derives the greatest advantages for regulating her internal police by being incorporated. **1791** *Boston Rec.* 266 The officers of Police in this town [shall] be directed to Prosecute those who shall be guilty of Violating the Laws against Monopoly. **1830** ROYALL *Southern Tour* I. 26 The police of the boat is superior to the best regulated tavern. **1843** in *Atlantic Mo.* XV. 155/1 It had not been supposed necessary . . . to refer them to the questionable powers of internal and local police. **1883** SHIELDS *S. S. Prentiss* 97 After they [the new counties] were organized, the *boards of police* issued writs of election.

+**b.** The cleaning of a camp; the condition of a camp with respect to cleanliness.

1893 *Outing* May 158/1 The police of the camp was found to be excellent. **1894** *Ib.* July 312/2 The camp was at all times in good police.

2. *collect.* The body of officers intrusted with the duty of maintaining order, detecting crime, etc. {1800–}

See also INDIAN POLICE.

1810 *Columbian Centinel* 2 May 2/2 Some of the villains who headed the mob . . . are now undergoing an examination before the Police of the city. **1873** *Newton Kansan* 13 Feb. 2/3 The police in Topeka are making things lively for the gamblers, thieves, pimps and prostitutes. **1883** *Rep. Indian Affairs* 2 When the police approached the white men they escaped on the opposite side of the river. **1916** DU PUY *Uncle Sam* 205 Gard immediately called upon the Chicago police to throw out a dragnet.

+**3.** A policeman. *colloq. Obs.*

1839 *Chicago American* 5 Sept., There is a police in attendance . . . in the theatre. **1856** 'MARK TWAIN' *Adv. Snodgrass* 8 He was a police.

II. *attrib.* **4.** Designating various authorizations, powers, etc., connected with the exercise of the police power.

1831 PECK *Guide* 232 St. Louis had then no police regulations—the streets were filthy in the extreme. **1837** *S. Lit. Messenger* III. 644 We regret that Miss Martineau had not looked more closely into the negro quarters and into the various police trials of negro offenders in the different cities of the free states. **1852** EASTMAN *Aunt Phillis's Cabin* 71 You have other laws, police-laws, which deprive them of the most innocent recreations. **1856** MACLEOD *F. Wood* 214 Let us get a bill passed by our inspired men at Albany—a new Police Bill, which will strip this on-going man of his authority. **1883** *Century Mag.* Oct. 949/2 [Citizens should collect facts and] present them, in an official communication, to the police authorities.

5. Designating things connected with, or used by, the police, esp. in a police headquarters or police court.

1840 *Picayune* 8 Aug. 2/6 [They] were brought into the Police Prison of the Second Municipality. **1855** M. THOMPSON *Doesticks* 58 My name would positively have appeared in the Police Reports some morning. **1861** *Rep. Comm. Patents 1860* I. 261 John L. Rowe, of New York. . . . Improved Police Club. **1876** INGRAM *Centennial Exp.* 701 [In] the telegraphic department . . . were exhibited and in use all the telegraphic appliances of the day—police and fire-alarm, etc. **1882** MCCABE *New York* 520 If pressed too hard by the police boat, . . . they at once open fire upon it. **1883** SWEET & KNOX *Through Texas* 50 He began blowing a police-whistle. **1887** *Courier-Journal* 31 Jan. 5/4 The police-wagon . . . conveyed him to his home . . . in an insensible condition. **1898** *McClure's Mag.* X. 547/2 He was still in the infirmary attached to the police-cells. **1907** FIELD *Six-Cylinder Courtship* 57 To be charged with burglary and grand larceny, to have it entered in the police blotter by a goat of a sergeant, . . . was too screamingly absurd! **1922** PARRISH *Case & Girl* 271 I've looked him up in the police records.

6. a. Designating persons or groups of persons connected with or representing a police force.

1852 HALE *If, Yes, & Perhaps* 44, I had told the police agent he might send it to the St. Nicholas. **1856** MACLEOD *F. Wood* 205 The law gives the police corps to the Mayor to fill these positions. **1861** *Army Regulations* 76 The advanced post of the police guard is 200 paces in rear of the line of its field and staff. **1865** KELLOGG *Rebel Prisons* 253 They had a police squad, who made their appearance twice a day to see that the requisite order was maintained to secure this result. **1894** FORD *P. Stirling* 356 After a consultation with the police captain, the companies were told off, and filing out of the various doors, they began work. **1904** STEFFENS in *McClure's Mag.* April 587/1 No wonder Minneapolis, having cleaned out its police ring of vice grafters, now discovers boodle in the council! **1913** *Lit. Digest* 23 Aug. 271/1 Chicago's latest novelty in the establishment of a squad of policewomen on the regular force is not an innovation so real as apparent.

b. Designating persons who preside over police courts.

1852 *Harper's Mag.* Aug. 418/1 A rude fellow, while before the police-magistrate for some misdemeanor, was fined nine dollars. **1878** *Mich. Gen. Statutes* I. (1882) 601 Whenever complaint shall be made to any justice of the peace, or police justice, of any violation of any of the provisions of this act, he shall not require security [etc.]. **1894** *Columbus Dispatch* 5 Jan., He has been relieved of his duty as Acting Police Judge.

c. Designating groups of persons in control of the policies of municipal police or local vigilante organizations.

1856 MACLEOD *F. Wood* 208 The whole Police Board was elected at the late election. **1890** LANGFORD *Vigilante Days* (1912) 382 The wretched man had confessed to a leader of one of the police committees, . . . that he was the murderer of Dillingham.

Police commissioner. An officer or a member of a commission, appointed by the state or, usually, by the municipality, who determines or helps determine the policy and conduct of the police department. — **1857** *Harper's Mag.* Aug. 401/2 The Police Commissioners were busy in organizing their force in the various wards of the city. **1868** *N.Y. Herald* 1 July 8/6 Police Commissioner Brennan and that sweet tempered John A. Kennedy had conversation. **1898** *Kansas City Star* 18 Dec. 2/5 R. L. Gregory and H. C. Ward, police commissioners, each received a letter from Governor Stephens.

Police court. {1823–} A court of record having jurisdiction over certain minor offenses. Also attrib.

'Police courts in American cities are of two types. In some there are municipal courts with magistrates who are either appointed by the mayor or elected by popular vote. In others the police courts are merely the lowest tribunals in the hierarchy of the regular state courts' (1914 *Cycl. Amer. Govt.* I. 504).

1848 *Knickerb.* XXXI. 37 She has reared the sugar-cane, and refreshed herself with its rich pith, without the faintest shadowing-forth of . . . hospitals and almshouses, of town-paupers or police-courts. **1873** 'MARK TWAIN' & WARNER *Gilded Age* 487 Judge O'Shaunnessy . . . became the office and errand boy of a law firm, picked up knowledge enough to get some employment in police courts, was admitted to the bar [etc.]. **a1882** in McCabe *New York* 122 There are eleven police justices . . . each of whom has power to hold a police court in either of the six police-court districts. **1890** DAVIS *Gallegher* 93 He knew that the history of his life was written on Police Court blotters from the day that he was ten years old. **1913** LONDON *Valley of Moon* 330 The third [son] was a police court reporter in San Francisco.

+**Police department.** A department of a city or municipal government charged with maintaining order, detecting crime, etc.; collectively, the police force.

1810 *Boston Selectmen* 459 In the estimate of expences for the present year, a sum was named for the police department . . . and was adopted. **1855** in MacLeod *F. Wood* 230 It is the exclusive privilege of the Mayor, as head of the Police Department, to detail policemen [etc.]. **1894** *Harper's Mag.* Sept. 640/1 Members of the New York police department protected gamblers, keepers of disorderly houses, and 'green goods' men. **1916** DU PUY *Uncle Sam* 139 McCord would not have been in New Beaufort but for the ramifications of the New York police department in keeping track of these middle class criminals who live through the trade of burglary.

Police force. *collect.* The body of policemen and their officers of any community. {1840–} — **1875** *N. Amer. Rev.* CXX. 127 A henchman of [Tweed's] . . . had a place on the police force. **1882** MCCABE *New York* 371 The Legislature of the State passed a law in March, 1844, abolishing the old night watch and organizing a regular police force. **1901** 'FLYNT' *World of Graft* 17 By this it must not be understood, however, that every member of the Chicago police force is 'crooked.' **1922** FOSTER *Adv. Tropical Tramp* 184, I haven't seen Red since we beat it out of Iquique that night we cleaned up the police force.

Police headquarters. The headquarters of a police force. — **1898** *Kansas City Star* 20 Dec. 10/3 Bowen was taken to police headquarters, where Dr. Monahan, assistant police surgeon, sewed up a knife wound in his side. **1922** PARRISH *Case & Girl* 207 This is police headquarters calling.

+**Police jury.** *La.* (See quot. 1890.) — **1840** *Picayune* 22 Aug. 2/1 Will our friends . . . tell us what is meant in their city by the police jury? **1890**

Cent. 4592/3 *Police jury*, . . . the local authority in each parish (corresponding nearly to the board of supervisors of each county in many other States), invested with the exercise of ordinary police powers within the limits of the parish, such as prescribing regulations for ways, fences, cattle, taverns, drains, quarantine, support of the poor. **1914** *Cycl. Amer. Govt.* II. 705/2.

+**Police-jury ward.** 'In Louisiana, the chief subdivision of the parish' (*Cent.* 6821/2).

Policeman. A member of a police force. {1829–} — **1846** CORCORAN *Pickings* 26, I'll point you out to a policeman if you don't at once sit down. **1880** *Harper's Mag.* July 262/2 The policeman on this beat says he saw a man . . . come in this evening at your front door. **1904** STRATTON-PORTER *Freckles* 187 Will you come, or must I call a policeman to bring you? **1910** *N.Y. Ev. Post* 24 Dec. 6 Happily, in this city the situation has improved as between the citizen and the policeman.

Police office. The office or headquarters of a police force. {1798–} — **1820** *N.Y. Spectator* 2 May 3/3 We are requested to invite those merchants who have missed goods to call at the Police Office. **1846** CORCORAN *Pickings* 20 As the election excitement increases, so does the sale of whiskey punches, and so do the prisoners at the police office. **1882** PECK *Sunshine* 35 All the time this discussion was going on we sat by the safe in the police office.

Police officer. A civil officer charged with police duties; a policeman. {1794– (*Ann. Reg.* 159/1)} — **1812** *Boston Selectmen* 54 Charles Bulfinch Esq. was declared to be chosen Superintendent, & Mr. Jeremh. Bridge assistant Police officer. **1837** NEAL *Charcoal Sk.* (1838) 19 The temperament which, had she been a man, would, in an extended field, have made her a conqueror of nations, or, in a more limited field, a distinguished thief-catching police officer. **1873** *Mich. Gen. Statutes* I. (1882) 646 The city marshal, . . . as police officer, . . . shall be subject to the direction of the mayor. **1911** *Okla. Session Laws* 3 Legisl. 278 The Chief Factory Inspector, and Deputy FactoryInspector, are hereby empowered to act as police officers.

Police power. +The power of government to regulate its police affairs, esp. to advance the public welfare through restraint and compulsion exercised over private rights; the power to limit civil liberties.

The meaning of the term is not definitely fixed. The Supreme Court first used it to cover certain undefined powers reserved to the states. Now considerably narrowed in meaning, it differs from other powers, as the power of taxation, corporate power, judicial power, and military power, by being restricted to the legitimate protection of the public against the abuse of individual liberty.

1827 *Supreme Ct. Rep.* XXV. 442 The power to direct the removal of gunpowder is a branch of the police power, which unquestionably remains . . . with the states. **1842** *Ib.* XLI. 625 The police power belonging to the states in virtue of their general sovereignty . . . extends over all subjects within the territorial limits of the states, and has never been conceded to the United States. **1861** in Logan *Great Conspiracy* 364, I, M. Jeff. Thompson, Brigadier-General of the First Military District of Missouri, having . . . certain police powers granted by Acting-Governor Thomas C. Reynolds, . . . do most solemnly promise [etc.]. **1895** *N.Y. Dramatic News* 23 Nov. 3/2 That tribunal . . . decided that the legislature in passing the law had acted within the 'police powers' of the state. **1914** *Cycl. Amer. Govt.* II. 706/1 Congress is using the commerce power to accomplish the same objects which the state pursues through the police power.

‖**Policer.** One who polices. — **1837** NEAL *Charcoal Sk.* (1838) 221 Besides, you've no respect for functionaries . . . in wishing to 'bolish laws, and policers, and watchmen.

+**Police reporter.** A newspaper reporter who covers the police department. — **1870** MAVERICK *Raymond & N.Y. Press* 96 Every man in the company, from the chief to the police reporter, gave his whole mind to the preparation of the initial sheet. **1890** DAVIS *Gallegher* 4 His morbid interest in the doings of all queer characters . . . rendered him a valuable ally to our police reporter.

Police station. A local headquarters for the police force. {1865–} Also attrib. — **1851** ROSS *In New York* 27 Each Ward has a Police Station House. **1882** MCCABE *New York* 316 The basement [of the Grand Central Depot] contains a police station, barber shop, and restaurant. **1905** 'O. HENRY' *Trimmed Lamp* 112 His objections came to be spread finally upon some police station blotter or hospital register.

+**Police surgeon.** A surgeon connected with a police department. — **1868** *N.Y. Herald* 2 July 8/3 Dr. Waterman, police surgeon, was called and dressed the wounds. **1895** *Denver Times* 5 March 5/4 Police Surgeon Wheeler sewed up a big gash in his head.

***Policing.** +The action of cleaning or putting a camp in order. — **1865** *Atlantic Mo.* March 289/1 The sickening, pestilential odor of a huge camp without sewerage or system of policing, made the air a horror. **1887** BILLINGS *Hardtack* 101 All the labors of the service distinct from strict military duty, such as the 'policing' or clearing up of camp. **1893** LELAND *Memoirs* II. 60 There was no drill now . . . no special care of us, and no 'policing,' or keeping clean.

***Policy,** *n.*

***1.** A contract made by an insurance company with a person insuring life, property, etc.; a certificate of insurance.

1740 FRANKLIN *Writings* II. 360, I have not insured for anybody. . . . I will send the policy, that you may see it. **1784** in H. M. Brooks *Gleanings* II. 62 Hurd's Insurance-Office . . . , where Policies of Insurance are underwritten upon the most moderate premiums. **1865** *Nation* I. 157 This plan of paying for a policy by a definite number of annual instalments . . . obviates one of the greatest objections to life insurance. **1904** 'O. HENRY' *Roads of Destiny* 360, I don't believe any life-insurance company in the country would have issued me a policy on the strength of 'em.

+**2.** A game in which the players bet upon a number or a series of numbers to be drawn in a lottery or otherwise determined. Hence *to play policy.*

1877 [see POLICY *v.*]. **1878** DALY in J. F. Daly *A. Daly* 254 'Policy' rules the day here [in New Orleans], I fear, rather than Politics. **1882** C. B. LEWIS *Lime-Kiln Club* 89 You war well 'nuff to play policy. **1902** GHENT *Our Benevolent Feudalism* 172 Policy and race-betting, the special refuges of the desperately poor and the desperately fatuous, win new and lasting converts day by day.

3. Attrib. and comb. in sense 2. +**a.** Designating actions, tickets, etc., connected with the game of policy.

1851 *N.Y. Tribune* 20 March (Ernst), Policy gambling. **1872** BRACE *Dangerous Classes N.Y.* 99 Their money is unfortunately apt to slip away, especially for gambling and petty lotteries, called 'policy-tickets.' **1887** *Courier-Journal* 8 May 12/8 [He] thought he could increase his income somewhat by selling Louisiana lottery tickets and policy gigs. **1904** *N.Y. Times* 14 July 1 The 'peco' or policy joint [at Memphis, Tenn.] where the negroes had been wont to congregate and gamble. **1904** 'O. HENRY' *Roads of Destiny* 294 He was manager at different times of a skating-rink, a livery-stable, a policy game, a restaurant [etc.].

+**b.** Designating persons who operate, or are otherwise connected with, the game.

1875 *Chicago Tribune* 21 Nov. 13/1 The policy-dealers hide themselves in out of the way places, but their haunts must be known to the police. **1882** MCCABE *New York* 551 The policy managers are equal to the emergency. **1882** WHITMAN *Spec. Days* 259 The members . . . were expell'd gamblers, policy-backers, monte-dealers. **1899** *Chicago Record* 2 Jan. 5/1 Alleged Policy Men Arrested—Five men alleged to be connected with policy shops were arrested Saturday. **1901** HARRIGAN *Mulligans* 66 The colored people consider it a sacrilege to awaken a professional policy dreamer.

+**Policy,** *v. tr.* and *intr.* (See quotation.) — **1877** BARTLETT 479 Combined with the sale of lottery tickets, there is carried on an extensive game known by the name of *Policy.* To *policy* is to bet on certain numbers coming out in lottery drawings. A person can take any of the numbers in the scheme and *policy* them.

+**Policyholder.** A person to whom an insurance policy has been issued. — **1851** CIST *Cincinnati* 98 Penn Mutual Life Insurance Co. of Philadelphia. . . . All the profits divided among the policy holders every year. **1890** *Stock Grower & Farmer* 15 March 7/2 The Mutual Life Insurance Company, since its organization in 1843, has paid its policy-holders $287,681,948.20. **1911** *Okla. Session Laws* 3 Legisl. 203 He is satisfied that they are worth one hundred thousand dollars ($100,000), and that the deposit is made with him by the company for the protection of all his policy-holders.

+**Policy office.** =POLICY SHOP. — **1851** *Whig Almanac* 25 An election district . . . whose voters subsist mainly by keeping policy-offices, gambling-houses, grog-shops and darker dens of infamy. **1901** HARRIGAN *Mulligans* 63 The policy office was filled with poorly dressed negroes and negresses.

+**Policy-player.** A person who gambles on the policy game. — **1847** C. WHITE (*title*), The Policy Players. An Ethiopian Sketch. **1901** HARRIGAN *Mulligans* 65 A policy player's chances are a hundred to one against him.

+**Policy shop.** A place where bets are made in the game of policy. — **1875** *Chicago Tribune* 21 Nov. 13/2 The greatest number of the policy shops were on the South Side. **1882** C. B. LEWIS *Lime-Kiln Club* 89 De odder day I happened to pass a policy shop an' I saw you gwine in. **1901** HARRIGAN *Mulligans* 40 The floor over the basement was employed as a policy shop, in charge of a consumptive negro. **1914** KEATE *Destruction Mephisto's Web* 84 The Chinese and Mexican Lotteries, and in some cities Policy Shops, are now about the only ones in operation.

+**Policy slip.** (See quotation 1890.) Also attrib. — **1890** *Cent.* 4593/2 *Policy slip*, . . . the ticket given on a stake of money at a policy-shop. **1901** HARRIGAN *Mulligans* 71 The policy slip runner . . . gave Allup two slips of paper upon which were written the drawn numbers of the afternoon lotteries. **1903** *N.Y. Ev. Post* 22 Aug., We have had in this city policy slips which masqueraded as laundry lists and as menu cards.

***Poling.** +The action of propelling a boat with poles. — **1814** BRACKENRIDGE *Views La.* 205 The water is generally too deep to admit of poling. **1845** *Knickerb.* XXV. 193 The swift current . . . would not admit of the ordinary means of 'poling' against the stream.

***Polishing.** The action of making a surface smooth and glossy. Used attrib. with *shop, stick, stone, wheel.* — **1790** *Penna. Packet* 7 May 3/3 Imported and to be Sold by John Wood, Clock and Watch Maker, . . . polishing stones, hammers [etc.]. **1872** *Rep. Comm. Patents 1871* I. 374 Polishing-stick, Emery, G. C. Taft. **1885** *Harper's Mag.* March 559/1 After a vain attempt to see the steam-cutter, they entered the polishing-shops. **1911** PERSONS, etc. *Mass. Labor Laws* 280 Which of the following points in factory inspection do you feel especially well qualified to inspect: . . . emery wheels, polishing wheels, etc.

***Political,** *a.*

I. *1. Of or pertaining to the exercise of government; concerned with the responsibilities of government.

1776 *Decl. Independence,* When, in the course of human events, it becomes necessary for one people to dissolve the political bonds which have connected them with another. **1825** *Austin P.* II. (1924) 1123 Fees imposed by the Political Chief of the Province. **1884** *Century Mag.* April 863/1 Where, then, lies the hope for the political education which the negro can acquire only by the use of the ballot? **1894** ROBLEY *Bourbon Co., Kansas* 139 Everybody was in favor of a State government, except a few bad smelling politicians, . . . whose 'political principles' had degenerated into the sole desire to see the country kept embroiled and the field kept open for plundering, thieving and guerrilla warfare.

II. Of or pertaining to practical politics. {1769–}

2. Of persons: **a.** Possessed of skill and practical sense in politics; motivated by politics; engaged in politics. Freq. derogatory.

1806 *Balance* V. 161/3 It would seem almost incredible, that a nation . . . should in so short a space of time, sink to the vile posture, of a cowardly, political jockey. **1838** MAYO *Polit. Sk. Washington* (1839) 16 The *Democratic Firm* . . . have been succeeded by a conspiracy of political black-legs, who well know the value of the *old sign board* of an honourable party. **1868** *N.Y. Herald* 4 July 4/6 Perhaps there are not a few political dead beats here looking after the Democratic Convention. Oh, no! **1877** BARTLETT 436 'He's an old coon,' is said of one who is very shrewd; often applied to a political manager. **1893** *Chicago Tribune* 26 April 6/4 It looks as though that political groundhog, the Hon. Bill Springer, had seen his own shadow about March 4, and had gone back into his hole to stay for four years. **1905** N. DAVIS *Northerner* 279 He should himself become the tool of unscrupulous political tricksters in a deal whose object was to line their own pockets! **1913** LAFOLLETTE *Autobiog.* 133 [McKinley] stood unwaveringly by Bristow against the persistent importunity of many of his most intimate political advisers.

b. Appointed as a result of politics.

1868 *Ore. State Jrnl.* 1 Aug. 2/1 Blair is known as . . . a 'political general,' who held two offices, Major general in the Army and member of Congress, and drew pay for both at the same time.

3. Of an organization: Having for its object the control of elections and appointments to public office.

1806 *Repertory* 4 March (Th.), New York is now divided into four distinct political parties. **1882** SALA *Amer. Revisited* (1885) 138 For some mysterious reason . . . , the Consumers' Ice Company figured as a political organization in this astounding Parade. **1886** LOGAN *Great Conspiracy* 597 President Lincoln was serenaded by a Pennsylvania political club. **1892** DALY *Test Case* (1893) 21 We're not so far behind the times as you think. We have a political ring and a boss.

4. Of contests and campaigns: Having candidates or parties contending for control of an election.

1844 *Lexington Observer* 1 June 2/4 The commencement of another great political campaign has at length arrived. **1854** *Harper's Mag.* July 268/2 After some severe political struggle, in which he had dared to handle '"Old Hickory" without gloves,' . . . Mr. Bell unexpectedly met the old soldier on the street. **1865** PIKE *Scout & Ranger* (1932) 137, I was soon far away in the solitudes of the wilderness, where political contests are unknown. **1885** *Mag. Amer. Hist.* March 296/1 In 1826 . . . it was alleged that one Morgan was murdered by the Masons, and a bitter political war followed.

5. Of a meeting: Called or conducted for some party or partisan purpose.

1855 Hambleton *H. A. Wise* 276 The whole political destinies of the country may be controled [*sic*] by secret oath-bound organizations, a hybrid mixture of masonry, and a political caucus. **1898** PAGE *Red Rock* 15 A young countryman . . . happened to come along on his way home from a political gathering somewhere. **1912** NICHOLSON *Hoosier Chron.* 362 She wanted this Garrison girl to see a political convention.

6. Of graft and patronage: Controlled or made possible by politics.

1873 *Republic* I. 46 Thus public men are not merely tempted with free passes . . . but also by political promotion. **1884** *Century Mag.* April 808/2 With the growth of the country and of the political patronage system, the proper use of the building [the White House] as a dwelling for the chief magistrate has been more and more subordinated to its official use as a bureau of appointments. **1913** LAFOLLETTE *Autobiog.* 139 One of the political grafts of Wisconsin, ancient and time honored, was the farming out of the public funds to favored banks.

7. In special combinations.

Political assessment, an assessment made on officeholders for the support of a political organization; *p. bargain,* (see quotation); *p. editor,* a news editor who covers matters concerned with politics; *p. fence,* =FENCE *n.* 2; *p. headquarters,* the headquarters of a political organization; *p. speech,* a speech the purpose of which is to gain support for a particular party.

1882 *Nation* 6 July 4/2 The Revised Statutes prohibit any such contributions as are asked for in Congressman Jay A. Hubbell's recent 'political-assessment' circular addressed to the employees of the Government. **1914** *Cycl. Amer. Govt.* II. 710/2 *Political Bargain,* an agreement, usually corrupt, between contending political factions or individuals by which support is given a measure or candidate in return for a like favor. **1859** *La Crosse Daily Union & Democrat* 17 Nov. 2/1 Wanted. . . . Some individual with a truly philanthropic and Christian spirit, to 'talk Turkey' to the political editor. **1900** *Congress. Rec.* 5 Feb. 1522/1 The gentleman from Missouri has been running with the McKinley Administration until his political fences have got into very bad order. **1868** *N.Y. Herald* 4 July 4/5 The Fifth Avenue Hotel last night was . . . the grand political headquarters of the democracy of the country. **1847** ROBB *Squatter Life* 26 Some one said he would make a first rate stump speaker, and to prove his capability he commenced a political speech.

+Political capital. (See CAPITAL 2 b.)

Political influence. +The power to influence voters or to secure political offices for others. (Cf. INFLUENCE.) — **1838** [see next]. **1852** EASTMAN *Aunt Phillis's Cabin* 237 She had more political influence than any woman in our country has had, before or since. **1873** 'MARK TWAIN' & WARNER *Gilded Age* 223 The night watchmen of the public buildings and the darky boy who purifies the Department spittoons—represents Political Influence.

+Political machine. =MACHINE 1. — **1838** *N.Y. Advertiser & Exp.* 21 March 3/5 Mr. Benton's prominent head to-day was to prove that the United States Bank was a great political machine, and as such exerted great political influence. **1866** CARPENTER *At White House* 275 Mr. Lincoln . . . said with grim earnestness of tone and manner: 'Well, I cannot run the political machine; I have enough on my hands without that.' **1887** *Nation* 24 Feb. 16/3 Members [of Congress] are not chosen for what they do at Washington . . . , but on account of their management of the political machine at home.

+Political pull. Power or ability to get things done in politics; political influence. (Cf. PULL *n.* 3) — **1887** *Harper's Mag.* March 497 Political 'pulls' have lost much of their ancient power. **1895** COUES ed. Pike *Sources Miss,* I. p. lxiii, Pike was less fortunate than Lewis and Clark. The difference did not all depend upon merit; simply, he had no political 'pull.' **1918** LINCOLN *Shavings* 12 But he's been cal'latin', I cal'late, to use his political pull to get Leander exempted off.

***Politician.**

***1.** One versed in the science and art of government; a statesman. *Obs.*

1676 B. TOMPSON *Poetical Works* 99 A Funeral Tribute to the Honourable Dust of that most Charitable Christian, Unbiassed Politician [John Winthrop]. **1818** CLAY *Speeches* (1860) I. 58 That there are two classes of power in the constitution, I believe has never been controverted by an American politician.

2. One engaged in practical politics; one who makes politics his profession or livelihood. {1628–}

Various writers, such as James Bryce, have noted the disparaging tone that sometimes accompanies the use of this word by American speakers, but, as the quotations show, the word may have an uncolored or even complimentary significance. (Cf. PRACTICAL POLITICIAN.)

1796 WASHINGTON *Writings* XIII. 307 The mere Politician, equally with the pious man, ought to respect and to cherish [religion and morality]. **1807** J. ADAMS *Works* IX. 593, I do not say when I became a politician, for that I never was. **1849** *Commercial* (Wilmington, N.C.) 27 Jan. 2/2 (Th.) The Buncombe politicians—those who go for reëlection merely. **1862** O. W. NORTON *Army Lett.* 123 McClellan is a Democrat, though not a politician. **1870** *Nation* 13 Jan. 20/2 The office-seeker and his friend and patron, the politician, have come to be a byword and a shaking of the head in American society. **1883** *Harper's Mag.* Sept. 613/1 The cities . . . are still at the mercy of politicians at the Capitol. **1893** *Scribner's Mag.* June 711/1 The veteran lumberman and politician, Hon. Philetus Sawyer. **1912** NICHOLSON *Hoosier Chron.* 194 The active politicians who crossed his horizon interested Allen greatly; the rougher and more uncouth they were the more he admired them.

+3. The white-eyed vireo, *Vireo griseus.*

1844 *Nat. Hist. N.Y., Zoology* II. 122 The White-Eyed Greenlet. *Vireo noveboracensis.* . . . From its habit of using bits of newspapers in the construction of its nest, Wilson says that it is sometimes called the Politician; intending thereby a sly allusion to feathering its nest by the use of even the commonest materials. **1865** J. G. WOOD *Homes without Hands* (1866) 247 The White-Eyed Flycatcher . . . uses so much newspaper in the construction of its home, that it has gone by the name of the *Politician.* **1917** *Birds of Amer.* III. 109 White-eyed Vireo. . . . Other Names. —White-eyed Greenlet; Politician.

+Politicianer. =POLITICIAN 2. *colloq.* — **1837** NEAL *Charcoal Sk.* (1838) 137 It isn't saying much for your boss politicianer that he chose you. **1842** *Life in West* 306 The *politicianers,* as they are called here, expressed their sentiments freely. **1889** *Century Mag.* Jan. 409/1, I ain't no politicianer, an' I allays votes the Whig ticket, like my daddy did afo' me.

***Politics.**

1. The theory and practice of managing the affairs of a community, esp. as conditioned by the control of these affairs by political parties and political leaders; political life. {1693–} Cf. PRACTICAL POLITICS.

1729 FRANKLIN *Representative Selections* (1936) 138 Sometimes I propose to deliver Lectures of Morality or Philosophy, and (because I am naturally enclin'd to be meddling with Things that don't concern me) perhaps I may sometimes talk Politicks. **1840** *Diplom. Corr. Texas* I. (1908) 462 The more I mingle in Politics the more hateful they appear. **1885** CRAWFORD *Amer. Politician* 18 You always say that gentlemen should not touch anything so dirty as politics, Mrs. Wyndham. **1903** ELY *Evolution Indust. Soc.* 235 It is furthermore known that these corporations are now generally in politics. **1923** HERRICK *Lilla* 217 He thinks it might hurt his career—though that can't matter so much now that he is out of politics.

+**b.** *To play politics*, to engage in any activity for purely political purposes; to use means not always regarded as dignified or honorable in order to gain political advantage.

1907 *Springfield Republican* 13 May 6 Mr. Balfour has seized the opportunity [of the Colonial Conference] to play politics, and has apparently come out squarely in favor of trade preference. **1911** *N.Y. Ev. Post* 17 March 4 The people of the country as a whole are tired of seeing political parties trying to 'play politics.'

2. Political principles or opinions. {1769–}

1801 HAMILTON *Works* VIII. 581, I admit that his politics are tinctured with fanaticism; that he is too much in earnest in his democracy. **1898** PAGE *Red Rock* 246 Why, Cary, I even learnt my politics from you. **1905** N. DAVIS *Northerner* 52 Humph, Betty seems to have inherited old Ben Archer's politics!

Polka, *n.*[1]

1. A lively dance of Bohemian origin performed by two persons. {1844–}

1845 HONE *Diary* II. 253 Cotillons, waltzes, and polkas were danced in the house, on the lawn, and on the promenade-deck of the steamer. **1857** GUNN *N.Y. Boarding-Houses* 169 A young wife is not in the best of health or temper on the morning subsequent to six hours' active performance of polkas, cotillions, quadrilles, schottisches, etc. **1897** HOWELLS *Open-eyed Conspiracy* xv, [I] saw my charges through the dreadful half-dreams of such a state whirling in the waltz, hopping in the polka, sliding in the galop [etc.].

+**2.** (See quotation.)

1883 *Century Mag.* July 378/1 He looped [to the end of the leader], for a stretcher or tail-fly, what is known, technically, as the 'polka,' with scarlet body, red hackle, brown and white tail, and wings of the spotted feathers of the guinea-fowl.

3. Attrib. in sense 1 with *dance, gallopade, glide.*

1850 JUDD *R. Edney* 30 Their thoughts . . . fell into groups and circles and a sort of wild polka gallopade. **1851** BUSHNELL *Work & Play* (1864) 380 The apple-paring and quilting frolics, you may set down if you will, as the polka-dances and masquerades of homespun. **1885** BAYLOR *On Both Sides* 371 Mr. Ketchum . . . found all the young people assembled there practising steps, the 'two-and-a-half,' the 'polka-glide,' and other cheerful evolutions.

Polka, *n.*[2] A tight-fitting cloth or knitted jacket worn by women. In full *polka jacket.* {1844–} — **1850** *Harper's Mag.* June 143/1 Opera polkas are worn short, with wide sleeves, trimmed with large bands of ermine. **1857** STROTHER *Virginia* 102 Fanny's [doll] is to have a black velvet polka! **1860** E. COWELL *Diary* 34 There is only one girl here . . . and she is an oddity. A light colored silk skirt, and a bright scarlet Polka-jacket.

Polka, *v. intr.* To dance the polka. {1859–} — **1852** EASTMAN *Aunt Phillis's Cabin* 228 After a while we reached the dancing-room, where, in a very confined circle, a number were waltzing and Polka-ing. **1902** WISTER *Virginian* x, He polkas like a landslide.

Polka dot. [POLKA *n.*[1] 1.] One of the round dots arranged in regular patterns on textile fabrics; a pattern made of these dots. Also attrib. — **1884** BOURKE *Snake-Dance Moquis* 119 Covered with white spots which . . . resolved themselves into white arrow-heads and polka-dots, the latter arranged longitudinally, two and two. **1894** BANKS *Camp. Curiosity* 160, I bought a black and white polka-dot blouse and apron for work in the laundry. **1914** E. STEWART *Lett. Woman Homesteader* 91 Mrs. O'Shaughnessy brought a piece of crossbar with a tiny forget-me-not polka dot.

+**Polkery.** [James K. *Polk* (1795–1849), eleventh president of the United States (1845–9).] The supporters in general of James K. Polk, or their political principles and practices. *colloq. Obs.* — **1844** *N.Y. Morning Courier* 3 Dec. 2/2 The students of the University of Virginia . . . had a bonfire in glorification of Polkery, on Friday night. *Ib.*, As soon as Polkery speaks out and avows itself.

+**Polkism.** [See POLKERY.] The principles or characteristics of the political followers of James K. Polk. *colloq. Obs.* — **1844** *Lexington Observer* 2 Oct. 3/5 Van Burenism not Polkism. . . . Dr. Fairchild . . . is the second of the 'Democratic' electors of this State in 1840, who honorably refused to be sold to Polk.

+**Polkite.** [See POLKERY.] One holding political views similar to those of James K. Polk. *colloq. Obs.* — **1852** *Knickerb.* XXXIX. 281 A friend of mine heard an enthusiastic *Polkite* holding forth in a grocery concerning Clay and the Tariff.

+**Polkocracy.** =POLKERY. *Obs.* — **1845** *Xenia Torch-Light* 23 Oct. 2/3 Whig majority on joint ballot, 22! Last year the Whig majority was 16. So goes Polkocracy. *Ib.* 2/6 The township, . . . which has heretofore been locofoco, this year gives a Whig majority. What a *licking* for Polkocracy!

***Poll.**

***1.** The head of a human being; hence, a person or individual, esp. one subject to taxation.

1650 *Md. Council Proc.* III. 261 They are to bring in and pay unto me at my dwelling house at St. Maries aforsaid half a bushell of Corne per poll for every taxable person within this County. **1695** *Dedham Rec.* V. 235 A Rate made to defray the Towns debts of twelve pence on the poll. **1704** *Boston News-Letter* 17 July 2/2 An Act for Granting unto Her Majesty a Tax upon Polls and Estates of 22613 l. 10 s. **1794** *Mass. H. S. Coll.* 1 Ser. III. 200 In 1793 there were in Truro three hundred and thirty polls, which, allowing four persons to one poll, make thirteen hundred and twenty inhabitants. **1832** WILLIAMSON *Maine* II. 186 From the census of the taxable polls, the population of the whole Province, was estimated to be about 142,000 souls.

+**2.** *pl.* A place at which votes are cast in an election.

1802 *Ann. 7th Congress.* 1 Sess. 1377 The polls shall be kept open from eight o'clock in the morning till seven o'clock in the evening. **1843** 'CARLTON' *New Purchase* I. 212 A long line of *independent* voters marching past him with drum and fife to the polls. **1898** PAGE *Red Rock* 200 Most of the disfranchised whites stayed away, haughtily or sullenly, from the polls, where ballots were cast under a guard of soldiers. **1911** *Okla. Session Laws* 3 Legisl. 213 The polls shall be open at seven o'clock A.M. and closed at six o'clock P.M.

***Pollack, Pollock.** Any one of various marine fishes of the genera *Pollachius* and *Theragra*, esp. *P. virens.*
Cf. COALFISH.

1668 *Mass. Bay Rec.* IV. II. 400 No man shall henceforth kill any codfish, hake, haddock, or pollucke, to be drjed for sale, in the month of December or January. **1794** *Mass. H. S. Coll.* 1 Ser. III. 199 The sturgeon, . . . frost fish, pollock, cusk, flounder, . . . and alewife, are most of them caught in great plenty. **1832** WILLIAMSON *Maine* I. 80 Here Cod, haddock, pollock and halibut, are taken plentifully. **1880** *Harper's Mag.* Aug. 339/2 The pollock is known by his white stripes, to which the haddock has dark stripes corresponding. *a***1884** JORDAN in Goode, etc. *Fisheries* I. 232 [The Alaska pollack] is known as Pollack to those who have seen the Atlantic species. **1911** *Rep. Fisheries 1908* 313/2 Pollack (*Pollachius virens*).—A food fish of importance, found mainly off the New England coast.

Poll book. A register containing the names of those who have voted or are entitled to vote. {1681–} Also attrib. — **1840** *Niles' Nat. Reg.* 25 April 119/1 [Here] are the records or poll books of the election. **1856** *Harper's Mag.* Aug. 403/1 Of the 2905 whose names are found in the census, only 831 appear on the poll-books. **1911** *Okla. Session Laws* 3 Legisl. 82 The challenger, poll book holder and watcher shall perform duties as provided by law.

Polled Angus. A breed of black, hornless cattle developed in Scotland. Also attrib. {1842– (Low *Breeds Dom. Animals* I. 13)} — **1880** *Cimarron News & Press* 30 Sept. 2/4 Polled Angus Cattle . . . hold their own with the best families of the Shorthorn breed. **1885** *Wkly. New Mexican Rev.* 1 Jan. 4/1 W. B. Slaughter . . . has just received 100 fine Durham, Hereford and Polled Angus bulls. **1902** WISTER *Virginian* xxiii, That dead Polled Angus cow . . . was still warm when we got to her. **1913** BARNES *Western Grazing Grounds* 95 The Polled Angus, now called Aberdeen Angus, and Galloways were tried by the western rangemen.

Polling place. In an election, a place at which votes are cast. {1832–} Cf. POLL 2. — [**1841** BUCKINGHAM *America* I. 29, I was taken by several friends to the different polling places of the wards.] **1884** *Fargo (Dak.) Broadaxe* 7 April, With dodgers of warning distributed at the different polling-places. **1910** *Atlantic Mo.* Sept. 292 There is in the American nation a fixed hostility to the employment of troops at polling-places.

Polliwog, Pollywog.
'*Dial.* and *U.S.*' (*O.E.D.*).

1. A tadpole. {*polwygle, *polwigge; pollywog, 1892}

1838 HALIBURTON *Clockmaker* 2 Ser. xix. 294 Little ponds never hold big fish, there is nothing but pollywogs, tadpoles, and minims in them. **1848** N. AMES *Childe Harvard* 151, I sat me on the grassy brink . . . and thus addressed a *Polliwog.* **1878** BEADLE *Western Wilds* 262 The water . . . was green, slimy, [and] full of vile pollywogs. **1889** CUSTER *Tenting on Plains* 76 Our rain-water was . . . full of gallinippers and pollywogs.

+**2.** (See quot. 1854.) *Obs.* Also attrib.

1854 A. M. MURRAY *Lett. from U.S.* (1856) I. 197 Party terms, . . . such as Adamantines, Hard-shells, Soft-shells, Loco-focos, Rick-burners, and Pollywogs, . . . have originated in casual expressions made use of by public speakers which have happened to hit the fancy of the hearers, so that they became cant terms. **1864** SALA in *Daily Telegraph* 27 Sept., 'The slimy machinations of the pollywog politicians have usurped the government of our city,' said Poer.

+**Poll list.** A list of those eligible to vote. {1889} — **1824** *Ann. 18th Congress* 1 Sess. 947 It is by law imperatively made the duty of inspectors to destroy such double ballots as, on a comparison with the poll lists, . . . clearly appear to be fraudulent. **1848** *Knickerb.* XVIII. 520 A poll-list of the votes of both political parties was presented by Scribble. **1877** *Mich. Gen. Statutes* I. (1882) 148 It shall be the duty of the inspectors of election of each voting precinct, to cause to be numbered in figures, and in numerical order, the name of every person entered upon the poll lists required by law to be kept at such election.

***Pollock.** (See POLLACK.)

+**Poll parish.** A group of persons formally associated for ecclesiastical purposes, without regard to definite territorial limits: (see quot. 1792). So called in distinction from *territorial parish.* Now hist. — **1792** *Mass. H. S. Coll.* 1 Ser. I. 115 These [parishes] have no distinct territories, both meeting houses being in the central or compact part of the town. They are called poll parishes; each inhabitant having a right by law to belong to which parish he pleases; only signifying his choice, by leaving his name for that purpose with the town clerk. **1821** *Ib.* 2 Ser. X. 32 An unhappy controversy arose between him and Noah Sprague, Esq. which terminated in the erection of a poll parish.

Poll tax. A tax of so much per person or head, usually upon men over a certain age or between certain ages. {1694–}

1692 *Mass. Province Acts & Resolves* I. 30 All persons who through age or infirmity are unable to manage their affairs are to be free of the poll-tax, at the discretion of the selectmen. **1772** *Muddy River & Brookline Rec.* (1875) 236 Voted to abate to ye Hired men that are not Inhabitants in said Town the Sum Eight Shillings & Eight pence of their Poll Tax for the year 1772. **1804** *Steele P.* I. 443 As well almost might the legislature amuse itself and its constituents by attempting to equalize our poll tax. **1884** *Century Mag.* April 861/1 In the Southern States poll-taxes are required of all voters under the age of sixty. **1900** *Congress. Rec.* 22 Jan. 1034/2, 50,000 negroes . . . will be entitled to vote . . . provided they can pay their poll tax on or before the 1st day of March in each election year.

Polo. A game somewhat like hockey but played on horseback. {1872–} Also attrib. and transf. — **1878** *Harper's Mag.* Jan. 258/1 'Duck on the rock' . . . is far ahead of polo, pallone, lawn tenis [*sic*], or Aunt Sally. **1882** *Wheelman* I. 5 The blue polo caps . . . were remarked. **1885** *South Fla. Sentinel* (Orlando) 8 April 3/2 The first game of [roller] polo was played at the rink on Thursday evening. **1893** SANBORN *S. Calif.* 13 Every recreation of city or country is found in this little world [at Coronado Beach]: thirty billiard-tables, pool, bowling, tennis, polo, bathing. **1902** ALDRICH *Sea Turn* 18 Their athletic figures and bronzed faces told of polo and golf and sea weather.

Polo club. A group organized to play polo. — **1879** *Scribner's Mo.* June 309/2 Three summers ago, some young men in New York formed the Polo Club, and built a sumptuous house at Fordham, with grounds especially laid out for the game. **1883** *Wheelman* I. 412 Our club . . . had been a dramatic club, a sketch club, . . . a polo club [etc.].

+**Polonay.** A woman's gown made up of a bodice and a skirt looped back to show an elaborate petticoat; a polonaise. *colloq.* — **1880** *Scribner's Mo.* April 921/1, I wish I hed the pattern o' that white polonay o'hern. **1887** *Courier-Journal* 16 Jan. 14/3 A skimp and much-made over black silk was required to be made into a modern 'polonay.' **1897** STUART *Simpkinsville* 159 That black polonay she's got on, it was fo' dollars a yard.

Polygala. 1. =FLOWERING WINTERGREEN. **2.** (See quot. and cf. GAY-WINGS.) — **(1) 1814** BIGELOW *Florula Bostoniensis* 166 *Polygala paucifolia.* Few leaved Polygala. **1887** BURROUGHS in *Century Mag.* July 334, I must not forget to mention that delicate and lovely flower of May, the fringed polygala. **(2) 1833** EATON *Botany* (ed. 6) 271 *Polygala . . . polygama,* ground flower, bitter polygala.

Polygamist. The husband in a plural marriage. {1637–} Used with reference to the Mormons. (Cf. PLURAL *a.*) — **1860** *Harper's Mag.* May 833/1 The closing speech against the bill was made by Mr. Hooper, the delegate from Utah, who said that he himself was not a polygamist. **1869** BOWLES *Our New West* 254 Brigham, Jr., and Joseph A. [Young] have set up as polygamists and prophets for themselves. **1886** *Advance* XXI. 99/4 The American Bluebeard [*i.e.*, a Mormon] is quite as dangerous in his character of a disloyalist as that of a polygamist. **1900** *Congress. Rec.* 23 Jan. 1072/2 Brigham H. Roberts is, and has been for many years, a polygamist, in defiant practice of the habit and condition, with full knowledge of the laws of the land.

***Polygamy.** The practice of having plural wives. Used with reference to the Mormons. — **1851** *Harper's Mag.* June 66/2 [Joseph Smith] in his book prohibits polygamy and priestcraft. **1870** BEADLE *Utah* 225 Polygamy would be all right, Bill, if they only wouldn't pull hair. But the women will pull hair anyway you fix it. **1893** in *Congress. Rec.* 23 Jan. (1900) 1081/2 Polygamy had been forbidden by the Mormon Church. **1900** *Ib.* 3 Jan. 628/1 Mr. Martin presented the petitions . . . praying for the adoption of an amendment to the Constitution to prohibit polygamy.

***Polypod(y).** Any one of various ferns of the genus *Polypodium,* esp. *P. vulgare,* commonly growing among rocks. Also attrib. — **1643** *Rowley Rec.* 37 Certaine vplands laid out in the ffield called Pollipod ffield. **1814** BIGELOW *Florula Bostoniensis* 252 *Polypodium vulgare.* Common Polypody. . . . A handsome fern. **1821** *Mass. H. S. Coll.* 2 Ser. IX. 154 Plants, which are indigenous in the township of Middlebury, [Vermont, include] . . . *Polypodium vulgare,* Polypod.

Polytechnic, *a.* and *n.*

1. *adj.* Pertaining to various branches of the applied sciences. Usually with reference to schools. {1805–}

1865 *Ore. State Jrnl.* 23 Dec. 1/5 The museum will contain . . . a polytechnic department, for the exhibition of working models of new inventions. **1869** *Polytechnic* 25 Sept. 12/1 We have established a corps of correspondents at the various Polytechnic and Scientific Schools. **1905** *Ib.* 19 July 199/2 The past reputation of the Rensselaer Polytechnic Institute [is] a glorious heritage.

2. *n.* A polytechnic school; a school offering instruction in the applied sciences. {1881–}

1893 *Harper's Mag.* April 666/1 The four courses of instruction at the Polytechnic lead to collegiate degrees. **1894** *Polytechnic Institute Soc. of Ky. Proc. 1893* 19 He was an early and earnest friend of the Polytechnic. **1920** *Brooklyn Polytechnic Institute Cat.* 12 The location of the Polytechnic in the heart of the city affords facilities for the examination and study of engineering works, machine shops, and chemical and industrial processes.

***Pomace.** Also †**pumice.**

***1.** The mass of crushed apples produced in making cider.

1786 WASHINGTON *Diaries* III. 137 Beat about one Bushel of the Wild Crab into pumice, and sowed it in the hop Inclosure. **1857** *Ill. Agric. Soc. Trans.* III. 488 [The seeds] of the apple are usually washed out of the pomace at the cider mill, before it ferments. **1885** 'CRADDOCK' *Prophet* 297 Jacob tole him whar the cave war, an' 'bout haulin' the apples fur pomace.

+**2.** =FISH POMACE.

1861 *Maine Agric. Rep.* VI. 44 The residuum left after expressing the oil, that is the cake, pumice, or as commonly called, the *chum,* . . . contains nearly the whole fertilizing portions of the fish. **1887** GOODE, etc. *Fisheries* V. I. 26 Large quantities of fish were also pressed for the oil, the pomace being used locally as a fertilizer. **1898** *Rep. Comm. Fisheries* XXII. 479 The 'fish cuttings' and refuse fish which accumulate at the canneries are made into pomace and sold for fertilizer.

+**3.** The crushed seeds of the castor-oil plant after the oil has been extracted.

1878 *Conn. Bd. of Agric. Rep. 1877* 395 In some [fertilizers], castor pomace, leather scraps, and other cheaper materials are used. **1896** *Dept. Agric. Yrbk. 1895* 192 Castor-oil plants have been cultivated to some extent in the United States for over twenty years. . . . The pomace is considered valuable for fertilizing purposes.

***Pomatum.** A scented ointment for the hair; a pomade. — **1784** *Mass. Centinel* 2 June 4/3 Lane and Gould, have for sale, . . . hard and soft Pomatum of different scents. **1808** HITCHCOCK *Poet. Dict.* 87 And scent their sconces with pomatum. **1878** *Decorum* 316 In the way of a pomatum bear's grease is as pleasant as anything.

***Pome-citron.** The citron tree or its fruit. *Obs.* — **1699** J. DICKENSON *God's Protecting Prov.* 77 They have [in Fla.] large Orchards, in which are plenty of Oranges, Lemmons, Pome-Citrons, Lymes [etc.]. **1711** *Boston News-Letter* 12 March 2/2 Good green Tea, Pomcitron . . . ; To be Sold by Zabdiel Boylston, at his Shop at the Head of Dock-Square in Boston. **1715** *Ib.* 19 Dec. 2/2 To be sold by Mr. Zabdiel Boylston at his Apothecaries Shop in Cornhill Boston, all sorts of Fruit and Spice, fine new Pomcitron and Capers at reasonable rates.

***Pomegranate.** A tropical fruit about the size of an orange, with a reddish, leathery rind enclosing numerous seeds, having crimson, pulpy coats; a tree (*Punica granatum*) producing this fruit.

1682 ASH *Carolina* 6 Fruit Trees there are in abundance of various and excellent kinds, the Orange, Lemon, Pomegranate, Fig and Almond. **1751** WASHINGTON *Diaries* I. 24 After Dinner was the greatest Collection of Fruits I have yet seen on the Table there was Granadello the Sappadilla Pomgranate Sweet Orange Water [etc.]. **1789** MORSE *Amer. Geog.* 447 In this state [Ga.] are produced . . . oranges, figs, pomegranates, &c. **1812** STODDARD *Sk. Louisiana* 168 The Delta produces various kinds of excellent fruit; such as . . . citrons, and shaddock; . . . pomegranates and strawberries. **1858** *Texas Almanac 1859* 185 Even now figs and pomegranates grow well in some of the gardens. **1894** *Scribner's Mag.* May 603/1 There are bananas, figs, grapes, pomegranates . . . proving, in the most eloquent way, the owner's boast that anything can be produced on this rich soil [in Texas]. **1910** TOMPKINS *Mothers & Fathers* 96 Trellises of jasmine vied with scarlet heaps of pomegranate.

attrib. **1686** SEWALL *Letter-Book* I. 29 A glass of Pomgranat Juice and syrrup Cinnamon mixt for Hull.

Pomologist. One skilled in the science of fruit-growing. {1839–} — **1850** *Rep. Comm. Patents 1849: Agric.* 430 C. R. Overman, pomologist, of Canton, Ill., writes me. **1862** *Ib. 1861: Agric.* 234 One of the best pear growers of our country . . . has fruited more original seedling varieties than any other pomologist of the age.

+**Pomona wine.** (See quot. 1814.) *Obs.* — **1788** *Mass. Centinel* 18 Oct. 40/2 The drink with this should be beer, cyder, pomona wine, milk and water, or simple water. **1814** *Henderson's N.C. Almanack* 14 *Pomona Wine* is made by adding to new cider strained or scummed in the above manner, about one 5th or 6th of good spirits and keeping it until old and ripe.

Pompadour. {1752–} +A style followed by men and boys of combing the hair straight back from the forehead without a part; hair combed in this way. Also as adverb. — **1895** *Wkly. Examiner* (San Francisco) 19 Sept. 1/7 Henry Jacob has a pompadour and a profile not unlike Durrant's. **1905** *Westminster Gaz.* 7 Nov. 12/1 Because Congressman Roberts has been so successful a campaigner and still had his hair cut pompadour, it does not follow that General Bartlett can win with his hair cut banged. **1920** LEWIS *Main Street* 76 The meek ambitiousness . . . clouded like an aura his pale face, flap ears, and sandy pompadour.

+**Pompano, Pampano.** [Sp. *pámpano.*] A fish of the genus *Trachinotus* found along the Atlantic and Gulf coasts of the United States, esp. the Carolina pompano (*T. carolinus*), highly valued as a food fish.

1840 *Picayune* 1 Sept. 2/1 There was a tall dinner party at the New Brighton Hotel, Pass Christian, on Sunday. Pompanos were plentiful, and sparkling hock flew about. **1894** *Scribner's Mag.* May 603/2 The epicure from the States would go wild with the display . . . of June fish, rock, sheep's-head, pompano [caught in the Rio Grande R.]. **1906** *N.Y. Ev. Post* 2 Nov. 16 Fresh mackerel, 50 cents; pompano, 45 cents; Spanish mackerel, 45 cents. **1911** *Rep. Fisheries 1908* 313–4 Pompano, or Pampano (*Trachinotus carolinus*).—An excellent food fish, found on the Atlantic coast from Cape Cod to the Gulf, being very common on the Florida coasts. . . . Other species found on our eastern coast are the 'old-wife,' or 'gaff-topsail pompano;' the 'round pompano,' or 'Indian River permit;' the 'permit' or 'great pompano,' which is frequently not distinguished from the 'common pompano' (*T. carolinus*) by the fishermen. *attrib.* **1851** HALL *Manhattaner* 161 We forgot our military sighings in the discussion . . . of the momentous question whether it was orthodox to eat rum-omelette with 'pompano'-fish. **1881** INGERSOLL *Oyster-Industry* 247 *Pompano-Shells.*—Mollusks of the genus *Donax.* (Florida gulf.) Eaten by the pompano.

b. *California pompano,* the poppy fish (*Palometa simillima*) of the Pacific coast.

1896 JORDAN & EVERMANN *Check-List Fishes* 351 California Pompano. Pacific Coast of United States, Puget Sound to San Diego. **1911** *Rep. Fisheries 1908* 314/1.

***Pompion.** A pumpkin. *Obs.* — **1588** [see MACOCK]. **1607** in Smith *Works* I. p. xliii, He sowes his wheate, . . . tobacco, pompions [etc.]. **1678** WINTHROP in *Phil. Trans.* XII. 1067 In the vacant places between the Hills [of corn] they will Plant Squashes and Pompions; loading the Ground with as much as it will bear. **1704** S. KNIGHT *Journal* 37 But his worship (it seems) was gone into the feild, with a Brother in office, to gather in his Pompions. **1788** WASHINGTON *Diaries* III. 407 The rest of the hands were about finishing . . . pulling the large weeds from among the Pompions. **1832** *N.H. Hist. Soc. Coll.* III. 205 Melons, squashes and pompions flourish well.

+**Pompion berry.** (See quotations.) *Obs.* (Cf. HACKBERRY.) — **1833** EATON *Botany* (ed. 6) 86 *Celtis occidentalis,* nettle tree, pompion berry. **1859** BARTLETT 331 *Pompion Berry,* another name for the fruit of *Celtis occidentalis.*

+**Ponca.** An Indian of a tribe belonging to the Dhegiha group of the Siouan family; also, pl., the tribe. Also collect. and attrib. — **1858** BUCHANAN in *Pres. Mess. & P.* V. 484, I transmit herewith . . . a treaty negotiated with the Ponca tribe of Indians on the 12th of March, 1858. **1888** WHITMAN *Nov. Boughs* 409 There were Omahas, Poncas, Winnebagoes. **1910** HODGE, etc. *Amer. Indians* II. 278/2 The Ponca crossed the Missouri and went on to Little Missouri r. and the region of the Black hills.

Poncho. A piece of heavy cloth or a blanket having a slit in the center to permit its use as a cloak or raincoat. {1748–} — **1847** HENRY *Campaign Sk.* 232 The Mexicans were bundled up in their panchos [*sic*], and looked frozen to death. **1862** Moore *Rebellion Rec.* V. II. 67 The men carrying nothing but their arms, canteens, haversacks, and rubber *ponchos.* **1897** *Outing* XXX. 284/1 For active service . . . the two regiments would need to be supplied with . . . rubber blankets or 'ponchos,' which can be used as a garment or blanket. **1910** DOUGLAS ed. Parkman *Oregon Trail* 357 *Ponchos,* Garments worn by Spanish-Americans, having the shape of a blanket and with a slit for the head to pass through.

***Pond,** *n.*

***1.** A naturally formed pool or lake.

This use of *pond,* although known only locally in England, is very common in the United States, esp. in New England. The second group of examples indicates that in the early nineteenth century the use of the term with reference to large bodies of water was regarded as distinctively American.

(1) **1622** 'MOURT' *Relation* 82 Master Carver with fiue other went to the great Ponds, which seeme to be excellent fishing-places. **1696** *Providence Rec.* XIV. 292 A Pond . . . with in the Limetts of the aforesd Towne of Providence. **1700** *Conn. Rec.* IV. 340 A tract of land bounded south upon a great pond, beginning at a grey oak. **1792** IMLAY *Western Territory* 47 The country is flat, and interspersed with small lakes or ponds, occasioned by the lowness of the banks of the Ohio in this fork. **1843** TALBOT *Journals* 17 We reached a pond of the most execrable water. **1856** *Harper's Mag.* Sept. 449/2 Lake Drummond lies on the Virginia side, and . . . is a pond of eighteen or twenty miles in circuit. **1884** GOODE, etc. *Fisheries* I. 617 The Horned Dace . . . abounds in all small streams and ponds from Western Massachusetts to Nebraska and southward.

(2) **1809** KENDALL *Travels* II. 39 [There are] lakes or pools, in New England always denominated ponds. There are in the town sixty-eight of these ponds that supply fish, and that are consequently permanent bodies of water. **1818** COBBETT *Year's Residence* I. 11 There are *ponds,* as they call them here; but, in England, they would be called *lakes.* **1842** BUCKINGHAM *E. & W. States* I. 90 We passed also some pretty lakes, called here, almost invariably, ponds, though some of them were many miles in extent. **1848** COOPER *Oak Openings* I. 160 This is one of the proofs of the convertible nature of our language . . . which has changed the smaller sized 'rivers' into 'creeks,' 'lakes' into 'ponds,' 'squares' into 'parks,' public promenades on the water into 'batteries.'

2. =BIG POND. {great pond, 1641–}

1780 in W. Sargent *Loyalist Poetry* 110 Then Jack was sent across the Pond To take her in the rear, Sir. **1853** *Knickerb.* XLII. 52, 'I am going over the pond,' said he, meaning thereby the Atlantic. **1890** *Stock Grower & Farmer* 5 April 4/3 Mr. Hoyt . . . will cross the pond and spend some months in merry old England.

3. *attrib.* **a.** Designating land or pieces of land adjacent to ponds.

1649 *Essex Probate Rec.* I. 110, I give her two acres of ground during her naturall life in the pond feild next mr. Rogers. **1784** *N.H. Probate Rec.* III. 708 We have set off . . . one Acre of land in the Pond Pasture near the Hay-Market. **1883** SMITH *Geol. Survey Ala.* 248 *Pond-land soil* (exhausted), near Mulberry, Autauga county. . . . Vegetation, mostly sweet gum.

b. In the names of trees or plants that grow in or near ponds.

See also PONDBUSH, POND DOGWOOD, etc.

1884 SARGENT *Rep. Forests* 23 *Anona laurifolia.* . . . Pond apple. . . . Common and reaching its greatest development within the United States on the low islands and shores of the Everglades in the neighborhood of bay Biscayne. **1894** *Amer. Folk-Lore* VII. 90 *Cephalanthus occidentalis,* pond buttonwood, crouper-bush. Ferrisburgh, Vt. *Ib.* 103 *Agropyrum glaucum,* . . . slough-grass, pond-grass, Colorado blue-grass, blue-grass, S.W. Neb.

c. In the names of birds or classes of birds that frequent ponds.

1877 WHITMAN *Spec. Days* 100, I find here [in N.J.]: . . . Pond snipes (plenty). **1917** *Birds of Amer.* I. 112 Hooded Merganser. *Lophodytes cucullatus.* . . . [Also called] Pond, Mud, Pickax, or Summer, Sheldrake. *Ib.* 113 Wild Ducks fall naturally into the two groups known as River or Pond Ducks and Sea or Bay or Diving Ducks.

d. In special combinations.

Pond fresh, a freshet or sudden influx of water in a shallow stream caused by the opening of a milldam; *p. gate,* a gate or barrier for controlling the escape of water from a mill pond; *p. man,* (see quotation); *p. manure,* muck obtained from a pond for use as fertilizer; *p. tortoise,* (see quotation).

1865 *Atlantic Mo.* XV. 398/2 Last May, for instance, occurred a pond-fresh, long to be remembered on Oil Creek, when the stream rose with such furious rapidity that the loaded boats became unmanageable. **1850** *Knickerb.* XXXV. 23 An acquaintance of mine, one day slipped into the race while raising the pond-gate, and the swift water carried him a quarter of a mile to the floom. **1905** *Forestry Bureau Bul.* No. 61, 43 *Pond man,* one who collects logs in the mill pond and floats them to the gang-way. **1847** in Commons, etc. *Doc. Hist.* I. 195 Getting out pond manure. **1884** GOODE, etc. *Fisheries* I. 157 Three species of genus *Chrysemys,* the Pond Tortoises, inhabit the United States.

***Pond,** *v.*

1. *tr.* To obstruct (a stream) so that it forms a pond. {1742–}

1673 *Springfield Rec.* II. 119 This grant is on condition . . . it be not prejudiciall to the high way nor to any mans propriety by ponding up of water w[i]thout reasonable satisfaction. **1694** *Ib.* 283 Increase Sikes . . . did desire of the Town the stream of Pacowseek Brooke to set a Saw mil on, & the Low land for ponding. **1793** B. LINCOLN in *Mass. H. S. Coll.* 3 Ser. V. 120 Our boats and stores being all in Wood Creek, . . . and very little water running in it, being ponded above, for the use of mills.

2. *intr.* Of water: To form a pond. {1857–}

1787 WASHINGTON *Diaries* III. 274 The other hands were making drains to let of the water (wch. was ponding in wet weather). **1818** *Niles' Reg.* XV. 135/1 Through these embankments must be made culverts, or passages for the water, from the upper tides, under the canal, to prevent its ponding there.

+**Pondbush.** **1.** The spicebush, *Benzoin aestivale.* (Cf. POND SPICE 2.) **2.** =POND SPICE 1. — (1) **1859** HILLHOUSE tr. Michaux *Sylva* II. 118 [The red bay] is seen . . . round the ponds covered with the *Laurus æstivalis,* (Pond-bush.) (2) **1860** CURTIS *Woody Plants N.C.* 92 Pond Bush. (*Tetranthera geniculata,* Nees.)—Occupies small ponds in the Lower District, giving a gray smoky aspect to these localities.

+**Pond dogwood.** =BUTTONBUSH. — **1784** [see POND HOLE]. **1813** MUHLENBERG *Cat. Plants* 15 *Cephalanthus occidentalis,* Pond dogwood. **1833** EATON *Botany* (ed. 6) 87 *Cephalanthus occidentalis,* button bush, pond dog-wood. . . . Swamps.

Pondfish. {1677–} +Any one of various small sunfishes of the family Centrarchidae. (See also BLACK-EARED *a.*) — **1842** *Nat. Hist. N.Y., Zoology* IV. 31 The Common Pond Fish. *Pomotis vulgaris.* . . . This beautiful little fish has derived one of its popular names, viz. Sun-fish, from the glittering colors it displays while basking in the sun. **1883** *Nat. Museum Bul.* No. 27, 463 *Lepomis gibbosus.* . . . Common Sun-fish; . . . Moccasin; Tobacco-box; Pond-fish. . . . Eastern United States. **1903** T. H. BEAN *Fishes N.Y.* 484 The common sunfish, or sunny, pumpkin seed, bream, tobacco box, and pondfish is one of the best known fishes of the United States.

+**Pond frog.** Any one of various frogs found in or near ponds. *Obs.* — **1672** JOSSELYN *New Eng. Rarities* 38 The Indians will tell you, that up in the Country there are Pond Frogs as big as a Child of a year old. **1832**

WILLIAMSON *Maine* I. 169 Of the Frog kind are six species:—1. the Toad; 2. the pond Frog; 3. the speckled Frog; 4. the tree Toad; 5. the bull Frog; and 6. the green Frog.

+**Pond hole.** A comparatively small but deep pond. — **1784** CUTLER in *Amer. Acad. Mem.* I. 409 *Cephalanthus.* . . . Globe-Flower Shrub. Pond Dogwood. Button Bush. . . . Common in watery swamps and pond-holes. **1850** *Rep. Comm. Patents 1849: Agric.* 90 The quantity is much increased by drawing muck from the pond-holes, which are abundant. **1872** HOLMES *Poet* 94 Some of these little stagnant pond-holes are a good deal deeper than you think.

+**Pond lily.** A water lily, esp. the yellow water lily or spatterdock, *Nuphar advena.*

1748 ELIOT *Field-Husb.* i. 5 A natural Pond . . . over grown with Pond Lillies. **1778** CARVER *Travels* 520 Heart's Ease, Lilies red and yellow, Pond Lilies, Cowslips. **1817–8** EATON *Botany* (1822) 363 *Nymphaea odorata*, pond lily. . . . Var. *rosea* has the flower purplish beneath, and the hind lobes of the leaves acutish. Water. **1868** GRAY *Field Botany* 47 *Nymphæa*, Water-Lily, Pond-Lily . . . : the fruit ripens under water. **1905** WIGGIN *Rose* 46 They said I smoked right along, jest as cool an' placid as a pond-lily.

b. *Pond-lily begonia*, the shell begonia, *Begonia conchaefolia.*

1892 *Amer. Folk-Lore* V. 96 *Begonia Warscewiczii*, pond-lily begonia. Cambridge, Mass.

+**Pond moss.** Any one of various water mosses of the genus *Fontinalis.* — **1874** LONG *Wild-Fowl* 204 [They] live chiefly upon acorns, pond-moss . . . and insects. **1875** *Fur, Fin & Feather* (ed. 3) 117 Widgeon . . . feed more by night than day, chiefly upon pond-moss, the blades, roots, and seeds of various water-grasses, insects, &c.

+**Pond perch.** =FRESH-WATER SUNFISH. — **1765** ROWE *Diary* 82 We caught at least ten dozn. of Pond Perch. **1807** *Mass. H. S. Coll.* 2 Ser. III. 57 The pond perch is small and lean. **1814** MITCHILL *Fishes N.Y.* 403 Fresh-water Sunfish, or Pond Perch (*Labrus auritus*). . . . Lives in fresh water altogether, and is taken both by the hook and seine, for pastime and food. **1839** STORER *Mass. Fishes* 11 *P[omotis] vulgaris.* Fresh water Sun Fish. Pond Perch. . . . Though seldom brought to market, it is considered by many, an excellent edible fish.

+**Pond pine.** A pine (*Pinus serotina*) found in sandy, swampy regions in the southern states. — **1810** MICHAUX *Arbres* I. 17 *Pond pine* (Pin des mares), nom donné par moi à cette espèce, qui n'en a aucun dans les Etats méridionaux. **1832** BROWNE *Sylva* 241 The Pond Pine frequently recurs in the maritime parts of the Southern States. **1880** ENGELMANN *Revision of Genus Pinus* 23 *P[inus] serotina* . . . [is] apt to grow on wet places (whençe the name *Pond-pine*). **1897** SUDWORTH *Arborescent Flora* 27.

+**Pond spice. 1.** A shrub (*Litsea geniculata*) found in ponds in the pine barrens from Virginia to Florida. (Cf. PONDBUSH 2.) **2.** The spice-bush (*Benzoin aestivale*) or a related species. (Cf. PONDBUSH 1.) — **(1) 1857** GRAY *Botany* 380 *T[etranthera] geniculata.* (Pond Spice.) . . . Swamps, Virginia and southward. April. **1861** WOOD *Botany* 621 *Tetranthera.* Pond Spice. . . . *T. geniculata.* . . . In sandy swamps, borders of lagoons, Va. to Fla. **(2) 1901** MOHR *Plant Life Ala.* 519 *Benzoin.* . . . Pond Spice. . . . Eastern North America, 2 [species]. *Benzoin benzoin.* . . . Spicewood. Feverbush. . . . *Benzoin melissaefolium.*

***Pondweed.** Any one of various aquatic plants or species of plants of the genus *Potamogeton.* — **1791** MUHLENBERG *Index Florae* 162 *Potamogeton*, Pond-weed. **1814** BIGELOW *Florula Bostoniensis* 41 *Potamogeton natans.* Floating pond weed. . . . A very common species of pond weed, growing near the muddy banks of deep waters. **a1862** THOREAU *Maine Woods* 310 In the water, *Nuphar advena* (yellow pond-lily), some *potamogetons* (pond-weed), *Sagittaria variabilis* (arrow-head), *Sium lineare?* (water-parsnip). **1874** LONG *Wild-Fowl* 185 The seeds of . . . pond weeds . . . are accepted by them as food. **1901** MOHR *Plant Life Ala.* 327 *Potamogeton.* . . . Pondweed. . . . Europe, Asia, North America, 37 species; endemic in Atlantic North America, 14.

+**Pondy,** *a.* Abounding in ponds; marshy, swampy. — **1686** *Springfield Rec.* II. 266 The Revd. Mr. Pelatiah Glover desires . . . thirty or forty acres of wet Pondy Land at poor brooke. **1770** WASHINGTON *Diaries* I. 427 The Kanhawa . . . in many places very rich; in others somewhat wet and pondy. **1805** CLARK in *Lewis & C. Exped.* III. (1905) 236 A low pondey Countrey, maney places open with small ponds.

+**Pone.** *S.* [Algonquian.]

1. =CORN PONE.

[**1612** SMITH, etc. *Virginia* I. 17 Eating the broth with the bread which they call Ponap.] **1634** *Relation of Beginnings of Md.* 17 Their ordinary diet is Poane and Omine, both made of Corne, to which they adde at times, Fish, Fowle, and Venison. **1683** PENN *Let. Descr. Penna.* 5 Of words of Sweetness, *Anna*, is Mother, . . . *pone*, Bread, *metse*, eat. **1705** BEVERLEY *Virginia* IV. 55 The Bread in Gentlemen's Houses, is generally made of Wheat, but some rather choose the Pone, which is the Bread made of *Indian* Meal. **1744** *Mass. H. S. Coll.* 1 Ser. VII. 172 [The dinner] consisted of six eggs fried with six pieces of bacon, with some clammy pone or Indian bread. **1824** DODDRIDGE *Notes* 109 Jonny cake and pone were at the outset of the settlements of the country, the only forms of bread in use for breakfast and dinner. **1877** *Congress. Rec.* 19 Nov. 534/2 Is it possible that we can teach such a fastidious people [as the French] to eat mush and pone? **1916** THOBURN *Stand. Hist. Okla.* I. 262 The ripened grain, ground [by the Indians] into meal, either at the grist-mill or by means of a hand-mill, was made into the simple, nutritious and always palatable 'hoe-cake' or 'pone.'

attrib. **1884** Z. F. Smith *Kentucky* (1886) 122 There was corn bread in pone, in hoe cake, and in batter cake form. **1894** *Harper's Mag.* Sept. 628/1 His wife makes it into big rocklike 'dodgers' or pone-cakes with salt and water and 'no rising.'

2. A patty or cake of corn, or wheat, bread.

1796 LATROBE *Journal* 16 The same cask also contains cherries, a few biscuits, and pones of Indian and wheat bread. **1843** 'CARLTON' *New Purchase* I. 63 The cabin lady kept on . . . all the time cleaning and cutting up chickens, making pones [etc.]. **1865** KELLOGG *Rebel Prisons* 315 An old darkey woman came out with several 'pones' of corn-bread for sale. **1880** 'MARK TWAIN' *Tramp Abroad* 575 Mix well together, knead into the form of a 'pone.' **1903** FOX *Little Shepherd* i, No more would he take, however, than what he thought he could get along with— . . . a little bacon and a pone of corn-bread.

+**Pone bread.** Corn bread in the form of pones. (Cf. PONE 2.) — **a1785** *Md. Hist. Mag.* II. 258, I procured some milk and excellent pone bread from a hut. **1833** NEAL *Down-Easters* I. 47, I should like to know . . . what upon irth he means by . . . hoe-cakes, an pone bread. **1879** *Scribner's Mo.* June 223/1 Now that the wagons were up and 'pone' bread and beef stews had re-appeared in the menu, the Foot Cavalry, feeling its keep, waxed fat and kicked.

Pongee. A thin, soft, silk fabric; a piece or bolt of such cloth; a handkerchief or garment made of it. {1711–} Also attrib. — **1820** *Columbian Centinel* 1 Jan. 3/4 Just received and for sale by Joseph Eustis, Jr. . . . 36 yd. Pongees. **1828** ROYALL *Black Book* II. 125 The poor old man . . . [scattered] the crumbs over . . . my new pongee. **a1855** J. F. KELLY *Humors* 195 Closing his box, and wiping his face with his *pongee*, the Major continued. **a1882** in McCabe *New York* 205 There are traveling dresses in black silk, in pongee, in velvet, in piquè. **1891** 'THANET' *Otto the Knight* 234 [He was] quite a typical figure of a planter sitting there, with his dainty linen and cool pongee coat. **1923** WYATT *Invis. Gods* 111 Persons driving on the boulevard . . . often saw the artist reclining [on the porch], lightly clad in pongee pajamas.

Pontoon. 1. A flat-bottomed boat or other floating vessel used esp. as one of the supports of a temporary bridge over a stream. {1676–} +**2.** (See quotation.) — **(1) 1819** W. T. TONE *Nec. of Improving Nat. Forces* 100 Manoeuvred with their pontoons at the word of command, rapidly deploying and reploying them. **1856** WHIPPLE *Explor. Ry. Route* I. 116 Many of the holes in the canvass were mended, the air was replenished, and the pontoon again danced lightly upon the water. **1865** *Nation* I. 558 Two out of five I found right here by the pontoon. **(2)** *Forestry Bureau Bul.* No. 61, 33 *Catamaran.* A small raft carrying a windlass and grapple, used to recover sunken logs. (Gen.) . . . [Also called] pontoon (P[acific] C[oast] F[orest]).

Pontoon bridge. A bridge built upon pontoons. {1796–} — **1862** in McClellan *Own Story* 238 These vessels transported . . . pontoon bridges, telegraph materials, and the enormous quantity of equipage, etc., required for an army. **1881–5** MCCLELLAN *Ib.* 343 The army could easily have crossed the Chickahominy . . . at Coles's ferry and Barret's ferry by pontoon bridges. **1907** ANDREWS *Recoll.* 180 General Steele . . . built a pontoon bridge.

Pontoon train. *Mil.* A train of wagons carrying materials for erecting pontoon bridges: (see also first quot.). {1834–} — **1858** *New Amer. Cycl.* III. 691/2 A pontoon train contains, beside the pontoons, the oars, boat-hooks, anchors, cables, &c., . . . the balks and planks . . . to form the platform of the bridge. **1867** Goss *Soldier's Story* 18 The Williamsburg road . . . was crowded with baggage wagons, ammunition, pontoon trains, and all the indescribable material of a vast army. **1885** *Century Mag.* July 466/1 The mules belonging to an engineer ponto[o]n train were being watered at the swamp.

Pony, *n.* Also †**poney.**

1. A small horse; an Indian pony. {1659–}

1804 FESSENDEN *Orig. Poems* (1806) 33 Fops too proud to ride on ponies. **1825** *Austin P.* II. (1924) 1074 They say that you must keep their poneys for them. **1880** *Cimarron News & Press* 22 Jan. 2/1 Two men . . . with six or eight ponies, can profitably manage 500 head of cattle. **1925** TILGHMAN *Dugout* 13 The chief ordered a pony to be killed.

+**2.** A literal translation of a Latin or Greek text used by students to avoid study; any translation or key so used. *colloq.*

1827 *Harvard Reg.* Sept. 194, I'll tell you what I mean to do. Leave off my lazy habits . . . and stick to the law, Tom, without a *Poney.* **1850** *Yale Banger* 2 Dec., The tutors with ponies, their lessons were learning. The Sophs the dead body of Euclid were burning. **1876** TRIPP *Student-Life* 34 He was the only man in the class who never took advantage of translations, or 'ponies' as they call them. **1906** *Nation* 2 Aug. 95 An edict against 'cribs'—the words 'pony' and 'trot' are more common in this country—has been issued by the head master of Eton.

transf. **1869** TOURGEE *Toinette* (1881) 290 It became one of my tasks to learn and repeat her lessons to her until she partly understood them. She used to boast of me among her companions as her 'pony.'

+**3.** A small glass of beer; a small glass for other drinks. *slang.*

1849 G. G. FOSTER *N.Y. in Slices* 81 The game is kept up, mollified now and then by a choice swig at the 'poney.' **1884** (clipping from newspaper), In England a 'pony' is a £25 note; in America a glass of beer; in the dictionary a small horse. **1893** *Voice* 3 Aug., At this official 'joint' five cents purchases a very small glass of beer known as a 'pony.' **1913** London *Valley of Moon* 392 Some drink rain and some champagne Or brandy by the pony.

attrib. **1885** *Santa Fé Wkly. New Mexican* 30 July 4/2 It's the exclusive pony-glass dealers who harvest the nickles these warm days.

+**4.** In special combinations.

Pony grass, (see quotation); *p. post,* the transportation of mail by pony riders (cf. Pony express); *p. purse,* (see quot. 1859); *p. truck,* on locomotives of certain types, a two-wheeled truck under the front end.

1883 Allen *New Farm Book* 112n., The pony grass may perhaps be mentioned as one of the principal of the winter grasses in that region [near Green Bay]. **1893** Cushing *Story of P.O.* 420 Before railroads led to every part of the country the only communication was by pony post. **1859** Bartlett 332 *Pony-purse,* a subscription collected upon the spot, or from a few persons. **1865** *Harper's Mag.* Aug. 322/2 A pony purse was made up among the members to buy candles. **1883** Knight *Suppl.* 613/2 [The Mogul locomotive] is made in several sizes, but with the typical three pairs of connected drivers and a swinging pony truck in front.

+**Pony,** *v.*

1. *tr.* To pay or give *up* (something). *slang.* Also absol.

1824 *Atlantic Mag.* I. 343 (F. and H.), Every man . . . vociferously swore that he had ponied up his 'quarter.' **1848** Burton *Waggeries* 117 The celestial feminines . . . insisted upon poneying their share. **1856** *Porter's Spirit of Times* 18 Oct. 117/3 There are several little traps set for the unwary, which seldom fail to induce him to pony up. **1907** London *Road* 211 Before I got done with him he had ponied up a silver quarter.

2. *intr.* and *tr.* Of a student: To use a pony in preparing or reciting a lesson; to prepare (a lesson) with the aid of a pony. *slang.*

1851 Hall *College Words* 235 *Pony,* to use a translation. **1852** *Yale Tomahawk* May, We learn that they do not poney their lessons. **1853** *Songs of Yale* 23 If you poney he will see.

‖**b.** *tr.* To tutor (a student).

1865 *Harper's Mag.* July 213/2 A classmate, whom . . . I had ponied through term after term in Latin, Greek, and mathematics.

Pony carriage. A light carriage suitable for ponies to draw. — **1872** *Atlantic Mo.* May 539 Lucy . . . had gone to order the pony carriage, for a visit to the post office. **1888** Daly *Lottery of Love* 30 And I'll drive you to the beach in my pony-carriage. **1905** Pringle *Rice Planter* 150 I sent Chloe to Gregory in the pony carriage, and she brought back the money.

+**Pony engine.** (See quot. 1864.) — **1864** Webster 1012/1 *Pony-engine,* a locomotive used for switching cars from one track to another. [*U.S.*]. **1877** McCabe *Hist. Great Riots* 344 All was quiet there on the 23d, only an occasional pony engine being allowed to move along the track.

+**Pony express.** In 1860–1, a rapid mail service using relays of ponies from Missouri to California; a rider in this service; any mail service similarly operated. Now hist.

1860 *Jrnl. of Discourses* VIII. 240 (Th.), Are we not receiving news every few days by the Pony Express? **1880** *Harper's Mag.* March 556/1 He rode the Pony Express, springing from horse to horse, and making his hundred miles per diem. **1892** *S. Dak. Hist. Coll.* I. 66 Outside news came by pony express, at the rate of fifty cents a letter. **1900** in Handsaker *Pioneer Life* 13 No pony express, stage lines or railroads then. What a change! **1910** J. Hart *Vigilante Girl* 326 In the main street there was little sign of life except when the 'pony express' flashed through.

b. Attrib. with *line, rider, route, service.*

1869 J. R. Browne *Adv. Apache Country* 481 In May, 1862, William Talcott, an employé in the Pony Express service, went to look for his ponies in the nearest ranges of mountains. **1880** *Scribner's Mo.* July 456/1 Both offices established pony-express lines to the principal camps in the mountains. **1890** Langford *Vigilante Days* (1912) 29 Tracy & Co., of Lewiston, had a pony express route from that town to Salmon River. **1893** Majors *70 Years on Frontier* 180 'Pony Bob' was employed by Wells, Fargo & Co., as a pony express rider, in the prosecution of their transportation business.

Pony phaeton. A light phaeton, the body usually of basketwork. {1838–} — **1871** *Scribner's Mo.* II. 634 You and Frances can go in the pony-phaeton, and I will send Thomas down on foot. **1885** *Harper's Mag.* Aug. 420/2 Aunt Fanny was embracing her pretty niece on the steps of a pony-phaeton. **1887** Perry *Flock of Girls* 62 Miss Violet . . . was standing on the lawn of her summer home at Newport, waiting for her pony-phaeton.

+**Pony report.** (See quotations.) — **1877** *Harper's Mag.* Dec. 57/1 Condensed abstracts, known as 'pony' reports, are made and forwarded to smaller towns. **1904** *Bookman* Nov. 201 To another class of papers it [the Associated Press] serves 'pony' reports of from 1,000 to 5,000 words a day.

Pony rider. +A pony-express rider. — **1877** W. Wright *Big Bonanza* 118 A Pony rider . . . reported that the Piute Indians . . . had murdered two or three men. **1893** *Chicago Tribune* 24 April 3/1 The tattered outfits of pony riders, and the numberless other relics . . . not only adorn but substantiate thrilling tales. **1913** G. D. Bradley *Story of Pony Express* 58 The saddle-bag used by the pony rider for carrying mail was called a *mochila.*

Poodle dog. One of a breed of dogs, usually small, having long curly hair, and freq. kept as pets. {1839–} — **1846** *Xenia Torch-Light* 2 April 1/5 The General conferred a particular favor upon me, by entrusting to my care a *rattle snake* . . . and a *poodle dog.* **1870** 'F. Fern' *Ginger-Snaps* 204 Now, a lock of hair has some significance—at least, I hope that man thought so, who received from me a curl clipped from a poodle-dog, which at this moment may be labelled with my name. **1898** *Boston Transcript* 19 Nov. 24/4 Sometimes a poodle-dog is employed to run along the shore, off which the canvas-backs are feeding, and 'tole' them within range by exciting their curiosity.

***Pool,** *n.*[1] +(See quotation.) — **1883** *Century Mag.* July 323/1 When once a new '*pool,*' or belt of [oil-]producing territory is found, the wells multiply rapidly.

Pool, *n.*[2] {1693–}

+**1.** Pocket billiards, a form of billiards played on a pool table, usually with numbered object balls and a cue ball. {of the Eng. game, 1848–}

1864 Dick *Amer. Hoyle* (1866) 427 A man may thus win an undecided game of fifteen ball pool by scoring one in the succeeding game, provided neither of his adversaries scored any thing at all. **1900** Munn *Uncle Terry* 119, [I] maybe play pool for an hour or two with some poor devil as lonesome as I am. **1916** Wilson *Somewhere* 348 They find him . . . playing pool in a saloon over on Eighth Avenue.

attrib. **1864** Dick *Amer. Hoyle* (1866) 420 It is optional with the adversary to make the player spot his ball on the pool spot, play it over again, or take the lead himself. **1920** Lewis *Main Street* 549 [She] spied Nat Hicks in the pool-parlor, being witty over bottle-pool.

2. The collective amount wagered on a horse race or other contest. Also attrib.

1868 *N.Y. Herald* 3 July 10/1 Let us take a glance at the pool stand before the races begin. **1875** 'Mark Twain' *Sk. New & Old* 310 No pools permitted on the run of the comet—no gambling of any kind. **1887** *Advance* 13 Oct. 641/1 Why is it claimed by the advocates of horse-racing that 'books' and 'pools' are essential to its maintenance? **1907** White *Arizona Nights* 236 We had pools on the results, gave odds, made books, and kept records.

+**3.** A common fund made up of contributions by several speculators united for sharing profits and losses; the group of speculators so united.

1870 Medbery *Men Wall St.* 137 *Pool.* The stock and money contributed by a clique to carry through a corner. **1885** *Harper's Mag.* Nov. 842/2 Some relief is afforded by a 'let up,' or the withdrawal from the market of the 'clique,' or 'pool,' or combination of operators that cornered him. **1910** *N.Y. Ev. Post* 31 Jan. (Th.), I told him I thought we could cancel all the Alaska claims; that a lot of prominent people had formed a pool, and that the evidence would prove it.

+**4.** A combination entered into by previously competing business companies, esp. railroads, to avoid injurious competition and to control prices and rates.

1875 *Chicago Tribune* 2 Nov. 7/1 The great pool or combination of the roads leading from this city to the East is now in working order, the agreement for a division of earnings having been signed by all the roads, except the Erie and Chicago Line. **1881** *Chicago Times* 1 June, The marine insurance men are still striving to form a pool, and expect soon to succeed. **1886** *Harper's Mag.* Aug. 455/2 It is asserted in favor of the pools, or railway combinations, that they prevent discriminations. **1887** *Courier-Journal* 5 May 4/4 The wall-paper pool has been abandoned, and the price of that very necessary commodity promises to take a tumble. **1904** Smith *Promoters* 40 We'll make one grand consolidated trust out of all the trusts and pools and combines of the world.

attrib. **1875** *Chicago Tribune* 8 Dec. 12/5 There are about as many more which send their coal to the company's yards, . . . which are known to the trade as 'pool' collieries. **1881** *Chicago Times* 4 June, The company will now compete with the other pool lines leading eastward.

+**Pool,** *v. tr.* To place (resources) in a pool or common fund. Also fig. {1884–} — **1872** *Chicago Tribune* 8 Dec., The receipts were to be 'pooled.' **1884** *Harper's Mag.* March 573/2 Small writers who pooled their wits to make a great one. **1888** Bryce *Amer. Commw.* III. vi. c. 403 If there were two lines they might have agreed to 'pool,' as it is called, their traffic receipts and work in harmony. **1903** E. Johnson *Railway Transportation* 229 In pooling their earnings from competitive business, it is customary for each road to retain a third or a half of the revenue it derives from that traffic, and to turn the remaining two thirds or half into the pool.

+**Pool box.** In horse racing, a box into which the wagers on a certain horse are placed. Also attrib. — **1887** *Courier-Journal* 1 May 13/5, I feel worse about such a race than when I have a lot of my own money in the pool-box. **1890** *Stock Grower & Farmer* 19 July 3/3 The attractions of the race track have dwindled down to local stock, with an occasional 'ringer' to help out the pool box receipts. **1902** McFaul *Ike Glidden* 171 The vehement cheers of those about the pool box seemed more deafening as the race progressed.

+**Pool gambling.** Gambling in which the wagers are pooled, those participating sharing proportionately in the gains and losses. Also attrib. — **1882** McCabe *New York* 548 The great evil of 'pool' gambling is that it encourages young men and boys to enter into the combinations. **1886** Chadwick *Art of Pitching* 7 The professional exemplars of the game were a few of them under the influence of the pool-gambling element. *Ib.*, They prohibited pool-gambling on all professional association club grounds.

Pooling. +Of railroads: Entering into a pool or combine to avoid competition and to control rates. Also attrib. — **1884** *American* VII. 229 A pooling combination to regulate prices. **1887** *1st Rep. Interst. Commerce Comm.* 34 When the pooling system was put in force by the Trunk Line Association. **1897** *Phila. Times* 23 May, In pooling, competing lines between competing points . . . agree that they will put into a common fund [etc.]. **1903** E. JOHNSON *Railway Transportation* 287 Pooling became unlawful in 1887, and all rate agreements illegal ten years later.

+**Pool room.** A room in which bets on races, prize fights, etc., are placed; a room in which pool is played. Also attrib. — **1875** *Chicago Tribune* 12 Aug. 7/4 Fox's Pool Room. . . . Pools sold at 11 A.M. sharp. **1882** McCABE *New York* 548 The commission on the sales charged by the proprietors of the pool rooms is from three to five per cent. **1895** J. L. FORD *Lit. Shop* 150 For three hours I sat with my two Israelitish friends—a pool-room keeper and a dime-museum keeper respectively—and talked. **1897** HOWELLS *Open-eyed Conspiracy* xiv, Bookmakers from the pool-rooms took the bets of the ladies. **1924** *Scribner's Mag.* Dec. 636/2 It is far better . . . to have young men and boys working in the gymnasium . . . than to have them loafing on the street corners, or in the pool-rooms.

+**Pool seller.** One who sells chances in a betting pool. — **1887** *Advance* 13 Oct. 6/1 No less than 15 poolsellers were in the grand stand. **1892** *Pall Mall Gaz.* 4 May 5/1 The New York police have steadfastly resisted the efforts of enterprizing 'pool-sellers' to make betting on horse racing as easy for women as for men.

+**Pool selling.** The selling of chances or shares in a betting pool. — **1869** J. H. BROWNE *Great Metropolis* 573 Pool selling is managed in this way. **1875** *Chicago Tribune* 22 July 5/3 There was lively pool-selling at the outset. **1886** CHADWICK *Art of Pitching* 7 There never has been, nor is now, a greater evil connected with all American sports than the curse of pool selling. **1893** *Chicago Tribune* 20 April 4/1 The Senate today by a decisive vote referred to the Committee on Judiciary three bills on the question of pool-selling and bookmaking.

Pool table. A form of billiard table, provided with pockets, on which pool is played. {1860–} Also attrib. — **1891** C. ROBERTS *Adrift Amer.* 133 The first thing I saw when I entered was two men lying under the pool table. **1894** *Harper's Mag.* May 974/2 A few days since, at the pool table, one of the players . . . turned to the boy and said [etc.]. **1909** WASON *Happy Hawkins* 250 Big white-faced fellers with pool-table backs an' stocky legs. **1914** STEELE *Storm* 81, I saw a long, shed-like structure . . . and the green of a pool-table showing through an open door.

Poop cabin. A cabin under the poop deck of a vessel. Hence *poop-cabined* a. — **1839** *S. Lit. Messenger* V. 9/1 The packets of the 'Dramatic Line,' [from N.Y. to Liverpool] . . . have no cabin below, but a long poop cabin reaching nearly to the mainmast. **1850** COLTON *Deck & Port* 14 Another order soon came for the construction of a poop-cabin. **1887** *Century Mag.* Aug. 483/2 A plain white-painted, three-hatched, and poop-cabined canal-boat.

Poop deck. Originally the top or covering of a poop cabin; the aftermost deck on a ship. — **1838** HAWTHORNE *Notebooks* (1932) 28 This cabin is on a level with the quarter-deck, and is covered by the poop-deck. **1840** DANA *Two Years* 159 With her topmasts stayed forward, and high poop-deck, [the ship] looked like an old woman with a crippled back. **1886** *Outing* May 166/2 He accordingly had an awning spread over the poop deck.

+**Pooquaw.** [See quot. 1902.] =QUAHOG. — **1848** MITCHELL *Nantucketisms* 41 *Pooquaw*, quahog or round clam. **1902** *Amer. Folk-Lore* XV. 254 *Pooquaw*. A Nantucket name for the round clam (hard clam), known in other parts of New England as *quahog*. The word, *pooqwaw*, as the earlier form *pequaock* shows, is a corruption of the Indian word revealed in the Narragansett *poquau hock*, Massachusetts *poquahoc*. The Indian term signifies literally 'tight *or* tightly closed shell,' from *poquau*, 'thick,' *hock*, 'that which covers.' **1910** HODGE *Amer. Indians* II. 332/2 The last half of the word [*quahog*] has survived in English, while in Nantucket the first part has come down as *pooquaw*.

*Poor, *a.*

+1. Sick, unwell, poorly. *Obs.*

1758 in A. Tomlinson *Military Jrnls.* 15 Corperal Carpenter was taken poor. *Ib.* 25 This day at knight Leiut. Smith came back & very poor he was the rest of the guard returned well. **1758** S. THOMPSON *Diary* (1896) 12 Our men are very poor, and we scarce could get men for work or for guard.

2. Provided for or serving those who are without financial means. {1621–} See also POOR BOX, FARM, etc.

1829 SHERWOOD *Gaz. Georgia* (ed. 2) 51 About thirty pupils at school on the poor fund in 1828. *Ib.*, The poor school and Academy Funds drawn by this county are amalgamated. **1885** JACKSON *Zeph* ii, I think it's a shame to have any such things 's poor-pews: it's a kind o' badge o' disgrace to sit there.

+3. In plant names.

Poor toe, =FLORIDA CLOVER; *p. pine*, any one of various southern pines found in poor, sandy regions.

1889 VASEY *Agric. Grasses* 103 *Richardsonia scabra* (Mexican Clover; Spanish Clover; Florida Clover; Water Parsley; Bell-fountain; Poor Toe; Pigeon-weed, etc.). **1897** SUDWORTH *Arborescent Flora* 29 *Pinus echinata.* Shortleaf Pine. . . . Poor Pine (Fla.). . . . *Pinus glabra.* Spruce Pine. . . . Poor Pine (Fla.).

Poor box. A box, usually in a church, for contributions for the poor. {poor's box, 1621–; 1852–} — **1653** *Boston Rec.* 2, I owe unto the poore boxe. **1837** NEAL *Charcoal Sk.* (1838) 191 Now I'm as hungry as a poor box, and as thirsty as a cart load of sand. **1869** HALE *Ingham P.* 179, [I could] have as much for the poor-box, or any poor rascal that had not thriven as well as I.

Poor farm. +A farm maintained at public expense for the care of the poor. — **1859** *Yale Lit. Mag.* XXIV. 418 (Th.), [He] let both his sisters go to the 'poor-farm.' **1875** *Chicago Tribune* 4 Sept., The Board were particularly attentive and regular in their visits to the poor-farm. **1895** A. BROWN *Meadow-Grass* 168 The latter had actually taken to her bed . . . , announcing that 'she'd ruther go to the poor-farm and done with it than resk her life there another night.' **1911** *Okla. Session Laws* 3 Legisl. 31 Nothing in this act shall affect any purchase of a poor farm, or the erection of buildings thereon.

+**Poor-folksy,** *a. S.* (See quot. 1859.) *colloq.* (Cf. POOR WHITE FOLKSY.) — **1859** BARTLETT 332 *Poor Folksy.* Like, or after the fashion of, poor people. **1904** GLASGOW *Deliverance* 358, I don't see what you want to traipse around with that little poor-folksy yaller dog for.

Poorhouse. A house or institution where the destitute are maintained at public expense. {1782–}

Cf. ALMSHOUSE.

1785 *Huntington Rec.* III. 128 In case there should be an Addition Built to the Poor House said Overseers Hath liberty to take away said Poor. **1809** *Ann. 10th Congress* 2 Sess. 428 During the present inclement season, hundreds of applicants for admittance into the poor-house have been denied. **1867** 'LACKLAND' *Homespun* 259 Secretly, but continually, I rejoiced that there was still a *something* between me and the poor-house. **1891** WILKINS *New Eng. Nun* 95, I shouldn't think your beautiful sister Liddy an' her husband would let you come to the poor-house. **1911** *Okla. Session Laws* 3 Legisl. 127 The council may . . . establish and regulate hospitals, work houses and poor houses.

attrib. **1805** PARKINSON *Tour* 335 They have also some other sorts [of potatoes], for which I know no names; having taken their names from some small cause, such as the poor-house potatoes, from coming from the poor-house at Baltimore. **1845** *Xenia Torch-Light* 31 July 2/3 The Delegates . . . will meet at the town Hall in Xenia, . . . for the purpose of nominating candidates . . . for the offices of Representative in the State Legislature, Treasurer, . . . and Poor House Director.

***Poor man.** Used in the possessive in the popular names of foods and plants: (see quotations).

1855 *Chicago W. Times* 4 Oct. 4/7 We had for dinner buffalo meat, soup, pork and beans, and to crown the whole, poor man's pudding. **1868** G. G. CHANNING *Recoll. Newport* 25, I was fed entirely upon bread and milk, and whitepot, pronounced *whitpot*. This last was strictly a Rhode-Island dish, and sometimes called the 'poor man's custard.' **1883** SMITH *Geol. Survey Ala.* 521 The Florida clover, or 'poor man's trouble,' is the greatest pest in the way of a weed. **1899** *Animal & Plant Lore* 118 *Pteris aquilina*, the bracken fern, is called [in Ala.] 'poor man's soap,' because its root stocks will make a lather with water.

+**Poor man's diggings.** (See quot. 1875 and cf. DIGGING *n.* 1.) — **1875** *Chicago Tribune* 14 Oct. 7/3 If it did pay, it would be what is called poor man's diggings, for it was no place where capital could be successfully employed. **1876** *Rocky Mt. News* 31 May, In fact, in miner's parlance, they said there were no 'poor-man's diggings' in that section of the country.

+**Poor master.** One having charge of administering public relief for the poor. — **1873** *Harper's Mag.* April 799/2 The 'prisoner' said he would prefer to pay the fine; and . . . he walked over to the poor-master of the town and paid the ten dollars. **1885** *Amer. Missionary* Jan. 8 The agent was to act as a sort of national poormaster and deal out rations [to the Indians]. **1894** ROBINSON *Danvis Folks* 291 Jake's goin' tu see the s'lec'-men, er the poormaster.

+**Poor-Robin's-plantain.** Any of various herbs used for medicinal purposes, as the rattlesnake weed, *Hieracium venosum*. — **1778** CARVER *Travels* 517 *Poor Robin's Plantain* is of the same species as the last [the rattlesnake plantain], but more diminutive in every respect; it receives its name from its size, and the poor land on which it grows. **1789** *Amer. Philos. Soc.* III. p. xx, The *Hieracium venosum* . . . grows from the north to Virginia inclusively; is called *poor Robins plantain;* and said to frustrate the bite both of the rattle snake, and of his supposed precursor the *pilote-snake.* **1791** *Ib.* 115 *Hieracium Kalmii* (*Rattle-Snake-Plantain, Poor-Robin's Plantain*).

Poor's house. =POORHOUSE. *Obs.* {1870–, *Sc.*} — **1756** *Bristol* (Va.) *Vestry Bk.* 164 Ordered That Stephen Dewey . . . agree in settleing the Terms of the Poors House. **1820** FLINT *Lett. from Amer.* 192 Some paupers in a poor's house at Cincinnati refused to carry water for their own use.

+**Poor trash.** =POOR WHITE TRASH. — **1863** 'E. KIRKE' *Southern Friends* 55 The poor trash who scratched a bare subsistence from a sorry patch of beans and collards. **1867** L. BAKER *U.S. Secret Service* 207 There was the lean, lank, sallow, dirty, hang-dog specimen of the 'poor trash' of the South.

Poor valley. *S.E.* +(See quot. 1925.) Also attrib. — **1792** in *Amer. Speech* XV. 299/1 Beginning on the South Side of the poor Valley knobs. **1925** *Va. Geol. Survey Bul.* No. 25, 13 The Devonian black shale is noted for the poor quality of its soil and the valleys carved in it are almost universally known throughout the middle and southern Appalachians as 'poor valleys.'

+Poor white. An ignorant, shiftless, poverty-stricken, southern white. Usually collective or plural.

'In discriminating southern speech, it was not used to include all white persons who were poor. . . . The "poor-whites" were those who were both poor and conspicuously lacking in the common social virtues and especially fell short of the standard in certain economic qualities' (W. T. Couch, ed., *Culture in the South* 414). Cf. CLAY EATER, CRACKER[2] 1, DIRT-EATER, MEAN WHITE.

1819 FAUX *Memorable Days* 118 The poor white, or white poor, in Maryland, . . . scarcely ever work. **1833** *Md. Hist. Mag.* XIII. 338 The poor whites at the South are not as well off in their physical condition as the slaves, and hardly as respectable. **1869** TOURGEE *Toinette* (1881) 195 Perhaps I was tired of being a 'pore white.' **1884** *Century Mag.* Nov. 153 The inhabitants of the Blue Ridge and great Cumberland ranges are a very different class from the poor whites of the lowlands. **1886** EBBUTT *Emigrant Life* 120 He was an emigrant from Tennessee, a 'poor white,' a man that the niggers looked down upon. **1911** ROLT-WHEELER *Boy with Census* 47 The po' white, in a few years, is goin' to be only a memory like the backwoodsman o' the time o' Dan'l Boone.

transf. **1903** HADLEY *Freedom & Responsib.* 79 The power of making contracts belonged chiefly to freemen, . . . the planters of Rome, as distinct from the poor whites.

b. Attrib. with *class, folks, people*, etc.

1853 'P. PAXTON' *Yankee in Texas* 279 His overseer . . . [was] despised by them [the Negroes], as coming within the list of 'poor white folks,' a class they think almost beneath contempt. **1869** TOURGEE *Toinette* (1881) 421 The 'poor white' woman really loved her whom she had nursed and petted as a slave girl. **1880** *Scribner's Mo.* June 293/1 Her parents were of the 'poor white' class and lived in some remote Virginian wild. **1898** DUNBAR *Folks from Dixie* 193 So's you wouldn't be eatin' off o' none o' these poor white people 'round here. **1900** *Everybody's Mag.* II. 599/2 Ten years of growth of such plants as those in operation at Pelzer and Piedmont ought to make the terms 'poor white planter,' 'white tenant farmer,' and 'poor white trash' disappear from the Southern vocabulary.

+Poor white folksy. =POOR WHITE TRASH. Also attrib. or as adj. (Cf. POOR-FOLKSY *a.*) — **1864** *Harper's Mag.* Aug. 412/2, I wouldn't do my hair in a three strand braid on no account; it is too poor-white-folksy for me. **1868** *Putnam's Mag.* June 704 That wretched caste commonly spoken of as the 'mean whites,' the 'poor white folksy.' **1902** G. C. EGGLESTON *D. South* 240 An' a mighty poor white folksey breakfas' he'll git too.

+Poor white trash. *collect.* The poor whites of the South. Also attrib. — **1833** KEMBLE *Journal* II. 112 The slaves themselves entertain the very highest contempt for white servants, whom they designate as 'poor white trash.' **1872** POWERS *Afoot & Alone* 105 Just as long as there are negroes in the South, whether bond or free, just so long will there be a 'poor white trash.' **1895** CHAMBLISS *Diary* 83 Stealing all that the 'poh white trash' raise. **1903** J. RALPH *Making of Journalist* 130 [The people in southern Ind.] were pure Anglo-Saxons, but were of the 'poor white trash' order.

+Poorwill. [Imitative.] A bird of the western states and Mexico (*Phalaenoptilus nuttalli*), resembling the whippoorwill, but lacking one syllable of its note. — **1878** *Nat. Museum Proc.* I. 427 '*Antrostomus' nuttali.* —Poor-will. **1887** ROOSEVELT in *Century Mag.* March 664/2 At nightfall the poor-wills begin to utter their boding call from the wooded ravines . . . ; not 'whip-poor-will,' as in the East, but with two syllables only. **1901** WHITE *Claim Jumpers* 115 Outside a poor-will began to utter its weird call. **1917** *Birds of Amer.* II. 171/1, I first heard the song of the Poor-will in a wild cañon in the mountains of New Mexico.

+Pop, *n.*[1] Short for *poppa*, a variant of *papa. colloq.* (Cf. PAP.[2]) — **1840** *Knickerb.* XVI. 207 'Pop!' screamed a white-headed urchin from the house, 'Mam says supper's ready.' **1904** H. R. MARTIN *Tillie* 69 And I don't see . . . where Tillie gets her fibbin' from. Certainly not from her pop.

***Pop,** *n.*[2] *S.* **+1.** A faulty peanut, one that has no nut or fruit in it. *colloq.* **2.** A carbonated soft drink. *colloq.* {1812–} — **(1) 1869** *Rep. Comm. Agric. 1868* 221 [The pods] turn out to be nothing more than what is popularly called 'pops.' **1906** PRINGLE *Rice Planter* 388, I would feel very proud of the yield [of peanuts] if there were not so many 'pops' in them. **(2) 1882** PECK *Sunshine* 167 He would be justified in going into the hotel and ordering a bottle of pop, and then refusing to pay for it. **1893** 'THANET' *Stories* 95 Harry . . . sold 'pop,' and candy and cakes to the boys. **1920** LEWIS *Main Street* 304 Boys . . . were wolfing sandwiches, [and] drinking strawberry pop out of bottles.

***Pop,** *v.*

+1. *tr.* To heat or roast (popcorn) till it pops or bursts open.

1853 *Harper's Mag.* May 853/1 A little boy sat by the kitchen-fire, A-popping corn in the ashes. **1865** A. D. WHITNEY *Gayworthys* 36 After they had popped corn, . . . they had all gone to bed, and to sleep. **1907** *St. Nicholas* May 614/1 Grandma lives on a farm and we used to have great fun popping corn whenever we went to see her.

+2. *Baseball.* To hit (a ball) *up* so that it flies high into the air.

1868 CHADWICK *Base Ball* 43 Popping one up . . . is done when a ball is hit high into the air and so as to fall into one of the in-fielder's hands. **1888** *Outing* May 119/2 Smith popped up an easy fly-ball, which George Wright put up his hands to catch. **1912** MATHEWSON *Pitching* 204 Then Doyle popped up a weak foul behind the catcher.

+Popcorn.

1. A variety of small-eared Indian corn (*Zea mays everta*), the mature grains of which pop open when exposed to dry heat.

1851 J. F. W. JOHNSTON *Notes N. Amer.* I. 152 In some the horny part is large, as in the varieties known by the names of brown, Canada, rice, and pop corns. **1885** 'CRADDOCK' *Prophet* 248 The long yellow and red strings of pop-corn . . . apparently swayed as the light rose and fell. **1891** CHASE & CLOW *Industry* II. 85 The color of the kernels ranges from white . . . to dark red and even purple; the shape, from the tiny rice grains of the pop-corn, to the long, sharp kinds of the South and West. **1906** *Springfield W. Repub.* 5 July 14 Eight acres have been sown with green corn, and one with popcorn for popping at open fires in the winter.

2. Popcorn that has been popped.

Cf. POPPED CORN.

1871 *Amer. Naturalist* V. 171 [The mouse] had filled an over-shoe from a basket of pop-corn which had been popped and placed in the closet. **1881** McLEAN *Cape Cod Folks* 180 Grandpa . . . stumbled across the little landing of the stairway, . . . bearing with him a pan of much scorched and battered pop-corn. **1897** BRODHEAD *Bound in Shallows* 208 Crowds of half-grown boys straggled along the tiers of the grandstand, scattering pop-corn. **1916** WILSON *Somewhere* 114 They had lured the kids off with candy and popcorn.

3. *attrib.* **a.** In sense 2 with *candy, merchant, party, stand.* (See also POPCORN BALL, POPCORN MAN.) **b.** In sense 1 with *meal.*

1855 M. THOMPSON *Doesticks* 257 [He] had just pawned his coat and a spare shirt to get money to set himself up in business again, as a pop-corn merchant. **1876** INGRAM *Centennial Exp.* 758 The total amount realized from concession contracts . . . is over $290,000, divided as follows . . . : the soda water venders, $20,000; . . . proprietors of the pop-corn stands, $8,000 [etc.]. **1891** *Scribner's Mag.* Dec. 770/1 A representative from every Spanish family in New Mexico joined the annual *conducta*, . . . his burros laden with . . . coffee, popcorn-meal and dried meat. **1904** 'O. HENRY' *Heart of West* 278 The old woman has got some popcorn candy and rag dolls. **1907** *St. Nicholas* May 615/1 The idea had come to them . . . to invite them up some evening for a popcorn party.

+Popcorn ball. A ball of popped corn made to cohere by the use of syrup. — **1875** *Chicago Tribune* 21 Nov. 2/6 Each one had grown tired of jaw-breakers and popcorn balls. **1891** 'THANET' *Otto the Knight* 45 He must . . . receive a miscellaneous array of tributes . . . [including] a bowie knife and a popcorn ball. **1924** CROY *R.F.D. No. 3* 215 They were . . . leading children gnawing at popcorn balls.

+Popcorn man. A vendor of popped corn. — **1855** M. THOMPSON *Doesticks* 78 A company . . . composed entirely of . . . stage-drivers, candy-peddlers, pop-corn men. **1891** *Pomona* (Calif.) *Progress* 12 Feb. 1/1 The popcorn-man, on the corner of Main and Second streets, is the latest street-novelty.

***Pope.**

1. An effigy of the pope used in celebrations on Pope Day or Pope Night. *Obs.* {1673–} Also attrib.

Cf. POPE DAY, POPE NIGHT.

1764 ROWE *Diary* 67 The wheel of the carriage that the Pope was fixed on run over a Boy's head & he died instantly. The Sheriff, Justices . . . were ordered to destroy both So. & North End Popes. **1776** *Ib.* 114 This is a Day of Confusion in Boston occasioned by a foolish Custom of carrying about the pope & the Devill &c on a large carriage thro' the Streets of this Town. [**1823** TUDOR *Life J. Otis* 26 The town was divided into two parties, called the *North-end* and *South-end*, who had each their 'pope,' as it was called.]

+2. Short for *Pope Day* (or *Night*) *celebration. Obs.* Also attrib.

1769 *Boston Chronicle* 6–9 Nov. 361/2 Description of the Pope, 1769. **1772** *Boston Gaz.* 3 Feb. 3/2 The ingenuity of some of those nocturnal Sley-frolickers, had added the Drum and Conk-shell, or Pope-horn, to their own natural, noisy, abilities.

3. a. The nighthawk (*Chordeiles minor*), sometimes mistaken for the whippoorwill. **b.** The painted bunting, *Passerina ciris.* **c.** The Labrador auk, *Fratercula arctica.* {1674–}

1781 PETERS *Hist. Conn.* (1829) 194 The whipperwill . . . is also called the pope, by reason of its . . . bawling out *Pope!* **1890** *Cent.* 4620/3 *Pope.* . . . The painted finch, or nonpareil. . . . (Louisiana.) **1917** *Birds of Amer.* I. 18 Puffin. *Fratercula arctica arctica.* . . . [Also called] Sea Parrot; Pope; Bottle-nose. *Ib.* III. 73 Painted Bunting. . . . [Also called] Painted Finch; Pope; Nonpareil.

+4. A nickname for the Rev. Timothy Dwight (1752–1817), president of Yale College (1795–1817). *Obs.*

1800 *Aurora* (Phila.) 12 Sept. (Th.), Dr. Dwight, the President of Yale College, [is] universally called the Pope. . . . Theodore Dwight, brother of the Pope, is a candidate for Congress. *Ib.* 16 Dec. (Th.), Long Allen and the Pope of Connecticut.

+**Pope Day.** The fifth of November, celebrated as the anniversary of the Gunpowder Plot. Now hist. — **1769** Rowe *Diary* 194 Nov. 6. Monday—The People have behaved Well, being Pope Day. **1821** *Columbian Centinel* 10 Nov. 1/4 Monday last, Nov. 5th, being 'Pope Day,' brought to my recollection scenes of former days. **1823** Tudor *Life J. Otis* 25 A custom of English origin, prevailed in Boston [a1774], and occasionally in other seaports of Massachusetts, of celebrating the fifth of November, the day of the well known Gunpowder plot, which was called *Pope day*.

+**Pope Night.** The night of Nov. 5, celebrated originally as the anniversary of the Gunpowder Plot. Now hist. — **1773** Rowe *Diary* 254 Very quiet for a Pope Night. **1842** *Lowell Offering* II. 111 But the little boys of Amesbury and Salisbury, have a celebration, which, so far as I know, is peculiar to themselves. It is the observance of Pope Night, or the Fifth of November, by bonfires upon the hills, shoutings, and all such demonstrations of rejoicing. **1907** *Nation* 24 Oct. 376 Until very recently, at least, the boys of Portsmouth, N.H., have celebrated Pope Night, without knowing or caring much about Guy Fawkes and the Gunpowder Plot.

+**Popeye.** A bulging or prominent eye. {1887} — **1828** Royall *Black Book* II. 377 But the lawyer of lawyers is his partner, . . . a shrimp in size, a sallow complexion, small face, and little blue pop eye, with a great deal of white. **1885** 'Craddock' *Prophet* 45 He had wide pop-eyes, and long ears, and a rabbit-like aspect. *c***1895** Norris *Vandover* (1914) 35 Besides Turner herself there was Henrietta Vance, a stout, pretty girl, with pop eyes and a little nose.

+**Pop-eyed,** *a.* Having popeyes; open-eyed with expectation, wonder, etc. — **1824** Royall *Lett. from Ala.* 176 The first countenance I caught was Senator Foot, of Connecticut—a handsome middle-sized black pop-eyed Yankee. **1866** C. H. Smith *Bill Arp* 54 Then all the pop-eyed folks run about and say 'Booh! Booh!!' **1906** *Atlantic Mo.* Oct. 573 The class was open-mouthed, and the professor pop-eyed with wonder. **1921** Paine *Comr. Rolling Ocean* 152 They are simply pop-eyed to hear all about the speedy apprentice.

+**Popgun bill.** A contemptuous term applied originally to a number of tariff bills each of which reduced the tariff on a single commodity. — **1894** *Congress. Rec.* App. 13 Aug. 1202/1, I propose to speak generally of these four 'popgun' bills which are . . . to be fired from this House into the country to try to give some sugarcoating to the action of the House . . . on the general tariff bill. *Ib.* 5 Dec. 47/1 Bills . . . which are shortly to come before the Senate, termed, irreverently, as I submit, the 'pop-gun bills.' **1895** *Ib.* 26 Dec. 322/2 [The Republicans] run in here a popgun, horizontal, revenue-only bill.

+**Popgun wood.** *local.* =Elder[1] 1. — **1861** *Harper's Mag.* Aug. 363/2 'Sambuca' . . . was quite too learned a name, however, for the Bakertown [Conn.] boys. Their own plain elder or pop-gun wood suited their tastes better.

***Poplar.** Also †pop(e)ler.
See also Popple.

***1.** Any one of various species of tall, straight-bodied, soft-wooded trees of the genus *Populus*.

The word is applied in the U.S., not only to the many native species of *Populus*, but also to the tulip tree (see 3 below), which belongs to a different genus. (See also American black poplar, Aspen poplar, etc., and cf. American aspen, Aspen, etc.)

1671 *S.C. Hist. Soc. Coll.* V. 333 This Land bears very good . . . Ash, Hickery, Popler, Beach [etc.]. **1755** L. Evans *Anal. Map Colonies* 28 This has fine Land, wide extended Meadows, lofty Timber; . . . Walnut, Chestnut and Poplar [fitted] for domestic Services. **1789** Morse *Amer. Geog.* 404 The soil is deep and black, and the natural growth, . . . black locust, poplar, elm [etc.]. **1834** Peck *Gaz. Illinois* 114 Alexander County . . . has a fertile soil, covered with . . . oaks of various kinds, especially white oak, cypress, poplar, walnut [etc.]. **1885** *Harper's Mag.* Dec. 70/2 The virescent drab of poplar, the rosy ash of young maple, . . . find their complement here.

b. Wood or lumber obtained from such trees.

1728 *Boston Rec.* 222 No Popler, Chestnut, . . . or Ceder Shall be Corded up or Exposed to Sale. **1816** Weems *Letters* III. 153 Give me boxes made of ½ inch poplar in place of pine. **1859** Jackson in M. A. Jackson *Gen. Jackson* 130 The coffin [of John Brown] was of black walnut, enclosed in a box of poplar of the same shape as the coffin.

***2.** A particular tree of one of these species.

1677 *Topsfield Rec.* 20 That popeler is his bound corner tree. **1705** Sewall *Diary* II. 129 Sam. Robinson sets four Poplars in the Foreyard. **1780** [see Hackberry tree]. **1835** Longstreet *Georgia Scenes* 79 The classic hut occupied a lovely spot, overshadowed by majestic hickorys, towering poplars, and strong armed oaks. **1884** Harris in *Century Mag.* Nov. 120 A large poplar grew in the woods some distance from the Staley cabin.

+**3.** The American tulip tree (*Liriodendron tulipifera*) or its wood.

1709 Lawson *Carolina* 93 The Tulip-Trees . . . are, by the Planters, call'd Poplar, as nearest approaching that Wood in Grain. **1824** Blane *Excursion U.S.* 244 The Plane, with its long white arms, and the Tulip-tree (*Liriodendron tulipifera*) called by the Americans the Poplar, attain to an enormous magnitude. **1868** Gray *Field Botany* 42 *L[iriodendron] Tulipifera.* A tall, very handsome tree, in rich soil, commonest W[est], where it, or the light and soft lumber (much used in cabinet-work), is called White-wood, and even Poplar. **1888** Warner *On Horseback* 91 It was a poplar, or tulip.

4. *attrib.* **a.** Designating things made of or consisting of poplar.

1670 *Essex Inst. Coll.* XXV. 296 The land [was] bounded . . . from the poplar tree upon a straite line to a poplar stake. **1838** *S. Lit. Messenger* IV. 220/2 The maples were tapped, poplar trays were dug out in which to catch the sugar water. *Ib.* 308/1 Hurrying to a large poplar chest, she drew there from a wooden box containing powder. **1845** *Xenia Torch-Light* 23 Oct. 3/4 The undersigned . . . will offer for sale . . . a lot of seasoned White Oak, Poplar and Black Walnut Lumber. **1884** *Boston Jrnl.* 9 June, Large quantities of poplar-wood, to be used in the manufacture of excelsior, are being delivered . . . at $4.50 a cord.

b. Designating areas or places where poplar trees occur naturally or are planted for ornament.

1716 *Manchester Rec.* I. 136 It is voted to give to mr Ames chever for a paster . . . ten accors in popler plain. **1754** *Georgia Col. Rec.* VI. 433 [He] prayed for three hundred and forty Acres of Land, situated on the West end of Lands laid out for James New on Poplar Swamp. **1773** Fithian *Journal* I. 77, I shall in a proper time describe . . . the Area, Poplar-Walk, Garden, & Pasture.

c. In the names of trees that resemble or suggest poplar.

1817–8 Eaton *Botany* (1822) 203 *Betula populifolia*, white birch, poplar birch. 30 to 40 feet high.

+**Poplar borer.** The larva of a beetle (*Saperda calcarata*) injurious to poplars. (Cf. Lindentree borer.) — **1884** *Rep. Comm. Agric.* 383 The Poplar-Borer . . . has been destructive to poplar trees on the shores of Casco Bay.

+**Poplar canoe.** A dugout canoe made from the trunk of a poplar tree. — **1775** Adair *Indians* 395 The enemy now and then passed the river in their light poplar canoes. **1893** Leland *Memoirs* I. 55 An occasional Maryland dug-out or poplar canoe.

+**Poplar-leaved birch.** The American gray birch. — **1813** Muhlenberg *Cat. Plants* 88 *Betulia populifolia*, Poplar-leaved birch. **1821** Nuttall *Travels Arkansa* 178 In places near the margin of the river, [was] the poplar-leaved birch. **1897** Sudworth *Arborescent Flora* 139.

***Poplar tree.** A tree belonging to any one of various species, or one of the species, of the genus *Populus;* also, a tulip tree.

Cf. Poplar 2.

1655 *Charlestown Land Rec.* 135 A poplar tree being within 3 or 4 foot of the stake, or bound mark of this Ground. **1708** E. Cook *Sot-Weed Factor* 3 A Canoo is an Indian Boat, cut out of the body of a Popular-Tree. **1797** F. Baily *Tour* 323 Enormous poplar-trees . . . line the banks of [the Mississippi R.]. **1809** A. Henry *Travels* 128 The beaver feeds in preference on young wood of the birch, aspen, and poplar-tree. **1905** Rice *Sandy* 183 They were friendly old poplar-trees on which the bark formed itself into all sorts of curious eyes.

+**b.** *Poplar-tree borer*, =Poplar borer.

1854 Emmons *Agric. N.Y.* V. 262 (*index*), Poplartree borer, 121, 133. [*Ib.* 121: The larvae of the *Saperda calcarata* infest lombardy poplars.]

+**Poplar worm.** The larva of any one of various insects injurious to poplar trees. — **1806** *Balance* V. 228/2 The scratch from a cat poisoned by the poplar worm was equally pernicious. **1807** Irving, etc. *Salmagundi* xiii. 327 Last year the poplar worm made its appearance.

Poplin. A fabric usually of silk and worsted having a ribbed or corded surface, or a garment made of such a fabric. {1710–} Also attrib. — **1714** *Essex Inst. Coll.* XLIII. 51, 10¾ green Poppling. **1737** *N.J. Archives* XI. 517 The other lin'd with light colour'd Silk Poplin that is pretty well worn. **1767** *Essex Inst. Coll.* II. 89/1 A Poplin Gound at Eleven Shillings. **1851** *Harper's Mag.* Jan. 287/1 Plain poplins are much worn. **1905** Lincoln *Partners* 22 [She] was gowned in what the boy learned later was her 'brown poplin.'

+**Pop(l)ocracy.** [Cf. Popocrat.] The policies of the Populist party; popular rule. — **1895** *Voice* 18 July 5/3 Our fight will be for poplocracy, popular rule. **1896** *Boston Jrnl.* 24 Oct. 7/3 He is ready to support Popocracy.

‖**Poplocratic,** *a.* =Popocratic *a.* — **1895** *Voice* 18 July 5/3, I think no more significant name could be found than the Poplocratic Party.

+**Popocrat.** [*Pop*ulist, Demo*crat.*] =Populist. Obs. — **1896** *Chicago Tribune* 4 Aug. 1/1 The first returns are always in favor of the Popocrats. **1898** *Congress. Rec.* 31 Jan. 1308/2 A man is a very mean man who would try to steal a piece of five minutes, and none but a Popocrat would do it.

+**Popocratic,** *a.* [Cf. prec.] Pertaining to the Populist party (q.v.). *Obs.* — **1896** *Chicago Tribune* 4 Aug. 1/1 Incomplete returns . . . indicate Popocratic gains. **1896** *Boston Jrnl.* 9 Nov. 5/7 It would be a happiness to offer congratulations to the Hon. George Fred Williams of Dedham, Mass., if one could only be sure that the Hon. G. F. Williams of Dedham, Mass., were the biggest fool in the Popocratic collection. **1904** *Omaha Bee* 16 Aug. 4 If it is so important that the people of Nebraska move cautiously in the selection of their chief executive this year, why did not the popocratic conventions discover the fact before?

+**Pop-over.** A puff made of thin flour batter rich in eggs and cooked quickly to insure lightness and puffiness. — **1876** M. F. Henderson *Cooking* 71 Breakfast Puffs, or Pop-overs . . . may be baked in roll-pans.

1879 PHELPS *Old Maid's Paradise* (1885) 166 It was a disappointment . . . that the pop-overs were light as silver clouds. **1918** LINCOLN *Shavings* 107 Some warmed-over pop-overs . . . had 'slumped' in the cooking.

+**Popped corn.** Popcorn that has been popped by heating. — **1842** THOREAU *Journal* I. 311 The popped corn is a perfect winter flower, hinting of anemones and houstonias. **1850** S. F. COOPER *Rural Hours* 388 A great deal of popped corn is now used in New York and Philadelphia by the confectioners, who make it up into sugar-plums, like *pralines*. **1904** *Charlotte Observer* 27 May 4 Popped corn is all the rage. Everybody is eating it.

***Popper.**

+**1.** A form of firecracker.

1841 *S. Lit. Messenger* VII. 219/2 Firing poppers in the drawing-room. **1844** W. T. THOMPSON *Major Jones's Courtship* (1872) 167 Every body tuck Crismus, specially the niggers, and sich other carryins on—sich dancin and singin, and shootin poppers and sky-rackets, you never did see.

+**2.** (See quot. 1876.)

1876 KNIGHT 1764/2 *Popper*, a domestic implement for popping corn. It is usually a wire basket, which is held over the fire and shaken or revolved so as to keep the corn moving. **1893** HOWELLS *Coast of Bohemia* 207 She bought a popper and three ears of corn. **1913** EMERSON *R. Fielding at now Camp* 98 There was a basket of popcorn and several 'poppers' and the crowd of young folk were soon shelling corn and popping it.

+**3.** A whip lash. *colloq.*

1876 CROFUTT *Trans-continental Tourist* 42 How often the sharp ring of the 'popper' aroused the timid hare or graceful antelope?

***Poppet.** A small figure in human form used for purposes of witchcraft or sorcery. — **1692** in Burr *Witchcraft Cases* (1914) 163 They are their own Image without any Poppits of Wax or otherwise. **1693** C. MATHER *Wonders Invis. World* (1862) 137 They did in holes of the said old Wall, find several Poppets, made up of Rags and Hogs-bristles, with headless Pins in them.

***Popple.** Also **pop(p)ell,** etc. =POPLAR. *dial.*

'Now *dial.* and *U.S.*' (*O.E.D.*).

1670 *Rowley Rec.* 214 The most northerlie angle is a poppell. **1724** *Braintree Rec.* 151 So on to a pople, thence to another pople which we marked. **1850** S. F. COOPER *Rural Hours* 62 The poplar, or poppels as the country people call them, are already half-leaved. **1879** in Cleaveland *Hist. Bowdoin College* 91 The green youth . . . secured, it might be after much 'dickering,' popple, or bass, or white maple. **1922** A. BROWN *Old Crow* 189 He droned on about 'popple,' the local word for poplar.

b. Attrib. with *bud, grindlet, staddle*, etc.

See also POPPLE BARK.

1687 *Waterbury Prop. Rec.* 207 Ye lo land up among ye hills in a kind of a popple swamp. *Ib.*, 234 Four acers for a pauster on ye north sd of joseph gaylards four acer lot up popell grinlet. **1739** in C. O. Parmenter *Hist. Pelham, Mass.* 36 From thence it Runs E. 152 Perch to a pople stadle. **1740** *Dudley Rec.* I. 86 From thense . . . to a popel stump with a heap of stons about it. **1774** *Conn. Rec.* XIV. 366 About 1650 acres of land was antiently sequestered and set apart for their use within the following boundaries: beginning at a popple tree. **1894** ROBINSON *Danvis Folks* 8 A pa'tridge is continerly a-feedin' on . . . blackberries, popple-buds, and birch-buds.

+**Popple bark.** The bark of the poplar tree, used in tonics. *colloq.* — **1891** GARLAND *Main-travelled Roads* (1922) 292 When they's anything the matter with me, I take a lunkin' ol' swig of popple-bark and bourbon. **1894** ROBINSON *Danvis Folks* 5 You must git some popple bark, and steep up a big han'f'l on't in a gallern o' water, an' hev her drink a ha' pint on' t most any time when she's dry. **1903** W. J. LONG *Beasts of Field* 120 The beaver eats only bark—the white inner layer of 'popple' bark is his chief dainty.

***Poppy.**

***1.** Any one of various plants of the genus *Papaver*. Also with defining terms.

1709 LAWSON *Carolina* 78 Poppies in the Garden, none wild yet discover'd. **1791** MUHLENBERG *Index Florae* 171 *Papaver*, Poppy. **1832** HALE *Flora* 134 White Poppy, *Papaver somniferum*. . . . The white Poppy is preferred for making opium. **1833** EATON *Botany* (ed. 6) 250 *Papaver rheas*, wild poppy. . . . Naturalized. **1857** GRAY *Botany* 25 [The] common poppy . . . [is found] near dwellings in some places. **1910** C. HARRIS *Eve's Husband* 236 The ell took up the space I had always given to poppies in the garden. **1915** ARMSTRONG & THORNBER *Western Wild Flowers* 164 Wind Poppy. *Papaver heterophyllum*. . . . [This] smells strong of opium when picked, and its flowers glow like jewels.

+**2.** Any of various plants of the poppy family, as the California poppy (*Eschscholtzia californica*), the state flower. Also with defining term.

1845 FRÉMONT *Exped.* 249 The Californian poppy, of a rich orange color, was numerous to-day. **1861** WOOD *Botany* 223 *Meconopsis*. . . . Yellow Poppy. Herbs with a yellow juice. **1878** B. F. TAYLOR *Between Gates* 67 There are poppies scattered abroad [in Calif.]. **1893** SANBORN *S. Calif.* 84 In April I found wild peas in blossom, harebells, morning-glories, poppies, and many varieties of yellow flowers. **1898** A. M. DAVIDSON *California Plants* 110 We have turned thousands of acres of poppies into grain fields, orchards or city lots, but we still have left in our foothills and upland valleys, glowing poppy fields. **1915** ARMSTRONG & THORNBER *Western Wild Flowers* 160 [The] Matilija Poppy . . . is often considered the handsomest flower in the West.

3. Attrib. with *field, head, oil, seed.*

1684 I. MATHER *Providences* (1856) iii. 68 Being still feaverish, an emulsion, made with poppy seed, millet, carduus benedictus, &c. was made use of. **1771** *Copley-Pelham Lett.* 140 Consigned to Mr. Henry Pelham at Boston . . . 1 [lb.] 2 [oz.] fine Poppy Oil. **1888** EGGLESTON in *Century Mag.* July 352/2 He plucked and rubbed out another poppy-head. **1898** Poppy field [see 2].

+**Poppycock.** [Du. *pappekak*, lit. 'soft dung.'] Nonsense, foolish talk, bosh. *colloq.* Also attrib. — **1865** BROWNE *A. Ward; His Travels* 35 You won't be able to find such another pack of poppycock gabblers as the present Congress of the United States. **1890** *Congress. Rec.* 9 June 5857/1 All their alleged wealth and respectability is poppycock. **1898** *Ib.* 20 Dec. 344/2 There is less superstition about me than any human being that ever lived, and less reverence for mere balderdash and poppycock. **1904** *McClure's Mag.* April 591/2 'Bosh!' cried the lawyers. 'Poppycock,' the cynics sneered, and the courts rule out the cases. **1922** A. BROWN *Old Crow* 60 Letter Dick sent you is all poppycock.

+**Poppy mallow.** Any one of various American plants of the genus *Callirrhoë* having poppylike flowers. — **1870** *Amer. Naturalist* III. 162 The Poppy-mallow (*Malva Papaver*) . . . forms one of the most brilliant figures in the prairie carpet [in Kan.].

+**Pop-squirt. a.** A toy squirt. **b.** (See quot. 1877.) *slang. Obs.* — **1848** N. AMES *Childe Harvard* 92, I will . . . meet thee, and thou shalt take 'Pop-squirts,' and fight with me on 'Cambridge Lake!' **1877** BARTLETT 484 *Pop-Squirt*, an insignificant, but pretentious fellow.

***Popular.** +**1.** (See quot. 1866.) **2.** Good. — **(1) 1848** LOWELL *Biglow P.* 1 Ser. i. 13 He see a cruetin Sarjunt a struttin round as popler as a hen with 1 chicking. **1867** *Ib.* 2 Ser. p. lviii, A few phrases not in Mr. Bartlett's book which I have heard [include] . . . *Popular:* conceited. **(2) 1884** *Sat. Rev.* 8 Nov. 590/2 [In] an out-of-the-way New York restaurant, . . . a young citizen observed, 'I don't call this very popular pie.' They have come to take popular quite gravely and sincerely as a synonym for good.

+**Popular sovereignty.** Sovereignty vested in the people as a whole.

A phrase applied specifically before the Civil War to the doctrine that Congress should leave the people of the territories, as well as the states, to regulate their own domestic matters, particularly in regard to the slavery question. (Cf. NONINTERVENTION.)

1848 *Whig Almanac 1840* 4/2 If you decide that we have not governed faithfully . . . , you prove yourself an enemy of Popular Sovereignty. **1858** DOUGLAS in Logan *Great Conspiracy* 72 Let us maintain the great principles of Popular Sovereignty, of State rights and of the Federal Union as the Constitution has made it. **1884** BLAINE *20 Years of Congress* I. 140 Mr. Douglas . . . had doubtless contrived some argument or fallacy by which he could reconcile that judicial edict [the Dred Scott decision] with his doctrine of 'popular sovereignty.' **1913** A. C. COLE *Whig Party in So.* 175 The great principle of popular sovereignty . . . had until recently been considered the quintessence of Democratic orthodoxy in the South.

Popular vote. The vote of the entire electorate thought of as including all the people. — **1840** *Politician's Register* 4 All the States but South Carolina choose their Electors by a popular vote. **1888** *Amer. Almanac* 268 Popular vote for President, 1884. **1893** *Harper's Mag.* April 803/1 Complete returns from the election gave the following result of the popular vote.

***Populate,** *v.* +*intr.* To become populous. *Obs.* — **1796** MORSE *Amer. Geog.* I. 556 Its [Lancaster's] trade is already great, and must increase, in proportion as the surrounding country populates. **1802** *Ann. 7th Congress* 2 Sess. 93 They have, I admit, attempted to show . . . that our empire is large, that it is populating fast. **1817** S. BROWN *Western Gazetteer* 80 The western section will populate fastest, owing to the extent of recently purchased lands. **1831** WITHERS *Chron. Border Warfare* 290 Lots were given away by lottery to intending actual settlers . . . and in a few months Judge Symmes was able to write that 'it populates considerably.'

+**Populism.** The principles and policy of the Populist party (q.v.). — [**1893** *19th Cent.* July 139 The politicians have been compelled . . . to pander to Populism.] **1894** *Advance* 10 May, Populism seems to have got control of the Illinois Prohibitionists. **1895** ROBINSON *Men Born Equal* 44, I could not have inherited Populism because it did not exist when I was born. **1900** *Congress. Rec.* 14 Feb. 1801/2 Much has been said by Republicans about the decay and infernality of Populism. **1903** A. T. HADLEY *Freedom & Responsibility* 2 Without such unselfish purpose and adherence to tradition, monarchy degenerates into tyranny, aristocracy into oligarchy, democracy into populism.

+**Populist.** A member of the Populist party. Also transf.

1892 *Nation* 17 Nov. 367/3 The Populists will hereafter 'flock by themselves.' **1895** *Chicago Tribune* 6 April 1 What the Populists and Socialists call the capitalistic class . . . lives on its income from rents and bonds. **1898** *Kansas City Star* 21 Dec. 2/6 Rule 30 gives a member five minutes to explain his vote. The Populists propose to give him two minutes instead. **1903** *Forum* Jan. 327 As soon as hard times come again, we shall have the Populist with his wail of woe. He may not flourish under the same name—he was a Greenbacker before.

b. Attrib., passing into adj., with *convention, handbook, leader, vote.*

1893 *Chicago Tribune* 26 April 10/6 The rank and file of the 'kickers' who made up the Populist vote are not for a third party. **1898** in *Congress. Rec.* 22 Jan. (1900) 1029/2 They become like the 'organized' being referred to in the Populist Handbook. **1898** *Kansas City Star* 18 Dec. 4/3 The Populist leaders . . . put this idea into effect. **1925** BRYAN *Memoirs* 117 Because of Mr. Watson's nomination by the Populist Convention, Mr. Sewall did not take an active part in the campaign.

+**Populistic,** *a.* Of or pertaining to the Populist party (q.v.). — **1894** *Advance* 4 Oct., It was Mr. Bryan & his populistic ideas which were the bone of contention. **1896** *N.Y. Dramatic News* 18 July 5/1 Even the democrats, who accuse the show's populistic managers of piracy and other high crimes, admit that the performance . . . was funnier than anything to be found at the theatres. **1902** *Nation* 19 June 490/2 The style is dithyrambic, the sentiment is populistic, and the treatment of materials is eclectic. **1904** *Booklovers Mag.* Jan. 4 In 1900 the Populistic support showed signs of ebbing in the face of better agricultural conditions.

+**Populist party.** The popular designation for the People's party (q.v.), organized (1891) to champion the interests of workers in general and the agrarian classes in particular against the moneyed interests of the country. Now hist.

1893 *Nation* 19 Jan. 43/2 The situation results from the rise of the Populist party. **1896** BRYAN *First Battle* 320 The Democratic, Populist, and Silver parties . . . have outlined the specific legislation necessary to restore silver to its ancient position by the side of gold. **1898** *Kansas City Star* 18 Dec. 4/4 Mr. Harvey . . . can easily secure strong backing within the Populist party. **1900** *Congress. Rec.* 15 Jan. 836/2 It is one of the fundamental principles of the Populist party to abolish not only alien landlordism but all landlordism. **1916** *N.Y. Times* 22 Nov. 9/2 [Nebraska] was said to be the last State in which the Populist Party existed.

+**Populite.** =POPULIST. *Obs.* Also attrib. — **1892** *Columbus Dispatch* 1 Nov., Why did I become a Populite? Simply because I think it is the party of the future. **1898** *Congress. Rec.* 8 Feb. 1553/1 Mr. Kolb . . . has been the head and shoulders of the Populite party of Alabama since its organization.

***Porcelain.** Also †**purslin.**

***1.** A fine, thin, translucent earthenware, or an article made of this.

1690 in Earle *Colonial Days N.Y.* 104 Holland cupboard furnished with earthenware and purslin. **1740** *Ga. Col. Rec.* IV. 670 Such as shall not be inferior to Porcelain itself. **1815–16** *Niles' Reg.* IX. Suppl. 185/1 In the district of Maine there is established a manufactory of fine porcelain. **1891** EGGLESTON in *Century Mag.* Feb. 547/2 What would be said of her set of old china if she inserted such a piece of new porcelain?

b. Attrib. with *clay, dinner service, earth, stove.*

1812 *Lit. & Philos. Repertory* (Middlebury, Vt.) April 65 Porcelain earth . . . was not known [in Amer.] till about three years since, when it was discovered at Monkton, in the state of Vermont. **1842** *Nat. Hist. N.Y. Geology* II. 159 In Pownal (Vt.), . . . a large bed of porcelain clay has been found. **1856** CURTIS *Prue & I* (1892) 23 [This] little event is inharmonious with the fine porcelain dinner-service, with the fragrant wines, the glittering glass [etc.]. **1907** ANDREWS *Recoll.* 211 The rooms were heated by porcelain stoves different from anything we had ever seen.

‖**2.** (See quotation.)

1709 LAWSON *Carolina* 191 The Hair of their [the Indians'] Heads is made into a long Roll like a Horses Tail, and bound round with Ronoak or Porcelan, which is a sort of Beads they make of the Conk-Shells.

***Porch.** +A veranda.

1832 KENNEDY *Swallow Barn* II. 41 Hafen Blok was regaling his circle of auditors in the porch at Swallow Barn. *a*1861 WINTHROP *Open Air* 131 Here are roses on the porch, a piano, or at least a melodeon, by the parlor-window. **1901** WHITE *Westerners* 251 Then there was the gambler, the faro man, who sat on the hotel 'porch.' **1916** WILSON *Somewhere* 195 Wilbur Todd had once endeavoured to hold her hand out on the porch at a country-club dance.

b. Attrib. with *frock, knocker, side, step.*

1835 BIRD *Hawks* I. 37 The coach . . . stopped at the porch-step. **1859** A. CARY *Country Life* 27 Two or three times he came to the porch-side to ask whether she was any better. **1916** WILSON *Somewhere* 183 Them riding pants fixed her good in the minds of our lady porch-knockers. **1925** *Sears, Roebuck & Co. Cat.* No. 150, 28 A neat, trim gingham house or porch frock is an asset to every woman's wardrobe.

***Porcupine.** +Any rodent of the family Erethizontidae, having long sharp spines loosely attached to the skin.

1634 WOOD *New Eng. Prospect* 22 The Porcupine is a small thing not much unlike a Hedgehog. **1672** JOSSELYN *New Eng. Rarities* 17 The Porcupine in some parts of the Countrey Eastward, towards the French, are as big as an ordinary Mungrel Cur. **1743** CATESBY *Carolina* II. xxx, These Porcupines are natives of New England, and the more Northern parts of America, and are sometimes, tho' rarely, found as far South as Virginia. **1789** MORSE *Amer. Geog.* 55 Beasts of the same genus, but of different species from the eastern continent [include]: The Panther, . . . Pole Cat, Porcupine, &c. **1809** A. HENRY *Travels* 146*n.*, The animal, which, in America, is called the porcupine, is a hedge-hog, or urchin. **1873** *Winfield* (Kan.) *Courier* 13 Nov. 3/1 A porcupine was captured near Wellington, Sumner county, last week. **1907** *St. Nicholas* May 623 [Illustration reading:] Father porcupine: 'There! I left a few quills in the tires, but I guess that's the last time that sight-seeing automobile will run down a poor old porcupine like me.'

attrib. **1665** *Narragansett Hist. Reg.* III. 71 [They sent] a porcupine bagg for a present to the Queene. **1845** DE SMET *Oregon Missions* (1847) 153, I overcame natural disgust, and assisted at their porcupine feast.

Porcupine grass. {1880– in Austral.} +A tall grass (*Stipa spartea*) found chiefly in the West, the flowering glume of which has long, strong awns. — **1857** GRAY *Botany* 549 Porcupine Grass. . . . Plains and prairies, from Illinois and N. Michigan northwestward. **1884** *Amer. Naturalist* XVIII. 929 You ask whether the fruits of porcupine grass . . . are ever a source of inconvenience or injury to living animals? This may be very emphatically answered in the affirmative. **1889** VASEY *Agric. Grasses* 42 *Stipa spartea* is called porcupine grass, . . . from the long, stiff, twisted awns inclosing the seed. **1913** BARNES *Western Grazing Grounds* 43 Owing to the presence in many portions of both these desert regions [in Ariz.] of a grass known as . . . porcupine grass . . . the sharp awns . . . of which work into the wool and finally into the very skin of the animals, sheep cannot be successfully grazed.

Porcupine quill. A quill of a porcupine, +freq. used by Indians for ornamental purposes. {1664–} — **1701** WOLLEY *Journal N.Y.* (1902) 36 They have an instinct of natural Pride, which appears in their circumstantial Ornaments, many of them wearing . . . Porcupine-quills through their Noses. **1765** TIMBERLAKE *Memoirs* 39 The stem [of the peace pipe] is about three feet long, finely adorned with porcupine quills, dyed feathers, . . . and such like gaudy trifles. **1827** *Western Mo. Rev.* I. 266 Painted porcupine quills are twisted in their hair. **1881** *Harper's Mag.* April 668/1 Poor Wolf, in . . . glory of porcupine quills and eagle feathers, had put [on a] . . . pair of huge gold-bowed spectacles.

Porcupine skin. The skin of a porcupine. — **1775** CRESSWELL *Journal* 116 Went over the River and bought a Porcupine Skin of an Indian. **1809** A. HENRY *Travels* 146 The fat of our bear was melted down, and the oil filled six porcupine-skins.

Porgee. =PORGY. (Cf. POGY.) — **1849** D. WEBSTER *Private Corr.* II. 337, [I] caught some fish, namely, tautog and skippog, the same, I suppose as are called 'Porgee' in New York. **1878** *Harper's Mag.* Feb. 335/2 The porgee . . . is taken with bait in July and August. **1911** *Rep. Fisheries 1908* 318/2 The name [white perch] is also applied . . . to the porgee (*Damalichthys argyrosomus*) on the California coast.

Porgy. [Of obscure origin.] Any one of various marine fishes, esp. any one of the various North American species of sea bream of the family Sparidae. {pargie, 1725, in W. Indies; porgy, 1734, in Bahamas}

For a discussion of the word and its applications see Hodge, etc. *Amer. Indians* II. (1910) 287. (See also PORGEE, POGY, PAUGIE.)

1775 ROMANS *Nat. Hist. Florida* App. p. xix, A little to the north hereof is a small reef . . . where vast quantities of groopers, snappers, amberfish, porgys, margate-fish, rock-fish, yellow-tails, Jew-fish, &c. may be taken. **1799** ELLICOTT in Mathews *Life A. Ellicott* 186 Along the Florida Reef . . . a great abundance and variety of fish may be taken: such as . . . porgys, turbots, stingr[a]ys. **1880** *Harper's Mag.* Sept. 504/2 It quite depended upon their choice of position whether porgies should even make an appearance on the coast at all. **1911** *Rep. Fisheries 1908* 317/1 Surf-fish (*Embiotocidæ*).—A food fish found in large numbers along the Pacific coast. . . . They are also called 'pogy' and 'porgy' on the Oregon coast.

b. Attrib. with *boat, fleet, steamer.*

1880 *Harper's Mag.* Sept. 510/1 Among the rest are two of the singular 'porgy steamers' turned to mackereling. **1906** *N.Y. Ev. Post* (Sat. Suppl.) 18 Aug. 1 The 'porgy' boats, dirty, snub-nosed, and half the time unfit to be afloat on anything bigger than a pond are far removed in standing from their fellows. **1914** STEELE *Storm* 191 For the first time that season the porgie fleet moved in around Long Point.

***Pork.**

***1.** The flesh of swine, esp. in a fresh condition, to be used as food.

1654 in Hutchinson *Coll. Papers Mass. Bay* 253 Wee have at present plenty of biskett, and some porke. **1698** THOMAS *Pensilvania* 24 Their Merchandize chiefly consists in Horses, Pipe-Staves, Pork and Beef Salted and Barrelled up. **1704** S. KNIGHT *Journal* 42 Pay is Grain, Pork, Beef, &c. at the prices sett by the General Court that Year. **1785** WASHINGTON *Diaries* II. 429 Began to put up my Hogs at the different Plantations, to fatten for Porke. **1816** *Bentley Diary* IV. 407 It is but lately we have seen a neighboring marketman attentive to the article of pork & bacon. **1895** *Dept. Agric. Yrbk. 1894* 9 It is the demand for wheat, the demand for beef, the demand for pork . . . which confers a money value upon them in markets. **1907** *St. Nicholas* Oct. 1136/2 Certain kinds of pork are called 'Beechnut,' as if that name signifies especially 'good eating.'

b. Used with the names of foods often eaten with pork. See also PORK AND BEANS.

1704 S. KNIGHT *Journal* 25 Ye woman bro't in a Twisted thing like a cable, but something whiter . . . ; [which] shee serv'd in a dish of Pork and Cabage. **1871** DE VERE 339 The vessels on the great lakes always lay in a goodly store of *pork and molasses*, when they undertake a longer voyage.

+**2.** *Politics.* Federal money granted for local improvements on a political patronage basis. *colloq.*

Cf. PORK BARREL 2.

1879 *Congress. Rec.* 28 Feb. 2131/1 St. Louis is going to have some of the 'pork' indirectly; but it will not do any good. **1888** *Congress. Rec.* 7 May 3793/1 Has the 'pork' been so cunningly divided amongst the members of the House in this bill [for rivers and harbors] that its final passage is assured? **1901** *Congress. Rec.* 2 March 3527/1 Every man who has a piece of pork in the bill is expected to keep his mouth shut. **1916** *N.Y. Ev. Post* 12 May, 'Pork' has hitherto stood for just one process, the parcelling out of Federal moneys for court houses, post offices, and waterways, not by States, but by Congressional districts.

3. Attrib. and comb. in sense 1 with *cask, chopping, crackling,* etc.; in sense 2 with *bill;* in transf. sense with *pot.*

1663 *Essex Probate Rec.* I. 426, 4 tun of pork cask. **1837** IRVING *Bonneville* I. 94 *Mangeurs de lard*, or pork eaters; as such new comers are superciliously called by the veterans of the wilderness. **1838** *N.Y. Advertiser & Exp.* 7 Feb. 3/3 The 'pork season' has just closed, and . . . the number of hogs slaughtered and packed in the city, is a fraction over *one hundred and ten thousand.* **1844** M. C. HOUSTOUN *Texas* (1845) 223 Our fare was not bad of its kind, there being 'pork dodgers' and 'dough doings,' (corn bread) chicken fixings and sausages. **1850** S. WARNER *Wide, Wide World* xxv, Miss Fortune had no idea of having pork-chopping or apple-paring done there. **1869** BROWNE *Adv. Apache Country* 440 When properly prepared by a skillful cook they resemble pork 'cracklings.' **1871** STOWE *Sam Lawson* 197 Old Cesar, he used to call the pond his pork-pot. He'd jest go down and throw in a line and ketch his dinner. **1887** *Courier-Journal* 3 Feb. 7/4 The brokers who stick to the pork pit day in and day out the year round. **1901** *Congress. Rec.* 2 March 3527/1 This bill [the river and harbor bill] has become known in the most remote corners of the United States . . . as the pork bill of Congress. **1917** MCCUTCHEON *Green Fancy* 22 'Ham and eggs, pork tenderloin, country sausage, rump steak and spring chicken,' said Mr. Bacon.

+**Pork and beans.** A dish consisting of beans cooked with and flavored by pork. (Cf. BOSTON (BAKED) BEANS.) — **1775** J. ANDREWS *Letters* 95 Pork and beans one day, and beans and pork another and fish when we can catch it. **1828** *Yankee* May 147/1 A husking supper was composed of Indian puddings, and pork-and-beans baked, and a dessert of apple-pie and cheese. **1864** *Wkly. New Mexican* 27 May 1/4 Gen. Grant . . . says he can maintain his physical integrity on pork and beans, as soldiers do out West. **1891** SALA in *Times* (London) 22 Feb. 2/3 Then I heard of the contemplated establishment of a London American club, the scheme of which seemed to comprise unlimited cocktails, . . . pork and beans, soft-shell crabs [etc.].

+**Pork barrel.**

1. A barrel in which pork is kept.

1830 in Kittredge *Old Farmer* (1904) 206, I know our crops will be short next season, . . . for the brine has all leaked out of the pork barrel! **1845** COOPER *Chainbearer* vii, I hold a family to be in a desperate way, when the mother can see the bottom of the pork barrel. **1886** BURROUGHS in *Century Mag.* Sept. 787/2 When the pork-barrel was empty they *shot* [a hog].

2. *Politics.* A governmental appropriation or bill which supplies funds for local improvements designed to ingratiate Congressmen with their constituents. *colloq.* Also attrib. (Cf. PORK 2.)

1913 *Stand.* 1932/3. **1916** *N.Y. Ev. Post* 12 May, The River and Harbor bill is the pork barrel par excellence, and the rivers and harbors are manipulated by Federal machinery and not by State machinery. **1921** BRYCE *Modern Democracies* II. 63 Every year sees the distribution from what is called 'the Pork Barrel' of grants of money to particular districts or cities for so-called 'local public works.' **1924** E. C. SMITH *Dict. Amer. Politics* 328. **1924** *Lit. Digest* 15 March 10/1 Congress seems to be running wild with its 'pork-barrel' legislation.

+**Pork business.** The business of curing and marketing pork. — **1838** ELLSWORTH *Valley of Wabash* 42 The pork business, in its various branches, has furnished the commencement and completion of many splendid fortunes. **1848** *Rep. Comm. Patents 1847* 549 In consequence of the rapid development of the pork business in western states . . . we have, in another place estimated the number of swine in the United States at 35,000,000.

+**Pork City.** Cincinnati, Ohio. A nickname. (Cf. PORKOPOLIS.) — **1847** ROBB *Squatter Life* 19 A streak of *fat* was waiting for his arrival in the pork city. **1855** M. THOMPSON *Doesticks* 309 Being in the vicinity of the Pork city (where they have a ham on the top of the tallest church spire in the place, pointing with the knuckle end to Heaven,) I had an opportunity to visit a large wine-cellar.

Porker. A hog or pig, esp. one fattened for pork. {1657-} — **1643** *Md. Archives* IV. 227 The Court found for the pl[aintif]f 1560 lb. tob[acco] and a good porker. **1716** *N.C. Col. Rec.* II. 219, I have no . . . sort of provisions Save 5 young porkers which weight about Quarter each. **1835** HOFFMAN *Winter in West* II. 117 The fated porker . . . hangs a stark and naked effigy among his immolated brethren. **1894** *Harper's Mag.* July 287/2 Except for . . . the confiscation now and then of a stray chicken or young porker, they [*i.e.*, the Indians] pretty steadily observed the law of *meum* and *tuum.*

+**Porkfish.** A name used locally for any one of various American fish of the family Haemulidae. (Cf. GRUNT, HOGFISH.) — [*c*1733 CATESBY *Carolina* II. 4 The Pork Fish . . . is broad and short, and somwhat flat. . . . The Bahamians esteem this a good Fish.] **1888** GOODE *Amer. Fishes* 81 The Norfolk Hog-fish, *Pomodasys fulvomaculatus*, . . . is the . . . 'Pork-fish' and 'Whiting' at Key West. **1911** *Rep. Fisheries 1908* 310/2 *Grunt.*—The name of several small *Hæmulidæ* quite common off the south Atlantic and Gulf coasts, and sometimes found on the California coast. Different species are known as . . . 'sargo,' 'pork-fish,' etc. *Ib.* 314/1 Pork-fish (*Anisotremus virginicus*).

+**Pork house.** A business house that deals in pork. — **1837** W. JENKINS *Ohio Gaz.* 171 Eaton contains . . . four pork houses. **1875** BURNHAM *Three Years* 220 A good-looking, well-dressed 'farmer from Missouri,' came up to Cincinnati . . . looking into the great pork-houses, and inquiring the price of hams. **1890** HOWELLS *Boy's Town* 36 Cooper-shops, where the barrels were made, alternated with the pork-houses.

Pork merchant. A merchant who deals in pork. — **1838** *N.Y. Advertiser & Exp.* 7 Feb. 3/3 Cincinnati has always enjoyed a high reputation for the superior quality of the pork, lard and bacon cured by her 'Pork Merchants.' **1872** *Harper's Mag.* Feb. 369/1 A pork merchant . . . received him kindly, being used to deal with hog-drovers.

+**Porkopolis.**

1. Cincinnati, Ohio. A nickname. Now hist.

1844 *Spirit of Times* (Phila.) 27 Sept. (Th.), Parson Miller has not entirely succeeded in regenerating the morals of *Porkopolis* yet. **1859** *Ladies' Repository* Jan. 51/1 Cincinnati is . . . 'Porkopolis' from the immense quantities of pork put up every winter in this place. **1880** *Harper's Mag.* Oct. 730/2 Did we not call Cincinnati 'Porkopolis' for many years? **1887** *Courier-Journal* 15 Feb. 6/6 Perhaps he expects to get a large vote in Porkopolis.

2. Chicago, Illinois. A nickname.

1869 L. SIMONIN *Grand-Ouest* 11 Chicago . . . fait concurrence à Cincinnati, et lui dispute le surnom de *Porcopolis*, ou la ville des porcs. **1908** LORIMER *J. Spurlock* 23, I was determined that, so long as I was in Porkopolis, I should do as the porkers did.

+**Porkopolitan.** [Cf. PORKOPOLIS 1.] A member of a Cincinnati baseball team. *colloq.*[2] — **1898** *N.Y. Tribune* 28 May 5/2 The Porkopolitans won as they pleased.

+**Pork-packer.** One engaged in the business of preparing and marketing pork. {1884-} Cf. PACKER 2. — **1838** *N.Y. Advertiser & Exp.* 7 Feb. 3/3 It is due to that enterprising class of citizens, the pork packers, that the error should be corrected. **1871** GROSVENOR *Protection* 260 They are permitted . . . to force every American pork-packer to pay $110. **1892** *Courier-Journal* 4 Oct. 5/5 All the present board, including Pork-packer John Cudahy, will be re-elected without opposition. **1910** WALCOTT *Open Door* i. 8 If you don't dance to the name of Spanetti, you're a pork-packer and maybe something worse.

+**Pork-packing.** The business of dressing, curing, and marketing pork. Also attrib. — **1851** CIST *Cincinnati* 228 Pork and Beef Packing. **1868** *Ill. Agric. Soc. Trans.* VII. 475 The only reliable statement of the pork-packing of the West we have any knowledge of. **1882** *Nation* 10 Aug. 105/1 Three thousand men have been thrown out of employment in Chicago by the temporary suspension of work in a pork-packing establishment. **1902** LORIMER *Lett. Merchant* 143 You've got to eat hog, think hog, dream hog—in short go the whole hog if you're going to win out in the pork-packing business.

Pork pie. {1732-} A woman's hat resembling in shape a deep round pie. In full *pork-pie hat.* {1860-} — **1870** O. LOGAN *Before Footlights* 261 But on the cars we see all the world and his wife, and children, too, particularly his marriageable daughters, who wear pork-pie hats and flirt. **1871** *Scribner's Mo.* II. 214 The sort of hat which we believe is called pork-pie. **1884** HARTE *In Carquinez Woods* 107 The hat thus procured, a few days later, became, by the aid of a silk handkerchief and a bluejay's feather, a fascinating 'pork pie.'

+**Pork-raiser.** One who raises hogs for the market. (Cf. CATTLE RAISER.) — **1839** *Indiana H. Rep. Jrnl.* 23 Sess. 231 The scarcity of [salt] . . . is likely to prove so mischievous to the interests of our pork raisers and dealers. **1872** *Ill. Dept. Agric. Trans.* IX. 390 Dark, cold, damp Piggeries are a nuisance to any farmer or pork raiser. **1880** INGHAM *Digging Gold* 203 Is this the *honor* of Western pork-raisers?

Porkwood. {1880-} *Florida.* +=PIGEONWOOD. — **1884** SARGENT *Rep. Forests* 117 *Pisonia obtusata.* . . . Pigeon Wood. Beef Wood. Cork Wood. Pork Wood. **1897** SUDWORTH *Arborescent Flora* 192.

Porous plaster. A medicinal plaster having many small holes. {*Syd. Soc. Lex.*} — **1881** *Ore. State Jrnl.* 1 Jan. 5/5 Our enterprising druggist, F. M. Wilkins, . . . [has] secured the agency for . . . Eucalyptus Porous Plasters. **1897** *Kissimmee* (Fla.) *Valley* 9 June 3/5 A porous plaster is successful because it sticks to one thing. **1900** *Century Mag.* Feb. 644/2 We received several quite unsolicited testimonials to the merits of Perkins' Patent Porous Plaster.

***Porpoise.** Any one of various cetacean mammals, mostly marine.

See also HARBOR PORPOISE and cf. GRAMPUS.

1612 SMITH, etc. *Virginia* I. 15 Of fish we were best acquainted with Sturgeon, Grampus, Porpus, Seales, Stingraies. **1709** LAWSON *Carolina* 154 Porpoises are frequent, all over the Ocean and Rivers that are Salt; nay, we have a Fresh-Water Lake in the Great Sound of North Carolina that has Porpoises in it. **1749** HEMPSTEAD *Diary* 527 They killed a Porpoise in the River here yesterday with Guns, Canoos & boats. **1819** *Henderson's N.C. Almanack 1820* 27, I have been accustomed to see Whales, Sharks, Grampusses, Porpoises, and other large fishes. **1880** *Harper's*

Mag. Sept. 504/1 The porpoise lunges from the right; dogfish, blue-fish, black-fish, from the left. **1911** *Rep. Fisheries 1908* 314/1 Porpoise (*Phocæna communis*). . . . It is known as 'harbor porpoise,' 'herring-hog,' 'puffer,' 'snuffer,' 'snuffing pig,' etc.

***Porridge.**

***1.** A soup or stew of vegetables, meat etc.; a mush made of boiled meal or cereal.

1684 I. MATHER *Providences* (1856) v. 105 Ashes were thrown into the porridge which they had made ready for their supper, so as that they could not eat it. **1731** J. SECOMB *Father Abbey's Will* x, Some Devil's weed, And burdock seed To season well your porridge. **1883** *Harper's Mag.* Aug. 461/2 With a few drops of this extract we can give the flavor of roast fowl to this vegetable, with a few drops of that turn our porridge into turtle soup. **1896** WILKINS *Madelon* 231, I've got to make some porridge for him.

+2. Slush of ice, snow, etc. Also attrib.

1700 SEWALL *Diary* II. 26 Because of the Porrige of snow, Bearers . . . rid to the grave. **1870** *Scribner's Mo.* I. 154 While the engineers were floundering in the porridge at the west end, they wisely resolved to . . . sink a shaft to grade. **1880** *Scribner's Mag.* Jan. 331/2 The water was full of porridge-ice.

***Porridge pot.** A pot in which porridge is cooked. — **1686** *Jamaica* (L.I.) *Rec.* I. 299 The afoersd. Richard is to give his brother John . . . an iron porige pot that was Johns mothers. **1827** in Kittredge *Old Farmer* (1904) 205 Just as old Mrs. Drizzle went to take up her dinner, there came a most terrifying gust, and swoop it carried porridge pot, pork, pud'n and mother Drizzle all up chimney.

***Porringer.** A small bowl or vessel from which porridge, broth, etc., is eaten. — **1633** *N.H. Prov. Papers* I. 77, 2 porringers. **1704** SEWALL *Diary* II. 116 Drunk a porringer of Sage Tea, upon which I sweat very kindly. **1842** *Knickerb.* XX. 350 The tin porringer dangling on a corner of the well-top seems to beckon to the dusty traveler to stay and quench his thirst. **1910** TOMPKINS *Mothers & Fathers* 84, I bought the baby a silver porringer.

***Port.** A place to which vessels come to load and unload; a harbor or haven.

1632 *Va. Statutes at Large* I. 163 Every shipp arivinge in this colony from England . . . shall . . . sayle upp to the porte of James Citty. **1636** *Plymouth Laws* 36 All that tract of land southward to the southerne ocean with all and singular lands rivers havens waters creeks ports fishings fowlings &c. **1696** *Conn. Rec.* IV. 160 The master of the vessel . . . will land and deliver it in some port in this Colonie, according as by the said act. **1735** *Boston Rec.* 120 Our whole Trade to the West Indies and back to this Port is reduced to so low an Ebb. **1790** *Ann. 1st Congress* II. 1817 Messrs. Lawrence, Seney [etc.] . . . were appointed a committee to bring in a bill to establish health offices in the principal ports of the Union. **1848** POLK in *Pres. Mess. & P.* IV. 587 The possession of the ports of San Diego and Monterey . . . will enable the United States to command the . . . commerce of the Pacific. **1882** MCCABE *New York* 302 The business of the port of New York is immense.

attrib. **1817** *Ann. 14th Congress* 2 Sess. 779 Boston must be the victim when anything like a port bill is in agitation. **1841** DANA *Two Years* 236 [We] engaged in the usual port duties of landing cargo, etc.

b. *Port of entry*, a port at which there is a customhouse for the entry of goods.

1840 *Niles' Nat. Reg.* 23 May 188/1 Mr. King . . . reported a bill for the establishment of ports of entry in the states of Missouri and Arkansas. **1861** COX *8 Yrs. in Congress* 192 Repeal here every law making ports of entry at the recusant cities or towns. **1873** COZZENS *Marvellous Country* 43 [Arizona's] complete isolation . . . with no port of entry, nor communication with the Gulf of California.

Portable soup. Soup in a congealed state so as to be more conveniently carried. {1758–} — **1800** *Columbian Centinel* 22 Jan. 3/3 He has . . . Gold Beater's Skin; Portable Soup; Liquid Powder [etc.]. **1807** GASS *Journal* 136 So Captain Lewis gave out some portable soup, which he had along, to be used in case of necessity. **1836** IRVING *Astoria* II. 33 [They had] about five pounds of portable soup, and a sufficient quantity of dried meat to allow each man a pittance of five pounds and a quarter.

Portage, *n.

+1. The carrying or transporting of canoes, goods, etc., overland from one stretch or body of navigable water to another, usually around rapids, falls, etc. {1857–}

Cf. CARRY *n.* 1.

1698 [see sense b]. **1759** *New Amer. Mag.* Aug. 577 The portage by land is both fatiguing and dangerous. **1790** PUTNAM in Cutler *Life & Corr.* II. 380 From Lake Erie, by a very easy navigation and short portages, an army may descend by the Alleghany, . . . or the Wabash rivers, into any part of the Ohio country. **1812** *Niles' Reg.* III. 53/1 A portage of 50 miles would then bring him to Bear creek. **1858** THOREAU *Maine Woods* 115 We were just completing our portage . . . when Joe exclaimed from the stream that he had killed a moose. **1921** *Outing* Feb. 212/3 A portage . . . would bring us to the shores of another lake.

+b. *To make a portage*, to carry or transport canoes, goods, etc., over a carrying place.

1698 tr. Hennepin *New Discov. Amer.* I. 74 [We] brought up our Bark to the great Rock of Niagara, . . . where we were oblig'd to make our Portage; that is, to carry over-land our Canow's and Provisions, and other Things, above the great Fall of the River, which interrupts the Navigation. **1755** L. EVANS *Anal. Map Colonies* 18 You are obliged to make a Portage up three pretty sharp Hills about eight Miles. **1805** LEWIS in *L. & Clark Exped.* II. (1904) 153 He might be enabled to give Capt. Clark an idea of the point at which it would be best to halt to make our portage. **1844** LEE & FROST *Oregon* 40 After making the portage they proceeded up the river. **1897** *Outing* XXX. 583/2 We camped at night, made our portages, and traveled rapidly.

+2. A land route or passageway along which canoes and goods are carried around obstructions in a stream or between navigable bodies of water.

Cf. CARRYING PLACE.

1698 tr. Hennepin *New Discov. Amer.* I. 75 The Portage was two Leagues long. **1755** L. EVANS *Anal. Map Colonies* 23 From Bohemia, where large Flats or small Shallops can come, there is a Portage of eight Miles to Cantwell's Bridge. **1792** *Ann. 2d Congress* 1038 The part of this territory occupied by Indians is north and west of the following lines, . . . beginning at the mouth of the Cuyahoga, and running up the river to the portage between that and the Tuscaroras branch of the Muskingum. **1887** TOURGEE *Button's Inn* 6 The portage left the bed of the stream, crept up the bank and skirted the edge of the cañon. **1903** WHITE *Forest* 6, I once met an outfit in the North Woods, plodding diligently across portage.

3. The postage or cost of carriage of letters sent by post. *Obs.* {1631}

1708 *Boston News-Letter* 27 Dec. 2/2 The Letter was not Sign'd nor the Portage paid. **1714** *Ib.* 15 March 2/2 Saturday last . . . was Quarter Day at Boston for Paying the Portage of Letters. **1715** *Ib.* 3 Jan. 2/2 All Persons that send Letters from Boston to Connecticut, are hereby Notified, first to Pay the Portage of the same.

+4. Attrib. in senses 1 and 2 with *collar, road, route, track.*

1817 S. BROWN *Western Gaz.* 262 In wet seasons the portage road is very bad. **1853** BOND *Minnesota* 240 Voyageurs . . . use the 'portage-collar,' which is a strap passing around the forehead, attached at each end to the burden . . . to be carried, which is also partly supported upon the back. **1887** TOURGEE *Button's Inn* 8 To have cut a wagon-road along the old portage route . . . would have required the services . . . of at least a thousand axemen. **1894** WINSOR *Cartier to Frontenac* 258 The party began to carry the material . . . along the portage track for twelve miles.

Portage, *v. tr.* To carry (boats, goods, etc.) over a portage; to avoid (falls or rapids) by making a portage. {1864–} — **1871** HUYSHE *Red River Exped.* 104*n.*, Boats, provisions, &c. &c., have to be 'portaged' or carried over this break [in the navigation]. **1880** *Harper's Mag.* Aug. 397 The canoe . . . must be light, that she may be easily portaged. **1888** *Century Mag.* Jan. 415/2 We portaged the boats around the falls the next day. **1896** *Harper's Mag.* June 119/1 All the chutes of these big rivers have to be portaged.

Portage bill. A list of the names of the crew of a ship with an indication of the amount owed each for wages, allowances, etc. {1795–} Now hist. (Cf. PORTLEDGE BILL.) — **1743** Weeden *Econ. Hist. New Eng.* II. 469*n.*, A Portage bill of mens Names and Wages due on board the Snow Jolly Bachelor. **1776** *R.I. Col. Rec.* VII. 553 Cargo, outfits and portage bill, of the schooner Eagle, by Joseph Stanton. **1807** *State P.* (1819) VI. 31 The following is extracted from the portage bill of the ship Caledonia.

+Portage path. A path along which boats and goods are portaged. — **1812** MELISH *Travels* II. 259 Hitherto I had seen nothing but *log houses* since I left Canton. . . . [I] was advised to go by the portage path. **1843** *Amer. Pioneer* II. 24 Its eastern limit was defined to be the course of the Cuyahoga, the Muskingum, and the old portage path.

+Portal. *S.W.* [A new borrowing from Sp.] A porch or veranda. — **1849** *31st Congress 1 Sess.* Sen. Ex. Doc. No. 64, 134 There are two or three buildings in the town with extensive fronts and *portales*, (porches,) which look, for this country, very well. **1872** *Republican Rev.* 3 Feb. 1/4 The pillars to the rear portal next to the *placita* [of the Pallacio] falling over and not more than half of them standing. **1910** J. HART *Vigilante Girl* 195 With the assistance of some *mozos*, Arthur's chair was taken to the *portal*.

***Porter.**[1]

***1.** Originally one employed to carry burdens or transport goods; now usually one who carries baggage at a railroad station or elsewhere.

1654 JOHNSON *Wonder-w. Prov.* 114 Having dispatch'd the Porters, they found the winding way in without a Guide. **1723** *Boston Rec.* 175 No Indian Negro or Molatto Bond or free Shal presume to work as a Porter in or about the Town. **1790** *Phila. Ordinances* (1812) 124 All porters . . . shall walk by the head of the shaft or wheel horse . . . within reach of the . . . halter of the said horse. **1835** HOFFMAN *Winter in West* I. 77 At the call of the porter I rose and descended to the bar-room. **1879** STOCKTON *Rudder Grange* vii, My package was wheeled to the express car, and two porters . . . hoisted it into the car. **1920** COOPER *Under Big Top* 139 A wandering porter suddenly would be frightened by the sight of two glaring green eyes.

+b. In certain railroad cars, esp. Pullmans, an attendant who waits upon passengers, makes up berths, etc.

1877 ROE *Army Lett.* 164 The porter in our car caught Hal, but Ryan told him to let the dog go. **1883** RITTENHOUSE *Maud* 188 He took us to the dressing-room in the sleeper, and the porter brought us towels. **1884** *Century Mag.* Oct. 944/1 The employments in which tips are regularly accepted, as those of servants in hotels and restaurants, porters, and stewards on ships and steam-boats and sleeping-cars, are almost wholly monopolized by foreigners and negroes. **1907** LONDON *Road* 2, I reached the millionaire at the same instant that the porter reached me.

+2. One who assists in carrying the coffin at a funeral. *Obs.*
1702 *Boston Rec.* 25 It being proposed . . . that there be a Moderation in the . . . wages of Porters for carrying the corps. **1774** CUTLER in *Life & Corr.* I. 45 Eight ministers were appointed as pall-bearers, and four under-bearers, or porters. **1780** *Essex Inst. Coll.* XV. 69 Elisabeth ye Daughter of Captn. Benja[min] West buryed with porters and paull holders. **1882** MCCABE *New York* 233 Porters to carry the coffin from the house to the hearse are paid $1.50 each.

3. A dark-colored malt beer. {1727-}
1769 ROWE *Diary* 191, The Merchants . . . gave me a pretty tight Lecture abo. the Importation of some Porter on board Jarvis. **1797** *Ann. 4th Congress* 2 Sess. 2031 There ought to be laid an additional duty . . . on all beer, ale, and porter, imported in bottles. **1811** MEASE *Philadelphia* 77 Beer was brewed in Philadelphia for several years before the revolutionary war, and soon after peace the more substantial porter was made by the late Wm. Robert Hare. **1891** G. EHRET *25 Years of Brewing* 28 A few brew-houses whose product had acquired an uncommon reputation —like the porters and ales of Philadelphia—remained in operation.

b. Attrib. with *beer, bottle, cellar, glass.*
1779 *York Co., Va., Rec.: Wills* XXII. 28 April, 2 pint porter glasses. **1796** *Boston Directory* 224 Baker, Joseph B., wine and porter cellar, south side market. **1823** JAMES *Exped.* I. 56 In one of these he had found two pieces of earthenware, one having nearly the form of a porter-bottle. **1845** *Xenia Torch-Light* 23 Oct. 4/3 J. Klein . . . has just received from the city . . . Porter Beer, Vinegar, and Wine in bottles.

+**Porter.**[2] [See first quotation.] A variety of apple; also, the tree on which it is grown. In full *Porter apple.* — **1847** IVES *New Eng. Fruit* 39 *Porter.*—Originated on the farm of the Rev. Samuel Porter, in Sherburne, Mass. The fruit is sometimes large, the shape oblong. **1849** *New Eng. Farmer* I. 54 My Porter apple has not been in bearing long enough for me to ascertain its bearing properties. **1870** *Rep. Comm. Agric. 1869* 521 J. F. C. Hyde . . . [recommends] the Gravenstein and Pumpkin Sweeting for baking, and Porter for fall. **1887** WILKINS *Humble Romance* 238 On the right of the garden were two old apple-trees, a Baldwin and a Porter.

Porterhouse.
'Chiefly *U.S.*' (*O.E.D.*).

1. A tavern or place at which porter, ale, etc., are sold. *Obs.* {1800-}
1786 FRANKS *N.Y. Directory* 41 Norris Rich. porter-house, 3, Broad-street. **1796** *Boston Directory* 288 Trench, George, porter house and tavern, No. 69, Ann street. **1807** IRVING, etc. *Salmagundi* xv. 409 Dabble was now very frequent . . . in his visits to those temples of politicks, popularity and smoke, the ward porter-houses. **1864** NICHOLS *Amer. Life* II. 152, I had occasion to go one day into a porter-house, or grog shop. *a***1882** WEED *Autobiog.* 54 Even porter-houses, as now constituted, were almost unknown [in 1815].

+2. Short for PORTERHOUSE STEAK.
1854 *Harper's Mag.* Jan. 269/2 Will you have it rare or well-done? Shall it be a porter-house? **1876** *Ib.* 147/1 Who would not prefer a well-broiled porter-house from the hand of a good cook. **1911** HARRISON *Queed* 14 There had been Porterhouse the last time. **1913** LONDON *Valley of Moon* 410 Good things all the way up from juicy porterhouse and the kind of coffee Mrs. Hall makes.

+**Porterhouse steak.** A choice beefsteak cut from the loin next to the sirloin. — **1841** MATHEWS *Writings* 206/2, I guess I'll take a small porter-house steak, without the bone. **1861** *Vanity Fair* 16 Feb. 73/1 Let it be a porter-house steak, rare, with Worcestershire sauce. **1883** *Harper's Mag.* Aug. 462/2 A porter-house steak learned to expect him on the noon of every day. **1904** *Nation* 31 March 245 The picture was drawn of the country stepping up to the butchers' block and demanding porterhouse and sirloin steaks in abundance.

Portfire. A form of match or fuse used formerly in firing cannons. *Obs.* {1647-} Also attrib. — **1775** *N.H. Prov. Papers* VII. 653 My whole time has been taken up . . . making Cartridges, Cannisters and Port Fires for the field Pieces. **1806** CLARK in *Lewis & C. Exped.* IV. (1905) 237, I had a small pece of port fire match in my pocket. **1835** HOFFMAN *Winter in West* I. 97 The artillerymen were standing with lighted portfires, when the order to retire within the fort caused them to fling their matches to the ground. **1867** EDWARDS *Shelby* 61 Captain Dunnington's quick, seaman eyes caught her outline in a moment, and, striking down the nearest port-fire to him, [he] shouted . . . : 'Hold on men.'

Portfolio.

1. A flat, portable case for papers, drawings, etc. {1722-}
1790 *Penna. Packet* 11 Dec. 3/2 Imported, . . . Travelling port folios and paper cases. **1840** *Knickerb.* XVI. 244 Now reach me my port-folio, and let me sign the check. **1891** WILKINS *New Eng. Nun* 146 Betsey . . . got an old black portfolio and pen and ink out of the chimney cupboard. **1907** *St. Nicholas* May 648/2 In the artist's portfolio they are the exception.

+2. A position in the cabinet of the president of the United States.
1884 BLAINE *20 Years of Congress* I. 40 Robert J. Walker . . . [was] already indicated for the portfolio of the Treasury in the new administration. **1886** ALTON *Among Law-Makers* 69 It is often a difficult question for a public man to decide whether or not to resign a seat in the Senate in order to accept a Cabinet portfolio. **1925** BRYAN *Memoirs* 408 Secretary Bryan . . . resigned his portfolio rather than sign the second note to Germany.

Portière. A curtain hung over a doorway. {1855-} — **1877** ROE *Army Lett.* 164 With face buried in a portiere, [I] was sobbing my very breath away. **1886** H. D. BROWN *Two College Girls* 240, I shall think you don't like the rugs, or the portières, or something about it. **1907** 'O. HENRY' *Strictly Business* 56 The gold portières parted and closed, and the mysterious automobilist entered the room.

Portland cement. A hydraulic cement of which the principal ingredients are pure limestone and clay. {1824-} Also attrib. — **1890** *Stock Grower & Farmer* 15 March 7/1 The irrigating dam on upper Cherry Creek [in Colo.] . . . is of rock laid in Portland cement. **1897** F. C. MOORE *How To Build a Home* 66 Only Portland cement mortar should be used in cisterns. **1915** *Boston Transcript* 30 Jan. III. 14/3 Reënforced concrete is made of sand, stone, and Portland cement, with steel bars placed in this.

+**Portlander.** A native or inhabitant of Portland, Maine. — **1861** *Vanity Fair* 25 May 250/1 'It is generally conceded here that Lincoln's Congress . . . will convene in Portland, Maine, or perhaps in Toronto—never in Washington City.' A terrible thing, if true, and one that will go far toward reconciling the Portlanders to their loss of the benefits that were to be reaped from the visit of the Great Eastern on her first trip.

+**Portland fancy.** A kind of dance. — **1898** WISTER *Lin McLean* 13 Do yu' know the Portland Fancy? **1904** LOVETT *R. Gresham* 63 Below, the couples . . . were circling the hall in the rapidly weaving figures of the Portland Fancy.

+**Portland tern.** The long-tailed or arctic tern, *Sterna paradisaea.* — **1874** COUES *Birds N.W.* 691 *Sterna Portlandica.* Portland Tern. . . . The subject of the present article differs materially from any other Tern I have seen. **1917** *Birds of Amer.* I. 62 Arctic Tern. *Sterna paradisæa.* . . . [Also called] Short-footed Tern; Portland Tern; Pike's Tern.

+**Portledge.** [From *portage* in same sense.] Orig., the freight or cargo furnished by a sailor taking part in a common venture; later, a mariner's wages. *Obs.* Also attrib. — **1636** *Maine Doc. Hist.* III. 97 There are 6 of them men which . . . would nott take them vnlesse Mr. Winter would giue them bills for the last yeares Portledge. **1639** *Ib.* 185 Eduard Trebie . . . Creditor for his ½ share for his portledge monye.

+**Portledge bill.** =PORTAGE BILL. — **1668** *Mass. Bay Rec.* IV. II. 390 The masters . . . shall make cleere agreem[en]ts wth. their marriners & officers for their wages, & those agreements enter into a booke, . . . a copy whereof the master, as a portlege bill, shall leaue wth. their owners. **1735** *Boston Rec.* 280 All his Hands . . . being number'd were found to be according to his Portlidge Bill. **1775** *Mass. Archives* CCVI. 94 To the am[ount] of Mens wages as per Portledg Bill 56. 17. 11½.

***Portmanteau.** Also †**portmantue, portmantua.** A bag or case, usually of leather, for carrying clothes and traveling necessities; a valise or suitcase.
See also PORTMANTLE.
1638 *Md. Archives* IV. 76 An old portmantue & p. boots. **1778** J. JONES *Letters* 7 It is probable the enemy have got possession of Mr. Pleasants' portmantua. **1805** *Ann. 8th Congress* 2 Sess. 1671 Expenses of prosecution, portmanteaus, mail locks, and other expenses incident to the Department . . . [were] paid for by the Postmaster General out of the funds of the office. **1870** RAE *Westward by Rail* 77 Frantic efforts are made to attract the attention of the baggage clerk, and to induce him to attach the necessary check to the trunk or portmanteau. **1907** *St. Nicholas* July 829 'My portmanteau, guide?' 'It's aboard sir—at the rear.'
attrib. **1770** WASHINGTON *Diaries* I. 404 My Portmanteau horse faild in his Stomach. **1790** *Penna. Packet* 9 April 2/2 [For sale:] Portmanteau trunks. . . . A variety of riding whips.

Portmantle. =prec. *Obs.* {1602-} — **1656** *Essex Probate Rec.* I. 232 A portmantle, two sives. **1711** T. BUCKINGHAM *Land Exped.* (1825) 106 A Portmantle with lock and key. **1778** *Jrnls. Cont. Congress* X. 312 For each trooper . . . a saddle, halters, curry-comb and brush, portmantle, picket cord, and pack saddle.

+**Port Orford cedar.** [*Port Orford*, Oregon.] A large and valuable evergreen tree, *Chamaecyparis lawsoniana*, found in western North America. — **1884** SARGENT *Rep. Forests* 8 The change from the northern to southern forest is marked by the . . . Port Orford Cedar (*Chamæcyparis Lawsonia*). **1897** SUDWORTH *Arborescent Flora* 82 Port Orford Cedar (Oreg., Cal.).

Portrait-painter. An artist who paints portraits. {1797-} — **1765** in Singleton *Social N.Y.* 333 At present there is no other portrait-painter in the city but himself. **1789** *Boston Directory* 185 Gullager Christian, portrait painter. **1846** *Knickerb.* XXVII. 275 We do not know when we have encountered a more forcible tribute to an American portrait-painter. **1872** ROE *Barriers* xxxi, Every glance at his face was that of a portrait-painter.

***Portugal.** Also †**portingale.** *attrib.* Designating various things brought from or associated with Portugal.
1658 *Essex Probate Rec.* I. 271 Hour glasse, portingale ware, morter & pestill. **1759** H. M. Brooks *Gleanings* II. 9 A Bill of Lading for two Boxes of Portugal Gold. **1779** *Essex Inst. Coll.* LVI. 25 Congress spent part of this day respecting a Portugal vessel taken by orders from Carter Broxten.

b. *spec.* In the names of fruit trees, vegetables, etc.
1739 W. STEPHENS *Proc. Georgia* I. 330 De Lyon . . . has planted some Hundreds of the Portugal Grape this Year. **1781-2** JEFFERSON *Notes Va.*

(1788) 38 Portugal bay. *Laurus indica.* **1785** WASHINGTON *Diaries* II. 349 Brought 9 scions of the Portugal Peach from Mr. Cockburn's with me. **1851** BUIST *Family Kitchen Gardener* 5 We have omitted a few vegetables of a coarse description, principally raised for cattle, by field culture. Among which are the *Portugal* [*Couve tronchuda*], and *Cow Cabbage*.

Portugal cap. A cap of a style worn in or thought to be worn in Portugal. *Obs.* — **1637** *Essex Inst. Coll.* I. 40/1 He ca——— [came] before ye x x [church] with a portugal cap on. **1647** *Conn. Rec.* I. 478 One Portingale cap begun made & vnlyned. **1663** *Essex Probate Rec.* I. 414 1 Hatt & Portugall capp.

Portugee, *n.* and *a.* Portuguese. *illiterate.* {1878–} — **1830** COOPER *Water Witch* II. 197 It being altogether unreasonable to suppose that a Portugee should do what an Englishman had not yet thought of doing. **1834** *N.Y. Mirror* 5 July 5/2 A Portugué breakfast is teasing to the imagination. **1867** *Atlantic Mo.* April 434/2 [A sailor boy:] Mother's a Portegee.... [The mother:] I am a Portuguese, sir. **1880** *Harper's Mag.* Sept. 505/1 At one place was a 'Portugee' of the Western Islands.

***Portulaca.** Any one of various cultivated tropical American herbs of a prostrate or ascending nature belonging to the genus *Portulaca.* — **1866** A. D. WHITNEY *L. Goldthwaite* x, These were flower-seeds,—bags labelled 'Petunia,' 'Candytuft,' 'Double Balsam,' 'Portulaca.' **1885** *Century Mag.* April 835 His wife had made a few flower-beds in which bachelor's-buttons, poppies, and portulacas flourished. **1912** N. WOODROW *Sally Salt* 13 Here, hand me that portulaca, Lucy.

Port warden. 'An officer invested with the chief authority in a port' (*Cent.*). Cf. HARBOR MASTER. — **1841** CIST *Cincinnati* 48 Joseph Pierce, Port-warden. **1873** *Mich. Gen. Statutes* I. (1882) 670 The council may also appoint a harbor-master, wharf-masters, port wardens, and such other officers as may be necessary. **1906** *N.Y. Globe* 20 Feb. 6 The following vessels are now under examination by the Port Wardens.

Port wine. A strong, dark-red wine made in Portugal, or a wine likened to this. {1700–} Also attrib. — **1805** PARKINSON *Tour* 44 He gave me some grape-juice to drink, which he called Port wine, and entertained me with saying he made it himself. **1845** POLK in *Pres. Mess. & P.* IV. 400 A duty of 15 cents per gallon was imposed on port wine in casks. **1863** A. D. WHITNEY *F. Gartney* x, She handed Mr. Gartney his port-wine tonic. **1878** *Amer. Home Cook Book* 23 Flavour with the catsup and port wine.

Posada. [Sp.] An inn. {1763–, in Spain and S. Amer.} — **1851** M. REID *Scalp Hunters* x, The miserable accomodations of New Mexican *posadas* vexed me to an excess of endurance. **1877** HARTE *Story of Mine* (1896) 400 Avoid the highway. Stop at no posada nor fonda. **1884** HARTE *On Frontier* 156 If you can't push through to-night, you can lie over at the posada on the summit.

+**Pose.** A point on a portage at which a voyageur puts down his load for resting. — **1832** S. HALL *Diary* Sept. (Archives of Amer. Bd. Comm. Foreign Missions LXXIV. No. 44) The men shouldered their burdens and went on to the next pose, and so on until all the poses had been passed.

***Posey.** (See POSY.)

+**Posish.** Abbrev. for *position. colloq.* {1927} — **1862** NORTON *Army Lett.* 113 Snorting their impatience to 'get into posish,' came the Monitor, the Galena and others. **1865** PIKE *Scout & Ranger* (1932) 7 Some of the managers and their wives, feeling the importance of their 'posish,' put on considerable 'style.' **1889** MUNROE *Golden Days* 69 All we've got to do is to get the cradle in posish. **1901** 'FLYNT' *World of Graft* 199, I'd give 'em exactly what they asked for, or t'row up the posish.

***Position. 1.** One's attitude or stand on a certain issue or question. {1905} **2.** A place of employment; a job. {1900–} — **(1) 1848** *N.Y. Tribune* 6 June (B.), We regret that unavoidable absence at Philadelphia will deprive us of the pleasure of hearing these gentlemen 'define their position.' **(2) 1868** *Rep. Comm. Educ.* 473 The same authority which commissions for a position is to receive also application for discharge. **1890** *Cent.* 4635/2 A *position* in a bank. **1898** *Kansas City Star* 20 Dec. 2/5 Morton Albaugh . . . has not said that he would refuse a good position in the federal service.

+**Positionist.** =POSTURE MASTER. — **1843** in Odell *Annals N.Y. Stage* V. 61 [On October 2nd, the popular and ubiquitous T. G. Booth joined (the circus), as well as Jenkins, Edwards, and Hamlin,] the astonishing positionist.

***Posnet.** A small metal kettle provided with a handle. {–1863} — **1640** *Conn. Rec.* I. 448 James Olmestead [owns] . . . a pott posnette, 1 dripping pan. **1642** *Essex Probate Rec.* I. 21, I doe give unto my wife . . . a great brasse posnett and a chafing dish. **1646** *Conn. Probate Rec.* I. 16 Three brasse posnetts, 10s. **1653** *Mayflower Descendant* XI. 101 One posnett and a frying pan.

+**Possau.** [? Amer. Indian.] The brew used in the physic dance (q.v.). — **1800** HAWKINS *Sk. Creek Country* 76 While they are dancing, the possau is brewed. This is a powerful emetic. *Ib.* 79 The youth, during this initiation, . . . drinks the possau.

***Posse.** A body of armed men, under the command of a sheriff or other officer of the law, raised on a given occasion to hunt for a criminal, suppress a riot, etc. {1691–}

1775 FITHIAN *Journal* II. 30 Mr. McGinnis . . . had apprehended a Fellow for the Suspicion of having stolen his Horse— . . . A *Posse* were dispatched for a Woman said to be his companion. **1799** *Ann. 7th Congress* 2 Sess. 1414 It was agreed to send express to Easton, in order to obtain the *posse* to aid him. **1840** *Niles' Nat. Reg.* 21 March 48/3 Sheriff Fitter, with a large *posse*, was on the ground and made many arrests. **1885** *Wkly. New Mexican Rev.* 12 Feb. 1/4 A heavy posse of ranchmen is scouring the country for the other divisions of the raiding bands [of Apaches]. **1917** MCCUTCHEON *Green Fancy* 77, The best thing for you to do, Abner, is to get a posse of men together and begin raking the woods up yonder for the men that did the shooting.

***Possessed,** *a.* +*Like all possessed*, as if driven by an evil spirit; furiously. — **1833** S. SMITH *Life J. Downing* 209 [He] struck his fists together like all possessed. **1852** STOWE *Uncle Tom* i, Some of your plantation niggers would be singing and whooping like all possessed. **1881** *Harper's Mag.* April 644 That old minister . . . is a-fiddling away like all possessed at the dance. **1898** WESTCOTT *D. Harum* 226, I had to scratch grav'l like all possessed. **1916** PORTER *David* 280 He danced and laughed and clapped his hands, . . . an' carried on like all possessed.

+**Possession house.** A house or hut built *c*1772 to bolster a land claim in the disputed territory of the New Hampshire Grants (q.v.). — **1772** *Doc. Hist. N.Y. State* IV. 803 [Certain people of Bennington] are artfully endeavoring to support a Claim to the intermediate Territory, under the Weak pretence of Hutts hastily Built on small Spotts of Ground which they Term possession Houses.

***Posset.** A drink of hot milk curdled with wine, beer, or other liquor, often spiced. Also attrib. — **1683** *Mass. H. S. Coll.* 4 Ser. V. 113 For change of drink, sometimes we take posset-drink, in which we boil feather-few. **1835** HOFFMAN *Winter in West* II. 220 [Like] the 'spiced posset' that is sometimes offered by mine host when about to retire for the night, it [*sc.* the julep] must be viewed as a relic of ancient manners. **1848** HOLMES *Poetical Works* (1895) 30/1 The little captain stood and stirred the posset with his sword. **1871** *Scribner's Mo.* II. 512/2 [Katrina] was making a goat's-milk posset.

+**Possible,** *interj.* (See quotations.) — **1835** TODD *Notes* 8 O my! with possible! [are] universal interjections [in America]. **1844** 'UNCLE SAM' *Peculiarities* I. 118 Mr. Pogue.—You knew Mr. Bompard? . . . He is in disgrace with his honour, Judge Murphy. Mr. Shippensburg.—Possible! —How so?

+**Possibles.** [Sp. *posibles* 'wealth, income.'] *pl.* The belongings and valuables of a trapper, mountaineer, or the like.

In view of the fact that all the evidence for this word appears in the West, it is unlikely that its use is an extension of the British slang term {1823, 1824} of a similar general meaning.

1841 FARNHAM *Travels* 55/1 The loss of their [*i.e.*, the horses'] services in transporting their traps and furs, and 'possibles,' (clothing, cooking utensils, &c.,) was severely felt. **1850** GARRARD *Wah-To-Yah* xxi. 255 Putting my 'possibles' in a wagon, I received my account of coffee, sugar, etc., from the affable Doctor Hempstead. **1853** 'P. PAXTON' *Yankee in Texas* 104 The river swept over our camp-ground, and was gradually creeping up the bank, but Joe said that our 'possibles' were now beyond its reach. **1886** *Outing* Dec. 198/2 Dick had a big tepé, . . . not ter speak uv a considerable lot of possibles ter make things comfortable.

+**Possible sack.** A bag in which camping provisions and personal belongings are carried; a haversack. (Cf. prec.) — **1846** W. G. WEBB *Altowan* I. 142 Auguste . . . , by dint of much search in his possible-sack, found a piece of tobacco. **1848** RUXTON *Life Far West* v, Many a gâge d'amour of cunning shape and device . . . he had packed in his 'possible' sack for the same destination. **1888** J. J. WEBB *Adventures* 121 The captain, or leader, of the company . . . [agreed] to haul our beds and 'possible sacks' for forty dollars each.

+**Possum,** *n.* Also †**possown.** [Shortening of OPOSSUM.]

1. =OPOSSUM.

1613 WHITAKER *Good Newes Va.* 41 The female possown . . . will let forth her young out of her bellie, and take them vp into her bellie againe. **1666** ALSOP *Maryland* (1869) 40 The Otter, the Possum, the Hare, . . . and several others . . . inhabit here in Mary-Land in several droves and troops, ranging the Woods. **1698** THOMAS *Pensilvania* 14 There are . . . Rabits, and that strange Creature, the Possam, she having a false Belly to swallow her Young ones, by which means she preserveth them from danger. **1735** *Ga. Hist. Soc. Coll.* II. 60 A possum . . . is very like a little pig. **1819** NOAH *She Would Be a Soldier* I. ii, I know all tracks—used to 'em when I hunt 'possums. **1838** DRAKE *Tales Queen City* 151 A fierce little junior . . . had often signalized himself on the banks of Licking river, as the 'real thing,' in hunting 'coons' and 'holeing possums.' **1880** 'MARK TWAIN' *Tramp Abroad* 38 He cocked his head to one side, shut one eye and put the other one to the hole, like a 'possum looking down a pig.

b. The flesh of the opossum.

1670 D. DENTON *Brief Descr. N.Y.* 7 They eat likewise Polecats, Skunks, Racoon, Possum, Turtles, and the like. **1851** *Polly Peablossom* 117, I'd eaten a matter of two pounds of side, and half ov a possum. **1905** N. DAVIS *Northerner* 156 Falls ate his possum with the appetite which the ride in the cold air had given him. **1917** *Mammals of Amer.* 297/2 Baked 'Possum and Sweet Potato are the joy of the Southern darky.

c. Pretense or deceit. (Cf. sense 3 c.)

1843 'CARLTON' *New Purchase* II. 201 Tim Scratch know'd better nor to come! he's not sick no how—it's all possum!

2. *transf.* A person who feigns or dissembles.

1856 *Yale Lit. Mag.* XXI. 147 (Th.), He's awful on possums; oh, I tell ye now, he's great. **1857** STROTHER *Virginia* 65 Mass' Porte, never mind dat ole possum. **1891** *Harper's Mag.* Dec. 49/2, I'm a 'possum for adapting myself to any odd hollows.

3. Phrases. **a.** *To play possum,* to dissemble; to pretend illness, inaction, etc.

1822 *Notices of East Florida* 40 (Th.S.), After being severely wounded, they have been known to lie for several hours as if dead. . . . Hence the expression of 'playing possum' is common among the inhabitants, being applied to those who act with cunning and duplicity. **1829** Sherwood *Gaz. Georgia* (ed. 2) 20 He is playing 'possum with you. **1840** Simms *Border Beagles* I. 170 He swears that I don't want he should have the girl—that I'm only playing 'possum. **1871** *Amer. Naturalist* IV. 715 This splendid 'Cock of the Rock' . . . 'plays 'possum,' falling apparently dead when shot at, but soon flies off. **1885** *Wkly. New Mexican Rev.* 4 June 2/4 The old party of liberty and union is not dead nor is it playing 'possum'! **1917** *Mammals of Amer.* 296/2 There is a belief among many naturalists that the Opossum never 'plays 'Possum,' in an attempt to deceive.

b. *Possum up a gum tree,* (see quotations).

1831 Peck *Guide* 156 The very woods and hills shake with the negro song of 'possum up a gum-tree.' **1840** Haliburton *Clockmaker* 3 Ser. xxi, Many's the time I have danced 'Possum up a gum tree' at a quiltin' frolic or huskin' party. **1848** G. E. Ellis *Let.* (Bartlett MS.), 'Possum up a gum tree' [is used] at the South & West, for *opossum.*

c. *To come the possum over* (someone), see Come *v.* 3 b.

4. *attrib.* and *comb.* **a.** Designating products made or taken from the opossum.

1709 Lawson *Carolina* 188 The Indian Womens Work is . . . to make Mats, Baskets, Girdles of Possum-Hair, and such-like. **1848** *Knickerb.* XXXI. 92 Molasses in the East is sweet, For Yankee urchins good to eat, But 'possum-oil far in the West I *reckon* still is thought the best.

b. Designating persons, dogs, etc., connected with hunting or eating opossums.

1855 Willis *Convalescent* 73 On our way through the woods, my 'possum-catcher stepped off to take a look at his steel-trap set at a hole in a rock. **1881** Tourgee *'Zouri's Christmas* iii, An ancient hound, whose fame as a 'possum-dog was unrivaled in the county. **1884** Harris *Mingo* 6 Many who read this will remember the ''possum suppers' which it was Mingo's delight to prepare for these young men. **1900** *Congress. Rec.* 11 Jan. 784/1 A 'possum hound or dog is a very trusty and tried friend of the colored person. **1903** Fox *Little Shepherd* xxi, 'Possum signs were plentiful. **1909** *N.Y. Ev. Post* 4 Jan. (Th.), Harry S. Fisher of Newman, Ga., [is] known as the 'possum king.

c. In the names of plants and trees.

1894 *Amer. Folk-Lore* VII. 90 *Viburnum nudum,* possum-berry, Ocean Springs, Miss. **1860** Curtis *Woody Plants N.C.* 90 Possum haw. . . . The fruit is a deep blue. **1884** Sargent *Rep. Forests* 152 *Quercus aquatica.* . . . Water Oak. Duck Oak. Possum Oak. **1897** Sudworth *Arborescent Flora* 321 *Diospyros virginiana.* . . . Possumwood (Fla.).

d. In special combinations.

Possum hunt, the act of hunting opossums; *possum playing,* the action of playing possum (used attrib.); *p. toddy,* (see quotation).

1853 Simms *Sword & Distaff* (1854) 117 With a 'coon and 'possum hunt, by night, we shall lay in sufficient store of venison for a week's entertainment. **1856** Kane *Arctic Explor.* I. 391 The Esquimaux . . . say that the dogs soon learn this 'possum-playing' habit. **1888** *Century Mag.* Sept. 766/1 A favorite small beer in those sections where the persimmon-trees flourished best was made of the fruit of that tree, and was called in the vernacular of at least one part of the Confederacy ''possum toddy.'

+**Possum,** *v. intr.* and *tr.* To feign death; to dissemble. *colloq.* — **1832** Flint *Geog. Mississippi Valley* (ed. 2) I. 67 In the common parlance of the country, any one, who counterfeits sickness . . . is said to be 'possuming' [ed. 1828 oppossuming]. **1835** Audubon *Ornith. Biog.* III. 456 It is only ''possuming,' and no sooner has its enemy withdrawn, than it . . . once more makes for the woods. **1853** Baldwin *Flush Times Ala.* 150 All this time I was possuming sleep . . . as innocent as a lamb. **1894** Cable *J. March* xxii, A dim shape . . . vanished before he could add, 'He was possuming!'

+**Possum fat.**

1. Fat taken from the opossum: (see also quot. 1847).

1847 T. Ford *Hist. Illinois* (1854) 89 The genius and humor of the times invented or imported a slang language, very expressive of the achievements of these political heroes. Such an operator in politics was said to carry 'a gourd of *possum fat,*' with which to 'grease' the members. **1851** *Polly Peablossom* 70 She looked up everything 'bout the house, an' all sorts of good things—bacon, an' possum fat. **1884** *Harper's Mag.* Dec. 169/2 The plantation negro with 'possum fat and 'coon . . . is just as much alive to the odor.

2. *Possum fat and hominy,* (see quot. 1824).

1824 Blane *Excursion U.S.* 134 'Possum fat and hommony' is a favourite dish with Western and Southern negroes. **1838** Drake *Tales Queen City* 91 [He was] born in a canebrake, rocked in a sugar trough, and raised upon 'possum fat and homony.' **1856** C. White *Oh, Hush!* 7, I'd gib you eberyting dat's nice, . . . Dar's possum fat an' hominy.

+**Possum-hunt,** *v. intr.* To hunt for opossums. — **1900** *Congress. Rec.* 11 Jan. 784/1, I used to 'possum hunt.

+**Possum-hunting.** The action of hunting opossums. — **1840** *S. Lit. Messenger* VI. 396/1 He is fond of possum, rabbit, and coon-hunting. **1847** *Knickerb.* XXIX. 433 [Getting out shingles is] a real salty business; . . . by heavens, it beats coon and possum-huntin' all holler. **1867** Crawford *Mosby* 277 The men . . . thought somebody was going out a 'possum hunting. **1904** Glasgow *Deliverance* 193 We'll go 'possum hunting one night.

+**Possuming.** **1.** The action of dissembling. *colloq.* **2.** The action of hunting opossums. *colloq.* Used attrib. — (1) **1846** Levinge *Echoes from Backwoods* II. 32 *'Possuming* is become an idiom; a term signifying any one who is humbugging or deceiving. **1862** *Harper's Mag.* Dec. 99/2 So you see you must endure it to the end—fur thar's no possumin' thar. (2) **1869** *Routledge's Every Boy's Annual* 607 To go out with him on a 'possuming expedition.

***Post,** *n.*[1] A stout piece of timber or metal used in a vertical position.

1. A fence post or gatepost.

1636 *Boston Rec.* 12 William Wilkes, Isaack Cullimore . . . shall raynge theire payle . . . straight from the corner of William Wilkes his house, or from the upper poast of his garding gap. **1657** *Southampton Rec.* I. 129 Every inhabitant of this towne that hath fenceing in or about the great and little plaines and oxpasture, shall at both ends of his fence put his railes in his owne posts. **1742** *Harvard Rec.* II. 716 His Account of Red Cedar Posts amounting to Thirty two pounds 10/ [shall] be allow'd. **1785** Marshall *Amer. Grove* 94 The timber [of the mulberry tree] affords very durable posts, for fencing, etc. **1807** Gass *Journal* 52 They set up 16 forked posts five or six feet high, and lay poles from one fork to another. **1905** N. Davis *Northerner* 33 Betty's shrinking figure endeavoring to conceal itself behind the slender iron post of the gate.

+**b.** In various phrases designating different kinds of fences. Freq. used attrib.

See also Post(s) and rail(s).

[**1658** *Boston Rec.* 145 All outside fences aboutt pastures or cornfeilds shall bee substantially fenced, either with five rayles, or posts and pales, or sufficient stone walls, or other wise.] **1858** Warder *Hedges & Evergreens* 107 We must raise timber for post-and-bar fence or depend upon the pines and cedars of distant regions. **1861** *Ill. Agric. Soc. Trans.* IV. 202, 509 acres, inclosed in a model manner with a substantial post and board fence. **1861** in Logan *Great Conspiracy* 295 They found a post-and-log fence across the Winchester turnpike. **1871** Bagg *At Yale* 145 The building . . . stands back a rod or more from the street, being separated from it by a post-and-chain fence.

***2.** A timber used as a support of a superstructure; a whipping post; a stand for public notices, etc.

1663 *Portsmouth Rec.* 120 Any such person . . . [shall] make due and true publication . . . by a writinge upon the publicke post or at the mill. **1683** *N.H. Hist. Soc. Coll.* VIII. 147 [He] procured of said judge the shameful sentence of ten stripes, to be laid upon me at a post. **1759** *Essex Inst. Coll.* XIX. 189 Ye said Cort marshull Sentenced him to ye Post and then ye Coll forgave him. **1837** Peck *New Guide* 127 A band-mill is the most simple [form of mill]. A large upright post is placed on a gudgeon [etc.]. **1894** *Outing* XXIV. 213/1 Each band halted, saluted, and wheeling their horses rode back to their own goal post. Circling around the posts, each party shouted its war cry.

3. *attrib.* **a.** In sense 1 with *fence, head, iron.*

1647 *Essex Probate Rec.* I. 77 One Postiron, a hale & a how. **1850** in Commons, etc. *Doc. Hist.* I. 201 February . . . 26, 27, 28, making post fence. **1857** *Atlantic Mo.* I. 94/1 The topmost rails and post-heads of this fence have been [notched].

b. In special combinations.

Post bedstead, =Four-poster; *p. odds,* the betting odds of a horse race at the starting post.

1852 Eastman *Aunt Phillis's Cabin* 114 A very high post bedstead, over which were suspended white cotton curtains, gave an air of grandeur to one side of the room. **1887** *Courier-Journal* 5 May 5/2 The Post odds were: Editor and Minch, even money; Sam Harper 8 to 1.

***Post,** *n.*[2]

***1.** One who carries letters, packets, etc., on a fixed route between towns or communities. *Obs.*

1674 *Conn. Rec.* II. 244 All posts their ferridge shall be on the country account. **1704** S. Knight *Journal* 21, I on a suden was Rous'd . . . by the Post's sounding his horn. **1715** *Boston News-Letter* 3 Jan. 2/2 The Western Post this Turn goes to Saybrook, to Exchange his Mayl of Letters with the New-York Post. **1757** *Lett. to Washington* II. 191 What the Post will take for carrying them to Lancaster I don't know. As he is a private Post, he makes his own Bargain I suppose. **1796** Morse *Univ. Geog.* I. 484 A post regularly rides from Albany to the Chenessee river, once a fortnight. **1833** *Niles' Reg.* XLIV. 365/2 If the defendants employed a person to carry letters from New York to Providence regularly, such person was to be deemed a post.

+**b.** *Flying post,* a mail carrier traveling by relays of horses.

1697 Sewall *Diary* I. 464, I visited Unkle Quinsey, met Mr. Torrey . . . Flying Post or Post-Master.

***2.** The service given by a carrier or carriers of letters, dispatches, etc., over a fixed route; an instance of delivery or service by such carriers. *Obsolescent.*

The more usual term in the United States is *mail.* See also *Constitutional post* and *Ministerial post* under the adjectives.

1697 SEWALL *Letter-Book* I. 186, I met him there with an order by the Post. 1704 *Boston News-Letter* 14 Aug. 2/2 His Excellency our Governour receiving Intelligence on Saturday night by the Post from N. York of the French Privateer . . . his coming upon our Coast. 1777 J. ADAMS *Familiar Letters* 252 Do you write by the post? If you do, there must be some legerdemain. 1801 *Austin P.* I. (1924) 61, I wrote you a few posts since in answer to your letter. 1860 CLAIBORNE *Sam. Dale* 85 [Between] Washington, in Adams County, . . . and Tombigbee there was only a monthly post.

3. A station on a route over which letters, etc., are regularly conveyed by a carrier. {1768-}

1775 *Jrnls. Cont. Congress* II. 208 That a line of posts be appointed under the direction of the Postmaster general, from Falmouth in New England to Savannah in Georgia, with as many cross posts as he shall think fit. 1792 *Ann. 2d Congress* 58 It shall . . . be lawful for the Postmaster General to enter into contracts . . . for extending the line of posts.

4. *ellipt.* =POST PAPER. {1711-}

1790 *Penna. Packet* 8 March 1/3 A General Assortment of American Manufactured Writing Paper . . . [including] thick and thin folio and quarto Post. 1846 MACKENZIE *Van Buren* 262 The above was written on a sheet of gilt post, from Washington, Dec., 1836.

5. *attrib.* Designating persons, things, etc., connected with the mails.

Many of these compounds are now obsolete.

1753 in Singleton *Social N.Y.* 38 All letters for persons living in town that remain uncalled for on post nights, will on Monday morning be sent out by a penny post provided for that purpose. 1774 FINLAY *Journal* 91 There's no Post boat. 1856 CURTIS *Prue & I* (1892) 60 'It's nearly post-time, sir,' said the clerk. 1884 W. SHEPHERD *Prairie Exper.* 100 A little before noon the boy came in riding with the post-bag from the other side. 1892 A. E. LEE *Hist. Columbus, Ohio* I. 341/2 Col. Andrew McElvain . . . the first postcarrier under Hosac [postmaster & contractor for carrying the mails]. 1898 WESTCOTT *D. Harum* 22 [The letter] should be put into the very first post-box he came to.

***Post,** *n.*[3]

1. =MILITARY POST. {1703-}

1779 JEFFERSON *Writings* II. (1893) 276 Intending to fix a post and small Garrison in Powell's valley, we have ordered part of a battalion thither to erect a stockade. 1789 MORSE *Amer. Geog.* 464 This post is established to cover the country from the incursions of the Indians. 1812 MARSHALL *Kentucky* 317 The Indians could but observe that the British still held the posts on the Lakes. 1848 *Santa Fe Republican* 3 May 2/4 Capt. Cunningham is now left in command of this Post. 1897 CLOVER *Paul Travers' Adv.* 24 You won't see much activity at this post. . . . It is to be abandoned shortly. 1909 STERNBERG *Life of Fossil Hunter* 219, I had obtained from the Secretary of War a letter of introduction to the commanders of western posts.

+b. The soldiers who occupy such a post.

1867 CRAWFORD *Mosby* 138 All the post were soon the other side of the Hazel in a safe place.

+2. An establishment in a sparsely settled area for carrying on trade; a trading post.

1796 HAWKINS *Letters* 15, I believe a small post might be kept to advantage. 1801 *Spirit Farmers' Mus.* 268 [Twelve dollars might] save the favourite mare, or the likely two year old, from being . . . sold for half their value at the Post. 1836 IRVING *Astoria* II. 13 The post, however, was deserted. 1847 PARKMAN in *Knickerb.* XXX. 284 Fort Laramie is one of the posts established by the 'American Fur Company.' 1893 *Harper's Mag.* May 813/2 When the post ceased to be profitable, it would be abandoned. 1905 COLE *Early Oregon* 9 Near the site of the post of the Hudson Bay Company . . . was Elkton.

+3. (See quotation; perhaps =sense 2.)

1818 DARBY *Emigrant's Guide* 4 Like all other establishments made in America, the first settlements of Louisiana were detached, and known by the term of 'posts.'

+4. A local chapter of a veterans' organization, esp. of the G.A.R. and the American Legion.

1868 in *Nat. Memorial Day 1869* (G.A.R.) 7 Posts and comrades will in their own way arrange such fitting services and testimonials of respect as circumstances may permit. 1874 *G.A.R.* (Mass.) *Ann. Encampment Proc.* 9 Pains must be taken in the working of Posts . . . in the Grand Army of the Republic. 1893 *Congress. Rec.* 30 Sept. 1971/1, I do not wonder that there is great dissatisfaction among the boys in blue, . . . and that in their posts and other organizations they have passed resolutions condemning the conduct of the Commissioner of Pensions. 1922 *Outlook* 27 Dec. 735/3 There are Legion posts that stand sponsor for the Boy Scout movement in their cities.

5. *attrib.* **a.** Designating persons connected with a military post.

1862 CUMMING *Hospital Life* (1866) 51/1 Mr. Denniston . . . is post chaplain here [at Chattanooga, Tenn.]. 1867 in Fleming *Hist. Reconstruction* I. 428 Post commanders will cause to be arrested persons charged with the commission of crimes and offenses. 1873 BEADLE *Undevel. West* 525 Mr. B. M. Thomas, post farmer, constitutes a department by himself.

b. Designating various establishments connected with a military post.

1861 *Army Regulations* 35 The saving on the flour ration . . . by baking the soldiers' bread at a post bakery. 1871 *Rep. Indian Affairs* (1872) 402 Cadetta . . . requested to have a coffin made for Chatto and have him buried in the post cemetery. 1881 *Ib.* 83 Books had been opened at the post-trading store for some time for the entry of claims. 1882 *Nation* 23 Nov. 434/1 Considerable progress has been made in the work of organizing and establishing post-schools and reading-rooms.

+c. Designating persons associated with a trading post.

1890 *Harper's Mag.* Oct. 654/1 The post factor, Mr. Rankin, was sick in bed, and the Indians were on a spree. 1904 WHITE *Silent Places* 5 These men lounging on the river bank were the Company's post-keepers and runners.

+d. *Post meeting,* a chapter meeting of a veterans' organization.

1903 ADE *In Babel* 251 You ought to heard old Cap Nesbit the other night after post-meetin'.

***Post,** *v.*[1]

1. *tr.* To make known the status or condition of (a person) by putting up, or, later, by publishing in a newspaper, a public notice. {1633-} Also with *up.*

1711 *Boston Rec.* 126 The Sel. men will proceed to post up Reputed drunkards & comon Tiplers as the Law directs. 1718 *Mass. H. Rep. Jrnl.* II. 71 He was Posted as a Souldier in pay. 1749 *N.J. Archives* XII. 518 Sarah . . . eloped from her Husband's Bed and Board about ten Years ago, and thereon her said Husband posted her, forbidding all Persons to trust her on his Account. 1871 *Harper's Mag.* Sept. 796/1 My husband . . . has thought proper to post me, and accuse me of having left his bed and board without cause.

2. To furnish (a place) with posts. {1716}

1781 *Baltimore Rec.* 43 Such sum as may be sufficient to pay [?pave] and Post the Market House and arround it. 1874 *Vermont Bd. Agric. Rep.* II. 514 In 1868 I built me a large and commodious cattle barn, one hundred by forty-five feet, seventeen feet posted.

+3. To protect (land) from trespass by putting up a notice.

1907 *Springfield W. Repub.* 22 Aug. 6 The ranch was eventually reached, after opening and closing several gates, all marked 'Posted.' 1910 *Ib.* 24 Nov. 10 Farmers have posted their land in all directions and are expressing dissatisfaction at the slaughter of deer.

Post,** *v.*[2] **+tr.* To inform (a person or one's self) on some subject. {1886} Often with *up.* (See also POSTED *a.*)

1863 HOPLEY *Life in South* I. 5 But politics were altogether too perplexing, and to 'post' oneself up on names and principles which seemed to change more frequently than the fashions, appeared a hopeless task. 1883 SWEET & KNOX *Through Texas* 45, I posted some of the boys, and told them to be handy in the evening. 1905 A. ADAMS *Outlet* 17 Several of the boys who were friendly to my interests posted me that the older foremen were going to claim first choice. 1912 WASON *Friar Tuck* 152 He began to post me upon Olaf the Swede.

absol. 1902 *Kan. State Hist. Soc. Trans.* VII. 427, I thought you would like something fresh to read and post up on what is going on in the country.

***Postage.**

***1.** The conveyance of letters, etc., by post; a postal-delivery service. *Obs.* {*Obs.*}

1691 *Mass. H. S. Coll.* 3 Ser. VII. 52 It shall . . . be lawful to and for the Post Master General . . . to demand, have, receive and take for the postage and conveyance of all such letters . . . according to the several rates [etc.]. 1749 W. DOUGLASS *Summary* I. 466 From Piscataqua or Portsmouth, to Philadelphia, is a regular Postage. 1755 L. EVANS *Anal. Map Colonies* 23 From Frederick . . . there is a Postage to Cantwell's Bridge.

2. The charge made for the conveyance of mail. {1654-}

1686 SEWALL *Letter-Book* I. 25 N. sent per Jno. Perry, and paid 3d. Postage. 1775 *Amer. Hist. Review* I. 293 The Postage should be 20 per cent less than the Kings Postage. 1792 *Ann. 2d Congress* 58 The person or persons so contracting to receive . . . all the postage which shall arise on letters, newspapers, and packets, conveyed by any such post. 1821 *Ann. 17th Congress* 1 Sess. I. 22 Mr. Williams . . . asked and obtained leave . . . to bring in a bill authorizing the transmission of certain documents free of postage. 1842 *Niles' Nat. Reg.* 30 July 348/2 The bill relating to the reduction of postage . . . was taken up, amended . . . and ordered to be engrossed. 1903 *Churchman* 14 Nov. 608 The domestic postage on this copy of the Churchman is 2 cents. The foreign postage is 3 cents.

+3. *concrete.* Postage stamps.

1862 NORTON *Army Lett.* 130 Paper, ink, pen and postage is forthcoming.

4. Attrib. in sense 2 with *bill, bounty, charge.*

1851 *N. Amer. Miscellany* I. 188/1 The new postage-bill, and a change in the tariff are still subjects of discussion. 1855 HOLBROOK *Among Mail Bags* 386 Let it go without Postage Bounty, To Union Valley, Cortland County. 1893 CUSHING *Story of P.O.* 664 In case of the refusal or neglect of addressees of such dutiable books, . . . to pay the customs duties and any postage charges, the postmaster specially returns the same.

+**Postage currency.** =POSTAL CURRENCY. Now hist. — **1862** *Washington Republican* 6 Sept. 2/1 The Assistant Treasurer is . . . using his best endeavors to procure . . . the 'Postage Currency,' in order to relieve the whole community from the embarrassment consequent upon the scarcity of 'silver change.' **1862** (Inscription on five-cent bill), Postage Currency, Furnished only by the Assistant Treasurers and designated Depositaries of the U.S. U.S. Postage, Five Cents. [On back:] Act approved July 17, 1862. **1863** *Statutes at Large* XII. 711 Be it further enacted, That in lieu of postage stamps for fractional currency, and of fractional notes, commonly called postage currency . . . , the Secretary of the Treasury may issue fractional notes of like amounts. **1864** *N. Mex. Press* 2 Aug. 1/2 Many traders refuse to receive patched or worn postage currency; and whenever they do happen to have one, they shove it off on to somebody else.

+**Postage-due stamp.** A postage stamp affixed to a piece of mail to indicate the amount in which the postage is deficient. — **1893** CUSHING *Story of P.O.* 425 The postage due stamps . . . used . . . by postmasters or clerks only . . . are supposed never to come into possession of the public.

Postage stamp.

1. Any of a great variety of stamps having specified face values, sold by the Post Office Department, to be affixed to a piece of mail in prepayment of the postage; a design of such a stamp embossed or printed on an envelope, card, etc. {1840-}

1847 *Statutes at Large* IX. 201 The Postmaster-General [shall] be authorized to prepare postage stamps, which, when attached to any letter or packet, shall be evidence of the payment of the postage chargeable on such letter. **1852** *Harper's Mag.* Sept. 693/1 Small newspapers and periodicals . . . prepaid by affixing postage-stamps thereto, are to be charged only half a cent for each ounce. **1872** [see POSTAL CARD]. **1885** CRAWFORD *Amer. Politician* 163 The man at the hotel this morning had no postage stamps. **1902** *Harper's Mag.* May 969/1 But one must collect something, even postage-stamps and book-plates.

attrib. **1852** (*title* [cited by Ernst]), Postage Stamp Album, for the Stamps of all Nations.

+**2.** An ungummed stamp used as currency during the Civil War.

1862 *Boston Transcript* 18 July 2/2 Postage Stamps as a Legal Tender. It is said that the Treasury Department will issue a large quantity of stamps for general circulation. . . . They will be printed on thick paper without gum. **1863** [see FRACTIONAL NOTE].

+**Postage(-stamp) currency.** =POSTAL CURRENCY. — **1862** *Boston Transcript* 22 July 2/4 The Postage Stamp Currency. . . . The demand already is immense. **1862** *Washington Republican* 6 Aug. 1/2 The New Postage Stamp Currency. . . . They are to be of four denominations, viz.: Five, ten, twenty-five, and fifty cents. **1862** *37th Congress 3 Sess.* H. R. Ex. Doc. No. 1, 133 The issue of 'postage currency' by the Treasury Department will doubtless soon displace postage stamps from circulation.

+**Postal,** *n.* [Absol. of POSTAL *a.*]

1. Short for POSTAL CARD.

1871 W. DRYSDALE *Let.* (*O.E.D.*), I have already, by postal, . . . acknowledged receipt of your late favour. **1881** RITTENHOUSE *Maud* 7 Wrote postals to Mama and Elmer. **1893** *Harper's Mag.* Dec. 60/2 She was thinking of Sally Ann's postal. **1911** FERBER *Dawn O'Hara* 103 She wrote picture postals like mad. **1920** HOWELLS *Vacation of Kelwyns* 208 Just drop a postal.

2. Short for POSTAL CAR.

1891 *Rep. Postmaster-Gen.* 583, 2 daily lines of 50-foot postals superseding 2 lines of 40-foot.

Postal, *a.* Of or pertaining to the carriage of the mails. {1843-} — **1844** TYLER in *Pres. Mess. & P.* IV. 315, I transmit to the Senate . . . a postal convention between the United States and the Republic of New Granada, signed in the city of Bogota on the 6th of March last. **1849** *Whig Almanac 1850* 34/1 On the 21st of Dec., 1848, a letter . . . [proposed] an excellent practical system of postal reform. **1872** *Statutes at Large* XVII. 201 The postmaster . . . is hereby authorized . . . to issue, or to cause to be issued, . . . postal money-orders payable at any other money-order office. **1887** *Postal Laws* 417 Postal officers . . . will place within the outer mail bag a registered package card-receipt. **1894** *Congress. Rec.* 8 Aug. 8326/2 Chicago is today easily the second great postal point in the Union.

+**Postal car.** A railway mail car. Also attrib. — **1868** *N.Y. Herald* 17 July 5/6 A postal car is attached . . . to the express trains from New York to Buffalo. **1878** *45th Congress 2 Sess.* Sen. Misc. Doc. No. 14, p. xxviii, The limited mail-train over the Pennsylvania Central consisted of two postal-cars and four or five passenger-cars. **1879** *Statutes at Large* XX. 357 The Postmaster General shall separate the estimate for postal-car service from the general estimates. **1903** E. JOHNSON *Railway Transportation* 176 The postal cars now being put into service are models of the builder's art.

+**Postal card. a.** A post card with a postage stamp printed upon it that is issued by the Post Office Department. **b.** A picture post card. (Cf. POSTAL *n.* 1.)

1872 *Statutes at Large* XVII. 304 The Postmaster-General . . . [is] authorized and directed to furnish and issue to the public, with postage-stamps impressed upon them, 'postal cards,' manufactured of good stiff paper. **1884** NYE *Baled Hay* 178 No one denies that the postal card is a great thing, and yet it makes people mad to get one. **1896** *Vt. Agric. Rep.* XV. 69 A postal card addressed to the Station asking to be placed on its mailing list [is] sufficient. **1903** ELY *Evolution Indust. Soc.* 244 A postal card is put in the post office addressed as the parcel is. **1916** WILSON *Somewhere* 345, I wanted to send a postal card to the North American Cleaning and Dye Works.

+**Postal clerk.** A railway mail clerk. Also attrib. — **1872** *Statutes at Large* XVII. 310 Every route-agent, postal clerk, or other carrier of the mail shall receive any mail-matter presented to him, if properly prepaid by stamps. **1887** *Postal Laws* 408 The Registered-Pouch Service, for the exchange of registered mail . . . between terminal post-offices on postal-clerk lines. **1900** *Congress. Rec.* 3 Jan. 641/1 House bill No. 4351, for the reclassification of postal clerks.

+**Postal currency.** A paper currency authorized July 17, 1862, the notes of which bore the facsimiles of postage stamps. Now hist.

Issued to take the place of actual postage stamps, which had been used instead of coins, and superseded by the fractional currency (q.v.) authorized in 1863. (Cf. POSTAGE CURRENCY, POSTAGE-STAMP CURRENCY.)

1862 *Washington Republican* 15 Aug. 2/3 The five and twenty-five cents stamps are printed on yellow bank note paper, and the tens and fifties on white paper. Their technical denomination is 'postal currency.' **1867** LOCKE *Swingin' Round* 172 Our wallets is barren uv postal currency. **1868** *40th Congress 2 Sess.* H. R. Ex. Doc. No. 218, 1 The *postal* currency was the first government issue representing fractional parts of a dollar, and was commenced in August, 1862, and closed in April, 1863. **1894** LEAVITT *Our Money Wars* 203 Postal Currency Gone [in 1876].

+**Postal note.** A money order bearing the name of the payee. *Obs.* — **1882** *Nation* 27 July 64/1 A bill providing for the issue of postal notes for sums not exceeding five dollars was passed in the House on Friday. **1887** *Postal Laws* 477 A money-order issued on such new form shall be designated and known as a 'postal note,' and a fee of three cents shall be charged for the issue thereof. **1893** CUSHING *Story of P.O.* 213 A postal note may be drawn for any amount less than $5.

Postal savings bank. A savings bank operated by the Post Office Department. {1885 (*Encycl. Brit.* XIX. 572/2)} Also attrib. — **1891** *Atlantic Mo.* June 814/2 A school savings bank or postal savings bank system, as recommended by the Mohonk Negro conference, would be of great benefit to the colored people. **1893** CUSHING *Story of P.O.* 746 A letter from the Postmaster General . . . accompanied fourteen bills (advocating postal savings banks, a postal telegraph and postal telephone, pneumatic tubes [etc.]). **1900** *Congress. Rec.* 11 Jan. 760/1 A petition . . . praying for the establishment of postal savings banks throughout the country. **1902** J. H. HAMILTON *Savings* 425 The postal savings banks are . . . an invaluable supplement to any other system.

Postal telegraph. A proposed telegraph system to be operated under the authority of the Post Office Department. {1869- (*Act 32 & 33 Vict.* c. 73 § 23)} Freq. attrib. — **1868** *N.Y. Herald* 11 July 4/1 A bill establishing the postal telegraph system and incorporating a company for the purpose was introduced and referred. **1883** *Harper's Mag.* Oct. 790/1 The strike has turned public attention to the question of a postal telegraph. **1888** *Solid Muldoon* (Ouray, Colo.) (F.), The Eastern press is a dead unit against the passage of the postal telegraph bill. **1900** *Congress. Rec.* 8 Jan. 664/2 The Senator from North Carolina asks unanimous consent for the printing of a paper touching the postal telegraph system.

+**Post and rail.** See POST(S) AND RAIL(S).

+**Post auger.** An instrument for boring post holes. — **1819** *Plough Boy* I. 123 Hoxie's patent post auger for digging post holes. **1869** *Rep. Comm. Agric. 1868* 354 Its practicability can always be ascertained by digging a well, or by boring with a pile or post auger. **1901** MERWIN & WEBSTER *Calumet 'K'* 269 A swarm of men with spades, post augers, picks, and shovels had invaded the C. & S.C. right-of-way.

Post-bellum. {1883-} *attrib.* +After the Civil War (1861-5). Cf. ANTE-BELLUM. — **1900** *Congress. Rec.* 1 Feb. 1413/2 Every glowing fact in her [N. Carolina's] glorious history and development—colonial, Revolutionary, ante-bellum and post-bellum—proclaims the greatness . . . of her people. **1904** PAGE in *McClure's Mag.* April 622/1 Then came the worst enemy that either race had ever had: the post-bellum politician. **1911** HARRISON *Queed* 276 No writer has yet done anything like justice to the old soldier cult in the post-bellum South. **1912** NICHOLSON *Hoosier Chron.* 75 She continued her efforts . . . , summoning from the shadows all the Hoosier statesmen of the post-bellum period to aid her.

+**Post bill.** 'A bill of letters mailed by a postmaster' (W. '41). — **1792** *Ann. 2d Congress* 62 The deputy postmasters . . . [shall] answer to him, for all by or way letters, and shall specify the same . . . in the post bill. **1794** *Ann. 3d Congress* 1438 The Postmaster shall duly enter the same, and specify the number and rate or rates in the post-bill. **1833** *Niles' Reg.* XLIV. 371/2 It appears from the post bill that this mail had been received at the post office in Cincinnati. **1855** HOLBROOK *Among Mail Bags* 375 As the post-bill was missing, the Hartford post master expressed the opinion that the letter had very probably fallen into the hands of the mail robber.

Post card. A correspondence card sent through the mail without an envelope. {1870-} In recent years often distinguished from the postal card (q.v.) issued by the Post Office Department. — **1879** WEBSTER

Suppl. 1573/3 *Postal-card, Post-card.* A card sold by the government for transmission through the mails, at a lower rate of postage than a sealed letter. The message is written on one side of the card, and the direction on the other. **1903** *Booklovers Mag.* Oct. 403 All stores handle post-cards as side lines. **1908** 'O. HENRY' *Options* 132 Not a chalk-mark on the gate-post nor a post-card in the post-office to give us a clew.

+**Post cedar. 1.** An incense cedar, *Libocedrus decurrens.* **2.** The white cedar, *Chamaecyparis thyoides.* — **(1) 1884** SARGENT *Rep. Forests* 176 *Libocedrus decurrens.* . . . White Cedar. Bastard Cedar. Post Cedar. Incense Cedar. **1897** SUDWORTH *Arborescent Flora* 64 *Libocedrus decurrens.* . . . Post Cedar (Cal., Nev., Idaho). **(2) 1897** SUDWORTH *Arborescent Flora* 77 *Chamæcyparis thyoides.* . . . Post Cedar (Del.).

Post chaise. A closed, horse-drawn carriage for travelling, esp. one hired from one stage to another. {1712-} — **1765** *Mass. Gazette* 5 June 4/2 Chariots, post chaises, phaetons, curricles. **1791** BENTLEY *Diary* I. 277 Expences of a Hackney Coach or Post Chaise, 12/. **1818** *Niles' Reg.* XIV. 168/1 The post chaise between New-York and Philadelphia makes the trip in a little more than *eleven hours.*

Post coach. A stagecoach, esp. one carrying mail. {1673-}

1790 *Penna. Packet* 1 Jan. 3/3 Establishment of the Post Coaches. **1823** J. M. DUNCAN *Travels U.S.* II. 316 Post coaches, as they are called, which have been recently introduced on the roads between New York and Baltimore, . . . are beginning to make their appearance in some other places. **1834** PECK *Gaz. Illinois* 322 Here is a post office where the mail is received in post coaches six times a week. **1841** PARK *Pantology* 480 The chariot, and post coach, have only one seat, for two or more persons, inside; but, like the preceding, are drawn by two or more horses.

+**Post croaker.** =LAFAYETTE 1. — **1896** JORDAN & EVERMANN *Checklist Fishes* 399 *Leiostomus Xanthurus.* . . . Spot; Goody; Post-croaker; Oldwife; Lafayette.

Post day. The day on which mail arrives at or leaves a place. *Obs.* {1670-} Cf. MAIL DAY. — **1776** in *S. Lit. Messenger* XXVII. 326/2 The Rider . . . refused to set out a day sooner than he used to do before the alteration of the Post day. **1780** *Essex Inst. Coll.* XIII. 222, I was unable on the last postday to thank you for yr. favor of Novr. 23d. **1784** *Belknap P.* I. 51 As it is post day, I am in the midst of business and hurry.

+**Post-driver. 1.** An implement for driving posts into the ground. **2.** =AMERICAN BITTERN. — **(1) 1857** *Rep. Comm. Patents 1856* I. 128 Sampson, Junium M. Post-driver Mar. 25, 1856. **(2) 1888** *Harper's Mag.* Sept. 509/1 The call of the caribou . . . is a hoarse pumping sound, very much of the character emitted by that species of bittern called by some a 'post-driver,' or 'stake-driver,' only vastly louder.

Posted, *a.* {1602-} +Well-informed; supplied with the latest news. Used in both predicate and attrib. positions. Also with *up.* (Cf. POST *v.*[2])

1847 *National Encycl.* I. 619 *Posted-up* is an Americanism for well-informed, thoroughly conversant with. **1855** MITCHELL *Fudge Doings* I. 54 She is 'well posted' in regard to all these matters. **1875** *Chicago Tribune* 8 July 7/4 It is their intention to look over the ground and become fully posted before they attempt to talk with the Indians. **1880** 'MARK TWAIN' *Tramp Abroad* 354 He was shrewd, prompt, posted, and punctual. **1898** *Kansas City Star* 20 Dec. 5/1 Clem Fairchild, one of the best posted members of the majority, declared that no amendment of the rules is necessary. **1914** 'BOWER' *Flying U Ranch* 61 We'll keep you posted, and I'll write all the particulars as soon as I can.

Poster.[1] A placard or bill displayed, or intended to be displayed, in public; also, copy for one. {1838-}

1845 J. W. NORRIS *Chicago Directory* 136 Bill Heads, Hand Bills, Posters, and all other printing in this branch. **1869** 'MARK TWAIN' *Innocents* 167 The tall van, plastered with fanciful bills and posters, that follows the band-wagon of a circus. **1901** MERWIN & WEBSTER *Calumet 'K'* 112 So we got up a poster and had it printed, telling what they all think of the G. & M. **1920** LEWIS *Main Street* 112 [She was] grateful for the protection of a billboard covered with ragged posters.

+**Poster.**[2] *Football.* A drop kick or place kick for a goal in which the ball touches the goalposts. *Obs.* — **1876** in P. H. Davis *Football* 462 Whether it touch such cross-bar or the posts it is called a poster and is not a goal.

Post-free, *a.* Free from a postage charge. {1882-; cf. postage-free, 1692} — **1723** *Boston News-Letter* 7 March 2/2 The Publisher . . . Desires them to send their Accounts Post-Free.

+**Postgraduate,** *n.* A person taking a course of study or reading after graduation; a graduate. Also fig. — **1890** *Cent.* 4641/3 *Postgraduate,* . . . a graduate; one studying after graduation. **1900** *Congress. Rec.* 19 Feb. 1917/1 Now, the Senator is a senior, a post-graduate of great distinction of the academy of which he is now a member. **1904** WALLER *Wood Carver* 178 Marking out the work for the post-graduates . . . has filled my time.

+**Postgraduate,** *a.* Pertaining to a course of study carried on after graduation. — **1858** *N.Y. Tribune* 12 Nov. 5/5 Prof. Francis Lieber gave yesterday . . . a lecture introductory to a series on the History of Commerce, forming a portion of the Post-Graduate Course of Columbia College. **1877** PHELPS *Story of Avis* 62 Avis . . . [had] finished, as one was careful to say in Harmouth, her *school* education, thus delicately expressing the true Harmouth compassion for those types of society in which post-graduate courses of reading were not added to a young lady's accomplishments. **1896** *Century Mag.* March 798/2 There is scarcely one [university] that does not now provide an annex or postgraduate opportunities for [women].

+**Post guide.** *Conn.* A post serving as a guide to travelers; a guide-post. *Obs.* — **1796** *Conn. Acts & Laws* 344 The Select-men in the several Towns . . . [shall] erect, and keep up Post-Guides . . . [indicating] the principal Road, or Roads, from the Towns wherein they are erected, to the Town . . . adjoining. **1839** *Conn. Statute Laws* 637 Any person or persons [who] shall pull down, break, or deface any mile-stone, post-guide, or other monument for the direction of travellers . . . shall pay . . . treble damages.

Post hole. A hole dug in the ground for a post. {1703} Also attrib. — **1722** *New-Eng. Courant* 2 April 2/2 A Man's Bones were taken up in a Garden . . . by some Carpenters who were digging Post-Holes for a Fence. **1863** *Rep Comm. Patents 1861* I. 588 Improvement in Post-hole Excavators. **1869** *Ib. 1868* I. 743/2 James K. Miller, New York, N.Y.—Post Hole Borer. **1891** HOLMES *Over Teacups* 219, I engaged him, I say, to dig some post-holes.

Post horn. A straight, conical horn formerly used by mail carriers or mail-coach drivers. {1675-} — **1746** FRANKLIN *Writings* II. 298 Please to send me . . . a dozen of post horns of different sizes. **1773** FINLAY *Journal* 22 Mr. Emerson thinks that the want of Post-horns is a loss to the office, for by warning given by the horn many letters wou'd go by Post which are now sent by other oportunity's. **1835** *S. Lit. Messenger* I. 546 This impression is not diminished by the winding of the post horn from the 'western stage' as it rattles over the crags of the mountain above. **1876** INGRAM *Centennial Exp.* 416 We fancied we could hear the silvery note of the old 'post-horn.' **1904** WALLER *Wood-Carver* 299 The scream of the locomotive . . . sounded forever the doom of the Hornet's post-horn.

***Post horse.** A horse used for traveling post. — **1712** HEMPSTEAD *Diary* 6, I keep ye Post horse. **1815** *N. Amer. Rev.* I. 15 There being no post-horses on the roads, almost all our journeying is in these vehicles.

Posthouse. A post office. *Obs.* {1635-; now *obs.* or *dial.*} — **1697** SEWALL *Diary* I. 465 Letters are at the Posthouse. **1701** in Dexter *Doc. Hist. Yale Univ.* 25, I haue a letter at the post house in wch I can putt this.

***Postilion.** One who rides the near lead horse when four or more horses are used with a post chaise or other carriage; the rider of a near horse of any team. {1623-33-} Also appositive. Now hist. — **1705** SEWALL *Diary* II. 122 The Govr, his Lady, Driver, Postilion, Troopers escaped all safe. **1830** BRECK in *Recoll.* (1877) 181 A coach-and-four with two postilions, and an out-rider in handsome livery stood at the door. **1853** POYAS *Peep into Past* 123 Peter became the Postilion boy. **1895** G. KING *New Orleans* 262 The postilion would gallop his horses in a sweeping circle through the great courtyard.

+**Postilion basque.** (See quot. 1890.) — **1871** *Scribner's Mo.* II. 209 Bodices are pointed in front and lengthened into postillion basques behind. **1890** *Cent.* 4642/3 *Postilion-basque,* a woman's basque having its skirt cut at the back into short square tabs or coat-tails, after the fashion of a postilion's coat.

Posting. {1656-} +The action of putting down fence posts. — **1788** WASHINGTON *Diaries* III. 321 In the Neck, the Posting, Railing, and ditching was compleated this Morning up to the Gate.

***Postman.** A mailman; a mail-carrier.

1691 *Mass. H. S. Coll.* 3 Ser. VII. 54 Any ferryman . . . [who] shall at any time neglect, or refuse, or delay the conveying over his . . . ferry, any post-man or his horse, . . . shall forfeit the sum of five pounds. **1842** *Diplom. Corr. Texas* III. (1911) 1001 Your favor of the 29th Inst. . . . has just been handed in by the Postman. **1885** HOWELLS *S. Lapham* xxii, The morning postman brought Mrs. Lapham a letter from Irene. **1912** NICHOLSON *Hoosier Chron.* 9 A certain day . . . found her meeting the postman far across the campus.

Postmark. Any mark officially put on a piece of mail, esp. one which indicates the time and place of mailing. {1678-} — **1825** NEAL *Bro. Jonathan* II. 158 Mr. Ashley . . . [looked] at the date—post-mark—signature. **1856** M. J. HOLMES *L. Rivers* 260 He brought one . . . which bore the post-marks of several places. **1881** STODDARD *E. Hardery* 159 The post-mark is San Francisco.

Postmarking stamp. An instrument for stamping a postmark on a piece of mail. — **1859** *Postal Regulations* § 397 The use of the office dating or post-marking stamp as a canceling instrument is prohibited.

***Postmaster.** (See also DEPUTY POSTMASTER.)

1. A man in charge of a post office {1603-}, +esp., since the establishment of the United States, a civil officer under the Postmaster-General.

In early colonial times, some postmasters carried mail: (see quot. 1697 and RIDING POSTMASTER.)

1680 *Mass. Bay Rec.* V. 273 It is ordered that he be continued for postmaster. **1697** [see POST *n.*[2] 1 b]. **1703** *Mass. H. S. Coll.* VII. 62 In regard that the Post Master General . . . is incapacitated to give such salaries to the several Post Masters, as is requisite [etc.]. **1740** W. STEPHENS *Proc. Georgia* I. 649 A new Post-Master being lately appointed, he suffered no Letters to be brought ashore. **1776** *Jrnls. Cont. Congress* IV. 107 Resolved, That . . . Dr. Franklin be directed to write to post masters and enquire on what terms expresses can be procured. **1821** *Ann. 17th Congress* 1 Sess. I. 43 To permit the Postmasters, in the Western country, to receive, for postages on letters, the currency of the State in which the said offices are located. **1890** *Stock Grower & Farmer* 1 Feb. 4/4 We would establish a postal telegraph system, and have the postmasters elected by the people. **1900** *Congress. Rec.* 3 Jan. 635/1 Charles N. Cooper, to be postmaster at Huron, in the county of Beadle and State of South Dakota. **1924** MULFORD *Rustler's Valley* 139 The postmaster . . . reached for the cancelling hammer, filling the small room with swift and regular thuddings.

+**2.** *Colonial.* A deputy postmaster-general.

1704 *Boston News-Letter* 24 April 2/2 All Persons in Town and Country, may have said News-Letter . . . Agreeing with John Campbell, Postmaster for the same. **1717** *Mass. H. Rep. Jrnl.* I. 214 A letter of John Campbell, post-master of New-England.

Postmaster-general.

1. The administrative head of a postal system. {1626-}

+**a.** Of a colony or colonies.

1691 *Mass. H. S. Coll.* 3 Ser. VII. 52 The said Post Master general, shall settle or cause to be settled posts or running messengers for that purpose. **1693** *Mass. Province Laws* I. 117 The postmaster-general . . . shall continue constant posts for the carriage of letters to the several places and stages above mentioned. **1694** *Conn. Rec.* IV. 123 This Court . . . doe order and enact that all such persons as shall be imployed by the Post Master Generall in the severall stages within this Colony of Conecticutt shall and may pass and repass all and every ferry . . . without payeing any rate. **1712** *N.J. Archives* 1 Ser. IV. 154 John Hamilton, Postmaster Generall of North America. **1756** *Md. Gazette* 4 March, By command of the Postmasters-General.

+**b.** Of the United States under the Continental Congress and later under the Constitution.

The Postmaster-General became a member of the president's cabinet in 1829.

1775 *Amer. Hist. Review* I. 291 Dr Franklin the PostMaster General desired the Delegates of New Jersey to nominate Deputy PostMasters throughout that Colony. **1789** *Ann. 1st Congress* I. 90, I [Washington] likewise nominate . . . Samuel Osgood, for Postmaster General. **1792** *Ann. 2d Congress* 59 There shall be one Postmaster General, who shall have authority to appoint an assistant and deputy postmasters, at all places where such shall be found necessary. **1840** *Niles' Nat. Reg.* 28 March 58/3 A letter from the postmaster general, transmitting a report. **1900** *Congress. Rec.* 16 Jan. 873/1 It is highly important, that the Postmaster-General should obey the law.

2. *Deputy postmaster-general,* a regional administrative officer under the postmaster-general.

1715 *Boston News-Letter* 11 April 2/2 Complaint being made to the Deputy Post Master General of New England . . . [that] the said Letters are long detain'd from the Owners, several often lost and never delivered, others Imbezell'd and Open'd, to the great loss and prejudice of the Merchants.

Postmistress. A woman in charge of a post office. {1697-} — **1824** *Boston D. Advertiser* 7 Aug. 2/4 Postmistress. A New-Jersey paper announces that Mrs. Jane Wilson . . . received a commission . . . appointing her postmaster at Trenton in the place of her deceased husband. **1865** *Atlantic Mo.* Feb. 148/2 The postmistress *ex officio* . . . proceeds to assort the Ashfield mail. **1890** *Century Mag.* Aug. 510/1 If the door still refuses to yield . . . probably the postmistress 'has battened down the hatches' and gone 'gamming.' **1905** *N.Y. Ev. Post* 27 Oct. 6 [President Roosevelt] is one of the blackest of black Republicans. For example, he had closed a Mississippi post-office because some whites had made trouble for the colored postmistress.

+**Post note.** [L. *post* 'after' and *note.*] A promissory note payable to order at a specified future date. Distinguished from a note payable to bearer on demand. Now hist.

Issued by banks and other financial institutions before the Civil War as a circulating medium and especially 'resorted to by many banks during the great commercial revulsions in 1836-7' (B. '48).

1791 JEFFERSON in *Harper's Mag.* LXX. 534/2 Recd. from bank a post note . . . for 116⅔ D. **1804** *New York Herald* 9 June 3/4 Lost. . . . The following post notes: . . . no. 1238, payable to Joseph Roberts, dated Philadelphia, Sep. 23, 1801. **1836** *Mass. Laws* XIII. 967 The banks . . . may borrow money, and issue therefor post notes upon time, and bearing interest at not less than four and one half per cent, per annum. **1839** RAGUET *On Currency & Banking* 112n., The banks of New York are prohibited from issuing post-notes. **1844** *Maine Reports* XXIV. 37 The defendant's intestate . . . put into the hands of the plaintiffs' cashier, J. R. Groton, certain post notes, issued by the Mississippi Shipping Company. **1852** GOUGE *Fiscal Hist. Texas* 97 The money . . . consisted of United States Bank post-notes. **1912** DREISER *Financier* 20 Steemberger . . . used to come to the elder Cowperwood's bank . . with . . . post-notes of the United States Bank in denominations of one thousand, five thousand, and ten thousand dollars.

+**Post oak.**

1. One of various species of oak, the wood of which is suitable for posts; a tree of any of these species, or its wood.

Applied chiefly to the iron oak (*Quercus stellata*) of the eastern states and the swamp post oak (*Q. lyrata*) of the South.

[**1764** REUTER *Wachau* 559 Post Oak.] **1775** ROMANS *Nat. Hist. Fla.* 18 The principal however are the following: . . . Virginian white oak. . . . Dwarf white oak, or post oak. **1819** E. DANA *Geog. Sketches* 239 Extensive flats, however, occur, of post oak, always growing on a poor, wet soil. **1835** IRVING *Tour Prairies* 126 Straggling forests of the kind of low scrubbed trees . . . called 'post-oaks,' and 'black-jacks.' **1852** MARCY *Explor. Red River* (1854) 6 The country adjoining is high, rolling prairie, interspersed here and there with groves of post-oak, and presents to the eye a most pleasing appearance. **1884** SARGENT *Rep. Forests* 139 *Quercus obtusiloba.* . . . Post Oak. Iron Oak. **1901** W. L. JEPSON *Flora of W. Middle Calif.* 142 *Q[uercus] Garryana.* Pacific Post Oak. . . . In the mountains at lower or middle elevations.

2. Attrib. with *acorn, land, prairie land, wood.*

1800 HAWKINS *Sk. Creek Country* 20 Between these rivers, there is some good post and black oak land. **1819** SCHOOLCRAFT *Mo. Lead Mines* 37 The wild turkey is still very common . . . during the heat of the day in the open post oak woods. **1847** DEWEES *Lett. from Texas* 302 There is almost always enough [mast] to fatten hogs. We have the post-oak acorn, the black-jack [etc.]. **1868** *Rep. Comm. Agric. 1867* 61 In Lowndes county, Alabama, . . . great havoc was committed . . . in the post oak prairie lands.

+**Post-oak flat.** A flat stretch of land covered with post oaks. — **1844** GREGG *Commerce of Prairies* II. 193 Some of the uplands, . . . known usually as 'post-oak flats,' . . . seem to be based upon quick-sand. **1862** *Ill. Agric. Soc. Trans.* V. 567 [Sugar cane] brought from the post-oak flats and red clay soil along the edge of the timber, has far excelled, in quality of sirup, that grown in the deep, black mold of the center of the prairie. **1882** *Econ. Geol. Illinois* II. 105 We find some regular post-oak flats, with white soil and level surface. **1905** 'O. HENRY' *Four Million* 58 Joe Larrabee came out of the post-oak flats of the Middle West.

+**Post-oak grape.** The summer grape, *Vitis aestivalis.* — **1845** F. B. PAGE *Prairiedom* 83 The post-oak grape . . . grows abundantly on the high-lands bordering on the western rivers [in Texas]. **1891** COULTER *Bot. W. Texas* I. 62 Summer grape. . . . Abounding in the sandy post-oak woods of eastern Texas it is called 'post-oak grape' or 'sand-grape.'

Post office. {1652-}

1. a. A place from which mail is either transmitted to various destinations or distributed locally; a building in which mail is handled. {1679-} **b.** The local organization for handling mail.

1680 *Mass. Bay Rec.* V. 273 It is ordered, . . . that all masters of ships or other vessells doe, vpon their arrivall, send their letters that come in the bagg to the sajd post office. **1704** *Boston News-Letter* 13 Nov. 2/2 A Negro Woman Slave . . . to be Sold by Mr. Nicholas Boone Bookseller, and to be seen at the London Coffee-House, next door to the Post-Office in Boston. **1708** *Ib.* 11 Oct. 4/2 Several persons do refuse to take up, receive and pay for their Letters that come and go by Post, to the great detriment of the Post-Office. **1758** FRANKLIN *Writings* III. 440 The Post-Office, if 'tis agreable to you, may be removed to Mr. Dunlap's House, it being propos'd by our good Friend Mr. Hughes. **1775** *Virginia Gaz.* 4 March, A Few Boxes Of Keyser's Famous Pills To Be Sold At The Post Office. **1787** [see POST ROAD]. **1837** W. JENKINS *Ohio Gaz.* 59 *Andrew's,* a post office at the site of a newly laid out town of the same name. **1871** *Harper's Mag.* Oct. 655 The post-office was in the Rotunda building and in the house of a hook-and-ladder company adjoining. **1905** 'O. HENRY' *Strictly Business* 37 The crop of farmers is never so short out there but what you can get a few of 'em to sign a petition for a new post office that you can discount for $200 at the county bank.

2. The organization or department of government charged with conveying and distributing the mails; the service provided by this organization. {1652-}

The first post-office organization was set up by the General Court of Massachusetts in 1639; an intercolonial post office was established in 1692. (Cf. GENERAL POST OFFICE.)

1692 *N.Y. Legisl. Council Jrnl.* I. 26 Col. Hamilton having presented some proposalls concerning a Post Office to be Erected & Established throughout their Ma[jes]tyes Territoryes upon the Main of America [etc.]. **1694** *Conn. Rec.* IV. 123 Their most excelent Ma[jes]ties King Wm. and Queen Mary . . . have granted a Post Office to be set up in these parts of New England. **1732** *N.Y. Gazette* 31 July 1/2 The Post-Office that was first begun in America, by Col. Hamilton of New-Jersey, about 38 years ago, has never yet been established to the Southward of Philadelphia. **1774** S. ADAMS in *Warren-Adams Lett.* I. 25 Mr. Watson will inform you what Steps our Committee of Correspondence have taken with Regard to the Establishment of a Post Office upon constitutional Principles. **1789** *Ann. 1st Congress* I. 893 They have passed a bill for the temporary establishment of the Post-Office. **1853** STOWE *Key* 126/2 This very man would not send a fifty-dollar bill through the post-office, in an unsealed letter. **1872** *Atlantic Mo.* Feb. 253 The Post-Office announces that it desires to assume the business of telegraphy. **1909** PARKER *G. Cleveland* 94 When Mr. Cleveland came into power the Post-Office was growing with great rapidity.

+**3.** With identifying words.

Branch post office, a branch of a main city post office, providing services connected with the mails; *distributing p.,* a post office set up for the distribution of local mail; *inferior p.,* in colonial times, one of the provincial post offices (q.v., sense 1); *private p.,* a privately controlled place or organization for handling private mail, as that of a company; *volunteer p.,* a post office run by volunteer help.

1871 BAGG *At Yale* 213 A branch post-office was connected with the Bookstore, the 'boxes' whereof were rented for a dollar each, or one half the price of those in the general office. **1819** E. Dana *Geogr. Sk.* 78 The distributing post-office is kept here. **1711** *Boston News-Letter* 16–23 April 2/2 The Inferiour Post-Offices in this Province of the Massachusetts-Bay, New-Hampshire, Rhode-Island and Connecticut will also take in Letters to go by the said Pacquet. **1848** *Whig Almanac 1849* 47/2 Private post-offices, as in New York, ought not to be required, with a surplus cent levied on each letter. **1860** Greeley *Overland Journey* 125 A volunteer post-office is just established, to which an express-office will soon attach itself.

+**4.** A place or town with a post office.

1860 Greeley *Overland Journey* 39 Our next post-office above Jones's was Hickory Grove. **1872** Tice *Over Plains* 122 A short distance southeast of Middle Boulder Post-office, rich lodes have been discovered.

+**5.** A kind of kissing game.

1904 Darrow *Farmington* 163 We had to keep still, and couldn't go outdoors, and had to play 'needle's eye' and 'post-office.'

6. *attrib.* **a.** Designating things handled by, or used in, the post office.

1827 *Amer. State P.: Post Office* 304 William J. Stone, [for] Post office stamps, [$]128.49. **1860** *36th Congress 1 Sess.* H.R. Rep. No. 648, 43 With regard to the printing of the post office blanks, Mr. Brown testifies [etc.]. **1867** *Ore. State Jrnl.* 18 May 3/1, I have received instructions from the Post Office Department authorizing the issuing of 'Post Office Money Orders.' **1880** Whitman *Spec. Days* 162 To-day [I received] a letter from Mrs. E. S. L., Detroit, accompanied in a little post-office roll by a rare old engraved head of Elias Hicks. **1881** *Ore. State Jrnl.* 15 Jan. 1/2 Remittances by Draft, Postoffice Order, Wells Fargo & Co's Express, and Registered Letter at our risk.

b. Designating governmental acts, actions, or legislation respecting the post office.

1774 J. Adams *Diary* Works II. 389 The Post-office Act was before the year 1763. **1840** *Log Cabin* (N.Y.) 26 Dec. 2/5 Post Office Reform. . . . There must be a modification of the Rates of Postage. **1854** Benton *30 Years' View* I. 23/1 The post-office and post-road grant.

c. Designating persons connected, or hoping to be connected, with the post office.

1855 Holbrook *Among Mail Bags* 280 It had somehow leaked out that the 'Post-Office Agent' was there. **1866** Moore *Women of War* 251 Sceptical as the soldier had become of army agents and post-office clerks, he felt certain [etc.]. **1887** *Postal Laws* 218 Every post-office inspector carries a commission signed by the Postmaster-General. **1897** *Chicago Tribune* 25 July 15/2 Jo Bristow flocks by himself when he meets a crowd of fourth class postoffice aspirants on a Washington street.

+**Post-office address.** The name or address of a place to which mail will be delivered by the post office. — **1861** *Army Regulations* 373 Post-office address for October, Fort Jay. **1883** *Century Mag.* Aug. 635/1 He has been known even to leave his post-office address behind. **1901** *Chicago Tribune* 16 Feb., Give postoffice address in full, including county and State.

+**Post-office box.** One of many pigeonholes in a post office, in which private mail is put, to be either asked for or taken out by the renter of the box. Also attrib. and transf. — **1875** Burnham *Three Years* 244 A close watch was set at the Post Office Box named, in East Liberty. **1900** *Congress. Rec.* 17 Feb. 1902/1 For rent of office for the surveyor-general, . . . post-office box rent, . . . and other incidental expenses, $500. **1907** *St. Nicholas* May 645 It's our own little Post-office box!

Post-office building. 1. A building that houses a local post office. +**2.** A building in Washington, D.C., from which the Post-Office Department is administered. — **(1) 1870** *Republican Rev.* 16 April 2/2 Found . . . in front of the Post Office Building, a sum of money Federal currency. **(2) 1878** *Nation* XXVII. 93/1 The Congressional Committee now holding sessions in the Post-office building to enquire into the causes and remedy of the existing business depression have commenced work.

+**Post-office car.** A railroad mail car, esp. one designed for sorting mail. — **1857** *Mich. Gen. Statutes* I. (1882) 869 The prices shall not be less for carrying said mails in the regular passenger trains than the amount which said corporation would receive as freight on a like weight of merchandise transported on their merchandise train, and a fair compensation for their post-office car. **1867** *Western R.R. Ann. Rep.* 19 (Ernst), 3 Post Office cars, built for the government, which have not been used. **1903** E. Johnson *Railway Transportation* 180 The additional pay received by the railroads that supply and haul full-sized railway post-office cars is as follows.

Post-Office Department. +The department of the United States government charged with handling the mails. — **1782** *Jrnls. Cont. Congress* XXIII. 672 If any postmaster, post-rider, or other person employed in the Post Office Department, shall be guilty of a breach of the said oath . . . [he] shall forfeit and pay three hundred dollars. **1834** Jackson in *Pres. Mess. & P.* III. 117 The importance of the Post-Office Department and the magnitude to which it has grown . . . seem to demand its reorganization by law. **1901** *Chicago Tribune* 16 Feb., The laws of the Post-office department are strict, and newspapers insufficiently prepaid cannot be forwarded.

+**Post-office paper.** ? =Post paper. — **1842** *Cultivator* IX. 160 If young men . . . who lack wherewithal to amuse themselves . . . would procure a few quires of paper, (that called 'post office paper' is suitable,) and stitch them neatly together, and commence saving *scraps* from the newspapers . . . they would . . . gather a large bundle of Odds and Ends.

Post-office window. 1. An outside window of a post-office building. **2.** A window through which customers are served in a post office. — **(1) 1708** *Boston News-Letter* 15–22 March 2/2 Before Candle lighting if no Post be come in; The same is to be seen on a little Board hanging out at the Post-Office Window. **(2) 1892** *Harper's Mag.* March 636/2 Only one thing she has not learned, and that is, not to break into the head of a line waiting at the ticket-office or the post-office window.

Postpaid, *a.* With postage prepaid. {1653–} — **1708** *Boston News-Letter* 11 Oct. 4/2 Several persons do write upon their Letters Post paid, . . . without ever paying the Postage of the said Letters. **1814** *Niles' Reg.* V. 369/1 Letters to the editor must be post-paid. **1885** *Gentlemen Coon's Parade* 1 A Complete Descriptive Catalogue of DeWitt's Acting Plays, and Dewitt's Ethiopian and Comic Dramas . . . mailed free and post-paid.

Post paper. A writing paper of such a size that a half sheet folded forms the ordinary letter paper. {1648–} Cf. Post *n.*[2] 4. — **1754** *S.C. Gazette* 19 Feb. 3/1 Lately Imported, . . . white fustians and dimities, patterns of English chints, worsted damasks, post paper. **1770** *Md. Hist. Mag.* XIII. 62 Direct the Copies to be wrote on post paper & let me Have them. **1790** *Penna. Packet* 8 May 4/4 Thick and thin post paper gilt, black edges and plain. **1876** Knight 1773/2 Post paper is seldom sold in the *folio*, . . . but is cut in halves, folded, and forms quarto post, or common letter-paper.

+**Postrider.** One who rides post, either as a private or as a post-office employee. (Cf. Mail rider.)

1705 *Boston News-Letter* 19 Nov. 2/2 Whoever can give any true Intelligence of her to . . . the Post-Rider . . . shall be sufficiently Rewarded. **1759** *Penna. Gazette* 3 May 4/3 Ludwick Bierley, Lancaster Post-Rider, hereby informs his employers that it is now upwards of 12 months since he began to ride that stage. **1775** *Mass. H. S. Coll.* 3 Ser. VII. 89 It is recommended accordingly, to make an establishment for post riders between the Massachusetts forces and the town of Worcester. **1791** *Ann. 1st Congress* II. 2107 Stage drivers and private post riders may have been the carriers of many letters which ought to have gone in the mail. **1855** Barnum *Life* 130, [I] sent out tickets on commission by postriders. **1888** *Experiences of Forty-Niner* 28 He proved to be the mail post-rider from Santa Fé.

Post road. A road over which mail-carriers travel, or used to travel. Formerly provided with stations for post horses. {1657–}

1691 *Mass. H. S. Coll.* 3 Ser. VII. 52 For the post of each single letter from the post road in Connecticut Colony to Boston, nine pence. **1720** *Amer. Wkly. Mercury* 1 Dec. 2/1 An Act for keeping in Repair the Post Road from New York to Kingsbridge. **1787** *Constitution* i. § 8 The Congress shall have Power . . . To establish Post Offices and post Roads. **1819** R. M. Johnson *Broadside* (MS.), The whole length of the Post Roads in the United States is about 50,000 miles. **1856** *Harper's Mag.* June 117/2 A vigorous effort is on foot to induce the General Government to open a post-road and establish a line of weekly posts between California and Missouri. **1904** Waller *Wood-Carver* 3 The four-horse coach . . . lunges along the post-roads of Northern and Central Vermont.

b. With qualifying terms.

1751 in Kittredge *Old Farmer* (1904) 264 These are to signify to all Persons that travel the great Post-Road South-West from Boston, That I keep a House of Publick Entertainment. **1790** *Steele P.* I. 65, I have been using my utmost exertions to get the continental post road to pass through Fayetteville. **1815** *Niles' Reg.* IX. 92/1 The main post-road from the eastern to the southern states crosses the Brandywine on a hanging bridge of 148 feet chord. **1893** *Harper's Mag.* May 828, 1 The base-line for further development was the Boston Post Road—a blithe and bustling highway, along which ebbed and flowed constantly a strong tide of travel.

+**Post route.** A route by which a mail carrier travels. Also attrib. — **1773** Finlay *Journal* (1867) 1 The post route by lake Champlain was tedious and subject to retardments. **1831** *Congress. Deb.* 9 Feb. 159 Why do all his [Mr. McLean's] friends in both Houses oppose the passage of the post route bill? **1843** *P. O. Laws* I. 11 (*marginal note*), No letters to be carried on post routes, either by land or water. **1872** *Statutes at Large* XVII. 200 For preparing and publishing post-route maps, twenty-two thousand dollars. **1877** Hodge *Arizona* 204 Two great stage lines have been in operation in Arizona for many years, and several minor ones, and horseback post routes.

Post(s) and rail(s).

1. Fence posts and rails, once commonly used for the construction of fences. {1616–}

1641 *New Haven Col. Rec.* 54 Fencing wth. . . . strong and substantiall posts and rales . . . nott above 18d. **1657** *East-Hampton Rec.* I. 111 Begininge at a percell of post and railes vpon hoggnecke w[hi]ch post and railes the natives informed me was made formerly by Southhampton men. **1663** *Harvard Rec.* I. p. lxxv (*note*), [The town] granted Liberty To the Colledge for posts & rayles to fence in the yds. & a clapbord tree. **1779** E. Parkman *Diary* 107 He goes to ye Ministerial Lot to get Posts and Rails. **1818** Cobbett *Year's Residence* I. 13 The fences are of post and rail.

b. *ellipt.* =sense 2.

1671 *Portsmouth Rec.* 160 And for post and rayles it Shall be of the Same hight of the Virginia ffence. **1886** Roosevelt in *Century Mag.* July 338/1 It is impossible to come up at full speed and 'fly' a high post-and-rails, in the way a hedge, brook, or low fence can be gone at.

2. a. *Post-and-rail fence*, a fence constructed of rails attached to a series of posts. (Cf. POST *n.*[1] 1 b.)

1684 *Conn. Rec.* III. 512 Great parte of my post and rayle fences being feched and burnt by the sowders. **1765** WASHINGTON *Diaries* I. 216 Sowing . . . 19 Bushls in ye large cut within the Post and Rail fence. **1785** *Ib.* II. 360 The Post and Rail fences running from the Kitchen to the South Haw ha! and from the Servts. Hall to the North Haw ha! **c1835** FOBES *Arnold's Exped.* 8 We advanced to a post and rail fence through a shower of musket-balls. **1858** WARDER *Hedges & Evergreens* 115 He also has a post-and-rail-fence, that has stood for twenty-seven years. **1880** *Scribner's Mo.* Feb. 507/2 The fence which is half wall and half board has a homely, rural look, as has the low wall topped with rails, . . . which is as much of a 'post and rail' fence as we often find in northern New England.

b. *Post-and-rail fencing*, fencing made of posts and rails.

1786 WASHINGTON *Diaries* III. 30 [Spaded] a piece of ground No. West of the green House, adjoining thereto, the garden Wall, and Post and rail fencing lately erected as yards for my Stud horses.

Post stage. 1. A stopping place on a post road. {1642–} **+2.** A stagecoach. *Obs.* — **(1) 1732** *N.Y. Gazette* 31 July 1/2 Any one likewise, who wants Advertisements . . . dispersed, may have them fixt up at any, or all the Post-Stages. **(2) 1738** *Va. Gazette* 28 April, Alexander Spotswood, Esq.; . . . lately formed a new Regulation for carrying on the several Post-Stages with greater Expedition and Certainty than hitherto. **1771** *Essex Inst. Coll.* XI. 39 Benj. Hart . . . now drives the post stage lately improved by John Noble.

+Post stamp. A piece of postage currency. — **1863** *Merchants' Mag.* Feb. 133 It is no doubt the case, if the government paper money was discredited like post stamps or the shinplasters of individuals and corporations, a severe pressure would result for the moment.

Post town. A town in which a (main) post office is established. {1635–}

1703 *Mass. H. S. Coll.* 3 Ser. VII. 63 All towns in this Province, . . . where no Post office is settled, [should] be obliged to call for their letters at the next post town. **1796** HAWKINS *Letters* 14 He is in 4 miles of Pendleton Court House, a post town. **1809** CUMING *Western Tour* 302 Wilkinsonburg does not prosper, notwithstanding it is the capital of a county, and is a post town. **1851** A. CARY *Clovernook* 128 One day when her father was going to the post-town, . . . Annie asked him if he would inquire at the post-office for a letter for her. **1863** *Rio Abajo Press* 13 Oct. 2/2 The Press has subscribers in every post-town in the Territory. **1880** *Harper's Mag.* Nov. 891/1 The old mail-coach came lumbering in from the post-town.

+Post township. A town or township in which a post office is established. *Obs.* — **1837** W. JENKINS *Ohio Gaz.* 55 *Alexander*, a post township on the south line of Athens county. *Ib.* 85 *Boardman*, a flourishing post township of Trumbull county. **1842** *Popular Encycl.* V. 304/1 *Onondaga;* a post-township and capital of Onondaga county, New York.

+Post trader. A trader at a military or trading post. — **1871** *Republican Rev.* 1 April 2/1 Indians stole Levinsky's buggy horses from the Post trader's corral. **1882** *Nation* 7 Sept. 192 Reports that the Crow Indians of Montana have been committing depredations are denied by a post-trader, who asserts that they never were more peaceable than now. **1898** WISTER *Lin McLean* 8 [The Bishop] held the Episcopal service this Sunday morning for some brightly glittering army officers and their families, . . . the agency doctor, the post-trader [etc.].

Posture master. An expert in the art of assuming different bodily postures; a professional acrobat. {1691–} — **1752** *N.Y. Post-Boy* 4 May, Richard Brickell, with the famous Posture-Master lately arrived here, has taken the Theatre in Nassau-Street.

Posture woman. An adult female entertainer, expert in the art of assuming striking postures. — **1855** WOOD *Recoll. Stage* 456 For those who cared for neither negro singers, nor Italian ones, for dancing girls, nor posture women, new resorts have been multiplied in gaming houses.

+Post village. A village with an independent post office. {in Canada, 1907} — **1827** SHERWOOD *Gazetteer of Georgia* p. v, Post Village. **1837** W. JENKINS *Ohio Gaz.* 253 The post village of West Alexandria is situated on the north line of the township. **1857** DANA *Great West* 243 St. Paul. Post village and capital of Ramsay county, Minnesota Territory, on the left bank of the Mississippi. **1874** ALDRICH *P. Palfrey* vi, The letter . . . was dated at an obscure little post-village with a savage name somewhere on the frontiers of Montana.

***Posy.** In attrib. and comb. uses. — **1839** KIRKLAND *New Home* (1840) 145 Our vase of flowers usually a broken-nosed pitcher, is a 'posy-pot.' **1862** *N.Y. Tribune* 30 May 1/1 The sweet bells jingled all night in the Erbey posey-yard, 'mid altheas, honeysuckles, and roses. **1880** *Harper's Mag.* Sept. 586 The white-rose trees were pruned and trained, and a 'posy bed' by the south door made the yard gay and fragrant. **1887** *Ib.* July 306/1, I used to shet myself up here all day an' think I couldn't have no posy-gard'n. **1891** *Scribner's Mag.* Sept. 347 Old blue and white 'apothecary jars' . . . form for us nowadays a fine 'posy-holder.'

+Posy ball, dance. *Florida.* A festive ball of which the queen and king are chosen by the offer and acceptance of a bouquet. — **1837** WILLIAMS *Florida* 116 The Posey Dance, of St. Augustine is introduced in a different manner. *Ib.*, The lady selects from her visitors, some happy beau, . . . and presents him with a boquet [*sic*]. . . . If he accepts . . . , he is king of the ball, which shortly after succeeds, and the posey lass becomes queen, as a matter of course. The posey ball is a mixed assembly.

+Posy pea. (See quotation.) — **1893** *Amer. Folk-Lore* VI. 140 *Lathyrus odoratus*, posy peas. Franconia, N.H.

+Posy-watcher. (See quotation.) — **1843** *Congress. Globe* 29 Dec. 81/3 Mr. Wright presented a petition from James Wilson, the keeper of the gate at the Capitol (commonly called the posey-watcher.)

***Pot.**

***1.** A vessel of a rounded form, usually one employed in boiling or cooking.

1637 *Conn. Rec.* I. 12 If there be any . . . kittles, pottes, tooles, or any thinges els that belonges to the commonwealth, . . . they are to be delivered into the handes of the saide Constables. **1701** *Boston Rec.* 10 This order shall not be understood . . . to debarr . . . any tradesmen or others from kindling charcole in a pot or pan out of doore. **1792** *Ann. 2d Congress* 1043 This was a common pot with a wooden lid of the usual form, in the centre of which a hole was bored. **1805** *Pocumtuc Housewife* 20 (Ernst), A pot of Beans can be baking back side, out of the way, with the rest. **1889** COOKE *Steadfast* 13 On one side of the fire stood a bake-kettle and a four-legged pot. **1911** VANCE *Cynthia* 163 The several cooks responsible for its concoction hovered solicitously round the pot, exceedingly jealous of its ultimate perfection.

transf. **1880** *Harper's Mag.* Dec. 63 In these furnaces . . . there stand eight hundred big queer 'pots' . . . holding a syrupy mass that is molten glass.

+b. *To be pot and can in*, to be of one mind with respect to; *to boil pot*, to prepare a meal by boiling vegetables and meat together in a pot. (Cf. BOILED *ppl. a.* 2.)

1789 *Amer. Museum* V. 297/2, I suppose we shall be pot and can in the general conviction, that the kingdom cannot be supported by keeping clear consciences. **1850** S. WARNER *Wide, Wide World* xxxv, I tell you what, Ellen, we'll just boil pot for to-day; somebody else will send us something by to-morrow most likely.

***2.** An earthenware jar or crock in which butter is kept.

1680 *N.H. Hist. Soc. Coll.* VIII. 40 She bid her daughter Deborah take the pot of butter from her husband. **1684** I. MATHER *Providences* (1856) i. 21 They were forced . . . to betake themselves to their boat, taking with them a good supply of bread and a pot of butter. **1690** *Plymouth Laws* 232 Butter in firkin or pott at 6 *d.* p'r pound.

***3.** A hollow vessel for taking fish, crabs, or lobsters.

1765 *Mass. Province Laws* IV. 741 No person . . . [shall] catch any salmon, shad or alewives, with seines, nets or pots, . . . on pain of forfeiting for each offence the sum of three pounds. **1881** MCLEAN *Cape Cod Folks* 244 The boys were out in the bay 'setting pots.' **1911** *Rep. Fisheries 1908* 308 Crabs . . . are caught with scrap nets, dip nets, pots, seines [etc.].

b. The circular bowl or crib of a pound net.

1865 *Mich. Laws* 717 The size of the meshes of all the pot of said nets, shall not be less than two and a half inches in extension.

+4. =JACK POT 1 b. Also transf.

To open the pot, (see OPEN *v.* 3).

1856 BAGBY *Old Va. Gentleman* 228 He has no great faith in 'cases,' but believes in betting on three cards at a time, and has a special hankering for 'the pot.' **1880** *Congress. Rec.* 27 Feb. 1182/1 On another occasion the amount of money to be paid was by the same Senator called a 'pot.' *Ib.* 1186/1 It has been spoken of as a grab, or as this fund being one that was going into a common pot to be divided. **1884** CARLETON *Thompson St. Poker Club* (1889) 37 With this the Elder showed four aces, swept the pot into his hat and left the room. **1914** KEATE *Destruction Mephistos' Web* 72 They net the same results—that is, win the pot.

5. In special combinations.

Pot closet, a closet in which pots used in cooking are kept; *p. hound*, a hound of a worthless or nondescript breed; *p. roast*, a roast of meat suitable for cooking in a pot; *p. shell*, a potsherd; *potware*, pottery {1766}; *potworks*, a pottery.

1890 S. HALE *Letters* 245 This morning arrived the dusky band . . . who will . . . finish the *odds* and *ends* of cleaning, the bottom of the pot closet and the top of the front door. **1903** A. ADAMS *Log Cowboy* 238 Common old pot hounds and everyday yellow dogs have gone out of style entirely. **1882** F. E. OWENS *Cook Book* 59 Pot Roast of Beef. Get a solid piece from the round [etc.]. **1889** *Harper's Mag.* July 248 The pots are made of fire-clay . . . mixed in varying proportions of raw and burned clay and pieces of the broken pots called 'pot shells,' freed from glass and ground fine. **1661** *Southampton Rec.* II. 9, I give my children Sarah Mary and Josiah 18 parcels of pot ware. **1765** in *Harper's Mag.* LXII. 358/1 New pott-works in South Carolina.

Pot amaranth. (See quot. 1840.) — **1817–8** EATON *Botany* (1822) 170 *Amaranthus oleraceus*, pot amaranth. Sometimes the flowers are pentandrous. **1821** *Mass. H. S. Coll.* 2 Ser. IX. 146. **1840** DEWEY *Mass. Flowering Plants* 95 *A[maranthus] oleraceus.* Pot Amaranth. A smaller weed about gardens, with insignificant flowers; rarely used as a pot-herb.

Potash.

1. a. *pl.* Crude potassium carbonate obtained by leaching wood ashes in pots. {1648–} (Cf. BLACK SALTS.)

1624 *Va. House of Burgesses* 28 Most [of the passengers were] gentlemen . . . except some Polanders to make Pitch, tarre, Potashes. **1698** THOMAS *Pensilvania* 25 Their merchandize chiefly consists in . . . Tobacco, or Pot-Ashes, Wax, &c. **1708** *N.J. Archives* 1 Ser. III. 345 Ye Salt that the Pans produce will be a constant Supply for raising me Effects for making of ye said Pot-ashes. **1808** in *Niles' Reg.* XV. 57/2 Let us look at the rich productions of our interior country: . . . Pot and pearl ashes, tanners' bark. **1845** COOPER *Chainbearer* xiii, Ten acres of land, cropped for the first time, . . . [would] make a ton of pot-ashes, which would sell for at least two hundred dollars. **1884** ROE *Nature's Story* 102 He sent to New York for his phosphates, his potashes, [and] his muriates.

b. *sing.* =prec. {1751–}

1766 *Boston Ev.Post* 4 Aug. 2/3 Price current of merchantable potash in New York. **1796** *Boston Directory* 288 Townsend David, inspector of nails and pot-ash, Middle street. **1806** *Balance* V. 68/1 Let me again . . . call the public attention to a cheap and easy method of extinguishing the greatest flame by the application of pot-ash. **1921** *Dept. Agric. Yrbk. 1920* 365 Render the potash soluble before applying it as a fertilizer.

2. Attrib. and comb. with *house, maker, manufactory.*

1766 ROWE *Diary* 117 A fire . . . burnt Mr. Snow's potash house down. **1789** *Boston Directory* 178 Blair Victor, soap-boiler, pot-ash-maker. **1796** WANSEY *Excursion U.S.* 56, I heard there was a potash manufactory established [in Conn.].

+**Potashery.** (See quot. 1882.) — [**1846** G. WARBURTON *Hochelaga* I. 263 Potasheries, tanneries, breweries, iron-works, paper-works, and others.] **1882** THAYER *From Log-Cabin* 150 A pot-ashery was an establishment containing vats for leeching ashes, and large kettles for boiling the lye.

Potash kettle. A large vessel used in making potash. — **1790** *Penna. Packet* 2 Jan. 3/3 He can furnish pot-ash kettles, sugar boilers, . . . or any other kind of castings on a reasonable notice. **1819** *Plough Boy* I. 8 Constantly on hand, Potash Kettles, from 18 to 55 dollars. **1878** *Vermont Bd. Agric. Rep.* V. 105 The sap was . . . boiled in large potash kettles, with nothing but green wood, and seldom, if ever, any protection from the storms.

Potash work(s). An establishment where potash is made. — **1704** *Boston News-Letter* 4 Dec. 2/2 There is lately set up at Charlstown Ferry in Boston, a Pottash-work, at the house of John Russell Ferryman. **1708** *N.J. Archives* 1 Ser. III. 345 This would be a Constant support to me in Carrying on of the Pot-ash Works. **1734** *Doc. Hist. N.Y. State* I. 724 When the Dutch were in possession of this Collony they sett up a Pottash work at vast expence. **1801** BENTLEY *Diary* II. 394 Was called to attend a funeral below Ashe Street upon the Bank of the river, in Gen. Abbott's building where his potash works lately stood.

***Potato.**

I. ***1. a.** The sweet potato (q.v.). **b.** The Irish potato (q.v.).

See also KIDNEY POTATO, SMALL POTATO, SPANISH POTATO and cf. BLUE-NOSE 2.

[**1565** HAWKINS *Voyages* (1878) 27 Certaine Indians . . . brought downe to vs . . . Hennes, Potatoes and pines.] **1610** *True Declaration Va.* 13 What should I speake of cucumbers, muske melons, pompions, potatoes . . . which our gardens yeelded. **1698** THOMAS *Pensilvania* 20 Also several sorts of eating Roots, as Turnips, Potatoes, Carrats. **1709** LAWSON *Carolina* 77 The Garden-Roots that thrive well in Carolina, are . . . Potatoes, of several delicate sorts, Ground Artichokes, Radishes. *c***1790** T. COXE *View U.S.* 62 The produce, manufactures, and exports of Pennsylvania . . . [include] spelts, onions, potatoes. **1804** J. ROBERTS *Penna. Farmer* 62 Potatoes boiled and mixed with a small quantity of Indian, pea, bean or buckwheat meal, is a good fattener for them [*i.e.*, hogs]. **1885** *Santa Fé Wkly. New Mexican* 20 Aug. 1/2 The potato . . . can not be grown successfully from land that is irrigated by the clear mountain streams. **1909** *Indian Laws & Tr.* III. 419 For annual amount for the purchase of beef, mutton, wheat, flour, beans, and potatoes, . . . thirty thousand dollars.

+2. In colloq. phrases.

To tell that to the potatoes, an expression of disbelief; *to hold one's potato*, to be patient.

1856 SIMMS *Charlemont* 321 Would you, indeed? Tell that to the potatoes. Don't I know better. **1892** *Congress. Rec.* 27 Jan. 600/1 Now let me beg of the gentleman to hold his potato.

II. *attrib.* and *comb.* **3.** Designating dishes and drinks prepared from potatoes.

1815 in Kittredge *Old Farmer* (1904) 184 Potatoe coffee.—From a Philadelphia Paper. **1817** *Yankee Traveller* 75 Wrangle . . . drove a lucrative trade in the sale of potatoe whisky, and adulterated New-England rum. **1839** *S. Lit. Messenger* V. 377/1 Master Billy taking a piece of potato pone daintily between his fingers . . . [said] 'This *patella poon* is exceeding fine.' **1841** *Ib.* VII. 39/1 [These] are succeeded by a dessert of potato custard, stewed fruit and buttermilk. **1852** EASTMAN *Aunt Phillis's Cabin* 56, I jist wanted some brandy to put in these potato puddins. **1867** *Common Sense Cook Book* 10 [Recipe for] Potato Rolls. **1876** M. F. HENDERSON *Cooking* 194 Potato Croquettes. Add to four or five mashed potatoes . . . the beaten yolk of one egg. **1882** GODFREY *Nantucket* 64 To be sure, the Nantucketers make what they call a 'potato chowder'; but then, a potato chowder without fish or clams . . . [is] a flat and insipid dish.

4. Designating farm implements used in cultivating or harvesting potatoes.

1819 *Plough Boy* I. 123 Young's potatoe harrow made to order. **1858** WARDER *Hedges & Evergreens* 63 Boys then gather up the plants, either by hand, or aided by that useful implement the potato-rake. **1868** *Rep. Comm. Patents 1867* I. 367 Potato plow, J. P. Stanton.

5. Designating one having to do with potatoes.

1851 *Harper's Mag.* April 662/2 The poultry-woman must be changed, the potato-man discarded. **1868** HAWTHORNE *Notebooks* II. 13, I, after all, was the . . . cow-milker, potato-hoer and hay-raker. **1868** *N.Y. Herald* 3 July 3/6 On or about the 1st of June . . . a potato dealer despatched one of his men named Michael O'Brien with a wagon load of potatoes.

6. Designating places or receptacles in which potatoes are kept or stored.

1849 N. KINGSLEY *Diary* 10 Worked at makeing potatoe bin in round house. **1864** STOWE *House & Home P.* 258 Biddy rushes to her potato-basket. **1865** *Atlantic Mo.* June 659/1 [A letter] was laid on the potato-chest. **1898** *McClure's Mag.* X. 272 [The] potato cellar . . . was used only for storing those edible tubers in winter.

7. In the names of insects injurious to potatoes.

See also POTATO BEETLE, POTATO BUG, POTATO FLY.

1705 BEVERLEY *Virginia* IV. 63 The troublesome Vermine . . . [are] Musketa's, Chinches, Seedticks, or Red-worms, by some call'd Potato-lice. **1854** EMMONS *Agric. N.Y.* V. 218 *Sphinx convolvuli.* Potato Hawk-moth. . . . The larva feeds upon the sweet-potato vine. *Ib.* 219 *Sphinx quinquemaculatus* . . . is the common potato-moth, the larva of which descends into the earth to transform. **1874** *Rep. Comm. Agric. 1873* 159 Another species . . . is also said to kill the caterpillar of the potato-sphinx.

8. In special combinations.

Potato bed, a plot of well-prepared ground where sweet potatoes are placed to sprout; *p. chip*, a thin slice of Irish potato fried until crisp; *p. clay*, a substance used by the Hopi Indians in making pigments; *p. fire*, a fire at which potatoes are roasted; *p. gospel*, (see quotation); *p.-grabbler*, the hand (*slang*); *p. land*, land suitable for growing potatoes; *p.-masher*, a utensil for mashing potatoes after they have been cooked; *p. money*, potatoes used as currency; *p. ridge*, a ridge upon which the slips or draws of sweet potatoes are set out; *p.-stealer*, (see quotation). *slang.*

1775 CRESSWELL *Journal* 95 Found a Potato bed and I ate about a dozen of them raw. **1878** *Amer. Home Cook Book* 67 Put around potato chips prepared as follows. **1902** *Rep. Smithsonian Inst. 1900* 469 Some of the talc-like substance, called potato-clay . . . is then produced, and the operator puts a piece about the size of a walnut in his mouth. **1836** GILMAN *Recoll.* (1838) 254 Sometimes I even strayed, for companionship, to the potato-fire, which, though in the open air, was rarely extinguished, and usually found some one roasting or eating [potatoes]. **1883** BURROUGHS in *Century Mag.* Aug. 531/1 Your rose-colored philanthropies, your potato gospels (vegetarianism) . . . and the like. **1851** *Polly Peablossom* 60, I'd jest doubled up these pertater grabblers, calculatin' to plant one of 'em on the tip of his nose. **1855** *Amer. Inst. N.Y. Trans. 1854* 168 Salt . . . will kill grubs, and may be used to advantage on potato land. **1855** *Chicago Times* 16 Jan. 4/1 Butter moulds and stamps, ladles, rolling pins, potato mashers, . . . wholesale and retail at Hollister's Bazaar. **1691** *Mass. Bay Currency Tracts* 31 Why may not Paper-mony be as good as Tobacco-mony, Potato-mony, and Sugar-mony? **1851** *Fla. Plantation Rec.* 381, 15 [slaves] hoing Cotton at Cars half the day and Rakeing up Potatoe Ridges in the afternoon. **1835** LONGSTREET *Ga. Scenes* 127 Let your Uncle Johnny put his potato-stealer, (hand,) into that hat, and tickle the chins of them . . . shiners.

Potato apple. The small round berry or seed ball of the potato plant. {1825– (Loudon *Encycl. Agric.* 782)} — **1798** *N.Y. State Soc. Arts* I. 261, I gathered what are commonly called the potatoe-apples, when they were fully ripe. **1819** *Plough Boy* I. 168 Take the potatoe apple, as it is called, from the best potatoes, when fully ripe. **1844** LEE & FROST *Oregon* 93 My neighbor found his field being covered with young potato tops, which proved to have sprung from the seeds, or potato apples, as they are sometimes called, which had dropped into the ground the preceding year. **1877** BARTLETT 809 He doesn't know enough to throw potato-apples over a fence.

+**Potato ball.** **1.** =prec. **2.** A ball or croquette of mashed potatoes. — **(1)** **1850** *Rep. Comm. Patents 1849: Agric.* 198 In 1847, he planted a single potato-ball or apple. **1855** *Amer. Inst. N.Y. Trans. 1854*, 206 The vines cease to bear potato balls or seeds. **1877** *Vermont Bd. Agric. Rep.* IV. 33 Nature can make potato balls, but she couldn't make the Early Rose. **(2)** **1882** F. E. OWENS *Cook Book* 102 Potato Balls. Take the remains of mashed potatoes; make into flat balls, dip in beaten egg and fry a nice brown in drippings. **1887** I. ALDEN *Little Fishers* xi, Mrs. Decker . . . was serving three lovely fish and a bowl of potato balls for 'Decker' and herself.

+**Potato beetle.** The Colorado beetle (*Leptinotarsa decemlineata*) which destroys the leaves of the Irish potato. (See also COLORADO 2 and cf. POTATO BUG.) — **1868** *Amer. Naturalist* III. 129 The New Potato-beetle . . . was long ago known at the base of the Rocky Mountains. **1874** *Rep. Comm. Agric. 1873* 153 The much-dreaded western potato-beetle . . . made its appearance in the immediate neighborhood of Washington, D.C. **1877** *Vermont Bd. Agric. Rep.* IV. 109 Thus this Potato-beetle has made a steady progress, . . . until it has now arrived in our midst.

+Potato bug.

1. =POTATO FLY. Also attrib.

1799 E. DRINKER *Journal* (1889) 347 They call them here . . . the Potato-Bug, being numerous on the potato tops. **1806** in Kittredge *Old Farmer* (1904) 186 The potatoe fly, or bug, appears about the first of July. **1838** *Hesperian* (Columbus, Ohio) I. 42/1 This company, formed for the praiseworthy purpose of encouraging the growth of potatoe-bugs, and manufacturing potato-bug oil. **1907** Bailey *Cycl. Amer. Agric.* II. 524/1 The old-fashioned potato-bug or blister-beetle (*Epicauta vittata*) is combated in the same way as the Colorado potato-beetle. It is now rarely seen.

2. =POTATO BEETLE.

1867 *Mich. Agric. Rep.* VI. 71 We were startled with the announcement that the Colorado potato-bug was in Michigan. **1908** *Springfield Repub.* 2 Sept. 14/6 Potato bugs on the rails at Lazy lane stalled eight trolly cars laden with excursionists.

Potato-digger. A horse-drawn implement for digging and gathering potatoes. (Cf. DIGGER 3.) — **1847** *Rep. Comm. Patents 1846* 18 A patent has been granted for a potato digger. **1868** *Mich. Agric. Rep.* VII. 346 Your committee gave as good a trial to the potato-digger as was possible. **1887** *Scientific Amer.* LVII. 74/1 A combined cultivator and potato digger. . . . It has a plow or ditcher shovel formed from a plate of metal.

Potato disease. Any one of various potato blights caused by parasitic fungi. {1845-} (Cf. POTATO ROT.) — **1846** *Niles' Nat. Reg.* 29 Aug. 416/1 *Potato disease.* The Burlington *Press*, of the 21st states that this disease has attacked the potato *earlier*, certainly than last season. **1855** *Amer. Inst. N.Y. Trans. 1854* 204, I shall not enter into any lengthy discussion relative to the potato disease.

Potato field. A field in which potatoes are grown. {1822-} — **1800** BROWN *A. Mervyn* xxx, On one side was a potato-field, on the other a *melon-patch.* **1836** GILMAN *Recoll.* 39 That thing, sir, with wheels, out by the potato-field. **1855** WILLIS *Convalescent* 51 On a slight elevation in the potato-field, behind the barn, Jemmy was soon at work with his pick-axe. **1861** NORTON *Army Lett.* 35 We don't care much for their *phelinks* when we get out of camp and into a rebel's potato-field. **1887** WILKINS *Humble Romance* 72 She was just up from the potato-field herself.

+**Potato fly.** Any one of various soft-bodied beetles of the family Meloidae which are injurious to potatoes. (Cf. POTATO BEETLE, POTATO BUG.) — **1806** in Kittredge *Old Farmer* (1904) 186 The potatoe fly, or bug, appears about the first of July. **1832** WILLIAMSON *Maine* I. 172 *Lytta bittata;* Potato fly, (looks like a Spanish Fly.). **1854** EMMONS *Agric. N.Y.* V. 96 *Cantharidae.* . . . They are at times abundant upon potato vines, whence they have acquired the name of potato fly, particularly the *Epicauta vittata.*

Potato ground. Ground upon which potatoes are grown. {1753-} Also transf. — **1742** *Mass. Col. Soc. Publ.* VI. 24, [I promise] to give him one half of all the ingles grain I rese Evrey year Except what I rese on old putatou ground or turnip yeards. **1789** W. DUNLAP *Darby's Return* I. i, He had, *like me*, Return'd his own *potatoe ground* to see. **1868** HAWTHORNE *Notebooks* I. 90 It is agreeable to look down at the square patches of cornfield, or of potato-ground.

+**Potato heap.** A conical heap or pile of potatoes protected against the weather with a covering of straw or earth. — **1858** *Texas Almanac 1859* 85 He should carefully examine his potato-heaps, and know that every thing has been done to secure this crop from decay. **1886** *Congress. Rec.* 10 June 5749/1 Instances are related in which potato heaps covered with earth and left out during winter have been entered by the gophers and the tubers carried off.

+**Potato hill. a.** The hill in which potatoes are planted. (Cf. HILL 2.) **b.** =POTATO HEAP. Also transf. — **1821** NUTTALL *Travels Arkansa* 148 To the west continued a proximate chain of piney hills, with remarkable serrated summits, known by the familiar name of the Potatoe hills. **1856** SIMMS *Charlemont* 27 They walk as if perpetually in the faith that their corn-rows and potatoe-hills were between their legs. **1888** *Harper's Mag.* April 705/1 When Jones watched his potato hill, his smoke-house was sure to be entered.

+**Potato hole.** A hole or excavation, usually covered with a mound of straw and earth, in which potatoes are stored in winter. (Cf. POTATO HEAP, POTATO HILL.) — *c*1775 BOUCHER *Glossary* p. 1, All the 'moodies I For Mollsey, in my 'tatoe-hole, put by. **1839** *Knickerb.* XIII. 305 Under a part of the floor, was a small excavation in the earth, which the host called his potato-hole, since, being near the fire, it served in winter to keep his potatoes from freezing. **1852** J. B. JONES *Col. Vanderbomb* 61 History nowhere shows that Clodius ever descended into such a hole as this—a potato hole, I believe.

+**Potato hook.** An agricultural implement with bent tines for digging potatoes. — **1856** *Mich. Agric. Soc. Trans.* VII. 53 D. O. & W. S. Penfield . . . [exhibited] six Patridge's potatoe hooks. **1874** *Vermont Bd. Agric. Rep.* II. 551 Then with axes, potato hooks, and bog hoes, the turf was all peeled off.

Potato house. A house for storing potatoes. — **1791** W. BARTRAM *Travels* 192 The lowest or ground part is a potatoe house. **1920** *3d Nat. Country Life Conf. Proc.* 155 Potato houses . . . are isolated and located with special reference to the good of the products involved.

Potato onion. A variety of onion producing many underground bulbs as multipliers or offsets of the parent bulb. {1855-} — **1859** *Ill. Agric. Soc. Trans.* III. 507 The potatoe onion is planted as the potatoe, and grows in clusters under ground. **1870** *Rep. Comm. Agric. 1869* 222 The Potato Onion . . . is a variety of the common onion. . . . Its bulbs grow just below the surface of the ground, somewhat after the manner of the potato.

+**Potato patch.** A comparatively small field or area in which potatoes are planted. (Cf. PATCH *n.* 1.) — **1807** IRVING, etc. *Salmagundi* xvi. 421 Some . . . enjoy the varied and romantic scenery of . . . potato patches, and log huts. **1834** C. A. DAVIS *Lett. J. Downing* 23 Mr. Van Buren . . . came down on the horse's rump jist as he kicked up behind, and that sent him clean over the fence into the Deacon's potato-patch. **1913** LONDON *Valley of Moon* 404 Hall put Billy to work on the potato patch—a matter of three acres which the poet farmed erratically.

Potato-planter. A person or a device that plants potatoes. — **1788** WASHINGTON *Diaries* III. 363 At the Ferry the Potatoe planters having overtaken the Plows and Harrows, went to Weeding Corn with their hoes. **1859** *Rep. Comm. Patents 1858* I. 441 Improvement in Potato Planters.

Potato rot. Any one of various rots caused by blight, blackleg, etc., which attack potato tubers. {1858-} Cf. POTATO DISEASE. — **1848** *Rep. Comm. Patents 1847* 136 The potato rot seems likewise to have been felt to a considerable extent among the common potato. **1854** SHILLABER *Mrs. Partington* 43 A more disastrous havoc of potato rot has never since transpired than assailed her crops. **1884** *Rep. Comm. Agric.* 314 Harris was equally ignorant of the appearance of the potato-rot.

Potato salad. A salad made of small pieces of boiled potato, and dressing and other ingredients. — **1876** M. F. HENDERSON *Cooking* 224 New small onions sliced, mixed with cold boiled potatoes cut into dice. French dressing. This potato salad is very nice. **1897** CRANE *Third Violet* 142 Who is going for the potato salad?

Potato tops. *pl.* The parts of the potato plant, esp. of the Irish potato, which grow above ground. (Cf. POTATO VINE.) — *c*1801 FESSENDEN *Orig. Poems* (1806) 17 And add fragrant crops Of potatoe tops. **1802** ELLICOTT *Journal* 4 A very heavy hoar frost, vines, potato tops and corn leaves killed in the vallies between the mountains. **1852** ELLET *Pioneer Women* 369 Her family had lived on potato tops, . . . till something better could be raised. **1896** JEWETT *Pointed Firs* 67 There was a great square patch of rough, weedy potato-tops and tall ragweed.

+**Potato vine.** The foliage of the potato plant. — **1777** FITHIAN *Journal* I. 257, I took a Walk thro' the Pumpkin & Potatoe Vines. **1787** WASHINGTON *Diaries* III. 211 When the Potatoe vines had risen 6 Inches through this bed of straw another of equal thickness . . . was spread between the rows. **1870** WARNER *Summer in Garden* xv, It would take a sharp eye to see the potato vines amid the rampant grass and weeds.

+**Potato worm.** The larva of a sphinx or hawk moth injurious to potatoes. Also attrib. — **1850** S. F. COOPER *Rural Hours* 202 The common green potato, or tobacco-worm, is said to become a moth of this kind. **1872** *Vermont Bd. Agric. Rep.* I. 319 The large night-flying moths, which come from and in turn produce, the large larvæ, as the potato-worm and tobacco-worm. **1879** *Scribner's Mo.* July 395/1 You would be surprised to see the tongue of the potato-worm sphinx, when it is uncoiled. *Ib.* Dec. 242/1 This white grub, which the farmers often call the 'potato worm' is . . . the strawberry's most formidable foe.

+**Potawatomi(e).** Also **Potawatami,** †**Pottowatema,** etc.

1. *pl.* An Algonquian Indian tribe first encountered by Europeans on the islands of Green Bay, Wisconsin.

[**1640** *Relat. des Jésuites* (1858) 35/1 Es enuirons de cette nation sont les Nadvesiv, les Assinipour, les Erinioua j, . . . et les Pouutouatami.] **1722** COXE *Descr. Carolana* 48 The Nations who dwell on this River, are Outogamis, Malominis, . . . Sacky, and the Poutouatomis beforementioned. **1807** *Ann. 10th Congress* 1 Sess. 575 All hopes of the speedy recovery of their prisoners from the hands of the Pattawatamies . . . [are] at an end. **1831** WITHERS *Chron. Border Warfare* 256 [At] a grand council convened at Chilicothe, . . . The Mingoes, the Tawas, Pottawatomies, and various other tribes were represented. **1835** HOFFMAN *Winter in West* I. 276 The Indians that frequent the neighbourhood of Chicago . . . are chiefly Pottawattamies and Ottawas. **1868** *N.Y. Herald* 31 July 5/4 The Senate . . . ratified treaties with the Potawatamies. **1910** HODGE, etc. *Amer. Indians* 290/1 Polygamy was common among the Potawatomi when they were visited by the early missionaries.

2. Short for POTAWATOMI(E) INDIAN.

1825 W. BIGGS *Narr. Captivity* 12 He was a young fellow about 19 years of age and of a different nation, being a Pottowatema. **1835** HOFFMAN *Winter in West* I. 244 Two painted Pottawattamies were crouched on the hearth. **1848** BRYANT *California* iii. 37 The Potawattomie was a tall, athletic young man.

3. Attrib. with *chief, nation, redskin, town.*

1789 *Ann. 1st Congress* I. 41 The treaties of Fort Harmar, . . . with the sachems and warriors of the Wyandot, Delaware, Ottawa, Chippawa, Pattiwatima, and Sac nations, . . . appear to have been negotiated . . . so as to unite the interests of the United States with the justice due the said Indian nations. **1799** J. SMITH *Acct. Captivity* 44 The warriors were preparing to go to war, in the Wiandot, Pottowatomy, and Ottawa towns. **1811** *Ann. 12th Congress* 1 Sess. II. 2115 This answer had been despatched by the Potawatimie Chief Winemac. **1864** *Harper's Mag.* Nov. 736/1 It wasn't everybody that had the tastes of a Pottawatomie redskin.

+**Potawatomi(e) Indian.** An Indian of the Potawatomi tribe. — **1808** *Ann. 12th Congress* 1 Sess. II. 1857 A young man from the Delaware towns came to inform me that a Pottawatomie Indian had arrived at the towns. **1900** *Congress. Rec.* 5 Feb. 1503/1, I ask unanimous consent for the immediate consideration of the bill . . . for the relief of John Anderson, a Pottawatomie Indian, and his adult children. **1907** in Blair *Indian Tribes Upper Miss.* II. 287 Out on the bare prairies of Kansas I lived with the Pottawatomi Indians for four years.

+**Pot cheese.** (See quot. 1859.) — **1812** PAULDING *J. Bull & Bro. Jon.* 115 Tell me, thou heart of cork, . . . and brain of pot cheese. **1859** BARTLETT 420 *Smear-case*, . . . a preparation of milk; . . . otherwise called Cottage-Cheese. In New York it is called Pot-cheese. **1878** *Rep.*

Indian Affairs 19 They learn to milk and make butter and pot-cheese which they relish highly.

*****Pothanger.** A device for suspending a pot over a fire. *Obs.* Usually pl. — **1644** *Conn. Rec.* I. 460, 5 pair of tongs & iron spitts, pothangers, . . . a Fornace. **1647** *Essex Probate Rec.* I. 87 One paire of pott hangers. **1675** *Maine Wills* 62, I giue vnto my sd sonn . . . one spitt, with Andirons & pott hangers.

*****Potherb.** An herb which is boiled for use as food; also, an herb used as flavoring for food. — **1630** HIGGINSON *New-England* 9 Diuers excellent Pot-herbs grow abundantly. **1709** LAWSON *Carolina* 77 Our Pot-herbs and others . . . are Angelica wild and tame, Balm, Buglos. **1792** IMLAY *Western Territory* 90 That country produces also all the pot-herbs which are common in Europe. **1871** HOWELLS *Wedding Journey* 84 In the garden full of worthy pot-herbs, [are] such idlers in the vegetable world as hollyhocks and larkspurs. **1882** SALA *Amer. Revisited* (1885) 328 The cooks and *bonnes* of the Creole households making their purchases of . . . pot herbs for soup.

Pothole. A hole in the ground or rock shaped somewhat like a pot, esp. one formed by the rotation of stones in running water. {1839–} — **1827** MCKENNEY *Tour to Lakes* 54 The waters were once, in many places, some fifty feet above their present level; for their action upon the rocks is plainly seen in the *pot holes*, as the excavations are called. **1875** *Amer. Naturalist* IX. 174 There are well-worn cavities in the sides of the mountains, showing how the running waters . . . formed the cavity much as a 'pot hole' is made in our streams at the present time. **1902** WHITE *Blazed Trail* 6 The pines stood on a country rolling with hills, deep with potholes.

*****Pothook.** A hook for suspending a pot over a fire in cooking. Usually pl. — **1633** *N.H. Prov. Papers* I. 77, 1 pr. of pott-hookes. **1694** *Conn. Probate Rec.* I. 414, I give to Hannah Hough, my gr. Child, a brass Box with pott hooks. **1733** *N.H. Probate Rec.* II. 471, I Give . . . to my Doughter . . . my Large Bible and a pot and pot hooks. **1841** *Congress. Globe* App. 25 Jan. 153/1 Pot hooks and kettles, with scythes and wash tub.

+**Pothouse politician.** A frequenter of pothouses who talks politics. — **1809** IRVING *Knickerb.* IV. vi, [He was] distracted by petitions of 'numerous and respectable meetings,' consisting of some half a dozen scurvy pot-house politicians. **1834** *Congress. Deb.* 14 Feb. 561 From the dense crowds of your populous cities you may have the 'miserable petitions' of 'pot-house politicians.' **1860** MORDECAI *Virginia* 57 He was more useful to the city than a host of loud-mouthed, pot-house politicians. **1871** *Scribner's Mo.* II. 624 By annexing Newfoundland it is to be feared we should also annex a body of voters and pot-house politicians. **1873** MILLER *Amongst Modocs* 105 A pot-house politician should represent us at the court of St. James's, if such an Indian is to be taken as a representative of his race.

+**Potlatch.** *N.W.* [Chinook *patshatl* 'a gift, giving.']

1. A gift or present.

*a***1861** WINTHROP *Canoe & Saddle* 57 [The Klickatat Indians] expressed the friendliest sentiments, perhaps with a view to a liberal 'potlatch' of trinkets.

2. (See quot. 1910.) Also attrib.

1884 *San Francisco Chron.* Sept., A potlatch is . . . a sort of grand reunion and general gathering, lasting sometimes for weeks. [**1907** C. HILL-TOUT *Brit. N. Amer.* 52 [Roofs were used as] platforms upon occasions of public festivity such as 'potlatch' gatherings, naming feasts, etc.] **1910** HODGE, etc. *Amer. Indians* II. 293/2 Although varying considerably in different parts of the coast, these potlatches were mainly marked . . . by the giving away of quantities of goods, commonly blankets. . . . During the festival in which the gifts were made, houses and carved poles were raised, chiefs' children were initiated into the secret societies [etc.]. *transf.* **1902** WILSON *Spenders* 357 This life of idleness you been leadin'—one continual potlatch the whole time—it wa'n't doin' you a bit of good.

+**Pot lead,** *n.* [Du. *potlood.*] (See quot. 1890.) — **1890** *Cent.* 4652/3 *Pot-lead,* . . . black-lead or graphite: as, a *pot-lead* crucible. (The word is now used chiefly of graphite in stove-polish applied to the hulls of racing-yachts below the water-line to diminish the friction of the water by giving a smooth surface.) **1894** *Outing* XXIV. 194/1 [I used] very fine sandpaper and pot lead till my boat's bottom was beautifully burnished.

+**Pot-lead,** *v.* [f. noun.] (See quot. 1890.) Also *ppl. a.* — **1890** *Cent.* 4652/3 *Pot-lead,* . . . to coat with pot-lead: as, to *pot-lead* a yacht. **1894** *Outing* XXIV. 72/1 The racing shell, used only three times, its bottom pot-leaded, is brought out.

Pot liquor. The liquid in which meat, usu. pork or bacon, or vegetables have been cooked. {1773–} — **1819** *Amer. Farmer* I. 68 The common pot liquor, from the boiling of pork or bacon, . . . [is] injurious to confined hogs. **1839** BRIGGS *H. Franco* I. 225 [We] swallowed the scalding hot pot liquor. *c***1866** BAGBY *Old Va. Gentleman* 47 A true Virginian . . . [must] begin on pot-liquor, and keep it up until he sheds his milk-teeth. **1895** A. BROWN *Meadow-Grass* 269 'Such cold potatoes—' 'B'iled in the pot-liquor!' she whispered, a knowing gleam in her blue eyes. *c***1910** in *Chicago Tribune* 31 May (1940) 12/3 Real pot-licker, the only variety worthy of discussion, is distilled—preferably in an iron kettle over wood fire—from hog jowl and *wild* greens.

*****Pot marjoram.** A variety of marjoram used in cookery. {(Lyte *Dodoens* 474)} — **1637** MORTON *New Canaan* 66 The Country there naturally affordeth very good pot-herbes and sallet herbes; . . . as Potmarioram, Tyme, Alexander, Angellica, . . . in very great abundance. **1709** LAWSON *Carolina* 77 Our pot-herbs and others of use [include] . . . Marigold, Pot-Marjoram, and other Marjorams, Summer and Winter Savory [etc.]. **1806** MCMAHON *Amer. Gardener's Cal.* 583. **1863** F. BURR *Field & Garden Veg.* 428 Pot Marjoram. . . . The crop in all respects should be treated, as directed for Common Marjoram.

Pot metal.

1. a. A lead and copper alloy formerly used in making pots. {1693–} **b.** A grade of cast iron suitable for casting hollow ware.

1697 *Mayflower Descendant* X. 13 Brass Iron and pott metle. **1792** BRACKENRIDGE *Mod. Chivalry* (1937) 75 Some [should claim] brass, some copper, pewter, a bit of tin, or pot-metal, just as the specific value of their services might entitle them. **1819** SCHOOLCRAFT *Mo. Lead Mines* 141 The recent invention and introduction into general use, of Britannia and other wares, has now almost superseded the use of pot-metal. **1880** DEMING *Adirondack Stories* 24 A bell, composed of a cheap patent mixture of pig-iron, pot-metal, and lead, was sending forth its dismal metallic clangor.

+**2.** *attrib.* Designating work shoes made of a hard, coarse, black leather.

1845 *Knickerb.* XXVI. 415 The butcher's apprentice . . . wears 'pot-metal brogans.' **1853** 'P. PAXTON' *Yankee in Texas* 25 He had . . . divested his feet of a heavy pair of 'pot metal' boots, and invested them in two old, worn-out, slip-shod brogans.

Potpie. A pie made with meat; now, usually, a baked dish of diced meat and vegetables with a top crust of pastry; also, a fricassee of meat and dumplings. {1895–} — **1824** DODDRIDGE *Notes* 109 The standard dinner dish for every log rolling, house raising, and harvest day, was a pot pye, or what in other countries is called 'Sea pye.' **1857** *Rep. Comm. Patents 1856: Agric.* 134 Though their [the purple grackles'] flesh is eaten by many, especially in pot-pies, it is really little better than that of the crow. **1892** S. HALE *Letters* 270 Here I found that if I ordered pot-pie,—they would throw in bread and butter.

Pot rack, *n.*[1] A set of bars or iron fixtures used to support or suspend a pot used in cooking. *Obs.* Usually pl. — **1634** *N.H. Prov. Papers* I. 93 One pare of pott-rackes. **1678** *New Castle Court Rec.* 361, 2 paire of Pott Racks. **1791** in Imlay *Western Territory* (1797) 470 Sixteen kettles of 15 gallons each, to boil the sap, with pot racks for each kettle. **1818** WEEMS *Letters* III. 226 Dick soon found a substitute in a heavy iron pot-rack that hung very conveniently over the fire place.

+**Potrack,** *n.*[2] [Imitative.] The cry of a guinea fowl. — **1840** *S. Lit. Messenger* VI. 386/2 The guinea-fowls make a great racket, with their pot-rack.

+**Potracking.** [See prec.] The uttering of a 'potrack' (q.v.). — **1883** HARRIS *Nights Uncle Remus* (1911) 193 The squawking and *pot-racking* went on at such a rate that the geese awoke. **1886** *Pop. Science Mo.* XXVIII. 640 That the dusting of chickens, cackling of geese, and the 'pot-racking' of Guinea-hens have not given rise to an elaborate series of weather proverbs is, I think, surprising.

*****Pottage.** A dish of cereal, vegetables, or vegetables and meat cooked to softness and appropriately seasoned. Also attrib. — **1624** *Va. House of Burgesses* 28 They fell into extreame want, not havinge anything left to sustein them save a little ill conditioned Barley, which ground to meal & pottage made thereof. **1662** *Essex Probate Rec.* I. 403 One pottage pot, one kettle, a smothing Iron. **1877** *Harper's Mag.* March 562/2 The old parson's daughter went her way absorbed in the savory pottages and unsavory tempers of the sick room. **1899** GOING *Flowers* 17 The garden grew only bitter herbs for fast-day pottage.

*****Potter.**

1. One who makes pots and other earthenware vessels.

1741 W. STEPHENS *Proc. Georgia* II. 153 Mr. Duchee, the Potter, had now accomplish'd his Intention of making China Ware. **1771** FRANKLIN *Autobiog.* 288 Her friends . . . persuaded her to marry another, one Rogers, a potter, which was done in my absence. **1818** FLINT *Lett. from Amer.* 62 [In Pittsburgh] 1 Potter (fine ware). **1881** *Harper's Mag.* Feb. 369/2 The United States Potters' Association . . . has effected much in the . . . development of the industry.

2. The red-bellied terrapin, *Pseudemys rubriventris.*

1884 GOODE, etc. *Fisheries* I. 154 The 'Red-bellied Terrapin,' *Pseudemys rugosa,* . . . is also known under the names 'Potter,' 'Red-fender,' and 'Slider.'

+**Pottering time.** (See quotation.) — **1791** BENTLEY *Diary* I. 254 After *pottering time* is over, which is running upon the broken ice without falling into the water & requires great activity, comes on *marble time.*

Potter's clay. Clay of a kind used by potters. {1616–} — **1789** MORSE *Amer. Geog.* 88 Horses grind the tanners bark, and potters clay. **1815** DRAKE *Cincinnati* 39 Beds of brick and potter's clay are common. **1843** *Nat. Hist. N.Y., Geology* I. 250 The clay beds at this locality are an impure potter's clay. **1883** *Gringo & Greaser* 1 Dec. 1/1 We have also gypsum (plaster of paris) beds, sulphur deposits and beds of kaolin or potters clay.

*****Potter's field.** [Cf. Matt. 27:7.] +A field in which paupers, strangers, and criminals are buried. Also transf. — **1777** J. ADAMS *Familiar Letters* 259, I took a walk into the Potter's Field, a burying ground between the new stone prison and the hospital. **1820** *Niles' Reg.* XVIII. 361/2 The bodies of hundreds of honest men are every year boxed up roughly and consigned to the 'Potter's field,' without ceremony. **1882** MCCABE *New York* 430 A little more than sixty years ago the pretty Square was used by the city as a Potter's Field, the last resting-place of the poor and wretched. **1906** 'MARK TWAIN' in *Westminster Gaz.* 26 Nov. 4/2 You did not put it in the respectable part of the magazine, but interred it in that 'potter's field,' the Editor's Drawer.

Potter's ware. *collect.* Articles made by potters. — **1789** MORSE *Amer. Geog.* 90 Of the long list of articles which we now make ourselves, we will mention . . . bricks, tiles, potters ware [etc.]. **1794** T. COXE *View U.S.* 25 Potters ware, mill-stones, and other stone work, cabinet work . . . are tending to greater perfection, and will soon be sold so cheap as to throw foreign goods of the same kind entirely out of the market. **1806** *Ann. 9th Congress* 2 Sess. 1124 The soil around them is a white, tenacious clay, probably fit for potter's ware.

+**Potter wasp.** A wasp, as *Eumenes fraterna*, which constructs small potlike or vaselike cells of mud. (Cf. DIRT-DAUBER, MUD-DAUBER, MUD WASP.) — **1880** ALLAN-OLNEY *New Virginians* I. 99 The little potter-wasp makes a nest of clay, shaped like an ancient pot, which it fills with caterpillars.

* **Pottery.**

* **1.** A factory or place where earthenware is made.

1809 CUMING *Western Tour* 223 Pittsburgh [has] five coopers; thirteen weavers; . . . six hatters; two potteries of earthen ware; eight straw bonnet makers [etc.]. **1860** ABBOTT *South & North* 318 But look . . . [at] glass factories, and potteries, and cutlery. **1882** [see MATCH SAFE].

2. *collect.* Articles produced by potters. {1785–}

1741 W. STEPHENS *Proc. Georgia* II. 199 He was exceedingly caress'd by the General &c. which I could easily give credit to, on Account of his Pottery. **1823** JAMES *Exped.* I. 33 We found some fragments of pottery, arrow points, and other articles of Indian manufacture. **1865** *Atlantic Mo.* March 313/1 It was not till about the time they [the Indian mound builders] reached the Ohio Valley that they manufactured pottery. **1885** *Wkly. New Mexican Review* 29 Jan. 4/1 The exhibit [of the territory at New Orleans] could be improved fifty per cent by the addition of filigree work, pottery, amole soaps, etc.

3. Attrib. with *stuff, ware, work.*

1740 *Georgia Col. Rec.* IV. 670 A Pottery Work is carried on with Success. **1873** COZZENS *Marvellous Country* 189 All over the plain we found hundreds of branch acequias, together with marks of former habitations, broken pottery ware, and stone *mettates.* **1888** STOCKTON *Dusantes* 146 Now, sir, . . . we ask you to . . . have a ginger-jar built, jus' the size an' shape and gen'ral trim of that other one, but of no pottery-stuff.

***Pottle.** A measure of capacity equal to two quarts. *Obs.* Also attrib. — **1636** *Plymouth Laws* 56 [He] shall have a pottle of Corne toule upon every bushell. **1659** *Conn. Rec.* I. 331 There shalbe provided for every Mill in this Collony . . . a Pottle dish of 2 Quarts. **1670** *Harvard Rec.* I. 49, 3 pottle pots, at 6s a peice. **1766** in Chalkley *Scotch-Irish Settlement Va.* I. 131 One wig, two fiddles, one pottle noggin—attached. **1788** WASHINGTON *Diaries* III. 341 About a pottle of the Naked Barley.

* **Pouch.**

1. A bag, usually of leather, in which hunters formerly carried bullets; a bullet pouch. {1669–}

1827 COOPER *Prairie* iii, I had much better have kept my powder in the horn and the lead in its pouch. **1838** J. MCDONALD *Biog. Sketches* 38 His gun-rack was examined, and there hung his rifle and his pouch in their usual place. **1848** COOPER *Oak Openings* I. 58 The powder had been taken from his horn, and the bullets from his pouch. **1894** *Harper's Mag.* Sept. 614/1 Powder-horns and pouches and a dog-horn—the very sort of curios the hunter was seeking—hung upon other rafters.

+**2.** A bag for carrying goods to be sent by mail or express. Cf. MAIL POUCH.

1833 *Niles' Reg.* XLIV. 337/2 The letter mail bag, or 'Pouch,' was missed between New Brunswick, (N.J.) and New York. **1879** *Postal Laws* 106 Letter and circular mail must always be . . . placed in the pouch loose. **1889** *Century Mag.* Aug. 606/2 The pouches put on board the *Aller* carried the usual copies for the foreign circulation. **1903** *Chicago Chronicle* 11 April 1/4 This is the second theft . . . , two pouches having been stolen on the night of March 13.

attrib. **1874** PINKERTON *Expressman & Detective* 207, [I will get] you to have a key made similar to a pouch-key. **1887** *Postal Laws* 408 The postmaster is at once provided with the necessary pouches, locks, keys, pouch bills, and labels.

‖**3.** =POCKET *n.* 2.

1873 MILLER *Amongst Modocs* 256 We began to have a strong suspicion that we had only chanced upon a pouch in the rock.

+**Pouched rat. a.** =POCKET GOPHER. **b.** =KANGAROO RAT. — **1849** *Sk. Nat. Hist., Mammalia* IV. 96 The Camas pouched rat is common in N. America, on the banks of the Columbia river. **1856** WHIPPLE *Explor. Ry. Route* I. 90 New species of pouched rats, an owl, and magnificent antlers of a mountain sheep, had been secured. [**1867** *Amer. Naturalist* I. 395 The Pouched Kangaroo Rat . . . is one of the most abundant of the Rodents about Fort Whipple [in Ariz.], where it more nearly takes the place of the house rat.] **1874** COUES *Birds N.W.* 366 In the stomachs of those [buzzards] examined I found the remains of burrowing pouched-rats (*Thomomys fulvus*).

+**Pouchong.** (See quotation.) — **1835** *Encycl. Amer.* XII. 161 The black teas, usually imported by Europeans and Americans, are . . . bohea, congo, campo, souchong, pouchong, pekoe.

Poudrette. A fertilizer made from dried, deodorized, night soil, mixed with charcoal, gypsum, etc. {1840–} — **1846** *Spirit of Times* 16 May 141/1 The six rows on which poudrette was used, gave *two bushels* of ears more than the other six rows. **1850** *Rep. Comm. Patents 1849: Agric.* 21 The best method of preparing poudrette can be published in the next annual report. **1857** *Harper's Mag.* July 203/1 His vegetables cost him middling dear . . . by the accounts he gave me of gardeners' pay, poudrette, clearing up of stones, and so on. **1883** ALLEN *New Farm Book* 77 *Poudrette* is the name given to the human fœces after it has been mixed with charcoal dust or charred peat.

Poulterer. One whose business is selling poultry. {1638–} — **1763** in Singleton *Social N.Y.* 356 Hyam Myers at the sign of the Poulterers in Broad Street . . . intends to keep a proper poulterer's shop in the same manner as they are kept in London. **1883** *Harper's Mag.* Aug. 457/1 The sight of the wild duck, . . . at a poulterer's door, almost broke his heart.

* **Poultry.**

* **1.** *collect.* Domestic fowls, as chickens, ducks, turkeys, etc.

1624 SMITH *Gen. Hist. Va.* IV. 164 Many more Powltry, what was brought or bred. **1701** WOLLEY *Journal N.Y.* (1902) 73, I faired very plentifully with . . . Poultry coop'd up and corn'd and cram'd, which made the common Sea men so long for a novelty. **1797** IMLAY *Western Territory* (ed. 3) 253 Even poultry thrive but little where indigo is made. **1822** WOODS *English Prairie* (1904) 302 Broom-corn . . . is useful for poultry. **1885** JACKSON *Zeph* iv, [On] a small ranch . . . she raised vegetables and kept poultry and cows.

transf. **1846** *Spirit of Times* (N.Y.) 4 July 223/2 A '*Squatter*' . . . sustains himself in killing Bear, Deer and other *poultry!*

2. *attrib.* and *comb.* **a.** Designating persons who have to do with poultry.

1851 *Harper's Mag.* April 662/2 The poultry-woman must be changed. **1852** *Knickerb.* April 344 The arrival of a steam-boat from the upper country brings together the 'Poultry-Dealers,' a class of population unknown in any other city of the Union [than New Orleans]. **1865** *Atlantic Mo.* June 661/2 My experiments with chickens have been attended with a success so brilliant that unfortunate poultry-fanciers have appealed to me for assistance. **1889** *Opelousas* (La.) *Democrat* 7 Dec. 2/5 Mr. Felch, the well-known poultryman, has a Scotch collie dog. **1894** *Vt. Agric. Rep.* XIV. 167 The poultry specialist, like all others, is a public benefactor.

b. Designating various contrivances and structures used in raising poultry.

1867 EDWARDS *Shelby* 359 The soldiers on this expedition plundered every house, barnyard, poultry-roost, and cabin on the line of march. **1876** KNIGHT 1780/2 *Poultry-feeder*, a device to feed grain to fowls in quantity as used. It is upon the principle of the fountain-inkstand or the water-bottle for bird-cages, grain falling down into the trough as the latter is emptied. **1880** *Harper's Mag.* Aug. 356/2 After one stare . . . he led the horses under his poultry shed. **1884** ROE *Nature's Story* 225 A pole . . . forms the corner of a little poultry-coop.

***Poultry house.** A house in which poultry is kept, esp. at night. — **1819** *Amer. Farmer* I. 46 Respecting the cleansing of poultry-houses from vermin, or chicken-lice. **1842** *Nat. Hist. N.Y., Zoology* I. 30 The skunk . . . is regarded as a fit subject for extermination, on account of the havoc which he causes in the poultry-house and barn-yard. **1871** LEWIS *Poultry Book* 120 Here is another house, designed to meet the wants of a person who cannot afford to put up a poultry house. **1920** *3d Nat. Country Life Conf. Proc.* 155 No argument is necessary to justify poultry houses.

Poultry-raising. The raising of poultry for the market. — **1850** in Browne *Poultry Yard* 304 There is profit attending poultry raising, when undertaken on a moderate scale. **1870** 'MARK TWAIN' *Sk., New & Old* 81 From early youth I have taken an especial interest in the subject of poultry-raising. **1896** *Vt. Agric. Rep.* XV. 28 Poultry raising has of late years attracted the attention of the farmer.

Poultry show. A public gathering or fair where choice specimens of poultry are exhibited. (Cf. CAT SHOW, CATTLE SHOW, etc.) — **1868** M. H. SMITH *Sunshine & Shadow* 597 He has gotten up baby-shows, poultry-shows, and dog-shows. **1871** LEWIS *Poultry Book* 77 A specimen of this turkey . . . was shown at the New York State Poultry Show in 1869.

Poultry yard. A yard in which poultry is kept or raised. — **1831** HOLLEY *Texas* (1833) 117 It is an evil which persons . . . who would open . . . poultry yards . . . could very soon remedy. **1871** LEWIS *Poultry Book* 135 Either of these designs will answer all purposes of a drinking fountain for the poultry yard. **1885** *Harper's Mag.* Jan. 210/1 He and Polly made enthusiastic plans . . . for a great poultry-yard. **1904** PRINGLE *Rice Planter* 140 They are anxious to start a poultry yard.

* **Pound.**[1]

* **1.** A unit of weight formerly varying locally but now containing 16 ounces or 7,000 grains.

In the U.S. the weight of a person is stated in pounds, as in quot. 1907; in Britain in stones (14 lbs.) and pounds, e.g. ten stone seven.

1623 in Neill *Virginia Carolorum* 69 Mr. Bolton shall receive for his salary . . . ten pound of tobacco, and one bushel of corn, for every planter and tradesman, above the age of sixteen years, alive at the crop. **1657** *Brookhaven Rec.* 3 Ten pound of powder, ten pound of lead. **1780** *Va. State P.* I. 377, I hope and expect that Your Excellency . . . [will] fix my pay on the first footing of ten shillings old money, or Fifty pounds of Tobacco pr: day. **1843** N. BOONE *Journal* (1917) 209 A ball, of about 12 to the pound, passed through his foot. **1907** LONDON *Road* 34, I weigh only one hundred and sixty pounds.

b. Attrib. with *apple, ball, pippin, rate, sweet.*

1794 in J. Hall *Statistics of West* 224 Each of the boats are armed with six pieces carrying a pound ball; also a number of good muskets. **1815** *Niles' Reg.* IX. 172/1, I was presented with an apple, called pound pipen. **1817** W. COXE *Fruit Trees* 118 Pound apple. This is a large fair apple, very showy. **1893** CUSHING *Story of P.O.* 410 The pound rate was established by the Congressional Act of 1874. **1904** WALLER *Wood-Carver* 34 The tanned russets, the noble pound-sweets—forty-five to a bushel!

*2. **a.** =POUND STERLING. **b.** A unit in a standard of monetary value set up by different colonies or states before the adoption of the dollar and cents system of currency; a note of one of these values. Now hist.

The values of the colonial or state pounds varied according to the degree of depreciation that prevailed at any given time. At the time when the dollar and cents currency was adopted, the pound in New York was worth about $2.50, in Georgia, about $4.50.

1645 *New Haven Col. Rec.* 175 [He] set him a prise, namely 12 l. **1702** C. MATHER *Magnalia* I. 69 The passage of the persons that peopled New-England, cost at least ninety-five thousand pound. **1782** *Essex Inst. Coll.* XXI. 282 Voted Sixty Pound hard Money to Defray Preching this year. **1784** JEFFERSON *Writings* I. 243, I know of no Unit which can be proposed in competition with the Dollar, but the Pound. But what is the Pound? 1547 grains of fine silver in Georgia; 1289 grains in Virginia, Connecticut, [etc.]; . . . 966¾ grains in North Carolina and New York. **1789** *Ann. 1st Congress* I. 229 A cargo and outfits of a vessel worth £1000, lawful money, would bring in return 22,000 gallons of molasses.

***Pound.**[2]

*1. An enclosure built and maintained at public expense for impounding stray or trespassing stock.

1633 *Plymouth Laws* 34 Every Cunstablericke [shall] have a sufficient pound to impound cattle that shall transgresse any such orders as are or shalbe made. **1677** *Boston Rec.* 115 Libertie is granted them to Erect two pounds. **1709** *Providence Rec.* VIII. 9 There being no Pound in the Towne. **1840** *Picayune* 5 Sept. 2/6 [A horse] was brought to the pound of the Second Municipality. **1902** LORIMER *Lett. Merchant* 119 Chauncey lolled in the best room of every house in our town, and we used to wonder how he managed to browse up and down the streets that way without getting into the pound.

attrib. and *comb.* **1662** *Conn. Rec.* I. 379 Whosoeuer for the future shal complaine of and prosecute to effect in a legal way, any pound-breach or rescue, . . . he or they shalbe paid one quarter part of the fine. **1675** *Plymouth Laws* 175 It shalbee lawful for such an one to impound the beast that hath treaspased in a pound house or place of restraint. **1685** *East-Hampton Rec.* II. 159 Two hooks for ye pound gate.

+**b.** An enclosure in which wild animals, as buffalo, are entrapped.

1817 S. BROWN *Western Gazetteer* 199 A small party is sent out to decoy the animals into the pound. **1876** ALLEN *Amer. Bisons* 472 The rushing of a herd over a precipice or into a pound prepared especially to entrap them.

+2. Short for POUND NET.

1870 *Amer. Naturalist* IV. 403 These fish being caught in gill-nets and 'pounds,' are generally taken from the water some hours after being actually entrapped. **1885** *N.Y. Ev. Post* 28 Aug. (*Cent.*), We concluded the day by accompanying the fisherman and a neighbor as they went to 'lift' their pounds.

+**Poundable,** *a.* Of stock: Subject to being placed in a pound. — **1657** *Hempstead Rec.* I. 26 All yonge Cattell . . . that shall bee found in the filld ore hard after the abovesaid day shall bee poundabell by aney that will pound them. **1660** *Ib.* 91 Hooges to bee poundable. **1687** *East-Hampton Rec.* II. 207 All swine that goe in the Towne or Limits thereof unyoaked are poundable by any parson that shall soe find them.

***Poundage.** The action of impounding stray or trespassing stock; the charge made upon the owner of such stock. — **1641** *Ipswich Rec.* 3 Dec., Mr. Wilson . . . shall have a penny a head for poundage out of the forfeits. **1658** *Hempstead Rec.* I. 38 Swine . . . shall then be soulde by outcry and payment being made for the damage and chardge of the poundage. **1759** *Huntington Rec.* II. 445 Any person shall have Power . . . to pound any creatures in case his fence be Judged sufficient . . . & recover Damage & ye poundage. **1845** JUDD *Margaret* II. 284 She has brought in the strays, and many is the poundage she has saved Uncle Ket.

+**Pound boat.** [f. POUND[2] 2.] A flat-bottomed, centerboard boat used in the pound fisheries of the Great Lakes. — **1884** *Nat. Mus. Bul.* No. 27, 700 Lake Erie pound boat. . . . Their peculiar construction enables them to carry large quantities of fish in shallow water and to lift the bowl of the pounds without upsetting.

Poundcake. A plain cake made with a pound, or an equal part, measured by weight, of each of its principal ingredients. {1841–} Also transf. — **1805** *Pocumtuc Housewife* (1906) 31 Pound Cake. **1829** ROYALL *Pennsylvania* I. 197 If any student is deficient in the qualifications for a degree, only give Miss C. a piece of poundcake, and that matter is settled. **1889** COOKE *Steadfast* 73 Nobody in Trumbull could make . . . such short-cakes, 'lection cake, or pound cake. **1904** *N.Y. Sun* 17 Aug. 4 Most of the members of the New York county committee have been very well provided for in the matter of political pound cake. **1910** C. HARRIS *Eve's Husband* 180 A wagon loaded with seventy-eight fried chickens, six hundred biscuit and forty-two enormous pound-cakes rolled out of the town.

Pounded, *a.* Reduced to fine particles or powder by pounding. {1600–} — **1805** *Ann. 9th Congress* 2 Sess. 1066 Buffalo robes, tallow, dried and pounded meat and grease. **1836** IRVING *Astoria* I. 165 Their packages of pounded salmon entered largely into the system of barter. **1866** *Rep. Indian Affairs* 259 While the ignorant and uncivilized are content to live upon pounded corn, raised mostly by the female portion of their families. **1885** *Harper's Mag.* June 70/1 Pounded corn was their only bread, their only meat game brought down by their rifles.

Pounder. An official chosen to impound cattle. {1622–} — **1644** *Ipswich Rec.* 4 April, The Comon Pounder or any other party shall have ijd a pecce for all piggs, or any other Cattell, that they shall impound. **1685** *East-Hampton Rec.* II. 165 Jacob Daighton and John Miller Juno are Choasen pounders for this present year. **1727** *Smithtown Rec.* 81 Lieutenant Richard Smith chosen pounder.

***Pounding.** *attrib.* Designating objects used in the action of pounding or beating. — **1657** *East-Hampton Rec.* I. 112, 2 barrels one poundeinge tubb one churne [etc.]. **1673** *Essex Inst. Coll.* L. 28 A halfe bushel & gallon & a pounding trough. **1867** *Atlantic Mo.* March 366/2 The mixture looked like a family wash after an unusual course of rubbing-board, pounding-stick, and Hibernian muscle.

+**Pounding barrel.** A barrel in which clothes are pounded in water to clean them. — **1853** *Mich. Agric. Soc. Trans.* IV. 87 One pounding barrel, for clothes. **1869** STOWE *Oldtown Folks* 340 The thunder of the pounding-barrel, announced that the washing was to be got out of the way before daylight. **1894** ROBINSON *Danvis Folks* 176, I don't see . . . haow father ever got holt o' his boots when I'd hid 'em in the paoundin' berril.

+**Pounding mill.** A powdermill; a stamping mill; a mill for cleaning rice. — **1789** MORSE *Amer. Geog.* 369 They might avail themselves of a good situation on a creek, for a pounding mill. **1815** *Niles' Reg.* VIII. 291/1 The pounding mill, belonging to the great establishment of the Messrs. Duponts, . . . was accidentally blown up. **1849** LANMAN *Lett. from Alleghany Mts.* 17 The vein gold is brought to light by means of what is called a pounding mill. **1905** PRINGLE *Rice Planter* 142 The cows and pigs are fed on the flour, a gray substance that comes from the grain as the chaff is removed in the pounding mill.

Poundkeeper. =next. {1783–} — **1643** *Ipswich Rec.* 25 March, Every owner of such cattell shall pay for every head soe impounded . . . 2d to the Poundkeeper. **1695** *Huntington Rec.* II. 175 Samuell Smith should stand & Remaine pound keeper for this present yeare. **1766** *Essex Inst. Coll.* XXI. 233 John Rowe Pound Keeper this year. **1841** CIST *Cincinnati* 163 Levi M'Lean . . . figures at different periods as jailer, pound-keeper, butcher and constable.

Poundmaster. One who has charge of a public pound. — **1792** *Southampton Rec.* III. 335 John Couper Samuel Cooper Henry Corwithe Poundmasters. **1841** *Knickerb.* XVII. 289 The pound-master struggled in vain to 'head him off.' **1875** [see FIREWARDEN]. **1897** *Outing* XXIX. 537/1 You get my vote the next time you run for poundmaster.

+**Pound net.** A net arranged to serve as a trap in taking fish. Also attrib. — **1865** *Mich. Gen. Statutes* I. (1882) 577 The penalties of this section shall not apply or work injury to persons who are the present owners of pound or trap nets. **1897** *Outing* XXX. 362/1 The run from Cleveland to South Bass Island was marked . . . by the encountering of one of the greatest nuisances . . . that a seafaring man can meet with, and that is pound-nets. **1904** *Newark Ev. News* 13 June 6 The charges against the pound net fishermen are that by using nets of too small mesh they destroy tons upon tons of young food fishes. **1911** *Rep. Fisheries 1908* 316/2 Monterey Spanish mackerel . . . are caught on troll lines and in gill nets and pound nets.

+**Pound party.** A donation party, usually for a minister or a bride, to which the guests bring provisions, originally in pound packages. — **1877** BARTLETT 487. **1883** DE VERE in *Encycl. Brit.* (ed. 9) *Amer. Suppl.* I. 200/1 Of late a new word, pound party, has been coined to indicate meetings where each person attending is by a tacit understanding expected to bring a pound of some commodity to be used. **1889** *Boston Jrnl.* 22 Jan. 2/3 The old-fashioned pound party has become this winter a fashionable city entertainment. **1909** *Dialect Notes* III. 359.

***Pound sterling.** A British monetary unit equivalent normally to about $4.85. — **1632** *Plymouth Col. Rec.* I. 5 That if any were elected to the office of Councell, and refused to hold the place, that then he be amerced in ten pounds sterling fine. **1654** *Suffolk Deeds* III. 251 The some of one hundred three score & fower pounds sterljng Agreed to be pajd in Cashe. **1784** JEFFERSON *Writings* I. 243 Or shall we hang the pound sterling, as a common badge, about all their necks? **1823** THACHER *Military Jrnl.* 572 The British general . . . immediately closed with him for the stipulated sum of ten thousand pounds sterling.

+**Pound sweet.** =next. — **1859** F. R. ELLIOTT *Western Fruit Book* 102 Pumpkin Sweet. Pound Sweet, Lyman's Pumpkin Sweet [etc.]. . . . An old Connecticut fruit, valued for baking. **1923** *Standardized Plant Names* 539/1.

+**Pound sweeting.** A variety of apple. Also attrib. — **1853** *Knickerb.* XLII. 172 A wood-pecker . . . was drumming away upon a decayed limb of the old 'pound-sweeting' apple-tree. **1879** B. F. TAYLOR *Summer-Savory* 116 One was a fine specimen of a lean deacon, and the other as rotund as one of his own Pound Sweetings, for he was the man who gave me Rhode Island Greenings out of his Sunday-noon lunch. **1895** A. BROWN *Meadow-Grass* 211 There were great pound sweetings, full of the pride of mere bigness.

Pout.** +Any one of various American fresh-water catfishes; an eel-pout. (Cf. BULLPOUT, EELPOUT 2, HORN POUT.) — **1707** J. WILLIAMS *Redeemed Captive* (1758) 18 There seven of us supped on the Fish, called Bull-head or Pout, and did not eat it up, the Fish was so large. **1778** CARVER *Travels* 171 There is also [in L. Ontario] a sort called the Cat-head or Pout, which are in general very large, some of them weighing eight or ten pounds. [**1809** A. HENRY *Travels* 252 We took pouts, cat-fish, or cat-heads, of six pounds weight.] *a1862** THOREAU *Maine Woods* 210 He would not touch a pout . . . and said that neither Indians nor whites thereabouts ever ate them, which I thought was singular, since they are esteemed in Massachusetts.

+Pouty, *a.* and *adv.* **1.** *adj.* Inclined to pout; sullen. **2.** *adv.* In a pouting manner. — **(1) 1863** 'G. HAMILTON' *Gala-Days* 221 They never were tired when anything was to be done, or . . . peevish, or pouty, or 'offish.' **1897** STUART *Simpkinsville* 23 This stove's ez dull-eyed and pouty ez any other woman ef she's neglected. **1912** WASON *Friar Tuck* 77 With a pouty look on his face, Tank sez: 'It's time we fixed up an' moved out into the dark.' **(2) 1897** BRODHEAD *Bound in Shallows* 99, I had acted kind of pouty that night.

***Poverty.** In the names of trees and plants: (see quotations). {1847–} — **1880** TOURGEE *Bricks* 94 His rider's feet just . . . [brushed] the low 'poverty-pines' which grew by the roadside. **1894** *Amer. Folk-Lore* VII. 90 *Anaphalis margaritacea*, . . . poverty-weed, Penobscot Co., Me. **1897** SUDWORTH *Arborescent Flora* 139 White Birch. . . . Common Names. . . . Old Field Birch. Poverty Birch (Me.).

+Poverty grass. Any one of various grasses, as *Aristida dichotoma*, that grow in poor, sandy soil. — **1833** EATON *Botany* (ed. 6) 27 *Aristida dichotoma*, beard grass, poverty grass. **1878** Killebrew *Tenn. Grasses* 232 *Aristida Dichotoma* . . . is called poverty grass because it is seldom seen except on old barren fields, too poor for cultivation, and contains no nutriment. **1894** *Amer. Folk-Lore* VII. 103 *Eleocharis tenuis*, . . . poverty-grass, kill-cow, West Va. **1920** LINCOLN *Mr. Pratt* 95 He owned the sheds and barn . . . and the poverty grass.

***Powder.**

***1.** =GUNPOWDER 1.

The examples in (1) reflect the efforts made by the American colonists to prevent the Indians from securing gunpowder.

(1) **1619** *Va. House of Burgesses* 13 That no man do sell or give any Indians any piece shott, or poulder, or any other armes offensive or defensive. **1658** GORGES *Briefe Narration* 28 Disorderly Persons . . . sell unto the Savages, Musquets, Fowling-Pieces, Powder, Shot, . . . and other Armes. **1675** in Easton *Indian War* 91 The Constables of the severall Tounes [shall] take Care no Powder or Lead bee sold to the Indyans. **1691** *Mass. Ct. of Assistants Rec.* I. 356 He would sweare point blank that he knew some men that had sold the Indians Powder & shot.

(2) **1632** *Plymouth Laws* 31 That for each able person aforesaid, he be at all times after the last of May next ensuing furnished with two pounds of powder and ten pounds of bullets. **1690** *Ib.* 225 The Town Councils . . . [shall] take care that such as are Impressed . . . be each one fitted with . . . not less than three charges of powder and shot for each man. **1707** *Boston Rec.* 57 Ordered that Capt. Timothy Clark do deliver two barrells of the Townes Powder to . . . the Committee for a fire meeting in Boston. **1827** COOPER *Prairie* iii, My character against a horn of powder, that the bird would be hanging head downwards, in five minutes. **1907** *St. Nicholas* July 788/1 There shall be heaps of powder burned, and every bell shall ring.

2. *Powder and ball*, powder and bullets as used in rifles, +hence, shooting. Also attrib.

*c***1695** MILLER *Desc. of New York* (1843) 35 Twenty pieces of ordnance, . . . shells, bombs, carcasses, spades, mattocks, and also powder and ball. **1791** W. BARTRAM *Travels* 74 Having fishing tackle, a neat light fusee, powder and ball, I found myself well equipped for my voyage. **1833** COKE *Subaltern's Furlough* vii, The American light troops carry powder and ball flasks suspended across their shoulders in place of a cartridge-box. **1857** *Lawrence* (Kan.) *Republican* 11 June 3 If these [peaceable means] failed, he would try powder and ball. **1873** *Newton Kansan* 3 July 1/7 [The duel] was a real, *bona fide* powder-and-ball affair. **1903** FOX *Little Shepherd* xxi, A little interchange of powder-and-ball civilities followed.

3. In special combinations.

Powder boat, a boat used as a storage place for gunpowder; *p. charger*, a small measure holding just enough gunpowder to charge a firearm (cf. CHARGER); *p. committee*, a committee charged with providing a military force with gunpowder; *p. fever*, (see quotation); *p.-maker*, one who makes gunpowder; *p. man*, in mining, one in charge of blasting, usually with gunpowder; *p. pan*, the part of a gunlock which holds the priming; *p. train*, a train of wagons hauling gunpowder.

1882 *Century Mag.* Sept. 678/2 The old steamer . . . is turned into a store-ship, a powder-boat, or a floating hospital. **1868** *Putnam's Mag.* May 592/2 [An alligator's] hollow tooth makes a good powder-charger. **1775** *Jrnls. Cont. Congress* II. 191 The President [shall] be desired to write to the powder committees or committees of safety in this city and New York . . . to forward to the camp as much good gunpowder as they can spare. **1856** OLMSTED *Slave States* 200 Among sailors and soldiers, when men suddenly find themselves ill and unable to do their duty in times of peculiar danger, or when unusual labor is required, they are humorously said to be suffering under an attack of the powder-fever, the cape-fever, the ice-fever [etc.]. **1775** *S.C. Hist. Soc. Coll.* III. 87 In consequence of the order of yesterday, . . . Mr. Bartie, the powder-maker attended [the meeting of the council of safety]. **1886** *Scientific Amer.* LIV. 85/2 In driving the heading, each of the three shifts is made up of a boss, 4 drill men, 4 helpers on drills, 1 powder man, 1 car man, and 2 laborers. **1851** MELVILLE *Moby-Dick* 542 That Parsee smells fire like a fusee; and smells of it himself, like a hot musket's powder-pan. **1867** *Ore. State Jrnl.* 19 Jan. 1/2 One wagon of a powder train . . . blew up near Green River, Utah, on the 12th of October.

Powder barrel. A barrel for gunpowder. {1769–} — **1689** SEWALL *Diary* I. 289, 1 fishing net Called a Seyne, put up in a powther barrell. **1776** *N.H. Comm. Safety Rec.* 62 Ordered . . . to pay . . . for 30 Powder Barrels.

+Powder-burn, *v. tr.* To burn (an object) with the hot gases that issue from a firearm when discharged. — **1846** W. G. STEWART *Altowan* I. 125 That he might powder-burn the bear by the nearness of the shot. **1847** in Howe *Hist. Coll. Ohio* 99 In this struggle, Lytle . . . [had] his face powder burnt. **1853** *S. Lit. Messenger* XIX. 463/1, I got in pursuit with another officer . . . , determined this time to powder-burn my game.

Powder canister. A canister or keg of gunpowder. — **1847** *Knickerb.* XXX. 14 He did not know the alphabet until he was twenty-three, and . . . he acquired it then from the printed advertisements of his powder-canisters. **1874** LONG *Wild-fowl* 113 The powder-canister is of tin, square, and made to fit in proper place. **1911** WHITE *Bobby Orde* xi, In the bunks themselves lay powder canisters, shotbags, wad-boxes.

Powder cask. A cask or keg for gunpowder. — **1758** *Essex Inst. Coll.* XVIII. 196 He beat in ye Powder Casks and threw 'm into ye wells. **1778** *N.H. Comm. Safety Rec.* 168 Ordered Doctr. Josiah Gilman to Deliver Colo. Samuel Hobart . . . all the powder casks. **1862** LOWELL *Biglow P.* 2 Ser. iii. 103 Ther' 's nothin' like a powder-cask f'r a stiddy corner-stone.

Powdered sugar. Sugar that has been pulverized or reduced to a powder. {1765–} — **1761** *Newport Mercury* 19 May 4/1 To be Sold by Public Vendue, . . . A quantity of Prize Goods, consisting of Powder'd Sugar and Coffee. **1816** *Ann. 14th Congress* 1 Sess. 1873 [Duty] on white, clayed, or powdered sugar, four cents per pound. **1907** *St. Nicholas* May 670/1 Add one-half cup of powdered sugar.

Powderflask. A flask used by hunters, soldiers, etc., for carrying gunpowder. {1753–} — **1765** ROGERS *Acct. N. Amer.* 106 His powder-flask, by some accident, took fire, which wounded him to that degree as to put him to exquisite pain. **1834** *S. Lit. Messenger* I. 157/2 Their arms were of divers descriptions; double barrelled guns, deer guns, ducking guns, and a blunderbuss, with powderflasks and horns swung round their shoulders. **1890** HOWELLS *Boy's Town* 153 Then he made himself a powder-flask out of an ox-horn that he got and boiled till it was soft, . . . and then scraped thin with a piece of glass. **1905** BELASCO *Girl of Golden West* (1925) I. 61 Wearing a pale, faded beaver hat and a heavy overcoat, his pistol and powder flask in his belt.

+Powder gourd. A gourd used by hunters as a container for powder. — **1775** in Pusey *Road to Ky.* (1921) 42 My hors . . . threw Down the Saddel Bags & Broke three of our powder goards. **1845** HOOPER *Simon Suggs' Adv.* 201, I finds the big powder gourd they all kept their powder in.

***Powderhorn.** The horn of an ox or cow suitably prepared as a container for gunpowder.

1645 *Conn. Probate Rec.* I. 21 A file, a butter tube, a powder horn, a prre of old Stockings. **1707** *Boston News-Letter* 17 Feb. 2/1 He threw away his Blanket, Breeches and Powder Horn, to further his flight. **1788** MAY *Jrnl. & Lett.* 75, I put powder-horn and shot-bag onto him. **1833** J. HALL *Harpe's Head* 36 Under one arm hung a large powder-horn, on the other side was suspended a square pouch. **1897** BRODHEAD *Bound in Shallows* 235 A great log fireplace . . . [lighted] up the beamed ceiling and four-posted bed and turkey-red hangings and array of rifles and powder-horns. **1916** EASTMAN *From Deep Woods* 31, [I took] my Hudson Bay flintlock gun, . . . with my shot-pouch and a well-filled powder-horn.

Powder house. A building for storing gunpowder. {1774–} Also attrib. — **1720** *Mass. H. Rep. Jrnl.* II. 288 *Daniel Powning*, Keeper of the Powder-House in Boston. **1767** *Charlestown Land Rec.* 244 There are eight Range Ways between the Common and the Powder House. **1789** *Boston Directory* 183 Foster Thomas, powder-house-keeper. **1832** WATSON *Hist. Tales N.Y.* 99 The powder house he remembered. **1896** SHINN *Story of Mine* 211 There is a powder house.

***Powdering tub.** (See quot. 1884.) — **1638** *Md. Archives* IV. 48 1. litle powdring tubb. **1657** *East-Hampton Rec.* I. 122 Two barrels & one powdering tub. **1724** *New-Eng. Courant* 9–16 Nov. 1/2 If the former [the gentlemen's Negroes] rob the Brandy-Bottle, 'tis no doubt thought reasonable among them that the latter [the tradesmen's Negroes] should be as free with the Poudering-Tub, in order to compleat their Collations. **1884** *Century Mag.* Jan. 444/1 In New England, each family had, after the old English custom, its 'powdering tub,'—not yet everywhere disused,—in which the pork for the family table was salted, and from which it was taken to be smoked by hanging in the ample chimney.

Powder keg. A keg for gunpowder. Also fig. — **1855** SIMMS *Forayers* 39 Sinclair . . . drew up an old powder-keg by a rope-hitch. **1876** 'MARK TWAIN' *Tom Sawyer* xxxiii. 260 It was the treasure-box, sure enough, occupying a snug little cavern, along with an empty powder-keg, a couple of guns in leather cases. **1893** POST *Harvard Stories* 6 One reason why they do it . . . is to make you flare up, you little powder keg.

Powder magazine. A place in a fort or a ship where gunpowder is stored. {1769–} — **1762** FRANKLIN *Writings* IV. 186 [To secure] a powder magazine from lightning, . . . I think they cannot do better than to erect a mast not far from it. **1796** *Ann. 4th Congress* 2 Sess. 2572 Governor's Island has been fortified with a fort made of earth, and two batteries under its protection, partly lined with brick masonry, two air-furnaces, a large powder magazine, and barrack for the garrison. **1832** DUNLAP *Hist. Amer. Theatre* 44 Pearl-street, not long since called Magazine-street (from a powder magazine which stood there in former days). **1895** G. KING *New Orleans* 43 The powder magazine was placed on what would now be the neutral ground in front of the custom house.

Powdermill. A mill for making gunpowder. {1650–} — **1676** in Hutchinson *Coll. Papers Mass. Bay* 487 At Dorchester, 7 miles from Boston, is a powder mill in good repair, well wrought. **1774** in Peyton *Adv. Grandfather* (1867) 151 About a half-mile below the Fall, there is a powder-mill, protected by two stockade forts. *a***1817** DWIGHT *Travels* IV. 489 Manufacturing Establishments . . . in the District of Connecticut . . . [include] Powder Mills 7. **1878** H. H. JACKSON *Travel At Home* 59 Down in the bottom of the canyon is a little green meadow oasis, where there are a few white houses and a powder-mill.

+**Powder money.** Tax money for the purchase of gunpowder for common defense. *Obs.* — **1715** *Mass. H. Rep. Jrnl.* I. 8 All Ships or other Vessels that Load or Unload at the Port of Kittery . . . [shall] Pay the Duties of Impost and Powder Money according to Law. **1721** *Ib.* III. 208 The former Impositions of Powder Money, double Light Money, and double Duties on Wine.

+**Powder post.** {powder of post, 1769–} The powder of worm-eaten wood. Also fig. and attrib. — **1790** DEANE *New Eng. Farmer* 151/1 The smaller kind [of timber worm] eats only the sappy part of the wood, turning it to what is vulgarly called *powder-post.* **1845** JUDD *Margaret* I. 161, I can [tell the Latin] for the maggot that makes powder-post of our whole family, Didymus Hart. **1863** MITCHELL *My Farm* 83 A wild, sweeping, gallant blaze, that wrapped old powder-post timbers in its roar, . . . came crinkling through the roof in a hundred wilful jets.

Powderproof, *a.* Of locks, safes, etc.: Proof against being blown open with gunpowder. — **1856** *Porter's Spirit of Times* 8 Nov. 167/1 Robert M. Patrick, Sole Manufacturer in the United States, of the above celebrated Safes, and Patent Powder Proof Defiance Locks and Cross-Bars. **1859** *Programme* (N.Y.) 7 Feb. 4 Wilder's patent salamander safes, secured with the best patent powder and burglar-proof locks. **1886** *Harper's Mag.* July 195/2 Each outer door, hung on crane hinges, is forced bodily into position by an eccentric lever, and is thus made air-tight and powder-proof.

+**Powder rate.** In colonial times, a rate or assessment levied for providing gunpowder for common defense. *Obs.* — **1651** *Watertown Rec.* I. I. 22 The two Constables . . . gaue an acompt of the powder rate of the last yeare. **1681** *Springfield Rec.* II. 147 Voted by ye Town to ffree David ffrow ffrom a powder Rate & all other Town Rates.

Powder wagon. *Mil.* A wagon carrying gunpowder. — **1775** *Jrnls. Cont. Congress.* III. 337 For a guard over a powder waggon, the sum of 42 pounds. **1846** SAGE *Scenes Rocky Mts.* iv, While journeying across the grand prairies, the powder-waggon accidentally caught fire.

Powder works. A place at which gunpowder is made. — **1712** SEWALL *Letter-Book* II. 8 Near the house in which dwells Walter Everden tenant to the proprietors of the powder-works. **1861** *Army Regulations* 472 Inspection Report . . . of Cannon (or Musket) Powder, &c., at the Powder Works of A.B. **1913** LONDON *Valley of Moon,* The day the powder works blew up at Pinole, . . . he and she had not joined in the panic rush for out-of-doors.

Power. +Religious enthusiasm or frenzy. Also attrib. — **1862** *Harper's Mag.* Dec. 101 These exercises had been prolonged nearly an hour when several of the seekers were taken with 'the power.' *Ib.,* Elder Hill went on to another 'power' patient. **1899** *Mo. So. Dakotan* I. 141 One sister got the power in right good Methodist fashion. **1923** J. H. COOK *On Old Frontier* 231 A great revivalist of the shouting Methodist school, who could soon have great numbers of blind followers under the influence of 'the power.'

***Powerful,** *a.* Great in amount or quantity; impressive, mighty. *colloq.* {1862–} — **1822** WOODS *English Prairie* (1904) 346, I also have got some beefs, and a powerful chance of corn. **1839** *S. Lit. Messenger* V. 377/1 To be sure I did see a powerful sight of bear signs. **1867** GOSS *Soldier's Story* 255 The Yanks have got a powerful spite 'gainst us. **1916** PORTER *David* 132 Joe's father had 'played in the band' in his youth, and (according to the Widow Glaspell) had been a 'powerful hand for music.'

Powerful, *adv.* Very, exceedingly; to a great extent. *colloq.* {1876–} — **1833** HALL *Harpe's Head* 86 This has been a powerful hot day. **1882** *Century Mag.* April 884/1 You mout move around here more'n a year an' never need a pistol, but ef you *should* happen to need one, you'd need it powerful. **1917** MATHEWSON *Second Base Sloan* 40 Apples is powerful fillin' fruit, Mas' Wayne.

Power house. A house for machinery used in generating mechanical power. {1895–} — **1881** *Harper's Mag.* March 597/1 He found himself . . . at that 'Power House' of which he had heard . . . for many a year. **1905** N. DAVIS *Northerner* 96 Falls . . . struck across the outskirts of the town to the power-house. **1917** SINCLAIR *King Coal* 305 Let's go off quietly, and have our meeting on the dump in back of the power-house.

Power loom. A loom operated or driven by mechanical power. {1808–} Also attrib. — **1821** *Mass. H. S. Coll.* 2 Ser. IX. 128 The building contains . . . fifteen *power looms,* (or looms, which are moved by water). **1865** *Atlantic Mo.* May 616/2 There is a lower class of workers who find employment in the . . . power-loom factories that abound among us. **1914** *Smithsonian Inst. Ann. Rep.* 676 The new loom, which appears to me to be likely to revolutionize the construction of machines for weaving by power, . . . differs from the ordinary power loom.

+**Power press.** A printing press driven by mechanical power. — **1841** Cist *Cincinnati* Advt., They have in their Printing establishment . . . five Power Presses. **1851** CIST *Ib.* 232 Morgan & Overend, . . . with nine Adams power presses, . . . employ thirty-two hands. **1871** RINGWALT, etc. *Amer. Encycl. Printing* 172/1 *Fly,*—an invention for taking off or delivering the sheets from a power-press.

+**Powhatan pipe.** A tobacco pipe, supposedly of the type used by the Powhatan Indians. — **1866** COOKE *Surry* 61 On the table lay pipes of every form, chibouques, hookahs, narghilès, meerschaums carved into grotesque or beautiful figures, and the plain but excellent Powhatan pipe of Virginia. **1869** TOURGEE *Toinette* (1881) 221 Geoffrey . . . was fairly settled to a smoke with one of the old man's genuine 'Powhatan' pipes.

+**Powwow,** *n.* Also †**powah, powaw.** [Of Indian origin. Cf. Narraganset *powáw,* Massachuset *pauwaw.*] See also PAW(W)AW *n.*

1. An Indian medicine man, priest, wizard, or magician. **1624** WINSLOW *Good Newes* 22 The actor of this fact was a *Powah,* one of special note amongst them. **1697** C. MATHER *Magnalia* (1853) I. 55 The Indians employed their *sorcerers,* whom they call *powaws,* like Balaam, to curse them. **1744** BRAINERD *Journal* (1902) 256 Powwows . . . are supposed to have a power of enchanting, or poisoning them [*sc.* Indians] to death, or at least in a very distressing manner. **1764** HUTCHINSON *Hist. Mass.* I. 473 Upon him [God] they had their first dependence for recovery from sickness, but if he failed them they applied to their powows. **1850** HAWTHORNE *Scarlet Letter* xxii, Many a church-member saw I, walking behind the music, that has danced in the same measure with me, when Somebody was fiddler, and, it might be, an Indian powwow or a Lapland wizard changing hands with us! **1884** *Harper's Mag.* June 152/2 The ecstasies . . . of these conjurors and powows are survivals of a distorted tradition. **1907** *Springfield W. Repub.* 21 March 13 There were among them [the Indians of New England] men and women whom they called powaws. These were a combination of conjurer and physician, and were held in profound respect.

2. A noisy conjuring or ceremonial rite held or performed by Indians; a council or conference of Indians.

1647 SHEPARD *Clear Sun-shine* 18 [The Indians] have utterly forsaken all their *Powwaws,* and given over that diabolicall exercise, being convinced that it is quite contrary to praying unto God. **1788** MAY *Jrnl. & Lett.* 94 The Indians made one of their hellish pow-wows, which lasted till the hour of rising. **1809** *Mass. Spy* 9 Aug. (Th.), [They] regard it no more than they would an Indian Pow-wow upon the banks of the Missouri. **1890** CUSTER *Following Guidon* 46 We find it impossible to hurry the Indians much, they have so many powwows and ceremonies before determining upon any important action. **1903** WHITE *Forest* 208 They drift together up and down the North Country streams, or camp for big powwows and conjuring. **1919** *Maine My State* 142 Once the Indians held a pow-wow to keep up their courage.

attrib. **1843** WHITTIER *Writings* VII. 257 Without were 'dogs and sorcerers,' . . . Powah wizards, and 'the foul fiend.'

b. *transf.* The healing art; magic or witchcraft. Also attrib.

1856 KANE *Arctic Explor.* II. 126 My skill in pow-wow had given me a sort of correlative rank among [the Esquimaux angekoks]. **1901** *Scribner's Mag.* Nov. 525 The 'powwow-doctors' [among the Dunkers] still repeat over many bedsides the mysterious formulas.

3. A meeting, gathering, assemblage, esp. one thought of as noisy and demonstrative. *colloq.*

The first group of quotations illustrates the common use of the word to describe political meetings.

(1) **1812** *Salem Gazette* 5 June 3/3 The Warriors of the Democratic Tribe will hold a powow at Agawam on Tuesday next. **1865** *Daily Telegraph* 26 May, The Abolitionists are having a great pow-wow . . . as to whether they shall or not maintain their organisation, now that slavery is dead. **1885** *Wkly. New Mexican Rev.* 15 Jan. 4/4 Democratic Love-Feast. A Pow Wow at Chairman Gildersleeve's office Followed by a Banquet. **1906** *N.Y. Ev. Post* 8 May 2 No Democrats attended the pow-wows at which a settlement was reached.

(2) **1840** DANA *Two Years* xx. 198 The Catalina had several Kanakas on board, who were . . . carried up to the oven, where they had a long powwow, and a smoke. **1875** 'MARK TWAIN' *Old Times* i. 17 The riotous powwow of setting a spar was going on down on the forecastle. **1900** H. ROBERTSON *Red Blood & Blue* 287 They's a cannon . . . an' a gran' promenade . . . windin' up with a big powwow at the 'Cademy. **1904** PRINGLE *Rice Planter* 59 On the rice plantation the first of January is the time for the yearly powwow, which the negroes regard as a necessary function.

4. (See quot. 1871.) *Obs.* Also transf.

1852–3 *Burlesque Catalogue* (Yale) 35 The students are forbidden to occupy the State-House steps on the evening of Presentation day, since the Faculty design hereafter to have a Pow-wow there, as on the last. **1856** HALL *College Words* (ed. 2) 359. **1871** BAGG *At Yale* 275 About the year 1850, the custom arose among the Freshmen of celebrating their accession to sophomoric dignity by a performance called a 'Pow-wow,' upon the night of Presentation Day. It was held upon the State House steps, and consisted of burlesque speeches, songs and poems.

attrib. **1871** BAGG *At Yale* 276 Squads of muddy Freshmen . . . disappeared among the brick buildings, there to dream [of] . . . fair faces, morning flunk, and dunning Pow-wow committees.

+**Powwow,** *v.* [See prec.] (See also PAW(W)AW *v.*)

1. *intr.* **a.** Of Indians: To act as a conjuror; to engage in a powwow.

1648 Shepard *Clear Sun-Shine* 5 Both he that shall *Powwow*, & he that shall procure him to *Powwow*, shall pay 20*s.* apeece. **1685** *Plymouth Laws* 298 No Indian which shall dwell or come into our Jurisdiction shall presume at any time to *Powwow* or perform outward Worship to the Devil or other false God. **1702** C. MATHER *Magnalia* (1853) I. 58 Our rain . . . after our Powawing for it, breaks down the corn. **1788** DENNY *Journal* 129 Several days pass over. Indians pow-wowing. **1835** LATROBE *Rambler in N.A.* II. 204 Companies of old warriors might be seen sitting smoking under every bush; arguing, palavering, or 'pow-wowing.'

b. *transf.* To counsel, deliberate, or converse, esp. in a noisy or vehement manner.

1818 *Mass. Spy* 9 Sept. (Th.), The Indian fashion (unknown in England) of powowing and huzzaing in approbation of toasts, is generally unwelcome to a majority of those who are engaged in it. **1857** LONGFELLOW in S. Longfellow *H. W. Longfellow* II. 334 Senator Mason of Virginia was there, pow-wowing about the Union. **1884** 'MARK TWAIN' *H. Finn* iii, We would go to the cave and powwow over what we had done. **1911** SAUNDERS *Col. Todhunter* 189 Me and him ain't had a chance to pow-wow together for four or five years.

2. *tr.* To make (a person) the object of a powwow, esp. in sense 2 b.

1856 KANE *Arctic Explor.* II. 116, I gave him a piece of red flannel, and powwowed him. **1863** P. S. DAVIS *Young Parson* 154 His father . . . powwowed it [the child], and the doctor gave it some stuff, and now it's picking up agin. **1872** *Newton Kansan* 17 Oct. 1/4 The noble savages were willing to be feted and whiskeyed and pow-wowed.

+**Powwower.** =Powwow 1. *Obs.* — **1646** *Mass. Col. Rec.* III. 98 Ye p[ro]curer [shall be fined] five pounds, ye pawwawer five pounds. **1774** D. JONES *Journal* (1865) 79 This apparel is also used by their pou-wouers in their attempts of healing the sick. **1781** PETERS *Hist. Conn.* 68*n.*, The Savage Pawawwers, or Priests, never concern themselves with marriages, but leave them to the Paniesh, or Magistrates. **1812** PAULDING *J. Bull. & Bro. Jon.* 97 The *Essex Junta* . . . are undoubtedly the genuine descendants of the witches and the *Pow-wowers.* **1820** *Western Rev.* II. 163 The Powwowers or Priests were formerly in high estimation, as it is believed that they are the agents of the different powers, or great spirits that govern the universe.

+**Powwowing.** Also †**powaheing, powawing.** The action on the part of an Indian, or of Indians, of performing or taking part in a powwow. Also transf. (Cf. PAW(W)AWING.)

1642 LECHFORD *Plain Dealing* 117 They will have their times of Powaheing, which they will, of late, have called Prayers, according to the English word. **1764** HUTCHINSON *Hist. Mass.* I. 475*n.*, Their sweatings in their hot houses was a more rational remedy than the powowing. **1846** McKENNEY *Memoirs* I. 83 It was the medicine-man's drum over a sick child, accompanied by the usual pow-wowing. **1871** *Rep. Indian Affairs* (1872) 582 The potency seems to be in the blowing and 'pow-wow-ing.' **1905** LINCOLN *Partners* 8, I cal'late there must have been some high old pow-wowin' in the old house.

+**Pozo.** (See quot. 1877.) *Obs.* — **1854** BARTLETT *Personal Narr.* II. 465*n.*, *Noria* is properly a wheel or engine for drawing water from a well; the term is also applied to wells where wheels are so employed, to distinguish them from *pozos*, or common wells. **1863** *37th Congress Spec. Sess.* Sen. Ex. Doc. No. 1, 5, [I] left the boat in a gulley near the . . . 'Pozo,' partially filled with sand. **1877** BARTLETT 489 *Pozo.* (Span.) A spring or well. A word in use on the frontier of Mexico.

P. p. Abbrev. for *post position.* Used in reference to starting a horse race. — **1875** *Courier-Journal* 18 May 4/3 The second race was the event of the day—the Kentucky Derby, a dash of 1½ miles for three-year olds, fifty dollars entrance, p.p., the Association adding $1,000.

+**Practical politician.** One engaged in the actual problems of politics, spec. of controlling votes, working for a party, etc. Freq. depreciative. — **1812** *Ann. 12th Congress* 1 Sess. 2210 There were two circumstances, inherent in this system of coercing Great Britain by commercial restrictions, which ought to have made practical politicians very doubtful of its result. **1888** *Denver Repub.* 29 Feb. (F.), The heelers and strikers, bummers and stuffers, otherwise known as practical politicians, . . . do the work at the Democratic polls and manipulate the primaries. **1890** HOWELLS *Shadow of Dream* I. i, He was a 'practical' politician; he adhered to his party in all its measures.

+**Practical politics.** Politics involving actual work in a party, or attempts at actual control of an election. — **1868** BANCROFT in Howe *Life & Letters G. Bancroft* II. 185 These are the considerations that led me to the views that have governed my life in questions of practical politics. **1881–5** McCLELLAN *Own Story* 34, I knew nothing about 'practical politics.' **1904** A. FRENCH *Barrier* 163 Any campaign which they [*sc.* reformers] conduct would be the usual formal and ineffectual protest against 'practical politics.'

+**Practical printer.** (See PRINTER 2.)

+**Practice game.** *Athletics.* A game played for practice, usually prior to formally scheduled games. — **1885** *Wkly. New Mexican Rev.* 9 April 3/3 The clubs of Santa Fe, Las Vegas, Raton and Socorro have already had practice games.

+**Practice ship.** A ship used in the Naval Academy in giving the cadets practical instruction. — **a1861** WINTHROP *Open Air* 227 There they found the Naval Academy in danger of attack, and Old Ironsides—serving as a practice-ship for the future midshipmen—also exposed. **1888** DORSEY *Midshipman Bob* 188 The boys buckled down to hard work, which was not remitted until the June examinations were over, the practice-ships fitted out for a cruise [etc.]. **1898** *How to Gain Admission to Annapolis* 8 About the fifth of June each year, the members of the first, third and fourth classes embark on the Academy practice ship.

***Practiser.** **1.** A physician or surgeon. +**2.** (See quotation.) — **(1) 1767** HUTCHINSON *Hist. Mass.* II. 274 Another practiser, Laurence Dalhoude, . . . had been a surgeon in the French army. **(2) 1900** A. ALLEN *P. Brooks* I. 290 There were other similar [mission] stations in the vicinity, where [seminary] students officiated by reading service and extempore preaching. . . . The common name given to them was *practisers*, with the emphasis on the second syllable.

***Practitioner.**

***1.** A physician or surgeon.

1721 *Mass. H. S. Coll.* 4 Ser. II. 164 [In Boston] we abound with Practitioners, though no other graduate than myself. **1770** *Penna. Chronicle* 10–17 Sept. 138/2 Dr. Anthony Yeldall, Practioner [*sic*] in Physic and Surgery, . . . cures (by the blessing of God) all savable distempers. **1873** *Newton Kansan* 15 May 1/6 Dr. W. Parker, a widely-known practitioner of New York City, spent some time in studying the disease. **1890** LANGFORD *Vigilante Days* (1912) 159 Dr. Leavitt, also an able practitioner, . . . at the time, [was] engaged in the mining.

+**2.** *Christian Science.* An authorized or recognized healer.

1883 EDDY in *Christian Science Jrnl.* I. 3 The most of our practitioners have plenty to do and many more are needed. **1899** *Christian Science Jrnl.* XVII. 516 Finally a Christian Science practitioner was employed, and I was completely healed. **1915** DREISER *Genius* 710 Angela had somehow concluded . . . that Christian Science, as demonstrated by its practitioners, might help her through this crisis, though she had no real faith in it.

Praeses. {1637–50–} +*College slang.* A college president. — **1836** *Harvardiana* III. 98 Did not the Praeses, himself, most kindly and oft reprimand me? **1851** HOLMES *Poetical Works* (1895) 114/1 The good old Præses cries, . . . 'You have passed, and are classed With the *Boys of '29.*'

Pragmatism. {1863–} *Philos.* +An American philosophical movement founded by C. S. Peirce (1839–1914) and William James (1842–1910), characteristic doctrines of which are that the practical consequences of a conception are the expression of its whole meaning, and that the object of thinking is to develop general principles of conduct.

'As late as 1893, when I might have procured the insertion of the word pragmatism in the *Century Dictionary*, it did not seem to me that its vogue was sufficient to warrant that step' (1903 Peirce *Lectures on Pragmatism* V. 13). Peirce later adopted the word *pragmaticism* to distinguish his particular philosophy from other forms of pragmatism: 'So, then, the writer, finding his bantling "pragmatism" so promoted, . . . begs to announce the birth of the word "pragmaticism," which is ugly enough to be safe from kidnappers' (1905 Peirce in *Monist* XV. 165 f.).

1898 W. JAMES *Philos. Conceptions & Pract. Results* 5 The principle of practicalism or pragmatism, as he [C. S. Peirce] called it, when I first heard him enunciate it at Cambridge [Mass.] in the early '70s, is the clue . . . by following which . . . we may keep our feet upon the proper trail. *Ib.* 6 Our conception of these effects, then, is for us the whole of our conception of the object, so far as that conception has positive significance at all. This is the principle of Peirce, the principle of pragmatism. **1902** PEIRCE in Baldwin *Dict. Philosophy* II. 322/2 Pragmatism is really an attempt to construe all reality 'retrospectively'—as adequately given in the system of concrete practically derived truths. **1910** H. H. BAWDEN *Principles of Pragmatism* 43 It is not getting away from complexity that pragmatism recommends, but controlling complexity in relation to the attainment of the values of life. **1923** DEWEY in Peirce *Chance, Love & Logic* 302 There is a marked difference between his [Peirce's] pragmaticism and the pragmatism of, say, James.

+**Prairie.** [Fr., 'a meadow.']

The following quotations are significant as regards early pronunciations and spellings of the word. (See also PARARA).

1804 *Lewis & Clark Exped.* VII. (1905) 38 Got on our way at hard Scrable Perarie. **1805** PARKINGTON *Tour* 88 He offered to give me two hundred acres of land called priory, that is, rich meadow without wood upon it. **1823** DODDRIDGE *Logan* II. i, The grass of the prearie he mistakes for a large water. **1846** COOPER *Redskins* xxii, Then I spoke of the 'prer-ies,' as almost all western men pronounce the word. **1850** GARRARD *Wah-To-Yah* xix. 222, Good cigars ain't to be picked upon on the peraira every day. **1853** 'P. PAXTON' *Yankee in Texas* 98 You don't catch him showin' his profile in the perara tell dark.

I. 1. A level or rolling area of land, destitute of trees and usually covered with grass. {*a*1682, of a meadow in France}

This word has been applied to areas of different types in different parts of the country, giving rise to the following specific senses: **a.** A meadow, esp. one alongside a river; a relatively small area of low-lying grassland. (See also BOTTOM, SWAMP, WET PRAIRIE.) **b.** A grass-covered opening in a forest; a savanna. (See also HIGH, RIDGE, UPLAND PRAIRIE.) **c.** A level open area about a town, house, etc. **d.** A broad expanse of level or rolling land in the Indiana, Illinois, and Mississippi Valley country, covered by coarse grass. (See also GRAND, OPEN PRAIRIE.) **e.** An extensive plateau to the west of the Mississippi. In pl., frequently referring to the entire area between the Mississippi River and the Rocky Mountains. (See also GREAT, HOG-WALLOW, OPEN, ROLLING, WESTERN PRAIRIE.)

1773 in Hutchins *Va., Penna., Md., & N.C.* 55 The Prairies (Meadows) extend further from the [Illinois] river. **1787** E. DENNY *Mil. Jrnl.* 312 The prairies between . . . [Vincennes and Kaskaskia] are remarkable. One . . . is thirty miles in width, and near one hundred miles in length. They run north and south. **1792** *Amer. Philos. Soc.* III. 219 Some of these *Praires* are high lands, surrounded by an extensive timbered country, in many places much lower than the clear lands. **1807** GASS *Journal* 17 We encamped on the south side of the river at a prairie. **1808** PIKE *Sources Miss.* 7 Four hundred yards in the rear, there is a small prairie of 8 or 10 acres, which would be a convenient spot for gardens. **1814** BRACKENRIDGE *Views La.* 158 The prairies or savannas, and alluvia, scarcely constitute the other two-fifths of the state. **1816** U. BROWN *Journal* II. 361 Thence 13 Miles Crossing the great glades, which if in Ohio State would be a Prere to Wm. Jonsons. **1823** C. H. WILSON *Wanderer in Amer.* 111 Those *prairies*, being swampy, or in plain English, boggy land, exhale agues and fevers innumerable. **1832** CATLIN *Indians* I. 24 The buffalo . . . roams over the vast prairies. **1835** A. PARKER *Trip to Texas* 123 On a large prairie in front of his house, I saw two Indian mounds. **1838** C. NEWELL *Revol. Texas* 176 The prairies are natural pastures of Texas. **1852** REYNOLDS *Hist. Illinois* 28 [He] finally reached the Pawnees in a fine buffalo region in the Prairies four or five hundred miles from the Mississippi. **1873** BEADLE *Undevel. West* 353 [We] came out upon a rich prairie clothed with beautiful groves and bordered with fine timber, in the country of the Cherokees. **1886** POORE *Reminisc.* II. 522 The fertile prairies of the far West . . . supply the inhabitants of the Eastern States with food. **1908** Handsaker *Pioneer Life* 76 The Indians . . . had gone through a little prairie or opening, and ambushed by dividing and going back on the sides of the opening. **1925** TILGHMAN *Dugout* 15 North, west and south the dull brown prairie rose in rolling hills.

b. With specifying words.

1817 FORDHAM *Narr. Travels* 202 We then travelled . . . through part of the Long Prairie . . . ; and the *English Prairie*, with all its swelling hills, . . . opened at once upon our sight. **1826** in Peck *Guide* (1831) 209 The Big Prairie in Missouri, between Cape Girardeau and New Madrid, is . . . perhaps more properly barren land. **1835** SIMMS *Partisan* 330 The hammock was here quite bald, showing somewhat like what the western men call the 'Door Prairie'—that is, they come upon it as through a door in the woods. **1869** *Putnam's Mag.* May (De Vere), A trembling prairie, into which one would sink as into quicksand. **1869** *Overland Mo.* III. 310 [In] Texas . . . there is the 'chocolate' prairie, . . . the 'hummock,' (yielding principally small honey-locusts) and the 'wire-grass.'

c. With descriptive words.

Characterizing epithets of the type illustrated below are found over and over again. (See also OPEN PRAIRIE, ROLLING PRAIRIE.)

1846 SAGE *Scenes Rocky Mts.* xv, On the right lay a broad expanse of undulating prairie, covered with stately clusters of absinthe. **1868** *N.Y. Herald* 10 July 6/2 They displayed the true, manly spirit that seems . . . to spring up in the breast of the Western man as grass springs up on the broad prairies. **1882** *Wheelman* I. 138, I began to think . . . of leaving Wisconsin behind me, to roll across the limitless prairies and cornfields of Illinois. **1893** *Harper's Mag.* Jan. 318/1 The cottage in the river valley, the lonesome house on the wide prairie, the street that ran down to the wharf.

2. Quasi-adj. and generic: =PRAIRIE LAND.

1805 in Thoburn *Stand. Hist. Okla.* I. 32 We found the country all prairie, except small copses of wood, cedar, cotton and musketo. **1814** BRACKENRIDGE *Views La.* 50 The adjacent country is generally prairie. **1843** FRÉMONT *Explor. Rocky Mts.* 10 The ocean of prairie, . . . we were told, stretched without interruption almost to the base of the Rocky Mountains. **1901** DUNCAN & SCOTT *Allen & Woodson Co., Kansas* 580 About six per cent of the original surface of the county was covered with forest and the remainder was prairie.

3. *To break prairie*, to plow virgin prairie land.

1839 *Cultivator* VII. 33 Fancy, then, a plow . . . turning an unbroken sod, eighteen to twenty-six inches wide, . . . and you have a picture of 'breaking prairie.' **1857** *Lawrence* (Kan.) *Republican* 11 June 3 Probably not one fourth of those who are breaking prairie this year in Kansas, ever had any experience in this matter. **1873** *Winfield* (Kan.) *Courier* 18 Jan. 3/2 Several farmers south-west of town commenced breaking prairie Tuesday last. **1890** *Stock Grower & Farmer* 26 April 5/1, I have been absent a month, and find on my return 200 acres of prairie broke.

4. *On the prairie*, as a free gift. *colloq.*

1848 RUXTON *Life Far West* iv, The winner at the conclusion of the game sweeping the goods towards him, and often returning a small portion 'on the prairie,' with which the loser may again commence operations with another player. **1857** *Harper's Mag.* Oct. 644/2 Several of the chiefs now came up, and demanded something 'on the prairie,' and even attempted to seize sundry blankets.

II. *attrib.* and *comb.* **5. a.** Designating animals that live on the prairies; also, in specific and allusive names.

1806 LEWIS in *L. & Clark Exped.* V. (1905) 80 A speceis of Lizzard called by the French engages prarie buffaloe are native of these plains as well as of those of the Missouri. I have called them the horned Lizzard. **1843** FRÉMONT *Explor. Rocky Mts.* 12 A large prairie-snake . . . was occupied in eating young birds. **1844** GREGG *Commerce of Prairies* I. 54 The excitement that the first sight of these 'prairie beeves' [buffaloes] occasions . . . beggars all description. **1846** DE SMET *Oregon Missions* (1847) 241 In every one of their old encampments we observed great quantities of prairie-turtle shells, a proof of their being numerous and serving as food for the savages. **1846** *Spirit of Times* (N.Y.) 11 July 229/1 Couldn't kill a prairie rat on the whole route to save us from starvation. **1860** GREELEY *Overland Journey* 93 It is impossible for a stranger to the prairies to realize the impudence of these prairie-lawyers [gray wolves]. **1868** *Amer. Naturalist* II. 534 Prairie Mouse (*Hesperomys Sonoriensis*). This widely spread Mouse is common at Fort Benton [Mont.]. **1872** *Ill. Dept. Agric. Trans.* IX. 204 The old fashioned 'prairie rooter and elm peeler' are banished from the county. **a1885** in *Century Mag.* XXXII. 787/2 'Prairie-sharks' and 'razor-backs' were the local names for them. **1888** *Ipswich* (Mass.) *Chronicle* 15 Sept. 2/4 In some parts of the country . . . a gopher . . . [is] a striped squirrel or prairie chipmunk.

b. Designating horses used on, or habituated to, the prairies.

1837 IRVING *Bonneville* I. 69 [They] are generally well mounted on . . . short, stout horses, similar to the prairie ponies. **1847** ROBB *Squatter Life* 42 You look . . . tired as a prairie team, arter a hard day's ploughin'. **1860** HOLMES *E. Venner* xxiii, The prairie horse knew the trick of the cord. **a1861** WINTHROP *Canoe & Saddle* 50, I could not ride the leagues, . . . barebacking the bonyness of prairie nags.

6. Designating various natural features of the prairies, esp. with respect to soil, topography, and vegetable growth.

1808 PIKE *Sources Miss.* 18 Hills, or rather prairie knobs [were] on both sides. **1830** *Illinois Mo. Mag.* I. 24 [There is] fuel to propel the locomotive engines, should they be preferred to animal power, which the exuberant prairie plains . . . are so well adapted to support. **1831** HOLLEY *Texas* (1833) 118 Corn is obtained in the prairie cane-brakes. **1843** FRÉMONT *Explor. Rocky Mts.* 16 The road led across a high and level prairie ridge. **1847** FIELD *Drama in Pokerville* 110 The elk, reaching a prairie pond, or 'sink,' the hunters at their heels, plunged despairingly in. **1857** BRAMAN *Texas* 40 [The Old Caney River in Colo.] is very little else, above tidewater, than a large prairie drain. **1862** *Ill. Agric. Soc. Trans.* V. 203 The soil is a whitish prairie drift, similar to the land in the basin of Egypt. **1869** *Republican D. Jrnl.* (Lawrence, Kan.) 7 March, Even the prairie branches on which there are no trees or bushes always afford sufficient stock water. **1886** WINCHELL *Walks & Talks* 280 The prairie formation is a stratified deposit of fine clay, sand, and alluvial matter. **1891** WELCH *Recoll. 1830–40* 148 After a tedious, dismal, back-aching journey from Wisconsin Territory, . . . through prairie mud, . . . [we] reached [Detroit].

7. Designating towns and habitations on the prairies.

1838 ELLSWORTH *Valley of Wabash* 52 At considerable expense of time and labor, we have prepared a plan . . . of a house or 'Prairie cottage' for the western settler. **1857** UNDERHILL & THOMPSON *Elephant Club* 99 The cars had just left the flourishing prairie city of Scraggsville. **1862** *Harper's Mag.* Sept. 447/2 As Independence is the eastern, so may the Mora be considered the western prairie port of the great Santa Fé trail. **1867** *Atlantic Mo.* March 326/1 Chicago, for fifteen years after it began its rapid increase, was perhaps of all prairie towns the most repulsive to every human sense.

8. Designating roads or routes across the prairies.

1841 *Picayune* 10 Nov. 2/1, I should not be at all surprised if Kendall would reach here [St. Louis] by the great prairie route from Santa Fé. **1845** *Cultivator* ns. II. 142/2, I undertook to drive a dozen miles over a road that the very thoughts of is enough to make the bones ache, of one who is accustomed only to the smooth prairie roads. **1850** GARRARD *Wah-To-Yah* x. 136 He was . . . journeying the prairie trail . . . [to] the Platte purchase, in Missouri.

9. Designating persons who reside on or frequent the prairies.

1848 PARKMAN in *Knickerb.* XXXI. 484 He seemed the very model of a wild prairie-rider. **1867** DIXON *New America* I. 85 A prairie brave, mounted on a strong pony. **1857** F. HUNTER *Western Border Life* 232 [He] entered into animated conversation about the prairie-people. **1872** *Harper's Mag.* XLVI. 20 [In Colo.] rise Pike's and Long's Peaks . . . —the landmarks of prairie voyageurs in days gone by. **1895** *Outing* XXVI. 475/1 The Southern California clubs . . . express a positive dislike for bronchos, cayuses, cow-ponies and prairie rangers of any and all sorts.

10. Designating vehicles used on the prairies.

In these combinations, the prairie is imagined to be the ocean, the vehicles, ships. (See also PRAIRIE OCEAN, PRAIRIE SCHOONER.)

1851 M. REID *Scalp Hunters* iii, I do not remember a more striking picture than to see the long caravan of waggons, the 'prairie ships,' deployed over the plain. **1870** KEIM *Sheridan's Troopers* 49 The coaches or 'prairie clippers,' as they are called by the denizens of the country, pitched and jolted.

11. In specific names. **a.** Of plants and trees.

1847 WOOD *Botany* 336 *S[ilphium] Terebinthinaceum.* Prairie Burdock. . . . Prairies, Western! and Southern States. **1839** in *Mich. Agric. Soc. Trans.* VII. 419 *Silphium terebinthinaceum.* Prairie dock. **1846** Emory *Military Reconn.* 399 The other [plant] is what our men call prairie indigo, (*baptisia leucantha*). **1869** FULLER *Flower Gatherers* 90 Another species, called *Prairie Innocence*, has very branching stems, and flowers of pink or rosy whiteness. **1913** Barnes *Western Grazing Grounds* 64 The principal grasses are the bunch grasses of the wheat-grass group . . . , prairie June grass (*Koeleria cristata*) and blue joints. **1869** Fuller *Flower Gatherers* 247 One of the Lysimachias of the west is called *Prairie Money-wort.* **1822** Woods *English Prairie* (1904) 222 Prairie onions are common in moist situations. **a1885** in *Century Mag.* XXXII. 787/1 In July and August it [the Iowa prairie] is pink with the 'prairie pink,' dotted with scarlet lilies. **1893** *Amer. Folk-Lore* VI. 136 *Anemone patens*, var. *Nuttalliana*, . . . gosling, prairie smoke, crocus. Minnesota. **1894** *Ib.* VII. 98 *Croton monanthogynus*, . . . prairie tea, common from the Gila to the Rio Grande. **1837** Irving *Bonneville* I. 40 They had to eke out their scanty fare with . . . the Indian potato, the wild onion, and the prairie tomato. **1901** Mohr *Plant Life Ala.* 466 *Salix humilis*. . . . Prairie Willow. . . . In the barrens, flat gravelly ground.

b. Of birds.

1917 *Birds of Amer.* III. 76 Lark Bunting. *Calamospiza melanocorys*. . . . [Also called] Prairie Bobolink. **1874** Prairie falcon [see Falcon 2]. **1839** Audubon *Ornith. Biog.* V. 19 [The] Prairie Finch, *Fringilla Bicolor*, . . . inhabits a portion of the Platte country, in large flocks. **1917** *Birds of Amer.* II. 24/1 The Prairie Grouse weighs about two pounds and its flesh is tender, juicy, and delicious. **1887** Ridgway *Manual N.A. Birds* 348 Upper Mississippi Valley and region of the Great Lakes . . . *O[tocoris] alpestris praticola*. Prairie Horned Lark. **1917** *Birds of Amer.* III. 198/2 On the Great Plains and prairie districts, . . . [the long-billed marsh wren] is known as the Prairie Marsh Wren. **1888** *Pittsburg Despatch* (F.), Man has a friend in the Prairie Runner, which is the name of a bird whose mission in life is to supervise the centipede census. **1887** Ridgway *Manual N.A. Birds* 204 Great Plains of United States . . . *P[ediocœtes] phasianellus campestris*. Prairie Sharp-tailed Grouse. **1917** *Birds of Amer.* III. 171/1 Sprague's Pipit [*Anthus spraguei*], called the Missouri Skylark, or sometimes the Prairie Skylark. *Ib.* I. 247 Upland Plover. *Bartramia longicauda*. . . . [Also called] Prairie Snipe. **1828** Bonaparte *Ornithology* III. 55 There existed in the interior of America a very large species of Grous, called by the hunters of the west the Prairie Turkey.

c. Of insects.

1894 *Harper's Mag.* Feb. 456/1 The form [of walking stick] common over the greater part of the United States, . . . [called in some states] 'prairie alligators,' our *Diapheromera ferata* . . . may be compared to an animated straw. **1860** M. Reid *Odd People* 341 [The Yamparico] finds a resource, however, in the prairie cricket, an insect . . . of the *gryllus* tribe.

12. In special combinations.

Prairie belt, =Prairie region 2; *p. chip*, a buffalo or cow chip; *p. claim*, a land claim to prairie land; *p. cocktail*, (see quotation); *p. corn*, corn raised on prairie land; *p. down*, a breed of sheep; *p. forestry*, the action or process of getting trees to grow on prairie land; *p. island*, a part of the prairie cut off as an island by a river; *p. itch*, (see quotation); *p. law*, customs with the force of law among prairie people; *p. loo*, (see quotation); *p. man*, a man from Illinois (cf. Prairie state 2 a); *p. match*, a friction match suited for use on the prairies; *p. oyster*, a prairie cocktail (q.v.); *p.-renovator*, (see quotation).

1883 Smith *Geol. Survey Ala.* 265 North of the Prairie belt the Gravelly Pine Hills have great resemblance to this division. **1897** Hough *Story of Cowboy* 179 Some of the boys kicked together enough of the abundant prairie chips—the only fuel within sixty miles of that point. **1857** *Lawrence* (Kan.) *Republican* 4 June 2 Many untaken prairie claims are yet inviting the emigrant hither. **1890** *Cent.* 4668/1 *Prairie-cocktail*, a raw egg, peppered and salted, and drunk in vinegar or spirits. Also called *prairie-oyster*. [Western U.S.] **1853** *Knickerb.* XLII. 326 The abundant ears of the lofty prairie-corn . . . embellished the buck-horns in our town-sanctum during the fall and winter months! **1836** J. Hall *Statistics of West* 149 The prairie down, bearing a strong similarity to the celebrated breed of 'south downs,' in England, . . . should be kept exclusively upon high ground and pine herbage. **1890** *Stock Grower & Farmer* 8 Feb. 5/1, I regard the thorough fining of the soil before planting as one of the very important steps in prairie forestry. **1807** Gass *Journal* 246 We went down the [Mo.] river [in N.D.] upwards of 70 miles to day, and encamped on a prairie island. **1877** Bartlett 489 *Prairie-Itch*, a cutaneous eruption caused by the friction of the fine red dust of prairie countries in summer. **1827** Cooper *Prairie* vii, It is the usage of their people, and what may be called the prairie law. **1835** Hoffman *Winter in West* I. 221, I was contented to wrap myself as closely as possible in my buffalo robe, and join him in a game of *prairie loo*. . . . The game consists merely in betting upon the number of wild animals seen by either party towards the side of the vehicle on which he is riding, a wolf or deer counting ten, and a grouse one. The game is a hundred. **1863** *Ladies' Repository* Aug. 486/2 He said the prairie man's name was Job Smith. **1865** Pike *Scout & Ranger* (1932) 53, I drew a box of prarie matches from my pocket. **1905** Belasco *Girl of Golden West* I, Mix me a prairie oyster. . . . Crack the egg —I'll stand [the cost]. **1883** Knight *Suppl.* 717/2 *Prairie Renovator*, . . . an implement with tearing harrow teeth, drawn over the surface of grass land to loosen the roots and the soil, dislodge moss, uproot weeds, and break up the matted vegetation.

+**Prairie bean.** A forage plant (*Phaseolus metcalfei*) of the Southwest; a bean of this plant. — **1805** Lewis in *L. & Clark Exped.* II. (1904) 29 The Indians of the Missouri make great use of this cherry, . . . mashing the seed boiling them with roots or meat, or with the prairie beans and white apple. **1885** Havard *Flora W. & S. Texas* 501 *Phaseolus retusus*. (Prairie Bean.) Common on prairies west of the Pecos.

+**Prairie bird. 1.** Generically, any bird that lives on the prairie. **2.** A specific name for different birds: (see quotations). — **(1) 1805** Clark in *Lewis & C. Exped.* II. (1904) 184 An emence number of Prarie burds now sitting of two kinds. **1873** *Amer. Naturalist* VII. 197 (*caption*), The Prairie Birds of Southern Illinois. **(2) 1917** *Birds of Amer.* I. 257 Golden Plover. *Charadrius dominicus dominicus*. . . . [Also called] Prairie-bird. *Ib.* II. 212 Horned Lark. *Otocoris alpestris alpestris*. . . . [Also called] Prairie Bird. *Ib.* III. 76/1 The name White-winged Prairiebird [for the lark bunting] . . . seems to avoid confusion with . . . the Lark Sparrow.

+**Prairie bitters.** (See quotation.) — **1848** Bartlett 260 *Prairie-bitters*, a beverage common among the hunters and mountaineers. It is made with a pint of water and a quarter of a gill of buffalo-gall, and is considered an excellent medicine.

+**Prairie bluff.** A bluff along a stream that runs through a prairie. — **1836** Edward *Hist. Texas* 30 Matagorda . . . [is] laid out on a prairie bluff. **1841** Catlin *N. Indians* I. 66 We launched off one fine morning, taking our leave of . . . the beautiful green fields, hills, and dales, and prairie bluffs, that encompass the enchanting shores of the Yellow Stone.

+**Prairie bottom.** Rich, level grassland alongside a stream, or once overflowed by a stream. — **1823** James *Exped.* I. 123 Our party encamped . . . in a narrow, but beautiful and level prairie bottom. **1834** A. Pike *Sketches* 12 It is bordered by a strip of timber, . . . and on the outside of this, a prairie bottom, . . . of exceeding rich land. **1843** Frémont *Explor.* 19 Along our road today the prairie bottom was more elevated and dry. **1868** *Iowa State Agric. Soc. Rep. 1867* 139 On strong prairie-bottom it [the Rio Grande bearded wheat] is liable to get down.

+**Prairie-breaker.** (See quot. 1883 and cf. Prairie plow.) — **1867** Dixon *New America* I. 44 When the ground is . . . cut by the prairie breaker, the rosin-weed disappears. **1883** Knight *Suppl.* 717/2 *Prairie-plow*, a plow with a broad, sharp share and long mold-board, for cutting a wide, shallow furrow, and completely inverting the furrow slice. A prairie breaker.

+**Prairie-breaking.** The action of plowing virgin prairie land; land so plowed. — **1859** *Ill. Agric. Soc.* IV. 37 The plows were running . . . too deep for ordinary prairie breaking. **1879** *Scribner's Mo.* Nov. 132/2 It is only by resorting to figures that one can reach a comprehension of the aggregate extent of these long, narrow, black strips of 'prairie-breaking.' **1886** Ebbutt *Emigrant Life in Kansas* 45 Will Hopkins . . . used to do a good deal of prairie-breaking, having a twenty-four inch plough and six yoke of oxen.

+**Prairie cattle. 1.** Cattle living on prairies. **2.** Buffaloes. — **(1) 1836** *Knickerb.* VIII. 287 There is not a more stirring sight than that of driving a herd of the prairie cattle over the river. **(2) 1844** Gregg *Commerce of Prairies* I. 97 While in the midst of the buffalo range, travellers usually take the precaution of laying up a supply of beef for exigencies in the absence of 'prairie cattle.'

+**Prairie chicken.**

1. One of three species of grouse native to prairie country; a bird of any such species. Also collect.

The species are: **a.** A rapidly disappearing grouse (*Tympanuchus cupido americanus*) of the Mississippi valley, ranging from Manitoba to Texas. (Cf. Heath hen 2, Pinnated grouse a, Prairie hen.) **b.** A smaller species (*T. pallidicinctus*) of western Texas; sometimes called the *lesser prairie chicken*. (Cf. sense 3.) **c.** The sharp-tailed grouse (*Pedioecetes phasianellus*) of the West; the prairie chicken of the Northwest. (Cf. sense 3.)

1847 *30th Congress 1 Sess.* H. R. Ex. Doc. No. 41, 545 The woods had been full of prairie chickens; in all directions we noticed their foot prints in the snow. **1850** Garrard *Wah-To-Yah* i. 6 We saw two deer, several prairie chickens. **1857** *Lawrence* (Kan.) *Republican* 18 June 4 [Beans] are a sure crop unless the prairie chickens destroy them. **1875** *Chicago Tribune* 6 Nov. 2/4 Prairie-chickens and quails were never more plentiful than now. **1886** Roosevelt in *Outing* Aug. 524 The proper name of the prairie chicken found with us is, the Sharp-tailed Grouse. **1890** *Opelousas* (La.) *Democrat* 8 Feb. 2/5 Not less than 1,000,000 of prairie-chickens are marketed in Chicago every year. **1917** *Birds of Amer.* II. 26/1 The Heath Hen possibly was once a smaller eastern race of the Prairie Chicken, but . . . it now stands as a distinct species.

attrib. **1897** *Kissimmee* (Fla.) *Valley Gazette* 1 Dec. 2/2 In the duck and prairie chicken season, eager and wealthy sportsmen shoot and hunt in special Pullman cars, which are side tracked on the prairie in the game region.

2. One of these birds used as food.

1840 *Picayune* 13 Sept. 2/2 The travelling public will find . . . a fine table covered with white fish . . . and prairie chickens. **1851** M. Reid *Scalp Hunters* ii, I need not describe a dinner at the Planters', with its venison steaks, its buffalo tongues, its 'prairie chicken.'

3. *Lesser prairie chicken*, =sense 1 b; *prairie chicken of the Northwest*, =sense 1 c.

1917 *Birds of Amer.* II. 26 The Lesser Prairie Chicken . . . occurs on the Great Plains, from Kansas south to west-central Texas; its plumage is similar to that of the Prairie Chicken but paler. *Ib.* 27 Sharp-tailed Grouse. *Pediœcetes phasianellus phasianellus*. . . . [Also called] Prairie Chicken of the Northwest; Northern Sharp-tailed Grouse.

+**Prairie clover.** Any species of the genus *Petalostemon;* a plant of this genus. — **1857** Gray *Botany* 95 *Petalostemon*, Prairie Clover. . . . Chiefly perennial herbs, . . . [with] small flowers. **1870** *Amer. Naturalist* IV. 581 The prairie clovers, or turban flowers, . . . are among the most interesting of the leguminose species. **1891** Coulter *Bot. W. Texas* I. 79. **1901** Mohr *Plant Life Ala.* 823 The so-called bald prairies . . . [present] white and purple flowered prairie clovers.

+Prairie cock. a. = COCK OF THE PLAINS. ?**b.** = PRAIRIE CHICKEN 1.

1805 CLARK in *Lewis & C. Exped.* III. (1905) 123 Send out Hunters to shute the Prarie Cock a large fowl which I have only Seen on this river. **1846** W. G. STEWART *Altowan* I. 31 The prairie cock (a large species of grouse, of a pepper-and-salt colour, and long, pointed tail), . . . rose at their feet. **1852** BAIRD in Stansbury *Gt. Salt Lake* 319 *Tetrao urophasianus*, Bp.—Cock of the Plains, or Prairie Cock; Sage Cock. . . . Its flesh is not usually considered edible. **1875** BURROUGHS *Winter Sunshine* 115 The prairie hens or prairie cocks set up that low musical cooing or crowing that defies the ear to trace or locate. **1900** GARLAND *Eagle's Heart* 107 A belated prairie cock began to boom.

+Prairie country. Country consisting of prairies or a prairie. — **1806** *Ann. 9th Congress* 2 Sess. 1136 The quality of the land is supposed superior to that on Red river, until it ascends to the prairie country, where the lands on both rivers are probably similar. **1848** BRYANT *California* iii. 34 Our march was . . . through an undulating prairie-country, occasionally dotted with a few trees and clumps of small hazel-bushes. **1873** *Newton Kansan* 20 Feb. 2/2 All prairie countries are subject to high winds. **1907** LILLIBRIDGE *Trail* 152 The darkness that precedes morning had the prairie country in its grip.

+Prairied, *a.* Having many prairies. — **1849** WHITTIER *Poetical Works* (1894) 371/2 The South-land boasts its teeming cane, The prairied West its heavy grain. **1859** *Ib.* 219/2 In sunny South and prairied West Are exiled hearts remembering still, . . . The homes of Haverhill.

+Prairie dog.

1. A burrowing rodent of the genus *Cynomys*, found on the great plains of the Louisiana Purchase and Texas, and in the Rocky Mountain region. Also collect.

The prairie dogs are of several species, the common one being *C. ludovicianus*. (Cf. DOG *n.* 3.)

1774 in Peyton *Adv. Grandfather* (1867) 121 One of the singular and interesting sights on my route was the villages of the Prairie dogs. **1806** *Balance* 29 July 235/2 It may have been brought from Louisiana, where are salt mountains, horned frogs and prairie dogs. **1838** S. PARKER *Tour Rocky Mts.* 59 A small animal called the prairie dog . . . takes its name, not from its appearance, but from its barking, which is like that of a very small dog. **1847** PALMER *Rocky Mts.* 21 The prairie-dog is something larger than a common sized gray squirrel, of a dun color. **1884** *Albany* (Tex.) *News* Aug., The prairie dog is a standing threat against the future prosperity of the grazing districts of the State. **1914** 'BOWER' *Flying U Ranch* 135 There ain't enough grass left in our lower field to graze a prairie dog.

b. With specifying words.

1867 *Amer. Naturalist* I. 362 The short-tailed Prairie Dog (*C[ynomys] Gunnisonii*) . . . is distinguished from the other by its smaller size [etc.]. **1917** *Mammals of Amer.* 202/2 Gunnison Prairie Dog.— . . . Darker in color; tail tipped with white. New Mexico and Colorado to Arizona. *Ib.* 205/2 Wherever White-tailed Prairie Dogs live in the neighborhood of cultivated ground they are very injurious to green crops.

2. Attrib. with *brown, country, hillock.*

1850 GARRARD *Wah-To-Yah* x. 138 The animals sank up to the fetlocks in the loamy bottom soil, . . . or shyed around the prairie dog hillocks. **1873** BEADLE *Undevel. West* 82 We next entered 'Dog-town,' eastern border of the prairie-dog country. **1902** WISTER *Virginian* xvi, There is a brown skunk down in Arkansaw. Kind of prairie-dog brown.

+Prairie-dog hole. A hole burrowed by prairie dogs. — **1890** CUSTER *Following Guidon* 210 A sergeant's horse, getting his foot into a prairie-dog hole, had thrown him. **1895** REMINGTON *Pony Tracks* 11, I could see the deep ruts in the road . . . and dodge the prairie-dog holes. **1913** CATHER *O Pioneers* 20 One of his plow horses broke its leg in a prairie-dog hole and had to be shot.

+Prairie-dog hunter. = FERRET[1] 2. — **1885** *Amer. Naturalist* XIX. 922 The long lost black-footed ferret, or prairie dog-hunter, of Western Kansas, whose rediscovery was recorded a few years since by Dr. Coues.

+Prairie-dog town. An area in which a colony of prairie dogs have dug their holes. — **1843** N. BOONE *Journal* (1917) 204 Passed great quantities of Prairie dog towns. **1860** GREELEY *Overland Journey* 95 There cannot be less than a hundred square miles of prairie-dog towns within the present buffalo range. **1880** *Cimarron News & Press* 23 Dec. 1/4 [The burrowing owl] lives in holes in the ground and in prairie dog towns. **1923** J. H. COOK *On Old Frontier* 104 Away they go, over bad-lands, prairie-dog towns—any- and everything that comes in their way.

+Prairie-dog village. = prec. — **1823** JAMES *Exped.* II. 142 We passed a number of prairie dog villages . . . along the [Platte] river. **1843** FRÉMONT *Explor.* 20 A prairie-dog village, so thickly settled that there were three or four holes in every twenty yards square, occupied the whole bottom for nearly two miles in length. **1890** CUSTER *Following Guidon* 206 [He] made his tortuous way through the prairie-dog village.

+Prairiedom. The region of the western prairies. — **1845** (*title*), Prairiedom: Rambles & Scrambles in Texas or New Estrémadura. **1851** M. REID *Scalp Hunters* vi, The famous city of Santa Fè; . . . the metropolis of all prairiedom. **1866** *Ill. Agric. Soc. Trans.* VI. 285 The day is coming rapidly which is to usher in general planting of them [*i.e.*, hardy varieties of evergreens] over all prairiedom.

+Prairie farm. A farm established on prairie land. — **1838** ELLSWORTH *Valley of Wabash* 49 A late and lamented brother of the writer . . . had just finished a prairie farm containing 800 acres. **1847** COYNER *Lost Trappers* 209, I have known farmers, in Illinois and Missouri, to . . . make a prairie farm infinitely easier than they could have opened a farm in the woods. **1884** 'MARK TWAIN' *H. Finn* vii, Hogs soon went wild in them bottoms after they had got away from the prairie-farms.

+Prairie fire. A fire that sweeps over a prairie, burning the grass.

1836 EDWARD *Hist. Texas* 70 Why should there be any lack of timber when by planting it as they do in Europe, and preserving it afterwards from the annual prairie fires, it would grow with such rapidity, as would . . . be sufficient to answer every useful demand. **1847** ROBB *Squatter Life* 73 He resolved to sweep the south, from that point, like a prairie fire. **1860** GREELEY *Overland Timber* 11 [The timber of Ill.] will increase still more rapidly as roads and plowing check the sweep of prairie-fires. **1875** *Chicago Tribune* 6 Nov. 2/4 Prairie fires are becoming very alarming. **1890** *Stock Grower & Farmer* 18 Jan. 5/1 This immediate section [San Angelo, Tex.] deserves congratulations for its lucky escape from prairie fires this fall. **1925** TILGHMAN *Dugout* 75 It was early for prairie fires, and her husband had plowed fire-guards about his hay stacks.

+Prairie flower.

1. A flower that grows wild on the prairies.

1836 J. HALL *Statistics of West* 56 The prairie-flower displays its diversified hues. **1847** ROBB *Squatter Life* 133 Her step was as light as a panter's, and her breath sweet as a prairie flower. **1873** *Newton Kansan* 22 May 3/2 The wild prairie flowers . . . are beginning to look beautiful. **1894** *Harper's Mag.* Aug. 422/1 To be sure there were patches of orange prairie flowers all about.

2. Abraham Lincoln. A nickname.

1861 *Vanity Fair* 23 Feb. 90/1 Mr. Lincoln . . . was called out at the next station and received applause and shouts of 'Hail to the Prairie Flower!' **1862** BROWNE *A. Ward His Book* 181 One man from Ohio . . . mistook me for Old Abe and addrest me as 'The Pra-hayrie Flower of the West!'

+Prairie fly. One of various flies common to the prairies, as *Tabanus lineola* or *T. costalis*. (Cf. GREENHEAD 2, HORSEFLY.) — **1822** WOODS *English Prairie* 278 We had no buffalo gnats, and but few prairie flies or musquetoes. **1831** *Illinois Mo. Mag.* I. 448 In the heat of summer they [*sc.* buffaloes] would be driven from the latter [*sc.* dry upland plains] by prairie flies. **1843** MARRYAT *M. Violet* xxviii, The wife and children . . . will stick to him as naturally as a prairie fly to a horse. **1852** REYNOLDS *Hist. Illinois* 332 A green prairie fly was the most numerous and annoying.

+Prairie fowl. 1. = PRAIRIE CHICKEN. **2.** = HEATH HEN 1. — (1) **1804** CLARK in *Lewis & C. Exped.* VI. (1905) 121 The Prarie Fowl common to the Illinois are found as high up as the River Jacque. **1807** GASS *Journal* 126 Our hunters killed 5 prairie fowls. **1831** PECK *Guide* 174 The prairie fowl . . . is the grouse of the New York market. **1893** ROOSEVELT *Wilderness Hunter* 92 When making long wagon trips over the great plains, antelope often offer the only source of meat supply, save for occasional water fowl, sage fowl, and prairie fowl—the sharp-tailed prairie fowl, be it understood. (2) **1866** *N.J. Laws* 681 No person shall . . . kill, or take, or destroy any pinnated grouse, commonly called prairie fowl.

+Prairie fox. = KIT FOX. — **1846** SAGE *Scenes Rocky Mts.* xxviii, For several nights I had a constant visitor in the shape of a prairie fox,—a creature about twice the size of a large red squirrel. **1847** Emory *Military Reconn.* 405 Amongst the animals, we have [near Fort Bent] . . . the silver-grey fox, (*canis cinerea argentus;*) and the prairie fox, (*canis velox*). **1875** BURROUGHS *Winter Sunshine* 108 The prairie fox, the cross fox, and the black or silver-grey fox, seem only varieties of the red fox.

+Prairie gopher. A ground squirrel of the genus *Citellus*. — **1875** *Amer. Naturalist* IX. 148, I elect to write about the prairie gopher—as I shall call that particular species known in the books as *Spermophilus Richardsoni* . . . for several reasons. **1907** LILLIBRIDGE *Trail* 15 The longitudinal stripes of a prairie gopher or on the back of a bobwhite.

+Prairie gourd. A gourd or gourdlike plant that grows on the prairie: (see quotations). — **1847** Emory *Military Reconn.* 405 We also have the prairie gourd, (*cucumis perennis;*) that is abundant also from Bent's fort to Santa Fé. **1847** EMORY *Ib.* 13 The principal growth is the buffalo grass, . . . prairie gourd (*cucurbita aurantia,*) and very rarely that wonderful plant, the *Ipomea leptophylla*.

+Prairie grass. a. Grass that grows upon the prairies. **b.** *spec.* Any of several species of such grass, as *Sporobolus asper, Eatonia obtusata, Bromus ciliatus*.

1812 *Conn. Courant* 24 Nov. 2/3 [They] were one night in danger, in consequence of the Indians setting the prairie grass on fire. **1822** WOODS *English Prairie* 198 Prairie-grass,—a very coarse strong grass; cattle are fond of it. **1843** N. BOONE *Journal* (1917) 194 Our march today was principally over the short buffalo grass, the prairie grass having almost entirely disappeared. **1872** TICE *Over Plains* 12 When the settlers first came these hills [in Kan.] were covered with prairie grass with no sign of any other growth. **1888** SHERIDAN *Memoirs* I. 26 The roof was put on—a thatched one of prairie grass. **1894** *Amer. Folk-Lore* VII. 104 *Eatonia obtusata*, . . . prairie-grass, Central Neb. **1894** COULTER *Bot. W. Texas* III. 519 *S[porobolus] asper*. . . . Prairie grass. . . . [Found in] Rich low land, Texas, and northward. **1903** WHITE *Forest* iv. 35, I once slept on a bed of prairie grass, before a fire of dried buffalo chips and mesquite.

+Prairie ground squirrel. = PRAIRIE DOG. — **1844** GREGG *Commerce of Prairies* II. 228 It was denominated the 'barking squirrel,' the 'prairie ground-squirrel,' etc., by early explorers.

+**Prairie hare.** **1.** The varying hare, *Lepus americanus*. **2.** The white-tailed jack rabbit, *L. townsendi*. — (1) **1840** EMMONS *Mass. Quadrupeds* 58 *Lepus Virginianus*. Harlan. Prairie Hare.... This species is common throughout the New England States, and is known generally as the White Rabbit. (2) **1868** *Amer. Naturalist* II. 536 Prairie Hare (*Lepus Townsendii*). This hare is common east of the Rocky Mountains. **1917** *Mammals of Amer.* 280/1 Although called the Prairie Hare, this species is found also on mountain slopes.

+**Prairie hawk.** A hawk that lives on the prairies, as the sparrow hawk, *Falco sparverius*. — **1817** FORDHAM *Narr. Travels* 143 Saw some prairie hawks, blue bodies, ash coloured belly and wings, tipped with black. **1832** BRYANT *Poetical Works* (1925) 131 [Breezes] pass the prairie-hawk that, poised on high, Flaps his broad wings, yet moves not. **1898** CANFIELD *Maid of Frontier* 201 With a swoop like the swoop of the prairie hawk down swooping for the quail, the Paint Horse was away. **1907** LILLIBRIDGE *Trail* 259 Answering, coercing, swift as the swoop of a prairie hawk, as a human being in abandon, the man's arms were about her.

+**Prairie hay.** Hay made from prairie grass. Also attrib. — **1845** *Cultivator* ns. II. 93 There are tens of thousands ... without any kind of forethought of preparation for shelter or comfort, except what they may gather from a poor supply of prairie hay. **1865** *Chicago Tribune* 10 April 1 Ashkun, ... 72 miles from Chicago, the finest upland Prairie Hay country in the State. **1872** *Newton Kansan* 26 Sept. 2/4 Western prairie hay sells in Philadelphia at $24 per ton. **1878** BEADLE *Western Wilds* 433 First rate prairie hay, on which stock will keep fat all winter, can be put up for two dollars per ton. **1898** *Mo. So. Dakotan* I. 45 Today we know of nothing so relished by sheep and that will make them thrive so well as our weedy upland prairie hay.

+**Prairie hen.** = PRAIRIE CHICKEN.

1806 LEWIS in *L. & Clark Exped.* IV. (1905) 121 The Grouse or Prairie hen is peculiarly the inhabitant of the Grait Plains of Columbia. **1808** PIKE *Sources Miss.* 44 Killed nothing but five prairie hens, which afforded us this day's subsistence: this bird I took to be the same as grouse. **1838** *S. Lit. Messenger* IV. 28/2 The prairie hen is commonly found in the northern and middle regions of Indiana and Illinois. **1842** *Life in West* 255 His wife soon spread out her store of good things before us ... prairie-hen, ... cheesecakes, cherry-pie. **1875** BURROUGHS *Winter Sunshine* 115 Wild ducks are taking the place of prairie-hens and quails. **1917** *Birds of Amer.* II. 24 Prairie Chicken. *Tympanuchus americanus americanus*.... Other Names.—Prairie Hen; Pinnated Grouse; Prairie Grouse.

+**Prairie hills.** *pl.* The hills of a rolling prairie. — **1807** GASS *Journal* 29 We went on about a mile to high prairie hills on the north side of the river. **1821** NUTTALL *Travels Arkansa* 205 Being a little recovered, we now ventured out some distance into the prairie hills. **1839** LEONARD *Adventures* (1904) 251 The country is generally composed of prairie hills, covered with excellent grass.

+**Prairie hunter.** One who hunts game on the prairies. — **1841** *S. Lit. Messenger* VII. 56/2 The author has conversed with a number of our prairy hunters, and Texan adventurers. **1847** PARKMAN in *Knickerb.* XXX. 289 He differs as much from the genuine 'mountain-man,' the wild prairie hunter, as a Canadian voyageur.

+**Prairie Indian.** An Indian who lives on the western prairies. — **1837** *Diplom. Corr. Texas* I. (1908) 261 The prairie Indians are unskillful in the use of fire arms. **1840** *Ib.* 464 The Caddo's are ... furnished with the means of ... supplying the Comanche, and other wild Prairie Indians with arms and ammunition. **1852** MARCY *Explor. Red River* (1854) 28, They say that they are not afraid to meet any of the prairie Indians. **1874** GLISAN *Jrnl. Army Life* 463 These men are never so happy as when ... in pursuit of a band of fleeing, horse-thieving, prairie Indians.

+**Prairie land.**

1. Land made up of prairies or a prairie; meadow land.

1807 GASS *Journal* 145 Back from the river the tops of the hills, to a great distance are prairie land. **1837** W. JENKINS *Ohio Gaz.* 94 Bucyrus ... is a large and populous township embracing considerable rich prairie land, under a high state of cultivation. **1843** *Cultivator* X. 37/1 In this section of the state [n.w. Iowa], there is much prairie land now subject to entry, and some timber land. **1883** SMITH *Geol. Survey Ala.* 468 A loose walnut prairie land makes up a small proportion of the country about Faunsdale. **1894** GARLAND in *Harper's Mag.* June 144/1 Toward noon they left the sunny prairie land of northern Illinois and southern Wisconsin.

2. A region of prairies; a prairielike expanse.

1862 *Rep. Comm. Patents 1861: Agric.* 548 Of the cultivated animals of prairie-land, ... it will be hard to find distinguishing traits. **1869** STOWE *Oldtown Folks* 155 The children travelled onward along the winding course of the river, through a prairie-land of wild-flowers.

+**Prairie lark.** **1.** = HORNED LARK. **2.** Sprague's pipit, *Anthus spraguei*. — (1) **1805** *Lewis & Clark Exped.* VI. (1905) 187 The Prarie lark, bald Eagle, & the large plover have returned. **1806** *Ib.* V. (1905) 176 The dove the black woodpecker ... the prairie lark, ... are found in this valley. (2) [**1885** *Encycl. Brit.* (ed. 9) XIX. 112/2 In North America [pipits] are represented by only two species—*Neocorys spraguii*, the Prairie-Lark of the north-western plains, and *Anthus ludovicianus*, the American Titlark.]

+**Prairie life.** Life on the western prairies. Also attrib. — **1843** FRÉMONT *Explor. Rocky Mts.* 9, I had collected ... twenty-one men, principally Creole and Canadian *voyageurs*, who had become familiar with prairie life in the service of the fur companies in the Indian country. **1847** PARKMAN in *Knickerb.* XXIX. 314 [My horse] had conceived a mortal aversion to the prairie life. **1886** *Century Mag.* May 238/2 He was doubtless the original of Dr. Battius, the naturalist of one of Cooper's prairie-life novels.

+**Prairie marmot.** = PRAIRIE DOG. — **1826** GODMAN *Nat. Hist.* II. 114 The Prairie Marmot. *Arctomys Ludovicianus*.... Commonly called Prairie-dog. **1888** *Ipswich Chronicle* 15 Sept. 2/4 Usually a country that is inhabited by prairie dogs, or more properly by prairie marmots, has a dry, thin atmosphere.

+**Prairie marmot squirrel.** = prec. — **1872** TICE *Over Plains* 253 *Cynomys* literally means Dog-mouse, or Dog-rat.... Those who have not fancied the latter, have proposed to call him the Prairie Marmot Squirrel.

+**Prairie mole.** The Canada pocket gopher, *Thomomys talpoides*. — **1808** PIKE *Sources Miss.* 31, [I] caught a curious little animal on the prairie, which my Frenchman termed a *prairie mole*, but it is very different from the mole of the States.

+**Prairie ocean.** The western prairies. — **1844** GREGG *Commerce of Prairies* I. 311 On our passage this time across the 'prairie ocean' which lay before us ... there was now a plain wagon trail. **1855** BOYNTON *Journey through Kansas* 159 [The] driver ... had lost his horses in the night, and in the morning the whole party found themselves '*becalmed*' on the prairie-ocean, and not a sail in sight.

+**Prairie owl.** **1.** The burrowing owl, *Speotyto cunicularia hypogaea*. **2.** (See quotation.) — (1) **1846** SAGE *Scenes Rocky Mts.* xii, The prairie-owl and rattlesnake maintain friendly relations with [prairie dogs]. **1867** MELINE *Santa Fé & Back* 276 The prairie owl found among them is the burrowing owl (*Strix cunicularia*), sometimes called the Coquimbo owl. **1872** TICE *Over Plains* 44 Defamers [of the prairie dog] even admit that he lives in amity and peace with the jackass-rabbit, the burrowing prairie owl, and even with the malicious rattlesnake. **1907** LILLIBRIDGE *Trail* 13 He would have watched the movement of a coyote or a prairie owl, for the simple reason that it was the only visible object endowed with life. (2) **1917** *Birds of Amer.* II. 101 Short-eared Owl. *Asio flammeus*.... Other Names.—Marsh Owl; Swamp Owl; Prairie Owl.

+**Prairie pea.** ? **a.** A species of milk vetch that grows on the western prairies; a plant of this species. **b.** The fruit of this plant. — **1848** BRYANT *California* ii. 28, I observed, also, a plant producing a fruit of the size of the walnut, called the prairie-pea.... In a raw state, it [the fruit] is eaten by travellers on the plains to quench thirst. **1869** *Amer. Naturalist* III. 162 One of the earliest flowers [of the Kansas plains] is the Prairie-pea (*Astragalus Mexicanus*).

+**Prairie pigeon.** **1.** The upland plover, *Bartramia longicauda*. **2.** = FRANKLIN'S (ROSY) GULL. **3.** = CURLEW 2 b. **4.** = GOLDEN PLOVER. — (1) **1874** COUES *Birds N.W.* 503 In most parts of the West, between the Mississippi and the Rocky mountains, this Tattler, commonly known as the 'Prairie Pigeon,' is exceedingly abundant during the migrations. (2) **1917** *Birds of Amer.* I. 51 The farmer ... calls them 'Prairie Pigeons,' a pretty and appropriate title, though in reality they are Franklin's Gulls. (3) *Ib.* 254 Eskimo Curlew.... [Also called] Prairie Pigeon. (4) *Ib.* 257 Golden Plover.... [Also called] Prairie-bird; Prairie Pigeon.

+**Prairie pillow.** ? A pillow stuffed with prairie grass. — **1840** *Crockett Almanac* 20 She got her living by making Prarie pillows.

+**Prairie plover.** **a.** The mountain plover, *Eupoda montana*. **b.** = PRAIRIE PIGEON 1. **c.** = GOLDEN PLOVER. — **1868** WATERS *Life among Mormons* 7 For the small birds—prairie plover, and meadow larks—it was not necessary to leave the road. **1888** TRUMBULL *Names of Birds* 173 *Bartramia longicauda*.... In Southern Wisconsin ... in 1851 this bird ... was known as the Prairie Plover, and also as the Prairie Snipe. **1890** *Cent.* 4668/2 The American golden plover, *Charadrius dominicus*. Also called *prairie-plover* and *prairie-snipe*. **1917** *Birds of Amer.* I. 267/1 Mountain Plover.... Its unofficial name of Prairie Plover is more appropriate.

+**Prairie plow.** A plow adapted to breaking prairie: (see quots. 1839, 1875). Cf. PRAIRIE-BREAKER. — **1839** in *Cultivator* VII. 33/1 It may be amusing to eastern readers, to hear a description of a 'prairie plow.' Fancy, then, a plow share weighing 125 lbs., the beam fourteen feet long, attached to a pair of cart wheels, to the tongue of which are hitched from three to seven yoke of oxen. **1861** *Ill. Agric. Soc. Trans.* IV. 392 The sod should be broken with a prairie plow. **1876** KNIGHT 1782/1 *Prairie-plow*, a large plow supported in front on wheels, and adapted to pare and overturn a very broad but shallow furrow-slice.

+**Prairie plum.** The Chickasaw plum, *Prunus angustifolia*, or a related species. Also attrib. — **1814** BRACKENRIDGE *Views La.* 62 Amongst the species of plums in Louisiana ... there is none more interesting than the prairie plum, (*prunus chickasa*) which literally covers tracts of ground. **1827** *Western Mo. Rev.* I. 323 Prairie plums are abundant in the prairies of Illinois and Missouri. **1851** *S. Lit. Messenger* XVII. 569/2 Having pretty thoroughly exhausted the prairie plumb crop, ... they were now prone to the land of pork and beans. **1901** MOHR *Plant Life Ala.* 551 *Prunus umbellata* ... Prairie plum.... Louisianian area. South Carolina to Florida, west to Mississippi, Louisiana, and southern Missouri.

+**Prairie potato.** Breadroot, *Psoralea esculenta*. (Cf. PRAIRIE TURNIP.) — **1828** *Western Mo. Rev.* II. 139 [The Shoshoni] lived indolently on dried venison and salmon, and prairie potatoes. **1845** FRÉMONT *Exped.* 107 On the heights above were five or six Kansas women, engaged in digging prairie potatoes, (*psoralea esculenta*.). **1848** E. BRYANT *California* iv. 54 This root is called the prairie potato.

+**Prairie rattler.** = next. — **1878** BEADLE *Western Wilds* 133 The only dangerous snakes are the little prairie rattlers, seldom over two feet long.

+**Prairie rattlesnake.** (See quot. 1890.)
1817 S. BROWN *Western Gazetteer* 31 The only venomous serpents, are the common and prairie rattlesnake, and copper-heads. **1831** BUTTRICK *Travels* 78 The prairie rattlesnake, a small but very poisonous reptile frequently . . . [is] seen in those parts. **1835** A. PARKER *Trip to Texas* 52 Then there is the prairie rattlesnake, about a foot long. Their bite is not considered very dangerous. **1873** 'MARK TWAIN' & WARNER *Gilded Age* 125 Prairie-rattlesnakes . . . never strike above the knee. **1883** *Amer. Naturalist* XVII. 1186 Since September last I have had a prairie rattlesnake (*Caudisona tergemina*) in confinement. **1890** *Cent.* 4668/3 *Prairie-rattlesnake*, . . . one of several different rattlesnakes inhabiting the prairies, as the massasauga, *Sistrurus catenatus*, and especially *Crotalus confluentus*.

+**Prairie region. 1.** A region of prairie land. **2.** *spec.* The black-belt region of central Alabama. — **(1) 1857** *Rep. Comm. Patents 1856: Agric.* 79 The grey prairie-squirrel . . . exists throughout the prairie regions of Wisconsin, Illinois, Missouri, Iowa, and probably Minnesota. **1865** PIKE *Scout & Ranger* (1932) 106 For days, we could not see a crow, or even one of those little brown birds, so plentiful in every prairie region. **1873** *Newton Kansan* 13 Feb. 3/4 We cannot compute the value it would add to the prairie region. **(2) 1883** SMITH *Geol. Survey Ala.* 304 Putting Chambers and Lee together with the counties which constitute the *Prairie region*, we have the nucleus of the Central cotton belt. **1901** MOHR *Plant Life Ala.* 99 The term 'prairie region,' applied to this plain, refers . . . to the black, calcareous, highly fertile soil of these uplands.

+**Prairie rose.** A climbing rose (*Rosa setigera*), usually with deep pink blossoms. — **1822** WOODS *English Prairie* 218 But the prairie-roses, balm, here called bergamot, and sassafras-wood . . . have all powerful scents. **1834** *Visit to Texas* 188 One of the first flowers which appears to deck the Prairie in the spring is the Prairie rose. **1891** COULTER *Bot. W. Texas* I. 106 *Rosa setigera.* Climbing or Prairie rose. A common eastern species extending into northern Texas. **1906** PITTMAN *Belle of Blue Grass C.* 91 Over the fence crept a luxurious trailing vine, the prairie rose, which was now covered with great clusters of buds.

+**Prairie sage.** A sagebrush, probably *Artemisia tridentata.* — **1843** FRÉMONT *Explor. Rocky Mts.* 14 The *artemisia*, absinthe, or prairie sage, as it is variously called. **1846** SAGE *Scenes Rocky Mts.* 108*n.*, H. Fremont in his report . . . of 1842, '3, '4, has designated three varieties of shrubs by the general term of artemisie, among which are greasewood and prairie sage.

+**Prairie schooner.** A large, canvas-covered wagon used especially by emigrants to cross the western prairies.
Cf. COVERED WAGON 2, FORE-AND-AFT WAGON, MOUNTAIN SCHOONER.
1845 *Xenia Torch-Light* 31 July 1/2 The Prairie schooners . . . [are] principally occupied in carrying lead from Mineral Point to the Lake ports. **1858** *N.Y. Tribune* 7 June 5/6 'Prairie schooners' . . . are generally drawn by oxen, otherwise by mules. **1860** *Ill. Agric. Soc. Trans.* IV. 510 When I came to Chicago, . . . Hoosier apples and peaches, brought in prairie schooners—from the Wabash, perhaps—sold for half the price now obtained. **1880** *Cimarron News & Press* 24 June 3/2 Trains of prairie schooners daily arrive from the eastern part of this county and the Panhandle of Texas. **1885** *Milnor* (Dak.) *Free Press* 4 April 8/1 A prairie schooner was visible on our streets yesterday, the first of the season. **1905** *Cincinnati Enquirer* 3 Feb. 1 Mrs. Augusta Miller to-day arrived here from Chamberlain, S.D., in a prairie schooner drawn by two white-faced cows. **1919** *Travel* Nov. 36 The prairie schooner is not yet obsolete. Many Western people use this type of covered wagon . . . for limited distance travel.

+**Prairie sod.** The sod of a virgin prairie or a square or slab of this sod.
1857 *Ill. Agric. Soc. Trans.* III. 414 It is well known that the 'up-turned prairie sod' is wanting in alumina (the base of clay,) and is too open in its texture by reason of vegetable fibres and excess of humus. **1861** *Ib.* IV. 37 The machine was put to work in prairie sod. **1873** EGGLESTON *Myst. Metrop.* 23 A house built of cakes of the tenacious prairie-sod. **1898** *Mo. So. Dakotan* I. 48 This stone house . . . was surrounded by a stockade built of prairie sods, impenetrable by arrows or bullets. **1914** 'BOWER' *Flying U Ranch* 222 And they had squandered all their ammunition on the prairie sod, to hurry a band of sheep.

+**Prairie soil.** A kind of soil found on prairies or land having such soil. — **1817** S. BROWN *Western Gazetteer* 66 The common field near the town contains nearly 5000 acres, of excellent prairie soil. **1849** KINGSLEY *Diary* 88 A large plain is in the rear of a rich praira soil back to the mountains. **1876** *Ill. Dept. Agric. Trans.* XIII. 288 The prairie soils are usually darker, more crude, coarser and wetter than the woodland.

+**Prairie squirrel.**

1. =PRAIRIE DOG.
1808 PIKE *Sources Miss.* 155 We returned and on our way, killed some prairie squirrels, or wishtonwishes. **1821** FOWLER *Journal* 23 The sand and gravel thrown up by the Prarie Squarrels is precisely the same of that in the river. **1857** *Rep. Comm. Patents 1856: Agric.* 81 The famous 'Prairie Dog,' or 'Prairie Squirrel,' exists in great abundance on the plains west of the Missouri River.

2. Any of various spermophiles of the western prairies, as *Citellus tridecemlineatus.*
1857 *Rep. Comm. Patents 1856: Agric.* 73 These are with great propriety called 'Prairie Squirrels,' for their true home is on the prairie. **1859** BARTLETT 181 *Ground squirrel*, a name sometimes erroneously given to the striped and spotted prairie squirrel.

+**Prairie state.**

1. One of the states on the prairies of the West and Middle West: (see quot. 1867).
1852 STOWE *Uncle Tom* xlv, Brave and generous men of New York, farmers of rich and joyous Ohio, and ye of the wide prairie states, answer, is this a thing for you to protect and countenance? **1864** *Maine Agric. Soc. Returns 1863* 55 These principles tend to establish the advantages of our county for wool growing . . . over the Prairie States. **1867** *Atlantic Mo.* March 333/1 Cattle from the prairie States,—Texas, Missouri, Kansas, Illinois, Iowa, Wisconsin, Minnesota. **1881** *Harper's Mag.* Jan. 225/1 The business had broadened, too, as the Prairie States became more thickly settled. **1890** *Stock Grower & Farmer* 4 Jan. 6/1 In the prairie states, . . . 'a dry season scares corn farmers, a wet season ruins them.'

2. a. (Both words usually capitalized.) The state of Illinois. A nickname.
1857 *Ill. Agric. Soc. Trans.* III. 414 Many of the best farmers of Kentucky were selling out old homes, long endeared to them, and settling in our Prairie State. **1867** *Trübner's Amer. Lit. Rec.* Aug. 41/1 Maine is popularly known as The Lumber or Pine Tree State; . . . Illinois as The Sucker or Prairie State. **1887** *Courier-Journal* 6 Feb. 12/3 Alas for the boys of the Prairie State. **1907** *Boston Transcript* 9 Nov., A list of the popular names of the States . . . [includes] Prairie—Illinois.

‖**b.** (See quotation.)
1867 DIXON *New America* I. 41 Of all the States and Territories which still exist on paper, Kansas may be described as the Prairie State.

+**Prairie titlark.** =PIPIT b. — **1831** AUDUBON *Ornith. Biog.* I. 408 The notes of the Prairie Titlark are clear and sharp, consisting of a number of *tweets*, the last greatly prolonged. **1917** *Birds of Amer.* III. 169.

+**Prairie traveler.** One who travels across the prairies. — **1844** GREGG *Commerce of Prairies* II. 32 But what attracted our attention most were the little dog settlements . . . so often alluded to by prairie travellers. **1856** WHIPPLE *Explor. y. Route* I. 28 Prairie travellers clarify muddy water by dropping into the vessel containing it pieces of mucillaginous cactus. **1891** EGGLESTON *Faith Doctor* 49 As he rose to go, like a prairie traveller protecting himself by back-firing, he said [etc.].

+**Prairie tribe.** An Indian tribe that lives on the prairies, esp. in the West. — **1846** SAGE *Scenes Rocky Mts.* ix, The mode of marriage prevalent among the mountain and prairie tribes would seem rather strange. **1849** *31st Congress 1 Sess.* Sen. Ex. Doc. No. 64, 215 [The Kickapoos] are brave warriors, good shots, and prepared to meet any of the prairie tribes, either in peace or war. **1866** *Rep. Indian Affairs* 173 There is . . . great ignorance concerning the location of the prairie or blanket tribes. **1887** *Scribner's Mag.* II. 505/2 The local prejudice against the prairie tribes . . . has probably discouraged any attempts to perpetuate Indian appellations.

+**Prairie turnip.** =BREADROOT. (Quot. 1859 probably misidentifies the plant as camass root.) Cf. PRAIRIE POTATO. — **1814** BRACKENRIDGE *Views La.* 249 The prairie turnip, is a root very common in the prairies, with something of the taste of the turnip, but more dry; this they eat dried and pounded, made into gruel. **1832** CATLIN *Indians* I. 56 The 'Pomme Blanche,' or prairie turnip, . . . is found in great quantities in these northern prairies, and furnishes the Indians with an abundant and nourishing food. **1859** BARTLETT 224 Kamas Root. (*Camassia esculenta*). Breadroot. The Pomme des Prairies or Pomme Blanche of the Canadians, and Prairie Turnip of the hunters and trappers of the West.

+**Prairie uplands.** The relatively high prairies of the West. — **1851** M. REID *Scalp Hunters* xxxv, A life spent beneath the blue heaven of the prairie-uplands and the mountain 'parks,' had made astronomers of these reckless rovers. **1892** *S. Dak. Hist. Coll.* I. 62 The prairie uplands must be settled along the railways.

+**Prairie wagon.** A wagon used especially on the prairies: (see quot. 1867). — **1856** BREWERTON *War in Kansas* 146 The vehicle, . . . like most ambulances, or 'prairie wagons,' as they call them here, proved rather airy. **1867** DIXON *New America* I. 37 Our big Concord coach has been exchanged for a light prairie waggon, smaller in size, frailer in build, without a door, with very bad springs, and with canvas blinds for windows.

+**Prairie warbler.** A small warbler (*Dendroica discolor*) chiefly of the eastern part of the country. — **1811** WILSON *Ornithology* III. 87 [The] Prairie Warbler . . . I first discovered in that singular tract of country in Kentucky, commonly called the Barrens. **1839** PEABODY *Mass. Birds* 311 The Prairie Warbler . . . is a small and quiet, but fearless bird. **1883** *Century Mag.* Sept. 652/2 The prairie warbler is . . . so bold that one can sit within a few feet of it, while it hunts for its food like the chickadees, often head down. **1917** *Birds of Amer.* III. 150/1 The Prairie Warbler is not very common on the prairies.

+**Prairie wolf. a.** A small-sized wolf (*Canis latrans*) of the western prairies and mountain plateau regions; the coyote. **b.** Any of several closely related species of coyote.
'Authorities recognize today no fewer than 12 to 14 species and subspecies exclusive of the larger wolves' (1917 *Mammals of Amer.* 66). Cf. MEDICINE WOLF.
1804 CLARK in *Lewis & C. Exped.* I. (1904) 108 A Prarie Wolf came near the bank and Barked at us this evening. **1823** JAMES *Exped.* I. 153 The prairie wolves roam over the plains in considerable numbers. **1836** HOLLEY *Texas* 95 The prairie wolf . . . is a very small species of the wolf, very

mischievous, but not so much to be feared as the large black wolf. **1858** PETERS *Kit Carson* 22 The Indian cur, by a casual observer, could be easily mistaken for a prairie wolf. **1885** *Amer. Naturalist* XIX. 896 In America the evidence tends to prove that the Eskimo, and other domestic varieties of dogs were domesticated . . . from the gray wolf or prairie wolf. **1898** CANFIELD *Maid of Frontier* 39 The long howl of the prairie wolf rose on the air and hung tremulant.

+**Prairillon.** [Amer. Fr., dim. of *prairie.*] A small prairie. — **1843** FRÉMONT *Explor. Rocky Mts.* 64 We were posted in a grove of beech, . . . with a narrow prairillon on the inner side. **1846** SAGE *Scenes Rocky Mts.* xxiii, The less elevated parts of these mountains are frequently covered with groves of small timber and openings of grass suitable for pasturage, while intermingled with them are occasional valleys and *prairillons* of diminutive space, favorable to the growth of grain and vegetables.

***Praise.** *attrib.* +Designating persons, places, etc., associated with the worship or praise of God. — **1862** E. W. Pearson *Lett. Port Royal* 20 I went with him to the praise-house, where he has his school. *Ib.* 36 He had been up to the praise-meeting by Uncle Peter's invitation. **1864** *Ib.* 253 It was not praise-night. **1866** CARPENTER *At White House* 209 Their place of worship was a large building which they called 'the praise house;' and the leader of the meeting, a venerable black man, was known as 'the praise man.' **1879** WEBSTER *Suppl.* 1574/1 *Praise-meeting.* [*U.S.*]

***Praiser.** =APPRAISER. *Obs.* — **1653** *Maine Doc. Hist.* IV. 99 Then the praisers went into the brewhouse to prayse such goods as weare leuied.

Praline. a. (See quot. 1809.) **b.** A confection, sometimes in the form of a cake, usually made by browning nut kernels, as almonds or pecans, in boiling sugar and water. {1727–}

'Chiefly *U.S.*' (*O.E.D.*).

1809 A. HENRY *Travels* 265, I left our fort on Beaver Lake . . . provided with dried meat, frozen fish, and a small quantity of praline, made of roasted maize, rendered palatable with sugar. **1850** S. F. COOPER *Rural Hours* 388 A great deal of popped corn is now used in New York and Philadelphia by the confectioners, who make it up into sugar-plums, like *pralines.* **1899** CHOPIN in Rankin *K. Chopin* (1932) 274 They played at a small table on which were a shaded lamp, a few magazines and a dish of *pralines.* **1904** STUART *River's Children* 76 The heaping confections . . . were always in evidence at the man-hour—bon-bons, kisses, pralines.

+**Prarow.** [Cf. BRARO, -OW.] The American badger. *Obs.* — **1807** GASS *Journal* 51 Captain Clarke and one of the men went to hunt and killed a deer and a prarow. **1812** J. CUTLER *Topogr. Descr. Ohio* 168 A species of badger, called prarow, inhabits these plains.

***Prawn.** Any one of various small crustaceans, esp. one of the larger shrimps, often used as food.

1682 ASH *Carolina* 26 The Seas and Rivers . . . [abound in] Plaice, Eels, Crabs, Prawns twice as large as ours in England. **1799** ELLICOTT in Mathews *Life A. Ellicott* 186 We likewise found a remarkable species of prawns. **1882** G. C. EGGLESTON *Wreck of Red Bird* 20 The net . . . came up after the first cast with about a hundred shrimps—of the large kind called prawn in the North—in it. **1911** *Rep. Fisheries 1908* 316/1 Prawns are generally larger than shrimps, often attaining a length of 7 inches.

attrib. **1883** *Nat. Museum Bul.* No. 27, 119 During the first few weeks of the Prawn fishery, it is one of the most profitable of all the fisheries in this section [near Charleston, S.C.]. *Ib.*, The number of shrimpers continues about the same as the prawn-catchers, in June, until near the close of the season.

***Prayer.** +In special combinations.

Prayer circle, a group of persons who pray together; *p. lodge,* =MEDICINE LODGE; *p. meal,* the meal used by the Indians in religious rites; *p. powder,* (see quotation); *p. ring,* a prayer circle.

1880 DEMING *Adirondack Stories* 25 As a preliminary to the sermon, a prayer-circle was formed. **1925** TILGHMAN *Dugout* 22 The medicine men of the Cheyennes had built prayer lodges and were industriously making medicine. **1882** *Century Mag.* Aug. 527/2 [The Indians] prayed aloud, each scattering a pinch of their prayer-meal, composed of corn-meal with an admixture of finely ground precious sea-shells, which they always carried with them in little bags. **1825** NEAL *Bro. Jonathan* I. 4 A silver bullet—a leaf o' the Bible, for wadding—and a charge of 'prayer-powder' —powder, over every 365 grains of which, the Lord's prayer has been said. **1846** *Knickerb.* XXVIII. 305 When a 'prayer ring' was to be formed, he announced it at the close of a sermon.

***Prayer book.** A book of prayers; the Book of Common Prayer. Also transf. — **1685** SEWALL *Diary* I. 68 By the Rule in the Prayer Book it [our election] should be a Week sooner [than Easter]. **1801** WEEMS *Letters* II. 164 As to the prayer books, they are the very books I delight to sell. **1840** DANA *Two Years* 225 Smaller hand-stones, which the sailors called 'prayer-books,' are used to scrub in among the crevices and narrow places, where the large holystone will not go. **1852** EASTMAN *Aunt Phillis's Cabin* 45 Here comes Mark with the Prayer Book. **1898** PAGE *Red Rock* 133 I'm a churchman, I am. I've got a prayer-book—somewhere.

+**Prayer cure.** Cure or healing brought about by prayer. — **1877** PHELPS *Story of Avis* 390 Should he try Colorado, the South, . . . Spiritualism, or the prayer-cure? **1888** *Pittsburg Dispatch* 29 July (F.), There is also a doctor of mystic philosophy from Boston, who advertises a course of instruction on faith cure, [and] prayer cure.

Prayer day. A day set apart for prayer. — **1745** FRANKLIN *Writings* II. 283 [In New England] you have a fast and prayer day for that purpose [praying for victory]. **1822** *Ann. 17th Congress* 1 Sess. 230 The prayer days were peculiarly agreeable to the Indians.

Prayerful, *a.* Devout, much given to prayer. {1626} — **1702** C. MATHER *Magnalia* (1853) I. 592 He was very pious in his childhood, and, because pious, therefore prayerful. **1829** *Va. Lit. Museum* 30 Dec. 459 *Prayerful—prayerfully,* used by some of the clergy—but not English. **1836** L. MATTHEWS *Lectures* 131 So *joyful, fearful, fearless, hopeless,* etc. came into use; and so *prayerful* and *heartless* are coming in. **1866** WHITTIER *Writings* VI. 153 Pious, sober, prayerful people . . . were derided by their neighbors as Puritans, precisians, and hypocrites.

Prayer house. {1852} +On a plantation, a small house or chapel resorted to by Negro slaves for prayer. *Obs.* — **1856** OLMSTED *Slave States* 450 On most of the large rice plantations . . . there is a small chapel, which the negroes call their prayer-house. **1859** *Harper's Mag.* Nov. 734/1 The religious services of the blacks . . . are held on some plantations, in little huts appropriated to that use under the name of 'prayer-houses.'

Prayer meeting. A meeting for prayer, esp. one held regularly each week. {1831–} — **1816** WILSON *Commonplace Bk.* 6, I attended a prayer-meeting at Mr. Waggoner's. **1823** *Baptist Mag.* IV. 32 It had been the practice of the church to hold weekly prayer-meetings. **1847** BRIGGS *Tom Pepper* I. 253 Old Gil attended the weekly prayer-meeting of his church. **1875** STOWE *We & Neighbors* 375 They hold weekly prayer-meetings, and seek to draw in the wretched people there. **1925** BRYAN *Memoirs* 450, I find his diversions to have been Sunday school, church, prayer meetings, . . . and at long intervals, a circus or an evening at the theater.

Prayer stick. (See quot. 1910.) — [**1865** TYLOR *Early Hist. Mankind* 89, I do not know whether any of these curious prayer-sticks are now to be seen.] **1894** *Nation* 13 Sept. 204/1 The prayer-sticks . . . are sent by a special courier, on the second day of the celebration, to the fanes of the rain-gods. **1910** HODGE, etc. *Amer. Indians* II. 304/1 *Prayer sticks,* sticks to which feathers are attached, used as ceremonial supplicatory offerings.

Prayer time. A time at which a prayer service is held. {1838–} — **1650** *Harvard Rec.* I. 35 The Butler henceforth shall receive . . . Twenty shillings in money . . . to provide Candles for the Hall, for prayer time & supper. **1677** SEWALL *Diary* I. 45 This was at prayer time, Feb. 19. **1707** *Ib.* II. 193 [Mr. Willard] was himself taken ill there, which oblig'd him to come from thence before Prayer-Time. **1871** STOWE *Sam Lawson* 206 Heven't you never heard how there was a council held to try Parson Morrel for laughin' out in prayer-time?

***Praying,** *a.* +In special combinations.

Praying circle, =*prayer circle* s.v. PRAYER; *p. man,* a man accustomed to pray, especially in public. {1892–}

1850 FOOTE *Sk. Virginia* 414 They began to hold praying circles, as they were called, in different parts of the congregation. **1845** *Indiana Mag. Hist.* XXIII. 40, I had been a praying man for some time.

+**Praying band.** A group who pray together, usually for a particular purpose. — **1883** *Century Mag.* Sept. 788/2 The Woman's Christian Temperance Union is the lineal descendant of the Woman's Crusade of 1874, whose first 'praying band' was led from the Presbyterian Church of Hillsboro' by Mrs. Thompson. **1900** WINCHESTER *W. Castle* 44 He had seen [him] years before, . . . conducting a revival meeting with a praying-band, of which he was leader.

+**Praying Indian.** An Indian converted to Christianity. Now hist.

1662 *Dedham Rec.* IV. 258 Being (through grace) now praying Indians, they have, in a sollemne fast, given up theire right in these lands. **1685** *Mass. H. S. Coll.* 4 Ser. V. 133 The Indians commonly called praying Indians . . . frequent their public meetings to worship God together on the Lord's days. **1720** D. NEAL *Hist. New-Eng.* I. 234 The new Converts were distinguish'd by the Name of the *Praying Indians,* who as soon as they had renounc'd their Old Religion, abandon'd their wild and barbarous Way of Living. **1764** HUTCHINSON *Hist. Mass.* I. 285 The war was hurried on by a piece of revenge, which Philip caused to be taken upon John Sausaman, a praying Indian. [**1891** EARLE *Sabbath* 82 He visited a 'praying' Indian's home wherein lay a sick papoose over whom a 'pow-wow' was being held by a medicine-man.]

+**Praying town.** A town or village composed of praying Indians. *Obs.* — **1670** ELIOT *Brief Narr.* 7 Both of them [were] to take care of the new Praying-Town beyond them. **1674** *Mass. H. S. Coll.* 1 Ser. I. 163 They killed but one or two of them [*i.e.*, praying Indians], about one praying town, called Wamesit. *Ib.*, They were at some other praying towns of Indians.

***Preacher.**

***1.** One whose occupation is to preach; a minister or clergyman. In full *preacher of the gospel(s).*

1648 SHEPARD *Clear Sun-Shine* 9, I could not tell how those old Indians should attain to such knowledge unlesse perhaps by means of the French Preacher cast upon those coasts many yeers since. **1714** *Boston News-Letter* 22 March 2/1 He was for many years a Preacher of the Gospels at the Isle of Shoals. **1787** *Discipline of M. E. Church* 8 [An elder's] Duty [is] . . . to take Charge of all Deacons, travelling and local Preachers and Exhorters. **1815** Mills & Smith *Missionary Tour* 19 Many of their preachers are exceedingly illiterate. **1844** *Indiana Senate Jrnl.* 29 Sess. 140 *Resolved,* That the judiciary committee be instructed to enquire into the expediency of passing a law exempting all licensed preachers of the Gospel . . . from working on public roads . . . when on their professional duties. **1898** HARPER *S. B. Anthony* I. 15 They always stopped at Grandfather Read's for . . . a drink of hard cider, but the elders and preachers were regaled with something stronger. **1920** *3d Nat. Country Life Conf. Proc.* 48 Teacher and preacher . . . can provide for the social life of the community in fairs [etc.].

‖**b.** (See quotation.)

1829 ROYALL *Pennsylvania* II. 38 You scarcely go a mile in Pennsylvania but you see a *Preacher*—as signboards are called. They point out the road, but never travel it.

+**2.** In special phrases and combinations.

Preacher in charge, in the Methodist church, a preacher who has charge of a particular station or circuit; *p. life*, life spent in preaching; *preacher of the day*, a preacher who has charge of the services on a particular day; *preacher's stand*, (see quotation).

1871 EGGLESTON *Hoosier Schoolm.* 220 The good minister . . . in Methodist parlance was called 'the preacher-in-charge of Lewisburg Station.' **1870** STEPHENS *Married in Haste* 101 How much of the old preacher life must cling about you. **a1817** DWIGHT *Travels* I. 268 At this entertainment the Preacher of the Day, and his successor, are present. **a1870** CHIPMAN *Notes on Bartlett* 339 *Preachers' Stand.* A pulpit in a church; a platform for a preacher at 'Camp Meetings.' The latter use occasioned the former, among certain people.—Southern and Western usage; but occasional, in N[ew] E[ngland].

+**Preacher in the pulpit.** The showy orchis. — **1884** MILLER *Plant-Names* 112/1 Preacher-in-the-pulpit. *Orchis spectabilis.* **1905** W. H. GIBSON *Our Native Orchids* 20 The white sepals unite in an arch bending over the Anther cells in such a way as to give the name 'Preacher in the Pulpit' to the orchid.

* **Preaching.**

* **1.** The delivering of a sermon; a public service consisting chiefly of a religious discourse. Also attrib.

1735 *Boston Rec.* 111 The Overseers of the Poor had . . . taken Care to Provide Preaching at the Alms-House. **1829** FLINT *G. Mason* 20 A 'preaching,' as it is called, that creates any excitement, is there not unlike an ordination. **1840** HOFFMAN *Greyslaer* II. 30 Pity the good man couldn't catch some droppings o' elequence from yonder preaching book to lifen his sarmints. **1862** NORTON *Army Lett.* 100 Sunday, July 13, 1862 . . . We have no preaching to-day. **1887** EGGLESTON in *Century Mag.* April 909/1 When it came to preaching the Public Friend had no pulpit, but mounted upon a preaching-stool. **1900** GARLAND *Eagle's Heart* 183 To the cowboy this sort of preaching came with surprise.

+**2.** In special phrases.

To go to preaching, to attend a public religious service at which a sermon is preached; *as certain as preaching*, very sure or certain. *colloq.*

1851 *Fla. Plantation Rec.* 388 Jno. Evans Went to Preaching. **1853** 'P. PAXTON' *Yankee in Texas* 116 To the latter [a southerner], drawing his comparison from his idolized rifle, a thing is '*as sure as shooting*,' while to the former [a Yankee], more pious or more hypocritical, it is '*as sartin as preachin*'.'

+**Preaching ground.** The area or grounds, as at a camp meeting, where public religious services are held. — **1820** FLINT *Lett. from Amer.* 232 This new arrangement made a striking change in the camp, the bustle being removed from the centre and distributed along the outskirts of the preaching ground. **1856** STOWE *Dred* I. 318 Before departing to the preaching ground, he had arranged a slow fire.

***Preaching place.** A place where preaching services are held; a position as a preacher. {1571, 1641} — **1845** *Indiana Mag. Hist.* XXIII. 21 Brother Oglesby went there to hunt a preaching place. **1856** CARTWRIGHT *Autobiog.* 85 We took in a new preaching-place, at a Mr. Moor's. **1863** P. S. DAVIS *Young Parson* 26 In addition to the Gainfield congregation, Mr. Meagre had two other 'preaching places,' as they were called. **1898** YOUNG *Jessamine Co., Ky.* 190 Previous to this [1820] the Presbyterian preaching place had been established about one and a half miles from Nicholasville.

+**Preaching stand.** A preacher's stand (q.v. under PREACHER 2). — **1860** *Harper's Mag.* Dec. 83/1 The preaching-stand . . . [was] neither cleaner nor more ornamental than the rest of the church.

***Preceptor.** An instructor or teacher, esp. one in charge of a school or academy. — **1784** *Mass. Centinel* 24 April 3/2 A Committee is also appointed to procure a Preceptor, who shall teach the Latin and Greek languages, Geography, Logick, etc. **1800** *Columbian Centinel* 25 Jan. 4/1 This work is much approved and highly spoken of by many teachers, preceptors, and others. **1825** NEAL *Bro. Jonathan* I. 12 Master Champlin [was] preceptor of an academy, to which boys and girls, quite grown up, would go. **1870** EGGLESTON *Duffels* 130 [He] had the good fortune to enter immediately into a partnership with his law preceptor.

Preceptress. A female preceptor, especially one in a girls' school. {1784-} — **1834** HAWTHORNE *Twice-told Tales* (1879) I. 126 Her speech . . . was so sensible and well worded, and delivered with such grace and propriety, that everybody thought her fit to be preceptress of the best academy in the State. **1896** WILKINS *Madelon* 149 She had married late in life, having been previously a preceptress in a young ladies' school. **1904** *N.Y. American* 4 May 5 Miss Frances Doughty, a preceptress, discovered the fire [at a girls' school].

* **Precinct.**

+**1.** One of the county divisions provided for by John Locke in his work on the Constitutions of Carolina. *Obs.*

1669 *Fundamental Constit. Carolina* iii, Each county shall consist of eight signories, eight baronies, and four precincts; each precinct shall consist of six colonies. **1702** *N.C. Col. Rec.* I. 559 There should be a standard of weights and measures sent for the use of the precinct. **1709** *Ib.* 712 This precinct was one of the two I attended. **c1773** in *S. Lit. Messenger* XI. 142/1 The Province of South Carolina is divided into 4 Counties . . . subdivided into very large Tracts of Land which go by the name of Precincts or Districts.

* **2.** A political subdivision of a town, township, county, or ward, +esp. such a division serving as an election district; also, the voting place of such a subdivision.

The quotations in the second group make specific mention of elections.

(1) **1706** *R.I. Col. Rec.* III. 562 Each town in this Collony is required . . . to state the Severall Constables' precincts in each town, for the gathering the rates and Taxes. **1728** [see COUNTER[1] 1]. **1802** *Mass. H. S. Coll.* 1 Ser. VIII. 201 In 1714, it was made a district or precinct, and put under the constablerick of that town. **1925** BRYAN *Memoirs* 85 The precinct in which our country home near Lincoln was located.

(2) **1833** *Sketches D. Crockett* 150 The store happened to be a precinct for holding elections. **1877** JOHNSON *Anderson Co., Kansas* 78 On the canvass of the vote the probate judge threw out all the returns except the Shannon precinct. **1897** BLISS, etc. *Encycl. Soc. Reform* 541/2 The ward politician knows every voter in his precinct. **1911** *Okla. Session Laws* 3 Legis. 77 The said special election board . . . [shall] see that each precinct, or voting place in the said county, is supplied with booths and other necessary conveniences.

+**3.** (See quot. *a*1870.) Now hist.

1713 SEWALL *Diary* II. 405 Ipswich Hamlet petitions the Genl. Court to give them the Powers of a Precinct. **1716** *Mass. H. Rep. Jrnl.* I. 89 Praying that . . . they may be vested with the Powers and Priviledges of a Precinct. **1722** *Ib.* III. 184 Voted That the —— Day of April, be Appointed a Day of Fasting and Prayer . . . throughout the several Towns and Precincts of this Province. **a1870** CHIPMAN *Notes on Bartlett, Precinct*, . . . a town whose corporate rights did not include sending deputies to the Col[onial] legislature.—Mass., before 1776.

+**4.** *New Eng.* An area or region under the spiritual care of a minister or clergyman. *Obs.*

1708 *Braintree Rec.* 70 It was then voted that there should be two distinct precincts or societies, in this Town for ye more regular & convenient upholding of ye worship of God. **1712** SEWALL *Diary* II. 331 Joseph and I retired . . . to ask direction from *God* about his Call to the new Precinct at Salem. **1793** *Mass. H. S. Coll.* 1 Ser. III. 1 In this town is one whole Congregational precinct, where the Rev. Joseph Barker is settled as minister.

+**5.** One of the districts into which a city is divided to facilitate the work of the police; also, transf., the police station in such a district.

Cf. DISTRICT *n.* 1 d.

1864 [see sense 6 c.]. **1882** MCCABE *New York* 374 The city is divided into thirty-five precincts, in each of which there is a station-house. **1894** FORD *P. Stirling* 142, I had to go with them . . . to the precinct and speak to the superintendent.

6. *attrib.* **a.** In sense 4 with *congregation.*

1717 *Canton* (Mass.) *Rec.* (1896) 4 It was voted . . . that ye sd Precinct Congregation would proceed to ordain mr Josiph morse.

b. In sense 3 with *line, meeting.*

1718 *Mass. H. Rep. Jrnl.* II. 101 A Draught of the Settlement of the Precinct Line between *Ipswich* & *Chebacco.* **1735** *Amherst Rec.* 5/1 Request of several freholders of the third or East Precinct of Hadley for the Calling of a precinct Meeting.

c. In sense 5 with *police, returns, station, station house.*

1864 *N.Y. Herald* 4 April, The body was removed to the Fourth precinct station house. **1899** WILLIAMS *Stolen Story* 25 The Police Head-quarters man sent in by telephone a bunch of precinct returns—arrests, accidents, and so on. **1902** ALDRICH *Sea Turn* 198 The keys were at the precinct station. **1904** *N.Y. Sun* 22 Aug. 4 A flat house robbery . . . never gets beyond the ken of the precinct police.

d. In sense 1 with *board of canvassers, election, election board*, etc.

1884 *Boston Jrnl.* 15 Sept., Precinct election officers need not necessarily vote in the precinct in which they are appointed. **1890** *Congress. Rec.* 3 June 5565/2 No man can be appointed [in Ala.] to hold a precinct election unless he is known to be a 'lightning man,' a ballot-box stuffer, a false counter. **1911** *Okla. Session Laws* 3 Legisl. 78 The precinct board of canvassers, shall canvass the vote. *Ib.* 227 The precinct election board shall be chosen for a term of four years.

+**Precinct court.** [PRECINCT 2.] A court in a precinct. *Obs.* — **1704** *N.C. Col. Rec.* I. 605 Ordered that the Marshall bring forth the body of Tho: Evans to the next pr[e]cinct Court to answer the compl[ain]t. **1715** *Ib.* II. 206 Said land shall be appraised by four honest men . . . appointed by the Precinct Court.

+**Precinct house.** A house serving as the headquarters of an election precinct. Also attrib. — **1863** Moore *Rebellion Rec.* V. I. 77 The Mayor of Philadelphia . . . called upon all able-bodied men to assemble next morning at the precinct-houses of the election districts. **1890** T. HALL *Tales* 171 He did very well to copy off the entries in a precinct house register or to discover the important arrivals at the hotels, but that was about all he could do.

***Predicate,** *v.* +*tr.* To found, affirm, base, etc. (an action, decision, etc.) *on* or *upon* some particular basis or data.
1766 CLAP *Hist. Yale-Coll.* 21 The Trustees . . . [passed] another Vote predicated upon sundry former ones, wherein they finally settled the College at New-Haven. **1796** WASHINGTON *Writings* XIII. 227 Was not the first application to you predicated on this information? **1803** JEFFERSON *Writings* X. 403 The other party saw the case now existing, on which our representations were predicated. **1839** SUMNER in E. L. Pierce *Mem. & Lett. C. Sumner* II. 105 This [opinion] . . . is predicated upon my confidence in his ability. **1888** CLEVELAND in *Daily News* (London) 10 Sept. 5/4 The reform we seek to inaugurate is predicated upon the utmost care for established industries and enterprises.

+**Pre-empt,** *v.*

1. *tr.* To secure (public land) by pre-emption. {1890-}
1850 LEWIS *La. Swamp Doctor* 87 A few hours' ride from town was one of these islands, 'pre-empted' by a man named Spiffle. **1872** *Congress. Globe* 12 Dec. 163/2 The man who desires to preëmpt land builds a shanty, scratches up a little bit of land, and gets two witnesses to swear that he has made an improvement. **1890** *Stock Grower & Farmer* 22 Feb. 4/4 Any head of family coming to the territory can homestead or pre-empt land under the government laws. **1900** GOODLANDER *Fort Scott* 14 If you wanted to pre-empt the land you had to build a house or a shanty . . . and live there off and on for six months before you could use your pre-emption right.
absol. **1867** RICHARDSON *Beyond Miss.* 138 Land is plenty and everybody preëmpts. **1873** BEADLE *Undevel. West* 75 Ike was a comin' out to pre-empt.

b. To obtain (a mining claim) by pre-emption.
1876 HARTE in *Scribner's Mo.* Jan. 373/2 Any other man but me couldn't hev bin sich a fool as to preëmpt sich a claim fur gold. **1877** JOHNSON *Anderson Co., Kansas* 59 He jumped the claim . . . and pre-empted it in the spring of 1856.

2. *transf.* To take as if by pre-emption.
1888 WILLARD in *Literature* 1 Sept. 276 [The Prohibition party] had unquestionably pre-empted for itself the proud position of the party of the future. **1908** 'O. HENRY' *Strictly Business* 179 Clearly, that spot in the moral vineyard was pre-empted. **1913** LONDON *Valley of Moon* 11 Many [tables and benches] . . . were already pre-empted by family parties.

+**Pre-emptible,** *a.* Of land: Available for purchase and settlement by pre-emptors. — **1857** *Lawrence* (Kan.) *Republican* 28 May 4 Any lands owned by government, not military or Indian reserves, are pre-emptible, whether surveyed or not. **1886** *N. Amer. Rev.* Jan. 54 As pre-emptible land recedes farther into the West, . . . it becomes more surely impossible for the man without means to establish himself.

Pre-emption.

1. The act of acquiring, or the right to acquire by purchase or otherwise, before others {1602-}, +used esp. of the preference or prior right of securing public lands, given by the government to settlers rather than to speculators.
Cf. PRE-EMPTION LAW, PRE-EMPTION RIGHT.
1747 *Baltimore Rec.* 21 Mr. Alexander Lawson applied also to enter his Preemption of making out Ground into the water. *c***1779** in Marshall *Kentucky* (1812) 125 Michael Stoner . . . claimed a right to a settlement and preemption to a tract of land lying on Stoner's fork. **1798** *Ann. 5th Congress* I. 495 The bill . . . for giving a pre-emption to certain purchasers and settlers, was read the second time. **1848** in Bryant *California* App. 458 Captain Sutter . . . would be perfectly satisfied with the simple promise of a pre-emption, on account of the mill which he has built there at considerable cost. **1878** *Harper's Mag.* Jan. 197 The land had been claimed by three parties—one by squatter rights, another by pre-emption, and the third by a 'New Madrid' claim. **1901** DUNCAN & SCOTT *Allen & Woodson Co., Kansas* 582 Finding that the Indians would not settle on the Reserve, the Government, in 1860, had all of these lands offered for sale and opened to pre-emption.
transf. **1855** HOLBROOK *Among Mail Bags* 288 His chair was appropriated by a fatigued neighbor, who 'squatted' on the vacant territory, regardless of 'pre-emption' or pre-session.

b. *The right of pre-emption*, the right of prior purchase of public lands.
1790 *Kentucky Petitions* 154 In the year 1786 he . . . aplied for his Right of preemtion but the Court would not admit of his proving his Right of preimtion. **1792** *Ann. 2d Congress* 1035 There remained to the United States the right of pre-emption of the lands westward and southward of the said lines. **1816** *Ann. 14th Congress* 2 Sess. 373 The right of pre-emption in the purchase of public lands in said Territory may be extended. **1864** *Wkly. New Mexican* 27 May 2/4 The right of pre-emption under the homestead act of May 20, 1862.

+**2.** A piece of land obtained or to be obtained by pre-emption.
1844 *Filson Club Hist. Q.* IX. 235 Each of these two men . . . had a pre-emption of 1400 acres. **1853** MCCONNEL *Western Char.* 137 Many a time . . . have I passed the 'clearing,' or 'pre-emption,' where, with nervous arm and sturdy heart, the 'squatter' cleaves out, and renders habitable, a home for himself and a heritage for his children. **1887** *Harper's Mag.* June 69/2 The 'claims' and 'pre-emptions' were marked to await the time when the owner could safely take possession.

+**3.** Attrib. with *act, bill, claimant*, etc.
1780 in *Travels Amer. Col.* 643 Received a Letter and Preemption Warrant. **1791** in Imlay *Western Territory* (1797) 463 The whole country to the eastward of the pre-emption line will be well and thickly inhabited. **1839** THOREAU *Journal* I. 98 A mere surveyor's report or clause in a preëmption bill contains matter of quite extraneous interest. **1842** *Amer. Pioneer* I. 43, I went to live with an elder brother on a pre-emption settlement, on the northeast side of the Alleghany river. **1845** *Xenia Torch-Light* 4 Dec. 3/5 West 24 poles to a stone in the west boundary line of said Preemption Lot. **1856** *Mich. Agric. Soc. Trans.* VIII. 730 The immediate north bank was squatted on by pre-emption claimants. **1867** *Ore. State Jrnl.* 5 Jan. 1/5 Mr. Ramsay introduced a bill making Agricultural College scrip receivable for pre-emption fees. **1871** *Rep. Indian Affairs* (1872) 513 [The Menomonees] had for some time been living away from the reservation among the Whites, or on land they claimed under the 'pre-emption' or 'homestead act.' **1880** *Cimarron News & Press* 11 March 3/4 Manuel Munis, of Madison, Colfax county, N.M., . . . made pre-emption declaratory statement 492.

+**Pre-emption certificate.** A certificate issued to one who has secured a pre-emption right. — **1780** in *Travels Amer. Col.* 642 My pre-emption certificates [were sent down] by James Brown. **1812** *Ann. 12th Congress* 1 Sess. II. 2352 Citizens . . . whose lands have not been . . . claimed in right of donation or pre-emption certificates . . . [are] confirmed in their respective claims.

+**Pre-emption claim.** A claim to public land made in accordance with pre-emption laws; the land embraced in such a claim. — **1783** in *Travels Amer. Col.* 671 Depositions proving Joh. Ross assignment of a Settlement and preemption claim to 1400 acres of land. **1857** *Lawrence* (Kan.) *Republican* 28 May 3 Particular attention paid to contested pre-emption claims. **1880** BURNETT *Old Pioneer* 71 The land was open to preëmption claims. **1900** DRANNAN *Plains & Mts.* 576 She asked if I had not told him to stay on the pre-emption claim that night.

+**Pre-emptioner.** =PRE-EMPTOR. *Obs.* Also transf. — **1841** *Knickerb.* XVII. 278 They amused themselves by calling the exclusives 'squatters,' 'preëmptioners,' etc. **1872** TICE *Over Plains* 80 The plain is dotted with new shanties of the homesteaders and pre-emptioners.

+**Pre-emptionist.** =PRE-EMPTOR. *Obs.* — **1850** LEWIS *La. Swamp Doctor* 24 Such is the character of the pioneers and pre-emptionists of the swamp. **1878** *Rev. Statutes* 415 (*margin*), Oath of pre-emptionist, where filed, penalty.

+**Pre-emption law.** Any one of various federal laws giving the first right in securing public land to actual occupants complying with certain prescribed conditions. — **1837** VAN BUREN in *Pres. Mess. & P.* III. 389 The limitations and restrictions to guard against abuses in the execution of a preemption law will necessarily attract the careful attention of Congress. **1855** Hambleton *H. A. Wise* 293 This may be done by such amendments to the preemption laws as experience may prove necessary for the purpose. **1872** *Newton Kansan* 26 Dec. 2/2 Can a man . . . prove up on 80 [acres] after fulfilling the requirements of the pre-emption law? **1890** *Stock Grower & Farmer* 25 Jan. 7/1 Thus secure the disposition of this vast area of public lands to actual settlers under our homestead and pre-emption laws.

+**Pre-emption right.** The right given an occupant to secure public land by compliance with pre-emption laws.
1784 FILSON *Kentucke* 37 The Settlement and pre-emption rights arise from occupation. **1797** *Ann. 4th Congress* 2 Sess. 2353 A bill from the Senate . . . to give a pre-emption right to certain purchasers, was read. **1824** DODDRIDGE *Notes* 99 Building a cabin and raising a crop of grain, however small, of any kind, entitled the occupant to four hundred acres of land, and a preemption right to one thousand acres more adjoining. **1848** in Brewster *Life J. D. Whitney* 99 Yet they have been beating each other's empty brain-cases in, . . . all about the preëmption-right to a parcel of land. **1873** EGGLESTON *Myst. Metrop.* 91, I have used my pre-emption right, or I would take that myself. **1900** [see PRE-EMPT *v.* 1].

b. Used with reference to mineral land.
1855 GLISAN *Jrnl. Army Life* 225 This only refers to pre-emption right, that is, the title to mineral land conferred by virtue of having first 'squatted on it.'

+**Pre-emption settler.** A settler or occupant of public land, having a pre-emption right. — **1858** *Texas Almanac 1859* 24 This act extends to preemption settlers or their assigns the time to return their field-notes to the Land Office for patent. **1873** *Republic* I. 51 Bills have been passed . . . for the relief of aged and infirm preëmption settlers. **1907** ANDREWS *Recoll.* 130 Preëmption settlers from various counties had conflicting claims before the land office.

Pre-emptive, *a.* {1855-} +Of or pertaining to the pre-emption of public land. — **1795** *Ann. 3d Congress* 2 Sess. 1154 The State had a right more positive than the pre-emptive one, to lands actually occupied and defended by hostile tribes of Indians. **1854** BENTON *30 Years' View* I. 12/2 Applications were made at that time for the establishment of the pre-emptive system. *Ib.*, Now the pre-emptive principle has become a fixed part of our land system. **1875** YOUNG *Hist. Chautauqua Co., N.Y.* 66 Robert Morris became seized of the preemptive title to all the lands in the state west of the eastern boundary of the Holland Purchase.

+**Pre-emptor.** One who secures public land in accordance with pre-emption laws. (Cf. PRE-EMPTIONER, PRE-EMPTIONIST.) — **1846** WORCESTER 557/1 *Pre-emptor*, one who practises pre-emption. **1855** *Kan. State Hist. Soc. Trans.* V. 168 A preemptor who complies with the requirements of the acts of congress cannot be prevented from obtaining his title. **1864**

Wkly. New Mexican 27 May 2/4 As to the right of pre-emptors under the homestead act of May 20, 1862. **1894** 'O. HENRY' *Rolling Stones* 219 The lordly cattle baron . . . stood at the Commissioner's desk side by side with the pre-ëmptor . . . and played the old game of 'freeze-out.'

+**Prefect.** [Sp. *prefecto.*] In regions of former Spanish influence, a magistrate, ruler, or governor. (In American use this word is a direct borrowing from Spanish and not a continuation of the earlier English *prefect.*) — **1847** *Santa Fe Republican* 11 Dec. 1/3 Accounts of the Prefects as disbursing officers of the funds for the different counties [shall] be made subject to the inspection of the grand juries or some competent tribunal. **1850** *31st Congress 1 Sess.* Sen. Ex. Doc. No. 76, 4 Prefects and alcaldes [in N.M.] impose fines and incarcerate, without the intervention of a jury. **1888** J. J. WEBB *Adventures* 192 He claimed four mules as stolen property, and we were notified to take them before the prefect's court for trial.

+**Preferred stock.** Stock which has priority over common stock in assignment of dividends and in distribution of assets. {preference stock or shares, 1842–} — **1850** *Mass. Acts & Resolves* 375 The Connecticut River Railroad Company are hereby authorized to issue . . . preferred stock. **1883** in Leavitt *Our Money Wars* 260 There would be issued . . . income bonds and common and preferred stock. **1895** E. CARROLL *Principles Finance* 212. **1919** R. W. BABSON *Bonds & Stocks* 172 An effort is then made only to ascertain . . . the amount remaining for dividends on the Preferred and Common stocks.

+**Prehaps,** *adv.* Variant of *perhaps. jocular.* — **1836** *Quarter Race Ky.* (1846) 24, I thought I'd make a rise on chuck-a-luck, but you *prehaps* never saw such a run of luck. **1847** FIELD *Drama in Pokerville* 73 '*Pre*haps,' Parson Hyme didn't put it into Pokerville for two mortal hours; and *pre*haps Pokerville didn't wiggle! **1856** DERBY *Phoenixiana* 125 You hear . . . the pleasant screak of the victim Whose been shot prehaps in his gizzard.

+**Prêle.** [Fr.] A plant or species of plant of the genus *Equisetum* found on the western prairies. (Cf. HORSETAIL.) — **1843** FRÉMONT *Explor. Rocky Mts.* 46, I encamped on a spot which afforded good grass and *prêle* (*equisetum*) for our animals. **1846** SAGE *Scenes Rocky Mts.* viii, An abundance of prelée [*sic*] and rushes afforded fine pasturage to our animals. **1852** STANSBURY *Gt. Salt Lake* 27 The grass is generally very abundant, and prêle (the common scouring-rush) is found in great plenty.

Premier. {1711–} +The Secretary of State in the president's cabinet. — **1878** *Harper's Mag.* March 490/2 The diplomatic anteroom, where foreign dignitaries await audience with the Premier, is handsome in its appointments. **1886** ALTON *Law-Makers* 68 The Secretary of State is sometimes (though not accurately) referred to as 'The Premier.' **1905** *Washington Post* 21 March 4 Elihu Root . . . is ideally equipped for the duties of the Department of State, but it is considered unlikely that he could be induced to return to the Cabinet, even as premier.

Premises.* *pl.* A piece of land, esp. the grounds about a building; a house or other building and any ground attached to it. {1730–} — **1640 in *Lechford's Note-Book* 245 The said Richard Parker shall & will finish the housing on the premises and build a new barne. **1719** *Mass. H. Rep. Jrnl.* II. 209 Voted . . . to pay the charge of necessary Surveys and the Committee, for their Service in and about the Premises. **1822** *Ann. 17th Congress* 1 Sess. I. 108 He shall pay for valuable improvements made upon his land before he shall oust the occupant and take possession of the premises. **1919** *Maine My State* 290 A stranger . . . sat regarding the premises with a smile of shrewd and pleasant contemplation.

Premium. {1661–}

1. A reward or bounty given by governmental authority. +**a.** For the killing of Indians or wild animals. Now hist.

Cf. BOUNTY *n.* 3.

1711 *Boston News-Letter* 12 Nov. 2/1 On Monday last Lieut. Hilton Brought here three Indian Scalps for which the Government paid him the premium. **1720** *Mass. H. Rep. Jrnl.* II. 273 A Petition . . . *Praying* That the *Premium* for Killing of Wolves may be paid otherwise than by Discount of the Tax. **1756** *Lett. to Washington* II. 4 There is no Exception in the Act of Assembly giving Premiums for Scalps.

b. For the production or manufacture of designated commodities. {1770–}

1720 *Boston Rec.* 148 [Voted] That a Premium be allowed by the Town of five pounds for the first peice of Linnen Spun and Wove here (provided it be worth four Shilling p'yd). **1734** *Mass. H. Rep. Jrnl.* XIII. 50 Voted, That for the further encouraging the raising of Hemp and Flax within this Province, the Premiums be doubled. **1792** *Ann. 2d Congress* 1012 Premiums serve to reward some particular excellence or superiority, some extraordinary exertion or skill, and are dispensed only in a small number of cases.

+**c.** Public land given as a reward for military service, or to encourage timber culture in the West. (Cf. BOUNTY LAND.)

'Any person who shall plant, protect, and keep in a healthy, growing condition for ten years forty acres of timber . . . on any quarter-section of any of the public lands of the United States shall be entitled to a patent for the whole of said quarter-section at the expiration of said ten years on making proof of such fact' (1873 *Statutes at Large* XVII. 605–6).

1836 *Diplom. Corr. Texas* I. (1908) 56 The pay and rations of the United States with a premium of six hundred and forty acres, will induce just as many to come. **1885** *Century Mag.* XXIX. 794/2 Nearly one-fifth of this vast area [the western plains] was 'entered' in 1882, which shows the growing influence of the princely premiums offered by Congress and by many of the Western States to encourage tree-planting.

2. A prize given for achievement in agriculture or domestic science, as determined by competition at a fair or exhibition. {1797–}

1805 *Nat. Intelligencer* 24 April 3/2 It is, indeed, greatly to be desired that . . . the premiums offered, may be an inducement to graziers and farmers to bring their cattle and other effects to the city. **1842** *N.Y. Agric. Soc. Trans.* I. 27 All animals will be examined and premiums awarded on the first day of the fair. **1857** *Mich. Agric. Soc. Trans.* IX. 316 We found no premium offered in the printed list for Buggy Harness. **1898** E. C. HALL *Aunt Jane* 6, I took the premium on my salt-risin' bread and sponge cake.

3. a. (See quot. 1895.) +**b.** Something given as payment or as a reward to agents selling or people buying specified commodities.

(**a**) **1870** MEDBERY *Men Wall St.* 291 Men paid 35 as a premium for United Mexican mining shares in December. **1895** E. CARROLL *Principles Finance* 300 *Premium on shares*, the price beyond the face value. (**b**) **1887** *Youth's Companion* 26 May 239/3 We have made a specialty since 1877 of giving as Premiums to those who get up clubs or purchase Tea and Coffee, in large quantities, Dinner and Tea Sets. **1890** *Fireside Visitor* (Augusta, Me.) 15 Nov. 13/1 If you will send me two new yearly subscribers to the Fireside Visitor and premium pictures, I will send the Mozart Music Box free as a premium. **1903** WIGGIN *Rebecca* 132 The young Simpsons groped about for some inexpensive form of excitement, and settled upon the selling of soap for a premium. **1923** *Youth's Companion* 29 Nov. 731/4 Four other beautiful dinner sets, silverware, aluminum-ware and other choice premiums.

4. *attrib.* **a.** In various senses with *crop, list, picture*, etc.

1840 *Niles' Reg.* 5 Dec. 210/2 Whig premium flags. . . . Majorities in the several states for their candidate, are now casting about to find out which state, county, city and township are entitled to flags, for having given the largest federal majority in proportion to their population. **1845** *Lowell Offering* V. 281 The 'premium' system has its modifying influence. . . . Premiums are awarded to those overseers [in the weaving rooms] who accomplish most. **1850** *Rep. Comm. Patents 1849* 169 Having thus described the construction and arrangement of my improved premium stove. **1857** *Ill. Agric. Soc. Trans.* II. 94 The three classes named in your premium list, viz.: 'Thoroughbred horses,' 'horses of allwork,' (roadsters) and 'draught horses.' **1863** MITCHELL *My Farm* 245 The estimate of labor and other expenses on premium-crops is so various. **1890** Premium picture [see 3 b]. **1907** *St. Nicholas* Sept. 1019/2 He didn't say much—just looked over his eye-glasses and talked about premium pigs and mowing-machines.

+**b.** *Premium land*, in Texas under Mexican rule, land granted to certain empresarios as a reward for fulfilling contracts concerning the colonization of the empresario grants. (Cf. sense 1 c.)

1838 C. NEWELL *Revol. Texas* 186 [These grants] consisted . . . in a claim . . . to a certain amount of premium land. *Ib.* 187 If they [the empresarios] had introduced ninety-nine families, and not the hundredth, they were entitled to no proportion of premium land whatever.

+**Premonitories.** *pl.* Premonitory symptoms. — **1834** *Knickerb.* IV. 307 The premonitories seize me before I have time to run to the doctors for relief. **1853** KANE *Grinnell Exped.* 308, I am down myself today with all the premonitories.

Prentice.* =APPRENTICE 1. Also attrib. with *boy.* — **1653 *Boston Rec.* 48, I was a Prentice. **1686** *Conn. Probate Rec.* I. 528, I give to my Prentice boy my Hanger or short Sword. **1713** C. MATHER *Diary* II. 199 My kinsmen, that are prentices, must have my frequent counsils and charges, to serve their masters with all possible fidelity. **1846** MELVILLE *Typee* 162, I felt in some sort like a 'prentice-boy who, going to the play in the expectation of being delighted with a cut-and-thrust tragedy, is almost moved to tears of disappointment at the exhibition of a genteel comedy. **1884** 'MARK TWAIN' *H. Finn* xi, You're a runaway 'prentice, that's all.

+**Prep.** [Abbrev. of *preparatory.*] A student in a preparatory school. *colloq.* Also attrib. in sense of the school. — **1890** *Cent.* 4695/1 *Prep*, a student who is taking a preparatory course of study; especially, one who is preparing for college. (College slang, U.S.) **1895** WILLIAMS *Princeton Stories* 244 Charlie Symington was a well-built prep. boy who had been known to strike out three men with the bases full. **1899** QUINN *Penna. Stories* 117 He was going to tell all those people, from the Governor down to the prep in the gallery, . . . just what the college had done for him.

+**Preparatory department.** In a school, a department which prepares students for collegiate work. — **1848** *Indiana Gen. Ass. Doc. 1848–9* II. 279 Connected with the Institution is a flourishing Grammar School, which serves the double purpose of a Normal School and a Preparatory Department. **1851** CIST *Cincinnati* 69 The Classes in the course of study in the Preparatory Department, are divided among the Adjunct Professors of Mathematics and Languages and the Professor of Modern Languages. **1881** *Ore. State Jrnl.* 8 Jan. 5/3 The preparatory department numbers between sixty and seventy pupils.

Preparatory school. A school, often privately owned, in which students receive preparatory training, usually for entering college. {1828–} — **1841** *S. Lit. Messenger* VII. 551/1 In its preparatory school, there are about four hundred boys. **1879** *Scribner's Mo.* Dec. 207 The Johns Hopkins is seeking . . . to penetrate downward into the preparatory schools. **1903** *World's Work* Sept. 3884 The preparatory school . . . take[s] boys from 12 to 14 years of age to fit them in from 3 to 6 years for entrance to our best colleges. **1917** COMSTOCK *Man* 40 Brace during preparatory school and college had formed a deep and sincere attachment for Conning Truedale.

+**Prep school.** Short for PREPARATORY SCHOOL. Also attrib. — **1895** WILLIAMS *Princeton Stories* 128 After awhile he found himself walking with the freshman way out toward the Prep. school. **1899** QUINN *Penna. Stories* 93 The admission of such prep schools was against the constitution. **1905** *McClure's Mag.* June 123/2 The commercial class of prep school athletes admire their prototypes in the colleges. **1921** PAINE *Comr. Rolling Ocean* 99 He had trouble in prep school and was canned.

Prerevolutionary, *a.* +Belonging to the time before the American Revolutionary War (1775–83). — **1868** BEECHER *Norwood* 328 Planted in 1646, it was more than a hundred years old when the pre-revolutionary excitements were taking place in Boston. **1868** *Putnam's Mag.* Jan. 21 Short legs—long pipe—style very Pre-Revolutionary. **1874** ALDRICH *P. Palfrey* x, Since the hanging of a witch or two in the pre-revolutionary days, the office of sheriff there has been virtually a sinecure.

Prerogative court. {1603–} +A probate court. *Obs.* except in New Jersey. — **1711** *Conn. Rec.* V. 283 Mary Wakeman, an orphan, has made application to this Assembly for liberty to appeal from an act or sentence of the prerogative court in the county of Fairfield. **1793** *N.J. Rep.* (1901) 180 The Orphans' Court is . . . a court partaking of the powers of a chancery and prerogative jurisdiction, instituted by law to remedy and supply the defects in the powers of the Prerogative Court, with regard to the accountability of executors, administrators, and guardians. **1917** *N.J. Equity Rep.* LXXXVIII. 263 An appeal was taken to the prerogative court.

+**Presbygational.** [*Presby*terian and Congre*gational*.] Characterized by features of both Presbyterian and Congregational methods of church government, with specific reference to the Plan of Union (1801–52) of these two denominations. — **1895** R. E. THOMPSON *Hist. Presb. Churches* 72 This 'Presbygational' system, as it afterward was nicknamed, . . . had respect especially to the settlement of western New York from New England. *Ib.* 183 The Presbyterians . . . [urged] these Presbygational churches to become thoroughly Presbyterian.

+**Presbygationalism.** The combination of features of both Presbyterian and Congregational methods of church government, as in the Plan of Union (1801–52). — **1892** *Advance* 10 Nov. 927/3 It was recommended that their [Congregational] churches be associated with presbytery. . . . The result was Presbygationalism, a composite creature, symbolic of little else than the folly of its progenitor. **1893** *Ib.* 30 March 249 An ecclesiasticism wherein delegates duly elected by vote of the local churches are required to sit with a teaching eldership that are not thus delegated, and to share ecclesiastical power with them, is Presbygationalism.

***Presbyter.** +In the early Congregational churches, a ruling elder. — **1666** *Conn. Rec.* II. 55 Whether the laying on of hands in ordination of Elders belong to Presbiters or Brethren. **1722** FRANKLIN in *N.-E. Courant* 1–8 Oct. 1/1 [The ministers in Conn. who have embraced Anglicanism] have deny'd the Validity of Ordination by the Hands of Presbyters.

***Presbyterial,** *a.* =PRESBYTERIAN *a.* — **1674** JOSSELYN *Two Voyages* 179 The Governments of their Churches are Independent and Presbyterial, every Church . . . [has] one Pastor, one Teacher, Ruling Elders and Deacons. **1799** in *Constit. of Associate Reformed Church in N.A.* (1850) 329 They do hereby declare . . . the aforesaid form of Presbyterial church-government . . . to be the true and genuine government . . . of the Associate-Reformed Church. **1815** DWIGHT *Remarks on Review of Inchiquin's Lett.* 56 In order to obtain a license, and afterwards to be admitted to ordination, they [*sc.* students in divinity] must in each case pass through the Associational or Presbyterial examination, mentioned above. **1856** W. S. KENNEDY *Plan of Union* 229 Many . . . expect to see the Presbyterial element return perhaps to the Old School body, and the Congregational come out as pure Congregationalists.

‖**Presbyterialized,** *a.* Made to conform to Presbyterian polity. — **1856** W. S. KENNEDY *Plan of Union* 144 The last half century has . . . developed a new type or modification of ecclesiasticism . . . which we may call co-operative Presbyterianism, Plan of Unionism, or Presbyterialized Congregationalism.

Presbyterian, *n.* One favoring church government by presbyters; a member of the Presbyterian church. {1641–}

1690 I. MATHER in *Andros Tracts* II. 37 In the same Church [*i.e.*, the church of New England] there have been Presbyterians, Independents, Episcopalians and Antipædobaptists, all welcome to the same Table of the Lord. **1700** C. MATHER *Diary* I. 364, I adjoin a savoury little Discourse . . . to confute our pretended Presbyterians. **1765** ROGERS *Acct. N. Amer.* 72 The religious persuasions here [in N.Y.] are very numerous; there being Episcopalians, Lutherans, Presbyterians, Anabaptists. **1808** BENTLEY *Diary* III. 365 The Presbyterians are different in the Middle States. **1895** *Boston Jrnl.* 10 April 8/1 Many of the settlers . . . were Scotch-Irish (so-called) Presbyterians. **1907** T. C. JOHNSON *Va. Presbyterianism* 8 An attempt is made to indicate some of the services of Presbyterians in behalf of religious liberty, during colonial and revolutionary days.

Presbyterian, *a.* Of or pertaining to church government by presbyters or presbyteries, and specifically to the Presbyterian church. {1641–} — **1714** *Brookhaven Rec.* 104 The aforesayd building [was dedicated] . . . in the purity of holy Relegion & in quallyte of a Presbeterian Meeteing House. **1768** *Boston Gazette* 9 May, The young Women of the Presbyterian Congregation . . . generously gave Mrs. Parsons the spinning of two hundred and seventy Skeins of good Yarn. **1814** in Mills & Smith *Missionary Tour* 8 Only one place, Wheeling, is supplied with Presbyterian preaching half the time. **1871** *Republican Rev.* 18 March 1/3 Messrs. Roberts and Menaul are both Presbyterian clergymen, attached to the Navajo Mission. **1925** *Presbyterian Hist. Soc. Jrnl.* XII. 193 Another phase of Presbyterian influence in early American education is evident in the production of the tools for knowledge.

Presbyterian church. The organized body of Christians who adhere to Presbyterian doctrines and church government; the building in which a local group of these Christians worships. {1692– (*Sc. Presb. Eloquence* 53)}

1773 *Huntington Rec.* II. 522 The money to be applied towards Buying a New Parsonage House and Lott in or near Town for the use of the Presbyterian church and Congregation. *a***1817** DWIGHT *Travels* II. 31 The Presbyterian church . . . is fronted with two towers. **1861** *Congregationalist* 27 Dec. (Chipman), The first time I attended the Presbyterian Church [in Darnestown, Md.], . . . a prayer-meeting was in progress. **1880** *Cimarron News & Press* 9 Sept. 2/5 Mr. Valdez, of Las Vegas, had the contract for building the Presbyterian church here and I think it will be the best building in town when finished. **1925** BRYAN *Memoirs* 455 He was long an elder . . . in the Presbyterian Church.

Presbyterianism. The system of church government by presbyters and presbyteries; the doctrine and polity characteristic of the Presbyterian church: (see also quot. 1878). {1644–}

1735 COLMAN in Turell *Life B. Colman* 107 The Consociation of Churches, is the very Soul and Life of the Congregational Scheme . . . ; without which we must be Independent, and with which all the Good of Presbyterianism is attainable. **1767** [see CONGREGATIONALISM]. *a***1840** in E. A. Park *Memoir N. Emmons* (1861) 163 Associationism leads to Consociationism; Consociationism leads to Presbyterianism. **1878** STOWE *Poganuc People* 25 Congregationalism—or, as it was then called by the common people, Presbyterianism—was the religion established by law in New England. **1883** R. P. KERR *Presbyterianism for the People* 10 Presbyterianism . . . may be described as ecclesiastical republicanism combined with Calvinistic theology. **1907** T. C. JOHNSON (*title*), Virginia Presbyterianism.

***Presbytery.** A church court consisting of ministers and elders representing churches of a given area, or the area so represented; church government by courts of this type, characteristic of the Presbyterian church.

1648 in W. Walker *Creeds of Congregationalism* 218 This Government of the church . . . in respect of the Presbyetry & powr comitted to them, it is an Aristocracy. **1654** JOHNSON *Wonder-w. Prov.* 32 Yee Presbytery, Lord it not over them or any Churches, but feed every one. **1712** *N.J. Archives* 1 Ser. IV. 154, [I] find there is not one of 'em inclinable to Presbytery, but all well affected to Church & State. **1791** *Presb. Church Constitution* 387 A presbytery consists of all the ministers, and one ruling elder from each congregation, within a certain district. **1811** MEASE *Philadelphia* 212 The members of the two presbyteries, who formed the union, denounced the minority as schismatics. *a***1817** DWIGHT *Travels* II. 112 He lived within the bounds of the Presbytery of Albany. **1852** in W. Walker *Creeds of Congregationalism* 540 It is not deemed expedient that new Congregational Churches . . . become connected with Presbyteries. **1872** *Newton Kansan* 12 Dec. 2/2 The session of Presbytery on Saturday evening was opened with a sermon by your humble servant, the moderator.

***Prescription.** In special combinations.

Prescription book, a book used in writing prescriptions; *p. clerk*, a druggist who fills prescriptions; *p. room*, a room in a drug store where prescriptions are filled.

1887 HARRIS in *Century Mag.* XXXIV. 541/2 Dr. Buxton, prescription-book in hand, gazed at her quizzically. **1910** C. HARRIS *Eve's Husband* 155 It was his custom to ignore the proprietor and to order what he wanted directly from the prescription clerk. **1900** DIX *Deacon Bradbury* 27 He had . . . conducted countless small experiments by himself in the rear prescription-room.

Prescription glass. 1. A lens made according to an oculist's prescription. **2.** (See quotation.) — (1) **1888** *Scientific Amer.* LVIII. 259/1 The lens-grinding room . . . is devoted almost exclusively to making what are known as 'prescription glasses.' (2) **1890** *Cent.* 4701/3 *Prescription-glass*, . . . a glass vessel with measures, as of a tablespoonful, teaspoonful, etc., marked on it.

Present,** *n.* +A gift made to or received from Indians, usually as a pledge or token of amicable relations. — *a1656** BRADFORD *Hist.* 519 The comissioners thought it meete before any hostile acte was performed, to cause a presente to be returned, which had been sente to ye gove[rno]r of the Massachusetts from the Narigansett sachems. **1711** *Boston News-Letter* 26 March 1/2 The Indian . . . departed before night well pleas'd with his entertainment and Presents. **1747** *Penna. Col. Rec.* V. 139 He had . . . call'd for the Goods design'd as a Present to the Indians. **1837** *Diplom. Corr. Texas* I. (1908) 178 Genl Urea paid the said Chiefs at that time one thousand dollars in money and presents. *a*1918 G. STUART *On Frontier* II. 84 When they were refused presents they became insolent.

∗**Present,** *v.* or *a.* +(See quots.) {cf. *O.E.D.*, *Present* v. 11*d*, quot. 1720} — **1848** BARTLETT 261 *Present*, put on the back of letters to persons residing in the place where the letter is written. Peculiar to the United States. The Spanish equivalent *presente* is also used in Central America. **1905** *Dialect Notes* III. 16 *Present*, adj. The word is put on the envelope of letters to persons residing in the town where the letters are written, and which are not sent through the post.

∗**Presentation.** A ceremony at Yale University at which the students recommended for the B.A. degree were presented to the president. Now hist. {1683–, at English universities} Also attrib. — **1843** BELDEN *Sk. Yale Coll.* 131*n.*, At the middle of the third term . . . certificates are presented by the Faculty to the Corporation recommending those who have passed a satisfactory examination as worthy of a degree. This gave rise to the term 'Presentation Day.' **1864** *Harper's Mag.* Sept. 497/1 [Article on] Presentation week at Yale. *Ib.* 498/2 First, we go with the Faculty to the Presentation Dinner. **1871** BAGG *At Yale* 531 At the earlier presentations a huge bowl of punch is said to have been provided.

Preservatory. {1654–} +A place or apparatus for preserving meat, vegetables, etc., by keeping them cool. — **1853** FOWLER *Home for All* 116 My ice-house consists of *two stories*—the upper one for ice, the lower, a room kept cool by the ice and its drippings, a preservatory for keeping fruit, butter, eggs, fresh meat, fish, bacon, pies, etc. **1876** KNIGHT 1783/2 *Preservatory*, an apparatus for preserving substances to be used as foods.

∗**Preserve.** Fruit or other vegetable products preserved by being cooked with sugar. Often pl. {1600–}

1789 MORSE *Amer. Geog.* 54 The fruit is small and sour, and makes an excellent preserve, or sweet-meat. **1852** STOWE *Uncle Tom* x, The poor soul had . . . brought out . . . some preserves that were never produced except on extreme occasions. **1893** *Harper's Mag.* March 595 The New England women, before the war, were knitting and putting up famous preserves. *a*1918 G. STUART *On Frontier* I. 129 The menu . . . [included] a preserve made from choke-cherries.

attrib. **1854** THOREAU *Walden* 235 She [goes] to her preserve-pot. **1856** M. J. HOLMES *L. Rivers* 108 The big preserve dish got broken.

Preserve jar. A jar in which preserves are kept: (see quot. 1876). — **1867** HARRIS *Sut Lovingood* 92 Perserve jars, vinegar jugs, seed bags, yarb bunches, . . . all mix'd. **1876** KNIGHT 1784/1 *Preserve-jar*, a jar the mouth of which may be hermetically closed, both to insure the better preservation of the fruit and to prevent evaporation. **1884** ROE *Nature's Story* 307 Raccoons . . . will uncover preserve-jars . . . , and with the certainty of a toper uncork a bottle and get drunk on its contents.

∗**Presidency.**

∗**1.** The office held by the president of a court, college, or business.

1718 SEWALL *Letter-Book* II. 90, I presume it cannot be said that I exercised the Presidency [of the superior court] immoderately or unfairly. **1780** *N.H. Hist. Soc. Coll.* IX. 111 The affairs of the Presidency [of Dartmouth Coll.] I esteem too delicate for me to make any particular mention of. **1853** *Knickerb.* XLII. 104 Benjamin Loder, Esq., has retired from the presidency of the New York and Erie Rail-Road. **1856** *S. Lit. Messenger* XXII. 68/2 Mr. Cadwell was again elected to the presidency [of the Univ. of N.C.]. **1901** MERWIN & WEBSTER *Calumet 'K.'* 63, I had ambitions to be promoted to the presidency [of the railroad], but it didn't seem very likely.

+**2. a.** The office or position of the president of the United States.

*a*1800 TWINING *Visit* (1894) 136 General Washington . . . remained there till 1789, when the general voice of his country called him from his pastoral pursuits to the Presidency of the Government. **1816** *Nat. Intelligencer* 9 April 1/1 The Nomination of candidates for the Presidency and Vice Presidency by the Republican Congressional Meeting, appears to have received the approbation of a large majority of the Republican party. **1864** *Wkly. New Mexican* 24 June 2/1 That Fremont would be the nominee for the presidency was a foregone conclusion. **1896** *Congress. Rec.* 24 March 3159/1 As a War Democrat I voted for General Grant, the nominee for the Presidency in 1868.

+**b.** The office of the presiding officer or president of the United States Senate.

Cf. PRESIDENT 8.

1804 CUSHING in Cutler *Life & Corr.* II. 176 Can they submit to the degradation of the presidency of a man [Aaron Burr] lying under the legal imputation of murder?

+**3.** *Mormon Ch.* A board consisting of a president (q.v., sense 12) and two counselors. *First presidency*, the highest board of this kind, consisting of the head of the hierarchy of the church and two counselors, and having jurisdiction over the entire church organization.

*a*1853 in Gardner *Faiths of World* II. 492/2 The hierarchy of the Mormon church has many grades of offices and gifts. The first is the presidency of three persons. **1867** DIXON *New America* I. 293 Brigham Young, Heber Kimball, and Daniel Wells, [were] the three members of what is here called the First Presidency. **1882** WAITE *Adv. Far West* 250 Brigham Young and his two Counselors form the First Presidency, under the title of the Gods, or Grand Archees.

∗**President.**

∗**I.** The chief magistrate or executive head of a government. +**1.** The highest or ruling officer in an American colony or 'province.' *Obs.*

Cf. GOVERNOR 1 a.

1608 SMITH *Works* (1910) 6 The Counsell was sworn, and the President elected [at Jamestown], . . . where was made choice for our scituation. **1647** *R.I. Col. Rec.* I. 191 The Generall Officers for the whole Colonie shall be these, Sci: One President, foure Assistants [etc.]. **1654** *United Colony Rec.* II. (1859) 442 Roger Williams of Prouidence Colony Presidt. **1681** *Maine Doc. Hist.* IV. 401 The majestrates haue ellected & Appointed the Honored Thomas Danforth Esqr our present Deputy Gouernor to be President of the Province of Maine for the yeare ensuing. **1705** BEVERLEY *Virginia* IV. 201 The first Constitution of Government appointed by them, was by a President and Council, which Council was nominated by the Corporation, . . . and the President annually chosen by the People.

+**2.** The executive head or governor of a state government.

The use of *president* in these early examples, and the election procedure indicated in them, are reflections of the fact that chief executives of the colonies had been called 'presidents' (cf. sense 1) and had been elected by councils. By 1800 *president* had yielded place, in popular use, to *governor*. Cf. FIRST MAGISTRATE 1.

1776 *Del. Constitution* § 7 A President or Chief Magistrate shall be chosen by joint ballot of both Houses. **1776** *Penna. Constitution* § 3 The supreme executive power shall be vested in a president and council. **1780** *Va. State P.* I. 371 When the Governors or Presidents of two or more States act in the field together, he who has been longest in office shall take rank of all other Governors or presidents. **1792** IMLAY *Western Territory* 165 The President of the State [of Ky.] is chosen annually. *a*1817 DWIGHT *Travels* II. 154 Bartlett derived its name from his Excellency Josiah Bartlett, some years since President of [N.H.].

+**b.** The chief magistrate or governor of the Republic of Texas. *Obs.*

1836 *Diplom. Corr. Texas* I. (1908) 144 Remember me to the President and Cabinet. **1837** DEWEES *Lett. from Texas* 216 After General Houston became President of this Republic, he made preparations for sending Santa Anna back to his country. **1840** *Diplom. Corr. Texas* III. (1911) 1277 Be kind enough to have it signed by the President and yourself. **1846** POLK *Diary* I. 309 At 6 O'Clock this evening Gen'l Samuel Houston, late President of Texas and now a Senator in Congress, called.

+**3.** The highest executive officer of the United States government. In full *President of the United States.*

The employment of this term in the Constitution (see quot. 1787) was a continuation of the earlier usage, in which the officer designated was the presiding officer of the Continental Congress (cf. sense 7, quots. 1783, 1784). Cf. CHIEF EXECUTIVE, CHIEF MAGISTRATE 2, FIRST MAGISTRATE 2.

1787 *Constitution* ii. § 4 The President, Vice-President, and all civil Officers of the United States shall be removed from office on Impeachment for, and conviction of, Treason. **1798** F. AMES *Works* (1854) I. 218 The fear of the Executive power is still as lively as if the President were a king. **1808** *Ann. 10th Congress* 1 Sess. I. 335 The President of the United States is Commander-in-chief of the Army and Navy. **1845** *Lexington Observer* 5 Feb. 3/2 With such Presidents as we have had for the past sixteen years . . . the Constitution is a dead letter. **1873** *Republic* I. 45 An election by the House . . . virtually places the election of President in the hands of the representatives. **1912** *St. Louis Globe-Dem.* 6 Nov. 1/6 Woodrow Wilson was elected president of the United States yesterday by a vote of landslide proportions.

+**b.** As a title.

1855 PIERCE in *Pres. Mess. & P.* V. 312 These long-continued efforts had brought upon the Government . . . such indignities as to induce President Adams . . . to speak of it in terms of the highest indignation. **1886** LOGAN *Great Conspiracy* 658 Soon they actually began, themselves, to believe, that President Hayes had been 'counted in,' by improper methods! **1924** *Lit. Digest* 23 Aug. 6/1 President Coolidge says he favors economy.

+**4.** In some states, the chief officer of a village or a town: (see quot. 1914).

1844 *Indiana Senate Jrnl.* 29 Sess. 211 A bill for the relief of the president and trustees of the town of Greencastle. **1897** HOWELLS *Open-eyed Conspiracy* vii, Her father is not only the president, as they call it, of the village, but he's the president of the bank. **1904** *N.Y. Times* 16 March 1 Larchmont, N.Y. . . . E. L. Hopkins was elected President of the village. **1914** *Cycl. Amer. Govt.* III. 47/2 *Presidents of Villages*, the official title of the chief officer of a village in New York, Vermont, Michigan, Illinois, Wisconsin, and Minnesota. More often the title mayor is used.

+**5.** The chief executive officer of the Confederate States of America. Now hist. Also as title.

1861 *Constit. Confed. States* vii. § 1 The Congress . . . shall prescribe the time for holding the election of President and Vice-president. **1863** J. R. BALME *Amer. States* (1864) 185 Jefferson Davis, the Confederate President, whom Lincoln's soldiers intended to have hung. **1866** 'F. KIRKLAND' *Bk. Anecdotes* 114/2 Some of the Sixth Missouri Cavalry visited the former residence of 'President' Davis.

II. A presiding officer or chairman. ***6.** A person appointed or elected to preside over a legislative assembly or a meeting; the ranking officer of a judicial court.

1638 *Md. Archives* I. 4 Every one that is to speake to any matter, shall . . . direct his speech to the Lieutent. g[ene]rall as President of the Assembly. **a1649** WINTHROP *Hist.* I. 178 Henry Vane, by his place of governor, was president of this council for his year. **1655** *R.I. Court Rec.* I. 8 The Generall Court of Tryalls at Portsmouth: June 26: 1655. Mr. Roger Williams President. **1685** *Plymouth Laws* 294 The eldest magistrate shall be President of the Court. **1757** *General Orders* 77 All Genll. & Field Offrs. Serving by Commission from ye Governor, Lt. or Deputy Governor or Presidents of ye Counsel for ye time being of our sd. Provences. **1776** *N.H. Constitution*, Precepts . . . signed by the President of the Council . . . shall issue annually. **1812** JAY *Correspondence* IV. 362 The president of every county, State, or national convention should be a person fitted to receive and employ *authority*, consistent with the laws and constitution. **1861** *Army Regulations* 125 The President of a court-martial . . . is the organ of the court.

+7. The chairman or presiding officer at the meetings of the Continental Congress. In full *president of the United States in Congress assembled. Obs.*

1775 *Jrnls. Cont. Congress* II. 255 *Resolved*, That the president write to the provincial Congress of New York . . . directing them immediately to send forward the whole of the troops ordered to be raised. **1776** A. ADAMS *Familiar Letters* 149 The mansion-house of your President [John Hancock] is safe, and the furniture unhurt. **1777** *Jrnls. Cont. Congress* VII. 8 Resolved, That a letter be written by the President to the president and council of the state of Georgia. **1778** *Ib.* X. 37 Agreed. . . . That the President inform the President of the State of Pennsylvania that Congress approve the measure they propose. **1783** in Hildeburn *Century of Printing* II. 409 Proclamation. By His Excellency Elias Boudinot, Esquire, President of the United States in Congress Assembled. **1784** *Jrnls. Cont. Congress* 23 April, The preceding articles shall be . . . duly executed by the president of the United States in Congress assembled, under his hand, and the seal of the United States.

+8. The officer, normally the vice president of the United States, who presides at the meetings of the United States Senate. In full *President of the Senate.*

Cf. PRESIDENCY 2 b.

1787 *Constitution* i. § 3 The Vice President of the United States shall be President of the Senate, but shall have no vote. **1846** *Whig Almanac 1847* 3 Senate. George M. Dallas, of Pennsylvania, President. **1850** *31st Congress 1 Sess.* Sen. Ex. Doc. No. 64, 3 [To] Hon. Wm. R. King, President pro tem. of the Senate. **1886** ALTON *Among Law-Makers* 20 The Vice-President of the United States . . . is termed the 'presiding officer' or 'President' of the Senate. **1900** *Congress. Rec.* 22 Feb. 2062/2 Mr. President, yesterday I gave notice to the Senate that to-day, at the completion of the reading of the Farewell Address, . . . I would [speak].

+b. *spec.* The president of the Senate chosen by that body in 1789: (see quotation).

This action was taken in order to conform with the requirements of the Constitution ii. § 1.

1789 *Annals 1st Congress* I. 17 The Senate proceeded, by ballot, to the choice of a President, for the sole purpose of opening and counting the votes for President of the United States. John Langdon was elected.

+9. The chief executive officer of a business or industrial company, as a bank, railroad, etc.

1781 *Jrnls. Cont. Congress* XXI. 1188 It is hereby ordained, . . . that those who are . . . subscribers to the said bank be . . . a corporation and body politic to all intents and purposes, by the name and stile of 'the President, Directors, and Company of the Bank of North America.' **1798** *Mass. Statutes* 1 March, The Massachusetts mutual fire insurance Company . . . shall have power to choose a President, Treasurer & fifteen Directors. **1811** MEASE *Philadelphia* 105 There are twenty-five directors [of the Bank of Penna.] including the president. **1853** *Knickerb.* XLII. 104 No President of this great road has ever done more. **1909** *Nation* 11 March 251 One is a little irritated to learn that President, meaning the chairman of a business concern, is branded as an Americanism [in the *O.E.D.*].

+10. One of the chief officers of The First Church of Christ, Scientist, in Boston, Massachusetts, and of some branch churches.

1895 M. B. EDDY in *Church Manual* 17 The President of this Church shall hold his office one year only, and is eligible to this office once in three years. **1922** *Boston Transcript* 5 June 12/1 Mr. Tomlinson [t]urned and welcomed to the readers' desk the new president of the Church. **1924** *Christian Science Jrnl.* July 203 He is a member of Third Church of Christ, Scientist, Los Angeles, where he has served as President.

III. The administrative head of an educational or religious establishment. ***11.** The principal executive of a college +or university.

See COLLEGE 1 note and cf. RECTOR 1.

1643 *New Eng. First Fruits* (1896) 2 Over the Colledge [Harvard] is master Dunster placed, as President, a learned conscionable and industrious man. **c1764** in Woolsey *Hist. Disc. Yale* (1850) 54 The Freshmen . . . are forbidden to wear their hats . . . in the front door-yard of the President's or Professor's house. **1780** *N.H. Hist. Soc.Coll.* IX. 111 Respecting the College what accounts you have received officially from the President I am unable to say. **1807** *Laws Union Coll.* 37–8 (Hall), No class meetings shall be held without special license from the President. **1884** *American* VIII. 233, I see the president of Harvard tells his neighbors that the platform is immoral and demagogical. **1894** *Univ. Chicago Register* 35 William Rainey Harper, . . . President of the University, and Head Professor of the Semitic Languages and Literature. **1920** *Rev. of Reviews* Oct. 409/2 In the nineteenth century Yale College had several great presidents.

+12. The chief executive official of the Mormon church, or a subordinate official with similar powers and responsibilities.

a1853 in J. Gardner *Faiths of World* II. 493/1 The president [of the Mormon church] . . . gives the decision . . . to which all must yield implicit obedience. **1883** Schaff *Religious Encycl.* II. 1578/2 In practical administration the president of the church, with his two counsellors, forming the First Presidency, is the sovereign authority. *Ib.*, Every city, or 'stake,' including a chief town and surrounding towns, has its president, with two counsellors.

IV. +13. *President's* (*official*) *family*, the members of the president's cabinet.

1790 MACLAY *Deb. Senate* 193 As I came out from the Hall, all the President's family were there—Humphreys, Jackson, Nelson, etc., etc. **1905** *Independent* 2 March 470/1 There will be but one change in the President's official family,—that of the Postmaster-General.

Presidentess. a. A female president. {1782–} ||**b.** The wife of the president of the United States. — **1819** *Amer. Farmer* I. 280*n.*, [This Leghorn braid is] fine enough . . . for the Presidentess of this Republick. **1838** COOPER *Homeward B.* x, They formed a tea society, with the parson's wife for presidentess. **a1870** CHIPMAN *Notes on Bartlett* 340 *Presidentess*, a woman who presides—N.Y.

+President-general. A president who outranks or is superior to all minor presidents in a system, society, or federation. {1897} — **1754** *Mass. H. S. Coll.* 3 Ser. V. 70 [It is proposed] that the said general government be administered by a President-General, to be appointed and supported by the crown. **1784** *Mass. Centinel* 27 March 3/1 His Excellency George Washington, Esq., is *President-General* of that society [the Cincinnati]. **1809** J. ADAMS *Works* IX. 620 At the meeting of the Cincinnati at New York, . . . they choose Hamilton their President-General. **1858** BANCROFT *Hist. U.S.* VII. 140 Galloway, of Pennsylvania, . . . proposed for the government of the colonies a president-general, to be appointed by the king.

Presidential, *a.* {1603–}

+1. Of or pertaining to the president of the United States or his office.

1799 C. LEE in J. Adams *Works* IX. 22 The offenders . . . experienced the presidential clemency, and not a traitor suffered the punishment of law. **1838** *U.S. Mag.* Jan. 144 Have we not heard . . . of a President, whose wont it was, . . . at his presidential dinners, to speak of *'that old fool*, Franklin?' **1866** CARPENTER *At White House* 56 [Gen. Grant] attended the Presidential levee, entering the reception room unannounced. **1904** G. CLEVELAND (*title*), Presidential Problems.

+2. Of or pertaining to the president of a college or to his position.

1816 DWIGHT in E. Baldwin *Annals Yale Coll.* 96 The only serious defect in his Presidential character was, that he was prone to consider boys as being men. **1831** E. BALDWIN *Ib.* 135 Those duties, (as being distinct from Presidential obligations,) . . . were blended . . . with those of other Professorships. **1895** W. S. TYLER *Hist. Amherst Coll.* 210 A committee was appointed to take into consideration the presidential vacancy.

+3. In special combinations.

Presidential candidate, a candidate for the presidency of the United States; *p. count*, the count of presidential electoral votes, made by the Senate; *p. governor*, during or immediately after the Civil War, a governor appointed by President Lincoln or President Johnson for one of the Southern states; *p. plan*, the plan of Presidents Lincoln and Johnson for restoring the Southern states to statehood in the Union after the Civil War; *p. term*, the period of four years for which a president of the United States is elected; *p. timber*, men who would make good candidates for the presidency of the United States.

1893 *McClure's Mag.* I. 493/2 He was to be four years later the successful presidential candidate of his party. **1877** *Harper's Mag.* Dec. 148/1 Scenes of tumult . . . signalized the closing hours of our last Congress in the endeavor to prevent the consummation of the Presidential count. **1866** in Fleming *Hist. Reconstruction* I. 195 Then came the appointment of Presidential Governors, an anomaly heretofore unknown in a Government composed of states which were once supposed to possess some at least of the attributes of sovereignty. **1879** TOURGEE *Fool's Errand* 49 The plan . . . was what has since been known as the 'presidential plan.' **1839** *26th Congress. 1 Sess.* Sen. Doc. No. 2, 15 Losses appear to have occurred from defaults among officers in every 'administration' or presidential term. **1903** *Washington Post* 10 Nov. 1 For a few moments yesterday there stood in the centre aisle of the Senate enough Presidential timber of both political parties to keep the government running a quarter of a century.

+**Presidential campaign.** A political campaign leading up to and culminating in the election of a president of the United States. Also attrib. (Cf. CAMPAIGN *n.* 2.) — **1835** C. P. BRADLEY *I. Hill* 60 He finally thought the time had arrived for taking an active part in the presidential campaign. **1883** 'MARK TWAIN' *Life on Miss.* xxxviii, Other bric-a-brac: . . . pewter presidential-campaign medal. **1889** *Voice* 2 May, Re-read the talk for Local Option and High License in the late Presidential campaign. **1909** PARKER *G. Cleveland* 114 Colonel Lamont was casting about for a title to the first pamphlet issued during the Presidential campaign.

+**Presidential canvass.** =prec. — **1844** *Lexington Observer* 25 Sept. 2/5 The Presidential Canvass. . . . Henry Clay will be elected. **1854** BENTON *30 Years' View* I. 126/2 That dissatisfaction . . . became a point of attack on Mr. Adams's administration, and an element in the presidential canvass which ended in his defeat. **1891** WELCH *Recoll. 1830–40* 356 Mass meetings, political processions and pilgrimages then first came into general adoption as features of a Presidential canvass. **1900** *Congress Rec.* 26 Jan. 1234/2, I saw much of him at the national headquarters of the committee which managed Mr. Blaine's Presidential canvass.

+**Presidential chair.** The office or position of a president, esp. that of the president of the United States. — **1792** HAMILTON *Works* VIII. 261 Mr. Jefferson aimed with ardent desire at the Presidential chair. **1807** JANSON *Stranger in Amer.* 125 The two presidential chairs were taken [by Jefferson & Burr] without farther resistance. **1854** *N.J. Hist. Coll.* II. 408 Dr. Carnahan has occupied the presidential chair of this College longer than any of his distinguished predecessors. **1900** *Congress. Rec.* 31 Jan. 1341/1 There was a Jackson in the Presidential chair to take that bank by the throat and compel it to go into liquidation.

+**Presidential convention.** A convention held by a political party for nominating candidates for president and vice president of the United States. (Cf. CONVENTION 2 c.) — **1872** *Atlantic Mo.* May 640 The time for the Presidential convention draws near. **1879** *Nation* 15 May 332/1 The Democrats suggest the men who will do most to promote the nomination of Mr. Samuel J. Tilden at the next Presidential Convention.

+**Presidential election.** A quadrennial election in which a president and vice president of the U.S., or, more exactly, presidential electors, are chosen by popular vote. (Cf. ELECT *v.* 2 a, note.) — **1812** *Niles' Reg.* II. 235/1 [If] it were consistent to express a wish on the ensuing presidential election, we would say . . . it were well, that De Witt Clinton had been nominated vice-president. **1837** *Whig Almanac 1838* 3 In the late Presidential Election, it [the Whig party] polled 730,203 votes, exclusive of South Carolina and Michigan. **1851** *Harper's Mag.* Dec. 120/1 In several of the States, . . . the elections of this year do not afford any substantial ground for predicting their votes in the Presidential election. **1890** *Congress. Rec.* 28 June 6730/2 The last Presidential election, with its . . . multifarious questionable methods, is too fresh in the minds of the people.

+**Presidential elector.** =ELECTOR 2. — **1820** *Niles' Reg.* XVIII. 432/1 We lately noticed an alleged defect in the law of this state, as to the election of presidential electors. **1844** CLAY in *Whig Almanac 1845* 41/1, I am greatly obliged . . . by the kindness . . . which has prompted this visit from the Governor, the Presidential Electors of Kentucky and some of my fellow-citizens in private life. **1884** *Century Mag.* Nov. 128 The emancipation of the country from the evils of the spoils system . . . needs to be supplemented by an emancipation of the people and the Presidential electors from the thralldom which confines the choice of a President to designated candidates. **1907** ANDREWS *Recoll.* (1928) 144 In 1860 the Douglas Democratic state convention placed me at the head of the ticket for presidential electors.

+**Presidential fever.** (See quot. 1914.) — **1882** *Century Mag.* Jan. 435/1 This honor comes to me unsought. I have never had the presidential fever. **1914** *Cycl. Amer. Govt.* III. 47/1 *Presidential Fever*, a phrase used to denote the eager desire for, and ambition to gain, the presidency of the United States, prevalent among prominent political leaders and 'favorite sons' in the several states.

+**Presidential message.** =PRESIDENT'S MESSAGE. — **1839** *S. Lit. Messenger* V. 752/2 Our bachelor . . . was poring over one of those long presidential messages. **1859** WILMER *Press Gang* 193 Martin Van Buren, in one of his Presidential messages, proposed to make embezzlement of the public money a felony punishable by confinement in the State's Prison.

+**Presidential office. 1.** An office or suite of offices occupied by a president; the position of a president. **2.** (See quotation.) — **(1) 1798** WASHINGTON *Writings* XIV. 24 From the want of the list, which I left in the Presidential office, . . . it would be hazardous . . . to give a decided opinion. **1841** TYLER in *Pres. Mess. & P.* IV. 38 The patronage incident to the Presidential office, already great, is constantly increasing. **1846** N. F. MOORE *Hist. Sk. Columbia Coll.* 75 The professorship which for about three years had been annexed to the presidential office, should be detached therefrom. **(2) 1882** *Nation* 2 Nov. 370/2, 1,951 of these [post] offices are filled by appointment of the President, and are known as Presidential offices, and the remainder—44,280—are filled by appointment of the Postmaster-General.

+**Presidential year. 1.** A year spent in the office of president. **2.** A year in which a presidential election occurs. — **(1) 1785** R. H. LEE in J. Adams *Works* IX. 544 My presidential year [in Congress] being ended, I had left New York for this place. **1877** in W. S. Tyler *Hist. Amherst Coll.* 207 The class that graduates to-morrow carries with it the memory of your first presidential year [at Amherst]. **(2) 1876** *Scribner's Mo.* Jan. 432/2 It is 'Presidential year,' and the great question concerning the currency is to be settled. **1900** *Congress. Rec* 14 Feb. 1802/1 The Democratic vote maintained itself at 40,000, coming within 10,000 of its great vote in 1896, a Presidential year. **1903** *N.Y. Ev. Post* 5 Sept., Every merchant knows that the buying demand is exceedingly sensitive. It is traditionally so in a Presidential year.

+**President judge.** (See quot. 1914 and cf. PRESIDING JUDGE.) — **1833** *Indiana Mag. Hist.* XXII. 64 Hon. Gustavus A. Everts, president judge [of the Circuit Court of Elkhart Co., Ind.]. **1840** *Niles' Nat. Reg.* 30 May 199/2 A bill to allow associate judges of the courts of common pleas, as well as president judges, to admit persons to bail . . . was then taken up and passed. **1849** CHAMBERLAIN *Ind. Gazetteer* 65 The President Judges are chosen by the Legislature, and the Associate and Probate Judges by the people. **1914** BOUVIER *Law Dict.* 2676/2 *President Judge*, a title sometimes given to the presiding judge. It . . . is now used in the courts of common pleas in Pennsylvania. So in the old Virginia court of appeals.

+**President-making.** The choosing of a president, esp. a president of the United States. Also attrib. or as adj. — **1833** *Congress. Deb.* 31 Jan. 1560 If we look into our legislation before all other considerations were absorbed in president making, we shall find [etc.]. **1844** *U.S. Mag.* June 561/2 The great free North and the great free West will then take the matter of President-making into their own steadier and trustier hands. **1857** STROTHER *Virginia* 13 So fully was the public mind occupied with filibustering and president-making [in 1852], that the notes of preparation for this important expedition were scarcely heard. **1868** *N.Y. Herald* 10 July 6/5 The cliques and combinations, the trading and log rolling . . . in most cases have determined the nominations of these President-making conventions.

***Presidentship.** The office of a president, as of a college or of the United States. — **1695** in Quincy *Hist. Harvard* I. 76 The Reverend President . . . is settled in his presidentship by an act of the great and general Assembly. **1720** in Peirce *Hist. Harvard Univ.* 93*n.*, [He] took his degrees in the presidentship of Mr. Charles Chauncy. **1757** *N.J. Archives* XX. 142 The Reverend Mr. Jonathan Edwards is chosen to succeed him in the Presidentship [of the College of N.J.]. **1891** *Scribner's Mag.* Sept. 293/1 If you offered him . . . the president-ship of the United States, he wouldn't take it.

President's house. +The official residence of the president of the United States, now the White House. (Cf. EXECUTIVE MANSION, MANSION c.) — **1799** WELD *Travels* 6 The president's house, as it is called, was erected for the residence of the president, before the removal of the seat of the federal government from Philadelphia was agitated. **1802** *Ann. 7th Congress* 2 Sess. 1316 The appropriations, except as to the Capitol and President's House, [were] struck out. **1828** COOPER *Notions* II. 11 The Americans familiarly call the exceedingly pretty little palace in which their chief magistrate resides, the 'White House,' but the true appellation is the President's House. **1881** *Harper's Mag.* March 544/2 From the park east of the Capitol to the President's House . . . there is a long stretch of government land.

+**President's message.** An address or communication delivered before or sent to Congress by the president of the United States.

1834 HAWTHORNE *Twice-told Tales* (1879) I. 118 The fellow ought to be hired to go express with the President's Message. **1846** *Whig Almanac 1847* 13/2 The Tariff of 1846 . . . was confessedly based on a portion of the President's Message of December last. **1862** NORTON *Army Lett.* 128 I have been much interested in the President's message. **1874** COLLINS *Kentucky* I. 42 President's message . . . reaches Maysville by express mail and steamboat. **1915** *Amer. Rev. of Reviews* Jan. 13/2 The President's Message. . . . Mr. Wilson appeared in person on the second day of the session, and delivered his message to Congress.

b. A communication from the president of the republic of Texas to the Texas congress. *Obs.*

1840 *Picayune* 18 Nov. 2/4 The President's Message to the Texian Congress of 1840–41, was delivered in 'manuscript.'

+**Presiding elder.** In the Methodist church, a minister who has supervision over the churches and preachers in a certain district. — **1831** PECK *Guide* 258 There are three districts, over each of which is a presiding Elder. **1844** Rupp *Relig. Denominations* 447 A presiding elder, although no higher as to order than an elder, has charge of several circuits and stations, called collectively a district. **1887** *Century Mag.* XXXIV. 339/1 On that day the Presiding Elder was to deliver a sermon. **1925** TILGHMAN *Dugout* 7 The presiding elder was goin' home with my folks for dinner.

Presiding judge. =PRESIDENT JUDGE. — **1802** *Ann. 7th Congress* 1 Sess. 117 The constant changing of presiding judges . . . hung up the business. **1869** TOURGEE *Toinette* (1881) 245 Geoffrey's counsel . . . called the attention of His Honor, the Presiding Judge of the Court, to the fact that [etc.].

+**Presidio.** *S.W.* [Sp.] A fortress, garrison, or military post, now, spec., the post at San Francisco. {a prison fort in Africa, 1853}

1808 PIKE *Sources Miss.* 111. App. 28 The presidio of . . . Rio Grande is situated on that river. **1849** *31st Congress 1 Sess.* Sen. Ex. Doc. No. 64, There being no prospect of our seeing the much-talked-of *presidio* or fort of the Navajos, . . . the expedition returned to camp. **1875** HARTE in *Scribner's Mo.* Dec. 241/2 A fervid May sun had been baking the adobe walls of the Presidio of San Ramon. **1904** *San Francisco Chron.* 1 Oct. 16 The monthly muster and inspection of the artillery was held yesterday at the Presidio.

attrib. **1840** DANA *Two Years* xviii, 160 A bull was expected down from the country, to be baited in the presidio square. **1898** ATHERTON *Californians* 204 At one of the Presidio hops she spent the evening . . . in a boat on the bay with an officer who was as accomplished a flirt as herself.

** **Press,** *n.*[1] The impressing of men for the army or navy, or a warrant for such impressment. *Obs.* Also attrib.

1637 MORTON *New Canaan* 119 They injoyne him to come to their needeles watch howse in person, and for refusinge give him a cracked Crowne for presse money. **1640** *Mass. Bay Rec.* I. 296 Henry Chapman, for not obeying a presse, was fined 5 sh[illing]s. **1676** I. MATHER *K. Philip's War* (1862) 139 At Boston there is a Press in order to sending forth another Army to pursue the enemy. **1743** *Md. Hist. Mag.* XX. 369 Endeavor to keep the men Sober and clear of Press. **1776** FITHIAN *Journal* II. 210 Press warrants are issued to draught three men out of every five of the militia. **1803** *State P.* (1819) V. 18 There has been a hot press throughout this island. In this port about sixty seamen have been taken out of American vessels. **1807** *Ib.* VI. 14 From conjectures that she was a press vessel, . . . I concluded to go on board . . . alone.

* **Press,** *n.*[2]

* **1.** An apparatus for exerting great pressure, used in extracting the juices from fruits and in making cheese.

Cf. CHEESE PRESS, CIDER PRESS.

1680 *Conn. Probate Rec.* I. 303 My eldest son John shall have . . . the Press and Mill in the Barne. **1703** *N.H. Probate Rec.* I. 504, I give to my beloved Son . . . Cellars[,] Cyder mill, press. **1848** *Rep. Comm. Patents 1847* 462, [I] gathered the grapes as soon as ripe, put them on the press as soon as gathered. **1865** A. D. WHITNEY *Gayworthys* 65 Get the cows home, and the milkin' done, while I get this cheese into the press. **1924** *Sears, Roebuck & Co. Cat.* No. 148, 840 Fruit and Vegetable Press. Made of steel.

b. = COTTON PRESS.

1835 INGRAHAM *South-West* II. 289 Immediately under the room containing ginned cotton, is the press. **1884** 'CRADDOCK' *Where Battle Was Fought* 100 The gin-house and the press were burned.

* **2.** A machine for printing; a printing press.

1654 JOHNSON *Wonder-w. Prov.* 206 The Court . . . committed them [*i.e.*, the laws] to the Press, and . . . they were printed. **1725** *New-Eng. Courant* 4 Jan. 1/2 You Illit-rate Slaves that work at Press. **1857** *Lawrence* (Kan.) *Republican* 9 July 2 A Kansas editor . . . is glad . . . to get out of sight and hearing of exchanges, types, presses, compositors, devils, and all. **1903** SHUMAN *Pract. Journalism* 11 With steam-power hitched to such a press the possibilities of journalism were becoming great.

3. *collect.* Newspapers or journals, often those of a specified area, regarded as a source of information and a means of expression of opinion. {1797-}

See also NEWSPAPER PRESS.

1780 J. ADAMS *Works* VII. 182 The press, the towns, the juries, and the assemblies are four sources, from whence an unerring demonstration of the true sentiments of the people of America may be drawn. **1806** *Balance* V. 3/3 The press has been contaminated by the foulest polutions. **1861** in Logan *Great Conspiracy* 250 They have possessed themselves of all the avenues of information in the South—the telegraph, the press, and the general control of the postmasters. **1900** *Congress. Rec.* 19 Jan. 980/1 It is studiously circulated throughout the press east of the Alleghany Mountains that the Populist party has gone to pieces. **1925** BRYAN *Memoirs* 480 The press asserted that Mr. Bryan had worked for the introduction of this bill.

4. *attrib.* **a.** In sense 1 with *house;* in sense 2 with *mate.*

1744 *N.J. Archives* XII. 211 To Be Sold, . . . A new Fulling-Mill, Press-House and Dye-House. **1833** *Niles' Reg.* XLIV. 404/1 In 1816, the editor of this journal was a press-mate to James Harper.

b. In special combinations.

Press box, a booth or stall at an athletic contest, etc., for the convenience of newspaper reporters; *p. boy,* a boy who assists a pressman in a printing establishment; *p. congress,* a congress or convention of representatives of the press; *p. service,* an organization which collects and distributes news items to newspapers; *p. stuff,* material suitable for newspapers; *p. ticket,* a ticket given to a reporter or other representative of the press.

1890 H. PALMER *Stories of Base Ball Field* 43 Time and again, when sitting in the press-box behind the catcher, I have been . . . lost in admiration of the Bostonian's skill. **1890** *Cent.* 3560/3 *Machine-boy.* . . . In the United States known as *feeder* or *press-boy.* **1894** SHUMAN *Steps into Journalism* 17 Joe Howard, a New York writer, . . . was one of the speakers at the World's Fair Press Congress in Chicago. **1917** SINCLAIR *King Coal* 212 'Won't the story go to other papers?' . . . 'Yes, we have a press service.' **1917** MCCUTCHEON *Green Fancy* 251, I wouldn't repeat this story to Mr. Lyndon Rushcroft. . . . He would blab it all over the county. The greatest press stuff in the world. **1868** *N.Y. Herald* 4 July 4/1 Somebody connected with a democratic journal in this city had control of the press tickets.

* **Press,** *v. tr.* To force (a man) to serve in the army or navy; to take or commandeer (a horse, boat, etc.) during an emergency. Also transf. absol. Also *vbl. n.* (Cf. IMPRESS *v.*)

1636 *Plymouth Laws* 44 In case . . . there be not volunteers sufficient offered for the service, then it [shall] be lawfull for the Govr. and assistants to presse in his Ma[jes]ties name by their warrant directed to the Constables. **1682** *Ib.* 199 The Govr. or any of the Assistants shall have power to presse men Artificers or others to make or repaire prisons or other Instruments of Justice. **1717** SEWALL *Diary* III. 118 Capt. Cayley's men make a Rout in the Town at night by Pressing without Orders. **1776** *Jrnls. Cont. Congress* VI. 862 Resolved. That the quarter masters in every department be ordered to avoid pressing horses and carriages, as much as possible. **1809** J. ADAMS *Works* IX. 327 A few words more on the subject of pressing. **1850** COLTON *3 Years Calif.* 64 He had a permit from the American Alcade to press horses wherever found. **1889** P. BUTLER *Recollections* 271 They were continually riding around the country, frightening the people, and 'pressing' horses—which was another name for stealing them.

Press agent. One employed to secure favorable advertising or publicity for a town, business, individual, etc. — **1885** *Santa Fé Wkly. New Mexican* 20 Aug. 1/5 The careless Las Vegas press agent . . . seems likely to get into hot water. **1895** *N.Y. Dramatic News* 7 Dec. 3/2 The Castle square had decided to abolish the post of press agent. **1908** SINCLAIR *Metropolis* 113 He has a regular press agent for her, a chap he loads up with jewellery and checks whenever he gets her picture into the papers. **1920** HOWELLS *Vacation of Kelwyns* 179 He is her press agent, as they call it.

+**Press association.** An organization for collecting news and supplying it to newspapers. — **1877** *Harper's Mag.* Dec. 58/2 The American Press Association is an organization similar to the Associated Press. **1893** Philips *Making of Newspaper* 8 The 'manifolded' despatches . . . come in yellow envelopes from the press associations. **1896** *Internat. Typogr. Union Proc.* 41/1 Had we been . . . in a position to secure a franchise from one of the great press associations, the outlook would undoubtedly have been brighter. **1917** SINCLAIR *King Coal* 212 We limit the amount of news the Western press association can suppress.

Pressboard. = IRONING BOARD. — **1861** STOWE *Pearl Orr's Isl.* I. 28 That dignitary sits . . . looking majestically over the press-board on her knee. **1871** — *Sam Lawson* 144 Cinthy she sot by the fire in the front parlor with her goose and her press-board and her work. **1882** PECK *Sunshine* 124 The boy and his mother and a press board paid a visit to the back kitchen. **1896** HARRIS *Sister Jane* 17, I've got this press-board on my lap.

+**Press clipping.** = CLIPPING 2. Also attrib. with *bureau.* — **1894** [see CLIPPING 2]. **1924** *Publisher's Weekly* CVI. 121/2 *Press clipping bureau*—An organization which makes a business of collecting personal notices, book reviews, etc., from current periodicals and furnishing them for a fixed sum per clipping to the persons concerned. **1925** *Scribner's Mag.* Oct. 438/2, I used to subscribe many years ago to a press-clipping bureau. *Ib.*, 'Papa, what is a press-clipping bureau?' 'My son, you pay five dollars, and receive one hundred insults.'

+**Press club.** An organization made up of those engaged in printing, publishing, or writing. — **1896** *Peterson Mag.* ns. VI. 311/1 The Pittsburg Women's Press Club made a wise choice in selecting for a secretary Miss Marie de Sayles Coyle. **1925** *Lit. Digest* 27 June 27/2 And so for press clubs everywhere, intent on ideals, here is a Danielle come to judgment.

Pressed brick. Brick subjected to pressure, for improving the shape and texture, before burning. {1850- (Dobson *Manuf. Tiles & Bricks* 32)} Also attrib. — **1875** KNIGHT 823/1. **1888** *Harper's Mag.* June 47/2 Several wells yield quantities [of rock-gas] that have displaced a considerable amount of coal . . . at the pressed-brick works. **1914** ATHERTON *Perch of Devil* 24 When I have a . . . pressed brick house . . . nobody'll be too good for me.

Press-feeder. One who feeds sheets of paper into a printing press. — **1886** CARNEGIE *Triumphant Democracy* 435 Fifty proof-readers are constantly employed [in the Government printing-office], besides one hundred and fifteen press-feeders. **1896** *Internat. Typogr. Union Proc.* 16/1 The International Typographical Union recognizes the right of the International Printing Pressman's Union to charter, regulate, and control printing pressmen, pressfeeders, and helpers in press rooms.

Press gang.[1] A body of men authorized to press men for the army or navy. *Obs.* {1693-} — **1721** *Mass. H. Rep. Jrnl.* III. 30 That which most surprizes us is the Sum . . . paid to Mary Smith, Innholder for Sundries, supplied the Press Gangs Impressing Sailors for His Majesties Ship. **1813** CLAY *Speeches* (1842) 55 The naked truth is, she [*i.e.*, England] comes, by her press-gangs, on board of our vessels. **1886** ALCOTT *Jo's Boys* iii, Aren't they [*i.e.*, girls] worse than a press-gang to carry a fellow out of his moorings?

+**Press gang.**[2] Newspapers collectively; representatives of newspapers, as reporters. — **1859** L. WILMER (*title*), Our Press Gang; or, a Complete Exposition of the Corruptions and Crimes of the American Newspapers. **1887** *Courier-Journal* 20 Jan. 1/7 Sam Morse, of the Chicago *Times,* announced that he had perfected an arrangement by which the press gang could get into the hall of the House.

* **Pressing iron.** An iron used when heated to smooth seams, cloth, etc. (Cf. GOOSE *n.* 2.) — **1644** *Essex Probate Rec.* I. 33 Shers and presing iron and yard. **1658** *Southold Rec.* I. 449 The personall estate whereof Elizabeth Payne widdow dyed [includes]: . . . A painted platter—a pressing Iron—a small cleever. **1698** in Burr *Witchcraft Cases* (1914) 65 Also a pressing-Iron lying on the ledge of the Chimney back, was convey'd invisibly into the Yard.

* **Pressman.**

* **1.** A man who operates a printing press.

1771 FRANKLIN *Autobiog.* 302 Meredith was no compositor, a poor pressman, and seldom sober. **1791** FRENEAU *Poems* (1795) 421 Who, year from year, . . . Is author, pressman, devil—and what not? **1857** *Lawrence* (Kan.) *Republican* 25 June 3 A pressman can find a good situation by applying immediately at the *Republican* office. **1896** *Typographical Jrnl.* IX. 352 Subordinate unions shall receive applications for membership from such pressmen, stereotypers, electrotypers and bookbinders as meet the requirements of law.

2. One who does pressing in a tailor's shop.

1840 *Picayune* 13 Oct. 2/6 A young man . . . wishes a situation as a cutter, trimmer, pressman, or coat maker in a tailor's shop. **1857** *Harper's Mag.* July 284/2 Nehemiah . . . fell kerslap upon the goose of the pressman.

+**3.** One who works at a cotton press.

1869 *Overland Mo.* III. 10 The pressmen and ginners, too, like the fields, have been snowed upon.

+**Press paper.** {1821–} Heavy paper or pasteboard used in binding books. — **1760** *Boston Gazette* 16 June, Ink Horns, . . . writing and press paper, . . . knitting needles. **1791** *Ann. 2d Congress* 1000 [Manufactures include] Pasteboards, fullers or presspapers, paperhangings.

+**Press report.** A report or news item given to or appearing in the press or newspapers. — **1868** *N.Y. Herald* 10 July 4/2 Another Question of Privilege—The Press Reports. **1899** *N.Y. Journal* 10 Aug. 14/4 How can they, with all press reports censored as they are?

Pressroom. The room in a printing establishment where the presses are. {1683–} — **1868** BAGBY *Old Va. Gentleman* 190 The printing floor, the press-room, the sale and distribution of papers, mailing [etc.] . . . were all attended to by R. F. Walker, the manager. **1882** MCCABE *New York* 596 The press-rooms . . . are connected with the composing-rooms by elevators. **1916** SEITZ *Training for Newsp. Trade* 108 The ordinary press-hand in a press room receives by the New York standard $25 per week for six night hours, and 7½ day.

Presswork.

1. The printing off at a printing press of what has been set up in type. {1771–}

1771 FRANKLIN *Autobiog.* 280 In America . . . presswork is mix'd with composing. **1860** *36th Congress 1 Sess.* H. R. Rep. No. 249, 36 Twenty-six cents per page per thousand impressions, of sixteen pages, presswork. **1882** WHITMAN *Spec. Days* 195, [I] did most of the work myself, including the press-work.

2. Work done in connection with advertising.

Freq. in theatrical use and usually two words. (Cf. PRESS AGENT.)

1895 *N.Y. Dramatic News* 9 Nov. 5/4 He has now been relieved of the press work by M. J. Keating, formerly of The Traveler and press agent of the Plant steamers. *Ib.* 7 Dec. 17/1 Mr. Meyer . . . did some excellent press work for the company.

Pretty. {1773–} ?An ornament or article of clothing. {1882} — **1736** *Boston News-Letter* (Earle), Children's Silver Peaks & Flowers, Dutch Prettys.

+**Pretty-by-night.** The marvel-of-Peru (*Mirabilis julapa*), which blooms late in the afternoon. (Cf. FOUR-O'CLOCK 1.) — **1872** EGGLESTON *End of World* 169 She planted some pretty-by-nights in an old cracked blue-and-white tea-pot. **1892** *Amer. Folk-Lore* V. 102 *Mirabilis Jalapa*, pretty-by-night. Fort Worth, Tex. **1910** C. HARRIS *Eve's Husband* 275 The 'pretty by nights' under the windows . . . refused to consider the tragedy of Adam's unfaithfulness.

+**Pretzel.** [G. *prezel.*] A kind of brittle, salted bread or German biscuit, often made in the form of a knot or ring. — **1874** PINKERTON *Expressman & Detective* 64 He laid in . . . an abundance of 'pretzels.' **1883** SWEET & KNOX *Through Texas* 228 Fritz . . . [turned] over to his creditors half a gross of *pretzels* and a grindstone. **1901** WHITE *Westerners* 116 She seized a pretzel from a tin pan at her side and threw it at Peter.

***Previous,** *adv.* and *a. colloq.* +**1.** *adv.* Hastily, precipitously. +**2.** *Too previous*, too hasty, premature. — **(1) 1883** PECK *Bad Boy* 85 When I saw Pa feeling under the bed for a bed slat I got up stairs pretty previous now. **(2) 1890** *Boston Jrnl.* 21 June 2/3 The grumbling in this matter has been too previous. **1895** *Boston Herald* 11 May 6/6 Summer is too previous. **1900** HALE *Letters* 356 Carla Atkinson is coming here to lunch with me, . . . but I'm too previous, and she won't be here for half an hour.

Previousness. {1677–} +The state of being 'too previous'; improper haste. *colloq.* — **1884** *Boston Jrnl.* 4 March 2/1 (*caption*), A Case of Previousness. **1885** *Ib.* 16 April 2/1 Mr. Peck seems to be the victim of his own over-confidence and indiscreet previousness. **1892** *Law Times* XCIII. 413/1 His previousness, however, is not always effective.

Previous question. {1700–} +In a deliberative body, the question of whether the immediately pending question or questions shall be voted on at once with little or no further debate.

In the U.S. the previous question is now used as a device to limit debate and bring the immediate question to a vote. In England it is used to postpone action on the main question.

[**1710** SEWALL *Diary* II. 288 After reading papers and debates, at last they who were against the precinct, mov'd that a previous Vote might be put; whether would vote it now, or no; and the Council was divided, so nothing was done. [Ed. note (1879): This is an old form of the Previous Question, which is still in use in England.]] **1739** *Boston Rec.* 220 A previous Question was put. . . . Voted in the Affirmative. **1814** *Mass. Spy* 28 Dec. 3/2 The last nail [in the adoption of the conscription bill] was driven by that infernal hammer, the previous question. **1835** CROCKETT *Tour* 24 Having been cut out of my speech in Congress, by the 'previous question,' . . . I owe the country a speech. **1867** *Congress. Globe* 20 Feb. 1639/1 It is not filibustering when gentlemen . . . vote against the call for the previous question. **1896** *Internat. Typogr. Union Proc.* 2/1 Upon the previous question being ordered, [they] were unanimously adopted by a rising vote.

+**Prex.** A students' term for a college president. *slang.* — **1828** *Yankee* I. 232/1 Our Prex says this:—You surely miss [etc.]. **1851** *Amherst Indicator* III. 228 Good old Prex used to get the students together and advise them on keeping their faces clean. **1871** BAGG *At Yale* 655 The students, among themselves, rarely mention his name unless preceded with the title 'Prex,' which is oftener used alone to designate him. **1906** *N.Y. Evening Post* 11 June 6 If the various unpopular 'Prexes' would study the grounds of their unpopularity, they would find it in the quasi-servile position they have forced upon many of their faculty.

+**Prexy.** =prec. Also as title. *slang.* — **1871** BAGG *At Yale* 655 The title 'Prex' . . . is oftener used alone to designate him [the president] among the Seniors, the modified form of 'Prexy' is somewhat in vogue, in familiar talk. **1896** MOE *Hist. Harvard* 34 When Prexy Chauncy took hold of Harvard in 1654, the financial grab-bags of the College had big holes in their bottoms. **1905** *N.Y. Ev. Post* 1 Sept. 7 Scores of entering classes are lined up in chapel to listen to good advice from the dean or 'Prexie.'

+**Price catalogue.** A catalogue that lists the prices of certain goods. — **1861** *Chicago Tribune* 26 May 1/9 Illustrated price Catalogues of Pianos and Melodeons sent free of charge.

Price current. {1696–}

1. The current price of a given commodity. *Obs.*

1649 *Boston Rec.* 95 [Rent is] to be payd . . . in corne or porke at the prize curant. **1666** *Plymouth Laws* 149 All damages . . . shalbee payed in any good current Countrey pay at prise current. **1766** *Boston Ev. Post* 4 Aug. 2/3 Price current of merchantable potash in New York.

2. A statement of prevailing prices of commodities; a price list. {1696–}

Both *prices current* and *price currents* are used as the plural in America; only the latter is common in Britain.

1815 *Niles' Reg.* IX. 3/2 This account of the *selling prices* of the several stocks mentioned, is taken from the *public prices current* of the two places. **1828** *Yankee* I. 145/2 Of most of our large papers, seven eighths are made up either of advertisements or of ship-news, and commercial-news, price-currents, etc. **1856** *Mich. Agric. Soc. Trans.* VII. 533 A glance at our 'prices current' might suffice to satisfy the most incredulous. **1877** *Harper's Mag.* Dec. 37/2 They had cut out scraps from price-currents, and pieced them together.

+**Price Raid.** [Sterling *Price* (1809–67), Confederate general who raided Kansas in October, 1864.] **1.** *Price Raid commission*, a commission appointed to inquire into the validity of the Price Raid claims. **2.** *Price Raid claim*, one of the claims made for money by volunteers who had taken part in resisting the Price Raid. (See next.) — **(1) 1867** in D. W. Wilder *Annals of Kan.* (1886) 458 These forged or fabricated claims purport to have been sworn to before the Secretary of the Price Raid Commission. **(2) 1869** *Ib.* 510 The State of Kansas has . . . assumed Price Raid claims to the amount of half a million, . . . which ought to be paid by the General Government.

+**Price Raid scrip.** Scrip issued by the Kansas government, and redeemed in part by Congress in 1872, to satisfy the Price Raid claims. — **1872** in D. W. Wilder *Annals of Kan.* (1886) 565 There have been audited claims for which the scrip commonly known as the Price Raid Scrip has been issued or ordered to be issued. **1873** *Winfield* (Kan.) *Courier* 11 Jan. 3/4 Price raid scrip wanted.

+**Price tag.** A tag marked with a price and attached to a commodity for sale. — **1881** *Harper's Mag.* Sept. 587/1 He . . . busied his hands nervously in untying a little green price tag from the handle of the umbrella. **1888** *Chautauquan* VIII. 422 Accordingly they attached 'etiquettes,' or price-tags, to their articles. **1907** 'O. HENRY' *Roads of Destiny* 74 If the beauty of Fergus McMahan gained any part of our reception . . . , I'll eat the price-tag in my Panama.

***Prick,** *n.* +A pricker or priming wire. — **1859** *Kan. State Hist. Soc. Trans.* V. 581 Ordnance stores this day turned over to Samuel Medary, . . . 100 cap pouches and pricks, worn.

***Prick,** *v.* +**1.** *tr.* To prod (powder) into a touch-hole with a pricker. *Obs.* +**2.** To pierce or cut the tail of (a horse) in such a way as to cause him to carry the tail high. (Cf. NICK-TAILED *a.*) +**3.** (See quotation.) — **(1) 1775** *Mass. H. S. Coll.* 2 Ser. II. 292, I order'd my men . . . to prick dry Powder into the Touchholes. **(2) 1868** WOODRUFF *Trotting Horse* 228 It was the fashion to have horses pricked and docked. **(3) 1862** *Army Lett.* 89, I've been in the service over a year now and I've never been 'pricked' (marked absent without leave).

***Pricker.** An instrument for piercing or pricking, esp. a sharp, wirelike instrument for keeping open the touchhole of an old-time musket; a priming wire.

1645 *Conn. Rec.* I. 464 Goods prysed by Gyles Smith . . . 1 priker. **1775** *Jrnls. Cont. Congress* III. 460 *Resolved*, That the battalion . . . be supplied with gun brushes, prickers [etc.]. **1781** *Va. State P.* I. 416, 2 Priming Horns and Prickers. **1876** KNIGHT 1787/2 *Pricker*, . . . a tool used to mark stitch-holes so as to render them uniform in distance. **1884** *Nat. Museum Bul.* No. 27, 778 Splicer or pricker. . . . Used for splicing trawl-lines.

Prickleback. Any of several small fishes of the family Gasterosteidae having two or more spines on the back; a stickleback. {1746-} — **1860** *Harper's Mag.* March 488/2 Did you ever, when you were a boy, catch a little fish that goes by the name of Stickleback, Prickleback, . . . and a few others?

***Prickly, *a.* In the specific names of plants and trees.**

Only a selection of examples is given. (See also PRICKLY ASH, PRICKLY GOOSEBERRY, etc.)

1737 BRICKELL *N. Carolina* 22 Prickly Bind-Weed . . . groweth in North Carolina. **1858** WARDER *Hedges & Evergreens* 250 *Pinus sabiniana,* or Prickly-coned Pine, has long leaves. **1784** Prickly devil's-bit [see DEVIL'S-BIT]. **1860** CURTIS *Woody Plants N.C.* 20 Prickly pine. (*P. pungens.*) . . . I have never learned that the timber of this tree is of any special value. **1847** EMORY *Military Reconn.* 11 The low grounds abound in prickly rush. **1802** DRAYTON *S. Carolina* 65 Carolinian Glasswort or prickly salt wort, . . . Jerusalem oak. (*Chenopodium Anthelminticum.*) A noxious weed, growing in dry grounds. **1819** E. DANA *Geogr. Sk.* 238 In addition to the larger growth, is an indefinite variety of vines, underwood, and shrubbery—such as Spanish mulberry, prickly sumach, [and] mascadine.

+Prickly ash.

1. a. =ANGELICA TREE. (Cf. HERCULES'-CLUB.) **b.** A prickly aromatic shrub, *Zanthoxylum americanum.* **c.** A similar shrub (*Z. clava-herculis*) of the South.

1709 LAWSON *Carolina* 101 Prickly-Ash grows up like a Pole; of which the Indians and English make Poles to set their Canoes along in Shoal-Water. **1743** CLAYTON *Flora Virginica* 150 *Aralia,* . . . Gambriar & Prickly-ash. **1808** PIKE *Sources Miss.* 31 The whole bottom [is] covered with the prickly ash. **1821** NUTTALL *Travels Arkansa* 76, I saw here a prickly-ash (*Zanthoxylion Clava Herculis*), the size of an ordinary ash. **1843** TORREY *Flora N.Y.* I. 132 *Zanthoxylum Americanum.* Common Prickly Ash. . . . Banks of rivers and lakes and in rocky woods. **1860** CURTIS *Woody Plants N.C.* 91 Prickly ash. (*Aralia spinosa.*) . . . The berries . . . are thought by some to be also a valuable remedy for the bite of a rattlesnake. **1899** GOING *Flowers* 74 Prickly-ash, and hackberry . . . are thus unsystematic in their mode of conducting their affairs.

2. Used as the source of medicines. Also attrib.

Cf. TOOTHACHE BUSH.

1778 CARVER *Travels* 393 The chief . . . prepared for him a decoction of the bark of the roots of the prickly ash. **1792** POPE *Tour S. & W.* 97 A Decoction from the Root of prickly Ash, is a good Purgative. **1817** *N. Amer. Rev.* IV. 176 This day purchased of a man on the road, two cents worth of prickly ash bark, an infallible remedy for all diseases. **1824** E. PETTIGREW *Let. to J. H. Bryan* 5 Oct. (Univ. N.C. MS.), I think I have been benefited by the Prickly ash bark and Gin.

+Prickly beaver. The porcupine. — **1845** DE SMET *Oregon Missions* (1847) 155 The American porcupine, the *Hystrix dorsata,* is called by modern Zoologists, the *Prickly Beaver.*

+Prickly gooseberry. The wild gooseberry, *Grossularia cynosbati.* — — **1795** WINTERBOTHAM *Hist. View* III. 393 Prickly gooseberry, *Ribes cynosbati.* **1833** EATON *Botany* (ed. 6) 305 Prickly gooseberry. . . . Berries prickly, dark brown, . . . Catskill Mt. **1860** CURTIS *Woody Plants N.C.* 84 Prickly gooseberry. . . . Distinguished from the others by its prickly fruit, which is brownish when ripe, and eatable.

+Prickly heat. (See quot. 1859.) {1898-} — **1736** WESLEY *Works* I. (1829) 36, I found she had only the prickly heat, a sort of rash, very common here [Savannah, Ga.] in summer. **1774** CRESSWELL *Journal* 18 [The Americans] call it the Prickly heat and say it is very wholesome. **1818** FLINT *Lett. from Amer.* 10 For two days past, the skin of my face has been spotted, accompanied with blotches, and with partial swelling. This is called the prickly heat, from the pungent feeling that attends it. **1859** BARTLETT 342 *Prickly Heat,* a cutaneous eruption or rash which appears during the excessive heat of summer.

+Prickly pear. Also †**prickle pear.**

1. a. The pear-shaped fruit of any flat-jointed cactus of the genus *Opuntia.* **b.** Any cactus of this genus. {1760-}

Cf. INDIAN FIG, OPUNTIA.

*c*1618 STRACHEY *Virginia* 119 Here is a cherry-redd fruict both within and without . . . which wee call the prickle peare. **1737** [see INDIAN FIG]. **1775** ROMANS *Nat. Hist. Florida* App. p. xxxvi, *Sandy Key* is a low key covered with some bushes and prickly-pears. **1802** DRAYTON *S. Carolina* 6 Their soil is of very sandy nature; producing . . . tooth-ache tree, prickly pear. **1834** A. PIKE *Sketches* 57 Finding some very large, deep purple, prickly pears, Lewis and myself ate of them. **1858** *Los Angeles Star* 8 Jan., [The camels lived] upon bushes, prickly pears and whatever they could pick up on the route. **1893** ROOSEVELT *Wilderness Hunter* 356 Mixed among them were prickly pears, standing as high as our heads on horseback. **1923** J. H. COOK *On Old Frontier* 27 When the acorn crop was good and the mesquite beans and prickly pears were abundant, horses, cattle, hogs, and turkeys would get very fat.

2. Attrib. with *bush, leaf, shrub.*

1739 *Ga. Hist. Soc. Coll.* I. 188 The islands in Georgia are full of the prickly pear shrubs which feed flies. **1846** in Claiborne *Life Quitman* I. 286 There were still the same stunted chapparal, disagreeable prickly-pear bushes, and infinity of stones of all sizes. **1923** Prickly-pear leaf [see FREIGHTER 2].

+Prickly-pear cactus. =prec., sense 1. — **1857** GRAY *Lessons Botany* 96 We discern the stem . . . in the flattened joints of the Prickly-Pear Cactus. **1897** *Outing* XXIX. 582/1 Temescal Wash is a mile wide and composed of sand and prickly pear cactus. **1923** J. H. COOK *On Old Frontier* 29 The cattle seemed to be very fond of the prickly-pear cactus, and would eat them in spite of thorns.

+Prickly poppy. Any plant of the genus *Argemone,* esp. the Mexican poppy (q.v.). — **1836** EATON *Botany* (ed. 7) 168 *Argemone mexicana,* prickly poppy. . . . Platte River. **1869** *Amer. Naturalist* III. 163 The Prickly Poppy (*Argemone*) looks now like a common thistle. **1898** A. M. DAVIDSON *Calif. Plants* 112 In sandy washes, later in the season, the prickly poppy will send out great white flowers with crumpled petals and a great many yellow stamens.

+Prickly ray. A species of skate, *Raja eglanteria.* — **1842** *Nat. Hist. N.Y., Zoology* IV. 368 The Prickly Ray. . . . I have never seen but the single specimen . . . found on the shore of Staten Island, Richmond county.

+Pride of China. =next. Also attrib. — **1785** WASHINGTON *Diaries* II. 383 Next 3 rows of the Seed of the Pride of China. **1831** ROYALL *Southern Tour* II. 83 The pride of China . . . in full bloom, . . . the genial sunshine, and the pleasant shade [in Savannah]—I have no name for the scene! **1835** INGRAHAM *South-West* II. 101 The 'pride of China,'—the universal shade tree in the south-west. **1865** RICHARDSON *Secret Service* 79 The Pride of China tree was very abundant about the dwellings. **1901** MOHR *Plant Life Ala.* 588 Pride of China. Bead Tree. . . . Of some value for lumber.

+Pride of India. The China tree, *Melia azedarach.*

Cf. prec., BEAD TREE, CHINA TREE 1.

1803 J. DAVIS *Travels* 79 The mocking-bird . . . was warbling, close to my window, from a tree called by some the Pride of *India,* and by others the Poison-berry Tree. **1810** LAMBERT *Travels* II. 365 A tree, called the *pride of India,* (*melia azedarach*) is planted in rows along the foot-paths of the streets in Charleston. **1847** DARLINGTON *Weeds & Plants* 69 Pride of India [or] Bead-tree. . . . This tree has been introduced into the Southern States as an ornamental shade tree. **1892** APGAR *Trees Northern U.S.* 75.

b. Attrib. with *tree.*

1841 *S. Lit. Messenger* VII. 37/2, The spring-house . . . [stands] under the fostering patronage of a cluster of catalpas, a solitary cedar, and a Pride-of-India tree. **1893** *Harper's Mag.* April 756/2 This causeway broadened into a sandy street under huge pride-of-India trees, whose branches met overhead.

+Pride of Ohio. (See quotation and cf. AMERICAN COWSLIP, COWSLIP 1 b.) — **1861** WOOD *Botany* 503 *Dodecatheon.* . . . Pride of Ohio. . . . *D. Meadia.* . . . A singularly elegant herb, on prairies, dry or rocky soils, Penn. to Ind., Ill., Wisc. and throughout the Western States.

+Pride of the West. Cincinnati, Ohio. A nickname. — **1835** HOFFMAN *Winter in West* II. 120, I could not but admit that the amphitheatre of green hills opposite me did really shut in 'The Pride of the West.'

+Prideweed. The horseweed, *Leptilon canadense.* (Cf. COLT'S-TAIL 2, FIREWOOD 2, FLEABANE.) — **1817-8** EATON *Botany* (1822) 273 *Erigeron canadense,* fleabane, pride-weed. . . . Powdered leaves useful in stopping blood. **1821** *Mass. H. S. Coll.* 2 Ser. IX. 150 *Erigeron canadense,* Prideweed. **1845** LINCOLN *Botany* App. 101/2.

***Priest.**

***1.** A Christian clergyman; a member of the clerical profession.

In the strict usage of hierarchical churches, a priest stands above a deacon and below a bishop.

***a.** A Catholic clergyman.

Now the usual sense unless otherwise indicated.

1649 *Md. Archives* I. 245 [Whoever shall call anyone a] Prespiterian popish prest, Jesuite, Jesuited papist, . . . in a reproachfull manner . . . [shall] loose the somme of tenne shillings. **1721** *Mass. H. Rep. Jrnl.* III. 117 Resolved, . . . that Monsieur Rallee, and any other French Priest Residing among them [the Indians], be seized, secured, and sent to Boston. **1808** PIKE *Sources Miss.* III. App. 7 The third side [of the Santa Fe plaza] is occupied by the priests and their suit. **1847** D. VIGIL in *Santa Fe Republican* 11 Dec. 1/4 The Priests wish to control them [*sc.* burial grounds] entirely, and they frequently exact enormous sums from the poor for the privilege of burying their relatives. **1883** *Harper's Mag.* Aug. 338/2 There is . . . a boys' school carried on by priests. **1909** H. C. SHELDON *Sacerdotalism* 276 A priest of the coarser grain occupies the confessional.

***b.** A Protestant clergyman.

Often used to designate a clergyman of a different faith from the one held by the speaker or writer, e.g., a Congregational clergyman, formerly called a priest by the Quakers.

1786 *New Haven Gazette* 5 Oct. 267/2 (Th. S.), The priest [a married 'minister'] took the hint. **1800** *Aurora* (Phila.) 23 Dec. (Th.), All the priests of the state [of Conn.]. **1808** [see INSTITUTOR]. **1856** *Congress. Globe* 10 April 862/3 'What was the preacher's name?' . . . 'Beecher. . . . He is a priest; but, of course, he does not worship as Christ worshiped.' **1925** *Const. & Canons P.E. Ch. Montana* 20 Any Priest or Deacon of the Diocese may, for himself, request of the Bishop the inquiry provided for in this Canon.

+2. An Indian conjurer or medicine man. {a pagan minister, *c*1250-}

1676 GLOVER *Va.* in *Phil. Trans.* XI. 633 The Indians . . . have Priests, which are generally thought to be Conjurers. **1812** WILSON *Ornithology*

VI. 54 The priests, or conjurers, among some of our Indian nations, . . . have adopted the Great Horned Owl . . . as the symbol . . . of their office. **1849** *31st Congress 1 Sess.* Sen. Ex. Doc. No. 64, 68 From this Indian [at Jemez] I also learned . . . that they have priests to administer their own religion. **1873** MILLER *Amongst Modocs* 39 Their priest or medicine man . . . chaunts the death-song.

***3.** A rabbi.

1689 SEWALL *Diary* I. 269 This 29th July the Jews have great joy by reason of a Priest come to Town in the Harwich Coach, they having not had one a long time.

Priestly. A variety of apple tree or its fruit. Also in possessive. — **1806** *Balance* V. 140/1 Plant the largest growing trees, such as priestly's on the north side. **1818** *Amer. Monthly Mag.* II. 428/2 Table Apples [include] . . . Priestly, November.

***Prim. a.** The privet (*Ligustrum vulgare*), widely planted for hedges. **+b.** One of various related American species. — **1709** LAWSON *Carolina* 90 We have a Prim or Privet, which grows on the dry, barren, sandy Hills, by the Sound side. **1784** *Amer. Acad. Mem.* I. 402 *Ligustrum.* . . . Prim. Privet. A shrub . . . not very common in a wild state. **1814** BIGELOW *Florula Bostoniensis* 5 *Ligustrum vulgare*, Privet or Prim. . . . Frequent in woods and near fences, particularly in Roxbury. **1857** GRAY *Botany* 356 *L[igustrum] vulgare.* (Common Privet or Prim.) . . . Used for low hedges: naturalized in copses by the agency of birds in E. New England and New York.

***Primage.** A customary sum allowed to the master and crew of a vessel for loading and care of a cargo: (see also quot. 1895). — **1643** *Maine Doc. Hist.* III. 357 Pd the master for primage. **1755** *R.I. Commerce* I. 63 You shall have in lieu of Primage [etc.]. **1895** E. CARROLL *Principles Finance* 300 *Primage*, a percentage allowed by shippers to the owners or charterers of a vessel for the loading of goods.

‖**Primarian.** *Educ.* A pupil in a primary school. — **1883** *Education* July 637 It is . . . important for a primarian to develop a keen perception of relations in respect to the words of his reader.

Primary, *n.* {*a*1721– in various ellipt. uses}

This word, short for PRIMARY ASSEMBLY OR MEETING and PRIMARY ELECTION, has exclusively American currency in the senses that follow.

+1. =PRIMARY MEETING.

***a*1861** WINTHROP *Open Air* 147, I accepted the office of Orator of the Day at our primary. **1873** 'MARK TWAIN' & WARNER *Gilded Age* 530 The nation of good and worthy people . . . continued to sit comfortably at home and leave the true source of our political power (the 'primaries') in the hands of saloon-keepers. **1882** *Nation* 28 Sept. 256/1 The decision of the question, who should be the Republican candidate for the Governorship . . . was in the hands of the politicians who 'fix' and 'run' primaries. **1900** *Congress. Rec.* 16 Feb. 1873/1 The political hack . . . by handling primaries or manipulating political conventions, has ingratiated himself into the favor of some political boss. **1912** NICHOLSON *Hoosier Chron.* 326 He had personally led the fight in the Fraser County primaries and had vanquished Bassett!

+2. A direct primary: (cf. sense 3).

The rules under which such primaries are held vary; e.g., in the closed primary the voter must be a member of the party whose ticket he votes; in an open primary such membership is not necessary.

1901 *Outlook* 2 March 477/2 The recent trial of direct primaries in Minneapolis, Minn., has forced every one to recognize that disinterested citizens will attend primaries . . . if they are allowed to vote directly for candidates. **1913** WILSON in *N.Y. Times* 3 Dec. 2/4 This legislation should provide for the retention of party conventions, but only for the purpose of declaring and accepting the verdict of the primaries and formulating the platforms of the parties. **1924** *Lit. Digest* 6 Sept. 7/1 In Democratic Texas success in the Democratic primary is equivalent to election.

+b. *Run-off primary*, (see quotation).

1924 *Lit. Digest* 6 Sept. 8/2 Texas . . . has a double primary. If no one has a majority in the first primary election, a later 'run-off' primary is held, in which the voters choose between the two candidates receiving the highest number of votes at the first balloting.

+3. *Direct primary*, a preliminary election in which the people vote for the nomination of party candidates; the method or system of such an election. Also attrib.

1900 *Outlook* 8 Sept. 91/2 The important political news last week was all connected . . . with the issue of direct primaries. **1902** MEYER *Nominating Systems* 71 Several [reforms], the 'Clark system,' the scheme of the 'open book,' and the direct primary, will be reviewed. **1913** *N.Y. Times* 11 Nov. 7/1 The matter of direct primaries as an issue was revived to-day when Gov. Glynn told Senate Leader Wagner . . . that the Legislature ought to pass a genuine direct primaries bill.

+4. Attrib. in senses 1 and 2 with *campaign, convention, law, system.*

1900 *Congress. Rec.* 22 Jan. 1036/2 The nomination of the primary convention settles the whole business. *Ib.* 31 Jan. 1369/1 It was in a Democratic primary campaign. **1902** MEYER *Nominating Systems* 19 The primary . . . is summoned by the local party managing committee or some other prescribed authority . . . under statutory law, where caucus or primary laws have been enacted. **1913** *Forum* July 53 The remedy for all the evils of every known primary system is direct elections.

***Primary,** *a.* Of or pertaining to education in a primary school. {1802–} — **1837** PECK *New Guide* 347 Number of students in collegiate, academical and primary departments [of Augusta College, Ky.], about 200. **1842** MANN *Oration 4 July* 33 For every dollar given by the wealthy, . . . to cultivate the higher branches of knowledge, a hundred should have been given for primary education. **1883** *Harper's Mag.* Sept. 648/1 A teacher in one of the primary classes at Malden, Massachusetts, had been teaching the little ones under her care the meaning of horizontal and vertical lines. **1894** *Ib.* May 942/1 The outcome of the movement was the building of three large school-houses . . . having each one accommodations for primary and grammar departments.

Primary assembly. =PRIMARY MEETING. {1789, of French politics} — **1801** *Spirit Farmers' Mus.* 61 The Editor of the Gazette of the United States . . . notices the 'Primary Assemblies' of our towns. **1817** *Niles' Reg.* XIII. 210/1 Another *caucus* called the '*Primary assembly*,' . . . directed that Mr. *Ritchie*, and not Mr. *Mason*, should be supported. **1833** *Knickerb.* I. 291 With all his power over the people in their primary assemblies—he seems to lack certain of the gifts of a great practical politician. **1884** *Century Mag.* Nov. 127 The primary assemblies which appoint the delegates to the nominating conventions notoriously embrace but a small part of the voters of a party.

+Primary caucus. =PRIMARY MEETING. — **1821** *Mass. Spy* 11 April (Th.), And this was all the hocus-pocus of a primary caucus. **1902** MEYER *Nominating Systems* 7 A new institution, the 'representative caucus,' [was] composed of delegates selected in primary caucuses held in case of cities in the wards, and in case of counties in the townships.

Primary court. A court of first jurisdiction. — **1880** *Harper's Mag.* Sept. 647/2 In one of these primary courts in that state [S.C.] . . . a case was on trial.

+Primary ditch. =LATERAL. — **1890** *Stock Grower & Farmer* 22 Feb. 8/2 The company undertakes to construct the primary ditches from the canals to the highest point on the line of each section.

Primary election. {1789, of French politics}

+1. An election at a primary meeting (q.v.); a caucus election.

1835 C. P. BRADLEY *I. Hill* 54 The freemen of the State were called upon to give, at their primary elections, an expression of their opinion. **1847** T. FORD *Hist. Illinois* (1854) 88 Personal politics . . . [was] carried from the primary elections into the legislature. **1895** *Century Mag.* Oct. 831/1 In a primary election held in Louisville . . . some voters in one district were openly paid as much as seventy-five dollars each.

+2. An election by a direct primary. Also attrib.

Etymologically derived from PRIMARY *n.* 2 used attrib. with *election.*

1901 *Amer. Rev. of Reviews* Oct. 465/1 The Minnesota primary election law, passed by the State Legislature during the session of 1899 . . . was extended . . . so as to make the nominations of candidates for all except State offices matters of direct popular choice. **1911** *Okla. Session Laws* 3 Legisl. 231 The secretary of the State Election Board shall . . . certify to the auditor of the state all the necessary expenses incurred in conducting . . . primary elections.

+Primary meeting. A meeting in a precinct, county, or other election district, at which voters belonging to the same political party take the first steps towards the nomination of party candidates, as by the selection of delegates to a convention; a caucus for choosing candidates.

1829 *Niles' Reg.* XXXVI. 363/2 The battle is in reality fought in the primary meetings, and not on the day appointed by law for the election. **1850** in Claiborne *Life Quitman* II. 39 These should be chosen by the Legislature, and the people in their primary meetings. **1872** *Newton Kansan* 17 Oct. 3/3 It is desired that there be a full attendance at the primary meetings, that the delegates chosen may fairly represent the voice of the people of Harvey county. **1885** *Century Mag.* April 825 Nine out of ten of our wealthy and educated men . . . are really ignorant of the nature of a caucus, or a primary meeting, and never attend either.

Primary school. The first school in which children are instructed; the first three or four grades of an elementary school. {1802–}

'In the broad meaning of the term, kindergarten classes are also included among the primary grades' (1913 Monroe, etc. *Cycl. Educ.* V. 29).

1817 in J. M. Wightman *Annals Boston Primary Sch. Com.* (1860) 22 Primary schools for children under the age of seven years. **1835** *S. Lit. Messenger* I. 275 Others classify them into 1st *primary* schools, where only spelling, reading, and writing are taught. **1879** *Scribner's Mo.* Dec. 202/1 The young men of Baltimore have open to them 'a well-considered system of instruction from the primary school to the university.' **1902** G. M. MARTIN *Emmy Lou* 107 And Miss Jenny was sent away to examine a Primary School in another district.

***Prime,** *a.*

1. Of a slave: First-class; the best quality. *Obs.*

1792 *Fayetteville* (N.C.) *Gaz.* 25 Sept., Thirteen Prime Slaves, Belonging to the same Estate. **1835** A. PARKER *Trip to Texas* 97, I was told that one prime hand on good land would *make* ten bales of cotton a year, and raise corn enough to support himself. **1852** in Stowe *Key* 135/2, 110 Prime and Likely Negroes, belonging to the Estate of the late John Robinson, of South Carolina.

2. Of live stock, meats, and fish: Of the best quality. {1884–; in generic sense, 1628–}

1819 *Amer. Farmer* I. 142 Salt Beef, prime pieces, 10. **1850** *Rep. Comm. Patents 1849: Agric.* 426 Prime Mess Pork has been a losing article. **1890** *Stock Grower & Farmer* 22 Feb. 4/2 *The Gazette* is a firm believer in a good steady market for prime cattle from this out. **1895** JEWETT *Nancy* 293, I shouldn't have bothered you so late about a mere fish, but they was such prime mackerel.

+**Prime,** *v.*[1] [?f. PRIME *a.* 2. Cf. PRIMING 1.] *tr.* To cut off the best parts of the carcass of (an animal). — **1738** BYRD *Dividing Line* (1901) 199 We only prim'd the Deer, being unwilling to be encumbered with their whole Carcasses.

***Prime,** *v.*[2] +*tr.* To pull off the lower leaves of (growing tobacco). — **1792** POPE *Tour S. & W.* 63 [The Creeks] scarcely ever weed, hill, prime, top or succour their Tobacco.

***Primer.**[1] Also †**primmer.**

***1.** A small elementary book for teaching children to read; a textbook for elementary instruction.

Cf. NEW ENGLAND PRIMER.

1645 *New Haven Col. Rec.* 176 She sold primmers at 9d. apeece. **1724** SEWALL *Letter-Book* II. 177 Delivered Thomas Umpas of the Vinyard, going a Fishing Voyage, One Primer English and Indian. **1772** TRUMBULL *Progress of Dulness* (1794) I. 5 [He] scorns to hesitate or faulter In primer, spelling book or psalter. **1809** WEEMS *Letters* II. 391 If they cou'd they wd get a guinea a piece for their John Rogers Primer. **1865** *Atlantic Mo.* XV. 243 Go from bed to bed, and you see in their hands primers, spelling-books, and Bibles. **1902** G. M. MARTIN *Emmy Lou* 10 But this morning he was at his desk copying from his Primer on to his slate.

2. Attrib. with *book, class, songbook, teacher.*

1856 SIMMS *Charlemont* 103 He died, like that blessed man, John Rogers, that we see in the primer-books, leaving a wife with eleven children. **1883** WILDER *Sister Ridnour* 191, I noticed the same in that beautiful little primer song-book Aunt Maria bought for Bessie. **1902** G. M. MARTIN *Emmy Lou* 3 Neither did she know any of the seventy other little boys and girls making the Primer Class. *Ib.* 5 The way of the Primer teacher was not made easy in a public school of twenty-five years ago.

***Primer.**[2] [f. *prime* v. 'to charge or load.'] +*transf.* An aperitif or appetizer. — **1862** *Harper's Mag.* Aug. 312/1 Notwithstanding the refreshment of a dozen on the half shell at Washington Market, and a primer, . . . which primer was simply a gill of Bourbon straight.

***Priming.**

‖**1.** A choice cut of meat. (Cf. PRIME *v.*[1])

1753 BYRD *Journey to Eden* (1901) 312 The Primeings of a young Doe . . . were slighted amidst these Daintys.

2. The gunpowder, usually superior in quality, used in the pan of a gun and ignited by a spark or flame. {1625–}

1775 *R.I. Hist. Soc. Coll.* VI. 3, I observed the flash of the priming of a gun. **1788** FRANKLIN *Autobiog.* 409 His and his companions' guns would not go off, the priming being wet with the rain. **1827** COOPER *Prairie* iii, He raised his rifle while he spoke, and assured himself of the state of its flint, as well as of the priming by manual examination. **1857** HAMMOND *Northern Scenes* 212, I had spattered water into the canoe, wettin' the primin' and makin' the gun of no more use than a stick.

+**b.** *fig.* and *allusive.* A small or trivial thing; a small part.

'As the *priming* bears but a small proportion to the charge of a gun, so this word is used in the West to denote any thing trivial' (B. '59).

1833 J. HALL *Harpe's Head* 88 You aint no part of a priming to me. **1843** STEPHENS *High Life N.Y.* I. 10, I can't begin to write more than a priming of what a feller may see as he goes up Broadway. **1847** *Knickerb.* July 14 It was 'all-nation hot inside the clap-boards,' but not a 'priming' to what it was 'down where the rich man is crying for water.'

+**3.** *pl.* The tobacco leaves pulled off the growing plant.

Cf. PRIME *v.*[2]

1899 M. L. FLOYD *Cultivation of Cigar-Leaf Tobacco* 14 The first priming, which means the first four leaves taken from the stalk, also the last priming, which means the last four or six leaves taken from the top of the stalk, are kept separate. **1904** GLASGOW *Deliverance* 166 The very primings ought to be as good as some top leaves.

4. Attrib. in sense 2 with *horn, iron, needle.*

1702 *Essex Inst. Coll.* XLII. 162 Inventory of Ship . . . a parcell of priming Irons, wire, &c for great gunns. **1781** *Va. State P.* I. 417, 2 Sponges & Rammers, 2 Priming Horns. **1838** *N.Y. Advertiser & Exp.* 12 May 1/5 The Fuse . . . [supersedes] the use of the metallic priming-needle.

***Priming wire.** A sharp wire put through the touchhole of a gun to clear it and to penetrate the powder cartridge before priming; a priming iron. — **1709** *Conn. Rec.* XV. 565 Agreed, That the souldiers of the train bands . . . [meet] with a good firelock, a cartouch box, priming-wire [etc.]. **1776** *N.H. Laws* IV. (1916) 42 Every Officer and private Soldier . . . shall equip himself . . . with a good Fire Arm, good Ramrod, a Worm, Priming Wire and Brush. **1824** DODDRIDGE *Notes* 169 Even the want of any article of war equipments, such as ammunition, a sharp flint, a priming wire, a scalping knife or tomahawk was thought highly disgraceful.

+**Primitive Baptist.** =OLD SCHOOL BAPTIST. Also attrib. — **1851** *Polly Peablossom* 143 Brethren Crump and Noel were both members of the Primitive Baptist Church. **1872** MORRELL *Flowers & Fruits* 72 There was also an organization calling themselves 'Primitive Baptists,' on the Colorado River. **1901** *Harper's Mag.* Dec. 99, I am ashamed of being a Primitive Baptist! **1910** *Census: Religious Bodies 1906* II. 151 Colored Primitive Baptists. . . . The rite of foot-washing is observed.

Primp, *v.* {1801–} +*intr.* To dress or 'fix' up smartly; to 'spruce up.' — **1881** RITTENHOUSE *Maud* 1 Eva . . . pulled down her basque, 'primped' at her hair, . . . and looked expectantly towards the door. **1896** HARRIS *Sister Jane* 160 Mandy had withdrawn to primp a little, as women will do. **1904** *N.Y. Tribune* 31 July, Miss Nellie herself was puff-powdering and primping before the mirror. **1906** F. LITTLE *Lady of Decoration* 49 Those old fellows . . . giggled and primped like a lot of school girls!

Primpy, *a.* (See quotation.) — **1859** BARTLETT 342 *Primpy,* fastidious in the duties of the toilet, finical. A woman's word.

***Primrose. a.** =EVENING PRIMROSE. **b.** Any plant or flower of the genus *Primula.* (Cf. BIRD'S-EYE PRIMROSE.)

1784 *Amer. Acad. Mem.* I. 438 *Oenothera.* . . . Primrose. Common in old fields. **1791** MUHLENBERG *Index Florae* 163 *Primula, veris,* Primrose. **1818** BRYANT *Poetical Works* 4 On the infant's little bed, . . . Nestled the lowly primrose. **1898** A. M. DAVIDSON *Calif. Plants* 113 This primrose appears rather early in the spring.

***Prince.**

+**1. a.** A wealthy business man or industrialist. (Cf. KING 3 b.) **b.** A paragon *of* something.

(a) 1841 BUCKINGHAM *America* III. 427 Capitalists and merchants [of Boston] . . . are here called 'princes.' **1884** *Century Mag.* Sept. 796 At a shady end of the veranda, are seen the railroad king, . . . the bonanza mine owner, the Texas rancher, and the Pennsylvania iron prince. **(b) 1852** EASTMAN *Aunt Phillis's Cabin* 230 Mark was a perfect prince of a driver.

2. Used in the possessive: **a.** In the names of a certain corduroy fabric. {1810–}

1784 *Mass. Centinel* 16 June 3/3 Tomorrow, will be sold . . . Calimancoes, Princes Stuff. **1841** Cist *Cincinnati* 179 Among other goods advertised [in 1801], I notice muslinets, japaned muslins, princes rib [etc.].

+**b.** In the names of various apples and berries.

Possibly from a personal surname.

1817 W. COXE *Fruit Trees* 101 Princes Harvest . . . is a very fine apple for stewing when green, and when ripe is a very pleasant eating apple. *Ib.* 109 Fall, or Holland Pippin . . . appears to be the same with Princes large Pippin of New-York. **1862** *Rep. Comm. Patents 1861: Agric.* 198 *Prince's Scarlet Climax.* . . . Bright scarlet, fine flavor, very productive, a splendid market berry.

Prince Albert. [From *Prince Albert,* Prince Consort of England (1819–61).] (See quot. 1890.) In full *Prince Albert coat.* — **1890** WEBSTER 1138/2 *Prince Albert coat,* a long double-breasted frock coat for men. **1896** NORRIS *Stories & Sk.* (1931) 211 He wears an inexpensive 'Prince Albert' invariably unbuttoned to show the flowered design of his waistcoat. **1902** FITCH *Captain Jinks* (1915) II. 314 'What do you want this hundred for?' 'For a new Prince Albert and a swallow-tail suit.' **1920** COOPER *Under Big Top* 127 An elderly gentleman . . . affected a silk hat, Prince Albert and cane.

Prince's-feather. {1629–} One of various plants, as the gentleman's cane (*Persicaria orientalis*), the annual *Amaranthus hybridus hypochondriacus,* etc. {1721–}

1817–8 EATON *Botany* (1822) 401 *Polygonum orientale,* prince's feather. . . . It has become naturalized in many places. **1845** *Lowell Offering* V. 257 We must not forget . . . the prince's feathers, to say nothing of the tansy in the corners of the yard. **1847** WOOD *Botany* 471 *A[maranthus] hypochondriacus.* Prince's Feather. . . . This species is native in the Middle States, and cultivated often as a garden annual. **1885** 'CRADDOCK' *Prophet* 175 The 'prince's feathers' bloomed in great clumsy crimson tufts close by the step. **1893** 'MARK TWAIN' *P. Wilson* i, Each . . . had a garden . . . stocked with hollyhocks, marigolds, touch-me-nots, prince's-feathers, and other old-fashioned flowers. **1919** STURTEVANT *Notes on Edible Plants* 43 *A[maranthus] paniculatus.* . . . Prince's Feather . . . North America and naturalized in the Orient.

+**Prince's pine.**

1. The pipsissewa, *Chimaphila corymbosa.* {1891}

1817–8 EATON *Botany* (1822) 236 *Chimaphila umbellata,* prince's pine, bitter wintergreen. . . . Both species are tonics and diuretics. **1840** DEWEY *Mass. Flowering Plants* 107 Prince's Pine. . . . A decoction of the plant has been supposed to be a remedy for cancer. **1869** FULLER *Flower Gatherers* 156, I like the Indian name, though the more common one is 'Prince's Pine.' **1899** VAN DYKE *Fisherman's Luck* 73 Prince's Pine and golden loose-strife and pink laurel . . . and a score of lovely flowers were all abloom.

2. (See quotation.)

1884 SARGENT *Rep. Forests* 201 *Pinus Banksiana.* . . . Gray Pine. Scrub Pine. Prince's Pine.

+**Prince's piny.** ? = prec., sense 1. *colloq.* — **1858** COOKE in *Atlantic Mo.* March 526/2 [We were] always out in the woods between schools, huntin' checker-berries, and young winter-greens, and prince's piney. **1861** *Harper's Mag.* Oct. 652/1 [She] hung the shelf above the chimney with bundles of . . . sweet fern, sweet-cicely, prince's piny, sassafras root [etc.].

+**Prince's pride.** =PRINCE'S PINE 1. — **1859** BARTLETT 323 *Pipsissewa*, . . . a popular domestic remedy, much used by the Indians and now of the U.S. Pharmacopœia. Also called Prince's Pride and Wintergreen.

***Principal.** {of a college, 1563–} +The head, or one of the heads, of a primary or secondary school.

1833 in *Century Mag.* XXX. 780/1, I am, sir, . . . permitted to be the Principal of the Canterbury (Conn.) Female Boarding School. **1851** CIST *Cincinnati* 55 Each of the school districts, occupying a School Building, has a Male Principal and a Female Principal. **1881** *Ore. State Jrnl.* 1 Jan. 5/2 Prof. Gatch . . . [has] accepted the position of principal of The Dalles Academy. **1901** HARTE in *Harper's Mag.* Dec. 70 'No! no!' interrupted the horrified principal.

+**Principal chief.** =HEAD CHIEF. — **1866** *Rep. Indian Affairs* 89 To attempt to conclude a treaty of peace with Howlock, principal chief of a tribe of Snake Indians not treated with. **1891** O'BEIRNE *Leaders Ind. Territory* 43/2 Her brother-in-law is ex-Principal Chief of the Choctaws. **1916** THOBURN *Stand. Hist. Okla.* I. 330 [The Choctaws] had selected for Peter P. Pitchlynn the office of principal chief of the nation.

+**Principal meridian.** *Surveying.* Any of the true meridians established under the authority of the Surveyor-General, used as reference lines in subdividing public lands in different parts of the country. — **1831** PECK *Guide* 294 The town is laid out in fractional sections, thirteen and fourteen, in township 5 north, in range 10, west of the third principal meridian. **1837** — *Gaz. Illinois* 75 There are five principal meridians in the land surveys in the west. **1890** *Manual Surveying Instructions* (Gen. Land Office) 36 Guide meridians shall be extended north and south from the base line, at intervals of every 24 miles east and west from the principal meridian.

+**Principe.** [Sp., 'a prince.'] A kind of small cigar. Also fig. — **1838** *Yale Lit. Mag.* III. 268 And I am here . . . ! for the last time at liberty here unquestionably *ex fumo dare lucem*, as my principe might say. **1844** *Knickerb.* XXIII. 441 Here's a dozen Principes to use as occasion may offer, and especially after dinner. *a***1846** *Quarter Race Ky.* 168 After a good substantial supper, I lit a 'York County Principe,' (the like of which sell in these regions [Penna.] at the rate of four for a penny.) **1869** J. R. BROWNE *Adv. Apache Country* 350 Posters . . . displaying to the public eye the prodigious assortments of Regalias, Principes, Cheroots, etc., . . . to be had within the limits of their cigar and tobacco emporium.

***Principle.** *Christian Science.* +A synonym for God. Freq. in phrase *divine Principle.* — **1883** M. B. EDDY in *Christian Science Jrnl.* 2 June 2 God is no longer a mystery to the Christian Scientist, but a divine Principle. **1898** S. J. HANNA in *Progress* June 640 God is the Principle of the Universe and man—of all that really is. **1914** *New England Mag.* April 57 Convinced that this healing was not a miracle, but the operation of divine Principle, she [Mrs. Eddy] searched the Scriptures for the explanation of that Principle.

Prinos. The Linnaean name for a group of plants which includes the winterberry. — [**1866** LINDLEY & MOORE *Treas. Botany* 927/2 *Prinos.* . . . The species are natives of North America. . . . Some of them are evergreen, while others are deciduous.] **1883** *Harper's Mag.* April 728/2 In this belt is a group of rhododendrons, another of kalmias, evergreen prinos.

***Print.**

***1.** A printed publication; a newspaper; an issue of a newspaper.

The *O.E.D.* regards this as 'now chiefly U.S.' It appears, however, to be obsolescent. (Cf. PUBLIC PRINT.)

1680 SEWALL *Diary* II. 14* John Russell, the Anabaptist minister is buried, scarce having time to read his Print in favour of that Sect. **1690** *Ib.* I. 333 Print of the Governour and Council comes out shewing their disallowance of the Public Occurrences. **1705** *Boston News-Letter* 5 March 2/2 All which we shall enlarge upon in our succeeding Prints. **1714** *Ib.* 22 March 2/1 By the first [sloop] they have Prints to the latter end of November. **1732** *Boston Rec.* 35 The Committe are Directed to advertise in the weekly Prints. **1783** JAY *Correspondence* III. 97, I have received the prints of the rise and fall of the balloon. **1857** *Lawrence Republican* 23 July 1 A great deal has been said in the Pro-Slavery prints about the application of donations. **1892** *Nation* 22 Dec. 470/3 Of course, the Government prints take in each case the opposite view.

2. A printed cotton goods or other fabric. {1837–}

The first quotation may belong to sense 3.

1756 *Holyoke Diaries* 16 Put Prints out to whiten. **1845** *Xenia Torch-Light* 31 July 4/5 Adams & Cooper Have just received . . . a large lot of Fancy Prints 6¼ cts and upwards. **1867** 'LACKLAND' *Homespun* 167 The girls flock . . . to finger, for the twentieth time, the limited stock of berages, prints, and mousselin de laines. **1911** *Sears, Roebuck & Co. Cat.* No. 122, 59/3 Extra Quality Solid Turkey Red Print.

3. An impression printed from an engraving. {1662–}

1779 *York Co., Va., Rec.: Wills* 28 April, 11 prints. **1885** EGGLESTON in *Century Mag.* April 879/1 The prints which adorned the rooms in that day were of several sorts. **1907** HARRIS *Tents of Wickedness* 308 A set of coloured French prints . . . would make this corner, just *make* it.

4. *attrib.* and *comb.* **a.** In sense 2 with *apron, cloth, dress,* etc.

1845 *Lowell Offering* V. 109*n.*, The print-yard watchman's bell—that often rings. **1865** *Atlantic Mo.* April 403/2 A lady in a soiled print dress and much jewelry kindly played at them upon a gorgeous piano. **1866** A. D. WHITNEY *L. Goldthwaite* xvi, Nobody would think . . . [that the] common print apron of dark blue . . . meant anything beyond the ordinary adjuncts of a traditional old woman's dress. **1886** *Pop. Science Mo.* Feb. 480 A yard of cotton cloth of the kind called print-cloth . . . is less than four cents. **1900** *Everybody's Mag.* II. 426/1 Getting up in a hurry, she caught the hem of her print skirt with her foot.

b. In sense 1 and 3 with *paper, publisher.*

1851 *Harper's Mag.* Jan. 276/2 Booksellers, Print-publishers, Jewelers, . . . reserve for December their finest and most elaborate productions. **1903** SHUMAN *Practical Journalism* 13 If print paper were still made of rags the modern press could not exist.

***Printed,** *a.* Of various fabrics: Colored or figured by the process of printing. — **1711** *Boston News-Letter* 22 Oct. 2/2 To be Sold on reasonable Terms . . . Woolen and worsted Hose, printed Linnen, Felt Hats [etc.]. **1787** *Md. Gazette* 1 June 3/3 A few pieces Printed Linens and Cottons; Corduroys [etc.]. **1893** *Chicago Tribune* 23 April 44/3, 30-inch Printed Lawns, 30-inch Printed Crepe.

***Printer.**

***1.** One whose trade or business is to print books, etc.; an owner of or a workman in a printing office.

1654 JOHNSON *Wonder-w. Prov.* 129 M. Jos. Glover . . . provided . . . a Printer, which hath been very usefull in many respects. **1681** *Boston Rec.* 71 Samuel Sewall became surety to the town for Samuel Greene, printer. **1733** FRANKLIN *Poor Richard's Almanac 1734* 23 Sold by the Printer, . . . common blank Bonds for money. **1767** *Boston Gazette* 23 Nov., The Printers of this Paper . . . have lately purchas'd a new Set of Types, at a very great Expence. **1841** CIST *Cincinnati* Advt., R. P. Brooks, Book & Job Printer, . . . Is prepared to execute . . . every variety of Fancy or Plain Job Printing. **1869** *Ore. State Jrnl.* 2 Jan. 1/6 My printer's bill was in his paw and blood was in his eye. **1915** *Atlantic Mo.* Dec. 812/2 The accents . . . were not cast with the type, but inserted separately and laboriously by the printer.

+**2.** *Practical printer*, a printer who has had practical experience.

1839 *Indiana H. Rep. Jrnl.* 23d Sess. 553 In the opinion of Messrs. Douglass Maguire and D. V. Culley, practical printers, the time allowed Douglass & Noel to complete the public printing was insufficient. **1874** *Internat. Typogr. Union Proc.* 88 A practical printer is one who has had the four years' experience. **1892** *York County Hist. Rev.* 74 Charles H. Sprenkel, Justice of the Peace and Practical Printer.

Printer's devil. =DEVIL *n.* 2. {1763–} — **1838** *N.Y. Advertiser & Exp.* 9 May 2/1 We can send 'a devil'—a Printer's Devil, we mean, over to him with a bundle at a time. **1863** NORTON *Army Lett.* 144 A Corporal . . . occupies about as responsible a position as a printer's devil. **1893** *Harper's Mag.* May 854/2 Much of his prose was written with the printer's devil waiting in the hall for the unfinished page.

Printer's ink. {1820–} *fig.* +Printed matter; advertising through print. — **1855** BARNUM *Life* 316 'Printer's ink' was employed, in every possible form, to put and keep Jenny Lind before the people.

Printery. A printing office. {1657–} 'Chiefly *U.S.*' (*O.E.D.*). — **1638** *Mass. H. S. Coll.* 4 Ser. VI. 99 Wee haue a printery here. **1848** BARTLETT 262 *Bakery, bindery*, have long been in use amongst us, and in New York even *paintery* and *printery.* **1895** *Voice* 16 May 3/4 A temporary printery had been erected at Tennessee City. **1906** *Washington Post* 29 April 17 The bindery division of the public printery.

Print house. A printing office. *Obs.* {1629–} — **1636** *Essex Inst. Coll.* IX. 36 [Town orders are unknown] for want of a print howse or some other meanes whereby to publish them. **1655** in Quincy *Hist. Harvard* I. 463 The revenue of the press . . . must at present be improved for the finishing of the print-house.

***Printing.** In attributive uses.

1. Designating various activities and places connected with printing.

1789 *Ann. 1st Congress* I. 43 It should be left to the Secretary of the Senate and Clerk of the House of Representatives, to contract with such person as shall engage to execute the printing and binding business on the most reasonable terms. **1796** WEEMS *Letters* II. 37 Being in the Printing-line, . . . I thought it an advantageous offer. **1820** *Columbian Centinel* 26 Jan. 2/3 The fire reached the bay . . . taking the brick building occupied by us with our printing establishment. **1845** SOL. SMITH *Theatr. Apprent.* 33 The roof fell in while I was passing from the printing room, through a small entry, into the street. **1904** 'O. HENRY' *Roads of Destiny* 295, I was coming out of a printing-shop one afternoon.

2. Designating various instruments and tools used in printing.

1801 *Ann. 7th Congress* 2 Sess. 1225 Articles paying twelve and a half per cent. ad valorem . . . [include] anvils, vises, and printing type. **1829** *20th Congress 2 Sess.* H. R. Doc. No. 59, 8 Improvement in the printing machine, or roller press, April 29 [1828], George W. Cartright. **1868** *Mich. Agric. Rep.* VII. 363 Mechanics' & Inventors' Association, Detroit, [exhibited] Flester's printing wheel. **1873** PHELPS *Trotty's Wedding* vi, Max carried Trotty up into the attic, and fixed his chair by the printing-table. **1876** INGRAM *Centennial Exp.* 183 The printing rollers were of wood.

Printing house.** A house in which printing is done; a printing office. {–1721} — *a1649** WINTHROP *Hist.* 293 A printing house was begun at

Cambridge by one Daye, at the charge of Mr. Glover. **1743** FRANKLIN *Writings* II. 237, I have already three printing-houses in different colonies. **1916** DU PUY *Uncle Sam* 52 The areaway upon which its single window looked faced the wall of a printing house.

Printing office. An establishment in which printing is done. {1827–}

1733 FRANKLIN *Poor Richard's Almanac 1734* t.-p., Printed and sold by B. Franklin, at the New Printing-office. **1751** *New York Post-Boy* 29 April, Tickets to be had at the Theatre, and at the New Printing Office in Bever-Street. **1809** CUMING *Western Tour* 195 There are [in Chillicothe, O.,] fourteen stores, a post-office, and two printing-offices. **1872** *Newton Kansan* 10 Oct. 3/2 Sociable this evening at the residence of the editor of this paper, upstairs, over the printing office. **1916** SEITZ *Training for Newsp. Trade* 21 The printing office is a very inviting place.

Printing paper. {1892–} Paper to be used in printing books, newspapers, etc. — **1789** *Ann. 1st Congress* I. 106 The articles enumerated for duty were . . . blank books, writing, printing, and wrapping paper. **1810** *Columbian Centinel* 20 Jan. 3/2, 250 reams fine Demi Printing Paper . . . will be sold on a liberal credit. **1873** PHELPS *Trotty's Wedding* vi, Then they cut out the pages, out of white printing-paper that Lill had bought for three cents a sheet.

* **Printing press.** An instrument for printing on paper from type, plates, etc.; a printing machine.

1762 *Md. Gazette* 12 Aug., New printing press. **1809** CUMING *Western Tour* 223 Pittsburgh [has] . . . one copper-plate printing press. **1857** *Lawrence* (Kan.) *Republican* 4 June 3 Wanted, . . . one Printing Press, one Grist Mill [etc.]. **1869** *Boyd's Business Directory* 597, 50 per cent . . . may be saved By Using Maurice's Patent Autographic Printing Press. **1902** *Harper's Mag.* May 1003/1 My youngest son . . . persuaded me, a year ago, to buy him a printing-press.

fig. **1798** JEFFERSON *Writings* X. 36 The sedition bill . . . may be meant to put the printing presses under the *imprimatur* of the executive. **1857** *Lawrence* (Kan.) *Republican* 11 June 2 She has sent over large bodies of her most gallant . . . sons, to abate certain serious 'nuisances' in our midst such as printing presses, elegant hotels, and private residences.

b. A press for printing cotton cloth.

1876 INGRAM *Centennial Exp.* 183 It was upon the same principle as the calico printing press.

+**Printing telegraph.** (See quot. 1890.) — **1847** *Rep. Comm. Patents 1846* 351, I therefore characterize my invention as the first recording or printing telegraph by means of electro-magnetism. **1860** PRESCOTT *Telegraph* 402 The printing telegraph . . . was proposed in September, 1837. **1890** *Cent.* 4733/3 *Printing-telegraph*, . . . any form of automatic self-recording telegraph, as the 'ticker' of a stock-reporting telegraph.

Print-seller. One who sells engraved prints. {1710–} — **1837** *S. Lit. Messenger* Jan. 26/1 As well one might attempt to teach an apprentice the art of engraving, by employing him constantly in working at the press, or bearing the impressions to the print-sellers. **1864** NICHOLS *Amer. Life* I. 96 The windows of the book and print-sellers . . . [were] attractive.

Print shop. A shop in which engraved prints are sold. {*a*1697–} Also attrib. — ***a*1861** WINTHROP *Open Air* 314 The print-shops had taken down their battle-scenes and death-bed scenes. **1865** *Atlantic Mo.* Jan. 57/2 James Gillray, the renowned delineator of . . . hundreds of political cartoons . . . now to be found only in old print-shops. **1883** HOWELLS *Woman's Reason* ix, As she passed a print-shop window she saw that pretty series of engravings.

Print works. *pl.* A factory where fabrics are printed. Also attrib. in sing. — **1836** *Niles' Nat. Reg.* 1 Oct. 80/3 *Silk print works.* . . . A new brick building . . . [has] been erected for the printing of silks and ginghams. **1888** *Amer. Almanac* 275 Occupations of the People of the United States. . . . Print-work operatives. **1891** CHASE & CLOW *Industry* II. 29 The color house at the print-works is an important place.

Prismatic compass. *Surveying.* (See quot. 1876.) {1859} — **1853** MARCY *Explor. Red River* p. iii, We succeeded in obtaining . . . a prismatic compass, . . . but could not procure a chronometer. **1876** KNIGHT 1804/1 *Prismatic Compass*, an instrument for measuring horizontal angles by means of the magnetic meridian. It is principally employed in reconnoissance or in sketching the general features of a country.

* **Prison.**

* **1. a.** A building or set of buildings used for the safe custody of persons lawfully committed to it; a penitentiary. **b.** A military prison camp.

'It is usually specifically applied to the place of confinement of convicted criminals' (W. '09). See also STATE('S) PRISON.

1638 *R.I. Col. Rec.* I. 59 It is ordered that a Howse for a prison . . . shall forthwith be built. **1698** MATHER *Diary* I. 271 There are many Miserables, at this Time, in our Prison. **1772** A. G. WINSLOW *Diary* 66 There were 10 corn baskets of the feast (at the Hall) sent to the prison & almshouse. **1851** *Harper's Mag.* July 277/1 In San Francisco a prison is in the course of erection by the labor of felons. **1865** KELLOGG *Rebel Prisons* 370 The officers of nearly all the Southern prisons seem to have imbibed the spirit of the prime leaders of the rebellion. **1907** ANDREWS *Recoll.* 176 It was a matter of humanity . . . to send them to a better prison . . . , as the Columbus prison was very unsanitary. **1914** *Cycl. Amer. Govt.* III. 64/2 Public sentiment in favor of separate prisons for women is rapidly growing.

2. *attrib.* **a.** Designating parts or departments of a prison and its grounds.

1646 *Suffolk Deeds* I. 60 Valentine Hill of Boston granted to William Davies a house & garden bounded with . . . the prison garden on the west [etc.]. **1782** TRUMBULL *M'Fingal* 136, [I saw] Our spacious prison-walls arise. **1820** BRYANT *Poetical Works* 39 Does he whom thy kind hand dismissed to peace, Upbraid the gentle violence that took off His fetters, and unbarred his prison-cell? **1830** COOPER *Water Witch* I. i, No doubt the prison door, as you have so clearly expressed it, might be opened. **1853** STOWE *Key* 58/2 He was soon promoted to be steward of the prison hospital. **1865** KELLOGG *Rebel Prisons* 299, I took my position near the prison-gate, with two of my comrades.

b. Designating money charges made against the inmates of a prison.

1704 *Boston News-Letter* 26 June 1/2 The Witnesses proving no matter of Fact upon them, . . . [they] were acquitted by the Court, paying Prison Fees. **1777** *N.H. Comm. Safety Rec.* 81 Ordered the Keeper of the Goal . . . to discharge Francis Weeks from Confinement, said Weeks paying all prison charges.

c. Designating people or groups concerned with prison administration or reform.

1790 *Penna. Packet* 6 Jan. 3/2 A stated Meeting of the Philadelphia Prison Society . . . will be held at the German School-House, in Cherry alley. ***a*1859** *N.Y. Express* (B.), The Prison Association held its monthly meeting last night. **1865** KELLOGG *Rebel Prisons* 379 If the prison authorities had permitted them . . . to cut logs within two miles of the prison, the men would gladly have built comfortable and ample barracks in one week. **1887** *Courier-Journal* 1 May 20/6 On that occasion the prison officials only were present. **1892** Prison warden [see PENOLOGIST]. **1914** *Cycl. Amer. Govt.* III. 62/1 Prison matrons have been found exceedingly useful in caring for children.

d. In special combinations.

Prison break, an escape from prison; *p. competition*, the competition arising from the use of cheap prison labor; *p. contractor*, one who contracts for prison labor; *p. fever*, a fever endemic in crowded prisons; *p. hole*, a dungeon; *p. shirt*, a regulation shirt worn by prisoners; *p. stocks*, stocks set up in a prison to be used in punishment.

1643 *Md. Archives* IV. 247 Of this prison-break . . . the said attorny impeacheth the said [Richard Ingle]. **1900** *Congress. Rec.* 8 Jan. 693/1 A bill . . . to protect free labor from prison competition. **1875** in W. M. Fisher *Californians* 64 The prison contractors have been latterly undersold in the market. **1782** TRUMBULL *M'Fingal* 139 [He] ordered out with like endeavour, Detachments of the prison-fever. **1677** *New Castle Court Rec.* 131 Capt: Billop Comanded ye deponant to help to take him out of ye stokes againe and to put him into the Prizon hole. **1907** LONDON *Road* 90 Our new clothes were brought to us—stout prison shirts, and coats and trousers conspicuously striped. **1680** *Doc. Col. Hist. N.Y.* XII. 654 We have ordered A prisson stocks and wheeping post, forth with to be built.

* **Prison base.** =PRISONERS' BASE. {–1707} — **1781** DENNY *Journal* 41 This business reminds me of a play among the boys, called Prison-base. **1789** MORSE *Amer. Geog.* 148 Quoits, wrestling, . . . foot races, and prison-bass are universally practised in the country. **1806** LEWIS in *L. & Clark Exped.* V. (1905) 117 The men divided themselves into two parties and played prison base, by way of exercise. **1848** DRAKE *Pioneer Life Ky.* 149 Prison base, as Webster calls it, known by us, however, as prisoner's base, was racing in high and complex perfection.

* **Prisoner.**

* **1.** A person who is in legal custody, as a convicted criminal or a person awaiting trial; an inmate of a prison.

1653 *Boston Rec.* 26 My thoughts . . . have beene about . . . the setting up of a Bridewell or Workehouse for Prisonrs Malefactors & some sort of poore people. **1693** C. MATHER *Wonders Invis. World* (1862) 142 At another time this Deponent was desired by the Prisoners to come unto an Husking of Corn. **1704** *Boston News-Letter* 26 June 1/2 The Council for the Prisoner, and the Prisoner himself being fairly heard, The Court was cleared. **1836** [see PENITENTIARY 1]. **1883** *Ill. Rev. Statutes* 431 Upon the arraignment of a prisoner, it shall be sufficient . . . to declare orally . . . that he is not guilty. **1904** *Chicago Tribune* 9 Aug. 3 County jail officers blocked a delivery after the prisoners had sawed several bars of an outside window.

* **2.** *Mil.* In time of war, a person captured or held by the enemy.

1705 *Boston News-Letter* 14 May 2/1 He would so serve all therein, and the Prisoners that he had taken. **1777** *Jrnls. Cont. Congress* VIII. 421 Resolved, That Congress approve General Washington's conduct as to the cartel for exchange of prisoners. **1848** *Whig Almanac 1849* 41/2 All prisoners of war . . . shall be restored as soon as practicable after the exchange of ratifications of this Treaty. **1862** NORTON *Army Lett.* 83 We took several prisoners. **1901** R. A. ALGER *Sp.-Amer. War* 297 This capture of the Spanish army . . . was accomplished without the loss of a prisoner.

3. In the possessive with *box*, *counsel*.

1840 *Niles' Nat. Reg.* 4 April 80/3 His wife and son were . . . conducted to the prisoner's box where he was sitting. **1845** *Xenia Torch-Light* 31

July 2/6 The called Court of Virginia sustained these doctrines, refusing the motion of the prisoners' counsel to bail them.

Prisoners' base. A game in which the members of the two opposing teams try to capture their opponents while they are off their own territories, called 'bases.' {1855-}

Cf. PRISON BASE.

1806 CLARK in *Lewis & C. Exped.* V. (1905) 118 Our party devided and played at prisoners base untill night. **1848** [see PRISON BASE]. **1881** *Harper's Mag.* Jan. 184/2 The young folks would shout in many-pitched voices as they played at 'prisoners' base.' **1897** STUART *Simpkinsville* 166 The children played . . . 'prisoners' base.'

+**Prisoner's dance.** (See quotation.) — **1791** J. LONG *Voyages* 35 The dances among the Indians [include] . . . 7. The prisoner's dance. 8. The spear dance.

***Prison house.** A house or building serving as a prison; a jail. — **1658** *Suffolk Deeds* III. 131c, A dwelling house . . . [bounded] westward with the ground belonging to the prison howse. **1756** HEMPSTEAD *Diary* 674, [I] went to the Prisonhouse to take an Evidence for Capt. Boardman. **1865** *Atlantic Mo.* April 433/1, I remember the unutterable loathing with which I leaned against the door of that prison-house.

Prison-keeper. One who has charge of a prison. {1881} — **1663** *Mass. Bay Rec.* IV. II. 89 It is the duty of all prison keepers from tjme to tjme to present a true list of all the prisoners [etc.]. **1692** in Burr *Witchcraft Cases* (1914) 160 Mr. Corwin, and Mr. Higison were at the Prison-Keepers House. **1721** *Mass. H. Rep. Jrnl.* III. 22 The Petition of Seth Smith, Prison-Keeper, praying for an allowance, for keeping Ovid Rushbrook and John Blin. **1777** *N.H. Comm. Safety Rec.* 72 The prison keeper at Exeter had a permit to release said persons.

Prison labor. Labor done by prisoners. Also attrib. — **1845** *Xenia Torch-Light* 4 Dec. 2/7 So far as practicable without a violation of old contracts for prison labor, the employment of the convicts has . . . been directed to those objects which do not conflict with the interests of any of the existing mechanical pursuits of the State. **1901** 'FLYNT' *World of Graft* 188, I can beat the workin' man figurin' out this prison-labor business just the same.

+**Prison lot.** A lot of land on which a prison is built. *Obs.* — **1678** *Conn. Hist. Soc. Coll.* VI. 184 A peice of the land in the prisson Lott. **1795** in Chalkley *Scotch-Irish Settlement Va.* I. 404 Two orders of the Augusta Court, March, 1788, granting to Hum[phreys] to build an *Elaboratory* on the prison lot [etc.].

+**Prison pen.** In the Civil War, a penlike prison. (Cf. PEN² 4 a.) — **1865** WHITMAN *Spec. Days* 79 Blackest and loathsomest of all, the dead and living burial-pits, the prison-pens of Andersonville. **1867** GOSS *Soldier's Story* 161 Major Bogle . . . commanded the respect of others amid all the accumulated misery of the 'prison pen.' **1888** GRIGSBY *Smoked Yank* 16 Perhaps some old soldier . . . may let it lead him back to the old camp ground, or prison pen.

Prison ship. A ship fitted out or used as a prison. {1795} Also fig.

1780 *N.J. Archives* 2 Ser. IV. 284 The Good-Hope prison ship . . . was entirely consumed. **1790** *Ann. 1st Congress* I. 1133 Again our brave and unhappy brethren were doomed to miserable deaths, in gaols and prison ships. **1832** DUNLAP *Hist. Amer. Theatre* 43 The prison-ships, those charnel houses of the living, had a greater share in the human victims. **1865** *Atlantic Mo.* Feb. 195/1 He describes the settlement of the English colonies, and narrates . . . the American Revolution, with the customary episodes,—Saratoga, Yorktown, Major André, Miss McCrea, and the prison ships. **1902** HULBERT *Forest Neighbors* 110 They journeyed on for nearly an hour longer, she on her prison-ship, and he on land.

Prison yard. An enclosure about a prison. — **1642** *Boston Rec.* 70 The Constables are appointed . . . to take care for the building a salt peter house in the prison yarde. **1776** *Jrnls. Cont. Congress.* IV. 121 Resolved, That the said G. Connolly be allowed . . . to walk in the prison yard or hall. **1867** L. BAKER *U.S. Secret Service* 512 About 11 A.M., the prison-yard was thrown open to those having passes. **1901** E. E. SPARKS *Expansion of Amer. People* 168 In 1793, Blanchard, 'the bold aeronaut,' made an ascent from the prison yard in Philadelphia.

***Private,** *n.*

1. A soldier without any rank; a common soldier. {1781-}

1775 *Jrnls. Cont. Congress* II. 188 Regular companies of Militia . . . consist of one Captain, . . . one drummer, one fifer, and about 68 privates. **1815** *Niles' Reg.* VII. 381 Many of these officers entered the revolutionary army as privates. **1849** *Whig Almanac 1850* 26/2 The American private is denied even the lowest commission in the army—beyond the rank of sergeant-major he can never rise. **1872** *Newton Kansan* 17 Oct. 2/3 Col. Wm. Irving . . . enlisted as a private in the 14th Ohio Volunteer Infantry, in April, 1861. **1892** *Aberdeen* (S.D.) *Sun* 3 June 2/1 The decent private in the United States army is a good deal more of a gentleman than the drinking, gambling, tyrannical officer who endeavors to fix a great social gulf between them. **1918** *Outlook* 29 May 186/2 Schools for officers and privates, and for special branches of service, are frequent.

+**2.** *College slang.* A personal and private admonition.

1848 *Oration before H[arvard] L[odge] I.O.O.F.* (Hall), Reckon on the fingers of your mind the reprimands, deductions, parietals, and privates in store for you. **1851** HALL *College Words* 245 At Harvard College, one of the milder punishments is what is called *private admonition,* by which a deduction of thirty-two marks is made from the rank of the offender. . . . Often abbreviated into *private.*

***Private,** *a.*

American usage does not differ from British usage. The following categories are illustrated because of their special American contexts.

1. a. Of an armed vessel: Owned and operated by a private person or persons.

1704 *Boston News-Letter* 7 June 2/2 Captain Ebenezer Coffin in the Sloop Anne, a Private Man of War, came in on Thursday the 1st. Currant. **1817** *Ann. 14th Congress* 2 Sess. 75 To Mr. Tait was referred the memorial of Frederick Jenkins . . . in behalf of the owners, officers, and crew of the late private armed brig General Armstrong.

b. Conducted, sponsored, or controlled by a person or persons not acting in a public capacity.

1740 *Holyoke Diaries* 6 A private Fast at Cambridge on account of the throat distemper. **1836** in Mackenzie *Van Buren* 176 If the fetters are knocked off by the repeal of the Restraining Law, private banking associations may be formed. **1854** PIERCE in *Pres. Mess. & P.* V. 233 The responsibility of this Government is thus pledged for a long series of years to the interests of a private company established for purposes of internal improvement in a foreign country. **1877** *Rep. Indian Affairs* 34 The burden of the expense was to be borne by private enterprise. **1881** *Ib.* 196 Their tuition . . . is met by annual scholarship donations of that amount from private charity. **1888** *Economist* 20 Oct. 4/1 But new roads are now particularly interesting as affecting private investments along their lines.

2. Of persons: Hired to serve a particular person or persons; not employed in public service.

1773 *Md. Hist. Mag.* XV. 286 Read my letter to Lewis, seal & forward it by the 1st Private post. **1901** 'FLYNT' *World of Graft* 182 Do you think that the private detective agencies are a necessity in policing the country? **1923** WATTS *L. Nichols* 199 Picking up a job of driving now and then from some trucking or private-expressman.

3. Of houses, rooms, and other property: For the use of a particular person or persons.

1828 SHERBURNE *Memoirs* 184 Our meetings were holden in private houses. **1841** BUCKINGHAM *America* I. 15 We took up our quarters at the adjoining house, which was what is called a private boarding-house. **1845** *Xenia Torch-Light* 23 Oct. 3/7 J. H. Cromwell, Proprietor of the Broadway Hotel, . . . has made a large addition to his house, in which are contained bedrooms and private parlors. **1850** GLISAN *Jrnl. Army Life* 30 As the private conveyance and the stage were too much crowded, some of the passengers remained aboard the boat. **1898** PAGE *Red Rock* 524 Senator Rockfield was admitted to the study or private office of the Secretary. **1903** *N.Y. Ev. Post* 12 Sept., The sumptuous private dormitories that have sprung up around our large universities. **1913** LONDON *Valley of Moon* 114 The four were to go to a private room in Barnum's Restaurant for the wedding supper.

4. In special combinations.

Private banker, a banker who directs a private bank; *p. levee, wharf,* a levee or wharf privately built or owned.

1837 in Mackenzie *Van Buren* 178 The Bills of the banks of this State only shall be circulated as Money by private bankers. **1883** *Ill. Rev. Statutes* 262 An Act . . . to regulate and control private levees, private wharves and landing places or embankments.

Private bank. A bank conducted by private individuals, neither authorized, nor subject to supervision, by the government. {1834-} +With special reference to the Massachusetts currency problem in the eighteenth century. Also attrib. (Cf. LAND BANK 1.) — **1714** *Mass. Bay Currency Tracts* 115 Whether it imports to their advantage or disadvantage, and which does most of all import them, the Publick or the Private Bank? **1720** *Ib.* 282 This hath always been the great Argument with me why a Private Bank must be better than a Publick. **1734** *Mass. H. Rep. Jrnl.* 93 And I wish the Government had no reason to fear that this will be the Consequence of what is called the Private Bank, or Merchants Notes. **1846** MACKENZIE *Van Buren* 175 Flagg on Free, Private, and Privileged Banks—General Maison and the Restraining Act.

Private bill. A legislative bill affecting the interests of a particular individual, place, or corporation. {1844-} — **1840** *Niles' Nat. Reg.* 6 June 220/3 Mr. Russell appealed to the house not thus to give the go-by to private bills. **1900** *Congress. Rec.* 19 Jan. 1004/2 Gentlemen would not make some of these speeches against private bills.

+**Private bill(s) day.** (See quot. 1914.) — **1881** *Harper's Mag.* March 552/1 At almost any moment except in the 'morning hour' and on 'private bill day,' an exciting and masterly discussion may begin. **1914** *Cycl. Amer. Govt.* III. 65/2 Private-bills day in the federal House of Representatives is the day regularly set apart for the consideration of private business—especially of claims against the government, and pension bills. This day is Friday in every week, but may be devoted to other business by a majority vote of the House.

+**Private car.** A railroad car fitted up for occupancy by a single person or party. Also attrib. — **1887** GEORGE *40 Years on Rail* 223 President Vanderbilt's private car . . . contains a state room, card-room, sitting and dining-room. **1908** LORIMER *J. Spurlock* 332 Between the Governor's cheque and this private car they've rather managed to turn our little problem play into a comic opera. **1917** SINCLAIR *King Coal* 258 He took others of his private-car friends and introduced them to his North Valley friends.

+**Private entertainment.** Accommodations such as are offered by an inn or a tavern; a wayside place for the accommodation of travelers. *To keep private entertainment*, to operate a tavern.

1789 in V. W. Howard *Bryan Sta. Heroes* 42 Andrew Gatewood . . . has opened private entertainment for man and horse on the road from Lexington. **1809** CUMING *Western Tour* 188, I stopped to rest, as it was a house of private entertainment. **1839** C. A. MURRAY *Travels* I. 95 The owners and occupants of land (being generally two or three miles apart) are most of them tavern-keepers, or, as it is there [in western Va.] termed, they keep 'private entertainment.' **1870** NOWLAND *Indianapolis* 173 As there were no hotels at that time, they were all 'taverns,' or 'private entertainments.' **1897** *Outing* XXX. 65/2 This time we had come up from Richmond through the Peninsula, . . . sometimes taking pot-luck at typical 'private entertainments.'

Privateer. {1664–}

+**1.** A free-lance soldier.

1676 I. MATHER *K. Philip's War* (1862) 58 Hearing many profane oaths among some of our Souldiers (namely those Privateers, who were also Volunteers). **1677** HUBBARD *Narrative* I. 18 Our Horseman with the whole Body of the Privateers . . . ran violently down upon them over the said Bridg.

2. An armed vessel, owned and controlled by private individuals and commissioned by a sovereign power to cruise against the merchantmen and war vessels of the enemy. {1664–}

The United States, though not a signatory to the Declaration of Paris (April 16, 1856), has commissioned no privateers since that date.

1678 *Doc. Hist. N.Y. State* I. 89 There are no privateers about our Coasts. **1685** SEWALL *Diary* I. 86 Samson Waters, Capt., to go with Mr. Patteshal's Brigenteen to fetch in two Privateers that this morn are said to be in the Bay, a Sloop and Shalop. **1708** *R.I. Col. Rec.* IV. 58 Very few of the enemy's privateers . . . will run or outsail one of our laded vessels. **1778** *Amer. Pioneer* II. 75 There is at this time *five* privateers fitting out here, which, I suppose, will take four hundred men. **1812** *Niles' Reg.* II. 380/2 Many stout privateers from 18 to 22 guns, are nearly prepared for service in the eastern states. **1836** *Diplom. Corr. Texas* I. (1908) 81 Do try to start off a Privateer from New York to capture . . . the vessel lately bought by the Mexicans. **1866** 'F. KIRKLAND' *Bk. Anecdotes* 379/2 The intelligence that the Confederate privateer Alabama was cruising about the Cape of Good Hope, created much excitement.

3. The commander or crew of such a vessel, or a member of its crew. {*a*1674–}

Like other nautical terms, in which ships are often personified, *privateer* is frequently ambiguous.

1684 *Plymouth Laws* 203 An act for the restraining and punishing privateers and pirates. **1706** *Boston News-Letter* 14 Jan. 2/2 The Privateer presently boarded him. **1720** *Amer. Wkly. Mercury* 11 Aug. 2/2 The said Capt. *Holland* designs when he cant act as a Privateer, to fit out a ship of 24 guns as a *Guard de la Coast*. **1778** *Mass. Spy* 15 Oct. 4/1 Major-General Gray turned his thoughts towards New-London, where he hoped to surprize a number of privateers. **1860** MORDECAI *Virginia* 323 Our privateers were numerous, daring and frequently successful in getting their prizes into those ports which the enemy could not easily blockade. **1881** *Ore. State Jrnl.* 1 Jan. 2/2 Our commerce would immediately become the prey of privateers.

4. *French privateer*, a privateer commissioned by the French government.

1704 *Boston News-Letter* 28 Aug. 2/2 The Briganteen Society belonging to Milford in Connecticut . . . was taken by a French Privateer of 14. Guns. **1707** SEWALL *Diary* II. 194 At Dinner had the good News brought of the French privateer being Taken. **1711** HEMPSTEAD *Diary* 3 A sloop att anchor near Watch point. . . . Sopposed to be a french privateer.

5. *attrib.* Designating ships used as privateers.

1705 *Boston News-Letter* 12 March 2/1 Captain Balling Commander of a Privateer Briganteen from Jamaica of 12 Guns. *Ib.* 17 Sept. 2/2 A Guinea Man . . . that arrived here met with a Martinico Privateer Sloop. **1726** PENHALLOW *Indian Wars* 30 They fitted out a privateer shallop with twenty seven men. **1758** *Newport Mercury* 26 Dec. 3/1 Ready to sail on a Cruise against His Majesty's Enemies, the Privateer Brig Defiance.

Privateering. The action of cruising against the enemy in a privateer. Frequently *a-privateering.* {1664–} Also attrib.

1704 *Boston News-Letter* 22 May 2/2 Captain Peter Lawrence is going a Privateering from Rhode Island, in a good Sloop, . . . for Canada. **1756** *N.J. Archives* XX. 71 William Day . . . has gone a privateering in the brig Johnson. **1776** J. ADAMS *Familiar Letters* 155 Read our privateering laws and our commercial laws. **1828** SHERBURNE *Memoirs* 19 My father, though a high whig, disapproved the practice of privateering. **1861** in E. Cowell *Diary* 367 It will be said that in surrendering the right of privateering, the U.S. having a small Navy, places its commerce at the mercy of the European powers.

+**Privateersman.** A seaman on a privateer. Also transf. — **1779** *Narragansett Hist. Reg.* I. 40 The privateersmen took the fish boats. **1817** *Niles' Reg.* XIII. 290/1 The establishment of Galvezton is nothing more or less than one of privateersmen. **1862** Moore *Rebellion Rec.* V. II. 184, I was to endeavor to effect the release of our officers held as hostages by the rebels, by delivering their privateersmen within their lines on parole. **1885** *Century Mag.* Nov. 65/1 In and out among the craft of heavier burden shuffled the small, tough bronchos. Their riders . . . were the doughty privateers-men, returning with a convoy of pack-animals.

+**Private land claim. a.** A claim of a private individual to land allegedly subject to the federal land laws. **b.** *Committee on Private Land Claims*, a Congressional committee authorized to investigate such claims. — **1868** *N.Y. Herald* 2 July 3/4 Mr. Orth . . . from the Committee on Private Land Claims, reported the Senate bill. **1880** *Cimarron News & Press* 11 March 1/7 The McGarraghan claim is once more being argued before the committee on private land claims. **1891** *Statutes at Large* XXVI. 854 An act to establish a court of private land claims, and to provide for the settlement of private land claims in certain States and Territories.

Private man. =PRIVATE *n.* 1. *Obs.* {1691–; now *obs.*} — **1740** *S.C. Hist. Soc. Coll.* IV. 154 A detachment of Two hundred and fifty private Men of the Carolina Regiment. **1757** *Lett. to Washington* II. 150 Send me a Muster Roll . . . with the Names of each private Man, Serjt. Corporal & Drums.

Private sale. A sale by private negotiation rather than by public auction. — **1777** *N.J. Archives* 2 Ser. I. 435 To be sold at private sale, by the Subscriber, that valuable tract of land called Mount Penn. **1851** CIST *Cincinnati* 270 In the northern section of Cincinnati . . . lies a well located property . . . which is selling out at private sale only. **1911** *Okla. Session Laws* 3 Legisl. 214 Such bonds . . . shall be sold at a public or private sale, as the township board may deem it advisable.

Private school. A school privately owned and directed; a school not supported by taxation. {a school operated for private profit as opposed to an English public school, 1857} — **1830** *Illinois Mo. Mag.* I. 112 All the inhabitants of a country should have the means of education placed within their reach. . . . Can this ever be done by *private schools* established and supported by individuals? **1847** *Santa Fe Republican* 11 Dec. 2/1 Where there are no private schools or academies, . . . the means of obtaining an education are exceedingly limited. **1890** HOWELLS *Boy's Town* 55 The other school was another private school . . . called the Academy. **1915** *Independent* 14 June 479 The private school differs from the public school essentially in that it has the power to select its students.

Private secretary. A secretary employed to assist one person exclusively. — **1790** WASHINGTON in *Pres. Mess. & P.* I. 70, I have directed Mr. Lear, my private secretary, to lay before you a copy of the adoption [etc.]. **1809** *Ann. 10th Congress* 2 Sess. 432 The Private Secretary of the President is to be the bearer of the despatches. **1836** *Diplom. Corr. Texas* I. (1908) 144, I shall take Wolfe as my private secretary at all events if he is not appointed Secy of Legation. **1884** *Century Mag.* April 809/1 Now there are four rooms occupied by the private secretary and his staff of clerks. **1900** *Congress. Rec.* 15 Feb. 1838/1 All of us have private secretaries to do our own work as members.

***Privet.** (See also PRIVY.[2])

***1.** =PRIM. Also attrib.

1709 LAWSON *Carolina* 90 We have a Prim or Privet, which grows on the dry, barren, sandy Hills, by the Sound side. **1784** CUTLER in *Mem. Academy* I. 403 Privet . . . makes excellent hedges. **1836** J. HALL *Statistics of West* 138 April 8. Buds of the privet beginning to open. **1890** HARRIS in *Century Mag.* Dec. 287 A privet hedge . . . gave promise of rare sweetness in the spring. **1908** *Outing* April 126 Privet makes a splendid hedge wherever hardy—indeed, it would no doubt be considered our best plant for this purpose.

+**2.** *S.* An oleaceous shrub, *Forestiera acuminata.*

1884 SARGENT *Rep. Forests* 112 *Forestiera acuminata*. . . . Privet. . . . Borders of swamps and streams, in low, wet soil.

3. One or other of several species of *Ilex.* Freq. with defining terms.

1901 MOHR *Plant Life Ala.* 603 *Ilex decidua*. . . . Privet. Deciduous Holly. *Ib.*, *Ilex longipes*. . . . Long-peduncled Privet. *Ib.*, *Ilex caroliniana*. . . . Carolina Privet. *Ib.*, *Ilex monticola*. . . . Mountain Privet.

***Privilege.** (See also MILL, WATER PRIVILEGE.)

***1.** A right to use certain properties, +esp. as arising from the ownership or occupancy of adjacent or nearby properties. Now hist.

1632 *Plymouth Laws* 31 The former priviledges of the said acres should be laid downe. **1654** *Suffolk Deeds* II. 57, I Richard Carter . . . [have] sold unto Jeames Johnson of Boston all that my Dwelling howse in Boston . . . , with the Barne fence & all the priveledges there to belongeing. **1661** *Topsfield Rec.* I. 5 The said Zacheas Gould . . . doth giue in the aforesaid farme into the sad Towne for euer with all the prieuledges and apurtinances thereunto belonging. **1725** *New-Eng. Courant* 10–17 July 2/2 A large double House and Wharff, . . . with the Priviledge of the Flatts, to be sold. **1772** in C. Hazard *Thos. Hazard* 249 A Priviledge in the Well for Water.

attrib. **1767** *Charlestown Land Rec.* 222 There is a Privilege Way belonging to the Town.

2. *concrete.* +**a.** The land used by the exercise of such a right. Also in place names.

1700 *Md. Hist. Mag.* XX. 287 Benjors Priviledge. **1882** Godfrey *Nantucket* 92 Every fractional part of a common or privilege was noted.

+**b.** A waterfall that furnishes power to a mill, etc.

1835 *Knickerb.* April 272 There was also a great business done at a tilt-hammer forge, over a fine 'privilege,' where 'the sweet waters meet.' **1845** KIRKLAND *Western Clearings* 195 He paced the bank of the noisy little 'privilege' that turned the grist-mill. **1865** *Maine Bd. Agric. Rep.* X. 138 Bond Brook . . . furnishes an excellent privilege for considerable machinery.

+**3.** *Stock market.* (See quot. 1890.)

1870 MEDBURY *Men Wall St.* 101 'Privileges' approach very nearly to the nature of a bet. Privileges are either *puts* or *calls*. **1890** *Cent.* 4738/3 *Privilege*, . . . a speculative contract covering a 'put' or a 'call,' or both a put and a call (that is, a 'straddle').

***Privy.**[1] A hole dug into the ground and nearly always covered by seats and a shelter, used as a toilet; a water-closet. — **1708** SEWALL *Diary* II. 238 A very pretty Boy . . . fell into a scurvy open Privy before night; of which loathsom Entertainment he died in a day or two. **1750** *Harvard Rec.* II. 818 [Voted] that the South Privy be clear'd. **1856** HALL *College Words* (ed. 2) 46 *Burlington.* At Middlebury College, a water-closet; privy. **1879** *Harper's Mag.* June 133/1 Most of the smaller houses had common privies.

***Privy.**[2] **1.** Obs. or dial. variant of PRIVET. {-1593; now *dial.*} **2.** *local.* =MATRIMONY VINE. — **(1) 1786** WASHINGTON *Diaries* III. 37 Took the covering off the Plants in my Botanical garden, and found none living . . . except some of the Acasce or Acacia, flower fence, and privy. **(2) 1892** *Amer. Folk-Lore* V. 101 *Lycium vulgare*, privy; Jackson vine; jasmine. . . . Mansfield, O.

***Privy councilor.** +A member of a royal governor's council. Now hist. — **1692** *N.H. Prov. Papers* II. 75 The oaths of a privy Councilor were administered to each of the said Council this day. **1699** *Ib.* 315 Lieut. Govern[o]r Wm. Partridge . . . also took the oath of Privy Councillor.

***Prize,** *n.*[1]

***1.** A ship legally captured under the rights of war.

1658 *Suffolk Deeds* III. 133 The ship. being a flemish bottom & seuerall of the seamen dutch seuerall persons questioning whither shee was not a prize The Gouernor & depty Governor . . . sent for the s[ai]d mr. Thomas Coartman. **1671** in Neill *Virginia Carolorum* 331 In twenty-eight yeares there has never been one prize brought into the country. **1704** *Boston News-Letter* 3 July 2/2 There's Arriv'd here another Prize . . . Taken a Trading with the Spaniards, her loading consists of about 30 or 40 boxes of Steel, 102 double bars of Iron [etc.]. **1711** *Ib.* 4 June 1/2 There arrived at Nantasket two of Her Majesty's Ships of War from the West-Indies with four French Prizes. **1778** *Warren-Adams Lett.* II. 29 By this Means our prizes and Merchantmen have a fine Chance to get in. **1815** *Md. Hist. Mag.* I. 226 At 8 P.M. discharged two of the Vessels, on board of which by permission of the Captain put 7 Prisoners, officers of Different Prizes. **1846** POLK in *Pres. Mess. & P.* IV. 496 Besides, in case prizes should be made of American vessels, the utmost vigilance will be exerted by our blockading squadron. **1862** FARRAGUT in *Navy in Civil War* I. 145, I don't know how many escape, but we certainly make a good many prizes. **1883** [see PRIZE CREW]. **1916** [see PRIZE MASTER].

2. Attrib. with *case, claim, goods*, etc.

1704 *Boston News-Letter* 12 June 2/2 The Prize Sloop . . . had on board . . . 30 Cases of Liquors. **1705** *Ib.* 12 March 2/1 A Privateer Sloop call'd the Sea-flower . . . was Cast away . . . , with divers Prize Goods. **1812** *Ann. 12th Congress* 2 Sess. 433 The Committee of Ways and Means are . . . in possession of three statements of prize sales. **1875** *Chicago Tribune* 2 Nov. 5/4, 2,842 prize claims, amounting to $358,598 in the aggregate. **1883** *Navy in Civil War* I. 193 Its suggestion of a remedy for the owners, in view of the character of prize proceedings in the Confederacy, was little less than a mockery. **1914** *Cycl. Amer. Govt.* III. 70/1 *Prize Cases.*

***Prize,** *n.*[2] *attrib.* and *comb.*

1. Passing into adj.: That has gained a reward or a prize; excellent; first-class. {1803-}

1840 DANA *Two Years* xviii. 164 Two monstrous prize-cocks were brought on. **1842** *Chicago American* 1 Sept., 1st night of the Prize Comedy, written by John Adams, Esq. **1869** ALCOTT *Little Women* II. 156 The prize-story experience had seemed to open a way. **1873** PHELPS *Trotty's Wedding* xiii, But I got some prize-candy, when it came my turn.

2. Designating various things and actions connected with giving or competing for prizes.

1790 *Columbian Centinel* 9 Oct. 32/3 Prize Tickets in Charlestown Lottery exchanged for any of the above. **1856** *Porter's Spirit of Times* 4 Oct. 85/2 Annual Prize Match of the 'Prairie Shooting Club' of Cincinnati, held Sept. 20th, 1856. **1887** *Courier-Journal* 16 Jan. 16/4 She lost the prize at prize-speaking, and Ben lost the race at Yale.

Prize, *v.* {1686-} *S.* +*tr.* To compress (cured tobacco) into a hogshead or other container.

1724 JONES *Virginia* 40 [They] by Degrees *prize* or press it with proper Engines into great Hogsheads. **1759** in Commons, etc. *Doc. Hist.* I. 112 The Tobacco will be all prised before Christmas. **1775** *Amer. Husbandry* I. 226 The greatest part of the tobacco is prized, or put up into hogsheads by the planters themselves. **1863** *Ill. Agric. Soc. Trans.* V. 669 Tobacco of this description should be . . prized lightly in the casks so as to admit of a free and open leaf. **1902** *Farmers' Bul.* No. 60, 17 The leaves . . . are tied into hands and bulked down for a short time, after which they are 'prized' into hogsheads.

Prize court. A court that adjudicates marine captures in time of war {1810-}; +a U.S. district court sitting as such a court. — **1795** *Supreme Ct. Rep.* III. 54 All persons, in every part of the world, are concluded by the sentence of a prize court, in a case coming clearly within its jurisdiction. **1861** E. COWELL *Diary* 406 They are not lawful prizes till they are brought into port and condemned by a prize Court, either in the jurisdiction of the C.S. or in that of an ally. **1883** *Navy in Civil War* I. 192 The prize-court of the Confederacy now sat in Semmes's cabin, and all questions of law and fact were settled by the captain's decision. **1914** *Cycl. Amer. Govt.* III. 70/1 In the United States the district courts are invested with the power of prize courts with appeal to the Supreme Court.

Prize crew. A crew put on a captured ship to bring her into port. {1830} — **1815** *Md. Hist. Mag.* I. 225 Put Mr. Coffin and a prize Crew on board and ordered her to keep company with us. **1861** *Chicago Tribune* 26 May 1/3 The brig Hiawatha . . . was sent home in charge of Lieut. Russell and a prize crew. **1883** *Navy in Civil War* I. 227 The Tuscaloosa, a prize of the Alabama, entered the harbor at the Cape with a prize crew. **1916** *Outlook* 9 Aug. 823/1 The Appam is a British steamship which was . . . put into the charge of a German prize crew, and taken into . . . Norfolk, Virginia.

Prize fight. A public fight between two pugilists for a wager or money. {1824-} — **1849** G. G. FOSTER *N.Y. in Slices* 47 Put down these prize-fights and fire-riots, and abolish three-quarter of the groggeries and other vile haunts of rowdyism. **1856** MacLeod *F. Wood* 295 The prize-fight between John Leese and Frank McIntyre, which was to come off that day at Parker's Island, in the East River, was effectually stopped, and Leese safely locked up in a prison. **1923** *Lit. Digest* 6 Oct. 36/1 The prize-fight . . . is nothing but commercialism appealing not to the instincts of sportsmanship but to the fighting instinct.

Prize fighter. A professional pugilist or boxer. {1703-} — **1825** NEAL *Bro. Jonathan* I. 259 So will the crowd behave . . . especially when they are gathered about prize-fighters, or wrestlers. **1860** E. COWELL *Diary* 209 All this bloodthirsty City mad about the prize-fighter, Heenan. **1907** LONDON *Road* 161 He is now a manager of prize-fighters and proud of it.

Prize master. An officer put in charge of a prize ship. {1800-} — **1760** *Essex Inst. Coll.* XLVII. 125 He put a Prize Master (as he called him) and three more of his hands on board the sloop. **1793** *State P.* (1819) I. 116 A prize master was ordered on board. **1802** ELLICOTT *Journal* 247 The prize master was to furnish us with a supply of meat. **1860** MORDECAI *Virginia* I. 27, A Yankee prize-master was placed over my Scotch captain. **1916** *Outlook* 9 Aug. 823/2 Prizes cannot be brought into the waters of the United States for the purpose of laying up by a prize master.

Prize money. Money realized from the sale of captured goods, esp. a prize ship; a share of this as distributed to a crew. {1748-} — **1749** *N.H. Probate Rec.* III. 733, I give to Doctor Robert Ratsey all my Waidges, Prize money [etc.]. **1839** BIRD *Robin Day* 25 'Curse the prize-money,' said Dicky Dare, . . . 'I go for the glory!' **1880** LAMPHERE *U.S. Govt.* 95/1 Prize-money is distributed to the officers and crew of the capturing vessel in proportion to their respective rates of pay in the service.

***Prizer.** =APPRAISER. — **1652** *Mayflower Descendant* XI. 9 Hee left a smale house . . . which was vallued by the prissers of his said estate. **1670** *Watertown Rec.* I. I. 99 John Bigullah is chosen a prisser for the town of all such goods. **1693** *Boston Rec.* 213 Prizers of Grane—Thomas Harod, Henry Dearing. **1749** *Smithtown Rec.* 94 Shubal Marchant chosen fence viewer and prizer of damages.

Prize ring. A space, usually square and roped off, in which a prize fight is held. {1840-} Also attrib. — **1865** *Nation* I. 815 Why does he have recourse to a threadbare verbal vulgarity worthy only of the pot-house or the prize-ring? **1885** *Santa Fé Wkly. New Mexican* 3 Sept. 4/2 No little interest has developed here at home in prize ring matters since the meeting of Sullivan and McCaffrey near Cincinnati on Saturday. **1893** POST *Harvard Stories* 184 Don't ever try fair prize-ring methods with him.

Prize ship. A ship captured as a prize of war. {a1722-} — **1710** *Boston News-Letter* 26 June 2/2 On the said day arrived Her Majesties Ship the Feversham . . . with Col. Hunter, our Governour, and with him a Prize Ship of 300 Tons. **1776** CUTLER in *Life & Corr.* I. 55 [We] went on board the Lady Juliana, a prize ship of 400 tons, taken by one of our privateers. **1863** DICEY *6 Mos. Federal States* I. 87 The officer in command of the 'Erie' when sent as a prize-ship to New York.

Prizing. +The action of compressing tobacco into a container. — **1793** *Md. Hist. Mag.* VI. 214 [Tobacco] underwent a repacking and priseing preparatory to shipping. **1820** *Amer. Farmer* I. 395 We must defer to another number some remarks on *prizing*, and the manufacturing of chewing tobacco. **1864** *Maine Agric. Soc. Returns 1863* 164 In prizing, the different qualities should not be mixed.

Pro-. {1645-; 'favoring,' 1828-} Used in expressions relating to the northern or southern states, esp. during or in allusion to the Civil War. — **1856** in L. W. Spring *Kansas* (1885) 48, I tell you I'm pro-slave. **1862** *N.Y. Tribune* 7 April (Chipman), Jackson's force is said to be in part composed of Pro-Union men who have been impressed into the Rebel service. **1866** 'F. KIRKLAND' *Bk. Anecdotes* 65/1 Some one was discussing the character of a pro-Southern clergyman—a time-serving Washington domine. **1868** *Ore. State Jrnl.* 31 Oct. 1/3 The pro-rebel Democracy have chimed in. **1883** *Century Mag.* July 426/1 The 'Commercial Review of the South and West,' was circulating its invaluable statistics and its pro-Southern deductions.

*Probabilities. *pl.* +Weather forecasts. *colloq.* (Cf. OLD PROBABILITIES.) — **1886** *Pop. Science Mo.* Aug. 546 The official publications embrace the 'probabilities' and the so-called 'weather-maps.'

*Probate, *n.* Also †probat.

*1. The official proving of the validity or genuineness of a will; documentary evidence of such proving.

1650 in W. S. Perry *Hist. Coll. Amer. Col. Church* I. (1870) 2 It shall be lawful, as it hath been used heretofore, to make Probates of wills . . . in the Colony. **1704** *N.C. Col. Rec.* I. 64 A Will of Wm. Lacy. . . .Ordered that the Execut[o]r have probat of the Sd Will. **1835** *S. Lit. Messenger* I. 423/2 The probat of wills . . . [in Mass. is] confided to an officer, called the *Judge of Probat.* **1869** TOURGEE *Toinette* (1881) 237 If she offered the will for probate it would be sustained, and she would be allowed to qualify as Executrix. **1911** *Okla. Session Laws* 3 Legisl. 64 There shall be but one general record of probate, guardianship, or other estate matters.

2. Attrib. with *business, district, matter,* etc.

1718 SEWALL *Diary* III. 178 Had much Business in the probat office. **1809** KENDALL *Travels* I. 178 Courts of probate . . . are fixed in probate-districts. **1839** *Indiana H. Rep. Jrnl.* 23d Sess. 273 The petition of sundry citizens of Switzerland county [was presented] . . . for an act to authorize the associate judges for said county to transact probate business. **1875** *Mich. Gen. Statutes* I. (1882) 216 The judge of probate of the county of Washtenaw shall have power to appoint a probate register for said county. **1911** *Okla. Session Laws* 3 Legisl. 240 The court . . . may make an order with regard to probate matters at said town.

*Probate, *v. tr.* To prove (a will) by legally establishing its validity. {1837-} ('Chiefly *U.S.*' *O.E.D.*) — **1791** CHIPMAN *Reports & Dissertations* (1871) 52 Cruger's will has never been probated in any proper office in this State [Vt.]. **1858** *N.Y. Tribune* 2 Oct. 6/2 The will of Mr. Ebenezer Francis has been 'probated' in Norfolk County [Mass.]. **1907** *N.H. State P.* XXXI. p. vii, A few wills were probated and estates settled in all these counties.

+Probate court. A court having jurisdiction of probate and administration.

Probate jurisdiction was at first vested in colonial governors and their councils, but is now in most of the states a function of county administration, many of the states having established probate courts, variously designated, in each county. (Cf. COURT 1 m, ORPHANS' COURT.)

1726 *Mass. H. S. Coll.* 6 Ser. V. 426, I never gave any inventory into the Probate Court at Boston. **1843** in Hines *Voyage* 428 The judicial power shall be vested in a Supreme Court, consisting of the Supreme Judge and two Justices of the Peace, a Probate Court, and in Justices of the Peace. **1864** *Wkly. New Mexican* 17 June 2/2 This certificate . . . he must deliver to the clerk of the Probate Court for the county in which the marriage was celebrated. **1877** JOHNSON *Anderson Co., Kansas* 89 The Territorial Legislature, in 1855, attempted to confer civil and criminal jurisdiction on the probate court, concurrent with the district court. **1914** *Cycl. Amer. Govt.* I. 504/2 Jurisdiction and powers [of orphans' courts] are similar to those of probate courts in other states.

+Probate judge. A judge who presides over a probate court. (Cf. JUDGE 2 b.) — *c***1844** *Indiana Mag. Hist.* XXII. 379 In the summer of 1823 the offic[e] of Probate Judge became vacant. **1877** JOHNSON *Anderson Co., Kansas* 70 A. Simons was appointed county clerk, and Samuel Anderson, probate judge. **1890** LANGFORD *Vigilante Days* (1912) 479 A writ of *habeas corpus* was issued by the probate judge of the county.

*Probation.

1. *Educ.* (See quotations.) *Obsolescent.* {1706-}

'Now only in U.S.' (*O.E.D.*).

1851 HALL *College Words* 245 *Probation*, in colleges and universities, the examination of a student as to his qualifications for a degree. *Ib., Probation*, . . . the time which a student passes in college from the period of entering until he is matriculated and received as a member in full standing. In American colleges, this is usually six months, but can be prolonged at discretion. **1895** *Stand.* 1418/3 *Probation.* . . . In universities, examination of a student for degrees.

+b. The status of a student who has been given a limited period of time in which to improve his scholastic standing or be dismissed.

1897 FLANDRAU *Harvard Episodes* 235 The next day the Office put Billy 'on probation.'

+2. *Law.* A system of tutelage under court supervision and control provided in some cases for convicted defendants, usually young persons or first offenders in misdemeanor cases, who are not imprisoned but released on suspended sentences; also, the status of such a defendant. {1897-}

1878 *Mass. Acts & Resolves* 147 The mayor of the city of Boston shall appoint, annually . . . a suitable person . . . to recommend . . . the placing on probation of such persons as may reasonably be expected to be reformed without punishment. **1900** *N.J. Laws* 291 Any person . . . who shall violate the condition of his probation . . . , [may] be taken into custody and sentenced for his original offense. **1909** *Colo. Laws* 482 In no case shall any period of probation under this act exceed two years from the entry of the decree of the court. **1914** *Cycl. Amer. Govt.* III. 63/1 Although adult probation has made great progress, it has not kept pace with juvenile probation.

attrib. **1908** (*title*), First Report of the State Probation Commission [of N.Y.]. **1908** *N.Y. State Probation Comm. Rep. 1907* 10 Hon. Dennis McCarthy . . . [was appointed] a member of the State Probation Commission.

Probationer. 1. In some churches, one licensed to preach but not yet ordained. {1645-} +2. One who has joined a church on a probationary basis and is not yet a full member. +3. A convicted delinquent responsible to the convicting court and under the supervision of a probation officer. — **(1) 1845** *Indiana Mag. Hist.* XXIII. 31, I find he traveled nine years as a probationer and member of the Western and Tennessee conferences. **(2) 1856** CARTWRIGHT *Autobiog.* 39 There were in the entire bounds of the Western Conference, of members, probationers, colored and all, two thousand, four hundred and eighty-four. **1867** DIXON *New America* II. 132 The [Shaker] family at North House contains two orders of members (1) Probationers, (2) Covenanters. **1871** EGGLESTON *Duffels* 169, I believe he became a 'probationer,' but his creed was never quite settled enough for him to accept 'full membership.' **(3) 1907** in *N.Y. State Probation Comm. Rep.* (1908) 78 Whenever a probationer is reported to the judge as having violated the terms of his probation the judge uses his discretion as to the subsequent disposition of the case. **1910** *Ib.* 1909 35 Fines have been collected in instalments from probationers chiefly in the Buffalo Morning Courts.

+Probationist. 1. A candidate for church membership. 2. One who believes in the doctrine of future probation. *Obs.* — **(1) 1885** *Congregationalist* (*Cent.*), What portion of the probationists uniting with the M[ethodist] E[piscopal] church become full members? **(2) 1898** *Advance* 5 May 601/1, I am satisfied the probationists among us are an extremely small minority.

+Probation officer. An officer of a municipal criminal court appointed to assist in the exercise of its probationary functions. {1897-} — **1880** *Mass. Acts & Resolves* 87 The aldermen of any city, except the city of Boston, . . . may establish the office of probation officer. **1887** *Nat. Prison Assoc. Proc.* 215 Our Massachusetts probation officers . . . are appointed by cities or towns to take charge of persons placed by the courts on probation. **1900** *N.J. Laws* 289 Each probation officer shall, in the execution of his official duties, have all the powers of a constable under the laws of this state. **1920** *3d Nat. Country Life Conf. Proc.* 199 Probation officers are now reaching a large number of rural districts.

+Proc, Prock. Short for PROCLAMATION MONEY. *Obs.* Also attrib. — **1755** J. MURRAY *Letters* (1901) 78 The Money I get since the Presidents Currency came out is all proc. **1768** *N.C. Col. Rec.* VII. 775 To the amount of Five Pounds Prock. **1806** WEEMS *Letters* II. 335 Can I remit silver, or North Carolina Proc?

*Proceed, *v. intr.* To graduate from college +as a bachelor of arts. *Obs.* 'One is said to graduate B.A., to proceed M.A., B.D., etc. (in U.S. also to proceed B.A.)' (*O.E.D.*). — **1650** Quincy *Hist. Harvard* I. 518 They, that expect to proceed Bachelors that year, to be examined of their sufficiency according to the laws of the College. **1755** *Ib.* II. 93 To take effectual measures to prevent those, who proceeded Bachelors of Arts, from having entertainments of any kind, . . . after the Commencement day. **1833** PEIRCE *Hist. Harvard* 52 In 1656 he proceeded Bachelor of Arts. **1850** WOOLSEY *Hist. Discourse Yale* 38 (*Cent.*), The oldest [surviving graduate] proceeded Bachelor of Arts the very Commencement at which Dr. Stiles was elected to the Presidency.

*Process.

*1. A warrant, summons, or writ by which a person is brought to court.

1635 *Mass. Bay Rec.* I. 140 Mr Allerton shalbe sent for, by processe, to the nexte Court of Assistants. **1749** *N.J. Archives* 1 Ser. VII. 447 Thomas Clauson . . . was a person indicted of high treason, against whom he had delivered several processes to the Sheriff for apprehending him. **1799** *Ann. 7th Congress* 2 Sess. 1420, I remained while he served the process at Mr. Trexler's. **1904** T. E. WATSON *Bethany* 5 [To] have the Sheriff riding about serving Process . . . would create . . . a sensation.

+2. *comb.* Designating persons having, or professing to have, methods for extracting precious metal from ore.

1876 RAYMOND *8th Rep. Mines* 3 The process-owner [is interested], because it may enlarge the field of his operations. **1877** W. WRIGHT *Big Bonanza* 139 'Process-peddlers,' with little vials of chemicals in their vest pockets, went from mill to mill to show what they could do and would do, provided they received from $5,000 to $20,000 for their secret.

*Procession, *n.* =PERAMBULATION. *Obs.* {1693} — **1662** *Va. Statutes at Large* II. 102 Each county court shall appoint and order the vestrys of each parish . . . to appoint certaine dayes betweene Easter and Whitsunday to goe the said processions. **1673** *Ib.* 304 The act for processions hath been hindred to be put in execution. **1705** *Ib.* III. 327 The procession of the bounds of any persons land . . . shall be held . . . sufficient to settle the bounds.

Procession, *v.*

+1. *S. tr.* To perambulate (a boundary). Now hist.

1691 *Va. Statutes at Large* III. 82 The time for processioning lands hereafter [shall] be between the last day of 7ber [Sept.] and the last day of March. **1705** *Ib.* 325 Once in every four years the bounds of every person's land shall be processioned, (or gone round) and the land marks renewed. **1747** in Chalkley *Scotch-Irish Settlement Va.* II. 434 Edward Hall's land not processioned. **1796** in Summers *Ann. S.W. Va.* 861 The precincts formerly laid off for processioning the lands within this County are so large that [etc.]. **1885** E. INGLE *Local Institutions Va.* 64 Once in every four years the vestry, by order of the county court, divided the parish into precincts, and appointed two persons in each precinct to 'procession' the lands.

2. *S. intr.* To perambulate the bounds of a precinct. *Obs.* {1671}

Cf. PERAMBULATE *v.* 1.

1724 *Bristol* (Va.) *Vestry Bk.* 15 Whereas the precinct belonging unto Mr. Tho. Bott jun[io]r is thought too large for them it is ordered that they procession up to Noon[ing] Creek. **1747** [see next]. **1795** in Summers *Ann. S.W. Va.* 859 [The] said processioners are to proceed to procession within their respective precincts on the first Monday in October.

* **Processioner.** *S.* +One appointed to examine and renew the landmarks of a precinct or area: (see also quot. 1890).

Cf. PERAMBULATOR 1.

1731 *Bristol* (Va.) *Vestry Bk.* 59 Order'd that George Tucker be Prosessioner in the Stead of Robert Tucker jun[io]r who is Lame and cannott Officiate as prosessioner. **1747** in Chalkley *Scotch-Irish Settlement Va.* II. 433 [from parish vestry book] Processioners' Returns: Robert Huston and Alex. McClure: Processioned for Wm. Hall, Robert Allison present. **1795** in Summers *Ann. S.W. Va.* 463 The said Processioners to examine their business the first day of February next. **1859** BARTLETT 342 *Processioner,* an officer in Kentucky, and possibly in other States, whose duty it is to determine and mark out the bounds of lands. **1890** *Cent.* 4747/2 *Processioner,* a county officer in North Carolina and Tennessee charged with the duty of surveying lands at the request of an occupant claiming to be owner.

* **Processioning.** *S.* (See quot. 1896.) {1663-} Now hist.—**1691** *Va. Statutes* III. 82 Soe much of the said act as appoints the time of processioning [shall] be, and is hereby repealed. **1705** *Ib.* 327 Processionings [shall] be made by the consent of the owners of the said lands. **1896** BRUCE *Econ. Hist. Virginia* I. 543 The Assembly adopted . . . the law of processioning. According to this law, the people in every neighborhood were required once in the course of every four years to assemble at a designated spot, and from that point march in a body to examine and, if necessary, to renew the terminal marks of every plantation in their precinct.

+**Process kettle.** A kettle used in processing meats, vegetables, etc., for preserving them. — **1883** *Nat. Museum Bul.* No. 27, 222 The 'process kettle' or 'tub' . . . is then closed . . . and the oysters again steamed. **1892** *York County Hist. Rev.* 59/2 [They] make a specialty of . . . tools of every description, pump, 'process kettle' for canners [etc.].

+**Prock.**[1] Variant of PROC.

+**Prock.**[2] A fabulous quadruped having two short legs opposite two long ones, so as to be able to browse on mountain sides. *Obs.* — **1840** *Picayune* 8 Sept. 2/1 Koch, the proprietor [of a St. Louis Museum], . . . first discovered the prock. **1853** *Harper's Mag.* Oct. 708/2 An animal, known in that remote and seldom-visited region [the Rocky Mts.] as the 'Prock'; a creature that was only caught . . . on the side of a mountain, along which, and nowhere else, could he graze. **1896** *Advance* 4 June 823/1 That fabulous 'prock,' an animal whose two right legs were only half the length of the left legs.

* **Proclamation.**

***1.** The giving of public notice by an official; that which is proclaimed by such an official.

1675 EASTON *Indian War* 27 The War [began] without Proclamation, and sum of our Peopell did not kno [it]. **1705** *Boston News-Letter* 30 April 2/1 On the 17th Currant was Emitted by his Excellency . . . a Proclamation, Prohibiting the Importation of any clipt Money of Bitts or double Bitts into this Colony. **1794** *State P.* (1819) II. 83 My proclamation of the 7th of August last was accordingly issued. **1806** *Balance* 27 May 162/3 The proclamation of the President is a very proper thing. **1864** *Wkly. New Mexican* 3 June 2/2 Gov. Goodwin has issued a proclamation defining the judicial districts, and assigning the judges. **1912** NICHOLSON *Hoosier Chron.* 534 The Great Seal of the Hoosier Commonwealth . . . was affixed to a proclamation of the governor convening the legislature in special session.

+**b.** *Proclamation of Emancipation,* =EMANCIPATION PROCLAMATION.

1862 LINCOLN in Logan *Great Conspiracy* 435 What good would a Proclamation of Emancipation from me do? **1866** 'F. KIRKLAND' *Bk. Anecdotes* 652 [Lincoln's] place in history would centre chiefly in the memorable Proclamation of Emancipation. **1884** *Century Mag.* April 810/1 The President receives in the Cabinet Room—not the historic room where Lincoln signed the Proclamation of Emancipation. **1900** *Congress. Rec.* 15 Jan. 806/2 [Lincoln's] greatest title is that of the Emancipator, earned by issuing . . . the proclamation of emancipation.

2. =next.

1751 *N.J. Archives* XIX. 110 Lands pay already 2s. 6d. Proclamation, for every 100 Acres.

+**Proclamation money. a.** Colonial money valued according to a standard for use in American colonies prescribed by Queen Anne in 1704 in which the Spanish dollar of 17½ dwt. was rated at six shillings. **b.** A form of paper currency issued in some of the states during or soon after the Revolutionary War. *Obs.* — **1716** *N.J. Archives* 1 Ser. IV. 271 Annuall payment . . . must not be paid in bills but in currant silver money of the easterne divesion, or proclamation money. **1748** *N.H. Prov. Papers* V. 905 His Majesty has recommended that my salary should be fixed & Paid in Sterling or Proclamation money. **1778** *N.C. State Rec.* XIII. 375 According to law valued said negro James at eighty pounds Procklamation Money. **1860** MORDECAI *Virginia* 279 This money was called *proc.* (*i.e.,* proclamation money,) and was issued on bits of thick paper about the size of a playing card, and for various sums, from sixpence up to forty shillings. **1896** [see PROC MONEY].

+**Proc money.** Short for PROCLAMATION MONEY. — **1776** *N.J. Archives* 2 Ser. I. 94 Joseph Archer . . . has this day obtained of me . . . a Note of Hand for Twelve Pounds proc. money. **1896** H. WHITE *Money & Banking* 16 Six shillings was considered by the home government a fair average of the colonial valuations of the Spanish dollar. This valuation came to be known by the term proclamation money, or proc. money.

* **Proctor.** An officer in a college or university whose duty is to supervise the conduct of students, especially in dormitories and during examinations.

1817 *N. Amer. Rev.* Nov. 147 The officers of the University [Harvard] are, at present, twenty Professors, . . . Regent, five Proctors. **1836** GILMAN *Recoll.* (1838) 176 Then came the stale jokes . . . of the rolling of hot iron balls down entry stairs, to be taken up by some poor unsuspecting martyr proctor. **1893** POST *Harvard Stories* 84 He learned not to growl at the proctor on his staircase. **1902** CORBIN *Amer. at Oxford* 276 In each building in which students lived [at Harvard], a proctor resided who was supposed to see that the regent's orders were enforced.

+**b.** *Proctor's freshman,* a freshman who does errands for a proctor. *Obs.*

1851 [see FRESHMAN 1 b]. **1876** TRIPP *Student-Life* 15 If you can manage to be tutor's or proctor's Freshman, you have a first-rate room.

* **Produce.** *collect.* Natural products; the products of the farm, dairy, etc. {1719-} Also attrib.

See also COUNTRY PRODUCE, FARM PRODUCE.

1695 *York Deeds* IV. 81, I giue . . . ye produce of ye fruites of ye Earth as corn apples Cyder butter cheese. **1738** *Georgia Col. Rec.* III. 422 None . . . have been able to raise sufficient Produce to maintain their Families in Bread-kind only. **1821** *Ann. 17th Congress* 1 Sess. I. 46 When a farmer obtains his judgment against this very merchant for the sale of his produce, the force of his execution may be arrested for three months. **1872** *Vermont Bd. Agric. Rep.* I. 161 B. F. Rugg, who was then engaged largely in the produce trade, . . . undertook to carry out a plan for controlling the Boston butter market. **1912** IRWIN *Red Button* 140, I came here to found a great commercial career—as bill-clerk in a produce house.

Produce merchant. A merchant who deals in country produce. — **1841** Cist *Cincinnati* Advt., Produce, Forwarding, and Commission Merchants. **1869** *Boyd's Business Directory* 12 Fuller E. R. produce merchant, 707. **1870** M. H. SMITH *20 Years Wall St.* 398 The oyster-beds yield a supply as certainly as the farm of the produce merchant.

Prof, Proff. A students' abbreviation of PROFESSOR. *slang.* — **1838** *Yale Lit. Mag.* III. 144 For Proffs and Tutors too, Who steer our big canoe, Prepare their lays. **1849** *Gallinipper* Dec. 6 Alas! how dearly for the fun they paid, Whom the Proffs. gobbled, and the Tutors too! *a***1860** E. C. Porter *Songs of Yale* 13 He . . . Lines with guns the chapel, Gives the Prof. a thump, sir! **1925** *Scribner's Mag.* July 62/1 'Profs are always old,' Thorpe asserted.

Professional, *n.* {1811-} +(See quotations.) — **1868** CHADWICK *Base Ball* 44 *Professionals.*—This is the term applied to all ball players who play base-ball for money, or as a means of livelihood. **1900** NELSON *A B C Wall St.* 156 Room traders, scalpers and others who speculate for their own account are called professionals.

* **Professional,** *a.* Engaged in an occupation or activity as a profession or means of livelihood. Often applied disparagingly. {1793-}

1798 in *Ann. 10th Congress* 1 Sess. 2741 The solemn air and dictatorial manner of a professional schoolmaster may have contributed much to establish his character. **1859** WILMER *Press Gang* 224 There are certain idle and worthless fellows, sometimes called 'professional jurymen,' who hang about the purlieus of the Court House, and are always willing to be employed as jurors. **1884** *Century Mag.* March 654/2 There are professional lobbyists who go there in numbers every winter; their doings . . . can be traced by the aid of a detective reporter. **1891** C. ROBERTS *Adrift Amer.* 68, I only wanted to see if you would work, I don't believe in feeding professional bums.

+**b.** With reference to baseball. {1850-, in cricket}

1871 (*title*), National Association of Professional Base Ball Players. Proceedings of Convention, March, 1871. **1878** *De Witt's Base Ball Guide* 17 In 1869 the first regular professional club—the Cincinnati Red Stockings—took their place upon the field. **1889** CAMP *College Sports* (1893) 170 The first sensation of a college in-field on meeting a professional nine is one of hurry.

+**Professional school.** A school in which students are prepared for a profession. — **1881** *Harper's Mag.* March 628/1 Degrees shall yet be lawful certificates of proficiency to be accepted at their 'face value' by professional schools. **1893** *Rep. Comm. Education 1889-90* 875 In taking up in order the several classes of professional schools, the requisites for admission to them will be considered first. **1914** *Cycl. Amer. Govt.* III. 635/2 The Division of Higher Education [of the Bureau of Educ.] has charge of the statistics . . . regarding universities, colleges, technological schools, normal schools, and professional schools.

***Professor.**

*1. One who professes or openly avows Christianity. 'Now chiefly *Sc.* and *U.S.*' (*O.E.D.*).

a1656 BRADFORD *Hist.* 472 Againe, when adultrie or sodomie is committed by professors or church members, I fear it comes too near ye sine of ye preists daughters. **1714** SEWALL *Letter-Book* II. 32 Give warning to professors, that they beware of worldlymindedness. **1824** *Baptist Mag.* IV. 429 Old professors acknowledged to their brethren and the world their backslidings from God. **1881** McLEAN *Cape Cod Folks* 53 Grandma and Grandpa Keeler, by the way, were good Methodists, but Madeline was not a 'professor.' **1903** WIGGIN *Rebecca* 213 Mrs. Burch . . . was about to open her lips to ask if Rebecca was not a 'professor.'

*2. A teacher or instructor, especially one of college or university rank. Also as a title.

1736 *Harvard Rec.* I. 130 The President, Professors & Tutors, shall advise them what Books are most proper for their reading. **1780** E. PARKMAN *Diary* 224 Mr. Samuel Williams of Bradford is chose professor instead of ye late Dr. Winthrop. **1844** *Whig Almanac 1845* 34/1, 23 Professors of Mathematics, (on duty), $1,200. **1892** *Boston Transcript* 21 April, Professors from small fresh-water colleges are much surprised at this absence of professional insistence. **1906** FREEMAN *By Light of Soul* 385 The principal of the Normal School in Westbridge had been a certain Professor Lane.

+b. *Professor of dust and ashes*, (see quot. 1851). *Obs.*

1847 WELLS & DAVIS *Sk. Williams Coll.* 77 Was interrupted a moment just now, by the entrance of Mr. C—, the gentleman who makes the beds, sweeps, takes up the ashes, and supports the dignity of the title, 'Professor of dust and ashes.' **1851** HALL *College Words* 247 *Professor of Dust and Ashes*, a title sometimes jocosely given by students to the person who has the care of their rooms.

3. In jocular or grandiose use, applied to a person assumed or claiming to be learned, experienced, or skilled in some vocation or profession, as auctioneering, dancing, etc. {1864-}

For some discussion of this use see *Amer. Speech* III. (1928) 256-7.

1774 in Hildeburn *Century of Printing* II. 182 Catalogue of New and Old Books, to be sold by Auction, by Robert Pell, Bookseller, and Professor of Book-Auctioneering. **1859** BARTLETT 343 *Professor*. . . . The application of the word to dancing-masters, conjurers, banjo-players, etc., has been called an Americanism. **1870** O. LOGAN *Before Footlights* 91 There are quite a number of these 'professors of symmetry' in this country, but they are most numerous in Philadelphia. **1896** SHINN *Story of Mine* 56 They were never out of sight of pilgrims—Irishmen with wheelbarrows, . . . 'professors' with divining rods and electric 'silver detectors.'

Professorship. The office or position of a college professor. {1641-} — **1704** SEWALL *Letter-Book* I. 302 As to your Professorship, . . . considering the way in which you obtain it, it will be hurtfull to yourself, to the College and to the province. **1846** *Knickerb.* XXVIII. 10 The professorships in our colleges are in the main filled by men who are in every respect competent. **1900** WINCHESTER *W. Castle* 30 Of course he lost the professorship of Greek in the University of California. **1903** *N.Y. Herald* 5 June 7/1 A donation of $10,000 [was announced] to endow a professorship in the School of Commerce . . . which shall be known as the Charles Waldo Haskins professorship of auditing and the history of accountancy.

***Progress,** *v.*

'Common in England *c*1590-1670. . . . In 18th c. obs. in England, but app. retained (or formed anew) in America, where it became very common *c*1790. . . . Thence readopted in England after 1800 (Southey 1809); but often characterized as an Americanism, and much more used in America than in Great Britain, in sense 3, in which ordinary English usage says "go on," "proceed"' (*O.E.D.*).

1. *fig. intr.* To improve or advance; to make progress. {1610-}

1789 FRANKLIN *Writings* X. 77 Another [verb] is formed from the Substantive *Progress*, the most awkward and abominable of the three; *The committee, having* Progressed, *resolved to adjourn.* **1791** WASHINGTON *Writings* XII. 24 Our country . . . is fast progressing in its political importance and social happiness. **1816** PICKERING 155 *To Progress.* This obsolete English word . . . has had an extraordinary currency for the last twenty or thirty years.

+2. To go forward, to proceed.

1808 C. SCHULTZ *Travels* II. 170 In this manner . . . the head [of an island] is continually progressing up the [Miss.] river. **1832** VIGNE *6 Mos. in Amer.* II. 266 Groups of lank thin-jawed personages may be seen 'progressing' towards the door. **a1862** THOREAU *Maine Woods* 286 We had been busily progressing all day. **1888** DORSEY *Midshipman Bob* 177 The boats were so evenly ahead of the ship that they couldn't be seen by the Englishmen, and she just quietly 'progressed' away from them.

Progressive, *a.* {1607-} +Designating card games, as euchre and poker, played by groups at separate tables, the players changing tables in accordance with prescribed rules. Also transf. — **1886** RITTENHOUSE *Maud* 366 So we had a jolly little time, playing progressive eucher, and indulging in some music. **1887** KELLER *Draw Poker* 79 The latest development of Draw Poker is known as Progressive Poker and doubtless owes its origin to the popularity of progressive euchre. **1890** S. HALE *Letters* 24 The lunch was at little tables, made a sort of 'progressive' one, for after each course *I* was moved. **1892** DALY *Test Case* (1893) 21 We have a progressive euchre club—penny a point. **1898** NICHOLS *Idyl of Wabash* 69 Her daughter . . . now and then indulged in that perilous frivolity, progressive euchre, and attended the theater.

Progressivist. One who favors or aims at progress or reform; a progressive. {1904} — **1885** *Advance* 1 Jan. 867/2 There are . . . no more impracticable progressivists than those who clamor for a repeal of all laws.

***Prohibition.**

1. The forbidding by law of the importation of certain commodities. {1670-}

1711 SEWALL *Diary* II. 305 Col. Byfield argues the Case of Prohibition. **1794** *Ann. 3d Congress* 1448 Any of the aforesaid articles, . . . which, during the continuance of this prohibition, shall be found on board of any vessel, . . . shall be forfeited. **1822** *Ann. 17th Congress* I. 245 Many objections might be made to the contemplated prohibition.

+2. The prohibiting by law of the manufacture and sale of spirituous liquors for general use. {1897-, in Canada}

1851 *Amer. Temp. Union Ann. Rep.* 27 The State of Vermont has struggled arduously to arrive at the summit level of entire prohibition. **1855** in MacLeod *F. Wood* 258 The penalties of prohibition will go into effect. **1889** P. BUTLER *Recollections* 46 Kansas . . . has been the first State in the Union . . . to incorporate prohibition into its fundamental law. **1925** BRYAN *Memoirs* 186 His views on the initiative and referendum and prohibition had not altered.

3. Attrib. in sense 2 with *convention, liquor, system, town.*

1877 *Harper's Mag.* Dec. 146/2 He argues the license system a failure and the prohibition system a success. **1883** *Ib.* Aug. 480/1 The New Jersey State Prohibition Convention, May 22, nominated Dr. Isaac N. Quimby for Governor. **1891** 'THANET' *Otto the Knight* 183 It's a prohibition town; and prohibition in Grinnell does prohibit. **1924** *Scribner's Mag.* Dec. 646/1, I would have enlarged every Justice of the peace in Vermont and hung him in a Mexican silver frame, if I hadn't drunk prohibition liquor and gone to Boston.

+**Prohibition amendment.** 1. An amendment to a state constitution prohibiting the manufacture and sale of spirituous liquors for common use. 2. The Eighteenth Amendment (1919) to the Constitution of the United States, prohibiting the manufacture, sale, and transportation of spirituous liquors, except for certain specified purposes. — **(1) 1883** *Harper's Mag.* Dec. 162/1 The prohibition amendment was defeated [in Ohio]. **1886** *Ib.* June 157/1 The Prohibition amendment was carried [in R.I.] by a decisive majority. **(2) 1917** *Nation* 9 Aug. 138/2 Some wild things are said about last week's vote in the Senate in favor of a prohibition amendment of the Constitution. **1919** *Lit. Digest* 15 Feb. 32/1 Protestant church papers are loudest among the religious press in laudation of the passing of the prohibition amendment. **1924** E. R. SHAW *Prohibition* 34 The Prohibition Amendment was the first to be submitted by a Senate elected directly by the people.

+**Prohibition candidate.** A candidate for political office endorsed or sponsored by the Prohibition party. — **1877** *Harper's Mag.* Dec. 146/1 The monograph of Hon. Robert C. Pitman, . . . Prohibition candidate for Governor of [Mass.] . . . possesses a value to the student of sociology. **1893** *Ib.* May 978/2 Judge Cox, late Prohibition candidate for County Auditor.

Prohibitionist. One who favors prohibition {*a*1846}, +esp. of the manufacturing and selling of spirituous liquors. {1883} — **1854** (*title*), The Prohibitionist. **1877** *Scribner's Mo.* July 391 The strict prohibitionist will . . . not admit this to be a gain; he looks upon all liquor-selling alike. **1883** *Harper's Mag.* Aug. 480/1 The Ohio Prohibitionists, June 14, nominated for . . . Auditor of State, Gresham Lease. **1894** 'MARK TWAIN' *Those Twins* Introd., Her half was a prohibitionist and had never drunk a drop in his life. **1912** NICHOLSON *Hoosier Chron.* 311, I've never taken any stock in this clamor of the Prohibitionists and temperance cranks generally.

+**Prohibition law.** A law prohibiting the manufacture and sale of intoxicating liquors for general use. (Cf. LIQUOR LAW, MAINE LAW.) — **1886** *Century Mag.* March 728/2 The prohibition law was strictly enforced. **1890** *Harper's Mag.* Nov. 961/2 A prohibition law would stop drinking. **1911** *Okla. Session Laws* 3 Legisl. 165 Such special enforcement shall have the power and authority of the sheriffs throughout the state of Oklahoma, for the enforcement of the prohibition laws of this state.

+**Prohibition party.** A political party having as its fundamental principle opposition to the manufacture and sale of intoxicating liquors for common consumption. (Cf. NARROW GAUGE 2 c.) — **1869** in D. L. Colvin *Prohibition in U.S.* 73 We adopt the name of the National Prohibition Party, as expressive of our primary object. **1884** in Porter *Nat. Party Platforms* 128 The Prohibition party, in National Convention assembled. **1891** WELCH *Recoll. 1830-40* 84 There were no 'Prohibition Parties,' at that time, nor 'Maine' nor 'Scott' laws. **1896** *Voice* 19 Nov. 4 The Prohibition Party is in the field: it can be depended upon to do what it can. **1914** *Cycl. Amer. Govt.* III. 77 The Prohibition party has been the longest-lived of all third parties in this country.

Prohibitory law. {1602-} + = PROHIBITION LAW. In full *prohibitory liquor law.* — **1854** *La Crosse Democrat* 11 April 2/2 Gov. Seymore, of New York, vetoes the Prohibitory Liquor Law. **1856** MACLEOD *F. Wood* 43 It was before the passage of the Prohibitory Liquor Law. **1883** *Century Mag.* July 337/2 The beer-seller went on to say that he voted for prohibitory laws every time. **1889** P. BUTLER *Recollections* 25 Those who have watched the progress of the temperance reform in Iowa have noticed that, while the prohibitory law is enforced almost throughout the State [of Iowa], there are yet exceptions.

***Project,** *v. S.* +*intr.* To experiment, trifle, play tricks *with;* to saunter, meander, loiter *around.* Also *vbl. n. colloq.*

1820 J. HALL *Lett. fr. West* 290 A man who goes into the woods . . . has a . . . great deal of *projecking* to do, as well as hard work. **1845** W. T. THOMPSON *Chron. Pineville* 107 You see what comes of your projectin' about town, when you ought to be gwine home. **1848** W. T. THOMPSON *Major Jones's Travels* (1880) 76, I didn't know whether he was projectin with me or not. **1891** 'THANET' *Otto the Knight* 66 Quality liked projeckin' roun' de kitchin. **1906** LYNDE *Quickening* 135 Don't you know you oughtn't to go projecting around in the woods all alone?

+Prom. =PROMENADE 3. Also attrib. — **1894** *Outing* XXIV. 68/2 For two days . . . in January the room is crowded with 'Prom' girls and their escorts. **1899** QUINN *Penna. Stories* 170 All you children can get tickets of me for the Senior Prom right now. **1912** NICHOLSON *Hoosier Chron.* 187, I went up there once to see a girl I had met at a Prom. **1924** MARKS *Plastic Age* 136 No freshman was allowed to attend the Prom. . . . There was a tea-dance at the fraternity house during Prom week.

***Promenade.**

1. A place, as a paved public walk, suitable for promenading. {1648–} Also attrib.

1827 [see PUBLIC 2 a]. **1854** CUMMINS *Lamplighter* 507 In the public promenade-ground, on the shore of Saratoga lake, and on board the steamboat at Albany, did I both see and recognise you. **1878** *Decorum* 280 It should . . . be the plainest of promenade-dresses. **1894** HOWELLS in *Harper's Mag.* May 823/1, I stood on the Promenade at Portland.

+2. =PROMENADE DECK. {1882}

1845 *Knickerb.* XXV. 61 On the upper deck the engineers and sailors, ladies, emigrants and gentlemen, sat side by side upon the single seat which ran all round the promenade. **1873** HOWELLS *Chance Acquaintance* i, On the forward promenade of the Saguenay boat . . . Miss Kitty Ellison sat.

+3. A ball or dance given by students, usually of a particular class. Also attrib.

1871 BAGG *At Yale* 664 The Junior Promenade Concert is not a very ancient affair. **1887** *Lippincott's Mag.* Aug. 298 The most important society event of the year is the Junior Promenade. . . . During 'Promenade week' the three upper classes hold germans. **1905** *N.Y. Herald* 22 Jan. 10 Yale men assumed the rôle of host . . . for the vanguard of the fair guests invited to the Junior Promenade, the gayest event of the college year.

+Promenade deck. An upper deck of a vessel on which passengers are accustomed to promenade. — **1829** *Amer. Traveller* 14 Sept. (Ernst), The engraving above exhibits what may emphatically be called a Land Barge . . . with a Cabin, Births, etc. below . . . [with] a promenade deck, awning, seats, etc. above. **1845** HONE *Diary* II. 253 Cotillons, waltzes, and polkas were danced . . . on the promenade-deck of the steamer. **1898** WESTCOTT *D. Harum* 375 He was sitting there . . . , looking idly over the sea, with an occasional glance at the people who were walking on the promenade-deck below. **1911** VANCE *Cynthia* 148 They paused by the after rail of the promenade deck.

Promenader. One who promenades. {1830–} — **1838** *U.S. Mag.* I. 301 You will scarcely meet any groups of promenaders throughout the day-time. **1871** HOWELLS *Wedding Journey* 266 The promenaders . . . paced back and forth upon the planking. **1898** WESTCOTT *D. Harum* 28 The deck began to fill with promenaders.

Promissory note. A written promise to pay a specified amount of money under prescribed conditions to bearer or to a designated payee. {1710–} — **1719** *Mass. H. Rep. Jrnl.* II. 133 A Promissory note of Thomas Tarbol. **1784** FRANKLIN *Autobiog.* 322 The library was opened one day in the week for lending to the subscribers, on their promissory notes to pay double the value if not duly returned. **1833** CROCKETT *Sketches* 121 Upon asking for an explanation, I found out that bonds, or promissory notes, were termed dogs. **1911** *Okla. Session Laws* 3 Legisl. 216 If any such promissory note or assessment is not paid when due, action may be brought thereon.

***Promontory.** A cape, headland, or point of land jutting out into a sea, bay, etc. — **1789** MORSE *Amer. Geog.* 169 This promontory circumscribes Barnstable Bay. **1815** DRAKE *Cincinnati* 64 The rocks of the celebrated reef, bordering that promontory [in east Florida], are calcareous. **1896** JEWETT *Country of Pointed Firs* 129 The small island with its low whitish promontory lay in full view before us.

***Promote,** *v. Educ.* +*tr.* To advance (a pupil) from one class or grade to another. — **1876** *Scribner's Mo.* Feb. 584/1 Their mother holds them back; will not let them be 'promoted,' or dragged through at high-pressure speed from class to class. **1902** *Forum* June 471 Because of the manner of grading and promoting, the graded school tends to keep all the children of each grade in intellectual lock-step.

***Promoter.** One who promotes or aids in promoting some financial scheme or enterprise. Often opprobrious. {1876–} — **1873** *Republic* March App. p. xiv, He joined himself with the promoters of a scheme whereby the Government was to be defrauded. **1890** *Stock Grower & Farmer* 4 Jan. 3/1 The 'promoters' of the Rio Grande Ditch company have already received a dividend. **1902** MCFAUL *Ike Glidden* 127 Each day brought its new characters, fakirs, peddlers, schemers and promoters.

***Prompter.** One employed to follow the script of a play, offstage, and remind actors of forgotten lines during a dramatic performance. — **1812** *Niles' Reg.* I. 340/2 There was only one *paper* scene hanging, which Mr. Utt the prompter declares . . . was removed six or eight feet behind the lamp. **1832** DUNLAP *Hist. Amer. Theatre* 54 The office of prompter, so essential in a theatre, was filled by Mrs. Hemsworth, who occasionally played. **1889** BRAYLEY *Boston Fire Dept.* 220 There were two thousand volumes of prompter's books . . . destroyed.

***Prong.** *S.* +A branch or fork of a stream, swamp, road, etc. — **1725** in *Amer. Speech* XV. 300 To a Gum on the south side of the north prong of the Spring Swamp. **1747** in *Ib.*, A long one of the Prongs of the said Dam. **1784** WASHINGTON *Diaries* II. 311 Carpenters Creek, a branch of Jackson's, which is the principal prong of James River. **1796** HAWKINS *Letters* 27 [Cross] a branch and take up one prong, the lands rich tho' broken, the timber large. **1834** PECK *Gaz. Illinois* 241 Fraziers Creek . . . falls into the south prong of Bear creek. **1913** MORLEY *Carolina Mts.* 177 When a stream or a road forks, the two divisions are 'prongs.'

+Prongbuck. A male prong-horned antelope.

1834 *Penny Cycl.* II. 71/2 The prongbuck inhabits all the western parts of North America from the 53° of north latitude to the plains of Mexico and California. **1882** BAILLIE-GROHMAN *Camps in Rockies* 46 For even the prongbuck (or antelope) has deserted his usual runs. **1893** ROOSEVELT *Wilderness Hunter* 62 They saw me at once and ran, but I held well ahead of a fine young prong-buck, and rolled him over like a rabbit, with both shoulders broken. **1902** WHITE *Blazed Trail* 126 By and by a prongbuck joined them. **1917** *Mammals of Amer.* 35/1 The American Pronghorn, known also as the 'Prongbuck,' 'Pronghorned Antelope,' or, simply, 'Antelope,' has the distinction of being the sole representative of a family.

+Prongdoe. The female of the prong-horned antelope (q.v.). — **1890** *Cent.* 4771/1 The prongdoe regularly drops twins.

+Pronghorn. *ellipt.* =next. — **1826** GODMAN *Amer. Nat. Hist.* II. 324 The prong-horn . . . is usually called a goat by the Canadians. **1871** DE VERE 371 The Pronghorn (*Antilocapre americana*) . . . is called *Cabrée* by the Canadian voyageurs, and the *Goat* by the fur-traders. **1877** ALLEN *Amer. Bison* 581 The tact and caution required in the successful pursuit of the watchful pronghorn. **1917** *Mammals of Amer.* 35/1 The Pronghorn is strictly a North American animal, and is the most graceful and the fleetest of all our quadrupeds.

+Prong-horn(ed) antelope. A deerlike ruminant (*Antilocapra americana*), found on the western prairies and popularly called an antelope.

Cf. ANTELOPE 1, CABRI.

(*a*) **1815** ORD *N. Amer. Zool.* (1894) 308 The Prong-Horned Antelope is found in great numbers on the plains and the high-lands of the Missouri. **1823** JAMES *Exped.* I. 262. **1852** MARCY *Explor. Red River* (1854) 67 [The] prong-horned antelope of the plains, is very much swifter. **1867** *Amer. Naturalist* I. 537 The Prong-horned Antelope . . . , the swiftest animal of America, runs races [over the Ariz. plains] with the winds.

(*b*) **1826** GODMAN *Nat. Hist.* II. 321 The prong-horn antelope is an animal of wonderful fleetness. **1868** *Amer. Naturalist* II. 131 He describes the . . . Prong-horn Antelope. **1902** ROOSEVELT, etc. *Deer Family* 98 The prongbuck or pronghorn antelope, known throughout its range simply as antelope, is a very extraordinary creature.

+Pronto, *adv.* [Sp.] At once, promptly. *colloq.* — **1850** GARRARD *Wah-To-Yah* xi. 146 Me be off *pronto.* **1925** TILGHMAN *Dugout* 103 [He] cut short his hearty welcome by a request for a horse 'pronto.'

Pronunciamento. *S.W.* [Sp. *pronunciamiento.*] A proclamation or manifesto. {1845–} — **1836** *Diplom. Corr. Texas* I. (1908) 121 Pronunciamentos are taking place, in favor of Federalism . . . without any molestation from the government. **1875** *Scribner's Mo.* July 275/1 The 'Emperor Norton,' a harmless creature who firmly believes that he is the legitimate sovereign of the United States and Mexico; issues frequent pronunciamentos.

***Proof. 1.** *attrib.* Designating containers used in testing the strength of alcoholic liquors. **+2.** Conclusive evidence showing that the requirements for obtaining a patent for government land have been fulfilled. — **(1) 1834** CARRUTHERS *Kentuckian* I. 97, I thought in a minute about our old still-house, and the school-master, and the miller, and the blacksmith, and the stiller, talkin politics . . . and takin a swig every now and then out of the old proof-vial. **1848** *Knickerb.* XVIII. 380 Isaac was a first-rate judge of liquors. . . . With what profound deliberation he drew his proof-glass from the bung-hole of a brandy-pipe. **(2)** [**1862** *Statutes at Large* XII. 393 Nothing in this act shall . . . prevent any person . . . [from] obtaining a patent therefor from the government, . . . on making proof of settlement and cultivation.] **1907** *Indian Laws & Tr.* III. 628 Two Dollars and Fifty Cents per acre in cash payable at date of final proof upon entries made.

+Proof-reader. One whose profession is reading printers' proof for detecting and indicating errors. — **1855** I. C. PRAY *Mem. J. G. Bennett* 41 From this post he was transferred to that of a proof-reader in the printing-house of Wells & Lilly. **1877** *Harper's Mag.* Dec. 44/2 More telegraph boys, compositors, proof-readers, and reporters passed the visitors on the stairs. **1892** *Harper's Wkly.* 9 Jan. 42/4 The proof-readers are expected to catch and correct it.

Proof text. A passage of Scripture regarded as proving a doctrinal or theological point. {1874–} Also attrib. — **1847** WEBSTER 877/3 *Proof-text,* a passage of Scripture relied upon for proving a doctrine, &c. **1859** STOWE *Minister's Wooing* xl, Taking his Concordance, [he] began busily tracing out and numbering all the proof-texts for one of the chapters of his theological system. **1869** — *Oldtown Folks* 381 The Bible was mostly read by ministers and proof-texts quoted from it. **1874** BUSHNELL *Forgiveness* 164 The man who should . . . draw out his conclusion that we are to forgive just four hundred and ninety times, would even raise a smile among proof-text scholars.

Proof whisky. Whisky of standard proof or strength. — **1801** in Cist *Cincinnati 1841* 177 Advertisement. Much wanted by the subscriber. Good cows, proof whiskey, well cured bacon [etc.]. **1867** *Congress. Globe* App. 21 Jan. 60/1 These backings . . . come out doublings or proof whiskey.

+**Prop.**[1] A settling or precipitating tank used in making sugar or syrup. — **1862** *Rep. Comm. Patents 1861: Agric.* 304 Nothing but a neutral sediment remains, which generally attaches to the pan, or pipes, or settles in the 'prop,' if allowed to do so. **1887** *Century Mag.* Nov. 116/1 In the course of the boiling [the syrup] is ladled successively into . . . 'the prop' or 'proy,' 'the flambeau,' 'the sirop,' and 'the battery.'

+**Prop.**[2] [Origin unknown.] In pl., a game played with four shells or counters, shaken and thrown like dice; also, sing., a counter used in this game.

1833 SNELLING *Exposé of Gaming in New Eng.* 11 [We] threw the *props* upon the table. **1857** *Knickerb.* XLIX. 38 In those days Mace had got just a *leetle* too old and too genteel to play props with the boys. **1893** HALE *New Eng. Boyhood* 70 Among others [of the foreign customs introduced by seafaring men] was the use of 'props,' a gambling game which the boys had introduced perfectly innocently as an element in playing marbles. **1908** *Boston Transcript* 5 Sept. III. 6/5 Props was a very common gambling game in the country in the forties and fifties.

attrib. **1833** SNELLING *Exposé of Gaming in New Eng.* 11 We advanced to the prop table and held forth our hand for the props between two infamous blackguards. **1868** *How Gamblers Win* (N.Y.) 97 It is said that there is not a Prop-house in the city of New York.

Prop.[3] Any of the movable articles used in acting a play or in setting the stage; also, transf., a property man. {1854- (Scott & Howard *Life Blanchard* I. 125)} Chiefly pl. — **1896** *N.Y. Dramatic News* 15 Aug. 3 Improvements have been made at the Academy of music, Scranton; . . . new stage, new property room full of new furniture and 'props.' **1902** PATTERSON & BATEMAN *By Stage Door* 192 While he was 'Props' he was discharged . . . for not yelling 'Fire!' at the right time. **1911** C. POLLOCK *Footlights* 257 By-play with small articles, rehearsed twenty times, is blundered over when the player finds the 'prop' actually in his hands.

Propagandist, *n.* One who spreads propaganda. {1829-} — **1852** FILLMORE in *Pres. Mess. & P.* V. 180 [Patriots of the Revolution knew] that it was not possible for this nation to become a 'propagandist' of free principles without arraying against it the combined powers of Europe. **1876** LOWELL *Among My Books* 2 Ser. 114 Evil is a far more cunning and persevering propagandist than Good. **1900** *Congress. Rec.* 24 Jan. 1146/2 The claimant is a propagandist of a system of social order that is destructive of the Christian family. **1917** MCCUTCHEON *Green Fancy* 179 He was certain that she was the fair propagandist described by Sprouse.

Propagandist, *a.* Having to do with propaganda. {1885-} — **1824** D. WEBSTER *Works* III. 62 It may be easy to call this resolution *Quixotic*, the emanation of a crusading or propagandist spirit. **1856** PIERCE in *Pres. Mess. & P.* V. 354 [Slavery men] had recourse . . . to the extraordinary measure of propagandist colonization of the Territory of Kansas.

Propeller. {1780-}

1. An appliance actuated by machinery for propelling a vessel through the water, now usually a screw propeller. {1838-} Also attrib.

1809 FULTON *U.S. Patent Specif.*, The successful construction of steam boats depends on their parts being well proportioned, whether wheels or any other propellers be used. **1843** *N.Y. Semi-Weekly Exp.* 10 Jan. 1/5 The U.S. steamer Union made the *first* trial trip of her propellers yesterday afternoon, in a short run down the river. **1849** W. WILLIS in Smith & Deane *Journal* App. 465 A few gentlemen . . . formed a company in 1843 for the purpose of putting *Propeller* Steamboats on to the route [from Portland to Boston]. **1862** Moore *Rebellion Rec.* V. II. 179 The timbers, or shape of the hull, is there, together with the chimney and propeller-wheel or flanges. **1869** *Causes Reduct. Tonnage* (1870) 49, I was told that on the Atlantic a wooden vessel cannot stand the action of the propeller. **1876** KNIGHT 1809/1 The propeller may be made to rise out of the water when the ship is under canvas alone.

+**2.** A steamboat, esp. one for lake service, propelled by a screw propeller.

1845 J. W. NORRIS *Chicago Directory* 113 They have the agency of several responsible lines on the Erie Canal and forward by Steamboats, Propellers, or vessels on the Lakes. **1862** MCCLELLAN in *Own Story* 499 We have some propellers here, but they are laden with commissary supplies. **1876** *Harper's Mag.* Dec. 125/1 The captain of the *Flying Arrow* was captain of a propeller which brought passengers and merchandise from the upper lakes.

+**b.** In appositive use.

1845 *Niles' Wkly. Reg.* 25 Oct. 128/3 The propeller 'Massachusetts,' left New York on the 15 Sep. **1889** *Kansas City Star* 7 Oct. 1/6 Wheelsman Thomas Rowland of the propeller Rosedale was killed during the storm. **1894** *Harper's Mag.* Jan. 318/2 The propeller *Dean Richmond*, with a crew of eighteen men, sank in Lake Erie October 15th.

+**3.** (See quotations.)

1875 KNIGHT 1488/2 One other mode of draft is to be noticed, and that is the *propeller*, in which the cutting apparatus [of the mower] is ahead of the horses, which push the implement before them. **1883** KNIGHT *Suppl.* 724/2 *Propeller*, . . . a kind of trolling bait, having oblique wings which cause it to rotate in the water. **1905** *Hartford Courant* 2 Feb. 1 [In] the big propellers—the fire engines that furnish their own power— . . . the power is applied to the rear wheels.

***Property.**

***1.** That which is owned. With reference to a slave or slaves.

*a*1800 TWINING *Visit* (1894) 33 She was the *property*, I understood, of Mr. Francis, who had *bought* her some time before. **1835** CHANNING *Works* (1886) 722/1 Freemen . . . talk of the slave as 'property,' with the same confidence as if this were the holiest claim. **1857** BENTON *Exam. Dred Scott* 16 The Constitution could be so extended [to the territories], and . . . carry along with it protection to persons and property, *to wit*, the owner and his slaves.

2. In special combinations.

Property book, a book in which a record of property is kept; *p. law*, a law specifying the conditions under which the property of a debtor may be sold by a creditor; *p. line*, a boundary line between adjacent landed properties; *p. theory*, the theory according to which Negro slaves were regarded as the property of their masters. *Obs.*

1855 A. Lawrence *Diary & Corr.* 278 On the first of January, 1850, Mr. Lawrence, as usual, reviews, in his property-book, the state of his affairs during the preceding year. **1854** BENTON *30 Years' View* I. 5/2 Stop laws—property laws— . . . the intervention of the legislator between the creditor and the debtor: this was the business of legislation. **1885** *Century Mag.* Oct. 914 The drive breaks from the walk and side road which skirts the property line on the eastern boundary of the park. **1888** *Ib.* Dec. 284/2 The rejection and condemnation of . . . the subversive 'property theory' of Jefferson Davis [had called the Republican party into being].

Property-holder. A holder or owner of property, usually real estate. — **1824** *Ann. 18th Congress* 1 Sess. II. 3129 The memorial of the . . . property-holders of the city of Baltimore. **1851** CIST *Cincinnati* 73 There is no city in the world . . . in which so large a share of the community are property holders. **1898** PAGE *Red Rock* 228 Hiram Still had become the largest property-holder in the county. **1911** *Okla. Session Laws* 3 Legisl. 187 Any such lands . . . shall be detached therefrom when a petition therefor, signed by two-thirds of the property-holders thereof, is filed.

Property-owner. =prec. {1902-} — **1865** *Harper's Mag.* July 154/2 It is the nightmare of property-owners. **1884** *Century Mag.* March 648/1 The rights of property-owners were disregarded, and they were assessed for 'improvements' when their property was ruined. **1905** WIGGIN *Rose* 166 Surely no property-owner in the universe could . . . observe his corn leveled to the earth, his sign removed, his house open, . . . without going in to surprise the rogue and villain who could be guilty of such vandalism.

Property qualification. A qualification for office or for voting based upon the ownership of a certain amount of property. {1862-} — **1807** *Ann. 10th Congress* 1 Sess. I. 916 The Constitution of the United States requires no property qualification in the elected. **1844** *Whig Almanac 1845* 6/2 The vote for Polk exceeds the whole number of white males of all ages in the Parish in 1840, although Louisiana exacts a Property qualification of her voters! **1900** *Congress. Rec.* 19 Feb. 1920/2 A property qualification is required of the voter who seeks to vote for any candidate for the senate.

Property room. A room in which stage properties or accessories are kept. {1830- (Bernard *Retrosp. Stage* I. 252)} — **1839** in Northall *Curtain* 31 A complete list of the company [includes] . . . *Property Room*, Dejonge, Williams. **1855** I. C. PRAY *Mem. J. G. Bennett* 44 In the property room of the theatre was an old Dutch clock. **1877** *Harper's Mag.* Feb. 466/2 The great spaces, the open draughts, the inflammable scenery, the oils and paints and varnishes of the property-rooms . . . supply every condition favorable to sudden, swift, and resistless fire. **1896** [see PROP3].

***Prophet.**

+**1.** Among American Indians, a religious leader, freq. one who advocated return to uncorrupted ancestral customs and beliefs. Now hist.

1800 HAWKINS *Sk. Creek Country* 84 This last town has taken the war club, and dance the prophets dances, and are used as spies on the war party. **1810** *Ann. 12th Congress* 1 Sess. II. 1858 An agent from the British arrived at the Prophet's town . . . to urge the Prophet to unite as many tribes as he could against the United States. **1896** *Bureau Amer. Ethnol. 14th Rep.* 764 When Tävibo, the prophet of Mason valley, died, about 1870, he left a son named Wovoka.

+**2.** A term applied to Joseph Smith, founder of the Mormon church, and to subsequent leaders and high priests in the organization. Also as a title.

1843 MARRYAT *M. Violet* xlii, It contains . . . a splendid suite of apartments for the particular accommodation of the prophet Joe Smith. **1848** *S. Lit. Messenger* XIV. 646/2 On the present occasion, the Prophet [Joseph Smith] was unwilling to trust the Gentile Judiciary. **1867** DIXON *New America* I. 249 [Brigham] Young's house is called the Beehive; in it no drone ever finds a place; for the Prophet's wives are bound to support themselves. **1892** GUNTER *Miss Dividends* 121 'The prophet up there,' he nods his head in the direction of Brigham Young's private residence, 'and some of the other leaders of the Church are beginning to be afraid of Tranyon.' **1900** *Congress. Rec.* 24 Jan. 1129/2 A sworn complaint charging Prophet Snow with adultery with his ninth wife was made.

***Proposition.**

+1. A matter requiring attention; something to be dealt with. Usually preceded by an adjective modifier. *colloq.*

1893 *Scribner's Mag.* June 756/1 'Aren't you ashamed to tell me this?' 'Of course I am, but that isn't the proposition just now.' **1896** ADE *Artie* 168, I'm goin' against a tough proposition. **1902** WHITE *Blazed Trail* 168 You bet we did 'em, . . . but it looked like a hard proposition for a while.

b. Preceded by a noun used attributively. *colloq.*

1877 BURDETTE *Rise of Mustache* 258 For a long time the good lady held out stoutly against the chicken proposition. **1902** WISTER *Virginian* 19 The biggest tobacco proposition for five cents got out yet. **1910** WHITE *Rules of Game* 181 We're the only two business propositions in this country.

+2. With characterizing adjective applied to a person. *colloq.*

1899 ADE *Fables in Slang* 9 In her own Town he had the Name of being a Cold Proposition. **1901** — *40 Modern Fables* 7 You are Dead Wise in your Theory that one who is a Parsimonious Papa during Courtship will prove to be a Close Proposition as a Husband. **1921** PAINE *Comr. Rolling Ocean* 12 As a chum this studious expert in English literature was a hopeless proposition.

***Propound,** *v. tr.* To propose or nominate (a person) for citizenship in a colony, membership in a church, or election to an office. *Obs.* {–1673}

1638 *Essex Inst. Coll.* IX. 71 Daniell Baxter propoundeth himselfe to be an Inhabitant. **1643** *Conn. Rec.* I. 99 Mr. Fenwicke is propownded to stand in election for a Magistrate. **1655** *Portsmouth Rec.* 69 Goodman Parent propounded himself for inhabitant. **1828** WEBSTER s.v., In *congregational churches* . . . persons intending to make public profession of their faith, and thus unite with the church, are *propounded* before the church and congregation; that is, their intention is notified some days previous, for the purpose of giving opportunity to members of the church to object to their admission. **1864** KIMBALL *Was He Successful?* 25 In due course he was propounded and admitted into the church.

+**Proprietarian.** A stickler for propriety. — **1866** HOWELLS *Venetian Life* xx, The *Conversazioni* of the rigid proprietarians where people sit down to a kind of hopeless whist . . . and say nothing.

***Proprietary,** *n.* +The owner or one of the owners, by royal grant, of any one of various American colonies. Also *lord proprietary.* Now hist.

1637 *Md. Archives* I. 23 Insolencies, mutinies and contempts against the Lord Proprietary and the government of this place. **1666** *Ib.* II. 130 Bee itt Enacted by the Right Hon[ora]ble the Lord Proprietary by and with the Assent of . . . this present General Assembly That [etc.]. **1683** *Penna. Col. Rec.* I. 57 Wm. Penn, proprietery and Governer of Pensilvania. **1757** FRANKLIN *Writings* III. 372 No part of these monies was ever paid by the *proprietaries* or ever raised on their estates. **1788** — *Autobiog.* 391 These public quarrels were all at bottom owing to the proprietaries, our hereditary governors. **1808** WILSON *Ornithology* I. 23 The Baltimore bird, so named . . . from its colors, . . . being those of the arms or livery of lord Baltimore, formerly proprietary of Maryland. **1854** BANCROFT *Hist. U.S.* I. 243 Some other rights were conferred on the proprietary—the . . . power of creating manors and courts baron.

***Proprietary,** *a.* +Of or pertaining to a proprietor or owner of an American colony. Now hist.

1704 PENN in *Gt. Brit. Hist. MSS. Comm. 15th Rep.* App. IV. 79 How much better the Colonies thrive in proprietary hands than under the immediate government of the crown. **1789** MORSE *Amer. Geog.* 97 The second [type of government in the Amer. colonies] was a proprietary government, in which the proprietor of the province was governor. **1914** *Cycl. Amer. Govt.* I. 315/2 The charters of the British colonies in America are usually divided into three groups; corporation, proprietary, and royal.

Proprietor.

'Anomalously formed and substituted in 17th c. for the etymological word *Proprietary.* . . . App. first used of the "proprietors" of the North American colonies' (*O.E.D.*).

1. =PROPRIETARY *n. Obs.* Also *lord proprietor.*

1637 *Md. Archives* IV. 4 To answere the severall crimes of sedition, pyracie and murther w[hi]ch shalbe on the Lord Proprietors behalfe. **1725** *New-Eng. Courant* 5 April 1/2 The Governour's Message to this House . . . relating to the private Instructions sent him from the late Honourable Proprietor, *William Penn* Esq. **1737** in Scharf *Hist. Maryland* I. 401 Commissioners were appointed by the Lord Baltimore and the Proprietors of Pennsylvania. **1851** DIXON *W. Penn* (1872) 291 The latter now his heir, and, as it seemed, the future lord proprietor of Pennsylvania.

2. One who owns or has exclusive legal right to land {*a*1667–}; +spec. (usually pl.), one of a group of landowners acting together in certain regulatory or governmental capacities in a colonial town. Now hist.

1645 *Mass. Col. Rec.* II. 115 A committee [is] appointed to lay out ye way through Roxberry . . . , & to judge what is meete satisfaction to ye propriet[o]rs. **1665** *Cambridge Prop. Rec.* 145 Also before the drawing of the lotts tis by all the proprietors agreed [etc.]. **1680** *Mass. H. S. Coll.* 4 Ser. V. 36 Some of the proprietors of the township of Taunton, in this Colony, purchasing a certain parcel of land. **1704** *Cambridge Prop. Rec.* 222 Ye Proprietors of Cambridge . . . Did impower us. **1753** *Brookhaven Rec.* 168 That peice or parsel of land called the Gore peice of land . . . shall belong to the propriators of the town of brookhaven. **1819** MCMURTRIE *Sk. Louisville* 166 The town [New Albany, Ind.] was laid out by the Messrs. Scribners who were the proprietors in 1814. **1841** CIST *Cincinnati* 16 As an inducement to settlers the new proprietors agreed to give an in lot six rods by twelve . . . and an out lot. **1882** Godfrey *Nantucket* 87 In the olden time all the land, except such pieces as were set aside for homesteads, . . . was held in common by the twenty-seven original proprietors.

+b. Used of Indians. *Obs.*

1664 *Brookhaven Rec.* 12 Massetewse and Sunke squaw, Native proprieters and owners of all the lands. **1667** *Oyster Bay Rec.* I. 80 We the Indian propriators of Matinecock . . . [have] Made Over Unto John Dyer . . . a parcel of Land Containing forty Acres of Woodland. **1689** *Huntington Rec.* II. 48 Wee the above named Indians beeing the sole and true proprietors of the premises . . . doe putt the said samuell cetcham in the Lawfull and Pecable possession of the said Island.

3. An owner of a house or an established business. {1681–}

1659 *Suffolk Deeds* III. 418 A wharfe to land Goods vpon but meinteined by the proprietors of the sajd Bargained House for saffe guard thereof. **1770** *Penna. Gaz.* 11 Jan. 1/3 The Proprietors of the China works, now erecting in Southwark. **1818** FEARON *Sketches* 58 The barber enquired if he wanted the proprietor or his *boss*, as he termed him, who was also a black. **1845** *Xenia Torch-Light* 31 July 1/1 Mr. Fillmore, the proprietor of the Milwaukee Sentinel, . . . offered me a seat in his wagon which I gladly accepted. **1869** *Boyd's Business Directory* 280 Eldredge House! C. H. Robinson, Proprietor. **1922** PARRISH *Case & Girl* 133 It was plainly evident the proprietor of the saloon felt no enthusiasm over his unknown customers.

Proprietorship. The right or condition of proprietor.

This word first came into use with reference to the North American colonies. After Locke (1669) the next known English use is 1817.

1669 *Fundamental Constit. Carolina* v, Those who are then Lords Proprietors shall not have power to alienate or make over their proprietorships. **1790** *Lunenburg* (Mass.) *Proprietors' Rec.* (1897) 304 An act . . . for the finial Settlement of the Proprietorship of the Town of Lunenburg. **1836** JACKSON in *Pres. Mess. & P.* III. 250 [The measure requiring payment in specie for the public lands] has tended to save the new States from a nonresident proprietorship. **1857** BENTON *Exam. Dred Scott Case* 127 Sovereignty, and Proprietorship, and a right to make rules and regulations respecting the territory of the United States. **1880** *Harper's Mag.* Aug. 376 He heard of the change in the proprietorship of the library.

***Propriety. a.** A piece of land owned by an individual; a private estate. **b.** A settlement or township owned by proprietors. {1661} Now hist.

'*Obs.* exc. in *Amer. Hist.*' (*O.E.D.*).

1635 *Watertown Rec.* I. I. 1 Whoever being an Inhabitant in the Towne shall receive any person . . . upon their propriety . . . shall maintain the said persons at their owne charges. **1651** *Essex Inst. Coll.* V. 265/1 William Baylie is graunted to cvtt what grass he Can find . . . that is not in any mans proprietie. **1701** *Conn. Rec.* IV. 367 The dividing line to alter no mans proprietye of land now laid out. **1790** *Lunenburg* (Mass.) *Proprietors' Rec.* 304 Voted to Chuse a man to lay the Case of this Propriety before Some Sutable person. [**1832** WILLIAMSON *Maine* II. 158 Town privileges were not fully allowed to North-Yarmouth, till January, 1732. It had been only a 'propriety.' **1894** *Nation* 19 July 51/1 Early in 1774 he removed to Lenox, Mass., was at once elected clerk of that 'Propriety,' and was sent as its delegate to the General Court of the colony.]

attrib. **1682** *Hartford Land Distrib.* 469 He passed over . . . his propriety lott in the west diuission. **1721** *Mass. H. Rep. Jrnl.* III. 42 Touching the Divisions of their Propriety Land.

+**Props.** (See PROP.[2])

+Prorate, *v.*

1. *tr.* To allot or divide (fares, dividends, business, etc.) proportionately.

1860 *Congress. Globe* 21 Dec. 180/1 The amendment . . . requires this company to pro-rate passenger fare with all railroad companies or lines which terminate either at Alexandria, Washington or Baltimore. **1881** *Chicago Times* 17 June, The basis [has been established] for pro-rating business between the subsidized and unsubsidized portions of the railroad. **1892** A. E. Lee *Hist. Columbus, Ohio* II. 262 The Baltimore & Ohio to operate and maintain the road, . . . and prorate sixty-five per cent. of the gross earnings . . . ; that is, to pay the Central Ohio thirtyfive per cent. of the gross earnings. **1911** *Okla. Session Laws* 3 Legisl. 205 The said company's capital stock, or surplus, when prorated between two or more classes of business the company desires to write, shall be sufficiently large when divided . . . to give to each character of business one hundred thousand dollars of capital.

2. *intr.* or *absol.* To make an agreement or arrangement based proportionately on a given rate, *with* another company.

1867 *Chicago Times* 21 March 4/1 The Hannibal and St. Jo road . . . is bound to 'pro-rate' with any and all roads coming to Hannibal. **1878** *Congress. Rec.* App. 8 June 424/2 Both companies are bound to prorate with other roads. **1890** *N.Y. Tribune* 6 June 2/6 The Santa Fe [Railroad] . . . will hereafter refuse to prorate with them on shipments of grain and live stock. **1906** *N.Y. Ev. Post* 17 May 2 The New England roads ought to pro-rate, but refuse to do so.

*****Prorogue,** *v. tr.* To dismiss or adjourn the meetings of (a legislative assembly). *Obs.* — **1619** *Va. House of Burgesses* 16 Sir George Yeardly the Govern[o]r prorogued the said Generall Assembly till the first of Marche. **1684** *N.H. Hist. Soc. Coll.* VIII. 199 Governor to have a negative voice in making laws, with power to dissolve and prorogue general assemblies at pleasure. **1704** *Boston News-Letter* 21 Aug. 2/2 On Saturday his Excellency Prorogu'd the General Assembly to the 25th day of October next. **1789** MORSE *Amer. Geog.* 465 The governor shall have power to convene, prorogue, and dissolve the general assembly. **1854** BANCROFT *Hist. U.S.* VI. 328 Hutchinson most unwisely for himself, and still more so for England, prorogued it [the Mass. Assembly] to the middle of March.

Proscenium. {1606–} *Theater.* The part of the stage in front of the curtain, or the curtain and its supporting arch or framework. {1807–} Also attrib. — **1828** *Yankee* I. 295/2 The decorations and painting of the boxes, the procenium, and the drop scene, are . . . magnificent. **1870** O. LOGAN *Before Footlights* 197 A pictured representation of the Father of his Country hung over one proscenium box. **1912** P. MCKEON *Fire Prevention* 153 The proscenium arch has a fire curtain.

+**Prosecuting attorney.** An attorney chosen or designated by a state or county to conduct the prosecution in court proceedings, usually involving cases of a criminal nature. (Cf. DISTRICT ATTORNEY.) — **1838** *Indiana H. Rep. Jrnl.* 23 Sess. 42 John W. Payne . . . was . . . declared duly elected Prosecuting Attorney of the second Judicial Circuit of the State of Indiana. **1890** *Mich. Gen. Statutes* III. 2858 The prosecuting attorney . . . is . . . empowered to appoint two assistant prosecuting attorneys. **1900** *Congress. Rec.* 27 Jan. 1244/2 We find him to have filled all the important positions of prosecuting attorney, judge, State senator, and twice elected to this body. **1912** NICHOLSON *Hoosier Chron.* 180 The Republican prosecuting attorney of Ranger County joined with the local bank in certifying to Miles's probity.

Proselyte, *v. tr.* and *absol.* To make a proselyte of; to proselytize or convert. {1624–} Also *vbl. n.*

1805 *Ann. 9th Congress* 2 Sess. 1078 Their priests took much pains to proselyte these Indians to the Roman catholic religion. **1869** BEECHER *Sermons* I. 365, I never lifted my hand to proselyte a person. **1905** GARLAND *Tyranny of Dark* 2 Some of the women had embraced Christian Science, but they did not esteem it necessary to proselyte. **1922** LIPPMANN *Pub. Opinion* 47 The older proselyting worked more slowly, perhaps more surely, but never so inclusively.

+**Proslaver.** One favoring the retention or extension of the institution of slavery. — **1858** *N.Y. Tribune* 29 Dec. 6/4 The Pro-Slavers all went home without any action.

+**Proslavery.** The advocacy of slavery. Usually attrib., passing into adj. Now hist. (Cf. ANTI-SLAVERY.)

1839 *Corr. R. W. Griswold* (1898) 24 Their delinquent, office-seeking, pro-slavery brethren of this benighted region [central N.Y.]. **1862** *Congress. Globe* 12 May 2067/2 The ultraism and madness of pro-slavery in the border States. **1877** JOHNSON *Anderson Co., Kansas* 41 He and William Sherman . . . and a few other Pro-Slavery men in the neighborhood had always been violent and bad men. **1884** BLAINE *20 Years of Congress* I. 86 General Cass ran as the distinctively pro-slavery candidate. **1906** *N.Y. Ev. Post* 24 March, The Rev. Ambrose Converse, a Northern man with Southern principles, made his pro-slavery Philadelphia *Christian Observer* so 'coppery' during the civil war that Seward suppressed it.

b. Used predicatively as an adjective.

1855 in Hambleton *H. A. Wise* 305 The party is accused of being pro-slavery. **1865** *Congress. Globe* 22 Feb. 1001/1 This bill . . . will not prevent . . . [Mr. Mallory] from passing upon it in such manner as he may deem best, whether it be anti-slavery or pro-slavery. **1865** RICHARDSON *Secret Service* 140, I am pro-slavery—I own niggers.

||**Proslaveryish,** *a.* Favoring slavery. — **1856** S. ROBINSON *Kansas* 115 The governor, with very pro-slaveryish leanings, replied [etc.].

+**Proslaveryism.** The forces and principles favoring or upholding slavery. Now hist. (Cf. FREE-SOILISM.) — **1856** W. A. PHILLIPS *Conquest of Kan.* 409 The power it gained for pro-slaveryism has been jealously guarded. **1856** BREWERTON *War in Kan.* 124 'The hour and man' of Free-State-ism, or Pro-Slavery-ism, for we can scarce say which, is yet to come. **1858** *N.Y. Tribune* 8 May 5/4 The whole of this is merely an adroit attempt of Pro-Slaveryism and Hunkerism to get up a new issue in the canvass. **1861** *Ib.* 15 July 6/4 The intense Pro-Slaveryism of that city [Baltimore] . . . is simply the sign of a caste. It is aristocratic to be Pro-Slavery. **1885** L. W. SPRING *Kansas* 26 The border experienced a boisterous revival of pro-slaveryism.

+**Proslavery party.** A party or faction interested in upholding or extending slavery, esp. the group opposed to the free-soilers in the Kansas struggle (1854–58). Now hist. — **1856** in Robinson *Kansas* 23 We severely condemn those pro-slavery men who, from mercenary motives, are calling upon the pro-slavery party to submit. **1866** *Ore. State Jrnl.* 14 April 2/1 He denied . . . that the 'Democratic party' is or ever has been a pro-slavery party. **1877** JOHNSON *Anderson Co., Kansas* 55 The roads to Missouri were blockaded by the Pro-Slavery party. **1894** ROBLEY *Bourbon Co., Kansas* 50 The migratory hordes of the Pro-slavery party had, under the faint pretense of 'election,' taken possession of the Territory.

* **Prospect,** *n.*

+**1.** A spot or location giving indications of the presence of minerals.

1839 [see FINDER]. **1882** *47th Congress 1 Sess.* H. R. Ex. Doc. No. 216, 180 There are also a number of prospects being opened up in the vicinity. **1901** WHITE *Westerners* 208 He led them . . . from prospect to prospect, from shaft to shaft.

2. A specimen or sample of mineral obtained from a small amount of pay dirt or ore. {1852–}

1859 *Humboldt* (Calif.) *Times* 18 June (Chipman), C. A. Robinson . . . exhibited a prospect, which he stated he procured from one pan of dirt. **1872** 'MARK TWAIN' *Roughing It* 443 A '*prospect*' is what one finds in the first panful of dirt—and its value determines whether it is a good or a bad prospect.

+**3.** (See quotation.)

1890 BLAIKIE *Summer Suns in Far West* 39 At one place [in Colo.] you change into what is called a 'prospect' or open carriage, in order to have a better view of the wonderful scenery.

4. Attrib. and comb. in senses 1 and 2 with *camp, holder, operation, work.*

1876 RAYMOND *8th Rep. Mines* 196 Hence our prospect-operations for the past year have been confined exclusively to the western portion. **1882** *47th Congress 1 Sess.* H. R. Ex. Doc. No. 216, 290 Prospect work is all that has thus far been done. **1885** *Santa Fé Wkly. New Mexican* 31 Dec. 4/3 Every prospect holder in the district feels that he is banking his time and money on 'a sure thing.' **1894** *Harper's Mag.* Jan. 323/2 Nothing but bad whiskey can 'rile' the humor of a prospect camp.

* **Prospect,** *v.*

+**1.** *intr.* To explore or examine a region: (1) for gold or other precious minerals or (2) for oil or water.

(1) **1850** AUDUBON *Western Jrnl.* 201 We tried to 'prospect' for ourselves, and we lost three days. **1875** *Chicago Tribune* 8 July 7/4 No man had attempted to prospect on the bank of the creek without finding more or less gold. **1890** LANGFORD *Vigilante Days* (1912) 389, I froze my feet while prospecting at the head of Rattlesnake Creek. **1902** 'O. HENRY' *Roads of Destiny* 197 We prospected together for gold and silver over Arizona, New Mexico, and a good part of California. **1916** THOBURN *Stand. Hist. Okla.* I. 21 The Wichita Mountains were again visited in 1650, . . . the object being to prospect for gold, and silver.

(2) **1880** *Cimarron News & Press* 23 Dec. 3/1 Mr. Francis Clutton . . . is prospecting for water on a good cattle range 70 miles from Cimarron. **1897** BRODHEAD *Bound in Shallows* 105 Paw, I see the paper states they're prospectin' for ile over in Wayne.

+**b.** *transf.* To search or look about for something.

1867 CRAWFORD *Mosby* 296 Montjoy, who was ahead some distance *prospecting*, came back and reported the enemy advancing. **1875** *Chicago Tribune* 6 July 8/2 A delegation of producers from Florida arrived . . . to prospect in reference to sending a share of their products to this office. **1884** *New Eng. Hist. & Gen. Reg.* XXXVIII. 340 Wherever I have prospected in the records [in Eng.], . . . I have found indications of [genealogical material of] great richness.

+**2.** Of a mine or pay dirt: To yield, promise, or turn out *well* (or in some stated manner) upon actual test. Also *tr.*

1851 KINGSLEY *Diary* 167 They say it does not prospect verry well. **1867** *Wkly. New Mexican* 23 Feb. 1/3 [A pan of] black dirt . . . prospected sixteen colors. **1876** RAYMOND *8th Rep. Mines* 60 The dirt on the bed-rock is very rich, having prospected from $5 to $10 to the pan in places. **1882** *47th Congress 1 Sess.* H. R. Ex. Doc. No. 216, 77 The Hunter mine . . . is prospecting well.

+**3.** *tr.* To work (a mine, ledge, etc.) experimentally in order to ascertain its richness in precious minerals.

1851 CLAPPE *Lett. from Calif.* 92 There is a deep pit in front of our cabin, and another at the side of it, though they are not worked, as, when 'prospected,' they did not 'yield the color.' **1865** *Wkly. New Mexican* 26 May 2/1 The miners are prospecting other ledges. **1871** RAYMOND *3d Rep. Mines* 221 The only thing now wanting . . . is capital, to enable the miners to prospect their lodes and erect smelting furnaces. **1891** *Century Mag.* Feb. 533 It is only where there is a steep grade that the rich stratum on the bed-rock can be conveniently prospected and washed.

b. *transf.* To examine or explore (something).

1865 'MARK TWAIN' *Sketches* (1926) 159 You can get that book and prospect her. **1866** — *Lett. Sandwich Islands* (1938) 2 He liked to prospect curious foreign dishes and find out what they were like. **1887** HARTE *Millionaire & Devil's Ford* 147 There's nothin' now left to prospect but your story of your strike. **1889** 'MARK TWAIN' *Conn. Yankee* 132 These donkeys didn't prospect these liars for details.

+**4.** To explore or search (a region) for indications of gold or other minerals. {1865–, in Canada}

1858 *N.Y. Tribune* 20 Sept. 7/2 [He] left Cherry Creek, near Pike's Peak, on the 27th of July, having satisfactorily 'prospected' a rich gold region. **1866** *Wkly. New Mexican* 27 April 2/2 Parties of prospectors are leaving town daily to prospect the mountains both near and far. **1870**

RAE *Westward by Rail* 337 He purposed returning in the course of a few weeks in order to 'prospect' certain parts of the Territory of Utah which had not, in his opinion, received sufficient attention. **1883** RITCH *Illust-N. Mex.* 98 These mountains have never yet been thoroughly prospected.

b. *fig.* and *transf.* To survey or examine as to prospects. {1867–}

1864 WELLS *Our Burden & Strength* 10 Let us now cautiously prospect the resources of the future. **1880** *Cimarron News & Press* 9 Sept. 3/2 The D. & R. G. railroad surveyors are here prospecting this valley.

Prospect glass. A telescope or field glass. *Obs.* {1617–} — **1711** *Springfield Rec.* II. 42 A Prospect Glass, (6 d). **1769** J. ADAMS *Diary* Works II. 217 You can see with a prospect-glass, every ship, sloop, schooner, and brigantine. **1783** E. PARKMAN *Diary* 299 Prospect Glass 6/.

+**Prospect hole.** A hole or excavation made in prospecting for gold or silver deposits. — **1868** *Ore. State Jrnl.* 11 July 3/1 They sunk several prospect holes on Cayote Creek. **1880** INGHAM *Digging Gold* 339 There are many prospect holes and several good mines in the vicinity of Alpine. **1896** SHINN *Story of Mine* 141 Besides the five thousand actual claims there were many more prospect holes a few feet across. **1905** CROTHERS *Pardoner's Wallet* 178 On the mountain side were hoisting works and hundreds of prospect holes which menaced the lives of the unwary.

+**Prospecting.**

1. Searching for new mineral deposits, esp. of gold or silver. {1887–, of Australia}

1850 COLTON *3 Years Calif.* 292 Half their time is consumed in what they call prospecting; that is, looking up new deposits [of gold]. **1871** RAYMOND *3d Rep. Mines* 283 In Grant County little real mining has been carried on, while much prospecting has taken place. **1880** BURNETT *Old Pioneer* 271 Some practical, sensible, economical man called the whole process 'prospecting.' **1892** *Harper's Mag.* Dec. 140 Prospecting means hunting gold, and is the fourth and greatest of the learned professions.

2. Attrib. with *horn, shaft, trip, work.*

1869 *Overland Mo.* March 279/1 Over one of the hoisting shafts there is a large wooden bucket with a rope and rude windlass such as you might see on the prospecting shaft of the poorest miner. **1876** RAYMOND *8th Rep. Mines* 21 Constant prospecting-work is maintained in advance. **1883** RITCH *Illust. N. Mex.* 72 Three years ago a miner by the name of Lufkin . . . started out on a prospecting trip in the foot-hills of the southern extremity of the Black Range. **1896** SHINN *Story of Mine* 46 His return to pick, pan, and prospecting horn, his death under the cloud of partial insanity . . . are among the dramatic elements of this strange life history.

+**Prospecting pan.** =GOLD PAN. — **1872** MCCLELLAN *Golden State* 124 Ten million dollars in gold had been extracted from the mines, . . . the rocker, shovel, prospecting-pan, and crevice-knife, being the only machinery employed. **1886** HARTE *Millionaire & Devil's Ford* 169 The flour pan . . . stood on the rude table side by side with the 'prospecting pans,' half full of gold washed up from their morning's work. **1889** MUNROE *Golden Days* 102 The other mule bore a pack . . . containing a small tent, . . . iron prospecting pan [etc.].

+**Prospecting tour.** A tour or journey of exploration made in seeking regions or deposits rich in minerals, esp. gold or silver. — **1850** TYSON *Diary in Calif.* 73 He had been on a 'prospecting' tour, or examining the deep canons of the rivers and ravines for a suitable place to dig. **1869** BROWNE *Adv. Apache Country* 39 A few extra mules and jacks to lend to intimate friends going on prospecting tours. **1872** TICE *Over Plains* 119, I had just got . . . into Denver from a very successful prospecting tour through New Mexico. **1890** *Stock Grower & Farmer* 24 May 8/1, I had simply gone down to that country [Roswell, N.M.] on . . . a prospecting tour.

+**Prospector.** One who prospects, esp. one who explores a region for gold or silver deposits. {1862–}

1857 BORTHWICK *3 Years in Calif.* 124 A 'prospecter' goes with a pick and shovel, and a wash-pan; and . . . he digs down untill he reaches the dirt in which it may be expected that the gold will be found. **1871** *Republican Rev.* 23 Sept. 1/4 Miners, prospectors, and people generally, of the entire Territory are more than ever satisfied of the richness and permanency of our mines. **1883** RITCH *Illust. N. Mex.* 67 The mountains seem to be full of rich veins which only wait the labor of the prospector and miner to be discovered and developed. **1896** SHINN *Story of Mine* 75 The old quartz prospectors . . . tried to trace every scattered fragment of 'float rock' back to the ledge from which it came. **1923** 'BOWER' *Parowan Bonanza* 5 Your orthodox prospector promises himself a bath and a clean shave when he strikes it rich.

+**Prospect shaft.** A shaft sunk in connection with prospecting operations. — **1876** RAYMOND *8th Rep. Mines* 56 As determined by the prospect-shafts, the channel falls toward this end on a steep grade. **1882** *47th Congress 1 Sess.* H. R. Ex. Doc. No. 216, 324 There are besides several prospect and incline shafts. **1901** WHITE *Westerners* 194 He took Lafond down every prospect shaft.

***Protect,** *v. tr.* To encourage or safeguard (a domestic industry or product) by a protective tariff. {1827–} Also *ppl. a.*

1789 *Ann. 1st Congress* I. 111 [Measures] calculated to encourage the productions of our country, and protect our infant manufactures. **1802** JEFFERSON *Writings* III. 348 [To] maintain commerce and navigation in all their lawful enterprises; . . . and protect the manufactures adapted to our circumstances; . . . these, fellow citizens, are the landmarks by which we are to guide ourselves in all our proceedings. **1820** *Ann. 16th Congress* 1 Sess. II. 2308 If American manufactures were duly protected, they create for agriculture an extensive . . . home market. **1890** *Stock Grower & Farmer* 17 May 6/2 Sugar goes on the free list. . . . Wool is protected. **1905** *McClure's Mag.* XXIV. 353 Governor Garvin was defeated . . . because a Republican President had to be elected, and a legislature to return to the United States Senate the arch-representative of protected, privileged business!

Protecting duty. A duty or tariff levied to protect domestic enterprise or products. {1821–} — **1789** *Ann. 1st Congress* I. 110 If the committee delay levying and collecting an impost until a system of protecting duties shall be perfected, there will be no importations [etc.]. **1802** *Ann. 7th Congress* 1 Sess. 230 They have probably caused this protecting duty to impede . . . progress. **1826** in Benton *30 Years' View* I. 216/2 Too long an adherence to the opposition to her right of laying protecting duties. **1833** *Ib.* 315/2 They wished to try the constitutionality of protecting duties.

***Protection.**

1. The system of safeguarding domestic producers from foreign competition by the imposition of import duties. {1828–}

Protection is sometimes used more generally to include all the measures, including payments of bounties, adopted by a country to promote what it regards as its best economic interests with respect to productions, trade, and native resources. (Cf. FREE TRADE.)

1789 *Ann. 1st Congress* I. 150 He conceived it the duty of the committee to pay as much respect to the encouragement and protection of husbandry as they did to manufactures. **1806** *Ann. 9th Congress* 1 Sess. 620 Mr. F. said the protection secured by the Constitution to commerce was well stated and enforced by his colleague. **1833** *Congress. Deb.* 26 Feb. 1781 This [R.I.] General Assembly views with alarm, and with unqualified disapprobation, the propositions . . . for abandoning . . . the principle of protection to domestic industry. **1884** *Century Mag.* Nov. 150 Writers and speakers who wish to be read and understood of men must cease to use the word 'protection' as synonymous with 'high tariff.' **1912** NICHOLSON *Hoosier Chron.* 162 Most . . . were Republicans and devout believers that the furnace fires of America's industries were brought down from Heaven by Protection, a modern Prometheus.

attrib. **1884** *Boston Jrnl.* 25 Oct. 2/4 Connecticut and New York will show gains for the protection party which will bury Cleveland under greater majorities than those by which Mr. Greeley was overcome. **1887** *Courier-Journal* 5 Jan. 4/4 The State of Rhode Island is a protection State, and Mr. Aldrich is a protection Senator. *Ib.* 8 Jan. 4/2 The difference between a Pennsylvania protection Democrat and a Republican seems to be the difference between two bay mules.

***2.** A writing or statement that gives protection, +esp. a certificate issued by the United States custom authorities to seamen who are American citizens; the holder of such a certificate. Also attrib.

1803 *State P.* (1819) V. 12 It is not stated that . . . they had protections. **1814** *Ann. 13th Congress* 2 Sess. 1557 An industrious farmer noticed in the number of the slain one of his own name. He exclaimed, there goes one of my protections. **1865** A. D. WHITNEY *Gayworthys* 127 Gershom was to . . . sign his shipping articles, and go with his uncle to get his 'protection,' and his sea rig. **1866** 'F. KIRKLAND' *Bk. Anecdotes* 152/2, I'm a good l'yal citizen. I've got my pertection papers. **1870** WATSON *Camp-Fires Revol.* 141 General Howe gave them papers, which he called 'protections.'

Protectionist. A supporter or advocate of the economic theory of protection. {1844–} Also attrib. or as adj. (Cf. FREE TRADER 1.) — **1844** *Lexington Observer* 16 Oct. 2/2 John C. Calhoun . . . informed his friends . . . that the game playing in Pennsylvania and elsewhere, to make it appear that Mr. Polk is a *protectionist*, is well understood to be a kind of justifiable deception. **1867** *Atlantic Mo.* March 342/2 The young Republican, on the contrary, is a thorough-going protectionist. **1897** *Pop. Science Mo.* April 84/2 Every protectionist system is dominated by the sentiments of fear and enmity. **1913** LA FOLLETTE *Autobiog.* 103 Domestic competition did not prove the strong regulator of commerce that the early protectionists believed it would.

Protective, *a.*

1. Of or pertaining to the economic policy or doctrine of protection. {1820– (*Ann. Reg.* 772)}

1820 [see PROTECTIVE DUTY]. **1841** GREELEY in *Log Cabin* 30 Jan. 2/1 The *Protective* party of this country. **1842** *S. Lit. Messenger* VIII. 273/1 The subject of the protective policy, at all times one of deep interest to the country, has [now] assumed . . . the most commanding importance. **1842** *Whig Almanac 1843* 8/2 This article cannot be advantageously produced at home, and is not a proper subject of Protective legislation.

2. Designed to secure or safeguard the rights and interests of individuals. Often in the names of organizations.

1872 MCCLELLAN *Golden State* 400 In San Francisco alone there are one hundred and fifty benevolent and eighty protective societies. **1890** *Stock Grower & Farmer* 18 Jan. 3/2 Horse and cattle thieves are rampant in Dona Ana county, New Mexico. . . . The stockmen of that section have found it necessary to organize a protective association. **1894** ROBLEY

Bourbon Co., Kansas 86 The killing of Hedrick and Denton . . . caused Mr. Hopkins and his neighbor, Mr. Denison, to start out and organize a 'Protective Society.' **1904** A. DALE *Wanted, a Cook* 118 At first I refused to give her any wages, and she threatened some Protective Women's Association on me.

Protective duty. A tax, usually high, levied on imported articles that would compete with domestic products. {1820– (*Ann. Reg.* 771)} — **1820** *Ann. 16th Congress* 2 Sess. 2023 The resort to high protective duties for the encouragement or preservation of the domestic manufacture [etc.]. **1835** C. P. BRADLEY *I. Hill* 114 He warmly opposed high protective duties as being inconsistent with true republican principles. **1842** *Whig Almanac 1843* 9/2 A Protective Duty in aid of Home Manufactures . . . will inevitably and largely increase the price of Agricultural products. **1871** GROSVENOR *Protection* 21 The accompanying decrease of exports has left the balance of trade against us larger in each period of high duties than in a corresponding period of lower protective and non-protective duties.

Protective system. The economic system of protection by tariffs on imports. {1820–} (Cf. AMERICAN SYSTEM.) — **1820** *Ann. 16th Congress* 2 Sess. 2023 The principal reliance, however, of the argument in favor of the protective system, rested on its tendency to the formation of a domestic market for agricultural productions. **1839** GREELEY in *Merchants' Mag.* I. 54 It has ever been the special effort of the foes of the protective system, to enlist the mercantile interest, as such, in the support of their cause. **1871** GROSVENOR *Protection* 95 It is claimed that the protective system will create 'a home market' for agricultural products. **1893** *Harper's Mag.* March 640/1 The President expressed the opinion that the protective system had been largely instrumental in promoting the prosperity of the country.

Protective tariff. A tariff designed to protect domestic producers, as distinguished from a tariff for revenue.

1838 *U.S. Mag.* Feb. 291 [Legislative power] exerts the infinitely more important power of making laws and creating systęms—witness . . . its Protective Tariff. **1866** *Ore. State Jrnl.* 14 April 2/1 He was opposed to a protective tariff . . . and to everything that was anti Democratic. **1900** *Congress. Rec.* 22 Jan. 1035/2 A protective tariff is the proper thing to have and undertake. **1905** *McClure's Mag.* Feb. 337/2 Senator Aldrich, . . . our leading legislative authority on protective tariff, . . . speaks for privileged business.

***Protector.** +A title used for or in connection with George Washington. *Obs.* — **1777** HUTCHINSON *Diary & Lett.* II. 145 Nothing of news except that the Congress have appointed Washington Protector of the United States, and established a Military Order of Independence, of which he is to be Sovereign. **1789** *Ann. 1st Congress* I. 35 His Highness, the President of the United States of America, and Protector of their Liberties.

Pro tem, *a.* [Abbrev. of *pro tempore*.] Temporary, or operating for a limited time only. Usu. applied to presiding officers. {1846–} — **1828** *Jamestown* (N.Y.) *Journal* 13 Feb. 2/2 Leave was accordingly granted, when, on the suggestion of the Speaker, the house proceeded to the choice of a Speaker pro tem. **1832** *Ib.* 21 Nov. 1/3 He [Speaker] has also power to depute a member, by the rules of the house, to act as speaker pro tem. **1856** *Democratic Conv. Proc.* 15 The Convention was called to order precisely at ten o'clock, by the *pro tem.* President, Samuel Medary. **1857** *Lawrence* (Kansas) *Republican* 11 June 2 Hon. Lyman Allen was elected President *pro tem.*

***Protestant,** *n.* One who protests; a Christian not a member of the Roman Catholic church.

Although the usual distinction is one between members of the Roman Catholic church and other Western Christians, other groups have been excluded, or have chosen to exclude themselves, from the implications of the word. *Protestant* is not used to designate members of the Orthodox and Old Catholic churches, and is rejected by many members of the Protestant Episcopal church. (Cf. CATHOLIC *n.* and *a.*)

1789 MORSE *Amer. Geog.* 453 [The trustees of Ga.] wisely opened a door for the indigent and oppressed protestants. **1846** HUGHES *Diary* 63 Our Govt. has no connexion with Religion—all Religions are equal—the one has no preference over another, the Catholic and Protestant are esteemed alike. **1870** LAMY in *Republican Rev.* 29 Oct. 2/2 What is most remarkable is, that the officers from whom we [Catholics] received these favors were Protestants. **1910** C. HARRIS *Eve's Husband* 261 She was the kind of person who, being a Protestant, would have taken pleasure in poking the altar cloth in a Catholic cathedral with the muddy end of her umbrella. **1921** Mathews & Smith *Dict. Religion & Ethics* 356/2 Certain non-Catholic groups, especially the Baptists, have sometimes refused to be called Protestants on the ground that they originated in the N.T. period rather than in that of the Reformation.

***Protestant,** *a.*

***1.** Owned by or belonging to a religious denomination other than the Roman Catholic church.

1689 *Huntington Rec.* II. 32 It would be well accepted by our Train bands that every Town would send us two known Protestant, trusty souldiers. **1857** DAVIS *El Gringo* 194 The opposition of the priesthood to the children being educated in Protestant schools is so great that they [*sc.* American missionaries] could not accomplish much. **1895** G. KING *New Orleans* 287 The young Protestant minister, now an old one in the community, writes [etc.]. *a***1918** G. STUART *On Frontier* I. 268 Rev. A. M. Tarbett arrived early in 1864 and was the first protestant minister in Montana.

b. *spec.* Of or pertaining to the Methodist Protestant church as distinguished from the Methodist Episcopal church (q.v.). Cf. METHODIST PROTESTANT.

1846 *Indiana Mag. Hist.* XXIII. 320 Our Protestant brethren did not keep up any regular public worship in the house; . . . the Methodist Episcopal Church had the occupancy of the house more than two years.

+**2.** In special combinations.

Protestant Episcopal, belonging to the Protestant Episcopal church; *P. Episcopalian,* a member of the Protestant Episcopal church; *P. Episcopalism,* the doctrines and polity of the Protestant Episcopal church; *P. Methodist,* a member of the Methodist Protestant church; *P. Methodist church,* the Methodist Protestant church (cf. METHODIST PROTESTANT).

1894 *Harper's Mag.* March 642/2 Obituary. . . . Theodore B. Lyman, Protestant Episcopal Bishop of North Carolina, aged seventy-eight years. **1814** in J. Adams *Works* X. 87 The opposition consisted chiefly of the Friends or Quakers, the Menonists, the Protestant Episcopalians. **1836** *S. Lit. Messenger* II. 282 In regard to Protestant Episcopalism in America it may be safely said that . . . there were no written memorials extant. **1846** *Indiana Mag. Hist.* XXIII. 320, I believe the Protestant Methodists are trying to resuscitate their church in the town. **1844** Rupp *Relig. Denominations* 424 Some of the preachers and people . . . thought it best to unite with a body of seceders from the Methodist Episcopal Church, who held a convention in Baltimore, and took the name of Protestant Methodist Church.

+**Protestant Episcopal church.** The official name of the Anglican church in the United States. (Cf. EPISCOPAL CHURCH.) — **1780** in W. S. Perry *Hist. Amer. Episcopal Ch.* II. 21 On motion of the Secretary it was proposed that the Church known in the province as Protestant be called 'the Protestant-Episcopal Church,' and it was so adopted. **1785** *Ib.* 99 A general Convention of the Protestant Ep[iscopa]l church in ye U[nite]d States of America . . . shall be held in ye City of Philadelphia. **1836** *S. Lit. Messenger* II. 282 More than five years ago, the author . . . conceived the idea of gathering together such materials for the History of the Protestant Episcopal Church in the United States, as might still exist. **1903** *Nation* 22 Jan. 79/2 The present Protestant Episcopal Church in the United States owes its origin in a preëminent degree [to Bishop Compton].

***Prothonotary.**

***1.** A register or clerk of a court.

1682 *N.H. Hist. Soc. Coll.* VIII. 122 Fees of Court. To the prothonotary, or clerk, 2 s. 6 d. **1709** *N.J. Archives* 1 Ser. III. 460, I Jeremiah Bass, Esq. Secretary of her Majestys Province of New Jersy, and Prothonetary of the said Supream Court, have hereunto set my Hand. **1802** *Ann. 7th Congress* 1 Sess. 1331 Every court of record in any individual State, having common law jurisdiction, and a seal, and clerk or prothonotary, shall be considered as a district court. **1859** *Harper's Mag.* Oct. 707/1 The Prothonotary of the Court was John Mulhollan, Esq. **1914** *Cycl. Amer. Govt.* III. 84/1 *Prothonotary,* the clerk of the court of common pleas in Pennsylvania and Delaware.

+**2.** =COUNTY CLERK. *Obs.*

1776 J. ADAMS *Familiar Letters* 216 Mr. Francis Hopkinson, . . . it seems, is . . . a son of a prothonotary of this county. **1794** WASHINGTON *Diaries* IV. 221 Quarters were provided for me at the House of a Mr. Espy. Prothonotary of the County of Bedford. *a***1821** BIDDLE *Autobiog.* 195 There were a number of applicants for the office of Prothonotary for the county of Dauphin.

+**3.** Short for next.

1811 WILSON *Ornithology* III. 72 The Blue-winged Yellow Warbler . . . greatly resembles this in its general appearance; but the bill of the Prothonotary is rather stouter, and the yellow much deeper.

+**Prothonotary warbler.** A handsome southern orange- or golden-colored warbler (*Protonotaria citrea*) frequenting regions near streams and swamps. — **1790** LATHAM *Index Ornithologicus* II. 542 Prothonotary Warbler. . . . Habitat in *Louisiana.* **1811** WILSON *Ornithology* III. 72 Prothonotary Warbler. *Sylvia Protonotarius.* . . . They are abundant in the Mississippi and New Orleans territories, near the river. **1874** COUES *Birds N.W.* 47 Prothonotary Warbler. . . . This species was noticed by neither Expedition; it only reaches the lowermost Missouri. **1917** *Birds of Amer.* III. 113/1 The Prothonotary Warbler is a southern Warbler whose range does not extend as far as Canada.

***Protocol.** A diplomatic agreement signed by friendly powers, or the document embodying such an agreement; a document preliminary to the opening of a diplomatic transaction. Also attrib.

1825 CLAY *Speeches* (1860) I. 213 It is already known by the publication of the British and American projets, the protocols, and the correspondence [etc.]. **1845** POLK *Diary* (1929) 16 A protocol might be signed which would open the negotiation again. **1898** *Kansas City Star* 18 Dec. 2/4 [The peace treaty] includes a statement of the contentions of the Spaniards over the provisions of the protocol agreement. **1916** THOBURN *Stand. Hist. Okla.* I. 359 This was not done, however, until the Union Cherokee delegates had signed the protocol or preliminary treaty.

+**b.** (See quotation.)

1890 *Cent.* 4797/2 *Protocol,* . . . in the parts of the United States acquired from Mexico, the original record of the transfer of land.

*** Protract**, *v. Surveying. tr.* To make (a plat); to draw to scale; to plot out (a course or piece of land). {1607–} Also *ppl. a.* — **1696** *Penna. Rec.* I. 498 Ordered, that . . . a Return in words, of the Courses and protracted figure thereof be made Into the Secries office. **1715** *Mass. H. Rep. Jrnl.* I. 5 A petition of *Joseph Morse*, . . . Praying that a Plot of Four Thousand Acres of Land, . . . laid out and protracted by *Thomas White*, . . . may be confirmed. **1718** *Ib.* II. 32 Ordered, That Samuel Thaxter Esq; . . . Return, the Plot he shall protract to this Court, for Allowance and Confirmation. **1719** *Ib.* 154 Resolved, That the Land Protracted and Delineated in the said Plat, be Granted and confirmed. **1816** U. Brown *Journal* II. 233 [He] said it would hinder too much time for him to lay the Course we had run & protract the true one.

Protracted meeting. +A series of religious services held during the morning, afternoon, and evening for a number of days. (Cf. Big meeting.) — **1835** Reed & Matheson *Visit* II. 14 Sometimes a whole day, or more, in connexion with the Sabbath, is set apart for the purpose; and, in that case, it would receive the modern appellation of a protracted meeting. **1855** *Harper's Mag.* XI. 422/2 In the year 1831 a great excitement prevailed in the western part of the State of New York on the subject of religion, and 'protracted meetings' were very common. **1891** Welch *Recoll. 1830–40* 244 It was sometime in the thirties that a popular preacher named Phinney, held a protracted meeting at the 'Old First.' **1925** Bryan *Memoirs* 17 A protracted meeting held in a Christian Church.

*** Prove**, *v.* With *up.*

+1. *Mining. tr.* To test or try out (a vein).

1853 *Harper's Mag.* March 444/1 Copper mining is however in its infancy, and all that has as yet been done is hardly more . . . than may be expressed by the phrase, common among the miners, of 'proving up' the veins.

+2. To validate (a title) or substantiate (a claim) to government land by complying with the regulations for securing it by pre-emption.

1883 *Gringo & Greaser* 1 Sept. 1/1 They should be rigidly required to prove up their titles within a given time. **1892** *Harper's Mag.* June 95/2 As they 'prove up' those claims in the fulness of time, each will get her one hundred dollars.

+3. *intr.* To complete the requirements under which government land is secured.

1857 *Lawrence* (Kan.) *Republican* 28 May 2 A man buying a claim with a house already on it, must himself erect one before he can prove up and take the duplicate for his land. **1872** *Newton Kansan* 26 Dec. 2/2 Can a man . . . prove up on 80 [acres] after fulfilling the requirements of the pre-emption law? **1893** *Kan. State Hist. Soc. Trans.* V. 91 'Money to loan to prove up' was the device on many a little board building. **1911** J. F. Wilson *Land Claimers* 140 He's going to prove up in April.

+b. *transf. To prove up on*, to make good one's claim to (something).

1878 Beadle *Western Wilds* 43 My wife proved up on her Cherokee blood.

Providence. An event regarded as an act of God. {1643–} Freq. with adjectives denoting disaster or calamity. — **1645** *New Haven Col. Rec.* 162 The judgm[en]t of the Court was thatt itt was an afflicting providence of God w[hi]ch the said Barnes was to beare himselfe. **1721** *Essex Inst. Coll.* LI. 289 Mr. Nathl. Higginson . . . Dyed on March 10. . . . An awfull Providence this is to . . . Madm. Higginson & the family of Higginson. **1809** Kendall *Travels* III. 292 In England, the phrase *a providence* . . . is always applied to an occurrence that is happy, and in a human view desirable; but in New England, it appears to be more frequently used for that which is disastrous, but which is at the same time to be regarded, and submitted to, as the act of God. **1814** *Conn. Courant* 1 March 3/2 Distressing Providence.—On Wednesday last . . . John N. Olcott . . . broke in [the ice] and drowned.

*** Provider.** *A good* (*excellent*, etc.) *provider*, a person who makes a good (excellent, etc.) income with which to support a family. — **1862** Browne *A. Ward His Book* 226 Then I axed him. was Lewis a good provider? **1863** Taylor *H. Thurston* 24 He was an excellent 'provider,' especially for his guests. **1895** Wiggin *Village Watch-Tower* 110 Jot ain't a very good provider.

*** Province.**

*** 1.** An administrative division of a country. **a.** One of the former British colonies which after the Revolutionary War united to form the United States. Now hist.

Strictly applicable only to those colonies that were so called in their charters, but in time used of other colonies as well.

1622 *Prince Society Publ.* XVII. 180 All that part of ye maine land in New England . . . w[hi]ch the said Sr. Ferdinando Gorges and Capt. John Mason . . . intend to name ye Province of Maine. **1638** *Md. Archives* I. 2 Capt: Robert wintour Esq, one of the Counsell of this Province. **1699** *Conn. Rec.* IV. 301 A committee [shall] be appointed, to treat with the goverment of the Province of the Massachusetts Bay. **1705** *Boston News-Letter* 23 July 2/2 All Persons in Town and Country, in this and Neighbouring Provinces, . . . are hereby desired [etc.]. **1776** *N.J. Archives* 2 Ser. I. 116 The mercenary aid of neighboring powers, threatens the rights and liberties of the thirteen United Provinces with ruin and destruction. **1832** Dunlap *Hist. Amer. Theatre* 22 Perth Amboy, then the capital of the province of New-Jersey, . . . occasionally received the visits of the Thespians. **1898** E. B. Greene *Provincial Governor* 15 When James Duke of York became king, New York ceased to be a proprietary colony and became a royal province.

+b. (See quotations 1809, 1879.) *colloq.* Usually pl.

1809 Kendall *Travels* III. 259 The earlier counterfeiters . . . had commenced their business in Canada, or as it is here called . . . in *the province*. **1879** Webster *Suppl.* 1574/3 *The Provinces*, the Dominion of Canada; the states under the government of Great Britain, north and northeast of the United States. **1888** *Boston Jrnl.* 28 July 3/1 Reports from the Provinces.

+c. One of the districts or divisions in the Southwest under the rule of Mexico.

1808 Pike *Sources Miss.* (1810) 201, 50 dragoons and 50 mounted militia of the province, armed in the same manner, viz: Lances, escopates and pistols. **1834** A. Pike *Sketches* 169 Santiago Abreu, the present Governor of the Province of New Mexico, is . . . the most distinguished man in it. **1847** Polk in *Pres. Mess. & P.* IV. 540 The Provinces of New Mexico and the Californias are contiguous to the territories of the United States. **1855** Glisan *Jrnl. Army Life* 200 Province after province has revolted against Santa Anna. **1880** *Cimarron News & Press* 22 Jan. 3/3 The Beaubien and Miranda Grant . . . [was] conceded unto the said Charles Beaubien and Guadaloupe Miranda . . . by the then civil and military governor of New Mexico, then a province or department of the Republic of Mexico.

+d. The Louisiana territory.

1857 Benton *Exam. Dred Scott Case* 87 [The vote] was given on the principle of total exclusion of slavery from the whole province of Louisiana. **1880** Cable *Grandissimes* 362, I know that Congress has divided the province into two territories. **1888** — in *Century Mag.* Dec. 254/1 Agents of the Revolution had come from France and so 'contaminated,' as he says, 'the greater part of the province.'

+2. One of the districts or divisions of the Invisible Empire or Ku-Klux Klan. *Obs.*

1867 [see Grand *a.* 1]. **1877** Beard *K.K.K. Sketches* 74 The Grand Division, or Empire, was subdivided into Realms, Provinces, and Dens. *Ib.*, The ruler of a Province was termed a Grand Giant.

3. Attrib. in sense 1 a. **a.** Designating officials serving in provinces.

1685 *N.H. Hist. Soc. Coll.* VIII. 260 Thomas Thurton, Province marshal, and deputy searcher of his Majesty's customs in the said province. **1721** *Braintree Rec.* 105 Bills of Credit now Lodged in ye hands of ye Province Treasurer for the use of ye town. **1762** in Peirce *Hist. Harvard* 268 The further sum of five hundred pounds sterling, in bills of exchange, drawn on the Province Agent.

b. Designating things owned by or serving the needs of a province. Often with reference to financial affairs.

1720 *Mass. Bay Currency Tracts* 384 That a Province Bank be setled. . . . That there be proper Offices, Province Bank-Books, &c. **1721** *Mass. H. Rep. Jrnl.* III. 49 The above-named *A.B.* is . . . Directed to Account with, and pay into the Province Treasury, all such Sums. *Ib.* 115 For Repairing the Province-House. **1739** *Boston Rec.* 233 The Province Galley, and Sloop, . . . were for the Defence of Our Coast. **a1772** Woolman *Journal* 199 Job was going down the river to the province-store at Shamokin. **1776** *N.J. Archives* 2 Ser. I. 69 The province road from Amboy to Salem runs through it. **1777** in Jenkins *B. Gwinnett* 235 £50 of the province Money . . . is all I have had since Mr. Gwinnetts Death.

+Province bill. A paper bill or note issued by the government of the province of Massachusetts Bay. In full *province bill of* (*public*) *credit*. *Obs.* Usually pl. — **1711** *Essex Inst. Coll.* IV. 186/2 Fifty pounds in Province Bills. **1715** *Boston News-Letter* 3 Jan. 2/2 All such Persons . . . may agree with the said Campbell, on reasonable Terms, . . . to be paid in Province Bills of Credit. **1739** W. Douglass *Discourse Currencies* 7 Some are . . . in Paper Money called Colony or Province Bills of public Credit. **a1756** *Mass. H. S. Coll.* 2 Ser. IV. 99 Some time about the year 1703, upon the occasion of the Indian War, came forth 'Province Bills,' which we call Paper Money.

+Province line. The boundary line between the United States and Canada. *Obs.* — **1798** I. Allen *Hist. Vermont* 67 Some Green Mountain Boys, undertook to carry those gentlemen over the province line, to some settlements in Lower Canada. **1809** Kendall *Travels* III. 277 The bay itself . . . is intersected by what is called the *province-line* . . . , which is the southern boundary of Lower Canada.

+Province tax. A tax levied on property within a province. *Obs.* — **1703** *Boston Rec.* 34 Agreed that the Select men . . . do this weeke take ye Lists of the Polls, . . . in order to ye Apportioning the Province Tax. **1721** *Mass. H. Rep. Jrnls.* III. 133 That the several Families in Controversie . . . be for the present excused from all Province Taxes. **1774** *Manchester Rec.* II. 147 Voted that the select-men be a Committee: forthwith to Hire the province Tax for the year 1774.

*** Provincial**, *n.* +A soldier of one of the British provinces which later became the United States. Now hist. (Cf. Provincial troops.) — **1756** *Lett. to Washington* I. 205 Nor will I ever Serve in the provincialls below the Rank I bear. **1775** Cutler in *Life & Corr.* I. 49 We obtained an exact account of the number of Provincials that were killed and wounded. **1852** Reynolds *Hist. Illinois* 46 General Braddock landed [with] . . . 2,000 men, regulars and provincials.

*Provincial, *a.* +Of or pertaining to one of the former British colonies in what is now the United States. +**a.** Used of a governmental or legislative group.

1683 *Penna. Col. Rec.* I. 72 Consideration arising whether ye Govrs. three Voyces should stand in Prov[incia]ll Councill as by ye ould Charter. **1775** *Jrnls. Cont. Congress* II. 84 The Provincial Convention of New York [shall] be requested to convey . . . five thousand barrels of flour for the use of the Continental Army.

+**b.** Used of an officer in a province.

1689 *Penna. Col. Rec.* I. 253 Possession . . . had been formerly given to ye said Woollaston, persuant to a Decretall order of ye Provin[cia]ll Judges. **1776** *Amer. Hist. Review* I. 308 A Letter from Owen Jones Provincial Treasurer here to a County Treasurer was read.

+**c.** Used of a military force or establishment in a province.

1757 *General Orders* 39 The Men Belonging to ye Provensial Reg[imen]ts who are Appointed to Do ye Duty of Rangers are to Be Emmediately Supplyed with Leather Shot Bags. *Ib.* 127 Souldiers belonging to ye Several Provensial Corps on ye Island to hold them Selves in Readiness to turn out at a Minuts warning. *Ib.* 129 Any person who Shall be found Guilty of fireing off Crackers or Squibs in ye Provensial Camp Shall be Emediately Confin.d. **1775** FITHIAN *Journal* II. 135 Many are inlisting in the provintial service.

+**Provincial congress.** A legislative assembly in one of the British provinces which later formed the United States. — **1775** *Amer. Hist. Review* VI. 311 Read p.m. Proclamation f[ro]m Provincial Congress. **1775** in H. M. Brooks *Gleanings* IV. 51 Measures that have been recommended by the Continental and Provincial Congresses. **1776** *N.J. Archives* 2 Ser. I. 55 John Demarest, . . . and Jacobus Post, . . . were elected . . . to represent the County of Bergen in Provincial Congress, to be held at Trenton.

+**Provincial court.** A court in one of the British provinces that later became the United States. *Obs.* — **1669** *Md. Archives* II. 172 The Matter . . . is only examinable & punishable by the honourable Justices of the Provincial Court. **1671** *Ib.* 261 That the Word or County Court might be inserted . . . next after the Words Clerk of the Provin[cia]l Court. **1689** *Penna. Col. Rec.* I. 252 A sentence of Death had passed vpon her in a Provinc[ia]ll Court held in ye County of Kent. **1732** FRANKLIN *Poor Richard's Almanac 1733* 22 Provincial Courts in Maryland.

+**Provincial troops.** Troops belonging to or recruited from the British provinces which later became the United States. Now hist. — **1747** *Georgia Col. Rec.* VI. 187 The Provincial or Extra Troops [have] been lately discharged. **1757** *General Orders* 86 All ye Provensial Troops are Emmediately to move out of ye Camp. **1775** JEFFERSON *Writings* I. (1892) 460 Washington set out from here on Friday last as generalissimo of all the provincial troops in North America.

*Provision.

1. Food or food supplies. {1610–} Usually pl.

1630 in WINTHROP *Hist.* (1853) I. 449 If money be brought to you . . . for goodman Lockwood, let Mr. Peirce be paid his bill of provisions for him. **1680** *Conn. Rec.* III. 53 Packer's Oath. . . . You shall pack no kinds of goods or provissions but such as are good and sound. **1701** *Boston Rec.* 14 No person . . . [shall buy] any other sort of provision . . . before two of the clock in the afternoon. **1792** PUTNAM in *Memoirs* 284 Not one of them will serve any valuable purpus for transporting by water the bagage stores & provision of an army. **1821** *Ann. 17th Congress* 1 Sess. I. 28 It was the interest of the contractor to issue the cheapest provisions which could be had. **1907** *St. Nicholas* July 832/2 They brought back loads of clothing, stores, provisions and the commander's baggage and private papers.

2. Attrib. with *bag, car, depot,* etc.

1791 *Ky. Petitions* 168 [He] supplied them with the necessary arms Provision Bags and pack Horses. **1830** *Congress. Deb.* 11 May 429/2 Mr. B. could not quit this part of his subject, without endeavoring to fix the attention of the Senate upon the provision trade of the West. **1847** *Santa Fe Republican* 20 Nov. 3/1 Provision Warehouse. . . . Will open on Monday next, in the store opposite to Mr. Coleman's corner. **1865** Fleming *Hist. Reconstruction* I. 18 There remained fit for use . . . 1 baggage car, 1 provision car, 2 stock and 2 flat cars. **1877** BARTLETT 173 We have also provision depots, butter depots, &c. **1898** CANFIELD *Maid of Frontier* 88 Cavin was . . . bound and borne shrieking to the ragged provision tent.

3. In special combinations.

Provision broker, a broker who deals in provisions; *p. horse,* a pack horse that carries provisions; *p. land,* land upon which vegetables used as provisions are or may be grown; *p.-packer,* a packer who puts up or processes provisions; *p. state,* (see quotation).

1875 *Chicago Tribune* 22 July 1/1 Underwood & Co. Grain & Provision Brokers. 170 Washington-St. **1783** in *Travels Amer. Col.* 674 Maj. Mosebys lost his provision horse and provisions. **1825** in Commons, etc. *Doc. Hist.* I. 252 This tract contains . . . excellent cotton and provision land. **1871** GROSVENOR *Protection* 259 The attempt to shut it [*i.e.,* salt from the W. Indies] out is simply an endeavor to deny to our provision-packers the benefit of that tropical sunlight. **1872** *Congress. Globe* 8 March 1527/1 [In 1778, the people of Conn.] produced flour, grain, and other commissary supplies, . . . [securing] to the State the honorable distinction of being called 'the provision State.'

Provisional army. An army assembled for temporary service, as in an emergency. — **1797** *Ann. 5th Congress* I. 16 So much of the President's Speech as relates to . . . making arrangements for forming a provisional army, [shall] be referred to Messrs. Tracy, Sedgwich . . . and Vining. *Ib.* 239 Provision [shall] be made by law, for empowering the President to raise a provisional army. **1798** *Ib.* II. 1525 A bill from the Senate, authorizing the President of the United States to raise a provisional army of 20,000 men, was read the first time. **1861** LEE in M. A. Jackson *Gen. Jackson* 166, I have the pleasure of sending you a commission of brigadier-general in the Provisional Army.

Provisional government. +A temporary government, as in a territory of the United States, established to function until the organization of another government. — **1803** CUTLER in *Life & Corr.* II. 148 Look at the power given to the President by the provisional government of Louisiana. **1836** *Diplom. Corr. Texas* I. (1908) 103, I must conclude . . . with the expression of my entire approbation . . . of the various efforts of the agents of the Provisional Government. **1852** GOUGE *Fiscal Hist. Texas* 25 The chief reliance of the Provisional Government was . . . on loans. **1880** TOURGEE *Bricks* 175 The period of actual reconstruction had passed, and independent, self-regulating States had taken the place of Military Districts and Provisional Governments.

Provisional governor. A temporary governor {1617–}, +esp. one appointed by the president of the United States for one of the Southern states during the reconstruction of the South after the Civil War. Now hist. — [**1864** in Fleming *Hist. Reconstruction* I. 120 The provisional governor shall canvass such returns and declare the person having the highest number of votes elected.] **1900** *Congress. Rec.* 25 Jan. 1171/2 Will the Senator tell me who was the provisional governor appointed by President Johnson? **1907** ANDREWS *Recoll.* 153 The President had appointed provisional-governors for some other southern states.

Provision dealer. One who deals in provisions. {1834–} — **1877** *Harper's Mag.* Jan. 284/2 They sold some grapes and apples and pears to the provision dealer in exchange for beef and chicken. **1881** *Ib.* March 598/2 He made his home with . . . a provision dealer across the street.

Provisioner. +One who supplies or deals in provisions. — **1866** HOWELLS *Venetian Life* 102 Among other provisioners who come to your house in Venice, are those ancient *contadine,* who bring fresh milk in bottles carefully packed in baskets filled with straw. **1887** *Council Bluffs Herald* 17 Jan., Every article of staple and fancy goods in the provisioner's line. **1894** *Cosmopolitan* XVII. 58 The display was on either side of the provisioner's door.

Provision house. A house for the storing of provisions; a business establishment that deals in provisions. — **1804** ORDWAY in *Jrnls. of Lewis & O.* 166 Raised a provision & Smoak house. **1903** *N.Y. Times* 15 Oct. 1 Deacon Cotten . . . was dickering with representatives of meat and provision houses for supplies. [**1906** *Daily Chronicle* (London) 20 April 7/2 Food is very scarce [in San Francisco], as the provision houses are all destroyed.]

Provision man. One who sells provisions. — **1872** *Boston Ordinances* 25 July (Ernst), The vehicle of market or provision men. **1875** STOWE *We & Neighbors* 8 Simons, the provision man at the corner, told me that the house had been bought by a young editor.

+**Provision pay.** Pay in produce or commodities. *Obs.* — **1683** *East-Hampton Rec.* II. 131 Agreed . . . with mr. peter Benson to teach school the Next yeare . . . and for his Wages hee is to be payd the some of thirty five pound in probision pay. **1692** SEWALL *Letter-Book* I. 7 Some of the Provision-Pay was Wheat, which I sold, for Indian Corn; being inform'd 't would greatly gratify the poor.

+**Provision pit.** The part of an exchange devoted to trading in provisions. (Cf. CORN PIT, PIT[1] 4.) — **1887** *Courier-Journal* 3 Feb. 7/4 Within a very few minutes after the opening the crowd in the provision pit increased. **1902** LORIMER *Lett. Merchant* 178 Four or five years ago little Jim Jackson had the bears in the provision pit hibernating.

+**Provision store.** A store in which provisions, esp. for domestic animals, are sold. — **1796** *Boston Directory* 245 Fletcher Jonathan, provision store Torry's wharf, house Middle street. **1845** *Xenia Torch-Light* 31 July 3/7 The subscriber has just opened a Grocery and Provision Store. **1875** STOWE *We & Neighbors* 21 Dinah met their girl in at the provision store and struck up an acquaintance. **1881** *Ore. State Jrnl.* 1 Jan. 8/2 Callison & Osburn is prepared to furnish . . . everything usually kept in a first class Grocery and Provision Store.

Provision train. A train of wagons carrying provisions. — **1850** GARRARD *Wah-To-Yah* v. 75 He was in charge of a provision train. **1862** Moore *Rebellion Rec.* V. II. 369 Send back and bring up your provision-trains to your command. **1896** *Harper's Mag.* April 764/1 Blücher . . . found that he had captured . . . all the enemy's hospital outfit, his field-smithies, and his provision-train.

Provision wagon. A wagon used to convey provisions. — **1765** ROGERS *Journals* p. viii, I tarried till August 26th, and was then ordered with 100 men to escort the provision-waggons. **1846** HUGHES *Diary* 77 Twelve Provision wagons came in. **1855** SIMMS *Forayers* 550 He will bring us gifts from Parnassus not unworthy of those which we have enjoyed from the provision-wagon of Lord Rawdon. *a***1918** G. STUART *On Frontier* I. 97 Three days were consumed in getting together the equipment of men and horses with provision wagons and everything necessary.

***Proviso.** A provision or clause, as in a law or legal enactment, which makes a stipulation or condition.

1718 *Mass. H. Rep. Jrnl.* II. 103 The following Proviso added to the said Vote, *viz. Provided* [etc.]. **1781** PETERS *Hist. Conn.* (1829) 173 They made a law . . . with this proviso, that no one should be holden to pay a note, bond, or vote, made or given to support the Gospel. **1831** BENTON *30 Years' View* I. 202/2 With a proviso for the District of Columbia. **1865**

Atlantic Mo. XV. 745/1 It was hampered by a proviso submitting it to the people for ratification. **1884** BLAINE *20 Years of Congress* I. 67 He thereupon . . . moved a *proviso* to the two-million bill.

+b. =WILMOT PROVISO. Also attrib.

1846 POLK *Diary* II. 76 Had there been time, there is but little doubt the Senate would have struck out the slavery proviso & that the House would have concurred. **1848** *Whig Almanac 1849* 8/2 Long ere this, however, the Proviso or Free Soil question had become a potent element in the feud which divided the party in New York.

Provo. {1675–1746} **+1.** =PROVOST 3. *Obs.* **2.** =PROVOST 2. {1692–1746} — **(1) 1779** *N.J. Archives* 2 Ser. III. 226 Two of them made their escape, and the other two are safely lodged in the provo of the continental troops. **1832** DUNLAP *Hist. Amer. Theatre* 43 The Jail, then called the provo, where American prisoners suffered for asserting the rights of their country, scowled on the east. **(2) 1866** W. REID *After the War* 419 We've got a Provo', in our town that settles their hash mighty quick. He's a downright high-toned man, that Provo', if he is a Yankee.

***Provost.**

***1.** The head or president of a college.

1775 *Penna. Packet* 22 May, The Honorable Members of the Continental Congress were pleased to proceed in a body from the State-House to the College, where they were received at the gate by the Provost. **1832** DUNLAP *Hist. Amer. Theatre* 33 The Reverend Dr. Cooper, provost of King's (now Columbia) College, wrote the following prologue. **1851** HALL *College Words* 248 *Provost*, the President of a college. **1920** *Univ. of Pa. Bul.* XXI. 6 Nov. 18 Under other Provosts as well as in the present administration, [friends] have . . . faithfully and generously supported the University.

+b. In some colleges and universities, an officer of high rank charged with various executive or administrative duties.

1835 *Knickerb.* V. 137 It was thought expedient to divide the duties and powers of the President between that officer and another, to be called the *Provost.* **1846** N. F. MOORE *Hist. Sk. Columbia Coll.* 78 In the following month [*i.e.*, June, 1811], the Trustees determined to divide the powers and duties of the presidential office between a president and an officer to be styled Provost, who, in the absence of the President, should supply his place. **1922** *Who's Who in Amer.* XII. 702/2 Claxton, Philander Priestley, univ. provost; . . . provost Univ. of Ala. since 1921.

2. A military officer having police duties. {1799–} Also attrib.

1776 ROWE *Diary* 302 This Party consisted of . . . a Refugee, Mr. Welsh the Provost Deputy . . . & abo. fifteen soldiers. **1863** WHITMAN *Spec. Days* 49 There are one or two general directories of the hospitals kept at provost's headquarters. **1898** PAGE *Red Rock* 121 The Provost officer might consult some friend who would insist on his taking up the insult. **1903** FOX *Little Shepherd* xxii, Morgan's great raid in June, '61, spread consternation . . . [and] every district and county were at the mercy of a petty local provost.

+3. (See quot. 1890.)

1780 *Heath P.* III. 112 He has flung into the provost many of our friends. **1890** *Cent.* 4807/2 *Provost*, . . . a temporary prison in which the military police confine prisoners until they are disposed of.

‖**4.** (See quotation.)

1852 REYNOLDS *Hist. Illinois* 53 Two aged discreet persons are chosen, who are called Provosts; one to select the ladies for the dance, and the other for the gentlemen.

+Provost guard. A detail of soldiers appointed to perform police duties; the quarters occupied by such a detail. — **1778** *Jrnls. Cont. Congress* X. 74 About thirty [officers] . . . have been confined in the provost guard and in the most loathsome gaols. **1862** Moore *Rebellion Rec.* V. II. 151 Major Fisher . . . was left in Corinth with a provost-guard, to prevent pillage and protect the public stores. **1877** W. WRIGHT *Big Bonanza* 249 An old military post [was] occupied during the rebellion by a provost guard. **1883** SWEET & KNOX *Through Texas* 595 We may be caught by the provost-guard, and put in the bull-pen.

***Provost marshal.**

+1. The chief police officer in some of the American colonies. *Obs.* {1737–, in W. Indies}

1619 *Va. House of Burgesses* 9 If any private person be found culpable . . . [of drunkenness, he is] to lye in bottes 12 houres in the House of the Provost Marshall. **1676** *Conn. Rec.* II. 488 The Councill doe appoynt Capt. George Denison to be Provost Marshall of the Narragancet country, pro tempore. **1683** *Mass. H. S. Coll.* 4 Ser. V. 115 To James Sherlock, Gentleman, Provost-Marshal and Sheriff of said Province, or his Deputy. **1765** ROGERS *Acct. N. Amer.* 133 In South Carolina they have an officer, called the Provost Marshal, who acts as Sheriff of the whole province.

***2.** *Mil.* An officer appointed to have charge of soldiers detailed to police duties in a district, town, camp, etc.

1775 *Jrnls. Cont. Congress* II. 221 [Resolved,] That the appointment of provost Marshal . . . be left to the commander in chief of the army. **1862** CUMMING *Hospital Life* 41/2 We had procured them from the provost marshal in Mobile, but they did not amount to any thing, as an order had just been received from head-quarters at Chattanooga prohibiting any one going in there without a special permit. **1884** BLAINE *20 Years of Congress* I. 385 General McClellan directed the provost marshall of the district . . . 'to arrest Brigadier-General Charles P. Stone at once.' **1907** ANDREWS *Recoll.* 155 At Pikeville we were in the midst of Union people who wanted to take the oath of allegiance, and as provost-marshal I administered the oath to many citizens.

+Prox, *n. local.* [Short for PROXY.] A ticket or ballot in an election: (see also quot. 1885). Also in attrib. use to designate a vote cast by a deputy or substitute.

1669 *R.I. Col. Rec.* II. 242 Mr. Peleg Sanford and Mr. John Coggeshall are to assist for the opening of the proxes. **1698** *Ib.* III. 333 Capt'n Nathaniel Coddington, Capt'n Robert Carr, are appointed to open the prox votes on the day of Election. **1768** *Ib.* VI. 551 Upon this plan, . . . only one prox will be printed. **1816** PICKERING 157 The abbreviation *Prox* is also used in *Rhode Island*, for the *Ticket;* (as it is called elsewhere) that is, the *List* of Candidates at Elections. **1843** *R.I. Hist. Soc. Coll.* V. 64 Such of the colony as could not attend the General Assembly, had the right to send their votes for these officers by some other persons; hence the origin of the terms prox, and proxy votes, as applied to the present mode of voting for state officers in Rhode Island. **1868** G. G. CHANNING *Recoll. Newport* 186, I placed in the hand least affected the State 'prox,' so called, which he retained. **1885** *Mag. Amer. Hist.* March 298/1 *Prox* or *proxy.*—Formerly used in Rhode Island and Connecticut to denote an election at which voting by proxy was allowed under certain conditions.

+Prox, *v. intr.* To vote by means of a prox or as a proxy. — **1758** *Narragansett Hist. Reg.* IV. 39 There is some of the frinds of Smithfield that has not yet proxed for Governor.

***Proxy.**

***1.** A document authorizing a person to vote in the place of another; a vote or voter in such a plan.

1641 *Mass. Bay Rec.* I. 333 The way of proxies (as it is called) is found subject to many miscarriages. **1658** *Mass. H. S. Coll.* 4 Ser. VII. 496 The votes of the present freemen & some few proxies carryed the election for Governour to Mr. Newman. **1792** *Ann. 2d Congress* 466 Shall we . . . search whence this right of proxy? **1887** *Courier-Journal* 6 May 2/1 Cast the vote of Cumberland and Clinton counties, for which he held proxies, for Thompson. **1902** MEYER *Nominating Systems* 56 The difficulty of binding delegates with definite instructions; the use of proxies.

+2. (See quot. 1816.) Also attrib.

1660 *Conn. Rec.* I. 346 The remote Plantations that use to send Proxies at the Election by their Deputies. **1679** *R.I. Col. Rec.* III. 30 Voted, . . . that Capt'n Samuell Gorton and Mr. Caleb Carr shall open the proxies. **1760** *Narragansett Hist. Reg.* II. 109, I am 200 ahead in the proxies. **1816** PICKERING 156 This use of the term *proxies* [for written votes or ballots] is not known, I believe, in any of the States, except *Rhode Island*, and *Connecticut*. It is also used sometimes as equivalent to *election*, or *election-day*. **1828** WEBSTER, *Proxy*, . . . in *popular use*, an election or day of voting for officers of government. **1843, 1885** [see PROX *n.*].

+3. Among Mormons, one who substitutes for another, esp. one who takes the place, in a marriage, of a dead husband or wife, to whom the other party in the marriage is regarded as actually united in wedlock. Also attrib.

1882 WAITE *Adv. Far West* 89, I must raise up seed for my dead brother and you must be sealed to your husband while I act as proxy. *Ib.* 123 Another case illustrating the Proxy doctrine as it is called came to my knowledge a few days ago. *Ib.* 215 *Proxy Women.* This is a common term in Utah, and signifies that a woman is married to one man for 'time,' and sealed to another for eternity.

Prudential. {1648–} *pl. New Eng.* +Matters of local government or administration calling for the exercise of prudent care and management.

1646 *Mass. Bay Rec.* II. 180 Every township, or such as are deputed to order the prudentialls thereof, shall have power to present to the Quarter Court all idle and unprofitable persons. **1660** *Conn. Rec.* I. 350 Al defects in Armes or neglects in traineing . . . shalbe determined by any one Magestrate . . . and by two of them yt order the prudentials of ye Towne. **1697** *Boston Rec.* VII. 228 Voted that the prudentials of the town is left to the judgment and Discretion of the Selectmen. **1721** *Canton* (Mass.) *Rec.* 7 The Assassars was Chosen a committee for To manege the Prodanshals of This precinct. **1755** *Amherst Rec.* 18/2 Voated 4 that the present Assessors be a Committy to take Care of the prudentials of this precinct. **1774** in F. Chase *Hist. Dartmouth Coll.* I. 263 Agreed with Frederick Earnest . . . to take the care of the kitchen, and inspect and conduct the prudentials of it. **1891** CHASE *Ib.* 565 The condition of the College in its prudentials was such as might well have led any one to hesitate to take the helm.

Prudential affairs. *New Eng.* +The business and administrative affairs of a colonial town requiring the exercise of prudence and discretion in their management. *Obs.* (Cf. PRUDENTIAL.) — **1644** *Springfield Rec.* I. 175 Power to order in all the prudentiall affaires of the Towne. **1661** *Topsfield Rec.* 6 They are chosen for selectmen . . . to order the prudentiall afaires of the towne. **1718** *Mass. H. Rep. Jrnl.* II. 91 The said Families, to have the Privilege of a Town, as to the ordering the Prudential Affairs thereof. **1738** *R.I. Col. Rec.* IV. 547 The prudential affairs of the said town.

+Prudential committee. An advisory committee. — **1822** *Missionary Herald* XVIII. 1 American Board of Commissioners for Foreign Missions. Report of the Prudential Committee. **1823** *Baptist Mag.* IV. 24 Monday evening was assigned for the missionaries to receive the instructions of the Prudential Committee. **1851** HALL *College Words* 248 *Prudential committee*, in Yale College, a committee to whom the discretionary concerns of the College are intrusted. **1910** *N.Y. Ev. Post* 26 Nov. Suppl. 10 During his 30 years of service—25 years as member of the prudential committee [at Yale]—he has missed but one meeting.

Prudential man. *New Eng.* {1642–} +A man selected with others to have charge of the prudential affairs of a colonial town. *Obs.* — **1647** *Ipswich Rec.* 7 Feb., There was chosen for the prudentiall men for this year, Major Denison, John Tuttle [etc.]. **1651** *Rowley Rec.* 71 Chosen for prudentiall men Francis Parratt William Asie [etc.]. **1669** *Boston Rec.* 49 Wee judge it doth not belonge to vs as prudentiall men to determine the placeinge of it.

***Prune. a.** The dried fruit of any one of several varieties of plum. **+b.** A plum of a variety suitable for drying, or the tree on which it grows. {a plum or plum tree, –1698}

1633 *N.H. Prov. Papers* I. 73, 12 pound of prunes. **1761** in Singleton *Social N.Y.* 364 To be sold, . . . Currants, Figgs and Prunes. **1872** McCLELLAN *Golden State* 331 So far the cultivation of prunes has been very limited. **1899** *Dept. Agric. Yrbk. 1898* 311 Plums or prunes are treated somewhat differently from most other fruits. **1900** W. H. BARNES *Plum in Kansas* 137 The prune was first planted or grafted in California in 1856. **1904** A. DALE *Wanted, a Cook* 205 How different was the reality to the anticipation of boiled mutton and stewed prunes!

attrib. **1856** *Rep. Comm. Patents 1855: Agric.* 301 Mr. Pfeiffer . . . also raises prune-trees in great numbers. **1924** R. CUMMINS *Sky-High Corral* 64 Shasta was very busy concocting an enormous prune pie.

Prunella. Also †**prunelloe.** =EVERLASTING *n.* 1. {1656–} Also attrib.

1745 in Watson *Philadelphia* 179 [For sale:] Tandems, . . . prunelloe, barragons, druggets. **1857** *Harper's Mag.* July 168/1 [The Shaker women's] shoes . . . were made of prunella, of a brilliant ultramarine blue. **1882** *Century Mag.* Oct. 827/1 Captain Bennett was remarking from the rocking-chair, while his prunella shoes went up and down. **1891** WELCH *Recoll. 1830–40* 173 Lasting or prunella boots with an Indian embroidered moccasin for the outside.

+b. *pl.* Shoes made in part of prunella.

1833 *Sketches D. Crockett* 147 With forms not screwed into fashion's mould, nor feet encumbered with light prunellas, they trip the fairy dance. **1840** *Knickerb.* XV. 387 The very girl whom I had seen . . . scamper upon the flanks of the mountain, bare-foot, . . . now walked out in prunellas. **1891** F. H. SMITH in *Century Mag.* March 735 He had changed his shoes, his white stockings now being incased in low prunellas tied with a fresh ribbon. **1914** E. STEWART *Lett. Woman Homesteader* 38 Little Mandy, . . . I am afraid, was a selfish little beast since she had to have her prunellas when all the rest of the 'young uns' had to wear shoes that old Uncle Buck made out of rawhide.

***Pruning knife.** A knife used in pruning. Also fig. — **1797** HAWKINS *Letters* 97 You can also order up . . . hand saws, pruning knives [etc.]. **1822** *Ann. 17th Congress* 1 Sess. I. 142 Mr. O. did not think this was the branch of service to which the pruning knife ought to be first applied. **1839** *S. Lit. Messenger* V. 802/2 Hedges, which long unvisited by the pruning knife, had grown rough and irregular, told of the degeneration. **1871** *Harper's Mag.* Aug. 385/2 There was Uncle Nathan feeling the edge of a pruning-knife with his thumb. **1904** GLASGOW *Deliverance* 165 Taking his pruning-knife . . . [he] went out alone to begin work on his ripest plants.

Pruning shears. Shears having strong blades and long handles, used in pruning hedges, shrubbery, etc. {1822–} — **1809** *Amer. State P.: Misc.* II. 138 [Improvement in] pruning shears, July 13, Simeon Jocelin, New Haven, Connecticut. **1862** *Rep. Comm. Patents 1861: Agric.* 645. **1866** W. REID *After the War* 205 The shrubbery was . . . a little more luxuriant indeed, since the pruning-shears had perforce been idle. **1884** ROE *Nature's Story* 131 Amy often observed Webb . . . in the tops of apple and other trees, with saw and pruning shears or nippers.

Pry, *n.* A lever or instrument for prying. {1823–}

'Dial. and *U.S.'* (*O.E.D.*).

1827 COOPER *Prairie* xiv, Put in another pry, girls. **1851** SPRINGER *Forest Life* 156 All hands are . . . lifting with heavy pries, hand-spikes, and cant-dogs, to roll these massive sticks into the brook channel. **1905** *Forestry Bureau Bul.* No. 61, 38 *Grab skipper*, a short iron pry or hammer. **1924** MULFORD *Rustlers' Valley* xxvii., Mitt was searching the scantily timbered slope above the ledge for a pry to set the boulders rolling.

attrib. **1858** WILLIS *Convalescent* 386 The long end of the pry-stick was beginning to quiver with the first stir of the oxen.

Pry, *v. tr.* To lift or raise with a lever. {1823–}

'Dial. and *U.S.'* (*O.E.D.*).

1806 *Webster* 240/2 *Pry*, . . . to raise with a lever. **1839** *S. Lit. Messenger* V. 378/1 Do let us get some long poles and *pry* him out. **1876** 'MARK TWAIN' *Tom Sawyer* 89 They pried the lid off with their shovels. **1885** JACKSON *Zeph* vi, Nat pried the grate out with an iron bar. **1904** *N.Y. Ev. Post* 17 Sept. 4 The Republicans refused to pry up the lid that conceals these iniquities.

***Psalm book.** A book containing the Psalms, esp. for public worship. — [**1689** SEWALL *Diary* I. 250 Writt to Dr. Grew, inclosing my Psalm-Book, in Turkey-Leather, and 4 of Mr. Cotton Mather's Sermons.] **1706** *Boston News-Letter* 6 May 4/2 A New Edition of the New-England Psalm-Book, Printed with a New Fair Character, and on good fine Paper; with a New Set of most Common Tunes, more free from Errors than heretofore. **1865** *Atlantic Mo.* Feb. 150/1 He relieves himself by constructing a small meeting-house out of the psalm-books and Bible.

***Psalter.** An edition or a selection of the Psalms. — **1633** *N.H. Prov. Papers* I. 78, 1 psalter. **1685** *Plymouth Laws* 301 Every such School-Master . . . shall receive children after they are fit to begin in their Psalter. **1733** FRANKLIN *Poor Richard's Almanac 1734* 23 Sold by the Printer, . . . Psalters. **1890** (*title*), The Psalter of the United Presbyterian Church of North America.

Psyche. {1647–} A mirror that swings in a frame; a cheval glass. In full *psyche glass.* {1838–} — **1838** *S. Lit. Messenger* IV. 59/2 When completely dressed, he surveyed his figure fully reflected in a psyche glass. **1839** *Ib.* V. 35/2 To M. . . . was assigned the only carpetted apartment as compensation for their French couches, psyches, mirrors. **1856** CURTIS *Prue & I* (1892) 9 My fancy . . . looks at the vast mirror, and surveys her form at length in the Psyche-glass.

‖**Psychometrician.** A person allegedly having the faculty of divining the qualities or properties of an object from mere physical contact or proximity. — **1867** *Ore. State Jrnl.* 19 Jan. 4/4 The Great English Astrologist, Clairvoyant, and Psychometrician . . . has now located herself at Hudson, N.Y.

Psychometrist. =prec. {1900–} — **1864** NICHOLS *Amer. Life* II. 20 Then came psychometrists, who could tell the lives, characters, fortunes, and diseases of people they had never seen.

***Ptarmigan.**

***1.** The willow ptarmigan (*L. lagopus*) of the arctic regions: (see quotation).

Though the writer of quot. 1872 identifies the bird as belonging to this species, it may actually be the white-tailed ptarmigan.

1872 *Harper's Mag.* Dec. 33/1 It was a flock of the rare willow-grouse, or ptarmigan (*Tetrao* [*lagopus*] *saliceti*), another habitant of subarctic regions, here [in the Rocky Mts.] finding a congenial home. **1917** *Birds of Amer.* II. 20 Willow Ptarmigan. . . . [Also called] Ptarmigan; Common Ptarmigan. . . . Accidental in Wisconsin, Michigan, New York, Maine, and Massachusetts.

+2. The white-tailed ptarmigan (*Lagopus leucurus*) of the Rocky Mountains; a bird of this species.

1874 Coues *Birds N. W.* 427 Once, while walking near the summit of the range, I chanced to look down, and saw a Ptarmigan in the grass, at my very feet. **1886** *Outing* Dec. 201/1 A small covey of ptarmigan (mountain grouse) whirred up and settled at such provokingly short distance that I could not resist a couple of shots. **1917** *Birds of Amer.* II. 23/2 In few birds is protective coloration exhibited to such an extent as in these Ptarmigans that live along 'the top of the world.'

Public, *n.* {1611–}

+1. *College slang.* An admonition or rebuke given in public.

1837 *Knickerb.* IX. 244, I was reported to the government . . . and received a 'public.' **1842** *Ib.* XIX. 439 Prayers he has cut, to the extent of a 'public.' **1851** HALL *College Words* 249 At Harvard College, the punishment next higher in order to a *private admonition* is called a *public admonition*. . . . It is often called *a public*. **1876** TRIPP *Student-Life* 133 If we make a noise . . . we shall get publics, if nothing worse.

+2. (See quotation.)

1823 I. HOLMES *Account* 341 These publics are generally weekly assemblies by dancing-masters, free for all his scholars and their parents, and nearly so for all females.

***Public,** *a.* Also †**publicke.**

American usage of this adjective does not differ from British usage. The following categories are illustrated because of their special American contexts.

***I.** Of or pertaining to the people of a community with reference to their will and activities as expressed through government. **1.** Referring to the fiscal matters of a community as a whole.

See also PUBLIC BANK, PUBLIC DEBT.

1637 *Plymouth Laws* 57 There shalbe a watch of foure men hyred to keepe watch at New Plymouth at the publicke charge. **a1647** GORGES *Briefe Narration* 46, I ordained a Treasurer for receipt of the Publique Revenue. **1691** *Mass. Bay Currency Tracts* 27 For themselves to bring these Bills to the Publick Treasury . . . is a crying Opression. **1790** *Ky. Petitions* 163 Warrants which he may receive from the Aud. of public accounts. **1806** *Balance* 22 April 127/1 He accused Mr. Madison of unconstitutional views in wishing to draw from the Treasury . . . public monies. **1852** *Harper's Mag.* Dec. 120 Instructions sent out from the Treasury Department to the collector not to receive the ingots stamped by the Assay Office, in payment of public dues. **1923** *New Republic* 7 Nov. 3/2 If a country district is to have any high school at all, it will have to be an expensive public investment.

***2. a.** Referring to roads, bridges, parks, etc., owned by, or open to the use of, the public.

In this connection sense II is also implied. (See also PUBLIC ROAD, PUBLIC SQUARE.)

1638 *Conn. Rec.* I. 17 There may be a publique highway for Carte & horse vppon the vpland. **1738** W. STEPHENS *Proc. Georgia* I. 80 Bailiff Parker and Mr. Hugh Anderson . . . took a Walk, first to the Publick

Garden. **1796** F. BAILY *Tour* 120 [The Battery] is the only public walk the New Yorkers can boast of. **1827** DRAKE & MANSFIELD *Cincinnati* 93 The municipal authorities . . . [may] establish a Public Promenade, for pleasure, ornament, and recreation. **1871** *Mich. Gen. Statutes* I. (1882) 424 Ferry landings shall be deemed public highways, and may be laid out . . . in the same manner . . . as other public highways and bridges. **1904** *Indian Laws & Tr.* III. 87 The President is also authorized to reserve a tract . . . in the northeastern portion of the abandoned military reservation, . . . as a public park.

b. Referring to things owned and used by the general public.

See also PUBLIC LIBRARY.

1718 *Boston Rec.* 129 The Projection of an Act for a Publick Market in Boston . . . at a former meeting of the Inhabts was Continued untill now. **1737** *Va. Gazette* 29 April, [Richmond] lies near the 'Publick Warehouse' at Shoecoe's. **1746** *Md. Gazette* 5 Aug., By a late Act of Assembly in Virginia, a public Ferry is erected at the Plantation of William Clifton. **1789** MORSE *Amer. Geog.* 177 The public granary is converted into a store. **1789** *Statutes at Large* I. 53 An Act for the establishment and support of Lighthouses, Beacons, Buoys, and Public Piers. **1840** *Picayune* 24 Sept. 2/5 A letter . . . asking the use of the public carts to fill up the lot of the St. Patrick Female Orphan Asylum, was read. **1851** CIST *Cincinnati* 168 There are eighty-three public cisterns, and seventy-nine fire-plugs, employed for the extinguishment of fires exclusively. **1851** ROSS *In New York* 42 There are fountains of health and life, in the streets, called '*public hydrants*.' **1904** *N.Y. Ev. Post* 30 June 3 The excavation for the public comfort station in Chatham Square. **1911** *Okla. Session Laws* 3 Legisl. 191 Any city or town, having acquired possession . . . of a reservoir for public water supply, is hereby authorized [etc.].

3. Referring to documents containing matters of record of the general or local government.

1646 *N.H. Prov. Papers* I. 186 Mr. George Smith & Edw[ar]d Starbuck are appointed to survey . . . such publick registers as belong to the Courts at Pascataque. **1677** *N.C. Col. Rec.* I. 249 Riseing in armes, breaking sundry locks, stealing the publicke Records [etc.]. **1839** *4th Congress of Texas Jrnls.* I. 6 The act of the last Congress directing the removal of the Public Archives from the city of Houston was an expression of legislative will too decisive to permit me one moment to falter in carrying it out.

***4.** Referring to persons acting as officers of the government.

See also PUBLIC PRINTER, PUBLIC SERVANT.

1644 *R.I. Col. Rec.* I. 197 The Publick Treasurer shall only receive such fines [etc.]. **1648** *New Haven Col. Rec.* 406 John Copper [shall] be publique powndér for ye towne. **1700** *Conn. Rec.* IV. 325 There shall be . . . appointed one person in each countie . . . to be a Publick Surveyour. **1712** *N.C. Col. Rec.* I. 902 The sum of Sixty pounds [shall] be presented to the said Col. John Barnwell, by the Publick Receiver. **1851** CIST *Cincinnati* 55 The Public Teachers now number about one hundred and thirty-eight. **1909** PARKER *G. Cleveland* 54 [He condemned] the interference of public officials in the making of nominations for State offices.

***5.** Referring to schools supported and conducted under the authority of the local government.

In this connection sense II is also implied. (See also PUBLIC SCHOOL.)

1710 *Boston Rec.* 73 [A town committee] now propose to Erect a Brick Building . . . to be let out for the Support of a Publick writeing School in the Town. **1715** *Ib.* 113 Real Estate for the use of the Publick Lattin School. **1775** BURNABY *Travels* 70 In each county throughout this province [Md.], there is a public free-school. **1832** WILLIAMSON *Maine* II. 537 It was insisted by the eastern people, that a public Seminary planted among them, would enlarge and spread the benefits of education. **1911** *Amer. Phys. Ed. Rev.* XVI. 390 The department of physical training in a public high school exists primarily for the promotion of health . . . among the mass of students.

***II.** Of or pertaining to things available to, actions done by or for, opinions entertained by, etc., the people generally.

***6. a.** Referring to meetings, social events, etc., that are open to the public.

See also PUBLIC MEETING, PUBLIC WORSHIP.

1639 *Watertown Rec.* I. I. 5 If any of ye Freemen be absent from any Publick Towne meeting . . . , he shall forfett for every time 2*s*. 6*d*. **1671** in S. Smith *Down East* (1854) 11 [It was] ordered that a cage be made, or some other means be invented . . . *to punish such as sleep* or *take tobacco* on the Lord's day, at meeting, in the time of the public exercise. **1827** DRAKE & MANSFIELD *Cincinnati* 90 Throughout the winter season, there are public balls, assemblies, and cotillion parties. **1854** BENTON *30 Years View* I. 217/1 He sent me a manuscript copy of a speech . . . to be delivered in New-York, at some 'public dinner.'

b. Referring to actions or activities participated in by, or open to, the public.

Some of these activities are initiated or authorized by government action. (Cf. general sense I.)

1736 *Holyoke Diaries* 4 Public Fast on account of unusually mortal diseases. **1759** *Ib.* 21 Public rejoycing, fire works &c. at Boston for taking Quebeck. **1780** STILES *Diary* II. 485 December. . . . 7. This day is public Continental Thanksgiving recommended by Congress & authorised in each State by their respective Legislatures. **1806** *Balance* V. 387/1 Patriotism would certainly prefer its continuance, and application to . . . public education. **1815** *Holyoke Diaries* 164 Mr. T(urner) had public dancing. **1868** BEECHER *Norwood* 452 One day in three hundred and sixty-five for public fasting could not seem unreasonable. **1884** *Century Mag.* Feb. 583/2 Society . . . recognized them [*i.e.*, hospitals and schools] not as public charities, but as public interests.

7. Referring to things that may be used or hired by the general public; not private. {1617–}

See also PUBLIC BATH, PUBLIC HALL, etc.

1715 *N.C. Col. Rec.* II. 206 All such mills as are or shall be built as afores[ai]d shall be deemed Publick Mills and the owner . . . shall be obliged . . . to grind wheat and Indian Corn for all such persons as shall require the same. **1803** CUTLER in *Life & Corr.* II. 119 He dines at the public table. **1844** FEATHERSTONHAUGH *Slave States* 28 [The] sharpers . . . keep a public gaming-table, that is open day and night, where faro, roulette, rouge et noir, and other desperate games are played. **1883** 'MARK TWAIN' *Life on Miss.* xxxviii, There were also public towels, public combs and public soap. **1891** *Ohio Bur. Labor Statistics 14th Rep.* 14 The superintendents of the 'Free Public Employment Offices' are required by law to report to this Bureau. **1893** POST *Harvard Stories* 31 The public wards are chuck-full. **1893** *McClure's Mag.* I. 394/2 There were even days when the Joneses questioned whether they were not running a public telephone, so often did the bell ring.

8. Referring to various conditions, expressions, and psychological attitudes of the people. {1812–}

1792 JEFFERSON *Writings* VIII. 444 The occasion of electing a Vice-President has been seized as a proper one for expressing the public sense on the doctrines of the monocrats. **1806** in Commons, etc. *Doc. Hist.* III. 67 The newspaper called the *Aurora*, has teemed with false representations . . . to poison the public mind. **1854** BENTON *30 Years' View* I. 37/1 The electors . . . from the beginning . . . have stood pledged to vote for the candidates indicated . . . by the public will. **1884** *Century Mag.* March 655/2 The prominent men of society in Washington are the prominent men of the country at large, and their morals and their character, their honesty and dishonesty, are a faithful reflection of the tone of public sentiment in regard to morality throughout the country.

9. Referring to newspapers, pamphlets, etc., intended to be read by the public. {*a*1641–}

1737 *Boston Rec.* 164 Advertise the same in the Public News Papers. **1776** FITHIAN *Journal* II. 178 We received the public papers. **1838** COOPER *Amer. Democrat* 129 This fearful change must, in a great measure, be ascribed to the corruption of the publick press.

III. 10. In special combinations.

Public creditor, one who holds government securities; *p. crib*, the federal or a state treasury; *p. utility*, a private or public corporation that performs some vital service for the public such as providing water or transportation facilities.

1798 *Ann. 5th Congress* I. 707 He did not think these of sufficient weight to prevent justice from being done to this class of public creditors. **1853** *La Crosse Democrat* 8 Nov. 1/5 [The delegates have] no other view . . . than to get one elected who will . . . give them a key to the public crib. **1903** ELY *Evolution Indust. Soc.* 225 The principal classes of these public utilities are water, light and transportation.

Public auction. An auction sale open to the public. — **1803** *Indian Laws & Tr.* III. 704 No lease shall be made, but by public auction. **1848** *Santa Fe Republican* 15 Jan. 2/4 The Subscribers will sell at Public Auction, on Wednesday the 19th inst., at their stand in Santa Fe, Dry Goods, Clothing and Hardware. **1911** *Okla. Session Laws* 3 Legisl. 243 Said blocks and the improvements thereon shall be appraised and the blocks shall be sold at public auction.

Public bank. A bank conducted by the government or subject to its regulations. Distinguished from a private bank (q.v.). — **1714** *Mass. Bay Currency Tracts* 136, I wonder then how it consisted with his Consciencious regard to it [the law], to advise the Publick to Erect a Publick Bank of Credit! **1715** *Boston Rec.* 115 A Town Meeting [shall] be appointed to debate & declare whether they are for a Publick or Private Bank. **1720** *Mass. Bay Currency Tracts* 275 We have found by the unhappy Experience of the Publick Bank, that [etc.].

Public bath(s). A building or place providing baths for the general public. {public swimming baths, 1878– (*Encycl. Brit.* III. 438/2)} — **1811** SUTCLIFF *Travels* 42 This morning I was conducted . . . to one of the Public Baths [in N.Y. City]. **1827** MCKENNEY *Tour to Lakes* 86 We see here . . . a court house and jail; and *public baths!* **1899** NORRIS *McTeague*, She could see . . . the glass skylights and water tanks of the big public baths.

Public bill. +**1.** A government note issued by a public bank. **2.** A legislative bill concerning public matters. (Cf. PRIVATE BILL.) — **(1)** **1714** *Mass. Bay Currency Tracts* 105 We have had Twelve Years Experience already of Publick Bills, with great Honour, Safety, and Success. **1720** *Ib.* 336 Let now the Publick Bills of Credit be thus Supported, which They ought to be. **(2)** **1886** ALTON *Among Law-Makers* 47 It is by public bills that measures designed for enforcement throughout the country and involving the legal rights of the people, are enacted. **1914** *Cycl. Amer. Govt.* I. 202/2 Calendar Wednesday is the day set apart by a rule of the House of Representatives . . . for the consideration of public bills, excepting those that are privileged under the rules.

***Public building. a.** A building owned or controlled by the public, or, loosely, by any agency authorized by the government. **b.** A private building open to the public. — **1742** *Maryland Hist. Mag.* XX. 170 Iron wire Lattices or Casements to be made Double Work or Strong, . . . to defend the outside of the Windows of a Public Building. **1789** MORSE *Amer. Geog.* 427 The public buildings [in Charleston, S.C.] are an exchange, state house [etc.]. **1837** PECK *New Guide* 192 The public buildings of Detroit are a state-house, a council-house, an academy, and two or three banking-houses. **1849** [see ESTUFA 1]. **1900** *Congress. Rec.* 3 Jan. 637/1 A bill . . . to provide for the erection of a public building at Eagle Pass, Tex.

+**Public day.** A day employed in public business; a day when the public may be heard, participate in, or witness, some activity.

1722 FRANKLIN *Writings* II. 20 An honest Neighbour . . . [was] in Town some time since on a publick Day. **1723** *Boston Rec.* 173 No free Indian Negro or Molatto Shal on Training dayes, or any other Publick dayes carry into the Common or Training field . . . any Strong drink Cakes or any other Provision. **1797** BOWNE *Life* 12, I go to Boston every public day. **1866** 'F. KIRKLAND' *Bk. Anecdotes* 644/1 Once, on what was called 'a public day'—when Mr. Lincoln received all applicants in their turn—the first thing he saw [etc.]. **1901** *Harper's Mag.* Dec. 205/1 Tim and his wife used to go to school public days to see him.

+**b.** *College.* Commencement day.

1829 *Va. Lit. Museum* 95 *Public Day.*—On Saturday last, the 18th, instant, the following exercises took place in the Rotunda [at the Univ. of Va.], in the presence of the Rector and Visiters and a numerous assemblage of the public. **1847** *S.Lit. Messenger* XIII. 567/2 The exercises of the 'Public Day' at William and Mary, have long been closed with a dinner, at which the Declaration of Independence is read. **1851** HALL *College Words* 249 *Public day,* in the University of Virginia, the day on which the certificates and diplomas are awarded to the successful candidates.

Public debt. A debt incurred or assumed by the public, esp. the national debt (q.v.) as represented by formal instruments of indebtedness. {1653–}

1721 *Mass. H. Rep. Jrnl.* III. 9 Acts have been Passed . . . for Striking Bills of Credit, and Issuing out the same, in order to discharge their Publick Debts. **1787** CUTLER in *Life & Corr.* I. 127 Congress would pay more than four millions of the public debt. **1792** JEFFERSON *Writings* VIII. 401 No man is more ardently intent to see the public debt . . . paid off than I am. **1836** *Diplom. Corr. Texas* I. (1908) 153 Send me on an estimate of our public debt. **1848** *Santa Fe Republican* 24 Aug. 2/1 The public debt of the U. States, July 1, 1847, was $39,000,000. **1868** *14th Amendment,* § 4 The validity of the public debt of the United States . . . shall not be questioned. **1918** *Current Hist.* Aug. 277/2 The public debt of the . . . United States . . . At Most Recent Date [in millions of dollars] $15,008.

+**Public domain.** Lands belonging to a state, or, more commonly, to the general government; public lands.

1832 in *Whig Almanac 1844* 38/1 Within a few years . . . restless men have thrown before the public their visionary plans for squandering the public domain. **1839** [see CONFEDERATED *a.* 2]. **1852** REYNOLDS *Hist. Illinois* 279 He surveyed much of the public domain in St. Clair, and Randolph counties. **1873** *Republic* I. 35 Congress has supreme power over the public domain. **1909** *Indian Laws & Tr.* III. 389 The Secretary of Interior . . . is authorized . . . to allot any Indian on the public domain who has not heretofore received an allotment, . . . eighty acres of agricultural [land].

Public hall. A hall that is used for public gatherings. {1855–} — **1831** PECK *Guide* III. 289 *Belleville* [contains] . . . a public hall for literary purposes. **1873** *Winfield* (Kan.) *Courier* 18 Jan. 3/2 The upper room [will be used] as a public hall. **1893** *Harper's Mag.* April 669/2 Its public hall was the scene of many social and historic gatherings.

***Public house.**

1. A house for the accommodation or entertainment of any member of the public; a hotel; a licensed saloon. {1669–}

In England a public house 'rarely accommodates lodgers, and . . . has for its chief business the selling of beer and other liquors' (*Cent.*). In the United States, the sense is more general.

1658 *Boston Rec.* 148 Itt was voted that the Gen. Court bee desired to make a law against publick houses entertainment of any inhabitants to drink on the night after the Sabbath is ended. **1682** *Mass. H. S. Coll.* 4 Ser. V. 60 In the middle of the town, one public house is very sufficient for the entertainment of travellers. **1732** in Singleton *Social N.Y.* 41 Finely situated either for a gentlemen's country-seat or a Publick House. **1784** SMYTH *Tour* I. 49 Taverns, public-houses, or ordinaries, . . . in the general acceptance of the names here are synonymous terms. **1819** E. DANA *Geogr. Sk.* 78 In Jan. 1817, were 130 [houses], of which six are licensed public houses. **1847** *Santa Fe Republican* 17 Sept. 2/3 When Genl. Kearney one year ago entered Santa Fe, at that time there was but one Public House. **1873** BEADLE *Undevel. West* 784 The Alamo Hotel . . . unites the characteristics of the Yankee hotel, the Southern 'public house,' and the foreign *hostelrie.* **1925** *Amer. Mercury* June 212/2 There was a vast difference in architectural form between the stately King's Arms in Boston and the rude wooden shack which served as a public-house in the back country of North Carolina.

comb. **1723** *Amer. Wkly. Mercury* 21 Nov. 2/2 Notice is hereby given to all Publick House-keepers, and other Persons Licensed to Retail Liquors . . . who have neglected to make due Entryes and Accounts.

b. In full *public house of entertainment.*

1673 *Dorchester Rec.* 193 The same day Nicholas George was allowed to kepe an publique house of entertainement. **1690** *Plymouth Laws* 231, 50lb excise [shall] be . . . raysed upon the publique houses of Entertainment.

***2.** =PUBLIC BUILDING a.

1675 *Plymouth Laws* 175 It is enacted by the Court that there be a publicke house erected in every Towne of this Government for the Towne comfortably to meet in to worship God.

Publicist. a. (See quot. 1828.) {1792–} **b.** Loosely, a journalist. {1833–} — **1795** A. HAMILTON *Ann. 3rd Congress* 1 Sess. 1366 Some of the most approved publicists . . . say [the income of lands] may be sequestered 'to hinder the remittance of it to the enemy's country.' **1818** CLAY *Speeches* (1860) I. 94 Martens and other publicists lay down these principles. **1828** WEBSTER, *Publicist,* a writer on the laws of nature and nations; one who treats of the rights of nations. *Kent, Du Ponceau.* **1898** *Kansas City Star* 18 Dec. 2/2 It will not unite itself with any last dog movement of politics as that . . . fathered by such trust-engineering publicists.

+**Public land.**

1. a. *pl.* Lands owned by the public, most commonly by the national government.

1789 *Ann. 1st Congress* I. 61 These troops were raised . . . to prevent all intrusions on the public lands. **1812** CLAY *Speeches* (1860) I. 29 The general government receives annually for the public lands, about $600,000. **1831** PECK *Guide* 57 The public lands in all the states and territories, when owned by the general government, are all surveyed and sold on one general plan. **1852** GOUGE *Fiscal Hist. Texas* 27 The public lands the Provisional Government [of Texas] bestowed very freely. **1873** *Harper's Mag.* April 785/2 Mr. Stewart introduced a bill . . . granting the State of Nevada 1,000,000 acres of the public lands for common-school purposes. **1903** E. JOHNSON *Railway Transportation* 312 In making these grants to railroads the United States sought, among other purposes, to increase the accessibility and value of the public lands not given away. **1917** *Statutes at Large* XL. I. 248 Any settler upon the public lands . . . [who] enlists . . . [shall] have his services . . . construed to be equivalent . . . to residence and cultivation.

b. *sing.* Land on the public domain.

1832 CLAY *Speeches* (1842) 220 There is public land enough to found an empire. **1836** *Diplom. Corr. Texas* I. (1908) 91 Liberal appropriations of public land shall be made for the endowment of Seminaries of learning, Colleges, and other institutions of public utility. **1900** *Congress. Rec.* 17 Feb. 1903/1 The surveyor-general of the State writes me that there are more inquiries for public land than there have been for years.

2. Attrib. and comb. with *bill, debtor, law,* etc.

1846 *Niles' Nat. Reg.* July 11 304/3 Public Land Bill. The debate in the house of representatives on the graduation bill, terminated at 2 o'clock yesterday. **1854** BENTON *30 Years' View* I. 11/2 Among these was the great and prominent class of the public land purchasers. *Ib.* 12/2 Many members of Congress were among the public land debtors. **1860** GREELEY *Overland Journey* 178 Let me . . . illustrate the military and public land systems of the United States. **1900** *Congress. Rec.* 10 Jan. 754/1 A bill (H. R. 5763) to extend the public-land laws to the district of Alaska.

+**Public-land state.** A state containing public land belonging to the federal government. — **1900** *Congress. Rec.* 4 Jan. 648/1 The bill . . . declaring the character of the accounts between the United States and the several public-land States. **1910** PINCHOT *Fight for Conservation* 93 We are facing in the public-land States west of the Mississippi the great question whether the Western people are to be predominately a people of tenants . . . or freeholders and free men.

Public letter. A letter concerned with public matters. — **1775** *Warren-Adams Lett.* I. 56 You will collect from the publick Letter by this Express our Sentiments with regard to the necessity of assuming civil Government constantly increasing upon us. **1848** *Santa Fe Republican* 15 Jan. 4/1 After marching three miles we met Kit Carson direct on express from California with a mail of public letters for Washington.

Public library. A library for the general use of the pubic; the building that houses such a library. {1614–}

1712 *N.C. Col. Rec.* I. 860 Dr. Brays public library is all dispersed and lost by those wretches. **1764** in Peirce *Hist. Harvard* 282 The repository of our most valuable treasures, the public Library and Philosophical Apparatus, was seen in flames. **1815** DRAKE *Cincinnati* 160 It was not until the year 1809 that any efforts were made towards the establishment of a public library. **1899** *Mo. So. Dakotan* I. 148 Even in our public libraries, the pride and boast of our country, lurks a pitfall for the unwary. **1905** *Current Lit.* Jan. 99/2 Mr. Horace White . . . [presented] the first complete and authoritative account of Mr. Andrew Carnegie's remarkable list of benefactions in the way of founding public libraries.

Public man. A man actively participating in public affairs. {1817–} — **1822** *Ann. 17th Congress* 1 Sess. I. 147 He alluded to his liberality as a public man, not to personal or private liberality. **1850** in Claiborne *Life Quitman* II. 38 The desire of our public men is, that the Nashville Convention . . . should recommend the call of a Southern congress. **1907** ANDREWS *Recoll.* (1928) 44 Mr. Ayer . . . was one of the best lawyers and one of the most promising public men in New Hampshire. **1925** BRYAN *Memoirs* 99 By this time I had become acquainted with a good many public men.

Public meeting. A meeting open to the community at large. {1821-30-} — **1639** *Portsmouth Rec.* 10 It is granted at a publike mettinge [of the inhabitants] of portsmouth. **1661** *Boston Rec.* 1 Att a Publick meeting of all ye Inhabitants vpon lawful warning from house to house, were chosen [etc.]. **1820** *Columbian Centinel* 1 Jan. 2/3 A Public Meeting was held in Salem yesterday, on the subject of the proposition before Congress to abolish Drawbacks. **1883** E. M. BACON *Dict. Boston, Mass.* 304 All sorts of public meetings, balls, cat-shows, dog-shows, foot-races, walking-matches, and wrestling-matches.

***Public notary.** (See NOTARY.)

Public office.

1. A room or set of rooms wherein matters relating to the public are conducted. {1792-}

1796 *Aurora* (Phila.) 3 Dec. (Th.), [A man] wants employment in a Bookstore, Compting House, or Public Office. **1817** S. BROWN *Western Gazetteer* 98 The public offices are on the first floor [of the statehouse in Frankfort, Ky.]. **1884** *Century Mag.* April 809/2 Here are all the paraphernalia of a busy public office.

2. A position of trust or authority held by an official of the community.

1844 *Mass. Acts & Resolves* 363 Public offices are public trusts, created for the benefit of the whole people, and not for the benefit of those who may fill them. **1885** CLEVELAND in *Pres. Mess. & P.* VIII. 364 Conservative and sober men ..., in fear of the confusion and risk attending an arbitrary and sudden change in all the public offices with a change of party rule, cast their ballots against such a chance. **1902** E. C. MEYER *Nominating Systems* 425 Eligibility to public office is determined, not by competence, but by political influence.

Public opinion. The collective opinion of the people. Often thought of as a single force in politics. {1781-} — **1801** JEFFERSON *Writings* X. 229 The great extent of our republic is new.... The mighty wave of public opinion which has rolled over it, is new. **1806** FESSENDEN *Democracy Unveiled* I. 23 In America public opinion must, in a great measure, supply the place of long established precedents, and form the chain which binds together society. **1857** BENTON *Exam. Dred Scott Case* 85 Public opinion at home, and town-meeting resolves, were bearing down the moderate members from the free States. **1875** C. F. WINGATE *Views & Interviews* 85 The public are apt to suppose that newspapers create public opinion?

Public print. A newspaper or pamphlet printed for the general public. (Cf. PRINT 1.) — **1705** *Boston News-Letter* 24 Sept. 2/1 We know not the certainty of any others besides those mentioned in the Publick Print. **1797** *Ann. 5th Congress* I. 215 They were told by the public prints that the President had appointed negotiators. **1832** DUNLAP *Hist. Amer. Theatre* 24 The oppositionists continued their attacks though the medium of the public prints. **1900** *Congress. Rec.* 17 Jan. 905/2 Every little while you see in public prints a reference to 'prophecies unrealized.'

Public printer. A printer officially designated to print government documents, forms, etc. — **1835** J. HALL *Sk. of West* II. 193 The state treasurer, auditor, attorney general, and public printer, are, under the constitution, elected by the general assembly. **1900** *Congress. Rec.* 18 Jan. 953/2 The Report on Agriculture ... was retained by the Public Printer for nine months and one day.

Public reception. A reception open to the public. Also attrib. — **1866** CARPENTER *At White House* 87 It was just after the public reception, and three hours' hand-shaking is not calculated to improve a man's chirography. **1884** *Century Mag.* April 812/2 Now one or two public receptions during a session of Congress are thought a sufficient concession to the democratic principle. **1902** A. MACGOWAN *Last Word* 141 Miss Salem remarked that it was public reception day at the White House.

Public road. A road open to, or used and maintained by, the general public. {1819-} — **1716** *N.C. Col. Rec.* II. 265 Thos. Lee praying yt the main Road ... may be his established Bounds to Maintain and keep as a publick road at his own Costs. **1785** *Mass. Hist. Soc. Proc.* V. 480 It is agreeable to the *taste* of Southern gentlemen to live off from the public road. **1834** in *Atlantic Mo.* XXVI. 742 A by-path carried me through fields into a public road. **1911** *Okla. Session Laws* 3 Legisl. 136 Any person [who] shall willfully or maliciously disturb ... the peace and quiet of any city of the first class ... by running any horse at unusual speed along any street, alley, highway or public road ... shall be deemed guilty of a misdemeanor.

Public room. *spec.* A room in a hotel or inn open to the general public. {1855-} — **1762** in Earle *Customs Old New Eng.* 247 At the Public Room of the above Inn will be delivered a series of Moral Dialogues. **1835** *Harvardiana* I. 155, I was seated in the public room of the principal hotel. **1887** TOURGEE *Button's Inn* 19 The voice came from the public-room, the doors of which opened on the porch. **1904** *N.Y. Sun* 21 Aug. 5 The process of paging Mr. Smith consists in calling out his name in the dining and other public rooms of the hotel.

Public sale. A sale open to the public; a public auction. {1678- (s.v. *Auction* sb. 2 in *O.E.D.*)}

1686 *Boston Rec.* 84 What goods by you shall be distrained upon, you are to expose to pu[b]lique Saile. **1714** *Boston News-Letter* 20 Sept. 2/2 To be Sold by Publick Sale or Vendue ..., The Hull of the Ship Hanover. **1812** *Amer. Review of Hist.* Oct. 370 Let there be a horse race, or a cock fight, or a public sale, or a camp meeting of a week's duration, and notice the multitudes of able bodied individuals who attend them. **1852** in Stowe *Key* 134/2, I will sell ... 50 of as likely Negroes as have ever been exposed to public sale, belonging to the estate of A. P. Vinson. **1911** *Okla. Session Laws* 3 Legisl. 214 Such bonds when issued under this act shall be sold at a public or private sale, as the township board may deem it advisable.

***Public school.**

+**1.** A free elementary or secondary school maintained by taxation or by funds accruing from public lands, and usually managed by the local government; a building housing such a school. {1872-, in Scottish and colonial use}

In England *public school* usually refers to an endowed school, such as Rugby and Charterhouse. (Cf. COMMON SCHOOL, FREE SCHOOL, PUBLIC *a.* 5.)

1636 *Harvard Rec.* I. 171 The Court voted for the erecting a publick Schooll or Colledge in Cambridge. *c***1649** *Boston Rec.* 81 He was chosen to be Feofee of the Publick Schoole in Roxbury. **1683** *Penna. Frame of Govt.* § 10 The Governor and provincial Council shall erect and order all public schools. **1773** *License to Teach* 23 June (Pettigrew P.), I do hereby Licence and appoint you the said Charles Pettigrove Master of the Publick School in Edenton. **1785** *Jrnls. Cont. Congress* XXVIII. 378 There shall be reserved the lot N 16, of every township, for the maintenance of public schools, within the said township. **1833** *Ind. Laws 1832-3* 78 An Act incorporating Congressional Townships, and providing for Public Schools therein. **1848** *Santa Fe Republican* 24 May 2/3 Why is it that the public schools are not established; we believe there was an act passed by our Assembly providing for such. **1873** *Penna. Constitution* § 10 The general assembly shall provide for the maintenance and support of a thorough and efficient system of public schools. **1903** HART *Actual Govt.* 549 The public school is the greatest democratic influence in our country. **1925** *New Republic* 24 June 115/1 The public schools are associated in the public mind with representative government and universal suffrage.

2. Attrib. with *children, desk, kindergarten*, etc.

1870 O. LOGAN *Before Footlights* 274 A procession in the West would not be complete without the presence of the inevitable public school children. **1872** 'MARK TWAIN' *Roughing It* 299 He could get the monthly public-school report. **1873** *Harper's Mag.* March 627/1 Such technical education ... must be inwrought with our public-school system. **1912** NICHOLSON *Hoosier Chron.* 435 She was ... a public school-teacher, they believed, the daughter of an old friend. **1919** *Rep. Comm. Educ.* 85 In many places there are no public-school kindergartens. **1920** HOWELLS *Vacation of Kelwyns* 115 [She brought] out what was best in the twenty-five or thirty children ... answering from their regulation public-school desks.

Public schoolhouse. A schoolhouse maintained by the local government. — **1857** *Mass. Acts & Resolves* 712 The sum expended for *building and repairing* public school-houses during the past year, reached ... $588,214. **1872** TICE *Over Plains* 12 All the towns and villages along the road have good public school houses, and one or more churches. **1912** NICHOLSON *Hoosier Chron.* 377 She was not a woman to harbor in her home a girl who labored in a public school-house.

+**Public-school land.** Land set aside by the public-land laws for public schools. — **1900** *Congress. Rec.* 31 Jan. 1353/2 We are leasing not only our public-school lands, but our public domain. **1905** *Forestry Bureau Bul.* No. 62, 36 Of these latter grants there are four classes—public school lands, university lands, asylum lands, and county school lands.

Public servant. One who holds a public office. {1676-} — **1825** CLAY *Speeches* (1860) I. 209 The portion of the public servants who make up the general assembly have no right to instruct that portion of them who constituted the Kentucky delegation in the House of Representatives. **1828** COOPER *Notions* I. 95 *Public servants*, as the officers are here [in N.Y. City and suburbs] emphatically called, must pay the utmost deference to the public will. **1885** *Century Mag.* April 822 The public servants of comparatively small importance are protected by their own insignificance from the consequences of their bad actions. **1910** PINCHOT *Fight for Conservation* 145 One step in this direction ... is a law forbidding any Senator or Member of Congress or other public servant to perform any services for any corporation engaged in interstate commerce.

Public service. Service conducted for the general public under the agency of government. {1709-}

1645 *New Haven Col. Rec.* 168 The farmers that have butter and cheese were desired to keepe it in their hands, that in case the publicque service require it, they may be furnished. **1719** *Mass. H. Rep. Jrnl.* II. 127 An old, blind Indian ... received the hurt which occasioned his blindness in the Public Service. **1900** *Congress. Rec.* 11 Jan. 764/1 The business of the House [will] be ... suspended to enable his associates to pay proper tribute of regard to his high character and distinguished public services.

+**b.** *Public-service corporation*, a corporation that operates a public utility.

1908 STEVENS *Liberators* 187 The public service corporation had dictated the nomination of the entire Republican State and Legislative ticket. **1911** *Okla. Session Laws* 3 Legisl. 179 Any public service corporation ... may contract for the construction and maintenance of bridges. **1912** NICHOLSON *Hoosier Chron.* 79 This capable firm was retained by most of the public service corporations.

Public speaking. The action or art of speaking in public. {1828-} — **1762** W. SMITH *Discourses* (ed. 2) App. 113 This attention to public speaking, which is begun here [in the College of Phila.] with the very rudiments of the mother-tongue, is continued down to the end. **1856** EMERSON *Eng. Traits* 132 A kind of pride in bad public speaking is noted in the

House of Commons, as if they were willing to show that they did not live by their tongues. **1875** STOWE *We & Neighbors* 116 The church . . . was entirely unadapted for any purposes of public speaking. **1923** *Univ. of Mich.Catalogue* 350 Those preparing to teach Public Speaking should take at least twenty hours of work in the department.

Public square. A square or rectangular area in a town used as a park, market place, etc.; a plaza.

1786 in Durrett *Louisville* 174 [Lots] 224, 225, 226, Public Square. **1792** POPE *Tour S. & W.* 55 In the public Square . . . also they hold their War Dances . . . and keep their annual Festival called the *Busk.* **1817** S. BROWN *Western Gazetteer* 54 The public square and a great part of the town stands on a beautiful level. **1835** HOFFMAN *Winter in West* I. 69 The great defect in the town [of Pittsburgh] is the total want of public squares, and, indeed, of an agreeable promenade of any kind. **1899** CHESNUTT *Conjure Woman* 3 There was a red brick market-house in the public square. **1925** BRYAN *Memoirs* 27 [She] began housekeeping in the home on Broadway, about half-way between the public square and the railroad.

Public trust. An obligation to serve the people assumed by one who accepts public office. — **1835** D. WEBSTER *Works* I. 335 Offices, created for the people, are public trusts, not private spoils. **1844** [see PUBLIC OFFICE 2]. **1900** *Congress. Rec.* 11 Jan. 785/1.

+Public vendue. A public sale or auction by outcry.

Frequently in phrases *at (a) public vendue, by public vendue.*

1686 in Munsell *Annals Albany* II. 93 Which said lotts of grounde ye common councill will dispose of at a publike vendu or out cry. **1705** *Boston News-Letter* 23 April 2/2 On Tuesday the 15th of May next will be Exposed to Sale by Publick Vendue . . . one quarter part of a Farm at the South-end of Quananicut Island. **1750** *Baltimore Rec.* 27 The Commissioners have therefore resolved to put the same Lotts up to public Vendue on Saturday the sixth day of October. **1802** *Ann. 7th Congress* 2 Sess. 1227 He was compelled to expose them to sale, at public vendue, in the city of New York. **1851** A. CARY *Clovernook* 231 Bills posted in front of the Clovernook Hotel, . . . stating, in large printed letters, that there 'would be sold at public vendue, . . . all the following property.'

attrib. **1710** *S.C. Statutes* II. 348 The person herein after appointed publick vendue master, or his deputy.

Public work. An architectural or engineering structure or improvement, as a building, canal, or park, built with government funds. Usually pl.

1676 in Neill *Virginia Carolorum* 361 For haveing upon specious pretences of publique works raised great unjust taxes [etc.]. **1777** *N.H. Comm. Safety Rec.* 69, £4-5-6 for working & finding Tools . . . , on the publick works at New Castle. **1818** *N. Amer. Rev.* VIII. 11 Upon an application of the citizens of Petersburg [Va.], the Board of Public Works directed their Engineer to make a survey. **1850** GLISAN *Jrnl. Army Life* 29 The most important public work in the vicinity is the United States Navy Yard. **1903** E. JOHNSON *Railway Transportation* 16 The opening of the Erie Canal roused Pennsylvania to action, and in 1826 she began her system of 'public works,' the main feature of which was a composite rail and water route.

Public worship. Worship done in public; an occasion or meeting open to the public for worshiping God. {1644-} — **1720** D. NEAL *Hist. New-Eng.* I. 303 T. Harris of Barbadoes disturbed the publick Worship again. **1772** A. G. WINSLOW *Diary* 22 Yesterday was very bad weather, neither aunt, nor niece at publick worship. **1835** J. MARTIN *Descr. Virginia* 162/2 There are 7 houses of public worship [in Petersburg, Va.]. **1882** THAYER *From Log-Cabin* 236 He was at public worship, when the contribution-box was passed through the audience.

Publish,** *v.* **+tr.* To announce or make public the names of (persons intending marriage). {to publish the banns, 1488-}

1651 *Essex Antiquarian* VII. 45 Mr. Phillips of Rowley, having been published, writes to the General Court saying that there is no one [*i.e.*, no clergyman] to marry him. **1682** *N.H. Hist. Soc. Coll.* VIII. 117 My son and Sarah were legally published, and took each other before one of his Majesty's council. **1724** *Essex Inst. Coll.* XXXVI. 332 Mary Flint & Saml. Wainwright publishd Nov. 29 & married January 27. **1751** MACSPARRAN *Diary* 65, [I] read Prayers at Home, and published Tom Weeks & Ruth Browne ye 2d time. *c***1840** NEAL *Beedle's Sleigh Ride* 24 The next Sunday morning she was published. **1886** STAPLETON *Major's Christmas* 124 Then say you will marry me, and we will be published to-day.

***Publisher.**

***1.** =CRIER 2.

1695 SEWALL *Diary* I. 411 Robt. Williams the Bell-Ringer, Publisher (Crier) and Grave-digger died this morn.

2. a. One who owns and operates a newspaper. {an author or editor, 1654-1775} **b.** One whose business is to issue books, newspapers, engravings, etc. {1740-}

'The word *publisher* for *newspaper owner* confuses our people' (1920 Lord Northcliffe quoted in Horwill).

1724 *New-Eng. Courant* 6-13 July 2/1 A certain Publisher in the World, has a soft and weak Head. **1838** *U.S. Mag.* I. 466 A New York publisher . . . had already given currency to many of the infidel works most in vogue abroad. **1853** *Knickerb.* XLII. 434 Some enterprising publisher . . . would 'find his account' in collecting these admirable letters into a volume. **1896** *Internat. Typogr. Union Proc.* 29/1 The union got into trouble with the publishers of that city over the question of apprentices. **1907** *St. Nicholas* June 680/1 Publishers besought Mr. Aldrich to write more such tales. **1911** *Springfield W. Repub.* 6 April 11 Connecticut Publisher Dead. F. R. Swift, owner of the Bridgeport and Waterbury Herald, died last week.

Publishing house. A business organization that issues books, music, catalogues, etc.; a building housing such an organization. {1828-} — **1862** NEWELL *Orpheus C. Kerr* I. 380, I'm agent for the great American publishing house of Rushem & Jinks. **1864** NICHOLS *Amer. Life* I. 158 There are . . . four daily newspapers, several large publishing houses, libraries [etc.]. **1882** MCCABE *New York* 147 Several of the leading publishing houses of the country . . . [are] quartered in magnificent buildings. **1916** DU PUY *Uncle Sam* 53 The expected summons brought him to the publishing house in five minutes.

***Publishment.** **+**The action of making public the banns or the names of persons intending marriage.

1692 *Mass. Province Laws* I. 61 The fee to be paid for every marriage shall be three shillings, and for publishment and certificate thereof, one shilling. **1722** SEWALL *Diary* III. 303 Possibly you have heard of our Publishment last Thorsday. **1745** HEMPSTEAD *Diary* 442, 3 publishments up. **1788** *Mayflower Descendant* XI. 41 Levi Young Entred his Intentions of Marriage with Molly Godfrey Both of Chatham in order for Publishment. **1837** in Martineau *Society* III. 331 Mrs. Prudence Bates, . . . after the regular publishment on the church-doors for three Sundays, was united to me in the holy bands of wedlock. **1898** *Hist. Northampton, Mass.* I. 104 The publishment, when not posted, is . . . supposed to have been made by announcement.

+Puccoon. [Algonquian. Cf. POKE *n.*[3]] Any of various American plants, or their roots, yielding red or yellow pigment; the pigment itself.

Specific plants are the bloodroot (q.v., sense 1), the goldenseal (q.v.), and any plant of the genus *Lithospermum.* Variant spellings are numerous. See also POCONES. 'In s.w. Virginia puccoon is locally abbreviated "coon"' (1910 Hodge etc. *Amer. Indians* II. 315).

*c***1618** STRACHEY *Virginia* 64 Their heads and shoulders they paint oftennest, and those red, with the roote pochone. *Ib.* 192 Poughkone, the red paint or die. **1705** BEVERLEY *Virginia* II. 23 They have the Puccoon and Musquaspen, Two Roots, with which the Indians use to paint themselves red. **1796** MORSE *Univ. Geog.* I. 189 Among the native and uncultivated plants of New England, the following have been employed for medicinal purposes: . . . Cohush (*Actæa spicata*). . . . Blood root, or Puccoon (*Sanguinaria canadensis*). **1817-8** EATON *Botany* (1822) 203 *Batschia canescens*, puccoon, false bugloss. . . . A red substance covering the root is the puccoon of the Indians. **1864** BRYANT *Let. to F. Bryant* 30 May (MS.), On my way hither [to Ill.] I saw . . . the golden flower of the puccoon or red root. **1893** [see next]. **1912** NICHOLSON *Hoosier Chron.* 125 To-day Mrs. Bassett rejoiced in the discovery of the season's first puccoon, showing its orange-yellow cluster on a sandy slope.

+Puccoon root. =prec. — **1709** LAWSON *Carolina* 172 For want of this Root, they sometimes use Pecoon-Root, which is of a Crimson Colour, but it is apt to die the Hair of an ugly Hue. *c***1866** BAGBY *Old Va. Gentleman* 60 An exceedingly strange whim . . . accompanied by preposterous vagaries about the virtues of puccoon-root, 'jimson' weed, white oak bark. **1893** *Amer.Folk-Lore* VI. 137 *Sanguinaria Canadensis*, puccoon, Banner Elk, N.C.; puccoon root, Anderson, Ind.

Puck. A rubber disk used in playing ice hockey. — [**1891** *Field* March 334/3 The ball (or 'puck,' as it is called) is a flat piece of india-rubber, circular in shape, about two inches thick. . . . No striking with the stick is allowed, only pushing the 'puck' along the ice.] **1907** *St. Nicholas* July 780/2 Harris, who played point on the home team, got away with the puck for a long race down the rink.

+Puckerbush. (See quotation.) — **1897** SUDWORTH *Arborescent Flora* 117 *Myrica cerifera.* Wax Myrtle. . . . Puckerbush (Fla.).

+Puckermouth. The summer flounder, *Paralichthys dentatus.* — **1884** GOODE, etc. *Fisheries* I. 178 In Rhode Island the names Brail and Puckermouth are used.

Puckery, *a.* **1.** Marked with puckers. {1858-} **+2.** Of fruit or other food: That makes the mouth pucker. — (1) **1830** *Mass. Spy* 10 Feb. (Th.), I diddn't like the set of the shoulders, they were so dreadful puckery; but the man said it was alright. (2) **1834** S. SMITH *Major Downing* 47, I guess he'll find the apple-sauce full as puckery when he gets down into it. **1858** HAWTHORNE *Fr. & Ital. Note-Books* II. 150 Grapes are better than puckery cider apples. **1887** *Harper's Mag.* Feb. 451/1 But to the human palate it is dry, insipid, and puckery. **1916** PORTER *David* 274 You know what she is—sour as a lemon an' puckery as a choke-cherry.

+Puckery-hickory. (See quotation.) — **1724** JONES *Virginia* 145 Such [dealers] have often doubly cheated the Government; first by running Tobacco, or entering all light Hogsheads at Importation, which in their Language is called *Hickory-puckery;* and then again by getting a Debenture for Tobacco that has been run, or entering all heavy Hogsheads for Exportation, which they term *Puckery-hickory.*

***Pudding.**

***1.** A food preparation using various ingredients and formerly boiled in a cloth; now usually a dessert with a cereal basis to which is added milk, eggs, fruit, etc.

See also CORNSTARCH, HASTY, HUCKLEBERRY, INDIAN PUDDING.

1622 'MOURT' *Relation* 84 We gave him strong water, and bisket, and butter, and cheese, & pudding, and a peece of a mallerd. **1654** JOHNSON *Wonder-W. Prov.* 109* [The Indians] strive for variety after the English manner, boyling Puddings made of beaten corne [etc.]. **1789** MACLAY *Deb. Senate* 129 The desert was *first* apple pies, puddings, etc.; then iced creams, jellies, etc. **1867** *Common Sense Cook Book* 69 [Recipe for] beefsteak pudding. **1881** STODDARD *E. Hardery* 233 Mrs. Lawrence made the announcement with a face to which a knowledge of the triumph won over turkeys, puddings, and all kindred trials and tribulations had restored its accustomed placidity. **1907** *St. Nicholas* May 662/2 She was just going to get some milk for the pudding.

b. *transf.* A dinner. *dial.* (Cf. PUDDING TIME.)

1825 NEAL *Bro. Jonathan* I. 3 He was a regular visitor at Mr. Harwood's; took his 'pudding' there, three times a week; and supper, almost every night.

*__2.__ *pl.* (See quotation.)

1869 *Overland Mo.* III. 129 In most of the Atlantic Southern States there is a dish to be found about hog-slaughtering time, named 'puddings.' It consists of swine's flesh, bread, sage, and other matters of nourishment and seasoning, chopped fine, and then squirted out into links from the end of a sausage-gun.

+**3.** (See quot. 1860.)

*c*__1840__ NEAL *Beedle's Sleigh Ride* 13 His cravat had a pudding in it. **1860** MORDECAI *Virginia* 185 Those who could afford neither the valet, nor so extensive an investment of muslin, resorted to a substitute for its bulk, in what was called a pudding, or . . . a pad, which formed the foundation on which the cravat was built. **1868** G. G. CHANNING *Recoll. Newport* 241 The collar of the shirt . . . was inclosed by what was called either a cravat or stock or neckcloth or 'pudding.'

4. *To turn a pudding*, of a kite, to turn down and upward in one revolution.

1844 *Knickerb.* XXIV. 260 There is one which has just 'turned a pudding' twenty times.

5. Attrib. with *bag, boiler, cloth*, etc.

1638 *Md. Archives* IV. 48, 1. old pudding panne. **1723** *New-Eng. Courant* 16 Sept. 1/2 She knows . . . who makes Broth of Salt Pork and a Pudding Bag. **1828** LESLIE *Receipts* 15 Dip your pudding-cloth in boiling water. **1852** STOWE *Uncle Tom* xviii, Dinah . . . [gave] a poke, or rap on the head, to some of the young operators, with the pudding-stick that lay by her side. **1879** A. D. WHITNEY *Just How* 203 Keep the outer kettle covered, that the steam may surround the pudding-boiler.

Pudding dish. A dish for making or serving a pudding. Also fig. and attrib. — **1776** *Penna. Ledger* 20 April, Joseph Stansbury . . . is selling off . . . his baking dishes, compotiers, pudding dishes [etc.]. **1829** LONGFELLOW in S. Longfellow *H. W. Longfellow* I. 163 The Devil, dressed like a collier, with smutty face and pudding-dish hat. **1907** *St. Nicholas* July 798/2 The little old dumpling of a woman in the . . . inverted pudding-dish of a bonnet . . . sighed regretfully.

***Pudding time.** Dinner time. *local.* {1840; now *dial.*} (See *Amer. Speech* I. 45 and 616.) — **1839** TOWNSEND *Narrative* 252 As it was pudding time with us, our visitor was of course invited to sit and eat. **1853** SIMMS *Sword & Distaff* (1854) 429 Get out, my dear fellow, and let us hurry in to dinner. You are just in pudding-time.

***Puddle,** *v.*

1. *tr.* To render the lining of (an embankment, pond, etc.) water-tight by coating it with a soft or semi-liquid mixture of clay or soil. {1844–}

1808 in *Niles' Reg.* XV. 55/2 The embankments are well puddled, and the piers of the bridges are of hewn stone. **1896** *Boston Transcript* 4 Aug. 3/5 Another great use of water is made by the sewer department for flushing sewers and puddling trenches.

2. (See quot. 1905.) {1825– (Loudon *Encycl. Agric.* 577)}

1861 *Ill. Agric. Soc. Trans.* IV. 116 Mr. Bebb . . . planted 400 trees in 1851, . . . puddled them before he took them from the nursery. **1905** *Forestry Bureau Bul.* No. 61, 17 *Puddle*, to dip the roots of young trees in thin mud.

3. *Gold mining.* (See quotation.) {1859–, in Australia}

1877 W. WRIGHT *Big Bonanza* 32 The gold was in clay, which was so tough that before it could be washed out in rockers it was necessary to 'puddle' it—that is, put it into a large square box or a hole in the ground, and dissolve it by adding a proper quantity of water and working it about with hoes or shovels.

Puddler.

1. A workman who puddles or stirs and turns over molten iron. {1831–}

1861 *Atlantic Mo.* April 431/2 The old man, like many of the puddlers and feeders of the mills, was Welsh. **1869** *Causes Reduct. Tonnage* (1870) 163 So in our foundries, puddlers . . . get about sixty dollars. **1902** PHILLIPS *Woman Ventures* 102 [Those killed] were a puddler named Jack Farron, and his son Tom, and Tom's wife.

2. An implement for puddling iron.

1876 KNIGHT 1815/1 Mechanical puddlers have assumed two forms. 1. The Mechanical Rabble. . . . 2. The rotary puddling-furnace. **1894** *Harper's Mag.* Feb. 421/1 Among these [successful machines] are the so-called rotary 'puddlers.'

Puddling furnace. A furnace in which molten iron is decarbonized. {1825–} — **1854** BROMWELL *Locomotive Sk.* 122 Pig iron is always converted into blooms, and this is done either in the forge-fire or the puddling furnace. **1880** *Harper's Mag.* Dec. 57 In Pittsburgh . . . eight hundred puddling furnaces are seething. **1894** *Ib.* Feb. 424/2 The introduction of regular puddling-furnaces . . . occurred in 1816.

+**Pudjicky,** *a.* Fussy; sensitive. *dial.* — **1866** A. D. WHITNEY *L. Goldthwaite* iii, She's dreadfully *pudjicky*, Emma Jane is; she won't have anything without it's exactly right. **1890** JEWETT *Strangers* 13 Women folks is dreadful pudjicky about their cookin'. **1891** *Amer. Folk-Lore* IV. March 71 *Pudgicky*, similar to preceding [*pernickety*], but with a notion of being cross and fretful. . . . *Cambridge, Mass.* **1911** *Dialect Notes* III. 546 *Pudjiky, putchy*, . . . sullen, or pettish. 'Mary's acting a little pudjiky today.' [Neb.]

+**Pueblo.** [Sp.]

1. In the Southwest, either an Indian village made up of several separate adobe or stone buildings, or a large, many-storied, terraced building serving to house the members of the whole community; generically, any town.

[**1818** *Amer. St. P. For. Relations* IV. 307 There was in almost every valley [in Chile] a pueblo of peaceful and submissive Indians.] **1836** EDWARD *Hist. Texas* 162 When the Alcaldes or the citizens of the *pueblo* are plaintiffs or defendants, the conciliation shall be had . . . before the first Corregidor. **1844** GREGG *Commerce of Prairies* I. 273 The cacique . . . collects together the principal chiefs of the Pueblo in an *estufa*. **1848** *Santa Fe Republican* 31 Aug. 2/3 They raised the white flag and begged for mercy, but not until our colors were streaming from the top of one of the [Taos] Pueblos, (a house some five stories high). **1873** ARNY *Items regarding N. Mex.* 31 Within the limits of New Mexico there are 19 pueblos (towns) entirely occupied by Indians who are civilized so far as to maintain themselves. **1878** BEADLE *Western Wilds* 190 The white cross of the chapel, without which no Mexican town can be called a *pueblo*, spoke peace to all. **1885** *Wkly. New Mexican Rev.* 29 Jan. 2/5 [The Indians] almost all speak Spanish, besides the language of the pueblo to which they belong. **1903** *N.Y. Ev. Post* 19 Dec. 7 An Indian 'pueblo' perched high on barren cliffs in desert Arizona.

2. (cap.) An Indian belonging to a tribe that lives in one of these villages or buildings; in pl., the tribe.

'Several linguistic stocks are represented,—the Uto-Aztecan, Tanoan, Keresan, and Zuñian' (W. '34).

1834 A. PIKE *Sketches* 141 These Pueblos, (a word which signifies tribes—of Indians) are in fact, all handsome, athletic men. **1844** GREGG *Commerce of Prairies* I. 268 Most of these Pueblos call themselves the descendants of Montezuma. **1870** *Republican Rev.* 21 May 2/3 The Utes are known to be the best Indians in the Territory—always, of course, excepting the Pueblos. **1893** T. C. DONALDSON *Moqui Pueblo Indians of Arizona* 10 The beautiful legend of the Pueblo looking from the roof of his house for the coming of Montezuma. **1913** *Amer. Rev. of Reviews* April 493/1 You can still see the old mission church pitted with cannon ball and bullet, when General Price shelled it in the uprising of the pueblos after American occupation.

collect. **1834** A. PIKE *Sketches* 145 As the Pueblo were unprepared for this manœuvre, they broke through, and again charged back.

b. Any Indian who lives in a town.

1864 *Wkly. New Mexican* 29 July 2/1 We hope . . . that these [Navajo] Indians will be speedily converted again into 'Pueblos.'

3. Attrib. in sense 2 with *blood, faith, force*, etc.

1849 *31st Congress 1 Sess.* Sen. Ex. Doc. No. 64, 64 The Pueblo and Mexican force . . . is to join us at this point. **1870** *Republican Rev.* 3 Dec. 2/2 There are nineteen Pueblo villages in New Mexico who have lands granted to them by the Spanish and Mexican governments. **1880** *Cimarron News & Press* 15 July 3/1 Major Brooks . . . [is] purchasing Pueblo pottery, Navajo blankets and Mexican curiosities. **1884** *Century Mag.* Nov. 57 He also had Pueblo faith deep down in his heart, because of the Pueblo blood which flowed in his veins. **1890** *Stock Grower & Farmer* 18 Jan. 6/3 The warlike (?) Pueblo squaws drove them off.

+**Pueblo Indian.** =PUEBLO 2. — **1844** GREGG *Commerce of Prairies* I. 132 Two thousand of the insurgent mob, including the Pueblo Indians, pitched their camp in the suburbs of the capital [Santa Fe]. **1850** *31st Congress 1 Sess.* Sen. Ex. Doc. No. 64, 57 Among the 10,000 (estimated) Pueblo Indians who inhabit New Mexico, as many as *six* distinct *dialects* obtain. **1890** *Stock Grower & Farmer* 11 Jan. 3/2 The preliminary surveyors of the Rio Grande ditch have been stopped in their work by the Pueblo Indians. **1905** *Indian Laws & Tr.* III. 145 The lands now held by the various villages or pueblos of Pueblo Indians . . . shall be free and exempt from taxation.

+**Pueblo town.** A town inhabited by Pueblo Indians. — **1849** *31st Congress 1 Sess.* Sen. Ex. Doc. No. 64, 63, I notice here [at Jemez], on the outskirts of the village, the usual accompaniments of Mexican and pueblo towns. **1858** PETERS *Kit Carson* 31 On their route, the company passed through Zuni, a Pueblo town.

***Puff,** *n.* A downy pad for applying powder to the hair or skin. {1712–} Also attrib.

1732 FRANKLIN *Writings* II. 188 Dashing the Puff into the Powder-Box. **1790** *Columbian Centinel* 9 Oct. 31/2 For Sale, . . . Silk, and Down Puffs, Wash Balls. **1850** LEWIS *La. Swamp Doctor* 121 He puts quick-lime into the young ladies' puff-box. **1923** *Ladies Home Jrnl.* May 58 (*advt.*), To lovely women the exquisite Gainsborough Puff is the very utmost in puff daintiness.

Puff, *v.* **1.** *tr.* To smoke (a pipe or cigar) with intermittent puffs. {1861} **2.** To emit (smoke) from a pipe. {1867} — **(1) 1809** IRVING *Knickerb.* III. iii, Here the old burgher would sit, puffing his pipe. **1875** JAMES *R. Hudson* i, Rowland . . . lighted a cigar and puffed it awhile in silence. **(2) 1823** JAMES *Exped.* I. 188 The chiefs and magi are seated in front of their people, puffing smoke from their pipes.

Puff adder. {1824-} +=HOG-NOSE(D) SNAKE. — **1882** *Amer. Naturalist* XVI. 566 Twice afterward I noticed this strange habit of the puff adders. **1888** *Pop. Science Mo.* XXXIII. 660 The blow-snake of Illinois is variously known in other localities as hog-nose, flat-head, viper and puff-adder. **1896** BRUCE *Econ. Hist. Virginia* I. 129 Other varieties of snakes were common, such as the puff adder, the moccasin, the corn, the black, the water, and the horn.

Puffball. Any of various globose fungi of the families Lycoperdaceae and Sclerodermaceae, having the property of discharging ripe spores in a puff when struck. {1649-} — **1817-8** EATON *Botany* (1822) 454 *Sclerotium semen*, barked puff-ball. . . . On dead potato stems in autumn. **1848** THOREAU *Maine Woods* 34 Such delicate puff-balls seemed a singular diet for backwoodsmen. **1907** *St. Nicholas* July 846/1 Toadstools are common fungi, as also are puffballs.

Puffer. {1629-}

+1. Any of several fishes of the family Tetraodontidae, esp. the globefish (*Sphoeroides maculatus*) of the Atlantic coast.

1814 MITCHILL *Fishes N.Y.* 473 Puffer. . . . He is called in some places, *toad-fish*, because his back is mottled with yellow and dark. **1842** *Nat. Hist. N.Y., Zoology* IV. 327 The Common Puffer. . . . This species is scarcely ever eaten. **1883** *Nat. Museum Bul.* No. 27, 428 *Tetrodon nephelus*. . . . Rough Swell-fish; Puffer; Blower; Swell Toad. Gulf of Mexico, abundant; east coast of Florida (Indian River). **1897** *N.Y. Forest, Fish, & Game Comm. 2d Rep.* 244 Puffer; Swell-Fish. . . . Found in Gravesend Bay at all times except the cold months. **1911** *Rep. Fisheries 1908* 317/1 Swell-fish (*Tetraodontidae*).—The different species are known as 'globe-fishes,' 'puffers,' 'swell-toad,' etc.

+2. (See quotations.)

1864 WEBSTER 1059/1 *Puffer*, . . . a fish of the genus *Diodon;* globe-fish. **1884** GOODE, etc. *Fisheries* I. 170 The Porcupine Fishes—Diodontidæ. Swell Fishes and Puffers.—There are four species of this family inhabiting the Atlantic coast, and two on the coast of California.

+3. =HARBOR PORPOISE.

1884 GOODE, etc. *Fisheries* I. 14 On the Atlantic coast occurs most abundantly the little Harbor Porpoise *Phocæna brachycion* Cope, known to the fishermen as 'Puffer,' 'Snuffer' [etc.]. **1911** *Rep. Fisheries 1908* 314/1 Porpoise (*Phocæna communis*).—A cetacean found on the north Atlantic and north Pacific coasts, ascending rivers. It is known as 'harbor porpoise,' 'herring-hog,' 'puffer' [etc.].

Puff fish. Any of various fishes of the families Tetraodontidae and Diodontidae. {1885} — **1807** *Mass. H. S. Coll.* 2 Ser. III. 55 The puff fish, or swell fish, or bellows fish, is a cartilaginous fish. **1884** GOODE, etc. *Fisheries* I. 170 These fishes [of the family Diodontidae] are commonly known by such names as 'Burr Fish,' 'Ball Fish' [etc.] . . . ; while in Southern Florida the names 'Porgy,' 'Puffer,' and 'Puff Fish' are sometimes used.

***Puffin.** **1.** The Labrador auk, *Fratercula arctica*. **2.** The sea parrot (*Lunda cirrhata*) of the Pacific coast. Also *tufted puffin*. — **(1) 1835** AUDUBON *Ornith. Biog.* III. 105 On my voyage to Labrador I observed Puffins every day. **1839** PEABODY *Mass. Birds* 401 The Puffin, *Mormon arcticus*, commonly called the sea parrot. . . . They breed in holes. **1917** *Birds of Amer.* I. 18 Puffin. . . . [Also called] Labrador Auk. **(2) 1858** BAIRD *Birds Pacific R.R.* 902 *Mormon Cirrhata*. . . . The Tufted Puffin. . . . Western coast of America. **1917** *Birds of Amer.* I. 18/1 On the Farallons, off the California coast, . . . these Puffins nest on barren rocks.

+Puffing grubby. A sculpin: (see quot. 1884). Cf. GRUBBY. — **1884** GOODE, etc. *Fisheries* I. 258 On our Atlantic coast are found several species of . . . [the Cottidae], generally known by the name 'Sculpin,' and also by such titles as 'Grubby,' 'Puffing-grubby,' 'Daddy Sculpin' [etc.]. **1911** *Rep. Fisheries 1908* 315/1.

Puffing pig. =HARBOR PORPOISE. {1845, in S. Amer.} — **1884** *Nat. Museum Bul.* No. 27, 640 *Phocæna brachycion*, Cope. Puffing Pig. Herring Hog. Atlantic coast of the United States. This is one of the commonest species, frequenting the harbors and ascending the rivers.

+Pugasaing. [Amer. Ind., see last quot.] =BOWL. — **1848** SCHOOLCRAFT *Indians* 188 Pugasaing; or, the game of the bowl . . . is the principal game of hazard among the northern tribes. *Ib.* 189 The term pugasaing denotes this act of throwing. It is the participial form of the verb.

+Pug brandy. [f. s.w. Eng. dial. *pug*, 'apple pulp.'] A low grade of brandy, supposedly made from the refuse of a cider press. — **1857** *Harper's Mag.* Nov. 859/1 He was addicted to the use of the low wines of distilleries, bald-face whisky, pug brandy, hard cider, etc.

Pug mill. A machine for mixing and working clay. {1824-} — **1856** *Mich. Agric. Soc. Trans.* VII. 162 The clay must be properly mixed, or amalgamated in a pug mill. **1873** *Pat. Off. Gazette* III. 509/1 Pug-Mill. . . . Has a shaft provided with a fixed rack placed between two grinders.

+Puim. [Amer. Indian.] (See quotations.) — **1634** WOOD *New Eng. Prospect* 85 The Indians . . . have two sorts of games, one called *Puim*, the other *Hubbub*, not much unlike Cards and Dice, being no other than Lotterie. **1764** T. HUTCHINSON *Hist. Mass.* I. 470 They had two principal games of chance, one they called puim, this was much the same with a game Charlevoix mentions among the Miamis, which he calls jeu des pailles, or the game of straws.

Puke. {1737-}

+1. A native Missourian; one who has emigrated from Missouri. A nickname.

Cf. PIKE *n.*[4]

1835 A. PARKER *Trip to Texas* 87 The inhabitants . . . of Michigan are called *wolverines;* . . . of Missouri, *pukes*, &c. **1843** 'CARLTON' *New Purchase* II. 47 This Protestant assembly was a gathering of delegates principally from the land of Hoosiers . . . [with] a small chance of Pukes from beyond the father of floods. **1847** T. FORD *Hist. Illinois* (1854) 68 Analogies always abound with those who desire to be sarcastic; so the Illinoians . . . called the Missourians 'Pukes.' . . . Missouri had sent up to the Galena country whole hoards of uncouth ruffians, from which it was inferred that Missouri had taken a 'puke.' **1867** RICHARDSON *Beyond Miss.* 132 Early Californians christened as 'Pukes' the immigrants from Missouri, declaring that they had been vomited forth from that prolific State. **1893** *Chicago Tribune* 26 April 6/4, I have noticed . . . a great many learned and owl-like explanations of why Illinoisans are called 'Suckers' and Missourians 'Pukes.'

+2. A ruffian or obnoxious person.

1847 ROBB *Squatter Life* 152 Captain and all hands are a set of cowardly *pukes!* **1853** BALDWIN *Flush Times Ala.* 287 Sir William Blackstone . . . he regarded as 'something between a sneak and a puke.'

+Pukeweed. (See quotation.) — **1848** DUNGLISON *Med. Lexicon* 510/1 *Lobelia Inflata*, Indian Tobacco, Wild Tobacco, Puke Weed [etc.].

***Pull,** *n.*

1. An act of moving or traveling, as over a difficult terrain or up a steep grade. {1861-}

1816 U. BROWN *Journal* II. 143 Two pulls today, one 7, the other 8 miles, without seeing a house. **1834** C. A. DAVIS *Lett. J. Downing* 191 The squire is a pretty good horse for a tight pull.

+2. A jest. *colloq.*

1817 *Mass. Spy* 21 May (Th.), Our Jehu was a butt of wit and raillery for every one he met on the road; to use a Georgian phrase, every man, woman, and child that he passed had a pull at him.

+3. Influence capable of being used for one's advantage; a particular species of such influence. *colloq.*[2]

See also POLITICAL PULL.

1887 *Courier-Journal* 1 May 10/2 A man with cash in this place has a big pull. **1893** *Chicago Tribune* 24 April 2/6 Young aristocrats from the East, sons of army officers, . . . have been put over my head, not from merit but by pull. **1900** ADE *More Fables* 62 Finally his Father worked a Pull and got him a Job with a Steel Company. **1923** HERRICK *Lilla* 102 There were teachers who had secret 'pull,' and were carried on the rolls in spite of their incompetence.

***Pull,** *v.*

1. *intr.* To come *into* or *in* a place; to travel *on* to a place. *colloq.*[2] {pull down, 1877}

1885 *Wkly. New Mexican Rev.* 16 April 2/5 Hull . . . pulled into Santa Fe with a prairie-schooner. **1895** REMINGTON *Pony Tracks* 176 We will pull in about there. **1900** DRANNAN *Plains & Mts.* 548 Pulling on for the mountains, . . . we saw the ruins of two wagons that had been burned. **1916** EASTMAN *From Deep Woods* 62 It was a crisp winter morning when the train pulled into Chicago.

b. *To pull out*, to leave or depart. *colloq.* {1891}

1855 SIMMS *Forayers* 257 Two or three of you, must scout day and night . . . till you find the coast is clear—then put in and pull out. **1880** 'MARK TWAIN' *Tramp Abroad* 287 [We] pulled out for the summit again. **1887** GEORGE *40 Yrs. on Rail* 63 As we pulled out of Bennington about nine o'clock, I warned my engineer. **1913** LONDON *Valley of Moon* 445 It'd run us pretty well along into summer before we could pull out. **1925** TILGHMAN *Dugout* 90 She seemed to remember, dimly, her mother's saying that they had 'just pulled out and left.'

+2. *tr.* To draw (a gun). Also absol.

1883 'MARK TWAIN' *Life on Miss.* xxvi, When they happened to meet, they pulled and begun. **1895** *Century Mag.* June 282/1 He pulled a pistol on me. **1903** *N.Y. Sun* 2 Dec. 3 (*headline*), He Thought Simms Was Going To Pull A Gun.

+3. In various special and colloq. senses. (See also FREIGHT *n.* 7, LEATHER 2.)

a. *tr.* To stretch and draw (candy) until it is ready to set. **b.** To 'fix' (a race). **c.** To play (a trick of some kind). **d.** *intr.* Of a log jam: To break. **e.** To work hard or exercise influence *for* someone. **f.** To attract.

(a) 1886 [see PULLING HOOK]. **1893** *Harper's Mag.* Feb. 442 He pulled the candy with glee, but also with eager industry, covering platter after platter with his braided sticks. **(b) 1902** WISTER *Virginian* xxxv, 'This race will not be pulled,' said McLean. **(c) 1916** WILSON *Somewhere* 353 But Pete had pulled this too often before when in difficulties. **(d) 1902** WHITE *Blazed Trail* 329 When the logs began to cave under them . . . the foreman set the example of hunting safety. 'She "pulls," boys,' he yelled. **(e) 1903** *Forum* Oct. 311 Such committees are exposed to all kinds of influence— . . . all pulling for this or that applicant. **(f) 1914**

S. H. ADAMS *Clarion* 33 Talk about ads. that pull! It pulled like a mule-team and a traction engine and a fifty-cent painless dentist all in one.

+**4.** In phrases.

To pull it, to run away; *to pull a boner*, to commit an error.

1804 FESSENDEN *Orig. Poems* (1806) 79 And then she flew straight out of sight, As fast as she could pull it. **1917** MATHEWSON *Second Base Sloan* 203 You'll get bawled out when you pull a boner.

***Pullback.**

1. A kind of skirt in which the fullness is drawn to the back. {1885}

1875 *Chicago Tribune* 15 Nov. 8/1 He was just fastening the strings of his pull-back. [Note—'He' is a woman.] **1882** HOWELLS *Modern Instance* xiv, Pale, plain girls . . . in fashionable bangs and pull-backs, went about taking orders. **1887** *Courier-Journal* 6 Feb. 9/4 From this, as from the pull-back of later times, there was a quick recoil to voluminous drapery and the bell hoop.

attrib. **1875** *Chicago Tribune* 18 Sept. 6/5 Glancing at the low part of the young lady's form, which her 'pull-back' skirt displayed to excellent advantage. *Ib.* 16 Oct. 6/7, I have a little invention . . . which will allow you to wear the new style of pull-back dresses as easily as the breeches.

+**2.** (See quotation.)

1905 *Forestry Bureau Bul.* No. 61, 39 *Haul back*, a small wire rope, traveling between the donkey engine and a pulley set near the logs to be dragged, used to return the cable. (P[acific] C[oast] F[orest].) . . . [Also called] back line, pull back, trip line.

+**Pulldoo.** *local.* [Fr. *poule d'eau* 'water hen.'] =AMERICAN COOT. — **1859** BARTLETT 347 *Pull-doo*, a small black duck found in the bays and inlets of the Gulf of Mexico. **1917** *Birds of Amer.* I. 214.

+**Pulled wool.** Wool taken from the skin of a dead sheep. — **1832** *Niles' Reg.* 29 Sept. 67/1 There continues a good demand for fleece and pulled wool. **1863** RANDALL *Pract. Shepherd* 175 Pulled wool is not as well adapted to some purposes as sheared wool. **1884** *Century Mag.* Feb. 519/2 The 'tag-locks' and pulled wool were mostly worked up in the neighboring small factories into stocking-yarn, flannel, and blankets for the farmer's use. **1890** *Stock Grower & Farmer* 5 April 5/1 At Boston pulled wools are quiet.

Pullicat. Colored material out of which bandannas are made; a bandanna handkerchief. {1794-} — **1768** FRENEAU *Poems* (1795) 12 Hum-hums are here—and muslins. . . . Bandanas, baftas, pullcats, India teas. **1790** *Penna. Packet* 19 Oct. 3/2 Richard and James Potter are rapidly disposing of . . . Two yard pullicats, Cossacs [etc.]. **1841** CIST *Cincinnati* 179 Among other goods advertised [in 1801], I notice . . . pullicats, seersuckers, madrapores.

+**Pullikins.** *pl.* Pincers or forceps. *slang.* Also fig. — **1845** *Big Bear Ark.* 171 He sings out for the pinchers—swore they were his favorite insterments—always used 'em—beat pullicans to h——! **1850** LEWIS *La. Swamp Doctor* 23 The swamp doctor . . . practises dentistry with a gum lancet and a pair of pullikens. **1860** MORDECAI *Virginia* 272 As a preacher he drew the fangs of Satan with his spiritual pullikins.

***Pulling.** +The action of traveling over difficult terrain. Also fig. — **1816** U. BROWN *Journal* II. 360 Butler so far exhausted that it was hard pulling to save him. **1846** MAGOFFIN *Down Santa Fé Trail* 84 This morning the pulling has been worse than ever.

+**Pulling bone.** *local.* A wishbone. — **1877** BARTLETT 502 *Pulling-Bone*, the common name in Maryland, Virginia, &c., for the yoke-like breast-bone of chickens, by pulling which till it breaks children and young ladies settle which will be the first married.

***Pulling hook.** +A hook on which taffy is pulled. — **1886** *Harper's Mag.* June 93/2 The paste [for candy] then goes to the 'pulling-hooks,' where for five or six minutes it is pulled and twisted and repulled and retwisted.

+**Pullman.** [G. M. *Pullman* (1831-97), the designer.]

1. A railroad passenger car built by the Pullman Company, esp. a sleeping car. {1875-}

1873 BEADLE *Undevel. West* 743 The company have discarded the Pullman, on account, as they allege, of its extortionate charges. **1883** HALE in *Harper's Mag.* Jan. 276/2 [He] had slept in the Pullman. **1891** SWASEY *Early Days Calif.* 347 The traveler . . . speeds over the same ground now in a luxuriously-appointed Pullman. **1895** *N.Y. Dramatic News* 7 Dec. 2/4 While it is true that the Pullman is a vast improvement upon the sleeper that preceded it, there is still a wide margin of betterment to be adopted. **1910** RAINE *B. O'Connor* 11 Through the window of her Pullman the young woman in Section 3 had glimpsed a bevy of angry train officials. **1920** LEWIS *Main Street* 20 There is no smug Pullman attached to the train.

2. In the possessive: The Pullman Company's. *Obs.*

1868 H. M. FLINT *Railroads of U.S.* 406 We left Albany . . . in a Pullman's saloon parlor car. **1870** RAE *Westward by Rail* 77 [They] proceed to the office in order to secure berths in Pullman's sleeping car. **1872** TICE *Over Plains* 7 Back into one of Pullman's sleeping cars, I was soon stowed away in one of its ample berths.

3. *attrib.* **a.** Designating various kinds of railroad passenger cars built by the Pullman Company.

See also PULLMAN CAR, PULLMAN PALACE CAR.

1875 *Chicago Tribune* 11 Sept. 1/7 Pullman hotel cars are also run on the western part of the road. **1880** *Cimarron News & Press* 13 May 3/1 Pullman sleepers are running through to Albuquerque on the N.M. & S.P. **1882** SALA *Amer. Revisited* (1885) 88 The Pullman 'parlor'—or, as it is called in England, 'drawing-room car.' **1890** *Stock Grower & Farmer* 12 April 7/4 Through Pullman vestibule sleepers from Los Angeles to Chicago. **1894** *Harper's Mag.* Sept. 616/2 Through some of these [passes] are run latter-day railroads, with Pullman coaches, 'diners,' and the accompaniments of telephone and telegraph. **1907** *St. Nicholas* July 771/2 This route ain't as popular as if it had Pullman sleeping cars.

b. Designating various services or accommodations offered by or in connection with Pullman cars.

1885 *Harper's Mag.* April 698/2 The traveller . . . goes to sleep in his Pullman berth. **1903** E. JOHNSON *Railway Transportation* 151 The development of a second-class, as here suggested, would in reality mean three classes: the Pullman service and the first and second classes. **1906** LYNDE *Quickening* 178 He had engaged Pullman reservations for six persons to New York.

c. In special combinations.

Pullman porter, a porter who works on a Pullman car; *P. train*, a railroad train made up of Pullman cars.

1890 *Harper's Mag.* Jan. 327/1 Samson is a former Pullman porter, and a most efficient servitor. **1905** RICE *Sandy* 129 When the Pullman train came into the Clayton station, he was leaning against a truck in a pose of studied indifference.

+**Pullman car.** =PULLMAN 1.

1870 RAE *Westward by Rail* 29 No Royal personage can be more comfortably housed than the occupant of a Pullman car, provided the car be an hotel one. **1876** A. D. WHITNEY *Sights & Insights* I. 2, [I] was safely off in a big arm-chair in the Pullman car, with my parcels all put up. **1877** BARTLETT 447 *Palace Car*, an elegantly fitted car or railway carriage. . . . They were first introduced by Mr. Pullman of Chicago, and for a time were called Pullman cars. **1895** CHAMBLISS *Diary* 296 The section opposite to mine in the Pullman car was occupied last night by a lady and two small children. **1905** N. DAVIS *Northerner* 100 The second army of invasion came down in Pullman cars to wage a new war of conquest in this lovely land of their desire.

attrib. **1904** in Whitman *Diary* 54 Sprinkled through all Whitman's pocket-book diaries are names of men to whom he was attracted, *e.g.*, a Pullman-car conductor, a policeman, a 'bus driver.

+**Pullman conductor.** An official representing the Pullman Company, in charge of the Pullmans of a train. — **1887** *Courier-Journal* 6 Feb. 4/1 The body of Pullman Conductor Burgess was one of the first taken out. **1894** WISTER in *Harper's Mag.* Aug. 386/2 Bill, Abe, the train conductor, the Pullman conductor, the engineer, and fireman abandoned their duty. **1907** 'O. HENRY' *Roads of Destiny* 338 The third bartender used to be a Pullman conductor.

+**Pullman palace car.** A palace car built by the Pullman Company. (Cf. PALACE CAR.) — **1870** *Republican Rev.* 6 Aug. 1/2 The road [from Kansas to Denver] now carries four of the Pullman Palace Cars. **1877** MINTURN *Travels West* 3 We had a compartment in one of the Pullman Palace cars. **1883** RITTENHOUSE *Maud* 188 Going to Mobile tonight per Pullman Palace car and all sorts of style. **1897** *Outing* XXX. 628/2 The Pennsylvania Railroad Company has arranged for a two weeks' tour to this most interesting section of the United States, leaving New York by special train of Pullman palace cars Sept. 2, 1897.

***Pulp.** *attrib.* Designating various things, persons, and actions connected with the making of paper pulp. {1853-}

1832 *22d Congress. 2 Sess.* H. R. Ex. Doc. No. 130, 10 Pulp strainer, James Sawyer, Newbury, Vt., Jan. 21. **1857** E. STONE *Life of Howland* 120 The accumulations of more than a hundred years . . . had found their way to the paper maker's pulp vat. **1883** WELLS *Practical Economics* (1885) 107 He thinks that even the pulp-makers, 'with 15 new pulp-mills started during the past year,' 'will find difficulty in marketing their pulp in the immediate future.' **1885** *N.H. Forestry Comm. Rep.* June 10 Telegraph-poles, pulp-wood, bark, etc., . . . [must] amount to five millions of dollars, and probably more. **1887** *Courier-Journal* 1 May 2/4 The pulp-mill bridge has started, and unless held the other bridges will be endangered. **1891** *Fur, Fin, & Feather* March 150/2 A fishway will be constructed in the dam of the pulp company at Mechanicsville. **1892** *Vt. Agric. Rep.* XII. 123 Last year the poplar was cut and sold for pulp making. **1893** AULD *Picturesque Burlington* 164 They also manufacture fire engines, pulp machinery [etc.]. **1897** BRODHEAD *Bound in Shallows* 50 He had, indeed, some sort of silent partnership in a pulp factory below the hill.

+**Pulpería.** *W.* [Sp.] A grocery and liquor store. — **1840** DANA *Two Years* 108 [The grog-shop] was kept by a Yankee, . . . [who] came to California and set up a 'Pulperia.' **1850** COLTON *Deck & Port* 402 Do you see that pulperia, with its gathered group of soldiers and sailors, poets and politicians? **1869** DANA *Two Years* (new ed.) 451 Tom Wrightington, who kept the rival pulpería, fell from his horse when drunk.

***Pulpit.**

***1.** A raised structure from which a preacher delivers a sermon; the high desk at which a preacher stands while delivering a sermon. Also fig.

1688 SEWALL *Diary* I. 203 [The corpse was] carried in at the western dore, and set in the Alley before the pulpit. **1749** *Georgia Col. Rec.* VI. 247 It wants Nothing to compleat it, but the Seats Pulpit and Communion Table. **1779** E. PARKMAN *Diary* 171 Mr. Gale came up to ye Pulpit to desire me to read ye Congress's Circular Letter. **1836** HAWTHORNE *Twice-*

told Tales (1879) I. 45 He was to have exchanged pulpits with Parson Shute, of Westbury. **1898** YOUNG *Jessamine Co., Ky.* 195 In this old building are the straight-benches and the white painted pulpit which were used for more than fifty years. **1904** HARBEN *Georgians* 67 [They] were in their places in the 'amen corner,' at the right of the crude pulpit.

+2. A raised platform from which a machine can be observed and controlled.

1880 *Harper's Mag.* Dec. 62 Another shout, and the boy touches another lever in the gallery of levers, irreverently termed the 'pulpit.' **1903** *Electrical World* 26 Dec. 1051/2 The operator of the hoisting motor stands in a pulpit above the floor.

3. Attrib. and comb. with *cushion, floor, stairs,* etc.

1698 SEWALL *Diary* I. 471 Pulpit cushion taken away, fired, but quenched. **1725** *New-Eng. Courant* 3–10 July 2/2 Some evil minded Persons carry'd into the Presbyterian Meeting House . . . a stinking Sturgeon of about 8 foot in Length, and laid it on the Pulpit Floor. **1772** A. G. WINSLOW *Diary* 15 [Aunt] saw Dr P. roll up the pulpit stairs. **1876** HABBERTON *Jericho Road* 59 There was an unusual commotion among the small boys on the pulpit-steps. **1903** LEWIS *Boss* 313, I'll have no pulpit-thumper doggin' me!

***Pulpit cloth.** An ornamented cloth for covering the desk of a pulpit. {–1711} — **1748** *Bristol* (Va.) *Vestry Bk.* 132 [Ordered] That the Church Wardens provide two surplices a pulpit Cloth. **1763** *Md. Hist. Mag.* X. 40 Ordered, That there be a Crimson Velvet Cushion and Pulpit Cloth procured for the Church. **1872** *Atlantic Mo.* March 317 Fragments of richly colored altar-pieces, fine pulpit-cloths, and pieces of old carving used to be preserved in farm-houses, and shown to visitors.

Pulpit rock. A rock having the appearance of a pulpit. — **1841** BARBER & HOWE *Hist. Colls. N.Y. State* 201 One mile west of the village [Oxbow] is a rock called 'pulpit rock.' **1888** *Harper's Mag.* June 41/1 Its side ravines have fantastic pulpit rocks and pinnacles.

Pulque. [Sp., prob. from a Mex. Indian language.]

1. *S.W.* A fermented drink made from various species of *Agave*, esp. *A. atrovirens.* {1693, of Mexico}

Cf. MESCAL 1.

[**1796** MORSE *Univ. Geog.* I. 729 *n.*, *Pulque* is the usual wine or beer of the Mexicans, made of the fermented juice of the Maguei.] **1836** EDWARD *Hist. Texas* 118 Pulque, or the beer of Maguey, is not stronger than spruce beer, and merely renders them heavy or stupid. **1847** RUXTON *Adv. Rocky Mts.* (1848) 183 Frijoles and chile colorado comprise their daily bill of fare, with a drink of pulque when passing through the land of the maguey. **1888** SHERIDAN *Memoirs* I. 28 To prevent scurvy we used the juice of the maguey plant, called pulque.

||**2.** A food made from the maguey plant.

Probably an error.

1873 ARNY *Items regarding N. Mex.* 22 A species of the maguey plant grows in the Caballo Mountains . . . from which a sweet wholesome and palatable food as well as drink is made by the Mexicans and Indians, . . . The food is called 'Pulque' and the liquor 'Mescal.'

3. Attrib. with *shop, stand, whisky, woman.*

1838 'TEXIAN' *Mexico v. Texas* 280 Padre don Roque . . . undertook to say mass with *pulque* whiskey. **1845** GREEN *Texian Exped.* 201 He would stop with us at the pulque stands on the roadside. *Ib.* 227 In passing a pulque woman, we had only to flatter this lieutenant [etc.]. **1847** RUXTON *Adv. Rocky Mts.* (1848) 79, I was detected as a stranger by a knot of idle rascals standing at the door of a pulque-shop.

Pulsant, *a.* Pulsating. {1891; *rare*} — **1709** *Essex Inst. Coll.* XXXV. 131 The Toules pulsant artery and nerves [were] laid bare.

***Pulse.** The edible seeds of various leguminous plants, as beans and peas; a plant that yields such seeds. — **1674** in Alvord & Bidgood *Trans-Allegheny Region* 213 And aboundance of corne [was brought] and all manner of pulse with fish, flesh and beares oyle. **1737** BRICKELL *N. Carolina* 70 The first [sort of black gum tree] bears a black Berry . . . which the Indians commonly mix with their Pulse. **1789** MORSE *Amer. Geog.* 414 Oats and flax grow well in the back hilly country, . . . and pulse of all kinds in all parts. **1836** EDWARD *Hist. Texas* 132 The other agricultural products [include] . . . maize, wheat, [and] pulse.

Pulse-warmer. A wristlet. — **1876** BOURKE *Journal* 1 March, 'Pulse warmers' about 6 inches long will preserve the wrists. **1896** E. HIGGINSON *Land of Snow Pearls* 223 Mother, where's my Sund'y pulse-warmers at?

Pult. (See quot. 1877.) *Obs.* {1880–, Cornish dial.} — **1862** *N.Y. Tribune* 29 July 2/2 Next morning, pult quicker and weaker; . . . the disease was very obstinate, pult increasing in quickness and symptoms more aggravating. **1877** BARTLETT 503 Some country doctors think *pulse* is plural, and say, 'A very good pult.'

Pulverizer. {1836–}

1. A machine for pulverizing soil. {1847–}

1858 *Rep. Comm. Patents 1857* II. 334 Improvement in Clay Pulverizers. . . . The clay enters the grated cylinder, . . . and the pulverized clay drops through the openings. **1868** *Rep. Comm. Agric. 1867* 279 There are also included . . . one six-furrow balance-wheeled plough, one seven-tine pulverizer or sub-soiler, balanced and on wheels. **1874** *Ib. 1873* 269 The 'circular pulverizer,' applied before the harrow, shortens the labor.

2. A machine for pulverizing ores. {1888}

1874 RAYMOND *6th Rep. Mines* 499 The mining laboratory now contains . . . a little hand-jigger, a rotary pulverizer, and a fan-blower. **1885** *Wkly. New Mexican Rev.* 9 April 4/3 Hatch & Koneman . . . will have their patent concentrator, pulverizer and amalgamator in operation at the Cash Entry mine May 1.

Puma. [Sp., from native name in S. Amer.] =COUGAR. {1777–} — **1840** EMMONS *Mass. Quadrupeds* 35 The Puma, or American Lion, . . . preys of course upon all the animals weaker than itself. **1901** STILLMAN *Autobiog. Journalist* I. 291, I remembered that the cry was that of a puma. **1923** J. H. COOK *On Old Frontier* 26 Then there were pumas, or mountain lions, as they were commonly called.

***Pumice.** Lava of a porous, spongy structure. Also *pumice stone.* — **1767** in H. M. Brooks *Gleanings* IV. 31 Borax & Salt-Petre. Pommice and Rottenstone. **1781–2** JEFFERSON *Notes Va.* (1788) 18 A substance supposed to be pumice, found floating on the Missisipi, has induced a conjecture, that there is a volcano on some of its waters. **1804** LEWIS in *L. & Clark Exped.* VI. (1905) 164 The tract of Country which furnishes the Pummice Stone seen floating down the Missouri, is rather burning or burnt plains than burning mountains. **1837** PECK *New Guide* 26 Pumice stone, and other volcanic productions, occasionally float down [the Missouri R.]. **1897** F. C. MOORE *How To Build a Home* 62 Two coats of good quality of wood-varnish, neatly rubbed down with pumice-stone and water.

***Pump.**[1]

***1.** A mechanical contrivance for raising water, usually from a well or a cistern.

1659 *Suffolk Deeds* III. 311 To Haue and to Hold the aboue menconed dwelling house Gatehouse bakehouse yard Garden pump trees fences &c. **1699** E. WARD *Trip New Eng.* 45, I was mightily pleas'd one Morning with a Contention between two Boys at a Pump in Boston. **1734** *Harvard Rec.* I. 153 When any damage is done, to any Other parts of the College, or to any of its Appurtenances, Such as fences, pump, Clock &c the same shall be made good. **1796** *Ann. 4th Congress* 2 Sess. 2571 Leveling the earth round the works, fencing the land pertaining to them, a pump for the well, painting the wood work, and rendering the whole perfectly complete. **1815** *View N.Y. State Prison* 14 In this yard there is . . . a store-house for brushes . . . ; also an excellent saw-pit, a cellar, . . . fire-engine-house, pump, &c. **1891** WILKINS *New Eng. Nun* 91, I had a pump in my kitchen sink, an' things real handy.

2. In special combinations.

Pump boat, a boat well provided with pumps; *p. ladder*, a ladder used in connection with pumping operations, as in a mine; *p. mule*, a mule used for operating a pump; *p. station*, in mining operations, an enlargement in a shaft or tunnel to facilitate pumping operations; *p. tree*, a tree used or suitable for use as a pump log (q.v.).

1878 *N. Amer. Rev.* Sept. 227, I brought to the assistance of her commanding officer two heavy pump-boats. **1883** M. H. FOOTE *Led-Horse Claim* 55, I've been waltzing up five hundred feet of pump-ladders. **1907** WHITE *Arizona Nights* 263 There, at the long troughs filled by the windmill or the blindfolded pump mule, they drank. **1877** W. WRIGHT *Big Bonanza* 187 The bodies of the poor fellows were discovered at the pump station—a recess some feet square in one side of the shaft. **1871** BURROUGHS *Wake-Robin* (1886) 11 One sees them [*i.e.*, bluebirds] hovering with a saucy, inquiring air about barns and out-buildings, . . . inspecting knot-holes and pump-trees.

***Pump.**[2] A low, snugly fitting shoe or slipper without fastenings, used chiefly for dress wear or dancing. — **1726** *Boston News-Letter* 18 Aug. 2/2 [A runaway] had on . . . a pair of Pumps with Silver Buckles in them. **1790** *Penna. Packet* 5 Feb. 3/3 Nathaniel Prentiss [sells] . . . Lined & bound spring-heel'd Pumps [for girls]. **1807** IRVING *Salmagundi* 459 Right goodlie morocco pumps decorated with clasps or buckles. **1891** WELCH *Recoll. 1830–40* 179 Pumps were worn, sometimes light French boots. **1916** WILSON *Somewhere* 217 She gets up and goes over to her horse, picking her way daintily in the silly little tan pumps.

+Pumpage. The total amount or quantity pumped. — **1881** *Scientific Amer.* XLIV. 361 The pumpage for last year amounted to 21,120, 792,786 gallons. **1893** *Columbus Dispatch* 6 Nov., The total average pumpage is given as 9,071,835 gallons.

Pump chain. The chain serving as a conveyer for the water cups or disks of a chain pump. — **1853** *Mich. Agric. Soc. Trans.* IV. 108 Lot of pump chain and tubes, of galvanized iron. **1856** *Ib.* VII. 55 D. O. & W. S. Penfield . . . [exhibited] sample of pump chains.

Pump hook. A long iron rod with a hook at one end used for removing a valve from a pump. {1867–} — **1640** *Md. Archives* IV. 112 A pumpho[ok]. **1702** *Essex Inst. Coll.* XLII. 161 Inventory of ship: . . . a pump Hooke. **1781** *Md. Hist. Mag.* VI. 312 Invoice of Schooner Nautilus's Materials: . . . 1 pump Hook.

***Pumping,** *n.* and *a.*

+1. *n.* (See quot. 1887.)

1875 *Chicago Tribune* 8 Dec. 3/2 They thought of a hand-car, and then shudderingly considered the job of pumping 200 miles. **1887** M. ROBERTS *Western Avernus* 241 A hand-car coming along . . . with some section hands working it along by means of the lever, 'pumping,' as it is commonly called.

2. *attrib.* or *adj.* That raises or removes water.

1850 *Rep. Comm. Patents 1849* 448 Two other patents have been granted for modifications of the so termed pumping windlass. **1875** in Raymond *8th Rep. Mines* 80 The mill, hoisting and pumping machinery, although getting old, are in fair working-order. **1883** *Century Mag.* July 335/1 On the main lines there is on an average a pumping engine every twenty-five miles. **1912** *Ib.* 534 For continuing the construction of necessary channels and laterals . . . , and for maintaining and operating the pumping plow, thirty-five thousand dollars.

***Pumpion.** =next. Also attrib. (Cf. POMPION.) — **1616** SMITH *New England* 10 The hearbes and fruits are of many sorts and kindes: as . . . pumpions, gourds, strawberries [etc.]. **1699** J. DICKENSON *God's Protecting Prov.* 58 [It was] full of Pumpion Vines and some small Pumpions on them. **1786** WASHINGTON *Diaries* III. 49 Conversing with General Spotswood on the growth, and preservation of the Pumpion, he informed me that a person in his neighbourhood who had raised of them many years had preserved them by splitting them in two. **1816** Clipping in *Pettigrew P.* (Univ. N.C. MS.), A brace of pigs and a tub of pumpions.

Pumpkin. Also **pumkin, punkin, †pomkin.** [f. POMPION.]

1. The large globular fruit of the vine *Cucurbita pepo*, or of one of the numerous varieties of this. {1706–}

The characteristically American form 'punkin,' representing a common pronunciation, occurs relatively seldom in writing, and then usually in contexts which suggests its colloquial nature. See particularly sense 3 below.

1654 JOHNSON *Wonder-w. Prov.* 56 And let no man make a jest at Pumpkins, for with this fruit the Lord was pleased to feed his people to their good content, till Corne and Cattell were increased. **1676** *Hempstead Rec.* I. 304 Jeames beat is to have for his Pains a third Part of what Corn an puumkins that is prodused of the land. **1717** SEWALL *Diary* III. 141 Bastion . . . help'd to bring some Pumpkins &c. **1790** DENNY *Journal* 147 The army all engaged burning and destroying . . . corn, beans, pumpkins, stacks of hay, fencing and cabins, etc. **1825** PICKERING *Inquiries Emigrant* (1831) 63 Pumpkins (Americans call them *punkins*) are very large. **1881** *Cimarron News & Press* 24 Feb. 1/6 A pumpkin grown on the Vermejo . . . weighed 80 pounds. **1924** RAINE *Land of Saddle-Bags* 28 If we growed punkins up in yan cove, they'd break loose and roll down and kill somebody.

b. This fruit prepared as food or used as an ingredient in food. {1833–}

1699 E. WARD *Trip New-Eng.* 16 Their Diet is Fish, . . . Indian-Corn, and Kidney-Beans boil'd, Earth-Nuts, Chest-Nuts, Lilly-Roots, Pumpkins, Milions [etc.]. **1807** GASS *Journal* 141 Bread . . . tastes like that sometimes made of pumpkins. **1808** PIKE *Sources Miss.* 128 At the quarters of the chief . . . we were regaled with boiled pumpkins. **1818** FORDHAM *Narr. Travels* 204, I like corn or hoe cakes . . . and stewed pumpkins very well. **1836** GILMAN *Recoll.* (1838) 52, I tell them you eat punkins biled like squash.

+c. The color, orange, of a ripe pumpkin.

1850 LEWIS *La. Swamp Doctor* 73 He described the awful effects it [*sc.* ague] had upon our gals, developing their spleens, and bringing the punkin to their blessed faces.

+d. In figurative and exclamatory expressions.

1847 ROBB *Squatter Life* 82 Your head is swelled as big as a *pumkin!* **1868** BEECHER *Norwood* 100 Scissors and pumpkins! if that ain't a spree! **1906** FITZGERALD *Sam Steele's Adv.* 237 We're rich, nevvy—rich as punkins!

+e. *Dried pumpkin*, pumpkin preserved by drying. Cf. DRIED *a.* 2.

1821 J. FOWLER *Journal* 15 Camped near the Indeans from them got some dryed meet corn beens and dryed pumkins. **1850** GARRARD *Wah-To-Yah* iv. 64 Their mules packed with dried pumpkin, corn, etc. **1853** B. F. TAYLOR *Jan. & June* 252 Festoons of dried pumpkin adorned the ceiling.

+2. A chump or dolt. *colloq.* {1830–, in Canada}

1768 in Buckingham *Newspaper Lit.* I. 148 Come shake your dull noddles, ye Pumpkins, and bawl. **1788** *Mass. Convention* (1856) 303 If a southern man heard it, he would call us pumpkins.

+3. *Some pumpkins*, a person regarded as of unusual importance or as possessing superior attainments in some indicated direction. *slang.*

1846 *Spirit of Times* 18 April 91/2 Tom is 'some punkins.' **1851** BYRN *Life Ark. Doctor* 97 (Th.), We went on until the third or fourth set, and I thought I was 'some pumpkins' at dancing. **1889** *Century Mag.* Jan. 407/1 He's a do-less kind of a devil, . . . but he's some punkins with the gang in the Holler. **1913** LONDON *Valley of Moon* 380 Say, friend, you're some punkins at a hundred yards dash, ain't you?

+b. A thing of rare or superior excellence or importance. *slang.*

1846 *Spirit of Times* 25 April 97/1 The skins, Indian relics, etc. are 'some punkins' and no mistake. **1853** *La Crosse Democrat* 8 Nov. 2/3 The Minnesota country about St. Anthony is 'some pumpkins.' **1855** *Herald of Freedom* (Lawrence, Kan.) 26 May 1/3 See them 'ere water-melons as big as a bushel basket—an' them 'are squashes bigger'n a flour barrel—wouldn't they call 'em 'sum punkins' down east? **1869** BARNUM *Struggles & Triumphs* 569 You had better not wager too much on your fast horse, for you know mine is some pumpkins.

+4. A person of fancied or assumed consequence. *slang.* Usu. pl. even in sing. sense.

1852 BRISTED *Upper Ten Th.* 216 She gave a big ball, and we, being punkins, were of course among the invited. **1861** NEWELL *Orpheus C. Kerr* I. 79 You're sticking rather too thick to the rear of that house to be much punkins in a muss. Why don't you go to the front like a man? **1899** T. HALL *Tales* 14 The other two are troops of the Eleventh that think themselves particular pumpkins.

5. *attrib.* and *comb.* **a.** Designating foods or other things made of pumpkins.

1704 S. KNIGHT *Journal* 67 Had Rost Beef and Pumpkin sause for supper. **1827** J. BERNARD *Retrosp.* 150 Between twelve and one his throat would require another emulsion, and he would sip half a pint of some mystery termed bumbo, apple-toddy, or pumpkin flip. **1848** LOWELL *Biglow P.* 1 Ser. v. 64 Something more than a pumpkin-lantern is required to scare manifest and irretrievable Destiny out of her path. **1865** HOLLAND *Plain Talk* 16 The music of a corn-stalk fiddle or a pumpkin trumpet may not be overwhelmingly ravishing in itself; but we are expected to admire it.

b. Designating places or areas on which pumpkins are planted.

1787 WASHINGTON *Diaries* III. 213, 139 pumpkin hills were Planted. **1799** — *Writings* XIV. 223 The large lot . . . is to have oats sown on the potato and pumpkin ground.

c. Designating persons having to do with pumpkins.

1869 J. R. BROWNE *Adv. Apache Country* 128 Toward the shades of evening the pumpkin-venders [Indians] had sufficiently warmed their backs and were about to depart. **1898** HAMBLEN *Gen. Manager's Story* 27, I thought so—another Walton punkin husker.

+Pumpkin bread. Bread made of pumpkin and Indian meal. *Obs.*— [**1704** S. KNIGHT *Journal* 47 But the Pumpkin and Indian mixt Bred had such an Aspect, and the Bare-legg'd Punch so awkerd or rather Awfull a sound, that we left both.] **1819** *Western Rev.* I. 185 Pumpkin bread and cakes are as much used in the interior of Kentucky, as pumpkin pies in New-England. **1843** *Amer. Pioneer* II. 452 To save meal, we often made pumpkin bread, in which when meal was scarce, the pumpkin would so predominate as to render it next to impossible to tell our bread from that article.

+Pumpkin butter. A preserve or thick sauce made by boiling down pumpkins. (Cf. BUTTER[1] 2.)— **1885** *Buckeye Cookery* 250 Pumpkin Butter. **1893** M. A. OWEN *Voodoo Tales* 6 The place of the vegetables was taken by . . . little jars of a villainous sweet compound of pumpkin stewed with watermelon-juice and known to all as 'punkin-butter.'

+Pumpkin head. 1. (See quotation.) **2.** A stupid fellow, a dolt. *colloq.* — **(1) 1781** PETERS *Hist. Conn.* 195 Newhaven is celebrated for having given the name of *pumkin-heads* to all the New-Englanders. It originated from the Blue Laws, which enjoin every male to have his hair cut round by a cap. When caps were not to be had, they substituted the hard shell of a pumkin. **(2) 1848** IRVING *Knickerb.* IV. xi, Beside each pumpkin-head peered the end of a rusty musket. **1876** SCUDDER *Dwellers* 87 'Pumpkin head!' said the Doctor, more vigorously than politely. **1884** 'MARK TWAIN' *H. Finn* xviii, Ef we hadn' . . . ben sich punkin-heads, as de sayin' is, we'd a seed de raf. **1898** FREDERIC *Deserter* 143 You can't raise a plug [of tobacco] in a whole regiment of 'em. Regular pumpkin-heads!

+Pumpkin hood. A snugly fitting hood or helmet of a shape somewhat suggestive of a pumpkin. *Obs.* — **1863** A. D. WHITNEY *F. Gartney* xv, Aunt Faith, in her pumpkin hood and Rob Roy cloak. **1876** — *Sights & Insights* I. 27 What will they all say [on the ship] when they see Emery Ann's 'pumpkin hood?' **1899** A. BROWN *Tiverton Tales* 239 The sled was empty, save for a rocking-chair where sat an enormous woman enveloped in shawls, her broad face surrounded by a pumpkin hood.

+Pumpkin pie. A pie made with pumpkin or a substitute.

1654 JOHNSON *Wonder-w. Prov.* 174 This poor Wilderness hath . . . plenty of wine and sugar, . . . and quince tarts instead of their former Pumpkin Pies. **1784** FRENEAU *Poems* (1786) 389 Systems they built on pumpkin pies, And prov'd that every thing went round. **1818** PALMER *Travels U.S.* 241 One or two dishes are peculiar to New England, and always on the table, toast dipped in cream and pumpkin pie. **1845** COOPER *Chainbearer* viii, Even the pumpkin-pies of the Middle States are vastly better than those usually found in New England. **1907** *St. Nicholas* May 615/2 Pumpkin pies and strawberry short-cake were also introduced to the French palate and found good.

+Pumpkin pine. The white pine (*Pinus strobus*) of the eastern United States, or a tree of this variety. (Cf. APPLE PINE.) — **1809** KENDALL *Travels* III. 145 Of the white pine, the lumberers distinguish two varieties, one of which they call *punkin pine* . . . on account of the softness and fine grain of the wood. **1832** [see APPLE PINE]. **1851** SPRINGER *Forest Life* 41 The pumpkin Pine is generally found on flat land and in ravines; also on abrupt ridges, called horsebacks, where the forest is dense. **1907** *Springfield W. Repub.* 29 Aug. 15 The virgin white pine has practically disappeared from New England and huge 'pumpkin pines' four and five feet in diameter are now a matter of tradition.

+Pumpkin porridge. A porridge made of pumpkin. *Obs.* — **1657** *East-Hampton Rec.* I. 120 Mrs. Gardiner spoke to Mary & Arther about pomkin porrage. **1699** E. WARD *Trip New. Eng.* 9 Pumpkin Porrage being as much in esteem with New-England Saints, as Jelly Broth with Old-England Sinners.

+Pumpkin pudding. A pudding made of boiled pumpkin. — **1805** *Indep. Chronicle* 26 Dec. 3/1 Clams and oysters, succatouch and pumpkin puddings, turkies, ducks [etc.]. **1828** LESLIE *Receipts* 21 Sweet Potato Pudding. . . . Pumpkin Pudding. **1840** A. M. MAXWELL *Run through U.S.* I. 81 My opposite neighbour to-day at dinner urged me to make an experiment on some 'real, genu*ine*, Yankee, New England, pumpkin pudding.'

Pumpkin seed.

1. The seed of the pumpkin.

1781 PETERS *Hist. Conn.* 243 Maize . . . is planted in hillocks three feet apart, five kernels and two pumkin-seeds in a hillock. **1787** WASHINGTON *Diaries* III. 159, 6 Quarts Pumpkin Seeds. **1793** in E. E. F. Ford *Notes N. Webster* I. 325 Will you be so kind as to procure me from Col[one]l Wadsworth a few Pompkin seed, of a very large Sort. **1873** LELAND *Egyptian Sketch Book* 126 How they contrived to be so laughy and smily on pumpkin-seeds and cold water I cannot conjecture.

+**2. a.** Any one of various small, flat, fresh-water sunfishes, esp. *Eupomotis gibbosus.*

1814 *Mass. H. S. Coll.* 2 Ser. III. 102 There are, however, various kinds of smaller fish, viz. . . . bill fish; pumpkin seed, or flat fish, &c. **1842** *Nat. Hist. N.Y., Zoology* IV. 32 The numerous spots on its body has occasioned it to be called by the whimsical name of *Pumpkin-seed.* **1884** GOODE, etc. *Fisheries* I. 405 The common 'Sun-fish,' 'Pumpkin-seed,' or 'Sunny' of the brooks of New York and New England . . . is everywhere abundant in the Great Lake region and in the coastwise streams from Maine to Georgia. **1911** *Rep. Fisheries 1908* 314/1 *Pumpkin-seed.*—A name applied to the sunfish (*Eupomotis gibbosus*) of the brooks of New York and New England, and to the butterfish (*Poronotus triacanthus*) in Connecticut.

+**b.** The butterfish, *Poronotus triacanthus.*

1884 GOODE, etc. *Fisheries* I. 333 The 'Butter-fish' of Massachusetts and New York, sometimes known . . . in Connecticut as the 'Pumpkin-seed,' . . . is common between Cape Cod and Cape Henry. **1911** [see sense 2 a].

+**3.** A small, shallow, round-bottomed sailboat.

1884 J. A. HENSHALL *Camping in Fla.* 15 There are . . . the 'pumpkin-seed,' and the 'flat-iron' models [of sailing boats].

+**Pumpkin vine.** The coarse, decumbent vine of *Cucurbita pepo*, which bears pumpkins. — **1810** CUTLER in *Life & Corr.* II. 343 The cactus grandiflora, or night-flowering cereus, . . . has a long stem, resembling a pumpkin-vine, but no leaves. **1824** DODDRIDGE *Notes* 101, I remember how narrowly the children watched the potatoe tops, pumpkin and squash vines. **1868** *Mich. Agric. Rep.* VII. 349 A. Lapham, Dearborn, [exhibited] 1 pumpkin vine. **1909** CALHOUN *Miss Minerva* 106 How's he going to sit under a pumpkin vine when he's inside of a whale?

+**Pump log.** A log suitably bored or hollowed out for making a pump or for a water pipe. — **1816** *N. Amer. Rev.* III. 429 The mill for grinding apples . . . is an overshot, and is fed by a pump log. **1844** *Knickerb.* XXIII. 443 The cool spring water . . . was conveyed the whole distance in 'pump-logs.' **1879** STOCKTON *Rudder Grange* 197 He looked like he'd been drawn through a pump-log.

Pump-maker. One whose occupation is making pumps. {1623-} **1654** JOHNSON *Wonder-w. Prov.* 209 Turners, Pumpmakers, and Wheelers, . . . are orderly turn'd to their trades. **1789** *Boston Directory* 175 Brewer, John, block and pump-maker, Summer-street. **1820** FLINT *Lett. from Amer.* 213 [There are] a plough maker; pump and block maker; . . . and one fanning mill maker [in Cincinnati]. **1888** *Amer. Almanac* 275 Pump-makers, . . . Quarrymen.

Pump man. One who operates a pump or has charge of pumping operations. {1776-} — **1877** WRIGHT *Big Bonanza* 443 [In the mines] the engineers, station-tender, pump-men, and the watchmen on the lower levels, all occupy positions to which are attached grave responsibilities. **1885** *Century Mag.* Jan. 435 The cry ran through the boat that we were on fire, and my duty as pump-man called me to the pumps. **1896** SHINN *Story of Mine* 226 The pump men and engineers see to their respective duties.

***Pump nail.** A nail used in connection with a ship's pump. {-1626} — **1805** *State P.* (1819) V. 241 They robbed the brig of . . . all her candles, pump nails, locks, and gimblets.

Pump spout. In a pump, the spout or lip from which the water flows. — **1867** 'LACKLAND' *Homespun* 321 He washes his ruddy face under the pump-spout. **1890** HOWELLS *Boy's Town* 72 He put his mouth to the pump-spout. **1891** WILKINS *New Eng. Nun* 160 When he had filled his pail he took it carefully from the pump spout, and started back to the house.

***Punch,** *n.*[1] An instrument or tool for making a hole in or stamping an object. — **1646** *Essex Probate Rec.* I. 49, 7 forging hott punches, 2 Iron wrenches. **1750** FRANKLIN *Exper. on Electricity* (1769) 63 A silversmith's iron punch, inch thick, is what I use. **1790** *Ann. 1st Congress* II. 1395 The engrossed bill to vest in Frances Bailey the exclusive privilege of making and vending certain punches, for stamping the matrices of types, &c., was read the third time and passed. **1812** *Niles' Reg.* II. 9/2 A smooth punch of the right taper is driven in [the plate] to smooth and form them. **1902** 'O. HENRY' *Rolling Stones* 67 Specially designed and constructed were the implements— . . . the collection of curiously fashioned keys, the blued drills and punches of the finest temper.

Punch, *n.*[2] A beverage variously prepared but usually consisting principally of wine, spirits, or fruit juices suitably flavored and sweetened. {1632-}

1666 *Md. Archives* II. 127 Hee hath charged the Burgesses this Assembly for Liquors: As Wine, Rumme, Brandy, Punch. **1718** SEWALL *Diary* III. 197, I Treated with a Bowl of Punch. **1796** A. BARTON *Disappointment* II. iii, I make a bowl of punch, your master loves punch. **1827** *Md. Hist. Mag.* XVII. 245 Took a glass of Curaçoa, and another of Whiskey punch with them and returned to my own house at 11. **1882** MCCABE *New York* 323 A table is spread, provided with all the delicacies of the season, and rare and costly wines, and punch.

attrib. **1771** in *New Eng. Mag.* ns. XII. 345/2 It being very near punch time, we steered to Captain Service's house. **1790** *Penna. Packet* 7 Dec. 3/3 Joseph Anthony, Junior, . . . Has Imported. . . . Punch ladles and strainers.

***Punch,** *v. W.* +*To punch cattle* (or *cows*), to drive cattle as if by prodding them on; to work on a cattle ranch as a cowboy. *colloq.* {1886-, in Australia} Also with object omitted.

Since *bullpuncher* occurs in 1874 and *cow-puncher* in 1879, it is assumed that this meaning of *punch* originated in the U.S.

1890 *Stock Grower & Farmer* 21 June 4/1 J. O. Phillips . . . will be initiated into the business of punching cattle. **1894** WISTER in *Harper's Mag.* Jan. 296/1 Why don't you . . . quit punching cows, which is too much physical exercise for you? **1902** — *Virginian* 167, I was goin' back to punch cattle or fight Indians. **1910** RAINE *B. O'Connor* 30 We used to punch together on the Hashknife. **1923** 'BOWER' *Parowan Bonanza* 276 In that case . . . you'd still be punchin' cows for your dad, most likely.

Punch bowl. A bowl from which punch is served. {1692-} — **1716** CHURCH *Philip's War* 41 Capt. Church . . . was now better imploy'd in taking his Prisoners & running them into a Valley, in form of something shap'd like a Punch-bole. **1850** MITCHELL *Lorgnette* I. 58 Another sort of celebrity at the balls is the diner-out, who is . . . stupified with a new lift at the punch-bowl. **1872** *Atlantic Mo.* March 317 An ancient font was found doing duty as a tavern punch-bowl. **1923** STANARD *Richmond* 144 A Temperance Society is born [*c*1840] in Richmond whose pledge seems to presage the death knell of the free punch-bowl at the Governor's Mansion.

***Puncheon.**[1] Also †**punchin, punchun, puntion.**

+**1.** A thick, heavy piece of rough timber, usually split from a log and having at least one hewed surface. Also in generic sense.

1725 in *Travels Amer. Col.* 150 [We] went to Old Estotoe a large Town and very well ffortifyed all round with Punchins and also ditched on the Outside of the sd Punchins. **1791** in Jillson *Dark & Bl. Ground* 109 It is kept covered from the weather by a deer skin and some pieces of puncheon. **1804** *Md. Hist. Mag.* IV. 9 Houses or cabins . . . are generally made of heavy timber logs covered with split timbers called 'puncheons' which they pin to the rafters with wooden pins. **1843** *Amer. Pioneer* II. 445 Puncheons were planks made by splitting logs to about two and a half or three inches in thickness, and hewing them on one or both sides with the broad-axe. Of such our floor, doors, tables and stools were manufactured. **1887** KIRKLAND *Zury* 21 'Puncheons,' or 'slabs,' are the side-cuts from logs squared for sawing. *a*1918 G. STUART *On Frontier* I. 189 Gold Tom and Jacobs hauled puncheons for Burr's floor.

+**2.** Attrib. with *bench, fence, fort,* etc.

1754 *Lett. to Washington* I. 48, I have erected a puntion Fort. **1784** WASHINGTON *Diaries* II. 295 A dwelling House and barn (of midling size) with Puncheon Roofs. **1823** JAMES *Exped.* I. 145 [The Indians] arranged themselves, agreeably to their tribes, on puncheon benches. **1829** FLINT *G. Mason* 11 Their 'puncheon' shutters . . . had excluded the uncertain light. **1845** HOOPER *Simon Suggs' Adv.* 141 It's got a punchun fence in the place of a rale one. **1853** RAMSEY *Tennessee* 717 Never were the story, the joke, the song and the laugh, better enjoyed than upon . . . the puncheon stools, around the roaring log fire of the early Western settler. **1886** Z. F. SMITH *Kentucky* 39 We have the tradition of the border schoolhouse of rude logs and puncheon seats on the dirt floor.

***Puncheon.**[2] A large cask serving as a container, usually for liquids. — **1760** *Newport Mercury* 22 April 3/3 Choice old Jamaica Rum by the Puncheon, or any Quantity above ten Gallons. **1789** MORSE *Amer. Geog.* 112 The sloop . . . was laden with one hundred and nineteen puncheons of Jamaica spirits. **1841** *Knickerb.* XVII. 382 It is said that a sloop is arrived there which has been bound from Grenada to New-York, with seventy puncheons of rum. **1853** 'P. PAXTON' *Yankee in Texas* 401 A hundred . . . huge boats all lie with their bows . . . pointing to . . . the unwieldy sugar puncheons.

+**Puncheon door.** A door made of puncheons. *Obs.* — **1827** *Western Mo. Rev.* I. 447 [There] was a log pen, roofed, ten feet square, with three wooden windows, and a white washed puncheon door. **1833** FLINT *D. Boone* 14 A ponderous puncheon door . . . completed the appendages of this primeval seminary of learning. **1886** Z. F. SMITH *Kentucky* 150 The outlet was a puncheon door with a bar to secure it.

||**Puncheoned,** *a.* Made of puncheons. — **1843** 'CARLTON' *New Purchase* 109 And first, the puncheoned area was separated into two grand parts.

+**Puncheon floor.** A floor made of puncheons. — **1791** in Jillson *Dark & Bl. Ground* 111 Puncheon floors are all right as long as it is cold enough to let them be covered with furs. **1838** DRAKE *Tales Queen City* 64 They danced merrily over the puncheon floor of their rustic cabins. **1877** W. WRIGHT *Big Bonanza* 29 The enthusiastic Johntowners went forth in the dance with ardor and filled the air with splinters from the puncheon floor. **1920** Lewis *Main Street* 151 She wanted to be swinging across a puncheon-floor with a dancing fiddler.

+**Puncheon table.** A table made of a puncheon or of puncheons. — **1843** 'Carlton' *New Purchase* 199 Adjoining the bureau was the puncheon table with its white oak legs. **1847** Howe *Hist. Coll. Ohio* 274 At their [the early settlers'] weddings, a puncheon table, formed like a bench, without a cloth, was covered with refreshments.

Puncher. {1681–} + =Cow-puncher. (See also Bull-puncher.)

1890 *Stock Grower & Farmer* 28 June 3/4 There were . . . hundreds of expert 'punchers' where you can't count them by tens—tenderfeet and all. **1894** *Harper's Mag.* March 515/1 The 'punchers' were squatting about in groups in front of the straggling log and adobe buildings. **1898** Wister *Lin McLean* 1 Lin's brother punchers slept about him on the ground. **1924** C. E. Mulford *Rustlers' Valley* iv, At the far end of the bar a tipsy puncher insisted on singing 'Home, Sweet Home.'

b. In appositive use.

1897 *Outing* XXX. 164/2 Cautiously picking his way . . . appeared the picturesque figure of an old 'puncher' friend from Colorado. **1898** Wister *Lin McLean* 78 The appearance of the puncher bridegroom also interested Ogden.

Punching bag. A stuffed or inflated leather bag, usually pear-shaped, to be hung up and punched with the fists for exercise. Also attrib. — **1896** Ade *Artie* 4 If they'll put in a punchin'-bag and a plunge they can have my game. **1897** *Outing* XXX. 182/2 The use of chest-weights, the traveling-rings and punching-bag, may be taken to develop different groups of muscles. **1909** 'O. Henry' *Options* 258, I've done nothing but a little punching-bag work. **1911** Harrison *Queed* 89 He went around like a museum guide, introducing the beloved apparatus . . . under its true names and uses, the chest-weights, . . . the punching-bag and trapeze.

Punching machine. A machine for punching holes in materials. — **1850** *Rep. Comm. Patents 1849* 185 Having thus fully described my improved punching machine [etc.]. **1878** *Harper's Mag.* April 645/2 The bar then goes to the punching-machine, that . . . bites a hole through the iron. **1911** Rolt-Wheeler *Boy with Census* 256 He settled back at his work on the punching machine.

+**Punch room.** A room in which punch is served or dispensed. — **1827** Drake & Mansfield *Cincinnati* 30 [The theater has] a spacious gallery, with commodious lobbies, punch room, &c. **1841** *S. Lit. Messenger* VII. 764/1 If you wont go home with me, you can take me down to the punch-room.

+**Punch ticket.** *Railroad.* A ticket designed to be punched by a conductor or gateman on the occasion of each trip. — **1887** George *40 Yrs. on Rail* 227 Many cases have been reported where in punch-tickets the bits of pasteboard punched out have been saved and carefully glued in the old places. **1890** *Harper's Mag.* May 908/1 A person . . . who by many punch-tickets builds up the fortunes of the stockholders.

+**Pung.** *New Eng.* [Short for Tom Pung.]

1. A form of box sleigh usually drawn by one horse.

1825 Cooper *L. Lincoln* xxv, He was in the act of seating himself in the pung. **1855** M. Thompson *Doesticks* 183 The streets were filled with sleighs, cutters, pungs, and every variety of sled. **1881** McLean *Cape Cod Folks* 187 My father had one of those 'ere pungs, as we used to call 'em, that he used to ride around in. **1922** A. Brown *Old Crow* 71 Seeing his passenger, he lifted his whip-stock in salute and stepped out of the pung to meet him.

attrib. **1835** *Knickerb.* VI. 564, I remember a pung-ride one evening to an inn. **1858** *Ib.* LII. 539 Two young 'Suckers' . . . jumped into a one-horse pung wagon.

2. =Pungy.

1901 *Scribner's Mag.* April 503/1 This old pung'll do to carry home fish in a pinch.

+**Punger gourd.** [Origin obscure.] A variety of gourd. — **1884** *Tenn. Code* 526 The following property shall be exempt from execution, seizure or attachment— . . . Heads of Families. . . . Two gourds, two punger gourds, One carpet [etc.].

+**Punging.** Jumping on and off a moving pung; hitching a sled to, or stealing a ride on, a pung. — **1891** Howells *Quality of Mercy* 90 Small boys . . . observed his haste in their intervals of punging.

+**Pungle,** *v. tr.* To contribute, pay, or hand over (money). Usually with *down* or *up. slang.* Also absol. or intr. — **1851** *Alta Californian* 19 July, A singular genius . . . was 'pongling down' huge piles of gold at a monte table. **1854** *Journal* (Wilmington, N.C.) 21 April 2/3 (Th.S.), Gamblers 'pungling down' their dust. **1884** 'Mark Twain' *H. Finn* v, I'll make him pungle, too, or I'll know the reason why. **a1910** *Chicago Tribune* (Th.S.), Mr. Fuddleston at once pungled up to the extent of $5. **1910** E. S. Field *Sapphire Bracelet* 141, I'll have him arrested, and then make him pungle up something handsome before I'll agree not to appear against him.

+**Pungy.** [Origin obscure. Cf. Pung.] **1.** A boat used in the oyster trade in Chesapeake Bay. **2.** (See quotation.) — **(1) 1880** G. A. Townsend *Tales Chesapeake* 29 They launched the pungy, not alone. **1884** *Nat. Museum Bul.* No. 27, 220 The average sized 'pungy' in the Chesapeake has a crew of seven or eight. **1893** *Outing* XXII. 150/2 Craft of all kinds, from the stately merchantman to the pungy loaded with fruit from the 'Eastern sho',' dotted the bay. **(2) 1890** *Cent.* 4848/2 *Pungy,* a small boat like a sharpey. [Massachusetts.]

***Punish,** *v. Baseball.* +*tr.* (See quotations.) — **1868** Chadwick *Base Ball* 44 The pitcher is said to be 'punished' when the batsmen find no difficulty in hitting away the balls he delivers to them. **1875** *Chicago Tribune* 16 Sept. 8/4 The home nine . . . punished the parabolic curve with a relish pleasant to see. **1885** Chadwick *Art of Pitching* 44 A pitcher is only 'punished' in the technical application of the term, when runs are really earned off his pitching.

***Punishment.** +A fine imposed upon a student for violation of college rules. *Obs.* Also attrib. — **1686** *Harvard Rec.* I. 260 The Steward . . . [shall] be accountable . . . to the College Treasurer for all Study rents, Detriments, Punishments, Gallery Money [etc.]. **1738** *Ib.* II. 680 (in margin), Butler & Steward allow'd 20/ per year for making up &c the punishment Bills.

+**Punk.** [Lenape *punk, ponk,* 'fine ashes, powder.'] {1862}

1. Partially decayed wood, esp. of the pine, hickory, or maple, capable of being used as touchwood or tinder.

1705 Beverley *Virginia* III. 49 Or else they take Punck, (which is a Sort of a soft Touchwood, cut out of the knots of Oak or Hiccory Trees, but the Hiccory affords the best,) this they shape like a Cone, . . . and apply the Basis of it to the parts affected. **1756** Bartram in Darlington *Mem. Bartram & Marshall* 206 [The Indians] shoot red-hot iron slugs, or punk, into the roof, and fire the house over their heads. **1792** Belknap *Hist. New-Hampshire* III. 94 [The Indians] raised a blister by burning *punk* or touchwood on the skin. **a1817** Dwight *Travels* II. 197 They made a fire with the aid of a flint . . . and some punk; a substance, formed by a partial decomposition of the heart of the maple tree. **1888** Bittinger *Hist. Haverhill, N.H.* 357n., The tinder was a soft, dry, spongy substance called 'punk,' found in wood. **1923** Cook *On Old Frontier* 15 Each man carried a flint and steel, together with a piece of punk or prepared cotton tape.

2. A slow-burning preparation sold in long pencil-like pieces and used chiefly in igniting fireworks.

1869 Aldrich *Bad Boy* 92 Here and there were tables at which could be purchased the smaller sort of fireworks, such as pin-wheels, serpents, double-headers, and punk warranted not to go out. **1907** London *Road* 92 It would last for hours, and my cell-mate called it a 'punk.'

3. A form of incense.

1870 in De Vere 157 A Chinese lady of rank in San Francisco walks attended by three maids of honor, bearing lighted sticks of punk highly perfumed. **1880** *Harper's Mag.* Dec. 73 Before the ancestral tablets or household idol, incense was consumed, punk or joss-sticks, mock money and pieces of red paper covered with printed prayers were burned. **1890** *Boston Jrnl.* 10 May 5/8 The burning of innumerable sticks of bamboo punk, which sent forth a faint, sickening odor.

4. Attrib. in names of trees. (Cf. Punk oak.)

1902 White *Blazed Trail* 128 Thorough smoking in the fumes of punk maple would obviate this. **1903** — *Forest* 111 It should be bright and glowing, so that the punk birch . . . will not smother it entirely.

+**Punkie.** [Du. *punki,* fr. Lenape. Cf. Punk.] Any one of various minute biting flies or midges of the family Chironomidae, esp. those of the genus *Culicoides.* (Cf. No-see-'em.) — **1840** *Knickerb.* Sept. 270 Of all the tortures of this nature, that inflicted by the *gnat* (sand-flies, punkies, brulos, for they bear all these appellations,) is the least endurable. **1859** *Harper's Mag.* July 169/2 Our good hostess . . . gathered up a large piece of bark, threw a few live coals upon it . . . remarking, 'There's a "smudge" to keep off the punkies.' **1903** White *Forest* 108 The midge, again—or punkie, or—'no see-'um,' just as you please—swarms down upon you suddenly. **1910** Hodge *Amer. Indians* II. 328/1 *Punkie* (also *punky, punk*), a minute gnat, called also sand-fly or midge (*Simulium nocivum*), the bite of which produces an intolerable itching and smarting sensation as if a spark of fire had dropped upon the naked skin.

+**Punk oak.** The water oak, *Quercus nigra.* — **1884** Sargent *Rep. Forests* 152 *Quercus aquatica.* . . . Possum Oak. Punk Oak. . . . Probably not used except as fuel. **1897** Sudworth *Arborescent Flora* 175 Common names [of the water oak include] . . . Duck Oak, Possum Oak, Punk Oak.

+**Punk wood.** =Punk 1. — **1883** *Harper's Mag.* Feb. 427/2 She opened a flint-and-tinder box and struck a spark into the punk-wood. **1903** White *Forest* 180 Sometimes a faint rounded shell . . . swelled above the level, to crumble to punkwood at the lightest touch of our feet.

+**Punky,** *a.* [Punk.] Of wood: Partially decayed, resembling punk. Also fig. — **1872** Huntington *Road-Master's Assistant* 117 A bridge may . . . have a small knot partially decayed, or 'punky,' as it is termed. **1880** *Northwestern Lumberman* 24 Jan., For punky knots the general rule is to allow the whole scale of the log for defects. **1886** *Harper's Mag.* Dec. 105/2 George's mother's folks did have a kind of a punky spot somewhere in their heads. **1904** *N.Y. Times* 5 May 8 Written by another man Mr. Austin would doubtless find these verses as amusing as the rest of us do, . . . would appreciate their punky pretentiousness.

***Punt.**[1] A small boat, skiff, dugout, etc., esp. a shallow, flat-bottomed boat square at the ends.

1746 E. Kimber *Itinerant Observer* 53 We ourselves step'd into a small *Punt,* and put off to the *Shallop.* **1835** Ingraham *South-West* I. 142 A hundred skiffs, wherries, punts, dug-outs, and other non-descript craft, with equally euphonic denominations, were darting about in all directions. **1872** Powers *Afoot & Alone* 23 One of those gigantic negroes . . . sat in the stern of a frail punt, and wafted me over the river. **1883** *Century*

Mag. Sept. 731/2 One may see anchored in the little cove behind Castle Hill . . . a trim sloop or two, and various dories and punts.

attrib. **1861** *Ohio Acts* LVIII. 125 It shall also be unlawful for any person, . . . by the aid or use of any swivel, punt gun, . . . or any gun other than the common shoulder gun, or by the aid or use of any punt boat, or sneak boat used for carrying such gun, to catch, kill [etc.].

Punt.[2] *Football.* A kick given the ball before it reaches the ground after being dropped from the hands. {1845-} Also transf. (Cf. DROP KICK, PLACE KICK *n.*) — **1876** in P. H. Davis *Football* (1911) 462 A goal may be obtained by any kind of kick except a punt. **1887** *Century Mag.* Oct. 889/1 To score a goal, the ball must pass . . . over the cross-bar, . . . from a 'place-kick,' or from a 'drop-kick,' . . . not from a 'punt,' a kick made while the ball is in the air. **1898** *N.Y. Journal* 23 Sept. 8 The drop kick differs from the punt in that when the ball is dropped from the hands it is allowed to touch the ground. **1907** *St. Nicholas* May 589/1 A hammering of soft fists, with an occasional punt from a slipper toe, added themselves to the uproar.

+**Punt gun.** A shotgun of large gauge mounted on a swivel in a punt and used for shooting waterfowl. — **1861** [see PUNT[1]]. **1871** *N.Y. Laws* 1670 No person shall at any time kill any wild duck, goose or brant, with . . . a swivel or punt gun.

∗**Pup.**

∗**1.** A contemptuous term for a person {1589}; +a young blood; a boy.

1856 *Porter's Spirit of Times* 15 Nov. 172/3 There were three pups—bless me!—what a speech for a woman; but what can you call a parcel of supercilious fellows, who, with a piece of glass stuck in their eye, survey the crowd as if contamination dwelt amongst them. **1870** MEDBERY *Men Wall St.* 31 Down in the cock-pit the Commodore's 'pups,' as the merciless, cacophonic 'street' argot denominates the broker friends of Vanderbilt, are making an ineffective rally. **1902** LORIMER *Lett. Merchant* 118 Chauncey thought that he was something of a pup himself. **1903** LEWIS *Boss* 48 'Here's a pup,' cried Big Kennedy.

+**2.** (See quotations.)

1898 W. B. HASKELL *2 Yrs. in Klondike & Alaskan Gold-Fields* 253. **1902** *Pop. Science Mo.* July 232 The principal streams [in the Klondike region] are known as creeks; the short steep tributaries which flow into them as 'gulches'; and the streamlets which feed these as 'pups.' **1904** E. ROBINS *Magn. North* II. 137 Little creek; call 'em pups here.

+**3.** *Pup tent*, a low, small tent.

1902 *Kan. Hist. Coll.* VII. 413*n.*, For over four years I slept under the same 'pup-tent,' shared hard-tack and literally drank from the same canteen with Nobel Prentis.

+**Pupelo.** *New Eng.* Cider brandy. — **1806** *Salem Register* 7 April (Th.), Do you not deny to the poor labourer the common refreshment of a little toddy, and stint him with a glass of pupelo? **1845** JUDD *Margaret* I. 42 In Livingston there were five distilleries for the manufacture of cider-brandy, or what was familiarly known as pupelo. **1885** EGGLESTON in *Century Mag.* April 884/2 Cider they reenforced by distilling it into 'pupelo,' or brandy.

∗**Pupil.** One who is taught by another. Also attrib. — **1747** *Harvard Rec.* II. 777 That the Mathematical Professor do receive . . . Such a Summ as shall make up his whole Jncome from the College, . . . including the Pupil Money, Mr. Hollis's Salary & Mr. Thomas Brattle's Legacy. **1851** CIST *Cincinnati* 328 Four buildings have already been erected for the accommodation of the pupils. **1885** *Wkly. New Mexican Rev.* 2 July 3/6 Ten pupils [of St. Michael's College] were presented with rich gold pendant medals. **1911** *Okla. Session Laws* 3 Legisl. 122 Said board shall have [power to] . . . adopt courses of study for pupils' reading circles.

Puppet show. A dramatic show of puppets. {1650-} Also fig. — **1774** J. HARROWER *Diary* 87 This night finishes the Puppet shows, roape dancings &c. which has continowed every night this week in town. **1783** *Holyoke Diaries* 109 We went to the Puppet Show. **1807** IRVING, etc. *Salmagundi* xi., 262, I have seen that great political puppet-show—an Election. **1914** *Amer. Rev. of Reviews* Jan. 102/1 The puppet show does not flourish in our American cities.

∗**Puppy.** +A coin of little value: (see quotations). It is not known just what coin this was. *Obs.* — **1800** *Columbian Centinel* 1 Feb. 2/4 If tugging a man's cloak costs '*damn'd puppy*' how much will writing an insolent letter to the President of the United States, come to? **1846** COOPER *Redskins* xxx, The debtors of the deceased can meet his obligations with a coin technically called 'puppies.'

+**Puppy love.** Sentimental and transitory affection between a boy and a girl. — **1834** CARRUTHERS *Kentuckian* I. 175 Oh! it is nothing more than puppy love! **1867** HARRIS *Sut Lovingood* 82 Hits a cure fur puppy luv. **1912** DREISER *Financier* 38 This was just one of the early love affairs, or puppy loves.

+**Purbelo, Purbulo, Purblo.** Variants of PUEBLO. Also attrib. — **1846** ROBINS in *Santa Fe Exped.* (1932) 31 On the 21st day of September, 1846, we . . . encamped at St. Domingo, a Purbelo village on the Rio del Norte. **1847** COYNER *Lost Trappers* 171 The governor . . . ordered a Captain Viscarro with sixty men, ten of whom were brave Purbulo Indians, living near Santa Fe, to conduct these exiles. **1850** GARRARD *Wah-To-Yah* xix. 212 Them Purblos have *cached* our cavyard, I spect.

∗**Purchase.**

∗**1.** That which is bought or traded for: +spec., a tract of land acquired by a colony, a private person or company, a state, or by the central government, either directly from the Indians or from some agency that has extinguished Indian claims. Freq. in place names.

See also NEW PURCHASE, PLATTE PURCHASE, and cf. GADSDEN PURCHASE, LOUISIANA PURCHASE, wherein a change of sovereignty is involved.

1670 *Derby Rec.* 308 A parcel of Land . . . bounded with a littel brooke and with English purches on ye south side. **1725** *Huntington Rec.* II. 354 It was voated and agreed to make a new division in the old purchass between the Cold Spring and Cow harbour. **1757** *Doc. Hist. N.Y. State* I. 523 Four Families . . . fled from Henderson's Purchase. **1777** *Va. State P.* I. 287 He asked . . . for a path to the Kentucky purchase. **1813** *Ann. 12th Congress* 2 Sess. 930 Thence . . . to the western boundary of the Osage purchase. **1821** W. DALTON *Travels U.S.* 135 The eastern boundary of the Holland Company's purchase is crossed six miles east of Batavia. . . . This 'purchase' is part of the tract ceded to Massachusetts. **1839** PLUMBE *Sk. Iowa* 27 Those . . . have never cast their eyes upon the 'Black Hawk Purchase.' **1894** *Harper's Mag.* April 676/2 The bride . . . is well known and much admired, not only in the Purchase, but in this city.

+**2.** (See quotation.)

1909 WEBSTER 1737/2 *Purchase*, . . . in New Hampshire, an unorganized minor territorial division consisting of land which was originally laid off and sold by the State to an individual or individuals.

Purchase money. The money paid or to be paid for a thing purchased. {a1763-} Also fig. — **1720** *Boston Rec.* 146 [The] purchace money is to be Invested, in Some Real Estate for the use of this Town. **1782** CRÈVECŒUR *Letters* 92, I found myself under the necessity of going to Philadelphia, in order to pay the purchase money. **1858** VIELÉ *Following Drum* 102 It is . . . wronging generations yet unborn, by allowing them to forget how precious the purchase-money that bought their freedom. **1892** M. A. JACKSON *Gen. Jackson* 114 He might be permitted to emancipate himself by a return of the purchase-money.

∗**Purchaser.** One who acquires land through purchase. — **1627** *Plymouth Laws* 29 After the purchasers are served as afore[sai]d . . . then such planters as are heirs [etc.]. **1655** *Brookhaven Rec.* 1 The Sachem . . . [has] granted unto sayd purchasers, free liberty. **1704** *Providence Rec.* XIV. 283 Some part of which sd Rights [were] not . . . yet laid out, nor devided from the Gennerall Comon belonging to the Generall Purchassers of the sd Towne & Towneshipp. **1904** *Indian Laws & Tr.* III. 593 All lands . . . remaining undisposed of at the expiration of four years . . . shall be sold . . . not more than six hundred and forty acres to any one purchaser.

Purchasing, *a.* That or who buys; authorized to buy. — **1780** *Heath P.* III. 18 Inability of the purchasing commissaries to discharge the debt. **1863** *Horticulturist* Oct. Advt. 2 Purchasing and Information Agency. Articles of every description purchased. **1866** *Ore. State Jrnl.* 15 Sept. 4/4 San Francisco Purchasing Agency.

+**Purchasing agent.** An agent authorized to purchase something for his principal. — **1823** in McKenney *Memoirs* I. 302, I supplanted none of . . . the purchasing agents, in our cities, by others of my own selecting. **1836** *Diplom. Corr. Texas* I. (1908) 58 We have appointed . . . Edward Hall purchasing agent. **1877** *Harper's Mag.* April 726/2 The accessions to the library are first made by the judgment of the regular purchasing agents of the library. **1906** LYNDE *Quickening* 212 We have to monkey with the purchasing agent of a corporation.

+**Pure-blood,** *n.* **1.** An Indian with only Indian blood in his veins. **2.** A pure-bred animal. — (1) **1882** *Harper's Mag.* May 895/1 The half and quarter breeds, though a mongrel race, seem to have . . . greater powers of resistance than the pure-bloods. **1889** *Congress. Rec.* 9 Feb. 1714/1 Out of the pure-bloods I suppose it would be almost impossible to find a single man qualified . . . to perform the duties of a juryman. (2) **1894** *Vt. Agric. Rep.* XIV. 166, I do not wish to speak as a specialist, although having bred pure bloods for almost thirty years. **1903** *Kan. State Bd. Agric. Bienn. Rep.* XIII. 63 Likewise fifty per cent. can be added to the value if pure-bloods only are used in the northern half of this territory.

+**Pure-blood,** *a.* =next. — **1859** *Mich. Agric. Trans.* X. 355 All the theory in the world . . . cannot convince our people that the Durham cattle will keep as easy . . . as the pure blood, elegantly-constructed sprightly Devon. **1871** *Rep. Indian Affairs* (1872) 247 Augustus Chenguay . . . says that he is a pure blood Indian without any admixture of white blood. **1888** *Vt. Agric. Rep.* X. 49 Why don't you get some pure blood Holsteins?

+**Pure-blooded,** *a.* Pure-bred. {1886} — **1821** in Morse *Rep. Indian Affairs* II. 69 The number of pure blooded Indians is extremely small, say fifty or sixty, and is rapidly decreasing. **1850** GARRARD *Wah-To-Yah* vii. 99 The unfair horsetrader might have taken my scalp for presuming to dictate to him, a pure-blooded Cheyenne. **1887** *Nation* 10 March 214/1 He adds that the Spaniards are likewise without any desire for knowledge, and declares there is no *avenir* for the pure-blooded race. **1903** *Kan. State Bd. Agric. Bienn. Rep.* XIII. 63 A quarter of a billion acres of grass, nurturing 10,000,000 head of cattle, . . . [can] be doubled in value in a single decade, if only pure-blooded sires are used in all the cow herds.

+**Pure-bred,** *a.* Having blood of only one strain. Also absol.

'The terms "thoroughbred," "full-blood," and "pure-bred," are generally used in this country as practically synonymous' (1894 *Vt. Agric. Rep.* XIV. 104).

1869 *Rep. Comm. Agric. 1868* 10 Specimens of pure-bred domestic fowls. **1881** *Cimarron News & Press* 17 Feb. 2/2 A pure bred bull . . . should be purchased. **1894** *Vt. Agric. Rep.* XIV. 105 A pure bred . . . is an animal eligible to record in the pedigree register of its breed. **1925** BRYAN *Memoirs* 34 My parents were not fanciers of pure-bred stock.

Pure-food. *attrib.* +Designating enactments, persons, etc., connected with regulating the contents of canned or compounded foods. — **1894** *Jrnl. Franklin Inst.* April 267 Senator Paddock, of Nebraska, . . . after years of futile struggle, succeeded in having the Senate pass what is known as the Pure Food Bill. **1900** *Amer. Rev. of Reviews* Jan. 69/1 A national pure-food law . . . could only regulate interstate traffic in adulterated and misbranded products. **1911** *Outlook* 13 May 48/1 Many pure-food experts . . . desired that the use of benzoate in foods should be forbidden altogether. **1913** *Collier's Wkly.* 16 Aug. 24 Idaho [is] a pure food state.

+**Pure quill.** The real thing. *slang.* — **1888** *Detroit Free Press* Aug. (F.), When religun is religun, an' it's the pure quill an' no water in it, there's never one of us but kin take it in large doses.

* **Purgatory.**

+**1.** *New Eng.* **a.** A cavern or narrow walled ravine. Also in place names. **b.** (See quot. 1902.)

1766 CUTLER in *Life & Corr.* I. 12 Hunted in Purgatory with Mr. Dean and Mr. Penniman [for botanical specimens] this afternoon, but found nothing. **1797** MORSE *Amer. Gazetteer*, Sutton, a township in Worcester co., Massachusetts, . . . The cavern, commonly called *Purgatory*, . . . is a natural curiosity. **1888** WHITNEY *Names & Places* 160 Along the coast of New England, and in the interior, narrow ravines with nearly perpendicular walls are called 'purgatories.' **1902** A. MATTHEWS *Purgatory River* 1n., There are in New England several small brooks to which the name of Purgatory is given, either because they drain swamps, or flow through or near rock chasms which are called Purgatories.

+**2.** *local.* (See quot. 1831.) Also attrib.

1831 PECK *Guide* 308 In the low prairies near the Wabash, are swamps, called by the people *purgatories*, which are almost impassable in the wet season. **1834** — *Gaz. Illinois* 172 The eastern part of Allison's Prairie, towards the Wabash, contains some wet land and purgatory swamps.

+**Purgery.** (See quot. 1876.) — **1853** *Harper's Mag.* VII. 763/1 The cane juice . . . is removed into the 'purgery,' where it is, as sugar, placed in hogsheads. **1862** *Rep. Comm. Patents 1861: Agric.* 310 The hogsheads filled with the moist sugar are wheeled off to the 'purgery.' **1876** KNIGHT 1836/1 *Purgery*, the portion of a sugar-house where the sugar from the coolers is . . . allowed to drain off its molasses.

+**Purging house.** =prec. — **1862** *Rep. Comm. Patents 1861: Agric.* 310 Better attention to the cultivation and seasons favorable to the maturation of the cane, . . . together with well-arranged purging-houses, . . . [will] result in a fair yield.

* **Puritan,** *n.* One of the Calvinistic members of the English Protestant church advocating simpler forms of faith and worship than those established by law, +who settled in the New England colonies, esp. in Massachusetts Bay, or was born into the early New England church; also, a Pilgrim of Plymouth colony.

As shown by A. Matthews in *Mass. Col. Soc. Publ.* XVII. (1914) 372–84, the distinction drawn between *Pilgrim* and *Puritan* in respect to the settlers of Plymouth and Massachusetts Bay is of comparatively recent date: (see quot. 1866 and cf. PILGRIM 2 a, note, and PILGRIM FATHER, note.)

1723 *Harvard Rec.* II. 480 Our Fathers were some of the Old Puritans, so called from the Purer Church-State and way of Worship and manner of Godly Discipline. **1777** S. WEST *Anniv. Sermon* (1778) 38 [Their adversaries] called them [our fathers], *Fanaticks, Schismaticks*, and, in scorn, *Puritans;* and they doubtless thought that God would be glorified by their thus cruelly persecuting their brethren. **1794** BELKNAP in *Mass. Col. Soc. Publ.* XVII. 373 A company of English Puritans, who had resided twelve years in Holland, began a colony in New England, which they called *New Plymouth.* **1847** DILLINGHAM *Ib.* 376 A step in advance of their brother Puritans, had entitled them [*i.e.*, the Mayflower passengers] to the designation of Separatists. **1855** FELT *Eccles. Hist. New Eng.* I. 38 The undertaking of the Leyden Puritans to found a commonwealth . . . is one of brighter, sublimer ends. *a***1861** WINTHROP *Canoe & Saddle* 105, I now recall how godly Puritans once brandished ruder axes and bill-hooks. [**1866** B. SCOTT in *Mass. Col. Soc. Publ.* XVII. 377, I propose first to show that the Pilgrim Fathers of Plymouth Colony . . . were not *Puritans*, as is often carelessly and erroneously reported, but *Separatists*.] **1870** GOODWIN *Ib.* 378 Let me speak of the difference between the *Puritans* and the *Pilgrims.* **1891** in B. S. Heath *Labor & Finance Revol.* p. vii, Josiah Heath and Abigail Smith, were from New Hampshire, and were descendants of the early Puritans. **1907** ROOSEVELT in *Boston Transcript* 20 Aug. 1/7 The coming hither of the Puritan three centuries ago shaped the destinies of this continent.

* **Puritan,** *a.*

+**1.** Of persons: Belonging to, or descended from, the New England Puritans.

See PURITAN *n.*, note.

1820 in *Mass. Col. Soc. Publ.* XVII. 373 The Puritan Pilgrims of New England landed on the soil of the new world [in 1620]. **1854** BANCROFT *Hist. U.S.* III. 68 In Connecticut . . . the Puritan Clergy, who were there, . . . consociated with the legislature. **1881** PIERSON *In the Brush* 282 The hardy Puritan pioneers, in the absence of a minister, had what were called 'deacon-meetings.' **1900** DIX *Deacon Bradbury* 32 All the old, stern, passionate fire of devotion . . . would flame out on his countenance, as it had flamed on those of his Puritan forefathers. **1913** LA FOLLETTE *Autobiog.* 223 Combined with the Puritan Yankee of New England, these sturdy immigrants have produced a courageous, progressive race of men in whom the spirit of democracy dominates.

+**2.** Of movements, places, etc.: Made up of, characteristic of, or belonging to the Puritans of New England.

1847 *Mass. H. S. Coll.* 3 Ser. X. 171 Those who followed Governor Winthrop from his own country may not improperly be designated the *Second Puritan Emigration*,—the *First* being formed of those who had been of Mr. Robinson's church. **1858** LONGFELLOW *M. Standish* III. 31 The musical voice of Priscilla Singing the hundredth Psalm, the grand old Puritan anthem. **1868** *N.Y. Herald* 2 July 4/1 The delegates from the Puritan region . . . have wisely decided to refrain from coming. **1885** CRAWFORD *Amer. Politician* 23 His friends . . . put it in the clouds as a kind of rainbow—a promise that Puritan blood could not go wrong. **1896** WILKINS *Madelon* 320 Dorothy, in spite of his stern Puritan creed, was yet dearer to him than that abstraction of her which he deemed her soul. **1903** *Boston Transcript* 22 Dec. 10 We shall not be surprised if the Forefather's Day addresses this year hark back to Pilgrim and Puritan ideals.

+**Puritan Father.** A founding father of New England. **1.** A Plymouth father. **2.** In later use, an early Puritan of Massachusetts Bay: (see also quot. 1878). — **(1) 1806** in Thacher *Hist. Plymouth* (1832) 232 December 22.—This is the 186th anniversary of the first landing of our puritan fathers. **1851** BANVARD *Plymouth & Pilgrims* 273 Iron castings, in imitation of heraldry curtains, . . . [bear] the names in bas-relief of the forty-one Puritan fathers who signed the memorable compact, while in the cabin of the Mayflower. **(2) 1870** R. C. WINTHROP *Oration on Landing of Pilgrims* 39, I rejoice, too, that the Puritan Fathers of Massachusetts, who followed them [*i.e.*, the Pilgrim Fathers] to these shores ten years afterwards, . . . were, if not technically and professedly, yet to all intents and purposes, Separatists, also. **1878** I. N. TARBOX in *Mass. Col. Soc. Publ.* XVII. 380 The Puritan Fathers are the men of the Massachusetts Bay and the colonies that grew directly out of that. **1894** LEAVITT *Our Money Wars* 15 The Boston Puritan Fathers got . . . a share of the buccaneering plunder.

* **Puritanism.** The doctrines and principles of the Puritans.

[**1702** MATHER *Magnalia* (1853) I. 257 The Bishop of the Diocess, having understood that Mr. Cotton was infected with Puritanism, set himself immediately to discourage his being there.] **1775** BURNABY *Travels* 82 The character of the inhabitants of this province [Mass.] is much improved . . . : but puritanism and a spirit of persecution is not yet totally extinguished. **1832** DUNLAP *Hist. Amer. Theatre* 46 The accomplished Burgoyne . . . now produced his second drama in that strong hold of Puritanism and unconquerable liberty. **1858** BUCHER *Life Thoughts* 27 New Englandism is but another word for Puritanism in the Independent sense. **1920** HOWELLS *Vacation of Kelwyns* 227 It's about the only remnant of Puritanism left them in *this* neighborhood.

+**Puro.** *S.W.* [Sp.] A cigar of pure tobacco. *Obs.* — **1844** GREGG *Commerce of Prairies* I. 243 The puro or cigarro is seen in the mouths of all. **1844** KENDALL *Narr. Santa Fé Exped.* II. 244, I took everything that was offered—loaves of bread, . . . fruits, puros, . . . and all. **1880** *Cimarron News & Press* 18 March 3/1 He promises to send us some *puros* when he gets down into Sonora, if he can do so without the duty coming too high.

Purp. Humorous variant of *pup.* — **1869** Dumont *Benedict's Congress Songster* 40 And that's what's the matter with the purp. **1876** *Fur, Fin & Feather* Sept. 134/1 A fine-looking specimen of a thorough-bred shepherd dog, and a finer 'purp,' . . . seemed to be his only companions.

* **Purple,** *a.*

1. In the specific names of plants, fruits, and trees. **a.** As simple modifier.

There are other examples in books on botany.

*c*1729 CATESBY *Carolina* I. 35 *Convulvulus Caroliniensis.* . . . The Purple Bindweed of Carolina. **1805** LEWIS in *L. & Clark Exped.* I. (1904) 338 [The] under brush is the same with that of the low timbered bottoms with the addition of the . . . choke cherry, purple currant, and honeysuckle bushis. **1806** *Ib.* IV. (1905) 274 Near the river we find the Cottonwood, . . . the purple haw, . . . and whiteburry honeysuckle. **1814** BIGELOW *Florula Bostoniensis* 153 *Gerardia purpurea.* Purple Gerardia. . . . Common in pastures. **1840** DEWEY *Mass. Flowering Plants* 102 *Polygonum coccineum.* Purple Knotweed. Named from the color of both the leaves and the dense spikes of flowers. *Ib.* 133 *Aster puniceus.* Purple Aster. . . . Fields and woods in rather wet soils. **1843** TORREY *Flora N.Y.* I. 272 *Thaspium atropurpureum.* . . . Purple Alexanders. . . . Rocky hill-sides and borders of woods. *Ib.* II. 20 *Utricularia purpurea.* Purple Bladderwort. . . . It is common in the neighboring parts of New-Jersey. **1845** JUDD *Margaret* I. 143 She gathered the . . . red cohosh, purple bush-trefoil, . . . and other flowers. **1857** Purple trillium [see BIRTHROOT]. **1892** APGAR *Trees Northern U.S.* 161 Among the most useful varieties are *atropurpurea* (Purple Beech), . . . and *argentea variegata* (Silver Variegated Beech). *Ib.* 165 *Salix purpurea.* (Purple Willow.) . . . Often cultivated for the twigs, which are used in basket-making. **1897** SUDWORTH *Arborescent Flora* 294 *Æsculus octandra hybrida.* . . . Purple Buckeye. **1901** MOHR *Plant Life Ala.* 129 The grasses [along the shores of Mobile and

Peridido bays] are: . . . *Cenchrus megacephalus* (sand bur), *Sieglingia purpurea* (purple sand grass).

b. In combination with adjectives in *-ed.*

See also PURPLE-LEAVED *a.*

*c*1730 CATESBY *Carolina* I. 61 *Ligustrum Laurifolio, fructu violaceo.* The Purple-berried Bay. . . . The fruit which succeeds are globular berries. **1843** TORREY *Flora N.Y.* II. 488 *Plotyloma atropupurea.* . . . Purple-stalked Rock-brake. . . . Limestone rocks: not common. **1846** BROWNE *Trees Amer.* 22 *Magnolia purpurea,* The Purple-flowered Magnolia. **1850** S. F. COOPER *Rural Hours* 168 The handsome, large purple-fringed orchis is also found here. **1856** *Rep. Comm. Patents 1855: Agric.* 273 Varieties of cane which have hitherto been most cultivated in Louisiana [include] . . . the 'Purple-banded'; the 'Grey'; the 'Greyish-white.' **1923** WYATT *Invis. Gods* 16 The departing prairie had dropped a clump or two of golden-rod, of black-eyed Susan and purple-panicled timothy.

2. In the names of varieties of fruits and grains.

See also PURPLE CANE, PURPLE POTATO.

1850 *Rep. Comm. Patents 1849: Agric.* 132 The purple straw, greatly admired in some neighborhoods, . . . has not succeeded well in my own. **1862** *Ib. 1861: Agric.* 541 Of plums, Jefferson, imperial gage and purple gage [succeeded best].

3. In the specific names of birds.

See also PURPLE FINCH, PURPLE GALLINULE, etc.

1869 *Amer. Naturalist* III. 188 On returning in June I found here [in Cal.] the Purple-throat Humming Bird. **1895** *Outing* XXVI. 69/2 The purple linnet . . . had vied with the summer tanager and the Carolina wren. **1917** *Birds of Amer.* III. 5/1 Purple finch. *Carpodacus purpureus purpureus.* . . . [Also called] Purple Grosbeak.

4. In special uses with *bug, fever, quartz, shore crab, veil:* (see quotations).

1854 EMMONS *Agric. N.Y.* V. 270 *Purpuricenus,* or Purplebug: . . . *Purpuricenus humeralis.* **1808** A. McV. GRANT *Mem. Amer. Lady* I. 287 It was called the purple or spotted fever, and was probably of the putrid kind. **1896** *Cosmopolitan* XX. 450 The fluor-spar is locally known as 'purple quartz.' **1883** *Nat. Museum Bul.* No. 27, 112 Six species of Crabs are regarded as edible on the Pacific coast . . . [including the] Purple Shore Crab (*H[eterographus] nudus*). **1905** *Nat. Geographic Mag.* July 337/1 Off the New England coast a curious object is often found floating on the water, somewhat resembling a lady's veil . . . of a violet or purple color. The fishermen allude to it generally as the 'purple veil.' . . . On examining the substance with a magnifying glass . . . it was obvious that the purple veil, as a whole, was the egg-mass of a fish.

+**Purple cane.** **1.** A variety of raspberry. **2.** A variety of sugar cane the mature stalks of which are purple or purplish in color; also, a stalk of such cane. Also with defining term. — **(1) 1862** *Rep. Comm. Patents 1861: Agric.* 167 The *Purple Cane,* or American Red Cane, . . . [is] a very valuable variety of raspberry. **1871** *Ill. Agric. Soc. Trans.* VIII. 173 The varieties in common use are Purple-cane, a very prolific, light-purple, soft berry, valuable for family use only, . . . Doolittle Black-cap [etc.]. **(2) 1897** W. C. STUBBS *Sugar Cane* 79 The purple cane is conspicuous for its increased powers of germination and multiplication. **1917** *Dept. Agric. Bul.* No. 486, 6 Cases are also reported of plain Louisiana Purple cane throwing off sports of striped cane.

+**Purple finch.** An American finch, *Carpodacus purpureus.*

*c*1730 CATESBY *Carolina* I. 41 The Purple Finch. . . . They feed on the berries of Juniper. **1808** WILSON *Ornithology* I. 119 [The] Purple Finch . . . is a winter bird of passage. **1842** THOREAU *Journal* I. 449 A little girl has just brought me a purple finch or American linnet. **1869** *Amer. Naturalist* III. 292 Among the birds who are thus victimized are the . . . Purple Finch and Baywinged Bunting. **1903** WHITE *Forest* 91 You will hear . . . purple finches or some of the pine sparrows warbling high and clear. **1917** *Birds of Amer.* III. 5/1 The haunts of the Purple Finch are the low green forests.

Purple gallinule. +A gallinule (*Ionornis martinica*) of the southern states. — **1813** WILSON *Ornithology* IX. 71 The Purple Gallinule [was seen] in a thick swamp, a short distance from Savannah, Georgia. **1839** PEABODY *Mass. Birds* 375 The Purple Gallinule, *Gallinula Martinica,* and the Florida Gallinule, *G. galeata,* . . . [are] rare and accidental visiters in the State. **1883** *Nat. Museum Bul.* No. 27, 155 *Ionornis martinica.* Purple Gallinule. Warmer parts of North and South America. **1917** *Birds of Amer.* I. 211/1 The Purnle Gallinule has been richly endowed with beautiful feathers.

+**Purple grackle.** A crow blackbird, *Quiscalus quiscula.* — [**1782** LATHAM *Gen. Syn. Birds* I. II. 462 Purple Grakle. . . . This inhabits Carolina.] **1811** WILSON *Ornith.* III. 44 The Purple Grakles visit Pennsylvania from the south. **1831** AUDUBON *Ornith. Biog.* I. 35 The flesh of the Purple Grakle is little better than that of the Crow, being dry and ill-flavoured. **1895** *Dept. Agric. Yrbk. 1894* 233 The common purple grackle (*Quisqualus quiscula*) . . . [has] two subspecies, the bronzed grackle (*Quiscalus q. æneus*) and the Florida grackle (*Quiscalus q. aglæus*). **1917** *Birds of Amer.* II. 268/1 The Purple Grackle is like a small edition of the Crow.

+**Purple jackdaw.** (See JACKDAW.)

Purple-leaved, *a.* In the specific names of plants and trees. {1759-} — **1843** TORREY *Flora N.Y.* I. 232 *Epilobium coloratum.* Purple-leaved Willow-herb. . . . Wet thickets; common, except in the western part of the State. **1863** *Horticulturist* XVIII. 258/1 To this list might be added the Purple-leaved Beech. **1869** *Rep. Comm. Agric. 1868* 197 A pleasing variety of color may be introduced by forming a hedge of the purple-leaved berberry (*Berberis vulgaris,* var. *purpurea*). **1892** APGAR *Trees Northern U.S.* 146 European White Birch. . . . Cultivated in this country, under many names . . . ; among them may be mentioned *pendula* (weeping) . . . , *atropurpurea* (purple-leaved).

+**Purple martin.** A large North American swallow, *Progne subis.*

1743 CATESBY *Carolina* II. p. xxxvi, Land-Birds which breed and abide in Carolina in the Summer, and retire in Winter: . . . The yellow Titmouse. The purple Martin. The humming Bird. **1828** BONAPARTE *Synopsis* 64 The Purple Martin . . . inhabits the whole continent of America. **1839** PEABODY *Mass. Birds* 343 The Purple Martin . . . is more intimate with man than any other native bird. **1892** TORREY *Foot-Path Way* 182 Purple martins, cliff swallows, . . . and chimney sweeps . . . breed to the northward of us in incalculable numbers. **1917** *Birds of Amer.* III. 83/1 Of all the species [of the swallows] the Purple Martin is undoubtedly the most popular.

+**Purple potato.** A variety of potato. — **1775** ROMANS *Nat. Hist. Florida* 123 *Purple potatoe,* having that colour throughout except a very little of the heart. **1790** S. DEANE *Newengland Farmer* 224/2.

Purple sandpiper. A sandpiper (*Arquatella maritima*) of the northeastern coast. {1824} — **1828** BONAPARTE *Synopsis* 319 The Purple Sandpiper. . . . Inhabits both continents on rocky shores only. **1839** PEABODY *Mass. Birds* 368 The Purple Sandpiper . . . is sold in the market at Boston. **1858** BAIRD *Birds Pacific R.R.* 717 The purple sandpiper . . . is frequently met with on the shores of the Atlantic, where it is diffused throughout the extent of temperate North America. **1884** *Nat. Museum Bul.* No. 27, 149. **1917** *Birds of Amer.* I. 233/1, I have seen Purple Sandpipers on the rocky Maine coast in December.

Purpose novel. A novel written for the purpose of discussing or exposing some social or economic problem. — **1893** *Forum* Jan. 594 The purpose-novel is an odious attempt to lecture people who hate lectures, to preach at people who prefer their own church, and to teach people who think they know enough already. **1894** *Harper's Mag.* Oct. 797/1 There is an analogy to this feeling in the present reaction against the domestic, the pathological, and the 'purpose' novels.

***Purse,** *n.*[1]

***1.** A pouch or bag for carrying money.

1700 SEWALL *Letter-Book* I. 237 The money . . . is in a little Linnen Purse. **1774** J. ANDREWS *Letters* 27 The Gentleman oblig'd him to accept of a purse containing about 15 or 20 Johannes. **1854** M. J. HOLMES *Tempest & Sunshine* 48, I have been knitting on your purse. **1907** *St. Nicholas* June 736/1 [She] put the change in her purse. **1910** J. HART *Vigilante Girl* 378 The women . . . had put their hand-satchels and purses on the table.

2. A sum of money made up as a prize or present. {1650-} Also attrib.

1688 SEWALL *Diary* I. 240 This day a Gannet was seen, and a Purse made for him that should first see Land. **1786** WASHINGTON *Diaries* III. 124 Mr. Lear went up to Alexandria to see the Jockey club purse run for. **1804** *Steele P.* II. 791 The entry money for each coalt shall . . . compose a purse to be set apart for this days races. **1884** *Gringo & Greaser* 15 Feb. 1/2 The good ladies of Taylorville, Ill., are getting up a handsome purse for Miss Emma Bond. **1898** *Kansas City Star* 19 Dec. 3/1 Bingen's share of the purse money amounted to only $4,650. **1919** *Lit. Digest* 26 July 44/1 They collected a purse for him.

+**Purse,** *n.*[2] [Abbrev. of PURSE SEINE.] *attrib.* Designating boats and various devices used in connection with purse seines.—**1879** *Rep. Comm. Fisheries* V. 126 The captain of the gang is in charge of the 'purse-boat.' **1884** *Nat. Museum Bul.* No. 27, 1000 Davit-iron. . . . Used in Cape Ann seine-boats. The purse-blocks hook into it. *Ib.* 1001 Seine purse-ring. . . . Made of brass, with roller, to prevent chafing of purse-line. **1889** K. MUNROE *Dorymates* 40 Through these [rings] ran a second stout line, known as the 'purse rope.' **1890** *Cent.* 4860/1 *Purse-ring,* a metal ring attached to the bridle-rope on the foot of a purse-seine, for the pursing-line to run through.

***Purse,** *v.* +*tr.* To draw the mouth of (a purse seine) together. — **1880** *Harper's Mag.* Sept. 510/1 The two ends are brought together, and the net pursed up. **1889** MUNROE *Dorymates* 40 Hauling on this rope and 'pursing' the seine is the hardest part of the entire job.

***Purser.** A ship's officer who keeps the accounts. — **1643** *Suffolk Deeds* I. 51 He received a letter from Edward Bennett the purser of the Marye Rose. **1711** *Boston News-Letter* 19 Nov. 1/2 Capt. Paston, Mr. Hyde the Chaplain, Purser and several other Officers, in all upwards of 90 were all drown'd. **1794** *Ann. 3d Congress* 1426 There shall be employed, in each of the said ships, . . . one sailing-master, one purser, . . . and eight midshipmen. **1840** *Niles' Nat. Reg.* 21 March 44/3 Mr. Williams . . . reported the bill to regulate the pay and emoluments of pursers in the navy. **1866** 'MARK TWAIN' *Lett. Sandwich Islands* 15 Hite, the Purser, served under General Sherman.

+**Purse seine.** A seine that may be drawn into the form of a bag. Also attrib.

1870 *Amer. Naturalist* IV. 515 Purse-seines are used to the best advantage in capturing [mackerel]. **1880** *Harper's Mag.* Aug. 351/1 The great purse seines of the fleet take everything . . . and tend toward rapid extinction of the fish. **1884** *Nat. Museum Bull.* No. 27, 697 Purse-seine boat. . . . This model represents the class of boats exclusively used in the mackerel purse-seine fisheries of New England. *Ib.* 1000 Purse-Seine

Block. Original design of Merchant's patent, 1882. **1907** *Daily News* (London) 9 Sept. 7 The United States Government waives the use of purse seines by American fishermen during the term governed by the agreement. **1911** *Rep. Fisheries 1908* 312/1 [Mackerel] are caught in purse seines, pounds, weirs, gill nets, etc., and with hook and line.

Purse-seiner. (See quotation.) — **1890** *Cent.* 4860/1 *Purse-seiner*, a vessel employed in the menhaden or the mackerel purse-seine fishery.

Pursing. [f. PURSE *v.*] *attrib.* and *adj.* Designating things used in drawing together the mouth of a purse seine. {1883-} — **1884** *Nat. Museum Bul.* No. 27, 996 The pursing weight varies from 100 to 150 pounds. *Ib.* 1001 These rings are fitted on the foot of a mackerel-seine and the pursing line passes through them. **1890** *Cent.* 4860/2 *Pursing-block*, a block used in hauling in the pursing-line or bridle of a purse-seine.

***Purslane.** Any plant of the family Portulacaceae, esp. *Portulaca oleracea*.

1612 SMITH, etc. *Virginia* I. 12 Many hearbes in the spring time there are commonly dispersed throughout the woods, good for brothes, and sallets, as Violets, Purslin, Sorrell, &c. **1698** THOMAS *Pensilvania* 21 [They have] most sorts of Saladings, besides what grows naturally Wild in the Country, and that in great plenty also, as . . . Penny-Royal and Purslain. **1737** BRICKELL *N. Carolina* 18 The Sallads are . . . Cresses of several sorts, . . . and many more; French and English Sorrel, Purslain two sorts, viz. the Tame and the Wild. **1837** WILLIAMS *Florida* 30 [It] produces nothing but grass, sea cress and purslain. **1854** THOREAU *Walden* 67, I have made a satisfactory dinner . . . simply off a dish of purslane (*Portulaca oleracea*) which I gathered in my cornfield, boiled and salted. **1877** *Harper's Mag.* Jan. 287/1 We had only wished that we had some of her purslane to go with it. **1902** HARBEN *A. Daniel* 1 The polished ploughshare cut into the mellow soil and sped onward, . . . burying the tenacious crab-grass and succulent purslane.

+Purslane speedwell. An annual herb (*Veronica peregrina*) of North America. — **1817-8** EATON *Botany* (1822) 508 *Veronica peregrina*, purslane-speedwell. **1847** DARLINGTON *Weeds & Plants* 227 Foreign Veronica. Purslane Speedwell. Neckweed. **1898** CREEVEY *Flowers of Field* 250 Neckweed. Purslane Speedwell. . . . A common weed throughout the United States.

Puseyite. (See quotation.) {1838-} — **1864** NICHOLS *Amer. Life* I. 371 The Episcopal Church . . . is divided into High Churchmen, or Puseyites, Moderate Churchmen, and Low Churchmen.

Push-, stem of *push* v. {1686-} Designating various vehicles and instruments operated by pushing. — **1834** *S. Lit. Mess.* I. 181/1 My poor Missis your aunt, has nothin to ride in, but a nasty, pitiful push phaton. **1855** *Amer. Inst. N.Y. Trans. 1854* 198 The ordinary hand hoe is not so good a tool for getting rid of weeds as the push or scuffle hoe. **1879** STOCKTON *Rudder Grange* xiii, Sunday afternoon, Captain Atkinson and Mrs. Atkinson and their little girl in a push-wagon, come here. **1881** *Congress. Rec.* 15 Feb. 1685/1 They want to have the stream made so that it can be navigable for . . . old-fashioned stern-wheel steamers, push-boats, or whatever they may desire. **1902** CLAPIN 324 *Push-buggy*, baby-carriage.

+Push ball. A game in which contesting sides try to push a massive ball to opposite goals; the ball used in this game. Also attrib. and fig. — **1896** MOE *Hist. Harvard* 62 The Faculty . . . stuck to the Freshmen—since the upper three classes were on the other side of the push-ball. [**1898** *Encycl. Sport* II. 168/2 Pushball was developed . . . into an organized game about the year 1895 by the Newtown Athletic Club near Boston.] **1905** *Brooklyn Eagle*, 20 Feb. 16 A feature of the relay meet will be the pushball game, between teams of 20 men each.

+Push button. A button which, when pressed, serves as a control for one device or another, as to close or open an electric circuit. — **1878** G. B. PRESCOTT *Speaking Telephone* 376 The push button or key used in short circuits serves to close the latter in a very simple manner. **1881** *Century Mag.* Dec. 319/1 The bellows . . . is closed by pressure of the finger on a push-button. **1889** *Scientific Amer.* LX. 313/2 The push buttons are located in the attendants' rooms and are operated at that point. **1897** F. C. MOORE *How to Build a Home* 59 It is well to have an electric bell to the servants' bedrooms . . . with a push-button near the head of the bed of the mistress. **1911** VANCE *Cynthia* 207 He stopped by the push-button for the annunciator in the main saloon.

+Push car. *Railroad.* **1.** A hand car. **2.** (See quot.) — **(1) 1884** NYE *Baled Hay* 225 A section-crew . . . riding down that mountain on a push-car. **(2) 1890** *Cent.* 4862/3 *Push-car*, . . . a car used at a ferry-slip to connect an engine with a train on a ferry-boat. (U.S.)

Pushcart. A cart pushed by hand. {1899} Also attrib. — **1898** *Imported Bridegroom* 229 He would seek refuge from identification in closer communion with the crockery on his push-cart. **1903** *N.Y. Times* 16 Aug., Three pushcart men, none of whom could speak a word of English, stood trembling before the magistrate. **1908** 'O. HENRY' *Options* 87 Then you turn . . . right, dodge a push-cart, . . . and hop, skip, and jump to a granite ledge.

+Pushing pole. =POLE *n.* 1 b. — **a1811** HENRY *Camp. Quebec* 195 The pushing-pole was of the same kind of materials [ash or birch], . . . and if iron could be had, was shod at the but-end.

***Pushpin.** A child's game played with pins. — **1832** KENNEDY *Swallow Barn* I. 37 Sometimes it [a boy's skullcap] is devoted to push-pin. **1843** 'CARLTON' I. 49 We . . . played away the intervals at checkers with white and red corns, and then tried push-pin and tee-totum. **1854** *S. Lit. Messenger* XX. 607/1 We had suffered . . . whippings for neglected lessons—the time . . . having been occupied in the other and more delightful operations of blackberry hunting, [and] push-pin.

+Pus(s)ley. Colloq. variant of PURSLANE. Often in phrase *meaner than pusley*. Also with defining term.

1833 A. GREENE *Life D. Duckworth* II. 71 All their writin is like pussly and witch-grass—you never can know where to find it. **1854** PAIGE *Dow's Sermons* IV. 14 (Th.), I flourish, professionally, like pussley in a deserted pig pasture. **1878** COOKE *Happy Dodd* 323 It's meaner'n pusley to keep you here, and be a livin' on your int'rest money. **1892** *Amer. Folk-Lore* V. 93 *Portulaca grandiflora*, French pusley. So. Vt. **1907** FREEMAN *By Light of Soul* 399 He treated her as mean as pusley.

+Pusstail. [*Puss* 'a cat' and *tail*.] (See quotation.) — **1890** *Cent.* 4863/2 *Pusstail*, a common grass of the genus *Setaria:* so called on account of the bristly cylindrical spikes. More often called *foxtail*.

Pussy. {1726-} *+attrib.* In the names of American plants. Also possessive. — **1892** *Amer. Folk-Lore* V. 98 *Antennaria plantaginifolia*, . . . pussy's toes. Worcester, Mass. **1915** ARMSTRONG & THORNBER *Western Wild Flowers* 124 The flower-clusters are like pink cushions, so the pretty little name of Pussy-paws is appropriate. *Ib.* Pussy-tails. *Stellariopsis santolinoides* (*Ivesia*). . . . The leaves of this odd little plant look like catkins.

+Pussy-footed, *adv.* Quietly, noiselessly. — **1893** *Scribner's Mag.* Nov. 653 Men who were beginning to walk pussy-footed and shy at shadows.

Pussy willow. Any willow with silky catkins, esp. the glaucous willow. Also attrib. and fig. {1893, *Wilts. dial.*} — **1869** FULLER *Flower Gatherers* 52 The aments . . . are covered with hairs so soft and silken that children often call them 'Pussy-Willows.' **1885** *Outing* Nov. 177/1 We must not forget those gladly-welcomed harbingers of spring, the pussy-willows. **1906** *N.Y. Ev. Post* 19 May 9 A fat pussy-willow is dangling in the March sun. **1917** McCUTCHEON *Green Fancy* 345 He knew what all Europe was saying about the pussy-willow attitude of the United States.

***Put,** *v.*

I. 1. *tr.* To convey (a person, etc.) across a river. {1893-}

a1649 WINTHROP *Hist.* 178 Cattle . . . which came late, and could not be put over the river, lived very well all the winter without any hay. **1805** LEWIS in *L. & Clark Exped.* II. (1904) 184, [I] sent Shannon down the opposite side to bring the canoe over to me and put me across the Missouri.

+2. *intr.* To extend. *Obs.* (Cf. senses 9 a, 11 c.)

1822 J. FOWLER *Journal* 102 Heare the mountain Puts a Cross the Plain to the River Delmort about 6 miles to our right. **1853** McCONNEL *Western Char.* 137 Upon some point of timber which puts a mile or two within the plain . . . the 'squatter' cleaves out, and renders habitable, a home for himself.

***3.** To start, set out, make off. *colloq.* (Cf. senses 8, 9 b, 13.)

'Obs. exc. *U.S. colloq.'* (*O.E.D.*).

1839 MARRYAT *Diary in Amer.* II. 231 Clear out, quit, and put—all mean 'be off.' 'Captain, now, you *hush* or *put*.' **1845** SOL. SMITH *Theatr. Apprent.* 138, I'll quietly take old Copp [a horse] and put. **1865** TROWBRIDGE *Three Scouts* 351 He can raise a white rag on a stick, and put. **1887** HARRIS in *Century Mag.* Sept. 718/1 He humped up his arm this away, an' the gal tuck it, an' off they put.

II. In combination with adverbs.

‖**4.** *To put along*, to linger about, to tarry.

1775 *Essex Inst. Coll.* XIII. 163 If you cannot find a comfortable Retirement, I would have you put along here & take up for a few days at Folsoms.

***5.** *To put back*, +to demote or turn back (a pupil).

1887 PERRY *Flock of Girls* 78, I don't want to lose anything, and have to be put back when school begins.

***6.** *To put down.* **+a.** To cure or preserve (meat, etc.) for future use. Also *vbl. n.* (Cf. sense 11 b.)

1843 *Knickerb.* XXI. 436 Daniel Gilbert's property . . . *cut up* very handsomely, (to borrow the common figure upon such occasions, derived from the putting down of pork for the winter). **1881** JEWETT *Country By-Ways* 40 He's put down a kag of excellent beef. **1889** COOKE *Steadfast* 229 Who'll put down my pork and beef as Almiry did?

+b. To build or construct by laying down.

1887 *Courier-Journal* 2 Feb. 3/6 For furnishing the material and putting down new footway crossings in the Eastern and Western districts of the city.

c. To bore or sink (a well). {1875-}

1890 *Stock Grower & Farmer* 8 Feb. 6/2 None of the flock owners seem inclined to put down wells. **1906** *Indian Laws & Tr.* III. 239 The sum of five thousand dollars . . . [is] appropriated . . . to enable the Secretary of the Interior to put down an artesian well.

***7.** *To put in.* **+a.** Of a stream: To come or flow in.

1809 CUMING *Western Tour* 97 The creek . . . puts in from the Virginia side. **1816** U. BROWN *Journal* II. 144 The falls of Licking directly putting in on the West side of said River. **1873** BEADLE *Undevel. West* 737 On a stream known as Quaking Asp River, putting in on the north side of the Missouri in latitude 48½ degrees; . . . we were overtaken by a terrific snow-storm. **1903** A. ADAMS *Log of Cowboy* 347 The trail on leaving the river led up Many Berries, one of the tributaries of the Yellowstone putting in from the north side.

b. To intervene or interfere. {1614–*a*1713}

1845 SIMMS *Wigwam & Cabin* 1 Ser. 43, I thought how soon . . . I might see without being able to put in, the long yellow hair of Betsey and the babies twirling on the thumbs of some painted devil of the tribe. **1855** *Harper's Mag.* Oct. 602/1 The unfortunate victim hollowed out, 'Oh, Moses, if you have any love for your brother, *put in*, and divide this fight!' **1901** HARBEN *Westerfelt* 290 You wus tellin' me . . . 'at the lan' an' house wus in yore name an' her'n, an' 'at I had no right to put in.

+c. To deliver (logs) at a mill or landing.

1902 WHITE *Blazed Trail* 96 We contracted last fall . . . to put in five million feet of our timber. *Ib.* 99 Besides you still own the million and a half which, if you do not care to put them in yourself, you can sell for something in the skids. **1905** *Forestry Bureau Bul.* No. 61, 44.

***8.** *To put off*, +to depart, make off, leave. *colloq.* (Cf. senses 3, 9 b, 14.)

1803 C. PETTIGREW *MS. Let. to E. P.* (Univ. N.C. MS.), [His impudence] made me threaten him, on which he put off. *c*1845 [see HOLLOW *n.* 1]. **1858** *Nat. Intelligencer* 22 July (B.), Over fifteen thousand persons have deserted their homes in California, and put off by every means of conveyance for Fraser's river.

***9.** *To put out.* **+a.** To stretch away or extend. (Cf. sense 2.)

1755 *N.J. Archives* XIX. 532 To be sold . . . A Plantation . . . about three Quarters of a Mile from a good Landing that puts out of said River. **1840** HOFFMAN *Greyslaer* I. 116 A ledge of bald rock to the left yonder . . . puts out from the ridge. **1878** BEADLE *Western Wilds* 311 Commenced the ascent of the Buckskin, a low range of partially-wooded hills, putting out across the plateau nearly to the Colorado.

+b. To depart, go away, make off. (Cf. senses 3, 8, 14.)

1835 *Niles' Reg.* XLVIII. 436 Apprehending judge Lynch's law, he put out in a hurry. **1853** 'P. PAXTON' *Yankee in Texas* 39 Joe . . . ordered the bully to hold his tongue or to 'put out'; and the bully put out for home, all alone, and very much put out indeed. **1885** *Century Mag.* Nov. 36/1 He sent home his animals and put out for Salt Lake. **1895** *Ib.* Sept. 674/2 The Old Man puts out for London.

+c. *Baseball.* To cause (a player) to be out. {1735–, of cricket} Cf. PUT-OUT *n.* 2.

1845 in *Appletons' Ann. Cycl.* XXV. 77/2 A runner can not be put out in making one base, when a balk is made by the pitcher. **1868** CHADWICK *Base Ball* 44 The fielder who touches him with the ball has the credit of putting him out. **1880** N. BROOKS *Fairport Nine* 180 High was caught between the bases and so put out. **1891** N. CRANE *Baseball* 79 *Assist*, the credit given by the scorer to a fielder who handles the ball in assisting to put out a player. **1912** C. MATHEWSON *Pitching* 107 Snodgrass was put out trying to get to third base.

+d. To cause or permit (a horse) to show his best speed.

1868 G. A. MCCALL *Lett. from Frontiers* 345 After a mile's gentle trot, I '*put him out*,' and he went as steadily as ever.

+e. To spend or hand out (money). (Cf. sense 11 d.)

1884 *Boston Jrnl.* 13 Sept., 'McKinley would be elected,' says an Ohio correspondent, 'if the opposing candidate did not have a rich father-in-law, who will put out money freely.'

10. *To put through*, to carry, push on, get successfully through with (an undertaking). {1891–, *dial.*}

'Chiefly *U.S.*' (*O.E.D.*).

1861 *Ill. Agric. Soc. Trans.* IV. 115 The reply was . . . indicative of the strength of will with which he 'puts through' whatever he undertakes. **1875** HOLLAND *Sevenoaks* 143 Put it through, Sarah; you have the floor, and I'm ready to take it all now. **1889** 'MARK TWAIN' *Conn. Yankee* 272 The holy community was in good shape to make a night of it; so we . . . put it through on that line.

***11.** *To put up.* **+a.** *New Eng.* To send a note to be read from the pulpit. *Obs.*

1685 SEWALL *Diary* I. 68, I put up a Note to pray for the Indians. **1724** *Ib.* III. 341 In the Afternoon I put up this Note at the Old South, 'Samuel Sewall desires prayers [etc.].'

b. To can or preserve (foodstuffs); to save (hay.) Also *vbl. n.* (Cf. sense 6 a.) {of liquor, 1651–}

1837 PECK *Gaz. Illinois* 147 Alton contained . . . four large slaughtering and packing houses for putting up pork. **1851** SPRINGER *Forest Life* 54 Among other preliminaries which anticipate the winter operations of lumbermen is the 'putting up' of large quantities of meadow hay. **1881** *Rep. Indian Affairs* 155 Salt and dried salmon are still put up, but in diminishing quantities. **1896** *Voice* 13 Feb. 3/3 The same cannery could put up our fruits & vegetables in their season.

+c. To extend or lead up *from.* (Cf. sense 2.)

1847 HOWE *Hist. Coll. Ohio* 539 They came to a deep ravine, putting up from the river in a southerly direction.

+d. To stake, deposit, provide (money). Also absol. (Cf. sense 9 e.)

1865 'MARK TWAIN' *Sk., New & Old* 34 The feller took the box, and put up his forty dollars. **1884** *Boston Jrnl.* 16 Aug., A wealthy Bostonian yesterday wagered $1000, and put up the money, that Mr. Blaine's majority in New York State would exceed 40,000. **1898** *Kansas City Star* 18 Dec. 3/1 They must put up cash enough. **1902** WILSON *Spenders* 176 Young Burman of the Chicago Board of Trade had been pinched in his own wheat corner for four millions—'put up' by his admiring father. **1911** LINCOLN *Cap'n Warren's Wards* 337 You're putting up for it, and I ought to be much obliged.

+e. To build, fashion, or construct.

1866 *Ill. Agric. Soc. Trans.* VI. 79 These plows are put up in a substantial manner. **1912** NICHOLSON *Hoosier Chron.* 219 Sylvia was as well 'put up' as any of the girls.

+f. To put in jail. *colloq.*[2]

1872 BRACE *Dangerous Classes N.Y.* 289 He kept himself drunk for three weeks, and smashed a number of policemen, and was 'put up.' **1901** HARBEN *Westerfelt* 289 'Ef I was you-uns,' she called back from the door, "I'd have 'er put up!' **1902** — *A. Daniel* 71 Jake Lynan . . . stold Thad Wilson's stump-suckin' hoss an' was ketched an' put up.

+g. To size up, estimate, 'figure out.'

1880 'MARK TWAIN' *Tramp Abroad* 192 Say, didn't I put you up right? . . . I spotted you for my kind the minute I heard your clack. **1894** — *P. Wilson* xv, I'm bound to say I put it up the way Tom does. **1895** *Century Mag.* Sept. 674/2 'What is to be will be.' That's about the way I put it up.

III. In combination with prepositions.

‖**12.** *To put after*, to keep company with, court, woo. *colloq.*

1838 *Lexington Observer* 2 June, I have been putting after that gal considerable time.

***13.** *To put for*, +to make for; to set out in desperate haste towards. *colloq.* (Cf. sense 3.)

1845 HOOPER *Daddy Biggs' Scrape* 198 Both on us put for the bank quick. **1854** M. J. HOLMES *Tempest & Sunshine* 24 Of course they've put for the river. **1863** NORTON *Army Lett.* 183 Colonel Chamberlain mounted and put for the brigade post-haste. **1903** *N.Y. Times* 24 Sept. 7 He never spied a little fellow in dresses but what, with pointed beak and flapping wings, he put for him.

+14. *To put from*, of a stream, to make off or flow *from.* (Cf. senses 7 a, 15.)

1773 FITHIAN *Journal* I. 56 From his house we see the Potowmack, and a fine River putting from it.

15. *To put into* {1604–}, +of a stream or ravine, to flow, empty, or lead into. (Cf. sense 2.)

1807 GASS *Journal* 172 A small river . . . puts into a large bay on the south side of the Columbia. **1834** PECK *Gaz. Illinois* 19 Rock River . . . puts into the Mississippi. **1847** HOWE *Hist. Coll. Ohio* 366 In many of the little ravines putting into the valleys, the scenery is in all the wildness of untamed nature. **1903** A. ADAMS *Log of Cowboy* 362 Our pilot led us up the divide . . . , weaving in and out around the heads of creeks putting into either river.

IV. In various colloq. phrases.

16. *To put it to* (someone), or variants of this {1747–}: +To get the better of (someone); to chastise or berate; to beat.

1835 LONGSTREET *Ga. Scenes* 29 Dod drot my soul if he's put it to daddy as bad as he thinks he has. **1840** *Picayune* 12 Aug. 2/1 The next time we find ourselves served such a trick we will give the editor 'goss.' We will 'put it to him low.' **1845** KIRKLAND *Western Clearings* 211 The wolf grinned, but Jake he never stopped to grin, but put it on to him as cool as a cowcumber, till he got so he could see his brains, and then he was satisfied. **1875** STOWE *We & Neighbors* 100 You ought to hear me expound the commandments, and put it into them about stealing and lying.

+17. *To put the joke* (or *laugh*) (*up*)*on* (someone), to get off a joke (or laugh) at the expense of (someone).

1853 HAWTHORNE *Works* (1883) IV. 289 Cadmus suspected . . . that he was putting a joke upon him. **1902** LORIMER *Lett. Merchant* 271 It was a month after that before Bud could go down Main Street without some man . . . reaching out and fetching him a clip on the ear for having come back and put the laugh on him.

‖**18.** *To be hard put up for*, to be hard put to it for.

1879 TOURGEE *Fool's Errand* 29 [They] was mighty hard put up for excuses.

+19. *To put up or shut up*, to make good, produce proof, etc., or cease talking; to come out openly or stop objecting. *colloq.*

1887 *Courier-Journal* 26 Jan. 1/7 Put Up or Shut Up. **1889** 'MARK TWAIN' *Conn. Yankee* 512 This was a plain case of 'put up or shut up.' **1894** FORD *P. Stirling* 301 Now, put up or shut up. No more beating about the bush. **1902** HARBEN *A. Daniel* 308 Me'n Alan will pull fer you like a yoke o' steers. . . . What you say? Put up or shet up.

+20. *To put* (someone) *on to* (something), to acquaint (someone) with little known facts about (something); *to put* (someone) *on*, to inform (someone).

1895 *N.Y. Dramatic News* 12 Oct. 5/3 Mr. Jack is always a newspaper man's friend, and only too pleased to put one on to 'a good thing' in the shape of news. **1899** QUINN *Penna. Stories* 46 Field had put him on to the game. **1904** W. H. SMITH *Promoters* 308, I'll put you on, and tell you all about it when you get here.

+**21.** In miscellaneous phrases.

To put the law on (someone), to bring legal action against (someone); *to put oneself into* (something), to devote oneself wholeheartedly to (something); *to put the run on* (someone), to force (someone) to run away.

1888 STOCKTON *Dusantes* 104 If he dares to open a package of mine, I'll put the law on him! **1889** *Century Mag.* March 778/2 She had put herself into it for all she was worth. **1914** 'BOWER' *Flying U Ranch* 188, I wouldn't be hopeful of putting the run on this Dunk person by telling him ghost stories.

+**Put-in.** Turn or place to speak; affair; intrusion. *colloq.* — **1853** 'MARK TWAIN' *Hannibal Jrnl.* 25 May, Never speak when it's not your 'put-in.' **1883** EGGLESTON *Hoosier School-Boy* 28 It's your put-in now, Riley. **1891** GARLAND *Main-travelled Roads* (1922) 53 Oh, you shet up, who wants your put-in? **1902** HARBEN *A. Daniel* 301 This ain't no put-in o' mine, gracious knows!

+**Put-out,** *n.*

1. An annoyance or inconvenience.

1833 NEAL *Down-Easters* I. 83, I shouldn't think twould be any put-out to you to take somebody else. **1843** STEPHENS *High Life N.Y.* II. 32 Don't be oneasy about the trouble, it won't be no put out to Captin Doolittle.

2. *Baseball.* The act of retiring or putting out a player. Cf. PUT *v.* 9 c.

1887 *Courier-Journal* 26 May 2/6 McClellan . . . went to third on a put-out and scored on Pinckney's sacrifice hit. **1910** *Spalding's Base Ball Guide* 382 An assist should be given to each player who handles . . . the ball from the time it leaves the bat until it reaches the player who makes the put-out. **1912** MATHEWSON *Pitching* 189 Merkle was under the shower bath when the alleged put-out was made.

***Putter,** *n.* *Putter-out*, one who puts an animal out to graze (*Obs.*); *putter-up*, one who cures or puts up pork. (Cf. PUT *v.* 11 b.) — **1639** *Dedham Rec.* III. 65 The sayd owner or putter out of ye said Swyne . . . shall paye all Dammages that shall happen by the same. **1848** *Rep. Comm. Patents 1847* 527 The price of lard . . . tempts the putter up of pork to trim very close.

Putter, *v.* ['*Dial.* and *U.S.* var. of *potter* v.' (*O.E.D.*).] *intr.* To work in a desultory or lackadaisical manner; to waste time or energy on trifles. Often with *around.* {1823, *Suffolk dial.*}

1877 BARTLETT 487 *To potter round*, to busy one's self with trifles . . . '*to putter round*.' **1881** STODDARD *E. Hardery* 171, I jest love to putter 'round. **1893** S. HALE *Letters* 284 'Twas a sight to see the two old darkies clumsily puttering away with the mops and towels. **1904** CRISSEY *Tattlings* 333 He's entitled to putter around with his pet theory of legislation.

b. Hence *putterer*, *puttering* a., *putteringly* adv.

1887 *Harper's Mag.* Aug. 479/2 The great Goethe . . . might oftener be called the good Goethe in the worst sense of that epithet, so wanderingly, putteringly benevolent are some of his letters. **1895** S. M. H. GARDNER *Quaker Idyls* 85 He was a hard-workin' kind of a putterer. **1897** KIPLING *Captains Courageous* iii. 100 But it's a putterin' job all the same.

Putty. A doughlike paste or cement, usually compounded from whiting and linseed oil. {1706–} Also attrib. — **1798** I. ALLEN *Hist. Vermont* 270 Putty . . . even in its native state, equals in tenacity and induration the composite material of that article in your country [England]. **1838** *Mass. Agric. Survey 1st Rep.* 71 The bee moth is to be guarded against by making the crevices of the hive tight with putty or glue. **1866** *Rep. Indian Affairs* 244, I sent to Agent Stone some glass and nails and putty. **1907** *St. Nicholas* June 747/1 Honey-bees fill all the cracks in their home and smear the interior with propolis . . . in a manner similar to a painter's use of putty, paint and varnish. **1917** MATHEWSON *Second Base Sloan* 89 All they needed were points, a putty knife, and some glass!

+**Putty-blower.** A blowtube for shooting pellets of putty. (Cf. BEAN-, PEA-SHOOTER.) — **1861** NEWELL *Orpheus C. Kerr* I. 156 [The muskets] are inferior to the putty-blowers of our innocent childhood. **1878** HARTE *Drift from Two Shores* 160 The bootblack drew a tin putty-blower from his pocket, took unerring aim, and nailed in a single shot the minute-hand to the dial. **1897** *Outing* April 60/1, [I] thought of barn-yard cleaning in a wet-spring, and ejected the morsel as a pellet leaveth the putty-blower.

+**Putty head.** A soft-headed, stupid person. Also in appositive use. (Cf. LUNKHEAD, PUMPKIN HEAD 2.) — **1856** M. J. HOLMES *L. Rivers* 370 He got so engaged about the darned 'liquor law,' and the putty-heads that made it, that he'd no idee 'twas so late. **a1861** WINTHROP *Open Air* 148 We was about sick of putty-heads and sneaks that . . . didn't dare to make us stand round and bone in. **1864** TROWBRIDGE *Cudjo's Cave* 399 We must fight it through, or go back, like that putty-head Deslow. **1892** *Amer. Folk-Lore* V. 145 *Putty-head.*—A term of reproach. Soft head, stupid.

+**Puttyroot.** An American orchid (*Aplectrum hyemale*) producing a corm filled with a glutinous matter that may be used as a cement. — **1817–8** EATON *Botany* (1822) 250 *Corallorhiza hyemalis*, adam and eve, putty root. . . . A cement resembling putty may be made of the root. **1858** R. HOGG *Veg. Kingdom* 779 The tubers of *Aplectrum hyemale* are so viscid that they are called *Putty-root* in the United States, and are used for cementing broken earthenware.

***Pygmy,** *a.* (See PIGMY *a.*)

***Pyramid.** In the specific names of plants and trees.

1817–8 EATON *Botany* (1822) 282 *Frasera caroliniensis*, pyramid flower, columbo root. **1894** *Amer. Folk-Lore* VII. 92 *Solidago*, sp., pyramid golden-rod, N.Y. **1897** SUDWORTH *Arborescent Flora* 260 *Robinia pseudacacia pyramidalis*. . . . Pyramid Locust. **1915** ARMSTRONG & THORNBER *Western Wild Flowers* 228 Pyramid Bush. *Spiraea pyramidata*. . . . This grows in the mountains.

***Pyramidal,** *a.* In the names of, or with reference to, various trees the foliage of which grows somewhat in the form of a pyramid. {1796–} — **1879** *Scribner's Mo.* Nov. 38 And close by are arranged erect, pyramidal dark green, Irish Yews. **1892** APGAR *Trees Northern U.S.* 146 [Names for the] European White Birch . . . extensively cultivated in this country [include] . . . *laciniata* (cut-leaved), *fastigiata* (pyramidal). **1897** SUDWORTH *Arborescent Flora* 199 *Liriodendron tulipifera pyramidalis* Dippel. Pyramidal Tulip-tree.

***Pyrites.** Any one of various sulphides and arsenides of iron, cobalt, nickel, etc., esp. fool's gold.

a1817 DWIGHT *Travels* IV. 484 Copperas was extracted in large quantities from Pyrites in Vermont, New-Jersey and Tennessee. **1823** JAMES *Exped.* I. 64 The smell of sulphur is very perceptible along the bank of the river, occasioned doubtless by the decomposition of pyrites, in the exposed parts of the coal beds. **1877** HARTE *Story of Mine* (1896) 127, 'I dipped a little west today,' Ruth went on, without heeding the brotherly remonstrance, 'and struck quartz and pyrites.' **1894** *Harper's Mag.* Feb. 410/2 Pyrites, or 'fool's gold,' is an ore frequent in America.

transf. **1889** MUNROE *Golden Days* 270, I mistrust he's only pyrites after all.

+**Pyrography.** [Gr. *pyro* 'fire' and *graphy*. Presumably a new coinage.] (See quotations.) {1891–} — **1876** KNIGHT 1837/2 *Pyrography*, a mode of printing by a system of heated metallic cylinders, which burn into the wood any design required. **1895** *Conv. Amer. Instructors of Deaf Proc.* 366 The 'Legend of Sleepy Hollow,' done in pyrography on the wood-work of a fire-place. **1900** *Boston Ev. Globe* 18 Dec. 3/6 Pyrography is the art of making striking pictures upon calf and sheepskin with the red-hot point of a platinum needle. **1901** *Boston Globe* 6 Jan. 25/5 'Poker drawing' has become a fashionable fad and as it must have a newer and more elegant name it is now known as 'pyrography.'

***Pyrola.** A genus of perennial herbs of the family Pyrolaceae, or a species or a plant of this genus. Also with defining term. — **1672** JOSSELYN *New Eng. Rarities* 67 Pirola, or Winter Green, that kind which grows with us in England is common in New-England, but there is another plant which I judge to be a kind of Pirola, and proper to this Country. **1785** MARSHALL *Amer. Grove* 117 *Pyrola umbellata.* Umbellated Pyrola. . . . The roots are said to give ease in the tooth ach. **1818** *Mass. H. S. Coll.* 2 Ser. VIII. 170 In July the lover of plants is gratified with . . . two species of pyrala, the small geranium, [and] several species of hypericum or John's wort. **a1862** THOREAU *Maine Woods* 207 Of smaller plants, there were . . . *Pyrola secunda*, apparently the commonest Pyrola in those woods, now out of bloom, *Pyrola elliptica*, and *Chiogenes hispidula.* **1903** *Yale Lit. Mag.* Oct. 18 Tom brought in a fragrant armload of pyrolas.

+**Pyxie.** [*Pyxi*danthera.] (See quot. 1882.) Also *pyxie moss.* — **1882** *Harper's Mag.* June 65 The delicate pyxie (*Pyxidanthera barbulata*), a little prostrate trailing evergreen, forming dense tufts or masses, . . . is strictly a pine-barren plant, and its locality is confined to New Jersey and the Carolinas. **1892** *Amer. Folk-Lore* V. 100 *Pyxidanthera barbulata*, pyxie moss. N.J.

Q

+**Qua-bird.** =NIGHT HERON. — **1796** MORSE *Univ. Geog.* I. 212 Quaw-Bird or Frog Catcher. *Ardea Clamator.* **1813** WILSON *Ornithology* VII. 105 The food of the Night Heron, or Qua-bird, is chiefly composed of small fish, which it takes by night. **1835** AUDUBON *Ornith. Biog.* III. 275 [In S.C. the night heron] is named 'the Indian Pullet,' . . . and in our Eastern States its usual appellation is 'Qua Bird.' **1917** *Birds of Amer.* I. 194 Black-crowned Night Heron. *Nycticorax nycticorax nævius.* . . . [Also called] American Night Heron; Qua-bird; Quawk.

Quack.[1] *attrib.* passing into *adj.* Of or pertaining to any ignorant but pretentious practice. {1653–} See also QUACK DOCTOR. — **1721** *New-Eng. Courant* 7 Aug. 1/2 [They] very lavishly bestow all the fulsome common Place of *Quack Advertisements.* **1804** FESSENDEN *Terrible Tractoration* 154 Dr. B. has absolutely himself become the proprietor of a quack medicine. **1865** *Atlantic Mo.* April 403/2 Upon the frowning front of a cliff, . . . some Vandal has daubed the advertisement of a quack nostrum. **1876** 'MARK TWAIN' *Tom Sawyer* xii. 109 She calculated his capacity as she would a jug's, and pilled him up every day with quack cure-alls.

+**Quack.**[2] Short for QUACK GRASS. — **1839** BUEL *Farmer's Companion* 144 To clean the ground of the roots of foul plants, as dock, quack, etc. **1868** *Rep. Comm. Agric. 1867* 347 Quack produces better hay than timothy for cattle. **1909** *N.Y. Ev. Post* (s.-w. ed.) 11 March 5 In conquering the quack he did the one thing that could have enabled him to get a crop from that unfertilized soil.

Quack doctor. An ignorant pretender to the skill and qualifications of a doctor. {1751–} — **1775** FITHIAN *Journal* II. 66, I brought it out to try a ragged, blustering, Quack Doctor, who was boasting of his ability & success in drawing teeth. **1813** in Kittredge *Old Farmer* (1904) 100 From quack lawyers, quack doctors, quack preachers, mad dogs and yellow fever, good Lord, deliver us! **1865** BROWNE *A. Ward; His Travels* 68 The num'ris quack doctors she called in didn't help her any.

+**Quack grass.** [Eng. *quick-grass*, Du. *kweekgras*, Da. *kvækgræs*.] The European couch grass (*Agropyron repens*), naturalized throughout the United States. — **1817–8** EATON *Botany* (1822) 494 *Triticum repens*, wheat-grass, couch-grass, quack-grass. . . . Very troublesome in fertile soil, and useful in barren sand. **1839** BUEL *Farmer's Companion* 151 One of our neighbors has been enabled completely to eradicate quack-grass in his Indian corn. **1884** VASEY *Agric. Grasses* 108 Quack grass. . . . There has been a good deal of discussion relative to this grass, some pronouncing it one of the vilest of weeds.

* **Quadrant.** An instrument used for measuring altitudes or for making other angular measurements, variously mounted for navigation, surveying, etc. Often with name of an inventor or manufacturer.

1678 *New Castle Court Rec.* 351, 1 quadrant. **1710** *N.C. Col. Rec.* I. 742 Then we proceeded again to take the latitude at the same place as yesterday having fixed the quadrant very firm. **1737** *Harvard Rec.* II. 673 Voted. . . . That Mr. Prince's Account of Expences (for Two quadrants of Altitude & Journeys to Boston for them) . . . be allowed. **1799** in H. M. Brooks *Gleanings* IV. 43, 1 best brass Sextant, latest improvement; Hadley's Quadrants, Davis' do. **1833** *Niles' Reg.* XLIV. 1/1 The fog is so thick, and the water so much disturbed, that neither the quadrant nor the lead-line renders accustomed service. **1884** *Nat. Museum Bul.* No. 27, 728 Quadrant. . . . Used for obtaining altitudes of the sun, moon, or stars, from which the position of a vessel can be determined when at sea.

Quadrille.[1] A once-fashionable card game played by four people with a deck of forty cards. *Obs.* {1726–} — **1757** in Singleton *Social N.Y.* 172 She had no notion at her age of sacrificing all the dear pleasures of routs, hops, quadrille for a philosophical husband. **1773** [see LOO 1]. **1781** PETERS *Hist. Conn.* 325 They are not permitted to read plays; cannot converse about whist, quadrille, or opera. **1790** *Holyoke Diaries* 123 Playd Quadrille.

Quadrille.[2] A square dance of five figures, each a complete dance in itself, performed by four couples. {1773–} See COTILLION, note.

[**1832** TROLLOPE *Domestic Manners* I. 215 They call their dances cotillions instead of quadrilles, and the figures are called from the orchestra in English.] **1835** [see FASHIONIST]. **1841** *Knickerb.* XVII. 277 One of the party played the violin . . . , to the extent of two country dances and half a quadrille. **1860** in Christy *Ethiopian Joke Book No. 3* 70, I always knew you could dance *quadrilles.* **1903** FOX *Little Shepherd* xviii, The dance was a quadrille, and the figure was 'Grand right and left.' **1914** 'BOWER' *Flying U Ranch* 181 The Happy Family knew those ways as they knew the most complicated figures of the quadrilles they danced so lightfootedly with the girls of the Bear Paw country.

attrib. **1839** *Chicago American* 2 Nov., Mrs. Ingersoll . . . employs the winter here in giving dancing lessons and quadrille and cotillion parties. **1844** in H. M. Brooks *Gleanings* IV. 152 The enchanting music of the Salem Quadrille Band.

Quadroon. Also **quadron.** (See also QUARTERO(O)N and QUATROON.)

1. A person born of a white person and a mulatto; a person of one quarter Negro blood. {1796–}

1832 FERRALL *Ramble* 192 The Louisianians are prohibited by law from marrying with quadroons, although this *caste* is free. **1846** CHILD *Fact & Fiction* 62 The edicts of society had built up a wall of separation between her and them; for she was a quadroon. **1863** DICEY *6 Mos. Federal States* I. 78 For every quadroon you meet, you see two or three mulattoes. **1899** CHESNUTT *Wife of His Youth* 160 A pretty quadroon whispered to her neighbor;—'I don't b'liebe she's natch'ly ez white ez dat.'

+**2.** A child of a Spaniard and a mestizo.

1833 NEAL *Down-Easters* I. 194 Her grand-father was a Spaniard; her grand-mother a native Creek; she is a quadroon, therefore.

3. *attrib.* passing into *adj.* **a.** In sense 1, designating persons who are, or appear to be, quadroons.

1837 MARTINEAU *Society* II. 323 A New Hampshire gentleman . . . followed another custom there [in La.]; taking a Quadroon wife. **1852** STOWE *Uncle Tom* i, A small quadroon boy . . . entered the room. **1852** *Knickerb.* XL. 201, I had no Creole family who took an interest in me, and as a consequence was left to the remaining alternative of a quadroon-nurse and physician. **1895** G. KING *New Orleans* 348 Many of the quadroon belles, however, attained honourable marriage, and, removing to France, obtained full social recognition for themselves and their children.

b. Designating groups, places, etc., composed of or inhabited by quadroons.

1856 OLMSTED *Slave States* 597 A gentleman, of New England education, gave me the following account of his acquaintance with the quadroon society. **1880** CABLE *Grandissimes* 71 There advanced into the light of his hanging lamp . . . a woman of the quadroon caste, of superb stature and poise. **1883** *Century Mag.* July 421/1 One could take a skiff . . . and row . . . throughout the rear suburbs, now the Quadroon quarter.

+**c.** In sense 2 with *Choctaw.*

1891 O'BEIRNE *Leaders Ind. Territory* 68/1 Mr. Lowery's father was a white man and his mother a quadroon Choctaw.

+**Quadroon (fancy) ball.** A ball attended by part-Negro women and white men. — **1880** CABLE *Grandissimes* 19, I saw the same old man, at a quadroon ball a few years ago. **1888** DALY *Lottery of Love* 18, A brace of my men . . . were jugged for kicking up a rumpus at a quadroon fancy-ball. **1895** G. KING *New Orleans* 343 The celebrated quadroon balls . . . divided the nights of the week with the balls given to the white ladies.

***Quagmire.** A wet, boggy place. — **1608** SMITH *Works* (1910) 15 Minding them more than my steps, I stept fast into the quagmire, and also the Indian in drawing me forth. **1713** *N.C. Col. Rec.* II. 45 About 50 or 60 men of them got together between Machepungo River and Roanoke Island which is . . . all in a manner lakes, quagmires, and cane swamps. **1821** WEEMS *Letters* III. 319 Within 5 miles of this village I was completely ingulphed in a Quagmire. **1831** PECK *Guide* 94 What is known in New England by the name of *swamp* can scarcely be found in Illinois, and a quagmire is of still rarer occurrence. **1887** CUSTER *Tenting on Plains* 381 Coming from Michigan, where there is a liberal dispensation of swamp and quagmire, . . . very naturally I guided my horse around any lands that had even a depression.

+**Quahog, Quahaug.** Also **quohaug,** etc. [Algonquian. Cf. Pequot *p'quaughhaug* 'hard clam.'] See also COHOG, POQUAW.

1. The hard or round clam, *Venus mercenaria.*

1799 BENTLEY *Diary* II. 312 They are not the long large Clams of our Beaches, nor the Quahoag, but really a larger species of the Hog or Common Clam, differing from the long or large Clams. **1826** ed. N. Morton *New England's Mem.* App. 388 The characters of the shell, here described, and which is denominated a *clam-shell*, are applicable to the *quahawg.* **1845** *Knickerb.* XXV. 88 With bass on one day, halibut the next, tautog on the third, etc., varied now and then with clams, quahogs and other shell-fish, the inhabitants generally appeared contented with their fare. **1903** *N.Y. Ev. Telegram* 20 Oct. 4 Shall we eventually get down to nothing but quohaugs and chowder? **1911** *Rep. Fisheries 1908* 314/1 Quahaug

(*Venus mercenaria*).—An edible clam, found very abundantly from Cape Cod to Florida.

2. Attrib. and comb. with *bed, clam, clamming*, etc.

1815 *Mass. H. S. Coll.* 2 Ser. IV. 289 The quahaug clam is common, and the oyster is taken in two or more places. **1870** *Amer. Naturalist* III. 354 Fragments of Quahaug valves . . . are quite abundant. **1883** Goode *Fishery Industries U.S.* 45 The Clam and Quahaug Fishery. **1894** *Youth's Companion* 22 Nov. 562/3 The bulk of the eeling and quahaug clamming as well as the lobstering was done in its vicinity. **1920** Lincoln *Mr. Pratt* 133 You've cleaned out somebody's private quahaug bed.

*** Quail.**

+1. Any of several small game birds of the family Odontophoridae. Also collective.

In the northern and eastern states, the bobwhite or American partridge of the genus *Colinus*, esp. *C. virginianus*, is the commonest quail; in the West and Southwest, the most common species are the California quail of the Pacific coast, the Massena quail of Arizona, the plumed partridge or mountain quail of the Pacific coast, the blue quail of the Southwest, etc. (qq. v.). Besides these latter, the bobwhite has been introduced into the Rocky Mountain and Pacific coast areas. (Cf. Partridge 1.)

1637 Morton *New Canaan* 70 There are quailes also, but bigger than the quailes in England. **1701** Wolley *Journal N.Y.* 40 They have great store of wild-fowl, as Turkys, Heath-hens, Quails, Partridges, Pigeons. **1782** Crèvecœur *Letters* 29, I draw a great fund of pleasure from the quails which inhabit my farm [in Carlisle, Penna.]. **1803** *Lit. Mag.* (Phila.) Nov. 154 For several days past this city [New Haven] has been the resort of a very extraordinary number of quails. **1812** Wilson *Ornithology* VI. 26 The Quail, as it is called in New England, or the Partridge, as in Pennsylvania, is nine inches long, and fourteen inches in extent. **1836** Edward *Hist. Texas* 75 Among the birds fit for food, are the wild turky, . . . the partridge and the quail. **1846** Farnham *Prairie Land* 195 The quail dodges about farm-yards, grain-fields, and woodland [in Ill.]. **1849** *31st Congress 1 Sess.* Sen. Ex. Doc. No. 64, 183 Quails or partridges are found at all places upon our road [along the Canadian R.]. **1869** J. R. Browne *Adv. Apache Country* 76 Quail were very abundant as we drew near our first camping-place on the Gila. **1872** McClellan *Golden State* 211 There is abundance of trout in the adjacent streams, and of bear, deer, and quail in the hills. **1894** *Scribner's Mag.* May 603/2 The Rio Grande is at nearly all seasons full of . . . quails. **1917** *Birds of Amer.* II. 1 With few exceptions our Quails welcome the extension of agriculture, and the added food supply in farmed areas results in an increase of their numbers.

+b. With specifying terms.

See also Blue quail, California quail, etc., and cf. Marsh quail, Sea quail.

1849 *31st Congress 1 Sess.* Sen. Ex. Doc. No. 64, 52 Four different kinds of quails were killed: the common quail; the tufted quail, slightly ash-colored; the California quail, with a long plume from the top of its head; and another variety. **1874** Coues *Birds N.W.* 434 Plumed Quail.—*Lophortyx Gambeli*. . . . Gambel's Quail may be looked for in every kind of cover. **1917** *Birds of Amer.* II. 10 Mearns's Quail. *Cyrtonyx Montezumæ mearnsi*. . . . [Also called] Montezuma Quail; . . . Fool Quail; Fool Hen; Black Quail.

+2. A girl: (see esp. quot. 1901). *College slang.*

1859 *Yale Lit. Mag.* XXIV. 291 (Th.), The freshman heareth of 'Quails,' he dresseth himself in fine linen, he seeketh to flirt with ye 'quails,' but they know him not. **1901** *Dialect Notes* II. 146 *Quail*, a young lady student at co-educational institution. Wesleyan Univ. **1904** *Hartford Courant* 4 Oct. 1 Because she was hazed by the young women students at Wesleyan, one 'quail,' as the boys call them, who was a freshman here last year did not return to Wesleyan this fall. **1909** *N.Y. Ev. Post* 11 March (Th.), The 'quails' have been barred at Wesleyan—'quails' is the Middletown University's name for her 'co-eds.'

3. *attrib.* and *comb.* **a.** In sense 1 with *bagger, bagging, dog*, etc.

1807 Irving, etc. *Salmagundi* xv. 395 He was particularly adroit in making our quail-traps and fishing-rods. **1856** *Porter's Spirit of Times* 22 Nov. 193/1 It is not long since that we replied, to a query where good quail shooting can be had, within three hundred miles of our city: 'No where!' *Ib.* 27 Dec. 269/1 'Don' is as good a quail dog as man ever shot over. **1865** 'Mark Twain' *Sk., New & Old* 34 He got the frog out and prized his mouth open and took a teaspoon and filled him full of quail shot. **1879** *Harper's Mag.* Oct. 703/1 Advice [was] offered by a circle of quail-baggers and other by-standers. *Ib.* 703/2 A quail-bagging expedition was regarded as an event of considerable importance. **1897** *Outing* April 94/2 Ever since last quail-time I have been casting rather dubious glances at a certain old gun.

b. In the specific names of other birds.

1895 *Dept. Agric. Yrbk. 1894* 211 Among the birds [in southern Fla.] may be mentioned the white-crowned pigeon, Zenaida dove, quail doves [etc.]. **1917** *Birds of Amer.* II. 67 Cooper's Hawk. *Accipiter cooperi*. . . . [Also called] Quail Hawk. **1844** *Nat. Hist. N.Y., Zoology* II. 164 The Quail-Head. *Ammodramus Caudacutus*. . . . It is found only in salt marshes where it breeds. **1917** *Birds of Amer.* III. 26 Grasshopper Sparrow. *Ammodramus savannarum australis*. . . . [Also called] Quail Sparrow.

Quail track. +1. Scribbled handwriting resembling birds' tracks. *Obs.* +2. *Quail-track corn*, a variety of Indian corn. — (1) **1842** *Yale Lit. Mag.* VIII. 96, I can't always decipher *quail tracks*. **1855** Holbrook *Among Mail Bags* 404 The most skilful interpreters of the species of chirography known as 'quail tracks,' are often taxed to their utmost capacity. (2) **1855** *Mich. Agric. Soc. Trans.* VI. 495 One acre of quail track corn; planted on muck land.

Quake grass. 1. =Quaking grass. {1814 (*E.D.D.*)} +2. =Quack grass. — (1) **1821** Schoolcraft *Narr. Travels* 93 The margin of the lake [Huron] is skirted with bull-rushes, quake grass, (*briza canadensis*,) and other aquatic plants. (2) **1840** Dewey *Mass. Flowering Plants* 250 *Triticum repens*. Quake, or Quack, or Couch Grass. Sometimes from its resemblance to wheat, it is called Wheat-Grass.

+Quakenasp. =Quaking asp. — **1822** J. Fowler *Journal* 143 The timber on the mountains Heare is Pitch Pine Spruce Pine Hemlock and quakenasp the latter of which there are vast quantityes. **1905** *N.Y. Ev. Post* 2 Sept., I have seen quakenasp groves on the summer range, where you could walk miles and miles through these bluebells.

*** Quaker.**

1. A member of the Society of Friends, the religious body founded by George Fox. {1653-}

See also Hicksite, Shaking, Singing Quaker and cf. Friend, Orthodox *a.*

1655 in Neill *Virginia Carolorum* 155n., As for the 'Countess' I can tell you heavie news of her, for she is turned quaker, and preaches every day in a tubb. **1656** *Conn. Rec.* I. 283 No towne wthin this Jurisdiction shall entertaine any Quakers, Ranters, Adamites, or such like notorious heritiques. **1678** *Mass. H. S. Coll.* 4 Ser. V. 18 We whose names are hereunder written, called Quakers in your said jurisdiction, . . . cannot give maintenance to your present established preachers. **1732** Franklin *Poor Richard's Almanac 1733* 22 Quakers General Meetings are kept, at Philadelphia, March 18. **1756** Washington *Writings* I. 302, The Quakers . . . chose rather to be whipped to death than to bear arms. **1797** *Ann. 5th Congress* I. 664 This memorial . . . had been treated as coming from an Abolition Society—it was a memorial of the General Meeting of the people called Quakers. **1825** Neal *Bro. Jonathan* II. 166 Of all the puritans, . . . the quakers were beyond doubt perhaps the most ignorant, obstinate, and foolishly presumptuous. **1848** Burton *Waggeries* 74 An orthodox Quaker, with an undeniable and buttonless shad-bellied coat and drab continuations. **1900** *Congress. Rec.* 4 Jan. 646/2 Some of the writers of these letters are Quakers, members of the Society of Friends.

+2. *ellipt.* =Quaker gun.

1830 N. Ames *Mariner's Sk.* 7 Our six iron six-pounders and six *quakers*, (wooden guns,), were, like the millenial lion and lamb, lying down together in the hold. **1840** Dana *Two Years* xxvii. 291 The only other vessel in the port was a Russian government bark, . . . mounting eight guns, (four of which we found to be Quakers). **1844** *Cincinnati Misc.* I. 26 The ship was the Louisa, a letter of marque, mounting twelve guns, but appearing to have eighteen, six of them being what the sailors called Quakers; that is, very pacific ones, made of wood. **1862** *N.Y. Tribune* 13 Some of our soldiers cried when they found that 'quakers' were mounted on the Rebel breastworks.

+3. A citizen of Philadelphia or of the state of Pennsylvania. Also transf.

Cf. Quaker City.

1846 *Porter's Spirit of Times* 4 July 217/3 What strikes a 'plain coated Quaker,' on strolling through the business streets of Boston, is the extreme beauty and elegance of the buildings. **1919** *N.Y. Times* 12 Oct. x. 2/7 The versatile University of Pennsylvania football team . . . resorted to its second string for a rapid overhead attack which closed with . . . the score of 89 to 0. It was the largest score put up by the Quakers here in ten years.

4. *attrib.* **a.** Designating persons who are Quakers.

1676 *Boston Rec.* 193 Were drowned . . . a quaker maide, and a young man a factor. **1723** *New-Eng. Courant* 6–13 May 1/2 Who ever saw a Quaker-Slut? . . . 'Tis a Contradiction in Terms. **1771** Franklin *Autobiog.* 255, I met a young Quaker man whose countenance I lik'd. **1864** *Ladies' Repository* Sept. 538/1 But we were intending to give a sketch of our Quaker Poet [*i.e.*, Whittier]. **1864** Trowbridge *Cudjo's Cave* 472 This Quaker schoolmaster, turned fighting man, was the last person Augustus would have wished to see. **1872** *Atlantic Mo.* Jan. 18 There was a Quaker farmer near Philadelphia, . . . named William Bartram. **1885** *Century Mag.* Sept. 783 The struggle between the modest and heroic young Quaker woman and the town lasted for nearly two years.

b. Designating garments, styles, etc., worn by Quakers.

See also Quaker bonnet, cap, hat.

1705 *Boston News-Letter* 12 Nov. 2/2 His Under Garments were of the well-known Quaker Cut. **1833** S. Smith *Life J. Downing* 46 He call'd 2 or 3 chaps in Quaker coats. **1835** *S. Lit. Messenger* I. 551 He hurried off, in his Quaker dress, as fast as his *legs* could carry him. **1880** *Harper's Mag.* June 70 The pert cat-bird in his Quaker garb is here. **1898** Harper *S. B. Anthony* I. 6 [She] was noted for the beauty and elegance of her Quaker attire, her bonnets always being made in New York.

c. Designating things, policies, etc., owned, occupied, or sponsored by Quakers.

1708 Sewall *Diary* II. 232 A Petition for building a Quaker Meeting house with Wood, in Brattle's Close. **1790** Maclay *Deb. Senate* 169 The whole day was spent on the Quaker memorial for the abolition of slavery. **1808** *Ann. 10th Congress* 2 Sess. 787, I do not like this Quaker policy. **1881**

Harper's Mag. Jan. 181/1 From the time of its settlement Wilmington was essentially a Quaker community.

d. Passing into adj.: Plain, quiet, or subdued in color. {1818}

1804 Lewis in *L. & Clark Exped.* VI. (1905) 125 The upper part of the neck, back, and wings [of the least tern] are of a fine, quaker coulour. **1830** Holmes *Poetical Works* (1895) 323/2 But she comes as the saintly sisters do, In modest suit of a Quaker hue. **1880** *Harper's Mag.* Nov. 906/1 The powders are most deceptive in color; . . . black appears a purplish-gray; Vandyck brown, Quaker gray.

Quaker bonnet. **1.** A plain, close-fitting bonnet. {1859} **2.** *pl.* (See quotations.) — (1) **1803** Bowne *Life* 151 The little white satin quaker bonnets, cap-crowns, are the most fashionable. **1877** *Harper's Mag.* Feb. 478/2 Among those who attended the New England yearly Meeting . . . was Martha H——, . . . whose 'Quaker bonnet' did not conceal her wavy hair, bright eyes, and regular features. (2) **1898** Britton & Brown *Illus. Flora* III. 212 *Houstonia coerulea.* Bluets. . . . Called also Quaker Ladies, Quaker bonnets, Venus' Pride. **1915** Armstrong & Thornber *Western Wild Flowers* 252 Quaker Bonnets. *Lupinus laxiflorus.* . . . This is very common in Utah, handsome and conspicuous.

Quaker cap. A cap of a style worn by Quaker women. — **1852** Stowe *Uncle Tom* xiii, 'Nicely,' said Ruth, taking off her little drab bonnet, and . . . [displaying] a round little head, on which the Quaker cap sat with a sort of jaunty air. **1856** M. J. Holmes *Homestead* iv. viii, Grandma, in rich black silk and plain Quaker cap, was hovering near her favorite child.

+Quaker City.

1. Philadelphia, Pennsylvania. A nickname. Also attrib.

1841 Bache *Fire-Screen* 127 A *millioniare* of the Quaker city, *marrying* a little mantua-maker! **1852** *Harper's Mag.* Sept. 537/1 Mr. Randolph passed on to Philadelphia, and placed himself under the competent medical hands of the celebrated Dr. Parish, . . . of the 'Quaker City.' **1878** Pinkerton *Strikers* 239 By their revolutionary action [the regiments] certainly assisted greatly in creating the general desire for revenge upon the Quaker City militia. **1888** W. Lawrence *A. A. Lawrence* 19 The new invention [the steam carriage] did not seem to have brought civilization into the filthy streets of the Quaker city. **1903** *Critic* Aug. 190 A New York woman who becomes a resident [in Phila.] . . . does not find the Quaker city so 'slow' as it is generally represented.

2. (See quotation.)

1859 *Ladies' Repository* Jan. 51/2 Richmond, Indiana, is the 'Quaker City of the West,' as it is one of the principal settlements of Friends.

Quakeress. A female Quaker. {1764-} — **1721** *New Eng. Hist. & Gen. Reg.* XXX. 61 [Baptism of] John Rennolds, the little child of John Rennolds, his wife a Quakeress, not consenting. **1859** *Ladies' Repository* Jan. 35/1 My boarding-house was . . . kept by an old Quakeress.

+Quaker gun. A dummy gun. So called because of the doctrine of nonresistance held by the Quakers. — **1809** *Ann. 10th Congress* 2 Sess. 1367 Our vessels bound to England will, if they make any show of resistance, do it by *Quaker* guns. **1884** *Century Mag.* Dec. 284 Then the Quaker guns! Who has not heard of the 'Quaker guns' at Manassas? **1888** Dorsey *Midshipman Bob* 88 'He's like a Quaker gun,' said Haxall—'piles of appearance, but no damage done.'

+Quaker gunboat. A sham gunboat. — **1864** *Nat. Almanac* (Phila.) 76/2 (Ernst), A quaker gunboat made of logs, with funnels of pork barrels.

+Quaker hat. A broad-brimmed hat of a type worn by Quakers. — **1849** *Whig Almanac 1850* 25/2 Dr. Franklin, with his Quaker hat, when in Paris, received $12,000 a year. **1853** 'P. Paxton' *Yankee in Texas* 110 He wore a huge flap-eared Quaker hat.

Quakerish, *a.* Characteristic of Quakers; resembling Quakers. {1822-} — **1743** in F. Chase *Hist. Dartmouth Coll.* I. 5 [He] made a great show of sanctity, by means whereof he was under advantage to propagate his Quakerish notions. **1787** Cutler in *Life & Corr.* I. 210 We were very Quakerish, every man attending close to the business of eating, without uttering scarcely a word. **1837** *S. Lit. Messenger* III. 664/1 He is a small man—dresses in black—his habiliments staid and Quakerish. **1890** Howells *Boy's Town* 13 [She] always wore a dress of Quakerish plainness, with a white kerchief crossed upon her breast.

Quakerism. The principles or practices of the Quakers. {1656-} — **1708** *N.C. Col. Rec.* I. 700 The people of North Carolina . . . are now (covered) with the dark clouds of Quakerism. **1752** J. MacSparran *Amer. Dissected* 29 As Quakerism prevailed, Learning was decried, Ignorance and Heresy . . . increased. **1819** F. Wright *Soc. & Manners in Amer.* 49 Though we found some *quietism* in the society [of Phila.] we have found less absolute *quakerism* than we expected. **1870** Whittier *Writings* VII. 306, [I have] an unshaken faith in the one distinctive doctrine of Quakerism—the Light within—the immanence of the Divine Spirit in Christianity.

+Quaker-ladies. *pl.* The small pale-blue flowers of the bluet, *Houstonia caerula.* — **1871** *Scribner's Mo.* II. 102 Tenderest of all in yonder woods, where hepatica, and May blossoms, and Quaker ladies twinkle into life. **1878** *Harper's Mag.* April 778/2 How could she climb down and gather 'Quaker ladies,' or climb up for columbine among the rocks? **1892** *Amer. Folk-Lore* V. 97 *Houstonia cærulea,* Quaker ladies, Concord, Mass.; Boston. **1900** S. Day *From Mayflowers to Mistletoe* 22 In their little grey-blue bonnets Chatting, brim to brim, Half a million Quaker ladies, Straight and small and slim.

Quaker meeting. A religious meeting of Quakers; also, in allusion to the Quakers' custom of remaining silent until moved by the spirit, a silent meeting. {1751-} — **1659** *Plymouth Laws* 125 Others thinke it meet to p[er]mitt some p[er]sons to frequent the Quaker meetings to endeavor to reduce them form [*sic*] the error of their wayes. **1704** Sewall *Diary* II. 102 Convers'd with Mr. Noyes, told him of the Quaker Meeting at Sam. Sawyers. **1797** *Steele P.* II. 773 Indian and negro rights are fine things to talk about in a quaker meeting. **1822** *Ann. 17th Congress* 1 Sess. 273 Was Congress . . . to transform itself into a Quaker meeting? **1891** Earle *Sabbath* 47 In all the Puritan meetings, as then and now in Quaker meetings, the men sat on one side of the meeting-house and the women on the other.

***Quaking,** *a.* Of a piece of ground: Not firm; trembling. {1728-} — **1676** *Doc. Col. Hist. N.Y.* XII. 556, [I] could not make the s[ai]d way Sufficient for Cattle to goe over; by Reason of the Rottenness of the ground, being a Quaking mire w[hi]ch hath noe foundation for a way. **1790** Deane *New-Eng. Farmer* 229/2 *Quaking Meadow,* or *Marish,* low boggy land that shakes and settles under any one in passing over it. **1846** Lyell *Second Visit* II. 136 [The low country of La.] contains, he said, wide 'quaking prairies.'

+Quaking ash. =next. Also attrib. — **1846** W. G. Stewart *Altowan* I. 221 He crossed [the road] among some birch and quaking ash. **1897** Lewis *Wolfville* 285 Thar ain't no grass none for the little hoss, but I peels him about a bushel of quakin'-ash bark, an' he's doin' well 'nough.

+Quaking asp. Any of several species of aspen, esp. the American aspen, *Populus tremuloides;* a tree of one of these species. Also attrib.

1845 Frémont *Exped.* 112 Quaking asp (*populus tremuloides*) was mixed with the cottonwood. **1858** A. Jackson *Diary* (MS.) 1 Camped at a spring in quakingasps. **1878** Beadle *Western Wilds* 168 The town is in a grove of quaking asp, and was in no danger. **1888** *Harper's Mag.* Nov. 858/1, I have stood on the margin of a quaking-asp thicket. **1919** Hough *Sagebrusher* 4 A few quaking asps standing near the cabin door likewise gave motion and brightness to the scene.

+Quaking aspen. =prec. — **1847** Palmer *Rocky Mts.* 76 Occasionally there is a grove of quaking aspen. **1850** Sawyer *Way Sketches* 46 There are some groves of small Quaking Aspen a short distance to the left of the road. *a***1918** G. Stuart *On Frontier* I. 169 The cottonwoods, alders, quaking-aspens, and willows are only commencing to leaf out.

***Quaking grass.** **1.** Any of several grasses of the genus *Briza.* **+2.** *Fall quaking grass,* rattlesnake grass. — (1) **1791** Muhlenberg *Index Florae* 161 *Briza,* Quaking-grass. **1832** Williamson *Maine* I. 124 To these may be added Brome, Bent, Cock's-foot, Hair, Quaking, Panic, and Soft Grasses. **1850** S. F. Cooper *Rural Hours* 124 Some of the most troublesome weeds . . . are naturalized . . . ; quaking-grass, quitch-grass, yard-grass, and crab-grass, also. **1901** Mohr *Plant Life Ala.* 383 *Briza media.* . . . Quaking Grass. Introduced and escaped from cultivation in the Atlantic States from Ontario southward. (2) **1889** Vasey *Agric. Grasses* 109 Rattlesnake Grass; Fall Quaking Grass. . . . Cattle are fond of it, both green and when made into hay.

*** Qualify,** *v.*

1. *intr.* To take an oath of office, provide sureties, etc. {1790-}

1772 *Va. House of Burgesses* 229 The said *Dandridge* has never yet qualified [as a vestryman for St. John's parish]. **1857** *Baltimore Sun* 1 Oct. (Th.), The new Auditor of the Treasury . . . qualified, and entered upon the duties of his office. **1868** *Congress. Globe* 13 Feb. 1145/2 The question arises, if Philip F. Thomas can be permitted to take oath, or, in other words, to 'qualify' as a Senator of the United States. **1901** Duncan & Scott *Allen & Woodson Co., Kansas* 15 On the 19th of January they had another meeting and appointed Nimrod Hankins assessor, Sherlock having refused to qualify.

+b. To swear *to;* to make oath. *Obs.*

1827 Cooper *Red Rover* viii. 216 A seafaring man, by your dress? and one in search of a ship, as I am ready to qualify to. **1840** *S. Lit. Messenger* VI. 507/2 Why, it is cousin Liddy he's sparking—but it's no use, I can qualify. **1848** Bartlett 267, I am ready to *qualify* to what I have asserted!

+2. *passive.* To be sworn in.

[**1723** *Penna. Statutes* III. 382 Every such brewer . . . shall be qualified by oath . . . that he or she will not . . . use any of the said ingredients.] **1797** *Ann. 5th Congress* I. 281 Stephen Bullock, from Massachusetts, appeared, produced his credentials, was qualified, and took his seat. **1800** Cutler in *Life & Corr.* II. 37 [The gov. of Mass.] met the two Houses at 12, and was qualified. **1867** *Congress. Globe* App. 16 Feb. 165/3 [He] said he had come to file his bond and be qualified.

+Quamas(h). Variant of Camas. Also attrib. — **1806** Lewis in *L. & Clark Exped.* V. (1905) 170 Immediately above the springs on the creek there is a handsome little quamas plain of about 10 acres. **1831** R. Cox *Adv. Columbia R.* 228 Camas or quamash roots . . . are found. **1839** Townsend *Narrative* 124 Captain W. . . . finally bought of them a small quantity of dried salmon, and a little fermented kamas or *quamash* root. **1896** *Garden & Forest* IX. 253/1 *Camass.* . . . Variants: Camas, Cammas, Quamash, and Quamish.

+Quapaw. An Indian of a southwestern Siouan tribe. Also collective. — **1772** in *Travels Amer. Col.* 520 The Quarpas . . . or Arkansaws (a small nation on the west side of Mississippi.) **1821** Nuttall *Travels Arkansa* 223 In the spring and autumn the Quapaws have a custom of making a contribution dance. **1900** *Congress. Rec.* 1 Feb. 1420/2 The Quapaws have had their lands completely allotted to them. **1910** Hodge, etc. *Amer. Indians* II. 334/1 The Quapaw are known historically and from other evidence to have been mound builders.

Quarantinable, *a.* Subject to quarantine. — **1863** *N.Y. Laws* 576 With existing quarantinable disease on board, . . . merchandise of the first class shall be landed at the quarantine warehouse. **1894** *Harper's Wkly.* 7 April 315/2 Protection against cholera and other quarantinable disease . . . is secured [by the Marine Hospital Service].

Quarantine, *n.* {1609–}

1. The period during which a ship or persons are kept isolated as a precaution against possible spread of disease; an enforced detention or prohibition of intercourse for a definite period or the observance of this period. {1663–}

1721 *Mass. H. Rep. Jrnl.* III. 70 A Bill effectually to Oblige all Vessels coming from infected Places to perform their Quarantine. **1799** Bentley *Diary* II. 310 Endeavours are used to get a law of quarantine to embarass the Merchants. **1883** *Century Mag.* July 424/2 In 1821, a quarantine of some sort was established.

b. A place where a ship quarantine is carried out. {1892}

1809 Irving *Knickerb.* III. v, Now it skirts the long shore . . . spreading its wide shadows from the high settlements of Weehawk quite to the lazaretto and quarentine. **1861** in E. Cowell *Diary* 376 Two steamers were despatched to the quarantine, or lower side of the Mississippi river. **1884** Matthews & Bunner *In Partnership* 196 We dropped anchor off Quarantine at three o'clock on Monday morning.

2. An enforced isolation of livestock for a certain period or +a restriction of their movement in order to prevent the spread of disease.

1879 *Diseases of Swine* 151 All strange hogs must be kept in quarantine for fourteen days before being allowed to run with healthy herds. **1890** *Stock Grower & Farmer* 1 Feb. 3/3 The rigid quarantine maintained by the board has prevented the cattlemen of Texas from using the Pecos valley for a trail to drive stock to Montana and Wyoming. **1901** *Amer. Rev. of Reviews* XXIV. 309/2 Most of the ranches are beyond the imaginary line of quarantine which separates the Southern herds from the Northern. **1915** *Hoard's Dairyman* 22 Jan. 774/1 The hoof and mouth disease is not necessarily fatal and can be stamped out by quarantine.

+3. Any prohibition or restriction.

1891 *Boston Jrnl.* 7 Jan. 2/3 A rigid quarantine against firearms and firewater on the reservations of the Northwest is one of the prime requirements of the Indian problem.

4. *attrib.* **a.** In sense 1 with *hospital, island, mob,* etc.

1846 *Mich. Gen. Statutes* I. (1882) 468 The said quarantine regulations . . . shall be observed and complied with by all persons. **1855** in A. Lawrence *Diary & Corr.* 139 One of his family . . . had experienced a light attack of varioloid; and . . . was obliged to be transported to the Quarantine Hospital, situated in Boston Harbor. **1859** Wilmer *Press Gang* 358 The New York Quarantine Mob. In August, 1858, a brutal mob attacked the Quarantine Station on Staten Island. **1861** E. Cowell *Diary* 340 Mr. Chester . . . was invited by Sam to accompany us to Hoboken, in hopes of seeing the Great Eastern, reported off the bar at Quarantine Island. **a1882** in McCabe *New York* 102 Usually vessels are boarded from the quarantine tug.

b. In sense 2 with *district, inspector, order, station.*

1884 *Rep. Comm. Agric.* 203 A committee of prominent cattle-men went to Frankfort to-day to endeavor to procure quarantine orders. **1885** *Wkly. New Mexican Rev.* 25 June 3/6 These are Texas herds which came in via the Pecos trail recently, during Mr. William's tenure of the office of quarantine inspector. **1891** O'Beirne *Leaders Ind. Territory* 56/2 Jackson was appointed . . . commissioner of the quarantine district. **1892** *Statutes at Large* XXVII. 80 To establish and maintain quarantine Stations and to provide proper shelter for and care of neat cattle imported, . . . fifteen thousand dollars.

Quarantine, *v.* {1850–}

1. *tr.* To put into quarantine. {1860–}

1804 Irving in P. M. Irving *Life W. Irving* I. (1862) 89, I should be detained, quarantined, smoked, and vinegared. **1858** Holmes *Autocrat* 207, I was quarantined once at Marseilles. **1869** 'Mark Twain' *Innocents* 254 We propose to go . . . by rail to Naples. They do not quarantine the cars, no matter where they get their passengers from.

transf. **1860** *Harper's Mag.* June 137/2 The entire body of reefers were 'quarantined,' i.e. confined to the limits of the [navy] yard.

+2. To isolate (a disease).

1879 *Diseases of Swine* 163, I desired to make an effort to quarantine the disease and confine it to his herd.

+3. To protect (a place) by restricting access to it.

1890 *Stock Grower & Farmer* 24 May 7/3 The state [of Neb.] is strictly quarantined against all cattle from Texas.

4. *intr.* To institute a quarantine.

1888 Hearn in *Harper's Mag.* Oct. 738/1 Only two cases had been reported when every neighboring British colony quarantined against Martinique.

+Quarantine ground. An area in which ships, live stock, etc., are quarantined. — **1808** *Ann. 10th Congress* 1 Sess. 1753 The ship arrived at the quarantine ground, near the harbor of Boston. **1814** *Niles' Reg.* VI. 184/1 His line commences in the rear of the quarantine ground. **1846** *Mich. Gen. Statutes* I. (1882) 468 Any township may establish a quarantine ground in any suitable place. **1885** *Wkly. New Mexican Rev.* 29 Jan. 3/6 There is a deep and determined feeling among Lincoln county cattlemen that this region, at least, shall not become the quarantine ground for the whole state of Texas.

Quarantine law. 1. A law authorizing a quarantine at a port. {1805} **+2.** A similar law quarantining live stock. — **(1) 1801** *Steele P.* I. 230 The amount [was] expended in purchasing of Land & erecting wharves & buildings under the act respecting quarantine & health laws. **1868** *N.Y. Herald* 8 July 3/6 Several persons . . . were arrested . . . for alleged violation of the Quarantine Law. **(2) 1885** *Wkly. New Mexican Rev.* 29 Jan. 2/2 The quarantine law . . . if rightly enforced, will keep out diseased cattle. **1916** Thoburn *Stand. Hist. Okla.* II. 702 Important measures which passed both houses of the Fourth Legislative Assembly . . . were the following: A comprehensive banking law; a general election law; . . . and a general live stock quarantine law.

+Quarantine line. =Fever line. — **1890** *Stock Grower & Farmer* 19 April 4/2 Thousands of cattle are going daily into the Creek, Chickasaw and Choctaw country from points in Texas below the quarantine line. **1911** *Okla. Session Laws* 3 Legisl. 255 The excises board of any county situated above the state quarantine line as fixed by the State Board of Agriculture, shall have power to levy a tax on all taxable property.

Quarantiner. 1. A person who is put in quarantine. {1831} **2.** One who enforces a quarantine. — **(1) 1835** in *S. Lit. Messenger* IV. 303/2 The surrounding country is full of *quarantiners*, waiting for admission. **(2) 1888** *Columbus Dispatch* 19 Sept., The men are simply volunteer quarantiners hunting for bilious looking subjects.

Quarantine station. A place where people or ships are put in quarantine. {1841} — **1815** *Niles' Reg.* IX. 172/2 There were detained at the quarantine stations 40 [vessels]. **1833** Coke *Subaltern's Furlough* i, The ship . . . anchored half a mile above the quarantine station, nineteen miles from Philadelphia. **1882** McCabe *New York* 98 Below the narrows, are Dix and Hoffman Islands, occupied by the State of New York as a Quarantine Station.

***Quarrel.**[1] A stone quarry. *Obs.* {*dial.*} — **1666** *Oyster Bay Rec.* I. 21 Of timber pasters or pastareges, ferem Marshes en Mashes Mines Minerals Quarells.

***Quarrel.**[2] (See quot. 1876.) — **1672** *Dedham Rec.* IV. 225 Mr. Man sent 6*d* in money in satisfaction for three quarrells of glase broken by the schollers while he keept the schole. **1685** Sewall *Diary* I. 87 The Window of Mothers Bed-Chamber next the Street hath many Quarrels broken in it. **1719** *Ib.* III. 235 Something was thrown forcibly against the uper part of the North Window, and five or six Quarrels broken. **1876** Knight 1842/1 *Quarrel*, . . . a pane of glass of a diamond or rhombal shape.

*** Quarry.**[1]

***1.** A place, usually an open-air excavation, from which stone for building and other purposes is obtained.

1649 *Va. Hist. Reg. & Lit. Adv.* II. 70 Stones, and rocks, and quarries of several kinds, . . . are in divers places found in Virginia. **1666** *Brookhaven Rec.* 18 Creekes, Quarrys, woodlands [etc.]. **1685** *Charlestown Land Rec.* 196 One Acre of Land left for A Quarry. **1740** W. Stephens *Proc. Georgia* I. 603 [He] found in it a plentiful Quarry of Iron Stone. **1809** Kendall *Travels* I. 90 A mile or two above the city . . . is a quarry of free-stone. **1831** Peck *Guide* 24 Towards the sources of this river the quarries exist from which are made the red stone pipes of the Indians. **1883** *Harper's Mag.* Nov. 823/2 The whole hill-side seems to be ridged and furrowed with quarries. **1907** *St. Nicholas* July 849/1 Across the street from our house is a quarry, from which a great deal of stone had been taken for building.

b. With the name of the stone obtained in a quarry. (See also Marble quarry.)

1788 May *Jrnl. & Lett.* 50 This morning . . . viewed a grindstone quarry. **1834** [see Freestone *n.*[1] 1 b]. **1849** Chamberlain *Ind. Gazetteer* 274 A millstone quarry, near Scipio, has also at times been worked extensively. **1885** *Wkly. New Mexican Rev.* 19 March 3/5 Contractor Donoghue has opened up a new sand stone quarry near the city.

‖**2.** The stone that is quarried.

1883 *Harper's Mag.* Oct. 719/1 The Kentucky blue-limestone too is a quarry for the turnpike-roads.

3. Attrib. with *company, man, place, worker.*

1685 *Charlestown Land Rec.* 198 A Quarry place Cont. bounded north Eastrly by the Country rode. **1857** Vaux *Villas* 26 All the quarry-workers . . . live by the constant demand for the exercise of this art of building. **1880** *Harper's Mag.* Aug. 348/1 His audience was made up of young fishermen . . . and quarrymen, or ex-quarrymen. **1893** *Ib.* April 656/2 It was one of the cities that seem to have been turned out by a quarry company and a saw-mill.

Quarry.[2] =Quarrel.[2] {1611–} — **1698** Thomas *Pensilvania* 30 The Glaziers . . . will have Five Pence a Quarry for their Glass. **1728** *Md. Hist. Mag.* VIII. 151 18 Quaries put in and Nails. **1876** Knight 1842/1 The *quarries* are fixed in *cames*, which are tied by leaden strips to *saddle-bars* running transversely across the iron frame of the casement window.

* **Quart.** Two pints, a quarter of a gallon; +(see quot. 1890). Also attrib. (See GALLON, note.)

1630 HIGGINSON *New-England* 7 In our Plantation we have already a quarte of Milke for a penny. **1643** *Conn. Rec.* I. 456 A Inuentory of the goods of Tho: Scott: . . . 1 quart pot, 2 porringers [etc.]. **1645** *Plymouth Laws* 81 Every Miller [shall] have two toul dishes . . . so made that upheaped they will hold no more than a quart and a pottle. **1786** in Summers *Hist. S.W. Va.* 416 He drank a share of a quart bowl of whiskey grog. **1835** LONGSTREET *Ga. Scenes* 209 The old folks used to tell me, that when I was born, they put me in a quart-mug. **1872** *Ill. Dept. Agric. Trans.* IX. 63 Seed [should be] sown at the rate of from twelve to sixteen quarts to the acre, in the spring, in good corn-planting time. **1890** *Cent.* 4896/1 In the United States there is a quart of dry measure . . . 1 United States dry quart = 1.1017 liters. **1896** *Internat. Typogr. Union Proc.* 63/2 Coffee Mill, $6; 3 paring knives, 45¢; quart measure, 25¢. **1913** LONDON *Valley of Moon* 336 She also had a special private market, receiving five cents more a quart than was fetched by the best dairy milk.

Quart cup. A cuplike vessel holding a quart. — **1856** STOWE *Dred* I. 82 You can't fill a quart-cup out of a thimble. **1880** *Harper's Mag.* June 24/1 He absent-mindedly raised the quart cup to his lips.

+**Quartel.** *S.W.* [Sp. *cuartel.*] Barracks or quarters for soldiers. *Obs.* — **1832** DEWEES *Lett. from Texas* 142 Seven hundred Mexicans . . . were at the quartel or barracks. **1844** KENDALL *Narr. Santa Fé Exped.* II. 135 One of the buildings we passed was a large quartel, filled apparently with convicts destined to swell the ranks of Santa Anna's army. **1848** BRYANT *California* xxvii. 335 The quartel, a barn-like adobe house, faces the public square.

* **Quarter.**

+**1.** *New Eng.* A particular section, tract, or district regarded as a unit of settlement; the settlers on such an area. *Obs.*

1640 *New Haven Col. Rec.* 42 Every one of the 5 quarters whose proportion of meadow is under 8 acres, shall have itt in the iland in the east riuer. **1649** *Ib.* 477 William Bassett passeth ouer to Robert Emry . . . 6 acrs. & ½ of vpland . . . in ye subverbes quarter. **1674** *Conn. Probate Rec.* 294, I give to my Daughter Elizabeth Hall one peice of upland Lying in the Boggy meadow quarter. **1702** *Derby Rec.* 338 The first quarter is from an heap off stones between his barn & my house eastward. **1761** in C. O. Parmenter *Hist. Pelham, Mass.* 225 Voted that Each quarter Build their own Scole Houses.

attrib. **1649** *New Haven Col. Rec.* 478 Mr. Crane complained of Samuel Whitehead for leaving open ther quarter gate.

+**2.** = NEGRO QUARTER. Freq. pl. Now hist.

1724 JONES *Virginia* 36 The Negroes live in small Cottages called Quarters. **1745** *Va. Gazette* 16 May 4/2 Ran away from the Subscriber's Quarter . . . the following Negro's, . . . Sambo, . . . Aaron, . . . Berwick. **1799** WELD *Travels* 84 Their quarters . . . are usually situated one or two hundred yards from the dwelling house. **1803** J. DAVIS *Travels* 382, I walked away to the Quarter. **1898** CHOPIN in Rankin *K. Chopin* (1932) 259 Dimple . . . made herself unpopular in the kitchen and down at the quarters. **1916** THOBURN *Stand. Hist. Okla.* I. 261 'The quarters' . . . formed a picturesque feature of the old time plantation life.

+**3.** A fourth of a mile.

In English use only with *mile* expressed, as *a quarter of a mile, a mile and a quarter.*

1827 COOPER *Prairie* iv, His camp is but a short quarter from us. **1878** *Western Wilds* 31 It was weeks before I could walk a quarter.

attrib. **1845** HOOPER *Simon Suggs' Adv.* 14 He Stole . . . his father's plow-horses to enter them in 'quarter' matches. **1884** HARRIS in *Century Mag.* Nov. 118 There was a quarter-track . . . if he chose to enjoy the pleasures of horse-racing.

‖**4.** A quarterly exhibition in a school.

1782 in S. Baldwin *Simeon Baldwin* 103 Heard our Pupils rehearse a Tragedy preparing for Quarter.

+**5.** A fourth of a dollar. In full *quarter of a dollar.*

1783 *Md. Gazette* 5 Sept. 3/3 Price half a dollar to grown people, and a quarter to children. **1789** *Ann. 1st Congress* I. 228 A gallon of molasses is worth a quarter of a dollar before it is distilled. **1850** LEWIS *La. Swamp Doctor* 29, I will give you a quarter if you will carry one of these bundles down to that steamboat. **1897** *Outing* XXX. 121/2 The fare was a quarter apiece. **1903** 'O. HENRY' *Roads of Destiny* 162 He tossed a quarter into the hat of a blind man sitting by the door.

attrib. **1876** MILLER *First Fam'lies* 227 This last adventure wore him down to about the condition of an old quarter-coin. **1886** STAPLETON *Major's Christmas* 35 When I want a five-cent meal, I goes to a five-cent concern; simularly when I goes to a quarter house, I calkerlate to pay the cash.

6. The fourth part of a school year; a term. {1836–}

1827 DRAKE & MANSFIELD *Cincinnati* 42 The price of tuition . . . is from four to ten dollars a quarter. **1846** *Ind. Hist. Soc. Publ.* III. 412 They must pay their portion of the whole expense of the quarter. **1891** *Univ. of Chic. Official Bul.* No. 1, 12 The year shall be divided into four quarters, beginning respectively on the first day of October, January, April and July. **1905** COLE *Early Oregon* 22 He said he had not got all the pupils they required . . . for the quarter of thirteen weeks.

+**7.** = QUARTER SECTION.

1831 PECK *Guide* 257 Each quarter may be divided . . . , leaving eighty acres as the smallest tract. **1845** HOOPER *Simon Suggs' Adv.* 36 Many a long and hard race was run by rival land-hunters, intent upon the acquisition of the same . . . 'tip-top quarter.' **1872** *Newton Kansan* 12 Sept. 3/3 [He] had homesteaded the southeast quarter of sec. 14, rg. 5 west, tn. 21. **1890** *Stock Grower & Farmer* 21 June 8/2 The southeastern quarter of section eight [8] township seven [7] north, range twenty-eight [28] east, containing 160 acres. **1905** *Indian Laws & Tr.* III. 144 Josephine Lillie is hereby given . . . the west half of the northwest quarter of section ten.

8. (See quot. 1876.) Also attrib.

1859 G. W. PERRY *Turpentine Farming* 157 Quarter hoops require to be made large enough to pass easily over the head hoop. **1876** KNIGHT 1843/1 *Quarter,* . . . (*Coopering,*) the portion of the side of a cask intermediate between the *chime* and the *bulge.*

+**9.** A quarter back; also, the position played by this man.

1893 CAMP *College Sports* 120 The criss-cross or double pass is another excellent example of a disguised play, the ball being passed by the quarter to one of the backs. **1899** QUINN *Penna. Stories* 27 Then Frank was sent in to quarter to run the team. **1907** *St. Nicholas* Sept. 1013/2 There was some discussion last year as to whether a line man could run from his position in the line and take the ball from the quarter.

+**10.** In special combinations.

Quarter-hand, (see quotation and cf. HALF-HAND 1); *q. pitch,* a pitch or slope of a roof equal to one-fourth of the measurement from ridge to eaves; *q. pole,* a pole that marks the quarter mile in a race course; *q. sawing,* (see quotation); *q. tackey,* = QUARTER HORSE; *q. timber,* (see quotation); *q. township,* one-fourth of a township.

1856 OLMSTED *Slave States* 433 The field-hands are all divided into four classes, according to their physical capacities. The children beginning as 'quarter-hands' . . . [finally become] 'full hands.' **1842** KIRKLAND *Forest Life* II. 79 It took a full hour to make our principal architect acknowledge that water would run off a roof which sloped at any less than 'quarter-pitch.' **1868** WOODRUFF *Trotting Horse* 259 At the quarter-pole she had recovered her stroke. **1898** S. B. GREEN *Forestry in Minn.* 299 Quarter-sawing. . . . The log is first quartered and then sawed into boards, cutting them alternately from each face of the quarter of the log. **1851** *Polly Peablossom* 174 It'll be 'the old quarter tackey word.' **1876** KNIGHT 1844/1 *Quarter-timber,* (*Carpentry,*) scantling from 2 to 6 inches deep. **1832** WILLIAMSON *Maine* II. 572 In 1798, the residue was offered for sale in quarter townships at a dollar by the acre.

+**Quarter back.** *Football.* A backfield player, formerly stationed directly behind the center to receive the ball and pass it to a runner. Also attrib. — **1879** in P. H. Davis *Football* (1911) 468 The man who first receives the ball from the snap-back shall be called the quarter-back. **1887** *Century Mag.* Oct. 891/1 The 'center rush,' kicks the ball backward, or 'snaps it back,' to the quarter-back. **1903** *McClure's Mag.* Feb. 428/1 Henry was a quarter-breed, quarter-back Cherokee, educated East in the idioms of football, and West in contraband whisky. **1910** *St. Nicholas* Oct. 1073/1 The quarter-back may run with the ball and cross the line of scrimmage at any point.

Quarter bill. +A bill or account rendered a student at the end of a quarter. — **1734** in Peirce *Hist. Harvard* App. 126 Every scholar, in the first quarter-bill made up after his admission, shall be charged six shillings to the use of the College for Gallery money. **1790** *Harvard Laws* 6 The parents . . . [shall] give bond . . . in the sum of two hundred ounces of silver, to pay their several quarter-bills.

+**Quarter blood.** One who is one-quarter Indian. In full *quarter-blood Indian.* (Cf. FULL BLOOD *n.* 1, HALF-BLOOD 2.) — **1845** *Knickerb.* XXV. 236 Of this description was a quarter-blood, of great beauty. **1878** BEADLE *Western Wilds* 26 The straight black hair, and nose just aquiline enough to give piquancy to the countenance, indicated the quarter-blood. **1890** LANGFORD *Vigilante Days* (1912) 24 Cherokee Bob . . . received his name from the fact that he was a quarter-blood Indian.

+**Quarter-breed.** The offspring of a half-breed and a white person; a quarter blood. Also attrib. (Cf. HALF-BREED *n.* 1.) — **1827** MCKENNEY *Tour to Lakes* 387 Three were full blood, the remainder half breeds, and quarter breeds. **1853** J. W. BOND *Minnesota* 211 A work upon the Chippewas was prepared by the late W. W. Warren, himself a quarter-breed of this nation. **1880** *Harper's Mag.* Dec. 35/1 Douglas was soon to marry . . . a French quarter-breed girl.

Quarter cask. A cask containing a fourth of a hogshead. {1711–} — **1654** *Conn. Rec.* I. 255 Every ancor of Liquors that is landed . . . shall pay to the publique treasury 10ss. & every . . . quarter cask 10ss. wheather they are full or noe. **1683** *N.H. Hist. Soc. Coll.* VIII. 150 One butt and one quarter cask of Malaga wine . . . was lately seized. **1704** *Boston News-Letter* 21 Aug. 2/2 There's good Fyall Wine to be Sold by the Pipe, Quarter Cask, or smaller Quantities. **1862** *Trial C. M. Jefferds* 47 A quarter cask do you mean?

+**Quarter court.** A court sitting quarterly, as a court of quarter sessions. *Obs.* (Cf. COURT 3 n.) — **1622** in W. M. West *Source Book Amer. Hist.* (1913) 76 At a great and generall Quarter Courte held for Virginia in the Afternoone the 22 of May 1622. **1639** *Portsmouth Rec.* 4 The quarter courts ar to bee . . . the first thursday in december. **1641** *Mass. Bay Rec.* I. 325 There shalbee 4 Quarter Courts kept yearly by the ma[gis]trats of Ipswich & Salem. **1680** *N.H. Hist. Soc. Coll.* VIII. 41 You are hereby required to summon Wilmot Oliver to appear tomorrow . . . at the quarter court to be held at Dover.

*** Quarter day.** One of the four days during the year fixed by custom as the time when tenancy of houses begins and ends and quarterly changes fall due. *Obsolescent.*

1637 *R.I. Col. Rec.* I. 30 The 5 disposers shall from the date hereof, meete every month-day . . . and at the quarter-day. **1746** *Holyoke Diaries* 38 Quarter Day kept in ye hall. **1837** *Baltimore Commerc. Transcript* 2 Aug. 2/3 (Th.), Tuesday will be a slim 'quarter day' to many of the landlords. **1869** FULLER *Flower Gatherers* 282 Being quarter-day, there had been several removals.

+b. *Educ.* (See quot. 1851.) *Obs.*

1764 in Peirce *Hist. Harvard* 217 The undergraduates [shall] be obliged to observe the studying hours and to perform the College exercises on quarter-day . . . as at other times. **1851** HALL *College Words* 250 *Quarter-Day.* The day when quarterly payments are made. The day that completes three months.

+Quarter dollar. A silver coin having one-fourth the value of a dollar. — **1794** *Amer. Calendar* 59 Silver Coins: . . . Quarter Dollars. Dismes. Half Dismes. **1832** WATSON *Hist. Tales N.Y.* 151 [Buttons] made out of real quarter dollars, with the coinage impression still retained, . . . were used for the coats. **1852** [see HALF DIME]. **1873** *Rev. Statutes* (1878) 696 The silver coins of the United States shall be a trade-dollar, a half-dollar, or fifty-cent piece, a quarter-dollar [etc.].

+Quarter eagle. A gold coin worth $2.50, or one-fourth of an eagle. (Cf. EAGLE 3.) — **1792** *Ann. 2d Congress* 71 Quarter eagles; each to be of the value of two dollars and a half dollar. **1837** *P.O. Laws & Reg.* (1843) I. 59 The quarter eagle, [shall be] sixty-four and one-half grains. **1887** *Courier-Journal* 17 Feb. 2/5 The banking-firm of Zimmerman & Forshay . . . received yesterday . . . $10,000 in quarter eagles.

+Quarter horse. A horse trained to run quarter-mile races. Often in figurative expressions. (Cf. QUARTER NAG.) — **a1846** *Quarter Race Ky.* 121 Anybody that has seen a 'quarter-horse' run by a 'dunghill' knows how this was. **1857** [see BREAK *v.* 13 c]. **1883** HOWE *Country Town* (1926) 169 It was one of their greatest accomplishments to drive a quarter-horse to a wood wagon to some out-of-the-way neighborhood. **1893** ROOSEVELT *Wilderness Hunter* 45 The frightened deer . . . sped off across the grassy slopes like a quarter horse.

Quarterly meeting. A meeting held approximately every three months, esp. in certain religious denominations, as among the Methodists and the Quakers. {1750-} Also attrib.

1713 *N.C. Col. Rec.* II. 37 Friends appoint John Morris & Henry White to represent the state of this meeting to the Quarterly Meeting. **1805** [see CAMPER 1]. **1832** WILLIAMSON *Maine* II. 697 Two or more Stewards are appointed in each circuit, who attend all quarterly meetings. **1881** PIERSON *In the Brush* 181 As we were about to leave to attend a quarterly-meeting at the court-house, she called him back. **1905** VALENTINE *H. Sandwith* 76 The young Quaker seer . . . , now Quarterly Meeting sessions were over, was about to leave Dunkirk.

+b. *M.E. Ch. Quarterly meeting conference,* (see quot. 1844).

1844 Rupp *Relig. Denominations* 448 A *quarterly meeting conference* is composed of all the travelling and local preachers, exhorters, stewards, and leaders, belonging to any particular circuit or station. **1846** *Indiana Mag. Hist.* XXIII. 284 The objection to a union with the circuit grew out of an unfortunate want of harmony in the quarterly meeting conference.

***Quartermaster.** A petty officer in a naval or military organization. Also as a title. — **1630** WINTHROP in R. C. Winthrop *Life J. Winthrop* II. 38 Be sure they [*i.e.*, provisions] be bestowed in the ship where they may be readyly come by, (w[hi]ch the boatswaine will see to, & the quarter masters, if they be rewarded beforehande). **1700** *Topsfield Rec.* 107 At a lawfull meeting of ye Towne of Topsfield ye 7th of May 1700 quortermaster Tobiiah Pirkins is chosen Representitive for to sarue at ye grate and Genarall court to be houlden at Boston. **1807** *Ann. 10th Congress.* I Sess. 673 This corn [was sold] . . . , and the avails placed in the quartermaster's hands. **1910** J. HART *Vigilante Girl* 12 What is that curious tinkling noise, Quartermaster?

Quartermaster-general. *Mil.* A staff officer having charge of supplies, equipment, etc. {1701-}, +esp., in the United States army since 1916, an officer of the rank of major general in charge of the Quartermaster Corps.

[**1757** *General Orders* 35 The Name of which Person So Appointed [as sutler] is to Be Given In to Mr. Lesley Assisting Debuty Quarter Master General.] **1781** *Va. State P.* I. 550 Certain information of Colo. Porterfield's death, necessitates the appointment of a Quarter Master Genl: for this State. **1812** *Military Laws* (1858) 183 The quartermaster general shall be entitled to the rank, pay and emoluments of a brigadier general. **1862** TUCKER in McClellan *Own Story* 238 That evening the quartermaster-general was informed of the decision. **a1892** M. A. Jackson *Gen. Jackson* 319, I stated in some instances that he thought of me as his quartermaster-general. **1916** *Statutes at Large* XXXIX. 170 The Quartermaster Corps shall consist of one Quartermaster General with the rank of major general; two assistants [etc.].

Quartermaster's department. *Mil.* The department having charge of supplies and equipment. — **1777** *Jrnls. Cont. Congress* IX. 191 Ordered, That General Mifflin's plan . . . for regulating the duty of the quarter-master's department, be referred to the committee. **1812** *Military Laws* (1858) 183 That there be, and hereby is, established a quartermaster's department for the army of the United States. **1866** W. REID *After the War* 17 The parents of the children have been . . . [employed as laborers in the Quarter-master's Department. **1884** HEDLEY *Marching through Ga.* (1890) 268 These supplies were turned over to the commissary and quartermaster's department for issue in the regular way.

Quartermaster sergeant. A non-commissioned officer appointed to assist a quartermaster. {1869-} — **1865** O. W. NORTON *Army Lett.* 260, I send you a photo of my quartermaster-sergeant James Duty.

+Quarter meeting. A meeting, as of a court or religious body, held quarterly. *Obs.* — **1639** *Portsmouth Rec.* 7 At a quarter Meeting ye first Thursd 1639 Nicholas Browne doth dismisse himself [etc.]. **1669** *R.I. Col. Rec.* II. 273 The Councill adjourned till four of the clock in the afternoon, to give way for the Quarter Meeting. **1708** SEWALL *Diary* II. 231 Elder Bridgham . . . [and others] earnestly solicited me to speak to a place of Scripture at their privat Quarter-Meeting in the room of Mr. Chiever.

+Quarter nag. =QUARTER HORSE. *colloq.* Also fig. — **1834** BRACKENRIDGE *Recollections* 225 Cunning is the wisdom of fools; but it is only a quarter nag. **1851** *Polly Peablossom* 112 The way that bar broke into a canter 'ud hev distanced any quarter nag in Christendom! **1878** in Summers *Ann. S.W. Va.* 1547, I dropped out of my perch and took to my heels like a quarter-nag.

Quartero(o)n. Also **quartroon.** =QUADROON. *Obs.* {1707, in W. Indies; 1819-} — **1793** JEFFERSON *Writings* IX. 276 Castaing is described as a small dark mulatto, and La Chaise as a Quarteron. **1805** *Amer. Pioneer* II. 236 The colored women have . . . their weekly balls, (called quartroon balls) at which none but white gentlemen attend. **1808** C. SCHULTZ *Travels* II. 195 The whites, the quarteroons or coloured people, and the blacks, have each [in New Orleans] their separate amusements. **1812** STODDARD *Sk. Louisiana* 321 The dancing assemblies of the *quarterons*, or free people of color, in New-Orleans, are not the least interesting in point of beauty and dress. **1832** VIGNE *6 Mos. in Amer.* II. 14 The preacher was a half-cast, or quarteroon, as the negroes call them. **1878** in Summers *Ann. S.W. Va.* 1518 Wilburn is one-fourth Indian—what is called a quarteroon.

+Quarter post. *Surveying.* A post or marker set up at a corner of a quarter section of land. Also attrib. — **1849** *31st Congress 1 Sess.* H. R. Ex. Doc. No. 5, II. 508 After descending the precipice, the descent was gradual till we came to the quarter-post, which is in a cedar swamp. **1877** *Mich. Gen. Statutes* I. (1882) 210 The boards of supervisors of the several counties are hereby authorized to establish and perpetuate any government section corners or quarter-posts in their respective counties. **1881** *Ib.*, The surveyor as above employed shall sink into the earth at all section and quarter-post corners from the surface to a depth of at least three feet, a column of broken brick.

+Quarter race. A horse race over a quarter-of-a-mile course. — **1792** TOULMIN *Descr. Kentucky* 12 His time is employed in quarter-races, cock-fights. **1835** LONGSTREET *Ga. Scenes* 24 Away went Bullet, as if in a quarter race, with all his beauties spread in handsome style. **1856** *Porter's Spirit of Times* 22 Nov. 195/3 A quarter race was to have come off there. **1889** *Harper's Mag.* Aug. 386/2 [They] had foot-races for themselves, and quarter-races for their horses.

+Quarter racing. The action or practice of racing horses over a course a quarter of a mile long. — **1784** SMYTH *Tour* I. 22 In the southern part of the colony, and in North Carolina, they are much attached to *quarter-racing.* **1827** J. BERNARD *Retrosp.* 155 More fun, however, prevailed at another species of this diversion peculiar to the interior, called 'quarter-racing.' **1877** CAMPION *On Frontier* 91 An account . . . will afford an opportunity to describe 'quarter-racing,' a style of 'running' horses but little, if at all, practised out of North America. **1892** ALLEN *Blue-Grass Region* 130 From the first, there had stood out among the Kentuckians broad exhibitions of exuberant animal vigor . . . —foot-racing for the men, and quarter-racing for the horses.

+Quarter section. A tract of land, containing 160 acres and forming one-fourth of a section. (Cf. QUARTER 7.) — **1804** *Statutes at Large* II. 281 Public lands of the United States, the sale of which is authorized by law, may . . . be purchased . . . in entire sections, in half sections, or in quarter sections. **1846** *Ind. Hist. Soc. Publ.* III. 413 Who will complain? Certainly not the poor man nor the owner of a quarter section. **1885** *Santa Fé Wkly. New Mexican* 1 Oct. 1/2 The great railroad companies have appraised and sold their land grants, fixing a price on every quarter-section. **1925** TILGHMAN *Dugout* 80 Every quarter section was taken.

*** Quarter sessions. a.** An inferior court of record sitting quarterly. *Obsolescent.* **+b.** (See quot. 1914.) Also attrib. (See also COURT 3 n.)

1641 *R.I. Col. Rec.* I. 113 The Quarter Session Courts shall always be kept the first, the first Tuesday in March; the second, the first Tuesday in June. **1701** *Phila. Ordinances* (1812) 5 Justices of the county courts, quarter sessions, oyer and terminer and gaol delivery. **1811** MEASE *Philadelphia* 58 These brands [for flour casks] are to be registered with the clerk of the Quarter Sessions of the County. **1898** YOUNG *Jessamine Co., Ky.* 164 In earliest times the quarter session judges who represented the Circuit Court held their sessions in sheds or stables. **1914** *Cycl. Amer. Govt.* I. 504/2 In Pennsylvania the sessions of the local courts of original jurisdiction for the trial of criminal cases, the creation of local districts and the granting of liquor licenses are called quarter sessions.

+**Quarter stretch.** A race course, or part of a race course, a quarter of a mile long. Also transf. — **1834** *S. Lit. Messenger* I. 182, I pulled and pulled till I got out of sight, and turned down the quarter stretch. **1836** *Quarter Race Ky.* 14 Bay still disclaimed racing, but would run the quarter stretch. **c1875** BAGBY *Old Va. Gentleman* 306 He run a quarter-stretch down the low-grounds of the base.

Quarter ticket. One-fourth part or share of a lottery ticket. *Obs.* — **1790** *Columbian Centinel* 9 Oct. 31/2 Whole and quarter Tickets in the Monthly State Lottery, may be had of David West. **1845** SOL. SMITH *Theatr. Apprent.* 85, I went to a lottery-office with a quarter ticket I had purchased.

+**Quarter-yearly,** *adv.* Once in a quarter of a year; quarterly. *Obs.* — **1791** *Ann. 1st Congress* 2012 The interest of the debt should be paid quarter-yearly. **1795** HAMILTON *Works* VII. 95 His allowance is at the rate of 25,000 dollars per annum, 6,250 dollars quarter-yearly. **1803** *Steele P.* I. 373, I will, quarter yearly, apply for and remit to you such interest as shall hereafter become due on this stock. **1861** *Army Regulations* 154 Every officer having public money to account for, and failing to render his account thereof quarter-yearly, . . . will be promptly dismissed.

+**Quartet(te) table.** A nest of four small tables, or a table belonging to such a nest. — **1856** COZZENS *Sparrowgrass P.* 89 In one door-way stood a tray of delicate confections, upon two slender quartette tables. **1857** *Harper's Mag.* March 453/1 On this quartette-table we will lay the portfolio.

+**Quartillo.** *S.W.* [Sp. *cuartillo.*] The fourth part of a real. *Obs.* — **1844** KENDALL *Narr. Santa Fé Exped.* II. 190 A galopina, or kitchen girl, . . . soon explained the business of the holy brother by dropping a quartillo into the box. **1878** BEADLE *Western Wilds* 190 Even the boys took their first lesson by pitching for *quartillas*.

Quartroon. (See QUARTERO(O)N.)

Quartz.

1. a. A common form of silica occurring in nature in massive or crystallized form, often as a constituent of various rocks. {1756–} **b.** (See quot. 1881.)

1804 CUTLER in *Life & Corr.* I. 172 The rocks of the [White] mountains are mostly granite, mixed with some quartz, mica, and a silicious stone of a dark brownish color. **1832** WILLIAMSON *Maine* I. 178 Quartz is used for watch seals and ornamental jewelry. **1867** *Wkly. New Mexican* 23 Feb. 1/4 As yet I have no means of knowing whether the quartz proves rich in gold or not. **1881** RAYMOND *Mining Gloss., Quartz,* . . . any hard or silver ore, as distinguished from gravel or earth. **1893** M. HOWE *Honor* 45 Richard Cole was . . . stroking the rough rich quartz, and giving vent to inarticulate cries of almost bestial joy.

2. *attrib.* **a.** Consisting of or containing quartz.

1831 PECK *Guide* 132 Quartz crystals exist in Gallatin county. **1850** *Rep. Comm. Patents 1849: Agric.* 89 Its western and southern material is composed to a very great extent of quartz rock intermingled occasionally with chlorite, steatite, and gneiss. **1864** *Ore. State Jrnl.* 7 May 2/2 The mountains for fifty miles around . . . are full of quartz ledges. **1867** *Wkly. New Mexican* 23 Feb. 1/4 There are hardly any persons in this part of the country, who are able to raise money enough to work quartz-veins. **1876** RAYMOND *8th Rep. Mines* 131 Auriferous quartz-lodes were known to abound in this county. **1881** *Harper's Mag.* Feb. 359/2 The freight trains come, with their tonnage of spars, quartz clays, and coals.

b. In special combinations.

Quartz battery, a quartz mill or stamp mill; *q. camp,* a camp of quartz miners; *q. gold,* (see quotation).

1869 J. R. BROWNE *Adv. Apache Country* 346 Quartz-batteries are battering; hammers are hammering. **1910** *Haines* (Alaska) *Pioneer Press* 18 March 2/3 For Conrad City, located in the heart of the newly discovered and fabulously rich quartz camp of the Windy Arm District, take our daily trains to Caribou. **1874** RAYMOND *6th Rep. Mines* 317 The gold found in it . . . is largely 'quartz gold,' that is, not rounded and water-worn, but irregular and frequently twisted in form, usually very bright, and always of fine quality, as is the gold of the quartz-veins.

+**Quartz claim.** A mining claim where valuable mineral-bearing quartz occurs or is thought to occur. (Cf. PLACER CLAIM.) — **1876** RAYMOND *8th Rep. Mines* 220 The discovery . . . of quartz-claims in the district . . . gave an impetus to quartz-prospecting. **1884** *Century Mag.* Oct. 843/2 Locating a quartz claim on a mountain-side . . . is not a short cut to wealth.

+**Quartz-crusher.** A machine for crushing or pulverizing quartz. — **1859** *Rep. Comm. Patents 1858* I. 562 Improvement in Quartz Crushers. **1864** *Ore. State Jrnl.* 30 July 3/1 Parties who arrived from San Francisco . . . brought with them a quartz crusher. **1892** *Harper's Mag.* Dec. 140 The Rocky Mountain method of prospecting is by means of the gold-pan or the quartz-crusher.

+**Quartz mill.** A machine for pulverizing quartz; a stamp mill. — **1861** *Chicago Tribune* 15 April 1 The Scoville Quartz Mill . . . was exhibited at the Mechanics Fair last fall. **1872** MCCLELLAN *Golden State* 266 There are about four hundred and fifty quartz-mills . . . in the State. **1880** INGHAM *Digging Gold* 122 The First Quartz-mill was built in California . . . in 1851. **1898** *McClure's Mag.* X. 248 Jim went over into the valley where the quartz mills were.

+**Quartz mine.** A mine from which gold or silver is obtained by quartz mining. — **a1861** WINTHROP *J. Brent* 7 They depended upon me and the quartz mine to set them up again. **1876** RAYMOND *8th Rep. Mines* 80 The Idaho Mine of Grass Valley has for several years been considered the leading quartz-mine of the State. **1891** *Century Mag.* Feb. 533/2 This auriferous region [in Calif. has] . . . the most productive quartz mines.

+**Quartz mining.** (See quot. 1890.) Also attrib. — **1851** *Whig Almanac 1852* 19/1 Quartz-mining has been attempted in many places. **1853** *Harper's Mag.* Feb. 420/2 It will yield equally well with any of the Sonora or Quartz-mining companies. **1860** HARTE *Luck of Roaring Camp* 143 Then Smith went into quartz-mining; . . . then into hydraulics and ditching. **1876** RAYMOND *8th Rep. Mines* 42 The most extensive quartz-mining operation of the county at present is the Gwin or Paloma Mine. **1890** *Cent.* 4900/1 In California and other gold-mining regions mining in the solid rock is commonly called *quartz-mining,* in contradistinction to *placer* and *hydraulic mining.*

+**Quatroon.** =QUADROON. {quatron, 1748} Also attrib. — **1808** PIKE *Sources Miss.* III. App. 20 Three-twentieths may be Spaniards from Europe, five-twentieths Creoles, five-twentieths Metifs and Quatroons, and seven-twentieths Indians. **1823** I. HOLMES *Account* 333 In New Orleans, there is a description of coloured persons whom they name quatroons, that is, the colour between a mulatto and a white. **1840** *Knickerb.* XVI. 416 Stepton's ring at the door was immediately responded to by a pretty quatroon servant.

Quawk. [Imitative.] **1.** The cry of a duck or a heron. +**2.** =NIGHT HERON. (Cf. QUA-BIRD.) — **(1) 1863** 'G. HAMILTON' *Gala-Days* 73 For the heavy booming of cannon rose the 'quauk!' of ducks. **1895** CHAPMAN *Handbk. Birds* (1904) 137 Occasionally they [*i.e.,* black-crowned night herons] utter a loud, hoarse *quawk,* the origin of their common name. **(2) 1844** *Nat. Hist. N.Y., Zoology* II. 227 The Black-crowned Night Heron, or Quawk, . . . derives its popular name from the deep guttural cry. **1867** *Amer. Naturalist* I. 344 Many . . . were all agog to cover themselves with glory by shooting a quawk. **1877** WHITMAN *Spec. Days* 100, I find [in N.J.] . . . Cheewinks, Quawks, Ground robins. **1917** *Birds of Amer.* I. 194.

+**Quebrada.** [Sp.] (See quot. 1890 and cf. BARRANCA.) — **a1861** WINTHROP *J. Brent* 211 We took breakneck leaps across dry quebradas in the clay. **1890** *Cent.* 4903/1 *Quebrada,* . . . a gorge; a ravine; a defile: a word occasionally used by writers in English on Mexican and South American physical geography, and by the Spanish Americans themselves, with about the same meaning as *barranca.*

* **Queen.**

+**1.** An Indian woman having the rank of a chief in her tribe. *Obs.*

1675 *Conn. Rec.* II. 403 They say the Indyans are scattered; the two sachems Suikquens, Nononanto, & ye Queene beeing neere ye Nipmug Country. **1675** *Mass. H. S. Coll.* 4 Ser. VI. 300 [He] sent post . . . to the Old Queen, . . . to give vs a meeting at Mr. Smiths. **1822** MORSE *Rep. Indian Affairs* I. 31 A woman of this tribe [the Nottoways], about sixty years old, named Edie Turner, is its present reigning Queen.

2. Used in the possessive to designate various things associated in some way with queens: (see also quot. 1830).

See also QUEEN'S WARE.

1779 *York Co., Va., Rec.: Wills* XXII. 28 April, 1 lot of Queens china. 17/4/0. **1830** WATSON *Philadelphia* 176 Among the caps was the 'queen's night cap,' the same always worn by Lady Washington. **1845** *Cincinnati Misc.* I. 138 Their dresses were chiefly of *silk,* of various colors, and some of them were of good old fashioned *Queen's gray.*

‖**b.** *Queen's-lace,* ?Queen Anne's lace.

1907 FREEMAN *By Light of Soul* 52 She walked slowly between the fields, which were white and gold with queen's-lace and golden-rod.

+**3.** *Queen Elizabeth's bone,* the cramp bone or patella of a sheep.

1846 *Knickerb.* XXVII. 17 From the Pope's Eye, to Queen Elizabeth's bone, each preferable and available slice . . . was apparent to his practised eye.

Queen Anne. Attrib. and possessive in names of various things associated with Queen Anne of England (1702–14). — **1775** in Rauck *Boonesborough* 186 [We] fixed Mr. Cocke off with a good queen Ann's musket. **1884** *Century Mag.* March 651/1 Many of these alleged 'Queen Anne' houses, with their rooms cut up into all sorts of angles, are reputed to be most uncomfortable places to live in. **1887** STOCKTON *Hundredth Man* x, His thoughts went immediately forth to a medium-sized frame house, probably in the Queen Anne style, somewhere in the suburbs of the city. **1894** *Amer. Folk-Lore* VII. 89 *Daucus Carota,* Queen Anne's lace, somewhat general.

+**Queen City.**

1. Cincinnati, Ohio. A nickname.

Cf. QUEEN OF THE WEST.

1838 B. DRAKE (*title*), Tales and Sketches from the Queen City. **1854** HOLMES *Tempest & Sunshine* 113 As they neared the Queen City, they noticed . . . a tall, intelligent, but rather reckless looking young man. **1896** *N.Y. Dramatic News* 18 July 15/1 This has been a gala week for the Queen City.

2. Used with an *of* phrase to designate a particular city: (see quotations).

1843 MARRYAT *M. Violet* xli, St. Louis has been described by so many travellers, that it is quite useless to mention anything about this 'queen city of the Mississippi.' **1851** WORTLEY *Travels in U.S.* 63 Buffalo [is called] the Queen City of the Lakes. **1879** WHITMAN *Spec. Days* (1892) 147 So much for my feeling toward the Queen city of the plains and peaks

[Denver, Colo.]. **1880** *Harper's Mag.* Dec. 70 Local prejudice . . . and proverbial procrastination . . . unite to keep 'Chinatown' practically a sealed book to the better-class denizens of the 'Queen City of the Pacific' [San Francisco]. **1892** *Vt. Agric. Rep.* XII. 120 Burlington, the 'queen city' of Vermont, offers inducements to people of various tastes.

+**Queenfish.** (See quot. 1911.) — **1884** GOODE, etc. *Fisheries* I. 380 This species is known as 'King-fish' or 'Queen fish.' **1911** *Rep. Fisheries 1908* 314/1 Queen-fish (*Seriphus politus*).—A small food fish of excellent quality found on the Pacific coast south of Tomales Bay. It is also called 'kingfish.'

****Queen of the meadow(s).** **1.** One of several species of *Spiraea*, esp. *S. alba* or *S. latifolia.* +**2.** =JOE-PYE('S) WEED. — **(1) 1784** *Amer. Acad. Mem.* I. 451 Queen of the Meadows. Blossoms red or purple. In moist pastures. **1843** TORREY *Flora N.Y.* I. 198 *Spirea salicifolia*. . . . Queen-of-the-meadow. . . . Wet bushy meadows; also in dry elevated situations. **1898** CREEVEY *Flowers of Field* 484 Meadow-sweet. Queen-of-the-meadows. . . . A slender, reddish-stemmed shrub, 2 to 6 feet high. **(2) 1892** *Amer. Folk-Lore* V. 98 *Eupatorium purpureum*, Queen-of-the-meadow. Worcester Co., Mass. **1901** MOHR *Plant Life Ala.* 761 *Eupatorium maculatum*. . . . Spotted Trumpet-weed. Queen of the Meadow. . . . Alleghenian to Louisianian area.

+**Queen of the prairie.** A tall perennial American herb (*Filipendula rubra*) found in meadows and prairies. — **1857** GRAY *Botany* 114 *S[piraea] lobata.* (Queen of the Prairie.) Meadows and prairies, Penn. to Michigan, Illinois, and Kentucky. **1898** CREEVEY *Flowers of Field* 146 Queen-of-the-prairie. . . . A stately, beautiful plant adorning the meadows and prairies south and west of Pennsylvania.

+**Queen of the West.** A designation usually applied to Cincinnati, Ohio, but sometimes to St. Louis, Mo. *Obs.* (Cf. QUEEN CITY 1.) — **1835** HOFFMAN *Winter in West* I. 130 It is in vain for thriving Pittsburg or flourishing Louisville . . . to dispute with Cincinnati her title of 'Queen of the West.' **1835** A. PARKER *Trip to Texas* 76 St. Louis will . . . remain in all time to come, the undisputed 'Queen of the West.' **1840** *Knickerb.* XVI. 157 In this way we glided in our broad-horn past Cincinnati, the Queen of the West' as she is now called.

+**Queen's arm.** A musket of a type originally used by British soldiers in the time of Queen Anne (1702–14). *Obs.* — **1829** *Mass. Spy* 20 May (Th.), One of the party returned the salute with an old queen's arm. **1851** *Knickerb.* XXXVIII. 472 Captain Tinker . . . had advanced his company to a high state of 'theoretical practice,' through the aid of broom-sticks and corn-stalks, interspersed here and there with a rusty old 'Queen's-arm.' **1898** N. BROOKS *Boys of Fairport* 196 Ned Martin carried the heavy 'Queen's arm' that had belonged to his grandfather, who fought at Bunker Hill and Concord.

+**Queen's-delight.** A herbaceous plant (*Stillingia sylvatica*) of the southern states. — **1868** GRAY *Field Botany* 295 *Stillingia sylvatica*, Queen's Delight. Dry soil from Virginia S[outh]. **1901** MOHR *Plant Life Ala.* 594 Queen's Delight. . . . Southeastern Virginia to Florida, west to Louisiana, Arkansas, and Texas.

+**Queen snake.** (See quot. 1909.) — **1902** *Smithsonian Rep. 1900* 104/2 Specimen of Queen snake, *Natrix leberis*, from Great Falls, Md. **1909** *Cent. Suppl.* 1098/2 *Queen snake*, a water-snake, *Natrix leberis*, of the central and eastern United States.

Queen's ware. Wedgwood ware of a distinctive cream color; any cream-colored earthenware, esp. glazed earthenware. Also attrib.

Invented by Wedgwood 1761–63 and named by him after Queen Charlotte.

1773 in Singleton *Social N.Y.* 130 [Imported goods include] pencil'd china, blue and white Queen's ware, Delph, and stone enamelled black. **1809** CUMING *Western Tour* 92 Mr. Bakewell from England . . . politely shewed us his manufactury of pottery and queensware. **1850** *Annual of Sci. Discovery* 96 The manufacture of Queensware, like that of glass, is rapidly advancing in this country. **1851** *S. Lit. Messenger* XVII. 30/1 She then poured the black, bitter liquid into her queensware bowl with blue flowers pictured on it. **1892** *York County Hist. Rev.* 76/2 Jacob Miller, General Store, [sells] . . . queens ware, agate and hollow ware [etc.].

attrib. **1831** ROYALL *Southern Tour* III. 202 The queensware factory [in Louisville, Ky.,] belongs to a Mr. Lewis.

Quercitron. The quercitron oak; also, a dyestuff prepared from the bark of this. {1794–} — **1832** BROWNE *Sylva* 291 From the cellular integument of the black oak is obtained the quercitron, of which great use is made in dyeing wool, silk and paper hangings. **1843** TORREY *Flora N.Y.* II. 188 Black Oak, Quercitron. . . . The bark . . . yields the valuable dye called *quercitron*, and is also much used in tanning. **1847** DARLINGTON *Weeds & Plants* 315 Quercitron. Yellow-barked Oak. . . . The inner bark is an article of commerce, under the name of Quercitron.

Quercitron bark. The bark of the quercitron oak, used in tanning and dyeing. {1794–} — **1806** *Ann. 9th Congress* 2 Sess. 1113 The foliage of the hickory, and oak, which produces the quercitron bark, is changed before its fall into a beautiful yellow. **1832** BROWNE *Sylva* 289 There are several varieties of this species of oak, all of which afford the quercitron bark, so highly esteemed in dyeing, staining, tanning etc. **1840** *Niles' Nat. Reg.* 16 May 167/3 She has near 100 hhds. of tobacco and quercitron bark.

Quercitron oak. The N.A. black oak, *Quercus velutina.* {1852–} — **1810** MICHAUX *Arbres* I. 25 Q[uercus] tinctoria. . . . *Black oak*, seule dénomination dans tous les Etats du milieu, de l'ouest et du midi. *Quercitron oak*, nom du commerce. **1832** BROWNE *Sylva* 289 Black or Quercitron Oak. . . . Except the state of Maine, the northern part of New Hampshire, Vermont and Tennessee, this species is found throughout the United States on both sides of the Alleghanies. **1897** SUDWORTH *Arborescent Flora* 169 Yellow Oak. . . . [Also called] Quercitron Oak (Del., S.C., La., Kans., Minn.).

+**Querida.** *S.W.* [Sp.] Darling, sweetheart. — **1834** A. PIKE *Sketches* 105 Querida, when the turtle dove is attacked by the hawk . . . , she has been known to take refuge in the bosom of man. **1925** BURNS *Saga of Billy the Kid* 185 In every placeta in the Pecos some little senorita was proud to be known as his querida.

+**Querl, Quirl.** [Origin obscure.] (See quot. 1879.) *colloq.* — **1853** B. F. TAYLOR *Jan. & June* 23 [The grapevine's] aspirations were soon manifested in the display of divers mermaidish-looking ringlets, with two or three dainty 'quirls' therein. **1879** WEBSTER *Suppl.* 1575/2 *Querl*, . . . a coil; a twirl; as the *querl* of hair on the fore leg of a blooded horse. **1889** COOKE *Steadfast* 162 A hundred resolute little quirls above the low forehead.

****Questionist.** At Harvard College, during the term in which final examinations are held, a candidate for the bachelor's degree. *Obs.* {1574–1887, of Cambridge} — **1650** *Harvard Rec.* I. 28 In Case any of ye Sophisters Questionists or Inceptors faill in ye premises required . . . they shall be deferred to ye following Year. **1654** *Ib.* III. 293 The approved Questionists, . . . after the usual examination, . . . are made Bachelors at the beginning of Lent.

Questionnaire. A series of questions about a subject under investigation, usually printed and submitted to a number of persons. {1901–} — **1899** *Educational Rev.* XVIII. 87 By means of questionnaires the writer obtained . . . data bearing on the . . . characteristics of more than ten thousand children. **1899** *Pop. Science Mo.* May 106 Various *questionnaires* [have been] sent out by Dr. G. Stanley Hall and others who are interested in the scientific study of children. **1923** *Harper's Mag.* July 276/2 Neither in college offices nor in any other, are returned questionnaires ever opened.

****Quick.** +Short for QUICKSILVER. — **1882** *47th Congress 1 Sess.* H. R. Ex. Doc. No. 216, 651 As fast as it collects the 'quick' passes by an inverted siphon to the strainers.

+**Quickhatch.** [Algonquian.] =CARCAJOU 1. Now *rare.* (Cf. GLUTTON.) — **1743** CATESBY *Nat. Hist.* II. xxx, The Quickhatch . . . inhabits the very Northern Parts of *America* and has not been observed by any Author, or known in *Europe* till the year 1737, one was sent to Sir *Hans Sloane* from *Hudson's Bay.* [**1752** J. ROBSON *Acct. Hudson's Bay* 47 But before morning a quiquihatch or wolverine, a very strong, cunning and rapacious creature, had broke through the fence.] **1789** MORSE *Amer. Geog.* 55 Beasts of different *genus* from any known in the old world [include] . . . the Opossum, the Racoon, the Quickhatch.

** **Quicksand.** Loose wet sand that yields readily to pressure and swallows up any heavy object that comes upon it.

1672 LEDERER *Discoveries* 11, I was almost swallowed in a quicksand. **1802** ELLICOTT *Journal* 120 When the water is low, you have high muddy banks, quick-sands, and sand bars. **1822** J. FOWLER *Journal* 156 But for feer of the quick Sand it Was thaught best take all the Bagage over In the Boat. **1863** *Rio Abajo Press* 20 Jan. 2/1 Not so the Rio del Norte, as can testify every one who has stalled in the quicksands when crossing. **1923** J. H. COOK *On Old Frontier* 98 The Niabrara River . . . was about fifty yards wide and four feet deep, with a very quick current and plenty of quicksand.

b. Attrib. with *bed, bottom, river.*

1854 MARCY *Explor. Red River* 29 Red river . . . is eighty yards wide, with but a very small portion covered with water, running over the quicksand bed. **1869** HALE *Sybaris* 91 These people . . . have known enough to dam this river, where there is a quicksand bottom. **1925** TILGHMAN *Dugout* 26 When I've got to swim a quicksand river I'd ruther have daylight.

** **Quicksilver.** The metal mercury.

1731 FRANKLIN in W. Pepper *Medical Side B. Franklin* 20 An imprudent use of quicksilver in the cure of the itch. **1819** E. DANA *Geogr. Sk.* 203 Iron ore, copper, quicksilver, and pit-coal, are produced in the country. **1914** KEATE *Destruction Mephisto's Web* 52 These dice are bored into and the holes thus made are filled with a preparation containing quicksilver.

attrib. **1848** in Bryant *California* App. 463 The quicksilver mine of Mr. Alexander Forbes . . . is in a spur of mountains. **1876** RAYMOND *8th Rep. Mines* 260 By means of a rude but clever arrangement of quicksilver-tanks, steam is generated and the pulp submitted to its action.

+**Quicksilver weed.** The early meadow rue, *Thalictrum dioicum.* — **1893** *Amer. Folk-Lore* VI. 136 *Thalictrum dioicum*, quicksilver weed. Penobscot Co., Me.

Quick stock. + =LIVE STOCK 1. *Obs.* {*quick good(s), –1745} — **1677** *East-Hampton Rec.* I. 405, I Thomas Diament sen[io]r doe oblige my selfe . . . to give & bequeath unto my sonn . . . a double Share of ye Quick Stock w[hi]ch I shall Leave behind me. **1696** *N.H. Probate Rec.* I. 425, I doe giue and bequeath . . . meddow quick stock household goods. **1714** *Essex Inst. Coll.* XLIII. 85 To Inventory on file in Quick Stock £329 05. **1740** *N.H. Probate Rec.* III. 1, I give and bequeath to my loveing Wife Ann hodsdon all my quick stock.

Quick water. +(See quot. 1905.) — **a1862** THOREAU *Maine Woods* 276 The Indian navigator naturally distinguishes by a name those parts of a stream where he has encountered quick water and forks. **1894** WISTER in *Harper's Mag.* April 782/1 That quick water's the Mahkin

Rapids. **1905** *Forestry Bureau Bul.* No. 61, 44 *Quickwater*, that part of a stream which has fall enough to create a decided current.

***Quid.** +[Abbrev. of *tertium quid.*] (See quot. 1914.) Now hist. — **1805** JEFFERSON *Writings* (1830) IV. 45 That I have avowed . . . any predilection for those called the third party, or Quids, is . . . false. **1818** FEARON *Sketches* 139 The political parties [in Penna. include] at present . . . no party men, called 'Quids.' **1914** *Cycl. Amer. Govt.* III. 128/1 The Quids were the John Randolph . . . men, opposed to Jefferson and Madison. They formed the first 'third party' in the United States. Randolph claimed that his were the Republican principles of 1798, and that Jefferson and Madison had departed from them.

+**Quiddism.** The political philosophy of the Quids. *Obs.* — **1806** *Ann. 9th Congress* 1 Sess. 775 There is another question relative to what is generally called *quiddism*. . . . If we belong to the third party, be it so.

Quiddle, *n.* **1.** *pl.* (See second quot.) **2.** A fussy person. *local.* {1893–, *dial.*} — **(1) 1815** HUMPHREYS *Yankey* 30 Blind staggers! Quiddles! I vow. *Ib.* 107 *Quiddles*, disorder in the head, moping disease in horses, dizziness. **(2) 1829** [see QUIDDLE *v.*]. **1856** EMERSON *English Traits* 108 The Englishman is very petulant and precise about his accommodation at inns, . . . a quiddle about his toast and his chop.

***Quiddle,** *v. intr.* To trifle, to waste time *with. local.* {1883–, *dial.*} — **1829** *Va. Lit. Museum* 30 Dec. 460 To *quiddle.* 'To busy one's self about trifles.' The word is also used as a substantive. *New England.* **1869** STOWE *Oldtown Folks* 240 Who's a going to stop to quiddle with young uns? **1891** WILKINS *New Eng. Nun* 428 You've been quiddlin' out there all the mornin'.

Quiddler. (See quotation.) — **1841** WEBSTER 407/2 *Quiddler*, one who spends time in trifling niceties.

Quiddling. *n.* and *a.* **1.** *n.* Spending time on trifles **2.** *adj.* Fussy, trifling. — **(1) 1841** WEBSTER 407. **(2) 1860** EMERSON *Conduct of Life* 133 Neither will we be driven into a quiddling abstemiousness. **1869** BOWLES *Our New West* 157 A quiddling Secretary of the Interior or Indian Commissioner refuses to carry it out. **1880** *Scribner's Mo.* June 227/1 Bold, strong, free from quiddling lines, they hold with a firm grasp the conceptions of the artist.

***Quill,** *n.*

***1.** A writing pen made from the feather of a goose or other large bird. Also transf.

1676 B. TOMPSON *Poetical Works* 63 What meanes this silence of Harvardine quils While *Mars* triumphant thunders on our hills. **1722** *New-Eng. Courant* 6 Aug. 1/1 Thou only canst express with fluent Quill, The mighty Product of Harvardine Skill. **1790** *Penna. Packet* 21 April 4/4 Robert Campbell, Bookseller and Stationer, . . . has just received . . . Bonnet Papers, Quills, Wax & Wafers. **1820** *Columbian Centinel* 15 Jan. 3/1 For sale: . . . Quills, of all prices; Ink Powder. **1880** CABLE *Grandissimes* 137 Paper, quills, and ink were handed down from a shelf and Joseph retired into the shop.

‖**b.** *Head quill*, the chief editor of, or writer for, a newspaper. *slang.*

1873 BEADLE *Undevel. West* 35 The Head Quill of the Indianapolis Journal briefly declined.

2. One of the large hollow spines of a porcupine. {1602–}

1789 MORSE *Amer. Geog.* 57 These quills the porcupine darts at his enemy. **1805** LEWIS in *L. & Clark Exped.* III. (1905) 4 The breast [of the Indian women's robes] is usually ornament[e]d with various figures of party colours rought with the quills of the Porcupine. **1907** [see PORCUPINE].

+**3.** (See quotation and cf. next.)

1855 in Hambleton *H. A. Wise* 426 [Uncle Sam] and his wife [Miss Know-Nothing] . . . married each other for money, at first, or for 'quills' as they say.

***4.** The tube or barrel of a feather +used as a container for gold dust.

1858 PETERS *Kit Carson* 424 We have seen quills full of gold dust which has been collected there.

+**5.** *pl.* A simple musical instrument made of pieces of reed or cane of different lengths.

1886 *Century Mag.* Feb. 521/2 But to show how far the art of playing the 'quills' could be carried . . . see this 'quill tune' . . . from a gentleman who heard it in Alabama.

6. Attrib. with *manufactory, toothpick, tune, work.*

1836 *Phila. Public Ledger* 25 March 3/4 Quill manufactory and dealers in stationery. **1843** *Knickerb.* XXII. 164 The Indians prepare it in bark, . . . curiously ornamented with quill work and beads. **1886** Quill tune [see sense 5]. **1888** CABLE *Bonaventure* 154, I never use a quill toothpick.

Quill, *v.* [Origin obscure.] *intr.* To go or move rapidly. *colloq.* — **1869** *Overland Mo.* III. 127 A trig, smirk little horse . . . often has to 'june,' or 'quill,' or 'get up and quill.'

+**Quillback.** The spearfish, *Carpiodes velifer.* — **1884** GOODE, etc. *Fisheries* I. 615 The Carp Sucker—*Carpiodes cyprinus.* The different species . . . known as 'Carp,' 'Carp Suckers,' 'Spear-fish,' 'Sail-fish,' 'Quillback,' etc., abound in all the larger bodies of water south and west of New York as far as the Rio Grande. **1911** *Rep. Fisheries 1908* 314/1 *Quillback.*—A sucker (*Ictiobus velifer*) found abundantly in the Mississippi Valley.

+**Quill pig.** A porcupine. *colloq.* — **1885** *Harper's Mag.* July 225/2 The cabin was . . . tenanted only by an interesting family of what the guides quaintly call 'quill pigs.' **1905** *N.Y. Ev. Post* 30 Jan. 6 Two years ago the 'quill pig,' as it is familiarly known in the Maine woods, was convicted of girdling and killing valuable forest trees. **1917** *Mammals of Amer.* 217/1 Anyone who has traveled in the woods of the northern United States is familiar with the Porcupine, or Quill Pig.

+**Quilltail (coot).** The ruddy duck, *Erismatura jamaicensis rubida.* Also *quill-tailed coot.* — **1888** TRUMBULL *Names of Birds* 112 Ruddy Duck of Wilson 1814. . . . At Tuckerton N.J., [called] Quill-tail coot. **1890** *Cent.* 4913/2 *Quilltail*, . . . the ruddy duck, *Erismatura rubida.* Also called *quilltail coot.* (New Jersey.) **1917** *Birds of Amer.* I. 152 Ruddy Duck. *Erismatura jamaicensis.* . . . [Also called] Bumblebee Coot; Quill-tailed Coot; Heavy-tailed Coot.

+**Quillwood.** (See quotation.) — **1806** LEWIS in *L. & Clark Exped.* IV. (1905) 59 There is a shrub which grows commonly in this neighbourhood which is precisely the same with that in Virginia sometimes called the quill-wood.

Quillwort. 1. Any one of various plants of the genus *Isoetes.* {1787–} +**2.** (See quotation and cf. JOE-PYE('S) WEED.) — **(1) 1817–8** EATON *Botany* (1822) 321 *Isoetes lacustris*, quill-wort . . . colour green: growing immersed, or at the margin of ponds.—Resembles a zophyte. **1843** TORREY *Flora N.Y.* II. 514. **1882** *Amer. Naturalist* XVI. 506 The grass-like or rush-like plants commonly designated as the quillworts, and included in the genus *Isoëtes*, . . . belong to the great group of plants lying next below the Phanerogams. **(2) 1894** *Amer. Folk-Lore* VII. 92 *Eupatorium purpureum*, . . . quill-wort, Indian gravel root, West Va.

***Quilt,** *n.*

***1.** A bed covering consisting essentially of two thicknesses of material with some soft substance, as cotton or wool, between them. Also attrib.

See also BEDQUILT.

1638 *Md. Archives* IV. 43 A true and perfect Inventary of all the goods & debts w[hi]ch were Andrew Baker's, . . . piece of beare skin . . . a quilt bedd. **1727** *Boston News-Letter* 29 June 2/2 To be Sold, . . . All sorts of European Goods, Consisting of . . . Feather-Beds, Ruggs, Quilts, Blankets [etc.]. **1787** BENTLEY *Diary* I. 78 [I received] a letter from my father, shewing his proceedings respecting the Legacy of a Quilt and Pillow Cases, & Adams' refusal. **1803** [see COTTONADE]. **1847** ROBB *Squatter Life* 119 Close by stood a small wagon, with a quilt cover, to which was harnessed a horse. **1885** 'CRADDOCK' *Prophet* 268 There was . . . a bed, too, draped with a gay quilt. **1902** WISTER *Virginian* iii, Medicine Bow was quiet as I went my way to my quilts.

+**2.** An article of apparel worn by women. *Obs.*

1774 FITHIAN *Journal* I. 184 She appears to Day in a Chintz cotton Gown with an elegant blue Stamp, a Sky-Blue silk Quilt, spotted Apron. *Ib.* 185 [Miss Hale] is drest in a white Holland Gown, cotton Diaper Quilt very fine, a Lawn apron. **1778** *Holyoke Diaries* 99 Bought a Blue Sarsnet quilt.

3. In special combinations.

Quilt pattern, a pattern or design according to which a quilt is made (cf. LOG CABIN 2); *q. piece*, one of the small pieces or scraps of cloth used in making a quilt; *q. piecing*, the action of sewing together small pieces of cloth for a quilt.

1891 EARLE *Sabbath* 110 [The women discussed] their patterns in quilt-piecing, and sometimes they slyly exchanged quilt-patterns. **1883** 'S. BONNER' *Dialect Tales* 115, I'll give you a whole bagful of quilt pieces.

***Quilt,** *v.* +**1.** *intr.* To make a quilt or quilts. **2.** *tr.* To secure or fix (a needle) in needlework by taking incompleted quilting or running stitches. — **(1) 1838** *U.S. Mag.* I. 342 She could knit, spin, weave, and quilt. **1861** STOWE *Pearl Orr's Isl.* I. 21 Miss Roxy and Miss Ruey Toothacre . . . could upholster and quilt. **1881** WARNER *W. Irving* 32 A number of girls were quilting. **(2) 1908** FREEMAN *Shoulders of Atlas* 236 As she spoke, she quilted her needle into her work and tossed it on a table.

Quilting. {1611–} =next. {1819 *dial.*} (Cf. QUILTING FROLIC, PARTY.) — **1768** *Essex Inst. Coll.* XIV. 260 [August] 18, quilting at my house. **1825** NEAL *Bro. Jonathan* I. 175 'Where is Edith?' . . . 'Gone to a quiltin'.' **1878** in Summers *Ann. S.W. Va.* 1524 A corn-shucking and quilting at Mr. Bryants . . . drew together a large number of the men and women of the neighborhood. **1914** E. STEWART *Lett. Woman Homesteader* 102 Zobbie often met Pauline at the quiltings and other gatherings at the homes of non-partisans.

+**Quilting bee.** A social gathering of the women of a neighborhood to engage in quilting. (Cf. BEE[2] 1.) — **1832** GOODRICH *System of Univ. Geog.* 107 The females also have similar meetings called 'quilting bees,' when many assemble to work for one, in padding or *quilting* bed coverings or *comforters.* **1836** WESTON *Visit* 213 This lady told me that a Mr. Aldridge, her next neighbour, was to have a 'Quilting Bee' that night. **1848** IRVING *Knickerb.* VII. ii, Now were instituted 'quilting bees' . . . and other rural assemblages. **1881** *Harper's Mag.* Oct. 725/2 He has his corn-shuckings, his log-rollings, his quilting bees. **1907** *St. Nicholas* Oct. 1145/2 Grandmother . . . often rode five and ten miles to visit her distant friends, attending quilting bees and corn-huskings.

Quilting frame. A light, collapsible wooden frame in which material to be quilted is held flat and taut. — **1739** *Penna. Gazette* 15 Nov. 4/1 (Ernst). **1779** *York Co., Va., Rec.: Wills* XXII. 28 April, 1 quilting frame 20/. **1856** [see APPLE-BUTTER 2]. **1891** *Harper's Mag.* Oct. 824/1 The quilting frames were hung there also.

+**Quilting frolic.** =QUILTING BEE. (Cf. FROLIC 2.) — **1819** NOAH *She Would Be a Soldier* I. i, I'm the boy for a race, for an apple-paring or quilting frolic. **1839** *S. Lit. Messenger* V. 377/2 A parcel of her friends had got together at a quilting frolic. **1868** Lossing *Hudson* 349 The old Dutch house . . . [was] the very dwelling wherein occurred Katrina Van Tassel's memorable quilting frolic.

+**Quilting match.** =Quilting bee. — **1837** *S. Lit. Messenger* III. 297 Arrayed like the cover produced by the united efforts of a quilting match. **1845** *Lowell Offering* V. 87 My mind involuntarily reverted to the merry-making scenes, the tea parties, the quilting matches [etc.].

+**Quilting party.** =Quilting bee. — **1835** *Knickerb.* VI. 180 There was a great quilting-party invited to Tecumseh-Place, which assembled all the principal young people of the county. **1848** Drake *Pioneer Life Ky.* 186 Another kind of gathering was the quilting party. **1907** *St. Nicholas* Sept. 1044/2 She had gone, with her grandmother whom she was visiting, to a quilting-party.

*__Quince.__

*__1.__ The fruit of the quince tree, or the tree itself.

1649 *Perfect Descr. Va.* 14 The Governour in his new Orchard hath 15 hundred fruit-trees, besides his Apricocks, Peaches, Mellicotons, Quinces, Wardens, and such like fruits. **1674** *Cal. State P., Amer. & W.I.* VII. 581 Maine [has] . . . quinces, apricots, plums, cherries, currants, strawberries [etc.]. **1762** *Holyoke Diaries* 56 Preserved quinces. Made syrup of cores and parings. **1781–2** Jefferson *Notes Va.* (1788) 40 The orchards produce apples, pears, cherries, quinces, peaches [etc.]. **1838** C. Newell *Revol. Texas* 168 The Quince, a very valuable fruit, is said to produce remarkably well in Texas. **1872** McClellan *Golden State* 327 Most of the quinces raised come from Los Angeles, Santa Clara, and Yuba counties. **1898** Harper *S. B. Anthony* I. 7 On all the farms were fine orchards of apples, plums, pears, cherries and quinces. **1922** Hesler & Whetzel *Man. Fruit Diseases* 395 Quinces affected with bitter-rot show symptoms very similar to those exhibited by the apple.

2. *attrib.* **a.** With *cutting, root, stock.*

1629 *Mass. Bay Rec.* I. 24 Peare, aple, quince kernells, pomegranats. **1852** *Horticulturist* VII. 292/2, I have pear trees on the quince root which are twenty-five years old. **1857** *Lawrence* (Kan.) *Republican* 28 May 3 John B. Wood has for sale . . . 1,000 Pears, on Quince stocks, choice selections. **1858** Warder *Hedges & Evergreens* 73, I have seen quince-cuttings and willows planted by dropping them in a furrow.

b. With *butter, jam, jelly,* etc.

1654 [see Pumpkin pie]. **1832** Child *Frugal Housewife* 118 Quince Marmalade.—To two pounds of quince put three quarters of a pound of nice sugar. **1862** in Gray & Ropes *War Letters* 61 The woman fed us on pies, 'apple and quince butter' . . . and coffee. **1867** *Common Sense Cook Book* 99 [Recipe for] quince jam puree. **1880** *Harper's Mag.* Oct. 780/2 The royal jelly . . . has a very rich taste—'some thing between cream, quince jelly, and honey.' **1887** Wilkins *Humble Romance* 51 [She] put on . . . a little dish of quince sauce, and some custard-pie.

Quince apple. {1600–} A variety of apple. {1664, an Eng. apple} — **1817** W. Coxe *Fruit Trees* 138 Quince apple . . . came originally from the state of New-York. **1847** Ives *New Eng. Fruit* 46 *Quince Apple.*—The tree of this variety is of vigorous growth; the size of the fruit large. **1849** S. W. Cole *Amer. Fruit Book* 115 Fall Apples. . . . *Quince* of Coxe. Large; flattish; yellow; flesh yellowish, juicy, crisp, of a very pleasant flavor.

+**Quince drink.** (See quotations.) — **1666** *Md. Archives* II. 149 Quince drink thirty per gallon. **1676** Glover *Va.* in *Phil. Trans.* XI. 628 Here are also great stores of Quinces, which are larger and fairer than those of England, and not so harsh in taste; of the juice of these [quinces] they also make Quince-drink. **1709** Lawson *Carolina* 109 Of this Fruit, they make a Wine, or Liquor, which they call Quince-Drink, and which I approve of beyond any Drink which that Country affords.

*__Quince tree.__ A central Asiatic fruit tree (*Cydonia oblonga*) or a related species. — **1737** Brickell *N. Carolina* 100 The Quince-Tree thrives well, and is in plenty. **1842** Hawthorne *Notebooks* (1932) 152 There are . . . one or two quince trees. **1860** *Ladies' Repository* June 338/2 The small quince-trees . . . grew on one side of the old brown homestead of Deacon Palmer. **1892** Apgar *Trees Northern U.S.* 102 *Pyrus vulgaris.* (Quince. Common Quince-tree.) . . . From Europe. Several varieties in cultivation.

+**Quincy granite.** Granite quarried in Quincy, Massachusetts. — **1857** Vaux *Villas* 63 A range of stores, called Commercial Block, . . . is now erected in Quincy granite on Commercial Wharf, Boston. **1882** McCabe *New York* 236 Quincy granite is extensively used.

Quindar. A species of duck. — **1832** Williamson *Maine* I. 142 There [are] . . . in all no less than nineteen species [of ducks]. . . . 14. Quindar; 15. red head Quindar.

Quinine. An alkaloid extracted from the bark of various species of cinchona and used as a medicine. {1826–} — **1839** Townsend *Narrative* 343 My stock of quinine being exhausted, I determined to substitute an extract of the bark of the dogwood. **1852** *Fla. Plantation Rec.* 80 It seames Like Nothing will brake the Fever hear Except Calomel, Ippecac and Qinine. **1905** Pringle *Rice Planter* 235, I found Mr. C. unprovided with the medicines we think necessary . . . , so I put up phials of quinine, calomel, and soda.

Quinine and whisky. A drink used as a tonic. — **1864** Norton *Army Lett.* 229 Three times a day my tormentor comes with quinine and whisky disguised as 'tonic solution.' **1900** Stockton *Afield & Afloat* 315 I mixed him a dose of quinine and whiskey.

+**Quinine tree.** =Hop tree. — **1897** Sudworth *Arborescent Flora* 267 *Ptelea trifoliata.* Hoptree. . . . [Also called] Quinine-tree (Mich.).

+**Quinnat.** [Amer. Indian. Cf. Chinook *ikwána.*] =Chinook salmon. (Cf. King salmon.)

1836 Richardson *Fauna Bor.-Amer.* III. 219 This salmon . . . is known by the name of quinnat. **1859** Cooper & Suckley *Nat. Hist. Washington Terr.* 322 The quinnat . . . is by far the most valuable salmon of any species found in Oregon. **1881** *Amer. Naturalist* XV. 178 Only the quinnat has been noticed south of San Francisco. **1911** *Rep. Fisheries 1908* 315/1 The California salmon, . . . or quinnat (*O[ncorhynchus] tschawytscha*), is found from Monterey to Alaska.

+**Quinnat salmon.** =prec. — **1879** *Nat. Museum Proc.* I. 69 *Oncorhynchus Quinnat.* . . . Quinnat Salmon. **1881** *Amer. Naturalist* XV. 183 The quinnat salmon, from its great size and abundance is more valuable than all other fishes on our Pacific coast together. **1883** *Nat. Museum Bul.* No. 27, 395. **1896** Jordan & Evermann *Check-List Fishes* 290 Quinnat Salmon; Chinook Salmon. . . . Alaska, Oregon, and California, southward to Ventura River.

Quinoa. An Andean species of goosefoot (*Chenopodium quinoa*) introduced into the United States from France. {1625–, in Peru and Chili} — **1855** Browne in *Amer. Inst. N.Y. Trans. 1854* 592 White Quinoa (*Chenopodium quinoa*) from France, but originally from Peru. . . . The leaves . . . are eaten like spinach; but the seeds are the parts most generally used as food. **1890** *Amer. Naturalist* XXIV. 320 Quinoa. *Chenopodium quinoa.* . . . In 1853 seeds from France were distributed from the U.S. Patent Office.

Quint. {1659–} +A bicycle for five riders. — **1896** *Boston M. Journal* 26 June 3/7 The quint made its first appearance on Memorial Day.

*__Quintal.__ A weight of 100 or 112 pounds; a hundredweight, used esp. in measuring fish. (See also Kental.)

In England, commonly 112 pounds; in the United States, commonly 100 pounds.

1651 *Suffolk Deeds* II. 126 Thirty two quintalls of merchantable Codd. **1671** *Plymouth Laws* 284 And whosoever shall take any Basse . . . shall pay to the colonies use six pence per Quintal. **1708** *Boston News-Letter* 18 Oct. 3/2 Another Ship . . . had on board 16 hundred Quintals of Fish. **1759** Rowe *Letters* 335, I will send you two quintails of the Best Fish. **1779** *Essex Inst. Coll.* XXI. 279 Voted the Parish Rate to be 80 quintals of scale fish for the Present year. **1806** Webster 245/1 *Quintal,* a hundred pounds, a kentle. **1833** Wyeth *Oregon* 51 We would advise them to pack up a few quintals of salt fish. **1884** *N.Y. Herald* 27 Oct. 6/2 Havana Markets. . . . Butter—Superior American, $59 & $61, currency, per quintal. **1903** *McClure's Mag.* Nov. 49/1 'Tis as much as a quintal o' fish.

+**Quirl.** (See Querl.)

+**Quirlicue.** A curlicue. — **1885** *Home Missionary* April 459 The Rocky Mountains . . . always seemed like little feather quirlicues on a map.

+**Quirt,** *n.* [Mex. Sp. *cuarta,* orig. a long whip for striking the lead mule of a four-mule team.] A whip, esp. a riding whip with a braided lash of rawhide or leather. Chiefly *S.W.*

1845 *Amer. Rev.* Feb. 127/2 The 'quirt,' with its long heavy lash of knotted raw-hide [was] in his hand. **1881** *Cimarron News & Press* 17 March 1/4 Unused until the last moment remains the heavy cowhide 'quirt.' **1894** Wister in *Harper's Mag.* June 124/1 Whirling the leather quirt, [he] drove them [*sc.* the horses] cowed before him and out of the stream. **1903** A. Adams *Log of Cowboy* 15 If a rider carried a quirt, he usually dispensed with spurs. **1924** Mulford *Rustlers' Valley* x, Lose your quirt, Boss?

+**Quirt,** *v. tr.* To strike with a quirt. — **1888** Roosevelt in *Century Mag.* April 854/2 A first-class rider will sit throughout it all without moving from the saddle, quirting his horse all the time. **1903** A. Adams *Log of Cowboy* 164 Rod Wheat was quirting up the cattle. **1925** Tilghman *Dugout* 27 Pike quirted two [ponies] till they struggled on to safety.

*__Quit,__ *v.*

'Exc. in the legal term *notice to quit* and in its reflexive use . . . the verb *quit* is nowadays almost obs. in Eng.' (Horwill.)

1. *intr.* To discontinue doing something {*a*1641–1868}; +to resign or refuse to work longer on a job.

Cf. Quitting.

1773 Fithian *Journal* I. 54, I was introduced to one Mr Walker . . . , lately a School-master but has quit. **1785** Washington *Diaries* II. 334 The Ice unexpectedly leaving the Shore, [I] was obliged to quit. **1807** *Ann. 10th Congress* 1 Sess. I. 478 [Robert A. New] inquired of them whether they would stand by Colonel Burr and go on, or quit. **1896** *Columbus Dispatch* 13 April 7/5 The waiters who quit at the Chittenden hotel Friday night are still out. **1911** Lincoln *Cap'n Warren's Wards* 204 If I can't turn out better stuff than that, I'd better quit. **1920** Alsaker *Maintaining Health* 249 If the muscles get a little sore and stiff at first do not quit, for by continuing the exercises the soreness soon leaves.

b. To go away; also, fig., to die.

'*Dial.* and *U.S.*' (*O.E.D.*).

1833 *Md. Hist. Mag.* XIII. 370 If I could have got my trunk I would quit for good. **1839** Marryat *Diary in Amer.* II. 231 Clear out, quit, and put—all mean 'be off.' **1879** Tourgee *Fool's Errand* 90 Uncle Jerry'll quit in some of dem spells yit!

2. *tr.* To stop (doing something). {1754}
'Now *U.S.*' (*O.E.D.*).
1837 IRVING *Bonneville* II. 29 They followed on his trail, nor quit hovering about him on his march until they had stolen a number of his best horses and mules. **1867** *Ill. Agric. Soc. Trans.* VII. 58, I quit feeding my cows anything but grass. **1892** GUNTER *Miss Dividends* 208 Quit calling him bishop. **1920** ALSAKER *Eating for Health* 237 Quit lunching. Quit taking eggs and milk and olive oil between meals.

+3. *To quit off*, to cease; to stop. *colloq.*
1874 EGGLESTON *Circuit Rider* 249 That's what every body thought . . . until you quit off going with her so suddenly. **1894** *Advance* 1 March, I don't see how you ever made up your mind to quit off [from study].

***Quitch grass.** =QUACK GRASS. (Cf. COUCH GRASS.) — **1790** S. DEANE *New-Eng. Farmer* 230/2 *Quitch-Grass*, . . . a most obstinate and troublesome weed. **1850** S. F. COOPER *Rural Hours* 124 Some of the most troublesome weeds of this tribe are naturalized, as . . . quaking-grass, quitch-grass, yard-grass, and crab-grass. **1866** LOWELL *Biglow P.* 2 Ser. p. lx, I believe that words, or even the mere intonation of them, have an astonishing vitality and power of propagation by the root, like the gardener's pest, quitch-grass.

***Quitclaim.** An instrument by which an interest or claim in or to an estate is released to another. Also fig. — **1743** *Huntington Rec.* II. 398 He would Give the town the sum of thirty Pounds if they Would give Him a Quit Claim. **1879** T. D. PRICE *Diary* (M.S.) 31 Dec., Signed quit claims to Josiah for Liberty land owned by Father. **1924** MULFORD *Rustlers' Valley* xi, He rang a coin on the bar, waved a quitclaim to any change, and walked to the door.

Quitclaim deed. A deed that carries a quitclaim. — **1756** HEMPSTEAD *Diary* 667, I rid out . . . to take the acknowledgmt of a quit claim deed to Samll Bills from Sd. Darrow & wife to her father's farm in Groton. **1802** *Mass. H. S. Coll.* 1 Ser. VIII. 201 Building spots now sell at a high price: they are transferred by quit-claim deeds. **1892** GUNTER *Miss Dividends* 182, I have . . . received from Tranyon a quit-claim deed to you of the Mineral Hill locations. **1912** NICHOLSON *Hoosier Chron.* 183, I have a quitclaim deed for Mrs. Owen to sign.

***Quitrent.** A rent, usually small, payable by a freeholder or copyholder in lieu of services. Now chiefly hist.
1651 *Va. House of Burgesses* 80 That the quittrents granted unto us by the late Kinge for seaven yeares bee confirmed. **1678** *Doc. Hist. N.Y. State* 92 There are some few quitt-rents, as also Excise or license monys. **1707** *N.J. Archives* 1 Ser. III. 199 This deponent . . . was in hopes they shou'd be clear'd from paying Quitrents by their raising this money. **1733** *Md. Hist. Mag.* XIX. 393 We are all obliged to pay our Quit Rents. **1787** TYLER *Contrast* I. ii, An't you going to have the quit-rent of twenty miles square? **1836** EDWARD *Hist. Texas* 132 In Oaxaca . . . Indians are land holders upon a moderate quit rent. **1909** WEBSTER 1758/2 *Quitrent.* Often written *quit rent*. . . . In the United States they survive to some extent in Pennsylvania.

Quitter, *n.* {1611-} +That which, or one who, quits or shirks. — [**1881** *Standard* (London) 7 Sept. 5/2 They may perhaps have a right to the term 'quitter,' to stigmatise an animal that will not make a fight.] **1887** *Columbus Dispatch* 31 May, The mighty pressure gives confidence that the [gas] well will not be a quitter. **1896** ADE *Artie* 3 You guys must think I'm a quitter. **1906** *Churchman* 22 Sept. 435 A man may shirk and be a 'quitter,' as they call him, in the class room, if he pleases, but he cannot be a 'quitter' on the football field and retain his position on the team. **1921** PAINE *Comr. Rolling Ocean* 5 The college can call me a quitter if it wants to.

***Quitter,** *v. intr.* To twitter. {1513} — **1871** STOWE *Sam Lawson* 64 There was the old tom-turkey a struttin' and a sidlin' and a quitterin,' and a floutin' his tail-feathers in the sun. *Ib.* 156 You might as well 'a' tried to get it out an old tom-turkey, that'll strut and gobble and quitter, . . . but won't say nothin'.

***Quitting.** *attrib.* +With reference to the action of ceasing work for the day. — **1850** WATSON *Camp-Fires Revol.* 111 Every day, he'd come into the workshop, about quitting time. **1898** *McClure's Mag.* X. 248, I have acted as his quitting-bell, and called in on him when it was time for him to cease working. **1917** SINCLAIR *King Coal* 134 When the quitting-whistle blew, Mike Sikoria came quickly to join Hal.

***Quiver.** A case for carrying arrows. — **1634** WOOD *New Eng. Prospect* 66 A Sagamore with . . . his bow in his hand, his quiver at his back. **1705** BEVERLEY *Virginia* III. 4 His Quiver is of a thin Bark. **1808** BARKER *Indian Princess* II. i, Their arrows rested in their quivers. **1846** THORPE *Myst. Backwoods* 85 The rider, dropping his rein, plucks an arrow from his quiver. **1892** *Harper's Mag.* March 497/1 The Sioux . . . each carried a fire-bag, a quiver, and a brightly painted shield.

Quixotic. **1.** Of persons: Idealistic but visionary. {1857-} **2.** Of actions, qualities, etc.: Characteristic of a quixotic person. {1851-} — **(1) 1815** J. ADAMS *Works* X. 157, I considered Miranda as a vagrant, a vagabond, a Quixotic adventurer. **(2) 1824** D. WEBSTER *Works* III. 62 It may be easy to call this resolution *quixotic*, the emanation of a crusading or propagandist spirit. **1844** EMERSON *Politics* Ess. 2 Ser., All public ends look vague and quixotic beside private ones. **1869** 'MARK TWAIN' *Innocents* 540 The pilgrims . . . keep themselves in a constant state of Quixotic heroism.

Quixotical, *a.* =prec., sense 2. {1850} — **1808** *Ann. 10th Congress* 2 Sess. 651 Suppose the Emperor of China . . . were to declare the whole European Continent in a state of blockade, would it be required . . . that we should go on a Quixotical expedition to compel him to repeal the decree?

+Quiz. [f. dial. *quiz* v.] An oral or written examination. Also attrib.
1867 *Atlantic Mo.* Oct. 468/2, I attended the quizzes, as they call them, pretty closely. **1883** *Harvard Coll. Ann. Rep.* 102 (Ernst), The daily 'quizzes' on preceding lectures. **1895** *Conv. Amer. Instructors of Deaf Proc.* 314 My first lesson should be in the form of a quiz. **1907** *Springfield W. Repub.* 7 Feb. 16 For the food chemists the quiz included a study of both French and German. **1915** CAMPBELL *Proving Virginia* 226 The black-robed Seniors assembled . . . to perform the last holy rites over their antique manuscripts, quiz papers, precious testimonials of midnight toil.

Quizzing glass. A monocle. {1802-} — **1828** H. FINN, etc. *Whimwhams* 107 No man of sense or property wears a quizzing glass. **1850** COLTON *Deck & Port* 59 An Englishman . . . [was] promenading Broadway in white kid gloves, with gold-headed cane and quizzing-glass. **1886** *Harper's Mag.* July 202/1 A cockney, 'just come hover, ye know,' lighted pipe in mouth, and quizzing-glass screwed into one eye.

+Quoddy boat. *Maine.* (See quotation.) — **1884** *Nat. Museum Bul.* No. 27, 694 The Quoddy boat is sloop-rigged, and is largely employed in the herring and other shore fisheries in Passamaquoddy Bay and vicinity. It is celebrated for speed and seaworthiness.

+Quoddy salmon. The pollack, *Pollachius virens*. — **1884** GOODE, etc. *Fisheries* I. 230 At Eastport these fish are often called 'Quoddy Salmon.'

***Quoit.** *pl.* A game in which the players pitch flat iron rings, called *quoits*, at a pin. — **1775** FITHIAN *Journal* II. 114 The men, for exercise, play at quoits, hunt deer, turkeys, pheasants, etc. **1832** WILLIAMSON *Maine* I. 507 The principal amusements of the natives are dancing; foot-racing; wrestling; quoits; chequers. **1855** LONGFELLOW *Hiawatha* 145 Skilled was he in sports and pastimes, . . . In the play of quoits and ball-play.

+Quondy. (See quotation.) — **1875** *Fur, Fin & Feather* (ed. 3) 119 Along the coast of New England it [*i.e.*, the long-tailed duck] is generally called the quondy.

Quota, *n.* That part or share given or paid, or expected to be given or paid, by one party to an amount or stock contributed to by all. {1668-} **+a.** In respect to the number of soldiers or recruits contributed by the colonies or states.
1696 *N.J. Archives* II. 115 Nor will it ever be otherwise untill the Crowne . . . put an indisputable command upon every Colony to furnish a Quota and pay them. **1711** *N.H. Prov. Papers* III. 497 That which imports us is . . . to make provision for the just Payment of ye subsistance and wages due to our Quota. **1720** *Mass. H. Rep. Jrnl.* II. 346 His Excellency the Governour [shall] be desired to Write to the Government of *Piscataqua*, to furnish their Quota [of soldiers]. **1776** *Ky. Petitions* 38 [We are] willing . . . to support the . . . cause, by raising our Quoto [*sic*] of men. **1822** *Ann. 17th Congress* 1 Sess. I. 144 Requisitions were made on the different States for their respective quotas of 195,500 men. **1862** *Huntington Rec.* III. 472 We, the citizens of the Town of Huntington, . . . to avoid the stigma of having its quota of men raised by a draft instead of voluntary recruits, . . . authorize a vote by ballot [to raise thirty thousand dollars].

+b. In respect to moneys paid to the central government by individual colonies or states.
1775 *Jrnls. Cont. Congress* II. 222 That each Colony pay its respective quota in four equal annual payments. **1796** *Ann. 4th Congress* 2 Sess. 2699 An act of Congress should be passed, declaring the quotas of the different States. **1821** JEFFERSON *Writings* I. 39 Those articles were debated which determined the proportion, or quota, of money which each state should furnish to the common treasury.

+Quota, *v. tr.* To impose in accordance with a quota. Also *vbl. n.* — **1784** E. GERRY in *New Eng. Hist. & Gen. Reg.* XLIX. 431 Their places should be speedily supplied by Troops to be *required* & quotied [*sic*] on the several States by Congress. **1786** JEFFERSON *Writings* (1905) V. 367 A convention might be formed between Portugal, Naples and the United States, by which the burthen of the war might be quota-ed on them, according to their respective wealth. **1798** *Ib.* VII. (1896) 267 They shall be free hereafter to tax houses separately, as by an indirect tax. This is to avoid the quotaing of which they cannot bear the idea.

Quotation marks. *pl.* Inverted commas and apostrophes used to mark off a quotation, a slang expression, etc. — **1888** CABLE in *Century Mag.* Nov. 112/2 But at the close of the last century . . . quotation marks were just beginning to come into use. **1895** *Nation* 14 March 191 It is the ordinary rule to put quotation-marks about any word used in an odd, affected, or ludicrous or mysterious fashion. **1897** *Century Mag.* Feb. 563/1, I put play in quotation-marks to express the sarcasm of it, for I never saw anything more nearly approaching war in my life.

***Quote,** *v. tr.* To state the price of (a commodity or stock). {1866-} — **1815** *Niles' Reg.* 29 April 140/1 *Ballast stones* were humorously 'quoted' in one of the papers . . . as being in great demand at $150 per ton. **1865** *Atlantic Mo.* May 575/1 The artist is like the stock which is to be quoted at the board and thrown upon the market. **1888** *Economist* 3 Nov. 4/3 The effect of quoting Gas Trust upon the ticker . . . has been to stimulate trade in this stock here.

R

∗**Rabbi.** A Jewish teacher or doctor of the law. Often as a personal title. — [**1722** J. MONIS *Truth* (t.-p.), Dedicated to the Jewish Nation. . . . By R. Judah Monis.] **1773** E. STILES *Literary Diary* I. 354 [At] the Synagogue . . . I saw Rabbi Carigal. **1892** *Central Conf. Amer. Rabbis Yrbk.* 3 The second annual convention of the Central Conference of American Rabbis opened its session at Baltimore . . . on Sunday, July 5, 1891. **1921** in H. Berkowitz *Intimate Glimpses Rabbi's Career* 6 Four graduates [of Hebrew Union College] . . . have made their mark by creating a new type of rabbi in accordance with the needs of American Jewry.

∗**Rabbit.**

I. ∗**1. a.** Any of various well-known burrowing rodents of the family Leporidae characterized by long ears and legs. **b.** A hare.

See also JACKASS RABBIT, JACK RABBIT.

1634 WOOD *New Eng. Prospect* 22 The Rabbets be much like ours in England. The Hares be some of them white, and a yard long. **1743** CATESBY *Carolina* II. p. xxviii, *Marmota Americana*. The Monax. This Animal is about the bigness of a wild rabbet. **1831** AUDUBON *Ornith. Biog.* I. 268 Small Hares, or, as we usually call them, *Rabbits*, are also frequently caught. **1856** *Porter's Spirit of Times* 11 Oct. 97/2 The hare sits in *forms* . . . ; while the rabbit lives in burrows dug in sandy soil. **1897** *Outing* Jan. 379/2 Drag your old rabbit, and I'll drag this. **1907** *St. Nicholas* July 835/1 Sometimes rabbits and prairie-dogs scampered among the bushes.

+**2.** (See quotation.) *slang. Obs.*

See also DEAD RABBIT.

1859 MATSELL *Vocabulum* 72 *Rabbit*, a rowdy. 'Dead rabbit,' a very athletic rowdy fellow.

II. *attrib.* and *comb.* **3.** Designating places or paths frequented by rabbits.

1853 'P. PAXTON' *Yankee in Texas* 58 Something that might have been a trail, or might have been a rabbit-path. **1854** THOREAU *Walden* 302 Around every swamp may be seen the partridge or rabbit walk. **1884** ROE *Nature's Story* 41 The boy concealed them [*sc.* traps] in the copse where the rabbit-tracks were thickest.

4. Designating dishes prepared from rabbit meat.

1867 *Common Sense Cook Book* 71 [Recipe for] rabbit curry. **1910** WALCOTT *Open Door* 146 You know I'm . . . content with the humble rabbit sauté . . . when I can afford nothing better.

5. Designating the action of hunting rabbits, or things associated with this action.

See also RABBIT ROUND-UP.

1867 EDWARDS *Shelby* 405 Tired children [were] dreaming of . . . rabbit-snares out in the woods where the frosts have fallen. **1873** *Ill. Dept. Agric. Trans.* X. 65 They prevailed on him to suspend his rabbit-hunting, and 'show them 'round.' **1887** *Lisbon* (Dak.) *Star* 23 Dec. 7/1 Several hundred people . . . assembled to engage in the rabbit drive. **1897** *Outing* XXIX. 456/1 Rabbit-chasing is a form of equestrian sport, generally participated in by the young men and women of Southern California. **1899** CHESNUTT *Conjure Woman* 90 He had sa'ntered up in de woods . . . ter look atter a rabbit-trap. **1904** 'O. HENRY' *Roads of Destiny* 294 Once he went rabbit-shooting in Yonkers. **1909** *Cent. Suppl.* 1102/2 *Rabbit-stick*, . . . a throwing-stick, similar to the Australian boomerang, used by the Indians of the southwestern United States in hunting rabbits and other small game. **1925** BRYAN *Memoirs* 37 A part of each Saturday was given over to some kind of sport, usually a rabbit hunt.

+**6.** *Rabbit ear*, (see quotation).

1881 INGERSOLL *Oyster-Industry* 247 *Rabbit Ear.*—A long, slender oyster.

+**Rabbit berry.** =BUFFALO BERRY 1 and 2. Also *rabbit's-berry*. — **1804** *Lewis & Clark Exped.* VII. (1905) 52 We found Some red berreys which they call Rabbit berrys. **1839** *Knickerb.* XIII. 432 We found, on the west bank, a kind of large whortleberry, called *wabosimin*, or rabbits'-berry, by the Odjibwas. **1846** BROWNE *Trees Amer.* 429 The Silvery-Leaved Shepherdia. . . . Missouri Silver-leaf, Buffalo-tree, . . . Buffalo Berry-tree, Rabbit Berry. **1892** APGAR *Trees Northern U.S.* 132 *Shepherdia argentea.* (Buffalo-berry. Rabbit-berry.) . . . A small handsome tree, 5 to 20 ft. high, wild in the Rocky Mountains, and sometimes cultivated east.

+**Rabbit bush.** A western shrub (*Chrysothamnus graveolens*), or a related species, used as a retreat by jack rabbits. Also *rabbit brush*. — **1852** STANSBURY *Gt. Salt Lake* 235 The only vegetation today has been a little dwarf artemisia, grease-bush, rabbit-bush, . . . and an occasional dwarf cedar on the bluffs. **1861** R. F. BURTON *City of Saints* 591 An expanse of white sage and large rabbit-bush. **1890** *Cent.* 4924/2 *Rabbit-brush*, a tall shrubby composite plant, . . . growing abundantly in alkaline soils of western North America. **1914** STEWART *Lett. of Woman Homesteader* 18 Our horse was midside deep in rabbit-brush, a shrub just covered with flowers that look and smell like goldenrod.

Rabbit fish. {1848–} +**1.** The smooth puffer (*Lagocephalus laevigatus*), having teeth resembling those of a rabbit. +**2.** The spotted balloonfish, *Cyclichthys schoepfi*. — **(1) 1842** *Nat. Hist. N.Y., Zoology* IV. 330 The Lineated Puffer . . . is called Rabbit-fish, according to Schoepfi, on account of the whiteness of its flesh. **1884** GOODE, etc. *Fisheries* I. 170 The Rabbit Fish . . . is known in New England waters through the occasional visits of stragglers. **1897** *N.Y. Forest, Fish, & Game Comm. 2d Rep.* 244 Rabbit-Fish; Smooth Puffer.—Occasionally taken in the fall in Gravesend Bay. **(2) 1883** *Nat. Museum Bul.* No. 27, 428 *Chilomycterus geometricus*. . . . Spiny Box-fish; Rabbit-fish; Swell Toad. East coast of the United States from Southern Massachusetts to Texas.

Rabbit foot. Also **rabbit's(-)foot.**

+**1.** A clover (*Trifolium arvense*) with soft, furry flower heads. In full *rabbit-foot clover*. (Cf. HARE 2.)

1817–8 EATON *Botany* (1822) 491 Rabbit-foot, field clover. . . . Grows in dry pastures or barren fields. **1850** S. F. COOPER *Rural Hours* 125 The downy 'rabbit-foot,' or 'stone-clover,' the common red variety . . . [are] introduced. **1878** JACKSON *Travel at Home* 186 [There grows] Rabbit's foot, May-weed, shepherd's purse [&c.]. **1889** *Cent.* 1060/1 Other species, mostly weeds of little value, are the yellow or hop clover, . . . the stone, hare's-foot, or rabbit-foot clover [etc.].

+**2.** The foot of a rabbit, carried as a charm or good-luck token. Also fig.

1887 *Courier-Journal* 20 Feb. 7/4 Some of the railroad engineers . . . firmly believe in the charm of the rabbit foot. **1902** HARBEN *A. Daniel* 309 Pole worked the rabbit-foot on them back there. **1912** *Commoner* 15 Nov. 7 Mrs. Wade Mountfort . . . presented him with a rabbit's foot.

+**Rabbit hawk.** The red-tailed hawk, *Buteo borealis*. — **1880** CABLE *Grandissimes* 43 A great rabbit-hawk sat alone in the top of a lofty pecan-tree. **1890** A. W. BUTLER *Birds of Indiana* 47 *Buteo borealis*. Red-Tailed Hawk. . . . This is the common 'Hen Hawk,' or 'Rabbit Hawk' of the farmers. **1903** 'O. HENRY' in *McClure's Mag.* Dec. 144/1 [I] noticed a rabbit-hawk sitting on a dead limb in a water-elm.

+**Rabbit moth.** A flannel moth, *Megalopyge opercularis:* (see quotation). — **1890** *Cent.* 4924/3 *Rabbit-moth* . . . : so called from its soft furry appearance and rabbit-like coloration.

+**Rabbitmouth (sucker).** =CUTLIPS b. (Cf. HARELIP SUCKER.) — **1882** *Nat. Museum Bul.* No. 16, 144 Hare-lip Sucker . . . Rabbit-mouth Sucker. **1884** GOODE, etc. *Fisheries* I. 614 The Rabbit-mouth Sucker . . . is found in abundance in many rivers of Tennessee and in some streams in Ohio. **1911** *Rep. Fisheries 1908* 317 The different species [of sucker] are known as . . . 'rabbit-mouth,' 'harelip,' 'split-mouth,' 'red horse' [etc.].

+**Rabbit round-up.** The hunting and driving together of the jack rabbits of a given area for extermination. — **1887** *Lisbon* (Dak.) *Star* 23 Dec. 7/1 A California Rabbit Roundup. **1911** *N.Y. Ev. Post* 21 Dec. 7/2 Twelve hundred jack rabbits . . . were bagged in a big rabbit round-up of the sort now popular in western Kansas, where the 'jacks' have been causing much trouble for farmers.

Rabbit's(-)foot. (See RABBIT FOOT.)

+**Rabbit tobacco.** The balsamweed, *Gnaphalium obtusifolium*. — **1894** *Amer. Folk-Lore* VII. 92 *Gnaphalium polycephalum*, rabbit-tobacco, N.C. **1908** 'O. HENRY' *Options* 200, I don't give a pipeful of rabbit tobacco whether Queen Sophia Christina or Charlie Culberson rules these fairy isles.

Rabbit weed. {1750–} +A woody plant with small yellow flowers (*Gutierrezia sarothrae*) of the Middle West and Southwest. — **1884** *Harper's Mag.* Sept. 502/2 The prairies—middle lands, . . . covered with sorry bunch-grass and sad rabbit-weed—were neglected.

Rabble, *n.* A piece of iron bent at the end, used for stirring and skimming molten iron in the process of puddling. {1864–} — **1874** RAYMOND *6th Rep. Mines* 423 The charge . . . is spread out evenly over the surface with an iron rabble. **1876** — *8th Rep. Mines* 385 The slag is now drawn with a rabble into molds prepared for it. **1905** VALENTINE *H. Sandwith* 5 Rabbles, tapping bars, fosses and other furnace tools lay about or were cooling in the troughs of running water.

Rabble, *v.*[1] {1644–} ‖*intr.* To move off in a loose, disorderly group. — *a***1861** WINTHROP *J. Brent* 93 He dismissed his audience with . . . an injunction to keep closer to the train . . . and not be rabbling off to catch grasshoppers.

Rabble, *v.*[2] *tr.* To stir or skim with a rabble. — **1874** RAYMOND *6th Rep. Mines* 423 One of the furnace-doors is opened and the charge is rabbled. **1894** *Harper's Mag.* Jan. 420/2 The molten metal is thoroughly stirred, or 'rabbled' to make it uniform.

Rabbler. **1.** A person who uses a rabble. **2.** (See quotation.) {1883} — (1) **1877** RAYMOND *8th Rep. Mines* 398 The upper hearths are not very accessible to the rabblers. (2) **1876** KNIGHT 1850/1 *Rabbler*, . . . a scraper.

Rabble-rouser. A demagogue. {rabble-rousing, 1802} — **1843** 'CARLTON' *New Purchase* I. 211 Can any thing come up to the cant and whine of a selfish, godless rabblerouser? **1906** *Dialect Notes* III. 152 He can get votes; he's a *rabble-rouser*. [n.w. Ark.] **1920** MENCKEN *Prejudices* 2 Ser. 116 On the other side was a ready-made issue, . . . so far unembraced by any other rabble-rouser of the first magnitude.

+Rac(c)oon, *n.* Also †**rackoon.** ['Of Algonquian origin; cf. Virginian *ärä'kun*, fr. *ärä'kunĕm*, lit., he scratches with his hands' (W. '34).] Cf. COON *n.*

1. A grayish brown, furry animal (*Procyon lotor*) common to the whole of North America. {1619-}

The sound of the native Indian word is approximated in the first two quotations. With the first of these cf. *rarowcun* s.v. RACCOON SKIN.

1608 SMITH *Works* (1910) 23 The Empereur *Powhatan*, each weeke once or twice, sent me many presents of Deare, bread, *Raugroughcuns*. **1610** *Estate of Virginia* (1844) 13 There are Arocouns, and Apossouns, in shape like to pigges.

(*a*) **1634** WOOD *New Eng. Prospect* (1865) 24 The Rackoone is a deepe furred beast. **1654** JOHNSON *Wonder-w. Prov.* 83 As for flesh they looked not for any in those times . . . unlesse they could barter with the Indians for Venison or Rockoons. **1701** WOLLEY *Journal N.Y.* (1902) 37 The Skins of . . . Bears, Bevers, Rackoons, Foxes [etc., the Indians] . . . bring upon their backs to New-York. **1765** ROGERS *Acct. N. Amer.* 161 This wide extended plain is covered with tall grass, among which are deer, elks, bears, rackoons, &c. in great plenty. **1834** *S. Lit. Messenger* I. 121 [There is] an ample supply of wolves, . . . foxes, rackoons, and squirrels.

(*b*) **1634** *Relation of Beginnings of Md.* 22, I haue seene Deere, Racounes, and Squirrells. **1647** ELIOT *Day-Breaking* 6 [We] asked them [*sc.* Indians] if they saw a great *Wigwam*, or a great house, would they thinke that *Racoones* or Foxes built it that had no wisedome? **1674** JOSSELYN *Two Voyages* 85 The *Racoon* or *Rattoon* is of two sorts, gray *Rattoons*, and black *Rattoons*. **1791** J. LONG *Voyages* 41 The country every where abounds with wild animals, particularly . . . wood cats, racoons, wolves, musquashes, &c. **1808** PIKE *Sources of Miss.* 30 Killed three geese and one racoon, also a *brelaw*, an animal I had never before seen. **1882** *Vt. Agric. Rep.* VII. 69 He believes the racoon and the skunk are beneficial to the farmers.

(*c*) **1672** JOSSELYN *New Eng. Rarities* 17 The Raccoon liveth in hollow trees, and is about the size of a Gib Cat. **1699** E. WARD *Trip to New-Eng.* 14 The Raccoon . . . is a Creature about the bigness of a Cat. **1709** LAWSON *Carolina* 121 The raccoon is of a dark-gray Colour. **1745** E. KIMBER *Itinerant Observer* 11 The Raccoon is delicate eating. **1817** S. BROWN *Western Gazetteer* 30 Foxes, oposum, and raccoon, remain in considerable numbers. **1880** *Scribner's Mo.* April 877/1 In winter a few wild cats, raccoons, opossums, foxes, and wolves had been known to take refuge there. **1907** ANDREWS *Recoll.* 128 They saw an animal they supposed to be a raccoon. **1916** THOBURN *Stand. Hist. Okla.* I. 6 Raccoon, opossum, . . . muskrat and prairie dog were the principal animals.

2. *fig.* A member of the New Jersey militia in the American Revolution.

1779 *N.J. Archives* 2 Ser. III. 703 Each *devoted racoon* [is] to receive down forty *soft* or *paper* dollars.

3. Attrib. and comb. in sense 1 with *bridge, fat, fur*, etc.

1667 *Oyster Bay Rec.* I. 81 The S[ai]d bounds [begin] from Raccoon Swamp. **1779** *N.J. Archives* 2 Ser. III. 170 An apprentice lad . . . [is] supposed to have taken out of his master's hatter's shop . . . about half a pound of raccoon furr cut off the skins. **1791** W. BARTRAM *Travels* 445 We were obliged to carry every article of our effects, and this by no other bridge than a sapling felled across it, which is called a raccoon bridge. **1809** A. HENRY *Travels* 131 Racoon-hunting was my more particular and daily employ. **1832** *Louisville Directory* 98 [The ground-wheat flour] was shortened with racoon fat. **1858** VIELÉ *Following Drum* 82 [They] recounted . . . an exciting raccoon hunt.

b. *spec.* With *cap, coat*, in sense: Made of raccoon skin or fur.

1649 *Conn. Rec.* I. 497 An Inventory of the Estate of Mr. William Whiting: . . . 2 Racoone coats, 1 Wolf skin coate [etc.]. **1840** *Knickerb.* XVI. 163 He then made me a rakish raccoon-cap, with a flaunting tail to it.

c. In the specific names of plants.

1834 AUDUBON *Ornith. Biog.* II. 80 The Racoon Grape is characterized by . . . the small size of the bluish-black fruit. **1860** DARLINGTON *Weeds & Plants* 38 May-apple . . . is known in some parts of the country as Wild Lemon and Raccoon Berry.

+Raccoon, *v. intr.* To hunt raccoons. — **1834** C. A. DAVIS *Lett. J. Downing* 265 The Gineral . . . tell'd a plaguy long story about his goin out once with a gang of his niggers a rakoonin. *Ib.* 267 It would a gone all round the country that I know'd nothin about rakoonin.

+Raccoon fox. = CIVET CAT. (Cf. MOUNTAIN CAT c.) — **1859** COOPER & SUCKLEY *Nat. Hist. Washington Terr.* 114 The ring-tailed bassaris, often called raccoon fox, is common in California, where the people tame it. **1873** *Amer. Naturalist* VII. 115 The 'Raccoon Fox,' as the miners called it, had occasionally been tamed. **1917** *Mammals of Amer.* 108 Ring-tailed Cat. . . . [Also called] Mountain Cat, Raccoon Fox.

+Raccoon oyster. (See quots. 1884 and 1857; cf. COON OYSTER.) Also attrib. — **1835** AUDUBON *Ornith. Biog.* III. 181 Oysters on what are called in the Southern States and the Floridas 'Racoon oyster beds.' **1835** SIMMS *Partisan* 417 This bed is as hard as a bed of racoon oysters. **1857** *Rep. Comm. Patents 1856: Agric.* 132 [Crow-blackbirds] frequently seize on shrimps, . . . or on 'Raccoon oysters,' a kind of shell-fish, so named under the idea that it is eaten by the raccoon. **1884** GOODE, etc. *Fisheries* I. 752 From this cause, overcrowding, the shells of the individual oysters become very narrow and greatly elongated; the peculiar forms which result are known to oystermen as 'Raccoon Oysters,' or 'Cat's-tongues.'

+Raccoon perch. (See quot. 1896.) — **1896** JORDAN & EVERMANN *Check-List Fishes* 357 *Perca flavescens*. . . . Yellow Perch, American Perch; Ringed Perch; Raccoon Perch. Fresh waters of the eastern United States. **1902** *Amer. Folk-Lore* XV. 256.

+Raccoon skin. The skin or fur of the raccoon, often used for garments, etc. (Cf. COONSKIN.)

1624 Smith *Gen. Hist. Va.* III. 48 He sat covered with a great robe, made of *Rarowcun skinnes*. **1670** D. DENTON *Descr. New York* 3 The Inhabitants . . . have a considerable Trade with the Indians, for Bevers, Otter, Raccoon skins, with other Furrs. **1701** WOLLEY *Journal N.Y.* (1902) 35 Many of them [*i.e.*, Indians] wear . . . Rackoon skins sewed or scuered together. **1789** MAY *Jrnl. & Lett.* 146, I have taken other things: upwards 500 raccoon-skins, some beaver, and 120 deer-skins. **1807** *Ann. 10th Congress* 1 Sess. 635 May be I had a few deer skins and some racoon skins left. **1839** *S. Lit. Messenger* V. 99/1 His father . . . had suffered him to raise pocket money . . . by selling hare-skins and rackoon-skins.

b. Attrib. with *bag, coat, haversack.*

1643 WILLIAMS *Key* (1866) 144 *Mohĕwonck*, a Rakoone-skin coat. **1723** *New-Eng. Courant* 14 Oct. 2/2 One of the Mohawks lately come to Town, has lost a Rackoon-Skin Bag, with some small Things in it. **1903** FOX *Little Shepherd* i, A small raccoon-skin haversack hung from one of the prongs.

***Race.**[1]

***1.** An artificial channel for water made to drain an area or to supply water power; also, the water in the channel. {-1805; 1890 Australia}

'Now chiefly *U.S.*' (*O.E.D.*), except in *head-, mill-, tail-race*.

1674 *Conn. Rec.* II. 232 From the sayd stone, a strayt line to a white oak tree upon Homes his race [shall be a boundary]. **1738** W. STEPHENS *Proc. Georgia* I. 162 They were mending the Race for the back Water to go off quick. **1768** WASHINGTON *Writings* II. 241 My Carpenter & House People went to work at my Mill repairing the Dams, . . . & opening the Race. **1817** S. BROWN *Western Gazetteer* 105 A little above the harbor is a mill turned by the Ohio, by means of a race. **1883** ZEIGLER & GROSSCUP *Alleghanies* 104 A small volume of water . . . pours through the flume, by means of a race,—a long, small trough, made of boards, rotten and moss-grown, and elevated on log foundations, about ten feet above the ground.

***2.** A contest, as in running, sailing, or trotting; a season's competition.

See also FOOT RACE, HORSE RACE.

1674 *Plymouth Laws* 171 Whatsoever person shall run a race with any horse kind in any street or comon road shall forfeite five shillings in money. **1722** in Buckingham *Newspaper Lit.* I. 61 How will you look at Cambridge Races, 'Mongst idle fops and gaping asses? **1798** WEEMS *Letters* II. 98 They are to have great races at Petersburg sometime in next month. **1840** *Picayune* 15 Oct. 2/2 Nashville Fall Races . . . commenced on Monday. **1886** CHADWICK *Art of Batting* 38 [They] go in for a style of batting which . . . proves costly . . . to the success of a team in taking the lead in a championship race. **1886** *Outing* Nov. 167/2 The first of the race was straight to windward. **1894** *Vt. Agric. Rep.* XIV. 96 He trotted in seventeen races . . . ; won nine first moneys.

+b. *spec. Polit.* A competition or contest for public office.

1855 I. C. PRAY *Mem. J. G. Bennett* 288 He had been the first to start many of them upon the ground for a successful political race. **1881** PIERSON *In the Brush* 133 This pursuit of office was always spoken of as a 'race.' **1900** *Congress. Rec.* 17 Jan. 915/2 Being publicly notified that I am out of the Vice-Presidential race would have been somewhat humiliating. **1903** *N.Y. Ev. Post* 17 Sept. 1 Mr. Cutting ran up stairs to tell Dr. Gould . . . that Mr. Grout would make the race. **1905** *N.Y. Ev. Post* 28 Dec. 1 Assemblyman Rogers . . . withdrew from the speakership race and re-entered it. **1912** COBB *Back Home* 279 See if there ain't . . . something definite . . . on the race for state senator!

3. *attrib.* **a.** With *colt, course, field*, etc., with reference to horse racing.

See also RACE GROUND, RACE HORSE, etc.

1785 WASHINGTON *Diaries* II. 427 All returned, except Mr. Jno. Bassett, who got hurt in the race field. **1809** CUMING *Western Tour* 225 Houses, trees, and cultivated fields, are seen for three miles to Mr. Davis's . . . house, about half a mile beyond the race course. **1850** LEWIS *La. Swamp Doctor* 47 She couldn't 'tend races, and have a race-colt of her own to comfort her 'clinin' years. **1853** *S. Lit. Messenger* XIX. 70/1 He brought with him a small race mare which excited the acquisitiveness of his father. **1891** O'BEIRNE *Leaders Ind. Territory* 40/2 [He] has always kept the best race stock in the district. **1893** *Outing* XXII. 101/1 Goldsmith Maid left the turf with a race record never equaled. **1896** *N.Y. Dramatic News* 4 July 14/4 Tom Stewart . . . handled the crowd very well at the D. W. C. race meet last week.

b. +*Race-about,* a small racing boat (cf. KNOCKABOUT 1); *race boat,* a boat built for or used in racing. {1866}

1858 HOLMES *Autocrat* 189 My own particular water-sulky, a 'skeleton' or 'shell' raceboat. **1905** *St. Nicholas* Aug. 865 There were . . . pennants for the raceabouts and halfraters.

*** Race.**[2]

***1.** An ethnic group. **a.** Used of American Indians or of a particular tribe or nation of these Indians.

1774 *Doc. Hist. N.Y. State* I. 765 River Indians . . . are understood by the Delawares being originally of the same Race. **1826** COOPER *Last of Mohicans* xiii, The brothers and family of the Mohican formed our war-party; and you see before you all that are now left of his race. **1835** JACKSON in *Pres. Mess. & P.* III. 171 The plan of removing the aboriginal people who yet remain within the settled portions of the United States to the country west of the Mississippi . . . was adopted on the most mature consideration of the condition of this race. **1869** 'MARK TWAIN' *Sk., New & Old* 69 Does she mourn over the extinguished council-fires of her race?

b. Used of the Negroes.

1839 KEMBLE *Residence in Ga.* 11 The blessed unconsciousness and ignorance of childhood keeps them for a few years unaware of the conventional proscription under which their whole race is placed. **1865** COX *8 Yrs. in Congress* 69 [Mr. Hutchins] talked the language of love to the black race only to hide his hate for the white race who people our southern States. **1881** *Boston Commonwealth* 5 March 2 The Washington *Post* sends up an agonized wail for the incoming administration to recognize the colored citizens by putting a representative of the race in the cabinet. **1918** C. B. JOHNSON *Songs of My People* 17 With you agone Who'll stir with mighty voice the Race?

c. Used of the Japanese and other orientals.

1901 [see sense 2 b]. **1924** *Lit. Digest* 12 Jan. 14/1 The Japanese themselves reported two years ago that 58 per cent. of their race in this State [Calif.] were employed in agricultural pursuits.

+2. *attrib.* **a.** In sense 1 b with *conflict, consciousness, feeling,* etc.

See also RACE PREJUDICE, PROBLEM, QUESTION, RIOT.

1867 *Atlantic Mo.* Nov. 608/2 As a national or 'race' illustration, behind the footlights, might not 'Jim Crow' and a black face tickle the fancy of pit and circle? *c***1875** in J. S. Reynolds *Reconstruction in S.C.* 304 The government is wholly composed of negroes elected on the race issue, asserted even against white Republicans. **1880** TOURGEE *Invisible Empire* xii, Any one who asked the support of colored men as against a Democratic nominee was precipitating a race-conflict. **1891** *Congress. Rec.* App. 17 Jan. 101/1 At Marion, Ind., . . . when the Democrats were attempting to have a rally, . . . they were attacked by the colored people, the race line being distinctly drawn by that race. **1897** *Chicago Tribune* 28 July 3/7 Race riot in the jail. . . . This gave the negroes an excellent chance to start a 'race' war. **1904** PAGE in *McClure's Mag.* March 549/2 [With] race-feeling growing, . . . it is time that all sensible men should endeavor . . . [to] look at the subject frankly. **1905** *N.Y. Ev. Post* 11 Oct. 4 If the white race are permeated with race consciousness, there is no danger of amalgamation.

b. *Race suicide,* in a race, voluntary restriction of births to such a point that the population cannot maintain its numbers.

1901 *Amer. Acad. Pol. Sci. Annals* July 88 The American farm hand, mechanic and operative might wither away before the heavy influx of a prolific race from the Orient. . . . For a case like this I can find no words so apt as 'race suicide.'

Race ginger. (See quot. 1828.) {race of ginger, 1547–} — **1781** *R.I. Commerce* II. 157 Race Ginger 22 d. **1828** WEBSTER, *Race-ginger,* ginger in the root or not pulverized.

Race ground. A ground used for racing. {1802–} — **1727** *Md. Hist. Mag.* VII. 400 This Vestry resolve to meet on Thursday . . . at the race ground near Mr. Bensons. **1835** AUDUBON *Ornith. Biog.* III. 324 Between that city and the race-ground, which is scarcely a mile distant. **1858** VIELÉ *Following Drum* 150 It was a beaten cattle-track . . . forming part of what had once been a race-ground.

Race horse. A horse bred and kept for racing. {*a*1626–} Also attrib. — **1753** HEMPSTEAD *Diary* 601 Hemp sold his Race Horse. **1835** A. PARKER *Trip to Texas* 107 Good race-horses are of great value. **1868** WOODRUFF *Trotting Horse* 47, I do not undertake to disparage the method pursued by the race-horse men. **1896** WILKINS *Madelon* 104 Her great blue eyes were fixed fearfully upon the bounding heels and flanks of the old white race-horse.

+Race path. 1. (See quotation.) **2.** =RACE TRACK. — **(1) 1828** *Western Mo. Rev.* I. 512 The 'Devil's' race paths, tea table, oven, etc., are places of difficult or hazardous navigation, that frequently occur. (2) **1832** J. HALL *Legends of West* 46 He 'swapped' horses, bred fine colts; and attended at the race paths. **1847** HOWE *Hist. Coll. Ohio* 555 There was the very race-path still existing.

Race prejudice. Bias against people of another race, esp. in America against Negroes. — **1899** CHESNUTT *Wife of His Youth* 7, I have no race prejudice, . . . but we people of mixed blood are ground between the upper and the nether millstone. **1915** *New Republic* 13 March 146/2 America is full of race prejudice. **1924** E. F. YOUNG *Race Prejudice* 195 The problem of race prejudice is the problem of demonstrating in actual life the actual or potential worth of Negroes, individually and collectively.

+Race problem. The social problem created by the presence of the Negro race in the United States. — **1891** *Congress. Rec.* 16 Jan. 1431/1 If they would allow us to proceed it would be but a short time until what is called 'the race problem,' in my opinion, would settle itself. **1899** CHESNUTT *Wife of His Youth* 94 What our country needs most in its treatment of the race problem . . . is a clearer conception of the brotherhood of man.

+Race question. =prec. — **1889** *Boston Jrnl.* 26 Dec. 2/4 The Wilmington, N.C., Star (Dem.) thinks that time only can solve the race-question in the South. **1900** *Congress. Rec.* 22 Jan. 1034/2 There is a race question so long as any number of negroes vote against the Democratic party.

*** Racer.**

+1. The common black snake (*Coluber constrictor*) or a related species.

See also BLACK RACER, BLUE RACER.

1823 JAMES *Exped.* I. 267 *Coluber constrictor*—Racer. **1842** *Nat. Hist. N.Y., Zoology* III. 37 The Pilot Black-snake . . . is manifestly the snake . . . to which they gave the name of *Racer* and *Pilot.* **1866** GREGG *Life in Army* 18 This species, were called *racers* on account of their great speed. **1908** *Dialect Notes* III. 291 *Black-runner,* a black snake noted for fleetness. Also called *black racer,* or simply *racer.* [e. Ala.]

+2. A poor or thin fish: (see also quots. 1884). Also attrib.

1832 WILLIAMSON *Maine* I. 159 [The salmon] then stay till the next May, when they return with their young to the sea; these are 'the racers' so called. **1884** GOODE, etc. *Fisheries* I. 488 About Grand Traverse Bay, Lake Michigan, two varieties [of lake trout] are also recognized, one being long, slim, and coarse-meated, . . . and are known as 'Reef Trout,' or when very large are called 'Racers.' *Ib.*, In the vicinity of Thunder Bay, Lake Huron, . . . another form [of lake trout] is known by the name of 'Racer.' *Ib.*, The Lake Trout has other appellatives, such as . . . 'Silver Lunge,' 'Racer Lunge,' 'Black Salmon,' and 'Lake Salmon.' **1911** *Rep. Fisheries 1908* 314/1 *Racer.*—A shad that has spawned and is lean and worthless.

+3. An automobile designed for great speed.

1903 *Scientific Amer.* LXXXIX. 96/1 Barney Oldfield, on the Ford-Cooper racer, . . . has been steadily lowering track records. **1916** WILSON *Somewhere* 289 Once she'd tramped on the gas of a ninety-horsepower racer and socked him against a stone wall at a turn some fool had made in the road.

+Race riot. An outbreak of disorder caused by feeling between the Negroes and the white population. — **1890** *Our Day* May 406 Race Riots in the South. **1896** *N.Y. Herald* 24 Dec. 8/2 Another negro has been shot down by a mob in Mayfield, Ky., and a big race riot seems imminent. **1899** *Kansas City Star* 16 March 12/1 Atlanta Sends a Militia Company to Prevent a Race Riot. **1919** *N.Y. Times* 28 July 10/2 The outbreak of race riots in Chicago, following so closely on those reported from Washington, shows clearly enough that the thing is not sporadic.

Race track. A race course. Also attrib. — **1859** MATSELL *Vocabulum* 113 Men are only caught, or put in hock, on the race–tracks, or on the steamboats down South. **1885** *Santa Fé Wkly. New Mexican* 24 Sept. 4/3 A very large crowd attended the races at Agua Fria race track on Saturday. **1907** *Sunday Oregonian* 15 Sept. (Th.), Race-track Fans drop much coin. **1913** LONDON *Valley of Moon* 27 The band led the way to the race track for the games.

+Raceway. A mill race.

1837 *Knickerb.* IX. 254, I was . . . thrown into the race-way. **1850** *Ib.* XXXV. 23 This race-way, from long use, had become slippery with moss and slime on the inside. **1872** MCCLELLAN *Golden State* 256 In the newly made race-way of the saw-mill . . . gold has been found. **1904** *N.Y. Ev. Post* 8 June 2 Several men were assaulted, and some were thrown into the raceway.

b. A passage or conduit: (see quotations).

1875 KNIGHT 1355/2 In the lay [of the power loom] . . . is a raceway for the shuttle. **1897** MOORE *How to Build a Home* 58 Raceways for carrying wires through the house should be of iron or other metal. **1898** *Inland Printer* Nov. 178/1 This machine will select the type, place them in a raceway and move them along until a line is set up.

*** Rack.**[1]

***1.** A bar or a number of bars used as a support for a spit or a cooking utensil. *Obs.* Usually pl.

1633 *N.H. Prov. Papers* I. 77 In the Little Roome [were left] . . . 1 grid-iron, 1 pr. of pott. hookes, 1 pr. of racks. **1649** *Conn. Rec.* I. 497 An Inventory of the Estate of Mr. William Whiting: . . . 3 spitts, a jack, racks [etc.]. **1674** *Harvard Rec.* I. 61 Kitchins Utensils: . . . 2 Iron racks.

***2.** A frame for fodder for horses and cattle.

1652 *Suffolk Deeds* I. 137 In the stable [are] one Rack & manger. **1771** *Md. Hist. Mag.* XIV. 127 Hay . . . may be let into the Racks of the sheds. **1845** *Cultivator* ns. II. 93 He fodders his sheep without racks. **1871** *Harper's Mag.* Dec. 51/1 [He] supplied . . . the rack with corn fodder. **1883** *Ib.* Oct. 719/2 Little or no fancy iron-work in the way of stable fittings is used, wooden racks and mangers being preferred.

+b. *To stand up to the rack* (and variants), to accept one's duty or one's fortune.

1834 CROCKETT *Narr. Life* 61, I was determined to stand up to my rack, fodder or no fodder. **1837** BIRD *Nick* II. 128 Up to the rack, fodder or no fodder; that's the work; there's no 'scaping them consequences. **1840** *Knickerb.* XVI. 227 So, gentlemen, 'stand up to the rack, fodder or no fodder,' as John Randolph used to say, when a political hack was made to run for office in a district where he stood no chance of election. **1854** [see BUNKUM *a.*]. **1890** *Stock Grower & Farmer* 12 July 4/2 For several years cattlemen have been severe losers but most of them have stood pluckily to the rack.

+3. In a river, a framework to obstruct the passage of fish.

1735 *Penna. Col. Rec.* IV. 24 Racks are a much greater Obstruction to Navigation than Wears.

+4. =HORSE RACK.

1827 *Mass. Spy* 24 Oct. (Th.), I reckon in futur you'll hitch your creter to the rack afore Patty Pott's door. **1834** NOTT *Novellettes* II. 154 Their horses were attached to the *rack* until they could be taken care of by the servants. **1843** 'CARLTON' *New Purchase* II. 211 One dozen horses [were] at Carlton's rack. **1907** *St. Nicholas* Aug. 912/1 Which of you kids took Mr. Gordon's horse away from the hitching rack last night?

+5. (See quotation and cf. BAGGAGE-RACK.)

1843 'CARLTON' *New Purchase* I. 5 The stages of that day wore no boots. In place of that leathern convenience, was a cross-barred ornament projecting in the rear to receive the baggage or at least half of it. This receptacle was called the 'Rack.'

+6. (See quotations.)

1903 *Nation* 6 Aug. 115/2 Another Americanism we miss under Racks, the technical name for the side plankings or buffers of our ferry slips. **1905** *N.Y. Ev. Post* 20 Dec. 1 Three of the Lackawanna 'racks,' as the arrangements of piles to fit the ferryboats are called, were left intact.

***Rack.**[2] A gait of a horse: **a.** The pace. ('Now only *U.S.' O.E.D.*) **+b.** The single-foot. — **1734** *N.J. Archives* XI. 395 Stolen . . . a black Horse. . . . Paces at the rate of 6 or 7 Miles an Hour and goes pretty fast on a Rack. **1832** KEMBLE *Rec. of Girlhood* (1879) 549 The Americans . . . prefer a shambling sort of half-trot, half-canter, which they judiciously call a rack. **1864** LOWELL *Fireside Trav.* 202 [The horse] had the rudiments of four [paces]—walk, trot, rack, and gallop. **1895** *Century Mag.* Aug. 626/1 He prefers to go in a 'rack,' or a running walk.

***Rack.**[3] A reach of a river. {1838, *dial.*} — **1832** WATSON *Hist. Tales N.Y.* 27 The 'Racks,' so called, along the [Hudson] river, were Dutch names for Reaches.

+Rackabone. [Cf. RACK OF BONES.] A lean person or animal. Often used of horses. *colloq.* — **1854** M. J. HOLMES *Tempest & Sunshine* 59 Turn that old rackerbone of yourn straight round, and turn down that ar street. **1900** *Congress. Rec.* App. 6 March 117/2 A Western farmer had a college-bred son who went off preaching. . . . He came back with an old rackabone.

+Racker. A horse which moves with a racking gait. (Cf. RACK.[2]) — **1829** *Sporting Mag.* XXIII. 266 The racker comes to us from our North Western territory. **1849** NASON *Journal* 52 The horses are what we call 'rackers.' **1862** *Rep. Comm. Patents 1861: Agric.* 558 Of the rackers I may remark that Thomas E. Turnner . . . imported from Narragansett bay a light chestnut. **1902** MCFAUL *Ike Glidden* 108 Lickety got ter puffn' up his ole hoss, soze you'd a thought it was the Millbridge Racker.

***Racket.** Also **racquette, raquet.**

+1. A snowshoe constructed of a light wooden frame and a network of cords.

[**1613** PURCHAS *Pilgrimage* VIII. iv. 630 Their Dogges . . . haue rackets tyed vnder their feet, the better to runne on the snow.] **1677** HUBBARD *Narrative* II. 27 It was not possible for any to have travelled that Way, unless they carried Rackets under their Feet, wherewith to walk upon the Top of the Snow. **1704** *N.H. Prov. Papers* II. 419 They have upwards of 30 pr. of Snow Shoes and Racketts already made. **1763** *Boston Ev. Post* 7 March, Several persons who have come . . . were obliged to travel with Rackets. **1808** PIKE *Sources Miss.* 61 Mr. Grant fell through the ice with his rackets on. **1897** *Outing* XXIX. 362/1 When the racquette is fastened the heel and toe are free.

attrib. **1780** E. PARKMAN *Diary* 199, I was drawn by a number of Rackettmen, in a very handsome Sleigh. *Ib.* 207 Another snowstorm . . . covers ye Rackett Tracks and fills ye Roads again.

+2. a. A similar shoe for walking over marshy ground. **b.** (See quotation.)

(a) 1846 DE SMET *Oregon Missions* (1847) 193 The savages travel over these marshy places in *Rackets.* **(b) 1864** WEBSTER 1080/2 *Racket,* . . . a broad wooden shoe or patten for a horse, to enable him to step on marshy or soft ground.

+3. A kind of dance employing the slide and the shift or change. Also attrib. and with defining term.

1881 RITTENHOUSE *Maud* 30 Do you dance the raquet? **1885** DODWORTH *Dancing* 51 Racket Waltz (One-Slide Racket in Waltz Time). *Ib.* 52 Changes are made . . . by alternating the one-slide racket with the three-slide.

Racketing. {1753-} +The performance of the dance known as the racket. — **1882** RITTENHOUSE *Maud* 127 Mr. Menager must needs add his share to praise my grace in raqueting.

+Rack heap. A mass of rubbish. Also transf. — **1883** *Amer. Philol. Ass. Trans.* 55 *Wrack-heap,* as it probably should be spelled, or *rack-heap,* as it is spelled commonly, means in West Virginia 'a confused mass of logs and other rubbish, usually accumulated by high water.' **1883** 'MARK TWAIN' *Life on Miss.* xxiii, There was only one boat advertised. . . . She was a venerable rack-heap. **1889** P. BUTLER *Recollections* 72 There were in the river heaps of drift-wood, called 'rack-heaps,' dangerous places into which the water rushed with great violence.

Rack of bones. [Probably from RACK.[1]] A skeleton; hence, a thin or wretched person. (Cf. RACKABONE.) — **1804** ORDWAY in *Jrnls. of Lewis & O.* 128 We Saw the rack of Bones of a verry large fish. **1876** HABBERTON *Jericho Road* 146 Ain't it bad enough to be a good-for-nothin' rack of bones that's no comfort to myself? **1889** 'MARK TWAIN' *Conn. Yankee* 220 This poor rack of bones was a woman of middle age, apparently. **1911** LINCOLN *Cap'n Warren's Wards* 140 If she fell on that poor rack-o'-bones, . . . 'twould be a final smash.

Racoon. (See RAC(C)OON *n.* and *v.*)

Racquette, *n.* (See RACKET.)

Rad. {1831-} Short for RADICAL. — **1824** in Mackenzie *Van Buren* 195 Wend you with the *Rads* to-night, Sixty-five perchance they'll muster. **1871** *Harper's Mag.* July 319/1 But the war is now over, says the Rads, we're prospering well. **1898** PAGE *Red Rock* 411 He was abusing Leech and Still and pretty much all the Rads.

***Raddle.**[1] (See quot. 1841.) {1883-, *n. dial.*} — **1841** WEBSTER II. 413/1 In *New England,* an instrument consisting of a wooden bar, with a row of upright pegs set in it, which is employed by domestic weavers, to keep the warp of a proper width, and prevent it from becoming entangled, when it is wound upon the beam of the loom. **1876** KNIGHT 1852/1.

+Raddle.[2] (See quot. 1876.) — **1876** KNIGHT 1852/1 *Raddle,* . . . an iron bar with an end bent at right angles, used by puddlers in stirring the iron in the furnace, and also in making up the balls for the tilt or squeezer. A *rabble.* **1890** *Cent.* 4931/1.

Radiated asbestos. (See ASBESTOS 2.)

Radiator. {1836-} +A fixture through which steam or hot water from a central heating plant circulates in order to warm a room. — **1851** CIST *Cincinnati* 213 By the introduction of evaporatory radiators and registers, the air is kept moist. **1876** KNIGHT 1853/2 In Fig. 4103 the radiator is made in sections. **1899** ADE *Doc' Horne* 10 They knew the radiator was the coldest thing in the room. **1906** *N.Y. Ev. Post* 29 Dec. Sat. Suppl. 1 There are still thousands who stay by their own firesides—or radiators—on that day.

Radical. {1641-}

1. An advocate of basic change in politics or religion: (see also quot. 1830). {1802-} Freq. disparaging.

1822 J. Q. ADAMS *Diary* 282 General Scott . . . said Archer was a Radical and inclined to be Jacobinical. **1829** *Western Mo. Rev.* II. 593 The schism in the Methodist Church . . . exists between the sticklers for the ancient structure of episcopalianism . . . and the *radicals,* who seem to be contending for a more democratic form of church government. **1830** *Congress. Deb.* 26 Feb. 208/2 After the election of President Monroe, three or four republican parties rose upon the ruins of the federalists. Amongst them was the Crawford party. . . . The Washington Republican . . . denominated Mr. Crawford the radical chief, and those who supported him radicals. **1830** D. WEBSTER *Ib.* 27 Jan. 67/1 The name of Radicals, as a term of distinction, applicable and applied to those who denied the liberal doctrines of Internal Improvements, originated [*c*1822], . . . somewhere between North Carolina and Georgia. **1838** in Buckingham *America* I. 176 In a city of 300,000 inhabitants, 2000 radicals, agrarians, Fanny-Wright men, and *Locofocos* can be found. **1921** *N. Amer. Rev.* Aug. 316 Liberals are merely terror-stricken Radicals.

+2. a. In the Civil War, a member of the group in the North who favored extreme measures against the South, as abolition of slavery, confiscation of property, etc. **b.** After the Civil War, one who favored a policy of reconstruction based on full recognition of the political and social equality of Negroes and white citizens; one who supported the carpet-bag governments in the South.

1862 NORTON *Army Lett.* 129, I suppose the radicals have got enough of Burnside now. **1865** *Amer. Annual Cycl.* 14/2 Nothing would satisfy the Radicals of the North. **1867** *Congress. Rec.* 16 April 848/2 Somebody who is not the choice of the Senate, but a sort of compromise man, who is neither Democrat nor Radical. **1868** *Ore. State Jrnl.* 18 July 1/4, I had rather be called a Radical than a rebel, at any time. **1870** *Republican Rev.* 31 Sept. 3/1 The Governor's . . . record as a radical of the advanced school, running back to the organization of the Republican party, has not been marred by any action of his in this Territory.

3. *attrib.* or as *adj.* **a.** In sense 1 with *Democracy, wing.*

1843 *Whig Almanac 1844* 19/2 William H. Crawford of Georgia . . . [was] the leader and champion of the Radical Democracy, and its candidate for President in 1824. **1848** *Ib. 1849* 8/2 The Wright or Radical wing had never cordially approved the policy of Annexation.

+b. In sense 2 b with *abolitionist, candidate, Congress,* etc.

1868 in Fleming *Hist. Reconstruction* I. 468 Hence you find that another rebellion was commenced, having its origin in the radical Congress. **1868** *N.Y. Herald* 4 July 5/2 The radical candidate for Governor . . . hurries back to Vicksburg. *Ib.*, The snug little sum of $37,321.40 has already been paid to four radical papers. **1874** COLLINS *Kentucky* I. 217, 7 Radical negroes at 2 A.M. called out of his house one who voted the Democratic ticket, and Kukluxed him by shooting him with bird-shot. **1882** A. JOHNSTON *Amer. Politics* 193 A Convention of Radical Men . . . wished to deal with rebellion and rebels more harshly. **1883** *Century Mag.* Oct. 957/2 'A Radical Abolitionist' . . . puts a false interpretation on the language used by Chief-Justice Taney in the Dred Scott Case. **1888** M. LANE in *America* 11 Oct. 15 *Liberal party.*—A portion of the Republican party in Missouri, headed by Carl Schurz in 1870, as distinguished from the radical wing. It was shortlived.

Radicalism. {1820–} +The political principles of radicals (q.v., sense 2). — **1865** *Nation* I. 66 The particular aversion of the Golden Circle was radicalism of every sort, and hence no lodges were erected in South Carolina or Massachusetts. **1865** *Amer. Annual Cycl.* 512/1 The National Democracy of the United States . . . [is] the only agent by which radicalism can be successfully met. **1874** in Fleming *Hist. Reconstruction* II. 152 If that body [Congress] and the President show a disposition to . . . maintain Radicalism in Louisiana, then Wells, Anderson & Co. will, no doubt, rule accordingly.

Radical party. +(See quot. 1914.) Also attrib. — **1866** G. WELLES *Diary* II. 612 The last long session of Congress was devoted chiefly to Radical party organization. **1868** *N.Y. Herald* 4 July 5/1 The great majority . . . are weary of the rule of the radical party. **1871** *Republican Rev.* 3 June 2/2 In the meantime the Radical party has pledged itself to the right, and trusted the people. **1914** *Cycl. Amer. Govt.* III. 131/1 A name sometimes given to the Republican party especially soon after the Civil War, and, while often applied generally to the whole party by its opponents, more commonly applicable to the extreme element and its leaders in determined opposition to the policy and acts of President Johnson.

+**Radical Republican.** A member of the Republican party who favored drastic measures against the South. Also attrib. Hence *Radical Republicanism.* (Cf. RADICAL 2 b.) — **1865** *Amer. Annual Cycl.* 512/2 We invite all law-abiding citizens . . . to join us in our opposition to the Radical Republican party. **1868** *N.Y. Herald* 1 July 7/5 The radical republican associations in the various Assembly districts . . . elected delegates. **1868** *Ore. State Jrnl.* 24 Oct. 1/6 Your example is of rare value as a contribution to the assailed cause of Radical Republicanism. **1900** *Congress. Rec.* 14 Feb. 1799/2 An election law . . . put the election machinery into the hands of three unequivocal radical Republicans appointed in each county.

Radiograph. {1881} An image produced on a sensitive plate by some means other than light, as X rays. {1896–} — **1896** *Columbus Dispatch* 27 Feb. 8/4 F. L. Woodward . . . has devised a new ray lamp by means of which excellent cathodic radiographs have been obtained. **1898** *Pop. Science Mo.* 569 The radiograph of the normal chest shows the clearly marked out lungs. **1903** *N.Y. Herald* 17 May 4/6 Photographs made by radium are called radiographs.

* **Radish.**

* **1.** A well-known garden plant, *Raphanus sativus,* or its edible root.

1634 WOOD *New Eng. Prospects* (1865) 15 The ground affoards very good kitchin Gardens, for Turneps, Parsnips, Carrots, Radishes, and Pumpions. **1709** LAWSON *Carolina* 77 The Garden-Roots that thrive well in Carolina, are . . . Radishes, Horse-Radish, Beet, both sorts. **1803** *Lit. Mag.* (Phila.) Dec. 170 A radish in the landlord's garden . . . proved to be twenty-two and an half inches in circumference. **1860** E. COWELL *Diary* 58 Here we have also radishes, cucumbers, etc., a very fine table. **1914** 'BOWER' *Flying U Ranch* 169 You can pull the weeds out of his radishes.

+**2.** Attrib. in the names of insects.

1854 EMMONS *Agric. N.Y.* V. 262 (*index*), Radish-bugs, 135. [*Ib.* 135 *Halticides.* Genus *Haltica.* . . . They feed upon the leaves of vegetables.] **1873** *Amer. Naturalist* VII. 242 The cabbage web moth . . . is noticed; also the radish weevil. **1891** *Cent.* 4935/2 *Radish-fly,* . . . an American dipterous insect, *Anthomyia raphani,* injurious to the radish.

* **Raft,** *n.*[1]

* **1.** A float of lumber fastened together for easy transportation.

1644 *Conn. Rec.* I. 460 A Rafte of Planke is goeing downe. **1713** *Essex Inst. Coll.* XLII. 348 [They were] bound up to Salem with a raft of timber or pieces for Masts. **1817** S. BROWN *Western Gazetteer* 104 The boards, plank and shingles used, are mostly brought in rafts from the mills of Allegany county. **1856** ANDREWS *Recoll.* 277 Large logs are transported as rafts. **1877** W. WRIGHT *Big Bonanza* 243 The rafts of logs are towed across the lake by small steamboats.

* **2.** A flat structure of logs or boards, used for navigation.

1676 *New Eng. Hist. & Gen. Reg.* XXXVIII. 224 The Indians made two great rafte of board & rayles. **1750** T. WALKER *Journal* 47 We then made a Raft and carried over one Load of Baggage. **1854** BROMWELL *Locomotive Sk.* 187 We see the glories of the broad Alleghany on both sides, strewn with arks, rafts, and flat-boats. *a*1918 G. STUART *On Frontier* II. 17 The boats . . . were little better than rafts.

+**3.** A mass of driftwood impeding or completely obstructing navigation. Freq. found in western rivers.

1772 B. ROMANS in P. L. Phillips *Notes on B. Romans* 122, I Could not Proceed any farther not being provided with any Tools, to Clear the River, of the Rafts a little higher up. **1804** CLARK in *Lewis & C. Exped.* I. (1904) 68 The Boat turned twice on the quick Sand & once on a raft of Drift. **1834** PECK *Gaz. Illinois* 336 At a trifling expense, in clearing out the trees and rafts of timber, it [*sc.* the Spoon R.] might be made navigable.

+**b.** With reference to the large obstruction in the Red River between Oklahoma and Texas.

1825 *Austin P.* II. (1924) 1077 This has opened the Eyes of Govt. Relative to the Raft in Red River and measures are about to be taken to open it. **1833** *Niles' Reg.* 29 June 286/1 He had succeeded in removing twenty-six miles of the great raft on the Red River. **1840** *Ib.* 18 July 309/2 A channel has been cut through the raft, so as to permit the passage of any of the boats. **1878** *Congress. Rec.* 16 Jan. 370/2, I am told that trees have been found growing from the vegetable mold, which had formed upon that raft.

+**c.** *transf.* A dense flock of waterfowl.

Cf. RAFT DUCK.

1709 LAWSON *Carolina* 150 Raft-Fowl includes all the sorts of small Ducks and Teal, that go in Rafts along the Shoar. **1872** *Fur, Fin & Feather* (ed. 2) 26 These great collections [of ducks] are termed rafts.

4. Attrib. and comb. with *boat, bridge, fowl,* etc.

1709 Raft-fowl [see sense 3 c.]. **1753** WASHINGTON *Writings* I. 38, I fortunately saved myself by catching hold of one of the Raft Logs. **1799** *Wilmington* (N.C.) *Gazette* 5 Sept., For Sale. My Mills on the raft swamp. **1833** CATLIN *Indians* I. 72 Soon ran upon the head of an island, that was covered with immense quantities of raft and drift wood. **1862** in Moore *Rebellion Rec.* V. II. 478 Over this stream there is a floating or raft-bridge. **1876** *Nat. Museum Bul.* No. 6, 43 Methods of Transportation. . . . Indian raft-boats, Launches.

Raft, *n.*[2] [Variant of earlier *raff* (*a*1677–).] A quantity of persons or things. *colloq.* {1887–, *dial.*} — **1833** *Jamestown* (N.Y.) *Jrnl.* 25 Sept. 2/1 Only think what an everlasting raft of fellows we should have. **1845** COOPER *Chainbearer* xviii, A raft of the critturs you did get atween you. **1853** 'P. PAXTON' *Yankee in Texas* 123 Two days after, a raft of people came along, and stopped at Old Charley's. **1870** 'MARK TWAIN' *Sk., New & Old* 248 He had me measure him and take a whole raft of directions. **1906** *Springfield W. Republican* 20 Dec. 11 This bill will be rushed through on some 'claims day' with a raft of other bills.

Raft, *v.*[1]

1. *tr.* To transport (logs or boards) in the form of rafts. {1706–}

1768 in F. Chase *Hist. Dartmouth Coll.* I. 104 The stream, called Baker's River (a branch of Merrimack, by which logs are rafted to the sea), runs through it. **1817** S. BROWN *Western Gazetteer* 91 [Boards] rafted down the Allegany and Ohio rivers. **1864** NICHOLS *Amer. Life* I. 22 Pine-trees . . . [had been] rafted down the river. **1890** *Century Mag.* Dec. 181/1 On the Sacramento River or some of its tributaries, . . . the lumber could be rafted down to the fort.

2. To move or transport on a raft. {1845}

1766 W. SMITH *Hist. Acct. Exped. Bouquet* 126 The carts, provisions and baggage, may be rafted over, or a bridge built. **1847** PARKMAN in *Knickerb.* XXIX. 314 We crossed it on the following day, rafting over our horses and equipage with much difficulty.

3. To form into a raft; to bind together as a raft. {1745–}

1822 *Mass. Spy* 1 May (Th.), [He] was instantly killed by the fall of a pile of dock-logs, which he was assisting to raft. **1857** CHANDLESS *Visit Salt Lake* 69 He was . . . up to most work, driving a team or a plough, rafting logs, and what not. **1870** *Maine Rep.* LVI. 567 He caused the whole quantity [of logs] to be . . . rafted for sale. **1905** WIGGIN *Rose* 144 [Her lover] had floated down stream to her . . . on a couple of logs rafted together.

+**4.** To cross (a stream) by means of a raft.

1765 ROGERS *Journals* 177 The river St. Francis . . . is very still water, and may be easily rafted where you cross it. **1804** CLARK in *Lewis & C. Exped.* I. (1904) 38 They were obliged to raft or Swim many Creeks. **1806** PIKE *Exped.* (1895) II. 373 We found the Indians on the west shore, they having rafted the river. **1845** FRÉMONT *Exped.* 251 We had expected to raft the river.

+**5.** *intr.* To use a raft; to travel on a raft. {1840–}

1741 *New. Eng. Hist. & Gen. Reg.* XXXIII. 330 We met with great difficulty in passing that River, first attempting to wade . . . , then tried to Raft but it was so shallow in some places we could not use it. **1753** WASHINGTON *Diaries* I. 57 Sent our Horses a little way up French Creek to raft over and encamp.

6. *To raft off* {trans. vb., 1745–}, +to begin a voyage on a raft; to push *off* on a raft.

1841 COOPER *Deerslayer* vi, These foxes will be rafting off to storm your castle. *Ib.* viii, Vagabonds will have to swim for it, or raft off, to come near this place.

‖**Raft,** *v.*[2] [f. RAFT *n.*[2]] To go *with.* — **1888** DELAND *J. Ward* 173 He hadn't no trade learned, neither,—just rafted with men as bad as him.

+**Raft duck.**

1. The scaup duck (*Nyroca marila*), or a related species. (Cf. BLACK-HEAD 1 a, BLUEBILL.)

1824 LATHAM *Gen. Hist. Birds* X. 302 [The] Scaup Duck . . . is known in Georgia, and called by some the Raft Duck. **1844** *Nat. Hist. N.Y., Zoology* II. 323 The Broadbill *Fuligula Marila* . . . on the Chesapeake . . . is called Blackhead, and in Virginia Raft-duck. **1889** [see Flock duck]. **1917** *Birds of Amer.* I. 135.

2. The redhead, *Nyroca americana.* Also *red-headed raft duck.*

1888 Trumbull *Names of Birds* 51 *Aythya americana.* . . . From Pamlico Sound to South Carolina commonly known as the Red-Headed Raft Duck. **1917** *Birds of Amer.* I. 131.

*__Rafter.__[1] **1.** A sloping beam in a roof. +**2.** (See quotation.) — **(1)** **1674** *Md. Archives* II. 406 There [shall] be a state house and Prison built . . . the principall Rafters of the porch & staire Case to be seven & five Inches. **1797** Graham *Pres. State of Vt.* 162 The rafters are then made for the roof. **1885** 'Craddock' *Prophet* 249 The peltry hanging from the rafters, apparently swayed as the light rose and fell. **1920** Howells *Vacation of Kelwyns* 101 He suspected that the small chirpings and squeakings from the rafters were the vigils of bats. **(2)** **1889** *Cent.* 825/3 *Carline,* . . . a transverse iron or wooden bar placed across the top of a railroad-car from side to side to support the roof-boards. Sometimes called a *rafter.*

Rafter.[2] One who rafts timber. {1851-} — **1809** Kendall *Travels* III. 305 What was now demanded by the law, was . . . that the rafters should relinquish . . . the earnings of their immediate hands. **1851** Springer *Forest Life* 43 The amount of employment it furnishes to lumbermen, mill-men, rafters, coasters, truckmen, merchants, and mechanics, exceeds that furnished by any other single product in Maine. **1891** C. Robert *Adrift Amer.* 206 The rafters were engaged in making the rafts up.

Rafter level. A level made of wooden rails. — **1786** Washington *Diaries* III. 106 After doing this, and levelling part of the ground (with a Rafter level) . . . I intended to have run a course or two of Fencing. **1834** J. F. Burke *Brit. Husbandry* I. 534 In America, where it is much used for ascertaining the declination of land, it is called a rafter-level.

Raftsman. One who works on a raft. {1883-} Also *raft man.*

[**1776** C. Carroll *Jrnl. Visit to Canada* (1845) 67 A small current begins here, and the raftsmen are not obliged to row.] **1828** Sherburne *Memoirs* 237 The raft men had the privilege of cooking, and sleeping under cover, in the boat. **1841** Cooper *Deerslayer* xiv, The vagabonds can make logs sarve their turn, as well as the best raftsmen on the rivers. **1859** Wilmer *Press Gang* 34 The raftsmen who were engaged in floating timber down the Susquehanna. **1887** *Courier-Journal* 16 Feb. 4/5 Raftmen from the mountains near the headwaters of Roaring river tell a tale of disaster and loss. **1913** London *Valley of Moon* 265 He was bully of the raftsmen of the Susquehanna.

*__Rag,__ *n.*

1. Jocular uses: +**a.** *pl.* Paper money, esp. depreciated bank notes.

1816 *Ann. 14th Congress* 1 Sess. 775, I say cash, sir, for we there [in Mass.], have nothing of that circulating medium which the gentleman from Virginia (Mr. Randolph) denominates rags. **1818** Flint *Lett. from Amer.* 106 Small bills are in circulation of a half, a fourth, an eighth, and even a sixteenth part of a dollar. These small rags are not current at a great distance from the places of their nativity. **1838** *N.Y. Advertiser & Exp.* 10 Jan. 2/1 The Yarmouth Register states that the Cape Cod and Cape Ann Fishermen have been compelled to take their bounty . . . in '*rags*,' called 'checks,' on certain 'Rag Factories' in the city of Boston. **1857** *Knickerb.* XLIX. 35 You'll find it [*sc.* pay] here—cash or check—slugs, rags, or dollars—according to order.

+**b.** A piece of clothing.

1855 *Knickerb.* XLV. 502 Oh! the robe was of *moire antique,* (a very expensive 'rag'). **1862** Browne *A. Ward His Book* 130, [I] put on a clean biled rag to attend Miss Picklehomony's grate musical sorry at the Melodeon. **1883** 'Mark Twain' *Life on Miss.* iii, I stood up and shook my rags off and jumped into the river.

2. Phrases. +**a.** *To take the rag off,* to do something just right; to excel. (See Bush *n.* 3.)

1810 *Norfolk Gazette* 19 Sept. 2/3 (Th. S.), This 'takes the rag off the bush' so completely, that we suppose we shall hear no more . . . about the Chesapeake business. **1836** *Crockett's Yaller Flower Almanac* 20 He takes the rag off. **1858** *Harper's Mag.* Jan. 281/1 A number of farmers were . . . telling stories about their work, . . . when one of them took the rag off the whole of them by relating his experience.

+**b.** *To chew the rag,* to talk; to argue; to talk at length. Also *rag-chewing. slang.*

1885 *Santa Fé Weekly New Mexican* 1 Oct. 1/3 After a few minutes rag-chawing a verdict of 'came to his death from unknown causes,' is promptly rendered. **1901** *McClure's Mag.* April 576/2 There are a few soreheads . . . who chew the rag about corruption an' the way the town's run.

3. *attrib.* and *comb.* +**a.** In sense 1 a with *capital, currency,* etc.

1817 Paulding *Lett. from South* II. 122 This comfortable dog palmed upon us a bank-note of some distant Rag-Manufactory. **1834** *Congress. Deb.* 26 Feb. 729 Instead of hard money, we shall have a miserable rag currency, not worth the paper out of which it is made. **1838** Rag factory [see sense 1 a]. **1870** M. H. Smith *20 Years Wall St.* 366 They denounced the certificates as rag capital, and would have nothing to do with the investment.

b. Designating persons who work or deal literally or figuratively with rags.

*a***1841** Hawes *Sporting Scenes* II. 168 Their reporter—horrid office! Rag-picker! Street-sweeper! Kennel-cleaner! **1851** Hall *Manhattaner* 103 Not far off a brace of 'rag hookers' are disputing the middle of the street with a couple of quarrelling negro garçons. **1887** I. Alden *Little Fishers* ix, If Sarah Jane has begged me once to let her sell it to the rag pedlars, I believe she has twenty times.

+**c.** Designating habitations made chiefly of canvas or places composed of such habitations.

1851 L. Clappe *Lett. from Calif.* 94 The first artificial elegance which attracts your vision is a large rag shanty, roofed, however, with a rude kind of shingles. **1890** Custer *Following Guidon* 220, I envied that [a dug-out] for the wind would not toy with his habitation . . . as it did our 'rag houses.' *a***1916** Webster *Gold Seekers of '49* (1917) 123 Sacramento City at this time was built principally of cloth houses and tents. . . . It was generally known as the 'Rag City.'

d. *Rag lamp,* a lamp consisting of a rag lying in a bath of oil or lard; *r. wick,* a rag used as a wick in such a lamp.

1889 'Mark Twain' *Conn. Yankee* xlii. 531 He had re-instituted the ancient rag-lamp. *a***1918** G. Stuart *On Frontier* 31 A tin lamp holding about a quart of lard with a rag wick in its spout which, when lighted, would cast a strong light for several yards.

*__Rag,__ *v.* +*To rag out,* to dress up. *slang.* — **1865** Browne *A. Ward; His Travels* 180 Don't make fun of our clothes. . . . We ain't goin' to *rag out* till we git to Nevady! **1894** Hoyt *Texas Steer* (1925) II. 20 Speaking of clothes, don't you think me and ma are ragged out pretty well for folks right off a ranch?

+**Rag baby.**

1. A doll made of rags. Also fig.

1809 *Ann. 10th Congress* 2 Sess. 1165 If they insist upon dressing up, in their own way, their rag-babies, and will shake and beat them about for their own amusement, it is not for me to interfere. **1848** *Ladies' Repository* VIII. 75 Susy . . . made them a rag-baby's head, and Jim put his old hat on it. **1876** *Wide Awake* 74/1 She remembered a large rag-baby which her mother had begun to make the spring before.

2. (See quot. 1892 and cf. Rag *n.* 1 a.) Also attrib.

1875 *Chicago Tribune* 8 Nov. 4/2 The rag-baby policy has been rejected, and has proved fatally disastrous wherever presented. **1876** *Congress. Rec.* 8 April 2317/2 The chief end and purpose of the eastern moneyed power is . . . to secure the uninterrupted reign of 'rag money' and the 'rag baby.' **1892** Walsh *Literary Curiosities* 947 *Rag-Baby,* . . . a humorous personification of the greenback currency. It was used with great effect by speakers and caricaturists in the Presidential campaign of 1876. **1895** Myers *Bosses & Boodle* 111 The Democrats of Ohio adopted a platform in favor of the 'rag baby.'

Rag-bag. A bag in which rags are kept. {1861-} — **1833** *New Eng. Mag.* IV. 523 Every good housewife keeps a rag-bag . . . to serve as a receptacle for rags. **1854** M. J. Holmes *Tempest & Sunshine* 112 Mrs. Stanley then turned her rag bag inside out. **1887** I. Alden *Little Fishers* ix, It didn't seem quite the thing to throw such pretty soft stuff into the rag-bag.

+**Rag baron.** A financial magnate operating in paper money. (Cf. Rag *n.* 1 a.) — **1818** *Niles' Reg.* XIV. 226/1 The name of a *Jew* and '*rag-baron*' is synonimous. **1838** Clay *Speeches* (1842) 343 We hear . . . denunciations against banks, corporations, rag barons, the spirit of monopoly, etc. **1855** *Chicago Times* 8 March 2/1 He advocates . . . treating the hostility of the 'rag barons' with the contempt it deserves.

+**Rag carpet.** A carpet made of rags, esp. one made by weaving the rags together. — **1837** *S. Lit. Messenger* III. 333 There was a snug little bedroom . . . and a comfortable good-sized one for Charlotte, with a neat rag carpet. **1850** S. F. Cooper *Rural Hours* 313 In Europe these rag carpets are not seen, at least not on the common track of travellers. **1861** Stowe *Pearl Orr's Isl.* I. 10 'The best room,' with its low studded walls, white dimity window curtains, [and] rag carpet. **1885** *Harper's Mag.* March 592/2 There was a worn rag-carpet, some cane-seated chairs, and one black wooden rocker. **1920** Howells *Vacation of Kelwyns* 26 They had given them the rag carpets and the hooked rugs, the high-post bedsteads and splint chairs.

+**Rag-carpeted,** *a.* Covered or furnished with a rag carpet. — **1845** Kirkland *Western Clearings* 185, I led the young gentleman through the shop into the rag-carpeted sitting-room of Mrs. Larkins. **1889** *Century Mag.* Jan. 410/2 The fire . . . flung strange shadows over the rag-carpeted floor.

+**Rag carpeting.** Carpeting woven or otherwise made of rags. — **1813** *Niles' Reg.* III. 329/1 Articles manufactured by Mrs. Webster, . . . a laudable example of female industry, and economy [include] 22 yards of bottle green and black cloth, . . . 24 do. rag carpeting. **1843** [see Cadder]. **1873** 'Mark Twain' *Gilded Age* 60 The parlor carpet was from St. Louis —though the other rooms were clothed in the 'rag' carpeting of the country. **1887** I. Alden *Little Fishers* ix, Her hands had been busy over long seams of rag carpeting.

*__Ragged,__ *a.*

1. In the specific names of plants.

1814 Bigelow *Florula Bostoniensis* 206 *Orchis psycodes.* Ragged Orchis. . . . This is our common species. **1817-8** Eaton *Botany* (1822) 459 *Silphium perfoliatum,* ragged cup. **1847** Darlington *Weeds & Plants*

279 Oriental Polyonum. Ragged Sailor. Prince's Feather. . . . This showy species . . . has become sparingly naturalized. **1868** GRAY *Field Botany* 40 *Nigella Damascena*, Common Fennel-flower or Ragged-Lady.

+**2.** *The ragged edge*, the verge.

1878 BEADLE *Western Wilds* 91 He is constantly in trouble, and sometimes on the ragged edge of starvation. **1889** 'MARK TWAIN' *Conn. Yankee* 196 He was always on the ragged edge of apprehension. **1911** LINCOLN *Cap. Warren's Wards* 254 The Dunns are dangerously close to the ragged edge.

Ragging. {1875-} +(See quotation.) — **1890** *Cent.* 4939/1 *Ragging*, . . . a method of fishing for the striped-bass, etc., in which a red rag is used as a fly.

+**Rag money.** =RAG *n.* 1 a. {1893} — **1833** *Congress. Deb.* 18 Dec. 2219 We had nothing but a metallic currency—no swindling shops—no rag money. **1856** GOODRICH *Recoll.* I. 493 This whole mass [of questionable bills] acquired the title of 'rag money,' 'shin-plasters,' &c. **1875** *Chicago Tribune* 29 July 4/3 Blanton Duncan . . . helped to beat the South by supplying its de-facto Government with measureless quantities of rag-money.

+**Ragocrat.** An advocate of rag money; a banker who issues rag money. *Obs.* — **1838** *N.Y. Advertiser & Exp.* 18 April 3/1 The Government of this country has . . . called them [the merchants and the banks] all sorts of 'Rag Barons,' 'Ragocrats' and 'Aristocrats,' and the like. **1842** H. W. BEESON *Speech* 9 July 12/2 (Th. S.), 'Pauper labor' indeed—and we have now, thanks to the ragocrats, got some of that blessing here.

+**Ragshag.** (See quot. 1909.) *colloq.* — **1887** *Conn. Courant* 7 July (*Cent.*), While the Ragshags were marching, . . . [he] caught his foot in his ragged garment and fell. **1909** WEBSTER 1764/4 *Ragshag*, . . . a ragged person, esp. a masquerader.

***Ragstone.** Any of various hard stones used as whetstones. {1840-} — **1707** *Boston News-Letter* 25 Aug. 2/2 Grindstones & Ragstones. . . . To be Sold by Mr. John George, Merchant, at his Ware House. **1759** *Newport Mercury* 26 June 4/3 Imported . . . and to be sold by Jacob Richardson; . . . Rub and Norway Rag Stones.

+**Ragtime.** Music characterized by frequent syncopation, as in many Negro melodies, with a regularly accented accompaniment. Also attrib.

1897 ADE *Pink Marsh* 159 He told of his belief that the angels in heaven played 'rag-time' music. **1899** *Chicago Record* 11 Jan. 4/4 This is the reason, also, for the popularity of 'rag time,' 'stop time' and all other ingenious rhythmical contrivances of the vaudeville music-maker. **1910** E. S. FIELD *Sapphire Bracelet* 65 Sadie allowed herself to be led to the piano, where she plunged, with a splendid splash, into a raging torrent of ragtime. **1922** SANDBURG *Slabs of Sunburnt West* 12 Trucks . . . [are] steered by drivers whistling ragtime against the sunsets.

Ragweed. {1658-} +A hardy weed of grayish-green color, belonging to the genus *Ambrosia*.

1790 DEANE *New-Eng. Farmer* 176/1 The milk of cows in summer is sometimes made very bitter by their feeding on rag-weed. **1840** DEWEY *Mass. Flowering Plants* 142 *Ambrosia elatior.* Rag Weed. Wild Wormweed. . . . The bruised leaves were formerly in popular use as an application to wounds and bruises. **1870** *Amer. Naturalist* IV. 582 Prominent among [the flora of the Prairies are] . . . the rag-weeds (*Ambrosia*), the wormwoods (*Artemisia*), . . . and the psoraleas. **1899** TARKINGTON *Gentleman from Ind.* iii, The green tangle of rag and iron weed and long grass in the corners of the snake fence.

Rag wheel. A chain wheel. {1829, 1830} — **1812** *Niles' Reg.* II. 393/2 A rag wheel [of a mill machine] of three feet diameter is kept in complete motion. **1873** BAILEY *Life in Danbury* 9 He employed a carpenter from a place twenty miles distant to make a new rag-wheel.

***Ragwort.** Any species of Senecio, +esp. *S. aureus.* Also with defining term. — **1790** DEANE *New-Eng. Farmer* 313/2 Of the upland weeds those which have proved to be the most troublesome are . . . rag-weed, ragwort [etc.]. **1818** *Mass. H. S. Coll.* 2 Ser. VIII. 169 The most interesting are . . . two species of veronica or speedwell, the golden senecio or ragwort, [and] the columbine. **1857** GRAY *Botany* 231 Golden Ragwort. . . . Common everywhere. *Ib.*, Woolly Ragwort. . . . Mountains of Penn. . . . and southward. **1915** ARMSTRONG & THORNBER *Western Wild Flowers* 564 Ragwort. *Senecio perplexus var. dispar.* . . . Utah, Idaho. A conspicuous plant and quite handsome.

+**Rah,** *interj.* Short for *hurrah:* (see also quot. 1877). — **1872** *Harper's Mag.* Jan. 319/1 The other [battery] flashed in the pan, and a few voices piped, 'Rah for Seymour!' **1877** BARTLETT 792 *'Rah! 'rah! 'rah!* The formula for a cheer by the students of Harvard College, Cambridge. **1889** 'MARK TWAIN' *Conn. Yankee* 421 'Rah for protection—to Sheol with free-trade! **1905** *Century Mag.* Aug. 483/1 A pavilion filled with American visitors exploded in barbaric 'rah-rah-rahs.'

***Raid.** A military foray, +with special reference to the Civil War. (See also PRICE RAID.) — **1862** MCCLELLAN in *Own Story* 511, I did not prevent the raid upon Manassas. **1877** JOHNSON *Anderson Co., Kansas* 82 When Quantrell made his raid on Lawrence, . . . the records of this office being in Lawrence, were destroyed. **1895** M. A. Jackson *Gen. Jackson* 598 Nor was Jackson led away by the specious advantages of the so-called 'raids.'

Raider. One who goes on a raiding expedition {1870-}, +with special reference to the Civil War. Also appositive.

1863 *Commonwealth* (Boston) 30 Oct., Governor Bramlette of Kentucky . . . telegraphs that the rebel raiders are within forty miles of his capital. **1865** BOUDRYE *Fifth N.Y. Cavalry* 43 Stuart's raiders came through our lines. **1867** EDWARDS *Shelby* 42 Captain John H. Morgan afterward the celebrated raider-general, had a fine company in his native city of Lexington. **1878** *Harper's Mag.* March 526/1 As the raider chief came up alongside, Kate trembled. **1887** *Courier-Journal* 6 Feb. 13/7 Col. John S. Mosby, the famous Confederate raider, was at the Fifth Avenue Hotel today.

+**b.** (See quotation.)

1867 Goss *Soldier's Story* 102 Where a thief had the boldness to steal in open daylight and by a dash, grab and run, to get off with his booty, he was termed a 'raider,' which was considered one grade above the sneaking 'flanker.'

+**Raiding-party.** A party of raiders. — **1865** KELLOGG *Rebel Prisons* 98 We concluded all communications were interrupted by our 'raiding parties.' **1885** *Harper's Mag.* March 611/1 Washington detailed soldiers to guard them from British raiding parties. **1892** M. A. JACKSON *Gen. Jackson* 462 The raiding-parties of the enemy were operating all through the intervening country.

***Rail,** *n.*[1]

I. ***1.** A bar split from a piece of timber, chiefly used horizontally in a rail fence.

See also CEDAR RAIL, FENCE RAIL.

1631 SMITH *Adv. Planters* 25 You have so many great and small growing trees for your mainposts, to fix hedges, palisados, houses, rales, or what you will. **1653** *Watertown Rec.* I. 32 Fouer good Rayles well set to three foot and ahalfe hie or any thing answerable thereto shall be accounted asufficient fence. **1737** W. STEPHENS *Proc. Georgia* I. 50 The Land begins at the Rails near the Town's End. **1784** SMYTH *Tour* I. 335 Trees cut or sawed into lengths of eleven or twelve feet . . . are mauled or split into rails from four to six inches thick. **1797** [see FORK(ED) FENCE]. **1866** *Rep. Indian Affairs* 217 We are now going to work making rails and other preparations for fencing and other improvements. **1901** DUNCAN & SCOTT *Allen & Woodson Co., Kansas* 281 [He] began the task of making the rails with which to fence forty acres of his farm.

+**b.** A bar used in the process of riding a person on a rail. (See sense 2 c.)

1818 *Niles' Reg.* XV. 126/1 She was way-laid in the evening by the ruffians, placed upon a *rail*, and rode in that manner quite a mile and a half. **1853** 'MARK TWAIN' in *Hannibal Jrnl.* 26 May, A fellow who whips his wife is not a man, and . . . can be excused properly from a 'ride on a rail.' **1902** LORIMER *Lett. Merchant* 218 They had Lem on a rail headed for the county line.

2. Phrases. +**a.** *To split rails*, to split pieces of timber into rails. Also *to split a rail.*

1714 HEMPSTEAD *Diary* 38, I was at home al day spliting Railes & holing Posts. **1820** *Niles' Reg.* XVIII. 256/1 At 97 he went into the woods and split 100 chesnut rails in less than a day. **1897** *Kissimmee* (Fla.) *Valley* 3 March 1/6 T. P. Howard is having a ruxious old time splitting rails for T. H. Anier as the timber is so tough. **1907** *St. Nicholas* Oct. 1078/1 You never split a rail in your life.

+**b.** *To ride a rail*, (see quotation). *Obs.*

1836 T. POWER *Impressions* I. 299 Here I enjoyed my first lesson in what is familiarly termed riding a rail. . . . The term is derived from a fence-rail being occasionally used to supply the place of a broken thoro'-brace, by which all these stages are hung.

+**c.** *To ride* (someone) *on a rail*, to punish (someone) by placing him astride a rail and carrying him about as an object of derision.

1837 HAWTHORNE *Twice-told Tales* (1879) I. 126 The millmen . . . [hesitated whether to] ride him on a rail, or refresh him with an ablution at the town-pump. **1840** *Picayune* 19 Sept. 2/5 Charles Conrad . . . has been ridden on a rail in Richmond, Va. for expressing abominable abolition sentiments. **1853** 'MARK TWAIN' in *Hannibal D. Jrnl.* 23 May, The gentleman ought to be ducked, ridden on a rail, tarred and feathered. **1875** *Chicago Tribune* 22 July 8/4 Said ambitious reporter ought to be tarred and feathered and rode on a rail out of decent society. **1900** *Congress. Rec.* 5 Feb. 1521/2 Up in Maine, . . . they mobbed two preachers, tarred and feathered them, and rode them on a rail because they preached the doctrine of Jesus Christ.

II. 3. One of a continuous line of bars used to guide the wheels of a vehicle {*a*1734-}, esp. an iron or steel bar used on a railroad. {1834-}

1808 in *Niles' Reg.* XV. 55/2 The most durable . . . rail roads, consist of iron *rails* let down on stone foundations. **1854** GLISAN *Jrnl. Army Life* 158 This entire extent of country will be bound together . . . by iron rails. **1888** CABLE *Bonaventure* 148 He showed them the rails of the track, . . . how they rested on their cross-ties. **1917** MATHEWSON *Sec. Base Sloan* 4 A wan gleam of approaching daylight fell on one burnished rail of the track which lay a few rods distant.

b. *By rail*, by means of a railroad. Usually *to go* (*travel*, etc.) *by rail.* {1872}

1844 GODLEY *Letters from A.* II. 139 After leaving Boston I travelled by 'rail' to Hudson. **1869** 'MARK TWAIN' *Innocents Abroad* 21 They can by rail go on to Florence. **1874** PINKERTON *Expressman & Detective* 10 The Adams Express Company . . . had established its agencies at all points with which there was communication by rail, steam or stage. **1920** C. R.

COOPER *Under Big Top* 7 Men depart by rail, buggy and automobile for the 'country routes.'

III. 4. *attrib.* and *comb.* **a.** In sense 1 with *hook, length, maker,* etc.

See also RAIL-SPLITTER, -SPLITTING, TIMBER.

1644 *Essex Inst. Coll.* L. 324 Inventory of estate of John Mattackes, . . . ould hatt, 4 s.; 4 Raile hoockes, 4 s. **1647** *Boston Rec.* 90 It is ordered that their shalbe a hygh way . . . along the rayle side. **1650** *Rowley Rec.* 61 Number 1 to Mr Carlton; thirty rail Lengths. **1676** *Jamaica Rec.* I. 182 They are to have Liberty to take any timber . . . in our commons exsept Clappborde trees and Rayle trees under eightene inches. **1787** WASHINGTON *Diaries* III. 280 At Dogue Run cutting Rail Stuff with the Men. **1836** EDWARD *Hist. Texas* 68 This tree is good . . . for making the best rail posts in the country. **1842** *Cultivator* IX. 160 *Buckwheat* may be thrashed upon just such a rail pen, covered over with rails, much better than upon the ground. **1860** G. W. Bungay *Bobolink Minstrel* 72 They'll find what, by felling and mauling, Our rail-maker statesman can do.

b. In sense 3 with *frog, mill, spike.*

1871 GROSVENOR *Protection* 195 The first rail-mill was built, it is stated, in 1841. **1872** HUNTINGTON *Road-Master's Asst.* 88 The ordinary cast-steel plated frogs . . . are rapidly going out of use, giving place to elastic frogs and what are known as *rail* frogs. **1887** *Courier-Journal* 20 Jan. 5/3 An attempt was made Monday night to ditch the eastbound passenger train by pulling the rail-spike near San Jose.

c. In sense of a railroad with *bed, portage, rate,* etc.

1855 WILLIS *Convalescent* 56 *Polypus Island* . . . makes a break for us in the music of every rail-train. **1856** D. MACLEOD *F. Wood* 180 So far as rail-travel in this city can affect them, the present roads may be said to have a monopoly. **1880** 'MARK TWAIN' *Tramp Abroad* 306 The railbed was as steep as a roof. **1882** *Harper's Mag.* Dec. 4/1 Another stretch of river reaches to the Dalles, the second cataract, passed by a rail portage fifteen miles long. **1903** E. JOHNSON *Railway Transportation* 81 Existing roads are becoming of greater value with the progress of the country and the growing volume of rail traffic. **1905** *Scientific Amer.* 478 'Rail-sickness' may claim its victims. **1925** BRYAN *Memoirs* 463 Mr. Bryan advocated rail-rate regulation.

***Rail,** *n.*[2] A neckerchief worn by a woman. *Obs.* — **1634** *Mass. Bay Rec.* I. 126 Men & women shall haue liberty to weare out such app[ar]ell as they are nowe proveded of, (except . . . immoderate greate rayles, longe wings, &c.). **1639** *Ib.* 274 Other superfluities, w[hi]ch may easily bee redressed . . . [as] knots of ryban, broad shoulder bands, & rayles.

***Rail,** *n.*[3] Any of numerous wading birds of the family Rallidae. Often with specifying terms.

The American species include the *Carolina, clapper, king, Virginia,* etc., *rail* (qq.v.). Cf. FRESH-WATER MARSH HEN, ORTOLAN a., RAILBIRD,[1] SORA.

1796 MORSE *Amer. Geog.* I. 214 Soree. Brown Rail. Widgeon. *Rallus Virginianus.* **1812** WILSON *Ornithology* VI. 27 The natural history of the Rail . . . is to the most of our sportsmen involved in profound and inexplicable mystery. **1836** AUDUBON in *Harper's Mag.* LXI. 669/1 Titian Peale has given me a rail new to our fauna. **1862** *N.H. Laws* 2609 Any person [who] shall . . . take, kill or destroy any of the birds called snipes, woodcocks, plovers, rails, yellow-legs or sand-pipers . . . , shall forfeit for every [bird] . . . the sum of one dollar. **1917** *Birds of Amer.* I. 210/1 The Black Rail, the smallest Rail in America, is believed to be a very rare bird in New England.

attrib. **1876** *Fur, Fin & Feather* Sept. 164 In the rail boat you generally stand across a seat.

***Rail,** *v.* +*tr.* To lay (a railroad track) with rails. — **1888** *Harper's Mag.* June 125/2 One hundred and fifty miles of new road graded last year, which was to receive its rails this spring, will not be railed.

***Railbird.**[1] + =RAIL *n.*[3] — **1808** ASHE *Travels* 160 [Among the birds described by Catesby is] Soree. Rail-bird. *Rallus Virginianus.* **1859** *Penna. Laws* 640 It shall be unlawful for any person or persons to shoot, kill, trap, or destroy rail birds or reed birds. **1865** *Atlantic Mo.* XV. 95 Gunners congregated in numbers dangerous to themselves, shooting rail and reed-birds.

+**Rail bird.**[2] A spectator who perches on a rail. — **1892** *Columbus Dispatch* 24 Nov., The 'rail birds,' that is, those who are clinging to the pine boards forming the press box, began to shout, 'Left, right, left, right.'

+**Rail car.** A railroad coach. Also attrib. — **1834** *Knickerb.* III. 112 My time sped again at the rate of rail-car travel. **1839** *Holyoke Diaries* 183 Went to Boston in the rail Car first time. **1860** ABBOTT *South & North* 206 Thence, in rail-cars, [I] passed through the heart of Alabama. **1890** LANGFORD *Vigilante Days* (1912) 517 The coach began gradually to disappear from the haunts of busy life, and the swift-winged rail-car to usurp its customary duties.

+**Rail cut.** A rail of a certain length; the length of such a rail. — **1836** EDWARD *Hist. Texas* 69 The farmers often get it measuring two rail cuts in length. **1847** DRAKE *Pioneer Life Ky.* 42 The helve was made of shell-bark hickory . . . having always scratched upon it a one or two foot measure, for the purpose of measuring off the 'rail cuts.' **1880** *Scribner's Mo.* Feb. 503/2 The pole fence was laid after the same fashion of a rail fence, only the poles were longer than rail-cuts.

+**Rail fence.** A fence made of wooden rails, usually constructed either in zigzag fashion or straight with posts at the joints; fencing made of rails.

See also FIVE-RAIL FENCE, FOUR-RAIL FENCE, POST(S) AND RAIL(S) 2 a. and cf. SNAKE FENCE, WORM FENCE.

1649 *Charlestown Land Rec.* 110, I doe sell . . . five Akers of planting Land . . . [bounded] on the North by the ould raile fence. **1672** *Springfield Rec.* II. 244 There is grannted to the Major that little peece of land at the Southeast of the Round hill as far as . . . John Stewarts raile fence on his ditch. **1761** *Boston Selectmen* 161 Mr. Cushing is desired to repair the Rail Fence round the Common. **1790** S. DEANE *New-Eng. Farmer* 90/2 Rail fence is perhaps as much used as any. **1839** *S. Lit. Messenger* V. 377/1, I never stopped to fetch breath till a high rail fence brought me up. **1883** [see BLACKBERRY 2]. **1919** HOUGH *Sagebrusher* 66 This is a sort of ally, like, down along between the willers and the rail fence.

b. *Crooked rail fence,* =WORM FENCE.

1831 J. FOWLER *Tour New York* 79 The usual description of fences are *worm,* or crooked rail fences. **1844** *Knickerb.* XXIV. 188 You require for this purpose a walnut-grove . . . with a crooked rail fence running through it. **1856** *Rep. Comm. Patents 1855: Agric.* 20 Formerly, cattle were kept here through the winter with very little protection except a crooked rail fence.

+**Rail-ride,** *v. tr.* To ride (a person) on a rail. Also *vbl. n.* — **1861** *N.Y. Tribune* 22 Oct. 4/6 A dozen scamps . . . will be hired by the well-supplied Aristocrat to tar-and-feather, rail-ride, shoot or stab or hang, the poor Man with One Nigger. **1902** CLAPIN 328 *Rail-riding,* a savage punishment, which consists . . . in placing the culprit upon the sharp edge of a rail, to be carried through the streets.

Railroad, *n.*

Railroad and *railway* 'are used interchangeably in the United States. . . . In the British Empire, *railway* is used in preference to *railroad'* (1940 *Quiz on Railroads & Railroading* § 64). Cf. ELECTRIC RAILROAD, ELECTRIC RAILWAY, ELEVATED *a.*

I. 1. A wagon road laid with wooden or iron rails for the support of the wagon wheels {1775–}; a road laid with wooden rails to guide the wheels of a vehicle.

Cf. POLE ROAD.

1818 *Niles' Reg.* XV. 45/1 Iron, and even timber rail roads, may however sometimes be substituted in those level parts of the country. **1839** HOFFMAN *Wild Scenes* 19 Upon the outlet of this lake was a saw-mill; and we here saw a model of a wooden railroad, contrived by a forester.

2. A track consisting of parallel lines of iron or steel rails for the conveyance of cars drawn by a locomotive or, in early use, by horses; the transportation company and its services connected with such a track or tracks. {1831–56; now northern and Sc.} Also collective.

See also CABLE RAILROAD, ELEVATED *a.* 1 b.

1825 *Niles' Reg.* XXIX. 35/1 Railroads. . . . At the ensuing session, it is intended to make a railway of 1,000 yards in length, on Capitol Hill, Harrisburg. **1832** HONE *Diary* I. 47 The railroad is just finished, and is an excellent substitute for the bad roads which travellers had formerly to encounter. . . . The cars are . . . drawn at present by horses. **1842** *Whig Almanac 1843* 17/1 In New Hampshire, the party has taken decided ground . . . against any direct aid to Railroads by the State. **1848** *Ib. 1849* 46/1 The railroad, steamboat and canal have been of infinite service. **1853** PIERCE in *Pres. Mess. & P.* V. 221 The surveys . . . were designed to ascertain the most practicable and economical route for a railroad from the river Mississippi to the Pacific Ocean. **1869** [see GOLDEN SPIKE]. **1873** *Republic* I. 54 In the last forty years 61,480 miles of railroad have been built. **1881** CHASE *Editor's Run in N. Mex.* 111 Since the advent of the A. T. & S. F. railroad, two and a half years ago, the territory [of N. Mex.] has been steadily gaining in population. **1895** *Columbus Dispatch* 10 Oct. 1/2 At many points railroads are being forced to haul water for their engines. **1913** LONDON *Valley of Moon* 196, I guess the railroad paid him pretty well. **1925** BRYAN *Memoirs* 217 The railroads were at once a curse and a blessing to the country.

b. With defining terms.

1833 in Commons, etc. *Doc. Hist.* I. 216 Grading for a plantation railroad. **1836** NICKLIN *Peregrination* xiv, The Portage Rail Road across the Allegheny mountain . . . will also claim a portion of our epistolary labours. **1884** 'CRADDOCK' *Where Battle Was Fought* 210 The young man did run down to Graftenburg, . . . setting out for that city *via* the Chattalla branch railroad.

3. *transf.* and *fig.* +**a.** A kind of liquor. +**b.** A railroad train; a procession in a general sense. +**c.** A college cheer that imitates the sound of a railroad locomotive.

(a) **1837** NEAL *Charcoal Sk.* (1838) 63 A fluid sometimes termed 'railroad,' from the rapidity with which it hurries men to the end of their journey. **(b)** **1856** 'MARK TWAIN' *Adv. Snodgrass* 26 Drat my buttons, if I wasn't astonished at the way that rail road was a gittin over the ground. **1873** [see DOG-GONE *v.* 2 *b*]. **(c)** **1902** BELL *Hope Loring* 170 'Now a railroad for Poe,' cried Hope, when the first [cheer] had ceased.

II. *attrib.* and *comb.* {1825–} **4. a.** Designating various kinds of rolling stock.

See also RAILROAD CAR.

1828 *Niles' Reg.* XXXV. 212/2 Improved rail road wagon. . . . Mr. William Howard . . . has invented an improved rail way wagon. **1833** *Ib.* XLIV. 98/2 Comfortable naps may be taken in the rail-road coaches, if desired. **1865** *Atlantic Mo.* XV. 737 He knows every railroad-engine, its power, speed, and hours of coming and going. **1885** *Century Mag.* July 460/1 General Lee's famous railroad monitor was approaching.

b. Designating various things on the right of way of a railroad.

1835 *Knickerb.* V. 53 Rail-road tracks are projecting in all directions. **1840** *Niles' Nat. Reg.* LVIII. 32/1 The rail road bridge over the North Anna river, Va. was burnt on the night of the 7th instant. **1851** *Polly Peablossom* 91 [He had] lips resembling a railroad embankment. **1870** M. H. SMITH *20 Years Wall St.* 87 They represent immense franchises, railroad beds, rolling stock, real estate, and business. **1882** LATHROP *Echo of Passion* xiii, It was a solemn group that wound up the highway from the railroad crossing, coming back. **1894** ROBLEY *Bourbon Co., Kansas* 14 The pike, or grade, like a railroad grade, was constructed across all river and creek bottoms.

5. Designating persons, groups of persons, or gatherings connected in some way with railroads. **a.** With the construction of railroads.

1851 CIST *Cincinnati* 178 Eshelby makes . . . a substantial calf-skin boot, . . . designed for winter wear, especially of persons whose business exposes them to travel through the snow or water—surveyors and railroad parties, for example. **1855** HOLBROOK *Among Mail Bags* 57, [I] inquired for a letter for Robert Marshall, railroad contractor. **1868** *Ore. State Jrnl.* 17 Oct. 1/6 The *Oregonian* says about 100 additional railroad hands, Chinese, arrived by the *John L. Stephens.* **1872** HUNTINGTON *Road-Master's Asst.* 12 An important matter in connection with track-laying, too often overlooked by railroad managers, is the selection of cross-ties. **1880** *Cimarron News & Press* 9 Sept. 3/2 The D. & R. G. railroad surveyors are here prospecting this valley. **1894** CABLE *J. March* xx, Two or three Northern capitalists—railroad prospectors—were on the following Friday, at the Swanee Hotel.

b. With the operation or management of a railroad or railroads.

See also RAILROAD KING, MAGNATE, MAN.

1856 *Knickerb.* XLVII. 275 Musings of a City Rail-road Conductor. **1869** *Boyd's Business Directory* 50/2 Railroad Ticket Agent. Murray A., Erie railway office. **1881** *Chicago Times* 14 May, Twelve days ago the railroad switchmen in all but one of the freight-yards in this city struck. **1883** *Harper's Mag.* Nov. 942/1 That veteran railroad financier and manager, Thomas A. Scott. **1898** *Kansas City Star* 18 Dec. 2/3 Grant Meade became a railroad brakeman. **1913** LONDON *Valley of Moon* 190 Up Pine street . . . was coming a rush of railroad police and Pinkerton's, firing as they ran.

c. With legislative, legal, or promotional activities of railroads.

1835 HOFFMAN *Winter in West* I. 158, I was, therefore, not at all surprised to find among these notices a call for 'a rail-road meeting' in the evening, especially as nearly eighteen months had elapsed since the first white man erected his cabin in this section of the country. **1850** *Amer. Almanac 1851* 329 A railroad jubilee at Burlington, Vt., celebrates the union by railroad of the waters of the Lakes and the Atlantic. **1857** *Harper's Mag.* Feb. 425/2 While he was in office, a railroad celebration was held. **1868** Railroad committee [see sense 7 b]. **1887** *Nation* 10 March 199/1 [Mr. Blodgett] is in one sense a 'railroad man.' . . . But it is said that he will not be a 'railroad Senator.' **1888** *Boston Globe* 5 Feb. 1/3 If any 'railroad lobbyist' cast reflections on his character he would wipe out the whole kit and caboodle of them. **1890** DAVIS *Gallegher* 6 Richard F. Burrbank was one of the most prominent of New York's railroad lawyers. **1913** LA FOLLETTE *Autobiog.* 124 The railroad lobby outside and the railroad members inside would have prevented any action.

d. With the manipulation of railroads for purposes of monopoly.

1870 *Nation* 12 May 296/2 The performance may be considered the greatest raid ever yet made by a railroad Ring on a State Government. **1886** A. T. HADLEY *Railroad Transportation* 91 The earliest railroad pools were probably developed in New England, but they were on a small scale.

e. With governmental regulation of railroads.

See also RAILROAD COMMISSIONER.

1898 *Kansas City Star* 18 Dec. 4/3 There is a good prospect that the Populists will continue to hold the control of the railroad board. **1913** LA FOLLETTE *Autobiog.* 238 He was now making a dogged fight for a railroad commission to regulate rates.

6. Designating various things, actions, and places that relate to the conveyance of passengers and their convenience at various stops.

See also RAILROAD DEPOT, EATING HOUSE.

1856 BAGBY *Old Va. Gentleman* 222 In the waistcoat pocket may be found a free railroad ticket. **1865** STOWE *House & Home P.* 266 A nice little bit of land in a rural district half an hour's railroad-ride from Boston. **1869** *Boyd's Business Directory* 407 Railroad House, Frederick Allen, Prop'r, Oneida, Madison County, N.Y. **1880** *Harper's Mag.* July 194/1 The store established in a 'dug-out' contrasts curiously with the new railroad dining hall. **1885** HOWELLS *S. Lapham* xvi, The mountains and cañons of the West, which the Colonel and his wife had visited on one of the early official railroad excursions. **1895** CHAMBLISS *Diary* 48, I did not come out on one of those railroad passes especially designed for the accommodation of senators. **1910** *N.Y. Ev. Post* 17 Dec. 7 The round-trip railroad fare will be $6.80.

7. a. Designating stocks, bonds, etc., related to the financing or capitalization of railroads.

1855 HOLBROOK *Among Mail Bags* 341 A letter was once sent from the Dead Letter Office at Washington, containing rail road scrip to a considerable amount. **1857** *Mass. Acts & Resolves* 725 By the provisions of an Act of the legislature of 1854, 2,944 shares of the Western Railroad stock were transferred to the School Fund. *Ib.* 726 Western Railroad Bonds, due July 15, 1857, $995,000. **1863** A. D. WHITNEY *F. Gartney* xi, I've heard you talk about railroad dividends. *Ib.*, I haven't been obliged to sell *all* my railroad stocks, wifey. **1875** in Leavitt *Our Money Wars* (1894) 187 There were hard times in 1840 and 1857, and at other times; but then there . . . were no railroad debts.

b. Designating legislation and related matters affecting railroads.

1868 *Ore. State Jrnl.* 8 June 2/3 The Oregon people are still grinding away on the railroad bill, but have not been able to get it out of the Pacific railroad committee yet. *Ib.* 10 Oct. 2/5 The afternoon was spent in discussing Gazley's railroad memorial. **1873** *Harper's Mag.* XLVI. 745 The action was brought under the 'Railroad law.' **1898** *Kansas City Star* 20 Dec. 5/1 There is strong talk today that nothing must be attempted except railroad legislation.

8. Designating or referring to towns important for their railroads.

1859 *Ladies' Repository* Jan. 51/2 Indianapolis is the 'Railroad City, from the number of railroads centering at that point. **1860** E. COWELL *Diary* 216 Indianapolis is the great railroad centre for the West and of great growing importance. **1872** *Newton Kansan* 10 Oct. 2/2, I saw no rowdyism or drunkenness such as is witnessed in many railroad towns. **1873** *Ib.* 5 June 3/3 As a railroad point we have always been one of the best.

9. In special combinations.

Railroad camp, a construction camp for a railroad; *r. fire*, a grass or forest fire ignited by a train locomotive; *r. land grant*, =RAILROAD GRANT; *r. plow*, a snow plow; *r. shop*, a machine shop for the repair of locomotives, etc.; *r. stagecoach*, a stagecoach that makes connections with a railroad; *r. time*, clock time observed by a railroad.

*c***1908** CANTON *Frontier Trails* 33 Stolen cattle were driven into railroad camps and sold to contractors at half their value. **1892** *Vt. Agric. Rep.* XII. 122 The railroad fires have been most destructive in this County, having burned over thousands of acres. **1890** *Stock Grower & Farmer* 8 March 5/3 The intervening sections of the Atlantic & Pacific railroad land grant [in Ariz.] are owned by the cattle men and are not fenced. **1854** *Penna. Agric. Rep.* 425 R. Hall, for railroad plow and boy's plow. **1867** G. W. HARRIS *Sut Lovingood* 232 He tuck a noshun tu work a spell down tu Ataylanty, in the railroad shop. **1873** *Winfield* (Kansas) *Courier* 19 June 2/3 A ride over muddy roads . . . brought us to Wichita again: and thence by the railroad stage coach home. **1880** *Cimarron News & Press* 22 July 3/1 Local time is 55 minutes slower than railroad time.

+**Railroad,** *a.* (See quotation.) — **1835** ABDY *Journal* III. 65 The road was hilly and bad; great part of it being what is vulgarly called 'corduroy,' or 'bang-up,' or 'rail-road.' The term alludes to the planks or rails, which are placed transversely; so that the road presents the appearance of [corduroy].

Railroad, *v.*

1. *tr.* To supply (a country) with railroads. {*a*1847}

1829 ROYALL *Pennsylvania* I. 123 They are canaling and rail-roading the whole country. **1878** BEADLE *Western Wilds* 432 Kansas had been, in the expressive language of the border, 'railroaded to death.'

+**2.** *fig.* **a.** To rush (something).

1850 MATHEWS *Moneypenny* 125 Teddy hurried through his pie, railroading it down his throat at a high velocity.

+**b.** To send (a person) to a place of punishment with immoderate speed and often by means of manufactured or false evidence.

1877 *N.Y. Herald* 9 March 8/4 'Railroaded!' Joe Coburn Takes the Cars for His Ten Years' Home [*i.e.*, Sing Sing]. **1884** *Advance* 14 Feb. 102/4 The Law and Order Leagues . . . have 'railroaded' seven [liquor] dealers into the House of Correction. **1901** 'FLYNT' *World of Graft* 183 I've been railroaded (convicted, sentenced, and punished) four times since I've been on the turf. **1914** S. H. ADAMS *Clarion* 132 They got the wrong girl, and, to cover themselves, they tried to railroad her.

+**c.** To send or carry *into, out,* or *through* in a high-handed manner; to dispatch with undue speed or fraud.

1889 *Boston Jrnl.* 25 Jan. 2/2 The Supreme and Superior Judges in Connecticut . . . are paid only a moderate salary, and are railroaded out of office at the age of seventy. **1900** *Congress. Rec.* 24 Jan. 1129/1 They railroaded their State [Utah] into this Union. **1903** *N.Y. Times* 18 Sept. 3 At the meeting in which the trust proposition was 'railroaded through,' the book agents were excluded. **1923** WYATT *Invis. Gods* 176 Herman C. Riley . . . railroaded the infamous anti-civil-service act through the State legislature.

+**d.** To transport by railroad.

1891 ELLIS *Check 2134* 263 They were 'railroaded' thither. **1893** C. S. LELAND *Memoirs* 69 We were marched and railroaded back to Philadelphia.

+**3.** *intr.* To travel by rail. Also *to railroad it.*

1858 *Harper's Mag.* Dec. 1/2 Railroading it through northern Georgia . . . they arrived at Montgomery. **1889** *Lit. World* (Boston) 8 June 190/3 From Auckland the party traversed New Zealand . . . now steaming along the coast, now railroading along the shore. **1908** 'O. HENRY' *Options* 171 From Washington we railroaded it to New Orleans.

+**4.** To work on a railroad.

1877 BARTLETT 512 *To railroad*, to be a conductor on a railroad. Pennsylvania. **1887** GEORGE *40 Yrs. on Rail* 176, I have railroaded for forty years. **1898** HAMBLEN *Gen. Manager's Story* 22, I had never railroaded in any capacity before.

+**Railroad car.** One of the separate coaches or carriages of a railroad train. (Cf. CAR 1 b.) — **1833** *Niles' Reg.* XLIV. 193/2 The *body and contents* of a wagon . . . [were] placed upon a rail road car. **1855** *Knickerb.* XLVI. 273 The rail-road car is the true republican carriage. **1920** COOPER *Under Big Top* 4 A circus . . . has its own railroad cars.

+**Railroad commissioner.** A member of any of certain commissions set up by different states to deal with the railroads. — **1845** *Mass. Acts & Resolves* 582 The Governor . . . shall appoint . . . five persons, who shall, together, constitute 'the Board of Rail-road Commissioners.' **1873** *Harper's Mag.* May 943/1 The annual election in New Hampshire for Governor, Railroad Commissioners, three members of Congress, and members of the Legislature took place March 11. **1898** *Kansas City Star* 18 Dec. 4/3 Mr. Stanley is disposed to favor the election of railroad commissioners by the people.

Railroad company. A company organized to construct or operate a railroad. {1825} — **1815** *N.J. Acts* 68 (Ernst), The New Jersey Rail Road Company. **1852** *Harper's Mag.* June 118/1 [The Whigs of N.C.] disapproved the action of Congress by which so large a portion of the public lands is given to new States, or to railroad companies. **1866** *Rep. Indian Affairs* 286 Liberal grants of lands, in alternate sections, [shall] be made to railroad companies, to build a road through the territory. **1903** E. JOHNSON *Railway Transportation* 73 The railroad company derives its powers from a charter granted to it by the State.

+**Railroad connection.** Communication by rail; railroad facilities. — **1865** KELLOGG *Rebel Prisons* 47 [Tarboro, N.C.] is in railroad connection with the South by a short branch road. **1883** *Harper's Mag.* Oct. 715/2 Lexington . . . has fine important railroad connections. **1884** *Gringo & Greaser* 15 Jan. 1/1 The 'Democrat Pictorial Annual for 1884' . . . has a map showing Albuquerque's railroad connections, present and prospective.

+**Railroad depot.** =DEPOT 2. — **1836** J. HANCOCK *Merchant's Guide Boston* 63 (Ernst). **1849** CHAMBERLAIN *Ind. Gazetteer* 298 The public buildings in the City [of Madison] are the Court House, . . . a large Railroad Depot [etc.]. **1866** 'F. KIRKLAND' *Bk. Anecdotes* 141 The train from Corinth arrived at the Memphis and Charleston railroad depot. **1881** *Harper's Mag.* Jan. 184/1 Old Joel Zane . . . [lived] at a spot now occupied by a railroad dépôt.

+**Railroad eating house.** A restaurant at a railroad station. — **1873** *Newton Kansan* 5 June 3/2 Wm. Pierce is having the old age Saloon entirely remodeled for a railroad eating house. **1898** WISTER *Lin McLean* 52 [She] got a position in the railroad eating-house at Sidney. **1902** 'O. HENRY' *Roads of Destiny* 186 [The passengers] slouched limberly over to the railroad eating-house.

+**Railroader.** A person working in some capacity on or with a railroad. — **1857** *Mag. of Travel* April 179, I'd like to git one of them ere railroaders [construction men] to go home with me. **1877** MCCABE *Hist. Great Riots* 133 Several railroaders . . . demanded that the engineers and firemen should leave their engines. **1887** *Courier-Journal* 30 Jan. 4/5 There is not a better known railroader in the city than Edwin J. Elliott, Assistant Ticket Agent of the Louisville and Nashville railroad. **1904** *Springfield W. Repub.* 10 June 2 Our railroads . . . are managed or operated by professional railroaders who have come here from other parts of the country. **1906** *N.Y. Ev. Post* 19 Nov. 1 The skill shown by the men in handling the locomotive convinced the detectives that they were railroaders of considerable experience.

+**Railroad grant.** A land grant made to a railroad. — **1857** *Lawrence Republican* 4 June 4 There is . . . the question of Railroad grants made by Congress to all the new States but one. **1890** *Stock Grower & Farmer* 22 Feb. 4/4 Railroad grants [in N.M.] include about two and one-half millions [of acres]. **1913** *Indian Laws & Tr.* III. 560 (in margin), Relinquishment to Indian occupants of lands in railroad grants, Arizona, New Mexico, and California.

Railroading. {1882}

+**1.** Traveling by rail.

1855 LOWELL *Letters* I. 224, I hoped also to have a quiet Sunday . . . after a week's railroading. **1869** 'MARK TWAIN' *Innocents* 106 It is hard to make railroading pleasant, in any country. **1880** *Harper's Mag.* Aug. 485 [She had] about a hundred miles more of railroading to do alone.

+**2.** The activity or action of building or operating a railroad.

1870 in Tarbell *Hist. Standard Oil Co.* I. 78 The South Improvement Company . . . may seize upon the lands of other parties for railroading. **1882** MCCABE *New York* 185 The New York Elevated made it its business . . . to secure men who were thoroughly accustomed to railroading. **1904** *N.Y. Ev. Post* 9 May 7 His coal-shipping interests took him into railroading.

+**3.** The action of rushing something through. Used attrib.

1884 *American* VIII. 104 A conviction [was] secured in an hour or two. . . . The 'railroading' feature . . . produces a painful feeling.

+**Railroad iron.** Iron rails; iron for rails. — **1827** SHERWOOD *Gaz. Georgia* 40 Hollow ware is made in abundance, and some railroad iron. **1831** *Congress. Deb.* App. 14 Jan. p. ci, An act . . . regulating the importation of railroad iron . . . expressly confines the application of its provisions to iron imported for railroads. *Ib.* p. cv, Your memorialists . . . now earnestly pray: . . . That the duty now imposed on railroad iron, when punched in the United States, be remitted. **1868** *N.Y. Herald* 6 July 12/3 The La Crosse Company violated their agreement . . . for the purchase of railroad iron. **1887** *Courier-Journal* 3 Feb. 3/3 Eight young men . . . were set at work unloading railroad iron from the steamer Lake Winnipeg.

+**Railroad king.** A leader in the railroad industry. (Cf. KING 3 b.) — **1871** HOWELLS *Wedding Journey* 219 The American traveller . . . [forgets] the swindling railroad kings whose word is law to the whole land. **1883** FULTON *Sam Hobart* 33 He was familiar with the history of Tom Scott, the railroad king of the Pennsylvania Central. **1904** TARBELL *Hist. Standard Oil Co.* I. 93 The acquiescence of the 'railroad kings' . . . was followed by an unwilling promise to break the contracts with the company.

+**Railroad land.** Public land given to railroads to help finance their construction. (Cf. RAILROAD GRANT and *railroad land grant* under RAILROAD *n.* 9.) — **1872** *Newton Kansan* 17 Oct. 3/3 Mr. Wm. B. Blake . . . having purchased railroad land east of town, is about building a fine residence thereon. **1877** *Statutes at Large* XIX. 404 An act to secure the rights of settlers upon certain railroad-lands. **1890** *Stock Grower & Farmer* 8 Feb. 3/3 The Buford property is odd-numbered sections of railroad land. **1897** in *Congress. Rec.* 4 Jan. (1900) 647/2 The act of September 29, 1890, . . . restoring to settlement forfeited railroad lands.

+**Railroad magnate.** A powerful railroad-owner or operator. — **1885** CRAWFORD *Amer. Politician* 174 Great railroad magnates . . . found in him a character and intelligence precisely suited to their ends. **1890** *Boston Jrnl.* 9 Jan. 2/1 This control may place [great power] in the hands of railroad magnates should they take an interest in deciding the political fortunes of the State.

+**Railroad man.**

1. =RAILROADER.

1863 'G. HAMILTON' *Gala-Days* 70 The railroad-men at Saratoga tell you that you can go straight from there to the foot of Lake George. **1870** M. H. SMITH *20 Years Wall St.* 437 His practical acquaintance with railroads . . . gave him great influence with railroad men. **1887** *Courier-Journal* 3 Feb. 3/3 The railroad men and coal heavers were very reticent as to what action they would take. **1911** LINCOLN *Cap'n Warren's Wards* 6 Darn a railroad man's job anyhow!

2. A man well disposed toward a railroad or toward the construction of a railroad; a lawyer representing a railroad.

1870 RAE *Westward by Rail* 191 Throughout the state of California the scheme [of putting through a railroad] became so popular, that to be a 'railroad man' was one of the best claims wherewith to secure the votes of electors. **1885** CRAWFORD *Amer. Politician* 19 He is a lawyer, don't you know?—great railroad man.

Railroad station. A place where a train stops for the discharge or taking on of passengers, etc. {1837-} — **1854** HAMMOND *Hills, Lakes* 42 Having no . . . railroad station to reach by a given minute, we resigned ourselves to our fate, and floated quietly on. **1863** 'G. HAMILTON' *Gala-Days* 22 Its railroad-station is a magnificent piece of architecture. **1923** HERRICK *Lilla* 172 She passed the county building on her way from the railroad station.

+**Railroad tie.** A transverse support to which the rails of a railroad are spiked. — **1856** [see DOUGLAS(S) SPRUCE]. **1874** B. F. TAYLOR *World on Wheels* 109 Those railroad ties flew out from under his feet at a lively rate. **1908** 'O. HENRY' *Strictly Business* 9 All shows walk back to New York on tan oxford and railroad ties.

Railroad train. A series of railway cars connected end to end with a locomotive to draw them. — **1836** *Amer. Jrnl. Science* XXX. 382 The vibrating effects of a passing . . . rail road train. **1890** *Nation* 10 April 241/2 There is not a particle of politics in the concern any more than in any combination of Western brigands to 'hold up' a railroad train. **1922** SANDBURG *Slabs Sunburnt West* 55 The little flivs of women, ready to throw themselves in front of railroad trains for men they love, can have a chance.

+**Rail-splitter.**

1. One who splits rails; a nickname for Abraham Lincoln.

1860 *Congress. Globe* App. 19 June 462/2 They call him 'Uncle Abe,' 'Old Abe,' 'Honest old Abe,' 'The old rail-splitter,' 'The flat-boatman,' &c. **1862** 'E. KIRKE' *Among Pines* 75 No, he's not a mulatto; he's a rail-splitter. **1868** *Ore. State Jrnl.* 22 Aug. 2/2 Lincoln was a rail splitter, and Grant is a wood chopper. **1901** CHURCHILL *Crisis* 150 What they seemed proudest of was that he had been a rail-splitter.

2. (See quotations.)
1885 *Mag. Amer. Hist.* March 298/1 Clubs of 'Rail-Splitters' were formed during the campaign. **1887** BILLINGS *Hardtack* 19, I had taken an active part in the torchlight parades of the 'Wide-awakes' and 'Rail-splitters,' as the political clubs of the Republicans [during the 1860 campaign] were called.

+**Rail-splitting.** The action of splitting rails. Also attrib. — **1826** FLINT *Recoll.* 34, I find I am chartered on a rail-splitting Yankee. **1845** C. M. KIRKLAND *Western Clearings* 93 Farmers . . . may see deer tracks in every direction round the scene of their daily rail-splitting. **1887** J. KIRKLAND *Zury* 21 Gluts are wooden wedges used in rail-splitting.

+**Rail timber.** Timber suitable for making rails. — **1662** *Portsmouth Rec.* 396 He is to presarve all the Rayle timbar. **1681** *Topsfield Rec.* 30 Take any raile timber that is apon ye Common that has bin feled one yeare. **1737** WASHINGTON *Diaries* III. 282 Men [were] cutting Rail timber except those who were at the Mansn. House abt. the Hogs. **1816** U. BROWN *Journal* I. 281 A poor stony rocky Country . . . abound[s] plentifully with good Water, with an abundance of good Chestnut rail Timber. **1860** GREELEY *Overland Journey* 65 The squatter can give you a hundred good excuses for his miserable condition: . . . he has no good rail-timber [etc.].

Railway. (See RAILROAD *n.* note.)

I. 1. =RAILROAD 1. {1776–}
1813 *Niles' Reg.* IV. 111/1 The velocity of carriages on smooth level roads or rail-ways, will greatly exceed that of boats in water. **1827** SHERWOOD *Gaz. Georgia* 136 The chief Engineer . . . recommends a rail way of pine timber, rather than a canal. **1837** PECK *New Guide* 181 Coal . . . is dug from the adjacent mountains, and brought to the works on wooden rail-ways.

2. =RAILROAD 2. {1832–}
See also COG RAILWAY, ELECTRIC RAILWAY, etc.
1825 *Niles' Reg.* 21 May 192/2 We have iron in abundance, timber and stone in abundance, land is cheap, therefore every advantage in making iron rail ways is thrown in our way. **1835** INGRAHAM *South-West* I. 171 The length of this rail-way [from New Orleans to Lake Pontchartrain] is about five miles. **1839** *Knickerb.* XIII. 67 No post-routes or rail-ways can ever come. **1865** *Atlantic Mo.* June 731/2 The railway, the steamboat, and many other important improvements and discoveries . . ., have all come since that day [1815]. **1873** *Republic* I. 25 If the Government should take the telegraph, why not the railways? **1890** *Harper's Mag.* May 888/1 Across this ditch two old 'cross-ties' made a bridge to the railway. **1912** *Lit. Digest* 13 April 747/1 The vice-president of the Great Northern Railway . . . made this public statement.

+**3.** (See quotations.)
1824 *Mass. Laws* 319 Stephen Phillips, William P. Richardson, [and others] . . . are made a body politic . . ., for the purpose of making and supporting a marine railway in the town of Salem. *a***1870** CHIPMAN *Notes on Bartlett* 353 *Railway* is, in the U.S., applied to a 'marine railway.' **1899** *Boston Transcript* 28 Jan. 14/1 In Massachusetts the steam lines are legally designated 'railroads' while 'railways' refers to the lines operated by animal or electric power.

II. *attrib.* and *comb.* **4.** Designating companies and securities connected with the organization of railroads.
1868 *N.Y. Herald* 6 July 9/5 The railway share market was strong and active during the past week. **1871** in Johnson *Anderson Co., Kansas* 167 No bonds shall be delivered until the Paola & Fall River railway company shall give good and sufficient guarantees. **1882** in *Century Mag.* XXVI. 301/2 A contract is a contract, whether it concerns flour or railway bonds.

5. Designating various pieces of railroad rolling stock or equipment used by railroads.
1838 *Civil Engineer* I. 390/1 A new Railway Truck, the invention of Mr. Robert Grant, of Maine, . . . is guided by the carbody with such ease [etc.]. **1864** WEBSTER 270/3 To cone the tires of railway-carriage wheels. **1875** KNIGHT 1014/1 *Gravel-car*, a railway ballast-wagon. **1892** *S. Dak. Hist. Coll.* I. 75 The whistle of the railway engine at Pierre had its response in the cheers that rang in the Black Hills. **1897** *McClure's Mag.* X. 19 These photographs exhibit the great transfer railway ferryboats.

6. Designating things on the right of way of a railroad.
1851 CIST *Cincinnati* 108 A portion of the vertical wall and the roof, strongly framed together and mounted on wheels on a railway track, may . . . be rolled either north or south, when the entire heavens falls within the sweep of the telescope. **1862** in Kettell *Hist. Rebellion* II. 448 Block houses should be built at all the railway bridges occupied by grand guard. **1873** 'MARK TWAIN' & WARNER *Gilded Age* 440 The hole could be used for a railway-tunnel. **1881** 'MARK TWAIN' *Tramp Abroad* 155 The heavy work in . . . the new railway gradings is done mainly by Italians.

7. Designating that part of the postal service carried on aboard trains, and persons and things connected with it.
1879 *Statutes at Large* XX. 357 In making his estimates for railway mail service, the Postmaster General shall separate the estimate for postal-car service from the general estimates. **1900** *Congress. Rec.* 3 Jan. 628/1 Mr. Sewell presented a petition of sundry railway mail clerks of Asbury Park, N.J. **1914** *63d Congress 2 Sess.* H. R. Doc. No. 1155, 11 Compensation for railway mail pay is based partially on space and partially on weight. **1924** *Railway Post Office* June 5 The Dr. Egan Manufactory . . . Extends Greetings to the Railway Mail Association.

8. Designating persons connected with the operation or management of railroads.
1883 in Fulton *Sam Hobart* 150 What did this railway officer do? **1883** *Century Mag.* Aug. 574/1 Azalea . . . [had] found a stout and bald-headed railway conductor, whose adoration made amends for his lack of romance. **1892** *Harper's Mag.* Feb. 487/1 A famous railway president . . . noticed a son of toil digging a ditch.

9. In special combinations.
Railway depot, =RAILROAD DEPOT; *r. freight yard*, =FREIGHT YARD; *r. guard*, a military guard for protecting a railroad; *r. guide*, a book or folder giving travel information about railroads; *r. plow*, (see quotation); *r. shop*, a railroad shop (q.v. under RAILROAD *n.* 9).
1863 Moore *Rebellion Rec.* V. I. 60 At Richmond, La., they destroyed the railway dépôt, together with its contents. **1883** *Harper's Mag.* June 75/1 Below is the great railway freight yard. **1862** MCCLELLAN in *Own Story* 521 Couch's infantry are almost (too) good to use as railway guards. **1856** *Porter's Spirit of Times* 22 Nov. 197/1 *Appleton's Railway and Steam Navigation Guide for the Fall and Winter Season* . . . contains some important changes in the arrangement of several of the lines. **1883** KNIGHT *Suppl.* 741/2 *Railway Plow* 1. A plow attached to a car or locomotive and used in excavating or ditching alongside the track. . . . 2. A snow plow. **1903** *Scientific Amer. Suppl.* LV. 22934/1 The following general classification of railway shops may be made.

+**Railway car.** =RAILROAD CAR. — **1828** *Congress. Deb.* 9 April 2249 The rail way car at Charleston, South Carolina, . . . weighs upwards of one ton. **1867** *Atlantic Mo.* April 479/2 The American railway-car is popular, it cannot be denied. **1894** *Harper's Mag.* July 316/1 Railway cars for transporting the army were appropriated at Omaha.

+**Railway king.** =RAILROAD KING. (Cf. KING 3 b.) — **1847** E. D. BANCROFT *Lett. from England* 113 We both went to a concert at Mr. Hudson's, the great railway 'king,' who has just made an immense fortune from railway stocks. **1873** *Ill. Dept. Agric. Trans.* X. 228 Railway kings . . . have learned to flank competition by combination. **1886** *Harper's Mag.* July 255/1 This is the condition to which our railway kings have brought us. **1904** TARBELL *Hist. Standard Oil Co.* I. 73 Mr. Archbold . . . and his colleagues had gone to the railway kings to remonstrate.

+**Railway postal clerk.** A clerk in the railway mail service of the U.S. post office. (Cf. POSTAL CLERK.) — **1887** *Courier-Journal* 6 Feb. 16/6 Many seek appointment under the impression that the position of railway postal clerk is a 'soft snap.' **1901** G. C. TUNELL *Railway Mail Service* 18 The compensation . . . must be regarded in part a payment for hauling them [post-office cars] with their load and the railway postal clerks in them. **1924** *Railway Post Office* June 7/3 The average salary of railway postal clerks for 1923 was $2,107.

+**Railway post office.** A post office in a mail car. Also attrib. — **1874** *Rep. Postmaster-General* 209 Each railway post-office clerk . . . is required to attach to each package of letters he makes up a facing or label. **1903** E. JOHNSON *Railway Transportation* 173 Sometimes the railway post-offices occupy an entire car . . . and sometimes they occupy a part of a car, usually the baggage-car, in which an apartment is fitted up as a post-office.

Railway station. =RAILROAD STATION. {1838} — **1862** Moore *Rebellion Rec.* V. II. 196 By the time of their arrival at the railway station, more than one million dollars' worth of Federal property must have been captured and destroyed. **1872** HOLMES *Poet* 127 Why did not you think of a railway-station, where the cars stop five minutes for refreshments? **1883** 'MARK TWAIN' *Life on Miss.* xxii, At the railway-stations the loafers carry both hands in their breeches pockets. **1918** LINCOLN *Shavings* 10 The Orham band . . . had serenaded them at the railway station.

***Rain,** *n.* +In special combinations.
Rain belt, a belt or region subject to rain; *r.-belter*, 'a farmer, in the western part of the United States, who settles on the semi-arid plains during a wet season, relying upon a continuance of sufficient rainfall' (*Cent. Suppl.*); *r. dog*, (see quotation); *r. frog*, a tree frog or spring peeper; *r. owl*, *r. table*, (see quotations).
1894 *Congress. Rec.* 11 Aug. 8434/2 In the rain belts of the East the vegetation comes up in the spring. **1902** *N.Y. Tribune* 30 Sept. 5/5 There is again an influx of the 'rainbelters,' a venturesome and foolhardy class of settlers. **1872** 'MARK TWAIN' *Roughing It* 513 What the sailors call 'rain-dogs'—little patches of rainbow—are often seen drifting about the heavens. **1827** MCKENNEY *Tour to Lakes* 158 We found the few people who live near its mouth, . . . [with] rain frogs on the logs of their huts to sing them to repose. **1917** *Birds of Amer.* II. 103 Barred Owl. *Strix varia varia.* . . . Other Names.—Hoot Owl; Rain Owl; Wood Owl [etc.]. **1873** RAYMOND *Silver & Gold* 30 Rain table for Sacramento, . . . arranged according to the seasons, showing the amount in inches of each month, during twenty-three years, and for each rainy season; also the mean . . . annual amount of rain.

Rain, *v.* +*intr. To know enough to go in when it rains* (and variants), to be at least ordinarily intelligent. Often in negative and allusive contexts. *colloq.* — **1857** *Knickerb.* XLIX. 95 When it commences to rain, the celerity with which he 'comes in' would do credit to maturer years. **1906** *Springfield W. Repub.* 12 July 2 Every citizen of Vermont who is capable of going in when it rains ought to understand [etc.]. **1923** WYATT *Invis. Gods* 19 Hetherington Marshfield . . . [doesn't] know enough to go in when it rains!

+**Rain barrel.** =RAIN-WATER BARREL. — **1884** 'CRADDOCK' *Tenn. Mts.* 17 The ash-hopper was visible close in the rear; the rain-barrel affiliated with the damp wall. **1893** *Harper's Mag.* April 791/2 Lucy's recollection of him was that of a dirty lad fussing with frogs and tadpoles in a rain-barrel. **1902** LORIMER *Lett. Merchant* 271 The Widow found her 'lost lamb' hiding behind a rain-barrel.

+**Rainbow cactus.** A cactus (*Echinocereus rigidissimus*) of the Southwest having red and white spines. — **1893** *Garden & Forest* 11 Oct. 429/2 One [booth] sells the 'Rainbow Cactus,' which is a good species of Echinocactus. **1897** *Ib.* 10 March 98/2 It is usually known as Rainbow Cactus, on account of the bright-colored spines.

+**Rainbow-chaser.** A visionary; one who strives for impossible or impractical things. *colloq.* — **1892** *Courier-Journal* 1 Oct. 1/8 The rainbow chasers of the Administration are not idle these days. **1904** *N.Y. Evening Post* 18 July 1 Senator Gorman is anything but a 'rainbow-chaser.'

+**Rainbow darter.** The blue johnny or soldier fish (*Oligocephalus caeruleus*) of the Mississippi Valley, or a related fish. (Cf. DARTER 2, JOHNNY 4.) — **1882** *Nat. Museum Bul.* No. 16, 514 *Pœcilichthys.* . . . Rainbow Darters. *Ib.* 517, *P. cœruleus.* . . . Blue Darter; Rainbow Darter; Soldier-fish. **1903** T. H. BEAN *Fishes N.Y.* 518 The blue darter, blue Johnny, rainbow darter, or soldier fish, is found in the Ohio valley and in some parts of the Mississippi valley.

Rainbow fish. =prec. — **1890** *Cent.* 4943/2 *Rainbow-fish,* . . . the blue darter.

+**Rainbow trout.** A trout (*Salmo irideus*), native to the coastwise mountain streams of California, or a species (*S. shasta*) closely allied to this. — **1882** *Nat. Museum Bul.* No. 16, 312 *S[almo] irideus.*—California Brook Trout; Rainbow Trout. **1892** *Vt. Agric. Rep.* XII. 159 Some twelve years ago a few thousand rainbow trout escaped from a private pound into East Creek. **1897** *N.Y. Forest, Fish, & Game Comm. 2d Rep.* 224 Rainbow Trout . . . are inveterate fighters, and the strongest invariably rules the rest. **1911** *Rep. Fisheries 1908* 316/2 The rainbow trout . . . of California and the Dolly Varden trout (*Salvelinus malma*) of the mountains are sometimes known as 'speckled trout.'

+**Rain butt.** A butt or tub used to catch rain water from the eaves of a house. (Cf. RAIN BARREL.) — **1861** *Atlantic Mo.* April 430/1, I can see a narrow brick-yard sloping down to the river-side, strewed with rain-butts and tubs. **1886** MITCHELL *R. Blake* 197 The rain-butt was right under the window.

+**Rain check.** A check or ticket issued to a spectator at an outdoor performance, to be used on a subsequent occasion if the performance is stopped by rain. Also fig. — **1890** (rain check issued by Detroit Base Ball Ass.), Rain-check. In case rain interrupts game of this date before 3 innings are played, this Check will admit Bearer to Grounds for next League Game only. **1911** HARRISON *Queed* 316 No charge f'r lookin', and . . . rain checks given in case of wet grounds.

Raincoat. A waterproof coat worn as a protection against rain. — **1830** [see CAMBET 1 b]. **1870** M. H. SMITH *20 Years Wall St.* 36 Umbrellas were unknown, but ladies and gentlemen wore 'rain-coats.' **1908** 'O. HENRY' *Options* 85 Put this raincoat on. **1917** MCCUTCHEON *Green Fancy* 58 The gaudy rose-coloured skirt [was] hanging below the bottom of the long rain-coat.

+**Rain crow. a.** The yellow-billed cuckoo, *Coccyzus americanus.* (Cf. COWBIRD 2.) **b.** The black-billed cuckoo, *C. erythrophthalmus.* — **1806** LEWIS in *L. & Clark Exped.* V. (1905) 205, I saw both yesterday and today the Cookkoo or as it is sometimes called the *rain craw.* **1844** [see COWBIRD 2]. **1885** 'CRADDOCK' *Prophet* 235 A rain-crow was huskily cawing. **1917** *Birds of Amer.* II. 130/1 Both species are known as the 'Rain Crow' because of the belief—especially among farmers—that their guttural cry predicts rain.

+**Raines Law.** [John *Raines*, Amer. lawyer and politician (1840–1909).] Used attrib. with reference to a law passed in 1896 in New York State, restricting Sunday liquor sales to hotels: **a.** *Raines (Law) hotel,* a saloon provided with rooms in order to comply with the law. Often used as a place of assignation. **b.** *R. L. sandwich,* a sandwich served with liquor in order to meet the legal requirement that liquor should be served only with food. — **1896** *N.Y. Dramatic News* 11 July 3 Even the hardened court interpreter fled trembling to the nearest Raines hotel. **1901** 'FLYNT' *World of Graft* 154 There's the Raines law hotel people for one. **1904** *N.Y. Times* 9 May 5 The various saloons along Surf Avenue where Police Capt. Dooley killed the Raines Law sandwich last season. **1908** *Amer. Acad. Pol. Sci. Annals* XXXII. 566 The community itself . . . has been, to a shameful degree, *particeps criminis,* in creating and encouraging 'Raines Law Hotels' and the vice for which they stand.

Rain-maker. One who endeavors to produce or cause rain {1856–}; +spec., among American Indians, one who professes to bring rain by incantation. — **1775** ADAIR *Indians* 85 When the ground is parched, their *rain-makers,* (as they are commonly termed) are to mediate for the beloved red people, with the bountiful holy Spirit of fire. **1833** CATLIN *Indians* I. 134 Well, I introduce you to a new character . . . a *medicine-man,* and one of the highest and most respectable order, a '*Rain Maker!*' **1845** *Pop. Science Mo.* Sept. 643 Rain-makers of our time bang and thrash the air. **1899** CUSHMAN *Hist. Indians* 258 The Choctaws had several classes of dignitaries among them who were held in the highest reverence: The Medicine Man or Prophet, the Rain Maker, the Doctor.

Rain-making. {as adj., 1889–} +Among American Indians, the bringing of rain by incantation. — **1775** ADAIR *Indians* 87 Rain-making, in the Cheerake mountains, is not so dangerous an office, as in the rich level lands of the Chikkasah country, near the Mississippi. **1899** CUSHMAN *Hist. Indians* 261 Umba Ikbi's mind must be free of all contending emotions while engaged in the mystic ceremony of rain-making.

Rain squall. A sudden and violent gust or storm of rain. — **1849** KINGSLEY *Diary* 80 A few rain squalls headed off this forenoon to the NE. **1860** GREELEY *Overland Journey* 188 We had a rain-squall—just rain enough to lay the dust.

* **Rain-water.** *attrib.* and *comb.* Designating storage places, etc., for water that falls as rain.

1857 VAUX *Villas* 124 The rain-water cistern . . . is so placed that it may be sunk in the upper part of the linen-press. **1864** *Wkly. New Mexican* 23 Sept. 1/3, [I] camped at 3 o'clock at some rain-water holes which I found near Cerro Alto. **1884** *Century Mag.* April 872/1 Holes for rain-water leaders have been hacked through the cornice. *Ib.* Nov. 47/2 It is a usual practice to connect the under-drains of a house with . . . the rain-water conductors from the roof.

+**b.** *Rain-water fish,* (see quotation).

1897 *N.Y. Forest, Fish, & Game Comm. 2d Rep.* 232 *Lucania parva.* . . . Rainwater-Fish.—This killifish is abundant in Peconic, Shinnecock and Great South Bays.

Rain-water barrel. A barrel in which rain water from the eaves of a house is caught. — **1869** *Rep. Comm. Agric. 1868* 317 Musquitoes . . . may be seen by thousands in old rain-water barrels. **1871** EGGLESTON *Hoosier Schoolm.* 84 For there, right before them, was Granny Sanders's log cabin, . . . with its rain-water barrel by the side of the low door. **1895** *Outing* XXVI. 393/1 A blazing bonfire . . . threw a flickering warm light on . . . the rain-water barrel.

Rainy season. The time of year when rain is most abundant. {1719–} — **c1730** [see BITTERN[1]]. **1817** S. BROWN *Western Gazetteer* 13 The rainy season . . . commences after midsummer. **1872** MCCLELLAN *Golden State* 294 December . . . and the succeeding months until May are termed winter, or the 'rainy season,' in California. **1910** TOMPKINS *Mothers & Fathers* 269 Never had the rainy season earned its title so thoroughly.

* **Raise,** *n.*

+**1.** A steep or vertical passage connecting one working place in a mine with another at a different level.

1876 RAYMOND *8th Rep. Mines* 197 We are . . . engaged in running a raise up from west drift on eighth level. **1883** BEADLE *Western Wilds* 576 Over twelve thousand linear feet of drifts, raises, and winzes, were made during the year.

2. An increase in the amount of a bet or a stake. {1894–} Also in figurative context.

1883 'MARK TWAIN' *Life on Miss.* xxxix, France and Italy . . . cracked on such a rattling impost that cotton-seed olive-oil couldn't stand the raise. **1887** KELLER *Draw Poker* 11 Limit, a condition made at the beginning of the game limiting the amount of any single bet or raise. **1891** WELCHER *Wild West* 21 By continued raises Potlatch had everything which he possessed . . . at stake.

+**3.** An increase in wages or pay. *colloq.*

1898 *Scribner's Mag.* Oct. 489/1 A. J. Packer . . . had begun to ponder doubts of his wisdom in agreeing to the second 'raise.' **1900** DIX *Deacon Bradbury* 186 Father's promised me a raise, th' first o' January. **1923** WATTS *L. Nichols* 76 Luther himself . . . could not get up the courage to touch Schulte for a raise.

+**4.** *To make a raise,* to secure money or something else of value or importance; to get a loan. *slang.*

1837 NEAL *Charcoal Sketches* (1838) 96, I made a raise of a horse and saw. **1840** *Picayune* 18 Oct. 2/2 Two young women went round peddling sugar made up in four pound paper parcels, by which they made considerable of a raise. **1846** W. G. STEWART *Altowan* I. 189 They were all to proceed next day to 'make a raise,' as they termed it, on the stranger camp, where their debts to others would be unknown. **1878** BEADLE *Western Wilds* 41 At last I made a little raise . . . and concluded to come home. **1900** HANDSAKER in *Pioneer Life* 35 The two brothers 'made quite a raise' in the California mines soon after their discovery.

* **Raise,** *v.*

+**1.** *tr.* To erect or set up (a building).

Cf. RAISING.

1657 *Essex Inst. Coll.* VII. 40/1 The said John norman is . . . to be paid in corne & cattell the one halfe att or before the house be raised. **1701** *Ib.* VIII. 220 Our people began to raise ye Meeting House. **1788** MAY *Jrnl. & Lett.* 66, I am in hopes to raise [the house] in eight or ten days. **1846** *Knickerb.* XXVIII. 338 After the usual amount of eating, drinking, swearing, and joking, the house . . . was raised and covered in. **1879** *Harper's Mag.* June 142/1 If a man raised a house or barn, the rum flowed freely.

+**b.** To set up the frame of (a ship).

1772 *Essex Inst. Coll.* XLIII. 285 Robert Jenkins ship raised. **1777** *Ib.* Frigate raised in my brothers yard.

+**2.** To form or appoint (a committee). *Obs.*

1711 *Boston Rec.* 80 The Summe of Thirteen hundred pounds . . . [shall be] Layd out in Some Real Estate for the use of the Publick Lattin School, . . . by Such other Committee as the Town may hereafter raise . . . for that Service. **1816** PICKERING 160 A member moves that a committee should be raised . . . ; and a committee is accordingly raised. **1823** *Boston School Com. Minutes* 8 Nov., The Committee raised . . . to consider the state of the E. Cl. School, reported by their Chairman.

3. To grow or promote the growth of (field crops, vegetables, etc.) {1669–} Also *vbl. n.*

1729 FRANKLIN *Writings* II. 143 A may be skilful in the Art of making Cloth, and B understands the raising of Corn. **1789** *Gazette of U.S.* 25 April 1/1 The soil I chuse for raising Hemp, is a light rich mould. **1812** MARSHALL *Kentucky* 319 General Wilkinson . . . had previously encouraged the raising of tobacco. **1887** *Century Mag.* Nov. 104/1 Cane planting and grinding require a stricter and more systematic labor organization than raising cotton or rice. **1903** *N.Y. Tribune* 18 Oct. 6 The officers had a cultivated garden, in which they raised their own vegetables.

4. To rear, nurture, bring up (a family or person). {1744–1795}

This sense became obsolete in British usage about 1800. It has survived in the United States despite much comment, chiefly from British sources, of the kind shown in the second group of examples below.

(1) **1762** J. ADAMS *Diary* Works II. 140 The story of Pratt's death was told. His Honor said it would be a loss to his family; he was in a fair way to have raised it. **1797** J. PETTIGREW *Let.* 22 March (Univ. N.C. MS.), The thoughts of ingratitude or disobedience to a parent who has rased one up from the cradle. **1824** *Catawba Journal* 19 Oct., I understood he was raised by a man by the name of Williams. **1881** *Phila. Times* No. 2228, Dr. Whitehead was born and raised in New Jersey. **1891** O'BEIRNE *Leaders Ind. Territory* 193/2 He was raised by his uncle, Anonchubba. **1925** BRYAN *Memoirs* 94, I have not yet been able to understand how a man could raise twenty-six children.

(2) **1818** *N. Amer. Rev.* March 323 This use of the word *raise*, we believe, is not to be found in any correct writer. It is a provincialism, and, if we mistake not, confined almost exclusively to Virginia, and perhaps some of the neighbouring states. **1824** HODGSON *Letters from N.A.* II. 208 One of my young Canadian female companions . . . was *raised*, as they say here, in Portsmouth. **1882** G. C. EGGLESTON *Wreck of Red Bird* 3 Maum Sally . . . was born and 'raised,' as she would have said, in 'Ole Firginny.' *a***1892** in W. S. Walsh *Literary Curiosities* 948 'You should not say *raised*. *Bred* is better; we say so in England.' 'Do you? . . . In Kentucky we breed cattle and horses and mules, and raise children.'

+5. (See quotation.) *Obs.*

1775 BURNABY *Travels* 151 When the trees are fallen, they yoke seventy or eighty pair of oxen, and drag them along the snow. It is exceedingly difficult to put them first in motion, which they call raising them.

6. To breed or rear live stock. {1767–}

1789 *Ann. 1st Congress* 167 The people . . . in the back parts raised cattle. **1817** S. BROWN *Western Gazetteer* 16 [They] raise stock, and cultivate the soil. **1831** PECK *Guide* 171 This [mast-fed] kind of pork is by no means equal to that raised and fatted on corn. **1876** *Vermont Bd. Agric. Rep.* III. 167 We cannot raise large horses for the team and carryall. **1894** *Vt. Agric. Rep.* XIV. 93 [The] demand for all kinds of horses has influenced almost everyone who has a mare, to try to raise a colt.

+7. To surmount or gain the top of (a hill or slope).

1804 ORDWAY in *Jrnls. of Lewis & O.* 168 We raised a Steep bank back of this bottom. **1869** 'MARK TWAIN' *Innocents* 387, I 'raised the hill' and stood in Odessa for the first time. **1872** — *Roughing It* 287 As I 'raised the hill' overlooking the town, it lacked fifteen minutes of twelve.

8. To kindle or start (a fire). *Obs.*

In Eng. use only with reference to incendiarism.

1813 *Niles' Reg.* IV. 167/1 It was with difficulty we could raise fires. **1843** HAWKS *D. Boone* 45 At night they would return to their camp, raise a fire [etc.]. **1847** COYNER *Lost Trappers* 26 Fires were not raised.

9. To pitch (a tune or hymn) by leading off in singing the opening verse or part.

Cf. HIST *v.*

1856 OLMSTED *Slave States* 25 An old negro . . . raised a hymn, which soon became a confused chant. **1871** *Harper's Mag.* Aug. 474 As there was no one present to 'raise the tune,' [he] commenced the singing himself. **1898** WESTCOTT *D. Harum* xxxi, I guess it would floor him to try an' raise a tune. **1905** PRINGLE *Rice Planter* 274, I knew I would have to 'raise' the hymn—that means stand up in your pew and sing it without accompaniment.

10. To increase (a bet or stake) in a poker game: (see also quot. 1887); to increase one's bet above the amount staked by (another player). Also fig.

1864 W. B. DICK *Amer. Hoyle* (1866) 177 *Raising a Bet.*—The same as going better. **1885** *Weekly New Mexican Rev.* 11 June 4/3 The Capital sees her envious competitors and raises 'em one in the industrial line. **1887** KELLER *Draw Poker* 69 This, of course, does not apply if any one has 'raised,' that is more than doubled the ante before it comes around to the starting point. **1922** T. A. MCNEAL *When Kansas was Young* 188 The Texan drew more cards, 'saw' the twelve cows and raised the Major fifty steers.

b. *To raise out*, to make (a player) withdraw from a game by increasing the stake. {1894}

1872 'MARK TWAIN' *Roughing It* 332, 'I have to pass, I judge.' 'How?' 'You've raised me out, pard.'

+11. To cause (someone) to appear.

1875 'MARK TWAIN' *Sk., New & Old* 90 But I can't raise anybody with this bell. **1891** WILKINS *New-Eng. Nun* 254 Guess I'll . . . see if I can raise anybody.

***Raised,** *a.* Of bread or cake: +Leavened with yeast or made from yeast dough. — **1805** *Pocumtuc Housewife* (1906) 30 Raised Cake. **1837** CORAHAM *Treatise on Bread* 29 (Ernst), Loaf or raised bread. **1889** COOKE *Steadfast* 189 [The election cake] wore only the style of 'raised cake.'

+**Raised biscuit.** Biscuit leavened with yeast. — **1805** *Pocumtuc Housewife* (1906) 20 Raised Biscuit are made much like bread. **1907** *N.Y. Ev. Post* (s.-w. ed.) 18 July 5 The everlasting repetition of salt meats, potatoes, and raised biscuit in their bill of fare, makes them especially susceptible to rheumatism. **1914** ATHERTON *Perch of Devil* 28, I've got fried chicken . . . and raised biscuit.

***Raiser.** +One who takes part in raising a house. — **1705** SEWALL *Diary* II. 139 Drove a Pin in the Ministers House which I found Raising; bolted on the Raisers out of Bishop's Lane before I was aware. **1854** THOREAU *Walden* 49 No man was ever more honoured in the character of his raisers than I.

* **Raisin.** A grape of a special variety dried in the sun or by artificial heat.

1643 WILLIAMS *Key* (1866) 44 *Wenómeneash*, Grapes or Raysins. **1699** SEWALL *Diary* I. 492 Betty . . . serv'd Almonds and Raisins. **1705** *Boston News-Letter* 20 Aug. 2/1, 400 Baskets of Rezins, some Currants. **1849** T. T. JOHNSON *Sights Gold Region* 206 A box of raisins sold also weight for weight. **1886** H. D. BROWN *Two College Girls* 224 Good rich frosting, too, and plenty of raisins in the cake.

b. Attrib. and comb. with *camp, making, stoning.*

1873 'G. HAMILTON' *Twelve Miles* 316 Think of the 'week before Thanksgiving' free from suet and the sound of the chopping-knife and the dread ordeal of raisin-stoning. **1883** *Century Mag.* Oct. 814/2 Many grape-growers believe that in raisin-making will ultimately be found the greatest profit. **1895** GRAHAM *Stories of Foot-Hills* 215, I'm going over to Bassett's raisin-camp to pick grapes..

* **Raising.** +The erecting or setting up of a house or the framework of a structure; formerly done by communal effort, and made the occasion for a social merrymaking.

See also BARN-RAISING, HOUSE-RAISING.

1651 *Watertown Rec.* I. I. 29 [For] raising of the howse . . . 14£: 15s: 0. **1699** *Brookhaven Rec.* 63 It was agreed by the majority of all those that weare present att the Raising of the frame of the towne's well. **1714** *Essex Inst. Coll.* X. I. 104, I went to ye raising ye Meeting House at Horse Bridge. **1772** CUTLER in *Life & Corr.* I. 38 At Robert Dodge's, at a raising. **1780** PARKMAN *Diary* 238 Rec'd a Letter from Rev. Whitney to request me . . . to attend the Raising a New House for him. **1825** COOPER *L. Lincoln* xv, Next you'll see what a raising they'll invite the people to! **1891** EARLE *Sabbath* 8 The village doctor got '£3 for setting . . . Ebenezer Burt's thy' which had somehow through the rum or the raising . . . gotten broken. **1903** W. E. CURTIS *True A. Lincoln* 94 The neighbors seldom gathered for a 'raising,' or a 'quilting,' or a 'paring,' or a 'husking-bee,' without [etc.].

attrib. **1779** E. PARKMAN *Diary* 162 In Northboro [I] was compelled to go into Deacon Paul Newton's to raising Supper.

+**Raising bee.** A house-raising and the social festivity occasioned by this. (Cf. prec. and BEE[2] I.) — [**1836** TRAILL *Backwoods of Canada* (1846) 93 Neighbours who assemble at your summons to raise the walls of your house . . . : this is termed a 'raising bee.'] **1848** IRVING *Knickerb.* (rev. ed.) v. ii, 'Raising-bees' also were frequent. **1848** [see BUILDING BEE]. **1887** KIRKLAND *Zury* 13 When the 'raising bee' took place, the refreshments . . . had to be cooked by Selina.

Raisin grape. A grape from which raisins are made. Also *raisin grapevine.* {1676–} See also MALAGA 2. — **1855** BROWNE in *Amer. Inst. N.Y. Trans. 1854* 628 Raisin Grape vines . . . [have been] imported from France, and principally distributed in the middle and western States. **1886** *Congress. Rec.* 10 June 5749/1 Gophers are passionately fond of ripe raisin grapes. **1891** WARNER in *Harper's Mag.* Jan. 169/2 Some [lands] . . . are better adapted to citrus fruits, others to the raisin grape. **1895** *Dept. Agric. Yrbk. 1894* 211 The raisin grape, olive, and almond are among the most important agricultural products [in the S. Atlantic and Gulf States].

* **Rake,** *n.* A farm and garden tool consisting of a long handle and a crossbar provided with teeth or tines, used for bringing together hay, leaves, etc. Also attrib.

1644 *Essex Probate Rec.* I. 39 Rakes and rake hedds, 7s. 8d. **1721** HEMPSTEAD *Diary* 111, I was at home al day fitting Sythes & Rakes & Staking ye Meadow-hay. **1731** J. SECCOMB *Father Abbey's Will* vi, An old Sword Blade, A Garden Spade, A Hoe, a Rake, a Ladder. *a***1817** DWIGHT *Travels* IV. 487, 1 Rake factory, 11,000 rakes, [$]1,870. **1841** *Lowell Offering* I. 16 All the neighbors . . . were expected to bring with them some implements of husbandry, such as ploughs, . . . scythe-snaths, rakes, [and] goads. **1880** *Harper's Mag.* Dec. 83/2 Her husband . . . sat by the fire fitting a rake-tail more firmly into a hay rake. **1907** *St. Nicholas* June 719/2 Some brought rakes to clear the field carefully.

* **Rake,** *v.*

***1.** *To rake after*, +to follow reapers or mowers and rake up the grain or hay they have cut.

1879 B. F. TAYLOR *Summer-Savory* 68 Yonder in the meadow is a man 'raking after' and he is eighty. **1884** *Century Mag.* July 457/2 Through the long summer days he followed his father, dropping corn or hoeing potatoes, and later carrying the men their dinners in the hay-field, or 'raking after.'

2. *To rake down* {1854-}, +to haul in or win (money or property), as at cards. *slang.* Also fig.

1845 SOL. SMITH *Theatr. Apprent.* 151 With one hand he gracefully turned over four Kings and a Jack, and with the other tremblingly 'raked down' the pile of bank notes, gold and silver. **1853** BALDWIN *Flush Times Ala.* 8 What lots of 'Ethiopian captives' and other plunder he *raked down* vexed Arithmetic to count. **a1861** WINTHROP *J. Brent* 75, I ked rake down yer dimes, ef I chose. **1877** HARTE *Story of Mine* (1896) 373 You kin rake down the pile now.

***Raking.** +**1.** *pl. fig.* Refuse or leavings. +**2.** A rebuke, scolding, dressing *down.* — **(1) 1868** *Ill. Agric. Soc. Trans.* VII. 434 The supply of hogs . . . appeared to be made up of the rakings and sweepings of the country. **(2) 1854** *La Cross Democrat* 17 Jan. 2/4 Mr. Wright . . . gave Smith a small raking down. **1883** SHIELDS *S. S. Prentiss* 125 The 'raking down' which Prentiss had given his prosecutor was worth that. **1907** *Black Cat* June 7, I'll bet somebody has got a raking for losing it.

***Rally.** +A political mass meeting for arousing enthusiasm for a particular candidate or cause.

1840 *Niles' Nat. Reg.* LIX. 20/2 *Rally of the democracy of Niagara.* . . . More voters were brought together, than upon any previous occasion in Niagara county! **1884** R. GRANT *Average Man* 260 It would be necessary to have some enthusiastic rallies, with speeches and music. **1903** ADE *In Babel* 342, I got acquainted with him when they had the rally over at Ransom. **1904** *N.Y. Tribune* 21 Dec. (*Cent.*), At the last Presidential Election, at a great Republican rally, there were two speeches made. **1906** *Springfield W. Repub.* 13 Sept. 16 The work that is being done in behalf of Eugene N. Foss . . . will culminate this evening in a rally in the Court Square theater.

transf. **1920** *3d Nat. Country Life Conf. Proc.* 48 Funds for the school are obtained through rallies held in the churches on the fifth Sunday.

***Ram.**

***1.** A male sheep.

1634 WOOD *New Eng. Prospect* 41 The inhabitants use to put their cattle in these [islands] for safety, viz. their Rammes, Goates, and Swine. **1706** *Boston Rec.* 34 Whosoever . . . Shall finde or take up any Ram going with his or their Sheep [out of season] . . . , Such Ram Shall be forfeited. **1855** HOLBROOK *Among Mail Bags* 77 The Squire put the ram into an empty hog-pen. **1906** PRINGLE *Rice Planter* 326 There is one splendid ram and the lambs are beauties.

attrib. **1743** *Southampton Rec.* III. 40 Ichabod Cooper sells to Nathaniel Halsey 1-5 of a 50 in . . . the Ram paster in Lot 17.

+**b.** A male bighorn or mountain sheep.

1847 RUXTON *Adv. Rocky Mts.* (1848) 263 The old ram bounded up the mountain.

2. An iron beak or projection on the bow of a war vessel enabling it to ram other ships. {1869-}

1863 Moore *Rebellion Rec.* V. I. 6 Four of the rebel boats had rams. **1865** W. J. TENNEY *Mil. Hist. Rebellion* 223/2 The Merrimac soon crushed her iron horn or ram into the frigate.

3. A warship fitted with a ram or specially constructed for ramming operations. {1869-}

1862 in W. J. Tenney *Mil. Hist. Rebellion* 169/1 The gunboats and one of my rams had passed below. **1865** RICHARDSON *Secret Service* 260 We had five iron-clads and several rams, which were then experimental. **1867** GOSS *Soldier's Story* 59 While endeavoring to throw a shell down the smoke-stack of the ram he was killed. **1897** [see IRONCLAD *a.* 1].

attrib. **1862** Moore *Rebellion Rec.* V. II. 167 Col. Ellet, of the ram-fleet, . . . had moved down the stream with two or three of his boats. **1878** *N. Amer. Rev.* CXXVII. 381 All fleets should be attended upon by ram-vessels.

+**Ramada.** *S.W.* [Sp.] An arbor or arborlike structure; a porch. — **1875** BOURKE *Journal* 2 April, Slept this night under the ramada. **1895** REMINGTON *Pony Tracks* 80 We stood under the *ramada* of the ranch-house. **1919** J. S. CHASE *Calif. Desert Trails* 316 The family was already breakfasting . . . under the *ramada*, or brush-roofed shed, which is the general living-room during the hot months.

+**Ram beaver.** ? A hat in the style of a beaver but made of wool. — **1809** IRVING *Knickerb.* VI. vii, The biting steel clove through the stubborn ram-beaver. **1840** *Knickerb.* XV. 339 Having worn his eternal ram-beaver into greasy desuetude, he came to the conclusion to get a new one. **1853** *Ib.* XLII. 650 The rain, descending on Tom's ancient 'ram-beaver,' and drenching that 'helm to storm impermeable,' . . . had no power to disturb Tom's good-nature.

+**Rambo.** [Origin unknown.] A variety of winter apple; an apple of this variety.

1817 W. COXE *Fruit Trees* 116 Rambo, or Romanite. This apple is much cultivated in Delaware, Pennsylvania, and New-Jersey. **1847** IVES *New Eng. Fruit* 46 *Rambo, or Romanite.*—This apple is much cultivated in Pennsylvania [and] . . . is known by the name of Seek-no-farther, in the Philadelphia market. **1874** *Vermont Bd. Agric. Rep.* II. 313 Eating a Rambo in Western Pennsylvania or Eastern Ohio, many are very anxious to plant Rambos in Vermont. **1898** DELAND *Old Chester Tales* 178 Its apples . . . were poor enough—hard, gnarly russets, or small, bitter rambos. **1913** STRATTON-PORTER *Laddie* xi, There was a teasing fragrance in the spiced vinegar heating for pickles, a reminder of winesap and rambo in the boiling cider.

attrib. **1906** *N.Y. Ev. Post* 5 May, There were still the meetings of an evening . . . beneath the rambo apple tree.

+**Rambunctious,** *a.* Fierce, wild, uncontrollable, rampageous. *slang.* — **1835** KENNEDY *Horse Shoe Robinson* I. 78, I confess myself to be as weak in the flesh as e'er a rumbunctious fellow you mought meet on the road. **1866** C. H. SMITH *Bill Arp* 54 A plan was set on foot to procure a fierce and rambunkshus animal from the mountains of Hepsidam. **1904** E. ROBINS *Magn. North* I. 123 And it hasn't thought of sleetin' . . . or anything else rambunksious. **1914** 'BOWER' *Flying U Ranch* 131 You sure are a rambunctious person when you feel that way.

***Ram goat.** A male goat. *Obs.* {-1634} — **1634** *Boston Rec.* 2 A rate [shall be assessed] for the goates keeping and other charges in rambe goats. **1659** *Mass. H. S. Coll.* 4 Ser. VII. 233 Some 2 calues, 2 sheepe, & some few ram gotes are dead allredy. **1796** A. BARTON *Disappointment* III. i, He's got a beard like a ram-goat, and a nose like a bald-eagle!

Ramie. An Asiatic perennial plant (*Boehmeria nivea*) cultivated for its fiber, or a variety of this. {1873 (*Treas. Bot.* ed. 2, 153/1)} Also attrib. and comb. (Cf. GRASS-CLOTH.) — **1868** GRAY *Field Botany* 299 *B[oehmeria] nivea*, Ramie, or the Grass-Cloth Plant of China, . . . is recently planted S.W. for its very valuable textile fibres. **1874** *Dept. Agric. Rep.* *1873* 262 A treatise has been prepared by Emile Lefranc, of the 'Southern Ramie-Planting Association.' **1885** *South Fla. Sentinel* (Orlando) 15 April 1/6 To capitalists who are prepared to invest in growing ramie, jute or silk, there can be no risk. **1895** *Dept. Agric. Yrbk.* *1894* 451 What is the expense of establishing a ramie plantation?

***Rammer.** A rod for shoving home the charge in a cannon; a ramrod. — **1678** *New Castle Court Rec.* 241, 2 leadells, 3 sponges, 3 rammers. **1774** *Penna. Packet* 19 Sept. 3/3 The rammer [is] too short by three or four inches. **1815** *Niles' Reg.* VIII. 3/1 His desperate band . . . killed them with the rammers of their own guns! **1887** *Outing* X. 4/1 The rammer was stuck in his gun so that none of us could pull it out.

Ramrod. A rod of wood or metal used in charging a muzzle-loading firearm. {1797-} Also fig. (Cf. RAMMER.) — **1757** *General Orders* 49 Men Who are Worn.d for Guard [shall] Appear . . . with Ramrods a Proper Length for Their Guns. **1821** NUTTALL *Travels Arkansa* 187 [After] breaking his gun in pieces, and flogging him with the ram-rod, they [*sc.* the Osages] will turn him out into the wilderness. **1859** J. B. JONES *Southern Scenes* 39 The rattle of iron ramrods . . . in the immediate vicinity did not seem to attract his attention. **1884** *Century Mag.* Dec. 282 Inspection over, the last jingle of ramrod in resounding musket was heard, and we were dismissed. **1904** 'O. HENRY' *Four Million* 153 We are grown stiff with the ramrod of convention down our backs.

Ram's-head. {1601-} +A species of moccasin flower (*Cypripedium arietinum*) having a flower the shape of which suggests a ram's head. — **1843** TORREY *Flora N.Y.* II. 288 *Cypripedium arietinum.* . . . Ram's-head. . . . Near Oneida lake. **1869** FULLER *Flower Gatherers* 125 One species is called the 'Ram's Head,' from the very singular form of the flower. **1907** *St. Nicholas* Aug. 939/1 Only by rare good fortune will the ram's-head . . . reward our search.

Ramsted. (See RANSTE(A)D.)

+**Ramstugi(n)ous.** [Of fanciful origin.] Severe, wild, vicious. *slang. Obs.* — **1847** *Swim for a Deer* 120 (Th.), [An old he-bear] is as ramstugenous an animal as a log-cabin loafer in the dog-days. **1848** *Oquawka* (Ill.) *Spectator* 12 Feb. 6 Can you make a ramstugious speech and abuse all the har off a man's head? **1851** BYRN *Ark. Doctor* 81 (Th.), The old lady bawled out, 'There comes our ramstuginous little doctor.'

+**Ramus.** Formed from *ignoramus* by metanalysis. *slang. Obs.* — **1839** *Knickerb.* XIII. 450 The ignorant ramus! **1844** 'UNCLE SAM' *Peculiarities* II. 145 Tell your father not to make a 'ramus of himself. **1855** *Harper's Mag.* Aug. 290/2 The people are sich ignorant ramusses.

+**Rance sniffle.** *local.* (See quot.) — **1869** *Overland Mo.* III. 131 'Rance sniffle' is a strange combination of words to express a mean and dastardly piece of malignity. I have never heard it outside of Georgia.

+**Ranch,** *n.* Also **Ranche.** [f. RANCHO.]

1. *S.W.* and *W.* **a.** A private house for public entertainment. *Obs.* **b.** A ranch house, or the group of buildings of which it is a part; the headquarters of a cattle outfit. **c.** A village; an Indian rancheria. *Obs.*

1808 PIKE *Sources Miss.* 254 When we arrived at the Ranche, we soon had out a number of boys, who brought in the horse. **1841** *Picayune* 18 Feb. 2/3 A fierce and bloody conflict had been raging in the Ranch. **1847** HENRY *Campaign Sk.* 17 The village of Corpus Christi, or 'Kinney's Ranch' as it is generally called, is situated on the western shore of Corpus Christi Bay. **1850** TYSON *Diary in Calif.* 59 [We] walked to the ranch, a kind of private house for public entertainment. **1867** MELINE *Santa Fé & Back* 19 A ranche is not a dwelling, or a farm-house, nor a store, nor a tavern, but all of these, and more. **1872** 'MARK TWAIN' *Roughing It* 161 The Secretary and I took quarters in the 'ranch' of a worthy French lady by the name of Bridget O'Flannigan. **1881** *Cimarron News & Press* 17 Feb. 3/1 Mr. Lee was 4 miles from camp at the time but managed to remount his horse and ride to the ranch. **1883** [see FEUD 1]. **1886** *Outing* Nov. 104/1, I was just awakening from a siesta in the old ranche. **1889** F. BUTLER *Recollections* 229 We saw how the people had been murdered, the trains plundered and the ranches burned along our route.

2. *W.* **a.** A small cultivated farm or country place. **b.** An extensive establishment for grazing cattle, sheep, etc., including the land, corrals, ranch houses, and organization connected with it.

Quots. 1831, 1858, and 1866 may belong to senses 1 a and 1 b.

1831 PATTIE *Personal Narr.* 221, [At] a ranch . . . I procured a horse for three dollars. **1853** 'P. PAXTON' *Yankee in Texas* 117 The old Texan has no farm, it is a *ranche.* **1858** PETERS *Kit Carson* 277 At the first ranche they came to, they halted and made a rest of two or three days. **1866** *Wkly. New Mexican* 20 Oct. 2/1 The Indians wounded a man at the ranch of Miguel Romero. **1883** *Rep. Indian Affairs* 111 The portion of the tribe at Walker River . . . expect to farm it [*sc.* the arable land] in small ranches. **1885** *Wkly. New Mexican Rev.* 29 Jan. 3/6 The loss of cattle and sheep on the range and ranches was enormous. **1903** [see BUSTER 4]. **1925** TILGHMAN *Dugout* 70 A ten-thousand acre ranch in Texas, with cattle and horses.

3. With defining terms in sense 2.

See also BEE-RANCH, CATTLE RANCH, etc.

1880 *Cimarron News & Press* 15 April 3/1 M. W. Mills and family started for their fruit ranch in Red river cañon. **1888** *Century Mag.* Jan. 412/1 There are [in Mont.] hay ranches, grain ranches, milk ranches, horse ranches, cattle ranches, and chicken ranches. **1890** *Stock Grower & Farmer* 12 July 5/1 They are pasturing on the Alfalfa ranches. **1900** [see FOX *n.* 6 b]. **1904** *N.Y. Ev. Post* 26 Nov., An advertisement appeared in the San Francisco daily papers for 300 boys to work on a hop-ranch in the country.

4. *Vamoose the ranch,* (see VAMOOSE *v.*).

5. *attrib.* **a.** Designating persons or a group of persons who work, live on, or own ranches.

See also RANCHEMAN, RANCHMAN.

1879 ROE *Army Lett.* 219 It was surprising that so many of the Sun River and ranch people came. **1886** J. J. MCCLOSKEY (*title*), The Ranch King. **1887** *Outing* May 114/1 Bill, my ranch-hand, followed me on old Prince. **1888** *Century Mag.* Feb. 500 The ranch-owners differ more from each other than do the cowboys. **1894** HOYT *Texas Steer* (1925) I. 17 Oh, I do so want to be something besides a Texas ranch girl. **1897** HOUGH *Story of Cowboy* 221 The old and staid cowboy might not care to run his horse and rope his friends as the younger members of the ranch staff took delight in doing. **1902** WISTER *Virginian* xvii, It would be no more the Virginian who commanded him; it would be the real ranch foreman. **1919** HOUGH *Sagebrusher* 111 These here ranch Johns is handy with rope and lead.

b. Designating things produced on, or otherwise connected with, ranches.

See also RANCH HOUSE.

1880 *Cimarron News & Press* 26 Aug. 3/1 Fresh Ranch Butter at Porter's. **1886** ROOSEVELT in *Outing* July 387, I took along the ranch wagon, drawn by four shaggy horses. **1895** REMINGTON *Pony Tracks* 58 You can only go there if . . . 'Jack' will take you in the ranch coach. **1897** HOUGH *Story of Cowboy* 155 With each ranch outfit there must of course be the proper horse herd. **1908** 'O. HENRY' *Strictly Business* 17 [He] had $647,000 in cash in his (ranch) library just received for the sale of a drove of beeves. **1923** HERRICK *Lilla* 262 Lilla walked a little way down the ranch road.

c. Designating animals raised or used on ranches.

1897 HOUGH *Story of Cowboy* 227 In the Indian Nations the writer has been out with a pack of greyhounds, which included a good pack of ranch dogs. **1898** CANFIELD *Maid of Frontier* 41 He was a gray of unusual size for a ranch horse. *Ib.* 208 Some ranch chickens scratched busily in the sand outside. **1901** *Amer. Rev. of Reviews* XXIV. 307/2 Average ranch cows, for breeding purposes, are worth from eighteen to twenty-four dollars each.

+Ranch, *v.*

1. *intr.* To operate a ranch; to farm.

1872 'MARK TWAIN' *Roughing It* 242 He had been farming (or ranching, as the more customary term is) in Washoe District. **1890** *Stock Grower & Farmer* 29 March 6/3 Stockmen . . . have ranched there from ten to twenty years. **1906** LYNDE *Quickening* 322 He is ranching in Indian Territory. **1923** HERRICK *Lilla* 240, I am going to learn how to ranch and support myself.

quasi-tr. **1890** *Internat. Ann., Anthony's Photogr. Bul.* III. 32 Any enterprising young tourist . . . can find plenty of work and fun among the jolly fellows who 'ranch it' in the West.

2. *tr.* To put (an animal) on a ranch.

1873 BEADLE *Undevel. West* 663 Six hundred miles . . . had worn out my horse, and on the 16th instant I 'ranched him' twenty miles south of Beaver. **1890** LANGFORD *Vigilante Days* (1912) 481 In pursuance of that agreement, he immediately branded and ranched [the ponies].

+Ranch country. Cattle country suitable for ranches. — **1885** *Wkly. New Mexican Rev.* 22 Jan. 2/5 Texas . . . is still as good, if not a better ranch country, than New Mexico. **1895** *Rev. of Reviews* Aug. 167/2 Roosevelt says of the ranch country where his herds graze, the basin of the Upper Missouri, that it 'might be spoken of as one gigantic, unbroken pasture.'

+Rancheman. Variant of RANCHMAN. — **1872** TICE *Over Plains* 158 Many of these ranchemen have realized comfortable fortunes by their business. **1885** *Wkly. New Mexican Rev.* 12 Feb. 1/4 A heavy posse of ranchemen is scouring the country for the other division of the raiding bands. **1890** LANGFORD *Vigilante Days* (1912) 328 Near Lewiston they fell in with a rancheman.

+Rancher. *W.* [f. RANCH *n.* or *v.*, or ad. RANCHERO.]

1. a. A person who owns or operates a stock ranch. **b.** A cowboy.

1866 *Rep. Indian Affairs* 189 Teamsters, packers, herders, ranchers, and miners all over the country have become exasperated. **1877** BARTLETT 515 *Rancher.* See *Ranchman.* **1882** BAILLIE-GROHMAN *Camps in Rockies* 70 We would meet cavalcades of wild young Texan 'ranchers' or cowboys. **1890** LANGFORD *Vigilante Days* (1912) 227 My horse was immediately put in charge of a rancher, or person who made the care of horses a specialty. **1907** LILLIBRIDGE *Trail* 119 The hat in the rancher's hand started revolving again. **1916** WILSON *Somewhere* 365 After being a woman she is a rancher.

2. A farmer.

1884 W. SHEPHERD *Prairie Exper.* 125 If stock-owners are in power, they say to the small rancher, 'Fence your fields.' **1890** *Stock Grower & Farmer* 11 Jan. 6/3 The majority of ranchers, however, neglect the fruit trees.

+Ranchera. *W.* [Sp., fem. of RANCHERO.] A country-woman; a farm woman. — **1838** 'TEXIAN' *Mexico v. Texas* 302, I did not think . . . that she was more than a common ranchera. **1844** GREGG *Commerce of Prairies* I. 216 The ordinary apparel of the female peasantry and the *rancheras,* is the *enaguas* or petticoat of home-made flannel. **1884** *Advance* 14 Aug., So fearful are the dainty creatures of being considered rancheras or countrywomen.

Rancheria. *W.* An Indian village. Also transf. {1600, 1760–72 in S. Amer.}

[**1841** W. KENNEDY *Texas* II. 42 *Rancho,* and *Rancheria,* are used in Spanish America to signify a labourer's house, or a collection of peasant's huts, from one and upwards. Be the number great or small, if there be not a church, the aggregate is called *Rancheria.*] **1844** GREGG *Commerce of Prairies* I. 296 In a few days they reached a *rancheria* of about fifty warriors with their families. **1848** BARTLETT 270 *Rancheria,* the place, site, or house in the country where a number of rancheros collect together. **1856** *Porter's Spirit of Times* 20 Dec. 252/3, I am in hopes that many a grey hide . . . will find its way into my *rancheria* ere the returning spring. **1867** *Wkly. New Mexican* 20 July 2/3 Our command . . . burned the rancheria which seemed a permanent home of the Indians. **1889** MUNROE *Golden Days* 119 Rancheria . . . is the term applied to all Indian villages on the Pacific slope. **1914** A. H. FITCH *Junipero Serra* 222 There were many rancherias on the banks of the Colorado.

attrib. **1857** *Rep. Explorations Pacific R.R.* (War Dept.) VI. III. 92 *Elymus arenarius* . . . grows in all parts of California where there are deserted Indian lodges, and is, therefore, called . . . 'rancheria grass.'

+b. *Indian rancheria,* an Indian village.

1851 KINGSLEY *Diary* 170 We stoped at an Indian rancheria and amused ourselves. **1865** *Wkly. New Mexican* 26 May 2/1 Lieut. Barr . . . discovered and surprised an Indian rancheria.

+Ranchero. *W.* [Sp.] **a.** A man who owns or operates a stock ranch. **b.** A herdsman. **c.** A small farmer.

1827 DEWEES *Lett. from Texas* 66 A few wealthy rancheros dwell in the country, who own vast herds of stock, of all kinds. **1838** 'TEXIAN' *Mexico v. Texas* 163 He took with him three *rancheros* from the vicinity. **1844** GREGG *Commerce of Prairies* I. 109 A swarthy *ranchero* soon made his appearance. **1848** in Bryant *California* App. 461 The greater part of the farmers and rancheros had abandoned their fields to go to the mines. **1857** DAVIS *El Gringo* 173 During the summer and fall the rancheros come in [to Santa Fe] from the country every morning with newly-cut grass or hay. **1885** *Wkly. New Mexican Rev.* 5 Feb. 3/6 Sheriff Poe . . . with a posse of four men aided by Mr. J. M. Abercrombie, a ranchero near Chaperito, surrounded Aragon's house. **1891** HARTE *First Family of Tasajara* I. 92 He seemed to be an odd mingling of the sailor and ranchero. **1903** A. ADAMS *Log of Cowboy* 12 A number of different rancheros had turned in cattle making up the herd.

+Ranch house. A house belonging to a ranch; the living quarters of a rancher. — **1862** *Harper's Mag.* June 14/1, I rode on about five miles further, where I reached a small ranch-house. **1869** J. R. BROWNE *Adv. Apache Country* 186 A few abandoned ranch-houses and corrals on the wayside indicated that it was once a grazing region. **1884** *Gringo & Greaser* 1 Jan. 1/2 We have a Ranch for sale, . . . 7 good ranch houses and one adobe dwelling with 7 rooms. **1907** LILLIBRIDGE *Trail* 79, I eat at the ranch house sometimes. **1916** WILSON *Somewhere* 3 The walls of the big living-room in the Arrowhead ranch house are tastefully enlivened here and there with artistic spoils of the owner.

+Ranching. The operating of a ranch, esp. a cattle ranch; working on a ranch. {1882, in Canada} — **1873** BEADLE *Undevel. West* 267 'Ranching' came next and all this industry is not lost. **1885** *Wkly. New Mexican Rev.* 15 Jan. 2/5 Santiago L. Hubbell . . . married a Mexican lady and settled down to ranching on the Rio Grande below Isleta. **1902** *Harper's Mag.* May 877/1 After a heavy day's ranching a book soon grew heavy also in his hand. **1915** CAMPBELL *Proving Virginia* 161, I believe you did like ranching when you were at Dave's.

+Ranchito, -a. [Sp.] A small ranch or farm. — **1850** GARRARD *Wah-To-Yah* xvii. 208 To the Ranchito is something less than a mile. **1898** ATHERTON *Californians* 344, I wanted a small sum to pay off the mortgage on a ranchita.

+**Ranchman.** A man who owns or works on a ranch, esp. a cattle ranch. (See also RANCHEMAN.) — **1866** *Ore. State Jrnl.* 30 June 1/3 A number of ranchmen are selling out and moving before the approaching railroad whistle. **1873** 'MARK TWAIN' & WARNER *Gilded Age* 479 Ranchmen and farmers had come with their families from five miles around. **1890** *Stock Grower & Farmer* 8 Feb. 3/1 The beef breeders of the eastern and middle states are now blaming the western ranchmen for the low prices of beef. **1920** *Amer. Hist. Ass. Rep.* (1925) 320 The replacing of the ranchmen on the Cherokee Outlet with an agricultural population was but one chapter in the story of the struggle between the cattlemen of Oklahoma and the pioneer farmers of adjoining States.

Rancho. [Sp.] =RANCH *n.* in senses 1 and 2. {1845–, in S. Amer.}

1808 PIKE *Sources Miss.* 260 Marched early and at nine o'clock arrived at a Rancho. **1827** DEWEES *Lett. from Texas* 66 Their ranchos are kept under good cultivation. **1834** A. PIKE *Sketches* 40 Beyond, there are some deserted ranchos, as they are called—that is, sheep-pens and shepherd huts. **1838** 'TEXIAN' *Mexico v. Texas* 16 The Tata padre and the strange gentleman . . . drove away with great speed towards the *rancho*, or village of Larza. **1846** in Claiborne *Life Quitman* I. 284 For the additional purpose of mutual protection in this border country, several of these *labores* generally lie together, and the houses of their owners also together, forming a village, and this is called a rancho. **1851** *Harper's Mag.* Dec. 122/2 A large party of Mormons have purchased the rancho of San Bernardino, near Los Angelos. **1853** BREWERTON *With Kit Carson* (1930) 33 The town of San Pedro . . . consisted of only one *rancho*, or Mexican farm-house. **1863** MASSETT *Drifting About* 131 A man would buy a tract of land or a 'rancho' for perhaps $1000 or so. **1871** *Republican Rev.* 7 Jan. 2/1 There was a big time on Monday last, in the Ranchos of Albuquerque, it being the patronal feast day. **1897** HOUGH *Story of Cowboy* 4 At times they even crossed the Rio Grande and drove away herds to their *ranchos* to the north. **1910** J. HART *Vigilante Girl* 179 Occasionally a raid would be made on a great rancho, . . . and a herd of horses stolen.

+**Ranch woman.** **1.** A woman who lives on a ranch. **2.** A woman who operates a ranch. — **(1) 1880** *Scribner's Mag.* May 127 A charming little ranchwoman. **1919** HOUGH *Sagebrusher* 156 The big ranchwoman's heart went out to her in spite of all. **(2) 1894** *McClure's Mag.* III. 105/1 And speaking of successful ranchwomen, cattle of more than one brand . . . are owned and run by Mrs. S. E. Barber.

+**Randall.** *attrib.* Designating followers of Congressman S. J. Randall (1828–90), an advocate, in the Democratic party, of the protective tariff. — **1887** *Courier-Journal* 6 Feb. 2/1 Below is the tariff correspondence between the tariff reformers on one side and the Randall men . . . on the other. **1900** *Congress. Rec.* 31 Jan. 1365/2, I was a Randall Democrat.

Randall grass. =MEADOW FESCUE (GRASS). — **1884** VASEY *Agric. Grasses* 103 Meadow Fescue grass, Tall Fescue, Randall grass . . . is an introduced species, now frequently met with in meadows.

Randallite. +**1.** A follower of S. J. Randall: (see RANDALL). +**2.** (See quotation and cf. FREEWILL BAPTIST.) — **(1) 1887** *Courier-Journal* 6 Feb. 2/1 Speaker Carlisle's Efforts to Arrive At an Understanding With the Randallites. **(2) 1890** *Cent.* 4953/3 *Randallite.* (After Benjamin Randall (1749–1808), founder of the body of Freewill Baptists at New Durham, New Hampshire, in 1780.) A Freewill Baptist. (Rare.)

***Random.** *Surveying.* +A line run at random from which to start a survey. In full *random line.* — **1743** *N.J. Archives* 1 Ser. VI. 155 You are to chain eastward . . . untill the Point come to have the same bearing as the course which by your best judgement you conceive you ought to run for the random line. *Ib.* 159 You may then come back to the place where your random cutt Delaware & in your comeing you may compute the course of the true line. **1787** ELLICOTT in Mathews *Life A. Ellicott* 64 We prepared to proceed down the River to a proper place for correcting the random line by astronomical observations.

* **Range,** *n.*

+**1.** An area of uncultivated ground or wild country over which domestic or wild animals range for food; now, esp., a cattle range.

See also BUFFALO RANGE.

1640 *Essex Hist. Coll.* V. 170/1 The range of the cattle at the fforest river head. **1658** *East-Hampton Rec.* I. 148 This land and the grasse therof for a range or rune for to feede horses or Cattell on. **1724** JONES *Virginia* 35 The Uplands and Barrens . . . serve for Ranges for Stock. **1775** Rauck *Boonesborough* 179 Buffaloe had abandoned their range & were gone into other parts. **1817** S. BROWN *Western Gazetteer* 71 The prevailing timber being oak, the range for hogs is excellent. **1846** THORPE *Myst. Backwoods* 63, I hunted the gobbler always in the same 'range.' **1857** *Ill. Agric. Soc. Trans.* II. 359 The early settlers depended greatly on stock and the range to support the stock. **1880** *Cimarron News & Press* 19 Feb. 3/2 Mr. Porter has a valuable range enclosed in 28 miles of wire fence. **1898** *Farmers' Bul.* No. 72, 9 The range was overstocked, and a dozen cows and sheep were crowded on the 'free grass.' **1905** *Forestry Bureau Bul.* No. 62, 14 Ranges which formerly supported 100,000 head of cattle are not now carrying more than 10,000. **1913** BARNES *Western Grazing Grounds* 33 There are two distinct ranges—the southern or breeding range, and the northern or finishing range.

+**b.** Without article: Grazing or foraging ground; pasture; pasturage.

1626 *Va. Mag. Hist. & Biog.* II. 52, 300,000 acres of land, which will feed such nombers of people, with plentifull range for Cattle. **1724** JONES *Virginia* 41 In the Marshes, and woods, and old Fields is good Range for Stock. **1791** W. BARTRAM *Travels* 384 Low grounds and Cane swamp afforded excellent food and range for our horses. **1800** *Raleigh (N.C.) Register* 4 Nov., One thousand acres of back land . . . commands a large outlet of good range for hogs and cattle. **1898** CANFIELD *Maid of Frontier* 13 [He] had right of range over countless miles which belonged to nobody. **1924** R. CUMMINS *Sky-High Corral* 25 Make ol' settlers pay rent on range they've used free for thirty years.

+**c.** An area or the territory patrolled by rangers (sense 1).

1692 *Va. State P.* I. 38 Hoping yor Honrs will considr our duty was the harder, and that our Ranges being bad and Stony, are forst to be att ye charge of Shewing [our horses].

+**d.** The area ranged over by an Indian tribe.

1843 FRÉMONT *Explor. Rocky Mts.* 15 We were now in the range of the Pawnees. **1849** *31st Congress 1 Sess.* Sen. Ex. Doc. No. 64, 175 As we are now coming into the vicinity of the Comanche 'range,' I have given orders for cartridges to be issued to the command.

+**e.** Freq. in phrase *on* (or *off*) *the range.*

1831 PECK *Guide* 171 Thousands of hogs are raised without any expense, except a few breeders to start with, and a little attention in hunting them on the range, and keeping them tame. **1870** *Rep. Comm. Agric. 1869* 587 Fat beef cattle wintered and fattened on the 'range' have been shipped down the Columbia. **1897** LEWIS *Wolfville* 81 These yere Britons would be . . . a-stampedin' the cattle plum off the range. **1925** TILGHMAN *Dugout* 78 Most of his stock had been out on the range and escaped the Indians.

f. *To ride* (*look* or *comb*) *the range,* to look for or after cattle on a range.

1890 *Stock Grower & Farmer* 31 May 4/4 All the parties who have thus far ridden the range agree that the calf crop is light. **1907** WHITE *Arizona Nights* 77 We rode the range for upwards of two year. *Ib.* 262 All day long thus they would ride, without food or water for man or beast, looking the range. **1920** [see COMB *v.* 4].

+**g.** In special phrases.

At range, turned loose on a range; *to take the range,* to depart; *to run on a range,* to run cattle on a range.

1832 WATSON *Hist. Tales N.Y.* 84 All horses at range are ordered to be branded. **1834** SIMMS *Guy Rivers* 452 The sooner you 'take the range' the better. **1904** 'O. HENRY' *Heart of West* 4 We been runnin' on the same range, and ridin' the same trails since we was boys.

+**2.** A row *of* lots, usually fronting a river or other body of water. *Obs.*

1681 *Conn. Probate Rec.* I. 325 On halfe of my great Lott in the westermost Rang of Lotts. **1684** *Jamaica* (L.I.) *Rec.* I. 291 The proportion that did belong to Mr. Bryan Newtons lot [was] . . . ye 20th lot among ye rang of small lots that front to ye River. **1715** *Boston Rec.* 57 This List contains an accompt of the first Range of Lotts.

3. A chain of mountains or hills; a mountainous divide. {1705–}

1775 *Vt. Hist. Soc. Coll.* I. 9 At a meeting of the committees of the several townships of the New Hampshire Grants, west of the range of the Green Mountains, . . . [we] voted as follows. **1805** *Lewis & Clark Exped.* VII. (1905) 118 He would only go over the range of these mountains and wait our arival. **1823** [see COURSE *v.* 2]. **1872** MCCLELLAN *Golden State* 162 In the Coast Range, timber is confined chiefly to scattering trees. **1890** LANGFORD *Vigilante Days* (1912) 19 A small lake . . . is separated by the main range of the Rocky Mountains from the large lakes of the Yellowstone.

+**b.** *W. To go* (or *be helped*) *over the range,* to die or be killed.

1887 *Scribner's Mag.* II. 508/1 'To go over the range' is to die, as any reader of Bret Harte's frontier stories knows. **1901** RYAN *Montana* 6 There must have been some reason for the suspicion that she helped him 'over the range,' as they say out here.

+**4.** In the public land survey, a row of townships lying between two meridians six miles apart, the rows being numbered in order from east to west from the principal meridian.

1785 *Jrnls. Cont. Congress* XXVIII. 376 The geographer shall designate the townships . . . by numbers progressively from south to north; always beginning each range with number one. **1788** in Cutler *Life & Corr.* I. 438 We all concurred in an Order to extend four of our Town Lines to the 11th Range. **1817** *Niles' Reg.* XII. 97/2 A *range* consists of any number of townships, and embraces all those belonging to the same system, which lie north or south of each other. **1873** *Newton Kansan* 1 May 2/3 Section twenty-eight crosses said stream in township 24, range 2 east. **1884** *Lisbon* (Dak.) *Star* 22 Aug., The caucus for township 134, range 56, . . . was called to meet at the skating rink. **1910** *Okla. Session Laws* 3 Legisl. 5 The permanent capitol of the state shall be erected on . . . : Fifteen acres of land surrounding a point on the half-section line running north and south between the northeast fourth and the northwest fourth of section twenty-seven (27), township twelve (12) north, range three (3).

+**5.** *Mining.* (See quots. 1866 and 1919.)

1866 *Harper's Mag.* May 689/1 In the best mining grounds the veins run in an east and west, north and south direction, approximately. These are termed 'ranges,' whether applied to a mine or a district. **1871** RAY-

MOND *3d Rep. Mines* 81 The range is intersected by deep ravines and gulches emptying in Greenhorn Creek or Bear River. **1899** *Mich. Pol. Science Assn. Publ.* III. 149 All lands where iron was ever found before have furnished their quota [of miners], but the newer ranges got the most undesirable class. **1919** A. H. FAY *Glossary of Mining* 556 In the Lake Superior region, a term applied to a deposit of iron ore and the associated rocks. . . . Now the term simply means deposits of iron ore, which are all known as 'ranges,' even if the ground where they occur be low swamps.

6. A large cookstove provided with one or more ovens and other devices for cooking operations. {kitchen-range, 1807–; range, 1862–}

See also COOKING RANGE, GAS RANGE.

1875 *Scribner's Mo.* Dec. 287/1 It is a mistake to suppose that a kitchen must necessarily be uncomfortable, because it has not gas, hot and cold water, stationary wash-tubs, and an elevated range. **1881** *Rep. Indian Affairs* 66 The kitchen is furnished with a hotel range. **1920** COOPER *Under Big Top* 5 The ton of coal . . . will be consumed in the big traveling ranges.

+**7.** A tier or row of firewood. *Obs.*

1728 *Boston Rec.* 222 No Popler, Chestnut, [etc.] . . . Shall be Corded up or Exposed to Sale with or among any firewood . . . on Penalty of Twenty Shillings for Every Range that Shall haue the Quantity of Eight feet of Square Timber. *Ib.* 224 The Several Sealers of Wood . . . are hereby Directed not to Seal any Rang of wood not Corded as aforesaid.

8. *attrib.* and *comb.* **a.** Designating things connected with laying out a line of direction or with ranges (sense 2).

1669 *Providence Rec.* XVII. 215 [The] Line may be knowne by ye Range trees. **1693** *Manchester Rec.* 51 [We were appointed] to sett range bounds upon ye line betwen ye great white oake . . . & ye pine stump. **1700** *Providence Rec.* IV. 139 A heape of stones laid for a Range marke. **1834** *Huntington Rec.* III. 355 It shall commence at the northermost range pole on the south Beach. **1858** WARDER *Hedges & Evergreens* 71 Set these line-stakes to correspond exactly with the range-stakes.

+**b.** Designating animals fed on range.

1859 MARCY *Prairie Traveler* iv, For prairie service, horses which have been raised exclusively upon grass, . . . or 'range horses,' as they are called in the West, are decidedly the best. **1877** ROE *Army Lett.* 179 Both of our horses . . . were really range animals. **1890** *Stock Grower & Farmer* 29 March 5/1 A lot numbering 1,500 range sheep from New Mexico recently sold in Chicago at . . . $4.60 for averages of 73 pounds. **1894** *Outing* XXIV. 336/2 Their 'range' cows and razor-backed hogs climb the steep hills like goats. **1897** HOUGH *Story of Cowboy* 7 The buffalo grass and the sweet waters of the far North would fatten a range broadhorn to a stature far beyond any it could attain on a southern range. *Ib.* 335 Wyoming and Montana [were] furnishing the bulk of the range beef instead of Texas. **1898** *Mo. So. Dakotan* I. 67 The crop of ripe range steers will be lighter than last year. **1901** WHITE *Westerners* 2 Much of the range stock, on which the plainsman relied to draw his heavy 'schooners,' had died. **1909** WASON *Happy Hawkins* 30 He raised the colts just like range ponies.

+**c.** Designating rights and rules set up for the use of the range.

1885 *Santa Fé Wkly. New Mexican* 5 Nov. 4/1 Trail, range privileges and many things of interest to range men only, should be considered. **1890** *Stock Grower & Farmer* 21 June 5/1 Included with the cattle was a bunch of good saddle horses and some valuable land, which will add considerably to the range rights and possessions of Heckle and McDowell. **1914** 'BOWER' *Flying U Ranch* 158 They also wound them round and round with ropes . . . and gave them some very good advice upon the matter of range rules and the herding of sheep.

+**d.** Designating persons connected with an outfit running cattle on a range.

1890 *Stock Grower & Farmer* 22 Feb. 6/2 There is but one road for range cattle men to travel to reach prosperity, and that is by better breeding. *Ib.* 15 March 6/3 John Donahue, range foreman for the G-bar-outfit, came in on Monday. *Ib.* 5 April 3/2 Charles McMonigle . . . has been appointed range manager of the Rio Arriba Land and Cattle company. **1902** MACGOWAN *Last Word* 12, I have already told you that Mr. Pearsall (the most famous range cook in the West Texas cattle county) never came.

+**e.** Designating various actions and activities connected with raising cattle on a range.

1907 WHITE *Arizona Nights* 271 Under the shed were . . . curved short irons for the range branding. *Ib.* 274 In March began the spring branding, then the corralling and breaking of the wild horses, the summer range-riding. **1914** 'BOWER' *Flying U Ranch* 171 The petty meanness of range-stealing and nagging trespass may be harder to bear than the flourishing of a gun before one's face. *a***1918** G. STUART *On Frontier* II. 187 There was never a 'range war' between them [*sc.* the cattlemen and the sheepmen] in Montana.

+**f.** In special combinations.

Range country, country that offers range to live stock; *r. county*, a county in a range country; *r. line*, (see quotation).

1890 *Stock Grower & Farmer* 18 Jan. 4/4 The agricultural and live stock editor of the Fort Worth *Gazette* . . . says the *Stock Grower* is the best journal of its character published in range country. *a***1918** G. STUART *On Frontier* II. 224 Some very efficient sheriffs of the 'range counties' . . . enabled us to control the situation. **1817** *Niles' Reg.* XII. 97/2 The north and south lines dividing the townships are called *range* lines.

* **Range,** *v.*

* **1. a.** *tr.* To traverse (a country or place), +by way of protecting it or seeking out an enemy.

1645 *Mass. H. S. Coll.* 4 Ser. VI. 150, I purpose to-morrow . . . to range the woods with some more company. **1677** HUBBARD *Narrative* I. 89 The Forces . . . should be hastned out again to range the Woods. **1717** *N.C. Col. Rec.* II. 275 An Order of the Assembly [was given] to Range the Country after the Enemie Indians. **1726** PENHALLOW *Indian Wars* 107 Capt. Harmon drew off with about sixty men to range their corn fields. **1844** *Knickerb.* XXIII. 115 Our spies ranged the country for miles in advance and on either flank.

* **b.** *intr.* To move about a country, +to seek out enemies.

1676 *Mass. H. S. Coll.* 4 Ser. V. 9 The people in all our towns . . . are very desirous to be ranging after the enemy. **1788** in Ramsey *Tennessee* 518 Sevier . . . was out ranging, and came on the Indians' trail. **1837** *Diplom. Corr. Texas* I. (1908) 203 You will . . . urge the necessity of that Government's immediately mounting at least 500 men to range on the frontier.

+**2.** Of animals: To forage on a range.

1746 *Georgia Col. Rec.* VI. 155 All Cattle belonging to Ebenezer that he found ranging with those of the Trust should be drove up together. **1791** W. BARTRAM *Travels* 208 The cattle which only feed and range in the high forests and pine savannas are clear of this disorder. **1807** GASS *Journal* 238 Game of different kinds [can be found] ranging through the plains. **1849** [see DRIVE *v.* 1 b.]. **1885** *Century Mag.* April 841 The snow lies on them too deeply in winter for cattle to range, as in Montana, all the year round. **1897** HOUGH *Story of Cowboy* 5 A cow, . . . if driven north and allowed to range on the sun-cured short grasses, . . . might increase [in weight] fairly by one-third.

+**3.** *tr.* To put (cattle) on range. Also fig.

1857 OLMSTED *Journey through Texas* 184 They ranged their cattle over as much of the adjoining prairie as they chose. **1909** WASON *Happy Hawkins* 197, I got nine hundred dollars I wish you'd range out with the rest o' my herd.

+**Range bear.** =RANGER 4. — **1893** ROOSEVELT *Wilderness Hunter* 265 They insist on . . . others with names known only in certain localities, such as the range bear, the roach-back, and the smut-face. **1897** HOUGH *Story of Cowboy* 230 In a few instances the cowboy has ridden alongside and with his six-shooter killed the grizzly, cinnamon, or 'range bear.'

+**Range boss.** *W.* The boss of an outfit rounding up cattle on a range. — **1893** CHITTENDEN *Ranch Verses* 94 The range boss's outfit rides in through the herd Cutting out and inspecting. **1897** LEWIS *Wolfville* 110 Sorter as range-boss of the whole outfit is a lean gent in a black coat.

+**Range cattle.** Cattle raised or fed on a range.

1885 *Wkly. New Mexican Rev.* 9 April 3/3 The cattle are . . . one of the best bunches of range cattle in New Mexico. **1901** *Amer. Rev. of Reviews* XXIV. 305/1 The following official estimate of range cattle . . . in the Southwest is of interest. **1913** BARNES *Western Grazing Grounds* 286 There are but three diseases among western range cattle which can be considered general.

b. Attrib. with *business, industry.*

1889 *Rep. Secy. Agric.* 64 Trusted agents of the Bureau, well acquainted with the range-cattle industry, were sent into the field. **1890** *Stock Grower & Farmer* 8 Feb. 3/2 Notwithstanding the great depression of the range cattle business there are still some people who think that western cattlemen have a soft thing in their business.

+**Range man.** A cattleman who grazes his stock on a range. — **1885** [see RANGE *n.* 8 c]. **1890** *Stock Grower & Farmer* 25 Jan. 4/2 It is strange that our range men are so unreasonable as to kick against the big four. **1913** BARNES *Western Grazing Grounds* 95 The Polled Angus, now called Aberdeen Angus, and Galloways were tried by the western rangemen.

* **Ranger.**

+**1.** A member of a body of armed men, usually mounted, employed to range over an area for its protection; a person employed to protect the western frontier against the Indians.

See also FOREST RANGER 1, MOUNTED RANGER.

1670 *Mass. H. S. Coll.* 1 Ser. VI. 211, [I] saw one of captain Willet's rangers coming on post on horseback. **1692** *Va. State P.* I. 38. **1713** *N.C. Col. Rec.* II. 32, I have ordered all our Rangers . . . to march that way. **1740** *Ga. Hist. Soc. Coll.* II. 81 For the defense of the colony now, it is necessary to have . . . rangers who can ride the woods. **1776** *Jrnls. Cont. Congress* V. 606 The regiment of rangers, now in the pay of . . . South Carolina [shall] be placed upon continental establishment. **1812** *Niles' Reg.* II. 119/2 The several companies of rangers, authorised to be raised by a late act of congress for the protection of our north-western frontier against the Indians, are already in active service. **1838** C. NEWELL *Revol. Texas* 72 The General Council of the Provisional Government . . . had provided for . . . establishing and organizing a corps of rangers. **1848** *Santa Fe Republican* 18 March 2/2 We at any rate look for Skillman's Rangers to fetch us an express in ten or twelve days. **1885** *Wkly. New Mexican Rev.* 11 June 3/3 The rangers approached and demanded their arms. **1912** RAINE *Brand Blotters* 250 This graceless scamp . . . was not the lieutenant of rangers.

+**b.** With the name of the government employing the ranger.

See also TEXAN RANGER, TEXAS RANGER.

1810 WEEMS *Washington* (ed. 10) 40 The Virginia Rangers discovered signs of the Indians. **1833** S. SMITH *Major Downing* 191 They are the likeliest company [of soldiers] I've seen since I went with my Tennessee rangers to New Orleans. *c***1835** CATLIN *Indians* II. 71 Another demand, ... was for the restoration of an United States ranger, ... who had been captured. **1840** DANA *Two Years* xxviii. 311 There was but one man in the only house here, and him I shall always remember as a good specimen of a California ranger. **1861** *Chicago Tribune* 26 May 1/2 Capt. Frank Bennett, Illinois Rangers, ... offered himself. **1867** *Wkly. New Mexican* 4 May 2/2 The Arizona rangers ... were on the road from Santa Cruz to the mine when they were attacked.

+**2.** An officer employed to protect an area against, or to take charge of, strays.

1796 in Imlay *Western Territory* (1797) 553 [The county court] shall also have power to appoint one register and ranger for the county, who shall hold their offices during good behaviour. **1886** Buck *Ref. Handbook Med. Sciences* II. 304/1 In Mississippi the coroner is also the county ranger, and performs the duties of that office. **1891** O'BEIRNE *Leaders Ind. Territory* 44/2 He is now a candidate for Ranger of Blue county.

+**3.** A horse trained to serve a ranger.

1841 *S. Lit. Messenger* VII. 54/1 [We] clatter Our season'd rangers of a steady bound, Upon their fainting heels. **1855** F. MARRYAT *Mts. & Molehills* xi, I had two horses; one was an old grey 'Texian Ranger.'

+**4.** (See quotation.)

1868 *Amer. Naturalist* I. 657, I had at one time two tamed [black bears, *Ursus americanus*]. ... One was what is called the 'Ranger' Bear. ... The other was what is called a 'Hog Bear,' and was shorter-legged and blacker. So I am sure the Hog Bear and Ranger are of one species.

+**5.** A cow allowed to feed on a range.

1885 *Wkly. New Mexican Rev.* 7 May 3/6 Benjamin McLean, ... now a heavy cattle raiser in Socorro county, with 28,000 head of rangers there, is stopping at the Las Vegas springs. **1903** *Kan. State Bd. Agric. Rep. 1901–2* 15 The best rangers I ever saw on the Chicago market were high-grade Short-horns from Montana.

+**6.** A cattleman who ranges cattle.

1890 *Stock Grower & Farmer* 11 Jan. 4/2 The quarantine forced our people to market our stock direct in the stock yards and taught us that it was more profitable ... than to sell our yearlings to the northwestern rangers.

* **7.** An employee of a forest service who supervises forest improvements, issues grazing permits, etc.; a forest ranger (sense 2).

1905 *Forestry Bureau Bul.* No. 60, 28 The ranger or warden could do much work on the trails when there was no danger from fires. **1924** R. CUMMINS *Sky-High Corral* 15 No damn ranger was goin' to make a count on my stock.

+**8.** Attrib. in sense 1 with *band, force, service, system.*

1835 WHITTIER *Poetical Works* (1894) 504/1 The Indian points his hand To where across the echoing glen Sweep Harmon's dreaded ranger-band. **1857** *Harper's Mag.* 644/1 Let the *Ranger* system, then, be adopted in place of the old discipline—a system in which each man, acting in concert with his fellows, yet fights on his own. **1884** *N. Mex. Terr. Rep.* 86 This distribution [of the militia] is more available ... for exigencies that may arise, than a patrol or 'Ranger' service would be. **1898** CANFIELD *Maid of Frontier* 76 The ranger force of Texas is singular.

+**Ranger bear.** (See RANGER 4.)

+**Range rider.** A cowman who rides the range. — **1890** *Stock Grower & Farmer* 28 June 3/4 A few years more will see all the last of the range rider. **1897** HOUGH *Story of Cowboy* 39 The range riders are continual sentinels and pickets, besides being courier, fighting force, and commander, each for himself. **1923** J. H. COOK *On Old Frontier* 22 After a few weeks I learned ... to be a 'range rider.'

+**Range way.** A way for taking cattle to and from a range. — **1685** *Charlestown Land Rec.* 196 [The lot is bounded] South Eastrly by the range way two pole broad. **1707** *Cambridge Prop. Rec.* 236 We stated a way ... from ye Range way Near said Lawrences house to ye Range way where sd ffasset dwells.

+**Ranginess.** The quality of being rangy. — **1872** *Vermont Bd. Agric. Rep.* I. 213 A cross of a 900 or 1000 lb. mare with a 1100 or 1200 lb. horse, with bone, ranginess and endurance, is not too violent a cross.

Ranging. *attrib.* and *a.* {1622–} +Designating men and groups performing the work of a ranger. — **1758** Rogers *Jrnls.* 77 They are not to inlist any man ... but what are able-bodied, well acquainted with the woods, used to hunting, and in every way qualified for the Rangeing service. **1781** *Va. State P.* I. 495 The Ranging Man in open Council Declar'd against the War. **1790** WASHINGTON *Diaries* IV. 101 Out of these a fine Ranging Regiment might be enlisted.

+**Ranging bear.** =RANGER 4. — **1796** MORSE *Univ. Geog.* I. 196 The Ranging Bear ... is carnivorous.

+**Ranging company.** A military company of rangers. — **1756** WASHINGTON in *Lett. to Washington* II. 3n., I promised ... that a regular force may be established in lieu of the militia and ranging companies. **1779** in Sparks *Corr. Revol.* II. 285 Authorized the Lieutenants ... to raise a ranging company. **1836** EDWARD *Hist. Texas* 99 Let a ranging company or companies be organized in military form and order.

+**Ranging party.** A party or company made up of rangers; a party that ranges. — **1758** *Essex Inst. Coll.* XVIII. 115 The other two [companies were] ... left for Ranging Parties. **1799** J. SMITH *Acct. Captivity* 74 [He is] exceedingly fit for the command of a ranging or scouting party. **1836** CROCKETT *Exploits* 121 [He] headed a ranging party.

+**Ranging timber.** Timber suitable for use as cross timbers in the construction of a house or ship. — **1682** *Dorchester Rec.* 265 The same day was granted to Philip Withington liberty to get Rangeng timber for a dwelling house in the Commons. **1774** *Copley-Pelham Lett.* 234 Stones ... are neatly laid together, and ranged so that a peace of ranging timber of about 9 Inches broad on the Top and 4 Inches high on the side would well Imiatate. **1796** MORSE *Univ. Geog.* I. 394 Vast quantities of Ship timber, ranging timber, plank, deals ... are brought down in rafts. **1816** *Mass. H. S. Coll.* 2 Ser. VII. 114 Abington and its vicinity formerly afforded large supplies of square and ranging timber.

Rangy, *a.* {1880–, in Australia}

'Chiefly *U.S.*' (*O.E.D.*).

1. a. Of an animal: Long-limbed and capable of long, easy movements. {1886}

1868 WOODRUFF *Trotting Horse* 381 The latter was a fine, rangy gelding. **1876** *Rep. Vermont Bd. Agric.* III. 215 They were ... light colored, rather rangy sheep. **1885** ROOSEVELT *Hunting Trips of Ranchman* 21 The ponies ... used for the circle-riding in the morning have need rather to be strong and rangey. **1905** A. ADAMS *Outlet* 179 The steers were large and rangy, extremely uniform in ages and weights.

+**b.** Of a horse's gait: Long and adapted to ranging.

1891 *Harper's Mag.* July 206/2 He cannot ... sit close without pounding to the long rangy trot of a big thorough-bred.

+**c.** Of a person: Long of leg and arm.

1899 ADE *Doc' Horne* 42 He was considerably over six feet tall, raw boned and rangy. **1904** *N.Y. Sun* 28 Aug. 5 Physically, the Archbishop has the tall, rangy build of the English athlete. **1922** [see END 2].

+**2.** Of a place: Commodious; permitting range; extensive.

1880 LANIER *Poems* (1884) 5 Breathe it free, By rangy marsh, in lone sea-liberty. **1883** C. HALLOCK *Sportsman's Gazetteer* 452 The Toronto (Canada) Hunt Club has ... a large rangy shed for the horses.

+**3.** Of a person: (see quotation).

1890 *Cent.* 4956/1 *Rangy*, ... sometimes applied to a roving person, as a lad who wanders from home, or who has a predilection for a roving life, as that of a sailor. (U.S.)

* **Rank,** *v.*

+**1.** *tr.* To outrank; to have precedence over another by virtue of superiority in rank.

1841 *S. Lit. Messenger* VII. 766/1, I have Mr. Sanford under my command—I *rank* him. **1865** *Morning Star* (London) 27 May, That's right, ... the President ranks us both. **1888** CODY *Wild West* 551 General Carr ... took command of all the troops, he being the senior officer and ranking General Penrose. **1903** *Smart Set* IX. 75/1 All the ambassadors rank the ministers. **1904** *Delineator* Dec. 933 The Secretary of State ranks all the other members of the Cabinet.

+**b.** *Milit. To rank out*, to deprive (someone) of something by virtue of having superiority over him in rank. Also *ppl. a.*

1872 ROE *Army Lett.* 66 Faye has been turned out of quarters—'ranked out,' as it is spoken of in the Army. **1889** CUSTER *Tenting on Plains* 372 The colonel of the regiment arrived, and ranked us out of our quarters. **1917** J. A. MOSS *Officers' Manual* 485 *Ranked-out*, to be compelled to vacate by a senior, as 'to be ranked-out of quarters.'

+**2.** To pile (wood or bark) in regular rows or tiers; to cord.

1859 T. D. PRICE *Diary* (MS.) 25 Dec., Drew some firewood on sled to rank in shed. **1882** *Ib.* 3 Feb., Mark sledded some wood to top of hill to split and rank. **1888** KIRKLAND *McVeys* 335 All this time they were busy ranking up the wood the teamsters were throwing off. **1905** *Forestry Bureau Bul.* No. 61, 44 *Rank*, to haul and pile regularly, as, to rank bark or cord wood.

* **Ranking.** +Leading; foremost; superior in rank. — **1862** *Yale Lit. Mag.* XXIX. 80 (Th.), His two ranking officers were both gone. **1898** PAGE *Red Rock* 86 The ranking officer ... had been summoned that morning to the city. **1903** *N.Y. Times* 15 Aug., Steadiness on the part of the English lawn tennis players again resulted in their winning over the ranking American experts. **1912** HASKIN *Amer. Gov.* 11 The literary merit of McKinley's messages improved after John Hay became his ranking adviser.

+**Rank list.** *Educ.* A list showing the comparative standing of students on the basis of scholarship. — **1876** TRIPP *Student-Life* 129 It helps a man to be good at some one thing, either a splendid oar, or in the Nine, or the Glee Club, or the Pierian, or a good gymnast. It is a hundred times better than the rank-list. *Ib.* 270 The rank-list came out at last. **1884** R. GRANT *Average Man* 22 If Woodbury Stoughton only chose to work, he could have any place on the rank-list.

* **Ransom.** A sum or premium paid an Indian for the release of a captive. — *a***1649** WINTHROP *Hist.* I. 68 James Sagamore's wife, who had been taken away at the surprise at Agawam, ... writ that the Indians demanded ... ransom. **1719** *Mass. H. Rep. Jrnl.* II. 183 The Sum of Five Pounds, fifteen Shillings [shall] be allowed ... to John Bixby, the

Petitioner to Reimburse what he paid for his Ransom. **1841** Cooper *Deerslayer* xiii, They will give them two ivory creatur's as ransom; one for each scalp.

Ranste(a)d, Ramsted. [See quot. 1830.] +The common toadflax. In full *ranstead weed.* (Cf. Butter and eggs.) — **1830** Watson *Philadelphia* 642 The Ranstead weed . . . came first from Wales, being sent as a garden flower for Mr. Ranstead of Philadelphia, an upholsterer and a Welshman. **1843** Torrey *Flora N.Y.* II. 32 *Linaria Vulgaris.* Common Toad-flax, or Ransted. . . . Road-sides, fields, etc.; very common. **1847** [see Butter and eggs]. **1857** Gray *Botany* 284 Toad-Flax. Butter-and-eggs. Ramsted. . . . A showy but pernicious weed. **1901** Britton *Manual Flora* 821.

+**Rantankerous,** *a.* Cantankerous, perverse; quarrelsome; troublesome to deal with. *colloq.* — **1832** Paulding *Westward Ho!* I. 180 Not he, the rantanckerous squatter. **1845** W. T. Thompson *Chron. Pineville* 178 She better not come a cavortin' bout me with any of her rantankerous carryin's on! **1861** Newell *Orpheus C. Kerr* I. 18 Sal screamed out that I'd murdered the rantankerous critter. **1879** Tourgee *Fool's Errand* 102 He was jes' de rantankerousest Union man dat ever was, all tru de wah. **1898** Harris *Tales of Home Folks* 48 They never had such a rantankerous nigger to deal with.

Ranter. A member of a religious sect characterized by noisiness and extravagance in conduct and worship. Used orig. of a seventeenth-century sect of Antinomians, but later applied to Quakers and Methodists. {1651–} Now hist.

1656 *Conn. Rec.* I. 283 No towne wthin this Jurisdiction shall entertaine any Quakers, Ranters, Adamites, or such like notorious heritiques. **1668** *Ib.* II. 87 Such bookes or manuscripts as contayne the errors of Quakers, Ranters, Adamites or such like Notorious Heretiques, should not be kept. **1781** Peters *Hist. Conn.* (1829) 124 Quakers, baptists, adamites, ranters, episcopalians. **1832** Watson *Hist. Tales N.Y.* 31 About that time the public peace had been disturbed by those Quakers, whom the Friends themselves sometimes censured as 'ranters.' **1867** Dixon *New America* II. 143 The religious passion breaks out . . . always in a sect of extreme opinions, generally among the Ranters, the Tunkers, the Seventh-day Baptists, the Come-outers, and the Methodists.

***Rap.** +*fig.* A rebuke or reprimand; blame. *colloq.* — **1777** *Amer. Pioneer* II. 17 The post master general . . . has lately had a rap, which I hope will have a good effect. **1865** *Atlantic Mo.* March 297/2 He who has the bad taste to meddle with the caprices of believers . . . gets the rap and the orders of dismissal.

***Rape. a.** A turnip. *Obs.* **b.** An annual plant (*Brassica napus*) somewhat resembling the cabbage and grown chiefly as a forage or cover crop. Also *rapeseed.* — **1634** Wood *New Eng. Prospect* (1865) 15 This land likewise affoards Hempe and Flax . . . with Rapes if they bee well managed. **1666** in *Hist. Coll. S. Carolina* II. 13 The Meadows are very proper for Rice, Rape-seed, Lin-seed. **1705** Beverley *Virginia* IV. 56 It was formerly said of the Red-top Turnip, that there in three or four Years time, it degenerated into Rape; but that happen'd merely by an Error in saving the Seed. **1863** Randall *Pract. Shepherd* 58 The ram lambs are folded on rape. **1871** *Rep. Comm. Agric. 1870* 503 The culture of rape was introduced at Fond du Lac a dozen years ago by General Hamilton for the extraction of the oil. **1913** Britton & Brown *Illus. Flora* (ed. 2) II. 194.

Rape cake. (See quot. 1858.) {1660–} — **1825** Lorain *Pract. Husbandry* 120 Rape cake is also highly esteemed [as a manure]. **1858** C. Flint *Milch Cows* 197 Rape-cake . . . is the residuum after pressing the oil from rape-seed.

Rapeseed oil. Oil extracted from the seed of rape. {1816–} — **1751** [see Mill *n.*[1] 1]. **1819** *Western Rev.* I. 185 The Harmonists press this oil in the press used for rape seed oil.

+**Rapid.** A place in a river where the water descends rapidly but without waterfalls or cascades. Usually pl. {1820–}

1765 Croghan *Journal* 136 What is called the Fall here, is no more than rapids. **1792** Imlay *Western Territory* 47 The Rapids of the Ohio . . . are occasioned by a ledge of rocks which stretch across the bed of the river from one side to the other. **1802** Ellicott *Journal* 19 The rapids are occasioned by the water falling from one horizontal stratum of limestone, to another. **1848** Thoreau *Maine Woods* 25 Just above McCauslin's, there is a rocky rapid, where logs jam in the spring. **1890** Langford *Vigilante Days* (1912) 497 The last and most fearful rapid of the Yellowstone is near the mouth of the Tongue River. **1905** Wiggin *Rose* 33 We're well acquainted with that rock and them rapids.

+**Rapid transit.** Local passenger transportation. Sometimes restricted to modes of transportation faster than those operating in street traffic. {1895 (quoted in *Scientific Amer.* LXXIII. 250/1)} Also attrib. — **1882** McCabe *New York* 67 Rapid transit, too, now so fully developed, will . . . keep the present population resident in their own city. **1888** *Economist* 20 Oct. 9/3 The rival rapid transit companies on the South Side are unmistakably approaching a warm contest. **1908** Stevens *Liberators* 205 The rapid-transit company . . . applied to the Supreme Court for an injunction. **1914** *Cycl. Amer. Govt.* III. 151/1 Rapid transit facilities [can] be introduced . . . either by the construction of elevated or subway . . . lines, or a combination of elevated and subway lines.

***Rapier.** A long, narrow, two-edged sword suitable for thrusting or cutting. Also attrib. — **1631** *Mass. Hist. Proc.* XLV. 497 A parcell of a duzen and a halfe of rapier blades . . . he sould to the Indians . . . for a skin a peece. **1683** *Conn. Probate Rec.* I. 363, I give unto my son Thomas his son, Jarrad Spencer by name, my Rapier. **1855** Simms *Forayers* 373 He simply cast his eyes upon the pistols . . . convenient to his grasp, to say nothing of the rapier which had just been unbuckled from his side.

+**Rapist.** One guilty of rape. — **1889** *Columbus Dispatch* 13 June, Two horse thieves and a rapist were sentenced. **1901** *Nation* 18 April 313/1 A bill having been passed by the State [Ark.] legislators, March 20, 1901, 'providing for the public execution of convicted rapists,' the original plan was abandoned.

Rappee. A strong, pungent snuff made from the darker and coarser tobacco leaves, orig. by rasping. {1740–} — **1782** *Royal Gazette* (Charleston) 13 July 4/3 For Sale, per package . . . Rappee and Scots Snuff. *c*1800 J. Plummer *Life & Adv.* 232, [I] concluded it necessary to take what is called rappee, (I don't know that I spell the word right, having never seen it in print). *c*1850 A. Lawrence *Diary & Corr.* 25 The scented rappee of forty years ago had great charms for me.

Rapper. {1755–} +One who allegedly secures communications from the spirits of the dead, who announce their presence by raps or knocks. — **1852** *Harper's Mag.* Dec. 129/1 [The biologists'] province . . . does not as yet extend into the spirit world. Not so, however, of the rappers and table-movers. **1859** *Ib.* Aug. 422/2 'The Fox girls,' as the Rochester rappers were called, paid a visit to Philadelphia. **1875** *Chicago Tribune* 1 Oct. 7/3 Something of a sensation was excited by the appearance . . . of Margaret Fox Kane, one of the original rappers of Rochester a quarter of a century ago.

***Rapping.** +The action attributed to spirits supposed to announce their presence by raps or knocks. — **1852** Eastman *Aunt Phillis's Cabin* 275, I look upon it as one of the imaginary horrors of the times—a delusion like spiritual rappings, got up out of sheer timidity of disposition. **1860** Emerson *Conduct of Life* 182 In creeds never was such levity; witness the . . . maundering of Mormons, the squalor of Mesmerism, the deliration of rappings. **1901** Stillman *Autobiog. Journalist* I. 179 Society was largely occupied by the table-tippings and the 'rappings.'

+**Rappist.** A member of a communistic religious society founded by George (*i.e.*, Johann Georg) Rapp (1757–1847); a Harmonist (q.v., sense 1). Now hist. (Cf. Economist.) — **1845** *Essays on Christ. Union* 372 The following are the principal religious sects in America . . . : The Protestant Episcopal Church, . . . the Rappists, Shakers, Mormons, . . . and other small sects and parties. **1867** Dixon *New America* II. 217 The Rappists had to sell Harmony. **1884** Schaff *Religious Encycl.* III. The Rappists emigrated to Economy, seventeen miles northwest of Pittsburg. **1903** [see Harmonist 1].

+**Rappite.** =prec. *Obs.* (Cf. Economite, Harmonite.) — **1832** Ferrall *Ramble* 92 The Rappites had been in possession of the place [New Harmony, Ind.] for six years. **1837** Martineau *Society* II. 59 The co-operative methods of the Shakers and Rappites might be tried without any adoption of their spiritual pride and cruel superstition. **1864** Nichols *Amer. Life* II. 29 The Rappites . . . founded large communities and gathered wealth by industry.

Raquet, Raqueting. (See Racket, Racketing.)

Rare, *a.* {1655–} Of meat: Underdone. {1784–} Also absol.

'Now often regarded as an Americanism, but current in many English dialects . . . , and used by English writers in the first half of the 19th c.' (*O.E.D.*).

1832 Vigne *6 Mos. in Amer.* I. 128 The meat . . . should be sent to table underdone, or what in America is called 'rare.' **1854** *Harper's Mag.* May 845/2 You may hear any day at dinner, 'Ma! will you have a piece of the rare or well done.' **1885** *Century Mag.* Jan. 403 He had said . . . that rare roast beef was much improved by horse-radish. **1911** Ferber *Dawn O'Hara* 20, Y've devoured rare porterhouse and roast beef day after day.

+**Rare,** *v.* [Var. of *rear.*] *intr.* and *tr.* To rear or lift; to plunge or cavort. *colloq.* — **1833** *Sketches D. Crocket* 92 He just rared up upon his hind legs. **1850** Garrard *Wah-To-Yah* xix. 226 The old coon . . . rared his head back. **1891** 'Thanet' *Otto the Knight* 8 Ain't that Bassett a r'arin' and chargin'! **1898** Canfield *Maid of Frontier* 100 Break 'em with a curb an' they rare an' fall back on you.

Rareripe. {1799–}

+**1.** An early ripening variety of peach; a peach of such a variety. In full *rareripe peach.*

1722 *New-Eng. Courant* 3 Sept. 2/1 Having in his Garden a plentiful Crop of Rare-Ripes, he agreed with an Ethiopian Market-Man . . . to bring him an Horse-load of them to Town. **1854** *Mich. Agric. Soc. Trans.* V. 68 Seedling rareripe peaches [were exhibited]. **1854** *Harper's Mag.* Nov. 849/2 After eating a great number of these 'rare-ripes'—a very choice variety, . . . we filled our pockets.

+**b.** Attrib. with *flush* in sense: Of the color of a rareripe peach.

1861 Holmes *E. Venner* vi, *Rosa Milburn.* Sixteen. Brunette, with a rare ripe flush in her cheeks.

‖**2.** (See quotation.)

1890 Lowell *Biglow P.* 2 Ser. Introd. 239 President Lincoln said of a precocious boy that he was a *rareripe.*

+**Rareripe corn.** A variety of early Indian corn. *Obs.* — **1786** Washington *Diaries* III. 145 The Eastern rare-ripe Corn . . . had yielded . . . unproductively both at Muddy hole and in the Neck. **1799** — *Writings* XIV. 231 All that part . . . is to be planted with rare-ripe corn. **1835** J. Martin *Descr. Virginia* 59 In the year 1619 two crops of rare-ripe corn were made.

+**Rasher.** [Sp. *racio* a kind of fish.] A rockfish (*Rosicola miniatus*) found off the coast of California. — **1880** *Nat. Museum Proc.* III. 146 The following species of 'rock-fish' were obtained by us in Monterey Bay. The names used by the fishermen . . . [include]: Meron, Tom-cod, Jack-fish, . . . Rasher. **1884** GOODE, etc. *Fisheries* I. 265 This species is known to the Portuguese at Monterey as the 'Rasher,' a name of unknown origin and orthography. **1896** JORDAN & EVERMANN *Check-List Fishes* 429.

***Rasp.** A coarse file or rasping tool with teeth formed by indentations made with a punch. — **1768** in H. M. Brooks *Gleanings* IV. 39 Ink powder and sealing wax, files and rasps; horse fleams. **1826** COOPER *Last of Mohicans* xxvii, The savage grated his teeth together like rasps of iron. **1881** *Rep. Indian Affairs* 434 Rasps, horse, 16-inch.

Raspberry. Also †**rasberry.**

1. The fruit of any one of various plants of the genus *Rubus*, or a plant producing this, as *R. strigosus* or *R. occidentalis.* {1623–}

1630 HIGGINSON *New-England* 9 Plums, Raspberies, Corrance, . . . Hurtleberies & Hawes of Whitehorne [are] neere as good as our Cherries in England. **1698** THOMAS *Pensilvania* 17 Rasberries, Strawberries, Cramberries . . . are common and free for any to gather. **1767** in Singleton *Social N.Y.* 44 In a spacious garden . . . are great plenty of currants, gooseberries, raspberries and English strawberries. **1804** [see BOXBERRY]. **1883** *Practical Housekeeping* 428 Raspberries are in market from the middle of June till September. **1907** *St. Nicholas* Oct. 1060/1 While gathering a mess of raspberries along a bush-smothered foot-path, I noticed a black speck.

2. *attrib.* and *comb.* **a.** Designating foods or drinks prepared from raspberries or their juice.

1808 IRVING, etc. *Salmagundi* xx. 522 On the first of January [cakes are given] to all visitors, together with a glass of . . . raspberry-brandy. **1828** LESLIE *Receipts* 25 Raspberry and apple-pies are much improved by . . . pouring in a little cream. **1832** CHILD *Frugal Housewife* 118 Raspberry Jam.—Take an equal quantity of fruit and sugar. **1867** Goss *Soldier's Story* 29, I was treated to raspberry wine and baker's bread. **1868** A. D. WHITNEY *P. Strong* 138, I made her give up . . . the special raspberry-roll for dinner and the iced-cake for tea.

b. Designating insects injurious to raspberries.

1854 EMMONS *Agric. N.Y.* V. 264 (*index*), *Agrilus* or Raspberry beetle. **1892** KELLOGG *Kansas Insects* 4 No injury is done by . . . the four-winged hymenopterous insects (the Raspberry- and Rose-slug Saw-flies). *Ib.* 93 Raspberry slug (*Selandria rubi*). . . . The adults . . . insert their eggs beneath the skin of the raspberry leaf.

+**Raspberry shrub.** A drink prepared from the juice of raspberries, sugar, and vinegar. — **1832** CHILD *Frugal Housewife* 82 Raspberry shrub mixed with water is a pure, delicious drink for summer. **1880** *Harper's Mag.* March 573/1 Our ras'berry shrub is good, if I do say it. **1886** WARNER *Their Pilgrimage* xi, Mr. Glow and King and Forbes, sipping their raspberry shrub in a retired corner of the bar-room, were interested spectators of the scene.

Raspberry vinegar. =prec. {1713–} Also attrib. — **1805** *Pocumtuc Housewife* (1906) 30 [Recipe for] Raspberry Vinegar. **1867** *Common Sense Cook Book* 110 [Recipe for] Raspberry Vinegar Beverage. **1893** *Harper's Mag.* Feb. 456 Miss Sarey Mirandy passed around raspberry-vinegar and crullers on an old silver-plated tray. **1904** GLASGOW *Deliverance* 517 A bottle of Miss Saidie's raspberry vinegar was hidden in one corner.

+**Raster.** =ARRASTRE. — **1877** BARTLETT 515 *Rastra*, . . . an instrument used by the California gold-miners, consisting of two heavy stones attached by a strap to a horizontal bar. **1881** RAYMOND *Mining Gloss.*, *Arrastre.* Sp[anish]; Apparatus [etc.]. . . . Sometimes incorrectly written *arraster, arrastra*, or *raster.* **1885** *Wkly. New Mexican Rev.* 2 April 3/4 Messrs. Probst and Gonzales will construct an old style Mexican 'raster,' crushing the ore with heavy boulders and horse power.

***Rat,** *n.*

***1.** Any one of various well-known small rodents of the genus *Rattus*, or of some allied genera.

See also BLACK RAT, BROWN RAT, etc.

1622 'MOURT' *Relation* 110 One of the Savages had shot a Shad in the water, and a small Squirril as big as a Rat. **1738** *Boston Rec.* 215 Sundry Inhabitants [petition] that some method may be projected for the Destruction of Rats. **1824** DODDRIDGE *Notes* 71 Rats . . . were not known here for several years after the settlement of the country. **1907** *St. Nicholas* July 845/2 Besides mice and rats the house-snake catches many crickets.

+**2.** =MOUNTAIN RAT.

1805 ORDWAY in *Jrnls. of Lewis & O.* 242 We over halled the Baggage and killed a large curious kind of a rat with hair on his tail.

+**3.** =MUSKRAT 1 a.

1832 KENNEDY *Swallow Barn* I. 307, I have got no more than two rats. **1841** COOPER *Deerslayer* iii, A shallow bay . . . had got the name of the 'Rat's Cove,' from . . . its being a favorite haunt of the musk-rat. **1857** *Rep. Comm. Patents 1856: Agric.* 108 Old trappers . . . have never seen 'rat' more abundant than they have been on the prairies of Northern Illinois.

+**4.** A member of a certain religious sect in Indiana (*c*1824). A nickname.

1843 'CARLTON' *New Purchase* II. 88 When rumour declared we intended to elect a man nominally a Rat, . . . the wrath was roused of the people, religious, and irreligious, of all other sects. *Ib.* 89, The people . . . [were determined] to keep out a Rat.

+**5.** A student. *slang.*

1850 LEWIS *La. Swamp Doctor* 113 There were four or five brother 'Rats' besides myself residing in the hospital, all candidates for graduation, and all desirous of obtaining sufficient medical lore.

+**6.** A compositor or printer not in good standing with a trade union; a strike-breaker or scab. *slang.*

1848 BARTLETT 270 *Rat*, a contemptuous term used by printers, to denote a man who works under price. **1868** *Ore. State Jrnl.* 17 Oct. 1/6 The President of the National Typographical Union has pronounced a general amnesty, by virtue of which all expelled members, 'rats,' etc., will be admitted to the Unions. **1874** *Internat. Typogr. Union Proc.* 28 The custom of striking from the role of permanent members . . . the names of printers retiring from the business . . . practically places them in the same category with 'rats' and other 'unfair' printers. *a***1882** WEED *Autobiog.* 86 The journeymen 'struck' . . . because a 'rat' had been employed in our office. **1896** *Typographical Jrnl.* IX. 100 A force of rats were doubled up from the Evening Ledger to get out the paper.

+**7.** A pad used in certain styles of women's coiffure.

Cf. MOUSE *n.* 2.

1863 A. D. WHITNEY *F. Gartney* xi, The luminous tresses . . . rippled . . . after a style of their own that in these later days Fashion and Art have striven hopelessly to achieve with crimping-pins and—'*rats!*' **1888** [see MOUSE *n.* 2]. **1901** ADE *40 Modern Fables* 70 She carried plenty of Brown Hair that she Built Up by putting Rats under it. **1922** COURTENAY *Physical Beauty* 33 No young girl should use a rat.

+**8.** *To give* (someone) *rats*, to make trouble for (someone); to berate. *Obs.*

1863 *Boston Herald* 15 Feb. 4/1 Hooker is doing something in the way of giving the rebels rats. **1869** 'MARK TWAIN' *Sk., New & Old* 48 You may write a blistering article on the police—give the Chief Inspector rats.

9. Attrib. in sense 6 with *concern, office*, etc.

1824 *Microscope* (Albany, N.Y.) 6 March (Th.), Loren Webster, chief ink-dauber in a rat-printing office at the west; Ralph Walby, nothing at all but a rat-printer. **1859** BARTLETT 355 *Rat Office*, a printing office in which full prices are not paid. **1896** *Typographical Jrnl.* IX. 435 No. 80 selected the Hudson-Kimberly Company, a large rat concern, as the one upon which a fight should be made.

10. In special combinations.

Rat-baiting, the worrying of rats with small dogs; *r. fall*, a trap for killing rats by crushing them (cf. DEADFALL 1); *r. guard*, (see quotation); *r. house*, the lodge or den of muskrats; *r. joint*, a contemptuous designation for a low resort (cf. JOINT *n.* 3 b); *r.-licked*, smooth or glossy, as if by the licking of a rat.

1872 *Atlantic Mo.* May 558 Dog-fights and rat-baiting are the attractions held out to 'draw' custom to the whiskey-tap. **1897** *Dept. Agric. Yrbk. 1896* 164 A most excellent 'rat fall' may be made of a strong barrel, about half full of water. **1917** *Boston Sun. Globe Mag.* 20 May 8/3 (Ernst), Every vessel that lands at the wharves must have rat guards on any connection between it and the shore. These guards are discs of galvanized iron as big around as a dishpan. Each has a hole in the center and this is so fitted around the rope that no rat can pass. **1874** LONG *Wild-Fowl* 49 To build a blind in a rat-house, a large one like a small haystack should be selected. **1901** WHITE *Westerners* 122, I'll shoot up your old rat joint. **1839** BIRD *Robin Day* 33 A runt of a midshipman, with a head all ratlicked.

Rat, *v.* {1815–}

+**1.** *intr.* To hunt or catch muskrats.

1841 COOPER *Deerslayer* iii, Here the old fellow is! . . . ratting it away . . . ; up to his knees in mud and water, looking to the traps and the bait.

+**2.** *tr.* To dress (a person's) hair with a rat.

1866 A. D. WHITNEY *L. Goldthwaite* x, Next morning, at breakfast, Sin Saxon was as beautifully ruffled, ratted, and crimped . . . as ever.

+**3.** To denounce (a newspaper or printing office) as employing rat or scab labor; to relegate (a printer or compositor) to the status of a rat. *slang.*

1874 *Internat. Typogr. Union Proc.* 22 Attempt to force non-Union printers upon Union printers. Result: Unfavorable. Office 'ratted.' **1896** *Ib.* 29/1 The union 'ratted' the three daily papers. **1898** *Ib.* 60/1 Mr. Hotchkiss, who had refused to obey the call of the committee . . . , was ratted.

+**b.** To get out (a paper) with rat labor.

1896 *Internat. Typogr. Union Proc.* 28/1 The proprietor . . . was asked to discharge the compositor, which he refused to do, saying he would rat the paper first.

***Rate,** *n.*

1. A tax or assessment levied proportionally to raise money for local use; the money raised in this way. *Obs.* {1712–}

1633 *Dorchester Rec.* 4 [A pound shall be] made & set up. . . out of the publique rate. **1687** *Mass. H. S. Coll.* 4 Ser. V. 155 On a single rate (as they call it) for levying of a penny in the pound, some must pay 5 *d.* and some 2 *d.* in the pound to others' penny. **1704–5** [see COLLECTOR 2]. **1730**

SEWALL *Letter-Book* II. 285, I paid you a Ten shilling Rate for your Minister. **1799** *Ann. 7th Congress* 2 Sess. 1429 The rates certainly would be taken.

+b. *As sure as rates*, very sure or certain.

1815 HUMPHREYS *Yankey* 55 The man is . . . horn mad, as sure as rates. **1830** S. SMITH *Life J. Downing* 56 Last August, . . . according to the papers we were going to have two Governors right off, sure as rates. **1854** — *Down East* 238 But you'll kill that mare, colonel, as sure as rates.

2. A charge or price according to a fixed ratio or standard made by a railroad for its services. {1883–}

1878 PINKERTON *Strikers* 215 The constant diminution of receipts made a very great reduction of rates necessary to the retention of a class of through business. **1885** CUSTER *Boots & Saddles* 242 In order to induce immigration the railroads had reduced the rates. **1910** PINCHOT *Fight for Conservation* 32 The merchants . . . [want] satisfactory rates from railroads.

3. *attrib.* and *comb.* **a.** In sense 1 with *free, gatherer, list, money.*

1648 *N.H. Prov. Papers* I. 190 The petition of the inhabitants of Excetter for their rate & head money to be forborne . . . , the Court doth not thinke meete to grante. **1651** *East-Hampton Rec.* I. 16 Mr James shall haue for the worke of the Mynistry amonge us . . . the sum of 45£ & his land to lay Rate free. **1661** *Huntington Rec.* I. 34 All the rates now made shall be gathered and payed . . . upon the penalty of ten shillings to be forfeited to the rate gatherer. **1729** *Manchester Rec.* I. 175 The Select Men or assessors shall have 4s. pr Day . . . the time that they are a Making of the Rate Lists.

b. In sense 2 with *bill, clerk, law, sheet.*

1887 *Courier-Journal* 9 May 3/3 Shall second-class fares be placed in the rate-sheets generally? **1897** *Chicago Ev. Post* 15 May, The question of summer tourist rates has been under consideration . . . , but rate clerks were unable to agree on those that should be effective to Colorado points. **1898** *Kansas City Star* 20 Dec. 5/2 In Iowa there is a stringent rate law which has been held up as a model for Kansas. **1908** LORIMER *J. Spurlock* 249 Probably goin' to Washington to hire some blank Brutus to stab the rate bill in the back.

***Rate,** *v.* +*tr.* To carry or convey at a fixed rate. — **1881** *Chicago Times* 12 March, Large quantities of freight have been rated through to New York by this and other lines.

+**Rate-cutting.** The lowering of freight rates. {1919} — **1888** *Economist* 10 Nov. 8/3 One of the leading bear influences has been the old evil of rate-cutting by the railroad companies. **1897** *Boston Jrnl.* 14 Jan. 1/1 Prominent officials of the road say, however, that they know nothing about any rate cutting. **1903** E. JOHNSON *Railway Transportation* 253 In 1901 the competition of the lake lines with the trunk lines for the grain trade led to rate cutting.

+**Rate-maker.** =RATER. *Obs.* — **1660** *Mass. H. S. Coll.* 4 Ser. VII. 249 The rate makers think it is just that 18*li.* for a mans head should pay as many pence as 18*li.* for a horse. **1672** *Portsmouth Rec.* 173 Those then appointed to be the Rate-Makers . . . Neglected to make the Lard Rate. **1682** *Derby Rec.* 130 The Town have chosen Sar Johnson mr. John Hubbel & Abel Gun listers & rate makers. **1716** *Conn. Hist. Soc. Coll.* VI. 321 Voted that the Listers and Ratemakers distribute the New Law book in this Town.

+**Rate pay.** [RATE *n.* 1.] Money collected, or to be collected, as rates or taxes. *Obs.* — **1680** *Boston Rec.* 137 Allowed to James Euerall & his Daughtr Manninge 20ld. in rate pay in consideration of theire houses beinge burnt. **1686** *Ib.* 84 Ye Sume of Sixtye pounds . . . [is] to be p[ai]d as rate pay.

Rater. One selected to assess the rates or taxes in a town or colony. *Obs.* {1611–} — **1633** *Dorchester Rec.* 4 The Raters shall be mr. Woolcott, Mr. Johnson [etc.]. **1651** *Portsmouth Rec.* 53 The raters shall rate them according to their estates. **1690** *Plymouth Laws* 233 The Constable or Constables of each of these Towns [shall] forthwith warn the Inhabitants of their severall Towns to meet and choose their raters for each Town.

+**Rate war.** A struggle or competition over rates, esp. railroad rates. — **1893** [see HORN *n.* 5]. **1898** NICHOLAS *Idyl of Wabash* 11 A turn of fortune in the shape of a railroad rate war made it . . . possible for Miss Calistra to go to see her. **1903** E. JOHNSON *Railway Transportation* 218 In 1869 a 'rate war' carried the rates for a time to 25 cents a hundred [pounds] for all classes.

Rat fight. A fight arranged, for public amusement, between rats and small dogs, as terriers. *Obs.* — **1870** 'F. FERN' *Ginger-Snaps* 115 A woman couldn't go to report a rat-fight, or a prize-fight, or a dog-fight. **1876** *Wide Awake* 133/2 It is to our credit that a rat-fight is seldom publicly witnessed in America.

+**Ratfish.** A fish of the genus *Chimaera*, esp. *C. colliei* of the Pacific coast. (Cf. ELEPHANT FISH.) — **1882** *Nat. Museum Bul.* No. 16, 54 *Chimæra.* . . . Rat-fishes. . . . Mostly of the northern seas; not valued for food. *Ib.* 55 *C. coliæi.* . . . Rat-fish; Elephant-fish. . . . Pacific coast, from Monterey northward; very abundant. **1896** JORDAN & EVERMANN *Check-List Fishes* 226.

+**Ratherish,** *adv.* In a slight degree; somewhat. *colloq.* — **1862** *N.Y. Tribune* 22 April (*Cent.*), Levalette is ratherish against Popish temporality; Gen. Guyon is rather favorable to it. **1884** MATTHEWS & BUNNER *In Partnership* 175 She is ratherish pretty. **1887** *Library Mag.* 12 Feb. 422 Mr. Lang has a ratherish good opinion [of Longfellow's poems].

+**Rathskeller.** [Ger., 'town-hall cellar.'] A beer saloon or a restaurant serving drinks below the street level or in a basement. — **1900** ADE *More Fables* 159 Mr. Byrd . . . happened to be in a Rathskeller not far away. **1905** *N.Y. Ev. Post* 28 Dec. 7 In the rathskellers . . . even politicians talk with approximate frankness. **1909** [see FAN *n.*[1] 3]. **1912** NICHOLSON *Hoosier Chron.* 266 The Speaker of the House . . . had been dining in the rathskeller.

* **Ratification.**

+1. A formal act of approval of the federal constitution, or of amendments proposed to this, taken by a state or states.

1787 *Constitution* v, Amendments . . . shall be valid . . . when ratified by the Legislatures of three fourths of the several States, or by Conventions in three fourths thereof, as the one or other Mode of Ratification may be proposed by the Congress. *Ib.* vii, The ratification of the Conventions of nine States shall be sufficient for the establishment of this Constitution between the States so ratifying the same. **1788** [see CONSTITUTION 3]. **1886** ALTON *Among Law-Makers* 46 Proposed amendments to the Constitution are submitted to the States for ratification.

+b. A similar action performed by voters in a state, in approval of a constitution or an amendment.

1914 *Cycl. Amer. Govt.* III. 436/2 The process of ratification is in general more difficult than the proposing of amendments.

+2. The action taken by the president of the United States and the Senate in confirming or approving treaties.

'The President . . . shall have Power, by and with the Advice and Consent of the Senate, to make Treaties, provided two thirds of the Senators present concur' (*Constitution* ii. 2).

1789 *Steele P.* I. 42 After some Months the Treaties of Hopewell were entered on the Journal but no question of Ratification was taken on them as is always done with foreign Powers. **1803** CUTLER in *Life & Corr.* II. 139 Although the House had no voice in the ratification, the principles and probable consequences [of the Louisiana treaty] were pretty thoroughly discussed. **1840** *Niles' Nat. Reg.* 18 April 104/3 In the event of the senate not advising the ratification of the amended treaty, I invite [etc.]. **1900** *Congress. Rec.* 4 Jan. 642/2 Mr. Frye presented a memorial . . . remonstrating against the ratification of the reciprocity treaty with France. **1914** *Cycl. Amer. Govt.* III. 152/1 A treaty . . . is then transmitted to the President that he may complete the ratification and proclaim it.

+**Ratification meeting.** A public meeting to signify approval of a political action or proceeding, as the nomination of a party candidate. — **1848** *Congress. Globe* 3 July 893/3 Mr. Niles . . . compared the proceedings of the day with those of a ratification meeting. **1867** *Atlantic Mo.* June 662/1 When Frank Blair and his friends returned from nominating Mr. Lincoln . . . , a ratification meeting was held at St. Louis, which was assailed and broken up by a mob of 'Democrats.' **1868** *Congress. Globe* 14 Feb. 1169/3 On the 20th of December, 1860, the South Carolina convention passed an ordinance of secession. On the same day a grand ratification meeting . . . was held at Memphis. **1904** *N.Y. Ev. Post* 23 June 2 The first Roosevelt ratification meeting of the campaign will be held this evening, when the Republican Club of the 31st Assembly District will endorse the nominees of the Chicago convention.

***Ration.** +An allowance of provisions issued by United States authorities to an Indian or to Indians, as at an Indian agency. Usually pl. — **1846** MCKENNEY *Memoirs* I. 207 General Houston . . . [referred] to the intention of the Executive to supply rations to the emigrant Indians by contract. **1870** KEIM *Sheridan's Troopers* 164 The Indians . . . remained quietly in their villages, except during times of drawing rations. **1883** *Rep. Indian Affairs* 8 Under the plea that they were planting and needed rations until the ripening of their corn, they have drawn heavily on the agency. **1889** [see BREECHCLOUT].

Ratoon, *n.*

1. A shoot or sprout of any of various plants, esp. sugar cane, springing from the roots or stubbles of a previous growth. {1779–} Also attrib.

Cf. PLANT CANE.

1631 *Va. House of Burgesses* 63 Wee humbly intreate his Ma[jes]ty will bee pleased to add unto us the continuance of his princely assistance, . . . prohibiting all ratoones and second cropps. **1833** SILLIMAN *Man. Sugar Cane* 12 The canes, or rattoons, as they are called from such fields, are small and short. **1851** *Fla. Plantation Rec.* 367 Ploughed the Rattoon sugar Cain. **1887** *Century Mag.* Nov. 111/1 Next year the cane sprouts from the stubble, and is called first ratoons.

+2. A portion of a stalk of sugar cane suitable for planting; a sugar-cane stump.

1827 *Western Mo. Rev.* I. 82 It is propagated by cuttings or slips of the cane stalk, called rattoons. **1829** SHERWOOD *Gaz. Georgia* 255 Old stumps of cane left in the ground, and covered from frost, will vegetate on the next occurrence of spring . . . : these stumps are called rattoons. **1890** *Congress. Rec.* 9 May 4387/1 Sugar-cane is propagated from cuts called 'rattoons.'

***Ratoon,** *v. intr.* Of plants, esp. sugar cane: To send up a new shoot or sprout from the roots or stubble of a previous growth. {1756–, in Jamaica, etc.} — **1828** in Commons, etc. *Doc. Hist.* I. 289 The cotton . . . ratooned or grew from its roots the following year. **1833** SILLIMAN *Man. Sugar Cane* 14 The rattoons of even the heartiest varieties . . . are so deficient when suffered to rattoon a third year, that [etc.]. **1887** *Century Mag.* Nov. 111/1 On the Upper Coast, above New Orleans, it is customary to let the stubble ratoon but once. **1897** *Kissimmee* (Fla.) *Val-*

ley Gazette 19 May 1/4 Well cared for stubble will rattoon for three years in most parts of this state.

Ratooning. The raising of crops by allowing the plants to ratoon; the natural reproduction of such plants as sugar cane by the springing of new shoots from the old growth. {1790–, in W. Indies} — **1837** WILLIAMS *Terr. of Florida* 106 This rattoning cannot be practised in climates where the frost is sufficiently severe to kill the roots. **1856** OLMSTED *Slave States* 666 In Louisiana it is usual to plant once in three years, trusting to the ratooning for two crops only.

Rat pit. A pit or enclosure for rat fights. {1851–} — **1868** *N.Y. Herald* 28 July 5/4 The proprietor of a rat pit in the First ward held high social carnival with the sporting gentleman of an upper district. **1875** STOWE *We & Neighbors* 338 They bought a place that used to be kept for a rat-pit, and had it cleaned up. **1882** [see GAMBLING 2].

Rat-tail. {1705–}

1. A round, tapering file. In full *rat-tail file.* {1846–}

1744 *Md. Hist. Mag.* XXI. 251, 6 Ratt Tale Files. *a***1861** WINTHROP *J. Brent* 283 Trust him to gnaw himself free with that Connecticut rat-tail. **1891** SWASEY *Early Days Calif.* 128 He procured a . . . quantity of rat-tail files.

2. A fish of the family Macrouridae; a grenadier. Also *rat-tail fish.* (Cf. ONION FISH.)

1882 *Nat. Museum Bul.* No. 16, 811 *M[acrurus] fabricii.* . . . Rat-tail; Grenadier. . . . Massachusetts to Greenland and Norway. **1884** GOODE, etc. *Fisheries* I. 244 The largest species . . . is *Macrurus rupestris,* called 'Rat-tail Fish,' as well as 'onion-fish.'

+**3.** *attrib.* In plant names: (see quotations).

1892 *Amer. Folk-Lore* V. 97 *Mesembryanthemum* sp., dew plant. N. Ohio.; rat-tail pink. Dorchester, Mass. **1893** *Garden & Forest* 11 Oct. 429/1 Tasajo . . . and the Rat-tail Opuntia . . . are represented [in a display of cacti at the Columbian Exposition] by large plants.

Rattan. {1660–}

1. Any one of various climbing plants having tough, pliant stems, or a portion of the stem of such a plant for use in making wickerwork. {1681–}

Cf. SUPPLE-JACK.

1819 E. DANA *Geogr. Sk.* 90 The undergrowth is reed and cane, palmettos, rattan, grape vines and china brier. **1832** *Louisville Pub. Adv.* 1 March, 3 bales chair maker's rattans, just received and for sale. **1860** CURTIS *Woody Plants N.C.* 117 Rattan. Supple Jack. (*Berchemia volubilis.*)—A very tough flexible vine running up trees. . . . Grows from Virginia southward. **1897** *Outing* XXX. 100/2 The Mesinger saddles . . . retain the center opening, beneath which is a weaving of rattan, securing strength, durability and elasticity.

2. =next.

1913 LONDON *Valley of Moon* 492 Mrs. Hale took the tiny rattan beside the big Mission rocker.

Rattan chair. A chair made of the smooth reedlike stems of rattan. — **1879** *Harper's Mag.* July 211 In the large parlor . . . with rattan chairs galore . . . presided Karl Whitaker. **1903** *Smart Set* IX. 25/2 Peter Rathbawne was seated in a deep, rattan chair, watching his daughter.

Ratter. {1834–} A rat-catcher; a dog or cat that catches rats. Also transf. — **1857** S. H. HAMMOND *Northern Scenes* 121 Off at the right was an old spotted ratter [a cat]. **1866** *Ore. State Jrnl.* 24 Nov. 2/2 When a political ratter throws his rake into the stinking pool of the Five Points and brings up the black muck of the bottom, he makes it a point of policy to flatter the said soft matter. **1873** 'MARK TWAIN' & WARNER *Gilded Age* 311 [The dog's] mother had heart disease, but was . . . a wonderful ratter. **1887** *Century Mag.* Sept. 704/1 Against these ravages the company supply a special guardian in the person of the ratter.

Rat terrier. A small dog of any one of various breeds, originally used for hunting small game, esp. rats. {1851–} — **1855** M. THOMPSON *Doesticks* 284 The chief . . . pawned his uniform and star to get money to bet on a rat-terrier. **1865** [see CHICKEN COCK]. **1892** M. A. JACKSON *Gen. Jackson* 393 [His] walls were decorated with pictures of race-horses, fine stock, game-cocks, and a *famous rat-terrier!*

+**Rattinet.** (See quot. 1890.) — **1812** *Niles' Reg.* II. 9/1 Much of it [*i.e.,* wool] . . . may be wrought into *worsted* stuffs, such as shalloons, rattinets, durants. **1890** *Cent.* 4973/3 *Rattinet,* a woolen stuff thinner than ratteen.

***Rattle,** *n.*

+**1.** The jointed organ at the end of a rattlesnake's tail, or one of the articulated cells of which this is composed. Usually pl.

[**1624** SMITH *Gen. Hist. Va.* 30 Those Rattels are somewhat like the chape of a Rapier but lesse, which they take from the taile of a snake.] **1674** JOSSELYN *Two Voyages* 27 [The rattlesnake] had a rattle which is nothing but a hollow shelly bussiness joynted. **1733** BYRD *Journey to Eden* (1901) 293 We kill'd two very large Rattle-snakes, one of 15 and the other of 12 Rattles. **1815** *Niles' Reg.* IX. 152/1 A rattlesnake in the Alleghany mountains . . . had twenty-nine rattles, and must, therefore, have been thirty-two years old. **1890** CUSTER *Following Guidon* 114 When he discovered a snake with seven or more rattles he leaped from his horse. **1904** STRATTON-PORTER *Freckles* 25 He mastered an Irishman's inborn repugnance to snakes sufficiently to cut off his rattles to show to Duncan.

transf. and *attrib.* **1855** SIMMS *Forayers* 317 He is . . . a liquid serpent, who will glide into the porches of your dwelling, and coil himself in a corner, yet sound no rattle. **1869** J. R. BROWNE *Adv. Apache Country* 394, I inquired if these vicious reptiles, of which I had heard so much in Aurora, were of the rattle or copperhead species.

+**b.** The sound made by these when shaken or vibrated.

1851 GLISAN *Jrnl. Army Life* 70 My Comanche horse will jump ten feet at the sudden rattle of one of these reptiles.

***2.** An instrument for making a rattling sound, +used by Indians, esp. on festive occasions or in incantation ceremonies.

1705 BEVERLEY *Virginia* III. 7 In his right Hand is an Indian Rattle. **1809** [see MEDICINE SONG]. **1833** CATLIN *Indians* I. 242 *Rattles* . . . charged with pebbles or something of the kind . . . produce a shrill noise to mark the time in their dances and songs. **1881** *Rep. Indian Affairs* 9 The Indian doctor still holds his sway, with his singing, rattles, tom-toms, and dances.

+**3.** *pl.* A popular name for croup. *Obs.*

1744 HEMPSTEAD *Diary* 434 A Child . . . died of the Rattles or Throat Destemper. **1806** W. PETTIGREW *Let.* 26 Nov. (Univ. N.C. MS.), He was then taken very bad with the rattels.

+**4.** A mild expletive.

1787 TYLER *Contrast* v. i, But what the rattle makes you look so tarnation glum? *Ib.* ii, What the rattle ails you?

+**5.** *pl.* (See quotation.) *colloq.*

Cf. RATTLE *v.* 2.

1888 *Cosmopolitan* Oct. 452/2 The younger players are not infrequently attacked by what in base-ball vernacular is known as 'the rattles,' a complaint much akin to what sportsmen call the 'buck fever,' and actors 'stage fright.'

6. In special combinations.

Rattle bones, =BONE *n.* 2; *r. cap,* an empty-headed, noisy person; *r. dandy,* a fop; *r. gourd,* a gourd fashioned into a rattle.

1848 IRVING *Knickerb.* (rev. ed.) IV. vi, The procession was accompanied by a full band of boys and negroes, performing on the popular instruments of rattle-bones and clam-shells. **1805** *Amer. Pioneer* II. 231, I have never seen a presumptuous talkative rattle-cap or hoyden here. **1845** SIMMS *Wigwam & Cabin* 2 Ser. 156 The parting speech of the negro was not precisely the D.I.O. of the rattle-dandy of fashionable life but was very much like it. **1791** W. BARTRAM *Travels* 505 [The Indians'] music is both vocal and instrumental; but of the latter they have scarcely anything worth the name: the tambour, rattle-gourd, and a kind of flute.

***Rattle,** *v.*

+**1.** *intr.* and *tr.* Of a rattlesnake: To produce a noise by vibrating the rattles; to give (a warning) by this means.

1823 DODDRIDGE *Logan* II. ii, The large snake rattles, and bites. **1850** *Knickerb.* XXXV. 22 [Rattle-snakes] 'rattle' you a warning of their residence. **1888** ROOSEVELT *Century Mag.* June 201/1 One or two [rattle-snakes] coiled and rattled menacingly as I stepped near.

+**2.** *tr.* To confuse, embarrass, or disconcert (a person). *colloq.*

1869 J. R. BROWNE *Adv. Apache Country* 282, I think he was slightly rattled by the formidable appearance of our escort. **1882** PECK *Sunshine* 137 The young man might have been rattled, and powerless to grasp the situation. **1901** GRINNELL *Gold Hunting in Alaska* 58 The opposition was doing its best to 'rattle' me. **1913** RILEY *Eccentric Mr. Clark* 36 That's a thing that always rattles me. **1924** A. J. SMALL *Frozen Gold* 10 Henderson . . . begged his customers not to get rattled.

Rattlebox. {1780–}

+**1.** Any one of various species of *Crotalaria,* esp. *C. sagittalis,* the seeds of which rattle in the pod when ripe.

1817–8 EATON *Botany* (1822) 255 *Crotalaria sagittalis,* rattle-box. **1868** *Rep. Comm. Agric. 1867* 72 The caterpillars of the *Utetheisa* (*Deiopeia*) *bella* . . . feed upon the seeds of the rattle-box, (*Crotalaria.*) generally inside the pod. **1884** *Amer. Naturalist* XVIII. 1148 Experiments lately made . . . prove that *Crotalaria sagittalis,* the Rattle-box, is a 'loco-plant.'

+**2.** The silver-bell tree, *Halesia carolina.*

1884 SARGENT *Rep. Forests* 106 Rattlebox. Snow-drop tree. . . . Reaching its greatest development in the southern Alleghany mountains. **1897** SUDWORTH *Arborescent Flora* 323 Silverbell-tree. . . . Rattlebox (Tex.).

+**3.** The bladder campion, *Silene latifolia.*

1893 *Amer. Folk-Lore* VI. 138 *Silene cucubalus,* rattle-box. Berkshire Co., Mass.

‖**4.** *transf.* The rattles of a rattlesnake.

1913 STRATTON-PORTER *Laddie* i, The only things to be careful about were a little, shiny, slender snake, . . . and a big thick one with . . . a whole rattlebox on its tail.

+**Rattled snake.** +=RATTLESNAKE. *Obs.* — **1748** WASHINGTON *Writings* I. 6 This day see a Rattled snake, ye first we had seen in all our journey.

Rattle pod. +(See quotation.) — **1898** A. M. DAVIDSON *Calif. Plants* 133 There are the 'rattle-pods,' so common in sandy soil; this plant is called loco weed by the stockmen, and is believed to loco horses.

***Rattler.** +=RATTLESNAKE. — **1827** COOPER *Prairie* xxxiii, It would be no easy matter to judge of the temper of the rattler by considering the fashions of the moose. **1836** [see COACHWHIP SNAKE b]. **1880** *Scribner's Mo.* June 223/2 Out from the hole crawled a huge rattler. **1914** 'BOWER' *Flying U Ranch* 132 Say, they hang together like bull snakes and rattlers, don't they?

+Rattlesnake.

1. Any one of various American pit vipers of the family Crotalidae having a tail terminating in a rattle.

There are two genera, *Sistrurus* and *Crotalus*, and many species, all being confined to America. Rattlesnakes vary in size from the small ground rattlesnake or massassauga to the diamond-back, which sometimes attains a length of eight feet. (See also BANDED *a.* 2, quot. 1823, DIAMOND-BACK b, and DIAMOND, GROUND, PRAIRIE RATTLESNAKE.)

1630 HIGGINSON *New-England* 12 There are some Serpents called Rattle Snakes, that haue Rattles in their Tayles. **1672** JOSSELYN *New-Eng. Rarities* 38 The Rattle Snake . . . poysons with a Vapour that comes thorough two crooked Fangs in their Mouth. **1705** *Boston News-Letter* 18 June 2/2 4 of our English Prisoners at Mont-Real . . . were so put to it for Provisions by the way, that they were forced to eat Rattle Snakes. **1790** *Columbian Centinel* 15 Sept. 3/2 A child . . . was bitten by a rattlesnake, and expired the next morning. **1807** GASS *Journal* 113 A rattle-snake came among our canoes in the water. **1883** *Harper's Mag.* Oct. 707/1 The rattle snake recoiled itself. **1923** J. H. COOK *On Old Frontier* 28 There were . . . rattlesnakes too numerous to mention.

b. *transf.* (Cf. COPPERHEAD 5.)

1867 *Wkly. New Mexican* 2 March 2/1 [The] copperhead principle . . . hissed encouragement, in the North during the rebellion, to the less degraded rattlesnake of secession.

2. (See quotation.) *Obs.*

1862 E. McDERMOTT *Pop. Guide Internat. Exhib.* 185 [At] an American bar . . . visitors may indulge in 'juleps,' . . . 'cobblers,' 'rattlesnakes,' 'gum ticklers' [etc.].

3. *attrib.* and *comb.* **a.** In the names of places or objects associated with rattlesnakes.

1666 *Lancaster Rec.* 301 Northardly it is bounded by pine Land and sum Rocky Called Ratel Snake hill. **1724** SEWALL *Letter-Book* II. 172 The Head-Line . . . [runs] from Rattlesnake Rock to Philps's Brook.

b. In the names of, or with reference to, plants in some way suggestive of rattlesnakes or thought to be an antidote to rattlesnake bites.

See also RATTLESNAKE GRASS, RATTLESNAKE MASTER.

1736 FRANKLIN *Poor Richard's Almanac 1737* 3 (*caption*), Rattle-Snake Herb. **1817–8** EATON *Botany* (1822) 294 *Goodyera pubescens*, rattle-snake leaf, scrophula-weed. **1818** *Amer. Jrnl. Science* I. 368 May 15. Rattlesnake violet (*Viola primulifolia*) in full flower.

c. Designating places where rattlesnakes live or abound.

1834 *S. Lit. Messenger* I. 98 To the reputed wonders of rattlesnake dens . . . we cannot testify. **1844** *Knickerb.* XXIV. 188, I found myself in the centre of a large rattle snake patch.

d. In special combinations.

Rattlesnake grease, grease obtained from a rattlesnake; *r. note*, a musical note similar to the rattling or 'singing' of a rattlesnake; *r. oil*, (see quotation); *R. State*, South Carolina (a nickname). Cf. RATTLESNAKE 1 b.

1893 M. A. OWEN *Voodoo Tales* 105 Yo' kin brag on rattlesnake grease . . . twell yo' tongues is all wo' ter frazzles. **1835** LONGSTREET *Ga. Scenes* 134 The tambourine player . . . performed the rattle-snake note with his middle finger. **1847** RUXTON *Adv. Rocky Mts.* (1848) 203 An old crone was busy decocting simples. . . . She asked me to taste it, giving it the name of aciete de vivoras—rattlesnake-oil. . . . It was not really viper-oil, but was so called. **1861** *N.Y. Tribune* 16 Nov. (Chipman), The recent magnificent exploit [at Beaufort, S.C.] on the coast of the Rattlesnake State.

+Rattlesnake fern. A species of grape fern (*Botrychium virginianum*) having sporangia resembling the rattles of a rattlesnake. — **1814** PURSH *Flora Amer.* II. 656 *Botrychium virginicum*. . . . It is known by the name of Rattle Snake Fern. **1839** in *Mich. Agric. Soc. Trans.* VII. 401. **1845** LINCOLN *Botany* App. 82/2 *Botrychium . . . virginicum*, (rattlesnake fern, Ju.)

+Rattlesnake flag. *Hist.* (See quot. 1909.) — **1895** *Stand.* I. a690 (plate), Rattlesnake Flag of the Revolution. **1909** WEBSTER 2067/3 *Rattlesnake flag*, . . . any of several flags bearing a rattlesnake and, usually, the motto 'Don't Tread On Me,' used by the colonies at the outbreak of the Revolution. **1925** T. H. CUMMINGS *First Flag* 3 Some of the southern colonies used a rattlesnake flag with the motto 'Don't tread on me.'

+Rattlesnake grass. A handsome stout species of American grass (*Glyceria canadensis*), the spikelets of which suggest the rattles of the rattlesnake. — **1814** BIGELOW *Florula Bostoniensis* 25 *Briza Canadensis*. Rattlesnake grass. . . . A large grass found in meadows and readily recognized by its swelling spikelets. **1843** TORREY *Flora N.Y.* II. 466. **1878** Killebrew *Tenn. Grasses* 232 *Glyceria Canadensis*, Rattlesnake Grass, . . . resembles quaking grass very much.

+Rattlesnake master. Any of various plants reputed to cure the bite of a rattlesnake, as: **a.** A plant of the genus *Liatris*. (Cf. BLAZING STAR 1.) **b.** The button snakeroot, *Eryngium aquaticum*. **c.** The false aloe, *Manfreda virginica*. Also *rattlesnake master weed*, *rattlesnake's master*. (Cf. MASTER WEED.) — **1835** LATROBE *Rambler in N.A.* I. 126 Every where among the long grass, the *Liatris*, or rattlesnakes'-master shoots up, and displays its spike of red flowers. **1843** MARRYAT *M. Violet* xxiii, Close to my feet I beheld five or six stems of the rattlesnake master weed. **1870** [see BUTTON (RATTLE)SNAKEROOT]. **1890** *Cent.* 4975/1 *Rattlesnake-master*, . . . the false aloe, *Agave Virginica*, said to be so called in South Carolina. **1899** CUSHMAN *Hist. Indians* 229 [The ancient Choctaws] possessed an antidote for the bite and sting of snakes and insects, in the root of a plant called rattle snake's master, having a pungent yet not unpleasant odor.

+Rattlesnake money. Paper money displaying the device of a rattlesnake. *Obs.* — **1803** *Ann. 7th Congress* 2 Sess. 246 We never ought to lose sight of an old Revolutionary motto, on our *rattlesnake money*, 'United we stand, divided we fall.' **1804** *Ann. 8th Congress* 2 Sess. 1595 They were at liberty to pay in paper at that time current in Georgia, (except what was called rattlesnake money.)

+Rattlesnake plantain. Any one of various orchids of the genus *Peramium*, the coloration of whose leaves suggests a rattlesnake. — **1778** CARVER *Travels* 482 Remedies . . . Providence has bounteously supplied, by causing the Rattle Snake Plaintain, an approved antidote to the poison of this creature, to grow in great profusion where-ever they are to be met with. **1789** *Amer. Philos. Soc.* III. p. xix, A species of Jussiæa . . . [grows] in the northern counties near the haunts of rattle-snakes, called Rattle-snake plantain. **1836** EDWARD *Hist. Texas* 42 Then there are the herb varieties . . . [such as] the rattle-snake plantain, the toad plantain. **1897** ROBINSON *Uncle Lisha's Outing* 32 Tangles of hobble bush sprawled over the russet carpet of hemlock leaves, gayly flecked with variegated rattlesnake plantain.

+Rattlesnake-root. Any one of various plants regarded as efficacious in cases of rattlesnake bites.

This term is applied not only to various plants of the genus *Prenanthes* but also to the bugbane (*Cimicifuga racemosa*) and to the seneca (snake) root (*Polygala senega*). See also BUTTON (RATTLE)SNAKEROOT, FERN RATTLESNAKE ROOT.

1682 ASH *Carolina* 11 They have three sorts of the Rattle-Snake Root which I have seen; the Comous or Hairy, the Smooth, the Nodous, or Knotted Root: All which are lactiferous, or yielding a Milkie Juice. **1733** *Georgia Col. Rec.* III. 62 [Received] several Parcels of Sea Rod, Snake Root, Rattle Snake Root. **1792** POPE *Tour S. & W.* 97 Rattle-Snake Root, . . . from its strong aromatic Smell, the Rattle-Snake will never approach, and [it] is accordingly used by the Indians to banish that and other Serpents from their Lodgments. **1806** *Mass. Spy* 30 April (Th.), *Seneca*, or *rattle snake root:* . . . has been celebrated as a specific in the cure of croup. **1889** [see CANCERWEED 2].

+Rattlesnake's cousin. =RATTLESNAKE'S MATE. — **1819** *Niles' Reg.* XVII. 44/2 'A rattlesnake's mate, or cousin' was lately killed at Wilton, R.I.

+Rattlesnake's master. (See RATTLESNAKE MASTER.)

+Rattlesnake's mate. =COPPERHEAD 1. — **1818** *Amer. Jrnl. Science* I. 84 *Scytalus Cupreus*, or Copper-head Snake, . . . [is known] in New-England, by the names of *rattlesnake's mate* and *red adder*. **1819** [see RATTLESNAKE'S COUSIN].

+Rattlesnake's tail. **1.** The tail of a rattlesnake. **2.** A chiton. — (**1**) **1880** *Cimarron News & Press* 22 July 3/1 Hinsdale and Van Dyke are collecting a cabinet of specimens of rattlesnake's tails. (**2**) *a***1884** in Goode, etc. *Fisheries* I. 701 These shells have been called by different names, . . . such as 'Wood-louse,' 'Sea-boat,' 'Rattle-snake's Tail,' 'Lobster's Tail,' 'Sea-bug,' and 'Sea-caterpillar.'

Rattlesnake weed. Any one of various plants reputedly efficacious in the treatment of rattlesnake bites or associated with the rattlesnake in some other way.

The term has been applied to the following plants: the button snakeroot, the hawkweed, the rattlesnake plantain, the rattlebox (qq.v.), a prairie herb (*Daucus pusillus*), and others.

[**1760** J. LEE *Introd. Botany* App. 324 Rattlesnake Weed, *Eryngium*.] **1846** Emory *Military Reconn.* 387 The prairies were covered with tall stalks of the rattlesnake weed, (*rudebeckia purpurea*.) **1878** STOWE *Poganuc People* 214 The Indian doctor . . . brought a bag of rattlesnake-weed with him, and he made poultices of it. **1885** *Outing* Nov. 180/1 A pretty thing sends a creeping feeling down our backs, because it is rattle-snake weed. **1890** *Cent.* 4975/1 *Rattlesnake-weed*, . . . a hawkweed, *Hieracium venosum*, of the eastern half of the United States. . . . The leaves . . . and the root are thought to possess an astringent virtue. **1898** A. M. DAVIDSON *Calif. Plants* 177 One of . . . [the Calif. Euphorbias], rattle-snake weed, is common in the south.

‖**Rattletail snake.** =RATTLESNAKE 1. — **1867** COZZENS *Sayings* 106 A Enormous Rattletail Snake—a regular whopper!

+Rattle-te-bang, Rattlety-bang. A discordant, rattling, banging noise. Also used as *adv.* and *adj. colloq.* — **1824** *Old Colony Memorial* (Plymouth) 6 March (Th.), [He said] as how they had ten thousand rattletraps, and kept up a tarnation sort of rattlety bang. **1870** TALMAGE *Crumbs Swept Up* 194 [With] tin pails appended, . . . the miserable cur went down the street, rattle–te–bang. **1872** *Newton Kansan* 29 Aug. 4/2 The bells should be of the noisy, rattle-te-bang kind. **1889** *Boston Jrnl.* 16 Jan. 2/3 Rattletybang, crash, came a whole assortment of bottles, flasks and cigar boxes.

Rattleweed. {1893–, *dial.*} +The bugbane (*Cimicifuga racemosa*) or an allied plant; a plant of the genus *Astragalus*. — **1791** *Amer. Philos. Soc.* III. 114 *Actæa racemosa* (American Bane-berry, Black Snake-root, Rattle-weed). **1851** GLISAN *Jrnl. Army Life* 70 The rattle-weed . . . derives its name from the fact that its pod is full of loose seed and makes a rattling noise when dry, if touched by the passer-by. **1878** in Summers *Ann. S.W. Va.* 1567 These hill-sides . . . abound with Indian turnips, . . .

rattle-weed, spikenard and copper-head snakes. **1883** *Harper's Mag.* March 503/1 The loco, or rattle-weed, met with also in California, drives them [*sc.* horses] raving crazy. **1893** *Amer. Folk-Lore* VI. 136 *Cimicifuga racemosa*, rattle-weed. Banner Elk, N.C.

Rattoon, *n.* and *v.* (See RATOON *n.* and *v.*; also, RAC(C)OON *n.*)

***Rat trap.** A trap for catching rats. — **1790** *Penna. Packet* 1 March 1/1 This Day . . . Will commence the Sale of a Large and General Assortment of . . . rat traps, . . . gimblets, draw and lifting handles. **1845** *Knickerb.* XXV. 448 After breakfast I went out to look at the . . . long rat-trap, with the bait in the middle. **1897** F. C. MOORE *How to Build a Home* 47 A store-room thus constructed is like a rat-trap.

***Rave.** +(See quots. 1876 and 1905.) Also attrib. — **1847** *Rep. Comm. Patents 1846* 81 The raves are carried in front in such a form as to furnish a frame for the dash-board. **1851** SPRINGER *Forest Life* 106 It was astonishing to see how he [the man] had gnawed the rave of the sled. **1876** KNIGHT 1885/2 *Rave*, . . . one of the side pieces of a wagon-body frame or of a sleigh. **1886** *Scientific Amer.* 27 Feb. 130/2 The rave bolts [in a bobsleigh] extend upward from the runners in front and rear of the knees. **1905** *Forestry Bureau Bul.* No. 61, 44 *Rave*, a piece of iron or wood which secures the beam to the runners of a logging sled. (N[orth] W[oods], L[ake] S[tates Forest].)

* **Raven.** A large black bird of the genus *Corvus*, +as the northern raven, *C. corax principalis*, and the Mexican raven, *C. c. sinuatus*, of the Rocky Mountain region.

1709 LAWSON *Carolina* 139 Ravens, the same as in England, though very few. **1778** CARVER *Travels* 466 The whipperwill, the Raven, the Crow, the Owl, Parrots [etc.]. **1806** LEWIS in *L. & Clark Exped.* IV. (1905) 246 We saw . . . ravens, crows, eagles Vultures and hawks. **1874** COUES *Birds N.W.* 379 These [slaughterings] were high times for the Buzzards, Ravens, wolves, and all the dogs of the neighborhood. **1917** *Birds of Amer.* II. 228/1 One may see Ravens any summer about the garbage piles back of some of the hotels in the Yellowstone and Glacier national parks.

Raven's-duck. A superior quality of duck used for sailcloth. {ravenduck, 1753–} — **1761** *Newport Mercury* 28 April 4/3 Just Imported . . . Russia and ravens duck. **1788** *R.I. Commerce* II. 367 Captain Benjamin Pierce . . . will wait upon you with a letter of credit . . . to furnish him for our Account with . . . Forty eight Pieces of Ravens duck. **1816** *Ann. 14th Congress* 1 Sess. 1873 [The duty on] ravens duck [shall be] . . . one dollar and twenty-five cents. **1876** KNIGHT 1885/2.

***Ravine.** A long hollow, depression, gorge, etc., worn by a stream or torrents. Also attrib. — **1781** WASHINGTON *Diaries* II. 263 We also began two inclosed Works on the right of Pidgeon Hill—between that and the Ravine above Mores Mill. **1805** ORDWAY in *Jrnls. of Lewis & O.* 240 He observed a deep raveen in which was Shelving rocks. **1839** PLUMBE *Sk. Iowa* 31 There is a wild pea which grows on the bottom lands and in the ravines. **1850** SAWYER *Way Sketches* 118 In this region there is two classes of mines, the Coyota and the ravine and creek diggings. **1886** EBBUTT *Emigrant Life* 26 To an inexperienced eye all the little valleys or ravines, as they are called, were strangely alike. **1924** [see CROWD *v.* 2 b].

***Raw,** *n. W.* +An untrained pony. — **1895** *Outing* XXVI. 389/2 The animals are mostly from the Texan and New Mexican mustang herds. They pay for a 'raw' on an average fifty dollars. *Ib.* 476/2 The way to circumvent fancy prices is to buy a 'raw' and make him over into a 'trained.'

***Raw,** *a.* +Of land: Not cleared or opened for cultivation; virgin. Also transf. — **1883** SWEET & KNOX *Through Texas* 282 [He] came to Atascoso County, Texas, and bought a piece of raw land [etc.]. **1901** DUNCAN & SCOTT *Allen & Woodson Co., Kansas* 199 He moved into a board shanty on practically a raw piece of land.

Raw cotton. Cotton that has been ginned but not otherwise processed. {1863–} Cf. GINNED COTTON. — **1835** *S. Lit. Messenger* I. 260 [The Richmond Cotton Manufactory] consumes about 1,500 pounds of raw cotton per day. **1842** TYLER in *Pres. Mess. & P.* IV. 177 The United States consume large quantities of raw cotton. **1850** GARRARD *Wah-To-Yah* xiv. 175 In the pocket is carried a roll of raw cotton . . . bound with calico [for lighting cigarettes]. **1871** [see COTTON GOODS.]

* **Rawhide.**

*1. A fresh or green hide, esp. an untanned or partially tanned cattle skin.

1658 *Plymouth Laws* 119 After December 1658 noe raw hides . . . shalbee transported out of the Govrment. **1791** *Ann. 1st Congress* 2131 Duties [must] be laid on . . . raw hides, beaver, and all other furs. **1801** *Hist. Review & Directory* I. 110 The produce of North Carolina is . . . lumber, tallow, raw hides. **1865** NORTON *Army Lett.* 273 Most of them sleep on raw ox-hides. . . . One sees . . . the families reclining on these rawhides in all stages of dress below semi-nakedness. **1884** [see BOTTOM *v.* 1]. **1923** J. H. COOK *On Old Frontier* 12 It was not many months before I could work up rawhide into saddle rigging, ropes, quirts and reins.

+2. A whip made of rawhide.

Cf. COWHIDE *n.* 2.

1829 *Mass. Spy* 16 Sept. (Th.), She took down a raw hide, and kept the whip moving. **1854** GLISAN *Jrnl. Army Life* 131 He received fifty lashes on the bare back with a rawhide. **1875** *Chicago Tribune* 23 Nov. 7/3 She had a rawhide, and had standing near several who are said to have been invited to witness the cowhiding. **1896** HARRIS *Sister Jane* 273 The rawhide descended with a swishing sound.

+3. A shoe made of rawhide.

1887 *Scribner's Mag.* II. 512/1 Over a pair of stiff, straight boots—jacks, Bluchers, or raw-hides—an Indian is complacently and outrageously exultant.

4. *attrib.* Designating things made of rawhide. **a.** Used of ropes and cords.

See also RAWHIDE ROPE.

1833 CATLIN *Indians* I. 71 The raw-hide thong, with which it [*sc.* the boat] was tied to a stake, had been chewed. **1850** GARRARD *Wah-To-Yah* xvii. 198 He borrowed our rawhide lariats. **1872** MCCLELLAN *Golden State* 346 With the raw-hide reata stretched from the captured animal to the pummel of the saddle, [the horse will] lead the most refractory animal at will. **1907** WHITE *Arizona Nights* 163 The women had belts with raw-hide strings hanging to the knees. **1916** THOBURN *Stand. Hist. Okla.* I. 27 Pulling the cordelle (rawhide towing line) they laboriously ascended the courses of the rivers.

b. Used of receptacles or containers.

1848 Bryant *California* App. 463 The fragments of rock and ore are removed . . . in raw-hide sacks. **1877** HODGE *Arizona* 124 The water that entered the shafts and drifts was packed out by the Mexicans in rawhide buckets. **1885** *Santa Fé Wkly. New Mexican* 1 Oct. 2/6 On exhibition. . . . Two rawhide trunks and a wooden trunk stand 219 years old. **1888** J. J. WEBB *Adventures* 168 He brought out a rawhide bag full of honey.

c. Used of footwear.

1864 *Ladies' Repository* April 202/2 Feet were bare, and had probably never been . . . trammeled with raw-hide brogans. **1901** CHURCHILL *Crisis* 354 He had walked into the country, first providing himself with butternuts and rawhide boots and a bowie-knife.

5. In special combinations.

Rawhide artist, one who uses a branding iron; *R. State*, Texas (a nickname); *r. Texan*, a Texan used to frontier conditions; a 'wild and woolly' Texan.

1894 *Harper's Mag.* Feb. 356/1 A rawhide artist paints HF in the sizzling flesh. **1869** *Overland Mo.* Aug. 130/2 The Rawhide State particularly excels in that fusty savagery of idioms peculiar to the swaggering drawcansirs of the South-west. **1883** SWEET & KNOX *Through Texas* 18, I'm just pining away for a fight. I'm a raw-hide Texan, I am.

+**Rawhide-bottomed,** *a.* Of chairs: Having a bottom or seat made of rawhide. — **1850** LEWIS *La. Swamp Doctor* 149 On a raw-hide-bottomed chair, I sat in that log cabin. **1889** *Harper's Mag.* Dec. 119/1 Old Uncle Dicky Crawls, tilted back against the chimney jamb, in a rawhide-bottomed chair. **1898** CANFIELD *Maid of Frontier* 18 The rawhide-bottomed chairs slightly marked the dirt-floor.

+**Rawhide rope.** A rope made of rawhide. — **1841** FOOTE *Texas* II. 384 [A] lariat [is] a platted raw-hide rope. **1850** GARRARD *Wah-To-Yah* ii 32, I went with a piece of tobacco to an Indian, and by pointing to a neatly plaited rawhide rope, . . . we made an exchange. **1865** PIKE *Scout & Ranger* (1932) 54 One of the men threw a raw-hide rope over the top of the lodge. **1899** CUSHMAN *Hist. Indians* 235 Two of these [packs] were suspended across the saddle by means of rawhide rope one-fourth of an inch in diameter.

+**Rawhiding. 1.** A severe chastisement with a rawhide whip. **2.** (See quotation.) — (1) **1848** *Knickerb.* XVIII. 519 The editor, it was predicted, would catch a raw-hiding before sun-set. (2) **1890** *Columbus Dispatch* 1 July, Those Big Four yardmen . . . do more 'rawhiding' than the men in . . . any other yards. 'Rawhiding' means that they have very hard work to perform.

***Raw silk.** The strong lustrous thread reeled from the cocoons of the silkworm. Also attrib. — **1678** *New Castle Court Rec.* 350 An Inventory of ye goods Belonging to Richard Hunter. 1 Remnant of Sattin Ribbin . . . , a Parcell of Raw silk, 1 silver spone. **1734** *Georgia Col. Rec.* III. 97 [Received] A Trunk containing Eight large Pounds of Raw Silk. **1771** HABERSHAM *Letters* 146 Mr. Wertsch . . . has shipt on board the Snow Industry . . . , 438 lbs Raw Silk. **1866** A. D. WHITNEY *L. Goldthwaite* ii, Two pairs of bright brown raw-silk stockings . . . completed the mountain outfit. **1896** *Atlantic Mo.* May 597/1 Her form . . . was swathed in a clinging raw-silk dust-cloak.

+**Raw trotter.** (See quotation.) — **1843** MARRYAT *M. Violet* xxxvi, When the traveller is a 'raw trotter' or a 'green one' (Arkansas' denomination for a stranger), the host employs all his cunning to ascertain if his guest has any money.

***Ray.** Any of various fishes of the order Batoidei: (see quot. 1911). Also with defining terms. — **1588** HARRIOT *Briefe Rep. Va.* D3 There are also Troutes: Porpoises: Rayes. **1766** STORK *Acct. E. Florida* 52 Those mostly made use of, are the bass, mullet, different sorts of rays [etc.]. **1814** MITCHILL *Fishes N.Y.* 477 Ocellated Ray. *Raja ocellata*. . . . One of these fishes . . . was thirty inches long. **1842** *Nat. Hist. N.Y., Zoology* IV. 369 The Spotted Ray, *Raia ocellata*, . . . is caught with the hook on our sandy coast, in company with the Cod. **1911** *Rep. Fisheries 1908* 314/1 Ray (*Raiæ*).—A general name given to a large group of fishes found on all our coasts. They are also called 'skates,' 'torpedoes,' 'devil-fishes,' etc.

Ray grass. A perennial meadow and pasture grass, *Lolium perenne*. {1677–} Also attrib. and with defining term. (Cf. RYE GRASS.) — **1761** WASHINGTON *Diaries* I. 178 Sowed a Bushell of Ray grass seed. **1781–2** JEFFERSON *Notes Va.* (1788) 40 Our grasses are lucerne, . . . timothy, ray and orchard grass. **1814** BIGELOW *Florula Bostoniensis* 27 Ray grass. Darnel. . . . May, June. Perennial. **1855** BROWNE in *Amer. Inst. N.Y. Inst. 1854* 619 The 'Improved Ray grass' possesses several desirable properties. **1901** MOHR *Plant Life Ala.* 827 *Lolium perenne.* English Ray Grass.

*** Razor.**

***1.** A sharp-edged instrument used for shaving hair from the skin.

1678 *New Castle Court Rec.* 350 An Inventory of ye goods Belonging to Richard Hunter. . . . 1 Razer & a hoane [etc.]. **1711** *Springfield Rec.* II. 39 An Inventory of the Estate of John Maillefaud. . . . One Dozen of Raisors at one shilling 4 pence the raisor. **1798** HAWKINS *Letters* 301 If our beloved man had not taken my knife, raisor and moccasin all from me, I should have put myself to death. **1812** in J. Cutler *Descr. Ohio* 164, I was permitted to take . . . my papers, a razor and a lappo coat. **1872** McCLELLAN *Golden State* 127 Razors were out of use: no time to shave. **1904** WALLER *Wood-Carver* 20, I had never seen a razor.

+b. In figurative expression.

*c***1849** PAIGE *Dow's Sermons* I. 52 [The violet] is always blue—'blue as a razor'—though never intoxicated, except seemingly with delight.

+2. (See quot. 1848.) *slang. Obs.*

1848 *Yale Lit. Mag.* XIII. 283 (Th.), A pun, in the elegant College dialect, is called a razor, while an attempt at a pun is called a sick razor. **1849** *Yale Tomahawk* Nov., The meeting will be opened with razors by the Society's jester. **1849** *Gallinipper* Dec. (Hall), All armed with squibs, stale jokes, dull razors, puns.

3. *attrib.* and *comb.* **a.** With *box, case, factory,* etc.

1670 *R.I. Col. Rec.* II. 346 Your rasour case I have sent for. **1789** *Boston Directory* 184 Fillis William, razor-grinder. **1803** BOWNE *Life* 174, I saw the famous musician . . . this morning with the razor-box in his hand to shave some of the gentlemen. **1821** *Amer. Jrnl. Science* III. 26 A quarry of razor hones . . . has been opened for several years past. **1851** B. ALCOTT *Journals* 239 One might establish potteries and razor factories to advantage on these premises.

b. *Razor handle,* + = RAZOR CLAM.

1835 AUDUBON *Ornith. Biog.* III. 182, I have seen it [*i.e.*, the Oyster-Catcher] . . . take up a 'razor-handle' or solen, and lash it against the sands until the shell was broken and the contents swallowed.

Razorback. {1832–}

1. = RAZORBACK HOG. {1867–}

Cf. CAROLINA RACE-HORSE, LAND PIKE 2.

1879 *Diseases of Swine* 189, I have not learned of a single person [in St. Johns Co., Fla.] having an improved breed of pigs. All depend on the 'razor-back' or 'land pike.' **1897** *Outing* XXX. 377/2 He hath an appetite that can make a Florida razor-back jealous. **1901** *Munsey's Mag.* XXIV. 494/1 Queer hogs those would seem. . . . In the vernacular of the South, they were razor backs. **1906** PRINGLE *Rice Planter* 403 It is a complete razor back and I don't want it, but Jim . . . told me he would pay the dollar and take the hog. **1923** J. H. COOK *On Old Frontier* 27 There were numerous hogs in these jungles [in Texas] besides the javalinas—regular old razor-backs.

attrib. **1897** *Outing* XXIX. 542/1 Just fancy springing an old-gold shoat of the Florida razorback strain upon the astute gentlemen who are most interested in the big trails! **1916** THOBURN *Stand. Hist. Okla.* I. 262 In all parts of the country [were found] . . . the half-wild, 'razor-back' swine in great abundance.

+2. (See quotations.)

1886 *Nat. Museum Proc.* VIII. 13 *Ictiobus urus,* Agassiz. Razor-back Buffalo. **1888** GOODE *Amer. Fishes* 69 [The Strawberry Perch] is also called 'Bar-fish,' 'Razor Back.' **1896** JORDAN & EVERMANN *Check-List Fishes* 241 *Xyrauchen cypho.* Razor-back Sucker; Hump-backed Sucker.

Razorback hog. An inferior sharp-backed, long-legged hog or breed of hogs, usually neglected and living in a half-wild state in the woods. Also *razor-backed hog.* — **1882** SWEET & KNOX *Texas Siftings* 17 To the traveller through Texas one of the strangest and most peculiar features of the landscape is the razor-back hog. **1888** SHERIDAN *Memoirs* I. 52 [He] protected the camp from the intrusions and ravages of a drove of *razor-backed hogs* which belonged to Mr. Switzler. **1900** BRUNCKEN *N. Amer. Forests* 99 All this, of course, is done for the benefit of browsing cattle, and especially that pest of southern woodlands, the razor-back hog. **1912** COBB *Back Home* 301 The timber was full of razor back hogs stropping themselves against the tree boles. **1923** COOK *On Old Frontier* 187 A number of old razor-back hogs that were about the place located and feasted upon the dead Indians.

Razorbill. a. = RAZOR-BILLED AUK. {1674–} **b.** The black skimmer, *Rhynchops nigra.* — **1743** CATESBY *Carolina* II. p. xxxvi, European Water-Fowls, which I have observed to be also Inhabitants of America: . . . Razor-bill. The Woodcock. Snipes. **1791** BARTRAM *Travels* 295 *Rhynchops niger;* the shearwater or razor bill. **1828** BONAPARTE *Synopsis* 431 The Razor-bill . . . inhabits the north of both continents. **1844** *Nat. Hist. N.Y., Zoology* II. 284 The *Razorbill* appears along the coast of this State. *Ib.* 297 [The] Razor-bill, Cutwater, Flood Gull, . . . for it [the black skimmer, *Rhynchops nigra*] is known under all these names, reaches our coast from Tropical America in May. **1917** *Birds of Amer.* I. 29.

Razor-billed auk. An auk (*Alca torda*) sometimes found as far south as Virginia and North Carolina. {1824–} — **1835** AUDUBON *Ornith. Biog.* III. 112 The food of the Razor-billed Auk consists of shrimps, various other marine animals, and small fishes. **1858** BAIRD *Birds Pacific Ry.* 901 The razor-billed auk. . . . *Hab.* Northeastern coast of America; Newfoundland; Labrador, and south in winter to New Jersey. **1917** *Birds of Amer.* I. 29/1 The Razor-billed Auk presents a striking and interesting appearance in the water.

+Razor clam. One of various mollusks of the family Solenidae, esp. *Ensis directus,* having a long, narrow shell; a knife-handle or long clam (sense b). (Cf. RAZOR 3 b, RAZOR FISH 1.) — **1882** SIMMONDS *Dict. Useful Animals, Razor fish,* in America *Solen ensis* is called the razor clam. **1884** *Boston Jrnl.* 18 Oct. 2/3 The list of delicacies this year included alligator, razor-clams, octopus [and] king-crab. **1911** [see RAZOR FISH 1].

Razor fish. 1. = RAZOR CLAM. {1602–} **2.** The Bermuda chub (*Kyphosus sectatrix*). **3.** A fish of the West Indies, *Xyrichthys psittacus.* {1753, of a related fish in the Mediterranean.} — **(1) 1637** MORTON *New Canaan* 91 Raser fishes there are. **1883** [see KNIFE-HANDLE]. **1911** *Rep. Fisheries 1908* 314/1 Razor-shell (*Ensis directus*). . . . It is also called 'razor-fish,' 'razor-clam,' 'knife-handle,' etc. **(2) 1842** *Nat. Hist. N.Y., Zoology* IV. 100 The Razor-fish . . . appears along our southern shores. **(3) 1883** *Nat. Museum Bul.* No. 27, 436 *Xyrichthys lineatus.* . . . Razor-fish. West Indies; west Florida.

Razor shell. The razor clam or the shell of this. {1752–} — **1792** BELKNAP *Hist. New-Hampshire* III. 183 There are many other fresh and salt water fishes. . . . Hog Clam, *Mya arenaria.* Razor Shell Clam, *Solen ensis.* Long Shell Clam, *Solen radiatis.* **1843** *Nat. Hist. N.Y., Zoology* VI. 242 This is the common Razor-shell of our shores. **1884** [see KNIFE-HANDLE]. **1911** *Rep. Fisheries 1908* 314/1 [The] Razor-shell . . . is a common inhabitant of sand bars and sand flats in New England.

Razor strop. A strop or strap, usually of leather, used in sharpening a razor. {1789– (*Times* 28 Apr.)} — **1759** *Newport Mercury* 26 June 4/3 Hones, Razor-strops &c. **1800** *Columbian Centinel* 8 Feb. 3/4 Have you never used Hopkins Razor Strops? **1857** *Quinland* I. 119 A razor-strop [was] sticking out of one trousers pocket.

*** Reach.**

***1.** A long straight stretch in a river.

1607 in Smith *Works* p. xlii, Now we passed a Reach of. 3. mile ½. in length. **1685** *Conn. Rec.* III. 338 Our course . . . brought us to ye Northernmost end of a Reach of Hudson's River. **1765** CROGHAN *Journal* (1904) 129 We enter the long reach where the [Ohio] river runs a straight course for twenty miles. **1808** PIKE *Sources Miss.* 11 After making two short reaches, we commenced one, which is 30 miles in length. **1888** WARNER *On Horseback* 134 The stream winds through them [the hills], with many a pretty turn and 'reach.' **1907** *St. Nicholas* Oct. 1076/2 They ran down to Silver Cove in a series of long reaches and then came back up the river before the wind.

+b. The land or region along such a place in a river.

1808 ASHE *Travels* 119 The shrubs distinguishing the Reach, are the arbutus and the honey locust. *Ib.*, The reach (to use the old man's words) is moderate healthy.

+2. A peninsula-like piece of land in a bend in a river.

1844 FEATHERSTONHAUGH *Slave States* 131/1 Many long but narrow *reaches* of land, as they are called, are formed.

+3. The coupling pole of a wagon.

1876 KNIGHT 1887/1 *Reach,* . . . a pole connecting the rear axle to the *bolster* of a road-wagon. A *coupling-pole.* **1897** LEWIS *Wolfville* 173 At last I ups an' make a hammock outen a Navajo blanket, which is good an' strong, an' swings the Colonel to the reach of the trail wagon. **1903** A. ADAMS *Log of Cowboy* 330 He ordered the wagon unloaded and the reach lengthened.

+4. A well sweep.

1887 FREDERIC *Seth's Brother's Wife* 144 The fences had been rebuilt, the farm yard cleaned up and sodded, the old well-curb and reach removed.

*** Read,** *v.*

1. *To read out,* to expel from a church, political party, etc., as if by reading a sentence of expulsion. {1865}

1836 DUNLAP *Mem. Water Drinker* (1837) I. 201 He was left in possession of some property, which he dissipated even before he 'was read out of meeting.' **1870** *Nation* 3 Feb. 66/1 His attack on Mr. Dawes, . . . being in the nature of an attempt to 'read him out' of the Republican party, was . . . absurd as well as unseemly. **1890** *Harper's Mag.* Feb. 349/2 They said I wasn't no Christian; and so they got together and read me out o' the church.

2. *To read up,* to acquire information *on* a subject by reading. {1847} Also transf.

1851 HALL *College Words* 253 Students often speak of *reading up,* i.e. preparing themselves to write on a subject, by reading the works of authors who have treated of it. **1869** 'MARK TWAIN' *Innocents* 147, I shall throttle down my emotions hereafter, about this sort of people, until I have read them up, and know whether they are entitled to any tearful attentions or not. **1880** — *Tramp Abroad* 459, I am not so ignorant about glacial movement, now. . . . I have 'read up' since. **1889** *Century Mag.* March 660/2, I took the oldest of the local papers . . . and prepared . . . , to use a familiar phrase, to 'read up.'

*** Reader.**

***1.** One appointed to read the lessons or other parts of a church service. *Obs.*

1676 *New Castle Court Rec.* 28 Upon the Peticon of Emilius de Ring Reader in the Church—The Court ordered that [etc.]. **1701** *N.C. Col. Rec.* I. 544 Ordered that the Church Wardens provide a reader. **1708** *Ib.*

679 Ordered that Mr. Nicholas Crisp agree . . . to officiate as a Reader in the Chapel.

+**b.** *Christian Science.* One of the two members elected to conduct the services of a Christian Science church or society. See also FIRST READER 2, SECOND READER.

1895 EDDY in *Church Manual* 18 The readers must devote a suitable portion of their time to preparation for reading the Sunday lesson. **1900** *Granite Mo.* May, This lesson is read alternately from the books, the Bible and the textbook, by two readers, a man and a woman.

+**2.** One accustomed or trained to read or recite in public. Cf. ELOCUTIONIST.

1869 'MARK TWAIN' *Innocents* 92 The 'Reader' . . . rose up and read the same old Declaration of Independence. **1880** — *Tramp Abroad* 402 The public reciter or 'reader' . . . goes around trying to imitate the sounds of the various sorts of bells with his voice. **1915** J. R. SCOTT *Technic of Speaking Voice* 591 To the speaker, and much more to the reader, bearing takes precedence of gesture.

3. A book to assist children in learning to read by supplying exercises and directions suited to their capacities. Also attrib. {1799-}

1873 PHELPS *Trotty's Wedding* i, It was not until Miss Merle Higgins came into Fourth Reader that he went to Indiana to apply for a divorce. **1902** C. MORRIS *Stage Confidences* 165 [When] disaster in the way of missing blocks of rubber, broken slate pencils, or ink-stained reader covers sent floods of tears down small faces, this teacher always came to the rescue. **1912** [see BLUE BOOK 1].

* **Reading.** In special combinations.

Reading club, a club of those desirous of self-improvement through reading (cf. READING CIRCLE, READING SOCIETY); *r. master,* a master or teacher of reading; *r. party,* a party at which reading aloud is the chief diversion; *r. voice,* the voice or manner of expression used in reading aloud.

1877 PHELPS *Story of Avis* 9 What was the use of reading-clubs . . . if one could not tell whether one owed an idea to an old Greek, or an evening caller? **1686** *Boston Rec.* 191 The President & Councill doe Order . . . [that they] mainetaine an able reading and Writinge Master. **1871** STOWE *Pink & White Tyranny* 208 Lillie had declared that reading aloud was a bore, which was definitive against reading-parties. **1825** NEAL *Bro. Jonathan* I. 91 You have read it, without any consideration for us; . . . in your reading voice.

Reading circle. A group or society composed of those interested in reading for self-improvement. {1909-} — **1871** STOWE *Pink & White Tyranny* 124 They would get up their reading-circles, and he would set her to improving her mind. **1882** 'M. HARLAND' *Eve's Daughters* 67 Contrive tea-parties, charades, reading-circles, and the like pretty imitations of the amusements of their elders.

Reading class. A class made up of pupils in reading. — **1838** FULLER *Woman in 19th C.* (1855) 347 The forwardness of their minds has induced me to take both into my reading-class. **1848** *Knickerb.* XVIII. 67 The bustle of the reading-class returning to their seats had not subsided. **1883** *Harper's Mag.* Sept. 648/1 That rather old young reading class in District Number Three. **1901** *Ib.* Dec. 30/1 Yesterday they had held the same book in the reading-class.

Reading clerk. {1788-} In a legislative body, a clerk who reads aloud bills under consideration. — **1865** in Hart *Amer. Hist. Contemporaries* IV. 466 The roll is called over by the Reading Clerk.

Reading matter. In periodical literature, matter for continuous reading as distinguished from advertisements, notices, etc.; magazines, newspapers, etc. {1884} — **1875** 'MARK TWAIN' *Old Times* ix. 58 These were not pictures at all, but the grimmest and most dead-earnest of reading matter. **1920** *3d Nat. Country Life Conf. Proc.* 101 A literature table exhibited the best reading matter for the farm home.

Reading room. A room for reading, usually one provided with books, newspapers, etc., for public use. {1759-} — **1809** CUMING *Western Tour* 166 There is a coffee house here [in Lexington, Ky.], where is a reading room for the benefit of subscribers and strangers. **1852** *Harper's Mag.* Dec. 116/1 He is always in the reading-room of [the Society Library]. **1883** FULTON *Sam Hobart* 46 The time for free libraries and free reading-rooms had not come. **1911** *Okla. Session Laws* 3 Legisl. 201 The city council of any city of the first class in this state shall have power to establish and maintain a public library and reading room.

Reading school. A school in which attention is devoted wholly or chiefly to reading. — **1707** *Springfield Rec.* II. 74 The law of the Province obliges this Town to keep & maintain a Gramer School writing school & reading School. **1715** *Boston Rec.* 119 Voted. That the Motions made by Collo. Adam Winthrop abt. Reading Schools . . . , be Continued to ye next meeting. **1823** B. A. GOULD *System Educ. Free Schools Boston* 10 The Master of the grammar or reading school.

Reading society. =READING CIRCLE. {1797-} — **1822** *Missionary Herald* XVIII. 52 Gilmantown, N.H. Female Reading Society . . . [gave $]7.00. **1870** [see LITERARY CLUB]. **1883** *Century Mag.* May 156/1 Two book clubs, and several musical associations and reading societies keep . . . this one village from . . . intellectual stagnation.

Readjuster. {1862-} +A member of a political party in Virginia (1878-83) which sought legislative readjustment of the state debt. Now hist. Also attrib. (Cf. FUNDER.) — **1879** *Nation* 13 Nov. 317 Further news from Virginia indicates that the Repudiators, or Readjusters, as they call themselves, have elected a majority of the General Assembly. **1881** [see GRIPSACK b]. **1888** BRYCE *Amer. Commw.* II. II. xlvi. 202 In Virginia the question of repudiating the State debt gave birth a few years ago to a party which called itself the '*Readjusters*.' **1914** *Cycl. Amer. Govt.* I. 572/2 In Virginia [in 1880] there were two tickets, those of the 'regulars' and the 'readjusters.'

Readmission. {1655-} The action of admitting again; +the restoration of one of the seceding Southern states to its place in the Federal Union after the Civil War. — **1864** *Ore. State Jrnl.* 24 Dec. 3/1 A resolution was offered providing for the re-admission of Louisiana into the Union. **1865** C. SCHURZ in *39th Congress. 1 Sess.* Sen. Ex. Doc. No. 2, 44 The only manner in which, in my opinion, the southern people can be induced to grant to the freedman some measure of self-protecting power in the form of suffrage, is to make it a condition precedent to 'readmission.'

Ready. {1688-} +The state of being ready or prepared. *colloq.* — **1878** B. F. TAYLOR *Between Gates* 71 A time hardly long enough for a century plant to get a good ready for blossoming. **1883** 'MARK TWAIN' *Life on Miss.* li, We backed out and 'straightened up' for the start—the boat pausing for a 'good ready.' **1897** LEWIS *Wolfville* 2 So we begins to draw in our belts an' get a big ready.

Real, *n.* =RIAL. {1611-} Also attrib. — **1692** SEWALL *Letter-Book* I. 6 For loss in . . . Peru Reals, and want of weight, I charge but 9s. though 'twas more. **1705** — *Diary* II. 121, I admitted it: gave him 3 Reals. **1850** COLTON *3 Years Calif.* 35 Neither of them has a real in his pocket.

Real, *adv.* Very. *colloq.*[2] {1658-} 'Chiefly *Sc.* and *U.S.*' (*O.E.D.*). — **1827** [see BASKET 2 b]. *c***1849** PAIGE *Dow's Sermons* I. 147 One [girl] thought me real mean for uttering such super-diabolical sentiments. **1891** [see CHIPPER *v.* 2]. **1920** MULFORD *J. Nelson* 216 They're real handy—an' chute brandin' shore saves a lot of time.

Real estate.

1. Immovable or fixed property, as houses and lands. {1711-}

'In Eng. *real estate* is a legal term only. In Am. it is an everyday business term also' (Horwill).

1666 *Conn. Rec.* II. 39 Great inconvenience . . . may ensue to orphanes whose parents . . . were possessed wth a reall estate of houseing & lands. **1711** *Boston Rec.* 77 Voted . . . yt they Lay out . . . money in Some Real Estate for the use of the Publick Lattin School. **1788** *Mass. Spy* 3 April 3/4 To be sold, . . . Two thirds of the Real Estate of Capt. Adam Maynard. **1822** *Ann. 17th Congress* 1 Sess. I. 104 The effect is . . . to establish their municipal code as to real estate. **1880** *Harper's Mag.* Nov. 959/2 The Captain had acquired considerable experience in the business of managing real estate. **1918** [see ESCHEAT *n.* 2].

+**b.** (See quotation.) *Obs.*

1857 BENTON *Exam. Dred Scott Case* 19 In some States, as in Virginia, and others, slaves are only chattels: in others, as in Kentucky and Louisiana, they are real estate.

+**2.** *attrib.* and *comb.* **a.** Designating places, institutions, and commercial activities or pursuits connected with or dealing in real estate.

1843 *Niles' Nat. Reg.* 4 March 5 Real estate bank. . . . A committee of the legislature of Arkansas have reported the facts connected with the management of this institution. **1849** *Knickerb.* XXXIII. 174 His father had recently made some 'heavy' real-estate purchases. **1879** STOCKTON *Rudder Grange* i, Euphemia sometimes went with me on my expeditions to real estate offices. **1885** *Century Mag.* Aug. 600/1 Congress enacted the law which has served us ever since as an excuse and a precedent in our real-estate transactions with the red man. **1887** *Courier-Journal* 3 May 4/3 The leading dailies are publishing stunning accounts of the real-estate boom. **1888** *Economist* 20 Oct. 9/3 In addition to all the other advantages of this branch of the real-estate business, it is wise [etc.].

b. Designating persons having to do with real estate.

1856 MACLEOD *F. Wood* 191 Indeed, there are few real estate owners, with families, who cannot get their whole tax returned. **1903** *Chicago Chronicle* 11 April 1 For many years he was one of the prominent real estate dealers of Chicago. **1917** [see BOOMER[1] 1]. **1923** HERRICK *Lilla* 79 The real estate promoter . . . showed evidence of a certain indulgence.

c. Designating commercial securities and taxes based on real estate.

1871 GROSVENOR *Protection* 37 Enormous sums were loaned upon real-estate security. **1887** *Courier-Journal* 3 May 8/4 They will continue to buy and sell stocks, bonds and real estate paper. **1905** *Omaha Bee* 10 Jan. 3 In the city of O'Neill there is delinquent real estate taxes to the amount of more than $80,000.

+**Real-estate agent.** An agent concerned in the purchase or sale of real estate; a dealer in real estate. Often facetious or jocular. — **1850** SAWYER *Way Sketches* 114 The cities appear on maps suspended from the offices of 'real estate agents,' as large and as well as New York or London. **1872** *Billings' Farmer's Allminax* 8 The yung female born during this month . . . will finally marry a real estate agent. **1894** *Harper's Mag.* Oct. 806/2 'Ladies and gentlemen,' began Colonel Handy Polk, the well-known real-estate agent. **1908** 'O. HENRY' *Options* 5 He was a man about the size of a real-estate agent.

+**Real-estate broker.** A broker who deals in real estate. — **1857** *Lawrence Republican* 4 June 1 Ladd & Prentiss, Real Estate Brokers and General Land Agents. **1882** *Nation* 6 July 4/3 James E. Mallory, a real-estate broker, died soon after the accident. **1884** HOWELLS *Silas Lapham* v, It seems to me that it is about time for you to open out as a real-estate broker.

+**Real-estate man.** A man engaged in the buying and selling of real estate. — **1882** McCabe *New York* 278 Real estate men and diamond merchants like [Nassau St.]. **1892** *Courier-Journal* 4 Oct. 1/7 Buffalo real estate men are making every arrangement to take care of the gathering. **1896** *Home Missionary* Nov. 341 Immigration into that region was greatly stimulated by real estate men.

+**Real-estate speculator.** One who makes speculations in real estate. — **1873** *Harper's Mag.* Feb. 473/2 Samuel N. Pike, the well-known real estate speculator, died in New York city. **1878** [see Colony 7 c]. **1880** *Harper's Mag.* Sept. 562 This region . . . was seized upon by real-estate speculators.

Realize, *v.* {1611–}

+**1.** *tr.* To pass through or have actual experience of. *Obs.*

1776 A. Adams *Familiar Letters* 138 To-night we shall realize a more terrible scene still. **1791** Washington *Writings* XII. 62, [I hope] that you may find it [*i.e.*, national happiness] in your nation, and realize it yourself.

2. To conceive of as being real; to apprehend or understand clearly. {1775–}

Formerly chiefly American, and often condemned by English writers about the middle of the nineteenth century, as shown in the second group of examples.

(1) **1781** Schuyler in Sparks *Corr. Revol.* III. 281 My heart realizes your feelings on the occasion. **1795** Sullivan *Hist. Maine* 232 There was a peculiarity of thinking in that age, both in Europe and America, which we can hardly realize at this day. **1819** Irving *Sketch Bk.* No. 1, 49 She cannot realize the change we must undergo. **1866** H. Phillips *Hist. Sk. Paper Currency* II. 93 Congress scarcely realized the magnitude of the situation. **1918** Lincoln *Shavings* 329 Well, as I was saying, I realized it all, but I didn't care so much.

(2) **1841** G. Combe *Notes U.S.* I. 28 It is difficult to 'realize,' as the Americans express it, the idea of being so far from home. **1856** Martineau *Autobiog.* II. 438 They *must* be wrong in 'realizing' (as one would say in America) the First Cause.

Realizing, *a.* {1768–} +*Realizing sense*, a sense of actuality, reality, or familiarity. — **1806** Vaill in I. Parsons *Mem. J. Vaill* 95, I have . . . a fixed and realizing sense of the truths contained in the word of God. **1853** Motley *Correspondence* I. 163 It gives a 'realising sense,' as the Americans have it. **1883** *Harper's Mag.* April 688/2 [We] proceeded to get a realizing sense of the quaint . . . Market Square. **1898** H. Harland *Comedies & Errors* 87 (*Cent.*), Since he had no 'realizing sense' of men, how could he hold men?

***Realm.** +In the two Ku-Klux Klans, a district or state under the authority of a Grand Dragon. — **1868** in *Century Mag.* XXVIII. 409/1 By order of the G.D., Realm No. 1. **1877** [see Grand cyclops]. **1884** *Century Mag.* July 405 These officers [of the Ku-Klux Klan] were: . . . The Grand Dragon of the Realm and his eight Hydras [etc.]. **1924** [see Ku-Klux Klan b].

Reannexation. The action of reannexing {1866}, +with reference to the proposed acquisition by the United States in the annexation of Texas of several Mexican provinces on the left bank of the Rio Grande River. *Obs.* Also transf. — **1844** in *Whig Almanac 1846* 30/1 These former provinces of the Mexican Vice-royalty, . . . we now propose to incorporate, so far as they lie on the left bank of the river, into our Union, by virtue of a treaty of re-annexation with Texas. **1846** Corcoran *Pickings* 148 In fact, your honour, I'm as much in favour of reannexation as President Tyler himself.

***Reaper.** =Reaping machine. {1862–}

1851 *Living Age* XXXI. 239/2 It is wonderful how well the American reaper does its work. **1858** *Texas Almanac 1859* 75 Patent reapers are now coming into general use. **1870** *Republican Rev.* 10 Dec. 2/2 A bran new mower and reaper is for sale at Salvador Armijo's store, . . . and is the first we have ever seen in this part of the country. **1884** [see Director 2]. **1923** Herrick *Lilla* 238 But there are tractors and reapers and sprayers.

attrib. **1868** *Iowa State Agric. Soc. Rep. 1867* 237 By the folding arrangement the driver can fold the reaper-bar . . . rendering it perfectly portable.

b. *Reaper-and-binder*, a reaping machine that binds as well as cuts standing grain.

1894 Warner *Golden House* ix, He's got no more feeling in business than a reaper-and-binder.

***Reap hook.** A tool for reaping having a sharp, curved blade and a short handle.

1642 *Md. Archives* IV. 97 Inventary of mr John Cockshott's goods. . . . A reap hook, a mincing knife [etc.]. **1714** *Boston News-Letter* 18 Oct. 2/2 To be Sold by Mr. Jonathan Belcher . . . Sickles and Reap Hoops [*sic*]. **1786** Washington *Diaries* III. 83 Immediately set to cutting the heads with reap hooks. **1857** *Ill. Agric. Soc. Trans.* II. 354 The wheat crop [in the French settlements in s. Ill.] . . . was cut with the sickles, or reap hooks, as no cradles existed in those times. **1903** Pringle *Rice Planter* 36 Thursday the field was cut down by the hands with small reap-hooks.

+**Reaping frolic.** A social gathering of neighbors to assist one of their number in harvesting. *Obs.* (Cf. Frolic 2.) — **1774** Cresswell *Journal* 26 What they call a reaping frolic . . . is a Harvest Feast. **1822** Woods *English Prairie* (1904) 300 Reaping frolics, are parties to reap the whole growth of wheat, &c. in one day. **1833** Martineau *Illust. Polit. Econ.* VIII. 1. 18 They meant to have a reaping frolic when the corn should be ripe.

Reaping hook. =Reap hook. {1700–} — **1638** *Md. Council Proc.* I. 76, I have seised . . . a reaping hooke [and] 5. dozen of truck-knives. **1730** *Md. Hist. Mag.* XIX. 185 To Mr. Phil Smith merc[han]t . . . 1 Dozen. Reaping hooks. **1870** *Rep. Comm. Agric. 1869* 451 Those who don't mow with the hoe do so with the reaping hook. **1887** *Century Mag.* Oct. 863/2 He did not drive the work, but . . . led the cradles and the reaping-hooks.

Reaping machine. A horse-drawn machine for harvesting standing grain crops; a harvester. {1812–} Cf. Mowing machine. — **1826** *19th Congress 1 Sess.* H. R. Doc. No. 22, 19 Improvement . . . in the reaping and cutting machine. **1838** Ellsworth *Valley of Wabash* 68 Another material reduction, of the expense . . . , will be found in the use of some of the mowing and reaping machines recently invented. **1852** *Mich. Agric. Soc. Trans.* III. 156 A reaping machine . . . [is] almost a necessary implement to the farmer. **1870** *Rep. Comm. Agric. 1869* 326 The beginning of the year found reaping and mowing machines with numerous defects. **1887** [see Cotton gin].

Rear,** *v. To rear up*, +to act up or cause trouble. *colloq.* — *a1841** Hawes *Sporting Scenes* I. 74 Pardon, pardon, boys, for rearing up and caracoling, in this irregular fashion. **1886** James *Bostonians* 102 Mrs. Farrinder was liable to rear up, as they used to say down in Pennsylvania.

***Rear admiral.** A flag officer in the navy ranking next below a vice admiral: +**a.** As provided for in the Continental navy. +**b.** As actually commissioned in the United States Navy after the passage of the act of July 16, 1862. — **1776** [see Admiral 1]. **1862** *Rep. Secy. Navy* 39 The officers of our blockading squadrons and of the Mississippi flotilla were recognized flag-officers until the passage of the act of the 16th of July establishing the grade of rear admiral, when they received that appointment. **1900** *Congress. Rec.* 11 Jan. 787/2 Albert Kautz [was promoted] to be a rear-admiral in the Navy. **1918** *Current Opinion* Oct. 222/3 Rear-Admiral Niblack is in command of Squadron Two of the American Patrol Fleet.

‖**Rearage.** =Arrearage 2. — **1779** *Essex Inst. Coll.* XXI. 280 Voted the Parish Rates to be Two Hundred Pounds . . . to Pay of old Rearerges that the Parish ows.

+**Rear crew.** The men who work at the rear of a log drive. — **1893** *Scribner's Mag.* June 715/1 Behind them follows the 'rear crew,' the name indicating the work they do.

+**Rear-horse.** A mantis, esp. *Stagomantis carolina.* — **1869** *Rep. Comm. Agric. 1868* 308 The *Mantes* or 'rear-horses' prey upon other insects. **1876** *Field & Forest* I. 74 We were much interested in watching the hatching of the eggs in an egg-cluster of *Mantis Carolina*, commonly known in the Southern States as rear-horses. **1890** [see Devil's-coach-horse].

Rear yard. A yard to the rear of a dwelling. (Cf. Back yard.) — **1861** *Vanity Fair* 4 May 210/2 Gen. Beauregard was discovered in the White House rear-yard. **1893** *Harper's Mag.* April 656/2 [Brooklyn] always had long and pretty gardens or rear yards. **1923** Herrick *Lilla* 224 Everybody was raising vegetables on vacant lots and in rear yards, these war days.

+**Reata.** [Sp.] A rope or lariat, usually of rawhide. (See also Riata.) — **1853** *Harper's Mag.* Aug. 308/2 Each mule being secured by a long *reata* . . . , was permitted to graze until sunset. **1872** McClellan *Golden State* 344 The vaquero, reata in hand, mounted his fleet horse. **1890** *Century Mag.* Dec. 173 Their reatas . . . [were] fastened to the shafts and to the pommels of their saddles. **1910** Mulford *H. Cassidy* xii, Why in h——l can't you tell things in a herd, 'stead of stringin' em out like a stiff reata trailing to soften?

+**Reb.** =Rebel 2. (See also Johnny Reb.) — **1862** Norton *Army Lett.* 128 The mud will prevent the rebs from moving north. **1867** Goss *Soldier's Story* 41, I was mixed up in some 'right smart tall grass,' as the expression goes among the 'rebs.' **1894** *Harper's Mag.* Aug. 427/1 Rebels, or, for short, Rebs, was all that a Northern soldier's lips could shape themselves to utter. **1908** 'O. Henry' *Options* 96 The alleged aristocratic superiority of a 'reb' ought to be visible to him at once.

Rebate. {1656–} *Railroad.* +An allowance made to a shipper by which he is given transportation at rates lower than the legal ones: (see quot. 1914).

1872 in Tarbell *Hist. Standard Oil Co.* I. 93 No rebates, drawbacks, or other arrangements of any character shall be made or allowed. **1889** *N.Y. Times* 8 Sept., The dressed-beef combine . . . undoubtedly gets a rebate by shipping stock to Chicago, St. Louis, or Kansas City, and returning them in the shape of dressed beef. **1904** Tarbell *Hist. Standard Oil Co.* I. 34 All three of the roads began as early as 1868 to use secret rebates. **1908** Stevens *Liberators* 130 The chairman was exceptionally well posted on freight discriminations and rebates. **1914** *Cycl. Amer. Govt.* III. 156/1 A rebate . . . may be accomplished by such crude devices as underbilling the weight of freight, false classification or a return in cash of a portion of the freight charges.

attrib. **1907** *Pearson's Mag.* Jan. 21/2 The rebate system is ruinous as well as unfair.

***Rebel.**

I. 1. A supporter of the American cause during the Revolutionary War.

1775 *Mass. Spy* 3 May 3/1 The commanding officer accosted the militia in words to this effect, 'Disperse you damn'd rebels!' **1780** *N.J. Archives*

2 Ser. IV. 152 Major Lumm seized Possession of the Academy, which the Rebels had converted into a Barrack. **1832** DUNLAP *Hist. Amer. Theatre* 47 The audience supposing his words, 'The rebels have attacked the lines on the Neck,' belonged to the farce, applauded the very natural acting of the man. **1847** *Knickerb.* XXIX. 54 Mrs. Mowatt is . . . a great grand-daughter of one of those old 'rebels' who signed the Declaration of Independence.

+**2.** One who espoused the cause of the South during the Civil War. Now hist.

1861 E. COWELL *Diary* 290 [The] proceeding caused the necessary diversion of 'the rebels'' course. **1865** BOUDRYE *Fifth N.Y. Cavalry* 133 Another road was found . . . which the fleeing Rebels had taken. **1895** CHAMBLISS *Diary* 305 The malignant epithets, 'Yankee' and 'Rebels,' . . . were invented by fanatics and foreigners to aggravate our interstate quarrel. **1905** RICE *Sandy* 123 'Was he a rebel?' . . . 'He was a Confederate, sir! I never knew a rebel.'

+**b.** *pl.* The Southern Confederacy. *Obs.*

1863 *Cincinnati Gaz.* 5 Feb. 3/2 What the Rebels Hope of Northern Copperheads. **1864** *Wkly. New Mexican* 3 June 1/4 The Rebels are reported to have ordered an entire fleet from French builders. **1865** *Atlantic Mo.* March 285/2 The Rebels keep their best generals for their Home Guard.

II. *attrib.* and *comb.* **3.** In sense 1 with *arms, general, keg,* etc.

1776 TRUMBULL *M'Fingal* 67 They saw your rebel-rout Determin'd still to hold it out. **1777** HUTCHINSON *Diary & Lett.* II. 169 We credit the rebel newspapers, which are very unfavorable. **1778** *Amer. Museum* I. 56/2 The rebel kegs were either totally demolished, or obliged to fly. **1781** PETERS *Hist. Conn.* 411 David Wooster, the rebel General, . . . received a fatal ball through his bladder. **1782** TRUMBULL *M'Fingal* 152 Behold his chiefs . . . Spread thro' our camps their dread alarms, And swell the fears of rebel-arms.

4. In sense 2. **a.** Designating military units composed of Confederate soldiers.

1861 MCCLELLAN in *Own Story* 91 How did you learn that Buckner and Smith have joined the rebel army? **1862** Moore *Rebellion Rec.* V. II. 84 In front . . . several rebel regiments marched about dark. **1862** Rebel band [see DIXIE 2]. **1866** 'F. KIRKLAND' *Bk. Anecdotes* 279/1 They retreated . . . to a point where a whole rebel brigade had stacked their arms.

b. Designating places and institutions maintained for or by the Confederates during the Civil War.

1861 NORTON *Army Lett.* 24 The rebel camps are within two miles of us. **1865** KELLOGG *Rebel Prisons* p. vii, The multiplied woes of the battle-field . . . are almost the enjoyments of Paradise, in comparison with the fearful and prolonged agonies of Prisoners in *Rebel Stockades*. **1868** *Ore. State Jrnl.* 31 Oct. 2/3 Nearly every one [of the flags] bore the name of a battle, a rebel dungeon, a General, or some appropriate motto.

c. Designating individuals in the Confederate service or supporting the Confederate cause.

1862 NORTON *Army Lett.* 62 If rebel scouts discovered us they could not estimate our numbers. **1863** *Ib.* 157 If I was a picket here, and should see a rebel general across there, I couldn't resist the temptation to draw a bead on him. **1866** CARPENTER *At White House* 209 The famous 'peace' conference, . . . between President Lincoln and Secretary Seward, and the Rebel commissioners Stephens, Hunter, and Campbell, took place the 3d of February, 1865. **1868** *N.Y. Herald* 2 July 4/3 The old gentleman waxed warm in his eulogy of the rebel chief [R. E. Lee]. **1869** Rebel bushwhacker [see BUSHWHACKER 2]. **1870** O. LOGAN *Before Footlights* 213 This was a new character to me, the rebel Negro. I found plenty of them further South. **1880** *Harper's Mag.* July 262/2 There's a dangerous character at large in Baltimore—a rebel agent on secret service.

d. Designating things owned by the Confederates or by the Confederate authorities.

1864 *Wkly. New Mexican* 10 June 2/4 The honor of destroying the rebel ram Arkansas belongs to [Commodore Wm. D. Porter]. **1865** *Atlantic Mo.* April 430/2 A Rebel steamer . . . [was] said to be . . . awaiting her chance to run the blockade. **1866** 'F. KIRKLAND' *Bk. Anecdotes* 222/2 Those Union flags fluttered along the fringe where fifty rebel guns were kenneled.

5. In special combinations.

Rebel cabinet, the cabinet of the Southern Confederacy; *r. conch* (see CONCH 2, quot. 1861); *r. rag,* a contemptuous designation for the Confederate flag; *r. ticket,* a political ticket voted for or endorsed by the Confederates.

1884 *Century Mag.* April 826/1 These newspapers . . . would be in the hands of the rebel Cabinet next morning. **1862** NORTON *Army Lett.* 64 Our color guard . . . planted the flag of the Eighty-third on the fortifications so long disgraced by the rebel rag. **1866** W. REID *After the War* 144 We knows the difference between the Union ticket and the Rebel ticket.

+**Rebel brigadier.** (See quots. 1888, 1914.) — **1878** *N. Amer. Rev.* CXXVI. 93 Unlike the 'rebel brigadiers,' his presence is not a rock of offense to the loyal mind. **1888** BROWN & STRAUSS *Dict. Amer. Politics* (1907) 337 *Rebel Brigadiers* is a phrase applied to men in public life that served in the Confederate Army during the Civil War. The phrase is applied irrespective of the rank they held. It is a venomous phrase and used only by their opponents. **1914** *Cycl. Amer. Govt.* III. 156/2 *Rebel brigadiers,* an epithet of contempt applied by the radical Republicans in Congress about 1874 to Congressmen from the southern states because a larger portion of the Representatives had been officers in the Confederate army.

Rebeldom. {1859-} +The Confederate states during the Civil War. *Obs.* — **1862** GRAY *Letters* 480 As to Rebeldom, there is now hardly any State that we have not got some foothold in. **1865** KELLOGG *Rebel Prisons* 35 Our own regiment was over four hundred strong, . . . so that we were quite a company, doomed to the miseries of *rebeldom*. **1887** BILLINGS *Hardtack* 280 Afterwards [soldiers] went by thousands into other sections of Rebeldom.

+**Rebeless.** (See quotation.) *Obs.* — **1863** *Rocky Mt. News* (Denver) 29 Jan. (Th.), A new word appears in the newspapers, which had not been thought of by Lindly [*sic*] Murray when he wrote his grammar. We refer to the word 'rebeless,' a female rebel.

+**Rebel gray.** The gray cloth used in making uniforms for Southern soldiers during the Civil War. Also transf. and attrib. (Cf. BLUE *n.* 5, GRAY *n.* 1.) — **1866** GREGG *Life in Army* 172 If they had been dressed in rebel gray, . . . no doubt they would have met with a warm welcome. **1886** LOGAN *Great Conspiracy* 314 The 'Boys in Blue' are irresistibly advancing, driving the 'Rebel Gray' back and back. **1895** *Century Mag.* May 18/1 He stripped off his rebel-gray jacket.

+**Rebelism.** The spirit, practice, or polity of the Southerners during the Civil War. *Obs.* — **1862** *Constitution* (Middletown, Conn.) 26 March (Chipman), There is a good deal of rebelism in the *Old Bailie*. **1867** *Congress. Globe* 10 Dec. 103/3 The action of Congress can have no other effect than to embarrass the work of reconstruction, . . . to feed the spirit of rebelism and incite insubordination.

* **Rebellion.** Armed resistance to one's government. **a.** In the Revolutionary War.

1777 CRESSWELL *Journal* 264 A great deal of Peltry, Pot-Ashes and Naval stores was annually sent to England from New York before the Rebellion. **1778** *Penna. Mag.* VI. 288 The Calculation . . . of the Continental Debt towards supporting the Rebellion in America to this day May 31, 1778 is £23,970,000.10s 7½d, sterling.

b. In the Civil War.

See also WAR OF THE REBELLION.

1861 *Cincinnati Gaz.* 26 Sept. (Th.), O Lord, had the East done as well as the Hoosier State in furnishing men to put down this rebellion, we would not [etc.]. **1867** *Wkly. New Mexican* 2 March 2/1 This endeavor to foster the *Caste* spirit springs from the very copperhead principle that hissed encouragement, in the North during the rebellion, to the less degraded rattlesnake of secession. **1900** *Congress. Rec.* 20 Jan. 1021/1 A report on the claim of the State of Nevada for moneys advanced in aid of the suppression of the rebellion in the civil war [was referred] to the Committee on War Claims. **1914** [see IRONCLAD OATH].

attrib. and *comb.* **1864** NORTON *Army Lett.* 234 One of Uncle Samuel's rebellion smashers . . . was on his way home. **1865** *Ore. State Jrnl.* 23 Dec. 1/5 Mr. Barnum is receiving . . . rebellion record curiosities.

+**Rebellionist.** An advocate of the Southern cause during the Civil War. *Obs.* — **1862** *N.Y. Tribune* 19 June 4/6 A very large vote was polled [in Wilmington]. In this city, it reached to 1,434, which is only 80 votes less than the rebellionists polled in the whole county a week ago.

+**Rebel state.** One of the states composing the Confederate States of America. *Obs.* — **1861** in E. Cowell *Diary* 352 The rebel States have made proffers to purchase vessels in England and other European countries. **1868** *N.Y. Herald* 2 July 3/3 Congress should take some action on the subject of the votes of the late rebel States. **1894** LEAVITT *Our Money Wars* 40 In 1865, the legal tender and bank note circulation was $1,199,565,231 among 27,000,000 people (rebel States excluded).

+**Rebel yell.** A characteristic yell uttered by Southern soldiers, usually when going into action, during the Civil War. Also transf. — **1868** *Ore. State Jrnl.* 26 Sept. 2/5 It was the 'old rebel yell.' **1885** *Century Mag.* June 290/1 The 'rebel yell' from the cliffs turned them back. **1895** M. A. Jackson *Gen. Jackson* 642 It was answered by the veterans on the other side with an old-fashioned 'rebel yell.' **1908** MCGAFFEY *Show-Girl* 228 [We] turned loose a Rebel yell for help and pretty soon along comes a tugboat. **1912** COBB *Back Home* 283 This yell, which is shrill and very penetrating, has been described in print technically as the Rebel yell.

+**Reboso.** =next. — **1853** in *Wkly. New Mexican* 9 Dec. (1864) 2/2 Some blanketed, with sombreros and cigarritoes, . . . some with rebosos.

+**Rebozo.** Also **reboza.** [Sp.] A shawl or long scarf worn over the head and shoulders by Spanish American women. — **1844** GREGG *Commerce of Prairies* I. 216 A Mexican female is scarcely ever seen without her rebozo or shawl. **1857** DAVIS *El Gringo* 189 The *rebozo* . . . appears to be a fixture in the toilet of a New Mexican lady. **1895** GRAHAM *Stories of Foot-Hills* 134 The lake itself was not more placid than the señora's face under her black reboza. **1909** M. AUSTIN *Lost Borders* 167 Marguerita leaned her fat arms on the table, wrapped in her blue reboza.

+**Rebunch,** *v. tr.* and *absol.* To arrange or form into new groups or bunches. Also *vbl. n.* — **1881** *Harper's Mag.* Oct. 723 A sure though gradual rebunching of the small farms into large estates. **1888** Bryce *Amer. Commw.* II. III. lxvi. 500 They can destroy, rebunch, fail to distribute, and what not as they please.

+**Recede,** *v. tr.* To cede back or give up again to a former owner. (Cf. CEDE *v.*) — **1771** in F. Chase *Hist. Dartmouth Coll.* I. 435 The lands on the west side Connecticut river might be receded back to New Hampshire. **1805** M. CUTLER in *Life & Corr.* II. 185 The first step was to re-cede Alexandria to Virginia.

Receipt, *v.* {1848–} +**1.** *tr.* To give written acknowledgment of having received (money, etc.). +**2.** *intr.* To give a receipt *for* money, etc. — (1) **1787** CUTLER in *Life & Corr.* I. 376, [I] have delivered him one hundred and ten dollars . . . , which he has receipted to me as received on the account of the Ohio Company. **1798** I. ALLEN *Hist. Vermont* 233 In a short time forty prisoners were returned. . . . Major Fay, as Commissary of prisoners, receipted them. (2) **1832** *23d Congress 1 Sess.* Sen. Doc. No. 512, II. 829 [Stock] will be delivered . . . to an issuing officer, . . . who will receipt therefor. **1874** PINKERTON *Expressman & Detective* 21 These were receipted for by Maroney. **1913** LONDON *Valley of Moon* 503 These two assistants had . . . been receipted for by the local deputy sheriff.

+**Receiptor.** *Law.* A person who gives a receipt for property committed or bailed to him by the attaching officer. — **1814** *Mass. Supreme Ct. Rep.* XI. 319 The receiptors are precluded, by their own act, from calling in question the validity of the attachment. **1839** STORY *Law of Bailments* § 125 Upon bailments of this sort it may not be without use to consider . . . what are the rights and duties of the bailee, commonly called the receiptor. **1872** BOUVIER *Law Dict.* (ed. 14) II. 418/2 *Receiptor.* In Massachusetts. A name given to the person who, on a trustee process being issued and goods attached, becomes surety to the sheriff to have them forthcoming on demand. **1914** *Ib.* (ed. 8, Rawle) III. 2824/2 The officer taking the goods often, instead of retaining them in his own manual control, delivers them to some third person, termed the 'receiptor,' who gives his receipt for them.

+**Receivability.** Acceptability, esp. with ref. to bills or notes. — **1813** JEFFERSON *Writings* XIII. 276 These bills would make their way . . . by their receivability for customs and taxes. **1834** *Congress. Deb.* 2 Jan. 128 The receivability of the notes of the bank, in payment of all public dues, gave [the U.S.] another interest in the circulation and general management of the institution.

* **Receiver.**

+**1.** (See quot. 1793.) *Obs.*

1705 *Va. State P.* I. 98 The inconveniency of ignorant or negligent Receivers [will be] entirely removed. **1793** *Md. Hist. Mag.* VI. 214 Tobacco did not [*c*1750] undergo a public inspection as now—men skilled in that article were employed by the merchants (and who were called receivers) to view, weigh and give receipts to the planters.

+**2.** In a government land office, an official who receives the money for land that is sold.

1834 JACKSON in *Pres. Mess. & P.* III. 51 Upon his report . . . of the proceedings in the register's and receiver's offices at Indianapolis I deemed it proper to remove both of those officers. **1849** CHAMBERLAIN *Ind. Gazetteer* 24 The officers of each district are a Register and a Receiver, appointed by the President of the United States and confirmed by the Senate. **1873** EGGLESTON *Myst. Metrop.* 96 The lawyer . . . was brother-in-law to the receiver of the land-office. **1907** *Indian Laws & Tr.* III. 275 The amount at which . . . water rights shall be sold shall . . . be paid to the receiver of the local land office.

3. (See quot. 1914.) {1793–}

1857 *Harper's Mag.* Oct. 701/2 When you have a Fund and a Receiver you must know that questions of honesty or dishonesty . . . don't enter. **1883** *Ib.* Nov. 939/1 The railroad . . . went through the usual course, first passing into the hands of a receiver. **1893** M. HOWE *Honor* 123 The head of the firm . . . made over the contents of the great vaults beneath the counting-house to the receiver. **1903** *Chicago Chronicle* 11 April 1/5 An action [was] brought by the receiver of the company against Mr. Sage, E. V. Leow, . . . and Charles J. Obermayer. **1914** *Cycl. Amer. Govt.* III. 159/1 *Receiver*, a person (sometimes a corporation) appointed by a court of equity to take charge of and manage property, pending litigation, for the benefit of the litigant owners, stockholders or creditors, as they may prove themselves entitled.

* **Receiver-general.** A receiver of public revenues in general. — **1654** *Md. Council Proc.* I. 299 [The inhabitants shall] pay to his L[or]d[shi]ps receiver Generall here . . . all such arrears of Rent as are due. **1688** *N.J. Archives* 1 Ser. II. 31 [As for the office] of Treas: a receiver Gen. it is not worth your counting. **1705** *Boston News-Letter* 30 April 2/2 Thomas Byerley Esqr. late Receiver General of this Province is suspended. **1846** *Whig Almanac 1847* 35/1 The rooms . . . were directed to be prepared and provided . . . for the use of Receivers General of Public Moneys. **1858** BANCROFT *Hist. U.S.* VII. 155 The congress of Massachusetts . . . chose a receiver-general of their own and instituted a system of provisional taxation. **1923** *Mass. General Court Man. 1923–24* 459 Treasurer and Receiver-General. James Jackson (*R.*) of Westwood. *Ib.*, George B. Willard, Deputy Treasurer and Receiver-General, Waltham.

Receiving house. {1832–} +**1.** (See quot. 1900.) +**2.** (See quotation.) — (1) **1900** NELSON *A B C Wall St.* 157 *Receiving houses*, houses which make a business of receiving and selling cash grain. **1901** MERWIN & WEBSTER *Calumet 'K'* 288 Farmers were driving their wheat-laden wagons to the hundreds of local receiving houses. (2) **1854** in W. E. Connelley *Kansas* 343 It is recommended that, at such points as the Directors [of the Emigrant Aid Society] select for places of settlement, they shall at once construct a boarding house, or receiving house, in which 300 persons may receive temporary accommodation on their arrival.

Receiving ship. A ship moored at a navy yard or port for the temporary accommodation of recruits, men being transferred, etc. {1830–} — **1841** *S. Lit. Messenger* VII. 762/2 A couple of gentlemen . . . introduced themselves to me as Midshipmen of the Receiving-Ship. **1858** *Ib.* XXVI. 87/2 Three are in use as 'receiving ships,' in which recruits are entertained until required for service at sea. **1865** KELLOGG *Rebel Prisons* 351 The one first mentioned was styled the 'receiving ship.' **1886** *Harper's Mag.* June 5/2 She is in use as a receiving-ship.

+**Receiving vault.** A place in a cemetery where the bodies of the dead are placed temporarily before final interment. — **1872** *Amer. Naturalist* March 160 In excavating the 'receiving vault' of the Riverview Cemetery, . . . 'a bushel basket full of axes' were found. **1882** MCCABE *New York* 235 The cost of an interment in the receiving vault is $25. **1891** HOWELLS *Imperative Duty* xi, There was a terrible provisionality about the whole business, beginning with the provisional deposition of the dead in the receiving-vault at Mount Auburn. **1898** ATHERTON *Californians* 348 The house—it was like entering the receiving vault on Lone Mountain.

* **Reception,** *n.*

1. A social function at which a person or persons receive. {1882}

1842 *Diplom. Corr. Texas* III. (1911) 1412, I attended last night the reception of Mr Guizot the Minister for Foreign Affairs. **1860** E. COWELL *Diary* 203 Had a reception the next day. **1887** *Lippincott's Mag.* Oct. 578 During this [commencement] week come . . . society receptions. **1907** *St. Nicholas* Oct. 1119/1 The 'happy couple' . . . will hurry back to Red Feather's house to the reception.

2. *attrib.* +**a.** Designating times at which the president receives callers.

1846 POLK *Diary* (1929) 70 These informal reception evenings are very pleasant. **1866** CARPENTER *At White House* 146 Among the numerous visitors on one of the President's reception days, were a party of Congressmen.

b. Designating rooms where people are received, as patients at a doctor's office or visitors in a home.

1865 *Atlantic Mo.* June 723/1 We entered a side room—a sort of reception *salon*. **1872** *Chicago Ev. Jrnl.* 27 Aug., The play opens in the reception parlor of the physician. **1902** 'O. HENRY' *Roads of Destiny* 292 On a couch in the reception chamber Victory lay.

+**Reception,** *v. colloq.* **1.** *passive.* To be received at a reception. **2.** *intr.* To attend receptions. — (1) **1887** *New Orleans States* 8 May 6/2 Celebrities of one kind or another . . . have been teaed and receptioned to their own and everybody else's satisfaction. (2) **1889** LOWELL *Letters* II. 407 Here I am busy dining and receptioning again.

+**Reception committee.** A committee that formally welcomes a person or persons. — **1851** NORTHALL *Curtain* 89 We believe Mr. Marks consulted some members of the reception-committee. **1890** *Stock Grower & Farmer* 22 March 5/3 The reception committee at Fort Worth was evidently new at the business. **1898** *Kansas City Star* 19 Dec. 1/5 The reception committee entered the car.

Reception room. a. A room in a private house where visitors are received. {1829} **b.** A public waiting room connected with a hospital, lawyer's office, etc. +**c.** A room for a formal reception.

1846 MAGOFFIN *Down Santa Fé Trail* 70 My dirt-floored chamber, dining-room, parlour, reception room, &c. &c. is quite dessolated. **1876** INGRAM *Centennial Exp.* 600 The visitor first entered a hall used as a general reception-room. **1880** 'MARK TWAIN' *Tramp Abroad* 276, I never see you in the reception room. **1882** MCCABE *New York* 314 The second floor is occupied by the reception room, the social parlor, the office of the Secretary, . . . and the reading room. **1883** [see COATROOM]. **1892** M. A. JACKSON *Gen. Jackson* 474 The casket . . . was placed in the centre of the reception-room in the Executive Mansion. **1892** *York County Hist. Rev.* 26 The premises occupied comprise an operating room . . . and a reception room and office. **1904** STRATTON-PORTER *Freckles* 387 Ushering Lord and Lady O'More into the reception room, she said to McLean [etc.]. **1910** TOMPKINS *Mothers & Fathers* 143 With the other three [girls] filling both drawing-rooms and the reception room, I have to take to the dining room.

* **Recess.**

+**1.** An eating place or restaurant.

1850 S. F. COOPER *Rural Hours* 468 As for the eating-houses . . . there are some dozen of them—Lunches, Recesses, Restaurants, &c. **1891** WELCH *Recoll. 1830–40* 337 The town had an abundance of 'Restaurants,' 'Recesses' and 'Coffee Houses,' as they were variously called.

+**2.** A period of cessation from school work during which students play games, eat lunches, etc.

1860 HOLMES *E. Venner* xxvi, In the *recess* . . . or interval of suspended studies in the middle of the forenoon, this girl carried her autograph-book [to Elsie]. **1881** *Harper's Mag.* Sept. 557/2 Our chief amusement at 'recess' that winter . . . was sliding down hill upon a long board. **1885** *Santa Fé Weekly New Mexican* 8 Oct. 2/7 Rose Terry Cooke suggests that children should carry raw lunches to school and be taught to cook the same during the recess. **1904** M. KELLY *Little Citizens* 203 The First Reader Class filed down the yard for recess.

+**b.** *Big recess*, the period between the morning and afternoon sessions when students eat lunch.

1902 L. BELL *Hope Loring* 19 It was 'big recess,' as the children called it. **1903** FOX *Little Shepherd* iii, At noon—'big recess'—Melissa gave Chad some cornbread and bacon.

3. Attrib. in sense 2 with *bell, game, ground, time.*

1869 STOWE *Oldtown Folks* 431 At recess-time she strolled out with me into the pine woods back of the school-house. **1902** G. M. MARTIN *Emmy Lou* 60 The recess-bell rang. **1904** Recess game [see CHERMANY]. **1905** VALENTINE *H. Sandwith* 393 A high price would be paid that recess grounds might be secured for Dunkirk youth with bat and ball.

***Rechabite.** A member of a society of abstainers from alcoholic liquor, founded in England in 1835, and in the U.S. in 1842. *Obs.* — **1845** [see COME-OUTER]. **1861** E. COWELL *Diary* 236 A very grand Procession of Rechabites passed today, stretching out to a great length along Broadway.

+**Recharter,** *n.* The renewal of a charter, esp. with reference to the second Bank of the United States. — **1832** *Congress. Deb.* 9 Jan. 1515 The president and directors of the United States' Bank have petitioned for a recharter of that institution. **1834** C. A. DAVIS *Lett. J. Downing* 254 It looks plagy strange that folks who want a recharter of a Bank should be cut-throats and murderers. **1838** *U.S. Mag.* Feb. 289 The Bank was determined to wring a recharter perforce from the hands of the Federal Government. **1844** *Indiana Senate Jrnl.* 29 Sess. 51 The committee on education to whom was referred a memorial, and sundry petitions, praying the re-charter of Hanover college, have . . . had the same under consideration. **1853** *Harper's Mag.* Jan. 261/2 The Governor's Message recommends the re-charter of all private banks, under proper restrictions.

+**Recharter,** *v. tr.* To charter again, esp. to renew the charter of the Bank of the United States. Also *vbl. n.* — **1831** *Congress. Deb.* 13 Dec. 1431 The vote . . . will be far from disclosing the actual opinions of members in regard to rechartering the bank. **1833** JACKSON in *Pres. Mess. & P.* III. 6 At the session of 1831–32 an act was passed by a majority of both Houses of Congress rechartering the present bank. **1854** BENTON *30 Years' View* I. 187/2 The men of 1811 had committed a fatal error, when most wisely refusing to re-charter the institution of that day, they failed to provide a substitute for its currency, and fell back upon the local banks. **1884** *19th Cent.* Dec. 1005 The Vice-President . . . was found to be opposed to the rechartering of a United States Bank.

Reciprocity. {1766–} A policy or relation between the United States and another country whereby each grants the other reciprocal trade or other advantages. {1782–} Also attrib.

1778 *U.S. Treaties* (1910) I. 469 The Most Christian King [of France], and the thirteen United States of North America . . . [take] for the basis of their agreement the most perfect equality and reciprocity . . . respecting commerce and navigation. **1836** *Diplom. Corr. Texas* I. (1908) 127 A just reciprocity is our basis, in the full confidence that a similar one will influence the counsels of the United States. **1847** CLAY in *Whig Almanac 1848* 10/1 Out of these acts have sprung a class, and a large class, of treaties, . . . commonly called Reciprocity Treaties. **1904** *Providence Jrnl.* 28 July 6 Republicans who differ sharply with Senator Lodge on the question of reciprocity. **1911** *Springfield W. Republican* 31 Aug. 1 Its enactment into law would have ditched them in their present reciprocity campaign.

* **Recitation.**

+**1.** In a school, the action of answering questions on a prepared lesson or exercise; the occasion or class period when this is performed.

1770 FITHIAN *Journal* I. 8 At nine the Bell rings for Recitation. **1780** E. PARKMAN *Diary* 208 He has been absent from the Recitations. **1823** B. A. GOULD *System Educ. Free Schools Boston* 52 Recitations in this are made two or three times each half day. **1837** PECK *New Guide* 353 Two able professors . . . hear recitations and deliver lectures. **1893** POST *Harvard Stories* 149 Hudson and Gray went over to a recitation in University Hall. **1904** *Churchman* 6 Aug. 237 The recitations [at W. Point] are not merely occasional or scattered questions, but a demonstration of principle at the blackboard, or a solution of problems.

+**2.** Attrib. with *bell, bench, hall, hour.*

1834 PECK *Gaz. Illinois* 88 Lebanon Seminary has a commodious chapel, or recitation hall. **1855** *Knickerb.* XLV. 14, I resided . . . within hearing of the recitation-bell. **1882** 'M. HARLAND' *Eve's Daughters* 210 Or recitation-hour is upon you, and you have neither lesson, nor book. **1887** *Lippincott's Mag.* Aug. 293 [A student] never tires of inscribing his class numerals on recitation-benches.

+**Recitationist.** One who delivers a reading or recitation. — **1885** STEDMAN in *Century Mag.* Feb. 512/1 The youth . . . has heard this last of the recitationists deliver one of his poems. **1887** *Ohio State Jrnl.* (Columbus) 24 June, She is a clear, graceful recitationist.

+**Recitation room.** A room in which school recitations are heard. — **1827** [see CHAPEL 2]. **1849** *Knickerb.* XXXIII. 182, I am astonished that any student should render such a one in *my* recitation-room. **1897** *N.Y. Journal* 5 Sept. 41/4 Recitation rooms are opened for the year's exercises.

* **Recite,** *v.*

+**1.** *tr.* To repeat or reply to questions about (a lesson, etc.) in a school recitation.

1743 *Holyoke Diaries* 35 Wee Recited Tully's offices. **1823** B. A. GOULD *Syst. Educ. Free Schools Boston* 22 The boys come into school in the morning, prepared to recite a given portion. **1854** M. J. HOLMES *Tempest & Sunshine* 29 Her lessons, however, were generally well learned, and well recited. **1903** WIGGIN *Rebecca* 54 [She] recited . . . grammar after school hours to Miss Dearborn alone.

+**2.** *intr.* To answer a question in a school recitation; to repeat a lesson. Also *vbl. n.*

1759 *Essex Inst. Coll.* XLIX. 6 Finished reciting, the Dr. gave us good advice. **1815** *Niles' Reg.* IX. 18/1 Those not immediately engaged in reciting . . . remain in their own chambers. **1827** *Boston H. S. for Girls, Regulations* 6 Only half of the school can conveniently recite together. **1873** BEADLE *Undevel. West* 380 The sexes . . . do not even recite together. **1904** *Churchman* 6 Aug. 237 Each cadet [at W. Point] must be prepared to recite every day upon all the subjects of study upon which he is engaged.

Recke(n) hook. A hook for suspending pots in a chimney. *Obs.* {1856–, *dial.*} — **1645** *Essex Probate Rec.* I. 50 Estate of William Goog of Lynn. . . . One gridiron & recke hookes [etc.]. **1649** *Ib.* 99 Estate of John Jarrat of Rowley. . . . Reckon hooks & some small things, 4s. [etc.].

* **Reckon,** *v.*

* **1.** *local. tr.* To suppose or be of the opinion (*that*).

1707 SEWALL *Diary* II. 186, [I] reckon'd we were not to enquire any further. **1810** M. DWIGHT *Journey to Ohio* 47, I reckon we shall be unable to proceed on our journey. **1860** GREELEY *Overland Journey* 77, I reckon 'claims' will not be greedily hunted nor bought. **1885** 'CRADDOCK' *Prophet* 172 He 'reckoned' that they would not have left Him standing in the road. **1898** E. C. HALL *Aunt Jane* 68 Sam, what do you reckon? My quilt took the premium. **1917** MATHEWSON *Sec. Base Sloan* 47 Reckon you paid a heap of money.

2. *I reckon*, used parenthetically or as an affirmative reply. {1603–}

'Still common in Eng. dialects, and current in the southern States of America in place of the northern *I guess*' (*O.E.D.*).

1787 TYLER *Contrast* v, i, Something dang'd cute, I reckon. **1825** JOHN NEAL *Bro. Jonathan* I. 46 Only break yourself, will you, of those execrable Virginia-isms— . . . I reckon—jist [etc.]. **1828** FLINT *A. Clenning* I. 10 [I asked] whether he was in the habit of receiving strangers. 'I reckon so,' was the answer. **1834** SIMMS *Guy Rivers* I. 74, I know jist as well how to keep order, I reckon, as any on you. **1866** C. H. SMITH *Bill Arp* 33 There is not much margin for extortion on the Government at that price, I reckon. **1884** HARRIS in *Century Mag.* Nov. 120 Evans owns this place, I reckon. **1907** WHITE *Arizona Nights* 300 'Think you could teach him to eat sugar, Brent?' 'I reckon,' replied the cowboy.

***Reclaim,** *v. tr.* To bring (waste land) under cultivation or into practical use. {1764–} — **1865** *Ore. State Jrnl.* 29 April 1/5 We suggest that a premium be offered for the first one hundred acres of apparently worthless alkali desert reclaimed to the successful cultivation of grain. **1883** [see FAUBOURG]. **1909** *Indian Laws & Tr.* III. 385 Any such drainage district . . . is hereby authorized to assess the cost of reclaiming the tribal lands of the Omaha and Winnebago Indians.

***Reclamation.** The action or process of reclaiming waste lands. {1861–} Also attrib. — **1883** KNIGHT Suppl. 745/2 *Reclamation Plow*, a plow for breaking new land. **1890** *Stock Grower & Farmer* 25 Jan. 5/3 The reclamation of alkali lands is becoming a question of deep importance. **1900** *Congress. Rec.* 3 Jan. 628/2 A petition of the California Water and Forest Association . . . was referred to the Committee on Irrigation and Reclamation of Arid Lands. **1919** HOUGH *Sagebrusher* 250 The camp of the reclamation engineers and construction men lay upon a bench or plateau.

+**Reclining chair.** A chair so constructed that one may recline in it. — **1865** *Atlantic Mo.* Jan. 37/1 Mrs. Blake was sitting in her reclining-chair as Miss Pix entered. **1873** PHELPS *Trotty's Wedding* vii, Well, I've come to get a reclining-chair for my wife. **1892** *Harper's Mag.* Feb. 438/2 She had tilted her reclining chair almost into the lap of the lady behind her. **1903** WIGGIN *Rebecca* 139 The premiums . . . were three—a bookcase, a plush reclining chair, and a banquet lamp.

+**Reclining-chair car.** A railroad coach equipped with reclining chairs. — **1890** H. Palmer *Stories Base Ball Field* 223 Free Reclining Chair Cars between Chicago and Omaha.

* **Recognize,** *v.*

+**1.** *Law.* **a.** *tr.* To bind over by a recognizance. **b.** *intr.* To enter into a recognizance. *Obs.*

(a) 1699 *Penna. Col. Rec.* I. 563 The said Edward Robinson recognized himself in 300 *l.* **1809** TYLER *Vt. Rep.* I. 148 Mallery was recognised by Justice Seaton to appear in this court. **1839** *S. Lit. Messenger* V. 220/1 The witnesses also, for the commonwealth, . . . were *recognized* to attend and testify. **1898** PAGE *Red Rock* 561 He had had her recognized to appear. **(b) 1754** [see ASSIZE 1]. **1783** in Parmenter *Hist. Pelham Mass.* 250 Samuel Sampson as principal in behalf of said John recognizes to the Commonwealth in the sum of fifty pounds with sureties.

+**2.** *tr.* To acknowledge (a person) as having a right to the floor of an assembly.

1888 BRYCE *Amer. Commw.* I. I. xiii. 187 A recent Speaker . . . [was] universally condemned because he had usually 'recognized' (*i.e.* called on in debate) his own friends only. **1923** H. M. ROBERT *Parliamentary Law* 570 A member is said to have 'obtained the floor' when he has risen and addressed the chair . . . and has been 'recognized' by the chair.

Recommend. A recommendation. *colloq.*² '*Dial* and *U.S.*' (*O.E.D.*). — **1799** Dow *Travels* (1806) 103 This morning, I went on shore, having no proper recommends with me. **1827** *Mass. Spy* 28 Feb. (Th.), Have you got any blank recommends for scholars? **1891** RYAN *Told in Hills* 29 If Mr. Hardy wants a guide, give me a recommend, can't you? **1900** MUNN *Uncle Terry* 31, I am paying you seventy-five dollars a month on the recommend of an important client of mine.

***Reconsider,** *v.* +*tr.* In parliamentary usage: To consider (a vote, motion, etc.) a second time. — **1729** *Boston Rec.* 10 Voted To Reconsider, The Vote of the Sixth of May last past about placing the Grainery. **1746** *Ib.* 86 A Motion was made . . . that the Town would reconsider the motion of Mr. Jeremiah Allen. **1844** L. S. CUSHING *Rules of Proceeding* 134 It has now come to be . . . a principle of the common parliamentary law of this country, to reconsider a vote already passed. **1894** T. B. REED *Rules* 148 In England the motion to reconsider is not known.

Reconsideration. {1783-} +In parliamentary practice: A second consideration of a motion, vote, etc. — **1736** *Boston Rec.* 148 A Motion [was] Made and Seconded, For Reconsidering A Vote pass'd at this Meeting, . . . And thereupon a Reconsideration being had [etc.]. **1789** *Ann. 1st Congress* 350 The act would require the reconsideration of the Legislature in a short time. **1798** JEFFERSON *Manual* (1837) xliii, The votes of negative and reconsideration . . . destroy one another, and are as if they were expunged from the Journals. **1844** L. S. CUSHING *Rules of Proceeding* 133 The inconvenience of this rule . . . has led to the introduction into the parliamentary practice . . . of the motion for *reconsideration.* **1894** T. B. REED *Rules* 151 The practice of reconsideration has led to much waste of time.

Reconstruct, *v.* {1768-}

+**1.** *tr.* After the Civil War, to re-establish (the South and its different state governments) in conformity with the reconstruction program of the North. Also *ppl. a.*

1865 S. SCHURZ in Hart *Amer. Hist. Contemporaries* IV. 452 The people are willing to reconstruct their State Governments. **1866** *Rep. Joint Com. Reconstruction* III. 12 'Well,' said the governor, 'I agree to that; but let us wait until we get the State reconstructed.' **1867** EMERSON *Works* XI. (1904) 352 The aim of the hour was to reconstruct the South; but first the North had to be reconstructed. **1900** *Congress. Rec.* 25 Jan. 1172/1 Negro suffrage was brought upon the South solely by reason of the rejection, by the reconstructed South, of the fourteenth amendment to the Constitution.

+**b.** To bring (a Southerner) to a full acceptance of the reconstruction program of the North after the Civil War. Also *ppl. a.*

1865 *Ore. State Jrnl.* 21 Oct. 1/1 A returned rebel, but partially reconstructed, entered a saloon and ordered a Lieutenant to take his blouse off as he did not like blue coats. **1870** LOWELL *Among My Books* 141 They all came in, like reconstructed rebels. **1898** DUNBAR *Folks from Dixie* 191, I thought that I was reconstructed, but I'm not.

+**2.** To reconcile (a Filipino) to the government of the United States.

1904 *N.Y. Times* 13 June 2 Aguinaldo gives evidence of having been thoroughly 'reconstructed.'

+**Reconstructed state.** A Southern state restored to the Union after the Civil War in accordance with the program of Congress. — **1868** *N.Y. Herald* 4 July 5/2 The Mississippi delegation will at least insist on leaving the nomination to the delegations from the reconstructed States. **1878** BEADLE *Western Wilds* 418 Texas is the most tolerant and liberal of all the reconstructed States. *a***1880** in Tourgee *Invisible Empire* iv, The report of the committee of the Tennessee Legislature tells the results in . . . the then (1864-68) only Reconstructed State.

Reconstructing. +The remaking of Southern institutions after the Civil War in accordance with the plan of Congress. Also *ppl. a.* — **1865** *Nation* I. 386 The Reconstructing State Convention of Alabama has pronounced against the repudiation of the war debt of the state. **1866** LOWELL *Biglow P.* 2 Ser. xi. 244 We've gut an awful row to hoe In this 'ere job o' reconstructin'. **1879** BISHOP *4 Months in Sneak-Box* 280 His business was managed and the county funds handled by a white politician of the 'reconstructing' element then in power.

Reconstruction. {1791-}

+**1.** The reorganization of the government of the United States.

1861 *Cincinnati Commercial* 28 Jan. 2/3 The project of Re-construction is one by which the expression of the popular will in the election of the 6th of November, is to be revolutionized out of existence, and the Northern States to be converted into the subjugated provinces of King Cotton. *Ib.* The capacity for the re-construction of the Government does not exist among us.

+**2.** The reorganization and restoration of the seceding states of the South to the Union; the remodeling of the governments of the Southern states in accordance with the program of Congress.

1863 *Savannah Repub.* in *Boston Sun. Herald* 23 Aug. 3/7 He who advocates reconstruction advocates submission, and he knows it; but he thinks the word reconstruction is less objectionable than submission. **1865** LINCOLN *Works* II. 673 In the annual message of December, 1863, and in the accompanying proclamation, I presented a plan of reconstruction. **1866** in McPherson *Hist. Reconstruction* 243/1 [The President's] attempt to fasten his scheme of reconstruction upon the country is as dangerous as it is unwise. **1874** in Fleming *Hist. Reconstruction* II. 201, I have brought it through 'Reconstruction,' and now we have the 'Usurpation.' **1879** TOURGEE *Fool's Errand* 49 This was in the primary period of what has since become memorable as the era of 'reconstruction.' **1911** HARRISON *Queed* 45 The morning *Post* . . . had stood like a wall during the cruelties of Reconstruction; . . . had crucified carpet-baggism.

+**3.** Attrib. with *bill, committee, era,* etc.

1866 *Ore. State Jrnl.* 3 March 1/5 Congress has had a reconstruction committee of fifteen members. **1867** *Ib.* 2 March 2/4 The President will most undoubtedly veto the reconstruction bill. **1868** *N.Y. Herald* 3 July 4/6 The reconstruction policy of the radicals will be complete before the next election. **1873** *Newton Kansan* 15 May 4/2 It still desired the overthrow of the reconstruction laws. **1900** *Congress. Rec.* 25 Jan. 1162/2 The President of the United States during the progress of the reconstruction measures said, that no State had ever been out of the Union at all. **1904** *N.Y. Ev. Post* 12 May 7 Ever since the period of chaos known as the Reconstruction era, the negro has been the under dog in Southern Republicanism.

+**Reconstruction act.** An act of Congress, esp. one of 1867, setting forth the procedure and the conditions for the readmission of Southern states into the Union. — **1867** in Harrell *Brooks & Baxter War* 37/1 After a most careful and most thorough consideration of the *Reconstruction Act* itself, . . . we regard reconstruction under that act as an impossibility. **1868** *Democratic Conv. Proc.* 60 We regard the reconstruction acts, so called, of Congress, as . . . an usurpation.

+**Reconstructionary,** *a.* Of or pertaining to the reconstruction of the South. — **1879** TOURGEE *Fool's Errand* xxxix. 290 To overawe and suppress the Union, Federal, or Reconstructionary element of the South, was of itself an undertaking of no difficulty whatever to the trained leaders of that section.

+**Reconstructionist. a.** A southern advocate of reorganizing the South to restore it to the Union. **b.** An advocate of reconstruction, esp. in accordance with the plan of Congress. — **1863** *Savannah Repub.* in *Boston Sun. Herald* 23 Aug. 3/7 So much for the Submissionists. Now a word to the Reconstructionists; and let me tell you, Mr. Editor, that I do not consider them a whit better. **1866** W. REID *After the War* 404 There were 'reconstructionists' who believed, from the day of the defeat at Gettysburg, that Southern independence was hopeless. **1888** HARRIS in *Harper's Mag.* April 703/2 The Republican 'reconstructionists' . . . barred the way. **1898** *Kissimmee* (Fla.) *Valley Gazette* 28 Jan. 1/7 Mr. Vest . . . had been in Louisiana during the reign of the reconstructionists.

+**Reconstruction period.** The period after the Civil War in which the seceding states were reconstructed. — **1888** M. LANE in *America* 20 Sept. 15 In the 'Reconstruction' period, the Republican party insisted upon proof of reconstruction before the full restoration of rights and privileges to the seceding states. **1894** *Outing* XXIV. 472/1 During the reconstruction period, [Wait] resigned to engage in business in Chicago.

***Record.**

1. A document preserving an account of certain facts or events; freq., pl., a collection of such accounts. {1611-}

1634 *Watertown Rec.* I. 1. 1 One of them . . . shall keep the Records and Acts of the Towne. **1729** *Suffield Doc. Hist.* 242 Voted, to Improve Peter Roe, and Joseph Winchel, to search ye Records Relating to ye Breadth of High Street. **1866** MCCLELLAN in *Own Story* 220 He had his own adjutant-general and entirely distinct records. **1911** *Nation* 2 Feb. 109/2 The War Department permits no one to examine its records.

attrib. **1666** *Md. Archives* II. 137 No Cl[er]k of any County Court . . . shall exact any other ffee than is here prescribed for the entring any matter vpon Record not exceeding halfe a leafe in the Record books.

+**b.** *Congressional record,* the printed debates of Congress; since March 4, 1873, the official title of the printed record of these debates.

1831 *Congress. Deb.* 3 Feb. 606 We might go through the whole congressional record, and we should find Mr. Randolph . . . equally hostile to the administration of Mr. Madison. **1873** *Congress. Rec.* 21 March 137/1 *Resolved,* That the Congressional Printer be directed to have the same number of the *Congressional Record* for the present session printed as was printed of the *Globe* for the last session. **1906** O. O. STEALEY *20 Yrs. in Press Gallery* 11 The only advantage he derives from the discussion is the privilege to bury his remarks in the *Congressional Record.*

+**c.** Short for sense b.

1873 *Congress. Rec.* 21 March 135/1 No Senator now has a complete file of the *Record.* **1900** *Congress. Rec.* 10 Jan. 730/2 Why can not that be printed in the *Record?*

+**2.** The sum of what one has done; the leading facts or attitudes in the life of a person or a party.

'App. of American origin, but now in common Eng. use' (*O.E.D.*).

1856 *Greeley on Lincoln* (1893) 133 A candidate must have a slim record in these times. **1863** *Congress. Globe* 13 Feb. 935/2 My record . . . has been made before the country and the world; there let it stand. **1866** LOWELL *Writings* V. 266 Every public man is more or less in the habit of considering what he calls his 'record' as the one thing to be saved in the general deluge. **1888** *N. Amer. Rev.* June 685 Behind the record stands the man. **1922** J. F. RHODES *McKinley & Roosevelt Administrations* 292 Roosevelt . . . dilated on the 'Record of the Republican party,' on the currency and the tariff.

+**b.** A criminal record.

1908 BEACH *Barrier* 45 Maybe I've got a record—you don't know. **1918** A. WOODS *Crime Prevention* 87 The convict has a hard enough row to hoe when he gets out to overcome his record, even if he is mechanically capable.